KU-712-603

READER'S DIGEST

Wordpower
Dictionary

Reader's Digest Wordpower Dictionary
was edited and designed by Oxford University Press
for The Reader's Digest Association Limited, London.

First edition Copyright © 2001 The Reader's Digest Association Limited,
11 Westferry Circus, Canary Wharf, London E14 4HE.
www.readersdigest.co.uk

If you have any comments or suggestions about this book,
email us at: gbeditorial@readersdigest.co.uk

Copyright © 2001 Reader's Digest (Australia) Pty Limited.
Copyright © 2001 Reader's Digest (New Zealand) Limited.
Copyright © 2001 Reader's Digest Association Far East Limited.
Philippines Copyright © 2001 Reader's Digest Association Far East Limited.

All rights reserved.

No part of this book may be reproduced, stored in a retrieval system,
or transmitted in any form or by any means, electronic, electrostatic,
magnetic tape, mechanical, photocopying, recording or otherwise,
without permission in writing from the publishers.

® Reader's Digest, The Digest and the Pegasus logo
are registered trademarks of The Reader's Digest Association, Inc,
of Pleasantville, New York, USA.

Typeset in Bembo by Interactive Sciences Ltd, Gloucester
Printed by Brepols Fabrieken NV, Turnhout, Belgium

ISBN 0 276 42463 8

Note on trademarks and proprietary status

This dictionary includes some words which have, or are asserted to have, proprietary status as trademarks or
otherwise. Their inclusion does not imply that they have acquired for legal purposes a non-proprietary or
general significance, nor any other judgment concerning their legal status. In cases where the editorial staff
have some evidence that a word has proprietary status this is indicated in the entry for that word by the label
trademark, but no judgment concerning the legal status of such words is made or implied thereby.

READER'S DIGEST
Wordpower
Dictionary

Published by The Reader's Digest Association Limited

LONDON • NEW YORK • SYDNEY • MONTREAL • AUCKLAND

Contents

Editorial team

EDITOR	Bill Trumble
ASSOCIATE EDITORS	Angus Stevenson
	Catherine Soanes
SENIOR EDITOR	Julia Elliott
ASSISTANT EDITORS	Jonathan Blaney
	Judith Wood
EDITORIAL ASSISTANT	Richard Jones
ADMINISTRATIVE COORDINATOR	Sarah O'Connor
PRONUNCIATIONS	Susan Wilkin
GOOD ENGLISH SUPPLEMENT	Robert Allen
CONSULTANT	Judy Pearsall

For Reader's Digest

EDITOR	Julian Browne
ART EDITOR	Joanna Walker
EDITORIAL CONSULTANTS	Michael Janes
	Bruce Moore
PROOFREADER	Barry Gage

Reader's Digest General Books

EDITORIAL DIRECTOR	Cortina Butler
ART DIRECTOR	Nick Clark
EXECUTIVE EDITOR	Julian Browne
DEVELOPMENT EDITOR	Ruth Binney
PUBLISHING PROJECTS MANAGER	Alastair Holmes
STYLE EDITOR	Ron Pankhurst

About the Reader's Digest Wordpower Dictionary

The book in your hands is a uniquely user-friendly new type of dictionary. Gathered together in one volume you will find a treasure trove of practical information about our language. Whether you want to write or speak more clearly, ensure that you are using English correctly and sensitively, expand your vocabulary, understand technical terms or slang, play word games, or simply explore the wonderful richness of English for its own sake, everything you need is here.

Besides containing the full word coverage you would expect of a large family dictionary, *Wordpower* presents a wide range of additional features to give you quick access to the word or usage you want. It includes useful related words; notes giving guidance on spelling, pronunciation, grammar, and other points of usage; and illuminating facts about the origins of or connections between individual words or word groups. So it is much more than just a dictionary – it's a thesaurus, a reverse dictionary, and a style guide too.

The emphasis is always on clarity and accessibility, with easy-to-understand explanations and definitions that avoid technical terms or specialised abbreviations and symbols. A generous and open layout makes the page simple to navigate and ensures that you get directly to the information you require.

Wordpower is the result of more than four years' collaboration between Reader's Digest and Oxford University Press. Its text has been specially developed from that of the tenth edition of the *Concise Oxford Dictionary*, which derives from the *New Oxford Dictionary of English*. So it is directly shaped by the evidence of how our language is actually used today provided by the analysis of hundreds of millions of words of real English carried out for the *New Oxford Dictionary of English*.

Here, at your disposal, is all the expressiveness, beauty, and sheer variety of 21st-century English.

How to use this book

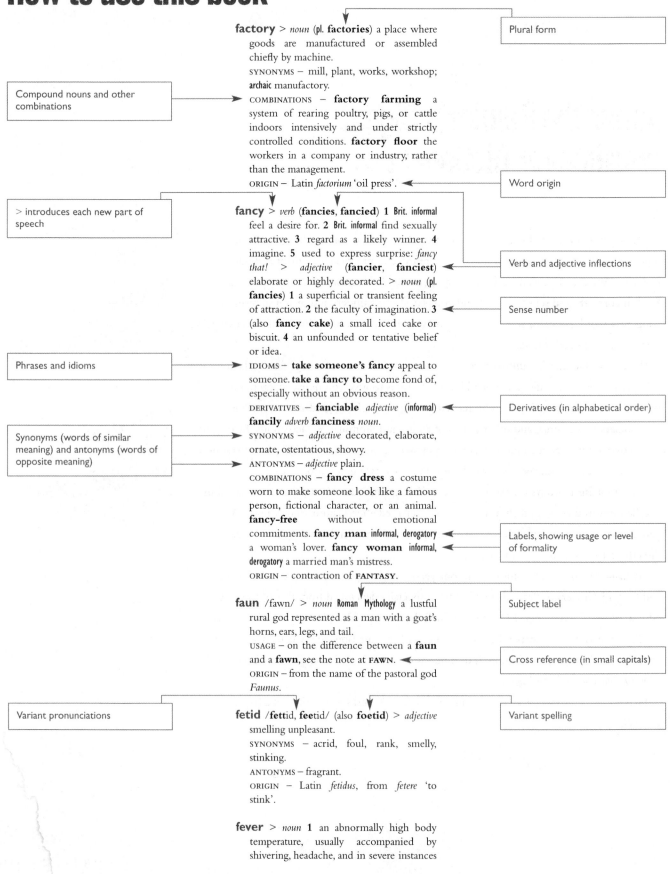

factory > *noun* (pl. **factories**) a place where goods are manufactured or assembled chiefly by machine.

SYNONYMS – mill, plant, works, workshop; archaic manufactory.

COMBINATIONS – **factory farming** a system of rearing poultry, pigs, or cattle indoors intensively and under strictly controlled conditions. **factory floor** the workers in a company or industry, rather than the management.

ORIGIN – Latin *factorium* 'oil press'.

fancy > *verb* (**fancies, fancied**) **1** Brit. informal feel a desire for. **2** Brit. informal find sexually attractive. **3** regard as a likely winner. **4** imagine. **5** used to express surprise: *fancy that!* > *adjective* (**fancier, fanciest**) elaborate or highly decorated. > *noun* (pl. **fancies**) **1** a superficial or transient feeling of attraction. **2** the faculty of imagination. **3** (also **fancy cake**) a small iced cake or biscuit. **4** an unfounded or tentative belief or idea.

IDIOMS – **take someone's fancy** appeal to someone. **take a fancy to** become fond of, especially without an obvious reason.

DERIVATIVES – **fanciable** *adjective* (informal) **fancily** *adverb* **fanciness** *noun*.

SYNONYMS – *adjective* decorated, elaborate, ornate, ostentatious, showy.

ANTONYMS – *adjective* plain.

COMBINATIONS – **fancy dress** a costume worn to make someone look like a famous person, fictional character, or an animal. **fancy-free** without emotional commitments. **fancy man** informal, derogatory a woman's lover. **fancy woman** informal, derogatory a married man's mistress.

ORIGIN – contraction of **FANTASY**.

faun /fawn/ > *noun* Roman Mythology a lustful rural god represented as a man with a goat's horns, ears, legs, and tail.

USAGE – on the difference between a **faun** and a **fawn**, see the note at **FAWN**.

ORIGIN – from the name of the pastoral god *Faunus*.

fetid /**fett**id, **fee**tid/ (also **foetid**) > *adjective* smelling unpleasant.

SYNONYMS – acrid, foul, rank, smelly, stinking.

ANTONYMS – fragrant.

ORIGIN – Latin *fetidus*, from *fetere* 'to stink'.

fever > *noun* **1** an abnormally high body temperature, usually accompanied by shivering, headache, and in severe instances

Labels on the right and left (diagram callouts):

- Plural form
- Compound nouns and other combinations
- Word origin
- > introduces each new part of speech
- Verb and adjective inflections
- Sense number
- Phrases and idioms
- Derivatives (in alphabetical order)
- Synonyms (words of similar meaning) and antonyms (words of opposite meaning)
- Labels, showing usage or level of formality
- Subject label
- Cross reference (in small capitals)
- Variant pronunciations
- Variant spelling

How to use this book

Wordfinder feature (list of related words, with meanings)

Pronunciation (for selected words)

Wordpower facts box (giving interesting information about the headword and related words)

Grammatical information

Label showing regional distribution

Homonym numbers (indicating different words with the same spelling)

Usage note

Problem spelling (shown by asterisk)

Spelling note

Example of use (taken from real evidence)

Typical pattern or form (in bold)

Part of speech and sense number in synonym section (corresponding to those in main definition section)

delirium. **2** a state of nervous excitement or agitation.

WORDFINDER – antipyretic (*used to prevent or reduce fever*), febrifuge (*medicine used to reduce fever*), febrile (*having or showing the symptoms of fever*).

COMBINATIONS – **fever pitch** a state of extreme excitement.

ORIGIN – Latin *febris*.

fiasco /fɪaskō/ > *noun* (pl. **fiascos**) a ludicrous or humiliating failure.

wordpower facts

Fiasco

Fiasco is an Italian word, meaning 'bottle' or 'flask', and it was briefly used in English in this sense (**flagon** and **flask** come from the same root, Latin *flaska*). However, **fiasco** was taken up more readily in English in the sense 'ludicrous or humiliating failure'; this came from the Italian phrase *far fiasco*, literally 'make a bottle', a phrase used figuratively in Italian theatre to mean 'fail in a performance'.

fives > *plural noun* (treated as sing.) a game in which a ball is hit with a gloved hand or a bat against a wall.

flack¹ N. Amer. informal > *noun* a publicity agent. > *verb* publicise or promote.

flack² > *noun* variant spelling of FLAK.

flaunt > *verb* display ostentatiously.

USAGE – do not confuse **flaunt** with **flout**; **flaunt** means 'display ostentatiously', while **flout** means 'openly disregard (a rule)'.

SYNONYMS – exhibit, parade, show off.

fluorescent* > *adjective* **1** having or showing fluorescence. **2** (of lighting) based on fluorescence from a substance illuminated by ultraviolet light. **3** vividly colourful.

*SPELLING – *fluor-*, not *flour-*: *fluor*escent.

COMBINATIONS – **fluorescent screen** a transparent screen coated with fluorescent material to show images from X-rays.

freak > *noun* **1** (**also freak of nature**) a person, animal, or plant which is abnormal or deformed. **2** (before another noun) unusual and unexpected: *a freak storm.* **3** informal a person who is obsessed with a particular activity or interest. > *verb* (usu. **freak out**) informal behave or cause to behave in a wild and irrational way.

DERIVATIVES – **freakish** adjective.

SYNONYMS – *noun* **1** aberration, abnormality, mutant, oddity.

Pronunciation system

Wordpower uses a respelling system for pronunciation in which specialised symbols are kept to a minimum, and stressed syllables are shown in bold. The dictionary's policy is to give pronunciations for words which may be less familiar or which can present problems even to native English speakers. *Wordpower* does not give pronunciations for ordinary everyday words assumed to be familiar to everyone, such as *bake*, *baby*, *boastful*, and *budget*.

List of respelling symbols

Vowels	Examples	Consonants	Examples
a	*as in* **pat**	b, bb	*as in* **bay, ebony**
aa	*as in* **palm**	ch	*as in* **church**
aar	*as in* **farm**	d, dd	*as in* **dog, adage**
air	*as in* **fair, mayor**	f, ff	*as in* **fit, coffee**
arr	*as in* **carry**	g, gg	*as in* **get, struggle**
aw	*as in* **law, caught**	h	*as in* **head**
awr	*as in* **warm**	j	*as in* **judge, carriage**
ay	*as in* **day**	k, kk	*as in* **kick, gecko**
e	*as in* **men**	<u>kh</u>	*as in* **loch**
ee	*as in* **feet**	ks	*as in* **mix**
eer	*as in* **hear, souvenir**	kw	*as in* **quick**
er	*as in* **fern**	l, ll	*as in* **like, cello**
err	*as in* **ferry**	'l	*as in* **bottle, candle**
ə	*as in* **along**	m, mm	*as in* **may, hammer**
ər	*as in* **parade, bitter**	'm	*as in* **chasm, idealism**
i	*as in* **pin**	n, nn	*as in* **nun, runner**
ī	*as in* **time, buy**	N	*as in* **en route, croissant**
īr	*as in* **fire, desire**	'n	*as in* **wooden, button**
irr	*as in* **lyrics**	ng	*as in* **sing, sink**
o	*as in* **rob**	ngg	*as in* **single, anger**
ō	*as in* **go, hotel**	p, pp	*as in* **pit, supper**
ö	*as in* **colonel, poseur**	r, rr	*as in* **run, fir, spirit**
oo	*as in* **unite, speculate**	s, ss	*as in* **sit, messy**
o͝o	*as in* **wood, sugar**	sh	*as in* **shut, passion**
o͞o	*as in* **food, music**	t, tt	*as in* **taste, butter**
oor	*as in* **tour, jury**	th	*as in* **thin, truth**
or	*as in* **door, corner**	<u>th</u>	*as in* **then, mother**
orr	*as in* **sorry, warrior**	v, vv	*as in* **vet, civil**
ör	*as in* **fleur de lys, voyeur**	w	*as in* **way**
ow	*as in* **mouse, coward**	y	*as in* **yet, tortilla**
owr	*as in* **powerful**	z, zz	*as in* **zero, fuzzy**
oy	*as in* **boy, noisy**	<u>zh</u>	*as in* **measure, vision**
u	*as in* **cut, blood**	–	–
ur	*as in* **curl, journey**	–	–
urr	*as in* **hurry**	–	–

Abbreviations used in the dictionary

adj.	adjective
Austral.	Australian
fem.	feminine
masc.	masculine
N. Amer.	North American
N. English	Northern English
NZ	New Zealand
pl.	plural
pronunc.	pronunciation
S. African	South African
sing.	singular
usu.	usually
W. Indian	West Indian

A¹ (also **a**) > *noun* (pl. **As** or **A's**) **1** the first letter of the alphabet. **2** denoting the first, best, or most important in a set. **3** Music the sixth note of the diatonic scale of C major. **4** the human blood type (in the ABO system) containing the A antigen and lacking the B.
IDIOMS – **from A to B** from one's starting point to one's destination. **from A to Z** over the entire range.
COMBINATIONS – **A level** (in the UK except Scotland) the higher of the two main levels of the GCE examination. [ORIGIN – short for *advanced level*.] **A-line** (of a garment) slightly flared from a narrow waist or shoulders. **A-side** the side of a pop single regarded as the main one.

A² > *abbreviation* **1** ampere(s). **2** (Å) ångstrom(s). **3** (in showing goals or points conceded) against. **4** answer. **5** (in names of sports clubs) Athletic.

a¹ (**an** before a vowel sound) > *determiner* **1** used when mentioning someone or something for the first time; the indefinite article. **2** one single: *a hundred*. **3** someone like (the name specified). **4** per: *typing 60 words a minute*.

a² > *abbreviation* **1** (in travel timetables) arrives. **2** (used before a date) before. [ORIGIN – from Latin *ante*.] **3** Brit. (with reference to sporting fixtures) away.

a-¹ (often **an-** before a vowel) > *prefix* not; without: *atheistic*.
ORIGIN – Greek.

a-² > *prefix* **1** to; towards: *aside*. **2** in the process of: *a-hunting*. **3** in a specified state: *aflutter*.

a-³ > *prefix* **1** of: *anew*. **2** utterly: *abash*.
ORIGIN – unstressed form of **OF** (sense 1); Old French, from Latin *ex* (sense 2).

A1 > *adjective* informal excellent.
ORIGIN – used at Lloyd's Register of Shipping of ships in first-class condition as to hull (A) and stores (1).

AA > *abbreviation* **1** Alcoholics Anonymous. **2** anti-aircraft. **3** Automobile Association.

aardvark /**aard**vaark/ > *noun* a badger-sized African burrowing mammal, with a tubular snout and a long tongue, feeding on ants and termites.
ORIGIN – South African Dutch, from *aarde* 'earth' + *vark* 'pig'.

Aaron's rod > *noun* the plant mullein.
ORIGIN – alluding to *Aaron* in the Bible, whose staff was said to have flowered.

AB¹ > *noun* the human blood type (in the ABO system) containing both the A and B antigens.

AB² > *abbreviation* **1** able seaman. **2** Alberta. **3** US Bachelor of Arts. [ORIGIN – from Latin *Artium Baccalaureus*.]

ab- (also **abs-**) > *prefix* away; from: *abdicate*.
ORIGIN – Latin.

aback > *adverb* archaic towards or situated to the rear.
IDIOMS – **take aback** shock or surprise (someone).

abacus /**abb**əkəss/ > *noun* (pl. **abacuses**) a frame with rows of wires or grooves along which beads are slid, used for calculating.
ORIGIN – Greek *abax* 'slab, drawing board'.

abaft /ə**baaft**/ > *adverb & preposition* Nautical in or behind the stern of a ship.
ORIGIN – from **a-²** + archaic *baft* 'in the rear'.

abalone /abbə**lō**ni/ > *noun* an edible mollusc with an ear-shaped shell lined with mother-of-pearl.
ORIGIN – from an American Indian language.

abandon > *verb* **1** desert or leave permanently. **2** give up (an action or practice) completely. **3** (**abandon oneself to**) indulge in (a desire or impulse) without restraint. > *noun* complete lack of inhibition or restraint.
DERIVATIVES – **abandonment** *noun*.
SYNONYMS – *verb* **1** desert, forsake, leave, quit. **2** drop, give up, refrain from, relinquish, renounce. *noun* recklessness, uninhibitedness.
ORIGIN – Old French *abandoner*, from *bandon* 'control'; related to **BAN¹**.

abandoned > *adjective* unrestrained; uninhibited.

abase /ə**bayss**/ > *verb* (**abase oneself**) behave in a way that lessens others' respect for one.
DERIVATIVES – **abasement** *noun*.
ORIGIN – Old French *abaissier* 'to lower'.

abashed > *adjective* embarrassed, disconcerted, or ashamed.
ORIGIN – from Old French *esbair* 'utterly astound'.

abate /ə**bayt**/ > *verb* **1** (of something bad) become less intense or widespread. **2** Law reduce or remove (a nuisance).
DERIVATIVES – **abatement** *noun*.
SYNONYMS – **1** die down, diminish, ease, recede.
ANTONYMS – **1** intensify.

ORIGIN – Old French *abatre* 'to fell', from Latin *battere* 'to beat'.

abattoir /**abb**ətwaar/ > *noun* a slaughterhouse.
ORIGIN – French, from *abattre* 'to fell'.

abbacy /**abb**əsi/ > *noun* (pl. **abbacies**) the office of an abbot or abbess.

abbatial /ə**bay**sh'l/ > *adjective* relating to an abbey, abbot, or abbess.

abbé /**abb**ay/ > *noun* (in France) an abbot or other cleric.
ORIGIN – French.

abbess /**abb**iss/ > *noun* a woman who is the head of an abbey of nuns.

abbey > *noun* (pl. **abbeys**) an establishment occupied by a community of monks or nuns.
ORIGIN – Latin *abbatia*, from *abbas* 'abbot'.

abbot > *noun* a man who is the head of an abbey of monks.
ORIGIN – Greek *abbas* 'father', from Aramaic.

abbreviate /ə**bree**viayt/ > *verb* shorten (a word, phrase, or text).
SYNONYMS – condense, cut, reduce, shorten.
ORIGIN – Latin *abbreviare*, from *brevis* 'short'.

abbreviation > *noun* **1** a shortened form of a word or phrase. **2** the process or result of abbreviating.
WORDFINDER – acronym (*abbreviation pronounced as a word, e.g. laser, NATO*), initialism (*abbreviation pronounced letter by letter, e.g. BBC, DNA*).

ABC¹ > *noun* **1** the alphabet. **2** an alphabetical guide. **3** the rudiments of a subject.

ABC² > *abbreviation* **1** American Broadcasting Company. **2** Australian Broadcasting Corporation.

abdabs (also **habdabs**) > *plural noun* (often in phrase **the screaming abdabs**) Brit. informal nervous anxiety or tension.

abdicate /**ab**dikayt/ > *verb* **1** (of a monarch) formally give up the throne. **2** fail to fulfil or undertake (a duty).
DERIVATIVES – **abdication** *noun*.
ORIGIN – Latin *abdicare* 'renounce'.

abdomen /**ab**dəmən/ > *noun* **1** the part of the body containing the digestive and reproductive organs; the belly. **2** Zoology the rear part of the body of an arthropod.
DERIVATIVES – **abdominal** /ab**domm**in'l/ *adjective* **abdominally** *adverb*.
ORIGIN – Latin.

abduct > *verb* take (someone) away by force or deception.
DERIVATIVES – **abductee** *noun* **abduction** *noun* **abductor** *noun*.
SYNONYMS – carry off, kidnap, seize, snatch.
ORIGIN – Latin *abducere* 'lead away'.

abeam > *adverb* at right angles to a ship's or an aircraft's length.

abed > *adverb* archaic in bed.

Aberdeen Angus > *noun* a breed of hornless black beef cattle originating in Scotland.

Aberdonian /abbərdōniən/ > *adjective* relating to Aberdeen. > *noun* a person from Aberdeen.

aberrant /əberrənt/ > *adjective* departing from an accepted standard or normal type.

DERIVATIVES – **aberrance** *noun* **aberrancy** *noun* **aberrantly** *adverb*.

aberration /abbəraysh'n/ > *noun* 1 a departure from what is normal or acceptable. 2 a mental or moral lapse. 3 Optics the failure of rays to converge at one focus because of a defect in a lens or mirror.

DERIVATIVES – **aberrational** *adjective*.

SYNONYMS – 1 anomaly, deviation, divergence, irregularity.

ORIGIN – Latin, from *aberrare* 'to stray'.

abet /əbet/ > *verb* (**abetted, abetting**) (usu. in phrase **aid and abet**) encourage or assist (someone) to do something wrong, in particular to commit a crime.

DERIVATIVES – **abetment** *noun* **abetter** (also **abettor**) *noun*.

ORIGIN – Old French *abeter*, from *beter* 'hound, urge on'.

abeyance /əbayənss/ > *noun* (in phrase **in** or **into abeyance**) temporarily suspended or not used.

ORIGIN – first used in the sense 'position of being without an owner or claimant': from Old French *abeance* 'aspiration to a title', from *abeer* 'aspire after'.

ABH > *abbreviation* actual bodily harm.

abhor /əbhor/ > *verb* (**abhorred, abhorring**) regard with disgust and hatred.

SYNONYMS – abominate, detest, hate, loathe.

ORIGIN – Latin *abhorrere*, from *horrere* 'to shudder'.

abhorrent > *adjective* inspiring disgust and loathing.

DERIVATIVES – **abhorrence** *noun*.

SYNONYMS – detestable, loathsome, repugnant, revolting.

abide > *verb* 1 (**abide by**) accept or observe (a rule or decision). 2 informal tolerate: *he could not abide conflict.* 3 (of a feeling or memory) endure. 4 archaic live; dwell.

abiding > *adjective* continuing through time; enduring.

DERIVATIVES – **abidingly** *adverb*.

ability > *noun* (pl. **abilities**) 1 the power or capacity to do something. 2 skill or talent.

SYNONYMS – 1 capability, capacity, faculty, potential, power. 2 accomplishment, expertise, prowess, skill, talent.

ab initio /ab inishiō/ > *adverb* & *adjective* from the beginning.

ORIGIN – Latin.

abject /abjekt/ > *adjective* 1 extremely unpleasant and degrading: *abject poverty.* 2 completely without pride or dignity: *an abject apology.*

DERIVATIVES – **abjection** *noun* **abjectly** *adverb* **abjectness** *noun*.

SYNONYMS – 1 appalling, miserable, wretched. 2 craven, grovelling, obsequious, servile.

ORIGIN – from Latin *abjectus* 'rejected'.

abjure /əbjoor/ > *verb* formal swear to give up (a belief or claim).

DERIVATIVES – **abjuration** *noun*.

ORIGIN – Latin *abjurare*, from *ab-* 'away' + *jurare* 'swear'.

ablation /əblaysh'n/ > *noun* 1 the loss of solid material by melting, evaporation, or erosion. 2 the surgical removal of body tissue.

ORIGIN – Latin, from *auferre* 'take away'.

ablative /ablətiv/ > *adjective* 1 Grammar (of a case) indicating an agent, instrument, or source, expressed by 'by', 'with', or 'from' in English. 2 involving ablation.

ablaze > *adjective* burning fiercely.

able > *adjective* (**abler, ablest**) 1 having the power, skill, or means to do something. 2 skilful and competent.

DERIVATIVES – **ably** *adverb*.

SYNONYMS – 1 (**able to**) capable of, fit to, qualified to, up to. 2 accomplished, competent, proficient, skilful, talented.

ANTONYMS – 1 (**able to**) unable to, incapable of. 2 incompetent, inept.

COMBINATIONS – **able seaman** a rank of sailor in the Royal Navy above ordinary seaman and below leading seaman.

ORIGIN – Latin *habilis* 'handy'.

-able > *suffix* forming adjectives meaning: 1 able to be: *calculable.* 2 subject to; relevant to: *taxable.* 3 having the quality to: *suitable.*

DERIVATIVES – **-ability** *suffix* **-ably** *suffix*.

able-bodied > *adjective* not physically unfit or disabled.

ablution /əblōōsh'n/ > *noun* 1 (**ablutions**) Brit. (in army slang) a room with washing places and toilets. 2 formal or humorous the act of washing oneself.

DERIVATIVES – **ablutionary** *adjective*.

ORIGIN – Latin, from *abluere* 'wash away'.

ABM > *abbreviation* anti-ballistic-missile.

abnegate /abnigayt/ > *verb* formal give up or reject (something desired or valuable).

DERIVATIVES – **abnegation** *noun*.

ORIGIN – Latin *abnegare*, from *negare* 'deny'.

abnormal > *adjective* deviating from what is normal.

DERIVATIVES – **abnormality** *noun* **abnormally** *adverb*.

SYNONYMS – atypical, irregular, odd, unusual.

ANTONYMS – normal, typical.

ORIGIN – Greek *anōmalos* 'uneven'; related to **ANOMALOUS**.

aboard > *adverb* & *preposition* on or into (a ship, train, or other vehicle).

abode > *noun* formal or literary 1 a house or home. 2 residence: *right of abode.*

ORIGIN – from **ABIDE**.

abolish > *verb* formally put an end to (a practice or institution).

SYNONYMS – cancel, end, rescind, scrap.

ORIGIN – Latin *abolere* 'destroy'.

abolition > *noun* the abolishing of a system, practice, or institution.

abolitionist > *noun* a person who favours the abolition of something, especially capital punishment or (formerly) slavery.

DERIVATIVES – **abolitionism** *noun*.

A-bomb > *noun* an atom bomb.

abominable > *adjective* 1 causing moral revulsion. 2 informal very bad; terrible.

DERIVATIVES – **abominably** *adverb*.

SYNONYMS – 1 despicable, detestable, obnoxious, repellent.

COMBINATIONS – **Abominable Snowman** the yeti.

ORIGIN – Latin *abominabilis*, from *abominari* 'deprecate', from *ab-* 'away from' + *omen* 'omen'.

abominate /əbomminayt/ > *verb* formal detest; loathe.

abomination > *noun* 1 an object of disgust or hatred. 2 a feeling of hatred.

aboriginal > *adjective* 1 inhabiting or existing in a land from the earliest times or from before the arrival of colonists; indigenous. 2 (**Aboriginal**) relating to the Australian Aboriginals. > *noun* 1 an aboriginal inhabitant. 2 (**Aboriginal**) a member of one of the indigenous peoples of Australia.

wordpower facts
Aboriginal
There are several hundred Aboriginal languages, most of which are now extinct. They are related to each other but not, apparently, to any other language family. The language that has given English the most words is probably *Dharuk*, formerly spoken in the area around Sydney, from which come **boomerang**, **dingo**, **koala**, **wallaby**, and **wombat**. Other languages include *Wiradhuri* (from which we get **billabong** and **kookaburra**), *Kamilaroi* (the source of **budgerigar**), *Nyungar*, *Warlpiri*, and *Adnyamadhanha*. **Didgeridoo** is from a language of Arnhem Land, while **kangaroo** comes from North Queensland.

aborigine /abbərijini/ > *noun* **1** an aboriginal person, animal, or plant. **2** (**Aborigine**) an Australian aboriginal.
ORIGIN – from Latin *ab origine* 'from the beginning'.

abort > *verb* **1** carry out or undergo the abortion of (a fetus). **2** Biology (of an embryonic organ or organism) remain undeveloped; fail to mature. **3** bring to a premature end because of a problem or fault.
SYNONYMS – **3** call off, discontinue, halt, suspend.
ORIGIN – Latin *aboriri* 'miscarry'.

abortifacient /əbortifaysh'nt/ Medicine > *adjective* (of a drug) causing abortion. > *noun* an abortifacient drug.

abortion > *noun* **1** the deliberate termination of a human pregnancy, before the fetus is able to survive independently. **2** the natural expulsion of a fetus from the womb before it is able to survive independently. **3** informal, derogatory something imperfectly planned or made.
WORDFINDER – miscarriage (*spontaneous loss of a fetus before the 28th week of pregnancy*), stillbirth (*spontaneous loss of a fetus after the 28th week*).

abortionist > *noun* chiefly derogatory a person who carries out abortions.

abortive > *adjective* failing to produce the intended result; unsuccessful.
DERIVATIVES – **abortively** *adverb*.

ABO system > *noun* a system of four basic types (A, AB, B, and O) into which human blood may be classified according to the presence or absence of particular antigens.

abound > *verb* **1** exist in large numbers or amounts. **2** (**abound in** or **with**) have in large numbers or amounts.
SYNONYMS – **1** be abundant, be numerous, be plentiful. **2** (**abound in or with**) be full of, overflow with, teem with.
ORIGIN – Latin *abundare* 'overflow', from *unda* 'a wave'.

about > *preposition & adverb* **1** on the subject of; concerning. **2** used to indicate movement within a particular area or location in a particular place. **3** approximately.
IDIOMS – **be about to** be on the point of.

about-turn (also chiefly N. Amer. **about-face**) > *noun* **1** Military a turn made so as to face the opposite direction. **2** informal a complete change of opinion or policy.

above > *preposition & adverb* **1** at a higher level than. **2** in preference to. **3** (in printed text) mentioned earlier.
IDIOMS – **above all** (**else**) more so than anything else. **above board** legitimate and honest. **above oneself** conceited. **not be above** be capable of doing (something unworthy).

abracadabra > *exclamation* a word said by conjurors when performing a magic trick.

abrade /əbrayd/ > *verb* scrape or wear away.
ORIGIN – Latin *abradere* 'scrape away'.

abrasion /əbrayzh'n/ > *noun* **1** the action or process of abrading or being abraded. **2** an area of scraped skin.

abrasive /əbraysiv/ > *adjective* **1** capable of polishing or cleaning a hard surface by rubbing or grinding. **2** harsh or rough in manner. > *noun* a substance used for abrading.
DERIVATIVES – **abrasively** *adverb* **abrasiveness** *noun*.

abreaction > *noun* Psychoanalysis the expression and consequent release of a previously repressed emotion, achieved through hypnosis or suggestion.

abreast > *adverb* **1** side by side and facing the same way. **2** alongside. **3** (**abreast of**) up to date with.

abridge > *verb* shorten (a text or film).
DERIVATIVES – **abridgement** (also **abridgment**) *noun* **abridger** *noun*.
ORIGIN – Latin *abbreviare*, from *brevis* 'short'.

abroad > *adverb* **1** in or to a foreign country or countries. **2** in different directions; over a wide area. **3** at large; in circulation. **4** archaic out of doors. > *noun* foreign countries collectively.

abrogate /abrəgayt/ > *verb* formal repeal or do away with (a law or agreement).
DERIVATIVES – **abrogation** *noun* **abrogator** *noun*.
ORIGIN – Latin *abrogare* 'repeal'.

abrupt > *adjective* **1** sudden and unexpected. **2** brief to the point of rudeness; curt. **3** steep.
DERIVATIVES – **abruptly** *adverb* **abruptness** *noun*.
SYNONYMS – **1** sudden, startling, unexpected, unforeseen. **2** blunt, brusque, curt, gruff, terse.
ORIGIN – from Latin *abruptus* 'broken off, steep', from *rumpere* 'break'.

ABS > *abbreviation* anti-lock braking system.

abscess* > *noun* a swollen area within body tissue, containing pus.
*SPELLING – remember *s* and *c*: ab*s*ce*s*s.
ORIGIN – Latin *abscessus*, from *abscedere* 'go away'.

abscissa /absissə/ > *noun* (pl. **abscissae** /absissee/ or **abscissas**) Mathematics the distance from a point on a graph to the vertical or *y*-axis; the *x*-coordinate.
ORIGIN – from Latin *abscissa linea* 'cut-off line'.

abscission /əbsizh'n/ > *noun* Botany the process by which parts of a plant, e.g. dead leaves, break off naturally.

abscond /əbskond/ > *verb* leave hurriedly and secretly to escape from custody or avoid arrest.
DERIVATIVES – **absconder** *noun*.
ORIGIN – Latin *abscondere* 'hide'.

abseil* /absayl/ > *verb* descend a near-vertical surface using a rope coiled round the body and fixed at a higher point.
DERIVATIVES – **abseiler** *noun* **abseiling** *noun*.
*SPELLING – ab*seil*, not -*sail*.
ORIGIN – German *abseilen*, from *ab* 'down' + *Seil* 'rope'.

absence > *noun* **1** the state of being away from a place or person. **2** (**absence of**) the non-existence or lack of.
IDIOMS – **absence makes the heart grow fonder** proverb you feel more affection for those you love when parted from them.

absent > *adjective* /abs'nt/ **1** not present. **2** showing a lack of attention. > *verb* /absent/ (**absent oneself**) stay or go away.
DERIVATIVES – **absently** *adverb*.
SYNONYMS – *adjective* **1** away, missing, out, unavailable. **2** distracted, dreamy, inattentive, preoccupied.
ANTONYMS – *adjective* **1** present. **2** attentive.
ORIGIN – from Latin *abesse* 'to be away'.

absentee > *noun* a person who is absent.

absenteeism > *noun* frequent absence from work or school without good reason.

absent-minded > *adjective* inattentive or forgetful.
DERIVATIVES – **absent-mindedly** *adverb* **absent-mindedness** *noun*.

absinth /absinth/ > *noun* **1** the shrub wormwood. **2** (usu. **absinthe**) a green aniseed-flavoured liqueur formerly made with wormwood.
ORIGIN – French, from Greek *apsinthion* 'wormwood'.

absolute > *adjective* **1** not qualified or diminished in any way; total. **2** having unlimited power: *an absolute ruler*. **3** not relative or comparative: *absolute moral principles*. **4** Grammar (of a construction) syntactically independent of the rest of the sentence, as in *dinner being over, we left the table*; (of a transitive verb) used without an expressed object (e.g. *guns kill*); (of an adjective) used without an expressed noun (e.g. *the brave*). **5** Law (of a decree) final. > *noun* Philosophy a value or principle which is universally valid or able to be viewed without relation to other things.
DERIVATIVES – **absoluteness** *noun*.
SYNONYMS – *adjective* **1** complete, outright, pure, total, utter. **2** autocratic, despotic, dictatorial, tyrannical. **3** incontrovertible, set, universal.
ANTONYMS – *adjective* **1** qualified, partial. **2** constitutional. **3** relative.
COMBINATIONS – **absolute majority** a majority over all rivals combined; more

3

than half. **absolute pitch** Music **1** perfect pitch. **2** pitch according to a fixed standard defined by the frequency of the sound vibration. **absolute temperature** a temperature measured from absolute zero in kelvins. **absolute zero** the lowest temperature theoretically possible (zero kelvins, −273.15°C).

ORIGIN − Latin *absolutus* 'freed, unrestricted', from *absolvere* 'set free, acquit'.

absolutely > *adverb* **1** with no qualification, restriction, or limitation. **2** used for emphasis or to express agreement. **3** not viewed in relation to other things or factors.

SYNONYMS − **1** completely, exactly, totally, utterly.

absolution > *noun* **1** formal release from guilt, obligation, or punishment. **2** formal declaration by a priest that a person's sins are forgiven.

SYNONYMS − **1** exoneration, forgiveness, pardon, reprieve.

absolutism > *noun* **1** the principle that those in government should have unlimited power. **2** belief in absolute principles in philosophy.

DERIVATIVES − **absolutist** *noun & adjective*.

absolve /əzolv/ > *verb* **1** declare (someone) free from guilt or responsibility. **2** give absolution for (a sin).

ORIGIN − Latin *absolvere* 'set free, acquit'.

absorb /əbzorb, -sorb/ > *verb* **1** soak up (liquid or another substance). **2** take in (information). **3** assimilate or swallow up (something less powerful). **4** use up (time or resources). **5** reduce the effect or intensity of (sound or an impact). **6** engross the attention of.

DERIVATIVES − **absorbable** *adjective* **absorbed** *adjective* **absorber** *noun* **absorbing** *adjective*.

SYNONYMS − **2** assimilate, digest, take in, understand. **4** consume, occupy, use up. **6** engross, immerse, preoccupy.

ORIGIN − Latin *absorbere* 'suck in'.

absorbent > *adjective* able to soak up liquid easily.

DERIVATIVES − **absorbency** *noun*.

absorption > *noun* the process of absorbing or the action of being absorbed.

DERIVATIVES − **absorptive** *adjective*.

abstain > *verb* **1** (often **abstain from**) restrain oneself from doing or indulging in something. **2** formally choose not to vote.

DERIVATIVES − **abstainer** *noun*.

SYNONYMS − **1** (**abstain from**) avoid, give up, refrain from.

ORIGIN − Latin *abstinere* 'hold from'.

abstemious /əbsteemiəss/ > *adjective* not self-indulgent, especially as regards eating and drinking.

DERIVATIVES − **abstemiously** *adverb* **abstemiousness** *noun*.

SYNONYMS − abstinent, moderate, restrained, sober, temperate.

ANTONYMS − intemperate.

ORIGIN − Latin *abstemius*, from *ab-* 'from' + a word related to *temetum* 'alcoholic liquor'.

abstention /əbstensh'n/ > *noun* **1** an instance of abstaining from a vote. **2** abstinence.

abstinence /abstinənss/ > *noun* the practice of abstaining, especially from drinking alcohol.

DERIVATIVES − **abstinent** *adjective*.

abstract > *adjective* /abstrakt/ **1** theoretical rather than physical or concrete. **2** (of art) achieving its effect through colour and shapes rather than attempting to represent recognisable reality. > *verb* /əbstrakt/ **1** extract or remove. **2** (**abstract oneself**) leave or withdraw. **3** consider theoretically or separately from something else. **4** make a written summary of. > *noun* /abstrakt/ **1** a summary of a book or article. **2** an abstract work of art.

DERIVATIVES − **abstractly** *adverb* **abstractor** *noun*.

SYNONYMS − *adjective* **1** conceptual, metaphysical, notional, theoretical.

ANTONYMS − *adjective* **1** actual, concrete.

COMBINATIONS − **abstract expressionism** a kind of abstract art aiming at subjective emotional expression with particular emphasis on spontaneous creativity (e.g. action painting).

ORIGIN − from Latin *abstrahere* 'draw off'.

abstracted > *adjective* not concentrating on what is happening; preoccupied.

DERIVATIVES − **abstractedly** *adverb*.

abstraction > *noun* **1** the quality of being abstract. **2** something which exists only as an idea. **3** a preoccupied state. **4** abstracting or removing something.

abstruse /əbstrooss/ > *adjective* difficult to understand; obscure.

DERIVATIVES − **abstrusely** *adverb* **abstruseness** *noun*.

SYNONYMS − complicated, confusing, incomprehensible, obscure.

ANTONYMS − clear, obvious.

ORIGIN − Latin *abstrusus* 'concealed'.

absurd > *adjective* completely unreasonable, illogical, or inappropriate.

DERIVATIVES − **absurdity** *noun* **absurdly** *adverb*.

SYNONYMS − illogical, inappropriate, nonsensical, ridiculous, unreasonable.

ORIGIN − Latin *absurdus* 'out of tune', hence 'irrational'; related to *surdus* 'deaf, dull'.

ABTA > *abbreviation* Association of British Travel Agents.

abundance /əbundənss/ > *noun* **1** a very large quantity of something. **2** plentifulness

or prosperity. **3** the amount of something present.

SYNONYMS − **1** copiousness, cornucopia, mass, plentifulness, profusion.

ANTONYMS − **1** scarcity, lack.

ORIGIN − Latin *abundantia*, from *abundare* 'overflow'.

abundant > *adjective* **1** existing or available in large quantities; plentiful. **2** (**abundant in**) having plenty of.

SYNONYMS − **1** copious, plentiful, profuse, rich.

abundantly > *adverb* **1** in large quantities; plentifully. **2** extremely.

abuse > *verb* /əbyooz/ **1** use improperly or to excess. **2** treat with cruelty or violence, in particular assault sexually. **3** speak to in an insulting and offensive way. > *noun* /əbyooss/ **1** the improper use of something. **2** cruel and violent treatment, in particular sexual assault. **3** insulting and offensive language.

DERIVATIVES − **abuser** *noun*.

SYNONYMS − *verb* **1** exploit, misuse. **2** assault, hurt, maltreat, molest. **3** insult, swear at, vilify. *noun* **3** invective, swearing, vilification.

ORIGIN − Latin *abuti* 'misuse'.

abusive > *adjective* **1** extremely offensive and insulting. **2** involving cruelty and violence.

DERIVATIVES − **abusively** *adverb* **abusiveness** *noun*.

abut /əbut/ > *verb* (**abutted**, **abutting**) **1** be next to or share a boundary with. **2** touch or lean on.

ORIGIN − Old French *abouter*, from *bouter* 'strike, butt'.

abutilon /əbyootilon/ > *noun* a herbaceous plant or shrub growing in warm climates, with showy yellow, red, or mauve flowers.

ORIGIN − Latin, from an Arabic word meaning 'Indian mallow'.

abutment > *noun* a structure supporting the side of an arch, especially at the end of a bridge.

abysmal > *adjective* **1** informal extremely bad. **2** literary very deep.

DERIVATIVES − **abysmally** *adverb*.

abyss /əbiss/ > *noun* **1** a very deep chasm. **2** (**the abyss**) a catastrophic situation:

ORIGIN − from Greek *abussos* 'bottomless'.

abyssal > *adjective* **1** relating to the depths of the ocean. **2** Geology plutonic.

Abyssinian /abissiniən/ > *adjective* historical relating to Abyssinia (the former name of Ethiopia). > *noun* **1** historical a person from Abyssinia. **2** a breed of cat having long ears and short brown hair flecked with grey.

AC > *abbreviation* **1** alternating current. **2** air conditioning. **3** Aircraftman. **4** appellation contrôlée. **5** athletic club.

Ac > *symbol* the chemical element actinium.

a/c > *abbreviation* **1** account. **2** (also **A/C**) air conditioning.

acacia /əkaysha/ > *noun* a tree or shrub of warm climates with yellow or white flowers.
ORIGIN – Greek *akakia*.

academe /akkədeem/ > *noun* (often in phrase **the groves of academe**) academia.

academia /akkədeemiə/ > *noun* the academic environment or community.

academic > *adjective* 1 relating to education and scholarship. 2 scholarly rather than technical or practical. 3 not of practical relevance. > *noun* a teacher or scholar in an institute of higher education.
DERIVATIVES – **academically** *adverb*.

academician /əkaddəmish'n/ > *noun* 1 a member of an academy. 2 N. Amer. an academic.

academicism /akkədemmisiz'm/ > *noun* adherence to formal or conventional rules and traditions in art or literature.

academy > *noun* (pl. **academies**) 1 a place of study or training in a special field. 2 a society or institution of distinguished scholars, artists, or scientists. 3 US & Scottish a secondary school.
COMBINATIONS – **Academy award** an award given by the Academy of Motion Picture Arts and Sciences for achievement in the film industry; an Oscar.
ORIGIN – Greek *akadēmeia*, from *Akadēmos*, the name of the garden where Plato taught.

Acadian /əkaydiən/ > *adjective* relating to the former French colony of Acadia (now Nova Scotia) in Canada. > *noun* a person from Acadia.

acanthus /əkanthəss/ > *noun* 1 a plant or shrub with bold flower spikes and spiny decorative leaves. 2 Architecture a representation of an acanthus leaf.
ORIGIN – Greek *akanthos*, from *akantha* 'thorn'.

a cappella /a kəpellə/ > *adjective & adverb* (of music) sung without instrumental accompaniment.
ORIGIN – Italian, 'in chapel style'.

acaricide > *noun* a substance poisonous to mites or ticks.
ORIGIN – from Greek *akari* 'mite, tick'.

ACAS /aykass/ > *abbreviation* Advisory, Conciliation, and Arbitration Service.

accede /əkseed/ > *verb* (usu. **accede to**) formal 1 assent or agree to a demand, request, or treaty. 2 take up an office or position.
ORIGIN – Latin *accedere* 'come to'.

accelerando /əksellərandō, əchel-/ > *adverb & adjective* Music with a gradual increase of speed.
ORIGIN – Italian.

accelerant > *noun* a substance used to help fire spread.

accelerate /əksellərayt/ > *verb* 1 begin or cause to move more quickly. 2 increase in rate, amount, or extent.
DERIVATIVES – **acceleration** *noun*.
SYNONYMS – 1 go faster, hasten, hurry up, speed up.
ANTONYMS – 1 decelerate, slow down.
ORIGIN – Latin *accelerare* 'hasten', from *celer* 'swift'.

accelerator > *noun* 1 a foot pedal which controls the speed of a vehicle's engine. 2 Physics an apparatus for accelerating charged particles to high velocities. 3 a substance that speeds up a chemical process.

accelerometer /əksellərommitər/ > *noun* an instrument for measuring acceleration.

accent > *noun* /aks'nt, aksent/ 1 a way of pronouncing a language, associated with a country, area, or social class. 2 an emphasis given to a syllable, word, or note. 3 a mark on a letter or word indicating how a sound is pronounced or stressed. 4 a particular emphasis: *the accent is on participation*. > *verb* /aksent/ 1 (**accented**) spoken with a particular accent. 2 stress (a word, syllable, or note). 3 emphasise (a feature).
DERIVATIVES – **accentual** *adjective*.

wordpower facts
Accent
The word **accent** comes from Latin *accentus* 'tone, signal, or intensity', which was formed from *ad-* 'to' + *cantus* 'song' and was a direct translation of the Greek word *prosōidia* 'a song sung to music, intonation', literally 'song added to (speech)'. In Greek and Latin the syllables of a word were pronounced with a distinct difference in musical pitch. Syllables marked with a *grave* accent (from Latin *gravis* 'heavy, serious') were spoken at a comparatively low pitch, those with an *acute* (from Latin *acutus* 'sharp, high') at a higher pitch, and those with a *circumflex* (from Latin *circumflexus*, 'bent around') began at the higher pitch and descended during the pronunciation of the syllable. This variation in pitch was eventually replaced by a system whereby accent was marked by greater or lesser stress, as in English.

accentuate /əksentyooayt/ > *verb* make more noticeable or prominent.
DERIVATIVES – **accentuation** *noun*.
SYNONYMS – emphasise, highlight, stress, underline.

accept > *verb* 1 agree to receive or undertake (something offered). 2 regard favourably or with approval. 3 believe to be valid or correct. 4 take on (a responsibility or liability). 5 tolerate or submit to.

DERIVATIVES – **acceptance** *noun* **acceptor** *noun*.
SYNONYMS – 2 approve of, embrace, greet, welcome. 3 believe, credit, trust. 4 acknowledge, adopt, recognise.
ORIGIN – Latin *acceptare*, from *capere* 'take'.

acceptable > *adjective* 1 able to be accepted. 2 adequate, though not outstanding or perfect.
DERIVATIVES – **acceptability** *noun* **acceptably** *adverb*.
SYNONYMS – 1 admissible, justifiable, welcome. 2 adequate, fair, satisfactory, sufficient, tolerable.

access > *noun* 1 the means or opportunity to approach or enter a place. 2 the right or opportunity to use something or see someone. 3 retrieval of information stored in a computer's memory. 4 an attack or outburst of an emotion: *an access of rage*. > *verb* 1 gain access to; make accessible. 2 approach or enter (a place).
ORIGIN – Latin *accessus*, from *accedere* 'come to'.

accessible > *adjective* 1 able to be accessed. 2 friendly and easy to talk to; approachable. 3 easily understood or appreciated.
DERIVATIVES – **accessibility** *noun* **accessibly** *adverb*.
SYNONYMS – 1 reachable. 2 affable, approachable, congenial, friendly, welcoming. 3 comprehensible, intelligible, understandable.
ANTONYMS – inaccessible.

accession > *noun* 1 the attainment of a position of rank. 2 the formal acceptance of a treaty or joining of an association. 3 a new item added to a library or museum collection.

accessorise (also **accessorize**) > *verb* add a fashion accessory to (a garment).

accessory (also **accessary**) > *noun* (pl. **accessories**) 1 a thing which can be added to something else to make it more useful, versatile, or attractive. 2 a small article carried or worn to complement a garment. 3 Law a person who helps someone commit a crime without taking part in it. > *adjective* chiefly technical subsidiary or supplementary.
SYNONYMS – *noun* 1 addition, attachment, extra, supplement.
ORIGIN – Latin *accessorius* 'additional thing'.

accident > *noun* 1 something unfortunate that happens unexpectedly and unintentionally. 2 something that happens by chance or without apparent cause. 3 chance.
IDIOMS – **accidents will happen in the best regulated families** proverb however careful you try to be, it is inevitable that unfortunate or unforeseen events will occur.

5

SYNONYMS – **1** calamity, misfortune, mishap, tragedy.

ORIGIN – from Latin *accidere* 'to fall or happen'.

accidental > *adjective* **1** happening by accident. **2** incidental; subsidiary. > *noun* Music a sign indicating a momentary departure from the key signature by raising or lowering a note.

DERIVATIVES – **accidentally** *adverb*.

accidie /aksidee/ > *noun* depression, apathy, or listlessness.

ORIGIN – Latin *accidia*, from Greek *akēdia* 'listlessness'.

acclaim > *verb* praise enthusiastically and publicly. > *noun* enthusiastic public praise.

SYNONYMS – *verb* celebrate, eulogise, extol, praise. *noun* acclamation, applause, plaudits, praise.

ORIGIN – Latin *acclamare*, from *clamare* 'to shout'.

acclamation > *noun* loud and enthusiastic approval or praise.

IDIOMS – **by acclamation** (of election, agreement, etc.) by shouting approval rather than by voting.

acclimate /aklimayt, əklī-/ > *verb* chiefly N. Amer. acclimatise.

DERIVATIVES – **acclimation** *noun*.

acclimatise (also **acclimatize**) > *verb* make or become accustomed to a new climate or new conditions.

DERIVATIVES – **acclimatisation** *noun*.

acclivity /əklivviti/ > *noun* (pl. **acclivities**) an upward slope.

ORIGIN – Latin *acclivitas*, from *clivus* 'a slope'.

accolade /akkəlayd, akkəlayd/ > *noun* something given as a special honour or in recognition of merit.

wordpower facts

Accolade

In English an **accolade** was originally a gesture performed by a monarch when knighting someone, in different periods an embrace, a kiss, and a touch on a person's shoulders with a sword. The word comes from Provençal *acolada*, which literally meant 'embrace around the neck' and was based on Latin *ad-* 'to' + *collum* 'neck'. Thus **accolade** is linked to words such as **col**, **collar**, and **décolletage**.

accommodate* > *verb* **1** provide lodging or space for. **2** adapt to or fit in with.

*SPELLING – double *c*, double *m*: ac**c**o**mm**odate.

SYNONYMS – **1** house, lodge, put up, take in.

ORIGIN – Latin *accommodare*, from *commodus* 'fitting'.

accommodating > *adjective* willing to help or fit in with someone's wishes.

DERIVATIVES – **accommodatingly** *adverb*.

accommodation > *noun* **1** a room, building, or space where someone may live or stay. **2** (**accommodations**) chiefly N. Amer. lodgings. **3** a settlement or compromise. **4** adaptation to changing circumstances.

SYNONYMS – **1** housing, lodgings, quarters.

COMBINATIONS – **accommodation address** Brit. an address used by a person unable or unwilling to give a permanent address.

accompaniment > *noun* **1** a musical part which accompanies an instrument, voice, or group. **2** something that supplements or complements something else.

accompanist > *noun* a person who provides a musical accompaniment.

accompany > *verb* (**accompanies, accompanied**) **1** go somewhere with (someone). **2** be present or occur at the same time as. **3** play musical support or backing for (an instrument, voice, or group).

SYNONYMS – **1** escort, partner, travel with. **2** appear with, attend, coexist with, coincide with.

ORIGIN – Old French *accompagner*, from *compaignon* 'companion'.

accomplice /əkumpliss/ > *noun* a person who helps another commit a crime.

ORIGIN – from obsolete *complice* 'an associate', from Latin *complex* 'allied'.

accomplish > *verb* achieve or complete successfully.

SYNONYMS – attain, carry out, fulfil, realise.

ORIGIN – Old French *acomplir*, from Latin *complere* 'fill up, finish, fulfil'.

accomplished > *adjective* highly trained or skilled.

accomplishment > *noun* **1** something that has been achieved successfully. **2** an activity that one can do well. **3** the successful achievement of a task.

SYNONYMS – **1** achievement, deed, feat, triumph. **2** ability, attainment, skill, talent.

accord > *verb* **1** give or grant someone (power or recognition). **2** (**accord with**) be in agreement or consistent with. > *noun* **1** an official agreement or treaty. **2** agreement in opinion or feeling.

IDIOMS – **of one's own accord** voluntarily or without outside intervention. **with one accord** in a united way.

SYNONYMS – *verb* **1** award, confer, give, grant. **2** (**accord with**) agree with, correspond with, harmonise with, tally with. *noun* **2** agreement, concord, harmony.

ORIGIN – Old French *acorder* 'reconcile', from Latin *cor* 'heart'.

accordance > *noun* (in phrase **in accordance with**) in a manner conforming with.

according > *adverb* **1** (**according to**) as stated by or in. **2** (**according to**) corresponding or in proportion to. **3** (**according as**) depending on whether.

accordingly > *adverb* **1** appropriately. **2** consequently.

accordion /əkordiən/ > *noun* a musical instrument played by stretching and squeezing with the hands to work a bellows, the melody and chords being sounded by buttons or keys.

DERIVATIVES – **accordionist** *noun*.

ORIGIN – from Italian *accordare* 'to tune'.

accost > *verb* approach and address boldly or aggressively.

ORIGIN – French *accoster*, from Latin *costa* 'rib, side'.

account > *noun* **1** a description of an event or experience. **2** a record of financial expenditure and receipts. **3** a service through a bank or similar organisation by which funds are held on behalf of a client or goods or services are supplied on credit. **4** importance: *money was of no account to her*. > *verb* **1** consider or regard in a specified way. **2** (**account for**) supply or make up (a specified amount). **3** (**account for**) give a satisfactory record or explanation of. **4** (**account for**) succeed in killing or defeating.

IDIOMS – **call** (or **bring**) **to account** require (someone) to explain a mistake or poor performance. **money of account** denominations of money used in reckoning but not current as coins. **on someone's account** for a specified person's benefit. **on account of** because of. **on no account** under no circumstances. **on one's own account** with one's own money or assets. **take account of** consider along with other factors before reaching a decision. **there's no accounting for tastes** (or **taste**) proverb it's impossible to explain why different people like different things, especially those things which the speaker considers unappealing. **turn to (good) account** turn to one's advantage.

SYNONYMS – *noun* **1** description, record, report, story, tale. **4** consequence, importance, significance. *verb* **1** consider, deem, regard, view as. **2** (**account for**) comprise, constitute, form, make up. **3** (**account for**) explain, justify.

ORIGIN – Old French *acont*, from *conter* 'to count'.

accountable > *adjective* **1** required or expected to justify actions or decisions. **2** understandable.

DERIVATIVES – **accountability** *noun* **accountably** *adverb*.

accountancy > *noun* the profession or duties of an accountant.

accountant > *noun* a person who keeps or inspects financial accounts.

accounting > *noun* the keeping of financial accounts.

accoutre /əkōōtər/ (US **accouter**) > *verb* (**accoutred, accoutring**; US **accoutered, accoutering**) clothe or equip.
ORIGIN – French *accoutrer*, from *couture* 'sewing'.

accoutrement /əkōōtrəmənt/ (US also **accouterment**) > *noun* **1** an additional item of dress or equipment. **2** (**accoutrements**) a soldier's outfit other than weapons and garments.

accredit > *verb* (**accredited, accrediting**) **1** (**accredit to**) attribute (something) to (someone). **2** give official authorisation to. **3** send (a diplomat or journalist) to a particular place or post.
DERIVATIVES – **accreditation** *noun*.

accrete /əkreet/ > *verb* grow or form by gradual accumulation.
ORIGIN – Latin *accrescere* 'grow'.

accretion /əkreesh'n/ > *noun* **1** growth or increase by gradual accumulation. **2** a thing formed or added in this way.

accrue /əkrōō/ > *verb* (**accrues, accrued, accruing**) **1** (of a benefit or sum of money) be received in regular or increasing amounts. **2** accumulate or receive (payments or benefits).
DERIVATIVES – **accrual** *noun*.
ORIGIN – Latin *accrescere* 'grow'.

acculturate /əkulchərayt/ > *verb* absorb and integrate into a different culture.
DERIVATIVES – **acculturation** *noun*.

accumulate* /əkyōōmyoolayt/ > *verb* **1** gather together a number or quantity of. **2** gather or build up.
DERIVATIVES – **accumulation** *noun* **accumulative** *adjective*.
*SPELLING – two *c*s, one *m*: *accumulate*.
SYNONYMS – **1** amass, assemble, collect, pile up.
ORIGIN – Latin *accumulare* 'heap up', from *cumulus* 'a heap'.

accumulator > *noun* **1** a person or thing that accumulates. **2** Brit. a large rechargeable electric cell. **3** Brit. a bet placed on a series of events, the winnings and stake from each being placed on the next.

accurate /akyoorət/ > *adjective* **1** correct in all details. **2** capable of or successful in reaching the intended target.
DERIVATIVES – **accuracy** *noun* **accurately** *adverb*.
USAGE – strictly speaking, **accurate** does not mean the same as **precise**. **Accurate** means 'correct in all details', while **precise** contains the idea of trying to specify details

exactly: if you say 'It's 4.04 and 12 seconds' you are being *precise*, but not necessarily *accurate* (your watch might be slow).
SYNONYMS – **1** correct, exact, right.
ORIGIN – from Latin *accurare* 'do with care', from *cura* 'care'.

accursed /əkursid, əkurst/ > *adjective* **1** literary under a curse. **2** informal horrible.

accusation > *noun* a charge or claim that someone has done something illegal or wrong.

accusative /əkyōōzətiv/ Grammar > *adjective* (of a case) expressing the object of an action or the goal of motion.
ORIGIN – from Latin *casus accusativus* 'the case showing cause'.

accuse > *verb* (often **accuse of**) **1** charge with an offence or crime. **2** claim that (someone) has done (something wrong).
DERIVATIVES – **accusatory** *adjective* **accuser** *noun*.
SYNONYMS – **2** (**accuse of**) blame for, charge with, implicate in.
ORIGIN – Latin *accusare* 'call to account', from *causa* 'reason, motive, lawsuit'.

accustom > *verb* **1** (**accustom to**) make used to. **2** (**be accustomed to**) be used to.
SYNONYMS – **2** (**be accustomed to**) be familiar with, be habituated to, be practised in, be used to.
ORIGIN – Old French *acostumer*, from *costume* 'custom'.

accustomed > *adjective* customary; usual.

AC/DC > *adjective* **1** alternating current/direct current. **2** informal bisexual.

ace > *noun* **1** a playing card with a single spot on it, the highest card in its suit in most games. **2** informal a person who is very good at a particular activity. **3** Tennis a service that an opponent is unable to return. **4** Golf a hole in one. > *adjective* informal very good. > *verb* informal (in tennis) serve an ace against (someone).
IDIOMS – **ace up one's sleeve** (or N. Amer. **in the hole**) a plan or piece of information kept secret until required. **hold all the aces** have all the advantages. **within an ace of** very close to.
ORIGIN – Latin *as* 'unity, a unit'.

acellular > *adjective* Biology **1** not divided into or containing cells. **2** consisting of one cell only.

-aceous > *suffix* **1** Botany forming adjectives from family names: *ericaceous*. **2** chiefly Biology & Geology forming adjectives describing similarity: *olivaceous*.
ORIGIN – from Latin *-aceus*.

acephalous /aysseffələss, -kef-/ > *adjective* without a head.
ORIGIN – Greek *akephalos*, from *kephalē* 'head'.

acerbic /əserbik/ > *adjective* **1** sharp and

forthright. **2** archaic or technical tasting sour or bitter.
DERIVATIVES – **acerbically** *adverb* **acerbity** *noun*.
ORIGIN – Latin *acerbus* 'sour-tasting'.

acetaldehyde /assitaldihīd/ > *noun* Chemistry a colourless volatile liquid aldehyde.

acetaminophen /əseetəminnəfen/ > *noun* North American term for **PARACETAMOL**.

acetate /assitayt/ > *noun* **1** Chemistry a salt or ester of acetic acid. **2** fibre or plastic made of cellulose acetate. **3** a transparency made of cellulose acetate film.

acetic acid /əseetik/ > *noun* the organic acid that gives vinegar its characteristic taste.
ORIGIN – from Latin *acetum* 'vinegar'.

acetone /assitōn/ > *noun* a colourless volatile liquid ketone used as a solvent and in chemical synthesis.

acetylene /əsettileen/ > *noun* a gas which burns with a bright flame, used in welding.

Achaean /əkeeən/ > *noun* **1** a person from Achaea in ancient Greece. **2** literary a Greek. > *adjective* relating to Achaea or the Achaeans.

ache > *noun* a continuous or prolonged dull pain. > *verb* **1** suffer from an ache. **2** (often **ache for**) feel an intense desire; yearn.
DERIVATIVES – **aching** *adjective* **achingly** *adverb*.
SYNONYMS – *verb* **1** be painful, hurt, throb. **2** (**ache for**) long for, pine for, yearn for.

wordpower facts

Ache

In Old English **ache** was spelled *æce* as a noun and *acan* as a verb. In Middle and early modern English the noun was spelled *atche* and rhymed with 'batch' and the verb was spelled and pronounced as it is today. The noun began to be pronounced like the verb around 1700; the modern spelling is largely due to the lexicographer and writer Samuel Johnson, who mistakenly assumed it to be derived from Greek *akhos* 'pain'.

achene /əkeen/ > *noun* Botany a small, dry one-seeded fruit that does not open to release the seed.
ORIGIN – Latin *achaenium*, from *a-* 'not' + Greek *khainein* 'to gape'.

achieve* > *verb* bring about or accomplish by effort, skill, or courage.
DERIVATIVES – **achievable** *adjective* **achiever** *noun*.
*SPELLING – the usual rule is *i* before *e* except after *c*: *achieve*.

SYNONYMS – accomplish, attain, fulfil, realise.

ORIGIN – Old French *achever* 'come or bring to a head', from *a chief* 'to a head'.

achievement > *noun* **1** a thing that is achieved. **2** the process or fact of achieving.

SYNONYMS – **1** accomplishment, attainment, deed, feat, triumph.

Achilles' heel /əkilleez/ > *noun* a weakness or vulnerable point.

ORIGIN – from the mythological Greek hero *Achilles*, whose mother plunged him into the River Styx when he was a baby, thus making his body invulnerable except for the heel by which she held him.

Achilles tendon > *noun* the tendon connecting calf muscles to the heel.

achondroplasia /əkondrōplayziə, aykon-/ > *noun* Medicine a hereditary condition in which the growth of long bones is retarded, resulting in short limbs.

ORIGIN – from A-¹ + Greek *khondros* 'cartilage' + *plasis* 'moulding'.

achromatic /akrōmattik/ > *adjective* **1** transmitting light without separating it into colours. **2** without colour.

achy > *adjective* (**achier, achiest**) suffering from an ache or aches.

acid > *noun* **1** a substance with chemical properties that include turning litmus red, neutralising alkalis, and dissolving some metals. **2** informal the drug LSD. > *adjective* **1** having the properties of an acid; having a pH of less than 7. **2** sharp-tasting or sour. **3** (of a remark) bitter or cutting.

WORDFINDER – alkali, base (*substance reacting with acids*), amphoteric (*reacting as either acid or alkali*), indicator (*substance showing acidity by colour change*), litmus test (*test for acid or alkali*), neutral (*neither acid nor alkaline*), pH (*scale of acidity or alkalinity*).

DERIVATIVES – **acidic** *adjective* **acidly** *adverb* **acidy** *adjective*.

COMBINATIONS – **acid drop** Brit. a boiled sweet with a sharp taste. **acid house** a kind of fast, repetitive synthesised dance music. **acid jazz** a kind of dance music incorporating elements of jazz, funk, soul, and hip hop. **acid rain** rainfall made acidic by sulphur and nitrogen oxides from the industrial burning of fossil fuels. **acid rock** a style of rock music popular in the late 1960s, associated with hallucinogenic drugs. **acid test** a conclusive test of success or value. [ORIGIN – from the original use denoting a test for gold using nitric acid.]

ORIGIN – Latin *acidus*, from *acere* 'be sour'.

acidify > *verb* (**acidifies, acidified**) make or become acid.

DERIVATIVES – **acidification** *noun*.

acidity > *noun* **1** the level of acid in something. **2** bitterness or sharpness in a person's remarks or tone.

acidulate /əsidyoolayt/ > *verb* make slightly acidic.

acidulous /əsidyooləss/ > *adjective* sharp-tasting; sour.

-acious > *suffix* (forming adjectives) inclined to; having as a capacity: *capacious*.

ORIGIN – from Latin *-ax, -ac-*.

-acity > *suffix* forming nouns of quality or state corresponding to adjectives ending in *-acious*.

ORIGIN – from Latin *-acitas*.

ack-ack > *noun* military slang anti-aircraft gunfire or guns.

ORIGIN – signallers' former name for the letters *AA*.

ackee /akkee/ (also **akee**) > *noun* the fruit of a West African tree, eaten as a vegetable.

ORIGIN – from Kru (a West African language).

ackers > *plural noun* Brit. informal money.

ORIGIN – probably from Arabic *fakka* 'small change, coins'; originally used by British troops in Egypt as a name for the piastre.

acknowledge > *verb* **1** accept or admit the existence or truth of. **2** confirm that one has received or is grateful for (something). **3** greet with words or gestures.

SYNONYMS – **1** accept, admit, concede, grant, recognise.

ANTONYMS – **1** deny, reject.

ORIGIN – from the obsolete verb *knowledge*.

acknowledgement (also **acknowledgment**) > *noun* **1** the action or fact of acknowledging. **2** an act or instance of acknowledging. **3** (**acknowledgements**) (in a book) a printed expression of the author's gratitude to others.

acme /akmi/ > *noun* the highest point of achievement or excellence.

SYNONYMS – apex, height, peak, pinnacle, zenith.

ANTONYMS – nadir.

ORIGIN – Greek *akmē* 'highest point'.

acne > *noun* a skin condition marked by numerous red pimples on the face.

ORIGIN – Greek *aknas*, a misreading of *akmas*, a plural of *akmē* 'highest point, peak, or facial eruption'; compare with ACME.

acolyte /akkəlīt/ > *noun* **1** an assistant or follower. **2** a person assisting a priest in a religious service.

ORIGIN – Latin *acolytus*, from Greek *akolouthos* 'follower'.

aconite /akkənīt/ > *noun* **1** a poisonous plant with hooded pink or purple flowers. **2** (also **winter aconite**) a small plant bearing yellow flowers in early spring.

ORIGIN – Greek *akoniton*.

acorn > *noun* the fruit of the oak, a smooth oval nut in a cup-like base.

ORIGIN – Old English, related to ACRE; later associated with OAK and CORN¹.

acoustic /əkōōstik/ > *adjective* **1** relating to sound or hearing. **2** (of popular music or musical instruments) not having electrical amplification. > *noun* **1** (also **acoustics**) the properties of a room or building that determine how sound is transmitted in it. **2** (**acoustics**) (treated as sing.) the branch of physics concerned with the properties of sound.

DERIVATIVES – **acoustical** *adjective* **acoustically** *adverb* **acoustician** *noun*.

ORIGIN – Greek *akoustikos*, from *akouein* 'hear'.

acquaint* > *verb* **1** (**acquaint with**) make (someone) aware of or familiar with. **2** (**be acquainted with**) know personally. **3** (**be acquainted**) (of two or more people) know each other personally.

*SPELLING – note that **acquaint**, **acquiesce**, **acquire**, **acquit**, and related words have a *c* before the *qu*: a**c**quaint.

ORIGIN – Latin *accognitare*, from *cognoscere* 'come to know'.

acquaintance > *noun* **1** familiarity with or knowledge of someone or something. **2** a person one knows slightly.

acquiesce /akwiess/ > *verb* (often **acquiesce in** or **to**) accept or consent to something without protest.

SYNONYMS – (**acquiesce in** or **to**) abide by, agree to, concur with, go along with.

ORIGIN – Latin *acquiescere*, from *quiescere* 'to rest'.

acquiescent > *adjective* ready to accept or do something without protest.

DERIVATIVES – **acquiescence** *noun*.

acquire > *verb* **1** come to possess. **2** learn or develop (a skill, quality, etc.).

DERIVATIVES – **acquirement** *noun* **acquirer** *noun*.

SYNONYMS – **1** come by, gain, get, obtain.

COMBINATIONS – **acquired taste** a thing that one learns to like over time.

ORIGIN – Latin *acquirere* 'get in addition', from *quaerere* 'seek'.

acquisition /akwizish'n/ > *noun* **1** an object that has recently been acquired. **2** the act of acquiring.

acquisitive > *adjective* excessively interested in acquiring money or material things.

DERIVATIVES – **acquisitively** *adverb* **acquisitiveness** *noun*.

SYNONYMS – avaricious, grasping, greedy, materialistic.

acquit > *verb* (**acquitted, acquitting**) **1** formally declare that (someone) is not guilty of a criminal charge. **2** (**acquit oneself**) behave or perform in a specified way.

DERIVATIVES – **acquittal** *noun*.

SYNONYMS – **1** absolve, clear, exonerate, find innocent.

ORIGIN – Latin *acquitare* 'pay a debt', from *quitare* 'set free'.

acre /**ay**kər/ > *noun* a unit of land area equal to 4,840 square yards (0.405 hectare).
DERIVATIVES – **acreage** *noun*.
ORIGIN – Old English, originally denoting the amount of land a pair of oxen could plough in a day.

acrid /**ak**rid/ > *adjective* unpleasantly bitter or pungent.
DERIVATIVES – **acridity** *noun* **acridly** *adverb*.
SYNONYMS – bitter, pungent, sharp, sour.
ORIGIN – Latin *acer* 'sharp, pungent'.

acrimonious /akri**mō**niəss/ > *adjective* angry and bitter.
DERIVATIVES – **acrimoniously** *adverb*.

acrimony /**ak**riməni/ > *noun* bitterness or ill feeling.
ORIGIN – first used in the sense 'bitter taste or smell': from Latin *acrimonia*, from *acer* 'pungent, acrid'.

acrobat > *noun* an entertainer who performs acrobatics.
ORIGIN – Greek *akrobatēs*, from *akrobatos* 'walking on tiptoe'.

acrobatic > *adjective* involving or adept at spectacular gymnastic feats.
DERIVATIVES – **acrobatically** *adverb*.

acrobatics > *plural noun* (usu. treated as sing.) spectacular gymnastic feats.

acromegaly /akrō**megg**əli/ > *noun* abnormal growth of the hands, feet, and face caused by overproduction of growth hormone by the pituitary gland.
DERIVATIVES – **acromegalic** /akrō-mi**gal**ik/ *adjective*.
ORIGIN – from Greek *akron* 'tip, extremity' + *megas* 'great'.

acronym /**ak**rənim/ > *noun* a word formed from the initial letters of other words (e.g. *laser*, *Aids*).
ORIGIN – from Greek *akron* 'end, tip' + *onoma* 'name'.

acrophobia /akrə**fō**biə/ > *noun* extreme or irrational fear of heights.
DERIVATIVES – **acrophobic** *adjective*.
ORIGIN – from Greek *akron* 'summit'.

acropolis /ə**kropp**əliss/ > *noun* a citadel or fortified part of an ancient Greek city, built on high ground.
ORIGIN – Greek, from *akron* 'summit' + *polis* 'city'.

across > *preposition & adverb* from one side to the other of (something).
IDIOMS – **across the board** applying to all.
ORIGIN – first meaning 'in the form of a cross': from Old French *a croix*, *en croix* 'in or on a cross'.

acrostic /ə**kros**tik/ > *noun* a poem or puzzle in which certain letters in each line form a word or words.
ORIGIN – Greek *akrostikhis*, from *akron* 'end' + *stikhos* 'row, line of verse'.

acrylic > *adjective* of or relating to polymers of **acrylic acid**, an organic acid used in making synthetic resins. > *noun* acrylic paint or textile fabric.
ORIGIN – from Latin *acer* 'pungent' + *oleum* 'oil'.

ACT > *abbreviation* **1** advance corporation tax. **2** Australian Capital Territory.

act > *verb* **1** take action; do something. **2** take effect or have a particular effect. **3** behave in a specified way. **4** (**act as**) fulfil the function of. **5** (**act for** or **on behalf of**) represent on a contractual or legal basis. **6** (**acting**) temporarily doing the duties of another. **7** perform a fictional role in a play or film. > *noun* **1** a thing done. **2** a law passed formally by a parliament. **3** a simulation or pretence: *putting on an act*. **4** a main division of a play, ballet, or opera. **5** a set performance or performing group. **6** dated a record of the decisions or proceedings of a committee or academic body.
IDIOMS – **act of contrition** (in the Roman Catholic Church) a prayer expressing regret for having done wrong. **act of God** an instance of uncontrollable natural forces in operation. **act of grace** a privilege or concession that cannot be claimed as a right. **act up** informal behave badly. **get in on the act** informal become involved in a particular activity to share its benefits.
SYNONYMS – *verb* **1** do something, move, take action, take steps. **2** function, operate, take effect, work. **3** bear oneself, behave, conduct oneself, function. *noun* **1** action, deed, move. **2** bill, law, statute. **3** pretence, sham, show, simulation. **5** performance, routine, turn.
ORIGIN – Latin *actus* 'event, thing done', from *agere* 'to do or act'.

actinic /ak**tinn**ik/ > *adjective* (of light) able to cause chemical reactions through having a significant short-wavelength or ultraviolet component.
ORIGIN – from Greek *aktis* 'ray'.

actinide /**ak**tinīd/ > *noun* Chemistry any of the series of fifteen radioactive metallic elements from actinium to lawrencium in the periodic table.

actinium /ak**tinn**iəm/ > *noun* a rare radioactive metallic chemical element found in uranium ores.

action > *noun* **1** the process of doing something to achieve an aim. **2** a thing done. **3** the effect or influence of something such as a chemical. **4** a legal process; a lawsuit. **5** armed conflict. **6** the way in which something works or moves. **7** informal exciting or notable activity. > *verb* take action on or deal with.
IDIOMS – **actions speak louder than words** proverb what someone actually does means more than what they say they will do. **in action** engaged in an activity; in operation. **out of action** not working.

SYNONYMS – *noun* **1** activity, endeavour, enterprise, measures, steps. **2** achievement, act, deed, move.
COMBINATIONS – **action painting** a style of painting in which paint is thrown or poured on to the canvas. **action replay** Brit. a playback of part of a television broadcast, especially one in slow motion. **action stations** chiefly Brit. the positions taken up by military personnel in preparation for action.

actionable > *adjective* Law giving sufficient reason to take legal action.

activate > *verb* **1** make active or operative. **2** convert (a substance, molecule, etc.) into a reactive form.
DERIVATIVES – **activation** *noun* **activator** *noun*.
SYNONYMS – **1** actuate, start off, start up, turn on.
COMBINATIONS – **activated carbon** (also **activated charcoal**) charcoal that has been treated to increase its ability to absorb gases and dissolved substances.

active > *adjective* **1** moving or tending to move about vigorously or frequently. **2** (of a person's mind) alert and lively. **3** participating in a particular sphere or activity. **4** working; operative. **5** (of an electric circuit) capable of automatic change in response to input or feedback. **6** (of a volcano) erupting or having erupted in historical times. **7** having a chemical or biological effect on something. **8** Grammar (of a verb) in which the subject is the person or thing performing the action and which can take a direct object (e.g. *she loved him* as opposed to the passive form *he was loved*).
DERIVATIVES – **actively** *adverb*.
SYNONYMS – *adjective* **1** energetic, lively, mobile, sprightly. **4** functioning, operational, operative, working.
ANTONYMS – passive, inactive.
COMBINATIONS – **active matrix** Electronics a display system in which each pixel is individually controlled. **active service** direct participation in military operations as a member of the armed forces.

activism > *noun* the use of vigorous campaigning to bring about political or social change.
DERIVATIVES – **activist** *noun & adjective*.

activity > *noun* (pl. **activities**) **1** a condition in which things are happening or being done. **2** busy or vigorous action or movement. **3** an action taken in pursuit of an objective. **4** a recreational pursuit. **5** the degree to which something displays its characteristic property or behaviour.
SYNONYMS – **2** bustle, hubbub, hustle and bustle, life. **4** hobby, interest, pastime, pursuit.

actor > *noun* **1** a person whose profession is acting. **2** a participant in an action or process.

WORDFINDER – histrionic, thespian (*of actors or drama*); protagonist, deuteragonist, tritagonist (*principal, second, third character, originally in Greek drama*).

actress > *noun* a female actor.

DERIVATIVES – **actressy** *adjective*.

actual > *adjective* **1** existing in fact. **2** existing now; current: *actual income*.

SYNONYMS – **1** factual, genuine, real, true.

COMBINATIONS – **actual bodily harm** Law minor injury inflicted on a person by the deliberate action of another, considered less serious than grievous bodily harm.

ORIGIN – Latin *actualis*, from *actus* 'event, thing done'.

actualise (also **actualize**) > *verb* make a reality of.

DERIVATIVES – **actualisation** *noun*.

actuality > *noun* (pl. **actualities**) **1** actual existence or fact, as opposed to what was intended or expected. **2** (**actualities**) existing conditions or facts.

actually > *adverb* **1** as the truth or facts of a situation. **2** as a matter of fact; even.

actuary /akchooəri/ > *noun* (pl. **actuaries**) a person who compiles and analyses statistics in order to calculate insurance risks and premiums.

DERIVATIVES – **actuarial** *adjective*.

ORIGIN – Latin *actuarius* 'bookkeeper'.

actuate /akchooayt/ > *verb* **1** cause to operate. **2** motivate to act in a particular way.

DERIVATIVES – **actuation** *noun* **actuator** *noun*.

acuity /əkyōoiti/ > *noun* sharpness or keenness of thought, vision, or hearing.

acumen /akyoomən, əkyōomən/ > *noun* the ability to make good judgements and take quick decisions.

SYNONYMS – acuity, astuteness, canniness, judgement, shrewdness.

ORIGIN – Latin, 'sharpness, point'.

acupressure /akyoopreshər/ > *noun* a system of complementary medicine in which manual pressure is applied to the body at specific points along supposed lines of energy.

acupuncture /akyoopungkchər/ > *noun* a system of complementary medicine in which very thin needles are inserted in the skin at specific points along supposed lines of energy.

DERIVATIVES – **acupuncturist** *noun*.

ORIGIN – from Latin *acu* 'with a needle' + PUNCTURE.

acute > *adjective* **1** (of something bad) critical; serious. **2** (of an illness) rapidly becoming severe. Contrasted with CHRONIC. **3** having or showing a perceptive understanding or insight. **4** (of a physical sense or faculty) highly developed. **5** (of an angle) less than 90°.

DERIVATIVES – **acutely** *adverb* **acuteness** *noun*.

SYNONYMS – **1** critical, grave, serious, severe. **3** perceptive, quick-witted, shrewd, wise. **4** keen, sensitive, sharp.

COMBINATIONS – **acute accent** a mark (´) placed over certain letters in some languages to indicate a feature such as altered sound quality (e.g. in *fiancée*).

ORIGIN – Latin *acutus* 'sharpened', from *acus* 'needle'.

-acy > *suffix* forming nouns of state or quality: *celibacy*.

AD > *abbreviation* Anno Domini (placed before a date, indicating that it comes the specified number of years after the traditional date of Christ's birth).

USAGE – AD is normally written in small capitals and should be placed before the numerals, as in AD *375*, whereas BC is normally placed after the numerals, as in *72* BC.

ORIGIN – from Latin *Anno Domini* 'in the year of the Lord'.

ad > *noun* informal an advertisement.

ad- (also **a-** before *sc, sp, st*; **ac-** before *c, k, q*; **af-** before *f*; **ag-** before *g*; **al-** before *l*; **an-** before *n*; **ap-** before *p*; **ar-** before *r*; **as-** before *s*; **at-** before *t*) > *prefix* **1** denoting motion or direction to: *advance*. **2** denoting reduction or change into: *adapt*. **3** denoting addition or increase: *adjunct*.

ORIGIN – from Latin *ad* 'to'.

adage /addij/ > *noun* a proverb or short statement expressing a general truth.

ORIGIN – Latin *adagium* 'saying', from *aio* 'I say'.

adagio /ədaazhiō/ Music > *adverb* & *adjective* in slow time. > *noun* (pl. **adagios**) an adagio passage.

ORIGIN – Italian, from *ad agio* 'at ease'.

Adam > *noun* (in the Bible and Koran) the name of the first man.

IDIOMS – **Adam's ale** dated, humorous water. **Adam's apple** a projection at the front of the neck formed by the thyroid cartilage of the larynx. [ORIGIN – so named from the notion that a piece of the forbidden fruit became lodged in Adam's throat.] **not know someone from Adam** not know or be completely unable to recognise the person in question.

ORIGIN – Hebrew, 'man', later taken to be a name.

adamant > *adjective* refusing to be persuaded or to change one's mind.

DERIVATIVES – **adamantly** *adverb*.

ORIGIN – Greek *adamas* 'untameable, invincible'; related to DIAMOND.

adamantine /adəmantīn/ > *adjective* literary unbreakable.

adapt > *verb* **1** make suitable for a new use or purpose. **2** become adjusted to new conditions.

DERIVATIVES – **adaptive** *adjective*.

SYNONYMS – **1** adjust, alter, convert, modify, tailor.

ORIGIN – Latin *adaptare*, from *aptus* 'fit'.

adaptable > *adjective* able to adjust to or be modified for new conditions or uses.

DERIVATIVES – **adaptability** *noun* **adaptably** *adverb*.

adaptation (also **adaption**) > *noun* **1** the action or process of adapting or being adapted. **2** a film or play adapted from a written work. **3** Biology a change by which an organism becomes better suited to its environment.

adaptogen /ədaptəjən/ > *noun* (in herbal medicine) a natural substance considered to help the body adapt to stress.

DERIVATIVES – **adaptogenic** *adjective*.

adaptor (also **adapter**) > *noun* **1** a device for connecting pieces of equipment. **2** Brit. a device for connecting more than one plug at a time or plugs of a non-standard type to an electrical socket.

ADC > *abbreviation* **1** aide-de-camp. **2** analogue to digital converter.

add > *verb* **1** join to or put with something else. **2** (also **add up**) put together (two or more numbers or amounts) to calculate their total value. **3** (**add up**) informal make sense. **4** say as a further remark. **5** (**add up**) increase in amount, number, or degree.

SYNONYMS – **1** attach, join, put on, put in. **2** count up, tally, total; Brit. tot up.

ORIGIN – Latin *addere*, from *ad-* 'to' + *dare* 'put'.

addendum /ədendəm/ > *noun* (pl. **addenda** /ədendə/) an extra item added at the end of a book or text.

ORIGIN – Latin, 'that which is to be added', from *addere* (see ADD).

adder > *noun* a poisonous snake with a dark zigzag pattern on its back.

addict > *noun* a person who is addicted to something.

addicted > *adjective* **1** (often **addicted to**) physically dependent on a particular substance. **2** devoted to a particular interest or activity.

SYNONYMS – **2** (**addicted to**) dedicated to, devoted to, fixated on.

ORIGIN – from Latin *addicere* 'assign'.

addiction > *noun* the fact or condition of being addicted.

DERIVATIVES – **addictive** *adjective*.

addition > *noun* **1** the action or process of adding something to something else. **2** a person or thing added.

SYNONYMS – **1** attachment, inclusion, incorporation, introduction. **2** adjunct, attachment, extra, supplement.

wordpower facts

Adder

Adder is an example of a word formed by *wrong division* of two elements. It comes from the Old English word *nædre*, but the initial *n* was lost in medieval times through *a naddre* being read as 'an addre'. Other words formed in such a way include **apron** (originally *a napron*) and **auger**; *orange*, from Old French *orenge*, is based on Arabic *nāranj*. The process sometimes works the other way, resulting in *n* being added to the beginning of a word: *a newt* was originally *an ewt*, and **nickname** and **nonce** developed in the same way.

additional > *adjective* added, extra, or supplementary.
DERIVATIVES – **additionally** *adverb*.

additive > *noun* a substance added to improve or preserve something. > *adjective* relating to or produced by addition.

addle > *verb* **1** confuse. **2** (of an egg) become rotten. > *adjective* unsound; muddled.
DERIVATIVES – **addled** *adjective*.

address* > *noun* **1** the particulars of the place where someone lives or an organisation is situated. **2** Computing a number identifying a location in a data storage system or computer memory. **3** a formal speech. **4** dated skill or dexterity. > *verb* **1** write someone's name and address on (an envelope or parcel). **2** speak formally to. **3** think about and begin to deal with.
DERIVATIVES – **addressee** *noun* **addresser** *noun*.
***SPELLING** – two *d*s: address.
SYNONYMS – *noun* **3** lecture, oration, speech, talk. *verb* **3** apply oneself to, attend to, see to, tackle.
ORIGIN – Old French, from Latin *ad-* 'towards' + *directus* (see **DIRECT**).

adduce /ədyōoss/ > *verb* cite as evidence.
ORIGIN – Latin *adducere* 'bring in'.

adenine /addineen/ > *noun* Biochemistry a compound which is one of the four constituent bases of DNA.
ORIGIN – from Greek *adēn* 'gland'.

adenoids /addinoydz/ > *plural noun* a mass of tissue between the back of the nose and the throat, concerned in producing antibodies and sometimes enlarged and hindering speech or breathing in the young.
DERIVATIVES – **adenoidal** *adjective*.
ORIGIN – from Greek *adēn* 'gland'.

adenosine /ədennəseen/ > *noun* Biochemistry a compound (adenine combined with ribose) which occurs in living cells in the form of phosphates (in particular **adenosine** triphosphate, ATP) whose breakdown provides energy for muscle action and other processes.

adept > *adjective* /addept, ədept/ very skilled or proficient. > *noun* /addept/ a person who is adept at something.
ORIGIN – Latin *adeptus* 'achieved', from *adipisci* 'obtain, attain'.

adequate > *adjective* fulfilling expectations or needs, though not outstanding or perfect.
DERIVATIVES – **adequacy** *noun* **adequately** *adverb*.
SYNONYMS – acceptable, passable, satisfactory, sufficient.
ORIGIN – from Latin *adaequare* 'make equal to'.

à deux /aa dö/ > *adverb* for or involving two people.
ORIGIN – French.

adhere /ədheer/ > *verb* (**adhere to**) **1** stick fast to. **2** remain faithful to.
DERIVATIVES – **adherence** *noun*.
ORIGIN – Latin *adhaerere* 'stick to'.

adherent > *noun* someone who supports a particular party, person, or set of ideas. > *adjective* sticking fast to an object or surface.

adhesion /ədheezh'n/ > *noun* **1** the action or process of adhering. **2** technical the sticking together of different substances. Compare with **COHESION**. **3** Medicine an abnormal joining of inflamed or injured parts.

adhesive /ədheessiv/ > *adjective* causing adherence; sticky. > *noun* an adhesive substance.

ad hoc /ad hok/ > *adjective & adverb* formed or done for a particular purpose only.
ORIGIN – Latin, 'to this'.

ad hominem /ad homminem/ > *adverb & adjective* (of an argument) personal rather than objective.
ORIGIN – Latin, 'to the person'.

adiabatic /aydiəbattik/ > *adjective* Physics **1** relating to a process or condition in which heat does not enter or leave the system concerned. **2** impassable to heat.
DERIVATIVES – **adiabatically** *adverb*.
ORIGIN – Greek *adiabatos* 'impassable', from *a-* 'not' + *dia* 'through' + *batos* 'passable'.

adieu /ədyōo/ > *exclamation* chiefly literary goodbye.
ORIGIN – Old French, from *a* 'to' + *Dieu* 'God'.

ad infinitum /ad infinītəm/ > *adverb* endlessly; forever.
ORIGIN – Latin, 'to infinity'.

adios /addioss/ > *exclamation* Spanish term for **GOODBYE**.
ORIGIN – Spanish, from *a* 'to' + *Dios* 'God'.

adipose /addipōz/ > *adjective* technical denoting body tissue used to store fat.
DERIVATIVES – **adiposity** *noun*.
ORIGIN – Latin *adiposus*, from *adeps* 'fat'.

adit /addit/ > *noun* an access or drainage passage leading horizontally into a mine.
ORIGIN – Latin *aditus* 'approach, entrance'.

adjacent /əjays'nt/ > *adjective* next to or adjoining something else.
DERIVATIVES – **adjacency** *noun*.
SYNONYMS – (**adjacent to**) adjoining, beside, bordering, next to.
ORIGIN – from Latin *adjacere* 'lie near to'.

adjective > *noun* Grammar a word used to describe or modify a noun, such as *sweet*, *red*, or *technical*.
DERIVATIVES – **adjectival** *adjective*.
ORIGIN – Old French *adjectif*, from Latin *adicere* 'add'.

adjoin > *verb* be next to and joined with.
ORIGIN – Old French *ajoindre*, from Latin *adjungere* 'join to'.

adjourn /əjurn/ > *verb* **1** break off (a meeting) with the intention of resuming it later. **2** postpone (a resolution or sentence).
DERIVATIVES – **adjournment** *noun*.
SYNONYMS – **1** break off, discontinue, halt, suspend.
ORIGIN – Old French *ajorner*, from *a jorn nome* 'to an appointed day'.

adjudge > *verb* decide or award judicially.
ORIGIN – Latin *adjudicare*, from *judex* 'a judge'.

adjudicate /əjōodikayt/ > *verb* **1** make a formal judgement on a disputed matter. **2** judge a competition.
DERIVATIVES – **adjudication** *noun* **adjudicative** *adjective* **adjudicator** *noun*.
ORIGIN – Latin *adjudicare* (see **ADJUDGE**).

adjunct /əjungkt/ > *noun* **1** an additional and supplementary part. **2** Grammar a word or phrase in a sentence other than the verb or predicate. > *adjective* connected in an auxiliary way.
DERIVATIVES – **adjunctive** *adjective*.
ORIGIN – from Latin *adjungere* (see **ADJOIN**).

adjure /əjoor/ > *verb* formal solemnly urge (someone) to do something.
ORIGIN – Latin *adjurare*, from *ad-* 'to' + *jurare* 'swear'.

adjust > *verb* **1** alter (something) slightly in order to achieve a desired result. **2** become used to a new situation. **3** assess (loss or damages) when settling an insurance claim.
DERIVATIVES – **adjustable** *adjective* **adjuster** *noun* **adjustment** *noun*.
SYNONYMS – **1** adapt, alter, modify, tune.
ORIGIN – Old French *ajoster* 'to approximate', from Latin *ad-* 'to' + *juxta* 'near'.

adjutant /əjoot'nt/ > *noun* a military officer acting as an administrative assistant to a senior officer.

ORIGIN – from Latin *adjutare* 'be of service to', from *adjuvare* 'help towards'.

adjuvant /**ad**joov'nt/ > *noun* chiefly Medicine **1** something which increases the effect of something else, especially a substance which enhances the body's immune response to an antigen. **2** (before another noun) (of chemotherapy) applied after initial treatment for cancer to suppress secondary tumour formation.
ORIGIN – from Latin *adjuvare* 'help towards'.

ad-lib > *verb* (**ad-libbed, ad-libbing**) speak or perform in public without preparing in advance. > *adverb & adjective* **1** spoken without advance preparation. **2** Music with free rhythm and expression. > *noun* an ad-lib remark or speech.
ORIGIN – abbreviation of Latin *ad libitum* 'according to pleasure'.

ad litem /ad **lī**tem/ > *adjective* Law acting in a lawsuit on behalf of people who cannot represent themselves.
ORIGIN – Latin, 'for the lawsuit'.

admin > *noun* informal, chiefly Brit. administration.

administer > *verb* **1** be responsible for managing or implementing (an organisation or policy). **2** dispense (a drug or remedy). **3** inflict (punishment).
DERIVATIVES – **administrable** *adjective*.
SYNONYMS – **1** direct, manage, organise, run.
ORIGIN – Latin *administrare*, from *ad-* 'to' + *ministrare* 'wait upon'.

administrate > *verb* administer; carry out administration.
DERIVATIVES – **administrative** *adjective* **administrator** *noun*.

administration > *noun* **1** the organisation and running of a business or system. **2** the action of administering. **3** the government in power. **4** chiefly N. Amer. the term of office of a political leader or government.

admirable /**ad**mirəb'l/ > *adjective* deserving respect and approval.
DERIVATIVES – **admirably** *adverb*.
SYNONYMS – commendable, estimable, laudable, praiseworthy.

admiral > *noun* **1** the most senior commander of a fleet or navy. **2** (**Admiral**) a naval officer of the second most senior rank, above vice admiral and below Admiral of the Fleet.
COMBINATIONS – **Admiral of the Fleet** the highest rank of admiral in the Royal Navy.
ORIGIN – first denoting an emir or Arab commander: from Old French *amiral*, from Arabic *'amīr* 'commander' (the root of **EMIR**).

Admiralty > *noun* (in the UK) the government department that formerly administered the Royal Navy, now used only in titles.

admire > *verb* **1** regard with respect or warm approval. **2** look at with pleasure.
DERIVATIVES – **admiration** *noun* **admirer** *noun* **admiring** *adjective*.
SYNONYMS – **1** esteem, look up to, respect, revere.
ORIGIN – Latin *admirari*, from *ad-* 'at' + *mirari* 'wonder'.

admissible > *adjective* **1** acceptable or valid. **2** having the right to be admitted to a place.
DERIVATIVES – **admissibility** *noun*.

admission > *noun* **1** a confession. **2** the process or fact of being admitted to a place. **3** a person admitted to hospital for treatment.

admit > *verb* (**admitted, admitting**) **1** confess to be true or to be the case. **2** allow to enter. **3** receive into a hospital for treatment. **4** accept as valid. **5** (**admit of**) allow the possibility of.
SYNONYMS – **1** acknowledge, allow, concede, confess.
ORIGIN – Latin *admittere*, from *ad-* 'to' + *mittere* 'send'.

admittance > *noun* the process or fact of entering or being allowed to enter.

admix > *verb* chiefly technical mix with something else.
DERIVATIVES – **admixture** *noun*.

admonish > *verb* **1** reprimand firmly. **2** earnestly urge or warn.
DERIVATIVES – **admonishment** *noun* **admonition** *noun* **admonitory** *adjective*.
ORIGIN – Latin *admonere* 'urge by warning'.

ad nauseam* /ad **naw**ziam/ > *adverb* to a tiresomely excessive degree.
*SPELLING – ad nause**am** , not *-eum*.
ORIGIN – Latin, 'to sickness'.

ado > *noun* (usu. in phrase **without much** (or **more**) **ado**) trouble; fuss.
ORIGIN – first used in the sense 'action, business': from northern *at do* 'to do'.

adobe /ə**dō**bi/ > *noun* a kind of clay used to make sun-dried bricks.
ORIGIN – from Spanish *adobar* 'to plaster', from an Arabic word meaning 'bricks'.

adolescent > *adjective* in the process of developing from a child into an adult. > *noun* an adolescent boy or girl.
DERIVATIVES – **adolescence** *noun*.
ORIGIN – from Latin *adolescere*, from *ad-* 'to' + *alescere* 'grow, grow up'.

Adonis /ə**dō**niss/ > *noun* an extremely handsome young man.
ORIGIN – from the name of a beautiful youth in Greek mythology.

adopt > *verb* **1** legally take (another's child) and bring it up as one's own. **2** choose to take up or follow (an option or course of action). **3** Brit. choose as a candidate for office. **4** assume (an attitude or position). **5** Brit. (of a local authority) accept responsibility for the maintenance of (a road). **6** formally approve or accept.
DERIVATIVES – **adoptable** *adjective* **adoptee** *noun* **adopter** *noun* **adoption** *noun*.
SYNONYMS – **2** back, endorse, espouse, support.
ORIGIN – Latin *adoptare*, from *ad-* 'to' + *optare* 'choose'.

adoptive > *adjective* **1** (especially of a parent) in that relationship by adoption. **2** (of a place) chosen as one's permanent place of residence.
USAGE – do not confuse **adoptive** with **adopted**: children are **adopted**, but parents are **adoptive**.

adorable > *adjective* inspiring great affection.
DERIVATIVES – **adorably** *adverb*.

adore > *verb* love and respect deeply.
DERIVATIVES – **adoration** *noun* **adorer** *noun* **adoring** *adjective* **adoringly** *adverb*.
SYNONYMS – cherish, dote on, hold dear, treasure.
ORIGIN – Latin *adorare* 'to worship', from *ad-* 'to' + *orare* 'speak, pray'.

adorn > *verb* make more attractive or beautiful.
DERIVATIVES – **adornment** *noun*.
SYNONYMS – bedeck, decorate, embellish, ornament.
ORIGIN – Latin *adornare*, from *ad-* 'to' + *ornare* 'deck, add lustre'.

adrenal /ə**dree**n'l/ > *adjective* relating to a pair of glands (the **adrenal glands**), situated above the kidneys and secreting adrenalin and other hormones.
ORIGIN – from **AD-** + **RENAL**.

adrenalin /ə**drenn**əlin/ (also **adrenaline**) > *noun* a hormone that increases rates of blood circulation, breathing, and carbohydrate metabolism, secreted by the adrenal glands (especially in conditions of stress).

adrenalised /ə**drenn**əlīzd/ (also **adrenalized**) > *adjective* excited, tense, or highly charged.

Adriatic /aydri**att**ik/ > *adjective* of the region of the **Adriatic Sea**, the arm of the Mediterranean between Italy and the Balkans.

adrift > *adjective & adverb* **1** (of a boat) drifting without control. **2** Brit. informal no longer fixed in position.

adroit /ə**droyt**/ > *adjective* clever or skilful in using the hands or mind.
DERIVATIVES – **adroitly** *adverb* **adroitness** *noun*.
SYNONYMS – adept, deft, dexterous, proficient, skilful.
ANTONYMS – clumsy.

ORIGIN – from French *à droit* 'according to right, properly'.

adsorb /ədˈzorb, -ˈsorb/ > *verb* (of a solid) hold (molecules of a gas, liquid, or dissolved substance) in a layer on its surface.

DERIVATIVES – **adsorbable** *adjective* **adsorption** *noun* **adsorptive** *adjective*.

adsorbent > *noun* a substance which adsorbs another. > *adjective* able to adsorb substances.

aduki /əˈdooki/ > *noun* variant of ADZUKI.

adulation /adyooˈlaysh'n/ > *noun* excessive admiration.

DERIVATIVES – **adulate** *verb* **adulatory** *adjective*.

SYNONYMS – adoration, hero worship, idolisation.

ORIGIN – Latin, from *adulari* 'fawn on'.

adult /ˈaddult, əˈdult/ > *noun* **1** a person who is fully grown and developed. **2** Law a person who has reached the age of majority. > *adjective* **1** fully grown and developed. **2** for or characteristic of adults.

DERIVATIVES – **adulthood** *noun*.

ORIGIN – Latin *adultus*, from *adolescere* (see ADOLESCENT).

adulterate > *verb* /əˈdultərayt/ make (something) poorer in quality by adding another substance.

DERIVATIVES – **adulterant** *adjective* **adulteration** *noun*.

ORIGIN – Latin *adulterare* 'corrupt'.

adulterer > *noun* (fem. **adulteress**) a person who has committed adultery.

adultery > *noun* voluntary sexual intercourse between a married person and a person who is not their husband or wife.

DERIVATIVES – **adulterous** *adjective*.

ORIGIN – from Latin *adulterare* 'debauch, corrupt'.

adumbrate /ˈaddumbrayt/ > *verb* formal **1** give a faint or general idea of. **2** foreshadow.

DERIVATIVES – **adumbration** *noun*.

ORIGIN – Latin *adumbrare*, from *ad-* 'to' + *umbrare* 'cast a shadow'.

advance > *verb* **1** move forwards. **2** make or cause to make progress. **3** put forward (a theory or suggestion). **4** hand over (payment) to (someone) as a loan or before it is due. > *noun* **1** a forward movement. **2** a development or improvement. **3** an amount of money advanced. **4** an approach made with the aim of initiating a sexual or amorous relationship. > *adjective* done, sent, or supplied beforehand.

DERIVATIVES – **advancer** *noun*.

SYNONYMS – *verb* **1** forge ahead, gain ground, proceed, push forward. **2** develop, further, progress, promote.

ANTONYMS – *verb* **1** retreat. **2** hinder.

ORIGIN – from Latin *abante* 'in front', from *ab* 'from' + *ante* 'before'.

advanced > *adjective* **1** far on in progress or life. **2** complex; not elementary. **3** very modern.

COMBINATIONS – **advanced level** fuller form of *A level*. **advanced supplementary level** (in the UK except Scotland) a GCE examination with a smaller syllabus than A level.

advancement > *noun* **1** the process of promoting a cause or plan. **2** the promotion of a person in rank or status. **3** a development or improvement.

advantage > *noun* **1** a condition or circumstance that puts one in a favourable position. **2** Tennis a score marking a point interim between deuce and winning the game. > *verb* be of benefit to.

IDIOMS – **take advantage of 1** make unfair use of for one's own benefit. **2** dated seduce. **3** make good use of the opportunities offered by.

DERIVATIVES – **advantageous** /advənˈtayjəss/ *adjective*.

SYNONYMS – *noun* **1** asset, benefit, bonus, merit, strength.

ANTONYMS – *noun* **1** disadvantage, handicap.

ORIGIN – Old French *avantage*, from *avant* 'in front', from Latin *abante* (see ADVANCE).

advent /ˈadvent/ > *noun* **1** the arrival of a notable person or thing. **2** (**Advent**) Christian Theology the coming or second coming of Christ. **3** (**Advent**) the first season of the Church year, leading up to Christmas.

COMBINATIONS – **Advent calendar** a calendar containing small numbered flaps, one of which is opened on each day of Advent to reveal a seasonal picture.

ORIGIN – Latin *adventus* 'arrival'.

Adventist > *noun* a member of a Christian sect emphasising belief in the imminent second coming of Christ.

DERIVATIVES – **Adventism** *noun*.

adventitious /adventˈishəss/ > *adjective* **1** happening according to chance. **2** Botany (of roots) growing directly from the stem or other upper part of a plant.

DERIVATIVES – **adventitiously** *adverb*.

ORIGIN – Latin *adventicius* 'coming to us from abroad'.

adventure > *noun* **1** an unusual, exciting, and daring experience. **2** excitement associated with danger or the taking of risks.

DERIVATIVES – **adventuresome** *adjective*.

SYNONYMS – **1** enterprise, escapade, exploit, venture.

ORIGIN – from Latin *adventurus* 'about to happen', from *advenire* 'arrive'.

adventurer > *noun* a person who enjoys or seeks adventure.

adventuress > *noun* **1** a woman who enjoys or seeks adventure. **2** a woman who seeks advancement by dishonest or unscrupulous methods.

adventurism > *noun* willingness to take risks in business or politics.

DERIVATIVES – **adventurist** *noun* & *adjective*.

adventurous > *adjective* open to or involving new or daring methods or experiences.

DERIVATIVES – **adventurously** *adverb* **adventurousness** *noun*.

SYNONYMS – bold, daring, enterprising, intrepid.

adverb > *noun* Grammar a word or phrase that modifies the meaning of an adjective, verb, or other adverb, or of a sentence (e.g. *gently*, *very*, *fortunately*).

ORIGIN – Latin *adverbium*, from *ad-* 'to' + *verbum* 'word, verb'.

adverbial Grammar > *noun* a word or phrase functioning as a major part of a clause and typically expressing place (*in the garden*), time (*in May*), or manner (*in a strange way*). > *adjective* relating to or functioning as an adverb or adverbial.

adversarial /advəˈsairiəl/ > *adjective* involving or characterised by conflict or opposition.

DERIVATIVES – **adversarially** *adverb*.

adversary /ˈadvərsəri/ > *noun* (pl. **adversaries**) an opponent.

ORIGIN – Latin *adversarius* 'opposed, opponent', from *adversus* (see ADVERSE).

adverse /ˈadverss/ > *adjective* preventing success or development; unfavourable: *adverse publicity*.

DERIVATIVES – **adversely** *adverb*.

USAGE – do not confuse **adverse** with **averse**, which means 'strongly disliking or opposed to', as in *I am not averse to helping out*.

SYNONYMS – bad, detrimental, harmful, unfavourable.

ANTONYMS – favourable.

ORIGIN – Latin *adversus* 'against, opposite', from *advertere* 'turn towards'.

adversity > *noun* (pl. **adversities**) difficulty; misfortune.

advert[1] /ˈadvert/ > *noun* Brit. informal an advertisement.

advert[2] /ədˈvert/ > *verb* (**advert to**) formal refer to.

ORIGIN – Latin *advertere* 'turn to'.

advertise* > *verb* **1** describe or draw attention to (a product, service, or event) in a public medium in order to promote sales or attendance. **2** make (a quality or fact) known. **3** seek to fill (a vacancy) by placing a notice in a newspaper or other medium.

DERIVATIVES – **advertiser** *noun* **advertising** *noun*.

*SPELLING – unlike most verbs ending in *-ise*, **advertise** cannot be spelled with an *-ize* ending.

SYNONYMS – **1** market, promote, publicise.

ORIGIN – Old French *advertir*, from Latin *advertere* 'turn to'.

advertisement > *noun* a notice or display advertising something.

advertorial /adver**tor**iəl/ > *noun* an advertisement in the style of an editorial or objective journalistic article.

advice > *noun* **1** guidance or recommendations offered with regard to future action. **2** a formal notice of a sale or other transaction.

ORIGIN – Old French *avis*, from Latin *ad* 'to' + *videre* 'to see'.

advisable > *adjective* to be recommended; sensible.

DERIVATIVES – **advisability** *noun*.

advise* > *verb* **1** recommend (a course of action). **2** offer advice to. **3** inform (someone) about a fact or situation.

DERIVATIVES – **adviser** (also **advisor**) *noun*.

***SPELLING – **advise** cannot be spelled with an *-ize* ending.

SYNONYMS – **1** advocate, call for, recommend, subscribe to. **2** counsel, recommend.

advised > *adjective* behaving as the speaker would recommend; sensible or prudent.

DERIVATIVES – **advisedly** *adverb*.

advisory > *adjective* having the power to make recommendations but not to enforce them.

advocaat /**ad**vəkaat/ > *noun* a liqueur made with eggs, sugar, and brandy.

ORIGIN – Dutch, 'advocate' (being originally considered a lawyer's drink).

advocate > *noun* /**ad**vəkət/ **1** a person who publicly supports or recommends a cause or policy. **2** a person who pleads a case on someone else's behalf. **3** Scottish term for **BARRISTER**. > *verb* /**ad**vəkayt/ publicly recommend or support.

DERIVATIVES – **advocacy** *noun*.

SYNONYMS – *noun* **1** backer, campaigner, champion, supporter. *verb* champion, endorse, press for, promote.

ORIGIN – Latin *advocare* 'call to one's aid'.

adze /adz/ (US **adz**) > *noun* a tool similar to an axe, with an arched blade at right angles to the handle.

adzuki /əd**zoo**ki/ (also **aduki**) > *noun* (pl. **adzukis**) a small dark-red edible bean.

ORIGIN – Japanese.

Aegean /i**jee**ən/ > *adjective* of the region of the **Aegean Sea**, the part of the Mediterranean between Greece and Turkey.

aegis /**ee**jiss/ > *noun* the protection, backing, or support of someone.

ORIGIN – Greek *aigis* 'shield of Zeus'.

-aemia (also **-haemia**, US **-emia** or **-hemia**) > *combining form* in nouns denoting that a substance is present in the blood: *septicaemia*.

ORIGIN – Greek *-aimia*, from *haima* 'blood'.

aeolian /ee**ō**liən/ (US **eolian**) > *adjective* chiefly Geology relating to or arising from the action of the wind.

COMBINATIONS – **aeolian harp** a stringed instrument that produces musical sounds when a current of air passes through it.

ORIGIN – from *Aeolus*, the name of the god of the winds in Greek mythology.

aeon /**ee**on/ (US or technical also **eon**) > *noun* **1** an indefinite and very long period of time. **2** a major division of geological time, subdivided into eras. **3** Astronomy & Geology a period of a thousand million years.

ORIGIN – Greek *aiōn* 'age'.

aerate /**air**ayt/ > *verb* introduce air into.

DERIVATIVES – **aeration** *noun* **aerator** *noun*.

ORIGIN – from Latin *aer* 'air'.

aerated > *adjective* **1** (of a liquid) made effervescent by being charged with carbon dioxide. **2** Brit. informal agitated, angry, or over-excited.

aerial > *noun* a structure that transmits or receives radio or television signals. > *adjective* **1** existing or taking place in the air. **2** involving the use of aircraft.

DERIVATIVES – **aerially** *adverb*.

aerie > *noun* US spelling of **EYRIE**.

aero- /**air**ō-/ > *combining form* **1** relating to air: *aerobic*. **2** relating to aircraft: *aerodrome*.

ORIGIN – from Greek *aēr* 'air'.

aerobatics > *plural noun* (treated as sing. or pl.) feats of flying performed for display.

DERIVATIVES – **aerobatic** *adjective*.

aerobic /air**ō**bik/ > *adjective* **1** relating to physical exercise intended to improve the absorption and transportation of oxygen. **2** Biology using or involving oxygen from the air.

DERIVATIVES – **aerobically** *adverb*.

ORIGIN – from **AERO-** + Greek *bios* 'life'.

aerobics > *plural noun* (treated as sing. or pl.) aerobic exercises.

aerodrome > *noun* Brit. a small airport or airfield.

aerodynamic > *adjective* **1** relating to aerodynamics. **2** having a shape which reduces the drag from air moving past.

DERIVATIVES – **aerodynamically** *adverb*.

aerodynamics > *plural noun* **1** (treated as sing.) the branch of science concerned with the interaction between the air and solid bodies moving through it. **2** (treated as pl.) aerodynamic properties.

DERIVATIVES – **aerodynamicist** *noun*.

aerofoil > *noun* Brit. the basic form of an aircraft wing or similar structure, designed to provide lift in flight.

aerogramme (US **aerogram**) > *noun* a letter for sending by airmail; an air letter.

aeronautics > *plural noun* (usu. treated as sing.) the study or practice of travel through the air.

DERIVATIVES – **aeronautic** *adjective* **aeronautical** *adjective*.

ORIGIN – Latin *aeronautica* 'matters relating to aeronautics', from Greek *aēr* 'air' + *nautēs* 'sailor'.

aeroplane > *noun* chiefly Brit. a powered flying vehicle with fixed wings and a weight greater than that of the air it displaces.

ORIGIN – from French *aéro-* 'air' + Greek *-planos* 'wandering'.

aerosol > *noun* **1** a substance enclosed under pressure and released as a fine spray. **2** Chemistry a suspension of submicroscopic particles dispersed in air or gas.

DERIVATIVES – **aerosolise** (also **aerosolize**) *verb*.

ORIGIN – from **AERO-** + **SOL**[2].

aerospace > *noun* the branch of technology and industry concerned with aviation and space flight.

aesthete /**eess**theet/ (US also **esthete**) > *noun* a person who is appreciative of art and beauty.

aesthetic /eess**thett**ik/ (US also **esthetic**) > *adjective* **1** concerned with beauty or the appreciation of beauty. **2** of pleasing appearance. > *noun* a set of principles underlying the work of a particular artist or artistic movement.

DERIVATIVES – **aesthetically** *adverb* **aestheticism** *noun*.

ORIGIN – Greek *aisthētikos*, from *aisthesthai* 'perceive'.

aesthetics (US also **esthetics**) > *plural noun* (usu. treated as sing.) **1** a set of principles concerned with the nature of beauty, especially in art. **2** the branch of philosophy concerned with questions of beauty and artistic taste.

aestival /**ee**stiv'l/ > *adjective* technical belonging to or appearing in summer.

ORIGIN – Latin *aestivalis*, from *aestus* 'heat'.

aether > *noun* variant spelling of **ETHER** (in senses 3 and 4).

aetiology /eeti**oll**əji/ (US **etiology**) > *noun* **1** Medicine the cause of a disease or condition. **2** the investigation of cause or a reason.

DERIVATIVES – **aetiological** *adjective*.

ORIGIN – Greek *aitiologia*, from *aitia* 'a cause'.

afar > *adverb* chiefly literary at or to a distance.

AFC > *abbreviation* **1** Air Force Cross. **2** Association Football Club.

affable > *adjective* good-natured and sociable.

DERIVATIVES – **affability** *noun* **affably** *adverb*.

ORIGIN – Latin *affabilis*, from *ad-* 'to' + *fari* 'speak'.

affair > *noun* **1** an event of a specified kind or that has previously been referred to. **2** a matter that is a particular person's responsibility. **3** a love affair. **4** (**affairs**) matters of public interest and importance.

SYNONYMS – **1** event, case, incident, matter. **2** concern, preserve, province, responsibility.

ORIGIN – from Old French *à faire* 'to do'.

affaire /a**fair**/ (also **affaire de** or **du cœur** /affair də/ /dyoo **kör**/) > *noun* a love affair.

ORIGIN – French, 'affair (of the heart)'.

affect¹ /ə**fekt**/ > *verb* **1** have an effect on; make a difference to. **2** touch the feelings of.

DERIVATIVES – **affecting** *adjective* **affectingly** *adverb*.

USAGE – do not confuse **affect** and **effect**. **Affect** means 'make a difference to', whereas **effect** means 'a result' or 'bring about (a result)'.

SYNONYMS – **1** act on, influence, shape, touch. **2** hurt, trouble, upset.

ORIGIN – Latin *afficere* (see AFFECT²).

affect² /ə**fekt**/ > *verb* **1** pretend to have or feel. **2** use, wear, or assume pretentiously or so as to impress.

ORIGIN – Latin *affectare* 'aim at', from *afficere* 'affect, influence'.

affect³ /**aff**ekt/ > *noun* Psychology emotion or desire regarded in terms of their influence on behaviour.

DERIVATIVES – **affectless** *adjective*.

ORIGIN – German *Affekt* from Latin *affectus* 'disposition', from *afficere* 'affect, influence'.

affectation /affek**tay**sh'n/ > *noun* behaviour, speech, or writing that is artificial and designed to impress.

SYNONYMS – ostentation, posturing, pretension.

affected > *adjective* artificial and designed to impress.

DERIVATIVES – **affectedly** *adverb*.

SYNONYMS – artificial, contrived, pretentious, studied.

ANTONYMS – natural, unaffected.

affection > *noun* a feeling of fondness or liking.

SYNONYMS – fondness, liking, love, warmth.

ORIGIN – Latin, from *afficere* (see AFFECT²).

affectionate > *adjective* readily showing affection.

DERIVATIVES – **affectionately** *adverb*.

SYNONYMS – caring, fond, loving, tender, warm.

ANTONYMS – cold, unfeeling.

affective > *adjective* chiefly Psychology relating to moods, feelings, and attitudes.

afferent /**aff**ərənt/ > *adjective* Physiology relating to the conduction of nerve impulses or blood inwards or towards something. The opposite of EFFERENT.

ORIGIN – from Latin *afferre* 'bring towards'.

affiance /ə**fī**ənss/ > *verb* (**be affianced**) literary be engaged to marry.

ORIGIN – Old French *afiancer*, from Latin *affidare* 'declare on oath'.

affidavit /affi**day**vit/ > *noun* Law a written statement confirmed by oath or affirmation, for use as evidence in court.

ORIGIN – Latin, 'he has stated on oath'.

affiliate > *verb* /ə**fill**iayt/ officially attach or connect to an organisation. > *noun* /ə**fill**iət/ an affiliated person or organisation.

DERIVATIVES – **affiliation** *noun*.

ORIGIN – Latin *affiliare* 'adopt as a son'.

affinity > *noun* (pl. **affinities**) **1** a spontaneous or natural sympathy. **2** a close relationship based on a common origin or structure. **3** relationship by marriage. **4** the tendency of a substance to combine with another.

SYNONYMS – **1** empathy, rapport, sympathy. **2** correspondence, identity, resemblance, similarity.

ORIGIN – Latin *affinitas*, from *affinis* 'related'.

affirm > *verb* **1** state emphatically or publicly. **2** Law make a formal declaration rather than taking an oath.

DERIVATIVES – **affirmation** *noun*.

ORIGIN – Latin *affirmare*, from *ad-* 'to' + *firmus* 'strong'.

affirmative > *adjective* agreeing with or consenting to a statement or request. > *noun* an affirmative statement or word. > *exclamation* chiefly N. Amer. yes.

IDIOMS – **in the affirmative** so as to accept or agree to a statement or request.

DERIVATIVES – **affirmatively** *adverb*.

COMBINATIONS – **affirmative action** chiefly N. Amer. action favouring those who tend to suffer from discrimination.

affix > *verb* /ə**fiks**/ attach or fasten to something else. > *noun* /**aff**iks/ Grammar an addition to a word in order to modify its meaning or create a new word.

DERIVATIVES – **affixation** *noun*.

ORIGIN – Latin *affixare*, from *ad-* 'to' + *figere* 'to fix'.

afflict > *verb* cause pain or suffering to.

DERIVATIVES – **affliction** *noun*.

SYNONYMS – burden, distress, torment, trouble.

ORIGIN – Latin *afflictare* 'knock about, harass', or *affligere* 'knock down, weaken'.

affluent > *adjective* wealthy.

DERIVATIVES – **affluence** *noun*.

ORIGIN – from Latin *affluere* 'flow towards, flow freely'.

afford > *verb* **1** (**can** or **could afford**) have sufficient money, time, or means for. **2** provide (an opportunity or facility).

DERIVATIVES – **affordability** *noun* **affordable** *adjective*.

ORIGIN – Old English, 'promote, perform', later 'manage to do'; related to FORTH.

afforest /ə**forr**ist/ > *verb* convert (land) into forest.

DERIVATIVES – **afforestation** *noun*.

affray > *noun* Law, dated a breach of the peace by fighting in a public place.

ORIGIN – from Old French *afrayer* 'disturb, startle'.

affront > *noun* an action or remark that causes offence. > *verb* offend the modesty or values of.

ORIGIN – Old French *afronter* 'to slap in the face, insult'.

Afghan /**af**gan/ > *noun* a person from Afghanistan. > *adjective* relating to Afghanistan.

COMBINATIONS – **Afghan coat** Brit. a kind of sheepskin coat with the skin outside. **Afghan hound** a silky-haired breed of dog used for hunting.

afghani /af**gaa**ni/ > *noun* (pl. **afghanis**) the basic monetary unit of Afghanistan, equal to 100 puls.

aficionado /əfissyə**naa**dō/ > *noun* (pl. **aficionados**) a person who is very knowledgeable and enthusiastic about an activity or subject; a devotee.

ORIGIN – first used in the sense 'devotee of bullfighting': from Spanish, 'amateur', from *aficionar* 'become fond of'.

afield > *adverb* to or at a distance.

AFL > *abbreviation* Australian Football League.

aflame > *adjective* in flames.

afloat > *adjective & adverb* **1** floating in water. **2** on board a ship or boat. **3** out of debt or difficulty.

AFM > *abbreviation* Air Force Medal.

afoot > *adverb & adjective* **1** in preparation or progress. **2** chiefly N. Amer. on foot.

afore > *preposition* archaic or dialect before.

afore- > *prefix* before; previously.

aforementioned (also **aforesaid**) > *adjective* formal denoting a thing or person previously mentioned.

a fortiori /ay forti**or**ī/ > *adverb* for an even stronger reason.

ORIGIN – Latin, from *a fortiori argumento* 'from stronger argument'.

afoul > *adverb* N. Amer. into conflict or difficulty with.

afraid > *adjective* feeling fear or anxiety.

IDIOMS – **I'm afraid** used to express polite apology or regret.

SYNONYMS – fearful, frightened, nervous, scared.

ORIGIN – past participle of the obsolete verb *affray*, from Old French *afrayer* 'disturb, startle'.

A-frame > *noun* a timber frame shaped like a capital letter A.

afresh > *adverb* in a new or different way.

African > *noun* **1** a person from Africa, especially a black person. **2** a person of black African descent. > *adjective* relating to Africa or people of African descent.

DERIVATIVES – **Africanise** (also **Africanize**) *verb*.

African American chiefly US > *noun* an American of African origin. > *adjective* relating to African Americans.

Afrikaans /afri**kaanss**/ > *noun* a language of southern Africa derived from Dutch, an official language of South Africa.

ORIGIN – Dutch, 'African'.

Afrikaner /afri**kaan**ər/ > *noun* an Afrikaans-speaking white South African.

DERIVATIVES – **Afrikanerdom** noun.

ORIGIN – from Dutch *Afrikaan* 'an African' + the personal suffix -*der*.

Afro > *noun* (pl. **Afros**) a hairstyle consisting of a mass of very tight curls all round the head, like the natural hair of some black people.

Afro- > *combining form* African: *Afro-Asiatic*.

Afro-American > *adjective & noun* another term for **AFRICAN AMERICAN**.

Afro-Caribbean > *noun* a person of African descent living in or coming from the Caribbean. > *adjective* relating to Afro-Caribbeans.

aft /aaft/ > *adverb & adjective* at, near, or towards the stern of a ship or tail of an aircraft.

after > *preposition* 1 in the time following (an event or another period of time). 2 behind. 3 in pursuit of. 4 next to and following in order or importance. 5 in allusion or reference to. > *conjunction & adverb* in the time following (an event). > *adjective* 1 archaic later. 2 nearer the stern of a ship.

IDIOMS – **after all** in spite of any indications to the contrary. **after hours** after normal working or opening hours.

afterbirth > *noun* the placenta and fetal membranes discharged from the womb after a birth.

afterburner > *noun* an auxiliary burner in the exhaust of a jet engine.

aftercare > *noun* care of a person after a stay in hospital or on release from prison.

after-effect > *noun* an effect that follows after the primary action of something.

afterglow > *noun* light remaining in the sky after the sun has set.

after-image > *noun* an impression of a vivid image retained by the eye after the stimulus has ceased.

afterlife > *noun* 1 (in some religions) life after death. 2 later life.

aftermath > *noun* the consequences of an unpleasant or disastrous event.

ORIGIN – from **AFTER** + dialect *math* 'mowing'.

afternoon > *noun* the time from noon or lunchtime to evening.

afters > *plural noun* Brit. informal the dessert course of a meal.

aftershave > *noun* a scented lotion for applying to the skin after shaving.

aftershock > *noun* a smaller earthquake following the main shock of a large earthquake.

aftertaste > *noun* a strong or unpleasant taste lingering in the mouth after eating or drinking.

afterthought > *noun* something thought of or added later.

afterwards (US also **afterward**) > *adverb* at a later or future time.

afterword > *noun* a concluding section in a book, typically by a person other than the author.

afterworld > *noun* a world entered after death.

Ag > *symbol* the chemical element silver.

ORIGIN – from Latin *argentum*.

again /əgen, əgayn/ > *adverb* 1 once more. 2 returning to a previous position or condition. 3 in addition to what has already been mentioned.

against > *preposition* 1 in opposition to. 2 to the disadvantage of. 3 in resistance to. 4 in anticipation of and preparation for (a difficulty). 5 in relation to (money owed, due, or lent) so as to reduce, cancel, or secure it. 6 in or into contact with. 7 (in betting) in anticipation of the failure of.

IDIOMS – **have something against** dislike or bear a grudge against.

agape¹ /əgayp/ > *adjective* (of a person's mouth) wide open.

agape² /aggəpay/ > *noun* Christian Theology Christian love as distinct from erotic love or simple affection.

ORIGIN – Greek, 'brotherly love'.

agar /aygaar/ (also **agar-agar** /aygaaraygaar/) > *noun* a jelly-like substance obtained from red seaweed and used in biological cultures and as a thickener in foods.

ORIGIN – Malay.

agaric /aggərik/ > *noun* a fungus with gills on the underside of the cap, e.g. a mushroom.

ORIGIN – Greek *agarikon* 'tree fungus'.

agate /aggət/ > *noun* an ornamental stone consisting of a hard variety of chalcedony.

ORIGIN – Greek *akhatēs*.

agave /əgayvi/ > *noun* an American plant with narrow spiny leaves and tall flower spikes.

ORIGIN – from Greek *Agauē*, the name of one of the daughters of Cadmus in Greek mythology.

age > *noun* 1 the length of time that a person or thing has existed. 2 a particular stage in someone's life. 3 the latter part of existence; old age. 4 a distinct period of history. 5 a division of geological time that is a subdivision of an epoch. 6 (**ages** or **an age**) informal a very long time: *I haven't seen her for ages.* > *verb* (**aged**, **ageing** or **aging**) 1 grow or cause to appear old or older. 2 (with reference to an alcoholic drink, cheese, etc.) mature.

IDIOMS – **act** (or **be**) **one's age** behave in a manner appropriate to someone of one's age. **come of age** reach adult status (in UK law at 18).

SYNONYMS – *noun* 4 aeon, epoch, era, time.

COMBINATIONS – **age of consent** the age at which a person's consent to sexual intercourse is legally valid. **age-old** having existed for a very long time.

ORIGIN – Latin *aetas*, from *aevum* 'age, era'.

-age > *suffix* forming nouns: 1 denoting an action or its result: *leverage*. 2 denoting an aggregate or number of: *mileage*. 3 denoting a place or abode: *vicarage*. 4 denoting fees payable for: *postage*.

ORIGIN – Latin -*aticum*.

aged > *adjective* 1 /ayjd/ of a specified age. 2 /ayjid/ old. 3 /ayjid/ having been subjected to ageing.

ageing* (also **aging**) > *noun* 1 the process of growing old. 2 the process of change in the properties of a material over a long period. > *adjective* growing old; elderly.

***SPELLING** – the standard spelling is **ageing**, although **aging** is very common.

ageism > *noun* prejudice or discrimination on the grounds of age.

DERIVATIVES – **ageist** adjective & noun.

ageless > *adjective* not ageing or appearing to age.

DERIVATIVES – **agelessness** noun.

agency > *noun* 1 an organisation providing a particular service. 2 a government office or department providing a specific service. 3 intervention to produce a particular result.

ORIGIN – Latin *agentia*, from *agere* 'to do'.

agenda > *noun* 1 a list of items of business to be discussed at a meeting. 2 a list of matters to be addressed.

USAGE – **agenda** is the plural of **agendum** in Latin, but in modern English it is normally used as a singular noun with a standard plural form (**agendas**). See also **DATA** and **MEDIA**.

ORIGIN – Latin, 'things to be done', from *agere* 'to do'.

agent > *noun* 1 a person that provides a particular service, typically one that involves liaising between two other parties. 2 a spy. 3 a person or thing that takes an active role or produces a specified effect.

SYNONYMS – 1 broker, go-between, representative. 3 instrument, means, mover, vehicle.

COMBINATIONS – **agent noun** a noun denoting a person or thing that performs the action of a verb, usually ending in -*er* or -*or*, e.g. *worker, accelerator*.

wordpower facts

Agent

Agent and **actor** are related: they both come from Latin *agere* (stem *agent-*) 'to do, act, or drive', from which a great number of important English words are formed. The majority begin with **a-**, for example **act**, **agenda**, **agile**, **agitate**, and **ambiguous**. Others include **cogent** (literally 'compelling, driving together'), **exact** ('completed, done thoroughly'), and **navigate** ('sail, 'drive' a ship').

agent provocateur /aazhoN prəvokkətör/ > *noun* (pl. **agents provocateurs** pronunc. same) a person employed to induce suspected offenders to commit criminal acts and thus be convicted.
ORIGIN – French, 'provocative agent'.

agglomerate > *verb* /əglommərayt/ collect or form into a mass. > *noun* /əglommərət/ a mass or collection of things.
DERIVATIVES – **agglomeration** *noun*.
ORIGIN – Latin *agglomerare* 'add to'.

agglutinate /əglootinayt/ > *verb* firmly stick together to form a mass.
DERIVATIVES – **agglutination** *noun*.
ORIGIN – Latin *agglutinare* 'cause to adhere'.

aggrandise /əgrandīz/ (also **aggrandize**) > *verb* **1** increase the power, status, or wealth of. **2** artificially enhance the reputation of.
DERIVATIVES – **aggrandisement** *noun*.
ORIGIN – French *agrandir*, from Latin *grandis* 'large'.

aggravate > *verb* **1** make worse. **2** informal annoy or exasperate.
DERIVATIVES – **aggravating** *adjective* **aggravation** *noun*.
USAGE – the use of **aggravate** to mean 'annoy or exasperate' is not regarded as good English, although it actually dates back to the 17th century.
SYNONYMS – **1** exacerbate, intensify, worsen.
ORIGIN – Latin *aggravare* 'make heavy', from *gravis* 'heavy, serious'.

aggravated > *adjective* Law (of an offence) made more serious by related circumstances.

aggregate > *noun* /agrigət/ **1** a whole formed by combining several different elements. **2** the total score of a player or team in a fixture comprising more than one game or round. > *adjective* /agrigət/ formed or calculated by the combination of many separate items. > *verb* /agrigayt/ combine into a whole.
DERIVATIVES – **aggregation** *noun* **aggregative** /agrigətiv/ *adjective*.
SYNONYMS – *noun* **1** amalgam, collection, jumble, mass.
ORIGIN – Latin *aggregare* 'herd together', from *grex* 'a flock'.

aggression > *noun* hostile or violent behaviour or attitudes.
ORIGIN – Latin, from *aggredi* 'to attack'.

aggressive* > *adjective* **1** characterised by or resulting from aggression. **2** unduly forceful.
DERIVATIVES – **aggressively** *adverb* **aggressiveness** *noun*.
*SPELLING – double g, double s: ag*gressive*.
SYNONYMS – **1** belligerent, combative, hostile, violent.
ANTONYMS – **1** friendly, submissive.

aggressor > *noun* a person or country that attacks another without being provoked.

aggrieved* > *adjective* resentful because of unfair treatment.
*SPELLING – remember, the usual rule is *i* before *e* except after *c*: aggr*ieved*.
SYNONYMS – affronted, indignant, irked, piqued.
ORIGIN – past participle of the obsolete verb *aggrieve*, from Latin *aggravare* 'make heavier'.

aggro > *noun* Brit. informal **1** aggressive behaviour. **2** difficulties.
ORIGIN – abbreviation of *aggravation*.

aghast /əgaast/ > *adjective* filled with horror or shock.
ORIGIN – from obsolete *gast* 'frighten'; spelling influenced by GHOST (compare with GHASTLY).

agile > *adjective* able to move quickly and easily.
DERIVATIVES – **agilely** *adverb* **agility** *noun*.
SYNONYMS – fit, lithe, nimble, supple.
ORIGIN – Latin *agilis*, from *agere* 'to do'.

agitate > *verb* **1** make troubled or nervous. **2** campaign to arouse public concern about an issue. **3** stir or disturb (a liquid) briskly.
DERIVATIVES – **agitation** *noun*.
SYNONYMS – **1** disquiet, disturb, perturb, upset, worry. **2** campaign, crusade, fight.
ORIGIN – Latin *agitare* 'agitate, drive', from *agere* 'to do or drive'.

agitator > *noun* a person who urges others to protest or rebel.

agitprop /ajitprop/ > *noun* political propaganda, especially in the arts.
ORIGIN – from Russian *agitatsiya* 'agitation' + *propaganda* 'propaganda'.

aglet /aglət/ > *noun* a metal or plastic tube fixed round each end of a shoelace.
ORIGIN – French *aiguillette* 'small needle'.

AGM > *abbreviation* annual general meeting.

agnostic /agnostik/ > *noun* a person who believes that nothing can be known concerning the existence of God. > *adjective* relating to agnostics.
DERIVATIVES – **agnosticism** *noun*.

ago > *adverb* before the present (used with a measurement of time).
USAGE – when **ago** is followed by a clause, the clause should be introduced by **that** rather than **since**, e.g. *it was sixty years ago that I left this place* (not *it was sixty years ago since I left this place*).
ORIGIN – past participle of the obsolete verb *ago* 'pass', used to express passage of time.

agog > *adjective* very eager to hear or see something.
ORIGIN – from Old French *en gogues*, from *en* 'in' + *gogue* 'fun'.

agonise (also **agonize**) > *verb* **1** worry greatly. **2** cause agony to.
DERIVATIVES – **agonising** *adjective* **agonisingly** *adverb*.

agony > *noun* (pl. **agonies**) extreme suffering.
SYNONYMS – anguish, pain, torment, torture.
COMBINATIONS – **agony aunt** (or **agony uncle**) Brit. informal a person who answers letters in an agony column. **agony column** Brit. informal a column in a newspaper or magazine offering advice on readers' personal problems.
ORIGIN – Greek *agōnia*, from *agōn* 'contest'.

agora[1] /aggərə/ > *noun* (pl. **agorae** /aggəree/ or **agoras**) (in ancient Greece) a public open space used for assemblies and markets.
ORIGIN – Greek.

agora[2] /aggəraa/ > *noun* (pl. **agorot** or **agoroth** /aggərōt/) a monetary unit of Israel, equal to one hundredth of a shekel.
ORIGIN – Hebrew, 'small coin'.

agoraphobia /aggərəfōbiə/ > *noun* irrational fear of open or public places.
DERIVATIVES – **agoraphobic** *adjective* & *noun*.
ORIGIN – from Greek *agora* 'marketplace'.

agrarian /əgrairiən/ > *adjective* relating to agriculture.
ORIGIN – Latin *agrarius*, from *ager* 'field'.

agree > *verb* (**agrees**, **agreed**, **agreeing**) **1** have the same opinion about something. **2** (**be agreed**) (of two or more parties) be in agreement. **3** (**agree to**) express willingness to comply with (a request, suggestion, etc.). **4** (also **agree on**) chiefly Brit. reach agreement about. **5** (**agree with**) be consistent with. **6** be good for: *hard-boiled eggs did not agree with her.*
SYNONYMS – **1** concur, see eye to eye. **3** (**agree to**) accede to, acquiesce in, assent to, consent to. **5** (**agree with**) conform to, correspond to, match.
ANTONYMS – **1** differ, disagree.

ORIGIN – Old French *agreer*, from Latin *ad-* 'to' + *gratus* 'pleasing'.

agreeable > *adjective* **1** pleasant. **2** willing to agree to something. **3** acceptable.

DERIVATIVES – **agreeableness** *noun* **agreeably** *adverb*.

agreement > *noun* **1** the state of agreeing with someone or something. **2** consistency. **3** a negotiated and typically legally binding arrangement.

SYNONYMS – **1,2** concurrence, harmony. **3** contract, pact, treaty.

ANTONYMS – **1** disagreement. **2** inconsistency.

agriculture > *noun* the science or practice of farming, including the growing of crops and rearing of animals.

DERIVATIVES – **agricultural** *adjective* **agriculturally** *adverb* **agriculturist** *noun*.

ORIGIN – Latin *agricultura*, from *ager* 'field' + *cultura* 'cultivation'.

agrimony /ˈagrɪməni/ > *noun* (pl. **agrimonies**) a plant with slender spikes of yellow flowers.

ORIGIN – Greek *argemōnē* 'poppy'.

agrochemical > *noun* a chemical used in agriculture.

agronomy /əˈgrɒnəmi/ > *noun* the science of soil management and crop production.

DERIVATIVES – **agronomic** *adjective* **agronomist** *noun*.

ORIGIN – from Greek *agros* 'field' + *-nomos* 'arranging'.

aground > *adjective & adverb* (with reference to a ship) on or on to the bottom in shallow water.

ague /ˈaygyoo/ > *noun* archaic **1** malaria or some other illness involving fever and shivering. **2** a fever or shivering fit.

ORIGIN – Old French, from Latin *acuta febris* 'acute fever'.

AH > *abbreviation* in the year of the Hegira (used in the Muslim calendar for reckoning years).

ORIGIN – from Latin *anno Hegirae*.

ahead > *adverb* **1** further forward in space or time. **2** in advance. **3** in the lead.

IDIOMS – **ahead of 1** before. **2** earlier than planned or expected.

ahistorical > *adjective* lacking historical perspective or context.

ahoy > *exclamation* Nautical a call to attract attention.

AI > *abbreviation* artificial intelligence.

AID > *abbreviation* artificial insemination by donor.

aid > *noun* **1** help or support. **2** material help given to a country in need. > *verb* help.

IDIOMS – **in aid of** chiefly Brit. in support of.

ORIGIN – Old French *aide*, from Latin *adjuvare*, from *juvare* 'help'.

aide /ayd/ > *noun* an assistant to a political leader.

aide-de-camp /ˌayd də ˈkoN/ > *noun* (pl. **aides-de-camp** pronunc. same) a military officer acting as a confidential assistant to a senior officer.

ORIGIN – French, 'camp adjutant'.

aide-memoire /ˌaydmemˈwaar/ > *noun* (pl. **aides-memoires** or **aides-memoire** pronunc. same) **1** a note, object, or device used to aid the memory. **2** a diplomatic memorandum.

ORIGIN – French, from *aider* 'to help' and *mémoire* 'memory'.

Aids > *noun* a disease, caused by the HIV virus and transmitted in body fluids, in which the sufferer loses immunity to infection and some forms of cancer.

ORIGIN – acronym from *acquired immune deficiency syndrome*.

aikido /īˈkeedō/ > *noun* a Japanese form of self-defence and martial art that uses locks, holds, throws, and the opponent's own movements.

ORIGIN – Japanese, 'way of adapting the spirit'.

ail > *verb* archaic trouble or afflict in mind or body.

aileron /ˈayləron/ > *noun* a hinged surface in the trailing edge of an aircraft's wing, used to control the roll of the aircraft about its longitudinal axis.

ORIGIN – French, 'small wing'.

ailing > *adjective* in poor health.

ailment > *noun* a minor illness.

ailurophobia /īˌlyoorəˈfōbiə/ > *noun* extreme or irrational fear of cats.

DERIVATIVES – **ailurophobe** *noun*.

ORIGIN – from Greek *ailuros* 'cat'.

aim > *verb* **1** point (a weapon or camera) at a target. **2** direct at someone or something. **3** try to achieve something. > *noun* **1** a purpose or intention. **2** the aiming of a weapon or missile.

IDIOMS – **take aim** point a weapon or camera at a target.

SYNONYMS – *verb* **1,2** direct, focus, level, train. **3** (**aim for**) aspire to, seek, work towards. *noun* **1** goal, objective, target.

ORIGIN – Old French *amer*, from Latin *aestimare* 'assess, estimate'.

aimless > *adjective* without purpose or direction.

DERIVATIVES – **aimlessly** *adverb* **aimlessness** *noun*.

SYNONYMS – pointless, purposeless.

ANTONYMS – purposeful.

ain't > *contraction* informal **1** am not; are not; is not. **2** has not; have not.

USAGE – **ain't** is not acceptable in formal contexts, although it is widespread in many dialects and in informal speech.

aioli /īˈōli/ > *noun* mayonnaise seasoned with garlic.

ORIGIN – French, from Provençal *ai* 'garlic' + *oli* 'oil'.

wordpower facts
Air
Air is interesting as a word in which different meanings come from different sources. The main modern meanings, senses 1 to 5, entered English via Old French and Latin from Greek *aēr*. Senses 7 and 8 are probably from a completely different word, Old French *aire* 'site, disposition', which derives from the Latin word *ager* 'field', the root of English words such as **agriculture**. The Italian word *aria* (used in English to denote a long operatic solo song) gave English sense 6, 'tune or melody', although the Italian form actually goes back to the same Latin base as senses 1 to 5.

air > *noun* **1** the invisible gaseous substance surrounding the earth, a mixture mainly of oxygen and nitrogen. **2** the open space above the surface of the earth. **3** (before another noun) indicating the use of aircraft: *air travel*. **4** the earth's atmosphere as a medium for transmitting radio waves. **5** one of the four elements (air, earth, fire, and water) in ancient and medieval philosophy and in astrology. **6** Music a tune or short melodious composition. **7** an impression or manner. **8** (**airs**) an affected and condescending manner. > *verb* **1** express (an opinion or grievance) publicly. **2** broadcast (a programme) on radio or television. **3** expose to fresh or warm air.

IDIOMS – **airs and graces** an affectation of superiority. **in the air** noticeable all around. **on** (or **off**) **the air** being (or not being) broadcast on radio or television. **take the air** go out of doors. **up in the air** unresolved. **walk** (or **tread**) **on air** feel elated.

DERIVATIVES – **airless** *adjective*.

COMBINATIONS – **air bag** a safety device in a vehicle, that inflates rapidly when there is a sudden impact, so cushioning the occupant. **airbase** a base for military aircraft. **air bed** Brit. an inflatable mattress. **air bladder** an air-filled bladder or sac found in certain animals and plants. **air brake 1** a brake worked by air pressure. **2** a movable flap or other device on an aircraft to reduce its speed. **airbrick** Brit. a brick perforated with small holes for ventilation. **airburst** an explosion in the air, especially of a nuclear bomb. **air chief marshal** a high rank of RAF officer, above air marshal and below Marshal of the RAF. **air commodore** a rank of RAF officer, above group captain and below air vice-marshal. **air cushion 1** an inflatable cushion. **2** the layer of air supporting a hovercraft or similar vehicle. **airdrop** an act of dropping supplies, troops, or equipment by parachute. **airfield** an area of land set aside for the take-off, landing, and maintenance of aircraft. **air force** a branch of the armed forces concerned with fighting or defence in the air. **airframe** the body of an aircraft as distinct from its engine. **airfreight** the carriage of goods by aircraft. **air-freshener** a scented substance or device for masking unpleasant odours in a room. **air gun 1** a gun which uses compressed air to fire pellets. **2** a tool using very hot air to strip paint. **airhead** informal a stupid person. **air hostess** Brit. a stewardess in a passenger aircraft. **air kiss** a restrained embrace, in which the lips are pursed as if kissing but without making contact. **air letter** a sheet of light paper folded and sealed to form a letter for sending by airmail. **airlift** an act of transporting supplies by aircraft, typically in an emergency. **airlock 1** a stoppage of the flow in a pump or pipe, caused by an air bubble. **2** a compartment with controlled pressure and parallel sets of doors, to permit movement between areas at different pressures. **airmail** a system of transporting mail overseas by air. **airman** (or **airwoman**) **1** a pilot or member of the crew of an aircraft in an air force. **2** a member of the RAF below commissioned rank. **air marshal** a high rank of RAF officer, above air vice-marshal and below air chief marshal. **air mile 1** a nautical mile used as a measure of distance flown by aircraft. **2** (**Air Miles**) trademark points (equivalent to miles of free air travel) accumulated by buyers of airline tickets and other products. **air pistol** (also **air rifle**) a gun which uses compressed air to fire pellets. **air plant** a tropical American epiphytic plant with long, narrow leaves that absorb water and nutrients from the atmosphere. **airplay** broadcasting time devoted to a particular record, performer, or musical genre. **air pocket 1** a cavity containing air. **2** a region of low pressure causing an aircraft to lose height suddenly. **air quality** the degree to which the air is pollution-free. **air raid** an attack in which bombs are dropped from aircraft on to a ground target. **air-sea rescue** a rescue from the sea using aircraft. **airspace** the part of the air above and subject to the jurisdiction of a particular country. **airspeed** the speed of an aircraft relative to the air through which it is moving. **airstream** a current of air. **airstrip** a strip of ground for the take-off and landing of aircraft. **airtime** time during which a broadcast is being transmitted. **air traffic control** the ground-based personnel and equipment concerned with controlling and monitoring air traffic within a particular area. **air vice-**

marshal a high rank of RAF officer, above air commodore and below air marshal. **airwaves** the radio frequencies used for broadcasting.

airborne > *adjective* **1** carried or spread through the air. **2** (of an aircraft) flying.

airbrush > *noun* an artist's device for spraying paint by means of compressed air. > *verb* **1** paint with an airbrush. **2** alter or conceal (a photograph or a part of a photograph) using an airbrush.

air conditioning > *noun* a system for controlling the humidity, ventilation, and temperature in a building or vehicle.

DERIVATIVES – **air-conditioned** *adjective* **air conditioner** *noun*.

aircraft > *noun* (pl. same) an aeroplane, helicopter, or other machine capable of flight.

WORDFINDER – aileron, flaps, fuselage, rudder, spoiler, stabiliser, tailplane, undercarriage (*parts of aeroplane*); jet, piston engine, ramjet, turbofan, turbojet, turboprop (*kinds of aircraft engine*); aerodynamics, aeronautics (*science of aircraft flight*), aviation (*business of operating aircraft*), avionics (*aircraft electronics*).

COMBINATIONS – **aircraft carrier** a large warship from which aircraft can take off and land. **aircraftman** (or **aircraftwoman**) the lowest RAF rank, below leading aircraftman (or leading aircraftwoman).

aircrew > *noun* **1** the crew of an aircraft. **2** a member of an aircraft's crew.

Airedale > *noun* a large rough-coated black-and-tan breed of terrier.

ORIGIN – from *Airedale*, a district in Yorkshire.

airer > *noun* Brit. a frame or stand for airing or drying laundry.

airing > *noun* **1** an exposure to warm or fresh air. **2** a public expression of an opinion or discussion of a subject.

airline > *noun* **1** an organisation providing a regular passenger air service. **2** (**air line**) a pipe or tube supplying air.

airliner > *noun* a large passenger aircraft.

airplane > *noun* North American term for **AEROPLANE**.

airport > *noun* a complex of runways and buildings for the take-off, landing, and maintenance of civil aircraft, with facilities for passengers.

airship > *noun* a power-driven aircraft kept buoyant by a body of gas (usually helium) which is lighter than air.

WORDFINDER – blimp (*small airship or barrage balloon*), dirigible (*steerable airship*), envelope (*gas container of airship*), gondola (*cabin beneath an airship's body*), Zeppelin (*early German airship*).

airtight > *adjective* **1** not allowing air to escape or pass through. **2** unassailable: *an airtight alibi*.

airway > *noun* **1** the passage by which air reaches the lungs. **2** a tube for supplying air to the lungs in an emergency. **3** a recognised route followed by aircraft.

airworthy > *adjective* (of an aircraft) safe to fly.

DERIVATIVES – **airworthiness** *noun*.

airy > *adjective* (**airier**, **airiest**) **1** spacious and well ventilated. **2** light as air; delicate. **3** casual; dismissive.

DERIVATIVES – **airily** *adverb* **airiness** *noun*.

airy-fairy > *adjective* informal, chiefly Brit. foolishly idealistic and vague.

aisle /īl/ > *noun* **1** a passage between rows of seats. **2** a passage between sets of shelves in a supermarket, bookshop, etc. **3** Architecture a side part of a church parallel to, and divided by pillars from, a nave, choir, or transept.

IDIOMS – **lead up the aisle** get married to (someone).

ORIGIN – Old French *ele*, from Latin *ala* 'wing'.

aitch > *noun* the letter H.

IDIOMS – **drop one's aitches** fail to pronounce the letter *h* at the beginning of words.

ORIGIN – Old French *ache*.

aitchbone > *noun* **1** the buttock or rump bone of cattle. **2** a cut of beef lying over this.

ORIGIN – from dialect *nache* 'rump' (from Latin *natis* 'buttock') + **BONE**; the initial *n* was lost by wrong division of *a nache bone*.

ajar > *adverb & adjective* (of a door or window) slightly open.

ORIGIN – from obsolete *char*, from Old English *cerr* 'a turn'.

AK > *abbreviation* Alaska.

aka > *abbreviation* also known as.

Akan /aakən/ > *noun* (pl. same) **1** a member of a people inhabiting southern Ghana and adjacent parts of Ivory Coast. **2** the language of this people.

ORIGIN – the name in Akan.

akee > *noun* variant spelling of **ACKEE**.

akimbo > *adverb* with hands on the hips and elbows turned outwards.

akin > *adjective* **1** of similar character; alike. **2** related by blood.

akvavit /akvəvit/ > *noun* variant spelling of **AQUAVIT**.

AL > *abbreviation* Alabama.

Al > *symbol* the chemical element aluminium.

-al > *suffix* **1** (forming adjectives) relating to; of the kind of: *tidal*. **2** forming nouns chiefly denoting verbal action: *arrival*.

alabaster /aləbaastə, aləbaastər/ > *noun* a translucent form of gypsum, typically white, often carved into ornaments. > *adjective* literary smooth and white: *her pale, alabaster skin*.

ORIGIN – Latin, from Greek *alabastros*.

à la carte /aa laa **kaart**/ > *adjective & adverb* offering or ordered as dishes that are separately priced, rather than part of a set meal.
ORIGIN – French, 'according to the card'.

alack (also **alack-a-day**) > *exclamation* archaic an expression of regret or dismay.

alacrity > *noun* brisk and cheerful readiness.
ORIGIN – Latin *alacritas*, from *alacer* 'brisk'.

Aladdin's cave > *noun* a place filled with precious or interesting items.
ORIGIN – from *Aladdin* in the *Arabian Nights* who finds a magic lamp in a cave.

à la mode /aa laa **mōd**/ > *adverb & adjective* up to date; fashionable.
ORIGIN – French, 'in the fashion'.

alanine /**al**əneen/ > *noun* Biochemistry an amino acid which is a constituent of most proteins.
ORIGIN – from ALDEHYDE.

alarm > *noun* **1** anxious or frightened awareness of danger. **2** a warning of danger. **3** a warning sound or device. > *verb* **1** frighten or disturb. **2** (**be alarmed**) be fitted or protected with an alarm.
DERIVATIVES – **alarming** *adjective* **alarmingly** *adverb*.
SYNONYMS – *noun* **1** anxiety, apprehension, fear. **2** alert. *verb* **1** disturb, frighten, panic, scare.
COMBINATIONS – **alarm clock** a clock that can be preset to sound an alarm at a particular time to wake someone from sleep.
ORIGIN – from Italian *all' arme!* 'to arms!'

alarmist > *noun* a person who exaggerates a danger, so causing needless alarm. > *adjective* creating needless alarm.
DERIVATIVES – **alarmism** *noun*.

alarum /əl**aar**əm/ > *noun* archaic term for **ALARM**.
IDIOMS – **alarums and excursions** humorous confused activity and uproar.

alas > *exclamation* literary or humorous an expression of grief, pity, or concern.
ORIGIN – Old French *a las, a lasse*, from Latin *lassus* 'weary'.

alb > *noun* a white robe reaching to the feet, worn by clergy and servers in some Christian Churches.
ORIGIN – from Latin *tunica alba* 'white garment'.

albacore /**al**bəkor/ > *noun* a tuna of warm seas which travels in shoals.
ORIGIN – Arabic, probably from a word meaning 'premature, precocious'.

Albanian > *noun* **1** a person from Albania. **2** the language of Albania. > *adjective* relating to Albania.

albatross > *noun* (pl. **albatrosses**) **1** a very large seabird with long, narrow wings, found chiefly in the southern oceans. **2** a burden or encumbrance (in allusion to Coleridge's *The Rime of the Ancient Mariner*).
ORIGIN – alteration (influenced by Latin *albus* 'white') of *alcatras*, a 16th-century word applied to various seabirds; from an Arabic word meaning 'the diver'.

albedo /al**bee**dō/ > *noun* (pl. **albedos**) chiefly Astronomy the proportion of the light shining on a surface that is reflected by it.
ORIGIN – Latin, 'whiteness'.

albeit /awl**bee**it/ > *conjunction* though.
ORIGIN – from *all be it*.

albino /al**bee**nō/ > *noun* (pl. **albinos**) a person or animal having a congenital absence of pigment in the skin and hair (which are white) and the eyes (which are usually pink).
DERIVATIVES – **albinism** /**al**biniz'm/ *noun*.
ORIGIN – from Latin *albus* 'white'.

Albion > *noun* literary Britain or England.
ORIGIN – Latin, probably of Celtic origin and related to Latin *albus* 'white' (in allusion to the white cliffs of Dover).

album > *noun* **1** a blank book for the insertion of photographs, stamps, or other items forming a collection. **2** a collection of recordings issued as a single item.
ORIGIN – Latin, 'blank tablet', from *albus* 'white'; originally used in the Latin phrase *album amicorum* 'album of friends', referring to a blank book in which autographs, drawings, poems, etc. were collected.

albumen /**al**byoomin/ > *noun* egg white, or the protein contained in it.
ORIGIN – Latin, from *albus* 'white'.

albumin /**al**byoomin/ > *noun* Biochemistry a water-soluble form of protein found especially in blood serum and egg white and able to be coagulated by heat.
DERIVATIVES – **albuminous** /al**byoo**minəss/ *adjective*.

alcazar /alkə**zaar**/ > *noun* a Spanish palace or fortress of Moorish origin.
ORIGIN – Spanish, from an Arabic word meaning 'the castle'.

alchemy /**al**kəmi/ > *noun* **1** the medieval forerunner of chemistry, concerned particularly with attempts to convert common metals into gold or to find a universal elixir. **2** a mysterious or paradoxical process.
WORDFINDER – alkahest (*universal solvent*), elixir of life (*substance able to prolong life*), philosopher's stone (*substance able to change base metals into gold*), transmutation (*process of changing metals into gold*).
DERIVATIVES – **alchemical** *adjective*

alchemise (also **alchemize**) *verb* **alchemist** *noun*.
ORIGIN – from an Arabic word based on Greek *khēmia, khēmeia* 'art of transmuting metals'.

alcheringa /alchə**ring**gə/ > *noun* (in Australian Aboriginal mythology) a 'golden age' when the first ancestors were created.
ORIGIN – Aranda (an Aboriginal language), 'in the dreamtime'.

alcohol > *noun* **1** a colourless volatile liquid compound which is the intoxicating ingredient in drinks such as wine, beer, and spirits. **2** drink containing this. **3** Chemistry any organic compound containing a hydroxyl group —OH: *propyl alcohol*.
WORDFINDER – abstinence, teetotalism, temperance (*refusal to drink alcohol*), alcoholism, dipsomania (*addiction to alcohol*), delirium tremens (*alcoholic tremors*), libation (*a drink of alcohol*).
SYNONYMS – **1** Chemistry ethanol, ethyl alcohol.

wordpower facts

Alcohol

Perhaps surprisingly, the word **alcohol** is related to **kohl**, a black powder used as eye make-up. **Alcohol** entered English in the 16th century from French or medieval Latin, from Arabic *al-kuḥl* 'the kohl'. In early use the term referred to powders, specifically kohl, and especially to pure substances prepared by sublimation. In the 17th century it came to mean 'a distilled spirit or essence', the most familiar example being 'alcohol of wine', later shortened simply to 'alcohol'.

alcoholic > *adjective* **1** of or containing alcohol. **2** relating to the consumption of alcohol. > *noun* a person suffering from alcoholism.

alcoholism > *noun* addiction to alcoholic liquor.

alcopop > *noun* Brit. informal a ready-mixed soft drink containing alcohol.

alcove > *noun* a recess, typically in the wall of a room.
ORIGIN – Arabic, 'the vault'.

aldehyde /**al**dihīd/ > *noun* Chemistry an organic compound containing the group —CHO, formed by the oxidation of alcohols.
ORIGIN – from Latin *alcohol dehydrogenatum* 'alcohol deprived of hydrogen'.

al dente /al **den**tay/ > *adjective & adverb* (of food, especially pasta) cooked so as to be still firm when bitten.
ORIGIN – Italian, 'to the tooth'.

alder > *noun* a catkin-bearing tree of the birch family with toothed leaves, found especially on damp ground and riverbanks.

alderman > *noun* **1** chiefly historical a co-opted member of an English county or borough council, next in status to the mayor. **2** (also **alderwoman**) N. Amer. & Austral. an elected member of a city council.
ORIGIN – Old English, 'chief, patriarch', from *ald* 'old'.

ale > *noun* **1** chiefly Brit. beer other than lager, stout, or porter. **2** N. Amer. beer brewed by a fermentation process in which the yeast rises to the top.

aleatory /**ay**liətəri/ (also **aleatoric** /**ay**liə**torr**ik/) > *adjective* **1** depending on the throw of a dice or on chance. **2** (of music or other forms of art) involving elements of random choice during their composition or performance.
ORIGIN – from Latin *aleator* 'dice player'.

alembic /ə**lem**bik/ > *noun* an apparatus formerly used for distilling, consisting of a gourd-shaped container and a cap with a long spout.
ORIGIN – Arabic, from Greek *ambix* 'cup'.

alert > *adjective* **1** quick to notice and respond to danger or unusual circumstances. **2** quick-witted. > *noun* **1** (often in phrase **on the alert**) the state of being alert. **2** a warning of danger. > *verb* warn of a danger or problem.
DERIVATIVES – **alertly** *adverb* **alertness** *noun*.
SYNONYMS – *adjective* **1** attentive, aware, observant, vigilant. *verb* caution, warn.
ANTONYMS – *adjective* **1** inattentive.
ORIGIN – French *alerte*, from Italian *all' erta* 'to the watchtower'.

Alexander technique > *noun* a system designed to promote well-being through the control of posture.
ORIGIN – named after the Australian-born actor and elocutionist Frederick Matthias *Alexander* (1869–1955).

alexandrine /alig**zan**drīn/ Poetry > *adjective* (of a line of verse) having six iambic feet. > *noun* an alexandrine line.
ORIGIN – French, from the name of Alexander the Great, the subject of an Old French poem in this metre.

alfalfa /al**fal**fə/ > *noun* a plant with clover-like leaves and bluish flowers, grown in warm climates for fodder.
ORIGIN – Spanish, from an Arabic word meaning 'a green fodder'.

alfresco /al**fres**kō/ > *adverb* & *adjective* in the open air.
ORIGIN – Italian *al fresco* 'in the fresh (air)'.

alga /**al**gə/ > *noun* (pl. **algae** /**al**gee, **al**jee/) any of a large group of simple plants containing chlorophyll but lacking true stems, roots, and leaves, e.g. seaweed.
DERIVATIVES – **algal** *adjective*.
ORIGIN – Latin, 'seaweed'.

algebra /**al**jibrə/ > *noun* the branch of mathematics in which letters and other symbols are used to represent numbers and quantities in formulae and equations.
DERIVATIVES – **algebraic** /alji**bray**ik/ *adjective* **algebraist** *noun*.

wordpower facts
Algebra
The word **algebra** comes from Arabic *al-jabr* 'the reunion of broken parts', 'bone-setting', and in English it originally meant 'the surgical treatment of fractures'. The modern mathematical sense comes from the title of a book, *'ilm al-jabr wa'l-muḳābala* 'the science of restoring what is missing and equating like with like', by the 9th-century Muslim mathematician Abū Jaʿfar Muhammad ibn Mūsa, known as al-Ḵwārizmī (literally 'the man from Ḵwārizm', now Khiva in Uzbekistan); this nickname is the root of the word **algorithm**.

Algerian > *noun* a person from Algeria. > *adjective* relating to Algeria.

-algia > *combining form* denoting pain in a specified part of the body: *neuralgia*.
DERIVATIVES – **-algic** *combining form*.
ORIGIN – from Greek *algos* 'pain'.

Algonquian /al**gong**kwiən/ (also **Algonkian**) > *noun* **1** a large family of North American Indian languages. **2** a speaker of any of these languages. > *adjective* relating to this family of languages or its speakers.
NOTE – the terms **Algonquin** and **Algonquian** do not mean the same thing: **Algonquian** refers to a family of languages, of which **Algonquin** is a specific member. Other Algonquian languages include Arapaho, Cree, Blackfoot, Cheyenne, Mahican, and Ojibwa.

Algonquin /al**gong**kwin/ (also **Algonkin** /al**gong**kin/) > *noun* **1** a member of an American Indian people living in Canada along and westwards of the Ottawa River. **2** the Algonquian language of this people. > *adjective* relating to this people or their language.
ORIGIN – French, from a Micmac word meaning 'at the place of spearing fish and eels'.

algorithm /**al**gərithəm/ > *noun* a process or set of rules used in calculations or other problem-solving operations.
DERIVATIVES – **algorithmic** *adjective*.
ORIGIN – from the name of a 9th-century mathematician (see box at **ALGEBRA**).

alias /**ay**liəss/ > *adverb* also known as. > *noun* **1** a false identity or assumed name. **2** Computing an identifying label used to access a file, command, or address.
ORIGIN – Latin, 'at another time, otherwise'.

alibi /**al**ibī/ > *noun* (pl. **alibis**) a claim or piece of evidence that one was elsewhere when an alleged act took place. > *verb* (**alibis, alibied, alibiing**) informal provide an alibi for.
USAGE – the word **alibi** means 'an assertion by a person that he or she was elsewhere'; avoid using it simply to mean 'an excuse'.
ORIGIN – Latin, 'elsewhere'.

Alice band > *noun* a flexible band worn to hold back the hair.
ORIGIN – named after the heroine of *Alice's Adventures in Wonderland* by Lewis Carroll.

alien > *adjective* **1** belonging to a foreign country. **2** unfamiliar and disturbing. **3** (of a plant or animal species) introduced from another country and later naturalised. **4** relating to beings from other worlds. > *noun* **1** a foreigner. **2** an alien plant or animal species. **3** a being from another world.
DERIVATIVES – **alienness** *noun*.
SYNONYMS – *adjective* **1** foreign, non-native, overseas. **2** strange, unnatural. **4** extraterrestrial, unearthly.
ANTONYMS – *adjective* **1,3** native.
ORIGIN – Latin *alienus*, from *alius* 'other'.

alienate > *verb* **1** cause to feel isolated. **2** lose the support or sympathy of.
DERIVATIVES – **alienation** *noun*.

alight¹ > *verb* **1** formal, chiefly Brit. descend from a vehicle. **2** (**alight on**) chance to notice.

alight² > *adverb* & *adjective* **1** on fire. **2** shining brightly.

align > *verb* **1** place or arrange in a straight line or into correct relative positions. **2** (**align oneself with**) ally oneself to.
DERIVATIVES – **alignment** *noun*.
SYNONYMS – **1** arrange, line up, put in order. **2** (**align oneself with**) ally oneself with, associate with, side with.
ORIGIN – French *aligner*, from *à ligne* 'into line'.

alike > *adjective* similar. > *adverb* in a similar way.

alimentary > *adjective* providing nourishment or sustenance.
COMBINATIONS – **alimentary canal** the passage along which food passes through the body.
ORIGIN – Latin *alimentarius*, from *alimentum* 'nourishment'.

alimony > *noun* chiefly N. Amer. maintenance for a husband or wife after separation or divorce.
ORIGIN – first used in the sense 'nourishment, means of subsistence': from Latin *alimonia*, from *alere* 'nourish'.

aliphatic /alifattik/ > *adjective* Chemistry (of an organic compound) containing an open chain of carbon atoms in its molecule (as in the alkanes), not an aromatic ring.
ORIGIN – from Greek *aleiphar* 'fat'.

aliquot /alikwot/ > *noun* **1** a portion of a larger whole, especially a sample taken for chemical analysis or other treatment. **2** (also **aliquot part** or **portion**) Mathematics a quantity which can be divided into another a whole number of times. > *verb* divide into aliquots; take aliquots from.
ORIGIN – Latin, 'some, so many'.

alive > *adjective* **1** living; not dead. **2** continuing in existence or use. **3** alert and active. **4** having interest and meaning. **5** (**alive with**) swarming or teeming with.
DERIVATIVES – **aliveness** noun.
SYNONYMS – **1** animate, breathing, existing, extant, live, living. **2** active, extant, functioning.
ANTONYMS – dead; inactive, lifeless.

alkali /alkǝlī/ > *noun* (pl. **alkalis** or US also **alkalies**) a substance, such as lime or caustic soda, with particular chemical properties including turning litmus blue and neutralising or effervescing with acids.
ORIGIN – first used to denote a saline substance derived from the ashes of plants: from an Arabic word meaning 'fry or roast'.

alkaline > *adjective* containing an alkali or having the properties of an alkali; having a pH greater than 7.
DERIVATIVES – **alkalinity** noun.

alkaloid /alkǝloyd/ > *noun* Chemistry any of a class of nitrogenous organic compounds of plant origin which have pronounced physiological actions on humans.

alkane /alkayn/ > *noun* Chemistry any of the series of saturated hydrocarbons including methane, ethane, propane, and higher members.

alkene /alkeen/ > *noun* Chemistry any of the series of unsaturated hydrocarbons containing a double bond, including ethylene and propene.

alkyl /alkīl/ > *noun* Chemistry a hydrocarbon radical derived from an alkane by removal of a hydrogen atom.

alkyne /alkīn/ > *noun* Chemistry any of the series of unsaturated hydrocarbons containing a triple bond, including acetylene.

all > *predeterminer & determiner* **1** the whole quantity or extent of: *all her money.* **2** any

whatever: *he denied all knowledge.* **3** the greatest possible: *with all speed.* > *pronoun* everything or everyone. > *adverb* **1** completely. **2** indicating an equal score: *one-all.*
IDIOMS – **all along** from the beginning. **all and sundry** everyone. **all but 1** very nearly. **2** all except. **all for** informal strongly in favour of. **all in** informal exhausted. **all in all** on the whole. **all out** using all one's strength or resources: *going all-out to win.* **all over 1** everywhere. **2** typical of the person mentioned: *that's our management all over!* **all over the place** informal **1** everywhere. **2** in a state of disorder. **all round 1** in all respects. **2** for or by each person: *drinks all round.* **all told** in total. **at all** in any way. **in all** in total. **one's all** one's whole strength or resources.
COMBINATIONS – **all-clear** a signal that danger or difficulty is over. **All Saints' Day** a Christian festival in honour of all the saints, held (in the Western Church) on 1 November. **All Souls' Day** a Catholic festival with prayers for the souls of the dead in purgatory, held on 2 November. **all-time** hitherto unsurpassed: *the all-time record.* **all-wheel drive** N. Amer. four-wheel drive.

Allah /alǝ/ > *noun* the name of God among Muslims (and Arab Christians).
ORIGIN – Arabic.

allay /ǝlay/ > *verb* **1** diminish or end (fear or concern). **2** alleviate (pain or hunger).

allegation > *noun* a claim that someone has done something illegal or wrong, typically made without proof.
SYNONYMS – accusation, assertion, claim.

allege /ǝlej/ > *verb* claim that someone has done something illegal or wrong, typically without proof.
DERIVATIVES – **alleged** adjective **allegedly** adverb.
SYNONYMS – assert, claim, contend.
ORIGIN – first used in the sense 'declare on oath': from Old French *esligier*, from Latin *lis* 'lawsuit'; confused in sense with Latin *allegare* 'allege'.

allegiance /ǝleejǝnss/ > *noun* loyalty of a subordinate to a superior or of an individual to a group or cause.
SYNONYMS – loyalty, obedience.
ORIGIN – Old French *ligeance*; related to **LIEGE**.

allegorical > *adjective* constituting or containing allegory.
DERIVATIVES – **allegoric** adjective **allegorically** adverb.

allegory /aligǝri/ > *noun* (pl. **allegories**) a story, poem, or picture which can be interpreted to reveal a hidden meaning.
DERIVATIVES – **allegorist** noun.

ORIGIN – Greek *allēgoria*, from *allos* 'other' + *-agoria* 'speaking'.

allegretto /aligrettō/ > *adverb & adjective* Music at a fairly brisk speed.
ORIGIN – Italian, from **ALLEGRO**.

allegro /ǝlegrō/ Music > *adverb & adjective* at a brisk speed. > *noun* (pl. **allegros**) an allegro movement, passage, or composition.
ORIGIN – Italian, 'lively'.

allele /aleel/ > *noun* Genetics one of two or more alternative forms of a gene that arise by mutation and are found at the same place on a chromosome.
DERIVATIVES – **allelic** adjective.
ORIGIN – German *Allel*, abbreviation of **ALLELOMORPH**.

allelomorph /ǝleelōmorf/ > *noun* an allele.
DERIVATIVES – **allelomorphic** adjective.
ORIGIN – from Greek *allēl-* 'one another' + *morphē* 'form'.

alleluia /alilōōyǝ/ > *exclamation & noun* variant spelling of **HALLELUJAH**.

Allen key > *noun* trademark a spanner designed to fit into and turn an Allen screw.

Allen screw > *noun* trademark a screw with a hexagonal socket in the head.
ORIGIN – from the name of the *Allen* Manufacturing Company, Connecticut.

allergen /alǝrjǝn/ > *noun* a substance that causes an allergic reaction.

allergenic > *adjective* likely to cause an allergic reaction.

allergic > *adjective* **1** caused by or relating to an allergy. **2** having an allergy.

allergy > *noun* (pl. **allergies**) an adverse reaction by the body to a substance to which it has become hypersensitive.
WORDFINDER – allergen (*substance causing allergy*), anaphylaxis (*extreme allergic reaction*), histamine (*substance released by cells in allergic reaction*), hypo-allergenic (*unlikely to cause allergy*), urticaria (*allergic rash*).
DERIVATIVES – **allergist** noun.
ORIGIN – from Greek *allos* 'other'.

alleviate /ǝleeviayt/ > *verb* make (pain or difficulty) less severe.
DERIVATIVES – **alleviation** noun **alleviator** noun.
SYNONYMS – allay, assuage, ease, reduce, relieve.
ANTONYMS – aggravate.
ORIGIN – Latin *alleviare* 'lighten'.

alley > *noun* (pl. **alleys**) **1** a narrow passageway between or behind buildings. **2** a path in a park or garden. **3** a long, narrow area in which skittles and bowling are played.
COMBINATIONS – **alley cat** a stray urban cat. **alleyway** an alley between or behind buildings.

wordpower facts

Alley

The word **alley** comes, via Old French *alee* 'walking or passage', from the Latin verb *ambulare* 'to walk', which is at the root of many English words. Most are to do with walking, such as **amble** and the formal verbs **circumambulate** and **perambulate** 'walk through or round'. Several are rather rare or technical words, such as **ambulant** 'able to walk', **noctambulist** 'sleepwalker', and **somnambulism** 'sleepwalking'. Perhaps surprisingly, the word **ambulance** is also from *ambulare*: this entered English via French *hôpital ambulant* 'mobile field hospital'.

alliance > *noun* **1** the state of being allied or associated. **2** a union or association between countries or organisations. **3** a relationship or connection.
SYNONYMS – **1,2** affiliation, association, confederation, league, union.

allied > *adjective* **1** joined by or relating to an alliance. **2** (**Allied**) relating to Britain and its allies in the First and Second World Wars. **3** (**allied to** or **with**) in combination or working together with.

alligator > *noun* a large semiaquatic reptile similar to a crocodile but with a broader and shorter head.
COMBINATIONS – **alligator pear** North American term for **AVOCADO**.
ORIGIN – from Spanish *el lagarto* 'the lizard'.

all-in > *adjective* Brit. (especially of a price) inclusive of everything.
COMBINATIONS – **all-in wrestling** wrestling with few or no restrictions.

alliteration > *noun* the occurrence of the same letter or sound at the beginning of adjacent or closely connected words.
DERIVATIVES – **alliterate** *verb* **alliterative** *adjective* **alliteratively** *adverb*.
ORIGIN – Latin, from *littera* 'letter'.

allium /ˈaliəm/ > *noun* (pl. **alliums**) a plant of a genus that includes onion, garlic, leek, and chives.
ORIGIN – Latin, 'garlic'.

allocate > *verb* distribute (resources or duties) for a particular purpose.
DERIVATIVES – **allocable** *adjective* **allocation** *noun* **allocative** *adjective* **allocator** *noun*.
SYNONYMS – allot, apportion, assign, distribute, share out.
ORIGIN – Latin *allocare*, from *locare* 'to place'.

allopathy /əˈlopəthi/ > *noun* the treatment of disease by conventional means, i.e. with drugs having effects opposite to the symptoms. Contrasted with **HOMEOPATHY**.
DERIVATIVES – **allopath** *noun* **allopathic** *adjective*.

allosaurus /aləˈsorəss/ > *noun* a large bipedal carnivorous dinosaur of the late Jurassic period.
ORIGIN – from Greek *allos* 'other' + *sauros* 'lizard'.

allot > *verb* (**allotted**, **allotting**) give or apportion (something) to someone.
SYNONYMS – allocate, apportion, assign, share out.
ORIGIN – Old French *aloter*, from Latin *loter* 'divide into lots'.

allotment > *noun* **1** Brit. a plot of land rented by an individual from a local authority, for growing vegetables or flowers. **2** the action of allotting. **3** an amount of something allotted.

allotrope /ˈalətrōp/ > *noun* Chemistry each of two or more different physical forms in which an element can exist (e.g. graphite, charcoal, and diamond as forms of carbon).
DERIVATIVES – **allotropic** *adjective* **allotropy** /əˈlotrəpi/ *noun*.
ORIGIN – from Greek *allotropos* 'of another form'.

allow > *verb* **1** admit as legal or acceptable. **2** permit to do something. **3** (**allow for**) take into consideration when making plans or calculations. **4** provide or set aside for a particular purpose. **5** admit the truth of.
DERIVATIVES – **allowable** *adjective* **allowedly** *adverb*.
SYNONYMS – **1,2** authorise, consent to, permit, sanction.
ANTONYMS – **1,2** forbid.
ORIGIN – Old French *alouer*, from Latin *allaudare* 'to praise', reinforced by Latin *allocare* 'allocate'.

allowance > *noun* **1** the amount of something allowed. **2** a sum of money paid regularly to a person. **3** an amount of money that can be earned or received free of tax.
IDIOMS – **make allowances for 1** take into consideration. **2** treat (someone) leniently because of their difficult circumstances.
SYNONYMS – **1** allocation, quota, share.

alloy > *noun* /ˈaloy/ **1** a metal made by combining two or more metallic elements, especially to give greater strength or resistance to corrosion. **2** an inferior metal mixed with a precious one. > *verb* /əˈloy/ **1** mix (metals) to make an alloy. **2** spoil by adding something inferior.
WORDFINDER – *some common alloys:* amalgam (*mercury with other metals*), brass (*copper and zinc*), bronze (*copper and tin*), German silver (*nickel, zinc, and copper*), ormolu (*copper, zinc, and tin*), pewter (*tin with copper and antimony*), pinchbeck (*copper*

and zinc), solder (*usually lead and tin*), steel (*iron with carbon and other metals*), white metal (*usually tin with other metals*).
ORIGIN – Old French *aloier*, *aleier* 'combine', from Latin *alligare* 'bind'.

all right > *adjective* **1** satisfactory; acceptable. **2** permissible. > *adverb* fairly well. > *exclamation* expressing or asking for agreement or acceptance.
USAGE – the preferred form in formal writing is **all right** rather than **alright**.

all-round (US **all-around**) > *adjective* **1** having a great many abilities or uses. **2** in many or all respects.

all-rounder > *noun* Brit. a person competent in a range of activities.

allspice > *noun* the dried aromatic fruit of a Caribbean tree, used as a culinary spice.

allude > *verb* (**allude to**) **1** hint at. **2** mention in passing.
ORIGIN – Latin *alludere*, from *ad-* 'towards' + *ludere* 'to play'.

allure > *noun* powerful attractiveness or charm. > *verb* strongly attract or charm.
DERIVATIVES – **allurement** *noun*.
ORIGIN – Old French *aleurier*, from Latin *luere* 'a lure'.

alluring > *adjective* having a powerful attraction or charm.
DERIVATIVES – **alluringly** *adverb*.
SYNONYMS – beguiling, enticing, glamorous, inviting, tempting.

allusion > *noun* an indirect reference to something.

allusive > *adjective* working by or employing allusion rather than explicit statement.
DERIVATIVES – **allusively** *adverb* **allusiveness** *noun*.

alluvium /əˈloōviəm/ > *noun* a fertile deposit of clay, silt, and sand left by river flood water.
DERIVATIVES – **alluvial** *adjective*.
ORIGIN – Latin, from *luere* 'to wash'.

ally > *noun* /ˈalī/ (pl. **allies**) **1** a person, organisation, or country that cooperates with another. **2** (**the Allies**) the countries that fought with Britain in the First and Second World Wars. > *verb* /əˈlī/ (**allies**, **allied**) (**ally to** or **with**) **1** beneficially combine (a resource or commodity) with. **2** (**ally oneself with**) side with.
SYNONYMS – *noun* **1** associate, colleague, friend, partner.
ORIGIN – Old French *alier*, from Latin *alligare* 'bind'.

-ally > *suffix* forming adverbs from adjectives ending in *-al* (such as *radically* from *radical*).

alma mater /ˈalmə ˈmaatər, ˈmaytər/ > *noun* the school, college, or university that one once attended.
ORIGIN – Latin, 'bountiful mother'.

almanac /ˈawlmənak/ (also **almanack**) > *noun* **1** a calendar giving important dates and information, such as the phases of the moon. **2** an annual handbook containing information of general or specialist interest.

ORIGIN – Greek *almenikhiaka*.

almighty > *adjective* **1** having unlimited power; omnipotent. **2** *informal* enormous. > *noun* (**the Almighty**) a name or title for God.

almond > *noun* **1** the oval edible nut-like kernel of the almond tree. **2** the tree that produces this, related to the peach and plum.

COMBINATIONS – **almond eyes** eyes that are narrow and oval with pointed ends. **almond paste** marzipan.

ORIGIN – Greek *amugdalē*.

almoner /**aa**mənər/ > *noun* historical an official distributor of alms.

DERIVATIVES – **almonry** *noun*.

almost > *adverb* very nearly.

alms /aamz/ > *plural noun* historical charitable donations of money or food to the poor.

COMBINATIONS – **almshouse** a house built originally by a charitable person or organisation for poor people to live in.

ORIGIN – Old English, from Greek *eleēmosunē* 'compassion'.

aloe /**al**ō/ > *noun* **1** a succulent tropical plant with thick tapering leaves and bell-shaped flowers. **2** (**aloes** or **bitter aloes**) a strong laxative obtained from the bitter juice of various kinds of aloe. **3** (also **American aloe**) the century plant. **4** (also **aloes wood**) the heartwood of a tropical Asian tree, yielding a fragrant resin.

ORIGIN – Greek.

aloe vera > *noun* a jelly-like substance obtained from a kind of aloe, used as a soothing treatment for the skin.

ORIGIN – Latin, 'true aloe', probably in contrast to the American agave, which the aloe plant closely resembles.

aloft > *adjective & adverb* up in or into the air.

alone > *adjective & adverb* **1** on one's own; by oneself. **2** isolated and lonely. **3** only; exclusively.

DERIVATIVES – **aloneness** *noun*.

SYNONYMS – **1** lone, single, solitary, unaccompanied.

along > *preposition & adverb* **1** moving in a constant direction on (a more or less horizontal surface). **2** extending in a more or less horizontal line on. **3** in or into company with others.

IDIOMS – **along with** in company with or at the same time as. **be** (or **come**) **along** arrive.

alongside > *preposition* (N. Amer. also **alongside of**) **1** close to the side of; next to. **2** at the same time as or in coexistence with.

aloof > *adjective* not friendly or forthcoming.

DERIVATIVES – **aloofly** *adverb* **aloofness** *noun*.

SYNONYMS – cool, distant, haughty, unapproachable.

ANTONYMS – approachable, friendly.

wordpower facts

Aloof

Aloof is one of a number of familiar English words and phrases that originated in nautical use. It comes from the verb **luff**, 'to steer a boat nearer the wind', and originally meant 'away and to windward!', i.e. with the ship's head kept close to the wind away from a lee shore or other hazard. Other words and phrases with nautical origins include **busk**, **chock-a-block**, **batten down the hatches**, **go by the board**, **heave into sight**, **swing the lead**, and **up sticks**.

alopecia /alə**pee**shə/ > *noun* Medicine the abnormal loss of hair.

ORIGIN – Greek *alōpekia* 'fox mange'.

aloud > *adverb* not silently; audibly.

ALP > *abbreviation* Australian Labor Party.

alp > *noun* **1** a high mountain. **2** (the **Alps**) a high range of mountains in Switzerland and adjoining countries. **3** (in Switzerland) an area of green pasture on a mountainside.

ORIGIN – Latin *Alpes*, from Greek *Alpeis*.

alpaca /al**pakk**ə/ > *noun* (pl. same or **alpacas**) **1** a long-haired domesticated South American mammal related to the llama. **2** the wool of the alpaca.

ORIGIN – Spanish, from Aymara (an American Indian language).

alpenhorn /**al**pənhorn/ > *noun* a very long valveless wooden wind instrument played like a horn and used for signalling in the Alps.

ORIGIN – German, 'Alp horn'.

alpenstock /**al**pənstok/ > *noun* a long iron-tipped stick used by hillwalkers.

ORIGIN – German, 'Alp stick'.

alpha /**al**fə/ > *noun* **1** the first letter of the Greek alphabet (A, α), transliterated as 'a'. **2** Brit. a first-class mark given for a piece of work.

IDIOMS – **alpha and omega** the beginning and the end.

COMBINATIONS – **alpha particle** (also **alpha ray**) Physics a helium nucleus, especially as emitted by some radioactive substances. **alpha rhythm** Physiology the normal electrical activity of the brain when conscious and relaxed. **alpha testing** trials of a new product carried out before beta testing.

ORIGIN – Greek.

alphabet > *noun* an ordered set of letters or symbols used to represent the basic speech sounds of a language.

WORDFINDER – Braille (*alphabet for the blind*), cuneiform (*ancient Middle Eastern alphabet with wedge-shaped characters*), Cyrillic (*used for Russian*), Devanagari (*used for Sanskrit*), futhark (*alphabet of runes*), hieroglyphics, pictographs (*writing with pictures, as in ancient Egypt*), Kufic (*early Arabic*), ogham (*ancient Celtic alphabet*), Roman (*used for writing English*), syllabary (*characters representing syllables*).

DERIVATIVES – **alphabetise** (also **alphabetize**) *verb*.

ORIGIN – from Greek *alpha* and *bēta*, the first two letters of the Greek alphabet.

alphabetical > *adjective* in the order of the letters of the alphabet.

DERIVATIVES – **alphabetic** *adjective* **alphabetically** *adverb*.

alphanumeric /alfənyoo**merr**ik/ > *adjective* consisting of or using both letters and numerals.

alphorn /**al**phorn/ > *noun* another term for ALPENHORN.

alpine > *adjective* **1** relating to high mountains. **2** growing or found on high mountains. **3** (**Alpine**) relating to the Alps. > *noun* an alpine plant.

alpinist /**al**pinist/ > *noun* a climber of high mountains, especially in the Alps.

already > *adverb* **1** before the time in question. **2** as surprisingly soon or early as this.

alright > *adjective, adverb, & exclamation* variant spelling of ALL RIGHT.

USAGE – although **alright** is very common, in formal writing it is better to use the standard form **all right**.

Alsatian > *noun* **1** Brit. a German shepherd dog. **2** a person from Alsace, a region of NE France. > *adjective* relating to Alsace.

also > *adverb* in addition.

COMBINATIONS – **also-ran** a loser in a race or contest.

altar > *noun* **1** a table or flat-topped block on which religious offerings are made. **2** the table in a Christian church at which the bread and wine are consecrated in communion services.

WORDFINDER – baldachin, ciborium (*canopy over an altar*), diptych (*altarpiece with two panels*), dossal (*cloth hung behind an altar*), frontal (*cloth covering the front of an altar*), parclose (*rail around an altar*), piscina (*basin near altar*), reredos (*screen behind altar*), triptych (*altarpiece with three panels*).

IDIOMS – **lead to the altar** marry (a woman).

COMBINATIONS – **altar boy** a boy who acts as a priest's assistant during a service. **altarpiece** a painting or other work of art set above and behind an altar.

ORIGIN – Latin, from *altus* 'high'.

alter > *verb* change in character, appearance, direction, etc.; make or become different.

DERIVATIVES – **alterable** *adjective* **alteration** *noun*.

SYNONYMS – adapt, adjust, amend, change, modify, revise.

ORIGIN – Latin *alterare*, from *alter* 'other'.

altercation > *noun* a noisy argument or disagreement.

ORIGIN – Latin, from *altercari* 'to wrangle'.

alter ego /altər eegō, awltər eggō/ > *noun* (pl. **alter egos**) 1 a person's secondary or alternative personality. 2 a close friend who is very like oneself.

ORIGIN – Latin, 'other self'.

alternate > *verb* /awltərnayt/ 1 occur or do in turn repeatedly. 2 change repeatedly between two contrasting conditions. > *adjective* /awlternət/ 1 every other. 2 (of two things) each following and succeeded by the other in a regular pattern. 3 chiefly N. Amer. another term for ALTERNATIVE.

DERIVATIVES – **alternately** *adverb* **alternation** *noun*.

USAGE – do not use **alternate** to mean **alternative**: this use is primarily North American.

SYNONYMS – *verb* 2 fluctuate, oscillate, rotate, switch.

COMBINATIONS – **alternate angles** two equal angles formed on opposite side of a line crossing two parallel lines. **alternating current** an electric current that reverses its direction many times a second. Compare with *direct current*.

ORIGIN – Latin *alternare* 'do by turns', from *alter* 'other'.

alternative > *adjective* 1 (of one or more things) available as another possibility. 2 (of two things) mutually exclusive. 3 departing from or challenging traditional practices. > *noun* one of two or more available possibilities.

DERIVATIVES – **alternatively** *adverb*.

USAGE – some people maintain that you can have a maximum of two alternatives (because the word **alternative** comes from Latin *alter* 'other of two'), and that references to more than two alternatives are wrong. Such uses are, however, normal in modern standard English.

COMBINATIONS – **alternative energy** energy fuelled in ways that do not use up natural resources or harm the environment.

alternative medicine > *noun* a form of medical treatment regarded as unorthodox by the medical profession.

WORDFINDER – *forms of alternative and complementary medicine:* acupressure, acupuncture, chiropractic, herbalism, homeopathy, iridology, naturopathy, osteopathy, radionics, reflexology, shiatsu.

alternator > *noun* a dynamo that generates an alternating current.

although > *conjunction* 1 in spite of the fact that. 2 but.

altimeter /altimeetər/ > *noun* an instrument which indicates the altitude reached, especially in an aircraft.

altiplano /altiplaanō/ > *noun* the high tableland of central South America.

ORIGIN – Spanish.

altitude > *noun* the height of an object or point relative to ground or sea level.

DERIVATIVES – **altitudinal** *adjective*.

COMBINATIONS – **altitude sickness** illness resulting from shortage of oxygen at high altitude.

ORIGIN – Latin *altitudo*, from *altus* 'high'.

alto /altō/ > *noun* (pl. **altos**) 1 the highest adult male or lowest female singing voice. 2 (before another noun) referring to the second or third highest of a family of instruments: *an alto sax*.

ORIGIN – from Italian *alto canto* 'high song'.

altocumulus > *noun* rounded masses of cloud with a level base, at medium altitude.

altogether > *adverb* 1 completely. 2 in total. 3 on the whole.

IDIOMS – **in the altogether** informal naked.

altostratus > *noun* cloud forming a continuous uniform layer at medium altitude.

altruism /altroo-iz'm/ > *noun* 1 unselfish concern for others. 2 Zoology behaviour of an animal that benefits another at its own expense.

DERIVATIVES – **altruist** *noun* **altruistic** *adjective* **altruistically** *adverb*.

SYNONYMS – 1 selflessness, self-sacrifice, unselfishness.

ANTONYMS – 1 selfishness.

ORIGIN – from Italian *altrui* 'somebody else', from Latin *alteri huic* 'to this other'.

alum /aləm/ > *noun* a crystalline compound consisting of a sulphate of aluminium and potassium, used in dyeing and tanning.

ORIGIN – Latin *alumen*.

alumina /əloōminə/ > *noun* aluminium oxide, a constituent of many clays and found crystallised as corundum and sapphire.

aluminise /əloōminīz/ (also **aluminize**) > *verb* coat with aluminium.

aluminium /alyoominniəm/ (US **aluminum** /əloōminəm/) > *noun* a strong, light, corrosion-resistant silvery-grey metallic chemical element.

DERIVATIVES – **aluminous** *adjective*.

alumnus /əlumnəss/ > *noun* (pl. **alumni** /əlumnī/; fem. **alumna** /əlumnə/, pl. **alumnae** /əlumnee/) a former pupil or student of a particular school, college, or university.

ORIGIN – Latin, 'pupil', from *alere* 'nourish'.

alveolus /alveeələss, alviōləss/ > *noun* (pl. **alveoli** /alveeələli, alviōlī/) Anatomy 1 any of the many tiny air sacs in the lungs. 2 the bony socket for the root of a tooth.

DERIVATIVES – **alveolar** *adjective*.

ORIGIN – Latin, 'small cavity'.

always > *adverb* 1 on all occasions; at all times. 2 forever. 3 repeatedly. 4 failing all else.

ORIGIN – from *all way*.

alyssum /alisəm/ > *noun* (pl. **alyssums**) a herbaceous plant with small white or yellow flowers.

ORIGIN – Greek *alusson*, from *a-* 'without' + *lussa* 'rabies' (referring to its former use in herbalism).

Alzheimer's disease /alts-hīmərz/ > *noun* a form of progressive mental deterioration occurring in middle or old age.

ORIGIN – named after the German neurologist Alois *Alzheimer* (1864–1915).

AM > *abbreviation* amplitude modulation.

Am > *symbol* the chemical element americium.

am first person singular present of BE.

a.m. > *abbreviation* before noon.

ORIGIN – from Latin *ante meridiem*.

amah /aamə/ > *noun* a nursemaid or maid in the Far East or India.

ORIGIN – Portuguese *ama*.

amalgam /əmalgəm/ > *noun* 1 a mixture or blend. 2 Chemistry an alloy of mercury with another metal, especially one used for dental fillings.

ORIGIN – Greek *malagma* 'an emollient'.

amalgamate /əmalgəmayt/ > *verb* 1 combine or unite to form one organisation or structure. 2 Chemistry alloy (a metal) with mercury.

DERIVATIVES – **amalgamation** *noun*.

SYNONYMS – 1 combine, merge, integrate, unite.

amanuensis /əmanyooensiss/ > *noun* (pl. **amanuenses** /əmanyooenseez/) a literary assistant, in particular one who takes dictation.

ORIGIN – Latin, from *servus a manu* 'slave at handwriting, secretary'.

amaranth /amməranth/ > *noun* love-lies-bleeding (*Amaranthus caudatus*) or a related plant.

ORIGIN – Latin *amaranthus*, from Greek *amarantos* 'not fading'.

amaretti /amməretti/ > *plural noun* Italian almond-flavoured biscuits.

ORIGIN – Italian, from *amaro* 'bitter'.

amaretto /ammərettō/ > *noun* a brown almond-flavoured liqueur produced in Italy.

amaryllis /ammərilliss/ > *noun* a plant with large trumpet-shaped flowers.

ORIGIN – from Greek *Amarullis*, a name for a country girl in pastoral poetry.

amass > *verb* accumulate over time.
DERIVATIVES – **amasser** noun.
SYNONYMS – accumulate, assemble, collect, gather.
ORIGIN – Latin *amassare*, from *massa* 'lump'.

amateur > *noun* **1** a person who takes part in a sport or other activity without being paid. **2** a person who is incompetent at a particular activity. > *adjective* **1** non-professional. **2** incompetent; inept.
DERIVATIVES – **amateurism** noun.
ORIGIN – French, 'lover'.

amateurish > *adjective* incompetent; inept.
DERIVATIVES – **amateurishly** adverb **amateurishness** noun.

amatory /**amm**ətəri/ > *adjective* relating to or induced by sexual love or desire.
ORIGIN – Latin *amatorius*, from *amare* 'to love'.

amaze > *verb* surprise greatly; astonish.
DERIVATIVES – **amazement** noun.
SYNONYMS – astonish, astound, dumbfound, stagger, stun.

amazing > *adjective* **1** causing great surprise or wonder; astonishing. **2** informal very good or impressive.
DERIVATIVES – **amazingly** adverb.
SYNONYMS – astonishing, astounding, staggering, stunning.

Amazon /**amm**əz'n/ > *noun* **1** a member of a race of female warriors believed by the ancient Greeks to live somewhere on the borders of the known world. **2** a very tall, strong woman.

wordpower facts
Amazon
The English word **Amazon** comes from Greek, and was explained by the Greeks as meaning 'breastless', as if it came from *a-* 'without' + *mazos* 'breast'. This was a reference to the fable that the Amazons cut off the right breast so as not to interfere with the use of a bow and arrow, but the story was probably a folk etymology of an unknown foreign word. The River Amazon was named by the 16th-century Spanish conquistador Francisco de Orellana, who encountered bands of female warriors on its banks.

Amazonian /amməzōniən/ > *adjective* **1** relating to the River Amazon. **2** (of a woman) very tall and strong.

ambassador > *noun* **1** a diplomat sent by a state as its permanent representative in a foreign country. **2** a representative or promoter of an activity.
WORDFINDER – attaché, chargé d'affaires,

consul, emissary, envoy (*ambassadors and other representatives*), credentials (*ambassador's letter of introduction*), embassy (*ambassador's residence*), legate, nuncio (*papal representatives*).
DERIVATIVES – **ambassadorial** adjective **ambassadress** noun.
ORIGIN – Italian *ambasciator*, based on Latin *ambactus* 'servant'.

amber > *noun* **1** hard translucent fossilised resin, typically yellowish in colour, used in jewellery. **2** a honey-yellow colour.
ORIGIN – Old French, from an Arabic word originally meaning 'ambergris'.

ambergris /**amb**ərgreess/ > *noun* a wax-like substance secreted from the intestines of the sperm whale, found floating in tropical seas and used in perfume manufacture.
ORIGIN – from Old French *ambre gris* 'grey amber'.

ambidextrous /ambi**deks**trəss/ > *adjective* able to use the right and left hands equally well.
DERIVATIVES – **ambidexterity** noun **ambidextrously** adverb **ambidextrousness** noun.
ORIGIN – from Latin *ambi-* 'on both sides' + *dexter* 'right-handed'.

ambience /**amb**iənss/ (also **ambiance**) > *noun* **1** the character and atmosphere of a place. **2** character given to a sound recording by the space in which the sound occurs.

ambient /**amb**iənt/ > *adjective* **1** relating to the immediate surroundings of something. **2** (of music) electronic and having no vocals or persistent beat, used to create atmosphere.
ORIGIN – Latin, from *ambire* 'go round'.

ambiguity /ambi**gyōo**iti/ > *noun* (pl. **ambiguities**) uncertain or inexact meaning.

ambiguous /am**big**yōoəss/ > *adjective* **1** (of language) having more than one meaning. **2** not clear or decided.
DERIVATIVES – **ambiguously** adverb.
USAGE – do not confuse **ambiguous** with **ambivalent**. **Ambiguous** is primarily used to mean 'having more than one meaning, open to different interpretations', while **ambivalent** means 'having mixed feelings'.
SYNONYMS – equivocal, inconclusive, unclear.
ORIGIN – Latin *ambiguus* 'doubtful', from *ambigere* 'waver, go around'.

ambit > *noun* the scope, extent, or bounds of something.
ORIGIN – Latin *ambitus* 'circuit', from *ambire* 'go round'.

ambition > *noun* **1** a strong desire to do or achieve something. **2** desire for success, wealth, or fame.

ORIGIN – Latin, from *ambire* 'go around (canvassing for votes)'.

ambitious > *adjective* **1** having or showing ambition. **2** intended to meet a high standard and therefore difficult to achieve.
DERIVATIVES – **ambitiously** adverb **ambitiousness** noun.
SYNONYMS – **1** aspiring, determined, enterprising, purposeful. **2** bold, challenging, demanding, exacting, grandiose.

ambivalent /am**bivv**ələnt/ > *adjective* having mixed feelings or contradictory ideas about something or someone.
DERIVATIVES – **ambivalence** noun **ambivalently** adverb.
ORIGIN – from Latin *ambi-* 'on both sides' + *valere* 'be strong'.

amble > *verb* walk or move at a leisurely pace. > *noun* a leisurely walk.
ORIGIN – Latin *ambulare* 'to walk'.

ambrosia > *noun* **1** Greek & Roman Mythology the food of the gods. **2** something very pleasing to taste or smell. **3** another term for **bee bread**.
DERIVATIVES – **ambrosial** adjective.
ORIGIN – Greek, 'elixir of life', from *ambrotos* 'immortal'.

ambulance > *noun* a vehicle equipped for taking sick or injured people to and from hospital.
COMBINATIONS – **ambulance-chaser** derogatory, chiefly N. Amer. a lawyer who specialises in bringing cases seeking damages for personal injury.
ORIGIN – French, from *hôpital ambulant* 'mobile field hospital', from Latin *ambulare* 'walk'.

ambulant /**amb**yoolənt/ > *adjective* Medicine able to walk about; not confined to bed.

ambulatory /**amb**yoolətəri/ > *adjective* **1** relating to walking or able to walk. **2** moving from place to place; mobile. > *noun* (pl. **ambulatories**) an aisle or cloister in a church or monastery.

ambuscade /ambə**skayd**/ > *noun* an ambush.
ORIGIN – French *embuscade*, from a Latin word meaning 'to place in a wood'.

ambush > *noun* a surprise attack by people lying in wait in a concealed position. > *verb* attack in such a way.
ORIGIN – Old French *embusche*, from a Latin word meaning 'to place in a wood'; related to **BUSH**¹.

ameba > *noun* (pl. **amebae** or **amebas**) US spelling of **AMOEBA**.

ameliorate /ə**mee**liərayt/ > *verb* formal make (something) better.
DERIVATIVES – **amelioration** noun **ameliorative** adjective.
ORIGIN – alteration of **MELIORATE**.

amen /**aa**men, **ay**men/ > *exclamation* said at

the end of a prayer or hymn, meaning 'so be it'.

ORIGIN – Greek, from a Hebrew word meaning 'truth, certainty'.

amenable /əˈmeenəb'l/ > *adjective* **1** willing to respond to persuasion or suggestions. **2** (**amenable to**) capable of being acted on.

DERIVATIVES – **amenability** *noun* **amenably** *adverb*.

ORIGIN – from Old French *amener* 'bring to', from Latin *minari* 'threaten'.

amend > *verb* make minor improvements to (a proposal, document, etc.).

DERIVATIVES – **amendable** *adjective*.

USAGE – **amend** and **emend** have similar, but not identical, meanings: **amend** means 'make minor improvements to (a proposal, document, etc.)', while **emend** means 'correct and revise (a text)'.

SYNONYMS – alter, change, revise.

ORIGIN – Old French *amender*, from Latin *emendare* 'correct'.

amendment > *noun* **1** a minor improvement. **2** (**Amendment**) an article added to the US Constitution.

amends > *plural noun* (in phrase **make amends**) compensate or make up for a wrongdoing.

amenity /əˈmeeniti/ > *noun* (pl. **amenities**) a useful or desirable feature of a place.

SYNONYMS – convenience, facility, resource, service.

ORIGIN – Latin *amoenitas*, from *amoenus* 'pleasant'.

amenorrhoea /əmennəˈreeə/ (US **amenorrhea**) > *noun* abnormal failure to menstruate.

Amerasian /amməˈrayzh'n, amməˈraysh'n/ > *adjective* having one American and one Asian parent. > *noun* an Amerasian person.

American > *adjective* relating to the United States or to the continents of America. > *noun* a person from the United States or any of the countries of North, South, or Central America.

DERIVATIVES – **Americanisation** (also **Americanization**) *noun* **Americanise** (also **Americanize**) *verb* **Americanness** *noun*.

COMBINATIONS – **the American dream** the ideal of equality of opportunity associated with the US. **American football** a kind of football played in the US with an oval ball on a field marked out as a gridiron.

Americana /əmerriˈkaanə/ > *plural noun* things associated with the United States.

American Indian > *noun* a member of the indigenous peoples of America, especially North America.

USAGE – in the US the term **American Indian** is usually replaced by **Native American**, especially in official contexts; **American Indian** is still widespread in the UK, however, and is generally acceptable to American Indians themselves.

Americanism > *noun* **1** a word or phrase used or originating in the US. **2** the qualities typical of America and Americans.

americium /amməˈrissiəm/ > *noun* a radioactive metallic chemical element made by high-energy atomic collisions.

ORIGIN – from *America*, where it was first made.

Amerindian /amməˈrindiən/ (also **Amerind** /amməˈrind/) > *noun & adjective* another term for **AMERICAN INDIAN**.

amethyst /amməˈthist/ > *noun* a precious stone consisting of a violet or purple variety of quartz.

ORIGIN – Greek *amethustos* 'not drunken' (because the stone was believed to prevent intoxication).

Amharic /amˈharrik/ > *noun* the Semitic official language of Ethiopia.

ORIGIN – from *Amhara*, a region of central Ethiopia.

amiable > *adjective* friendly and pleasant in manner.

DERIVATIVES – **amiability** *noun* **amiably** *adverb*.

SYNONYMS – affable, amicable, friendly, good-natured.

ANTONYMS – unfriendly.

ORIGIN – Old French, from Latin *amicabilis* 'friendly, amicable'.

amicable /amˈmikəb'l/ > *adjective* done or conducted in a friendly way and without disagreement.

DERIVATIVES – **amicably** *adverb*.

SYNONYMS – civil, cordial, cooperative, friendly, harmonious.

ORIGIN – Latin *amicabilis*, from *amicus* 'friend'.

amice /amˈmiss/ > *noun* a white cloth worn on the neck and shoulders by a priest celebrating the Eucharist.

ORIGIN – Latin *amicia*.

amid > *preposition* surrounded by; in the middle of.

amidships (US also **amidship**) > *adverb & adjective* in the middle of a ship.

amidst > *preposition* literary variant of **AMID**.

amigo /əˈmeegō/ > *noun* (pl. **amigos**) informal, chiefly N. Amer. a friend.

ORIGIN – Spanish.

amine /ˈaymeen/ > *noun* Chemistry an organic compound derived from ammonia by replacement of one or more hydrogen atoms by organic radicals.

amino acid > *noun* any of a class of about twenty organic compounds which form the basic constituents of proteins and contain both acid and amine groups.

amir /əˈmeer/ > *noun* variant spelling of **EMIR**.

Amish /ˈaamish, ˈay-/ > *plural noun* a strict US Protestant sect living mainly in Pennsylvania and Ohio. > *adjective* relating to this sect.

ORIGIN – from the name of the Swiss preacher Jakob *Amman* (c.1645–c.1730).

amiss > *adjective* not quite right; inappropriate. > *adverb* wrongly or inappropriately.

IDIOMS – **not go amiss** be welcome and useful. **take amiss** be offended by (something said).

ORIGIN – probably from Old Norse *á mis* 'so as to miss'.

amity /ˈammiti/ > *noun* friendly relations.

ORIGIN – Old French *amitie*, from Latin *amicus* 'friend'.

ammeter /ˈammitər/ > *noun* an instrument for measuring electric current in amperes.

ammo > *noun* informal ammunition.

ammonia /əˈmōniə/ > *noun* a colourless, intensely pungent gas, forming a strongly alkaline solution in water which is used as a cleaning fluid.

DERIVATIVES – **ammoniacal** /amməˈnīək'l/ *adjective*.

wordpower facts
Ammonia
The English word **ammonia** has an interesting and unexpected origin. It comes in the first instance from **sal ammoniac**, an old-fashioned term for ammonium chloride, which derives from Latin *sal ammoniacus* 'salt of Ammon'. This name refers to the salt obtained in ancient times near the temple of Jupiter *Ammon* (a Romanised version of the supreme Egyptian god *Amun*) at Siwa in Egypt. **Ammonite** is also connected with Jupiter Ammon: the word comes from Latin *cornu Ammonis* 'horn of Ammon', because of the fossil's resemblance to the ram's horn associated with the god.

ammonite /ˈammənīt/ > *noun* an extinct marine mollusc with a spiral shell, found as a fossil.

ammonium /əˈmōniəm/ > *noun* Chemistry the ion NH_4^+, present in solutions of ammonia and in salts derived from ammonia.

ammunition > *noun* **1** a supply or quantity of bullets and shells. **2** points used to support one's case in argument.

ORIGIN – from French *la munition* 'the fortification'.

amnesia /amˈneeziə/ > *noun* loss of memory.

DERIVATIVES – **amnesiac** noun & adjective **amnesic** adjective & noun.

ORIGIN – Greek *amnēsia* 'forgetfulness'.

amnesty-amputate

amnesty > *noun* (pl. **amnesties**) **1** an official pardon for people convicted of political offences. **2** a period where no action is taken against people admitting to particular offences. > *verb* (**amnesties**, **amnestied**) grant an amnesty to.
ORIGIN – Greek *amnēstia* 'forgetfulness'.

amniocentesis /amniōsenteesiss/ > *noun* (pl. **amniocenteses** /amniōsenteeseez/) a procedure to take a sample of amniotic fluid from the womb, to check for abnormalities in the fetus.
ORIGIN – from **AMNION** + Greek *kentēsis* 'pricking'.

amnion /amniən/ > *noun* (pl. **amnions** or **amnia**) the innermost membrane surrounding an embryo.
DERIVATIVES – **amniotic** *adjective*.
COMBINATIONS – **amniotic fluid** the fluid surrounding a fetus within the amnion.
ORIGIN – Greek, 'caul'.

amoeba /əmeebə/ (US also **ameba**) > *noun* (pl. **amoebas** or **amoebae** /əmeebee/) a microscopic single-celled animal which is able to change shape.
DERIVATIVES – **amoebic** *adjective* **amoeboid** *adjective*.
ORIGIN – from Greek *amoibē* 'change, alternation'.

amok /əmok/ (also **amuck** /əmuk/) > *adverb* (in phrase **run amok**) behave uncontrollably and disruptively.
ORIGIN – Malay, 'rushing in a frenzy'.

among (chiefly Brit. also **amongst**) > *preposition* **1** surrounded by; in the middle of. **2** included or occurring in. **3** shared by; between.

amontillado /əmontilaadō/ > *noun* (pl. **amontillados**) a medium dry sherry.
ORIGIN – Spanish, from *Montilla*, a town in southern Spain.

amoral /aymorrəl/ > *adjective* having no moral sense; unconcerned with right or wrong.
DERIVATIVES – **amoralist** *noun* **amorality** *noun* **amorally** *adverb*.
USAGE – do not confuse **amoral** with **immoral**: **amoral** means 'not concerned with morality', while **immoral** means 'not conforming to accepted standards of morality'.

amorous > *adjective* showing or feeling sexual desire.
DERIVATIVES – **amorously** *adverb* **amorousness** *noun*.
SYNONYMS – carnal, erotic, lustful, passionate, sexual.
ORIGIN – Latin *amorosus*, from *amor* 'love'.

amorphous /əmorfəss/ > *adjective* **1** without a definite shape or form. **2** technical not crystalline.
ORIGIN – from Greek *a-* 'without' + *morphē* 'form'.

amortise /əmortīz/ (also **amortize**) > *verb* gradually write off (a cost) or reduce (a debt).
DERIVATIVES – **amortisation** *noun*.
ORIGIN – Old French *amortir*, from Latin *mors* 'death'.

amount > *noun* **1** the total number, size, value, or extent of something. **2** a quantity. > *verb* (**amount to**) **1** come to be (a total) when added together. **2** be the equivalent of.
SYNONYMS – *noun* aggregate, quantity, sum, total.
ORIGIN – from Old French *amont* 'upward', literally 'uphill', from Latin *ad montem*.

amour /əmoor/ > *noun* a lover or love affair, especially a secret one.
ORIGIN – Old French, from Latin *amor* 'love'.

amour propre /amoor proprə/ > *noun* self-respect.
ORIGIN – French.

amp¹ > *noun* short for **AMPERE**.

amp² > *noun* informal short for **AMPLIFIER**.

Ampakine /ampəkīn/ > *noun* (trademark in the US) any of a class of synthetic compounds which facilitate transmission of nerve impulses in the brain and appear to improve memory and learning capacity.
ORIGIN – from *AMPA* (an acronym denoting certain receptors in the brain) + Greek *kinein* 'to move'.

amperage /ampərij/ > *noun* the strength of an electric current in amperes.

ampere /ampair/ > *noun* the SI base unit of electric current, equal to a flow of one coulomb per second.
ORIGIN – named after the French physicist André-Marie *Ampère* (1775–1836).

ampersand /ampərsand/ > *noun* the sign &, standing for *and* or the Latin *et*.
ORIGIN – alteration of *and per se and* '& by itself is *and*', formerly chanted as an aid to learning the sign.

amphetamine /amfettəmin, -meen/ > *noun* a synthetic drug used illegally as a stimulant.

amphibian > *noun* **1** a cold-blooded animal of a class that breathes using gills when young and through lungs when adult, e.g. a frog, toad, or newt. **2** an aircraft or vehicle that can operate on land and on water.
WORDFINDER – herpetology (study of reptiles and amphibians), metamorphosis (transformation of amphibian larva to adult).
ORIGIN – Greek *amphibion*, from *amphi* 'both' + *bios* 'life'.

amphibious /amfibbiəss/ > *adjective* **1** living in or suited for both land and water. **2** (of a military operation) involving forces landed from the sea.
DERIVATIVES – **amphibiously** *adverb*.

amphibole /amfibōl/ > *noun* a mineral with fibrous or columnar crystals, found in many rocks.
ORIGIN – from Latin *amphibolus* 'ambiguous' (because of the varied structure of the minerals).

amphitheatre (US **amphitheater**) > *noun* **1** a round building consisting of tiers of seats surrounding a central space for dramatic or sporting events. **2** a semicircular seating gallery in a theatre.
ORIGIN – Greek *amphitheatron*, from *amphi* 'on both sides' + *theatron* 'theatre'.

amphora /amfərə/ > *noun* (pl. **amphorae** /amfəree/ or **amphoras**) a tall ancient Greek or Roman jar or jug with two handles and a narrow neck.
ORIGIN – Latin, from Greek *amphi-* 'on both sides' + *phoreus* 'bearer'.

amphoteric /amfəterrik/ > *adjective* Chemistry able to react both as a base and as an acid.
ORIGIN – Greek *amphoteros*, comparative of *amphō* 'both'.

ample > *adjective* (**ampler**, **amplest**) **1** enough or more than enough; plentiful. **2** large and accommodating.
DERIVATIVES – **amply** *adverb*.
SYNONYMS – **1** abundant, copious, generous, plentiful, sufficient. **2** capacious, sizeable, substantial.
ANTONYMS – **1** insufficient, meagre.
ORIGIN – Latin *amplus* 'large, abundant'.

amplifier > *noun* **1** an electronic device for increasing the strength of electrical signals. **2** a device of this kind combined with a loudspeaker, used to amplify electric guitars and other musical instruments.

amplify > *verb* (**amplifies**, **amplified**) **1** increase the volume or strength of (sound or electrical signals). **2** add detail to (a story or statement).
DERIVATIVES – **amplification** *noun*.
ORIGIN – Latin *amplificare*, from *amplus* 'large, abundant'.

amplitude > *noun* **1** Physics the maximum extent of a vibration or oscillation from the point of equilibrium. **2** breadth, range, or magnitude.
COMBINATIONS – **amplitude modulation** the modulation of a wave by varying its amplitude, used as a means of broadcasting an audio signal by radio.

ampoule /ampool/ (US also **ampul** or **ampule** /ampyool/) > *noun* a small sealed glass capsule containing a measured quantity of liquid ready for injecting.
ORIGIN – Latin *ampulla* (see **AMPULLA**).

ampulla /ampoollə/ > *noun* (pl. **ampullae** /ampoollee/) **1** a roughly spherical ancient Roman flask with two handles. **2** a flask for holding consecrated oil.
ORIGIN – Latin, related to **AMPHORA**.

amputate /ampyootayt/ > *verb* cut off (a limb) in a surgical operation.
DERIVATIVES – **amputation** *noun*.
ORIGIN – Latin *amputare* 'lop off'.

amputee > *noun* a person who has had a limb amputated.

amuck > *adverb* variant spelling of **AMOK**.

amulet /**am**yoolit/ > *noun* an ornament or small piece of jewellery worn as protection against evil.

ORIGIN – Latin *amuletum*.

amuse > *verb* **1** cause (someone) to laugh or smile. **2** provide enjoyment or occupation for (someone).

DERIVATIVES – **amused** *adjective* **amusedly** *adverb* **amusing** *adjective* **amusingly** *adverb*.

SYNONYMS – **1** delight, gladden, please, tickle. **2** divert, entertain, occupy.

ORIGIN – Old French *amuser* 'entertain, deceive', from *muser* 'stare stupidly'.

amusement > *noun* **1** the state of finding something funny. **2** the provision or enjoyment of entertainment. **3** Brit. a game machine or other device for providing entertainment.

SYNONYMS – **1** hilarity, merriment, mirth. **2** diversion, entertainment, leisure.

COMBINATIONS – **amusement arcade** Brit. an indoor area containing coin-operated game machines.

amyl /**ay**mīl/, **amm**il/ > *noun* Chemistry the straight-chain pentyl radical —C_5H_{11}.

ORIGIN – from Latin *amylum* 'starch'.

amylase /**amm**ilayz/ > *noun* Biochemistry an enzyme found in saliva and pancreatic fluid that converts starch into simple sugars.

amyl nitrite > *noun* a synthetic liquid used medicinally to dilate blood vessels and sometimes inhaled as a stimulant.

an > *determiner* the form of 'a' (the indefinite article) used before words beginning with a vowel sound.

USAGE – **an** should be used with words beginning with h in cases where the h is not pronounced, such as *an heir* and *an hour*, and French words such as *an hors d'oeuvre*. Cases like *an historical document* and *an hotel* reflect 18th or 19th-century speech; as the *h* in these words is now pronounced, it is better to use **a**.

an- > *prefix* variant spelling of **A-**[1] before a vowel (as in *anaemia*).

-an > *suffix* **1** forming adjectives and nouns, especially from names of places, systems, or zoological classes: *Cuban | crustacean*. **2** Chemistry forming names of organic compounds, chiefly polysaccharides.

ORIGIN – from Latin *-anus, -ana, -anum*.

ana- (usu. **an-** before a vowel) > *prefix* **1** up. **2** back. **3** again.

ORIGIN – from Greek *ana* 'up'.

-ana > *suffix* forming plural nouns denoting things associated with a person, place, or interest: *Victoriana*.

ORIGIN – from Latin, neuter plural of the adjectival ending *-anus*.

Anabaptism /**ann**ə**bap**tiz'm/ > *noun* the doctrine that baptism should only be administered to believing adults.

DERIVATIVES – **Anabaptist** *noun* & *adjective*.

anabolic steroid > *noun* a synthetic hormone used to promote muscle growth and illegally to enhance performance in sport.

anabolism /ə**nabb**əliz'm/ > *noun* Biochemistry the synthesis of complex molecules in living organisms from simpler ones together with the storage of energy. The opposite of **CATABOLISM**.

DERIVATIVES – **anabolic** *adjective*.

ORIGIN – from Greek *anabolē* 'ascent'.

anachronism /ə**nak**rəniz'm/ > *noun* **1** a thing belonging to a period other than the one in which it exists. **2** the placing of something in the wrong historical period.

DERIVATIVES – **anachronistic** *adjective* **anachronistically** *adverb*.

ORIGIN – from Greek *ana-* 'backwards' + *khronos* 'time'.

anaconda /annə**kon**də/ > *noun* a very large snake of the boa family, native to tropical South America.

ORIGIN – Sinhalese: first used to denote a kind of Sri Lankan snake.

anaemia /ə**nee**miə/ (US **anemia**) > *noun* a shortage of red cells or haemoglobin in the blood, resulting in pallor and weariness.

ORIGIN – Greek *anaimia*, from *an-* 'without' + *haima* 'blood'.

anaemic (US **anemic**) > *adjective* **1** suffering from anaemia. **2** lacking spirit or vitality.

anaerobic /annair**ō**bik/ > *adjective* Biology relating to or requiring the absence of oxygen.

DERIVATIVES – **anaerobically** *adverb*.

ORIGIN – from **AN-** + **AEROBIC**.

anaesthesia /anniss**thee**ziə/ (US **anesthesia**) > *noun* insensitivity to pain, especially as induced by an anaesthetic before a surgical operation.

ORIGIN – Greek *anaisthēsia*, from *an-* 'without' + *aisthēsis* 'sensation'.

anaesthesiology /anniss-theezi**oll**əji/ (US **anesthesiology**) > *noun* the branch of medicine concerned with anaesthetics.

DERIVATIVES – **anaesthesiologist** *noun*.

anaesthetic* /anniss**thett**ik/ (US **anesthetic**) > *noun* a drug or gas that causes insensitivity to pain. > *adjective* inducing or relating to anaesthesia.

*SPELLING – unlike words of similar form such as **encyclopedia** and **medieval**, **anaesthetic** is generally spelled with *-ae-* rather than *-e-* in the middle; the spelling **anesthetic** is American.

anaesthetise (also **anaesthetize**, US **anesthetize**) > *verb* administer an anaesthetic to.

anaesthetist (US **anesthetist**) > *noun* a medical specialist who administers anaesthetics.

anagram /**ann**əgram/ > *noun* a word or phrase formed by rearranging the letters of another.

ORIGIN – from Greek *ana-* 'back, anew' + *gramma* 'letter'.

anal /**ay**n'l/ > *adjective* **1** relating to the anus. **2** anal-retentive.

DERIVATIVES – **anally** *adverb*.

COMBINATIONS – **anal-retentive** Psychoanalysis excessively orderly and fussy (supposedly because of conflict over toilet-training in infancy).

analgesia /annəl**jee**ziə/ > *noun* Medicine relief of pain.

ORIGIN – Greek *analgēsia* 'painlessness', from *an-* 'not' + *algein* 'feel pain'.

analgesic /annəl**jee**zik/ Medicine > *adjective* relieving pain. > *noun* a pain-relieving drug.

analogous /ə**nal**əgəss/ > *adjective* comparable in certain respects.

DERIVATIVES – **analogously** *adverb*.

ORIGIN – Greek *analogos* 'proportionate'.

analogue /**ann**əlog/ (US also **analog**) > *noun* an analogous person or thing. > *adjective* (also **analog**) based on a continuously variable physical quantity (e.g. voltage) rather than digital information.

analogy /ə**nal**əji/ > *noun* (pl. **analogies**) **1** a comparison between one thing and another made to explain or clarify. **2** a correspondence or partial similarity.

DERIVATIVES – **analogical** *adjective*.

analysand /ə**nal**isand/ > *noun* a person undergoing psychoanalysis.

analyse* (US **analyze**) > *verb* **1** examine the elements or structure of (something) in detail. **2** psychoanalyse.

DERIVATIVES – **analysable** *adjective* **analyser** *noun*.

*SPELLING – in British English **analyse** cannot be spelled with a *-ze* ending.

SYNONYMS – **1** dissect, evaluate, inspect, investigate, scrutinise.

analysis /ə**nal**isiss/ > *noun* (pl. **analyses** /ə**nal**iseez/) **1** a detailed examination of the elements or structure of something. **2** the separation of something into its constituent elements. **3** psychoanalysis.

SYNONYMS – **1** evaluation, investigation, study.

ORIGIN – Greek *analusis*, from *analuein* 'unloose'.

analyst > *noun* **1** a person who conducts analysis. **2** a psychoanalyst.

analytical (also **analytic**) > *adjective* relating to or using analysis or logical reasoning.

DERIVATIVES – **analytically** *adverb*.

analyze > *verb* US spelling of **ANALYSE**.

anamnesis /annəm**nee**siss/ > *noun* (pl. **anamneses** /annəm**nee**seez/) recollection, especially of a supposed previous existence.

ORIGIN – Greek, 'remembrance'.

anamorphosis /annəˈmorfəsiss/ > *noun* a distorted image which appears normal when viewed from a particular point or with a suitable mirror or lens.

DERIVATIVES – **anamorphic** *adjective*.

ORIGIN – Greek, 'transformation'.

anaphora /əˈnaffərə/ > *noun* **1** Grammar the use of a word referring back to a word used earlier, for example the pronouns *he, she, it,* and *they* and the verb *do* in *I like it and so do they.* **2** the repetition of a word or phrase at the beginning of successive clauses.

DERIVATIVES – **anaphoric** /annəˈforrik/ *adjective.*

ORIGIN – Greek, 'repetition'.

anaphylactic shock /annəfiˈlaktik/ > *noun* Medicine a dangerous allergic reaction to something that the body has become hypersensitive to.

ORIGIN – from Greek *ana-* 'again' + *phulaxis* 'guarding'.

anarchic > *adjective* with no controlling rules or principles.

DERIVATIVES – **anarchical** *adjective* **anarchically** *adverb.*

anarchism > *noun* belief in the abolition of all government and the organisation of society on a cooperative basis.

DERIVATIVES – **anarchist** *noun & adjective* **anarchistic** *adjective.*

anarchy > *noun* **1** a state of disorder due to lack of government or control. **2** a society founded on the principles of anarchism.

SYNONYMS – **1** chaos, disorder, lawlessness.

ANTONYMS – **1** order.

ORIGIN – Greek *anarkhia,* from *an-* 'without' + *arkhos* 'chief, ruler'.

Anasazi /annəˈsaazi/ > *noun* (pl. same or **Anasazis**) a member of an ancient American Indian people of the south-western US.

ORIGIN – Navajo, 'ancient one' or 'enemy ancestor'.

anastigmatic /annəstigˈmattik/ > *adjective* (of a lens system) constructed so that the astigmatism of each element is cancelled out.

anastomosis /əˌnastəˈmōsiss/ > *noun* (pl. **anastomoses** /əˌnastəˈmōseez/) technical a connection between channels, blood vessels, etc.

ORIGIN – Greek, from *anastomoun* 'provide with a mouth'.

anathema /əˈnathəmə/ > *noun* **1** something that one vehemently dislikes: *racism was anathema to her.* **2** a Church decree excommunicating a person or denouncing a doctrine.

ORIGIN – Greek, 'thing dedicated', later 'thing devoted to evil'.

anathematise /əˈnathəmətīz/ (also **anathematize**) > *verb* curse; condemn.

Anatolian /annəˈtōliən/ > *adjective* relating to Anatolia in western Asia Minor. > *noun* a person from Anatolia.

anatomise (also **anatomize**) > *verb* **1** dissect (a body). **2** examine and analyse in detail.

anatomy > *noun* (pl. **anatomies**) **1** the scientific study of bodily structure. **2** the bodily structure of a person, animal, or plant. **3** a detailed examination or analysis.

DERIVATIVES – **anatomical** *adjective* **anatomically** *adverb* **anatomist** *noun.*

ORIGIN – from Greek *ana-* 'up' + *tomia* 'cutting'.

ANC > *abbreviation* African National Congress.

-ance > *suffix* forming nouns: **1** denoting a quality or state: *perseverance.* **2** denoting an action: *utterance.*

ORIGIN – French, from Latin *-antia, -entia.*

ancestor > *noun* **1** a person, typically one more remote than a grandparent, from whom one is descended. **2** something from which a later species or version has evolved.

DERIVATIVES – **ancestral** *adjective* **ancestrally** *adverb* **ancestress** *noun.*

SYNONYMS – antecedent, forebear, forefather, predecessor, progenitor.

ANTONYMS – descendant.

ORIGIN – Latin *antecessor,* from *antecedere* 'go before'.

ancestry > *noun* (pl. **ancestries**) a person's ancestors or ethnic origins.

SYNONYMS – blood, descent, extraction, lineage, parentage.

anchor > *noun* a heavy object used to moor a ship to the sea bottom, typically having a metal shank with a pair of curved, barbed flukes. > *verb* **1** moor with an anchor. **2** secure firmly in position. **3** be the anchorman or anchorwoman of (a programme).

COMBINATIONS – **anchorman** (or **anchorwoman**) a person who presents a live television or radio programme involving other contributors.

ORIGIN – Greek *ankura.*

anchorage > *noun* **1** a place where ships may anchor safely. **2** the state of anchoring or being anchored.

anchorite /ˈangkərīt/ > *noun* historical a religious recluse.

ORIGIN – Greek *anakhōrētēs,* from *anakhōrein* 'retire'.

anchovy /ˈanchəvi, anˈchōvi/ > *noun* (pl. **anchovies**) a small fish of the herring family, with a strong flavour.

ORIGIN – Spanish and Portuguese *anchova.*

ancien régime /ˌonsyaN reˈzheem/ > *noun* (pl. **anciens régimes** pronunc. same) a

political or social system that has been replaced by a more modern one.

ORIGIN – French, 'old rule'.

ancient > *adjective* **1** belonging to or originating in the very distant past. **2** chiefly humorous very old. > *noun* **1** (**the ancients**) the people of ancient times. **2** archaic or humorous an old man.

DERIVATIVES – **anciently** *adverb.*

SYNONYMS – *adjective* **1** bygone, olden, prehistoric, primeval, primordial.

COMBINATIONS – **ancient lights** English Law the established right of access to light of a property, used to prevent the construction of buildings which would obstruct such access. **the Ancient of Days** God.

ORIGIN – Old French *ancien,* from Latin *ante* 'before'.

ancillary /anˈsilləri/ > *adjective* **1** providing subsidiary support. **2** additional; supplementary.

ORIGIN – Latin *ancillaris,* from *ancilla* 'maidservant'.

-ancy > *suffix* forming nouns denoting a quality or state: *expectancy.*

ORIGIN – from Latin *-antia.*

and > *conjunction* **1** used to connect words, clauses, or sentences. **2** used to connect two identical words to emphasise progressive change or great duration: *getting better and better.* **3** (connecting two numbers) plus. **4** informal (after a verb) to: *try and do it.*

USAGE – it is often said to be bad writing style to begin a sentence with a conjunction such as **and** (or **but** or **because**). However, writers down the centuries, including Shakespeare, have used **and** and other conjunctions to start a sentence, typically for rhetorical effect. Provided there is a good reason for it, this should not be seen as a mistake.

COMBINATIONS – **AND gate** Electronics a gate circuit which produces an output only when there are signals on all of the input connections.

-and > *suffix* (forming nouns) denoting a person or thing to be treated in a specified way: *analysand.*

ORIGIN – from Latin gerundive ending *-andus.*

Andalusian /andəˈlooziən/ > *noun* a person from Andalusia in southern Spain. > *adjective* relating to Andalusia.

andante /anˈdantay/ Music > *adverb & adjective* in a moderately slow tempo. > *noun* an andante passage.

ORIGIN – Italian, literally 'going'.

Andean /anˈdeeən, ˈandiən/ > *adjective* relating to the Andes, a mountain system running the length of the Pacific coast of South America.

andiron /ˈandīən/ > *noun* a metal support,

typically one of a pair, for wood burning in a fireplace.

ORIGIN – Old French *andier*.

Andorran /anˈdorən/ > *noun* a person from Andorra, a small autonomous principality in the southern Pyrenees. > *adjective* relating to Andorra.

andouille /oNˈdōōi/ > *noun* **1** (in France) a pork sausage made from chitterlings. **2** (in Cajun cooking) a spicy smoked-pork sausage.

ORIGIN – French.

androgen /ˈandrəjən/ > *noun* Biochemistry a male sex hormone, such as testosterone.

ORIGIN – from Greek *anēr* 'man' + **-GEN**.

androgyne /ˈandrəjīn/ > *noun* **1** an androgynous individual. **2** a hermaphrodite.

androgynous /anˈdrojinəss/ > *adjective* partly male and partly female; of indeterminate sex.

DERIVATIVES – **androgyny** *noun*.

ORIGIN – from Greek *androgunos*, from *anēr* 'man' + *gunē* 'woman'.

android /ˈandroyd/ > *noun* (in science fiction) a robot with a human appearance.

ORIGIN – from Greek *anēr* 'man' + **-OID**.

-ane > *suffix* Chemistry forming names of saturated hydrocarbons.

anecdotage /ˈannikdōtij/ > *noun* **1** anecdotes collectively. **2** humorous old age in someone who likes to tell anecdotes.

anecdote /ˈannikdōt/ > *noun* **1** a short entertaining story about a real incident or person. **2** an account regarded as unreliable or as being hearsay.

DERIVATIVES – **anecdotal** *adjective* **anecdotalist** *noun* **anecdotally** *adverb*.

ORIGIN – Greek *anekdota* 'things unpublished'.

anechoic /ˈannikōik/ > *adjective* technical free from echo; tending to absorb or deaden sound.

anemia > *noun* US spelling of **ANAEMIA**.

anemic > *adjective* US spelling of **ANAEMIC**.

anemometer /ˈannimommitər/ > *noun* an instrument for measuring the speed of the wind or other flowing gas.

ORIGIN – from Greek *anemos* 'wind'.

anemone* /əˈnemməni/ > *noun* **1** a plant with brightly coloured flowers and deeply divided leaves. **2** short for *sea anemone*.

*SPELLING – anemone, not anenome: remember *m* for *middle*!

ORIGIN – Greek, 'windflower', apparently because the flowers open only when the wind blows.

aneroid /ˈannəroyd/ > *adjective* (of a barometer) measuring air pressure by the action of the air in deforming the lid of a box in which a vacuum has been created.

ORIGIN – from Greek *a-* 'without' + *nēros* 'water'.

anesthesia etc. US spelling of **ANAESTHESIA** etc.

aneurysm /ˈanyooriz'm/ (also **aneurism**) > *noun* Medicine an excessive localised swelling of the wall of an artery.

DERIVATIVES – **aneurysmal** *adjective*.

ORIGIN – Greek *aneurusma* 'dilatation'.

anew > *adverb* chiefly literary **1** in a new or different way. **2** once more; again.

angel > *noun* **1** a spiritual being believed to act as an attendant or messenger of God, conventionally represented as being of human form with wings. **2** a person of great beauty, kindness, or virtue. **3** theatrical slang a financial backer. **4** a former English coin bearing the figure of the archangel Michael killing a dragon.

WORDFINDER – *the traditional Christian hierarchy of angels (from lowest to highest):* seraph, cherub, throne, domination, virtue, power, principality, archangel, angel.

IDIOMS – **on the side of the angels** on the side of what is right.

COMBINATIONS – **angel cake** a very light, pale sponge cake typically baked in a ring shape and covered with soft icing. **angel dust** informal the hallucinogenic drug phencyclidine hydrochloride. **angelfish** a fish with a deep, laterally compressed body and large dorsal and anal fins, often vividly coloured or patterned. **angel hair** a type of pasta consisting of very fine long strands. **angels on horseback** Brit. an appetiser consisting of oysters individually wrapped in bacon and served on toast.

ORIGIN – Greek *angelos* 'messenger'.

Angeleno /anjəˈleenō/ (also **Los Angeleno**) > *noun* (pl. **Angelenos**) a person from Los Angeles.

ORIGIN – American Spanish.

angelic > *adjective* **1** relating to angels. **2** exceptionally beautiful, innocent, or kind.

DERIVATIVES – **angelically** *adverb*.

angelica /anˈjellikə/ > *noun* a tall aromatic plant, the candied stalks of which are used in confectionery and cake decoration.

ORIGIN – from Latin *herba angelica* 'angelic herb', so named because it was believed to be effective against poisoning and disease.

angelus /ˈanjələss/ > *noun* **1** a Roman Catholic devotion commemorating the Incarnation of Jesus and including the Hail Mary. **2** a ringing of bells announcing this.

ORIGIN – from the Latin phrase *Angelus domini* 'the angel of the Lord', the opening words of the devotion.

anger > *noun* a strong feeling of annoyance, displeasure, or hostility. > *verb* provoke anger in.

SYNONYMS – *noun* fury, rage, wrath. *verb* enrage, incense, infuriate.

ORIGIN – Old Norse, 'grief'.

angina /anˈjīnə/ (also **angina pectoris** /ˈpektəriss/) > *noun* a condition marked by severe pain in the chest, arising from an inadequate blood supply to the heart.

ORIGIN – Latin, 'quinsy', from Greek *ankhonē* 'strangling'; *pectoris* means 'of the chest'.

angiography /anjiˈogrəfi/ > *noun* radiography of blood or lymph vessels, carried out after introduction of a substance that is opaque to X-rays.

DERIVATIVES – **angiogram** *noun* **angiographic** *adjective*.

ORIGIN – from Greek *angeion* 'vessel'.

angioplasty /ˈanjiōplasti/ > *noun* (pl. **angioplasties**) a surgical operation to repair or unblock a blood vessel, especially a coronary artery.

ORIGIN – from Greek *plastos* 'formed'.

angiosperm > *noun* Botany a plant of a large group that have flowers and produce seeds enclosed within a carpel, including herbaceous plants, shrubs, grasses, and most trees. Compare with **GYMNOSPERM**.

Angle > *noun* a member of an ancient Germanic people that founded English kingdoms in Mercia, Northumbria, and East Anglia.

wordpower facts

Angle

The word **Angle** comes from Latin *Anglus* 'inhabitant of *Angul*'. *Angul* was a district of Schleswig (now in northern Germany), so named because it formed an *angle* in shape. The word **English** was formed in Old English from **Angle** and **-ish**. The fishing term **angle** is also related: the obsolete noun **angle**, from which the verb derives, denoted a fish hook, later extending to the rod and line.

angle¹ > *noun* **1** the space (usually measured in degrees) between two intersecting lines or surfaces at or close to the point where they meet. **2** a corner in a building or other structure, especially an external projection or internal recess. **3** a position from which something is viewed or along which it travels or acts. **4** a particular way of approaching an issue or problem. **5** angle iron or a similar constructional material. > *verb* **1** direct, move, or incline at an angle. **2** present (information) to reflect a particular view or have a particular focus.

WORDFINDER – acute (*less than 90°*), obtuse (*more than 90° and less than 180°*), reflex (*more than 180°*), right angle (*exactly 90°*); goniometry (*the precise measurement of angles*), trigonometry (*branch of mathematics concerned with angles*).

DERIVATIVES – **angled** *adjective*.

SYNONYMS – **3,4** perspective, standpoint, viewpoint.

COMBINATIONS – **angle bracket 1** either of a pair of marks in the form < >, used to enclose words or figures so as to separate them from their context. **2** a right-angled support projecting from a wall. **angle grinder** a device with a rotating abrasive disc, used to grind, polish, or cut metal and other materials. **angle iron** a constructional material consisting of pieces of iron or steel with an L-shaped cross section, able to be bolted together. **angle of attack** Aeronautics the angle between the line of the chord of an aerofoil and the relative airflow. **angle of incidence** Physics the angle which an incoming line or ray makes with a perpendicular to the surface at the point of incidence.

ORIGIN – Latin *angulus* 'corner'.

angle² > *verb* **1** fish with a rod and line. **2** seek something desired by indirectly prompting someone to offer it: *she was angling for sympathy.*

DERIVATIVES – **angler** *noun* **angling** *noun.*

ORIGIN – from the obsolete noun *angle* 'a fish hook'.

anglepoise > *noun* trademark a type of desk lamp with a jointed arm and counterbalancing springs that hold it in any position to which it is adjusted.

anglerfish > *noun* a marine fish that lures prey within reach of its mouth with a fleshy filament arising from its snout.

Anglican > *adjective* relating to the Church of England or any Church in communion with it. > *noun* a member of any of these Churches.

DERIVATIVES – **Anglicanism** *noun.*

ORIGIN – Latin *Anglicanus*, from *Anglus* 'Angle'.

anglicise (also **anglicize**) > *verb* make English in form or character.

DERIVATIVES – **anglicisation** *noun.*

Anglicism > *noun* **1** a word or phrase that is peculiar to British English. **2** the quality of being typically English or of favouring English things.

Anglo- > *combining form* **1** English: *anglophone.* **2** English or British and …: *Anglo-Latin.*

ORIGIN – from Latin *Anglus* 'English'.

Anglo-Catholicism > *noun* a tradition within the Anglican Church which is close to Catholicism in its doctrine and worship and is broadly identified with High Church Anglicanism.

DERIVATIVES – **Anglo-Catholic** *adjective* & *noun.*

Anglocentric > *adjective* centred on or considered in terms of England or Britain.

Anglo-Indian > *adjective* **1** relating to or involving both Britain and India. **2** of mixed British and Indian parentage. **3** chiefly

historical of British descent or birth but having lived long in India. > *noun* an Anglo-Indian person.

Anglo-Irish > *adjective* **1** relating to both Britain and Ireland (or specifically the Republic of Ireland). **2** of mixed English and Irish parentage. **3** of English descent but born or resident in Ireland.

Anglophile > *noun* a person who is fond of or greatly admires England or Britain.

DERIVATIVES – **Anglophilia** *noun.*

anglophone > *adjective* English-speaking.

Anglo-Saxon > *noun* **1** a Germanic inhabitant of England between the 5th century and the Norman Conquest. **2** a person of English descent. **3** chiefly N. Amer. any white, English-speaking person. **4** the Old English language. **5** informal plain English, in particular vulgar slang.

Angolan /ang**gō**lən/ > *noun* a person from Angola, a country in SW Africa. > *adjective* relating to Angola.

angora /ang**gor**ə/ > *noun* **1** a cat, goat, or rabbit of a breed having long and very soft hair or fur. **2** the hair of the angora goat or rabbit, typically blended with wool to make a soft yarn.

ORIGIN – from *Angora* (now Ankara) in Turkey.

angostura /anggə**styoor**ə/ > *noun* **1** an aromatic bitter bark from South America, used as a flavouring. **2** (also **Angostura bitters** trademark) a kind of tonic.

ORIGIN – from *Angostura* (now Ciudad Bolívar) in Venezuela.

angry > *adjective* (**angrier, angriest**) **1** feeling or showing anger. **2** (of a wound or sore) red and inflamed.

DERIVATIVES – **angrily** *adverb.*

SYNONYMS – **1** furious, irate, irked, vexed.

ANTONYMS – **1** content.

angst /angst/ > *noun* a profound feeling of generalised anxiety or dread.

DERIVATIVES – **angsty** *adjective.*

SYNONYMS – apprehension, foreboding, trepidation.

ORIGIN – German, 'fear'.

angstrom /**ang**strəm/ (also **ångström** /**ong**strerm/) > *noun* Physics a unit of length equal to one hundred-millionth of a centimetre, 10^{-10} metre.

ORIGIN – named after the Swedish physicist A. J. *Ångström* (1814–74).

anguish > *noun* severe mental or physical pain or suffering.

SYNONYMS – agony, torment, torture.

ORIGIN – Latin *angustia* 'tightness', (in plural) 'straits, distress', from *angustus* 'narrow'.

anguished > *adjective* experiencing or expressing anguish.

angular /**ang**gyoolər/ > *adjective* **1** having angles or sharp corners. **2** (of a person) lean and having a prominent bone structure. **3**

placed or directed at an angle. **4** Physics measured with reference to angles, especially those associated with rotation.

DERIVATIVES – **angularity** *noun* **angularly** *adverb.*

anhydrous /an**hī**drəss/ > *adjective* Chemistry containing no water.

ORIGIN – from Greek *an-* 'without' + *hudōr* 'water'.

aniline /**ann**ileen, **ann**ilin/ > *noun* an oily liquid found in coal tar, used in the manufacture of dyes, drugs, and plastics.

ORIGIN – from Arabic *an-nīl* 'indigo' (from which it was originally obtained).

anima /**ann**imə/ > *noun* Psychoanalysis **1** (in Jungian psychology) the feminine part of a man's personality. Compare with **ANIMUS**. **2** the part of the psyche which is directed inwards, in touch with the subconscious. Compare with **PERSONA**.

ORIGIN – Latin, 'air, life, soul'.

animadvert /anniməd**vert**/ > *verb* (**animadvert on** or **against**) formal criticise or censure.

DERIVATIVES – **animadversion** *noun.*

ORIGIN – Latin *animadvertere*, from *animus* 'mind' + *advertere* 'to turn'.

animal > *noun* **1** a living organism which feeds on organic matter, has specialised sense organs and nervous system, and is able to move about and to respond rapidly to stimuli. **2** a mammal, as opposed to a bird, reptile, fish, or insect. **3** a very cruel, violent, or uncivilised person. **4** (before another noun) physical rather than spiritual or intellectual: *animal lust.* **5** a particular type of person or thing: *a political animal.*

WORDFINDER – fauna (*animals of a particular region*), invertebrates (*animals without backbones*), vertebrates (*animals with backbones*), zoology (*scientific study of animals*).

SYNONYMS – **1** beast, creature. **3** beast, brute, monster.

COMBINATIONS – **animal liberation** the freeing of animals from exploitation and cruel treatment by humans. **animal magnetism 1** a quality of powerful sexual attractiveness. **2** historical a supposed physical force to which the action of mesmerism was ascribed.

ORIGIN – Latin, from *animalis* 'having breath', from *anima* 'life, breath'.

animalcule /**ann**imalkyōol/ > *noun* archaic a microscopic animal.

animalism > *noun* behaviour characteristic of animals; animality.

DERIVATIVES – **animalistic** *adjective.*

animality > *noun* human behaviour characteristic of animals, especially in being physical and instinctive.

animate > *verb* /**ann**imayt/ **1** bring to life or activity. **2** give (a film or character) the

appearance of movement using animation. > *adjective* /**ann**imət/ alive; having life.
DERIVATIVES – **animator** *noun*.
SYNONYMS – *verb* **1** activate, enliven, excite, stimulate.

wordpower facts

Animate

The root of the verb **animate**, the Latin word *anima*, meaning 'wind, air', hence 'life, breath', is shared by a number of words. The adjective *animalis*, 'having breath', gave us **animal**, and the notion of the fundamental 'breath of life' lies behind the processes of film **animation**. An extension of the sense of *life* into the notion of *soul* has occurred in the term **animism**, and with accompanying ideas of femininity and masculinity in the terms **anima** and **animus**, used in psychoanalysis.

animated > *adjective* **1** lively. **2** (of a film) made using animation.
DERIVATIVES – **animatedly** *adverb*.

animation > *noun* **1** the state of being full of life or vigour. **2** the technique of filming a sequence of drawings or positions of models to create an illusion of movement. **3** (also **computer animation**) the creation of moving images by means of a computer.
SYNONYMS – **1** liveliness, spirit, vivacity, zest.
ANTONYMS – **1** inertia, lethargy.

animatronics /animə**tronn**iks/ > *plural noun* (treated as sing.) the creation and operation of lifelike robotic models, especially for use in films.
DERIVATIVES – **animatronic** *adjective*.

anime /**ann**imay, **ann**imə/ > *noun* Japanese animated films, typically having a science fiction theme.
ORIGIN – Japanese.

animism /**ann**imiz'm/ > *noun* the belief that plants and inanimate objects have souls.
DERIVATIVES – **animist** *noun* **animistic** *adjective*.
ORIGIN – from Latin *anima* 'life, soul'.

animosity /anni**moss**iti/ > *noun* (pl. **animosities**) strong hostility.
SYNONYMS – antagonism, antipathy, enmity, hostility, ill will.
ANTONYMS – friendliness, goodwill.
ORIGIN – Latin *animositas*, from *animus* 'spirit, mind'.

animus /**ann**iməss/ > *noun* **1** hostility or ill feeling. **2** Psychoanalysis (in Jungian psychology) the masculine part of a woman's personality. Compare with ANIMA.
ORIGIN – Latin, 'spirit, mind'.

anion /**ann**īən/ > *noun* Chemistry a negatively charged ion. The opposite of CATION.
DERIVATIVES – **anionic** *adjective*.
ORIGIN – from ANODE + ION.

anise /**ann**iss/ > *noun* a plant grown for its aromatic seeds (aniseed).
ORIGIN – Greek *anison* 'anise, dill'.

aniseed > *noun* the seed of the plant anise, used as a flavouring.
WORDFINDER – *drinks flavoured with aniseed*: absinthe, ouzo, pastis, Pernod (trademark), Ricard (trademark), sambuca.

ankh /angk/ > *noun* an ancient Egyptian symbol of life in the shape of a cross with a loop instead of the top arm.
ORIGIN – Egyptian, 'life, soul'.

ankle > *noun* **1** the joint connecting the foot with the leg. **2** the narrow part of the leg between this and the calf.
WORDFINDER – tarsus (*the group of bones in the ankle*).

anklet > *noun* an ornamental chain or band worn round the ankle.

ankylosaur /**ang**kiləsor/ > *noun* a heavily built plant-eating dinosaur of the Cretaceous period, armoured with bony plates.
ORIGIN – from Greek *ankulos* 'crooked' + *sauros* 'lizard'.

ankylosing spondylitis > *noun* see SPONDYLITIS.

ankylosis /angki**lō**siss/ > *noun* Medicine abnormal stiffening and immobility of a joint due to fusion of the bones.
ORIGIN – from Greek *ankuloun* 'make crooked'.

anna > *noun* a former monetary unit of India and Pakistan, equal to one sixteenth of a rupee.
ORIGIN – Hindi.

annal /**ann**'l/ > *noun* **1** (**annals**) a history of events year by year. **2** a record of the events of one year.
DERIVATIVES – **annalist** *noun*.
ORIGIN – from Latin *annales libri* 'yearly books'.

annatto /ə**natt**ō/ > *noun* (pl. **annattos**) an orange-red dye obtained from a tropical fruit, used for colouring foods.
ORIGIN – Carib.

anneal /ə**neel**/ > *verb* heat (metal or glass) and allow it to cool slowly, so as to remove internal stresses.
ORIGIN – Old English, 'set on fire'.

annelid /**ann**əlid/ > *noun* a worm with a segmented body, such as an earthworm or leech.
ORIGIN – from Latin *annelus* 'small ring'.

annex > *verb* /ə**neks**/ **1** seize (territory) and add it to one's own. **2** add as an extra or subordinate part. > *noun* /**ann**eks/ (chiefly Brit. also **annexe**) (pl. **annexes**) **1** a building joined to or associated with a main building. **2** an addition to a document.
DERIVATIVES – **annexation** *noun*.
SYNONYMS – *verb* **1** seize, take over. **2** append, tack on. *noun* **1** addition, extension, wing.
ORIGIN – Latin *annectere* 'connect'.

annihilate /ə**nī**ilayt/ > *verb* **1** destroy completely. **2** informal defeat completely.
DERIVATIVES – **annihilation** *noun* **annihilator** *noun*.
SYNONYMS – **1** destroy, eradicate, obliterate.
ORIGIN – Latin *annihilare* 'reduce to nothing'.

anniversary > *noun* (pl. **anniversaries**) the date on which an event took place in a previous year.
ORIGIN – from Latin *anniversarius* 'returning yearly', from *annus* 'year' + *versus* 'turning'.

Anno Domini /annō **domm**inī/ > *adverb* full form of AD.

annotate /**ann**ətayt/ > *verb* add explanatory notes to.
DERIVATIVES – **annotation** *noun* **annotator** *noun*.
ORIGIN – Latin *annotare* 'to mark'.

announce > *verb* **1** make a public declaration about. **2** be a sign of: *lilies announce the arrival of summer*.
DERIVATIVES – **announcer** *noun*.
SYNONYMS – **1** declare, make known, proclaim, state.
ORIGIN – Latin *annuntiare*, from *nuntius* 'messenger'.

announcement > *noun* **1** a public declaration. **2** the action of announcing something.
SYNONYMS – **1** declaration, proclamation, pronouncement, statement.

annoy > *verb* **1** make slightly angry. **2** pester or harass. **3** archaic harm or attack repeatedly.
DERIVATIVES – **annoyance** *noun* **annoying** *adjective* **annoyingly** *adverb*.
SYNONYMS – **1** irk, irritate, peeve, vex.
ORIGIN – Old French *anoier*, from Latin *in odio*, in the phrase *mihi in odio est* 'it is hateful to me'.

annoyed > *adjective* rather angry.
SYNONYMS – angry, cross, irate, irritated, vexed.

annual > *adjective* **1** occurring once a year. **2** calculated over or covering a year. **3** (of a plant) living for a year or less. > *noun* **1** a book or magazine of a series published once a year. **2** an annual plant.
DERIVATIVES – **annually** *adverb*.
ORIGIN – Latin *annualis*, from *annus* 'year'.

annualised (also **annualized**) > *adjective* (of a rate of return or inflation) recalculated as an annual rate.

annuity > *noun* (pl. **annuities**) a fixed yearly allowance, especially one provided by a form of investment.

ORIGIN – Latin *annuitas*, from *annuus* 'yearly'.

annul /ənul/ > *verb* (**annulled, annulling**) declare (a law, marriage, or other legal contract) invalid.

DERIVATIVES – **annulment** *noun*.

SYNONYMS – cancel, nullify, repeal, revoke.

ORIGIN – Latin *annullare*, from *nullum* 'nothing'.

annular /anyoolər/ > *adjective* technical ring-shaped.

ORIGIN – Latin *annularis*, from *anulus* 'small ring'.

annulate /anyoolət/ > *adjective* chiefly Zoology marked with or formed of rings.

annunciation > *noun* **1** (**the Annunciation**) the announcement of the Incarnation by the angel Gabriel to Mary (Luke, chapter 1). **2** a Church festival commemorating this, held on 25 March.

ORIGIN – Latin, from *annuntiare* 'announce'.

annus horribilis /annəs horeebiliss/ > *noun* a year of disaster or misfortune.

ORIGIN – Latin, suggested by ANNUS MIRABILIS.

annus mirabilis /annəss miraabiliss/ > *noun* a remarkable or auspicious year.

ORIGIN – Latin, 'wonderful year'.

anode /annōd/ > *noun* a positively charged electrode. The opposite of CATHODE.

ORIGIN – Greek *anodos* 'way up'.

anodised /annədīzd/ (also **anodized**) > *adjective* (of metal, especially aluminium) coated with a protective oxide layer by electrolysis.

anodyne /annədīn/ > *adjective* unlikely to cause offence or disagreement; bland. > *noun* a painkilling drug or medicine.

ORIGIN – Greek *anōdunos* 'painless'.

anoint* > *verb* **1** smear or rub with oil, especially as part of a religious ceremony. **2** ceremonially confer office on (a priest or monarch) by anointing them.

*SPELLING – only one *n*: anoint.

ORIGIN – Old French *enoindre*, from Latin *inungere*.

anomalous > *adjective* differing from that which is standard or normal.

DERIVATIVES – **anomalously** *adverb* **anomalousness** *noun*.

SYNONYMS – abnormal, atypical, irregular, non-standard.

ORIGIN – from Greek *an-* 'not' + *homalos* 'even'.

anomaly /ənomməli/ > *noun* (pl. **anomalies**) something that deviates from what is standard or normal.

SYNONYMS – deviation, exception, inconsistency, oddity.

anomie /annəmi/ (also **anomy**) > *noun* lack of the usual social or moral standards.

ORIGIN – Greek *anomia*, from *anomos* 'lawless'.

anon > *adverb* archaic or informal soon; shortly.

ORIGIN – Old English, 'in or into (one state or course)'.

anonymity /annənimmiti/ > *noun* the state of being anonymous.

anonymous > *adjective* **1** not identified by name; of unknown identity. **2** lacking character; featureless.

DERIVATIVES – **anonymously** *adverb*.

SYNONYMS – **1** nameless, unidentified, unsigned. **2** characterless, featureless, nondescript, unremarkable.

ORIGIN – Greek *anōnumos* 'nameless', from *onoma* 'name'.

anopheles /ənoffileez/ > *noun* a mosquito of a genus which includes the species that transmits malaria.

ORIGIN – Greek, 'unprofitable, useless'.

anorak > *noun* **1** a waterproof jacket, usually with a hood. **2** Brit. informal a socially inept person with an obsessive interest in something.

ORIGIN – Greenland Eskimo.

anorexia /annəreksiə/ (also **anorexia nervosa**) > *noun* an emotional disorder characterised by an obsessive desire to lose weight by refusing to eat.

ORIGIN – from Greek *an-* 'without' + *orexis* 'appetite'.

anorexic (also **anorectic**) > *adjective* relating to or suffering from anorexia. > *noun* **1** a person suffering from anorexia. **2** (**anorectic**) a medicine which produces a loss of appetite.

another > *determiner & pronoun* **1** one more; a further. **2** denoting a different person or thing from one already mentioned.

answer > *noun* **1** something said or written in reaction to a question or statement. **2** the solution to a problem. > *verb* **1** respond with an answer. **2** (**answer back**) respond impudently. **3** (**answer to** or **for**) be responsible to or for. **4** satisfy (a need). **5** defend oneself against (a charge or accusation).

SYNONYMS – *noun* **1** rejoinder, reply, response, retort. *verb* **1** reply, respond, retort. **5** counter, rebut, refute.

COMBINATIONS – **answering machine** a device which supplies a pre-recorded answer to a telephone call and can record a message from the caller. **answerphone** Brit. an answering machine.

ORIGIN – Old English, from *and-* 'against, in reply' and a base shared by SWEAR.

answerable > *adjective* (**answerable to** or **for**) responsible to or for.

ant > *noun* a small insect, usually wingless, living in a complex social colony.

WORDFINDER – formic acid (*acid secreted by some ants*), formicarium (*ants' nest*), myrmecology (*scientific study of ants*).

IDIOMS – **have ants in one's pants** informal be fidgety.

COMBINATIONS – **anthill** a mound-shaped nest built by ants or termites.

-ant > *suffix* **1** (forming adjectives) having a quality or state: *arrogant*. **2** (forming nouns) performing a function: *deodorant*.

ORIGIN – Latin.

antacid /antassid/ > *adjective* preventing or correcting acidity in the stomach.

antagonise (also **antagonize**) > *verb* make hostile.

SYNONYMS – alienate, anger, annoy, provoke.

ANTONYMS – appease, placate.

ORIGIN – first used in the sense 'struggle against': from Greek *antagōnizesthai*, from *ant-* 'against' + *agōnizesthai* 'struggle'.

antagonism /antaggəniz'm/ > *noun* open hostility or opposition.

SYNONYMS – enmity, friction, hostility, opposition.

ANTONYMS – goodwill, rapport.

antagonist > *noun* an open opponent or enemy.

DERIVATIVES – **antagonistic** *adjective*.

ORIGIN – Greek *antagōnistēs*, from *antagōnizesthai* 'struggle against'.

Antarctic > *adjective* relating to the regions around the South Pole. > *noun* (**the Antarctic**) the regions around the South Pole.

ORIGIN – Greek *antarktikos* 'opposite to the north'.

ante /anti/ > *noun* a stake put up by a player in poker or brag before receiving cards. > *verb* (**antes, anted, anteing**) (**ante up**) put up (an amount) as an ante.

IDIOMS – **up** (or **raise**) **the ante** increase what is at stake or under discussion.

ORIGIN – Latin, 'before'.

ante- /anti/ > *prefix* before; preceding: *antecedent*.

ORIGIN – Latin *ante* 'before'.

anteater > *noun* a mammal with a long snout, feeding on ants and termites.

antebellum /antibelləm/ > *adjective* occurring or existing before a particular war.

ORIGIN – Latin, from *ante* 'before' + *bellum* 'war'.

antecedent /antiseed'nt/ > *noun* **1** a thing that existed before or precedes another. **2** (**antecedents**) a person's ancestors and family background. **3** Grammar an earlier word, phrase, or clause to which a following pronoun refers back. > *adjective* preceding in time or order.

ORIGIN – from Latin *antecedere* 'go before'.

antechamber > *noun* an ante-room.

antedate > *verb* **1** come before in time. **2** indicate that (a document or event) belongs to an earlier date.

antediluvian /antidiloōviən/ > *adjective* **1**

belonging to the time before the biblical Flood. **2** chiefly humorous ridiculously old-fashioned.

ORIGIN – from Latin *ante* 'before' + *diluvium* 'deluge'.

antelope > *noun* a swift-running deer-like animal with upward-pointing horns.

ORIGIN – Greek *antholops*.

antenatal > *adjective* before birth; during or relating to pregnancy.

antenna /antennə/ > *noun* (pl. **antennae** /antennee/) **1** each of a pair of long, thin sensory appendages on the heads of insects, crustaceans, etc. **2** (pl. also **antennas**) an aerial.

ORIGIN – Latin, alteration of *antemna* 'yard' (of a ship's mast).

antepartum /antipaartəm/ > *adjective* Medicine occurring not long before childbirth.

ORIGIN – Latin, 'before birth'.

antepenultimate > *adjective* last but two in a series.

ante-post > *adjective* Brit. (of a bet) placed before the runners are known, on a horse thought likely to be entered.

anterior > *adjective* **1** technical at or nearer the front. The opposite of **POSTERIOR**. **2** (**anterior to**) formal before.

ORIGIN – Latin, comparative of *ante* 'before'.

ante-room > *noun* a small room leading to a more important one.

anthelmintic /anthelmintik/ Medicine > *adjective* used to destroy parasitic worms. > *noun* an anthelmintic medicine.

ORIGIN – from Greek *anth-* 'against' + *helmins* 'worm'.

anthem > *noun* **1** an uplifting song associated with a group or cause, especially a patriotic one adopted as an expression of national identity. **2** a musical setting of a religious text to be sung by a choir during a church service.

DERIVATIVES – **anthemic** *adjective*.

ORIGIN – Latin *antiphona* 'antiphon'.

anther > *noun* the part of a flower's stamen that contains the pollen.

ORIGIN – Greek *anthos* 'flower'.

anthology > *noun* (pl. **anthologies**) a collection of poems or other pieces of writing or music.

DERIVATIVES – **anthologise** (also **anthologize**) *verb* **anthologist** *noun*.

SYNONYMS – collection, compendium, compilation, selection.

ORIGIN – Greek *anthologia*, from *anthos* 'flower' + *-logia* 'collection'.

anthracite /anthrəsīt/ > *noun* hard coal that burns with little flame and smoke.

ORIGIN – first used in reference to a stone resembling coal, described by the Roman scholar Pliny: from Greek *anthrakitēs*, from *anthrax* 'coal'.

anthrax /anthraks/ > *noun* a serious bacterial disease of sheep and cattle, able to be transmitted to humans.

ORIGIN – Greek *anthrax* 'coal, carbuncle'.

anthropocentric > *adjective* regarding humankind as the most important element of existence.

DERIVATIVES – **anthropocentrism** *noun*.

ORIGIN – from Greek *anthrōpos* 'human being'.

anthropogenic > *adjective* (chiefly of pollution) originating in human activity.

DERIVATIVES – **anthropogenically** *adverb*.

anthropoid > *adjective* referring to the higher primates including monkeys, apes, and humans.

anthropology /anthrəpolləji/ > *noun* the study of humankind, including the study of different societies and cultures and the study of human origins and evolution.

DERIVATIVES – **anthropological** *adjective* **anthropologist** *noun*.

anthropomorphic /anthrəpəmorfik/ > *adjective* **1** attributing human form or feelings to a god, animal, or object. **2** having human characteristics.

DERIVATIVES – **anthropomorphism** *noun*.

ORIGIN – from Greek *anthrōpos* 'human being' + *morphē* 'form'.

anthropophagi /anthrəpoffəgī/ > *plural noun* (in legends or fables) cannibals.

ORIGIN – from Greek *anthrōpophagos* 'man-eating'.

anthropophagy /anthrəpoffəji/ > *noun* cannibalism.

anti > *preposition* opposed to; against.

anti- > *prefix* **1** opposed to; against: *anti-aircraft*. **2** preventing or relieving: *antibacterial*. **3** the opposite of: *anticlimax*.

ORIGIN – from Greek *anti* 'against'.

antibacterial > *adjective* active against bacteria.

antibiotic > *noun* a medicine that inhibits the growth of or destroys bacteria.

ORIGIN – from Greek *biōtikos* 'fit for life'.

antibody > *noun* (pl. **antibodies**) a protein produced in the blood to counteract an antigen.

Antichrist > *noun* a supposed enemy of Christ expected by the early Church to appear before the end of the world.

anticipate > *verb* **1** be aware of (a future event) and prepare for it. **2** regard as probable. **3** look forward to. **4** act as a precursor to.

DERIVATIVES – **anticipator** *noun* **anticipatory** *adjective*.

SYNONYMS – **1,2** expect, forecast, foresee. **4** antedate, foreshadow, precede.

ORIGIN – Latin *anticipare*, from *ante-* 'before' + *capere* 'take'.

anticipation > *noun* the action of anticipating; expectation or prediction.

SYNONYMS – expectancy, expectation, hope, prediction.

anticlimax > *noun* a disappointing end to an exciting series of events.

DERIVATIVES – **anticlimactic** *adjective*.

SYNONYMS – comedown, disappointment, let-down, non-event.

anticline /antiklīn/ > *noun* a ridge or fold of stratified rock in which the strata slope downwards from the crest. Compare with **SYNCLINE**.

ORIGIN – from **ANTI-** + Greek *klinein* 'lean'.

anticlockwise > *adverb & adjective* Brit. in the opposite direction to the way in which the hands of a clock move round.

anticoagulant > *adjective* preventing the blood from clotting. > *noun* an anticoagulant drug.

anticonvulsant > *adjective* preventing or reducing the severity of epileptic fits or other convulsions. > *noun* an anticonvulsant drug.

antics > *plural noun* foolish, outrageous, or amusing behaviour.

SYNONYMS – buffoonery, capers, escapades, frolics, high jinks.

ORIGIN – from Italian *antico* 'antique', also 'grotesque'.

anticyclone > *noun* an area of high atmospheric pressure around which air slowly circulates, usually resulting in calm, fine weather.

DERIVATIVES – **anticyclonic** *adjective*.

antidepressant > *adjective* used to alleviate depression. > *noun* an antidepressant drug.

antidote > *noun* **1** a medicine taken to counteract a poison. **2** something that counteracts an unpleasant feeling or situation: *laughter is a good antidote to stress*.

SYNONYMS – **1** antiserum, antitoxin, antivenin, remedy. **2** corrective, cure, remedy, solution.

ORIGIN – Greek *antidoton*, from *anti-* 'against' + *didonai* 'give'.

anti-emetic > *adjective* preventing vomiting. > *noun* an anti-emetic drug.

antifreeze > *noun* a liquid added to water to prevent it from freezing, especially as used in the radiator of a motor vehicle.

antigen > *noun* a harmful substance which causes the body to produce antibodies.

DERIVATIVES – **antigenic** *adjective*.

Antiguan /anteegwən/ > *noun* a person from Antigua in the West Indies. > *adjective* relating to Antigua.

anti-hero (or **anti-heroine**) > *noun* a central character in a story, film, or play who lacks conventional heroic qualities.

antihistamine /antihistəmeen/ > *noun* a drug that counteracts the effects of histamine, used in treating allergies.

anti-inflammatory > *adjective* acting to reduce inflammation. > *noun* (pl. **anti-**

inflammatories) an anti-inflammatory drug.

antilogarithm > *noun* the number of which a given number is the logarithm.

antimacassar /antimə**kass**ər/ > *noun* a piece of cloth put over the back of a chair to protect it from grease and dirt.

ORIGIN – from **ANTI-** + **MACASSAR**, a kind of hair oil formerly used by men.

antimatter > *noun* matter consisting of the antiparticles of the particles making up normal matter.

antimony /**an**timəni/ > *noun* a brittle silvery-white metallic chemical element.

ORIGIN – Latin *antimonium*.

antinomian /antin**ō**miən/ > *adjective* believing that Christians are released by grace from obeying moral laws. > *noun* a person with such a belief.

DERIVATIVES – **antinomianism** *noun*.

antinomy /an**tinn**əmi/ > *noun* (pl. **antinomies**) a paradox.

ORIGIN – from Greek *anti* 'against' + *nomos* 'law'.

antioxidant > *noun* a substance that counteracts oxidation.

antiparticle > *noun* a subatomic particle with the same mass as a given particle but an opposite electric charge or magnetic effect.

antipasto /anti**past**ō/ > *noun* (pl. **antipasti** /anti**past**i/) an Italian hors d'oeuvre.

ORIGIN – Italian, from *anti-* 'before' + *pasto* 'food'.

antipathy /an**tipp**əthi/ > *noun* (pl. **antipathies**) a strong feeling of dislike.

DERIVATIVES – **antipathetic** *adjective*.

SYNONYMS – aversion, dislike, hostility, ill will.

ANTONYMS – affinity, liking.

ORIGIN – Greek *antipatheia*, from *anti-* 'against' + *pathos* 'feeling'.

anti-personnel > *adjective* (of weapons) designed to kill or injure people rather than to damage buildings or equipment.

antiperspirant > *noun* a substance applied to the skin to prevent or reduce perspiration.

antiphon /**an**tif'n/ > *noun* a short chant sung before or after a psalm or canticle.

ORIGIN – Greek *antiphōna* 'harmonies'.

antiphonal /an**tiff**ən'l/ > *adjective* (of church music) sung, recited, or played alternately by two groups.

Antipodes /an**tipp**ədeez/ > *plural noun* **1** (**the Antipodes**) Australia and New Zealand (in relation to the northern hemisphere). **2** (**antipodes** or **antipode**) the direct opposite of something.

DERIVATIVES – **antipodal** *adjective* **Antipodean** *adjective & noun*.

ORIGIN – from Greek *antipodes* 'having the feet opposite'.

antipyretic > *adjective* used to prevent or reduce fever. > *noun* an antipyretic drug.

antiquarian /anti**kwair**iən/ > *adjective* relating to the collection or study of antiques, rare books, or antiquities. > *noun* (also **antiquary**) a person who studies or collects antiquarian items.

DERIVATIVES – **antiquarianism** *noun*.

antiquated > *adjective* old-fashioned or outdated.

antique > *noun* a decorative object or piece of furniture that is valuable because of its age. > *adjective* **1** valuable because of its age. **2** old-fashioned or outdated. **3** literary ancient.

ORIGIN – Latin *antiquus* 'former, ancient'.

antiquity > *noun* (pl. **antiquities**) **1** the distant past, especially before the Middle Ages. **2** an object from the distant past. **3** great age.

antirrhinum /anti**rī**nəm/ > *noun* (pl. **antirrhinums**) a snapdragon.

ORIGIN – Greek *antirrhinon*, from *anti-* 'counterfeiting' + *rhis* 'nose' (from the flower's resemblance to an animal's snout).

antiscorbutic > *adjective* preventing or curing scurvy.

anti-Semitism > *noun* hostility to or prejudice against Jews.

DERIVATIVES – **anti-Semite** *noun* **anti-Semitic** *adjective*.

antiseptic > *adjective* **1** preventing the growth of micro-organisms that cause disease or infection. **2** so clean or pure as to lack character. > *noun* an antiseptic compound or preparation.

antiserum > *noun* (pl. **antisera**) a blood serum containing antibodies against specific antigens.

antisocial > *adjective* **1** contrary to accepted social customs and causing annoyance. **2** avoiding the company of others.

DERIVATIVES – **antisocially** *adverb*.

USAGE – the meaning of the core sense of **antisocial** is quite distinct from that of **unsociable**, which means 'not enjoying the company of or engaging in activities with others', and **unsocial**, which means 'socially inconvenient'.

SYNONYMS – **1** disorderly, disruptive, lawless, rebellious.

antithesis /an**tith**əsiss/ > *noun* (pl. **antitheses** /an**tith**əseez/) **1** a person or thing that is the direct opposite of another. **2** the putting together of contrasting ideas or words to produce a rhetorical effect.

ORIGIN – Greek, from *antitithenai* 'set against'.

antithetical /anti**thett**ikk'l/ > *adjective* **1** mutually opposed or incompatible. **2** (in rhetoric) using antithesis.

antitoxin > *noun* an antibody that counteracts a toxin.

antitrust > *adjective* chiefly US (of legislation) preventing or controlling monopolies.

antivenin /anti**venn**in/ > *noun* an antiserum containing antibodies against poisons in the venom of snakes.

antivivisection > *adjective* opposed to the use of live animals for scientific research.

DERIVATIVES – **antivivisectionist** *noun & adjective*.

antler > *noun* each of a pair of branched horns on the head of an adult deer.

ORIGIN – Old French *antoillier*.

antonym /**an**tənim/ > *noun* a word opposite in meaning to another.

ORIGIN – from Greek *anti-* 'against' + *onoma* 'a name'.

anus /**ay**nəss/ > *noun* the opening at the end of the digestive system through which solid waste matter leaves the body.

ORIGIN – Latin.

anvil > *noun* a heavy iron block on which hot metal can be hammered and shaped.

anxiety > *noun* (pl. **anxieties**) an anxious feeling or state.

SYNONYMS – apprehension, concern, nervousness, unease, worry.

anxious > *adjective* **1** experiencing worry or unease. **2** (**anxious to do**) very eager and concerned to do something.

DERIVATIVES – **anxiously** *adverb* **anxiousness** *noun*.

SYNONYMS – **1** apprehensive, concerned, nervous, worried, uneasy. **2** desirous, eager, impatient, keen.

ANTONYMS – **1** carefree, unconcerned.

ORIGIN – Latin *anxius*, from *angere* 'to choke'.

any > *determiner & pronoun* **1** one or some of a thing or number of things, no matter how much or how many. **2** whichever or whatever one chooses. > *adverb* at all; in some degree.

IDIOMS – **any more** to any further extent; any longer. **any time** at whatever time. **any time** (or **day** or **minute**) **now** informal very soon.

USAGE – when used as a pronoun **any** can be used with either a singular or a plural verb, depending on the context: *we needed more sugar but there wasn't any left* (singular verb) or *are any of the new videos available?* (plural verb).

anybody > *pronoun* anyone.

anyhow > *adverb* **1** anyway. **2** in a careless or haphazard way.

anyone > *pronoun* any person or people.

USAGE – the two-word phrase **any one** is not the same as the word **anyone** and the two forms cannot be used interchangeably. **Any one** means 'any single (person or thing)', as in: *not more than twelve new members are admitted in any one year*.

anything > *pronoun* a thing of any kind, no matter what.

IDIOMS – **anything but** not at all.

anyway > *adverb* **1** used to emphasise something just said. **2** used in conversations to change the subject or to resume after interruption. **3** nevertheless.

anywhere > *adverb* in or to any place. > *pronoun* any place.

Anzac /**an**zak/ > *noun* **1** a soldier in the Australian and New Zealand Army Corps (1914–18). **2** informal a person from Australia or New Zealand.

AOB > *abbreviation* Brit. (at the end of an agenda for a meeting) any other business.

aorta /ay**or**tə/ > *noun* the main artery supplying blood from the heart to the rest of the body.

DERIVATIVES – **aortic** *adjective*.

ORIGIN – Greek *aortē*, from *aeirein* 'raise'.

apace > *adverb* literary swiftly; quickly.

Apache /ə**pa**chi/ > *noun* (pl. same or **Apaches**) a member of an American Indian people living chiefly in New Mexico and Arizona.

ORIGIN – probably from a word in an American Indian language meaning 'enemy'.

apart > *adverb* **1** separated by a distance in time or space. **2** to or on one side. **3** into pieces.

IDIOMS – **apart from 1** except for. **2** as well as.

ORIGIN – from Latin *a parte* 'at the side'.

apartheid /ə**paar**tīd/ > *noun* historical the official system of segregation or discrimination on racial grounds formerly in force in South Africa.

ORIGIN – Afrikaans, 'separateness'.

apartment* > *noun* **1** chiefly N. Amer. a set of rooms forming one residence; a flat. **2** (**apartments**) a private suite of rooms in a very large house.

***SPELLING** – note that there is only one *p*: apartment.

ORIGIN – Italian *appartamento*, from *appartare* 'to separate'.

apathetic > *adjective* not interested or enthusiastic.

DERIVATIVES – **apathetically** *adverb*.

SYNONYMS – indifferent, lethargic, unenthusiastic, uninterested.

apathy /**ap**əthi/ > *noun* lack of interest or enthusiasm.

SYNONYMS – indifference, lassitude, lethargy, passivity, torpor.

ORIGIN – Greek *apatheia*, from *apathēs* 'without feeling'.

apatosaurus /ə**patt**ə**sawr**əss/ > *noun* scientific name for **BRONTOSAURUS**.

ORIGIN – from Greek *apatē* 'deceit' (because of a deceptive similarity between some of its bones and those of other dinosaurs) + *sauros* 'lizard'.

APC > *abbreviation* armoured personnel carrier.

ape > *noun* **1** a large tailless primate of a group including gorillas, chimpanzees, and gibbons. **2** informal an unintelligent or clumsy person. > *verb* imitate in an absurd or unthinking way.

aperçu /appər**syoo**/ > *noun* (pl. **aperçus**) a comment which makes an illuminating or entertaining point.

ORIGIN – French, 'thing perceived'.

aperient /ə**peer**iənt/ Medicine > *adjective* used to relieve constipation. > *noun* an aperient drug.

ORIGIN – from Latin *aperire* 'to open'.

aperitif /ə**perri**teef/ > *noun* an alcoholic drink taken before a meal to stimulate the appetite.

ORIGIN – French, from Latin *aperire* 'to open'.

aperture /**app**ərtyoor/ > *noun* **1** an opening, hole, or gap. **2** the variable opening by which light enters a camera.

Apex /**ay**peks/ > *noun* a system of reduced fares for air or rail journeys booked in advance.

ORIGIN – from *Advance Purchase Excursion*.

apex /**ay**peks/ > *noun* (pl. **apexes** or **apices** /**ay**piseez/) the top or highest part, especially one forming a point.

SYNONYMS – peak, pinnacle, summit.

ORIGIN – Latin, 'peak, tip'.

aphasia /ə**fay**ziə/ > *noun* inability to understand or produce speech, as a result of brain damage.

DERIVATIVES – **aphasic** *adjective & noun*.

ORIGIN – from Greek *aphatos* 'speechless'.

aphelion /ap**heel**iən/ > *noun* (pl. **aphelia** /ap**heel**iə/) the point in a planet's orbit at which it is furthest from the sun. The opposite of **PERIHELION**.

ORIGIN – from Greek *aph' hēlion* 'from the sun'.

aphid /**ay**fid/ > *noun* a greenfly or similar small insect feeding on the sap of plants.

ORIGIN – Greek *aphis*.

aphorism /**aff**əriz'm/ > *noun* a concise witty remark which contains a general truth.

DERIVATIVES – **aphoristic** *adjective*.

ORIGIN – Greek *aphorismos* 'definition'.

aphrodisiac /afrə**dizz**iak/ > *noun* a food, drink, or drug that arouses sexual desire.

ORIGIN – Greek *aphrodisiakos*, from *Aphrodite*, the goddess of love.

apiary /**ay**piəri/ > *noun* (pl. **apiaries**) a place where bees are kept.

DERIVATIVES – **apiarist** *noun*.

ORIGIN – Latin *apiarium*, from *apis* 'bee'.

apical /**ay**pik'l, **ap**ik'l/ > *adjective* technical relating to or forming an apex.

apices plural of **APEX**.

apiculture /**ay**pikulchər/ > *noun* technical bee-keeping.

ORIGIN – from Latin *apis* 'bee'.

apiece > *adverb* to, for, or by each one.

aplenty > *adjective* in abundance: *he has work aplenty*.

aplomb /ə**plom**/ > *noun* self-confidence or calm assurance.

SYNONYMS – assurance, confidence, poise, self-confidence.

ORIGIN – French, from *à plomb* 'according to a plumb line, perpendicularly'.

apnoea /ap**nee**ə/ (US **apnea**) > *noun* a medical condition in which a person has a tendency to stop breathing for a few seconds while sleeping.

ORIGIN – Greek *apnoia*, from *apnous* 'breathless'.

apocalypse /ə**pokk**əlips/ > *noun* **1** an event involving great and widespread destruction. **2** (**the Apocalypse**) the final destruction of the world, as described in the biblical book of Revelation.

ORIGIN – Greek *apokalupsis*, from *apokaluptein* 'uncover, reveal'.

apocalyptic > *adjective* resembling the end of the world in being momentous or catastrophic.

DERIVATIVES – **apocalyptically** *adverb*.

Apocrypha /ə**pok**rifə/ > *plural noun* (treated as sing. or pl.) those books of the Old Testament not accepted as part of Hebrew scripture and excluded from the Protestant Bible at the Reformation.

ORIGIN – Latin *apocrypha scripta* 'hidden writings'.

apocryphal > *adjective* **1** (of a story or statement) widely circulated but unlikely to be true. **2** of or belonging to the Apocrypha.

apogee /**app**əjee/ > *noun* **1** Astronomy the point in the orbit of the moon or a satellite at which it is furthest from the earth. The opposite of **PERIGEE**. **2** a culmination or climax.

ORIGIN – from Greek *apogaion diastēma* 'distance away from earth'.

apolitical > *adjective* not interested or involved in politics.

apologetic > *adjective* regretfully acknowledging an offence.

DERIVATIVES – **apologetically** *adverb*.

SYNONYMS – contrite, penitent, repentant, sorry.

ANTONYMS – defiant, unrepentant.

apologetics > *plural noun* (treated as sing. or pl.) reasoned arguments defending a theory or doctrine.

apologia /appə**lō**jiə/ > *noun* a formal written defence of one's opinions or conduct.

ORIGIN – Latin, 'apology'.

apologise (also **apologize**) > *verb* express regret for something that one has done wrong.

SYNONYMS – beg someone's pardon, repent, say sorry.

apologist > *noun* a person who offers an argument in defence of something controversial.

apology > *noun* (pl. **apologies**) 1 a regretful acknowledgement of an offence or failure. 2 (**an apology for**) a very poor example of. 3 a justification or defence.

ORIGIN – Greek *apologia* 'a speech in one's own defence'.

apophthegm /**app**əthem/ (US **apothegm**) > *noun* a concise saying stating a general truth.

ORIGIN – Greek *apothegma*, from *apophthengesthai* 'speak out'.

apoplectic /appə**plek**tik/ > *adjective* 1 informal overcome with anger. 2 dated relating to apoplexy (stroke).

apoplexy /**app**əpleksi/ > *noun* (pl. **apoplexies**) 1 dated unconsciousness or incapacity resulting from a cerebral haemorrhage or stroke. 2 informal extreme anger.

ORIGIN – Greek *apoplexia*, from *apoplēssein* 'disable by a stroke'.

apoptosis /appəp**tō**siss/ > *noun* Biology the death of cells which occurs as a normal part of an organism's development.

ORIGIN – Greek *apoptōsis* 'falling off'.

aporia /ə**por**iə/ > *noun* an irresolvable internal contradiction in a text, argument, or theory.

ORIGIN – Greek, from *aporos* 'impassable'.

apostasy /ə**post**əsi/ > *noun* abandonment of a belief or principle.

ORIGIN – Greek *apostasis* 'desertion'.

apostate /**app**əstayt/ > *noun* a person who renounces a belief or principle.

apostatise /ə**post**ətīz/ (also **apostatize**) > *verb* abandon a belief or principle.

a posteriori /ay posterri**or**ī/ > *adjective & adverb* involving reasoning based on known facts to deduce causes.

ORIGIN – Latin, 'from what comes after'.

apostle > *noun* 1 (**Apostle**) each of the twelve chief disciples of Jesus Christ. 2 an enthusiastic and pioneering supporter of an idea or cause.

WORDFINDER – *the Apostles of Jesus Christ:* Andrew, Bartholomew, James son of Alphaeus, James son of Zebedee, John, Judas Iscariot, Matthew, Matthias (*replaced Judas Iscariot*), Judas/Thaddeus son of James, Peter, Philip, Simon.

ORIGIN – Greek *apostolos* 'messenger'.

apostolate /ə**post**əlayt/ > *noun* 1 the position or authority of a religious leader. 2 evangelistic activity.

apostolic /appə**stoll**ik/ > *adjective* 1 relating to the Apostles. 2 relating to the Pope,

regarded as the successor to the Apostle St Peter.

apostrophe /ə**post**rəfi/ > *noun* 1 a punctuation mark (') used to indicate either possession (e.g. *Harry's book*) or the omission of letters or numbers (e.g. *can't*; *the summer of '69*). 2 Rhetoric a passage that turns away from the subject to address an absent person or thing.

ORIGIN – Greek *apostrophos*, from *apostrephein* 'turn away'.

apostrophise (also **apostrophize**) > *verb* 1 Rhetoric address an apostrophe to. 2 punctuate with an apostrophe.

apothecary /ə**poth**əkəri/ > *noun* (pl. **apothecaries**) archaic a person who prepared and sold medicines.

COMBINATIONS – **apothecaries' measure** a system of units formerly used in pharmacy for liquid volume (or weight), based on the fluid ounce and the ounce troy.

ORIGIN – Latin *apothecarius*, from Greek *apothēkē* 'storehouse'.

apothegm > *noun* US spelling of **APOPHTHEGM**.

apotheosis /əpothi**ō**siss/ > *noun* (pl. **apotheoses** /əpothi**ō**seez/) 1 the culmination or highest point: *science is the apotheosis of the intellect.* 2 elevation to divine status.

DERIVATIVES – **apotheosise** (also **apotheosize**) *verb*.

ORIGIN – Greek, from *apotheoun* 'make a god of'.

appal* (US **appall**) > *verb* (**appalled**, **appalling**) greatly dismay or horrify.

*****SPELLING – one *l* in *appal* and *appals*, two in *appalled* and *appalling*.

SYNONYMS – dismay, horrify, shock.

ORIGIN – Old French *apalir* 'grow pale'.

appalling > *adjective* informal very bad or displeasing.

DERIVATIVES – **appallingly** *adverb*.

apparatchik /appə**raat**chik/ > *noun* (pl. **apparatchiks** or **apparatchiki** /appə**raat**chikee/) 1 chiefly historical a member of the administrative structure of a communist party. 2 derogatory or humorous an official in a large political organisation.

ORIGIN – Russian, from German *Apparat* 'apparatus'.

apparatus /appə**ray**təss/ > *noun* (pl. **apparatuses**) 1 the equipment needed for a particular activity or purpose. 2 a complex structure within an organisation: *the apparatus of government.*

SYNONYMS – 1 devices, equipment, tools.

ORIGIN – Latin, from *apparare* 'make ready for'.

apparel /ə**parr**əl/ > *noun* formal clothing. > *verb* (**apparelled**, **apparelling**; US **appareled**, **appareling**) archaic clothe.

ORIGIN – Old French *apareillier* 'make fit', from Latin *ad-* 'to' + *par* 'equal'.

apparent > *adjective* 1 clearly seen or understood; obvious. 2 seeming real, but not necessarily so.

DERIVATIVES – **apparently** *adverb*.

SYNONYMS – 1 clear, evident, manifest, obvious. 2 ostensible, outward, seeming.

ORIGIN – from Latin *apparere* 'appear'.

apparition > *noun* a remarkable thing appearing suddenly, especially a ghost.

appeal > *verb* 1 make a serious or heartfelt request; ask urgently. 2 be attractive or interesting: *activities that appeal to all.* 3 Law apply to a higher court for a reversal of a lower court's decision. 4 Cricket (of the bowler or fielders) call on the umpire to declare a batsman out. > *noun* 1 an act of appealing. 2 the quality of being attractive or interesting.

SYNONYMS – *verb* 1 beg, call, plead. *noun* 2 allure, attraction, charm, interest.

ORIGIN – Latin *appellare* 'to address'.

appealing > *adjective* attractive or interesting.

DERIVATIVES – **appealingly** *adverb*.

appear > *verb* 1 become visible or evident. 2 give a particular impression; seem. 3 present oneself publicly or formally, especially on television or in a law court. 4 be published.

SYNONYMS – 1 be seen, emerge, be manifested, materialise.

ANTONYMS – 1 disappear, vanish.

ORIGIN – Latin *apparere*, from *parere* 'come into view'.

appearance > *noun* 1 the way that someone or something looks or seems. 2 an act of appearing.

IDIOMS – **keep up appearances** maintain an impression of wealth or well-being.

SYNONYMS – 1 aspect, look, mien. 2 advent, arrival, emergence, manifestation.

appease > *verb* placate (someone) by agreeing to their demands.

DERIVATIVES – **appeasement** *noun* **appeaser** *noun*.

SYNONYMS – conciliate, mollify, placate.

ORIGIN – Old French *apaisier*, from *pais* 'peace'.

appellant /ə**pell**ənt/ > *noun* Law a person who appeals against a court ruling.

appellate /ə**pell**ət/ > *adjective* Law (of a court) dealing with appeals.

appellation /appə**lay**sh'n/ > *noun* formal a name or title.

ORIGIN – Latin, from *appellare* 'to address'.

appellation contrôlée /appelassyoN kən**trō**lay/ (also **appellation d'origine** /dorri**zheen**/ **contrôlée**) > *noun* a guarantee that a French wine was produced in the region stated and in the approved manner.

ORIGIN – French, 'controlled appellation'.

append > *verb* add to the end of a document or piece of writing.
ORIGIN – Latin *appendere* 'hang on'.

appendage > *noun* a thing attached to or projecting from something larger or more important.

appendectomy /appen**dek**təmi/ (Brit. also **appendicectomy** /əpendi**sek**təmi/) > *noun* (pl. **appendectomies**) a surgical operation to remove the appendix.

appendicitis > *noun* inflammation of the appendix.

appendix > *noun* (pl. **appendices** or **appendixes**) 1 a small tube of tissue attached to the lower end of the large intestine. 2 a section of additional information at the end of a book.
ORIGIN – Latin, from *appendere* 'hang on'.

appertain /appə**tayn**/ > *verb* 1 (**appertain to**) relate to. 2 be appropriate.
ORIGIN – Latin *appertinere*, from *pertinere* 'pertain'.

appetiser (also **appetizer**) > *noun* a small dish of food or a drink taken before a meal to stimulate the appetite.

appetising (also **appetizing**) > *adjective* stimulating the appetite.

appetite > *noun* 1 a natural desire to satisfy a bodily need, especially for food. 2 a liking or inclination: *her appetite for study*.
DERIVATIVES – **appetitive** *adjective*.
SYNONYMS – craving, desire, hunger, urge.
ORIGIN – Latin *appetitus* 'desire for', from *appetere* 'seek after'.

applaud > *verb* 1 show approval by clapping; clap. 2 express approval of: *the world applauded his courage*.
SYNONYMS – 2 acclaim, approve of, praise, salute.
ORIGIN – Latin *applaudere*, from *plaudere* 'to clap'.

applause > *noun* approval shown by clapping.
SYNONYMS – acclaim, acclamation, clapping, cheering.

apple > *noun* the rounded fruit of a tree of the rose family, with green or red skin and crisp flesh.
WORDFINDER – *varieties of apple:* Blenheim Orange, Braeburn, Bramley, Cox, Discovery, Golden Delicious, Granny Smith, Royal Gala, russet.
IDIOMS – **the apple never falls far from the tree** proverb salient family characteristics are usually inherited. **the apple of one's eye** a person of whom one is extremely fond and proud. [ORIGIN – first denoting the pupil of the eye, extended as a symbol of something cherished.] **apples and pears** Brit. rhyming slang stairs. **a rotten** (or **bad**) **apple** informal a corrupt person in a group, likely to have a detrimental influence on the others. **upset the apple cart** spoil a plan or disturb the status quo.
DERIVATIVES – **appley** *adjective*.

apple-pie order > *noun* perfect order.

applet /**app**lit/ > *noun* Computing a small application running within a larger program.

appliance > *noun* 1 a device designed to perform a specific task, especially in the home. 2 Brit. the application of a method or skill.
SYNONYMS – 1 apparatus, device, gadget, machine.

wordpower facts
Appliance
The use of **appliance** to mean 'the application of something' had become rare if not obsolete until it was reintroduced into British English in the 1970s in the advertising slogan 'the appliance of science', used by the household appliance manufacturer Zanussi.

applicable /ə**plikk**əb'l, **app**likəb'l/ > *adjective* relevant or appropriate.
DERIVATIVES – **applicability** *noun*.

applicant > *noun* a person who applies for something.

application > *noun* 1 a formal request to an authority. 2 the action of applying something. 3 practical use or relevance. 4 sustained effort. 5 a computer program designed to fulfil a particular purpose.
SYNONYMS – 1 appeal, approach, petition. 2 applying, employment, exercise, use. 3 bearing, pertinence, relevance. 4 commitment, diligence, effort, industry, perseverance.

applicator > *noun* a device for inserting something or applying a substance to a surface.

applied > *adjective* practical rather than theoretical: *applied chemistry*.

appliqué /ə**plee**kay/ > *noun* decorative needlework in which fabric shapes are sewn or fixed on to a fabric background.
DERIVATIVES – **appliquéd** *adjective*.
ORIGIN – French, 'applied'.

apply > *verb* (**applies**, **applied**) 1 make a formal request for something to be done, such as asking to be considered for a job. 2 bring into operation or use. 3 be relevant. 4 put (a substance) on a surface. 5 (**apply oneself**) put all one's efforts into a task.
SYNONYMS – 2 employ, implement, operate, put into effect, use. 4 put on, spread. 5 (**apply oneself**) concentrate, knuckle down, pay attention.
ORIGIN – Latin *applicare* 'fold, fasten to'.

appoint > *verb* 1 assign a job or role to. 2 decide on (a time or place).
DERIVATIVES – **appointee** *noun*.
SYNONYMS – 1 choose, elect, nominate, select. 2 arrange, decide, determine, fix, ordain.
ORIGIN – Old French *apointer*, from *a point* 'to a point'.

appointed > *adjective* 1 (of a time or place) pre-arranged. 2 equipped or furnished: *a luxuriously appointed lounge*.

appointment > *noun* 1 an arrangement to meet. 2 a job or position. 3 the action of appointing or the process of being appointed. 4 (**appointments**) furniture or fittings.
IDIOMS – **by appointment** (**to the Queen**) selling goods or services to the Queen.
SYNONYMS – 1 engagement, rendezvous.

apportion > *verb* share out; assign.
DERIVATIVES – **apportionment** *noun*.
ORIGIN – Latin *apportionare*, from *portionare* 'divide into portions'.

apposite /**app**əzit/ > *adjective* very appropriate; apt.
ORIGIN – from Latin *apponere* 'apply'.

apposition > *noun* 1 chiefly technical the positioning of things next to each other. 2 Grammar a relationship in which a word or phrase is placed next to another in order to qualify or explain it (e.g. *my friend Sue*).
DERIVATIVES – **appositive** *adjective* & *noun*.

appraisal > *noun* 1 the action or an instance of assessing. 2 a formal assessment of an employee's performance at work.

appraise > *verb* 1 assess the quality or nature of. 2 give (an employee) an appraisal. 3 (of an official valuer) set a price on.
DERIVATIVES – **appraisee** *noun* **appraiser** *noun* **appraising** *adjective* **appraisingly** *adverb*.
USAGE – do not confuse **appraise** with **apprise**: **appraise** means 'assess', while **apprise** means 'inform'.
SYNONYMS – 1 assess, evaluate, gauge.
ORIGIN – alteration of obsolete *apprise* 'put a price on'.

appreciable > *adjective* large or important enough to be noticed.
DERIVATIVES – **appreciably** *adverb*.

appreciate /ə**pree**shiayt, ə**pree**siayt/ > *verb* 1 recognise the value or significance of. 2 be grateful for. 3 (often **appreciate that**) understand or recognise the implications of. 4 rise in value or price.
DERIVATIVES – **appreciator** *noun*.
SYNONYMS – 1 esteem, prize, recognise, respect, value.
ANTONYMS – 1 neglect, undervalue. 4 depreciate.
ORIGIN – Latin *appretiare* 'appraise', from *pretium* 'price'.

appreciation > *noun* **1** recognition of the value or significance of something. **2** gratitude. **3** a favourable written assessment of a person or their work. **4** increase in monetary value.

appreciative > *adjective* feeling or showing gratitude or pleasure.

DERIVATIVES – **appreciatively** *adverb* **appreciativeness** *noun*.

SYNONYMS – grateful, responsive, thankful.

ANTONYMS – ungrateful.

apprehend > *verb* **1** intercept or stop (someone) when they are doing something unlawful or wrong. **2** seize or arrest. **3** understand; perceive. **4** archaic anticipate with fear or unease.

ORIGIN – Latin *apprehendere*, from *prehendere* 'lay hold of'.

apprehension > *noun* **1** uneasy or fearful anticipation. **2** understanding. **3** the action of arresting someone.

SYNONYMS – **1** anxiety, disquiet, tension, unease, uneasiness.

apprehensive > *adjective* anticipating something with anxiety or fear.

DERIVATIVES – **apprehensively** *adverb* **apprehensiveness** *noun*.

SYNONYMS – anxious, fearful, nervous, tense, uneasy.

ANTONYMS – assured, confident.

apprentice > *noun* a person learning a skilled practical trade from an employer. > *verb* employ as an apprentice.

DERIVATIVES – **apprenticeship** *noun*.

SYNONYMS – beginner, learner, novice, starter, tyro.

ANTONYMS – master, veteran.

ORIGIN – Old French *aprentis*, from Latin *prehendere* 'lay hold of'.

apprise* > *verb* inform; tell.

USAGE – do not confuse **apprise** with **appraise**: **apprise**, often used in the structure *apprise someone of something*, means 'inform', while appraise means 'assess'.

*SPELLING – **apprise** cannot be spelled with an *-ize* ending.

ORIGIN – French, from *apprendre* 'learn, teach', from Latin *prehendere* 'lay hold of'.

approach > *verb* **1** come near to in distance, time, or standard. **2** go to (someone) with a proposal or request. **3** start to deal with in a certain way. > *noun* **1** a way of dealing with something. **2** an initial proposal or request. **3** the action of approaching. **4** a way leading to a place.

SYNONYMS – *verb* **1** come near to, near, proceed towards, resemble, verge on. **2** address, apply to, make overtures to, sound out. **3** begin, embark on, deal with, set about, tackle. *noun* **1** means, method, mode, modus operandi, procedure. **2** appeal, application, overture, proposal, request. **3** advance, arrival, coming.

ANTONYMS – *verb* **1** recede.

ORIGIN – Old French *aprochier*, from Latin *appropiare* 'draw near'.

approachable > *adjective* **1** friendly and easy to talk to. **2** able to be reached from a particular direction or by a particular means.

DERIVATIVES – **approachability** *noun*.

approbation > *noun* approval; praise.

DERIVATIVES – **approbative** *adjective* **approbatory** *adjective*.

ORIGIN – Latin, from *approbare* 'approve'.

appropriate > *adjective* /əprōpriət/ suitable, expected, or proper in particular circumstances. > *verb* /əprōpriayt/ **1** take for one's own use without permission. **2** devote (money) to a special purpose.

DERIVATIVES – **appropriately** *adverb* **appropriateness** *noun* **appropriation** *noun* **appropriator** *noun*.

SYNONYMS – *adjective* expected, fitting, proper, right, suitable. *verb* **1** annex, commandeer, hijack, requisition, seize.

ORIGIN – from Latin *appropriare* 'make one's own', from *proprius* 'own, proper'.

approval > *noun* **1** a person's opinion that something is good. **2** official acknowledgement that something is satisfactory.

IDIOMS – **on approval** (of goods) able to be returned if unsatisfactory.

SYNONYMS – **1** appreciation, approbation, favour, regard. **2** authorisation, backing, blessing, go-ahead, sanction.

ANTONYMS – disapproval, rejection.

approve > *verb* **1** (often **approve of**) believe that someone or something is good or acceptable. **2** officially acknowledge as satisfactory.

DERIVATIVES – **approving** *adjective* **approvingly** *adverb*.

SYNONYMS – **1** (**approve of**) commend, esteem, like, value. **2** authorise, confirm, ratify, sanction.

ANTONYMS – **1** (**approve of**) condemn, disapprove of. **2** refuse, turn down.

COMBINATIONS – **approved school** Brit. historical a residential institution for young offenders.

ORIGIN – Old French *aprover*, from Latin *approbare*.

approximate > *adjective* /əproksimət/ fairly accurate but not totally precise. > *verb* /əproksimayt/ **1** come close in quality or quantity. **2** estimate fairly accurately.

DERIVATIVES – **approximately** *adverb* **approximation** *noun* **approximative** *adjective*.

SYNONYMS – *adjective* estimated, inexact, rough. *verb* **1** approach, border on, near, verge on.

ANTONYMS – *adjective* exact, precise.

ORIGIN – Latin, from *proximus* 'very near'.

appurtenance /əpurtinənss/ > *noun* an accessory associated with a particular activity.

ORIGIN – Old French *apertenance*, from Latin *appertinere* 'belong to'.

APR > *abbreviation* annual (or annualised) percentage rate.

apraxia /əpraksiə/ > *noun* Medicine inability to perform particular activities as a result of brain damage.

ORIGIN – Greek, 'inaction'.

après-ski /aprayskee/ > *noun* social activities following a day's skiing.

ORIGIN – French, 'after skiing'.

apricot > *noun* an orange-yellow fruit resembling a small peach.

wordpower facts

Apricot

The word **apricot** comes from Portuguese *albricoque* or Spanish *albaricoque*, from an Arabic word based on Latin *praecox*, meaning 'early-ripe' (from *prae* 'before' and *coquere* 'to cook'). The adjective **precocious** comes from the same Latin root. **Apricot** is also interesting as a further example of wrong division (see box at **ADDER**), the Arabic root consisting of the two words *al-* 'the' + *barkūk*, from *praecox*.

April > *noun* the fourth month of the year.

COMBINATIONS – **April Fool's Day** 1 April, traditionally an occasion for playing tricks.

ORIGIN – Latin *Aprilis*.

a priori /ay prīorī/ > *adjective & adverb* based on theoretical reasoning rather than actual observation.

ORIGIN – Latin, 'from what is before'.

apron > *noun* **1** a protective garment covering the front of one's clothes and tied at the back. **2** an area on an airfield used for manoeuvring or parking aircraft. **3** (also **apron stage**) (in the theatre) a strip of stage projecting in front of the curtain. **4** an endless conveyor made of overlapping plates.

IDIOMS – **tied to someone's apron strings** under someone's influence and control to an excessive extent.

DERIVATIVES – **aproned** *adjective*.

ORIGIN – Old French *naperon*, from *nape*, *nappe* 'tablecloth', from Latin *mappa* 'napkin'; the *n* was lost by wrong division of *a napron*.

apropos /aprəpō/ > *preposition* with reference to.

IDIOMS – **apropos of nothing** having no relevance to any previous discussion or situation.

ORIGIN – French *à propos*.

apse /aps/ > *noun* a large semicircular or polygonal recess with a domed roof, typically at a church's eastern end.
DERIVATIVES – **apsidal** /apsid'l/ *adjective*.
ORIGIN – Greek *apsis* 'arch, vault'.

apt > *adjective* **1** appropriate or suitable in the circumstances. **2** (**apt to**) having a tendency to. **3** quick to learn.
DERIVATIVES – **aptly** *adverb* **aptness** *noun*.
SYNONYMS – **1** appropriate, expected, fitting, proper, suitable. **2** inclined, liable, likely, prone. **3** bright, quick, sharp.
ANTONYMS – **1** inappropriate. **2** unlikely. **3** slow.
ORIGIN – Latin *aptus* 'fitted'.

aptitude > *noun* a natural ability or inclination.
SYNONYMS – ability, bent, flair, inclination, talent.
ORIGIN – Old French, from Latin *aptus* 'fitted'.

aqua- /akwə/ > *combining form* relating to water: *aqualung*.
ORIGIN – Latin *aqua* 'water'.

aqualung > *noun* a portable breathing apparatus for divers.

aquamarine > *noun* **1** a light bluish-green variety of beryl. **2** a light bluish-green colour.
ORIGIN – Latin *aqua marina* 'seawater'.

aquanaut > *noun* a diver.
ORIGIN – Latin *aqua* 'water' + Greek *nautēs* 'sailor'.

aquaplane > *noun* a board for riding on water, pulled by a speedboat. > *verb* **1** ride on an aquaplane. **2** (of a vehicle) slide uncontrollably on a wet surface.

aqua regia /akwə **ree**jiə/ > *noun* Chemistry a highly corrosive mixture of concentrated nitric and hydrochloric acids.
ORIGIN – Latin, 'royal water': so called because it is able to dissolve gold.

aquarelle /akwərel/ > *noun* the technique of painting with thin, transparent watercolours.
ORIGIN – French, from Italian *acquarella* 'watercolour'.

aquarist /akwərist/ > *noun* a person who keeps an aquarium.

aquarium > *noun* (pl. **aquaria** or **aquariums**) a water-filled glass tank for keeping fish and other aquatic life.
ORIGIN – Latin, from *aquarius* 'of water'.

Aquarius /əkwairiəss/ > *noun* **1** Astronomy a large constellation (the Water Bearer), said to represent a man pouring water from a jar. **2** Astrology the eleventh sign of the zodiac, which the sun enters about 21 January.
DERIVATIVES – **Aquarian** *noun* & *adjective*.

aquatic /əkwattik/ > *adjective* **1** relating to water. **2** living in or near water. > *noun* an aquatic plant or animal.

aquatint > *noun* a print resembling a watercolour, made using a copper plate etched with nitric acid.
ORIGIN – French, from Italian *acqua tinta* 'coloured water'.

aquavit /**ak**wəveet/ (also **akvavit** /**ak**vəveet/) > *noun* an alcoholic spirit made from potatoes.
ORIGIN – Norwegian, Swedish, and Danish *akvavit* 'water of life'.

aqua vitae /akwə **vee**tee/ > *noun* archaic strong alcoholic spirit, especially brandy.
ORIGIN – Latin, 'water of life'.

aqueduct* /**ak**widukt/ > *noun* a long channel or elevated bridge-like structure, used for channelling water over a distance.
***SPELLING** – *aque-*, not *aqua-*: *aque*duct.
ORIGIN – Latin *aquae ductus*.

aqueous /**ay**kwiəss/ > *adjective* relating to or containing water.
COMBINATIONS – **aqueous humour** the clear fluid in the eyeball in front of the lens.

aquifer /**ak**wifər/ > *noun* a body of rock that holds water or through which water flows.

aquilegia /akwi**lee**jə/ > *noun* a plant bearing showy flowers with backward-pointing spurs.
ORIGIN – probably from Latin *aquilegus* 'water-collecting'.

aquiline /**ak**wilīn/ > *adjective* **1** like an eagle. **2** (of a nose) curved like an eagle's beak.
ORIGIN – Latin *aquilinus*, from *aquila* 'eagle'.

AR > *abbreviation* Arkansas.

Ar > *symbol* the chemical element argon.

-ar > *suffix* **1** (forming adjectives) of the kind specified: *molecular*. **2** forming nouns: *scholar* | *pillar*.

Arab > *noun* **1** a member of a Semitic people inhabiting much of the Middle East and North Africa. **2** a breed of horse originating in Arabia.
DERIVATIVES – **Arabisation** (also **Arabization**) *noun* **Arabise** (also **Arabize**) *verb*.
ORIGIN – Arabic.

arabesque /arrə**besk**/ > *noun* **1** Ballet a posture in which one leg is extended horizontally backwards and the arms are outstretched. **2** an ornamental design consisting of intertwined flowing lines. **3** Music a passage with a highly ornamented melody.
ORIGIN – French, from Italian *arabesco* 'in the Arabic style'.

Arabian > *noun* **1** historical a person from Arabia. **2** an Arab horse. > *adjective* relating to Arabia or its people.

Arabic > *noun* the Semitic language of the Arabs. > *adjective* relating to the Arabs or Arabic.
COMBINATIONS – **Arabic numeral** any of the numerals 0, 1, 2, 3, 4, 5, 6, 7, 8, and 9.

wordpower facts

Arabic

The literary language of Arabic, written from right to left in a cursive script, formed the basis of a number of languages, including Urdu and Malay. It was also the source of a large number of English words (which often entered English through Greek, Latin, French, or Spanish). These include **alcohol**, **algebra**, **assassin**, **aubergine**, **candy**, **coffee**, **cotton**, **ghoul**, **giraffe**, **lemon**, **mattress**, **mohair**, **orange**, **safari**, **saffron**, **sequin**, **sofa**, **sugar**, **tariff**; and many more.

arabica /ərabbikə/ > *noun* beans from a coffee plant widely grown in tropical Asia and Africa (*Coffea arabica*).
ORIGIN – Latin, 'Arabic'.

Arabism > *noun* **1** Arab culture or identity. **2** an Arabic word or phrase.
DERIVATIVES – **Arabist** *noun* & *adjective*.

arable > *adjective* **1** (of land) able to be ploughed and used for the cultivation of crops. **2** (of crops) cultivated on ploughed land.
ORIGIN – Latin *arabilis*, from *arare* 'to plough'.

arachnid /əraknid/ > *noun* a member of a class of arthropods including the spiders, scorpions, mites, and ticks.
ORIGIN – from Greek *arakhnē* 'spider'.

arachnophobia /əraknəf**ō**biə/ > *noun* extreme fear of spiders.
DERIVATIVES – **arachnophobe** *noun* **arachnophobic** *adjective*.

arak /ərak/ > *noun* variant spelling of **ARRACK**.

Aramaic /arrəmayik/ > *noun* a Semitic language used as a lingua franca in the Near East from the 6th century BC and still spoken in some communities. > *adjective* relating to this language.
ORIGIN – Greek *Aramaios* 'of *Aram*' (the biblical name of Syria).

Aran > *adjective* (of knitwear) featuring patterns of cable stitch and diamond designs, as made traditionally in the Aran Islands off the west coast of Ireland.

Arapaho /ərappəhō/ > *noun* (pl. same or **Arapahos**) a member of a North American Indian people living on the Great Plains.
ORIGIN – Crow, 'many tattoo marks'.

Arawak /arrəwak/ > *noun* (pl. same or **Arawaks**) **1** a member of a group of native peoples of the Greater Antilles and northern and western South America. **2** any of the languages of these peoples.
DERIVATIVES – **Arawakan** *adjective* & *noun*.
ORIGIN – Carib.

arbiter > *noun* **1** a person who settles a dispute. **2** a person who has influence over something.
ORIGIN – Latin, 'judge, supreme ruler'.

arbitrage /**aar**bitraazh, **aar**bitrij/ > *noun* Economics the simultaneous buying and selling of assets in different markets or in derivative forms, taking advantage of the differing prices.
DERIVATIVES – **arbitrageur** /aarbitraa**zhör**/ *noun*.
ORIGIN – French, from *arbitrer* 'give judgement'.

arbitrary /**aar**bitrəri/ > *adjective* **1** based on random choice or personal whim. **2** (of power or authority) used without constraint; autocratic.
DERIVATIVES – **arbitrarily** *adverb* **arbitrariness** *noun*.
SYNONYMS – **1** capricious, casual, chance, indiscriminate, random.
ANTONYMS – **1** planned, reasoned.
ORIGIN – Latin *arbitrarius*, from *arbiter* 'judge, supreme ruler'.

arbitrate > *verb* act as an arbitrator to settle a dispute.
SYNONYMS – adjudicate, decide, intercede, judge, mediate.
ORIGIN – Latin *arbitrari*, from *arbiter* 'judge, supreme ruler'.

arbitration > *noun* the use of an arbitrator to settle a dispute.

arbitrator > *noun* an independent person or body officially appointed to settle a dispute.

arbor¹ > *noun* **1** an axle on which something revolves. **2** a device holding a tool in a lathe.
ORIGIN – French *arbre* 'tree, axis', influenced by Latin *arbor* 'tree'.

arbor² > *noun* US spelling of ARBOUR.

arboreal /aar**bor**iəl/ > *adjective* **1** relating to trees. **2** living in trees.
DERIVATIVES – **arboreality** *noun*.
ORIGIN – from Latin *arbor* 'tree'.

arboretum /aarbə**ree**təm/ > *noun* (pl. **arboretums** or **arboreta**) a garden devoted to the study and display of trees.

arboriculture /**aar**bərikulchər/ > *noun* the cultivation of trees and shrubs.

arbour (US **arbor**) > *noun* a shady recess in a garden, with a canopy of trees or climbing plants.
DERIVATIVES – **arboured** *adjective*.
ORIGIN – Old French *erbier*, from Latin *herba* 'grass, herb'; influenced by Latin *arbor* 'tree'.

arc > *noun* **1** a curve forming part of the circumference of a circle. **2** a curving trajectory. **3** a luminous electrical discharge between two points. > *verb* (**arced**, **arcing**) **1** move with a curving trajectory. **2** (**arcing**) the forming of an electric arc.
COMBINATIONS – **arc lamp** (also **arc light**) a light source using an electric arc.
ORIGIN – Latin *arcus* 'bow, curve'.

arcade > *noun* **1** a covered passage with arches along one or both sides. **2** chiefly Brit. a covered walk with shops along one or both sides. **3** Architecture a series of arches supporting a wall.
DERIVATIVES – **arcaded** *adjective* **arcading** *noun*.
ORIGIN – French, from Latin *arcus* 'bow, curve'.

Arcadian > *noun* **1** a person from Arcadia, a mountainous region of southern Greece. **2** literary an idealised country dweller. > *adjective* **1** relating to Arcadia in Greece. **2** rustic in an idealised way.

Arcady /**aar**kədi/ > *noun* literary an ideal rustic paradise.
ORIGIN – Greek *Arkadia* 'Arcadia'.

arcane /aar**kayn**/ > *adjective* understood by few; mysterious.
DERIVATIVES – **arcanely** *adverb*.
ORIGIN – Latin *arcanus*, from *arca* 'chest'.

arcanum /aar**kayn**əm/ > *noun* (pl. **arcana**) a hidden thing; a mystery or profound secret.
ORIGIN – Latin, from *arca* 'chest'.

arch¹ > *noun* **1** a curved structure spanning an opening or supporting the weight of a bridge, roof, or wall. **2** the inner side of the foot. > *verb* form or cause to form an arch.
WORDFINDER – *parts of an arch:* abutment (*structure supporting the lateral pressure of an arch*), architrave (*moulding round an arch's exterior*), extrados (*outer curve of an arch*), intrados (*inner curve of an arch*), keystone (*central stone at the summit of an arch*), pier (*pillar of an arch*), springer (*lowest stone in an arch, where the curve begins*), voussoir (*wedge-shaped stone used in an arch's construction*).
DERIVATIVES – **arched** *adjective*.
COMBINATIONS – **archway** a curved structure forming a passage or entrance.
ORIGIN – Old French *arche*, from Latin *arcus* 'bow'.

arch² > *adjective* self-consciously playful or teasing.
DERIVATIVES – **archly** *adverb* **archness** *noun*.
ORIGIN – from ARCH-, by association with the sense 'rogue' in combinations such as *arch-scoundrel*.

arch- > *combining form* **1** chief; principal: *archbishop*. **2** pre-eminent of its kind: *an arch-enemy*.
ORIGIN – Greek *arkhi-*, from *arkhos* 'chief'.

archaea /aar**kee**ə/ > *plural noun* Biology micro-organisms which are similar to bacteria in size and simplicity of structure but constitute an ancient group intermediate between the bacteria and eukaryotes.
ORIGIN – from Greek *arkhaios* 'primitive'.

Archaean /aar**kee**ən/ (US **Archean**) > *adjective* Geology relating to the earlier part of the Precambrian aeon (before about 2,500 million years ago) when there was no life on the earth.
ORIGIN – from Greek *arkhaios* 'ancient'.

archaeology* /aarki**oll**əji/ (US also **archeology**) > *noun* the study of human history and prehistory through the excavation of sites and the analysis of physical remains.
DERIVATIVES – **archaeologic** *adjective* **archaeological** *adjective* **archaeologist** *noun*.
*SPELLING – remember the *a* in front of the *e*: archaeology. The spelling with just an *e* is American.
ORIGIN – from Greek *arkhaios* 'ancient'.

archaeopteryx /aarki**op**təriks/ > *noun* the oldest known fossil bird, of the late Jurassic period, which had feathers and wings like a bird, but teeth and a bony tail like a dinosaur.
ORIGIN – from Greek *arkhaios* 'ancient' + *pterux* 'wing'.

archaic /aar**kay**ik/ > *adjective* **1** belonging to former or ancient times. **2** old or in an old-fashioned style.
DERIVATIVES – **archaically** *adverb*.
ORIGIN – Greek *arkhaios* 'ancient'.

archaism > *noun* **1** the use of archaic features in language or art. **2** an archaic word or style.

archangel /**aark**aynjəl/ > *noun* an angel of high rank.
DERIVATIVES – **archangelic** *adjective*.

archbishop > *noun* the chief bishop responsible for a large district.

archdeacon > *noun* a senior Christian cleric to whom a bishop delegates certain responsibilities.

archduchess > *noun* **1** the wife or widow of an archduke. **2** historical a daughter of the Emperor of Austria.

archduke > *noun* **1** a chief duke. **2** historical a son of the Emperor of Austria.
DERIVATIVES – **archducal** *adjective* **archduchy** *noun*.

Archean > *adjective* US spelling of ARCHAEAN.

arch-enemy > *noun* a chief enemy.

archeology > *noun* US spelling of ARCHAEOLOGY.

archer > *noun* a person who shoots with a bow and arrows.
WORDFINDER – Sagittarius (*constellation and zodiac sign, the Archer*).
COMBINATIONS – **archerfish** an Asian and Australasian freshwater fish that knocks insect prey off vegetation by shooting water from its mouth.

ORIGIN – Old French *archier*, from Latin *arcus* 'bow'.

archery > *noun* shooting with a bow and arrows.

WORDFINDER – bolt (*heavy arrow shot from a crossbow*), fletch (*provide (an arrow) with feathers*), fletching (*feathers of an arrow*), longbow (*large bow drawn by hand*), nock (*notch at the end of a bow or of an arrow*), quiver (*case for arrows*), toxophilite (*student or lover of archery*), toxophily (*study or practice of archery*).

archetypal > *adjective* 1 very typical of a certain kind of person or thing. 2 relating to an original which has been imitated. 3 recurrent as a motif in literature, art, or mythology.

DERIVATIVES – **archetypally** *adverb*.

archetype /**aar**kitīp/ > *noun* 1 a very typical example. 2 an original model. 3 a recurrent motif in literature or art.

DERIVATIVES – **archetypical** *adjective*.

SYNONYMS – 1 ideal, model, paradigm, standard.

ORIGIN – Greek *arkhetupon*, from *arkhe-* 'primitive' + *tupos* 'a model'.

archiepiscopal /aarki-i**pis**kəp'l/ > *adjective* relating to an archbishop.

DERIVATIVES – **archiepiscopacy** (pl. **archiepiscopacies**) *noun* **archiepiscopate** *noun*.

Archimedean screw > *noun* a device invented by Archimedes for raising water by means of a helix rotating within a tube.

Archimedes' principle > *noun* Physics a law stating that a body immersed in a fluid is subject to an upward force equal to the weight of fluid the body displaces.

ORIGIN – discovered by the Greek mathematician and inventor Archimedes (*c.*287–212 BC), according to legend while he was taking a bath; he is supposed then to have run through the streets shouting 'Eureka!' ('I have found it!').

archipelago /aarki**pell**əgō/ > *noun* (pl. **archipelagos** or **archipelagoes**) an extensive group of islands.

ORIGIN – first used as a name for the Aegean Sea, notable for its large number of islands: from Greek *arkhi-* 'chief' + *pelagos* 'sea'.

architect > *noun* 1 a person who designs buildings and supervises their construction. 2 a person responsible for the invention or realisation of something. > *verb* Computing design and make (a program or system).

ORIGIN – Greek *arkhitektōn* 'chief builder'.

architectonic /aarkitekt**onn**ik/ > *adjective* 1 relating to architecture or architects. 2 having a clearly defined and artistically pleasing structure. > *noun* (**architectonics**) (**treated as sing.**) 1 the scientific study of architecture. 2 musical, literary, or artistic structure.

DERIVATIVES – **architectonically** *adverb*.

architecture > *noun* 1 the art or practice of designing and constructing buildings. 2 the style in which a building is designed and constructed. 3 the complex structure of something.

WORDFINDER – *architectural styles:* art deco, baroque, classical, Gothic, international, neoclassical, Palladian, Regency, rococo, Romanesque.

DERIVATIVES – **architectural** *adjective*.

architrave /**aar**kitrayv/ > *noun* 1 (in classical architecture) a main beam resting across the tops of columns. 2 the frame around a doorway or window.

ORIGIN – Italian, from *archi-* 'chief' + *-trave*, from Latin *trabs* 'a beam'.

archive /**aar**kīv/ > *noun* a collection of historical documents or records. > *verb* 1 place in an archive. 2 Computing transfer (data) to a less frequently used storage medium.

DERIVATIVES – **archival** *adjective*.

ORIGIN – French *archives* (plural), from Greek *arkheia* 'public records'.

archivist /**aar**kivist/ > *noun* a person who is in charge of archives.

archosaur /**aar**kəsor/ > *noun* a reptile of a large group that includes the crocodilians together with the extinct dinosaurs and pterosaurs.

ORIGIN – from Greek *arkhos* 'chief' or *arkhōn* 'ruler' + *sauros* 'lizard'.

-archy /**aar**ki/ > *combining form* forming nouns denoting a type of rule or government, corresponding to nouns ending in *-arch: monarchy.*

Arctic* > *adjective* 1 relating to the regions around the North Pole. 2 living or growing in such regions. 3 (**arctic**) informal (of weather) very cold. > *noun* (**the Arctic**) the regions around the North Pole.

***SPELLING – *Arc*tic, not *Ar*tic.

ORIGIN – Greek *arktos* 'bear, Ursa Major, pole star'.

ardent > *adjective* 1 very enthusiastic; passionate. 2 archaic or literary burning; glowing.

DERIVATIVES – **ardency** *noun* **ardently** *adverb*.

SYNONYMS – 1 fervent, passionate, zealous.

ardour (US **ardor**) > *noun* great enthusiasm; passion.

SYNONYMS – fervour, passion, zeal.

ORIGIN – Latin *ardor*, from *ardere* 'to burn'.

arduous > *adjective* involving strenuous or difficult work.

DERIVATIVES – **arduously** *adverb* **arduousness** *noun*.

SYNONYMS – back-breaking, demanding, exhausting, gruelling.

ANTONYMS – easy, effortless.

ORIGIN – Latin *arduus* 'steep, difficult'.

are[1] second person singular present and first, second, third person plural present of **BE**.

are[2] /aar/ > *noun* historical a metric unit of measurement, equal to 100 square metres.

ORIGIN – Latin *area* 'piece of level ground'.

area > *noun* 1 a part of an expanse or surface. 2 the extent or measurement of a surface. 3 a space allocated for a specific use. 4 a subject or range of activity. 5 a sunken enclosure giving access to a basement.

DERIVATIVES – **areal** *adjective*.

SYNONYMS – 1 acreage, expanse, region, stretch, tract.

COMBINATIONS – **area code** a dialling code.

ORIGIN – Latin, 'piece of level ground'.

arena > *noun* 1 a level area surrounded by seating, in which public events and entertainments are held. 2 a sphere of activity.

ORIGIN – Latin *harena*, *arena* 'sand, sand-strewn place of combat'.

aren't > *contraction* 1 are not. 2 am not (only used in questions).

USAGE – **aren't** was first used in questions to mean 'am not' as a way of avoiding **ain't**, which is now thought to be bad English (although in fact it is simply a contraction of the logical form **amn't**, now restricted to Scottish, Irish, and dialect use). Constructions such as *I'm right, aren't I* are now standard. It is not good English, however, to use **aren't** to mean 'am not' outside questions: *I aren't going* is incorrect.

areola /ə**ree**ələ/ > *noun* (pl. **areolae** /ə**ree**əlee/) Anatomy a small circular area, in particular the pigmented skin surrounding a nipple.

DERIVATIVES – **areolar** *adjective* **areolate** *adjective*.

ORIGIN – Latin, 'small open space'.

arête /ə**ret**/ > *noun* a sharp mountain ridge.

ORIGIN – French, from Latin *arista* 'ear of corn, spine'.

wordpower facts

Argent

The word **argent** comes through Old French from Latin *argentum* 'silver' (*argent* is modern French for 'money'). The country *Argentina* is so-called because of the silver found there, especially in the region of the River Plate (in Spanish *Río de la Plata*, the 'silver river', from *plata* 'silver').

argent > *adjective* & *noun* literary & Heraldry silver.

Argentine > *noun & adjective* another term for **ARGENTINIAN**.

argentine /**aar**jəntīn/ > *adjective* archaic of or resembling silver.
ORIGIN – Old French, from Latin *argentum* 'silver'.

Argentinian > *noun* a person from Argentina. > *adjective* relating to Argentina.

arginine /**aar**jineen/ > *noun* Biochemistry an amino acid which is an essential nutrient in the diet.
ORIGIN – German *Arginin*, perhaps from Greek *arginoeis* 'bright-shining, white'.

argon /**aar**gon/ > *noun* an inert gaseous chemical element, present in small amounts in the air.
ORIGIN – Greek, from *argos* 'idle'.

argosy > *noun* (pl. **argosies**) literary a large merchant ship, originally one from Ragusa (now Dubrovnik) or Venice.
ORIGIN – Italian *Ragusea nave* 'vessel of *Ragusa*'.

argot /**aar**gō/ > *noun* the jargon or slang of a particular group.
ORIGIN – French.

arguable > *adjective* 1 able to be argued or asserted. 2 open to disagreement.
DERIVATIVES – **arguably** *adverb*.

argue > *verb* (**argues, argued, arguing**) 1 exchange diverging or opposite views heatedly. 2 give reasons or cite evidence in support of something.
IDIOMS – **argue the toss** informal, chiefly Brit. dispute a decision already made.
DERIVATIVES – **arguer** *noun*.
SYNONYMS – **1** disagree, dispute, fight, quarrel, row. **2** assert, claim, contend.
ORIGIN – Latin *argutari* 'prattle', from *arguere* 'make clear, prove, accuse'.

argument > *noun* 1 a heated exchange of diverging or opposite views. 2 a set of reasons given in support of something.
SYNONYMS – **1** altercation, disagreement, fight, quarrel, row. **2** case, contention, hypothesis, thesis.

argumentation > *noun* systematic reasoning in support of something.

argumentative > *adjective* 1 given to arguing. 2 using or characterised by systematic reasoning.
DERIVATIVES – **argumentatively** *adverb* **argumentativeness** *noun*.

argy-bargy /**aar**jibaarjī/ > *noun* informal, chiefly Brit. noisy quarrelling.

argyle /**aar**gīl/ > *noun* a pattern used in knitwear, consisting of coloured diamonds on a plain background.
ORIGIN – from *Argyll*, the name of the Scottish clan on whose tartan the pattern is based.

aria /**aar**iə/ > *noun* Music an accompanied song for a solo voice in an opera or oratorio.
ORIGIN – Italian, from Latin *aer* 'air'.

Arian /**air**iən/ (also **Arien**) > *noun* a person born under the sign of Aries. > *adjective* relating to a person born under the sign of Aries.

arid > *adjective* 1 very dry; having little or no rain. 2 uninteresting; unsatisfying.
DERIVATIVES – **aridity** *noun* **aridly** *adverb* **aridness** *noun*.
SYNONYMS – **1** barren, dry, parched, waterless.
ANTONYMS – **1** fertile, lush, wet.
ORIGIN – Latin *aridus*, from *arere* 'be dry or parched'.

Aries /**air**eez/ > *noun* 1 Astronomy a small constellation (the Ram), said to represent the ram whose Golden Fleece was sought by Jason and the Argonauts. 2 Astrology the first sign of the zodiac, which the sun enters about 20 March.
ORIGIN – Latin, 'ram'.

aright > *adverb* dialect correctly; properly.

aril /**arr**il/ > *noun* Botany an extra covering around a seed, e.g. the red fleshy cup of a yew berry.
ORIGIN – Latin *arillus*, of unknown origin.

arise > *verb* (past **arose**; past participle **arisen**) 1 originate or become apparent. 2 (**arise from** or **out of**) occur as a result of. 3 formal or literary get or stand up.
SYNONYMS – **1** appear, become apparent, crop up, emerge, originate.

aristocracy > *noun* (pl. **aristocracies**) a class comprising people of noble birth with hereditary titles.

wordpower facts
Aristocracy
The word **aristocracy** comes from Greek *aristokratia*, from *aristos* 'best' and *-kratia* 'power, rule' (from *kratos* 'strength'). It originally referred to the government of a state by its best citizens, later by the rich and well born. From this developed the sense 'nobility', regardless of the form of government. The suffix *-kratia* lies at the roots of such words as *democracy* and *meritocracy*, in which the sense 'power, rule' is preserved.

aristocrat > *noun* a member of the aristocracy.
SYNONYMS – lord, noble, patrician, peer.

aristocratic > *adjective* belonging to or having the characteristics of the aristocracy.
DERIVATIVES – **aristocratically** *adverb*.
SYNONYMS – high-born, noble, patrician, titled, upper-class.
ANTONYMS – lower-class, plebeian.

Aristotelian /**arri**stəteeliən/ > *adjective* relating to the theories of the Greek philosopher Aristotle (384–322 BC). > *noun* a student or follower of Aristotle or his philosophy.

arithmetic > *noun* /ə**rith**mətik/ 1 the branch of mathematics concerned with the properties and manipulation of numbers. 2 the use of numbers in counting and calculation. > *adjective* /arrith**mett**ik/ relating to arithmetic.
DERIVATIVES – **arithmetical** *adjective* **arithmetically** *adverb* **arithmetician** *noun*.
COMBINATIONS – **arithmetic progression** (also **arithmetic series**) a sequence of numbers in which each differs from the preceding one by a constant quantity (e.g. 1, 2, 3, 4, etc.; 9, 7, 5, 3, etc.).
ORIGIN – Greek *arithmētikē tekhnē* 'art of counting', from *arithmos* 'number'.

-arium > *suffix* forming nouns denoting a place: *planetarium*.

ark > *noun* 1 (in the Bible) the ship built by Noah to save his family and two of every kind of animal from the Flood. 2 (**Ark** or **Holy Ark**) a chest or cupboard housing the Torah scrolls in a synagogue. 3 (**Ark of the Covenant**) the chest which contained the tablets of the laws of the ancient Israelites.
IDIOMS – **out of the ark** informal very old or old-fashioned.
ORIGIN – Latin *arca* 'chest'.

arm¹ > *noun* 1 each of the two upper limbs of the human body from the shoulder to the hand. 2 a side part of a chair supporting a sitter's arm. 3 a narrow body of water or land projecting from a larger body. 4 a branch or division of an organisation.
WORDFINDER – brachial (*of the arm*); *bones of the arm:* humerus, radius, ulna.
IDIOMS – **arm in arm** with arms linked. **cost an arm and a leg** informal be extremely expensive. **in arms** (of a baby) too young to walk. **keep at arm's length** avoid intimacy or close contact with. **with open arms** with great affection or enthusiasm.
COMBINATIONS – **armband 1** a band worn around the upper arm to hold up a shirtsleeve or as a form of identification. **2** an inflatable plastic band worn around the upper arm as a swimming aid. **armlock** a method of restraining someone by holding their arm bent tightly behind their back. **armpit** the hollow under the arm at the shoulder. **armrest** an arm of a chair or sofa or an equivalent support in a vehicle. **arm-wrestling** a contest in which two people engage hands and try to force each other's arm down on to a surface.

arm² > *verb* 1 supply with weapons. 2 provide

with essential equipment for a task or situation. **3** activate the fuse of (a bomb) so that it is ready to explode.

ORIGIN – Latin *armare*, from *arma* 'armour, arms'.

armada /aar**maa**də/ > *noun* **1** a fleet of warships. **2** (**the** (**Spanish**) **Armada**) the Spanish invasion fleet defeated by the English fleet in 1588.

ORIGIN – Spanish, from Latin *armare* 'to arm'.

armadillo > *noun* (pl. **armadillos**) a nocturnal insectivorous mammal native to Central and South America, with large claws and a body covered in bony plates.

ORIGIN – Spanish *armado* 'little armed man'.

Armageddon /aarmə**gedd**'n/ > *noun* **1** (in the New Testament) the last battle between good and evil before the Day of Judgement. **2** a catastrophic conflict.

ORIGIN – Greek, from a Hebrew phrase meaning 'hill of Megiddo' (Revelation, chapter 16).

Armagnac /**aar**mənyak/ > *noun* a type of brandy made in Aquitaine in France.

ORIGIN – from the former name of a district in Aquitaine.

armament /**aar**məmənt/ > *noun* **1** (also **armaments**) military weapons and equipment. **2** the process of equipping military forces for war.

armature /**aar**məchər/ > *noun* **1** the rotating coil of a dynamo or electric motor. **2** any moving part of an electrical machine in which a voltage is induced by a magnetic field. **3** a piece of iron acting as a keeper for a magnet. **4** a framework on which a clay sculpture is moulded. **5** Biology the protective covering of an animal or plant. **6** archaic armour.

armchair > *noun* **1** a large, upholstered chair with side supports for the sitter's arms. **2** (before another noun) experiencing something through reading, television, etc. rather than at first hand: *an armchair traveller.*

armed > *adjective* equipped with or involving a firearm.

COMBINATIONS – **armed forces** a country's army, navy, and air force.

Armenian /aar**mee**niən/ > *noun* **1** a person from Armenia. **2** the Indo-European language of Armenia. > *adjective* relating to Armenia.

armistice /**aar**mistiss/ > *noun* a truce.

ORIGIN – French, from Latin *arma* 'armour, arms' + *-stitium* 'stoppage'.

armlet > *noun* a bracelet worn round the upper arm.

armoire /arr**mwaar**/ > *noun* a cupboard or wardrobe.

ORIGIN – French, from Latin *armarium* 'closet'.

armor > *noun* US spelling of **ARMOUR**.

armorer > *noun* US spelling of **ARMOURER**.

armory¹ > *noun* heraldry.

DERIVATIVES – **armorial** *adjective*.

ORIGIN – Old French *armoierie*, from *armoier* 'to blazon', from Latin *arma* 'arms'.

armory² > *noun* US spelling of **ARMOURY**.

armour (US **armor**) > *noun* **1** the metal coverings formerly worn to protect the body in battle. **2** (also **armour plate**) the tough metal layer covering a military vehicle or ship. **3** military vehicles collectively. **4** the protective layer or shell of some animals and plants.

WORDFINDER – *parts of a suit of armour:* cuirass (*breastplate and backplate*), cuisse (*protecting the thigh*), gauntlet (*protecting the hand*), gorget (*protecting the throat*), greave (*protecting the shin*), vambrace (*protecting the arm*), visor (*protecting the face*).

DERIVATIVES – **armoured** *adjective*.

COMBINATIONS – **armour-plated** covered with armour plate.

ORIGIN – Old French *armure*, from Latin *armatura*, from *arma* 'armour, arms'.

armourer (US **armorer**) > *noun* **1** a maker or supplier of weapons or armour. **2** an official in charge of the weapons of a warship or regiment.

armoury (US **armory**) > *noun* (pl. **armouries**) **1** a store or supply of arms. **2** a set of resources available for a particular purpose.

SYNONYMS – **1** arsenal, depot, magazine.

arms > *plural noun* **1** guns and other weapons. **2** emblems originally displayed on the shields of knights to distinguish them in battle, surviving today as coats of arms.

IDIOMS – **a call to arms** a call to make ready for fighting. **up in arms** protesting vigorously.

COMBINATIONS – **arms control** international agreement to limit the production and accumulation of arms. **arms race** a situation in which nations compete for superiority in the development and accumulation of weapons.

ORIGIN – Latin *arma*.

army > *noun* (pl. **armies**) **1** an organised military force equipped for fighting on land. **2** a large number of similar people or things.

ORIGIN – Old French *armee*, from Latin *armare* 'to arm'.

arnica /**aar**nikə/ > *noun* a plant bearing yellow daisy-like flowers, used medicinally for the treatment of bruises.

aroha /**aar**ohə/ > *noun* NZ **1** love; affection. **2** sympathy.

ORIGIN – Maori.

aroma > *noun* a pleasant and distinctive smell.

SYNONYMS – bouquet, fragrance, perfume, scent.

ORIGIN – Greek, 'spice'.

aromatherapy > *noun* the use of aromatic plant extracts and essential oils for healing and cosmetic purposes.

DERIVATIVES – **aromatherapeutic** *adjective* **aromatherapist** *noun*.

aromatic > *adjective* **1** having an aroma. **2** Chemistry (of an organic compound) containing a flat ring of atoms in its molecule (as in benzene). > *noun* an aromatic plant, substance, or compound.

DERIVATIVES – **aromatically** *adverb*.

SYNONYMS – fragrant, perfumed, scented, sweet-smelling.

arose past of **ARISE**.

around > *adverb* **1** located or situated on every side. **2** so as to face in the opposite direction. **3** in or to many places throughout a locality. **4** here and there. **5** available or present. **6** approximately. > *preposition* **1** on every side of. **2** in or to many places throughout (a locality). **3** so as to encircle or embrace. **4** following an approximately circular route round.

USAGE – on the difference in use between **around** and **round**, see note at **ROUND**.

arouse > *verb* **1** bring about (a feeling or response) in someone. **2** excite sexually. **3** awaken from sleep.

DERIVATIVES – **arousal** *noun*.

SYNONYMS – **1** induce, provoke. **2** excite, stimulate, thrill, titillate, turn on.

ARP > *abbreviation* Brit. historical air-raid precautions.

arpeggio /aar**pej**iō/ > *noun* (pl. **arpeggios**) Music the notes of a chord played in rapid succession.

ORIGIN – Italian, from *arpeggiare* 'play the harp', from *arpa* 'harp'.

arrack /**arr**ək/ (also **arak**) > *noun* an alcoholic spirit made from the sap of the coco palm or from rice.

ORIGIN – from an Arabic word meaning 'sweat'.

arraign /ə**rayn**/ > *verb* call before a court to answer a criminal charge.

DERIVATIVES – **arraignment** *noun*.

ORIGIN – Old French *araisnier*, from Latin *ad-* 'to' + *ratio* 'reason, account'.

arrange > *verb* **1** put tidily or in a particular order. **2** organise or plan. **3** Music adapt (a composition) for performance with instruments or voices other than those originally specified.

DERIVATIVES – **arrangeable** *adjective* **arranger** *noun*.

SYNONYMS – **1** array, lay out, position, range. **2** organise, plan, settle, set up.

ORIGIN – Old French *arangier*, from *rang* 'rank'.

arrangement > *noun* **1** the result of arranging things in an attractive or ordered way. **2** a plan for a future event. **3** Music an arranged composition.

SYNONYMS — **1** alignment, disposition, distribution, layout, organisation, positioning. **2** agreement, deal, plan.

arrant /**arr**ənt/ > *adjective* utter; complete: *what arrant nonsense!*

DERIVATIVES — **arrantly** *adverb*.

ORIGIN — variant of **ERRANT**, originally in phrases such as *arrant thief*, meaning 'outlawed, roving thief'.

arras /**arr**əs/ > *noun* a tapestry wall hanging.

ORIGIN — named after the French town of *Arras*, where tapestries were made.

array > *noun* **1** an impressive display or range of a particular thing. **2** an ordered arrangement of troops. **3** literary elaborate or beautiful clothing. > *verb* **1** display or arrange in a neat or impressive way. **2** (**be arrayed in**) be elaborately clothed in.

SYNONYMS — *noun* **1** display, line-up, panoply, parade. **3** attire, garb. *verb* arrange, display, lay out. **2** (**be arrayed in**) be accoutred in, be decked in, be garbed in, be rigged out in.

ORIGIN — Old French *arei*.

arrears > *plural noun* money owed that should already have been paid.

IDIOMS — **in arrears 1** behind with paying money that is owed. **2** (of wages or rent) paid at the end of each period of work or occupation.

ORIGIN — Old French *arere*, from Latin *retro* 'backwards'.

arrest > *verb* **1** seize by legal authority and take into custody. **2** stop or check (progress or a process). **3** (**arresting**) attracting attention. > *noun* **1** the action of arresting someone. **2** a sudden cessation of motion.

DERIVATIVES — **arrestingly** *adverb*.

SYNONYMS — *verb* **1** apprehend, capture, catch, detain. **3** (**arresting**) conspicuous, eye-catching, impressive, striking.

ORIGIN — Old French *arester*, from Latin *restare* 'remain, stop'.

arrhythmia /ə**rith**miə/ > *noun* Medicine a condition in which the heart beats with an irregular rhythm.

DERIVATIVES — **arrhythmic** *adjective*.

ORIGIN — Greek *arruthmia* 'lack of rhythm'.

arris > *noun* Architecture a sharp edge formed by the meeting of two flat or curved surfaces.

ORIGIN — French *areste* 'sharp ridge'.

arrival > *noun* **1** the action or process of arriving. **2** a newly arrived person or thing.

arrive > *verb* **1** reach a destination. **2** be brought or delivered. **3** (of a particular moment) come about. **4** (**arrive at**) reach (a conclusion or decision). **5** informal become successful and well known.

SYNONYMS — **1,2** come, get there, turn up.

ANTONYMS — **1** depart.

wordpower facts
Arrive

The earliest meaning of **arrive** was 'bring a ship to shore', then 'come to shore, or to a port'. It comes, through Old French *ariver*, from Latin *ripa* 'shore'. The term **riparian**, used in law and ecology to refer to regions adjacent to a river, comes from the same stem, as does the word **river** itself.

arriviste /arree**veest**/ > *noun* often derogatory a person who has recently gained social or financial status or is ambitious to do so.

ORIGIN — French.

arrogant > *adjective* having an exaggerated sense of one's own importance or abilities.

DERIVATIVES — **arrogance** *noun* **arrogantly** *adverb*.

SYNONYMS — egotistical, superior, vain.

ANTONYMS — humble, meek, modest.

ORIGIN — Old French, from Latin *arrogare* 'claim for oneself'.

arrogate /**arr**əgayt/ > *verb* take or claim for oneself without justification.

DERIVATIVES — **arrogation** *noun*.

ORIGIN — Latin *arrogare* 'claim for oneself'.

arrondissement /a**ron**deessmon/ > *noun* **1** (in France) a subdivision of a local government department. **2** an administrative district of Paris.

ORIGIN — French, from *arrondir* 'make round'.

arrow > *noun* **1** a stick with a sharp pointed head and usually with feathers or vanes at the tail, designed to be shot from a bow. **2** a symbol resembling this, used to show direction or position. > *verb* move swiftly and directly.

DERIVATIVES — **arrowed** *adjective*.

arrowroot > *noun* a plant that yields a fine-grained starch used in cookery and medicine.

ORIGIN — Arawak *aru-aru* 'meal of meals'; altered by association with *arrow* and *root* (the plant's tubers were used to absorb poison from arrow wounds).

arroyo /ə**roy**ō/ > *noun* (pl. **arroyos**) US a deep and usually dry gully cut by an intermittent river or stream.

ORIGIN — Spanish.

arse > *noun* Brit. vulgar slang a person's bottom.

arsenal > *noun* a store of weapons and ammunition.

SYNONYMS — **1** armoury, depot, magazine.

ORIGIN — French, or obsolete Italian *arzanale*, from an Arabic phrase meaning 'house of industry'.

arsenic > *noun* a brittle steel-grey chemical element with many highly poisonous compounds.

DERIVATIVES — **arsenical** *adjective* **arsenide** *noun*.

ORIGIN — Greek *arsenikon*, from Arabic.

arson > *noun* the criminal act of deliberately setting fire to property.

DERIVATIVES — **arsonist** *noun*.

ORIGIN — Old French, from Latin *ardere* 'to burn'.

art¹ > *noun* **1** the expression of creative skill through a visual medium such as painting or sculpture. **2** the product of such a process; paintings, drawings, and sculpture collectively. **3** (**the arts**) the various branches of creative activity, such as painting, music, and drama. **4** (**arts**) subjects of study primarily concerned with human culture (as contrasted with scientific or technical subjects). **5** a skill: *the art of conversation.*

WORDFINDER — *art schools and styles:* art deco, art nouveau, baroque, classicism, cubism, Dada, expressionism, Fauvism, Impressionism, Mannerism, minimalism, Pre-Raphaelitism, rococo, surrealism, Vorticism.

SYNONYMS — **1** artistry, creativity. **5** craft, skill.

COMBINATIONS — **art deco** a decorative style prominent in the 1920s and 1930s, characterised by precise geometric shapes. [ORIGIN — French *art décoratif* 'decorative art'.] **art house** a cinema which shows artistic or experimental films. **artwork** illustrations or other non-textual material prepared for inclusion in a publication.

ORIGIN — Latin *ars*.

art² archaic or dialect second person singular present of **BE**.

artefact* /**aar**tifakt/ (US **artifact**) > *noun* a functional or decorative man-made object.

*SPELLING — use an *e*, not an *i*: art*e*fact. The spelling with an *i* is American.

ORIGIN — from Latin *arte* 'using art' + *factum* 'something made'.

arteriole /aar**teer**iōl/ > *noun* Anatomy a small branch of an artery leading into capillaries.

DERIVATIVES — **arteriolar** *adjective*.

arteriosclerosis /aarteeriōskleer**ō**siss/ > *noun* Medicine thickening and hardening of the walls of the arteries.

artery > *noun* (pl. **arteries**) **1** any of the muscular-walled tubes through which blood flows from the heart around the body. **2** an important route in a transport system.

DERIVATIVES — **arterial** *adjective*.

ORIGIN — Greek *artēria*.

artesian /aar**teezh**'n/ > *adjective* (of a well) bored vertically into a layer of water-bearing rock that is lying at an angle, with the result that natural pressure forces the water upwards.

ORIGIN – from *Artois*, a region in France.

artful > *adjective* cunningly clever.

DERIVATIVES – **artfully** *adverb* **artfulness** *noun*.

SYNONYMS – crafty, cunning, ingenious, sly.

ANTONYMS – ingenuous, straightforward.

arthritis /aar**thrī**tis/ > *noun* painful inflammation and stiffness of the joints.

DERIVATIVES – **arthritic** *adjective & noun*.

ORIGIN – Greek, from *arthron* 'joint'.

arthropod /**aar**thrəpod/ > *noun* Zoology an invertebrate animal with a segmented body, external skeleton, and jointed limbs, such as an insect, spider, or crustacean.

ORIGIN – from Greek *arthron* 'joint' + *pous* 'foot'.

arthroscope > *noun* Medicine an instrument for inspecting or operating on the interior of a joint.

DERIVATIVES – **arthroscopic** *adjective* **arthroscopy** *noun*.

Arthurian /aar**thoor**iən/ > *adjective* relating to the reign of the legendary King Arthur of Britain (perhaps a 5th- or 6th-century Romano-British chieftain or general).

artichoke > *noun* (also **globe artichoke**) the unopened flower head of a thistle-like plant, eaten as a vegetable.

ORIGIN – Italian *articiocco*, from Spanish *alcarchofa*, from Arabic.

article > *noun* **1** a particular object. **2** a piece of writing included in a newspaper or magazine. **3** a separate clause or paragraph of a legal document. **4** (**articles**) a period of professional training as a solicitor, architect, surveyor, or accountant. **5** Grammar the definite article (*the*) or indefinite article (*a* or *an*). > *verb* employ under contract as a trainee.

SYNONYMS – *noun* **1** item, object, thing.

COMBINATIONS – **articled clerk** a law student employed as a trainee. **article of faith** a firmly held belief.

articulate > *adjective* /aar**tik**yoolət/ **1** fluent and clear in speech. **2** having joints or jointed segments. > *verb* /aar**tik**yoolayt/ **1** pronounce (words) distinctly. **2** clearly express (an idea or feeling). **3** form a joint. **4** (**articulated**) having two or more sections connected by a flexible joint.

DERIVATIVES – **articulacy** *noun* **articulately** *adverb* **articulateness** *noun* **articulation** *noun*.

SYNONYMS – *adjective* **1** clear, coherent, eloquent, fluent, lucid. *verb* **2** air, communicate, express, give voice to.

ANTONYMS – *adjective* **1** inarticulate.

artifact > *noun* US spelling of **ARTEFACT**.

artifice /**aar**tifiss/ > *noun* the use of cunning plans or devices in order to trick or deceive.

ORIGIN – Latin *artificium*, from *ars* 'art' + *facere* 'make'.

artificer /aar**tiff**issər/ > *noun* **1** a person skilled in making or contriving things. **2** a skilled mechanic in the armed forces.

artificial > *adjective* **1** made as a copy of something natural. **2** contrived or affected.

DERIVATIVES – **artificiality** *noun* **artificially** *adverb*.

SYNONYMS – **1** fake, false, imitation, man-made, manufactured.

ANTONYMS – **1** natural, real.

COMBINATIONS – **artificial insemination** the veterinary or medical procedure of injecting semen into the vagina or uterus. **artificial intelligence** the performance by computer systems of tasks normally requiring human intelligence. **artificial respiration** the restoration or maintenance of someone's breathing by manual, mechanical, or mouth-to-mouth methods.

ORIGIN – from Latin *artificium*, from *ars* 'art' + *facere* 'make'.

artillery > *noun* **1** large-calibre guns used in warfare on land. **2** a branch of the armed forces trained to use artillery.

ORIGIN – Old French *artillerie*.

artisan > *noun* a skilled worker who makes things by hand.

DERIVATIVES – **artisanal** *adjective*.

ORIGIN – French, from Latin *artire* 'instruct in the arts'.

artist > *noun* **1** a person who paints or draws as a profession or hobby. **2** a person who practises or performs any of the creative arts. **3** informal a habitual practitioner of a specified activity: *a con artist*.

DERIVATIVES – **artistry** *noun*.

ORIGIN – French *artiste*, from Latin *ars* 'art'.

artiste /aar**teest**/ > *noun* a professional entertainer, especially a singer or dancer.

ORIGIN – French 'artist'.

artistic > *adjective* **1** having or revealing creative skill. **2** relating to or characteristic of art or artists: *an artistic temperament*. **3** aesthetically pleasing: *artistic designs*.

DERIVATIVES – **artistically** *adverb*.

SYNONYMS – **1** creative, imaginative, inventive. **3** aesthetic, attractive, decorative, tasteful.

artless > *adjective* **1** without guile or pretension. **2** clumsy.

DERIVATIVES – **artlessly** *adverb*.

art nouveau /aar noo**vō**/ > *noun* a style of decorative art and architecture prominent in the late 19th and early 20th centuries, characterised by intricate linear designs and flowing curves.

ORIGIN – French, 'new art'.

arty (chiefly N. Amer. also **artsy**) > *adjective* (**artier**, **artiest**) informal overtly artistic or interested in the arts.

DERIVATIVES – **artiness** *noun*.

arugula /ə**roo**gyoolə/ > *noun* N. Amer. the salad vegetable rocket.

ORIGIN – Italian *rucola*, from *ruca* 'rocket'.

arum /**air**əm/ > *noun* cuckoo pint (*Arum maculatum*) or a related plant.

COMBINATIONS – **arum lily** a tall lily-like African plant of the arum family.

ORIGIN – Greek *aron*.

arvo > *noun* (pl. **arvos**) Austral./NZ informal afternoon.

-ary > *suffix* **1** forming adjectives such as *budgetary* or *capillary*. **2** forming nouns such as *dictionary*.

Aryan /**air**iən/ > *noun* **1** a member of a people speaking an Indo-European language who spread into northern India in the 2nd millennium BC. **2** the language of this people. **3** (in Nazi ideology) a person of Caucasian race not of Jewish descent. > *adjective* relating to the Aryan people.

ORIGIN – Sanskrit, 'noble'.

As > *symbol* the chemical element arsenic.

as > *adverb* used in comparisons to refer to the extent or degree of something. > *conjunction* **1** used to indicate simultaneous occurrence. **2** used to indicate by comparison the way that something happens. **3** because. **4** even though. > *preposition* **1** used to refer to the function or character of someone or something: *it came as a shock*. **2** during the time of being.

IDIOMS – **as for** with regard to. **as from** (or **of**) chiefly Brit. from a particular time or date.

asafoetida /assə**fett**idə/ (US **asafetida**) > *noun* an unpleasant-smelling gum obtained from the roots of a plant of the parsley family, used in herbal medicine and Indian cooking.

ORIGIN – Latin, from *asa* (from a Persian word meaning 'mastic') + *foetida* (stinking).

asap > *abbreviation* as soon as possible.

asbestos > *noun* a highly heat-resistant fibrous silicate mineral, used in fire-resistant and insulating materials.

asbestosis /asbes**tō**siss/ > *noun* a serious lung disease, often accompanied by cancer, resulting from breathing asbestos dust.

ascend > *verb* **1** go up; climb or rise. **2** rise in status. **3** (of a voice or sound) rise in pitch.

ORIGIN – Latin *ascendere*.

ascendant* (also **ascendent**) > *adjective* **1** holding a position of increasing status or influence. **2** Astrology (of a planet, zodiacal sign, etc.) on or close to the intersection of the ecliptic with the eastern horizon. > *noun* **Astrology** the ascendant point.

IDIOMS – **in the ascendant** rising in power or influence.

DERIVATIVES – **ascendancy** *noun*.

*SPELLING – the standard spelling is with an *a*: ascend*ant*.

ascension > *noun* **1** the action of ascending in status. **2** (**Ascension**) (in Christian belief) the ascent of Christ into heaven on the fortieth day after the Resurrection.

DERIVATIVES – **ascensional** *adjective*.

ascent > *noun* **1** an instance of ascending. **2** a climb up a mountain. **3** an upward slope.

SYNONYMS – **1** ascension, climb, rise. **3** climb, gradient, incline, rise.

ANTONYMS – descent.

ascertain /assərtayn/ > *verb* find out for certain.

DERIVATIVES – **ascertainable** *adjective* **ascertainment** *noun*.

SYNONYMS – determine, establish, verify.

ORIGIN – Old French *acertener*, from Latin *certus* 'settled, sure'.

ascetic /əsettik/ > *adjective* strictly self-disciplined and abstemious. > *noun* an ascetic person.

DERIVATIVES – **ascetically** *adverb* **asceticism** *noun*.

SYNONYMS – *adjective* abstemious, austere, frugal, puritanical.

ANTONYMS – *adjective* decadent, sybaritic. *noun* sybarite.

ORIGIN – from Greek *askētēs* 'monk', from *askein* 'to exercise'.

ASCII /aski/ > *abbreviation* **Computing** American Standard Code for Information Interchange.

ascites /əsīteez/ > *noun* **Medicine** the accumulation of fluid in the peritoneal cavity, causing abdominal swelling.

ORIGIN – Greek *askitēs*, from *askos* 'wineskin'.

ascorbic acid /əskorbik/ > *noun* vitamin C, a compound found in citrus fruits and green vegetables, essential in maintaining healthy connective tissue.

ORIGIN – from Latin *scorbutus* 'scurvy'.

ascribe > *verb* (**ascribe to**) **1** attribute (a particular cause, person, or period) to. **2** regard (a quality) as belonging to.

DERIVATIVES – **ascribable** *adjective* **ascription** *noun*.

ORIGIN – Latin *ascribere*.

asdic > *noun* a form of sonar developed by the British in the Second World War to detect submarines.

ORIGIN – acronym from *Allied Submarine Detection Investigation Committee*.

aseptic /ayseptik/ > *adjective* marked by the absence of bacteria, viruses, and other micro-organisms. Compare with **ANTISEPTIC**.

asexual > *adjective* **1** **Biology** without sex or sexual organs. **2** (of reproduction) not involving the fusion of gametes. **3** without sexual feelings or associations.

DERIVATIVES – **asexuality** *noun* **asexually** *adverb*.

ASH > *abbreviation* Action on Smoking and Health.

ash[1] > *noun* **1** the powder remaining after something has been burned. **2** (**ashes**) the remains of a human body after cremation. **3** (**the Ashes**) a cricket trophy awarded for winning a test match series between England and Australia. [ORIGIN – from a mock obituary referring to the symbolic remains of English cricket after an Australian victory in 1882.]

WORDFINDER – *relating to ashes:* cinerary.

IDIOMS – **ashes in one's mouth** something that is bitterly disappointing.

DERIVATIVES – **ashy** *adjective*.

COMBINATIONS – **ash blonde** (also **ash blond**) (of hair) very pale blonde. **ashcan** US a dustbin. **ashtray** a small receptacle for tobacco ash and cigarette ends. **Ash Wednesday** the first day of Lent in the Western Christian Church. [ORIGIN – from the custom of marking the foreheads of penitents with ashes on that day.]

ash[2] > *noun* **1** a tree with compound leaves, winged fruits, and hard pale wood. **2** an Old English letter, ᚠ.

ashamed > *adjective* feeling embarrassed or guilty.

DERIVATIVES – **ashamedly** *adverb*.

Ashanti /əshanti/ (also **Asante**) > *noun* (pl. same) a member of a people of south central Ghana.

ORIGIN – the name in Akan.

ashen > *adjective* very pale through shock, fear, or illness.

Ashkenazi /ashkənaazi/ > *noun* (pl. **Ashkenazim** /ashkənaazim/) a Jew of central or eastern European descent. Compare with **SEPHARDI**.

ORIGIN – from *Ashkenaz*, a grandson of Noah (in the Bible).

ashlar /ashlər/ > *noun* large square-cut stones used as the surface layer of a wall.

ORIGIN – Old French *aisselier*, from Latin *axilla* 'little plank'.

ashore > *adverb* to or on the shore or land.

ashram /ashrəm/ > *noun* an Indian religious retreat or community.

ORIGIN – Sanskrit, 'hermitage'.

Asian /aysh'n, ayzh'n/ > *noun* a person from Asia or of Asian descent. > *adjective* relating to Asia.

USAGE – in Britain **Asian** is used to refer to people who come from (or whose parents came from) the Indian subcontinent, while in North America it is used to refer to people from the Far East.

Asiatic /ayshiattik, ayziattik/ > *adjective* relating to Asia.

USAGE – the accepted term when referring to individual people is **Asian** rather than **Asiatic**. However, **Asiatic** is the accepted term in scientific and technical use, for example in biological classifications.

aside > *adverb* **1** to one side; out of the way. **2** in reserve. > *noun* **1** an actor's remark addressed to the audience rather than the other characters. **2** an incidental remark.

IDIOMS – **aside from** apart from. **set aside 1** temporarily remove (land) from agricultural production. **2** annul (a legal decision or process).

asinine /assinīn/ > *adjective* extremely stupid or foolish.

DERIVATIVES – **asininity** *noun*.

ORIGIN – Latin *asininus*, from *asinus* 'ass'.

-asis (also **-iasis**) > *suffix* forming the names of diseases: *psoriasis*.

ORIGIN – Greek.

ask > *verb* **1** say something in order to get an answer or some information. **2** say that one wants someone to do, give, or allow something. **3** (**ask for**) request to speak to. **4** expect or demand (something) of someone. **5** invite to a social occasion. **6** (**ask out**) invite out on a date. **7** (**ask after**) enquire about the well-being of.

IDIOMS – **a big ask** Austral./NZ informal a difficult demand to fulfil. **for the asking** for little or no effort or cost.

SYNONYMS – **1** enquire, question, quiz. **2** apply for, call on, demand, request.

COMBINATIONS – **asking price** the price at which something is offered for sale.

askance /əskanss, əskaanss/ > *adverb* with a suspicious or disapproving look.

askari /əskaari/ > *noun* (pl. same or **askaris**) (in East Africa) a soldier or police officer.

ORIGIN – Arabic, 'soldier'.

askew /əskyoo/ > *adverb* & *adjective* not straight or level.

SYNONYMS – awry, crooked, off centre.

aslant > *adverb* at a slant. > *preposition* across at a slant.

asleep > *adjective* & *adverb* **1** in or into a state of sleep. **2** not attentive or alert. **3** (of a limb) numb.

asp /asp/ > *noun* **1** a small viper with an upturned snout. **2** the Egyptian cobra.

ORIGIN – Greek *aspis*.

asparagine /əsparrəjeen/ > *noun* **Biochemistry** an amino acid which is a constituent of most proteins.

ORIGIN – from **ASPARAGUS** (which contains it) + **-INE**[4].

asparagus /əsparrəgəss/ > *noun* a vegetable consisting of the tender young shoots of a tall plant.
ORIGIN – Greek *asparagos*.

aspartame /əspaartaym/ > *noun* a low-calorie artificial sweetener.

aspartic acid /əspaartik/ > *noun* an acidic amino acid present in many proteins and in sugar cane.
ORIGIN – from Latin *asparagus* 'asparagus'.

aspect > *noun* **1** a particular part or feature of something. **2** appearance or quality. **3** the side of a building facing a particular direction.
DERIVATIVES – **aspectual** *adjective*.
SYNONYMS – **1** angle, element, facet, feature. **2** air, appearance, character, quality. **3** elevation, facade, face.
COMBINATIONS – **aspect ratio 1** the ratio of the width to the height of an image on a television screen. **2** Aeronautics the ratio of the span to the mean chord of an aerofoil.
ORIGIN – Latin *aspectus*, from *aspicere* 'look at'.

aspen > *noun* a poplar tree with small rounded long-stalked leaves.

Asperger's syndrome /asperjərz/ > *noun* Psychiatry a mild autistic disorder characterised by awkwardness in social interaction, pedantry in speech, and preoccupation with very narrow interests.
ORIGIN – named after the Austrian psychiatrist Hans *Asperger* (1906–80).

asperity /əsperriti/ > *noun* (pl. **asperities**) **1** harshness of tone or manner. **2** a rough edge on a surface.
ORIGIN – Latin *asperitas*, from *asper* 'rough'.

aspersion /əspersh'n/ > *noun* (often in phrase **cast aspersions on**) an attack on someone's character or reputation.
ORIGIN – first used in reference to the sprinkling of water at baptism: Latin, from *aspergere* 'sprinkle'.

asphalt* /asfalt/ > *noun* a dark tar-like substance used in surfacing roads or waterproofing buildings. > *verb* surface with asphalt.
DERIVATIVES – **asphaltic** *adjective*.
*SPELLING – there is no ash in asphalt.
ORIGIN – Greek *asphalton*.

asphodel /asfədel/ > *noun* a plant of the lily family with long, slender leaves and flowers borne on a spike.
ORIGIN – Greek *asphodelos*, related to **DAFFODIL**.

asphyxia /əsfiksiə/ > *noun* a condition caused by the body being deprived of oxygen, leading to unconsciousness or death.
DERIVATIVES – **asphyxiant** *adjective* & *noun*.
ORIGIN – Greek *asphuxia*, from *a-* 'without' + *sphuxis* 'pulse'.

asphyxiate > *verb* kill or be killed by asphyxia; suffocate.
DERIVATIVES – **asphyxiation** *noun*.

aspic > *noun* a savoury jelly made with meat stock.
ORIGIN – French, 'asp', from the colours of the jelly as compared with those of the snake.

aspidistra /aspidistrə/ > *noun* a plant of the lily family with broad tapering leaves.
ORIGIN – from Greek *aspis* 'shield' (because of the shape of the stigma).

aspirant /əspīrənt/ > *adjective* aspiring towards a particular achievement or status. > *noun* a person who has such aspirations.

aspirate > *verb* /aspərayt/ **1** pronounce with an exhalation of breath. **2** pronounce the sound of *h* at the beginning of a word. **3** Medicine draw (fluid) by suction from a vessel or cavity. **4** technical inhale. > *noun* /aspərət/ an aspirated consonant or sound of *h*.
ORIGIN – Latin *aspirare*, from *spirare* 'breathe'

aspiration > *noun* **1** a hope or ambition. **2** the action of aspirating.
DERIVATIVES – **aspirational** *adjective*.

aspirator > *noun* Medicine an instrument or apparatus for aspirating fluid from a vessel or cavity.

aspire > *verb* (usu. **aspire to** or **to do**) have ambitions to be or do something.
DERIVATIVES – **aspiring** *adjective*.
SYNONYMS – (**aspire to**) aim for, hanker after, hope for, pursue.
ORIGIN – Latin *aspirare*, from *spirare* 'breathe'.

aspirin > *noun* (pl. same or **aspirins**) a medicine used in tablet form to relieve pain and reduce fever and inflammation.
ORIGIN – from the chemical name, *acetylated salicylic acid*.

ass¹ > *noun* **1** a donkey or similar wild horse with long ears and a braying call. **2** informal a foolish or stupid person.
ORIGIN – from a Celtic word based on Latin *asinus*.

ass² > *noun* North American form of **ARSE**.

assail > *verb* **1** attack violently. **2** (of an unpleasant feeling) come upon (someone) strongly.
ORIGIN – Latin *assalire*, from *salire* 'to leap'.

assailant > *noun* a person who attacks another.
SYNONYMS – aggressor, attacker.

assassin > *noun* a person who assassinates someone.
SYNONYMS – killer, murderer; informal hit man.

wordpower facts
Assassin
In the literal sense an **assassin** was a person who used cannabis, or hashish. The root of the word, which entered English from either French or medieval Latin, is the Arabic *ḥašīšī* 'hashish-eater', and it was first used in reference to the Nizari branch of Ismaili Muslims who ruled part of northern Persia in the 12th and 13th centuries, during the time of the Crusades. Renowned as militant fanatics, they were popularly reputed to use hashish before going on their murder missions, despite the fact that it would be more likely to subdue their militant zeal.

assassinate > *verb* murder (a political or religious leader).
DERIVATIVES – **assassination** *noun*.
SYNONYMS – execute, kill, murder.

assault > *noun* **1** a physical attack on a person or (Law) an act that threatens physical harm to a person. **2** an act of sexual molestation. **3** a military attack on an enemy position. **4** a concentrated attempt to do something difficult. > *verb* **1** subject to a physical or sexual assault. **2** make a military assault on.
DERIVATIVES – **assaultive** *adjective*.
SYNONYMS – *noun* **3** attack, offensive, raid, strike. *verb* **1** attack, molest, violate. **2** attack, raid, storm, strike at.
COMBINATIONS – **assault and battery** Law the action of threatening a person together with making physical contact with them. **assault course** Brit. a course providing a series of physical challenges, used for training soldiers.
ORIGIN – Old French *assauter*, from Latin *saltare* 'to leap'.

assay /assay, əsay/ > *noun* the testing of a metal or ore to determine its ingredients and quality. > *verb* **1** carry out an assay on. **2** archaic attempt.
DERIVATIVES – **assayer** *noun*.
COMBINATIONS – **assay office 1** a place where ores and metals are tested. **2** Brit. an institution which awards hallmarks to things made of precious metals.
ORIGIN – Old French *assai* 'trial'.

assegai /assigī/ > *noun* (pl. **assegais**) a slender iron-tipped spear used by southern African peoples.
ORIGIN – Arabic, 'the spear'.

assemblage > *noun* **1** a collection or gathering of things or people. **2** something made of pieces fitted together.

assemble > *verb* **1** come or bring together. **2** fit together the component parts of.
DERIVATIVES – **assembler** *noun*.

SYNONYMS – **1** collect, congregate, convene, gather, rally. **2** build, construct, erect, piece together.

ANTONYMS – **1** disperse. **2** dismantle.

ORIGIN – Old French *asembler*, from Latin *ad-* 'to' + *simul* 'together'.

assembly > *noun* (pl. **assemblies**) **1** a group of people gathered together. **2** a body with powers to make decisions and laws. **3** a regular gathering of teachers and pupils in a school. **4** the action of assembling component parts. **5** a unit consisting of assembled parts.

SYNONYMS – **1** congregation, convocation, gathering, meeting, rally. **2** congress, convention, council.

COMBINATIONS – **assembly line** a series of machines by which identical items are assembled in successive stages.

assent /əsent/ > *noun* the expression of approval or agreement. > *verb* (usu. **assent to**) express assent.

DERIVATIVES – **assenter** (also **assentor**) *noun*.

SYNONYMS – *noun* acceptance, acquiescence, agreement, approval, consent, endorsement.

ORIGIN – from Latin *assentire*, from *sentire* 'feel, think'.

assert > *verb* **1** state (a fact or belief) confidently and forcefully. **2** cause others to recognise (something) by confident and forceful behaviour. **3** (**assert oneself**) be confident and forceful.

SYNONYMS – **1** argue, aver, contend, declare, maintain, pronounce.

ORIGIN – Latin *asserere* 'claim, affirm'.

assertion > *noun* **1** a confident and forceful statement. **2** the action of asserting.

assertive > *adjective* confident and forceful.

DERIVATIVES – **assertively** *adverb* **assertiveness** *noun*.

SYNONYMS – assured, commanding, confident, forceful.

ANTONYMS – submissive.

assess > *verb* **1** evaluate or estimate the nature, value, or quality of. **2** set the value of a tax, fine, etc. for (a person or property) at a specified level.

DERIVATIVES – **assessable** *adjective* **assessment** *noun* **assessor** *noun*.

SYNONYMS – **1** estimate, evaluate, gauge, judge.

ORIGIN – Old French *assesser*, based on Latin *assidere* 'sit by'.

asset > *noun* **1** a useful or valuable thing or person. **2** (**assets**) property owned by a person or company.

SYNONYMS – **1** advantage, benefit, forte, strength.

ANTONYMS – **1** liability, handicap.

COMBINATIONS – **asset-stripping** the taking over of a company in financial

difficulties in order to sell each of its assets at a profit.

ORIGIN – first used in the sense 'sufficient estate to allow discharge of a will': from Old French *asez* 'enough'.

asseveration /əsevvəraysh'n/ > *noun* formal a solemn or emphatic declaration or statement.

DERIVATIVES – **asseverate** *verb*.

ORIGIN – Latin, from *asseverare*, from *severus* 'serious'.

assiduous /əsidyooəss/ > *adjective* showing great care and perseverance.

DERIVATIVES – **assiduity** /assidyo͞oiti/ *noun* **assiduously** *adverb* **assiduousness** *noun*.

SYNONYMS – careful, conscientious, diligent, meticulous.

ORIGIN – Latin *assiduus*, from *assidere* 'sit by'.

assign > *verb* **1** allocate (a task or duty) to someone. **2** give (someone) a job or task. **3** regard (something) as belonging to or being caused by. **4** transfer (legal rights or liabilities).

DERIVATIVES – **assignable** *adjective* **assigner** *noun*.

SYNONYMS – **1** allocate, allot, charge with. **2** appoint, commission, delegate, designate. **3** apportion, ascribe, attribute.

ORIGIN – Latin *assignare*, from *signare* 'to sign'.

assignation > *noun* **1** a secret arrangement to meet, especially by lovers. **2** the action of assigning.

SYNONYMS – rendezvous, tryst.

assignee > *noun* chiefly Law **1** a person to whom a right or liability is legally transferred. **2** a person appointed to act for another.

assignment > *noun* **1** a task allocated to someone as part of a job or course of study. **2** the action of assigning.

SYNONYMS – **1** commission, duty, project, task.

assimilate > *verb* **1** take in and understand (information or ideas). **2** absorb and integrate into a people or culture. **3** absorb and digest (food or nutrients). **4** regard as or make similar.

DERIVATIVES – **assimilable** *adjective* **assimilation** *noun* **assimilative** *adjective* **assimilator** *noun*.

SYNONYMS – **1** absorb, acquire, digest, grasp, imbibe, take in.

ORIGIN – Latin *assimilare* 'absorb, incorporate', from *similis* 'like'.

assist > *verb* help (someone). > *noun* chiefly N. Amer. **1** an act of helping. **2** (in sport) an act of touching the ball in a play in which a teammate scores or an opposing batter is put out.

SYNONYMS – *verb* aid, attend, help, support.

ANTONYMS – *verb* hinder.

ORIGIN – Old French *assister*, from Latin *assistere* 'stand by'.

assistance > *noun* help or support.

SYNONYMS – aid, backing, help, support.

assistant > *noun* **1** a person who ranks below a senior person. **2** a person who helps in particular work.

SYNONYMS – **1** aide, deputy, number two, second. **2** attendant, helper.

assize /əsīz/ (also **assizes**) > *noun* historical a court which sat at intervals in each county of England and Wales.

ORIGIN – Old French, from Latin *assidere* 'sit by'.

associate > *verb* /əsōsiayt, əsōshiayt/ **1** connect in the mind. **2** frequently meet or have dealings. **3** (**be associated with** or **associate oneself with**) be involved with. > *noun* /əsōsiət, əsōshiət/ **1** a work partner or colleague. **2** (before another noun) connected with an organisation or business: *an associate company*. **3** (before another noun) denoting shared function or membership but with lower status: *an associate member*.

SYNONYMS – *verb* **1** connect, equate, link, relate.

association > *noun* **1** a group of people organised for a joint purpose. **2** a connection or link between people or organisations. **3** a mental connection between ideas.

DERIVATIVES – **associational** *adjective*.

SYNONYMS – **1** affiliation, alliance, confederation, consortium, league, union.

COMBINATIONS – **Association Football** more formal term for SOCCER.

associative > *adjective* **1** of or involving association. **2** Mathematics unchanged in result by varying the grouping of quantities, as long as their order is the same, such that for example $(a \times b) \times c = a \times (b \times c)$.

assonance /assənənss/ > *noun* resemblance of sound between words arising from the rhyming of vowels only (e.g. *sonnet*, *porridge*) or from use of identical consonants with different vowels (e.g. *cold*, *culled*).

DERIVATIVES – **assonant** *adjective*.

ORIGIN – Latin *assonare* 'respond to'.

assorted > *adjective* of various sorts put together.

SYNONYMS – diverse, miscellaneous, mixed, varied, various.

ORIGIN – from Old French *assorter*, from *sorte* 'sort, kind'.

assortment > *noun* a miscellaneous collection.

assuage /əswayj/ > *verb* **1** make (an unpleasant feeling) less intense. **2** satisfy (an appetite or desire).

DERIVATIVES – **assuagement** *noun*.

SYNONYMS – **1** alleviate, ease, palliate, relieve, soothe.

ANTONYMS – **1** aggravate.

ORIGIN – Old French *assouagier*, based on Latin *suavis* 'sweet'.

assume > *verb* **1** accept (something) as true without proof. **2** take (responsibility or control). **3** begin to have (a quality, appearance, or extent). **4** pretend to have; adopt falsely.

USAGE – **assume** and **presume** both mean 'suppose something to be true', but while **assume** implies something is taken for granted without proof, **presume** is used especially when the supposition is based on evidence.

SYNONYMS – **1** deduce, presume, reckon, suppose. **2** bear, shoulder, take on, undertake.

ORIGIN – Latin *assumere*, from *sumere* 'take'.

assuming > *conjunction* based on the assumption that.

assumption > *noun* **1** a thing that is assumed to be true. **2** the action of assuming responsibility or control. **3** (**Assumption**) the reception of the Virgin Mary bodily into heaven, according to Roman Catholic doctrine.

assurance > *noun* **1** a positive declaration intended to give confidence. **2** confidence or certainty. **3** chiefly Brit. life insurance.

NOTE – in the context of life insurance, **assurance** and **insurance** do not mean the same thing. **Assurance** is used of policies under whose terms a payment is guaranteed, either after a fixed term or on the death of the insured person; **insurance** is the general term, and is used in particular of policies under whose terms a payment would be made only in certain circumstances (e.g. accident or death within a limited period).

assure > *verb* **1** tell someone something positively to dispel doubts. **2** make (something) certain to happen. **3** chiefly Brit. cover by assurance (life insurance).

DERIVATIVES – **assurer** *noun*.

SYNONYMS – **1** convince, persuade, reassure. **2** ensure, guarantee, secure.

ORIGIN – Old French *assurer*, based on Latin *securus* 'free from care'.

assured > *adjective* **1** confident. **2** protected against change or ending.

DERIVATIVES – **assuredly** *adverb*.

Assyrian /əsirriən/ > *noun* an inhabitant of Assyria, an ancient country in what is now Iraq. > *adjective* relating to Assyria.

astatine /astəteen/ > *noun* a very unstable radioactive chemical element belonging to the halogen group.

ORIGIN – from Greek *astatos* 'unstable'.

aster /astər/ > *noun* a Michaelmas daisy or related plant, typically with purple or pink rayed flowers.

ORIGIN – Greek, 'star'.

asterisk* > *noun* a symbol (*) used in text as a pointer to an annotation or footnote. > *verb* mark with an asterisk.

*****SPELLING – aster*isk*, not *-ix* (Astérix is a character in a comic cartoon strip).

ORIGIN – Greek *asteriskos* 'small star'.

asterism /astəriz'm/ > *noun* a group of three asterisks (⁂) drawing attention to following text.

astern > *adverb* behind or towards the rear of a ship or aircraft.

asteroid /astəroyd/ > *noun* a small rocky body orbiting the sun.

ORIGIN – from Greek *asteroeidēs* 'starlike'.

asthma /asmə/ > *noun* a medical condition marked by difficulty in breathing.

DERIVATIVES – **asthmatic** *adjective* & *noun* **asthmatically** *adverb*.

ORIGIN – Greek, from *azein* 'breathe hard'.

astigmatism /əstigmətiz'm/ > *noun* a distortion in the curve of the eyeball or a lens, resulting in an imprecise focus.

DERIVATIVES – **astigmatic** /astigmattik/ *adjective*.

ORIGIN – from **A-¹** + Greek *stigma* 'point'.

astilbe /əstilbi/ > *noun* a plant with plumes of tiny white, pink, or red flowers.

ORIGIN – Latin, from Greek *a-* 'not' + *stilbē* 'glittering'.

astir > *adjective* **1** in a state of excited movement. **2** awake and out of bed.

astonish > *verb* surprise or impress greatly.

DERIVATIVES – **astonished** *adjective* **astonishing** *adjective* **astonishingly** *adverb* **astonishment** *noun*.

SYNONYMS – amaze, astound, dumbfound, stagger.

ORIGIN – Old French *estoner* 'stun, stupefy', from Latin *ex-* 'out' + *tonare* 'to thunder'.

astound > *verb* shock or greatly surprise.

DERIVATIVES – **astounded** *adjective* **astounding** *adjective* **astoundingly** *adverb*.

ORIGIN – related to **ASTONISH**.

astrakhan /astrəkan/ > *noun* the dark curly fleece of young karakul lambs from central Asia.

ORIGIN – named after the city of *Astrakhan* in Russia.

astral /astrəl/ > *adjective* relating to the stars.

ORIGIN – Latin *astralis*, from *astrum* 'star'.

astray > *adverb* away from the correct path or direction.

astride > **1** *preposition* & *adverb* with a leg on each side of. **2** *adverb* (of a person's legs) apart.

astringent /əstrinjənt/ > *adjective* **1** causing the contraction of body tissues. **2** (of taste or smell) sharp or bitter. **3** harsh or severe. > *noun* an astringent lotion applied for medical or cosmetic purposes.

DERIVATIVES – **astringency** *noun* **astringently** *adverb*.

SYNONYMS – **2** acid, bitter, sharp. **3** acerbic, caustic, cutting, harsh, severe.

ANTONYMS – emollient.

ORIGIN – from Latin *astringere* 'pull tight'.

astro- /astrō/ > *combining form* relating to the stars or to outer space.

ORIGIN – from Greek *astron* 'star'.

astrodome > *noun* **1** chiefly US an enclosed stadium with a domed roof. **2** a domed window in an aircraft for astronomical observations.

astrolabe /astrəlayb/ > *noun* an instrument formerly used for making astronomical measurements and in navigation for calculating latitude.

ORIGIN – Latin *astrolabium*, from Greek *astrolabos* 'star-taking'.

astrology > *noun* the study of the movements and relative positions of celestial bodies and their supposed influence on human affairs.

WORDFINDER – *astrological terms:* ascendant, conjunction, cusp, horoscope, zodiac.

DERIVATIVES – **astrologer** *noun* **astrological** *adjective* **astrologically** *adverb*.

astronaut > *noun* a person trained to travel in a spacecraft.

ORIGIN – from Greek *astron* 'star' + *nautēs* 'sailor'.

astronautics > *plural noun* (treated as sing.) the science and technology of space travel and exploration.

astronomical > *adjective* **1** relating to astronomy. **2** informal (of numbers or quantities) extremely large: *astronomical fees.*

DERIVATIVES – **astronomic** *adjective* **astronomically** *adverb*.

COMBINATIONS – **astronomical unit** a unit of measurement equal to the mean distance from the earth to the sun, 149.6 million kilometres.

astronomy > *noun* the science of celestial objects, space, and the physical universe.

DERIVATIVES – **astronomer** *noun*.

astrophysics > *plural noun* (treated as sing.) the branch of astronomy concerned with the physical nature of celestial bodies.

DERIVATIVES – **astrophysical** *adjective* **astrophysicist** *noun*.

AstroTurf > *noun* trademark an artificial grass surface, used for sports fields.

astute > *adjective* good at making accurate judgements; shrewd.

DERIVATIVES – **astutely** *adverb* **astuteness** *noun*.

SYNONYMS – discerning, insightful, perspicacious, shrewd.

ORIGIN – Latin *astutus*, from *astus* 'craft'.

asunder > *adverb* archaic or literary apart.

asylum > *noun* **1** shelter or protection. **2** protection granted by a state to a political refugee. **3** dated an institution for the mentally ill.

ORIGIN – Greek *asulon* 'refuge'.

asymmetrical > *adjective* not symmetrical; without symmetry.
DERIVATIVES – **asymmetric** *adjective* **asymmetrically** *adverb*.

asymmetry /ay**simm**itri/ > *noun* (pl. **asymmetries**) lack of symmetry.

asymptomatic > *adjective* Medicine producing or showing no symptoms.

asymptote /**ass**imptōt/ > *noun* a straight line that continually approaches a given curve but does not meet it.
DERIVATIVES – **asymptotic** /assimp**tott**ik/ *adjective* **asymptotically** *adverb*.
ORIGIN – from Latin *asymptota linea* 'line not meeting'.

asynchronous > *adjective* not existing or occurring at the same time.
DERIVATIVES – **asynchronously** *adverb*.

At > *symbol* the chemical element astatine.

at¹ > *preposition* **1** expressing location or arrival. **2** expressing the time when an event takes place. **3** denoting a value, rate, or point on a scale. **4** expressing a state or condition. **5** expressing the object or target of a look, shot, action, or plan. **6** expressing the means by which something is done.
IDIOMS – **at that** in addition; furthermore. **where it's at** informal the focus of fashion.

at² > *noun* a monetary unit of Laos, equal to one hundredth of a kip.
ORIGIN – Thai.

atavistic /attə**vist**ik/ > *adjective* returning to something ancient or ancestral.
DERIVATIVES – **atavism** *noun* **atavistically** *adverb*.
ORIGIN – from Latin *atavus* 'forefather'.

ataxia /ə**tak**siə/ > *noun* Medicine the loss of full control of bodily movements.
DERIVATIVES – **ataxic** *adjective*.
ORIGIN – Greek, from *a-* 'without' + *taxis* 'order'.

ATC > *abbreviation* **1** air traffic control or controller. **2** Air Training Corps.

ate past of EAT.

-ate¹ > *suffix* forming nouns denoting: **1** status, office, or function: *doctorate*. **2** a group: *electorate*. **3** Chemistry a salt or ester: *chlorate*. **4** a product of a chemical process: *condensate*.
ORIGIN – Old French *-at* or Latin *-atus*.

-ate² > *suffix* **1** forming adjectives and nouns such as *associate*. **2** forming verbs such as *fascinate*.
ORIGIN – Latin *-atus*.

atelier /ə**tell**iay/ > *noun* a workshop or studio.
ORIGIN – French, from Old French *astelle* 'splinter of wood'.

atheism /**ay**thi-iz'm/ > *noun* disbelief in the existence of a god or gods.
DERIVATIVES – **atheist** *noun* **atheistic** *adjective* **atheistical** *adjective*.
ORIGIN – from Greek *a-* 'without' + *theos* 'god'.

atheling /**ath**əling/ > *noun* a prince or lord in Anglo-Saxon England.

Athenian /ə**thee**niən/ > *noun* a person from Athens in Greece. > *adjective* relating to Athens.

atherosclerosis /athərōsklee**rō**siss/ > *noun* a disease of the arteries in which fatty material is deposited on their inner walls.
DERIVATIVES – **atherosclerotic** *adjective*.
ORIGIN – from Greek *athērē* 'groats' + *sklērōsis* 'hardening'.

athlete > *noun* **1** a person who is good at sports. **2** a person who competes in athletics events.
COMBINATIONS – **athlete's foot** a form of ringworm infection affecting the skin between the toes.

wordpower facts

Athlete
Athlete comes from the Greek word *athlētēs*, from *athlein* 'compete for a prize', from *athlon* 'contest, prize'. The word *athlon* also occurs in the group of names for multiple sets of athletics events, including **decathlon** (ten events), **heptathlon** (seven), **pentathlon** (five), and **tetrathlon** (four).

athletic > *adjective* **1** fit and good at sport. **2** relating to athletics.
DERIVATIVES – **athletically** *adverb* **athleticism** *noun*.

athletics > *plural noun* (usu. treated as sing.) **1** chiefly Brit. the sport of competing in a series of events including running, jumping, and throwing. **2** N. Amer. physical sports and games.
WORDFINDER – *athletics events:* discus, hammer, high jump, hurdling, javelin, long jump, marathon, pole vault, relay race, shot put, steeplechase, triple jump.

at-home > *noun* a social gathering in a person's home.

athwart /ə**thwawrt**/ > *preposition & adverb* from side to side of something; across.

-ation > *suffix* (forming nouns) denoting an action or its result: *exploration*.
ORIGIN – French *-ation* or Latin *-ation-*.

Atlantic > *adjective* of or adjoining the Atlantic Ocean.
ORIGIN – from the name of the Greek god *Atlas*; the term originally referred to Mount Atlas in Libya.

atlas > *noun* **1** a book of maps or charts. **2** Anatomy the topmost vertebra of the backbone.
ORIGIN – from the name of the Greek god *Atlas*, who held up the pillars of the universe: his picture appeared at the front of early atlases.

ATM > *abbreviation* automated teller machine.

atmosphere > *noun* **1** the envelope of gases surrounding the earth or another planet. **2** the quality of the air in a place. **3** a pervading tone or mood. **4** a unit of pressure equal to mean atmospheric pressure at sea level, 101,325 pascals (roughly 14.7 pounds per square inch).
WORDFINDER – *layers of the earth's atmosphere* (*from lowest to highest*): troposphere, stratosphere, mesosphere, thermosphere, ionosphere (exosphere).
SYNONYMS – **3** ambience, feeling, mood.
ORIGIN – from Greek *atmos* 'vapour' + *sphaira* 'globe'.

atmospheric > *adjective* **1** relating to the atmosphere of the earth or another planet. **2** creating a distinctive mood, typically of romance, mystery, or nostalgia.
DERIVATIVES – **atmospherically** *adverb*.

atmospherics > *plural noun* electrical disturbances in the atmosphere, that interfere with telecommunications.

ATOL /**att**ol/ > *abbreviation* (in the UK) Air Travel Organiser's Licence.

atoll /**att**ol/ > *noun* a ring-shaped reef or chain of islands formed of coral.
ORIGIN – Maldivian.

atom > *noun* **1** the smallest particle of a chemical element, consisting of a positively charged nucleus surrounded by negatively charged electrons. **2** an extremely small amount: *there isn't an atom of truth in it.*
COMBINATIONS – **atom bomb** a bomb whose explosive power comes from the fission of heavy atomic nuclei.
ORIGIN – from Greek *atomos* 'indivisible'.

atomic > *adjective* **1** relating to an atom or atoms. **2** of or forming a single indivisible unit or component in a larger system. **3** relating to nuclear energy.
DERIVATIVES – **atomically** *adverb*.
COMBINATIONS – **atomic bomb** an atom bomb. **atomic clock** an extremely accurate type of clock which is regulated by the vibrations of an atomic or molecular system such as caesium. **atomic mass** the mass of an atom of a chemical element expressed in atomic mass units. **atomic mass unit** a unit of mass used to express atomic and molecular weights, equal to one twelfth of the mass of an atom of carbon-12. **atomic number** the number of protons in the nucleus of a chemical element's atom, which determines its place in the periodic table. **atomic theory** the theory that all matter is made up of tiny indivisible particles (atoms). **atomic weight** another term for *relative atomic mass*.

atomicity > *noun* **1** the number of atoms in the molecule of an element. **2** the state or fact of being composed of atoms.

atomise (also **atomize**) > *verb* **1** convert (a substance) into very fine particles or droplets. **2** fragment.

DERIVATIVES – **atomisation** *noun* **atomiser** *noun*.

atonal /aytōn'l/ > *adjective* Music not written in any key or mode.

DERIVATIVES – **atonality** *noun*.

atone /ətōn/ > *verb* (**atone for**) make amends for.

ORIGIN – from *at one*.

atonement > *noun* **1** amends for a wrong or injury. **2** (**the Atonement**) Christian Theology the reconciliation of God and mankind through the death of Jesus Christ.

SYNONYMS – amends, expiation, redemption, reparation.

atop > *preposition* literary on the top of.

atopic /aytoppik/ > *adjective* of or relating to a form of allergy in which a hypersensitivity reaction (such as eczema or asthma) occurs away from the part of the body in contact with the allergen.

DERIVATIVES – **atopy** /attəpi/ *noun*.

ORIGIN – from Greek *atopia* 'unusualness'.

ATP > *abbreviation* **1** Biochemistry adenosine triphosphate. **2** Brit. automatic train protection.

atrabilious /atrəbilliəss/ > *adjective* literary melancholy or ill-tempered.

ORIGIN – from Latin *atra bilis* 'black bile'.

atrium /aytriəm/ > *noun* (pl. **atria** /aytriə/ or **atriums**) **1** a central hall rising through several storeys and having a glazed roof. **2** an open central court in an ancient Roman house. **3** Anatomy each of the two upper cavities of the heart.

DERIVATIVES – **atrial** *adjective*.

ORIGIN – Latin.

atrocious > *adjective* **1** horrifyingly wicked. **2** informal extremely bad or unpleasant.

DERIVATIVES – **atrociously** *adverb*.

SYNONYMS – **1** heinous, monstrous, vile. **2** abominable, execrable, ghastly, intolerable.

ORIGIN – Latin *atrox* 'cruel'.

atrocity > *noun* (pl. **atrocities**) an extremely wicked or cruel act.

SYNONYMS – abomination, barbarity, outrage.

atrophy /atrəfi/ > *verb* (**atrophies**, **atrophied**) **1** (of body tissue or an organ) waste away. **2** gradually become less effective or vigorous. > *noun* the condition or process of atrophying.

DERIVATIVES – **atrophic** /ətroffik/ *adjective*.

ORIGIN – Greek *atrophia* 'lack of food'.

atropine /atrəpeen, atrəpin/ > *noun* a poisonous compound found in deadly nightshade, used in medicine as a muscle relaxant.

ORIGIN – from *Atropos*, the name of one of the Fates in Greek mythology.

attach* > *verb* **1** fasten; join. **2** include (a condition) as part of an agreement. **3** assign or attribute. **4** appoint (someone) for special or temporary duties. **5** Law, archaic seize (a person or property) by legal authority.

DERIVATIVES – **attachable** *adjective*.

*SPELLING – -*ach*, not -*atch*: att*ach*.

SYNONYMS – append, connect, fasten, fix, join.

ORIGIN – Old French *atachier* 'fasten, fix'.

attaché /ətashay/ > *noun* a person on an ambassador's staff with specialised duties.

COMBINATIONS – **attaché case** a small, flat briefcase for carrying documents.

ORIGIN – French, 'attached'.

attached > *adjective* affectionate; fond.

attachment > *noun* **1** an extra part or extension attached to something. **2** the action of attaching. **3** affection or fondness. **4** Brit. temporary secondment to an organisation.

attack > *verb* **1** take aggressive action against. **2** (of a disease, chemical, etc.) act harmfully on. **3** criticise or oppose fiercely and publicly. **4** begin to deal with (a problem or task) in a determined way. **5** (in sport) attempt to score goals or points. > *noun* **1** an instance of attacking. **2** a sudden short bout of an illness. **3** the players in a team whose role is to attack.

DERIVATIVES – **attacker** *noun*.

SYNONYMS – *verb* **1** assail, assault, fight, lay into, strike at. **3** censure, condemn, denigrate, lambaste, vilify.

ORIGIN – Italian *attaccare* 'join battle'.

attain > *verb* **1** succeed in accomplishing. **2** reach (a specified age, size, or amount).

DERIVATIVES – **attainable** *adjective*.

SYNONYMS – **1** accomplish, achieve, gain, secure. **2** arrive at, reach, realise.

ORIGIN – Latin *attingere*, from *tangere* 'to touch'.

attainder /ətayndər/ > *noun* historical the forfeiting of land and civil rights as a consequence of a death sentence.

ORIGIN – from Old French *ateindre* 'accomplish, convict, bring to justice'.

attainment > *noun* **1** the action of achieving. **2** an achievement.

attar /attaar/ > *noun* a fragrant essential oil made from rose petals.

ORIGIN – Arabic, 'perfume, essence'.

attempt > *verb* make an effort to achieve or complete (something). > *noun* an act of attempting.

ORIGIN – Latin *attemptare*, from *temptare* 'to tempt'.

attend > *verb* **1** be present at. **2** go regularly to (a school, church, etc.) **3** (**attend to**) deal with or pay attention to. **4** occur at the same time as or as a result of. **5** escort and wait on (an important person).

DERIVATIVES – **attendee** *noun* **attender** *noun*.

ORIGIN – Latin *attendere*, from *tendere* 'stretch'.

attendance > *noun* **1** the action of attending. **2** the number of people present at a particular occasion.

attendant > *noun* **1** a person employed to provide a service to the public. **2** an assistant to an important person. > *adjective* occurring at the same time as or as a result of something.

SYNONYMS – **1** assistant, steward. **2** aide, assistant, retainer.

attention > *noun* **1** the mental faculty of considering or taking notice. **2** special care or consideration. **3** (**attentions**) attentive treatment or sexual advances. **4** an erect posture assumed by a soldier, with the feet together and the arms straight down the sides of the body.

DERIVATIVES – **attentional** *adjective*.

SYNONYMS – **1,2** attentiveness, concentration, consideration, heedfulness, regard.

COMBINATIONS – **attention deficit disorder** a condition found in children, marked by concentration, hyperactivity, and learning difficulties.

attentive > *adjective* **1** paying close attention. **2** considerately attending to the comfort or wishes of others.

DERIVATIVES – **attentively** *adverb* **attentiveness** *noun*.

SYNONYMS – **1** alert, focused, vigilant, watchful. **2** conscientious, considerate, solicitous, thoughtful.

attenuate /ətenyooayt/ > *verb* **1** reduce the strength, effect, or value of. **2** make thin or thinner.

DERIVATIVES – **attenuation** *noun*.

ORIGIN – Latin *attenuare* 'make slender'.

attest /ətest/ > *verb* **1** provide or serve as clear evidence of. **2** declare that something exists or is the case.

DERIVATIVES – **attestation** *noun*.

SYNONYMS – affirm, confirm, corroborate, substantiate, verify.

ORIGIN – Latin *attestari*, from *testari* 'to witness'.

Attic /attik/ > *adjective* relating to Attica in Greece, or to ancient Athens.

attic > *noun* a space or room inside the roof of a building.

ORIGIN – first used in classical architecture to denote a small column and entablature built above a larger one: from Latin *Atticus* 'Attic'.

attire > *noun* clothes, especially fine or formal ones. > *verb* (**be attired**) be dressed in clothes of a specified kind.

ORIGIN – from Old French *atirer* 'equip', from *a tire* 'in order'.

attitude > *noun* **1** a settled way of thinking or feeling. **2** a posture of the body. **3** informal,

53

chiefly N. Amer. self-confident or aggressively uncooperative behaviour.

DERIVATIVES – **attitudinal** adjective.

SYNONYMS – **1** approach, outlook, position, viewpoint. **2** pose, position, posture.

ORIGIN – Italian attitudine 'fitness, posture'.

attitudinise (also **attitudinize**) > verb adopt or express a particular attitude for effect.

atto- > combining form used in units of measurement to indicate a factor of one million million millionth (10^{-18}).

ORIGIN – from Danish or Norwegian atten 'eighteen'.

attorney /əturni/ > noun (pl. **attorneys**) **1** a person appointed to act for another in legal matters. **2** chiefly US a lawyer.

IDIOMS – **power of attorney** Law the authority to act for another person in specified legal or financial matters.

COMBINATIONS – **Attorney-General** (pl. **Attorneys-General**) the principal legal officer of the Crown or a state.

ORIGIN – from Old French atorner 'assign'.

attract > verb **1** draw in by offering something interesting or advantageous. **2** cause (a specified reaction). **3** (often **be attracted to**) cause to have a liking for or interest in. **4** draw (something) closer by exerting a force.

DERIVATIVES – **attractor** noun.

SYNONYMS – **1,3** engage, enthral, entice, fascinate.

ANTONYMS – repel.

ORIGIN – Latin attrahere 'draw near'.

attractant > noun a substance which attracts. > adjective tending to attract.

attraction > noun **1** the action or power of attracting. **2** something that attracts interest. **3** Physics a force which tends to make objects move towards each other.

SYNONYMS – **1** allure, appeal, charm, desirability.

ANTONYMS – **1,3** repulsion.

attractive > adjective **1** pleasing or appealing to the senses. **2** arousing interest. **3** relating to attraction between physical objects.

DERIVATIVES – **attractively** adverb **attractiveness** noun.

SYNONYMS – **1,2** alluring, appealing, engaging, fascinating, pleasing.

attribute > verb /ətribyoot/ (**attribute to**) regard as belonging to or being caused by. > noun /atribyoot/ **1** a characteristic or inherent quality or feature. **2** an object that represents a person, status, or office.

DERIVATIVES – **attributable** /ətribyootəb'l/ adjective **attribution** noun.

SYNONYMS – verb ascribe, assign, charge, impute. noun **1** characteristic, feature, property, quality.

ORIGIN – Latin attribuere 'assign to'.

attributive /ətribyootiv/ > adjective Grammar (of an adjective) preceding the word that it relates to, as old in the old dog. Contrasted with PREDICATIVE.

DERIVATIVES – **attributively** adverb.

attrition /ətrish'n/ > noun **1** gradual wearing down through sustained attack or pressure. **2** wearing away by friction.

DERIVATIVES – **attritional** adjective.

ORIGIN – Latin, from atterere 'to rub'.

attune > verb adjust or accustom to a particular situation.

atypical > adjective not typical.

DERIVATIVES – **atypically** adverb.

Au > symbol the chemical element gold.

ORIGIN – from Latin aurum.

aubade /ōbaad/ > noun a poem or piece of music appropriate to the dawn.

ORIGIN – French, from Spanish albada, from alba 'dawn'.

auberge /ōbairzh/ > noun an inn in French-speaking countries.

ORIGIN – French, from Provençal alberga 'lodging'.

aubergine /ōbərzheen/ > noun chiefly Brit. a purple egg-shaped fruit eaten as a vegetable.

WORDFINDER – dishes featuring aubergines: baba ganoush, caponata, moussaka, ratatouille.

ORIGIN – French, from Arabic.

aubretia /awbreeshə/ (also **aubrietia**) > noun a trailing plant with dense masses of foliage and purple, pink, or white flowers.

NOTE – aubretias belong to the genus Aubrieta, but in popular use the spellings **aubretia** and **aubrietia** have become more frequent than the strictly correct form **aubrieta**.

ORIGIN – named after the French botanist Claude Aubriet (1668–1743).

auburn /awbərn/ > noun a reddish-brown colour.

wordpower facts

Auburn

Auburn is from Old French auborne, from Latin alburnus 'whitish', from albus 'white'. The original sense was 'yellowish white', but the word became associated with brown because in the 16th and 17th centuries it was often written abrune or abroun. Another example of a word referring to colour that has changed its meaning is **baize**.

au courant /ō kooron/ > adjective up to date and well informed.

ORIGIN – French, 'in the (regular) course'.

auction /awksh'n/ > noun a public sale in which goods or property are sold to the highest bidder. > verb sell at an auction.

ORIGIN – Latin, 'increase, auction', from augere 'to increase'.

auctioneer > noun a person who conducts auctions.

audacious /awdayshəss/ > adjective **1** showing a willingness to take bold risks; recklessly daring. **2** impudent.

DERIVATIVES – **audaciously** adverb **audaciousness** noun **audacity** noun.

SYNONYMS – **1** bold, daring, fearless, intrepid. **2** brazen, cheeky, impertinent, impudent.

ANTONYMS – **1** timid.

ORIGIN – Latin audax 'bold'.

audible > adjective able to be heard.

DERIVATIVES – **audibility** noun **audibly** adverb.

wordpower facts

Audible

Audible is one of a number of related words stemming from Latin audire 'to hear'. An **audience** is a group of assembled listeners; an **audit** was originally presented orally, to be heard; a performer is heard presenting their skills in an **audition**; the combining form **audio-** relates to hearing and sound.

audience > noun **1** the assembled spectators or listeners at an event. **2** a formal interview with a person in authority.

audio- > combining form relating to hearing or sound, especially when recorded, transmitted, or reproduced: audio-visual.

audio frequency > noun a frequency capable of being perceived by the human ear, generally between 20 and 20,000 Hz.

audiology /awdiolləji/ > noun the branch of science and medicine concerned with the sense of hearing.

DERIVATIVES – **audiological** adjective **audiologist** noun.

audio tape > noun magnetic tape on which sound can be recorded.

audio typist > noun a typist who transcribes from recorded dictation.

audio-visual > adjective using both sight and sound, typically in the form of slides or video and speech or music.

audit /awdit/ > noun an official inspection of an organisation's accounts. > verb (**audited**, **auditing**) make an audit of.

audition > noun an interview for a performer in which they give a practical demonstration of their skill. > verb assess or be assessed by an audition.

auditor > noun **1** a person who conducts an audit. **2** a listener.

auditorium > noun (pl. **auditoriums** or **auditoria**) **1** the part of a theatre or hall in

which the audience sits. **2** chiefly N. Amer. a large public hall.
ORIGIN – Latin.

auditory > *adjective* relating to the sense of hearing.

au fait /ō **fay**/ > *adjective* (**au fait with**) having a good or detailed knowledge of.
ORIGIN – French, 'to the point'.

auger /**aw**gər/ > *noun* a tool resembling a large corkscrew, for boring holes.
ORIGIN – Old English *nafogār*; the *n* was lost by wrong division of *a nauger*.

aught /awt/ (also **ought**) > *pronoun* archaic anything at all.

augment /awg**ment**/ > *verb* make greater by addition; increase.
DERIVATIVES – **augmentation** *noun*.
SYNONYMS – boost, increase, supplement, top up.
ORIGIN – Latin *augmentare*, from *augere* 'to increase'.

augmented > *adjective* Music (of an interval) one semitone greater than the corresponding major or perfect interval.

au gratin /ō **gra**taN/ > *adjective* (after a noun) sprinkled with breadcrumbs or grated cheese and browned.
ORIGIN – French, 'by grating'.

augur /**aw**gər/ > *verb* be a sign of (a likely outcome). > *noun* (in ancient Rome) a religious official who interpreted the significance of natural signs.
USAGE – do not confuse **augur** with **auger** (a tool used for boring).
SYNONYMS – *verb* betoken, bode, herald, signal.
ORIGIN – Latin, 'diviner'.

augury /**aw**gyəri/ > *noun* (pl. **auguries**) **1** an omen. **2** the interpretation of omens.

August > *noun* the eighth month of the year.
ORIGIN – named after *Augustus* Caesar, the first Roman emperor.

august /aw**gust**/ > *adjective* inspiring respect and admiration.
SYNONYMS – distinguished, exalted, illustrious, venerable.
ORIGIN – Latin *augustus* 'consecrated, venerable'.

Augustan /aw**gus**tən/ > *adjective* **1** relating to the reign of the Roman emperor Augustus (27 BC–AD 14), a notable period of Latin literature. **2** relating to a classical style of 17th- and 18th-century English literature. > *noun* a writer of the Augustan age.

Augustinian /awgə**stin**iən/ > *adjective* **1** relating to St Augustine (354–430). **2** relating to a religious order observing a rule derived from St Augustine's writings. > *noun* a member of an Augustinian order.

auk /awk/ > *noun* a short-winged black and white diving seabird of a family including the guillemot and puffin.
ORIGIN – Old Norse.

auld /awld/ > *adjective* Scottish form of **OLD**.
IDIOMS – **auld lang syne** times long past (literally 'old long since').

aumbry /**awm**bri/ > *noun* (pl. **aumbries**) a small recess or cupboard in the wall of a church.
ORIGIN – Latin *armarium* 'closet'.

au naturel /ō natyoo**rel**/ > *adjective & adverb* in the most simple or natural way.
ORIGIN – French.

aunt > *noun* the sister of one's father or mother or the wife of one's uncle.
COMBINATIONS – **Aunt Sally** (pl. **Aunt Sallies**) **1** a game in which players throw sticks or balls at a wooden dummy. **2** an easy target for criticism.
ORIGIN – Old French *ante*, from Latin *amita*.

auntie (also **aunty**) > *noun* (pl. **aunties**) informal **1** an aunt. **2** (**Auntie**) Brit. the BBC.

au pair /ō **pair**/ > *noun* a foreign girl employed to help with housework and childcare in exchange for board and lodging.
ORIGIN – French, 'on equal terms'.

aura /**aw**rə/ > *noun* (pl. **auras** or **aurae** /**aw**ree/) **1** the distinctive atmosphere or quality associated with someone or something. **2** a supposed invisible force surrounding a living creature.
SYNONYMS – **1** air, feeling, mood, spirit.
ORIGIN – Greek, 'breeze, breath'.

aural /**aw**rəl/ > *adjective* relating to the ear or the sense of hearing.
DERIVATIVES – **aurally** *adverb*.
NOTE – the words **aural** and **oral** (which means 'spoken rather than written' or 'relating to the mouth') have the same pronunciation and this can be confusing. A distinctive pronunciation for **aural** has been proposed, in which the first syllable rhymes with *cow*, but it has not become standard.
ORIGIN – from Latin *auris* 'ear'.

auralise /**aw**rəlīz/ (also **auralize**) > *verb* **1** imagine or hear in the mind. **2** make aurally perceptible.

aurar plural of **EYRIR**.

aureole /**aw**riōl/ (also **aureola** /aw**ree**ələ/) > *noun* **1** (in paintings) a radiant circle surrounding a person to represent holiness. **2** a circle of light around the sun or moon.
ORIGIN – from Latin *aureola corona* 'golden crown'.

au revoir /ō rə**vwaar**/ > *exclamation* goodbye.
ORIGIN – French, 'to the seeing again'.

auricle /**aw**rik'l/ > *noun* **1** the external part of the ear. **2** an atrium of the heart.
ORIGIN – Latin *auricula* 'little ear'.

auricular /aw**rik**yoolər/ > *adjective* **1** relating to the ear or hearing. **2** relating to or shaped like an auricle.

aurochs /**aw**roks/ > *noun* (pl. same) a large extinct wild ox that was the ancestor of domestic cattle.
ORIGIN – German.

aurora /aw**ror**ə/ > *noun* (pl. **auroras** or **aurorae** /aw**ror**ee/) the northern lights (**aurora borealis**) or southern lights (**aurora australis**), streamers of coloured light seen in the sky near the earth's magnetic poles, caused by particles from the sun interacting with atoms in the upper atmosphere.
ORIGIN – Latin, 'dawn, goddess of the dawn'.

auscultation /awskəl**taysh**'n/ > *noun* listening to sounds from the heart, lungs, or other organs with a stethoscope.
ORIGIN – Latin, from *auscultare* 'listen to'.

auspice /**aw**spiss/ > *noun* archaic an omen.
IDIOMS – **under the auspices of** with the support or protection of.

---

wordpower facts

Auspice

Derived from Latin *auspicium*, which comes from *avis* 'bird' and *specere* 'to look', **auspice** is related to such words as **aviary** and **aviation**. It originally referred to the observation of the flight of birds, which was used in ancient Rome as a way of supposedly foretelling the future.

---

auspicious /aw**spi**shəss/ > *adjective* indicating a good chance of success; favourable.
DERIVATIVES – **auspiciously** *adverb*.
SYNONYMS – favourable, promising, propitious.

Aussie (also **Ozzie**) > *noun* (pl. **Aussies**) & *adjective* informal Australia or Australian.

austere /o**steer**/ > *adjective* (**austerer**, **austerest**) **1** severe or strict in appearance or manner. **2** lacking comforts and luxuries. **3** plain and simple in style; unadorned.
DERIVATIVES – **austerely** *adverb* **austerity** *noun*.
SYNONYMS – **1** dour, forbidding, sober, stern. **2** frugal, harsh, spartan, strict. **3** functional, plain, stark, unadorned.
ANTONYMS – **1** genial. **2** lavish.
ORIGIN – Latin *austerus*, from Greek *austēros* 'severe'.

austral /**aw**strəl/ > *adjective* technical of the southern hemisphere.
ORIGIN – Latin *australis*, from *Auster* 'the south, the south wind'.

Australasian /ostrə**layzh**'n, ostrə**lays**h'n/ > *adjective* relating to Australasia, a region consisting of Australia, New Zealand, and islands of the SW Pacific. > *noun* a person from Australasia.

Australian > *noun* a person from Australia. > *adjective* relating to Australia.

COMBINATIONS – **Australian Rules** a form of football played on an oval field with an oval ball by teams of eighteen players.

Australopithecus /ostrəlō**pith**ikəss/ > *noun* a genus of fossil primates with both ape-like and human characteristics, found in Pliocene and Lower Pleistocene deposits in Africa.

DERIVATIVES – **australopithecine** /ostrəlō**pith**iseen/ *noun* & *adjective*.

ORIGIN – from Latin *australis* 'southern' + Greek *pithēkos* 'ape'.

Austrian > *noun* a person from Austria. > *adjective* relating to Austria.

COMBINATIONS – **Austrian blind** a ruched blind extending part-way down a window.

autarchy /**aw**taarki/ > *noun* (pl. **autarchies**) **1** another term for AUTOCRACY. **2** variant spelling of AUTARKY.

autarky (also **autarchy**) > *noun* **1** economic independence or self-sufficiency. **2** an economically independent state or society.

DERIVATIVES – **autarkic** *adjective*.

ORIGIN – Greek *autarkeia*, from *autarkēs* 'self-sufficiency'.

auteur /ō**tör**/ > *noun* a film director regarded as the author of his or her films.

ORIGIN – French, 'author'.

authentic > *adjective* of undisputed origin; genuine.

DERIVATIVES – **authentically** *adverb* **authenticity** *noun*.

SYNONYMS – bona fide, genuine, real, valid.

ANTONYMS – fake.

ORIGIN – Greek *authentikos* 'principal, genuine'.

authenticate > *verb* prove or show to be authentic.

DERIVATIVES – **authentication** *noun* **authenticator** *noun*.

SYNONYMS – endorse, validate, verify, vouch for.

author > *noun* **1** a writer of a book or article. **2** a person who originates a plan or idea. > *verb* be the author of.

DERIVATIVES – **authoress** *noun* **authorial** /aw**thor**iəl/ *adjective* **authorship** *noun*.

SYNONYMS – **2** creator, founder, initiator, originator.

ORIGIN – Latin *auctor*, from *augere* 'increase, originate'.

authorise (also **authorize**) > *verb* give official permission for or approval to.

DERIVATIVES – **authorisation** *noun*.

SYNONYMS – allow, approve, permit, sanction.

COMBINATIONS – **Authorised Version** an

English translation of the Bible made in 1611, at the order of James I.

authoritarian /awthorri**tair**iən/ > *adjective* favouring or enforcing strict obedience to authority. > *noun* an authoritarian person.

DERIVATIVES – **authoritarianism** *noun*.

SYNONYMS – *adjective* autocratic, dictatorial, disciplinarian, illiberal.

ANTONYMS – permissive.

authoritative /aw**thorr**itətiv/ > *adjective* **1** reliable because true or accurate. **2** commanding and self-confident. **3** supported by authority; official.

DERIVATIVES – **authoritatively** *adverb* **authoritativeness** *noun*.

SYNONYMS – **1** dependable, reliable, sound, trustworthy. **2** assertive, assured, commanding, imposing.

ANTONYMS – **1** unreliable. **2** diffident.

authority > *noun* (pl. **authorities**) **1** the power or right to give orders and enforce obedience. **2** a person or organisation having official power. **3** recognised knowledge or expertise. **4** an authoritative person or source of information.

SYNONYMS – **1** command, control, jurisdiction, power.

autism /**aw**tiz'm/ > *noun* a mental condition characterised by great difficulty in communicating with others and in using language and abstract concepts.

DERIVATIVES – **autistic** *adjective* & *noun*.

ORIGIN – from Greek *autos* 'self'.

auto > *adjective* & *noun* short for AUTOMATIC.

auto-[1] (usu. **aut-** before a vowel) > *combining form* **1** self: *autocrat*. **2** one's own: *autograph*. **3** automatic; spontaneous: *autoxidation*.

ORIGIN – from Greek *autos* 'self'.

auto-[2] > *combining form* relating to cars: *autocross*.

ORIGIN – from AUTOMOBILE.

Autobahn /**aw**tōbaan/ > *noun* a motorway in a German-speaking country.

ORIGIN – German, from *Auto* 'motor car' + *Bahn* 'path, road'.

autobiography > *noun* (pl. **autobiographies**) an account of a person's life written by that person.

DERIVATIVES – **autobiographer** *noun* **autobiographic** *adjective* **autobiographical** *adjective*.

autochthon /aw**tok**thən/ > *noun* (pl. **autochthons** or **autochthones** /aw**tok**thəneez/) an indigenous inhabitant of a place.

ORIGIN – Greek, from *autos* 'self' + *khthōn* 'earth'.

autochthonous /aw**tok**thənəss/ > *adjective* **1** indigenous. **2** having always existed in its present location.

autoclave /**aw**təklayv/ > *noun* a strong container employed in processes using high

pressures and temperatures, e.g. steam sterilisation.

ORIGIN – from Greek *auto-* 'self' + Latin *clavus* 'nail' or *clavis* 'key' (because it is self-fastening).

autocracy /aw**tok**rəsi/ > *noun* (pl. **autocracies**) **1** a system of government by one person with absolute power. **2** a state governed in this way.

ORIGIN – from Greek *autos* 'self' + *kratos* 'power'.

autocrat > *noun* **1** a ruler who has absolute power. **2** a domineering person.

DERIVATIVES – **autocratic** *adjective* **autocratically** *adverb*.

autocue > *noun* trademark (in television) a device used as a prompt in which a script is projected on to a screen visible only to the speaker or performer.

auto-da-fé /awtōdaa**fay**/ > *noun* (pl. **autos-da-fé** /awtōzdaa**fay**/) the burning of a heretic by the Spanish Inquisition.

ORIGIN – Portuguese, 'act of the faith'.

autodidact /**aw**tōdidakt/ > *noun* a self-taught person.

DERIVATIVES – **autodidactic** *adjective*.

auto-erotic > *adjective* relating to sexual excitement generated by stimulating one's own body.

DERIVATIVES – **auto-eroticism** *noun*.

autogenic /awtə**jenn**ik/ > *adjective* technical self-generated.

autogenous /aw**toj**inəss/ > *adjective* **1** arising from within or from a thing itself. **2** (of welding) done either without a filler or with a filler of the same metal as the pieces being welded.

autogiro (also **autogyro**) > *noun* (pl. **autogiros**) a form of aircraft with unpowered rotors and a propeller.

ORIGIN – Spanish, from *auto-* 'self' + *giro* 'gyration'.

autograph > *noun* **1** a person's signature written for an admirer or friend. **2** a manuscript or musical score in an author's or composer's own handwriting. > *verb* write one's signature on.

DERIVATIVES – **autographic** *adjective*.

ORIGIN – from Greek *autographos* 'written with one's own hand'.

autoharp > *noun* a kind of zither on which chords may be played by damping selected strings.

autoimmune > *adjective* (of disease) caused by antibodies or lymphocytes produced against substances naturally present in the body.

autolysis /aw**toll**ississ/ > *noun* Biology the destruction of cells or tissues by their own enzymes.

DERIVATIVES – **autolytic** *adjective*.

automate > *verb* convert (a process or facility) to operation by automatic equipment.

DERIVATIVES – **automation** *noun*.

COMBINATIONS – **automated teller machine** a machine that provides cash and other banking services on insertion of a special card.

automatic > *adjective* **1** operating with little or no direct human control. **2** (of a vehicle) using gears that change by themselves according to speed and acceleration. **3** (of a firearm) self-loading and able to fire continuously. **4** done or occurring without conscious thought. **5** (of a penalty) imposed inevitably as a result of a fixed rule. > *noun* an automatic machine, vehicle, or device.

DERIVATIVES – **automatically** *adverb* **automaticity** *noun*.

SYNONYMS – *adjective* **4** instinctive, involuntary, knee-jerk, unthinking.

COMBINATIONS – **automatic pilot** a device for keeping an aircraft on a set course. **automatic writing** writing said to be produced by a spiritual, occult, or subconscious means.

ORIGIN – Greek *automatos* 'acting by itself'.

automatism /awtommətiz'm/ > *noun* Psychiatry action which does not involve conscious thought or intention.

automaton /awtommət'n/ > *noun* (pl. **automata** /awtommətə/ or **automatons**) **1** a moving mechanical device resembling a human being. **2** a machine which operates according to coded instructions.

automobile > *noun* chiefly N. Amer. a motor car.

automotive /awtəmōtiv/ > *adjective* relating to motor vehicles.

autonomic /awtənommik/ > *adjective* relating to the part of the nervous system that controls bodily functions not consciously directed, e.g. breathing, circulation, and digestion.

autonomous > *adjective* self-governing or independent.

DERIVATIVES – **autonomously** *adverb*.

autonomy /awtonnəməss/ > *noun* **1** self-government. **2** freedom of action.

ORIGIN – Greek *autonomia*, from *autonomos* 'having its own laws'.

autopilot > *noun* short for **automatic pilot**.

autopsy /awtopsi/ > *noun* (pl. **autopsies**) an examination of a dead body to discover the cause of death or the extent of disease.

ORIGIN – Greek *autopsia*, from *autoptēs* 'eyewitness'.

autoroute > *noun* a French motorway.

ORIGIN – French.

auto-suggestion > *noun* the hypnotic or subconscious adoption of an idea which one has originated oneself.

autumn > *noun* chiefly Brit. the season after summer and before winter.

DERIVATIVES – **autumnal** *adjective*.

ORIGIN – Latin *autumnus*.

auxiliary /awgzillyəri/ > *adjective* providing supplementary or additional help and support. > *noun* (pl. **auxiliaries**) an auxiliary person or thing.

COMBINATIONS – **auxiliary verb** a verb used to form the tenses, moods, and voices of other verbs (e.g. *be*, *do*, and *have*).

ORIGIN – Latin *auxiliarius*, from *auxilium* 'help'.

avail > *verb* **1** (**avail oneself of**) use or take advantage of. **2** help or benefit. > *noun* use or benefit: *our scheming was to no avail*.

ORIGIN – Latin *valere* 'be strong, be of value'.

available > *adjective* **1** able to be used or obtained. **2** not otherwise occupied.

DERIVATIVES – **availability** *noun*.

SYNONYMS – **1** accessible, obtainable. **2** at one's disposal, free, unoccupied, vacant.

avalanche /avvəlaansh/ > *noun* **1** a mass of snow and ice falling rapidly down a mountainside. **2** an overwhelming deluge.

ORIGIN – French (Alpine dialect).

avant-garde /avvoN gaard/ > *adjective* (in the arts) new and experimental. > *noun* (**the avant-garde**) avant-garde ideas or artists.

DERIVATIVES – **avant-gardism** *noun* **avant-gardist** *noun*.

ORIGIN – French, 'vanguard'.

avarice > *noun* extreme greed for wealth or material gain.

DERIVATIVES – **avaricious** *adjective*.

SYNONYMS – cupidity, greed, rapacity.

ORIGIN – from Latin *avarus* 'greedy'.

avast /əvaast/ > *exclamation* Nautical stop; cease.

ORIGIN – Dutch *hou'vast* 'hold fast!'

avatar /avvətaar/ > *noun* **1** chiefly Hinduism a deity appearing in bodily form on earth. **2** an incarnation or embodiment of something.

ORIGIN – Sanskrit, 'descent'.

Ave Maria /aavay məreeə/ > *noun* a prayer to the Virgin Mary, used in Catholic worship.

ORIGIN – the opening words in Latin, 'hail, Mary!'

avenge > *verb* inflict harm in return for (a wrong).

DERIVATIVES – **avenger** *noun*.

ORIGIN – Old French *avengier*, from Latin *vindicare* 'vindicate'.

avenue > *noun* **1** a broad road or path. **2** a means of approach.

ORIGIN – from French *avenir* 'arrive, approach'.

aver /əver/ > *verb* (**averred**, **averring**) formal assert to be the case.

ORIGIN – Old French *averer*, from Latin *verus* 'true'.

average > *noun* **1** the result obtained by adding several amounts together and then dividing the total by the number of amounts. **2** a usual amount or level. > *adjective* **1** constituting an average. **2** usual or ordinary. **3** mediocre. > *verb* **1** amount to or achieve as an average. **2** calculate the average of.

ORIGIN – French *avarie* 'damage to ship or cargo', from Arabic; the modern sense arose from the equitable sharing of liability for losses at sea between the owners of the vessel and the cargo.

averse > *adjective* (**averse to**) strongly disliking or opposed to.

USAGE – do not confuse **averse** with **adverse**, which means 'preventing success or development; unfavourable'. It is correct to say *I am not averse to helping out*, not *I am not adverse to helping out*.

aversion > *noun* a strong dislike or disinclination.

DERIVATIVES – **aversive** *adjective*.

avert > *verb* **1** turn away (one's eyes, face, or thoughts). **2** prevent or ward off (an undesirable occurrence).

ORIGIN – Latin *avertere*, from *ab-* 'from' + *vertere* 'to turn'.

avian /ayviən/ > *adjective* relating to birds.

ORIGIN – from Latin *avis* 'bird'.

aviary /ayviəri/ > *noun* (pl. **aviaries**) a large enclosure for keeping birds in.

aviation > *noun* the activity of operating and flying aircraft.

ORIGIN – French, from Latin *avis* 'bird'.

aviator > *noun* dated a pilot.

aviculture /ayvikulchər/ > *noun* the keeping and breeding of birds.

DERIVATIVES – **aviculturist** *noun*.

avid > *adjective* keenly interested or enthusiastic.

DERIVATIVES – **avidity** *noun* **avidly** *adverb*.

SYNONYMS – eager, fervent, passionate, wholehearted.

ORIGIN – Latin *avidus*, from *avere* 'crave'.

avionics > *plural noun* (usu. treated as sing.) electronics used in aviation.

avocado > *noun* (pl. **avocados**) a pear-shaped fruit with a rough skin, pale green flesh, and a large stone.

ORIGIN – Spanish, from Nahuatl.

avocation /avvəkaysh'n/ > *noun* a hobby or minor occupation.

ORIGIN – Latin, from *avocare* 'call away'.

avocet /avvəset/ > *noun* a long-legged wading bird with an upturned bill.

ORIGIN – French, from Italian *avosetta*.

avoid > *verb* **1** keep away or refrain from. **2** prevent from doing or happening.

DERIVATIVES – **avoidable** *adjective* **avoidably** *adverb* **avoidance** *noun*.

SYNONYMS – **1** circumvent, dodge, evade, refrain from, steer clear of.

ORIGIN – Old French *evuider* 'clear out, get rid of'.

avoirdupois /**av**vərdəpoyz/ > *noun* a system of weights based on a pound of 16 ounces or 7,000 grains. Compare with TROY.
ORIGIN – from Old French *aveir de peis* 'goods of weight'.

avow > *verb* assert or confess openly.
DERIVATIVES – **avowal** *noun* **avowed** *adjective*.
ORIGIN – Old French *avouer* 'acknowledge', from Latin *advocare* 'summon in defence'.

avuncular /əˈvʊŋkyoolər/ > *adjective* like an uncle in being friendly towards a younger person.
ORIGIN – from Latin *avunculus* 'maternal uncle'.

AWACS /**ay**waks/ > *abbreviation* airborne warning and control system.

await > *verb* wait for.

awake > *verb* (past **awoke**; past participle **awoken**) **1** stop sleeping. **2** make or become active again. > *adjective* not asleep.

awaken > *verb* **1** awake. **2** rouse (a feeling).
DERIVATIVES – **awakening** *noun*.

award > *verb* give as an official payment, compensation, or prize to. > *noun* **1** something awarded. **2** the action of awarding something.
SYNONYMS – *verb* bestow, confer, give, grant. *noun* grant, honour, prize.
ORIGIN – Old French *awarder*, variant of *esguarder* 'consider, ordain', of Germanic origin; related to WARD.

aware > *adjective* having knowledge or perception of a situation or fact.
DERIVATIVES – **awareness** *noun*.
SYNONYMS – cognisant, conscious, informed, mindful.
ANTONYMS – oblivious, unaware.

awash > *adjective* covered or flooded with water.

away > *adverb* **1** to or at a distance. **2** into an appropriate place for storage. **3** towards or into non-existence. **4** constantly, persistently, or continuously. > *adjective* (of a sports fixture) played at the opponents' ground.

awe > *noun* a feeling of great respect mixed with fear or wonder. > *verb* inspire with awe.
SYNONYMS – amazement, reverence, veneration, wonder.

aweigh > *adjective* Nautical (of an anchor) raised just clear of the seabed.

awesome > *adjective* **1** inspiring awe. **2** informal excellent.

SYNONYMS – **1** amazing, astounding, breathtaking, formidable, spectacular.

awful > *adjective* **1** very bad or unpleasant. **2** used for emphasis: *an awful lot*. **3** archaic inspiring awe.
DERIVATIVES – **awfully** *adverb* **awfulness** *noun*.

awhile > *adverb* for a short time.

awkward > *adjective* **1** hard to do or deal with. **2** causing or feeling embarrassment. **3** causing inconvenience. **4** clumsy in movement or action.
SYNONYMS – **1** cumbersome, difficult, tricky, unwieldy. **3** inconvenient, inopportune, unfortunate.
ORIGIN – from obsolete *awk* 'clumsy'.

awl > *noun* a small pointed tool used for piercing holes.

awn /awn/ > *noun* Botany a stiff bristle growing from the ear or flower of barley, rye, and grasses.

awning > *noun* a sheet of canvas on a frame, sheltering a window or doorway.

awoke past of AWAKE.

awoken past participle of AWAKE.

AWOL /**ay**wol/ > *abbreviation* Military absent without official leave.

awry > *adverb* & *adjective* away from the expected course or position.

axe (US also **ax**) > *noun* **1** a heavy-bladed tool used for chopping wood. **2** (**the axe**) severe cost-cutting action. > *verb* cancel or dismiss suddenly and ruthlessly.
IDIOMS – **have an axe to grind** have a private reason for doing something.

axel /**ak**s'l/ > *noun* a jump in skating with one (or more) and a half turns in the air.
ORIGIN – named after the Norwegian skater *Axel* R. Paulsen (1885–1938).

axes plural of AXIS.

axial /**ak**sial/ > *adjective* forming, relating to, or around an axis.
DERIVATIVES – **axially** *adverb*.

axil /**ak**sil/ > *noun* Botany the upper angle where a leaf joins a stem.
ORIGIN – Latin *axilla*.

axiom /**ak**siəm/ > *noun* a proposition regarded as self-evidently true.
DERIVATIVES – **axiomatic** *adjective*.
ORIGIN – Greek *axiōma*, from *axios* 'worthy'.

axis > *noun* (pl. **axes** /**ak**seez/) **1** an imaginary line through a body, about which it rotates. **2** an imaginary line about which a regular figure is symmetrically arranged. **3** Mathematics

a fixed reference line for the measurement of coordinates. **4** (**the Axis**) the alliance between Germany and Italy in the Second World War.
ORIGIN – Latin, 'axle, pivot'.

axle /**ak**s'l/ > *noun* a rod or spindle passing through the centre of a wheel or group of wheels.
ORIGIN – Old Norse.

axolotl /**ak**səlott'l/ > *noun* a Mexican salamander which retains its aquatic newt-like larval form throughout life.
ORIGIN – Nahuatl, 'water servant'.

axon > *noun* the long thread-like part of a nerve cell.
ORIGIN – Greek *axōn* 'axis'.

ayah /**ī**ə/ > *noun* a nanny employed by Europeans in the former British Empire, especially India.
ORIGIN – Portuguese *aia* 'nurse'.

ayatollah /īəˈtollə/ > *noun* a Shiite religious leader in Iran.
ORIGIN – Arabic, 'token of God'.

aye[1] /ī/ (also **ay**) > *exclamation* archaic or dialect yes. > *noun* a vote for a proposal.

aye[2] /ay, ī/ > *adverb* archaic or Scottish always; still.
ORIGIN – Old Norse.

AZ > *abbreviation* Arizona.

azalea /əˈzayliə/ > *noun* a deciduous shrub with brightly coloured flowers.
ORIGIN – from Greek *azaleos* 'dry'.

Azerbaijani /azzərbīˈjaani/ > *noun* (pl. **Azerbaijanis**) a person from Azerbaijan. > *adjective* relating to Azerbaijan.

azimuth /**azz**iməth/ > *noun* Astronomy the horizontal direction of a celestial object, measured from the north or south point of the horizon.
ORIGIN – Arabic, 'the way, direction'.

azo dye /**ay**zō/ > *noun* Chemistry a synthetic dye whose molecule contains two adjacent nitrogen atoms between carbon atoms.
ORIGIN – from French *azote* 'nitrogen', from Greek *a-* 'without' + *zōē* 'life'.

Aztec /**az**tek/ > *noun* a member of the American Indian people dominant in Mexico before the Spanish conquest.
ORIGIN – Nahuatl, 'person of Aztlan', their legendary place of origin.

azure /**az**yər/ > *adjective* bright blue in colour like a cloudless sky. > *noun* a bright blue colour.
ORIGIN – Old French *azur*, from a Persian word meaning 'lapis lazuli'.

B¹ (also **b**) > *noun* (pl. **Bs** or **B's**) **1** the second letter of the alphabet. **2** denoting the second item in a set. **3** Music the seventh note of the diatonic scale of C major. **4** the human blood type (in the ABO system) containing the B antigen and lacking the A antigen.

COMBINATIONS – **B-movie** a low-budget film used as a supporting feature in a cinema programme. **B-side** the side of a pop single regarded as the less important one.

B² > *abbreviation* **1** (in chess) bishop. **2** black (used in describing grades of pencil lead). > *symbol* the chemical element boron.

b > *abbreviation* **1** (**b.**) born. **2** Cricket bowled by. **3** Cricket bye(s).

BA > *abbreviation* **1** Bachelor of Arts. **2** British Airways.

Ba > *symbol* the chemical element barium.

baa > *verb* (**baas**, **baaed**, **baaing**) (of a sheep or lamb) bleat. > *noun* the cry of a sheep or lamb.

baba /baabaa/ (also **rum baba**) > *noun* a rich sponge cake, soaked in rum-flavoured syrup.
ORIGIN – Polish, 'married peasant woman'.

baba ganoush /baabə ganoōsh/ (also **baba ghanouj** /baabə ganoōzh/) > *noun* a thick dip made from puréed aubergines, tahini, lemon, and garlic.
ORIGIN – Arabic, from *bābā* 'father' + *ghannūj*, perhaps a personal name.

babble > *verb* **1** talk rapidly in a foolish, excited, or incomprehensible way. **2** (of a stream) make a continuous murmur as the water flows over stones. > *noun* the sound of babbling.
DERIVATIVES – **babbler** *noun*.
SYNONYMS – *verb* **1** gabble, jabber, prate, prattle.

babe > *noun* **1** literary a baby. **2** informal a sexually attractive young woman.

babel /bayb'l/ > *noun* a confused noise made by a number of voices.
ORIGIN – from the biblical Tower of *Babel*, where God made the speech of the builders unintelligible.

baboon > *noun* a large ground-dwelling monkey with a long snout.
ORIGIN – first used in reference to a grotesque figure used in architecture: from Old French *babuin* or Latin *babewynus*.

babushka /bəbooshkə/ > *noun* (in Russia) an old woman or grandmother.
ORIGIN – Russian, 'grandmother'.

baby > *noun* (pl. **babies**) **1** a child or animal that is newly or recently born. **2** a timid or childish person. **3** informal a person with whom one is having a romantic relationship. **4** (**one's baby**) one's particular responsibility or achievement. > *adjective* comparatively small or immature of its kind. > *verb* (**babies**, **babied**) be overprotective towards.
IDIOMS – **be left holding the baby** informal be left with an unwelcome responsibility. **throw the baby out with the bathwater** discard something valuable along with things that are undesirable.
DERIVATIVES – **babyhood** *noun* **babyish** *adjective*.
COMBINATIONS – **baby blue** a pale shade of blue. **baby walker** a device for helping a baby learn to walk, consisting of a harness set into a frame on wheels.

baby boom > *noun* informal a temporary marked increase in the birth rate, especially the one following the Second World War.
DERIVATIVES – **baby boomer** *noun*.

baby doll > *noun* a girl or woman with pretty, childlike looks. > *adjective* referring to a style of women's clothing resembling that traditionally worn by a young child.

Babylonian /babilōniən/ > *noun* **1** an inhabitant of Babylon or Babylonia, an ancient city and kingdom in Mesopotamia. **2** the language of ancient Babylon. > *adjective* relating to Babylon or Babylonia.

babysit > *verb* (**babysitting**; past and past participle **babysat**) look after a child or children while the parents are out.
DERIVATIVES – **babysitter** *noun*.

baccalaureate /bakkəlawriət/ > *noun* **1** an examination qualifying candidates for higher education. **2** a university bachelor's degree.
ORIGIN – Latin *baccalaureatus*, from *baccalaureus* 'bachelor'.

baccarat /bakkəraa/ > *noun* a gambling card game in which players bet against a banker.
ORIGIN – French *baccara*.

bacchanal /bakkən'l/ chiefly literary > *noun* **1** a wild and drunken party or celebration. **2** a follower of Bacchus, the Greek or Roman god of wine.
ORIGIN – Latin *bacchanalis*, named after the god *Bacchus*.

Bacchanalia /bakkənayliə/ > *plural noun* (also treated as sing.) **1** the ancient Roman festival of the god Bacchus. **2** (**bacchanalia**) drunken revelry.
DERIVATIVES – **bacchanalian** *adjective*.

bacchant /bakkənt/ > *noun* (pl. **bacchants**; fem. **bacchante** /bəkanti/, pl. **bacchantes** /bəkanteez/) a priest or follower of Bacchus.

baccy > *noun* Brit. informal tobacco.

bachelor > *noun* **1** a man who has never been married. **2** a person who holds a first degree from a university.
DERIVATIVES – **bachelorhood** *noun*.
ORIGIN – Old French *bacheler* 'a young man aspiring to knighthood'.

bachelorette > *noun* N. Amer. a young unmarried woman.

bacillus /bəsilləss/ > *noun* (pl. **bacilli** /bəsillī/) a rod-shaped bacterium.
DERIVATIVES – **bacillary** *adjective*.
ORIGIN – Latin, 'little stick'.

back > *noun* **1** the rear surface of the human body from the shoulders to the hips. **2** the corresponding upper surface of an animal's body. **3** the side or part of something away from the viewer. **4** the side or part of an object that is not normally seen or used. **5** a player in a team game who plays in a defensive position behind the forwards. > *adverb* **1** in the opposite direction from that in which one is facing or travelling. **2** so as to return to an earlier or normal position. **3** into the past. **4** in return. > *verb* **1** give support to. **2** walk or drive backwards. **3** (of the wind) change direction anticlockwise around the points of the compass. The opposite of VEER. **4** bet money on (a person or animal) winning a race or contest. **5** (**back on** or **on to**) (of a building or other structure) have its back facing or adjacent to. **6** cover the back of. **7** provide musical accompaniment to (a singer or musician). > *adjective* **1** of or at the back. **2** in a remote or subsidiary position. **3** relating to the past.
WORDFINDER – dorsal (*on the back or upper side*), lumbar (*relating to the lower back*), posterior (*further back in position*), spinal (*relating to the backbone*), supine (*lying down on one's back*); lumbago (*back pain*).
IDIOMS – **back and forth** to and fro. **the back of beyond** a very remote place. **back down** concede defeat. **back off** draw back from confrontation. **back out** withdraw from a commitment. **back to front** Brit. with the back at the front and the front at the back. **back up** Computing make a spare copy of (data or a disk). **behind someone's back** without a person's knowledge. **get** (or **put**) **someone's back up** annoy someone. **put one's back into** approach (a task) with vigour. **turn one's back on** ignore; reject. **with one's back to** (or **up against**) **the wall** in a desperate situation.

DERIVATIVES – **backer** *noun* **backless** *adjective*.

COMBINATIONS – **back boiler** Brit. a boiler supplying hot water, built in behind a fireplace or integral to a gas fire.

backbeat > *noun* Music a strong accent on one of the normally unaccented beats of the bar.

back bench > *noun* (in the UK) any of the benches in the House of Commons occupied by MPs who do not hold office.

DERIVATIVES – **back-bencher** *noun*.

backbiting > *noun* malicious talk about an absent person.

backblocks > *plural noun* Austral./NZ land in the remote and sparsely inhabited interior.

backbone > *noun* 1 the spine. 2 the chief support of a system or organisation. 3 strength of character.

SYNONYMS – 3 fortitude, mettle, moral fibre, resolve.

back-breaking > *adjective* (of manual labour) physically demanding.

backchat > *noun* Brit. informal rude or impudent remarks.

backcloth > *noun* Brit. a backdrop.

backcomb > *verb* chiefly Brit. comb (the hair) towards the scalp to make it look thicker.

backdate > *verb* Brit. 1 make retrospectively valid. 2 put an earlier date to (a document or agreement) than the actual one.

back door > *noun* the door or entrance at the back of a building. > *adjective* (**back-door**) underhand; clandestine.

IDIOMS – **by** (or **through**) **the back door** in a clandestine or underhand way.

backdrop > *noun* 1 a painted cloth hung at the back of a theatre stage as part of the scenery. 2 the setting or background for a scene or event.

backfire > *verb* 1 (of a vehicle or its engine) undergo a mistimed explosion in the cylinder or exhaust. 2 (of a plan or action) go wrong, having the opposite effect to what was intended.

back-formation > *noun* a word that is formed from what appears to be its derivative (e.g. *edit* from *editor*).

backgammon > *noun* a board game in which two players move their pieces around triangular points according to the throw of dice.

ORIGIN – from *gammon*, apparently from Old English *gamen* or *gamenian* 'game'.

background > *noun* 1 part of a scene or description that forms a setting for the main figures or events. 2 information or circumstances that influence or explain something. 3 a person's education, experience, and social circumstances. 4 a persistent low level of radiation, noise, etc. present in a particular environment. 5 Computing tasks or processes running on a computer that do not need input from the user.

backhand > *noun* (in racket sports) a stroke played with the back of the hand facing in the direction of the stroke. > *verb* strike with a backhanded blow or stroke.

backhanded > *adjective* 1 made with the back of the hand facing in the direction of movement. 2 indirect or ambiguous: *a backhanded compliment*.

backhander > *noun* 1 a backhand stroke or blow. 2 Brit. informal a bribe.

backhoe (Brit. also **backhoe loader**) > *noun* a mechanical digger with a bucket attached to a hinged boom.

backing > *noun* 1 support. 2 a layer of material that forms or strengthens the back of something. 3 (especially in popular music) accompaniment to the main singer.

COMBINATIONS – **backing track** a recorded musical accompaniment.

backlash > *noun* 1 a strong and adverse reaction by a large number of people. 2 recoil or degree of play arising between parts of a mechanism.

SYNONYMS – 1 counteraction, reaction, retaliation.

backlist > *noun* a publisher's list of books published before the current season and still in print.

backlog > *noun* an accumulation of matters needing to be dealt with.

backlot > *noun* an outdoor area in a film studio where large exterior sets are made and some outside scenes are filmed.

backpack > *noun* a rucksack. > *verb* travel or hike carrying one's belongings in a rucksack.

DERIVATIVES – **backpacker** *noun*.

back passage > *noun* Brit. euphemistic a person's rectum.

back-pedal > *verb* 1 move the pedals of a bicycle backwards in order to brake. 2 hastily reverse one's previous action or opinion.

back room > *noun* a place where secret planning work is done. > *adjective* (**back-room**) relating to secret work or planning.

backscratching > *noun* informal mutual exchange of favours or help.

back-seat driver > *noun* informal a passenger in a car who gives the driver unwanted advice about the driving.

backside > *noun* informal a person's bottom.

backslapping > *noun* the action of offering hearty congratulations or praise.

backslash > *noun* a backward-sloping diagonal line (\).

backslide > *verb* (past **backslid**; past participle **backslid** or **backslidden**) relapse into bad ways.

DERIVATIVES – **backslider** *noun* **backsliding** *noun*.

backspace > *noun* a key on a typewriter or computer keyboard used to move the carriage or cursor backwards. > *verb* move a typewriter carriage or computer cursor backwards.

backspin > *noun* a backward spin given to a moving ball, causing it to stop more quickly or rebound at a steeper angle.

back-stabbing > *noun* the action of criticising someone while pretending to be friendly. > *adjective* behaving in such a way.

backstage > *adverb* in or to the area behind the stage in a theatre. > *adjective* relating to this area in a theatre.

backstairs > *plural noun* 1 stairs at the back or side of a building. 2 (before another noun) underhand; clandestine: *backstairs deals*.

backstitch > *noun* a method of sewing with stitches formed end to end. > *verb* sew using backstitch.

backstreet > *noun* 1 a minor street. 2 (before another noun) secret, especially because illegal.

backstroke > *noun* a swimming stroke performed on the back with the arms lifted out of the water in a backward circular motion.

back-to-back > *adjective* 1 chiefly Brit. (of houses) built in a terrace backing on to another terrace, with a wall or a narrow alley between. 2 following consecutively.

backtrack > *verb* 1 retrace one's steps. 2 reverse one's previous position or opinion.

back-up > *noun* 1 support. 2 a person or thing held in reserve. 3 Computing the procedure for making a spare copy of data.

backward > *adjective* 1 directed behind or to the rear. 2 having made less progress than is normal or expected. > *adverb* variant of BACKWARDS.

IDIOMS – **not backward in** not lacking the confidence to do.

DERIVATIVES – **backwardly** *adverb* **backwardness** *noun*.

backwards (also **backward**) > *adverb* 1 in the direction of one's back. 2 back towards the starting point. 3 in reverse of the usual direction or order.

WORDFINDER – palindrome (*word or sentence that reads the same backwards*), reciprocate (*move backwards and forwards*), recoil (*spring backwards*), regardant (*Heraldry, looking backwards*), retroflex (*turned backwards*), retrograde (*moving backwards*).

IDIOMS – **bend over backwards** informal make every effort to be fair or helpful. **know backwards** be entirely familiar with.

backwash > *noun* receding waves flowing outwards behind a ship.

backwater > *noun* 1 a part of a river not reached by the current, where the water is stagnant. **2** a place or state in which no development is taking place.

backwoods > *plural noun* chiefly N. Amer. **1** remote uncleared forest land. **2** a remote or sparsely inhabited region.

COMBINATIONS – **backwoodsman** chiefly N. Amer. an inhabitant of backwoods.

backyard > *noun* **1** Brit. a yard at the back of a house or other building. **2** N. Amer. a back garden. **3** (**one's own backyard**) informal the area close to where one lives.

bacon > *noun* salted or smoked meat from the back or sides of a pig.

IDIOMS – **bring home the bacon** informal achieve material success.

ORIGIN – Old French.

bacteria plural of BACTERIUM.

bactericide /bak**tee**risīd/ > *noun* a substance which kills bacteria.

DERIVATIVES – **bactericidal** *adjective*.

bacteriological > *adjective* **1** relating to bacteriology or bacteria. **2** relating to germ warfare.

bacteriology > *noun* the study of bacteria.

DERIVATIVES – **bacteriologist** *noun*.

bacterium > *noun* (pl. **bacteria**) a member of a large group of microscopic single-celled organisms which have cell walls but lack an organised nucleus, and include many kinds which can cause disease.

WORDFINDER – bacillus (*rod-shaped bacterium*), coccus (*spherical bacterium*), sepsis, septicaemia (*presence of bacteria in tissues or blood*); *kinds of bacteria:* campylobacter, chlamydia, clostridium, E. (= Escherichia) coli, legionella, listeria, meningococcus, pneumococcus, rickettsia, salmonella, shigella, staphylococcus, streptococcus, vibrio.

DERIVATIVES – **bacterial** *adjective*.

USAGE – **bacteria** is plural; the singular is **bacterium**. A disease can be caused *by bacteria* or *by a bacterium*, but not *by a bacteria*.

ORIGIN – Greek *baktērion* 'little rod' (because the first ones to be discovered were rod-shaped).

Bactrian camel > *noun* the two-humped camel, native to central Asia.

ORIGIN – named after *Bactria*, an ancient empire in central Asia.

bad > *adjective* (**worse**, **worst**) **1** of poor quality or a low standard. **2** creating a situation that is unwelcome or unpleasant. **3** (of something causing pain, danger, etc.) severe or serious. **4** offending moral standards or accepted conventions. **5** (**bad for**) harmful to. **6** injured, ill, or diseased. **7** (of food) decayed. **8** guilty; ashamed. **9** (**badder**, **baddest**) informal, chiefly N. Amer. good; excellent.

IDIOMS – **too bad** informal regrettable but unable to be changed.

DERIVATIVES – **badness** *noun*.

SYNONYMS – **1** defective, inferior, poor, unsatisfactory. **2** disagreeable, undesirable, unpleasant, unwelcome. **3** intense, serious, severe. **4** immoral, offensive, sinful, wicked. **5** damaging, deleterious, detrimental, disadvantageous, harmful.

ANTONYMS – good; agreeable, beneficial, virtuous.

COMBINATIONS – **bad blood** ill feeling. **bad debt** a debt that cannot be recovered. **bad faith** intent to deceive. **bad form** behaviour that offends against social conventions. **bad hair day** informal, chiefly US a day on which everything goes wrong. **bad-mouth** informal criticise maliciously. **bad-tempered** easily angered.

ORIGIN – perhaps from Old English *bǣddel* 'hermaphrodite, womanish man'.

baddy (also **baddie**) > *noun* (pl. **baddies**) informal a villain in a book, film, etc.

bade /bayd, bad/ past of BID[2].

badge > *noun* a small flat object sewn or pinned to one's clothing in order to display identification, affiliation, etc., or as a decoration.

badger > *noun* a heavily built nocturnal mammal, typically having a grey and black coat and a white-striped head. > *verb* repeatedly and annoyingly ask (someone) to do something.

ORIGIN – perhaps from BADGE, with reference to its distinctive head markings.

badinage /**badd**inaazh/ > *noun* witty conversation.

ORIGIN – French, from *badiner* 'to joke'.

badlands > *plural noun* heavily eroded land on which little can grow or be grown.

badly > *adverb* (**worse**, **worst**) **1** in an unsatisfactory or incompetent way. **2** severely; seriously. **3** very much.

IDIOMS – **badly off** poor.

badminton > *noun* a game with rackets in which a shuttlecock is hit back and forth across a net.

ORIGIN – named after *Badminton* in SW England, where the game was first played.

baffle > *verb* totally bewilder. > *noun* a device used to restrain or regulate the flow of sound, light, gas, or a fluid.

DERIVATIVES – **bafflement** *noun* **baffling** *adjective*.

SYNONYMS – *verb* bemuse, bewilder, confound, perplex, puzzle.

ORIGIN – perhaps related to French *bafouer* 'ridicule'.

bag > *noun* **1** a flexible container with an opening at the top. **2** (**bags**) loose folds of skin under a person's eyes. **3** (**bags of**) informal, chiefly Brit. plenty of. **4** informal an unpleasant or unattractive woman. **5** (**one's bag**) informal one's particular interest or taste. > *verb* (**bagged**, **bagging**) **1** put in a bag. **2** succeed in killing or catching (an animal). **3** succeed in obtaining. **4** (of clothes) form loose bulges. **5** Austral. informal criticise.

IDIOMS – **bags** (or **bags I**) Brit. informal a child's expression used to make a claim to something. **in the bag** informal as good as secured.

DERIVATIVES – **bagful** *noun* **bagger** *noun*.

COMBINATIONS – **bag lady** informal a homeless woman who carries her possessions in shopping bags.

bagasse /bə**gass**/ > *noun* the dry pulpy residue left after the extraction of juice from sugar cane.

ORIGIN – French, from Spanish *bagazo* 'pulp'.

bagatelle /baggə**tel**/ > *noun* **1** a game in which small balls are hit into numbered holes on a board. **2** something unimportant.

ORIGIN – Italian *bagatella*.

bagel /**bayg**'l/ > *noun* a dense, ring-shaped bread roll that is simmered before baking.

ORIGIN – Yiddish *beygel*.

baggage > *noun* **1** personal belongings packed in suitcases for travelling. **2** experiences or long-held opinions perceived as encumbrances: *emotional baggage*.

ORIGIN – Old French *bagage*, from *baguer* 'tie up' or *bagues* 'bundles'.

baggy > *adjective* (**baggier**, **baggiest**) **1** (of clothing) loose and hanging in folds. **2** (of eyes) with folds of puffy skin below them. > *noun* (**baggies**) loose, wide-legged trousers or shorts.

DERIVATIVES – **baggily** *adverb* **bagginess** *noun*.

SYNONYMS – **1** full, loose, roomy, voluminous.

ANTONYMS – **1** tight.

bagman > *noun* **1** Brit. informal, dated a travelling salesman. **2** US & Austral. informal an agent who collects or distributes the proceeds of illicit activities.

bagpipe > *noun* a musical instrument with reed pipes that are sounded by wind squeezed from a bag.

WORDFINDER – chanter (*pipe on which the melody is played*), drone (*pipe sounding a continuous low note*), pibroch (*elaborate Scottish music for bagpipes*), skirl (*shrill sound of bagpipes*), uillean pipes (*Irish bagpipes played using bellows worked by the elbow*).

DERIVATIVES – **bagpiper** *noun*.

baguette /ba**get**/ > *noun* a long, narrow French loaf.

ORIGIN – French, from Italian *bacchetto* 'little rod'.

Baha'i /baa**hī**/ (also **Bahai**) > *noun* (pl. **Baha'is**) **1** a religion founded in Persia in the 19th century, emphasising the essential oneness of humankind and of all religions and seeking world peace. **2** an adherent of the Baha'i faith.

ORIGIN – Persian, from an Arabic word meaning 'splendour'.

Bahamian /bəˈhaymiən/ > *noun* a person from the Bahamas. > *adjective* relating to the Bahamas.

Bahraini /baaˈrayni/ > *noun* a person from Bahrain. > *adjective* relating to Bahrain.

baht /baat/ > *noun* (pl. same) the basic monetary unit of Thailand, equal to 100 satangs.

ORIGIN – Thai.

Bahutu plural of **HUTU**.

bail[1] > *noun* **1** the temporary release of an accused person awaiting trial, sometimes on condition that a sum of money is lodged to guarantee their appearance in court. **2** money paid by or for such a person as security. > *verb* release or secure the release of (an accused person) on payment of bail.

IDIOMS – **go** (or **stand**) **bail** act as surety for an accused person. **jump bail** informal fail to appear for trial after being released on bail.

ORIGIN – Old French, 'custody, jurisdiction'.

bail[2] > *noun* **1** Cricket either of the two crosspieces bridging the stumps. **2** a bar on a typewriter or computer printer which holds the paper steady. **3** a bar separating horses in an open stable. **4** Austral./NZ a framework for securing the head of a cow during milking. > *verb* Austral./NZ **1** secure (a cow) during milking. **2** confront with intent to rob. **3** detain in conversation.

ORIGIN – Old French *baile* 'palisade, enclosure'.

bail[3] (Brit. also **bale**) > *verb* **1** scoop water out of (a ship or boat). **2** (**bail out**) make an emergency parachute descent from an aircraft. **3** (**bail out**) rescue (someone or something) from a difficulty.

ORIGIN – French *baille* 'bucket'.

bailey > *noun* (pl. **baileys**) the outer wall of a castle, or the area enclosed by this.

ORIGIN – probably from Old French *baile* (see **BAIL**[2]).

Bailey bridge > *noun* a prefabricated lattice steel bridge designed for rapid assembly, especially in military operations.

ORIGIN – named after the English engineer Sir Donald *Bailey* (1901–85).

bailiff > *noun* **1** chiefly Brit. a sheriff's officer who serves writs, seizes property to clear rent arrears, and carries out arrests. **2** Brit. the agent of a landlord.

ORIGIN – Old French *baillif*, from Latin *bajulus* 'carrier, manager'.

bailiwick /ˈbayliwik/ > *noun* Law the district or jurisdiction of a bailiff.

ORIGIN – from **BAILIFF** + Old English *wick* 'dwelling place'.

Baily's beads > *plural noun* Astronomy a string of bright points seen at the edge of the darkened moon at the beginning or end of

totality in an eclipse of the sun, caused by the uneven lunar surface.

ORIGIN – named after the English astronomer Francis *Baily* (1774–1844).

bain-marie /baNmərˈee/ > *noun* (pl. **bains-marie** or **bain-maries** pronunc. same) a pan of hot water in which a cooking container is placed for slow cooking.

ORIGIN – French, 'bath of Maria' (*Maria* is said to be the name of an alchemist).

bairn > *noun* chiefly Scottish & N. English a child.

bait > *noun* **1** food put on a hook or in a trap to entice fish or other animals. **2** variant spelling of **BATE**. > *verb* **1** taunt or tease. **2** set dogs on (a trapped or restrained animal). **3** put bait on or in.

IDIOMS – **rise to the bait** react to a provocation exactly as intended.

ORIGIN – Old Norse.

baiza /ˈbīzaa/ > *noun* (pl. same or **baizas**) a monetary unit of Oman, equal to one thousandth of a rial.

baize > *noun* a felt-like material, typically green, used for covering billiard and card tables.

---

wordpower facts

Baize

Despite the fact that it is generally green in colour today, **baize** is from the French word *bai* 'chestnut-coloured', presumably from the original colour of the cloth. *Bai* is also the root of the English word **bay**, used to describe a brown horse with black mane and tail. For another example of a word denoting colour that has changed its meaning, see **AUBURN**.

---

bake > *verb* **1** cook (food) by dry heat in an oven. **2** heat, especially so as to dry or harden. **3** informal be or become extremely hot in the sun or in hot weather. > *noun* a dish consisting of a number of ingredients mixed together and baked.

baked Alaska > *noun* a dessert consisting of sponge cake and ice cream in a meringue covering, cooked briefly in a hot oven.

baked beans > *plural noun* baked haricot beans, typically cooked in tomato sauce and canned.

Bakelite > *noun* trademark an early brittle form of plastic.

ORIGIN – named after Leo H. *Baekeland* (1863–1944), the Belgian-born American chemist who invented it.

baker > *noun* a person whose trade is making bread and cakes.

IDIOMS – **baker's dozen** a group of thirteen. [ORIGIN – from the bakers' former

custom of adding an extra loaf to a dozen sold to a retailer.]

DERIVATIVES – **bakery** *noun*.

Bakewell tart > *noun* Brit. a baked open tart consisting of a pastry case lined with jam and filled with almond sponge cake.

ORIGIN – named after the town of *Bakewell* in Derbyshire.

baking powder > *noun* a mixture of sodium bicarbonate and cream of tartar, used as a raising agent in baking.

baking soda > *noun* sodium bicarbonate.

baklava /ˈbakləvə/ > *noun* a Middle Eastern dessert made of filo pastry filled with chopped nuts and soaked in honey.

ORIGIN – Turkish.

baksheesh /bakˈsheesh/ > *noun* (in some eastern countries and the Indian subcontinent) a small sum of money given as alms, a tip, or a bribe.

ORIGIN – Persian.

balaclava > *noun* a close-fitting woollen hat covering the head and encircling the neck.

ORIGIN – named after the village of *Balaclava* in the Crimea: the balaclava was worn originally by soldiers in the Crimean War.

balalaika /baləˈlīkə/ > *noun* a Russian musical instrument like a guitar with a triangular body and three strings.

ORIGIN – Russian.

balance > *noun* **1** an even distribution of weight ensuring stability. **2** mental or emotional stability. **3** a condition in which different elements are equal or in the correct proportions. **4** an apparatus for weighing, especially one with a beam and central pivot. **5** a preponderance. **6** a figure representing the difference between credits and debits in an account. > *verb* **1** be or put in a steady position. **2** compare the value of (one thing) with another. **3** establish equal or appropriate proportions of elements in.

WORDFINDER – Libra (*constellation and zodiac sign, the Balance*).

IDIOMS – **balance of payments** the difference in total value between payments into and out of a country over a period. **balance of power 1** a situation in which states of the world have roughly equal power. **2** the power held by a small group when larger groups are of equal strength. **balance of trade** the difference in value between a country's imports and exports. **be** (or **hang**) **in the balance** be in an uncertain or critical state. **on balance** when all factors are taken into consideration.

DERIVATIVES – **balancer** *noun*.

SYNONYMS – **1** equilibrium, stability. **2** calmness, composure, equanimity, stasis. **3** comparability, correspondence, equivalence.

ANTONYMS – imbalance, instability.

COMBINATIONS – **balance sheet** a written statement of the assets, liabilities, and capital of a business.

ORIGIN – from Latin *libra bilanx* 'balance having two scale-pans'.

balboa /balbōə/ > *noun* the basic monetary unit of Panama, equal to 100 centésimos.

ORIGIN – named after the Spanish explorer Vasco Núñez de *Balboa* (1475–1519).

balcony > *noun* (pl. **balconies**) **1** an enclosed platform on the outside of a building. **2** the highest tier of seats in a theatre or cinema.

DERIVATIVES – **balconied** *adjective*.

ORIGIN – Italian *balcone*.

bald > *adjective* **1** having a scalp wholly or partly lacking hair. **2** (of an animal) not covered by the usual fur, hair, or feathers. **3** (of a tyre) having the tread worn away. **4** plain or blunt: *the bald facts*.

DERIVATIVES – **balding** *adjective* **baldish** *adjective* **baldly** *adverb* **baldness** *noun*.

COMBINATIONS – **bald eagle** a white-headed North American eagle, the national bird of the US.

baldachin /bawldəkin/ (also **baldaquin** /bawldəkin/) > *noun* a ceremonial canopy over an altar, throne, or doorway.

ORIGIN – from Italian *Baldacco* 'Baghdad', place of origin of the brocade originally used.

balderdash > *noun* senseless talk or writing.

baldric /bawldrik/ > *noun* historical a belt for a sword, worn over one shoulder and reaching down to the opposite hip.

ORIGIN – Old French *baudre*.

bale¹ > *noun* a large wrapped or bound bundle of paper, hay, or cotton. > *verb* make up into bales.

DERIVATIVES – **baler** *noun*.

ORIGIN – probably from Dutch.

bale² > *noun & verb* Brit. variant spelling of **BAIL³**.

baleen > *noun* whalebone.

COMBINATIONS – **baleen whale** any of the kinds of whale that have plates of whalebone in the mouth for straining plankton from the water.

ORIGIN – Latin *balaena* 'whale'.

baleful > *adjective* **1** menacing. **2** having a harmful effect.

DERIVATIVES – **balefully** *adverb*.

SYNONYMS – **1** menacing, sinister, threatening. **2** destructive, injurious, malign.

ORIGIN – Old English *balu* 'evil'.

Balinese /baalineez/ > *noun* (pl. same) a person from Bali. > *adjective* relating to Bali.

balk > *verb & noun* chiefly US variant spelling of **BAULK**.

Balkan /bawlkən/ > *adjective* relating to the countries occupying the part of south-east Europe bounded by the Adriatic, Ionian, Aegean, and the Black Seas. > *noun* (**the Balkans**) the Balkan countries.

ORIGIN – Turkish.

Balkanise (also **Balkanize**) > *verb* divide (a region or body) into smaller mutually hostile states or groups.

DERIVATIVES – **Balkanisation** *noun*.

balky /bawlki/ > *adjective* (**balkier, balkiest**) chiefly N. Amer. awkward; uncooperative.

ball¹ > *noun* **1** a solid or hollow sphere, especially one that is kicked, thrown, or hit in a game. **2** a single throw or kick of the ball in a game. **3** N. Amer. a game played with a ball, especially baseball. > *verb* squeeze or form into a ball.

IDIOMS – **the ball is in your court** it is up to you to make the next move. **the ball of the foot** the rounded part of the foot at the base of the big toe. **keep one's eye on** (or **take one's eye off**) **the ball** keep (or fail to keep) one's attention focused on the matter in hand. **on the ball** alert to new ideas, methods, and trends. **play ball** informal cooperate. **start** (or **get** or **set**) **the ball rolling** make a start.

COMBINATIONS – **ball bearing 1** a bearing in which the parts are separated by a ring of small metal balls which reduce friction. **2** a ball used in such a bearing. **ballboy** (or **ballgirl**) a boy (or girl) who retrieves balls that go out of play during a tennis match or baseball game. **ball game 1** a game played with a ball. **2** informal a situation that is completely different from a previous one.

ORIGIN – Old Norse.

ball² > *noun* a formal social gathering for dancing.

IDIOMS – **have a ball** informal enjoy oneself greatly.

ORIGIN – French *bal* 'a dance'.

ballad > *noun* **1** a poem or song telling a popular story. **2** a slow sentimental or romantic song.

DERIVATIVES – **balladeer** *noun* **balladry** *noun*.

ORIGIN – from Provençal *balada* 'dance, song to dance to'.

ball-and-socket joint > *noun* a joint in which a rounded end lies in a socket, allowing movement in all directions.

ballast > *noun* **1** a heavy substance carried by a ship or hot air balloon to keep it stable. **2** gravel or coarse stone used to form the base of a railway track or road. **3** a passive component used in an electric circuit to moderate changes in current.

ballcock > *noun* a valve which automatically tops up a cistern when liquid is drawn from it.

ballerina > *noun* a female ballet dancer.

ORIGIN – from Italian *ballerino* 'dancing master'.

ballet > *noun* **1** an artistic dance form performed to music, using formalised steps and gestures. **2** a creative work of this form or the music written for it.

WORDFINDER – arabesque, bourrée, entrechat, glissade, jeté, pirouette, plié (*ballet steps and movements*), barre (*bar used during exercises*), choreography (*design of dance movements*), pas de deux (*dance for two*), pas seul (*dance for one*), pointe (*tips of the toes*), répétiteur (*ballet tutor*), tutu (*ballet dancer's bodice and skirt*).

DERIVATIVES – **balletic** *adjective*.

ORIGIN – Italian *balletto* 'a little dance'.

balletomane /balitōmayn/ > *noun* a ballet enthusiast.

ballistic /bəlistik/ > *adjective* **1** relating to projectiles or their flight. **2** moving under the force of gravity only.

IDIOMS – **go ballistic** informal fly into a rage.

COMBINATIONS – **ballistic missile** a missile which is initially powered and guided but falls under gravity on to its target.

ORIGIN – from Greek *ballein* 'to throw'.

ballistics > *plural noun* (**treated as sing.**) the science of projectiles and firearms.

ballocks > *plural noun* variant spelling of **BOLLOCKS**.

balloon > *noun* **1** a small rubber sac which is inflated and used as a toy or a decoration. **2** a large bag filled with hot air or gas to make it rise in the air, from which is suspended a basket for carrying passengers. **3** a rounded outline in which the words or thoughts of characters in a comic strip or cartoon are written. > *verb* **1** swell out in a spherical shape. **2** Brit. lob or be lobbed high in the air.

IDIOMS – **when the balloon goes up** informal when the action or trouble starts.

DERIVATIVES – **ballooning** *noun* **balloonist** *noun*.

COMBINATIONS – **balloon angioplasty** Medicine surgical widening of a blood vessel by means of a catheter incorporating a small inflatable balloon.

ORIGIN – French *ballon* or Italian *ballone* 'large ball'.

ballot > *noun* **1** a procedure by which people vote secretly on an issue. **2** (**the ballot**) the total number of votes cast in such a process. **3** a lottery held to decide the allocation of tickets or other things among a number of applicants. > *verb* (**balloted, balloting**) **1** obtain a secret vote from (members). **2** cast one's vote on a particular issue.

ORIGIN – first used with reference to a ball placed in a container to register a vote: from Italian *ballotta* 'little ball'.

ballpark chiefly N. Amer. > *noun* **1** a baseball ground. **2** informal a particular area or range. > *adjective* informal approximate: *the ballpark figure*.

ballpoint pen > *noun* a pen with a tiny ball as its writing point.

ballroom > *noun* a large room for formal dancing.

COMBINATIONS – **ballroom dancing** formal social dancing in couples.

balls vulgar slang > *plural noun* **1** testicles. **2** courage; nerve. **3** (treated as sing.) Brit. nonsense; rubbish. > *verb* (**balls up**) bungle.

balls-up > *noun* Brit. vulgar slang a bungled task or action.

ballsy > *adjective* (**ballsier**, **ballsiest**) informal bold and confident.

bally /**bal**i/ > *adjective & adverb* Brit. old-fashioned euphemism for BLOODY (in sense 3).

ballyhoo informal > *noun* extravagant publicity or fuss. > *verb* (**ballyhoos**, **ballyhooed**) chiefly N. Amer. praise extravagantly.

balm > *noun* **1** a fragrant ointment used to heal or soothe the skin. **2** something that soothes or heals.

SYNONYMS – **1** emollient, liniment, ointment, salve, unguent. **2** comfort, palliative, relief, solace.

ORIGIN – Latin *balsamum* 'balsam'.

balmy > *adjective* (**balmier**, **balmiest**) (of the weather) pleasantly warm.

SYNONYMS – clement, gentle, mild, temperate.

baloney /bə**lō**ni/ (also **boloney**) > *noun* informal nonsense.

ORIGIN – perhaps from BOLOGNA.

balsa /**bol**sə/(also **balsa wood**) > *noun* very lightweight timber obtained from a tropical American tree, used chiefly for making models and rafts.

ORIGIN – Spanish, 'raft'.

balsam /**bol**səm/ > *noun* **1** an aromatic resin obtained from certain trees and shrubs, used in perfumes and medicines. **2** a herbaceous plant grown for its pink or purple flowers.

DERIVATIVES – **balsamic** *adjective*.

ORIGIN – Greek *balsamon*.

balsamic vinegar > *noun* dark, sweet Italian vinegar that has been matured in wooden barrels.

balti /**bol**ti/ > *noun* (pl. **baltis**) a type of Pakistani cuisine in which the food is cooked in a small two-handled pan.

ORIGIN – Urdu, 'pail'.

Baltic > *adjective* **1** relating to the Baltic sea or those states on its eastern shores. **2** relating to the Baltic languages. > *noun* an Indo-European branch of languages consisting of Lithuanian, Latvian, and Old Prussian.

ORIGIN – Latin *Balthae* 'dwellers near the Baltic Sea'.

baluster /**bal**əstər/ > *noun* a short pillar forming part of a series supporting a rail.

ORIGIN – Italian *balaustro*, from *balaustra* 'wild pomegranate flower' (because of the resemblance to part of the flower).

balustrade /balə**strayd**/ > *noun* a railing supported by balusters.

DERIVATIVES – **balustraded** *adjective*.

bambino /bam**bee**nō/ > *noun* (pl. **bambini** /bam**bee**ni/) a baby or young child.

ORIGIN – Italian, diminutive of *bambo* 'silly'.

bamboo > *noun* a giant tropical grass with hollow woody stems.

COMBINATIONS – **bamboo shoot** a young shoot of bamboo, eaten as a vegetable.

ORIGIN – Malay.

bamboozle /bam**bōō**z'l/ > *verb* informal **1** cheat or deceive. **2** confuse.

ban¹ > *verb* (**banned**, **banning**) officially prohibit. > *noun* an official prohibition.

SYNONYMS – *verb* bar, disallow, embargo, forbid, outlaw, proscribe, veto. *noun* embargo, interdict, moratorium, proscription, veto.

ORIGIN – Old English, 'summon by a public proclamation'.

ban² /baan/ > *noun* (pl. **bani** /**baa**ni/) a monetary unit of Romania, equal to one hundredth of a leu.

ORIGIN – Romanian.

banal /bə**naal**/ > *adjective* tediously unoriginal or ordinary.

DERIVATIVES – **banality** (pl. **banalities**) *noun* **banally** *adverb*.

SYNONYMS – clichéd, hackneyed, pedestrian, trite, vapid.

ANTONYMS – striking.

ORIGIN – French, from *ban* 'proclamation, summons' (originally meaning 'compulsory', hence 'common').

banana > *noun* a long curved fruit with yellow skin and soft flesh, which grows on a tropical or subtropical tree-like plant.

IDIOMS – **go** (or **be**) **bananas** informal become (or be) mad or angry.

COMBINATIONS – **banana republic** derogatory a small politically unstable country whose economy is dependent on a single export controlled by foreign concerns. **banana split** a sweet dish made with bananas cut down the middle and filled with ice cream, sauce, and nuts.

ORIGIN – Mande (an African language).

band¹ > *noun* **1** a flat, thin strip or loop of material used for reinforcement, to hold things together, or as decoration. **2** a stripe or strip of a different colour or composition from its surroundings: *a band of cloud.* **3** a range of values or a specified category within a series: *the lower-rate tax band.* **4** a range of frequencies or wavelengths in a spectrum. **5** a belt or strap transmitting motion between two wheels or pulleys. > *verb* **1** fit a band on or round. **2** mark with a band of a different colour or composition. **3** allocate to a range or category.

DERIVATIVES – **banding** *noun*.

COMBINATIONS – **bandbox** a circular cardboard box for carrying hats. **bandsaw** a saw consisting of an endless moving steel belt with a serrated edge. **bandwidth 1** a range of frequencies, especially one used in telecommunications. **2** the transmission capacity of a computer network or other telecommunication system.

ORIGIN – Old English, related to BIND.

band² > *noun* **1** a small group of musicians and vocalists who play pop, jazz, or rock music. **2** a group of musicians who play brass, wind, or percussion instruments. **3** a group of people with a common purpose or sharing a common feature. > *verb* form a group for a common purpose.

SYNONYMS – *noun* **1** combo, ensemble, group. **2** ensemble, orchestra. **3** circle, company, set; informal bunch. *verb* collaborate, join forces, team up, unite.

COMBINATIONS – **bandstand** a covered outdoor platform for a band to play on.

ORIGIN – Old French *bande*.

bandage > *noun* a strip of material used to bind up a wound or to protect an injury. > *verb* bind with a bandage.

ORIGIN – French, from *bande* 'band'.

bandanna /ban**dann**ə/ > *noun* a large coloured handkerchief or neckerchief.

ORIGIN – Hindi.

B. & B. > *abbreviation* bed and breakfast.

bandeau /**ban**dō/ > *noun* (pl. **bandeaux** /**ban**dōz/) **1** a narrow band worn round the head to hold the hair in position. **2** a woman's strapless top consisting of a band of fabric fitting around the bust.

ORIGIN – Old French *bandel* 'small band'.

banderilla /bandə**ril**yə/ > *noun* a decorated dart thrust into a bull's neck or shoulders during a bullfight.

ORIGIN – Spanish, 'small banner'.

banderillero /bandərily**air**ō/ > *noun* (pl. **banderillos**) a bullfighter who uses banderillas.

ORIGIN – Spanish.

bandicoot /**ban**dikōōt/ > *noun* a mainly insectivorous marsupial native to Australia and New Guinea.

COMBINATIONS – **bandicoot rat** an Asian rat that is a destructive pest.

ORIGIN – Telugu (an Indian language), 'pig-rat'.

bandit > *noun* (pl. **bandits** or **banditti** /ban**dee**ti/) a member of a gang of armed robbers.

DERIVATIVES – **banditry** *noun*.

SYNONYMS – brigand, highwayman, marauder, outlaw.

ORIGIN – from Italian *bandito* 'banned'.

bandog > *noun* a fighting dog bred for its strength and ferocity.

ORIGIN – because the dog was originally kept on a chain or 'band'.

bandolier /bandə**leer**/ (also **bandoleer**)

> *noun* a shoulder belt with loops or pockets for cartridges.

ORIGIN – French *bandoulière*, perhaps from Spanish *banda* 'sash' or Catalan *bandoler* 'bandit'.

bandwagon > *noun* an activity or cause that has suddenly become fashionable or popular: *the company is jumping on the Green bandwagon.*

ORIGIN – from the former use of a wagon to carry a band in a parade.

bandy¹ > *adjective* (**bandier, bandiest**) (of a person's legs) curved outwards so that the knees are wide apart.

ORIGIN – perhaps from obsolete *bandy* 'curved hockey stick'.

bandy² > *verb* (**bandies, bandied**) (usu. **bandy about** or **around**) pass on or mention (an idea, term, or rumour) in a casual or uninformed way.

IDIOMS – **bandy words** exchange angry remarks.

ORIGIN – first meaning 'pass a ball to and fro': perhaps from French *bander* 'take sides at tennis'.

bane > *noun* a cause of great distress or annoyance.

SYNONYMS – blight, burden, scourge.

bang > *noun* 1 a sudden loud sharp noise. 2 a sudden painful blow. 3 (**bangs**) chiefly N. Amer. a fringe of hair cut straight across the forehead. > *verb* 1 strike or put down forcefully and noisily. 2 make or cause to make a bang. 3 vulgar slang (of a man) have sexual intercourse with. > *adverb* informal, chiefly Brit. exactly: *bang on time.*

IDIOMS – **bang goes —** informal a plan or hope is suddenly destroyed. **bang on** Brit. informal exactly right. **bang on about** informal talk at tedious length about. **bang up** Brit. informal imprison. **bang-up** N. Amer. informal excellent. **with a bang** suddenly or spectacularly.

banger > *noun* chiefly Brit. 1 informal a sausage. 2 informal an old car. 3 a loud explosive firework.

Bangladeshi /bangglədeshi/ > *noun* (pl. same or **Bangladeshis**) a person from Bangladesh. > *adjective* relating to Bangladesh.

bangle > *noun* a rigid ornamental band worn around the arm.

ORIGIN – Hindi.

bani plural of **BAN²**.

banish > *verb* 1 make (someone) leave a place, especially as an official punishment. 2 get rid of; drive away.

DERIVATIVES – **banishment** *noun.*

SYNONYMS – 1 cast out, deport, drive out, evict, exile, oust. 2 allay, dismiss, dispel.

ORIGIN – Old French *banir.*

banister* (also **bannister**) > *noun* 1 (also **banisters**) the uprights and handrail at the side of a staircase. 2 a single upright at the side of a staircase.

*SPELLING – the usual spelling is **banister**, with one *n*.

ORIGIN – from **BALUSTER**.

banjax /banjaks/ > *verb* informal ruin or incapacitate.

ORIGIN – Anglo-Irish.

banjo > *noun* (pl. **banjos** or **banjoes**) a stringed musical instrument with a circular body and a long neck.

DERIVATIVES – **banjoist** *noun.*

ORIGIN – from a black American alteration of *bandore*, meaning a kind of lute.

bank¹ > *noun* 1 the land alongside or sloping down to a river or lake. 2 a long, raised mound or mass: *a mud bank.* 3 a set of similar things grouped together in rows. 4 a tier of oars. > *verb* 1 heap or form into a mass or mound. 2 (of an aircraft or vehicle) tilt sideways in making a turn. 3 build (a road, railway, or sports track) higher at the outer edge of a bend.

SYNONYMS – *noun* 1 brink, edge, shore, side. 2 embankment, ridge. *verb* 1 heap up, mound. 2 lean, list, slant, tip.

wordpower facts
Bank

The two words **bank¹** and **bank²** are related to each other and also to **bench**. **Bank** meaning 'land beside water' derives from the Old Norse word *bakki*, although the sense 'set of similar things grouped together in rows' entered English from French *banc* 'bench': the sense arose from the use of the word to refer to the bench occupied by the men pulling each oar in a galley, and hence to a line of oars set at the same height. **Bank** meaning 'financial organisation' is from Latin *banca* 'bench', and originally referred to a table on which a moneylender carried out his business, the forerunner of the modern financial institution.

bank² > *noun* 1 an organisation offering financial services, especially the safekeeping of customers' money until required and making loans at interest. 2 a stock or supply available for use: *a blood bank.* 3 a site or container where something may be left for recycling: *a paper bank.* 4 (**the bank**) the store of money or tokens held by the banker in some gambling or board games. > *verb* 1 deposit in a bank. 2 have an account at a bank. 3 (**bank on**) rely on.

IDIOMS – **break the bank** informal cost more than one can afford.

COMBINATIONS – **bank card** a cheque card. **bank holiday** Brit. a public holiday, when banks are officially closed. **banknote** a piece of paper money issued by a central bank. **bank rate** another term for *base rate* or *discount rate*.

bankable > *adjective* certain to bring profit and success.

DERIVATIVES – **bankability** *noun.*

banker¹ > *noun* 1 a person who manages or owns a bank. 2 the person who keeps the bank in some gambling or board games.

banker² > *noun* Austral./NZ informal a river that is flooded to the top of its banks.

banking¹ > *noun* the business conducted or services offered by a bank.

banking² > *noun* an embankment or artificial bank.

bankroll > *noun* N. Amer. 1 a roll of banknotes. 2 available funds. > *verb* informal support financially.

bankrupt > *adjective* 1 declared in law unable to pay one's debts. 2 completely lacking in a particular good quality or value: *morally bankrupt.* > *noun* a person legally declared as bankrupt. > *verb* reduce to a bankrupt state.

WORDFINDER – receiver (*official managing bankrupt business*), sequestrate (*take possession of assets of bankrupt person*).

DERIVATIVES – **bankruptcy** (pl. **bankruptcies**) *noun.*

ORIGIN – from Italian *banca rotta* 'broken bench'.

banksia /bangksiə/ > *noun* an evergreen Australian shrub with flowers resembling bottlebrushes.

ORIGIN – named after the English botanist Sir Joseph *Banks* (1743–1820).

banner > *noun* a long strip of cloth bearing a slogan or design, hung up or carried on poles. > *adjective* N. Amer. excellent; outstanding: *a banner year.*

ORIGIN – Old French *baniere.*

bannister > *noun* variant spelling of **BANISTER**.

bannock /bannək/ > *noun* Scottish & N. English a round, flat loaf.

banns > *plural noun* an announcement of an intended marriage read out in a parish church, allowing the opportunity for objections.

ORIGIN – plural of **BAN¹**.

banoffi pie /bənoffee/ (also **banoffee pie**) > *noun* a flan filled with bananas, toffee, and cream.

ORIGIN – from **BANANA** + **TOFFEE**.

banquet /bangkwit/ > *noun* an elaborate and formal meal for many people. > *verb* (**banqueted, banqueting**) entertain with a banquet.

ORIGIN – French, 'little bench'.

banquette /bangket/ > *noun* an upholstered bench along a wall.

ORIGIN – French, from Italian *banchetta* 'little bench'.

banshee /ban**shee**/ > *noun* (in Irish legend) a female spirit whose wailing warns of a death in a house.
ORIGIN – Old Irish *ben síde* 'woman of the fairies'.

bantam > *noun* a chicken of a small breed.
COMBINATIONS – **bantamweight** a weight in boxing and other sports between flyweight and featherweight.
ORIGIN – apparently named after the province of *Bantam* in Java.

banter > *noun* the good-humoured exchange of teasing remarks. > *verb* engage in banter.
SYNONYMS – *noun* badinage, chaff, raillery, repartee; formal persiflage. *verb* jest, joke.

Bantu /ban**too**/ > *noun* (pl. same or **Bantus**) 1 a member of a large group of peoples of central and southern Africa. 2 the group of languages spoken by these peoples.
USAGE – **Bantu** is a strongly offensive word in South Africa, especially if used of individual people, but is still used elsewhere to refer to the group of languages and their speakers collectively.
ORIGIN – Bantu, 'people'.

banyan /**ban**yən/ (also **banian**) > *noun* an Indian fig tree, whose branches produce aerial roots which later become new trunks.
ORIGIN – Gujarati, 'trader' (originally applied by Europeans to a tree under which traders had built a pagoda).

banzai /baan**zi**/ > *exclamation* a cry used by the Japanese when going into battle or in greeting their emperor. > *adjective* informal fierce and reckless.
ORIGIN – Japanese, 'ten thousand years (of life to you)'.

baobab /**bay**ōbab/ > *noun* a short African tree with a very thick trunk and large edible fruit.
ORIGIN – probably from an African language.

bap > *noun* Brit. a soft, round, flattish bread roll.

baptise (also **baptize**) > *verb* 1 administer baptism to. 2 give a name or nickname to.
ORIGIN – Greek *baptizein* 'immerse, baptise'.

baptism > *noun* the Christian rite of sprinkling a person with water or immersing them in it, symbolising purification and admission to the Christian Church.
WORDFINDER – catechumen (*a Christian preparing for baptism or confirmation*), chrism (*oil used for anointing in baptism*), font (*receptacle used for baptism*), sponsor (*godparent at a child's baptism*).
IDIOMS – **baptism of fire** a difficult experience undergone at the outset of a new undertaking.
DERIVATIVES – **baptismal** *adjective*.

Baptist > *noun* a member of a Protestant Christian denomination believing that baptism should be by total immersion and of adult believers only.

baptistery (also **baptistry**) > *noun* (pl. **baptisteries**) a building or part of a church used for baptism.

bar¹ > *noun* 1 a long rigid piece of wood, metal, etc. 2 a counter, room, or place where alcoholic drinks or refreshments are served. 3 a small shop or counter serving refreshments or providing a service: *a snack bar*. 4 a barrier or obstacle. 5 any of the short units into which a piece of music is divided, shown on a score by vertical lines. 6 (**the bar**) a partition in a court room, now usually imaginary, at which an accused person stands. 7 (**the Bar**) the profession of barrister. 8 (**the Bar**) Brit. barristers collectively. 9 Brit. a metal strip added to a medal as an additional distinction. > *verb* (**barred**, **barring**) 1 fasten with a bar or bars. 2 prohibit from doing something or going somewhere. > *preposition* chiefly Brit. except for.
IDIOMS – **be called** (or **go**) **to the Bar** Brit. be admitted as a barrister. **behind bars** in prison.
DERIVATIVES – **barred** *adjective*.
SYNONYMS – *noun* 2 inn; Brit. pub; US saloon; archaic hostelry, taproom, tavern. 4 barricade, barrier, impediment, obstacle, obstruction.
COMBINATIONS – **bar billiards** Brit. a form of billiards in which balls are struck into holes guarded by pegs. **bar chart** (also **bar graph**) a diagram in which different quantities are represented by rectangles of varying height. **bar code** a code in the form of a set of stripes of varying widths that can be read by a computer, printed on a product and identifying it for pricing and stock control. **barmaid** 1 a female bartender. 2 N. Amer. a waitress who serves drinks in a bar. **barman** chiefly Brit. a man who serves drinks in a bar or public house. **bartender** a person serving drinks at a bar.
ORIGIN – Old French *barre*.

bar² > *noun* a unit of pressure equivalent to a hundred thousand newtons per square metre.
ORIGIN – Greek *baros* 'weight'.

barathea /barrə**thee**ə/ > *noun* a fine woollen cloth.

barb > *noun* 1 a sharp projection near the end of an arrow, fish hook, etc., which is angled away from the main point so as to make extraction difficult. 2 a deliberately hurtful remark.
DERIVATIVES – **barbless** *adjective*.
ORIGIN – Latin *barba* 'beard'.

Barbadian /baar**bay**diən/ > *noun* a person from Barbados. > *adjective* relating to Barbados.

barbarian > *noun* 1 (in ancient times) a member of a people not belonging to the Greek, Roman, or Christian civilisations. 2 a person who behaves in a rough, uncivilised, or uncultured manner. > *adjective* 1 relating to the ancient barbarians. 2 behaving in an uncivilised manner; rough or uncultured.
SYNONYMS – *noun* 2 boor, brute, lout, oaf, ruffian. *adjective* 2 brutish, coarse, rough, uncivilised, uncultured.
ORIGIN – Old French *barbarien* or Latin *barbarus*, from Greek *barbaros* 'foreign'.

barbaric > *adjective* 1 savagely cruel. 2 primitive; unsophisticated.
DERIVATIVES – **barbarically** *adverb*.
SYNONYMS – 1 barbarous, brutal, cruel, savage. 2 primitive, savage, uncivilised, uncultured, unsophisticated.

barbarism > *noun* 1 extreme cruelty. 2 an uncivilised or primitive state. 3 a word or expression which is badly formed according to traditional rules, e.g. the word *breathalyser*, which is formed from two different languages (English and Greek).
DERIVATIVES – **barbarity** (pl. **barbarities**) *noun*.
SYNONYMS – 1 brutality, mercilessness, monstrousness, savagery.

barbarous > *adjective* 1 exceedingly cruel. 2 primitive; uncivilised.
DERIVATIVES – **barbarously** *adverb*.

barbecue > *noun* 1 an outdoor meal or party at which food is grilled on a rack over a charcoal fire. 2 a grill used at a barbecue. > *verb* (**barbecues**, **barbecued**, **barbecuing**) cook (food) on a barbecue.
COMBINATIONS – **barbecue sauce** a highly seasoned sauce containing vinegar, spices, and usually chillies.
ORIGIN – Spanish *barbacoa* 'wooden frame on posts', perhaps from Arawak.

barbed > *adjective* 1 having a barb or barbs. 2 (of a remark) deliberately hurtful.
SYNONYMS – 2 cutting, hurtful, mean, spiteful, wounding.
COMBINATIONS – **barbed wire** wire with clusters of short, sharp spikes set at intervals along it.

barbel /**baar**b'l/ > *noun* 1 a fleshy filament growing from the mouth or snout of certain fish. 2 a large freshwater fish with barbels hanging from the mouth.
ORIGIN – Latin *barbellus* 'small barbel', from *barba* 'beard'.

barbell /**baar**bel/ > *noun* a long metal bar to which discs of varying weights are attached at each end, used for weightlifting.

barber > *noun* a person who cuts men's hair and shaves or trims beards as an occupation. > *verb* cut or trim (a man's hair).
COMBINATIONS – **barbershop** a style of unaccompanied close harmony singing, typically for four male voices.

[ORIGIN – from the custom in the 16th and 17th centuries, to help pass the time spent at the barber's, of singing harmony to music provided by a lute.] **barber's pole** a red and white striped pole mounted outside a barber's shop as a business sign.

ORIGIN – Old French *barbe* 'beard'.

barberry > *noun* another term for BERBERIS.

barbican /baarbikən/ > *noun* a double tower above a gate or drawbridge of a castle or fortified city.

ORIGIN – Old French *barbacane*.

barbiturate /baarbityoorət/ > *noun* any of a class of sedative drugs related to a synthetic compound (**barbituric acid**) derived from uric acid.

ORIGIN – from *barbituric acid*, from German *Barbitursäure*, from the name *Barbara* + *Ursäure* 'uric acid'.

Barbour /baarbər/ (also **Barbour jacket**) > *noun* trademark a type of green waxed outdoor jacket.

ORIGIN – named after John *Barbour* & Sons Ltd., English clothing manufacturers.

bard[1] > *noun* **1** archaic or literary a poet, traditionally one reciting epics. **2** (**the Bard**) the English playwright William Shakespeare. **3** (**Bard**) the winner of a prize for Welsh verse at an Eisteddfod.

DERIVATIVES – **bardic** *adjective*.

ORIGIN – Celtic.

bard[2] > *verb* cover (meat or game) with rashers of fat bacon before roasting.

ORIGIN – from French *barde*, formerly also meaning 'armour for the breast of a warhorse'.

Bardolino /baardəleenō/ > *noun* a red wine from the Veneto region of Italy.

ORIGIN – Italian.

bare > *adjective* **1** not clothed or covered. **2** without the appropriate or usual covering or contents: *a big, bare room*. **3** without elaboration; basic: *the bare facts*. **4** very small or only just sufficient: *a bare majority*. > *verb* uncover and reveal.

IDIOMS – **with one's bare hands** without using tools or weapons.

DERIVATIVES – **barely** *adverb* **bareness** *noun*.

SYNONYMS – *adjective* **1** naked, nude. **2** empty, spartan, unadorned. *verb* expose, uncover, unmask, unveil.

COMBINATIONS – **bareback** on an unsaddled horse. **bareboat** (of a boat or ship) hired without a crew. **barefaced** shameless and undisguised.

barf > *verb* informal, chiefly N. Amer. vomit.

bargain > *noun* **1** an agreement made between people as to what each will do for the other. **2** a thing bought or offered for sale for a low price. > *verb* **1** negotiate the terms of an agreement. **2** (**bargain for** or **on**) be prepared for.

IDIOMS – **drive a hard bargain** press forcefully for a deal in one's favour. **into the bargain** in addition.

DERIVATIVES – **bargainer** *noun*.

SYNONYMS – *noun* **1** arrangement, deal, understanding. *verb* **1** barter, haggle, negotiate. **2** (**bargain for**) allow for, anticipate, envisage, expect.

ORIGIN – Old French *bargaine*.

barge > *noun* **1** a long flat-bottomed boat for carrying freight on canals and rivers. **2** a large ornamental boat used for pleasure or on ceremonial occasions. > *verb* **1** move forcefully or roughly. **2** (**barge in**) intrude on or interrupt a situation rudely or awkwardly.

ORIGIN – Old French, perhaps from Greek *baris* 'Egyptian boat'.

bargeboard > *noun* an ornamental board fixed to the gable end of a roof to hide the ends of the roof timbers.

ORIGIN – from *barge-* (used in terms relating to the gable of a building), perhaps from Latin *bargus* 'gallows'.

bargee /baarjee/ > *noun* chiefly Brit. a person in charge of or working on a barge.

bargepole > *noun* a long pole used to propel a barge and fend off obstacles.

IDIOMS – **would not touch with a bargepole** informal would refuse to have anything to do with.

barite > *noun* variant spelling of BARYTE.

baritone > *noun* **1** an adult male singing voice between tenor and bass. **2** (before another noun) denoting an instrument that is second lowest in pitch in its family: *a baritone sax*.

ORIGIN – Greek *barutonos*, from *barus* 'heavy' + *tonos* 'tone'.

barium /bairiəm/ > *noun* a soft, reactive metallic chemical element.

COMBINATIONS – **barium meal** a preparation containing barium sulphate, opaque to X-rays, which is swallowed so that the stomach or intestines can be studied radiologically.

ORIGIN – from BARYTE.

bark[1] > *noun* the sharp explosive cry of a dog, fox, or seal. > *verb* **1** give a bark. **2** utter (a command or question) abruptly or aggressively.

IDIOMS – **one's bark is worse than one's bite** one is not as ferocious as one seems. **be barking up the wrong tree** informal be pursuing a mistaken line of thought or course of action.

bark[2] > *noun* the tough protective outer sheath of the trunk and branches of a tree or woody shrub. > *verb* **1** strip the bark from. **2** scrape the skin off (one's shin) by accidentally hitting it.

WORDFINDER – angostura, cinchona, cinnamon, cork, mastic, sassafras (products obtained from bark), decorticate (remove the bark from), tannin (bitter substance in bark).

ORIGIN – Old Norse.

bark[3] > *noun* archaic or literary a ship or boat.

ORIGIN – variant of BARQUE.

barker > *noun* informal a tout at an auction or sideshow who calls out to passers-by to attract custom.

barking > *adjective* Brit. informal completely mad.

barley > *noun* a hardy cereal with coarse bristles extending from the ears, used chiefly in brewing and animal feed.

COMBINATIONS – **barley sugar** an amber-coloured sweet made of boiled sugar. **barley water** a drink made from water and a boiled barley mixture. **barley wine** a strong English ale.

barm > *noun* the froth on fermenting malt liquor.

bar mitzvah /baa mitsvə/ > *noun* the religious initiation ceremony of a Jewish boy who has reached the age of 13.

ORIGIN – Hebrew, meaning 'son of the commandment'.

barmy > *adjective* (**barmier, barmiest**) informal, chiefly Brit. extremely foolish; mad.

DERIVATIVES – **barmily** *adverb* **barminess** *noun*.

barn > *noun* a large farm building used for storage or for housing livestock.

COMBINATIONS – **barn dance 1** an informal social gathering for country dancing (originally held in a barn). **2** a dance for a number of couples moving round a circle. **barn owl** a pale-coloured owl with a heart-shaped face, typically nesting in farm buildings. **barnyard** N. Amer. a farmyard.

ORIGIN – Old English, 'barley house'.

barnacle /baarnək'l/ > *noun* a marine crustacean which attaches itself permanently to underwater surfaces.

DERIVATIVES – **barnacled** *adjective*.

COMBINATIONS – **barnacle goose** a goose with a white face and black neck, breeding in arctic tundra. [ORIGIN – from the former belief that the bird hatched from barnacles.]

ORIGIN – Latin *bernaca*.

barnet /baarnit/ > *noun* Brit. informal a person's hair.

ORIGIN – from rhyming slang *barnet fair* (a horse fair held at *Barnet*, Herts).

barney > *noun* (pl. **barneys**) Brit. informal a noisy quarrel.

barnstorm > *verb* chiefly N. Amer. **1** tour rural districts giving theatrical performances (formerly often in barns). **2** make a rapid tour as part of a political campaign.

DERIVATIVES – **barnstorming** *adjective*.

barograph > *noun* a barometer that records its readings on a moving chart.

barometer > *noun* **1** an instrument measuring atmospheric pressure, used especially in forecasting the weather. **2** an indicator of change: *new car registrations are a barometer of consumer confidence.*
DERIVATIVES – **barometric** *adjective.*
ORIGIN – from Greek *baros* 'weight'.

baron > *noun* **1** a member of the lowest order of the British nobility. **2** historical a person who held lands or property from the sovereign or an overlord. **3** a powerful person in business or industry: *a press baron.*
DERIVATIVES – **baronial** /bərōniəl/ *adjective.*
COMBINATIONS – **baron of beef** Brit. a joint of beef consisting of two sirloins joined at the backbone.
ORIGIN – Latin *baro* 'man, warrior'.

baronage > *noun* (treated as sing. or pl.) barons or nobles collectively.

baroness > *noun* **1** the wife or widow of a baron. **2** a woman holding the rank of baron.

baronet > *noun* a member of the lowest hereditary titled British order.
DERIVATIVES – **baronetcy** (pl. **baronetcies**) *noun.*

barony > *noun* (pl. **baronies**) the rank and estates of a baron.

baroque /bərok/ > *noun* a highly ornate and complex style of European architecture, art, and music of the 17th and 18th centuries. > *adjective* **1** in or relating to this style or period. **2** highly ornate and extravagant in style.

┌ wordpower facts ─
Baroque
The word **baroque** comes from Portuguese *barroco*, meaning 'irregularly shaped pearl'. It entered English from French in the mid 18th century as a derogatory term meaning 'grotesque, odd', and was first used to refer to the style of highly ornate architectural decoration which arose in Italy in the late Renaissance and which by the 18th century had fallen out of favour. Today **baroque** is the usual name for the dominant style of European art of the 17th and 18th centuries, between the mannerist and rococo periods.

barouche /bərōosh/ > *noun* historical a four-wheeled horse-drawn carriage with a collapsible hood over the rear half.
ORIGIN – Italian *baroccio* 'two-wheeled carriage'.

barque /baark/ > *noun* **1** a sailing ship in which the foremast and mainmast are square-rigged and the mizzenmast is rigged fore and aft. **2** literary a boat.
ORIGIN – Latin *barca* 'ship's boat'.

barrack[1] > *verb* provide (soldiers) with accommodation.
COMBINATIONS – **barrack-room lawyer** Brit. a person who speaks with apparent authority on subjects in which they are not qualified.

barrack[2] > *verb* **1** Brit. & Austral./NZ jeer loudly at (a performer or speaker). **2** (**barrack for**) Austral./NZ support and encourage.
SYNONYMS – **1** heckle, jeer at, taunt.
ORIGIN – probably from Northern Irish dialect.

barracks > *plural noun* (often treated as sing.) a large building or group of buildings for housing soldiers.
ORIGIN – Italian *baracca* or Spanish *barraca* 'soldier's tent'.

barracouta /barrəkōotə/ > *noun* (pl. same or **barracoutas**) **1** a long, slender fish of southern oceans, used as food. **2** NZ a long loaf of bread.
ORIGIN – alteration of **BARRACUDA**.

barracuda /barrəkōodə/ > *noun* (pl. same or **barracudas**) a large, slender predatory fish of tropical seas.

barrage /barraazh/ > *noun* **1** a concentrated artillery bombardment over a wide area. **2** an overwhelming succession of questions or complaints. **3** Brit. an artificial barrier across a river to control the water level. > *verb* bombard with questions or complaints.
COMBINATIONS – **barrage balloon** a large anchored balloon, typically with netting suspended from it, used as an obstacle to low-flying enemy aircraft.
ORIGIN – French, from *barrer* 'to bar'.

barramundi /barrəmundi/ > *noun* (pl. same or **barramundis**) a large, chiefly freshwater fish of Australia and SE Asia.
ORIGIN – probably from an Aboriginal language.

barre /baar/ > *noun* a horizontal bar at waist level used by ballet dancers as a support during exercises.
ORIGIN – French.

barrel > *noun* **1** a large cylindrical container bulging out in the middle and with flat ends. **2** a measure of capacity for oil and beer (36 imperial gallons for beer and 35 for oil). **3** a cylindrical tube forming part of an object such as a gun or a pen. > *verb* (**barrelled, barrelling;** US **barreled, barreling**) **1** informal, chiefly N. Amer. drive or move very fast. **2** put into a barrel or barrels.
WORDFINDER – cooper (*maker of barrels*), hogshead, keg, tun (*kinds of barrel*), hoop (*metal band around a barrel*), spigot (*plug for a barrel vent*), stave (*plank from which barrels are made*).

IDIOMS – **over a barrel** informal in a severely disadvantageous position.
COMBINATIONS – **barrel organ** a small pipe organ that plays a preset tune when a handle is turned. **barrel vault** Architecture a vault forming a half cylinder.
ORIGIN – Latin *barriclus* 'small cask'.

barren > *adjective* **1** (of land) too poor to produce vegetation. **2** (of a female animal) unable to bear young. **3** empty of meaning or value.
DERIVATIVES – **barrenness** *noun.*
SYNONYMS – **1** sterile, unproductive. **2** childless, infertile, sterile. **3** empty, futile, hollow, worthless.
ANTONYMS – **1,2** fertile, productive.
ORIGIN – Old French *barhaine*.

barrette /baret/ > *noun* a hairslide.
ORIGIN – French, 'small bar'.

barricade /barrikayd/ > *noun* an improvised barrier erected to block a road or entrance. > *verb* block or defend with a barricade.
ORIGIN – French, from Spanish *barrica* 'cask, barrel' (barrels being used to build the first barricades in 17th-century Paris); related to **BARREL**.

barrier > *noun* **1** an obstacle that prevents movement or access. **2** an obstacle to communication or progress: *a language barrier.*
SYNONYMS – **1** bar, barricade, fence, railing. **2** hindrance, impediment, obstacle.
COMBINATIONS – **barrier cream** Brit. a cream used to protect the skin from damage or infection. **barrier method** a method of contraception using a device or preparation which prevents sperm from reaching an ovum. **barrier reef** a coral reef close to the shore but separated from it by a channel of deep water.
ORIGIN – Old French *barriere*.

barring > *preposition* except for; if not for.

barrio /barriō/ > *noun* (pl. **barrios**) **1** (in a Spanish-speaking country) a district of a town. **2** (in the US) the Spanish-speaking quarter of a town or city.
ORIGIN – Spanish.

barrister > *noun* chiefly Brit. a lawyer who has the right to speak and argue a case in a higher court. Compare with **SOLICITOR**.
ORIGIN – from **BAR**[1].

barrow[1] > *noun* Brit. a two-wheeled handcart used by street traders.
ORIGIN – Old English, 'stretcher, bier'.

barrow[2] > *noun* Archaeology an ancient burial mound.

Barsac /baarsak/ > *noun* a sweet white wine from the district of Barsac in SW France.

Bart > *abbreviation* Baronet.

barter > *verb* exchange (goods or services) for other goods or services. > *noun* trading by bartering.
SYNONYMS – *verb* deal, exchange, swap.

ORIGIN – probably from Old French *barater* 'deceive'.

baryon /**barr**ion/ > *noun* Physics a subatomic particle with a mass equal to or greater than that of a proton, such as a nucleon.
ORIGIN – from Greek *barus* 'heavy'.

baryte /**barīt**/ (also **barytes** /bə**rī**teez/, **barite**) > *noun* a colourless or white mineral consisting of barium sulphate.
ORIGIN – earlier as *barytes*: from Greek *barus* 'heavy' + **-ITE**.

basal /**bays**'l/ > *adjective* forming or belonging to a base.
COMBINATIONS – **basal metabolic rate** the rate at which the body uses energy while at rest to maintain vital functions such as breathing and keeping warm.

basalt /**bass**awlt/ > *noun* a dark fine-grained volcanic rock that sometimes displays a columnar structure.
DERIVATIVES – **basaltic** /bə**sawl**tik/ *adjective*.
ORIGIN – Latin *basaltes*, from Greek *basanos* 'touchstone'.

bascule bridge /**bas**kyōōl/ > *noun* a type of bridge with a section which can be raised and lowered using counterweights.
ORIGIN – French *bascule* 'see-saw', from *battre* 'to bump' + *cul* 'buttocks'.

base¹ > *noun* **1** the lowest part or edge of something, especially the part on which it rests. **2** a foundation, support, or starting point: *the town's economic base collapsed.* **3** the main place where a person works or stays. **4** a centre of operations: *a military base.* **5** a main element or ingredient to which others are added. **6** Chemistry a substance capable of reacting with an acid to form a salt and water. **7** the root or stem of a word. **8** Mathematics a number used as the basis of a numeration scale. **9** Baseball each of the four stations that must be reached in turn to score a run. > *verb* **1** (**base on**) use as a foundation or starting-point for. **2** situate at a centre of operations.
IDIOMS – **get to first base** informal, chiefly N. Amer. achieve the first step towards one's objective. **touch base** informal briefly make or renew contact.
DERIVATIVES – **based** *adjective*.
SYNONYMS – *noun* **1** bottom, foot, support, stand. **2** basis, ground, premise, principle. **4** camp, headquarters, station. *verb* **2** locate, position, post, station.
COMBINATIONS – **base jump** a parachute jump from a fixed point, e.g. a high building or promontory. [ORIGIN – from *b*uilding, *a*ntenna-tower, *s*pan, *e*arth (denoting the types of structure used).] **base rate** the interest rate set by the Bank of England for lending to other banks, used as the basis for interest rates generally.
ORIGIN – Greek *basis* 'base, pedestal'.

base² > *adjective* **1** without moral principles; ignoble. **2** archaic of low social class. **3** (of coins) not made of precious metal.
DERIVATIVES – **basely** *adverb* **baseness** *noun*.
SYNONYMS – **1** ignoble, immoral, low, sordid, unprincipled.
COMBINATIONS – **base metal** a common non-precious metal such as copper, tin, or zinc.
ORIGIN – Latin *bassus* 'short'; early senses in English included 'low, short' and 'of inferior quality'.

baseball > *noun* a game between two teams played with a bat and ball on a diamond-shaped circuit of four bases, around all of which a batsman must run to score.
COMBINATIONS – **baseball cap** a cotton cap with a large peak.

baseless > *adjective* not based on fact; untrue.

baseline > *noun* **1** a minimum or starting point used for comparisons. **2** (in tennis, volleyball, etc.) the line marking each end of a court.

basement > *noun* a part of a building built partly or entirely below ground level.

bases plural of **BASE¹** and **BASIS**.

bash informal > *verb* **1** strike hard and violently. **2** (**bash out**) produce rapidly and carelessly. > *noun* **1** a heavy blow. **2** a party or social event. **3** Brit. an attempt: *she'll have a bash at anything.*
ORIGIN – perhaps a blend of **BANG** and **SMASH**.

bashful > *adjective* shy and easily embarrassed.
DERIVATIVES – **bashfully** *adverb* **bashfulness** *noun*.
SYNONYMS – diffident, reserved, reticent, shy, timid.
ANTONYMS – bold, confident.
ORIGIN – from obsolete *bash* 'make or become abashed'.

BASIC > *noun* a simple high-level computer programming language.
ORIGIN – from *Beginners' All-purpose Symbolic Instruction Code.*

basic > *adjective* **1** forming an essential foundation; fundamental. **2** consisting of the minimum required or offered, without elaboration or luxury: *the bedrooms are basic but comfortable.* **3** Chemistry containing or having the properties of a base; alkaline. > *noun* (**basics**) essential facts or principles.
SYNONYMS – **1** elementary, fundamental, key, primary. **2** limited, modest, rudimentary.
ANTONYMS – **1** secondary, unimportant.

basically > *adverb* **1** fundamentally. **2** in fact; essentially: *I basically did the same thing every day.*

basil > *noun* an aromatic plant of the mint family, used as a culinary herb.
ORIGIN – from Greek *basilikos* 'royal', from *basileus* 'king'.

basilica /bə**zill**ikə/ > *noun* **1** a large oblong building with double colonnades and an apse, used in ancient Rome as a law court or for public assemblies. **2** a Christian church of a similar plan.
ORIGIN – Latin, 'royal palace', from Greek *basilikos* 'royal'.

basilisk /**bazz**ilisk/ > *noun* **1** a mythical reptile with a lethal gaze or breath. **2** a long, slender Central American lizard, the male of which has a crest running from the head to the tail.
ORIGIN – Greek *basiliskos* 'little king, serpent'.

basin > *noun* **1** a large bowl or open container for preparing food or holding liquid. **2** a broadly circular valley or natural depression. **3** an area drained by a river and its tributaries. **4** an enclosed area of water for mooring boats.
ORIGIN – Latin *bacinus*, from *bacca* 'water container'.

basis > *noun* (pl. **bases** /**bay**seez/) **1** the foundation or underlying structure of a theory or process. **2** the way in which something is arranged or organised: *she needed coaching on a regular basis.*
SYNONYMS – **1** base, foundation, grounds, premise, principle. **2** arrangement, footing, system.
ORIGIN – Greek, 'step, pedestal'; related to **BASE¹**.

bask > *verb* **1** lie exposed to warmth and sunlight for pleasure. **2** (**bask in**) revel in (something pleasing).
SYNONYMS – **2** (**bask in**) lap up, revel in, savour, wallow in.
COMBINATIONS – **basking shark** a large shark which feeds on plankton and typically swims slowly close to the surface.

basket > *noun* **1** a container for holding or carrying things, made from interwoven strips of cane or wire. **2** Basketball a net fixed on a hoop, used as the goal. **3** a group, category, or range: *a basket of currencies.*
COMBINATIONS – **basket case** informal **1** a person who is incapacitated, especially one who is emotionally unstable. **2** something that is failing or functioning badly. [ORIGIN – US slang, denoting a soldier who had lost all four limbs.]
ORIGIN – Old French.

basketball > *noun* a team game in which goals are scored by throwing a ball through a netted hoop fixed at each end of the court.

basketry > *noun* **1** the craft of basket-making. **2** baskets collectively.

basmati rice /baz**maa**ti/ > *noun* a kind of long-grain Indian rice with a delicate fragrance.
ORIGIN – Hindi, 'fragrant'.

Basque /bask, baask/ > *noun* **1** a member of a people living in the western Pyrenees in France and Spain. **2** the language of this people.
ORIGIN – Latin *Vasco* 'inhabitant of Gascony' (in SW France).

basque /bask/ > *noun* a woman's close-fitting bodice, typically shaped to extend just below waist level.
ORIGIN – from BASQUE, referring to traditional Basque dress.

bas-relief /**bas**rileef/ > *noun* Art low relief moulding or carving.
ORIGIN – Italian *basso-rilievo*.

bass¹ /bayss/ > *noun* **1** the lowest adult male singing voice. **2** (before another noun) denoting the member of a family of instruments that is the lowest in pitch: *a bass clarinet*. **3** *informal* a bass guitar or double bass. **4** the low-frequency output of transmitted or reproduced sound.
DERIVATIVES – **bassist** *noun*.
COMBINATIONS – **bass clef** Music a clef placing F below middle C on the second-highest line of the stave.
ORIGIN – alteration of BASE².

bass² /bass/ > *noun* (pl. same or **basses**) a fish with a spiny dorsal fin, related to or resembling the perch.
ORIGIN – alteration of dialect *barse*.

basset (also **basset hound**) > *noun* a breed of sturdy hunting dog with a long body, short legs, and long, drooping ears.
ORIGIN – French, from *bas* 'low'.

bassinet /bassi**net**/ > *noun* a child's wicker cradle.
ORIGIN – French, 'little basin'.

basso /**bass**ō/ > *noun* (pl. **bassos** or **bassi** /**bass**i/) a bass voice or vocal part.
ORIGIN – Italian, 'low'.

bassoon > *noun* a large bass woodwind instrument of the oboe family.
DERIVATIVES – **bassoonist** *noun*.
ORIGIN – Italian *bassone*, from *basso* 'low'.

basso profundo /prə**fun**dō/ > *noun* (pl. **bassos profundos** or **bassi profundi** /prə**fun**di/) a bass singer with an exceptionally low range.

bast /bast/ > *noun* fibre obtained from plants and used for matting and cord.

bastard /**baa**stərd/ > *noun* **1** archaic or derogatory an illegitimate person. **2** informal an unpleasant or despicable person. **3** informal a person of a specified kind: *the poor bastard*. > *adjective* **1** archaic or derogatory illegitimate. **2** no longer in its pure or original form.

wordpower facts
Bastard
The word **bastard** came into English from Old French in the medieval period and derives from medieval Latin *bastardus*, which is probably from *bastum* 'packsaddle'. The reason for such a dramatic change of meaning is uncertain: however, there could be a parallel in the Old French term for an illegitimate child, *fils de bast*, literally 'packsaddle son', i.e. the son of a mule driver who uses a packsaddle for a pillow and is gone by morning.

bastardise (also **bastardize**) > *verb* **1** debase by adding new elements. **2** archaic declare (someone) illegitimate.
DERIVATIVES – **bastardisation** *noun*.

bastardy > *noun* archaic illegitimacy.

baste¹ > *verb* pour fat or juices over (meat) during cooking.
DERIVATIVES – **baster** *noun*.

baste² > *verb* tack with long, loose stitches in preparation for sewing.
ORIGIN – Old French *bastir* 'sew lightly'.

bastinado /basti**nay**dō/ > *noun* chiefly historical a form of punishment or torture that involves caning the soles of someone's feet.
ORIGIN – Spanish *bastonada*, from *bastón* 'stick, cudgel'.

bastion /**bast**iən/ > *noun* **1** a projecting part of a fortification allowing an increased angle of fire. **2** something protecting or preserving particular principles or activities: *the town was a bastion of Conservatism*.
ORIGIN – Italian *bastione*, from *bastire* 'build'.

bat¹ > *noun* an implement with a handle and a solid surface, used in sports for hitting the ball. > *verb* (**batted, batting**) **1** (in sport) take the role of hitting rather than throwing the ball. **2** hit with the flat of one's hand. **3** (**bat around** or **about**) informal, chiefly N. Amer. casually discuss (an idea).
IDIOMS – **off one's own bat** Brit. informal of one's own accord.

bat² > *noun* **1** a flying nocturnal mammal with membranous wings that extend between the fingers and limbs. **2** (**old bat**) informal an unattractive and unpleasant woman.
WORDFINDER – chiropteran (*of bats*), echolocation (*use of sound by bats*), fruit bat, horseshoe bat, noctule, pipistrelle, vampire (*kinds of bat*).
IDIOMS – **have bats in the belfry** informal be eccentric or mad.
COMBINATIONS – **batwing** (of a sleeve) having a deep armhole and a tight cuff.
ORIGIN – Scandinavian; sense 2 is from *bat*,

an old slang term for 'prostitute', or from BATTLEAXE.

bat³ > *verb* (**batted, batting**) flutter (one's eyelashes).
IDIOMS – **not bat an eyelid** informal show no surprise or concern.
ORIGIN – variant of obsolete *bate* 'to flutter'.

batch > *noun* **1** a quantity of goods produced at one time. **2** a quantity of loaves or rolls baked together. **3** Computing a group of records processed as a single unit. > *verb* arrange in batches.
SYNONYMS – *noun* **1** bunch, collection, lot, set.
COMBINATIONS – **batch file** a computer file containing a list of instructions to be carried out in turn.
ORIGIN – Old English; related to BAKE.

bate (also **bait**) > *noun* Brit. informal, dated an angry mood.
ORIGIN – from BAIT.

bated* > *adjective* (in phrase **with bated breath**) in great suspense.
*SPELLING – the spelling is b*a*ted not b*ai*ted.
ORIGIN – from obsolete *bate* 'restrain', from ABATE.

bath > *noun* **1** a large tub that is filled with water for immersing and washing one's body. **2** an act of washing in a bath. **3** (also **baths**) a building containing a public swimming pool or washing facilities. **4** a container holding a liquid in which an object is immersed in chemical processing. > *verb* wash in a bath.
WORDFINDER – balneal (*of baths or bathing*).
IDIOMS – **take a bath** informal suffer a heavy financial loss.
COMBINATIONS – **bathrobe** a dressing gown made of towelling. **bathroom 1** a room containing a bath and usually also a washbasin and toilet. **2** N. Amer. a room containing a toilet. **bath salts** crystals that are dissolved in bathwater to soften or perfume it.

Bath bun > *noun* Brit. a round currant bun topped with icing or sugar.
ORIGIN – named after the city of *Bath* in SW England.

bath chair > *noun* dated an invalid's wheelchair.
ORIGIN – named after *Bath* in SW England, frequented for its supposedly curative hot springs.

bathe /bayth/ > *verb* **1** wash by immersing one's body in water. **2** chiefly Brit. take a swim. **3** soak or wipe gently with liquid to clean or soothe. **4** suffuse or envelop: *my desk is bathed in sunlight*. > *noun* a swim.
DERIVATIVES – **bather** *noun*.
COMBINATIONS – **bathing costume** (or chiefly N. Amer. **bathing suit**) a swimming costume. **bathing machine** historical a

wheeled hut drawn to the edge of the sea, for changing in and bathing from.

batholith /bathəlith/ > *noun* Geology a very large igneous intrusion extending to an unknown depth in the earth's crust.

ORIGIN – from Greek *bathos* 'depth' + *lithos* 'stone'.

bathos /baythoss/ > *noun* (in literature) an unintentional change in mood from the important and serious to the trivial or ridiculous.

DERIVATIVES – **bathetic** /bəthettik/ *adjective*.

ORIGIN – Greek, 'depth'.

bathysphere > *noun* a manned spherical chamber for deep-sea observation.

ORIGIN – from Greek *bathus* 'deep'.

batik /bəteek/ > *noun* a method (originating in Java) of producing coloured designs on cloth by waxing the parts not to be dyed.

ORIGIN – Javanese, 'painted'.

batiste /bəteest/ > *noun* a fine linen or cotton fabric.

ORIGIN – French; probably related to *battre* 'to beat'.

batman > *noun* dated (in the British armed forces) an officer's personal valet or attendant.

ORIGIN – from Old French *bat* 'packsaddle'; the word originally referred to an orderly in charge of the *bat horse* which carried the officer's baggage.

bat mitzvah /bat mitsvə/ > *noun* a religious initiation ceremony for a Jewish girl at the age of twelve years and a day.

ORIGIN – Hebrew, 'daughter of commandment'.

baton > *noun* **1** a thin stick used to conduct an orchestra or choir. **2** a short stick passed from runner to runner in a relay race. **3** a stick carried and twirled by a drum major. **4** a police officer's truncheon. **5** a staff of office or authority.

IDIOMS – **pass** (or **take up**) **the baton** hand over (or take up) a duty or responsibility.

COMBINATIONS – **baton round** Brit. a large rubber or plastic bullet used in riot control.

ORIGIN – French, from Latin *bastum* 'stick'.

batrachian /bətraykiən/ > *noun* a frog or toad.

ORIGIN – Greek *batrakhos* 'frog'.

bats > *adjective* informal mad.

ORIGIN – from *have bats in the belfry* (see BAT²).

batsman > *noun* a player who bats in cricket.

battalion* /bətaliən/ > *noun* a large body of troops, forming part of a brigade.

*SPELLING – two *t*s, one *l*: ba*tt*a*l*ion.

ORIGIN – from Italian *battaglia* 'battle'.

batten¹ > *noun* a long, flat wooden or metal strip for strengthening or securing something. > *verb* strengthen or fasten with battens.

IDIOMS – **batten down the hatches 1** secure a ship's tarpaulins. **2** prepare for a difficulty or crisis.

ORIGIN – Old French *batant*, from *batre* 'to beat'.

batten² > *verb* (**batten on**) thrive or prosper at the expense of.

ORIGIN – Old Norse, 'get better'.

Battenberg > *noun* chiefly Brit. an oblong marzipan-covered sponge cake in two colours.

ORIGIN – named after the town of *Battenberg* in Germany.

batter¹ > *verb* strike repeatedly with hard blows.

DERIVATIVES – **batterer** noun.

SYNONYMS – bludgeon, pound, pummel, thrash.

COMBINATIONS – **battering ram** a heavy object swung or rammed against a door to break it down. [ORIGIN – from the original design of the object, which was in the form of a heavy beam with a carved ram's head at the end.]

ORIGIN – Old French *batre* 'to beat'.

batter² > *noun* a mixture of flour, egg, and milk or water, used for making pancakes or coating food before frying.

ORIGIN – from Old French *batre* 'to beat'.

batter³ > *noun* a player who bats in baseball.

battered > *adjective* (of food) coated in batter and fried.

---

wordpower facts

Battery

Why does **battery** mean both 'a source of electrical power' and 'the infliction of violence'? The word comes from Old French *baterie*, from Latin *battuere* 'to strike' (from which the words **batter** and **battle** are derived). Early senses in English were 'metal articles made by hammering' and 'a collection of pieces of artillery'. From this idea came the sense of a number of Leyden jars (an early device used to store electric charge) connected up so as to discharge simultaneously, the predecessor of the modern electric battery.

---

battery > *noun* (pl. **batteries**) **1** a device containing one or more electrical cells, for use as a source of power. **2** an extensive series or range: *a battery of tests.* **3** chiefly Brit. a series of small cages for the intensive rearing of poultry. **4** Law the infliction of unlawful personal violence on another person. **5** a fortified emplacement for heavy guns. **6** an artillery subunit of guns, men, and vehicles.

battle > *noun* **1** a sustained fight between organised armed forces. **2** a lengthy and difficult struggle or contest: *a battle of wits.* > *verb* fight or struggle tenaciously.

IDIOMS – **battle royal** (pl. **battles royal**) a fiercely contested fight or dispute.

DERIVATIVES – **battler** noun.

SYNONYMS – *noun* **1** combat, conflict, engagement. **2** competition, contest, dispute, fight, struggle. *verb* fight, struggle, wrestle.

COMBINATIONS – **battlecruiser** an early 20th-century warship that was faster and more lightly armoured than a battleship. **battledress** a uniform designed for battle, worn by soldiers. **battlefield** (also **battleground**) the piece of ground on which a battle is fought. **battleship** a heavily armoured warship with large-calibre guns. **battle stations** chiefly US the positions taken by military personnel in preparation for battle.

ORIGIN – Old French *bataille*, from Latin *battuere* 'to beat'; compare with **BATTERY**.

battleaxe > *noun* **1** a large axe used in ancient warfare. **2** informal a formidably aggressive older woman.

battledore /batt'ldor/ > *noun* **1** (also **battledore and shuttlecock**) a game played with a shuttlecock and rackets, a forerunner of badminton. **2** the small racket used in this.

ORIGIN – perhaps from Provençal *batedor* 'beater'.

battlement > *noun* a parapet with gaps at intervals for firing from, forming part of a fortification.

DERIVATIVES – **battlemented** *adjective*.

ORIGIN – from Old French *bataillier* 'fortify with movable defence turrets'.

batty > *adjective* (**battier**, **battiest**) informal mad.

DERIVATIVES – **battiness** noun.

ORIGIN – from BAT².

bauble > */bawb'l/* > *noun* **1** a small, showy trinket or decoration. **2** a decorative glass or plastic ornament hung on a Christmas tree.

SYNONYMS – **1** knick-knack, novelty, trifle; rare bibelot.

ORIGIN – Old French *baubel* 'child's toy'.

baud /baud/ > *noun* (pl. same or **bauds**) Computing a unit of transmission speed for electronic signals, corresponding to one information unit or event per second.

ORIGIN – named after the French engineer Jean M. E. *Baudot* (1845–1903).

baulk /bawlk, bawk/ (chiefly US also **balk**) > *verb* **1** (**baulk at**) hesitate to accept (an idea). **2** thwart or hinder (a plan or person). **3** (of a horse) refuse to go on. > *noun* a roughly squared timber beam.

SYNONYMS – *verb* **1** (**baulk at**) be reluctant to, eschew, resist. **2** curb, frustrate, hinder, impede, obstruct, thwart.

wordpower facts

Baulk

The senses of **baulk** have developed through the centuries in an interesting way. The word comes from Old English *balc*, meaning 'ridge, mound', 'unploughed ridge', and 'ridge left unploughed by mistake'. From these ideas came the senses 'blunder, omission' and 'ridge in one's way, obstacle' and the verb uses 'miss a chance', 'hesitate', and 'hinder'.

baulky > *adjective* British spelling of **BALKY**.

bauxite /**bawk**sīt/ > *noun* a clayey rock that is the chief ore of aluminium.
ORIGIN – from *Les Baux*, a village in SE France, where it was first found.

Bavarian /bə**vair**iən/ > *noun* a person from Bavaria, a region in southern Germany. > *adjective* relating to Bavaria.

bavarois /bavvə**waa**/ (also **bavaroise** /bavvə**waaz**/) > *noun* a dessert containing gelatin and whipped cream.
ORIGIN – French, 'Bavarian'.

bawd /bawd/ > *noun* archaic a woman in charge of a brothel.
ORIGIN – Old French *baudestroyt* 'procuress', from *baude* 'shameless'.

bawdy > *adjective* (**bawdier**, **bawdiest**) humorously indecent.
DERIVATIVES – **bawdily** *adverb* **bawdiness** *noun*.
SYNONYMS – earthy, ribald, risqué.
COMBINATIONS – **bawdy house** archaic a brothel.

bawl > *verb* **1** shout out noisily. **2** (**bawl out**) reprimand angrily. **3** weep noisily. > *noun* a loud shout.
SYNONYMS – *verb* **1** bellow, roar, yell. **2** (**bawl out**) berate, castigate, lambaste; informal give an earful. **3** howl, sob, wail. *noun* cry, roar; N. Amer. informal holler.

bay¹ > *noun* a broad curved inlet of the sea.
ORIGIN – Old Spanish *bahia*.

bay² (also **bay laurel** or **sweet bay**) > *noun* an evergreen Mediterranean shrub, with aromatic leaves that are used in cookery.
ORIGIN – Old French *baie*, from Latin *baca* 'berry'.

bay³ > *noun* **1** a window area that projects outwards from a wall. **2** a section of wall in a church or large hall, between two buttresses or columns. **3** an area, compartment, etc. specially allocated or marked off: *a loading bay*.
COMBINATIONS – **bay window** a window built to project outwards from a wall.

ORIGIN – Old French *baie*, from Latin *batare* 'to gape'.

bay⁴ > *adjective* (of a horse) reddish-brown with black points. > *noun* a bay horse.
ORIGIN – Old French *bai*, from Latin *badius*.

bay⁵ > *verb* (of a dog) howl loudly. > *noun* the sound of baying.
IDIOMS – **at bay** trapped or cornered. **bay for blood** demand retribution. **hold** (or **keep**) **at bay** prevent from approaching or having an effect.
ORIGIN – Old French *(a)baiier* 'to bark'.

bayberry > *noun* (pl. **bayberries**) a North American shrub with aromatic leathery leaves and waxy berries.

bayonet > *noun* **1** a long blade fixed to the muzzle of a rifle for hand-to-hand fighting. **2** (before another noun) denoting a type of fitting for a light bulb which is pushed into a socket and then twisted into place. > *verb* (**bayoneted**, **bayoneting**) stab with a bayonet.
ORIGIN – first used in reference to a short dagger: French *baïonnette*, from *Bayonne*, a town in SW France, where the daggers were made.

bayou /**bī**oo/ > *noun* (pl. **bayous**) (in the southern US) a marshy outlet of a lake or river.
ORIGIN – Louisiana French, from Choctaw.

bay rum > *noun* a perfume for the hair, distilled originally from rum and bayberry leaves.

bazaar /bə**zaar**/ > *noun* **1** a market in a Middle-Eastern country. **2** a fund-raising sale of goods.
ORIGIN – Persian, 'market'.

bazooka > *noun* **1** a short-range rocket launcher used against tanks. **2** a kazoo shaped like a trumpet.

BBC > *abbreviation* British Broadcasting Corporation.

bbl. > *abbreviation* barrels (especially of oil).

BBQ > *abbreviation* informal a barbecue.

BC > *abbreviation* **1** (placed after a date) before Christ. **2** British Columbia.
USAGE – BC is normally written in small capitals and should be placed after the numerals, as in *375* BC, whereas AD is normally placed before the numerals, as in AD *124*.

bcc > *abbreviation* blind carbon copy.

BCE > *abbreviation* before the Common Era (indicating dates before the Christian era, used especially by non-Christians).

BCG > *abbreviation* Bacillus Calmette-Guérin, an anti-tuberculosis vaccine.

BD > *abbreviation* Bachelor of Divinity.

BE > *abbreviation* **1** Bachelor of Education. **2** Bachelor of Engineering.

Be > *symbol* the chemical element beryllium.

be > *verb* (sing. present **am**; **are**; **is**; pl. present **are**;

1st and 3rd sing. past **was**; 2nd sing. past and pl. past **were**; present subjunctive **be**; past subjunctive **were**; present participle **being**; past participle **been**) **1** (usu. **there is** or **there are**) exist; be present. **2** occur; take place. **3** have the specified state, nature, or role. **4** come; go; visit. > *auxiliary verb* **1** used with a present participle to form continuous tenses. **2** used with a past participle to form the passive voice. **3** used to indicate something that is due to, may, or should happen.
IDIOMS – **the be-all and end-all** informal the most important aspect of something. **-to-be** of the future: *his bride-to-be*.

be- > *prefix* forming verbs: **1** all over; all round: *bespatter*. **2** thoroughly; excessively: *bewilder*. **3** expressing transitive action: *bemoan | befriend*. **4** affect with or cause to be: *befog*. **5** (forming adjectives ending in *-ed*) having; covered with: *bejewelled*.

beach > *noun* a pebbly or sandy shore at the edge of the sea or a lake. > *verb* bring or come on to a beach from the water.
WORDFINDER – littoral (*of beaches or shorelines*).
SYNONYMS – *noun* seashore, seaside, strand.

beachcomber > *noun* **1** a person who searches beaches for articles of value. **2** a long wave rolling in from the sea.

beachhead > *noun* a fortified position on a beach taken by landing forces.

beacon > *noun* **1** a fire lit on the top of a hill as a signal. **2** a light serving as a signal for ships or aircraft. **3** a radio transmitter signalling the position of a ship or aircraft.
ORIGIN – Old English, 'sign, portent, ensign'.

bead > *noun* **1** a small piece of glass, stone, etc., threaded in a string with others to make a necklace or rosary. **2** a drop of liquid on a surface. **3** a small knob forming the foresight of a gun. **4** the reinforced inner edge of a tyre. > *verb* **1** decorate or cover with beads. **2** form into a string like beads.
IDIOMS – **draw a bead on** chiefly N. Amer. take aim at with a gun.
DERIVATIVES – **beaded** *adjective*.
ORIGIN – Old English, 'prayer'; current senses derive from the use of a rosary, each bead of which represents a prayer.

beadle > *noun* Brit. **1** a ceremonial officer of a church, college, etc. **2** historical a parish officer dealing with petty offenders.

beady > *adjective* (of a person's eyes) small, round, and observing things clearly.
DERIVATIVES – **beadily** *adverb*.

beagle > *noun* a small, short-legged hound, originally used for hunting hares.
ORIGIN – perhaps from Old French *beegueule* 'open-mouthed'.

beagling > *noun* hunting with beagles.

beak > *noun* **1** a bird's horny projecting jaws;

a bill. **2** a projection at the prow of an ancient warship, used in attacking enemy ships. **3** Brit. informal a magistrate or schoolmaster.

DERIVATIVES – **beaked** adjective **beaky** adjective.

ORIGIN – Latin *beccus*.

beaker > noun Brit. **1** a tall plastic cup. **2** a cylindrical glass container used in laboratories.

ORIGIN – first used in the sense 'large drinking container': from Old Norse.

beam > noun **1** a long piece of timber or metal used as a support in building. **2** a narrow horizontal length of timber for balancing on in gymnastics. **3** a ray or shaft of light or particles. **4** a radiant smile. **5** a ship's breadth at its widest point. **6** a sideways direction from a ship. *there was land in sight on the port beam.* > verb **1** transmit (a radio signal). **2** shine brightly. **3** smile radiantly.

IDIOMS – **a beam in one's eye** a fault that is greater in oneself than in the person one is criticising. [ORIGIN – with biblical allusion to the Gospel of Matthew, chapter 7.] **off beam** informal on the wrong track. **on her** (or **its**) **beam ends** (of a ship) on its side.

bean > noun **1** an edible seed growing in long pods on certain plants. **2** the hard seed of a coffee or cocoa plant. **3** informal a very small amount or nothing at all: *they survived for a fortnight without spending a bean.* **4** informal, dated a person's head. > verb informal, chiefly N. Amer. hit on the head.

WORDFINDER – *kinds of bean:* adzuki, haricot, lima, mung (*source of bean sprouts*), soya; borlotti, cannellini, flageolet, pinto (*kinds of kidney bean*).

IDIOMS – **full of beans** informal lively; in high spirits. **old bean** Brit. informal, dated a friendly form of address.

COMBINATIONS – **beanbag 1** a small bag filled with dried beans and used in children's games. **2** a large cushion filled with polystyrene beads. **bean counter** informal an excessively careful accountant or bureaucrat. **bean curd** tofu. **beanfeast** Brit. informal a party with plentiful food and drink. [ORIGIN – first used in reference to an annual dinner given to employees, typically featuring beans and bacon.] **beanpole** informal a tall, thin person. **bean sprouts** the edible sprouting seeds of certain beans.

beanery > noun (pl. **beaneries**) N. Amer. informal a cheap restaurant.

beanie > noun (pl. **beanies**) a small close-fitting hat worn on the back of the head.

beano > noun (pl. **beanos**) Brit. informal a party.

bear[1] > verb (past **bore**; past participle **borne**) **1** carry. **2** have as a quality or visible mark. **3** support (a weight). **4** (**bear oneself**)

behave in a specified manner: *she bore herself with dignity.* **5** manage to tolerate: *I can't bear it.* **6** give birth to (a child). **7** (of a tree or plant) produce (fruit or flowers). **8** turn and proceed in a specified direction: *bear left.*

IDIOMS – **bear down on** approach in a purposeful or intimidating manner. **bear fruit** yield positive results. **bear someone a grudge** nurture a feeling of resentment against someone. **bear in mind** remember and take into account. **bear on** be relevant to. **bear out** support or confirm. **bear up** remain cheerful in difficult circumstances. **bear with** be patient or tolerant with. **bear witness** (or **testimony**) **to** testify to. **be borne in upon** come to be realised by. **bring to bear 1** prepare and use to effect. **2** aim (a weapon).

SYNONYMS – **1** bring, carry, convey, transport. **2** display, exhibit, possess. **3** hold, shoulder, support. **5** abide, endure, stand, suffer, tolerate. **7** generate, produce, yield. **8** swing, turn, veer.

bear[2] > noun **1** a large, heavy mammal with thick fur and a very short tail. **2** Stock Exchange a person who sells shares hoping to buy them back later at a lower price. Contrasted with **BULL**[1]. [ORIGIN – said to be from a proverb warning against 'selling the bear's skin before one has caught the bear'.] **3** a rough or bad-mannered person.

WORDFINDER – ursine (*of or like a bear*); Ursa Major (*constellation, the Great Bear*), Ursa Minor (*constellation, the Little Bear*).

IDIOMS – **like a bear with a sore head** Brit. informal very irritable.

COMBINATIONS – **bear-baiting** historical a form of entertainment which involved setting dogs to attack a captive bear. **bear garden** (also **bear pit**) a scene of uproar and confusion. [ORIGIN – first meaning 'place used for bear-baiting'.] **beargrass** a North American plant with long, coarse, grass-like leaves. **bear hug** a rough, tight embrace. **bear market** Stock Exchange a market in which share prices are falling. **bear's breech** a plant with large deep-cut leaves and tall spikes of purple and white flowers. **bearskin** a tall cap of black fur worn ceremonially by certain troops.

bearable > adjective able to be endured.

DERIVATIVES – **bearably** adverb.

SYNONYMS – acceptable, endurable, manageable, tolerable.

beard > noun **1** a growth of hair on the chin and lower cheeks of a man's face. **2** a tuft of hairs or bristles on certain animals or plants. > verb boldly confront or challenge (someone formidable).

DERIVATIVES – **beardless** adjective.

bearded > adjective having a beard.

COMBINATIONS – **bearded dragon** an Australian lizard with a large throat pouch bearing sharp spines.

bearer > noun **1** a person or thing that carries something. **2** a person who presents a cheque or other order to pay money.

bearing > noun **1** a person's way of standing, moving, or behaving. **2** relation; relevance: *the case has no bearing on the issues.* **3** (**bearings**) a device that allows two parts to rotate or move in contact with each other. **4** direction or position relative to a fixed point. **5** (**one's bearings**) awareness of one's position relative to one's surroundings. **6** Heraldry a device or charge.

SYNONYMS – **1** carriage, demeanour, manner, posture.

bearish > adjective **1** resembling or likened to a bear. **2** Stock Exchange characterised by falling share prices.

Béarnaise sauce /bayaar**nayz**/ > noun a rich sauce thickened with egg yolks and flavoured with tarragon.

ORIGIN – named after *Béarn*, a region of SW France.

beast > noun **1** an animal, especially a large or dangerous mammal. **2** a very cruel or wicked person.

SYNONYMS – **1** animal, brute, creature. **2** brute, fiend, monster, ogre, savage.

COMBINATIONS – **beast of burden** an animal used for carrying loads. **beast of prey** an animal that kills and eats other animals.

ORIGIN – Latin *bestia*.

beastie > noun (pl. **beasties**) Scottish or humorous a small animal or insect.

beastly Brit. informal > adjective very unpleasant. > adverb dated to an extreme and unpleasant degree.

DERIVATIVES – **beastliness** noun.

beat > verb (past **beat**; past participle **beaten**) **1** strike (someone) repeatedly and violently. **2** strike repeatedly to flatten or make a noise. **3** do better or be stronger than. **4** informal baffle. **5** (of the heart) pulsate. **6** (of a bird) move (the wings) up and down. **7** stir (cooking ingredients) vigorously. **8** move across (land) to raise game birds for shooting. > noun **1** a main accent in music or poetry. **2** a pulsation of the heart. **3** a movement of a bird's wings. **4** a brief pause or moment of hesitation. **5** an area patrolled by a police officer. **6** a stretch of water fished by an angler. > adjective informal completely exhausted.

IDIOMS – **beat about the bush** discuss a matter without coming to the point. **beat the bounds** historical mark parish boundaries by walking round them and striking certain points with rods. **beat down** force (someone) to reduce the price of something. **beat it** informal leave. **beat off** succeed in resisting (an attacker). **beat up** attack (someone) and hit them repeatedly. **beat a retreat** withdraw. **off the beaten track** isolated.

DERIVATIVES – **beatable** adjective **beater** noun.

SYNONYMS – verb **1** batter, bludgeon, pound, thrash. **3** conquer, defeat, outdo, overcome, surpass, trounce. **5** palpitate, pound, pulsate, race, throb. **6** flap, flutter. **7** mix, whip, whisk. noun **1** rhythm, stress, tempo. **2** pulse, throb.

COMBINATIONS – **beatbox** informal **1** a drum machine. **2** a radio or radio cassette player for playing loud music. **beat generation** a movement of young people in the 1950s and early 1960s who rejected conventional society. **beat-up** informal worn out by overuse.

beatific /beeətiffik/ > adjective **1** feeling or expressing blissful happiness. **2** Christian Theology bestowing holy bliss.

DERIVATIVES – **beatifically** adverb.

beatify* /beeattifī/ > verb (**beatifies, beatified**) (in the Roman Catholic Church) proclaim (a dead person) to be in a state of bliss, the first step towards making them a saint.

DERIVATIVES – **beatification** noun.

***SPELLING** – do not confuse with **beautify**: **beatify** has no u before the t.

ORIGIN – Latin beatificare, from beatus 'blessed'.

beatitude /biattityo͞od/ > noun **1** supreme blessedness. **2** (**the Beatitudes**) the blessings listed by Jesus in the Sermon on the Mount (Gospel of Matthew, chapter 5).

beatnik > noun a young man or woman associated with the beat generation.

beau /bō/ > noun (pl. **beaux** or **beaus** /bōz, bō/) dated **1** a boyfriend or male admirer. **2** a dandy.

ORIGIN – French, 'handsome'.

Beaufort scale /bōfərt/ > noun a scale of wind speed ranging from force 0 to force 12.

ORIGIN – named after the English admiral Sir Francis Beaufort (1774–1857).

Beaujolais /bōzhəlay/ > noun a light red wine produced in the Beaujolais district of SE France.

Beaujolais Nouveau /no͞ovō/ > noun a Beaujolais sold in the first year of a vintage.

ORIGIN – French, 'new Beaujolais'.

beau monde /bō mond/ > noun fashionable society.

ORIGIN – French, 'fine world'.

Beaune /bōn/ > noun a red burgundy wine from the region around Beaune in eastern France.

beauteous > adjective literary beautiful.

beautician > noun a person whose job is to give beauty treatments.

beautiful* > adjective **1** very pleasing to the senses or mind aesthetically. **2** of a very high standard; excellent.

DERIVATIVES – **beautifully** adverb.

***SPELLING** – remember the u before the t: beautiful.

SYNONYMS – **1** exquisite, gorgeous, lovely, ravishing. **2** excellent, superb.

ANTONYMS – **1** ugly.

beautify > verb (**beautifies, beautified**) make beautiful.

DERIVATIVES – **beautification** noun.

beauty > noun (pl. **beauties**) **1** a combination of qualities that delights the aesthetic senses. **2** (before another noun) intended to make someone more attractive: beauty treatment. **3** a beautiful woman. **4** an excellent example. **5** an attractive feature or advantage.

IDIOMS – **beauty is in the eye of the beholder** proverb something which one person finds beautiful or admirable may not appeal to another. **beauty is only skin-deep** proverb a pleasing appearance is not a guide to character.

SYNONYMS – **1** loveliness, pulchritude.

COMBINATIONS – **beauty contest** a contest in which the winner is the woman judged the most beautiful. **beauty queen** the winner of a beauty contest. **beauty salon** (also **beauty parlour**) an establishment in which hairdressing and cosmetic treatments are carried out. **beauty sleep** humorous sleep that helps one remain young and attractive. **beauty spot 1** a place with beautiful scenery. **2** a small artificial mole worn by a woman on the face.

ORIGIN – Old French beaute, from Latin bellus 'beautiful, fine'.

beaux plural of BEAU.

beaver > noun (pl. same or **beavers**) **1** a large semiaquatic rodent noted for gnawing through trees in order to fell them to make dams. **2** a hat made of felted beaver fur. **3** a very hard-working person. > verb (often **beaver away**) informal work hard.

bebop /beebop/ > noun a type of jazz originating in the 1940s and characterised by complex harmony and rhythms.

becalm > verb (**be becalmed**) (of a sailing ship) be unable to move through lack of wind.

became past participle of BECOME.

because > conjunction for the reason that; since.

IDIOMS – **because of** by reason of.

USAGE – on starting a sentence with **because**, see note at AND.

ORIGIN – from the phrase by cause.

béchamel /beshəmel/ > noun a rich white sauce made with milk infused with herbs and other flavourings.

ORIGIN – named after the Marquis Louis de Béchamel (died 1703).

beck¹ > noun N. English a stream.

ORIGIN – Old Norse.

beck² > noun (in phrase **at someone's beck and call**) always having to be ready to obey someone's orders.

ORIGIN – abbreviated form of BECKON.

beckon > verb **1** make a gesture to encourage or instruct someone to approach or follow. **2** seem appealing or inviting.

SYNONYMS – **1** motion, signal, summon, wave. **2** appeal, attract, entice, invite, tempt.

become > verb (past **became**; past participle **become**) **1** begin to be. **2** turn into. **3** (**become of**) happen to. **4** (of clothing) look good when worn by (someone). **5** be appropriate to.

SYNONYMS – **1,2** come to be, get, grow, turn into. **4** flatter, suit.

ORIGIN – Old English, from BE- + COME.

becoming > adjective **1** (of clothing) looking good on someone. **2** decorous; proper.

DERIVATIVES – **becomingly** adverb.

becquerel /bekkərel/ > noun Physics a unit of radioactivity used in the SI system, corresponding to one disintegration per second.

ORIGIN – named after the French physicist A-H. Becquerel (1852–1908).

BEd > abbreviation Bachelor of Education.

bed > noun **1** a piece of furniture incorporating a mattress or other surface for sleeping or resting on. **2** informal a bed as a place for sexual activity. **3** an area of ground where flowers and plants are grown. **4** a flat base or foundation. **5** a layer of rock. **6** the bottom of the sea or a lake or river. > verb (**bedded, bedding**) **1** provide with or settle in sleeping accommodation. **2** informal have sexual intercourse with. **3** (often **bed in** or **down**) fix or be fixed firmly. **4** (**bed out**) transfer (a plant) from a pot to the ground.

WORDFINDER – decumbiture (action of taking to one's bed).

IDIOMS – **a bed of roses** a comfortable or easy situation or activity. **get out of bed on the wrong side** start the day in a bad mood, which continues all day long. **put to bed** informal make (a newspaper) ready for press.

DERIVATIVES – **bedded** adjective.

COMBINATIONS – **bed and board** lodging and food. **bed and breakfast 1** sleeping accommodation and breakfast in a guest house or hotel. **2** a guest house. **bedbug** a wingless bug which sucks the blood of sleeping humans. **bedchamber** archaic a bedroom. **bedclothes** coverings for a bed, such as sheets and blankets. **bedfellow 1** a person sharing a bed with another. **2** a person or thing closely associated with another. **bedjacket** a soft loose jacket worn when sitting up in bed. **bedlinen** sheets, pillowcases, and duvet covers. **bedpan** a receptacle used as a toilet by a bedridden patient. **bedpost** any of the four upright supports of a bedstead. **bedrock 1** solid rock underlying loose deposits such as soil. **2** the fundamental principles on which something is based. **bedroom** a room for sleeping in. **bedside manner** the manner in which a doctor attends a patient. **bedsocks** chiefly Brit. thick socks worn in bed. **bedsore** a sore that develops as a result of lying in bed in one position for a prolonged period. **bed-wetting** involuntary urination during the night.

bedazzle > *verb* greatly impress with brilliance or skill.

beddable /beddəb'l/ > *adjective* informal sexually attractive or available.

bedding > *noun* **1** bedclothes. **2** straw or similar material for animals to sleep on. **3** a base or bottom layer.

COMBINATIONS – **bedding plant** an annual plant cultivated for planting in a bed in the spring.

bedeck > *verb* decorate lavishly.

bedevil > *verb* (**bedevilled, bedevilling;** US **bedeviled, bedeviling**) cause continual trouble to.

bedhead > *noun* Brit. an upright board or panel fixed at the head of a bed.

bedizen /bidīz'n/ > *verb* literary dress up or decorate gaudily.

ORIGIN – from obsolete *dizen* 'deck out'.

bedlam /bedləm/ > *noun* **1** a scene of uproar and confusion. **2** archaic an asylum.

SYNONYMS – **1** chaos, mayhem, pandemonium; informal hullabaloo.

ANTONYMS – **1** calm, order.

ORIGIN – early form of *Bethlehem*, referring to the hospital of St Mary of Bethlehem in London, used as an asylum for the insane.

Bedouin /beddoo-in/ (also **Beduin**) > *noun* (pl. same) a nomadic Arab of the desert.

ORIGIN – Old French, from an Arabic word meaning 'dwellers in the desert'.

bedraggled > *adjective* made wet, dirty, or untidy by rain, wind, etc.

SYNONYMS – dishevelled, rumpled, scruffy, unkempt, untidy.

bedridden > *adjective* confined to bed by sickness or old age.

bedsit (also **bedsitter** or **bed-sitting room**) > *noun* Brit. informal a rented room consisting of a combined bedroom and living room, with cooking facilities.

bedspread > *noun* a decorative cloth used to cover a bed.

bedstraw > *noun* a plant with small flowers and slender leaves, formerly used for stuffing mattresses.

Bedu /beddoo/ > *noun* another term for **BEDOUIN**.

bee > *noun* **1** a stinging winged insect which collects nectar and pollen from flowers and produces wax and honey. **2** a meeting for communal work or amusement: *a sewing bee.*

WORDFINDER – ambrosia (*bee bread*), apian (*of bees*), apiary (*place where bees are kept*), apiculture (*keeping of bees*), drone (*male bee*), hymenopteran (*bee, wasp, ant, or related insect*), royal jelly (*food for queen bee larvae*).

IDIOMS – **the bee's knees** informal an outstandingly good person or thing. **have a bee in one's bonnet** informal be obsessed with something.

COMBINATIONS – **bee bread** honey or pollen used as food by bees. **bee-eater** a brightly coloured insect-eating bird with a curved bill and long tail. **bee-stung** informal (of a woman's lips) full and red.

beech > *noun* a large tree with smooth grey bark and hard, pale wood.

COMBINATIONS – **beechmast** the angular brown nuts of the beech tree, pairs of which are enclosed in a prickly case.

beef > *noun* **1** the flesh of a cow, bull, or ox, used as food. **2** (pl. **beeves** /beevz/ or US also **beefs**) a cow, bull, or ox fattened for its meat. **3** informal flesh with well-developed muscle. **4** (pl. **beefs**) informal a complaint or grievance. > *verb* informal **1** (**beef up**) give (something) more substance or strength. **2** complain.

COMBINATIONS – **beefburger** a fried or grilled cake of minced beef eaten in a bun. **beefcake** informal men with well-developed muscles. **beefeater** a Yeoman Warder or Yeoman of the Guard in the Tower of London. [ORIGIN – first used as a derogatory term for a well-fed servant.] **beefsteak** a thick slice of steak, especially rump steak. **beef tea** Brit. a hot drink made with a beef extract. **beef tomato** (chiefly N. Amer. also **beefsteak tomato**) a large, firm variety of tomato. **beef Wellington** a dish consisting of beef coated in pâté and wrapped in puff pastry.

ORIGIN – Old French *boef*, from Latin *bos* 'ox'.

beefy > *adjective* **1** informal muscular or robust. **2** tasting like beef.

DERIVATIVES – **beefily** *adverb* **beefiness** *noun*.

beehive > *noun* **1** a structure in which bees are kept. **2** a woman's domed and lacquered hairstyle, popular in the 1960s.

bee-keeping > *noun* the occupation of owning and breeding bees for their honey.

DERIVATIVES – **bee-keeper** *noun*.

beeline > *noun* (in phrase **make a beeline for**) hurry directly to.

ORIGIN – with reference to the straight line supposedly taken instinctively by a bee when returning to the hive.

Beelzebub /bielzibub/ > *noun* the Devil.

ORIGIN – Hebrew, 'lord of flies', the name of a Philistine god.

been past participle of **BE**.

beep > *noun* a short, high-pitched sound made by electronic equipment or a vehicle horn. > *verb* produce a beep.

DERIVATIVES – **beeper** *noun*.

beer > *noun* an alcoholic drink made from malt fermented with yeast and flavoured with hops.

WORDFINDER – bitter (*strongly flavoured with hops*), cask beer, real ale (*brewed and stored traditionally*), draught beer (*served from a cask*), keg beer (*stored with carbon dioxide*), lager (*light effervescent beer*), malt (*grain prepared for use in brewing*), mash (*malt and water for brewing*), mild (*not strongly flavoured with hops*), porter (*dark beer made with roasted malt*), shandy (*beer mixed with lemonade*), stout (*dark beer made with charred malt*), wort (*infusion of malt used in brewing*).

IDIOMS – **beer and skittles** Brit. amusement or enjoyment.

COMBINATIONS – **beer belly** (also **beer gut**) informal a man's protruding stomach, supposedly caused by drinking too much beer. **beer cellar 1** an underground room for storing beer. **2** a basement bar where beer is served. **beer garden** a garden attached to a public house, where beer is served. **beer mat** a small cardboard mat for resting glasses on in a public house.

ORIGIN – Latin *biber* 'a drink', from *bibere* 'to drink'.

beery > *adjective* informal **1** drinking a lot of beer. **2** smelling or tasting of beer.

beeswax > *noun* **1** wax secreted by bees to make honeycombs, used for wood polishes and candles. **2** N. Amer. informal a person's concern: *that's none of your beeswax.*

beeswing /beezwing/ > *noun* a filmy crust on old port.

beet > *noun* a plant with a fleshy root, cultivated as food and for processing into sugar.

ORIGIN – Latin *beta*.

beetle¹ > *noun* **1** an insect with the forewings modified into hard wing cases that cover the hindwings and abdomen. **2** Brit. a dice game in which a picture of a beetle is drawn or assembled. > *verb* informal hurry along with short, quick steps.

WORDFINDER – coleopteran (*insect of the beetle order*), coleopterist (*student of beetles*), coleopterous (*of beetles*).

COMBINATIONS – **beetle-crusher** Brit. humorous a large boot or shoe.

ORIGIN – Old English, from a word meaning 'to bite'.

beetle² > *noun* **1** a very heavy mallet. **2** a machine used for making cloth more lustrous by pressing it with rollers.

beetle³ > *verb* (of rock or a person's eyebrows) project or overhang.

COMBINATIONS – **beetle-browed** having projecting eyebrows.

beetroot > *noun* chiefly Brit. the edible dark-red root of a variety of beet.

beeves plural of BEEF (in sense 2 of the noun).

beezer > *adjective* Brit. informal, dated excellent.

BEF > *abbreviation* historical British Expeditionary Force.

befall > *verb* (past **befell**; past participle **befallen**) literary (especially of something bad) happen to.

befit > *verb* (**befitted**, **befitting**) be appropriate for.
DERIVATIVES – **befitting** *adjective*.

before > *preposition, conjunction, & adverb* **1** during the period of time preceding. **2** in front of. **3** in preference to; rather than.
ORIGIN – Old English, from BY + FORE.

beforehand > *adverb* in advance.

befriend > *verb* become a friend to.

befuddle > *verb* muddle or confuse.
DERIVATIVES – **befuddled** *adjective* **befuddlement** *noun*.

beg > *verb* (**begged**, **begging**) **1** ask earnestly or humbly for something. **2** ask for food or money as charity. **3** (of a dog) sit up with the front paws raised in the hope of a reward.
IDIOMS – **beg off** withdraw from a promise or undertaking. **beg the question 1** (of a fact or action) invite a question or point that has not been dealt with. **2** assume the truth of a proposition without arguing it. **go begging** be available because unwanted by others.
SYNONYMS – **1** beseech, entreat, implore, plead.

began past of BEGIN.

begat archaic past of BEGET.

beget /bi**get**/ > *verb* (**begetting**; past **begot**; past participle **begotten**) archaic or literary **1** produce (a child). **2** cause.
DERIVATIVES – **begetter** *noun*.
SYNONYMS – **1** father, procreate, sire. **2** create, engender, generate, spawn.

beggar > *noun* **1** a person who lives by begging for food or money. **2** informal a person of a specified type: *lucky beggar!* > *verb* reduce to poverty.
IDIOMS – **beggar belief** (or **description**) be too extraordinary to be believed or described. **beggars can't be choosers** proverb people with no other options must be content with what is offered.
SYNONYMS – **1** down-and-out, mendicant, tramp, vagrant.

beggarly > *adjective* **1** meagre and ungenerous. **2** poverty-stricken.

beggary > *noun* a state of extreme poverty.

begin > *verb* (**beginning**; past **began**; past participle **begun**) **1** perform or undergo the first part of (an action or activity). **2** come into being. **3** have as its starting point. **4** (**begin on**) set to work on. **5** informal have

any chance of doing: *circuitry that Karen could not begin to comprehend.*
DERIVATIVES – **beginner** *noun* **beginning** *noun*.
SYNONYMS – **1** commence, initiate, start, undertake. **2** appear, emerge, happen, materialise.

begone > *exclamation* archaic go away at once!

begonia /bi**gō**niə/ > *noun* a plant having flowers with brightly coloured sepals but no petals.
ORIGIN – named after the French botanist Michel *Bégon* (1638–1710).

begorra /bi**gorr**ə/ > *exclamation* an exclamation of surprise traditionally attributed to the Irish.
ORIGIN – alteration of *by God*.

begot past of BEGET.

begotten past participle of BEGET.

begrudge > *verb* **1** feel envious that (someone) possesses or enjoys (something). **2** give reluctantly or resentfully.
SYNONYMS – **1** envy, grudge, resent.

beguile > *verb* **1** charm, enchant, or trick. **2** archaic or literary help (time) pass pleasantly.
DERIVATIVES – **beguiling** *adjective*.

beguine /bay**geen**/ > *noun* a popular dance of Caribbean origin, similar to the foxtrot.
ORIGIN – from French *béguin* 'infatuation'.

begum /**bay**gəm/ > *noun* Indian **1** a Muslim woman of high rank. **2** (**Begum**) the title of a married Muslim woman.
ORIGIN – Urdu, from Turkish *bigim* 'princess'.

begun past participle of BEGIN.

behalf > *noun* (in phrase **on** (US also **in**) **behalf of** or **on someone's behalf**) **1** in the interests of a person, group, or principle. **2** as a representative of.
ORIGIN – from a mixture of the earlier phrases *on his halve* and *bihalve him*, both meaning 'on his side'.

behave > *verb* **1** act in a specified way. **2** (also **behave oneself**) act in a polite or proper way.
SYNONYMS – **1** function, operate, perform, react. **2** be good, be on one's best behaviour.

behaved > *adjective* acting in a specified way: *a well-behaved child.*

behaviour (US **behavior**) > *noun* the way in which someone or something behaves.
DERIVATIVES – **behavioural** *adjective*.
SYNONYMS – actions, conduct, manners.

behaviourism (US **behaviorism**) > *noun* Psychology the theory that behaviour can be explained in terms of conditioning or training, and that psychological disorders are best treated by altering behaviour patterns.
DERIVATIVES – **behaviourist** *noun* & *adjective*.

behead > *verb* execute (someone) by cutting off their head.

beheld past and past participle of BEHOLD.

behemoth /bi**hee**moth/ > *noun* a huge or monstrous creature.
ORIGIN – Hebrew, 'monstrous beast'.

behest /bi**hest**/ > *noun* (usu. in **at the behest of**) literary a person's order or command.

behind > *preposition & adverb* **1** at or to the back or far side of. **2** further back than other members of a moving group. **3** in support of. **4** responsible for (an event or plan). **5** less advanced than. **6** late in accomplishing or paying something. **7** remaining after the departure or death of. > *noun* informal a person's bottom.

behindhand > *adjective* late or slow in doing something.

behold > *verb* (past and past participle **beheld**) archaic or literary see or observe.
DERIVATIVES – **beholder** *noun*.
SYNONYMS – descry, discern, espy.

beholden > *adjective* (usu. **beholden to**) owing a debt; indebted.

behove /bi**hōv**/ (US **behoove** /bi**hōōv**/) > *verb* (**it behoves someone to do**) formal it is a duty, responsibility, or appropriate response for someone to do.

beige > *noun* a pale sandy fawn colour.
ORIGIN – French.

being > *noun* **1** existence. **2** the nature or essence of a person. **3** a living creature: *alien beings.*
SYNONYMS – **1** actuality, essence, existence, life, reality. **3** animal, creature, individual, person.

bejabers /bi**jay**bərz/ (also **bejabbers** /bi**jabb**ərz/) > *exclamation* Irish expressing surprise.
ORIGIN – alteration of *by Jesus*.

bejewelled (US **bejeweled**) > *adjective* adorned with jewels.

belabour (US **belabor**) > *verb* **1** attack physically or verbally. **2** argue or discuss in excessive detail.

belated > *adjective* coming late or too late.
DERIVATIVES – **belatedly** *adverb* **belatedness** *noun*.
SYNONYMS – behindhand, delayed, overdue, tardy.

belay /**bee**lay, bi**lay**/ > *verb* **1** fix (a rope) round a rock, pin, or other object to secure it. **2** nautical slang stop! > *noun* **1** an act of belaying. **2** something used for belaying.

bel canto /bel **kan**tō/ > *noun* a style of operatic singing using a full, rich tone.
ORIGIN – Italian, 'fine song'.

belch > *verb* **1** noisily emit wind from the stomach through the mouth. **2** forcefully emit (smoke or flames). > *noun* an act of belching.

beldam /beldəm/ (also **beldame**) > *noun* archaic an old woman.
ORIGIN – from Old French *bel* 'beautiful' + DAM[2].

beleaguered > *adjective* **1** under siege. **2** in difficulties; harassed.
ORIGIN – from Dutch *belegeren* 'camp round'.

belemnite /belləmnīt/ > *noun* an extinct marine cephalopod mollusc with a bullet-shaped internal shell, found as a fossil.
ORIGIN – from Greek *belemnon* 'dart'.

belfry > *noun* (pl. **belfries**) the place in a bell tower or steeple in which bells are housed.
ORIGIN – Old French *belfrei*.

Belgian > *noun* a person from Belgium. > *adjective* relating to Belgium.

Belial /beeliəl/ > *noun* the Devil.
ORIGIN – Hebrew, 'worthlessness'.

belie > *verb* (**belied, belying**) **1** fail to give a true idea of. **2** show to be untrue or unjustified.
ORIGIN – Old English, 'deceive by lying'.

belief > *noun* **1** a feeling that something exists or is true, especially where there is no proof. **2** a firmly held opinion or conviction. **3** (**belief in**) trust or confidence in. **4** religious faith.
IDIOMS – **beyond belief** astonishing; incredible.
SYNONYMS – **1** confidence, faith, trust. **2** conviction, creed, principle.
ANTONYMS – **1** disbelief, doubt.

believe* > *verb* **1** accept that (something) is true or (someone) is telling the truth. **2** (**believe in**) have faith in the truth or existence of. **3** have religious faith. **4** think or suppose.
DERIVATIVES – **believable** *adjective* **believer** *noun*.
*SPELLING – *i* before *e* except after *c*: bel*ie*ve.
SYNONYMS – **1** credit, trust. **2** (**believe in**) accept, count on, support. . **4** assume, consider, hold, presume.
ANTONYMS – disbelieve, doubt.

Belisha beacon /bəleeshə/ > *noun* (in the UK) an orange ball containing a flashing light, mounted on a post at each end of a zebra crossing.
ORIGIN – named after Leslie Hore-*Belisha* (1893–1957), UK Minister of Transport when the beacons were introduced.

belittle > *verb* dismiss as unimportant.
SYNONYMS – denigrate, deprecate, depreciate, disparage, slight.
ANTONYMS – magnify, praise.

Belizean /beleeziən/ (also **Belizian**) > *noun* a person from Belize, a country on the Caribbean coast of Central America. > *adjective* relating to Belize.

bell > *noun* **1** a deep inverted metal cup that

sounds a clear musical note when struck. **2** a device that buzzes or rings to give a signal. **3** (**bells**) a musical instrument consisting of a set of metal tubes, played by being struck. **4** Nautical the time as indicated every half-hour of a watch by the striking of the ship's bell one to eight times: *at five bells in the forenoon of June 11.* **5** something bell-shaped, in particular the end of a trumpet. > *verb* **1** summon or indicate with a bell. **2** flare outwards in the shape of a bell.
WORDFINDER – campanile (*bell tower*), campanology (*bell-ringing*), carillon (*set of bells sounded from a keyboard*), change-ringing (*ringing church bells in varying orders*), knell (*sound of bell, especially at funeral*), peal (*ringing of bells, or set of bells*), ropesight (*skill in change-ringing*), tocsin (*alarm bell*).
IDIOMS – **bell the cat** take the danger of a shared enterprise upon oneself. [ORIGIN – an allusion to a fable in which the mice suggest hanging a bell around the cat's neck to have warning of its approach.] **bells and whistles** attractive additional features or trimmings. **give someone a bell** Brit. informal telephone someone. **ring a bell** informal sound vaguely familiar.
COMBINATIONS – **bell-bottoms** trousers with a marked flare below the knee. **bellboy** (also **bellhop**) chiefly N. Amer. a porter in a hotel or club. **bell curve** Statistics a graph of a normal distribution, with a large rounded peak which tapers away at each end. **bellflower** a plant with blue, purple, or white bell-shaped flowers. **bell jar** a bell-shaped glass cover for use in a laboratory. **bell metal** an alloy of copper and tin for making bells. **bell-ringing** the activity or pastime of ringing church bells or handbells.

belladonna /belládonnə/ > *noun* **1** deadly nightshade. **2** a drug made from deadly nightshade.
ORIGIN – Italian *bella donna* 'fair lady', perhaps from the cosmetic use of its juice to dilate the pupils.

belle /bel/ > *noun* a beautiful girl or woman.
ORIGIN – French, 'beautiful, fine', feminine of *beau*.

belle époque /bel epok/ > *noun* the period of settled and comfortable life before the First World War.
ORIGIN – French, 'fine period'.

belles-lettres /bel letrə/ > *plural noun* literary works written and read for their elegant style.
ORIGIN – French, 'fine letters'.

bellicose /bellikōs/ > *adjective* aggressive and ready to fight.
DERIVATIVES – **bellicosity** /bellikossiti/ *noun*.

wordpower facts

Bellicose

Bellicose and **belligerent** are both from Latin *bellum* 'war', which is the root of some other English words expressing combat or conflict. **Duel** is from *duellum*, an archaic and literary form of *bellum*, which was used in medieval Latin with the meaning 'combat between two persons', partly influenced by *dualis* 'of two'. **Rebel** comes from Latin *rebellis* (ultimately from *bellum*), and was used originally with reference to a fresh declaration of war by the defeated. Also from *bellum* are the words **antebellum** and **postbellum**, which mean 'before' and 'after a war'.

belligerence /bəlijərənss/ (also **belligerency**) > *noun* aggressive or warlike behaviour.
SYNONYMS – aggression, antagonism, hostility, truculence; Brit. informal bolshiness.

belligerent > *adjective* **1** hostile and aggressive. **2** engaged in a war or conflict. > *noun* a nation or person engaged in war or conflict.
DERIVATIVES – **belligerently** *adverb*.
SYNONYMS – *adjective* **1** aggressive, antagonistic, bellicose, hostile, pugnacious, quarrelsome. **2** fighting, hostile, warring.
ANTONYMS – **1** friendly. **2** neutral, peaceful.
ORIGIN – from Latin *belligerare* 'wage war'.

Bellini /beleeni/ > *noun* (pl. **Bellinis**) a cocktail consisting of peach juice mixed with champagne.
ORIGIN – named after the Venetian painter Giovanni *Bellini* (c.1430–1516); the cocktail was said to have been invented in Venice.

bellow > *verb* **1** emit a loud, deep roar of pain or anger. **2** shout or sing very loudly. > *noun* a loud, deep shout or sound.

bellows > *plural noun* **1** a device with a bag that emits air when squeezed together with two handles, used for blowing air into a fire. **2** an object or device with sides that allow it to expand and contract.

Bell's palsy > *noun* paralysis of the facial nerve causing muscular weakness in one side of the face.
ORIGIN – named after the Scottish anatomist Sir Charles *Bell* (1774–1842).

bellwether > *noun* **1** the leading sheep of a flock, with a bell on its neck. **2** a leader or indicator.

belly > *noun* (pl. **bellies**) **1** the front part of the human body below the ribs, containing the stomach and bowels. **2** a person's stomach. **3** the rounded underside of a ship or aircraft. **4** the top surface of a violin or similar instrument, over which the strings are placed. > *verb* (**bellies, bellied**) swell or bulge.

IDIOMS – **go belly up** informal go bankrupt.

DERIVATIVES – **bellied** adjective.

COMBINATIONS – **belly button** informal a person's navel. **belly laugh** a loud unrestrained laugh.

ORIGIN – Old English, 'bag'.

bellyache informal > *noun* a stomach pain. > *verb* complain noisily or persistently.

bellyflop informal > *noun* a dive into water, landing flat on one's front. > *verb* (**bellyflopped, bellyflopping**) perform a bellyflop.

bellyful > *noun* a sufficient amount to eat.

IDIOMS – **have a bellyful of** informal have more than enough of (something).

belong > *verb* **1** be rightly put into a particular position or class. **2** fit or be acceptable in a particular place or environment. **3** (**belong to**) be a member of. **4** (**belong to**) be the property or possession of.

belongings > *plural noun* a person's movable possessions.

Belorussian /bellōrush'n/ (also **Byelorussian**) > *noun* a person from Belarus. > *adjective* relating to Belarus.

beloved > *adjective* dearly loved. > *noun* a much loved person.

SYNONYMS – *adjective* adored, cherished, treasured. *noun* darling, sweetheart.

below > *preposition & adverb* **1** at a lower level than. **2** (in printed text) mentioned further down.

IDIOMS – **below stairs** Brit. dated in the basement of a house (occupied by servants).

Bel Paese /bel paa-**ay**zay/ > *noun* trademark a rich, mild, creamy white cheese from Italy.

ORIGIN – Italian, 'fair country'.

belt > *noun* **1** a strip of leather or other material worn round the waist to secure clothes or to carry things. **2** a continuous band in machinery that transfers motion from one wheel to another. **3** a strip or encircling area: *the asteroid belt.* **4** informal a heavy blow. > *verb* **1** fasten or secure with a belt. **2** beat or hit very hard. **3** (**belt out**) informal sing or play (something) loudly and forcefully. **4** informal rush or dash. **5** (**belt up**) informal be quiet.

IDIOMS – **below the belt** unfair; disregarding the rules. [ORIGIN – from the notion of an unfair and unlawful blow in boxing.] **belt and braces** Brit. providing double security, by using more than one means to the same end. **tighten one's belt** cut one's spending. **under one's belt** safely or satisfactorily achieved or acquired.

DERIVATIVES – **belted** adjective.

SYNONYMS – *noun* **1** girdle, sash, strap. **3** band, stretch, tract, zone.

COMBINATIONS – **beltway** US a ring road.

ORIGIN – Latin *balteus* 'girdle'.

Beltane /**bel**tayn/ > *noun* an ancient Celtic festival celebrated on May Day.

ORIGIN – Scottish Gaelic.

belter > *noun* informal **1** an outstanding example of something. **2** a loud, forceful singer or song.

beluga /bə**lōō**gə/ > *noun* (pl. same or **belugas**) **1** a small white toothed whale of Arctic waters. **2** a very large sturgeon from which caviar is obtained.

ORIGIN – Russian, 'white'.

belvedere /**bel**videer/ > *noun* a summer house or open-sided gallery positioned to command a fine view.

ORIGIN – Italian, literally 'fair sight'.

belying present participle of BELIE.

BEM > *abbreviation* British Empire Medal.

bemoan > *verb* lament or express sorrow for.

bemuse > *verb* cause to feel confused.

DERIVATIVES – **bemused** adjective **bemusement** noun.

SYNONYMS – befuddle, bewilder, confuse, perplex, puzzle.

ben > *noun* Scottish a high mountain.

ORIGIN – Scottish Gaelic and Irish.

bench > *noun* **1** a long seat for more than one person. **2** a long, sturdy work table in a workshop or laboratory. **3** (**the bench**) the office of judge or magistrate. **4** (**the bench**) a seat at the side of a sports field for coaches and players not taking part in a game.

COMBINATIONS – **bench press** an exercise in which one lies on a bench with feet on the floor and raises a weight with both arms. **bench test** (also **bench run**) a test carried out on a product before it is released.

ORIGIN – Old English, related to BANK[1].

bencher > *noun* Law (in the UK) a senior member of any of the Inns of Court.

benchmark > *noun* **1** a standard or point of reference. **2** a surveyor's mark cut in a wall and used as a reference point in measuring altitudes.

bend[1] > *verb* (past and past participle **bent**) **1** give or have a curved or angled shape, form, or course. **2** lean or curve the body downwards; stoop. **3** force or be forced to give in. **4** interpret or modify (a rule) to suit oneself. **5** direct (one's attention or energies) to a task. > *noun* **1** a curved or angled part or course. **2** a kind of knot used to join two ropes together, or one rope to another object. **3** (**the bends**) (treated as sing.) decompression sickness.

IDIOMS – **bend someone's ear** informal talk to someone at length or in an unwelcome way. **round the bend** informal mad.

DERIVATIVES – **bendable** adjective **bendy** adjective.

SYNONYMS – *verb* **1** arch, buckle, curl,

curve, flex. **2** bow, duck, lean over, stoop. *noun* **1** angle, arc, corner, curve, loop, turn.

bend[2] > *noun* Heraldry a broad diagonal stripe from top left to bottom right of a shield.

COMBINATIONS – **bend sinister** a broad diagonal stripe from top right to bottom left of a shield (a supposed sign of bastardry).

ORIGIN – Old French *bende* 'flat strip'.

bender > *noun* informal **1** a drinking bout. **2** Brit. a shelter made by covering a framework of bent branches with canvas. **3** derogatory a male homosexual.

beneath > **1** *preposition & adverb* extending or directly underneath. **2** *preposition* of lower status or worth than.

Benedictine /benni**dik**tin/ > *noun* **1** a monk or nun of a Christian religious order following the rule of St Benedict. **2** /benni**dik**teen/ trademark a liqueur based on brandy, originally made by Benedictine monks in France. > *adjective* of St Benedict or the Benedictines.

benediction > *noun* **1** the utterance of a blessing. **2** the state of being blessed.

ORIGIN – Latin, from *benedicere* 'bless'.

benefaction /benni**fak**sh'n/ > *noun* formal a donation or gift.

ORIGIN – Latin, from *bene facere* 'do good (to)'.

benefactor > *noun* a person who gives money or other help.

DERIVATIVES – **benefactress** noun.

SYNONYMS – backer, donor, patron, sponsor.

benefice /**benni**fiss/ > *noun* a Church office whereby a member of the clergy receives accommodation and income in return for pastoral duties.

ORIGIN – Latin *beneficium* 'favour, support', from *bene facere* 'do good'.

beneficent /bi**neff**iss'nt/ > *adjective* doing or resulting in good.

DERIVATIVES – **beneficence** noun **beneficently** adverb.

beneficial > *adjective* favourable or advantageous.

DERIVATIVES – **beneficially** adverb.

beneficiary > *noun* (pl. **beneficiaries**) a person who benefits from something, especially a trust or will.

benefit* > *noun* **1** an advantage gained from something. **2** a payment made by the state or an insurance scheme to someone entitled to receive it, e.g. an unemployed person. **3** a public performance to raise money for a charity. > *verb* (**benefited** or **benefitted, benefiting** or **benefitting**) **1** receive an advantage; profit. **2** bring advantage to.

IDIOMS – **benefit of clergy 1** historical exemption of the English clergy and nuns from the jurisdiction of the ordinary civil courts. **2** ecclesiastical sanction or approval.

the benefit of the doubt a concession that a person must be regarded as correct or innocent if the opposite has not been proven.

***SPELLING** – note that there is usually a single *t* in **benefited** and **benefiting**; spelling with a double *t* is commoner in American English.

SYNONYMS – *noun* **1** advantage, asset, gain, help, profit. **2** aid, allowance, grant. *verb* **1** gain, profit. **2** aid, assist, boost, help, improve.

ANTONYMS – *noun* **1** disadvantage, drawback. *verb* **2** damage, harm.

ORIGIN – Latin *benefactum* 'good deed', from *bene facere* 'do good'.

benevolent > *adjective* **1** well meaning and kindly. **2** (of an organisation) charitable rather than profit-making.

DERIVATIVES – **benevolence** *noun* **benevolently** *adverb*.

SYNONYMS – **1** altruistic, caring, compassionate, kind, sympathetic.

ANTONYMS – **1** mean, unkind.

ORIGIN – from Latin *bene volent-* 'well wishing'.

Bengali /beng**gaw**li/ > *noun* (pl. **Bengalis**) **1** a person from Bengal in the north-east of the Indian subcontinent. **2** the language of Bengal. > *adjective* relating to Bengal.

benighted > *adjective* **1** ignorant or unenlightened. **2** *archaic* unable to travel further because darkness has fallen.

benign > *adjective* **1** genial and kindly. **2** favourable; not harmful. **3** (of a tumour) not malignant.

DERIVATIVES – **benignity** *noun* **benignly** *adverb*.

SYNONYMS – **1** amiable, cordial, friendly, genial, mild. **2** advantageous, auspicious, favourable, harmless. **3** harmless.

ANTONYMS – **1** unfriendly, unkind. **2** harmful. **3** cancerous, malignant.

ORIGIN – Latin *benignus*, probably from *bene* 'well' + *-genus* '-born'.

benignant /bə**nig**nənt/ > *adjective* less common term for **BENIGN**.

DERIVATIVES – **benignancy** *noun*.

Beninese /benni**neez**/ > *noun* a person from Benin, a country in West Africa. > *adjective* relating to Benin.

benison /**benn**iz'n/ > *noun literary* a blessing.

ORIGIN – Old French *beneiçun*, from Latin *benedictio* 'benediction'.

bent¹ past and past participle of **BEND¹**. > *adjective* **1** having an angle or sharp curve. **2** *informal, chiefly Brit.* dishonest; corrupt. **3** *Brit. informal, derogatory* homosexual. **4** (**bent on**) determined to do or have. > *noun* a natural talent or inclination.

bent² > *noun* a stiff grass used for lawns and in hay grasses.

benthos > *noun* Biology the flora and fauna found on the bottom of a sea or lake.

DERIVATIVES – **benthic** *adjective*.

ORIGIN – Greek, 'depth of the sea'.

bentonite > *noun* a kind of absorbent clay formed by breakdown of volcanic ash, used especially as a filler.

ORIGIN – named after Fort *Benton* in Montana, US, where it was first found.

benumb > *verb* deprive of feeling.

Benzedrine /**ben**zidreen/ > *noun* trademark for **AMPHETAMINE**.

benzene /**ben**zeen/ > *noun* Chemistry a volatile liquid hydrocarbon present in coal tar and petroleum.

ORIGIN – from *benzoic acid*, from an Arabic word meaning 'incense of Java'.

benzine /**ben**zeen/ > *noun* a mixture of liquid hydrocarbons obtained from petroleum.

benzodiazepine /benzōdī**ay**zipeen/ > *noun* Medicine any of a class of organic compounds used as tranquillisers, such as Librium and Valium.

benzoic acid > *noun* Chemistry a white crystalline compound present in some plant resins and used as a food preservative.

DERIVATIVES – **benzoate** *noun*.

bequeath /bi**kweeth**/ > *verb* **1** leave (property) to someone by a will. **2** hand down or pass on.

ORIGIN – Old English, related to **QUOTH**.

bequest > *noun* **1** the action of bequeathing. **2** something that is bequeathed.

SYNONYMS – inheritance, legacy, settlement.

berate > *verb* scold or criticise angrily.

SYNONYMS – admonish, rebuke, reproach, scold, upbraid.

Berber /**ber**bər/ > *noun* a member of the indigenous people of North Africa.

ORIGIN – Arabic, from Greek *barbaros* 'foreigner'.

berberis /**ber**bəriss/ > *noun* a spiny shrub with yellow flowers and red berries.

ORIGIN – Latin *barbaris*.

bereave > *verb* (**be bereaved**) be deprived of a close relation or friend through their death.

DERIVATIVES – **bereavement** *noun*.

bereft > *adjective* **1** (**bereft of**) deprived of; without. **2** lonely and abandoned.

ORIGIN – archaic past participle of **BEREAVE**.

beret /**berr**ay/ > *noun* a flattish round cap of felt or cloth.

ORIGIN – French, 'Basque cap'.

bergamot /**ber**gəmot/ > *noun* **1** an oily substance extracted from a variety of Seville orange, used as flavouring in Earl Grey tea. **2** an aromatic herb of the mint family.

ORIGIN – named after *Bergamo* in northern Italy.

beriberi /berri**berr**i/ > *noun* a disease

causing inflammation of the nerves and heart failure, due to a deficiency of vitamin B_1.

ORIGIN – Sinhalese, from a word meaning 'weakness'.

berk /berk/ > *noun* Brit. informal a stupid person.

ORIGIN – abbreviation of *Berkeley* or *Berkshire Hunt*, rhyming slang for 'cunt'.

berkelium /ber**kee**liəm/ > *noun* a radioactive metallic chemical element made by high-energy atomic collisions.

ORIGIN – named after the University of *Berkeley* in California (where it was first made).

berm /berm/ > *noun* a raised bank or flat strip of land bordering a river, canal, or road.

ORIGIN – French *berme*.

Bermudan /bər**myoo**dən/ (also **Bermudian**) > *noun* a person from Bermuda. > *adjective* relating to Bermuda.

Bermuda shorts (also **Bermudas**) > *plural noun* casual knee-length shorts.

berry > *noun* (pl. **berries**) **1** a small roundish juicy fruit without a stone. **2** Botany a fruit that has its seeds enclosed in a fleshy pulp, e.g. a banana or tomato.

berserk /bər**zerk**/ > *adjective* out of control; wild and frenzied.

SYNONYMS – crazed, demented, frenzied, manic, wild.

wordpower facts

Berserk

The word **berserk** was first used in English in the early 19th century, in reference to ancient Norse warriors. These warriors, **berserkers**, fought with furious violence, literally 'going berserk'. The word derives from Old Norse, but its original meaning is uncertain: it may be from *bjorn* 'bear' + *serkr* 'coat', or possibly from *berr* 'bare' (i.e. without armour).

berserker > *noun* an ancient Norse warrior who fought with a wild frenzy.

berth > *noun* **1** a ship's place at a wharf or dock. **2** a fixed bunk on a ship or train. > *verb* **1** moor in a berth. **2** provide a berth for (a passenger).

IDIOMS – **give a wide berth to** stay well away from.

ORIGIN – probably from a nautical use of **BEAR¹** + **-TH²**.

beryl /**berr**il/ > *noun* a transparent pale green, blue, or yellow mineral used as a gemstone.

ORIGIN – Greek *bērullos*.

beryllium /bəˈrilliəm/ > *noun* a hard, grey, lightweight metallic chemical element of which the mineral beryl is a compound.

beseech > *verb* (past and past participle **besought** or **beseeched**) chiefly literary ask (someone) fervently for something.
DERIVATIVES – **beseeching** *adjective* **beseechingly** *adverb*.
SYNONYMS – entreat, implore, importune, plead.
ORIGIN – from Old English *sēcan* 'seek'.

beset > *verb* (**besetting**; past and past participle **beset**) trouble or harass persistently.

beside > *preposition* **1** at the side of; next to. **2** compared with. **3** in addition to; apart from.
IDIOMS – **beside oneself** distraught.

besides > *preposition* in addition to; apart from. > *adverb* in addition; as well.

besiege* > *verb* **1** surround (a place) with armed forces in order to capture it or force it to surrender. **2** harass or oppress with requests or complaints.
DERIVATIVES – **besieger** *noun*.
*SPELLING – the usual rule is *i* before *e* except after *c*: besiege.
SYNONYMS – **1** blockade, encircle. **2** assail, beset, harass, overwhelm, pester.

besmirch /biˈsmurch/ > *verb* **1** damage (someone's reputation). **2** literary make dirty; soil.
SYNONYMS – **1** blacken, drag through the mud, sully, tarnish.

besom /ˈbeez'm/ > *noun* **1** a broom made of twigs tied round a stick. **2** derogatory, chiefly Scottish & N. English a woman or girl.

besotted /biˈsottid/ > *adjective* strongly infatuated.
ORIGIN – from obsolete *besot* 'make foolishly affectionate', from SOT.

besought past and past participle of BESEECH.

bespatter > *verb* spatter with liquid.

bespeak > *verb* (past **bespoke**; past participle **bespoken**) **1** be evidence of. **2** order or reserve in advance.

bespectacled > *adjective* wearing glasses.

bespoke > *adjective* Brit. (of goods) made to order.

best > *adjective* **1** of the most excellent or desirable type or quality. **2** most suitable, appropriate, or sensible. > *adverb* **1** to the highest degree; most. **2** to the highest standard. **3** most suitably, appropriately, or sensibly. > *noun* **1** (**the best**) that which is the most excellent or desirable. **2** (**one's best**) the highest standard one can reach. **3** (in sport) a record performance. > *verb* informal outwit or defeat.
IDIOMS – **at best** taking the most optimistic view. **be for the best** be desirable in the end, although not at first seeming so. **the best-laid plans of mice and men gang aft agley** proverb even the most careful planning doesn't necessarily ensure success. [ORIGIN – see GANG².] **the best of three** (or **five** etc.) victory achieved by winning the majority of a specified odd number of games. **the best part of** most of. **get the best of** overcome. **give someone best** Brit. admit that someone is superior. **had best** find it most sensible to. **make the best of** derive what limited advantage one can from. **six of the best** Brit. a caning as a punishment, traditionally with six strokes of the cane.
SYNONYMS – *adjective* **1** finest, greatest, optimum, superlative, supreme.
ANTONYMS – *adjective* **1** worst.
COMBINATIONS – **best boy** the assistant to the chief electrician of a film crew. **best end** Brit. the rib end of a neck of lamb or other meat. **best man** a male friend or relative chosen by a bridegroom to assist him at his wedding. **best-seller** a book or other product that sells in very large numbers.

bestial /ˈbestiəl/ > *adjective* **1** of or like a beast. **2** savagely cruel and wicked.
DERIVATIVES – **bestially** *adverb*.
ORIGIN – Latin *bestialis*, from *bestia* 'beast'.

bestiality > *noun* **1** savagely cruel and wicked behaviour. **2** sexual intercourse between a person and an animal.

bestiary /ˈbestiəri/ > *noun* (pl. **bestiaries**) a book describing animals, especially a moralising medieval work.

bestir > *verb* (**bestirred**, **bestirring**) (**bestir oneself**) exert or rouse oneself.

bestow > *verb* give or grant (an honour, right, or gift).
DERIVATIVES – **bestowal** *noun*.
SYNONYMS – award, confer, donate, grant, present.
ORIGIN – from Old English *stōw* 'place'.

bestrew > *verb* (past participle **bestrewed** or **bestrewn**) literary scatter or lie scattered over (a surface).

bestride > *verb* (past **bestrode**; past participle **bestridden**) stand astride over; span or straddle.

bet > *verb* (**betting**; past and past participle **bet** or **betted**) **1** risk money or property against another's on the basis of the outcome of an unpredictable event such as a race or game. **2** informal feel sure. > *noun* **1** an act of betting. **2** a sum of money staked. **3** informal a candidate or option with a specified likelihood of success: *Allen looked a good bet for victory*. **4** (**one's bet**) informal one's opinion.
IDIOMS – **you bet** informal you may be sure; certainly.
DERIVATIVES – **bettor** (also **better**) *noun*.
SYNONYMS – *verb* **1** gamble, hazard, risk, wager. *noun* **1** gamble. **2** ante, stake.
ORIGIN – perhaps a shortening of obsolete *abet* 'abetment'.

beta /ˈbeetə/ > *noun* **1** the second letter of the Greek alphabet (Β, β), transliterated as 'b'. **2** Brit. a second-class mark given for a piece of work.
COMBINATIONS – **beta particle** (also **beta ray**) Physics a fast-moving electron emitted by some radioactive substances. **beta rhythm** Physiology the normal electrical activity of the brain when conscious and alert. **beta testing** independent trials of a new product carried out in the final stages of development (after alpha testing).
ORIGIN – Greek.

beta blocker > *noun* a drug which prevents increased activity by the heart, used to treat angina and reduce high blood pressure.
ORIGIN – so called because such drugs *block* a group of receptors in the nervous system (denoted *beta*) which increase heart activity.

betake > *verb* (past **betook**; past participle **betaken**) (**betake oneself to**) literary go to.

betatron /ˈbeetətron/ > *noun* Physics an apparatus for accelerating electrons in a circular path by magnetic induction.

betel /ˈbeet'l/ > *noun* the leaf of an evergreen plant related to pepper, which in the East is chewed and used as a mild stimulant.
COMBINATIONS – **betel nut** the bitter-tasting seed of an areca palm, chewed with betel leaves.
ORIGIN – Portuguese, from a Dravidian language.

bête noire /bet ˈnwaar/ > *noun* (pl. **bêtes noires** pronunc. same) (**one's bête noire**) a person or thing that one particularly dislikes.
ORIGIN – French, 'black beast'.

bethink > *verb* (past and past participle **bethought**) (**bethink oneself**) formal come to think.

betide > *verb* literary happen; befall.

betimes > *adverb* literary in good time; early.

bêtise /beˈteez/ > *noun* a foolish remark or action.
ORIGIN – French, from *bête* 'foolish'.

betoken > *verb* literary be a warning or sign of.

betony /ˈbettəni/ > *noun* a plant of the mint family bearing spikes of purple flowers.
ORIGIN – Latin *betonica*.

betook past of BETAKE.

betray > *verb* **1** act treacherously towards (a person, country, etc.) by revealing information to or otherwise aiding the enemy. **2** be disloyal or unfaithful to. **3** unintentionally reveal; be evidence of.
DERIVATIVES – **betrayal** *noun* **betrayer** *noun*.
SYNONYMS – **1,2** double-cross, give away. **3** expose, give away, reveal.
ANTONYMS – **1,2** be loyal to, stick by. **3** conceal, hide.

ORIGIN – from **BE-** + obsolete *tray* 'betray', based on Latin *tradere* 'hand over'.

betrothed ▷ *adjective* formally engaged to be married. ▷ *noun* (**one's betrothed**) the person to whom one is engaged.

DERIVATIVES – **betrothal** *noun*.

better ▷ *adjective* **1** more desirable, satisfactory, or effective. **2** partly or fully recovered from illness or injury. ▷ *adverb* **1** more satisfactorily or effectively. **2** to a greater degree; more. ▷ *noun* **1** that which is better; the better one. **2** (**one's betters**) chiefly dated or humorous one's superiors in social class or ability. ▷ *verb* **1** improve on or surpass. **2** make (something) better; improve. **3** (**better oneself**) achieve a higher social position or status.

IDIOMS – **better the devil you know than the devil you don't know** proverb it's wiser to deal with an undesirable but familiar person or situation than to risk a change that might lead to something worse. **better off** in a more advantageous position, especially in financial terms. **the better part of** almost all of; most of. **better safe than sorry** proverb it's wiser to be cautious and careful than to be hasty or rash and so do something you may later regret. **for better or worse** whether the outcome is good or bad. **get the better of** defeat or overcome. **had better** would find it wiser to.

USAGE – in the phrase **had better do something** the word **had** is often dropped in informal speech, as in *you better not come tonight*. In writing, the **had** may be contracted to **'d** but it should not be dropped altogether.

SYNONYMS – *adjective* **1** preferable, superior. **2** cured, healed, healthier, recovered, well. *verb* **1** beat, improve on, surpass, top. **2** improve, raise; formal ameliorate, meliorate.

ANTONYMS – *adjective* worse.

betterment ▷ *noun* improvement.

bettong /**bett**ong/ ▷ *noun* a short-nosed Australian rat-kangaroo.

ORIGIN – Dharuk (an Aboriginal language).

between ▷ *preposition & adverb* **1** at, into, or across the space separating (two objects, places, or points). **2** in the period separating (two points in time). **3** (as preposition) indicating a connection or relationship involving (two or more parties). **4** (as preposition) by combining the resources or actions of (two or more parties).

IDIOMS – **between ourselves** (or **you and me**) in confidence.

USAGE – it is correct to say **between you and me** but incorrect to say **between you and I**, because a preposition such as **between** should be followed by an object pronoun such as **me**, **him**, **her**, and **us**

rather than a subject pronoun such as **I**, **he**, **she**, and **we**.

betwixt ▷ *preposition & adverb* archaic term for **BETWEEN**.

IDIOMS – **betwixt and between** informal neither one thing nor the other.

bevel ▷ *noun* **1** (in carpentry) a surface or edge which slopes away from a horizontal or vertical surface. **2** (also **bevel square**) a tool for marking angles in carpentry and stonework. ▷ *verb* (**bevelled, bevelling**; US **beveled, beveling**) cut a bevel on.

ORIGIN – Old French, from *baif* 'open-mouthed', from *baer* 'gape'.

beverage ▷ *noun* a drink, other than water.

ORIGIN – Old French *bevrage*, from Latin *bibere* 'to drink'.

bevvy ▷ *noun* (pl. **bevvies**) Brit. informal an alcoholic drink.

DERIVATIVES – **bevvied** *adjective*.

ORIGIN – abbreviation of **BEVERAGE**.

bevy /**bevv**i/ ▷ *noun* (pl. **bevies**) a large group of people or things.

bewail ▷ *verb* greatly regret or lament.

DERIVATIVES – **bewailer** *noun*.

SYNONYMS – bemoan, deplore, lament, mourn, regret.

beware ▷ *verb* be cautious and alert to risks or dangers.

SYNONYMS – be careful, look out, take care, watch out.

ORIGIN – from the phrase *be ware* 'be aware'.

bewilder ▷ *verb* perplex or confuse.

DERIVATIVES – **bewildered** *adjective* **bewildering** *adjective* **bewilderingly** *adverb* **bewilderment** *noun*.

SYNONYMS – baffle, confound, confuse, perplex, puzzle.

ORIGIN – from obsolete *wilder* 'lead or go astray'.

bewitch ▷ *verb* **1** cast a spell over. **2** enchant and delight.

DERIVATIVES – **bewitcher** *noun* **bewitching** *adjective* **bewitchment** *noun*.

SYNONYMS – **1** enchant, entrance, hex. **2** captivate, delight, enchant, entrance.

beyond ▷ *preposition & adverb* **1** at or to the further side of. **2** more extensive or extreme than. **3** happening or continuing after. **4** having reached or progressed further than (a specified level or amount). **5** to or in a degree where a specified action is impossible. **6** apart from; except. ▷ *noun* (**the beyond**) the unknown, especially in references to life after death.

bezel /**bezz**'l/ ▷ *noun* a groove holding a gemstone or the glass cover of a watch in position.

ORIGIN – Old French.

bezique /bi**zeek**/ ▷ *noun* a trick-taking card game for two, played with a double pack of 64 cards.

ORIGIN – French *bésigue*, perhaps from a Persian word meaning 'juggler'.

Bh ▷ *symbol* the chemical element bohrium.

bhaji /**baa**ji/ (also **bhajia** /**baa**jə/) ▷ *noun* (pl. **bhajis, bhajia**) (in Indian cooking) a small flat cake or ball of vegetables, fried in batter.

ORIGIN – Hindi, 'fried vegetables'.

bhang /bang/ (also **bang**) ▷ *noun* (in India) the leaves and flower-tops of cannabis, used as a narcotic.

ORIGIN – Hindi.

bhangra /**baang**grə/ ▷ *noun* a type of popular music combining Punjabi folk traditions with Western pop music.

ORIGIN – Punjabi, denoting a type of folk dance.

b.h.p. ▷ *abbreviation* brake horsepower.

Bhutanese /boōtə**neez**/ ▷ *noun* a person from Bhutan, a small kingdom in the Himalayas. ▷ *adjective* relating to Bhutan.

Bi ▷ *symbol* the chemical element bismuth.

bi- (also **bin-** before a vowel) ▷ *combining form* **1** two; having two: *biathlon*. **2** occurring twice in every one or once in every two: *bicentennial*. **3** lasting for two: *biennial*.

ORIGIN – Latin, 'doubly, having two'.

biannual ▷ *adjective* occurring twice a year. Compare with **BIENNIAL**.

DERIVATIVES – **biannually** *adverb*.

bias ▷ *noun* **1** an inclination or prejudice in favour of a particular person, thing, or viewpoint. **2** a slanting direction across the grain of a fabric. **3** the tendency of a ball in the game of bowls to swerve because it is slightly flattened on one side. **4** Electronics a steady voltage, applied to an electronic system or device, that can be adjusted to change the way the device operates. ▷ *verb* (**biased, biasing**) influence unfairly; prejudice.

SYNONYMS – *noun* **1** favouritism, partiality, predisposition, prejudice.

ANTONYMS – *noun* **1** impartiality, objectivity.

COMBINATIONS – **bias binding** a narrow strip of fabric cut on the bias, used to bind edges.

ORIGIN – first used in the sense 'oblique' or 'oblique line': from French *biais*.

biased* ▷ *adjective* having a bias; unfairly influenced or prejudiced.

*SPELLING – only one *s*: biased.

SYNONYMS – one-sided, partial, partisan, slanted.

biathlon ▷ *noun* a sporting event in which the competitors combine cross-country skiing and rifle shooting.

DERIVATIVES – **biathlete** *noun*.

bib¹ ▷ *noun* **1** a piece of cloth or plastic fastened under a child's chin to keep its clothes clean while it is eating. **2** the upper front part of an apron or pair of dungarees.

IDIOMS – **one's best bib and tucker** informal one's smartest clothes.

wordpower facts
Bib
The relationship between the words is unclear, but it seems likely that the three English words **bib** are related to each other and also to **beer**, **beverage**, **bibulous**, and **imbibe**. The common root is the Latin verb *bibere*, meaning 'to drink'. Of the three forms of **bib**, the archaic verb meaning 'to drink' arose first, in the Middle Ages: it probably came from *bibere*, although it may have originated in imitation of repeated movements of the lips made while drinking. **Bib**[1] is thought to have developed from this verb, either because it is worn by a child while it is drinking or because the bib 'drinks' moisture that is spilled on it. **Bib**[3], the fish, seems to have got its name from the membrane that it can distend to cover its head.

bib[2] > *verb* (**bibbed**, **bibbing**) archaic drink (an alcoholic drink).
DERIVATIVES – **bibber** *noun*.

bib[3] > *noun* a common inshore fish of the cod family.

bibelot /**beeb**əlō/ > *noun* a small ornament or trinket.
ORIGIN – French, from *bel* 'beautiful'.

Bible > *noun* **1** the Christian scriptures, consisting of the Old and New Testaments. **2** the Jewish scriptures. **3** (**bible**) informal a book regarded as authoritative.
ORIGIN – Greek *biblion* 'book'.

biblical > *adjective* relating to or contained in the Bible.
DERIVATIVES – **biblically** *adverb*.

bibliography /bibli**og**rəfi/ > *noun* (pl. **bibliographies**) **1** a list of books or documents relevant to a particular subject or author. **2** the study of books in terms of their classification, printing, and publication. **3** a list of the books referred to in a scholarly work.
DERIVATIVES – **bibliographer** *noun* **bibliographic** *adjective*.

bibliomania > *noun* passionate enthusiasm for collecting and possessing books.
DERIVATIVES – **bibliomaniac** *noun* & *adjective*.

bibliophile /**bibl**iōfīl/ > *noun* a person who collects or has a great love of books.
DERIVATIVES – **bibliophilic** *adjective* **bibliophily** *noun*.

bibulous /**bib**yooləss/ > *adjective* formal very fond of drinking alcohol.

DERIVATIVES – **bibulously** *adverb* **bibulousness** *noun*.
ORIGIN – Latin *bibulus* 'freely drinking'.

bicameral /bī**kamm**ərəl/ > *adjective* (of a legislative body) having two chambers.
DERIVATIVES – **bicameralism** *noun*.
ORIGIN – from Latin *camera* 'chamber'.

bicarbonate /bī**kaar**bənayt/> *noun* **1** Chemistry a salt containing the anion HCO_3^-. **2** (also **bicarbonate of soda**) sodium bicarbonate.

bicentenary > *noun* (pl. **bicentenaries**) the two-hundredth anniversary of a significant event.
DERIVATIVES – **bicentennial** *noun* & *adjective*.

biceps /**bī**seps/ > *noun* (pl. same) **1** a large muscle in the upper arm which flexes the arm and forearm and turns the hand to face palm uppermost. **2** (also **leg biceps**) a muscle in the back of the thigh which helps to flex the leg.
ORIGIN – Latin, 'two-headed' (because the muscle has two points of attachment).

bichon frise /beeshən **freez**/ > *noun* a breed of toy dog with a fine, curly, white coat.
ORIGIN – from French *barbichon* 'little water spaniel' + *frisé* 'curly-haired'.

bicker > *verb* argue about trivial matters.
SYNONYMS – quarrel, squabble, wrangle.

bicuspid > *adjective* having two cusps or points. > *noun* a tooth with two cusps, especially a human premolar tooth.
ORIGIN – from Latin *cuspis* 'sharp point'.

bicycle > *noun* a vehicle consisting of two wheels held in a frame one behind the other, propelled by pedals and steered with handlebars attached to the front wheel. > *verb* ride a bicycle.
DERIVATIVES – **bicyclist** *noun*.
ORIGIN – from Greek *kuklos* 'wheel'.

bid[1] > *verb* (**bidding**; past and past participle **bid**) **1** offer (a certain price) for something, especially at an auction. **2** (**bid for**) (of a contractor) tender for (work). **3** (usu. **bid for** or **to do**) make an effort to obtain or achieve: *they are bidding for places in the England side.* > *noun* **1** an offer to buy something. **2** an offer to do work or supply goods at a stated price. **3** an effort to obtain or achieve something.
DERIVATIVES – **bidder** *noun* **bidding** *noun*.
SYNONYMS – *verb* **1** offer, submit, tender.

bid[2] > *verb* (**bidding**; past **bid** or **bade**; past participle **bid**) **1** utter (a greeting or farewell) to. **2** archaic command (someone) to do something.

biddable > *adjective* meekly ready to accept and follow instructions.

bidden archaic or literary past participle of **BID**[2].

biddy > *noun* (pl. **biddies**) informal a woman, especially an old one.

bide > *verb* archaic or dialect remain or stay in a certain place.
IDIOMS – **bide one's time** wait quietly for a good opportunity to do something.

bidet /**bee**day/ > *noun* a low oval basin for washing one's genital and anal area.
ORIGIN – French, 'pony'.

Biedermeier /**bee**dərmīər/ > *adjective* denoting a 19th-century German style of furniture and decoration characterised by restraint and utilitarianism.
ORIGIN – from the name of a fictitious German schoolmaster created by L. Eichrodt (1854).

biennial > *adjective* **1** taking place every other year. Compare with **BIANNUAL**. **2** (of a plant) taking two years to grow from seed to fruition and die. > *noun* **1** a biennial plant. **2** an event celebrated or taking place every two years.
DERIVATIVES – **biennially** *adverb*.
ORIGIN – from Latin *annus* 'year'.

bier /beer/ > *noun* a movable platform on which a coffin or corpse is placed before burial.

biff informal > *verb* strike roughly with the fist. > *noun* a sharp blow with the fist.

bifid /**bī**fid/ > *adjective* Botany & Zoology divided by a deep cleft or notch into two parts.
ORIGIN – Latin *bifidus* 'doubly split'.

bifocal > *adjective* (of a lens) having two parts each with a different focal length, one for distant and one for near vision. > *noun* (**bifocals**) a pair of glasses with bifocal lenses.

bifurcate > *verb* /**bī**fərkayt/ divide into two branches or forks. > *adjective* /bī**fur**kət/ forked; branched.
DERIVATIVES – **bifurcation** *noun*.
ORIGIN – Latin *bifurcare* 'divide into two forks'.

big > *adjective* (**bigger**, **biggest**) **1** of considerable size, physical power, or extent. **2** of considerable importance or seriousness. **3** informal exciting great interest or popularity. **4** informal, often ironic generous: *'That's big of you!'*
IDIOMS – **big with child** archaic advanced in pregnancy. **in a big way** informal to a great extent or high degree. **talk big** informal talk confidently or boastfully. **think big** informal be ambitious. **too big for one's boots** informal conceited.
DERIVATIVES – **bigness** *noun*.
SYNONYMS – **1** considerable, large, sizeable, substantial. **2** major, significant, substantial.
ANTONYMS – little, small; insignificant, minor.
COMBINATIONS – **big band** a large group of musicians playing jazz or swing music. **big bang** the rapid expansion of matter from a state of extremely high density and

temperature which, according to current theories, marked the origin of the universe. **Big Brother** a person or organisation exercising total control over people's lives. [ORIGIN – from the name of the fictitious head of state in George Orwell's *Nineteen Eighty-four* (1949).] **big business** large-scale financial or commercial activity. **big cheese** informal an important person. [ORIGIN – *cheese* is probably from a Persian word meaning 'thing': the phrase *the cheese* was used earlier to mean 'first-rate' (i.e. *the* thing).] **big crunch** a contraction of the universe to a state of extremely high density and temperature (a hypothetical opposite of the big bang). **big dipper 1** Brit. a roller coaster. **2** (**the Big Dipper**) North American term for PLOUGH (in sense 2). **big end** (in a piston engine) the larger end of the connecting rod, encircling the crankpin. **big game** large animals hunted for sport. **big-head** informal a conceited person. **big mouth** informal an indiscreet or boastful person. **the big screen** informal the cinema. **the big time** informal the highest or most successful level in a career. **big top** the main tent in a circus. **big wheel 1** a Ferris wheel. **2** N. Amer. an important person. **bigwig** (also **big gun** or **big shot**) informal an important person.

bigamy > *noun* the offence of marrying someone while already married to another person.

DERIVATIVES – **bigamist** *noun* **bigamous** *adjective*.

ORIGIN – from Latin *bi-* 'twice' + Greek *-gamos* 'married'.

Bigfoot > *noun* (pl. **Bigfeet**) a large, hairy ape-like creature, supposedly found in NW America.

bight /bīt/ > *noun* **1** a curve or recess in a coastline or other geographical feature. **2** a loop of rope.

ORIGIN – Old English, 'a bend or angle'.

bigot /**bigg**ət/ > *noun* a person who is prejudiced in their views and intolerant of the opinions of others.

DERIVATIVES – **bigotry** *noun*.

ORIGIN – French.

bigoted > *adjective* prejudiced against and intolerant of those who hold different opinions.

SYNONYMS – illiberal, intolerant, narrow-minded, prejudiced.

ANTONYMS – liberal, open-minded.

bijou /**bee**zhoo/ > *adjective* small and elegant. > *noun* (pl. **bijoux** pronunc. same) archaic a jewel or trinket.

ORIGIN – French, 'jewel', from Breton *bizou* 'finger-ring'.

bike informal > *noun* a bicycle or motorcycle. > *verb* ride a bicycle or motorcycle.

DERIVATIVES – **biker** *noun*.

bikini > *noun* (pl. **bikinis**) a women's two-piece swimsuit.

ORIGIN – named after *Bikini*, an atoll in the western Pacific, where an atom bomb was exploded in 1946 (because of the supposed 'explosive' effect created by the garment).

bilateral > *adjective* **1** having two sides. **2** involving two parties.

DERIVATIVES – **bilaterally** *adverb*.

bilberry > *noun* (pl. **bilberries**) the small blue edible berry of a hardy dwarf shrub found on heathland and high ground.

bilby /**bil**bi/ > *noun* (pl. **bilbies**) a burrowing Australian bandicoot with long ears.

Bildungsroman /**bil**dooongzrōmaan/ > *noun* a novel dealing with someone's formative years or spiritual education.

ORIGIN – German, from *Bildung* 'education' + *Roman* 'a novel'.

bile > *noun* **1** a bitter fluid which aids digestion, secreted by the liver and stored in the gall bladder. **2** anger or resentment.

COMBINATIONS – **bile duct** the tube which conveys bile from the liver and the gall bladder to the duodenum.

ORIGIN – Latin *bilis*; sense 2 arose because in medieval medicine bile—the cardinal humour 'yellow bile' or *choler*—was associated with an irritable temperament (see box at HUMOUR).

bilge > *noun* **1** the area on the outer surface of a ship's hull where the bottom curves to meet the vertical sides. **2** (**bilges**) the lowest internal portion of the hull. **3** (also **bilge water**) dirty water that collects inside the bilges. **4** informal nonsense; rubbish. > *verb* archaic break a hole in the bilge of (a ship).

bilharzia /bil**haart**siə/ > *noun* a chronic disease caused by infestation with blood flukes, endemic in parts of Africa and South America.

ORIGIN – named after the German physician Theodor *Bilharz* (1825–62), who discovered the parasite.

bilingual > *adjective* **1** speaking two languages fluently. **2** expressed in or using two languages.

DERIVATIVES – **bilingualism** *noun*.

bilious > *adjective* **1** relating to bile. **2** affected by nausea or vomiting. **3** bad-tempered or resentful.

DERIVATIVES – **biliously** *adverb* **biliousness** *noun*.

bilk > *verb* informal **1** cheat or defraud. **2** obtain (money) fraudulently.

DERIVATIVES – **bilker** *noun*.

ORIGIN – perhaps a variant of BAULK.

Bill > *noun* (**the Bill** or **the Old Bill**) Brit. informal the police.

bill¹ > *noun* **1** a printed or written statement of the money owed for goods or services. **2** a draft of a proposed law presented to parliament for discussion. **3** a programme of entertainment at a theatre or cinema. **4** a poster or handbill. **5** N. Amer. a banknote. > *verb* **1** list (a person or event) in a programme. **2** (**bill as**) proclaim as. **3** send a bill to. **4** charge (a sum of money).

IDIOMS – **bill of exchange** a written order requiring a person to make a specified payment to the signatory or to a named payee. **bill of lading** a detailed list of a ship's cargo given by the master of the ship to the person consigning the goods. **a clean bill of health** a declaration or confirmation of good health or condition. [ORIGIN – from *bill of health*, a certificate relating to the incidence of infectious disease on a ship or in the port from which it has sailed.] **fit the bill** be suitable for a particular purpose.

DERIVATIVES – **billable** *adjective* **billing** *noun*.

COMBINATIONS – **billboard** a hoarding. **billfold** N. Amer. a wallet. **bill of rights** a statement of rights, in particular the English constitutional settlement of 1689 and the first ten amendments to the Constitution of the US, ratified in 1791. **billposter** (also **billsticker**) a person who pastes up advertisements or other notices on hoardings.

ORIGIN – Old French *bille*, probably from Latin *bulla* 'seal, sealed document'.

bill² > *noun* **1** the beak of a bird. **2** a narrow promontory. > *verb* (of birds, especially doves) stroke bill with bill during courtship.

IDIOMS – **bill and coo** informal behave or talk in a loving and sentimental way.

billabong > *noun* Austral. a branch of a river forming a backwater or stagnant pool.

ORIGIN – Wiradhuri (an Aboriginal language).

billet¹ > *noun* a civilian house where soldiers are lodged temporarily. > *verb* (**billeted**, **billeting**) lodge (soldiers) in a civilian house.

ORIGIN – first used in reference to a short document, later a written order requiring a householder to lodge the bearer; from Old French *billette*; related to BILL¹.

billet² > *noun* **1** a thick piece of wood. **2** a small bar of metal for further processing.

ORIGIN – Old French *billette* 'little tree trunk', from Latin *billa*, *billus* 'branch, trunk'.

billet-doux /billi**doo**/ > *noun* (pl. **billets-doux** /billi**dooz**/) dated or humorous a love letter.

ORIGIN – French, 'sweet note'.

billhook > *noun* a tool having a sickle-shaped blade with a sharp inner edge, used for pruning or lopping branches.

billiards > *plural noun* (treated as sing.) a game played on a billiard table, for two people using three balls.

COMBINATIONS – **billiard table** a smooth cloth-covered rectangular table used in billiards, snooker, and some forms of pool, with six pockets at the corners and sides into which balls are struck with cues.

ORIGIN – French *billard*, from Old French *bille* 'tree trunk'.

billion > *cardinal number* **1** a thousand million; 1,000,000,000 or 10^9. **2** dated, chiefly Brit. a million million (1,000,000,000,000 or 10^{12}). **3** (**billions**) informal a very large number or amount.

DERIVATIVES – **billionth** *ordinal number*.

ORIGIN – from *million*, by substitution of the prefix *bi-* 'two' for the initial letters.

billionaire > *noun* a person possessing assets worth at least a billion pounds or dollars.

billow > *noun* **1** a large undulating mass of cloud, smoke, or steam. **2** archaic a large sea wave. > *verb* **1** (of fabric) fill with air and swell outwards. **2** (of smoke, cloud, or steam) move or flow outward with an undulating motion.

DERIVATIVES – **billowy** *adjective*.

SYNONYMS – *verb* **1** balloon, belly, bulge out, float. **2** pour, swirl.

ORIGIN – Old Norse.

billy (also **billycan**) > *noun* (pl. **billies**) a tin or enamel cooking pot with a lid and folding handle, used in camping.

ORIGIN – perhaps from an Aboriginal word meaning 'water'.

billy goat > *noun* a male goat.

ORIGIN – from *Billy*, familiar form of the given name *William*.

bimbo > *noun* (pl. **bimbos**) informal, derogatory an attractive but unintelligent or frivolous young woman.

DERIVATIVES – **bimbette** *noun*.

wordpower facts

Bimbo

Although the word **bimbo** has a contemporary feel it has quite a long history. It comes from an Italian word meaning 'little child, baby', and is first recorded in English in 1919. The *Oxford English Dictionary* defines its first use as 'a fellow, chap; usu. contemptuous', and gives the example 'Nothing but the most heroic measures will save the poor bimbo'. About a decade later it developed the new meaning 'a woman, especially a prostitute'. It was not until the late 1980s that the word acquired its modern sense and enjoyed a new vogue in the media.

bimonthly > *adjective & adverb* appearing or taking place twice a month or every two months.

USAGE – the meaning of **bimonthly** (and other similar words such as **biweekly** and **biyearly**) is ambiguous. The only way to avoid this ambiguity is to use alternative expressions such as *every two months* and *twice a month*.

bin Brit. > *noun* **1** a receptacle in which rubbish is placed for disposal. **2** a large container for storing a specified substance. **3** a partitioned container for storing wine. > *verb* (**binned**, **binning**) **1** throw (something) away by putting it in a bin. **2** store (wine) in a bin.

COMBINATIONS – **bin-end** one of the last bottles from a bin of wine.

binary /bīnəri/ > *adjective* **1** composed of or involving two things. **2** using or denoting a system of numbers with two as its base, employing the digits 0 and 1. > *noun* (pl. **binaries**) **1** the binary system of notation. **2** Astronomy a system of two stars revolving round their common centre.

ORIGIN – Latin *binarius*, from *bini* 'two together'.

bind > *verb* (past and past participle **bound**) **1** tie or fasten tightly together. **2** restrain (someone) by tying their hands and feet. **3** wrap or encircle tightly. **4** hold in a united or cohesive group or mass. **5** impose an obligation on. **6** (**be bound by**) be hampered or constrained by. **7** (**bind over**) (of a court of law) require (someone) to fulfil an obligation, typically by paying a sum of money as surety. **8** secure (a contract), typically with a sum of money. **9** fix together and enclose (the pages of a book) in a cover. **10** trim (the edge of a piece of material) with a fabric strip. **11** (of a food or medicine) make (someone) constipated. > *noun* **1** informal an annoyance. **2** a statutory constraint. **3** Music another term for TIE.

SYNONYMS – *verb* **1** fasten, lash together, tie. **2** restrain, tie up, truss.

binder > *noun* **1** a cover for holding magazines or loose sheets of paper together. **2** a reaping machine that binds grain into sheaves. **3** a bookbinder.

bindery > *noun* (pl. **binderies**) a workshop or factory in which books are bound.

bindi /bindee/ > *noun* (pl. **bindis**) a decorative mark worn in the middle of the forehead by Indian women.

ORIGIN – Hindi.

binding > *noun* **1** a strong covering holding the pages of a book together. **2** fabric cut or woven in a strip, used for binding the edges of a piece of material. **3** a device fixed to a ski to grip a ski boot. > *adjective* (of an agreement) involving a contractual obligation.

SYNONYMS – *adjective* compulsory, obligatory, unbreakable.

bindweed > *noun* a twining plant with trumpet-shaped flowers, several kinds of which are invasive weeds.

bine /bīn/ > *noun* a long, flexible stem of a climbing plant.

ORIGIN – a dialect form of BIND.

binge > *noun* a period of excessive indulgence in something, especially eating or drinking. > *verb* (**binged**, **bingeing** or US also **binging**) indulge in an activity, especially eating, to excess.

DERIVATIVES – **binger** *noun*.

SYNONYMS – *noun* debauch, drinking bout, spree.

bingo > *noun* a game in which players mark off randomly called numbers on printed cards, the winner being the first to mark off all their numbers. > *exclamation* **1** a call by someone who wins a game of bingo. **2** used to express satisfaction at a sudden positive event or outcome.

binnacle > *noun* a built-in housing for a ship's compass.

ORIGIN – first as *bittacle*, from Spanish *bitácula* or Portuguese *bitacola*, from Latin *habitaculum* 'dwelling place'.

binocular /binokyoolər/ > *adjective* adapted for or using both eyes.

COMBINATIONS – **binocular vision** vision using two eyes with overlapping fields of view, allowing good perception of depth.

ORIGIN – from Latin *bini* 'two together' + *oculus* 'eye'.

binoculars > *plural noun* an optical instrument with a separate lens for each eye, used for viewing distant objects.

binomial /binōmiəl/ > *noun* **1** Mathematics an algebraic expression of the sum or the difference of two terms. **2** Biology the two-part Latin name of a species (the genus followed by the species name). > *adjective* consisting of two terms.

ORIGIN – from Latin *bi-* 'having two' + Greek *nomos* 'part, portion'.

bint > *noun* Brit. informal, derogatory a girl or woman.

ORIGIN – Arabic, 'daughter, girl'.

bio- > *combining form* **1** of or relating to life: *biosynthesis*. **2** biological; relating to biology: *biohazard*. **3** of living beings: *biogenesis*.

ORIGIN – from Greek *bios* 'human life', the sense being extended in modern scientific usage to mean 'organic life'.

biochemistry > *noun* the branch of science concerned with the chemical processes which occur within living organisms.

DERIVATIVES – **biochemical** *adjective* **biochemist** *noun*.

biochip > *noun* a device acting like a silicon chip, with components made from biological molecules or structures.

biocide > *noun* **1** a substance that is poisonous to living organisms, such as a pesticide. **2** the destruction of life.

DERIVATIVES – **biocidal** *adjective*.

biodegradable > *adjective* capable of being decomposed by bacteria or other living organisms.
DERIVATIVES – **biodegradability** *noun* **biodegradation** *noun* **biodegrade** *verb*.

bio-diesel > *noun* a biofuel intended as a substitute for diesel.

biodiversity > *noun* the variety of plant and animal life in the world or in a particular habitat.

bioengineering > *noun* **1** genetic engineering. **2** the use of artificial tissues or organs in the body. **3** the use in engineering or industry of organisms or biological processes.
DERIVATIVES – **bioengineer** *noun & verb*.

biofeedback > *noun* the use of electronic monitoring of a normally automatic bodily function in order to train someone to acquire voluntary control of that function.

bioflavonoid > *noun* any of a group of compounds occurring mainly in fruit, sometimes regarded as vitamins.

biofuel > *noun* fuel derived directly from living matter.

biogas > *noun* gaseous fuel, especially methane, produced by the fermentation of organic matter.

biogeography > *noun* the branch of biology concerned with the geographical distribution of plants and animals.
DERIVATIVES – **biogeographer** *noun* **biogeographic** *adjective* **biogeographical** *adjective*.

biography > *noun* (pl. **biographies**) an account of someone's life written by someone else.
DERIVATIVES – **biographer** *noun* **biographic** *adjective* **biographical** *adjective* **biographically** *adverb*.

biohazard > *noun* a risk to human health or the environment arising from biological research.

bioinformatics /bīōinfəmattiks/ > *plural noun* (treated as sing.) the science of collecting and analysing complex biological data such as genetic codes.

biological > *adjective* **1** relating to biology or living organisms. **2** (of a parent or child) related by blood; natural. **3** relating to the use of micro-organisms or toxins of biological origin as weapons of war. **4** (of a detergent) containing enzymes to assist the process of cleaning.
DERIVATIVES – **biologically** *adverb*.
COMBINATIONS – **biological clock** a natural mechanism that controls the recurring bodily activities of an organism. **biological control** the control of a pest by the introduction of a natural enemy or predator.

biology > *noun* **1** the scientific study of living organisms. **2** the plants and animals of a

particular area. **3** the features of a particular organism or class of organisms.
WORDFINDER – cytology (*biology of cells*), ecology (*study of interrelations of organisms*), ethology (*study of animal behaviour*), exobiology (*extraterrestrial biology*), histology (*study of living tissue*), morphology (*study of forms of organisms*), physiology (*study of normal functions of organisms*), systematics, taxonomy (*classification of living organisms*).
DERIVATIVES – **biologist** *noun*.

bioluminescence > *noun* the biochemical emission of light by living organisms such as glow-worms and deep-sea fishes.
DERIVATIVES – **bioluminescent** *adjective*.

biomass > *noun* **1** the total quantity or weight of organisms in a given area or volume. **2** organic matter used as a fuel, especially in the generation of electricity.

biome > *noun* a large naturally occurring community of flora and fauna occupying a major habitat, such as forest or tundra.

biomorph > *noun* **1** a decorative form or object resembling a living organism. **2** a graphical representation of an organism generated on a computer.
DERIVATIVES – **biomorphic** *adjective*.

bionic > *adjective* **1** relating to the use of electrically operated artificial body parts. **2** informal having ordinary human powers increased by or as if by the aid of such devices.
DERIVATIVES – **bionically** *adverb* **bionics** *plural noun*.

biophysics > *plural noun* (treated as sing.) the science of the application of the laws of physics to biological phenomena.
DERIVATIVES – **biophysical** *adjective* **biophysicist** *noun*.

biopic > *noun* informal a biographical film.

biopiracy > *noun* bioprospecting regarded as a form of exploitation of developing countries.

bioprospecting > *noun* the search for plant and animal species from which medicinal drugs and other commercially valuable compounds can be obtained.
DERIVATIVES – **bioprospector** *noun*.

biopsy > *noun* (pl. **biopsies**) an examination of tissue taken from the body, to discover the presence, cause, or extent of a disease.
ORIGIN – from Greek *bios* 'life' + *opsis* 'sight'.

biorhythm > *noun* a recurring cycle in the physiology or functioning of an organism, such as the daily cycle of sleeping and waking.
DERIVATIVES – **biorhythmic** *adjective*.

biosphere > *noun* the regions of the surface and atmosphere of the earth occupied by living organisms.
DERIVATIVES – **biospheric** *adjective*.

biosynthesis > *noun* the production of

complex molecules within living organisms or cells.
DERIVATIVES – **biosynthetic** *adjective*.

biota > *noun* the animal and plant life of a particular region, habitat, or geological period.
ORIGIN – Latin, from Greek *biotē* 'life'.

biotechnology > *noun* the exploitation of biological processes for industrial and other purposes, especially the genetic manipulation of micro-organisms for the production of antibiotics, hormones, etc.
DERIVATIVES – **biotechnological** *adjective* **biotechnologist** *noun*.

biotic > *adjective* relating to living things and the effect they have on each other.
ORIGIN – Greek *biōtikos*, from *bios* 'life'.

biotin /bīətin/ > *noun* a vitamin of the B complex, found in egg yolk, liver, and yeast, involved in the synthesis of fatty acids and glucose.

biotype > *noun* a group of organisms having an identical genetic constitution.

bipartisan > *adjective* involving the agreement or cooperation of two political parties.
DERIVATIVES – **bipartisanship** *noun*.

bipartite > *adjective* **1** involving two separate parties. **2** technical consisting of two parts.

biped /bīped/ > *noun* an animal that walks on two feet.
DERIVATIVES – **bipedal** /bīpeed'l/ *adjective*.
ORIGIN – from Latin *bi-* 'having two' + *pes* 'foot'.

biplane > *noun* an early type of aircraft with two pairs of wings, one above the other.

bipolar > *adjective* having or relating to two poles or extremities.
DERIVATIVES – **bipolarity** *noun*.

birch > *noun* **1** a slender hardy tree having a peeling, typically silver-grey or white bark and yielding a hard fine-grained wood. **2** (**the birch**) chiefly historical a punishment in which a person is flogged with a bundle of birch twigs. > *verb* chiefly historical punish with the birch.

bird > *noun* **1** a warm-blooded egg-laying vertebrate animal which has feathers, wings, and a beak, and typically is able to fly. **2** informal a person of a specified kind or character: *she's a sharp old bird*. **3** Brit. informal a young woman or girlfriend.
WORDFINDER – avian (*of birds*), aviary (*place where birds are kept*), aviculturist (*breeder of birds*), oology (*study of birds' eggs*), ornithology (*study of birds*), rara avis ('*rare bird*', *something or someone exceptional*), twitcher (*obsessively dedicated birdwatcher*); *fossil bird: archaeopteryx*.
IDIOMS – **the bird has flown** the person one is looking for has escaped or left. **a bird in the hand is worth two in the bush** proverb it's better to be content with

what you have than to risk losing everything by seeking to get more. **birds of a feather flock together** proverb people of the same sort or with the same tastes and interests will be found together. **do (one's) bird** Brit. informal serve a prison sentence. [ORIGIN – *bird* from rhyming slang *birdlime* 'time'.]

COMBINATIONS – **birdbrain** informal a stupid person. **bird dog** N. Amer. **1** a gun dog trained to retrieve birds. **2** informal a talent scout in the field of sport. **birdlime** a sticky substance spread on to twigs to trap small birds. **bird of paradise** (pl. **birds of paradise**) a tropical bird, the male of which is noted for the brilliance of its plumage and its spectacular courtship display. **bird of passage 1** dated a migratory bird. **2** a person who passes through a place without staying for long. **bird of prey** a bird that feeds on animal flesh, typically having a hooked bill and sharp talons (e.g. an eagle, hawk, or owl). **bird's-eye view** a general view from above. **birdshot** the smallest size of shot for sporting rifles or other guns. **bird's nest soup** (in Chinese cookery) a soup made from the dried gelatinous coating of the nests of swifts and other birds. **bird table** Brit. a small raised platform in a garden on which food for birds is placed. **birdwatching** a hobby involving the observation of birds in their natural environment.

wordpower facts

Bird

The word **bird** is from Old English *brid* 'chick, fledgling'. As well as denoting a feathered flying creature it is of course a slang term for a girl or young woman. Although this seems a modern use, in fact it dates back to the Middle Ages. In this sense **bird** was confused with the now-obsolete word *burd*, a poetic term for a woman, and perhaps also with **bride**. The medieval work *Cursor Mundi* refers to the Virgin Mary as 'that blisful bird of grace', i.e. 'that blessed woman of grace'. The use was revived in the twentieth century.

birder > *noun* informal a birdwatcher.

birdie > *noun* (pl. **birdies**) **1** informal a little bird. **2** Golf a score of one stroke under par at a hole. > *verb* (**birdied**, **birdying**) Golf play (a hole) with a score of one under par.
ORIGIN – the golf term is from US slang *bird*, meaning any first-rate thing.

birding > *noun* informal birdwatching.

birdsong > *noun* the musical vocalisations of birds.

biretta /birettə/ > *noun* a square cap with three flat projections on top, worn by Roman Catholic clergymen.
ORIGIN – Italian *berretta* or Spanish *birreta*, from Latin *birrus* 'hooded cape'.

biriani /birriaani/ (also **biriyani** or **biryani**) > *noun* an Indian dish made with highly seasoned rice and meat, fish, or vegetables.
ORIGIN – Urdu, from a Persian word meaning 'fried or grilled'.

biro > *noun* (pl. **biros**) Brit. trademark a kind of ballpoint pen.
ORIGIN – named after László József *Biró* (1899–1985), Hungarian inventor of the ballpoint.

birr /bur/ > *noun* the basic monetary unit of Ethiopia, equal to 100 cents.
ORIGIN – Amharic.

birth > *noun* **1** the emergence of a baby or other young from the body of its mother; the start of life as a physically separate being. **2** the beginning of something. **3** origin or ancestry: *he is of noble birth*. > *verb* chiefly N. Amer. give birth to.
WORDFINDER – antenatal, antepartum (*before birth*), Caesarean section (*operation to deliver child*), congenital (*present from birth*), dystocia (*difficulty in giving birth*), epidural (*spinal anaesthetic giving in childbirth*), episiotomy (*surgical cutting of vagina to assist childbirth*), natal (*of the place and time of birth*), natality (*birth rate*), neonate (*newborn child*), obstetrics (*branch of medicine concerned with childbirth*), perinatal (*near to the time of birth*), postpartum (*following birth*), puerperal (*of childbirth*), viviparous (*giving birth to live young*).
IDIOMS – **give birth** bear a child or young.
SYNONYMS – *noun* **1** childbirth, delivery, nativity, parturition. **2** beginning, creation, dawn, genesis, origin. **3** ancestry, blood, descent, lineage, origin.
COMBINATIONS – **birth certificate** an official document recording a person's place and date of birth and the names of their parents. **birth control** the prevention of unwanted pregnancies, especially through the use of contraception. **birthing pool** a large circular tub in which a woman is able to give birth to her baby while lying in water. **birthmark** a coloured mark on the body which is there from birth. **birth mother** a woman who has given birth to a child, as opposed to an adoptive mother. **birthplace** the place where a person was born. **birth rate** the number of live births per thousand of population per year. **birth sign** Astrology the zodiacal sign through which the sun is passing when a person is born.

birthday > *noun* the annual anniversary of the day on which a person was born.

birthright > *noun* **1** a particular right or privilege that a person has from birth, especially as an eldest son. **2** a natural or moral right, possessed by everyone.

birthstone > *noun* a gemstone popularly associated with the month or astrological sign of a person's birth.
WORDFINDER – *traditional birthstones:* garnet (*January*), amethyst (*February*), bloodstone (*March*), diamond (*April*), emerald (*May*), pearl (*June*), ruby (*July*), sardonyx (*August*), sapphire (*September*), opal (*October*), topaz (*November*), turquoise (*December*).

biryani > *noun* variant spelling of **BIRIANI**.

bis /bis/ > *adverb* Music to be repeated.
ORIGIN – Latin, 'twice'.

biscuit > *noun* **1** Brit. a small, flat, crisp unleavened cake. **2** N. Amer. a small, soft round cake like a scone. **3** porcelain or other pottery which has been fired but not glazed.
IDIOMS – **take the biscuit** (or chiefly N. Amer. **cake**) informal be the most remarkable or foolish of its kind.
DERIVATIVES – **biscuity** adjective.
ORIGIN – Old French *bescuit*, based on Latin *bis* 'twice' + *coctus*, from *coquere* 'to cook' (because biscuits were originally cooked in a twofold process: first baked and then dried out in a slow oven).

bisect > *verb* divide into two parts; cut in half.
DERIVATIVES – **bisection** noun **bisector** noun.
SYNONYMS – bifurcate, cleave, divide, halve.
ORIGIN – from **BI-** + Latin *secare* 'to cut'.

bisexual > *adjective* **1** sexually attracted to both men and women. **2** Biology having characteristics of both sexes. > *noun* a person who is sexually attracted to both men and women.
DERIVATIVES – **bisexuality** noun.

bishop > *noun* **1** a senior member of the Christian clergy, usually in charge of a diocese and empowered to confer holy orders. **2** a chess piece, typically having a top shaped like a mitre, that can move in any direction along a diagonal.
WORDFINDER – episcopal (*of bishops*); crozier (*bishop's hooked staff*), diocese (*district under a bishop*), episcopacy (*government by bishops*), mitre (*bishop's headdress*), prelate (*bishop or other Church dignitary*), Right Reverend (*title given to bishop*), see (*seat of authority of a bishop or archbishop*), suffragan (*bishop assisting a diocesan bishop*).
ORIGIN – Old English, from Greek *episkopos* 'overseer'.

bishopric > *noun* **1** the office or rank of a bishop. **2** a diocese.

bismuth /bizməth/ > *noun* a brittle reddish-tinged grey metallic chemical element resembling lead.
ORIGIN – from German *Wismut*.

bison > *noun* (pl. same) a humpbacked shaggy-haired wild ox.
ORIGIN – Latin.

bisque¹ /bisk/ > *noun* a rich soup made from lobster or other shellfish.
ORIGIN – French.

bisque² > *noun* another term for BISCUIT (in sense 3).

bistable /bīstayb'l/ > *adjective* (chiefly of an electronic circuit) having two stable states.

bistro /beestro/ > *noun* (pl. **bistros**) a small, inexpensive restaurant.
ORIGIN – French.

bisulphate (US **bisulfate**) > *noun* Chemistry a salt containing the anion HSO_4^-.

bit¹ > *noun* 1 a small piece, quantity, or extent of something. 2 (**a bit**) a short time or distance. 3 (also **bit of fluff** or **stuff**) informal a girl or young woman.
IDIOMS – **a bit** somewhat. **bit by bit** gradually. **bit on the side** informal 1 a person with whom one is unfaithful to one's partner. 2 money earned outside one's normal job. **do one's bit** informal make a useful contribution. **to bits** 1 into pieces. 2 informal very much; to a great degree.
SYNONYMS – 1 chunk, crumb, fragment, morsel, piece, scrap.
COMBINATIONS – **bit part** a small acting role in a play or a film.
ORIGIN – Old English, 'bite, mouthful'.

bit² past of BITE.

bit³ > *noun* 1 a metal mouthpiece attached to a bridle, used to control a horse. 2 a tool or piece for boring or drilling. 3 the part of a key that engages with the lock lever. > *verb* put a bit into the mouth of (a horse).
IDIOMS – **get the bit between one's teeth** begin to tackle something in a determined way.

bit⁴ > *noun* Computing a unit of information expressed as either a 0 or 1 in binary notation.
COMBINATIONS – **bitmap** a representation in which each item corresponds to one or more bits of information, especially the information used to control the display of a computer screen. **bitstream** Electronics a stream of data in binary form.
ORIGIN – blend of BINARY and DIGIT.

bitch > *noun* 1 a female dog, wolf, fox, or otter. 2 informal a woman whom one considers to be malicious or unpleasant. 3 black English a woman (used in a non-derogatory sense). 4 (**a bitch**) informal a difficult or unpleasant thing or situation. > *verb* informal make spiteful comments.

bitchy > *adjective* (**bitchier, bitchiest**) informal malicious; spiteful.
DERIVATIVES – **bitchily** adverb **bitchiness** noun.

bite > *verb* (past **bit**; past participle **bitten**) 1 use the teeth to cut into something. 2 (of a snake, insect, or spider) wound with a sting,

pincers, or fangs. 3 (of a tool, tyre, boot, etc.) grip or take hold on a surface. 4 (of a fish) take the bait or lure on the end of a fishing line into the mouth. 5 (of a policy or situation) take effect, with unpleasant consequences. 6 (**bite back**) refrain with difficulty from saying (something). 7 informal annoy or worry: *what's biting you today?* > *noun* 1 an act or instance of biting or being bitten. 2 a piece cut off by biting. 3 Dentistry the bringing together of the teeth when the jaws are closed. 4 informal a quick snack. 5 a sharpness or pungency in flavour. 6 a feeling of cold in the air.
IDIOMS – **bite the bullet** decide to do something difficult or unpleasant that one has been hesitating over. [ORIGIN – from the old custom of giving wounded soldiers a bullet to bite on when undergoing surgery without anaesthetic.] **bite the dust** informal die or be killed. **bite the hand that feeds one** deliberately hurt or offend a benefactor. **bite off more than one can chew** take on a commitment one cannot fulfil. **bite one's tongue** make a desperate effort to avoid saying something. **once bitten, twice shy** an unpleasant experience causes one to be cautious when in a similar situation again.
DERIVATIVES – **biter** noun.
SYNONYMS – *verb* 1,2 gnaw at, nip, sink one's teeth into. *noun* 1 nibble, nip, sting. 2 morsel, mouthful, piece. 5 piquancy, sharpness, spiciness, tang, zest.

biting > *adjective* 1 (of a wind or the air) painfully cold. 2 (of wit or criticism) harsh or cruel.
DERIVATIVES – **bitingly** adverb.
SYNONYMS – 1 arctic, chilly, freezing, icy, penetrating. 2 acerbic, caustic, cutting, scathing, stinging.

bitten past participle of BITE.

bitter > *adjective* 1 having a sharp, pungent taste or smell; not sweet. 2 feeling angry hurt and resentment. 3 causing pain or unhappiness. 4 (of a conflict) harsh and acrimonious. 5 (of wind or weather) intensely cold. > *noun* 1 Brit. beer that is strongly flavoured with hops and has a bitter taste. 2 (**bitters**) (treated as sing.) liquor that is flavoured with bitter plant extracts and used as an additive in cocktails.
IDIOMS – **to the bitter end** to the very end, in spite of harsh difficulties.
DERIVATIVES – **bitterly** adverb **bitterness** noun.
SYNONYMS – *adjective* 1 acrid, harsh, sharp, tart. 2 aggrieved, embittered, jaundiced, rancorous, resentful, sour. 3 distressing, galling, painful, upsetting. 4 acrimonious, fierce, rancorous, vicious, virulent. 5 arctic, chilly, freezing, wintry.
ANTONYMS – *adjective* 1 sweet. 2 content,

magnanimous. 3 pleasing, welcome. 4 amicable. 5 balmy.
COMBINATIONS – **bitter lemon** Brit. a carbonated semi-sweet soft drink flavoured with lemons. **bitter orange** a Seville orange.

bittern > *noun* a marshbird of the heron family, noted for the male's deep booming call.
ORIGIN – Old French *butor*, from Latin *butio* 'bittern' + *taurus* 'bull' (because of its call).

bittersweet > *adjective* 1 sweet with a bitter aftertaste. 2 arousing pleasure tinged with sadness or pain. > *noun* the plant woody nightshade.

bitty > *adjective* (**bittier, bittiest**) informal 1 chiefly Brit. made up of small parts that seem unrelated. 2 N. Amer. (with another adjective) tiny: *a little-bitty girl.*
DERIVATIVES – **bittily** adverb **bittiness** noun.

bitumen /bityoomən/ > *noun* a black viscous mixture of hydrocarbons obtained naturally or as a residue from petroleum distillation, used for road surfacing and roofing.
DERIVATIVES – **bituminous** adjective.
ORIGIN – Latin.

bituminous coal > *noun* a kind of black coal that burns with a characteristically bright smoky flame.

bitzer > *noun* Austral./NZ informal 1 a contraption made from previously unrelated parts. 2 a mongrel dog.
ORIGIN – abbreviation of the phrase *bits and pieces.*

bivalve > *noun* an aquatic mollusc which has a compressed body enclosed within two hinged shells, such as an oyster, mussel, or scallop. > *adjective* 1 (also **bivalved**) having a hinged double shell. 2 Botany having two valves.

bivouac /bivvoo-ak/ > *noun* a temporary camp with limited cover, used especially by climbers or soldiers. > *verb* (**bivouacked, bivouacking**) stay in such a camp.
ORIGIN – French, probably from Swiss German *Biwacht* 'additional guard at night'.

bivvy informal > *noun* (pl. **bivvies**) a small tent or temporary shelter. > *verb* (**bivvies, bivvied**) use such a tent or shelter.
ORIGIN – abbreviation of BIVOUAC.

biweekly > *adjective & adverb* appearing or taking place every two weeks or twice a week.
USAGE – the meaning of **biweekly**, **biyearly**, and **bimonthly** is ambiguous. The only way to avoid this ambiguity is to use alternative expressions such as *every two weeks* and *twice a week.*

biyearly > *adjective & adverb* appearing or taking place every two years or twice a year.

biz > *noun* informal business.

bizarre* /biᴢ**aar**/ > *adjective* very strange or unusual.

DERIVATIVES – **bizarrely** *adverb* **bizarreness** *noun*.

***SPELLING** – one *z*, two *r*s: biᴢ*arre*.

SYNONYMS – curious, odd, outlandish, peculiar, strange, weird.

ANTONYMS – normal, ordinary.

ORIGIN – French, from Italian *bizzarro* 'angry'.

Bk > *symbol* the chemical element berkelium.

blab informal > *verb* (**blabbed, blabbing**) reveal secrets by indiscreet talk. > *noun* a person who blabs.

blabber informal > *verb* talk indiscreetly or excessively. > *noun* **1** a person who blabbers. **2** indiscreet or excessive talk.

COMBINATIONS – **blabbermouth** informal a person who talks indiscreetly or excessively.

black > *adjective* **1** of the very darkest colour owing to the absence of or complete absorption of light. **2** deeply stained with dirt. **3** (of coffee or tea) served without milk. **4** relating to or denoting a human group having dark-coloured skin, especially of African or Australian Aboriginal ancestry. **5** characterised by tragedy, disaster, or despair. **6** (of humour) presenting tragic or harrowing situations in comic terms. **7** full of anger or hatred. > *noun* **1** black colour or pigment. **2** a member of a dark-skinned people, especially one of African or Australian Aboriginal ancestry. **3** Brit. informal blackcurrant cordial. > *verb* **1** make black, especially with black polish or make-up. **2** Brit. dated refuse to handle (goods) or have dealings with (a person or business) as a way of taking industrial action.

WORDFINDER – *shades of black:* coal-black, ebony, jet, nigrescent, sable.

IDIOMS – **black someone's eye** hit someone in the eye so as to cause bruising. **black out 1** make (a room or building) dark by extinguishing lights and covering windows. **2** obscure completely. **3** suddenly lose consciousness; faint. **in the black** not owing any money. **in someone's black books** informal in disfavour with someone. **look on the black side** informal view a situation from a pessimistic angle.

DERIVATIVES – **blackish** *adjective* **blackly** *adverb* **blackness** *noun*.

USAGE – to refer to African peoples and their descendants, **black** is the word most generally accepted in Britain today, in preference to **coloured** or **Negro**. In the US **African American** and **Afro-American** are often used.

SYNONYMS – *adjective* **5** calamitous, catastrophic, fateful, terrible, tragic. **6** cynical, ghoulish, grim, macabre, sick.

COMBINATIONS – **black and tan 1** a breed of terrier with a black back and tan markings on the face, flanks, and legs. **2** Brit. a drink composed of stout and bitter. **3** (**Black and Tans**) an armed force recruited by the British government to fight Sinn Fein in Ireland in 1921. [ORIGIN – so named because of the colours of their uniform.] **black and white** (of a situation or debate) involving clearly defined opposing principles or issues. **black art** (also **black arts**) black magic. **black bean** a cultivated variety of soya bean. **black belt** a black belt worn by an expert in judo, karate, and other martial arts. **blackbird 1** a thrush of which the male has all-black plumage and a yellow bill. **2** an American songbird with largely black plumage. **blackboard** a large board with a dark surface for writing on with chalk. **black box** a flight recorder in an aircraft. **blackcap** a warbler of which the male has a black cap. **blackcurrant** the small round edible black berry of a shrub. **black economy** the part of a country's economic activity which is not recorded or taxed by its government. **black eye** an area of bruised skin around the eye resulting from a blow. **black-figure** a type of ancient Greek pottery in which figures are painted in black, details being added by cutting through to the red clay background. Compare with *red-figure*. **blackfly 1** a black or dark green aphid which is a common pest of crops. **2** a small black bloodsucking fly. **black hole** Astronomy a region of space having a gravitational field so intense that no matter or radiation can escape. **black ice** a transparent coating of ice on a road surface. **black magic** magic involving the supposed summoning of evil spirits. **Black Maria** informal a police vehicle for transporting prisoners. [ORIGIN – said to be named after a black woman, *Maria* Lee, who kept a boarding house in Boston and helped police in escorting drunk and disorderly customers to jail.] **black mark** informal a note of a person's misdemeanour or discreditable action. **black mass** a travesty of the Roman Catholic Mass in worship of the Devil. **black pudding** Brit. a black sausage containing pork, dried pig's blood, and suet. **Black Rod** (in the UK) the chief usher of the Lord Chamberlain's department of the royal household, who is also usher to the House of Lords. [ORIGIN – short for *Gentleman Usher of the Black Rod*.] **black sheep** informal a member of a family or group who is regarded as a disgrace to it. **black spot 1** Brit. a place marked by a particular trouble. **2** a plant disease producing black blotches on the leaves. **the black stump** Austral. informal the last outpost of civilisation. **black swan** a mainly black swan with white flight feathers, native to Australia. **black tie** men's formal evening wear. **black widow** a highly poisonous American spider having a black body with red markings.

blackamoor /**blakk**əmor/ > *noun* archaic a black African or a very dark-skinned person.

ORIGIN – from **BLACK** + **MOOR**.

blackball > *verb* reject or vote against (a candidate applying to become a member of a private club).

ORIGIN – from the practice of registering an adverse vote by placing a black ball in a ballot box.

blackberry > *noun* (pl. **blackberries**) the edible soft fruit of a prickly climbing shrub, consisting of a cluster of purple-black drupels. > *verb* (**blackberries, blackberried**) gather blackberries.

blacken > *verb* **1** become or make black or dark. **2** damage or destroy (someone's reputation).

Blackfoot > *noun* (pl. same or **Blackfeet**) a member of a confederacy of North American Indian peoples of the north-western plains consisting of three closely related tribes: the Blackfoot proper or Siksika, the Bloods, and the Peigan.

blackguard /**blagg**aard/ > *noun* dated a man who behaves in a dishonourable or contemptible way.

DERIVATIVES – **blackguardly** *adjective*.

ORIGIN – first used to denote a body of servants, especially the menials in charge of kitchen utensils; the exact significance of 'black' is uncertain.

blackhead > *noun* a plug of oily matter in a hair follicle.

blacking > *noun* black paste or polish.

blackjack > *noun* **1** chiefly N. Amer. a gambling card game in which players try to acquire cards with a face value totalling exactly 21. **2** N. Amer. a flexible lead-filled truncheon.

blackleg > *noun* Brit. derogatory a person who continues working when fellow workers are on strike.

blacklist > *noun* a list of people or groups regarded as unacceptable or untrustworthy. > *verb* put on a blacklist.

SYNONYMS – *verb* ban, bar, boycott, embargo, ostracise.

blackmail > *noun* **1** the action of demanding money from someone in return for not revealing discreditable information. **2** the use of threats or manipulation in an attempt to influence someone's actions. > *verb* subject to blackmail.

DERIVATIVES – **blackmailer** *noun*.

ORIGIN – first used to denote protection money levied by Scottish chiefs: from obsolete *mail* 'tribute, rent'.

black market > *noun* an illegal trade in officially controlled or scarce commodities.
DERIVATIVES – **black marketeer** *noun*.

blackout > *noun* **1** a period when all lights must be turned out to prevent them being seen by the enemy during an air raid. **2** a temporary loss of consciousness. **3** a sudden failure or dimming of electric lights. **4** an official suppression of information.

blackshirt > *noun* a member of a Fascist organisation, in particular an Italian paramilitary group founded by Mussolini, the Nazi SS, or Oswald Moseley's British Union of Fascists.
ORIGIN – so named because of the colour of the Italian fascist uniform.

blacksmith > *noun* **1** a person who makes and repairs things in iron by hand. **2** a person who shoes horses; a farrier.

blackthorn > *noun* a thorny shrub which bears white flowers, followed by blue-black fruits (sloes).

blackwater fever > *noun* a severe form of malaria in which blood cells are rapidly destroyed, resulting in dark urine.

bladder > *noun* **1** a sac in the abdomen which receives urine from the kidneys and stores it for excretion. **2** an inflated or hollow flexible bag or chamber.
WORDFINDER – cystic (*of the bladder or gall bladder*), cystitis (*inflammation of the bladder*), ureter, urethra (*ducts conveying urine into, out of, the bladder*).

bladderwort > *noun* an aquatic plant with small air-filled bladders which keep the plant afloat and trap tiny animals.

bladderwrack > *noun* a brown seaweed with strap-like fronds containing air bladders.

blade > *noun* **1** the flat cutting edge of a knife or other tool or weapon. **2** the broad, flat part of an oar, leaf, or other object. **3** a long, narrow leaf of grass. **4** informal, dated a dashing young man. **5** a shoulder bone in a joint of meat, or the joint itself.
DERIVATIVES – **bladed** *adjective*.

blaeberry /**blay**bəri/ > *noun* Scottish and northern English term for **BILBERRY**.

blag Brit. informal > *noun* **1** a violent robbery. **2** an act of using clever talk or lying to obtain something. > *verb* (**blagged, blagging**) **1** steal in a violent robbery. **2** obtain by clever talk or lying.
DERIVATIVES – **blagger** *noun*.
ORIGIN – perhaps from French *blaguer* 'tell lies'.

blame > *verb* **1** hold (someone) responsible for a fault or wrong. **2** (**blame on**) assign the responsibility for something bad to (someone). > *noun* **1** responsibility for a fault or wrong. **2** criticism for a fault or wrong.
IDIOMS – **be to blame** be responsible for a fault or wrong.

DERIVATIVES – **blameable** (US also **blamable**) *adjective* **blameworthy** *adjective*.
SYNONYMS – *verb* **1** find culpable, hold accountable, hold liable, hold responsible. **2** (**blame on**) ascribe to, attribute to, lay at the door of. *noun* **1** culpability, fault, guilt, responsibility.
ORIGIN – Old French *blasmer*, from Greek *blasphēmein* 'blaspheme'.

blameless > *adjective* innocent of wrongdoing.
DERIVATIVES – **blamelessly** *adverb* **blamelessness** *noun*.
SYNONYMS – exemplary, guiltless, innocent, irreproachable, unimpeachable.
ANTONYMS – blameworthy, guilty.

blanch > *verb* **1** make or become white or pale. **2** prepare (vegetables) by immersing them briefly in boiling water. **3** peel (almonds) by scalding them.
ORIGIN – Old French *blanchir*, from *blanc* 'white'.

blancmange /bləˈmonj/ > *noun* a sweet jelly-like dessert made with cornflour and milk.
ORIGIN – from Old French *blanc mangier*, from *blanc* 'white' + *mangier* 'eat'.

blanco > *noun* Brit. a white substance used for whitening belts and other items of military equipment.

bland > *adjective* **1** (of food or drink) lacking flavour or seasoning. **2** lacking strong features or characteristics and therefore uninteresting.
DERIVATIVES – **blandly** *adverb* **blandness** *noun*.
SYNONYMS – **1** flavourless, insipid, tasteless. **2** dull, feeble, insipid, uninspiring.
ORIGIN – first used in the sense 'gentle in manner': from Latin *blandus* 'soft, smooth'.

blandishments > *plural noun* flattery intended to persuade or cajole.

blank > *adjective* **1** not marked, decorated, or filled in; bare or plain. **2** not comprehending or reacting. **3** complete; absolute: *a blank refusal*. > *noun* **1** a space left to be filled in a document. **2** a cartridge containing gunpowder but no bullet. **3** an empty space or period of time. **4** a roughly cut disc. > *verb* **1** cause to appear blank or empty. **2** N. Amer. defeat (an opponent) without allowing them to score. **3** Brit. informal deliberately ignore (someone).
IDIOMS – **draw a blank** fail to elicit a favourable response.
DERIVATIVES – **blankly** *adverb* **blankness** *noun*.
SYNONYMS – *adjective* **1** bare, featureless, plain, unmarked. **2** expressionless, impassive, inscrutable, uncomprehending.
COMBINATIONS – **blank cheque 1** a cheque with the amount left for the payee to fill in. **2** an unlimited freedom of action.
blank verse verse without rhyme.

wordpower facts

Blank

The words **blank** and **blanket** are both from Old French *blanc* 'white'. In English **blank** first meant 'pale, colourless', from which it was a short step to 'not marked, decorated, or filled in'. **Blanket** originally denoted undyed woollen cloth. Other words from *blanc* are **blanch** and **blancmange**.

blanket > *noun* **1** a large piece of woollen material used as a covering for warmth. **2** a thick mass or layer of a specified material: *a blanket of cloud*. > *adjective* covering all cases or instances; total: *a blanket ban*. > *verb* (**blanketed, blanketing**) cover completely with a thick layer.
IDIOMS – **born on the wrong side of the blanket** dated illegitimate.
DERIVATIVES – **blanketing** *noun*.
COMBINATIONS – **blanket bath** Brit. an all-over wash given to a person confined to bed. **blanket stitch** a buttonhole stitch used on the edges of material too thick to be hemmed. **blanket weed** a common green freshwater alga forming mats of long filaments.

blanquette /blonˈket/ > *noun* a dish consisting of white meat in a white sauce.
ORIGIN – French, from *blanc* 'white'.

blare > *verb* sound loudly and harshly. > *noun* a loud, harsh sound.
SYNONYMS – *verb* blast, bray, screech, squawk, trumpet.
ORIGIN – Dutch or Low German *blaren*.

blarney > *noun* talk intended to be charming or flattering.
ORIGIN – named after *Blarney* Castle in Ireland, where there is a stone said to bestow the gift of persuasive speech on anyone who kisses it.

blasé /ˈblaazay/ > *adjective* unimpressed with something because of over-familiarity.
SYNONYMS – casual, indifferent, jaded, nonchalant, unimpressed.
ANTONYMS – excited, impressed.
ORIGIN – French, from *blaser* 'cloy'.

blaspheme /blasˈfeem/ > *verb* speak irreverently about God or sacred things.
DERIVATIVES – **blasphemer** *noun*.
ORIGIN – Greek *blasphēmein*, from *blasphēmos* 'evil-speaking'.

blasphemous > *adjective* sacrilegious against God or sacred things; profane.
DERIVATIVES – **blasphemously** *adverb*.
SYNONYMS – impious, irreligious, irreverent, profane, sacrilegious, ungodly.

blasphemy /ˈblasfəmi/ > *noun* (pl. **blasphemies**) irreverent talk about God or sacred things.

SYNONYMS – impiety, irreligiousness, irreverence, profanity, sacrilege.

blast > *noun* **1** a destructive wave of highly compressed air spreading outwards from an explosion. **2** an explosion. **3** a strong gust of wind or air. **4** a single loud note of a horn or whistle. **5** informal a severe reprimand. **6** N. Amer. informal an enjoyable experience. > *verb* **1** blow up with explosives. **2** (**blast off**) (of a rocket or spacecraft) take off. **3** produce loud music or noise. **4** informal criticise fiercely. **5** kick or strike (a ball) hard. **6** literary (of wind) wither (a plant). > *exclamation* Brit. informal expressing annoyance.

IDIOMS – (**at**) **full blast** at maximum power or intensity.

DERIVATIVES – **blaster** noun.

COMBINATIONS – **blast furnace** an iron-smelting furnace in which a blast of hot compressed air is used.

blasted > *adjective* informal used to express annoyance.

blatant* > *adjective* open and unashamed; flagrant.

DERIVATIVES – **blatancy** noun **blatantly** adverb.

*SPELLING – -*ant*, not -*ent*: blat*ant*.

SYNONYMS – brazen, flagrant, open, overt, shameless.

ANTONYMS – inconspicuous, subtle.

wordpower facts
Blatant
The word **blatant** was apparently invented by the poet Edmund Spenser in his romance *The Faerie Queene* (1596), and was used by him to describe a thousand-tongued monster produced by Cerberus and Chimaera, a symbol of slander, which he called the *blatant beast*. Spenser perhaps derived it from Scots *blatand* 'bleating'. **Blatant** was subsequently used to mean 'clamorous, offensive to the ear'; the sense 'unashamedly conspicuous' arose in the late 19th century.

blather (also **blither**) > *verb* talk long-windedly without making much sense. > *noun* long-winded talk with no real substance.

ORIGIN – Old Norse.

blaze > *noun* **1** a very large or fiercely burning fire. **2** a very bright light or display of colour. **3** a conspicuous outburst: *a blaze of publicity*. **4** a white stripe down the face of a horse or other animal. **5** (**blazes**) informal a euphemism for 'hell': *go to blazes!* **6** a cut made on a tree to mark a route. > *verb* **1** burn or shine fiercely or brightly. **2** (often **blaze away**) shoot repeatedly or indiscriminately. **3** present (news) in a prominent or sensational manner.

IDIOMS – **blaze a trail 1** mark out a path or route. **2** be the first to do something; pioneer.

DERIVATIVES – **blazing** adjective.

SYNONYMS – *noun* **1** conflagration, inferno. *verb* **1** flame, flare, glare.

blazer > *noun* **1** a jacket worn by schoolchildren or sports players as part of a uniform. **2** a man's smart jacket not forming part of a suit.

blazon /**blay**z'n/ > *verb* **1** display or depict prominently or vividly. **2** Heraldry describe or depict (a coat of arms). > *noun* **1** a correct description of armorial bearings. **2** archaic a coat of arms.

ORIGIN – from Old French *blason* 'shield'.

bleach > *verb* **1** cause to become white or lighter by a chemical process or by exposure to sunlight. **2** clean or sterilise with bleach. > *noun* a chemical used to bleach things and also to sterilise drains, sinks, etc.

SYNONYMS – *verb* **1** blanch, fade, whiten.

COMBINATIONS – **bleaching powder** a powder containing calcium hypochlorite, used to bleach materials.

ORIGIN – Old English, 'paleness, whiteness'; related to **BLEAK**.

bleacher > *noun* **1** a person or thing that bleaches. **2** N. Amer. a cheap bench seat in an uncovered part of a sports ground.

bleak > *adjective* **1** bare and exposed to the elements. **2** charmless and inhospitable. **3** (of a situation) not hopeful or encouraging.

DERIVATIVES – **bleakly** adverb **bleakness** noun.

SYNONYMS – **1** bare, barren, desolate, exposed. **2** cheerless, desolate, dismal, grim, unwelcoming. **3** inauspicious, depressing, grim, sombre, unpromising.

ANTONYMS – **2** cheering, welcoming. **3** hopeful, promising.

ORIGIN – Old English, 'shining, white': related to **BLEACH**.

bleary > *adjective* (**blearier**, **bleariest**) (of the eyes) dull and unfocused from sleep or tiredness.

DERIVATIVES – **blearily** adverb.

SYNONYMS – blurry, filmy, muzzy, unfocused.

bleat > *verb* **1** (of a sheep or goat) make a weak, wavering cry. **2** speak or complain in a weak or foolish way. > *noun* **1** the weak, wavering cry of a sheep or goat. **2** a person's weak or foolish cry or complaint.

bleb > *noun* a small blister or bubble.

ORIGIN – variant of **BLOB**.

bleed > *verb* (past and past participle **bled**) **1** lose blood from the body as a result of injury or illness. **2** draw blood from (someone) as a former method of medical treatment. **3** informal drain of money or resources. **4** (of dye or colour) seep into an adjacent colour or area. **5** allow (fluid or gas) to escape from a closed system through a valve. > *noun* an instance of bleeding.

DERIVATIVES – **bleeder** noun.

COMBINATIONS – **bleeding heart 1** informal, derogatory a person considered to be excessively soft-hearted or liberal. **2** a plant with red heart-shaped flowers.

bleeding > *adjective* Brit. informal used for emphasis, or to express annoyance.

bleep > *noun* a short high-pitched sound made by an electronic device as a signal or to attract attention. > *verb* **1** make a bleep. **2** (in broadcasting) censor (a word or phrase) by substituting a bleep.

DERIVATIVES – **bleeper** noun.

blemish > *noun* **1** a small flaw which spoils the appearance of something. **2** a moral defect. > *verb* spoil the appearance of.

SYNONYMS – *noun* defect, fault, flaw, imperfection, mark. *verb* blight, disfigure, impair, mar, spoil.

ORIGIN – Old French *blesmir* 'make pale, injure'.

blench > *verb* make a sudden flinching movement because of fear or pain.

ORIGIN – Old English, 'deceive'.

blend > *verb* **1** mix and combine with something else. **2** form a harmonious combination or part of a whole. > *noun* a mixture of different things or people.

SYNONYMS – *verb* **1** amalgamate, combine, fuse, meld, merge, mingle. **2** coordinate, fit, harmonise. *noun* amalgam, combination, mixture, synthesis, union.

blender > *noun* an electric device used for liquidising or chopping food.

blenny > *noun* (pl. **blennies**) a small coastal fish with scaleless skin and spiny fins.

ORIGIN – from Greek *blennos* 'mucus' (because of its mucous coating).

bless > *verb* **1** call divine favour upon. **2** consecrate by a religious rite. **3** praise (God). **4** (**be blessed with**) be endowed with or granted (something greatly desired).

IDIOMS – **bless you!** said to a person who has just sneezed.

SYNONYMS – **1** consecrate, dedicate, hallow, sanctify. **3** adore, exalt, glorify, praise, worship.

ORIGIN – Old English; related to **BLOOD**, perhaps from the notion 'mark or consecrate with blood'.

blessed /**bless**id, blest/ > *adjective* **1** made holy. **2** endowed with divine favour and protection. **3** bringing pleasure or relief as a welcome contrast to a recent experience. **4** informal used in mild expressions of exasperation.

DERIVATIVES – **blessedness** noun.

SYNONYMS – **1** consecrated, hallowed, holy, sacred. **2** favoured, fortunate, happy, select.

blessing > *noun* **1** God's favour and protection. **2** a prayer asking for blessing. **3** a beneficial thing for which one is grateful. **4** a person's sanction or support.

IDIOMS – **a blessing in disguise** an apparent misfortune that eventually has good results.

SYNONYMS – **2** benediction, intercession. **3** boon, godsend.

blether > *verb & noun* chiefly Scottish another term for BLATHER.

blew past of BLOW¹.

blewit /blōoit/ (also **blewits**) > *noun* an edible mushroom with a pale buff or lilac cap.

ORIGIN – probably from BLUE¹.

blight > *noun* **1** a plant disease, especially one caused by fungi. **2** a thing that spoils or damages something. **3** ugly or neglected urban landscape. > *verb* **1** infect (plants) with blight. **2** spoil or harm. **3** subject (an urban area) to neglect.

SYNONYMS – *noun* **1** canker, mildew, rot, rust. **2** affliction, bane, curse, plague, scourge. *verb* **2** afflict, harm, mar, ruin, spoil.

blighter > *noun* Brit. informal a person regarded with contempt, irritation, or pity.

Blighty > *noun* Brit. informal Britain or England (as used by soldiers serving abroad).

ORIGIN – from an Urdu word meaning 'foreign, European'.

blimey > *exclamation* Brit. informal expressing surprise, excitement, or alarm.

ORIGIN – altered form of *God blind* (or *blame*) *me!*

blimp > *noun* informal **1** (also **Colonel Blimp**) Brit. a pompous, reactionary person. **2** a small airship or barrage balloon. **3** N. Amer. an obese person.

DERIVATIVES – **blimpish** adjective.

ORIGIN – sense 1 derives from a character invented by the cartoonist David Low.

blind > *adjective* **1** lacking the power of sight; unable to see. **2** done without being able to see or without necessary information. **3** lacking perception, judgement, or reason. **4** concealed, closed, or blocked off. **5** (of flying) using instruments only. **6** informal the slightest: *it didn't do a blind bit of good*. > *verb* **1** cause (someone) to be unable to see. **2** deprive of understanding or judgement. **3** (**blind with**) confuse or overawe (someone) with (something they do not understand). > *noun* **1** a screen for a window. **2** something designed to conceal one's real intentions. > *adverb* without being able to see clearly.

IDIOMS – **bake blind** bake (a pastry) without a filling. **blind drunk** informal extremely drunk. **turn a blind eye** pretend not to notice. [ORIGIN – said to be in allusion to Nelson, who lifted a telescope to his blind eye at the Battle of Copenhagen

(1801), thus not seeing the signal to 'discontinue the action'.] **when the blind lead the blind, both shall fall into a ditch** proverb those people without knowledge or experience should not try to guide others in a similar position.

DERIVATIVES – **blindly** adverb **blindness** noun.

SYNONYMS – *adjective* **1** partially sighted, sightless, unsighted, visually impaired. **3** blinkered, dim, obtuse, undiscerning, unperceptive.

ANTONYMS – *adjective* **1** sighted.

COMBINATIONS – **blind alley 1** a cul-de-sac. **2** a course of action leading nowhere. **blind date** a social engagement with a person one has not previously met, designed to have a romantic or sexual aim. **blind man's buff** (US also **blind man's bluff**) a game in which a blindfold player tries to catch others while being pushed about by them. [ORIGIN – from obsolete *buff* 'a blow'.] **blind side** a direction in which a person has a poor view. **blind spot 1** Anatomy the point of entry of the optic nerve on the retina, insensitive to light. **2** an area where a person's view is obstructed. **3** an area in which a person lacks understanding or impartiality. **4** Telecommunications a point within the normal range of a transmitter where there is unusually weak reception. **blindworm** a slow-worm.

blinder > *noun* Brit. informal an excellent performance in a game or race.

blindfold > *noun* a piece of cloth tied around the head to cover someone's eyes. > *verb* deprive of sight with a blindfold. > *adverb* with a blindfold covering the eyes.

ORIGIN – from obsolete *blindfell* 'strike blind, blindfold'.

blinding > *adjective* **1** (of light) very bright. **2** suddenly and overwhelmingly obvious. **3** informal (of an action) remarkably skilful and exciting.

DERIVATIVES – **blindingly** adverb.

SYNONYMS – **1** brilliant, dazzling, glaring.

blini /bleeni/ (also **blinis**) > *plural noun* (sing. **blin**) pancakes made from buckwheat flour.

ORIGIN – Russian.

blink > *verb* **1** shut and open the eyes quickly. **2** (often **blink at**) react with surprise or disapproval. **3** (of a light) shine unsteadily or intermittently. > *noun* an act of blinking.

IDIOMS – **on the blink** informal (of a machine) not working properly; out of order.

ORIGIN – Scots variant of BLENCH.

blinker > *noun* chiefly Brit. **1** (**blinkers**) a pair of small screens attached to a horse's bridle to prevent the horse seeing sideways. **2** (**blinkers**) a thing that prevents someone from understanding a situation fully. **3** a

vehicle indicator light that flashes on and off. > *verb* **1** put blinkers on (a horse). **2** cause to have a narrow outlook.

DERIVATIVES – **blinkered** adjective.

blinking > *adjective* Brit. informal used to express annoyance.

blintze /blints/ > *noun* a thin rolled pancake filled with cheese or fruit and then fried or baked.

ORIGIN – Russian *blinets* 'little pancake'.

blip > *noun* **1** a very short high-pitched sound made by an electronic device. **2** an unexpected, minor, and usually temporary deviation from a general trend. **3** a small flashing point of light on a radar screen. > *verb* (**blipped**, **blipping**) (of an electronic device) make a blip.

blipvert > *noun* a television advert of a few seconds' duration.

bliss > *noun* **1** perfect happiness; great joy. **2** a state of spiritual blessedness. > *verb* (**bliss out** or **be blissed out**) informal be in a state of perfect happiness, oblivious to everything else.

SYNONYMS – *noun* **1** ecstasy, elation, joy, rapture. **2** beatitude, benediction, blessedness.

ORIGIN – Old English, related to BLITHE.

blissful > *adjective* extremely happy; full of joy.

DERIVATIVES – **blissfully** adverb.

SYNONYMS – ecstatic, elated, euphoric, joyful, overjoyed, rapturous.

blister > *noun* **1** a small bubble on the skin filled with serum and typically caused by friction or burning. **2** a similar swelling, filled with air or fluid, on a surface. > *verb* be or cause to be affected with blisters.

ORIGIN – perhaps from Old French *blestre* 'swelling, pimple'.

blistering > *adjective* **1** (of heat) intense. **2** (of criticism) very vehement. **3** (in sport) extremely fast, forceful, or impressive.

DERIVATIVES – **blisteringly** adverb.

blithe /blīth/ > *adjective* **1** cheerfully or thoughtlessly indifferent. **2** literary happy or joyous.

DERIVATIVES – **blithely** adverb **blitheness** noun.

SYNONYMS – **1** careless, casual, cheerful, nonchalant.

ORIGIN – Old English, related to BLISS.

blither > *verb & noun* variant spelling of BLATHER.

blithering > *adjective* informal complete; utter: *a blithering idiot*.

BLitt > *abbreviation* Bachelor of Letters.

ORIGIN – from Latin *Baccalaureus Litterarum*.

blitz > *noun* **1** an intensive or sudden military attack. **2** (**the Blitz**) the German air raids on Britain in 1940. **3** informal a sudden and concerted effort. > *verb* **1** attack or seriously damage in a blitz. **2** succeed in overwhelming or defeating utterly.

ORIGIN – abbreviation of **BLITZKRIEG**.

blitzkrieg /**blits**kreeg/ > *noun* an intense military campaign intended to bring about a swift victory.

ORIGIN – German, 'lightning war'.

blizzard > *noun* a severe snowstorm with high winds.

bloat > *verb* cause to swell with fluid or gas.

bloated > *adjective* **1** swollen with fluid or gas. **2** excessively large or wealthy.

SYNONYMS – **1** bulging, distended, puffed up, swollen.

bloater > *noun* a herring cured by salting and light smoking.

blob > *noun* **1** a drop of a thick liquid or viscous substance. **2** an indeterminate roundish mass or shape.

DERIVATIVES – **blobby** *adjective*.

bloc > *noun* a group of countries or political parties who have formed an alliance.

ORIGIN – French, 'block'.

block > *noun* **1** a large solid piece of material with flat surfaces on each side. **2** chiefly Brit. a large single building subdivided into separate flats or offices. **3** a group of buildings bounded by four streets. **4** a large quantity of things regarded as a unit. **5** an obstacle to the normal progress or functioning of something. **6** a flat area of something, especially a solid area of colour. **7** a starting block. **8** a large metal moulding containing the cylinders of an internal-combustion engine. **9** a pulley or system of pulleys mounted in a case. > *verb* **1** prevent movement or flow in. **2** impede or prevent (an action or movement). **3** (**block out** or **in**) mark out (an outline) or shade in roughly.

IDIOMS – **knock someone's block off** informal hit someone about the head. **put one's head** (or **neck**) **on the block** informal put one's standing or reputation at risk.

DERIVATIVES – **blocker** *noun* **blocky** *adjective*.

SYNONYMS – *verb* **1** choke, clog, plug, stop up. **2** hamper, hinder, impede, obstruct, prevent.

COMBINATIONS – **block and tackle** a lifting mechanism consisting of ropes, a pulley block, and a hook. **block capitals** plain capital letters. **blockhead** informal a very stupid person. **blockhouse 1** a reinforced concrete shelter used as an observation point. **2** US a house made of squared logs. **block release** Brit. a system of allowing employees the whole of a stated period off work for education. **block vote** Brit. a vote proportional in power to the number of people a delegate represents.

ORIGIN – Old French, from Dutch.

blockade > *noun* an act of sealing off a place to prevent goods or people from entering or leaving. > *verb* set up a blockade of.

IDIOMS – **run a blockade** (of a ship) manage to enter or leave a blockaded port.

blockage > *noun* an obstruction which makes movement or flow difficult or impossible.

SYNONYMS – hindrance, impediment, jam, obstruction, stoppage.

blockbuster > *noun* informal a film or book that is a great commercial success.

DERIVATIVES – **blockbusting** *adjective*.

ORIGIN – first used in the Second World War to denote a huge aerial bomb capable of destroying a whole block of buildings.

blockish > *adjective* **1** bulky or crude in form. **2** unintelligent; stupid.

bloke > *noun* Brit. informal a man.

ORIGIN – Shelta.

blokeish (also **blokish** or **blokey**) > *adjective* Brit. informal stereotypically male in behaviour and interests.

blonde > *adjective* (also **blond**) **1** (of hair) fair or pale yellow. **2** having fair hair and a light complexion. > *noun* **1** a woman with blonde hair. **2** the colour of blonde hair.

USAGE – the alternative spellings **blonde** and **blond** correspond to the feminine and masculine forms in French. However, in English, which does not have such distinctions of grammatical gender, the differentiation is not always made, and the adjective in either spelling may be used of both women and men. The word is more commonly used of women, though, and as a noun the spelling is invariably **blonde**.

ORIGIN – French, feminine of *blond*, from Latin *blondus* 'yellow'.

Blood /blud/ > *noun* (pl. same or **Bloods**) a member of a North American Indian people belonging to the Blackfoot Confederacy.

blood > *noun* **1** the red liquid that circulates in the arteries and veins, carrying oxygen and carbon dioxide. **2** family background: *she must have Irish blood.* **3** violence involving bloodshed. **4** fiery or passionate temperament. **5** dated a fashionable and dashing young man. > *verb* **1** initiate in a particular activity. **2** Hunting smear the face of (a novice hunter) with the blood of the kill.

WORDFINDER – haemal (*relating to blood*), haematology (*study of blood*); *components of blood:* corpuscle, erythrocyte, haemoglobin, leucocyte, plasma, platelet, rhesus factor, serum.

IDIOMS – **blood and thunder** informal unrestrained and violent action or behaviour. **blood is thicker than water** proverb family relationships are the most important ones. **blood, sweat, and tears** extremely hard work. **first blood 1** the first shedding of blood in a fight. **2** the first point or advantage gained in a contest. **give blood** allow blood to be removed medically from one's body for use in transfusions. **have blood on one's hands** be responsible for someone's death. **make someone's blood boil** informal infuriate someone. **make someone's blood run cold** horrify someone. **new** (or **fresh**) **blood** new members admitted to a group.

DERIVATIVES – **blooded** *adjective*.

COMBINATIONS – **blood brother** a man who has sworn to treat another man as a brother. **blood count** a determination of the number of corpuscles in a specific volume of blood. **blood-curdling** horrifying; very frightening. **blood feud** a lengthy conflict between families involving a cycle of retaliatory killings. **blood group** any of various types of human blood classified according to their compatibility in transfusion, especially by means of the ABO system. **bloodhound** a large hound with a very keen sense of smell, used in tracking. **bloodletting 1** historical the surgical removal of some of a patient's blood for therapeutic purposes. **2** violence during a war or conflict. **bloodline** a pedigree or set of ancestors. **blood money 1** money paid in compensation to the family of someone who has been killed. **2** money paid to a hired killer. **blood orange** an orange of a variety with red flesh. **blood poisoning** a diseased state due to the presence of micro-organisms or their toxins in the blood. **blood pressure** the pressure of the blood in the circulatory system, which is closely related to the force and rate of the heartbeat. **blood pudding** (also **blood sausage**) black pudding. **blood relation** (also **blood relative**) a person who is related to another by birth rather than by marriage. **blood sport** a sport involving the hunting, wounding, or killing of animals. **bloodstock** thoroughbred horses considered collectively. **bloodstream** the blood circulating through the body of a person or animal. **blood sugar** the concentration of glucose in the blood. **blood vessel** a tubular structure carrying blood through the tissues and organs; a vein, artery, or capillary.

bloodbath > *noun* an event in which many people are killed violently.

bloodless > *adjective* **1** (of a conflict) without violence or killing. **2** (of the skin) drained of colour. **3** lacking in vitality; feeble. **4** (of a person) cold or ruthless.

DERIVATIVES – **bloodlessness** *noun*.

bloodshed > *noun* the killing or wounding of people.

bloodshot > *adjective* (of the eyes) inflamed or tinged with blood.

bloodsucker > *noun* **1** an animal or insect that sucks blood. **2** informal a person who extorts money or otherwise lives off other people.

DERIVATIVES – **bloodsucking** adjective.

bloodthirsty > adjective (**bloodthirstier**, **bloodthirstiest**) eager to kill and maim.

bloody > adjective (**bloodier**, **bloodiest**) 1 covered with or composed of blood. 2 involving much violence or cruelty. 3 informal, chiefly Brit. used to express anger or shock, or for emphasis. 4 informal, dated, chiefly Brit. unpleasant: don't be too bloody to Nigel. > verb (**bloodies**, **bloodied**) cover or stain with blood.

DERIVATIVES – **bloodily** adverb **bloodiness** noun.

SYNONYMS – adjective 2 brutal, cruel, gory, sanguinary.

COMBINATIONS – **Bloody Mary** (pl. **Bloody Marys**) a drink consisting of vodka and tomato juice.

wordpower facts
Bloody

Although widely believed to be a profane reference to the blood of God or Christ, as in the archaic oath 'S-blood or God's blood, the informal use of **bloody** was probably, in the first place, simply a reference to young bloods (that is 'young aristocrats', or children of 'good blood'), who behaved in a rowdy manner; the phrase bloody drunk meant 'drunk as a blood' or 'drunk as a lord'. Nevertheless, the word was regarded as very offensive from the mid 1700s right up until the beginning of the 20th century: its use in 1914 by George Bernard Shaw in the play Pygmalion ('Walk! Not bloody likely.') was considered very daring.

bloom > verb 1 produce flowers; be in flower. 2 be or become very healthy. > noun 1 a flower, especially one cultivated for its beauty. 2 the state or period of blooming. 3 a youthful or healthy glow in a person's complexion. 4 a delicate powdery surface deposit on fruits. 5 a scum on the surface of water caused by the rapid growth of microscopic algae.

SYNONYMS – verb 2 blossom, flourish, thrive. noun 3 glow, lustre, radiance, sheen.

ORIGIN – Old Norse.

bloomer¹ > noun Brit. informal, dated a stupid mistake.

ORIGIN – equivalent to blooming error.

bloomer² > noun Brit. a large loaf with diagonal slashes on a rounded top.

bloomers > plural noun 1 women's loose-fitting knee-length knickers. 2 historical women's loose-fitting trousers, gathered at the knee or ankle.

ORIGIN – named after Mrs Amelia J. Bloomer (1818–94), an American social reformer who advocated a similar garment.

blooming > adjective Brit. informal used to express annoyance or for emphasis.

bloop informal, chiefly N. Amer. > verb (of an electronic device) emit a short low-pitched noise. > noun a short low-pitched noise emitted by an electronic device.

blooper > noun informal, chiefly N. Amer. an embarrassing error.

blossom > noun 1 a flower or mass of flowers on a tree or bush. 2 the state or period of flowering. > verb 1 (of a tree or bush) produce blossom. 2 develop in a promising or healthy way.

SYNONYMS – verb 2 bloom, burgeon, flourish, thrive.

blot > noun 1 a dark mark or stain, especially one made by ink. 2 a thing that mars something that is otherwise good; a blemish. > verb (**blotted**, **blotting**) 1 dry with an absorbent material. 2 mark, stain, or mar. 3 (**blot out**) obscure (a view). 4 (**blot out**) obliterate or ignore (a painful memory or thought).

IDIOMS – **blot one's copybook** Brit. tarnish one's good reputation.

blotch > noun a large irregular patch or unsightly mark. > verb cover or mark with blotches.

DERIVATIVES – **blotchy** adjective.

blotter > noun a frame holding a piece of blotting paper.

blotting paper > noun absorbent paper used for soaking up excess ink when writing.

blotto > adjective informal extremely drunk.

blouse > noun 1 a woman's upper garment resembling a shirt. 2 a loose smock or tunic. 3 a type of jacket worn as part of military uniform. > verb make (a garment) hang in loose folds.

IDIOMS – **big girl's blouse** Brit. informal a weak, cowardly, or over-sensitive man.

ORIGIN – French.

blouson /blooʹzon/ > noun a short loose-fitting jacket.

ORIGIN – French.

blow¹ > verb (past **blew**; past participle **blown**) 1 (of wind) move creating an air current. 2 be driven by the wind. 3 expel air through pursed lips. 4 force air through the mouth into (an instrument) to make a sound. 5 sound (the horn of a vehicle). 6 (of an explosion) displace violently. 7 burst or burn out through pressure or overheating. 8 force air through a tube into (molten glass) to create an artefact. 9 informal spend (money) recklessly. 10 informal completely bungle (an opportunity). 11 informal expose (a stratagem): his cover was blown. > noun 1 a strong wind. 2 an act of blowing.

IDIOMS – **blow a fuse** (or **gasket**) informal lose one's temper. **blow away** informal kill (someone) using a firearm. **blow hot and cold** alternate between different opinions or actions; vacillate. **blow someone's mind** informal impress or affect someone very strongly. **blow one's nose** clear one's nose of mucus by blowing through it. **blow off** informal break wind noisily. **blow over** (of trouble) fade away without serious consequences. **blow one's top** informal lose one's temper. **blow up 1** explode. **2** inflate. **3** (of a wind or storm) begin to develop. **4** lose one's temper. **5** (of a scandal or dispute) emerge or become public.

COMBINATIONS – **blow-dry** arrange (the hair) while drying it with a hand-held dryer. **blowfish** a fish that is able to inflate its body when alarmed. **blowfly** a bluebottle or similar large fly which lays its eggs on meat and carcasses. **blowhard** N. Amer. informal a person who blusters and boasts in an unpleasant way. **blowhole 1** the nostril of a whale or dolphin on the top of its head. **2** a hole in ice for breathing or fishing through. **3** a vent for air or smoke in a tunnel. **blowlamp** Brit. a blowtorch. **blowpipe 1** a weapon consisting of a long tube through which an arrow or dart is blown. **2** a long tube by means of which molten glass is blown. **blowtorch** a portable device producing a hot flame, used to burn off paint.

blow² > noun 1 a powerful stroke with a hand or weapon. 2 a sudden shock or disappointment.

IDIOMS – **blow-by-blow** (of a description of an event) giving all the details in the order in which they occurred. **come to blows** start fighting after a disagreement.

SYNONYMS – 1 punch, smack, strike, stroke, thump. 2 bombshell, jolt, setback, shock.

blower > noun 1 a device for creating a current of air to dry or heat something. 2 informal, chiefly Brit. a telephone.

blown past participle of BLOW¹.

blowout > noun 1 an occasion when a vehicle tyre bursts or an electric fuse melts. 2 N. Amer. informal an argument or outburst of anger. 3 informal a large, lavish meal.

blowsy /blowzi/ (also **blowzy**) > adjective (of a woman) coarse, untidy, and red-faced.

ORIGIN – from obsolete blowze 'beggar's female companion'.

blowy > adjective (**blowier**, **blowiest**) windy or windswept.

BLT > noun a sandwich filled with bacon, lettuce, and tomato.

blub > verb (**blubbed**, **blubbing**) informal sob noisily.

blubber¹ > noun the fat of sea mammals, especially whales and seals.

DERIVATIVES – **blubbery** adjective.

blubber² > *verb* informal sob noisily and uncontrollably.

bludge Austral./NZ informal > *verb* **1** live off the efforts of others. **2** cadge or scrounge. > *noun* an easy job or assignment.

bludgeon > *noun* a thick stick with a heavy end, used as a weapon. > *verb* **1** beat with a bludgeon. **2** bully into doing something.

bludger > *noun* Austral./NZ informal a scrounger or idler.

ORIGIN – abbreviation of *bludgeoner*: originally British slang denoting a pimp who robbed his prostitute's clients.

blue¹ > *adjective* (**bluer, bluest**) **1** of a colour intermediate between green and violet, as of the sky on a sunny day. **2** informal melancholy or depressed. **3** informal (of a film, joke, or story) with sexual or pornographic content. **4** (of a cat, fox, or rabbit) having fur of a smoky grey colour. **5** Brit. informal politically conservative. > *noun* **1** blue colour, pigment, or material. **2** Brit. a person who has represented Cambridge University or Oxford University in a particular sport. **3** Austral./NZ informal a nickname for a redheaded person. **4** Austral./NZ informal an argument or fight.

WORDFINDER – *shades of blue:* azure, cerulean, cyan, indigo, lavender, navy, petrol, sapphire, saxe, teal, turquoise, ultramarine.

IDIOMS – **once in a blue moon** informal very rarely. [ORIGIN – because a 'blue moon' is a phenomenon that never occurs.] **out of the blue** informal without warning; unexpectedly.

DERIVATIVES – **blueness** *noun.*

COMBINATIONS – **blue baby** a baby with cyanosis. **blueberry** the small blue-back berry of a North American dwarf shrub. **bluebird** an American songbird, the male of which has a blue head, back, and wings. **blue-blooded** of noble birth. **blue book** (in the UK) a report bound in a blue cover and issued by Parliament or the Privy Council. **blue cheese** cheese containing veins of blue mould, such as Stilton. **blue-collar** chiefly N. Amer. relating to manual work or workers. **blue-eyed boy** Brit. informal, chiefly derogatory a person highly regarded and treated with special favour. **bluegrass 1** (also **Kentucky bluegrass**) a meadow grass grown in North America for fodder. **2** a kind of country music characterised by skilled playing of banjos and guitars. **blue-green algae** cyanobacteria. **blue-pencil** censor or make cuts in (a manuscript, book, etc.). **Blue Peter** a blue flag with a white square in the centre, raised by a ship about to leave port. **blue tit** a common titmouse with a blue cap and yellow underparts. **blue whale** a bluish-grey rorqual which is the largest living animal.

ORIGIN – Old French *bleu.*

blue² > *verb* (**blues, blued, bluing** or **blueing**) Brit. informal, dated squander or spend recklessly.

bluebell > *noun* **1** a woodland plant which produces clusters of blue bell-shaped flowers. **2** Scottish term for HAREBELL.

bluebottle > *noun* a common blowfly with a metallic-blue body.

blue-chip > *adjective* (of companies or their shares) considered to be a reliable investment.

ORIGIN – from the *blue chip* used in gambling games, which usually has a high value.

blue heeler > *noun* Austral./NZ a cattle dog with a dark speckled body.

blueish > *adjective* variant spelling of BLUISH.

blueprint > *noun* **1** a design plan or other technical drawing. **2** something which acts as a plan, model, or template.

ORIGIN – from the former process in which plans were printed photographically using white lines on a blue ground or blue lines on a white ground.

blue riband > *noun* (also **blue ribbon**) a ribbon of blue silk given to the winner of a competition or as a mark of great distinction. > *adjective* (**blue-ribbon**) N. Amer. of the highest quality; first-class.

blues > *plural noun* **1** (treated as sing. or pl.) melancholic music of black American folk origin. **2** (**the blues**) informal feelings of melancholy or depression.

DERIVATIVES – **bluesy** *adjective.*

ORIGIN – from *blue devils* 'depression or delirium tremens'.

bluestocking > *noun* often derogatory an intellectual or literary woman.

wordpower facts
Bluestocking
The word **bluestocking** was originally used to describe a man wearing casual grey-blue worsted (instead of formal black silk) stockings. Later it was used in reference to those who attended a series of literary parties held around 1750 by three London society ladies, where some of the men wore informal dress. The women who attended became known as *blue-stocking ladies* or *blue-stockingers.*

bluey > *adjective* almost or partly blue. > *noun* (pl. **blueys**) Austral./NZ informal **1** archaic a bundle of possessions carried by a bushman. [ORIGIN – so named because the covering was generally a blue blanket.] **2** a nickname for a red-headed person.

bluff¹ > *noun* an attempt to deceive someone into believing that one can or will do

something. > *verb* try to deceive someone into believing that one can or will do something.

IDIOMS – **call someone's bluff** challenge someone to carry out a stated intention, in the expectation of being able to expose it as a pretence.

DERIVATIVES – **bluffer** *noun.*

ORIGIN – first used in the sense 'blindfold, hoodwink'; from Dutch *bluffen* 'brag'. The current sense originally referred to bluffing in the game of poker.

bluff² > *adjective* good-naturedly frank and direct.

DERIVATIVES – **bluffly** *adverb* **bluffness** *noun.*

SYNONYMS – blunt, direct, downright, forthright, frank.

ANTONYMS – evasive, sly.

bluff³ > *noun* a steep cliff, bank, or promontory. > *adjective* (of a cliff or a ship's bows) having a broad vertical or steep front.

bluish (also **blueish**) > *adjective* having a blue tinge.

blunder > *noun* a stupid or careless mistake. > *verb* **1** make a blunder. **2** move clumsily or as if unable to see.

SYNONYMS – *noun* error, gaffe, mistake, slip. *verb* **1** bungle, err, slip up. **2** fumble, grope, lurch, stagger.

blunderbuss > *noun* **1** historical a short large-bored gun. **2** an unsubtle and imprecise action or method.

ORIGIN – Dutch *donderbus* 'thunder gun'.

blunt > *adjective* **1** lacking a sharp edge or point. **2** having a flat or rounded end. **3** uncompromisingly forthright in manner. > *verb* **1** make or become less sharp. **2** weaken or reduce the force of.

DERIVATIVES – **bluntly** *adverb* **bluntness** *noun.*

SYNONYMS – *adjective* **1** dull, blunted, worn. **3** bluff, direct, forthright, frank. *verb* **1** dull, wear. **2** deaden, dull, mitigate, soften.

ANTONYMS – *adjective* **1** sharp. **3** mealy-mouthed, subtle. *verb* **1** hone, sharpen. **2** intensify, sharpen.

blur > *verb* (**blurred, blurring**) make or become unclear or less distinct. > *noun* something that cannot be seen, heard, or recalled clearly.

DERIVATIVES – **blurry** (**blurrier, blurriest**) *adjective.*

SYNONYMS – *verb* dim, fog, obscure.

ANTONYMS – *verb* focus, sharpen.

blurb > *noun* a short description of a book, film, or other product written for promotional purposes.

ORIGIN – coined by the American humorist Gelett Burgess (died 1951).

blurt > *verb* say suddenly and without careful consideration.

blush > *verb* become red in the face through

shyness or embarrassment. > *noun* **1** an instance of blushing. **2** literary a pink or pale red tinge.

IDIOMS – **at first blush** at the first glimpse or impression.

DERIVATIVES – **blushing** *adjective*.

SYNONYMS – *verb* colour, crimson, flush, redden.

blusher > *noun* a cosmetic used to give a warm reddish tinge to the cheeks.

bluster > *verb* **1** talk in a loud or aggressive way with little effect. **2** (of wind or rain) blow or beat fiercely and noisily. > *noun* blustering talk.

DERIVATIVES – **blusterer** *noun* **blustery** *adjective*.

BM > *abbreviation* **1** Bachelor of Medicine. **2** British Museum.

BMA > *abbreviation* British Medical Association.

BMX > *abbreviation* bicycle motocross.

boa > *noun* **1** a large snake which kills its prey by constriction. **2** a long, thin stole of feathers or fur worn around a woman's neck.

ORIGIN – Latin.

boab /bōab/ > *noun* Austral. another term for **BAOBAB**.

boar > *noun* (pl. same or **boars**) **1** (also **wild boar**) a wild pig with tusks. **2** an uncastrated domestic male pig.

board > *noun* **1** a long, thin, flat piece of wood used in building. **2** a thin, flat, rectangular piece of stiff material. **3** the decision-making body of an organisation. **4** the provision of regular meals in return for payment. **5** (**the boards**) informal the stage of a theatre. > *verb* **1** get on or into (a ship, aircraft, or other vehicle). **2** receive meals and accommodation in return for payment. **3** (of a pupil) live in school during term time. **4** (**board up** or **over**) cover or seal with pieces of wood. **5** (**be boarding**) (of an aircraft) be ready for passengers to get on.

IDIOMS – **go by the board** (of a plan or principle) be abandoned or rejected. [ORIGIN – from nautical use meaning 'fall overboard', the *board* meaning the side of a ship.] **on board** on or in a ship, aircraft, or other vehicle. **take on board** informal fully consider or assimilate (a new idea or situation). **tread the boards** informal appear on stage as an actor.

SYNONYMS – *verb* **1** catch, embark, get on, go aboard. **2** lodge, be put up, reside, stay.

COMBINATIONS – **board foot** a unit of volume for wood equal to 144 cubic inches. **board game** a game that involves the movement of counters or other objects around a board.

boarder > *noun* **1** a person who boards, in particular a pupil who lives in school during

term time. **2** a person who forces their way on to a ship in an attack.

boarding house > *noun* a private house providing food and lodging for paying guests.

boarding school > *noun* a school in which the pupils live during term time.

boardroom > *noun* a room in which a board of directors meets regularly.

boardsailing > *noun* another term for **WINDSURFING**.

DERIVATIVES – **boardsailor** *noun*.

boardwalk > *noun* **1** a wooden walkway across sand or marshy ground. **2** N. Amer. a promenade along a beach or waterfront.

boast > *verb* **1** talk about oneself with excessive pride. **2** possess (a feature that is a source of pride). > *noun* an act of boasting.

DERIVATIVES – **boaster** *noun* **boasting** *adjective & noun*.

SYNONYMS – *verb* **1** brag, crow, show off.

boastful > *adjective* showing excessive pride and self-satisfaction in oneself.

DERIVATIVES – **boastfully** *adverb* **boastfulness** *noun*.

SYNONYMS – bragging, conceited, egotistical, proud; informal big-headed.

ANTONYMS – modest, unassuming.

boat > *noun* **1** a vessel for travelling on water. **2** a boat-shaped serving dish for sauce or gravy. > *verb* travel or transport in a boat.

IDIOMS – **be in the same boat** informal be in the same difficult circumstances as others. **push the boat out** Brit. informal be extravagant. **rock the boat** informal disturb an existing situation.

DERIVATIVES – **boatload** *noun*.

SYNONYMS – *noun* **1** craft, ship, vessel; literary barque.

COMBINATIONS – **boathook** a long pole with a hook and a spike at one end, used for moving boats. **boatman** a person who provides transport by boat. **boat people** refugees who have left a country by sea. **boat train** a train scheduled to connect with the arrival or departure of a boat.

boatel > *noun* **1** a waterside hotel with facilities for mooring boats. **2** a moored ship used as a hotel.

boater > *noun* **1** a flat-topped straw hat with a brim. [ORIGIN – so called because originally worn while boating.] **2** a person who travels in a boat.

boating > *noun* rowing or sailing in boats as a sport or recreation.

boatswain /bōs'n/ (also **bosun** or **bo'sun**) > *noun* a ship's officer in charge of equipment and the crew.

ORIGIN – from **BOAT** + **SWAIN**.

Bob > *noun* (in phrase **Bob's your uncle**) Brit. informal used to express the ease with which a particular task can be achieved.

bob¹ > *verb* (**bobbed**, **bobbing**) **1** make a

quick, short movement up and down. **2** curtsy briefly. > *noun* **1** a quick, short movement up and down. **2** a brief curtsy.

IDIOMS – **bob for apples** try to catch floating apples with one's mouth, as a game.

bob² > *noun* **1** a short hairstyle hanging evenly all round. **2** a weight on a pendulum, plumb line, or kite tail. **3** a bobsleigh. > *verb* (**bobbed**, **bobbing**) cut (hair) in a bob.

bob³ > *noun* (pl. same) Brit. informal a shilling.

bobbin > *noun* a cylinder, cone, or reel holding thread.

ORIGIN – French *bobine*.

bobble¹ > *noun* a small ball made of strands of wool.

DERIVATIVES – **bobbly** *adjective*.

ORIGIN – from **BOB²**.

bobble² informal > *verb* **1** move with an irregular bouncing motion. **2** N. Amer. mishandle (a ball). > *noun* **1** an irregular bouncing motion. **2** N. Amer. a mishandling of a ball.

ORIGIN – from **BOB¹**.

bobby > *noun* (pl. **bobbies**) Brit. informal, dated a police officer.

ORIGIN – after Sir *Robert* Peel (1788–1850), the British Prime Minister who established the Metropolitan Police.

bobcat > *noun* a small North American lynx with a barred and spotted coat and a short tail.

ORIGIN – from **BOB²**, with reference to its short tail.

bobsleigh (N. Amer. **bobsled**) > *noun* a mechanically steered and braked sledge used for racing down an ice-covered run.

bobsy-die /bobzidī/ > *noun* dialect & NZ a great deal of fuss or trouble.

ORIGIN – contraction of *Bob's-a-dying*.

bobtail > *noun* a docked tail of a horse or dog.

bod > *noun* informal **1** a body. **2** chiefly Brit. a person.

bodacious /bōdayshəss/ > *adjective* N. Amer. informal excellent, admirable, or attractive.

ORIGIN – perhaps a variant of south-western dialect *boldacious*, blend of **BOLD** and **AUDACIOUS**.

bode > *verb* (**bode well** or **ill**) be a sign or portent that something good or bad will happen.

SYNONYMS – augur, portend, presage.

bodega /bədaygə/ > *noun* (in Spanish-speaking countries) a cellar or shop selling wine and sometimes food.

ORIGIN – Spanish, via Latin from Greek *apothēkē* 'storehouse'; related to **BOUTIQUE**.

bodge > *verb* Brit. informal make or repair badly or clumsily.

DERIVATIVES – **bodger** *noun*.

ORIGIN – alteration of **BOTCH**.

bodgie > *noun* (pl. **bodgies**) Austral./NZ informal a flawed or worthless thing.

bodhrán /**bow**raan/ > *noun* a shallow one-sided Irish drum usually played with a short stick.

ORIGIN – Irish.

bodh tree > *noun* variant of **BO TREE**.

bodice > *noun* **1** the upper front part of a woman's dress. **2** a woman's sleeveless undergarment, often laced at the front.

COMBINATIONS – **bodice-ripper** humorous a sexually explicit historical novel or film.

ORIGIN – first as *bodies*, from **BODY**.

bodiless > *adjective* **1** lacking a body. **2** incorporeal; insubstantial.

bodily > *adjective* **1** relating to the body. **2** material or physical. > *adverb* by taking hold of a person's body with force.

bodkin > *noun* **1** a thick, blunt needle with a large eye, used for drawing tape or cord through a hem. **2** historical a long pin used to fasten women's hair.

ORIGIN – perhaps Celtic.

body > *noun* (pl. **bodies**) **1** the physical structure, including the bones, flesh, and organs, of a person or animal. **2** the torso. **3** a dead body. **4** the main or central part of something. **5** a mass or collection of something. **6** an organised group of people with a common function: *a regulatory body*. **7** technical a piece of matter; a material object: *a falling body*. **8** a full flavour in wine. **9** fullness of a person's hair. **10** a bodysuit. > *verb* (**bodies, bodied**) (**body forth**) formal give material form to.

WORDFINDER – *relating to the body:* corporal, corporeal, somatic; *body types:* ectomorphic (*lean and delicate*), endomorphic (*round and plump*), mesomorphic (*compact and muscular*).

IDIOMS – **keep body and soul together** stay alive in difficult circumstances. **over my dead body** informal used to express strong opposition.

DERIVATIVES – **bodied** adjective.

SYNONYMS – *noun* **3** cadaver, carcass, corpse. **6** association, group, organisation.

COMBINATIONS – **body bag** a bag used for carrying a corpse from a battlefield or the scene of an accident or crime. **body blow 1** a heavy punch to the body. **2** a severe setback. **bodyboard** a short, light surfboard ridden in a prone position. **body clock** a person's biological clock. **body double** a stand-in for a film actor during stunt or nude scenes. **body language** the conscious and unconscious bodily movements by which feelings are communicated. **body politic** the people of a nation or society considered as an organised group of citizens. **body-popping** a kind of dancing characterised by jerky robotic movements of the joints. **body shop** a garage where repairs to the bodywork of vehicles are

carried out. **bodysnatcher** historical a person who illicitly dug up corpses for dissection. **body stocking** a woman's one-piece undergarment covering the torso and legs. **bodysuit** a woman's close-fitting stretch garment for the upper body. **bodysurf** surf without using a board. **body warmer** a sleeveless padded jacket. **bodywork** the metal outer shell of a vehicle.

bodybuilder > *noun* a person who strengthens and enlarges their muscles through exercise such as weightlifting.

DERIVATIVES – **bodybuilding** noun.

bodyguard > *noun* a person employed to protect a rich or famous person.

Boer /**bō**ər, boor/ > *noun* a member of the Dutch and Huguenot population which settled in southern Africa in the late 17th century.

ORIGIN – Dutch, 'farmer'.

boeuf bourguignon /berf **boor**ginyoN/ > *noun* a dish consisting of beef stewed in red wine.

ORIGIN – French, 'Burgundy beef'.

boff N. Amer. informal > *verb* **1** hit or strike. **2** have sexual intercourse with. > *noun* **1** a blow or punch. **2** an act of sexual intercourse.

boffin > *noun* informal, chiefly Brit. a person engaged in complex scientific or technical research.

boffo N. Amer. informal > *adjective* **1** (of a play or film) resoundingly successful. **2** (of a laugh) deep and unrestrained. > *noun* (pl. **boffos**) a success.

ORIGIN – from **BOFF** in the sense 'roaring success'.

bog > *noun* **1** an area of soft, wet, muddy ground. **2** Brit. informal a toilet. > *verb* (**bogged, bogging**) **1** (**bog down**) cause to become stuck; hinder the progress of. **2** (**bog in**) Austral./NZ informal start a task enthusiastically.

DERIVATIVES – **bogginess** noun **boggy** adjective.

SYNONYMS – *noun* **1** marsh, mire, quagmire, swamp.

COMBINATIONS – **bog-standard** informal ordinary; basic.

ORIGIN – Irish or Scottish Gaelic *bogach*, from *bog* 'soft'.

bogey[1] Golf > *noun* (pl. **bogeys**) a score of one stroke over par at a hole. > *verb* (**bogeys, bogeyed**) play (a hole) in one stroke over par.

ORIGIN – perhaps from *Bogey*, a name for the Devil, regarded as an imaginary player.

bogey[2] (also **bogy**) > *noun* (pl. **bogeys**) **1** an evil or mischievous spirit. **2** a cause of fear or alarm: *the bogey of recession*. **3** US military slang an enemy aircraft. **4** Brit. informal a piece of nasal mucus.

ORIGIN – a name applied to the Devil.

bogeyman (also **bogyman**) > *noun* an

imaginary evil being evoked to frighten children.

boggle > *verb* informal **1** be startled or baffled. **2** (**boggle at**) hesitate to do; be anxious about.

ORIGIN – probably related to **BOGEY**[2].

bogie /**bō**gi/ > *noun* (pl. **bogies**) chiefly Brit. **1** a structure with four or six wheels pivoted beneath the end of a railway vehicle. **2** chiefly N. English a low truck on four small wheels.

bogus > *adjective* not genuine or true.

DERIVATIVES – **bogusly** adverb **bogusness** noun.

SYNONYMS – counterfeit, fake, false, forged, fraudulent, sham.

ANTONYMS – authentic, genuine.

---

wordpower facts

Bogus

The word **bogus** first appeared in American English in the late 18th century in reference to an apparatus used for making counterfeit coins. It has been suggested that it came from *tantrabogus*, a word used in New England to denote any strange-looking apparatus or object. It has further been suggested that this may be related to *tantarabobs*, a term used in Devonshire dialect for the devil. There may be a link between **bogus** and **bogey** (or **bogy**) and **bogeyman**, both of which are based on *Bogey*, an old dialect name for the Devil.

---

bogy > *noun* (pl. **bogies**) variant spelling of **BOGEY**[2].

Bohemian /bō**hee**miən/ > *noun* **1** a person from Bohemia, a region of the Czech Republic. **2** a socially unconventional person, especially an artist or writer. [ORIGIN – French *bohémien* 'gypsy' (because gypsies were thought to come from Bohemia).] > *adjective* **1** relating to Bohemia. **2** socially unconventional.

DERIVATIVES – **Bohemianism** noun.

SYNONYMS – *adjective* **2** alternative, arty, unconventional, unorthodox.

ANTONYMS – *adjective* **2** conventional.

bohrium /**bor**iəm/ > *noun* a very unstable chemical element made by high-energy atomic collisions.

ORIGIN – named after the Danish physicist Niels *Bohr* (1885–1962).

boil[1] > *verb* **1** (with reference to a liquid) reach or cause to reach the temperature at which it bubbles and turns to vapour. **2** (with reference to food) cook or be cooked by immersing in boiling water. **3** seethe like boiling liquid. **4** (**boil down to**) amount to. > *noun* **1** the act or process of boiling. **2** boiling point. **3** a state of vigorous activity or excitement: *the team have gone off the boil this season.*

COMBINATIONS – **boiled sweet** Brit. a hard sweet made of boiled sugar.

ORIGIN – Old French *boillir*, from Latin *bullire* 'to bubble'.

boil² > *noun* an inflamed pus-filled swelling on the skin.

boiler > *noun* 1 a fuel-burning apparatus for heating water, especially a device providing a domestic hot-water supply or serving a central heating system. 2 Brit. informal a chicken suitable for cooking only by boiling.

COMBINATIONS – **boilerplate 1** rolled steel plates for making boilers. **2** N. Amer. stereotyped or clichéd writing. **3** N. Amer. standardised pieces of text for use as clauses in contracts or as part of a computer program. **boiler suit** Brit. a one-piece suit worn as overalls for heavy manual work.

boiling > *adjective* 1 at or near boiling point. 2 informal extremely hot.

COMBINATIONS – **boiling point** the temperature at which a liquid boils.

boisterous > *adjective* 1 noisy, energetic, and cheerful. 2 literary (of weather or water) wild or stormy.

DERIVATIVES – **boisterously** *adverb* **boisterousness** *noun*.

SYNONYMS – **1** animated, exuberant, high-spirited, lively.

ANTONYMS – **1** restrained, subdued.

bolas /bōləss/ > *noun* (treated as sing. or pl.) (especially in South America) a missile consisting of a number of balls connected by strong cord, thrown to entangle the limbs of cattle or other animals.

ORIGIN – Spanish and Portuguese, plural of *bola* 'ball'.

bold > *adjective* 1 confident and courageous. 2 dated audacious; impudent. 3 (of a colour or design) strong or vivid. 4 (of type) having thick strokes. > *noun* a typeface with thick strokes.

IDIOMS – **be so bold as to** dare to. **as bold as brass** confident to the point of impudence.

DERIVATIVES – **boldly** *adverb* **boldness** *noun*.

SYNONYMS – **1** audacious, brave, courageous, daring.

ANTONYMS – **1** timid.

COMBINATIONS – **boldface** a typeface with thick strokes.

bole > *noun* a tree trunk.

ORIGIN – Old Norse.

bolero /bəlairō/ > *noun* (pl. **boleros**) **1** a Spanish dance in simple triple time. **2** /bollərō/ a woman's short open jacket.

ORIGIN – Spanish.

boletus /bəleetəss/ (also **bolete**) > *noun* (pl. **boletuses**) a toadstool with pores rather than gills on the underside of the cap, and a thick stem.

ORIGIN – Greek *bōlitēs*.

bolide /bōlīd/ > *noun* a large meteor which explodes in the atmosphere.

ORIGIN – French, from Latin *bolis* 'missile'.

bolivar /bolivaar/ > *noun* the basic monetary unit of Venezuela, equal to 100 centimos.

ORIGIN – named after the Venezuelan Simon *Bolívar* (1783–1830), who liberated Venezuela from the Spanish.

Bolivian > *noun* a person from Bolivia. > *adjective* relating to Bolivia.

boliviano > *noun* (pl. **bolivianos**) the basic monetary unit of Bolivia, equal to 100 centavos or cents.

ORIGIN – Spanish, 'Bolivian'.

boll /bōl/ > *noun* the rounded seed capsule of plants such as cotton or flax.

COMBINATIONS – **bollworm** a moth caterpillar which is a pest of cotton and other crops.

ORIGIN – Dutch *bolle* 'rounded object'; related to BOWL¹.

bollard > *noun* 1 Brit. a short post used to prevent traffic from entering an area. 2 a short post on a ship or quayside for securing a rope.

bollocking (also **ballocking**) > *noun* Brit. vulgar slang a severe reprimand.

DERIVATIVES – **bollock** *verb*.

bollocks (also **ballocks**) > *plural noun* Brit. vulgar slang 1 the testicles. 2 (treated as sing.) nonsense; rubbish.

ORIGIN – related to BALL¹.

Bollywood > *noun* informal the Indian popular film industry, based in Bombay.

bologna /bəlōnyə/ > *noun* a smoked sausage made from bacon, veal, and pork suet.

ORIGIN – named after *Bologna*, a city in northern Italy.

bolometer /bəlommitər/ > *noun* Physics an electrical instrument for measuring radiant energy.

DERIVATIVES – **bolometric** *adjective*.

ORIGIN – from Greek *bolē* 'ray of light'.

boloney > *noun* variant spelling of BALONEY.

bolo tie /bōlō/ > *noun* N. Amer. a tie consisting of a cord around the neck with a large ornamental fastening at the throat.

ORIGIN – alteration of *bola tie*, from its resemblance to the BOLAS.

Bolshevik /bolshivik/ > *noun* historical **1** a member of the majority faction of the Russian Social Democratic Party, which seized power in the Revolution of 1917. **2** a person with politically subversive or radical views. > *adjective* relating to or characteristic of Bolsheviks or Bolshevism.

DERIVATIVES – **Bolshevism** *noun* **Bolshevist** *noun*.

ORIGIN – Russian, from *bol'she* 'greater'; the name was coined by Lenin, who described his own faction as *Bolsheviks* and the other, less extreme faction as *Mensheviks* (from *men'she* 'less').

bolshie (also **bolshy**) Brit. informal > *adjective* deliberately combative or uncooperative.

DERIVATIVES – **bolshiness** *noun*.

ORIGIN – from BOLSHEVIK.

bolster > *noun* 1 a long, firm pillow. 2 a part in a tool, vehicle, or structure providing support or reducing friction. > *verb* support or strengthen.

DERIVATIVES – **bolsterer** *noun*.

bolt¹ > *noun* 1 a long pin with a head that screws into a nut, used to fasten things together. 2 a bar that slides into a socket to fasten a door or window. 3 the sliding piece of the breech mechanism of a rifle. 4 a short, heavy arrow shot from a crossbow. 5 a flash of lightning across the sky. > *verb* fasten with a bolt.

IDIOMS – **a bolt from** (or **out of**) **the blue** a sudden and unexpected event. **bolt upright** with the back very straight. **have shot one's bolt** informal have done everything possible but still not succeeded.

bolt² > *verb* 1 run away suddenly. 2 (of a plant) grow quickly upwards and stop flowering as seeds develop. 3 eat (food) quickly.

IDIOMS – **make a bolt for** try to escape by running suddenly towards.

DERIVATIVES – **bolter** *noun*.

COMBINATIONS – **bolt hole** chiefly Brit. an escape route or hiding place.

ORIGIN – from BOLT¹, expressing the sense 'fly like an arrow'.

bolt³ > *noun* a roll of fabric, originally as a measure.

bolus /bōləss/ > *noun* (pl. **boluses**) 1 a small rounded mass of something, especially of food being swallowed. 2 a large pill used in veterinary medicine. 3 Medicine a single dose of a drug given all at once.

ORIGIN – Greek *bōlos* 'clod'.

bomb > *noun* 1 a container of explosive or incendiary material, designed to explode on impact or when detonated by a timer or remote control. 2 (**the bomb**) nuclear weapons collectively. 3 (**a bomb**) Brit. informal a large sum of money. > *verb* 1 attack with a bomb or bombs. 2 Brit. informal move very quickly. 3 informal fail badly.

IDIOMS – **go down a bomb** Brit. informal be very well received. **go like a bomb** Brit. informal 1 be very successful. 2 move very fast.

ORIGIN – French *bombe*, probably from Latin *bombus* 'booming, humming', from Greek *bombos*.

bombard /bombaard/ > *verb* 1 attack continuously with shells or other missiles. 2 subject to a continuous flow of questions or information. 3 Physics direct a stream of high-speed particles at (a substance). > *noun* /**bom**baard/ an early form of cannon.

DERIVATIVES – **bombardment** *noun*.

SYNONYMS – *verb* **1** blitz, bomb, pound, shell.

ORIGIN – first used as a noun: from Old French *bombarde*, probably from Latin *bombus* 'booming'.

bombardier /bombər**deer**/ > *noun* **1** a rank of non-commissioned officer in certain artillery regiments, equivalent to corporal. **2** a member of a bomber crew in the US air force responsible for sighting and releasing bombs.

COMBINATIONS – **bombardier beetle** a beetle that discharges an irritant vapour from its anus with an audible pop when alarmed.

bombast /**bom**bast/ > *noun* high-sounding language with little meaning.

SYNONYMS – bluster, hot air, orotundity.

ORIGIN – first denoting cotton wool used as padding: from Old French *bombace*, from Latin *bombyx* 'silkworm'.

bombastic /bom**bas**tik/ > *adjective* high-sounding but with little meaning.

DERIVATIVES – **bombastically** *adverb*.

SYNONYMS – blustering, grandiloquent, pompous, verbose.

Bombay duck > *noun* dried bummalo fish eaten as an accompaniment with curries.

ORIGIN – alteration of **BUMMALO** by association with the city of *Bombay* in India, from which bummalo were exported.

Bombay mix > *noun* an Indian spiced snack consisting of lentils, peanuts, and deep-fried strands of gram flour.

bombazine /**bom**bəzeen/ > *noun* a twilled dress fabric of worsted and silk or cotton.

ORIGIN – French *bombasin*, from Latin *bombycinus* 'silken'.

bombe /boNb/ > *noun* a frozen dome-shaped dessert.

ORIGIN – French, 'bomb'.

bombed > *adjective* **1** subjected to bombing. **2** *informal* intoxicated by drink or drugs.

bomber > *noun* **1** an aircraft that drops bombs. **2** a person who plants bombs, especially as a terrorist. **3** *informal* a large cannabis cigarette.

COMBINATIONS – **bomber jacket** a short jacket gathered at the waist and cuffs by elasticated bands and having a zip front.

bombora /bom**bor**ə/ > *noun* Austral. a wave which forms over a submerged offshore reef or rock.

ORIGIN – from an Aboriginal word.

bombshell > *noun* **1** something that comes as a great surprise and shock. **2** *informal* a very attractive woman.

bona fide /**bō**nə **f**ī**di**/ > *adjective* genuine; real. > *adverb* chiefly Law without intention to deceive.

ORIGIN – Latin, 'with good faith'.

bona fides /**bō**nə **f**ī**deez**/ > *noun* **1** honest and sincere intentions. **2** (treated as pl.) *informal* a person's credentials.

ORIGIN – Latin, 'good faith'.

bonanza > *noun* a source of wealth, profit, or good fortune.

ORIGIN – Spanish, 'fair weather, prosperity', from Latin *bonus* 'good'.

bon appétit /bon appe**tee**/ > *exclamation* used to wish someone an enjoyable meal.

ORIGIN – French, 'good appetite'.

bonbon > *noun* a sweet.

ORIGIN – French, from *bon* 'good'.

bonce > *noun* Brit. informal a person's head.

ORIGIN – first used to denote a large marble.

bond > *noun* **1** a thing used to tie or fasten things together. **2** (**bonds**) physical restraints used to hold someone prisoner. **3** a force or feeling that unites people. **4** a binding agreement. **5** a certificate issued by a government or a public company promising to repay borrowed money at a fixed rate of interest at a specified time. **6** (also **chemical bond**) a strong force of attraction holding atoms together in a molecule. **7** Building any of the various patterns in which bricks are laid to ensure strength in the resulting structure. > *verb* **1** join or be joined securely to something else. **2** establish a relationship based on shared feelings or experiences. **3** join or be joined by a chemical bond. **4** lay (bricks) in a strong overlapping pattern. **5** place (dutiable goods) in bond.

IDIOMS – **in bond** (of dutiable goods) stored by customs until duty is paid.

SYNONYMS – *noun* **2** (**bonds**) chains, fetters, irons, shackles. **3** fellowship, friendship, relationship. *verb* **1** attach, connect, join.

COMBINATIONS – **bond paper** high-quality writing paper. **bondsman 1** a person who guarantees a bond or agreement to make payment for a bond. **2** archaic a slave or feudal serf.

ORIGIN – variant of **BAND**¹.

bondage > *noun* **1** the state of being a slave or feudal serf. **2** sexual practice that involves the tying up or restraining of one partner.

bonded > *adjective* **1** joined securely together, especially by adhesive, heat, or pressure. **2** bound by a legal agreement. **3** (of imported dutiable goods on which duty has not yet been paid) held by customs.

COMBINATIONS – **bonded warehouse** a customs-controlled warehouse where bonded goods are held.

bone > *noun* **1** any of the pieces of hard, whitish tissue making up the skeleton in vertebrates. **2** the material of which bones consist. **3** a thing resembling a bone, such as a strip of stiffening for an undergarment. > *verb* **1** remove the bones from (meat or fish) before cooking. **2** (**bone up on**) informal study (a subject) intensively.

WORDFINDER – orthopaedics (*branch of medicine concerned with bone deformities*), osseous (*consisting of bone*), osteoporosis (*brittleness of the bones*), osteoarthritis (*degeneration of joint cartilage*).

IDIOMS – **bone of contention** a source of continuing disagreement. **close to the bone 1** (of a remark) accurate to the point of causing discomfort. **2** (of a joke or story) near the limit of decency. **have a bone to pick with** informal have reason to disagree or be annoyed with. **in one's bones** felt or believed deeply or instinctively. **make no bones about** be straightforward in stating or dealing with. **off** (or **on**) **the bone** (of meat or fish) having had the bones removed (or left in). **what's bred in the bone will come out in the flesh** (or **blood**) proverb a person's behaviour or characteristics are determined by their heredity. **work one's fingers to the bone** work very hard.

DERIVATIVES – **boneless** *adjective*.

COMBINATIONS – **bone china** white porcelain containing the mineral residue of bones that have been heated in a kiln. **bone dry** extremely dry. **bonehead** informal a stupid person. **bone idle** extremely idle. [ORIGIN – expressing *idle through to the bone*.] **bonemeal** ground bones used as a fertiliser. **boneshaker** Brit. informal **1** an old vehicle with poor suspension. **2** an early type of bicycle without rubber tyres. **boneyard** informal a cemetery.

boner > *noun* N. Amer **1** informal a stupid mistake. **2** vulgar slang an erection of the penis.

bonfire > *noun* an open-air fire lit to burn rubbish or as a celebration.

COMBINATIONS – **Bonfire Night** (in the UK) 5 November, on which fireworks are displayed, bonfires lit, and effigies of Guy Fawkes burnt, in memory of the Gunpowder Plot of 1605.

ORIGIN – from **BONE** + **FIRE**: originally denoting a fire on which bones were burnt, or for burning heretics.

bong > *noun* a water pipe used for smoking cannabis.

ORIGIN – Thai, 'cylindrical wooden tube'.

bongo > *noun* (pl. **bongos** or **bongoes**) each of a pair of small drums that are held between the knees and played with the fingers.

ORIGIN – Latin American Spanish.

bonhomie /bonnə**mee**/ > *noun* good-natured friendliness.

DERIVATIVES – **bonhomous** *adjective*.

ORIGIN – French, from *bonhomme* 'good fellow'.

bonito /bəˈneetō/ > *noun* (pl. **bonitos**) a small tuna with dark stripes, important as a food and game fish.

ORIGIN – Spanish.

bonk informal > *verb* **1** hit so as to cause a reverberating sound. **2** Brit. have sexual intercourse. > *noun* **1** a reverberating sound. **2** Brit. an act of sexual intercourse.

bonkers > *adjective* informal mad; crazy.

bon mot /bon mō/ > *noun* (pl. **bons mots** pronunc. same or /bon mōz/) a clever or witty remark; a quip or witticism.

ORIGIN – French, 'good word'.

bonne femme /bon fam/ > *adjective* (of fish, stews, and soups) cooked in a simple way: *sole bonne femme*.

ORIGIN – from French *à la bonne femme* 'in the manner of a good housewife'.

bonnet > *noun* **1** a woman's or child's hat tied under the chin and having a brim framing the face. **2** a soft brimless hat like a beret, worn by men and boys in Scotland. **3** Brit. the hinged metal canopy covering the engine of a motor vehicle. **4** a cowl on a chimney.

DERIVATIVES – **bonneted** adjective.

ORIGIN – Old French *bonet*, from Latin *abonnis* 'headgear'.

bonny (also **bonnie**) > *adjective* (**bonnier**, **bonniest**) chiefly Scottish & N. English **1** physically attractive; healthy-looking. **2** sizeable; considerable.

DERIVATIVES – **bonnily** adverb **bonniness** noun.

ORIGIN – perhaps related to Old French *bon* 'good'.

bonsai /bonsī/ > *noun* (pl. same) **1** (also **bonsai tree**) an ornamental tree or shrub grown in a pot and artificially prevented from reaching its normal size. **2** the art of growing trees or shrubs in such a way.

ORIGIN – Japanese, 'tray planting'.

bonus > *noun* **1** a sum of money added to a person's wages for good performance. **2** Brit. an extra dividend or issue paid to shareholders. **3** an unexpected and welcome event or addition.

ORIGIN – Latin, 'good'.

bon vivant /bon veeˈvon/ > *noun* (pl. **bon vivants** or **bons vivants** pronunc. same) a person indulging in a sociable and luxurious lifestyle.

ORIGIN – French, 'person living well'.

bon viveur /bon veeˈvör/ > *noun* (pl. **bon viveurs** or **bons viveurs** pronunc. same) another term for **BON VIVANT**.

ORIGIN – pseudo-French, from French *bon* 'good' and *viveur* 'a living person'.

bon voyage /bon vwaaˈyaazh/ > *exclamation* have a good journey.

ORIGIN – French, 'good journey'.

bony > *adjective* (**bonier**, **boniest**) **1** of, like, or containing bones. **2** so thin that the bones can be seen.

DERIVATIVES – **boniness** noun.

COMBINATIONS – **bony fish** a fish with a skeleton of bone, as opposed to a cartilaginous fish.

bonzer > *adjective* Austral./NZ informal excellent.

ORIGIN – perhaps an alteration of **BONANZA**.

boo > *exclamation* **1** said suddenly to surprise someone. **2** said to show disapproval or contempt. > *verb* (**boos**, **booed**) say 'boo' to show disapproval or contempt.

IDIOMS – **wouldn't say boo to a goose** is very shy or reticent.

booay /bōoˈi/ (also **booai**) > *noun* (**the booay**) NZ remote rural districts.

IDIOMS – **up the booay** informal completely wrong or astray.

ORIGIN – perhaps from the place name *Puhoi* in North Auckland, New Zealand.

boob¹ informal > *noun* **1** Brit. an embarrassing mistake. **2** N. Amer. a stupid person. > *verb* Brit. make an embarrassing mistake.

ORIGIN – from **BOOBY¹**.

boob² > *noun* informal a woman's breast.

ORIGIN – from **BOOBY²**.

boo-boo > *noun* informal a mistake.

boob tube > *noun* informal **1** Brit. a woman's tight-fitting strapless top. **2** N. Amer. television; a television set.

booby¹ > *noun* (pl. **boobies**) **1** informal a stupid person. **2** a large tropical seabird of the gannet family.

ORIGIN – probably from Spanish *bobo*, from Latin *balbus* 'stammering'.

booby² > *noun* (pl. **boobies**) informal a woman's breast.

ORIGIN – from dialect *bubby*; perhaps related to German dialect *Bübbi* 'teat'.

booby prize > *noun* a prize given to the person who comes last in a contest.

booby trap > *noun* an object containing a concealed explosive device designed to detonate when someone touches it. > *verb* (**booby-trap**) place a booby trap in or on (an object or area).

boodle > *noun* informal money, especially that gained or spent dishonestly.

ORIGIN – first used in sense 'a pack or crowd': from Dutch *boedel*, *boel* 'possessions, disorderly mass'.

boogie > *noun* (also **boogie-woogie**) (pl. **boogies**) **1** a style of blues played on the piano with a strong, fast beat. **2** informal a dance to pop or rock music. > *verb* (**boogied**, **boogieing**) informal dance to pop or rock music.

COMBINATIONS – **boogie board** a short, light surfboard ridden in a prone position.

book > *noun* **1** a written or printed work consisting of pages glued or sewn together along one side and bound in covers. **2** a main division of a literary work or of the Bible. **3** (**books**) a set of records or accounts. **4** a bookmaker's record of bets accepted and money paid out. **5** a set of tickets, stamps, matches, etc., bound together. > *verb* **1** reserve (accommodation, a ticket, etc.). **2** (**book in**) register one's arrival at a hotel. **3** (**be booked up**) have all places or dates reserved. **4** engage (a performer or guest) for an event. **5** make an official note of the details of (someone who has broken a law or rule).

WORDFINDER – bibliography (*list of books*), bibliophile (*collector or lover of books*), incunabulum (*early printed book*), recto (*right-hand page of an open book*), verso (*left-hand page of an open book*).

IDIOMS – **bring to book** officially call (someone) to account for their behaviour. **by the book** strictly according to the rules. **in someone's bad** (or **good**) **books** in disfavour (or favour) with someone. **in my book** in my opinion. **on the books** contained in a list of members, employees, or clients. **take a leaf out of someone's book** imitate someone's behaviour in a particular area. **you can't judge a book by its cover** proverb outward appearances are not a reliable indication of the true character of someone or something.

DERIVATIVES – **bookable** adjective **booker** noun **booking** noun.

COMBINATIONS – **bookbinder** a person skilled in the craft of binding books. **bookcase** an open cabinet containing shelves on which to keep books. **book club** an organisation which sells its subscribers selected books by mail order at reduced prices. **bookmark 1** a strip of leather or card used to mark a place in a book. **2** Computing a record of the address of a file, Internet page, etc., that enables quick access by a user. **bookplate** a decorative label pasted in the front of a book, bearing the name of its owner. **book token** Brit. a voucher which can be exchanged for books costing up to a specified amount. **book value** the value of a security or asset as entered in a firm's books. Contrasted with *market value*. **bookworm** informal a person who enjoys and spends much time reading.

ORIGIN – Old English, 'to grant by charter'.

bookend > *noun* a support placed at the end of a row of books to keep them upright.

bookie > *noun* (pl. **bookies**) informal a bookmaker.

bookish > *adjective* **1** devoted to reading and studying. **2** (of language) literary in style.

DERIVATIVES – **bookishly** adverb **bookishness** noun.

SYNONYMS – **1** academic, erudite, scholarly, studious, well-read.

bookkeeping > *noun* the activity of keeping records of financial affairs.
DERIVATIVES – **bookkeeper** *noun*.

booklet > *noun* a small, thin book with paper covers.

bookmaker > *noun* a person whose job is to take bets, calculate odds, and pay out winnings.

Boolean /ˈboōliən/ > *adjective* denoting a system of notation used to represent logical propositions by means of the binary digits 0 (false) and 1 (true), especially in computing and electronics.
ORIGIN – named after the English mathematician George *Boole* (1815–64).

boom¹ > *noun* a loud, deep, resonant sound. > *verb* make this sound.
DERIVATIVES – **boominess** *noun* **booming** *adjective* **boomy** *adjective*.

boom² > *noun* a period of great prosperity or rapid economic growth. > *verb* experience a boom.

boom³ > *noun* 1 a pivoted spar to which the foot of a vessel's sail is attached. 2 a movable arm carrying a microphone or film camera. 3 a floating beam used to contain oil spills or to form a barrier across the mouth of a harbour.
ORIGIN – Dutch, 'beam, tree, pole'; related to BEAM.

boomerang > *noun* a curved flat piece of wood that can be thrown so as to return to the thrower, used by Australian Aboriginals as a hunting weapon.
ORIGIN – Dharuk (an Aboriginal language).

boon > *noun* 1 a thing that is helpful or beneficial. 2 archaic a favour or request.
ORIGIN – Old Norse.

boon companion > *noun* a close friend.
ORIGIN – *boon* from Old French *bon* 'good'.

boondocks > *plural noun* (**the boondocks**) N. Amer. informal rough or isolated country.
ORIGIN – from a Tagalog word meaning 'mountain'.

boondoggle N. Amer. informal > *noun* an unnecessary, wasteful, or fraudulent project. > *verb* waste money or time on such projects.

boonies > *plural noun* N. Amer informal short for BOONDOCKS.

boor /boor/ > *noun* a rough and bad-mannered person.
DERIVATIVES – **boorish** *adjective* **boorishly** *adverb* **boorishness** *noun*.
SYNONYMS – lout, oaf.

boost > *verb* help or encourage to increase or improve. > *noun* a source of help or encouragement.

booster > *noun* 1 a dose of a vaccine that increases or renews the effect of an earlier one. 2 the part of a rocket or spacecraft used to give initial acceleration. 3 a source of help or encouragement. 4 a device for increasing electrical voltage or signal strength.

boot¹ > *noun* 1 a sturdy item of footwear covering the foot and ankle, and sometimes the lower leg. 2 informal a hard kick. 3 Brit. a space at the back of a car for carrying luggage. > *verb* 1 kick hard. 2 (**boot out**) informal force to leave. 3 start (a computer) and put it into a state of readiness for operation. [ORIGIN – from BOOTSTRAP.]
IDIOMS – **the boot is on the other foot** the situation is now reversed. **give** (or **get**) **the boot** informal dismiss (or be dismissed) from a job. **old boot** informal an ugly or disliked old woman. **put the boot in** Brit. informal kick or attack someone when they are already on the ground. **with one's heart in one's boots** very depressed or anxious.
DERIVATIVES – **bootable** *adjective* **booted** *adjective*.
COMBINATIONS – **bootboy** informal a rowdy youth with close-cropped hair and heavy boots. **boot camp** chiefly N. Amer. 1 a military training camp with very harsh discipline. 2 a prison for young offenders, run on military lines. **bootlace** a cord or leather strip for lacing boots. **bootlicker** informal an obsequious person.

boot² > *noun* (in phrase **to boot**) as well.
ORIGIN – Old English, 'advantage, remedy'.

bootblack > *noun* a person who makes their living by polishing boots and shoes.

bootee (also **bootie**) > *noun* 1 a baby's soft shoe. 2 a woman's short boot.

booth > *noun* 1 a small temporary structure used for selling goods or staging shows at a market or fair. 2 an enclosed compartment allowing privacy when telephoning, voting, etc.
ORIGIN – first used in the general sense 'temporary dwelling or shelter': Old Norse, from *búa* 'dwell'.

bootleg > *adjective* (of alcoholic drink or a recording) made or distributed illegally. > *noun* an illegal musical recording.
DERIVATIVES – **bootlegger** *noun* **bootlegging** *noun*.
ORIGIN – from a former practice among smugglers of hiding bottles in their boots.

bootless > *adjective* archaic (of an action) ineffectual; useless.

bootstrap > *noun* 1 a loop at the back of a boot, used to pull it on. 2 Computing the action of loading a program into a computer by means of a few initial instructions which enable the introduction of the rest of the program from an input device.
IDIOMS – **pull oneself up by one's bootstraps** improve one's position by one's own efforts.

booty > *noun* valuable stolen goods.
SYNONYMS – loot, plunder, spoils.
ORIGIN – Low German *būte*, *buite* 'exchange, distribution'.

booze informal > *noun* alcoholic drink. > *verb* drink large quantities of alcohol.
DERIVATIVES – **boozy** (**boozier, booziest**) *adjective*.
COMBINATIONS – **booze-up** a heavy drinking session.

boozer > *noun* informal 1 a person who drinks large quantities of alcohol. 2 Brit. a pub.

bop¹ informal > *noun* chiefly Brit. 1 a dance to pop music. 2 a social occasion with dancing. > *verb* (**bopped, bopping**) dance to pop music.
DERIVATIVES – **bopper** *noun*.
ORIGIN – shortening of BEBOP.

bop² informal > *verb* (**bopped, bopping**) hit or punch quickly. > *noun* a quick blow or punch.

bora /ˈborə/ > *noun* a cold, dry NE wind blowing in the upper Adriatic.
ORIGIN – Italian dialect, from *Boreas*, the Roman god of the north wind.

boracic /bəˈrassik/ > *adjective* 1 consisting of, containing, or denoting boric acid. 2 Brit. informal having no money. [ORIGIN – from *boracic lint*, rhyming slang for 'skint'.]

borage /ˈborrij/ > *noun* a herbaceous plant with bright blue flowers and hairy leaves.
ORIGIN – Latin *borrago*, perhaps from an Arabic word meaning 'father of roughness' (referring to the leaves).

borax /ˈboraks/ > *noun* a white mineral consisting of hydrated sodium borate, found in some alkaline salt deposits and used in making glass and as a metallurgical flux.
ORIGIN – Latin, from Aramaic.

Bordeaux /borˈdō/ > *noun* (pl. same /borˈdōz/) a wine from Bordeaux, a district of SW France.

bordello /borˈdellō/ > *noun* (pl. **bordellos**) chiefly N. Amer. a brothel.
ORIGIN – Italian, probably from Old French *bordel*, from *borde* 'small farm or cottage'.

border > *noun* 1 a boundary between two countries or other areas. 2 a decorative band around the edge of something. 3 a strip of ground along the edge of a lawn for planting flowers or shrubs. > *verb* 1 form a border around or along. 2 (of a country or area) be adjacent to (another). 3 (**border on**) come close to (an extreme condition).
SYNONYMS – *noun* 1 boundary, frontier. 2

edge, edging, margin. *verb* **1,2** abut, adjoin, neighbour.

borderer > *noun* a person living near the border between two countries.

borderline > *noun* **1** a line marking a boundary. **2** a position between or bridging different groups or categories. > *adjective* only just acceptable in quality or as belonging to a category: *borderline cases.*

bore[1] > *verb* **1** make (a hole) in something with a drill or other tool. **2** hollow out (a gun barrel or other tube). > *noun* **1** the hollow part inside a gun barrel or other tube. **2** the diameter of this.
DERIVATIVES – **borer** *noun*.
COMBINATIONS – **borehole** a deep, narrow hole in the ground made to locate water or oil.

bore[2] > *noun* a dull and uninteresting person or activity. > *verb* cause to feel weary and uninterested by being dull and tedious.
DERIVATIVES – **boredom** *noun*.

bore[3] > *noun* a steep-fronted wave caused by the meeting of two tides or by a tide rushing up a narrow estuary.

bore[4] past of BEAR[1].

boreal /**bor**iəl/ > *adjective* of the North or northern regions.
ORIGIN – from the name of *Boreas*, the Roman god of the north wind.

bored > *adjective* feeling weary and impatient because one is unoccupied or has no interest in one's current activity.
USAGE – use the constructions **bored by** or **bored with** rather than **bored of**. **Bored of**, although it mirrors the accepted construction **tired of**, is not considered to be good English.

boreen /**bo**reen/ > *noun* Irish a narrow country road.
ORIGIN – Irish.

boric acid > *noun* Chemistry a weakly acid crystalline compound derived from borax, used as a mild antiseptic.

boring > *adjective* not interesting; tedious.
DERIVATIVES – **boringly** *adverb*.

borlotti bean /**bor**lotti/ > *noun* a type of kidney bean with a pink speckled skin that turns brown when cooked.
ORIGIN – Italian *borlotti* 'kidney beans'.

born > *adjective* **1** existing as a result of birth. **2** (**born of**) existing as a result of (a situation or feeling). **3** having a natural ability to do a particular job or task. **4** (**-born**) having a specific nationality.
IDIOMS – **born and bred** by birth and upbringing. **in all one's born days** throughout one's life (used for emphasis). **not know one is born** not realise how easy one's life is. **I** (or **he**, etc.) **wasn't born yesterday** I am (or he, etc. is) not foolish or gullible.

wordpower facts

Born

Until the 18th century **borne** and **born** were simply variant forms of the past participle of **bear**, used interchangeably with no distinction in meaning. By around 1775, however, the present distinction in use had become established. At that time **borne** became the standard past participle, e.g. *she has borne you another son*, *the findings have been borne out*, and so on. **Born** became restricted to just one very common use, in reference to birth, which remains the case today: *she was born in 1965*, or *I was born and bred in Gloucester*.

born-again > *adjective* **1** (of a person) having converted to a personal faith in Christ. **2** newly converted to and very enthusiastic about (an idea, cause, etc.).

borne past participle of BEAR[1].

-borne > *adjective* carried by the thing specified.

Bornean /**bor**niən/ > *noun* a person from Borneo. > *adjective* relating to Borneo or its people.

boron /**bor**on/ > *noun* a non-metallic chemical element which can be prepared as a brown powder or (if pure) a black crystalline semiconductor.
DERIVATIVES – **boric** *adjective* **boride** *noun*.
ORIGIN – from BORAX.

boronia /bə**rō**niə/ > *noun* a sweet-scented Australian shrub, cultivated for its perfume and flowers.
ORIGIN – named after the Italian botanist Francesco *Borone* (1769–94).

borough /**burr**ə/ > *noun* **1** Brit. a town (as distinct from a city) with a corporation and privileges granted by a royal charter. **2** an administrative division of London. **3** a municipal corporation in certain US states. **4** each of five divisions of New York City.
ORIGIN – Old English, 'fortress, citadel'.

borrow > *verb* **1** take and use (something belonging to someone else) with the intention of returning it. **2** take and use (money) from a person or bank under agreement to pay it back later.
IDIOMS – **be (living) on borrowed time** be surviving against expectations.
DERIVATIVES – **borrower** *noun*.

borscht /borsht/ (also **borsch** /borsh/) > *noun* a Russian or Polish soup made with beetroot.
ORIGIN – Russian *borshch*.

borstal /**bor**st'l/ > *noun* Brit. historical a custodial institution for young offenders.
ORIGIN – named after the village of *Borstal*

in southern England, where the first of these was established.

borzoi /**bor**zoy/ > *noun* (pl. **borzois**) a breed of large Russian wolfhound with a narrow head and silky coat.
ORIGIN – Russian, from *borzyǐ* 'swift'.

bosh > *noun* informal nonsense.
ORIGIN – from Turkish *boş* 'empty, worthless'.

bosky /**bos**ki/ > *adjective* literary covered by trees or bushes.
ORIGIN – from *bosk*, obsolete variant of BUSH[1].

Bosnian /**boz**niən/ > *noun* a person from Bosnia. > *adjective* relating to Bosnia.

bosom > *noun* **1** a woman's breast or chest. **2** the chest as the seat of emotions. **3** a person's loving care or protection. > *adjective* (of a friend) very close.
DERIVATIVES – **bosomy** *adjective*.

boson /**bō**zon/ > *noun* Physics a subatomic particle, such as a photon, which has a spin of zero or a whole number.
ORIGIN – named after the Indian physicist S. N. *Bose* (1894–1974).

boss[1] informal > *noun* a person who is in charge of an employee or organisation. > *verb* give orders in a domineering manner. > *adjective* N. Amer. excellent.
ORIGIN – Dutch *baas* 'master'.

boss[2] > *noun* **1** a projecting knob or stud on the centre of a shield, propeller, or similar object. **2** Architecture an ornamental carving at the point where the ribs in a ceiling cross.
ORIGIN – Old French *boce*.

bossa nova /bossə **nō**və/ > *noun* a dance like the samba, originating in Brazil.
ORIGIN – Portuguese, 'new tendency'.

boss-eyed > *adjective* Brit. informal cross-eyed; squinting.
ORIGIN – probably related to dialect *boss* 'miss, bungle'.

bossy > *adjective* (**bossier, bossiest**) informal fond of giving orders; domineering.
DERIVATIVES – **bossily** *adverb* **bossiness** *noun*.
COMBINATIONS – **bossyboots** Brit. informal a bossy person.

bosun /**bō**s'n/ (also **bo'sun**) > *noun* variant spelling of BOATSWAIN.

bot > *noun* Computing an autonomous program on a network which can interact with systems or users.
ORIGIN – shortening of ROBOT.

botanical > *adjective* relating to botany. > *noun* a substance obtained from a plant and used as an additive.
DERIVATIVES – **botanic** *adjective* **botanically** *adverb*.
COMBINATIONS – **botanical garden** (also **botanic garden**) a place where plants are grown for scientific study and display to the public.

botany /bottəni/ > *noun* the scientific study of plants.
DERIVATIVES – **botanist** *noun*.
ORIGIN – from Greek *botanē* 'plant'.

botch informal > *verb* perform (an action or task) badly or carelessly. > *noun* (also **botch-up**) a badly performed action or task.
DERIVATIVES – **botcher** *noun*.
ORIGIN – first used in the sense 'repair' and not implying clumsiness.

both > *predeterminer, determiner, & pronoun* two people or things, regarded and identified together. > *adverb* applying equally to each of two alternatives.
USAGE – when **both** is used in constructions with **and**, the structures following the two words should be symmetrical: *both at home and at work* is better than *both at home and work*.

bother > *verb* 1 take the trouble to do something. 2 cause worry, concern, or inconvenience to. 3 (**bother with** or **about**) feel concern about or interest in. > *noun* trouble and fuss, or their cause. > *exclamation* chiefly Brit. used to express mild irritation.
SYNONYMS – *verb* 2 concern, disturb, inconvenience, trouble, worry. *noun* effort, inconvenience, trouble.
ORIGIN – Anglo-Irish: originally in the dialect sense 'noise, chatter'.

bothersome > *adjective* annoying; troublesome.
SYNONYMS – annoying, irritating, troublesome, trying, vexing.

bothy /bothi/ (also **bothie**) > *noun* (pl. **bothies**) (in Scotland) a small hut or cottage for farm labourers or as a mountain refuge.

bo tree /bō/ (also **bodh tree**) > *noun* a fig tree native to India and SE Asia, regarded as sacred by Buddhists because it was under such a tree that Buddha's enlightenment took place.
ORIGIN – from a Sinhalese word meaning 'tree of knowledge'.

botrytis /bətrītiss/ > *noun* a greyish powdery mould of plants, deliberately cultivated on the grapes for certain wines.
ORIGIN – from Greek *botrus* 'cluster of grapes'.

Botswanan /botswaanən/ > *noun* a person from Botswana, a country of southern Africa. > *adjective* relating to Botswana.

bottle > *noun* 1 a container with a narrow neck, used for storing liquids. 2 Brit. informal courage or confidence. > *verb* 1 place in bottles for storage. 2 (**bottle up**) repress or conceal (one's feelings). 3 (**bottle out**) Brit. informal lose one's nerve and decide not to do something. 4 informal hit with a glass bottle.
WORDFINDER – *bottle sizes in relation to the standard wine bottle:* magnum (*twice as large*), jeroboam (*four times as large*), rehoboam (*six times*), methuselah (*eight times*), salmanazar (*twelve times*), balthazar (*sixteen times*), nebuchadnezzar (*twenty times*).
IDIOMS – **hit the bottle** informal start to drink alcohol heavily.
COMBINATIONS – **bottle bank** Brit. a place where used glass bottles may be deposited for recycling. **bottlebrush 1** a cylindrical brush for cleaning inside bottles. **2** an Australian shrub or small tree with spikes of flowers resembling bottlebrushes. **bottle-feed** feed (a baby) with milk from a bottle. **bottle green** dark green.
ORIGIN – Old French *boteille*, from Latin *butticula* 'small cask'; related to BUTT⁴.

bottleneck > *noun* 1 the neck or mouth of a bottle. 2 a narrow section of road or a junction where traffic flow is restricted.

bottom > *noun* 1 the lowest point or part of something. 2 the furthest point or part of something. 3 the lowest position in a competition or ranking. 4 (also **bottoms**) the lower half of a two-piece garment. 5 chiefly Brit. a person's buttocks. > *adjective* 1 in the lowest position. 2 in the furthest position away in a downhill direction. > *verb* 1 (of a ship) touch the bottom of the sea. 2 (**bottom out**) (of a situation) reach the lowest point before stabilising or improving.
IDIOMS – **at bottom** fundamentally. **be at the bottom of** be the fundamental cause or origin of. **the bottom falls** (or **drops**) **out of something** something suddenly fails or collapses. **bottoms up!** informal said as a toast before drinking. **get to the bottom of** find an explanation for (a mystery).
DERIVATIVES – **bottomless** *adjective* **bottommost** *adjective*.
COMBINATIONS – **bottom drawer** Brit. dated household linen and other items stored by a woman in preparation for her marriage. **bottom feeder 1** any marine creature that lives on the seabed and feeds by scavenging. **2** N. Amer. informal a member of a group of very low social status who survives by whatever means possible. **bottom line** informal **1** the final total of an account or balance sheet. **2** the underlying and most important factor.

botty > *noun* (pl. **botties**) Brit. informal a person's bottom.

botulism /botyooliz'm/ > *noun* a dangerous form of food poisoning caused by a bacterium growing on improperly sterilised foods.
ORIGIN – German *Botulismus* 'sausage poisoning', from Latin *botulus* 'sausage'.

bouclé /bōōklay/ > *noun* yarn with a looped or curled ply.
ORIGIN – French, 'buckled, curled'.

boudin /bōōdaN/ > *noun* (pl. same) a French type of black pudding.
ORIGIN – French.

boudoir /bōōdwaar/ > *noun* a woman's bedroom or small private room.
ORIGIN – French, 'sulking place', from *bouder* 'pout, sulk'.

bouffant /bōōfoN/ > *adjective* (of hair) styled so as to stand out from the head in a rounded shape. > *noun* a bouffant hairstyle.
ORIGIN – French, 'swelling'.

bougainvillea /bōōgənvillia/ (also **bougainvillaea**) > *noun* an ornamental climbing plant widely cultivated in the tropics, with brightly coloured papery bracts surrounding the flowers.
ORIGIN – named after the French explorer L. A. de *Bougainville* (1729–1811).

bough > *noun* a main branch of a tree.
ORIGIN – Old English, 'bough or shoulder'; related to BOW³.

bought past and past participle of BUY.

bouillabaisse /bōōyəbess/ > *noun* a rich fish stew or soup, as made originally in Provence.
ORIGIN – French.

bouillon /bōōyoN/ > *noun* thin soup or stock made by stewing meat, fish, or vegetables.
ORIGIN – French, from *bouillir* 'to boil'.

boulder > *noun* a large rock.
DERIVATIVES – **bouldery** *adjective*.
COMBINATIONS – **boulder clay** clay containing many large stones, formed by deposition from melting glaciers.
ORIGIN – shortened from earlier *boulderstone*, of Scandinavian origin.

boule /bōōl/ (also **boules** pronunc. same) > *noun* a French game similar to bowls, played with metal balls.
ORIGIN – French, 'bowl'.

boulevard /bōōləvaard/ > *noun* a wide street, typically one lined with trees.
ORIGIN – French, 'a rampart' (later 'a promenade on the site of a rampart'), from German *Bollwerk* 'bulwark'.

boulevardier /bōōləvaardeer/ > *noun* a wealthy, fashionable socialite.
ORIGIN – French, 'person who frequents boulevards'.

boulle /bōōl/ (also **buhl**) > *noun* brass, tortoiseshell, or other material used for inlaying furniture.
ORIGIN – from the name of the French cabinetmaker André *Boulle* (1642–1732).

bounce > *verb* 1 spring quickly up or away from a surface after hitting it. 2 move or jump up and down repeatedly. 3 (of light or sound) reflect back from a surface. 4 (**bounce back**) recover well after a setback or problem. 5 informal (of a cheque) be returned by a bank when there are insufficient funds in an account to meet it.

6 Brit. informal pressurise (someone) into doing something. **7** informal, chiefly N. Amer. dismiss from a job. > *noun* **1** a rebound of a ball or other object. **2** an act of jumping or moving up and down. **3** exuberant self-confidence. **4** health and body in a person's hair.

IDIOMS – **bounce an idea off** informal discuss an idea with (another person) in order to test or improve it.

SYNONYMS – *verb* **1** rebound, ricochet, spring back. **2** bound, leap, spring. **4** (**bounce back**) rally, recover, revive.

bouncer > *noun* a person employed by a nightclub to prevent troublemakers entering or to eject them from the premises.

bouncing > *adjective* (of a baby) vigorous and healthy.

bouncy > *adjective* (**bouncier, bounciest**) **1** able to bounce or making something bounce well. **2** confident and lively.

DERIVATIVES – **bouncily** *adverb* **bounciness** *noun*.

SYNONYMS – **1** elastic, flexible, springy.

COMBINATIONS – **bouncy castle** a large inflatable structure on which children can jump and play.

bound¹ > *verb* walk or run with leaping strides. > *noun* a leaping movement towards or over something.

SYNONYMS – jump, leap, spring.

wordpower facts

Bound

There is a surprising link between the words **bound**, **bomb**, and **bombard**. All three come, via French, from Latin *bombus*, which means 'booming, humming'. **Bound** entered English from the French verb *bondir*, which originally meant 'resound', but then developed the sense 'rebound'.

bound² > *noun* **1** a boundary. **2** a limitation or restriction. > *verb* **1** form the boundary of. **2** restrict.

IDIOMS – **out of bounds 1** (in sport) beyond the field of play. **2** beyond the acceptable or permitted limits.

ORIGIN – Old French *bodne*, from Latin *bodina*.

bound³ > *adjective* going towards a specified place: *a train bound for Edinburgh*.

ORIGIN – from Old Norse *búinn*, past participle of *búa* 'get ready'.

bound⁴ past and past participle of **BIND**. > *adjective* **1** (**-bound**) restricted or confined to or by a place or situation: *his job kept him city-bound*. **2** destined or certain to be, do, or have something: *there is bound to*

be a change of plan. **3** obliged to do something.

IDIOMS – **I'll be bound** I am sure.

boundary > *noun* (pl. **boundaries**) **1** a line marking the limits of an area. **2** Cricket a hit crossing the limits of the field, scoring four or six runs.

SYNONYMS – **1** border, edge, frontier, margin, perimeter.

bounden /**bown**dən/ archaic past participle of **BIND**.

IDIOMS – **bounden duty** an obligatory responsibility.

bounder > *noun* Brit. informal, dated a dishonourable man.

boundless > *adjective* unlimited; limitless.

DERIVATIVES – **boundlessly** *adverb* **boundlessness** *noun*.

bounteous > *adjective* archaic bountiful.

DERIVATIVES – **bounteously** *adverb* **bounteousness** *noun*.

ORIGIN – Old French *bontif* 'benevolent', from *bonte* 'bounty, goodness'.

bountiful > *adjective* **1** large in quantity; abundant. **2** giving generously.

IDIOMS – **Lady Bountiful** a woman who engages in ostentatious acts of charity. [ORIGIN – from the name of a character in *The Beaux' Stratagem* (1707) by George Farquhar.]

DERIVATIVES – **bountifully** *adverb*.

SYNONYMS – **1** abundant, ample, plentiful. **2** generous, munificent, open-handed.

ANTONYMS – **1** meagre. **2** mean.

bounty > *noun* (pl. **bounties**) **1** a reward paid for killing or capturing someone. **2** historical a sum paid by the state to encourage trade. **3** chiefly historical a sum paid by the state to enlisting army or navy recruits. **4** literary something given or occurring in generous amounts. **5** literary generosity: *people along the Nile depend on its bounty*.

SYNONYMS – **1** prize, remuneration, reward.

COMBINATIONS – **bounty hunter** a person who pursues a criminal for a reward.

ORIGIN – Old French *bonte* 'goodness', from Latin *bonitas*, from *bonus* 'good'.

bouquet /boo**kay**, bō**kay**/ > *noun* **1** a bunch of flowers. **2** the characteristic scent of a wine or perfume.

SYNONYMS – **1** bunch, garland, posy, spray. **2** aroma, fragrance, nose, scent.

ORIGIN – French, from an earlier sense 'clump of trees', from Old French *bos*, variant of *bois* 'wood'.

bouquet garni /bookay **gaar**ni, bōkay/ > *noun* (pl. **bouquets garnis**) a bunch of herbs used for flavouring a stew or soup.

ORIGIN – French, 'garnished bouquet'.

bourbon /**bur**b'n/ > *noun* a kind of American whisky distilled from maize and rye.

ORIGIN – named after *Bourbon* County, Kentucky, where it was first made.

bourgeois /**boor**zhwaa/ (also **bourgeoise** /**boor**zhwaaz/) > *adjective* **1** characteristic of the middle class, especially in being materialistic or conventional. **2** (in Marxist contexts) capitalist. > *noun* (pl. same) a bourgeois person.

ORIGIN – French, from Latin *burgus* 'castle, fortified town'; related to **BOROUGH** and **BURGESS**.

bourgeoisie /boorzhwaa**zee**/ > *noun* (treated as sing. or pl.) **1** the middle class. **2** (in Marxist contexts) the capitalist class.

ORIGIN – French.

bourn¹ /born/ > *noun* dialect a small stream.

ORIGIN – Southern English variant of **BURN²**.

bourn² /born/ (also **bourne**) > *noun* literary **1** a boundary. **2** a goal or destination.

ORIGIN – French *borne*, from Old French *bodne* (see **BOUND²**).

bourrée /**boo**ray/ > *noun* **1** a lively French dance like a gavotte. **2** Ballet a series of very fast little steps performed on the tips of the toes with the feet close together.

ORIGIN – French, 'faggot of twigs' (the dance originally being performed around a twig fire).

bourse /boorss/ > *noun* a stock market in a non-English-speaking country, especially France.

ORIGIN – French, 'purse'.

bout /bowt/ > *noun* **1** a short period of illness or intense activity. **2** a wrestling or boxing match.

SYNONYMS – **1** attack, fit, spell.

ORIGIN – from dialect *bought* 'bend, loop'.

boutique /boo**teek**/ > *noun* a small shop selling fashionable clothes.

ORIGIN – French, 'small shop'.

bouzouki /boo**zoo**ki/ > *noun* (pl. **bouzoukis**) a long-necked Greek form of mandolin.

ORIGIN – modern Greek *mpouzouki*, perhaps related to Turkish *bozuk* 'spoilt' (with reference to roughly made instruments).

bovine /**bō**vīn/ > *adjective* **1** relating to or resembling cattle. **2** sluggish or stupid. > *noun* an animal of the cattle group, which also includes buffaloes and bisons.

DERIVATIVES – **bovinely** *adverb*.

ORIGIN – Latin *bovinus*, from *bos* 'ox'.

bovine spongiform encephalopathy > *noun* see **BSE**.

bovver > *noun* Brit. informal hooliganism or trouble-making.

ORIGIN – cockney pronunciation of **BOTHER**.

bow¹ /bō/ > *noun* **1** a knot tied with two loops and two loose ends. **2** a weapon for shooting arrows, made of curved wood joined at both ends by a taut string. **3** a rod with horsehair stretched along its length, used for playing some stringed instruments. > *verb* play (a stringed instrument) using a bow.

IDIOMS – **have another string to one's bow** Brit. have a further resource available.

COMBINATIONS – **bow-fronted** having a convexly curved front. **bow-legged** having legs that curve outwards at the knee. **bow tie** a necktie in the form of a bow. **bow window** a curved bay window.

bow² /bow/ > *verb* **1** bend the head or upper body as a sign of respect, greeting, or shame. **2** bend with age or under a heavy weight. **3** (often **bow to**) submit to pressure or demands. **4** (**bow out**) withdraw or retire from an activity. > *noun* an act of bowing.

IDIOMS – **bow and scrape** behave in an obsequious way. [ORIGIN – from the practice of performing an elaborate bow and drawing the foot back at the same time.] **take a bow** acknowledge applause by bowing.

SYNONYMS – *verb* **2** bend, buckle, stoop. **3** give in, give way, yield.

bow³ /bow/ (also **bows**) > *noun* the front end of a ship.

IDIOMS – **shot across the bows** a warning statement or gesture.

ORIGIN – German *boog*, Dutch *boeg* 'shoulder or ship's bow'; related to **BOUGH**.

bowdlerise /bowdlərīz/ (also **bowdlerize**) > *verb* remove improper or offensive material from (a text); censor or expurgate.

ORIGIN – from the name of Dr Thomas *Bowdler* (1754–1825), an American who published an expurgated edition of Shakespeare.

bowel /bowəl/ > *noun* **1** (often **bowels**) the lower part of the alimentary canal below the stomach; the intestines. **2** (**bowels**) the deepest inner parts of something: *the bowels of the earth.*

COMBINATIONS – **bowel movement** an act of defecation.

ORIGIN – Latin *botellus* 'little sausage'.

bower /bowr/ > *noun* **1** a pleasant shady place under trees. **2** literary a summer house or country cottage. **3** literary a lady's private room.

bowerbird > *noun* an Australasian bird noted for the male's habit of constructing an elaborate bower adorned with feathers, shells, etc. to attract the female.

bowie knife /bō-i/ > *noun* a long knife with a blade double-edged at the point.

ORIGIN – named after the American frontiersman Jim *Bowie* (1799–1836).

bowl¹ > *noun* **1** a round, deep dish or basin. **2** a rounded, concave part of an object. **3** a

natural basin. **4** chiefly N. Amer. a stadium for sporting or musical events.

bowl² > *verb* **1** roll (a round object) along the ground. **2** Cricket (of a bowler) propel (the ball) towards the wicket for the batsman to attempt to hit, or dismiss (a batsman) by hitting the wicket with a bowled ball. **3** move rapidly and smoothly. **4** (**bowl over**) knock (someone) down. **5** (**bowl over**) informal completely overwhelm or astonish (someone). > *noun* **1** a wooden or hard rubber ball used in the game of bowls. **2** a large ball used in tenpin bowling or skittles.

WORDFINDER – *types of delivery bowled in cricket:* beamer, bouncer, chinaman, flipper, googly, leg break, leg cutter, long hop, off break, off cutter, shooter, top spinner, yorker.

ORIGIN – Old French *boule*, from Latin *bulla* 'bubble'.

bowler¹ > *noun* **1** Cricket a member of the fielding side who bowls. **2** a player at bowls, tenpin bowling, or skittles.

bowler² > *noun* a man's hard felt hat with a round dome-shaped crown.

ORIGIN – named after the 19th-century English hatter William *Bowler*.

bowline /bōlin/ > *noun* **1** a rope attaching the weather side of a square sail to a ship's bow. **2** a simple knot for forming a non-slipping loop at the end of a rope.

bowling > *noun* the game of bowls, tenpin bowling, or skittles.

COMBINATIONS – **bowling alley** a long, narrow track along which balls are rolled in skittles or tenpin bowling. **bowling green** an area of closely mown grass on which the game of bowls is played.

bowls /bōlz/ > *plural noun* (treated as sing.) a game played with heavy wooden bowls, the object of which is to propel one's bowl as close as possible to a small white ball (the jack).

bowser /bowzər/ > *noun* trademark **1** a tanker used for fuelling aircraft or supplying water. **2** Austral./NZ a petrol pump.

ORIGIN – from the name of a company of oil storage engineers.

bowsprit /bōsprit/ > *noun* a spar running out from a ship's bow, to which the forestays are fastened.

Bow Street Runners /bō/ > *plural noun* (in the early 19th century) the London police.

ORIGIN – named after *Bow Street* in London, site of the chief metropolitan magistrates' court.

bowyer /bōyər/ > *noun* a person who makes or sells archers' bows.

box¹ > *noun* **1** a container with a flat base and sides and a lid. **2** an area enclosed within straight lines on a page or computer screen. **3** an enclosed area in a theatre or sports

ground, or for witnesses or the jury in a law court. **4** a facility at a newspaper office for receiving replies to an advertisement, or at a post office for keeping letters until collected. **5** Brit. a shield for protecting a man's genitals in sport. **6** Brit. a small country house used when shooting or fishing. **7** (**the box**) informal, chiefly Brit. television. **8** (**the box**) Soccer, informal the penalty area. > *verb* **1** put in a box. **2** (**box in**) restrict or confine.

COMBINATIONS – **boxcar** N. Amer. an enclosed railway freight wagon. **box girder** a hollow girder with a square cross section. **box junction** Brit. a road area at a junction marked with a yellow grid, which a vehicle should enter only if its exit is clear. **box number** a number identifying an advertisement in a newspaper, used as an address for replies. **box pleat** a pleat consisting of two parallel creases forming a raised band. **boxroom** Brit. a very small room.

ORIGIN – probably related to **BOX³**.

box² > *verb* take part in the sport of boxing. > *noun* a slap on the side of a person's head.

IDIOMS – **box clever** Brit. informal outwit someone. **box someone's ears** slap someone on the side of the head.

box³ > *noun* a slow-growing evergreen shrub with small glossy leaves and hard wood.

ORIGIN – Greek *puxos*.

box⁴ > *verb* (in phrase **box the compass**) recite the compass points in correct order.

ORIGIN – perhaps from Spanish *bojar* 'sail round', from Low German *bōgen* 'bend'.

boxer > *noun* **1** a person who boxes as a sport. **2** a medium-sized breed of dog with a smooth brown coat and pug-like face.

COMBINATIONS – **boxer shorts** men's underpants resembling shorts.

boxing > *noun* the sport of fighting with the fists wearing padded gloves and according to prescribed rules.

WORDFINDER – *main weight divisions in boxing (lightest to heaviest):* flyweight, bantamweight, featherweight, lightweight, welterweight, middleweight, heavyweight.

Boxing Day > *noun* chiefly Brit. a public holiday on the first day after Christmas Day.

ORIGIN – from the former custom of giving tradespeople a Christmas box on this day.

box office > *noun* a place at a theatre, cinema, etc. where tickets are sold.

boxy > *adjective* (**boxier, boxiest**) **1** squarish in shape. **2** (of a room or space) cramped.

boy > *noun* **1** a male child or youth. **2** (**boys**) informal men who mix socially or belong to a particular group. > *exclamation* informal used to express strong feelings.

DERIVATIVES – **boyhood** noun **boyish** *adjective.*

COMBINATIONS – **boyfriend** a person's regular male companion in a romantic or sexual relationship. **Boy Scout** old-fashioned term for **SCOUT** (in sense 3).

boyar /bōyaar/ > *noun* a member of the old aristocracy in Russia, next in rank to a prince.
ORIGIN – Russian *boyarin*.

boycott > *verb* refuse to have commercial or social dealings with (a person, organisation, or country) as a punishment or protest. > *noun* an act of boycotting.
SYNONYMS – ban, bar, blacklist, embargo.
ORIGIN – from the name of Captain Charles C. *Boycott*, an Irish land agent so treated in 1880 in an attempt to get rents reduced.

Boyle's law > *noun* Chemistry a law stating that the pressure of a given mass of an ideal gas is inversely proportional to its volume at a constant temperature.
ORIGIN – from the name of the English scientist Robert *Boyle* (1627–91).

boyo > *noun* (pl. **boyos**) Welsh & Irish informal a boy or man.

boysenberry /boyz'nberi/ > *noun* (pl. **boysenberries**) a large red edible blackberry-like fruit.
ORIGIN – named after the American horticulturalist Rudolph *Boysen* (1895–1950).

bozo /bōzō/ > *noun* (pl. **bozos**) informal, chiefly N. Amer. a stupid or insignificant person.

BP > *abbreviation* 1 before the present (era). 2 blood pressure. 3 British Petroleum.

Bq > *abbreviation* becquerel.

BR > *abbreviation* historical British Rail (or Railways).

Br > *symbol* the chemical element bromine.

bra > *noun* a woman's undergarment worn to support the breasts.
DERIVATIVES – **braless** *adjective*.
ORIGIN – abbreviation of **BRASSIERE**.

brace > *noun* 1 (**braces**) Brit. a pair of straps passing over the shoulders and fastening to the top of trousers to hold them up. 2 a strengthening or supporting piece or part. 3 a wire device fitted in the mouth to straighten the teeth. 4 (also **brace and bit**) a drilling tool with a crank handle and a socket to hold a bit. 5 a rope attached to the yard of a ship for trimming the sail. 6 (pl. same) a pair of things, especially birds or mammals killed in hunting. 7 either of two connecting marks { and }, used in printing and music. > *verb* 1 make stronger or firmer with a brace. 2 press (one's body) firmly against something to stay balanced. 3 (**brace oneself**) prepare for something difficult or unpleasant.
ORIGIN – from Old French *bracier* 'embrace', from *brace* 'two arms', from Latin *bracchium* 'arm'.

bracelet > *noun* an ornamental band or chain worn on the wrist or arm.
ORIGIN – Old French, from *bras* 'arm'.

brachial /braykiəl/ > *adjective* Anatomy of or relating to the arm.
ORIGIN – Latin *brachialis*, from *brachium* 'arm'.

brachiopod /brakiəpod/ > *noun* Zoology a marine invertebrate resembling a bivalve mollusc, with tentacles used for filter-feeding.
ORIGIN – from Greek *brakhiōn* 'arm' + *pous* 'foot'.

brachiosaurus /brakiəsawrəss/ > *noun* a huge herbivorous dinosaur with forelegs much longer than the hind legs.
ORIGIN – from Greek *brakhiōn* 'arm' + *sauros* 'lizard'.

bracing > *adjective* fresh and invigorating.
DERIVATIVES – **bracingly** *adverb*.

bracken > *noun* a tall fern with coarse lobed fronds.
ORIGIN – Scandinavian.

bracket > *noun* 1 each of a pair of marks ( ) [ ] { } < > used to enclose words or figures. 2 a category of similar people or things. 3 a right-angled support projecting from a wall. > *verb* (**bracketed**, **bracketing**) 1 enclose (words or figures) in brackets. 2 place in the same category or group. 3 hold or attach by means of a bracket.
ORIGIN – Spanish *bragueta* 'codpiece, bracket', from Latin *bracae* 'breeches'.

brackish > *adjective* (of water) slightly salty, as in river estuaries.
ORIGIN – from obsolete *brack* 'salty'.

bract > *noun* Botany a modified leaf with a flower or flower cluster in its axil.
ORIGIN – Latin *bractea* 'thin metal plate'.

brad > *noun* a nail with a rectangular cross section and a small asymmetrical head.
ORIGIN – Old Norse *broddr* 'spike'.

bradawl /braddawl/ > *noun* a tool for boring holes, resembling a screwdriver.

bradycardia /braddikaardiə/ > *noun* Medicine abnormally slow heart action.
ORIGIN – from Greek *bradus* 'slow' + *kardia* 'heart'.

brae /bray/ > *noun* Scottish a steep bank or hillside.
ORIGIN – from Old Norse *brá* 'eyelash'; related to **BROW**[1].

brag > *verb* (**bragged**, **bragging**) boast. > *noun* 1 a simplified form of poker. 2 an act of bragging.
DERIVATIVES – **bragger** *noun*.
SYNONYMS – *verb* boast, crow, show off.

braggadocio /braggədōchiō/ > *noun* boastful or arrogant behaviour.
ORIGIN – from the name of *Braggadocchio*, a boastful character in Edmund Spenser's *The Faerie Queene* (1590).

braggart /braggərt/ > *noun* a person who brags.
SYNONYMS – boaster, bragger, show-off.

Brahman /braamən/ > *noun* (pl. **Brahmans**) 1 (also **Brahmin**) a member of the highest Hindu caste, that of the priesthood. 2 (also **Brahma**) the ultimate reality underlying all phenomena in the Hindu scriptures.
ORIGIN – Sanskrit.

Brahmin /braamin/ > *noun* 1 variant spelling of **BRAHMAN** (in sense 1). 2 US a socially or culturally superior person.
DERIVATIVES – **Brahminical** *adjective*.

braid > *noun* 1 threads woven into a decorative band. 2 a length of hair made up of interlaced strands. > *verb* 1 form a braid with (hair). 2 edge or trim with braid.

Braille /brayl/ > *noun* a written language for the blind, in which characters are represented by patterns of raised dots.
ORIGIN – named after the blind French educationist Louis *Braille* (1809–52).

brain > *noun* 1 an organ of soft nervous tissue contained in the skull, functioning as the coordinating centre of sensation and intellectual and nervous activity. 2 intellectual capacity. 3 (**the brains**) informal the main organiser or planner within a group. > *verb* informal hit hard on the head with an object.
WORDFINDER – *parts of the brain:* cerebellum, dura mater, forebrain, hippocampus, hypothalamus, medulla oblongata, meninges, parietal lobe, pia, pineal gland, pituitary gland, pons, temporal lobe, thalamus, ventricle.
IDIOMS – **have on the brain** informal be obsessed with (something).
DERIVATIVES – **brained** *adjective*.
COMBINATIONS – **brainbox** Brit. informal a very clever person. **brain-dead** 1 having suffered brain death. 2 informal extremely stupid. **brain death** irreversible brain damage causing the end of independent breathing. **brain drain** informal the emigration of highly skilled or qualified people from a country. **brainpan** informal, chiefly N. Amer. a person's skull. **brainstem** the central trunk of the brain, consisting of the medulla oblongata, pons, and midbrain. **brains trust** a group of experts who give impromptu answers to questions. **brain-teaser** informal a problem or puzzle.

brainchild > *noun* informal an idea or invention originated by a specified person.

brainiac > *noun* N. Amer. informal a very intelligent person.
ORIGIN – from the name of a superintelligent alien character in the Superman comic strip.

brainless > *adjective* stupid; very foolish.
DERIVATIVES – **brainlessly** *adverb* **brainlessness** *noun*.

brainstorm > *noun* **1** informal a moment in which one is suddenly unable to think clearly. **2** a spontaneous group discussion to produce ideas. > *verb* have a spontaneous discussion to produce ideas.

brainwash > *verb* subject (someone) to a prolonged process to transform their attitudes and beliefs totally; indoctrinate.

brainwave > *noun* **1** an electrical impulse in the brain. **2** informal a sudden clever idea.

brainy > *adjective* (**brainier, brainiest**) informal clever; intelligent.

DERIVATIVES – **braininess** *noun*.

braise > *verb* fry (food) lightly and then stew it slowly in a closed container.

ORIGIN – French *braiser*, from *braise* 'live coals' (in which the container was placed).

brake¹ > *noun* a device for slowing or stopping a moving vehicle. > *verb* slow or stop a vehicle with a brake.

COMBINATIONS – **brake drum** a broad, short cylinder attached to a wheel, against which the brake shoes press to cause braking. **brake horsepower** an imperial unit equal to one horsepower, used in expressing the power available to an engine. **brake shoe** a long curved block which presses on to a brake drum.

brake² > *noun* historical an open horse-drawn carriage with four wheels.

brake³ > *noun* **1** a toothed instrument for crushing flax and hemp. **2** (also **brake harrow**) a heavy machine formerly used for breaking up large lumps of earth.

ORIGIN – perhaps related to BREAK.

brake⁴ > *noun* archaic or literary a thicket.

bramble > *noun* **1** a prickly scrambling shrub of the rose family, especially a blackberry. **2** chiefly Brit. the fruit of the blackberry.

brambling > *noun* a northern finch with a white rump, related to the chaffinch.

Bramley (also **Bramley's seedling**) > *noun* (pl. **Bramleys**) a variety of large English cooking apple with green skin.

ORIGIN – named after the 19th-century English butcher Matthew *Bramley*, in whose garden it first grew.

bran > *noun* pieces of grain husk separated from flour after milling.

COMBINATIONS – **bran tub** Brit. a lucky dip in which items are buried in bran.

ORIGIN – Old French.

branch > *noun* **1** a part of a tree which grows out from the trunk or a bough. **2** a river, road, or railway extending out from a main one. **3** a division of a large organisation, group, etc. > *verb* **1** divide into or send out one or more branches. **2** (**branch out**) extend one's activities or interests in a new direction.

WORDFINDER – brachiate, dendritic (*branched*), ramify (*be divided into branches*).

SYNONYMS – *noun* **1** bough, limb, offshoot.

3 department, division, section, sector. *verb* **1** bifurcate, fork. **2** (**branch out**) diversify.

ORIGIN – Old French *branche*, from Latin *branca* 'paw'.

brand > *noun* **1** a type of product manufactured by a company under a particular name. **2** an identifying mark common to the products of a particular company. **3** an identifying mark burned on livestock with a heated iron. **4** a piece of burning or smouldering wood. > *verb* **1** mark with a branding iron. **2** mark out as having a particular shameful quality. **3** assign a brand name to.

COMBINATIONS – **brand name** a name given by the maker to a product or range of products. **brand new** completely new.

wordpower facts

Brand

The word **brand** existed in Old English in the senses 'burning' and 'a piece of burning wood'. The sense 'mark permanently with a hot iron' gave rise to 'a mark of ownership made by branding', hence the current sense 'a type of product manufactured by a company under a particular name'. The phrase **brand new** arose from the idea of something being hot and glowing from a fire: Shakespeare used the similar phrase *fire-new*.

brandish > *verb* wave or flourish (something) as a threat or in anger or excitement.

ORIGIN – Old French *brandir*, related to BRAND.

brandling > *noun* a red earthworm with rings of a brighter colour, used in compost and as bait by anglers.

brandy > *noun* (pl. **brandies**) a strong alcoholic spirit distilled from wine or fermented fruit juice.

WORDFINDER – *kinds of brandy:* Armagnac, Calvados, cognac, eau de vie, grappa, kirsch, slivovitz.

COMBINATIONS – **brandy butter** Brit. a stiff sauce of brandy, butter, and sugar. **brandy snap** a crisp rolled gingerbread wafer.

ORIGIN – from earlier *brandwine*, from Dutch *branden* 'burn, distil' + *wijn* 'wine'.

brash > *adjective* self-assertive in a rude, noisy, or overbearing way.

DERIVATIVES – **brashly** *adverb* **brashness** *noun*.

SYNONYMS – arrogant, cocksure, full of oneself, thrusting.

ANTONYMS – diffident, meek.

ORIGIN – perhaps a form of RASH¹.

brass > *noun* **1** a yellowish alloy of copper and zinc. **2** (also **horse brass**) a flat brass

ornament for the harness of a draught horse. **3** Brit. a memorial consisting of a flat piece of inscribed brass in the wall or floor of a church. **4** brass wind instruments forming a band or section of an orchestra. **5** (also **top brass**) informal people in authority. [ORIGIN – from military slang, in allusion to the gold or brass insignia on officers' caps; compare with **brass hat**.] **6** Brit. informal money.

WORDFINDER – *brass musical instruments:* bugle, cornet, euphonium, flugelhorn, French horn, horn, sousaphone, trombone, trumpet, tuba.

IDIOMS – **brassed off** Brit. informal disgruntled. **cold enough to freeze the balls off a brass monkey** informal extremely cold. [ORIGIN – from a type of brass rack or 'monkey' in which cannonballs were stored and which contracted in very cold weather, ejecting the balls.] **get down to brass tacks** informal start to consider the basic facts.

COMBINATIONS – **brass band** a group of musicians playing brass instruments. **brass hat** Brit. informal a high-ranking military officer. **brass rubbing** reproduction of the design on an engraved brass by rubbing heelball or chalk over paper laid on it.

brasserie /brassəri/ > *noun* (pl. **brasseries**) an inexpensive French or French-style restaurant.

ORIGIN – French, 'brewery'.

brassica /brassikə/ > *noun* a plant of a family that includes cabbage, swede, rape, and mustard.

ORIGIN – Latin, 'cabbage'.

brassiere /brazziər/ > *noun* full form of BRA.

ORIGIN – French, 'bodice, child's vest'.

brassy > *adjective* (**brassier, brassiest**) **1** resembling brass in colour. **2** harsh or blaring like a brass instrument. **3** tastelessly showy or loud.

SYNONYMS – **3** flashy, ostentatious, vulgar.

brat > *noun* informal a badly behaved child.

DERIVATIVES – **brattish** *adjective*.

COMBINATIONS – **brat pack** informal a rowdy and ostentatious group of young celebrities.

bratwurst /bratvurst/ > *noun* a type of fine German pork sausage.

ORIGIN – German, from *Brat* 'a spit' + *Wurst* 'sausage'.

bravado > *noun* boldness intended to impress or intimidate.

SYNONYMS – bluster, boldness, swagger.

ORIGIN – Spanish *bravada*, from *bravo* 'brave'.

brave > *adjective* having or showing courage. > *noun* dated an American Indian warrior. > *verb* endure or face (unpleasant conditions) with courage.

DERIVATIVES – **bravely** adverb **bravery** noun.

SYNONYMS – adjective bold, courageous, valiant. verb confront, endure, withstand.

ANTONYMS – adjective cowardly, timid.

ORIGIN – Italian or Spanish bravo 'bold, untamed', from Latin barbarus 'foreign, barbarous, savage'.

bravo¹ /braavō/ > exclamation shouted to express approval for a performer.

bravo² /braavō/ > noun (pl. **bravos** or **bravoes**) a thug or hired assassin.

bravura /brəvyoorə/ > noun **1** great skill and brilliance. **2** the display of great daring.

ORIGIN – Italian, from bravo 'bold'.

braw /braw/ > adjective Scottish fine; splendid.

ORIGIN – variant of **BRAVE**.

brawl > noun a rough or noisy fight or quarrel. > verb take part in a brawl.

DERIVATIVES – **brawler** noun.

SYNONYMS – altercation, fight, scuffle.

brawn > noun **1** physical strength as opposed to intelligence. **2** Brit. cooked meat from a pig's or calf's head, pressed with jelly.

DERIVATIVES – **brawny** adjective.

SYNONYMS – **1** burliness, muscle, strength.

ORIGIN – Old French braon 'fleshy part of the leg'.

Braxton Hicks contractions /brakstən hiks/ > plural noun Medicine intermittent weak contractions of the uterus occurring during pregnancy.

ORIGIN – named after the English gynaecologist John Braxton Hicks (1823–97).

bray > noun the loud, harsh cry of a donkey. > verb make such a sound.

ORIGIN – from Old French braire 'to cry'.

braze > verb solder with an alloy of copper and zinc. > noun a brazed joint.

ORIGIN – French braser 'solder'.

brazen > adjective **1** bold and shameless. **2** chiefly literary made of brass. > verb (**brazen it out**) endure a difficult situation with apparent confidence and lack of shame.

DERIVATIVES – **brazenly** adverb.

SYNONYMS – adjective **1** barefaced, bold, presumptuous, shameless, unabashed.

ANTONYMS – adjective **1** modest, shy.

ORIGIN – Old English, 'made of brass'.

brazier¹ /brayziər/ > noun **1** a portable heater holding lighted coals. **2** N. Amer. a barbecue.

ORIGIN – French brasier, from braise 'hot coals'.

brazier² /brayziər/ > noun a person who makes brass articles.

Brazilian > noun a person from Brazil. > adjective relating to Brazil.

brazil nut > noun the large three-sided nut of a South American forest tree.

breach > verb **1** make a gap or hole in; break through. **2** break (a rule or agreement).

> noun **1** a gap made in a wall or barrier. **2** an act of breaking a rule or agreement. **3** a break in relations.

IDIOMS – **breach of the peace** chiefly Brit. violent or noisy behaviour that causes a public disturbance. **breach of promise** the breaking of a sworn assurance. **step into the breach** replace someone who is suddenly unable to do a job.

SYNONYMS – verb **1** burst, rupture, split. **2** contravene, infringe, violate. noun **2** contravention, infringement, violation. **3** rift, schism, separation.

ORIGIN – Old French breche; related to **BREAK**.

bread > noun **1** food made of flour, water, and yeast mixed together and baked. **2** informal money.

WORDFINDER – breads: bagel, baguette, bap, brioche, bruschetta, bun, chapatti, ciabatta, cob, focaccia, nan, panettone, paratha, pitta, poppadom, pumpernickel, puri, rye bread, soda bread.

IDIOMS – **bread and butter** a person's livelihood or main source of income. **bread and circuses** entertainment or political policies intended to keep the masses happy and docile. **break bread** celebrate the Eucharist. **cast one's bread upon the waters** do good without expecting gratitude or reward. [ORIGIN – with biblical allusion to the Book of Ecclesiastes, chapter 11.] **know which side one's bread is buttered** informal know where one's advantage lies.

COMBINATIONS – **breadcrumb** a small fragment of bread. **breadfruit** a large round starchy fruit native to Pacific islands, used as a vegetable and to make a substitute for flour. **bread sauce** sauce made with milk and breadcrumbs, eaten with roast turkey. **breadwinner** a person who supports their family with the money they earn.

breaded > adjective (of food) coated with breadcrumbs and fried.

breadline > noun **1** (usu. in phrase **on the breadline**) Brit. the poorest condition in which it is acceptable to live. **2** N. Amer. a queue of people waiting to receive free food.

breadth > noun **1** the distance or measurement from side to side of something; width. **2** wide range: breadth of experience. **3** dated a piece of cloth of standard or full width.

break > verb (past **broke**; past participle **broken**) **1** separate into pieces as a result of a blow, shock, or strain. **2** make or become inoperative; stop working. **3** interrupt (a continuity, sequence, or course). **4** fail to observe (a law, regulation, or agreement). **5** crush the strength or spirit of. **6** surpass (a record). **7** succeed in deciphering (a code). **8** make a sudden rush or dash. **9** lessen the

impact of (a fall). **10** suddenly make or become public. **11** (of a person's voice) falter and change tone. **12** (of a boy's voice) change in tone and register at puberty. **13** (of the weather) change suddenly, especially after a fine spell. **14** (of a storm) begin violently. **15** (of dawn or a day) begin as the sun rises. **16** use (a banknote) to pay for something and receive change. **17** make the first stroke at the beginning of a game of billiards, pool, or snooker. > noun **1** an interruption, pause, or gap. **2** a short rest or pause in work. **3** an instance of breaking, or the point where something is broken. **4** a sudden rush or dash. **5** informal an opportunity or chance. **6** (also **break of serve** or **service break**) Tennis the winning of a game against an opponent's serve. **7** Snooker & Billiards a consecutive series of successful shots. **8** a short solo in jazz or popular music.

IDIOMS – **break away** escape from control or influence. **break one's back** (or **neck**) put great effort into achieving something. **break the back of** accomplish the main or hardest part of. **break cover** (of game being hunted) emerge into the open. **break down 1** suddenly cease to function or continue. **2** lose control of one's emotions when in distress. **break in 1** force entry to a building. **2** interject. **3** accustom a horse to being ridden. **4** make (new shoes) comfortable by wearing them. **breaking and entering** (in North American, and formerly also British, law) the crime of entering a building by force to commit burglary. **break into** burst forth into (laughter, song, or faster movement). **break a leg!** theatrical slang good luck! **break of day** dawn. **break off** abruptly end or discontinue. **break out 1** (of something undesirable) start suddenly. **2** escape. **3** informal open and start using (something). **break out in** be suddenly affected by (an unpleasant sensation or condition). **break someone's serve** win a game in a tennis match against an opponent's service. **break up 1** (of a gathering or relationship) end or part. **2** Brit. end the school term. **break wind** release gas from the anus. **break with 1** quarrel with. **2** go against (a custom or tradition). **give someone a break** informal stop putting pressure on someone.

DERIVATIVES – **breakable** adjective **breakage** noun.

SYNONYMS – verb **1** crack, fragment, shatter, smash, snap. **4** contravene, infringe, violate. noun **1** gap, hiatus, interruption, interval, pause. **2** lull, pause, respite, rest.

COMBINATIONS – **break-dancing** an energetic and acrobatic style of street dancing, developed by US blacks. **break-in** an illegal forced entry in order to steal something.

breakaway > *noun* **1** a withdrawal from something established or long-standing. **2** a sudden rush away from a main group.

breakdown > *noun* **1** a failure or collapse. **2** an explanatory analysis, especially of statistics.

breaker > *noun* **1** a heavy sea wave that breaks on the shore. **2** a person that breaks up old machinery.

breakfast > *noun* a meal eaten in the morning, the first of the day. > *verb* eat this meal.

IDIOMS – **have for breakfast** informal deal with or defeat with contemptuous ease.

breakneck > *adjective* dangerously fast.

breakthrough > *noun* a sudden important development or success.

COMBINATIONS – **breakthrough bleeding** bleeding from the uterus occurring abnormally between menstrual periods.

breakwater > *noun* a barrier built out into the sea to protect a coast or harbour from the force of waves.

bream > *noun* (pl. same) a deep-bodied greenish-bronze freshwater fish.

ORIGIN – Old French *bresme*.

breast > *noun* **1** either of the two soft, protruding organs on a woman's chest which secrete milk after pregnancy. **2** a person's or animal's chest region. > *verb* **1** face and move forwards against or through. **2** reach the top of (a hill).

DERIVATIVES – **breasted** *adjective*.

COMBINATIONS – **breastbone** a thin flat bone running down the centre of the chest and connecting the ribs; the sternum. **breastfeed** feed (a baby) with milk from the breast. **breastplate** a piece of armour covering the chest. **breaststroke** a style of swimming in which the arms are pushed forwards and then swept back while the legs are alternately tucked in and kicked out. **breastwork** a low temporary defence or parapet.

breath > *noun* **1** air taken into or expelled from the lungs. **2** an instance of breathing in or out. **3** a slight movement of air. **4** a sign, hint, or suggestion: *he avoided the slightest breath of scandal*.

IDIOMS – **breath of fresh air** a refreshing change. **catch one's breath 1** cease breathing momentarily in surprise or fear. **2** rest after exercise to restore normal breathing. **draw breath** breathe in. **hold one's breath** cease breathing temporarily. **out of breath** gasping for air. **take breath** pause to recover normal breathing. **take someone's breath away** astonish or inspire someone. **under one's breath** in a very quiet voice.

COMBINATIONS – **breath test** a test in which a driver is made to blow into a breathalyser.

breathable > *adjective* **1** (of air) fit to breathe. **2** (of clothing) admitting air to the skin and allowing sweat to evaporate.

breathalyser (US trademark **Breathalyzer**) > *noun* a device used by police for measuring the amount of alcohol in a driver's breath.

DERIVATIVES – **breathalyse** (US **breathalyze**) *verb*.

ORIGIN – blend of BREATH and ANALYSE.

breatharian /breeTHair'iən/ > *noun* a person who believes that it is possible, through meditation, to reach a level of consciousness where one can exist on air alone.

breathe > *verb* **1** take air into the lungs and then expel it as a regular physical process. **2** say with quiet intensity. **3** admit or emit air or moisture. **4** give an impression of.

IDIOMS – **breathe down someone's neck 1** follow closely behind someone. **2** constantly check up on someone. **breathe one's last** die.

SYNONYMS – **1** draw breath, inhale and exhale, respire.

COMBINATIONS – **breathing space** an opportunity to pause, relax, or decide what to do next.

breather > *noun* informal a brief pause for rest.

breathless > *adjective* **1** gasping for breath. **2** feeling or causing great excitement or fear.

DERIVATIVES – **breathlessly** *adverb* **breathlessness** *noun*.

breathtaking > *adjective* astonishing or awe-inspiring.

DERIVATIVES – **breathtakingly** *adverb*.

breathy > *adjective* (of a voice) having an audible sound of breathing.

DERIVATIVES – **breathily** *adverb*.

breccia /brechə/ > *noun* Geology rock consisting of angular fragments cemented by finer chalky material.

ORIGIN – Italian, 'gravel'.

bred past and past participle of BREED.

breech > *noun* the back part of a rifle or gun barrel.

COMBINATIONS – **breech birth** a birth in which the baby's buttocks or feet are delivered first.

ORIGIN – Old English, 'garment covering the loins and thighs', later 'the buttocks', hence 'the hind part' of something.

breeches > *plural noun* short trousers fastened just below the knee, now worn for riding or as part of ceremonial dress.

COMBINATIONS – **breeches buoy** a lifebuoy on a rope with a canvas support by means of which a person may be held and transported.

breed > *verb* (past and past participle **bred**) **1** (of animals) mate and then produce offspring. **2** keep (animals) for the purpose of producing young. **3** bring up (someone) to behave in a particular way. **4** produce or lead to. > *noun* **1** a distinctive type within a species of animals or plants, especially one deliberately developed. **2** a sort or kind.

SYNONYMS – *verb* **1** procreate, mate, propagate, reproduce. **2** raise, rear.

breeder > *noun* **1** a person or animal that breeds. **2** a nuclear reactor which creates another fissile material (plutonium-239) as a by-product of energy production by fission of uranium-238.

breeding > *noun* upper-class good manners regarded as being passed on by heredity.

breeze > *noun* **1** a gentle wind. **2** informal something easy to do. > *verb* informal come or go in a casual or light-hearted manner.

ORIGIN – first used in the sense 'NE wind': probably from Old Spanish and Portuguese *briza*.

breeze block > *noun* Brit. a lightweight building brick made from cinders mixed with sand and cement.

ORIGIN – *breeze* from French *braise* 'live coals'.

breezy > *adjective* (**breezier, breeziest**) **1** pleasantly windy. **2** relaxed, informal, and cheerily brisk.

DERIVATIVES – **breezily** *adverb* **breeziness** *noun*.

SYNONYMS – **1** blowy, fresh, windy.

Bren gun > *noun* a lightweight quick-firing machine gun used by the Allies in the Second World War.

ORIGIN – blend of *Brno* in the Czech Republic (where it was originally made) and *Enfield* (where it was later made).

brethren archaic plural of BROTHER. > *plural noun* fellow Christians or members of a male religious order.

Breton /brett'n/ > *noun* **1** a person from Brittany. **2** the Celtic language of Brittany, derived from Cornish.

ORIGIN – Old French, 'Briton'.

breve > *noun* **1** Music a note twice as long as a semibreve, represented as a semibreve with two short bars either side, or as a square. **2** a written or printed mark (˘) indicating a short or unstressed vowel.

ORIGIN – variant of BRIEF: the musical term was originally used in a series where a *long* was of greater time value than a *breve*.

brevet /brevvit/ > *noun* a former type of military commission by which an officer was promoted to a higher rank without the corresponding pay.

ORIGIN – first used to denote an official letter: from Old French *brievet* 'little letter'.

breviary /breeviəri/ > *noun* (pl. **breviaries**) a book containing the service for each day, recited by those in orders in the Roman Catholic Church.

ORIGIN – Latin *breviarium* 'summary, abridgement'.

brevity /**brevv**iti/ > *noun* **1** concise and exact use of words. **2** shortness of time.

IDIOMS - **brevity is the soul of wit** proverb the essence of a witty statement lies in its concise wording and delivery. [ORIGIN - from Shakespeare's *Hamlet* (II. ii. 90).]

SYNONYMS - **1** conciseness, concision, pithiness, succinctness.

ANTONYMS - **1** verbosity.

ORIGIN - Latin *brevitas*, from *brevis* 'brief'.

brew > *verb* **1** make (beer) by soaking, boiling, and fermenting grain, hops, and other ingredients. **2** make (tea or coffee) by mixing it with hot water. **3** (of an unwelcome situation) begin to develop. > *noun* something brewed.

DERIVATIVES - **brewer** *noun*.

brewery > *noun* (pl. **breweries**) a place where beer is made commercially.

briar¹ (also **brier**) > *noun* a prickly scrambling shrub, especially a wild rose.

briar² (also **brier**) > *noun* a tobacco pipe made from the woody nodules of a white-flowered shrub of the heather family.

ORIGIN - French *bruyère* 'heath, heather'.

bribe > *verb* dishonestly persuade (someone) to act in one's favour by paying them or giving other inducement. > *noun* an inducement offered in an attempt to bribe someone.

DERIVATIVES - **bribery** *noun*.

SYNONYMS - *verb* buy off, corrupt, pay off, suborn.

ORIGIN - Old French *briber*, *brimber* 'beg'; the original sense was 'rob, extort', hence 'theft, stolen goods', also 'money extorted or demanded', later 'offer money as an inducement'.

bric-a-brac > *noun* miscellaneous objects and ornaments of little value.

ORIGIN - French, from obsolete *à bric et à brac* 'at random'.

brick > *noun* **1** a small rectangular block of fired or sun-dried clay, used in building. **2** Brit. a child's toy building block. **3** Brit. informal, dated a generous, helpful, and reliable person. > *verb* (often **brick up**) block or enclose with a wall of bricks.

WORDFINDER - bond (*arrangement of bricks*), course (*horizontal layer of bricks*), header (*brick laid at right angles to the face of the wall*), stretcher (*brick laid with its long side along the face of the wall*).

IDIOMS - **bricks and mortar** buildings, especially housing. **like a ton of bricks** informal with crushing weight, force, or authority. **you can't make bricks without straw** proverb nothing can be made or accomplished without adequate material or information.

COMBINATIONS - **brickfield** an area of ground where bricks are made. **bricklayer** a person whose job is to build structures with bricks. **brick red** a deep brownish red.

ORIGIN - Low German, Dutch *bricke*, *brike*.

brickbat > *noun* **1** a piece of brick used as a missile. **2** a critical remark or reaction.

brickie > *noun* (pl. **brickies**) Brit. informal a bricklayer.

bricolage /brikkə**laazh**/ > *noun* (pl. same or **bricolages**) **1** (in art or literature) construction or creation from a diverse range of available things. **2** something created in this way.

ORIGIN - French.

bridal > *adjective* of or concerning a bride or a newly married couple.

---

wordpower facts

Bridal

The word **bridal** was originally not an adjective but a noun, meaning 'wedding feast'. It comes from the Old English word for **bride**, *brȳd*, and *ealu* 'ale-drinking'. **Bridegroom** comes from *brȳd* and *guma* 'man' (not from **groom** 'a person employed to take care of horses').

---

bride > *noun* a woman on her wedding day or just before and after the event.

bridegroom > *noun* a man on his wedding day or just before and after the event.

bridesmaid > *noun* a girl or woman who accompanies a bride on her wedding day.

bridewell > *noun* archaic a prison or reform school for petty offenders.

ORIGIN - named after *St Bride's Well* in London, near which such a building stood.

bridge¹ > *noun* **1** a structure carrying a road, path, or railway across a river, road, etc. **2** the platform on a ship from which the captain and officers direct operations. **3** the upper bony part of a person's nose. **4** a partial denture supported by natural teeth on either side. **5** the part on a stringed instrument over which the strings are stretched. **6** (also **bridge passage**) Music a transitional section or middle eight in a composition. > *verb* be or make a bridge over or between.

WORDFINDER - aqueduct (*bridge carrying water*), Bailey bridge (*prefabricated bridge used by army*), bascule bridge (*with section raised using counterweights*), cantilever bridge (*built using projecting girders*), suspension bridge (*bridge suspended from cables*).

COMBINATIONS - **bridging loan** chiefly Brit. a sum of money lent by a bank to cover an interval between two transactions, typically the buying of one house and the selling of another.

bridge² > *noun* a card game related to whist, played by two partnerships of two players.

COMBINATIONS - **bridge roll** Brit. a small, soft bread roll with a long, thin shape.

bridgehead > *noun* a strong position secured by an army inside enemy territory.

bridie > *noun* (pl. **bridies**) Scottish a meat pasty.

ORIGIN - perhaps from obsolete *bride's pie*.

bridle > *noun* the headgear used to control a horse, consisting of buckled straps to which a bit and reins are attached. > *verb* **1** put a bridle on. **2** bring under control. **3** show resentment or anger, especially by throwing up one's head and drawing in one's chin.

COMBINATIONS - **bridleway** (also **bridle path**) Brit. a path or track along which horse riders have right of way.

Brie /bree/ > *noun* a kind of soft, mild, creamy cheese with a firm, white skin.

ORIGIN - named after *Brie* in northern France.

brief > *adjective* **1** lasting a short time. **2** concise; using few words. **3** (of clothing) not covering much of the body. > *noun* **1** chiefly Brit. a summary of the facts in a case given to a barrister to argue in court. **2** informal a solicitor or barrister. **3** chiefly Brit. a set of instructions about a task. **4** a letter from the Pope on a matter of discipline. > *verb* instruct or inform thoroughly in preparation for a task.

IDIOMS - **hold a brief for** Brit. be retained as counsel for. **hold no brief for** not support.

DERIVATIVES - **briefly** *adverb*.

SYNONYMS - *adjective* **1** fleeting, momentary, short. **2** concise, pithy, succinct. **3** revealing, scanty, skimpy.

ANTONYMS - *adjective* **1** long. **2** long-winded.

---

wordpower facts

Brief

The adjective **brief** comes from the Latin word *brevis*, meaning 'short', a root shared by **abbreviate** and the musical note **breve**. The noun sense of **brief** derives from late Latin *breve*, meaning 'note, dispatch': it was first used in English in the sense 'official letter' or 'royal mandate'.

---

briefcase > *noun* a flat rectangular case for carrying books and documents.

briefing > *noun* a meeting for giving information or instructions.

briefs > *plural noun* short, close-fitting underpants or knickers.

brier¹ > *noun* variant spelling of BRIAR¹.

brier² > *noun* variant spelling of BRIAR².

brig[1] > *noun* **1** a two-masted square-rigged ship. **2** informal a prison on a warship.

ORIGIN – abbreviation of BRIGANTINE.

brig[2] > *noun* Scottish & N. English a bridge.

brigade > *noun* **1** a subdivision of an army, typically consisting of a small number of battalions and forming part of a division. **2** informal, often derogatory a particular group of people: *the anti-smoking brigade.*

ORIGIN – French, from Italian *brigata* 'company'.

brigadier > *noun* a rank of officer in the British army, above colonel and below major general.

COMBINATIONS – **brigadier general** a similar rank of officer in the US army, air force, and marine corps.

brigalow /**brigg**əlō/ > *noun* an Australian acacia tree.

ORIGIN – from an Aboriginal word.

brigand /**brigg**ənd/ > *noun* a member of a gang that ambushes and robs people in forests and mountains.

DERIVATIVES – **brigandage** *noun.*

SYNONYMS – bandit, outlaw, robber.

ORIGIN – Italian, related to BRIGADE.

brigantine /**brigg**ənteen/ > *noun* a two-masted sailing ship with a square-rigged foremast and a mainmast rigged fore and aft.

ORIGIN – Italian *brigantino*, from *brigante* 'brigand'.

bright > *adjective* **1** giving out much light, or filled with light. **2** (of colour) vivid and bold. **3** intelligent and quick-witted. **4** (of sound) clear and high-pitched. **5** cheerfully lively. **6** (of prospects) good.

IDIOMS – **bright-eyed and bushy-tailed** informal alert and lively.

DERIVATIVES – **brighten** *verb* **brightly** *adverb* **brightness** *noun.*

SYNONYMS – **1** brilliant, dazzling, shining. **2** brilliant, intense, vivid.

ANTONYMS – dull.

COMBINATIONS – **bright spark** ironic a clever or witty person.

Bright's disease > *noun* a disease involving chronic inflammation of the kidneys.

ORIGIN – named after the English physician Richard *Bright* (1789–1858).

brill > *noun* a flatfish similar to the turbot.

brilliant > *adjective* **1** (of light or colour) very bright or vivid. **2** exceptionally clever or talented. **3** Brit. informal excellent; marvellous.

DERIVATIVES – **brilliance** (also **brilliancy**) *noun* **brilliantly** *adverb.*

SYNONYMS – **1** blazing, bright, dazzling, vivid.

ANTONYMS – **1** dull.

ORIGIN – French *brillant*, from *briller* 'shine', probably from Latin *beryllus* 'beryl'.

brilliantine > *noun* dated scented oil used on men's hair to make it look glossy.

brim > *noun* **1** the projecting edge around the bottom of a hat. **2** the lip of a cup, bowl, etc. > *verb* (**brimmed**, **brimming**) fill or be full to the point of overflowing.

DERIVATIVES – **brimful** *adjective* **brimmed** *adjective.*

brimstone /**brim**stōn/ > *noun* **1** archaic sulphur. **2** a large bright yellow or greenish-white butterfly.

ORIGIN – Old English, probably from *bryne* 'burning' + *stān* 'stone'.

brindle (also **brindled**) > *adjective* (of a domestic animal) brownish or tawny with streaks of other colour.

brine > *noun* water saturated or strongly impregnated with salt, e.g. seawater.

bring > *verb* (past and past participle **brought**) **1** carry or accompany to a place. **2** cause to be in a particular state or condition. **3** cause (someone) to receive (specified income or profit). **4** (**bring oneself to do**) force oneself to do (something unpleasant). **5** initiate (legal action).

IDIOMS – **bring about 1** cause (something) to happen. **2** cause (a ship) to head in a different direction. **bring forward 1** move (something scheduled) to an earlier time. **2** propose (an idea) for consideration. **bring the house down** make an audience laugh or applaud very enthusiastically. **bring off** achieve (something) successfully. **bring on 1** encourage or help (someone) to develop or improve. **2** cause (something unpleasant) to occur. **bring out 1** produce and launch (a new product or publication). **2** emphasise (a feature). **3** encourage (someone) to feel more confident. **bring round 1** restore (someone) to consciousness. **2** persuade (someone) to adopt one's own point of view. **bring to 1** restore (someone) to consciousness. **2** cause (a boat) to stop, especially by turning into the wind. **bring to bear** exert (influence or pressure). **bring to pass** chiefly literary cause (something) to happen. **bring up 1** look after (a child) until it is an adult. **2** raise (a matter) for discussion. **3** (of a ship) come to a stop.

DERIVATIVES – **bringer** *noun.*

SYNONYMS – **1** carry, conduct, convey, fetch, take.

COMBINATIONS – **bring and buy sale** Brit. a charity sale at which people donate things to sell.

brink > *noun* **1** the extreme edge of land before a steep slope or a body of water. **2** the verge of a state or situation, typically a bad one.

SYNONYMS – **2** edge, threshold, verge.

ORIGIN – Scandinavian.

brinkmanship /**bringk**mənship/ (US also **brinksmanship**) > *noun* the pursuit of a dangerous policy to the limits of safety before stopping.

briny /**brī**ni/ > *adjective* of salty water or the sea; salty. > *noun* (**the briny**) Brit. informal the sea.

brio /**bree**ō/ > *noun* vigour or vivacity.

ORIGIN – Italian.

brioche /**bree**osh/ > *noun* a small, round, sweet French roll.

ORIGIN – French, from *brier* 'split up into small pieces'.

briquette /**bri**ket/ (also **briquet**) > *noun* a block of compressed coal dust or peat used as fuel.

ORIGIN – French, 'small brick'.

brisk > *adjective* **1** active and energetic. **2** slightly brusque.

DERIVATIVES – **briskly** *adverb* **briskness** *noun.*

SYNONYMS – **1** active, energetic, quick, rapid, vigorous. **2** abrupt, blunt, brusque, businesslike, no-nonsense.

ANTONYMS – **1** sluggish.

ORIGIN – probably from French *brusque* (see BRUSQUE).

brisket > *noun* meat from the chest of a cow.

ORIGIN – perhaps from Old Norse *brjósk* 'cartilage, gristle'.

brisling /**briz**ling/ > *noun* (pl. same or **brislings**) a sprat, especially one seasoned, smoked, and canned.

ORIGIN – Norwegian and Danish.

bristle > *noun* **1** a short, stiff hair on an animal's skin or a man's face. **2** a stiff animal or artificial hair, used to make a brush. > *verb* **1** (of hair or fur) stand upright away from the skin. **2** react angrily or defensively. **3** (**bristle with**) be covered with or abundant in.

DERIVATIVES – **bristly** *adjective.*

Bristol fashion > *adjective* Brit. informal, dated in good order.

ORIGIN – from a nautical use, referring to the prosperity brought to the English city and port of Bristol from its shipping.

bristols > *plural noun* Brit. informal a woman's breasts.

ORIGIN – from rhyming slang *Bristol Cities* 'titties'.

Brit > *noun* informal a British person.

Britannia* /bri**tan**yə/ > *noun* the personification of Britain, usually depicted as a helmeted woman with shield and trident.

*SPELLING – note that there is one *t* and two *nn*s: Bri*tann*ia.

ORIGIN – the Latin name for Britain.

Britannic /bri**tann**ik/ > *adjective* dated of Britain or the British Empire.

British > *adjective* relating to Great Britain or the United Kingdom.

DERIVATIVES – **Britishness** *noun.*

COMBINATIONS – **British thermal unit** a unit of heat equal to the amount of heat needed to raise 1 lb of water at maximum density through one degree Fahrenheit.

ORIGIN – Old English, from *Bret* 'Briton', from Latin or Celtic.

Britisher > *noun* informal (especially in North America) a British person.

Briton > *noun* 1 a British person. 2 a native of southern Britain before and during Roman times.

ORIGIN – Old French *Breton*, from Latin or Celtic.

brittle > *adjective* 1 hard but liable to break or shatter easily. 2 hard or superficial in a way that masks nervousness or instability. > *noun* a brittle sweet made from nuts and set melted sugar.

DERIVATIVES – **brittleness** *noun*.

COMBINATIONS – **brittle bone disease** a disease in which the bones become brittle, especially osteoporosis.

broach > *verb* 1 raise (a sensitive subject) for discussion. 2 pierce or open (a cask or container) to draw out liquid.

ORIGIN – Old French *brochier*, from Latin *brocchus* 'projecting'.

broad > *adjective* 1 having a distance larger than usual from side to side. 2 of a specified distance wide. 3 large in area or scope. 4 without detail. 5 (of a hint) clear and unambiguous. 6 (of a regional accent) very noticeable and strong. 7 somewhat coarse and indecent. > *noun* N. Amer. informal a woman.

IDIOMS – **broad daylight** full daylight; day.

DERIVATIVES – **broaden** *verb* **broadly** *adverb* **broadness** *noun*.

SYNONYMS – *adjective* 1 expansive, sweeping, wide.

ANTONYMS – *adjective* 1 narrow.

COMBINATIONS – **broad bean** a large flat green bean which is usually eaten without the pod. **broad-brush** lacking in detail and finesse. **Broad Church** a tradition or group within the Anglican Church favouring a liberal interpretation of doctrine. **broadcloth** a fine cloth of wool or cotton. **broad gauge** a railway gauge which is wider than the standard gauge of 4 ft 8½ in (1.435 m). **broadleaved** (also **broadleaf**) (of trees or herbaceous plants) having relatively wide flat leaves, as opposed to conifers or grasses. **broad-minded** tolerant or liberal. **broadsheet** 1 a large piece of paper printed with information on one side only. 2 a newspaper with a large format. **broadsword** a sword with a wide blade, used for cutting rather than thrusting.

broadcast > *verb* (past **broadcast**; past participle **broadcast** or **broadcasted**) 1 transmit by radio or television. 2 tell to many people. 3 scatter (seeds) rather than placing in drills or rows. > *noun* a radio or television programme or transmission.

DERIVATIVES – **broadcaster** *noun*.

broadloom > *noun* carpet woven in wide widths.

broadside > *noun* 1 historical a firing of all the guns from one side of a warship. 2 the side of a ship above the water between the bow and quarter. 3 a strongly worded critical attack.

IDIOMS – **broadside on** sideways on.

Brobdingnagian /brobding**nagg**iən/ > *adjective* gigantic.

ORIGIN – from *Brobdingnag*, a land in Jonathan Swift's *Gulliver's Travels* (1726) where everything is of huge size.

brocade > *noun* a rich fabric woven with a raised pattern, usually with gold or silver thread.

DERIVATIVES – **brocaded** *adjective*.

ORIGIN – Spanish and Portuguese *brocado*, from Italian *brocco* 'twisted thread'.

broccoli* /**brokk**əli/ > *noun* a vegetable with heads of small green or purplish flower buds.

*SPELLING – two *c*s, one *l*: bro*cc*o*li*.

ORIGIN – Italian, plural of *broccolo* 'cabbage sprout, head'.

brochette /bro**shet**/ > *noun* a dish of meat or fish chunks barbecued, grilled, or roasted on a skewer.

ORIGIN – French, 'little skewer'.

brochure /**brō**shər/ > *noun* a magazine containing pictures and information about a product or service.

ORIGIN – French, 'something stitched'; related to BROACH and BROOCH.

broderie anglaise /brōdəri o**ng**glayz/ > *noun* open embroidery on fine white cotton or linen.

ORIGIN – French, 'English embroidery'.

brogue > *noun* 1 a strong outdoor shoe with ornamental perforated patterns in the leather. 2 a marked accent, especially Irish or Scottish, when speaking English.

wordpower facts

Brogue

The word **brogue** (from Scottish Gaelic and Irish *bróg*) was originally used in reference to rough shoes made from untanned leather that were worn in the wilder regions of Ireland and the Scottish Highlands. The 'accent' sense probably arose as an allusion to the footwear worn by those having a strong regional accent.

broil > *verb* chiefly N. Amer. 1 cook (meat or fish) by exposure to direct heat. 2 become very hot.

ORIGIN – Old French *bruler* 'to burn'.

broiler > *noun* 1 a young chicken suitable for roasting, grilling, or barbecuing. 2 N. Amer. a gridiron or grill for broiling meat or fish.

broke past (and archaic past participle) of BREAK. > *adjective* informal having completely run out of money.

IDIOMS – **go for broke** informal risk everything in an all-out effort.

broken past participle of BREAK. > *adjective* (of a language) spoken falteringly and with many mistakes, as by a foreigner.

DERIVATIVES – **brokenly** *adverb* **brokenness** *noun*.

COMBINATIONS – **broken-down** 1 worn out and dilapidated. 2 not working. **broken-hearted** overwhelmed by grief or disappointment. **broken home** a family in which the parents are divorced or separated.

broker > *noun* a person who buys and sells goods or assets for others. > *verb* arrange or negotiate (a deal or plan).

DERIVATIVES – **brokerage** *noun*.

NOTE – the term **broker** was officially replaced in the UK Stock Exchange by **broker-dealer** in 1986, broker-dealers being entitled to act both as agents and principals in share dealings.

COMBINATIONS – **broker-dealer** (in the UK) a person combining the former functions of a broker and jobber on the Stock Exchange.

ORIGIN – Old French *brocour*.

broking > *noun* Brit. the business or service of buying and selling goods or assets for others.

brolga /**brol**gə/ > *noun* a large grey Australian crane with an elaborate courtship display.

ORIGIN – from Kamilaroi (an Aboriginal language).

brolly > *noun* (pl. **brollies**) Brit. informal an umbrella.

bromeliad /brə**mee**liad/ > *noun* a plant of a tropical American family (Bromeliaceae), typically having short stems with rosettes of stiff, spiny leaves.

ORIGIN – from Latin *Bromelia*, a genus named after the Swedish botanist Olaf *Bromel* (1639–1705).

bromide > *noun* 1 Chemistry a compound of bromine with another element or group. 2 dated a sedative preparation containing potassium bromide. 3 a trite and unoriginal idea or remark, especially one intended to placate.

bromine /**brō**meen/ > *noun* a dark red liquid chemical element of the halogen group, with a choking irritating smell.

ORIGIN – from Greek *brōmos* 'a stink'.

bronchi plural of BRONCHUS.

bronchial /**brong**kiəl/ > *adjective* relating to the bronchi or bronchioles.

bronchiole /**brong**kiōl/ > *noun* Anatomy any of the minute branches into which a bronchus divides.

bronchitis > *noun* inflammation of the mucous membrane in the bronchial tubes.
DERIVATIVES – **bronchitic** *adjective* & *noun*.

bronchopneumonia /brongkŏnyŏŏ-mŏniə/ > *noun* a common form of pneumonia in which the small passages of the lungs become inflamed and filled with pus.

bronchoscope > *noun* a fibre-optic cable that is passed into the windpipe in order to view the bronchi.
DERIVATIVES – **bronchoscopy** *noun*.

bronchus /brongkəss/ > *noun* (pl. **bronchi** /brongkī/) any of the major air passages of the lungs which diverge from the windpipe.
ORIGIN – Greek *bronkhos* 'windpipe'.

bronco > *noun* (pl. **broncos**) a wild or half-tamed horse of the western US.
ORIGIN – Spanish, 'rough, rude'.

brontosaurus /brontəsawrəss/ > *noun* a huge herbivorous dinosaur of the late Jurassic period, with a long neck and tail.
NOTE – the name *Brontosaurus* is no longer used by palaeontologists; the current name for this dinosaur genus is *Apatosaurus*.
ORIGIN – from Greek *brontē* 'thunder' + *sauros* 'lizard'.

bronze > *noun* **1** a yellowish-brown alloy of copper and tin. **2** a yellowish-brown colour. **3** a sculpture or other object made of bronze. > *verb* **1** give a bronze surface to. **2** make suntanned.
DERIVATIVES – **bronzy** *adjective*.
COMBINATIONS – **Bronze Age** a period that followed the Stone Age and preceded the Iron Age, when weapons and tools were made of bronze. **bronze medal** a medal made of or coloured bronze, customarily awarded for third place in a race or competition.
ORIGIN – Italian *bronzo*, probably from a Persian word meaning 'brass'.

brooch > *noun* an ornament fastened to clothing with a hinged pin and catch.
ORIGIN – Old French *broche* 'spit for roasting', from Latin *brocchus* 'projecting'.

brood > *noun* **1** a family of young animals produced at one hatching or birth. **2** *informal* all the children in a family. > *verb* **1** think deeply about something distressing. **2** appear darkly menacing. **3** (of a bird) sit on (eggs) to hatch them. > *adjective* (of an animal) kept to be used for breeding.
DERIVATIVES – **brooding** *adjective* **broodingly** *adverb*.
SYNONYMS – *verb* **1** (**brood on** or **over**) dwell on, fret about, mope about, mull over, ponder.

brooder > *noun* a heated house for chicks or piglets.

broody > *adjective* (**broodier, broodiest**) **1** (of a hen) inclined to incubate eggs. **2** *informal* (of a woman) having a strong desire to have a baby. **3** thoughtful and unhappy.
DERIVATIVES – **broodiness** *noun*.

brook[1] > *noun* a small stream.
DERIVATIVES – **brooklet** *noun*.

brook[2] > *verb* *formal* tolerate or allow (opposition): *she would brook no criticism.*
ORIGIN – Old English 'use, possess' or 'digest, stomach'.

broom > *noun* **1** a long-handled brush used for sweeping. **2** a shrub typically having many yellow flowers and small or few leaves.
IDIOMS – **a new broom sweeps clean** *proverb* people newly appointed to positions of responsibility tend to make far-reaching changes.
COMBINATIONS – **broomball** N. Amer. a game similar to ice hockey in which players use rubber brooms or broom handles to manoeuvre a ball. **broomstick** the handle of a broom, on which witches are said to fly.

broomrape > *noun* a leafless parasitic plant with tubular flowers, which attaches itself to the roots of its host plant.
ORIGIN – from **BROOM** + Latin *rapum* 'tuber'.

Bros > *plural noun* brothers (in names of companies).

brose /brōz/ > *noun* *chiefly Scottish* a kind of porridge made with oatmeal or dried peas.
ORIGIN – Old French.

broth > *noun* **1** a thin soup of meat or vegetable stock. **2** *Microbiology* a liquid nutrient medium for the culture of bacteria.

brothel > *noun* a house where men visit prostitutes.
ORIGIN – first as *brothel-house*: from *brothel* 'worthless man, prostitute'.

brother > *noun* **1** a man or boy in relation to other children of his parents. **2** (pl. also **brethren**) *Christian Church* a member of a religious order of men. **3** a male associate or fellow member of an organisation. **4** a thing which resembles or is related to another. **5** N. Amer. *informal* a black man. > *exclamation* used to express annoyance or surprise.
WORDFINDER – fraternal (*relating to a brother*), fratricide (*murder of one's own brother or sister*), sibling (*brother or sister*).
DERIVATIVES – **brotherly** *adjective*.
COMBINATIONS – **brother-in-law** (pl. **brothers-in-law**) **1** the brother of one's wife or husband. **2** the husband of one's sister or sister-in-law.

brotherhood > *noun* **1** the relationship between brothers. **2** a feeling of kinship and closeness. **3** an association or community of people.
SYNONYMS – **2** camaraderie, comradeship, fellowship, kinship. **3** affiliation, association, community, fraternity, society.

brougham /brŏŏəm, brŏŏm/ > *noun* *historical* **1** a horse-drawn carriage with a roof, four wheels, and an open driver's seat in front. **2** a motor car with an open driver's seat.
ORIGIN – named after Lord *Brougham* (1778–1868), who designed the carriage.

brought past and past participle of **BRING**.

brouhaha /brŏŏhaahaa/ > *noun* a noisy and overexcited reaction.
ORIGIN – French.

brow > *noun* **1** a person's forehead. **2** an eyebrow. **3** the summit of a hill or pass.

browbeat > *verb* (past **browbeat**; past participle **browbeaten**) intimidate with words or looks.
SYNONYMS – bully, coerce, dragoon, hector, intimidate.

brown > *adjective* **1** of a colour produced by mixing red, yellow, and blue, as of dark wood or rich soil. **2** dark-skinned or suntanned. > *noun* brown colour, pigment, or material. > *verb* **1** make or become brown by cooking. **2** (**be browned off**) *informal* be irritated or depressed.
WORDFINDER – *shades of brown:* auburn, bronze, chestnut, chocolate, cinnamon, copper, dun, ebony, fallow, fawn, hazel, mahogany, rufous, russet, rust, sepia, sorrel, tan, tawny.
DERIVATIVES – **brownish** *adjective* **browny** *adjective*.
COMBINATIONS – **brown ale** Brit. dark, mild beer sold in bottles. **brown bear** a large bear with a coat colour ranging from cream to black. **brown belt** a belt of a brown colour marking a level of proficiency below that of a black belt in judo, karate, or other martial arts. **brown coal** lignite. **brown dwarf** Astronomy a celestial object intermediate in size between a giant planet and a small star. **brownfield** (of a site for building) having had previous development on it. Contrasted with *greenfield*. **brown goods** television sets, audio equipment, and similar household appliances. Compare with *white goods*. **brownout** chiefly N. Amer. a partial blackout. **brown rice** unpolished rice with only the husk of the grain removed. **brown sauce** a commercially prepared relish containing vinegar and spices. **brownstone** N. Amer. **1** a kind of reddish-brown sandstone used for building. **2** a building faced with such sandstone. **brown sugar** unrefined or partially refined sugar.

Brownian motion > *noun* Physics the erratic movement of microscopic particles in a fluid, as a result of collisions with the surrounding molecules.
ORIGIN – named after the Scottish botanist Robert *Brown* (1773–1858).

Brownie > *noun* (pl. **Brownies**) **1** (Brit. also **Brownie Guide**) a member of the junior branch of the Guides Association. **2** (**brownie**) a small square of rich chocolate cake. **3** (**brownie**) a benevolent elf that supposedly does housework secretly.

IDIOMS – **brownie point** informal, humorous a notional award given for an attempt to please.

browning > *noun* Brit. darkened flour for colouring gravy.

brown-nose N. Amer. informal > *noun* (also **brown-noser**) a person who acts in a grossly obsequious way. > *verb* ingratiate oneself with (someone) by acting in such a way.

Brownshirt > *noun* a member of a Nazi militia founded by Hitler in 1921 and suppressed in 1934, with brown uniforms.

brown trout > *noun* (pl. same) the common trout of European lakes and rivers, typically with dark spotted skin.

browse > *verb* **1** survey goods or text in a leisurely way. **2** Computing read or survey (data files) via a network. **3** (of an animal) feed on leaves, twigs, etc. > *noun* an act of browsing.

DERIVATIVES – **browsable** *adjective*.

ORIGIN – from Old French *brost* 'young shoot'.

browser > *noun* **1** a person or animal that browses. **2** Computing a program with a graphical user interface for displaying HTML files, used to navigate the World Wide Web.

brucellosis /brōōssəlōsiss/ > *noun* a bacterial disease chiefly affecting cattle and causing undulant fever in humans.

ORIGIN – from *Brucella*, the name of the bacterium responsible.

bruise > *noun* **1** an injury appearing as an area of discoloured skin on the body, caused by a blow rupturing underlying blood vessels. **2** a similar area of damage on a fruit, vegetable, or plant. > *verb* **1** inflict a bruise on. **2** be susceptible to bruising.

bruiser > *noun* informal, derogatory a tough, aggressive person.

bruit /brōōt/ > *verb* literary spread (a report or rumour) widely.

ORIGIN – Old French *bruire* 'to roar'.

brumby /brumbi/ > *noun* (pl. **brumbies**) (in Australia) a wild or unbroken horse.

brume > *noun* literary mist or fog.

DERIVATIVES – **brumous** *adjective*.

ORIGIN – French, from Latin *bruma* 'winter'.

Brummie (also **Brummy**) > *noun* (pl. **Brummies**) Brit. informal a person from Birmingham. > *adjective* informal **1** Brit. relating to Birmingham. **2** (**brummy**) Austral./NZ counterfeit, showy, or cheaply made.

brunch > *noun* a late morning meal eaten instead of breakfast and lunch.

Bruneian /brōōnīən/ > *noun* a person from

the sultanate of Brunei, in NW Borneo. > *adjective* relating to Brunei.

brunette (US also **brunet**) > *noun* a woman or girl with dark brown hair.

ORIGIN – from French *brun* 'brown'.

brunt > *noun* the chief impact of something bad: *education will bear the brunt of the cuts.*

bruschetta /brŏŏskettə/ > *noun* toasted Italian bread drenched in olive oil.

ORIGIN – Italian.

brush¹ > *noun* **1** an implement with a handle and a block of bristles, hair, or wire, used especially for cleaning, smoothing, or painting. **2** an act of brushing. **3** a slight and fleeting touch. **4** a brief encounter with something bad or unwelcome. **5** a drumstick with long wire bristles. **6** the bushy tail of a fox. **7** a drumstick with long wire bristles. **8** a piece of carbon or metal serving as an electrical contact with a moving part in a motor or alternator. > *verb* **1** clean, smooth, or apply with a brush. **2** touch or push lightly. **3** (**brush off**) dismiss in an abrupt, contemptuous way. **4** (**brush up** (**on**)) work to regain a previously learned skill.

ORIGIN – Old French *broisse*.

brush² > *noun* chiefly N. Amer. & Austral./NZ undergrowth, small trees, and shrubs.

DERIVATIVES – **brushy** *adjective*.

COMBINATIONS – **brushwood** undergrowth, twigs, and small branches.

ORIGIN – Old French *broce*.

brushed > *adjective* **1** (of fabric) having a soft raised nap. **2** (of metal) finished with a non-reflective surface.

brushtail > *noun* a tree-dwelling Australian marsupial with a pointed muzzle and a furred tail with a naked tip.

brusque /brŏŏsk/ > *adjective* abrupt in speech or manner.

DERIVATIVES – **brusquely** *adverb* **brusqueness** *noun*.

SYNONYMS – abrupt, brisk, curt, offhand, peremptory, short, unceremonious.

ORIGIN – French, 'lively, fierce', from Italian *brusco* 'sour'.

Brussels sprout (also **Brussel sprout**) > *noun* a vegetable consisting of the small compact bud of a variety of cabbage.

brut /brŏŏt/ > *adjective* (of sparkling wine) very dry.

ORIGIN – French, 'raw, rough'.

brutal > *adjective* **1** savagely violent. **2** without any attempt to disguise unpleasantness.

DERIVATIVES – **brutalism** *noun* **brutality** *noun* **brutally** *adverb*.

SYNONYMS – **1** barbaric, cold-blooded, cruel, ruthless, savage, vicious. **2** blunt, stark, unsparing.

ANTONYMS – gentle, kind.

ORIGIN – Latin *brutalis*, from *brutus* 'dull, stupid'.

brutalise (also **brutalize**) > *verb* **1** make brutal by frequent exposure to violence. **2** treat brutally.

DERIVATIVES – **brutalisation** *noun*.

SYNONYMS – **1** degrade, dehumanise, harden, inure.

brute > *noun* **1** a violent or savage person or animal. **2** informal a cruel or insensitive person. > *adjective* **1** unreasoning and animal-like. **2** merely physical. **3** harsh or inescapable.

DERIVATIVES – **brutish** *adjective*.

SYNONYMS – *noun* beast, monster, savage. *adjective* **1** bestial, boorish, inhuman, unfeeling, unreasoning.

ORIGIN – from Latin *brutus* 'dull, stupid'.

bryony /brīəni/ > *noun* (pl. **bryonies**) a climbing hedgerow plant with red berries.

ORIGIN – Greek *bruōnia*.

bryophyte /brīəfīt/ > *noun* Botany a member of the division of plants (Bryophyta) which comprises the mosses and liverworts.

ORIGIN – from Greek *bruon* 'moss' + *phuton* 'plant'.

bryozoan > *noun* Zoology a minute colonial aquatic animal found encrusting rocks or seaweed or forming stalked fronds.

ORIGIN – from Greek *bruon* 'moss' + *zōia* 'animals'.

BS > *abbreviation* **1** Bachelor of Surgery. **2** British Standard(s). **3** N. Amer. vulgar slang bullshit.

BSc > *abbreviation* Bachelor of Science.

BSE > *abbreviation* bovine spongiform encephalopathy, a fatal disease of cattle which affects the central nervous system and is believed to be related to Creutzfeldt–Jakob disease in humans.

BSI > *abbreviation* British Standards Institution.

BST > *abbreviation* **1** bovine somatotrophin, especially as an additive in cattle feed. **2** British Summer Time.

BT > *abbreviation* British Telecom.

Btu (also **BTU**) > *abbreviation* British thermal unit(s).

btw > *abbreviation* by the way.

bubble > *noun* **1** a thin sphere of liquid enclosing air or another gas. **2** an air- or gas-filled spherical cavity in a liquid or a solidified liquid such as glass. **3** a transparent domed cover. > *verb* **1** (of a liquid) be agitated by rising bubbles of air or gas. **2** (**bubble with**) be filled with (an irrepressible positive feeling). **3** (**bubble up**) (of a feeling) intensify to the point of being expressed.

COMBINATIONS – **bubble and squeak** Brit. a dish of cooked cabbage fried with cooked potatoes. **bubble bath** fragrant liquid added to bathwater to make it foam. **bubble wrap** (trademark in the US) protective plastic packaging in sheets containing numerous small air cushions.

bubblegum > *noun* **1** chewing gum that can be blown into bubbles. **2** (before another noun) chiefly N. Amer. simplistic or adolescent in style: *bubblegum pop music*.

bubbly > *adjective* (**bubblier, bubbliest**) **1** containing bubbles. **2** cheerful and high-spirited. > *noun* informal champagne.

bubo /byoōbō/ > *noun* (pl. **buboes**) a swollen inflamed lymph node in the armpit or groin.

DERIVATIVES – **bubonic** *adjective*.

ORIGIN – Greek *boubōn* 'groin or swelling in the groin'.

bubonic plague > *noun* a form of plague transmitted by rat fleas and characterised by the formation of buboes.

buccal /bukk'l/ > *adjective* technical relating to the cheek or mouth.

ORIGIN – from Latin *bucca* 'cheek'.

buccaneer /bukkəneer/ > *noun* **1** historical a pirate, originally one preying on ships in the Caribbean. **2** a recklessly adventurous and unscrupulous person.

DERIVATIVES – **buccaneering** *adjective*.

ORIGIN – first used of European hunters in the Caribbean: from French *boucanier*, from *boucan* 'a frame on which to cook or cure meat'.

buck¹ > *noun* **1** the male of some animals, especially deer and antelopes. **2** S. African an antelope (of either sex). **3** a vertical jump performed by a horse. **4** archaic a fashionable young man. > *verb* **1** (of a horse) perform a buck. **2** oppose or resist. **3** (**buck up**) informal make or become more cheerful.

IDIOMS – **buck up one's ideas** become more serious and hard-working.

COMBINATIONS – **buckhorn** deer horn used for knife handles and rifle sights. **buckshot** coarse lead shot used in shotgun shells. **buckskin 1** the skin of a male deer. **2** (**buckskins**) clothes or shoes made from buckskin. **3** thick smooth cotton or woollen fabric.

buck² > *noun* informal N. Amer. & Austral./NZ a dollar.

IDIOMS – **a fast buck** easily and quickly earned money.

buck³ > *noun* an object placed in front of a poker player whose turn it is to deal.

IDIOMS – **the buck stops here** informal the responsibility for something cannot be avoided. **pass the buck** informal shift responsibility to someone else.

buckaroo > *noun* N. Amer. dated a cowboy.

ORIGIN – alteration of VAQUERO.

buckboard > *noun* N. Amer. an open horse-drawn carriage with four wheels and seating that is attached to a plank between the front and rear axles.

ORIGIN – from *buck* 'body of a cart' + BOARD.

bucket > *noun* **1** a cylindrical open container

used to carry liquids. **2** (**buckets**) informal large quantities of liquid. **3** a scoop on a waterwheel, dredger, digger, etc. > *verb* (**bucketed, bucketing**) (**bucket down**) Brit. informal rain heavily.

DERIVATIVES – **bucketful** *noun*.

COMBINATIONS – **bucket seat** a vehicle seat with a rounded back to fit one person. **bucket shop** informal, derogatory **1** an unauthorised office speculating with the funds of unwitting investors. **2** Brit. a travel agency providing cheap air tickets.

ORIGIN – Old French.

buckeye > *noun* **1** an American tree or shrub related to the horse chestnut. **2** the shiny brown nut of the buckeye.

buckjump Austral./NZ > *verb* (of a horse) jump vertically with its head lowered, back arched, and legs drawn together. > *noun* an act of buckjumping.

DERIVATIVES – **buckjumper** *noun*.

buckle > *noun* a flat frame with a hinged pin, used for fastening a belt or strap. > *verb* **1** fasten with a buckle. **2** bend and give way under pressure. **3** (**buckle down**) tackle a task with determination.

SYNONYMS – *verb* **2** bend, crumple, distort, twist, warp.

ORIGIN – Latin *buccula* 'cheek strap of a helmet', from *bucca* 'cheek'; sense 2 of the verb is from French *boucler* 'to bulge'.

buckler > *noun* historical a small round shield held by a handle or worn on the forearm.

ORIGIN – from Old French *escu bocler* 'shield with a boss'.

Buckley's > *noun* (in phrase **have Buckley's chance**) Austral./NZ informal have little or no chance.

ORIGIN – perhaps from the name of William *Buckley* (died 1856), who, despite dire predictions as to his chances of survival, lived with the Aboriginals for many years.

buckram > *noun* coarse linen or other cloth stiffened with paste, used as interfacing and in bookbinding.

ORIGIN – Old French *boquerant*.

Bucks > *abbreviation* Buckinghamshire.

Buck's Fizz > *noun* Brit. a cocktail of champagne or sparkling white wine mixed with orange juice.

ORIGIN – from the name of *Buck's Club*, in London, and FIZZ.

buckshee > *adjective* informal, chiefly Brit. free of charge.

ORIGIN – alteration of BAKSHEESH.

buckthorn > *noun* a thorny shrub or small tree which bears black berries.

buck tooth > *noun* an upper tooth that projects over the lower lip.

DERIVATIVES – **buck-toothed** *adjective*.

buckwheat > *noun* a plant producing

starchy seeds used for fodder or milled into flour.

ORIGIN – Dutch, 'beech wheat'.

bucolic /byookollik/ > *adjective* relating to rural or pastoral life.

SYNONYMS – pastoral, rural, rustic, sylvan.

ORIGIN – Greek *boukolikos*, from *boukolos* 'herdsman'.

bud > *noun* **1** a knob-like growth on a plant which develops into a leaf, flower, or shoot. **2** Biology an outgrowth from an organism that separates to form a new individual asexually. > *verb* (**budded, budding**) form a bud or buds.

Buddhism /booddiz'm/ > *noun* a religion or philosophy, founded by Siddartha Gautama (Buddha; *c*.563–*c*.460 BC), which teaches that elimination of the self is the route to enlightenment.

WORDFINDER – *forms of Buddhism:* Mahayana, Theravada, Zen; bo tree (*fig tree sacred to Buddhists*), koan (*enlightening Buddhist anecdote or riddle*), nirvana (*transcendent state which is final goal of Buddhism*), stupa (*dome-shaped Buddhist shrine*), sutra (*Buddhist scripture*).

DERIVATIVES – **Buddhist** *noun* & *adjective* **Buddhistic** *adjective*.

budding > *adjective* beginning and showing signs of promise: *their budding relationship*.

SYNONYMS – burgeoning, developing, emergent, evolving.

buddleia /budliə/ > *noun* a shrub with clusters of fragrant lilac, white, or yellow flowers.

ORIGIN – named after the English botanist Adam *Buddle* (died 1715).

buddy informal, chiefly N. Amer. > *noun* (pl. **buddies**) **1** a close friend. **2** a working companion with whom close cooperation is required.

ORIGIN – perhaps an alteration of BROTHER.

budge > *verb* **1** make or cause to make the slightest movement. **2** change an opinion.

SYNONYMS – **1** give way, move, shift, stir. **2** acquiesce, yield.

ORIGIN – French *bouger* 'to stir', from Latin *bullire* 'to boil'.

budgerigar > *noun* a small Australian parakeet which is green with a yellow head in the wild.

ORIGIN – from an Aboriginal language.

budget > *noun* **1** an estimate of income and expenditure for a set period of time. **2** the amount of money needed or available for a purpose. **3** (**Budget**) a regular estimate of national revenue and expenditure put forward by a finance minister. > *verb* (**budgeted, budgeting**) allow or provide for in a budget. > *adjective* inexpensive.

DERIVATIVES – **budgetary** *adjective*.

wordpower facts
Budget

The original sense of **budget** was 'a leather pouch or bag', which was later extended to 'the contents of a bag' and the figurative senses 'long letter' and 'news'. In the 18th century the British Chancellor of the Exchequer, in presenting his annual statement, was said to 'open the budget', thus giving rise to the modern financial sense. The word itself comes from Old French *bougette*, meaning 'small leather bag', from Latin *bulga* 'leather bag'. **Bulge**, which also comes from *bulga*, was similarly first used in the sense 'leather sack or bag'.

budgie > *noun* (pl. **budgies**) informal term for BUDGERIGAR.

buff¹ > *noun* 1 a yellowish-beige colour. 2 a dull yellow leather with a velvety surface. > *verb* 1 polish (something). 2 give (leather) a velvety finish.
IDIOMS – **in the buff** informal naked.
ORIGIN – probably from Latin *bufalus* (see BUFFALO).

buff² > *noun* informal a person who is very interested in and knowledgeable about a particular subject.
ORIGIN – from BUFF¹: first applied to fire-watchers, because of the buff uniforms worn by New York firemen.

buffalo > *noun* (pl. same or **buffaloes**) 1 a heavily built wild ox with backswept horns. 2 the North American bison.
ORIGIN – Latin *bufalus*, from Greek *boubalos* 'antelope, wild ox'.

buffer¹ > *noun* 1 (**buffers**) Brit. projecting shock-absorbing pistons at the end of a railway track or on a railway vehicle. 2 a person or thing that reduces a shock or forms a barrier between adversaries. 3 Computing a temporary memory area used when creating or editing text or transferring data.
SYNONYMS – 2 barrier, bulwark, cushion, shield.

buffer² > *noun* Brit. informal an old-fashioned or incompetent elderly man.

buffet¹ /boofay, buffay/ > *noun* 1 a meal consisting of several dishes from which guests serve themselves. 2 a room or counter selling light meals or snacks. 3 /buffit/ a sideboard or cupboard for crockery.
ORIGIN – Old French *bufet* 'stool'.

buffet² /buffit/ > *verb* (**buffeted, buffeting**) (especially of wind or waves) strike repeatedly and violently. > *noun* dated a blow.

SYNONYMS – *verb* batter, beat against, lash, pound.
ORIGIN – from Old French *bufe* 'a blow'.

buffoon > *noun* a ridiculous but amusing person.
DERIVATIVES – **buffoonery** *noun* **buffoonish** *adjective*.
SYNONYMS – clown, dolt, fool, idiot.
ORIGIN – Latin *buffo* 'clown'.

bug > *noun* 1 Entomology an insect of an order including aphids and many other insects. 2 informal any small insect. 3 informal a harmful micro-organism. 4 informal an illness caused by a micro-organism. 5 informal an intense enthusiasm for something: *they caught the sailing bug.* 6 a microphone used for secret recording. 7 an error in a computer program or system. > *verb* (**bugged, bugging**) 1 conceal a microphone in. 2 informal annoy; bother.
COMBINATIONS – **bug-eyed** with bulging eyes.

bugaboo > *noun* chiefly N. Amer. an object of fear.
ORIGIN – probably Celtic.

bugbear > *noun* a cause of anxiety or irritation.
SYNONYMS – bane, bête noire, bogey, pet hate.

bugger vulgar slang, chiefly Brit. > *noun* 1 derogatory a person who commits buggery. 2 a person regarded with contempt or pity. 3 an annoying or awkward thing. > *verb* 1 practise buggery with. 2 (often **bugger up**) cause serious harm or trouble to. 3 (**bugger off**) go away. 4 (**bugger about** (or **around**)) act stupidly or carelessly. > *exclamation* used to express annoyance.
IDIOMS – **bugger all** nothing.

wordpower facts
Bugger

The word **bugger** comes from Old French *bougre*, meaning 'heretic'. It was first used in English in reference to members of a heretical Christian sect based in Albi in southern France in the 12th and 13th centuries (the Albigensians). The word ultimately comes from Latin *Bulgarus*, meaning 'Bulgarian', in particular one belonging to the Orthodox Church, which was regarded by the Roman Catholic Church as heretical. The sexual use of the term arose in the 16th century from an association of heresy with forbidden sexual practices.

buggery > *noun* anal intercourse.
buggy > *noun* (pl. **buggies**) 1 a small motor vehicle with an open top. 2 a light collapsible pushchair. 3 historical a light

horse-drawn vehicle for one or two people.

bugle¹ > *noun* a brass instrument like a small trumpet, traditionally used for military signals. > *verb* sound a bugle.
DERIVATIVES – **bugler** *noun*.
ORIGIN – Old French, from Latin *buculus* 'little ox'; first used in the sense 'wild ox', from which came the compound *bugle-horn*, later shortened to *bugle*.

bugle² > *noun* a creeping plant with blue flowers on upright stems.
ORIGIN – Latin *bugula*.

bugloss /byoogloss/ > *noun* a bristly plant with bright blue flowers.
ORIGIN – Greek *bouglōssos* 'ox-tongued', from *bous* 'ox' + *glōssa* 'tongue'.

buhl /bool/ > *noun* variant spelling of BOULLE.

build > *verb* (past and past participle **built**) 1 construct by putting parts or materials together. 2 increase over time. 3 (**build on**) use as a basis for further progress or development. 4 (**build in** or **into**) incorporate (something) as a permanent part of. > *noun* 1 the proportions of a person's or animal's body. 2 the style or form of construction of something.
DERIVATIVES – **builder** *noun*.
SYNONYMS – 1 assemble, construct, erect, raise. 4 (**build in** or **into**) assimilate, include, incorporate.
COMBINATIONS – **build-up** 1 a gradual accumulation. 2 a period of excitement and preparation before an event.

building > *noun* 1 a structure with a roof and walls. 2 the process or trade of building houses and other structures.
SYNONYMS – 1 edifice, erection, pile, structure.
COMBINATIONS – **building society** Brit. a financial organisation which pays interest on members' investments and lends capital for mortgages.

built past and past participle of BUILD. > *adjective* of a specified physical build: *a slightly built woman.*
COMBINATIONS – **built-in** 1 forming an integral part of a structure. 2 inherent; innate. **built-up** (of an area) densely covered by buildings.

bulb > *noun* 1 a rounded underground organ present in some plants, consisting of a short stem surrounded by fleshy leaf bases. 2 a light bulb. 3 an expanded or rounded part at the end of something.
ORIGIN – Greek *bolbos* 'onion, bulbous root'.

bulbil > *noun* Botany a small bulb-like structure which may fall to form a new plant.

bulbous > *adjective* 1 round or bulging in shape. 2 (of a plant) growing from a bulb.
SYNONYMS – bulging, round, spherical, swollen.

Bulgar /**bul**gaar/ > *noun* a member of a Slavic people who settled in what is now Bulgaria in the 7th century.

ORIGIN – Latin *Bulgarus*, from Old Church Slavonic *Blŭgarinŭ*.

Bulgarian > *noun* **1** a person from Bulgaria. **2** the Slavic language spoken in Bulgaria. > *adjective* relating to Bulgaria or Bulgarian.

bulgar wheat > *noun* a cereal food made from whole wheat partially boiled then dried.

ORIGIN – Turkish, 'bruised grain'.

bulge > *noun* **1** a rounded swelling distorting a flat surface. **2** Military a piece of land projecting outwards from an otherwise regular line. > *verb* **1** swell or protrude to an unnatural extent. **2** (often **bulge with**) be full of and distended with something.

DERIVATIVES – **bulging** *adjective* **bulgy** *adjective*.

SYNONYMS – *noun* bump, distension, lump, protuberance, swelling. *verb* bag, balloon, be distended, protrude, swell.

bulimia /byoo**limm**iə/ (also **bulimia nervosa**) > *noun* an emotional disorder characterised by bouts of overeating, typically alternating with fasting or self-induced vomiting.

DERIVATIVES – **bulimic** *adjective* & *noun*.

ORIGIN – Greek *boulimia* 'ravenous hunger', from *bous* 'ox' + *limos* 'hunger'.

bulk > *noun* **1** the mass or magnitude of something large. **2** the greater part. **3** a large mass or shape. **4** (before another noun) large in quantity: *a bulk supplier*. **5** roughage in food. > *verb* **1** be of great size or importance. **2** treat (a product) so that its quantity appears greater than it is.

IDIOMS – **in bulk** (of goods) in large quantities.

SYNONYMS – *noun* **1** magnitude, mass, size, substance, volume.

ORIGIN – probably from Old Norse.

bulkhead > *noun* a barrier between separate compartments inside a ship, aircraft, etc.

ORIGIN – from Old Norse *bálkr* 'partition'.

bulky > *adjective* (**bulkier**, **bulkiest**) large and unwieldy.

SYNONYMS – big, cumbersome, large, unwieldy.

ANTONYMS – compact, slim.

bull¹ > *noun* **1** an uncastrated male bovine animal. **2** a large male animal, e.g. a whale or elephant. **3** Brit. a bullseye. **4** Stock Exchange a person who buys shares hoping to sell them at a higher price later. Contrasted with **BEAR²**.

WORDFINDER – taurine (*of or like a bull*); Taurus (*constellation and zodiac sign, the Bull*).

IDIOMS – **like a bull in a china shop** behaving clumsily in a delicate situation.

take the bull by the horns deal decisively with a difficult situation.

COMBINATIONS – **bull bar** a grille fitted to the front of a motor vehicle to protect against impact damage. **bullfinch** a finch with mainly grey and black plumage, of which the male has a pink breast. **bullfrog** a very large frog with a deep croak. **bullheaded** determined and obstinate. **bullhorn** N. Amer. a megaphone. **bull market** Stock Exchange a market in which share prices are rising. **bullring** an arena where bullfights are held.

bull² > *noun* a papal edict.

ORIGIN – Latin *bulla* 'seal or sealed document'.

bull³ > *noun* informal nonsense.

bulldog > *noun* a breed of dog with a protruding lower jaw, a flat wrinkled face, and a broad chest.

COMBINATIONS – **bulldog clip** Brit. trademark a sprung metal device with two flat plates, used to hold papers together.

bulldoze > *verb* **1** clear or destroy with a bulldozer. **2** informal coerce.

ORIGIN – from **BULL¹** + -*doze*, an alteration of the noun **DOSE**.

bulldozer > *noun* a tractor with a broad curved blade at the front for clearing ground.

bullet > *noun* **1** a projectile fired from a small firearm. **2** (the bullet) informal dismissal from employment. **3** Printing a solid circle printed before each in a list of items.

ORIGIN – French *boulet* 'small ball', from Latin *bulla* 'bubble'.

bulletin > *noun* **1** a short official statement or summary of news. **2** a regular newsletter or report.

SYNONYMS – **1** announcement, communiqué, newsflash, notice, report. **2** digest, journal, newsletter, report, review.

COMBINATIONS – **bulletin board 1** N. Amer. a noticeboard. **2** Computing an information storage system designed to permit any authorised user to access and add to it from a remote terminal.

wordpower facts

Bulletin

The word **bulletin** derives from Italian *bulletta*, meaning 'passport', from Italian and medieval Latin *bulla*, 'seal, sealed document'. *Bulla* is also the root of **bill** meaning 'written statement of charges', and of the papal edict, the **bull**. The original Latin meaning of *bulla* was 'bubble', and this is the root of **bowl** in the sense 'ball' and of **budge**, **bullet**, **bulletin**, **bullion**, and **ebullient**.

bullfighting > *noun* the sport of baiting and killing a bull as a public spectacle.

WORDFINDER – *kinds of bullfighter:* matador, picador, toreador, torero; aficionado (*devotee of bullfighting*), banderilla (*decorated dart used in bullfighting*), corrida (*bullfight*).

DERIVATIVES – **bullfight** *noun* **bullfighter** *noun*.

bullion > *noun* gold or silver in bulk before coining.

ORIGIN – Old French *bouillon*, based on Latin *bullire* 'to boil'.

bullish > *adjective* **1** aggressively confident and self-assertive. **2** Stock Exchange characterised or influenced by rising share prices.

DERIVATIVES – **bullishly** *adverb* **bullishness** *noun*.

SYNONYMS – **1** aggressive, autocratic, dominating, high-handed, imperious.

ANTONYMS – meek.

bullock > *noun* a castrated male bovine animal raised for beef. > *verb* Austral./NZ informal work very hard.

bullrush > *noun* variant spelling of **BULRUSH**.

bullseye > *noun* **1** the centre of the target in sports such as archery and darts. **2** a hard peppermint-flavoured sweet.

bullshit vulgar slang > *noun* nonsense. > *verb* (**bullshitted**, **bullshitting**) talk nonsense in an attempt to deceive.

DERIVATIVES – **bullshitter** *noun*.

bull terrier > *noun* a dog that is a cross-breed of bulldog and terrier.

bully¹ > *noun* (pl. **bullies**) a person who deliberately intimidates or persecutes those who are weaker. > *verb* (**bullies**, **bullied**) intimidate.

SYNONYMS – *verb* browbeat, harass, intimidate, persecute, torment.

ORIGIN – probably from Dutch *boele* 'lover': first used as a term of endearment for either sex, then as a form of address for a male friend.

bully² > *adjective* informal, chiefly N. Amer. excellent.

IDIOMS – **bully for you!** (or **him** etc.) often ironic an expression of admiration or approval.

ORIGIN – from **BULLY¹**.

bully³ > *noun* (pl. **bullies**) (also **bully off**) the start of play in field hockey. > *verb* (**bullies**, **bullied**) start play in this way.

bully⁴ (also **bully beef**) > *noun* informal corned beef.

ORIGIN – from French *bouilli* 'boiled'.

bulrush (also **bullrush**) > *noun* a reed mace or similar waterside plant.

ORIGIN – probably from **BULL¹** in the sense 'large, coarse'.

bulwark /**bool**wərk/ > *noun* **1** a defensive

wall. **2** an extension of a ship's sides above deck level.

ORIGIN – Low German and Dutch.

bum¹ > *noun* Brit. informal a person's bottom.

COMBINATIONS – **bumbag** a small pouch for holding valuables, worn on a belt round the hips.

bum² informal > *noun* N. Amer. **1** a vagrant. **2** a lazy or worthless person. **3** a devotee of a particular activity: *a surf bum*. > *verb* (**bummed**, **bumming**) **1** get by asking or begging. **2** (**bum around**) chiefly N. Amer. pass one's time idly. > *adjective* bad or wrong: *a bum note*.

IDIOMS – **give someone the bum's rush** chiefly N. Amer. forcibly eject someone.

ORIGIN – probably from BUMMER.

bumble > *verb* **1** act or speak in an awkward or confused manner. **2** (of an insect) buzz or hum.

DERIVATIVES – **bumbler** *noun*.

ORIGIN – first used in the sense 'hum, drone': from BOOM¹.

bumblebee > *noun* a large hairy bee with a loud hum.

bumf (also **bumph**) > *noun* informal, chiefly Brit. useless or tedious printed information.

ORIGIN – first used in the sense 'toilet paper': abbreviation of slang *bum-fodder*.

bummalo /ˈbumməlō/ > *noun* (pl. same) a small elongated South Asian fish, dried as food.

bummer > *noun* informal **1** an annoying or disappointing thing. **2** N. Amer. a vagrant or loafer.

ORIGIN – perhaps from German *Bummler*, from *bummeln* 'stroll, loaf about'.

bump > *noun* **1** a light blow or a jolting collision. **2** a protuberance on a level surface. **3** a swelling on the skin caused by illness or injury. > *verb* **1** knock or run into with a jolt. **2** move with much jolting. **3** (**bump into**) meet by chance. **4** (**bump off**) informal murder. **5** (**bump up**) informal make larger or apparently larger.

DERIVATIVES – **bumpy** (**bumpier**, **bumpiest**) *adjective*.

SYNONYMS – *noun* **1** blow, collision, jolt, knock. **2** bulge, hump, knob, lump, protuberance. *verb* **1** bang, hit, knock, strike. **2** bounce, jerk, jolt.

COMBINATIONS – **bump-start** start (a motor vehicle) by pushing it in order to make the engine turn.

ORIGIN – perhaps Scandinavian.

bumper > *noun* **1** a protective horizontal bar across the front or back of a motor vehicle. **2** (also **bumper race**) Horse Racing a flat race for horses intended for future steeplechases. **3** archaic a glass of an alcoholic drink. > *adjective* exceptionally large or successful: *a bumper crop*.

COMBINATIONS – **bumper car** a dodgem.

bumph > *noun* variant spelling of BUMF.

bumpkin > *noun* an unsophisticated rustic.

SYNONYMS – rustic, peasant, yokel; N. Amer hillbilly.

ORIGIN – perhaps from Dutch *boomken* 'little tree' or *bommekijn* 'little barrel', used to denote a dumpy person.

bumptious > *adjective* irritatingly self-assertive or conceited.

DERIVATIVES – **bumptiously** *adverb* **bumptiousness** *noun*.

SYNONYMS – arrogant, cocky, conceited, pompous, self-important.

ANTONYMS – self-effacing.

ORIGIN – from BUMP.

bun > *noun* **1** a small cake or bread roll. **2** a hairstyle in which the hair is drawn into a tight coil at the back of the head. **3** (**buns**) N. Amer. informal a person's buttocks.

IDIOMS – **have a bun in the oven** informal be pregnant.

COMBINATIONS – **bunfight** Brit. informal, humorous a grand or official tea party or other function.

bunch > *noun* **1** a number of things growing or fastened together. **2** informal a group of people. **3** informal, chiefly N. Amer. a lot. **4** (**bunches**) a hairstyle in which the hair is tied back into two clumps at the back or on either side of the head. > *verb* collect or form into a bunch.

IDIOMS – **bunch of fives** Brit. informal a punch.

DERIVATIVES – **bunchy** *adjective*.

bund > *noun* (in India and Pakistan) an embankment or causeway.

ORIGIN – Urdu, from Persian.

bundle > *noun* **1** a collection of things or quantity of material tied or wrapped up together. **2** a set of nerves, muscles, or other fibres running in parallel. **3** informal a large amount of money. > *verb* **1** tie or roll up in or as if in a bundle. **2** (**be bundled up**) be dressed in many warm clothes. **3** informal push or carry forcibly.

IDIOMS – **a bundle of fun** (or **laughs**) informal, often ironic something extremely amusing or pleasant. **go a bundle on** Brit. informal be very keen on.

SYNONYMS – *noun* **1** bunch, clump, roll, sheaf, wad. *verb* **1** bale, bind together, roll up, tie together. **2** (**be bundled up**) be enveloped, be muffled up, be swathed, be wrapped up. **3** hustle, jostle, manhandle, push, shove.

ORIGIN – perhaps from Old English *byndelle*, 'a binding'.

bung¹ > *noun* a stopper for a hole in a container. > *verb* **1** close with a bung. **2** (**bung up**) block up.

ORIGIN – Dutch *bonghe*.

bung² Brit. informal > *verb* put or throw somewhere casually. > *noun* a bribe.

bung³ > *adjective* Austral./NZ informal ruined or useless.

IDIOMS – **go bung** fail completely.

ORIGIN – Yagara (an extinct Aboriginal language).

bungalow > *noun* a house with only one main storey.

ORIGIN – Hindi, 'belonging to Bengal'.

bungee /ˈbunji/ > *noun* a long nylon-cased rubber band used for securing luggage and in the sport of bungee jumping.

bungee jumping > *noun* the sport of leaping from a high place while secured by a bungee around the ankles.

DERIVATIVES – **bungee jump** *noun* **bungee jumper** *noun*.

bungle > *verb* **1** perform (a task) clumsily or incompetently. **2** be prone to making mistakes. > *noun* a mistake or failure.

DERIVATIVES – **bungler** *noun* **bungling** *adjective*.

SYNONYMS – *verb* **1** botch, mess up, mishandle, spoil.

bunion > *noun* a painful swelling on the big toe.

ORIGIN – Old French *buignon*, from *buigne* 'bump on the head'.

bunk¹ > *noun* a narrow shelf-like bed. > *verb* chiefly N. Amer. sleep in a bunk or improvised bed in shared quarters.

COMBINATIONS – **bunk bed** a piece of furniture consisting of two beds, one above the other. **bunkhouse** a building with sleeping accommodation for workers.

bunk² > *verb* (often **bunk off**) Brit. informal take time off from school or work without permission.

IDIOMS – **do a bunk** make a hurried departure.

bunk³ > *noun* informal, dated nonsense.

ORIGIN – abbreviation of BUNKUM.

bunker > *noun* **1** a large container for storing fuel. **2** an underground shelter for use in wartime. **3** a hollow filled with sand, used as an obstacle on a golf course. > *verb* refuel (a ship).

bunkum (also **buncombe**) > *noun* informal, dated nonsense.

ORIGIN – named after *Buncombe* County in North Carolina, which was once mentioned in a speech made by its congressman solely to please his constituents.

bunny > *noun* (pl. **bunnies**) informal **1** a child's term for a rabbit. **2** (also **bunny girl**) a club hostess or waitress wearing a skimpy costume with ears and a tail.

ORIGIN – from dialect *bun* 'squirrel, rabbit'.

bunny-hop > *verb* jump forward in a crouched position. > *noun* a jump of this kind.

Bunsen burner > *noun* a small adjustable gas burner used in laboratories.

ORIGIN – named after the German chemist Robert *Bunsen* (1811–99).

bunting[1] > *noun* a seed-eating songbird of a large group typically having brown streaked plumage and a boldly marked head.

bunting[2] > *noun* flags and streamers used as festive decorations.

bunyip /**bun**yip/ > *noun* Austral. **1** a mythical monster said to inhabit inland waterways. **2** an impostor or pretender.

ORIGIN – from an Aboriginal language.

buoy* /boy/ > *noun* an anchored float serving as a navigation mark or for mooring. > *verb* **1** keep afloat. **2** (often **be buoyed up**) cause to become or remain cheerful and confident. **3** cause (a price) to rise to or remain high. **4** mark with a buoy.

***SPELLING** – the *u* comes before the *o*: b*u*oy.

ORIGIN – probably from Dutch; the verb is from Spanish *boyar* 'to float'.

buoyant* > *adjective* **1** able to keep afloat. **2** cheerful and optimistic. **3** (of an economy or market) engaged in much activity.

DERIVATIVES – **buoyancy** *noun* **buoyantly** *adverb*.

***SPELLING** – *u* before *o*: b*u*oyant.

ORIGIN – from Spanish *boyar* 'to float'.

BUPA /**boo**pə/ > *abbreviation* British United Provident Association, a private health insurance organisation.

bur > *noun* see BURR.

burble > *verb* **1** make a continuous murmuring noise. **2** speak unintelligibly and at length. > *noun* **1** continuous murmuring noise. **2** rambling speech.

SYNONYMS – *verb* **1** babble, gurgle, murmur, purl.

burbot /**bur**bət/ > *noun* an elongated bottom-dwelling freshwater fish.

ORIGIN – Old French, *borbete*, probably from *borbe* 'mud, slime'.

burden > *noun* **1** a heavy load. **2** a cause of hardship, worry, or grief. **3** the main responsibility for a task. **4** a ship's carrying capacity. **5** the main theme of a text or argument. > *verb* **1** load heavily. **2** cause worry, hardship, or grief to.

IDIOMS – **burden of proof** the obligation to prove an assertion.

SYNONYMS – *noun* **1** cargo, load, weight. **2** care, problem, trouble, worry. **3** charge, duty, obligation, onus, responsibility. *verb* **2** grieve, oppress, trouble, worry.

burdensome > *adjective* oppressive; wearisome.

burdock > *noun* a herbaceous plant of the daisy family, with large leaves and prickly flowers.

ORIGIN – from BUR + DOCK[3].

bureau /**byoo**rō/ > *noun* (pl. **bureaux** or **bureaus**) **1** Brit. a writing desk with drawers and an angled top opening downwards to form a writing surface. **2** N. Amer. a chest of drawers. **3** an office for transacting particular business. **4** a government department.

ORIGIN – French, originally 'baize' (covering writing desks).

bureaucracy /byoo**rok**rəsi/ > *noun* (pl. **bureaucracies**) **1** a system of government in which most decisions are taken by state officials rather than by elected representatives. **2** excessively complicated administrative procedure.

DERIVATIVES – **bureaucratisation** (also **bureaucratization**) *noun* **bureaucratise** (also **bureaucratize**) *verb*.

bureaucrat > *noun* an official perceived as being overly concerned with procedural correctness.

DERIVATIVES – **bureaucratic** *adjective*.

bureau de change /byoorō dəsho**nzh**/ > *noun* (pl. **bureaux de change** pronunc. same) a place where one can exchange foreign money.

ORIGIN – French, 'office of exchange'.

burette /byoo**ret**/ (US also **buret**) > *noun* a graduated glass tube with a tap at one end, for delivering measured volumes of a liquid.

ORIGIN – French, from *buire* 'jug'.

burgeon /**bur**jən/ > *verb* grow or increase rapidly.

SYNONYMS – flourish, multiply, proliferate, thrive.

ANTONYMS – diminish, dwindle.

ORIGIN – Old French *bourgeonner* 'put out buds', from Latin *burra* 'wool'.

burger > *noun* a hamburger.

burgess > *noun* **1** Brit. archaic a citizen of a town or borough. **2** Brit. historical a Member of Parliament for a borough, corporate town, or university. **3** (in the US and historically in the UK) a magistrate or member of the governing body of a town.

ORIGIN – Old French *burgeis*, from Latin *burgus* 'castle, fort, fortified town'.

burgh /**burr**ə/ > *noun* archaic or Scottish a borough or chartered town.

ORIGIN – Scots form of BOROUGH.

burgher /**bur**gər/ > *noun* archaic a citizen of a town or city.

burglar > *noun* a person who commits burglary.

burglarise (also **burglarize**) > *verb* North American term for BURGLE.

burglary > *noun* (pl. **burglaries**) illegal entry into a building with intent to commit a crime such as theft.

ORIGIN – French *burglarie*, from *burgler* 'burglar'; related to Old French *burgier* 'pillage'.

burgle > *verb* commit burglary in (a building).

burgundy > *noun* (pl. **burgundiies**) **1** a red wine from Burgundy, a region of east central France. **2** a deep red colour.

burial > *noun* **1** the burying of a dead body. **2** Archaeology a grave or the remains found in it.

burin /**byoo**rin/ > *noun* **1** a steel tool used for engraving. **2** Archaeology a flint tool with a chisel point.

ORIGIN – French.

Burkinan /bur**kee**nən/ > *noun* a person from Burkina Faso, a country in western Africa. > *adjective* relating to Burkina Faso.

burl > *noun* **1** a lump in wool or cloth. **2** N. Amer. a rounded knotty growth on a tree.

ORIGIN – Old French *bourle* 'tuft of wool', from Latin *burra* 'wool'.

burlap /**bur**lap/ > *noun* coarse canvas woven from jute or hemp, used for sacking.

burlesque > *noun* **1** a comically exaggerated imitation, especially in a literary or dramatic work. **2** N. Amer. a variety show, typically including striptease. > *verb* (**burlesques**, **burlesqued**, **burlesquing**) parody.

SYNONYMS – *noun* **1** lampoon, mockery, parody, pastiche.

ORIGIN – Italian *burlesco*, from *burla* 'mockery'.

burly > *adjective* (**burlier**, **burliest**) (of a person) large and strong.

DERIVATIVES – **burliness** *noun*.

SYNONYMS – hefty, sturdy, thickset, well built.

ANTONYMS – slender.

ORIGIN – first used to mean 'dignified, imposing', probably from an Old English word meaning 'stately, fit for the bower'.

Burman > *noun* (pl. **Burmans**) & *adjective* another term for BURMESE.

Burmese > *noun* (pl. same) **1** a member of the largest ethnic group of Burma (Myanmar) in SE Asia. **2** a person from Burma. **3** the official language of Burma. **4** (also **Burmese cat**) a cat of a short-coated breed originating in Asia. > *adjective* relating to Burma or the Burmese.

burn[1] > *verb* (past and past participle **burned** or chiefly Brit. **burnt**) **1** (of a fire) flame or glow while consuming a fuel. **2** be or cause to be harmed or destroyed by fire. **3** use (a fuel) as a source of heat or energy. **4** (of the skin) become red and painful through exposure to the sun. **5** (**be burning with**) be entirely possessed by (a desire or emotion). **6** (**burn out**) become exhausted through overwork. **7** informal drive very fast. > *noun* an injury caused by burning.

IDIOMS – **burn one's boats** (or **bridges**) do something which makes turning back impossible. **burn the candle at both ends** go to bed late and get up early. **burn a hole in one's pocket** (of money) tempt one to spend it. **burn the midnight oil** work late into the night. **burn rubber** informal drive very quickly.

burn[2] > *noun* Scottish & N. English a small stream.

burner > *noun* **1** a part of a cooker, lamp,

etc. that emits a flame. **2** an apparatus for burning something.

IDIOMS – **on the back burner** US having low priority.

burning > *adjective* **1** very deeply felt. **2** of urgent interest and importance.

DERIVATIVES – **burningly** *adverb*.

SYNONYMS – **1** ardent, consuming, fervent, intense, passionate. **2** compelling, crucial, pressing, urgent.

burnish > *verb* polish by rubbing. > *noun* the shine on a polished surface.

DERIVATIVES – **burnisher** *noun*.

SYNONYMS – *verb* buff, polish, shine. *noun* lustre, patina, sheen.

ORIGIN – Old French *brunir* 'make brown', from *brun* 'brown'.

burnous /burnōōss/ (US also **burnoose**) > *noun* a long hooded cloak worn by Arabs.

ORIGIN – Arabic, from Greek *birros* 'cloak'.

burnout > *noun* **1** the reduction of a fuel or substance to nothing. **2** overheating of an electrical device or component. **3** physical or mental collapse.

burnt chiefly Brit. past and past participle of **BURN**[1].

burp informal > *verb* **1** belch. **2** make (a baby) belch after feeding. > *noun* a belch.

burr > *noun* **1** a whirring sound. **2** a rough pronunciation of the letter *r*, as in some regional accents. **3** (also **bur**) a prickly seed case or flower head that clings to clothing and animal fur. **4** (also **bur**) a rough edge left on a metal object by the action of a tool. **5** (also **bur**) a small drill used in woodworking, dentistry, or surgery. > *verb* **1** make a whirring sound. **2** speak with a burr. **3** form a rough edge on (metal).

ORIGIN – probably Scandinavian.

burrito /bəreetō/ > *noun* (pl. **burritos**) a Mexican dish consisting of a tortilla rolled round a filling of minced meat or beans.

ORIGIN – Latin American Spanish, from Spanish *burro* 'donkey'.

burro /bŏŏrō/ > *noun* (pl. **burros**) chiefly US a small donkey used as a pack animal.

ORIGIN – Spanish.

burrow > *noun* a hole or tunnel dug by a small animal as a dwelling. > *verb* **1** make a burrow. **2** hide underneath or delve into something.

DERIVATIVES – **burrower** *noun*.

SYNONYMS – *noun* earth, hole, sett, tunnel, warren. *verb* delve, dig, tunnel.

bursa /bursə/ > *noun* (pl. **bursae** /bursee/ or **bursas**) Anatomy a fluid-filled sac or cavity, especially at a joint.

ORIGIN – Latin, 'bag, purse'.

bursar > *noun* **1** chiefly Brit. a person who manages the financial affairs of a college or school. **2** Scottish a student holding a bursary.

ORIGIN – from Latin *bursa* 'bag, purse'.

bursary > *noun* (pl. **bursaries**) chiefly Brit. a grant, especially one awarded to a student.

bursitis /bursītiss/ > *noun* Medicine inflammation of a bursa, typically in a shoulder joint.

burst > *verb* (past and past participle **burst**) **1** break suddenly and violently apart. **2** be very full. **3** (**be bursting with**) feel (an irrepressible emotion or impulse). **4** move or be opened suddenly and forcibly. **5** (**burst into** or **out**) suddenly begin doing (something) as an expression of a strong feeling. > *noun* **1** an instance or the result of bursting. **2** a sudden brief outbreak of something violent or noisy. **3** a period of continuous effort.

IDIOMS – **burst someone's bubble** shatter someone's illusions.

SYNONYMS – *verb* **1** erupt, explode, fragment, rupture, shatter. *noun* **1** blast, breach, explosion, rupture. **2** eruption, explosion, flare-up, outbreak, outburst.

burton > *noun* (in phrase **go for a burton**) Brit. informal be ruined, destroyed, or killed.

ORIGIN – RAF slang: perhaps referring to *Burton* ale, from Burton-upon-Trent.

Burundian /bŏŏrōōndiən/ > *noun* a person from Burundi, a country in central Africa. > *adjective* relating to Burundi.

bury > *verb* (**buries**, **buried**) **1** put or hide underground. **2** place (a dead body) in the earth or a tomb. **3** cause to disappear or become unnoticeable. **4** (**bury oneself**) involve oneself deeply in something.

IDIOMS – **bury one's head in the sand** ignore unpleasant realities.

SYNONYMS – **2** entomb, inter, lay to rest. **3** conceal, cover, embed, hide, submerge.

bus > *noun* (pl. **buses**; US also **busses**) **1** a large motor vehicle carrying customers along a fixed route. **2** Computing a distinct set of conductors within a computer system, to which pieces of equipment may be connected in parallel. > *verb* (**buses** or **busses**, **bused** or **bussed**, **busing** or **bussing**) **1** transport or travel in a bus. **2** chiefly N. Amer. clear (dirty crockery) in a restaurant or cafeteria.

ORIGIN – shortening of **OMNIBUS**.

busby > *noun* (pl. **busbies**) a tall fur hat with a cloth flap hanging down on the right-hand side, worn by certain regiments of hussars and artillerymen.

NOTE – the term **busby** is often applied to the tall fur cap worn ceremonially by the guards at Buckingham Palace in London, but this is correctly called a **bearskin**.

bush[1] > *noun* **1** a shrub or clump of shrubs with stems of moderate length. **2** (**the bush**) (in Australia and Africa) wild or uncultivated country. > *verb* spread out into a thick clump.

COMBINATIONS – **bush telegraph** a rapid informal network by which information or gossip is spread.

ORIGIN – Old French *bois* 'wood'.

bush[2] > *noun* Brit. **1** a metal lining for a round hole, especially one in which an axle revolves. **2** a sleeve that protects an electric cable where it passes through a panel.

ORIGIN – Dutch *busse*.

bushbaby > *noun* (pl. **bushbabies**) a small nocturnal African primate with large eyes.

bushed > *adjective* informal **1** exhausted. **2** Austral./NZ lost in the bush. **3** Canadian & Austral./NZ mad.

bushel > *noun* **1** Brit. a measure of capacity equal to 8 gallons (equivalent to 36.4 litres). **2** US a measure of capacity equal to 64 US pints (equivalent to 35.2 litres).

ORIGIN – Old French *boissel*.

bushido /bōōsheedō/ > *noun* the code of honour and morals of the Japanese samurai.

ORIGIN – from Japanese words meaning 'samurai' and 'way'.

bushing > *noun* another term for BUSH[2].

Bushman > *noun* **1** a member of any of several aboriginal peoples of southern Africa. **2** old-fashioned term for SAN (the languages of these people). **3** (**bushman**) a person who lives or travels in the Australian bush.

bushranger > *noun* **1** US a person living far from civilisation. **2** Austral./NZ historical an outlaw living in the bush.

bushwhack > *verb* **1** N. Amer. & Austral./NZ live or travel in the bush. **2** N. Amer. & Austral./NZ work clearing scrub and felling trees. **3** N. Amer. ambush.

DERIVATIVES – **bushwhacker** *noun*.

bushwhacked > *adjective* informal exhausted.

bushy[1] > *adjective* (**bushier**, **bushiest**) **1** growing thickly. **2** covered with bush or bushes.

DERIVATIVES – **bushily** *adverb* **bushiness** *noun*.

SYNONYMS – **1** fluffy, luxuriant, thick.

ANTONYMS – sparse.

bushy[2] > *noun* (pl. **bushies**) Austral./NZ informal a person who lives in the bush.

business > *noun* **1** a person's regular occupation or trade. **2** work to be done or matters to be attended to. **3** (**one's business**) one's affair or concern. **4** commercial activity. **5** a commercial organisation. **6** informal a difficult or problematic matter. **7** (**the business**) informal an excellent person or thing. **8** Theatre actions other than dialogue in a play.

IDIOMS – **in business** informal able to begin something. **like nobody's business** informal extraordinarily. **mind one's own business** avoid meddling in other people's affairs.

SYNONYMS – **1** calling, craft, line of work, occupation, profession, trade. **2** concerns, duties, matters, tasks, work. **4** commerce, dealing, trading. **5** company, concern, enterprise, firm, organisation.

COMBINATIONS – **business card** a small card printed with one's name, occupation, and business address. **business end** informal the functional part of a tool or device. **businessman** (or **businesswoman**) a person who works in commerce, especially at executive level.

ORIGIN – Old English: the first sense was 'anxiety', then 'appointed task'; the sense 'state of being busy' was used until the 18th century but is now differentiated as *busyness*.

businesslike > *adjective* efficient and practical.

busk > *verb* play music in the street for voluntary donations from the public.

DERIVATIVES – **busker** noun.

ORIGIN – Italian *buscare* or Spanish *buscar* 'to seek': originally a nautical word meaning 'cruise about, tack'.

buskin > *noun* historical a calf-high or knee-high boot, as worn by ancient Athenian tragic actors.

ORIGIN – probably from Old French *bouzequin*.

busman > *noun* a bus driver.

IDIOMS – **a busman's holiday** leisure time spent doing the same thing that one does at work.

bust[1] > *noun* **1** a woman's breasts. **2** a sculpture of a person's head, shoulders, and chest.

ORIGIN – French *buste*, from Latin *bustum* 'tomb, sepulchral monument'.

bust[2] informal > *verb* (past and past participle **busted** or **bust**) **1** break, split, or burst. **2** chiefly N. Amer. strike violently. **3** chiefly N. Amer. raid, search, or arrest. **4** chiefly US demote (a soldier). > *noun* **1** a period of economic difficulty or depression. **2** a police raid. > *adjective* **1** damaged; broken. **2** bankrupt.

COMBINATIONS – **bust-up** a serious quarrel or fight.

ORIGIN – variant of **BURST**.

bustard /**bus**tərd/ > *noun* a large swift-running bird of open country.

ORIGIN – Old French *bistarde* and *oustarde*, from Latin *avis tarda* 'slow bird'.

buster > *noun* informal, chiefly N. Amer. a form of address to a man or boy.

bustier /**bus**tiay/ > *noun* a close-fitting strapless top for women.

ORIGIN – French.

bustle[1] > *verb* **1** move energetically or noisily. **2** (of a place) be full of activity. > *noun* excited activity and movement.

DERIVATIVES – **bustling** adjective.

SYNONYMS – *verb* **1** busy oneself, dash about, fuss, hurry, rush. **2** buzz, hum, pulse, whirl. *noun* commotion, flurry, hubbub, hurly-burly.

bustle[2] > *noun* historical a pad or frame worn under a skirt to puff it out behind.

busty > *adjective* (**bustier, bustiest**) informal (of a woman) having large breasts.

busy > *adjective* (**busier, busiest**) **1** having a great deal to do. **2** currently occupied with an activity. **3** full of activity; crowded. **4** excessively detailed or decorated. > *verb* (**busies, busied**) (**busy oneself**) keep occupied.

DERIVATIVES – **busily** adverb **busyness** noun.

SYNONYMS – *adjective* **1** hard-pressed, occupied, rushed, snowed under. **2** engaged, occupied, tied up. **3** bustling, crowded, packed, swarming, thronged. **4** cluttered, elaborate, fussy, intricate, ornate.

COMBINATIONS – **busybody** a meddling or prying person. **busy Lizzie** Brit. a plant with abundant red, pink, or white flowers.

but > *conjunction* **1** nevertheless. **2** on the contrary. **3** other than; otherwise than. **4** archaic without it being the case that. > *preposition* except; apart from. > *adverb* **1** only. **2** Austral./NZ, Scottish & N. English though, however: *he was a nice bloke but.* > *noun* an objection.

IDIOMS – **but for 1** except for. **2** if it were not for. **but then** on the other hand.

USAGE – on starting a sentence with **but**, see note at **AND**.

butane /**byoo**tayn/ > *noun* a flammable hydrocarbon gas present in petroleum and natural gas and used as a fuel.

ORIGIN – ultimately from Latin *butyrum* 'butter'.

butch > *adjective* informal aggressively or ostentatiously masculine.

ORIGIN – perhaps an abbreviation of **BUTCHER**.

butcher > *noun* **1** a person who cuts up and sells meat. **2** a person who slaughters animals for food. **3** a person who kills brutally or indiscriminately. > *verb* **1** slaughter or cut up (an animal) for food. **2** kill (someone) brutally. **3** ruin deliberately or through incompetence.

IDIOMS – **have** (or **take**) **a butcher's** Brit. informal have a look. [ORIGIN – *butcher's* from *butcher's hook*, rhyming slang for a 'look'.]

DERIVATIVES – **butchery** noun.

COMBINATIONS – **butcher bird** a shrike, so called from its habit of impaling prey on thorns.

ORIGIN – Old French *bochier*, from *boc* 'he-goat'.

butler > *noun* the chief manservant of a house.

ORIGIN – Old French *bouteillier* 'cup-bearer', from *bouteille* 'bottle'.

butt[1] > *verb* **1** hit with the head or horns. **2** (**butt in**) interrupt or intrude on a conversation or activity. **3** (**butt out**) N. Amer.

informal stop interfering. > *noun* a rough push with the head.

SYNONYMS – *verb* **2** (**butt in**) cut in, interject, interrupt, intrude.

ORIGIN – Old French *boter*.

butt[2] > *noun* **1** an object of criticism or ridicule. **2** a target or range in archery or shooting. **3** a position taken up by a person shooting grouse.

ORIGIN – Old French *but*.

butt[3] > *noun* **1** the thicker end of a tool or a weapon. **2** the square end of a plank or plate meeting the end or side of another. **3** the stub of a cigar or a cigarette. **4** N. Amer. informal a person's bottom. > *verb* **1** meet end to end. **2** join (pieces of timber) with the ends or sides flat against each other.

ORIGIN – from Dutch *bot* 'stumpy'.

butt[4] > *noun* a cask used for wine, ale, or water.

ORIGIN – Latin *buttis*.

butte /byoot/ > *noun* N. Amer. & technical an isolated hill with steep sides and a flat top.

ORIGIN – French, 'mound'.

butter > *noun* a pale yellow fatty substance made by churning cream and used as a spread or in cooking. > *verb* **1** spread with butter. **2** (**butter up**) informal flatter (someone).

IDIOMS – **look as if butter wouldn't melt in one's mouth** informal appear innocent while being the opposite.

COMBINATIONS – **butter bean** a lima bean of a variety with large flat white seeds. **buttercream** (also **butter icing**) a mixture of butter and icing sugar used as a filling or topping for a cake. **butterfat** the natural fat contained in milk and dairy products. **butterfingers** informal a clumsy person, especially one who fails to hold a catch. **buttermilk** the slightly sour liquid left after butter has been churned.

ORIGIN – Latin *butyrum*, from Greek *bouturon*.

buttercup > *noun* a common plant with bright yellow cup-shaped flowers.

butterfly > *noun* **1** an insect with two pairs of large, typically colourful wings held erect when at rest, feeding on nectar and active by day. **2** a showy or frivolous person. **3** (**butterflies**) informal a fluttering and nauseous sensation felt in the stomach when one is nervous. **4** a stroke in swimming in which both arms are raised and lifted forwards together.

WORDFINDER – caterpillar (*butterfly larva*), chrysalis (*butterfly pupa*), lepidopteran (*of butterflies and moths*), lepidopterist (*student or collector of butterflies and moths*).

COMBINATIONS – **butterfly bush** a buddleia. **butterfly effect** (in chaos theory) the phenomenon whereby a tiny localised change in a complex system can have large effects elsewhere. [ORIGIN – from the idea that a butterfly flapping its wings in Brazil might cause a tornado in Texas.] **butterfly nut** a wing nut.

butterscotch > *noun* a brittle yellow-brown sweet made with butter and brown sugar.

buttery¹ > *adjective* containing, tasting like, or covered with butter.

buttery² > *noun* (pl. **butteries**) Brit. a room in a college where food is kept and sold to students.
ORIGIN – Old French *boterie* 'butt-store'.

buttock > *noun* either of the two round fleshy parts of the human body that form the bottom.

button > *noun* **1** a small disc or knob sewn on to a garment to fasten it by being pushed through a buttonhole. **2** chiefly N. Amer. a decorative badge pinned to clothing. **3** a knob on a piece of electrical or electronic equipment which is pressed to operate it. **4** Fencing a knob fitted to the point of a foil to make it harmless. > *verb* **1** fasten or be fastened with buttons. **2** (**button up**) informal complete (something) satisfactorily.
IDIOMS – **button one's lip** informal stop or refrain from talking. **buttoned-up** informal formal and inhibited in manner. **on the button** informal, chiefly N. Amer. precisely.
DERIVATIVES – **buttoned** adjective.
COMBINATIONS – **button mushroom** a young unopened mushroom.
ORIGIN – Old French *bouton*.

buttonhole > *noun* **1** a slit made in a garment to receive a button for fastening. **2** Brit. a flower or spray worn in a lapel buttonhole. > *verb* informal accost and detain (someone) in conversation.

buttress /butriss/ > *noun* **1** a projecting support built against a wall. **2** a projecting portion of a hill or mountain. > *verb* **1** support with buttresses. **2** support or strengthen.
ORIGIN – from Old French *ars bouterez* 'thrusting arch'.

butty > *noun* (pl. **butties**) informal, chiefly N. English a sandwich.

butyl /byōōtīl/ > *noun* Chemistry the radical $-C_4H_9$, derived from butane.

buxom /buksəm/ > *adjective* (of a woman) attractively plump and large-breasted.
ORIGIN – from Old English *būgan* 'to bend' + -SOME¹: originally meaning 'compliant', later 'lively and good-tempered'.

buy > *verb* (**buys**, **buying**; past and past participle **bought**) **1** obtain in exchange for payment. **2** get (something) by sacrifice or great effort. **3** informal accept the truth of. > *noun* informal a purchase.

IDIOMS – **buy it** informal be killed. **buy time** delay an event temporarily so as to have longer to improve one's own position. **buy out 1** pay (someone) to give up an interest or share in something. **2** (**buy oneself out**) obtain one's release from the armed services by payment.
SYNONYMS – *verb* **1** acquire, gain, pay for, procure, purchase.
COMBINATIONS – **buyout** the purchase of a controlling share in a company, especially by its own managers.

buyer > *noun* **1** a person who buys. **2** a person employed to select and purchase stock for a business.
COMBINATIONS – **buyer's market** an economic situation in which goods or shares are plentiful and buyers can keep prices down.

buzz > *noun* **1** a low, continuous humming or murmuring sound. **2** the sound of a buzzer or telephone. **3** an atmosphere of excitement and activity. **4** informal a thrill. **5** informal a rumour. > *verb* **1** make a humming sound. **2** signal with a buzzer. **3** move quickly. **4** (**buzz off**) informal go away. **5** have an air of excitement or purposeful activity. **6** informal (of an aircraft) fly very close to (something) at high speed.
COMBINATIONS – **buzz saw** N. Amer. a circular saw. **buzzword** a technical word or phrase that has become fashionable.

buzzard /buzzərd/ > *noun* **1** a large bird of prey typically seen soaring in wide circles. **2** N. Amer. a vulture.
ORIGIN – Old French *busard*, from Latin *buteo* 'falcon'.

buzzer > *noun* an electrical device that makes a buzzing noise to attract attention.

BVM > *abbreviation* Blessed Virgin Mary.

bwana /bwaanə/ > *noun* (in East Africa) a form of address for a boss or master.
ORIGIN – Swahili.

by > *preposition* **1** through the agency or means of. **2** indicating a quantity or amount, or the size of a margin. **3** expressing multiplication, especially in dimensions. **4** indicating the end of a time period. **5** near to; beside. **6** past and beyond. **7** during. **8** according to. > *adverb* so as to go past. > *noun* (pl. **byes**) variant spelling of BYE¹.
IDIOMS – **by and by** before long. **by the by** (or **bye**) incidentally. **by and large** on the whole. [ORIGIN – a nautical use, describing the handling of a ship both towards and away from the direction the wind is blowing it.] **by oneself 1** alone. **2** unaided.

by- (also **bye-**) > *prefix* subordinate; incidental; secondary: *by-election*.

bye¹ > *noun* **1** the transfer of a competitor directly to the next round of a competition because they have no opponent assigned to them. **2** Cricket a run scored from a ball that passes the batsman without being hit.

bye² (also **bye-bye**) > *exclamation* informal goodbye.

by-election > *noun* Brit. an election held in a single constituency to fill a vacancy arising during a government's term of office.

Byelorussian /byellōrush'n/ > *adjective* & *noun* variant spelling of BELORUSSIAN.

bygone > *adjective* belonging to an earlier time.
IDIOMS – **let bygones be bygones** forget past differences and be reconciled.

by-law (also **bye-law**) > *noun* **1** Brit. a regulation made by a local authority or corporation. **2** a rule made by a company or society to control its members.

byline > *noun* **1** a line in a newspaper naming the writer of an article. **2** (also **byeline**) (in soccer) the part of the goal line to either side of the goal.

bypass > *noun* **1** a road passing round a town for through traffic. **2** a secondary channel or connection to allow a flow when the main one is closed or blocked. **3** a surgical operation to make an alternative passage to aid the circulation of blood. > *verb* go past or round.

byplay > *noun* subsidiary action in a drama.

by-product > *noun* **1** an incidental or secondary product made in the manufacture of something else. **2** an unintended but inevitable secondary result.

byre /bīr/ > *noun* Brit. a cowshed.

byroad > *noun* a minor road.

Byronic /bīronnik/ > *adjective* **1** characteristic of Lord Byron (1788–1824) or his poetry. **2** (of a man) alluringly dark, mysterious, and moody.

bystander > *noun* a person who is present at an event or incident but does not take part.

byte /bīt/ > *noun* Computing a group of binary digits (usually eight) operated on as a unit.
ORIGIN – based on BIT⁴ and BITE.

byway > *noun* a minor road or path.

byword > *noun* **1** a notable example or embodiment of something. **2** a proverb or saying.

Byzantine /bizantīn, bī-, bizzən-, -teen/ > *adjective* **1** relating to Byzantium (later called Constantinople, now Istanbul), its empire, or the Eastern Orthodox Church. **2** very complicated and detailed. **3** devious or underhand. > *noun* a citizen of Byzantium or the Byzantine Empire.

C

C¹ (also **c**) > *noun* (pl. **Cs** or **C's**) **1** the third letter of the alphabet. **2** denoting the third item in a set. **3** Music the first note of the diatonic scale of C major. **4** the Roman numeral for 100. [ORIGIN – abbreviation of Latin *centum* 'hundred'.]

C² > *abbreviation* **1** (**C.**) Cape. **2** Celsius or centigrade. **3** (in names of sports clubs) City. **4** (©) copyright. **5** (in Britain) Conservative. **6** Physics coulomb(s). > *symbol* the chemical element carbon.

c > *abbreviation* **1** Cricket caught by. **2** cent(s). **3** circa. **4** (**c.**) century or centuries. > *symbol* Physics the speed of light in a vacuum. [ORIGIN – probably from Latin *celeritas* 'swiftness'.]

CA > *abbreviation* California.

Ca > *symbol* the chemical element calcium.

ca. > *abbreviation* circa.

CAA > *abbreviation* (in the UK) Civil Aviation Authority.

CAB > *abbreviation* Citizens' Advice Bureau.

cab > *noun* **1** (also **taxi cab**) a taxi. **2** the driver's compartment in a truck, bus, or train. **3** historical a horse-drawn vehicle for public hire.

ORIGIN – abbreviation of **CABRIOLET**.

cabal /kəbal/ > *noun* a secret political clique or faction.

SYNONYMS – caucus, cell, clique, coterie, faction, sect.

ORIGIN – from Latin *cabala* 'Kabbalah' (its original sense in English).

Cabala > *noun* variant spelling of **KABBALAH**.

cabaret /kabbəray/ > *noun* **1** entertainment held in a nightclub or restaurant while the audience sit at tables. **2** a nightclub or restaurant where such entertainment is performed.

ORIGIN – Old French, 'wooden structure, inn'.

cabbage > *noun* **1** a vegetable with thick green or purple leaves surrounding a spherical heart or head of young leaves. **2** Brit. informal, derogatory a person with a very dull or limited life. **3** Brit. informal, offensive a person who is severely handicapped or brain-damaged.

COMBINATIONS – **cabbage white** a white butterfly whose caterpillars are pests of cabbages and related plants.

ORIGIN – Old French *caboche* 'head'.

Cabbala > *noun* variant spelling of **KABBALAH**.

cabbalistic /kabbəlistik/ > *adjective* relating to or associated with mystical interpretations or esoteric doctrine.

SYNONYMS – arcane, esoteric, mystical, occult.

cabby (also **cabbie**) > *noun* (pl. **cabbies**) informal a taxi driver.

caber /kaybər/ > *noun* a roughly trimmed tree trunk used in the Scottish Highland sport of tossing the caber.

ORIGIN – Scottish Gaelic *cabar* 'pole'.

Cabernet Franc /kabbərnay froN/ > *noun* a variety of black wine grape grown chiefly in parts of the Loire Valley and NE Italy.

Cabernet Sauvignon /kabbərnay sōvinyoN/ > *noun* a variety of black wine grape originally from the Bordeaux area of France.

cabin > *noun* **1** a private room or compartment on a ship. **2** the passenger compartment in an aircraft. **3** a small wooden shelter or house.

COMBINATIONS – **cabin boy** chiefly historical a boy employed to wait on a ship's officers or passengers. **cabin class** the intermediate class of accommodation on a passenger ship. **cabin cruiser** a motor boat with living accommodation. **cabin fever** informal, chiefly N. Amer. depression and irritability resulting from long confinement indoors during the winter.

ORIGIN – Old French *cabane*, from Latin *capanna*.

cabinet > *noun* **1** a cupboard with drawers or shelves for storing or displaying articles. **2** a wooden box or piece of furniture housing a radio, television, or speaker. **3** a committee of senior ministers responsible for controlling government policy.

DERIVATIVES – **cabinetry** *noun*.

COMBINATIONS – **cabinetmaker** a skilled joiner who makes furniture or similar high-quality woodwork.

ORIGIN – diminutive of **CABIN**; sense 3 derives from an obsolete sense 'small private room'.

cable > *noun* **1** a thick rope of wire or hemp. **2** an insulated wire or wires for transmitting electricity or telecommunication signals. **3** a cablegram. **4** the chain of a ship's anchor. **5** Nautical a length of 200 yards (182.9 m) or (in the US) 240 yards (219.4 m). > *verb* dated send a cablegram to.

COMBINATIONS – **cable car** a small carriage suspended on a continuous moving cable and travelling up and down a mountainside. **cable stitch** a combination of knitted stitches resembling twisted rope.

cable television a system in which television programmes are transmitted to the sets of subscribers by cable.

ORIGIN – Old French *chable*, from Latin *capulum* 'halter'.

cablegram > *noun* historical a telegraph message sent by cable.

cabochon /kabbəshon/ > *noun* a gem that is polished but not given facets.

ORIGIN – French, 'small head'.

caboodle > *noun* (in phrase **the whole caboodle** or **the whole kit and caboodle**) informal the whole number or quantity of people or things in question.

caboose > *noun* **1** N. Amer. a wagon with accommodation for the crew on a freight train. **2** archaic a kitchen on a ship's deck.

ORIGIN – Dutch *kabuis*.

cabriole leg > *noun* a kind of curved leg characteristic of Chippendale and Queen Anne furniture.

ORIGIN – French, 'light leap': so named from its resemblance to the front leg of a leaping animal.

cabriolet /kabriōlay/ > *noun* **1** a car with a roof that folds down. **2** a light two-wheeled carriage with a hood, drawn by one horse.

ORIGIN – French, from *cabriole* 'light leap': so named because of the carriage's motion.

cacao /kəkayō/ > *noun* bean-like seeds from a tropical American tree, from which cocoa, cocoa butter, and chocolate are made.

ORIGIN – Nahuatl.

cache /kash/ > *noun* **1** a hidden store of things. **2** Computing an auxiliary memory from which high-speed retrieval is possible. > *verb* store in a cache.

ORIGIN – French, from *cacher* 'to hide'.

cache-sexe /kashseks/ > *noun* (pl. pronunc. same) a covering for a person's genitals, worn by erotic dancers or primitive peoples.

ORIGIN – French, from *cacher* 'to hide' and *sexe* 'genitals'.

cachet /kashay/ > *noun* **1** prestige. **2** a distinguishing mark or seal. **3** a flat capsule enclosing a dose of unpleasant-tasting medicine.

ORIGIN – French, from *cacher* in the sense 'to press'.

cachexia /kəkeksiə/ > *noun* Medicine weakness and wasting of the body due to severe chronic illness.

DERIVATIVES – **cachectic** *adjective*.

ORIGIN – Greek *kakhexia*, from *kakos* 'bad' + *hexis* 'habit'.

cacique /kəseek/ > *noun* **1** (in Latin America or the Spanish-speaking Caribbean) a native chief. **2** (in Spain or Latin America) a local political boss.

ORIGIN – Taino (an extinct Caribbean language).

cack > *noun* Brit. informal excrement.
ORIGIN – Old English, based on Latin *cacare* 'defecate'.

cack-handed > *adjective* Brit. informal **1** inept; clumsy. **2** derogatory left-handed.

cackle > *noun* a raucous clucking cry, as made by a hen or goose. > *verb* **1** give a cackle. **2** talk inconsequentially and at length.
IDIOMS – **cut the cackle** informal stop talking aimlessly and come to the point.

cacophony /kəkoffəni/ > *noun* (pl. **cacophonies**) a harsh discordant mixture of sounds.
DERIVATIVES – **cacophonous** *adjective*.
SYNONYMS – din, hubbub, noise, racket.
ORIGIN – Greek *kakophōnia*, from *kakophōnos* 'ill-sounding'.

cactus /kaktəss/ > *noun* (pl. **cacti** /kaktī/ or **cactuses**) a succulent plant with a thick fleshy stem bearing spines but no leaves.
WORDFINDER – cholla, opuntia, peyote, prickly pear, saguaro (*kinds of cactus*); mescaline (*drug from a Mexican cactus*).
ORIGIN – Greek *kaktos* 'cardoon'.

cad > *noun* dated or humorous a man who behaves dishonourably, especially towards a woman.
DERIVATIVES – **caddish** *adjective*.
ORIGIN – abbreviation of **CADDIE** or **CADET**: originally denoting a passenger picked up by the driver of a horse-drawn coach for personal profit.

cadaver /kədaavər, kədavvər/ > *noun* Medicine or literary a corpse.
ORIGIN – Latin, from *cadere* 'to fall'.

cadaverous > *adjective* resembling a corpse in being very pale, thin, or bony.
SYNONYMS – emaciated, gaunt, haggard, pallid, skeletal.
ANTONYMS – corpulent, robust.

caddie (also **caddy**) > *noun* (pl. **caddies**) a person who carries a golfer's clubs and provides other assistance during a match. > *verb* (**caddied**, **caddying**) work as a caddie.
ORIGIN – from French **CADET**: a Scots term denoting a gentleman who joined the army without a commission, later coming to mean 'odd-job man'.

caddis /kaddis/ (also **caddis fly**) > *noun* a small moth-like insect whose aquatic larvae build protective cases of sticks, stones, etc.

caddy > *noun* (pl. **caddies**) a small storage container, especially for tea.
ORIGIN – from earlier *catty*, denoting a unit of weight of 1⅓ lb (0.61 kg), from Malay.

cadence /kayd'nss/ > *noun* **1** a modulation or inflection of the voice. **2** Music a sequence of notes or chords comprising the close of a musical phrase. **3** rhythm.
DERIVATIVES – **cadenced** *adjective*.

wordpower facts
Cadence
Cadence, with its connotations of sweet music, is an unlikely relative of the word **cadaver**. However, both come from the same Latin verb, *cadere*, meaning 'to fall': the shared notion is that of the voice or a note 'falling' and of the body 'fallen' in death. Several other words, similarly wide-ranging in meaning, also come from *cadere*, including **accident**, **cadenza**, **case**, **chance**, **chute**, and **decay**.

cadenza /kədenzə/ > *noun* Music a virtuoso solo passage in a concerto or other work, typically near the end.
ORIGIN – Italian.

cadet > *noun* **1** a young trainee in the armed services or police. **2** formal or archaic a younger son or daughter.
DERIVATIVES – **cadetship** *noun*.
ORIGIN – French, from Gascon dialect *capdet* 'little head', from Latin *caput* 'head'; the notion 'little head' gave rise to that of 'younger, junior'.

cadge > *verb* informal ask for or obtain (something to which one is not entitled).
DERIVATIVES – **cadger** *noun*.
ORIGIN – from the noun *cadger*, in northern English and Scottish meaning 'itinerant dealer'.

cadmium /kadmiəm/ > *noun* a silvery-white metallic chemical element resembling zinc.
COMBINATIONS – **cadmium yellow** a bright yellow pigment containing cadmium sulphide.
ORIGIN – from Latin *cadmia* 'calamine': so named because it is found with calamine in zinc ore.

cadre /kaadər/ > *noun* **1** a small group of people trained for a particular purpose or profession. **2** /also kaydər/ a group of activists in a revolutionary organisation.
SYNONYMS – **1** caucus, corps, section, squad, unit. **2** arm, cell, faction.
ORIGIN – French, from Latin *quadrus* 'square'.

caduceus /kədyoōsiəss/ > *noun* (pl. **caducei** /kədyoōsi-ī/) an ancient Greek or Roman herald's wand, typically having two serpents twined round it, carried by the messenger god Hermes or Mercury.
ORIGIN – Latin, from Greek *kērux* 'herald'.

caecilian /sisilliən/ > *noun* a burrowing worm-like amphibian with poorly developed eyes and no limbs.
ORIGIN – from Latin *caecilia* 'slow-worm'.

caecum /seekəm/ (US **cecum**) > *noun* (pl. **caeca**) Anatomy a pouch connected to the junction of the small and large intestines.

DERIVATIVES – **caecal** *adjective*.
ORIGIN – from Latin *intestinum caecum* 'blind gut'.

Caerns. > *abbreviation* Caernarfonshire.

Caerphilly /kairfilli, kər-/ > *noun* a kind of mild white cheese, originally made in Caerphilly in Wales.

Caesar* /seezər/ > *noun* a title of Roman emperors, especially those from Augustus to Hadrian.
*SPELLING – -ae-, not -ea-: C*ae*sar.
ORIGIN – family name of the Roman statesman Gaius Julius *Caesar*.

Caesarean /sizairiən/ (also **Caesarian**) > *adjective* relating to Julius Caesar or the Caesars. > *noun* a Caesarean section.
COMBINATIONS – **Caesarean section** a surgical operation for delivering a child by cutting through the wall of the mother's abdomen. [ORIGIN – from the story that Julius Caesar was delivered by this method.]

caesium /seeziəm/ (US **cesium**) > *noun* a soft, silvery, extremely reactive metallic chemical element.
ORIGIN – from Latin *caesius* 'greyish-blue' (because it has characteristic lines in the blue part of the spectrum).

caesura /sizyoōrə/ > *noun* **1** (in Greek and Latin verse) a break between words within a metrical foot. **2** (in modern verse) a pause near the middle of a line.
ORIGIN – Latin, from *caedere* 'cut'.

cafard /kafaar/ > *noun* melancholia.
ORIGIN – French.

cafe /kaffay/ > *noun* **1** a small restaurant selling light meals and drinks. **2** N. Amer. a bar or nightclub.
COMBINATIONS – **cafe curtain** a curtain covering the lower half of a window. **cafe society** people who spend a lot of time in fashionable restaurants and nightclubs.
ORIGIN – French, 'coffee or coffee house'.

cafeteria > *noun* a self-service restaurant.
ORIGIN – Latin American Spanish, 'coffee shop'.

cafetière /kaffətyair/ > *noun* a coffee pot containing a plunger with which the grounds are pushed to the bottom before the coffee is poured.
ORIGIN – French.

caffeine /kaffeen/ > *noun* a substance which is found in tea and coffee plants and is a stimulant of the central nervous system.
DERIVATIVES – **caffeinated** *adjective*.
ORIGIN – French *caféine*, from *café* 'coffee'.

caftan > *noun* variant spelling of **KAFTAN**.

cage > *noun* **1** a structure of bars or wires in which birds or other animals are confined. **2** any similar structure, in particular the compartment in a lift. > *verb* confine in a cage or other enclosure.
ORIGIN – Old French, from Latin *cavea*.

cagey (also **cagy**) > *adjective* informal uncommunicative owing to caution or suspicion.
DERIVATIVES – **cagily** adverb **caginess** (also **cageyness**) noun.

cagoule /kəgōōl/ (also **kagoul**) > *noun* a lightweight waterproof jacket with a hood.
ORIGIN – French, 'cowl'.

cahoots /kəhōōts/ > *plural noun* (in phrase **in cahoots**) informal colluding or conspiring together secretly.

caiman /kaymən/ (also **cayman**) > *noun* a tropical American reptile similar to an alligator.
ORIGIN – Carib.

Cain > *noun* (in phrase **raise Cain**) informal create trouble or a commotion.
ORIGIN – from the name of *Cain*, eldest son of Adam and Eve and murderer of his brother Abel (Book of Genesis, chapter 4).

caique /kīeek/ > *noun* **1** a light rowing boat used on the Bosporus. **2** a small eastern Mediterranean sailing ship.
ORIGIN – Turkish *kayık*.

cairn > *noun* **1** a mound of rough stones built as a memorial or landmark. **2** (also **cairn terrier**) a small breed of terrier with a shaggy coat.
ORIGIN – Scottish Gaelic *carn*.

caisson /kays'n, kəsōōn/ > *noun* **1** a large watertight chamber in which underwater construction work may be carried out. **2** a vessel or structure used as a gate across the entrance of a dry dock or basin.
ORIGIN – French, 'large chest'.

caitiff /kaytif/ > *noun* archaic a contemptible or cowardly person.
ORIGIN – Old French *caitif* 'captive', from Latin *captivus*.

cajole /kəjōl/ > *verb* persuade (someone) to do something by sustained coaxing or flattery.
DERIVATIVES – **cajolery** noun.
SYNONYMS – coax, inveigle, persuade, talk into.
ORIGIN – French *cajoler*.

Cajun /kayjən/ > *noun* a member of a French-speaking community in the bayou areas of southern Louisiana. > *adjective* relating to the Cajuns.
ORIGIN – an alteration of *Acadian* 'relating to Acadia', a former French colony in Canada (now Nova Scotia).

cake > *noun* **1** an item of soft, sweet food made from baking a mixture of flour, fat, eggs, and sugar. **2** a flat, round item of savoury food that is baked or fried. **3** the amount of money available for sharing: *a fair slice of the education cake.* > *verb* (of a thick or sticky substance) cover and become encrusted on.
IDIOMS – **cakes and ale** dated merrymaking. **a piece of cake** informal something easily achieved. **sell like hot cakes** informal be sold

quickly and in large quantities. **take the cake** see *take the biscuit* at BISCUIT. **you can't have your cake and eat it (too)** proverb you can't enjoy both of two desirable but mutually exclusive alternatives.
COMBINATIONS – **cake flour** N. Amer. plain flour. **cakehole** Brit. informal a person's mouth.
ORIGIN – Scandinavian.

cakewalk > *noun* **1** informal a very easy task. **2** a strutting dance popular at the end of the 19th century, developed from an American black contest in graceful walking which had a cake as a prize.

Cal > *abbreviation* large calorie(s).

cal > *abbreviation* small calorie(s).

calabash /kaləbash/ > *noun* a water container, tobacco pipe, or other object made from the dried shell of a gourd.
ORIGIN – Spanish *calabaza*, perhaps from a Persian word meaning 'melon'.

calaboose /kaləbōōss/ > *noun* US informal a prison.
ORIGIN – Spanish *calabozo* 'dungeon'.

calabrese /kaləbreez/ > *noun* a bright green variety of broccoli.
ORIGIN – Italian, meaning 'from Calabria', a region of SW Italy.

calamari /kaləmaari/ (also **calamares** /kaləmaarayz/) > *plural noun* squid served as food.
ORIGIN – Italian, from Greek *kalamos* 'pen' (with reference to the squid's long tapering internal shell and its ink).

calamine /kaləmīn/ > *noun* a pink powder consisting of zinc carbonate and ferric oxide, used to make a soothing lotion or ointment.
ORIGIN – Latin *calamina*, from Greek *kadmeia gē* 'Cadmean earth', from the name of *Cadmus*, the legendary founder of Thebes.

calamity > *noun* (pl. **calamities**) an event causing great and sudden damage or distress.
DERIVATIVES – **calamitous** adjective **calamitously** adverb.
SYNONYMS – cataclysm, catastrophe, disaster, tragedy.
ORIGIN – Latin *calamitas*.

calando /kəlandō/ > *adverb* Music gradually decreasing in speed and volume.
ORIGIN – Italian, 'slackening'.

calash > *noun* variant spelling of CALECHE.

calcareous /kalkairiəss/ > *adjective* containing calcium carbonate; chalky.
ORIGIN – Latin *calcarius*, from *calx* 'lime'.

calceolaria /kalsiəlairiə/ > *noun* a South American plant with brightly coloured slipper- or pouch-shaped flowers.
ORIGIN – Latin *calceolus* 'little shoe'.

calciferol /kalsiffərol/ > *noun* vitamin D_2, a substance produced naturally in the skin by

sunlight and essential for the deposition of calcium in bones.

calciferous /kalsiffərəss/ > *adjective* containing or producing calcium salts, especially calcium carbonate.

calcify /kalsifī/ > *verb* (**calcifies, calcified**) harden by deposition of or conversion into calcium carbonate or other calcium salts.
DERIVATIVES – **calcification** noun.

calcine /kalsīn, kalsin/ > *verb* reduce, oxidise, or dry (a substance) by roasting or strong heat.
DERIVATIVES – **calcination** noun.
ORIGIN – Latin *calcinare*, from *calx* 'lime'.

calcite /kalsīt/ > *noun* a white or colourless mineral consisting of calcium carbonate.

calcium > *noun* a soft grey reactive metallic chemical element.
COMBINATIONS – **calcium carbonate** a white insoluble compound occurring naturally as chalk, limestone, marble, and calcite, and forming mollusc shells.
ORIGIN – from Latin *calx* 'lime'.

calculate > *verb* **1** determine mathematically. **2** (**calculate on**) include as an essential element in one's plans. **3** intend (an action) to have a particular effect.
DERIVATIVES – **calculable** adjective.
SYNONYMS – **1** compute, determine, reckon, quantify, work out. **2** (**calculate on**) bank on, bargain on, expect, reckon on. **3** aim, design, intend, plan.
ORIGIN – Latin *calculare* 'count', from *calculus* 'small pebble (as used on an abacus)'.

calculated > *adjective* done with awareness of the likely consequences.
DERIVATIVES – **calculatedly** adverb.
SYNONYMS – deliberate, intentional, planned, premeditated.
ANTONYMS – unintentional.

calculating > *adjective* selfishly scheming.
DERIVATIVES – **calculatingly** adverb.
SYNONYMS – conniving, devious, mercenary, scheming, sly, wily.
ANTONYMS – ingenuous.

calculation > *noun* **1** a mathematical determination of quantity or extent. **2** an assessment of the risks or effects of a course of action.
SYNONYMS – **1** computation, reckoning, sum. **2** assessment, estimation, evaluation, projection.

calculator > *noun* something used for making mathematical calculations, in particular a small electronic device with a keyboard and a visual display.

calculus /kalkjooləss/ > *noun* **1** (pl. **calculuses**) the branch of mathematics concerned with finding derivatives and integrals of functions by methods based on the summation of infinitesimal differences. **2** (pl. **calculi** /kalkyoolī/) Medicine a stone formed by deposition of minerals in the kidney, gall bladder, or other organ.

ORIGIN – Latin, 'small pebble' (as used on an abacus).

caldera /kaal**dair**ə/ > *noun* a large volcanic crater, especially one formed by the collapse of the volcano's mouth.

ORIGIN – Spanish, from Latin *caldaria* 'boiling pot'.

caldron > *noun* chiefly US variant spelling of CAULDRON.

caleche /kə**lesh**/ (also **calash**) > *noun* historical 1 a light low-wheeled carriage with a removable folding hood. 2 a woman's hooped silk hood.

ORIGIN – French, from Polish *koło* 'wheel'.

Caledonian /kali**dō**niən/ > *adjective* relating to Scotland or the Scottish Highlands.

ORIGIN – from *Caledonia*, the Latin name for northern Britain.

calendar /**kal**indər/ > *noun* 1 a chart or series of pages showing the days, weeks, and months of a particular year. 2 a system by which the beginning, length, and subdivisions of the year are fixed. 3 a list or schedule of special days, events, or activities.

WORDFINDER – Gregorian calendar (*introduced 1582 (1752 in England and Wales) and used today*), Julian calendar (*used before 1582*).

DERIVATIVES – **calendrical** /kal**en**drik'l/ *adjective*.

ORIGIN – Latin *kalendarium* 'account book', from *kalendae* (see CALENDS).

calender /**kal**indər/ > *noun* a machine in which cloth or paper is pressed by rollers to glaze or smooth it. > *verb* press in such a machine.

ORIGIN – French *calendre*.

calends /**kal**endz/ (also **kalends**) > *plural noun* the first day of the month in the ancient Roman calendar.

ORIGIN – Latin *kalendae*, *calendae* 'first day of the month' (when the order of days was proclaimed and debts became due).

calendula /kə**len**dyoolə/ > *noun* a plant of a family that includes the common marigold.

ORIGIN – Latin, from *calendae* (see CALENDS): perhaps because it flowers for most of the year.

calf[1] > *noun* (pl. **calves**) 1 a young bovine animal, especially a domestic cow or bull in its first year. 2 the young of some other large mammals, such as elephants. 3 a floating piece of ice detached from an iceberg.

COMBINATIONS – **calf love** puppy love.

calf[2] > *noun* (pl. **calves**) the fleshy part at the back of a person's leg below the knee.

ORIGIN – Old Norse *kálfi*.

calibrate /**kal**ibrayt/ > *verb* 1 mark (a gauge or instrument) with a standard scale of readings. 2 compare the readings of (an instrument) with those of a standard. 3 adjust (experimental results) to take external factors into account or to allow comparison with other data.

DERIVATIVES – **calibration** *noun* **calibrator** *noun*.

ORIGIN – from CALIBRE + -ATE[2].

calibre /**kal**ibər/ (US **caliber**) > *noun* 1 quality of character or level of ability. 2 the internal diameter of a gun barrel, or the diameter of a bullet or shell.

SYNONYMS – 1 ability, capability, proficiency, quality, stature.

ORIGIN – first used in the sense 'social standing': from French, perhaps from an Arabic word meaning 'mould'.

calico /**kal**ikō/ > *noun* (pl. **calicoes** or US also **calicos**) 1 Brit. a type of plain white or unbleached cotton cloth. 2 N. Amer. printed cotton fabric. > *adjective* N. Amer. (of an animal) multicoloured or piebald.

ORIGIN – alteration of *Calicut*, a seaport in SW India where the fabric originated.

Californian > *noun* a person from California. > *adjective* of or relating to California.

californium /kali**for**niəm/ > *noun* a radioactive metallic chemical element made by high-energy atomic collisions.

ORIGIN – named after *California* University (where it was first made).

caliper /**kal**ipər/ (also **calliper**) > *noun* 1 (also **calipers**) a measuring instrument with two hinged legs and in-turned or out-turned points. 2 a motor-vehicle or bicycle brake consisting of two or more hinged components. 3 a metal support for a person's leg.

ORIGIN – probably an alteration of CALIBRE.

caliph /**kay**lif/ > *noun* historical the chief Muslim civil and religious ruler, regarded as the successor of Muhammad.

DERIVATIVES – **caliphate** *noun*.

ORIGIN – Arabic, 'deputy of God'.

calisthenics > *plural noun* US spelling of CALLISTHENICS.

calix > *noun* variant spelling of CALYX.

calk > *noun & verb* US spelling of CAULK.

call > *verb* 1 cry out to (someone) in order to summon them or attract their attention. 2 telephone. 3 (of a bird or animal) make its characteristic cry. 4 pay a brief visit. 5 give a specified name or description to. 6 fix a date or time for (a meeting, election, or strike). 7 predict the result of (a vote or contest). 8 bring (a witness) into court to give evidence. 9 inspire or urge to do something. > *noun* 1 a cry made as a summons or to attract attention. 2 a telephone communication. 3 the characteristic cry of a bird or animal. 4 a summons. 5 a brief visit. 6 (**call for**) demand or need for: *there is little call for antique furniture.* 7 a shout by an official in a game indicating that the ball has gone out of play or that a rule has been breached.

IDIOMS – **call for** require; demand. **call in** require payment of (a loan). **call off** cancel (an event or agreement). **call on** turn to as a source of help. **call of nature** euphemistic a need to urinate or defecate. **call the shots** (or **tune**) take the initiative in deciding how something should be done. **call up** 1 summon (someone) to serve in the army or to play in a team. 2 bring (something stored) into use. **on call** 1 available to provide a professional service if necessary. 2 (of money lent) repayable on demand.

DERIVATIVES – **caller** *noun*.

SYNONYMS – *verb* 1 cry out, exclaim, shout, yell. 4 drop by, look in, pop in, visit. 5 designate, dub, label, name, style. 6 announce, convene, declare, summon. *noun* 1 cry, exclamation, shout, yell.

COMBINATIONS – **call centre** an office in which large numbers of telephone calls, especially from customers, are handled for an organisation. **call girl** a female prostitute who accepts appointments by telephone. **calling card** chiefly N. Amer. a visiting card or business card. **call sign** (also **call signal**) a message or tune broadcast on radio to identify the broadcaster or transmitter.

calligraphy > *noun* decorative handwriting or handwritten lettering.

DERIVATIVES – **calligrapher** *noun* **calligraphic** *adjective*.

ORIGIN – Greek *kalligraphia*, from *kalligraphos* 'person who writes beautifully'.

calling > *noun* 1 a profession or occupation. 2 a vocation.

calliope /kə**līə**pi/ > *noun* chiefly historical an American keyboard instrument resembling an organ but with the notes produced by steam whistles.

ORIGIN – from *Calliope*, the Greek Muse of epic poetry (literally 'beautiful-voiced').

calliper > *noun* variant spelling of CALIPER.

callipygian /kalipi**ji**ən/ (also **callipygean**) > *adjective* literary having well-shaped buttocks.

ORIGIN – from Greek *kallos* 'beauty' + *pūgē* 'buttocks'.

callisthenics /kaliss**thenn**iks/ (US **calisthenics**) > *plural noun* gymnastic exercises to achieve bodily fitness and grace of movement.

ORIGIN – from Greek *kallos* 'beauty' + *sthenos* 'strength'.

callosity /kə**loss**iti/ > *noun* (pl. **callosities**) technical a callus.

callous > *adjective* insensitive and cruel. > *noun* variant spelling of CALLUS.

DERIVATIVES – **callously** *adverb* **callousness** *noun*.

SYNONYMS – *adjective* cold, cruel, heartless, insensitive, unfeeling.

ANTONYMS – kind, sensitive.

ORIGIN – from Latin *callosus* 'hard-skinned'.

callow > *adjective* (of a young person) inexperienced and immature.

DERIVATIVES – **callowly** *adverb* **callowness** *noun*.

SYNONYMS – green, immature, inexperienced, naive.

ANTONYMS – experienced, mature.

ORIGIN – Old English, 'bald', probably from Latin *calvus* 'bald', later 'unfledged'.

callus /kaləss/ (also **callous**) > *noun* **1** a thickened and hardened part of the skin or soft tissue. **2** Botany a hard formation of tissue formed over a wound.

DERIVATIVES – **callused** *adjective*.

ORIGIN – Latin, 'hardened skin'.

calm > *adjective* **1** not showing or feeling nervousness, anger, or other emotions. **2** peaceful and undisturbed. > *noun* **1** a calm state or period. **2** (**calms**) an area of the sea without wind. > *verb* (often **calm down**) make or become tranquil and quiet.

DERIVATIVES – **calmly** *adverb* **calmness** *noun*.

SYNONYMS – *adjective* **1** collected, composed, equable, steady, unruffled, untroubled. **2** peaceful, serene, still, tranquil, undisturbed. *noun* **1** composure, peacefulness, quietude, serenity, stillness, tranquillity. *verb* lull, pacify, quieten, soothe.

ANTONYMS – *adjective* agitated, disturbed. *verb* disturb, trouble.

ORIGIN – from Greek *kauma* 'heat of the day'.

calmative > *adjective* having a sedative effect. > *noun* a calmative drug.

calomel /kaləmel/ > *noun* mercurous chloride, a white powder formerly used as a laxative.

ORIGIN – from Greek *kalos* 'beautiful' + *melas* 'black' (perhaps because it was originally obtained from a black mixture of mercury and mercuric chloride).

Calor gas /kalər/ > *noun* Brit. trademark liquefied butane stored under pressure in portable containers, used as a substitute for mains gas.

ORIGIN – from Latin *calor* 'heat'.

caloric /kəlorrik, kalərik/ > *adjective* chiefly N. Amer. or technical relating to heat; calorific.

calorie > *noun* (pl. **calories**) **1** (also **large calorie**) a unit of energy, often used in specifying the energy value of foods, equal to the energy needed to raise the temperature of 1 kilogram of water through 1 °C (4.1868 kilojoules). **2** (also **small**

calorie) a unit of energy equal to one-thousandth of a large calorie.

ORIGIN – French, from Latin *calor* 'heat'.

calorific > *adjective* chiefly Brit. **1** relating to the amount of energy contained in food or fuel. **2** high in calories.

calorimeter /kalərimmitər/ > *noun* an apparatus for measuring the amount of heat involved in a chemical reaction or other process.

DERIVATIVES – **calorimetric** *adjective* **calorimetry** *noun*.

caltrop /kaltrəp/ (also **caltrap**) > *noun* **1** a spiked metal ball thrown on the ground to impede wheeled vehicles or (formerly) cavalry horses. **2** a creeping plant with hard spines.

ORIGIN – from Latin *calx* 'heel' or *calcare* 'to tread' + a word related to **TRAP**[1].

calumet /kalyoomet/ > *noun* a North American Indian peace pipe.

ORIGIN – French, from Latin *calamellus* 'little reed'.

calumniate /kəlumniayt/ > *verb* formal make false and defamatory statements about.

DERIVATIVES – **calumniator** *noun*.

SYNONYMS – defame, denigrate, discredit, malign, slander, traduce, vilify.

calumny /kaləmni/ > *noun* (pl. **calumnies**) the making of false and defamatory statements about someone. > *verb* (**calumnies**, **calumnied**) formal calumniate (someone).

DERIVATIVES – **calumnious** /kəlumniəss/ *adjective*.

SYNONYMS – *noun* defamation, denigration, slander, vilification.

ORIGIN – Latin *calumnia*.

Calvados /kalvədoss/ > *noun* apple brandy, traditionally made in the Calvados region of Normandy.

calve > *verb* **1** give birth to a calf. **2** (of a mass of ice) split off from an iceberg or glacier.

calves plural of **CALF**[1], **CALF**[2].

Calvinism > *noun* the Protestant theological system of John Calvin (1509–64) and his successors, centring on the doctrine of predestination.

DERIVATIVES – **Calvinist** *noun & adjective* **Calvinistic** *adjective*.

calypso /kəlipsō/ > *noun* (pl. **calypsos**) a kind of West Indian music or song in syncopated African rhythm, typically with words improvised on a topical theme.

calyx /kayliks/ (also **calix**) > *noun* (pl. **calyces** /kayliseez/ or **calyxes**) **1** Botany the sepals of a flower, forming a protective layer around a flower in bud. **2** Zoology a cup-like cavity or structure.

ORIGIN – Latin, from Greek *kalux* 'case of a bud, husk'.

calzone /kaltsōnay/ > *noun* (pl. **calzoni** or **calzones**) a type of pizza that is folded in half before cooking to contain a filling.

ORIGIN – Italian dialect, probably a special use of *calzone* 'trouser leg'.

cam > *noun* **1** a projection on a rotating part in machinery, designed to make sliding contact with another part while rotating and to cause it to move. **2** a camshaft.

ORIGIN – Dutch *kam* 'comb'.

camaraderie /kamməraadəri/ > *noun* mutual trust and friendship.

ORIGIN – French, from *camarade* 'comrade'.

camber /kambər/ > *noun* **1** a slightly convex or arched shape of a road, aircraft wing, or other horizontal surface. **2** Brit. a tilt built into a road at a bend or curve. **3** the slight sideways inclination of the front wheels of a motor vehicle.

DERIVATIVES – **cambered** *adjective*.

ORIGIN – Old French *chambre* 'arched', from Latin *camurus* 'curved inwards'.

cambium /kambiəm/ > *noun* (pl. **cambia** or **cambiums**) Botany a layer of cells in a plant stem between the xylem and phloem, from which new tissue grows by cellular division.

ORIGIN – Latin, 'change, exchange'.

Cambodian /kambōdiən/ > *noun* **1** a person from Cambodia. **2** the Khmer language. > *adjective* relating to Cambodia.

Cambrian /kambriən/ > *adjective* **1** Welsh. **2** Geology relating to the first period in the Palaeozoic era (between the Precambrian aeon and the Ordovician period, about 570 to 510 million years ago), the earliest time in which fossils can be used for geological dating.

ORIGIN – from Latin *Cambria*, from Welsh *Cymru* 'Wales'.

cambric /kambrik/ > *noun* a lightweight, closely woven white linen or cotton fabric.

ORIGIN – named after the town of *Cambrai* in northern France, where it was originally made; compare with **CHAMBRAY**.

Cambs. > *abbreviation* Cambridgeshire.

camcorder > *noun* a portable combined video camera and video recorder.

came past tense of **COME**.

camel > *noun* a large, long-necked mammal of arid country, with long slender legs, broad cushioned feet, and either one or two humps on the back.

WORDFINDER – Arabian camel or dromedary (*species with one hump*), Bactrian camel (*two humps*).

COMBINATIONS – **camel hair 1** a fabric made from the hair of a camel. **2** fine, soft hair from a squirrel's tail, used in artists' brushes.

ORIGIN – Greek *kamēlos*, of Semitic origin.

camellia /kəmeeliə/ > *noun* an evergreen shrub with showy flowers and shiny leaves.

ORIGIN – named after the 17th-century

Moravian botanist Joseph *Kamel* (Latinised as *Camellus*).

camelopard /**kamm**ələpaard, kəmelə-paard/ > *noun* archaic a giraffe.

ORIGIN – from Greek *kamēlos* 'camel' + *pardalis* 'leopard'.

Camelot /**kamm**əlot/ > *noun* **1** the place where King Arthur held his legendary court. **2** a place associated with glittering romance and optimism.

Camembert /**kamm**əmbair/ > *noun* a kind of rich, soft, creamy cheese originally made near Camembert in Normandy.

cameo /**kamm**iō/ > *noun* (pl. **cameos**) **1** a piece of jewellery consisting of a portrait in profile carved in relief on a background of a different colour. **2** a short piece of writing which neatly encapsulates something. **3** a small, distinctive part in a play or film played by a distinguished actor.

ORIGIN – Old French *camahieu*, influenced by Italian *cameo, cammeo*.

camera > *noun* a device for recording visual images in the form of photographs, cinema film, or video signals.

IDIOMS – **in camera** chiefly Law in private, in particular in the private chambers of a judge.

DERIVATIVES – **cameraman** *noun*.

COMBINATIONS – **camera-ready** in the right form to be reproduced photographically on to a printing plate.

> **wordpower facts**
> ## Camera
> The Latin word *camera*, from which the English word derives, denotes an arched or vaulted roof or chamber. This sense survives in English in certain special uses, such as the name of a circular domed building, the *Radcliffe Camera*, which forms part of the Bodleian Library in Oxford. More generally the sense survives in the word **chamber**, which comes from the same root, and the Latin form is preserved in the phrase **in camera**. The development of sense that led to the name of the photographic device first arose in the 18th century, in the term **camera obscura**, or 'dark chamber', a device which was the precursor of the modern camera.

camera obscura /**kamm**ərə ob**skyoor**ə/ > *noun* a darkened box with a lens or aperture for projecting the image of an external object on to a screen inside.

Cameroonian /**kamm**ə**rōōn**iən/ > *noun* a person from Cameroon, a country on the west coast of Africa. > *adjective* relating to Cameroon.

camiknickers > *plural noun* Brit. a woman's one-piece undergarment which combines a camisole and a pair of French knickers.

camisole /**kamm**isōl/ > *noun* a woman's loose-fitting undergarment for the upper body.

ORIGIN – French, from Latin *camisia* 'shirt or nightgown'.

camomile > *noun* variant spelling of CHAMOMILE.

camouflage /**kamm**əflaazh/ > *noun* **1** the disguising of military personnel and equipment by painting or covering them to make them blend in with their surroundings. **2** clothing or materials used for such a purpose. **3** the natural colouring or form of an animal which enables it to blend in with its surroundings. > *verb* hide or disguise by means of camouflage.

ORIGIN – French, from *camoufler* 'to disguise'.

camp¹ > *noun* **1** a place where tents are temporarily set up. **2** a complex of huts and other buildings for soldiers, holidaymakers, or detainees. **3** the supporters of a particular party or doctrine regarded collectively. **4** a fortified prehistoric site, especially an Iron Age hill fort. > *verb* lodge in a tent or caravan while on holiday.

WORDFINDER – bivouac (*temporary camp with limited cover*).

IDIOMS – **break camp** take down a tent or the tents of an encampment ready to leave.

COMBINATIONS – **camp bed** Brit. a folding portable bed. **campfire** an open-air fire in a camp. **camp follower 1** a civilian working in or attached to a military camp. **2** a person who associates with a group without being a full member of it. **campsite** a place used for camping, especially one equipped for holidaymakers.

ORIGIN – Latin *campus* 'level ground'.

camp² informal > *adjective* **1** (of a man) ostentatiously and extravagantly effeminate. **2** deliberately exaggerated and theatrical in style. > *noun* camp behaviour or style. > *verb* (usu. **camp it up**) behave in a camp way.

DERIVATIVES – **campy** *adjective*.

campaign > *noun* **1** a series of military operations intended to achieve an objective in a particular area. **2** an organised course of action to achieve a goal. > *verb* work in an organised way towards a goal.

DERIVATIVES – **campaigner** *noun*.

SYNONYMS – *noun* crusade, drive, movement, offensive, operation. *verb* (**campaign for**) champion, lobby for, promote, push, work towards.

> **wordpower facts**
> ## Campaign
> The word **campaign** derives from the French *campagne*, meaning 'open country', which was the earliest sense in English. The change in meaning occurred in the 17th century, from the military practice of moving at the start of summer out from a fortress or town into open country. In June 1667 Samuel Pepys referred in his *Diary* to money needed for 'the present campagne', meaning the duration of time 'in the field'; the soldiers would be camped there for the summer season, or for the duration of one continuous series of operations. In modern times military activity is less dependent on the weather, and **campaign** denotes the operations themselves rather than their season. The French form *campagne* comes ultimately from Latin *campus*, meaning 'level ground', the root also of **camp** and **campus**.

campanile /kamp**ə**nee**lay**/ > *noun* a bell tower, especially a free-standing one.

ORIGIN – Italian, from *campana* 'bell'.

campanology > *noun* the art or practice of bell-ringing.

DERIVATIVES – **campanological** *adjective* **campanologist** *noun*.

ORIGIN – from Latin *campana* 'bell'.

campanula /kam**pan**yoolə/ > *noun* another term for **bellflower**.

ORIGIN – from Latin *campana* 'bell'.

camper > *noun* **1** a person who spends a holiday in a tent or holiday camp. **2** (also **camper van**) a large motor vehicle with living accommodation.

camphor /**kam**fər/ > *noun* a white volatile crystalline substance with an aromatic smell and bitter taste, occurring in certain essential oils.

ORIGIN – Old French *camphore* or Latin *camphora*, from Sanskrit.

campion > *noun* a plant of the pink family, typically having pink or white flowers with notched petals.

ORIGIN – perhaps related to CHAMPION: the word was originally applied to a plant of this kind which was said to have been used for victors' garlands in ancient times.

campo /**kam**pō/ > *noun* (pl. **campos**) **1** (**the campo**) (in South America, especially Brazil) a grass plain with occasional stunted trees. **2** a square in an Italian or Spanish town.

ORIGIN – Spanish, Portuguese, and Italian *campo* 'field'.

campus > *noun* (pl. **campuses**) **1** the grounds and buildings of a university or college. **2** N. Amer. the grounds of a college, school, hospital, or other institution.

ORIGIN – Latin, 'level ground'.

campylobacter /**kam**pilōbaktər/ > *noun* a genus of bacterium responsible for some food poisoning in humans and spontaneous abortion in animals.

ORIGIN – from Greek *kampulos* 'bent' + **BACTERIUM**.

camshaft /**kam**shaaft/ > *noun* a shaft with one or more cams attached to it, especially one operating the valves in an internal-combustion engine.

can¹ > *modal verb* (3rd sing. present **can**; past **could**) **1** be able to. **2** used to express doubt or surprise: *he can't have finished.* **3** used to indicate that something is typically the case: *he could be very moody.* **4** be permitted to.

USAGE – when expressing or asking for permission, it is regarded as less formal (and possibly less polite) to use **can** rather than **may**: in more formal contexts is better to say *May we leave now?* than *Can we leave now?* The verb **can** is generally used to express ability or capability (*can he move?* = is he physically able to move?; *may he move?* = is he allowed to move?).

ORIGIN – Old English, 'know'.

can² > *noun* **1** a cylindrical metal container, in particular one in which food or drink is hermetically sealed for storage over long periods. **2** (**the can**) N. Amer. informal prison. **3** (**the can**) N. Amer. informal the toilet. > *verb* (**canned, canning**) **1** preserve in a can. **2** N. Amer. informal dismiss from a job or reject as inadequate.

IDIOMS – **a can of worms** a complex matter that once acknowledged will prove difficult to manage. **in the can** informal on tape or film and ready to be broadcast or released.

DERIVATIVES – **canner** noun.

Canada goose > *noun* a common brownish-grey North American goose, introduced in Britain and elsewhere.

Canadian > *noun* a person from Canada. > *adjective* relating to Canada.

canaille /kanī/ > *noun* **derogatory** the common people; the masses.

ORIGIN – French, from Italian *canaglia* 'pack of dogs', from *cane* 'dog', from Latin *canis*.

canal > *noun* **1** an artificial waterway allowing boats to travel inland or conveying water for irrigation. **2** a tubular duct in a plant or animal conveying food, liquid, or air.

ORIGIN – Old French, from Latin *canalis* 'pipe, groove, channel', from *canna* 'cane'.

canalise /**kann**əlīz/ (also **canalize**) > *verb* **1** convert (a river) into a navigable canal. **2** convey through a duct or channel. **3** give a direction or purpose to.

DERIVATIVES – **canalisation** noun.

canapé /**kann**əpay/ > *noun* **1** a small piece of bread or pastry with a savoury topping, often served with drinks. **2** a sofa, especially a decorative French antique.

ORIGIN – French, 'sofa, couch': the first sense is a figurative extension of this (a 'couch' on which to place toppings); related to **CANOPY**.

canard /kənaard, kannaard/ > *noun* an unfounded rumour or story.

ORIGIN – French, 'duck', also 'hoax', from Old French *caner* 'to quack'.

canary > *noun* (pl. **canaries**) **1** a bright yellow finch with a melodious song, popular as a cage bird. **2** (also **canary yellow**) a bright yellow colour.

---

wordpower facts

Canary

The **canary** acquired its name from the *Canary* Islands, to which the species from which the cage birds were bred is native. The name of the islands themselves comes from Latin *canaria insula*, which means 'island of dogs', from *canis* 'dog', one of the islands having had a notable population of large dogs. Other words that come from *canis* include **canaille**, **canine**, **chenille**, and **kennel**.

---

canasta /kənastə/ > *noun* a card game resembling rummy, using two packs and usually played by two pairs of partners.

ORIGIN – Spanish, 'basket'.

cancan > *noun* a lively, high-kicking stage dance originating in 19th-century Parisian music halls.

ORIGIN – French, child's word for *canard* 'duck', from Old French *caner* 'to quack'.

cancel > *verb* (**cancelled, cancelling**; US also **canceled, canceling**) **1** decide that (a planned event) will not take place. **2** annul or revoke. **3** (**cancel out**) neutralise or negate the effect of. **4** mark (a stamp, ticket, etc.) to show that it has been used and is no longer valid.

DERIVATIVES – **cancellation** noun **canceller** noun.

SYNONYMS – **1** abandon, call off, scrap. **2** annul, countermand, repeal, rescind, revoke. **3** (**cancel out**) counteract, counterbalance, negate, neutralise, nullify, offset.

ORIGIN – Latin *cancellare*, from *cancelli* 'crossbars'.

Cancer > *noun* **1** Astronomy a constellation (the Crab), said to represent a crab crushed under the foot of Hercules. **2** Astrology the fourth sign of the zodiac, which the sun enters at the northern summer solstice (about 21 June).

DERIVATIVES – **Cancerian** /kanseeriən/ *noun & adjective*.

ORIGIN – Latin, 'crab'.

cancer > *noun* **1** a disease in which there is an uncontrolled growth of abnormal cells in a part of the body. **2** a malignant growth or tumour resulting from such a disease. **3** something evil or destructive that is hard to contain or eradicate.

WORDFINDER – carcinogen (*substance causing cancer*), oncology (*branch of medicine concerned with cancer*).

DERIVATIVES – **cancerous** adjective.

ORIGIN – Latin, 'crab or creeping ulcer', translating Greek *karkinos*, said to have been applied to tumours because the swollen veins around them resembled the limbs of a crab.

candela /kandellə/ > *noun* Physics the unit of luminous intensity in the SI system.

ORIGIN – Latin, 'candle'.

candelabrum /kandilaabrəm/ > *noun* (pl. **candelabra** /kandilaabrə/) a large branched candlestick or holder for several candles or lamps.

USAGE – strictly speaking, because of the Latin origin, the singular form is **candelabrum** and the plural is **candelabra**.

ORIGIN – Latin, from *candela* 'candle'.

candid > *adjective* truthful and straightforward; frank.

DERIVATIVES – **candidly** adverb **candidness** noun.

SYNONYMS – direct, forthright, frank, honest, straightforward, truthful.

ANTONYMS – guarded, insincere.

---

wordpower facts

Candid

The word **candid** was first used in English to mean simply 'white, glistening', this being the meaning of the Latin word from which it came, *candidus* (from *candere* 'be white, glisten'). It rapidly acquired a number of figurative senses based on associations between whiteness and qualities such as purity and goodness, such as 'pure, innocent', 'unbiased', and 'free from malice', before taking on its modern meaning. Other words coming from *candere* include **candle** and **incandescent**; and a **candidate** (from *candidatus* 'white-robed') is so called because a person seeking office in Roman times traditionally wore a white toga.

---

candida /kandidə/ > *noun* a yeast-like parasitic fungus that can cause thrush.

ORIGIN – from Latin *candidus* 'white'.

candidate /**kan**didət/ > *noun* **1** a person who applies for a job or is nominated for election. **2** a person taking an examination. **3** a person or thing regarded as suitable for a particular fate, treatment, or position: *she was the perfect candidate for a biography.*

DERIVATIVES – **candidacy** *noun* **candidature** *noun* (Brit.).

SYNONYMS – **1** applicant, contender, nominee, runner. **2** entrant, examinee.

Candide /koN**deed**/ > *noun* an ingenuous person who retains a hopeful and optimistic outlook in difficult circumstances.

ORIGIN – from the name of the hero of Voltaire's satire *Candide* (1759).

candle > *noun* a stick or block of wax or tallow with a central wick which is lit to produce light as it burns.

WORDFINDER – flambeau (*branched candlestick*), menorah (*Jewish branched candelabrum*), sconce (*ornamental candle holder on wall*).

IDIOMS – **be unable to hold a candle to** informal be not nearly as good as. **not worth the candle** not justifying the cost or trouble involved.

COMBINATIONS – **candlepower** the illuminating power of a light source. [ORIGIN – from the former use of *candle* for a unit of luminous intensity, superseded by the *candela*.] **candlestick** a support or holder for a candle.

ORIGIN – Latin *candela*, from *candere* 'be white or glisten'.

Candlemas /**kan**d'lməss, -mass/ > *noun* a Christian festival held on 2 February to commemorate the purification of the Virgin Mary (after childbirth, according to Jewish law) and the presentation of Christ in the Temple.

candlewick > *noun* a thick, soft cotton fabric with a raised, tufted pattern.

candour (US **candor**) > *noun* the quality of being candid.

SYNONYMS – candidness, frankness, honesty, openness, truthfulness.

C & W > *abbreviation* country and western (music).

candy > *noun* (pl. **candies**) (also **sugar candy**) **1** N. Amer. sweets; confectionery. **2** chiefly Brit. sugar crystallised by repeated boiling and slow evaporation. > *verb* (**candies**, **candied**) preserve (fruit) by coating and impregnating it with a sugar syrup.

COMBINATIONS – **candy-ass** N. Amer. informal a timid, cowardly, or weak person. **candy-striped** patterned with stripes of white and another colour, typically pink.

ORIGIN – from French *sucre candi* 'crystallised sugar', from Arabic.

candyfloss > *noun* Brit. **1** a mass of pink or white fluffy spun sugar wrapped round a stick. **2** something worthless or insubstantial.

candyman > *noun* N. Amer. informal a person who sells illegal drugs.

candytuft > *noun* a plant with small heads of white, pink, or purple flowers, grown as a garden or rockery plant.

ORIGIN – from *Candy*, obsolete form of *Candia*, former name of Crete.

cane > *noun* **1** the hollow jointed stem of tall reeds, grasses, etc., especially bamboo. **2** the slender, pliant stem of plants such as rattan. **3** a woody stem of a raspberry or related plant. **4** a length of cane or a slender stick used as a support for plants, a walking stick, or an instrument of punishment. > *verb* beat with a cane as a punishment.

DERIVATIVES – **caner** *noun*.

ORIGIN – Latin *canna*, from Greek *kanna*, *kannē*.

caned > *adjective* **1** (of furniture) made or repaired with cane. **2** Brit. informal intoxicated with drink or drugs.

canine /**kay**nīn/ > *adjective* relating to or resembling a dog. > *noun* **1** a dog or other animal of the dog family. **2** (also **canine tooth**) a pointed tooth between the incisors and premolars, often greatly enlarged in carnivores.

ORIGIN – Latin *caninus*, from *canis* 'dog'.

canister* > *noun* **1** a round or cylindrical container. **2** historical small bullets packed in cases that fit the bore of a gun.

***SPELLING** – one *n*: ca**n**ister.

ORIGIN – Latin *canistrum*, from Greek *kanastron* 'wicker basket', from *kanna* 'cane'.

canker > *noun* **1** a destructive fungal disease of trees that results in damage to the bark. **2** an open lesion in plant tissue caused by infection or injury. **3** fungal rot in parsnips, tomatoes, or other vegetables. **4** an ulcerous condition in animals, especially an inflammation of the ear caused by a mite infestation. **5** chiefly N. Amer. a small ulcer of the mouth or lips. > *verb* **1** become infected with canker. **2** (**cankered**) infected with a pervasive and corrupting bitterness.

DERIVATIVES – **cankerous** *adjective*.

ORIGIN – first denoting a tumour: from Old French *chancre*, from Latin *cancer* 'crab, creeping ulcer, cancer'.

canna > *noun* a lily-like tropical American plant with bright flowers and ornamental strap-like leaves.

ORIGIN – Latin, 'cane, reed'.

cannabis > *noun* **1** a dried preparation or resinous extract made from a plant, used, chiefly in cigarettes, as a narcotic drug. **2** the plant from which this substance comes, also used to produce hemp fibre.

WORDFINDER – bhang, ganja, hashish, hemp, kif, marijuana (*names for or kinds of cannabis*).

ORIGIN – Latin (used as the botanical name for hemp); from Greek *kannabis*.

canned > *adjective* **1** preserved in a sealed can. **2** informal, chiefly derogatory (of music, applause, etc.) pre-recorded.

cannellini bean /kannə**lee**ni/ > *noun* a kidney-shaped bean of a medium-sized creamy-white variety.

ORIGIN – Italian *cannellini* 'small tubes'.

cannelloni /kannə**lō**ni/ > *plural noun* rolls of pasta stuffed with a meat or vegetable mixture, usually cooked in a cheese sauce.

ORIGIN – Italian, 'large tubes', from *cannello* 'tube'.

cannery > *noun* (pl. **canneries**) a factory where food is canned.

cannibal > *noun* a person who eats the flesh of other human beings.

WORDFINDER – anthropophagi (*legendary cannibals*), anthropophagy (*eating human flesh*).

DERIVATIVES – **cannibalism** *noun* **cannibalistic** *adjective*.

ORIGIN – Spanish *Canibales*, a variant (recorded by Columbus) of *Caribes*, the name of a West Indian people reputed to eat humans; compare with CARIB.

cannibalise (also **cannibalize**) > *verb* **1** use (a machine) as a source of spare parts for another, similar machine. **2** (of an animal) eat (an animal of its own kind).

DERIVATIVES – **cannibalisation** *noun*.

cannon > *noun* (pl. usu. same) **1** a large, heavy piece of artillery formerly used in warfare. **2** an automatic heavy gun that fires shells from an aircraft or tank. > *verb* chiefly Brit. (**cannon into** or **off**) collide with forcefully or at an angle.

COMBINATIONS – **cannon bone** a long tube-shaped bone between a horse's fetlock and the knee or hock. **cannon fodder** soldiers regarded merely as material to be expended in war.

ORIGIN – French *canon*, from Italian *cannone* 'large tube', from Latin *canna* 'cane'.

cannonade /kannə**nayd**/ > *noun* a period of continuous heavy gunfire. > *verb* discharge heavy guns continuously.

cannonball > *noun* **1** a round metal or stone projectile fired from a cannon. **2** N. Amer. a jump into water feet first with the knees clasped to the chest.

cannot > *contraction* can not.

USAGE – both the one-word form **cannot** and the two-word form **can not** are acceptable; however, **cannot** is far more usual.

cannula /**kan**yoolə/ > *noun* (pl. **cannulae** /**kan**yoolee/ or **cannulas**) Surgery a thin tube inserted into the body to administer medication, drain off fluid, or introduce a surgical instrument.

ORIGIN – Latin, 'small reed'.

canny > *adjective* (**cannier**, **canniest**) **1** shrewd, especially in financial or business matters. **2** N. English & Scottish pleasant; nice.

DERIVATIVES – **cannily** *adverb* **canniness** *noun*.

SYNONYMS – **1** astute, perspicacious, sharp, shrewd.

ORIGIN – from CAN¹, in the obsolete sense 'know'.

canoe > *noun* a shallow, narrow boat with pointed ends, propelled with a paddle. > *verb* (**canoes**, **canoed**, **canoeing**) travel in or paddle a canoe.

DERIVATIVES – **canoeist** *noun*.

ORIGIN – Spanish *canoa*, from Arawak.

canon¹ > *noun* **1** a general rule or principle by which something is judged. **2** a Church decree or law. **3** a collection of authentic sacred books. **4** the authentic works of a particular author or artist. **5** a list of literary works considered to be permanently established as being of the highest quality. **6** Music a piece in which the same melody is begun in different parts successively.

IDIOMS – **in canon** Music with different parts successively beginning the same melody.

COMBINATIONS – **canon law** ecclesiastical law, especially that laid down by papal pronouncements.

ORIGIN – Greek *kanōn* 'rule'.

canon² > *noun* **1** a member of a cathedral chapter. **2** (also **canon regular** or **regular canon**) (fem. **canoness**) a member of certain orders of Roman Catholic clergy that live communally like monks or nuns.

ORIGIN – Latin *canonicus*, from Greek *kanon* 'rule'.

canonic /kənonnik/ > *adjective* **1** Music in the form of a canon. **2** another term for CANONICAL.

DERIVATIVES – **canonicity** *noun*.

canonical > *adjective* **1** according to or ordered by canon law. **2** accepted as being authentic, accurate, and authoritative. **3** of or relating to a cathedral chapter or a member of it. > *noun* (**canonicals**) the prescribed official dress of the clergy.

DERIVATIVES – **canonically** *adverb*.

canonise (also **canonize**) > *verb* **1** (in the Roman Catholic Church) officially declare (a dead person) to be a saint. **2** sanction by Church authority.

DERIVATIVES – **canonisation** *noun*.

canonry > *noun* (pl. **canonries**) the office or benefice of a canon.

canoodle > *verb* informal kiss and cuddle amorously.

canopy > *noun* (pl. **canopies**) **1** a cloth covering over a throne, bed, etc. **2** a roof-like projection or shelter. **3** the expanding, umbrella-like part of a parachute. **4** the uppermost branches of the trees in a forest, forming a roof-like cover of foliage. > *verb* (**canopies**, **canopied**) cover or provide with a canopy.

ORIGIN – Latin *conopeum* 'mosquito net over a bed', from Greek *kōnōpeion* 'couch with mosquito curtains', from *kōnōps* 'mosquito'.

cant¹ /kant/ > *noun* **1** hypocritical and sanctimonious talk. **2** derogatory language peculiar to a specified group. **3** (before another noun) (of a word or phrase) temporarily current: *the cant word of our day.* > *verb* dated talk hypocritically and sanctimoniously.

---

wordpower facts

Cant

Probably deriving from the Latin verb *cantare*, meaning 'to sing', the word **cant** was first used in English in the senses 'singing, musical sound' and 'accent or intonation'. From there it came to mean 'a whining manner of speaking', which was associated particularly with beggars. It was then used in reference not just to the tone of voice but to the words themselves, to the secret language of the underworld of beggars and thieves. It is easy to see how the modern meanings, with their negative associations, then arose.

---

cant² /kant/ > *verb* be or cause to be in a slanting or oblique position; tilt. > *noun* **1** a slope or tilt. **2** a wedge-shaped block of wood remaining after the better-quality pieces have been cut off.

ORIGIN – Low German *kant*, *kante*, Dutch *cant* 'point, side, edge', related to Latin *cantus* 'corner, side'.

can't > *contraction* cannot.

Cantab. /kantab/ > *abbreviation* of Cambridge University.

ORIGIN – from Latin *Cantabrigiensis*, from *Cantabrigia* 'Cambridge'.

cantabile /kantaabilay/ > *adverb & adjective* Music in a smooth singing style.

ORIGIN – Italian, 'singable'.

cantaloupe /kantəloōp/ > *noun* a small round variety of melon with orange flesh and ribbed skin.

ORIGIN – French *cantaloup*, from the name of *Cantaluppi* near Rome.

cantankerous > *adjective* bad-tempered, argumentative, and uncooperative.

DERIVATIVES – **cantankerously** *adverb* **cantankerousness** *noun*.

SYNONYMS – crotchety, curmudgeonly, disagreeable, irascible, quarrelsome, tetchy.

ORIGIN – perhaps a blend of Anglo-Irish *cant* 'auction' and *rancorous*.

cantata /kantaatə/ > *noun* a medium-length narrative or descriptive piece of music with vocal solos and normally a chorus and orchestra.

ORIGIN – from Italian *cantata aria* 'sung air', from *cantare* 'sing'.

canteen > *noun* **1** a restaurant in a workplace or educational establishment. **2** Brit. a specially designed case or box containing a set of cutlery. **3** a small water bottle, as used by soldiers or campers.

ORIGIN – first used to denote a shop selling provisions or alcohol in a barracks: from French *cantine*, from Italian *cantina* 'cellar'.

canter > *noun* **1** a pace of a horse between a trot and a gallop, with not less than one foot on the ground at any time. **2** a ride on a horse at such a speed. > *verb* move at this pace.

IDIOMS – **in** (or **at**) **a canter** Brit. without much effort; easily.

ORIGIN – short for *Canterbury pace*, from the supposed easy pace of medieval pilgrims to Canterbury.

Canterbury bell > *noun* a tall cultivated bellflower with large pale blue flowers.

ORIGIN – named after the bells on Canterbury pilgrims' horses.

canticle /kantik'l/ > *noun* a hymn or chant forming a regular part of a church service.

ORIGIN – Latin *canticulum* 'little song'.

cantilever /kantileevər/ > *noun* **1** a long projecting beam or girder fixed at only one end, used chiefly in bridge construction. **2** a bracket or beam projecting from a wall to support a balcony, cornice, etc. > *verb* support by a cantilever or cantilevers.

canto /kantō/ > *noun* (pl. **cantos**) each of the sections into which some long poems are divided.

ORIGIN – Italian, 'song', from Latin *cantus*.

canton /kanton/ > *noun* **1** a political or administrative subdivision of a country. **2** a state of the Swiss Confederation.

DERIVATIVES – **cantonal** /kantən'l/ *adjective*.

ORIGIN – Old French, 'corner', related to Latin *cantus* 'corner, side'.

Cantonese /kantəneez/ > *noun* (pl. same) **1** a person from Canton (another name for Guangzhou), a city in China. **2** a form of Chinese spoken mainly in SE China and Hong Kong. > *adjective* relating to Canton or Cantonese.

cantonment /kantonmənt, kantoōnmənt/ > *noun* a military station in British India.

ORIGIN – French *cantonnement*, from *cantonner* 'to quarter'.

cantor /kantor/ > *noun* **1** (in Jewish worship) an official who sings and leads prayer in a synagogue. **2** (in formal Christian worship) a person who sings solo verses to which the choir or congregation respond.

ORIGIN – Latin, 'singer'.

Canuck /kənuk/ > *noun* informal a Canadian, especially a French Canadian.

canvas > *noun* (pl. **canvases** or **canvasses**) 1 a strong, coarse unbleached cloth used to make sails, tents, etc. 2 a piece of canvas prepared for use as the surface for an oil painting. 3 (**the canvas**) the floor of a boxing or wrestling ring, having a canvas covering. 4 either of a racing boat's tapering ends, originally covered with canvas. > *verb* (**canvassed, canvassing;** US **canvased, canvasing**) cover with canvas.
IDIOMS – **under canvas 1** in a tent or tents. **2** with sails spread.

wordpower facts
Canvas
The raw material used in the production of **canvas** fabric was originally, and is sometimes still, the plant hemp. This is revealed in the history of the word, which comes through Old Northern French *canevas* from the Latin name for hemp, *cannabis*. Hemp is also the source of **cannabis** itself, so **cannabis** and **canvas** are related both botanically and etymologically! **Canvas** (which was earlier spelled with a double -s) is also linked with the verb **canvass**, which originally meant 'toss in a canvas sheet' (a practice carried out both in fun and as a punishment); **canvass** then came to mean 'subject to assault or attack' or 'pull to pieces, criticise', and later 'scrutinise in order to reject bad votes', from which developed the modern sense, 'visit (someone) in order to seek their vote'.

canvass > *verb* 1 visit (someone) in order to seek their vote in an election. 2 question (someone) in order to ascertain their opinion on something. 3 Brit. propose (an idea or plan) for discussion. > *noun* an act of canvassing.
DERIVATIVES – **canvasser** *noun.*
SYNONYMS – *verb* **1,2** poll, sound out, survey.

canyon > *noun* a deep gorge, especially one with a river flowing through it.
ORIGIN – Spanish *cañón* 'tube', from Latin *canna* 'cane'.

canyoning > *noun* the sport of jumping into a fast-flowing mountain stream and being carried downstream.

CAP > *abbreviation* Common Agricultural Policy.

cap > *noun* 1 a soft, flat hat without a brim and usually with a peak. 2 a soft, close-fitting head covering worn for a particular purpose. 3 a protective lid or cover for a bottle, pen, etc. 4 Dentistry an artificial protective covering for a tooth. 5 an upper limit imposed on spending or borrowing. 6 chiefly Brit. a cap awarded to members of a sports team. 7 (also **Dutch cap**) Brit. informal a contraceptive diaphragm. 8 the broad upper part of a mushroom or toadstool. 9 a percussion cap. > *verb* (**capped, capping**) 1 put or form a lid or cover on. 2 put a cap on (a tooth). 3 provide a fitting climax or conclusion to. 4 place a limit on (prices, expenditure, etc.). 5 (**be capped**) chiefly Brit. be chosen as a member of a sports team. 6 Scottish & NZ confer a university degree on.
IDIOMS – **cap in hand** humbly asking for a favour. **set one's cap at** dated (of a woman) try to attract (a man). **to cap it all** as the final unfortunate incident in a long series.
SYNONYMS – *verb* **1** cover, crown, top. **4** curb, limit, restrict.
COMBINATIONS – **cap sleeve** a short sleeve which tapers to nothing under the arm. **capstone** a stone placed on top of a wall, tomb, or other structure.
ORIGIN – Old English, 'hood', from Latin *cappa*, perhaps from *caput* 'head'.

capability > *noun* (pl. **capabilities**) the power or ability to do something.

capable > *adjective* 1 (**capable of**) having the ability or quality necessary to do. 2 (of a person) competent.
DERIVATIVES – **capably** *adverb.*
SYNONYMS – **1** (**capable of**) able to, equal to, up to. **2** able, adept, competent, efficient, proficient.
ANTONYMS – **2** incompetent, inept.
ORIGIN – French, from Latin *capere* 'take or hold'.

capacious > *adjective* having a lot of space inside; roomy.
DERIVATIVES – **capaciously** *adverb* **capaciousness** *noun.*
SYNONYMS – ample, commodious, roomy, spacious.
ANTONYMS – cramped.
ORIGIN – from Latin *capax* 'capable'.

capacitance /kəpassitənss/ > *noun* Physics the ability of a circuit or object to store electric charge, equivalent to the ratio of the change in electric charge to the corresponding change in electric potential.

capacitate > *verb* formal or archaic make (someone) capable or legally competent.
DERIVATIVES – **capacitation** *noun.*

capacitor > *noun* a device used to store electric charge, consisting of one or more pairs of conductors separated by an insulator.

capacity > *noun* (pl. **capacities**) 1 the maximum amount that something can contain or produce. 2 (before another noun) fully occupying the available space: *a capacity crowd.* 3 the total cylinder volume that is swept by the pistons in an internal-combustion engine. 4 the ability or power to do something. 5 a specified role or position: *I was engaged in a voluntary capacity.*
SYNONYMS – **1** limit, room, scope, volume. **4** ability, capability, potential, power.
ORIGIN – Latin *capacitas*, from *capere* 'take or hold'.

caparison /kəparris'n/ > *noun* an ornamental covering spread over a horse's saddle or harness. > *verb* (**be caparisoned**) be decked out in rich decorative coverings.
ORIGIN – Spanish *caparazón* 'saddlecloth', from *capa* 'hood'.

cape¹ > *noun* 1 a cloak, especially a short one. 2 a part of a longer coat or cloak that falls loosely over the shoulders from the neckband. 3 N. Amer. the pelt from the head and neck of an animal. > *verb* N. Amer. skin the head and neck of (an animal) to prepare a hunting trophy.
DERIVATIVES – **caped** *adjective.*
ORIGIN – French, from Latin *cappa* 'covering for the head'.

cape² > *noun* a headland or promontory.
SYNONYMS – head, headland, peninsula, point, promontory.
ORIGIN – Old French *cap*, from Latin *caput* 'head'.

Cape gooseberry > *noun* the soft edible yellow berry of a tropical South American plant, enclosed in a lantern-shaped husk.

capelin /kaplin/ (also **caplin**) > *noun* a small food fish of the smelt family, found in North Atlantic coastal waters.
ORIGIN – French, from Latin *cappellanus*, from *cappa* 'cap or cape'.

capellini /kappəleeni/ > *plural noun* pasta in the form of very thin strands.
ORIGIN – Italian, 'little hairs'.

caper¹ > *verb* skip or dance about in a lively or playful way. > *noun* 1 a playful skipping movement. 2 informal an illicit or ridiculous activity or escapade.
IDIOMS – **cut a caper** make a playful, skipping movement.
DERIVATIVES – **caperer** *noun.*
SYNONYMS – *verb* cavort, frisk, frolic, gambol.
ORIGIN – from *capriole*, denoting a movement performed in riding in which the horse leaps from the ground and kicks out with its hind legs, from Italian *capriola* 'leap', based on Latin *caper* 'goat'.

caper² > *noun* a flower bud of a southern European shrub, pickled for use in cooking.
ORIGIN – Greek *kapparis*.

capercaillie /kappəkayli/ (Scottish also **capercailzie** /kappəkaylzi/) > *noun* (pl. **capercaillies**) a large turkey-like grouse of pine forests in northern Europe.

ORIGIN – from Scottish Gaelic *capull coille* 'horse of the wood'.

capillarity > *noun* the tendency of a liquid in a narrow tube or pore to rise or fall as a result of surface tension.

capillary /kəpilləri/ > *noun* **1** Anatomy any of the fine branching blood vessels that form a network between the arterioles and venules. **2** (also **capillary tube**) a tube with an internal diameter of hair-like thinness. > *adjective* relating to capillaries or capillarity.

COMBINATIONS – **capillary action** capillarity.

ORIGIN – Latin *capillaris*, from *capillus* 'hair'.

capital¹ > *noun* **1** the most important city or town of a country or region, usually its seat of government and administrative centre. **2** wealth owned by a person or organisation or invested, lent, or borrowed. **3** the excess of a company's assets over its liabilities. **4** a capital letter. > *adjective* **1** (of an offence or charge) liable to the death penalty. **2** (of a letter of the alphabet) large in size and of the form used to begin sentences and names. **3** informal, dated excellent.

IDIOMS – **make capital out of** use to one's own advantage.

SYNONYMS – *noun* **2** finance, funds, money, resources, wealth.

COMBINATIONS – **capital gain** a profit from the sale of property or an investment. **capital goods** goods that are used in producing other goods, rather than being bought by consumers. **capital punishment** the legally authorised killing of someone as punishment for a crime. **capital sum** a lump sum of money payable to an insured person or paid as an initial fee or investment.

ORIGIN – first used as an adjective in the sense 'relating to the head or top', later 'standing at the head or beginning': from Latin *capitalis*, from *caput* 'head'.

capital² > *noun* Architecture the top part of a pillar or column.

ORIGIN – Latin *capitellum* 'little head'.

capitalise (also **capitalize**) > *verb* **1** (**capitalise on**) take the chance to gain advantage from. **2** provide with financial capital. **3** convert into capital. **4** write or print (a word or letter) in capital letters or with an initial capital.

DERIVATIVES – **capitalisation** *noun*.

capitalism > *noun* an economic and political system in which a country's trade and industry are controlled by private owners for profit, rather than by the state.

DERIVATIVES – **capitalist** *noun* & *adjective* **capitalistic** *adjective*.

capitation > *noun* the payment of a fee or grant to a doctor, school, etc., the amount being determined by the number of patients, pupils, etc.

ORIGIN – Latin, from *caput* 'head'.

capitol /kappit'l/ > *noun* **1** (in the US) a building housing a legislative assembly. **2** (**the Capitol**) the seat of the US Congress in Washington DC. **3** (**the Capitol**) the temple of Jupiter on the Capitoline Hill in ancient Rome.

ORIGIN – Old French *capitolie*, from Latin *caput* 'head'.

capitulate /kəpityoolayt/ > *verb* give in to an opponent or an unwelcome demand; surrender.

DERIVATIVES – **capitulation** *noun* **capitulator** *noun*.

SYNONYMS – submit, surrender, throw in the towel, yield.

ANTONYMS – resist.

ORIGIN – first used in the sense 'parley, draw up terms': from Latin *capitulare* 'draw up under headings', from *caput* 'head'.

caplet > *noun* trademark a coated oral medicinal tablet.

ORIGIN – blend of CAPSULE and TABLET.

caplin > *noun* variant spelling of CAPELIN.

cap'n /kapp'n/ > *noun* informal contraction of CAPTAIN.

capo¹ /kappō/ (also **capo tasto**) > *noun* (pl. **capos**) a clamp fastened across all the strings of a fretted musical instrument to raise their tuning.

ORIGIN – from Italian *capo tasto* 'head stop'.

capo² /kappō/ > *noun* (pl. **capos**) chiefly N. Amer. the head or branch head of a crime syndicate, especially the Mafia.

ORIGIN – Italian, from Latin *caput* 'head'.

capoeira /kappooayrə/ > *noun* a system of physical discipline and movement featuring elements from dance and the martial arts, originating among Brazilian slaves.

ORIGIN – Portuguese.

capon /kayp'n/ > *noun* a castrated domestic cock fattened for eating.

DERIVATIVES – **caponise** (also **caponize**) *verb*.

caponata /kappənaatə/ > *noun* a dish of aubergines, olives, and onions seasoned with herbs.

ORIGIN – Italian.

cappuccino* /kappoocheenō/ > *noun* (pl. **cappuccinos**) coffee made with milk that has been frothed up with pressurised steam.

*****SPELLING** – double *p*, double *c*: cappu*cc*ino.

ORIGIN – Italian, 'Capuchin', because its colour resembles that of a Capuchin friar's habit.

caprice /kəpreess/ > *noun* a sudden and unaccountable change of mood or behaviour.

SYNONYMS – fancy, notion, whim.

ORIGIN – French, from Italian *capriccio* 'head with the hair standing on end', later 'sudden start', from *capo* 'head' and *riccio* 'hedgehog'.

capricious /kəprishəss/ > *adjective* given to sudden and unaccountable changes of mood or behaviour.

DERIVATIVES – **capriciously** *adverb* **capriciousness** *noun*.

SYNONYMS – changeable, fickle, mercurial, unpredictable, whimsical.

ANTONYMS – consistent, constant.

Capricorn /kaprikorn/ > *noun* Astrology the tenth sign of the zodiac (the Goat), which the sun enters at the northern winter solstice (about 21 December).

DERIVATIVES – **Capricornian** *noun* & *adjective*.

ORIGIN – Latin *capricornus*, from *caper* 'goat' + *cornu* 'horn'.

caprine /kaprīn/ > *adjective* relating to or resembling a goat or goats.

ORIGIN – Latin *caprinus*, from *caper* 'goat'.

capri pants /kəpree/ (also **capris**) > *plural noun* close-fitting tapered trousers for women.

ORIGIN – named after the island of *Capri* in Italy.

capsicum /kapsikəm/ > *noun* (pl. **capsicums**) the fruit of a tropical American plant, of which sweet peppers and chilli peppers are varieties.

ORIGIN – Latin, perhaps from *capsa* 'container, case'.

capsize > *verb* (of a boat) be overturned in the water.

SYNONYMS – keel over, overturn, tip over, upset.

ORIGIN – perhaps based on Spanish *capuzar* 'sink (a ship) by the head', from *cabo* 'head' + *chapuzar* 'to dive or duck'.

capstan /kapstən/ > *noun* a broad revolving cylinder with a vertical axis, used for winding a rope or cable.

ORIGIN – Provençal *cabestan*, from *cabestre* 'halter', from Latin *capere* 'seize'.

capsule > *noun* **1** a small soluble case of gelatin containing a dose of medicine, swallowed whole. **2** a small case or container. **3** a space capsule. **4** Botany a dry fruit that releases its seeds by bursting open when ripe.

DERIVATIVES – **capsular** *adjective* **capsulate** *adjective*.

ORIGIN – Latin *capsula* 'small case or container'.

captain > *noun* **1** the person in command of a ship. **2** the pilot in command of a civil aircraft. **3** a rank of naval officer above commander and below commodore. **4** a rank of officer in the army and in the US and Canadian air forces, above lieutenant and below major. **5** (in the US) a police officer in charge of a precinct. **6** the leader of a team, especially in sports. > *verb* serve as the captain of.

DERIVATIVES – **captaincy** noun.

ORIGIN – Old French *capitain*, from Latin *capitaneus* 'chief', from *caput* 'head'.

caption > *noun* **1** a title or brief explanation attached to an illustration or cartoon. **2** a piece of text appearing on screen as part of a film or broadcast. > *verb* provide with a caption.

ORIGIN – Latin, from *capere* 'take, seize' (see box at CAPTURE).

captious /kapshəss/ > *adjective* formal tending to find fault or raise petty objections.

DERIVATIVES – **captiously** adverb **captiousness** noun.

ORIGIN – Old French *captieux*, from Latin *capere* 'take, seize'.

captivate > *verb* attract and hold the interest and attention of; charm.

DERIVATIVES – **captivating** adjective **captivation** noun.

SYNONYMS – beguile, charm, enchant, enthral, entrance.

ORIGIN – Latin *captivare* 'take captive'.

captive > *noun* a person who has been taken prisoner or held in confinement. > *adjective* **1** imprisoned or confined. **2** having no freedom to choose an alternative. **3** (of a facility or service) controlled by and reserved for a particular organisation.

DERIVATIVES – **captivity** noun.

SYNONYMS – *noun* convict, detainee, hostage, prisoner. *adjective* **1** caged, confined, imprisoned, incarcerated, locked up.

captor > *noun* a person who imprisons or confines another.

capture > *verb* **1** take into one's possession or control by force. **2** record or express accurately in words or pictures. **3** cause (data) to be stored in a computer. > *noun* **1** the action of capturing or of being captured. **2** a person or thing that has been captured.

DERIVATIVES – **capturer** noun.

SYNONYMS – *verb* **1** apprehend, catch, lay hold of, seize. *noun* **1** apprehension, arrest, seizure.

Capuchin /kappoͦochin/ > *noun* **1** a friar belonging to a strict branch of the Franciscan order. **2** a cloak and hood formerly worn by women. **3** (**capuchin**) a South American monkey with a cowl-like cap of hair on the head.

ORIGIN – obsolete French, from Italian *cappuccino* 'small hood or cowl', from Latin *cappa* 'covering for the head'.

capybara /kappibaarə/ > *noun* (pl. same or **capybaras**) a large South American rodent resembling a long-legged guinea pig.

ORIGIN – Spanish *capibara* or Portuguese *capivara*, from a Tupi word meaning 'grass-eater'.

---

wordpower facts

Capture

Capture is one of a number of words that come ultimately from the Latin verb *capere*, which means 'to take or seize'. Obviously related are **captive** and **captivity**. Also from the same root is **caption**, which originally meant 'seizing, capture', then 'warrant for arrest'; later it came to denote a statement, usually appended to a legal document, outlining where, when, and by whose authority a warrant was issued—hence the sense 'heading or appended wording'. Other words that come from *capere*, such as **capable**, **capstan**, **conceive**, and **receive**, are now widely divergent in meaning.

---

car > *noun* **1** a powered road vehicle designed to carry a small number of people. **2** a railway carriage or (N. Amer.) wagon.

COMBINATIONS – **car boot sale** Brit. an outdoor sale at which people sell things brought in the boots of their cars. **car wash** a place for washing vehicles automatically, consisting of a drive-through structure fitted with brushes and sprinklers.

---

wordpower facts

Car

Although the modern **car** is quite unlike the two-wheeled wagon of medieval times, the basic sense of the word, 'a wheeled vehicle', is little changed since its first use in English in 1382. It comes (via Old Northern French *carre*) from the Latin word *carrus*, which means 'wheeled vehicle' and is the root also of **cargo**, **charge**, **chariot**, and of the verb **carry**, from which **carriage** developed. Surprisingly, **career** also comes from *carrus* (through French *carrière*): its earliest use in English denoted a road or racecourse.

---

carabineer /karrəbineer/ (also **carabinier**) > *noun* historical a cavalry soldier whose principal weapon was a carbine.

carabiner > *noun* variant spelling of KARABINER.

carabiniere /karrəbinyairi/ > *noun* (pl. **carabinieri** pronunc. same) a member of the Italian paramilitary police.

ORIGIN – Italian, 'carabineer'.

caracul > *noun* variant spelling of KARAKUL.

carafe /kəraf/ > *noun* an open-topped glass flask typically used for serving wine in a restaurant.

ORIGIN – French, from Italian *caraffa*, probably based on an Arabic word meaning 'draw water'.

carambola /karrəmbōlə/ > *noun* a starfruit.

ORIGIN – Portuguese, probably from an Indian language.

caramel > *noun* **1** sugar or syrup heated until it turns brown, used as a flavouring or colouring for food or drink. **2** a soft toffee made with sugar and butter that have been melted and further heated.

DERIVATIVES – **caramelise** (also **caramelize**) verb.

ORIGIN – French, from Spanish *caramelo*.

carapace /karrəpayss/ > *noun* the hard upper shell of a tortoise or crustacean.

ORIGIN – French, from Spanish *carapacho*.

carat /karrət/ > *noun* **1** a unit of weight for precious stones and pearls, equivalent to 200 milligrams. **2** (US also **karat**) a measure of the purity of gold, pure gold being 24 carats.

ORIGIN – French, from Greek *keration* 'fruit of the carob', also denoting a unit of weight.

caravan > *noun* **1** Brit. a vehicle equipped for living in, usually designed to be towed. **2** N. Amer. a covered truck. **3** historical a group of people travelling together across a desert in Asia or North Africa.

DERIVATIVES – **caravanner** noun **caravanning** noun.

ORIGIN – French *caravane*, from Persian.

caravanserai /karrəvansərī, -ri/ (US also **caravansary**) > *noun* (pl. **caravanserais** or **caravansaries**) **1** historical an inn with a central courtyard for travellers in the desert regions of Asia or North Africa. **2** a group of people travelling together; a caravan.

ORIGIN – Persian, 'caravan palace'.

caravel /karrəvel/ > *noun* historical a small, fast Spanish or Portuguese ship of the 15th–17th centuries.

ORIGIN – Portuguese *caravela*, from Greek *karabos* 'horned beetle' or 'light ship'.

caraway /karrəway/ > *noun* the seeds of a plant of the parsley family, used for flavouring.

ORIGIN – Latin *carui*, from Arabic, probably from Greek *karon* 'cumin'.

carbide > *noun* Chemistry a compound of carbon with a metal or other element.

carbine > *noun* **1** a light automatic rifle. **2** historical a short rifle or musket used by cavalry.

ORIGIN – French *carabine*, from *carabin* 'mounted musketeer'.

carbohydrate > *noun* any of a large group of compounds (including sugars, starch, and cellulose) which contain carbon, hydrogen, and oxygen, occur in foods and living tissues, and can be broken down to release energy in the body.

carbolic (also **carbolic acid**) > *noun* the compound phenol, especially when used as a disinfectant.

carbon > *noun* a non-metallic chemical element which has two main forms (diamond and graphite), occurs in impure form in charcoal, soot, and coal, and is present in all organic compounds.

DERIVATIVES – **carbonaceous** *adjective*.

COMBINATIONS – **carbon black** a fine carbon powder used as a pigment. **carbon copy 1** a copy made with carbon paper. **2** a person or thing identical to another. **carbon dating** the determination of the age of an organic object from the relative proportions of the isotopes carbon-12 and carbon-14 that it contains. **carbon dioxide** a colourless, odourless gas produced by burning carbon and organic compounds and by respiration, and absorbed by plants in photosynthesis. **carbon fibre** a material consisting of thin, strong crystalline filaments of carbon. **carbon monoxide** a colourless, odourless toxic flammable gas formed by incomplete combustion of carbon. **carbon paper** thin paper coated with carbon, used for making a second impression as a document is being written or typed. **carbon tax** a tax on petrol and other fossil fuels.

ORIGIN – Latin *carbo* 'coal, charcoal'.

carbonara /kaarbə**naar**ə/ > *adjective* denoting a pasta sauce made with bacon or ham, egg, and cream.

ORIGIN – Italian, 'charcoal kiln', perhaps influenced by *carbonata*, a dish of charcoal-grilled salt pork.

carbonate /**kaar**bənayt/ > *noun* a salt of the anion CO_3^{2-}, typically formed by reaction of carbon dioxide with bases. > *verb* dissolve carbon dioxide in.

DERIVATIVES – **carbonation** *noun*.

carbonated > *adjective* (of a soft drink) effervescent because of the addition of carbon dioxide.

carbonic /kaar**bonn**ik/ > *adjective* relating to carbon or carbon dioxide.

COMBINATIONS – **carbonic acid** a very weak acid formed when carbon dioxide dissolves in water.

Carboniferous /kaarbə**niff**ərəss/ > *adjective* Geology relating to the fifth period of the Palaeozoic era (between the Devonian and Permian periods, about 363 to 290 million years ago), a time when extensive coal-bearing strata were formed.

carbonise (also **carbonize**) > *verb* convert into carbon, by heating or burning.

DERIVATIVES – **carbonisation** *noun*.

carborundum /kaarbə**run**dəm/ > *noun* a very hard black solid consisting of silicon carbide, used as an abrasive.

ORIGIN – blend of **CARBON** and **CORUNDUM**.

carboy > *noun* a large round glass bottle with a narrow neck, used for holding acids or other corrosive liquids.

ORIGIN – from a Persian word meaning 'large glass flagon'.

carbuncle /**kaar**bungk'l/ > *noun* **1** a severe abscess or multiple boil in the skin. **2** a bright red gem, in particular a polished garnet.

DERIVATIVES – **carbuncular** *adjective*.

ORIGIN – Latin *carbunculus* 'small coal', from *carbo* 'coal, charcoal'.

carburettor /kaarbə**rett**ər/ (also **carburetter**, US **carburetor**) > *noun* a device in an internal-combustion engine for mixing air with a fine spray of liquid fuel.

DERIVATIVES – **carburetted** (US **carbureted**) *adjective*.

ORIGIN – from archaic *carburet* 'combine or charge with carbon'.

carcass (Brit. also **carcase**) > *noun* **1** the dead body of an animal, especially one prepared for cutting up as meat. **2** the remains of a cooked bird after all the edible parts have been removed. **3** the structural framework of a building, ship, or piece of furniture.

SYNONYMS – **1** body, cadaver, corpse, remains.

ORIGIN – Old French *carcois*; in later use from French *carcasse*.

carcinogen /kaar**sinn**əjən/ > *noun* a substance capable of causing cancer.

ORIGIN – from **CARCINOMA**.

carcinogenic /kaarsinnə**jenn**ik/ > *adjective* having the potential to cause cancer.

DERIVATIVES – **carcinogenesis** *noun* **carcinogenicity** *noun*.

carcinoma /kaarsi**nō**mə/ > *noun* (pl. **carcinomas** or **carcinomata** /kaarsi**nō**mətə/) a cancer arising in the tissues of the skin or of the lining of the internal organs.

DERIVATIVES – **carcinomatous** *adjective*.

ORIGIN – Latin, from Greek *karkinos* 'crab'; compare with **CANCER**.

card[1] > *noun* **1** thick, stiff paper or thin cardboard. **2** a piece of card for writing on, especially a postcard or greetings card. **3** a business card or visiting card. **4** a small rectangular piece of plastic containing machine-readable personal data, e.g. a credit card or cash card. **5** a playing card. **6** (**cards**) a game played with playing cards. **7** (**cards**) Brit. informal documents relating to an employee, especially for tax and national insurance, held by the employer. **8** informal, dated or N. Amer. a person regarded as odd or amusing. > *verb* **1** write (something) on a card, especially for indexing. **2** N. Amer. check the identity card of (someone), especially to verify their age.

WORDFINDER – cartomancy (*fortune telling*

using cards), cartophily (*collecting of picture cards*), deltiologist (*collector of postcards*).

IDIOMS – **a card up one's sleeve** Brit. a plan or asset that is kept secret until it is needed. **give someone their cards** (or **get one's cards**) Brit. informal dismiss someone (or be dismissed) from employment. **hold all the cards** be in a very strong position. **on** (or N. Amer. **in**) **the cards** informal possible or likely. **play the —— card** exploit the specified issue or idea mentioned, especially for political advantage: *he saw an opportunity to play the peace card*. **play one's cards right** make the best use of one's assets and opportunities. **put** (or **lay**) **one's cards on the table** be completely open and honest in declaring one's intentions.

COMBINATIONS – **card-carrying** registered as a member of a political party or trade union. **card index** a catalogue in which each item is entered on a separate card. **card sharp** (also **card sharper**) a person who cheats at cards in order to win money. **card table** a table for playing cards on, typically folding flat for storage and having a baize surface. **card vote** Brit. a block vote.

---

wordpower facts
Card
The earliest use of the word **card** was in the 15th century, when it denoted each of a set of small oblong pieces of pasteboard, used in playing games of chance: that is, a **playing card**. The word itself comes, via Old French *carte*, from Latin *carta*, meaning 'papyrus leaf, paper', ultimately from the Greek word for a papyrus leaf, *khartēs*. The same root is shared by a number of words, including **cartel**, **carton**, **cartoon**, and **cartouche**. The alternative Latin spelling *charta* led to the formation of **chart** and **charter**.

---

card[2] > *verb* comb and clean (raw wool or similar material) with a sharp-toothed instrument to disentangle the fibres before spinning. > *noun* a toothed implement or machine for this purpose.

DERIVATIVES – **carder** *noun*.

ORIGIN – Provençal *carda*, from *cardar* 'tease, comb', from Latin *carduus* 'thistle'.

cardamom /**kaar**dəməm/ (also **cardamum**) > *noun* the aromatic seeds of a plant of the ginger family, used as a spice.

ORIGIN – Greek *kardamōmon*, from *kardamon* 'cress' + *amōmon*, the name of a kind of spice plant.

cardboard > *noun* **1** pasteboard or stiff paper. **2** (before another noun) (of a fictional character) lacking depth and realism.

COMBINATIONS – **cardboard city** chiefly Brit. an urban area where homeless people congregate under makeshift shelters.

cardiac /**kaar**diak/ > *adjective* of or relating to the heart.

ORIGIN – Greek *kardiakos*, from *kardia* 'heart'.

cardigan > *noun* a knitted jumper fastening with buttons down the front.

ORIGIN – named after the 7th Earl of *Cardigan*, whose troops fighting in the Crimean War first wore such garments.

cardinal > *noun* **1** a leading dignitary of the Roman Catholic Church, nominated by and having the power to elect the Pope. **2** a deep scarlet colour like that of a cardinal's cassock. **3** an American songbird of which the male is partly or mostly red and which typically has a crest. > *adjective* of the greatest importance; fundamental.

WORDFINDER – conclave (*assembly of cardinals gathered to elect a pope*), consistory (*council of cardinals*), his/your eminence (*title given to cardinal*).

DERIVATIVES – **cardinalate** *noun* **cardinally** *adverb*.

COMBINATIONS – **cardinal humour** see HUMOUR. **cardinal number** a number denoting quantity (one, two, three, etc.), as opposed to an ordinal number (first, second, third, etc.). **cardinal point** each of the four main points of the compass (north, south, east, and west). **cardinal virtue** each of the chief moral attributes of scholastic philosophy: justice, prudence, temperance, and fortitude.

ORIGIN – Latin *cardinalis*, from *cardo* 'hinge'; sense 1 arose from the function of such priests as 'pivots' of church life.

cardiogram > *noun* a record of muscle activity within the heart made by a cardiograph.

cardiograph > *noun* an instrument for recording heart muscle activity.

DERIVATIVES – **cardiographer** *noun* **cardiography** *noun*.

ORIGIN – from Greek *kardia* 'heart'.

cardiology > *noun* the branch of medicine concerned with diseases and abnormalities of the heart.

DERIVATIVES – **cardiological** *adjective* **cardiologist** *noun*.

cardiopulmonary > *adjective* Medicine of or relating to the heart and the lungs.

cardiovascular > *adjective* Medicine of or relating to the heart and blood vessels.

cardoon > *noun* a tall thistle-like plant related to the globe artichoke, with edible leaves and roots.

ORIGIN – French *cardon*, from *carde* 'edible part of an artichoke', from Latin *carduus* 'thistle, artichoke'.

cardy (also **cardie**) > *noun* (pl. **cardies**) Brit. informal a cardigan.

care > *noun* **1** the provision of what is necessary for the welfare and protection of someone or something. **2** Brit. protective custody or guardianship provided by a local authority for children whose parents are dead or unable look after them. **3** careful attention or consideration applied to an action or plan. **4** a feeling of or reason for anxiety. > *verb* **1** feel concern or interest. **2** feel affection or liking. **3** (**care for** or **to do**) like to have or be willing to do. **4** (**care for**) look after and provide for the needs of.

IDIOMS – **care of** at the address of. **take care 1** be cautious; keep oneself safe. **2** make sure of doing something. **take care of 1** keep safe and provided for. **2** deal with.

DERIVATIVES – **caring** *noun* & *adjective*.

SYNONYMS – *noun* **3** carefulness, caution, concentration, diligence, pains, thoroughness. **4** burden, concern, trouble, worry. *verb* **1** be concerned, bother, mind, trouble, worry.

careen /ka**reen**/ > *verb* **1** turn (a ship) on its side for cleaning or repair. **2** (of a ship) tilt; lean over. **3** move in an uncontrolled way; career.

ORIGIN – French *carène*, from Latin *carina* 'a keel'.

career > *noun* **1** an occupation undertaken for a significant period of a person's life, usually with opportunities for progress. **2** progress through history: *the organisation's chequered career*. **3** (before another noun) working with long-term commitment in a particular profession: *a career diplomat*. > *verb* move along swiftly and in an uncontrolled way.

SYNONYMS – *noun* **1** job, occupation, profession, vocation.

COMBINATIONS – **career woman** a woman who pursues a profession.

ORIGIN – first denoting a road or racecourse: from French *carrière*, from Latin *carrus* 'wheeled vehicle'.

careerist > *noun* a person whose main concern is gaining advancement in their profession.

DERIVATIVES – **careerism** *noun*.

carefree > *adjective* free from anxiety or responsibility.

DERIVATIVES – **carefreeness** *noun*.

SYNONYMS – casual, happy-go-lucky, light-hearted, nonchalant, untroubled.

ANTONYMS – anxious, worried.

careful > *adjective* **1** taking care to avoid harm or mistakes; cautious. **2** (**careful with**) prudent in the use of. **3** done with or showing thought and attention.

DERIVATIVES – **carefully** *adverb* **carefulness** *noun*.

SYNONYMS – **1** cautious, prudent, vigilant,

wary, watchful. **3** conscientious, diligent, meticulous, thorough.

ANTONYMS – careless.

careless > *adjective* **1** not giving sufficient attention or thought to avoiding harm or mistakes. **2** (**careless of** or **about**) not concerned or worried about. **3** showing no interest or effort; casual.

DERIVATIVES – **carelessly** *adverb* **carelessness** *noun*.

SYNONYMS – **1** inattentive, incautious, negligent, remiss, unwary. **3** casual, shoddy, slapdash, sloppy.

ANTONYMS – careful.

carer > *noun* Brit. a family member or paid helper who regularly looks after a sick, elderly, or disabled person.

caress > *verb* touch or stroke gently or lovingly. > *noun* a gentle or loving touch.

DERIVATIVES – **caressing** *adjective* **caressingly** *adverb*.

SYNONYMS – *verb* brush, fondle, stroke, touch. *noun* stroke, touch.

ORIGIN – French *caresser*, from Latin *carus* 'dear'.

caret /**karr**ət/ > *noun* a mark (^, ʌ) placed below a line of text to indicate a proposed insertion.

ORIGIN – Latin, literally 'is lacking'.

caretaker > *noun* **1** Brit. a person employed to look after a public building. **2** (before another noun) holding power temporarily: *a caretaker government*. **3** chiefly N. Amer. a person employed to look after people or animals.

careworn > *adjective* tired and unhappy because of prolonged worry.

SYNONYMS – drained, drawn, gaunt, haggard, strained.

cargo > *noun* (pl. **cargoes** or **cargos**) goods carried commercially on a ship, aircraft, or truck.

SYNONYMS – consignment, goods, freight, load, shipment.

ORIGIN – Spanish, from Latin *carricare* 'to load', from *carrus* 'wheeled vehicle'.

Carib /**karr**ib/ > *noun* **1** a member of an indigenous South American people living mainly in coastal regions of French Guiana, Suriname, Guyana, and Venezuela. **2** the language of the Caribs. **3** (also **Island Carib**) an unrelated language, now extinct, formerly spoken in the Lesser Antilles.

ORIGIN – Spanish *Caribe*, from Haitian Creole; compare with CANNIBAL.

Caribbean* /karri**bee**ən, kə**ribb**iən/ > *adjective* relating to the region consisting of the Caribbean Sea, its islands (including the West Indies), and the surrounding coasts.

NOTE – there are two acceptable pronunciations of **Caribbean**: the British pronunciation puts the stress on the **-be-**, while in the US and the Caribbean itself the stress is on the **-rib-**.

*SPELLING – one r and two bs: Ca*ribb*ean.

caribou /**karr**iboo/ > *noun* (pl. same) N. Amer. a reindeer.

ORIGIN – Canadian French, from a Micmac word meaning 'snow-shoveller'.

caricature /**karr**ikətyoor/ > *noun* a depiction of a person in which their distinguishing characteristics are exaggerated for comic or grotesque effect. > *verb* make a caricature of.

DERIVATIVES – **caricatural** *adjective* **caricaturist** *noun*.

SYNONYMS – *noun* burlesque, cartoon, parody, satire, send-up. *verb* burlesque, parody, send up, take off.

ORIGIN – Italian *caricatura*, from *caricare* 'load, exaggerate'.

caries /**kair**eez/ > *noun* decay and crumbling of a tooth or bone.

DERIVATIVES – **carious** *adjective*.

ORIGIN – Latin.

carillon /kə**ril**yən/ > *noun* **1** a set of bells sounded from a keyboard or by an automatic mechanism. **2** a tune played on such bells.

ORIGIN – French, from Old French *quarregnon* 'peal of four bells', from Latin *quattuor* 'four'.

carjacking > *noun* chiefly N. Amer. the action of stealing a car after violently ejecting its driver.

Carmelite /**kaar**məlīt/ > *noun* a friar or nun of an order founded at Mount Carmel in Israel during the Crusades. > *adjective* relating to the Carmelites.

carminative /**kaar**minətiv/ Medicine > *adjective* relieving flatulence. > *noun* a carminative drug.

ORIGIN – from Latin *carminare* 'heal by incantation', from *carmen* 'song, verse, incantation'.

carmine /**kaar**mīn/ > *noun* a vivid crimson pigment made from cochineal.

ORIGIN – French *carmin*, from an Arabic word meaning 'kermes': see box at **VERMILION**.

carnage /**kaar**nij/ > *noun* the killing of a large number of people.

SYNONYMS – bloodshed, butchery, massacre, slaughter.

ORIGIN – French, from Latin *caro* 'flesh'.

carnal > *adjective* relating to physical, especially sexual, needs and activities.

DERIVATIVES – **carnality** *noun* **carnally** *adverb*.

SYNONYMS – bodily, corporeal, fleshly, sensual, sexual.

COMBINATIONS – **carnal knowledge** dated, chiefly Law sexual intercourse.

ORIGIN – Latin *carnalis*, from *caro* 'flesh'.

carnation > *noun* a double-flowered cultivated variety of clove pink, with grey-green leaves and showy pink, white, or red flowers.

ORIGIN – perhaps based on a misreading of an Arabic word meaning 'clove or clove pink', influenced by French *carnation* 'flesh colour or rosy pink', from Latin *caro* 'flesh'.

carnelian /kaar**nee**liən/ (also **cornelian** /kor**nee**liən/) > *noun* a dull red or pink semi-precious variety of chalcedony.

ORIGIN – Old French *corneline*, the prefix *car-* being suggested by Latin *caro* 'flesh'.

carnival > *noun* **1** an annual period of public revelry involving processions, music, and dancing. **2** N. Amer. a travelling funfair or circus.

DERIVATIVES – **carnivalesque** *adjective*.

SYNONYMS – **1** fair, festival, fiesta, gala.

ORIGIN – Italian *carnevale*, from Latin *carnelevamen* 'Shrovetide', from *caro* 'flesh' + *levare* 'put away'.

carnivore /**kaar**nivor/ > *noun* a carnivorous animal.

carnivorous /kaar**nivv**ərəss/ > *adjective* (of an animal) feeding on flesh.

DERIVATIVES – **carnivorously** *adverb* **carnivorousness** *noun*.

ORIGIN – Latin *carnivorus*, from *caro* 'flesh'.

carnosaur > *noun* a large bipedal carnivorous dinosaur of a group including tyrannosaurus, allosaurus, and megalosaurus.

carob /**karr**əb/ > *noun* the edible brownish-purple pod of an Arabian tree, from which a powder is extracted for use as a substitute for chocolate.

ORIGIN – Old French *carobe*, from Arabic.

carol > *noun* a religious song or popular hymn associated with Christmas. > *verb* (**carolled**, **carolling**; US **caroled**, **caroling**) **1** (**go carolling**) sing carols in the streets. **2** sing or say happily.

DERIVATIVES – **caroller** (US **caroler**) *noun*.

ORIGIN – Old French *carole*.

Carolingian /karrə**lin**jiən/ (also **Carlovingian** /kaarlə**vin**jiən/) > *adjective* **1** relating to the Frankish dynasty founded by the emperor Charlemagne's father (Pepin III), which ruled in western Europe from 750 to 987. **2** denoting a script developed in France during the time of Charlemagne, on which modern lower-case letters are largely based. > *noun* a member of the Carolingian dynasty.

ORIGIN – alteration of earlier *Carlovingian* (from French *carlovingien*), by association with Latin *Carolus* 'Charles'.

carotene /**karr**əteen/ > *noun* an orange or red plant pigment found notably in carrots, important in the formation of vitamin A.

DERIVATIVES – **carotenoid** /kə**rott**inoyd/ *noun*.

ORIGIN – from Latin *carota* 'carrot'.

carotid /kə**rott**id/ > *adjective* Anatomy relating to the two main arteries carrying blood to the head and neck.

ORIGIN – from Greek *karōtides*, plural of *karōtis* 'drowsiness, stupor' (because compression of these arteries was thought to cause stupor).

carouse /kə**rowz**/ > *verb* drink alcohol and enjoy oneself with others in a noisy, lively way. > *noun* a noisy, lively drinking party.

DERIVATIVES – **carousal** *noun* **carouser** *noun*.

SYNONYMS – *verb* celebrate, make merry, overindulge, revel; archaic wassail. *noun* binge, party, shindig, spree.

ORIGIN – first used as an adverb meaning 'right out, completely' in the phrase *drink carouse*, from German *gar aus trinken*.

carousel /**karr**əsel/ > *noun* **1** a merry-go-round at a fair. **2** a rotating machine or device, in particular a conveyor system for baggage collection at an airport. **3** historical an equestrian tournament among knights.

ORIGIN – French *carrousel*, from Italian *carosello*, perhaps from *carro* 'chariot'.

carp[1] > *noun* (pl. same) a deep-bodied freshwater fish, often kept in ponds and sometimes farmed for food.

ORIGIN – Latin *carpa*.

carp[2] > *verb* complain or find fault continually.

DERIVATIVES – **carper** *noun*.

SYNONYMS – cavil, complain, grouse, grumble, moan.

ORIGIN – first used in the sense 'talk, chatter': from Old Norse *karpa* 'brag', later influenced by Latin *carpere* 'pluck at, slander'.

carpaccio /kaar**pach**iō/ > *noun* an Italian hors d'oeuvre consisting of thin slices of raw beef or fish served with a sauce.

ORIGIN – Italian, named after the Renaissance painter Vittore *Carpaccio* (from his use of red pigments, resembling raw meat).

carpal Anatomy & Zoology > *adjective* relating to the carpus. > *noun* a bone of the carpus.

COMBINATIONS – **carpal tunnel syndrome** a painful condition of the hand and fingers caused by compression of a nerve where it passes over the carpal bones.

carpe diem /**kaar**pay **dee**-em/ > *exclamation* make the most of the present time.

ORIGIN – Latin, 'seize the day!': a quotation from the Roman poet Horace (*Odes*).

carpel > *noun* Botany the female reproductive organ of a flower, consisting of an ovary, a stigma, and usually a style.

DERIVATIVES – **carpellary** *adjective*.

ORIGIN – Greek *karpos* 'fruit'.

carpenter > *noun* a person who makes wooden objects and structures. > *verb* make by shaping wood.

DERIVATIVES – **carpentry** *noun*.

COMBINATIONS – **carpenter trousers** loose-fitting trousers with many pockets of various sizes and loops for tools at the top or sides of the legs.

ORIGIN – Old French *carpentier*, from Latin *carpentarius artifex* 'carriage maker', from *carpentum* 'wagon'.

carpet > *noun* 1 a floor covering made from thick woven fabric. 2 a large rug. 3 a thick or soft expanse or layer of something. > *verb* (**carpeted**, **carpeting**) 1 cover with a carpet. 2 Brit. informal reprimand severely.

IDIOMS – **on the carpet** informal being severely reprimanded by someone in authority. **sweep under the carpet** conceal or ignore (a problem) in the hope that it will be forgotten.

DERIVATIVES – **carpeting** *noun*.

COMBINATIONS – **carpet bag** a travelling bag made of a thick woven material used for carpets or rugs. **carpet-bomb** bomb (an area) intensively. **carpet slipper** a soft slipper with an upper of wool or thick cloth.

ORIGIN – first used to denote a thick cover for a table or bed: from obsolete Italian *carpita* 'woollen counterpane', from Latin *carpere* 'pluck, pull to pieces'; the phrase 'on the carpet' and the related verb sense are in reference to the covering over the table before which one would be summoned for a reprimand.

carpetbagger > *noun* derogatory, chiefly N. Amer. 1 a politician who seeks election in an area where they have no local connections. 2 an unscrupulous opportunist.

carport > *noun* an open-sided shelter for a car, projecting from the side of a house.

carpus /kaarpəss/ > *noun* (pl. **carpi** /kaarpī/) the group of small bones in the wrist.

ORIGIN – Greek *karpos* 'wrist'.

carrack /karrək/ > *noun* a large European merchant ship of a kind operating from the 14th to the 17th century.

ORIGIN – Old French *caraque*.

carrageen /karrəgeen/ (also **carrageen moss**) > *noun* an edible red shoreline seaweed with flattened branching fronds.

ORIGIN – Irish.

carrel /karrəl/ > *noun* 1 a small cubicle with a desk for a reader in a library. 2 historical a small enclosure or study in a cloister.

ORIGIN – apparently related to CAROL in the obsolete sense 'a ring or enclosure'.

carriage > *noun* 1 a four-wheeled passenger vehicle pulled by two or more horses. 2 Brit. any of the separate vehicles of a passenger train. 3 Brit. the conveying of goods from one place to another. 4 a person's bearing or deportment. 5 a moving part of a machine that carries other parts into the required position. 6 a wheeled support for moving a heavy object such as a gun.

SYNONYMS – 4 bearing, demeanour, deportment, manner, posture.

COMBINATIONS – **carriage clock** Brit. a portable clock in a rectangular case with a handle on top.

ORIGIN – Old French *cariage*, from *carier* 'carry'.

carriageway > *noun* Brit. 1 each of the two sides of a dual carriageway or motorway. 2 the part of a road intended for vehicles.

carrier > *noun* 1 a person or thing that carries or holds something. 2 a person or company that transports goods or people for payment. 3 a person or animal that transmits a disease to others without suffering from it themselves.

SYNONYMS – 1 bearer, conveyer, courier, porter, transporter.

COMBINATIONS – **carrier bag** Brit. a plastic or paper bag with handles, for carrying shopping. **carrier pigeon** a homing pigeon trained to carry messages.

carrion > *noun* the decaying flesh of dead animals.

COMBINATIONS – **carrion crow** a common black crow.

ORIGIN – Old French *caroine, charoigne*, from Latin *caro* 'flesh'.

carrot > *noun* 1 the tapering orange root of a plant of the parsley family, eaten as a vegetable. 2 something enticing offered as a means of persuasion (as contrasted with the 'stick' or threat of punishment).

ORIGIN – Greek *karōton*.

carroty > *adjective* (of a person's hair) orange-red.

carry > *verb* (**carries, carried**) 1 move or transport from one place to another. 2 have on one's person wherever one goes. 3 support the weight of. 4 assume or accept (responsibility or blame). 5 have as a feature or consequence. 6 conduct or transmit. 7 take or develop (an idea or activity) to a particular point. 8 approve (a proposed measure) by a majority of votes: *the motion was carried by one vote.* 9 persuade to support one's policy. 10 publish or broadcast: *the paper carried an account of the crisis.* 11 (of a sound or voice) travel a specific distance: *his voice carried clearly across the room.* 12 (**carry oneself**) stand and move in a specified way. 13 be pregnant with. > *noun* (pl. **carries**) an act of carrying.

IDIOMS – **be** (or **get**) **carried away** lose self-control. **carry all before one** overcome all opposition. **carry the can** Brit. informal take responsibility for a mistake or misdeed. **carry the day** be victorious or successful. **carry forward** transfer (figures) to a new page or account. **carry off** 1 take away by force. 2 (of a disease) kill. 3 succeed in doing. **carry on** 1 continue. 2 engage in (an activity). 3 informal, chiefly Brit. be engaged in a love affair. **carry out** perform (a task). **carry over** 1 keep to use or deal with in a new context. 2 postpone. **carry through** bring to completion. **carry weight** be influential.

SYNONYMS – *verb* 1 bear, convey, ferry, haul, transport. 3 bear, hold up, sustain, support. 4 accept, assume, bear, shoulder, take on.

ORIGIN – Old French *carier*, from Latin *carrus* 'wheeled vehicle'; compare with CAR.

carryall > *noun* N. Amer. a large bag or case.

carrycot > *noun* Brit. a baby's small portable cot.

carry-on > *noun* Brit. informal 1 a fuss. 2 (also **carryings-on**) questionable or improper behaviour.

cart > *noun* 1 an open horse-drawn vehicle with two or four wheels, used for carrying loads or passengers. 2 a shallow open container on wheels, pulled or pushed by hand. > *verb* 1 convey in a cart or similar vehicle. 2 informal carry (a heavy or cumbersome object) somewhere with difficulty. 3 convey or remove unceremoniously: *the demonstrators were carted off by the police.*

IDIOMS – **put the cart before the horse** reverse the proper order or procedure.

DERIVATIVES – **carter** *noun*.

ORIGIN – Old Norse.

carte blanche /kaart blaansh/ > *noun* complete freedom to act as one wishes.

ORIGIN – French, 'blank paper'.

cartel /kaartel/ > *noun* an association of manufacturers or suppliers formed to restrict competition and maintain high prices.

ORIGIN – German *Kartell*, from Italian *cartello*, from Latin *carta* 'card': used originally with reference to the coalition of the Conservative and National Liberal parties in Germany (1887).

Cartesian /kaarteeziən/ > *adjective* relating to the French philosopher René Descartes (1596–1650) and his ideas. > *noun* a follower of Descartes.

DERIVATIVES – **Cartesianism** *noun*.

COMBINATIONS – **Cartesian coordinates** a coordinate system using two (or three) mutually perpendicular axes.

Carthaginian /kaarthəjinniən/ > *noun* a person from the ancient city of Carthage on the coast of North Africa. > *adjective* relating to Carthage or its people.

carthorse > *noun* Brit. a large, strong horse suitable for heavy work.

Carthusian /kaarthyōoziən/ > *noun* a monk or nun of an austere contemplative order founded by St Bruno in 1084. > *adjective* relating to this order.

ORIGIN – from *Carthusia*, the Latin name for *Chartreuse* in France, where the order was founded.

cartilage /**kaar**tilij/ > *noun* firm, flexible connective tissue which covers the ends of joints and forms structures such as the larynx and the external ear.

DERIVATIVES – **cartilaginous** /kaarti-**laj**inəss/ *adjective*.

ORIGIN – Latin *cartilago*.

cartilaginous fish > *noun* a fish with a skeleton of cartilage rather than bone, e.g. a shark or ray.

cartography /kaar**tog**rəfi/ > *noun* the science or practice of drawing maps.

DERIVATIVES – **cartographer** *noun* **cartographic** *adjective*.

ORIGIN – from French *carte* 'card, map'.

carton > *noun* a light cardboard box or container.

ORIGIN – French, from Italian *cartone*, from *carta* 'paper'; related to **CARTOON**.

cartoon > *noun* **1** a drawing executed in an exaggerated style for humorous or satirical effect. **2** (also **cartoon strip**) a narrative sequence of humorous drawings with captions in a comic, newspaper, or magazine. **3** a film made from a sequence of drawings, using animation techniques to give the appearance of movement. **4** a full-size drawing made as a preliminary design for a painting or other work of art. > *verb* represent in a cartoon.

DERIVATIVES – **cartoonish** *adjective* **cartoonist** *noun* **cartoony** *adjective*.

ORIGIN – Italian *cartone*, from Latin *carta*, *charta* 'card, map'.

cartouche /kaar**toosh**/ > *noun* **1** a drawing or carved decoration representing a scroll with rolled-up ends, often bearing an inscription. **2** an oval or oblong enclosing Egyptian hieroglyphs, typically representing the name and title of a monarch.

ORIGIN – Italian *cartoccio*, from Latin *carta*, *charta* 'card, map'.

cartridge > *noun* **1** a container holding a spool of film, a quantity of ink, or other item or substance, designed for insertion into a mechanism. **2** a casing containing a charge and a bullet or shot for small arms or an explosive charge for blasting.

COMBINATIONS – **cartridge paper** thick, rough-textured drawing paper originally used for making cartridge casings.

ORIGIN – variant of **CARTOUCHE**.

cartwheel > *noun* a circular sideways handspring with the arms and legs extended. > *verb* perform cartwheels.

cartwright > *noun* chiefly historical a person whose job is making carts.

carve > *verb* **1** cut into or shape (a hard material) to produce an object or design. **2** produce in such a way. **3** cut (cooked meat) into slices for eating. **4** (**carve out**) develop (a career, reputation, etc.) through painstaking effort. **5** (**carve up**) divide up ruthlessly. **6** (**carve up**) informal aggressively overtake (another driver).

SYNONYMS – **1** chisel, engrave, hew, sculpt, whittle.

carvel-built /**kaar**v'l/ > *adjective* (of a boat) having external planks which do not overlap. Compare with **CLINKER-BUILT**.

ORIGIN – *carvel* is variant spelling of **CARAVEL**.

carver > *noun* **1** a person or tool that carves. **2** Brit. the principal chair, with arms, in a set of dining chairs, intended for the person carving meat.

carvery > *noun* (pl. **carveries**) chiefly Brit. a buffet or restaurant where cooked joints are carved as required.

carving > *noun* an object or design carved from wood or stone as a work of art.

WORDFINDER – glyptic (*of carving or engraving*).

caryatid /karri**att**id/ > *noun* (pl. **caryatides** /karri**att**ideez/ or **caryatids**) Architecture a supporting pillar in the form of a draped female figure.

ORIGIN – Greek *karuatides* 'priestesses of Artemis at Caryae', from *Karuai* (Caryae) in Laconia (southern Greece).

Casanova /kassə**nō**və/ > *noun* a man notorious for seducing women.

ORIGIN – from the name of the Italian adventurer Giovanni Jacopo *Casanova* (1725–98).

casbah > *noun* variant spelling of **KASBAH**.

cascade > *noun* **1** a waterfall, especially one in a series. **2** a mass of something that falls, hangs, or occurs in large quantities. **3** a succession of devices or stages in a process, each of which triggers or initiates the next. > *verb* **1** pour downwards rapidly and in large quantities. **2** arrange in a series or sequence.

SYNONYMS – *verb* **1** gush, pour, spill, stream, tumble.

ORIGIN – Italian *cascata*, from *cascare* 'to fall'.

cascara /kas**kaar**ə/ (also **cascara sagrada** /sə**graa**də/) > *noun* a laxative made from the dried bark of a North American buckthorn.

ORIGIN – Spanish, '(sacred) bark'.

case[1] > *noun* **1** an instance of a particular situation or set of circumstances. **2** an instance of a disease, injury, or problem. **3** an incident under official investigation by the police. **4** a legal action that is to be or has been decided in a court of law. **5** a set of facts or arguments supporting one side of a debate or lawsuit. **6** a person or their situation as a subject of medical or official attention. **7** Grammar an inflected form of a noun, adjective, or pronoun expressing the semantic relation of the word to other words in the sentence: *the possessive case*.

IDIOMS – **be the case** be so. **in case** so as to provide for the possibility of something happening or being true. **on** (or **off**) **someone's case** informal continually (or no longer) criticising or harassing someone.

SYNONYMS – **1** example, instance, occasion, occurrence, specimen. **4** action, dispute, lawsuit, suit.

COMBINATIONS – **case history** a record of a person's background or medical history kept by a doctor or social worker. **case law** the law as established by the outcome of former cases rather than by legislation. **case study 1** a detailed study of the development of a particular person, group, or situation over a period of time. **2** a particular instance used to illustrate a thesis or principle. **casework** social work directly concerned with individuals and their personal circumstances.

ORIGIN – Latin *casus* 'fall, occurrence, chance'.

case[2] > *noun* **1** a container or protective covering. **2** Brit. a suitcase. **3** a box containing twelve bottles of wine or other drink, sold as a unit. **4** each of the two forms, capital or minuscule, in which a letter of the alphabet may be written or printed. > *verb* **1** enclose within a case. **2** informal survey (a place) before carrying out a robbery.

COMBINATIONS – **case-harden 1** harden the surface of (a material). **2** (**case-hardened**) made callous or tough by experience. **case-sensitive** Computing differentiating between capital and lower-case letters.

ORIGIN – Old French *casse*, from Latin *capsa* 'box, receptacle'; sense 4 derives from a container for holding type in printing: two cases were set on an angled stand, the higher one for capitals (upper case) and the lower for minuscule (lower case).

casebook > *noun* Brit. a written record of cases, kept by a doctor, lawyer, etc.

casein /**kay**seen/ > *noun* the main protein present in milk and in cheese.

ORIGIN – from Latin *caseus* 'cheese'.

caseload > *noun* the number of cases being dealt with by a doctor, lawyer, or social worker at one time.

casement > *noun* a window set on a vertical hinge so that it opens like a door.

ORIGIN – Latin *cassimentum*, from *capsa* 'box, receptacle'.

cash > *noun* **1** money in coins or notes. **2** money as an available resource: *he was always short of cash*. > *verb* **1** give or obtain notes or coins for (a cheque or money order). **2** (**cash in**) convert (an insurance policy, savings account, etc.) into money. **3** (**cash in on**) informal take advantage of (a situation). **4** (**cash up**) Brit. count and check takings at the end of a day's trading.

IDIOMS – **cash in one's chips** informal die. **cash in hand** payment in cash rather than by cheque or other means.

DERIVATIVES – **cashable** adjective **cashless** adjective.

SYNONYMS – noun **1** change, coins, currency, money, notes.

COMBINATIONS – **cash and carry** a system of wholesale trading whereby goods are paid for in full and taken away by the purchaser. **cash book** a book in which receipts and payments of money are recorded. **cash card** Brit. a plastic card issued by a bank or building society which enables the holder to withdraw money from a cash dispenser. **cash cow** informal a business or investment that provides a steady income or profit. **cash crop** a crop produced for its commercial value rather than for use by the grower. **cash desk** Brit. a counter or compartment in a shop or restaurant where payments are made. **cash dispenser** (also **cashpoint**) Brit. an automated teller machine. **cash flow** the total amount of money passing into and out of a business, especially as affecting availability of liquid assets. **cash register** a machine used in shops for totalling and recording the amount of each sale and storing the money received.

ORIGIN – first denoting a box for money: from Old French casse or Italian cassa, from Latin capsa 'box, receptacle'.

cashback > noun **1** a cash refund offered as an incentive to buyers. **2** a facility whereby a customer may withdraw cash when making a debit card purchase.

cashew /ka**shōō**/ > noun (also **cashew nut**) the edible kidney-shaped nut of a tropical American tree.

ORIGIN – Tupi.

cashier[1] > noun a person handling payments and receipts in a shop, bank, or business.

cashier[2] > verb dismiss from the armed forces because of a serious misdemeanour.

ORIGIN – French casser 'revoke, dismiss', from Latin quassare 'quash'.

cashmere > noun fine soft wool, originally that obtained from a breed of Himalayan goat.

ORIGIN – an early spelling of Kashmir, a region on the northern border of India and NE Pakistan.

casing > noun **1** a cover or shell that protects or encloses something. **2** the frame round a door or window.

casino > noun (pl. **casinos**) a public building or room for gambling.

ORIGIN – Italian, 'little house'.

cask > noun a large barrel for the storage of liquid, especially alcoholic drinks.

COMBINATIONS – **cask beer** draught beer left to mature naturally in the cask from which it is served. **cask-conditioned** (of beer) undergoing a secondary fermentation in the cask and not further processed before serving.

ORIGIN – French casque or Spanish casco 'helmet'.

casket > noun **1** a small ornamental box or chest for holding valuable objects. **2** chiefly N. Amer. a coffin.

ORIGIN – perhaps a variant of Old French cassette 'little box'.

Cassandra /kə**san**drə/ > noun a prophet of disaster.

ORIGIN – from Cassandra in Greek mythology: in revenge for being cheated by her, Apollo caused her prophecies, though true, to be disbelieved.

cassata /kə**saatə**/ > noun a Neapolitan ice cream dessert containing candied or dried fruit and nuts.

ORIGIN – Italian.

cassava /kə**saavə**/ > noun the starchy tuberous root of a tropical American tree, used as food.

ORIGIN – Taino (an extinct Caribbean language).

casserole > noun **1** a large dish with a lid, used for cooking food slowly in an oven. **2** a kind of stew cooked slowly in an oven. > verb cook slowly in a casserole.

ORIGIN – French, from Latin cattia 'ladle, pan'.

cassette > noun a sealed plastic case containing audio tape, videotape, or film, for insertion into a recorder or camera.

ORIGIN – French, 'little box'.

cassia /**kass**iə/ > noun **1** a tree or plant of warm climates, producing senna and other products. **2** the aromatic bark of an East Asian tree, yielding an inferior kind of cinnamon.

ORIGIN – Latin, from a Hebrew word meaning 'bark resembling cinnamon'.

cassis /ka**seess**/ (also **crème de cassis** /krem də ka**seess**/) > noun a syrupy blackcurrant liqueur.

ORIGIN – French, 'blackcurrant'.

cassock > noun a long garment worn by some Christian clergy and members of church choirs.

ORIGIN – Italian casacca 'riding coat'.

cassoulet /**kass**oolay/ > noun a stew made with meat and beans.

ORIGIN – French, 'small stew pan'.

cassowary /**kass**əwairi/ > noun (pl. **cassowaries**) a very large flightless bird related to the emu, native mainly to New Guinea.

ORIGIN – Malay.

cast > verb (past and past participle **cast**) **1** throw forcefully or so as to spread over an area. **2** cause (light or shadow) to appear on a surface. **3** direct (one's eyes or thoughts) towards something. **4** express: journalists cast doubt on this account. **5** register (a vote). **6** assign a part to (an actor) or allocate parts in (a play or film). **7** discard or shed. **8** throw the hooked and baited end of (a fishing line) out into the water. **9** shape (metal or other material) by pouring it into a mould while molten. **10** produce by casting: a figure cast in bronze. **11** arrange and present in a specified form or style. **12** cause (a magic spell) to take effect. **13** Hunting (of a dog) search around for a scent. > noun **1** the actors taking part in a play or film. **2** an object made by casting metal or other material. **3** (also **plaster cast**) a bandage stiffened with plaster of Paris, moulded to support and protect a broken limb. **4** an act of casting. **5** form, appearance, or character: minds of a philosophical cast. **6** a slight squint.

IDIOMS – **cast about** (or **around** or **round**) search far and wide. **be cast away** be stranded after a shipwreck. **be cast down** feel depressed. **cast off 1** Knitting take the stitches off the needle by looping each over the next. **2** set a boat or ship free from its moorings. **cast on** Knitting make the first row of loops on the needle.

SYNONYMS – verb **1** fling, hurl, launch, pitch, toss. noun **1** company, dramatis personae, performers, players, troupe.

COMBINATIONS – **casting vote** an extra vote used by a chairperson to decide an issue when votes on each side are equal. [ORIGIN – from an obsolete sense of cast 'turn the scale'.] **cast iron 1** a hard alloy of iron and carbon which can be readily cast in a mould. **2** (**cast-iron**) firm and unchangeable: cast-iron guarantees.

ORIGIN – Old Norse.

castanets > plural noun a pair of small concave pieces of wood, ivory, or plastic, clicked together by the fingers as an accompaniment to Spanish dancing.

ORIGIN – Spanish castañeta 'little chestnut'.

castaway > noun a person who has been shipwrecked and stranded in an isolated place.

caste > noun **1** each of the hereditary classes of Hindu society, distinguished by relative degrees of ritual purity or pollution and of social status. **2** any exclusive social class.

WORDFINDER – Brahman (member of highest caste), Dalit or (formerly) untouchable (member of lowest or no caste, officially known as the scheduled caste), Kshatriya (member of second (military) caste), pariah (member of low caste), Sudra (member of fourth (worker) caste), Vaisya (member of third (merchant) caste).

wordpower facts
Caste
The word **caste** comes from Spanish and Portuguese *casta*, meaning 'lineage, breed', apparently from the adjective *casto* 'pure or unmixed' as applied to stock or lineage. Ultimately it comes from the Latin word *castus*, meaning 'pure and unpolluted', which developed in English in the form **chaste**; **castigate, chasten,** and **chastise** all come from the same root.

castellated /ˈkastəlaytid/ > *adjective* having battlements.
DERIVATIVES – **castellation** *noun*.

caster > *noun* 1 a person or machine that casts. 2 variant spelling of CASTOR.
COMBINATIONS – **caster sugar** (also **castor sugar**) Brit. finely granulated white sugar. [ORIGIN – because suitable for sprinkling from a castor.]

castigate /ˈkastigayt/ > *verb* reprimand severely.
DERIVATIVES – **castigation** *noun* **castigator** *noun*.
SYNONYMS – berate, chastise, lambaste, rebuke, upbraid.
ORIGIN – Latin *castigare* 'reprimand', from *castus* 'pure, chaste'.

Castilian /kaˈstilian/ > *noun* 1 a person from the Spanish region of Castile. 2 the language of Castile, the standard spoken and literary form of Spanish. > *adjective* relating to Castile or Castilian.

casting > *noun* an object made by casting molten metal or other material.

castle > *noun* 1 a large fortified building or group of buildings, typically of the medieval period. 2 Chess old-fashioned term for ROOK².
WORDFINDER – *parts of a castle:* bailey, barbican, battlement, crenellation, curtain wall, drawbridge, donjon, dungeon, gatehouse, keep, machicolation, moat, motte, parapet, portcullis, rampart, turret, ward.
IDIOMS – **castles in the air** (or **in Spain**) unattainable schemes existing only in the imagination.
ORIGIN – Latin *castellum* 'little fort'.

cast-off > *adjective* abandoned or discarded. > *noun* a cast-off garment.

castor /ˈkaastər/ (also **caster**) > *noun* 1 each of a set of small swivelling wheels fixed to the legs or base of a piece of furniture. 2 a small container with holes in the top, used for sprinkling salt, sugar, etc.
COMBINATIONS – **castor sugar** variant spelling of *caster sugar*.

castor oil > *noun* a pale yellow laxative oil obtained from the seeds of an African shrub.
ORIGIN – perhaps so named because in medicinal use it succeeded an oily substance secreted by beavers, called *castor*.

castrate > *verb* 1 remove the testicles of. 2 deprive of power or vigour.
WORDFINDER – eunuch (*castrated person*); *castrated animals:* bullock, capon, gelding, hog, wether.
DERIVATIVES – **castration** *noun* **castrator** *noun*.
SYNONYMS – *verb* emasculate, geld, neuter, sterilise, unsex.
ORIGIN – Latin *castrare*.

castrato /kaˈstraatō/ > *noun* (pl. **castrati** /kaˈstraatee/) historical a male singer castrated in boyhood so as to retain a soprano or alto voice.
ORIGIN – Italian.

casual > *adjective* 1 relaxed and unconcerned. 2 showing insufficient care or forethought: *a casual remark.* 3 not regular or firmly established; occasional or temporary: *casual workers.* 4 happening by chance; accidental. 5 (especially of clothing) informal. > *noun* 1 a temporary or occasional worker. 2 (**casuals**) clothes or shoes suitable for informal everyday wear.
DERIVATIVES – **casually** *adverb* **casualness** *noun*.
SYNONYMS – *adjective* 1 easy-going, insouciant, nonchalant, relaxed, unconcerned. 2 careless, offhand, throwaway. 4 accidental, chance, coincidental, random.
ANTONYMS – *adjective* 1 concerned. 2 premeditated. 3 permanent. 4 intentional, planned.
ORIGIN – Latin *casualis*, from *casus* 'fall', 'occurrence, chance'.

casualisation (also **casualization**) > *noun* the replacement of a permanently employed workforce by casual workers.

casualty > *noun* (pl. **casualties**) 1 a person killed or injured in a war or accident. 2 a person or thing badly affected by an event or situation: *the firm was one of the casualties of the recession.* 3 (also **casualty department**) the department of a hospital providing immediate treatment for emergency cases.
SYNONYMS – 1 death, fatality, loss, victim.

casuarina /kassyooəˈreenə/ > *noun* a tree with slender, jointed, drooping twigs bearing tiny leaves, native to Australia and SE Asia.
ORIGIN – from Latin *casuarius* 'cassowary' (from the resemblance of the branches to the bird's feathers).

casuistry /ˈkazhoo-istri/ > *noun* the use of clever but false reasoning, especially in relation to moral issues.
DERIVATIVES – **casuist** *noun* **casuistic** *adjective* **casuistical** *adjective*.

ORIGIN – via French from Latin *casus* 'fall, occurrence, chance'.

casus belli /ˈkaysəss ˈbelli/ > *noun* (pl. same) an act or situation provoking or justifying war.
ORIGIN – from Latin *casus* 'case' and *belli* 'of war'.

CAT > *abbreviation* Medicine computerised axial tomography.

cat > *noun* 1 a small domesticated carnivorous mammal with soft fur, a short snout, and retractile claws. 2 a wild animal resembling this, in particular a lion, tiger, or other member of the cat family. 3 informal a malicious or spiteful woman.
WORDFINDER – feline (*of cats; catlike*), ailurophobia (*fear of cats*); *animals of the cat family:* cheetah, civet, jaguar, leopard, lion, lynx, ocelot, puma, tiger.
IDIOMS – **all cats are grey in the dark** proverb distinguishing qualities are obscured in some circumstances, and if they can't be perceived they don't matter. **a cat may look at a king** proverb even a person of low status or importance has rights. **let the cat out of the bag** informal reveal a secret by mistake. **like a cat on a hot tin roof** (Brit. also **on hot bricks**) informal very agitated or anxious. **put** (or **set**) **the cat among the pigeons** Brit. say or do something likely to cause trouble. **when** (or **while**) **the cat's away, the mice will play** proverb it is natural for people to do as they like in the absence of someone in authority.
DERIVATIVES – **catlike** *adjective*.
COMBINATIONS – **cat burglar** a thief who enters a building by climbing to an upper storey. **cat flap** a small hinged flap in an outer door through which a cat may pass. **cat's cradle** a child's game in which patterns are constructed in a loop of string held between the fingers of each hand. **cat's eye 1** a semi-precious stone. 2 (**catseye**) Brit. trademark each of a series of reflective studs marking the lanes or edges of a road. **cat's paw** a person used by another to carry out an unpleasant task. [ORIGIN – with reference to the fable of a monkey tricking a cat into extracting roasting chestnuts from a fire with its paw.] **catsuit** chiefly Brit. a woman's close-fitting one-piece garment with trouser legs.

cata- (also **cat-**) > *prefix* 1 down; downwards: *catabolism.* 2 wrongly; badly: *catachresis.* 3 completely: *cataclysm.* 4 against; alongside: *catechise.*
ORIGIN – from Greek *kata* 'down'.

catabolism /kəˈtabbəliz'm/ > *noun* the breakdown of complex molecules in living organisms to form simpler ones, together with the release of energy. The opposite of ANABOLISM.
DERIVATIVES – **catabolic** *adjective*.

ORIGIN – from Greek *katabolē* 'throwing down'.

catachresis /kattə**kree**siss/ > *noun* (pl. **catachreses** /kattə**kree**seez/) the incorrect use of a word.

ORIGIN – Greek, from *katakhrēsthai* 'misuse'.

cataclysm /**katt**əkliz'm/ > *noun* a violent upheaval or disaster.

DERIVATIVES – **cataclysmic** *adjective* **cataclysmically** *adverb*.

ORIGIN – Greek *kataklusmos* 'deluge'.

catacomb /**katt**əkoōm, **katt**əkōm/ > *noun* an underground cemetery consisting of a gallery with recesses for tombs.

ORIGIN – Latin *Catacumbas*, the name of the subterranean cemetery of St Sebastian near Rome.

catafalque /**katt**əfalk/ > *noun* a decorated wooden framework to support a coffin.

ORIGIN – Italian *catafalco*.

Catalan /**katt**əlan/ > *noun* 1 a person from Catalonia in NE Spain. 2 the language of Catalonia. > *adjective* relating to Catalonia.

catalepsy /**katt**əlepsi/ > *noun* a medical condition in which a person suffers a trance or seizure with a loss of sensation and consciousness accompanied by rigidity of the body.

DERIVATIVES – **cataleptic** *adjective & noun*.

ORIGIN – Greek, from *katalambanein* 'seize upon'.

catalogue (US also **catalog**) > *noun* 1 a complete list of items arranged in alphabetical or other systematic order. 2 a publication containing details of items for sale. 3 a series of bad things: *a catalogue of failures.* > *verb* (**catalogues**, **catalogued**, **cataloguing**; US also **catalogs**, **cataloged**, **cataloging**) list in a catalogue.

DERIVATIVES – **cataloguer** *noun*.

SYNONYMS – *noun* 1 directory, index, inventory, list. *verb* index, list, log, systematise.

ORIGIN – Greek *katalogos*, from *katalegein* 'pick out or enrol'.

Catalonian /kattə**lō**niən/ > *adjective & noun* another term for **CATALAN**.

catalpa /kə**tal**pə/ > *noun* a tree with heart-shaped leaves and trumpet-shaped flowers, native to North America and east Asia.

ORIGIN – Creek.

catalyse /**katt**əliz/ (US **catalyze**) > *verb* cause or accelerate (a reaction) by acting as a catalyst.

DERIVATIVES – **catalyser** *noun*.

catalysis /kə**tal**ississ/ > *noun* the acceleration of a chemical reaction by a catalyst.

DERIVATIVES – **catalytic** /kattə**litt**ik/ *adjective*.

ORIGIN – Greek *katalusis* 'dissolution'.

catalyst > *noun* 1 a substance that increases the rate of a chemical reaction without itself undergoing any permanent chemical change. 2 a person or thing that causes something to happen.

catalytic converter > *noun* a device in the exhaust system of a motor vehicle, containing a catalyst for converting pollutant gases into less harmful ones.

catamaran /**katt**əməran/ > *noun* a yacht or other boat with twin hulls in parallel.

ORIGIN – Tamil, 'tied wood'.

catamite /**katt**əmīt/ > *noun* archaic a boy kept for homosexual practices.

ORIGIN – Latin *catamitus*, from Greek *Ganumēdēs* 'Ganymede' (Zeus's cup-bearer in Greek mythology).

cataplexy /**katt**əpleksi/ > *noun* a medical condition in which strong emotion or laughter causes a person to suffer sudden physical collapse though remaining conscious.

ORIGIN – Greek *kataplēxis*, from *kata-* 'down' + *plēssein* 'strike'.

catapult > *noun* 1 chiefly Brit. a forked stick with an elastic band fastened to the two prongs, used for shooting small stones. 2 historical a military machine for hurling large stones or other missiles. 3 a mechanical device for launching a glider or aircraft. > *verb* 1 hurl or launch with a catapult. 2 move or hurl suddenly or at great speed.

SYNONYMS – *verb* hurl, hurtle, launch, let fly, propel, shoot.

ORIGIN – Greek *katapeltēs*, from *kata-* 'down' + *pallein* 'hurl'.

cataract /**katt**ərakt/ > *noun* 1 a large waterfall. 2 a medical condition in which the lens of the eye becomes progressively opaque, resulting in blurred vision.

wordpower facts

Cataract

The word **cataract** comes from the Latin *cataracta*, 'waterfall, floodgate, portcullis', which is from the Greek word *kataraktēs*, meaning 'down-rushing'. The medical sense is probably a figurative use of the idea of the portcullis: even when the eye is open, the cataract obstructs vision, as the portcullis does a gateway.

catarrh /kə**taar**/ > *noun* excessive discharge of mucus in the nose or throat.

DERIVATIVES – **catarrhal** *adjective*.

ORIGIN – Greek *katarrhous*, from *katarrhein* 'flow down'.

catastrophe /kə**tas**trəfi/ > *noun* an event causing great damage or suffering.

DERIVATIVES – **catastrophic** *adjective* **catastrophically** *adverb*.

SYNONYMS – calamity, cataclysm, disaster, tragedy.

ORIGIN – Greek *katastrophē* 'overturning, sudden turn'.

catatonia /kattə**tō**niə/ > *noun* 1 abnormality of movement and behaviour arising from a disturbed mental state. 2 informal a state of immobility and stupor.

DERIVATIVES – **catatonic** *adjective*.

ORIGIN – from **CATA-** 'badly' + Greek *tonos* 'tone or tension'.

catboat > *noun* a single-masted sailing boat with only one sail.

ORIGIN – perhaps from obsolete *cat* (a former type of merchant ship used in NE England).

catcall > *noun* a shrill whistle or shout of mockery or disapproval. > *verb* make a catcall.

catch > *verb* (past and past participle **caught**) 1 intercept and hold (something thrown, propelled, or dropped). 2 seize or take hold of. 3 capture after a chase or in a trap, net, etc. 4 be in time to board (a train, bus, etc.) or to see (a person, programme, etc.). 5 entangle or become entangled: *she caught her foot in the bedspread.* 6 (**be caught in**) unexpectedly find oneself in (an unwelcome situation). 7 surprise (someone) in an awkward or incriminating situation. 8 engage (a person's interest or imagination). 9 perceive, hear, or understand: *he said something Jess couldn't catch.* 10 strike (someone or a part of one's body). 11 become infected with (an illness). 12 ignite and start burning. 13 Cricket dismiss (a batsman) by catching the ball before it touches the ground. > *noun* 1 an act of catching. 2 a device for securing a door, window, etc. 3 a hidden problem or disadvantage. 4 an unevenness in a person's voice caused by emotion. 5 informal a person considered desirable as a partner or spouse. 6 an amount of fish caught.

IDIOMS – **catch one's breath 1** draw one's breath in sharply to express an emotion. **2** recover one's breath after exertion. **catch someone's eye 1** be noticed by someone. **2** attract someone's attention by making eye contact. **catch the light** shine in the light. **catch on** informal **1** (of a practice or fashion) become popular. **2** understand what is meant. **catch out** Brit. **1** discover that (someone) has done something wrong. **2** take unawares: *you might get caught out by the weather.* **catch the sun 1** be in a sunny position. **2** Brit. become tanned or sunburnt. **catch up 1** succeed in reaching a person ahead. **2** do tasks which one should have done earlier. **3** (**be or get caught up in**) become involved in.

DERIVATIVES – **catchable** *adjective* **catcher** *noun*.

SYNONYMS – *verb* 1 grab, intercept, seize. 2 grab, grasp, seize, take hold of. 3 apprehend, capture, ensnare, entrap, net. 7

discover, find, surprise, take unawares. **11** come down with, contract, get, pick up. *noun* **3** drawback, hitch, snag, twist.

ORIGIN – Old French *chacier*, from Latin *captare* 'try to catch'.

catch-all > *noun* a term or category intended to cover all possibilities.

catching > *adjective* informal (of a disease) infectious.

catchline > *noun* Brit. **1** a short, eye-catching headline or title. **2** an advertising slogan.

catchment (also **catchment area**) > *noun* **1** the area from which a hospital's patients or a school's pupils are drawn. **2** the area from which rainfall flows into a river, lake, or reservoir.

catchpenny > *adjective* having a cheap, superficial attractiveness designed to encourage quick sales.

catchphrase > *noun* a well-known sentence or phrase.

catch-22 > *noun* a difficult situation from which there is no escape because it involves mutually conflicting or dependent conditions.

ORIGIN – title of a novel by Joseph Heller (1961), in which the main character feigns madness in order to avoid dangerous combat missions, but his desire to avoid them is taken to prove his sanity.

catchword > *noun* **1** a word or phrase commonly used to encapsulate a particular concept. **2** a word printed or placed so as to attract attention.

catchy > *adjective* (**catchier**, **catchiest**) (of a tune or phrase) instantly appealing and memorable.

DERIVATIVES – **catchiness** *noun*.

catechesis /kattikeesiss/ > *noun* religious instruction given in preparation for Christian baptism or confirmation.

ORIGIN – Greek *katēkhēsis* 'oral instruction'.

catechetical /kattikettikk'l/ > *adjective* **1** relating to catechesis. **2** (of religious teaching) carried out by means of questions and answers.

catechise (also **catechize**) > *verb* instruct by questions and answers, especially by using a catechism.

ORIGIN – Greek *katēkhizein*, from *katēkhein* 'instruct orally'.

catechism /kattikiz'm/ > *noun* a summary of the principles of Christian religion in the form of questions and answers, used for teaching.

catechist > *noun* a Christian teacher, especially one using a catechism.

catechumen /kattikyoomen/ > *noun* a Christian preparing for baptism or confirmation.

ORIGIN – from Greek *katēkhoumenos* 'being instructed', from *katēkhein* 'instruct orally'.

categorical (also **categoric**) > *adjective* unambiguously explicit and direct.

DERIVATIVES – **categorically** *adverb*.

SYNONYMS – absolute, decisive, definite, emphatic, unequivocal.

categorise (also **categorize**) > *verb* place in a particular category; classify.

DERIVATIVES – **categorisation** *noun*.

SYNONYMS – class, classify, grade, group, label, rank.

category > *noun* (pl. **categories**) a class or division of people or things having shared characteristics.

SYNONYMS – class, classification, division, group, order, section, set.

ORIGIN – Greek *katēgoria* 'statement, accusation'.

catenary /kəteenəri/ > *noun* (pl. **catenaries**) a curve formed by a wire, chain, etc. hanging freely from two points on the same horizontal level. > *adjective* involving or denoting a catenary.

ORIGIN – from Latin *catena* 'chain'.

cater > *verb* chiefly Brit. **1** (**cater for**) provide food and drink at (a social event). **2** (**cater for** or **to**) provide with what is needed or required. **3** (**cater for**) take into account. **4** (**cater to**) satisfy (a need or demand).

DERIVATIVES – **caterer** *noun*.

SYNONYMS – **2** (**cater for** or **to**) meet the needs of, minister to, provide for, serve. **3** (**cater for**) allow for, bear in mind, consider. **4** (**cater to**) gratify, humour, indulge, pander to, satisfy.

ORIGIN – Old French *acater* 'buy', from Latin *captare* 'seize'.

cater-cornered /kaytərkornərd/ (also **kitty-corner**) > *adjective* & *adverb* N. Amer. situated diagonally opposite.

ORIGIN – from the dialect word *cater*, meaning 'diagonally' and also denoting the four on dice, from French *quatre* 'four'.

---

wordpower facts

Caterpillar

The word **caterpillar** is probably a variant of Old French *chatepelose*, meaning 'hairy cat', influenced by the obsolete English word *piller*, 'ravager'. This association between the caterpillar and the cat is found in other languages: Swiss German has *Teufelskatz*, literally 'devil's cat'; the Italian dialect of Lombardy has *gatta*, meaning simply 'cat'. A **catkin**, which resembles a hairy caterpillar, is similarly named after its resemblance to a cat, coming from the obsolete Dutch word for 'kitten', *kattekin*; and in French a catkin is called a *chaton*, a 'kitten'.

---

caterpillar > *noun* **1** the larva of a butterfly or moth. **2** (also **caterpillar track** or

tread) trademark an articulated steel band passing round the wheels of a vehicle for travel on rough ground.

caterwaul /kattərwawl/ > *verb* make a shrill howling or wailing noise. > *noun* a shrill howling or wailing noise.

ORIGIN – from **CAT** + *waul* 'wail'.

catfish > *noun* a freshwater or marine fish with whisker-like barbels round the mouth.

catgut > *noun* material used for the strings of musical instruments and for surgical sutures, made of the dried intestines of sheep or horses (but not cats).

catharsis /kəthaarsiss/ > *noun* the release of pent-up emotions, for example through drama.

DERIVATIVES – **cathartic** *adjective* & *noun*.

ORIGIN – Greek *katharsis*, from *kathairein* 'cleanse'.

cathedral > *noun* the principal church of a diocese.

---

wordpower facts

Cathedral

The word **cathedral** was first used as an adjective in the term **cathedral church**, that is 'a church containing the bishop's throne'. It comes from the Latin word for a seat or throne, *cathedra*, from Greek *kathedra*, and is closely related to **chair**, which comes through Old French from the same root. The term **ex cathedra**, meaning 'with the full authority of office', is a reference to the authority of the pope; its literal meaning in Latin is 'from the teacher's chair'.

Catherine wheel > *noun* Brit. a firework in the form of a spinning coil.

ORIGIN – named after St *Catherine*, who was martyred after being tortured on a spiked wheel.

catheter /kathitər/ > *noun* a flexible tube inserted into a body cavity, particularly the bladder, for removing fluid.

ORIGIN – Greek *kathetēr*, from *kathienai* 'send or let down'.

cathode /kathōd/ > *noun* a negatively charged electrode. The opposite of **ANODE**.

COMBINATIONS – **cathode ray** a beam of electrons emitted from the cathode of a high-vacuum tube. **cathode ray tube** a high-vacuum tube in which cathode rays produce a luminous image on a fluorescent screen, used in televisions and visual display units.

ORIGIN – Greek *kathodos* 'way down'.

catholic > *adjective* **1** including a wide variety of things: *catholic tastes*. **2** (**Catholic**)

Roman Catholic. **3** (**Catholic**) of or including all Christians. > *noun* (**Catholic**) a Roman Catholic.

DERIVATIVES – **Catholicise** (also **Catholicize**) *verb* **Catholicism** *noun* **catholicity** *noun*.

SYNONYMS – *adjective* **1** broad, eclectic, varied, wide-ranging.

ORIGIN – Greek *katholikos* 'universal'.

cation /**katt**īən/ > *noun* Chemistry a positively charged ion. The opposite of ANION.

DERIVATIVES – **cationic** /kattīonnik/ *adjective*.

ORIGIN – from CATHODE + ION.

catkin > *noun* a spike of small soft flowers hanging from trees such as willow and hazel.

catlick > *noun* a perfunctory wash.

catmint > *noun* a plant with a pungent smell attractive to cats.

catnap > *noun* a short sleep during the day. > *verb* (**catnapped**, **catnapping**) have a catnap.

catnip > *noun* another term for CATMINT.

cat-o'-nine-tails > *noun* historical a rope whip with nine knotted cords, used for flogging.

catoptric /ka**top**trik/ > *adjective* Physics relating to mirrors or reflection.

DERIVATIVES – **catoptrics** *plural noun*.

ORIGIN – Greek *katoptrikos*, from *katoptron* 'mirror'.

catsup /**kat**səp/ > *noun* US another term for KETCHUP.

cat's whisker > *noun* a fine adjustable wire in a crystal radio receiver.

IDIOMS – **the cat's whiskers** (also **the cat's pyjamas**) informal an excellent person or thing.

cattery > *noun* (pl. **catteries**) a boarding or breeding establishment for cats.

cattle > *plural noun* large ruminant animals with horns and cloven hoofs, domesticated for meat or milk or as beasts of burden; cows and oxen.

WORDFINDER – bovine (*of or like cattle*).

COMBINATIONS – **cattle cake** Brit. concentrated food for cattle in a compressed flat form. **cattle grid** (N. Amer. **cattle guard**) a metal grid covering a ditch, allowing vehicles and pedestrians to cross but not animals.

ORIGIN – Old French *chatel* 'chattel'.

catty (also **cattish**) > *adjective* (**cattier**, **cattiest**) **1** deliberately hurtful; spiteful. **2** informal relating to cats.

DERIVATIVES – **cattily** *adverb*.

CATV > *abbreviation* community antenna television (cable television).

catwalk > *noun* **1** a narrow walkway or open bridge, especially in an industrial installation. **2** a narrow platform along which models walk to display clothes.

Caucasian /kor**kay**ziən, kor**kayzh**'n/ > *adjective* **1** relating to a broad division of humankind covering peoples from Europe, western Asia, and parts of India and North Africa. **2** white-skinned; of European origin. **3** relating to the region of the Caucasus in SE Europe. > *noun* a Caucasian person.

caucus /**kaw**kəss/ > *noun* (pl. **caucuses**) **1** a meeting of the members of a legislative body of a political party, to select candidates or decide policy. **2** a group of people with shared concerns within a larger organisation.

ORIGIN – perhaps from an Algonquian word meaning 'adviser'.

caudal /**kaw**d'l/ > *adjective* **1** of or like a tail. **2** at or near the hind part of the body.

DERIVATIVES – **caudally** *adverb*.

ORIGIN – from Latin *cauda* 'tail'.

caught past and past participle of CATCH.

caul /kawl/ > *noun* **1** the amniotic membrane enclosing a fetus, part of which is occasionally found on a baby's head at birth. **2** Anatomy the omentum.

ORIGIN – perhaps from Old French *cale* 'head covering'.

cauldron (also **caldron**) > *noun* a large metal pot, used for cooking over an open fire.

ORIGIN – Old French *caudron*, from Latin *caldarium* 'hot bath', *caldaria* 'cooking pot'.

cauliflower > *noun* a variety of cabbage with a large flower head of small creamy-white flower buds, eaten as a vegetable.

COMBINATIONS – **cauliflower ear** a person's ear that has become thickened or deformed as a result of repeated blows.

ORIGIN – from obsolete French *chou fleuri* 'flowered cabbage'.

caulk /kawk/ (US also **calk**) > *noun* a waterproof filler and sealant, used in building work and repairs. > *verb* **1** seal with caulk. **2** make (a boat or its seams) watertight.

ORIGIN – Latin *calcare* 'to tread'.

causal > *adjective* relating to or acting as a cause.

DERIVATIVES – **causally** *adverb*.

causality > *noun* **1** the relationship between cause and effect. **2** the principle that everything has a cause.

causation > *noun* **1** the action of causing. **2** the relationship between cause and effect.

causative > *adjective* **1** acting as a cause. **2** Grammar expressing causation.

cause > *noun* **1** a person or thing that produces an effect. **2** reasonable grounds for a belief or action: *cause for concern*. **3** a principle or movement which one is prepared to support or advocate. **4** a lawsuit. > *verb* be the cause of; make happen.

WORDFINDER – aetiology (*investigation of causes, especially of disease*).

IDIOMS – **cause and effect** the principle of causation. **make common cause** unite in order to achieve a shared aim.

DERIVATIVES – **causeless** *adjective*.

SYNONYMS – *noun* **1** agent, origin, root, source. **2** basis, grounds, justification, reason. *verb* create, effect, engender, generate, give rise to.

ORIGIN – Latin *causa*.

cause célèbre /kawz se**leb**rə/ > *noun* (pl. **causes célèbres** pronunc. same) a controversial issue arousing great public interest.

ORIGIN – French, 'famous case'.

causeway > *noun* a raised road or track across low or wet ground.

ORIGIN – Old French *causee*, from Latin *calx* 'lime, limestone' (used for paving roads).

caustic /**kaws**tik/ > *adjective* **1** able to burn or corrode organic tissue by chemical action. **2** scathingly sarcastic. > *noun* a caustic substance.

DERIVATIVES – **caustically** *adverb*.

SYNONYMS – *adjective* **2** acerbic, biting, cutting, mordant.

COMBINATIONS – **caustic soda** sodium hydroxide.

ORIGIN – Greek *kaustikos*, from *kaustos* 'combustible'.

cauterise /**kaw**tərīz/ (also **cauterize**) > *verb* burn the skin or flesh of (a wound) to stop bleeding or prevent infection.

DERIVATIVES – **cauterisation** *noun*.

ORIGIN – Greek *kautēriazein*, from *kautērion* 'branding iron'.

cautery /**kaw**təri/ > *noun* (pl. **cauteries**) **1** an instrument or caustic substance used for cauterising. **2** the action of cauterising.

caution > *noun* **1** care taken to avoid danger or mistakes. **2** warning: *advisers sounded a note of caution*. **3** Law, chiefly Brit. an formal warning given to someone who has committed a minor offence but has not been charged. > *verb* **1** warn or advise. **2** chiefly Brit. issue a legal caution to. **3** chiefly Brit. (of a police officer) advise (someone) of their legal rights when arresting them.

IDIOMS – **throw caution to the wind** act in a reckless manner.

SYNONYMS – *noun* **1** care, carefulness, vigilance, watchfulness. *verb* **1** advise, counsel, forewarn, warn.

ORIGIN – Latin, from *cavere* 'take heed'.

cautionary > *adjective* serving as a warning.

cautious > *adjective* careful to avoid potential problems or dangers.

DERIVATIVES – **cautiously** *adverb* **cautiousness** *noun*.

SYNONYMS – attentive, careful, prudent, vigilant, wary, watchful.

ANTONYMS – inattentive, incautious.

cava /**kaa**və/ > *noun* a Spanish sparkling wine made in the same way as champagne.
ORIGIN – Spanish.

cavalcade /kavvəl**kayd**, **kavv**əlkayd/ > *noun* a procession of vehicles, riders, or people on foot.
ORIGIN – French, from Italian *cavalcare* 'to ride'.

cavalier > *noun* **1** (**Cavalier**) historical a supporter of King Charles I in the English Civil War (1642–9). **2** archaic or literary a courtly gentleman. > *adjective* showing a lack of proper concern.
DERIVATIVES – **cavalierly** *adverb*.
SYNONYMS – *adjective* casual, offhand, perfunctory, reckless.
ORIGIN – Italian *cavaliere*, from Latin *caballus* 'horse'.

cavalry > *noun* (pl. **cavalries**) soldiers who fight on horses or in armoured vehicles.
DERIVATIVES – **cavalryman** *noun*.
COMBINATIONS – **cavalry twill** strong woollen twill of a khaki or light brown colour.
ORIGIN – Italian *cavalleria*, from *cavallo* 'horse'.

cave > *noun* a large natural underground chamber. > *verb* (**cave in**) **1** subside or collapse. **2** submit under pressure.
WORDFINDER – grotto (*small picturesque cave*), potholer, speleologist (*explorer of caves*), stalactite, stalagmite (*rock formations within cave*), troglodyte (*cave-dweller*).
DERIVATIVES – **caver** *noun*.
ORIGIN – Latin *cava*, from *cavus* 'hollow'.

caveat /**kavv**iat/ > *noun* a warning or proviso of specific conditions.
ORIGIN – Latin, 'let a person beware'.

caveat emptor /kavviat **emp**tor/ > *noun* the principle that the buyer is responsible for checking the quality and suitability of goods before purchase.
ORIGIN – Latin, 'let the buyer beware'.

caveman (or **cavewoman**) > *noun* a prehistoric person who lived in caves.

cavern > *noun* **1** a large cave, or chamber in a cave. **2** a vast, dark space.

cavernous > *adjective* like a cavern in size, shape, or atmosphere; very large and spacious.

caviar /**kavv**iaar/ (also **caviare**) > *noun* the pickled roe of sturgeon or other large fish, eaten as a delicacy.
ORIGIN – Italian *cavial* or French *caviar*.

cavil /**kavv**'l/ > *verb* (**cavilled, cavilling**; US **caviled, caviling**) make petty objections; quibble. > *noun* a petty objection.
ORIGIN – Latin *cavillari*, from *cavilla* 'mockery'.

caving > *noun* exploring caves as a sport.

cavitation > *noun* the formation of bubbles in a liquid.

cavity > *noun* (pl. **cavities**) **1** a hollow space within a solid object. **2** a decayed part of a tooth.
SYNONYMS – **1** chamber, crater, hollow, pit, space.
COMBINATIONS – **cavity wall** a wall formed from two thicknesses of bricks with a space between them.
ORIGIN – Latin *cavitas*, from *cavus* 'hollow'.

cavort > *verb* jump or dance around excitedly.
SYNONYMS – caper, frisk, frolic, gambol, jig, romp.
ORIGIN – perhaps an alteration of **CURVET**.

cavy /**kay**vi/ > *noun* (pl. **cavies**) a guinea pig or related South American rodent.
ORIGIN – Latin *cavia*, from Carib.

caw > *noun* the harsh cry of a rook, crow, or similar bird. > *verb* utter a caw.

cayenne /kay**en**/ (also **cayenne pepper**) > *noun* a pungent, hot-tasting red powder prepared from dried chillies.
ORIGIN – Tupi, later associated with *Cayenne* in French Guiana.

cayman > *noun* variant spelling of **CAIMAN**.

Cayuga /kay**oo**gə, **kī**oogə/ > *noun* (pl. same or **Cayugas**) a member of an American Indian people formerly inhabiting part of New York State.
ORIGIN – from a place name.

Cayuse /**kī**yooss/ > *noun* (pl. same or **Cayuses**) a member of an American Indian people of Washington State and Oregon.
ORIGIN – the name in Chinook Jargon.

CB > *abbreviation* **1** Citizens' Band. **2** (in the UK) Companion of the Order of the Bath.

CBE > *abbreviation* (in the UK) Commander of the Order of the British Empire.

CBI > *abbreviation* Confederation of British Industry.

CC > *abbreviation* **1** Brit. City Council. **2** Brit. County Council. **3** Cricket Club.

cc (also **c.c.**) > *abbreviation* **1** carbon copy (an indication that a duplicate has been or should be sent to another person). **2** cubic centimetre(s).

CCTV > *abbreviation* closed-circuit television.

CD > *abbreviation* compact disc.

Cd > *symbol* the chemical element cadmium.

cd > *abbreviation* candela.

CD-ROM > *noun* a compact disc used in a computer as a read-only device for displaying data.
ORIGIN – from *compact disc read-only memory*.

CDT > *abbreviation* Central Daylight Time.

CDV > *abbreviation* compact disc video.

CE > *abbreviation* **1** Church of England. **2** Common Era.

Ce > *symbol* the chemical element cerium.

ceanothus /seeə**nō**thəss/ > *noun* a North American shrub with dense clusters of small blue flowers.
ORIGIN – Greek *keanōthos*, denoting a kind of thistle.

cease > *verb* come or bring to an end; stop.
IDIOMS – **without cease** without stopping.
SYNONYMS – desist, finish, halt, stop, terminate.
ANTONYMS – continue, start.
ORIGIN – Latin *cessare*, from *cedere* 'to yield'.

ceasefire > *noun* a temporary suspension of fighting.

ceaseless > *adjective* constant and unending.
DERIVATIVES – **ceaselessly** *adverb*.
SYNONYMS – constant, continual, endless, everlasting, never-ending, perpetual, unending.

cecum > *noun* (pl. **ceca**) US spelling of **CAECUM**.

cedar > *noun* a tall coniferous tree with hard, fragrant wood.
ORIGIN – Greek *kedros*.

cede /seed/ > *verb* give up (power or territory).
SYNONYMS – concede, relinquish, surrender, yield.
ORIGIN – Latin *cedere* 'to yield'.

cedi /**see**di/ > *noun* (pl. same or **cedis**) the basic monetary unit of Ghana, equal to 100 pesewas.
ORIGIN – perhaps an alteration of **SHILLING**.

cedilla /si**dill**ə/ > *noun* a mark (¸) written under the letter c, especially in French, to show that it is pronounced like an s (e.g. *façade*).
ORIGIN – obsolete Spanish, 'little 'z''.

ceilidh /**kay**li/ > *noun* a social event with Scottish or Irish folk music and singing, traditional dancing, and storytelling.
ORIGIN – Old Irish *céilide* 'visit, visiting'.

ceiling* > *noun* **1** the upper inside surface of a room. **2** an upper limit set on prices, wages, or expenditure. **3** the maximum altitude an aircraft can reach.
***SPELLING** – *i* before *e* except after *c*: ceiling.
ORIGIN – from obsolete *ceil* 'line or plaster the roof of (a building)', perhaps from Latin *celare* 'conceal'.

celandine /**sell**əndīn/ > *noun* **1** (also **lesser celandine**) a common yellow-flowered plant of the buttercup family. **2** (**greater celandine**) a yellow-flowered plant of the poppy family, with toxic sap.
ORIGIN – from Greek *khelidōn* 'swallow' (the flowering of the plant being associated with the arrival of swallows).

celebrant /**sell**ibrənt/ > *noun* **1** a person who performs a rite, especially a priest at the Eucharist. **2** a person who celebrates something.

celebrate > *verb* **1** mark (a significant occasion) with an enjoyable activity. **2** engage in festivities to mark a significant occasion. **3** honour or praise publicly. **4** perform (a religious ceremony), in particular officiate at (the Eucharist).

DERIVATIVES – **celebration** *noun* **celebrator** *noun* **celebratory** *adjective*.

SYNONYMS – **1** commemorate, honour, mark, observe. **2** make merry, rejoice, revel. **3** extol, honour, laud, praise.

ORIGIN – Latin *celebrare*, from *celeber* 'frequented or honoured'.

celebrity > *noun* (pl. **celebrities**) **1** a famous person. **2** the state of being famous.

SYNONYMS – **1** household name, personality, star, superstar. **2** fame, prominence, renown, stardom.

ANTONYMS – **2** obscurity.

celeriac /siˈlerriak/ > *noun* a variety of celery which forms a large swollen edible root.

celerity /siˈlerriti/ > *noun* archaic or literary swiftness of movement.

ORIGIN – Latin *celeritas*, from *celer* 'swift'.

celery > *noun* a garden plant with crisp juicy stalks, used in salads or as a vegetable.

ORIGIN – French *céleri*, from Greek *selinon* 'parsley'.

celesta /siˈlestə/ (also **celeste** /siˈlest/) > *noun* a small keyboard instrument in which felted hammers strike a row of steel plates suspended over wooden resonators.

ORIGIN – from French *céleste* 'heavenly' (with reference to the instrument's ethereal sound).

celestial > *adjective* **1** positioned in or relating to the sky or outer space. **2** belonging or relating to heaven.

DERIVATIVES – **celestially** *adverb*.

SYNONYMS – **1** astronomical, cosmic, extraterrestrial, galactic. **2** divine, ethereal, heavenly, immortal.

ANTONYMS – earthly, terrestrial.

COMBINATIONS – **celestial equator** the projection into space of the earth's equator. **celestial sphere** an imaginary sphere of which the observer is the centre and on which all celestial objects are considered to lie.

ORIGIN – Latin *caelestis*, from *caelum* 'heaven'.

celiac > *noun* US spelling of COELIAC.

celibate /ˈselibət/ > *adjective* **1** abstaining from marriage and sexual relations for religious reasons. **2** having or involving no sexual relations. > *noun* a person who is celibate.

DERIVATIVES – **celibacy** *noun*.

SYNONYMS – *adjective* abstinent, chaste, continent, self-restrained.

ORIGIN – from Latin *caelibatus* 'unmarried state'.

cell > *noun* **1** a small room for a prisoner, monk, or nun. **2** Biology the smallest structural and functional unit of an organism, consisting of cytoplasm and a nucleus enclosed in a membrane. **3** a small compartment in a larger structure such as a honeycomb. **4** a small group forming a nucleus of political activity. **5** a device or unit in which electricity is generated using chemical energy or light, or in which electrolysis takes place.

WORDFINDER – *kinds of cell:* erythrocyte (*red blood cell*), gamete (*sex cell*), leucocyte (*white blood cell*), neuron (*nerve cell*), zygote (*cell formed by fusion of gametes*); cytology (*branch of biology concerned with cells*); meiosis, mitosis (*division of cells*).

ORIGIN – Latin *cella* 'storeroom or chamber'.

cellar > *noun* **1** a storage space or room below ground level in a house. **2** a stock of wine.

ORIGIN – Latin *cellarium* 'storehouse', from *cella* 'storeroom or chamber'.

cello /ˈchellō/ > *noun* (pl. **cellos**) a bass instrument of the violin family, held upright on the floor between the legs of the seated player.

DERIVATIVES – **cellist** *noun*.

ORIGIN – shortening of VIOLONCELLO.

cellophane /ˈselləfayn/ > *noun* trademark a thin transparent wrapping material made from viscose.

ORIGIN – from CELLULOSE + *-phane* (from Latin *diaphanus* 'diaphanous').

cellphone > *noun* a mobile phone.

cellular /ˈselyoolər/ > *adjective* **1** relating to or consisting of living cells. **2** (of a mobile telephone system) using a number of short-range radio stations to cover the area it serves. **3** (of fabric) woven with an open mesh to trap air for extra insulation. **4** consisting of small compartments or rooms.

cellulite /ˈselyoolīt/ > *noun* persistent fat immediately under the skin, causing dimpling.

ORIGIN – French, from *cellule* 'small cell'.

cellulitis > *noun* Medicine inflammation of connective tissue immediately under the skin.

celluloid > *noun* **1** a transparent flammable plastic made from camphor and nitrocellulose, formerly used for cinematographic film. **2** films as a genre.

cellulose /ˈselyoolōz, ˈselyoolōss/ > *noun* **1** an insoluble substance which is a polysaccharide derived from glucose and is the main constituent of plant cell walls and of vegetable fibres such as cotton. **2** paint or lacquer consisting principally of cellulose acetate or nitrocellulose in solution.

DERIVATIVES – **cellulosic** *adjective*.

COMBINATIONS – **cellulose acetate** a non-flammable polymer made by chemical treatment of cellulose, used as the basis of artificial fibres and plastic.

Celsius /ˈselsiəss/ > *adjective* of or denoting a scale of temperature on which water freezes at 0° and boils at 100°; centigrade.

USAGE – it is accepted practice to use **Celsius** rather than **centigrade** when giving temperatures: *25° Celsius*, not *25° centigrade*.

ORIGIN – named after the Swedish astronomer Anders *Celsius* (1701–44).

Celt /kelt, selt/ > *noun* **1** a member of a group of peoples inhabiting much of Europe and Asia Minor in pre-Roman times. **2** a native of a modern nation or region in which a Celtic language is (or was) spoken.

ORIGIN – from Greek *Keltoi* 'Celts'.

Celtic /ˈkeltik, ˈseltik/ > *noun* a group of languages including Irish, Scottish Gaelic, Welsh, Breton, Manx, and Cornish. > *adjective* relating to Celtic or to the Celts.

NOTE – in referring to language, peoples, and culture, the more usual pronunciation for **Celt** and **Celtic** is with an initial **k-** sound. An initial **s-** sound is standard in the names of sports teams such as Celtic FC.

cement > *noun* **1** a powdery substance made by strongly heating lime and clay, used in making mortar and concrete. **2** a soft glue that hardens on setting. > *verb* **1** fix with cement. **2** establish or strengthen: *the occasion cemented our friendship*.

DERIVATIVES – **cementation** *noun*.

ORIGIN – Latin *caementum* 'quarry stone', from *caedere* 'hew'.

cemetery * > *noun* (pl. **cemeteries**) a large burial ground.

*SPELLING – the ending is *-tery*, not *-try* or *-tary*: ceme*tery*.

SYNONYMS – churchyard, graveyard, necropolis.

ORIGIN – Greek *koimētērion* 'dormitory'.

cenotaph /ˈsennətaaf/ > *noun* a monument to someone buried elsewhere, especially a war memorial.

ORIGIN – from Greek *kenos* 'empty' + *taphos* 'tomb'.

Cenozoic /seenəˈzōik/ (also **Cainozoic**) > *adjective* Geology of or relating to the era following the Mesozoic era (from about 65 million years ago to the present), a time when mammals, birds, and flowering plants evolved and became dominant.

ORIGIN – from Greek *kainos* 'new' + *zōion* 'animal'.

censer > *noun* a container in which incense is burnt.

ORIGIN – Old French *censier*, from *encens* 'incense'.

censor > *noun* an official who examines material that is to be published and suppresses parts considered offensive or a threat to security. > *verb* suppress or remove unacceptable parts of (a book, film, etc.).
DERIVATIVES – **censorship** *noun*.
SYNONYMS – *verb* blue-pencil, bowdlerise, cut, delete, expurgate, suppress.
ORIGIN – Latin (denoting a magistrate in ancient Rome who held censuses and supervised public morals), from *censere* 'assess'.

censorious /sensoriəss/ > *adjective* severely critical.
DERIVATIVES – **censoriously** *adverb* **censoriousness** *noun*.
SYNONYMS – condemnatory, fault-finding, hypercritical, reproving.

censure /senshər/ > *verb* express strong disapproval of. > *noun* strong disapproval or criticism.
DERIVATIVES – **censurable** *adjective*.
USAGE – do not confuse **censure** with **censor**: **censure** means 'express strong disapproval of', whereas **censor** means 'suppress unacceptable parts of (a book, film, etc.)'.
SYNONYMS – *verb* admonish, criticise, denounce, reprove. *noun* admonition, criticism, denunciation, disapproval, reproof.
ANTONYMS – *verb* praise. *noun* approval, praise.
ORIGIN – from Latin *censura* 'judgement, assessment', from *censere* 'assess'.

census > *noun* (pl. **censuses**) an official count or survey of a population.
ORIGIN – Latin, from *censere* 'assess'.

cent > *noun* a monetary unit equal to one hundredth of a dollar or other decimal currency unit.
ORIGIN – from Latin *centum* 'hundred'.

centas /sentass/ > *noun* (pl. same) a monetary unit of Lithuania, equal to one hundredth of a litas.
ORIGIN – Lithuanian.

centaur /sentawr/ > *noun* Greek Mythology a creature with the head, arms, and torso of a man and the body and legs of a horse.
ORIGIN – Greek *kentauros*, the Greek name for a Thessalonian tribe of expert horsemen.

centavo /sentaavō/ > *noun* (pl. **centavos**) a monetary unit of Portugal, Mexico, Brazil, and certain other countries, equal to one hundredth of the basic unit.
ORIGIN – Spanish and Portuguese, from Latin *centum* 'a hundred'.

centenarian > *noun* a person a hundred or more years old. > *adjective* a hundred or more years old.

centenary /senteenəri, sentennəri/ > *noun* (pl. **centenaries**) chiefly Brit. the hundredth anniversary of an event.

ORIGIN – from Latin *centenarius* 'containing a hundred', from *centum* 'a hundred'.

centennial > *adjective* relating to a hundredth anniversary. > *noun* a hundredth anniversary.

center etc. US spelling of CENTRE etc.

centesimo /chentessimō/ > *noun* (pl. **centesimos**) a monetary unit of Italy, worth one hundredth of a lira.
ORIGIN – Italian.

centésimo /sentessimō/ > *noun* (pl. **centésimos**) a monetary unit of Uruguay and Panama, equal to one hundredth of the basic unit.
ORIGIN – Spanish.

centi- > *combining form* **1** one hundredth: *centilitre*. **2** hundred: *centipede*.
ORIGIN – from Latin *centum* 'hundred'.

centigrade > *adjective* of or denoting the Celsius scale of temperature, with a hundred degrees between the freezing and boiling points of water.
USAGE – it is accepted practice to use **Celsius** rather than **centigrade** when giving temperatures: *25° Celsius*, not *25° centigrade*.
ORIGIN – from Latin *centum* 'a hundred' + *gradus* 'step'.

centigram (also **centigramme**) > *noun* a metric unit of mass equal to one hundredth of a gram.

centilitre (US **centiliter**) > *noun* a metric unit of capacity equal to one hundredth of a litre.

centime /soNteem/ > *noun* a monetary unit of France, Belgium, Switzerland, and certain other countries, equal to one hundredth of a franc or other decimal currency unit.
ORIGIN – from Latin *centesimus* 'hundredth', from *centum* 'a hundred'.

centimetre (US **centimeter**) > *noun* a metric unit of length equal to one hundredth of a metre.

centimo /sentimō/ > *noun* (pl. **centimos**) a monetary unit of Spain and a number of Latin American countries, equal to one hundredth of the basic unit.
ORIGIN – Spanish.

centipede > *noun* an arthropod with an elongated body having many segments, most of which bear a pair of legs.
ORIGIN – from Latin *centum* 'a hundred' + *pes* 'foot'.

central > *adjective* **1** in or near the centre. **2** very important; essential.
DERIVATIVES – **centrality** *noun* **centrally** *adverb*.
SYNONYMS – **1** mean, medial, median, middle. **2** crucial, essential, fundamental, pivotal, primary.
COMBINATIONS – **central bank** a national bank that provides services for its country's government and commercial banking

system, and issues currency. **central heating** a system for warming a building by heating water or air in one place and circulating it through pipes and radiators or vents. **central nervous system** the complex of nerve tissues that controls the activities of the body. **central processing unit** (also **central processor**) Computing the part of a computer in which operations are controlled and executed. **central reservation** Brit. the strip of land between the carriageways of a motorway or other major road.

centralise (also **centralize**) > *verb* concentrate (control or power) under a single authority.
DERIVATIVES – **centralisation** *noun* **centralism** *noun* **centralist** *noun* & *adjective*.

centre (US **center**) > *noun* **1** a point in the middle of something that is equally distant from all of its sides, ends, or surfaces. **2** a place where a specified activity is concentrated. **3** a point to or from which an activity or process is directed. **4** a political position that avoids extremes. **5** the middle player in some team games. > *verb* **1** place in the centre. **2** (**centre on** or **around**) have as a major concern or theme.
SYNONYMS – *noun* **1** core, middle, mid point. **2** focus, heart, hub, nub, nucleus. *verb* **2** (**centre on**) focus on, hinge on, pivot on, revolve around.
COMBINATIONS – **centre back** (also **centre half**) Soccer a defender who plays in the middle of the field. **centreboard** a pivoted board lowered through the keel of a sailing boat to reduce sideways movement. **centre forward** Soccer & Hockey an attacker who plays in the middle of the field. **centre of gravity** the point from which the weight of a body appears to act.
ORIGIN – Latin *centrum*, from Greek *kentron* 'sharp point, stationary point of a pair of compasses'.

centrefold > *noun* **1** the two middle pages of a magazine. **2** an illustration on such pages, especially a picture of a naked or scantily clad model.

centre of mass > *noun* a point representing the mean position of all the matter in a body (in uniform gravity, the same as the centre of gravity).

centrepiece > *noun* the most important item in a display.

centre stage > *noun* **1** the centre of a stage. **2** the most prominent position. > *adverb* in or towards this position.

-centric > *combining form* **1** having a specified centre: *geocentric*. **2** originating from a specified viewpoint: *Eurocentric*.
DERIVATIVES – **-centricity** *combining form*.

ORIGIN – from Greek *kentrikos*, on the pattern of words such as *concentric*.

centrifugal /sentri**fyoo**g'l, sen**trif**yoog'l/ > *adjective* Physics moving away from a centre.

DERIVATIVES – **centrifugally** *adverb*.

COMBINATIONS – **centrifugal force** a force, arising from the body's inertia, which appears to act on a body moving in a circular path and is directed away from the centre around which the body is moving.

ORIGIN – from Latin *centrum* 'centre' + *-fugus* 'fleeing' (from *fugere* 'flee').

centrifuge /**sen**trifyooj/ > *noun* a machine with a rapidly rotating container, used chiefly to separate liquids from solids. > *verb* subject to the action of a centrifuge.

DERIVATIVES – **centrifugation** /sentrifyoo**gay**sh'n/ *noun*.

centripetal /sen**tripp**it'l/ > *adjective* Physics moving towards a centre.

DERIVATIVES – **centripetally** *adverb*.

COMBINATIONS – **centripetal force** a force which acts on a body moving in a circular path and is directed towards the centre around which the body is moving.

ORIGIN – from Latin *centrum* 'centre' + *-petus* 'seeking' (from *petere* 'seek').

centrist > *noun* a person having moderate political views or policies.

DERIVATIVES – **centrism** *noun*.

centurion > *noun* the commander of a century in the ancient Roman army.

ORIGIN – Latin, from *centuria* 'century'.

century > *noun* (pl. **centuries**) **1** a period of one hundred years. **2** a period of a hundred years reckoned from the traditional date of Christ's birth (strictly speaking, from 01 to 100 and so on). **3** a batsman's score of a hundred runs in cricket. **4** a company of a hundred men in the ancient Roman army.

COMBINATIONS – **century plant** a large agave which produces a very tall flowering stem after many years of growth and then dies.

ORIGIN – Latin *centuria*, from *centum* 'hundred'.

CEO > *abbreviation* chief executive officer.

cep /sep/ > *noun* an edible mushroom with a smooth brown cap.

ORIGIN – French dialect, 'tree trunk, mushroom', from Latin *cippus* 'stake'.

cephalic /si**fal**ik, ke-/ > *adjective* relating to the head.

ORIGIN – Latin *cephalicus*, from Greek *kephalē* 'head'.

cephalopod /**sef**fəlopod/ > *noun* Zoology a mollusc of a class including octopuses and squids.

ORIGIN – from Greek *kephalē* 'head' + *pous* 'foot'.

ceramic > *adjective* **1** made of clay that is permanently hardened by heat. **2** relating to ceramics. > *noun* (**ceramics**) **1** ceramic articles. **2** (usu. treated as sing.) the art of making ceramics.

DERIVATIVES – **ceramicist** *noun*.

ORIGIN – Greek *keramikos*, from *keramos* 'pottery'.

ceratopsian /serrə**top**siən, kerrə**top**siən/ > *noun* a gregarious plant-eating dinosaur of a group including triceratops, with a bony frill around the neck.

ORIGIN – from Greek *keras* 'horn' + *ops* 'face'.

cere /seer/ > *noun* Ornithology a waxy fleshy covering at the base of the upper beak in some birds.

ORIGIN – Latin *cera* 'wax'.

cereal > *noun* **1** a grain used for food, for example wheat, maize, or rye. **2** a grass producing such grain. **3** a breakfast food made from a cereal grain or grains.

ORIGIN – Latin, from *Ceres*, the Roman goddess of agriculture.

cerebellum /serri**bell**əm/ > *noun* (pl. **cerebellums** or **cerebella**) Anatomy the part of the brain at the back of the skull, which coordinates muscular activity.

DERIVATIVES – **cerebellar** *adjective*.

ORIGIN – Latin, 'little brain'.

cerebral /**serr**ibrəl, sə**ree**brəl/ > *adjective* **1** relating to the cerebrum of the brain. **2** intellectual rather than emotional or physical.

DERIVATIVES – **cerebrally** *adverb*.

COMBINATIONS – **cerebral hemisphere** each of the two parts of the cerebrum (left and right) of the brain. **cerebral palsy** a condition marked by impaired muscle coordination and spastic paralysis, caused by damage to the brain before or at birth.

ORIGIN – from Latin *cerebrum* 'brain'.

cerebration /serri**bray**sh'n/ > *noun* the working of the brain; thinking.

cerebrospinal /serribro**spī**n'l/ > *adjective* Anatomy relating to the brain and spine.

cerebrum /**serr**ibrəm/ > *noun* (pl. **cerebra** /**serr**ibrə/) Anatomy the principal part of the brain, located in the front area of the skull.

ORIGIN – Latin, 'brain'.

cerecloth /**seer**kloth/ > *noun* historical waxed cloth, used especially for wrapping a corpse.

ORIGIN – from Latin *cerare* 'to wax', from *cera* 'wax'.

ceremonial > *adjective* **1** relating to or used for ceremonies. **2** (of a post or role) involving only nominal authority or power. > *noun* ritual procedures observed at a ceremony.

DERIVATIVES – **ceremonially** *adverb*.

SYNONYMS – *adjective* **1** celebratory, formal, official, ritualistic, solemn, stately.

ceremonious > *adjective* relating or appropriate to grand and formal occasions.

SYNONYMS – formal, grand, majestic, solemn, stately.

ceremony > *noun* (pl. **ceremonies**) **1** a formal occasion, typically one celebrating a particular event or anniversary. **2** the ritual procedures observed at such occasions.

IDIOMS – **stand on ceremony** observe formalities.

SYNONYMS – **1** observance, rite, service. **2** formalities, pageantry, pomp, ritual.

ORIGIN – Latin *caerimonia* 'religious worship', (pl.) 'ritual observances'.

cerise /sə**reess**/ > *noun* a light, clear red colour.

ORIGIN – French, 'cherry'.

cerium /**serr**iəm/ > *noun* a silvery-white metallic chemical element, the most abundant of the lanthanide series.

ORIGIN – named after the asteroid *Ceres*, which was discovered in 1801, shortly before cerium was identified.

cert > *noun* Brit. informal **1** an event regarded as inevitable. **2** a competitor, candidate, etc. regarded as certain to win.

cert. > *abbreviation* **1** certificate. **2** certified.

certain > *adjective* **1** able to be relied on to happen or be the case. **2** completely convinced of something. **3** specific but not explicitly named or stated. > *pronoun* (**certain of**) some but not all.

SYNONYMS – *adjective* **1** definite, incontrovertible, indubitable, sure, unquestionable. **2** confident, convinced, positive, sure, unwavering.

ANTONYMS – **1,2** doubtful, uncertain.

ORIGIN – Latin *certus* 'settled, sure'.

certainly > *adverb* **1** definitely; undoubtedly. **2** yes; by all means.

certainty > *noun* (pl. **certainties**) **1** the quality or state of being certain. **2** a true fact or an event that is definitely going to take place.

SYNONYMS – **1** assurance, confidence, conviction, reliability. **2** inevitability, necessity, reality, truth.

certifiable > *adjective* able or needing to be certified, especially as being insane.

certificate > *noun* /sər**tiff**ikət/ **1** an official document recording a particular fact, event, or level of achievement. **2** an official classification awarded to a cinema film, indicating its suitability for a particular age group. > *verb* /sər**tiff**ikayt/ provide with a certificate.

DERIVATIVES – **certification** *noun*.

SYNONYMS – *noun* **1** authentication, guarantee, licence, verification, warrant.

ORIGIN – Latin *certificare*, from *certus* 'certain'.

certify > *verb* (**certifies**, **certified**) **1** formally confirm. **2** officially recognise (something) as meeting certain standards. **3** officially declare someone insane.

SYNONYMS – **1,2** endorse, guarantee, ratify, validate, verify.

certiorari /sertiōraari/ > *noun* Law a writ by which a higher court reviews a case tried in a lower court.

ORIGIN – Latin, 'to be informed', a phrase originally occurring at the start of the writ.

certitude > *noun* a feeling of absolute certainty.

cerulean /sirŏŏliən/ > *adjective* deep blue in colour like a clear sky.

ORIGIN – Latin *caeruleus*, from *caelum* 'sky'.

cervical /**ser**vik'l, ser**vī**k'l/ > *adjective* Anatomy **1** relating to the cervix. **2** relating to the neck.

COMBINATIONS – **cervical smear** Brit. a specimen of cellular material from the cervix spread on a microscope slide for examination for cancerous cells or precancerous changes.

ORIGIN – Latin *cervicalis*, from *cervix* 'neck'.

cervix /**ser**viks/ > *noun* (pl. **cervices** /**ser**viseez/) **1** the narrow neck-like passage forming the lower end of the womb. **2** technical the neck.

ORIGIN – Latin.

Cesarean (also **Cesarian**) > *adjective & noun* US spelling of **Caesarean**.

cesium > *noun* US spelling of **caesium**.

cessation > *noun* the fact or process of ceasing.

SYNONYMS – ending, finishing, stoppage, termination.

ORIGIN – Latin, from *cessare* 'cease'.

cession > *noun* the formal giving up of rights, property, or territory by a state.

ORIGIN – Latin, from *cedere* 'cede'.

cesspit > *noun* a pit for the disposal of liquid waste and sewage.

ORIGIN – from *cess* in **cesspool**.

cesspool > *noun* an underground container for the temporary storage of liquid waste and sewage.

ORIGIN – probably from archaic *suspiral* 'vent, water pipe, settling tank', from Old French *souspirail* 'air hole'.

CET > *abbreviation* Central European Time.

cetacean /sitaysh'n/ Zoology > *noun* a marine mammal of an order including whales and dolphins. > *adjective* relating to these mammals.

ORIGIN – from Latin *cetus*, from Greek *kētos* 'whale'.

ceteris paribus /kaytəriss **parr**iboŏss/ > *adverb* other things being equal.

ORIGIN – Latin.

CF > *abbreviation* cystic fibrosis.

Cf > *symbol* the chemical element californium.

cf. > *abbreviation* compare with.

ORIGIN – from Latin *confer* 'compare'.

CFC > *abbreviation* chlorofluorocarbon, any of a class of synthetic compounds of carbon, hydrogen, chlorine, and fluorine used as refrigerants and aerosol propellants and harmful to the ozone layer.

CFE > *abbreviation* (in the UK) College of Further Education.

CFS > *abbreviation* chronic fatigue syndrome.

cg > *abbreviation* centigram(s).

CGT > *abbreviation* capital gains tax.

CH > *abbreviation* (in the UK) Companion of Honour.

ch. > *abbreviation* chapter.

Chablis /**shab**li/ > *noun* a dry white burgundy wine from Chablis in eastern France.

cha-cha > *noun* a ballroom dance with small steps and swaying hip movements, performed to a Latin American rhythm.

ORIGIN – Latin American Spanish.

chaconne /shə**kon**/ > *noun* Music **1** a composition in a series of varying sections in slow triple time. **2** a stately dance performed to such music.

ORIGIN – French, from Spanish *chacona*.

chacun à son goût /shakön a son **goō**/ > *exclamation* each to their own taste.

ORIGIN – French.

Chadian /**chad**diən/ > *noun* a person from Chad in central Africa. > *adjective* relating to Chad or Chadians.

chador /**chud**dər/ (also **chuddar**) > *noun* a piece of dark-coloured cloth that is wrapped around the head and upper body leaving only the face exposed, worn by Muslim women.

ORIGIN – Persian, 'sheet or veil'.

chafe > *verb* **1** make or become sore by rubbing. **2** (of an object) rub abrasively against another. **3** rub (a part of the body) to restore warmth or sensation. **4** become impatient because of a restriction or inconvenience. > *noun* wear or damage caused by rubbing.

SYNONYMS – *verb* **1,2** abrade, grate, rasp, rub, scrape.

ORIGIN – Old French *chaufer* 'make hot', from Latin *calere* 'be hot' + *facere* 'make'.

chafer > *noun* a large flying beetle of a group including the cockchafer and June bug.

chaff[1] /chaaf/ > *noun* **1** the husks of grain or other seed separated by winnowing or threshing. **2** chopped hay and straw used as fodder.

IDIOMS – **separate** (or **sort**) **the wheat from the chaff** distinguish valuable people or things from worthless ones.

chaff[2] /chaaf, chaff/ > *noun* light-hearted joking. > *verb* tease.

ORIGIN – perhaps from **chafe**.

chaffinch > *noun* a common finch, the male of which has a bluish head, pink underparts, and dark wings with a white flash.

chafing dish > *noun* **1** a cooking pot with an outer pan of hot water, used for keeping food warm. **2** a metal pan used for cooking at table.

chagrin /**sha**grin/ > *noun* annoyance or shame at having failed. > *verb* (**be chagrined**) feel annoyed or ashamed.

SYNONYMS – *noun* dismay, distress, mortification, regret, shame.

ORIGIN – French, 'rough skin, shagreen'.

chain > *noun* **1** a connected series of metal links used for fastening or pulling, or as jewellery. **2** a connected series, set, or sequence. **3** a part of a molecule consisting of a number of atoms bonded together in a series. **4** a measure of length equal to 66 ft (20.117 m). > *verb* fasten or confine with a chain.

WORDFINDER – concatenate (*link together in a chain*).

SYNONYMS – *noun* **2** progression, sequence, series, string, train.

COMBINATIONS – **chain gang** a group of convicts chained together while working outside the prison. **chain letter** one of a sequence of letters, each recipient in the sequence being requested to send copies to a number of other people. **chain mail** historical armour made of small metal rings linked together. **chain reaction 1** a chemical reaction in which the products themselves spread the reaction. **2** a series of events, each caused by the previous one. **chainsaw** a power-driven saw with teeth set on a moving chain. **chain-smoke** smoke cigarettes in continuous succession. **chain stitch** an ornamental embroidery or crochet stitch resembling a chain. **chain store** one of a series of shops owned by one firm and selling the same goods.

chair > *noun* **1** a separate seat for one person, with a back and four legs. **2** the person in charge of a meeting or an organisation. **3** a professorship. **4** (**the chair**) US the electric chair. > *verb* **1** act as chairperson of (a meeting or organisation). **2** carry aloft in a chair or sitting position to celebrate a victory.

COMBINATIONS – **chairlift** a series of chairs hung from a moving cable, used for carrying passengers up and down a mountain.

ORIGIN – Old French *chaiere*, from Greek *kathedra*; compare with **cathedral**.

chairman (or **chairwoman**) > *noun* a person in charge of a meeting, committee, company, or other organisation.

DERIVATIVES – **chairmanship** *noun*.

chairperson > *noun* a chairman or chairwoman (used as a neutral alternative).

chaise /shayz/ > *noun* **1** chiefly historical a horse-drawn carriage for one or two people, especially one with an open top and two wheels. **2** another term for **post-chaise**. **3** US term for **chaise longue**.

ORIGIN – French.

chaise longue /shayz **longg**/ (US also **chaise lounge**) > *noun* (pl. **chaises longues** pronunc. same) **1** a sofa with a backrest at only one end. **2** N. Amer. a sunbed or other chair with a lengthened seat.
ORIGIN – French, 'long chair'.

chakra /**chuk**rə/ > *noun* (in Indian thought) each of the centres of spiritual power in the human body, usually considered to be seven in number.
ORIGIN – Sanskrit, 'wheel or circle'.

chalcedony /kal**sedd**əni/ > *noun* quartz occurring in a microcrystalline form such as onyx and agate.
ORIGIN – Latin *chalcedonius*, from Greek *khalkēdōn*.

chalet /**shal**ay/ > *noun* **1** a wooden house with overhanging eaves, typically found in the Swiss Alps. **2** a small wooden cabin used by holidaymakers.
ORIGIN – Swiss French, from Old French *chasel* 'farmstead'.

chalice > *noun* **1** historical a goblet. **2** the wine cup used in the Christian Eucharist.
ORIGIN – Old French, from Latin *calix* 'cup'.

chalk > *noun* **1** a soft white limestone formed from the skeletal remains of sea creatures. **2** a similar substance (calcium sulphate), made into sticks and used for drawing or writing. > *verb* **1** draw or write with chalk. **2** Brit. charge (drinks bought in a pub or bar) to a person's account. **3** (**chalk up**) achieve (something) noteworthy. **4** (**chalk up**) ascribe (something) to a particular cause.
WORDFINDER – calcareous (*containing chalk; chalky*).
IDIOMS – **as different as chalk and cheese** Brit. fundamentally different. **by a long chalk** Brit. by far.
DERIVATIVES – **chalky** (**chalkier, chalkiest**) *adjective*.
COMBINATIONS – **chalkboard** N. Amer. a blackboard.
ORIGIN – Latin *calx* 'lime'.

challenge > *noun* **1** a call to someone to participate in a contest. **2** a call to someone to prove something. **3** a demanding task or situation. **4** an attempt to win a sporting contest. > *verb* **1** dispute the truth or validity of. **2** invite (someone) to engage in a contest. **3** Law object to (a jury member). **4** compete with. **5** test the abilities of. **6** (of a sentry) call on (someone) to prove their identity.
DERIVATIVES – **challenger** *noun* **challenging** *adjective*.
SYNONYMS – *noun* **1,2** confrontation, provocation, summons, test. **3** difficulty, problem, trial, tribulation. *verb* **1** defy, dispute, question, take issue with. **5** spur on, stimulate, tax, test, try.

ORIGIN – Old French *chalenger*, from Latin *calumnia* 'calumny'.

challenged > *adjective* **1** euphemistic suffering from impairment or disability in a specified respect: *physically challenged*. **2** humorous lacking or deficient in a specified respect: *vertically challenged*.

---

wordpower facts

challenged

The use of **challenged** with a preceding adverb (e.g. **physically challenged**) was adopted in the US in the 1980s (quickly spreading to the UK and elsewhere) because it was felt to have a more positive ring than terms such as **disabled** or **handicapped**. However, serious use of the term was quickly followed by mocking or ironical uses, such as **cerebrally challenged** ('unintelligent'), **conversationally challenged** ('boring'), and **follicularly challenged** ('bald'), which poked fun at the use of euphemism and at political correctness generally.

---

chalybeate /kə**libb**iət/ > *adjective* denoting natural mineral springs containing iron salts.
ORIGIN – Latin *chalybs*, from Greek *khalups* 'steel'.

chamaeleon > *noun* variant spelling of CHAMELEON.

chamber > *noun* **1** a large room used for formal or public events. **2** one of the houses of a parliament. **3** (**chambers**) Law, Brit. rooms used by a barrister or barristers. **4** literary or archaic a private room, especially a bedroom. **5** an enclosed space or cavity. **6** (before another noun) Music of or for a small group of instruments. **7** the part of a gun bore that contains the charge.
WORDFINDER – bicameral (*denoting a legislative body having two chambers*), unicameral (*having one chamber*).
DERIVATIVES – **chambered** *adjective*.
SYNONYMS – **1** hall, room. **5** cavity, cell, compartment, hollow.
COMBINATIONS – **chambermaid** a woman who cleans rooms in a hotel. **Chamber of Commerce** a local association to promote the interests of the business community. **chamber pot** a bowl kept in a bedroom and used as a toilet.
ORIGIN – Latin *camera* 'vault, arched chamber', from Greek *kamara* 'object with an arched cover'; compare with CAMERA.

chamberlain /**chaym**bərlin/ > *noun* historical **1** an officer who managed the household of a monarch or noble. **2** Brit. an officer who received revenue on behalf of a corporation or public body.

ORIGIN – Old French, from Latin *camera* (see CHAMBER).

chamber music > *noun* instrumental music played by a small ensemble, such as a string quartet.

chambray /**sham**bray/ > *noun* a type of fabric with a white weft and a coloured warp, producing a mottled appearance.
ORIGIN – from *Cambrai* (see CAMBRIC).

chameleon /kə**meel**iən/ (also **chamaeleon**) > *noun* **1** a small slow-moving lizard with a long extensible tongue, protruding eyes, and the ability to change colour. **2** a changeable or inconstant person.
DERIVATIVES – **chameleonic** *adjective*.
ORIGIN – Greek *khamaileōn*, from *khamai* 'on the ground' + *leōn* 'lion'.

chamfer /**cham**fər/ Carpentry > *verb* cut away (a right-angled edge or corner) to make a symmetrical sloping edge. > *noun* a chamfered edge or corner.
ORIGIN – French *chamfrain*, from *chant* (see CANT[2]) + *fraint* 'broken'.

chamois > *noun* (pl. same) **1** /**sham**waa/ (pl. pronunc. same or /**sham**waaz/) an agile goat-antelope found in mountainous areas of southern Europe. **2** /**sham**mi/ (pl. pronunc. /**sham**miz/) (also **chamois leather**) soft pliable leather made from the skin of sheep, goats, or deer.
ORIGIN – French.

chamomile /**kamm**əmīl/ (also **camomile**) > *noun* an aromatic plant with white and yellow flowers.
ORIGIN – Latin *chamomilla*, from Greek *khamaimēlon* 'earth-apple' (because of the apple-like smell of its flowers).

champ[1] > *verb* **1** munch enthusiastically or noisily. **2** fret impatiently.
IDIOMS – **champ at the bit** be very impatient.

champ[2] > *noun* informal a champion.

champagne /sham**payn**/ > *noun* a white sparkling wine from Champagne, a region in NE France.
WORDFINDER – coupe (*broad, shallow champagne glass*), flute (*tall, narrow champagne glass*), méthode champenoise (*method of making champagne and other sparkling wines*).

champers > *noun* informal, chiefly Brit. champagne.

champion > *noun* **1** a person who has won a sporting contest or other competition. **2** a defender of a cause or person. > *verb* support the cause of. > *adjective* Brit. informal or dialect excellent.
SYNONYMS – *noun* **1** conqueror, prizewinner, title holder, victor. **2** advocate, crusader, defender, promoter, proponent, upholder. *verb* advocate, crusade, defend, promote, uphold.

wordpower facts

Champion

In its earliest use in English the word **champion** denoted a fighting man, especially one who was strong and brave. It came from the Latin word *campio*, denoting a combatant in the *campus*, that is the 'field' of athletic or military endeavour. *Campus*, meaning 'field' or 'level ground', is the root also of **camp**, **campus**, and **campaign**.

championship > *noun* **1** a sporting contest for the position of champion. **2** the vigorous defence of a person or cause.

champlevé /shoNləvay/ > *noun* enamelwork in which hollows made in a metal surface are filled with coloured enamels.
ORIGIN – French, from *champ* 'field' + *levé* 'raised'.

chance > *noun* **1** a possibility of something happening. **2** (**chances**) the probability of something happening. **3** an opportunity. **4** the occurrence of events in the absence of any obvious design. > *verb* **1** do something by accident. **2** *informal* risk.
WORDFINDER – aleatory (*depending on chance*), stochastic (*following a random pattern describable by statistics*).
IDIOMS – **by any chance** possibly. **chance one's arm** Brit. *informal* risk doing something. **on the** (**off**) **chance** just in case. **stand a chance** have a prospect of success. **take a chance** (or **chances**) expose oneself to the risk of danger or failure.
SYNONYMS – *noun* **1,2** likelihood, possibility, probability, prospect. **4** accident, coincidence, destiny, fate, fortuity, luck.
ORIGIN – Old French *cheance*, from *cheoir* 'fall, befall'.

chancel /chaans'l/ > *noun* the part of a church near the altar, reserved for the clergy and choir.
ORIGIN – Old French, from Latin *cancelli* 'crossbars'.

chancellery /chaansələri/ > *noun* (pl. **chancelleries**) the position, office, or department of a chancellor.

chancellor > *noun* **1** a senior state or legal official of various kinds. **2** (**Chancellor**) the head of the government in some European countries.
DERIVATIVES – **chancellorship** *noun*.
COMBINATIONS – **Chancellor of the Exchequer** the finance minister of the United Kingdom.
ORIGIN – Latin *cancellarius* 'porter, secretary' (originally a court official stationed at the grating separating public from judges), from *cancelli* 'crossbars': compare with **CHANCEL**.

chancer > *noun* Brit. *informal* a person who fully exploits any opportunity.

chancery > *noun* (pl. **chanceries**) **1** (**Chancery** or **Chancery Division**) (in the UK) the Lord Chancellor's court, a division of the High Court of Justice. **2** *chiefly Brit.* an office attached to an embassy or consulate. **3** a public record office.
ORIGIN – contraction of **CHANCELLERY**.

chancre /shangkər/ > *noun* Medicine a painless ulcer, particularly one developing on the genitals in venereal disease.
ORIGIN – French, from Latin *cancer* 'creeping ulcer'.

chancroid /shangkroyd/ > *noun* a venereal infection causing ulceration of the lymph nodes in the groin.

chancy > *adjective* (**chancier, chanciest**) *informal* uncertain; risky.
DERIVATIVES – **chancily** *adverb*.

chandelier > *noun* a large hanging light with branches for several light bulbs or candles.
ORIGIN – French, from *chandelle* 'candle'.

chandler /chaandlər/ > *noun* **1** (also **ship chandler**) a dealer in supplies and equipment for ships. **2** *historical* a dealer in household items such as oil and groceries.
DERIVATIVES – **chandlery** *noun*.
ORIGIN – first denoting a candlemaker or candle seller: from Old French *chandelier*, from *chandelle* 'candle'.

change > *verb* **1** make or become different. **2** exchange for another. **3** move from one to (another). **4** (**change over**) move from one system or situation to another. **5** exchange (a sum of money) for the same sum in a different currency or denomination. > *noun* **1** the action of changing. **2** an instance of becoming different. **3** money returned to someone as the balance of the sum paid or given in exchange for the same sum in larger units. **4** coins as opposed to banknotes. **5** a clean garment or garments as replacement clothing. **6** an order in which a peal of bells can be rung.
IDIOMS – **change hands 1** (of a business or building) pass to a different owner. **2** (of money) pass to another person in the course of a business transaction. **a change is as good as a rest** *proverb* a change of work or occupation can be as refreshing as a period of relaxation. **change one's tune** express a very different attitude. **for a change** contrary to how things usually happen. **get no change out of** Brit. *informal* fail to get information or a desired reaction from. **ring the changes** vary the ways of doing something. [ORIGIN – with allusion to the different orders in which a peal of bells may be rung.]

DERIVATIVES – **changeless** *adjective* **changer** *noun*.
SYNONYMS – *verb* **1** adapt, adjust, alter, modify, transform. **2** exchange, replace, substitute, swap, switch. *noun* **1,2** adaptation, adjustment, alteration, conversion, modification, rearrangement, transformation.
ORIGIN – Old French *changer*, from Latin *cambire* 'barter'.

changeable > *adjective* **1** liable to unpredictable variation. **2** able to be changed.
DERIVATIVES – **changeability** *noun*.
SYNONYMS – **1** fluctuating, inconsistent, inconstant, mutable, unstable, variable. **2** adjustable, alterable, interchangeable.
ANTONYMS – **1** constant. **2** fixed.

changeling > *noun* a child believed to have been secretly substituted by fairies for the parents' real child.

changeover > *noun* a change from one system or situation to another.

channel > *noun* **1** a length of water wider than a strait, joining two larger areas of water, especially two seas. **2** (**the Channel**) the English Channel. **3** a passage along which liquid or a watercourse may flow. **4** an electric circuit which acts as a path for a signal. **5** a band of frequencies used in radio and television transmission. **6** a medium for communication or the passage of information. **7** a navigable passage in a stretch of water otherwise unsafe for vessels. > *verb* (**channelled, channelling; US channeled, channeling**) **1** direct towards a particular end. **2** cause to pass along or through a specified route or medium.
SYNONYMS – *noun* **1** passage, sound. **6** agency, conduit, course, path, route. *verb* conduct, convey, direct, route.
COMBINATIONS – **channel-hop** *informal* change frequently from one television channel to another.
ORIGIN – Latin *canalis* 'pipe, groove, channel', from *canna* 'cane, reed'.

chant > *noun* **1** a repeated rhythmic phrase, typically one shouted or sung in unison by a group. **2** a monotonous or repetitive song. **3** a tune to which the words of psalms or other works with irregular rhythm are fitted by singing several syllables or words to the same note. > *verb* say or shout repeatedly in a sing-song tone.
SYNONYMS – *noun* **1,2** chorus, incantation, mantra, recitation. *verb* chorus, intone, sing.
ORIGIN – Old French *chanter* 'sing', from Latin *canere* 'sing'.

chanter > *noun* the pipe of a bagpipe, having finger holes on which the melody is played.

chanterelle /chantərel/ > *noun* an edible

woodland mushroom with a yellow funnel-shaped cap.

ORIGIN – Latin *cantharellus*, from Greek *kantharos*, denoting a kind of drinking container.

chanteuse /shaan**töz**/ > *noun* a female singer of popular songs.

ORIGIN – French, from *chanter* 'sing'.

chantry > *noun* (pl. **chantries**) a chapel or other part of a church endowed for the celebration of masses for the donor's soul.

ORIGIN – Old French, from *chanter* 'to sing'.

chanty > *noun* variant spelling of **SHANTY²**.

Chanukkah > *noun* variant spelling of **HANUKKAH**.

chaos > *noun* **1** complete disorder and confusion. **2** the formless matter supposed to have existed before the creation of the universe.

SYNONYMS – **1** confusion, disorder, mayhem, pandemonium, turmoil.

ANTONYMS – **1** order.

COMBINATIONS – **chaos theory** the branch of science concerned with the behaviour of complex systems in which tiny changes can have major effects, and which therefore seem unpredictable.

ORIGIN – Greek *khaos* 'vast chasm, void'.

chaotic > *adjective* **1** in a state of complete confusion and disorder. **2** describable by chaos theory.

DERIVATIVES – **chaotically** *adverb*.

SYNONYMS – **1** confused, disordered, disorderly, topsy-turvy, tumultuous.

ANTONYMS – **1** orderly.

chap¹ > *verb* (**chapped**, **chapping**) **1** (of the skin) crack and become sore, typically through exposure to cold. **2** (of the wind or cold) cause (skin) to crack in this way.

chap² > *noun* informal, chiefly Brit. a man or a boy.

ORIGIN – abbreviation of **CHAPMAN**.

chaparral /shapp**əral**/ > *noun* N. Amer. vegetation consisting chiefly of tangled shrubs and thorny bushes.

ORIGIN – Spanish, from *chaparra* 'dwarf evergreen oak'.

chapatti /chə**paa**ti/ > *noun* (pl. **chapattis**) (in Indian cookery) a thin pancake of unleavened wholemeal bread cooked on a griddle.

ORIGIN – Hindi, from a word meaning 'roll out'.

chapbook > *noun* historical a small pamphlet containing tales, ballads, or tracts, sold by pedlars.

ORIGIN – from **CHAPMAN**.

chapel > *noun* **1** a small building for Christian worship, typically one attached to an institution or private house. **2** a part of a large church with its own altar and dedication. **3** Brit. a place of worship for

Nonconformist congregations. **4** Brit. the members or branch of a print or newspaper trade union at a particular place of work.

wordpower facts

Chapel

The first sanctuary to be called a chapel was named after the holy relic preserved within it, the cape of St Martin, which was highly valued as a sacred relic by the Frankish kings who conquered Gaul in the 6th century. The Latin word *cappella*, meaning 'little cape' (from *cappa*, 'cape'), was applied to the sanctuary itself, and eventually to any holy sanctuary, entering English in the 13th century (via Old French *chapele*) in the form **chapel**. The word **chaplain** comes from Latin *cappellanus*, that is, an attendant charged with guarding the cape. The Latin form remains unchanged in the musical term **a cappella**.

chaperone /shapp**ərōn**/ (also **chaperon** /shapp**əron**/) > *noun* dated an older woman who escorts an unmarried girl at social occasions. > *verb* accompany and look after (someone).

DERIVATIVES – **chaperonage** /shapp-ərənij/ *noun*.

SYNONYMS – *verb* accompany, attend, conduct, escort.

ORIGIN – French, from *chape* 'cap, hood'.

chaplain > *noun* a member of the clergy officially assigned to an institution, group, private chapel, etc.

DERIVATIVES – **chaplaincy** *noun*.

chaplet > *noun* **1** a circlet for a person's head. **2** a string of 55 beads for counting prayers.

ORIGIN – Old French, from *chapel* 'hat', from Latin *cappa* 'cap'.

chapman > *noun* archaic a pedlar.

ORIGIN – Old English, from *cēap* 'bargaining, trade' (see **CHEAP**).

chaps > *plural noun* N. Amer. leather trousers without a seat, worn by a cowboy over ordinary trousers to protect the legs.

ORIGIN – short for *chaparajos*, from Mexican Spanish; related to **CHAPARRAL**.

chaptalisation /chaptəl**ī**zaysh'n/ (also **chaptalization**) > *noun* (in winemaking) the correction or improvement of must by the addition of calcium carbonate or sugar.

DERIVATIVES – **chaptalise** (also **chaptalize**) *verb*.

ORIGIN – from the name of Jean A. *Chaptal* (1756–1832), the French chemist who invented the process.

chapter > *noun* **1** a main division of a book. **2** a particular period in history or in a

person's life. **3** the governing body of a cathedral or other religious community. **4** chiefly N. Amer. a local branch of a society.

IDIOMS – **chapter and verse** an exact reference or authority. **a chapter of accidents** a series of unfortunate events.

SYNONYMS – **1** division, part, section, segment. **2** episode, epoch, era, period, phase, stage.

ORIGIN – Old French *chapitre*, from Latin *capitulum* 'little head'.

char¹ > *verb* (**charred**, **charring**) partially burn so as to blacken the surface. > *noun* charred material.

SYNONYMS – *verb* burn, scorch, sear, singe.

ORIGIN – apparently from **CHARCOAL**.

char² Brit. informal > *noun* a charwoman. > *verb* (**charred**, **charring**) work as a charwoman.

char³ (also **cha** /chaa/ or **chai** /chī/) > *noun* Brit. informal tea.

ORIGIN – Chinese.

char⁴ > *noun* variant spelling of **CHARR**.

charabanc /sharr**ə**bang/ > *noun* Brit. an early form of bus.

ORIGIN – French *char-à-bancs* 'carriage with benches'.

character > *noun* **1** the qualities distinctive to an individual. **2** the distinctive nature of something. **3** a person in a novel, play, or film. **4** a part played by an actor. **5** a printed or written letter or symbol. **6** strength and originality in a person's nature. **7** a person's good reputation. **8** informal an eccentric or amusing person.

DERIVATIVES – **characterful** *adjective* **characterless** *adjective*.

SYNONYMS – **1,2** disposition, essence, identity, nature. **6** fortitude, moral fibre, resolve, strength, will power. **7** good name, reputation, standing.

COMBINATIONS – **character actor** an actor who specialises in playing unusual people rather than leading roles.

ORIGIN – first used in the sense 'distinctive mark': from Old French *caractere*, from Greek *kharaktēr* 'a stamping tool'.

characterise (also **characterize**) > *verb* **1** describe the distinctive character of. **2** (of a feature or quality) be characteristic of.

DERIVATIVES – **characterisation** *noun*.

SYNONYMS – **1** depict, describe, portray, represent. **2** distinguish, mark, typify.

characteristic > *adjective* typical of a particular person, place, or thing. > *noun* a feature or quality typical of a person, place, or thing.

DERIVATIVES – **characteristically** *adverb*.

SYNONYMS – *adjective* distinctive, particular, peculiar, representative, typical. *noun* attribute, feature, hallmark, quality, property, trait.

charade /shə**raad**/ > *noun* **1** an absurd pretence. **2** (**charades**) (treated as sing.) a game which involves guessing a word or phrase from written or acted clues.

SYNONYMS – **1** masquerade, mockery, sham.

ORIGIN – Provençal *charrado* 'conversation'.

charbroil > *verb* N. Amer. grill (food, especially meat) on a rack over charcoal.

charcoal > *noun* **1** a porous black form of carbon obtained when wood is heated in the absence of air. **2** a dark grey colour.

charcuterie /shaar**koo**tari/ > *noun* (pl. **charcuteries**) **1** cold cooked meats collectively. **2** a shop selling such meats.

ORIGIN – French, from obsolete *char* 'flesh' + *cuite* 'cooked'.

chard /chaard/ > *noun* (also **Swiss chard**) a beet of a variety with edible broad white leaf stalks and green blades.

ORIGIN – French *carde*.

Chardonnay /**shaar**dənay/ > *noun* **1** a variety of white wine grape used for making champagne and other wines. **2** a wine made from this grape.

ORIGIN – French.

charentais /**sharr**əntay/ > *noun* a small variety of melon with a green rind and orange flesh.

ORIGIN – French, meaning 'from the Charentes region'.

charge > *verb* **1** demand (an amount) as a price for a service rendered or goods supplied. **2** accuse (someone) of something, especially an offence under law. **3** rush forward in attack. **4** entrust with a task. **5** store electrical energy in (a battery). **6** technical or formal load or fill (a container, gun, etc.) to the full or proper extent. **7** fill with a quality or emotion. > *noun* **1** a price asked. **2** a formal accusation made against a person. **3** a financial liability or commitment. **4** responsibility for care or control. **5** a person or thing entrusted to someone's care. **6** a headlong rush forward, typically in attack. **7** a property of matter, existing in a positive or negative form, that is responsible for electrical phenomena. **8** energy stored chemically in a battery for conversion into electricity. **9** a quantity of explosive to be detonated in order to fire a gun or similar weapon.

IDIOMS – **press charges** accuse someone formally of a crime so that they can be brought to trial.

DERIVATIVES – **chargeable** *adjective*.

SYNONYMS – *verb* **1** ask for, bill, demand, exact. **2** accuse, arraign, indict, prosecute. **3** attack, rush, storm. **4** burden, encumber, entrust. **7** imbue, infuse, permeate, pervade, suffuse. *noun* **1** fee, price, rate, tariff. **2** accusation, allegation, arraignment, indictment. **3** cost, expense, liability, outlay. **4** care, control, custody, jurisdiction, protection. **5** protégé, ward. **6** assault, attack, onslaught, raid, rush, strike.

COMBINATIONS – **charge account** an account to which goods and services may be charged on credit. **charge card** a credit card for use with an account which must be paid in full when a statement is issued. **charge nurse** Brit. a nurse in charge of a ward in a hospital.

ORIGIN – Old French *charger*, from Latin *carricare* 'to load', from *carrus* 'wheeled vehicle'.

charged > *adjective* **1** having an electric charge. **2** filled with excitement, tension, or emotion.

chargé d'affaires /shaar**zhay** da**fair**/ > *noun* (pl. **chargés** pronunc. same) **1** an ambassador's deputy. **2** a state's diplomatic representative in a minor country.

ORIGIN – French, 'person in charge of affairs'.

chargehand > *noun* Brit. a worker with supervisory duties ranking below a foreman.

charger > *noun* **1** a device for charging a battery. **2** a horse ridden by a knight or cavalryman.

chargrill > *verb* grill (food, typically meat or fish) quickly at a very high heat.

chariot > *noun* a two-wheeled vehicle drawn by horses, used in ancient warfare and racing.

WORDFINDER – Auriga (constellation, the Charioteer).

DERIVATIVES – **charioteer** *noun*.

ORIGIN – Old French, from Latin *carrus* 'wheeled vehicle'.

charisma /kə**riz**mə/ > *noun* **1** compelling attractiveness or charm that can inspire devotion in others. **2** (pl. **charismata** /kə**riz**mətə/) Christian Theology a gift bestowed by God.

SYNONYMS – **1** allure, charm, glamour, magnetism, presence.

ORIGIN – Greek *kharisma*, from *kharis* 'favour, grace'.

charismatic /karriz**matt**ik/ > *adjective* **1** having charisma. **2** relating to a movement within certain Christian Churches that emphasises the inspirational power of the Holy Spirit. > *noun* an adherent of the charismatic movement.

DERIVATIVES – **charismatically** *adverb*.

SYNONYMS – *adjective* **1** captivating, charming, fascinating, magnetic.

charitable > *adjective* **1** relating to the assistance of those in need. **2** tolerant in judging others.

DERIVATIVES – **charitably** *adverb*.

SYNONYMS – **1** altruistic, humanitarian, philanthropic. **2** compassionate, generous, magnanimous, sympathetic, tolerant, understanding.

charity > *noun* (pl. **charities**) **1** an organisation set up to assist those in need. **2** the voluntary giving of money or assistance to those in need. **3** help or money given in this way. **4** tolerance in judging others.

IDIOMS – **charity begins at home** proverb a person's first responsibility is for the needs of their own family and friends.

SYNONYMS – **2** altruism, humanitarianism, munificence, philanthropy. **3** aid, assistance, handouts, relief; historical alms. **4** compassion, generosity, magnanimity, sympathy, tolerance, understanding.

ORIGIN – Latin *caritas*, from *carus* 'dear'.

charlatan /**shaar**lət'n/ > *noun* a person who falsely claims to have expertise in a certain area.

DERIVATIVES – **charlatanism** *noun* **charlatanry** *noun*.

SYNONYMS – fake, fraud, impostor, mountebank.

ORIGIN – Italian *ciarlatano*, from *ciarlare* 'to babble'.

Charles's law > *noun* Chemistry a law stating that the volume of an ideal gas at constant pressure is directly proportional to the absolute temperature.

ORIGIN – named after the French physicist Jacques A. C. *Charles* (1746–1823).

charleston > *noun* a lively dance of the 1920s which involved turning the knees inwards and kicking out the lower legs.

ORIGIN – named after the city of *Charleston* in South Carolina, USA.

charlie > *noun* (pl. **charlies**) **1** Brit. informal a fool. **2** informal cocaine.

charlotte > *noun* a pudding made of stewed fruit with a casing or covering of bread, sponge cake, biscuits, or breadcrumbs.

charm > *noun* **1** the power or quality of delighting or fascinating others. **2** a small ornament worn on a necklace or bracelet. **3** an object, act, or saying believed to have magic power. > *verb* **1** delight greatly. **2** use one's charm in order to influence someone.

DERIVATIVES – **charmer** *noun* **charmless** *adjective*.

SYNONYMS – *noun* **1** allure, attractiveness, charisma, fascination, seductiveness. **3** amulet, incantation, spell, talisman, totem. *verb* **1** captivate, dazzle, delight, enchant, enthral. **2** beguile, bewitch, coax, win over.

ANTONYMS – *noun* **1** repellence, unattractiveness. *verb* repel.

COMBINATIONS – **charm offensive** a campaign of flattery designed to achieve the support of others.

ORIGIN – Old French *charme*, from Latin *carmen* 'song, verse, incantation'.

charmed > *adjective* (of a person's life) unusually lucky as though protected by magic. > *exclamation* dated expressing polite pleasure at an introduction.

charming > *adjective* **1** delightful; very appealing. **2** very polite, friendly, and likeable. > *exclamation* used as an ironic expression of displeasure.

DERIVATIVES – **charmingly** *adverb*.

charnel house > *noun* historical a building or vault in which corpses or bones were piled.

ORIGIN – Old French, from Latin *carnalis* 'relating to flesh', from *caro* 'flesh'.

Charolais /**sharrə**lay/ > *noun* (pl. same) a breed of large white beef cattle.

ORIGIN – named after the *Monts du Charollais*, hills in eastern France where the breed originated.

charpoy /**chaar**poy/ > *noun* Indian a light bedstead.

ORIGIN – from an Urdu word meaning 'four-legged'.

charr /chaar/ (also **char**) > *noun* (pl. same) a trout-like northern freshwater or marine fish.

chart > *noun* 1 a sheet of information in the form of a table, graph, or diagram. 2 a geographical map, especially one used for navigation by sea or air. 3 (**the charts**) a weekly listing of the current best-selling pop records. > *verb* 1 make a map of. 2 plot (a course) on a chart.

ORIGIN – Latin *charta*, from Greek *khartēs* 'papyrus leaf'; related to CARD[1].

charter > *noun* 1 a written grant by a sovereign or legislature, by which a body such as a university is created or its rights defined. 2 a written constitution or description of an organisation's functions. 3 (in the UK) a written statement of the rights of a specified group of people. 4 the hiring of an aircraft, ship, or motor vehicle. > *verb* 1 grant a charter to (a city, university, etc.). 2 hire (an aircraft, ship, or motor vehicle).

DERIVATIVES – **charterer** *noun*.

SYNONYMS – *noun* 1 authorisation, concession, covenant, grant, sanction. 2 canon, code, constitution.

COMBINATIONS – **charter flight** a flight by an aircraft chartered for a specific journey, not part of an airline's regular schedule.

chartered > *adjective* Brit. (of an accountant, engineer, etc.) qualified as a member of a professional body that has a royal charter.

Chartism > *noun* a British parliamentary reform movement of 1837–48, the principles of which were set out in a manifesto called *The People's Charter*.

DERIVATIVES – **Chartist** *noun & adjective*.

chartreuse /shaar**tröz**/ > *noun* a pale green or yellow liqueur made from brandy.

ORIGIN – named after *La Grande Chartreuse*, the Carthusian monastery near Grenoble where the liqueur was first made.

charwoman > *noun* Brit. dated a woman employed as a cleaner in a house or office.

ORIGIN – from obsolete *char* or *chare* 'a chore', related to CHORE.

chary /**chair**i/ > *adjective* (**charier**, **chariest**) (often **chary of**) cautiously reluctant.

SYNONYMS – cautious, dubious, guarded, reluctant, wary.

ORIGIN – Old English, 'sorrowful, anxious'; related to CARE.

chase[1] > *verb* 1 pursue in order to catch. 2 rush or cause to go in a specified direction. 3 try to obtain (something owed or required). > *noun* 1 an act of chasing. 2 (**the chase**) hunting as a sport. 3 Brit. (in place names) an area of unenclosed land formerly reserved for hunting.

IDIOMS – **give chase** go in pursuit.

SYNONYMS – *verb* 1 hunt, pursue, run after, track, trail. 2 dash, hasten, rush, speed.

ORIGIN – Old French *chacier*, from Latin *captare* 'continue to take'.

chase[2] > *verb* decorate (metal) with engraving or inlay.

DERIVATIVES – **chased** *adjective*.

ORIGIN – apparently from earlier *enchase*, from Old French *enchasser* 'set gems, encase'.

chaser > *noun* 1 a person or thing that chases. 2 a horse for steeplechasing. 3 informal a strong alcoholic drink taken after a weaker one.

Chasid etc. variant spelling of HASID etc.

chasm > *noun* 1 a deep fissure. 2 a profound difference between people, viewpoints, feelings, etc.

SYNONYMS – 1 abyss, canyon, gorge, ravine. 2 breach, divide, gulf, rift.

ORIGIN – Greek *khasma* 'gaping hollow'.

chassé /**shass**ay/ > *noun* a gliding step in dancing in which one foot displaces the other. > *verb* (**chasséd**, **chasséing**) make such a step.

ORIGIN – French, 'chased'.

Chassid etc. variant spelling of HASID etc.

chassis /**shass**i/ > *noun* (pl. same /**shass**iz/) 1 the base frame of a motor vehicle or other wheeled conveyance. 2 the outer structural framework of a piece of audio, radio, or computer equipment.

ORIGIN – French, 'frame'.

chaste > *adjective* 1 refraining from sexual intercourse outside marriage. 2 without unnecessary ornamentation.

SYNONYMS – 1 abstinent, modest, pure, restrained.

ORIGIN – Latin *castus* 'morally pure'.

chasten > *verb* (of a reprimand or misfortune) have a restraining or demoralising effect on.

SYNONYMS – cow, dismay, humble, subdue.

ORIGIN – Old French *chastier*, from Latin *castigare* 'castigate'.

chastise* > *verb* reprimand severely.

DERIVATIVES – **chastisement** *noun* **chastiser** *noun*.

*SPELLING – **chastise** cannot be spelled with an *-ize* ending.

SYNONYMS – berate, castigate, censure, rebuke, reprimand.

chastity > *noun* chaste behaviour; avoidance of sexual intercourse outside marriage.

COMBINATIONS – **chastity belt** historical a garment designed to prevent the woman wearing it from having sexual intercourse.

ORIGIN – Latin *castitas*, from *castus* 'morally pure'.

chasuble /**chaz**yoob'l/ > *noun* a sleeveless outer vestment worn by a priest when celebrating Mass.

ORIGIN – Latin *casubla*, from *casula* 'hooded cloak or little cottage'.

chat > *verb* (**chatted**, **chatting**) 1 talk in an informal way. 2 (**chat up**) informal engage (someone) in flirtatious conversation. > *noun* an informal conversation.

SYNONYMS – *verb* 1 chatter, converse, gossip, talk. *noun* conversation, gossip, talk.

COMBINATIONS – **chatline** a telephone service which allows conversation among a number of separate callers. **chat room** an Internet site dedicated to conversation, usually on a particular topic. **chat show** Brit. a television or radio programme in which celebrities are invited to talk informally.

ORIGIN – shortening of CHATTER.

chateau /**shatt**ō/ > *noun* (pl. **chateaux** pronunc. same or /**shatt**ōz/) a large French country house or castle.

ORIGIN – French.

chatelaine /**shatt**əlayn/ > *noun* dated a woman in charge of a large house.

ORIGIN – French, from *châtelain* 'governor of a castle'.

chattel /**chatt**'l/ > *noun* a personal possession.

ORIGIN – Old French *chatel*, from Latin *caput* 'head'.

chatter > *verb* 1 talk at length about trivial matters. 2 (of a person's teeth) click repeatedly together from cold or fear. > *noun* 1 incessant trivial talk. 2 a series of short quick high-pitched sounds.

IDIOMS – **the chattering classes** derogatory educated people considered as a social group given to liberal opinions.

DERIVATIVES – **chatterer** *noun*.

chatterbox > *noun* informal a person who chatters.

chatty > *adjective* (**chattier**, **chattiest**) 1 fond of chatting. 2 (of a conversation, letter, etc.) informal and lively.

SYNONYMS – communicative, expansive, garrulous, talkative.

chauffeur > *noun* a person employed to drive someone around in a car. > *verb* drive (a passenger) as a chauffeur.

ORIGIN – French, 'stoker' (by association with steam engines), from *chauffer* 'to heat'.

chauvinism /shōviniz'm/ > *noun* **1** exaggerated or aggressive patriotism. **2** excessive or prejudiced support for one's own cause, group, or sex.

SYNONYMS – **1** jingoism, nationalism, patriotism, xenophobia. **2** bigotry, prejudice, sexism.

ORIGIN – named after Nicolas *Chauvin*, a Napoleonic veteran noted for his extreme patriotism.

chauvinist > *noun* a person displaying excessive or prejudiced support for their own country, cause, group, or sex. > *adjective* relating to such excessive or prejudiced support.

DERIVATIVES – **chauvinistic** *adjective*.

chayote /chayōti/ > *noun* **1** a succulent green pear-shaped tropical fruit resembling a cucumber in flavour. **2** the tropical American vine which yields this fruit, also producing an edible yam-like root.

ORIGIN – Nahuatl.

cheap > *adjective* **1** low in price. **2** charging low prices. **3** inexpensive because of poor quality. **4** of little worth because achieved in a discreditable way. **5** N. Amer. informal miserly. > *adverb* at or for a low price.

DERIVATIVES – **cheapish** *adjective* **cheaply** *adverb* **cheapness** *noun*.

SYNONYMS – *adjective* **1,2** affordable, economical, inexpensive, reasonable. **3** gimcrack, inferior, second-rate, tawdry. **4** base, discreditable, low, mean.

ANTONYMS – *adjective* **1,2** expensive.

wordpower facts

Cheap

If your name is **Chapman**, are you **cheap**? In a sense you are, because the adjective **cheap** and archaic noun **chapman**, meaning 'a pedlar', both derive from the Old English word *cēap* 'bargaining, trade, market, goods, value', which goes back to Latin *caupo* 'small trader, innkeeper'. Use of **cheap** as an adjective dates from the 16th century: before that it was frequently found in phrases such as **good** or **great cheap**, meaning 'a good deal, a bargain'. Old place names such as *Cheapside* and *Eastcheap*, and also the element *Chipping*, as in Chipping Norton and Chipping Campden, derive from the Old English meaning, 'market'.

cheapen > *verb* **1** lower the price of. **2** degrade the worth of.

SYNONYMS – **2** debase, degrade, demean, discredit.

cheapjack > *adjective* chiefly N. Amer. of inferior quality.

cheapskate > *noun* informal a miserly person.

ORIGIN – from *skate* 'a disreputable or contemptible person'.

cheat > *verb* **1** act dishonestly or unfairly in order to gain an advantage. **2** deprive of something by deceitful or unfair means. **3** avoid (something undesirable) by luck or skill: *she cheated death in a spectacular crash.* > *noun* **1** a person who cheats. **2** an act of cheating.

SYNONYMS – *verb* **2** deceive, defraud, dupe, swindle. *noun* **1** fraud, racketeer, swindler, trickster.

ORIGIN – shortening of ESCHEAT.

Chechen /chechen/ > *noun* (pl. same or **Chechens**) a person from Chechnya, an autonomous republic in SW Russia.

check¹ > *verb* **1** examine the accuracy, quality, or condition of. **2** stop or slow the progress of. **3** Chess move a piece or pawn to a square where it directly attacks (the opposing king). > *noun* **1** an examination to check accuracy, quality, or condition. **2** an act of checking progress. **3** Chess an act of checking the opposing king. **4** a means of control or restraint. **5** N. Amer. the bill in a restaurant. **6** (also **check mark**) N. Amer. a tick (✓) > *exclamation* informal, chiefly N. Amer. expressing agreement.

IDIOMS – **check in 1** register at a hotel or airport. **2** have (one's baggage) weighed and put into the hold of an aircraft. **check out 1** settle one's hotel bill before leaving. **2** establish the truth or inform oneself about. **check up on** investigate. **in check 1** under control. **2** Chess (of a king) directly attacked by an opponent's piece or pawn.

DERIVATIVES – **checkable** *adjective*.

SYNONYMS – *verb* **1** examine, inspect, monitor, test, verify. **2** arrest, halt, impede, restrain.

ORIGIN – first used in chess: from Old French *eschequier* 'play chess, put in check', ultimately from Persian *šāh* 'king'; related to EXCHEQUER.

check² > *noun* a pattern of small squares. > *adjective* (also **checked**) having such a pattern.

ORIGIN – probably from CHEQUER.

check³ > *noun* US spelling of CHEQUE.

checker¹ > *noun* **1** a person or thing that checks. **2** US a cashier in a supermarket.

checker² > *noun & verb* US spelling of CHEQUER.

checking account (Canadian **chequing account**) > *noun* N. Amer. a current account at a bank.

checklist > *noun* a list of items required or things to be done or considered.

checkmate > *noun* **1** Chess a position of check from which a king cannot escape. **2** a final defeat or deadlock. > *verb* **1** Chess put into checkmate. **2** defeat or frustrate totally.

ORIGIN – from a Persian phrase meaning 'the king is dead'.

checkout > *noun* a point at which goods are paid for in a supermarket or similar store.

checkpoint > *noun* a barrier where security checks are carried out on travellers.

check-up > *noun* a thorough medical or dental examination to detect any problems.

Cheddar > *noun* a kind of firm smooth cheese originally made in Cheddar in SW England.

cheek > *noun* **1** either side of the face below the eye. **2** either of the buttocks. **3** boldly disrespectful talk or behaviour. > *verb* speak impertinently to.

IDIOMS – **cheek by jowl** close together. **turn the other cheek** refrain from retaliating after an attack or insult. [ORIGIN – with biblical allusion to the Gospel of Matthew, chapter 5.]

DERIVATIVES – **cheeked** *adjective*.

SYNONYMS – *noun* **3** audacity, boldness, impertinence, insolence, temerity.

COMBINATIONS – **cheekbone** the bone below the eye.

cheeky > *adjective* (**cheekier**, **cheekiest**) boldly disrespectful in an endearing or amusing way.

DERIVATIVES – **cheekily** *adverb* **cheekiness** *noun*.

SYNONYMS – bold, disrespectful, forward, impertinent, impudent, irreverent.

ANTONYMS – respectful.

cheep > *noun* **1** a shrill squeaky cry made by a young bird. **2** informal the slightest sound: *there hasn't been a cheep from anybody.* > *verb* make a cheep.

cheer > *verb* **1** shout for joy or in praise or encouragement. **2** praise or encourage with shouts. **3** (**cheer up**) make or become less miserable. **4** give comfort or support to. > *noun* **1** a shout of joy, encouragement, or praise. **2** (also **good cheer**) cheerfulness; optimism. **3** food and drink provided for a festive occasion.

SYNONYMS – *verb* **1** exclaim, hurrah, shout. **2** acclaim, applaud, hail, salute. **3** (**cheer up**) brighten, enliven, perk up. **4** comfort, console, hearten, gladden, uplift. *noun* **1** bravo, hurrah, whoop. **2** cheerfulness, gladness, light-heartedness, jollity, joy, optimism.

ORIGIN – Old French *chiere* 'face' (its original sense in English), from Greek *kara* 'head', also 'expression, mood', later 'a good mood'.

cheerful > *adjective* **1** noticeably happy and optimistic. **2** bright and pleasant: *a cheerful room*.

DERIVATIVES – **cheerfully** *adverb* **cheerfulness** *noun*.

SYNONYMS – **1** bright, happy, joyful, optimistic, sunny. **2** bright, pleasant, uplifting, welcoming.

ANTONYMS – **1** miserable, sad. **2** cheerless, gloomy.

cheerio > *exclamation* Brit. informal goodbye.

cheerleader > *noun* (in North America) a member of a group of girls that perform organised chanting and dancing in support of a team at sporting events.

cheerless > *adjective* gloomy; depressing.

DERIVATIVES – **cheerlessly** *adverb* **cheerlessness** *noun.*

cheers > *exclamation* informal **1** expressing good wishes before drinking. **2** chiefly Brit. said to express gratitude or on parting.

cheery > *adjective* (**cheerier, cheeriest**) happy and optimistic.

DERIVATIVES – **cheerily** *adverb* **cheeriness** *noun.*

cheese¹ > *noun* a food made from the pressed curds of milk, having a texture either firm and elastic or soft and semi-liquid.

WORDFINDER – casein (*protein in cheese*), rennet (*curdled milk used in making cheese*).

IDIOMS – **hard cheese** Brit. informal, dated used to express sympathy over a petty matter.

COMBINATIONS – **cheeseboard 1** a board on which cheese is served and cut. **2** a selection of cheeses served as a course of a meal. **cheeseburger** a beefburger with a slice of cheese on it, served in a bread roll. **cheesecloth** thin, loosely woven cotton cloth. **cheese-paring** excessive care with money; parsimony. **cheese plant** a Swiss cheese plant.

ORIGIN – Latin *caseus.*

cheese² > *verb* (usu. **be cheesed off**) Brit. informal exasperate, frustrate, or bore.

cheesecake > *noun* **1** a rich, sweet tart made with cream and soft cheese on a biscuit base. **2** informal images portraying women according to a stereotyped ideal of sexual attractiveness.

cheesy > *adjective* (**cheesier, cheesiest**) **1** like cheese in taste, smell, or consistency. **2** informal cheap or blatantly artificial.

DERIVATIVES – **cheesiness** *noun.*

cheetah /chee**t**ə/ > *noun* a large swift-running spotted cat found in Africa and parts of Asia.

ORIGIN – Hindi.

chef > *noun* a professional cook, especially the chief cook in a restaurant or hotel.

ORIGIN – French, 'head'.

chef-d'œuvre /shay **d**övrə/ > *noun* (pl. **chefs-d'œuvre** pronunc. same) a masterpiece.

ORIGIN – French, 'chief work'.

chela /**kee**lə/ > *noun* (pl. **chelae** /**kee**lee/) a pincer-like claw, especially of a crab or other crustacean.

ORIGIN – Latin *chele* or Greek *khēlē* 'claw'.

Chelsea boot > *noun* an elastic-sided boot with a pointed toe.

ORIGIN – named after *Chelsea*, a district of London.

Chelsea bun > *noun* Brit. a flat, spiral-shaped currant bun sprinkled with sugar.

Chelsea pensioner > *noun* an inmate of the Chelsea Royal Hospital for old or disabled soldiers.

chemical > *adjective* relating to chemistry or chemicals. > *noun* a distinct compound or substance, especially one which has been artificially prepared or purified.

DERIVATIVES – **chemically** *adverb.*

COMBINATIONS – **chemical engineering** the branch of engineering concerned with the design and operation of industrial chemical plants.

ORIGIN – from Latin *alchimia* 'alchemy'.

chemin de fer /shəmaN də **fair**/ > *noun* a card game which is a variety of baccarat.

ORIGIN – French, 'railway'.

chemise /shə**meez**/ > *noun* **1** a dress hanging straight from the shoulders, popular in the 1920s. **2** a woman's loose-fitting undergarment or nightdress.

ORIGIN – Old French, from Latin *camisia* 'shirt or nightgown'.

chemist > *noun* **1** Brit. a person who is authorised to dispense medicinal drugs. **2** Brit. a shop where medicinal drugs are dispensed and toiletries and other medical goods are sold. **3** a person engaged in chemical research or experiments.

ORIGIN – from Latin *alchimista* 'alchemist'.

chemistry > *noun* (pl. **chemistries**) **1** the branch of science concerned with the properties and interactions of the substances of which matter is composed. **2** the chemical properties of a substance or body. **3** attraction or interaction between two people.

WORDFINDER – *branches of chemistry:* organic (*of carbon compounds, chiefly biological*), inorganic (*of other substances*), physical (*application of physics to chemistry*); biochemistry (*of life*), geochemistry (*of the earth*), photochemistry (*chemical effects of light*), radiochemistry (*of radioactive materials*); alchemy (*medieval chemistry*).

chemotherapy /keemə**therr**əpi/ > *noun* the treatment of disease, especially cancer, by the use of chemical substances.

chenille /shə**neel**/ > *noun* a tufted velvety cord or yarn, or fabric made from this, used in clothing and soft furnishings.

ORIGIN – French, 'hairy caterpillar', from Latin *canicula* 'little dog'.

cheongsam /chiong**sam**/ > *noun* a straight, close-fitting silk dress with a high neck, worn by Chinese and Indonesian women.

ORIGIN – Chinese.

cheque (US **check**) > *noun* a written order to a bank to pay a stated sum from an account to a specified person.

COMBINATIONS – **cheque card** Brit. a card issued by a bank to guarantee the honouring of cheques up to a stated amount.

ORIGIN – variant of **CHECK¹**, in the sense 'device for checking the amount of an item'.

chequer (US **checker**) > *noun* **1** (**chequers**) a pattern of alternately coloured squares. **2** (**checkers**) (treated as sing.) N. Amer. the game of draughts. > *verb* **1** (**be chequered**) be divided into or marked with chequers. **2** (**chequered**) marked by periods of fluctuating fortune.

COMBINATIONS – **chequerboard** (US **checkerboard**) a board for playing checkers and similar games, having a regular chequered pattern in black and white. **chequered flag** Motor Racing a flag with a black-and-white chequered pattern, displayed to drivers at the end of a race.

ORIGIN – from **EXCHEQUER**, originally in the sense 'chessboard'.

cherish > *verb* **1** protect and care for lovingly. **2** maintain (a hope or ambition) over a long period.

SYNONYMS – **1** care for, dote on, love, nurture, protect. **2** foster, harbour, nurse, nurture.

ORIGIN – Old French *cherir*, from *cher* 'dear'.

Cherokee /**cherr**əkee/ > *noun* (pl. same or **Cherokees**) a member of an American Indian people formerly inhabiting much of the southern US.

ORIGIN – the Cherokees' name for themselves.

cheroot /shə**root**/ > *noun* a cigar with both ends open.

ORIGIN – French *cheroute*, from a Tamil word meaning 'roll of tobacco'.

cherry > *noun* (pl. **cherries**) **1** a small, soft round stone fruit that is bright or dark red. **2** the tree that bears such fruit. **3** a bright, deep red colour. **4** (**one's cherry**) informal one's virginity.

IDIOMS – **a bite at the cherry** an attempt or opportunity. **a bowl of cherries** a very pleasant situation: *life is no bowl of cherries.* **the cherry on the cake** a desirable thing providing the finishing touch to something already good.

COMBINATIONS – **cherry brandy** a sweet liqueur made with brandy in which cherries have been steeped. **cherry-pick** selectively choose (the best things or people) from those available. **cherry tomato** a miniature tomato with a strong flavour.

ORIGIN – Old French *cherise*, from Latin *ceresia*, from Greek *kerasos.*

chert /chert/ > *noun* a brittle, fine-grained rock which consists largely of silica and of which flint is a dark, compact form.

cherub > *noun* **1** (pl. **cherubim** or **cherubs**) a winged angelic being represented as a chubby child with wings. **2** (pl. **cherubs**) a beautiful or innocent-looking child.

DERIVATIVES – **cherubic** *adjective* **cherubically** *adverb*.

ORIGIN – Hebrew.

chervil /**cher**vil/ > *noun* a plant with delicate fern-like leaves which are used as a herb in cookery.

ORIGIN – Greek *khairephullon*.

Ches. > *abbreviation* Cheshire.

Cheshire /**che**shər/ > *noun* a kind of firm crumbly cheese, originally made in Cheshire.

COMBINATIONS – **Cheshire cat** a cat depicted with a broad fixed grin, as in Lewis Carroll's *Alice's Adventures in Wonderland* (1865). [ORIGIN – uncertain, but it is said that *Cheshire* cheeses used to be marked with the face of a smiling cat.]

chess > *noun* a board game for two players, the object of which is to put the opponent's king under a direct attack, leading to checkmate.

WORDFINDER – *chess pieces* (*in conventional order of value*): pawn, knight, bishop, rook, queen, king.

COMBINATIONS – **chessboard** a square board divided into sixty-four alternating dark and light squares, used for playing chess or draughts.

ORIGIN – Old French *esches*, from Latin *scaccus*, from Persian *šāh* 'king'.

chest > *noun* **1** the front surface of a person's body between the neck and the stomach. **2** the circumference of a person's upper body. **3** a large, strong box for storage or transport. **4** Brit. the treasury or financial resources of an institution. > *verb* Soccer propel (the ball) by means of one's chest.

WORDFINDER – pectoral (*relating to the chest*).

IDIOMS – **get off** one's **chest** informal say (something) that one has wanted to say for a long time. **keep** (or **play**) one's **cards close to** one's **chest** informal be extremely secretive about one's intentions.

DERIVATIVES – **chested** *adjective*.

COMBINATIONS – **chest of drawers** a piece of furniture consisting of an upright frame into which drawers are fitted.

ORIGIN – Greek *kistē* 'box'.

chesterfield > *noun* **1** a sofa having padded arms and back of the same height and curved outwards at the top. **2** a man's plain straight overcoat, typically with a velvet collar.

ORIGIN – named after a 19th-century Earl of *Chesterfield*.

chestnut* > *noun* **1** a hard, glossy brown nut which develops within a bristly case and can be roasted and eaten. **2** (also **sweet chestnut** or **Spanish chestnut**) the large tree that produces these nuts. **3** a deep reddish-brown colour. **4** a horse of a reddish-brown or yellowish-brown colour. **5** (usu. **old chestnut**) a joke, story, or subject that has become uninteresting through constant repetition.

*SPELLING – remember the *t* in the middle: ches*t*nut.

ORIGIN – from Greek *kastanea* + NUT.

chesty > *adjective* informal **1** Brit. having a lot of catarrh in the lungs. **2** (of a woman) having large or prominent breasts. **3** N. Amer. conceited and arrogant.

DERIVATIVES – **chestiness** *noun*.

chetrum /**chet**rōōm/ > *noun* (pl. same or **chetrums**) a monetary unit of Bhutan, equal to one hundredth of a ngultrum.

ORIGIN – from Dzongkha, the official language of Bhutan.

cheval glass /shəval/ (also **cheval mirror**) > *noun* a tall mirror fitted at its middle to an upright frame so that it can be tilted.

ORIGIN – French *cheval* 'horse, frame'.

chevalier /shevvəleer/ > *noun* **1** historical a knight. **2** a member of certain orders of knighthood or of modern French orders such as the Legion of Honour.

ORIGIN – Old French, from Latin *caballus* 'horse'.

chevet /shəvay/ > *noun* (in a church) an apse with a series of chapels set in bays behind the high altar.

ORIGIN – French, 'pillow'.

Cheviot /**chev**viət, **chee**viət/ > *noun* a large breed of sheep with short, thick wool.

ORIGIN – from the *Cheviot* Hills in northern England and Scotland.

chèvre /shevrə/ > *noun* French cheese made with goat's milk.

ORIGIN – French, 'goat'.

chevron > *noun* **1** a V-shaped line or stripe, especially one on the sleeve of a uniform indicating rank or length of service. **2** Heraldry a broad inverted V-shape.

ORIGIN – Old French, from Latin *caper* 'goat'.

chevrotain /shevrətayn/ > *noun* a small deer-like mammal with small tusks, found in tropical rainforests.

ORIGIN – French, 'little goat'.

chew > *verb* **1** bite and work (food) in the mouth to make it easier to swallow. **2** (**chew over**) discuss or consider at length. **3** (**chew out**) N. Amer. informal reprimand severely. > *noun* **1** an instance of chewing. **2** a thing, especially a sweet, for chewing.

IDIOMS – **chew the fat** (or **rag**) informal chat in a leisurely way.

DERIVATIVES – **chewable** *adjective* **chewer** *noun*.

SYNONYMS – *verb* **1** champ, chomp, gnaw, masticate, munch. **2** (**chew over**) mull over, ponder, ruminate on.

COMBINATIONS – **chewing gum** flavoured gum for chewing.

chewy > *adjective* suitable for chewing, or requiring much chewing.

DERIVATIVES – **chewiness** *noun*.

Cheyenne /shīan/ > *noun* (pl. same or **Cheyennes**) a member of an American Indian people formerly living between the Missouri and Arkansas Rivers.

ORIGIN – from a Dakota word meaning 'speak incoherently'.

chez /shay/ > *preposition* chiefly humorous at the home of.

ORIGIN – French.

chi¹ /kī/ > *noun* the twenty-second letter of the Greek alphabet (X, χ), transliterated as 'kh' or 'ch'.

ORIGIN – Greek.

chi² /kee/ (also **qi** or **ki**) > *noun* the circulating life force whose existence and properties are the basis of much Chinese philosophy and medicine.

ORIGIN – Chinese, literally 'air, breath'.

Chianti /ki**an**ti/ > *noun* (pl. **Chiantis**) a dry red Italian wine produced in Tuscany.

ORIGIN – named after the *Chianti* Mountains, Italy.

chiaroscuro /ki-aarəskoorō/ > *noun* the treatment of light and shade in drawing and painting.

ORIGIN – Italian, from *chiaro* 'clear, bright' + *oscuro* 'dark, obscure'.

chiasma /kīazmə/ (also **optic chiasma**) > *noun* (pl. **chiasmata** /kīazmətə/) Anatomy the X-shaped structure below the brain where the optic nerves from the left and right eyes cross over each other.

ORIGIN – Greek, 'crosspiece, cross-shaped mark'.

chiasmus /kīazməss/ > *noun* the inversion in a second phrase or clause of the order of words in the first.

ORIGIN – Greek *khiasmos* 'crosswise arrangement'.

chic /sheek/ > *adjective* (**chicer**, **chicest**) elegantly and stylishly fashionable. > *noun* stylishness and elegance.

DERIVATIVES – **chicly** *adverb*.

ORIGIN – French.

chicane /shikayn/ > *noun* **1** a sharp double bend created to form an obstacle on a motor-racing track. **2** archaic chicanery. > *verb* archaic employ chicanery.

ORIGIN – from French *chicaner* 'quibble'.

chicanery > *noun* the use of trickery to achieve one's purpose.

SYNONYMS – duplicity, fraudulence, sophistry, subterfuge, trickery.

Chicano /chikaanō/ > *noun* (pl. **Chicanos**; fem. **Chicana**, pl. **Chicanas**) chiefly US a North American of Mexican origin or descent.

ORIGIN – from Spanish *mejicano* 'Mexican'.

chichi /**shee**shee/ > *adjective* over-elaborate and affected; fussy.
ORIGIN – French.

chick > *noun* 1 a young bird, especially one newly hatched. 2 *informal* a young woman.
ORIGIN – abbreviation of CHICKEN.

chickadee > *noun* N. Amer. a titmouse.
ORIGIN – imitative of its call.

chicken > *noun* 1 a domestic fowl kept for its eggs or meat, especially a young one. 2 *informal* a coward. 3 *informal* a game in which the first person to lose their nerve and withdraw from a dangerous situation is the loser. > *adjective informal* cowardly. > *verb* (**chicken out**) *informal* be too scared to do something.
IDIOMS – **chicken-and-egg** (of a situation) in which each of two things appears to be necessary to the other. [ORIGIN – from the question 'What came first, the chicken or the egg?'] **like a headless chicken** *informal* frenziedly.
COMBINATIONS – **chicken feed** *informal* a paltry sum of money. **chicken wire** light wire netting with a hexagonal mesh.

chickenpox > *noun* an infectious disease causing a mild fever and a rash of itchy inflamed pimples; varicella.
ORIGIN – probably so named because of its mildness, as compared to smallpox.

chickpea > *noun* a round yellowish seed which is a pulse of major importance as food.
ORIGIN – from Latin *cicer* 'chickpea' + PEASE.

chickweed > *noun* a small white-flowered plant, often growing as a garden weed.

chicle /**chikk**'l/ > *noun* the milky latex of the sapodilla tree, used to make chewing gum.
ORIGIN – Nahuatl.

chicory /**chikk**əri/ > *noun* (pl. **chicories**) 1 a blue-flowered plant with edible leaves and a root which is used as an additive to or substitute for coffee. 2 North American term for ENDIVE.
ORIGIN – Greek *kikhorion*.

chide /chīd/ > *verb* (past **chided** or **chid** /chid/; past participle **chided** or *archaic* **chidden** /**chidd**'n/) scold or rebuke.

chief > *noun* 1 a leader or ruler of a people. 2 the head of an organisation. > *adjective* 1 having the highest rank or authority. 2 most important: *the chief reason*.
DERIVATIVES – **chiefdom** *noun*.
SYNONYMS – *noun* 1 chieftain, headman, leader, ruler. 2 boss, director, head, principal. *adjective* 1 head, leading, premier, principal, supreme. 2 cardinal, pre-eminent, primary, principal.
ANTONYMS – subordinate.
COMBINATIONS – **chief constable** Brit. the head of the police force of a county or

other region. **chief of staff** the senior staff officer of a service or command.

---

wordpower facts

Chief

Chief is one of many words that come from the Latin word *caput*, meaning 'head'. Others include **biceps** ('two-headed', because the muscle has two points of attachment), **capital**, **captain**, **chapter**, and **decapitate**. **Capitulate** is also from the same root: originally used in the sense 'parley, draw up terms', it entered English from the Latin verb *capitulare* 'draw up under headings'.

---

chiefly > *adverb* mainly; mostly.

chieftain > *noun* the leader of a people or clan.
DERIVATIVES – **chieftaincy** (pl. **chieftaincies**) *noun* **chieftainship** *noun*.

chiffchaff > *noun* a common warbler with drab plumage and a repetitive call.

chiffon > *noun* a light, transparent fabric of silk or nylon.
ORIGIN – French, from *chiffe* 'rag'.

chiffonier /shiffə**neer**/ > *noun* 1 Brit. a low cupboard used as a sideboard or having a bookshelf on top. 2 N. Amer. a tall chest of drawers.
ORIGIN – French, 'ragpicker, chest of drawers for oddments'.

chigger /**chigg**ər/ (also **jigger**) > *noun* 1 a tropical flea, the female of which lays eggs beneath the host's skin, causing painful sores. 2 N. Amer. a harvest mite.
ORIGIN – variant of CHIGOE.

chignon /**sheen**yoN/ > *noun* a knot or coil of hair arranged on the back of a woman's head.
ORIGIN – French, 'nape of the neck'.

chigoe /**chigg**ō/ > *noun* another term for CHIGGER (in sense 1).
ORIGIN – French *chique*, from a West African language.

chihuahua /chi**waa**wə/ > *noun* a very small breed of dog with smooth hair and large eyes.
ORIGIN – named after *Chihuahua* in northern Mexico.

chilblain > *noun* a painful, itching swelling on a hand or foot caused by poor circulation in the skin when exposed to cold.
ORIGIN – from CHILL + *blain* 'inflamed swelling'.

child > *noun* (pl. **children**) 1 a young human being below the age of full physical development. 2 a son or daughter of any age. 3 *derogatory* an immature or irresponsible

person. 4 (**children**) *archaic* the descendants of a family or people.
IDIOMS – **child's play** a task which is easily accomplished. **with child** *archaic* pregnant.
DERIVATIVES – **childless** *adjective*.
SYNONYMS – 1 infant, junior, juvenile, minor, youngster.
COMBINATIONS – **child benefit** (in the UK) regular payment by the state to the parents of a child up to a certain age.

childbed > *noun archaic* childbirth.

childbirth > *noun* the action of giving birth to a child.

childhood > *noun* the state or period of being a child.

childish > *adjective* 1 of, like, or appropriate to a child. 2 silly and immature.
DERIVATIVES – **childishly** *adverb* **childishness** *noun*.
SYNONYMS – 2 immature, infantile, juvenile, puerile.

childlike > *adjective* (of an adult) having the good qualities, such as innocence, associated with a child.
SYNONYMS – ingenuous, innocent, naive.

childminder > *noun* Brit. a person who looks after children in their own house for payment.

childproof > *adjective* designed to prevent children from injuring themselves or doing damage.

children plural of CHILD.

Chilean /**chill**iən/ > *noun* a person from Chile. > *adjective* relating to Chile.

chili > *noun* US spelling of CHILLI.

chiliast /**kill**iast/ > *noun* another term for MILLENARIAN.
DERIVATIVES – **chiliasm** *noun* **chiliastic** *adjective*.
ORIGIN – Latin *chiliastes*, from Greek *khiliastēs*, from *khilias* 'a thousand years'.

chill > *noun* 1 an unpleasant feeling of coldness. 2 a feverish cold. > *verb* 1 make cold. 2 horrify or frighten. 3 (usu. **chill out**) *informal* calm down and relax. > *adjective* chilly.
DERIVATIVES – **chilling** *adjective* **chillingly** *adverb* **chillness** *noun*.
SYNONYMS – *noun* 1 bitterness, chilliness, coldness, rawness. *verb* 1 cool, freeze, refrigerate. 2 alarm, frighten, horrify, scare.
ANTONYMS – *noun* 1 warmth. *verb* 1 warm. 2 comfort.
COMBINATIONS – **chill factor** a perceived lowering of the air temperature caused by the wind.

chiller > *noun* 1 a cold cabinet or refrigerator for keeping stored food a few degrees above freezing point. 2 a story or film that inspires terror and excitement.

chilli (also **chilli pepper**, **chile**, US **chili**) > *noun* (pl. **chillies**, **chiles**, or US **chilies**) 1 a small hot-tasting pod of a variety of capsicum, used in sauces, relishes, and spice powders. **2** chilli powder or chilli con carne.

COMBINATIONS – **chilli powder** a hot-tasting mixture of ground dried red chillies and other spices.

ORIGIN – Nahuatl.

chilli con carne /chilli kon **kaar**ni/ > *noun* a stew of minced beef and beans flavoured with chilli powder.

ORIGIN – Spanish *chile con carne* 'chilli pepper with meat'.

chillum /**chill**əm/ > *noun* (pl. **chillums**) **1** a hookah. **2** a pipe used for smoking cannabis.

ORIGIN – Hindi.

chilly > *adjective* (**chillier**, **chilliest**) **1** unpleasantly cold. **2** unfriendly.

DERIVATIVES – **chilliness** *noun*.

SYNONYMS – **1** bleak, cold, freezing, raw.

chime > *noun* **1** a melodious ringing sound. **2** a bell or a metal bar or tube used in a set to produce chimes when struck. > *verb* **1** (of a bell or clock) make a melodious ringing sound. **2** (**chime with**) be in agreement with. **3** (**chime in**) say something abruptly or as an interruption.

SYNONYMS – *noun* **1** peal, ring, toll. *verb* **1** peal, ring, sound, toll. **2** (**chime with**) accord with, agree with, be consistent with, correspond to.

ORIGIN – probably from CYMBAL (interpreted as *chime bell*).

chimera /kī**meer**ə/ (also **chimaera**) > *noun* **1** Greek Mythology a fire-breathing female monster with a lion's head, a goat's body, and a serpent's tail. **2** something hoped for but illusory or impossible to achieve. **3** Biology an organism containing a mixture of genetically different tissues.

ORIGIN – Greek *khimaira* 'she-goat or chimera'.

chimerical /kī**merr**ik'l/ > *adjective* **1** like a mythical chimera. **2** illusory or impossible to achieve.

DERIVATIVES – **chimerically** *adverb*.

chimney > *noun* (pl. **chimneys**) **1** a vertical pipe which conducts smoke and gases up from a fire or furnace. **2** a glass tube protecting the flame of a lamp. **3** a very steep narrow cleft by which a rock face may be climbed.

COMBINATIONS – **chimney breast** a part of an interior wall that projects to surround a chimney. **chimney piece** Brit. a mantelpiece. **chimney pot** an earthenware or metal pipe at the top of a chimney. **chimney stack** the part of a chimney that projects above a roof.

ORIGIN – Old French *cheminee*, from Greek *kaminos* 'oven'.

chimp > *noun* informal a chimpanzee.

chimpanzee > *noun* a dark-haired great ape

native to the forests of west and central Africa.

ORIGIN – Kikongo (a language of the Congo and surrounding areas).

chin > *noun* the protruding part of the face below the mouth. > *verb* informal hit or punch (someone) on the chin.

IDIOMS – **keep one's chin up** informal remain cheerful in difficult circumstances. **take it on the chin** informal accept misfortune stoically.

DERIVATIVES – **chinned** *adjective*.

china > *noun* **1** a fine white or translucent ceramic material. **2** household objects made from china. **3** Brit. informal a friend. [ORIGIN – from rhyming slang *china plate* 'mate'.]

COMBINATIONS – **china blue** a pale greyish blue. **china clay** kaolin.

ORIGIN – from a Persian word meaning 'relating to China'.

chinagraph pencil > *noun* Brit. a waxy pencil used to write on china, glass, or other hard surfaces.

Chinaman > *noun* chiefly archaic or derogatory a Chinese man.

China tea > *noun* tea made from a small-leaved type of tea plant grown in China, often smoked or with flower petals added.

Chinatown > *noun* a district of a non-Chinese town in which the population is predominantly of Chinese origin.

chinchilla /chin**chill**ə/ > *noun* **1** a small South American rodent with soft grey fur and a long bushy tail. **2** a breed of cat or rabbit with silver-grey or grey fur.

ORIGIN – Aymara or Quechua (South American Indian languages).

chin-chin > *exclamation* Brit. informal, dated a toast made before drinking.

ORIGIN – representing a pronunciation of a Chinese phrase.

Chindit /**chin**dit/ > *noun* a member of the Allied forces behind the Japanese lines in Burma (Myanmar) in 1943–5.

ORIGIN – from the Burmese name for a mythical creature.

chine¹ /chīn/ > *noun* **1** the backbone of an animal, or a joint of meat containing part of it. **2** a mountain ridge.

ORIGIN – Old French *eschine*, from Latin *spina* 'spine'.

chine² /chīn/ > *noun* (in the Isle of Wight or Dorset) a deep, narrow ravine.

chine³ /chīn/ > *noun* the angle where the planks or plates at the bottom of a boat or ship meet the side.

Chinese > *noun* (pl. same) **1** the language of China. **2** a person from China. > *adjective* relating to China.

WORDFINDER – sinology (*study of China's culture*).

COMBINATIONS – **Chinese box** each of a nest of boxes. **Chinese burn** informal a burning sensation inflicted on a person by

placing both hands on their arm and then twisting it. **Chinese chequers** (US **Chinese checkers**) a board game in which players attempt to move marbles or counters from one corner to the opposite one on a star-shaped board. **Chinese lantern 1** a collapsible paper lantern. **2** a plant with white flowers and globular orange fruits enclosed in a papery orange-red calyx. **Chinese leaves** (also **Chinese cabbage**) an oriental variety of cabbage which does not form a firm heart. **Chinese puzzle** an intricate puzzle consisting of many interlocking pieces. **Chinese wall** an insurmountable barrier, especially to the passage of information. **Chinese whispers** a game in which a message is distorted by being passed around in a whisper.

wordpower facts
Chinese

Chinese is the world's most commonly spoken first language, having an estimated 1.2 billion native speakers worldwide. The official and literary form of Chinese is **Mandarin**, and there also several dialects, of which **Cantonese** is the most widely spoken. Chinese script employs a system of signs and characters, some having a pictorial value and some representing sounds and abstract concepts. A spelling system called **Pinyin** is used for representing Chinese in the Roman alphabet. Chinese words and phrases that have become familiar in English include **feng shui**, **kowtow**, **sampan**, **tea**, **yin** and **yang**, and the names of many Chinese dishes such as **chop suey**, **chow mein**, and **dim sum**.

Chink (also **Chinky**) > *noun* informal, offensive a Chinese person.

chink¹ > *noun* **1** a narrow opening or crack. **2** a beam of light admitted by a chink.

SYNONYMS – **1** aperture, crack, gap, hole, opening.

chink² > *verb* make a light, high-pitched ringing sound, as of glasses or coins striking together. > *noun* a high-pitched ringing sound.

SYNONYMS – clink, jingle, ring, tinkle.

chinless > *adjective* **1** lacking a well-defined chin. **2** informal lacking strength of character.

chino /**chee**nō/ > *noun* **1** a cotton twill fabric, typically khaki-coloured. **2** (**chinos**) casual trousers made from such fabric.

ORIGIN – Latin American Spanish, 'toasted' (referring to the typical colour).

chinoiserie /shin**waaz**əri/ > *noun* **1** the use of Chinese motifs and techniques in

Western art, furniture, and architecture. **2** objects or decorations in this style.

ORIGIN – French, from *chinois* 'Chinese'.

Chinook /chinōōk/ > *noun* (pl. same or **Chinooks**) a member of an American Indian people originally living in Oregon.

COMBINATIONS – **Chinook Jargon** an extinct pidgin composed of elements from Chinook, English, French, and other languages, formerly used in the Pacific North-West of North America.

ORIGIN – Salish.

chinook /chinōōk/ > *noun* **1** a warm, dry wind which blows down the east side of the Rocky Mountains at the end of winter. **2** a large North Pacific salmon which is an important commercial food fish.

chintz > *noun* printed multicoloured cotton fabric with a glazed finish, used for curtains and upholstery.

ORIGIN – Hindi, 'spattering, stain'.

chintzy > *adjective* (**chintzier**, **chintziest**) **1** decorated with or resembling chintz. **2** tasteless in a genteel way. **3** N. Amer. informal miserly.

chinwag > *noun* Brit. informal a chat.

chip > *noun* **1** a small, thin piece removed in the course of cutting or breaking a hard material. **2** a blemish left by the removal of such a piece. **3** chiefly Brit. a long rectangular piece of deep-fried potato. **4** (also **potato chip**) chiefly N. Amer. a potato crisp. **5** short for MICROCHIP. **6** a counter used in certain gambling games to represent money. **7** (in football or golf) a short lofted kick or shot. > *verb* (**chipped**, **chipping**) **1** cut or break (a chip) from a hard material. **2** break at the edge or on the surface. **3** (**chip away**) gradually and relentlessly make something smaller or weaker. **4** (in football or golf) strike (the ball) to produce a short lofted shot or pass. **5** (**chipped**) Brit. (of potatoes) cut into chips.

IDIOMS – **chip in 1** contribute one's share of a joint activity. **2** Brit. informal make an interjection. **a chip off the old block** informal someone who resembles their parent in character. **a chip on one's shoulder** informal a deeply ingrained grievance. **have had one's chips** Brit. informal be dead or out of contention. **when the chips are down** informal when a very serious situation arises.

SYNONYMS – *noun* **1** bit, fragment, piece, shard, sliver.

chipboard > *noun* material made from compressed wood chips and resin.

chipmunk > *noun* a burrowing ground squirrel with light and dark stripes running down the body.

ORIGIN – Ojibwa.

chipolata > *noun* Brit. a small, thin sausage.

ORIGIN – Italian *cipollata* 'dish of onions'.

Chippendale /chippəndayl/ > *adjective* (of furniture) designed by or resembling the work of the English furniture-maker Thomas Chippendale (1718–79), neo-classical with elements of French rococo and chinoiserie.

chipper > *adjective* informal cheerful and lively.

ORIGIN – perhaps from northern English dialect *kipper* 'lively'.

chipping > *noun* Brit. a small fragment of stone, wood, or similar material.

chippy informal > *noun* (also **chippie**) (pl. **chippies**) **1** Brit. a fish-and-chip shop. **2** Brit. a carpenter. **3** N. Amer. a prostitute. > *adjective* touchy and irritable.

chiral /kīrəl/ > *adjective* Chemistry (of a molecule) not able to be superimposed on its mirror image.

DERIVATIVES – **chirality** noun.

ORIGIN – from Greek *kheir* 'hand'.

chirography /kīrogrəfi/ > *noun* handwriting, especially as distinct from typography.

DERIVATIVES – **chirographic** adjective.

chiromancy /kīrəmansi/ > *noun* the prediction of a person's future from the lines on the palms of their hands; palmistry.

ORIGIN – from Greek *kheir* 'hand'.

chiropody /kiroppədi/ > *noun* the treatment of the feet and their ailments.

DERIVATIVES – **chiropodist** noun.

ORIGIN – from Greek *kheir* 'hand' + *pous* 'foot'.

chiropractic /kīrəpraktik/ > *noun* a system of complementary medicine based on the manipulation of misaligned joints, especially those of the spinal column.

DERIVATIVES – **chiropractor** noun.

ORIGIN – from Greek *kheir* 'hand' + *praktikos* 'practical'.

chirp > *verb* **1** (of a small bird or a grasshopper) utter a short, sharp, high-pitched sound. **2** say in a lively and cheerful way. > *noun* a chirping sound.

SYNONYMS – *verb* **1** cheep, chirrup, trill, tweet.

chirpy > *adjective* (**chirpier**, **chirpiest**) informal cheerful and lively.

DERIVATIVES – **chirpily** adverb **chirpiness** noun.

chirr /chur/ (also **churr**) > *verb* (of a bird or insect) make a prolonged low trilling sound. > *noun* a low trilling sound.

chirrup > *verb* (**chirruped**, **chirruping**) (of a small bird) make repeated short, high-pitched sounds. > *noun* a chirruping sound.

DERIVATIVES – **chirrupy** adjective.

chisel > *noun* a long-bladed hand tool with a bevelled cutting edge, used to cut or shape wood, stone, or metal. > *verb* (**chiselled**, **chiselling**; US **chiseled**, **chiseling**) **1** cut or shape with a chisel. **2** (**chiselled**) (of a

man's facial features) strongly defined. **3** informal, chiefly N. Amer. cheat or swindle.

DERIVATIVES – **chiseller** noun.

SYNONYMS – *verb* **1** carve, cut, hew, incise, shape.

ORIGIN – Old French, from Latin *caedere* 'to cut'.

chit[1] > *noun* derogatory an impudent or arrogant young woman.

ORIGIN – first used to mean 'whelp, cub, or kitten'; perhaps related to dialect *chit* 'sprout'.

chit[2] > *noun* a short official note recording a sum owed.

ORIGIN – Hindi, 'note, pass'.

chital /cheet'l/ > *noun* a deer with curved antlers and a white-spotted fawn coat, native to India and Sri Lanka.

ORIGIN – Hindi, from a Sanskrit word meaning 'spotted'.

chit-chat informal > *noun* inconsequential conversation. > *verb* talk about trivial matters.

chitin /kītin/ > *noun* Biochemistry a fibrous substance which forms the exoskeleton of arthropods and the cell walls of fungi.

DERIVATIVES – **chitinous** adjective.

ORIGIN – from Greek *khitōn* 'tunic'.

chiton /kīton/ > *noun* **1** a long woollen tunic worn in ancient Greece. **2** a marine mollusc that has an oval flattened body with a shell of overlapping plates.

ORIGIN – Greek *khitōn* 'tunic'.

chitter > *verb* **1** make a twittering or chattering sound. **2** Scottish & dialect shiver with cold.

chitterlings /chittərlingz/ > *plural noun* the smaller intestines of a pig, cooked for food.

chivalrous > *adjective* **1** (of a man) courteous and gallant, especially towards women. **2** relating to the historical notion of chivalry.

DERIVATIVES – **chivalrously** adverb.

chivalry > *noun* **1** the medieval knightly system with its religious, moral, and social code. **2** the combination of qualities expected of an ideal knight, especially courage, honour, courtesy, justice, and a readiness to help the weak. **3** courteous behaviour, especially that of a man towards women.

DERIVATIVES – **chivalric** adjective.

SYNONYMS – **3** courtesy, gallantry.

ORIGIN – Old French *chevalerie*, from Latin *caballarius* 'horseman'.

chives > *plural noun* a small plant with long tubular leaves, used as a herb in cookery.

ORIGIN – Old French, from Latin *cepa* 'onion'.

chivvy (also **chivy**) > *verb* (**chivvies**, **chivvied**) tell (someone) repeatedly to do something.

SYNONYMS – badger, hound, nag, pester.

ORIGIN – first used in the sense 'a hunting cry', probably from the ballad *Chevy Chase*, which celebrated a skirmish on the Scottish border.

chlamydia /kləmiddiə/ > *noun* (pl. same or **chlamydiae** /kləmiddi-ee/) a very small parasitic bacterium.
ORIGIN – from Greek *khlamus* 'cloak'.

chloral /klorəl/ > *noun* Chemistry a viscous liquid used as a sedative in the form of a crystalline derivative (**chloral hydrate**).
ORIGIN – French, blend of *chlore* 'chlorine' and *alcool* 'alcohol'.

chlorate > *noun* Chemistry a salt containing the anion ClO$_3^-$.

chloride /klorīd/ > *noun* a compound of chlorine with another element or group.

chlorinate /klorinayt/ > *verb* impregnate or treat with chlorine.
DERIVATIVES – **chlorination** *noun*.

chlorine /kloreen/ > *noun* a poisonous, irritant, pale green gaseous chemical element of the halogen group.
ORIGIN – from Greek *khlōros* 'green'.

chlorofluorocarbon /klorōfloorō-kaarb'n/ > *noun* see **CFC**.

chloroform > *noun* a sweet-smelling liquid used as a solvent and formerly as a general anaesthetic. > *verb* make unconscious with this substance.
ORIGIN – from **CHLORINE** + **FORMIC ACID**.

chlorophyll /klorrəfil/ > *noun* a green pigment which is responsible for the absorption of light by plants to provide energy for photosynthesis.
ORIGIN – from Greek *khlōros* 'green' + *phullon* 'leaf'.

chloroplast /klorrəplast/ > *noun* a structure in green plant cells which contains chlorophyll and in which photosynthesis takes place.
ORIGIN – from Greek *khlōros* 'green' + *plastos* 'formed'.

chlorosis /klərōsiss/ > *noun* 1 loss of the normal green coloration of the leaves of plants. 2 anaemia caused by iron deficiency, causing a pale, faintly greenish complexion.
DERIVATIVES – **chlorotic** *adjective*.

chocaholic > *noun* variant spelling of **CHOCOHOLIC**.

choc ice > *noun* Brit. a small block of ice cream with a thin coating of chocolate.

chock > *noun* 1 a wedge or block placed against a wheel to prevent it from moving. 2 a ring with a gap at the top, through which a rope or line is run. > *verb* support or make fast with a chock.
ORIGIN – Old French *çoche* 'block, log'.

chock-a-block > *adjective* informal crammed full.
ORIGIN – first in nautical use, with reference to blocks in tackle running close together.

chock-full > *adjective* informal filled to overflowing.

chocoholic (also **chocaholic**) > *noun* informal a person who is very fond of chocolate.

chocolate > *noun* 1 a food made from roasted and ground cacao seeds, typically sweetened and eaten as confectionery. 2 a sweet covered with chocolate. 3 a drink made by mixing milk or water with chocolate. 4 a deep brown colour.
DERIVATIVES – **chocolatey** (also **chocolaty**) *adjective*.
COMBINATIONS – **chocolate-box** (of a view or picture) pretty in a trite, conventional way.
ORIGIN – French *chocolat* or Spanish *chocolate*, from Nahuatl.

chocolatier /chokkəlattiər/ > *noun* (pl. pronunc. same) a maker or seller of chocolate.
ORIGIN – French.

Choctaw /choktaw/ > *noun* (pl. same or **Choctaws**) a member of an American Indian people now living mainly in Mississippi.
ORIGIN – the Choctaws' name for themselves.

choice > *noun* 1 an act of choosing. 2 something chosen. 3 the right or ability to choose. 4 a range from which to choose. > *adjective* 1 of very good quality. 2 (of language) rude and abusive.
SYNONYMS – *noun* 1,2 option, preference, say, selection, vote. *adjective* 1 high-quality, prime, select, superior.
ANTONYMS – *adjective* 1 inferior.

choir > *noun* 1 an organised group of singers, especially one that takes part in church services. 2 the part of a large church between the altar and the nave, used by the choir and clergy.
WORDFINDER – chorister (*member of a choir*).
COMBINATIONS – **choirboy** (or **choirgirl**) a boy (or girl) who sings in a church or cathedral choir.
ORIGIN – Old French *quer*, from Latin *chorus* (see **CHORUS**).

choisya /choyziə/ > *noun* an evergreen shrub with sweet-scented white flowers.
ORIGIN – named after the Swiss botanist Jacques D. *Choisy* (1799–1859).

choke[1] > *verb* 1 prevent (someone) from breathing by constricting or obstructing the throat or depriving of air. 2 have trouble breathing in such a way. 3 fill (a space) so as to hinder movement. 4 make speechless with strong emotion. > *noun* 1 a valve in the carburettor of a petrol engine used to reduce the amount of air in the fuel mixture. 2 an inductance coil used to smooth the variations of an alternating current or to alter its phase.
SYNONYMS – *verb* 1 smother, strangle, suffocate, throttle. 2 cough, gag, gasp, retch, suffocate.

choke[2] > *noun* the inedible mass of silky fibres at the centre of a globe artichoke.
ORIGIN – probably a confusion of the ending of *artichoke* with **CHOKE**[1].

choke-damp > *noun* choking or suffocating gas found in a mine.

choker > *noun* 1 a close-fitting necklace or ornamental neckband. 2 a clerical or other high collar.

chokey > *noun* Brit. informal, dated prison.
ORIGIN – Hindi, 'customs or toll house, police station'.

choko /chōkō/ > *noun* (pl. **chokos**) Austral./NZ the fruit of the chayote, eaten as a vegetable.
ORIGIN – Spanish *chocho*.

choky > *adjective* (**chokier, chokiest**) 1 having or causing difficulty in breathing. 2 breathless with emotion.

cholecalciferol /kollikalsiffərol/ > *noun* vitamin D$_3$, a compound produced naturally in the skin by the action of sunlight.

choler /kollər/ > *noun* 1 (in medieval science and medicine) one of the four bodily humours, identified with bile and believed to be associated with a peevish or irascible temperament. 2 archaic or literary anger or irascibility.
ORIGIN – Latin *cholera* from Greek *kholē* 'bile'.

cholera /kollərə/ > *noun* an infectious disease of the small intestine, typically contracted from infected water and causing severe vomiting and diarrhoea.
ORIGIN – Latin, 'diarrhoea, bile'.

choleric /kollərik/ > *adjective* bad-tempered or irritable.

cholesterol /kəlestərol/ > *noun* a compound of the steroid type which occurs normally in most body tissues and is believed to cause clogging of the arteries if present in high concentrations in the blood (e.g. as a result of a diet high in animal fat).
ORIGIN – from Greek *kholē* 'bile' + *stereos* 'stiff'.

chomp > *verb* munch or chew noisily or vigorously.

chook /chook/ > *noun* informal, chiefly Austral./NZ a chicken or fowl.

choose > *verb* (past **chose**; past participle **chosen**) 1 pick out as being the best of two or more alternatives. 2 decide on a course of action.
DERIVATIVES – **chooser** *noun*.
SYNONYMS – 1 elect, opt for, pick, select, vote for.

choosy > *adjective* (**choosier, choosiest**)

informal excessively fastidious in making a choice.

DERIVATIVES – **choosiness** noun.

SYNONYMS – discriminating, fussy, particular, picky.

chop¹ > verb (**chopped**, **chopping**) **1** cut with repeated sharp, heavy blows of an axe or knife. **2** strike with a short, heavy blow. **3** ruthlessly abolish or reduce in size. > noun **1** a downward cutting blow or movement. **2** (**the chop**) Brit. informal dismissal, cancellation, or killing. **3** a thick slice of meat, especially pork or lamb, adjacent to and usually including a rib.

IDIOMS – **chop logic** argue in a tiresomely pedantic way. [ORIGIN – from a dialect use of chop meaning 'bandy words'.]

SYNONYMS – verb **1** cleave, cut, hack, hew, split.

ORIGIN – variant of **CHAP¹**.

chop² > verb (**chopped**, **chopping**) (in phrase **chop and change**) Brit. informal repeatedly change one's opinions or behaviour.

ORIGIN – first in the sense 'barter, exchange'; related to **CHAPMAN**.

chop-chop > adverb & exclamation quickly.

ORIGIN – pidgin English, from Chinese dialect; related to **CHOPSTICK**.

chopper > noun **1** Brit. a short axe with a large blade. **2** (**choppers**) informal teeth. **3** informal a helicopter. **4** informal a type of motorcycle with high handlebars. **5** vulgar slang a man's penis.

choppy > adjective (**choppier**, **choppiest**) (of the sea) having many small waves.

DERIVATIVES – **choppily** adverb **choppiness** noun.

chops > plural noun informal **1** a person's or animal's mouth, jaws, or cheeks. **2** the technical skill of a jazz or rock musician.

chopstick > noun each of a pair of small, thin, tapered sticks held in one hand and used as eating utensils by the Chinese and Japanese.

ORIGIN – pidgin English, from a Chinese dialect term meaning 'nimble ones'.

chop suey /chop **soo**i/ > noun a Chinese-style dish of meat with bean sprouts, bamboo shoots, and onions.

ORIGIN – Chinese, 'mixed bits'.

choral > adjective of, for, or sung by a choir or chorus.

DERIVATIVES – **chorally** adverb.

chorale > noun **1** a simple, stately hymn tune, or a composition consisting of a harmonised version of one. **2** chiefly US a choir or choral society.

chord¹ > noun a group of three or more notes sounded together in harmony.

DERIVATIVES – **chordal** adjective.

ORIGIN – from **ACCORD**; the spelling was influenced by **CHORD²**.

chord² > noun **1** a straight line joining the ends of an arc. **2** the width of an aircraft's wing from leading to trailing edge. **3** Engineering each of the two principal members of a truss. **4** Anatomy variant spelling of **CORD**.

IDIOMS – **strike** (or **touch**) **a chord** affect or stir someone's emotions.

ORIGIN – a later spelling (influenced by Latin chorda 'rope') of **CORD**.

chordate /**kor**dayt/ > noun Zoology an animal of a large group (the phylum Chordata) which includes all the vertebrates together with the sea squirts and lancelets (which possess a notochord).

ORIGIN – from Latin chorda 'rope', on the pattern of words such as vertebrate.

chore > noun a routine or tedious task, especially a household one.

ORIGIN – variant of obsolete char or chare; compare with **CHARWOMAN**.

chorea /ko**ree**ə/ > noun a neurological disorder characterised by jerky involuntary movements.

ORIGIN – Greek khoreia 'dancing in unison'.

choreograph /**korr**iəgraaf/ > verb compose the sequence of steps and moves for (a dance performance).

DERIVATIVES – **choreographer** noun.

choreography /korri**og**rəfi/ > noun **1** the sequence of steps and movements in dance. **2** the practice of designing such sequences.

DERIVATIVES – **choreographic** adjective **choreographically** adverb.

ORIGIN – from Greek khoreia 'dancing in unison', from khoros 'chorus'.

chorine /**kor**een/ > noun a chorus girl.

chorion /**kor**iən/ > noun the outermost membrane surrounding an embryo.

ORIGIN – Greek khorion.

chorister > noun **1** a member of a choir, especially a choirboy or choirgirl. **2** US a person who leads the singing of a church choir or congregation.

chorizo /chə**ree**zō/ > noun (pl. **chorizos**) a spicy Spanish pork sausage.

ORIGIN – Spanish.

chortle > verb laugh in a breathy, gleeful way. > noun a breathy, gleeful laugh.

SYNONYMS – cackle, chuckle, crow, giggle, snigger.

ORIGIN – coined by Lewis Carroll in Through the Looking Glass; probably a blend of **CHUCKLE** and **SNORT**.

chorus > noun (pl. **choruses**) **1** a part of a song which is repeated after each verse. **2** something said at the same time by many people. **3** a group of singers or dancers having a supporting role in a show, musical, etc. **4** a large group of singers, especially one performing with an orchestra. **5** a piece of choral music in an opera, oratorio, etc. **6** (in ancient Greek tragedy) a group of performers who comment on the main action. > verb (**chorused**, **chorusing**) (of a group of people) say the same thing at the same time.

SYNONYMS – noun **1** hook, refrain, response. **3** choir, ensemble.

COMBINATIONS – **chorus girl** a young woman who sings or dances in the chorus of a musical.

ORIGIN – Latin, from Greek khoros.

chose past of **CHOOSE**.

chosen past participle of **CHOOSE**.

choucroute /**shoo**kroot/ > noun another term for **SAUERKRAUT**.

ORIGIN – French, from German dialect Surkrut.

chough /chuf/ > noun a black bird of the crow family with a red or yellow downcurved bill.

ORIGIN – probably from the bird's call.

choux pastry /shoo/ > noun very light pastry made with egg, used for eclairs and profiteroles.

ORIGIN – French, from chou 'cabbage, rosette'.

chow /chow/ > noun **1** informal, chiefly N. Amer. food. **2** (also **chow chow**) a Chinese breed of dog with a tail curled over its back, a bluish-black tongue, and a thick coat. > verb (**chow down**) N. Amer. informal eat.

ORIGIN – shortened from **CHOW CHOW**.

chow chow > noun **1** another term for **CHOW** (in sense 2). **2** a Chinese preserve of ginger and orange peel in syrup. **3** a mixed vegetable pickle.

ORIGIN – pidgin English.

chowder > noun a rich soup containing fish, clams, or corn with potatoes and onions.

ORIGIN – perhaps from French chaudière 'stew pot', related to caudron 'cauldron'.

chow mein /chow **mayn**/ > noun a Chinese-style dish of fried noodles with shredded meat or seafood and vegetables.

ORIGIN – Chinese, 'stir-fried noodles'.

chrism /**krizz**'m/ > noun a consecrated oil used for anointing in the Catholic, Orthodox, and Anglican Churches.

ORIGIN – Greek khrisma 'anointing'.

Christ > noun the title given to Jesus. > exclamation used to express irritation, dismay, or surprise.

DERIVATIVES – **Christlike** adjective **Christly** adjective.

ORIGIN – Greek Khristos 'anointed one', translating a Hebrew word meaning 'Messiah'.

Christadelphian /kristə**del**fiən/ > noun a member of a Christian sect claiming to return to the beliefs and practices of the earliest disciples and expecting a second coming of Christ. > adjective relating to this sect.

ORIGIN – from Greek Khristos 'Christ' + adelphos 'brother'.

christen > *verb* **1** name (a baby) at baptism as a sign of admission to a Christian Church; baptise. **2** informal use for the first time.
DERIVATIVES – **christening** *noun*.
ORIGIN – Old English, 'make Christian'.

Christendom > *noun* dated the worldwide body of Christians.

Christian > *adjective* relating to or professing Christianity or its teachings. > *noun* a person who has received Christian baptism or is a believer in Christianity.
WORDFINDER – *dates in the Christian calendar:* Advent, Ascension, Christmas, Easter, Epiphany, Lent, Pentecost, Whit Sunday.
DERIVATIVES – **Christianisation** (also **Christianization**) *noun* **Christianise** (also **Christianize**) *verb*.
COMBINATIONS – **Christian era** the era beginning with the traditional date of Christ's birth.
ORIGIN – Latin *Christianus*, from *Christus* 'Christ'.

Christianity > *noun* the religion based on the person and teachings of Jesus Christ.

Christian name > *noun* a forename, especially one given at baptism.
USAGE – in recognition of the fact that English-speaking societies have many religions and cultures, not just Christian ones, the term **Christian name** has been superseded in many contexts by terms such as **given name**, **first name**, or **forename**.

Christian Science > *noun* the beliefs and practices of the Church of Christ Scientist, a Christian sect whose members believe that sin and illness are illusions which can be overcome by prayer and faith.
DERIVATIVES – **Christian Scientist** *noun*.

Christingle /**kris**tingg'l/ > *noun* a lighted candle symbolising Christ, held by children especially at Advent services.
ORIGIN – probably from German dialect *Christkindl* 'Christ child, Christmas gift'.

Christmas > *noun* (pl. **Christmases**) **1** (also **Christmas Day**) the annual Christian festival celebrating Christ's birth, held on 25 December. **2** the period immediately before and after this.
SYNONYMS – Noel; archaic Yule, Yuletide.
COMBINATIONS – **Christmas box** Brit. a present given at Christmas to tradespeople and employees. **Christmas cake** Brit. a rich fruit cake covered with marzipan and icing, eaten at Christmas. **Christmas pudding** Brit. a rich pudding eaten at Christmas, made with flour, suet, and dried fruit. **Christmas rose** a small white-flowered winter-blooming hellebore. **Christmas tree** an evergreen tree decorated with lights and ornaments at Christmas.
ORIGIN – Old English, 'Mass of Christ'.

chromate /**krō**mayt/ > *noun* Chemistry a salt in which the anion contains both chromium and oxygen.

chromatic > *adjective* **1** Music relating to or using notes not belonging to the diatonic scale of the key of a passage. **2** Music (of a scale) ascending or descending by semitones. **3** relating to or produced by colour.
ORIGIN – Greek *khrōmatikos*, from *khrōma* 'colour, chromatic scale'.

chromatid /**krō**mətid/ > *noun* Biology each of the two thread-like strands into which a chromosome divides during cell division.

chromatin /**krō**mətin/ > *noun* Biology the material of which non-bacterial chromosomes are composed, consisting of DNA or RNA and proteins.

chromatography > *noun* Chemistry a technique for the separation of a mixture by passing it through a medium in which the components move at different rates.
DERIVATIVES – **chromatogram** *noun* **chromatograph** *noun* **chromatographic** *adjective*.

chrome > *noun* **1** chromium plate as a finish. **2** (before another noun) denoting compounds or alloys of chromium: *chrome steel*.
DERIVATIVES – **chromed** *adjective*.
COMBINATIONS – **chrome yellow** a bright yellow pigment made from lead chromate.
ORIGIN – Greek *khrōma* 'colour' (some chromium compounds having brilliant colours).

chromite > *noun* the main ore of chromium, a brownish-black oxide of chromium and iron.

chromium > *noun* a hard white metallic chemical element used in stainless steel and other alloys.

chromosome > *noun* Biology a thread-like structure found in the nuclei of most living cells, carrying genetic information in the form of genes.
DERIVATIVES – **chromosomal** *adjective*.
ORIGIN – from Greek *khrōma* 'colour' + *sōma* 'body'.

chromosphere > *noun* Astronomy a reddish gaseous layer immediately above the photosphere of the sun or another star.
DERIVATIVES – **chromospheric** *adjective*.

chronic > *adjective* **1** (of an illness or problem) persisting for a long time. **2** having a persistent illness or bad habit. **3** Brit. informal very bad.
DERIVATIVES – **chronically** *adverb* **chronicity** *noun*.
COMBINATIONS – **chronic fatigue syndrome** a medical condition of unknown cause, with fever, aching, and prolonged tiredness and depression.
ORIGIN – Greek *khronikos* 'of time', from *khronos* 'time'.

chronicle > *noun* a written account of historical events in the order of their occurrence. > *verb* record (a series of events) in a detailed way.
DERIVATIVES – **chronicler** *noun*.
SYNONYMS – *noun* annal, diary, record, register.
ORIGIN – Greek *khronika* 'annals', from *khronikos* (see CHRONIC).

chronograph > *noun* an instrument for recording time with great accuracy.

chronology /krə**noll**əji/ > *noun* (pl. **chronologies**) **1** the study of records to establish the dates of past events. **2** the arrangement of events or dates in the order of their occurrence.
DERIVATIVES – **chronological** *adjective* **chronologically** *adverb* **chronologist** *noun*.
ORIGIN – from Greek *khronos* 'time'.

chronometer /krə**nomm**itər/ > *noun* an instrument for measuring time accurately in spite of motion or varying conditions.

chronometry > *noun* the science of accurate time measurement.
DERIVATIVES – **chronometric** *adjective*.

chrysalid > *noun* another term for CHRYSALIS.

chrysalis /**kriss**əliss/ > *noun* (pl. **chrysalises**) **1** an insect pupa, especially of a butterfly or moth. **2** the hard outer case enclosing this.
ORIGIN – Greek *khrusallis*, from *khrusos* 'gold' (because of the metallic sheen of some pupae).

chrysanthemum /kri**zan**thiməm/ > *noun* (pl. **chrysanthemums**) a garden plant with brightly coloured flowers.
ORIGIN – from Greek *khrusos* 'gold' + *anthemon* 'flower'.

chthonic /**kthonn**ik/ (also **chthonian** /**kthō**niən/) > *adjective* relating to or inhabiting the underworld.
ORIGIN – from Greek *khthōn* 'earth'.

chub > *noun* a thick-bodied river fish with a grey-green back and white underparts.

chubby > *adjective* (**chubbier**, **chubbiest**) plump and rounded.
SYNONYMS – dumpy, fat, plump, podgy, roly-poly.
ORIGIN – from CHUB.

chuck[1] informal > *verb* **1** throw (something) carelessly or casually. **2** (often **chuck in**) give up (a job or activity) suddenly. **3** (**chuck up**) vomit.
IDIOMS – **chuck it down** rain heavily.
DERIVATIVES – **chucker** *noun*.
ORIGIN – from CHUCK[2].

chuck[2] > *verb* touch playfully under the chin. > *noun* a playful touch under the chin.
ORIGIN – probably from Old French *chuquer* 'to knock, bump'.

chuck[3] > *noun* **1** a device for holding a

workpiece in a lathe or a tool in a drill. **2** a cut of beef extending from the neck to the ribs.

ORIGIN – a variant of **CHOCK**.

chuck⁴ > *noun* N. English used as a familiar form of address.

ORIGIN – alteration of **CHICK**.

chuckle > *verb* laugh quietly or inwardly. > *noun* a quiet laugh.

SYNONYMS – chortle, giggle, snigger, titter.

ORIGIN – from *chuck*, meaning 'to cluck'.

chucklehead > *noun* informal a stupid person.

ORIGIN – from *chuckle* 'big and clumsy'.

chuddies /**chud**eez/ (also **chuddis** /**chud**iss/) > *plural noun* Indian underpants.

ORIGIN – perhaps an alteration of **CHADOR**.

chuff > *verb* (of a steam engine) move with a regular puffing sound.

chuffed > *adjective* Brit. informal delighted.

ORIGIN – from dialect *chuff* 'plump or pleased'.

chug > *verb* (**chugged**, **chugging**) emit a series of muffled explosive sounds, as of an engine running slowly. > *noun* a sound of this type.

chukka > *noun* each of a number of periods (typically six) into which play in a game of polo is divided.

ORIGIN – Hindi, from a Sanskrit word meaning 'circle or wheel'.

chum informal > *noun* a close friend. > *verb* (**chummed**, **chumming**) (**chum up**) form a friendship with someone.

DERIVATIVES – **chummy** adjective.

ORIGIN – 17th-century Oxford University slang for a room-mate; probably short for *chamber-fellow*; compare with **CRONY**.

chump > *noun* **1** informal a foolish person. **2** Brit. the thick end of something, especially a loin of lamb or mutton.

IDIOMS – **off one's chump** Brit. informal, dated mad.

ORIGIN – first used in the sense 'thick lump of wood'; probably a blend of **CHUNK¹** and **LUMP¹** or **STUMP**.

chunder > *verb & noun* informal, chiefly Austral./NZ vomit.

ORIGIN – probably from rhyming slang *Chunder Loo* 'spew', from the name of a cartoon character.

chunk¹ > *noun* **1** a thick, solid piece of something. **2** a large amount.

SYNONYMS – **1** bit, block, hunk, lump, mass.

chunk² > *verb* make a muffled, metallic sound.

chunky > *adjective* (**chunkier**, **chunkiest**) **1** (of a person) short and sturdy. **2** containing chunks.

chunter > *verb* Brit. informal **1** chatter or grumble monotonously. **2** move slowly and noisily.

church > *noun* **1** a building used for public Christian worship. **2** (**Church**) a particular Christian organisation with its own distinctive doctrines. **3** institutionalised religion as a political or social force.

WORDFINDER – *parts of a church:* aisle, apse, chancel, clerestory, crypt, narthex, nave, spire, steeple, transept, vestry.

COMBINATIONS – **churchman** (or **churchwoman**) a member of the Christian clergy or of a Church. **Church of England** the English branch of the Western Christian Church, which rejects the Pope's authority and has the monarch as its head. **Church of Scotland** the national (Presbyterian) Christian Church in Scotland. **churchyard** an enclosed area surrounding a church, especially as used for burials.

ORIGIN – from Greek *kuriakon dōma* 'Lord's house', from *kurios* 'master or lord'.

churchwarden > *noun* either of two elected lay representatives in an Anglican parish.

churchy > *adjective* **1** excessively pious. **2** resembling or appropriate to a church.

churinga /chu**ring**gə/ > *noun* (pl. same or **churingas**) (among Australian Aboriginals) a sacred amulet or other object.

ORIGIN – from Aranda (an Aboriginal language), literally 'object from the dreaming'.

churl > *noun* **1** a rude and mean-spirited person. **2** archaic a peasant.

churlish > *adjective* rude, mean-spirited, and surly.

churn > *noun* **1** a machine for making butter by agitating milk or cream. **2** Brit. a large metal milk can. > *verb* **1** agitate (milk or cream) in a churn to produce butter. **2** move (liquid) about vigorously. **3** (**churn out**) produce (something) mechanically in large quantities. **4** (**churned up**) upset or nervous.

chute¹ (also **shoot**) > *noun* **1** a sloping channel for conveying things to a lower level. **2** a water slide into a swimming pool.

ORIGIN – French, 'fall' (of water or rocks).

chute² > *noun* informal a parachute.

chutney > *noun* (pl. **chutneys**) a spicy condiment made of fruits or vegetables with vinegar, spices, and sugar.

ORIGIN – Hindi.

chutzpah /**kho͝ot**spə/ > *noun* informal shameless audacity.

ORIGIN – Yiddish.

chyle /kīl/ > *noun* Physiology a milky fluid which drains from the small intestine into the lymphatic system during digestion.

ORIGIN – Greek *khūlos* 'juice'.

chyme /kīm/ > *noun* Physiology the fluid which passes from the stomach to the small intestine, consisting of gastric juices and partly digested food.

ORIGIN – Greek *khūmos* 'juice'.

Ci > *abbreviation* curie.

CIA > *abbreviation* Central Intelligence Agency.

ciabatta /chə**baat**ə/ > *noun* a flattish Italian bread made with olive oil.

ORIGIN – Italian, 'slipper' (from its shape).

ciao /chow/ > *exclamation* informal used as a greeting at meeting or parting.

ORIGIN – Italian, from dialect *schiavo* 'I am your slave'.

cicada /si**kaad**ə/ > *noun* a large bug with long transparent wings, which makes a shrill droning noise.

ORIGIN – Latin.

cicatrise /**sikk**ətrīz/ (also **cicatrize**) > *verb* heal by scar formation.

cicatrix /**sikk**ətriks/ (also **cicatrice** /**sikk**ətriss/) > *noun* (pl. **cicatrices** /sikkə**trī**seez/) **1** a scar. **2** Botany a mark on a stem left after a leaf or other part has become detached.

DERIVATIVES – **cicatricial** /sikkə**trish**'l/ *adjective*.

ORIGIN – Latin.

cicely /**siss**əli/ (also **sweet cicely**) > *noun* (pl. **cicelies**) an aromatic white-flowered plant with fern-like leaves.

ORIGIN – Greek *seselis*.

cicerone /chichə**rō**ni, sissə**rō**ni/ > *noun* (pl. **ciceroni** pronunc. same) a guide who gives information to sightseers.

ORIGIN – Italian, from the name of the Roman writer *Cicero* (106–43 BC), apparently referring to the guides' knowledge.

cichlid /**sik**lid/ > *noun* Zoology a perch-like freshwater fish.

ORIGIN – from Greek *kikhlē*.

CID > *abbreviation* (in the UK) Criminal Investigation Department.

-cide > *combining form* **1** denoting a person or substance that kills: *insecticide*. **2** denoting an act of killing: *suicide*.

ORIGIN – from Latin *-cida*, *-cidium*, from *caedere* 'to kill'.

cider > *noun* **1** an alcoholic drink made from fermented apple juice. **2** N. Amer. a cloudy unfermented drink made by crushing apples.

ORIGIN – Old French *sidre*, ultimately from a Hebrew word meaning 'strong drink'.

ci-devant /seedə**von**/ > *adjective* former.
ORIGIN – French, 'heretofore'.

cigar > *noun* a cylinder of tobacco rolled in tobacco leaves for smoking.
WORDFINDER – *types of cigar:* cheroot, cigarillo, corona, Havana, Manila.
ORIGIN – probably from a Mayan word meaning 'smoking'.

cigarette (US also **cigaret**) > *noun* a cylinder of finely cut tobacco rolled in paper for smoking.
COMBINATIONS – **cigarette card** Brit. a collectable card with a picture on it, formerly included in packets of cigarettes. **cigarette paper** a thin paper for rolling around tobacco to make a cigarette.
ORIGIN – French, 'little cigar'.

cigarillo /siggə**rill**ō/ > *noun* (pl. **cigarillos**) a small cigar.
ORIGIN – Spanish, 'little cigar'.

ciliary /**sill**iəri/ > *adjective* 1 Biology relating to or involving cilia. 2 Anatomy relating to the eyelashes or eyelids.

cilium /**sill**iəm/ > *noun* (pl. **cilia** /**sill**iə/) 1 Biology a microscopic vibrating hair-like structure, occurring on the surface of certain cells. 2 Anatomy an eyelash.
ORIGIN – Latin.

cill > *noun* chiefly Building variant spelling of SILL.

C.-in-C. > *abbreviation* Commander-in-Chief.

cinch > *noun* informal 1 an extremely easy task. 2 a certainty. > *verb* secure (a garment) with a belt.
ORIGIN – from Spanish *cincha* 'girth'.

cinchona /sing**kō**nə/ > *noun* 1 a South American tree cultivated for its bark, which contains quinine and related compounds. 2 a medicinal extract of this bark.
ORIGIN – named after the Countess of *Chinchón* (died 1641), who brought the bark to Spain.

cinder > *noun* a piece of burnt coal or wood that has stopped giving off flames but still has combustible matter in it.

Cinderella > *noun* a person or thing whose beauty or merits are unrecognised or disregarded.
ORIGIN – from the name of a fairytale character who is exploited as a servant by her family but is helped by a fairy godmother to marry Prince Charming.

cine > *adjective* cinematographic.

cineaste /**sinn**iast/ > *noun* a person who is very interested in the cinema.
ORIGIN – French.

cinema > *noun* chiefly Brit. 1 a theatre where films are shown. 2 the production of films as an art or industry.

wordpower facts
Cinema
A **cinema** shows moving pictures, and movement is the root idea of the word. The Greek verb *kinein* 'to move' (the source of **kinetic** and other **kine-**words related to movement) is the base, via its related noun *kinēma* 'movement'. This was used by the French brothers Auguste and Louis Jean Lumière to form the word *cinématographe* for their invention of an apparatus that showed moving pictures, which they patented in 1895. *Cinématographe* was anglicised to **cinematograph**, which in turn was abbreviated to **cinema** (first recorded in English in 1909).

cinematic > *adjective* relating to or characteristic of the cinema.
DERIVATIVES – **cinematically** adverb.

cinematograph > *noun* historical, chiefly Brit. an apparatus for showing films.

cinematography > *noun* the art of photography and camerawork in film-making.
DERIVATIVES – **cinematographer** noun **cinematographic** adjective.

cinéma-vérité /sinimə **verr**itay/ > *noun* a style of film-making characterised by realistic films avoiding artistic effect.
ORIGIN – French, 'cinema truth'.

cinephile > *noun* a person who is very interested in the cinema.

cineraria /sinnə**rair**iə/ > *noun* a winter-flowering plant of the daisy family.
ORIGIN – from Latin *cinerarius* 'of ashes' (because of the grey down on the leaves).

cinerary urn /**sinn**ərəri/ > *noun* an urn for holding a person's ashes after cremation.
ORIGIN – from Latin *cinerarius* 'of ashes'.

cingulum /**sing**yooləm/ > *noun* (pl. **cingula** /**sing**yoolə/) Anatomy 1 a curved bundle of nerve fibres in the brain. 2 a ridge of enamel on the crown of a tooth.
DERIVATIVES – **cingulate** adjective.
ORIGIN – Latin, 'belt'.

cinnabar /**sinn**əbaar/ > *noun* 1 a bright red mineral consisting of mercury sulphide. 2 (also **cinnabar moth**) a day-flying moth with black and red wings.
ORIGIN – Greek *kinnabari*.

cinnamon > *noun* 1 an aromatic spice made from the bark of an Asian tree. 2 a yellowish-brown colour resembling cinnamon.
ORIGIN – Greek *kinnamōmon*.

cinquecento /chingkwi**chen**tō/ > *noun* the 16th century as a period of Italian art and literature.
ORIGIN – Italian, 'five hundred'.

cinquefoil /**singk**foyl/ > *noun* 1 a plant with compound leaves of five leaflets and five-petalled yellow flowers. 2 Art an ornamental design of five lobes arranged in a circle.
ORIGIN – Latin *quinquefolium*, from *quinque* 'five' + *folium* 'leaf'.

cipher (also **cypher**) > *noun* 1 a code. 2 a key to a code. 3 dated a zero. 4 a person or thing of no importance. > *verb* encode (a message).
ORIGIN – Old French *cifre*, from an Arabic word meaning 'zero'.

circa /**sur**kə/ > *preposition* (usually preceding a date) approximately.
ORIGIN – Latin.

circadian /sur**kay**diən/ > *adjective* (of biological processes) recurring on a twenty-four-hour cycle.
ORIGIN – from Latin *circa* 'about' + *dies* 'day'.

circle > *noun* 1 a round plane figure whose boundary consists of points at equal distances from the centre. 2 a group of people or things forming a circle. 3 a curved upper tier of seats in a theatre. 4 a group of people with a shared profession or interests. > *verb* 1 move in circles around. 2 form or mark a circle around; ring.
WORDFINDER – *parts of a circle:* arc, chord, circumference, diameter, radius, sector, segment.
IDIOMS – **come** (or **turn**) **full circle** return to a previous position or situation. **go** (or **run**) **round in circles** informal do something for a long time without achieving anything.
SYNONYMS – *noun* 1 disc, hoop, ring, round; technical annulus. 4 milieu, society, sphere, world. *verb* 1 gyrate, revolve, rotate, spiral, whirl. 2 encircle, orbit, ring, surround.
ORIGIN – Latin *circulus* 'small ring', from *circus* 'ring'.

circlet > *noun* an ornamental circular band worn on the head.

circlip > *noun* Brit. a metal ring sprung into a slot to hold something in place.
ORIGIN – blend of CIRCULAR and CLIP[1].

circuit > *noun* 1 a roughly circular line, route, or movement. 2 Brit. a track used for motor racing. 3 a system of conductors and components forming a complete path for an electric current. 4 an established series of sporting events or entertainments. 5 a series of physical exercises performed in one training session. 6 (in the UK) a regular journey by a judge around a district to hear court cases. > *verb* move all the way around.
SYNONYMS – *noun* 1 circle, lap, orbit, revolution.
COMBINATIONS – **circuit-breaker** an

automatic safety device for stopping the flow of current in an electric circuit.
ORIGIN – Latin *circuitus*, from *circumire* 'go round'.

circuitous /surˈkyooitəss/ > *adjective* (of a route) longer than the most direct way.
SYNONYMS – indirect, meandering, roundabout, serpentine, winding; rare anfractuous.
ANTONYMS – direct.

circuitry > *noun* (pl. **circuitries**) electric circuits collectively.

circular > *adjective* 1 having the form of a circle. 2 Logic (of an argument) false because already containing an assumption of what is to be proved. 3 (of a letter or advertisement) for distribution to a large number of people. > *noun* a circular letter or advertisement.
DERIVATIVES – **circularity** noun **circularly** adverb.
SYNONYMS – *adjective* 1 round; technical annular.
COMBINATIONS – **circular saw** a power saw with a rapidly rotating toothed disc.

circularise (also **circularize**) > *verb* distribute a large number of letters, leaflets, etc. to.

circulate > *verb* 1 move continuously through a closed area. 2 pass from place to place or person to person. 3 move around a social function and talk to many people.
DERIVATIVES – **circulator** noun.
SYNONYMS – 1 course, flow round, pass round. 2 distribute, disseminate, pass round, put about, spread. 3 mingle, socialise.

circulating library > *noun* historical a small library which lent out books for a fee.

circulation > *noun* 1 movement to and fro or around something. 2 the continuous motion of blood round the body. 3 the public availability of something. 4 the number of copies sold of a newspaper or magazine.
DERIVATIVES – **circulatory** adjective.

circum- > *prefix* about; around: *circumambulate* | *circumpolar*.
ORIGIN – from Latin *circum* 'round'.

circumambient /surkəmˈambiənt/ > *adjective* chiefly literary surrounding.

circumambulate /surkəmˈambyoolayt/ > *verb* formal walk all the way round.
DERIVATIVES – **circumambulation** noun.

circumcircle > *noun* Geometry a circle touching all the vertices of a triangle or polygon.

circumcise* > *verb* 1 cut off the foreskin of (a young boy or man), especially as a Jewish or Islamic rite. 2 (among some peoples) cut off the clitoris, and sometimes the labia, of (a girl or young woman).
DERIVATIVES – **circumcision** noun.

*SPELLING – **circumcise** cannot be spelled with an -ize ending.
ORIGIN – Latin *circumcidere* 'cut around'.

circumference > *noun* 1 the enclosing boundary of a circle. 2 the distance around something.
DERIVATIVES – **circumferential** adjective **circumferentially** adverb.
ORIGIN – Latin *circumferentia*, from *circum* 'around' + *ferre* 'carry'.

circumflex > *noun* a mark (ˆ) placed over a vowel in some languages to indicate contraction, length, or another quality.
ORIGIN – Latin *circumflexus*, from *circum* 'around' + *flectere* 'to bend'.

circumlocution /surkəmləˈkyoosh'n/ > *noun* the use of many words where fewer would do.
DERIVATIVES – **circumlocutory** adjective.
ORIGIN – Latin, from *circum* 'around' + *loqui* 'speak'.

circumnavigate > *verb* sail all the way around.
DERIVATIVES – **circumnavigation** noun.

circumpolar > *adjective* 1 situated or occurring around one of the earth's poles. 2 Astronomy (of a star) above the horizon at all times in a given latitude.

circumscribe > *verb* 1 restrict; limit. 2 Geometry draw (a figure) round another, touching it at points but not cutting it.
DERIVATIVES – **circumscription** noun.
ORIGIN – Latin *circumscribere*, from *circum* 'around' + *scribere* 'write'.

circumspect > *adjective* unwilling to take risks or speak freely; cautious.
DERIVATIVES – **circumspection** noun **circumspectly** adverb.
SYNONYMS – cautious, discreet, guarded, wary.
ANTONYMS – incautious, unguarded.
ORIGIN – Latin *circumspectus*, from *circumspicere* 'look around'.

circumstance > *noun* 1 a fact or condition connected with an event or action. 2 unforeseen events outside one's control: *a victim of circumstance*. 3 (one's **circumstances**) one's state of financial or material welfare.
IDIOMS – **circumstances alter cases** proverb one's opinion or treatment of someone or something may vary according to the prevailing circumstances. **under** (or **in**) **no circumstances** never.
SYNONYMS – (**circumstances**) 1 affairs, conditions, the facts, the situation, things. 3 finances, means, position, resources, status.
ORIGIN – Latin *circumstantia*, from *circumstare* 'encircle, encompass'.

circumstantial > *adjective* 1 (of evidence or a legal case) pointing indirectly towards someone's guilt. 2 (of a description) containing full details.

circumvent /surkəmˈvent/ > *verb* find a way around (an obstacle).
DERIVATIVES – **circumvention** noun.
ORIGIN – Latin *circumvenire* 'skirt around'.

circus > *noun* (pl. **circuses**) 1 a travelling company of acrobats, trained animals, and clowns. 2 (in ancient Rome) a rounded sporting arena lined with seats. 3 informal a scene of frenetic activity: *a media circus*.
ORIGIN – Latin, 'ring, circus'.

cirque /surk/ > *noun* Geology a steep-sided hollow at the head of a valley or on a mountainside; a corrie or cwm.
ORIGIN – French, from Latin *circus* 'ring, circus'.

cirrhosis /siˈrōsiss/ > *noun* a chronic liver disease marked by degeneration of cells and thickening of tissue.
DERIVATIVES – **cirrhotic** adjective.
ORIGIN – from Greek *kirrhos* 'tawny' (the colour of the liver in many cases).

cirrocumulus /sirrōˈkyoomyooləss/ > *noun* cloud forming a broken layer of small fleecy clouds at high altitude.

cirrostratus /sirrōˈstraatəss/ > *noun* cloud forming a thin, uniform semi-translucent layer at high altitude.

cirrus /ˈsirrəss/ > *noun* (pl. **cirri** /ˈsirrī/) 1 cloud forming wispy streaks at high altitude. 2 Zoology & Botany a slender tendril or hair-like filament.
ORIGIN – Latin, 'a curl'.

CIS > *abbreviation* Commonwealth of Independent States.

cisalpine /sisˈalpīn/ > *adjective* on the southern side of the Alps.
ORIGIN – Latin *cisalpinus*.

cisco /ˈsiskō/ > *noun* (pl. **ciscoes**) a northern freshwater whitefish, important as a food fish.

cissy > *noun* & *adjective* variant spelling of SISSY.

Cistercian /sisˈtersh'n/ > *noun* a monk or nun of an order that is a stricter branch of the Benedictines. > *adjective* relating to this order.
ORIGIN – from *Cistercium*, the Latin name of *Cîteaux* near Dijon in France, where the order was founded.

cistern > *noun* 1 a water storage tank, especially as part of a flushing toilet. 2 an underground reservoir for rainwater.
ORIGIN – Latin *cisterna*, from *cista* 'box'.

cistus > *noun* a shrub with large white or red flowers, the twigs of which yield ladanum.
ORIGIN – Greek *kistos*.

citadel > *noun* a fortress protecting or dominating a city.
ORIGIN – French *citadelle* or Italian *cittadella*, from Latin *civitas* (see CITY).

citation > *noun* 1 a quotation from or reference to a book or author. 2 a mention of a praiseworthy act in an official report. 3

a note accompanying an award, giving reasons for it.

cite > *verb* **1** quote (a book or author) as evidence for an argument. **2** praise for a courageous act in an official dispatch. **3** Law summon to appear in court.

SYNONYMS – **1** mention, quote, refer to.

ORIGIN – Latin *citare*, from *cire* 'to call'.

citified > *adjective* chiefly derogatory characteristic of or accustomed to a city.

citizen > *noun* **1** a legally recognised subject or national of a state or commonwealth. **2** an inhabitant of a town or city.

DERIVATIVES – **citizenry** *noun* **citizenship** *noun*.

SYNONYMS – inhabitant, national, native, resident, subject.

COMBINATIONS – **Citizens' Band** a range of radio frequencies allocated for local communication by private individuals.

ORIGIN – Old French *citezein*, from Latin *civitas* (see **CITY**).

citric > *adjective* derived from or related to citrus fruit.

ORIGIN – from Latin *citrus* 'citron tree'.

citric acid > *noun* Chemistry a sharp-tasting acid present in the juice of lemons and other sour fruits.

DERIVATIVES – **citrate** *noun*.

citrine /sitrin/ > *noun* a glassy yellow variety of quartz.

citron > *noun* **1** a shrubby Asian tree bearing large lemon-like fruits. **2** the fruit of this tree.

ORIGIN – French, from Latin *citrus* 'citron tree'.

citronella > *noun* a fragrant natural oil obtained from a South Asian grass, used as an insect repellent and in perfume.

citrus > *noun* (pl. **citruses**) **1** a tree of a genus that includes citron, lemon, lime, orange, and grapefruit. **2** (also **citrus fruit**) a fruit from such a tree.

DERIVATIVES – **citrusy** *adjective*.

ORIGIN – Latin, 'citron tree, thuja'.

cittern /sittərn/ > *noun* a lute-like stringed instrument with a flattened back, used in 16th- and 17th-century Europe.

ORIGIN – Latin *cithara*, from Greek *kithara*, denoting a kind of harp.

city > *noun* (pl. **cities**) **1** a large town, in particular (Brit.) a town created a city by charter and containing a cathedral. **2** (**the City**) the part of London governed by the Lord Mayor and the Corporation. **3** (**the City**) the financial and commercial institutions in this part of London.

WORDFINDER – urban (*relating to a city*).

SYNONYMS – **1** conurbation, metropolis.

COMBINATIONS – **city father** a person concerned with the administration of a city. **city hall** N. Amer. municipal offices or officers collectively. **city slicker** informal a person with the sophisticated tastes or

values associated with city dwellers. **city state** a city and surrounding territory that forms an independent state. **City Technology College** (in the UK) a type of secondary school set up to teach technology and science in inner-city areas.

wordpower facts

City

The Latin word *civitas* (from *civis*, meaning 'citizen') was applied by the Romans to the old states and tribes of Britain and Gaul and to their chief towns. This Latin form is recorded in use in English in the Domesday Book (1086), applied, as an equivalent to the term *borough*, to certain important towns having some municipal autonomy. Such towns corresponded to the *cités* of France, and by the 13th century the Old French form *cite* had also entered English. It was applied mainly to ancient or foreign cities (probably in translation from the French), but also to important English boroughs such as London and Lincoln.

cityscape > *noun* a city landscape.

civet > *noun* **1** a slender nocturnal cat native to Africa and Asia. **2** a strong musky perfume obtained from the scent glands of the civet.

ORIGIN – Arabic.

civic > *adjective* relating to the life or administration of a city or town.

DERIVATIVES – **civically** *adverb*.

SYNONYMS – civil, metropolitan, municipal, public.

COMBINATIONS – **civic centre 1** the area of a town where municipal offices are situated. **2** a building containing municipal offices.

ORIGIN – Latin *civicus*, from *civis* 'citizen'.

civics > *plural noun* (treated as sing.) the study of the rights and duties of citizenship.

civil > *adjective* **1** relating to ordinary citizens, as distinct from military or ecclesiastical matters. **2** Law non-criminal: *a civil court*. **3** courteous and polite.

DERIVATIVES – **civilly** *adverb*.

SYNONYMS – **1** civilian, secular. **3** courteous, pleasant, polite, well mannered.

ANTONYMS – **1** military, religious. **3** rude.

COMBINATIONS – **civil defence** the organisation and training of civilians for their protection during wartime. **civil disobedience** refusal to comply with certain laws or to pay taxes, as a political protest. **civil engineer** an engineer who designs roads, bridges, dams, etc. **civil law 1** law concerned with ordinary citizens, rather than criminal, military, or religious

affairs. **2** the system of law predominant on the European continent, influenced by that of ancient Rome. **Civil List** (in the UK) an annual allowance voted by Parliament for the royal family's household expenses. **civil marriage** a marriage without religious ceremony. **civil rights** the rights of citizens to political and social freedom and equality. **civil servant** a member of the civil service. **civil service** the branches of state administration, excluding military and judicial branches and elected politicians. **civil war** a war between citizens of the same country.

ORIGIN – Latin *civilis*, from *civis* 'citizen'.

civilian > *noun* a person not in the armed services or the police force. > *adjective* relating to civilians.

SYNONYMS – non-combatant, private citizen.

civilisation (also **civilization**) > *noun* **1** an advanced stage or system of human social development. **2** the process of achieving this. **3** a civilised nation or region.

SYNONYMS – **1,2** advancement, culture, progress. **3** culture, people, society.

civilise (also **civilize**) > *verb* bring to an advanced stage of social development.

DERIVATIVES – **civiliser** *noun*.

SYNONYMS – educate, elevate, enlighten, raise up, refine, socialise.

civilised (also **civilized**) > *adjective* polite and well mannered.

SYNONYMS – cultivated, cultured, polite, refined, well mannered.

ANTONYMS – rude, uncivilised.

civility > *noun* (pl. **civilities**) **1** politeness and courtesy. **2** (**civilities**) polite remarks used in formal conversation.

SYNONYMS – **1** courtesy, good manners, politeness.

ANTONYMS – **1** rudeness.

civil liberty > *noun* **1** freedom of action and speech subject to laws established for the good of the community. **2** (**civil liberties**) one's rights to this.

DERIVATIVES – **civil libertarian** *noun*.

civvy > *noun* (pl. **civvies**) informal **1** a civilian. **2** (**civvies**) civilian clothes.

IDIOMS – **Civvy Street** Brit. informal civilian life.

CJD > *abbreviation* Creutzfeldt–Jakob disease.

Cl > *symbol* the chemical element chlorine.

cl > *abbreviation* centilitre.

clabber > *noun* chiefly US milk that has clotted on souring.

ORIGIN – shortening of *bonny clabber*, from Irish *bainne clabair* 'thick milk for churning'.

clack > *verb* make a sharp sound as of a hard object striking another. > *noun* a clacking sound.

clad archaic or literary past participle of **CLOTHE**. > *adjective* **1** clothed. **2** provided with cladding. > *verb* (**cladding**; past and past participle **cladded** or **clad**) cover with cladding.

cladding > *noun* a covering or coating on a structure or material.

clade /klayd/ > *noun* Biology a group of organisms comprising all the evolutionary descendants of a common ancestor.

ORIGIN – Greek *klados* 'branch'.

cladistics /kləˈdistiks/ > *plural noun* (treated as sing.) Biology a method of classification of animals and plants based on clades.

DERIVATIVES – **cladistic** *adjective*.

claggy > *adjective* Brit. dialect tending to form sticky lumps.

claim > *verb* **1** assert that something is the case, without providing evidence or proof. **2** demand as one's property or earnings. **3** call for (someone's attention). **4** request (money) under the terms of an insurance policy. **5** cause the loss of (someone's life). > *noun* **1** an assertion of the truth of something. **2** a demand for something considered one's due. **3** a request for compensation under the terms of an insurance policy.

DERIVATIVES – **claimable** *adjective* **claimant** *noun*.

SYNONYMS – *verb* **1** allege, assert, contend, declare, maintain, profess. **2** demand, exact, insist on, lay claim to. *noun* **1** allegation, assertion, contention, declaration, profession. **2** call, demand, exaction, insistence.

ORIGIN – Latin *clamare* 'call out'.

clairvoyance /klairˈvoyənss/ > *noun* the supposed faculty of perceiving events in the future or beyond normal sensory contact.

SYNONYMS – ESP, extrasensory perception, psychic powers, second sight, sixth sense.

ORIGIN – French, from *clair* 'clear' + *voir* 'to see'.

clairvoyant > *noun* a person claiming to have clairvoyance. > *adjective* having clairvoyance.

SYNONYMS – *noun* fortune teller, psychic, seer.

clam > *noun* a marine bivalve mollusc having two large shells, each of the same size. > *verb* (**clammed**, **clamming**) **1** chiefly N. Amer. dig for or collect clams. **2** (**clam up**) informal abruptly stop talking.

ORIGIN – Old English, 'a bond or bondage'; related to CLAMP.

clambake > *noun* N. Amer. a social gathering outdoors, especially for eating seafood.

clamber > *verb* climb or move in an awkward and laborious way. > *noun* an act of clambering.

SYNONYMS – climb, crawl, scramble.

ORIGIN – probably from *clamb*, obsolete past tense of CLIMB.

clamdiggers > *plural noun* close-fitting calf-length trousers for women.

clammy > *adjective* (**clammier**, **clammiest**) **1** unpleasantly damp and sticky. **2** (of air) cold and damp.

DERIVATIVES – **clammily** *adverb* **clamminess** *noun*.

SYNONYMS – **1** damp, moist, sticky, sweaty. **2** close, damp, dank, humid.

ORIGIN – from dialect *clam* 'to be sticky or adhere', related to CLAY.

clamour (US **clamor**) > *noun* **1** a loud and confused noise. **2** a vehement protest or demand. > *verb* (of a group) make a clamour.

DERIVATIVES – **clamorous** *adjective*.

SYNONYMS – *noun* **1** din, hubbub, racket, uproar. **2** calls, complaints, demands, outcry, protests. *verb* call, lobby, press, push.

ORIGIN – Latin *clamor*, from *clamare* 'cry out'.

clamp > *noun* a brace, band, or clasp for strengthening or holding things together. > *verb* **1** fasten in place or together with a clamp. **2** hold or grip tightly. **3** (**clamp down**) suppress or prevent something. **4** fit a wheel clamp to (an illegally parked car).

DERIVATIVES – **clamper** *noun*.

SYNONYMS – *verb* **1** clip, fasten, fix, secure. **2** clench, clutch, grasp, grip.

clampdown > *noun* informal a concerted attempt to suppress something.

clan > *noun* **1** a group of close-knit and interrelated families, especially in the Scottish Highlands. **2** a group with a strong common interest.

SYNONYMS – **2** circle, clique, coterie, crowd, group, set.

ORIGIN – Scottish Gaelic *clann* 'offspring, family', from Latin *planta* 'sprout'.

clandestine /klanˈdestin/ > *adjective* kept secret or done secretively.

DERIVATIVES – **clandestinely** *adverb* **clandestinity** *noun*.

SYNONYMS – covert, furtive, secret, secretive, surreptitious.

ANTONYMS – open.

ORIGIN – Latin *clandestinus*, from *clam* 'secretly'.

clang > *noun* a loud metallic sound. > *verb* make a clang.

clanger > *noun* informal, chiefly Brit. a mistake.

clangour /ˈklanggər/ (US **clangor**) > *noun* a continuous clanging sound.

DERIVATIVES – **clangorous** *adjective*.

ORIGIN – Latin *clangor*, from *clangere* 'resound'.

clank > *noun* a loud, sharp sound as of pieces of metal being struck together. > *verb* make a clank.

DERIVATIVES – **clanking** *adjective*.

clannish > *adjective* (of a group or its activities) tending to exclude people outside the group.

DERIVATIVES – **clannishly** *adverb* **clannishness** *noun*.

clansman > *noun* a male member of a clan.

clap¹ > *verb* (**clapped**, **clapping**) **1** strike the palms of (one's hands) together repeatedly, especially to applaud. **2** slap (someone) encouragingly on the back. **3** place (a hand) briefly over one's face as a gesture of dismay. **4** (of a bird) flap (its wings) audibly. > *noun* **1** an act of clapping. **2** an explosive sound, especially of thunder.

IDIOMS – **clap in jail** (or **irons**) put (someone) in prison (or in chains).

ORIGIN – Old English, 'throb, beat'.

clap² > *noun* informal a venereal disease, especially gonorrhoea.

ORIGIN – Old French *clapoir*.

clapboard /ˈklapbord, ˈklabbərd/ > *noun* chiefly N. Amer. each of a series of long planks of wood with edges horizontally overlapping, covering the outer walls of a building.

ORIGIN – Low German *klappholt* 'barrel stave', from *klappen* 'to crack' + *holt* 'wood'.

clapped-out > *adjective* informal, chiefly Brit. worn out from age or heavy use.

clapper > *noun* the tongue or striker of a bell.

IDIOMS – **like the clappers** Brit. informal very fast or hard.

clapperboard > *noun* a pair of hinged boards that are struck together at the beginning of filming to synchronise the picture and sound machinery.

claptrap > *noun* nonsense.

ORIGIN – first denoting something designed to elicit applause.

claque /klak, klaak/ > *noun* **1** a group of people hired to applaud or heckle a performer. **2** a group of sycophantic followers.

ORIGIN – French, from *claquer* 'to clap'.

claret /ˈklarrət/ > *noun* **1** a red wine, especially one from Bordeaux. **2** a deep purplish red colour.

ORIGIN – Old French *vin claret*, from Latin *claratum vinum* 'clarified wine', from *clarus* 'clear'.

clarify > *verb* (**clarifies**, **clarified**) **1** make more comprehensible. **2** melt (butter) to separate out the impurities.

DERIVATIVES – **clarification** *noun* **clarifier** *noun*.

SYNONYMS – **1** elucidate, explain, illuminate, shed light on.

ANTONYMS – **1** obfuscate, obscure.

clarinet > *noun* a woodwind instrument with a single-reed mouthpiece, a cylindrical tube, and holes stopped by keys.

DERIVATIVES – **clarinettist** (US **clarinetist**) *noun*.

ORIGIN – French *clarinette*, denoting a kind of bell.

clarion /**klarrɪən**/ > *noun* chiefly historical a shrill war trumpet. > *adjective* literary loud and clear.

IDIOMS – **clarion call** a strongly expressed demand for action.

ORIGIN – Latin, from *clarus* 'clear'.

clarity > *noun* 1 the state or quality of being clear and easily perceived or understood. 2 the quality of transparency or purity.

SYNONYMS – 1 clearness, comprehensibility, intelligibility, lucidity. 2 clearness, limpidity, purity, transparency.

ANTONYMS – 1 obscurity, vagueness. 2 murkiness, opacity.

ORIGIN – Latin *claritas*, from *clarus* 'clear'.

clarsach /**klaarsəkh**/ > *noun* a small harp with wire strings, used in the folk music of Scotland and Ireland.

ORIGIN – Scottish Gaelic, perhaps based on *clar* 'table, board'.

clash > *verb* 1 (of two opposing people or groups) come into violent conflict or disagreement. 2 be incompatible. 3 (of colours) appear discordant when placed together. 4 (of dates or events) occur inconveniently at the same time. 5 strike (cymbals) together forcefully. > *noun* an instance of clashing.

SYNONYMS – *verb* 1 come to blows, conflict, fight. 3 be discordant, jar, not go, not match. 5 clang, crash, smash.

clasp > *verb* 1 grasp tightly with one's hand. 2 place (one's arms) around something so as to hold it tightly. 3 press (one's hands) together with the fingers interlaced. 4 fasten with a clasp. > *noun* 1 a device with interlocking parts used for fastening. 2 a bar on a medal ribbon. 3 an act of clasping.

IDIOMS – **clasp hands** (of two people) hold or shake hands warmly.

SYNONYMS – *verb* 1 clutch, grip, grasp. 2 embrace, enfold, hold, hug, squeeze.

COMBINATIONS – **clasp knife** a knife with a blade that folds into the handle.

class > *noun* 1 a set or category of things having a common characteristic and differentiated from others by kind or quality. 2 a system that divides members of a society into sets based on social or economic status. 3 a set in a society ordered by social or economic status. 4 a group of students or pupils who are taught together. 5 a lesson. 6 Biology a principal taxonomic category that ranks above order and below phylum or division. 7 informal impressive stylishness. 8 Brit. a division of candidates according to merit in a university examination. > *verb* assign to a particular category. > *adjective* informal showing stylish excellence: *a class player*.

SYNONYMS – *noun* 1 category, classification, division, grade, grouping, set. *verb* categorise, classify, grade, group, sort.

COMBINATIONS – **class action** Law, chiefly N. Amer. a law suit filed or defended by an individual acting on behalf of a group. **class struggle** (in Marxist ideology) the conflict of interests between the workers and the ruling class in a capitalist society.

ORIGIN – Latin *classis* 'a division of the Roman people, a grade, or a class of pupils'.

classic > *adjective* 1 judged over a period of time to be of the highest quality. 2 remarkably typical: *the classic symptoms of flu*. > *noun* 1 a work of art of established value. 2 (**Classics**) the study of ancient Greek and Latin literature, philosophy, and history. 3 (**the classics**) the works of ancient Greek and Latin writers. 4 a thing recognised to be an excellent example of its kind.

SYNONYMS – *adjective* 1 definitive, enduring, exemplary, masterly, outstanding. 2 archetypal, paradigmatic, prototypical, quintessential, typical. *noun* 1 masterpiece. 4 exemplar, model, paradigm, standard.

ORIGIN – Latin *classicus* 'belonging to a class or division', later 'of the highest class'.

classical > *adjective* 1 relating to ancient Greek or Latin literature, art, or culture. 2 (of a form of art or a language) representing an exemplary standard within a long-established form. 3 (of music) of long-established form or style or (more specifically) written in the European tradition between approximately 1750 and 1830. 4 relating to the first significant period of an area of study: *classical Marxism*.

DERIVATIVES – **classically** *adverb*.

classicising (also **classicizing**) > *adjective* imitating a classical style.

classicism > *noun* the following of ancient Greek or Roman principles and style in art and literature, generally associated with harmony and restraint.

classicist > *noun* 1 a person who studies Classics. 2 a follower of classicism.

classification > *noun* 1 the action or process of classifying. 2 a category into which something is put.

DERIVATIVES – **classificatory** *adjective*.

SYNONYMS – *noun* 2 category, class, division, grade, grouping, set.

classified > *adjective* 1 (of newspaper or magazine advertisements) organised in categories. 2 (of information or documents) designated as officially secret. > *noun* (**classifieds**) classified advertisements.

classify > *verb* (**classifies, classified**) 1 assign to a particular class or category. 2 arrange (a group) in classes or categories according to shared characteristics. 3 designate (documents or information) as officially secret.

DERIVATIVES – **classifiable** *adjective* **classifier** *noun*.

SYNONYMS – 1 categorise, class, grade, group, order, sort.

classless > *adjective* 1 (of a society) not divided into social classes. 2 not showing characteristics of a particular social class.

DERIVATIVES – **classlessness** *noun*.

classroom > *noun* a room in which a class of pupils or students is taught.

classy > *adjective* (**classier, classiest**) informal stylish and sophisticated.

DERIVATIVES – **classily** *adverb* **classiness** *noun*.

clatter > *noun* a loud rattling sound as of hard objects striking each other. > *verb* 1 make a clatter. 2 fall or move with a clatter.

clause > *noun* 1 a unit of grammatical organisation next below the sentence in rank, and in traditional grammar said to consist of a subject and predicate. 2 a particular and separate article, stipulation, or proviso in a treaty, bill, or contract.

DERIVATIVES – **clausal** *adjective*.

ORIGIN – from Latin *claudere* 'shut, close'.

claustrophobia /**klawstrəfōbɪə**/ > *noun* extreme or irrational fear of confined places.

DERIVATIVES – **claustrophobe** *noun* **claustrophobic** *adjective*.

ORIGIN – from Latin *claustrum* 'lock, bolt'.

clavichord /**klavvikord**/ > *noun* a small, rectangular keyboard instrument.

ORIGIN – from Latin *clavis* 'key' + *chorda* 'string'.

clavicle > *noun* technical the collarbone.

DERIVATIVES – **clavicular** *adjective*.

ORIGIN – Latin *clavicula* 'small key' (because of its shape).

claw > *noun* 1 a curved, pointed horny nail on each digit of the foot in birds, lizards, and some mammals. 2 the pincer of a crab, scorpion, or other arthropod. 3 a mechanical device resembling a claw, used for gripping or lifting. > *verb* 1 scratch or tear at with the claws or fingernails. 2 (**claw away**) try desperately to move (something) with the hands. 3 (**claw one's way**) haul oneself forward with one's hands. 4 (**claw back**) regain or recover (money, power, etc.) laboriously or harshly.

IDIOMS – **get one's claws into** informal have a controlling influence over.

DERIVATIVES – **clawed** *adjective*.

SYNONYMS – *verb* 1 lacerate, rake, scrape, scratch, tear.

COMBINATIONS – **claw hammer** a hammer with one side of the head split and curved, used for extracting nails.

clay > *noun* 1 a sticky impermeable earth that can be moulded when wet and baked to make bricks and pottery. 2 literary the substance of the human body.

DERIVATIVES – **clayey** *adjective*.

COMBINATIONS – **clay pigeon** a saucer-shaped piece of baked clay or other material thrown up in the air as a target for shooting. **clay pipe** a tobacco pipe made of hardened clay.

claymore > *noun* historical a type of broadsword used in Scotland.

ORIGIN – from Scottish Gaelic, literally 'great sword'.

clean > *adjective* 1 free from dirt, pollutants, or harmful substances. 2 morally pure: *clean living*. 3 not obscene. 4 showing or having no record of offences or crimes: *a clean driving licence*. 5 played or done according to the rules: *a good clean fight*. 6 free from irregularities; smooth: *a clean fracture*. 7 (of an action) smoothly and skilfully done: *a clean take-off*. > *adverb* 1 so as to be free from dirt. 2 informal completely. > *verb* 1 make free of dirt or mess. 2 (**clean out**) informal use up or take (all the money or resources of a person or place). 3 (**clean up**) informal make a substantial gain or profit. > *noun* chiefly Brit. an act of cleaning.

IDIOMS – **clean and jerk** a weightlifting exercise in which a weight is raised above the head following an initial lift to shoulder level. **clean sheet 1** (also **clean slate**) an absence of existing restraints or commitments. 2 the achievement of conceding no goals in a soccer match. **come clean** informal fully confess something. **keep one's hands clean** remain uninvolved in an immoral or illegal act. **make a clean breast of it** fully confess something. **make a clean sweep 1** remove all unwanted people or things ready to start afresh. 2 win all of a group of related sporting contests.

DERIVATIVES – **cleanable** *adjective* **cleaning** *noun* **cleanness** *noun*.

SYNONYMS – *adjective* 1 hygienic, pristine, pure, sanitary, unsullied. 2 decent, honourable, pure, unimpeachable, upright. 5 fair, chivalrous, sporting. *verb* 1 cleanse, decontaminate, disinfect, purge, purify.

ANTONYMS – *adjective* 1 dirty. 2 corrupt, immoral. 5 dirty, unfair.

COMBINATIONS – **clean-cut 1** sharply outlined. 2 (of a person) clean and neat. **clean-shaven** (of a man) without a beard or moustache.

cleaner > *noun* a person or thing that cleans.

IDIOMS – **take to the cleaners** informal 1 defraud (someone) of a large portion of money or resources. 2 inflict a crushing defeat on.

cleanly > *adverb* /kleenli/ in a clean manner. > *adjective* /klenli/ (**cleanlier**, **cleanliest**) archaic habitually clean.

DERIVATIVES – **cleanliness** *noun*.

cleanse > *verb* 1 make thoroughly clean. 2 archaic (in biblical translations) cure (a leper). > *noun* an act of cleansing.

DERIVATIVES – **cleanser** *noun* **cleansing** *adjective*.

SYNONYMS – *verb* 1 clean, decontaminate, disinfect, purge, purify.

clear > *adjective* 1 easy to perceive or understand. 2 leaving or feeling no doubt. 3 easy to see or hear. 4 transparent; unclouded. 5 free of any obstructions or unwanted objects. 6 (of a period of time) free of commitments. 7 free from disease, contamination, or guilt. 8 (**clear of**) not touching; away from: *clear of the ground*. 9 complete: *seven clear days' notice*. 10 (of a sum of money) net. > *adverb* 1 so as to be out of the way of or uncluttered by. 2 with clarity. > *verb* 1 make or become clear. 2 get past or over (something) safely or without touching it. 3 show or declare to be innocent. 4 give official approval or authorisation to or for. 5 cause people to leave (a building or place). 6 (of a cheque) pass through a clearing house so that the money enters the payee's account. 7 earn or gain (an amount of money) as a net profit. 8 pay the total amount of (a debt).

IDIOMS – **clear the air 1** make the air less sultry. 2 defuse a tense situation by frank discussion. **clear the decks** prepare for something by dealing beforehand with anything that might hinder progress. **clear off** informal go away. **clear out** informal 1 empty. 2 leave quickly. **clear up 1** tidy (something) by removing unwanted items. 2 solve or explain. 3 (of an illness or other medical condition) become cured. 4 (of the weather) become brighter; stop raining. **in the clear** no longer in danger or under suspicion.

DERIVATIVES – **clearness** *noun*.

SYNONYMS – *adjective* 1 comprehensible, explicit, intelligible, lucid, plain, understandable. 2 apparent, evident, manifest, obvious, sure, unmistakable. 3 definite, distinct, sharp, well-defined. 4 limpid, pellucid, see-through, translucent, transparent, unclouded. 5 empty, free, open, unblocked, unobstructed.

ANTONYMS – *adjective* 1,2 unclear, vague. 3 murky, opaque. 4 blocked, obstructed.

COMBINATIONS – **clear-cut** sharply defined; easy to perceive or understand. **clearing bank** Brit. a bank which is a member of a clearing house. **clearing house 1** a bankers' establishment where cheques and bills from member banks are exchanged. 2 an agency which collects and distributes information. **clear-sighted** thinking clearly; perspicacious.

ORIGIN – Old French *cler*, from Latin *clarus*.

clearance > *noun* 1 the action or process of clearing or of being dispersed. 2 official authorisation for something to proceed. 3 clear space allowed for a thing to move past or under another. 4 (in soccer) a kick that sends the ball out of a defensive zone.

clearing > *noun* an open space in a forest.

clearly > *adverb* 1 with clarity. 2 obviously; without doubt.

clearway > *noun* Brit. a main road other than a motorway on which vehicles are not permitted to stop.

cleat > *noun* 1 a T-shaped or similar projection to which a rope may be attached. 2 a projecting wedge on a spar, tool, etc., to prevent slippage.

DERIVATIVES – **cleated** *adjective*.

cleavage > *noun* 1 a sharp division; a split. 2 the cleft between a woman's breasts. 3 Biology cell division, especially of a fertilised egg cell. 4 the splitting of rocks or crystals in a preferred plane or direction.

cleave¹ > *verb* (past **clove** or **cleft** or **cleaved**; past participle **cloven** or **cleft** or **cleaved**) 1 split or sever along a natural grain or line. 2 divide; split.

cleave² > *verb* (**cleave to**) literary 1 stick fast to. 2 become strongly involved with or emotionally attached to.

cleaver > *noun* a tool with a heavy broad blade, used for chopping meat.

clef > *noun* Music any of several symbols placed on a stave, indicating the pitch of the notes.

ORIGIN – French, from Latin *clavis* 'key'.

cleft past participle of **CLEAVE¹**. > *adjective* split, divided, or partially divided into two. > *noun* 1 a fissure or split in rock or the ground. 2 an indentation in a person's forehead or chin, or a hollow between two parts of the body.

IDIOMS – **be** (or **be caught**) **in a cleft stick** chiefly Brit. be in a situation in which any action one takes will have adverse consequences.

COMBINATIONS – **cleft lip** a congenital split in the upper lip on one or both sides of the centre, often associated with a cleft palate. **cleft palate** a congenital split in the roof of the mouth.

clematis /klemmətiss, kləmaytiss/ > *noun* an ornamental climbing plant bearing white, pink, or purple flowers and feathery seeds.

ORIGIN – Greek *klēmatis*, from *klēma* 'vine branch'.

clement > *adjective* 1 (of weather) mild. 2 merciful.

DERIVATIVES – **clemency** *noun*.

ORIGIN – Latin *clemens*.

clementine /klemmənteen, klemməntīn/ > *noun* a deep orange-red variety of tangerine grown around the Mediterranean and in South Africa.

ORIGIN – French *clémentine*.

clench > *verb* **1** close or press together (one's fist or teeth) tightly, in response to stress or anger. **2** contract (a set of muscles) sharply. **3** grasp tightly. > *noun* the action or state of clenching or being clenched.

SYNONYMS – *verb* **3** clasp, clutch, grasp, squeeze.

ORIGIN – first used in the sense of *clinch* 'fix securely'; related to CLING.

clerestory /kleerstori/ (US also **clearstory**) > *noun* (pl. **clerestories**) the upper part of the nave, choir, and transepts of a large church, incorporating a series of windows which admit light to the central parts of the building.

ORIGIN – from CLEAR + STOREY.

clergy /klerji/ > *noun* (pl. **clergies**) (usu. treated as pl.) the body of people ordained for religious duties in the Christian Church.

WORDFINDER – *the non-clergy:* the laity; *members of the clergy:* bishop, canon, chaplain, curate, dean, legate, minister, parson, rector, vicar.

ORIGIN – Latin *clericus* 'cleric, clergyman'.

clergyman (or **clergywoman**) > *noun* a priest or minister of a Christian church.

cleric > *noun* a priest or religious leader.

ORIGIN – Latin *clericus*, from Greek *klērikos* 'belonging to the Christian clergy', from *klēros* 'lot, heritage'.

clerical > *adjective* **1** relating to the routine work of an office clerk. **2** relating to the clergy.

DERIVATIVES – **clericalism** *noun* **clericalist** *noun* **clerically** *adverb*.

SYNONYMS – **1** administrative, white-collar. **2** ecclesiastical, priestly.

COMBINATIONS – **clerical collar** a stiff upright white collar which fastens at the back, worn by the clergy in some churches. **clerical error** a mistake made in copying or writing out a document.

clerihew /klerrihyoo/ > *noun* a short comic verse consisting of two rhyming couplets with lines of unequal length, typically referring to a famous person.

ORIGIN – named after Edmund *Clerihew* Bentley (1875–1956), the English writer who invented it.

clerk > *noun* **1** a person employed in an office or bank to keep records or accounts and to undertake other routine administrative duties. **2** an official in charge of the records of a local council or court. **3** a senior official in Parliament. **4** a lay officer of a cathedral, church, or chapel. **5** (also **desk clerk**) N. Amer. a receptionist in a hotel. **6** N. Amer. an assistant in a shop; a sales clerk. > *verb* N. Amer. work as a clerk.

DERIVATIVES – **clerkish** *adjective* **clerkly** *adjective* **clerkship** *noun*.

ORIGIN – Latin *clericus* 'cleric, clergyman'; reinforced by Old French *clerc*, from the same source.

clever > *adjective* (**cleverer**, **cleverest**) **1** quick to understand, learn, and devise or apply ideas. **2** skilful; adroit.

DERIVATIVES – **cleverly** *adverb* **cleverness** *noun*.

SYNONYMS – **1** bright, intelligent, quick, smart; informal brainy.

ANTONYMS – **1** stupid, unintelligent.

ORIGIN – first used in the sense 'quick to catch hold': perhaps of Dutch or German origin, and related to CLEAVE².

clew > *noun* **1** the lower or after corner of a sail. **2** (**clews**) Nautical the cords by which a hammock is suspended. > *verb* (**clew a sail up** or **down**) draw a sail up or let it down by the clews when preparing for furling or when unfurling.

ORIGIN – first denoting a ball of thread; related to CLUE.

cliché /kleeshay/ (also **cliche**) > *noun* **1** a hackneyed or overused phrase or opinion. **2** a very predictable or unoriginal thing.

SYNONYMS – **1** commonplace, platitude, stock phrase, truism.

ORIGIN – French, from *clicher* 'to stereotype'.

clichéd (also **cliched**) > *adjective* showing a lack of originality; hackneyed.

SYNONYMS – hackneyed, overused, predictable, unoriginal.

ANTONYMS – fresh, original.

click > *noun* **1** a short, sharp sound as of two metallic or plastic objects coming smartly into contact. **2** Computing an act of pressing one of the buttons on a mouse. > *verb* **1** make or cause to make a click. **2** move or become secured with a click. **3** Computing press (a mouse button). **4** informal become suddenly clear and understandable. **5** informal become friendly and compatible.

DERIVATIVES – **clickable** *adjective* **clicker** *noun*.

client > *noun* a person using the services of a professional person or organisation.

DERIVATIVES – **clientship** *noun*.

SYNONYMS – customer, patron, user.

ORIGIN – first denoting a person under the protection and patronage of another: from Latin *cliens*, from *cluere* 'hear or obey'.

clientele /kleeontel/ > *noun* clients or customers collectively.

ORIGIN – French, from Latin *clientela* 'clientship'.

cliff > *noun* a steep rock face, especially at the edge of the sea.

DERIVATIVES – **cliffy** *adjective*.

cliffhanger > *noun* a dramatic story or climactic ending that leaves an audience in suspense.

climacteric /klīmaktərik, klīmakterrik/ > *noun* **1** a critical period or event. **2** Medicine the period of life when fertility is in decline; (in women) the menopause. > *adjective* **1** having extreme and far-reaching implications or results; critical. **2** Medicine occurring at, characteristic of, or undergoing a climacteric.

ORIGIN – Greek *klimaktērikos*, from *klimaktēr* 'critical period', from *klimax* 'ladder, climax'.

climactic /klīmaktik/ > *adjective* forming an exciting climax.

DERIVATIVES – **climactically** *adverb*.

USAGE – do not confuse **climactic**, 'forming a climax', with **climatic**, which means 'relating to climate'.

SYNONYMS – critical, culminating, decisive, dramatic, final.

climate > *noun* **1** the general weather conditions prevailing in an area over a long period. **2** a prevailing trend or public attitude.

DERIVATIVES – **climatical** *adjective*.

SYNONYMS – **2** atmosphere, ethos, feeling, mood.

ORIGIN – first denoting a zone of the earth between two lines of latitude: from Greek *klima* 'slope, zone'.

climatic /klīmattik/ > *adjective* relating to climate.

DERIVATIVES – **climatically** *adverb*.

climatology > *noun* the scientific study of climate.

DERIVATIVES – **climatological** *adjective* **climatologist** *noun*.

climax > *noun* **1** the most intense, exciting, or important point of something. **2** an orgasm. **3** Ecology the final stage in a succession, in which a community reaches a state of equilibrium. > *verb* reach or bring to a climax.

SYNONYMS – *noun* **1** crescendo, culmination, peak, pinnacle, zenith.

ORIGIN – Greek *klimax* 'ladder, climax'.

climb > *verb* **1** go or come up to a higher position. **2** go up or scale (a hill, rock face, etc.) **3** (of a plant) grow up (a supporting structure) by clinging to or twining round it. **4** move with effort into or out of a confined space. **5** increase in scale, value, or power. **6** (**climb down**) withdraw from a position taken up in argument or negotiation. > *noun* **1** an ascent made by climbing. **2** a recognised route up a mountain or cliff.

IDIOMS – **be climbing the walls** informal feel frustrated, helpless, and trapped.

DERIVATIVES – **climbable** *adjective*.

SYNONYMS – *verb* **1** ascend, go up, rise. **2** ascend, go up, mount, scale. **4** clamber, crawl, scramble. **5** advance, go up, increase, progress, rise. **6** (**climb down**) back down, capitulate, concede defeat, give way, yield.

COMBINATIONS – **climbing frame** Brit. a structure of joined bars for children to climb on.

ORIGIN – related to CLAY and CLEAVE².

climber > *noun* **1** a person who climbs rocks

or mountains as a sport. **2** a climbing plant.

clime > *noun* chiefly literary a region considered with reference to its climate: *sunnier climes.*

clinch > *verb* **1** conclusively settle (a contract or contest). **2** secure (a nail or rivet) by driving the point sideways when it has penetrated. **3** (of two people) grapple at close quarters. **4** come together in an embrace. **5** fasten (a rope or angling line) with a clinch knot. > *noun* **1** a struggle or scuffle at close quarters. **2** an embrace. **3** (also **clinch knot**) a knot used to fasten ropes or angling lines, using a half hitch with the end seized back on its own part.

SYNONYMS – *verb* **1** close, conclude, confirm, seal, secure, wrap up.

ORIGIN – from CLENCH.

clincher > *noun* informal a fact, argument, or event that settles a matter conclusively.

cline /klīn/ > *noun* a continuum with an infinite number of gradations from one end to the other.

ORIGIN – from Greek *klinein* 'to slope'.

cling > *verb* (past and past participle **clung**) (**cling to** or **on to**) **1** hold on tightly to. **2** adhere or stick to. **3** remain persistently faithful to. **4** be emotionally dependent on.

DERIVATIVES – **clinging** *adjective.*

SYNONYMS – (**cling to** or **on to**) **1** clutch, cuddle, embrace, hold on to, hug. **3** abide by, adhere to, hold to, stand by, stick to.

COMBINATIONS – **cling film** Brit. a thin clinging transparent plastic film used as a wrapping or covering for food.

ORIGIN – Old English, related to CLENCH.

clingy > *adjective* (**clingier, clingiest**) liable to cling; clinging.

DERIVATIVES – **clinginess** *noun.*

clinic > *noun* **1** a place where specialised medical treatment or advice is given. **2** a gathering at a hospital bedside for the teaching of medicine or surgery. **3** chiefly N. Amer. a conference or short course on a particular subject.

ORIGIN – Greek *klinikē tekhnē* 'bedside art', from *klinē* 'bed'.

clinical > *adjective* **1** relating to the observation and treatment of patients (rather than theoretical or laboratory studies). **2** efficient and coldly detached. **3** (of a place) bare, functional, and clean.

DERIVATIVES – **clinically** *adverb.*

SYNONYMS – **2** cold, detached, dispassionate, impersonal.

COMBINATIONS – **clinical psychology** the branch of psychology concerned with the assessment and treatment of mental illness.

clinician > *noun* a doctor having direct contact with and responsibility for treating patients, rather than one involved with theoretical or laboratory studies.

clink¹ > *noun* a sharp ringing sound, such as

that made when metal or glass are struck. > *verb* make or cause to make a clink.

ORIGIN – Dutch *klinken.*

clink² > *noun* informal prison.

clinker > *noun* **1** the stony residue from burnt coal or from a furnace. **2** a brick with a vitrified surface.

ORIGIN – from Dutch *klinken* 'to clink'.

clinker-built > *adjective* (of a boat) having external planks which overlap downwards and are secured with clinched nails. Compare with **carvel-built.**

ORIGIN – from CLINCH.

clip¹ > *noun* **1** a flexible or spring-loaded device for holding an object or objects together or in place. **2** a piece of jewellery that can be fastened on to a garment with a clip. **3** a metal holder containing cartridges for an automatic firearm. > *verb* (**clipped, clipping**) fasten or be fastened with a clip or clips.

COMBINATIONS – **clipboard** a small board with a spring clip, used for holding papers and providing support for writing.

clip² > *verb* (**clipped, clipping**) **1** cut, trim, or excise with shears or scissors. **2** trim the hair or wool of (an animal). **3** strike smartly or with a glancing blow. **4** informal, chiefly US move quickly in a specified direction. > *noun* **1** an act of clipping. **2** a short sequence taken from a film or broadcast. **3** informal a smart or glancing blow. **4** informal a rapid or specified speed.

DERIVATIVES – **clipping** *noun.*

SYNONYMS – *verb* **1** cut, prune, shear, trim. **3** box, cuff, slap, smack.

COMBINATIONS – **clip art** pre-drawn pictures and symbols provided with word-processing software and drawing packages. **clip joint** a nightclub or bar that charges exorbitant prices.

ORIGIN – Old Norse.

clipped > *adjective* (of speech) having short, sharp vowel sounds and clear pronunciation.

clipper > *noun* **1** (**clippers**) an instrument for clipping. **2** a fast sailing ship, especially one of 19th-century design with concave bows and raked masts.

clique /kleek/ > *noun* a small group of people who spend time together and do not readily allow others to join them.

DERIVATIVES – **cliquey** (**cliquier, cliquiest**) *adjective* **cliquish** *adjective* **cliquishness** *noun.*

SYNONYMS – circle, coterie, gang, group, set.

ORIGIN – French, from Old French *cliquer* 'make a noise'.

clitoridectomy /klittəri**dek**təmi/ > *noun* (pl. **clitoridectomies**) excision of the clitoris; female circumcision.

clitoris /**klitt**əriss/ > *noun* a small sensitive

and erectile part of the female genitals at the front end of the vulva.

DERIVATIVES – **clitoral** *adjective.*

ORIGIN – Greek *kleitoris.*

cloaca /klō**ay**kə/ > *noun* (pl. **cloacae** /klō**ay**see/) **1** Zoology (in some animals) a common cavity at the end of the digestive tract for the release of both excretory and genital products. **2** archaic a sewer.

DERIVATIVES – **cloacal** *adjective.*

ORIGIN – Latin, related to *cluere* 'cleanse'.

cloak > *noun* **1** an overgarment that hangs loosely from the shoulders over the arms to the knees or ankles. **2** something that hides or covers: *a cloak of secrecy.* **3** (**cloaks**) Brit. a cloakroom. > *verb* dress, envelop, or hide in a cloak.

SYNONYMS – *verb* envelop, hide, mask, obscure, screen, shroud, veil.

COMBINATIONS – **cloak-and-dagger** involving intrigue and secrecy. **cloakroom 1** a room in a public building where outdoor clothes and bags may be left. **2** Brit. a room that contains a toilet or toilets.

ORIGIN – Old French *cloke*, from *cloche* 'bell, cloak', from Latin *clocca* 'bell'; related to CLOCK.

clobber¹ > *noun* Brit. informal clothing and personal belongings.

clobber² > *verb* informal **1** hit hard. **2** defeat heavily.

cloche /klosh/ > *noun* **1** a small translucent cover for protecting or forcing outdoor plants. **2** (also **cloche hat**) a woman's close-fitting, bell-shaped hat.

ORIGIN – French, 'bell'.

wordpower facts

Clock

The word **clock** comes from the Latin *clocca*, meaning 'bell'. Old English already had the word *bell* for the general sense, but **clock** was adopted for bells used for sounding the hour. (This was probably because the sound of the word **clock** represented the rattling sound made by early square-shaped iron handbells, which was unlike the ringing of the cast circular bells of later date.) The sense was then extended to any instrument used for the measurement of time. The word **cloak** also comes from *clocca*, so-called because of its bell shape. The horticultural **cloche** comes from the French word for 'bell', *cloche*, which comes from the same Latin root.

clock > *noun* **1** an instrument that measures and indicates the time by means of a dial or a digital display. **2** informal a measuring device resembling a clock, such as a speedometer. > *verb* informal **1** attain or register (a specified time, distance, or speed). **2** (**clock in** or **out** or Brit. **on** or **off**) register one's arrival at or departure from work by means of an automatic recording clock. **3** Brit. see or watch. **4** chiefly Brit. hit on the head. **5** illegally wind back the milometer of (a car).

WORDFINDER – horology (*art of making clocks, or study and measurement of time*).

IDIOMS – **round** (or **around**) **the clock** all day and all night. **turn** (or **put**) **back the clock** return to the past or to a previous way of doing things.

COMBINATIONS – **clock radio** a combined bedside radio and alarm clock. **clock tower** a tower, especially that of a church or civic building, displaying a large clock. **clock-watch** work no longer than the hours prescribed.

clocker > *noun* informal **1** Brit. a person who illegally winds back the milometer on a car. **2** US a dealer in cocaine or crack.

clockwise > *adverb* & *adjective* in a curve corresponding in direction to the movement of the hands of a clock.

clockwork > *noun* a mechanism with a spring and toothed gearwheels, used to drive a mechanical clock, toy, or other device.

IDIOMS – **like clockwork** very smoothly and easily.

clod > *noun* **1** a lump of earth. **2** informal a stupid person.

ORIGIN – variant of **CLOT**.

cloddish > *adjective* foolish, awkward, or clumsy.

DERIVATIVES – **cloddishly** *adverb* **cloddishness** *noun*.

clodhopper > *noun* informal **1** a large, heavy shoe. **2** a foolish, awkward, or clumsy person.

clog > *noun* **1** a shoe with a thick wooden sole. **2** an encumbrance. > *verb* (**clogged**, **clogging**) (often **clog up**) block or become blocked with something thick or sticky.

SYNONYMS – *verb* block, choke, congest, jam, stop up.

ORIGIN – first used in the sense 'block of wood to impede an animal's movement': origin unknown.

cloisonné /klwaazonay/ > *noun* enamel work in which different colours are separated by strips of flattened wire placed edgeways on a metal backing.

ORIGIN – French, 'partitioned', from *cloison* 'a partition or division'.

cloister /kloystər/ > *noun* **1** a covered, and typically colonnaded, passage round an open court in a convent, monastery, college, or cathedral. **2** a convent or monastery. **3** (**the cloister**) monastic life.

> *verb* seclude or shut up in a convent or monastery.

DERIVATIVES – **cloistral** *adjective*.

ORIGIN – Old French *cloistre*, from Latin *claustrum* 'lock, enclosed place', from *claudere* 'to close'.

cloistered > *adjective* **1** having or enclosed by a cloister. **2** sheltered from the outside world.

clomp > *verb* walk with a heavy tread. > *noun* the sound of a heavy tread.

clompy > *adjective* variant spelling of **CLUMPY** (in sense 1).

clone > *noun* **1** Biology an organism produced asexually from one ancestor to which it is genetically identical. **2** a person or thing regarded as identical with another; a copy or double. > *verb* **1** propagate as a clone. **2** make an identical copy of.

DERIVATIVES – **clonal** *adjective*.

ORIGIN – Greek *klōn* 'twig'.

clonk > *noun* a sound made by an abrupt and heavy impact. > *verb* **1** move with or make a clonk. **2** informal hit.

DERIVATIVES – **clonky** *adjective*.

clop > *noun* a sound made by a horse's hooves on a hard surface. > *verb* (**clopped**, **clopping**) move with such a sound.

close¹ /klōss/ > *adjective* **1** only a short distance away or apart. **2** (of a connection or resemblance) strong. **3** (of a relative) part of one's immediate family. **4** (of a relationship or the people conducting it) very affectionate or intimate. **5** (of a contest) likely to be won by only a small margin; evenly matched. **6** uncomfortably humid or airless. **7** (of observation or examination) done in a careful and thorough way. **8** (of a person) not willing to give away money or information. > *adverb* so as to be very near; with very little space between. > *noun* **1** Brit. a residential street without through access. **2** Brit. the precinct surrounding a cathedral. **3** Scottish an entry from the street to a common stairway or to a court at the back of a building.

IDIOMS – **close-fisted** unwilling to spend money; mean. **close-knit** (of a group of people) united or bound together by strong relationships and common interests. **close-mouthed** reticent; discreet. **at** (or **from**) **close quarters** (or **range**) close to or from a position close to someone or something. **close-run** (of a contest or objective) won or lost by a very small margin. **close shave** (also **close call**) informal a narrow escape from danger or disaster.

DERIVATIVES – **closely** *adverb* **closeness** *noun*.

SYNONYMS – *adjective* **1** adjacent, near, nearby. **2** distinct, marked, pronounced, striking, strong. **4** devoted, intimate. **6** airless, humid, stuffy. **7** assiduous, careful,

detailed, meticulous, painstaking, thorough.

ANTONYMS – *adjective* **1** distant, far. **2** slight. **4** distant.

COMBINATIONS – **close harmony** Music harmony in which the notes of the chord are close together, typically in vocal music.

---

wordpower facts
Close

Close comes through Old French *clos* from the Latin verb *claudere*, meaning 'to close or enclose, to shut'. **Clause** and **cloister** come from the same root, as do the group of related words **conclude**, **exclude**, **preclude**, and **seclude**.

---

close² /klōz/ > *verb* **1** move so as to cover an opening. **2** (also **close up**) bring two parts of (something) together. **3** (often **close down** or **up**) (of a business or other organisation) cease to be open to the public or in operation. **4** bring or come to an end. **5** finish speaking or writing. **6** bring (a transaction or arrangement) to a conclusion. **7** (**close around** or **over**) encircle and hold. **8** (**close on** or **in on** or **up on**) gradually get nearer to or surround. **9** (**close in**) (of bad weather or darkness) gradually surround one. **10** (**close in**) (of days) become dark at an increasingly early hour with the approach of the winter solstice. > *noun* **1** the end of an event or of a period of time or activity. **2** a shut position.

DERIVATIVES – **closable** *adjective* **closer** *noun*.

SYNONYMS – *verb* **1** fasten, lock, pull to, shut. **4** end, finish. **6** clinch, confirm, conclude, ratify, seal, secure, wrap up. **8** catch up, gain on. *noun* **1** conclusion, end, finish.

COMBINATIONS – **close season** (also chiefly N. Amer. **closed season**) **1** a period between specified dates when fishing or the killing of particular game is officially forbidden. **2** Brit. a part of the year when a particular sport is not played.

ORIGIN – from Old French *clore*, from Latin *claudere*.

closed > *adjective* **1** not open or allowing access; shut. **2** not communicating with or influenced by others.

IDIOMS – **behind closed doors** taking place secretly. **a closed book** a subject or person about which one knows nothing.

COMBINATIONS – **closed-circuit television** a television system in which the video signals are transmitted from one or more cameras by cable to a restricted set of monitors. **closed shop** a place of work where all employees must belong to an agreed trade union.

closet > *noun* **1** chiefly N. Amer. a tall cupboard or wardrobe. **2** a small room. **3** archaic a toilet. **4** (**the closet**) (especially with reference to homosexuality) a state of secrecy or concealment. **5** (before another noun) secret; covert: *a closet socialist*. > *verb* (**closeted**, **closeting**) **1** shut away in private conference or study. **2** (**closeted**) keeping the fact of being homosexual secret.

ORIGIN – Old French, from *clos* 'close'.

close-up > *noun* a photograph or film sequence taken at close range and showing the subject on a large scale.

clostridium /kloˈstriddiəm/ > *noun* (pl. **clostridia**) Biology a bacterium which causes diseases such as tetanus and botulism.

ORIGIN – from Greek *klōstēr* 'spindle'.

closure > *noun* **1** an act or process of closing something. **2** a device that closes or seals something. **3** (in a legislative assembly) a procedure for ending a debate and taking a vote.

clot > *noun* **1** a thick mass of coagulated liquid, especially blood, or of material stuck together. **2** Brit. informal a foolish or clumsy person. > *verb* (**clotted**, **clotting**) form or cause to form into clots.

COMBINATIONS – **clotted cream** chiefly Brit. thick cream obtained by heating milk slowly and then allowing it to cool while the cream content rises to the top in coagulated lumps. **clotting factor** a substance in the blood which is involved in the clotting process, such as factor VIII.

cloth > *noun* (pl. **cloths**) **1** woven, knitted, or felted fabric made from a soft fibre such as wool or cotton. **2** a piece of cloth for a particular purpose. **3** (**the cloth**) the clergy; the clerical profession.

SYNONYMS – **1** fabric, material, stuff, textile.

COMBINATIONS – **cloth cap** Brit. **1** a man's flat woollen cap with a peak. **2** (**cloth-cap**) relating to the working class.

clothe > *verb* (past and past participle **clothed** or archaic or literary **clad**) **1** provide with clothes. **2** (**be clothed in**) be dressed in.

SYNONYMS – **1** attire, dress, garb, outfit.

clothes > *plural noun* items worn to cover the body.

SYNONYMS – attire, clothing, garb, garments; formal apparel.

COMBINATIONS – **clothes horse** a frame on which washed clothes are hung to dry. **clothes line** a rope or wire on which washed clothes are hung to dry. **clothes moth** a small brown moth whose larvae can be destructive to textile fibres. **clothes peg** (also N. Amer. **clothespin**) Brit. a clip or forked device for securing clothes to a clothes line.

clothier /ˈklōthiər/ > *noun* a person who makes or sells clothes or cloth.

clothing > *noun* clothes collectively.

cloud > *noun* **1** a visible mass of condensed watery vapour floating in the atmosphere high above the ground. **2** an indistinct or billowing mass of smoke, dust, or something consisting of numerous particles. **3** an opaque patch within a transparent substance. **4** a burden of gloom or anxiety. > *verb* **1** (usu. **cloud over**) (of the sky) become full of clouds. **2** make or become less clear or transparent. **3** (of someone's face or eyes) become expressive of sadness, anxiety, or anger. **4** make unclear or uncertain.

WORDFINDER – nephology (*study or contemplation of clouds*); *cloud formations:* altocumulus, altostratus, cirrocumulus, cirrostratus, cirrus, cumulonimbus, cumulus, nimbus, stratocumulus, stratus.

IDIOMS – **have one's head in the clouds** be full of idealistic dreams. **on cloud nine** (or **seven**) extremely happy. [ORIGIN – with reference to a ten-part classification of clouds in which 'nine' was next to the highest.] **under a cloud** under suspicion or discredited.

DERIVATIVES – **cloudless** *adjective*.

COMBINATIONS – **cloud cuckoo land** a state of unrealistic or absurdly over-optimistic fantasy. [ORIGIN – translation of Greek *Nephelokokkugia*, the name of a city built by the birds in Aristophanes' comedy *Birds*, from *nephelē* 'cloud' + *kokkux* 'cuckoo'.]

wordpower facts
Cloud

The earliest use of **cloud** is recorded in Old English, in the sense 'a mass of rock; a hill'. It is found in a few place names that make reference to this sense, such as *Thorp Cloud*, the hill at the entrance to Dovedale in Derbyshire. Later it was used in the same sense as **clod** to mean 'a consolidated mass of earth or clay'; indeed **cloud**, **clod**, and **clot** are likely to have come ultimately from the same root. The current sense, 'mass of watery vapour', is first recorded in 1300, in a reference in the medieval work the *Cursor Mundi* to the sun climbing the clouds.

cloudburst > *noun* a sudden violent rainstorm.

cloudy > *adjective* (**cloudier**, **cloudiest**) **1** covered with or characterised by clouds; overcast. **2** not transparent or clear. **3** uncertain; unclear.

DERIVATIVES – **cloudiness** *noun*.

clout > *noun* **1** informal a heavy blow. **2** informal influence or power. **3** archaic a piece of cloth or clothing. > *verb* informal hit hard.

IDIOMS – **ne'er cast a clout till May be out** proverb do not discard your winter clothes until the end of May.

ORIGIN – first used in the sense 'a patch or metal plate'; related to CLEAT and CLOT.

clove[1] > *noun* **1** the dried flower bud of a tropical tree, used as a pungent aromatic spice. **2** (**oil of cloves**) an oil extracted from these buds and used for the relief of dental pain. **3** (also **clove pink** or **clove gillyflower**) a clove-scented pink which is the original type from which the carnation and other double pinks have been bred.

ORIGIN – Old French *clou de girofle* 'nail of gillyflower' (from its shape), GILLYFLOWER being originally the name of the spice and later applied to the similarly scented pink.

clove[2] > *noun* any of the small bulbs making up a compound bulb of garlic, shallot, etc.

clove[3] past of CLEAVE[1].

COMBINATIONS – **clove hitch** a knot by which a rope is secured by passing it twice round a spar or another rope that it crosses at right angles in such a way that both ends pass under the loop of rope at the front. [ORIGIN – *clove*, past tense of CLEAVE[1] (because the rope appears as separate parallel lines at the back of the knot).]

cloven past participle of CLEAVE[1].

COMBINATIONS – **cloven hoof** (also **cloven foot**) the divided hoof or foot of ruminants such as cattle, sheep, goats, antelopes, and deer.

clover > *noun* a herbaceous plant with dense white or deep pink flower heads and leaves which are typically three-lobed.

IDIOMS – **in clover** in ease and luxury.

clown > *noun* **1** a comic entertainer, especially one in a circus, wearing a traditional costume and exaggerated make-up. **2** a playful, extrovert person. > *verb* act comically or playfully.

DERIVATIVES – **clownish** *adjective*.

cloy > *verb* disgust or sicken with an excess of sweetness, richness, or sentiment.

DERIVATIVES – **cloying** *adjective* **cloyingly** *adverb*.

ORIGIN – shortening of obsolete *accloy* 'stop up, choke', from Old French *encloyer* 'drive a nail into'.

club[1] > *noun* **1** an association dedicated to a particular interest or activity. **2** an organisation offering members social amenities, meals, and temporary residence. **3** a nightclub with dance music. > *verb* (**clubbed**, **clubbing**) **1** (**club together**) combine with others to do something, especially to collect a sum of money. **2** informal go out to nightclubs.

DERIVATIVES – **clubber** *noun*.

SYNONYMS – *noun* **1** association, guild, order, society. *verb* **1** (**club together**) band together, join forces, join together, pool resources, team up.

COMBINATIONS – **club class** Brit. the intermediate class of seating on an aircraft, designed especially for business travellers. **clubhouse** a building having a bar and other facilities for the members of a club. **club sandwich** a sandwich typically of chicken and bacon, tomato, and lettuce layered between three slices of bread.

club² > *noun* **1** a heavy stick with a thick end, used as a weapon. **2** (also **golf club**) a club used to hit the ball in golf, with a heavy wooden or metal head on a slender shaft. **3** (**clubs**) one of the four suits in a conventional pack of playing cards, denoted by a black trefoil. > *verb* (**clubbed**, **clubbing**) beat with a club or similar implement.

COMBINATIONS – **club foot** a deformed foot which is twisted so that the sole cannot be placed flat on the ground. **clubroot** a disease of cabbages, turnips, etc. in which the root becomes swollen and distorted.

ORIGIN – Old Norse; related to **CLUMP**.

clubbable > *adjective* sociable and popular.

DERIVATIVES – **clubbability** *noun*.

cluck > *noun* the characteristic short, guttural sound made by a hen. > *verb* **1** make a cluck. **2** (**cluck over** or **around**) express fussy concern about.

DERIVATIVES – **clucky** *adjective*.

clue > *noun* a fact or piece of evidence serving to reveal a hidden truth or solve a problem. > *verb* (**clues**, **clued**, **clueing**) (**clue in**) informal, chiefly N. Amer. inform (someone) about a particular matter.

IDIOMS – **not have a clue** informal know nothing about something or about how to do something.

SYNONYMS – *noun* hint, indication, lead, pointer, tip-off.

wordpower facts

Clue

The word **clue** began as a variant in spelling of **clew**, which in Old English denoted a round mass or ball, later 'a ball of thread'. In various myths and legends, notably the story of Theseus, the legendary Greek hero who killed the Minotaur, a ball of thread is used to mark a way taken through a labyrinth or maze and to ensure the exit route can be found. From this the word **clue** developed the broader sense, something serving to guide one through a situation of puzzling intricacy, or to reveal a hidden truth.

clued-up (also chiefly N. Amer. **clued-in**) > *adjective* informal well informed about a particular subject.

clueless > *adjective* informal having no knowledge, understanding, or ability.

DERIVATIVES – **cluelessly** *adverb* **cluelessness** *noun*.

clump > *noun* **1** a small group of trees or plants growing closely together. **2** a compacted mass or lump of something. **3** another term for **CLOMP**. > *verb* **1** form into a clump or mass. **2** another term for **CLOMP**.

SYNONYMS – *noun* **1** cluster, thicket. **2** clod, lump, mass.

ORIGIN – first denoting a heap or lump; related to **CLUB²**.

clumpy > *adjective* (**clumpier**, **clumpiest**) **1** (also **clompy**) (of shoes or boots) heavy and inelegant. **2** forming clumps.

clumsy > *adjective* (**clumsier**, **clumsiest**) **1** awkward in movement or performance. **2** difficult to use; unwieldy. **3** tactless.

DERIVATIVES – **clumsily** *adverb* **clumsiness** *noun*.

SYNONYMS – **1** awkward, fumbling, maladroit, ungainly, ungraceful.

ANTONYMS – **1** adroit, graceful.

ORIGIN – from obsolete *clumse* 'make or be numb', probably of Scandinavian origin.

clung past and past participle of **CLING**.

Cluniac /kloōniak/ > *noun* a monk of a reformed Benedictine monastic order founded at Cluny in eastern France.

clunk > *noun* a dull, heavy sound such as that made by thick pieces of metal striking together. > *verb* move with or make a clunk.

cluster > *noun* a group of similar things positioned or occurring closely together. > *verb* form a cluster.

SYNONYMS – *noun* agglomeration, bunch, clump, collection, group. *verb* assemble, congregate, crowd, flock, gather, press.

COMBINATIONS – **cluster bomb** a bomb which releases a number of projectiles on impact.

clutch¹ > *verb* grasp tightly. > *noun* **1** a tight grasp. **2** (**clutches**) power; control. **3** a mechanism for connecting and disconnecting the engine and the transmission system in a vehicle.

SYNONYMS – *verb* clasp, cling to, grasp, hang on to, hold.

COMBINATIONS – **clutch bag** a slim, flat handbag without handles or a strap.

ORIGIN – first used in the sense 'bend, crook': variant of obsolete *clitch* 'close the hand'.

clutch² > *noun* **1** a group of eggs fertilised at the same time and laid in a single session. **2** a brood of chicks. **3** a small group of people or things.

ORIGIN – Old Norse.

clutter > *noun* **1** things lying about untidily. **2** an untidy state. > *verb* cover or fill with clutter.

SYNONYMS – *noun* **1** jumble, litter, mess. **2** chaos, confusion, disarray, disorder, mess, muddle. *verb* disarray, disorder, jumble, litter, strew with.

Cm > *symbol* the chemical element curium.

cm > *abbreviation* centimetre or centimetres.

CMG > *abbreviation* (in the UK) Companion of the Order of St Michael and St George.

CMV > *abbreviation* cytomegalovirus.

CNAA > *abbreviation* Council for National Academic Awards.

CND > *abbreviation* Campaign for Nuclear Disarmament.

CO > *abbreviation* **1** Colorado. **2** Commanding Officer.

Co > *symbol* the chemical element cobalt.

Co. > *abbreviation* **1** company. **2** county.

c/o > *abbreviation* care of.

co- > *prefix* **1** (forming nouns) joint; mutual; common: *co-driver*. **2** (forming adjectives) jointly; mutually: *coequal*. **3** (forming verbs) together with another or others: *co-produce*.

ORIGIN – Latin, variant of **COM-**.

coach¹ > *noun* **1** chiefly Brit. a comfortably equipped single-decker bus used for longer journeys. **2** a railway carriage. **3** a closed horse-drawn carriage. > *verb* travel or convey by coach.

COMBINATIONS – **coach-built** Brit. (of a vehicle) having specially or individually built bodywork. **coach house** a building formerly used for the storage of coaches. **coaching inn** historical an inn along a route followed by horse-drawn coaches, at which horses could be changed. **coachwork** the bodywork of a road or railway vehicle.

ORIGIN – French *coche*, from Hungarian *kocsi szekér* 'wagon from *Kocs*', a town in Hungary.

coach² > *noun* **1** an instructor or trainer in sport. **2** a tutor who gives private or specialised teaching. > *verb* train or teach as a coach.

SYNONYMS – *verb* drill, guide, instruct, teach, train.

ORIGIN – from **COACH¹**, originally as 18th-century university slang: the connection between the words is the idea of a student being 'conveyed' through an examination by a tutor as if riding in a coach.

coagulant /kōagyoolənt/ > *noun* a substance that causes coagulation.

coagulate /kōagyoolayt/ > *verb* (of a fluid, especially blood) change to a solid or semi-solid state.

DERIVATIVES – **coagulable** *adjective* **coagulation** *noun* **coagulative** *adjective* **coagulator** *noun*.

SYNONYMS – cake, clot, congeal, dry, set.

ORIGIN – Latin *coagulare* 'curdle'.

coal > *noun* **1** a combustible black rock

consisting mainly of carbonised plant matter and used as fuel. **2 Brit.** a piece of coal. > *verb* provide with or extract coal.

WORDFINDER – anthracite, bituminous coal, lignite (*kinds of coal*), Carboniferous (*geological period when many coal deposits were laid down*), coke (*fuel made by heating coal to remove volatile components*).

IDIOMS – **coals to Newcastle** something supplied to a place where it is already plentiful. **haul over the coals** reprimand severely.

DERIVATIVES – **coaly** *adjective*.

COMBINATIONS – **coalfish** a North Atlantic food fish of the cod family. Also called SAITHE. **coal gas** a mixture of gases obtained by distilling coal and formerly used for lighting and heating. **coal tar** a thick black liquid distilled from coal, containing organic chemicals including benzene, naphthalene, phenols, and aniline. **coal tit** (also **cole tit**) a small titmouse with a grey back, black cap and throat, and white cheeks.

coalesce /kōəless/ > *verb* come or bring together to form one mass or whole.

DERIVATIVES – **coalescence** *noun* **coalescent** *adjective*.

SYNONYMS – amalgamate, combine, join, merge, unite.

ORIGIN – Latin *coalescere*, from *co-* + *alescere* 'grow up'.

coalface > *noun* an exposed surface of coal in a mine.

IDIOMS – **at the coalface** engaged in work at an active rather than theoretical level in a particular field.

coalfield > *noun* an extensive area containing a number of underground coal strata.

coalition /kōəlish'n/ > *noun* a temporary alliance, especially of political parties forming a government.

DERIVATIVES – **coalitionist** *noun*.

ORIGIN – Latin, from *coalescere*, from *co-* + *alescere* 'grow up'.

coarse > *adjective* **1** rough or harsh in texture. **2** consisting of large grains or particles; unrefined. **3** (of a person's features) not elegantly formed or proportioned. **4** (of a person or their speech) rude or vulgar. **5 Brit.** relating to the sport of angling for coarse fish.

DERIVATIVES – **coarsely** *adverb* **coarseness** *noun*.

SYNONYMS – **1** bristly, harsh, prickly, rough. **4** crude, rude, uncouth, unrefined, vulgar.

ANTONYMS – **1** fine, soft. **4** polite, refined.

COMBINATIONS – **coarse fish Brit.** any freshwater fish other than salmon and trout.

coarsen > *verb* make or become coarse.

coast > *noun* **1** land adjoining or near the sea. **2** the easy movement of a vehicle without

the use of power. > *verb* **1** move easily without using power. **2** make progress without much effort. **3** sail along the coast.

WORDFINDER – littoral (*relating to the coast or shore*).

IDIOMS – **the coast is clear** there is no danger of being observed or caught.

DERIVATIVES – **coastal** *adjective*.

SYNONYMS – *noun* **1** coastline, seaside, shore. *verb* **1** cruise, freewheel, glide, sail.

> ## wordpower facts
> ### Coast
> The word **coast** comes through Old French *coste* from Latin *costa* 'rib, flank, side'. This is the source of a number of English words, such as **accost** (which originally meant 'lie or go alongside'), the technical term **costal** (meaning 'relating to the ribs'), and **cutlet** (from French *côtelette*, earlier *costelette*). **Coast** originally meant 'side of the body'; its main modern sense arose from the phrase *coast of the sea* 'side of the sea'.

coaster > *noun* **1** a ship carrying cargo along the coast from port to port. **2** a small mat for a glass. **3 N. Amer.** a toboggan.

coastguard > *noun* an organisation or person that keeps watch over coastal waters to assist people or ships in danger and to prevent smuggling.

coastline > *noun* a length of coast, with reference to its shape or character: *a rugged coastline*.

coat > *noun* **1** a full-length outer garment with sleeves. **2** an animal's covering of fur or hair. **3** an enclosing or covering layer or structure. **4** a single application of paint or similar material. > *verb* provide with or form a layer or covering.

SYNONYMS – *noun* **2** fur, hair, hide, pelt. *verb* cover, encrust, mantle, overlay, plaster.

COMBINATIONS – **coat dress** a woman's tailored dress that resembles a coat. **coat of arms** the distinctive heraldic bearings or shield of a person, family, corporation, or country. **coat of mail** historical a jacket composed of metal rings or plates, serving as armour.

ORIGIN – Old French *cote*.

coati /kōaati/ > *noun* (pl. **coatis**) a raccoon-like animal of Central and South America, with a long snout and a ringed tail.

ORIGIN – Spanish and Portuguese, from a Tupi word incorporating elements meaning 'belt' and 'nose'.

coating > *noun* a thin layer or covering of something.

coat-tail > *noun* each of the flaps formed by the back of a tailcoat.

IDIOMS – **on someone's coat-tails** undeservedly benefiting from another's success.

coax /kōks/ > *verb* **1** persuade gradually or by use of flattery to do something. **2** manipulate carefully into a particular situation or position.

SYNONYMS – **1** cajole, persuade, prevail on, talk into.

ORIGIN – first used in the sense 'pet, fondle': from obsolete *cokes* 'simpleton'.

coaxial /kōaksiəl/ > *adjective* **1** having a common axis. **2** (of a cable or line) transmitting by means of two concentric conductors separated by an insulator.

DERIVATIVES – **coaxially** *adverb*.

cob > *noun* **1 Brit.** a loaf of bread. **2** a corncob. **3** (also **cobnut**) a hazelnut or filbert. **4** a powerfully built, short-legged horse. **5** a male swan. **6** a roundish lump of coal.

ORIGIN – first denoting a strong man or leader: of unknown origin.

cobalt /kōbawlt/ > *noun* a hard silvery-white metallic chemical element with magnetic properties, used in alloys.

COMBINATIONS – **cobalt blue** a deep blue pigment containing cobalt and aluminium oxides.

ORIGIN – German *Kobalt* 'imp, demon' (from the belief that cobalt was harmful to the ores with which it occurred).

cobber > *noun* **Austral./NZ informal** a companion or friend.

ORIGIN – perhaps related to English dialect *cob* 'take a liking to'.

cobble¹ > *noun* (also **cobblestone**) a small round stone used to cover road surfaces.

DERIVATIVES – **cobbled** *adjective*.

ORIGIN – from COB.

cobble² > *verb* **1** (**cobble together**) roughly assemble from available parts or elements. **2** dated repair (shoes).

SYNONYMS – **1** (**cobble together**) contrive, knock up, patch together, rig up.

cobbler > *noun* **1** a person whose job is mending shoes. **2 chiefly N. Amer.** a fruit pie with a rich, cake-like crust. **3** (**cobblers**) **Brit.** informal nonsense. [ORIGIN – from rhyming slang *cobbler's awls* 'balls'.]

IDIOMS – **let the cobbler stick to his last** proverb people should only concern themselves with things they know something about.

cobra /kōbrə/ > *noun* a highly poisonous snake that spreads the skin of its neck into a hood when disturbed.

ORIGIN – from Portuguese *cobra de capello* 'snake with hood'.

cobweb > *noun* a spider's web, especially an old or dusty one.

DERIVATIVES – **cobwebbed** *adjective* **cobwebby** *adjective*.

ORIGIN – first as *coppeweb*, from obsolete *coppe* 'spider'.

coca /kōkə/ > *noun* a tropical American shrub, the leaves of which are a source of cocaine.

ORIGIN – Spanish, from an American Indian word.

cocaine /kōkayn/ > *noun* an addictive drug derived from coca or prepared synthetically, used as an illegal stimulant and sometimes medicinally as a local anaesthetic.

coccus /kokkəss/ > *noun* (pl. **cocci** /kokk(s)ī/) Biology any spherical or roughly spherical bacterium.

DERIVATIVES – **coccal** *adjective* **coccoid** *adjective*.

ORIGIN – first denoting a scale insect: from Greek *kokkos* 'berry'; related to COCHINEAL.

coccyx /koksiks/ > *noun* (pl. **coccyges** /koksijeez/ or **coccyxes**) a small triangular bone at the base of the spinal column in humans and some apes, formed of fused vestigial vertebrae.

DERIVATIVES – **coccygeal** /koksijiəl/ *adjective*.

ORIGIN – Greek *kokkux* 'cuckoo' (because the shape of the human bone resembles the cuckoo's bill).

cochineal /kochineel/ > *noun* a scarlet dye used for colouring food, made from the crushed dried bodies of female scale insects.

ORIGIN – French *cochenille* or Spanish *cochinilla*, from Latin *coccinus* 'scarlet', from Greek *kokkos* 'berry': see box at VERMILION.

cochlea /kokliə/ > *noun* (pl. **cochleae** /kokli-ee/) the spiral cavity of the inner ear, containing an organ which produces nerve impulses in response to sound vibrations.

DERIVATIVES – **cochlear** *adjective*.

ORIGIN – Latin, 'snail shell or screw'.

cock > *noun* 1 a male bird, especially of a domestic fowl. 2 vulgar slang a man's penis. 3 Brit. informal nonsense. 4 a firing lever in a gun which can be raised to be released by the trigger. 5 a stopcock. > *verb* 1 tilt or bend (something) in a particular direction. 2 raise the cock of (a gun) to make it ready for firing. 3 (**cock up**) Brit. informal spoil or ruin.

IDIOMS – **cock one's ear** (of a dog) raise its ears to an erect position.

COMBINATIONS – **cock-a-doodle-doo** used to represent the sound made by a cock when it crows. **cock and bull story** informal a ridiculous and implausible story. **cockcrow** literary dawn.

ORIGIN – Latin *coccus*; reinforced by Old French *coq*.

cockabully /kokkəbŏolli/ > *noun* (pl. **cockabullies**) NZ a small blunt-nosed freshwater fish.

ORIGIN – Maori.

cockade /kokayd/ > *noun* a rosette or knot of ribbons worn in a hat as a badge of office or as part of a livery.

DERIVATIVES – **cockaded** *adjective*.

ORIGIN – French *cocarde*, from obsolete *coquard* 'saucy'.

cock-a-hoop > *adjective* extremely pleased.

ORIGIN – from the phrase *set cock a hoop*, apparently denoting the action of turning on a tap and allowing liquor to flow.

cock-a-leekie > *noun* a soup traditionally made in Scotland with chicken and leeks.

cockatiel /kokkəteel/ > *noun* a slender long-crested Australian parrot, mainly grey with a yellow and orange face.

ORIGIN – Dutch *kaketielje*, probably from *kaketoe* 'cockatoo'.

cockatoo /kokkətŏo/ > *noun* a parrot with an erectile crest.

ORIGIN – Dutch *kaketoe*, from Malay.

cockatrice /kokkətriss/ > *noun* 1 another term for BASILISK (in sense 1). 2 Heraldry a mythical animal depicted as a two-legged dragon with a cock's head.

ORIGIN – Old French *cocatris*, from Latin *calcatrix* 'tracker', translating Greek *ikhneumōn*, from *ikhneuein* 'to track'.

cockchafer /kokchayfər/ > *noun* a large brown flying beetle which is a destructive plant pest.

ORIGIN – from COCK (expressing size) + CHAFER.

cockerel > *noun* a young domestic cock.

cocker spaniel > *noun* a small breed of spaniel with a silky coat.

ORIGIN – from COCK, because the dog was bred to flush game birds such as woodcock.

cock-eyed > *adjective* informal 1 crooked or askew; not level. 2 absurd; impractical. 3 having a squint.

cockfighting > *noun* the sport (illegal in the UK and some other countries) of setting two cocks to fight each other.

DERIVATIVES – **cockfight** *noun*.

cockle¹ > *noun* 1 an edible burrowing bivalve mollusc with a strong ribbed shell. 2 (also **cockleshell**) literary a small shallow boat.

IDIOMS – **warm the cockles of one's heart** give one a comforting feeling of contentment.

DERIVATIVES – **cockler** *noun* **cockling** *noun*.

ORIGIN – Old French *coquille* 'shell', from Greek *konkhulion*, from *konkhē* 'conch'.

cockle² > *verb* wrinkle or pucker.

ORIGIN – French *coquiller* 'blister (bread in cooking)', from *coquille* (see COCKLE¹).

cockney /kokni/ > *noun* (pl. **cockneys**) 1 a person from the East End of London, traditionally one born within the sound of Bow Bells. 2 the dialect or accent prevailing in this area.

wordpower facts
Cockney
The word **cockney** entered English in medieval times, when it meant 'a pampered child'; it is possibly related to the obsolete verb **cocker**, meaning 'to indulge, pamper, or mollycoddle'. **Cockney** came to signify a squeamish or feeble person, and then a town-dweller regarded as affected or puny when compared to the hardier inhabitants of the country. The current sense arose in the 17th century. It is apparently not the same word as Middle English *cokeney* 'cock's egg', denoting a small misshapen egg.

cockpit > *noun* 1 a compartment for the pilot and crew in an aircraft or spacecraft. 2 the driver's compartment in a racing car. 3 a place where cockfights are held.

ORIGIN – from COCK + PIT¹: sense 1 derives from an 18th-century nautical use denoting an area in the aft lower deck where wounded sailors were taken.

cockroach > *noun* a beetle-like scavenging insect with long antennae and legs, some kinds of which are household pests.

ORIGIN – Spanish *cucaracha*.

cockscomb > *noun* the crest or comb of a domestic cock.

cocksure > *adjective* presumptuously or arrogantly confident.

DERIVATIVES – **cocksurely** *adverb* **cocksureness** *noun*.

ORIGIN – from archaic *cock* (a euphemism for *God*) + SURE; later associated with COCK.

cocktail > *noun* 1 an alcoholic drink consisting of a spirit mixed with other ingredients, such as fruit juice. 2 (before another noun) associated with cocktail drinking or formal social occasions: *a cocktail dress*. 3 a dish consisting of a medley of small pieces of food: *a prawn cocktail*. 4 a mixture of diverse substances or factors, especially when dangerous or unpleasant.

WORDFINDER – *kinds of cocktail:* Bellini, Buck's fizz, daiquiri, Harvey Wallbanger, margarita, Martini, pina colada, screwdriver, snowball, tequila sunrise, Tom Collins.

wordpower facts

Cocktail

The original use of the word **cocktail** was as an adjective describing a creature with a tail like that of a cock, specifically a horse with a docked tail. Because hunters and carriage horses were generally docked, the word came to refer to a racehorse which was not a thoroughbred, which had a 'cock-tailed' horse in its pedigree. The modern sense of a mixed alcoholic drink is perhaps based on a similar notion, from the idea of an adulterated spirit; it arose in the US in the early 19th century.

cock-up > noun Brit. informal something done badly or inefficiently.

cocky¹ > adjective (**cockier**, **cockiest**) conceited in a bold or cheeky way.

DERIVATIVES – **cockily** adverb **cockiness** noun.

ORIGIN – first used in the sense 'lecherous': from **COCK**.

cocky² > noun (pl. **cockies**) Austral./NZ informal a cockatoo.

cocoa > noun 1 a powder made from roasted and ground cacao seeds. 2 a hot drink made from cocoa powder mixed with milk or water.

COMBINATIONS – **cocoa bean** a cacao seed. **cocoa butter** a fatty substance obtained from cocoa beans, used in making confectionery and cosmetics.

ORIGIN – alteration of **CACAO**.

coco de mer /kōkō də **mair**/ > noun a tall palm tree native to the Seychelles, having an immense nut in a hard woody shell.

ORIGIN – French, 'coco from the sea' (because the tree was first known from nuts found floating in the sea).

coconut* > noun 1 the large brown seed of a tropical palm, consisting of a hard woody husk surrounded by fibre, lined with edible white flesh and containing a clear liquid (**coconut milk**). 2 the edible white flesh of a coconut.

WORDFINDER – coir (fibre from coconut husks), copra (dried coconut kernels).

*SPELLING – no a: coconut; the spelling with a, as in cocoa, is old-fashioned.

COMBINATIONS – **coconut ice** Brit. a sweet made from sugar and desiccated coconut. **coconut shy** Brit. a fairground sideshow where balls are thrown at coconuts in an attempt to knock them off stands.

ORIGIN – from Spanish and Portuguese coco 'grinning face' (because of the appearance of the base of the coconut).

cocoon /kəkōōn/ > noun 1 a silky case spun by the larvae of many insects for protection during the pupal stage. 2 a covering that prevents the corrosion of metal equipment. 3 something that envelops in a protective or comforting way. > verb 1 wrap in a cocoon. 2 N. Amer. retreat from the stressful conditions of public life.

DERIVATIVES – **cocooner** noun.

SYNONYMS – verb 1 insulate, protect, screen, shelter.

ORIGIN – French cocon, from Provençal coucoun 'eggshell, cocoon', from coca 'shell'.

cocotte /kəkot/ > noun (usu. in phrase **en cocotte**) a small casserole in which individual portions of food can be cooked and served.

ORIGIN – French, from Latin cucuma 'cooking container'.

COD > abbreviation cash on delivery.

cod¹ (also **codfish**) > noun (pl. same) a large marine fish with a small barbel on the chin, important as a food fish.

COMBINATIONS – **cod liver oil** oil pressed from the fresh liver of cod, which is rich in vitamins D and A.

cod² Brit. informal > adjective not authentic; fake. > noun a joke or hoax. > verb (**codded**, **codding**) play a joke on.

cod³ > noun Brit. informal, dated nonsense.

ORIGIN – abbreviation of **CODSWALLOP**.

coda /kōdə/ > noun 1 Music the concluding passage of a piece or movement, typically forming an addition to the basic structure. 2 a concluding event, remark, or section.

ORIGIN – Latin cauda 'tail'.

coddle > verb 1 treat in an indulgent or overprotective way. 2 cook (an egg) in water below boiling point.

DERIVATIVES – **coddler** noun.

SYNONYMS – 1 cosset, indulge, mollycoddle, pamper.

code > noun 1 a system of words, figures, or symbols used to represent others, especially for the purposes of secrecy. 2 a set of conventions governing behaviour. 3 a systematic collection of laws or statutes: the penal code. 4 a sequence of numbers dialled to connect a telephone line with another exchange. 5 Computing program instructions. > verb 1 convert into a code. 2 (usu. **coded**) express in an indirect or euphemistic way. 3 assign a code to for purposes of classification or identification. 4 (**code for**) Biochemistry be the genetic code for (an amino acid or protein).

WORDFINDER – cipher (simple kind of code), cryptanalysis (breaking of codes), cryptography, cryptology (art of writing or solving codes), decipher, decrypt (make code intelligible), encipher, encrypt (convert into code).

DERIVATIVES – **coder** noun.

ORIGIN – first denoting a collection of statutes in ancient Rome: from Latin codex 'block of wood' (see **CODEX**).

codeine /kōdeen/ > noun Medicine a sleep-inducing and painkilling drug derived from morphine.

ORIGIN – from Greek kōdeia 'poppy head'.

codependency > noun excessive emotional or psychological reliance on a partner, typically one with an illness or addiction who requires support.

DERIVATIVES – **codependence** noun **codependent** adjective & noun.

codex /kōdeks/ > noun (pl. **codices** /kōdiseez/ or **codexes**) 1 an ancient manuscript text in book form. 2 an official list of medicines, chemicals, etc.

ORIGIN – Latin, 'block of wood'; first used to denote a collection of statutes, later a block split into tablets for writing on, hence a book.

codger > noun informal, derogatory an elderly man.

ORIGIN – perhaps a variant of cadger (see **CADGE**).

codicil /kōdisil, kodisil/ > noun an addition or supplement that explains, modifies, or revokes a will or part of one.

DERIVATIVES – **codicillary** /koddisilləri/ adjective.

ORIGIN – Latin codicillus, from codex 'block of wood' (see **CODEX**).

codify /kōdifī/ > verb (**codifies**, **codified**) organise into a system or code.

DERIVATIVES – **codification** noun **codifier** noun.

codling¹ > noun an immature cod.

codling² > noun a variety of cooking apple having a long tapering shape.

COMBINATIONS – **codling moth** a small greyish moth whose larvae feed on apples.

ORIGIN – perhaps from the surname Codlin, from quer de lion 'lion-heart'.

codpiece > noun a pouch to cover the genitals on a pair of man's breeches, worn in the 15th and 16th centuries.

ORIGIN – from earlier cod 'scrotum'.

codswallop > noun Brit. informal nonsense.

co-ed informal > adjective co-educational. > noun N. Amer. dated a female student at a co-educational institution.

co-education > noun the education of pupils of both sexes together.

DERIVATIVES – **co-educational** adjective.

coefficient /kō-ifish'nt/ > noun 1 Mathematics a quantity placed before and multiplying the variable in an algebraic expression (e.g. 4 in $4x^2$). 2 Physics a multiplier or factor that measures some property.

coelacanth /seeləkanth/ > noun a large bony marine fish with a three-lobed tail fin, known only from fossils until one was found alive in 1938.

ORIGIN – from Greek koilos 'hollow' + akantha 'spine' (because its fins have hollow spines).

coelenterate /seelentərayt/ > noun Zoology a member of a large group of aquatic invertebrate animals (phylum Cnidaria), including jellyfish, corals, and sea anemones, which typically have a tube- or cup-shaped body with a single opening ringed with tentacles.

ORIGIN – from Greek *koilos* 'hollow' + *enteron* 'intestine'.

coeliac /**see**liak/ (US **celiac**) > *adjective* Anatomy & Medicine of or relating to the abdomen.

COMBINATIONS – **coeliac disease** a condition in which the small intestine cannot digest food, caused by a reaction to the protein gluten.

ORIGIN – Greek *koiliakos*, from *koilia* 'belly'.

coelurosaur /si**lyoo**rəsawr/ > *noun* a small slender carnivorous dinosaur with long forelimbs.

ORIGIN – from Greek *koilos* 'hollow' + *oura* 'tail' + *sauros* 'lizard'.

coenzyme > *noun* Biochemistry a non-protein compound that is essential for the functioning of an enzyme.

coequal > *adjective* having the same rank or importance. > *noun* a person or thing equal with another.

DERIVATIVES – **coequality** *noun*.

coerce /kō**erss**/ > *verb* persuade (an unwilling person) to do something by using force or threats.

DERIVATIVES – **coercible** *adjective* **coercion** *noun* **coercive** *adjective*.

SYNONYMS – bully, dragoon, intimidate, pressure, pressurise.

ORIGIN – Latin *coercere* 'restrain'.

coeval /kō**ee**v'l/ > *adjective* having the same age or date of origin; contemporary. > *noun* a person of roughly the same age as oneself; a contemporary.

DERIVATIVES – **coevality** *noun* **coevally** *adverb*.

ORIGIN – Latin *coaevus*, from *co-* 'jointly, in common' + *aevum* 'age'.

coexist > *verb* **1** exist at the same time or in the same place. **2** exist in harmony.

DERIVATIVES – **coexistence** *noun* **coexistent** *adjective*.

coextensive > *adjective* extending over the same area, extent, or time.

C. of E. > *abbreviation* Church of England.

coffee > *noun* **1** a hot drink made from the roasted and ground bean-like seeds of a tropical shrub. **2** the roasted and ground seeds used to make this drink. **3** the shrub yielding these seeds.

WORDFINDER – cappuccino, espresso, latte (*coffee drinks*); arabica, mocha, robusta (*kinds of coffee bean*), caffeine (*stimulant present in coffee*), Tia Maria (*coffee-flavoured liqueur*).

COMBINATIONS – **coffee table** a small, low table. **coffee-table book** a large, lavishly illustrated book.

ORIGIN – Turkish, from Arabic.

coffer > *noun* **1** a small chest for holding valuables. **2** (**coffers**) the funds or financial reserves of an institution. **3** a decorative sunken panel in a ceiling.

COMBINATIONS – **coffered ceiling** a ceiling decorated with a coffer or coffers.

ORIGIN – Old French *coffre* 'chest', from Greek *kophinos* 'basket'.

cofferdam > *noun* a watertight enclosure pumped dry to permit construction work below the waterline, as when building bridges or repairing a ship.

coffin > *noun* a long, narrow box in which a dead body is buried or cremated. > *verb* (**coffined**, **coffining**) place in a coffin.

WORDFINDER – bier (*movable support for coffin*), catafalque (*framework supporting coffin*), hearse (*vehicle carrying coffin*), pall (*cloth spread over coffin*), sarcophagus (*stone coffin*).

ORIGIN – Old French *cofin* 'little basket', from Greek *kophinus* 'basket'.

cog > *noun* **1** a wheel or bar with a series of projections on its edge, which transfers motion by engaging with projections on another wheel or bar. **2** any one of these projections.

DERIVATIVES – **cogged** *adjective*.

cogent /**kō**jənt/ > *adjective* (of an argument or case) clear, logical, and convincing.

DERIVATIVES – **cogency** *noun* **cogently** *adverb*.

SYNONYMS – coherent, convincing, plausible, logical, sound.

ORIGIN – from Latin *cogere* 'compel'.

cogitate /**koj**itayt/ > *verb* formal meditate or reflect.

DERIVATIVES – **cogitation** *noun* **cogitative** *adjective* **cogitator** *noun*.

ORIGIN – Latin *cogitare* 'to consider'.

cognac /**kon**yak/ > *noun* a high-quality brandy distilled in Cognac in western France.

cognate /**kog**nayt/ > *adjective* **1** (of a word) having the same etymological derivation as another (e.g. English *father*, German *Vater*, and Latin *pater*). **2** formal related; connected. > *noun* a cognate word.

ORIGIN – Latin *cognatus*, from *co-* 'together with' + *natus* 'born'.

cognisance /**kog**niz'nss/ (also **cognizance**) > *noun* formal knowledge or awareness.

IDIOMS – **take cognisance of** formal attend to; take account of.

DERIVATIVES – **cognisant** *adjective* **cognise** (also **cognize**) *verb*.

cognition /kog**nish**'n/ > *noun* the mental action or process of acquiring knowledge through thought, experience, and the senses.

DERIVATIVES – **cognitional** *adjective*.

wordpower facts

Cognition

The word **cognition** is from Latin *cognoscere* 'get to know', which is the root of the 'knowing' words **cognitive** and **cognisance** and also of **recognise** and, with a different English form, **acquaint**. **Quaint** also comes from *cognoscere*, via Old French: its original sense was 'wise, clever', also 'ingenious, cunningly devised', hence 'out of the ordinary' and the modern sense 'attractively unusual'. The **cognoscenti** are people who know a lot about a particular subject: this word entered English from Italian, in which it means literally 'people who know'.

cognitive /**kog**nitiv/ > *adjective* of or relating to cognition.

DERIVATIVES – **cognitively** *adverb*.

COMBINATIONS – **cognitive therapy** a type of psychotherapy in which negative patterns of thought about the self and the world are challenged.

cognomen /kog**nō**mən/ > *noun* an extra personal name given to an ancient Roman citizen, functioning rather like a nickname and often passed down from father to son.

ORIGIN – Latin, from *co-* 'together with' + *gnomen* 'name'.

cognoscenti /konyə**shen**ti/ > *plural noun* people who are well informed about a particular subject.

cohabit > *verb* (**cohabited**, **cohabiting**) **1** live together and have a sexual relationship without being married. **2** coexist.

DERIVATIVES – **cohabitant** *noun* **cohabitation** *noun* **cohabitee** *noun* **cohabiter** *noun*.

ORIGIN – Latin *cohabitare*, from *co-* 'together' + *habitare* 'dwell'.

cohere /kō**heer**/ > *verb* **1** hold firmly together; form a whole. **2** (of an argument or theory) be logically consistent.

SYNONYMS – **1** bind, hold together, stick together. **2** be coherent, bear scrutiny, hang together, hold water, make sense.

ORIGIN – Latin *cohaerere*, from *co-* 'together' + *haerere* 'to stick'.

coherent > *adjective* **1** (of an argument or theory) logical and consistent. **2** able to speak clearly and logically. **3** holding together to form a whole. **4** Physics (of light or other waves) having a constant phase relationship.

DERIVATIVES – **coherence** *noun* **coherently** *adverb*.

SYNONYMS – **1** clear, cogent, cohesive, consistent, logical, rational. **2** articulate, fluent, lucid.

ANTONYMS – **1** incoherent. **2** inarticulate, incoherent.

cohesion /kōheezh'n/ > *noun* **1** the action or fact of holding together or forming a united whole. **2** technical the sticking together of particles of the same substance. Compare with ADHESION.

cohesive > *adjective* characterised by or causing cohesion.

DERIVATIVES – **cohesively** *adverb* **cohesiveness** *noun*.

cohort /kōhort/ > *noun* **1** an ancient Roman military unit, comprising six centuries and equal to one tenth of a legion. **2** a number of people banded together or treated as a group. **3** derogatory, chiefly N. Amer. a supporter or companion.

ORIGIN – Latin *cohors* 'yard, retinue'.

coif /koyf/ > *noun* **1** a close-fitting cap worn by nuns under a veil. **2** /kwaaf/ informal, chiefly N. Amer. short for COIFFURE. > *verb* /kwaaf, kwof/ (**coiffed, coiffing**; US also **coifed, coifing**) style or arrange (someone's hair).

ORIGIN – Old French *coife* 'headdress', from Latin *cofia* 'helmet'.

coiffeur /kwaaför/ > *noun* (fem. **coiffeuse** /kwaaföz/) a hairdresser.

ORIGIN – French, from *coiffer* 'arrange the hair'.

coiffure /kwaafyoor/ > *noun* a person's hairstyle.

DERIVATIVES – **coiffured** *adjective*.

coign /koyn/ > *noun* a projecting corner or angle of a wall.

IDIOMS – **coign of vantage** a favourable position for observation or action.

ORIGIN – variant of COIN.

coil¹ > *noun* **1** a length of something wound in a joined sequence of concentric loops. **2** an intrauterine contraceptive device in the form of a coil. **3** an electrical device consisting of a coiled wire, for converting the level of a voltage, producing a magnetic field, or adding inductance to a circuit. > *verb* arrange or form into a coil.

SYNONYMS – *noun* **1** convolution, spiral, turn, twist. *verb* twine, twist, wind.

ORIGIN – Old French *coillir*, from Latin *colligere* 'gather together'.

coil² > *noun* archaic or dialect a confused disturbance.

IDIOMS – **shuffle off this mortal coil** chiefly humorous die. [ORIGIN – from Shakespeare's *Hamlet* (III. i. 67).]

coin > *noun* a flat disc or piece of metal with an official stamp, used as money. > *verb* **1** make (coins) by stamping metal. **2** (often **coin it**) Brit. informal earn (large amounts of money) quickly and easily. **3** invent (a new word or phrase).

WORDFINDER – numismatics (*study or collection of coins*), obverse (*side of coin bearing head or principal design*), reverse (*secondary side of coin*).

IDIOMS – **to coin a phrase** said when introducing a new expression or a variation on a familiar one.

DERIVATIVES – **coiner** *noun*.

---

wordpower facts

Coin

The word **coin** is from Old French *coin* 'wedge, corner, die', from Latin *cuneus* 'wedge'. The original sense was 'cornerstone of a wall or building', later 'angle or wedge': these senses are now spelled **quoin** or occasionally **coign**, and are regarded as separate English words. The modern sense of **coin** developed from the word's use to mean a die for stamping money, and hence a piece of money produced by such a die.

---

coinage > *noun* **1** coins collectively. **2** the action or process of producing coins. **3** a system or type of coins in use. **4** the invention of a new word or phrase. **5** a newly invented word or phrase.

coincide /kō-insīd/ > *verb* **1** occur at the same time or place. **2** correspond in nature; tally. **3** be in agreement.

SYNONYMS – **1** concur, synchronise. **2** agree, correspond, tally.

ORIGIN – Latin *coincidere*, from *co-* 'together with' + *incidere* 'fall upon or into'.

coincidence > *noun* **1** a remarkable incidence of events or circumstances happening at the same time, without any apparent connection. **2** the fact or state of two or more things being the same in nature, or happening at the same time.

SYNONYMS – **1** accident, chance, twist of fate.

coincident > *adjective* **1** occurring together in space or time. **2** in agreement or harmony.

DERIVATIVES – **coincidently** *adverb*.

coincidental > *adjective* **1** resulting from a coincidence; done or happening by chance. **2** happening or existing at the same time.

DERIVATIVES – **coincidentally** *adverb*.

Cointreau /kwuntrō/ > *noun* trademark a colourless orange-flavoured liqueur.

ORIGIN – named after the *Cointreau* family, liqueur producers based in Angers, France.

coir /koyər/ > *noun* fibre from the outer husk of the coconut, used in potting compost and for making ropes and matting.

ORIGIN – from a Dravidian word.

coitus /kōitəss/ > *noun* technical sexual intercourse.

DERIVATIVES – **coital** *adjective*.

ORIGIN – Latin, from *coire* 'go together'.

coitus interruptus /intəruptəss/ > *noun* sexual intercourse in which the penis is withdrawn before ejaculation.

cojones /kəhōnayz/ > *plural noun* informal, chiefly N. Amer. **1** a man's testicles. **2** courage; guts.

ORIGIN – Spanish.

coke¹ > *noun* **1** a solid fuel made by heating coal in the absence of air so that the volatile components are driven off. **2** carbon residue left after the incomplete combustion or distillation of petrol or other fuels. > *verb* convert (coal) into coke.

coke² > *noun* informal term for COCAINE.

Col. > *abbreviation* Colonel.

col > *noun* the lowest point of a ridge or saddle between two peaks; a high mountain pass.

ORIGIN – French, 'neck'.

cola > *noun* **1** a brown carbonated drink flavoured with an extract of cola nuts, or with a similar flavouring. **2** (also **kola**) a small evergreen tree cultivated in the tropics, whose seed (the **cola nut**) contains caffeine.

ORIGIN – Temne (an African language).

colander /kulləndər/ > *noun* a perforated bowl used to strain off liquid from food.

ORIGIN – from Latin *colare* 'to strain'.

colcannon /kolkannən/ > *noun* an Irish and Scottish dish of cabbage and potatoes boiled and mashed together.

ORIGIN – from COLE + perhaps CANNON (it is said that cannonballs were used to pound vegetables such as spinach).

colchicum /kolchikəm/ > *noun* (pl. **colchicums**) **1** a plant of a genus that includes meadow saffron or autumn crocus. **2** the dried corm or seed of meadow saffron, used medicinally.

ORIGIN – from Greek *kolkhikon* 'of Colchis' (an ancient region east of the Black Sea), with allusion to Medea in classical mythology, a woman from Colchis who was a skilled poisoner (meadow saffron is poisonous).

cold > *adjective* **1** of or at a low or relatively low temperature. **2** not feeling or showing emotion or affection; unemotional. **3** objective or starkly realistic. **4** (of a colour) containing blue or grey and giving no impression of warmth. **5** (of a scent or trail) no longer fresh and easy to follow. **6** without preparation or rehearsal; unawares. **7** informal unconscious. > *noun* **1** cold weather or surroundings. **2** a common infection in which the mucous membrane of the nose and throat becomes inflamed, causing running at the nose and sneezing.

WORDFINDER – cryogenics (*branch of physics concerned with producing very low temperatures*), cryosurgery (*surgical use of intense cold*), gelid (*extremely cold*), hypothermia (*dangerously low body temperature*).

IDIOMS – **cold comfort** poor or inadequate consolation. **get cold feet** lose one's nerve. **the cold shoulder** intentional unfriendliness or rejection. **in cold blood** without feeling or mercy.

DERIVATIVES – **coldly** adverb **coldness** noun.

SYNONYMS – adjective **1** chilly, cool, frigid, freezing, glacial, icy. **2** cool, distant, frosty, lukewarm, unemotional, unfriendly.

ANTONYMS – adjective **1** hot. **2** friendly, warm.

COMBINATIONS – **cold-blooded 1** (of animals, e.g. reptiles and fish) having a body whose temperature varies with that of the environment. **2** without emotion; callous. **cold-call** make an unsolicited visit or telephone call to (someone) in an attempt to sell goods or services. **cold chisel** a toughened chisel used for cutting metal. **cold cream** a cream for cleansing and softening the skin. **cold cuts** slices of cold cooked meats. **cold frame** a frame with a glass top in which small plants are grown and protected. **cold fusion** nuclear fusion supposedly occurring at or close to room temperature. **cold-hearted** lacking affection or warmth; unfeeling. **cold sore** an inflamed blister in or near the mouth, caused by infection with the herpes simplex virus. **cold sweat** a state of sweating induced by nervousness or illness. **cold turkey** informal **1** abrupt withdrawal from a drug to which one is addicted. **2** symptoms such as sweating and nausea caused by this. **cold war** a state of hostility between the Soviet bloc countries and the Western powers after the Second World War.

cole > noun chiefly archaic cabbage, kale, or a similar plant.

ORIGIN – Latin *caulis* 'stem, cabbage'; compare with **KALE**.

coleopteran /kollioptərən/ > noun an insect of the order Coleoptera, comprising the beetles.

DERIVATIVES – **coleopterous** adjective.

ORIGIN – from Greek *koleos* 'sheath' + *pteron* 'wing'.

coleslaw > noun a salad dish of shredded raw cabbage and carrots with mayonnaise.

ORIGIN – Dutch *koolsla*, from *kool* 'cabbage' + *sla* 'salad'.

cole tit > noun variant spelling of *coal tit*.

coleus /kōliəss/ > noun a tropical plant with brightly coloured variegated leaves.

ORIGIN – Greek *koleos* 'sheath' (because the stamens are joined, resembling a sheath).

coley /kōli/ > noun (pl. same or **coleys**) a coalfish or saithe.

colic > noun severe pain in the abdomen caused by wind or obstruction in the intestines.

DERIVATIVES – **colicky** adjective.

ORIGIN – Latin *colicus*, from *colon* (see **COLON²**).

coliform /kolliform/ > adjective belonging to a group of rod-shaped bacteria typified by E. coli.

ORIGIN – from Latin *coli* 'of the colon'.

coliseum /kolliseeəm/ (also **colosseum**) > noun (in names) a large theatre, cinema, or stadium.

ORIGIN – from the name of the *Colosseum*, the vast amphitheatre of ancient Rome, from Latin *colosseus* 'gigantic'.

colitis /kəlītiss/ > noun inflammation of the lining of the colon.

collaborate /kəlabbərayt/ > verb **1** work jointly on an activity or project. **2** cooperate traitorously with an enemy.

DERIVATIVES – **collaboration** noun **collaborationist** noun & adjective **collaborative** adjective **collaborator** noun.

SYNONYMS – **1** cooperate, join forces, team up. **2** collude, fraternise.

ORIGIN – Latin *collaborare* 'work together'.

collage /kollaazh/ > noun **1** a form of art in which various materials are arranged and stuck to a backing. **2** a combination or collection of various things.

ORIGIN – French, 'gluing'.

collagen /kolləjən/ > noun the main structural protein found in animal connective tissue, yielding gelatin when boiled.

ORIGIN – French *collagène*, from Greek *kolla* 'glue'.

collapse > verb **1** suddenly fall down or give way. **2** (of a person) fall or slump as a result of physical incapacity. **3** fail suddenly and completely. > noun **1** an instance of a structure collapsing. **2** a sudden failure or breakdown.

SYNONYMS – verb **1** cave in, disintegrate, subside.

ORIGIN – Latin *collabi*, from *labi* 'to slip'.

collapsible > adjective able to be folded down.

collar > noun **1** a band of material around the neck of a shirt or other garment, either upright or turned over. **2** a band put around the neck of a domestic animal. **3** a connecting band or pipe in a piece of machinery. **4** Brit. a piece of meat cut from the neck of an animal, typically rolled up and tied. > verb informal seize or apprehend (someone).

DERIVATIVES – **collared** adjective **collarless** adjective.

COMBINATIONS – **collarbone** either of the pair of bones joining the breastbone to the shoulder blades; the clavicle.

ORIGIN – Latin *collare* 'band for the neck', from *collum* 'neck'.

collate /kəlayt/ > verb **1** collect and combine (texts or information). **2** compare and analyse (two or more sources of information). **3** Printing examine (a book) to make sure the sheets are in the correct order.

DERIVATIVES – **collator** noun.

SYNONYMS – **1** assemble, collect, gather.

ORIGIN – Latin *conferre* 'bring together'.

collateral /kəlattərəl/ > noun **1** something pledged as security for repayment of a loan. **2** a person descended from the same ancestor as another but through a different line. > adjective **1** additional but subordinate; secondary. **2** descended from the same stock but by a different line. **3** situated side by side; parallel.

DERIVATIVES – **collaterally** adverb.

SYNONYMS – **1** guarantee, security, surety.

COMBINATIONS – **collateral damage** inadvertent casualties and destruction in civilian areas caused by military operations.

ORIGIN – Latin *collateralis*, from *latus* 'side'.

collation /kəlaysh'n/ > noun **1** the action of collating. **2** a light informal meal.

colleague > noun a person with whom one works.

SYNONYMS – associate, co-worker, fellow worker, workmate.

ORIGIN – Latin *collega* 'partner in office'.

collect¹ /kəlekt/ > verb **1** bring or gather together. **2** systematically acquire (items of a particular kind) as a hobby. **3** call for and take away; fetch. **4** call for and receive (something) as a right or due. **5** (**collect oneself**) regain control of oneself. **6** Austral./NZ informal collide with. > adverb & adjective N. Amer. (of a telephone call) to be paid for by the person receiving it.

SYNONYMS – **1** accumulate, amass, assemble, gather.

ORIGIN – Latin *colligere* 'gather together'.

collect² /kollekt/ > noun (in church use) a short prayer, especially one assigned to a particular day or season.

ORIGIN – Latin *collecta* 'a gathering', from *colligere* 'gather together'.

collectable (also **collectible**) > adjective **1** worth collecting; of interest to a collector. **2** able to be collected. > noun an item valued and sought by collectors.

DERIVATIVES – **collectability** noun.

collected > adjective **1** calm and unperturbed. **2** (of works) brought together in one volume or edition.

SYNONYMS – **1** calm, composed, cool, self-possessed.

collection > noun **1** the action of collecting. **2** a regular removal of mail for dispatch or of refuse for disposal. **3** an instance of collecting money, as in a church service. **4** a group of things collected or accumulated.

collective > adjective **1** done by or belonging to all the members of a group. **2** taken as a whole; aggregate. > noun an enterprise owned or operated cooperatively.

DERIVATIVES – **collectively** *adverb* **collectivity** *noun*.

SYNONYMS – **1** common, joint, mutual, shared.

COMBINATIONS – **collective bargaining** negotiation of wages and other conditions of employment by an organised body of employees. **collective farm** a jointly operated amalgamation of several smallholdings, especially one owned by the state. **collective noun** a noun that denotes a group of individuals (e.g. *assembly, family*).

collectivism > *noun* **1** the giving of priority to a group over each individual in it. **2** the ownership of land and the means of production by the people or the state.

DERIVATIVES – **collectivise** (also **collectivize**) *verb* **collectivist** *adjective & noun*.

collector > *noun* **1** a person who collects things of a specified type. **2** an official who is responsible for collecting money owed.

WORDFINDER – *collectors:* antiquarian (*collector of ancient objects*), bibliophile (*books*), deltiologist (*postcards*), lepidopterist (*butterflies and moths*), numismatist (*coins*), philatelist (*stamps*), phillumenist (*matchboxes*).

colleen /**koll**een/ > *noun* Irish a girl or young woman.

ORIGIN – Irish *cailín* 'country girl'.

college > *noun* **1** an educational establishment providing higher education or specialised training. **2** (in Britain) any of the independent institutions into which some universities are separated. **3** an organised group of professional people.

COMBINATIONS – **College of Arms** (in the UK) an incorporated body which officially records and grants armorial bearings.

ORIGIN – Latin *collegium* 'partnership', from *collega* 'partner'.

collegial /kə**lee**jət/ > *adjective* **1** relating to a college; collegiate. **2** involving shared responsibility.

collegian /kə**lee**jən/ > *noun* a member of a college.

collegiate /kə**lee**jət/ > *adjective* **1** relating to a college or college students. **2** (of a university) composed of different colleges.

COMBINATIONS – **collegiate church** a church endowed for a chapter of canons but without a bishop's see.

collide > *verb* **1** (**collide with**) hit by accident when moving. **2** come into conflict or opposition.

ORIGIN – Latin *collidere*, from *laedere* 'to strike'.

collie > *noun* (pl. **collies**) a breed of sheepdog with a long, pointed nose and thick long hair.

ORIGIN – perhaps from **COAL** (the breed originally being black).

collier /**koll**iər/ > *noun* chiefly Brit. **1** a coal miner. **2** a ship carrying coal.

colliery > *noun* (pl. **collieries**) a coal mine.

collimate /**koll**imayt/ > *verb* **1** make (rays of light or particles) accurately parallel. **2** align (an optical system) accurately.

DERIVATIVES – **collimation** *noun* **collimator** *noun*.

ORIGIN – from Latin *collimare*, a mistaken reading of *collineare* 'align or aim'.

collinear /kə**linn**iər/ > *adjective* Geometry (of points) lying in the same straight line.

DERIVATIVES – **collinearity** *noun*.

collision > *noun* an instance of colliding.

DERIVATIVES – **collisional** *adjective*.

collocate > *verb* /**koll**əkayt/ (of a word) form a collocation with another. > *noun* /**koll**əkət/ a word that forms a collocation with another.

collocation > *noun* the habitual placing of a particular word next to another word or words, or a group of words so placed.

ORIGIN – Latin, from *collocare* 'place together'.

colloid /**koll**oyd/ > *noun* **1** a homogeneous substance consisting of submicroscopic particles of one substance dispersed in another, as in an emulsion or gel. **2** a gelatinous substance.

DERIVATIVES – **colloidal** *adjective*.

ORIGIN – from Greek *kolla* 'glue'.

collop /**koll**əp/ > *noun* dialect & N. Amer. a slice of meat.

ORIGIN – Scandinavian.

colloquial /kə**lō**kwiəl/ > *adjective* (of language) used in ordinary or familiar conversation; not formal or literary.

DERIVATIVES – **colloquially** *adverb*.

ORIGIN – from Latin *colloquium* 'conversation', from *loqui* 'to talk'.

colloquialism > *noun* a colloquial word or phrase.

colloquium /kə**lō**kwiəm/ > *noun* (pl. **colloquiums** or **colloquia** /kə**lō**kwiə/) an academic conference or seminar.

colloquy /**koll**əkwi/ > *noun* (pl. **colloquies**) **1** a conversation. **2** a gathering for discussion of theological questions.

collude /kə**lōō**d/ > *verb* come to a secret understanding; conspire.

SYNONYMS – connive, conspire, intrigue, plot.

ORIGIN – Latin *colludere* 'have a secret agreement', from *ludere* 'to play'.

collusion > *noun* secret cooperation in order to cheat or deceive others.

DERIVATIVES – **collusive** *adjective*.

SYNONYMS – conspiracy, intrigue, plotting.

collywobbles > *plural noun* informal, chiefly humorous **1** stomach pain or queasiness. **2** intense anxiety.

ORIGIN – formed from **COLIC** and **WOBBLE**.

colobus /**koll**əbəss/ > *noun* (pl. same) a slender leaf-eating African monkey with silky fur.

ORIGIN – from Greek *kolobos* 'curtailed' (with reference to its shortened thumbs).

cologne /kə**lōn**/ > *noun* eau de cologne or similarly scented toilet water.

Colombian /kə**lom**biən/ > *noun* a person from Colombia. > *adjective* relating to Colombia.

colon¹ /**kō**lən/ > *noun* a punctuation mark (:) used to precede a list of items, a quotation, or an expansion or explanation.

ORIGIN – Greek *kōlon* 'limb, clause'.

colon² /**kō**lən/ > *noun* the main part of the large intestine, which passes from the caecum to the rectum.

ORIGIN – Greek *kolon* 'food, meat'.

colón /kolon/ > *noun* (pl. **colones**) the basic monetary unit of Costa Rica and El Salvador, equal to 100 centimos in Costa Rica and 100 centavos in El Salvador.

ORIGIN – from Cristóbal *Colón*, the Spanish name of Christopher Columbus.

colonel /**kön**'l/ > *noun* a rank of officer in the army and in the US air force, above a lieutenant colonel and below a brigadier or brigadier general.

DERIVATIVES – **colonelcy** (pl. **colonelcies**) *noun*.

ORIGIN – from Italian *colonnello* 'column of soldiers'.

colonial > *adjective* **1** relating to or characteristic of a colony or of colonialism. **2** in a style characteristic of the period of the British colonies in America before independence. **3** (of animals or plants) living in colonies. > *noun* a person who lives in a colony.

DERIVATIVES – **colonially** *adverb*.

colonialism > *noun* the practice of occupying another country with settlers and exploiting it economically.

DERIVATIVES – **colonialist** *noun & adjective*.

colonic /kə**lonn**ik/ > *adjective* Anatomy relating to or affecting the colon.

COMBINATIONS – **colonic irrigation** a therapeutic treatment in which water is inserted via the anus to flush out the colon.

colonise (also **colonize**) > *verb* **1** establish a colony in (a place). **2** take over (a place) for one's own use.

DERIVATIVES – **colonisation** *noun* **coloniser** *noun*.

colonist > *noun* an inhabitant of a colony.

colonnade /kollə**nayd**/ > *noun* a row of evenly spaced columns supporting a roof or other structure.

DERIVATIVES – **colonnaded** *adjective*.

ORIGIN – French, from Latin *columna* 'column'.

colonoscopy /kōlə**nos**kəpi/ > *noun* (pl. **colonoscopies**) examination of the colon with a fibre-optic instrument inserted through the anus.

colony > *noun* (pl. **colonies**) **1** a country or area under the control of another country and occupied by settlers from that country. **2** a group of people of one nationality, race, or kind in one place. **3** a community of animals or plants of one kind living close together.

---

wordpower facts

Colony

The word **colony** is from Latin *colonia* 'farm, settlement', from *colere* 'cultivate'. In Roman times a *colonia* was a settlement of veteran soldiers in a hostile or newly conquered country, where they received land and acted as a garrison. The term came to be applied to the place so occupied: among the nine Roman *coloniae* in Britain were London, Bath, Chester, and Lincoln. The root word, *colere* 'cultivate', is the source also of **cult**, **culture**, and **cultivate**.

---

colophon /koll**ə**fən/ > *noun* **1** a publisher's emblem or imprint. **2** historical a statement at the end of a book giving information about its authorship and printing.
ORIGIN – Greek *kolophōn* 'summit or finishing touch'.

color > *noun* & *verb* US spelling of **COLOUR**.

Colorado beetle > *noun* a yellow- and black-striped American beetle whose larvae are highly destructive to potato plants.

coloration (also **colouration**) > *noun* **1** arrangement or scheme of colour; colouring. **2** character or tone, especially of music.

coloratura /kollərə**tyoor**ə/ > *noun* **1** elaborate ornamentation of a vocal melody. **2** a soprano skilled in such singing.
ORIGIN – Italian, 'colouring'.

colossal > *adjective* extremely large.
DERIVATIVES – **colossally** *adverb*.
SYNONYMS – enormous, gigantic, huge, immense, massive.
ANTONYMS – tiny.

colosseum > *noun* variant spelling of **COLISEUM**.

colossus /kə**loss**əss/ > *noun* (pl. **colossi** /kə**loss**ī/ or **colossuses**) a person or thing of enormous size, in particular a statue that is much bigger than life size.
ORIGIN – Latin, from Greek *kolossos*.

colostomy /kə**lost**əmi/ > *noun* (pl. **colostomies**) a surgical operation in which the colon is shortened and the cut end diverted to an opening in the abdominal wall.

ORIGIN – from **COLON**[2] + Greek *stoma* 'mouth'.

colostrum /kə**lost**rəm/ > *noun* the first secretion from the mammary glands after giving birth.
ORIGIN – Latin.

colour (US **color**) > *noun* **1** the property possessed by an object of producing different sensations on the eye as a result of the way it reflects or emits light. **2** one, or any mixture, of the constituents into which light can be separated in a spectrum or rainbow. **3** the use of all colours, not only black and white, in photography or television. **4** pigmentation of the skin as an indication of someone's race. **5** redness of the complexion. **6** interest, excitement, and vitality. **7** (**colours**) chiefly Brit. an item of a particular colour worn for identification, especially by the members of a sports team. **8** (**colours**) the flag of a regiment or ship. > *verb* **1** give a colour to. **2** show embarrassment by becoming red; blush. **3** influence, especially in a negative way; distort.
IDIOMS – **show one's true colours** reveal one's real character or intentions, especially when these are disreputable.
SYNONYMS – *noun* **2** hue, shade, tint. *verb* **1** dye, stain, tint. **2** blush, flush, redden.
COMBINATIONS – **colour-blind** unable to distinguish certain colours. **colour-fast** dyed in colours that will not fade or be washed out. **colour scheme** an arrangement or combination of colours. **colour sergeant** a rank of non-commissioned officer in the Royal Marines, above sergeant and below warrant officer (responsible for carrying one of the regiment's colours in a guard of honour). **colour supplement** Brit. a magazine printed in colour, issued with a newspaper.
ORIGIN – Latin *color*.

colourant (US **colorant**) > *noun* a dye or pigment used to colour something.

colouration > *noun* variant spelling of **COLORATION**.

colour-blind > *adjective* unable to distinguish certain colours.
WORDFINDER – deuteranopia (*insensitivity to green light*), monochromatism (*complete colour blindness*), protanopia (*insensitivity to red light*), tritanopia (*insensitivity to blue light*).
DERIVATIVES – **colour blindness** *noun*.

coloured (US **colored**) > *adjective* **1** having a colour or colours. **2** dated or offensive wholly or partly of non-white descent. **3** S. African of mixed ethnic origin. > *noun* **1** dated or offensive a person who is wholly or partly of non-white descent. **2** S. African an Afrikaans- or English-speaking person of mixed descent. **3** (**coloureds**) clothes, sheets, etc. that are any colour but white.

USAGE – in reference to skin colour **coloured** was the accepted term until the 1960s, when it was superseded by **black**; it is now widely regarded as offensive except in historical contexts. In South Africa, on the other hand, the term is used to refer to people of mixed-race parentage rather than as a synonym for **black**, and in this context is not considered offensive or derogatory.

colourful (US **colorful**) > *adjective* **1** having many or varied colours. **2** lively and exciting; vivid.
DERIVATIVES – **colourfully** *adverb* **colourfulness** *noun*.
SYNONYMS – brilliant, vibrant, vivid.
ANTONYMS – colourless, drab.

colouring (US **coloring**) > *noun* **1** the process or art of applying colour. **2** visual appearance with regard to colour. **3** the natural hues of a person's skin, hair, and eyes. **4** a substance used to colour something, especially food.

colourist (US **colorist**) > *noun* an artist or designer who uses colour in a special or skilful way.

colourless (US **colorless**) > *adjective* **1** without colour. **2** lacking character or interest; dull.
SYNONYMS – drab, dull, grey, monotone.
ANTONYMS – colourful.

colourway (US **colorway**) > *noun* any of a range of combinations of colours in which something is available.

colposcopy /kol**pos**kəpi/ > *noun* surgical examination of the vagina and the cervix of the womb.
ORIGIN – from Greek *kolpos* 'womb'.

colt /kōlt/ > *noun* **1** a young uncastrated male horse, in particular one less than four years old. **2** a member of a junior sports team.

colter > *noun* US spelling of **COULTER**.

coltish > *adjective* energetic but awkward in one's movements or behaviour.

coltsfoot > *noun* a plant with yellow flowers and large leaves.

colubrine /**kol**yoobrīn/ > *adjective* of or resembling a snake.
ORIGIN – Latin *colubrinus*, from *coluber* 'snake'.

columbine /**koll**əmbīn/ > *noun* a plant with long-spurred, typically purplish-blue flowers.
ORIGIN – from Latin *columba* 'dove' (from the supposed resemblance of the flower to a cluster of five doves).

column > *noun* **1** an upright pillar supporting an arch or other structure or standing alone as a monument. **2** a line of people or vehicles moving in the same direction. **3** a vertical division of a page or text. **4** a regular section of a newspaper or magazine on a particular subject or by a particular person. **5** an upright shaft used for controlling a machine.

WORDFINDER – *five orders of classical architecture, with distinctive columns:* Doric, Ionic, Corinthian (*Greek*), Composite, Tuscan (*Roman*); architrave (*beam resting across tops of columns*), capital (*top part of column*), colonnade (*row of columns*), entablature (*upper part of building supported by columns*), peristyle (*row of columns around a space*), pilaster (*rectangular column*), plinth (*slab at base of column*), portico (*roof supported by columns*).

DERIVATIVES – **columnar** *adjective* **columned** *adjective*.

ORIGIN – Latin *columna* 'pillar'.

columnist /kolləm(n)ist/ > *noun* a journalist who writes a column in a newspaper or magazine.

com- (also **co-, col-, con-,** or **cor-**) > *prefix* with; together; jointly; altogether: *combine*.

ORIGIN – from Latin *cum* 'with'.

coma /kōmə/ > *noun* a state of prolonged deep unconsciousness.

ORIGIN – Greek *kōma* 'deep sleep'.

Comanche /kəmanchi/ > *noun* (pl. same or **Comanches**) a member of an American Indian people of the south-western US.

ORIGIN – the Comanches' name for themselves.

comatose /kōmətōz/ > *adjective* **1** of or in a state of coma. **2** humorous extremely tired or lethargic.

comb > *noun* **1** an article with a row of narrow teeth, used for untangling or arranging the hair. **2** a device for separating and dressing textile fibres. **3** the red fleshy crest on the head of a domestic fowl, especially a cock. **4** a honeycomb. > *verb* **1** untangle or arrange (the hair) by drawing a comb through it. **2** prepare (wool, flax, or cotton) for manufacture with a comb. **3** search carefully and systematically.

COMBINATIONS – **comb jelly** a marine animal with a jellyfish-like body bearing rows of fused cilia for propulsion.

combat > *noun* fighting, especially between armed forces. > *verb* (**combated** or **combatted, combating** or **combatting**) **1** take action to reduce or prevent (something bad or undesirable). **2** archaic engage in a fight with.

COMBINATIONS – **combat trousers** loose trousers with large patch pockets halfway down each leg, typically made of hard-wearing cotton.

ORIGIN – from Latin *combattere* 'to fight with'.

combatant /kombətənt/ > *noun* a person or nation engaged in fighting during a war. > *adjective* engaged in fighting during a war.

SYNONYMS – *noun* fighter, soldier, warrior.

combative /kombətiv/ > *adjective* ready or eager to fight or argue.

SYNONYMS – aggressive, antagonistic, belligerent, pugnacious.

ANTONYMS – peaceable, placid.

combe /kōōm/ (also **coomb** or **coombe**) > *noun* Brit. a short valley or hollow on a hillside or coastline.

ORIGIN – Old English, related to **CWM**.

comber /kōmər/ > *noun* **1** a long curling sea wave. **2** a person or machine that combs cotton or wool.

combination > *noun* **1** the action of combining two or more different things. **2** something in which the component elements are individually distinct. **3** a specific sequence of numbers or letters used to open a combination lock. **4** (**combinations**) dated a single undergarment covering the body and legs.

DERIVATIVES – **combinational** *adjective*.

COMBINATIONS – **combination lock** a lock that is opened by rotating a set of marked dials to show a specific sequence of letters or numbers.

combine > *verb* /kəmbīn/ **1** unite or merge to form a whole. **2** do or engage in simultaneously. **3** Chemistry unite to form a compound. > *noun* /kombīn/ a group of people or companies acting together for a commercial purpose.

DERIVATIVES – **combiner** *noun*.

SYNONYMS – *verb* **1** amalgamate, fuse, merge, unite.

COMBINATIONS – **combine harvester** an agricultural machine that reaps, threshes, and cleans a cereal crop in one operation. **combining form** Grammar a form of a word normally used in combination with another element to form a word (e.g. *bio-* 'life' in *biology*).

ORIGIN – Latin *combinare* 'join two by two', from *bini* 'two together'.

combo > *noun* (pl. **combos**) informal **1** a small jazz, rock, or pop band. **2** chiefly N. Amer. a combination.

combust /kəmbust/ > *verb* consume or be consumed by fire.

DERIVATIVES – **combustible** *adjective* & *noun*.

ORIGIN – Latin *comburere* 'burn up'.

combustion > *noun* **1** the process of burning. **2** Chemistry rapid chemical combination with oxygen, involving the production of heat and light.

come > *verb* (past **came**; past participle **come**) **1** move, travel, or reach towards or into a place thought of as near or familiar to the speaker. **2** arrive. **3** occur; happen; take place. **4** occupy or achieve a specified position in space, order, or priority. **5** pass into a specified state, especially one of separation. **6** be sold or available in a specified form. **7** (also **come, come**) said to correct, reassure, or urge on someone. **8** (**coming**) likely to be important or successful in the future: *a coming man.* **9** informal have an orgasm. > *preposition* informal when a specified time is reached or event happens. > *noun* informal semen ejaculated at an orgasm.

IDIOMS – **come about 1** happen; take place. **2** (of a ship) change direction. **come across 1** (also chiefly Brit. **come over** or US **come off**) give a specified impression. **2** meet or find by chance. **3** informal hand over what is wanted. **come back** chiefly N. Amer. reply or respond, especially vigorously. **come by** manage to acquire or obtain. **come down on 1** criticise or punish harshly. **2** reach a decision in favour of (one side or another). **come down to** be dependent on (a factor). **come forward** volunteer for a task or to give evidence. **come from** originate in; have as a source or place of birth. **come in** prove to be: *it came in handy.* **come in for** receive (a negative reaction). **come into** inherit (money or property). **come of 1** result from. **2** be descended from. **come off 1** succeed; be accomplished. **2** fare in a specified way. **come off it** informal said when vigorously expressing disbelief. **come on 1** (of a state or condition) start to arrive or happen. **2** (also **come upon**) meet or find by chance. **3** said to encourage or correct someone or hurry them up. **come on to** informal make sexual advances towards. **come out 1** (of a fact) emerge; become known. **2** declare oneself as being for or against something. **3** acquit oneself or fare in a specified way. **4** (of a photograph) be produced satisfactorily or in a specified way. **5** (of the result of a calculation or measurement) emerge at a specified figure. **6** informal openly declare that one is homosexual. **7** Brit. dated (of a young upper-class woman) make one's debut in society. **come out in** Brit. (of a person's skin) break out in (a rash or a similar condition). **come out with** say in a sudden, rude, or incautious way. **come over 1** (of a feeling) begin to affect. **2** Brit. informal suddenly start to feel a specified way. **come round** chiefly Brit. (chiefly US also **come around**) **1** recover consciousness. **2** be converted to another person's opinion. **3** (of a date or regular occurrence) recur; be imminent again. **come to 1** recover consciousness. **2** (of an expense) reach in total; amount to. **3** (of a ship) come to a stop. **come to pass** chiefly literary happen; occur. **come up 1** (of a situation or problem) occur or present itself. **2** (of a time or event) approach or draw near. **come up with** produce (something), especially when pressured or challenged. **come upon 1** attack by surprise. **2** see *come on* (sense 2). **come what may** no matter what happens. **have it coming (to one)** informal be due for retribution. **not**

know if one is coming or going informal be confused, especially through being very busy.

COMBINATIONS – **come-hither** informal flirtatious or coquettish.

comeback > *noun* **1** a return to prominence or fashionability. **2** informal a quick reply to a critical remark. **3** informal opportunity to seek redress.

comedian > *noun* (fem. **comedienne**) **1** an entertainer whose act is intended to arouse laughter. **2** a comic playwright.

comedown > *noun* informal **1** a loss of status or importance. **2** a feeling of disappointment or depression. **3** a lessening of the sensations generated by a narcotic drug as its effects wear off.

comedy > *noun* (pl. **comedies**) **1** entertainment consisting of jokes and sketches intended to make an audience laugh. **2** a film, play, or programme intended to arouse laughter. **3** a humorous or satirical play in which the characters ultimately triumph over adversity.

WORDFINDER – black comedy, burlesque, farce, satire, slapstick, stand-up, vaudeville (*kinds of comedy*).

DERIVATIVES – **comedic** /kəmeedik/ *adjective*.

COMBINATIONS – **comedy of manners** a play, novel, or film that satirises behaviour in a particular social group.

ORIGIN – Greek *kōmōidia*, based on *kōmos* 'revel' + *aoidos* 'singer'.

comely /kumli/ > *adjective* (**comelier**, **comeliest**) archaic or humorous pleasant to look at; attractive.

DERIVATIVES – **comeliness** *noun*.

ORIGIN – probably shortened from *becomely* 'fitting, becoming'.

come-on > *noun* informal a gesture or remark intended to attract someone sexually.

comestible /kəmestib'l/ formal or humorous > *noun* an item of food. > *adjective* edible.

ORIGIN – Latin *comestibilis*, from *comedere* 'eat up'.

comet /kommit/ > *noun* a celestial object moving around the solar system, consisting of a nucleus of ice and dust and, when near the sun, a diffuse tail.

WORDFINDER – coma (*cloud of gas and dust around comet*), Oort cloud (*reservoir of comets surrounding solar system*), perihelion (*point of closest approach of comet to sun*).

DERIVATIVES – **cometary** *adjective*.

ORIGIN – Greek *komētēs* 'long-haired star'.

comeuppance > *noun* informal a punishment or fate that someone deserves.

comfit /kumfit/ > *noun* archaic a sweet consisting of a nut, seed, or other centre coated in sugar.

ORIGIN – Old French *confit*, from Latin *conficere* 'put together'.

comfort > *noun* **1** a state of physical ease and freedom from pain or constraint. **2** (**comforts**) things that contribute to comfort. **3** consolation for grief or anxiety. > *verb* cause (someone) to feel less unhappy; console.

DERIVATIVES – **comforting** *adjective*.

SYNONYMS – *noun* **1** ease, well-being. **3** consolation, solace.

ANTONYMS – *noun* **1** discomfort, hardship.

COMBINATIONS – **comfort station** N. Amer. euphemistic a public toilet.

ORIGIN – Old French *confort*, from Latin *confortare* 'strengthen'.

comfortable > *adjective* **1** providing or enjoying physical comfort. **2** free from financial worry. **3** (of a victory) with a wide margin.

DERIVATIVES – **comfortably** *adverb*.

comforter > *noun* **1** a person or thing that provides consolation. **2** Brit. a baby's dummy. **3** N. Amer. a warm quilt.

comfrey /kumfri/ > *noun* (pl. **comfreys**) a plant with large hairy leaves and clusters of purplish or white bell-shaped flowers.

ORIGIN – Old French *cumfirie*, from Latin *confervere* 'heal' (referring to the plant's medicinal use).

comfy > *adjective* (**comfier**, **comfiest**) informal comfortable.

DERIVATIVES – **comfily** *adverb* **comfiness** *noun*.

comic > *adjective* **1** causing or meant to cause laughter. **2** relating to or in the style of comedy. > *noun* **1** a comedian. **2** a children's periodical containing comic strips.

SYNONYMS – *adjective* **1** funny, humorous, jocular.

ANTONYMS – *adjective* **1** serious.

COMBINATIONS – **comic opera** an opera that portrays humorous situations and characters, with much spoken dialogue. **comic relief** humorous content in a dramatic or literary work which offsets more serious parts. **comic strip** a sequence of drawings in boxes that tell an entertaining story.

ORIGIN – Greek *kōmikos*, from *kōmos* 'revel'.

comical > *adjective* causing laughter, especially through being ludicrous.

DERIVATIVES – **comically** *adverb*.

comity /kommiti/ > *noun* (pl. **comities**) **1** an association of nations for their mutual benefit. **2** (also **comity of nations**) the mutual recognition by nations of the laws and customs of others. **3** formal polite and considerate behaviour towards others.

ORIGIN – Latin *comitas*, from *comis* 'courteous'.

comma > *noun* **1** a punctuation mark (,) indicating a pause between parts of a sentence or separating items in a list. **2** a butterfly with orange and brown wings and a white comma-shaped mark on the underside of the hindwing.

ORIGIN – Greek *komma* 'piece cut off, short clause'.

command > *verb* **1** give an authoritative order. **2** be in charge of (a military unit). **3** dominate (a strategic position) from a superior height. **4** be in a position to receive (something such as respect). > *noun* **1** an authoritative order. **2** authority, especially over armed forces: *the officer in command*. **3** a group of officers exercising control over a particular group or operation. **4** the ability to use or control something: *his command of English*. **5** Computing an instruction causing a computer to perform one of its basic functions.

SYNONYMS – *verb* **1** direct, instruct, order. *noun* **1** decree, diktat, directive, instruction, order.

COMBINATIONS – **command economy** a planned economy. **Command Paper** (in the UK) a document laid before Parliament by order of the Crown, though in practice by the government. **command performance** a presentation of a play, concert, or film at the request of royalty.

ORIGIN – Latin *commandare*, from *mandare* 'commit, command'.

commandant /kommandant/ > *noun* an officer in charge of a force or institution.

commandeer /kommandeer/ > *verb* **1** officially take possession of (something) for military purposes. **2** seize for one's own purposes.

SYNONYMS – **1** expropriate, requisition.

ORIGIN – Afrikaans *kommandeer*, from Dutch *commanderen* 'command'.

commander > *noun* **1** a person in authority, especially in a military context. **2** a rank of naval officer next below captain. **3** an officer in charge of a Metropolitan Police district in London. **4** a member of a higher class in some orders of knighthood.

COMBINATIONS – **commander-in-chief** (pl. **commanders-in-chief**) an officer in charge of all of the armed forces of a country.

commanding > *adjective* **1** indicating or expressing authority; imposing. **2** possessing or giving superior strength: *a commanding lead*. **3** (of a position or prospect) giving a wide view.

DERIVATIVES – **commandingly** *adverb*.

SYNONYMS – **1** authoritative, imperious, imposing, masterful. **2** dominant, imposing, powerful.

commandment > *noun* an order issued by or in the name of a god, especially any of the **Ten Commandments** (in the Bible), the rules of conduct given by God to Moses on Mount Sinai according to the Book of Exodus.

commando > *noun* (pl. **commandos**) **1** a

soldier specially trained for carrying out raids. **2** a unit of such troops.

COMBINATIONS – **commando knife** a long, slender knife suitable for hand-to-hand combat.

ORIGIN – Portuguese, from *commandar* 'to command'.

comme ci, comme ça /kom see kom saa/ > *adverb* neither very good nor very bad.

ORIGIN – French, 'like this, like that'.

commedia dell'arte /koˈmaydiə dellˈaartay/ > *noun* a kind of improvised comedy popular in Italy in the 16th to 18th centuries, based on stock characters.

ORIGIN – Italian, 'comedy of art'.

comme il faut /kom eel fō/ > *adjective* correct in behaviour or etiquette.

ORIGIN – French, 'as is necessary'.

commemorate* > *verb* honour the memory of as a mark of respect.

DERIVATIVES – **commemoration** *noun* **commemorative** *adjective*.

* SPELLING – the first *m* is double, but not the second: *commemorate*.

ORIGIN – Latin *commemorare* 'bring to remembrance'.

commence > *verb* begin.

SYNONYMS – begin, get under way, start.

ANTONYMS – conclude.

ORIGIN – Old French *commencier*, from Latin *initiare* 'begin'.

commencement > *noun* **1** the beginning of something. **2** N. Amer. a ceremony in which degrees or diplomas are conferred.

SYNONYMS – **1** beginning, inception, outset, start.

commend > *verb* **1** praise formally or officially. **2** present as suitable or good; recommend. **3** (**commend to**) archaic or formal entrust to.

DERIVATIVES – **commendation** *noun* **commendatory** *adjective*.

SYNONYMS – **1** applaud, compliment, congratulate, praise. **2** advocate, endorse, recommend.

ORIGIN – Latin *commendare*, from *mandare* 'commit, entrust'.

commendable > *adjective* deserving praise.

DERIVATIVES – **commendably** *adverb*.

SYNONYMS – admirable, laudable, praiseworthy.

ANTONYMS – reprehensible.

commensal /kəˈmens'l/ > *adjective* Biology relating to an association between two organisms in which one benefits and the other derives neither benefit nor harm.

ORIGIN – Latin *commensalis*, from *com-* 'sharing' + *mensa* 'a table'.

commensurable /kəˈmensʃərəb'l, kəˈmensyoorəb'l/ > *adjective* **1** measurable by the same standard. **2** (**commensurable to**) proportionate to. **3** Mathematics (of

numbers) in a ratio equal to a ratio of integers.

ORIGIN – Latin *commensurabilis*, from *mensurare* 'to measure'.

commensurate /kəˈmensʃərət, kəˈmensyoorət/ > *adjective* corresponding in size or degree; in proportion.

DERIVATIVES – **commensurately** *adverb*.

comment > *noun* **1** a remark expressing an opinion or reaction. **2** discussion, especially of a critical nature, of an issue or event. > *verb* express an opinion or reaction.

ORIGIN – Latin *commentum* 'contrivance, interpretation', from *comminisci* 'devise'.

commentary > *noun* (pl. **commentaries**) **1** the expression of opinions or offering of explanations about an event or situation. **2** a spoken account of a sports match or other event that is broadcast as it happens. **3** a set of explanatory or critical notes on a text.

commentate > *verb* provide a commentary on a sports match or other event.

commentator > *noun* **1** a person who comments on events or texts, especially in the media. **2** a person who provides a commentary on a sports match or other event.

commerce > *noun* **1** the activity of buying and selling, especially on a large scale. **2** dated social dealings between people.

ORIGIN – Latin *commercium* 'trade, trading', from *merx* 'merchandise'.

commercial > *adjective* **1** concerned with or engaged in commerce. **2** making or intended to make a profit. **3** (of television or radio) funded by the revenue from broadcast advertisements. > *noun* a television or radio advertisement.

DERIVATIVES – **commerciality** *noun* **commercially** *adverb*.

SYNONYMS – *adjective* **1** mercantile, merchant, trading.

COMBINATIONS – **commercial traveller** Brit. dated a travelling sales representative.

commercialise (also **commercialize**) > *verb* manage or exploit in a way designed to make a profit.

DERIVATIVES – **commercialisation** *noun*.

commercialism > *noun* emphasis on the maximising of profit.

Commie > *noun* (pl. **Commies**) informal, derogatory a communist.

commingle /kəˈminggg'l/ > *verb* literary mix; blend.

comminuted /ˈkomminyōotid/ > *adjective* **1** technical reduced to minute particles or fragments. **2** Medicine (of a fracture) producing multiple bone splinters.

DERIVATIVES – **comminution** *noun*.

ORIGIN – from Latin *comminuere* 'break into pieces'.

commis chef /ˈkommi shef/ > *noun* a junior chef.

ORIGIN – French, 'deputy chief'.

commiserate /kəˈmizzərayt/ > *verb* express sympathy or pity; sympathise.

DERIVATIVES – **commiseration** *noun*.

ORIGIN – Latin *commiserari*, from *miserari* 'to lament'.

commissar /ˈkommisaar/ > *noun* a Communist official, especially in Soviet Russia or China, responsible for political education.

ORIGIN – Russian *komissar*, from Latin *commissarius* 'person in charge'.

commissariat /kommiˈsairiət/ > *noun* chiefly Military a department for the supply of food and equipment.

commissary /ˈkommissəri/ > *noun* (pl. **commissaries**) **1** a deputy or delegate. **2** N. Amer. a restaurant or food store in a military base or other institution.

commission > *noun* **1** an instruction, command, or duty given to an appointed person or group. **2** an order for something to be produced specially. **3** a group of people given official authority to do something. **4** a sum paid to an agent in a commercial transaction. **5** a warrant conferring the rank of military officer. **6** the action of committing a crime or offence. **7** archaic the authority to perform a task. > *verb* **1** order or authorise the production of. **2** bring into working order. **3** appoint to the rank of military officer.

IDIOMS – **in** (or **out of**) **commission** in (or not in) use or working order.

SYNONYMS – *noun* **1** assignment, mission, task. *verb* **1** appoint, contract, engage.

ORIGIN – Latin, from *committere* 'join, entrust'.

commissionaire /kəˈmishənair/ > *noun* chiefly Brit. a uniformed door attendant at a hotel, theatre, or other building.

ORIGIN – French.

commissioner > *noun* **1** a person appointed by, or as a member of, a commission. **2** a representative of the supreme authority in an area. **3** the head of the Metropolitan Police in London.

COMBINATIONS – **commissioner for oaths** Brit. a solicitor authorised to administer an oath to a person making an affidavit.

commissure /ˈkommisyoor/ > *noun* Anatomy a seam or join, especially between the hemispheres of the brain or the two sides of the spinal cord.

ORIGIN – Latin *commissura* 'junction'.

commit > *verb* (**committed, committing**) **1** carry out or perform (a crime, immoral act, or mistake). **2** pledge to a course, policy, or use. **3** transfer for safekeeping or permanent preservation. **4** send to prison or psychiatric hospital, or for trial in a higher court.

ORIGIN – Latin *committere* 'join, entrust', from *mittere* 'put or send'.

C commitment–communicate

commitment* > *noun* **1** dedication to a cause or policy. **2** a pledge or undertaking. **3** an engagement or obligation that restricts freedom of action.

*SPELLING – there is no double *t*: commit*t*ment.

SYNONYMS – **1** allegiance, dedication, devotion, loyalty. **2** pledge, promise, vow. **3** duty, obligation, responsibility.

committal > *noun* **1** the sending of someone to prison or psychiatric hospital, or for trial. **2** the burial of a corpse.

committed > *adjective* **1** dedicated to a cause, activity, job, etc. **2** in a long-term emotional relationship.

SYNONYMS – **1** devoted, loyal, staunch, steadfast.

committee* /kəmitti/ > *noun* **1** a group of people appointed for a specific function by a larger group. **2** /kommitee/ Law, Brit. a person to whom another person or another person's property is entrusted.

*SPELLING – double *m*, double *t*: commi*tt*ee.

COMBINATIONS – **committee stage** the third of five stages of a bill's progress through Parliament, when it may be debated and amended.

commode > *noun* **1** a piece of furniture containing a concealed chamber pot. **2** a chest of drawers of a decorative type popular in the 18th century.

ORIGIN – French, 'convenient, suitable'.

commodify /kəmoddifī/ > *verb* (**commodifies, commodified**) turn into or treat as a mere commodity.

DERIVATIVES – **commodification** noun.

commodious /kəmōdiəss/ > *adjective* formal roomy and comfortable.

ORIGIN – Latin *commodus* 'convenient'.

commodity /kəmodditi/ > *noun* (pl. **commodities**) **1** a raw material or agricultural product that can be bought and sold. **2** something useful or valuable.

commodore /kommədor/ > *noun* **1** a naval rank above captain and below rear admiral. **2** the president of a yacht club. **3** the senior captain of a shipping line.

ORIGIN – probably from Dutch *komandeur* 'commander'.

common > *adjective* (**commoner, commonest**) **1** occurring, found, or done often; not rare. **2** without special rank or position; ordinary. **3** of the most familiar type. **4** showing a lack of taste and refinement supposedly typical of the lower classes; vulgar. **5** shared by two or more people or things. **6** belonging to or affecting the whole of a community: *common land*. **7** Grammar of or denoting the gender of words which can refer to individuals of either sex (e.g. *teacher*). > *noun* **1** a piece of open land for public use. **2** a form of Christian service used for each of a group of occasions.

IDIOMS – **common or garden** Brit. informal of the usual or ordinary type. **in common** in joint use or possession; shared. **in common with** in the same way as.

DERIVATIVES – **commonness** noun.

SYNONYMS – *adjective* **1–3** normal, ordinary, typical. **4** uncouth, unrefined, vulgar. **6** communal, public.

ANTONYMS – *adjective* **1–3** rare, unusual. **4** refined.

COMBINATIONS – **common denominator 1** Mathematics a common multiple of the denominators of several fractions. **2** a feature shared by all members of a group. **Common Era** the Christian era (used as a neutral term). **common ground** views shared by each of two or more parties. **common law** law derived from custom and judicial precedent rather than statutes. **common-law husband** (or **wife**) **1** a partner in a marriage recognised in some jurisdictions (excluding the UK) as valid by common law, though not brought about by a civil or ecclesiastical ceremony. **2** a partner in a relationship in which a man and woman cohabit for long enough to suggest stability. **common market 1** a group of countries imposing few or no duties on trade with one another and a common tariff on trade with other countries. **2** (**the Common Market**) the European Economic Community or European Union. **common noun** Grammar a noun referring to a class of objects or a concept as opposed to a particular individual. **common room** chiefly Brit. a room in an educational institution for use of students or staff outside teaching hours. **common time** Music a rhythmic pattern in which there are two or four beats in a bar.

ORIGIN – Latin *communis*.

commonality > *noun* (pl. **commonalities**) **1** the sharing of features or attributes. **2** (**the commonality**) another term for COMMONALTY.

commonalty /kommənəlti/ > *noun* (treated as pl.) (**the commonalty**) chiefly historical people without special rank or position.

commoner > *noun* one of the ordinary or common people, as opposed to the aristocracy or to royalty.

commonly > *adverb* very often; frequently.

commonplace > *adjective* not unusual or original; ordinary. > *noun* **1** a usual or ordinary thing. **2** a trite saying or topic; a platitude.

SYNONYMS – *adjective* ordinary, run-of-the-mill, unremarkable.

ANTONYMS – *adjective* unusual.

commons > *plural noun* **1** (**the Commons**) short for HOUSE OF COMMONS. **2** (**the Commons**) historical the common people

regarded as a part of a political system. **3** archaic provisions shared in common; rations.

IDIOMS – **short commons** insufficient allocation of food.

common sense > *noun* good sense and sound judgement in practical matters.

commonsensical > *adjective* possessing or marked by common sense.

commonweal /kommənweel/ > *noun* (**the commonweal**) archaic the welfare of the public.

commonwealth > *noun* **1** an independent state or community, especially a democratic republic. **2** (**the Commonwealth** or in full **the Commonwealth of Nations**) an association consisting of the UK together with states that were previously part of the British Empire, and dependencies. **3** a grouping of states or other bodies. **4** (**the Commonwealth**) the republican period of government in Britain between the execution of Charles I in 1649 and the Restoration of Charles II in 1660. **5** (**the commonwealth**) archaic the general good.

commotion > *noun* a state of confused and noisy disturbance.

SYNONYMS – tumult, turmoil, uproar.

ORIGIN – Latin, from *com-* 'altogether' + *motio* 'motion'.

communal /komyoon'l, kəmyoon'l/ > *adjective* **1** shared or done by all members of a community. **2** (of conflict) between different communities, especially those having different religions or ethnic origins.

DERIVATIVES – **communality** noun **communally** adverb.

SYNONYMS – **1** common, joint, shared.

ORIGIN – Latin *communalis*, from *communis* 'common'.

communard /komyoonaard/ > *noun* **1** a member of a commune. **2** (**Communard**) historical a supporter of the Paris Commune.

commune¹ /komyoon/ > *noun* **1** a group of people living together and sharing possessions and responsibilities. **2** the smallest French territorial division for administrative purposes. **3** (**the Commune** or **the Paris Commune**) the government elected in Paris in 1871, advocating communal organisation of society.

SYNONYMS – **1** collective, cooperative.

commune² /kəmyoon/ > *verb* (**commune with**) share one's intimate thoughts or feelings with.

communicable > *adjective* (especially of a disease) able to be communicated to others.

communicant > *noun* a person who receives Holy Communion.

communicate > *verb* **1** share or exchange information or ideas. **2** pass on, transmit, or convey (something intangible). **3** (of two

186

rooms) have a common connecting door. **4** receive Holy Communion.

DERIVATIVES – **communicator** noun.

SYNONYMS – **2** convey, impart, pass on, relay, transmit.

ORIGIN – Latin *communicare* 'share', from *communis* 'common'.

communication > noun **1** the action of communicating. **2** a letter or message. **3** (**communications**) means of sending or receiving information, such as telephone lines or computers. **4** (**communications**) means of travelling or of transporting goods, such as roads or railways.

IDIOMS – **lines of communications** the connections between an army in the field and its bases.

DERIVATIVES – **communicational** *adjective*.

COMBINATIONS – **communication cord** Brit. a cord or chain which a train passenger may pull in an emergency, causing the train to brake.

communicative > *adjective* willing or eager to talk or impart information.

DERIVATIVES – **communicatively** adverb.

SYNONYMS – expansive, forthcoming, talkative.

communion > noun **1** the sharing or exchanging of intimate thoughts and feelings. **2** (also **Holy Communion**) the service of Christian worship at which bread and wine are consecrated and shared; the Eucharist. **3** an allied group of Christian Churches or communities: *the Anglican communion*.

communiqué /kəmyoonikay/ > noun an official announcement or statement, especially one made to the media.

SYNONYMS – bulletin, press release, statement.

ORIGIN – French, 'communicated'.

communism > noun **1** a system whereby all property is owned by the community and each person contributes and receives according to their ability and needs. **2** a system of this kind derived from Marxism, established in China and formerly in the Soviet Union.

DERIVATIVES – **communist** noun & adjective **communistic** adjective.

communitarianism /kəmyoonitairiəniz'm/ > noun **1** a system of social organisation based on small self-governing communities. **2** an ideology which emphasises the responsibility of the individual to the community and the importance of the family unit.

DERIVATIVES – **communitarian** adjective & noun.

community > noun (pl. **communities**) **1** a group of people living together in one place. **2** (**the community**) the people of an area or country considered collectively;

society. **3** a group of people with a common religion, race, or profession: *the scientific community*. **4** the holding of certain attitudes and interests in common. **5** a group of interdependent plants or animals growing or living together or occupying a specified habitat.

COMBINATIONS – **community care** long-term care for mentally ill, elderly, and disabled people within the community rather than in hospitals or institutions. **community centre** a place providing educational or recreational activities for a neighbourhood. **community charge** (in the UK) a tax levied locally on every adult in a community, replaced in 1993 by the council tax; the poll tax. **community service** socially useful work that an offender is required to do instead of going to prison. **community singing** singing by a large crowd.

commutate /komyootayt/ > verb regulate or reverse the direction of (an alternating electric current), especially to make it a direct current.

commutation > noun **1** the commuting of a judicial sentence. **2** the commutating of an electric current.

commutative /kəmyootətiv/ > adjective Mathematics unchanged in result by interchanging the order of quantities, such that for example $a \times b = b \times a$.

commutator /komyootaytər/ > noun an attachment connected with the armature of a motor or dynamo, through which electrical contact is made and which ensures the current flows as direct current.

commute > verb **1** travel some distance between one's home and place of work on a regular basis. **2** reduce (a judicial sentence, especially a sentence of death) to a less severe one. **3** change (one kind of payment or obligation) for (another).

DERIVATIVES – **commutable** adjective **commuter** noun.

ORIGIN – Latin *commutare*, from *mutare* 'to change'; sense 1 derives from *commutation ticket*, the US term for a season ticket (because the daily fare is commuted to a single payment).

compact¹ > adjective /kəmpakt/ **1** closely packed together. **2** having all the necessary components or features neatly fitted into a small space. > verb /kəmpakt/ exert force on to make more dense; compress. > noun /kompakt/ a small flat case containing face powder, a mirror, and a powder puff.

DERIVATIVES – **compaction** noun **compactly** adverb **compactness** noun **compactor** noun.

SYNONYMS – verb compress, condense, pack down.

COMBINATIONS – **compact disc** a small plastic disc on which music or other digital

information is stored as a pattern of metal-coated pits from which it can be read using laser light reflected off the disc.

ORIGIN – from Latin *compingere* 'fasten together'.

compact² /kompakt/ > noun a formal agreement or contract between two or more parties.

SYNONYMS – accord, arrangement, contract, pact, treaty.

ORIGIN – Latin *compactum*, from *compacisci* 'make a covenant with'.

compadre /kompaadray/ > noun (pl. **compadres**) informal, chiefly N. Amer. a friend or companion.

ORIGIN – Spanish, 'godfather'.

companion > noun **1** a person with whom one spends time or travels. **2** each of a pair of things intended to complement or match each other. **3** (**Companion**) a member of the lowest grade of certain orders of knighthood.

DERIVATIVES – **companionship** noun.

> ## wordpower facts
> ### Companion
> The word **companion** is from Old French *compaignon*, which means 'one who breaks bread with another'. The base of the Old French word is Latin *panis* 'bread', which is the root of **pantry** (from Old French *paneter* 'baker', from Latin *panarius* 'bread seller') and **pastille** (from *pastillus* 'little loaf, lozenge').

companionable > adjective friendly and sociable.

DERIVATIVES – **companionably** adverb.

companionate /kəmpanyənət/ > adjective formal (of a marriage or relationship) between partners or spouses as equal companions.

companionway > noun a set of steps leading from a ship's deck down to a cabin or lower deck.

ORIGIN – from obsolete Dutch *kompanje* 'quarterdeck'.

company > noun (pl. **companies**) **1** a commercial business. **2** companionship, especially of a specified kind: *she is excellent company*. **3** a guest or guests: *we're expecting company*. **4** a number of individuals gathered together. **5** a body of soldiers, especially the smallest subdivision of an infantry battalion. **6** a group of actors, singers, or dancers who perform together.

IDIOMS – **in company with** together with. **keep someone company** spend time with someone to prevent them feeling lonely or bored. **keep company with** associate with habitually.

SYNONYMS – **1** business, concern, corporation, firm.

ORIGIN – Old French *compainie*; related to *compaignon* (see the note at **COMPANION¹**).

comparable /**kom**pərəb'l/ > *adjective* **1** able to be likened to another; similar. **2** of equivalent quality.

DERIVATIVES – **comparability** *noun* **comparably** *adverb*.

NOTE – the correct pronunciation is with the stress on the first syllable rather than the second: **com**parable, not com**par**able.

comparative* /kəm**parr**ətiv/ > *adjective* **1** measured or judged by comparison; relative. **2** involving comparison between two or more subjects or branches of science. **3** Grammar (of an adjective or adverb) expressing a higher degree of a quality, but not the highest possible (e.g. *braver*; *more fiercely*). Contrasted with **POSITIVE** and **SUPERLATIVE**.

*SPELLING – compar*ative*, not *-itive*.

comparatively > *adverb* to a moderate degree as compared to something else; relatively.

comparator /kəm**parr**ətər/ > *noun* **1** a device for comparing something measurable with a reference or standard. **2** something used as a standard for comparison.

compare > *verb* **1** (often **compare to** or **with**) estimate, measure, or note the similarity or dissimilarity between. **2** (**compare to**) point out or describe the resemblances of (something) with; liken to. **3** (usu. **compare with**) be similar to or have a specified relationship with another thing or person.

IDIOMS – **beyond** (or **without**) **compare** surpassing all others of the same kind. **compare notes** exchange ideas or information about a particular subject.

ORIGIN – Latin *comparare*, from *compar* 'like, equal'.

comparison > *noun* **1** the action of comparing. **2** the quality of being similar or equivalent.

IDIOMS – **beyond comparison** surpassing all others; beyond compare.

SYNONYMS – **1** contrast, juxtaposition. **2** comparability, equivalence, likeness, resemblance, similarity.

compartment > *noun* **1** a separate section of a structure or container. **2** a section of a railway carriage.

DERIVATIVES – **compartmental** *adjective* **compartmentally** *adverb*.

ORIGIN – French *compartiment*, from Latin *compartiri* 'divide'.

compartmentalise (also **compartmentalize**) > *verb* divide into categories or sections.

DERIVATIVES – **compartmentalisation** *noun*.

compass > *noun* **1** an instrument containing a magnetised pointer which shows the direction of magnetic north and bearings from it. **2** (also **compasses**) an instrument for drawing circles and arcs and measuring distances between points, consisting of two arms linked by a movable joint. **3** range or scope. > *verb* archaic **1** circle or surround. **2** contrive to accomplish.

ORIGIN – Old French *compas*, from Latin *com-* 'together' + *passus* 'a step or pace'.

compassion > *noun* sympathetic pity and concern for the sufferings or misfortunes of others.

SYNONYMS – concern, pity, sympathy.

ORIGIN – Latin, from *compati* 'suffer with'.

compassionate > *adjective* feeling or showing compassion.

DERIVATIVES – **compassionately** *adverb*.

SYNONYMS – concerned, pitying, sympathetic.

COMBINATIONS – **compassionate leave** leave from work granted in recognition of personal circumstances, especially the death of a close relative.

compatible* > *adjective* **1** able to exist or be used together without problems or conflict. **2** (of two people) able to have a harmonious relationship; well suited. **3** (usu. **compatible with**) consistent or in keeping.

DERIVATIVES – **compatibility** *noun* **compatibly** *adverb*.

*SPELLING – compat*ible*, not *-table*.

SYNONYMS – **2** harmonious, in tune, well suited. **3** consistent, consonant.

ORIGIN – Latin *compatibilis*, from *compati* 'suffer with'.

compatriot /kəm**pat**riət, kəm**pay**triət/ > *noun* a person from the same country; a fellow citizen.

ORIGIN – from Latin *com-* 'together with' + *patriota* 'fellow countryman'.

compeer /kəm**peer**/ > *noun* **1** formal a person of equal rank, status, or ability. **2** archaic a companion or associate.

ORIGIN – Old French *comper*, from Latin *par* 'equal'; rel. to **PEER²**.

compel > *verb* (**compelled**, **compelling**) **1** force or oblige (someone) to do something. **2** bring about by force or pressure.

SYNONYMS – **1** coerce into, force, impel, oblige.

ORIGIN – Latin *compellere*, from *pellere* 'drive'.

compelling > *adjective* **1** powerfully evoking attention or admiration. **2** that must be accepted or agreed with; impossible to disprove.

DERIVATIVES – **compellingly** *adverb*.

SYNONYMS – **1** engrossing, enthralling, gripping, riveting, spellbinding. **2** conclusive, irrefutable.

compendious > *adjective* formal presenting the essential facts in a comprehensive but concise way.

DERIVATIVES – **compendiously** *adverb*.

ORIGIN – Latin *compendiosus* 'advantageous, brief'.

compendium /kəm**pen**diəm/ > *noun* (pl. **compendiums** or **compendia** /kəm**pen**diə/) **1** a collection of concise but detailed information about a particular subject. **2** a collection of similar items.

ORIGIN – Latin, 'profit, saving' (literally 'what is weighed together'), from *compendere* 'weigh together'.

compensate > *verb* **1** give (someone) something to reduce or balance the bad effect of loss, suffering, or injury. **2** (**compensate for**) make up for (something undesirable) by exerting an opposite force or effect.

DERIVATIVES – **compensator** *noun* **compensatory** *adjective*.

SYNONYMS – **1** indemnify, make amends, make restitution, recompense. **2** balance out, counteract, counterbalance, offset.

ORIGIN – Latin *compensare* 'weigh against'.

compensation > *noun* **1** something given to compensate for loss, suffering, or injury. **2** something that compensates for an undesirable state of affairs. **3** the action or process of compensating. **4** chiefly N. Amer. salary or wages.

SYNONYMS – **1** indemnification, recompense, redress, reparations.

compère /**kom**pair/ Brit. > *noun* a person who introduces the acts in a variety show. > *verb* act as a compère for.

ORIGIN – French, 'godfather'.

compete > *verb* strive to gain or win something by defeating or establishing superiority over others.

ORIGIN – Latin *competere*, from *petere* 'aim at, seek'.

competence (also **competency**) > *noun* **1** the quality or extent of being competent. **2** dated an income large enough to live on.

SYNONYMS – adequacy, capability, effectiveness, proficiency.

competent > *adjective* **1** having the necessary ability or knowledge to do something successfully. **2** satisfactory or adequate, rather than outstanding. **3** having legal authority to deal with a particular matter.

DERIVATIVES – **competently** *adverb*.

SYNONYMS – **1** able, adept, capable, proficient.

ORIGIN – from Latin *competere* in the sense 'be fit or proper'.

competition > *noun* **1** the activity of competing against others. **2** an event or contest in which people compete. **3** the person or people with whom one is competing.

SYNONYMS – **2** contest, match, tournament. **3** opponent, opposition, rival.

competitive > *adjective* **1** relating to or characterised by competition. **2** strongly desiring to be more successful than others. **3** as good as or better than others of a comparable nature.

DERIVATIVES – **competitively** *adverb* **competitiveness** *noun*.

competitor > *noun* **1** a person who takes part in a sporting contest. **2** an organisation engaged in commercial or economic competition with others.

compilation > *noun* **1** the action or process of compiling. **2** a thing, especially a book or record, compiled from different sources.

SYNONYMS – **2** anthology, collection, selection.

compile > *verb* **1** produce (a collection) by assembling material from other sources. **2** gather (material) to produce such a collection.

DERIVATIVES – **compiler** *noun*.

ORIGIN – Latin *compilare* 'plunder or plagiarise'.

complacent /kəm**play**sənt/ > *adjective* smug and uncritically satisfied with oneself or one's achievements.

DERIVATIVES – **complacency** (also **complacence**) *noun* **complacently** *adverb*.

USAGE – do not confuse **complacent** with **complaisant**, which means 'willing to please'.

SYNONYMS – pleased with oneself, self-satisfied, smug.

ORIGIN – from Latin *complacere* 'to please'.

complain > *verb* **1** express dissatisfaction or annoyance. **2** (**complain of**) state that one is suffering from (a symptom of illness).

DERIVATIVES – **complainer** *noun*.

SYNONYMS – **1** grumble, moan, protest, whine.

ORIGIN – Latin *complangere* 'bewail', from *plangere* 'to lament'.

complainant > *noun* Law a plaintiff in certain lawsuits.

complaint > *noun* **1** a statement that something is unsatisfactory. **2** the expression of dissatisfaction. **3** a reason for dissatisfaction. **4** an illness or medical condition, especially a relatively minor one.

SYNONYMS – **1-2** grumble, moan, objection, protest. **3** grievance. **4** disease, disorder, illness.

complaisant /kəm**play**z'nt/ > *adjective* willing to please others or to accept their behaviour without protest.

DERIVATIVES – **complaisance** *noun*.

USAGE – do not confuse **complaisant** with **complacent**, which means 'smug and self-satisfied'.

ORIGIN – French, from Latin *complacere* 'to please'.

compleat > *adjective & verb* archaic spelling of COMPLETE.

complected /kəm**plek**tid/ > *adjective* N. Amer. having a specified complexion.

complement > *noun* /**kom**plimənt/ **1** a thing that contributes extra features to something else so as to enhance or improve it. **2** the number or quantity that makes something complete. **3** Grammar a word, phrase, or clause governed by a verb that completes the meaning of the predicate. **4** Geometry the amount by which a given angle is less than 90°. > *verb* /**kom**pliment/ serve as a complement to.

USAGE – do not confuse **complement** with **compliment**, which means 'an expression of praise' or 'politely congratulate'.

ORIGIN – Latin *complementum*, from *complere* 'fill up, fulfil'.

complementarity > *noun* (pl. **complementarities**) a situation in which two or more different things enhance each other or form a balanced whole.

complementary > *adjective* **1** combining so as to form a complete whole or enhance each other. **2** relating to complementary medicine.

COMBINATIONS – **complementary angle** either of two angles whose sum is 90°. **complementary colour** a colour that combined with a given colour makes white or black.

complementary medicine > *noun* medical therapy that falls beyond the scope of scientific medicine but may be used alongside it, e.g. acupuncture and osteopathy. See also ALTERNATIVE MEDICINE.

complete > *adjective* **1** having all the necessary or appropriate parts. **2** having run its full course; finished. **3** to the greatest extent or degree; total. **4** skilled at every aspect of an activity: *the complete footballer.* **5** (**complete with**) having as an additional part or feature. > *verb* **1** finish making or doing. **2** provide with the items necessary to make (something) complete. **3** write the required information on (a form). **4** Brit. conclude the sale of a property.

DERIVATIVES – **completeness** *noun*.

USAGE – on the use of **complete** with *more*, *very*, etc., see the note at UNIQUE.

SYNONYMS – *adjective* **1** entire, full, total, whole. **2** concluded, ended, finished. **3** absolute, total, utter. *verb* **1** conclude, end, finish.

ANTONYMS – *adjective* **1,2** incomplete.

ORIGIN – from Latin *complere* 'fill up, finish, fulfil'.

completely > *adverb* totally; utterly.

SYNONYMS – absolutely, entirely, totally, utterly, wholly.

completion > *noun* **1** the action or state of completing or being completed. **2** Brit. the final stage in the sale of a property, at which point it legally changes ownership.

complex > *adjective* **1** consisting of many different and connected parts. **2** not easy to understand; complicated. > *noun* **1** a group of similar buildings or facilities on the same site. **2** an interlinked system; a network. **3** Psychoanalysis a related group of repressed feelings or ideas which lead to abnormal mental states or behaviour. **4** informal an obsession or preoccupation.

DERIVATIVES – **complexity** *noun* **complexly** *adverb*.

SYNONYMS – *adjective* **2** complicated, convoluted, difficult, intricate, involved.

COMBINATIONS – **complex number** Mathematics a number containing both a real and an imaginary part.

ORIGIN – Latin *complexus*, from *complectere* 'embrace, comprise', later associated with *complexus* 'plaited'.

complexion > *noun* **1** the natural tone and texture of the skin of a person's face. **2** the general aspect or character of something.

DERIVATIVES – **complexioned** *adjective*.

SYNONYMS – **2** angle, perspective, slant.

ORIGIN – Latin, 'combination', from *complectere* 'embrace, comprise'; the term originally denoted physical constitution or temperament determined by the combination of the four bodily humours, hence sense 1 as a visible sign of this.

compliance /kəm**plī**ənss/ > *noun* **1** the action or fact of complying. **2** excessive acquiescence.

SYNONYMS – **1** adherence, conformity, obedience.

compliant > *adjective* **1** tending to be excessively obedient or acquiescent. **2** complying with rules or standards.

DERIVATIVES – **compliantly** *adverb*.

SYNONYMS – **1** amenable, biddable, tractable.

ANTONYMS – recalcitrant.

complicate > *verb* **1** make more intricate or confusing. **2** Medicine introduce complications in (an existing condition).

ORIGIN – Latin *complicare* 'fold together'.

complicated > *adjective* **1** consisting of many interconnecting elements; intricate. **2** involving many confusing aspects.

SYNONYMS – complex, convoluted, intricate, involved.

ANTONYMS – simple, straightforward.

complication > *noun* **1** a circumstance that complicates something; a difficulty. **2** an involved or confused state. **3** Medicine a secondary disease or condition aggravating an already existing one.

complicit /kəm**pliss**it/ > *adjective* involved with others in an unlawful activity.

complicity > *noun* involvement with others in an unlawful activity.

SYNONYMS – abetment, collusion.

ORIGIN – from Old French *complice* 'an associate', from Latin *complicare* 'fold together'.

compliment > *noun* /**kom**plimənt/ **1** an expression of praise or admiration, either in words or by an action. **2** (**compliments**) formal greetings. > *verb* /**kom**pliment/ politely congratulate or praise.

IDIOMS – **return the compliment 1** give a compliment in return for one received. **2** retaliate or respond in kind. **with the compliments of** given without charge by (someone).

USAGE – do not confuse **compliment** with **complement**, which is a verb meaning 'add to in a way which enhances or improves' or a noun denoting something which does that.

complimentary > *adjective* **1** expressing a compliment; praising or approving. **2** given free of charge.

SYNONYMS – **1** appreciative, congratulatory, flattering, laudatory.

compline /**kom**plin/ > *noun* (in the Roman Catholic and High Anglican Church) an evening service.

ORIGIN – from Old French *complie* 'completed', from Latin *complere* 'fill up, finish, fulfil'.

comply /kəm**plī**/ > *verb* (**complies, complied**) (often **comply with**) **1** act in accordance with a wish or command. **2** meet specified standards.

SYNONYMS – abide by, adhere to, conform to, obey, observe.

wordpower facts
Comply
The word **comply** comes via Italian *complire* from Latin *complere* 'fulfil, fill up'. Other words deriving from *complere* include **accomplish**, **complement**, **compliment**, **complete**, and **compline**. The original sense of **comply** was 'fulfil, accomplish', later 'fulfil the requirements of courtesy', hence 'be agreeable, oblige or obey'. **Compliment** developed in a similar way: it entered English from French *compliment*, from Italian *complimento* 'fulfilment of the requirements of courtesy'.

component /kəm**pō**nənt/ > *noun* a part or element of a larger whole. > *adjective* being part of a larger whole.

ORIGIN – from Latin *componere* 'put together'.

comport /kəm**port**/ > *verb* (**comport oneself**) formal conduct oneself; behave.

ORIGIN – Latin *comportare*, from *portare* 'carry, bear'.

comportment > *noun* formal behaviour or bearing.

compose > *verb* **1** create (a work of art, especially music or poetry). **2** constitute or make up (a whole). **3** arrange in an orderly or artistic way. **4** calm or settle (one's features or thoughts). **5** prepare (a text) for printing by setting up the type.

DERIVATIVES – **composed** *adjective* **composedly** *adverb*.

USAGE – for an explanation of the differences between **compose** and **comprise**, see the note at COMPRISE.

ORIGIN – Latin *componere* 'put together'.

composer > *noun* a person who writes music.

composite /**kom**pəzit/ > *adjective* **1** made up of various parts or elements. **2** (**Composite**) relating to a classical order of architecture consisting of elements of the Ionic and Corinthian orders. **3** /**kom**pəzit/ (of a plant) having flower heads consisting of numerous florets, as in a daisy or chrysanthemum. > *noun* **1** a thing made up of several parts or elements. **2** /**kom**pəzīt/ a motion for debate composed of two or more related resolutions.

ORIGIN – from Latin *componere* 'put together'.

composition > *noun* **1** the constitution of something made up from different elements: *the molecular composition of cells*. **2** a work of music, literature, or art. **3** a thing composed of various elements. **4** the action of composing. **5** the artistic arrangement of the parts of a picture.

DERIVATIVES – **compositional** *adjective*.

compositor /kəm**pozz**itər/ > *noun* a person who arranges type for printing or who keys text into a composing machine.

compos mentis /komposs **men**tiss/ > *adjective* having full control of one's mental faculties.

ORIGIN – Latin.

compost > *noun* **1** decayed organic material used as a fertiliser for growing plants. **2** a mixture of compost with loam soil used as a growing medium. > *verb* make into or treat with compost.

ORIGIN – Latin *composita* 'something put together', from *componere* 'compose'.

composure > *noun* the state of being calm and self-controlled.

SYNONYMS – aplomb, poise, self-possession.

compote /**kom**pōt, kom**pot**/ > *noun* fruit preserved or cooked in syrup.

ORIGIN – French, related to COMPOST.

compound¹ > *noun* /**kom**pownd/ **1** a thing composed of two or more separate elements. **2** a substance formed from two or more elements chemically united in fixed proportions. **3** a word made up of two or more existing words. > *adjective* /**kom**pownd/ **1** made up or consisting of several parts or elements. **2** (of interest) payable on both capital and the accumulated interest. Compare with SIMPLE. > *verb* /kəm**pownd**/ **1** make up (a composite whole). **2** make (something bad) worse. **3** mix (ingredients or constituents). **4** Law decline to prosecute (a felony) in exchange for money or other consideration.

DERIVATIVES – **compounder** *noun*.

COMBINATIONS – **compound eye** an eye consisting of an array of numerous small visual units, as found in insects and crustaceans. **compound fracture** an injury in which a broken bone pierces the skin. **compound time** Music musical rhythm or metre in which each beat in a bar is subdivided into three smaller units, so having the value of a dotted note. Compare with *simple time*.

ORIGIN – from Latin *componere* 'put together'.

wordpower facts
Compound
The sense of the verb **compound** 'make (something bad) worse', as in *this compounds their problems*, arose through non-lawyers interpreting the legal phrase **compound a felony** to mean 'aggravate a felony'. Compounding actually refers to the agreement not to prosecute a felony, in return for money or other consideration. The 'incorrect' meaning has become widely used, even by lawyers.

compound² /**kom**pownd/ > *noun* **1** a large open area enclosed by a fence, e.g. around a factory or within a prison. **2** another term for POUND³.

ORIGIN – Malay, 'enclosure, hamlet'.

comprehend /kompri**hend**/ > *verb* **1** grasp mentally; understand. **2** formal include or encompass.

SYNONYMS – **1** assimilate, grasp, understand.

ORIGIN – Latin *comprehendere*, from *prehendere* 'to grasp'.

comprehensible > *adjective* able to be understood; intelligible.

DERIVATIVES – **comprehensibility** *noun*.

SYNONYMS – intelligible, understandable.

ANTONYMS – incomprehensible, opaque.

comprehension > *noun* **1** the action of

understanding. **2** the ability to understand; range of understanding: *the vastness of the universe is beyond our comprehension.*

SYNONYMS – conception, grasp, understanding.

ANTONYMS – incomprehension.

comprehensive > *adjective* **1** including or dealing with all or nearly all aspects of something. **2** Brit. (of a system of secondary education) in which children of all abilities are educated in the same school. **3** (of motor-vehicle insurance) providing cover for most risks. **4** (of a victory or defeat) by a large margin. > *noun* Brit. a comprehensive school.

DERIVATIVES – **comprehensively** *adverb* **comprehensiveness** *noun*.

SYNONYMS – *adjective* **1** all-embracing, inclusive, thorough.

ANTONYMS – *adjective* **1** partial, selective.

compress > *verb* /kəm**press**/ **1** flatten by pressure; force into less space. **2** squeeze or press (two things) together. > *noun* /**kom**press/ a pad of absorbent material pressed on to part of the body to relieve inflammation or stop bleeding.

DERIVATIVES – **compressibility** *noun* **compressible** *adjective* **compressive** *adjective*.

SYNONYMS – *verb* **1** flatten, press, squash, squeeze.

COMBINATIONS – **compressed air** air that is at more than atmospheric pressure.

ORIGIN – Old French *compresser*, from Latin *comprimere* 'press together'.

compression > *noun* **1** the action of compressing or being compressed. **2** the reduction in volume (causing an increase in pressure) of the fuel mixture in an internal-combustion engine before ignition.

DERIVATIVES – **compressional** *adjective*.

compressor > *noun* **1** an instrument or device for compressing something. **2** a machine used to supply air or other gas at increased pressure.

comprise* > *verb* **1** be made up of; consist of. **2** (also **be comprised of**) make up; constitute.

USAGE – traditionally, **comprise** means 'consist of' and should not be used to mean 'constitute or make up'. However, a passive use of **comprise**, formed by analogy with words like **compose**, is now common: this use (as in *the country is comprised of twenty states*) means the same as the traditional active sense (as in *the country comprises twenty states*). The active use of *comprise of*, e.g. in *the property comprises of three bedrooms*, is not standard English.

*****SPELLING – **comprise** cannot be spelled with an *-ize* ending.

ORIGIN – French, 'comprised', from *comprendre* 'comprehend'.

compromise* > *noun* **1** an agreement or settlement reached when each of two opposing parties is prepared to make concessions. **2** an intermediate state between conflicting opinions, reached by mutual concession. > *verb* **1** settle a dispute by mutual concession. **2** expediently accept standards that are lower than is desirable. **3** bring into disrepute or danger by indiscreet or reckless behaviour.

DERIVATIVES – **compromiser** *noun*.

*****SPELLING – unlike most words ending in *-ise*, **compromise** cannot be spelled with an *-ize* ending.

ORIGIN – Old French *compromis*, from Latin *compromittere*, from *promittere* 'promise'.

compromising > *adjective* revealing an embarrassing or incriminating secret.

comptroller /kən**trōl**ər/ > *noun* a controller (used in the title of some financial officers).

ORIGIN – variant of **controller**.

compulsion > *noun* **1** the action or state of compelling or being compelled. **2** an irresistible urge to behave in a certain way.

SYNONYMS – **1** coercion, duress, force, obligation.

compulsive > *adjective* **1** resulting from or acting on an irresistible urge. **2** irresistibly interesting or exciting.

DERIVATIVES – **compulsively** *adverb* **compulsiveness** *noun*.

compulsory > *adjective* required by law or a rule; obligatory.

DERIVATIVES – **compulsorily** *adverb*.

SYNONYMS – mandatory, obligatory.

ANTONYMS – voluntary.

COMBINATIONS – **compulsory purchase** Brit. the officially enforced purchase of privately owned land or property for public use.

compunction > *noun* a feeling of guilt or moral scruple that prevents or follows wrongdoing: *they had no compunction about deceiving him.*

DERIVATIVES – **compunctious** *adjective*.

SYNONYMS – guilt, misgivings, qualms, remorse, scruples.

ORIGIN – Latin, from *compungere* 'prick sharply'.

computation > *noun* **1** mathematical calculation. **2** the use of computers, especially as a subject of research or study.

DERIVATIVES – **computational** *adjective*.

compute > *verb* **1** reckon or calculate (a figure or amount). **2** informal seem reasonable; make sense: *the idea did not compute.*

DERIVATIVES – **computable** *adjective*.

ORIGIN – Latin *computare*, from *putare* 'to settle (an account)'.

computer > *noun* an electronic device capable of storing and processing information in accordance with a predetermined set of instructions.

WORDFINDER – cyberspace (*environment for communication by computer*); *kinds of computer:* desktop, laptop, mainframe, notebook, palmtop, word processor, workstation; *components of a computer:* CPU, disk drive, hard disk, hardware, keyboard, memory, microprocessor, monitor, motherboard, mouse, peripherals, RAM, software, VDU.

COMBINATIONS – **computer-literate** having sufficient knowledge and skill to be able to use computers.

computerate > *adjective* informal another term for **computer-literate**.

computerise (also **computerize**) > *verb* convert to a system or form which is controlled, stored, or processed by computer.

DERIVATIVES – **computerisation** *noun*.

computing > *noun* the use or operation of computers.

comrade > *noun* **1** a companion who shares one's activities or is a fellow member of an organisation. **2** (also **comrade-in-arms**) a fellow soldier. **3** a fellow socialist or communist.

DERIVATIVES – **comradely** *adjective* **comradeship** *noun*.

wordpower facts
Comrade

The word **comrade** comes via French *camarade* from Spanish *camarada* 'roommate', which is ultimately from Latin *camera* 'chamber' (the root of English **camera**). The slang term **chum** arose from a similar idea: it was originally Oxford University slang for a room-mate, and probably derived from *chamber-fellow*. Cambridge University's equivalent of **chum**, **crony**, came, in a suitably learned way, from Greek *khronios* 'long-lasting' (here used to mean 'contemporary'), from *khronos* 'time'.

con[1] informal > *verb* (**conned, conning**) deceive (someone) into doing or believing something by lying. > *noun* a deception of this kind.

ORIGIN – abbreviation of **CONFIDENCE**, as in *confidence trick*.

con[2] > *noun* (usu. in phrase **pros and cons**) a disadvantage of or argument against something.

ORIGIN – from Latin *contra* 'against'.

con[3] > *noun* informal a convict.

con[4] (US also **conn**) > *verb* (**conned, conning**) Nautical direct the steering of (a ship).

ORIGIN – apparently from obsolete *cond* 'conduct, guide', from Old French *conduire*.

con- > *prefix* variant spelling of **COM-** assimilated before *c, d, f, g, j, n, q, s, t, v,* and sometimes before vowels (as in *concord, confide,* etc.).

concatenate /kənkattinayt/ > *verb* formal or technical link together in a chain or series.
DERIVATIVES – **concatenation** noun.
ORIGIN – Latin *concatenare* 'link together'.

concave /konkayv/ > *adjective* having an outline or surface that curves inwards like the interior of a sphere. Compare with **CONVEX**.
DERIVATIVES – **concavity** noun.
ORIGIN – Latin *concavus*, from *cavus* 'hollow'.

conceal > *verb* prevent from being seen or known.
DERIVATIVES – **concealer** noun **concealment** noun.
SYNONYMS – cover up, disguise, hide, secrete.
ANTONYMS – expose.
ORIGIN – Latin *concelare*, from *celare* 'hide'.

concede > *verb* **1** finally admit or agree that something is true. **2** admit defeat; surrender. **3** surrender (a possession, advantage, or right). **4** admit defeat in (a match or contest). **5** fail to prevent an opponent scoring (a goal or point).
SYNONYMS – **1** acknowledge, admit, agree, confess. **2** capitulate, give in, surrender. **3** relinquish, surrender, yield.
ORIGIN – Latin *concedere*, from *cedere* 'yield'.

conceit > *noun* **1** excessive pride in oneself. **2** an elaborate metaphor or artistic effect. **3** a fanciful notion.
ORIGIN – from **CONCEIVE**.

conceited > *adjective* excessively proud of oneself.
SYNONYMS – arrogant, narcissistic, self-regarding, vain.
ANTONYMS – modest.

conceivable > *adjective* capable of being imagined or understood.
DERIVATIVES – **conceivably** adverb.

conceive* > *verb* **1** become pregnant with (a child). **2** devise in the mind; imagine.
***SPELLING** – *i* before *e* except after *c*: conceive.
ORIGIN – Latin *concipere*, from *capere* 'take'.

concentrate > *verb* **1** (often **concentrate on**) focus all one's attention or mental effort on an object or activity. **2** gather together in numbers or a mass at one point. **3** focus on: *the party should concentrate its strategy on developing countries.* **4** increase the strength of (a solution). > *noun* a concentrated substance or solution.
DERIVATIVES – **concentrator** noun.
SYNONYMS – *verb* **2** congregate, converge, mass.
ANTONYMS – *verb* **2** disperse.
ORIGIN – from Latin *con-* 'together' + *centrum* 'centre' or from French *concentrer* 'to concentrate'.

concentration > *noun* **1** the action or power of concentrating. **2** a close gathering of people or things. **3** the relative amount of a particular substance contained within a solution or mixture.
ANTONYMS – **1** inattention.
COMBINATIONS – **concentration camp** a camp for detaining political prisoners, especially in Nazi Germany.

concentric > *adjective* (of circles or arcs) sharing the same centre.
DERIVATIVES – **concentrically** adverb **concentricity** noun.
ORIGIN – Latin *concentricus*, from *con-* 'together' + *centrum* 'centre'.

concept > *noun* **1** an abstract idea. **2** an idea to help sell or publicise a commodity.
SYNONYMS – **1** conception, idea, notion.
ORIGIN – Latin *conceptum* 'something conceived'.

conception > *noun* **1** the action of conceiving a child or of one being conceived. **2** the devising of a plan or idea. **3** a concept. **4** ability to imagine or understand.

conceptual > *adjective* of or relating to mental concepts.
DERIVATIVES – **conceptually** adverb.

conceptualise (also **conceptualize**) > *verb* form a concept of.
DERIVATIVES – **conceptualisation** noun.

concern > *verb* **1** relate to; be about. **2** be relevant to; affect or involve. **3** make anxious or worried. > *noun* **1** worry; anxiety. **2** a matter of interest or importance. **3** a business.
IDIOMS – **have no concern with** have nothing to do with. **to whom it may concern** used to address a reader whose identity is unknown.
SYNONYMS – *noun* **1** anxiety, apprehension, disquiet, unease, worry.
ORIGIN – Latin *concernere*, from *cernere* 'sift, discern'.

concerned > *adjective* worried or anxious.
SYNONYMS – anxious, bothered, disturbed, perturbed, troubled, worried.
ANTONYMS – unconcerned.

concerning > *preposition* about.

concert > *noun* /konsert/ **1** a musical performance given in public, typically of several compositions. **2** formal agreement; harmony. > *verb* /kənsert/ formal arrange by mutual agreement or coordination.
IDIOMS – **in concert 1** acting jointly. **2** giving a live public performance.
COMBINATIONS – **concert performance** Brit. a performance of a piece of music written for an opera or ballet without the accompanying dramatic action. **concert pitch 1** a standard for the tuning of musical instruments, in which the note A above middle C has a frequency of 440 Hz. **2** a state of readiness and keenness.
ORIGIN – Italian *concerto*, from *concertare* 'harmonise'.

concerted > *adjective* **1** jointly arranged or carried out: *a concerted campaign.* **2** using exertion: *a concerted effort.*
SYNONYMS – **1** combined, coordinated, joint, united. **2** energetic, strenuous, vigorous.

concertina /konserteenə/ > *noun* a small musical instrument played by stretching and squeezing a central bellows between the hands to blow air over reeds, each note being sounded by a button. > *verb* (**concertinas, concertinaed** or **concertina'd, concertinaing**) compress in folds like those of a concertina.

concerto /kənchertō/ > *noun* (pl. **concertos** or **concerti**) a musical composition for an orchestra and one or more solo instruments.
ORIGIN – Italian.

concession > *noun* **1** a thing conceded. **2** a reduction in price for a certain category of person. **3** the right to use land or other property for a specified purpose, granted by a government or other controlling body. **4** a commercial operation set up within the premises of a larger concern.
DERIVATIVES – **concessionary** adjective **concessive** adjective.
ORIGIN – Latin, from *concedere* 'concede'.

concessionaire /kənseshənair/ (also **concessionnaire**) > *noun* the holder of a concession or grant, especially for the use of land or trading rights.

conch /kongk, konch/ > *noun* (pl. **conchs** /kongks/ or **conches** /konchiz/) a tropical marine mollusc with a spiral shell.
ORIGIN – Greek *konkhē* 'mussel, cockle, or shell-like cavity'.

conchology /kongkolləji/ > *noun* the scientific study or collection of mollusc shells.
DERIVATIVES – **conchologist** noun.

concierge /konsiairzh/ > *noun* **1** (especially in France) a resident caretaker of a block of flats or small hotel. **2** a hotel employee who assists guests by booking tours, making theatre and restaurant reservations, etc.
ORIGIN – French.

conciliate /kənsilliayt/ > *verb* **1** make calm and content; placate. **2** mediate in a dispute.
DERIVATIVES – **conciliation** noun **conciliator** noun **conciliatory** adjective.
SYNONYMS – **1** appease, assuage, mollify, pacify, placate, soothe.
ORIGIN – Latin *conciliare* 'combine, gain', from *concilium* 'assembly'.

concise > *adjective* giving a lot of information clearly and in few words.

DERIVATIVES – **concisely** *adverb* **conciseness** *noun* **concision** *noun*.

SYNONYMS – compendious, pithy, succinct.

ORIGIN – Latin *concisus* 'cut up, cut down'.

conclave /**kon**klayv/ > *noun* **1** a private meeting. **2** (in the Roman Catholic Church) an assembly of cardinals for the election of a pope.

ORIGIN – Latin, 'lockable room', from *clavis* 'key'.

conclude > *verb* **1** bring or come to an end. **2** arrive at a judgement or opinion by reasoning. **3** formally settle or arrange (a treaty or agreement).

SYNONYMS – **1** end, finish, terminate, wind up. **2** deduce, infer.

ORIGIN – Latin *concludere*, from *claudere* 'to shut'.

conclusion > *noun* **1** an end or finish. **2** the summing-up of an argument or text. **3** a judgement or decision reached by reasoning. **4** the settling of a treaty or agreement.

conclusive > *adjective* decisive or convincing.

DERIVATIVES – **conclusively** *adverb* **conclusiveness** *noun*.

SYNONYMS – decisive, convincing, incontestable, incontrovertible, irrefutable.

concoct /kənˈkokt/ > *verb* **1** make (a dish or meal) by combining ingredients. **2** invent or devise (a story or plan).

DERIVATIVES – **concocter** *noun* **concoction** *noun*.

ORIGIN – Latin *concoquere* 'cook together'.

concomitant /kənˈkommɪtənt/ *formal* > *adjective* naturally accompanying or associated. > *noun* a concomitant phenomenon.

DERIVATIVES – **concomitance** *noun* **concomitantly** *adverb*.

ORIGIN – from Latin *concomitari* 'accompany', from *comes* 'companion'.

concord > *noun* **1** *formal* agreement; harmony. **2** a treaty.

ORIGIN – Latin *concordia*, from *concors* 'of one mind'.

concordance /kənˈkord'ns/ > *noun* **1** an alphabetical list of the important words in a text, usually with citations of the passages concerned. **2** *formal* agreement.

ORIGIN – from Latin *concordare* 'agree on'.

concordant > *adjective* in agreement; consistent.

concordat /kənˈkordat/ > *noun* an agreement or treaty, especially one between the Vatican and a secular state.

concourse > *noun* **1** a large open area inside or in front of a public building. **2** *formal* a crowd of people.

ORIGIN – Latin *concursus*, from *concurrere* 'assemble in crowds'.

concrete > *adjective* **1** existing in a material

or physical form; not abstract. **2** specific; definite: *concrete proof.* > *noun* a building material made from gravel, sand, cement, and water, hardening into a stone-like mass. > *verb* cover or fix solidly with concrete.

DERIVATIVES – **concretely** *adverb* **concreteness** *noun*.

SYNONYMS – *adjective* **1** material, solid, tangible. **2** conclusive, definite, firm, specific.

ANTONYMS – **1** abstract.

COMBINATIONS – **concrete jungle** an urban area with a high density of large, unattractive, modern buildings.

wordpower facts

Concrete

The word **concrete** entered the language in the Middle Ages in the sense 'formed by cohesion, solidified'. It comes from Latin *concrescere* 'grow together'. Another early use was as a grammatical term designating a quality belonging to a substance (usually expressed by an adjective, such as *white* in *white paper*) as opposed to the quality itself (expressed by an abstract noun, such as *whiteness*); later *concrete* came to be used to refer to nouns embodying attributes (e.g. *fool*, *hero*), as opposed to the attributes themselves (e.g. *foolishness*, *heroism*), and this is the basis of its use as the opposite of 'abstract'. The sense 'building material' dates from the 19th century. The base of **concrete** is Latin *crescere* 'grow', which is at the root of **accrete**, **increase**, **decrease**, **excrescence**, **crescendo**, and **crescent**. It is also behind **crew** and **recruit**, both of which originally had the idea of 'reinforcements' or 'supplementary troops'.

concretion > *noun* a hard solid mass formed by accumulation of matter.

concubine /ˈkongkyoobīn/ > *noun* **1** *chiefly historical* (in polygamous societies) a woman who lives with a man but has lower status than his wife or wives. **2** *archaic* a mistress.

ORIGIN – Latin *concubina*, from *con-* 'with' + *cubare* 'to lie'.

concupiscence /kənˈkyoopis'ns/ > *noun* *formal* lust.

DERIVATIVES – **concupiscent** *adjective*.

ORIGIN – Latin *concupiscentia*, from *concupiscere* 'begin to desire'.

concur* /kənˈkur/ > *verb* (**concurred**, **concurring**) **1** (often **concur with**) agree. **2** happen at the same time.

***SPELLING** – note that there is a double *r* in **concurred** and **concurring**.

SYNONYMS – **1** agree, be in accord, be in agreement.

ANTONYMS – **1** disagree.

ORIGIN – Latin *concurrere* 'run together, assemble in crowds'.

concurrent > *adjective* **1** existing or happening at the same time. **2** *Mathematics* (of three or more lines) meeting at or tending towards one point.

DERIVATIVES – **concurrence** *noun* **concurrently** *adverb*.

concuss > *verb* (usu. **be concussed**) cause to become temporarily unconscious or confused as a result of a blow to the head.

ORIGIN – first used in the sense 'shake violently': from Latin *concutere*, from *con-* 'together' + *quatere* 'shake'.

concussion > *noun* **1** temporary unconsciousness or confusion caused by a blow to the head. **2** a violent shock as from a heavy blow.

DERIVATIVES – **concussive** *adjective*.

condemn > *verb* **1** express complete disapproval of. **2** (usu. **condemn to**) sentence to a punishment, especially death. **3** force (someone) to endure something unpleasant. **4** officially declare to be unfit for use. **5** prove the guilt of.

DERIVATIVES – **condemnation** *noun* **condemnatory** *adjective*.

SYNONYMS – **1** censure, denounce, deplore.

ANTONYMS – **1** condone.

ORIGIN – Latin *condemnare*, from *damnare* 'inflict loss on'.

condensation > *noun* **1** water from humid air collecting as droplets on a cold surface. **2** the conversion of a vapour or gas to a liquid. **3** a concise version of something.

condense > *verb* **1** make denser or more concentrated. **2** change from a gas or vapour to a liquid. **3** express (writing or speech) in fewer words; make concise.

COMBINATIONS – **condensed milk** milk that has been thickened by evaporation and sweetened.

ORIGIN – Latin *condensare*, from *condensus* 'very thick'.

condenser > *noun* **1** an apparatus for condensing vapour. **2** a lens or system of lenses for collecting and directing light. **3** another term for **CAPACITOR**.

condescend > *verb* **1** show that one feels superior. **2** do something despite regarding it as below one's dignity: *he condescended to see me at my hotel.*

DERIVATIVES – **condescension** *noun*.

SYNONYMS – **1** patronise. **2** deign.

ORIGIN – Latin *condescendere*, from *descendere* 'descend'.

condescending > *adjective* feeling or showing a patronising attitude.

DERIVATIVES – **condescendingly** *adverb*.

SYNONYMS – patronising, supercilious, superior.

condign /kəndīn/ > *adjective* formal (of punishment) fitting and deserved.
ORIGIN – Latin *condignus*, from *dignus* 'worthy'.

condiment > *noun* a seasoning or relish for food, such as salt or mustard.
ORIGIN – Latin *condimentum*, from *condire* 'to pickle'.

condition > *noun* 1 the state of something or someone, with regard to appearance, fitness, or working order. 2 (**conditions**) circumstances affecting the functioning or existence of something. 3 a state of affairs that must exist before something else is possible: *for me to agree, three conditions must be met.* 4 an illness or medical problem. > *verb* 1 have a significant influence on; determine. 2 bring into a good or desirable state or condition. 3 train or accustom to behave in a certain way: *the child is conditioned to dislike food.* 4 set prior requirements on (something) before it can occur.
IDIOMS – **in** (or **out of**) **condition** in a fit (or unfit) physical state. **on condition that** with the stipulation that.
ORIGIN – Latin *condicion* 'agreement', from *condicere* 'agree upon'.

conditional > *adjective* 1 subject to one or more conditions being met. 2 Grammar (of a clause, phrase, conjunction, or verb form) expressing a condition. > *noun* Grammar the conditional mood of a verb, for example *should* in *if I should die.*
DERIVATIVES – **conditionality** *noun* **conditionally** *adverb*.

conditioner > *noun* a thing used to improve the condition of something, especially a liquid applied to the hair.

condo > *noun* (pl. **condos**) N. Amer. informal short for CONDOMINIUM (in sense 2).

condole /kəndōl/ > *verb* (**condole with**) express sympathy for.
ORIGIN – Latin *condolere* 'grieve or suffer with'.

condolence > *noun* an expression of sympathy, especially on the occasion of a death.

condom > *noun* a thin rubber sheath worn on the penis during sexual intercourse as a contraceptive or to protect against infection.

condominium /kəndəminniəm/ > *noun* (pl. **condominiums**) 1 the joint control of a state's affairs by other states. 2 N. Amer. a building or complex containing a number of individually owned flats or houses. 3 N. Amer. a flat or house in such a building or complex.
ORIGIN – Latin, from *con-* 'together with' + *dominium* 'sovereignty, dominion'.

condone /kəndōn/ > *verb* accept or forgive (an offence or wrongdoing).
DERIVATIVES – **condonation** /kɒndə-naysh'n/ *noun*.
ORIGIN – Latin *condonare* 'refrain from punishing'.

condor > *noun* a very large American vulture with a bare head and mainly black plumage.
ORIGIN – Spanish, from Quechua.

conduce > *verb* (**conduce to**) formal help to bring about.
ORIGIN – Latin *conducere* 'bring together'.

conducive > *adjective* (**conducive to**) contributing or helping towards.

conduct > *noun* /kɒndukt/ 1 the manner in which a person behaves. 2 management or direction: *the conduct of foreign affairs.* > *verb* /kəndukt/ 1 organise and carry out. 2 direct the performance of (a piece of music or an orchestra or choir). 3 guide to or around a place. 4 (**conduct oneself**) behave in a specified way. 5 transmit (heat, electricity, etc.) by conduction.

---

wordpower facts

Conduct

The term **conduct** originally denoted something that gave provision for safe passage, such as an escort or pass, an idea which survives in **safe conduct**. Later the verb sense 'lead, guide' arose, from which came 'manage' and 'management', later 'management of oneself, behaviour'. The original form of the word, which came from Latin *conducere* 'bring together' via Old French, was *conduit*, which is now an English word in its own right, meaning 'channel'; in all other uses the spelling was influenced by Latin.

---

conductance > *noun* the degree to which a material conducts electricity.

conduction > *noun* the transmission of heat or electricity directly through a substance, without motion of the material.
DERIVATIVES – **conductive** *adjective*.

conductivity > *noun* the degree to which a material conducts electricity or heat.

conductor > *noun* 1 a person who conducts an orchestra or choir. 2 a material or device that conducts heat or electricity. 3 a person who collects fares on a bus. 4 N. Amer. a guard on a train.
DERIVATIVES – **conductorship** *noun* **conductress** *noun*.

conduit /kɒndoo-it/ > *noun* 1 a channel for conveying water or other fluid. 2 a tube or trough protecting electric wiring.
ORIGIN – Old French, from Latin *conductus*, from *conducere* 'bring together'.

cone > *noun* 1 an object which tapers from a circular or roughly circular base to a point. 2 (also **traffic cone**) a plastic cone used to separate off sections of a road. 3 the cone-shaped dry fruit of a conifer. 4 one of two types of light-sensitive cell in the retina of the eye, responsible for sharpness of vision and colour perception. Compare with ROD.
ORIGIN – Greek *kōnos*.

coney /kōni/ (also **cony**) > *noun* (pl. **coneys**, **conies**) Brit. a rabbit.
ORIGIN – Old French *conin*, from Latin *cuniculus*.

confab informal > *noun* an informal conversation or discussion. > *verb* (**confabbed**, **confabbing**) engage in such conversation.

confabulate /kənfabyoolayt/ > *verb* formal converse.
DERIVATIVES – **confabulation** *noun*.
ORIGIN – Latin *confabulari* 'chat together'.

confect /kənfekt/ > *verb* make (something elaborate or dainty).
ORIGIN – Latin *conficere* 'put together'.

confection > *noun* 1 an elaborate sweet dish or delicacy. 2 an elaborately constructed thing: *a confection of democracy, social reform, and sheer personality.*

confectioner > *noun* a person who makes or sells confectionery.

confectionery* > *noun* (pl. **confectioneries**) sweets and chocolates collectively.
*SPELLING – the ending is *-ery*, not *-ary*: confection*ery*.

confederacy > *noun* (pl. **confederacies**) 1 a league or alliance, especially of confederate states. 2 (**the Confederacy**) the Confederate states of the US.

confederate > *adjective* /kənfeddərət/ 1 joined by an agreement or treaty. 2 (**Confederate**) denoting the southern states which separated from the US in 1860–1. > *noun* /kənfeddərət/ an accomplice or fellow worker.
ORIGIN – Latin *confoederatus*, from *foedus* 'league'.

confederated > *adjective* in alliance; allied.

confederation > *noun* 1 an alliance of a number of parties or groups. 2 a union of states with some political power vested in a central authority. 3 the action of confederating or the state of being confederated.
SYNONYMS – 1,2 league, union.

confer /kənfer/ > *verb* (**conferred**, **conferring**) 1 grant (a title, degree, benefit, or right). 2 have discussions.
DERIVATIVES – **conferment** *noun* **conferral** *noun*.
SYNONYMS – 1 (**confer on**) award to,

bestow on, grant, present with. **2** consult, discuss.

ORIGIN – Latin *conferre* 'bring together'.

conferee > *noun* **1** a person who attends a conference. **2** a person on whom something is conferred.

conference > *noun* **1** a formal meeting for discussion or debate. **2** an association in commerce for regulation or exchange of information. **3** a league of sports teams or clubs.

SYNONYMS – **1** congress, forum, seminar.

confess > *verb* **1** admit to a crime or wrongdoing. **2** acknowledge reluctantly. **3** declare one's sins formally to a priest. **4** (of a priest) hear the confession of.

ORIGIN – Old French *confesser*, from Latin *confiteri* 'acknowledge'.

confessedly > *adverb* by one's own admission.

confession > *noun* **1** an act of confessing, especially a formal statement admitting to a crime. **2** a formal admission of one's sins privately to a priest. **3** (also **confession of faith**) a statement setting out essential religious doctrine.

confessional > *noun* **1** an enclosed stall in a church, in which a priest sits to hear confessions. **2** a confession. > *adjective* **1** (of speech or writing) in which a person admits to private thoughts or incidents in their past. **2** relating to religious confession.

confessor > *noun* **1** a priest who hears confessions. **2** a person who makes a confession.

confetti > *noun* small pieces of coloured paper traditionally thrown over a bride and groom after a marriage ceremony.

ORIGIN – Italian, 'sweets' (from the Italian custom of throwing sweets during carnivals); related to **CONFECT**.

confidant /**kon**fidant/ > *noun* (**fem. confidante** pronunc. same) a person in whom one confides.

confide /kənf**ī**d/ > *verb* **1** (often **confide in**) tell someone about a secret or private matter in confidence. **2** (**confide to**) dated entrust (something) to the care of.

ORIGIN – Latin *confidere* 'have full trust'.

confidence > *noun* **1** the belief that one can have faith in or rely on someone or something. **2** a feeling of self-assurance arising from an appreciation of one's abilities. **3** the telling of private matters or secrets with mutual trust. **4** a secret or private matter told to someone under a condition of trust.

IDIOMS – **in someone's confidence** in a position of trust with someone. **take into one's confidence** tell one's secrets to.

SYNONYMS – **1** conviction, faith, trust. **2** self-assurance, self-confidence.

ANTONYMS – **1** doubt. **2** self-doubt.

COMBINATIONS – **confidence trick** (**N. Amer.** also **confidence game**) an act of cheating someone by gaining their trust.

confident > *adjective* **1** feeling confidence in oneself. **2** feeling certainty about something.

DERIVATIVES – **confidently** *adverb*.

SYNONYMS – **1** assured, self-assured, self-confident.

confidential > *adjective* **1** intended to be kept secret. **2** entrusted with private information: *a confidential secretary.*

DERIVATIVES – **confidentiality** *noun* **confidentially** *adverb*.

SYNONYMS – **1** classified, private, privileged, secret.

configuration /kənfigyoo**ray**sh'n/ > *noun* an arrangement of parts or elements in a particular form or figure.

DERIVATIVES – **configurational** *adjective*.

SYNONYMS – arrangement, layout.

configure > *verb* **1** arrange in a particular configuration. **2** Computing arrange or order (a computer system) so as to fit it for a designated task.

DERIVATIVES – **configurable** *adjective*.

ORIGIN – Latin *configurare* 'shape after a pattern'; related to **FIGURE**.

confine > *verb* /kənf**ī**n/ **1** (**confine to**) restrict (someone or something) within certain limits of (space, scope, or time). **2** (**be confined to**) be unable to leave (one's bed, home, etc.) due to illness or disability. **3** (**be confined**) dated (of a woman) remain in bed for a period before, during, and after giving birth. > *noun* (**confines**) /**kon**fīnz/ limits or boundaries.

DERIVATIVES – **confinement** *noun*.

SYNONYMS – **1** (**confine to**) enclose within, limit to, restrict within.

ORIGIN – from Latin *confinis* 'bordering', from *finis* 'end, limit'.

confined > *adjective* (of a space) enclosed; cramped.

confirm > *verb* **1** establish the truth or correctness of. **2** state with assurance that something is true. **3** make definite or formally valid. **4** (**confirm in**) reinforce (someone) in (an opinion or feeling). **5** (usu. **be confirmed**) administer the religious rite of confirmation to.

DERIVATIVES – **confirmatory** *adjective*.

SYNONYMS – **1** bear out, corroborate, prove, verify. **2** affirm, assert. **3** endorse, ratify, validate.

ORIGIN – Latin *confirmare*, from *firmus* 'firm'.

confirmation > *noun* **1** the action of confirming or state of being confirmed. **2** the rite at which a baptised person affirms their belief and is admitted as a full member of the Christian Church. **3** the Jewish ceremony of bar mitzvah.

confirmed > *adjective* firmly established in a habit, belief, or way of life: *a confirmed bachelor.*

confiscate /**kon**fiskayt/ > *verb* **1** take or seize (property) with authority. **2** transfer the possession of (something, especially land) to the public treasury as a penalty.

DERIVATIVES – **confiscation** *noun* **confiscatory** *adjective*.

ORIGIN – Latin *confiscare* 'put away in a chest, consign to the public treasury', from *fiscus* 'chest, treasury'; compare with **FISCAL**.

confit /**kon**fi/ > *noun* duck or other meat cooked very slowly in its own fat.

ORIGIN – French, 'conserved'.

conflagration /konflə**gray**sh'n/ > *noun* an extensive and destructive fire.

ORIGIN – Latin, from *flagrare* 'to blaze'.

conflate > *verb* combine into one.

DERIVATIVES – **conflation** *noun*.

ORIGIN – Latin *conflare* 'kindle, fuse'.

conflict > *noun* /**kon**flikt/ **1** a serious disagreement or argument. **2** a prolonged armed struggle. **3** an incompatibility between opinions, principles, etc.: *a conflict of interests.* > *verb* /kən**flikt**/ be incompatible or at variance with.

DERIVATIVES – **conflictual** *adjective*.

SYNONYMS – **1** clash, dispute.

ORIGIN – Latin *conflictus* 'a contest'.

confluence /**kon**flooənss/ > *noun* **1** the junction of two rivers. **2** an act or process of merging.

DERIVATIVES – **confluent** *adjective*.

ORIGIN – from Latin *confluere* 'flow together'.

conform > *verb* **1** comply with rules, standards, or conventions. **2** be similar in form or type.

ORIGIN – Latin *conformare*, from *formare* 'to form'.

conformable > *adjective* (usu. **conformable to**) **1** disposed or accustomed to conform. **2** similar in nature; consistent.

conformance > *noun* another term for **CONFORMITY**.

conformation > *noun* the shape or structure of something.

DERIVATIVES – **conformational** *adjective*.

conformist > *noun* a person who conforms to accepted behaviour or established practices. > *adjective* conventional.

DERIVATIVES – **conformism** *noun*.

conformity > *noun* **1** compliance with conventions, rules, or laws. **2** similarity in form or type.

confound > *verb* **1** surprise or bewilder. **2** prove wrong. **3** defeat (a plan, aim, or hope).

SYNONYMS – **1** amaze, astonish, bewilder, stagger, surprise.

ORIGIN – Latin *confundere* 'pour together, mix up'.

confounded > *adjective* informal, dated used to express annoyance.

DERIVATIVES – **confoundedly** *adverb*.

confraternity > *noun* (pl. **confraternities**) a brotherhood, especially with a religious or charitable purpose.

ORIGIN – Latin *confraternitas*, from *confrater* 'confrère'.

confrère /**kon**frair/ > *noun* a fellow member of a profession.

ORIGIN – French, from Latin *confrater*, from *frater* 'brother'.

confront > *verb* **1** meet face to face in hostility or defiance. **2** (of a problem) present itself to. **3** face up to and deal with (a problem). **4** compel to face or consider something.

DERIVATIVES – **confrontation** *noun* **confrontational** *adjective*.

ORIGIN – Latin *confrontare*, from *frons* 'face'.

Confucian /kən**fyoo**sh'n/ > *adjective* relating to the Chinese philosopher Confucius (551–479 BC) or his philosophy. > *noun* a follower of Confucius or his philosophy.

DERIVATIVES – **Confucianism** *noun* **Confucianist** *noun & adjective*.

confuse > *verb* **1** make bewildered or perplexed. **2** make less easy to understand. **3** mistake (one for another).

DERIVATIVES – **confusable** *adjective* **confusing** *adjective* **confusingly** *adverb*.

SYNONYMS – **1** baffle, bemuse, bewilder, perplex. **2** garble, muddle.

ORIGIN – from Latin *confusus*, from *confundere* 'mingle together'.

confused > *adjective* **1** bewildered. **2** lacking order and so difficult to understand or distinguish.

DERIVATIVES – **confusedly** *adverb*.

confusion > *noun* **1** the state of being confused; uncertainty or bewilderment. **2** a situation or state of panic or disorder. **3** the mistaking of one person or thing for another.

confute > *verb* formal prove to be wrong.

DERIVATIVES – **confutation** *noun*.

ORIGIN – Latin *confutare* 'restrain, answer conclusively'.

conga /**kong**gə/ > *noun* **1** a Latin American dance of African origin, performed by people in single file and consisting of three steps forward followed by a kick. **2** (also **conga drum**) a tall, narrow drum beaten with the hands.

ORIGIN – Spanish, from *congo* 'Congolese'.

congeal /kən**jeel**/ > *verb* become semi-solid, especially on cooling.

DERIVATIVES – **congelation** *noun*.

ORIGIN – Latin *congelare*, from *gelare* 'freeze'.

congener /kən**jeen**ər/ > *noun* a person or thing of the same kind as another.

DERIVATIVES – **congeneric** /konji**nerr**ik/ *adjective*.

ORIGIN – Latin, from *con-* 'together with' + *genus* 'race, stock'.

congenial /kən**jee**niəl/ > *adjective* **1** pleasant because of qualities or interests similar to one's own: *congenial company*. **2** suited to one's taste or inclination.

DERIVATIVES – **congeniality** *noun* **congenially** *adverb*.

SYNONYMS – **1** compatible, kindred, like-minded, well suited.

ANTONYMS – disagreeable.

congenital /kən**jenn**it'l/ > *adjective* **1** (of a disease or abnormality) present from birth. **2** having a particular trait from or as if from birth: *a congenital liar*.

DERIVATIVES – **congenitally** *adverb*.

ORIGIN – Latin *congenitus* 'born together'.

conger /**kong**gə/ (also **conger eel**) > *noun* a large predatory eel of coastal waters.

ORIGIN – Greek *gongros*.

congeries /kon**jeer**eez/ > *noun* (pl. same) a disorderly collection.

ORIGIN – Latin, 'heap, pile'.

congested > *adjective* **1** so crowded as to hinder or prevent freedom of movement. **2** abnormally full of blood. **3** blocked with mucus.

DERIVATIVES – **congestion** *noun*.

ORIGIN – from Latin *congerere* 'heap up'.

congestive > *adjective* Medicine involving or produced by congestion of a part of the body.

conglomerate > *noun* /kən**glomm**ərət/ **1** something consisting of a number of different and distinct things. **2** a large corporation formed by the merging of separate firms. **3** Geology a coarse-grained sedimentary rock composed of rounded fragments cemented together. > *adjective* /kən**glomm**ərət/ relating to a conglomerate. > *verb* /kən**glomm**ərayt/ gather into or form a conglomerate.

DERIVATIVES – **conglomeration** *noun*.

ORIGIN – from Latin *conglomerare* 'roll or heap together'.

Congolese /konggə**leez**/ > *noun* (pl. same) **1** a person from the Congo or the Democratic Republic of Congo (formerly Zaire). **2** any of the languages spoken in the Congo region. > *adjective* relating to the Congo or the Democratic Republic of Congo.

congratulate > *verb* **1** express good wishes or praise at the happiness, success, or good fortune of. **2** (**congratulate oneself**) think oneself fortunate or clever.

DERIVATIVES – **congratulatory** *adjective*.

ORIGIN – Latin *congratulari* 'congratulate', from *gratus* 'pleasing'.

congratulation > *noun* **1** (**congratulations**) praise or good wishes on a special occasion. **2** the action of congratulating.

congregant /**kong**grigənt/ > *noun* a member of a congregation.

congregate > *verb* gather into a crowd or mass.

ORIGIN – Latin *congregare* 'collect (into a flock)', from *grex* 'a flock'.

congregation > *noun* **1** a group of people assembled for religious worship. **2** a gathering or collection of people or things. **3** the action of congregating.

congregational > *adjective* **1** relating to a congregation. **2** (**Congregational**) of or adhering to Congregationalism.

Congregationalism > *noun* a system of organisation among Christian churches whereby individual churches are largely self-governing.

DERIVATIVES – **Congregationalist** *noun & adjective*.

congress > *noun* **1** a formal meeting or series of meetings between delegates. **2** (**Congress**) a national legislative body, especially that of the US. **3** the action of coming together.

DERIVATIVES – **congressional** *adjective*.

COMBINATIONS – **congressman** (or **congresswoman**) a male (or female) member of the US Congress.

ORIGIN – Latin *congressus*, from *congredi* 'meet'.

congruent /**kong**grooənt/ > *adjective* **1** in agreement or harmony. **2** Geometry (of figures) identical in form.

DERIVATIVES – **congruence** *noun*.

ORIGIN – from Latin *congruere* 'agree, meet together'.

congruous /**kong**grooəss/ > *adjective* in agreement or harmony.

DERIVATIVES – **congruity** *noun*.

conic /**konn**ik/ > *adjective* of a cone.

COMBINATIONS – **conic section** the figure of a circle, ellipse, parabola, or hyperbola formed by the intersection of a plane and a circular cone.

conical > *adjective* shaped like a cone.

conifer /**konn**ifər, **kōn**ifər/ > *noun* a tree bearing cones and evergreen needle-like or scale-like leaves, e.g. a pine or cypress.

DERIVATIVES – **coniferous** *adjective*.

ORIGIN – Latin, 'cone-bearing'.

conjecture /kən**jek**chər/ > *noun* an opinion or conclusion based on incomplete information; a guess. > *verb* form a conjecture; guess.

DERIVATIVES – **conjectural** *adjective*.

SYNONYMS – *noun* guess, hypothesis, speculation, supposition. *verb* guess, hypothesise, speculate, surmise.

ORIGIN – Latin *conjectura*, from *conicere* 'put together in thought'.

conjoin > *verb* formal join; combine.

conjoint > *adjective* combined or united.

conjugal /**kon**joog'l/ > *adjective* relating to marriage or the relationship between husband and wife.
SYNONYMS – marital, matrimonial, nuptial.
COMBINATIONS – **conjugal rights** the rights, especially to sexual relations, regarded as exercisable in law by each partner in a marriage.
ORIGIN – Latin *conjugalis*, from *conjux* 'spouse'.

conjugate > *verb* /**kon**joogayt/ **1** Grammar give the different forms of (a verb). **2** Biology (of bacteria or unicellular organisms) become temporarily united in order to exchange genetic material. > *adjective* /**kon**joogət/ **1** technical joined or related as a pair. **2** Biology (of gametes) fused. > *noun* /**kon**joogət/ a conjugate thing.
DERIVATIVES – **conjugation** *noun*.
ORIGIN – Latin *conjugare* 'yoke together'.

conjunct > *adjective* /kən**jungkt**/ joined together, combined, or associated. > *noun* /**kon**jungkt/ **1** each of two or more joined or associated things. **2** Grammar an adverbial joining two sentences or clauses (e.g. *however*).
ORIGIN – Latin *conjunctus*, from *conjungere* 'conjoin'.

conjunction > *noun* **1** Grammar a word used to connect clauses or sentences or to coordinate words in the same clause (e.g. *and*, *if*). **2** an instance of two or more events occurring at the same point in time or space. **3** Astronomy & Astrology an alignment of two planets so that they appear to be in the same place in the sky.
IDIOMS – **in conjunction** together.

conjunctiva /konjungkt**ī**və, kən**jungk**tivə/ > *noun* the mucous membrane that covers the front of the eye and lines the inside of the eyelids.
DERIVATIVES – **conjunctival** *adjective*.
ORIGIN – from Latin *membrana conjunctiva* 'conjunctive membrane'.

conjunctive > *adjective* of, relating to, or forming a conjunction. > *noun* Grammar a conjunction.

conjunctivitis /kənjungktiv**ī**tiss/ > *noun* inflammation of the conjunctiva.

conjuncture > *noun* **1** a combination of events. **2** a state of affairs.

conjure /**kun**jər/ > *verb* (usu. **conjure up**) **1** cause to appear as if by magic. **2** call to the mind. **3** call upon (a spirit) to appear by magic. **4** /kən**joor**/ archaic implore to do something.
IDIOMS – **a name to conjure with** an important, significant, or striking name.
ORIGIN – Latin *conjurare* 'band together by an oath, conspire'.

conjuring > *noun* the performance of seemingly magical tricks, often involving sleight of hand.

conjuror (also **conjurer**) > *noun* a performer of conjuring tricks.

conk¹ > *verb* (**conk out**) informal **1** (of a machine) break down. **2** faint or go to sleep. **3** die.

conk² > *noun* Brit. informal a person's nose.

conker > *noun* Brit. **1** the hard shiny dark brown nut of a horse chestnut tree. **2** (**conkers**) (treated as sing.) a children's game in which each has a conker on a string and tries to break another's with it.

wordpower facts
Conker

Conker is first recorded in the 19th century as a dialect word denoting a snail shell, with which the game, or a similar form of it, was originally played. It perhaps comes from **conch**, but was associated with (and frequently spelled) **conquer** in the 19th and early 20th centuries: an alternative name for the game was *conquerors*.

con man > *noun* informal a man who cheats others using confidence tricks.

conn > *verb* US spelling of **CON⁴**.

connect > *verb* **1** bring together so as to establish a link. **2** join together so as to provide access and communication. **3** (**be connected**) be related in some respect. **4** put into contact by telephone. **5** (of a train, bus, etc.) arrive at its destination just before another departs so that passengers can transfer.
DERIVATIVES – **connectable** *adjective* **connector** *noun*.
SYNONYMS – **1** attach, couple, join, link.
ANTONYMS – **1** disconnect.
COMBINATIONS – **connecting rod** the rod connecting the piston and the crankpin in an engine or pump.
ORIGIN – Latin *connectere*, from *nectere* 'bind'.

connection (Brit. also **connexion**) > *noun* **1** a link or relationship. **2** the action of connecting. **3** (**connections**) people with whom one has contact, especially those with influence. **4** an opportunity for catching a connecting train, bus, etc.
IDIOMS – **in connection with** concerning. **in this** (or **that**) **connection** with reference to this (or that).

connective > *adjective* connecting. > *noun* something that connects.
COMBINATIONS – **connective tissue** bodily tissue that connects, supports, binds, or separates other tissues or organs, typically consisting of relatively few cells embedded in fibrous material or fat.

connectivity > *noun* **1** the state or extent of being connected. **2** Computing capacity for the interconnection of platforms, systems, and applications.

connexion > *noun* variant spelling of **CONNECTION**.

conning tower /**konn**ing/ > *noun* the superstructure of a submarine, containing the periscope.

connive /kə**nīv**/ > *verb* **1** (**connive at** or **in**) secretly allow (a wrongdoing). **2** (often **connive with**) conspire to do something harmful or illegal.
DERIVATIVES – **connivance** *noun* **conniving** *adjective*.
ORIGIN – Latin *connivere* 'shut the eyes (to)'.

connoisseur /konnə**sör**/ > *noun* an expert judge in matters of taste.
DERIVATIVES – **connoisseurship** *noun*.
ORIGIN – French, former spelling of *connaisseur*, from *connaître* 'know'.

connotation /konnə**tay**sh'n/ > *noun* an idea or feeling invoked by a word in addition to its primary or literal meaning.

connote /kə**nōt**/ > *verb* **1** (of a word) imply or suggest in addition to its primary or literal meaning. **2** imply as a consequence or condition.
DERIVATIVES – **connotative** /**konn**ətaytiv/ *adjective*.
USAGE – **connote** does not mean the same as **denote**: whereas **denote** refers to the literal, primary meaning of something, **connote** refers to other characteristics suggested or implied by that thing. Thus one might say that **mother** *denotes* 'a woman who is a parent' but *connotes* qualities such as protection and affection.
ORIGIN – Latin *connotare* 'mark in addition'.

connubial /kə**nyoo**biəl/ > *adjective* literary conjugal.
ORIGIN – Latin *connubialis*, from *connubium* 'marriage'.

conquer > *verb* **1** overcome and take control of by military force. **2** successfully overcome (a problem) or climb (a mountain).
DERIVATIVES – **conquerable** *adjective* **conqueror** *noun*.
ORIGIN – Latin *conquirere* 'gain, win'.

conquest > *noun* **1** the action of conquering. **2** a conquered territory. **3** a person whose affection or favour has been won.

conquistador /kon**kwis**tədor, kon**kis**tədor/ > *noun* (pl. **conquistadores** /konkwistə**dor**ayz, konkistə**dor**ayz/ or **conquistadors**) a Spanish conqueror of Mexico or Peru in the 16th century.
ORIGIN – Spanish.

consanguineous /konsang**gwinn**iəss/ > *adjective* descended from the same ancestor.
DERIVATIVES – **consanguinity** *noun*.

ORIGIN − Latin *consanguineus* 'of the same blood'.

conscience > *noun* a person's moral sense of right and wrong, chiefly as it affects their own behaviour.

IDIOMS − **in (all) conscience** in fairness.

DERIVATIVES − **conscienceless** *adjective*.

ORIGIN − Latin *conscientia* 'knowledge within oneself', from *scire* 'to know'.

conscientious /konshi**en**shəss/ *adjective* **1** diligent and thorough in carrying out one's work or duty. **2** relating to a person's conscience.

DERIVATIVES − **conscientiously** *adverb* **conscientiousness** *noun*.

SYNONYMS − **1** assiduous, diligent, industrious, sedulous, thorough.

COMBINATIONS − **conscientious objector** a person who refuses to serve in the armed forces for reasons of conscience.

conscious > *adjective* **1** aware of and responding to one's surroundings. **2** (usu. **conscious of**) aware. **3** realised by oneself; deliberate.

DERIVATIVES − **consciously** *adverb*.

ORIGIN − Latin *conscius* 'knowing with others or in oneself'.

consciousness > *noun* **1** the state of being conscious. **2** one's awareness or perception of something.

conscript > *verb* /kən**skript**/ call up for compulsory military service. > *noun* /**kon**skript/ a conscripted person.

DERIVATIVES − **conscription** *noun*.

ORIGIN − from Latin *conscriptus*, from *conscribere* 'enrol'.

consecrate /**kon**sikrayt/ > *verb* **1** make or declare sacred. **2** ordain to a sacred office, typically that of bishop. **3** (in Christian belief) make (bread or wine) into the body and blood of Christ.

DERIVATIVES − **consecration** *noun*.

ORIGIN − Latin *consecrare* 'dedicate, devote as sacred'.

consecutive /kən**sek**yootiv/ > *adjective* **1** following in unbroken or logical sequence. **2** Grammar expressing consequence or result.

DERIVATIVES − **consecutively** *adverb*.

ORIGIN − Latin *consecutivus*, from *consequi* 'follow closely'.

consensual /kən**sen**syooəl, kən**sen**shooal/ > *adjective* relating to or involving consent or consensus.

consensus* /kən**sen**səss/ > *noun* general agreement.

*SPELLING − con*sen*sus, not *-cen-*.

ORIGIN − Latin, 'agreement'.

consent > *noun* permission or agreement. > *verb* **1** give permission. **2** agree to do.

SYNONYMS − *noun* agreement, assent, permission.

COMBINATIONS − **consenting adult** an adult who willingly agrees to engage in a sexual act.

ORIGIN − from Latin *consentire* 'agree'.

consequence > *noun* **1** a result or effect of an action or condition. **2** importance or relevance: *the past is of no consequence*. **3** dated social distinction.

SYNONYMS − **1** effect, result, outcome.

ORIGIN − Latin *consequentia*, from *consequi* 'follow closely'.

consequent > *adjective* following as a consequence.

DERIVATIVES − **consequential** *adjective* **consequently** *adverb*.

conservancy /kən**ser**vənsi/ > *noun* (pl. **conservancies**) **1** an organisation concerned with the preservation of natural resources. **2** a commission controlling a port, river, or catchment area. **3** conservation.

conservation > *noun* **1** preservation or restoration of the natural environment and wildlife. **2** preservation and repair of archaeological, historical, and cultural sites and artefacts. **3** careful use of a resource: *energy conservation*. **4** Physics the principle by which the total value of a quantity (e.g. mass or energy) remains constant in a closed system.

DERIVATIVES − **conservationist** *noun*.

conservative > *adjective* **1** averse to change and holding traditional values. **2** (in a political context) favouring free enterprise, private ownership, and socially conservative ideas. **3** (**Conservative**) of or relating to a Conservative Party. **4** (of an estimate) purposely low for the sake of caution. > *noun* **1** a conservative person. **2** (**Conservative**) a supporter or member of a Conservative Party.

DERIVATIVES − **conservatism** *noun* **conservatively** *adverb*.

SYNONYMS − *adjective* **1** conventional, reactionary, traditional, traditionalist.

conservatoire /kən**ser**vətwaar/ > *noun* a college for the study of classical music or other arts.

ORIGIN − French.

conservator /kən**ser**vətər, **kon**sərvaytər/ > *noun* a person involved in conservation.

conservatory > *noun* (pl. **conservatories**) **1** Brit. a room with a glass roof and walls, attached to a house and used as a sun lounge or a greenhouse. **2** chiefly N. Amer. another term for **CONSERVATOIRE**.

conserve /kən**serv**/ > *verb* **1** protect from harm, destruction, or wasteful overuse. **2** Physics maintain (a quantity) at a constant overall total. > *noun* /also **kon**serv/ fruit jam.

SYNONYMS − *verb* **1** preserve, protect, safeguard, save.

ORIGIN − Latin *conservare* 'to preserve'.

consider > *verb* **1** think carefully about. **2** believe to be. **3** take into account when making a judgement. **4** look attentively at.

SYNONYMS − **1** contemplate, meditate on, mull over, ponder. **2** deem, hold to be, regard as.

ORIGIN − Latin *considerare* 'examine', perhaps from *sidus* 'star'.

considerable > *adjective* **1** notably large. **2** significant or notable.

DERIVATIVES − **considerably** *adverb*.

SYNONYMS − **1** sizeable, substantial.

ANTONYMS − **1** paltry. **2** trivial.

considerate > *adjective* careful not to harm or inconvenience others.

DERIVATIVES − **considerately** *adverb*.

SYNONYMS − mindful, sensitive, thoughtful, unselfish.

ANTONYMS − inconsiderate, selfish.

consideration > *noun* **1** careful thought. **2** a fact taken into account when making a decision. **3** thoughtfulness towards others. **4** a payment or reward.

IDIOMS − **in consideration of** in return for.

SYNONYMS − **1** contemplation, deliberation, meditation, reflection.

considering > *preposition & conjunction* taking into consideration. > *adverb* informal taking everything into account.

consign /kən**sīn**/ > *verb* **1** deliver to someone's possession or care. **2** send (goods) by a public carrier. **3** (**consign to**) put (someone or something) in (a place) so as to be rid of them.

DERIVATIVES − **consignee** *noun* **consignor** *noun*.

ORIGIN − Latin *consignare* 'mark with a seal'.

consignment > *noun* a batch of goods that are consigned or delivered.

consist > *verb* **1** (**consist of**) be composed of. **2** (**consist in**) have as an essential feature.

ORIGIN − Latin *consistere* 'stand firm or still, exist'.

consistency (also **consistence**) > *noun* (pl. **consistencies**) **1** the state of being consistent. **2** the degree of thickness or viscosity of a substance.

consistent > *adjective* **1** conforming to a regular pattern; unchanging. **2** (usu. **consistent with**) in agreement.

DERIVATIVES − **consistently** *adverb*.

consistory /kən**sist**əri/ > *noun* (pl. **consistories**) **1** (in the Roman Catholic Church) the council of cardinals, with or without the Pope. **2** (also **consistory court**) (in the Church of England) a court presided over by a bishop, to administer ecclesiastical law in a diocese.

consolation /konsə**lay**sh'n/ > *noun* **1** comfort received after a loss or disappointment. **2** a source of such comfort.

DERIVATIVES – **consolatory** /kənsollətri/ *adjective*.

SYNONYMS – **1** comfort, condolence, solace.

COMBINATIONS – **consolation prize** a prize given to a competitor who narrowly fails to win.

console¹ /kənsōl/ > *verb* comfort (someone) in a time of grief or disappointment.

SYNONYMS – comfort, condole with, solace.

ORIGIN – Latin *consolari*, from *solari* 'soothe'.

console² /konsōl/ > *noun* **1** a panel or unit accommodating a set of controls. **2** (also **games console**) a small machine for playing computerised video games. **3** the cabinet containing the keyboards, stops, etc. of an organ. **4** an ornamental bracket or corbel.

ORIGIN – French, from Latin *consolidare* (see **CONSOLIDATE**).

consolidate /kənsollidayt/ > *verb* **1** make stronger or more solid. **2** combine into a single unit.

DERIVATIVES – **consolidation** *noun* **consolidator** *noun*.

ORIGIN – Latin *consolidare*, from *solidus* 'solid'.

consommé /kənsommay/ > *noun* a clear soup made with concentrated stock.

ORIGIN – French, 'consummated, completed'.

consonance /konsənənss/ > *noun* **1** agreement or compatibility. **2** the recurrence of similar-sounding consonants, especially in poetry.

consonant /konsənənt/ > *noun* **1** a speech sound in which the breath is at least partly obstructed and which forms a syllable when combined with a vowel. **2** a letter representing such a sound. > *adjective* (**consonant with**) in agreement or harmony with.

DERIVATIVES – **consonantal** *adjective*.

ORIGIN – Latin, from *consonare* 'sound together', from *sonus* 'sound'.

consort¹ > *noun* /konsort/ **1** a wife, husband, or companion, especially the spouse of a monarch. **2** a ship sailing in company with another. > *verb* /kənsort/ (**consort with**) habitually associate with.

ORIGIN – Latin *consors* 'sharing, partner'.

consort² /konsort/ > *noun* a small group of musicians performing together, typically playing Renaissance music.

ORIGIN – earlier form of **CONCERT**.

consortium /kənsortiəm/ > *noun* (pl. **consortia** /kənsortiə/ or **consortiums**) an association, typically of several companies.

ORIGIN – Latin, 'partnership'.

conspectus /kənspektəss/ > *noun* a summary or overview of a subject.

ORIGIN – Latin, 'a view or survey'.

conspicuous /kənspikyooəss/ > *adjective* **1** clearly visible. **2** attracting notice; notable: *conspicuous bravery*.

DERIVATIVES – **conspicuously** *adverb*.

SYNONYMS – **1** clear, discernible, manifest, noticeable, prominent, visible.

ANTONYMS – **1** inconspicuous.

ORIGIN – Latin *conspicuus*, from *conspicere* 'look at attentively'.

conspiracist > *noun* a supporter of a conspiracy theory.

conspiracy > *noun* (pl. **conspiracies**) **1** a secret plan by a group to do something unlawful or harmful. **2** the action of conspiring.

COMBINATIONS – **conspiracy theory** a belief that some secretive but influential organisation is behind a particular event or events.

conspirator > *noun* a person who takes part in a conspiracy.

DERIVATIVES – **conspiratorial** *adjective* **conspiratorially** *adverb*.

conspire > *verb* **1** jointly make secret plans to commit a wrongful act. **2** (of circumstances) seem to be acting together in bringing unfortunate results.

SYNONYMS – **1** collude, connive, intrigue, plot, scheme.

ORIGIN – Old French *conspirer*, from Latin *conspirare* 'agree, plot'.

constable > *noun* **1** Brit. a police officer. **2** the governor of a royal castle.

ORIGIN – Old French *conestable*, from Latin *comes stabuli* 'count, or head officer, of the stable'.

constabulary /kənstabyooləri/ > *noun* (pl. **constabularies**) chiefly Brit. a police force.

constant > *adjective* **1** occurring continuously. **2** remaining the same. **3** faithful and dependable. > *noun* **1** an unchanging situation. **2** Mathematics & Physics a quantity that does not change its value.

DERIVATIVES – **constancy** *noun* **constantly** *adverb*.

SYNONYMS – *adjective* **1** ceaseless, continual, continuous, unremitting. **2** immutable, invariable, steady, unchanging. **3** dependable, faithful, loyal, steadfast.

ANTONYMS – **1** fitful, inconstant. **2** inconstant, variable. **3** fickle, inconstant.

ORIGIN – Old French, from Latin *constare* 'stand firm'.

constellation > *noun* a group of stars forming a recognised pattern and typically named after a mythological or other figure.

ORIGIN – Latin, from *stella* 'star'.

consternation > *noun* anxiety or dismay.

ORIGIN – Latin, from *consternare* 'terrify, prostrate'.

constipate > *verb* (usu. **be constipated**) affect with constipation.

ORIGIN – Latin *constipare* 'crowd or press together'.

constipation > *noun* difficulty in emptying the bowels.

constituency /kənstityooənsi/ > *noun* (pl. **constituencies**) **1** a body of voters in a specified area who elect a representative to a legislative body. **2** chiefly Brit. the area represented in this way.

constituent > *adjective* **1** being a part of a whole. **2** having the power to appoint or elect. **3** able to make or change a political constitution. > *noun* **1** a member of a constituency. **2** a component part.

constitute /konstityoot/ > *verb* **1** be (a part) of a whole. **2** be or be equivalent to. **3** (usu. **be constituted**) establish by law.

SYNONYMS – **1** compose, comprise, make up, represent. **2** embody, be equivalent to, be tantamount to. **3** (**be constituted**) be established, be chartered, be founded, be inaugurated.

ORIGIN – Latin *constituere* 'establish, appoint', from *con-* 'together' + *statuere* 'set up'.

constitution > *noun* **1** a body of fundamental principles or established precedents according to which a state or organisation is governed. **2** the composition or forming of something. **3** a person's physical or mental state.

constitutional > *adjective* **1** relating to or in accordance with a constitution. **2** of or relating to a person's physical or mental state. > *noun* dated a walk taken regularly to maintain good health.

DERIVATIVES – **constitutionality** *noun* **constitutionally** *adverb*.

constitutive > *adjective* **1** having the power to establish something. **2** forming a constituent of something.

DERIVATIVES – **constitutively** *adverb*.

constrain > *verb* **1** compel or force towards a course of action. **2** (**constrained**) appearing forced. **3** severely restrict the scope, extent, or activity of.

DERIVATIVES – **constrainedly** *adverb*.

SYNONYMS – **1** compel, drive, force, impel, oblige. **3** check, curb, limit, restrain.

ORIGIN – Old French *constraindre*, from Latin *constringere* 'bind tightly together'.

constraint > *noun* **1** a limitation or restriction. **2** stiffness of manner.

SYNONYMS – **1** control, curtailment, limitation, restraint, restriction. **2** formality, inhibition, restraint, stiffness.

constrict > *verb* **1** make or become narrower, especially by encircling with pressure. **2** deprive of freedom of movement.

DERIVATIVES – **constriction** *noun* **constrictive** *adjective*.

SYNONYMS – **1** compress, contract, narrow, squeeze, tighten. **2** hinder, impede, obstruct, restrict.

ORIGIN – Latin *constringere* 'bind tightly together'.

constrictor > *noun* **1** a snake that kills by constricting its prey, such as a boa or python. **2** Anatomy a muscle whose contraction narrows a vessel or passage.

construct > *verb* /kən**strukt**/ **1** build or erect. **2** form (a theory) from various conceptual elements. > *noun* /**kon**strukt/ **1** an idea or theory. **2** something constructed.

DERIVATIVES – **constructor** *noun*.

SYNONYMS – *verb* **1** assemble, build, erect, make. **2** create, devise, form, formulate.

ORIGIN – Latin *construere* 'heap together, build'.

construction > *noun* **1** the action or process of constructing. **2** a building or other structure. **3** the industry of erecting buildings. **4** an interpretation or explanation.

DERIVATIVES – **constructional** *adjective*.

constructive > *adjective* **1** serving a useful purpose. **2** Law derived by inference; not stated explicitly.

DERIVATIVES – **constructively** *adverb* **constructiveness** *noun*.

SYNONYMS – **1** helpful, practical, profitable, useful, worthwhile.

COMBINATIONS – **constructive dismissal** the changing of an employee's job with the aim of forcing their resignation.

construe > *verb* (**construes, construed, construing**) interpret in a particular way.

DERIVATIVES – **construable** *adjective* **construal** *noun*.

SYNONYMS – gloss, interpret, read, take, understand.

ORIGIN – Latin *construere* 'heap together, build'.

consubstantiation /konsəbstanshi**aysh**'n/ > *noun* Christian Theology the doctrine that the substance of the bread and wine coexists with the body and blood of Christ in the Eucharist. Compare with **TRAN-SUBSTANTIATION**.

consul /**kon**s'l/ > *noun* **1** a state official living in a foreign city and protecting the state's citizens and interests there. **2** (in ancient Rome) each of two elected chief magistrates who ruled the republic.

DERIVATIVES – **consular** /**kon**syoolər/ *adjective* **consulship** *noun*.

ORIGIN – Latin, related to *consulere* 'take counsel'.

consulate > *noun* **1** the place where a consul works. **2** (in ancient Rome) the period of office of a consul. **3** (in ancient Rome) the system of government by consuls.

consult > *verb* **1** seek information or advice from. **2** seek permission or approval from. **3**

(**consulting**) engaged in the business of giving advice to others in the same field.

DERIVATIVES – **consultation** *noun* **consultative** *adjective* **consultee** *noun*.

ORIGIN – Latin *consultare*, from *consulere* 'take counsel'.

consultancy > *noun* (pl. **consultancies**) a professional practice giving expert advice in a particular field.

consultant > *noun* **1** a person who provides expert advice professionally. **2** Brit. a hospital doctor of senior rank.

consumable > *adjective* intended to be used up and then replaced. > *noun* a consumable commodity.

consume > *verb* **1** eat, drink, or ingest. **2** use up (a resource). **3** (especially of a fire) completely destroy. **4** (of a feeling) absorb all of the attention and energy of (someone).

DERIVATIVES – **consuming** *adjective*.

SYNONYMS – **2** absorb, deplete, exhaust, expend, use up. **3** destroy, devastate, raze, wipe out. **4** absorb, devour, eat up, engross, preoccupy.

ORIGIN – Latin *consumere*, from *con-* 'altogether' + *sumere* 'take up'.

consumer > *noun* a person who buys a product or service for personal use.

consumerism > *noun* **1** the protection or promotion of the interests of consumers. **2** the preoccupation of society with the acquisition of goods.

DERIVATIVES – **consumerist** *adjective* & *noun*.

consummate > *verb* /**kon**səmayt/ **1** make (a marriage or relationship) complete by having sexual intercourse. **2** complete (a transaction). > *adjective* /kən**summ**ət, **kon**səmət/ showing great skill and flair.

DERIVATIVES – **consummately** *adverb* **consummation** *noun* **consummator** *noun*.

ORIGIN – Latin *consummare* 'bring to completion'.

consumption > *noun* **1** the action or process of consuming. **2** an amount consumed. **3** dated a wasting disease, especially tuberculosis.

DERIVATIVES – **consumptive** *adjective* & *noun* (dated).

contact > *noun* /**kon**takt/ **1** the state or condition of physical touching. **2** (before another noun) caused by or operating through physical touch: *contact dermatitis*. **3** the state or condition of communicating or meeting. **4** a meeting or communication set up with someone. **5** a person who may be asked for information or assistance. **6** a person who has associated with a patient with a contagious disease. **7** a connection for the passage of an electric current from one thing to another. > *verb* /**kon**takt, kən**takt**/ get in touch or communication with.

DERIVATIVES – **contactable** *adjective*.

SYNONYMS – *noun* **1** connection, joining, meeting, touch, union. **3** communication, connection, correspondence. *verb* approach, communicate with, reach.

COMBINATIONS – **contact lens** a thin plastic lens placed directly on the surface of the eye to correct visual defects. **contact print** a photographic print made by placing a negative directly on to sensitised paper, glass, or film and illuminating it. **contact sport** a sport in which the participants necessarily come into bodily contact with one another.

ORIGIN – Latin *contactus*, from *contingere* 'touch, border on'.

contagion /kən**tay**jən/ > *noun* the communication of disease from one person to another by close contact.

ORIGIN – Latin, from *con-* 'together with' + the base of *tangere* 'to touch'.

contagious > *adjective* **1** (of a disease) spread by direct or indirect contact between people or organisms. **2** having a contagious disease. **3** (of an emotion, attitude, etc.) likely to spread to and affect others.

DERIVATIVES – **contagiously** *adverb* **contagiousness** *noun*.

SYNONYMS – **1** catching, communicable, infectious, transmittable.

contain > *verb* **1** have or hold within. **2** control or restrain. **3** prevent (a problem) from becoming worse.

DERIVATIVES – **containable** *adjective*.

SYNONYMS – **1** accommodate, carry, comprise, hold, include. **2,3** control, curb, restrain, suppress, stifle.

ORIGIN – Latin *continere*, from *con-* 'altogether' + *tenere* 'to hold'.

container > *noun* **1** a box, cylinder, or similar object for holding something. **2** a large standard-sized metal box for the transport of goods by road, rail, sea, or air.

containerise (also **containerize**) > *verb* pack into or transport by container.

DERIVATIVES – **containerisation** *noun*.

containment > *noun* the action of keeping something harmful under control.

contaminate > *verb* make impure by exposure to or addition of a poisonous or polluting substance.

DERIVATIVES – **contaminant** *noun* **contamination** *noun*.

SYNONYMS – corrupt, infect, poison, pollute, taint.

ORIGIN – Latin *contaminare* 'make impure', from *contamen* 'contact, pollution'.

contemn /kən**tem**/ > *verb* archaic treat or regard with contempt.

ORIGIN – Latin *contemnere*, from *temnere* 'despise'.

contemplate /**kon**təmplayt/ > *verb* **1** look at thoughtfully. **2** think about. **3** think profoundly and at length. **4** have (something) in mind as a probable intention.

DERIVATIVES – **contemplator** noun.

SYNONYMS – **1** eye, observe, regard, study, view. **3** meditate, muse, ponder, reflect, ruminate.

ORIGIN – Latin *contemplari* 'survey, observe, contemplate', from *templum* 'place for observation'.

contemplation > noun **1** the action of contemplating. **2** religious meditation.

contemplative /kəntemplətiv/ > adjective expressing or involving contemplation. > noun a person whose life is devoted to prayer, especially in a monastery or convent.

DERIVATIVES – **contemplatively** adverb.

contemporaneous /kəntempərayniəss/ > adjective existing at or occurring in the same period of time.

DERIVATIVES – **contemporaneity** noun **contemporaneously** adverb **contemporaneousness** noun.

ORIGIN – Latin, from *con-* 'together with' + *temporaneus*, from *tempus* 'time'.

contemporary* /kəntempərəri/ > adjective **1** living, occurring, or originating at the same time. **2** belonging to or occurring in the present. **3** modern in style or design. > noun (pl. **contemporaries**) **1** a person or thing existing at the same time as another. **2** a person of roughly the same age as another.

*SPELLING – contem*porary*, not *-pory*.

SYNONYMS – adjective **1** coeval, coexistent, concurrent, contemporaneous, synchronous. **2** current, modern, present-day. **3** modern, trendy, up-to-date.

ORIGIN – Latin *contemporarius*, from *con-* 'together with' + *tempus* 'time'.

contempt > noun **1** the feeling that a person or thing is worthless or beneath consideration. **2** (also **contempt of court**) the offence of being disobedient to or disrespectful of a court of law.

IDIOMS – **beneath contempt** utterly worthless or despicable. **hold in contempt** despise.

SYNONYMS – **1** abhorrence, disdain, disgust, scorn.

ORIGIN – Latin *contemptus*, from *contemnere*, from *temnere* 'despise'.

contemptible > adjective deserving contempt.

DERIVATIVES – **contemptibly** adverb.

SYNONYMS – base, despicable, detestable, loathsome, worthless.

contemptuous > adjective showing contempt.

DERIVATIVES – **contemptuously** adverb **contemptuousness** noun.

SYNONYMS – disdainful, derisive, scathing, scornful, sneering.

contend > verb **1** (**contend with** or

against) struggle to surmount (a difficulty). **2** (**contend for**) engage in a struggle or campaign to achieve. **3** assert something as a position in an argument.

DERIVATIVES – **contender** noun.

SYNONYMS – **1** (**contend with** or **against**) cope with, face, grapple with. **2** (**contend for**) compete for, fight for, vie for. **3** assert, claim, hold, maintain.

ORIGIN – Latin *contendere*, from *con-* 'with' + *tendere* 'stretch, strive'.

content¹ /kəntent/ > adjective **1** happy and at ease. **2** willing to accept something; satisfied. > verb **1** satisfy or please (someone). **2** (**content oneself with**) accept (something) as adequate despite wanting something more or better. > noun **1** a state of satisfaction. **2** a member of the British House of Lords who votes for a motion.

IDIOMS – **to one's heart's content** to the full extent of one's desires.

DERIVATIVES – **contentment** noun.

SYNONYMS – adjective contented, gratified, happy, pleased, satisfied. verb **1** gratify, mollify, please, satisfy. noun **1** contentedness, contentment, happiness, satisfaction.

ANTONYMS – adjective discontented, dissatisfied. noun discontent.

ORIGIN – Latin *contentus* 'satisfied', from *continere*, from *con-* 'altogether' and *tenere* 'to hold'.

content² /kontent/ > noun **1** (**contents**) the things that are contained in something. **2** the amount of a particular thing occurring in a substance: *soya milk has a low fat content*. **3** (**contents** or **table of contents**) a list of chapters or sections at the front of a book or periodical. **4** the material dealt with in a speech or text as distinct from its form or style.

ORIGIN – Latin *contentum* 'thing contained', from *continere* (see **CONTAIN**).

contented > adjective happy or satisfied and at ease; content.

DERIVATIVES – **contentedly** adverb **contentedness** noun.

contention > noun **1** heated disagreement. **2** an assertion.

IDIOMS – **in contention** having a good chance of success in a contest.

SYNONYMS – **1** conflict, disagreement, discord, dispute. **2** allegation, argument, assertion, claim.

ORIGIN – Latin, from *contendere* 'contend'.

contentious > adjective **1** causing or likely to cause disagreement or controversy. **2** Law relating to or involving differences between contending parties. **3** given to provoking argument.

DERIVATIVES – **contentiously** adverb **contentiousness** noun.

SYNONYMS – **1** controversial, debatable, disputed, vexed.

ORIGIN – Latin *contentiosus*, from *contendere* 'strive with'.

conterminous /kontɜːminəss/ > adjective **1** sharing a common boundary. **2** having the same area, context, or meaning.

DERIVATIVES – **conterminously** adverb.

ORIGIN – Latin *conterminus*, from *con-* 'with' + *terminus* 'boundary'.

contest > noun /kontest/ **1** an event in which people compete for supremacy. **2** a dispute or conflict. > verb /kəntest/ **1** compete to attain (a position of power). **2** take part in (a competition or election). **3** challenge or dispute.

IDIOMS – **no contest 1** a decision to declare a boxing match invalid on the grounds that one or both of the boxers are not making serious efforts. **2** a competition or comparison of which the outcome is a foregone conclusion.

DERIVATIVES – **contestable** adjective **contester** noun.

SYNONYMS – noun **1** championship, competition, game, match, tournament. **2** conflict, dispute, fight, struggle. verb **1** compete for, contend for, vie for. **2** compete in, contend in, enter, take part in. **3** challenge, dispute, oppose, question.

ORIGIN – first used in the sense 'swear to, attest'; from Latin *contestari* 'call upon to witness, initiate an action (by calling witnesses)'.

contestant > noun a person who takes part in a contest.

context > noun **1** the circumstances that form the setting for an event, statement, or idea. **2** the parts that immediately precede and follow a word or passage and clarify its meaning.

DERIVATIVES – **contextual** adjective **contextually** adverb.

SYNONYMS – **1** background, circumstances, environment, setting, situation.

ORIGIN – first used to denote the construction of a text; from Latin *contextus*, from *con-* 'together' + *texere* 'to weave'.

contextualise (also **contextualize**) > verb place or examine (something) in its context.

DERIVATIVES – **contextualisation** noun.

contiguous /kəntigyooəss/ > adjective **1** sharing a common border. **2** next or together in sequence.

DERIVATIVES – **contiguity** noun **contiguously** adverb.

ORIGIN – Latin *contiguus* 'touching'.

continent¹ > noun **1** any of the world's main continuous expanses of land (Europe, Asia, Africa, North and South America, Australia, Antarctica). **2** (also **the Continent**) the mainland of Europe as distinct from the British Isles.

ORIGIN – from Latin *terra continens* 'continuous land'.

continent² > *adjective* **1** able to control movements of the bowels and bladder. **2** exercising self-restraint, especially sexually.
DERIVATIVES – **continence** *noun* **continently** *adverb*.
ORIGIN – Latin, from *continere*, from *con-* 'altogether' and *tenere* 'to hold'.

continental > *adjective* **1** forming or belonging to a continent. **2** (often **Continental**) coming from or characteristic of mainland Europe. > *noun* (often **Continental**) a person from mainland Europe.
COMBINATIONS – **continental breakfast** a light breakfast of coffee and bread rolls with butter and jam. **continental climate** a relatively dry climate with very hot summers and very cold winters, characteristic of the central parts of Asia and North America. **continental drift** the gradual movement of the continents across the earth's surface through geological time. **continental quilt** Brit. a duvet. **continental shelf** an area of seabed around a large land mass where the sea is relatively shallow.

contingency /kən**tin**jənsi/ > *noun* (pl. **contingencies**) **1** a future event or circumstance which is possible but cannot be predicted with certainty. **2** a provision for such an event or circumstance. **3** the absence of certainty in events.

contingent /kən**tin**jənt/ > *adjective* **1** subject to chance. **2** (**contingent on** or **upon**) dependent on. **3** (of losses, liabilities, etc.) that can be anticipated to arise if a particular event occurs. > *noun* **1** a group of people within a larger group. **2** a body of troops or police sent to join a larger force.
DERIVATIVES – **contingently** *adverb*.
ORIGIN – Latin, from *contingere* 'befall'.

continual > *adjective* constantly or frequently occurring.
DERIVATIVES – **continually** *adverb*.
SYNONYMS – constant, incessant, persistent, recurrent.
ANTONYMS – occasional, sporadic.
USAGE – **continual** should be distinguished from **continuous**: see the note at **CONTINUOUS**.
ORIGIN – Old French *continuel*, from Latin *continuare*, from *continuus* 'uninterrupted'.

continuance > *noun* formal **1** the state of continuing. **2** the time for which a situation or action lasts.

continuation > *noun* **1** the action of continuing or state of being continued. **2** a part that is attached to and is an extension of something else.

continue > *verb* (**continues, continued, continuing**) **1** persist in an activity or process. **2** remain in existence, operation, or a specified state. **3** carry on with. **4** carry on

travelling in the same direction. **5** recommence or resume.
DERIVATIVES – **continuator** *noun*.
SYNONYMS – **1** carry on, persevere, persist. **2** endure, last, remain, survive. **3** keep up, maintain, prolong, sustain. **5** pick up, recommence, resume.
ANTONYMS – cease, discontinue, stop.
ORIGIN – Latin *continuare*, from *continuus* 'uninterrupted'.

continuity /kontin**nyoo**iti/ > *noun* (pl. **continuities**) **1** the unbroken and consistent existence or operation of something. **2** a connection or line of development with no sharp breaks. **3** the maintenance of continuous action and self-consistent detail in the scenes of a film or broadcast. **4** the linking of broadcast items by a spoken commentary.

continuo /kən**tin**yoo-ō/ (also **basso continuo**) > *noun* (pl. **continuos**) (in baroque music) an accompanying part which includes a bass line and harmonies, typically played on a keyboard instrument.
ORIGIN – Italian *basso continuo* 'continuous bass'.

continuous > *adjective* **1** without interruption. **2** forming a series with no exceptions or reversals.
DERIVATIVES – **continuously** *adverb* **continuousness** *noun*.
USAGE – **continuous** and **continual** are not synonyms, although there is some overlap. **Continuous** primarily means 'without interruption', and can refer to space as well as time, as in *the cliffs form a continuous line along the coast*. **Continual**, on the other hand, typically means 'happening frequently, with intervals between', as in *the bus service has been disrupted by continual breakdowns*.
SYNONYMS – **1** constant, non-stop, uninterrupted, unremitting.
ANTONYMS – **1** intermittent.
COMBINATIONS – **continuous assessment** Brit. the evaluation of a pupil's progress throughout a course of study, rather than by examination.
ORIGIN – Latin *continuus*, from *continere* 'hang together'.

continuum > *noun* (pl. **continua**) a continuous sequence in which adjacent elements are not perceptibly different from each other, but the extremes are quite distinct.
ORIGIN – Latin, from *continuus* 'uninterrupted'.

contort > *verb* twist or bend (something) out of its normal shape.
DERIVATIVES – **contortion** *noun*.
ORIGIN – Latin *contorquere* 'twist round, brandish'.

contortionist > *noun* an entertainer who

twists and bends their body into strange and unnatural positions.

contour > *noun* **1** an outline, especially one representing or bounding the shape or form of something. **2** (also **contour line**) a line on a map joining points of equal height above or below sea level. > *verb* **1** mould into a specific shape. **2** (**contoured**) (of a map or diagram) marked with contours. **3** (of a road or railway) follow the outline of (a topographical feature).
SYNONYMS – *noun* **1** outline, profile, shape, silhouette.
ORIGIN – French, from Italian *contorno*, from *contornare* 'draw in outline'.

contra- > *prefix* **1** against; opposite: *contraception*. **2** Music (of instruments or organ stops) pitched an octave below: *contrabass*.
ORIGIN – from Latin *contra* 'against'.

contraband /**kon**trəband/ > *noun* **1** goods that have been imported or exported illegally. **2** trade in smuggled goods. > *adjective* **1** imported or exported illegally. **2** relating to traffic in illegal goods.
DERIVATIVES – **contrabandist** *noun*.
SYNONYMS – *noun* **2** bootlegging, smuggling, trafficking. *adjective* **1** black-market, bootleg, illicit, smuggled.
ORIGIN – Italian *contrabando*, from *contra-* 'against' + *bando* 'proclamation, ban'.

contraception > *noun* the use of contraceptives.

contraceptive > *adjective* **1** serving to prevent pregnancy. **2** relating to contraception. > *noun* a device or drug used to prevent conception.

contract > *noun* /**kon**trakt/ **1** a written or spoken agreement intended to be enforceable by law. **2** informal an arrangement for someone to be killed by a hired assassin. > *verb* /kən**trakt**/ **1** decrease in size, number, or range. **2** (of a muscle) become shorter and tighter in order to effect movement of part of the body. **3** shorten (a word or phrase) by omitting or merging letters or words. **4** enter into a formal and legally binding agreement. **5** (**contract in** or **out**) Brit. choose to be or not to be involved in. **6** (**contract out**) arrange for (work) to be done by another person or organisation. **7** catch or develop (a disease). **8** become liable to pay (a debt).
DERIVATIVES – **contractive** *adjective* **contractual** *adjective* **contractually** *adverb*.
SYNONYMS – *noun* **1** agreement, covenant, deal, pact, treaty. *verb* **1** decrease, diminish, shrink, shrivel. **2** constrict, flex, tense, tighten. **4** agree, pledge, promise, undertake.
COMBINATIONS – **contract bridge** the standard form of the card game bridge, in which only tricks bid and won count towards the game.

ORIGIN – Latin *contrahere* 'draw together, tighten'.

contractable > *adjective* (of a disease) able to be caught.

contractible > *adjective* able to be shrunk or capable of contracting.

contractile /kəntraktīl/ > *adjective* **Biology & Physiology** capable of or producing contraction.

DERIVATIVES – **contractility** *noun.*

contraction > *noun* **1** the process of contracting. **2** a shortening of the muscles of the womb occurring at intervals during childbirth. **3** a word or group of words resulting from contracting an original form.

contractor > *noun* a person who undertakes a contract to provide materials or labour for a job.

contradict > *verb* **1** deny the truth of (a statement) by asserting the opposite. **2** challenge (someone) by making a statement opposing one made by them.

DERIVATIVES – **contradictor** *noun.*

SYNONYMS – **1** controvert, counter, refute; formal gainsay. **2** challenge, oppose; formal gainsay.

ORIGIN – Latin *contradicere* 'speak against'.

contradiction > *noun* **1** a combination of statements, ideas, or features which are opposed to one another. **2** the statement of a position opposite to one already made.

IDIOMS – **contradiction in terms** a statement or group of words associating incompatible objects or ideas.

SYNONYMS – **1** clash, conflict, disagreement, incongruity, inconsistency. **2** countering, denial, rebuttal, refutation.

contradictory > *adjective* **1** mutually opposed or inconsistent. **2** containing inconsistent elements.

DERIVATIVES – **contradictorily** *adverb* **contradictoriness** *noun.*

SYNONYMS – **1** antithetical, discrepant, incompatible, inconsistent, opposed.

ANTONYMS – consistent.

contradistinction > *noun* distinction made by contrasting the different qualities of two things.

contraflow > *noun* Brit. a temporary arrangement by which the lanes of a dual carriageway or motorway normally carrying traffic in one direction become two-directional.

contraindicate > *verb* Medicine (of a condition or circumstance) suggest or indicate that (a particular technique or drug) should not be used.

DERIVATIVES – **contraindication** *noun.*

contralto /kəntraltō/ > *noun* (pl. **contraltos**) the lowest female singing voice.

ORIGIN – Italian, from *contra-* 'counter to' + **ALTO**.

contraption > *noun* a machine or device that appears strange or unnecessarily complicated.

ORIGIN – perhaps from **CONTRIVE**, by association with **TRAP**[1].

contrapuntal /kontrəpunt'l/ > *adjective* Music of or in counterpoint.

DERIVATIVES – **contrapuntally** *adverb* **contrapuntist** *noun.*

ORIGIN – from Italian *contrapunto.*

contrariety /kontrərīəti/ > *noun* opposition or inconsistency between two things.

contrariwise /kəntrairiwīz/ > *adverb* **1** in the opposite way. **2** on the other hand.

contrary /kontrəri/ > *adjective* **1** opposite in nature, direction, or meaning. **2** (of two or more statements, beliefs, etc.) opposed to one another. **3** /kəntrairi/ perversely inclined to do the opposite of what is expected or desired. > *noun* (**the contrary**) the opposite.

IDIOMS – **on** (or **quite**) **the contrary** said when one is emphatically denying what has just been implied or stated. **to the contrary** with the opposite meaning or implication.

DERIVATIVES – **contrarily** *adverb* **contrariness** *noun.*

SYNONYMS – *adjective* **1** converse, opposing, opposite. **2** antithetical, contradictory. **3** awkward, obstinate, perverse, stubborn.

ORIGIN – Latin *contrarius*, from *contra* 'against'.

contrast > *noun* /kontraast/ **1** the state of being strikingly different from something that is juxtaposed or closely associated. **2** a thing or person noticeably different from another. **3** the degree of difference between tones in a television picture, photograph, etc. **4** enhancement of appearance provided by the juxtaposition of different colours or textures. > *verb* /kəntraast/ **1** differ strikingly. **2** compare so as to emphasise differences.

DERIVATIVES – **contrastive** *adjective.*

SYNONYMS – *noun* **1** difference, disparity, dissimilarity, distinction. *verb* **1** differ, diverge. **2** compare, juxtapose, set against.

ORIGIN – Latin *contrastare*, from *contra-* 'against' + *stare* 'stand'.

contravene /kontrəveen/ > *verb* **1** commit an act that is not in accordance with (a law, treaty, etc.). **2** conflict with (a right, principle, etc.).

DERIVATIVES – **contravener** *noun* **contravention** *noun.*

SYNONYMS – **1** breach, break, flout, infringe, violate.

ORIGIN – Latin *contravenire*, from *contra-* 'against' + *venire* 'come'.

contretemps /kontrətoN/ > *noun* (pl. same or /kontrətoNz/) a minor dispute or disagreement.

ORIGIN – French, from *contre-* 'against' + *temps* 'time': originally meaning 'motion out of time', denoting a thrust in fencing made at an inopportune moment; .

contribute /kəntribyōot, kontribyōot/ > *verb* **1** give in order to help achieve or provide something. **2** (**contribute to**) help to cause or bring about.

DERIVATIVES – **contribution** *noun* **contributive** *adjective* **contributor** *noun.*

NOTE – the first pronunciation, which puts the stress on **-tri-**, is regarded as the correct one, despite the fact that the alternative, with the stress on **con-**, is older.

SYNONYMS – **1** bestow, donate, give, grant. **2** (**contribute to**) add to, aid, advance, further, play a part in.

ORIGIN – Latin *contribuere* 'bring together, add', from *tribuere* 'bestow'.

contributory > *adjective* **1** playing a part in bringing something about. **2** (of a pension or insurance scheme) operated by means of a fund into which people pay.

con trick > *noun* informal a confidence trick.

contrite /kəntrīt, kontrīt/ > *adjective* recognising that one has done wrong and feeling or expressing remorse.

DERIVATIVES – **contritely** *adverb* **contriteness** *noun* **contrition** *noun.*

SYNONYMS – penitent, regretful, remorseful, repentant, sorry.

ORIGIN – Latin *contritus*, from *conterere* 'grind down, wear away'.

contrivance > *noun* **1** the action of contriving something. **2** an ingenious device or scheme.

contrive /kəntrīv/ > *verb* **1** devise or plan (something) using skill and artifice. **2** manage to do something foolish.

DERIVATIVES – **contriver** *noun.*

SYNONYMS – **1** design, devise, engineer, orchestrate, plan, stage-manage.

ORIGIN – Old French *controver* 'imagine, invent', from Latin *contropare* 'compare'.

contrived > *adjective* deliberately created rather than arising spontaneously.

SYNONYMS – affected, artificial, laboured, manufactured, studied.

ANTONYMS – natural, spontaneous.

control > *noun* **1** the power to influence people's behaviour or the course of events. **2** the restriction of an activity, tendency, or phenomenon. **3** a means of limiting or regulating something: *exchange controls.* **4** a device by which a machine is regulated. **5** the place where something is verified or from which an activity is directed. **6** a person or thing used as a standard of comparison for checking the results of a survey or experiment. > *verb* (**controlled, controlling**) **1** have control or command of. **2** regulate (a mechanical or scientific process). **3** (**controlled**) (of a drug) restricted by law in respect of use and possession.

IDIOMS – **in control** able to direct a situation, person, or activity. **out of control** no longer manageable. **under control** (of a danger or emergency) being dealt with or contained successfully.

DERIVATIVES – **controllability** noun **controllable** adjective **controllably** adverb **controller** noun.

SYNONYMS – noun **1** authority, command, government, leadership, power. **2** constraint, limitation, regulation, restriction. verb **1** command, direct, govern, manage, rule.

COMBINATIONS – **controlling interest** the holding by one person or group of a majority of the stock of a business. **control tower** a tall building from which the movements of air traffic are monitored and directed.

ORIGIN – first used in the sense 'verify accounts': from Old French contreroller 'keep a copy of a roll of accounts', from Latin contrarotulus 'copy of a roll', from contra- 'against' + rotulus 'a roll'.

controversial > adjective causing or likely to cause controversy.

DERIVATIVES – **controversialist** noun **controversially** adverb.

SYNONYMS – contentious, debatable, emotive, questionable, vexed.

controversy /**kon**trəversi, kən**trov**versi/ > noun (pl. **controversies**) debate or disagreement within a society or a group of people.

NOTE – the second pronunciation, with the stress on –**trov**-, is sometimes regarded as incorrect, although both are widespread.

SYNONYMS – argument, contention, debate, disagreement, dispute.

ORIGIN – Latin controversia, from controversus 'turned against, disputed'.

controvert > verb deny the truth of.

DERIVATIVES – **controvertible** adjective.

ORIGIN – from Latin controversus 'turned against, disputed'.

contumacious /kontyoo**mays**həss/ > adjective archaic or Law stubbornly or wilfully disobedient to authority.

DERIVATIVES – **contumaciously** adverb **contumacy** noun.

ORIGIN – from Latin contumax, perhaps from tumere 'to swell'.

contumely /kon**tyoom**li/ > noun (pl. **contumelies**) archaic insolent or insulting language or treatment.

DERIVATIVES – **contumelious** /kontyoo**mee**liəss/ adjective.

ORIGIN – Latin contumelia, perhaps from tumere 'to swell'.

contusion /kən**tyooz**h'n/ > noun Medicine a bruise.

DERIVATIVES – **contuse** verb.

ORIGIN – Latin, from contundere, from con- 'together' + tundere 'to beat, thump'.

conundrum /kə**nun**drəm/ > noun (pl. **conundrums**) **1** a confusing and difficult problem or question. **2** a riddle.

SYNONYMS – **1** difficulty, dilemma, quandary.

conurbation /konnur**bay**sh'n/ > noun an extended urban area, typically consisting of several towns merging with the suburbs of a central city.

ORIGIN – from CON- 'together' + Latin urbs 'city'.

convalesce /konvə**less**/ > verb gradually recover one's health after an illness or medical treatment.

ORIGIN – Latin convalescere, from valescere 'grow strong'.

convalescent > adjective recovering from an illness or medical treatment. > noun a convalescent person.

DERIVATIVES – **convalescence** noun.

convection > noun transference of mass or heat within a fluid caused by the tendency of warmer and less dense material to rise.

DERIVATIVES – **convect** verb **convectional** adjective **convective** adjective.

ORIGIN – Latin, from convehere 'carry together, collect, store'.

convector > noun a heating appliance that circulates warm air by convection.

convene /kən**veen**/ > verb **1** call people together for (a meeting). **2** assemble for a common purpose.

DERIVATIVES – **convenable** adjective.

SYNONYMS – **1** summon; formal convoke. **2** assemble, congregate, gather, meet.

ORIGIN – Latin convenire 'assemble, come together'.

convener (also **convenor**) > noun **1** a person who convenes meetings of a committee. **2** Brit. a senior trade union official at a workplace.

convenience > noun **1** freedom from effort or difficulty. **2** a useful or helpful device or situation. **3** Brit. a public toilet.

IDIOMS – **at one's convenience** when or where it suits one. **at one's earliest convenience** as soon as one can without difficulty. **flag of convenience** a flag of a country in which a ship is registered in order to avoid higher costs or stricter regulations in the owner's country.

COMBINATIONS – **convenience food** a food that has been pre-prepared commercially and so requires little preparation by the consumer.

ORIGIN – Latin convenientia, from convenire 'assemble, come together'.

convenient > adjective **1** fitting in well with a person's needs, activities, and plans. **2** involving little trouble or effort.

DERIVATIVES – **conveniently** adverb.

SYNONYMS – **1** expedient, handy, opportune, suitable.

ANTONYMS – inconvenient.

convent > noun **1** a Christian community of nuns living under monastic vows. **2** (also **convent school**) a school attached to and run by a convent.

wordpower facts
Convent
The words **convent** and **coven** are from the same root! They both come ultimately from Latin convenire 'come together, assemble, agree, fit', the root also of **convene**, **convenient**, **convention**, and **covenant**. The original spelling of **convent** was covent, which survives in the London place name Covent Garden. **Coven** is a variant of the archaic word **covin** 'fraud, deception', which originally denoted a company or band.

conventicle /kən**ven**tik'l/ > noun historical a secret or unlawful religious meeting, typically of nonconformists.

ORIGIN – Latin conventiculum 'place of assembly'.

convention > noun **1** a way in which something is usually done. **2** socially acceptable behaviour. **3** an agreement between countries. **4** a large meeting or conference. **5** N. Amer. an assembly of the delegates of a political party to select candidates for office. **6** a body set up by agreement to deal with a particular issue.

SYNONYMS – **1** custom, habit, norm, practice, tradition. **2** etiquette, propriety, protocol. **3** agreement, contract, pact, treaty. **4** assembly, colloquium, conference, gathering, summit, symposium.

ORIGIN – Latin, 'meeting, covenant'.

conventional > adjective **1** based on or in accordance with convention. **2** support or uphold ideas or patterns of behaviour that are generally held to be acceptable. **3** (of weapons or power) non-nuclear.

DERIVATIVES – **conventionalise** (also **conventionalize**) verb **conventionality** noun **conventionally** adverb.

SYNONYMS – **1** accustomed, customary, established, orthodox, traditional. **2** commonplace, conformist, conservative, prosaic, unadventurous.

ANTONYMS – **1** unorthodox. **2** unconventional.

converge /kən**verj**/ > verb **1** come together from different directions so as eventually to meet. **2** (**converge on**) come from different directions and meet at (a place or point).

DERIVATIVES – **convergent** adjective.

ORIGIN – Latin *convergere*, from *con-* 'together'+ *vergere* 'incline'.

conversant > *adjective* (**conversant with**) familiar with or knowledgeable about.

DERIVATIVES – **conversance** *noun* **conversancy** *noun*.

ORIGIN – Old French, from *converser*, from Latin *conversari* 'keep company with'.

conversation > *noun* an informal spoken exchange of news and ideas between two or more people.

DERIVATIVES – **conversational** *adjective*.

SYNONYMS – chat, discussion, gossip, talk.

conversationalist > *noun* a person who is good at or fond of engaging in conversation.

converse[1] > *verb* /kən**verss**/ hold a conversation.

DERIVATIVES – **converser** *noun*.

SYNONYMS – chat, chatter, gossip, talk; formal confabulate.

ORIGIN – first used in the sense 'live among, be familiar with'; from Old French *converser*, from Latin *conversari* 'keep company with'.

converse[2] /**kon**verss/ > *noun* a situation, object, or statement that is the opposite of another. > *adjective* opposite.

DERIVATIVES – **conversely** *adverb*.

ORIGIN – from Latin *conversus* 'turned about'.

conversion > *noun* **1** the process or action of converting or of being converted. **2 Brit.** a building that has been converted to a new purpose. **3 Rugby** a successful kick at goal after a try, scoring two points.

SYNONYMS – **1** alteration, change, metamorphosis, transformation, translation.

convert > *verb* /kən**vert**/ **1** change in form, character, or function. **2** change (money, stocks, or units in which a quantity is expressed) into others of a different kind. **3** adapt (a building) to make it suitable for a new purpose. **4** change one's religious faith or other beliefs. **5 Rugby** score extra points after (a try) by a successful kick at goal. > *noun* /**kon**vert/ a person who has changed their religious faith or other beliefs.

DERIVATIVES – **converter** (also **convertor**) *noun*.

SYNONYMS – *verb* **1** alter, change, metamorphose, transform, translate. **3** adapt, alter, reconstruct, redevelop, renovate.

ORIGIN – Latin *convertere* 'turn about'.

convertible > *adjective* **1** able to be converted. **2** (of a car) having a folding or detachable roof. > *noun* a convertible car.

DERIVATIVES – **convertibility** *noun*.

convex /**kon**veks/ > *adjective* having an outline or surface curved like the exterior of a circle or sphere. Compare with **CONCAVE**.

DERIVATIVES – **convexity** *noun* **convexly** *adverb*.

ORIGIN – Latin *convexus* 'vaulted, arched'.

convey /kən**vay**/ > *verb* **1** transport or carry to a place. **2** communicate (an idea, impression, or feeling). **3 Law** transfer the title to (property).

DERIVATIVES – **conveyable** *adjective* **conveyor** (also **conveyer**) *noun*.

SYNONYMS – **1** bear, carry, ferry, transfer, transport. **2** communicate, express, impart, relay.

COMBINATIONS – **conveyor belt** a continuous moving band used for transporting objects from one place to another.

ORIGIN – Latin *conviare*, from *con-* 'together' + *via* 'way'.

conveyance > *noun* **1** the action or process of conveying. **2 formal** a means of transport; a vehicle. **3** the legal process of transferring property from one owner to another.

DERIVATIVES – **conveyancer** *noun* **conveyancing** *noun*.

convict > *verb* /kən**vikt**/ declare (someone) to be guilty of a criminal offence by the verdict of a jury or the decision of a judge in a court of law. > *noun* /**kon**vikt/ a person convicted of a criminal offence and serving a sentence of imprisonment.

ORIGIN – Latin *convincere*, from *con-* 'with' + *vincere* 'conquer'.

conviction > *noun* **1** an instance of being convicted of a crime. **2** the action or process of convicting someone. **3** a firmly held belief or opinion. **4** the quality of showing that one is firmly convinced of what one believes or says.

SYNONYMS – **3** belief, opinion, persuasion, principle, view. **4** assurance, certainty, firmness, sureness.

convince > *verb* **1** cause (someone) to believe firmly in the truth of something. **2** persuade to do something.

DERIVATIVES – **convincer** *noun* **convincible** *adjective*.

USAGE – some people deplore the use of **convince** as a synonym for **persuade**, as in *she convinced my father to branch out on his own*, maintaining that **convince** should be reserved for situations in which someone's belief is changed but no action is taken as a result, while **persuade** should be used for situations in which action results. However, this newer use of **convince** is well established and is used by well-respected writers.

SYNONYMS – **1** prove to, satisfy. **2** persuade, prevail on, sway, talk round.

ORIGIN – Latin *convincere*, from *con-* 'with' + *vincere* 'conquer'.

convincing > *adjective* **1** able to convince. **2** (of a victory or a winner) leaving no margin of doubt.

DERIVATIVES – **convincingly** *adverb*.

SYNONYMS – **1** cogent, compelling, credible, persuasive. **2** conclusive, decisive, emphatic, resounding.

convivial /kən**vivv**iəl/ > *adjective* **1** (of an atmosphere or event) friendly and lively. **2** (of a person) cheerfully sociable.

DERIVATIVES – **conviviality** *noun* **convivially** *adverb*.

ORIGIN – first used in the sense 'fit for a feast'; from Latin *convivialis*, from *convivium* 'a feast'.

convocation /konvə**kay**sh'n/ > *noun* a large formal assembly of people.

DERIVATIVES – **convocational** *adjective*.

ORIGIN – Latin, from *convocare* 'call together'.

convoke /kən**vōk**/ > *verb* formal call together (an assembly or meeting).

ORIGIN – Latin *convocare* 'call together'.

convoluted /konvə**lōō**tid/ > *adjective* **1** (of an argument, statement, etc.) extremely complex. **2** intricately folded, twisted, or coiled.

DERIVATIVES – **convolutedly** *adverb*.

ORIGIN – Latin *convolutus*, from *convolvere* 'roll together, intertwine'.

convolution > *noun* **1** a coil or twist. **2** the state or process of being or becoming coiled or twisted. **3** a complex argument, statement, etc.

DERIVATIVES – **convolutional** *adjective*.

ORIGIN – Latin, from *convolvere* 'roll together'.

convolvulus /kən**volv**yooləss/ > *noun* (pl. **convolvuluses**) a twining plant with trumpet-shaped flowers, some kinds of which are invasive weeds; bindweed.

ORIGIN – Latin, 'bindweed', from *convolvere* 'roll together'.

convoy /**kon**voy/ > *noun* a group of ships or vehicles travelling together, typically with armed protection. > *verb* (of a warship or armed troops) accompany (a group of ships or vehicles) for protection.

IDIOMS – **in convoy** travelling as a group.

ORIGIN – first used in the senses 'convey' and 'act as escort': from Latin *conviare*, from *con-* 'together' + *via* 'way'.

convulsant > *adjective* producing convulsions. > *noun* a convulsant drug.

convulse /kən**vulss**/ > *verb* **1** suffer convulsions. **2** (**be convulsed**) be caused by an emotion, laughter, or physical stimulus to make sudden, violent, uncontrollable movements.

DERIVATIVES – **convulsive** *adjective* **convulsively** *adverb*.

ORIGIN – Latin *convellere* 'pull violently, wrench'.

convulsion > *noun* **1** a sudden, violent, irregular movement of the body caused by involuntary contraction of muscles. **2**

(**convulsions**) uncontrollable laughter. **3** a violent social or natural upheaval.

cony > *noun* variant spelling of CONEY.

coo > *verb* (**coos**, **cooed**) **1** (of a pigeon or dove) make a soft murmuring sound. **2** (of a person) speak in a soft gentle voice. > *noun* a cooing sound.

cooee informal > *exclamation* used to attract attention. > *verb* (**cooees**, **cooeed**, **cooeeing**) make such a call.
IDIOMS – **within cooee** Austral./NZ within reach.
ORIGIN – imitative of a signal used by Australian Aboriginals and copied by settlers.

cook > *verb* **1** prepare (food or a meal) by mixing, combining, and heating the elements or ingredients. **2** (with reference to food) heat or be heated so as to reach an edible state. **3** informal alter dishonestly. **4** (**cook up**) informal concoct (a story, excuse, or plan). > *noun* a person who cooks.
IDIOMS – **cook someone's goose** informal spoil someone's plans. **too many cooks spoil the broth** proverb if too many people are involved in a task or activity, it will not be done well.
SYNONYMS – *verb* **1** concoct, make, prepare.
COMBINATIONS – **cookhouse** a building used for cooking, especially on a ranch, military camp, etc.
ORIGIN – Old English, from Latin *coquus* 'a cook'.

cooker > *noun* Brit. **1** an appliance for cooking food, typically consisting of an oven, hob, and grill. **2** informal an apple or other fruit more suitable for cooking than for eating raw.

cookery > *noun* (pl. **cookeries**) **1** the practice or skill of preparing and cooking food. **2** N. Amer. a kitchen.

cookie > *noun* (pl. **cookies**) **1** N. Amer. a sweet biscuit. **2** Brit. a type of crumbly sweet biscuit. **3** informal a person of a specified kind: *she's a tough cookie.* **4** Scottish a plain bun.
IDIOMS – **the way the cookie crumbles** informal, chiefly N. Amer. the way things turn out, especially when undesirable.
COMBINATIONS – **cookie cutter** N. Amer. **1** a device with sharp edges for cutting biscuit dough into a particular shape. **2** (**cookie-cutter**) mass-produced; nondescript: *cookie-cutter songwriting.*
ORIGIN – Dutch *koekje* 'little cake'.

cookout > *noun* N. Amer. a party or gathering where a meal is cooked and eaten outdoors.

Cook's tour > *noun* informal a rapid tour of many places.

ORIGIN – from the name of the English travel agent Thomas *Cook* (1808–92).

cool > *adjective* **1** of or at a fairly low temperature. **2** keeping one from becoming too hot. **3** unfriendly or unenthusiastic. **4** free from anxiety or excitement: *he kept a cool head.* **5** (of jazz) restrained and relaxed. **6** informal fashionably attractive or impressive. **7** informal excellent. **8** (**a cool ——**) informal used to emphasise a specified large amount of money: *a cool £50 million.* > *noun* (**the cool**) a fairly low temperature, or a place or time characterised by this: *the cool of the day.* > *verb* become or cause to become cool.
IDIOMS – **keep** (or **lose**) **one's cool** informal maintain (or fail to maintain) a calm and controlled attitude.
DERIVATIVES – **coolish** adjective **coolly** adverb **coolness** noun.
SYNONYMS – *adjective* **1** chilly, cold, fresh, unheated. **3** frosty, stand-offish, tepid, unenthusiastic, unfriendly. **4** calm, collected, composed, unruffled.
ANTONYMS – *adjective* **1** warm, hot.
COMBINATIONS – **cooling-off period 1** an interval during which the parties in a dispute can try to settle their differences before taking further action. **2** an interval after a sale contract is agreed during which the purchaser can decide to cancel without loss. **cooling tower** a tall, open-topped, cylindrical concrete tower, used for cooling water or condensing steam from an industrial process.

coolant > *noun* a fluid used to cool an engine, nuclear reactor, or other device.

cooler > *noun* **1** a device or container for keeping things cool. **2** N. Amer. a refrigerator. **3** a long drink, especially a mixture of wine, fruit juice, and soda water. **4** (**the cooler**) informal prison or a prison cell.

coolibah /koolibaa/ > *noun* a North Australian gum tree which grows near watercourses and has very strong, hard wood.
ORIGIN – Kamilaroi (an Aboriginal language).

coolie /kooli/ > *noun* (pl. **coolies**) **1** dated an unskilled native labourer in India, China, and some other Asian countries. **2** offensive a person from the Indian subcontinent or of Indian descent.
COMBINATIONS – **coolie hat** a broad conical hat as worn by labourers in some Asian countries.
ORIGIN – Hindi, 'day labourer'.

coolth /koolth/ > *noun* **1** pleasantly low temperature. **2** informal articles, activities, or people perceived as fashionable.

coombe (also **coomb**) > *noun* variant spelling of COMBE.

coon > *noun* **1** N. Amer. short for RACCOON. **2** informal, offensive a black person. [ORIGIN –

slang use of sense 1, from an earlier sense '(sly) fellow'.]

coop /koop/ > *noun* **1** a cage or pen for confining poultry. **2** Brit. a basket used in catching fish. > *verb* (usu. **be cooped up**) confine in a small space.
ORIGIN – Latin *cupa* 'cask, tub'.

co-op /kō op/ > *noun* informal a cooperative organisation.

cooper > *noun* a person who makes or repairs casks and barrels. > *verb* make or repair (a cask or barrel).
DERIVATIVES – **cooperage** noun **coopery** noun.
ORIGIN – Dutch, Low German *kūper*, from *kūpe* 'tub, vat', based on Latin *cupa* 'cask, tub'.

cooperate /kōopərayt/ (also **co-operate**) > *verb* **1** work jointly towards the same end. **2** comply with a request.
DERIVATIVES – **cooperation** noun **cooperator** noun.
SYNONYMS – **1** collaborate, combine, join forces, team up, unite.
ORIGIN – Latin *cooperari* 'work together'.

cooperative (also **co-operative**) > *adjective* **1** involving cooperation. **2** willing to be of assistance. **3** (of a farm, business, etc.) owned and run jointly by its members, with profits or benefits shared among them. > *noun* a cooperative organisation.
DERIVATIVES – **cooperatively** adverb **cooperativeness** noun.
SYNONYMS – *adjective* **1** collaborative, collective, communal, pooled, unified. **2** accommodating, compliant, helpful, obliging.

co-opt > *verb* **1** appoint (someone) to membership of a committee or other body by invitation of the existing members. **2** divert to a role different from the usual or original one. **3** adopt (an idea or policy) for one's own use.
DERIVATIVES – **co-optation** noun **co-option** noun **co-optive** adjective.
ORIGIN – Latin *cooptare*, from *co-* 'together' + *optare* 'choose'.

coordinate (also **co-ordinate**) > *verb* /kōordinayt/ **1** bring the different elements of (a complex activity or organisation) into a harmonious or efficient relationship. **2** (**coordinate with**) negotiate with (others) in order to work together effectively. **3** match or harmonise attractively. > *adjective* /kōordinət/ equal in rank or importance. > *noun* /kōordinət/ **1** Mathematics each of a group of numbers used to indicate the position of a point, line, or plane. **2** (**coordinates**) matching items of clothing.
DERIVATIVES – **coordinator** noun.
SYNONYMS – *verb* **1** dovetail, harmonise, integrate, synchronise. **2** (**coordinate with**) collaborate with, cooperate with,

join forces with, negotiate with. **3** blend, complement, harmonise, match.

ORIGIN – from **co-** + Latin *ordinare* 'put in order', from *ordo* 'row, series, order'.

coordination (also **co-ordination**) > *noun* **1** the action or process of coordinating. **2** the ability to move different parts of the body smoothly and at the same time.

coot > *noun* **1** (pl. same) an aquatic bird of the rail family with black plumage and a white bill that extends back on to the forehead as a horny shield. **2** (usu. **old coot**) *informal* a stupid or eccentric person.

ORIGIN – probably Dutch or Low German.

cop *informal* > *noun* a police officer. > *verb* (**copped**, **copping**) **1** catch or arrest (an offender). **2** incur (something unwelcome). **3** US obtain (an illegal drug). **4** N. Amer. strike (an attitude or pose). **5** (**cop off**) have a sexual encounter. **6** (**cop out**) avoid doing something that one ought to do.

IDIOMS – **cop hold of** Brit. take hold of. **cop it** Brit. **1** get into trouble. **2** be killed. **not much cop** Brit. not very good.

ORIGIN – perhaps from Old French *caper* 'seize', from Latin *capere*.

copal /**kō**p'l/ > *noun* resin from certain tropical trees, used to make varnish.

ORIGIN – Spanish, from a Nahuatl word meaning 'incense'.

cope¹ > *verb* (often **cope with**) deal effectively with something difficult.

DERIVATIVES – **coper** *noun*.

SYNONYMS – (**cope with**) come through, handle, manage, withstand.

ORIGIN – first used in the sense 'meet in battle, come to blows': from Old French *coper*, from *cop* 'a blow', from Greek *kolaphos* 'a blow with the fist'.

cope² > *noun* a long, loose cloak worn by a priest or bishop on ceremonial occasions. > *verb* (in building) cover (a joint or structure) with a coping.

ORIGIN – Latin *cappa* 'covering for the head', from *caput* 'head'.

copeck > *noun* variant spelling of **KOPEK**.

Copernican system /kə**per**nikən/ (also **Copernican theory**) > *noun* the theory proposed by the Polish astronomer Nicolaus Copernicus (1473–1543) that the sun is the centre of the solar system, with the planets (including the earth) orbiting round it. Compare with **PTOLEMAIC SYSTEM**.

copier > *noun* a machine that makes exact copies of something.

co-pilot > *noun* a second pilot in an aircraft.

coping > *noun* the top course of a brick or stone wall, typically rounded or sloping.

ORIGIN – from **COPE²**, originally meaning 'dress in a cope', hence 'to cover'.

copious > *adjective* abundant in supply or quantity; plentiful.

DERIVATIVES – **copiously** *adverb* **copiousness** *noun*.

SYNONYMS – abundant, bountiful, generous, lavish, liberal, plentiful.

ANTONYMS – scanty, sparse.

ORIGIN – Latin *copiosus*, from *copia* 'plenty'.

copolymer /kō**poll**imər/ > *noun* Chemistry a polymer made by linking molecules of two different monomers.

copper¹ > *noun* **1** a red-brown metallic chemical element which is used for electrical wiring and as a component of brass and bronze. **2** (**coppers**) Brit. coins of low value made of copper or bronze. **3** Brit. dated a large copper or iron container for boiling laundry. **4** a reddish-brown colour. > *verb* cover or coat with copper.

WORDFINDER – cupreous (*of or like copper*), verdigris (*green encrustation on copper*).

DERIVATIVES – **coppery** *adjective*.

COMBINATIONS – **copper beech** a variety of beech tree with purplish-brown leaves. **copper-bottomed** Brit. thoroughly reliable. [ORIGIN – with reference to copper sheathing applied to the bottom of ships.] **copper sulphate** a blue crystalline solid used in electroplating and as a fungicide.

ORIGIN – Latin *cuprum*, from *cyprium aes* 'Cyprus metal' (so named because Cyprus was the chief source).

copper² > *noun* Brit. informal a police officer.

ORIGIN – from **COP**.

copperplate > *noun* **1** a polished copper plate with a design engraved or etched into it. **2** an elaborate looped style of handwriting. [ORIGIN – the copybooks for this were originally printed from copperplates.]

coppice > *noun* an area of woodland in which the trees or shrubs are periodically cut back to ground level to stimulate growth and provide wood. > *verb* cut back (a tree or shrub) in this way.

ORIGIN – Old French *copeiz*, from Latin *colpus*, from Greek *kolaphus* 'a blow with the fist'.

copra /**kop**rə/ > *noun* dried coconut kernels, from which oil is obtained.

ORIGIN – Portuguese and Spanish, from an Indian word for 'coconut'.

coprolite /**kop**rəlīt/ > *noun* Palaeontology a piece of fossilised dung.

ORIGIN – from Greek *kopros* 'dung'.

coprophilia /koprə**fill**iə/ > *noun* abnormal interest and pleasure in faeces and defecation.

copse > *noun* a small group of trees.

ORIGIN – shortened form of **COPPICE**.

Copt /kopt/ > *noun* **1** a native Egyptian in the Hellenistic and Roman periods. **2** a member of the Coptic Church, the native Christian Church in Egypt.

ORIGIN – Coptic, from Greek *Aiguptios* 'Egyptian'.

Coptic > *noun* the language of the Copts, which survives only in the Coptic Church. > *adjective* relating to the Copts or their language.

copula /**kop**yoolə/ > *noun* Logic & Grammar a connecting word, in particular a form of the verb *be* connecting a subject and complement.

DERIVATIVES – **copular** *adjective*.

ORIGIN – Latin, 'connection, linking of words'.

copulate /**kop**yoolayt/ > *verb* have sexual intercourse.

DERIVATIVES – **copulation** *noun* **copulatory** *adjective*.

ORIGIN – Latin *copulare* 'fasten together'.

copy > *noun* (pl. **copies**) **1** a thing made to be similar or identical to another. **2** a single specimen of a particular book, record, etc. **3** matter to be printed. **4** material for a newspaper or magazine article. > *verb* (**copies**, **copied**) **1** make a copy of. **2** imitate the behaviour or style of.

SYNONYMS – *noun* **1** duplicate, facsimile, imitation, replica, reproduction. *verb* **1** duplicate, replicate, reproduce, transcribe. **2** ape, emulate, imitate, impersonate, mimic.

COMBINATIONS – **copy typist** a person whose job is to type transcripts of written drafts. **copywriter** a person who writes the text of advertisements or publicity material.

ORIGIN – Latin *copia* 'abundance', later 'transcript'.

copybook > *noun* **1** a book containing models of handwriting for learners to imitate. **2** (before another noun) exactly in accordance with established standards: *a copybook landing*.

copycat > *noun* informal **1** a person who copies another. **2** (before another noun) (of an action, especially a crime) carried out in imitation of another: *copycat attacks*.

copy-edit > *verb* edit (text) by checking its consistency and accuracy.

DERIVATIVES – **copy editor** *noun*.

copyist > *noun* **1** a person who makes copies. **2** a person who imitates the styles of others, especially in art.

copyright > *noun* the exclusive legal right, given to the originator or their assignee for a fixed number of years, to publish, perform, film, or record literary, artistic, or musical material, and to authorise others to do the same.

coq au vin /kok ō vaN/ > *noun* a casserole of chicken pieces cooked in red wine.
ORIGIN – French, 'cock in wine'.

coquette /kəket/ > *noun* a flirtatious woman.
DERIVATIVES – **coquetry** noun **coquettish** adjective **coquettishly** adverb **coquettishness** noun.
ORIGIN – French, feminine form of *coquet* 'wanton', from *coq* 'cock'.

coracle /korrək'l/ > *noun* a small, round boat made of wickerwork covered with a watertight material, propelled with a paddle.
ORIGIN – Welsh *corwgl*, related to Scottish Gaelic and Irish *curach* 'small boat'.

coral > *noun* **1** a hard stony substance secreted by certain marine animals as an external skeleton, typically forming large reefs. **2** precious red coral, used in jewellery. **3** the pinkish-red colour of red coral.
ORIGIN – Greek *korallion*, *kouralion*.

coralline /korrəlīn/ > *adjective* **1** derived or formed from coral. **2** of the pinkish-red colour of red coral. **3** resembling coral.

cor anglais /kor ongglay/ > *noun* (pl. **cors anglais** pronunc. same) an alto woodwind instrument of the oboe family, having a bulbous bell and sounding a fifth lower than the oboe.
ORIGIN – French, 'English horn'.

corbel /korb'l/ > *noun* a projection jutting out from a wall to support a structure above it.
DERIVATIVES – **corbelled** (US **corbeled**) adjective **corbelling** (US **corbeling**) noun.
ORIGIN – Old French, from *corp* 'crow', from Latin *corvus* 'raven'.

cord > *noun* **1** material made from several strands twisted together to form a length. **2** a piece of such material. **3** an anatomical structure resembling a cord (e.g. the spinal cord). **4** an electric flex. **5** corduroy. **6** (**cords**) corduroy trousers. **7** a measure of cut wood (usually 128 cu. ft, 3.62 cubic metres). > *verb* attach a cord to.
DERIVATIVES – **cording** noun.
ORIGIN – Greek *khordē* 'gut, string of a musical instrument'.

cordate /kordayt/ > *adjective* Botany & Zoology heart-shaped.
ORIGIN – Latin *cordatus*, from *cor* 'heart'.

cordial > *adjective* **1** warm and friendly. **2** heartfelt and sincere. > *noun* **1** Brit. a sweet fruit-flavoured drink, sold as a concentrate. **2** chiefly N. Amer. another term for LIQUEUR. **3** a pleasant-tasting medicine.
DERIVATIVES – **cordiality** noun **cordially** adverb.
SYNONYMS – *adjective* **1** amiable, friendly, genial, warm, welcoming. **2** ardent, fervent, heartfelt, sincere, whole-hearted.

---

wordpower facts
Cordial

The Latin word *cor* 'heart' is the source of both **cordial** and **courage**. In fact the English word **heart**, which is of Old English origin, comes ultimately from the same root as *cor* and as Greek *kēr* and *kardia*, the source of **cardiac**. *Cor* is also the basis of English words ending in *-cord* and relating to feelings and relations: **accord**, **concord**, **discord**, and **record** (which originally had a meaning 'repeat so as to commit to memory').

---

cordite > *noun* a smokeless explosive made from nitrocellulose, nitroglycerine, and petroleum jelly.
ORIGIN – from CORD, because of its appearance.

cordless > *adjective* (of an electrical appliance or telephone) working without connection to a mains supply or central unit.

cordoba /kordəbə/ > *noun* the basic monetary unit of Nicaragua, equal to 100 centavos.
ORIGIN – named after F. Fernández de *Córdoba*, a 16th-century Spanish governor of Nicaragua.

cordon* /kord'n/ > *noun* **1** a line or circle of police, soldiers, or guards forming a barrier. **2** a fruit tree trained to grow as a single stem. > *verb* (**cordon off**) prevent access to or from by means of a cordon.
*SPELLING – cordon, not -den.
ORIGIN – Italian *cordone* and French *cordon*; related to CORD.

cordon bleu* /kordon blö/ > *adjective* Cookery of the highest class. > *noun* (pl. **cordons bleus** pronunc. same) a cook of the highest class.
*SPELLING – *bleu* is spelled the French way, rather than as *blue*.
ORIGIN – French, 'blue ribbon' (once signifying the highest order of chivalry in the reign of the Bourbon kings).

cordon sanitaire /kordon sannitair/ > *noun* (pl. **cordons sanitaires** pronunc. same) **1** a line or circle of guards positioned around an area infected by disease, preventing anyone from leaving. **2** a measure designed to prevent the spread of undesirable influences.
ORIGIN – French, 'sanitary line'.

corduroy /kordəroy/ > *noun* a thick cotton fabric with velvety ribs.
ORIGIN – probably from CORD + *duroy*, denoting a former kind of lightweight worsted.

cordwainer /kordwaynər/ > *noun* Brit. archaic a shoemaker.
ORIGIN – Old French *cordewan*, from

Spanish *cordobán* 'from Cordoba', with reference to a soft leather originally produced there.

cordwood > *noun* wood cut into cords or uniform lengths.

core > *noun* **1** the tough central part of various fruits, containing the seeds. **2** the central or most important part of something. **3** the dense metallic or rocky central region of a planet. **4** the central part of a nuclear reactor, which contains the fuel. > *verb* remove the core from (a fruit).
IDIOMS – **to the core** to the depths of one's being.
DERIVATIVES – **corer** noun.
SYNONYMS – *noun* **2** centre, crux, essence, gist, heart, nub, nucleus.
COMBINATIONS – **core time** Brit. the central part of the working day in a flexitime system, when an employee must be present.

coreopsis /korriopsiss/ > *noun* a plant of the daisy family, typically with yellow flowers.
ORIGIN – Latin, from Greek *koris* 'bug' + *opsis* 'appearance' (because of the shape of the seed).

co-respondent (also **corespondent**) > *noun* a person cited in a divorce case as having committed adultery with the respondent.

corgi (also **Welsh corgi**) > *noun* (pl. **corgis**) a breed of dog with short legs and a foxlike head.
ORIGIN – Welsh, from *cor* 'dwarf' + *ci* 'dog'.

coriander /korriandər/ > *noun* an aromatic Mediterranean plant of the parsley family, the leaves and seeds of which are used as herbs in cookery.
ORIGIN – Latin *coriandrum*, from Greek *koriannon*.

Corinthian /kərinthiən/ > *adjective* **1** relating to Corinth, a city in southern Greece and a city state in ancient Greece. **2** denoting the most ornate of the classical orders of architecture, characterised by flared capitals with rows of acanthus leaves. > *noun* a person from Corinth.

Coriolis force /korriōliss/ > *noun* a force (perpendicular to the direction of motion and to the axis of rotation) which acts on a mass moving in a rotating system and tends to deflect moving objects on the earth (e.g. rotating weather systems) to the right in the northern hemisphere and to the left in the southern.
ORIGIN – named after the French engineer Gaspard *Coriolis* (1792–1843).

cork > *noun* **1** the buoyant, light brown substance obtained from the bark of the cork oak. **2** a bottle stopper made of cork. **3** a piece of cork used as a float for a fishing

line or net. > *verb* **1** close or seal (a bottle) with a cork. **2** (**corked**) (of wine) spoilt by tannin from the cork.
COMBINATIONS – **cork oak** an evergreen Mediterranean oak, the bark of which is the source of cork.
ORIGIN – Dutch and Low German *kork*, from Spanish *alcorque* 'cork-soled sandal', from an Arabic word derived from Latin *quercus* 'oak, cork oak'.

corkage > *noun* a charge made by a restaurant or hotel for serving wine that has been brought in by a customer.

corker > *noun* informal an excellent person or thing.
DERIVATIVES – **corking** *adjective*.

corkscrew > *noun* a device for pulling corks from bottles, consisting of a spiral metal rod that is inserted into the cork, and a handle. > *verb* move or twist in a spiral.

corm > *noun* a rounded underground storage organ present in plants such as crocuses and cyclamens, consisting of a swollen stem base covered with scale leaves.
DERIVATIVES – **cormlet** *noun*.
ORIGIN – Greek *kormos* 'trunk stripped of its boughs'.

cormorant /**kor**mərənt/ > *noun* a large diving seabird with a long neck, long hooked bill, and mainly black plumage.
ORIGIN – Old French *cormaran*, from Latin *corvus marinus* 'sea-raven'.

corn[1] > *noun* **1** chiefly Brit. the chief cereal crop of a district, especially (in England) wheat or (in Scotland) oats. **2** N. Amer. & Austral./NZ maize. **3** informal something banal or sentimental.
COMBINATIONS – **corn dolly** Brit. a symbolic or decorative model of a human figure, made of plaited straw. **cornflakes** a breakfast cereal consisting of toasted flakes made from maize flour. **corn on the cob** maize when cooked and eaten straight from the cob.

corn[2] > *noun* a small, painful area of thickened skin on the toes or foot, caused by pressure.
ORIGIN – Latin *cornu* 'horn'.

corncob > *noun* the central woody part of an ear of maize, to which the grains are attached.

corncrake > *noun* a secretive crake (bird) inhabiting coarse grasslands, with a distinctive double rasping call.

cornea /**kor**niə/ > *noun* the transparent layer forming the front of the eye.
DERIVATIVES – **corneal** *adjective*.
ORIGIN – from Latin *cornea tela* 'horny tissue', from *cornu* 'horn'.

corned > *adjective* preserved with salt or brine.
COMBINATIONS – **corned beef 1** Brit. beef preserved in brine, chopped and pressed and sold in cans. **2** N. Amer. beef brisket cured in brine and boiled, typically served cold.

cornelian > *noun* variant spelling of CARNELIAN.

corner > *noun* **1** a place or angle where two or more sides or edges meet. **2** a place where two streets meet. **3** a secluded or remote region or area. **4** a difficult or awkward position. **5** a position in which one dominates the supply of a particular commodity. **6** (also **corner kick**) Soccer a free kick taken by the attacking side from a corner of the field. **7** Boxing & Wrestling each of the diagonally opposite ends of the ring, where a contestant rests between rounds. > *verb* **1** force into a place or situation from which it is hard to escape. **2** control (a market) by dominating the supply of a particular commodity. **3** go round a bend in a road.
IDIOMS – **fight one's corner** defend one's position or interests.
COMBINATIONS – **corner shop** Brit. a small shop selling groceries and general goods in a mainly residential area.
ORIGIN – Old French, from Latin *cornu* 'horn, tip, corner'.

cornerstone > *noun* **1** a stone that forms the base of a corner of a building, joining two walls. **2** a vital part or basis: *sugar was the cornerstone of the country's economy*.

cornet /**kor**nit/ > *noun* **1** a brass instrument resembling a trumpet but shorter and wider. **2** Brit. a cone-shaped wafer for holding ice cream.
DERIVATIVES – **cornetist** /kor**nett**ist/ (also **cornettist**) *noun*.
ORIGIN – Old French, 'little horn', from Latin *cornu* 'horn'.

cornflour > *noun* Brit. finely ground maize flour, used for thickening sauces.

cornflower > *noun* a slender plant of the daisy family with deep blue flowers.

cornice /**kor**niss/ > *noun* **1** an ornamental moulding round the wall of a room just below the ceiling. **2** a horizontal moulded projection crowning a building or structure.
DERIVATIVES – **corniced** *adjective*.
ORIGIN – Italian *cornice*, perhaps from Latin *cornix* 'crow'; compare with CORBEL.

corniche /kor**neesh**/ > *noun* a road cut into the edge of a cliff, especially one running along a coast.
ORIGIN – French, 'cornice'.

Cornish > *adjective* relating to Cornwall. > *noun* the ancient Celtic language of Cornwall.
COMBINATIONS – **Cornish pasty** Brit. a pasty containing seasoned meat and vegetables, especially potato.

cornucopia /kornyoo**kō**piə/ > *noun* **1** a symbol of plenty consisting of a goat's horn overflowing with flowers, fruit, and corn. **2** an abundant supply of good things.
DERIVATIVES – **cornucopian** *adjective*.
ORIGIN – from Latin *cornu copiae* 'horn of plenty' (a mythical horn able to provide whatever is desired).

corny > *adjective* (**cornier, corniest**) informal trite or mawkishly sentimental.
DERIVATIVES – **cornily** *adverb* **corniness** *noun*.
ORIGIN – from an earlier sense 'rustic, appealing to country folk'.

corolla /kə**rollə**/ > *noun* the petals of a flower, typically forming a whorl within the sepals.
ORIGIN – Latin, 'little crown'.

corollary /kə**rollə**ri/ > *noun* (pl. **corollaries**) **1** a logical proposition that follows from one already proved. **2** a direct consequence or result. > *adjective* associated; supplementary.
ORIGIN – Latin *corollarium* 'money paid for a garland; gratuity' (later 'deduction').

corona /kə**rōnə**/ > *noun* (pl. **coronae** /kə**rō**nee/) **1** the rarefied gaseous envelope of the sun or a star. **2** (also **corona discharge**) Physics the glow around a conductor at high potential. **3** a small circle of light seen round the sun or moon. **4** Anatomy a crown or crown-like structure. **5** Botany the trumpet-shaped central part of a daffodil or narcissus flower. **6** a long, straight-sided cigar.
ORIGIN – Latin, 'wreath, crown'; sense 6 comes from a proprietary name of a Havana cigar.

coronal /kə**rōn**l, **korr**ən'l/ > *adjective* relating to the crown or corona of something.

coronary > *adjective* relating to or denoting the arteries which surround and supply the heart. > *noun* (pl. **coronaries**) (also **coronary thrombosis**) a blockage of the flow of blood to the heart, caused by a clot in a coronary artery.
ORIGIN – Latin *coronarius* 'resembling or forming a crown'.

coronation > *noun* the ceremony of crowning a sovereign or a sovereign's consort.
ORIGIN – Latin, from *coronare* 'to crown'.

coroner /**korr**ənər/ > *noun* an official who holds inquests into violent, sudden, or suspicious deaths, and (in Britain) inquiries into cases of treasure trove.
ORIGIN – first denoting an official responsible for safeguarding the private property of the Crown: from Old French *coruner*, from *corune* 'crown'.

coronet /korrənit/ > noun 1 a small or simple crown. 2 a decorative band encircling the head.

ORIGIN – Old French coronete 'little crown'.

corpora plural of CORPUS.

corporal[1] > noun a rank of non-commissioned officer in the army, above lance corporal or private first class and below sergeant.

ORIGIN – Italian caporale, probably from Latin corpus 'body (of troops)'.

corporal[2] > adjective relating to the human body.

COMBINATIONS – **corporal punishment** physical punishment, such as caning or flogging.

ORIGIN – Latin corporalis, from corpus 'body'.

corporate > adjective 1 relating to a business corporation. 2 of or shared by all members of a group: corporate responsibility. > noun a business corporation.

DERIVATIVES – **corporately** adverb.

ORIGIN – from Latin corporare 'form into a body', from corpus 'body'.

corporation > noun 1 a large company or group of companies authorised to act as a single entity and recognised as such in law. 2 Brit. a group of people elected to govern a city, town, or borough.

COMBINATIONS – **corporation tax** tax levied on companies' profits.

corporatism > noun the control of a state or organisation by large interest groups.

DERIVATIVES – **corporatist** adjective & noun.

corporeal /korporiəl/ > adjective relating to a person's body; physical rather than spiritual.

DERIVATIVES – **corporeality** /korporialiti/ noun.

SYNONYMS – bodily, carnal, corporal, fleshly, physical.

ORIGIN – Latin corporealis, from corpus 'body'.

corps /kor/ > noun (pl. **corps** /korz/) 1 a main subdivision of an army in the field, consisting of two or more divisions. 2 a branch of an army assigned to a particular kind of work. 3 a body of people engaged in a particular activity: the press corps.

corps de ballet /kor də bal**ay**/ > noun (treated as sing. or pl.) 1 the members of a ballet company who dance together as a group. 2 the lowest rank of dancers in a ballet company.

corpse > noun a dead body, especially of a human. > verb theatrical slang spoil a piece of acting by forgetting one's lines or laughing uncontrollably.

SYNONYMS – noun body, cadaver, carcass.

---

wordpower facts

Corpse

Corpse and **corps** were originally the same word. **Corpse** entered English in medieval times, when it denoted the living body of a person or animal. It was an alteration of the archaic word **corse**, which came from Old French **cors**; the þ was added by association with Latin **corpus**, a change which also took place in French (Old French **cors** becoming French **corps**). The þ was originally silent, as in French; the final e was rare before the 19th century, but now distinguishes **corpse** from **corps**. Latin **corpus** is the root of the words from **corporal** to **corpuscle**, and also of **corset** and **incorporate**.

---

corpulent /korpyoolənt/ > adjective (of a person) fat.

DERIVATIVES – **corpulence** noun.

ORIGIN – Latin corpulentus, from corpus 'body'.

corpus /korpəss/ > noun (pl. **corpora** /korpərə/ or **corpuses**) 1 a collection of written texts. 2 a collection of written or spoken material in machine-readable form.

ORIGIN – Latin, 'body'.

Corpus Christi /korpəss **kris**ti/ > noun a feast commemorating the institution of the Eucharist, observed on the Thursday after Trinity Sunday.

ORIGIN – Latin, 'body of Christ'.

corpuscle /korpus'l/ > noun a minute body or cell in an organism, especially a red or white blood cell.

DERIVATIVES – **corpuscular** adjective.

ORIGIN – Latin corpusculum 'small body'.

corpus delicti /diliktī/ > noun Law the facts and circumstances constituting a breach of a law.

ORIGIN – Latin, 'body of offence'.

corpus luteum /lōotiəm/ > noun (pl. **corpora lutea** /lōotiə/) Anatomy a hormone-secreting structure that develops in an ovary after an ovum has been discharged but degenerates after a few days unless pregnancy has begun.

ORIGIN – Latin, 'yellow body'.

corral /kəraal/ > noun N. Amer. a pen for livestock on a farm or ranch. > verb (**corralled, corralling**) 1 N. Amer. put or keep (livestock) in a corral. 2 gather (a group) together.

ORIGIN – Spanish and Old Portuguese; related to KRAAL.

correct > adjective 1 free from error; true; right. 2 conforming to accepted social standards. 3 conforming to a particular ideology or accepted set of ideas: environmentally correct. > verb 1 put right (an error or fault). 2 mark the errors in (a text). 3 tell (someone) that they are wrong. 4 adjust (something) so it functions accurately or accords with a standard.

DERIVATIVES – **correctable** adjective **correctly** adverb **correctness** noun **corrector** noun.

SYNONYMS – adjective 1 accurate, exact, precise, right, true. 2 appropriate, fitting, proper, seemly. verb 1 amend, emend, rectify, remedy.

ANTONYMS – adjective 1 incorrect, wrong. 2 improper.

ORIGIN – from Latin corrigere 'make straight, amend'.

correction > noun 1 the action or process of correcting. 2 a change that rectifies an error or inaccuracy.

DERIVATIVES – **correctional** adjective.

correctitude > noun correctness, especially conscious correctness in one's behaviour.

corrective > adjective designed to correct something undesirable. > noun a corrective measure.

correlate /korrəlayt/ > verb have or bring into a relationship in which one thing affects or depends on another. > noun each of two or more related or complementary things.

correlation > noun 1 a mutual relationship. 2 the process of correlating two or more things. 3 Statistics interdependence of variable quantities.

correlative /kərellətiv/ > adjective 1 having a correlation. 2 Grammar (of words such as neither and nor) corresponding to each other and regularly used together. > noun a correlative word or concept.

correspond > verb 1 match or agree almost exactly. 2 be analogous or equivalent in character or form. 3 communicate by exchanging letters.

SYNONYMS – 1 agree, correlate, match, parallel, tally. 2 be akin, be analogous, equate, be equivalent.

ORIGIN – Latin correspondere, from respondere 'answer'.

correspondence > noun 1 the action or fact of corresponding. 2 letters sent or received.

SYNONYMS – 1 affinity, agreement, congruity, correlation.

COMBINATIONS – **correspondence course** a course of study in which student and tutors communicate by post.

correspondent > noun 1 a person who writes letters, especially on a regular basis. 2 a journalist reporting on a particular subject or from a particular country. > adjective corresponding.

corrida /koreedə/ > noun a bullfight.

ORIGIN – from Spanish corrida de toros 'running of bulls'.

corridor* > noun 1 a passage in a building or

train, with doors leading into rooms or compartments. **2** a belt of land linking two other areas or following a road or river. **3** (also **air corridor**) a route, especially over a foreign country, to which aircraft are restricted.

IDIOMS – **corridors of power** the senior levels of government or administration. [ORIGIN – from the name of C. P. Snow's novel *The Corridors of Power* (1964).]
*SPELLING – there is no *door*: corri*dor*.
ORIGIN – first used as a military term denoting a strip of land along the outer edge of a ditch, protected by a parapet: from Italian *corridore*, alteration of *corridoio* 'running-place'.

corrie /**korr**i/ > *noun* (pl. **corries**) a steep-sided hollow at the head of a valley or on a mountainside, especially in the mountains of Scotland.
ORIGIN – Scottish Gaelic and Irish *coire* 'cauldron, hollow'.

corrigendum /korri**jen**dəm/ > *noun* (pl. **corrigenda** /korri**jen**də/) a thing to be corrected, especially an error in a book.
ORIGIN – Latin, 'thing to be corrected'.

corroborate /kə**robb**ərayt/ > *verb* confirm or give support to (a statement or theory).
DERIVATIVES – **corroboration** *noun* **corroborative** *adjective*.
SYNONYMS – confirm, endorse, testify to, validate, verify.
ORIGIN – Latin *corroborare* 'strengthen'.

corroboree /kə**robb**əri/ > *noun* an Australian Aboriginal dance ceremony in the form of a sacred ritual or informal gathering.
ORIGIN – Dharuk (an Aboriginal language).

corrode /kə**rōd**/ > *verb* **1** (with reference to metal or other hard material) wear or be worn away slowly by chemical action. **2** gradually weaken or destroy.
DERIVATIVES – **corrosion** *noun*.
SYNONYMS – **1** decay, erode, rust, tarnish, wear away.
ORIGIN – Latin *corrodere*, from *rodere* 'gnaw'.

corrosive > *adjective* tending to cause corrosion. > *noun* a corrosive substance.

corrugate /**korr**oogayt/ > *verb* contract into wrinkles or folds.
ORIGIN – Latin *corrugare* 'to wrinkle'.

corrugated > *adjective* shaped into alternate ridges and grooves.
DERIVATIVES – **corrugation** *noun*.

corrupt > *adjective* **1** willing to act dishonestly in return for money or personal gain. **2** evil or morally depraved. **3** (of a text or computer data) made unreliable by errors or alterations. **4** archaic rotten or putrid.
> *verb* **1** make corrupt. **2** archaic infect; contaminate.
DERIVATIVES – **corrupter** *noun*

corruptible *adjective* **corruption** *noun* **corruptive** *adjective* **corruptly** *adverb*.
SYNONYMS – *adjective* **1** bribable, dishonest, fraudulent, unscrupulous, venal. **2** debauched, degenerate, depraved, evil, perverted, wicked. *verb* **1** bribe, debase, deprave, pervert, warp.
ORIGIN – from Latin *corrumpere* 'mar, bribe, destroy'.

corsage /kor**saazh**/ > *noun* **1** a spray of flowers worn pinned to a woman's clothes. **2** the bodice of a woman's dress.
ORIGIN – French, from Old French *cors* 'body'.

corsair /**kor**sair/ > *noun* **1** archaic a pirate. **2** historical a privateer, especially one operating along the southern shore of the Mediterranean.
ORIGIN – French *corsaire*, from Latin *cursarius*, from *cursus* 'a raid, plunder'.

corselette /korsə**let**/ (also **corselet**) > *noun* a woman's garment combining corset and brassiere.

corset > *noun* **1** a woman's tightly fitting undergarment extending from below the chest to the hips, worn to shape the figure. **2** a similar garment worn to support a weak or injured back.
DERIVATIVES – **corseted** *adjective* **corsetry** *noun*.
ORIGIN – Old French, 'little body'.

Corsican > *noun* **1** a person from the island of Corsica. **2** the language of Corsica. > *adjective* relating to Corsica.

cortège /kor**tezh**/ > *noun* a solemn procession, especially for a funeral.
ORIGIN – French, from Italian *corteggio* 'entourage or retinue'.

cortex /**kor**teks/ > *noun* (pl. **cortices** /**kor**tiseez/) Anatomy the outer layer of an organ or structure, especially (**cerebral cortex**) the outer, folded layer of the brain.
DERIVATIVES – **cortical** *adjective*.
ORIGIN – Latin, 'bark'.

corticosteroid > *noun* Biochemistry any of a group of steroid hormones produced by the cortex of the adrenal glands.

cortisone /**kor**tizōn/ > *noun* a steroid hormone produced by the adrenal glands and used as an anti-inflammatory and anti-allergy agent.

corundum /kə**run**dəm/ > *noun* extremely hard crystallised alumina, used as an abrasive.
ORIGIN – Tamil.

coruscate /**korr**əskayt/ > *verb* literary (of light) flash or sparkle.
DERIVATIVES – **coruscant** *adjective* **coruscation** *noun*.
ORIGIN – Latin *coruscare* 'glitter'.

corvette /kor**vet**/ > *noun* a small warship designed for escorting convoys.

ORIGIN – French, from Dutch *korf*, denoting a kind of ship.

corvine /**kor**vīn/ > *adjective* of or like a raven or crow, especially in colour.
ORIGIN – from Latin *corvus* 'raven'.

corybantic /korri**bant**ik/ > *adjective* literary wild; frenzied.
ORIGIN – from Greek *Korubantes*, denoting the priests of the Phrygian goddess Cybele, who performed wild dances.

corymb /**korr**imb/ > *noun* Botany a flower cluster whose lower stalks are proportionally longer so that the flowers form a fairly flat head.
ORIGIN – Greek *korumbos* 'cluster'.

coryza /kə**rīz**ə/ > *noun* catarrhal inflammation of the mucous membrane in the nose, as caused by a cold.
ORIGIN – Greek *koruza* 'nasal mucus'.

cos[1] /koss/ > *noun* a variety of lettuce with crisp narrow leaves that form a tall head.
ORIGIN – named after the Greek island of *Cos*, where it originated.

cos[2] /koss, koz/ > *abbreviation* cosine.

cosec /**kō**sek/ > *abbreviation* cosecant.

cosecant /**kō**seekənt/ > *noun* Mathematics (in a right-angled triangle) the ratio of the hypotenuse to the side opposite an acute angle (the reciprocal of sine).

cosh Brit. > *noun* a thick, heavy stick or bar used as a weapon. > *verb* hit on the head with a cosh.

co-signatory > *noun* a person or state signing a treaty or other document jointly with others.

cosine /**kō**sīn/ > *noun* Mathematics (in a right-angled triangle) the ratio of the side adjacent to a particular acute angle to the hypotenuse.

cosmetic > *adjective* **1** relating to treatment intended to improve a person's appearance. **2** improving only the appearance of something: *the reform was just a cosmetic exercise*. > *noun* (**cosmetics**) cosmetic preparations, especially for the face.
DERIVATIVES – **cosmetically** *adverb*.
ORIGIN – Greek *kosmētikos*, from *kosmos* 'order or adornment'.

cosmic > *adjective* relating to the universe or cosmos, especially as distinct from the earth.
DERIVATIVES – **cosmical** *adjective* **cosmically** *adverb*.
COMBINATIONS – **cosmic dust** small particles of matter distributed throughout space. **cosmic rays** (also **cosmic radiation**) highly energetic atomic nuclei or other particles travelling through space at a speed approaching that of light.

cosmogony /koz**mogg**əni/ > *noun* (pl. **cosmogonies**) the branch of science concerned with the origin of the universe, especially the solar system.

DERIVATIVES – **cosmogonic** /kozməgonnik/ *adjective* **cosmogonist** *noun*.

ORIGIN – from Greek *kosmos* 'order or world' + *-gonia* '-begetting'.

cosmography > *noun* (pl. **cosmographies**) **1** the branch of science which deals with the general features of the universe, including the earth. **2** a description or representation of the universe or the earth.

DERIVATIVES – **cosmographer** *noun* **cosmographic** *adjective* **cosmographical** *adjective*.

cosmology > *noun* (pl. **cosmologies**) **1** the science of the origin and development of the universe. **2** an account or theory of the origin of the universe.

DERIVATIVES – **cosmological** *adjective* **cosmologist** *noun*.

cosmonaut > *noun* a Russian astronaut.

ORIGIN – Russian *kosmonavt*.

cosmopolitan /kozmə**poll**it'n/ > *adjective* **1** consisting of people from many different countries and cultures: *a cosmopolitan metropolis*. **2** familiar with and at ease in many different countries and cultures. > *noun* a cosmopolitan person.

DERIVATIVES – **cosmopolitanism** *noun*.

SYNONYMS – *adjective* **1** global, international, multicultural, multiracial. **2** seasoned, sophisticated, urbane, worldly, worldly-wise.

ANTONYMS – *adjective* **2** provincial.

ORIGIN – from Greek *kosmos* 'world' + *politēs* 'citizen'.

cosmos > *noun* the universe seen as a well-ordered whole.

ORIGIN – Greek *kosmos* 'order or world'.

Cossack /**koss**ak/ > *noun* a member of a people of southern Russia, Ukraine, and Siberia, noted for their horsemanship and military skill.

ORIGIN – Russian *kazak* 'vagabond, nomad'.

cosset > *verb* (**cosseted, cosseting**) care for and protect (someone) in an overindulgent way.

SYNONYMS – indulge, mollycoddle, pamper, spoil.

ORIGIN – first denoting a lamb brought up by hand, later a spoiled child: probably from Old French *coscet* 'cottager'.

cost > *verb* (past and past participle **cost**) **1** require the payment of (a specified sum) in order to be bought or obtained. **2** involve the loss of: *his heroism cost him his life*. **3** (past and past participle **costed**) estimate the cost of. > *noun* **1** an amount given or required as payment. **2** the effort or loss necessary to achieve something. **3** (**costs**) legal expenses.

IDIOMS – **at all costs** (or **at any cost**) regardless of the price or the effort needed. **at cost** at cost price. **to someone's cost** with loss or disadvantage to someone.

SYNONYMS – *verb* **1** amount to, come to, fetch, sell for. *noun* **1** charge, fee, levy, price, tariff. **2** expense, penalty, price, sacrifice.

COMBINATIONS – **cost-effective** (also **cost-efficient**) effective or productive in relation to its cost. **cost price** the price at which goods are bought by a retailer.

ORIGIN – Old French *couster*, from Latin *constare* 'stand firm, stand at a price'.

co-star > *noun* a performer appearing with another or others of equal importance. > *verb* **1** appear in a production as a co-star. **2** (of a production) include as a co-star.

Costa Rican /kostə **ree**kən/ > *noun* a person from Costa Rica, a republic in Central America. > *adjective* relating to Costa Rica.

costermonger /**kos**tərmunggər/ > *noun* Brit. dated a person who sells fruit and vegetables from a handcart in the street.

ORIGIN – from *costard* (a type of apple).

costing > *noun* the estimated cost of producing or undertaking something.

costive /**kos**tiv/ > *adjective* constipated.

DERIVATIVES – **costiveness** *noun*.

ORIGIN – Old French, from Latin *constipare* 'press together'.

costly > *adjective* (**costlier, costliest**) **1** expensive. **2** causing suffering, loss, or disadvantage: *a costly mistake*.

DERIVATIVES – **costliness** *noun*.

costume > *noun* **1** a set of clothes in a style typical of a particular country or historical period. **2** a set of clothes worn by an actor or performer for a role. **3** Brit. dated a woman's matching jacket and skirt. > *verb* dress in a costume.

SYNONYMS – *noun* **1,2** apparel, attire, clothing, dress, garb.

COMBINATIONS – **costume drama** a television or cinema production set in a historical period. **costume jewellery** jewellery made with inexpensive materials or imitation gems.

ORIGIN – French, from Italian *custume* 'custom, fashion, habit', from Latin *consuetudo* 'custom'.

costumier /kos**tyoo**miər/ (US also **costumer** /kos**tyoo**mər/) > *noun* a maker or supplier of theatrical or fancy-dress costumes.

ORIGIN – French.

cosy (US **cozy**) > *adjective* (**cosier, cosiest**) **1** comfortable, warm, and secure. **2** not seeking or offering challenge or difficulty: *the cosy belief that man is master*. > *noun* (pl. **cosies**) a cover to keep a teapot or a boiled egg hot. > *verb* (**cosies, cosied**) informal **1** make (someone) feel cosy. **2** (**cosy up to**) snuggle up to or ingratiate oneself with.

DERIVATIVES – **cosily** *adverb* **cosiness** *noun*.

SYNONYMS – *adjective* **1** comfortable, secure, snug, warm.

ORIGIN – Scots.

cot¹ > *noun* Brit. a small bed with high barred sides for a baby or very young child.

COMBINATIONS – **cot death** Brit. the unexplained death of a baby in its sleep.

ORIGIN – Hindi, 'bedstead, hammock'.

cot² > *noun* **1** a small shelter for livestock. **2** archaic a small, simple cottage.

ORIGIN – Old English, related to **COTE**.

cot³ > *abbreviation* Mathematics cotangent.

cotangent /kō**tan**jənt/ > *noun* Mathematics (in a right-angled triangle) the ratio of the side (other than the hypotenuse) adjacent to a particular acute angle to the side opposite the angle (the reciprocal of tangent).

cote > *noun* a shelter for mammals or birds, especially pigeons.

ORIGIN – Old English, related to **COT²**.

coterie /**kō**təri/ > *noun* (pl. **coteries**) a small exclusive group of people with shared interests or tastes.

ORIGIN – French, from Low German *kote* 'cote'.

coterminous /kō**ter**minəss/ > *adjective* having the same boundaries or extent.

ORIGIN – alteration of **CONTERMINOUS**.

cotillion /kə**til**yən/ > *noun* **1** an 18th-century French dance related to the quadrille. **2** US a formal ball, especially one at which debutantes are presented.

ORIGIN – French *cotillon* 'petticoat dance'.

cotoneaster /kə**tō**niastər/ > *noun* a small-leaved shrub with bright red berries, often grown as a hedging plant.

ORIGIN – from Latin *cotoneum* 'quince'.

cottage > *noun* a small house, typically one in the country.

DERIVATIVES – **cottagey** *adjective*.

COMBINATIONS – **cottage cheese** soft, lumpy white cheese made from the curds of skimmed milk. **cottage hospital** Brit. a small local hospital. **cottage industry** a business or manufacturing activity carried on in people's homes. **cottage loaf** Brit. a loaf made from two round pieces of dough, the smaller on top of the larger. **cottage pie** Brit. a dish of minced meat topped with browned mashed potato.

ORIGIN – Old French *cotage*, from **COT²** or **COTE**.

cottager > *noun* a person living in a cottage.

cottar /**kot**tər/ (also **cotter**) > *noun* historical (in Scotland and Ireland) a farm labourer or tenant occupying a cottage in return for labour.

cotter pin > *noun* **1** a metal pin used to fasten two parts of a mechanism together. **2** a split pin that is opened out after being passed through a hole.

cotton > *noun* a soft white fibrous substance which surrounds the seeds of a tropical and subtropical plant, used to make cloth or thread for sewing. > verb informal (**cotton on**) begin to understand.

DERIVATIVES – **cottony** adjective.

COMBINATIONS – **cotton bud** Brit. a small wad of cotton wool on a short, thin stick, used for cosmetic purposes or cleaning the ears. **cotton wool 1** Brit. fluffy wadding of a kind originally made from raw cotton, used for applying or removing cosmetics or bathing wounds. **2** US raw cotton.

ORIGIN – Old French coton, from Arabic.

cotyledon /kottileed'n/ > noun an embryonic leaf, the first leaf to grow from a germinating seed.

ORIGIN – Greek kotulēdōn 'cup-shaped cavity'.

couch[1] /kowch/ > noun **1** a long upholstered piece of furniture for several people to sit on. **2** a long seat with a headrest at one end on which a psychoanalyst's subject or doctor's patient lies while undergoing treatment. > verb **1** (usu. **be couched in**) express in language of a specified style. **2** literary lie down.

COMBINATIONS – **couch potato** informal a person who spends a great deal of time watching television.

ORIGIN – Old French couche, from Latin collocare 'place together'.

couch[2] /kowch, kōōch/ (also **couch grass**) > noun a coarse grass with long creeping roots.

ORIGIN – variant of QUITCH.

couchette /kōōshet/ > noun **1** a railway carriage with seats convertible into sleeping berths. **2** a berth in such a carriage.

ORIGIN – French, 'small couch'.

cougar /kōōgər/ > noun N. Amer. a puma.

ORIGIN – French couguar, from Guarani.

cough > verb **1** expel air from the lungs with a sudden sharp sound. **2** (of an engine) make a sudden harsh noise. **3** (**cough up**) informal give (something, especially money) reluctantly. **4** Brit. informal reveal information; confess. > noun **1** an act or sound of coughing. **2** a condition of the respiratory organs causing coughing.

DERIVATIVES – **cougher** noun.

COMBINATIONS – **cough mixture** Brit. liquid medicine taken to relieve a cough.

could > modal verb past of CAN[1].

couldn't > contraction could not.

coulis /kōōli/ > noun (pl. same) a thin fruit or vegetable purée, used as a sauce.

ORIGIN – French, from couler 'to flow'.

coulomb /kōōlom/ > noun Physics the unit of electric charge in the SI system, equal to the quantity of electricity conveyed in one second by a current of one ampere.

ORIGIN – named after the French military engineer Charles-Augustin de Coulomb (1736–1806).

coulter /kōltər/ (US colter) > noun a vertical

cutting blade fixed in front of a ploughshare.

ORIGIN – Latin culter 'knife or ploughshare'.

council > noun **1** a formally constituted advisory, deliberative, or administrative body. **2** a body elected to manage the affairs of a city, county, or district. **3** (before another noun) Brit. (of housing) provided by a local council.

USAGE – do not confuse **council**, an administrative or advisory body, with **counsel**, advice or guidance.

COMBINATIONS – **council of war 1** a gathering of military officers in wartime. **2** a meeting held to plan a response to an emergency. **council tax** a tax levied on households by local authorities in the UK, based on the estimated value of a property.

ORIGIN – Latin concilium 'convocation, assembly'; compare with COUNSEL.

councillor (US also **councilor**) > noun a member of a council.

counsel > noun **1** advice, especially that given formally. **2** (pl. same) a barrister or other legal adviser conducting a case. **3** archaic consultation, especially to seek advice. > verb (**counselled**, **counselling**; US **counseled**, **counseling**) **1** give advice to. **2** give professional help and advice to (someone) to resolve personal or psychological problems. **3** recommend (a course of action).

IDIOMS – **keep one's own counsel** not disclose one's plans or opinions.

SYNONYMS – noun **1** advice, guidance. verb **1** advise, direct, guide.

ORIGIN – Latin consilium 'consultation, advice'.

counsellor (US **counselor**) > noun **1** a person trained to give guidance on personal or psychological problems. **2** a senior officer in the diplomatic service. **3** (also **counselor-at-law**) US & Irish a barrister.

USAGE – do not confuse **counsellor** with **councillor**: a **counsellor** gives guidance on personal or psychological problems, whereas a **councillor** is a member of a council.

count[1] > verb **1** determine the total number of. **2** recite numbers in ascending order. **3** take into account; include. **4** regard or be regarded as possessing a quality or fulfilling a role: people she had counted as her friends. **5** be significant; matter: it's the thought that counts. **6** (**count on**) rely on. **7** (**count in** or **out**) include (or not include) in a planned activity. **8** (**count down**) recite numbers backwards to zero to indicate remaining time, especially before the launch of a rocket. **9** (**count out**) complete a count of ten seconds over (a fallen boxer) to indicate defeat. > noun **1** an act of counting. **2** the total determined by counting. **3** a point for

discussion or consideration. **4** Law a separate charge in an indictment.

IDIOMS – **count the days** (or **hours**) be impatient for time to pass. **don't count your chickens before they're hatched** proverb don't be too confident in anticipating success before it is certain. **keep** (or **lose**) **count** take note of (or forget) the number or amount when counting. **out for the count** Boxing defeated by being knocked to the ground and unable to rise within ten seconds.

DERIVATIVES – **countable** adjective.

SYNONYMS – verb **1** add up, calculate, compute, total. **4** consider, judge, regard, think. **5** carry weight, matter, signify. **6** (**count on**) bank on, depend on, rely on, trust. noun **1** calculation, enumeration, reckoning. **2** amount, number, total, tally.

COMBINATIONS – **count noun** Grammar a noun that can form a plural and, in the singular, can be used with the indefinite article (e.g. books, a book). Contrasted with **mass noun**.

ORIGIN – Old French counter, from Latin computare 'calculate'.

count[2] > noun a foreign nobleman whose rank corresponds to that of an earl.

ORIGIN – Old French conte, from Latin comes 'companion, attendant'.

countdown > noun **1** an act of counting down to zero, especially before the launch of a rocket. **2** the final moments before a significant event.

countenance /kowntənənss/ > noun **1** a person's face or facial expression. **2** formal support or approval. > verb admit (something) as acceptable or possible.

IDIOMS – **keep one's countenance** maintain one's composure. **out of countenance** disconcerted or unpleasantly surprised.

SYNONYMS – noun **1** appearance, aspect, demeanour, expression, face, look.

ORIGIN – Old French contenance 'bearing, behaviour', from contenir 'contain'.

counter[1] > noun **1** a long flat-topped fitting over which goods are sold or served or across which business is conducted with customers. **2** a small disc used in board games for keeping the score or as a place marker. **3** a token representing a coin. **4** a factor used to give one party an advantage in negotiations. **5** a person or thing that counts something.

IDIOMS – **over the counter** by ordinary retail purchase, with no need for a prescription or licence. **under the counter** (or **table**) (with reference to goods bought or sold) surreptitiously and illegally.

counter[2] > verb **1** speak or act in opposition or response to. **2** Boxing give a return blow while parrying. > adverb (**counter to**) in the opposite direction to or in conflict

with. > *adjective* responding to something of the same kind, especially in opposition: *argument and counter argument.* > *noun* an act or speech which counters something else.
ORIGIN – from Latin *contra* 'against'.

counter- > *prefix* **1** denoting opposition, retaliation, or rivalry: *counter-attack.* **2** denoting movement or effect in the opposite direction: *counterpoise.* **3** denoting correspondence, duplication, or substitution: *counterpart.*

counteract > *verb* act against (something) so as to reduce its force or neutralise it.
DERIVATIVES – **counteraction** *noun* **counteractive** *adjective.*
SYNONYMS – cancel out, counterbalance, neutralise, nullify, offset.

counter-attack > *noun* an attack made in response to one by an enemy or opponent. > *verb* attack in response.

counterbalance > *noun* /**kown**tərbalənss/ **1** a weight that balances another. **2** a factor having the opposite effect to that of another, so neutralising it. > *verb* /kowntər**bal**ənss/ have an opposing and balancing effect on.
SYNONYMS – *verb* balance, counteract, even out, nullify, offset.

counterblast > *noun* a strongly worded reply to someone else's views.

counterclockwise > *adverb & adjective* N. Amer. anticlockwise.

counterculture > *noun* a way of life and set of attitudes at variance with the prevailing social norm.

counter-espionage > *noun* activities designed to prevent or thwart spying by an enemy.

counterfeit /**kown**tərfit/ > *adjective* made in exact imitation of something valuable with the intention to deceive or defraud. > *noun* a forgery. > *verb* **1** imitate fraudulently. **2** pretend to feel or possess (an emotion or quality).
DERIVATIVES – **counterfeiter** *noun.*
SYNONYMS – *adjective* bogus, fake, forged, simulated. *noun* copy, fake, forgery, replica. *verb* **1** copy, fake, forge. **2** fake, feign, put on, simulate.
ORIGIN – Old French *contrefait* 'made in opposition'.

counterfoil > *noun* chiefly Brit. the part of a cheque, ticket, etc. that is kept as a record by the person issuing it.

countermand /kowntər**maand**/ > *verb* **1** revoke (an order). **2** declare (voting) invalid.
ORIGIN – Latin *contramandare*, from *contra-* 'against' + *mandare* 'to order'.

countermeasure > *noun* an action taken to counteract a danger or threat.

counterpane > *noun* dated a bedspread.
ORIGIN – Old French *contrepointe*, from Latin *culcitra puncta* 'quilted mattress'.

counterpart > *noun* a person or thing that corresponds to or has the same function as another.
SYNONYMS – equivalent, opposite number, peer, twin.

counterpoint > *noun* **1** the technique of writing or playing a melody or melodies in conjunction with another, according to fixed rules. **2** a melody played in conjunction with another. **3** an idea or theme contrasting with the main element. > *verb* **1** add counterpoint to (a melody). **2** emphasise by contrast.
ORIGIN – Old French *contrepoint*, from Latin *contrapunctum* 'song marked over against (the original melody)'.

counterpoise > *noun* a counterbalance. > *verb* counterbalance.
ORIGIN – Old French *contrepois*, from *contre* 'against' + *pois* 'weight'.

counterproductive > *adjective* having the opposite of the desired effect.

Counter-Reformation > *noun* a period in the 16th and 17th centuries during which the Roman Catholic Church sought to counter the effects of the Protestant Reformation.

counter-revolution > *noun* a revolution opposing a former one or reversing its results.
DERIVATIVES – **counter-revolutionary** *adjective & noun.*

countersign > *verb* sign (a document already signed by another person).

countersink > *verb* (past and past participle **countersunk**) **1** enlarge and bevel the rim of (a drilled hole) so that a screw or bolt can be inserted flush with the surface. **2** drive (a screw or bolt) into such a hole.

countertenor > *noun* the highest male adult singing voice.

countervail /kowntər**vayl**/ > *verb* offset the effect of (something) by countering it with something of equal force.
DERIVATIVES – **countervailing** *adjective.*
ORIGIN – Old French *contrevaloir*, from Latin *contra valere* 'be of worth against'.

counterweight > *noun* a counterbalancing weight.

countess > *noun* **1** the wife or widow of a count or earl. **2** a woman holding the rank of count or earl.

counting > *preposition* taking account of; including.

countless > *adjective* too many to be counted; very many.

countrified (also **countryfied**) > *adjective* characteristic of the country, especially in being unsophisticated.

country > *noun* (pl. **countries**) **1** a nation with its own government, occupying a particular territory. **2** districts outside large urban areas. **3** an area with regard to its physical features: *hill country.*

WORDFINDER – *relating to the country or the countryside:* bucolic, pastoral, rural, rustic.
IDIOMS – **across country** not keeping to roads. **go to the country** Brit. test public opinion by dissolving parliament and holding a general election. **line of country** Brit. a subject in which a person is skilled or knowledgeable.
SYNONYMS – **1** land, kingdom, nation, power, realm, state.
COMBINATIONS – **country and western** country music. **country club** a club with sporting and social facilities, set in a rural area. **country cousin** an unsophisticated and provincial person. **country dance** a traditional type of English dance, in particular one performed by couples facing each other in long lines. **countryman** (or **countrywoman**) **1** a person living or born in the country. **2** a person from the same country as someone else. **country music** a form of popular music originating in the rural southern US, characteristically featuring ballads and dance tunes played on guitars, fiddle, and banjo.
ORIGIN – Old French *cuntree*, from Latin *contrata terra* 'land lying opposite'.

countryside > *noun* the land and scenery of a rural area.

county > *noun* (pl. **counties**) **1** a territorial division of some countries, forming the chief unit of local administration. **2** US a political and administrative division of a state. **3** (before another noun) Brit. of or denoting the upper-class landed families of a county: *the Warwickshire county set.*
COMBINATIONS – **county court 1** (in England and Wales) a judicial court for civil cases. **2** (in the US) a court for civil and criminal cases. **county town** (N. Amer. **county seat**) the town that is the administrative capital of a county.
ORIGIN – Old French *conte*, from Latin *comitatus* 'domain of a count'.

county council > *noun* (in the UK) the elected governing body of an administrative county.
DERIVATIVES – **county councillor** *noun.*

coup /kōō/ > *noun* (pl. **coups** /kōōz/) **1** short for **COUP D'ÉTAT**. **2** an unexpected and notably successful act.
ORIGIN – French, from Latin *colpus* 'a blow'.

coup de grâce /kōō də **graass**/ > *noun* (pl. **coups de grâce** pronunc. same) a final blow or shot given to kill a wounded person or animal.
ORIGIN – French, 'stroke of grace'.

coup d'état /kōō day**taa**/ > *noun* (pl. **coups d'état** pronunc. same) a sudden violent seizure of power from a government.
ORIGIN – French, 'blow of state'.

coupe /kōōp/ > *noun* a shallow glass or glass

dish, typically with a stem, in which desserts or champagne are served.

ORIGIN – French, 'goblet'.

coupé /kōōpay/ (also **coupe** /kōōp/) > *noun* a car with a fixed roof, two doors, and a sloping rear.

ORIGIN – first denoting an enclosed carriage for two passengers and a driver: from French *carrosse coupé* 'cut carriage'.

couple > *noun* 1 two individuals of the same sort considered together. 2 two people who are married or otherwise closely associated romantically or sexually. 3 (**a couple**) informal an indefinite small number. 4 Mechanics a pair of equal and parallel forces acting in opposite directions and tending to cause rotation. > *verb* 1 (often **be coupled to** or **with**) connect or combine. 2 have sexual intercourse.

DERIVATIVES – **coupledom** *noun* **coupler** *noun*.

ORIGIN – Old French *cople*, from Latin *copula* 'connection'; related to **COPULATE**.

couplet > *noun* a pair of successive lines of verse, typically rhyming and of the same length.

coupling > *noun* a device for connecting railway vehicles or parts of machinery together.

coupon > *noun* 1 a voucher entitling the holder to a discount on a product or a quantity of something rationed. 2 a detachable form used to send for a purchase or information or to enter a competition.

ORIGIN – French, 'piece cut off'.

courage > *noun* 1 the ability to do something that frightens one. 2 strength in the face of pain or grief.

IDIOMS – **have the courage of one's convictions** act on one's beliefs despite danger or disapproval. **take one's courage in both hands** nerve oneself to do something that frightens one.

SYNONYMS – 1 bravery, daring, nerve, pluck, valour.

ANTONYMS – 1 cowardice.

ORIGIN – Old French *corage*, from Latin *cor* 'heart'.

courageous > *adjective* having courage; brave.

DERIVATIVES – **courageously** *adverb* **courageousness** *noun*.

SYNONYMS – bold, brave, daring, intrepid, plucky, valiant, valorous.

ANTONYMS – cowardly.

courgette /koorzhet/ > *noun* Brit. a variety of marrow harvested and eaten at an early stage of growth.

ORIGIN – French, 'little gourd'.

courier /koorriər/ > *noun* 1 a messenger who transports goods or documents. 2 a person employed to guide and assist a group of tourists. > *verb* send or transport by courier.

ORIGIN – Old French *coreor* or French *courrier*, from Latin *currere* 'to run'.

course > *noun* 1 a direction that is followed or intended: *the aircraft changed course.* 2 the way in which something progresses or develops: *the course of history.* 3 a procedure adopted to deal with a situation. 4 a dish forming one of the successive parts of a meal. 5 a series of lectures or lessons in a particular subject. 6 a series of repeated treatments or doses of medication. 7 an area of land or water prepared for racing, golf, or another sport. 8 Architecture a continuous horizontal layer of brick or stone. > *verb* 1 (of liquid) flow. 2 pursue (game, especially hares) with greyhounds using sight rather than scent.

IDIOMS – **in (the) course of** 1 in the process of. 2 during. **of course** 1 as expected. 2 used to give agreement or permission.

SYNONYMS – *noun* 1 direction, path, route, tack, way. 2 advance, development, evolution, progression. 3 approach, procedure, technique, way. 5 programme, schedule, sequence, series.

COMBINATIONS – **coursebook** Brit. a textbook designed for use on a particular course of study. **coursework** work done during a course of study, typically counting towards a final mark.

> **wordpower facts**
> ## Course
> **Course** (from Latin *cursus*) is one of a great many words that are derived ultimately from Latin *currere* 'to run' or its stem *curs-*. Currere provides the *-cur-* element of words such as **concur**, **current**, **cursive**, **excursion**, **incur**, **occur**, **precursor**, and **recur**. It is also the basis of **corridor**, which entered English from Italian as a military term denoting a strip of land along the outer edge of a ditch, protected by a parapet—a 'running place'. Fast-moving **corsairs**, **couriers**, and **coursers** also come from *currere*.

courser[1] > *noun* literary a swift horse.

ORIGIN – Old French *corsier*, from Latin *cursus* 'course'.

courser[2] > *noun* a person who goes coursing with greyhounds.

court > *noun* 1 (also **court of law**) a body of people before whom judicial cases are heard. 2 the place where such a body meets. 3 a quadrangular area marked out for ball games such as tennis. 4 a quadrangle surrounded by a building or group of buildings. 5 the establishment, retinue, and courtiers of a sovereign. > *verb* 1 dated be

involved with (someone) romantically, especially with a view to marriage. 2 attempt to win the support or favour of. 3 go to great lengths to win (favourable attention). 4 risk incurring (misfortune) because of the way one behaves. 5 (of a male bird or other animal) try to attract (a mate).

IDIOMS – **hold court** be the centre of attention. **out of court** before a legal hearing can take place. **pay court to** pay flattering attention to.

SYNONYMS – *verb* 2 cultivate, curry favour with. 3 pursue, seek, solicit, strive for. 4 invite, provoke, risk.

COMBINATIONS – **court circular** Brit. a daily report of the activities and public engagements of royal family members. **courthouse** 1 a building in which a judicial court is held. 2 US a building containing the administrative offices of a county. **court order** a direction issued by a court or a judge requiring a person to do or not do something. **courtroom** the room or building in which a court of law meets. **court shoe** Brit. a woman's plain, lightweight shoe that has a low-cut upper and no fastening.

ORIGIN – Old French *cort*, from Latin *cohors* 'yard or retinue'.

court card > *noun* Brit. a playing card that is a king, queen, or jack of a suit.

ORIGIN – alteration of *coat card*, from the decorative dress of the figures depicted.

courteous /kurtiəss/ > *adjective* polite, respectful, and considerate.

DERIVATIVES – **courteously** *adverb* **courteousness** *noun*.

SYNONYMS – civil, considerate, gallant, polite, respectful.

ANTONYMS – discourteous, rude.

ORIGIN – Old French *corteis* 'having manners fit for a royal court'.

courtesan /kortizan/ > *noun* a prostitute, especially one with wealthy or upper-class clients.

ORIGIN – French *courtisane*, from obsolete Italian *cortigiana* 'female courtier'.

courtesy /kurtisi/ > *noun* (pl. **courtesies**) 1 courteous behaviour. 2 a polite speech or action, especially one required by convention.

IDIOMS – (**by**) **courtesy of** given or allowed by.

SYNONYMS – 1 civility, courteousness, gallantry, good manners, respect.

COMBINATIONS – **courtesy light** a small light in a car that is automatically switched on when a door is opened. **courtesy title** a title given to someone, especially the son or daughter of a peer, that has no legal validity.

courtier /kortiər/ > *noun* a sovereign's companion or adviser.

courtly > *adjective* (**courtlier**, **courtliest**) very dignified and polite.

DERIVATIVES – **courtliness** *noun*.

court martial > *noun* (pl. **courts martial** or **court martials**) a judicial court for trying members of the armed services accused of breaking military law. > *verb* (**court-martial**) (**court-martialled**, **court-martialling**; US **court-martialed**, **court-martialing**) try (someone) by court martial.

courtship > *noun* 1 a period of courting. 2 the courting behaviour of male birds and other animals. 3 the action of courting.

courtyard > *noun* an open area enclosed by walls or buildings, especially in a castle or large house.

couscous /**koos**koos/ > *noun* a North African dish of steamed or soaked semolina, usually served with spicy meat or vegetables.

ORIGIN – Arabic.

cousin > *noun* 1 (also **first cousin**) a child of one's uncle or aunt. 2 a person of a kindred people or nation.

IDIOMS – **first cousin once removed** 1 a child of one's first cousin. 2 one's parent's first cousin. **second cousin** a child of one's parent's first cousin. **third cousin** a child of one's parent's second cousin.

DERIVATIVES – **cousinly** *adjective* **cousinship** *noun*.

ORIGIN – Old French *cosin*, from Latin *consobrinus* 'mother's sister's child'.

couture /koo**tyoor**/ > *noun* 1 the design and manufacture of fashionable clothes to a client's specific requirements. 2 clothes of this type.

ORIGIN – French, 'sewing, dressmaking'.

couturier /koo**tyoo**riay/ > *noun* (fem. **couturière** /kootyoo**riair**/) a person who designs and sells couture clothes.

covalent /kō**vay**lənt/ > *adjective* Chemistry (of a chemical bond) formed by the sharing of electrons between atoms. Contrasted with **IONIC**.

DERIVATIVES – **covalency** *noun* **covalently** *adverb*.

cove¹ > *noun* 1 a small sheltered bay. 2 Architecture a concave arch or arched moulding at the junction of a wall with a ceiling.

DERIVATIVES – **coved** *adjective* **coving** *noun*.

ORIGIN – Old English, 'chamber, cave'.

cove² > *noun* Brit. informal, dated a man.

ORIGIN – perhaps from a Romany word meaning 'thing or person'.

coven /**kuvv**'n/ > *noun* a group of witches who meet regularly.

ORIGIN – variant of archaic *covin* 'band of people', from Latin *convenire* 'come together'; compare with **CONVENT**.

covenant /**kuvv**ənənt/ > *noun* 1 a solemn agreement. 2 a contract by which one undertakes to make regular payments to a charity. 3 an agreement held to be the basis of a relationship of commitment with God. > *verb* agree or pay by covenant.

DERIVATIVES – **covenantal** *adjective*.

SYNONYMS – *noun* 1 agreement, bond, contract, indenture, pledge, promise.

ORIGIN – Old French, 'agreeing', from Latin *convenire* 'come together'.

Covenanter > *noun* (in 17th-century Scotland) a person who adhered to the National Covenant or the Solemn League and Covenant, in support of Presbyterianism.

Coventry > *noun* (in phrase **send to Coventry**) chiefly Brit. refuse to associate with or speak to (someone).

---

wordpower facts

Send to Coventry

The origins of the phrase *send someone to Coventry* are uncertain. The expression is sometimes said to derive from the treatment formerly suffered by soldiers stationed in Coventry: they were so unpopular that they, and those who associated with them, were cut off socially by the citizens. Alternatively, it may have arisen because Royalist prisoners were sent there during the English Civil War (1642-9), the city being held by Parliamentary forces and thus unlikely to give the prisoners a warm welcome.

---

cover > *verb* 1 put something over or in front of (someone or something) so as to protect or conceal. 2 spread or extend over. 3 deal with (a subject) in speech or writing. 4 travel (a specified distance). 5 (of money) be enough to pay for. 6 (of insurance) protect against a liability, loss, or accident. 7 (**cover up**) try to hide or deny the fact of (a wrongful action). 8 (**cover for**) temporarily take over the job of. 9 aim a gun at. 10 protect (an exposed person) by shooting at the enemy. 11 (in team games) take up a position ready to defend against (an opponent). 12 record or perform a cover version of (a song). 13 (of a male animal, especially a stallion) copulate with (a female animal). > *noun* 1 something that covers or protects. 2 a thick protective outer part or page of a book or magazine. 3 shelter. 4 military support for someone in danger. 5 a means of concealing an illegal or secret activity. 6 Brit. protection by insurance. 7 a place setting at a table in a restaurant. 8 (also **cover version**) a recording or performance of a song previously recorded by a different artist. 9 (also **cover point**) Cricket a fielding position a little in front of the batsman on the off side and halfway to the boundary.

IDIOMS – **break cover** suddenly leave shelter when being pursued. **cover one's back** informal take steps to avoid attack or criticism. **under cover of** 1 concealed by. 2 while pretending to do something. **under separate cover** in a separate envelope.

DERIVATIVES – **covering** *noun*.

SYNONYMS – *verb* 1 cloak, envelop, screen, shield, shroud. 3 deal with, embrace, include, incorporate. 4 cross, journey, travel, traverse. 6 insure, protect, underwrite. 7 (**cover up**) conceal, hush up, suppress, whitewash. 8 (**cover for**) fill in for, relieve, replace.

COMBINATIONS – **cover charge** a service charge per person added to the bill in a restaurant. **covering letter** (N. Amer. **cover letter**) a letter explaining the contents of an accompanying enclosure. **cover note** Brit. a temporary certificate showing that a person has a current insurance policy.

ORIGIN – Old French *covrir*, from Latin *cooperire*, from *operire* 'to cover'.

coverage > *noun* the extent to which something is covered.

coverlet > *noun* a bedspread.

ORIGIN – Old French *covrelet*, from *covrir* 'to cover' + *lit* 'bed'.

covert > *adjective* /**kuvv**ərt, **kō**vərt/ not openly acknowledged or displayed. > *noun* /**kuvv**ərt/ 1 a thicket in which game can hide. 2 a feather covering the base of a bird's main flight or tail feather.

DERIVATIVES – **covertly** *adverb*.

SYNONYMS – *adjective* clandestine, closet, hidden, secret, surreptitious.

ANTONYMS – *adjective* overt.

ORIGIN – Old French, 'covered'.

cover-up > *noun* an attempt to conceal a mistake or crime.

covet /**kuvv**it/ > *verb* (**coveted**, **coveting**) yearn to possess (something belonging to someone else).

DERIVATIVES – **covetable** *adjective*.

ORIGIN – Old French *cuveitier*, from Latin *cupiditas* 'cupidity'.

covetous > *adjective* longing to possess something that belongs to someone else.

DERIVATIVES – **covetously** *adverb* **covetousness** *noun*.

SYNONYMS – acquisitive, desirous, grasping, greedy, yearning.

covey /**kuvv**i/ > *noun* (pl. **coveys**) a small flock of birds, especially partridge.

ORIGIN – Old French *covee*, from *cover*, from Latin *cubare* 'lie down'.

cow¹ > *noun* 1 a fully grown female animal of a domesticated breed of ox. 2 the female of certain other large animals, such as the elephant or whale. 3 informal, derogatory an unpleasant or disliked woman. 4 Austral./NZ an unpleasant person or thing.

WORDFINDER – heifer (*cow that has not borne a calf, or has borne only one calf*).

IDIOMS – **till the cows come home** informal for an indefinitely long time.

COMBINATIONS – **cowbell** a bell hung round a cow's neck. **cowcatcher** a metal frame at the front of a locomotive for pushing aside obstacles on the line. **cow parsley** a hedgerow plant of the parsley family with large, lacy heads of tiny white flowers. **cowpox** a disease of cows' udders spread by a virus, which can be contracted by humans and resembles mild smallpox. **cowpuncher** N. Amer. informal a cowboy.

cow² > *verb* (usu. **be cowed**) intimidate (someone) into submitting to one's wishes.
ORIGIN – probably from Old Norse *kúga* 'oppress'.

coward > *noun* a person contemptibly lacking in courage.
DERIVATIVES – **cowardice** *noun*.
ORIGIN – Old French *couard*, from Latin *cauda* 'tail', perhaps with reference to an animal with its tail between its legs.

cowardly > *adjective* lacking courage.
DERIVATIVES – **cowardliness** *noun*.
SYNONYMS – craven, faint-hearted, spineless, timid, timorous.
ANTONYMS – brave, courageous.

cowboy > *noun* **1** a man on horseback who herds cattle, especially in the western US. **2** informal an unscrupulous or unqualified tradesman.
WORDFINDER – chaparajos (*cowboy's trousers*), charro (*Mexican cowboy*), gaucho (*South American cowboy*), rodeo (*display of cowboy skills*).

cower > *verb* crouch down or shrink back in fear.
SYNONYMS – cringe, crouch, flinch, recoil, shrink, wince.
ORIGIN – Low German *kūren* 'lie in wait'.

cowherd > *noun* a person who tends grazing cattle.

cowl > *noun* **1** a large, loose hood forming part of a monk's habit. **2** a hood-shaped covering for a chimney or ventilation shaft. **3** another term for COWLING.
DERIVATIVES – **cowled** *adjective*.
ORIGIN – Latin *cucullus* 'hood of a cloak'.

cowlick > *noun* a lock of hair hanging over the forehead.

cowling > *noun* a removable cover for a vehicle or aircraft engine.

cowpat > *noun* a flat, round piece of cow dung.

cowpoke > *noun* N. Amer. informal a cowboy.

cowrie /**kow**ri/ (also **cowry**) > *noun* (pl. **cowries**) a marine gastropod mollusc having a smooth, glossy, domed shell with a long, narrow opening.
ORIGIN – Hindi.

cowslip > *noun* a wild primula with clusters of drooping fragrant yellow flowers in spring.
ORIGIN – Old English, 'cow slime'.

Cox (in full **Cox's orange pippin**) > *noun* an eating apple of a variety with a red-tinged green skin.
ORIGIN – named after the English fruit grower R. *Cox* (*c*.1776–1845).

cox > *noun* a coxswain. > *verb* act as a coxswain for.
DERIVATIVES – **coxless** *adjective*.

coxcomb /**koks**kōm/ > *noun* **1** archaic a vain and conceited man; a dandy. **2** variant spelling of COCKSCOMB.

coxswain /**koks**'n/ > *noun* **1** the steersman of a boat. **2** the senior petty officer in a small ship or submarine in the Royal Navy.
ORIGIN – from obsolete *cock* 'small boat' + SWAIN.

coy > *adjective* (**coyer, coyest**) **1** pretending shyness or modesty. **2** reluctant to give details about something sensitive: *he's coy about his age.*
DERIVATIVES – **coyly** *adverb* **coyness** *noun*.
ORIGIN – Old French *coi*, from Latin *quietus* 'quiet'.

coyote /koy**ō**ti, **koy**ōt/ > *noun* (pl. same or **coyotes**) a wolf-like wild dog native to North America.
ORIGIN – Nahuatl.

coypu /**koy**pōō/ > *noun* (pl. **coypus**) a large semiaquatic beaver-like South American rodent, farmed for its fur.
ORIGIN – Araucanian (a Chilean language).

cozen /**kuzz**'n/ > *verb* literary trick or deceive.
ORIGIN – perhaps from obsolete Italian *cozzonare* 'to cheat'.

cozy > *adjective* US spelling of COSY.

CPR > *abbreviation* cardiopulmonary resuscitation.

CPS > *abbreviation* (in the UK) Crown Prosecution Service.

cps (also **c.p.s.**) > *abbreviation* **1** Computing characters per second. **2** cycles per second.

CPU > *abbreviation* Computing central processing unit.

Cr > *symbol* the chemical element chromium.

crab > *noun* **1** a marine crustacean, some kinds of which are edible, with a broad shell and five pairs of legs, the first of which are modified as pincers. **2** (**crabs**) informal an infestation of crab lice. > *verb* **1** move sideways or obliquely. **2** fish for crabs.
WORDFINDER – Cancer (*constellation and zodiac sign, the Crab*).
IDIOMS – **catch a crab** Rowing make a faulty stroke in which the oar is jammed under the water or misses the water completely.
DERIVATIVES – **crabber** *noun* **crablike** *adjective & adverb*.
COMBINATIONS – **crabgrass** N. Amer. a creeping grass that can become a serious weed. **crab louse** a louse that infests human body hair.

crab apple > *noun* a small, sour kind of apple.
ORIGIN – perhaps an alteration of Scots and northern English *scrab*.

crabbed > *adjective* **1** (of writing) hard to read or understand. **2** bad-tempered; crabby.
ORIGIN – from CRAB, because of the crab's sideways gait and habit of snapping.

crabby > *adjective* (**crabbier, crabbiest**) bad-tempered; morose.
DERIVATIVES – **crabbily** *adverb* **crabbiness** *noun*.
ORIGIN – from *crab* meaning 'grumble', originally (of hawks) 'claw or fight each other'.

crabwise > *adverb & adjective* (of movement) sideways, especially in an awkward way.

crack > *noun* **1** a narrow opening between two parts of something which has split or been broken. **2** a sudden sharp or explosive noise. **3** a sharp blow. **4** informal a joke or jibe. **5** informal an attempt to do something. **6** (also **craic**) Irish enjoyable entertainment; a good time. **7** (also **crack cocaine**) a potent hard crystalline form of cocaine broken into small pieces. > *verb* **1** break with little or no separation of the parts. **2** give way under pressure or strain. **3** make a sudden sharp or explosive sound. **4** hit hard. **5** (of a person's voice) suddenly change in pitch, especially through strain. **6** informal solve, interpret, or decipher. **7** informal break into (a safe). > *adjective* very good or skilful.
IDIOMS – **crack down on** informal take severe measures against. **crack of dawn** daybreak. **crack of doom** a thunder peal announcing the Day of Judgement. **crack of the whip** Brit. informal a chance to try or participate in something. **crack on** informal proceed or progress quickly. **crack up** informal **1** suffer an emotional breakdown under pressure. **2** burst into laughter. **be cracked up to be** informal be asserted to be: *acting is not as glamorous as it's cracked up to be.* **get cracking** informal act quickly and energetically.
SYNONYMS – *noun* **1** cleft, crevice, fissure. *verb* **1** fracture, rupture, splinter, split. **2** cave in, collapse, crumble.

crackbrained > *adjective* informal extremely foolish.

crackdown > *noun* a series of severe measures against undesirable or illegal behaviour.

cracked > *adjective* **1** having cracks. **2** informal crazy.
COMBINATIONS – **cracked wheat** grains of wheat that have been crushed into small pieces.

cracker > *noun* **1** a paper cylinder which, when pulled apart, makes a sharp noise and releases a small toy or other novelty. **2** a firework that explodes with a crack. **3** a thin dry biscuit of a kind eaten with cheese. **4** Brit. informal a fine example of something.

COMBINATIONS – **cracker-barrel** N. Amer. simple and unsophisticated. [ORIGIN – with reference to the barrels of soda crackers formerly found in country stores.]

crackerjack > *noun* informal, chiefly N. Amer. an exceptionally good person or thing.

crackers > *adjective* informal, chiefly Brit. insane; crazy.

cracking > *adjective* Brit. informal **1** excellent. **2** fast and exciting: *a cracking pace.*

crackle > *verb* make a rapid succession of slight cracking noises. > *noun* **1** a sound made up of a rapid succession of slight cracking noises. **2** a pattern of minute surface cracks.

DERIVATIVES – **crackly** *adjective.*

crackling > *noun* the crisp, fatty skin of roast pork.

cracknel /kraknəl/ > *noun* **1** a light, crisp, savoury biscuit. **2** a brittle sweet made from set melted sugar.

crackpot informal > *noun* an eccentric or foolish person. > *adjective* eccentric or impractical.

cracksman > *noun* informal, dated a thief who breaks into safes.

-cracy > *combining form* denoting a particular form of government or rule: *democracy.*

ORIGIN – from Greek *-kratia* 'power, rule'.

cradle > *noun* **1** a baby's bed or cot, especially one mounted on rockers. **2** a place or period in which a specified thing originates or flourishes: *the cradle of civilisation.* **3** a supporting framework resembling a cradle, in particular for a boat under repair or for workers on the side of high building. > *verb* **1** hold gently and protectively. **2** place in a cradle.

COMBINATIONS – **cradle-snatcher** humorous a person who has a sexual relationship with a much younger person.

craft > *noun* **1** an activity involving skill in making things by hand. **2** skill in carrying out one's work. **3** (**crafts**) things made by hand. **4** cunning. **5** (pl. same) a boat, ship, or aircraft. > *verb* make (something) skilfully.

DERIVATIVES – **crafter** *noun.*

SYNONYMS – *noun* **1** calling, pursuit, trade, vocation. **2** adroitness, dexterity, skill, technique.

ORIGIN – Old English; sense 5 perhaps comes from the idea of vessels requiring skill to handle.

craftsman (or **craftswoman**) > *noun* a worker skilled in a particular craft.

WORDFINDER – craftsmen and their products: bowyer (*maker of bows*), chandler (*candles*), cooper (*barrels*), cutler (*cutlery*), fletcher (*arrows*), glover (*gloves*), luthier (*stringed instruments*), milliner (*hats*), spurrier (*spurs*).

DERIVATIVES – **craftsmanship** *noun.*

craftwork > *noun* **1** the making of things by hand. **2** items or work produced in such a way.

DERIVATIVES – **craftworker** *noun.*

crafty > *adjective* (**craftier, craftiest**) clever at achieving one's aims through cunning or deceit.

DERIVATIVES – **craftily** *adverb* **craftiness** *noun.*

SYNONYMS – artful, cunning, deceitful, devious, guileful, wily.

crag > *noun* a steep or rugged cliff or rock face.

ORIGIN – Celtic.

craggy > *adjective* (**craggier, craggiest**) **1** having many crags. **2** (of a man's face) attractively rugged and rough-textured.

DERIVATIVES – **craggily** *adverb* **cragginess** *noun.*

crake > *noun* a bird of the rail family with a short bill, such as the corncrake.

ORIGIN – Old Norse, based on the corncrake's call.

cram > *verb* (**crammed, cramming**) **1** force (too many people or things) into a room or container. **2** fill (something) to the point of overflowing. **3** study intensively just before an examination.

SYNONYMS – **1,2** jam, pack, squash, stuff.

crammer > *noun* Brit. a college that gives intensive preparation for examinations.

cramp > *noun* **1** painful involuntary contraction of a muscle or muscles. **2** a tool for clamping two objects together. **3** (also **cramp-iron**) a metal bar with bent ends for holding masonry together. > *verb* **1** restrict or inhibit the development of. **2** fasten with a cramp or cramps. **3** suffer from cramp.

IDIOMS – **cramp someone's style** informal prevent a person from acting freely or naturally.

SYNONYMS – *verb* **1** hinder, impede, inhibit, restrict.

ORIGIN – Low German and Dutch *krampe.*

cramped > *adjective* **1** uncomfortably small or crowded. **2** (of handwriting) small and difficult to read.

SYNONYMS – **1** confined, constricted, poky, restricted.

ANTONYMS – **1** spacious.

crampon /krampon/ > *noun* a spiked device fixed to a boot for climbing on ice or rock.

ORIGIN – Old French.

cranberry > *noun* a small sour-tasting red berry used in cooking.

ORIGIN – German *Kranbeere* 'crane-berry'.

crane[1] > *noun* **1** a tall machine used for moving heavy objects by suspending them from a projecting arm. **2** a moving platform supporting a camera. > *verb* **1** stretch out (one's neck) in order to see something. **2** move (an object) by means of a crane.

ORIGIN – from CRANE[2].

crane[2] > *noun* a tall, long-legged, long-necked wading bird.

COMBINATIONS – **crane fly** a slender two-winged fly with very long legs; a daddy-long-legs.

cranesbill > *noun* a plant with lobed leaves and purple or violet flowers.

cranial /krayniəl/ > *adjective* relating to the skull or cranium.

cranium /krayniəm/ > *noun* (pl. **craniums** or **crania** /kraynia/) the skull, especially the part enclosing the brain.

ORIGIN – Latin, from Greek *kranion.*

crank[1] > *noun* a part of an axle or shaft bent out at right angles, for converting reciprocal to circular motion and vice versa. > *verb* **1** turn a crankshaft or handle. **2** (**crank up**) informal increase the intensity of. **3** (**crank out**) informal, derogatory produce (something) regularly and routinely.

ORIGIN – Old English, related to CRINGE.

crank[2] > *noun* **1** an eccentric or obsessive person. **2** N. Amer. a bad-tempered person. **3** literary a fanciful turn of speech.

crankcase > *noun* a case or covering enclosing a crankshaft.

crankpin > *noun* a pin by which a connecting rod is attached to a crank.

crankshaft > *noun* a shaft driven by a crank.

cranky > *adjective* (**crankier, crankiest**) informal **1** eccentric, odd. **2** chiefly N. Amer. bad-tempered; irritable. **3** (of a machine) working erratically.

DERIVATIVES – **crankily** *adverb* **crankiness** *noun.*

ORIGIN – first used in the sense 'sickly, in poor health': perhaps from Dutch or German *krank* 'sick'.

cranny > *noun* (pl. **crannies**) a small, narrow space or opening.

ORIGIN – from Latin *crena* 'notch'.

crap vulgar slang > *noun* **1** excrement; faeces. **2** nonsense; rubbish. > *verb* (**crapped, crapping**) defecate. > *adjective* extremely poor in quality.

DERIVATIVES – **crappy** *adjective.*

ORIGIN – first used in Middle English to mean 'chaff', later 'residue from rendering fat' and 'dregs of beer'; current uses date from the 19th century.

crape > *noun* **1** variant spelling of CRÊPE. **2** black silk, formerly used for mourning clothes.

crap game > *noun* N. Amer. a game of craps.

craps > *plural noun* (treated as sing.) a North American gambling game played with two dice.

ORIGIN – perhaps from CRAB or *crab's eyes,* denoting a throw of two ones.

crapshoot > *noun* N. Amer. a game of craps.

crapulent /**krap**yoolənt/ > *adjective* literary relating to the drinking of alcohol or to drunkenness.

DERIVATIVES – **crapulence** *noun* **crapulous** *adjective*.

ORIGIN – Latin *crapulentus*, from *crapula* 'drunkenness'.

crash > *verb* **1** (of a vehicle) collide violently with an obstacle or another vehicle. **2** (of an aircraft) fall from the sky and violently hit the land or sea. **3** move with force, speed, and sudden loud noise. **4** make a sudden loud, deep noise. **5** (of shares) fall suddenly in value. **6** Computing fail suddenly. **7** (also **crash out**) informal fall deeply asleep. **8** informal gatecrash (a party). > *noun* **1** an instance of crashing. **2** a sudden loud, deep noise. > *adjective* rapid and concentrated: *a crash course in Italian.*

COMBINATIONS – **crash-dive** (of an aircraft or submarine) dive rapidly or uncontrollably. **crash helmet** a helmet worn by a motorcyclist to protect the head. **crash-land** land roughly in an emergency. **crash pad** informal a place to sleep in an emergency. **crash-test** deliberately crash (a new vehicle) in order to evaluate and improve its ability to withstand impact.

crashing > *adjective* informal complete; total: *a crashing bore.*

DERIVATIVES – **crashingly** *adverb*.

crashworthiness > *noun* the degree to which a vehicle will protect its occupants from the effects of an accident.

crass > *adjective* grossly insensitive and unintelligent.

DERIVATIVES – **crassly** *adverb* **crassness** *noun*.

SYNONYMS – boorish, insensitive, oafish, stupid.

ORIGIN – first used in the sense 'dense or coarse': from Latin *crassus* 'solid, thick'.

-crat > *combining form* denoting a member or supporter of a particular form of government or rule: *democrat*.

ORIGIN – from French *-crate*, from Greek *-kratia* 'power, rule'.

crate > *noun* **1** a slatted wooden case for transporting goods. **2** a square container divided into small individual units for holding bottles. **3** informal an old and dilapidated vehicle. > *verb* pack in a crate for transportation.

crater > *noun* **1** a large bowl-shaped cavity, especially one caused by an explosion or impact or forming the mouth of a volcano. **2** a large bowl used in ancient Greece for mixing wine. > *verb* form a crater or craters in.

ORIGIN – Greek *kratēr* 'mixing bowl'.

-cratic > *combining form* relating to a particular kind of government or rule: *democratic*.

cravat > *noun* a strip of fabric worn by men round the neck and tucked inside an open-necked shirt.

ORIGIN – French *cravate*, from *Cravate* 'Croat', because of the scarves worn by Croatian mercenaries in 17th-century France.

crave > *verb* **1** feel a powerful desire for. **2** dated ask for: *I must crave your indulgence.*

SYNONYMS – **1** long for, yearn for.

craven > *adjective* contemptibly lacking in courage; cowardly.

DERIVATIVES – **cravenly** *adverb*.

ORIGIN – from obsolete *cravant* 'defeated', perhaps from Old French *cravanter* 'crush, overwhelm'.

craving > *noun* a powerful desire for something.

craw > *noun* dated the crop of a bird or insect.

IDIOMS – **stick in one's craw** see STICK².

crawfish > *noun* chiefly N. Amer. a crayfish.

crawl > *verb* **1** move forward on the hands and knees or by dragging the body close to the ground. **2** (of an insect or small animal) move slowly along a surface. **3** move unusually slowly. **4** (**be crawling with**) be unpleasantly covered or crowded with. **5** feel an unpleasant sensation resembling something moving over the skin. **6** informal behave obsequiously or ingratiatingly. > *noun* **1** an act of crawling. **2** an unusually slow rate of movement. **3** a swimming stroke involving alternate overarm movements and rapid kicks of the legs.

DERIVATIVES – **crawler** *noun*.

SYNONYMS – *verb* **3** creep, inch. **4** (**be crawling with**) overflow with, swarm with, teem with.

crayfish > *noun* a freshwater or marine crustacean resembling a small lobster.

ORIGIN – Old French *crevice*, related to German *Krebs* 'crab'.

crayon > *noun* a stick of coloured chalk or wax, used for drawing. > *verb* draw with a crayon or crayons.

ORIGIN – French, from *craie* 'chalk'.

craze > *noun* a widespread but short-lived enthusiasm for something. > *verb* develop or cover with a network of fine cracks.

crazed > *adjective* wildly insane; demented.

crazy > *adjective* (**crazier, craziest**) **1** insane or unbalanced, especially in a wild or aggressive way. **2** extremely enthusiastic about something. **3** absurdly unlikely: *a crazy angle.* **4** archaic full of cracks or flaws. > *noun* (pl. **crazies**) informal, chiefly N. Amer. an insane person.

IDIOMS – **like crazy** to a great degree.

DERIVATIVES – **crazily** *adverb* **craziness** *noun*.

SYNONYMS – *adjective* **1** crazed, demented, deranged, insane, mad.

COMBINATIONS – **crazy paving** Brit. paving made of irregular pieces of flat stone.

creak > *verb* **1** make a harsh high-pitched sound when being moved or when pressure is applied. **2** show weakness or frailty under strain. > *noun* a creaking sound.

creaky > *adjective* (**creakier, creakiest**) **1** making a creaking sound. **2** decrepit or dilapidated.

cream > *noun* **1** the thick white or pale yellow fatty liquid which rises to the top when milk is left to stand. **2** a dessert or other food containing cream or having a creamy consistency. **3** a thick liquid or semi-solid cosmetic or medical preparation. **4** the very best of a group of people or things: *the cream of American society.* **5** a very pale yellow or off-white colour. > *verb* **1** work (butter) to form a smooth, soft paste. **2** mash (a cooked vegetable) and mix with milk or cream. **3** (**cream off**) take away (the best part of a group of people or things).

SYNONYMS – *noun* **4** best, crème de la crème, elite, finest, pick.

COMBINATIONS – **cream cheese** soft, rich cheese made from unskimmed milk and cream. **cream cracker** Brit. a dry unsweetened biscuit eaten with cheese. **cream puff 1** a cake made of puff pastry filled with cream. **2** informal a weak or ineffectual person. **cream sherry** a full-bodied mellow sweet sherry. **cream soda** a carbonated vanilla-flavoured soft drink. **cream tea** Brit. an afternoon meal consisting of tea to drink with scones, jam, and cream.

ORIGIN – Old French *cresme*, from Latin *chrisma* 'oil for anointing'.

creamer > *noun* **1** a cream or milk substitute for adding to coffee or tea. **2** N. Amer. a jug for cream. **3** historical a flat dish for skimming the cream off milk.

creamery > *noun* (pl. **creameries**) a factory that produces butter and cheese.

creamy > *adjective* (**creamier, creamiest**) resembling or containing a lot of cream.

DERIVATIVES – **creamily** *adverb* **creaminess** *noun*.

crease > *noun* **1** a line or ridge produced on paper, cloth, etc. by folding, pressing, or crushing. **2** Cricket any of a number of lines marked on the pitch at specified places. > *verb* **1** make a crease in. **2** become creased. **3** (**crease up**) Brit. informal burst out laughing.

SYNONYMS – *verb* **1,2** crinkle, crumple, wrinkle.

ORIGIN – probably a variant of CREST.

create > *verb* **1** bring into existence. **2** make (someone) a member of the nobility. **3** Brit. informal make a fuss; complain.

SYNONYMS – **1** engender, generate, make, produce.

ORIGIN – Latin *creare* 'produce'.

creatine /**kree**əteen/ > *noun* Biochemistry a compound formed in protein metabolism and involved in the supply of energy for muscular contraction.

ORIGIN – from Greek *kreas* 'meat'.

creation > *noun* **1** the action or process of creating. **2** a thing which has been made or invented, especially something showing artistic talent. **3** (**the Creation**) the creating of the universe regarded as an act of God. **4** (**Creation**) literary the universe.

creationism > *noun* the belief that the universe and living creatures were created by God in accordance with the account given in the Old Testament.

DERIVATIVES – **creationist** *noun* & *adjective*.

creative > *adjective* involving the use of the imagination or original ideas in order to create something.

DERIVATIVES – **creatively** *adverb* **creativeness** *noun* **creativity** *noun*.

SYNONYMS – artistic, imaginative, innovative, inventive, original.

COMBINATIONS – **creative accountancy** (also **creative accounting**) informal the exploitation of loopholes in financial regulation to gain advantage or to present figures in a misleadingly favourable light.

creator > *noun* **1** a person or thing that creates. **2** (**the Creator**) God.

creature > *noun* **1** a living being, in particular an animal as distinct from a person. **2** a person or organisation under the complete control of another.

COMBINATIONS – **creature comforts** material comforts such as good food and accommodation.

ORIGIN – first used in the sense 'something created': from Latin *creatura*, from *creare* 'produce'.

crèche /kresh/ > *noun* Brit. a nursery where babies and young children are cared for during the working day.

ORIGIN – French, related to **CRIB**.

cred > *noun* informal short for **CREDIBILITY** (in sense 2).

credal /**kreed**'l/ (also **creedal**) > *adjective* relating to a creed.

credence /**kreed**'nss/ > *noun* **1** belief in or acceptance of something as true. **2** the likelihood of something being true; plausibility.

ORIGIN – Latin *credentia*, from *credere* 'believe'.

credential /kri**den**sh'l/ > *noun* **1** a qualification, achievement, etc., that gives an indication of suitability. **2** a document or certificate proving a person's identity or qualifications. **3** a letter of introduction given by a government to an ambassador before a new posting.

credibility > *noun* **1** the quality of being credible. **2** (also **street credibility**) acceptability among fashionable young urban people.

credible > *adjective* able to be believed; convincing.

DERIVATIVES – **credibly** *adverb*.

USAGE – do not confuse **credible** with **creditable**: **credible** means 'believable, convincing', whereas **creditable** means 'deserving acknowledgement and praise'.

SYNONYMS – believable, cogent, convincing, plausible.

credit > *noun* **1** the facility of being able to obtain goods or services before paying for them, based on the trust that payment will be made in the future. **2** an entry in an account recording a sum received. **3** public acknowledgement or praise given for an achievement or quality. **4** a source of pride: *the fans are a credit to the club.* **5** a written acknowledgement of a contributor's role displayed at the beginning or end of a film or programme. **6** a unit of study counting towards a degree or diploma. **7** Brit. a grade above a pass in an examination. > *verb* (**credited, crediting**) **1** (often **credit to**) publicly acknowledge that someone participated in the production of (something). **2** (**credit with**) ascribe (an achievement or good quality) to (someone). **3** add (an amount of money) to an account. **4** believe (something surprising or unlikely).

IDIOMS – **be in credit** (of an account) have money in it. **do someone credit** make someone worthy of praise or respect.

SYNONYMS – *noun* **3** acclaim, commendation, kudos, recognition.

COMBINATIONS – **credit card** a plastic card which allows the holder to make purchases on credit. **credit union** a non-profit-making cooperative whose members can borrow money at low interest rates.

ORIGIN – Latin *creditum*, from *credere* 'believe, trust'.

creditable > *adjective* deserving public acknowledgement and praise, although not necessarily outstanding or successful.

DERIVATIVES – **creditably** *adverb*.

USAGE – do not confuse with **credible**.

SYNONYMS – admirable, commendable, laudable, praiseworthy, respectable.

creditor > *noun* a person or company to whom money is owing.

creditworthy > *adjective* considered suitable to receive commercial credit.

DERIVATIVES – **creditworthiness** *noun*.

credo /**kray**dō/ > *noun* (pl. **credos**) **1** a statement of a person's beliefs or aims. **2** (**Credo**) a creed of the Christian Church in Latin.

ORIGIN – Latin, 'I believe'.

credulous /**kred**yooləss/ > *adjective* excessively ready to believe things; gullible.

DERIVATIVES – **credulity** /kri**dyoo**liti/ *noun* **credulously** *adverb*.

SYNONYMS – gullible, naive, unworldly.

ANTONYMS – sceptical.

Cree /kree/ > *noun* (pl. same or **Crees**) a member of an American Indian people of central Canada.

ORIGIN – Algonquian.

creed > *noun* **1** a system of religious belief; a faith. **2** a statement of beliefs or principles; a credo.

ORIGIN – from Latin *credo* 'I believe'.

creedal > *adjective* variant spelling of **CREDAL**.

Creek /kreek/ > *noun* (pl. same) a member of a confederacy of American Indian peoples of the south-eastern US.

ORIGIN – from **CREEK**, because they lived beside the waterways of the flatlands of Georgia and Alabama.

creek > *noun* **1** a small waterway such as an inlet in a shoreline or channel in a marsh. **2** N. Amer. & Austral./NZ a stream or minor tributary of a river.

IDIOMS – **up the creek** informal **1** in severe difficulty or trouble. **2** Brit. stupid or misguided.

ORIGIN – Old French *crique* or Old Norse *kriki* 'nook'.

creel > *noun* **1** a large basket for carrying fish. **2** a rack holding bobbins or spools when spinning.

creep > *verb* (past and past participle **crept**) **1** move slowly and carefully, especially to avoid being noticed. **2** move or progress very slowly and steadily. **3** (of a plant) grow along the ground or other surface by extending stems or branches. **4** (**creep to**) informal behave obsequiously towards (someone). > *noun* **1** informal a contemptible person, especially one who behaves obsequiously. **2** very slow, steady movement or progress.

IDIOMS – **give someone the creeps** informal make someone feel revulsion or fear. **make one's flesh creep** cause one to have an unpleasant sensation like that of something crawling over the skin.

COMBINATIONS – **creeping Jesus** Brit. informal an excessively or hypocritically pious person.

creeper > *noun* **1** any plant that grows along the ground or another surface by extending stems or branches. **2** (**creepers**) informal soft-soled suede shoes.

creepy > *adjective* (**creepier, creepiest**) informal causing an unpleasant feeling of fear or unease.

DERIVATIVES – **creepily** adverb **creepiness** noun.

creepy-crawly > noun (pl. **creepy-crawlies**) informal a spider, worm, or other small creature.

cremate > verb dispose of (a dead person's body) by burning it to ashes.

DERIVATIVES – **cremation** noun.

ORIGIN – Latin cremare 'burn'.

crematorium /kremmətoriəm/ > noun (pl. **crematoria** or **crematoriums**) a building where the dead are cremated.

crème anglaise /krem oNglayz/ > noun a rich egg custard.

ORIGIN – French, 'English cream'.

crème brûlée /krem broōlay/ > noun (pl. **crèmes brûlées** pronunc. same or **crème brûlées** /krem broōlayz/) a dessert of custard topped with caramelised sugar.

ORIGIN – French, 'burnt cream'.

crème caramel /krem karrəmel/ > noun (pl. **crèmes caramel** pronunc. same or **crème caramels**) a custard dessert made with whipped cream and eggs and topped with caramel.

ORIGIN – French.

crème de cassis > noun see CASSIS.

crème de la crème /krem də laa krem/ > noun the best person or thing of a particular kind.

ORIGIN – French, 'cream of the cream'.

crème de menthe /krem də month/ > noun a green peppermint-flavoured liqueur.

ORIGIN – French, 'cream of mint'.

crème fraiche /krem fresh/ > noun a type of thick cream with buttermilk, sour cream, or yogurt.

ORIGIN – French, 'fresh cream'.

crenellated /krennəlaytid/ (also **crenelated**) > adjective (of a building) having battlements.

ORIGIN – Old French créneler, from Latin crena 'notch'.

crenellations > plural noun battlements.

Creole /kreeōl/ > noun 1 a person of mixed European and black descent. 2 a descendant of European settlers in the Caribbean or Central or South America. 3 a white descendant of French settlers in Louisiana. 4 a vernacular language which has developed through the interaction of a European language with an African or other non-European language.

ORIGIN – French, from Spanish criollo, probably from Portuguese crioulo 'black person born in Brazil'.

creosote > noun 1 a dark brown oil distilled from coal tar, used as a wood preservative. 2 a liquid distilled from wood tar and used as an antiseptic. > verb treat with creosote.

ORIGIN – from Greek kreas 'flesh' + sōtēr 'preserver'.

crêpe /krayp/ (also **crape**) > noun 1 a light, thin fabric with a wrinkled surface. 2 hard-wearing wrinkled rubber used for the soles of shoes. 3 /also krep/ a thin pancake.

DERIVATIVES – **crêpey** (also **crêpy**) adjective.

COMBINATIONS – **crêpe paper** thin, crinkled paper used for making decorations. **crêpe Suzette** (pl. **crêpes Suzette** pronunc. same) a thin dessert pancake flamed and served in alcohol.

ORIGIN – French, from Old French crespe 'curled, frizzed'.

crêpe de Chine /krayp də sheen/ > noun a fine crêpe of silk or similar fabric.

ORIGIN – French, 'crêpe of China'.

crepitate /kreppitayt/ > verb rare make a crackling sound.

DERIVATIVES – **crepitation** noun.

ORIGIN – Latin crepitare, from crepare 'to rattle'.

crept past and past participle of CREEP.

crepuscular /kripuskyoolər/ > adjective resembling or relating to twilight.

ORIGIN – from Latin crepusculum 'twilight'.

crescendo /krishendō/ > noun 1 (pl. **crescendos** or **crescendi** /krishendi/) a gradual increase in loudness in a piece of music. 2 the loudest or climactic point of something. > adverb & adjective Music with a gradual increase in loudness. > verb (**crescendoes**, **crescendoed**) increase in loudness or intensity.

ORIGIN – Italian, from Latin crescere 'grow, increase'.

crescent > noun 1 the curved sickle shape of the waxing or waning moon. 2 a thing of this shape, in particular a street or terrace of houses forming an arc.

ORIGIN – from Latin crescere 'grow'.

cress > noun 1 a plant with small white flowers and pungent leaves. 2 young sprouts of garden cress eaten in salads.

crest > noun 1 a comb or tuft of feathers, fur, or skin on the head of a bird or other animal. 2 a plume of feathers on a helmet. 3 the top of a ridge, wave, etc. 4 a distinctive heraldic device representing a family or corporate body. > verb 1 reach the top of. 2 (**be crested with**) have (something) attached at the top.

IDIOMS – **on the crest of a wave** at a very successful point.

DERIVATIVES – **crested** adjective.

ORIGIN – Old French creste, from Latin crista 'tuft, plume'.

crestfallen > adjective sad and disappointed.

SYNONYMS – dejected, despondent, downcast, downhearted.

ANTONYMS – cheerful.

Cretaceous /kritayshəss/ > adjective relating to the last period of the Mesozoic era (between the Jurassic and Tertiary periods, about 146 to 65 million years ago), at the end of which dinosaurs and many other organisms died out.

ORIGIN – from Latin creta 'chalk'.

Cretan /kreet'n/ > noun a person from the Greek island of Crete. > adjective relating to Crete.

cretin /krettin/ > noun 1 informal, offensive a stupid person. 2 Medicine, dated a person who is deformed and mentally handicapped because of congenital thyroid deficiency.

DERIVATIVES – **cretinism** noun.

ORIGIN – from Swiss French crestin 'Christian', apparently used to convey a reminder that handicapped people are human.

cretinous > adjective informal very stupid.

cretonne /kreton/ > noun a heavy cotton fabric, typically with a floral pattern, used for upholstery.

ORIGIN – French.

Creutzfeldt–Jakob disease /kroytsfelt-yakkob/ > noun a fatal degenerative disease affecting the human brain, thought to be caused by a protein particle or prion.

IDIOMS – **new variant Creutzfeldt–Jakob disease** a form of the disease believed to be caused by the same agent as BSE in cattle.

ORIGIN – named after the German neurologists H. G. Creutzfeldt and A. Jakob, who first described the disease in the early 1920s.

crevasse /krivass/ > noun a deep open crack in a glacier or ice field.

ORIGIN – French, from Old French crevace (see CREVICE).

crevice /krevviss/ > noun a narrow opening or fissure in a rock or wall.

SYNONYMS – cleft, crack, fissure.

ORIGIN – Old French crevace, from crever 'to burst'.

crew[1] > noun 1 a group of people who work on and operate a ship, boat, aircraft, or train. 2 such a group other than the officers. 3 informal, often derogatory a group of people. > verb 1 provide with a crew. 2 act as a member of a crew.

DERIVATIVES – **crewman** noun.

COMBINATIONS – **crew cut** a very short haircut for men and boys. [ORIGIN – apparently first adopted by boat crews of Harvard and Yale universities.] **crew neck** a close-fitting round neckline.

ORIGIN – Old French creue 'augmentation, increase', from Latin crescere 'grow'.

crew[2] past of CROW[2].

crewel /kroōəl/ > noun a thin, loosely twisted, worsted yarn used for tapestry and embroidery.

crib > noun 1 chiefly N. Amer. a child's bed with barred or latticed sides; a cot. 2 a barred rack for animal fodder; a manger. 3 informal a translation of a text for use by students, especially in a surreptitious way. 4 informal, chiefly N. Amer. an apartment or house. **5** short for CRIBBAGE. **6** Austral./NZ a snack. > *verb* (**cribbed**, **cribbing**) **1** informal copy (something) illicitly or without acknowledgement. **2** archaic steal.

DERIVATIVES – **cribber** noun.

cribbage > *noun* a card game for two players, the objective of which is to play cards whose value reaches exactly 15 or 31.

crick > *noun* a painful stiff feeling in the neck or back. > *verb* twist or strain (one's neck or back), causing painful stiffness.

cricket[1] > *noun* an open-air game played on a large grass field with bat and ball between teams of eleven players, the batsmen attempting to score runs by hitting the ball and running between the wickets.

WORDFINDER – *fielding positions in cricket:* cover, fine leg, gully, long leg, long off, long on, mid-off, mid-on, midwicket, point, slip, square leg, third man, wicketkeeper.

IDIOMS – **not cricket** Brit. informal not fair or honourable.

DERIVATIVES – **cricketer** noun **cricketing** *adjective.*

cricket[2] > *noun* an insect related to the grasshoppers but with shorter legs, of which the male produces a characteristic musical chirping sound.

ORIGIN – Old French *criquet,* from *criquer* 'to crackle'.

cri de cœur /kree də kör/ > *noun* (pl. **cris de cœur** pronunc. same) a passionate appeal or complaint.

ORIGIN – French, 'cry from the heart'.

cried past and past participle of CRY.

crier > *noun* an officer who makes public announcements in a court of justice.

crikey > *exclamation* Brit. informal an expression of surprise.

ORIGIN – euphemism for CHRIST.

crime > *noun* **1** an offence against an individual or the state which is punishable by law. **2** such actions collectively. **3** informal something shameful or deplorable.

ORIGIN – Latin *crimen* 'judgement, offence'.

crime passionnel /kreem pasyo**nel**/ > *noun* (pl. **crimes passionnels** pronunc. same) a crime committed in a fit of sexual jealousy.

ORIGIN – French, 'crime of passion'.

criminal > *noun* a person who has committed a crime. > *adjective* **1** relating to or constituting a crime. **2** informal deplorable and shocking.

DERIVATIVES – **criminality** noun **criminally** adverb.

SYNONYMS – *noun* lawbreaker, offender, villain; formal malefactor, miscreant. *adjective* **1** illegal, illicit, unlawful.

criminalise (also **criminalize**) > *verb* make (an activity) illegal.

DERIVATIVES – **criminalisation** noun.

criminology /krimmi**noll**əji/ > *noun* the scientific study of crime and criminals.

DERIVATIVES – **criminological** adjective **criminologist** noun.

crimp > *verb* **1** compress into small folds or ridges. **2** make waves in (hair) with a hot iron. > *noun* a curl, wave, or folded or compressed edge.

DERIVATIVES – **crimper** noun.

crimplene /**krim**pleen/ > *noun* trademark a synthetic crease-resistant fibre and fabric.

ORIGIN – probably from CRIMP + TERYLENE.

crimson /**krimz**'n/ > *noun* a rich deep red colour inclining to purple. > *verb* become flushed, especially through embarrassment.

ORIGIN – Arabic, related to KERMES: see box at VERMILION.

cringe /krinj/ > *verb* (**cringed**, **cringing**) **1** bend one's head and body in fear or in a servile manner. **2** have a sudden feeling of embarrassment or disgust. > *noun* an act of cringing.

SYNONYMS – *verb* **1** cower, flinch, recoil, shrink. **2** squirm, wince.

ORIGIN – Old English, 'bend, yield, fall in battle'; related to CRANK[1], CRINKLE.

cringeworthy > *adjective* informal causing feelings of embarrassment.

crinkle > *verb* form small creases or wrinkles. > *noun* a small crease or wrinkle.

DERIVATIVES – **crinkly** adjective.

SYNONYMS – furrow, pucker, wrinkle.

crinoline /**krinn**əlin/ > *noun* a stiffened or hooped petticoat formerly worn to make a long skirt stand out.

ORIGIN – French, from Latin *crinis* 'hair' + *linum* 'thread'.

cripes /krīps/ > *exclamation* informal, dated an expression of surprise.

ORIGIN – euphemism for CHRIST.

cripple > *noun* archaic or offensive a person who is unable to walk or move properly through disability or injury. > *verb* **1** make (someone) unable to move or walk properly. **2** cause severe and disabling damage to (something).

USAGE – avoid using the word **cripple** as a noun, as it has acquired offensive connotations; use a term such as 'disabled person'.

ORIGIN – Old English, related to CREEP.

crisis > *noun* (pl. **crises**) **1** a time of intense difficulty or danger. **2** a turning point, especially one in the course of a disease, when it becomes clear whether the patient will recover or not.

SYNONYMS – **1** dilemma, disaster, plight, predicament, quandary.

ORIGIN – Greek *krisis* 'decision', from *krinein* 'decide'.

crisp > *adjective* **1** firm, dry, and brittle. **2** (of the weather) cool, fresh, and invigorating. **3** briskly decisive and matter-of-fact. > *noun* (also **potato crisp**) Brit. a wafer-thin slice of potato fried until crisp and eaten as a snack. > *verb* **1** give (food) a crisp surface by cooking in an oven or under a grill. **2** archaic curl into short, stiff, wavy folds or crinkles.

DERIVATIVES – **crisper** noun **crisply** adverb **crispness** noun **crispy** (**crispier**, **crispiest**) *adjective.*

ORIGIN – Latin *crispus* 'curled'.

crispbread > *noun* a thin crisp biscuit made from crushed rye or wheat.

criss-cross > *adjective* containing a number of intersecting straight lines or paths. > *noun* a criss-cross pattern. > *verb* **1** form a criss-cross pattern on (a place). **2** move or travel around (a place) by going back and forth repeatedly.

ORIGIN – from *Christ-cross*: first denoting a figure of a cross preceding the alphabet in a hornbook.

criterion /krī**teer**iən/ > *noun* (pl. **criteria** /krī**teer**iə/) a principle or standard by which something may be judged or decided.

DERIVATIVES – **criterial** adjective.

USAGE – the singular form is **criterion** and the plural form is **criteria**; do not use **criteria** as if it were singular, as in *a further criteria needs to be considered.*

ORIGIN – Greek *kritērion* 'means of judging', from *kritēs* 'a judge'.

critic > *noun* **1** a person who expresses an unfavourable opinion of something. **2** a person who reviews literary or artistic works.

SYNONYMS – **1** denigrator, detractor.

ORIGIN – Greek *kritikos*, from *kritēs* 'a judge'.

critical > *adjective* **1** expressing adverse or disapproving comments or judgements. **2** expressing or involving an analysis of the merits and faults of a literary or artistic work. **3** having a decisive importance in the success or failure of something; crucial. **4** extremely ill and at risk of death. **5** Mathematics & Physics relating to a point of transition from one state to another. **6** (of a nuclear reactor or fuel) maintaining a self-sustaining chain reaction.

DERIVATIVES – **critically** adverb.

SYNONYMS – **1** censorious, derogatory, disparaging, scathing, unfavourable. **3** crucial, essential, paramount, vital.

ANTONYMS – **1** complimentary, favourable.

COMBINATIONS – **critical mass 1** Physics the minimum amount of fissile material needed to maintain a nuclear chain reaction. **2** the minimum amount of resources required to start or maintain a venture. **critical path** the sequence of stages determining the minimum time needed for a complex operation.

criticise (also **criticize**) > *verb* **1** indicate the faults of in a disapproving way. **2** form and express a critical assessment of (a literary or artistic work).

SYNONYMS – **1** censure, condemn, denigrate, denounce, disparage, lambaste.

criticism > *noun* **1** expression of disapproval; finding fault. **2** the critical assessment of literary or artistic works.

SYNONYMS – **1** censure, condemnation, disapproval, disparagement.

critique /kriteek/ > *noun* a detailed analysis and assessment of something. > *verb* (**critiques**, **critiqued**, **critiquing**) evaluate in a detailed and analytical way.

SYNONYMS – *noun* analysis, appraisal, assessment, evaluation.

ORIGIN – French.

critter > *noun* informal or dialect, chiefly N. Amer. a living creature.

croak > *noun* a characteristic deep hoarse sound made by a frog or a crow. > *verb* **1** utter a croak. **2** informal die.

DERIVATIVES – **croaker** noun **croakily** adverb **croaky** (**croakier**, **croakiest**) adjective.

Croatian /krōaysh'n/ > *noun* (also **Croat** /krōat/) **1** a person from Croatia. **2** the language of the Croats, almost identical to Serbian but written in the Roman alphabet. > *adjective* relating to Croatia or Croatian.

crochet /krōshay/ > *noun* a handicraft in which yarn is made up into a patterned fabric by means of a hooked needle. > *verb* (**crocheted** /krōshayd/, **crocheting** /krōshaying/) make (a garment or piece of fabric) in this way.

ORIGIN – French, 'little hook'.

croci plural of CROCUS.

crock¹ informal > *noun* **1** a old person considered to be feeble and useless. **2** Brit. an old worn-out vehicle. > *verb* **1** Brit. cause an injury to. **2** (**crocked**) N. Amer. drunk.

ORIGIN – first denoting an old ewe or horse: probably related to CRACK.

crock² > *noun* **1** an earthenware pot or jar. **2** an item of crockery. **3** N. Amer. informal something considered to be complete nonsense.

crockery > *noun* plates, dishes, cups, and similar items made of earthenware or china.

crocodile > *noun* **1** a large predatory semiaquatic reptile with long jaws, long tail, short legs, and a horny textured skin. **2** leather made from crocodile skin. **3** Brit. a line of schoolchildren walking in pairs.

COMBINATIONS – **crocodile clip** chiefly Brit. a sprung metal clip with long, serrated jaws, used to connect an electric cable to a battery. **crocodile tears** insincere tears or

expressions of sorrow. [ORIGIN – said to be so named from a belief that crocodiles wept while devouring or luring their prey.]

ORIGIN – Old French cocodrille, from Greek krokodilos 'worm of the stones'.

crocus /krōkəss/ > *noun* (pl. **crocuses** or **croci** /krōkī/) a small spring-flowering plant with bright yellow, purple, or white flowers.

ORIGIN – Greek krokos.

Croesus /kreesəss/ > *noun* a person of great wealth.

ORIGIN – from the name of a famously wealthy king of Lydia c.560–546 BC.

croft Brit. > *noun* **1** a small rented farm in Scotland or northern England. **2** a small enclosed field attached to a house. > *verb* farm (land) as a croft or crofts.

DERIVATIVES – **crofter** noun.

Crohn's disease /krōnz/ > *noun* a chronic disease involving inflammation and ulceration of the intestines, especially the colon and ileum.

ORIGIN – named after the American pathologist Burrill B. Crohn (1884–1983).

croissant /krwussoN/ > *noun* a crescent-shaped French roll made of sweet flaky pastry.

ORIGIN – French, 'crescent'.

Cro-Magnon /krōmagnən, krōmənyon/ > *noun* the earliest form of modern human in Europe, appearing c.35,000 years ago.

ORIGIN – the name of a hill in the Dordogne, France.

cromlech /kromlek/ > *noun* **1** (in Wales) a megalithic tomb; a dolmen. **2** (in Brittany) a circle of standing stones.

ORIGIN – Welsh, 'arched flat stone'.

crone > *noun* an ugly old woman.

ORIGIN – from Old French caroigne 'carrion'.

crony /krōni/ > *noun* (pl. **cronies**) informal, often derogatory a close friend or companion.

ORIGIN – 17th-century Cambridge university slang: from Greek khronios 'long-lasting' (here used to mean 'contemporary'); compare with CHUM.

cronyism (also **croneyism**) > *noun* derogatory the improper appointment of friends and associates to positions of authority.

crook > *noun* **1** a shepherd's hooked staff. **2** a bishop's crozier. **3** a bend, especially at the elbow in a person's arm. **4** informal a criminal or dishonest person. > *verb* bend (something, especially a finger). > *adjective* Austral./NZ informal **1** bad, unsound, or unwell. **2** dishonest; illegal.

COMBINATIONS – **crookbacked** archaic hunchbacked.

ORIGIN – Old Norse krókr 'hook'.

crooked /kroŏkkid/ > *adjective* **1** bent or

twisted out of shape or position. **2** informal dishonest or illegal.

DERIVATIVES – **crookedly** adverb **crookedness** noun.

SYNONYMS – **1** bent, contorted, distorted, misshapen, twisted.

croon > *verb* hum, sing, or speak in a soft, low voice. > *noun* a soft, low voice or tone.

DERIVATIVES – **crooner** noun.

ORIGIN – Low German and Dutch krōnen 'groan, lament'.

crop > *noun* **1** a plant, especially a cereal, fruit, or vegetable, cultivated for food or other use. **2** an amount of a crop harvested at one time. **3** an amount of people or things appearing at one time: *the current crop of politicians.* **4** a very short hairstyle. **5** a riding crop or hunting crop. **6** a pouch in a bird's gullet where food is stored or prepared for digestion. > *verb* (**cropped**, **cropping**) **1** cut very short or trim off the edges of. **2** (of an animal) bite off and eat the tops of (plants). **3** (**crop up**) appear or occur unexpectedly. **4** harvest (a crop) from an area. **5** sow or plant (land) with plants that will produce a crop.

COMBINATIONS – **crop circle** an area of standing crops which has been flattened in the form of a circle or other pattern by unexplained means. **crop dusting** the spraying of powdered insecticide or fertiliser on crops from the air. **crop top** (also **cropped top**) a woman's casual garment for the upper body, cut short so that it reveals the stomach.

wordpower facts
Crop

The word **crop** has an interesting and complex history. In Old English it meant 'pouch in a bird's gullet' (modern sense 6) and 'flower head, ear of corn' (now obsolete); this latter sense gave rise to sense 1 and others referring to the top of something, from which came the use to mean the upper part of a whip, as in *hunting crop* and *riding crop*. In Old English **crop** was related to German, Dutch, and Scandinavian words with a common idea of 'swollen protuberance or excrescence, bunch'; it also shared a root with **group** and **croup** 'rump or hindquarters of a horse'.

cropper > *noun* **1** a plant which yields a specified crop. **2** a machine or person that cuts or trims something. **3** chiefly US a person who raises a crop, especially as a sharecropper.

IDIOMS – **come a cropper** informal **1** fall heavily. **2** suffer a defeat or disaster.

croque-monsieur /krok məsyör/ > *noun* a fried or grilled cheese and ham sandwich.

ORIGIN – French, 'bite a man'.

croquet /krōkay/ > *noun* **1** a game played on a lawn, in which wooden balls are driven through a series of hoops with a mallet. **2** an act of croqueting a ball. > *verb* (**croqueted** /krōkayd/, **croqueting** /krōkaying/) knock away (an opponent's ball) by holding one's own ball against it and striking one's own.

WORDFINDER – bisque (*extra shot allowed to a weak player*), peg out (*hit the peg as final stroke*), roque (*US form of croquet played on a hard court*), roquet (*strike another ball with one's own*), rover (*ball that has gone through the hoops but not pegged out*).

ORIGIN – perhaps a dialect form of French *crochet* 'hook'.

croquette /krəket/ > *noun* a small ball or roll of vegetables, minced meat, or fish, fried in breadcrumbs.

ORIGIN – French, from *croquer* 'to crunch'.

crosier > *noun* variant spelling of CROZIER.

cross > *noun* **1** a mark, object, or figure formed by two short intersecting lines or pieces (+ or ×). **2** an upright post with a transverse bar, as used in antiquity for crucifixion. **3** a cross-shaped decoration awarded for bravery or indicating rank in some orders of knighthood. **4** a thing that is unavoidable and has to be endured: *she's just a cross we have to bear*. **5** an animal or plant resulting from cross-breeding; a hybrid. **6** (**a cross between**) a mixture or compromise of (two things). **7** (in soccer) a pass of the ball across the field towards the centre close to one's opponents' goal. > *verb* **1** go or extend across or to the other side of (a path, obstacle, or area). **2** pass in an opposite or different direction; intersect. **3** place crosswise: *Michele crossed her legs.* **4** draw a line or lines across; mark with a cross. **5** Brit. mark or annotate (a cheque) with a pair of parallel lines to indicate that it must be paid into a named bank account. **6** Soccer pass (the ball) across the field towards the centre when attacking. **7** cause (an animal of one species, breed, or variety) to interbreed with one of another. **8** oppose or stand in the way of. > *adjective* slightly angry; annoyed.

WORDFINDER – cruciform (*cross-shaped*); Crux (*constellation, the Cross or Southern Cross*).

IDIOMS – **at cross purposes** misunderstanding or having different aims from one another. **cross one's fingers** put one finger across another as a sign of hoping for good luck. **cross the floor** Brit. join the opposing side in parliament. **cross my heart** (**and hope to die**) used to emphasise the truthfulness and sincerity of what one is saying. **cross off** delete (an item) from a list. **cross oneself** make the sign of the cross in front of one's chest as a sign of Christian reverence or to invoke divine protection. **cross out** (or **through**) delete (a word or phrase) by drawing a line through it. **cross over** (of an artist) begin to appeal to a wider audience. **cross someone's palm with silver** often humorous pay someone for a service, especially fortune telling. **cross swords** have an argument or dispute. **crossed line** a telephone connection that has been wrongly made with the result that another call can be heard. **get one's wires** (or **lines**) **crossed** have a misunderstanding.

DERIVATIVES – **crosser** *noun* **crossly** *adverb* **crossness** *noun*.

SYNONYMS – *adjective* angry, annoyed, irate, irritable, vexed.

COMBINATIONS – **crossbar** a horizontal bar, in particular one between the two upright posts of a football goal or between the handlebars and saddle on a bicycle. **cross bench** a seat in the House of Lords occupied by a member who is independent of any political party. **cross-current 1** a current in a river or sea which flows across another. **2** a process or tendency which is in conflict with another. **cross hairs** a pair of fine wires crossing at right angles at the focus of an optical instrument or gunsight. **cross-hatch** shade (an area) with many intersecting parallel lines. **cross-legged** (of a seated person) with the legs crossed at the ankles and the knees bent outwards. **cross ownership** the ownership by one corporation of different companies with related interests or commercial aims. **crosspiece** a beam or bar fixed or placed across something else. **cross-ply** Brit. (of a tyre) having fabric layers with their threads running diagonally across each other. **cross-pollinate** pollinate (a flower or plant) with pollen from another flower or plant. **cross-question** question in great detail. **cross reference** a reference to another text given in order to elaborate on a point. **cross section 1** a surface or shape exposed by making a straight cut through something at right angles to the axis. **2** a typical or representative sample of a larger group. **cross stitch** a stitch formed of two stitches crossing each other. **crosstalk 1** unwanted transfer of signals between communication channels. **2** witty conversation. **cross tie** US a railway sleeper. **crosstrees** a pair of horizontal struts attached to a sailing ship's mast to spread the rigging. **crosswalk** N. Amer. & Austral. a pedestrian crossing. **crosswind** a wind blowing across one's direction of travel.

ORIGIN – Old Norse *kross*, from Latin *crux*.

crossbill > *noun* a thickset finch with a crossed bill adapted for extracting seeds from the cones of conifers.

crossbow > *noun* a medieval bow fixed across a wooden support, having a groove for the bolt and a mechanism for drawing and releasing the string.

DERIVATIVES – **crossbowman** *noun*.

cross-breed > *noun* an animal or plant produced by mating or hybridising two different species, breeds, or varieties. > *verb* breed in this way.

cross-check > *verb* verify (figures or information) by using an alternative source or method. > *noun* an instance of cross-checking figures or information.

cross-country > *adjective* **1** across fields or countryside, as opposed to on roads or tracks. **2** across a region or country, in particular not keeping to main or direct routes. > *noun* the sport of cross-country running, riding, skiing, or motoring.

cross-cut > *verb* **1** cut (wood or stone) across its main grain or axis. **2** alternate (one sequence) with another when editing a film.

COMBINATIONS – **cross-cut saw** a saw with a handle at each end, used by two people for cutting across the grain of timber.

cross-dressing > *noun* the wearing of clothing typical of the opposite sex.

crosse /kross/ > *noun* the stick used in women's field lacrosse.

ORIGIN – French, from Old French *croce* 'bishop's crook'.

cross-examine > *verb* question (a witness called by the other party) in a court of law to check or extend testimony already given.

DERIVATIVES – **cross-examination** *noun*.

cross-eyed > *adjective* having one or both eyes turned inwards towards the nose, either temporarily or as a permanent condition.

cross-fertilise > *verb* **1** fertilise (a plant) using pollen from another plant of the same species. **2** stimulate the development of (something) with an exchange of ideas or information.

DERIVATIVES – **cross-fertilisation** *noun*.

crossfire > *noun* gunfire from two or more directions passing through the same area.

cross-grained > *adjective* **1** (of timber) having a grain that runs across the regular grain. **2** stubbornly contrary or bad-tempered.

crossing > *noun* **1** a place where things, especially roads or railway lines, cross. **2** a place at which one may safely cross a street or railway line. **3** the intersection of a church nave and the transepts.

crossover > *noun* **1** a point or place of crossing. **2** the production of work or achieving of success in a new field or style, especially in popular music.

crosspatch > *noun* informal a bad-tempered person.

ORIGIN – from obsolete *patch* 'fool, clown', perhaps from Italian *pazzo* 'madman'.

crossroads > *noun* **1** an intersection of two or more roads. **2** (**crossroad**) N. Amer. a road that crosses a main road or joins two main roads.

crosswise (also **crossways**) > *adverb* **1** in the form of a cross. **2** diagonally or transversely.

crossword > *noun* a puzzle consisting of a grid of squares and blanks into which words crossing vertically and horizontally are written according to clues.

crostini /kros*tee*ni/ > *plural noun* small pieces of toasted or fried bread served with a topping as a starter or canapé.

ORIGIN – Italian, 'little crusts'.

crotch > *noun* **1** the part of the human body between the legs where they join the torso. **2** a fork in a tree, road, or river.

ORIGIN – perhaps related to Old French *croche* 'shepherd's crook'; partly also a variant of CRUTCH.

crotchet /*kroch*it/ > *noun* **1** Music, chiefly Brit. a musical note having the time value of a quarter of a semibreve, represented by a large solid dot with a plain stem. **2** a perverse or unfounded belief or notion.

ORIGIN – Old French *crochet* 'little hook'.

crotchety > *adjective* irritable.

crouch > *verb* adopt a position where the knees are bent and the upper body is brought forward and down. > *noun* a crouching stance or posture.

ORIGIN – perhaps from Old French *crochir* 'be bent', from *croche* 'shepherd's crook'.

croup¹ /krōōp/ > *noun* inflammation of the larynx and trachea in children, causing breathing difficulties.

ORIGIN – from dialect *croup* 'to croak'.

croup² /krōōp/ > *noun* the rump or hindquarters of a horse.

ORIGIN – Old French, related to CROP.

croupier /*krōō*piay/ > *noun* the person in charge of a gaming table, gathering in and paying out money or tokens.

ORIGIN – first denoting a person standing behind a gambler to give advice: from Old French *cropier* 'pillion rider'.

crouton /*krōō*ton/ > *noun* a small piece of fried or toasted bread served with soup or used as a garnish.

ORIGIN – French, from *croûte* 'crust'.

Crow > *noun* (pl. same or **Crows**) a member of an American Indian people of eastern Montana.

crow¹ > *noun* **1** a large perching bird with mostly glossy black plumage, a heavy bill, and a raucous voice. **2** informal an old or ugly woman.

WORDFINDER – corvine (*relating to crows*).

IDIOMS – **as the crow flies** in a straight line across country.

COMBINATIONS – **crow's foot** a branching wrinkle at the outer corner of a person's eye. **crow's-nest** a platform for a lookout at the masthead of a ship.

crow² > *verb* (past **crowed** or **crew**) **1** (of a cock) utter its characteristic loud cry. **2** express pride or triumph in a tone of gloating satisfaction. > *noun* the cry of a cock.

crowbar > *noun* an iron bar with a flattened end, used as a lever.

crowd > *noun* **1** a large number of people gathered together. **2** a large audience, especially at a sporting event. **3** informal, often derogatory a group of people with a common interest. > *verb* **1** (of a number of people) fill (a space) almost completely. **2** move or come together as a crowd. **3** move or stand too close to. **4** (**crowd out**) exclude by taking the place of.

SYNONYMS – *noun* **1** flock, gathering, horde, mass, multitude, throng. *verb* **2** cluster, congregate, flock, gather.

COMBINATIONS – **crowd-puller** informal an event or celebrity that attracts a large audience.

crowded > *adjective* (of a place) filled almost completely by a large number of people.

SYNONYMS – busy, congested, cramped, packed, thronged.

crowfoot > *noun* an aquatic plant with lobed or divided leaves and white or yellow flowers.

crown > *noun* **1** a circular ornamental headdress worn by a monarch as a symbol of authority. **2** (**the Crown**) the monarchy or reigning monarch. **3** a wreath of leaves or flowers worn as an emblem of victory, especially in ancient Greece or Rome. **4** an award or distinction gained by a victory or achievement. **5** the top or highest part, in particular of a person's head or a hat. **6** the part of a tooth projecting from the gum. **7** an artificial replacement or covering for the upper part of a tooth. **8** a British coin with a face value of five shillings or 25 pence, now minted only for commemorative purposes. > *verb* **1** ceremonially place a crown on the head of (someone) to invest them as a monarch. **2** rest on or form the top of. **3** be the triumphant culmination of (an effort or endeavour). **4** fit a crown to (a tooth). **5** informal hit on the head.

COMBINATIONS – **Crown Colony** a British colony controlled by the Crown. **Crown Court** (in England and Wales) a court which deals with serious cases referred from the magistrates' courts. **Crown Derby** a kind of soft-paste porcelain made at Derby in England, often marked with a crown above the letter 'D'. **crowned head** a king

or queen. **crown green** Brit. a kind of bowling green which rises slightly towards the middle. **Crown jewels** the crown and other jewellery worn or carried by the sovereign on state occasions. **Crown prince** (in some countries) a male heir to a throne. **Crown princess 1** the wife of a Crown prince. **2** (in some countries) a female heir to a throne. **crown wheel** a gearwheel or cogwheel with teeth that project from the face of the wheel at right angles.

ORIGIN – Old French *corune*, from Latin *corona* 'wreath, chaplet'.

crozier /*krō*ziər/ (also **crosier**) > *noun* a hooked staff carried by a bishop.

ORIGIN – Old French *croisier* 'cross-bearer'.

CRT > *abbreviation* cathode ray tube.

cru /krōō/ > *noun* (pl. **crus** pronunc. same) (in France) a vineyard or group of vineyards, especially one of recognised superior quality.

ORIGIN – French, 'growth'.

cruces plural of CRUX.

crucial /*krōō*sh'l/ > *adjective* **1** decisive or critical in the success or failure of something. **2** informal very important. **3** informal excellent.

DERIVATIVES – **crucially** adverb.

SYNONYMS – **1** critical, decisive, key, pivotal.

wordpower facts
Crucial

In common with many other English words, **crucial** comes from Latin *crux* (stem *cruc-*) 'cross'. In English it originally had the sense 'cross-shaped'. The sense 'decisive' is from Francis Bacon's Latin phrase *instantia crucis* 'crucial instance', which Bacon explained as being a metaphor from a *crux* or fingerpost marking a fork at a crossroads: when one reaches a fork in the road one has to make a decision. Sir Isaac Newton and Robert Boyle took up the metaphor in *experimentum crucis* 'crucial experiment'. Other words from Latin *crux* include **cross**, **crozier**, **crucible**, **crucify**, **cruise**, **crusade**, and **excruciate**.

cruciate ligament > *noun* either of a pair of ligaments in the knee which cross each other and connect the femur to the tibia.

ORIGIN – from Latin *cruciatus* 'cross-shaped'.

crucible /*krōō*sib'l/ > *noun* **1** a container in which metals or other substances may be melted or subjected to very high temperatures. **2** a situation of severe trial, or in which different elements interact to produce something new.

ORIGIN – Latin *crucibulum* 'night lamp, crucible', from *crux* 'cross'.

cruciferous /krōōsiffərəss/ > adjective Botany of the cabbage family (Cruciferae), with four equal petals arranged in a cross.

ORIGIN – from Latin *crux* 'cross' + *-fer* 'bearing'.

crucifix /krōōsifiks/ > noun a representation of a cross with a figure of Christ on it.

ORIGIN – Latin *crucifixus*, from *cruci fixus* 'fixed to a cross'.

crucifixion > noun 1 the execution of a person by crucifying them. 2 (**the Crucifixion**) the killing of Jesus Christ in such a way.

cruciform /krōōsiform/ > adjective having the shape of a cross.

crucify /krōōsifī/ > verb (**crucifies, crucified**) 1 put (someone) to death by nailing or binding them to a cross. 2 cause anguish to. 3 informal criticise severely.

ORIGIN – from Latin *crux* 'cross' + *figere* 'fix'.

crud > noun informal 1 an unpleasantly dirty or messy substance. 2 nonsense; rubbish.

DERIVATIVES – **cruddy** adjective.

ORIGIN – variant of CURD.

crude > adjective 1 in a natural or raw state; not yet processed or refined. 2 (of an estimate or guess) likely to be only approximately accurate. 3 constructed in a rudimentary or makeshift way. 4 offensively coarse or rude. > noun natural mineral oil.

DERIVATIVES – **crudely** adverb **crudeness** noun **crudity** noun.

SYNONYMS – adjective 3 basic, makeshift, primitive, rough, rudimentary. 4 coarse, indecent, obscene, ribald, rude, vulgar.

ANTONYMS – adjective 1 refined. 3 sophisticated.

ORIGIN – Latin *crudus* 'raw, rough'.

crudités /krōōditay/ > plural noun mixed raw vegetables served with a sauce into which they may be dipped.

ORIGIN – plural of French *crudité* 'rawness, crudity'.

cruel > adjective (**crueller, cruellest** or US **crueler, cruelest**) 1 disregarding or taking pleasure in the pain or suffering of others. 2 causing great pain or suffering.

DERIVATIVES – **cruelly** adverb.

SYNONYMS – 1 barbaric, brutal, callous, merciless, sadistic, savage. 2 harsh, severe.

ANTONYMS – 1 compassionate. 2 mild.

ORIGIN – Latin *crudelis*, related to *crudus* 'raw, rough'.

cruelty > noun (pl. **cruelties**) cruel behaviour or attitudes.

cruet /krōōit/ > noun 1 a small container for salt, pepper, oil, or vinegar for use at a dining table. 2 Brit. a stand holding such

containers. 3 a small container for the wine or water used to celebrate the Eucharist.

ORIGIN – Old French, 'small pot'; related to CROCK².

cruise > verb 1 move slowly around without a precise destination, especially for pleasure. 2 travel smoothly at a moderate or economical speed. 3 achieve an objective with ease. 4 informal wander about in search of a sexual partner. > noun 1 an instance of cruising. 2 a voyage on a ship taken as a holiday and usually calling in at several places.

COMBINATIONS – **cruise control** a device in a motor vehicle which maintains a selected constant speed without requiring use of the accelerator pedal. **cruise missile** a low-flying missile which is guided to its target by an on-board computer.

ORIGIN – probably from Dutch *kruisen* 'to cross'.

cruiser > noun 1 a fast warship larger than a destroyer and less heavily armed than a battleship. 2 a yacht or motor boat with passenger accommodation. 3 N. Amer. a police patrol car.

COMBINATIONS – **cruiserweight** chiefly Brit. (in boxing and other sports) light heavyweight.

crumb > noun 1 a small fragment of bread, cake, or biscuit. 2 the soft inner part of a loaf of bread. 3 informal, chiefly N. Amer. an objectionable or contemptible person. > verb cover (food) with breadcrumbs.

crumble > verb 1 break or fall apart into small fragments. 2 gradually disintegrate or fail. > noun Brit. a pudding made with fruit and a topping of flour and fat rubbed to the texture of breadcrumbs.

SYNONYMS – verb collapse, deteriorate, disintegrate, fall apart.

crumbly > adjective (**crumblier, crumbliest**) easily crumbling; friable.

DERIVATIVES – **crumbliness** noun.

crumbs > exclamation Brit. informal used to express dismay or surprise.

ORIGIN – euphemism for *Christ*.

crumhorn > noun variant spelling of KRUMMHORN.

crummy (also **crumby**) > adjective (**crummier, crummiest**) informal bad, unpleasant, or of poor quality.

crumpet > noun 1 a thick, flat cake with a soft, porous texture, eaten toasted and buttered. 2 Brit. informal women regarded as objects of sexual desire.

crumple > verb 1 crush so as to become creased and wrinkled. 2 suddenly lose force, effectiveness, or composure. > noun a crushed fold, crease, or wrinkle.

COMBINATIONS – **crumple zone** a part of a motor vehicle designed to crumple easily in a crash and absorb the main force of an impact.

ORIGIN – from obsolete *crump* 'make or become curved'.

crunch > verb 1 crush (something hard or brittle) with the teeth, making a marked grinding sound. 2 make or move with such a sound. > noun 1 a crunching sound. 2 (**the crunch**) informal the crucial point of a situation. 3 a sit-up.

crunchy > adjective (**crunchier, crunchiest**) making a crunching noise when bitten or crushed.

DERIVATIVES – **crunchily** adverb **crunchiness** noun.

crupper /kruppər/ > noun a strap buckled to the back of a saddle and looped under the horse's tail to prevent the saddle or harness from slipping forward.

ORIGIN – Old French *cropiere*; related to CROUP².

crural /krōōrəl/ > adjective Anatomy & Zoology relating to the leg or the thigh.

ORIGIN – Latin *cruralis*, from *crus* 'leg'.

crusade > noun 1 any of a series of medieval military expeditions made by Europeans to recover the Holy Land from the Muslims. 2 an energetic organised campaign with a political, social, or religious aim: *a crusade against crime*. > verb 1 lead or take part in a crusade. 2 (**crusading**) energetically campaigning for a particular aim.

DERIVATIVES – **crusader** noun.

ORIGIN – French *croisade*, from *croisée* 'the state of being marked with the cross'.

cruse /krōōz/ > noun archaic an earthenware pot or jar.

crush > verb 1 deform, squash, or pulverise by compressing forcefully. 2 crease or crumple (cloth or paper). 3 violently subdue (opposition or a rebellion). 4 cause (someone) to feel overwhelming disappointment or embarrassment. > noun 1 a crowd of people pressed closely together. 2 informal an intense infatuation. 3 a drink made from the juice of pressed fruit.

DERIVATIVES – **crushable** adjective **crusher** noun.

COMBINATIONS – **crush bar** Brit. a bar in a theatre that sells drinks in the interval. **crush barrier** Brit. a barrier for restraining a crowd. **crushed velvet** velvet which has its nap pointing in different directions in irregular patches. **crush zone** another term for *crumple zone*.

ORIGIN – Old French *cruissir* 'gnash teeth or crack'.

crust > noun 1 the tough outer part of a loaf of bread. 2 a hard, dry scrap of bread. 3 informal a living or livelihood: *earning a crust*. 4 a hardened layer, coating, or deposit on something soft. 5 a layer of pastry covering a pie. 6 the outermost layer of rock of which a planet consists, especially the part of the earth above the mantle. 7 a deposit formed in wine or port aged in the bottle. > *verb* form into or cover with a crust.

ORIGIN – Latin *crusta* 'rind, shell, crust'.

crustacean /krustaysh'n/ > *noun* a creature belonging to a large group of arthropods (the Crustacea) with hard shells, including crabs, lobsters, shrimps, woodlice, and barnacles.

crusty > *adjective* (**crustier, crustiest**) 1 having or consisting of a crust. 2 (of an old person) conservative and easily irritated. > *noun* (pl. **crusties**) informal a young person of a subculture characterised by a shabby appearance and a nomadic lifestyle.

DERIVATIVES – **crustiness** *noun*.

crutch > *noun* 1 a long stick with a crosspiece at the top, used as a support by a lame person. 2 something used for support or reassurance. 3 the crotch of the body.

crux /kruks/ > *noun* (pl. **cruxes** or **cruces** /krōoseez/) 1 the decisive or most important point at issue. 2 a particular point of difficulty.

SYNONYMS – 1 essence, heart, nub.

ORIGIN – Latin, 'cross'.

cry > *verb* (**cries, cried**) 1 shed tears. 2 shout or scream loudly. 3 (of a bird or other animal) make a loud characteristic call. 4 (**cry out for**) demand as a self-evident requirement or solution. 5 (**cry off**) informal go back on a promise or fail to keep to an arrangement. > *noun* (pl. **cries**) 1 a spell of shedding tears. 2 a loud shout or scream. 3 a distinctive call of a bird or other animal.

IDIOMS – **cry for the moon** ask for what is unattainable or impossible. **for crying out loud** informal used to express irritation or impatience.

SYNONYMS – *verb* 1 sob, wail, weep. 2 call, exclaim, shout, yell. *noun* 2 call, shout, yell.

ORIGIN – Old French *crier*, from Latin *quiritare* 'raise a public outcry', literally 'call on the *Quirites* (Roman citizens) for help'.

crybaby > *noun* informal a person who sheds tears frequently or readily.

cryer > *noun* archaic spelling of CRIER.

crying > *adjective* very great: *it would be a crying shame.*

cryogenics /krīəjenniks/ > *plural noun* (treated as sing.) 1 the branch of physics concerned with the production and effects of very low temperatures. 2 another term for CRYONICS.

DERIVATIVES – **cryogenic** *adjective*.

ORIGIN – from Greek *kruos* 'frost'.

cryonics /krīonniks/ > *plural noun* (treated as sing.) the deep-freezing of the bodies of people who have died of an incurable disease, in the hope of a future cure.

DERIVATIVES – **cryonic** *adjective*.

cryosurgery > *noun* surgery using the local application of intense cold to destroy unwanted tissue.

crypt > *noun* an underground room or vault beneath a church, used as a chapel or burial place.

ORIGIN – Greek *kruptē* 'a vault', from *kruptos* 'hidden'.

cryptanalysis > *noun* the art or process of deciphering coded messages without being told the key.

DERIVATIVES – **cryptanalyst** *noun*.

cryptic > *adjective* 1 mysterious or obscure in meaning. 2 (of a crossword) having difficult clues which indicate the solutions indirectly. 3 Zoology serving to camouflage an animal in its natural environment.

DERIVATIVES – **cryptically** *adverb*.

SYNONYMS – 1 abstruse, arcane, enigmatic, mysterious, obscure.

ANTONYMS – 1 clear.

ORIGIN – Greek *kruptikos*, from *kruptos* 'hidden'.

cryptobiosis /kriptəbīōsis/ > *noun* Biology a state in which an organism's metabolic activity is reduced to an undetectable level without disappearing altogether.

DERIVATIVES – **cryptobiotic** *adjective*.

cryptogam /kriptəgam/ > *noun* Botany, dated a plant with no true flowers or seeds, such as a fern, moss, liverwort, lichen, or alga.

DERIVATIVES – **cryptogamic** *adjective*.

ORIGIN – from Greek *kruptos* 'hidden' + *gamos* 'marriage' (because the means of reproduction was not apparent).

cryptogram /kriptəgram/ > *noun* a text written in code.

cryptography > *noun* the art of writing or solving codes.

DERIVATIVES – **cryptographer** *noun* **cryptographic** *adjective*.

cryptology > *noun* the study of codes, or the art of writing and solving them.

DERIVATIVES – **cryptological** *adjective* **cryptologist** *noun*.

cryptosporidium /kriptōsporiddiəm/ > *noun* (pl. **cryptosporidia**) a single-celled parasite found in the intestines of many animals, where it sometimes causes disease.

ORIGIN – from Greek *kruptos* 'hidden' + Latin *sporidium* 'small spore'.

cryptozoology > *noun* the search for animals whose existence is disputed or unsubstantiated, such as the Loch Ness monster.

crystal > *noun* 1 a clear transparent mineral, especially quartz. 2 a piece of a solid substance having a natural geometrically regular form with symmetrically arranged plane faces. 3 highly transparent glass with a high refractive index. 4 the glass over a watch face. 5 (before another noun) clear and transparent: *the crystal waters of the lake.*

COMBINATIONS – **crystal ball** a solid globe of glass or rock crystal, used for crystal-gazing. **crystal-gazing** looking intently into a crystal ball with the aim of seeing images relating to future or distant events. **crystal set** a simple early form of radio receiver with a crystal touching a metal wire as the rectifier, lacking an amplifier or loudspeaker and necessitating headphones or an earphone.

ORIGIN – Greek *krustallos* 'ice, crystal'.

crystalline /kristəlīn/ > *adjective* 1 having the structure and form of a crystal. 2 literary very clear.

COMBINATIONS – **crystalline lens** the lens of the eye.

crystallise (also **crystallize**) > *verb* 1 form crystals. 2 (**crystallised**) (of fruit) coated and impregnated with sugar. 3 make or become definite and clear.

DERIVATIVES – **crystallisation** *noun*.

crystallography /kristəlogrəfi/ > *noun* the branch of science concerned with the structure and properties of crystals.

DERIVATIVES – **crystallographer** *noun* **crystallographic** *adjective*.

Cs > *symbol* the chemical element caesium.

c/s > *abbreviation* cycles per second.

CSA > *abbreviation* Child Support Agency.

CSE > *abbreviation* historical (in England and Wales) an examination for secondary-school pupils not taking O levels, replaced in 1988 by the GCSE.

ORIGIN – abbreviation for *Certificate of Secondary Education*.

CS gas > *noun* a powerful form of tear gas used in the control of riots.

ORIGIN – from the initials of the American chemists Ben B. *Corson* and Roger W. *Stoughton*.

CST > *abbreviation* Central Standard Time.

CT > *abbreviation* 1 computerised (or computed) tomography. 2 Connecticut.

ct > *abbreviation* 1 carat. 2 cent.

CTC > *abbreviation* City Technology College.

CTS > *abbreviation* carpal tunnel syndrome.

Cu > *symbol* the chemical element copper.

ORIGIN – from Latin *cuprum*.

cu. > *abbreviation* cubic.

cub > *noun* 1 the young of a fox, bear, lion, or other carnivorous mammal. 2 (also **Cub Scout**) a member of the junior branch of the Scout Association, for boys aged about 8 to 11. 3 archaic a young man. > *verb* (**cubbed, cubbing**) 1 give birth to cubs. 2 hunt fox cubs.

COMBINATIONS – **cub reporter** informal a young or inexperienced newspaper reporter.

Cuban /kyōobən/ > *noun* a person from Cuba. > *adjective* relating to Cuba.

COMBINATIONS – **Cuban heel** a moderately high straight-sided heel on a shoe or boot.

cubby > *noun* (pl. **cubbies**) chiefly N. Amer. a cubbyhole.

cubbyhole > *noun* a small enclosed space or room.

ORIGIN – first meaning 'straw basket': related to dialect *cub* 'stall, pen, hutch'.

cube > *noun* **1** a symmetrical three-dimensional shape contained by six equal squares. **2** Mathematics the product of a number multiplied by its square, represented by a superscript figure 3. > *verb* **1** Mathematics multiply (a number) by its square; find the cube of. **2** cut (food) into small cubes.

COMBINATIONS – **cube root** the number which produces a given number when cubed.

ORIGIN – Greek *kubos*.

cubic /**kyoo**bik/ > *adjective* **1** having the shape of a cube. **2** (of a unit of measurement) equal to the volume of a cube whose side is one of the linear unit specified: *a cubic metre.* **3** involving the cube (and no higher power) of a quantity or variable.

DERIVATIVES – **cubical** *adjective*.

cubicle > *noun* a small partitioned-off area of a room.

ORIGIN – first meaning 'bedroom': from Latin *cubiculum*, from *cubare* 'lie down'.

cubism > *noun* an early 20th-century style of painting making use of simple geometric shapes and interlocking planes.

DERIVATIVES – **cubist** *noun & adjective*.

cubit /**kyoo**bit/ > *noun* an ancient measure of length, approximately equal to the length of a forearm.

ORIGIN – Latin *cubitum* 'elbow, forearm, cubit'.

cuboid /**kyoo**boyd/ > *adjective* more or less cubic in shape. > *noun* a solid which has six rectangular faces at right angles to each other.

DERIVATIVES – **cuboidal** *adjective*.

cuckold /**kuk**kōld/ > *noun* the husband of an adulterous woman, regarded as an object of derision. > *verb* make (a married man) a cuckold.

DERIVATIVES – **cuckoldry** *noun*.

ORIGIN – Old French *cucuault*, from *cucu* 'cuckoo' (from the cuckoo's habit of laying its egg in another bird's nest).

cuckoo > *noun* a grey or brown bird known for the two-note call of the male and for the habit of laying its eggs in the nests of small songbirds. > *adjective* informal crazy.

COMBINATIONS – **cuckoo clock** a clock with a mechanical cuckoo that pops out on the hour making a sound like a cuckoo's call. **cuckoo pint** a plant, the common wild arum, that has a purple or green spadix followed by bright red berries. [ORIGIN – from earlier *cuckoo-pintle*, from **PINTLE** in the obsolete sense 'penis' (because of the shape of the spadix).] **cuckoo spit** whitish froth found on leaves and plant stems, exuded by the larvae of froghoppers.

cucumber > *noun* the long, green-skinned fruit of a climbing plant, which has watery flesh and is eaten raw in salads.

ORIGIN – Old French *cocombre, coucombre*, from Latin *cucumis*.

cud > *noun* partly digested food returned from the first stomach of cattle or other ruminants to the mouth for further chewing.

IDIOMS – **chew the cud** think or talk reflectively.

cuddle > *verb* **1** hold (someone) close in one's arms as a way of showing love or affection. **2** (often **cuddle up to**) lie or sit close; nestle. > *noun* a prolonged and affectionate hug.

SYNONYMS – *verb* **1** clasp, embrace, hug.

cuddly > *adjective* (**cuddlier**, **cuddliest**) pleasantly soft or plump.

cudgel /**kuj**əl/ > *noun* a short, thick stick used as a weapon. > *verb* (**cudgelled**, **cudgelling**; US **cudgeled**, **cudgeling**) beat with a cudgel.

IDIOMS – **cudgel one's brain** think hard about a problem. **take up cudgels** start to defend or support someone or something strongly.

cue¹ > *noun* **1** a signal to an actor to enter or to begin their speech or performance. **2** a signal or prompt for action. **3** a facility for playing through an audio or video recording very rapidly until a desired starting point is reached. > *verb* (**cues**, **cued**, **cueing** or **cuing**) **1** give a cue to or for. **2** set a piece of audio or video equipment in readiness to play (a particular part of a recording).

IDIOMS – **on cue** at the correct moment.

COMBINATIONS – **cue card** a card held beside a camera for a television broadcaster to read from while appearing to look into the camera.

cue² > *noun* a long, tapering wooden rod for striking the ball in snooker, billiards, etc. > *verb* (**cues**, **cued**, **cueing** or **cuing**) use a cue to strike the ball.

COMBINATIONS – **cue ball** the ball that is to be struck with the cue in snooker, billiards, etc.

ORIGIN – first meaning 'long plait or pigtail': variant of **QUEUE**.

cuff¹ > *noun* **1** the end part of a sleeve, where the material of the sleeve is turned back or a separate band is sewn on. **2** chiefly N. Amer. a trouser turn-up. **3** (**cuffs**) informal handcuffs. > *verb* informal secure with handcuffs.

IDIOMS – **off the cuff** informal without preparation. [ORIGIN – as if from notes jotted on one's shirt cuffs.]

DERIVATIVES – **cuffed** *adjective*.

cuff² > *verb* strike with an open hand, especially on the head. > *noun* a blow given with an open hand.

SYNONYMS – slap, smack, swat.

cufflink > *noun* a device for fastening together the sides of a shirt cuff.

cui bono? /kwee **bonn**ō/ > *exclamation* who stands to gain (i.e. from a crime, and so might have been responsible for it)?

ORIGIN – Latin, 'to whom (is it) a benefit?'

cuirass /kwi**rass**/ > *noun* historical a piece of armour consisting of breastplate and backplate fastened together.

ORIGIN – Old French *cuirace*, from Latin *corium* 'leather'.

cuirassier /kwirra**seer**/ > *noun* historical a cavalry soldier wearing a cuirass.

ORIGIN – French.

cuisine /kwi**zeen**/ > *noun* a style or method of cooking, especially as characteristic of a particular country or region.

ORIGIN – French, 'kitchen'.

cul-de-sac /**kul**dəsak/ > *noun* (pl. **culs-de-sac** pronunc. same) a street or passage closed at one end.

ORIGIN – French, 'bottom of a sack'.

-cule > *suffix* forming nouns such as *molecule* and *reticule*, which were originally diminutives.

ORIGIN – from French *-cule* or Latin *-culus*, *-cula*, *-culum*.

culinary > *adjective* of or for cooking.

DERIVATIVES – **culinarily** *adverb*.

ORIGIN – from Latin *culina* 'kitchen'.

cull > *verb* **1** reduce the numbers of (animals) by selective slaughter. **2** select or obtain from a large quantity or a variety of sources. > *noun* a selective slaughter of animals.

ORIGIN – Old French *coillier*, from Latin *colligere* 'gather together'.

culminate /**kul**minayt/ > *verb* **1** (usu. **culminate in** or **with**) reach a climax or point of highest development. **2** archaic or Astrology (of a celestial body) reach or be at the meridian.

DERIVATIVES – **culmination** *noun*.

ORIGIN – Latin *culminare*, from *culmen* 'summit'.

culottes /kyoo**lot(s)**/ > *plural noun* women's knee-length trousers, cut with very full legs to resemble a skirt.

ORIGIN – French, 'knee breeches', from *cul* 'rump'.

culpable /**kul**pəb'l/ > *adjective* deserving blame.

DERIVATIVES – **culpability** *noun* **culpably** *adverb*.

SYNONYMS – at fault, blameworthy, guilty, to blame.

ORIGIN – Latin *culpabilis*, from *culpa* 'fault, blame'.

culprit > *noun* a person who is responsible for a crime or offence.

wordpower facts

Culprit

The unusually formed word **culprit** first appeared in the 17th century, in the formula *Culprit, how will you be tried?*, which was said by the Clerk of the Crown to a prisoner pleading not guilty. It perhaps arose from a misinterpretation of the written abbreviation *cul. prist*, for Old French *Culpable: prest d'averrer notre bille* '(You are) guilty: (We are) ready to prove our indictment'. In later use it was influenced by Latin *culpa* 'fault, blame'.

cult > *noun* **1** a system of religious worship directed towards a particular figure or object. **2** a small religious group regarded as strange or as imposing excessive control over members. **3** something popular or fashionable among a particular section of society.

DERIVATIVES – **cultish** *adjective* **cultist** *noun*.

ORIGIN – Latin *cultus* 'worship'.

cultivar /**kul**tivaar/ > *noun* a plant variety that has been produced in cultivation by selective breeding.

cultivate > *verb* **1** prepare and use (land) for crops or gardening. **2** raise or grow (plants or crops). **3** grow or maintain (living cells or tissue) in an artificial medium containing nutrients. **4** try to acquire or develop (a quality or skill). **5** try to win the friendship or favour of. **6** (**cultivated**) refined and well educated; cultured.

DERIVATIVES – **cultivable** *adjective* **cultivatable** *adjective* **cultivation** *noun*.

SYNONYMS – **1** dig, farm, till, work.

ORIGIN – Latin *cultivare*, from *cultiva terra* 'arable land'.

cultivator > *noun* **1** a person or thing that cultivates something. **2** a mechanical implement for breaking up the ground.

cultural > *adjective* **1** relating to the culture of a society. **2** relating to the arts and to intellectual achievements.

DERIVATIVES – **culturally** *adverb*.

SYNONYMS – **2** aesthetic, artistic, intellectual.

culture > *noun* **1** the arts and other manifestations of human intellectual achievement regarded collectively. **2** a refined understanding or appreciation of this. **3** the customs, institutions, and achievements of a particular nation, people, or group. **4** the cultivation of plants, breeding of animals, or production of cells or tissues. **5** a preparation of cells grown in an artificial medium containing nutrients. > *verb* maintain (tissue cells, bacteria, etc.) in conditions suitable for growth.

WORDFINDER – apiculture (*bee-keeping*), aviculture (*rearing birds*), floriculture (*cultivation of flowers*), pisciculture (*breeding fish*), sericulture (*cultivation of silk*), silviculture (*growing trees*), viticulture (*cultivation of grapevines*).

COMBINATIONS – **culture shock** disorientation experienced when suddenly subjected to an unfamiliar culture or way of life. **culture vulture** informal a person who is very interested in the arts.

ORIGIN – Latin *cultura* 'growing, cultivation', from *colere* 'cultivate'.

cultured > *adjective* **1** refined and well educated. **2** (of a pearl) formed round a foreign body inserted into an oyster.

SYNONYMS – **1** civilised, cultivated, discerning, educated, polished, sophisticated.

culvert /**kul**vərt/ > *noun* a tunnel carrying a stream or open drain under a road or railway.

cum /kum/ > *preposition* combined with; also used as: *a study-cum-bedroom*.

cumber /**kum**bər/ > *verb* **dated** hamper, hinder, or obstruct.

ORIGIN – from **ENCUMBER**.

Cumberland sauce > *noun* a piquant sauce made from redcurrant jelly, served with game and cold meats.

Cumberland sausage > *noun* Brit. a type of sausage traditionally made in a continuous strip and cooked as a spiral.

cumbersome > *adjective* **1** difficult to carry or use because of size and shape; unwieldy. **2** slow or complicated and therefore inefficient.

DERIVATIVES – **cumbersomely** *adverb* **cumbersomeness** *noun*.

SYNONYMS – **1** awkward, clumsy, ungainly, unwieldy.

cumbia /**koo**ombiə/ > *noun* a kind of dance music of Colombian origin, similar to salsa.

ORIGIN – Colombian Spanish.

cumbrous /**kum**brəss/ > *adjective* literary cumbersome.

cum grano salis /kum graanō **saal**is/ > *adverb* with a pinch of salt.

ORIGIN – Latin.

cumin /**kumm**in/ (also **cummin**) > *noun* the aromatic seeds of a plant of the parsley family, used as a spice, especially in curry powder.

ORIGIN – Greek *kuminon*, probably of Semitic origin.

cummerbund /**kumm**ərbund/ > *noun* a sash worn around the waist, especially as part of a man's formal evening suit.

ORIGIN – Urdu and Persian.

cumquat > *noun* variant spelling of **KUMQUAT**.

cumulate > *verb* /**kyoo**myoolayt/ accumulate or be accumulated.

DERIVATIVES – **cumulation** *noun*.

ORIGIN – Latin *cumulare*, from *cumulus* 'a heap'.

cumulative > *adjective* increasing or increased by successive additions.

DERIVATIVES – **cumulatively** *adverb*.

SYNONYMS – accruing, accumulating, aggregate.

cumulonimbus /kyoomyoolō**nim**bass/ > *noun* (pl. **cumulonimbi** /-nimbī/) cloud forming a towering mass with a flat base at fairly low altitude, as in thunderstorms.

cumulus /**kyoo**myoolass/ > *noun* (pl. **cumuli** /**kyoo**myoolī/) cloud forming rounded masses heaped on each other above a flat base at fairly low altitude.

ORIGIN – Latin, 'heap'.

cuneiform /**kyoo**niform/ > *adjective* **1** denoting the wedge-shaped characters used in the ancient writing systems of Mesopotamia, Persia, and Ugarit. **2** chiefly Biology wedge-shaped. > *noun* cuneiform writing.

ORIGIN – from Latin *cuneus* 'wedge'.

cunnilingus /kunni**ling**gəss/ > *noun* stimulation of the female genitals using the tongue or lips.

ORIGIN – from Latin *cunnus* 'vulva' + *lingere* 'lick'.

cunning > *adjective* **1** skilled in achieving one's ends by deceit or evasion. **2** ingenious. **3** N. Amer. attractive; charming. > *noun* **1** cunning behaviour; craftiness. **2** ingenuity.

DERIVATIVES – **cunningly** *adverb*.

SYNONYMS – *adjective* **1** artful, crafty, devious, guileful, wily.

ANTONYMS – *adjective* **1** guileless, naive.

wordpower facts

Cunning

Cunning is an example of a word that used to have positive associations but is now regarded as uncomplimentary. It originally meant 'erudite or skilful', and is related to the verb **can**, 'be able to'. The negative modern sense developed from the obsolete meaning 'possessing magical knowledge or skill', which was often found in the phrase 'cunning man (or woman)', a fortune teller, magician, wizard, or witch. Other words whose negative connotations have been acquired over the centuries include **perpetrate**, which was formerly neutral, and **rank** (of vegetation), which used to mean 'proud, sturdy, fully grown'.

cunt > *noun* vulgar slang **1** a woman's genitals. **2** an unpleasant or stupid person.

cup > *noun* **1** a small bowl-shaped container for drinking from. **2** a cup-shaped trophy, usually with a stem and two handles, awarded as a prize in a sports contest. **3** a sports contest in which the winner is awarded a cup. **4** chiefly N. Amer. a measure of capacity used in cookery, equal to half a US pint (0.237 litre). **5** either of the two parts of a bra shaped to contain or support one breast. **6** a long mixed drink made from wine or cider and fruit juice. > *verb* (**cupped**, **cupping**) **1** form (one's hand or hands) into the curved shape of a cup. **2** place one's curved hand or hands around.

WORDFINDER – chalice (*cup used for the eucharist*), Grail (*cup used by Christ at the Last Supper*).

IDIOMS – **in one's cups** dated drunk. **not one's cup of tea** informal not what one likes or is interested in.

COMBINATIONS – **cup-tied** Brit. (of a soccer player) ineligible to play for one's club in a cup competition as a result of having played for another club in an earlier round.

ORIGIN – Latin *cuppa*, probably from *cupa* 'tub'.

cupboard > *noun* a piece of furniture or small recess with a door and usually shelves, used for storage.

COMBINATIONS – **cupboard love** affection that is feigned so as to obtain something.

ORIGIN – first denoting a table or sideboard on which cups, plates, etc. were displayed.

cupcake > *noun* a small iced cake baked in a cup-shaped foil or paper container.

Cupid > *noun* **1** Roman Mythology the god of love, represented as a naked winged boy with a bow and arrows. **2** (also **cupid**) a representation of a naked winged child carrying a bow.

COMBINATIONS – **Cupid's bow** a pronounced double curve at the top edge of a person's upper lip, resembling the shape of the bow carried by Cupid.

cupidity /kyoōpidditi/ > *noun* greed for money or possessions.

SYNONYMS – avarice, greed, rapacity.

ORIGIN – Latin *cupiditas*, from *cupidus* 'desirous'.

cupola /kyoōpələ/ > *noun* **1** a rounded dome forming or adorning a roof or ceiling. **2** a gun turret. **3** a cylindrical furnace for refining metals.

ORIGIN – Latin *cupula* 'small cask'.

cuppa > *noun* Brit. informal a cup of tea.

cuprammonium /kyoōprəmōniəm/ > *noun* Chemistry a complex ion containing copper bonded to ammonia, solutions of which are able to dissolve cellulose.

cupreous /kyoōpriəss/ > *adjective* of or like copper.

ORIGIN – Latin *cupreus*, from *cuprum* 'copper'.

cupro /kyoōprō/ > *noun* a type of rayon

made by dissolving cotton cellulose with cuprammonium salts and spinning the resulting solution into filaments.

cupro-nickel > *noun* an alloy of copper and nickel, especially in the proportions 3:1 as used in 'silver' coins.

cur /kur/ > *noun* **1** an aggressive dog, especially a mongrel. **2** informal a despicable man.

ORIGIN – perhaps from Old Norse *kurr* 'grumbling'.

curaçao /kyoorəsō/ > *noun* (pl. **curaçaos**) a liqueur flavoured with the peel of bitter oranges.

ORIGIN – named after *Curaçao*, a Caribbean island where bitter oranges are grown.

curacy > *noun* (pl. **curacies**) the office of a curate.

curare /kyooraari/ > *noun* a paralysing poison obtained from South American plants and traditionally used by Indian peoples as an arrow poison.

ORIGIN – Carib.

curate[1] /kyoorət/ > *noun* a member of the clergy engaged as assistant to a parish priest.

IDIOMS – **curate's egg** Brit. something that is partly good and partly bad. [ORIGIN – from a cartoon in *Punch* (1895) depicting a meek curate who, given a stale egg when dining with the bishop, assures his host that 'parts of it are excellent'.]

ORIGIN – Latin *curatus*, from *cura* 'care'.

curate[2] /kyoorayt/ > *verb* select, organise, and look after the items in (a collection or exhibition).

DERIVATIVES – **curation** *noun*.

curative > *adjective* able to cure disease. > *noun* a curative medicine or agent.

SYNONYMS – *adjective* healing, remedial, therapeutic.

curator > *noun* a keeper of a museum or other collection.

DERIVATIVES – **curatorial** *adjective*.

curb > *noun* **1** a check or restraint. **2** a type of bit with a strap or chain attached which passes under a horse's lower jaw, used as a check. **3** US variant spelling of KERB. > *verb* keep in check.

SYNONYMS – *noun* **1** brake, check, rein, restraint, restriction. *verb* hold back, keep back, repress, restrain.

ORIGIN – Old French *courber* 'bend, bow', from Latin *curvare* 'bend'.

curd > *noun* **1** (also **curds**) a soft white substance formed when milk coagulates, used as the basis for cheese. **2** the edible head of a cauliflower or similar plant.

COMBINATIONS – **curd cheese** a mild, soft, smooth cheese made from skimmed milk curd.

curdle > *verb* separate into curds or lumps.

IDIOMS – **make one's blood curdle** fill one with horror.

ORIGIN – from obsolete *curd* 'congeal'.

cure > *verb* **1** relieve (someone) of the symptoms of a disease or condition. **2** end (a disease, condition, or problem) by treatment or appropriate action. **3** preserve (meat, fish, etc.) by salting, drying, or smoking. > *noun* **1** something that cures a disease, condition, or problem. **2** restoration to health. **3** the process of curing meat, fish, etc. **4** a Christian minister's area of responsibility.

DERIVATIVES – **curable** *adjective* **curer** *noun*.

SYNONYMS – *verb* **1** heal. **2** heal, rectify, remedy, repair. *noun* **1** curative, remedy, restorative.

ANTONYMS – *verb* **1,2** aggravate, exacerbate.

ORIGIN – first used in the senses 'care, concern, responsibility', later 'medical care' and hence 'remedy': Old French, from Latin *cura* 'care'.

curé /kyooray/ > *noun* a parish priest in a French-speaking country.

ORIGIN – French.

cure-all > *noun* a remedy that will supposedly cure any ailment or problem.

curettage /kyoorettij, kyooritaazh/ > *noun* Surgery the use of a curette, especially on the lining of the uterus.

curette /kyooret/ > *noun* a small surgical instrument used to remove material by a scraping action. > *verb* clean or scrape with a curette.

ORIGIN – French, from *curer* 'cleanse'.

curfew /kurfyoo/ > *noun* **1** a regulation requiring people to remain indoors between specified hours, typically at night. **2** the time at which such a restriction begins.

ORIGIN – first denoting a regulation requiring fires to be extinguished at a fixed hour in the evening: from Old French *cuevrefeu*, from *cuvrir* 'to cover' + *feu* 'fire'.

Curia /kyooriə/ > *noun* the papal court at the Vatican, by which the Roman Catholic Church is governed.

DERIVATIVES – **Curial** *adjective*.

ORIGIN – Latin, denoting a division of an ancient Roman tribe, (by extension) the senate of cities other than Rome, and later a feudal or Roman Catholic court of justice.

curie /kyoori/ > *noun* (pl. **curies**) a unit of radioactivity, corresponding to 3.7×10^{10} (37 billion) disintegrations per second.

ORIGIN – named after the French physicists Pierre and Marie *Curie* (1867–1934 and 1859–1906).

curio /kyooriō/ > *noun* (pl. **curios**) a rare, unusual, or intriguing object.

curiosity > *noun* (pl. **curiosities**) **1** a strong

desire to know or learn something. **2** a unusual or interesting object or fact.

IDIOMS – **curiosity killed the cat** proverb being inquisitive about other people's affairs may get you into trouble.

curious > *adjective* **1** eager to know or learn something. **2** strange; unusual.

DERIVATIVES – **curiously** *adverb*.

SYNONYMS – **1** inquiring, inquisitive, interested. **2** bizarre, odd, peculiar, strange, unusual.

ANTONYMS – **1** uninterested. **2** ordinary.

ORIGIN – Latin *curiosus* 'careful', from *cura* 'care'.

curium /kyoorɪəm/ > *noun* a radioactive metallic chemical element made by high-energy atomic collisions.

ORIGIN – named after Marie and Pierre *Curie*.

curl > *verb* **1** form or cause to form a curved or spiral shape. **2** move in a spiral or curved course. **3** (**curl up**) informal writhe with embarrassment, shame, or amusement. **4** play at the game of curling. > *noun* **1** something in the shape of a spiral or coil, especially a lock of hair. **2** a curling movement.

IDIOMS – **make someone's hair curl** informal shock or horrify someone.

DERIVATIVES – **curly** (**curlier**, **curliest**) *adjective*.

COMBINATIONS – **curling tongs** (also **curling iron**) a device incorporating a heated rod around which hair can be wound so as to curl it.

ORIGIN – from obsolete *crulle* 'curly', from Dutch *krul*.

curler > *noun* **1** a roller or clasp around which a lock of hair is wrapped to curl it. **2** a player in the game of curling.

curlew /kurlyōō/ > *noun* a large wading bird with a long downcurved bill and brown streaked plumage.

ORIGIN – Old French *courlieu*, derived from the sound of the bird's call.

curlicue /kurlikyōō/ > *noun* a decorative curl or twist in calligraphy or in the design of an object.

ORIGIN – from *curly* + CUE² (in the sense 'pigtail'), or *-cue* representing the letter *q*.

curling > *noun* a game played on ice, in which large circular flat stones are slid across the surface towards a mark.

curmudgeon /kərmujən/ > *noun* a bad-tempered or surly person.

DERIVATIVES – **curmudgeonly** *adjective*.

currach /kurrə/ (also **curragh**) > *noun* Irish and Scottish term for CORACLE.

ORIGIN – Irish and Scottish Gaelic *curach* 'small boat'.

currant > *noun* **1** a dried fruit made from a small seedless variety of grape. **2** a shrub producing small edible black, red, or white berries.

ORIGIN – from Old French *raisins de Corauntz* 'grapes of Corinth' (the original source).

currawong /kurrəwong/ > *noun* an Australian songbird with mainly black or grey plumage and a resonant call.

ORIGIN – from an Aboriginal word.

currency > *noun* (pl. **currencies**) **1** a system of money in general use in a particular country. **2** the quality or period of being current.

current > *adjective* **1** happening or being used or done now. **2** in common or general use. > *noun* **1** a body of water or air moving in a definite direction through a surrounding body of water or air. **2** a flow of electrically charged particles.

SYNONYMS – *adjective* **1** contemporary, modern, present, topical. **2** common, prevalent, prevailing.

ANTONYMS – *adjective* **2** obsolete.

COMBINATIONS – **current account** Brit. an account with a bank or building society from which money may be withdrawn without notice. **current assets** cash and other assets that are expected to be converted to cash within a year (as opposed to *fixed assets*).

ORIGIN – Old French *corant*, from Latin *currere* 'run'.

currently > *adverb* at the present time.

curricle /kurrik'l/ > *noun* historical a light, open two-wheeled carriage pulled by two horses side by side.

ORIGIN – Latin *curriculum* 'course, racing chariot'.

curriculum /kərikyooləm/ > *noun* (pl. **curricula** or **curriculums**) the subjects comprising a course of study in a school or college.

DERIVATIVES – **curricular** *adjective*.

ORIGIN – Latin, 'course, racing chariot'.

curriculum vitae /kərikyooləm veetī/ > *noun* (pl. **curricula vitae** /kərikyoolə veetī/) a brief account of a person's education, qualifications, and previous occupations, sent with a job application.

ORIGIN – Latin, 'course of life'.

currier /kurriər/ > *noun* a person who curries leather.

curry¹ > *noun* (pl. **curries**) a dish of meat, vegetables, etc., cooked in an Indian-style sauce of strong spices. > *verb* (**curries**, **curried**) prepare or flavour with such a sauce.

COMBINATIONS – **curry powder** a mixture of finely ground spices, such as turmeric and coriander, used for making curry.

ORIGIN – Tamil.

curry² > *verb* (**curries**, **curried**) **1** chiefly N. Amer. groom (a horse) with a curry comb. **2** historical treat (tanned leather) to improve its properties.

IDIOMS – **curry favour** ingratiate oneself through obsequious behaviour.

wordpower facts
Curry
Curry in the sense 'groom a horse' has nothing to do with Indian food: the word derives from Old French *correier*. The rather odd phrase **curry favour** is an alteration of Middle English *curry favel*, which comes from the name (*Favel* or *Fauvel*) of a chestnut horse in a 14th-century French romance. The horse was a symbol of cunning and duplicity; hence 'to curry (or rub down) Favel' meant to use the cunning which he personified.

curry comb > *noun* a hand-held device with serrated ridges, used for grooming horses.

curse > *noun* **1** an appeal to a supernatural power to inflict harm on someone or something. **2** a cause of harm or misery. **3** an offensive word or phrase used to express anger or annoyance. > *verb* **1** use a curse against. **2** (**be cursed with**) be afflicted with. **3** utter offensive words; swear.

SYNONYMS – *noun* **1** execration, imprecation, malediction. **2** affliction, bane, blight, evil, scourge. **3** expletive, oath, profanity, swear word.

cursed /kursid, kurst/ > *adjective* informal, dated used to express annoyance or irritation.

cursive /kursiv/ > *adjective* written with the characters joined. > *noun* writing with such a style.

DERIVATIVES – **cursively** *adverb*.

ORIGIN – Latin *cursivus*, from *currere* 'run'.

cursor > *noun* **1** a movable indicator on a computer screen identifying the point that will be affected by input from the user. **2** the transparent slide, engraved with a hairline, that is used to locate points on a slide rule.

ORIGIN – Latin, 'runner' (the first sense in English).

cursory /kursəri/ > *adjective* hasty and therefore not thorough.

DERIVATIVES – **cursorily** *adverb* **cursoriness** *noun*.

SYNONYMS – desultory, perfunctory, sketchy, slapdash.

ANTONYMS – thorough.

curst > *adjective* archaic spelling of CURSED.

curt > *adjective* (of a person or their speech) rudely brief.

DERIVATIVES – **curtly** *adverb* **curtness** *noun*.

SYNONYMS – abrupt, brusque, terse.

ORIGIN – Latin *curtus* 'cut short, abridged'.

curtail /kur**tayl**/ > *verb* reduce in extent or quantity.

DERIVATIVES – **curtailment** *noun*.

SYNONYMS – cut down, reduce, shorten, truncate.

ORIGIN – from obsolete *curtal* 'horse with a docked tail', from Latin *curtus* 'cut short, abridged', influenced by TAIL¹.

curtain > *noun* **1** a piece of material suspended at the top to form a screen, hung at a window in pairs or between the stage and auditorium of a theatre. **2** (**the curtain**) the rise or fall of a stage curtain between acts or scenes. **3** (**curtains**) *informal* a disastrous outcome. > *verb* **1** provide with a curtain or curtains. **2** conceal with a curtain.

COMBINATIONS – **curtain call** the appearance of one or more performers on stage after a performance to acknowledge the audience's applause. **curtain-raiser** an entertainment or other event happening just before a longer or more important one. [ORIGIN – first used in the theatre, to mean a short opening piece performed before a play.] **curtain wall 1** a fortified wall around a medieval castle, typically one linking towers together. **2** a wall which encloses the space within a building but does not support the roof.

ORIGIN – Latin *cortina*, translation of Greek *aulaia*, from *aulē* 'court'.

curtilage /kur**ti**lij/ > *noun* an area of land attached to a house and forming one enclosure with it.

ORIGIN – Old French, from *courtil* 'small court'.

curtsy (also **curtsey**) > *noun* (pl. **curtsies** or **curtseys**) a woman's or girl's formal greeting, made by bending the knees with one foot in front of the other. > *verb* (**curtsies**, **curtsied** or **curtseys**, **curtseyed**) perform a curtsy.

ORIGIN – variant of COURTESY.

curvaceous /kur**vay**shəss/ > *adjective* (especially of a woman or a woman's figure) having an attractively curved shape.

curvature /**kur**vəchər/ > *noun* the fact of being curved or the degree to which something is curved.

curve > *noun* **1** a line or outline which gradually deviates from being straight for some or all of its length. **2** a line on a graph showing how one quantity varies with respect to another. > *verb* form or cause to form a curve.

WORDFINDER – concave (*curving inwards*), convex (*curving outwards*).

ORIGIN – from Latin *curvare* 'to bend'.

curvet /kur**vet**/ > *noun* a graceful or energetic leap. > *verb* (**curvetted**, **curvetting** or **curveted**, **curveting**) (especially of a horse) leap gracefully or energetically.

ORIGIN – Italian *corvetta* 'little curve'.

curvilinear /kurvi**linn**iər/ > *adjective* contained by or consisting of a curved line or lines.

curvy > *adjective* (**curvier**, **curviest**) **1** having many curves. **2** *informal* (of a woman) curvaceous.

DERIVATIVES – **curviness** *noun*.

cusec /**kyoo**sek/ > *noun* a unit of water flow equal to one cubic foot per second.

cushion > *noun* **1** a bag of cloth stuffed with a mass of soft material, used as a comfortable support for sitting or leaning on. **2** a source of support or protection against impact. **3** the elastic lining of the sides of a billiard table, from which the ball rebounds. > *verb* **1** soften the effect of an impact on. **2** lessen the bad effects of.

ORIGIN – Old French *cuissin*, from a Latin word meaning 'cushion for the hip', from *coxa* 'hip, thigh'.

cushy > *adjective* (**cushier**, **cushiest**) *informal* **1** (of a task or situation) easy and undemanding. **2** N. Amer. (of furniture) comfortable.

DERIVATIVES – **cushiness** *noun*.

ORIGIN – from an Urdu word meaning 'pleasure'.

cusp /kusp/ > *noun* **1** a pointed end where two curves meet. **2** each of the pointed ends of a crescent, especially of the moon. **3** a cone-shaped projection on the surface of a tooth. **4** *Astrology* the initial point of an astrological sign or house. **5** a point of transition between two different states: *those on the cusp of adulthood.*

DERIVATIVES – **cuspate** *adjective* **cusped** *adjective*.

ORIGIN – Latin *cuspis* 'point or apex'.

cuspidor /**kus**pidor/ > *noun* N. Amer. a spittoon.

ORIGIN – Portuguese, 'spitter'.

cuss *informal* > *noun* **1** an annoying or stubborn person or animal. **2** a source of harm of misery. > *verb* use offensive language; swear or curse.

cussed /**kuss**id/ > *adjective* *informal* awkward; annoying.

DERIVATIVES – **cussedly** *adverb* **cussedness** *noun*.

custard > *noun* a dessert or sweet sauce made with milk and eggs and thickened with cornflour, or milk and a proprietary powder.

COMBINATIONS – **custard apple** a large fleshy tropical fruit with a sweet yellow pulp. **custard pie** an open pie containing cold set custard, or a similar container of foam, as thrown in slapstick comedy.

wordpower facts

Custard

Custard originally denoted something very different from what we understand by the word today. In the Middle Ages a *custarde* or *crustarde* was a kind of open pie containing pieces of meat or fruit in a sauce thickened with eggs. The word entered English from Old French *crouste* 'crust'; the form *crustarde*, and the original nature of the dish, survives in **croustade**, a crisp piece of bread or pastry hollowed to receive a savoury filling. **Custard** seems to have taken on its modern form and sense around 1600.

custodian /ku**stō**diən/ > *noun* a person who has responsibility for or looks after something.

SYNONYMS – curator, guardian, keeper, warden.

custody /**kus**tədi/ > *noun* **1** protective care or guardianship. **2** *Law* parental responsibility, especially as allocated to one of two divorcing parents. **3** imprisonment.

DERIVATIVES – **custodial** /ku**stō**diəl/ *adjective*.

ORIGIN – Latin *custodia*, from *custos* 'guardian'.

custom > *noun* **1** a traditional way of behaving or doing something that is specific to a particular society, place, or time. **2** *Law* established usage having the force of law or right. **3** *chiefly Brit.* regular dealings with a shop or business by customers.

SYNONYMS – **1** convention, habit, practice, tradition, usage.

COMBINATIONS – **custom-built** (also **custom-made**) made to a particular customer's order. **custom house** (also **customs house**) *chiefly historical* the office at a port or frontier where customs duty is collected.

ORIGIN – Old French *coustume*, from Latin *consuetudo*, from *consuescere* 'accustom'.

customary > *adjective* in accordance with custom; usual.

DERIVATIVES – **customarily** *adverb*.

SYNONYMS – familiar, normal, routine, traditional, usual.

customer > *noun* **1** a person who buys goods or services from a shop or business. **2** a person or thing of a specified kind that one has to deal with: *he's a tough customer.*

SYNONYMS – **1** client, consumer, patron.

customise (also **customize**) > *verb* modify (something) to suit a particular individual or task.

customs > *plural noun* **1** the duties levied by a government on imported goods. **2** the official department that administers and collects such duties.

COMBINATIONS – **customs union** a group of states that have agreed to charge the same import duties as each other and usually to allow free trade between themselves.

ORIGIN – first meaning a customary due paid to a monarch, later duty levied on goods on their way to market.

cut > *verb* (**cutting**; past and past participle **cut**) **1** make an opening, incision, or wound in (something) with a sharp implement. **2** shorten or divide into pieces with a sharp implement. **3** make, form, or remove with a sharp implement. **4** make or design (a garment) in a particular way. **5** reduce the amount or quantity of. **6** end or interrupt the provision of (a supply). **7** (of a line) cross or intersect (another line). **8** stop filming or recording. **9** move to another shot in a film. **10** make (a sound recording). **11** divide a pack of playing cards by lifting a portion from the top. **12** strike or kick (a ball) quickly and abruptly. **13** chiefly N. Amer. absent oneself deliberately from: *Rod was cutting class.* **14** chiefly N. Amer. dilute or adulterate (alcohol or a drug) by mixing it with another substance. > *noun* **1** an act of cutting. **2** a result of cutting: *a cut on his jaw.* **3** a reduction in amount or size. **4** the way or style in which a garment or the hair is cut. **5** a piece of meat cut from a carcass in a particular way. **6** informal a share of profits. **7** a version of a film after editing: *the director's cut.*

IDIOMS – **be cut out for** (or **to be**) informal have exactly the right qualities for a particular role. **a cut above** informal noticeably superior to. **cut and dried** (of a situation) completely settled. [ORIGIN – formerly used to distinguish the herbs of herbalists' shops from growing herbs.] **cut and run** informal make a speedy departure from a difficult situation rather than deal with it. [ORIGIN – a nautical phrase, meaning 'cut the anchor cable because of an emergency and make sail immediately'.] **cut and thrust** a difficult or competitive atmosphere or environment. [ORIGIN – a fencing phrase.] **cut both ways 1** (of a point or statement) serve both sides of an argument. **2** (of an action or process) have both good and bad effects. **cut your coat according to your cloth** proverb undertake only what you have the money or ability to do and no more. **cut corners** do something in a perfunctory way to save time or money. **cut a dash** be stylish or impressive. **cut dead** completely ignore (someone). **be cut from the same cloth** be of the same nature. **cut in 1** interrupt. **2** pull in too closely in front of another vehicle. **3** (of a motor or other device) begin operating automatically. **4** informal include (someone) in a deal and give them a share of the profits. **cut it** informal, chiefly N. Amer. come up to expectations. [ORIGIN – shortened form of the idiom *cut the mustard*.] **cut it out** informal stop it. **cut the mustard** informal reach the required standard. **cut no ice** informal have no influence or effect. **cut off 1** block the usual means of access to (a place). **2** deprive of a supply of power, water, etc. **3** break a telephone connection with (someone). **4** disinherit. **cut out 1** exclude (someone). **2** (of an engine) suddenly stop operating. **cut and paste** (on a word processor or computer) move (an item) from one part of a text to another. **cut a** (or **the**) **rug** informal, chiefly N. Amer. dance. **cut one's teeth** acquire initial experience of an activity. **cut a tooth** (of a baby) have a tooth appear through the gum. **cut up** informal **1** (of a driver) overtake (someone) and pull in too closely. **2** very distressed. **cut up rough** Brit. informal behave in an aggressive or awkward way.

SYNONYMS – *verb* **1** gash, lacerate, pierce, slash, slit. **2** carve, chop, cut up, dice, slice. *noun* **1,2** gash, laceration, slash, slit. **3** cutback, decrease, reduction.

COMBINATIONS – **cut glass** glass ornamented by having patterns cut into it. **cut-price** (chiefly N. Amer. also **cut-rate**) for sale at a reduced price; cheap. **cut-throat razor** Brit. a razor with a long blade which folds like a penknife. **cutwater 1** the forward edge of a ship's prow. **2** a wedge-shaped projection on the pier of a bridge.

cutaneous /kyoōtayniəss/ > *adjective* relating to or affecting the skin.

ORIGIN – from Latin *cutis* 'skin'.

cutaway > *adjective* **1** (of a coat or jacket) having the front cut away below the waist. **2** (of a diagram of an object) having some external parts left out to reveal the interior.

cutback > *noun* a reduction, especially in expenditure.

cute > *adjective* **1** endearingly pretty. **2** N. Amer. informal sexually attractive. **3** informal, chiefly N. Amer. clever; shrewd.

DERIVATIVES – **cutely** adverb **cuteness** noun.

SYNONYMS – **1** appealing, enchanting, endearing, lovable, sweet.

ORIGIN – shortening of ACUTE.

cutesy > *adjective* informal cute to a sentimental or mawkish extent.

cuticle /kyoōtik'l/ > *noun* **1** the dead skin at the base of a fingernail or toenail. **2** the epidermis of the body. **3** a protective layer covering the epidermis of a plant or invertebrate.

DERIVATIVES – **cuticular** adjective.

ORIGIN – Latin *cuticula* 'little skin'.

cutis /kyoōtiss/ > *noun* Anatomy the true skin or dermis.

ORIGIN – Latin, 'skin'.

cutlass /**kut**ləss/ > *noun* a short sword with a slightly curved blade, formerly used by sailors.

ORIGIN – Latin *cultellus* 'little knife'.

cutler > *noun* a person who makes or sells cutlery.

ORIGIN – Old French *coutelier*, from Latin *cultellus* 'little knife, ploughshare'.

cutlery > *noun* knives, forks, and spoons used for eating or serving food.

cutlet > *noun* **1** a portion of meat, especially a chop from just behind the neck. **2** a flat croquette of minced meat, nuts, or pulses.

ORIGIN – French *côtelette*, from *coste* 'rib'.

cut-off > *noun* **1** a point or level marking a designated limit. **2** a device for interrupting a power or fuel supply. **3** (**cut-offs**) shorts made by cutting off the legs of a pair of jeans. **4** chiefly N. Amer. a short cut.

cut-out > *noun* **1** a shape cut out of board or another material. **2** a hole cut for decoration or to allow the insertion of something. **3** a device that automatically breaks an electric circuit for safety.

cutpurse > *noun* archaic a pickpocket.

ORIGIN – with reference to stealing by cutting purses suspended from a waistband.

cutter > *noun* **1** a person or thing that cuts. **2** a light, fast patrol boat or sailing boat. **3** a ship's boat used for carrying light stores or passengers. **4** Cricket & Baseball a ball that deviates sharply on pitching.

cutting > *noun* **1** a piece cut off from something, in particular an article cut from a newspaper or a piece cut from a plant for propagation. **2** an open passage excavated through higher ground for a railway, road, or canal. > *adjective* **1** capable of cutting. **2** (of a remark) hurtful.

DERIVATIVES – **cuttingly** adverb.

COMBINATIONS – **cutting edge 1** the latest or most advanced stage; the forefront. **2** (**cutting-edge**) innovative; pioneering.

cuttlebone > *noun* the flattened internal skeleton of the cuttlefish.

cuttlefish > *noun* a swimming marine mollusc that resembles a broad-bodied squid, having eight arms and two long tentacles that are used for grabbing prey.

ORIGIN – related to Old English *codd* 'bag', with reference to the sac containing ink which the cuttlefish ejects into the water when threatened.

cut up > *adjective* informal very distressed.

cutworm > *noun* a moth caterpillar that lives in the soil and eats through the stems of young plants at ground level.

cuvée /kyoōvay/ > *noun* a type, blend, or batch of wine, especially champagne.

ORIGIN – French, 'vatful'.

CV > *abbreviation* curriculum vitae.

CVO > *abbreviation* (in the UK) Commander of the Royal Victorian Order.

CVS > *abbreviation* chorionic villus sampling, a test made in early pregnancy to detect fetal abnormalities.

cwm /kōom/ > *noun* a steep-sided hollow at the head of a valley or on a mountainside, especially in the Welsh mountains.
ORIGIN – Welsh; related to COMBE.

cwt. > *abbreviation* hundredweight.
ORIGIN – from Latin *centum* 'a hundred'.

-cy > *suffix* **1** denoting state or condition: *bankruptcy*. **2** denoting rank or status: *baronetcy*.
ORIGIN – from Latin *-cia, -tia* and Greek *-keia, -teia*.

cyan /sīən/ > *noun* a greenish-blue colour which is one of the primary colours, complementary to red.
ORIGIN – Greek *kuaneos* 'dark blue'.

cyanide /sīanīd/ > *noun* a salt or ester of hydrocyanic acid, most kinds of which are extremely poisonous.

cyanobacteria /sīanōbakteeriə/ > *plural noun* micro-organisms of a group comprising the blue-green algae, related to bacteria but capable of photosynthesis.

cyanocobalamin /sīanōkəbaləmin/ > *noun* vitamin B$_{12}$, a cobalt-containing vitamin derived from liver, fish, and eggs, a deficiency of which causes pernicious anaemia.

cyanogen /sīannəjən/ > *noun* a highly poisonous gas made by oxidising hydrogen cyanide.

cyanosis /sīanōsis/ > *noun* a bluish discoloration of the skin due to poor circulation or inadequate oxygenation of the blood.
DERIVATIVES – **cyanotic** *adjective*.
ORIGIN – Greek *kuanōsis* 'blueness'.

cyber- /sībər/ > *combining form* relating to information technology, the Internet, and virtual reality: *cyberspace*.
ORIGIN – from CYBERNETICS.

cybernetics > *plural noun* (treated as sing.) the science of communications and automatic control systems in both machines and living things.
DERIVATIVES – **cybernetic** *adjective*.
ORIGIN – from Greek *kubernētēs* 'steersman'.

cyberphobia > *noun* extreme or irrational fear of computers or technology.
DERIVATIVES – **cyberphobe** *noun* **cyberphobic** *adjective & noun*.

cyberpunk > *noun* a genre of science fiction set in a lawless subculture of an oppressive society dominated by computer technology.

cyberspace > *noun* the notional environment in which communication over computer networks occurs.

cybersquatting > *noun* the practice of registering well-known names as Internet addresses, in order to resell them at a profit.

cyborg /sīborg/ > *noun* a fictional or hypothetical person whose physical abilities are extended beyond human limitations by mechanical elements built into the body.
ORIGIN – blend of CYBER- and ORGANISM.

cycad /sīkad/ > *noun* a tall, cone-bearing, palm-like plant of warm regions.
ORIGIN – from supposed Greek *kukas*, an error for *koikas* 'Egyptian palms'.

cyclamate /sikləmayt, sikləmayt/ > *noun* a salt of a synthetic organic acid, formerly used as an artificial sweetener.
ORIGIN – contraction of *cyclohexyl-sulphamate*.

cyclamen /sikləmən/ > *noun* (pl. same or **cyclamens**) a plant having pink, red, or white flowers with backward-curving petals.
ORIGIN – Greek *kuklaminos*, perhaps from *kuklos* 'circle', with reference to its bulbous roots.

cycle > *noun* **1** a series of events that are regularly repeated in the same order. **2** a complete sequence of changes associated with a recurring phenomenon such as an alternating current, wave, etc. **3** a series of musical or literary works composed around a particular theme. **4** a bicycle. > *verb* **1** ride a bicycle. **2** move in or follow a cycle of events.
DERIVATIVES – **cycling** *noun*.
SYNONYMS – **1** revolution, rotation, round, sequence, series.
ORIGIN – Greek *kuklos* 'circle'.

cyclic /sīklik/ > *adjective* **1** occurring in cycles. **2** Chemistry having a molecular structure containing one or more closed rings of atoms.
DERIVATIVES – **cyclical** *adjective* **cyclically** *adverb*.

cyclist > *noun* a person who rides a bicycle.

cyclo-cross > *noun* cross-country racing on bicycles.

cycloid /sīkloyd/ > *noun* Mathematics a curve traced by a point on a circle being rolled along a straight line.
DERIVATIVES – **cycloidal** *adjective*.

cyclometer /sīklommitər/ > *noun* **1** an instrument for measuring circular arcs. **2** an instrument attached to a bicycle for measuring distance.

cyclone /sīklōn/ > *noun* **1** a system of winds rotating inwards to an area of low barometric pressure; a depression. **2** a tropical storm.
DERIVATIVES – **cyclonic** *adjective*.
ORIGIN – probably from Greek *kuklōma* 'wheel, coil of a snake'.

cyclopean /sīkləpeeən, sīklōpiən/ (also **cyclopian**) > *adjective* **1** of or resembling a Cyclops. **2** (of ancient masonry) made with massive irregular blocks.

cyclopedia /sīkləpeediə/ (also **cyclopaedia**) > *noun* archaic (except in book titles) an encyclopedia.

Cyclops /sīklops/ > *noun* **1** (pl. **Cyclops**, **Cyclopses**, or **Cyclopes** /sīklōpeez/) Greek Mythology a member of a race of savage one-eyed giants. **2** (**cyclops**) a minute freshwater crustacean which has a cylindrical body with a single central eye.
ORIGIN – from Greek *Kuklōps* 'round-eyed'.

cyclorama /sīkləraamə/ > *noun* **1** a panoramic scene set on the inside of a cylindrical surface, to be viewed by a central spectator. **2** a cloth stretched tight in an arc around the back of a stage set, used to represent the sky.

cyclosporin /sīklōsporin/ (also **cyclosporine**) > *noun* a drug used in surgery to prevent the rejection of grafts and transplants by the recipients.
ORIGIN – from Latin *spora* 'spore' (because it is produced from a fungus).

cyclotron /sīklətron/ > *noun* an apparatus in which charged atomic and subatomic particles are accelerated by an alternating electric field while following an outward spiral or circular path in a magnetic field.

cyder > *noun* archaic spelling of CIDER.

cygnet /signit/ > *noun* a young swan.
ORIGIN – Old French, from Greek *kuknos* 'swan'.

cylinder /sillindər/ > *noun* **1** a three-dimensional shape with straight parallel sides and a circular or oval cross section. **2** a piston chamber in a steam or internal-combustion engine. **3** a cylindrical container for liquefied gas under pressure. **4** a rotating metal roller in a printing press.
DERIVATIVES – **cylindrical** /silindrik'l/ *adjective* **cylindrically** *adverb*.
COMBINATIONS – **cylinder head** the end cover of a cylinder in an internal-combustion engine, against which the piston compresses the cylinder's contents.
ORIGIN – Greek *kulindros* 'roller'.

cymbal /simb'l/ > *noun* a musical instrument consisting of a slightly concave round brass plate which is either struck against another one or struck with a stick.
ORIGIN – Greek *kumbalon*, from *kumbē* 'cup'.

cyme > *noun* Botany a flower cluster with a central stem bearing a single terminal flower that develops first, the other flowers in the cluster developing on side stems. Compare with RACEME.
ORIGIN – French, 'summit, unopened flower head', from Latin *cyma*.

Cymric /kimrik/ > *adjective* (of language or

culture) Welsh. > *noun* the Welsh language.

ORIGIN – from Welsh *Cymru* 'Wales'.

cynic /**sinn**ik/ > *noun* **1** a person who has little faith in the integrity or sincerity of others. **2** a sceptic. **3** (**Cynic**) (in ancient Greece) a member of a school of philosophers founded by Antisthenes, characterised by an ostentatious contempt for wealth and pleasure.

DERIVATIVES – **cynicism** *noun*.

ORIGIN – Greek *kunikos*; probably originally from *Kunosarges*, the name of a gymnasium where Antisthenes taught, but popularly taken to mean 'doglike, churlish', *kuōn* 'dog' becoming a nickname for a Cynic.

cynical > *adjective* **1** tending not to believe in the integrity or sincerity of others. **2** sceptical. **3** contemptuous; mocking. **4** concerned only with one's own interests.

DERIVATIVES – **cynically** *adverb*.

cynosure /**sīn**əzyoor, **sin**əzyoor/ > *noun* a person or thing that is the centre of attention or admiration.

ORIGIN – first used to denote the constellation Ursa Minor, or the pole star which it contains: from Greek *kunosoura* 'dog's tail' (also 'Ursa Minor').

cypher > *noun* variant spelling of **CIPHER**.

cypress > *noun* an evergreen coniferous tree with flattened shoots bearing small scale-like leaves, whose dark foliage is sometimes associated with mourning.

ORIGIN – Greek *kuparissos*.

Cypriot > *noun* **1** a person from Cyprus. **2** the dialect of Greek used in Cyprus. > *adjective* relating to Cyprus.

Cyrillic /siɾ**ill**ik/ > *adjective* denoting the alphabet used for Russian, Ukrainian, Bulgarian, Serbian, and some other Slavic languages, ultimately derived from Greek uncials. > *noun* the Cyrillic alphabet.

ORIGIN – named after the 9th-century Greek missionary St *Cyril*, its reputed inventor.

cyst /sist/ > *noun* **1** Medicine an abnormal thin-walled sac or cavity in the body, containing fluid. **2** Zoology a tough protective capsule enclosing the larva of a parasitic worm or the resting stage of an organism.

ORIGIN – Greek *kustis* 'bladder'.

cystectomy > *noun* (pl. **cystectomies**) **1** a surgical operation to remove the urinary bladder. **2** a surgical operation to remove an abnormal cyst.

cysteine /**sis**ti-een/ > *noun* Biochemistry a sulphur-containing amino acid which occurs in keratins and other proteins. Compare with **CYSTINE**.

cystic > *adjective* **1** chiefly Medicine relating to or characterised by cysts. **2** Zoology enclosed in a cyst. **3** relating to the urinary bladder or the gall bladder.

COMBINATIONS – **cystic fibrosis** a hereditary disorder which affects the exocrine glands, resulting in the production of abnormally thick mucus and leading to the blockage of the pancreatic ducts, intestines, and bronchi.

cystine /**sis**teen/ > *noun* Biochemistry an oxidised form of the amino acid cysteine.

ORIGIN – from Greek *kustis* 'bladder' (because it was first isolated from urinary calculi).

cystitis /si**stī**tis/ > *noun* inflammation of the urinary bladder, typically caused by infection and accompanied by frequent painful urination.

cytogenetics /sītōjə**nett**iks/ > *plural noun* (**treated as sing.**) the study of inheritance in relation to the structure and function of chromosomes.

DERIVATIVES – **cytogenetic** *adjective* **cytogeneticist** *noun*.

ORIGIN – from Greek *kutos* 'vessel'.

cytology /sī**toll**əji/ > *noun* the branch of biology concerned with the structure and function of plant and animal cells.

DERIVATIVES – **cytological** *adjective* **cytologist** *noun*.

ORIGIN – from Greek *kutos* 'vessel'.

cytomegalovirus /sītō**megg**əlōvīrəss/ > *noun* Medicine a kind of herpesvirus which usually produces very mild symptoms in an infected person but may cause severe neurological damage in people with weakened immune systems and in the newborn.

ORIGIN – from Greek *kutos* 'vessel' + *megas* 'great' + **VIRUS**: the virus enlarges infected cells.

cytoplasm /**sī**tōplaz'm/ > *noun* Biology the material or protoplasm within a living cell, excluding the nucleus.

DERIVATIVES – **cytoplasmic** *adjective*.

ORIGIN – from Greek *kutos* 'vessel' + *plasma*, from *plassein* 'to shape'.

cytosine /**sī**təseen/ > *noun* Biochemistry a compound which is one of the four constituent bases of DNA.

czar etc. variant spelling of **TSAR** etc.

Czech /chek/ > *noun* **1** a person from the Czech Republic or (formerly) Czechoslovakia. **2** the Slavic language spoken in the Czech Republic. > *adjective* relating to the Czech Republic.

Czechoslovak /chekkə**slō**vak/ (also **Czechoslovakian**) > *noun* a person from the former country of Czechoslovakia, now divided between the Czech Republic and Slovakia. > *adjective* relating to the former country of Czechoslovakia.

D¹ (also **d**) > *noun* (pl. **Ds** or **D's**) **1** the fourth letter of the alphabet. **2** denoting the fourth item in a set. **3** Music the second note of the diatonic scale of C major. **4** the Roman numeral for 500. [ORIGIN – understood as half of CIↃ, an earlier form of M (= 1,000).]

COMBINATIONS – **D-lock** a mechanism used to secure a bicycle or motorbike, consisting of a metal U-shaped bar and crosspiece. **D notice** (in the UK) a government notice requiring news editors not to publicise certain sensitive information. [ORIGIN – D for *defence*.]

D² > *abbreviation* **1** (in the US) Democrat or Democratic. **2** (with a numeral) dimension(s) or dimensional. **3** (in tables of sports results) drawn.

d > *abbreviation* **1** (in genealogies) daughter. **2** deci-. **3** (in travel timetables) departs. **4** (**d.**) died (used to indicate a date of death). **5** Brit. penny or pence (of pre-decimal currency). [ORIGIN – from Latin *denarius* 'penny'.]

'd > *contraction* **1** had. **2** would.

DA > *abbreviation* **1** US district attorney. **2** informal duck's arse (US duck's ass), denoting a man's hairstyle in which the hair is slicked back on both sides and tapered at the nape.

D/A > *abbreviation* Electronics digital to analogue.

dab¹ > *verb* (**dabbed**, **dabbing**) **1** press lightly with absorbent material. **2** apply with light quick strokes. > *noun* **1** a small amount lightly applied. **2** (**dabs**) Brit. informal fingerprints.

SYNONYMS – *verb* **1** blot, swab. **2** daub, stroke. *noun* **1** dash, spot, touch.

dab² > *noun* a small North Atlantic flatfish.

dabble > *verb* **1** move (one's hands or feet) around gently in water. **2** take part in an activity in a casual way. **3** (of a duck or other water bird) move the bill around in shallow water while feeding.

DERIVATIVES – **dabbler** *noun*.

SYNONYMS – **1** paddle, splash.

dabchick > *noun* the little grebe.

dab hand > *noun* Brit. informal a person who is very skilled in a particular activity.

da capo /daa **kaa**pō/ > *adverb & adjective* Music repeat or repeated from the beginning.

ORIGIN – Italian, 'from the head'.

dace /dayss/ > *noun* (pl. same) a freshwater fish related to the carp.

ORIGIN – Old French *dars*.

dacha /**dach**ə/ (also **datcha**) > *noun* (in Russia) a house or cottage in the country, used as a holiday home.

ORIGIN – Russian, originally meaning 'grant of land'.

dachshund /**daks**ənd, **daks**-hŏond/ > *noun* a breed of dog with a long body and very short legs.

ORIGIN – German, 'badger dog' (the breed was originally used to dig badgers out of their setts).

dacoit /də**koyt**/ > *noun* a member of a band of armed robbers in India or Burma (Myanmar).

ORIGIN – Hindi, from a word meaning 'robbery by a gang'.

dactyl /**dak**til/ > *noun* Poetry a metrical foot consisting of one stressed syllable followed by two unstressed syllables.

DERIVATIVES – **dactylic** *adjective*.

ORIGIN – Greek *daktulos* 'finger' (the three bones of the finger corresponding to the three syllables).

dad > *noun* informal one's father.

Dada /**daa**daa/ > *noun* an early 20th-century movement in the arts which mocked conventions and emphasised the illogical and absurd.

DERIVATIVES – **Dadaism** *noun* **Dadaist** *noun & adjective*.

ORIGIN – French, 'hobby horse', the title of a review which appeared in 1916.

daddy > *noun* (pl. **daddies**) informal one's father.

daddy-long-legs > *noun* Brit. informal a crane fly.

dado /**day**dō/ > *noun* (pl. **dados**) **1** the lower part of the wall of a room, when decorated differently from the upper part. **2** Architecture the cube of a pedestal between the base and the cornice.

COMBINATIONS – **dado rail** a waist-high moulding round the wall of a room, separating the dado from the upper part of the wall.

ORIGIN – Italian, 'dice or cube'.

daemon¹ /**dee**mən/ (also **daimon**) > *noun* **1** (in ancient Greek belief) a divinity or supernatural being of a nature between gods and humans. **2** archaic spelling of DEMON¹.

DERIVATIVES – **daemonic** *adjective*.

ORIGIN – Greek *daimon*.

daemon² > *noun* variant spelling of DEMON².

daffodil > *noun* a bulbous plant bearing bright yellow flowers with a long trumpet-shaped centre.

ORIGIN – first spelled as *affodill*, from Latin *affodilus*, variant of *asphodilus* 'asphodel'.

daffy > *adjective* (**daffier**, **daffiest**) informal silly; mildly eccentric.

ORIGIN – from northern English dialect *daff* 'simpleton'; perhaps related to DAFT.

daft > *adjective* informal, chiefly Brit. silly; foolish.

ORIGIN – Old English, 'mild, meek'.

dag¹ Austral./NZ > *noun* a lock of wool matted with dung hanging from the hindquarters of a sheep. > *verb* (**dagged**, **dagging**) cut dags from (a sheep).

dag² > *noun* Austral./NZ informal a socially conservative person.

ORIGIN – first denoting an eccentric person: transferred use of English dialect meaning 'a challenge'.

dagger > *noun* **1** a short pointed knife, used as a weapon. **2** Printing an obelus (†).

WORDFINDER – *kinds of dagger*: dirk (*formerly carried by Scottish highlanders*), kris (*Malay or Indonesian dagger*), misericord (*used to kill a wounded enemy*), poniard (*small, slim dagger*), skean (*formerly used in Ireland and Scotland*), skean-dhu (*worn as part of Highland dress*), stiletto (*short, with tapering blade*).

IDIOMS – **at daggers drawn** in bitter conflict. **look daggers at** glare angrily at.

ORIGIN – perhaps from obsolete *dag* 'pierce', influenced by Old French *dague* 'long dagger'.

daggy > *adjective* (**daggier**, **daggiest**) Austral./ NZ informal **1** (especially of clothes) scruffy. **2** not stylish; unfashionable.

dago /**day**gō/ > *noun* (pl. **dagos** or **dagoes**) informal, offensive a Spanish, Portuguese, or Italian-speaking person.

ORIGIN – from the Spanish forename *Diego* 'James'.

daguerreotype /də**gerr**ətīp/ (also **daguerrotype**) > *noun* a photograph taken by an early process using an iodine-sensitised silver-coated copper plate and mercury vapour.

ORIGIN – named after L.-J.-M. *Daguerre* (1789–1851), its French inventor.

dahlia /**day**liə/ > *noun* a garden plant with brightly coloured single or double flowers and tuberous roots, native to Mexico.

ORIGIN – named after the Swedish botanist Andreas *Dahl* (1751–89).

Dáil /doyl/ (in full **Dáil Éireann** /doyl **air**ən/) > *noun* the lower House of Parliament in the Republic of Ireland.

ORIGIN – Irish, 'assembly of Ireland'.

daily > *adjective* done, happening, or produced every day or every weekday. > *adverb* every day. > *noun* (pl. **dailies**) informal **1** a newspaper published every day except Sunday. **2** (also **daily help**) Brit. dated a domestic cleaner.

daimon /**dī**mōn/ > *noun* variant spelling of DAEMON¹.

dainty > *adjective* (**daintier**, **daintiest**) **1** delicately small and pretty. **2** fastidious and fussy when eating. > *noun* (pl. **dainties**) a small item of food; a delicacy.

DERIVATIVES – **daintily** *adverb* **daintiness** *noun*.

SYNONYMS – *adjective* **1** delicate, neat, petite.

ORIGIN – from Old French *daintie* 'choice morsel, pleasure', from Latin *dignitas* 'worthiness or beauty'.

daiquiri /dakkəri/ > *noun* (pl. **daiquiris**) a cocktail containing rum and lime juice.

ORIGIN – from *Daiquiri*, a rum-producing district in Cuba.

dairy > *noun* (pl. **dairies**) a building for the processing and distribution of milk and milk products. > *adjective* **1** made from milk. **2** involved in milk production.

DERIVATIVES – **dairying** *noun*.

COMBINATIONS – **dairymaid** *archaic* a woman employed in a dairy. **dairyman** a man who is employed in a dairy or who sells dairy products.

ORIGIN – from obsolete *dey* 'dairymaid' (in Old English 'female servant'); related to DOUGH, LADY.

dais /dayiss/ > *noun* a low platform for a lectern or throne.

ORIGIN – Old French *deis*, from Latin *discus*: see box at DISCUS.

daisy > *noun* (pl. **daisies**) a small grassland plant with flowers having a yellow centre and white rays.

IDIOMS – **pushing up (the) daisies** *informal* dead and buried.

COMBINATIONS – **daisy chain** a string of daisies threaded together by their stems. **daisy wheel** a spoked disc carrying printing characters, used in word processors and typewriters.

ORIGIN – Old English, 'day's eye' (because the flower opens in the morning and closes at night).

Dakota /dəkōtə/ > *noun* (pl. same or **Dakotas**) a member of a North American Indian people of the northern Mississippi valley and the surrounding plains.

ORIGIN – the Dakotas' name for themselves, literally 'allies'.

daks > *plural noun* Austral. informal trousers.

ORIGIN – a proprietary name.

Dalai Lama /dalī laamə/ > *noun* the spiritual head of Tibetan Buddhism and, until the establishment of Chinese communist rule, the spiritual and temporal ruler of Tibet.

ORIGIN – Tibetan, 'ocean monk' (because he is regarded as 'the ocean of compassion').

dalasi /daalaasee/ > *noun* (pl. same or **dalasis**) the basic monetary unit of Gambia, equal to 100 butut.

ORIGIN – a local word.

dale > *noun* a valley, especially in northern England.

ORIGIN – Old English, related to DELL.

Dalit /daalit/ > *noun* (in the traditional Indian caste system) a member of the lowest caste. See also UNTOUCHABLE.

ORIGIN – from a Sanskrit word meaning 'oppressed'.

dally > *verb* (**dallies**, **dallied**) **1** act or move slowly. **2** (**dally with**) have a casual sexual liaison with. **3** (**dally with**) show a casual interest in.

DERIVATIVES – **dalliance** *noun*.

SYNONYMS – **1** dawdle, delay, idle, linger, meander; archaic tarry.

ORIGIN – Old French *dalier* 'to chat'.

Dalmatian > *noun* **1** a breed of large dog with short white hair and dark spots. **2** a person from Dalmatia, a region in Croatia. > *adjective* relating to Dalmatia.

dal segno /dal senyō/ > *adverb & adjective* Music repeat or repeated from the point marked by a sign.

ORIGIN – Italian, 'from the sign'.

dam¹ > *noun* a barrier constructed across a river to hold back water, in order to form a reservoir or prevent flooding. > *verb* (**dammed**, **damming**) build a dam across.

dam² > *noun* the female parent of an animal.

ORIGIN – from DAME.

damage > *noun* **1** physical harm reducing the value, operation, or usefulness of something. **2** (**damages**) financial compensation for a loss or injury. > *verb* inflict damage on.

SYNONYMS – *noun* **1** harm, impairment, injury. *verb* harm, impair, injure, mar.

ANTONYMS – *verb* benefit, improve.

ORIGIN – Old French, from Latin *damnum* 'loss or hurt'; related to DAMN.

damaging > *adjective* harmful or undesirable.

Damascene /damməseen/ > *adjective* **1** relating to the city of Damascus, the capital of Syria. **2** (of a change of belief or opinion) dramatic and sudden. [ORIGIN – with reference to the account in the Bible of the conversion of St Paul on the road to Damascus.] > *noun* a person from Damascus.

damascened > *adjective* **1** (of iron or steel) given a wavy pattern by hammering and welding and repeated heating and forging. **2** (of metal) inlaid with gold or silver.

ORIGIN – from *Damascus*, a city famous for this metalwork.

damask /damməsk/ > *noun* a rich, heavy fabric with a pattern woven into it. > *adjective* literary pink or light red.

COMBINATIONS – **damask rose** a sweet-scented rose with pink velvety petals.

ORIGIN – from *Damascus*, where the fabric was first produced.

dame > *noun* **1** (**Dame**) (in the UK) the title of a woman awarded a knighthood, equivalent to *Sir*. **2** N. Amer. informal a woman. **3** (also **pantomime dame**) Brit. a comic female character in pantomime, played by a man.

ORIGIN – Old French, from Latin *domina* 'mistress'.

damn /dam/ > *verb* **1** (**be damned**) (in Christian belief) be condemned by God to eternal punishment in hell. **2** harshly condemn. **3** curse. > *exclamation* informal expressing anger or frustration. > *adjective* informal used to emphasise anger or frustration.

IDIOMS – **as near as damn it** informal as close to being accurate as makes no difference. **damn all** Brit. informal nothing. **damn with faint praise** praise so unenthusiastically as to suggest condemnation. **not be worth a damn** informal have no value.

ORIGIN – Latin *damnare* 'inflict loss on', from *damnum* 'loss, damage'.

damnable > *adjective* very bad or unpleasant.

DERIVATIVES – **damnably** *adverb*.

damnation /damnaysh'n/ > *noun* condemnation to eternal punishment in hell. > *exclamation* expressing anger or frustration.

damned /damd/ > *adjective* **1** used to emphasise anger or frustration. **2** (**damnedest**) used to emphasise the surprising nature of something.

IDIOMS – **do** (or **try**) **one's damnedest** do (or try) one's utmost.

damning > *adjective* strongly suggestive of guilt.

DERIVATIVES – **damningly** *adverb*.

damp > *adjective* slightly wet. > *noun* moisture in the air, on a surface, or in a solid. > *verb* **1** make damp. **2** (often **damp down**) control or restrain (a feeling or situation). **3** (**damp down**) make (a fire) burn less strongly by reducing its air supply. **4** reduce or stop the vibration of (the strings of a musical instrument).

DERIVATIVES – **dampish** *adjective* **damply** *adverb* **dampness** *noun*.

SYNONYMS – *adjective* clammy, dank, moist. *noun* dampness, humidity, moisture.

ANTONYMS – *adjective* dry. *noun* dryness.

COMBINATIONS – **damp course** (also **damp-proof course**) a layer of waterproof material in a wall near the ground, to prevent rising damp. **damp squib** Brit. something that turns out to be much less impressive than expected.

dampen > *verb* **1** make damp. **2** make less strong or intense.

DERIVATIVES – **dampener** *noun*.

SYNONYMS – **1** damp, moisten. **2** cool, diminish, lessen, subdue.

damper > *noun* **1** a pad silencing a piano string. **2** a device for reducing vibration or oscillation. **3** a movable metal plate in a flue or chimney, used to regulate the draught.

IDIOMS – **put a damper on** informal have a subduing effect on.

damp-proof > *adjective* impervious to damp. > *verb* make (a building) impervious to damp by using a damp course.

damsel /**damz**'l/ > *noun* archaic or literary a young unmarried woman.

ORIGIN – Old French *dameisele*, from Latin *domina* 'mistress'.

damselfly > *noun* (pl. **damselflies**) a slender insect related to the dragonflies.

damson /**damz**'n/ > *noun* a small purple-black plum-like fruit.

wordpower facts

Damson

The name of the fruit comes from Latin *damascenum prunum* 'plum of Damascus'. Other words connected with the Syrian city are **damask**, because the material was first produced there, and **damascened**, because in the Middle Ages Damascus was a famous market for steel weapons of this kind.

dan > *noun* **1** a grade of advanced proficiency in judo or karate. **2** a person who has achieved a dan.

ORIGIN – Japanese.

dance > *verb* **1** move rhythmically to music, typically following a set sequence of steps. **2** move in a quick and lively way. > *noun* **1** a series of steps and movements that match the rhythm of a piece of music. **2** a social gathering at which people dance. **3** (also **dance music**) music for dancing to, especially in a nightclub.

WORDFINDER – terpsichorean (*relating to dancing*).

IDIOMS – **dance attendance on** try hard to please. **dance to someone's tune** comply with someone's demands. **lead someone a merry dance** Brit. cause someone a great deal of trouble.

DERIVATIVES – **dancer** *noun* **dancing** *noun*.

ORIGIN – Old French *dancer*.

D and C > *abbreviation* dilatation and curettage.

dandelion > *noun* a weed with large bright yellow flowers followed by rounded heads of seeds with downy tufts.

COMBINATIONS – **dandelion clock** Brit. the downy spherical seed head of a dandelion.

ORIGIN – French *dent-de-lion* 'lion's tooth' (because of the jagged shape of the leaves).

dander > *noun* (in phrase **get** or **have one's dander up**) informal lose one's temper.

dandified > *adjective* **1** (of a man) showing excessive concern about his appearance. **2** self-consciously elaborate.

dandle > *verb* gently bounce (a young child) on one's knees or in one's arms.

dandruff > *noun* flakes of dead skin on a person's scalp and in the hair.

dandy > *noun* (pl. **dandies**) a man unduly concerned with a stylish and fashionable appearance. > *adjective* (**dandier, dandiest**) informal, chiefly N. Amer. excellent.

DERIVATIVES – **dandyish** *adjective*.

Dane > *noun* a person from Denmark.

danger > *noun* **1** the possibility of suffering harm. **2** a cause of harm. **3** the possibility of something unpleasant happening.

SYNONYMS – **1** endangerment, jeopardy, peril, risk. **2** hazard, menace, threat.

ANTONYMS – **1** safety.

COMBINATIONS – **danger list** Brit. a list of those who are very seriously ill in a hospital. **danger money** extra payment for working under dangerous conditions.

wordpower facts

Danger

The word **danger** is from Old French *dangier*, from Latin *dominus* 'lord'. The original sense was 'jurisdiction or power', specifically 'power to harm', hence the current meaning 'possibility of being harmed'. A number of other words are based on *dominus*, including **domain, dominate, dominion, domino, don,** and **dungeon**: all retain some connection with power in modern English, with the exception of **domino**, whose relationship with *dominus* remains a puzzle.

dangerous > *adjective* **1** likely to cause or lead to harm or injury. **2** likely to cause problems.

DERIVATIVES – **dangerously** *adverb* **dangerousness** *noun*.

SYNONYMS – **1** hazardous, perilous, risky, unsafe.

ANTONYMS – **1** safe.

dangle > *verb* **1** hang so as to swing freely. **2** informal offer (an incentive) to someone.

DERIVATIVES – **dangler** *noun* **dangly** *adjective*.

Danish /**day**nish/ > *adjective* relating to Denmark or the Danes. > *noun* the language of Denmark.

COMBINATIONS – **Danish blue** a salty, strong-flavoured blue-veined white cheese.

Danish pastry a cake of sweetened pastry topped with icing, fruit, and nuts.

dank > *adjective* damp and cold.

DERIVATIVES – **dankly** *adverb* **dankness** *noun*.

ORIGIN – probably Scandinavian.

daphne /**daf**ni/ > *noun* a small evergreen shrub with sweet-scented flowers.

ORIGIN – first denoting the laurel or bay tree; from *Daphne*, a nymph in Greek mythology who was turned into a laurel bush.

daphnia /**daf**niə/ > *noun* (pl. same) a minute semi-transparent freshwater crustacean.

ORIGIN – named after *Daphne*, a nymph in Greek mythology.

dapper > *adjective* (of a man) neat in dress and appearance.

SYNONYMS – smart, spruce, trim.

dapple > *verb* mark with spots or small patches. > *noun* a patch of colour or light.

SYNONYMS – dot, fleck, speckle, spot.

COMBINATIONS – **dapple grey** (of a horse) grey or white with darker ring-like markings.

Darby and Joan > *noun* Brit. a devoted old married couple.

ORIGIN – from a poem (1735) in the *Gentleman's Magazine*.

dare > *verb* (3rd sing. present usu. **dare** before an expressed or implied infinitive without 'to') **1** have the courage to do something. **2** defy or challenge (someone) to do something. > *noun* a challenge, especially to prove courage.

IDIOMS – **how dare you** used to express indignation. **I dare say** (or **daresay**) it is probable.

daredevil > *noun* a person who enjoys doing dangerous things.

DERIVATIVES – **daredevilry** *noun*.

daring > *adjective* audaciously or adventurously bold. > *noun* adventurous courage.

DERIVATIVES – **daringly** *adverb*.

SYNONYMS – *adjective* adventurous, audacious, bold, fearless, intrepid.

ANTONYMS – *adjective* timid.

Darjeeling /daar**jee**ling/ > *noun* a high-quality tea grown in northern India.

ORIGIN – from *Darjeeling*, a hill station in West Bengal.

dark > *adjective* **1** with little or no light. **2** of a deep or sombre colour. **3** (of skin, hair, or eyes) brown or black. **4** secret or mysterious. **5** (**darkest**) humorous most remote or uncivilised. **6** depressing or cheerless. **7** evil. > *noun* **1** (**the dark**) the absence of light. **2** nightfall. **3** a dark colour or shade.

IDIOMS – **the darkest hour is just before the dawn** proverb when things seem to be at their worst they are about to start improving. **in the dark** in a state of ignorance. **keep dark** keep (something) secret. **a shot** (or **stab**) **in the dark** a wild guess.

DERIVATIVES – **darkish** *adjective* **darkly** *adverb* **darkness** *noun*.

SYNONYMS – *adjective* **1** dim, gloomy, inky, murky. **4** arcane, hidden, mysterious, secret. **6** bleak, cheerless, depressing, gloomy, sombre.

COMBINATIONS – **Dark Ages 1** the period in Europe between the fall of the Roman Empire and the Middle ages, *c.*500–1100, regarded as unenlightened. **2** any period regarded as unenlightened. **dark chocolate** plain chocolate. **dark horse** a person about whom little is known, or who turns out to have unexpected talents. **dark matter** Astronomy non-luminous material believed to exist in space. **darkroom** a room for developing photographs, from which normal light is excluded.

darken > *verb* **1** make or become darker. **2** cast a shadow over; spoil. **3** become unhappy or angry.

IDIOMS – **never darken someone's door** keep away from someone's home.

darkie (also **darky**) > *noun* (pl. **darkies**) informal, offensive a black person.

darkling > *adjective* literary **1** characterised by darkness. **2** growing darker.

darling > *noun* **1** used as an affectionate form of address. **2** an endearing person. **3** a person popular with a particular group: *he is the darling of Labour's left wing.* > *adjective* **1** beloved. **2** pretty; charming.

ORIGIN – Old English, related to DEAR.

darn¹ > *verb* mend (knitted material) by interweaving yarn across it.

DERIVATIVES – **darning** *noun*.

COMBINATIONS – **darning needle** a long sewing needle with a large eye, used in darning.

darn² > *verb, adjective, & exclamation* informal euphemism for DAMN.

darned > *adjective* informal euphemism for DAMNED.

dart > *noun* **1** a small pointed missile thrown or fired as a weapon. **2** a small pointed missile with a flight, used in the game of darts. **3** (**darts**) (usu. treated as sing.) an indoor game in which darts are thrown at a dartboard. **4** a sudden rapid movement. **5** a tapered tuck in a garment. > *verb* move suddenly or rapidly.

SYNONYMS – *verb* dash, rush, shoot.

COMBINATIONS – **dartboard** a circular board used as a target in the game of darts.

ORIGIN – Old French, from a Germanic word meaning 'spear, lance'.

Darwinism > *noun* the theory of the evolution of species by natural selection, advanced by the English natural historian Charles Darwin (1809–82).

DERIVATIVES – **Darwinian** *noun & adjective* **Darwinist** *noun & adjective*.

dash > *verb* **1** run or travel in a great hurry. **2** strike or throw with great force. **3** destroy or frustrate (hopes). **4** (**dash off**) write hurriedly. > *exclamation* Brit. informal used to express mild annoyance. > *noun* **1** an act of dashing. **2** chiefly N. Amer. a sprint. **3** a small amount of something added. **4** a horizontal stroke in writing, marking a pause or omission. **5** the longer of the signals used in Morse code. **6** impressive style; flair.

SYNONYMS – *verb* **1** hare, race, rush, zoom. **2** crash, lash, slam, smash. **3** destroy, frustrate, shatter. *noun* **3** pinch, soupçon, touch, trace.

dashboard > *noun* **1** the panel of instruments and controls facing the driver of a vehicle. **2** historical a board of wood or leather in front of a carriage, to keep out mud.

dashed > *adjective* Brit. informal, dated used for emphasis: *it's a dashed shame.*

dashiki /daashiki/ > *noun* (pl. **dashikis**) a loose, brightly coloured shirt, originally from West Africa.

ORIGIN – Yoruba or Hausa (a West African language).

dashing > *adjective* excitingly attractive and stylish.

DERIVATIVES – **dashingly** *adverb*.

dastardly > *adjective* dated or humorous wicked and cruel.

ORIGIN – from *dastard* 'despicable person', probably from *dazed* and influenced by *dotard* and *bastard*.

DAT > *abbreviation* digital audiotape.

data /daytə/ > *noun* **1** facts and statistics used for reference or analysis. **2** the quantities, characters, or symbols on which operations are performed by a computer.

USAGE – traditionally and in technical use **data** is treated as a plural, as in Latin it is the plural of **datum**. In modern non-scientific use, however, it is often treated as a singular, and sentences such as *data was collected over a number of years* are now acceptable.

COMBINATIONS – **databank** Computing a large store of data. **data capture** Computing the action of gathering data from an automatic device, control system, or sensor. **data protection** Brit. legal control over access to data stored in computers.

ORIGIN – Latin, plural of DATUM.

database > *noun* a structured set of data held in a computer.

datable (also **dateable**) > *adjective* able to be dated to a particular time.

datcha > *noun* variant spelling of DACHA.

date¹ > *noun* **1** the day of the month or year as specified by a number. **2** a day or year when a given event occurred or will occur. **3** informal a social or romantic appointment.

4 a musical or theatrical performance, especially as part of a tour. > *verb* **1** establish or ascertain the date of. **2** mark with a date. **3** (**date back to**) start or originate at (a particular time in the past). **4** informal, chiefly N. Amer. go on a date or regular dates with.

IDIOMS – **to date** until now.

COMBINATIONS – **dating agency** a service which arranges introductions for people seeking romantic partners or friends.

ORIGIN – Latin *data*, from *dare* 'give'; from the formula used in dating letters, *data epistola* 'letter given or delivered'.

date² > *noun* the sweet, dark brown, oval fruit of a North African and West Asian palm tree, containing a hard stone and usually eaten dried.

ORIGIN – from Greek *daktulos* 'finger' (because of the finger-like leaves of the tree).

dateable > *adjective* variant spelling of DATABLE.

dated > *adjective* appearing old-fashioned.

SYNONYMS – old-fashioned, outdated, outmoded, passé.

date stamp > *noun* **1** a stamped mark indicating a date. **2** an adjustable stamp used to make such a mark. > *verb* (**date-stamp**) mark with a date stamp.

dative /daytiv/ Grammar > *adjective* (in Latin, Greek, German, etc.) denoting a case of nouns and pronouns indicating an indirect object or recipient. > *noun* a dative noun, pronoun, etc.

ORIGIN – from Latin *casus dativus* 'case of giving', from *dare* 'give'.

datum /daytəm/ > *noun* (pl. **data**) **1** a piece of information. **2** an assumption or premise from which inferences may be drawn. **3** a fixed starting point of a scale or operation.

ORIGIN – Latin, 'something given'.

datura /dətyoorə/ > *noun* a shrubby North American plant of a genus including the thorn apple.

ORIGIN – Hindi.

daub /dawb/ > *verb* **1** coat or smear carelessly or liberally with a thick substance. **2** spread (a thick substance) on a surface in such a way. > *noun* **1** plaster, clay, etc., especially when mixed with straw and applied to laths or wattles to form a wall. **2** a patch or smear of a thick substance. **3** a painting executed without much skill.

DERIVATIVES – **dauber** *noun*.

ORIGIN – Old French *dauber*, from Latin *dealbare* 'whiten, whitewash', from *albus* 'white'.

daube /dōb/ > *noun* a stew of meat, typically beef, braised in wine.

ORIGIN – French.

daughter > *noun* **1** a girl or woman in relation to her parents. **2** a female descendant.

WORDFINDER – filial (*relating to a daughter*), filicide (*murder of one's own daughter*).

DERIVATIVES – **daughterhood** *noun* **daughterly** *adjective*.

COMBINATIONS – **daughter-in-law** (pl. **daughters-in-law**) the wife of one's son.

daunt /dawnt/ > *verb* (usu. **be daunted**) cause to feel intimidated or apprehensive.

DERIVATIVES – **daunting** *adjective* **dauntingly** *adverb*.

ORIGIN – Old French *danter*, from Latin *domitare*, from *domare* 'to tame'.

dauntless > *adjective* fearless and determined.

DERIVATIVES – **dauntlessly** *adverb* **dauntlessness** *noun*.

dauphin /dōfaN/ > *noun* historical the eldest son of the king of France.

ORIGIN – French, from the family name of the lords of the province of Dauphiné, ultimately a nickname meaning 'dolphin'.

daven /daavən/ > *verb* (**davened**, **davening**) (in Judaism) pray.

ORIGIN – Yiddish.

davenport /davv'nport/ > *noun* **1** Brit. an ornamental writing desk with drawers and a sloping surface for writing. **2** N. Amer. a large upholstered sofa.

ORIGIN – sense 1 is named after a Captain *Davenport*, for whom a desk of this type was made in the late 18th century; sense 2 is probably named after a manufacturer.

davit /davvit, dāyvit/ > *noun* a small crane on a ship, especially one of a pair for lowering a lifeboat.

ORIGIN – Old French *daviot*, from *david*, denoting a kind of carpenter's tool.

Davy Jones's locker > *noun* informal the bottom of the sea, especially regarded as the grave of those who drown.

ORIGIN – from 18th-century nautical slang *Davy Jones*, denoting the evil spirit of the sea.

Davy lamp > *noun* historical a miner's portable safety lamp with the flame enclosed by wire gauze to reduce the risk of a gas explosion.

ORIGIN – named after the English chemist Sir Humphry *Davy* (1778–1829), who invented it.

dawdle > *verb* move slowly; take one's time.

DERIVATIVES – **dawdler** *noun*.

SYNONYMS – dally, delay, lag, linger.

dawn > *noun* **1** the first appearance of light in the sky in the morning. **2** the beginning of something. > *verb* **1** (of a day) begin. **2** come into existence. **3** (**dawn on**) become evident to.

COMBINATIONS – **dawn chorus** the early-morning singing of birds.

day > *noun* **1** a period of twenty-four hours as a unit of time, reckoned from midnight to midnight and corresponding to a rotation

of the earth on its axis. **2** the time between sunrise and sunset. **3** (usu. **days**) a particular period of the past. **4** (**the day**) the present time or the time in question. **5** (**one's day**) the youthful or successful period of one's life. **6** (before another noun) working or done during the day: *my day job*.

IDIOMS – **any day** informal **1** at any time. **2** under any circumstances. **call it a day** decide to stop doing something. **day by day** gradually and steadily. **day in, day out** continuously or repeatedly over a long period. **one day** (or **some day** or **one of these days**) at some time in the future. **one of those days** a day when things go badly. **that will be the day** informal that is very unlikely. **these days** at present.

COMBINATIONS – **daybed 1** a couch for daytime rest. **2** N. Amer. a couch that can be made into a bed. **day boy** (or **day girl**) Brit. a boy (or girl) who lives at home and attends a school that also takes boarders. **day centre** (also **day-care centre**) a place providing daytime care and recreation facilities for those who cannot be fully independent. **day lily** a lily which bears large yellow, red, or orange flowers, each lasting only one day. **day off** (pl. **days off**) a day's holiday from work or school. **Day of Judgement** the time of the Last Judgement. **day out** (pl. **days out**) Brit. a trip or excursion for a day. **daypack** chiefly N. Amer. a small rucksack. **day release** Brit. a system in which employees are granted days off work to go on educational courses. **day return** Brit. a ticket at a reduced rate for a return journey on public transport within one day. **day room** a communal room in an institution, used during the day. **day school 1** a non-residential school. **2** a short educational course. **day surgery** minor surgery that does not require an overnight stay in hospital. **daytime 1** the time between sunrise and sunset. **2** the period of time corresponding to normal working hours. **day-to-day 1** happening regularly every day. **2** of a routine nature; ordinary.

Dayak /dīak/ (also **Dyak**) > *noun* (pl. same or **Dayaks**) a member of a group of indigenous peoples inhabiting parts of Borneo.

ORIGIN – Malay, 'up-country'.

daybreak > *noun* dawn.

daydream > *noun* a series of pleasant thoughts that distract one's attention from the present. > *verb* indulge in a daydream.

DERIVATIVES – **daydreamer** *noun*.

Day-Glo > *noun* trademark a fluorescent paint or other colouring.

daylight > *noun* **1** the natural light of the day. **2** dawn. **3** visible distance between one person or thing and another.

IDIOMS – **beat** (or **scare** etc.) **the** (**living**) **daylights out of** informal beat, scare, etc.

very severely. **see daylight** begin to understand something.

COMBINATIONS – **daylight robbery** Brit. informal blatant and unfair overcharging.

day trip > *noun* a journey or excursion completed in one day.

DERIVATIVES – **day tripper** *noun*.

daze > *verb* cause (someone) to feel stunned or bewildered. > *noun* a state of stunned confusion or bewilderment.

DERIVATIVES – **dazed** *adjective* **dazedly** *adverb*.

SYNONYMS – *verb* bewilder, stun, stupefy. *noun* haze, spin, stupor.

ORIGIN – Old Norse *dasathr* 'weary'.

dazzle > *verb* **1** (of a bright light) blind (someone) temporarily. **2** overwhelm with an impressive quality. > *noun* blinding brightness.

DERIVATIVES – **dazzlement** *noun* **dazzler** *noun* **dazzling** *adjective* **dazzlingly** *adverb*.

ORIGIN – from **DAZE**.

Db > *symbol* the chemical element dubnium.

dB > *abbreviation* decibel(s).

DBE > *abbreviation* (in the UK) Dame Commander of the Order of the British Empire.

DBS > *abbreviation* **1** direct broadcasting by satellite. **2** direct-broadcast satellite.

DC > *abbreviation* **1** direct current. **2** District of Columbia.

DCB > *abbreviation* (in the UK) Dame Commander of the Order of the Bath.

DCC > *abbreviation* digital compact cassette.

DCM > *abbreviation* (in the UK) Distinguished Conduct Medal.

DCMG > *abbreviation* (in the UK) Dame Commander of the Order of St Michael and St George.

DCVO > *abbreviation* (in the UK) Dame Commander of the Royal Victorian Order.

DD > *abbreviation* Doctor of Divinity.

D-Day > *noun* **1** the day (6 June 1944) in the Second World War on which Allied forces invaded northern France. **2** the day on which something important is to begin.

ORIGIN – from *D* for *day* + **DAY**.

DDI > *abbreviation* dideoxyinosine.

DDR > *abbreviation* historical German Democratic Republic.

ORIGIN – abbreviation of German *Deutsche Demokratische Republik*.

DDT > *abbreviation* dichlorodiphenyl-trichloroethane, a synthetic organic compound used as an insecticide but now banned in many countries.

DE > *abbreviation* **1** Delaware. **2** (in the UK) Department of Employment.

de- > *prefix* **1** (forming verbs and their derivatives) down; away: *deduct*. **2** (forming verbs and their derivatives) completely: *denude*. **3** (added to verbs and their derivatives) denoting removal or reversal: *de-ice*.

ORIGIN – from Latin *de* 'off, from' or *dis-*, expressing reversal.

deacon /deek'n/ > *noun* **1** (in Catholic, Anglican, and Orthodox Churches) an ordained minister of an order ranking below that of priest. **2** (in some Protestant Churches) a lay officer assisting a minister. > *verb* appoint or ordain as a deacon.

DERIVATIVES – **deaconship** *noun*.

ORIGIN – Greek *diakonos* 'servant'.

deaconess > *noun* a woman with duties similar to those of a deacon.

deactivate > *verb* make (equipment or a virus) inactive by disconnecting or destroying it.

DERIVATIVES – **deactivation** *noun* **deactivator** *noun*.

dead > *adjective* **1** no longer alive. **2** devoid of living things. **3** (of a part of the body) numb. **4** displaying no emotion. **5** no longer relevant or important. **6** lacking activity or excitement. **7** (of equipment) not functioning. **8** complete; absolute: *dead silence*. > *adverb* **1** absolutely. **2** exactly. **3** straight; directly. **4** Brit. informal very.

IDIOMS – **dead and buried** over; finished. **the dead of night** the quietest, darkest part of the night. **the dead of winter** the coldest part of winter. **dead on one's feet** informal extremely tired. **dead to the world** informal fast asleep. **from the dead** from being dead; from death.

DERIVATIVES – **deadness** *noun*.

SYNONYMS – *adjective* **1** deceased, departed, expired, late, lifeless.

ANTONYMS – *adjective* **1** alive.

COMBINATIONS – **deadbolt** a bolt engaged by turning a knob or key, rather than by spring action. **dead centre 1** the position of a crank when it is in line with the connecting rod and not exerting torque. **2** exactly in the centre. **dead duck** informal an unsuccessful or useless person or thing. [ORIGIN – from the old saying 'never waste powder on a dead duck'.] **dead end** an end of a road or passage from which no exit is possible. **dead hand** an undesirable persisting influence. **dead heat** a race in which two or more competitors are exactly level. **dead letter 1** a law or treaty which has not been repealed but is defunct in practice. **2** a letter that has not been delivered or claimed. **dead loss** an unproductive or useless venture, person, or thing. **dead reckoning** the process of calculating one's position, especially at sea, by estimating the direction and distance travelled. **dead ringer** a person or thing closely resembling another. **dead set 1** firm in one's determination. **2** see SET² (sense 10). **dead wood** useless or unproductive people or things.

deadbeat > *adjective* (**dead beat**) informal completely exhausted. > *noun* informal **1** an idle or feckless person. **2** N. Amer. a person who tries to evade paying debts.

deaden > *verb* **1** reduce the strength or intensity of (a noise or sensation). **2** cause to be insensitive. **3** deprive of force or vitality.

DERIVATIVES – **deadener** *noun*.

deadhead chiefly Brit. > *noun* a faded flower head. > *verb* remove dead flower heads from (a plant).

deadline > *noun* the latest time or date by which something should be completed.

deadlock > *noun* **1** a situation in which no progress can be made. **2** Brit. a lock operated by a key, as distinct from a spring lock. > *verb* **1** cause to come to a deadlock. **2** Brit. secure with a deadlock.

deadly > *adjective* (**deadlier, deadliest**) **1** causing or able to cause death. **2** (of a voice, glance, etc.) filled with hate. **3** extremely accurate or effective. **4** informal extremely boring. > *adverb* **1** in a way that resembles or suggests death. **2** extremely: *she was deadly serious*.

DERIVATIVES – **deadliness** *noun*.

SYNONYMS – *adjective* **1** fatal, lethal, life-threatening, mortal, terminal.

COMBINATIONS – **deadly nightshade** a poisonous bushy plant with drooping purple flowers and black cherry-like fruit. **deadly sin** (in Christian tradition) a sin regarded as leading to damnation.

dead-nettle > *noun* a plant of the mint family, with leaves that resemble those of a nettle without stinging hairs.

deadpan > *adjective* deliberately impassive or expressionless.

deadweight > *noun* **1** the weight of an inert person or thing. **2** the total weight of cargo, stores, etc. which a ship can carry.

deaf > *adjective* **1** without the faculty of hearing, or having impaired hearing. **2** (**deaf to**) unwilling to listen or respond to.

IDIOMS – **fall on deaf ears** be ignored. **turn a deaf ear** refuse to listen or respond.

DERIVATIVES – **deafness** *noun*.

COMBINATIONS – **deaf aid** Brit. a hearing aid. **deaf-blind** having severely impaired hearing and vision.

deafen > *verb* **1** cause to become deaf. **2** (**deafening**) extremely loud.

DERIVATIVES – **deafeningly** *adverb*.

deaf mute > *noun* a person who is deaf and unable to speak.

USAGE – avoid **deaf mute**, as it has acquired offensive connotations; use a term such as **profoundly deaf**.

deal¹ > *verb* (past and past participle **dealt**) **1** distribute (cards) to players for a game or round. **2** (**deal out**) distribute or apportion.

3 take part in commercial trading of a commodity. **4** informal buy and sell illegal drugs. **5** (**deal with**) have commercial relations with. **6** (**deal with**) take measures concerning. **7** (**deal with**) cope with. **8** (**deal with**) have as a subject. **9** inflict (a blow) on. > *noun* **1** an agreement between two or more parties for their mutual benefit. **2** the process of dealing cards in a card game.

IDIOMS – **a big deal** informal **1** an important thing. **2** (**big deal**) used ironically to express contempt for something regarded as unimpressive. **it's a deal** informal used to express assent to an agreement. **a deal of** a large amount of. **a good** (or **great**) **deal 1** a large amount. **2** to a considerable extent: *a good deal better*. **a raw deal** informal unfair treatment. **a square deal** a fair bargain or treatment.

SYNONYMS – *verb* **2** (**deal out**) allot, apportion, dispense, distribute, dole out. **7** (**deal with**) cope with, handle, manage. **8** (**deal with**) consider, cover, discuss, explore, tackle. *noun* **1** agreement, arrangement, settlement, understanding.

deal² > *noun* fir or pine wood as a building material.

ORIGIN – Low German and Dutch *dele* 'plank'.

dealer > *noun* **1** a person who buys and sells goods. **2** a person who buys and sells shares or other financial assets as a principal (rather than as a broker or agent). **3** a player who deals cards in a card game.

DERIVATIVES – **dealership** *noun*.

dean > *noun* **1** the head of a cathedral chapter. **2** the head of a university faculty or department of a medical school. **3** a college officer with a disciplinary role.

WORDFINDER – decanal (*relating to a dean or deanery*).

DERIVATIVES – **deanery** *noun*.

ORIGIN – first used in the sense 'head of a division of ten (monks etc.)': from Old French *deien*, from Latin *decanus* 'chief of a group of ten'.

dear > *adjective* **1** regarded with deep affection. **2** used in the polite introduction to a letter. **3** costly; expensive. > *noun* **1** an endearing person. **2** used as an affectionate form of address. > *adverb* at a high cost. > *exclamation* used in expressions of surprise or dismay.

DERIVATIVES – **dearness** *noun*.

SYNONYMS – *adjective* **1** adored, beloved, esteemed, loved.

dearest > *adjective* **1** most loved or cherished. **2** most expensive. > *noun* used as an affectionate form of address.

Dear John letter > *noun* informal a letter from a woman to a man, ending a personal relationship.

dearly > *adverb* **1** very much. **2** at great cost.

dearth /derth/ > *noun* a scarcity or lack.

death > *noun* **1** the action or fact of dying. **2** an instance of a person or an animal dying. **3** the state of being dead. **4** the end of something.

WORDFINDER – autopsy (*examination of a corpse to discover cause of death*), in extremis (*at the point of death*), inquest (*inquiry into the cause of a death*), memento mori (*object kept as a reminder of death*), post-mortem (*examination of a corpse to discover cause of death*), rigor mortis (*stiffening of joints and muscles after death*), thanatology (*scientific study of death*).

IDIOMS – **at death's door** so ill that one may die. **catch one's death (of cold)** informal catch a severe cold. **die a death** fail utterly or come to an end. **do to death** repeat to the point of tedium. **like death warmed up** informal extremely tired or ill. **put to death** execute. **to death 1** until dead. **2** used to emphasise the extreme nature of a feeling or action.

DERIVATIVES – **deathless** *adjective*.

SYNONYMS – **1,2** demise, dying, end, passing away.

COMBINATIONS – **death camp** a prison camp in which many people die or are put to death. **death cap** a deadly poisonous toadstool with a pale olive-green cap and white gills. **death cell** a cell occupied by a prisoner condemned to death. **death certificate** an official statement, signed by a doctor, detailing a person's death. **death duty** former name for **inheritance tax**. **death knell 1** the tolling of a bell to mark a death. **2** an event that signals the end of something. **death mask** a plaster cast of a person's face, made just after their death. **death penalty** punishment by execution. **death rate** the number of deaths per one thousand people per year. **death rattle** a gurgling sound in a dying person's throat. **death row** a prison block for those sentenced to death. **death toll** the number of deaths resulting from a particular cause. **death trap** a dangerous building, vehicle, etc. **death wish** an unconscious desire for one's own death.

deathbed > *noun* the bed where someone is dying or has died.

deathly > *adjective* (**deathlier**, **deathliest**) resembling or suggestive of death.

death-watch beetle > *noun* a small beetle whose larvae bore into and damage dead wood and structural timbers, making a sound like a watch ticking which was formerly believed to be an omen of death.

deb > *noun* informal a debutante.

debacle /day**baa**k'l/ > *noun* an utter failure or disaster.

SYNONYMS – disaster, failure, fiasco.

ORIGIN – French, from *débâcler* 'unleash'.

debag /dee**bag**/ > *verb* (**debagged**, **debagging**) Brit. informal remove the trousers of (someone) as a joke or punishment.

debar > *verb* (**debarred**, **debarring**) exclude or prohibit.

DERIVATIVES – **debarment** *noun*.

ORIGIN – French *débarrer*, from Old French *desbarrer* 'remove the bars from'.

debark > *verb* leave a ship or aircraft.

ORIGIN – French *débarquer*.

debase /di**bayss**/ > *verb* lower the quality, value, or character of.

DERIVATIVES – **debasement** *noun*.

SYNONYMS – degrade, demean, devalue.

debatable > *adjective* open to discussion or argument.

DERIVATIVES – **debatably** *adverb*.

debate > *noun* **1** a formal public discussion. **2** an argument or controversy involving many people. > *verb* **1** discuss or argue about. **2** consider; ponder.

IDIOMS – **under debate** being discussed.

DERIVATIVES – **debater** *noun*.

SYNONYMS – *verb* **1** discuss, dispute, thrash out.

ORIGIN – Old French, from Latin *battere* 'to fight'.

debauch /di**bawch**/ > *verb* corrupt morally. > *noun* a bout of excessive indulgence in sensual pleasures.

ORIGIN – French *débaucher* 'turn away from one's duty'.

debauched > *adjective* indulging in sensual pleasures to an excessive degree.

SYNONYMS – degenerate, depraved, dissipated, dissolute, licentious, rakish.

debauchee /dibbaw**chee**/ > *noun* a debauched person.

debauchery > *noun* excessive indulgence in sensual pleasures.

SYNONYMS – depravity, dissipation, dissoluteness, libertinism, licentiousness.

debenture /di**ben**chər/ > *noun* Brit. a bond issued by a company, acknowledging a debt and yielding a fixed rate of interest.

ORIGIN – Latin *debentur* 'are owing', used as the first word of a certificate recording a debt, from *debere* 'owe'.

debilitate /di**bill**itayt/ > *verb* severely weaken.

DERIVATIVES – **debilitation** *noun*.

SYNONYMS – devitalise, enfeeble, fatigue, weaken.

ORIGIN – Latin *debilitare*, from *debilis* 'weak'.

debility > *noun* physical weakness.

debit > *noun* **1** an entry in an account recording a sum owed or paid. **2** a payment made or owed. > *verb* (**debited**, **debiting**) (of a bank) remove (money) from a customer's account.

COMBINATIONS – **debit card** a card allowing the holder to debit a bank account electronically when making a purchase.

ORIGIN – French, from Latin *debitum* 'something owed'.

debonair > *adjective* (of a man) confident, stylish, and charming.

SYNONYMS – stylish, suave, urbane.

ORIGIN – from Old French *de bon aire* 'of good disposition'.

debouch /di**bowch**, di**boosh**/ > *verb* emerge from a confined space into an open area.

DERIVATIVES – **debouchment** *noun*.

ORIGIN – French *déboucher*, from *bouche* 'mouth'.

debrief > *verb* question (someone) in detail about a completed mission.

DERIVATIVES – **debriefing** *noun*.

debris /**deb**ree, **day**bree/ > *noun* **1** scattered items or pieces of rubbish. **2** loose broken pieces of rock.

SYNONYMS – **1** detritus, remnants, rubble, wreckage.

ORIGIN – French, from *débriser* 'break down'.

debt > *noun* **1** money or services owed or due. **2** the state of owing money. **3** a feeling of gratitude for a favour or service.

IDIOMS – **be in someone's debt** owe gratitude to someone for a favour. **debt of honour** a debt dependent on a moral but not a legal obligation.

ORIGIN – Latin *debitum* 'something owed', from *debere* 'owe'.

debtor > *noun* a person who owes money.

debug > *verb* (**debugged**, **debugging**) remove errors from (computer hardware or software).

DERIVATIVES – **debugger** *noun*.

debunk > *verb* **1** discredit (a widely held opinion). **2** reduce the inflated reputation of.

DERIVATIVES – **debunker** *noun*.

deburr /dee**bur**/ (also **debur**) > *verb* (**deburred**, **deburring**) smooth the rough edges of.

debut /**day**byoo/ > *noun* **1** a person's first appearance in a capacity or role. **2** (before another noun) denoting the first recording or publication of a singer or writer. > *verb* make a debut.

ORIGIN – French, from *débuter* 'lead off'.

debutant /**deb**yootant/ > *noun* a person making a debut.

debutante /**deb**yootaant/ > *noun* a young upper-class woman making her first official appearance in society.

Dec. > *abbreviation* December.

deca- /**dekk**ə/ (also **dec-** before a vowel) > *combining form* ten; having ten.

ORIGIN – from Greek *deka* 'ten'.

decade /**dekk**ayd/ > *noun* a period of ten years.

NOTE – some traditionalists dislike the

alternative pronunciation with the stress on **-cade** (sounds like *decayed*).

ORIGIN – Old French, from Greek *deka* 'ten'.

decadent > *adjective* **1** characterised by moral or cultural decline. **2** luxuriously self-indulgent.

DERIVATIVES – **decadence** *noun* **decadently** *adverb*.

SYNONYMS – **1** corrupt, debauched, degenerate, dissolute. **2** hedonistic, sybaritic.

ORIGIN – French *décadent*, from Latin *decadentia*; related to DECAY.

decaf > *noun* informal (trademark in the UK) decaffeinated coffee.

decaffeinated /dee**kaff**inaytid/ > *adjective* (of tea or coffee) having had most or all of its caffeine removed.

decagon /**dekk**əgən/ > *noun* a plane figure with ten straight sides and angles.

decahedron /dekkə**hee**drən/ > *noun* (pl. **decahedra** or **decahedrons**) a solid figure with ten plane faces.

decal /**dee**kal/ > *noun* a design on prepared paper for transferring on to glass, porcelain, etc.

ORIGIN – abbreviation of *decalcomania* 'transfer of decals', from French *décalquer* 'transfer a tracing' + *-manie* '-mania'.

decalcified > *adjective* (of rock or bone) containing a reduced quantity of calcium salts.

DERIVATIVES – **decalcification** *noun*.

decalitre (US **decaliter, dekaliter**) > *noun* a metric unit of capacity, equal to 10 litres.

Decalogue /**dekk**əlog/ > *noun* the Ten Commandments.

ORIGIN – from Greek *dekalogos biblos* 'book of the Ten Commandments'.

decametre (US **decameter, dekameter**) > *noun* a metric unit of length, equal to 10 metres.

decamp > *verb* depart suddenly or secretly.

decanal /di**kayn**'l, **dekk**ən'l/ > *adjective* relating to a dean or deanery.

ORIGIN – Latin *decanalis*, from *decanus* (see DEAN).

decant /di**kant**/ > *verb* **1** pour from one container into another to separate liquid from sediment. **2** informal transfer (passengers) to another place.

ORIGIN – Latin *decanthare*, from *de-* 'away from' + *canthus* 'edge, rim'.

decanter > *noun* a stoppered glass container into which wine or spirit is decanted.

decapitate /di**kapp**itayt/ > *verb* cut off the head of.

DERIVATIVES – **decapitation** *noun*.

ORIGIN – Latin *decapitare*, from *caput* 'head'.

decapod /**dekk**əpod/ > *noun* a crustacean with five pairs of walking legs, such as a shrimp.

ORIGIN – from Greek *deka* 'ten' + *pous* 'foot'.

decarbonise (also **decarbonize**) > *verb* remove carbon deposits from (an engine).

decathlon /di**kath**lən/ > *noun* an athletic event in which each competitor takes part in the same ten events: 100 metres sprint, long jump, shot-put, high jump, 400 metres, 110 metres hurdles, discus, pole vault, javelin, and 1,500 metres.

DERIVATIVES – **decathlete** *noun*.

ORIGIN – from Greek *deka* 'ten' + *athlon* 'contest'.

decay > *verb* **1** rot through the action of bacteria and fungi. **2** decline in quality or vigour. **3** Physics (of a radioactive substance, particle, etc.) undergo change to a different form by emitting radiation. > *noun* **1** the state or process of decaying. **2** rotten matter or tissue.

SYNONYMS – *verb* **1** decompose, moulder, putrefy, rot. **2** decline, degenerate, deteriorate, go downhill. *noun* **1** decomposition, putrefaction, rot.

ORIGIN – Old French *decair*, from Latin *decidere* 'fall down or off'.

decease > *noun* formal or Law death. > *verb* archaic die.

ORIGIN – Latin *decessus* 'death', from *decedere* 'to die'.

deceased formal or Law > *noun* (**the deceased**) the recently dead person in question. > *adjective* recently dead.

deceit > *noun* **1** the action or practice of deceiving. **2** a deceitful act or statement.

SYNONYMS – **1** deceitfulness, deception, double-dealing, duplicity, trickery.

deceitful > *adjective* acting to deceive others.

DERIVATIVES – **deceitfully** *adverb* **deceitfulness** *noun*.

SYNONYMS – dishonest, double-dealing, duplicitous, fraudulent; literary perfidious.

deceive* > *verb* **1** deliberately mislead. **2** (of a thing) give a mistaken impression.

DERIVATIVES – **deceiver** *noun*.

***SPELLING** – *i* before *e* except after *c*: deceive.

SYNONYMS – **1** delude, dupe, fool, hoodwink, mislead.

ORIGIN – Old French *deceivre*, from Latin *decipere* 'ensnare, cheat'.

decelerate /dee**sell**ərayt/ > *verb* begin to move more slowly.

DERIVATIVES – **deceleration** *noun*.

December > *noun* the twelfth month of the year.

ORIGIN – Latin, from *decem* 'ten' (being originally the tenth month of the Roman year).

decency > *noun* (pl. **decencies**) **1** decent behaviour. **2** (**decencies**) standards of propriety.

decennial /di**senn**iəl/ > *adjective* lasting for or recurring every ten years.

decent > *adjective* **1** conforming with generally accepted standards of morality or respectability. **2** of an acceptable standard. **3** Brit. informal kind or generous.

DERIVATIVES – **decently** *adverb*.

SYNONYMS – **1** honourable, proper, respectable, seemly. **2** adequate, reasonable, satisfactory.

ORIGIN – from Latin *decere* 'to be fit'.

decentralise (also **decentralize**) > *verb* transfer (authority) from central to local government.

DERIVATIVES – **decentralisation** *noun* **decentralist** *noun* & *adjective*.

deception > *noun* **1** the action of deceiving. **2** a thing that deceives.

SYNONYMS – **1** deceit, duplicity, fraud, trickery. **2** fraud, hoax, ruse, trick.

deceptive > *adjective* giving an impression different from the true one.

SYNONYMS – deceiving, delusive, illusory, misleading.

deceptively > *adverb* **1** to a lesser extent than appears the case. **2** to a greater extent than appears the case.

USAGE – beware of confusion when using **deceptively**, as it can mean both one thing and also its complete opposite. A *deceptively smooth surface* is one which appears smooth but in fact is not smooth at all, while a *deceptively spacious room* is one that does not look spacious but is in fact more spacious than it appears.

deci- > *combining form* one tenth.

decibel /**dess**ibel/ > *noun* a unit of measurement expressing the relative intensity of a sound or the power of an electrical signal.

ORIGIN – from DECI- + *bel*, a unit (= 10 decibels) named after Alexander Graham *Bell* (1847–1922), inventor of the telephone.

decide > *verb* **1** resolve in the mind as a result of consideration. **2** settle (an issue or contest). **3** give a judgement concerning a matter or legal case.

DERIVATIVES – **decidable** *adjective* **deciding** *adjective*.

SYNONYMS – **1** choose, conclude, determine, elect, opt. **2** determine, resolve, settle.

ORIGIN – Latin *decidere* 'determine', from *caedere* 'cut'.

decided > *adjective* definite; clear.

DERIVATIVES – **decidedly** *adverb*.

decider > *noun* a contest that settles the winner of a series of contests.

deciduous /di**sid**yooəss/ > *adjective* **1** (of a tree or shrub) shedding its leaves annually. Contrasted with EVERGREEN. **2** (of teeth or horns) shed after a time.

ORIGIN – Latin *deciduus*, from *decidere* 'fall down or off'.

decilitre (US **deciliter**) > *noun* a metric unit of capacity, equal to one tenth of a litre.

decimal > *adjective* relating to or denoting a system of numbers based on the number ten. > *noun* a fraction, whose denominator is a power of ten, expressed by numbers placed to the right of a decimal point.

DERIVATIVES – **decimalise** (also **decimalize**) *verb* **decimally** *adverb*.

COMBINATIONS – **decimal place** the position of a digit to the right of a decimal point. **decimal point** a full stop placed after the figure representing units in a decimal fraction.

ORIGIN – from Latin *decimus* 'tenth'.

decimate /**dess**imayt/ > *verb* **1** kill or destroy a large proportion of. **2** drastically reduce the strength of.

DERIVATIVES – **decimation** *noun*.

USAGE – the earliest sense of **decimate** was 'kill one in every ten of', a reference to the ancient Roman practice of killing one in every ten of a group of soldiers as a collective punishment. This has been more or less totally superseded by the sense 'kill or destroy a large proportion of', although some traditionalists argue that this later sense is incorrect.

decimetre (US **decimeter**) > *noun* a metric unit of length, one tenth of a metre.

decipher /di**sī**fər/ > *verb* **1** convert from code into normal language. **2** succeed in understanding (something hard to interpret).

DERIVATIVES – **decipherable** *adjective* **decipherment** *noun*.

decision > *noun* **1** a conclusion or resolution reached after consideration. **2** the action or process of deciding. **3** the quality of being decisive.

SYNONYMS – **1** conclusion, finding, judgement, resolution, ruling.

decisive > *adjective* **1** settling an issue quickly. **2** able to make decisions quickly.

DERIVATIVES – **decisively** *adverb* **decisiveness** *noun*.

SYNONYMS – **1** conclusive, deciding, definitive, determining. **2** confident, definite, firm, resolute, unhesitating.

ANTONYMS – indecisive.

deck > *noun* **1** a floor of a ship, especially the upper level. **2** a floor or platform, as in a bus or car park. **3** chiefly N. Amer. a pack of cards. **4** a component in sound-reproduction equipment, incorporating a player or recorder for discs or tapes. > *verb* **1** decorate brightly or festively. **2** informal knock to the ground with a punch.

IDIOMS – **hit the deck** informal fall to the ground.

DERIVATIVES – **decked** *adjective*.

COMBINATIONS – **deckchair** a folding chair with a wooden frame and a canvas seat. **deckhand** a member of a ship's crew performing cleaning or manual work.

wordpower facts

Deck

The word **deck** comes from the Dutch words *dec* 'covering, roof, cloak' and *dekken* 'to cover' (which is related to English **thatch**). In English it originally referred to canvas used to make a covering, especially on a ship; the term came to mean the covering itself and eventually denoted a solid surface serving as roof and floor. The sense 'pack of cards' seems to have been used first by Shakespeare.

decking > *noun* material used in making a deck.

deckle /**dekk**'l/ > *noun* a continuous belt on either side in a papermaking machine, used for controlling the size of paper produced.

COMBINATIONS – **deckle edge** the rough uncut edge of a sheet of paper.

ORIGIN – German *Deckel*, 'small covering'.

declaim > *verb* speak or recite in an emphatic or dramatic way.

DERIVATIVES – **declamatory** *adjective*.

ORIGIN – Latin *declamare*, from *clamare* 'to shout'.

declamation > *noun* the action or art of declaiming.

declaration > *noun* **1** a formal statement or announcement. **2** an act of declaring.

SYNONYMS – **1** announcement, edict, proclamation, pronouncement.

declarative /di**klarr**ətiv/ > *adjective* **1** of the nature of a declaration. **2** (of a sentence or phrase) taking the form of a simple statement.

declare > *verb* **1** announce solemnly or officially. **2** formally announce the beginning of (a state or condition). **3** (**declare oneself**) reveal one's intentions or identity. **4** acknowledge possession of (income or goods on which tax or duty should be paid). **5** Cricket close an innings voluntarily with wickets remaining. **6** (**declared**) having admitted that one is the specified thing: *a declared atheist.*

DERIVATIVES – **declaratory** *adjective* **declaredly** *adverb* **declarer** *noun*.

SYNONYMS – **1** announce, proclaim, pronounce, report.

ORIGIN – Latin *declarare*, from *clarare* 'make clear'.

déclassé /day**klass**ay/ (also **déclassée**) > *adjective* having fallen in social status.

ORIGIN – French.

declassify > *verb* (**declassifies, declassified**) officially declare (information or documents) to be no longer secret.

DERIVATIVES – **declassification** *noun*.

declension /di**klen**sh'n/ > *noun* **1** the variation of the form of a noun, pronoun, or adjective that identifies its grammatical case, number, and gender. **2** the class to which a noun or adjective is assigned according to this variation.

ORIGIN – Old French *declinaison*, from *decliner* 'to decline'.

declination /dekli**nay**sh'n/ > *noun* **1** Astronomy the angular distance of a point north or south of the celestial equator. **2** the angular deviation of a compass needle from true north.

decline > *verb* **1** become smaller, weaker, or less in quality or quantity. **2** politely refuse. **3** (especially of the sun) move downwards. **4** Grammar form (a noun, pronoun, or adjective) according to case, number, and gender. > *noun* a gradual and continuous loss of strength, numbers, or value.

SYNONYMS – *verb* **1** decrease, diminish, dwindle, reduce, wane.

ORIGIN – Latin *declinare* 'bend down, turn aside', from *clinare* 'to bend'.

declivity /di**kliv**viti/ > *noun* (pl. **declivities**) a downward slope.

ORIGIN – Latin *declivitas*, from *clivus* 'a slope'.

declutch > *verb* disengage the clutch of a motor vehicle.

decoction > *noun* a liquor containing the concentrated essence of a substance, produced as a result of heating or boiling.

ORIGIN – Latin, from *decoquere* 'boil down'.

decode > *verb* **1** convert (a coded message) into intelligible language. **2** convert (audio or video signals), in particular from analogue to digital.

DERIVATIVES – **decodable** *adjective* **decoder** *noun*.

decoke > *verb* Brit. informal remove carbon or carbonaceous material from.

décolletage /daykol**taazh**/ > *noun* a low neckline on a woman's dress or top.

ORIGIN – French, from *décolleter* 'expose the neck'.

décolleté /daykol**tay**/ > *adjective* having a low neckline. > *noun* a décolletage.

decolonise (also **decolonize**) > *verb* withdraw from (a colony), leaving it independent.

DERIVATIVES – **decolonisation** *noun*.

decolorise (also **decolorize** or **decolourise**) > *verb* remove the colour from.

DERIVATIVES – **decolorisation** *noun*.

decommission > *verb* **1** take (a ship) out of service. **2** dismantle and make safe (a nuclear reactor or weapon).

decompose > *verb* **1** (of organic matter)

decay. **2** break down into component elements.

DERIVATIVES – **decomposable** *adjective* **decomposition** *noun*.

SYNONYMS – **1** decay, moulder, putrefy, rot.

decompress /deekəm**press**/ > *verb* **1** expand (compressed computer data) to its normal size. **2** subject (a diver) to decompression.

DERIVATIVES – **decompressor** *noun*.

decompression > *noun* **1** reduction in air pressure. **2** the process of decompressing.

COMBINATIONS – **decompression chamber** a small room in which the air pressure can be varied, used to allow deep-sea divers to adjust to normal air pressure. **decompression sickness** a serious condition that results when too rapid decompression causes nitrogen bubbles to form in the tissues of the body.

decongestant /deekən**jest**ənt/ > *adjective* (of a medicine) used to relieve nasal congestion. > *noun* a decongestant medicine.

deconsecrate > *verb* transfer (a building) from sacred to secular use.

DERIVATIVES – **deconsecration** *noun*.

deconstruct /deekən**strukt**/ > *verb* **1** analyse by deconstruction. **2** dismantle and expose the workings of.

DERIVATIVES – **deconstructive** *adjective*.

deconstruction > *noun* a method of literary criticism which focuses on the text itself rather than the author's intentions, and emphasises the assumptions implicit in forms of expression.

DERIVATIVES – **deconstructionism** *noun* **deconstructionist** *adjective & noun*.

decontaminate > *verb* remove dangerous substances from.

DERIVATIVES – **decontamination** *noun*.

decontextualise (also **decontextualize**) > *verb* consider (something) in isolation from its context.

DERIVATIVES – **decontextualisation** *noun*.

decontrol > *verb* (**decontrolled**, **decontrolling**) release (a commodity, market, etc.) from controls or restrictions. > *noun* the action of decontrolling.

decor /**day**kor/ > *noun* **1** the furnishing and decoration of a room. **2** stage scenery.

ORIGIN – French, from Latin *decorare* 'embellish'.

decorate > *verb* **1** add ornamentation to. **2** apply paint or wallpaper to. **3** confer an award or medal on. **4** (**Decorated**) denoting a stage of English Gothic church architecture of the 14th century.

SYNONYMS – **1** adorn, bedeck, embellish, garnish, ornament, trim.

ORIGIN – Latin *decorare* 'embellish', from *decus* 'honour or embellishment'.

decoration > *noun* **1** the process or art of decorating something. **2** an ornament. **3** ornamentation. **4** a medal or award conferred as an honour.

decorative /**dekk**ərətiv/ > *adjective* **1** serving to make something look more attractive; ornamental. **2** relating to decoration.

DERIVATIVES – **decoratively** *adverb* **decorativeness** *noun*.

decorator > *noun* a person who decorates, in particular (Brit.) a person whose job is to paint interior walls or hang wallpaper.

decorous /**dekk**ərəss/ > *adjective* in keeping with good taste and propriety; polite and restrained.

DERIVATIVES – **decorously** *adverb* **decorousness** *noun*.

SYNONYMS – appropriate, decent, proper, seemly, tasteful.

ORIGIN – Latin *decorus* 'seemly'.

decorum /di**kor**əm/ > *noun* **1** behaviour in keeping with good taste and propriety. **2** prescribed behaviour; etiquette.

SYNONYMS – **1** decency, politeness, propriety, seemliness. **2** etiquette, form, protocol.

ORIGIN – Latin, 'seemly thing'.

découpage /**day**koopaazh/ > *noun* the decoration of a surface with paper cut-outs.

ORIGIN – French, from *découper* 'cut out'.

decouple > *verb* separate or disengage one thing from another.

decoy > *noun* /**dee**koy/ **1** a bird or mammal, or an imitation of one, used to lure game. **2** a person or thing used to mislead or lure someone into a trap. **3** a pond from which narrow netted channels lead, into which wild duck may be enticed for capture. > *verb* /di**koy**/ lure by means of a decoy.

SYNONYMS – *noun* **2** bait, inducement, lure.

ORIGIN – from Dutch *de kooi* 'the decoy', from Latin *cavea* 'cage'.

decrease > *verb* /di**kreess**/ make or become smaller or fewer in size, amount, intensity, or degree. > *noun* /**dee**kreess/ **1** an instance of decreasing. **2** the process of decreasing.

DERIVATIVES – **decreasing** *adjective* **decreasingly** *adverb*.

SYNONYMS – *verb* decline, diminish, dwindle, lessen, reduce, shrink. *noun* **1** decline, downturn, drop, reduction.

ANTONYMS – increase.

ORIGIN – Latin *decrescere*, from *de-* 'down' + *crescere* 'grow'.

decree > *noun* **1** an official order that has the force of law. **2** a judgement or decision of certain law courts. > *verb* (**decrees**, **decreed**, **decreeing**) order by decree.

COMBINATIONS – **decree absolute** (pl. **decrees absolute**) English Law a final order by a court of law which officially ends a marriage. **decree nisi** (pl. **decrees nisi**) English Law an order by a court of law that states the date on which a marriage will end, unless a good reason to prevent a divorce is produced. [ORIGIN – Latin *nisi* 'unless'.]

ORIGIN – Latin *decretum* 'something decided', from *decernere* 'decide'.

decrement /**dek**rimənt/ > *noun* **1** a reduction or diminution. **2** Physics the ratio of the amplitudes in successive cycles of a damped oscillation.

ORIGIN – Latin *decrementum* 'diminution', from *decrescere* 'to decrease'.

decrepit /di**krepp**it/ > *adjective* **1** worn out or ruined because of age or neglect. **2** elderly and infirm.

DERIVATIVES – **decrepitude** *noun*.

SYNONYMS – **1** dilapidated, rickety, ramshackle, run down. **2** feeble, frail, infirm.

ORIGIN – Latin *decrepitus*, from *crepare* 'rattle, creak'.

decretal /di**kreet**'l/ > *noun* a papal decree concerning a point of canon law. > *adjective* of the nature of a decree.

ORIGIN – Latin *decretale*, from *decernere* 'to decide'.

decriminalise (also **decriminalize**) > *verb* cease to treat (something) as illegal.

DERIVATIVES – **decriminalisation** *noun*.

decry /di**krī**/ > *verb* (**decries**, **decried**) publicly denounce.

DERIVATIVES – **decrier** *noun*.

ORIGIN – first used in the sense 'decrease the value of coins by royal proclamation': from French *décrier* 'cry down'.

decrypt /dee**kript**/ > *verb* make (a coded or unclear message) intelligible.

DERIVATIVES – **decryption** *noun*.

decurved > *adjective* Biology (especially of a bird's bill) curved downwards.

dedicate > *verb* **1** devote to a particular subject, task, or purpose. **2** address (a book) to a person as a sign of respect or affection. **3** ceremonially assign (a church or other building) to a deity or saint.

DERIVATIVES – **dedicatee** *noun* **dedicator** *noun* **dedicatory** *adjective*.

SYNONYMS – **1** commit, devote, give, pledge. **2** address, inscribe.

ORIGIN – Latin *dedicare* 'to devote or consecrate'.

dedicated > *adjective* **1** devoted to a task or purpose. **2** exclusively assigned or allocated for a particular purpose.

DERIVATIVES – **dedicatedly** *adverb*.

SYNONYMS – **1** committed, devoted, stalwart, staunch.

dedication > *noun* **1** the quality of being dedicated. **2** the action of dedicating. **3** the words with which something is dedicated.

SYNONYMS – **1** commitment, devotion, faithfulness, staunchness.

deduce > *verb* arrive at (a fact or a conclusion) by reasoning.

DERIVATIVES – **deducible** *adjective*.

SYNONYMS – gather, infer, reason, work out.

ORIGIN – Latin *deducere* 'to take or lead away'.

deduct > *verb* subtract or take away from a total.

ORIGIN – Latin *deducere* 'to take or lead away'.

deductible > *adjective* able to be deducted, especially from taxable income. > *noun* chiefly N. Amer. the part of an insurance claim to be paid by the insured; an excess.

DERIVATIVES – **deductibility** *noun*.

deduction > *noun* **1** the action of deducting. **2** an amount that is or may be deducted. **3** Philosophy the inference of particular instances by reference to a general law or principle. Contrasted with **INDUCTION**.

DERIVATIVES – **deductive** *adjective* **deductively** *adverb*.

deed > *noun* **1** an action that is performed intentionally or consciously. **2** (usu. **deeds**) a legal document, especially one relating to property ownership or legal rights. > *verb* N. Amer. convey or transfer by legal deed.

COMBINATIONS – **deed of covenant** Brit. an agreement to pay a regular amount of money, particularly when this enables the recipient to reclaim any tax paid by the donor on the amount. **deed poll** English Law a legal deed made and executed by one party only, especially to formalise a change of a person's name. [ORIGIN – so named because the parchment was 'polled' or cut evenly, not indented as in the case of a deed made by two parties.]

deejay > *noun* informal a disc jockey.

deem > *verb* formal regard or consider in a specified way.

deemster > *noun* a judge (of whom there are two) in the Isle of Man.

deep > *adjective* **1** extending far down or in from the top or surface. **2** extending a specified distance from the top, surface, or outer edge. **3** (of sound) low in pitch and full in tone; not shrill. **4** (of colour) dark and intense; rich. **5** very intense, profound, or extreme. **6** difficult to understand. **7** (in ball games) far down or across the field. > *noun* **1** (**the deep**) literary the sea. **2** a deep part of something, especially the sea. > *adverb* far down or in; deeply.

IDIOMS – **go off** (or **go in off**) **the deep end** informal give way immediately to an emotional or irrational outburst. **in deep water** informal in trouble or difficulty. **jump** (or **be thrown**) **in at the deep end** informal face a difficult problem or undertaking with little experience.

DERIVATIVES – **deepness** *noun*.

SYNONYMS – *adjective* **1** bottomless, fathomless; archaic profound. **3** low, resonant, sonorous. **5** extreme, heartfelt, intense, profound, wholehearted. **6** abstruse, esoteric, profound, recondite.

ANTONYMS – *adjective* **1** shallow. **3** high.

COMBINATIONS – **deep-dyed** informal thoroughgoing; complete. **deep-fry** fry (food) in an amount of fat or oil sufficient to cover it completely. **deep-seated** (also **deep-rooted**) firmly established. **deep space** outer space.

ORIGIN – Old English, related to **DIP**.

deepen > *verb* make or become deep or deeper.

deep freeze (also **deep freezer**) > *noun* a freezer. > *verb* (**deep-freeze**) store in or freeze using a deep freeze.

deeply > *adverb* **1** far down or in. **2** intensely.

deep-six > *verb* N. Amer. informal get rid of; destroy utterly.

ORIGIN – first occurring as *the deep six* 'the grave': perhaps from the custom of burial at sea at a depth of six fathoms.

deer > *noun* (pl. same) a hoofed grazing or browsing animal, the male of which usually has branched bony antlers that are shed annually.

WORDFINDER – cervine (*relating to deer*); buck, hart, stag (*male deer*); doe, hind (*female deer*); fawn (*a young deer in its first year*).

COMBINATIONS – **deerhound** a large rough-haired breed of dog resembling the greyhound. **deerstalker** a soft cloth cap, originally worn for hunting, with peaks in front and behind and ear flaps which can be tied together over the top.

ORIGIN – Old English, originally also denoting any quadruped.

de-escalate > *verb* reduce the intensity of (a conflict or crisis).

DERIVATIVES – **de-escalation** *noun*.

def > *adjective* black slang excellent.

ORIGIN – an alteration of **DEATH**, or shortened from **DEFINITIVE** or **DEFINITE**.

deface > *verb* spoil the surface or appearance of.

DERIVATIVES – **defacement** *noun*.

SYNONYMS – blemish, disfigure, mar, spoil, vandalise.

de facto /day **fak**tō/ > *adverb* in fact, whether by right or not. Contrasted with **DE JURE**. > *adjective* existing in fact if not by right or design: *a de facto one-party system*.

ORIGIN – Latin, 'of fact'.

defalcate /**dee**falkayt/ > *verb* formal embezzle (funds).

DERIVATIVES – **defalcation** *noun*.

ORIGIN – first used in the sense 'deduct, subtract': from latin *defalcare* 'to lop'.

defame > *verb* damage the good reputation of.

DERIVATIVES – **defamation** *noun* **defamatory** *adjective*.

SYNONYMS – besmirch, blacken, discredit, libel, slander, smear.

ORIGIN – Latin *diffamare* 'spread evil report', from *fama* 'report'.

default > *noun* **1** failure to fulfil an obligation, especially to repay a loan or appear in a law court. **2** a pre-selected option adopted by a computer program or other mechanism when no alternative is specified. > *verb* **1** fail to fulfil an obligation, especially to repay a loan or to appear in court. **2** (**default to**) revert automatically to (a pre-selected option).

IDIOMS – **by default** because of a lack of opposition or positive action. **in default of** in the absence of.

ORIGIN – Old French *defaillir* 'to fail', from Latin *fallere* 'disappoint, deceive'.

defaulter > *noun* **1** a person who defaults. **2** chiefly Brit. a member of the armed forces guilty of a military offence.

defeasible /di**fee**zib'l/ > *adjective* Law & Philosophy open to revision, valid objection, forfeiture, or annulment.

defeat > *verb* **1** win a victory over. **2** prevent (an aim) from being achieved. **3** reject or block (a proposal or motion). > *noun* an instance of defeating or being defeated.

SYNONYMS – **1** beat, conquer, triumph over, trounce, vanquish. **2** confound, foil, frustrate, thwart.

ORIGIN – Old French *desfaire*, from Latin *disfacere* 'undo'.

defeatist > *noun* a person who gives in to failure too readily. > *adjective* showing ready acceptance of failure.

DERIVATIVES – **defeatism** *noun*.

defecate /**deffi**kayt/ > *verb* discharge faeces from the body.

DERIVATIVES – **defecation** *noun* **defecatory** *adjective*.

ORIGIN – first used in the sense 'clear of dregs, purify': from Latin *defaecare*, from *faex* 'dregs'.

defect¹ /**dee**fekt/ > *noun* a shortcoming, imperfection, or lack.

SYNONYMS – flaw, fault, imperfection, shortcoming, weakness.

ORIGIN – Latin *defectus*, from *deficere* 'desert or fail'.

defect² /di**fekt**/ > *verb* abandon one's country or cause in favour of an opposing one.

DERIVATIVES – **defection** *noun* **defector** *noun*.

ORIGIN – Latin *deficere* (see **DEFECT¹**).

defective > *adjective* **1** imperfect or faulty. **2** lacking or deficient.

DERIVATIVES – **defectively** *adverb* **defectiveness** *noun*.

defence (US **defense**) > *noun* **1** the action of defending from or resisting attack. **2**

military measures or resources for protecting a country. **3** (**defences**) fortifications against attack. **4** attempted justification or vindication. **5** the case presented by or on behalf of the party being accused or sued in a lawsuit. **6** (**the defence**) the counsel for the defendant in a lawsuit. **7** (in sport) the action of defending one's goal or wicket, or the players in a team who perform this role.

SYNONYMS – **1** guarding, protection, resistance, shielding. **4** advocacy, endorsement, support.

defenceless (US **defenseless**) > *adjective* without defence or protection; totally vulnerable.

DERIVATIVES – **defencelessness** *noun*.

SYNONYMS – exposed, helpless, undefended, unprotected, vulnerable.

defend > *verb* **1** resist an attack on; protect from harm or danger. **2** conduct the case for (the party being accused or sued) in a lawsuit. **3** attempt to justify. **4** compete to retain (a title or seat). **5** (in sport) protect one's goal or wicket rather than attempt to score against one's opponents.

DERIVATIVES – **defendable** *adjective* **defender** *noun*.

SYNONYMS – **1** guard, protect, safeguard, shield. **3** explain, support.

ANTONYMS – attack.

ORIGIN – Latin *defendere*, from *de-* 'off' + *-fendere* 'to strike'.

defendant > *noun* a person sued or accused in a court of law. Compare with **PLAINTIFF**.

defenestration /deefeni**stray**sh'n/ > *noun* formal or humorous the action of throwing someone out of a window.

DERIVATIVES – **defenestrate** *verb*.

ORIGIN – Latin, from *fenestra* 'window'.

defensible > *adjective* **1** justifiable by argument. **2** able to be defended or protected.

DERIVATIVES – **defensibility** *noun* **defensibly** *adverb*.

defensive > *adjective* **1** used or intended to defend or protect. **2** very anxious to challenge or avoid criticism.

IDIOMS – **on the defensive** expecting or resisting criticism or attack.

DERIVATIVES – **defensively** *adverb* **defensiveness** *noun*.

defer¹ /di**fer**/ > *verb* (**deferred**, **deferring**) put off to a later time; postpone.

DERIVATIVES – **deferment** *noun* **deferral** *noun*.

SYNONYMS – adjourn, delay, postpone, shelve, suspend.

ORIGIN – Latin *differre*, from *dis-* 'apart' + *ferre* 'bring, carry'.

defer² /di**fer**/ > *verb* (**deferred**, **deferring**) (**defer to**) submit humbly to.

ORIGIN – Latin *deferre* 'carry away, refer'.

deference > *noun* humble submission and respect.

deferential > *adjective* showing deference; respectful.

DERIVATIVES – **deferentially** *adverb*.

defiance > *noun* open resistance; bold disobedience.

SYNONYMS – disobedience, dissent, insubordination, non-compliance, rebellion, resistance.

defiant > *adjective* showing defiance.

DERIVATIVES – **defiantly** *adverb*.

SYNONYMS – disobedient, insubordinate, intransigent, rebellious, recalcitrant.

defibrillation /deefibri**lay**sh'n/ > *noun* Medicine the stopping of fibrillation of the heart by administering a controlled electric shock.

DERIVATIVES – **defibrillate** *verb* **defibrillator** *noun*.

deficiency > *noun* (pl. **deficiencies**) **1** a lack or shortage. **2** a failing or shortcoming.

COMBINATIONS – **deficiency disease** a disease caused by the lack of some essential element in the diet.

deficient /di**fish**'nt/ > *adjective* **1** (often **deficient in**) not having enough of a specified quality or ingredient. **2** insufficient or inadequate.

SYNONYMS – **1** inadequate, lacking, wanting.

ORIGIN – Latin, from *deficere* 'fail'.

deficit /**def**fisit/ > *noun* **1** the amount by which something, especially a sum of money, falls short. **2** an excess of expenditure or liabilities over income or assets.

ORIGIN – Latin, 'it is lacking', from *deficere*.

defilade /deffi**layd**/ > *noun* Military protection against enemy observation or gunfire.

ORIGIN – from French *défiler* 'protect from the enemy'.

defile¹ /di**fīl**/ > *verb* **1** make dirty; spoil or pollute. **2** desecrate or profane (something sacred).

DERIVATIVES – **defilement** *noun* **defiler** *noun*.

SYNONYMS – **1** debase, degrade, pollute, spoil, sully, taint.

ORIGIN – alteration of obsolete *defoul*, from Old French *defouler* 'trample down'.

defile² /di**fīl**, **dee**fīl/ > *noun* a steep-sided narrow gorge or passage (originally one requiring troops to march in single file).

ORIGIN – French, from *file* 'column, file'.

define > *verb* **1** state or describe the exact nature or scope of. **2** give the meaning of (a word or phrase). **3** mark out the limits of.

DERIVATIVES – **definable** *adjective* **definer** *noun*.

SYNONYMS – **1** clarify, describe, elucidate, specify, spell out. **3** delimit, determine, fix, limit, outline.

ORIGIN – Latin *definire*, from *finire* 'finish'.

definite* > *adjective* **1** clearly stated or decided; not vague or doubtful. **2** (of a person) certain or sure about something. **3** clearly true or real. **4** having exact and discernible physical limits.

DERIVATIVES – **definiteness** *noun*.

USAGE – do not confuse with **definitive**, which means 'decisive and with authority'.

*****SPELLING – *-ite*, not *-ate*: defin*ite*.

SYNONYMS – **1** concrete, exact, explicit, precise. **3** certain, conclusive, decisive, firm, unambiguous. **4** delimited, demarcated, fixed.

ANTONYMS – **1** indefinite, vague. **3** ambiguous.

COMBINATIONS – **definite article** Grammar a determiner (*the* in English) that introduces a noun and implies that the thing mentioned has already been mentioned, is common knowledge, or is about to be defined.

definitely* > *adverb* without any doubt; certainly.

*****SPELLING – *-itely* not *-ately*: defin*itely*.

definition > *noun* **1** a statement of the exact meaning of a word or the nature or scope of something. **2** the action or process of defining. **3** the degree of distinctness in outline of an object or image.

IDIOMS – **by definition** by its very nature; intrinsically.

DERIVATIVES – **definitional** *adjective*.

definitive > *adjective* **1** (of a conclusion or agreement) decisive and with authority. **2** (of a book or other text) the most authoritative of its kind. **3** (of a postage stamp) for general use, not special or commemorative.

DERIVATIVES – **definitively** *adverb*.

USAGE – do not confuse with **definite**.

deflate > *verb* **1** let air or gas out of (a tyre, balloon, etc.). **2** cause to feel suddenly dispirited. **3** Economics reduce price levels in (an economy).

DERIVATIVES – **deflator** *noun*.

deflation > *noun* **1** the action or process of deflating or being deflated. **2** Economics reduction of the general level of prices in an economy.

DERIVATIVES – **deflationary** *adjective*.

deflect > *verb* deviate or cause to deviate from a straight course.

DERIVATIVES – **deflector** *noun*.

SYNONYMS – avert, deviate, divert, sidetrack.

ORIGIN – Latin *deflectere*, from *flectere* 'to bend'.

deflection (also **deflexion**) > *noun* the action or process of deflecting or being deflected.

defloration /deeflo**ray**sh'n/ > *noun* dated or literary the taking of a woman's virginity.

deflower > *verb* dated or literary deprive (a woman) of her virginity.

defoliant > *noun* a chemical used to remove the leaves from trees and plants.

defoliate /deef**ō**liayt/ > *verb* remove leaves or foliage from (trees or plants).
DERIVATIVES – **defoliation** *noun*.

deforest > *verb* clear of forest or trees.
DERIVATIVES – **deforestation** *noun*.

deform > *verb* distort the shape or form of; make misshapen.
DERIVATIVES – **deformable** *adjective* **deformation** *noun*.

deformed > *adjective* having a distorted shape or form.
SYNONYMS – contorted, distorted, malformed, misshapen.

deformity > *noun* (pl. **deformities**) **1** a deformed part, especially of the body. **2** the state of being deformed.
SYNONYMS – abnormality, irregularity, malformation.

defraud > *verb* illegally obtain money from (someone) by deception.
DERIVATIVES – **defrauder** *noun*.
SYNONYMS – cheat, swindle.
ORIGIN – Latin *defraudare*, from *fraudare* 'to cheat'.

defray > *verb* provide money to pay (a cost).
DERIVATIVES – **defrayal** *noun*.
ORIGIN – French *défrayer*, from obsolete *frai* 'cost, expenses'.

defrock > *verb* deprive (a person in holy orders) of ecclesiastical status.

defrost > *verb* **1** free (something) of accumulated ice. **2** thaw (frozen food).

deft > *adjective* quick and neatly skilful.
DERIVATIVES – **deftly** *adverb* **deftness** *noun*.
SYNONYMS – adept, adroit, dexterous, nimble, skilful.
ORIGIN – variant of **DAFT**, in the obsolete sense 'meek'.

defunct /di**fungkt**/ > *adjective* no longer existing or functioning.
ORIGIN – Latin *defunctus* 'dead', from *defungi* 'carry out, finish'.

defuse > *verb* **1** remove the fuse from (an explosive device) in order to prevent it from exploding. **2** reduce the danger or tension in (a difficult situation).
USAGE – do not confuse with **diffuse**, which means 'spread over a wide area'.
SYNONYMS – **1** deactivate, disarm, disable. **2** alleviate, calm, ease, relieve.

defy > *verb* (**defies**, **defied**) **1** openly resist or refuse to obey. **2** challenge (someone) to do or prove something.
DERIVATIVES – **defier** *noun*.
SYNONYMS – **1** disobey, flout, rebel against, resist. **3** challenge, dare.
ORIGIN – Old French *desfier*, from Latin *dis-* + *fidus* 'faithful'.

dégagé /day**gaa**zhay/ > *adjective* unconcerned or unconstrained.
ORIGIN – French, 'set free'.

degauss /dee**gowss**/ > *verb* Physics remove unwanted magnetism from.
ORIGIN – from the name of the German physicist and mathematician Karl Friedrich *Gauss* (1777–1855).

degenerate > *adjective* /di**jenn**ərət/ having lost normal and desirable qualities; showing evidence of decline. > *noun* /di**jenn**ərət/ a morally degenerate person. > *verb* /di**jenn**ərayt/ decline or deteriorate physically or morally.
DERIVATIVES – **degeneracy** *noun* **degenerately** *adverb* **degeneration** *noun*.
ORIGIN – Latin *degeneratus* 'no longer of its kind', from *genus* 'race, kind'.

degenerative > *adjective* (of a disease) characterised by progressive deterioration.

deglaze > *verb* dilute meat sediments in (a pan) to make a gravy or sauce.

degrade > *verb* **1** cause (someone) to suffer a loss of dignity or self-respect. **2** lower the character or quality of. **3** archaic reduce (someone) to a lower rank. **4** cause to break down or deteriorate chemically. **5** Physics reduce (energy) to a less readily convertible form.
DERIVATIVES – **degradable** *adjective* **degradation** *noun* **degradative** *adjective*.
SYNONYMS – **1** debase, demean, dishonour, humiliate. **4** decay, deteriorate, degenerate.

degrading > *adjective* causing a loss of self-respect; humiliating.
SYNONYMS – demeaning, humiliating, ignominious, mortifying, shameful.

degree > *noun* **1** the amount, level, or extent to which something happens or is present. **2** a unit of measurement of angles, equivalent to one ninetieth of a right angle. **3** a unit in a scale of temperature, intensity, hardness, etc. **4** an academic rank conferred by a college or university after examination or completion of a course. **5** each of a set of grades (usually three) used to classify burns according to their severity. **6** chiefly N. Amer. a legal grade of crime, especially murder. **7** a step in direct genealogical descent. **8** archaic social or official rank.
IDIOMS – **by degrees** a little at a time; gradually. **to a degree 1** to some extent. **2** dated to a considerable extent.
ORIGIN – Old French, from Latin *de-* 'down' + *gradus* 'grade'.

de haut en bas /də ōt oɴ **baa**/ > *adverb* & *adjective* in a condescending or superior manner.
ORIGIN – French, 'from above to below'.

dehisce /di**hiss**/ > *verb* technical gape or burst open.
DERIVATIVES – **dehiscence** *noun* **dehiscent** *adjective*.

ORIGIN – Latin *dehiscere*, from *hiscere* 'begin to gape'.

dehumanise (also **dehumanize**) > *verb* deprive of positive human qualities.
DERIVATIVES – **dehumanisation** *noun*.

dehumidify > *verb* (**dehumidifies**, **dehumidified**) remove moisture from (the air or a gas).
DERIVATIVES – **dehumidification** *noun* **dehumidifier** *noun*.

dehydrate /dee**hī**drayt, deehī**drayt**/ > *verb* **1** cause (someone) to lose a large amount of water from their body. **2** remove water from (food) in order to preserve it.
DERIVATIVES – **dehydration** *noun*.
ORIGIN – from Greek *hudros* 'water'.

de-ice > *verb* remove ice from.
DERIVATIVES – **de-icer** *noun*.

deicide /**dee**isīd, **day**isīd/ > *noun* the killing of a god.
ORIGIN – from Latin *deus* 'god'.

deify /**dee**ifī, **day**ifī/ > *verb* (**deifies**, **deified**) make into or worship as a god.
DERIVATIVES – **deification** *noun*.

deign /dayn/ > *verb* (**deign to do**) do something that one considers to be beneath one's dignity.
SYNONYMS – condescend, lower oneself, stoop.
ORIGIN – Latin *dignare* 'deem worthy', from *dignus* 'worthy'.

deindustrialisation (also **deindustrialization**) > *noun* decline in industrial activity in a region or economy.
DERIVATIVES – **deindustrialised** *adjective*.

deinonychus /dī**nonn**ikəss/ > *noun* a fast-running predatory dinosaur of the mid Cretaceous period.
ORIGIN – from Greek *deinos* 'terrible' + *onux* 'claw'.

deionised /deeī-ən**īzd**/ (also **deionized**) > *adjective* having had the ions or ionic constituents removed.

deism /**dee**iz'm, **day**iz'm/ > *noun* belief in the existence of a supreme being, specifically of a creator who does not intervene in the universe. Compare with **THEISM**.
DERIVATIVES – **deist** *noun* **deistic** *adjective*.

deity /**dee**iti, **day**iti/ > *noun* (pl. **deities**) **1** a god or goddess. **2** divine status, quality, or nature.
ORIGIN – Latin *deitas*, from *deus* 'god'.

déjà vu /dayzhaa **voō**/ > *noun* a feeling of having already experienced the present situation.
ORIGIN – French, 'already seen'.

deject > *verb* make sad or dispirited.
DERIVATIVES – **dejection** *noun*.
ORIGIN – Latin *deicere* 'to throw down'.

dejected > *adjective* sad and dispirited.
DERIVATIVES – **dejectedly** *adverb*.
SYNONYMS – downcast, despondent, disconsolate, dispirited, sad.

de jure /day **joo**ray/ > *adverb* rightfully; by right. Contrasted with DE FACTO. > *adjective* rightful.
ORIGIN – Latin, 'of law'.

dekko /**dekk**ō/ > *noun* Brit. informal a quick look or glance.
ORIGIN – used by the British army in India: from a Hindi word meaning 'look!'

Delaware /**dell**əwair/ > *noun* (pl. same or **Delawares**) a member of an American Indian people formerly inhabiting the Delaware River valley of New Jersey and eastern Pennsylvania.

delay > *verb* **1** cause to be late or slow. **2** loiter or hesitate. **3** postpone or defer (an action). > *noun* an instance of delaying or being delayed.
SYNONYMS – **1** detain, hold up, keep back, retard.
ORIGIN – Old French *delayer*.

delayering > *noun* the reduction of the number of levels in the hierarchy of employees in an organisation.

dele /**dee**li/ > *noun* a proof-reader's sign (⸗) indicating matter to be deleted. > *verb* (**deled, deleing**) delete or mark for deletion.
ORIGIN – Latin, 'blot out! efface!'

delectable > *adjective* lovely, delightful, or delicious.
DERIVATIVES – **delectably** *adverb*.

delectation /deelek**tay**sh'n/ > *noun* formal, chiefly humorous pleasure and delight.
ORIGIN – Latin, from *delectare* 'to charm'.

delegacy /**dell**igəsi/ > *noun* (pl. **delegacies**) a body of delegates; a committee or delegation.

delegate > *noun* /**dell**igət/ **1** a person sent to represent others, in particular at a conference. **2** a member of a committee. > *verb* /**dell**igayt/ **1** entrust (a task or responsibility) to another person. **2** (**delegate to do**) authorise (someone) to do something as a representative.
DERIVATIVES – **delegator** *noun*.
ORIGIN – Latin *delegare* 'send away, assign'.

delegation > *noun* **1** a body of delegates; a deputation. **2** the process of delegating or being delegated.

delete > *verb* **1** remove or erase (text). **2** remove (a product) from the catalogue of those available for purchase.
DERIVATIVES – **deletion** *noun*.
ORIGIN – first used in the sense 'destroy': from Latin *delere* 'to blot out, destroy'.

deleterious /delli**tee**riəss/ > *adjective* causing harm or damage.
DERIVATIVES – **deleteriously** *adverb*.
ORIGIN – Greek *dēlētērios* 'noxious'.

delft /delft/ > *noun* glazed earthenware typically decorated in blue on a white background.
ORIGIN – named after the town of *Delft* in the Netherlands, where it originated.

deli > *noun* (pl. **delis**) informal a delicatessen.

deliberate > *adjective* /di**libb**ərət/ **1** done consciously and intentionally. **2** fully considered; not impulsive. **3** careful and unhurried. > *verb* /di**libb**ərayt/ engage in long and careful consideration.
DERIVATIVES – **deliberately** *adverb* **deliberateness** *noun*.
SYNONYMS – *adjective* **1** calculated, conscious, intended, planned, purposeful. **3** careful, cautious, measured, unhurried. *verb* contemplate, mull over, reflect, ruminate.
ANTONYMS – *adjective* **1** accidental, unintentional.
ORIGIN – from Latin *deliberare* 'consider carefully'.

deliberation > *noun* **1** long and careful consideration. **2** slow and careful movement or thought.
SYNONYMS – **1** consideration, contemplation, reflection, rumination. **2** care, caution, steadiness.

deliberative > *adjective* relating to or involving consideration or discussion.

delicacy > *noun* (pl. **delicacies**) **1** delicate texture or structure. **2** susceptibility to illness or adverse conditions. **3** discretion and tact. **4** a choice or expensive food.
SYNONYMS – **1** daintiness, exquisiteness, fineness, fragility. **2** frailty, sickliness, weakness. **3** care, diplomacy, discretion, sensitivity, tact.

delicate > *adjective* **1** very fine in texture or structure. **2** easily broken or damaged; fragile. **3** susceptible to illness or adverse conditions. **4** requiring sensitive or careful handling. **5** skilful; deft. **6** (of food or drink) subtly and pleasantly flavoured.
IDIOMS – **in a delicate condition** archaic, euphemistic pregnant.
DERIVATIVES – **delicately** *adverb*.
SYNONYMS – **1** dainty, exquisite, fine. **2** breakable, fragile, frail. **3** frail, sickly, weak.
ANTONYMS – **1** coarse. **2** durable, strong.

wordpower facts
Delicate

The word **delicate** entered English in the Middle Ages from French *délicat* or Latin *delicatus*. Its first sense in English was 'delightful, charming', an idea which survives in relation to food or drink that is subtly and pleasantly flavoured, and in the food sense of **delicacy**. Other senses in Middle English, which are now obsolete, included 'voluptuous', 'self-indulgent', 'fastidious', and 'effeminate'.

delicatessen /dellikə**tess**'n/ > *noun* a shop selling cooked meats, cheeses, and unusual or foreign prepared foods.

ORIGIN – German or Dutch, from French *délicatesse* 'delicacy'.

delicious > *adjective* **1** highly pleasant to the taste. **2** delightful: *a delicious irony*.
DERIVATIVES – **deliciously** *adverb* **deliciousness** *noun*.
SYNONYMS – **1** appetising, flavoursome, tasty.
ORIGIN – Latin *deliciosus*, from *deliciae* 'delight, pleasure'.

delight > *verb* **1** please greatly. **2** (**delight in**) take great pleasure in. > *noun* **1** great pleasure. **2** a cause or source of great pleasure.
SYNONYMS – *verb* **1** charm, enchant, gladden, gratify, thrill. **2** (**delight in**) glory in, luxuriate in, revel in, wallow in. *noun* **1** elation, euphoria, glee, happiness, joy, pleasure.
ORIGIN – Latin *delectare* 'to charm'.

delighted > *adjective* feeling or showing great pleasure.
DERIVATIVES – **delightedly** *adverb*.
SYNONYMS – ecstatic, elated, euphoric, overjoyed, thrilled.

delightful > *adjective* causing delight; very pleasing.
DERIVATIVES – **delightfully** *adverb*.
SYNONYMS – charming, enchanting, pleasing, thrilling.

delimit /di**limm**it/ > *verb* (**delimited, delimiting**) determine the limits or boundaries of.
DERIVATIVES – **delimitation** *noun* **delimiter** *noun*.

delineate /di**linn**iayt/ > *verb* describe or indicate precisely.
DERIVATIVES – **delineation** *noun*.
ORIGIN – Latin *delineare* 'to outline'.

delinquency > *noun* (pl. **delinquencies**) **1** minor crime, especially that committed by young people. **2** formal neglect of one's duty. **3** chiefly US a failure to pay an outstanding debt.

delinquent /di**ling**kwənt/ > *adjective* **1** (especially of young people) tending to commit crime. **2** formal failing in one's duty. **3** chiefly N. Amer. in arrears. > *noun* a delinquent person.
DERIVATIVES – **delinquently** *adverb*.
ORIGIN – from Latin *delinquere* 'to offend'.

deliquesce /delli**kwess**/ > *verb* **1** (of organic matter) become liquid, typically during decomposition. **2** Chemistry (of a solid) become liquid by absorbing moisture from the air.
DERIVATIVES – **deliquescence** *noun* **deliquescent** *adjective*.
ORIGIN – Latin *deliquescere* 'dissolve'.

delirious > *adjective* **1** suffering from delirium. **2** in a state of wild excitement or ecstasy.
DERIVATIVES – **deliriously** *adverb*.

SYNONYMS – **1** babbling, incoherent, raving. **2** ecstatic, euphoric, frenzied, jubilant, rapturous.

delirium /di**lirr**iəm/ > *noun* an acutely disturbed state of mind characterised by restlessness, illusions, and incoherent thought and speech.
ORIGIN – Latin, from *delirare* 'deviate, be deranged' (literally 'deviate from the furrow').

delirium tremens /**tree**menz/ > *noun* a condition typical of withdrawal in chronic alcoholics, involving tremors and hallucinations.
ORIGIN – Latin, 'trembling delirium'.

deliver > *verb* **1** bring and hand over (a letter or goods) to the appropriate recipient. **2** provide (something promised or expected). **3** save or set free. **4** state or present in a formal manner. **5** assist in the birth of. **6** (also **be delivered of**) give birth to. **7** launch or aim (a blow or attack).
IDIOMS – **deliver the goods** informal provide what is promised or expected.
DERIVATIVES – **deliverable** *adjective* **deliverer** *noun*.
ORIGIN – Old French *delivrer*, from Latin *liberare* 'set free'.

deliverance > *noun* **1** the process of being rescued or set free. **2** a formal or authoritative utterance.

delivery > *noun* (pl. **deliveries**) **1** the action of delivering something, especially letters or goods. **2** the process of giving birth. **3** an act of throwing or bowling a ball, especially a cricket ball. **4** the manner or style of giving a speech.

dell > *noun* literary a small valley.
ORIGIN – Old English, related to **DALE**.

Delphic /**del**fik/ > *adjective* **1** relating to the ancient oracle at Delphi in central Greece. **2** deliberately obscure or ambiguous.

delphinium /del**finn**iəm/ > *noun* (pl. **delphiniums**) a plant bearing tall spikes of blue flowers.
ORIGIN – Latin, from Greek *delphin* 'dolphin' (because of the shape of the spur, thought to resemble a dolphin's back).

delta¹ > *noun* **1** the fourth letter of the Greek alphabet (Δ, δ), transliterated as 'd'. **2** Brit. a fourth-class mark given for a piece of work.
COMBINATIONS – **delta rhythm** the typical electrical activity of the brain during sleep. **delta wing** a single triangular swept-back wing on some aircraft.
ORIGIN – Greek, from Phoenician.

delta² > *noun* a triangular area of sediment deposited at the mouth of a river where it diverges into several outlets.
ORIGIN – from the shape of the Greek letter *delta*: originally with reference to the River Nile.

deltiologist /delti**oll**əjist/ > *noun* a person who collects postcards as a hobby.
ORIGIN – from Greek *deltion*, from *deltos* 'writing tablet'.

deltoid /**del**toyd/ > *adjective* technical triangular. > *noun* (also **deltoid muscle**) a thick triangular muscle covering the shoulder joint and used for raising the arm away from the body.

delude /di**lood**/ > *verb* persuade (someone) of something incorrect; mislead.
SYNONYMS – deceive, dupe, fool, mislead.
ORIGIN – Latin *deludere* 'to mock', from *ludere* 'to play'.

deluded > *adjective* having a mistaken belief; misguided.

deluge /**del**yōōj/ > *noun* **1** a severe flood or very heavy fall of rain. **2** a great quantity of something arriving at the same time: *a deluge of complaints.* > *verb* **1** inundate or overwhelm. **2** flood.
ORIGIN – Old French, from Latin *diluvium*, from *diluere* 'wash away'.

delusion > *noun* a belief or impression that is not in accordance with reality.
DERIVATIVES – **delusional** *adjective* **delusive** *adjective* **delusory** *adjective*.

de luxe /di **luks**/ > *adjective* luxurious or sumptuous; of a superior kind.
ORIGIN – French, 'of luxury'.

delve > *verb* **1** reach inside a receptacle and search for something. **2** research intensively into something. **3** literary dig or excavate.

demagnetise (also **demagnetize**) > *verb* remove magnetic properties from.
DERIVATIVES – **demagnetisation** *noun*.

demagogue /**demm**əgog/ > *noun* **1** a political leader who appeals to popular desires and prejudices. **2** (in ancient Greece and Rome) an orator who supported the cause of the common people.
DERIVATIVES – **demagogic** /demmə**gogg**ik/ *adjective* **demagoguery** *noun* **demagogy** *noun*.
ORIGIN – Greek *dēmagōgos*, from *dēmos* 'the people' + *agōgos* 'leading'.

demand > *noun* **1** an insistent and peremptory request, made as of right. **2** (**demands**) pressing requirements. **3** the desire of purchasers or consumers for a particular commodity or service. > *verb* **1** ask authoritatively or brusquely. **2** insist on having. **3** require; need.
IDIOMS – **in demand** sought after. **on demand** as soon as or whenever required.
SYNONYMS – *noun* **1** command, order, request, stipulation. **3** appetite, call, desire. *verb* **1** command, enjoin, order, urge. **2** call for, insist on, order.
ORIGIN – Latin *demandare* 'hand over, entrust'.

demanding > *adjective* requiring much skill, effort, or attention.
DERIVATIVES – **demandingly** *adverb*.

SYNONYMS – challenging, difficult, exacting, taxing, testing.

demarcate /**dee**maarkayt/ > *verb* set the boundaries or limits of.

demarcation > *noun* **1** the action of fixing boundaries or limits. **2** a dividing line.

wordpower facts
Demarcation
The word **demarcation** entered English in the 18th century from Spanish *demarcación*, from *demarcar* 'mark the bounds of'. Originally used in the phrase *line of demarcation* (Spanish *línea de demarcación*, Portuguese *linha de demarcação*), the word referred to the lines dividing the New World between the Spanish and Portuguese, laid down by Pope Alexander VI in 1493. In effect Spanish colonies were confined to the hemisphere more than 47 degrees west of the Greenwich meridian (i.e. west of the coast of Brazil) and more than 133 degrees east (beyond the East Indies).

démarche /day**maarsh**/ > *noun* a political step or initiative.
ORIGIN – French, from *démarcher* 'take steps'.

dematerialise (also **dematerialize**) > *verb* become no longer physically present, or spiritual rather than physical.
DERIVATIVES – **dematerialisation** *noun*.

demean¹ /di**meen**/ > *verb* **1** cause (someone) to suffer a loss of dignity or respect. **2** (**demean oneself**) do something that is beneath one's dignity.
DERIVATIVES – **demeaning** *adjective*.
SYNONYMS – **1** cheapen, debase, degrade, discredit.
ORIGIN – from **DE-** + **MEAN²**, on the pattern of *debase*.

demean² /di**meen**/ > *verb* (**demean oneself**) archaic conduct oneself.
ORIGIN – Old French *demener* 'to lead'.

demeanour (US **demeanor**) > *noun* outward behaviour or bearing.
SYNONYMS – bearing, carriage, conduct, deportment, manner.
ORIGIN – from **DEMEAN²**.

demented > *adjective* **1** suffering from dementia. **2** informal wild and irrational.
DERIVATIVES – **dementedly** *adverb*.
ORIGIN – from earlier *dement* 'drive mad', from Latin *demens* 'insane'.

dementia /di**men**shə/ > *noun* a mental disorder marked by memory failures, personality changes, and impaired reasoning.
ORIGIN – Latin.

dementia praecox /preekoks/ > *noun* archaic schizophrenia.

ORIGIN – Latin, 'early insanity'.

demerara sugar /demmərairə/ > *noun* a kind of light brown cane sugar, originally from the region of Demerara in Guyana.

demerge > *verb* Brit. separate (a company) from another with which it was merged.

DERIVATIVES – **demerger** *noun*.

demerit > *noun* 1 something deserving blame or criticism; a fault. 2 N. Amer. a mark awarded against someone for a fault or offence.

demersal /dimers'l/ > *adjective* (of fishes) living close to the seabed.

ORIGIN – Latin *demersus*, from *demergere* 'submerge, sink'.

demesne /dimayn, dimeen/ > *noun* 1 historical land attached to a manor. 2 archaic a domain.

ORIGIN – from Old French *demeine* 'belonging to a lord', from Latin *dominus* 'lord, master'.

demi- > *prefix* 1 half: *demisemiquaver*. 2 partially; in an inferior degree: *demigod*.

ORIGIN – French, from Latin *dimidius* 'half'.

demigod (or **demigoddess**) > *noun* a partly divine being.

demijohn > *noun* a bulbous narrow-necked bottle holding from 3 to 10 gallons of liquid.

ORIGIN – probably an alteration of French *dame-jeanne* 'Lady Jane'.

demilitarise (also **demilitarize**) > *verb* remove all military forces from (an area).

DERIVATIVES – **demilitarisation** *noun*.

demi-mondaine /demmimondayn/ > *noun* a woman who belongs to the demi-monde.

ORIGIN – French.

demi-monde /demmimond/ > *noun* a group considered to be on the fringes of respectable society.

ORIGIN – French, 'half-world'.

demineralise (also **demineralize**) > *verb* remove salts or minerals from.

DERIVATIVES – **demineralisation** *noun*.

demi-pension /demmipoNsyoN/ > *noun* hotel accommodation with bed, breakfast, and one main meal per day.

ORIGIN – French, 'half board'.

demise /dimīz/ > *noun* 1 the end or failure of something. 2 a person's death.

ORIGIN – Old French, from *desmettre* 'dismiss'.

demi-sec /demmisek/ > *adjective* (of wine) medium dry.

ORIGIN – French, 'half-dry'.

demisemiquaver > *noun* Music a note having the time value of half a semiquaver.

demist /deemist/ > *verb* Brit. clear condensation from.

DERIVATIVES – **demister** *noun*.

demo informal > *noun* (pl. **demos**) 1 a public demonstration of protest or other feeling. 2 a demonstration recording or piece of software. > *verb* (**demos**, **demoed**) give a demonstration of.

demob /deemob/ Brit. informal > *verb* (**demobbed**, **demobbing**) demobilise. > *noun* demobilisation.

demobilise (also **demobilize**) > *verb* take (troops) out of active service.

DERIVATIVES – **demobilisation** *noun*.

democracy /dimokrəsi/ > *noun* (pl. **democracies**) 1 a form of government in which the people have a voice in the exercise of power, typically through elected representatives. 2 a state governed in such a way. 3 control of a group by the majority of its members.

wordpower facts

Democracy

The word **democracy** comes from Greek *dēmokratia*, from *dēmos* 'the people' + *-kratia* 'power, rule'. The concept of democracy originated in certain city states of ancient Greece in which power was exercised directly by the whole citizen body, rather than indirectly by voting for representatives. Such rule was possible because the population of city states was small, and women and slaves had no political rights. Greek *dēmos* 'the people' is the source of words such as **demagogue**, **demography**, **endemic**, and **epidemic**.

democrat > *noun* 1 a supporter of democracy. 2 (**Democrat**) (in the US) a member of the Democratic Party.

democratic > *adjective* 1 relating to or supporting democracy. 2 egalitarian. 3 (**Democratic**) (in the US) relating to the Democratic Party.

DERIVATIVES – **democratically** *adverb*.

democratise (also **democratize**) > *verb* introduce a democratic system or democratic principles to.

DERIVATIVES – **democratisation** *noun*.

démodé /daymōday/ > *adjective* out of fashion.

ORIGIN – French, from *démoder* 'go out of fashion'.

demodulate > *verb* Electronics reverse the modulation of.

DERIVATIVES – **demodulation** *noun* **demodulator** *noun*.

demography /dimogrəfi/ > *noun* the study of the structure of human populations using statistics of births, deaths, wealth, etc.

DERIVATIVES – **demographer** *noun*

demographic /demməgraffik/ *adjective* **demographically** *adverb*.

demoiselle /demwaazel/ > *noun* archaic or literary a young woman.

ORIGIN – French, related to DAMSEL.

demolish /dimollish/ > *verb* 1 pull or knock down (a building). 2 comprehensively refute or defeat. 3 humorous eat up (food) quickly.

SYNONYMS – 1 destroy, flatten, raze. 2 crush, destroy, rout, wreck.

ORIGIN – Latin *demoliri*, from *de-* (expressing reversal) + *moliri* 'construct'.

demolition /demməlish'n/ > *noun* the action or process of demolishing or being demolished.

demon[1] > *noun* 1 an evil spirit or devil. 2 (before another noun) very forceful or skilful: *a demon cook*. 3 often humorous an evil or destructive person or thing. 4 another term for DAEMON[1].

WORDFINDER – exorcise (*drive out an evil spirit*), incubus (*male demon thought to have intercourse with sleeping women*), succubus (*female demon thought to have intercourse with sleeping men*).

ORIGIN – Greek *daimōn* 'deity, spirit'.

demon[2] (also **daemon**) > *noun* Computing a background process that handles requests for services such as print spooling, and is dormant when not required.

ORIGIN – perhaps from *disk and execution monitor* or *device monitor*, or merely a transferred use of DEMON[1].

demonetise /deemunnitīz/ (also **demonetize**) > *verb* deprive (a coin or precious metal) of its status as money.

DERIVATIVES – **demonetisation** *noun*.

demoniac /dimōniak/ > *adjective* demonic. > *noun* a person supposedly possessed by an evil spirit.

DERIVATIVES – **demoniacal** /deemənīak'l/ *adjective*.

demonic /dimonnik/ > *adjective* of, resembling, or characteristic of demons or evil spirits.

DERIVATIVES – **demonically** *adverb*.

SYNONYMS – devilish, diabolic, fiendish, infernal, satanic.

demonise (also **demonize**) > *verb* portray as wicked and threatening.

DERIVATIVES – **demonisation** *noun*.

demonolatry /deemənollətri/ > *noun* the worship of demons.

demonology > *noun* the study of demons or demonic belief.

demonstrable /demmənstrəb'l, dimonstrəb'l/ > *adjective* clearly apparent or capable of being logically proved.

DERIVATIVES – **demonstrably** *adverb*.

demonstrate > *verb* 1 clearly show that (something) exists or is true. 2 give a practical exhibition and explanation of. 3 take part in a public demonstration.

DERIVATIVES – **demonstrator** noun.

SYNONYMS – **1** establish, indicate, show. **2** display, exhibit, illustrate, show.

ORIGIN – Latin demonstrare 'point out'.

demonstration > noun **1** the action or an instance of demonstrating. **2** a public meeting or march expressing protest or other opinion on an issue.

demonstrative /dimonstrətiv/ > adjective **1** tending to show one's feelings openly. **2** serving to demonstrate something. **3** Grammar (of a determiner or pronoun) indicating the person or thing referred to (e.g. this, that, those). > noun Grammar a demonstrative determiner or pronoun.

DERIVATIVES – **demonstratively** adverb **demonstrativeness** noun.

SYNONYMS – adjective **1** emotional, expressive, open, responsive, unreserved. **2** illustrative, indicative.

ANTONYMS – adjective **1** reserved.

demoralise (also **demoralize**) > verb cause (someone) to lose confidence or hope.

DERIVATIVES – **demoralisation** noun **demoralised** adjective **demoralising** adjective.

SYNONYMS – cast down, discourage, dishearten, dispirit.

ORIGIN – French démoraliser 'corrupt, deprave', originally used during the French Revolution.

demote > verb reduce (someone) to a lower rank or less senior position.

DERIVATIVES – **demotion** noun.

demotic /dimottik/ > adjective **1** (of language) used by ordinary people; colloquial. **2** relating to demotic Greek. > noun **1** the form of modern Greek used in everyday speech and writing. Compare with **KATHAREVOUSA**. **2** demotic language.

ORIGIN – Greek dēmotikos, from dēmos 'the people'.

demotivate > verb make (someone) less eager to work or make an effort.

DERIVATIVES – **demotivation** noun.

demountable > adjective able to be dismantled or removed and readily reassembled or repositioned.

demur /dimur/ > verb (**demurred**, **demurring**) raise doubts or objections; show reluctance. > noun the action of demurring: they accepted this ruling without demur.

DERIVATIVES – **demurral** noun.

ORIGIN – Old French demourer 'remain, stay', from Latin morari 'delay'.

demure /dimyoor/ > adjective (**demurer**, **demurest**) (of a woman) reserved, modest, and shy.

DERIVATIVES – **demurely** adverb **demureness** noun.

ORIGIN – perhaps from Old French demourer 'remain, stay', influenced by mur 'grave'.

demurrer /dimurrər/ > noun Law an objection that an opponent's point is irrelevant.

demutualise (also **demutualize**) > verb change (a mutual organisation such as a building society) to one of a different kind.

demystify > verb (**demystifies**, **demystified**) make (a subject) less difficult to understand.

DERIVATIVES – **demystification** noun.

demythologise (also **demythologize**) > verb reinterpret (a subject) so that it is free of mythical elements.

den > noun **1** a wild animal's lair or home. **2** informal a person's private room. **3** a place where people meet secretly or illicitly: an opium den.

denar /deenər/ > noun the basic monetary unit of Macedonia.

ORIGIN – Latin denarius; compare with **DINAR**.

denarius /dinairiəss/ > noun (pl. **denarii** /dinairi-ī/) an ancient Roman silver coin.

ORIGIN – Latin, 'containing ten', from deni 'in tens'.

denary /deenəri/ > adjective relating to or based on the number ten.

denationalise (also **denationalize**) > verb transfer from public to private ownership.

DERIVATIVES – **denationalisation** noun.

denature /deenaychər/ > verb **1** take away or alter the natural qualities of. **2** make (alcohol) unfit for drinking by adding poisonous or foul-tasting substances.

DERIVATIVES – **denaturation** noun.

dendrite /dendrīt/ > noun **1** a short extension of a nerve cell that conducts impulses to the cell body. **2** a marking or structure with a branched, tree-like form.

DERIVATIVES – **dendritic** /dendrittik/ adjective.

ORIGIN – from Greek dendritēs 'tree-like'.

dendrochronology /dendrōkrənolləji/ > noun a technique of dating material based on the investigation of annual growth rings in tree trunks.

DERIVATIVES – **dendrochronological** adjective **dendrochronologist** noun.

ORIGIN – from Greek dendron 'tree'.

dendrology > noun the scientific study of trees.

dene /deen/ (also **dean**) > noun Brit. a deep, narrow wooded valley.

ORIGIN – Old English, related to **DEN**.

dengue /denggi/ (also **dengue fever**) > noun a tropical disease transmitted by mosquitoes, causing sudden fever and acute pains in the joints.

ORIGIN – West Indian Spanish, from Kiswahili.

deniable > adjective able to be denied.

DERIVATIVES – **deniability** noun.

denial > noun **1** the action of denying something. **2** Psychology refusal to acknowledge an unacceptable truth or emotion.

denier /denyər/ > noun a unit by which the fineness of yarn is measured, equal to the weight in grams of 9,000 metres of the yarn.

ORIGIN – formerly the name of a small coin: from Latin denarius.

denigrate /dennigrayt/ > verb criticise unfairly; disparage.

DERIVATIVES – **denigration** noun **denigrator** noun.

SYNONYMS – belittle, deprecate, disparage, run down, vilify.

ORIGIN – first used in the sense 'blacken, make dark': from Latin denigrare, from niger 'black'.

denim > noun **1** a hard-wearing cotton twill fabric, typically blue. **2** (**denims**) jeans or other clothes made of such fabric.

ORIGIN – first as serge denim: from French serge de Nîmes, denoting serge from the manufacturing town of Nîmes.

denizen /denniz'n/ > noun **1** formal or humorous an inhabitant or occupant. **2** Brit. historical a foreigner allowed certain rights in their adopted country.

ORIGIN – from Old French deinz 'within'.

denominate /dinomminayt/ > verb **1** formal call; name. **2** (**be denominated**) (of sums of money) be expressed in a specified monetary unit.

ORIGIN – Latin denominare, from nominare 'to name'.

denomination > noun **1** a recognised branch of a church or religion. **2** the face value of a banknote, coin, postage stamp, etc. **3** formal a name or designation.

denominational > adjective relating to a particular religious denomination.

DERIVATIVES – **denominationalism** noun.

denominator > noun Mathematics the number below the line in a vulgar fraction; a divisor.

de nos jours /də nō zhoor/ > adjective contemporary.

ORIGIN – French, 'of our days'.

denote /dinōt/ > verb **1** be a sign of; indicate. **2** be a name or symbol for.

DERIVATIVES – **denotation** noun **denotational** adjective **denotative** /dinōtətiv/ adjective.

USAGE – whereas **denote** refers to the literal, primary meaning of something, **connote** refers to other characteristics suggested or implied by that thing. Thus, one might say that a word like **mother** denotes 'a woman who is a parent' but connotes qualities such as protection and affection.

ORIGIN – Latin denotare, from notare 'observe, note'.

denouement /daynōōmoN/ > noun the

final part of a play, film, or narrative, in which matters are explained or resolved.

ORIGIN – French, from *dénouer* 'unknot'.

denounce > *verb* publicly declare (someone or something) to be wrong or evil.

DERIVATIVES – **denouncement** *noun* **denouncer** *noun*.

SYNONYMS – accuse, attack, condemn, decry, fulminate against, revile.

ORIGIN – Latin *denuntiare* 'give official information', from *nuntius* 'messenger'.

de novo /day **nō**vō/ > *adverb* & *adjective* starting from the beginning; anew.

ORIGIN – Latin, 'from new'.

dense > *adjective* **1** closely compacted in substance. **2** crowded closely together. **3** informal stupid.

DERIVATIVES – **densely** *adverb* **denseness** *noun*.

SYNONYMS – **1** compacted, concentrated, heavy, solid. **2** crowded, packed, solid.

ANTONYMS – **1** light. **2** sparse.

ORIGIN – Latin *densus*.

density > *noun* (pl. **densities**) **1** the degree of compactness of a substance; mass per unit volume. **2** the quantity of people or things in a given area or space.

dent > *noun* a slight hollow in a surface made by a blow or pressure. > *verb* **1** mark with a dent. **2** have an adverse effect on.

ORIGIN – variant of **DINT**.

dental > *adjective* **1** relating to the teeth or to dentistry. **2** Phonetics (of a consonant) pronounced with the tip of the tongue against the upper front teeth (as *th*) or the alveolar ridge (as *n*, *d*, *t*).

DERIVATIVES – **dentally** *adverb*.

COMBINATIONS – **dental surgeon** a dentist. **dental technician** a person who makes and repairs artificial teeth.

ORIGIN – Latin *dentalis*, from *dens* 'tooth'.

dentate /**den**tayt/ > *adjective* Botany & Zoology having a tooth-like or serrated edge.

dentifrice /**den**tifriss/ > *noun* a paste or powder for cleaning the teeth.

ORIGIN – French, from Latin *dens* 'tooth' + *fricare* 'to rub'.

dentil /**den**til/ > *noun* Architecture each of a series of small tooth-like rectangular blocks used as a decoration under the moulding of a cornice.

ORIGIN – Italian *dentello* 'little tooth'.

dentine /**den**teen/ (US **dentin** /**den**tin/) > *noun* hard, dense bony tissue forming the bulk of a tooth.

dentist > *noun* a person who is qualified to treat the diseases and conditions that affect the teeth and gums.

WORDFINDER – *branches of dentistry:* orthodontics (*treatment of irregularities in teeth and jaws*), paedontics (*concerned with children's teeth*), periodontics (*concerned with the structures surrounding the teeth*),

prosthodontics (*design and fitting of artificial replacements for teeth*).

DERIVATIVES – **dentistry** *noun*.

dentition /den**tish**'n/ > *noun* the arrangement or condition of the teeth in a particular species or individual.

denture /**den**chər/ > *noun* a removable plate or frame holding one or more artificial teeth.

denude > *verb* (often **be denuded of**) strip of covering or possessions; make bare.

DERIVATIVES – **denudation** *noun*.

ORIGIN – Latin *denudare*.

denunciation /dinunsi**ay**sh'n/ > *noun* the action of denouncing.

DERIVATIVES – **denunciatory** *adjective*.

deny /din**ī**/ > *verb* (**denies, denied**) **1** refuse to admit the truth or existence of. **2** refuse to give (something requested or desired) to. **3** (**deny oneself**) go without.

SYNONYMS – **1** contradict, controvert, gainsay, refute, repudiate. **2** refuse.

ORIGIN – Latin *denegare*, from *negare* 'say no'.

deodorant /di**ō**dərənt/ > *noun* a substance which removes or conceals unpleasant bodily odours.

deodorise (also **deodorize**) > *verb* remove or conceal an unpleasant smell in.

DERIVATIVES – **deodoriser** *noun*.

deoxygenate /dee**ok**sijənayt/ > *verb* remove oxygen from.

DERIVATIVES – **deoxygenation** *noun*.

deoxyribonucleic acid /di-oksirībō-nyoo**klay**ik/ > *noun* see **DNA**.

depart > *verb* **1** leave, especially to start a journey. **2** (**depart from**) deviate from (a course of action).

SYNONYMS – **1** go away, go off, leave, take one's leave.

ANTONYMS – **1** arrive.

ORIGIN – Old French *departir*, from Latin *dispertire* 'to divide'.

departed > *adjective* deceased; dead.

department > *noun* **1** a division of a large organisation or building, dealing with a specific area of activity. **2** an administrative district in France and other countries. **3** (**one's department**) informal one's area of special expertise or responsibility. **4** informal a specified aspect or quality: *he was a bit lacking in the height department*.

DERIVATIVES – **departmental** *adjective* **departmentalise** (also **departmentalize**) *verb* **departmentally** *adverb*.

SYNONYMS – **1** branch, division, section, sector, unit.

COMBINATIONS – **department store** a large shop stocking many types of goods in different departments.

departure > *noun* the action or an instance of departing.

SYNONYMS – exit, going, leaving.

depend > *verb* (**depend on**) **1** be controlled or determined by. **2** put one's trust in.

IDIOMS – **depending on** according to.

SYNONYMS – (**depend on**) **1** be contingent on, be dependent on, hang on, hinge on, rely on. **2** bank on, count on, rely on, trust, trust in.

ORIGIN – Latin *dependere* 'hang down'.

dependable > *adjective* trustworthy and reliable.

DERIVATIVES – **dependability** *noun* **dependably** *adverb*.

SYNONYMS – constant, reliable, steadfast, trustworthy.

ANTONYMS – unreliable.

dependant (also **dependent**) > *noun* a person who relies on another, especially a family member, for financial support.

dependency* > *noun* (pl. **dependencies**) **1** a country or province controlled by another. **2** the state of being dependent.

*SPELLING – *-ency* not *-ancy*: depend*ency*.

dependent* > *adjective* **1** (**dependent on**) contingent on or determined by. **2** relying on someone or something for financial or other support. **3** (**dependent on**) unable to do without. **4** Grammar subordinate to another clause, phrase, or word. > *noun* variant spelling of **DEPENDANT**.

DERIVATIVES – **dependence** *noun* **dependently** *adverb*.

*SPELLING – The standard spelling of the adjective is with the ending *-ent*, not *-ant*: depend*ent*. This spelling is increasingly also used for the noun, more usually spelled with an *a*.

depersonalise (also **depersonalize**) > *verb* deprive of human characteristics or individuality.

DERIVATIVES – **depersonalisation** *noun*.

depict /di**pikt**/ > *verb* **1** represent by a drawing, painting, or other art form. **2** portray in words; describe.

DERIVATIVES – **depiction** *noun*.

SYNONYMS – **1** illustrate, picture, portray, represent, show.

ORIGIN – Latin *depingere*, from *pingere* 'to paint'.

depilate /**depp**ilayt/ > *verb* remove the hair from.

DERIVATIVES – **depilation** *noun* **depilator** *noun*.

ORIGIN – Latin *depilare*, from *pilus* 'hair'.

depilatory /di**pill**ətri/ > *adjective* used to remove unwanted hair. > *noun* (pl. **depilatories**) a depilatory cream or lotion.

deplete /di**pleet**/ > *verb* reduce the number, quantity, or amount of.

DERIVATIVES – **depletion** *noun*.

SYNONYMS – consume, drain, empty, exhaust, use up.

COMBINATIONS – **depleted uranium** uranium from which most of the fissile isotope uranium-235 has been removed.

ORIGIN – Latin *deplere* 'empty out'.

deplorable /di**plor**əb'l/ > *adjective* deserving strong condemnation; shockingly bad.

DERIVATIVES – **deplorably** adverb.

SYNONYMS – abominable, appalling, atrocious, dreadful, shocking, terrible.

deplore > *verb* feel or express strong disapproval of.

SYNONYMS – abhor, bemoan, disapprove of, lament, regret.

ANTONYMS – admire, applaud.

ORIGIN – Latin *deplorare*, from *plorare* 'bewail'.

deploy /di**ploy**/ > *verb* **1** bring or move into position for military action. **2** bring into effective action.

DERIVATIVES – **deployment** noun.

SYNONYMS – **1** position, post, station. **2** call on, employ, marshal, make use of, muster.

ORIGIN – French *déployer*, from Latin *displicare* 'unfold or explain'.

depoliticise (also **depoliticize**) > *verb* remove from political activity or influence.

DERIVATIVES – **depoliticisation** noun.

deponent /di**pō**nənt/ > *noun* Law a person who makes a deposition or affidavit under oath.

ORIGIN – from Latin *deponere* 'put down'.

depopulate > *verb* substantially reduce the population of.

DERIVATIVES – **depopulation** noun.

deport > *verb* **1** expel (a foreigner or immigrant) from a country. **2** (**deport oneself**) archaic behave in a specified manner.

DERIVATIVES – **deportation** noun **deportee** noun.

ORIGIN – Latin *deportare*, from *portare* 'carry'.

deportment > *noun* **1** chiefly Brit. the way a person stands and walks. **2** N. Amer. a person's behaviour or manners.

SYNONYMS – **1** bearing, carriage, gait, posture.

depose > *verb* **1** remove from office suddenly and forcefully. **2** Law testify to or give (evidence) on oath, especially in writing.

SYNONYMS – **1** dethrone, oust, overthrow, remove, topple, unseat.

ORIGIN – Old French *deposer*, from Latin *deponere* 'put down'.

deposit > *noun* **1** a sum of money placed in a bank or other account. **2** a sum payable as a first instalment or as a pledge. **3** a returnable sum paid to cover possible loss or damage. **4** a layer or body of accumulated matter. **5** the action or an act of depositing. > *verb* (**deposited**, **depositing**) **1** put down in a specific place. **2** leave (something) with someone for safekeeping.

3 pay as a deposit. **4** (of a natural agency) lay down (matter) as a layer or covering.

IDIOMS – **lose one's deposit** (of a candidate in a UK parliamentary election) receive less than a certain proportion of the votes (thereby forfeiting a statutory financial deposit).

DERIVATIVES – **depositor** noun.

SYNONYMS – *noun* **4** accumulation, deposition, layer. *verb* **1** lay down, place, put down, set down. **3** consign to, entrust to, leave with, lodge.

COMBINATIONS – **deposit account** chiefly Brit. a bank account that pays interest and may not usually be drawn on without notice.

ORIGIN – Latin *depositum*, from *deponere* 'put down'.

depositary (also **depository**) > *noun* (pl. **depositaries**) a person to whom something is entrusted.

deposition /deepə**zish**'n, depə**zish**'n/ > *noun* **1** the action of deposing someone from office. **2** Law the process of giving sworn evidence. **3** Law a sworn statement to be used as evidence. **4** the action of depositing.

depository > *noun* (pl. **depositories**) **1** a place where things are stored. **2** variant spelling of **DEPOSITARY**.

depot /**depp**ō/ > *noun* **1** a place for the storage of large quantities of goods. **2** a place where buses, trains, or other vehicles are housed and maintained. **3** N. Amer. /**dee**pō/ a railway or bus station. **4** the headquarters of a regiment.

ORIGIN – French, from Latin *depositum* 'deposit'.

deprave /di**prayv**/ > *verb* lead (someone) away from what is natural or right; corrupt.

SYNONYMS – corrupt, debase, degrade, pervert.

ORIGIN – Latin *depravare*, from *pravus* 'crooked, perverse'.

depraved > *adjective* morally corrupt.

SYNONYMS – corrupt, evil, immoral, perverted.

depravity /di**pravv**iti/ > *noun* (pl. **depravities**) **1** moral corruption. **2** a wicked or morally corrupt act.

deprecate /**depp**rikayt/ > *verb* **1** express disapproval of. **2** another term for **DEPRECIATE** (in sense 2).

DERIVATIVES – **deprecation** noun **deprecatory** adjective.

ORIGIN – first used in the sense 'pray to ward off evil': from Latin *deprecari*, from *precari* 'pray'.

depreciate /di**pree**shiayt/ > *verb* **1** make or become lower in value over a period of time. **2** disparage or belittle.

DERIVATIVES – **depreciation** noun **depreciatory** /di**pree**shiətəri/ adjective.

ORIGIN – Latin *depreciare* 'lower in price, undervalue'.

depredation /depri**day**sh'n/ > *noun* (usu. **depredations**) an act of attacking or plundering.

ORIGIN – Latin *depraedatio*, from *depraedari* 'to plunder'.

depress > *verb* **1** cause (someone) to feel utterly dispirited or dejected. **2** reduce the level of activity in (a system). **3** push or pull down.

DERIVATIVES – **depressing** adjective **depressingly** adverb.

SYNONYMS – **1** demoralise, dishearten, dismay, dispirit, sadden.

ANTONYMS – **1** cheer up.

ORIGIN – Latin *depressare*, from *deprimere* 'press down'.

depressant > *adjective* reducing functional or nervous activity. > *noun* a depressant drug or other agent.

depressed > *adjective* **1** severely despondent and unhappy. **2** suffering from clinical depression. **3** suffering the damaging effects of economic recession.

SYNONYMS – **1** despondent, gloomy, melancholy, miserable, sad, unhappy.

ANTONYMS – **1** cheerful.

depression > *noun* **1** severe despondency and unhappiness. **2** (also **clinical depression**) a condition of mental disturbance characterised by feelings of depression together with other symptoms. **3** a long and severe recession in an economy or market. **4** the action of depressing something. **5** a sunken place or hollow. **6** Meteorology a low-pressure weather system.

SYNONYMS – **1** despondency, gloom, low spirits, melancholy, sadness, unhappiness.

depressive > *adjective* tending to causing depression. > *noun* a person who tends to suffer from depression.

depressurise (also **depressurize**) > *verb* release the pressure inside (a compartment or container).

DERIVATIVES – **depressurisation** noun.

deprivation /depri**vay**sh'n/ > *noun* **1** hardship resulting from the lack of basic material benefits. **2** the action of depriving or the state of being deprived.

deprive > *verb* (usu. **deprive of**) prevent from possessing, using, or enjoying something.

SYNONYMS – dispossess, divest, rob, strip.

ORIGIN – Latin *deprivare*, from *privare* 'bereave, deprive'.

deprived > *adjective* suffering a detrimental lack of basic material and cultural benefits.

SYNONYMS – disadvantaged, impoverished, needy, underprivileged, very poor.

Dept > *abbreviation* Department.

depth > *noun* **1** the distance from the top down, from the surface inwards, or from front to back of something. **2** (**the depths**) the deepest, lowest, or inmost part of something. **3** complexity and profundity of thought. **4** comprehensiveness of study or detail. **5** creditable intensity of emotion.

IDIOMS – **out of one's depth 1** in water too deep to stand in. **2** in a situation beyond one's capabilities.

SYNONYMS – **3** complexity, gravity, moment, profundity, seriousness, weight. **4** comprehensiveness, detail, thoroughness.

COMBINATIONS – **depth charge** a kind of bomb designed to explode at a set depth under water, used to attack submarines.

depthless > *adjective* **1** unfathomably deep. **2** shallow and superficial.

deputation > *noun* a group of people who undertake a mission on behalf of a larger group.

depute > *verb* /dɪˈpyoot/ **1** appoint (someone) to perform a task for which one is responsible. **2** delegate (authority or a task). > *noun* /**dep**yoot/ Scottish a deputy.

deputise /**dep**yootīz/ (also **deputize**) > *verb* temporarily act on behalf of someone else.

deputy > *noun* (pl. **deputies**) **1** a person appointed to undertake the duties of a superior in the superior's absence. **2** a parliamentary representative in certain countries.

SYNONYMS – **1** adjutant, assistant, proxy, representative, second in command.

ORIGIN – Old French *depute*, from Latin *deputare* 'consider to be, assign'.

deracinate /deeˈrassinayt/ > *verb* **1** literary tear up by the roots. **2** (**deracinated**) displaced from one's environment.

DERIVATIVES – **deracination** *noun*.

ORIGIN – French *déraciner* 'uproot'.

derail > *verb* **1** cause (a train) to leave the tracks. **2** obstruct or thwart (a process).

DERIVATIVES – **derailment** *noun*.

derailleur /dɪˈraylər/ > *noun* a bicycle gear which works by lifting the chain from one sprocket wheel to another.

ORIGIN – French, from *dérailler* 'derail'.

derange > *verb* **1** make insane. **2** throw into disorder.

DERIVATIVES – **derangement** *noun*.

ORIGIN – French *déranger*, from Old French *desrengier* 'move from orderly rows'.

deranged > *adjective* mad; insane.

derate > *verb* reduce the rating of (a component or device).

Derby /**daar**bi/ > *noun* (pl. **Derbies**) **1** an annual flat race at Epsom in Surrey for three-year-old horses, founded in 1780 by the 12th Earl of Derby. **2** (in names) a similar race or other important sporting contest. **3** (**derby** or **local derby**) a sports match between two rival teams from the same area. **4** (**derby** /**der**bi/) N. Amer. a bowler hat.

deregulate > *verb* remove regulations or restrictions from.

DERIVATIVES – **deregulation** *noun* **deregulatory** *adjective*.

derelict > *adjective* **1** in a very poor condition as a result of disuse and neglect. **2** chiefly N. Amer. shamefully negligent. > *noun* **1** a destitute person. **2** a ship or other piece of property abandoned by its owner.

SYNONYMS – *noun* **1** crumbling, decrepit, dilapidated, neglected, tumbledown.

ORIGIN – from Latin *derelinquere* 'to abandon'.

dereliction > *noun* **1** the state of having been abandoned and become dilapidated. **2** (usu. **dereliction of duty**) shameful failure to fulfil one's obligations.

derestrict > *verb* remove restrictions from.

DERIVATIVES – **derestriction** *noun*.

deride /dɪˈrīd/ > *verb* express contempt for; ridicule.

SYNONYMS – jeer at, mock, ridicule, scoff at.

ORIGIN – Latin *deridere* 'scoff at'.

de rigueur /də rɪˈgör/ > *adjective* required by etiquette or current fashion.

ORIGIN – French, 'in strictness'.

derision /dɪˈrizh'n/ > *noun* contemptuous ridicule or mockery.

SYNONYMS – contempt, disdain, mockery, ridicule.

derisive /dɪˈrīsiv/ > *adjective* expressing contempt or ridicule.

DERIVATIVES – **derisively** *adverb*.

derisory /dɪˈrīsəri/ > *adjective* **1** ridiculously small or inadequate. **2** another term for DERISIVE.

USAGE – there is a difference between **derisory** and **derisive**. **Derisory** usually means 'ridiculously small or inadequate', whereas **derisive** means 'expressing contempt'.

derivation > *noun* **1** the deriving of something from a source or origin. **2** the formation of a word from another word or from a root in the same or another language.

DERIVATIVES – **derivational** *adjective*.

derivative /dɪˈrivvətiv/ > *adjective* **1** chiefly derogatory imitative of the work of another artist, writer, etc. **2** (of a financial product) having a value deriving from an underlying variable asset. > *noun* **1** something which is derived from another source. **2** a derivative future, option, or other financial product. **3** Mathematics an expression representing the rate of change of a function with respect to an independent variable.

DERIVATIVES – **derivatively** *adverb*.

SYNONYMS – *adjective* **1** copied, imitative, plagiarised, second-hand, unoriginal.

ANTONYMS – *adjective* **1** original.

derive /dɪˈrīv/ > *verb* (**derive from**) **1** obtain (something) from (a source). **2** base (something) on a modification of. **3** have as a root or origin; originate from.

DERIVATIVES – **derivable** *adjective*.

wordpower facts

Derive

The words **derive** and **rival** are related through the Latin word *rivus* 'a stream', the ultimate source of both words. **Derive** entered English from Old French *deriver* or Latin *derivare* 'draw off or divert' and originally meant 'draw a fluid through or into a channel'. **Rival** is from Latin *rivalis* 'person using the same stream as another'.

dermatitis /dermətītiss/ > *noun* inflammation of the skin as a result of irritation by or allergic reaction to an external agent.

ORIGIN – from Greek *derma* 'skin'.

dermatology > *noun* the branch of medicine concerned with skin disorders.

DERIVATIVES – **dermatological** *adjective* **dermatologically** *adverb* **dermatologist** *noun*.

dermatosis /dermətōsiss/ > *noun* (pl. **dermatoses** /dermətōseez/) a disease of the skin, especially one that does not cause inflammation.

dermis /**der**miss/ > *noun* Anatomy the thick layer of the skin below the epidermis, consisting of living tissue.

DERIVATIVES – **dermal** *adjective*.

ORIGIN – modern Latin, suggested by *epidermis*.

dernier cri /dairniay ˈkree/ > *noun* the very latest fashion.

ORIGIN – French, 'last cry'.

derogate /**derr**əgayt/ > *verb* formal **1** (**derogate from**) detract from. **2** (**derogate from**) deviate from (a set of rules or standard of behaviour). **3** disparage.

DERIVATIVES – **derogation** *noun*.

ORIGIN – Latin *derogare* 'abrogate'.

derogatory /dɪˈroggətri/ > *adjective* showing a critical or disrespectful attitude.

DERIVATIVES – **derogatorily** *adverb*.

SYNONYMS – critical, disparaging, pejorative.

derrick /**derr**ik/ > *noun* **1** a kind of crane with a movable pivoted arm. **2** the framework over an oil well, holding the drilling machinery.

ORIGIN – first used to denote a hangman, also the gallows: from *Derrick*, the surname of a London hangman.

derrière /derriˈair/ > *noun* euphemistic or humorous a person's buttocks.

ORIGIN – French, 'behind'.

derring-do /derringˈdoo/ > *noun* dated or humorous action displaying heroic courage.

wordpower facts

Derring-do

The expression **derring-do** arises from the Middle English phrase *dorryng do* 'daring to do', used by Chaucer and misprinted in 16th-century editions as *derrynge do*. This was misinterpreted by the Elizabethan poet Edmund Spenser to mean 'manhood, chivalry', and subsequently taken up and popularised in the historical novels of Sir Walter Scott.

derris /**derr**iss/ > *noun* an insecticide made from the roots of a tropical plant.
ORIGIN – Greek, 'leather covering' (referring to the plant's pods).

derv (also **DERV**) > *noun* Brit. diesel oil for motor vehicles.
ORIGIN – acronym from *diesel-engined road vehicle*.

dervish /**der**vish/ > *noun* a member of a Muslim fraternity sworn to poverty and known for their wild rituals.
ORIGIN – from a Persian word meaning 'poor'.

desalinate /dee**sal**inayt/ > *verb* remove salt from (seawater).
DERIVATIVES – **desalination** *noun* **desalinator** *noun*.

descale > *verb* remove deposits of scale from.
DERIVATIVES – **descaler** *noun*.

descant > *noun* /**des**kant/ an independent treble melody sung or played above a basic melody. > *verb* /dis**kant**/ talk tediously or at length: *I have descanted on this subject before.*
COMBINATIONS – **descant recorder** the most common size of recorder, with a range of two octaves above the C above middle C.
ORIGIN – Latin *discantus* 'part song, refrain'.

descend > *verb* **1** move down or downwards. **2** slope or lead downwards. **3** (**descend to**) lower oneself to commit (a shameful act). **4** (**be descended from**) be a blood relative of (an ancestor). **5** (usu. **descend to**) pass by inheritance. **6** (**descend on**) make a sudden attack on or unwelcome visit to.
DERIVATIVES – **descendent** *adjective* **descender** *noun*.
SYNONYMS – **1,2** come down, drop, go down. **3** (**descend to**) lower oneself to, resort to, sink so low as to, stoop to.
ORIGIN – Latin *descendere* 'climb down'.

descendant* > *noun* a person, animal, etc. that is descended from a particular ancestor.
*SPELLING – the correct spelling of the noun **descendant** is with *-ant*, not *-ent*, at the end; **descendent** is an adjective and means 'descending'.
SYNONYMS – heir, offspring, scion.

descent > *noun* **1** an act or the action of descending. **2** a downward slope. **3** a person's origin or nationality. **4** (**descent on**) a sudden violent attack.
WORDFINDER – genealogy (*line of descent; study of lines of descent*), matrilineal (*relating to the female line of descent*), patrilineal (*relating to the male line of descent*).

describe > *verb* **1** give a detailed account in words of. **2** mark out or draw (a geometrical figure).
DERIVATIVES – **describable** *adjective* **describer** *noun*.
SYNONYMS – **1** narrate, recount, relate.
ORIGIN – Latin *describere* 'write down'.

description > *noun* **1** a spoken or written account. **2** the process of describing. **3** a sort, kind, or class: *people of any description.*
SYNONYMS – **1** account, chronicle, narration, narrative, report.

descriptive > *adjective* **1** serving or seeking to describe. **2** describing or classifying without expressing judgement.
DERIVATIVES – **descriptively** *adverb*.

descry /dis**kri**/ > *verb* (**descries**, **descried**) literary catch sight of.
ORIGIN – Old French *descrier* 'publish, proclaim', perhaps confused with obsolete *descry* 'describe'.

desecrate /**dess**ikrayt/ > *verb* treat (something sacred) with violent disrespect.
DERIVATIVES – **desecration** *noun* **desecrator** *noun*.
SYNONYMS – defile, pollute, profane, violate.
ORIGIN – from **DE-** (expressing reversal) + **CONSECRATE**.

desegregate > *verb* end a policy of racial segregation in (a place).
DERIVATIVES – **desegregation** *noun*.

deselect > *verb* Brit. reject (an existing MP) as a candidate in a forthcoming election.
DERIVATIVES – **deselection** *noun*.

desensitise (also **desensitize**) > *verb* **1** make less sensitive. **2** make indifferent to cruelty or suffering.
DERIVATIVES – **desensitisation** *noun*.

desert¹ /di**zert**/ > *verb* **1** leave without help or support; abandon: *her husband deserted her long ago.* **2** leave (a place), causing it to appear empty. **3** illegally run away from military service.
DERIVATIVES – **desertion** *noun*.
SYNONYMS – **1,2** abandon, forsake, leave.
ORIGIN – Latin *desertare*, from *desertus* 'left waste' (related to **DESERT²**).

desert² /**dezz**ərt/ > *noun* **1** a waterless, desolate area of land with little or no vegetation, typically covered with sand. **2** a situation or area considered dull and uninteresting: *a cultural desert.* > *adjective* like a desert; uninhabited and desolate.
USAGE – do not confuse **desert** (a waterless area) with **dessert** (the sweet course)!
ORIGIN – Latin *desertum* 'something left waste', from *deserere* 'leave, forsake'.

deserted > *adjective* totally empty of people.
SYNONYMS – abandoned, empty, uninhabited, unoccupied, vacant.
ANTONYMS – crowded, populous.

deserter > *noun* a member of the armed forces who deserts.

desertification /dizertifi**kay**sh'n/ > *noun* the process by which fertile land becomes desert.

deserts /di**zerts**/ > *plural noun* (usu. in phrase **get** or **receive one's just deserts**) what a person deserves with regard to reward or punishment.
ORIGIN – Old French *desert*, from *deservir* 'deserve'.

deserve > *verb* do something or show qualities worthy of (a reward or punishment as appropriate).
DERIVATIVES – **deserved** *adjective* **deservedly** *adverb*.
SYNONYMS – justify, merit, rate, warrant, be worthy of.
ORIGIN – Latin *deservire* 'serve well or zealously'.

deserving > *adjective* worthy of favourable treatment or assistance.
SYNONYMS – commendable, laudable, meritorious, praiseworthy.
ANTONYMS – undeserving, worthless.

desex > *verb* **1** deprive of sexual qualities. **2** castrate or spay (an animal).

déshabillé /dezza**bee**ay/ (also **dishabille** /dissa**beel**/) > *noun* the state of being only partly or scantily clothed.
ORIGIN – French, 'undressed'.

desiccate* /**dess**ikayt/ > *verb* remove the moisture from.
DERIVATIVES – **desiccated** *adjective* **desiccation** *noun*.
*SPELLING – one s, two cs: de*si*ccate.
ORIGIN – Latin *desiccare* 'make thoroughly dry'.

desideratum /diziddə**raa**təm/ > *noun* (pl. **desiderata** /diziddə**raa**tə/) something that is needed or wanted.
ORIGIN – Latin, 'something desired'.

design > *noun* **1** a plan or drawing produced to show the look and function or workings of something before it is built or made. **2** the art or action of producing such a plan or drawing. **3** underlying purpose or planning: *the appearance of design in the universe.* **4** a decorative pattern. > *verb* **1** conceive and produce a design for. **2** plan or intend for a purpose: *the reforms were designed to stimulate economic growth.*
IDIOMS – **by design** intentionally. **have**

designs on aim to obtain (something desired), especially in an underhand way.

SYNONYMS – *noun* **1** blueprint, diagram, drawing, outline, plan. **4** decoration, device, motif, pattern. *verb* **1** draft, map out, outline, plan, plot. **2** aim, intend, mean, plan.

ORIGIN – from Latin *designare* 'mark out, designate'.

designate > *verb* /**dezz**ignayt/ **1** assign a name or quality to; describe as. **2** appoint to a specified position. > *adjective* /**dezz**ignət/ (after a noun) appointed to an office or position but not yet installed: *the Director designate*.

DERIVATIVES – **designator** *noun*.

ORIGIN – Latin *designare* (see DESIGN).

designation > *noun* **1** the action of designating. **2** an official title or description.

designedly > *adverb* intentionally.

designer > *noun* **1** a person who designs things. **2** (before another noun) made by a famous fashion designer: *designer jeans*.

COMBINATIONS – **designer drug** a synthetic substitute for an illegal drug, devised to circumvent drug laws.

designing > *adjective* acting in a calculating, deceitful way.

desirable > *adjective* **1** wished for as being attractive, useful, or necessary. **2** (of a person) arousing sexual desire. > *noun* a desirable thing.

DERIVATIVES – **desirability** *noun* **desirableness** *noun* **desirably** *adverb*.

SYNONYMS – **1** attractive, desired, sought-after, valuable. **2** alluring, attractive, beguiling, seductive, sexy.

ANTONYMS – unattractive, undesirable.

desire > *noun* **1** a strong feeling of wanting to have something or wishing for something to happen. **2** strong sexual feeling or appetite. > *verb* **1** strongly wish for or want. **2** want (someone) sexually. **3** archaic request or entreat.

SYNONYMS – *noun* **1** fancy, inclination, urge, wish. **2** lust, lustfulness, passion; formal concupiscence. *verb* **1** crave, want, wish for. **2** lust after, want.

ORIGIN – Latin *desiderare*.

desirous > *adjective* (often **desirous of**) having a desire or wish for something.

desist /di**zist**/ > *verb* (often **desist from**) stop; cease.

ORIGIN – Latin *desistere*, from *sistere* 'to stop'.

desk > *noun* **1** a piece of furniture with a flat or sloping surface and often with drawers, for writing, reading, or other work. **2** a counter in a hotel, bank, airport, etc. **3** a specified section of a news organisation: *the sports desk*. **4** a position in an orchestra at which two players share a music stand.

COMBINATIONS – **desk job** a clerical or administrative job.

ORIGIN – Latin *desca*, from *discus* 'plate' (later 'desk').

deskill > *verb* reduce the level of skill required to carry out (a job).

desktop > *noun* **1** the working surface of a desk. **2** a microcomputer suitable for use at an ordinary desk. **3** the working area of a computer screen regarded as representing a notional desktop.

COMBINATIONS – **desktop publishing** the production of high-quality printed matter by means of a printer linked to a desktop computer.

desolate > *adjective* /**dess**ələt/ **1** giving an impression of bleak and dismal emptiness. **2** utterly wretched and unhappy. > *verb* /**dess**əlayt/ make desolate.

DERIVATIVES – **desolately** *adverb* **desolation** *noun*.

SYNONYMS – *adjective* **1** bleak, dismal, grim, inhospitable. **2** dejected, despondent, devastated, disconsolate, inconsolable, wretched. *verb* destroy, devastate, ravage, ruin, wreck.

ORIGIN – from Latin *desolare* 'abandon', from *solus* 'alone'.

despair* > *noun* the complete loss or absence of hope. > *verb* lose or be without hope.

IDIOMS – **be the despair of** be the cause of despair in (someone else).

DERIVATIVES – **despairing** *adjective* **despairingly** *adverb*.

*SPELLING – des-, not dis-: despair.

SYNONYMS – *noun* dejection, desperation, despondency, hopelessness, misery. *verb* give up, lose hope, resign oneself.

ORIGIN – Latin *desperare*, from *sperare* 'to hope'.

despatch > *verb* & *noun* variant spelling of DISPATCH.

desperado /despə**raa**dō/ > *noun* (pl. **desperadoes** or **desperados**) dated a desperate or reckless criminal.

ORIGIN – pseudo-Spanish alteration of the obsolete noun *desperate* 'person in despair or in a desperate situation'.

desperate* > *adjective* **1** feeling, showing, or involving despair. **2** extremely bad or serious: *a desperate shortage*. **3** having a great need or desire for something: *desperate for a cigarette*. **4** violent or dangerous.

IDIOMS – **desperate diseases must have desperate remedies** proverb extreme measures are justified as a response to a difficult or dangerous situation.

DERIVATIVES – **desperately** *adverb*.

*SPELLING – desperate, not -parate.

SYNONYMS – **1** despairing, hopeless, reckless, wild.

ORIGIN – Latin *desperatus* 'deprived of hope', from *desperare* (see DESPAIR).

desperation > *noun* a state of despair, especially as resulting in reckless behaviour.

SYNONYMS – despair, hopelessness, recklessness, wildness.

despicable /di**spik**əb'l, **des**pikəb'l/ > *adjective* deserving hatred and contempt.

DERIVATIVES – **despicably** *adverb*.

SYNONYMS – base, contemptible, detestable, loathsome, worthless.

ORIGIN – Latin *despicabilis*, from *despicari* 'look down on'.

despise* /di**spīz**/ > *verb* feel contempt or repugnance for.

*SPELLING – **despise** cannot be spelled with an *-ize* ending.

SYNONYMS – disdain, dismiss, look down on, scorn.

ORIGIN – Latin *despicere* 'look down'.

despite /di**spīt**/ > *preposition* in spite of.

ORIGIN – occurring first as a noun, meaning 'contempt, scorn': from Latin *despectus* 'looking down on', from *despicere* 'look down'.

despoil /di**spoyl**/ > *verb* literary steal or violently remove valuable possessions from; plunder.

DERIVATIVES – **despoiler** *noun* **despoliation** /dispōliaysh'n/ *noun*.

ORIGIN – Latin *despoliare* 'rob, plunder'.

despondent > *adjective* in low spirits from loss of hope or courage.

DERIVATIVES – **despondency** *noun* **despondently** *adverb*.

SYNONYMS – despairing, disconsolate, disheartened, downcast, gloomy, miserable, sad.

ANTONYMS – cheerful, hopeful.

ORIGIN – from Latin *despondere* 'give up, abandon'.

despot /**des**pot/ > *noun* a ruler with absolute power, especially one who exercises it in a cruel or oppressive way.

DERIVATIVES – **despotic** *adjective* **despotically** *adverb* **despotism** *noun*.

ORIGIN – Greek *despotēs* 'master, absolute ruler'.

des res /dez **rez**/ > *noun* Brit. informal a desirable residence.

dessert /di**zert**/ > *noun* the sweet course eaten at the end of a meal.

USAGE – do not confuse **dessert** (the sweet course) with **desert** (a waterless area)!

COMBINATIONS – **dessertspoon** a spoon used for dessert, smaller than a tablespoon and larger than a teaspoon. **dessert wine** a sweet wine drunk with or following dessert.

ORIGIN – French, from *desservir* 'clear the table'.

destabilise (also **destabilize**) > *verb* upset the stability of.

DERIVATIVES – **destabilisation** *noun*.

destination > *noun* the place to which someone or something is going or being sent.

SYNONYMS – goal, journey's end.

destine /**des**tin/ > *verb* (**be destined**) **1** be bound for a particular destination. **2** be intended, chosen, or fated to have a particular purpose or end: *they were destined to be friends.*

SYNONYMS – (**be destined**) **1** be bound, be headed, be heading. **2** be fated, be intended, be ordained, be predetermined.

ORIGIN – Latin *destinare* 'make firm, establish'.

destiny > *noun* (pl. **destinies**) **1** the events that will happen to a person, regarded as predetermined by fate. **2** the hidden power believed to control this; fate.

SYNONYMS – **1** fate, fortune, future, lot; archaic portion.

ORIGIN – Latin *destinata*, from *destinare* 'make firm, establish'.

destitute /**des**tityoot/ > *adjective* **1** extremely poor and lacking the means to provide for oneself. **2** (**destitute of**) not having; lacking.

DERIVATIVES – **destitution** *noun*.

SYNONYMS – **1** down and out, impoverished, indigent, poverty-stricken.

ORIGIN – first meaning 'deserted, abandoned': from Latin *destituere* 'forsake'.

destrier /**des**trier/ > *noun* literary a medieval knight's warhorse.

ORIGIN – Old French, from Latin *dextera* 'the right hand' (because the squire led the knight's horse with his right hand).

destroy > *verb* **1** put out of existence by severe damage or attack. **2** completely ruin or spoil. **3** kill (an animal) by humane means.

SYNONYMS – **1,2** annihilate, devastate, ravage, ruin, smash, wreck.

ORIGIN – Latin *destruere*, from *struere* 'build'.

destroyer > *noun* **1** a person or thing that destroys. **2** a small fast warship equipped for a defensive role against submarines and aircraft.

destruct > *verb* cause the destruction of.

DERIVATIVES – **destructor** *noun*.

destructible > *adjective* able to be destroyed.

destruction > *noun* **1** the action of destroying or the state of being destroyed. **2** a cause of someone's ruin.

SYNONYMS – annihilation, devastation, ruin.

destructive > *adjective* **1** causing destruction. **2** negative and unhelpful: *destructive criticism.*

DERIVATIVES – **destructively** *adverb* **destructiveness** *noun*.

SYNONYMS – **1** cataclysmic, catastrophic,

damaging, devastating, ruinous. **2** critical, discouraging, negative.

ANTONYMS – constructive.

desuetude /di**syoo**ityood/ > *noun* formal a state of disuse.

ORIGIN – first meaning 'cessation': from Latin *desuetudo*, from *desuescere* 'make unaccustomed'.

desultory /**dezz**əltri/ > *adjective* **1** lacking purpose or enthusiasm. **2** going from one thing to another in an erratic and intermittent way: *a desultory conversation.*

DERIVATIVES – **desultorily** *adverb*.

SYNONYMS – **1** casual, cursory, half-hearted, perfunctory.

wordpower facts
Desultory
The word **desultory** is derived ultimately from Latin *salire* 'to leap', which is the source of a great many apparently unrelated words that include **assail**, **assault**, **exult**, **insult**, **result**, **salacious**, **salient**, and **sally**. **Desultory** entered English in the 16th century from Latin *desultorius* 'superficial' (literally 'relating to a vaulter'), from *desilire* 'leap down'. The modern sense 2, 'erratically going from one thing to another', was part of its original meaning, but it also had a literal meaning of 'jumping about unpredictably' that is today lost: in the past one could say, as did the naturalist Gilbert White in 1789, 'I shot at it but it was so desultory that I missed my aim'.

detach* > *verb* **1** disengage (something) and remove it. **2** (**detach oneself from**) leave or distance oneself from (a group or situation). **3** (**be detached**) Military be sent on a separate mission.

DERIVATIVES – **detachable** *adjective*.

*SPELLING – only one *t*: de**t**ach, not -*tch*.

SYNONYMS – **1** pull off, remove, take off, undo, unfasten.

ORIGIN – first meaning 'discharge a gun': from French *détacher*, from *attacher* 'attach'.

detached > *adjective* **1** separate or disconnected. **2** (of a house) not joined to another on either side. **3** aloof and objective.

DERIVATIVES – **detachedly** *adverb*.

SYNONYMS – **3** disinterested, dispassionate, distant, objective, remote, uninvolved.

ANTONYMS – **3** involved.

detachment > *noun* **1** the state of being objective or aloof. **2** a group of troops, ships, etc. sent away on a separate mission. **3** the action or process of detaching.

detail > *noun* **1** a small individual item or fact. **2** small items or facts regarded

collectively: *her attention to detail.* **3** a small part of a picture reproduced separately for close study. **4** a small detachment of troops or police officers given a special duty. > *verb* **1** describe item by item. **2** assign to undertake a particular task.

IDIOMS – **in detail** as regards every aspect; fully.

SYNONYMS – *noun* **1** particular, nicety, point, refinement.

ORIGIN – French *détail*, from *tailler* 'to cut'.

detailed > *adjective* having many details.

detailing > *noun* small decorative features on a building, garment, or work of art.

detain > *verb* **1** keep from proceeding; delay. **2** keep in official custody.

DERIVATIVES – **detainer** *noun* **detainment** *noun*.

SYNONYMS – **1** delay, hinder, hold up, impede. **2** arrest, confine, hold, imprison.

ORIGIN – Latin *detinere* 'keep back'.

detainee /deetay**nee**/ > *noun* a person detained in custody, especially for political reasons.

detect > *verb* **1** discover or notice the presence or existence of. **2** discover or investigate (a crime or its perpetrators).

DERIVATIVES – **detectable** *adjective* **detectably** *adverb* **detection** *noun*.

SYNONYMS – **1** become aware of, discern, discover, notice, perceive.

ORIGIN – Latin *detegere* 'uncover', from *tegere* 'to cover'.

detective > *noun* a person, especially a police officer, whose occupation is to investigate crimes.

detector > *noun* a device designed to detect the presence of something and to emit a signal in response.

détente /day**tont**/ > *noun* the easing of hostility or strained relations between countries.

ORIGIN – French, 'loosening, relaxation'.

detention > *noun* **1** the action of detaining or state of being detained. **2** the punishment of being kept in school after hours.

COMBINATIONS – **detention centre** an institution where people, especially refugees and people awaiting trial, are detained.

deter /di**ter**/ > *verb* (**deterred**, **deterring**) **1** discourage (someone) from doing something by making them fear or doubt the consequences. **2** prevent the occurrence of.

SYNONYMS – discourage, dissuade, prevent, put off, stop.

ORIGIN – Latin *deterrere*, from *terrere* 'frighten'.

detergent > *noun* a soluble cleansing agent which combines with impurities and dirt to make them more soluble. > *adjective* relating to detergents or their action.

ORIGIN – from Latin *detergere* 'wipe away'.

deteriorate /diteeriərayt/ > *verb* become progressively worse.
DERIVATIVES – **deterioration** *noun*.
SYNONYMS – decline, degenerate, get worse, worsen.
ANTONYMS – improve.
ORIGIN – Latin *deteriorare*, from *deterior* 'worse'.

determinant /diterminənt/ > *noun* **1** a factor which determines the nature or outcome of something. **2** Biology a gene determining the character and development of particular cells in an organism. **3** Mathematics a quantity obtained by adding products of the elements of a square matrix according to a given rule. > *adjective* serving to determine or decide.

determinate /diterminət/ > *adjective* of fixed and definite limits or nature.
DERIVATIVES – **determinacy** *noun*.

determination > *noun* **1** firmness of purpose; resoluteness. **2** the action or process of determining.
SYNONYMS – **1** dedication, persistence, resoluteness, resolution, resolve, tenacity.

determine > *verb* **1** be the decisive factor in: *it is biological age that determines our looks.* **2** firmly decide. **3** ascertain or establish by research or calculation.
DERIVATIVES – **determinable** *adjective*.
SYNONYMS – **1** control, decide, dictate, govern, shape. **2** decide, make up one's mind, resolve. **3** ascertain, discover, establish, find out.
ORIGIN – Latin *determinare* 'limit, fix'.

determined > *adjective* having firmness of purpose; resolute.
DERIVATIVES – **determinedly** *adverb*.
SYNONYMS – persistent, resolute, tenacious.

determiner > *noun* **1** a person or thing that determines. **2** Grammar a modifying word that determines the kind of reference a noun or noun group has, for example *a*, *the*, *every*.

determinism > *noun* Philosophy the doctrine that all events and actions are determined by external forces acting on the will.
DERIVATIVES – **determinist** *noun* & *adjective* **deterministic** *adjective*.

deterrent /diterrənt/ > *noun* a thing that deters or is intended to deter. > *adjective* able or intended to deter.
DERIVATIVES – **deterrence** *noun*.

detest > *verb* dislike intensely.
SYNONYMS – abhor, abominate, despise, hate, loathe.
ORIGIN – Latin *detestari* 'denounce, abhor', from *testari* 'witness'.

detestable* > *adjective* deserving intense dislike.
*SPELLING – detest**able**, not -**ible**.
SYNONYMS – abhorrent, despicable, obnoxious, repugnant.

detestation /deetestaysh'n/ > *noun* intense dislike.

dethrone > *verb* **1** remove (a monarch) from power. **2** remove from a position of authority or dominance.
DERIVATIVES – **dethronement** *noun*.

detonate /dettənayt/ > *verb* explode or cause to explode.
DERIVATIVES – **detonation** *noun*.
ORIGIN – Latin *detonare*, from *tonare* 'to thunder'.

detonator > *noun* a device or charge used to detonate an explosive.

detour /deetoor/ > *noun* a divergence from a direct or intended route. > *verb* take a detour.
ORIGIN – French, 'change of direction'.

detox informal > *noun* /deetoks/ detoxification. > *verb* /deetoks/ detoxify.

detoxicate /deetoksikayt/ > *verb* another term for DETOXIFY.
DERIVATIVES – **detoxication** *noun*.

detoxify > *verb* (**detoxifies, detoxified**) **1** remove toxic substances from. **2** abstain or help to abstain from drink or drugs until the bloodstream is free of toxins.
DERIVATIVES – **detoxification** *noun* **detoxifier** *noun*.

detract > *verb* (**detract from**) cause to seem less valuable or impressive.
DERIVATIVES – **detraction** *noun*.
SYNONYMS – (**detract from**) devalue, diminish, take away from.
ORIGIN – Latin *detrahere* 'draw away'.

detractor > *noun* a person who disparages someone or something.

detrain > *verb* leave a train, or cause or assist to leave a train.

detriment /detrimənt/ > *noun* harm or damage: *she dieted to the detriment of her health.*
ORIGIN – Latin *detrimentum*, from *deterere* 'wear away'.

detrimental > *adjective* causing harm.
DERIVATIVES – **detrimentally** *adverb*.
SYNONYMS – damaging, deleterious, harmful, injurious, prejudicial.

detritus /ditrītəss/ > *noun* debris or waste material.
DERIVATIVES – **detrital** *adjective*.
ORIGIN – Latin, from *deterere* 'wear away'.

de trop /də trō/ > *adjective* unwelcome because excessive or superfluous.
ORIGIN – French.

detumescence /deetyoomess'nss/ > *noun* the process of subsiding from a state of swelling or sexual arousal.
DERIVATIVES – **detumescent** *adjective*.
ORIGIN – Latin *detumescere*, from *tumescere* 'to swell'.

detune > *verb* **1** cause (a musical instrument) to become out of tune. **2** reduce the performance of (a motor vehicle or engine) by adjustment.

deuce¹ /dyooss/ > *noun* **1** chiefly N. Amer. the number two on dice or playing cards. **2** Tennis the score of 40 all in a game, at which two consecutive points are needed to win the game.
ORIGIN – from Latin *duos* 'two'.

deuce² /dyooss/ > *noun* (**the deuce**) informal used as a euphemism for 'devil' in exclamations or for emphasis.
ORIGIN – probably of the same origin as DEUCE¹ (two aces at dice being the worst throw).

deuced /dyoossid, dyoost/ > *adjective* informal used for emphasis, especially to express disapproval or frustration.
DERIVATIVES – **deucedly** *adverb*.

deus ex machina /dayəss eks makkinə/ > *noun* an unexpected event saving a seemingly hopeless situation, especially in a narrative.
ORIGIN – Latin, from Greek *theos ek mēkhanēs* 'god from the machinery' (referring to the actors representing gods suspended above the stage in ancient Greek theatre, who intervened in the play's outcome).

deuterium /dyooteeriəm/ > *noun* Chemistry a stable isotope of hydrogen with a mass approximately twice that of the usual isotope.
ORIGIN – Latin, from Greek *deuteros* 'second'.

Deutschmark /doychmaark/ (also **Deutsche Mark** /doychə maark/) > *noun* the basic monetary unit of Germany, equal to 100 pfennig.
ORIGIN – German, 'German mark'.

devalue > *verb* (**devalues, devalued, devaluing**) **1** reduce the worth of. **2** reduce the official value of (a currency) in relation to other currencies.
DERIVATIVES – **devaluation** *noun*.
SYNONYMS – **1** belittle, cheapen, depreciate, trivialise.

devastate /devvəstayt/ > *verb* **1** destroy or ruin. **2** overwhelm with shock or grief.
DERIVATIVES – **devastation** *noun* **devastator** *noun*.
SYNONYMS – **1** demolish, destroy, lay waste to, ravage, ruin. **2** prostrate, shatter, shock, stun, traumatise.
ORIGIN – Latin *devastare*, from *vastare* 'lay waste'.

devastating > *adjective* **1** highly destructive. **2** extremely distressing or shocking. **3** informal very impressive or attractive.
DERIVATIVES – **devastatingly** *adverb*.
SYNONYMS – **1** calamitous, cataclysmic, catastrophic, ruinous, shattering. **2** crushing, overwhelming, shattering, traumatic.

develop* > *verb* (**developed, developing**) **1** become or make larger or more advanced. **2** start to exist; begin. **3** begin to experience or possess. **4** convert (land) to a new purpose, especially by constructing buildings. **5** treat (a photographic film) with chemicals to make a visible image.

DERIVATIVES – **developable** *adjective* **developer** *noun*.

***SPELLING** – there is no *e* at the end: deve*lop*.

SYNONYMS – **1** evolve, grow, improve, progress, upgrade.

ANTONYMS – **1** decline, stagnate.

COMBINATIONS – **developing country** a poor country that is seeking to become more advanced economically and socially.

ORIGIN – first meaning 'unfold': from French *développer*, from Latin *dis-* 'un-' + a second element found also in **ENVELOP**.

development > *noun* **1** the action of developing or state of being developed. **2** a new product or idea. **3** a new stage in a changing situation. **4** an area of land with new buildings on it.

DERIVATIVES – **developmental** *adjective* **developmentally** *adverb*.

deviant > *adjective* diverging from normal standards, especially in social or sexual behaviour. > *noun* a deviant person.

DERIVATIVES – **deviance** *noun* **deviancy** *noun*.

SYNONYMS – *adjective* aberrant, abnormal, perverted, warped. *noun* misfit, pervert; informal freak, weirdo.

ANTONYMS – *adjective* normal.

deviate > *verb* /**dee**viayt/ diverge from an established course or from normal standards.

SYNONYMS – diverge, go astray, stray, turn aside.

ORIGIN – Latin *deviare* 'turn out of the way', from *via* 'way'.

deviation > *noun* **1** the action or an act of deviating. **2** Statistics the amount by which a single measurement differs from a fixed value.

device > *noun* **1** a thing made for a particular purpose, especially a mechanical or electronic one. **2** a plan, scheme, or trick. **3** a drawing or design.

IDIOMS – **leave someone to their own devices** leave someone to do as they wish.

SYNONYMS – **1** apparatus, appliance, gadget, instrument, tool.

ORIGIN – Old French *devis*, from Latin *dividere* 'to divide'; an early sense was 'desire or intention', now found only in *leave someone to their own devices*.

devil > *noun* **1** (often **the Devil**) (in Christian and Jewish belief) the supreme spirit of evil. **2** an evil spirit; a demon. **3** a very wicked or cruel person. **4** a mischievously clever or self-willed person. **5** informal a person with specified characteristics: *the poor devil*. **6** (**the devil**) fighting spirit; wildness. **7** (**the devil**) a thing that is very difficult to deal

with. **8** (**the devil**) expressing surprise or annoyance.

WORDFINDER – diabolical (*relating to the Devil*); *names for the Devil:* Beelzebub, Belial, Lord of the Flies, Lucifer, Mephistopheles, Moloch, Old Nick, Satan.

IDIOMS – **be a devil!** informal said to encourage a hesitant person. **between the devil and the deep blue sea** caught in a dilemma, when a decision either way will bring undesirable consequences. **the devil can quote scripture for his purpose** proverb people may conceal unworthy motives by reciting words that sound morally authoritative. **the devil finds work for idle hands to do** proverb if someone doesn't have enough work to occupy them, they are liable to cause or get into trouble. **the devil looks after his own** proverb success or good fortune often seem to come to those who least deserve it. **devil-may-care** cheerful and reckless. **the devil's in the detail** the details of a matter are its most problematic aspect. **the devil to pay** serious trouble to be dealt with. **give the devil his due** proverb if someone or something generally considered bad or undeserving has any redeeming features these should be acknowledged. **like the devil** with great speed or energy. **speak (or talk) of the devil** said when a person appears just after being mentioned.

COMBINATIONS – **devil's advocate** a person who expresses a contentious opinion in order to provoke debate. **devil's food cake** chiefly N. Amer. a rich chocolate cake.

wordpower facts

Devil

The word **devil** comes ultimately from Greek *diabolos* 'accuser, slanderer'. This came into Old English as *dēofol*, in which we can recognise the modern word **devil**. *Diabolos* was the word used in the Greek version of the Old Testament, the Septuagint, to translate Hebrew *śāṭān* 'Satan', which itself became one of the many English names for the Devil. The adjectives **diabolical** and **diabolic** are more recent entries into the language, coming through Old French *diabolique* from the Latin word for 'devil', *diabolus*.

devilish > *adjective* **1** like a devil in evil and cruelty. **2** mischievous. **3** very difficult to deal with. > *adverb* informal, dated very; extremely: *a devilish clever chap*.

DERIVATIVES – **devilishly** *adverb* **devilishness** *noun*.

devilled > *adjective* cooked with hot seasoning.

devilment > *noun* reckless mischief; wild spirits.

devilry > *noun* **1** wicked activity. **2** reckless mischief.

devious /**dee**viəss/ > *adjective* **1** skilful in using underhand tactics. **2** (of a route or journey) deviating from the most direct course; roundabout.

DERIVATIVES – **deviously** *adverb* **deviousness** *noun*.

SYNONYMS – **1** conniving, Machiavellian, underhand.

ANTONYMS – **1** honest, straightforward.

ORIGIN – Latin *devius* 'out of the way', from *via* 'way'.

devise* /di**vīz**/ > *verb* **1** plan or invent (a procedure or mechanism). **2** Law leave (property consisting of land or buildings) to someone in a will.

DERIVATIVES – **deviser** *noun*.

***SPELLING** – **devise** cannot be spelled with an *-ize* ending.

SYNONYMS – **1** contrive, formulate, invent, plan.

ORIGIN – Old French *deviser*, from Latin *dividere* 'force apart, remove'.

devitalise (also **devitalize**) > *verb* deprive of strength and vigour.

DERIVATIVES – **devitalisation** *noun*.

devoid /di**voyd**/ > *adjective* (**devoid of**) entirely lacking in.

ORIGIN – from Old French *devoidier* 'cast out'.

devolution /deevə**loo**sh'n/ > *noun* the transferring of power by central government to local or regional administration.

DERIVATIVES – **devolutionary** *adjective* **devolutionist** *noun*.

devolve /di**volv**/ > *verb* **1** transfer (power) to a lower level, especially from central government to local or regional administration. **2** (**devolve on** or **to**) (of duties or responsibility) pass to (a deputy or successor). **3** (**devolve on** or **to**) Law (of property) pass from one owner to (another), especially by inheritance.

ORIGIN – Latin *devolvere* 'roll down'.

Devonian /di**vō**niən/ > *adjective* Geology relating to the fourth period of the Palaeozoic era (about 409 to 363 million years ago), a time when the first amphibians appeared.

devoré /də**vo**ray/ > *noun* a velvet fabric with a pattern formed by burning the pile away with acid.

ORIGIN – French, 'devoured'.

devote > *verb* (**devote to**) give (time or resources) to.

SYNONYMS – allocate, assign, commit, dedicate, set aside.

ORIGIN – Latin *devovere* 'consecrate', from *vovere* 'to vow'.

devoted > *adjective* very loving or loyal.
DERIVATIVES – **devotedly** *adverb*.
SYNONYMS – committed, constant, loyal, steadfast.
ANTONYMS – disloyal, indifferent.

devotee /devvətee/ > *noun* **1** a person who is very enthusiastic about someone or something. **2** a follower of a particular religion or god.
SYNONYMS – **1** aficionado, connoisseur, enthusiast, fan.

devotion > *noun* **1** great love or loyalty. **2** religious worship. **3** (**devotions**) prayers or religious observances.
DERIVATIVES – **devotional** *adjective*.
SYNONYMS – **1** commitment, constancy, love, loyalty, steadfastness. **2** praise, reverence, veneration, worship.
ANTONYMS – **1** disloyalty, indifference.

devour /divowr/ > *verb* **1** eat greedily. **2** (of fire) consume destructively. **3** read quickly and eagerly. **4** (**be devoured**) be totally absorbed by an emotion.
DERIVATIVES – **devourer** *noun*.
SYNONYMS – **1** gobble, guzzle, wolf.
ORIGIN – Latin *devorare*, from *vorare* 'to swallow'.

devout /divowt/ > *adjective* **1** deeply religious. **2** earnestly sincere: *my devout hope*.
DERIVATIVES – **devoutly** *adverb* **devoutness** *noun*.
SYNONYMS – **1** God-fearing, holy, pious, religious.
ORIGIN – Latin *devotus* 'devoted', from *devovere* 'consecrate'.

dew > *noun* **1** tiny drops of water that form when atmospheric vapour condenses on cool surfaces at night. **2** beaded or glistening liquid.
COMBINATIONS – **dewberry** the edible blue-black fruit of a trailing bramble, with a dewy white bloom. **dew point** the atmospheric temperature below which dew can form.

Dewey decimal classification > *noun* a decimal system of library classification which uses a three-figure code from 000 to 999 to represent the major branches of knowledge.
ORIGIN – named after the American librarian Melvil *Dewey* (1851–1931).

dewlap > *noun* a fold of loose skin hanging from the neck or throat of an animal or bird, especially that present in many cattle.

dewy > *adjective* (**dewier, dewiest**) **1** wet with dew. **2** (of a person's skin) appearing soft and lustrous.
COMBINATIONS – **dewy-eyed** naively sentimental.

Dexedrine /deksədreen/ > *noun* trademark a form of amphetamine.

dexter /dekstər/ > *adjective* **Heraldry** on or towards the bearer's right-hand side and the observer's left of a coat of arms. The opposite of **SINISTER**.
ORIGIN – Latin, 'on the right'.

dexterity /deksterriti/ > *noun* skill in performing tasks, especially with the hands.
ORIGIN – Latin *dexteritas*, from *dexter* 'on the right'.

dexterous /dekstrəss/ (also **dextrous**) > *adjective* showing dexterity; adroit.
DERIVATIVES – **dexterously** *adverb*.
SYNONYMS – adept, adroit, deft, skilful.
ANTONYMS – clumsy.

dextrose > *noun* a naturally occurring form of glucose.
ORIGIN – from Latin *dexter* 'on the right' + **-OSE**², because solutions of dextrose rotate the plane of polarised light to the right (i.e. clockwise).

dextrous > *adjective* variant spelling of **DEXTEROUS**.

DFC > *abbreviation* (in the UK) Distinguished Flying Cross.

DFE > *abbreviation* Department for Education.

DFM > *abbreviation* (in the UK) Distinguished Flying Medal.

DG > *abbreviation* director general.

dhal /daal/ (also **dal**) > *noun* (in Indian cookery) split pulses.
ORIGIN – Hindi.

dhansak /dansak/ > *noun* an Indian dish of meat or vegetables cooked with lentils and coriander.
ORIGIN – Gujarati.

dharma /daarmə/ > *noun* (in Indian religion) the eternal law of the cosmos.
ORIGIN – Sanskrit, 'decree or custom'.

dhobi /dōbi/ > *noun* (pl. **dhobis**) (in the Indian subcontinent) a person whose occupation is washing clothes.
ORIGIN – Hindi.

dhoti /dōti/ > *noun* (pl. **dhotis**) a loincloth worn by male Hindus.
ORIGIN – Hindi.

dhow /dow/ > *noun* a lateen-rigged ship with one or two masts, used chiefly in the Arabian region.
ORIGIN – Arabic.

dhurrie /durri/ > *noun* (pl. **dhurries**) a heavy cotton rug of Indian origin.
ORIGIN – Hindi.

di- /dī, di/ > *combining form* twice; two-; double: *dioxide*.
ORIGIN – Greek *dis* 'twice'.

dia- (also **di-** before a vowel) > *prefix* **1** through; across: *diameter*. **2** apart: *diaeresis*.
ORIGIN – Greek *dia* 'through'.

diabetes /dīəbeeteez/ > *noun* a disorder of the metabolism causing the production of large amounts of urine.
COMBINATIONS – **diabetes mellitus** /militəss/ the commonest form of diabetes, caused by a deficiency of the pancreatic hormone insulin, which results in a failure to metabolise sugars and starch.
ORIGIN – Greek, 'siphon'; *mellitus* is Latin for 'sweet'.

diabetic > *adjective* having or relating to diabetes. > *noun* a person with diabetes.

diabolical > *adjective* **1** (also **diabolic**) of or like the Devil, especially in being evil or cruel. **2** informal very bad; terrible.
DERIVATIVES – **diabolically** *adverb*.
SYNONYMS – **1** demonic, devilish, fiendish, satanic, ungodly. **2** awful, dire, lousy, rotten, terrible.
ORIGIN – from Latin *diabolus* 'devil'.

diabolism /dīabbəliz'm/ > *noun* worship of the Devil.
DERIVATIVES – **diabolist** *noun*.

diachronic /dīəkronnik/ > *adjective* concerned with the way in which something, especially language, has developed through time. Contrasted with **SYNCHRONIC**.
DERIVATIVES – **diachronically** *adverb* **diachrony** /dīakrəni/ *noun*.
ORIGIN – from Greek *khronos* 'time'.

diaconal /dīakkən'l/ > *adjective* relating to a deacon or deacons.
ORIGIN – from Latin *diaconus* 'deacon'.

diaconate /dīakkənayt, dīakkənət/ > *noun* **1** the office of deacon. **2** a body of deacons.

diacritic /dīəkrittik/ > *noun* a sign, such as an accent, written above or below a letter to indicate a difference in pronunciation from the same letter when unmarked. > *adjective* (of a mark or sign) indicating a difference in pronunciation.
DERIVATIVES – **diacritical** *adjective*.
ORIGIN – Greek *diakritikos*, from *diakrinein* 'distinguish'.

diadem /dīədem/ > *noun* a jewelled crown or headband worn as a symbol of sovereignty.
ORIGIN – Greek *diadēma*, from *diadein* 'bind round'.

diaeresis /dīeerəsiss/ (US **dieresis**) > *noun* (pl. **diaereses** /dīeerəseez/) a mark (¨) placed over a vowel to indicate that it is sounded separately, as in *naïve*.
ORIGIN – Greek *diairesis* 'separation'.

diagnose /dīəgnōz/ > *verb* **1** make a diagnosis of (an illness). **2** identify the medical condition of (someone).
DERIVATIVES – **diagnosable** *adjective*.
ORIGIN – back-formation from **DIAGNOSIS**.

diagnosis /dīəgnōsiss/ > *noun* (pl. **diagnoses** /dīəgnōseez/) the identification of the nature of an illness or other problem by examination of the symptoms.
SYNONYMS – conclusion, identification, judgement, verdict.

ORIGIN – Greek, from *diagignōskein* 'distinguish, discern'.

diagnostic /dīəg**nos**tik/ > *adjective* **1** concerned with diagnosis. **2** distinctive, and so allowing identification: *infections which are diagnostic of Aids*. > *noun* **1** a distinctive symptom or characteristic. **2** (**diagnostics**) (treated as sing. or pl.) the practice or techniques of diagnosis.

DERIVATIVES – **diagnostically** *adverb* **diagnostician** *noun*.

diagonal /dī**agg**ən'l/ > *adjective* **1** denoting a straight line joining opposite corners of a rectangle, square, or other figure. **2** (of a line) straight and at an angle; slanting. > *noun* a diagonal line.

DERIVATIVES – **diagonally** *adverb*.

ORIGIN – Greek *diagōnios* 'from angle to angle'.

diagram > *noun* a drawing giving a schematic representation of the appearance or structure of something. > *verb* (**diagrammed**, **diagramming**; US **diagramed**, **diagraming**) represent by means of a diagram.

DERIVATIVES – **diagrammatic** *adjective* **diagrammatically** *adverb*.

ORIGIN – Greek *diagramma*, from *diagraphein* 'mark out by lines'.

dial > *noun* **1** a disc marked to show the time on a clock or indicate a reading or measurement by means of a pointer. **2** a disc with numbered holes on a telephone, turned to make a call. **3** a disc turned to select a setting on a radio, cooker, etc. **4** Brit. informal a person's face. > *verb* (**dialled**, **dialling**; US **dialed**, **dialing**) call (a telephone number) by turning a dial or using a keypad.

DERIVATIVES – **dialler** (also **dialer**) *noun*.

COMBINATIONS – **dialling code** Brit. a sequence of numbers dialled to connect a telephone to an exchange in another area or country. **dialling tone** (N. Amer. **dial tone**) a sound produced by a telephone that indicates that a caller may start to dial.

ORIGIN – Latin *diale* 'clock dial', from *dies* 'day'.

dialect /**dī**əlekt/ > *noun* a form of a language which is peculiar to a specific region or social group.

DERIVATIVES – **dialectal** *adjective*.

ORIGIN – Greek *dialektos* 'discourse, way of speaking'.

dialectic /dīə**lek**tik/ Philosophy > *noun* (also **dialectics**) (usu. treated as sing.) **1** the investigation of the truth of opinions, especially by logical discussion. **2** enquiry into metaphysical contradictions and their solutions. **3** the existence or action of opposing social forces, concepts, etc. > *adjective* of or relating to dialectic or dialectics.

ORIGIN – from Greek *dialektikē tekhnē* 'art of debate', from *dialegesthai* 'converse with'.

dialectical > *adjective* **1** relating to the logical discussion of opinions. **2** concerned with or acting through opposing forces.

DERIVATIVES – **dialectically** *adverb*.

COMBINATIONS – **dialectical materialism** the Marxist theory that political and historical events result from the conflict of social forces (as caused by material needs).

dialectician /dīəlek**tish**'n/ > *noun* a person skilled in philosophical debate.

dialectology /dīəlek**toll**əji/ > *noun* the branch of linguistics concerned with the study of dialects.

DERIVATIVES – **dialectological** *adjective* **dialectologist** *noun*.

dialogic /dīə**lo**jik/ > *adjective* relating to or in the form of dialogue.

DERIVATIVES – **dialogical** *adjective*.

dialogue (US also **dialog**) > *noun* **1** conversation between two or more people as a feature of a book, play, or film. **2** discussion directed towards exploration of a subject or resolution of a problem. > *verb* chiefly N. Amer. take part in dialogue.

SYNONYMS – *noun* **1** conversation, discourse, talk. **2** debate, discussion, negotiation, talks.

COMBINATIONS – **dialog box** (Brit. also **dialogue box**) a small area on a computer screen in which the user is prompted to provide information or select commands.

ORIGIN – Greek *dialogos*, from *dialegesthai* 'converse with'.

dialyse /**dī**əlīz/ (US **dialyze**) > *verb* purify (a mixture) or treat (a patient) by means of dialysis.

dialysis /dī**al**isiss/ > *noun* (pl. **dialyses** /dī**al**iseez/) **1** Chemistry the separation of particles in a liquid on the basis of differences in their ability to pass through a membrane. **2** the clinical purification of blood by this technique, as a substitute for the normal function of the kidney.

ORIGIN – Greek *dialusis*, from *dialuein* 'split, separate'.

diamanté /dīə**mon**tay/ > *adjective* decorated with artificial jewels. > *noun* fabric or costume jewellery decorated with artificial jewels.

ORIGIN – French, 'set with diamonds'.

diamantine /dīə**man**tin, dīə**man**teen/ > *adjective* made from or resembling diamonds.

ORIGIN – French *diamantin*, from *diamant* 'diamond'.

diameter /dī**amm**itər/ > *noun* a straight line passing from side to side through the centre of a circle or sphere.

ORIGIN – from Greek *diametros grammē* 'line measuring across'.

diametrical /dīə**met**rik'l/ > *adjective* **1** (of opposites) complete; absolute. **2** of or along a diameter.

DERIVATIVES – **diametric** *adjective* **diametrically** *adverb*.

diamond > *noun* **1** a precious stone consisting of a clear and colourless crystalline form of pure carbon, the hardest naturally occurring substance. **2** a figure with four straight sides of equal length forming two opposite acute angles and two opposite obtuse angles; a rhombus. **3** (**diamonds**) one of the four suits in a conventional pack of playing cards, denoted by a red figure of such a shape.

WORDFINDER – bort (*inferior diamonds used in cutting tools*), diamantine (*made from or like diamonds*), kimberlite (*rock containing diamonds*), rhinestone (*imitation diamond, used in jewellery*), solitaire (*single diamond set on its own in jewellery*).

DERIVATIVES – **diamondiferous** /dīəmən**diff**ərəss/ *adjective*.

COMBINATIONS – **diamond jubilee** the sixtieth anniversary of a notable event. **diamond wedding** the sixtieth anniversary of a wedding.

ORIGIN – Old French *diamant*, from Latin *adamas, adamant-* 'invincible', later denoting the hardest metal or stone.

diamorphine /dīə**mor**feen/ > *noun* technical term for heroin.

dianthus /dī**anth**əss/ > *noun* (pl. **dianthuses**) a flowering plant of a group that includes the pinks and carnations.

ORIGIN – from Greek *Dios* 'of Zeus' + *anthos* 'flower'.

diapason /dīə**pay**zən/ > *noun* **1** an organ stop sounding a main register of flue pipes. **2** a grand swelling burst of harmony.

ORIGIN – from Greek *dia pasōn khordōn* 'through all notes'.

diaper /**dī**əpər/ > *noun* **1** N. Amer. a baby's nappy. **2** a fabric woven in a pattern of small diamonds. **3** a repeating geometrical pattern. > *verb* **1** N. Amer. put a nappy on (a baby). **2** decorate with a repeating geometrical pattern.

ORIGIN – from Greek *diaspros*, from *dia* 'across' + *aspros* 'white'.

diaphanous /dī**aff**ənəss/ > *adjective* light, delicate, and translucent.

SYNONYMS – filmy, gauzy, gossamer, sheer.

ORIGIN – Greek *diaphanēs*, from *dia* 'through' + *phainein* 'to show'.

diaphoretic /dīəfə**rett**ik/ > *adjective* Medicine inducing perspiration.

DERIVATIVES – **diaphoresis** *noun*.

ORIGIN – Greek *diaphorētikos*, from *diaphorein* 'sweat out'.

diaphragm /**dī**əfram/ > *noun* **1** a dome-shaped muscular partition separating the thorax from the abdomen in mammals. **2** a taut flexible membrane in mechanical or acoustic systems. **3** a thin contraceptive cap fitting over the cervix. **4** a device for varying the effective aperture of the lens in a camera or other optical system.

DERIVATIVES – **diaphragmatic** adjective.

ORIGIN – Latin diaphragma, from Greek dia 'through, apart' + phragma 'a fence'.

diarist > noun a person who writes a diary.

diarrhoea* /dīəreeə/ (US **diarrhea**) > noun a condition in which faeces are discharged from the bowels frequently and in a liquid form.

DERIVATIVES – **diarrhoeal** adjective.

*SPELLING – two rs, and -hoea at the end: diarrhoea.

ORIGIN – Greek diarrhoia, from diarrhein 'flow through'.

diary > noun (pl. **diaries**) **1** a book in which one keeps a daily record of events and experiences. **2** a book marked with each day's date, in which to note appointments.

SYNONYMS – **1** archive, chronicle, journal, log, memoir. **2** calendar, timetable.

wordpower facts

Diary

As well as being synonyms, **diary** and **journal** come from the same Latin word: dies 'day'. **Dial** and **dismal** also derive from dies, the latter being a contraction of dies mali 'evil days'. The dissimilarity of dies and **journal** is explained by the changes the word underwent in Old French. Latin diurnalis 'daily' became Old French jurnal, which came into English with the meaning 'a book containing the times of daily prayers'. **Journey** (originally meaning 'a day's travel') and **journeyman** (a labourer paid by the day) also come from diurnalis. The English word **day**, however, comes from a Germanic root shared by German Tag, rather than from Latin.

diaspora /dīaspərə/ > noun **1** (**the diaspora**) the dispersion of the Jews beyond Israel, beginning in the 8th century BC. **2** the dispersion of any people from their traditional homeland.

ORIGIN – Greek, from diaspeirein 'disperse'.

diastole /dīastəli/ > noun the phase of the heartbeat when the heart muscle relaxes and the chambers fill with blood. Contrasted with **SYSTOLE**.

DERIVATIVES – **diastolic** adjective.

ORIGIN – Greek, 'separation, expansion'.

diathermy /dīəthermi/ > noun a medical and surgical technique involving the production of heat in a part of the body by high-frequency electric currents.

ORIGIN – from **DIA-** + Greek thermos 'heat'.

diatom /dīətəm/ > noun a single-celled alga which has a cell wall of silica.

DERIVATIVES – **diatomaceous** adjective.

ORIGIN – from Greek diatomos 'cut in two'.

diatomic /dīətommik/ > adjective Chemistry consisting of two atoms.

diatonic /dīətonnik/ > adjective Music involving only the notes of the major or minor scale, without chromatic alteration.

ORIGIN – Greek diatonikos 'at intervals of a tone'.

diatribe /dīətrīb/ > noun a harsh and forceful verbal attack.

SYNONYMS – broadside, denunciation, harangue, rant, tirade.

ORIGIN – Greek diatribē 'spending of time, discourse'.

diazepam /dīazzipam/ > noun a tranquillising drug used to relieve anxiety. Also called **VALIUM** (trademark).

dibber > noun Brit. a dibble.

dibble > noun a pointed hand tool for making holes in the ground for seeds or young plants. > verb dig or plant with a dibble.

dibs > plural noun (often in phrase **have first dibs**) N. Amer. informal the right to share or choose something.

ORIGIN – first denoting pebbles used in a children's game, from earlier dib-stones.

dice > noun (pl. same; sing. also **die**) a small cube with faces bearing from one to six spots, used in games of chance. See also **DIE²**. > verb cut (food) into small cubes.

IDIOMS – **dice with death** take serious risks. **no dice** informal, chiefly N. Amer. used to indicate an unsuccessful attempt or request.

USAGE – historically, **dice** is the plural of **die**, but in modern standard English **dice** is used as both the singular and the plural.

ORIGIN – Old French des, plural of de, from Latin datum 'something given or played'.

dicey > adjective (**dicier**, **diciest**) informal difficult or potentially dangerous.

dichotomise (also **dichotomize**) > verb regard or represent as divided or opposed.

dichotomy /dīkottəmi/ > noun (pl. **dichotomies**) a separation or contrast between two things.

DERIVATIVES – **dichotomous** adjective.

SYNONYMS – antithesis, duality, polarity.

ORIGIN – Greek dikhotomia, from dikho- 'in two, apart'.

dick¹ > noun vulgar slang **1** a penis. **2** Brit. a stupid or contemptible person.

dick² > noun informal, dated, chiefly N. Amer. a detective.

dickens /dikkinz/ > noun informal used to express annoyance or surprise when asking questions: what the dickens is going on?

ORIGIN – a euphemism for 'devil'.

Dickensian /dikenziən/ > adjective of or

reminiscent of the novels of Charles Dickens (1812–1870), especially in terms of the urban poverty that they portray.

dicker /dikkər/ > verb **1** engage in petty argument or bargaining. **2** toy or fiddle with something.

ORIGIN – perhaps from obsolete dicker 'set of ten hides', used as a unit of trade, based on Latin decem 'ten'.

dickhead > noun vulgar slang a stupid, irritating, or ridiculous man.

dicky > adjective (**dickier**, **dickiest**) Brit. informal not strong, healthy, or functioning reliably.

dicotyledon /dīkotileed'n/ > noun a plant with an embryo bearing two cotyledons (seed leaves).

dicta plural of **DICTUM**.

Dictaphone /diktəfōn/ > noun trademark a small cassette recorder used to record speech.

dictate > verb /diktayt/ **1** state or order authoritatively. **2** say or read aloud (words to be typed or written down). **3** control or determine. > noun /diktayt/ an order or principle that must be obeyed.

DERIVATIVES – **dictation** noun.

SYNONYMS – verb **1** decree, mandate, order, stipulate. noun declaration, decree, edict, order, proclamation, pronouncement.

ORIGIN – Latin dictare.

dictator > noun a ruler with total power over a country.

SYNONYMS – autocrat, despot, tyrant.

dictatorial > adjective characteristic or typical of a dictator.

DERIVATIVES – **dictatorially** adverb.

SYNONYMS – autocratic, despotic, tyrannical.

dictatorship > noun **1** government by a dictator. **2** a country governed by a dictator.

diction > noun **1** the choice and use of words in speech or writing. **2** the style of enunciation in speaking or singing.

wordpower facts

Diction

The word **diction** comes from Latin dicere 'to say'. Dicere is also the source of the dict- element in words such as **dictum** (literally 'something said'), **addicted**, **benediction**, **contradict**, **edict**, **jurisdiction**, and **predict**. It is also the root of **judge**, which comes from Latin judex, from jus 'law' + dicere. **Dictionary** is from medieval Latin dictionarium manuale or dictionarius liber 'manual or book of words'.

dictionary > noun (pl. **dictionaries**) a book that lists the words of a language and gives their meaning, or their equivalent in a different language.

WORDFINDER – gazetteer (*geographical dictionary*), lexicographer (*person who compiles dictionaries*), lexicon (*a dictionary, especially of Greek, Hebrew, Syriac, or Arabic*), thesaurus (*book of synonyms*).

dictum /diktəm/ > noun (pl. **dicta** /diktə/ or **dictums**) **1** a formal pronouncement from an authoritative source. **2** a short statement that expresses a general principle.

did past of DO[1].

didactic /didaktik/ > adjective **1** intended to teach or give moral instruction. **2** patronising or moralising.

DERIVATIVES – **didactically** adverb **didacticism** noun.

ORIGIN – Greek *didaktikos*, from *didaskein* 'teach'.

diddle > verb informal cheat or swindle.

ORIGIN – probably from the name of Jeremy *Diddler*, a character in the farce *Raising the Wind* (1803) who constantly borrowed small sums of money.

diddly-squat > pronoun N. Amer. informal anything at all.

diddums > exclamation Brit. informal used to express commiseration to a child.

ORIGIN – from *did 'em*, i.e. 'did they?'.

didgeridoo /dijəridoo/ > noun an Australian Aboriginal wind instrument in the form of a long wooden tube, blown to produce a deep resonant sound.

ORIGIN – from an Aboriginal language.

didn't > contraction did not.

didst archaic second person singular past of DO[1].

die[1] > verb (**died**, **dying**) **1** stop living. **2** (**die out**) become extinct. **3** (often **die away** or **down**) become less loud or strong. **4** (**be dying for** or **to do**) informal be very eager for or to do.

IDIOMS – **die hard** disappear or change very slowly. **never say die** do not give up hope. **to die for** informal extremely good or desirable.

SYNONYMS – **1** expire, pass away, perish. **3** diminish, dwindle, fade, recede, wane.

ORIGIN – Old Norse.

die[2] > noun **1** singular form of DICE. **2** (pl. **dies**) a device for cutting or moulding metal or for stamping a design onto coins or medals.

IDIOMS – **the die is cast** an event has happened that cannot be changed. **(as) straight as a die 1** completely straight. **2** entirely open and honest.

USAGE – in modern English the traditional singular **die** (rather than **dice**) for a small cube with numbered faces is now uncommon, and **dice** is used for both the singular and the plural.

COMBINATIONS – **die-cast** (of a metal object) formed by pouring molten metal into a mould.

ORIGIN – Old French *de*, from Latin *datum* 'something given or played'.

dieback > noun a condition in which a tree or shrub begins to die from the tip of its leaves or roots backwards.

diehard > noun a person who supports something loyally and uncompromisingly.

dielectric /dī-ilektrik/ Physics > adjective non-conducting of electricity; insulating. > noun an insulator.

dieresis > noun US spelling of DIAERESIS.

diesel /deez'l/ > noun **1** an internal-combustion engine in which the heat of compressed air is used to ignite the fuel. **2** a form of petroleum used to fuel diesel engines.

ORIGIN – named after the German engineer Rudolf *Diesel* (1858–1913).

diet[1] > noun **1** the kinds of food that a person, animal, or community habitually eats. **2** a restricted regime of eating, followed in order to lose weight or for medical reasons. **3** (before another noun) (of food or drink) with reduced fat or sugar content. > verb (**dieted**, **dieting**) restrict oneself to a special diet to lose weight.

DERIVATIVES – **dietary** adjective **dieter** noun.

SYNONYMS – noun **1** fare, food, intake, regimen.

ORIGIN – Greek *diaita* 'a way of life'.

diet[2] > noun **1** a legislative assembly in certain countries. **2** historical a regular meeting of the states of a confederation.

ORIGIN – Latin *dieta* 'day's work', also 'meeting of councillors'.

dietetics > plural noun (treated as sing.) the branch of knowledge concerned with the diet and its effects on health.

DERIVATIVES – **dietetic** adjective.

dietitian /dīətish'n/ (also **dietician**) > noun an expert on diet and nutrition.

differ > verb **1** be unlike or dissimilar. **2** disagree.

IDIOMS – **agree to differ** amicably stop arguing about something because agreement will clearly not be reached. **beg to differ** politely disagree.

SYNONYMS – **1** be different, diverge, vary.

ORIGIN – Latin *differre*, from *dis-* 'from, away' + *ferre* 'bring, carry'.

difference > noun **1** a way in which people or things differ. **2** the state or condition of being different. **3** a disagreement, quarrel, or dispute. **4** the remainder left after subtraction of one value from another.

SYNONYMS – **1,2** differential, discrepancy, disparity, dissimilarity, distinction.

ANTONYMS – **1,2** similarity.

different > adjective **1** not the same as another or each other; unlike in nature, form, or quality. **2** informal novel and unusual. **3** distinct; separate.

IDIOMS – **different strokes for different folks** proverb different things appeal to different people.

DERIVATIVES – **differently** adverb **differentness** noun.

USAGE – should you say **different from**, **different to**, or **different than**? In British English **different from** is generally regarded as the correct use, on the basis that one thing *differs from* another, but in actual use **different** is followed by **to** as often as by **from**; **different than** is largely American.

SYNONYMS – **1** disparate, dissimilar, distinct, distinguishable, unlike.

ANTONYMS – **1** similar.

differentia /diffərenshiə/ > noun (pl. **differentiae** /diffərenshi-ee/) a distinguishing mark or characteristic.

ORIGIN – Latin.

differentiable /diffərenshiəb'l/ > adjective able to be differentiated.

DERIVATIVES – **differentiability** noun.

differential /diffərensh'l/ > adjective chiefly technical constituting or depending on a difference; differing or varying according to circumstances or relevant factors. > noun **1** Brit. a difference in wages between industries or between categories of employees in the same industry. **2** Mathematics an infinitesimal difference between successive values of a variable. **3** a gear allowing a vehicle's driven wheels to revolve at different speeds in cornering. **4** chiefly technical a difference.

DERIVATIVES – **differentially** adverb.

COMBINATIONS – **differential calculus** Mathematics the part of calculus concerned with the derivatives of functions. **differential equation** Mathematics an equation involving derivatives of a function or functions.

differentiate /diffərenshiayt/ > verb **1** recognise or identify as different; distinguish. **2** cause to appear different or distinct. **3** Mathematics transform (a function) into its derivative.

DERIVATIVES – **differentiation** noun **differentiator** noun.

difficult > adjective **1** needing much effort or skill to accomplish, deal with, or understand. **2** not easy to please or satisfy; awkward.

SYNONYMS – **1** demanding, exacting, hard, tough, tricky. **2** awkward, intractable, intransigent, refractory, uncooperative.

ANTONYMS – **1** easy, straightforward. **2** amenable, cooperative.

difficulty > *noun* (pl. **difficulties**) **1** the state or condition of being difficult. **2** a difficult or dangerous situation or circumstance.

SYNONYMS − **1** awkwardness, complexity, intricacy, trickiness. **2** crisis, plight, predicament, problem, quandary.

ORIGIN − Latin *difficultas*, from *dis-* (expressing reversal) + *facultas* 'ability, opportunity'.

diffident > *adjective* lacking in self-confidence.

DERIVATIVES − **diffidence** *noun* **diffidently** *adverb*.

SYNONYMS − reticent, self-effacing, unassuming, unconfident.

ANTONYMS − confident, self-assured.

ORIGIN − Latin, from *diffidere* 'fail to trust'.

diffraction > *noun* Physics the process by which a beam of light or other system of waves is spread out as a result of passing through a narrow aperture or across an edge.

DERIVATIVES − **diffract** *verb* **diffractive** *adjective*.

diffuse > *verb* /difyooz/ **1** spread over a wide area. **2** Physics (of a gas or liquid) travel or spread by diffusion. > *adjective* /difyooss/ **1** spread out over a large area; not concentrated. **2** lacking clarity or conciseness.

DERIVATIVES − **diffusely** /difyoosli/ *adverb* **diffuser** (also **diffusor**) *noun*.

USAGE − do not confuse with **defuse**, which means 'remove the fuse from' or 'reduce the danger or tension in'.

SYNONYMS − *verb* **1** disperse, scatter, suffuse. *adjective* **2** digressive, prolix, rambling, verbose.

ANTONYMS − *adjective* **2** pithy, succinct.

ORIGIN − Latin *diffundere* 'pour out'.

diffusion > *noun* **1** the action or process of becoming spread over a wide area. **2** Physics the intermingling of substances by the natural movement of their particles.

DERIVATIVES − **diffusive** *adjective*.

dig > *verb* (**digging**; past and past participle **dug**) **1** break up and turn over or move earth. **2** make (a hole) by digging. **3** (often **dig up**) extract from the ground by digging. **4** poke or jab sharply. **5** (**dig into** or **through**) search or rummage in. **6** (**dig out** or **up**) discover (facts). **7** informal, dated like; appreciate. > *noun* **1** an act of digging. **2** an archaeological excavation. **3** a sharp push or poke. **4** informal a mocking or critical remark. **5** (**digs**) informal, chiefly Brit. lodgings.

IDIOMS − **dig in** begin eating heartily. **dig in one's heels** stubbornly refuse to compromise.

SYNONYMS − *verb* **3** (**dig up**) disinter, excavate, exhume, mine, quarry, unearth.

digerati /dijəraati/ > *plural noun* informal people with expertise in information technology.

ORIGIN − blend of **DIGITAL** and **LITERATI**.

digest > *verb* /dījest, dijest/ **1** break down (food) in the stomach and intestines into substances that can be absorbed by the body. **2** Chemistry treat (a substance) with heat, enzymes, or a solvent to break it down. **3** reflect on and assimilate (information). > *noun* /dījest/ **1** a compilation or summary of material or information. **2** Chemistry a substance or mixture obtained by digestion.

DERIVATIVES − **digestible** *adjective*.

SYNONYMS − **1** absorb, assimilate, break down, take in, take up. **3** absorb, assimilate, take in, understand.

ORIGIN − Latin *digerere* 'distribute, dissolve, digest'.

digestif /dījestif, deezhesteef/ > *noun* a drink taken before or after a meal in order to aid the digestion.

ORIGIN − French, 'digestive'.

digestion > *noun* **1** the process of digesting. **2** a person's capacity to digest food.

digestive > *adjective* relating to the process of digesting food. > *noun* **1** a food or medicine that aids the digestion of food. **2** Brit. a round semi-sweet biscuit made with wholemeal flour.

digger > *noun* **1** a person, animal, or large machine that digs earth. **2** Austral./NZ informal a friendly form of address for a man.

diggings > *plural noun* a site that has been excavated.

dight /dīt/ > *adjective* archaic clothed or equipped. > *verb* **1** literary make ready; prepare. **2** Scottish & N. English wipe clean or dry.

ORIGIN − from archaic *dight* 'order, deal with', from Latin *dictare* 'dictate'.

digit /**di**jit/ > *noun* **1** any of the numerals from 0 to 9, especially when forming part of a number. **2** a finger or thumb.

ORIGIN − Latin *digitus* 'finger, toe'; sense 1 arose from the practice of counting on the fingers.

digital > *adjective* **1** of or relating to information represented as digits using particular values of a physical quantity such as voltage or magnetic polarisation. **2** (of a clock or watch) showing the time by means of displayed digits. **3** of or relating to a finger or fingers.

DERIVATIVES − **digitally** *adverb*.

COMBINATIONS − **digital audiotape** magnetic tape used to make digital recordings.

digitalis /dijitayliss/ > *noun* a drug prepared from foxglove leaves, containing substances that stimulate the heart muscle.

ORIGIN − from *Digitalis*, the Latin genus name of the foxglove (itself from *digitalis herba* 'plant relating to the finger', with reference to the shape of the flowers).

digitalise (also **digitalize**) > *verb* another term for **DIGITISE**.

digitigrade /**di**jitigrayd/ > *adjective* walking on the toes, like a dog, cat, or rodent. Compare with **PLANTIGRADE**.

ORIGIN − from Latin *digitus* 'finger, toe' + *-gradus* '-walking'.

digitise (also **digitize**) > *verb* convert (pictures or sound) into a digital form that can be processed by a computer.

DERIVATIVES − **digitiser** *noun*.

dignified > *adjective* **1** conducted with solemn or stately ceremony. **2** behaving with or demonstrating a composure that invites respect.

SYNONYMS − **1** distinguished, imposing, solemn, stately. **2** composed, decorous, gracious, restrained.

dignify > *verb* (**dignifies**, **dignified**) cause to be or appear impressive or worthy of respect.

ORIGIN − Latin *dignificare*, from *dignus* 'worthy'.

dignitary /**dig**nitri/ > *noun* (pl. **dignitaries**) a person holding high rank or office.

SYNONYMS − grandee, luminary, notable, VIP, worthy.

dignity > *noun* (pl. **dignities**) **1** the state or quality of being worthy of respect. **2** a composed or serious manner. **3** a sense of pride in oneself.

IDIOMS − **stand on one's dignity** insist on being treated with respect.

SYNONYMS − **1** grandeur, majesty, nobility, solemnity, stateliness. **2** composure, poise.

ORIGIN − Latin *dignitas*, from *dignus* 'worthy'.

digraph /**dī**graaf/ > *noun* a combination of two letters representing one sound, as in *ph*.

digress /dīgress/ > *verb* leave the main subject temporarily in speech or writing.

DERIVATIVES − **digression** *noun* **digressive** *adjective*.

SYNONYMS − deviate, diverge, go off at a tangent, ramble.

ORIGIN − Latin *digredi* 'step away'.

dihedral /dīheedrəl/ > *adjective* having or contained by two plane faces. > *noun* **1** an angle formed by two plane faces. **2** Aeronautics upward inclination of an aircraft's wing.

dike¹ > *noun* variant spelling of **DYKE¹**.

dike² > *noun* variant spelling of **DYKE²**.

diktat /**dik**tat/ > *noun* an order given by a ruler or foreign power, that people are forced to obey.

ORIGIN − German.

dilapidated* /diˈlappidaytid/ > *adjective* (of a building, vehicle, etc.) in a state of disrepair or ruin.
DERIVATIVES – **dilapidation** *noun*.
*SPELLING – *dil-*, not *del-*: di**lap**idated.
SYNONYMS – decrepit, derelict, neglected, ramshackle, tumbledown.
ORIGIN – from Latin *dilapidare* 'demolish, scatter as if throwing stones'.

dilatation /dīləˈtaysh'n/ > *noun* chiefly Medicine the action of dilating a vessel or opening or the process of becoming dilated.
COMBINATIONS – **dilatation and curettage** a surgical procedure involving dilatation of the cervix and curettage (scraping) of the uterus.

dilate /dīˈlayt/ > *verb* **1** become or cause to become wider, larger, or more open. **2** (**dilate on**) speak or write at length on.
DERIVATIVES – **dilation** *noun*.
ORIGIN – Latin *dilatare* 'spread out'.

dilator > *noun* **1** (also **dilator muscle**) Anatomy a muscle whose contraction dilates an organ or opening. **2** a surgical instrument for dilating a tube or cavity.

dilatory /ˈdilləˌtri/ > *adjective* **1** slow to act. **2** intended to cause delay.
DERIVATIVES – **dilatoriness** *noun*.
ORIGIN – Latin *dilatorius*, from *dilator* 'delayer', from *differre* 'defer'.

dildo > *noun* (pl. **dildos** or **dildoes**) an object shaped like an erect penis, used for sexual stimulation.

dilemma /diˈlemmə, dīˈlemmə/ > *noun* a situation in which a difficult choice has to be made between two alternatives, especially where both have drawbacks.
USAGE – **dilemma** should not be used to mean simply 'a difficult situation or problem'.
SYNONYMS – predicament, quandary.
ORIGIN – Greek, from *di-* 'twice' + *lēmma* 'premise'.

dilettante /dilliˈtanti/ > *noun* (pl. **dilettanti** /dilliˈtanti/ or **dilettantes**) a person who dabbles in a subject for enjoyment but without serious study.
DERIVATIVES – **dilettantish** *adjective* **dilettantism** *noun*.
SYNONYMS – amateur, dabbler, trifler.
ORIGIN – Italian, 'person loving the arts'.

diligence¹ /ˈdillijənss/ > *noun* care and conscientiousness in one's work.
SYNONYMS – application, assiduousness, conscientiousness, industry.

diligence² /ˈdillijənss/ > *noun* historical a public stagecoach.
ORIGIN – French, from *carrosse de diligence* 'coach of speed'.

diligent > *adjective* careful and conscientious in a task or duties.

DERIVATIVES – **diligently** *adverb*.
SYNONYMS – assiduous, conscientious, hard-working, industrious, sedulous.
ANTONYMS – casual, lazy.
ORIGIN – from Latin *diligere* 'love, take delight in'.

dill¹ > *noun* an aromatic culinary and medicinal herb with yellow flowers.
COMBINATIONS – **dill pickle** pickled cucumber flavoured with dill.

dill² > *noun* Austral./NZ informal a naive or foolish person.
ORIGIN – probably from dated *dilly* 'odd, foolish'.

dillybag > *noun* Austral. an Aboriginal bag or basket made from woven grass or fibre.
ORIGIN – from an Aboriginal word meaning 'coarse grass or reeds' + **BAG**.

dilly-dally > *verb* (**dilly-dallies**, **dilly-dallied**) informal dawdle or vacillate.

dilophosaurus /dīˌlōfəˈsawrəss/ > *noun* a large bipedal dinosaur of the early Jurassic period, with two long crests on the head.
ORIGIN – from Greek *dilophos* 'two-crested' + *sauros* 'lizard'.

diluent /ˈdilyoōənt/ technical > *noun* a substance used to dilute something. > *adjective* acting to cause dilution.

dilute /dīˈlyoōt/ > *verb* **1** make (a liquid) thinner or weaker by adding water or another solvent. **2** weaken by modifying or adding other elements. > *adjective* /also dīˈlyoōt/ **1** (of a liquid) diluted. **2** Chemistry (of a solution) having a relatively low concentration of solute.
DERIVATIVES – **diluter** *noun* **dilution** *noun* **dilutive** *adjective*.
SYNONYMS – *verb* **2** adulterate, thin, water down, weaken.
ORIGIN – Latin *diluere* 'wash away, dissolve'.

dim > *adjective* (**dimmer**, **dimmest**) **1** (of a light or illuminated object) not shining brightly or clearly. **2** made difficult to see by darkness, shade, or distance. **3** (of the eyes) not able to see clearly. **4** not clearly remembered. **5** informal stupid or slow to understand. > *verb* (**dimmed**, **dimming**) make or become dim.
IDIOMS – **take a dim view of** regard with disapproval.
DERIVATIVES – **dimly** *adverb* **dimness** *noun*.
SYNONYMS – *adjective* **1** faint, muted, subdued.
ANTONYMS – *adjective* **1** bright.

dime /dīm/ > *noun* N. Amer. a ten-cent coin.
IDIOMS – **a dime a dozen** informal very common and of little value.
COMBINATIONS – **dime store** a shop selling cheap merchandise.

wordpower facts
Dime
The words **dime** and **decimal** are related: both come from Latin *decimus* 'tenth'. **Dime** comes via Old French *disme* from Latin *decima pars* 'tenth part'. In medieval times it referred to a tenth part, in particular to a tithe (a word which itself means 'tenth part') paid to the Church or to a ruler. The modern meaning of a ten-cent coin (one tenth of a dollar) arose very early in the life of the United States, being first recorded in 1786.

dimension /dīˈmensh'n, diˈmensh'n/ > *noun* **1** a measurable extent, such as length, breadth, or height. **2** an aspect or feature.
DERIVATIVES – **dimensional** *adjective*.
SYNONYMS – **1** (**dimensions**) extent, measurements, proportions, size. **2** aspect, element, facet, feature, side.
ORIGIN – Latin, from *dimetiri* 'measure out'.

dimer /ˈdīmər/ > *noun* Chemistry a molecule consisting of two identical smaller molecules linked together.
DERIVATIVES – **dimeric** *adjective* **dimerise** (also **dimerize**) *verb*.

dimetrodon /dīˈmeetrədon/ > *noun* a large extinct carnivorous reptile of the Permian period, with long spines on its back supporting a sail-like crest.
ORIGIN – from Latin *di-* 'twice' + Greek *metron* 'measure' + *odous* 'tooth'.

diminish > *verb* make or become less.
IDIOMS – (**the law of**) **diminishing returns** the principle that as expenditure or investment increases each further increase produces a proportionately smaller return.
SYNONYMS – **1** decline, decrease, dwindle, fall, lessen, reduce.
COMBINATIONS – **diminished responsibility** English Law an unbalanced mental state considered as grounds to reduce a charge of murder to that of manslaughter.
ORIGIN – from Latin *minutia* 'smallness' and *deminuere* 'lessen'.

diminuendo /dimiˌnyoōˈendō/ > *adverb* & *adjective* Music with a decrease in loudness.
ORIGIN – Italian, 'diminishing'.

diminution /dimiˈnyoōsh'n/ > *noun* a reduction.

diminutive /diˈminyootiv/ > *adjective* **1** extremely or unusually small. **2** (of a word, name, or suffix) implying smallness (e.g. *-let* in *booklet*). > *noun* a shortened form of a name, typically used informally.
DERIVATIVES – **diminutively** *adverb* **diminutiveness** *noun*.

ORIGIN – Latin *diminutivus*, from *deminuere* 'lessen'.

dimity /**dimm**iti/ > *noun* a hard-wearing cotton fabric woven with stripes or checks.

ORIGIN – Greek *dimitos*, from *di-* 'twice' + *mitos* 'warp thread'.

dimmer > *noun* (also **dimmer switch**) a device for varying the brightness of an electric light.

dimorphic /dīˈmorfik/ > *adjective* chiefly Biology occurring in or representing two distinct forms.

DERIVATIVES – **dimorphism** *noun*.

ORIGIN – Greek *dimorphos*, from *di-* 'twice' + *morphē* 'form'.

dimple > *noun* **1** a small depression formed in the fleshy part of the cheeks when one smiles. **2** any small depression in the skin or flesh. > *verb* produce a dimple or dimples in the surface of.

DERIVATIVES – **dimply** *adjective*.

dim sum /dim **sum**/ (also **dim sim** /dim **sim**/) > *noun* a Chinese dish of small dumplings containing various fillings.

ORIGIN – Chinese, from *tim* 'dot' and *sam* 'heart'.

dimwit > *noun* informal a stupid or silly person.

DERIVATIVES – **dim-witted** *adjective*.

DIN > *noun* any of a series of international technical standards, used especially for electrical connections and film speeds.

ORIGIN – acronym from German *Deutsche Industrie-Norm* 'German Industrial Standard'.

din > *noun* a prolonged loud and unpleasant noise. > *verb* (**dinned, dinning**) (**din into**) instil (information) into by constant repetition.

SYNONYMS – *noun* cacophony, clamour, hubbub, racket, row, uproar.

dinar /**dee**naar/ > *noun* **1** the basic monetary unit of the states of Yugoslavia, equal to 100 paras. **2** the basic monetary unit of certain countries of the Middle East and North Africa.

ORIGIN – Latin *denarius* 'containing ten', from *decem* 'ten'.

dine > *verb* **1** eat dinner. **2** (**dine out on**) regularly entertain friends with (a particular anecdote).

COMBINATIONS – **dining car** a railway carriage equipped as a restaurant.

ORIGIN – Old French *disner*, probably from *desjëuner* 'to break fast'.

diner > *noun* **1** a person who dines. **2** a dining car on a train. **3** N. Amer. a small roadside restaurant.

dinette /dīˈnet/ > *noun* a small room or part of a room used for eating meals.

ding > *verb* make the metallic ringing sound of a bell.

dingbat > *noun* informal **1** N. Amer. & Austral./NZ a stupid or eccentric person. **2** (**dingbats**) Austral./NZ delusions or feelings of unease.

ding-dong > *noun* Brit. **1** the sound of a bell ringing with simple alternate chimes. **2** informal a fierce argument or fight. > *adjective* (of a contest) evenly matched and intensely fought.

dinghy /**ding**gi, **ding**i/ > *noun* (pl. **dinghies**) **1** a small open boat with a mast and sails, for recreation or racing. **2** a small inflatable rubber boat.

ORIGIN – first denoting a rowing boat in India; from Hindi.

dingle > *noun* literary or dialect a deep wooded valley.

dingo /**ding**gō/ > *noun* (pl. **dingoes** or **dingos**) a wild or semi-domesticated Australian dog with a sandy-coloured coat.

dingy /**din**ji/ > *adjective* (**dingier, dingiest**) gloomy and drab.

DERIVATIVES – **dingily** *adverb* **dinginess** *noun*.

SYNONYMS – dismal, drab, dreary.

dinkum /**ding**kəm/ > *adjective* Austral./NZ informal genuine.

IDIOMS – **fair dinkum** used to emphasise that or query whether something is genuine or true.

COMBINATIONS – **dinkum oil** the honest truth.

dinky > *adjective* (**dinkier, dinkiest**) Brit. informal attractively small and neat.

ORIGIN – Scots and northern English dialect *dink* 'neat, trim'.

dinky-di > *adjective* Austral./NZ informal dinkum; genuine.

dinner > *noun* **1** the main meal of the day, taken either around midday or in the evening. **2** a formal evening meal.

COMBINATIONS – **dinner jacket** a man's short jacket without tails, worn with a bow tie for formal evening occasions. **dinner lady** a woman who supervises children at mealtimes in a school.

ORIGIN – Old French *disner* (see DINE).

dinosaur /**dī**nəsawr/ > *noun* **1** an extinct reptile of the Mesozoic era, of which there were many kinds including large bipedal and quadrupedal forms. **2** a thing that is outdated or has become obsolete.

WORDFINDER – *dinosaurs*: apatosaurus (or brontosaurus), brachiosaurus, diplodocus, hadrosaur, iguanodon, stegosaur, triceratops, tyrannosaurus, velociraptor.

ORIGIN – from Greek *deinos* 'terrible' + *sauros* 'lizard'.

dint > *noun* an impression or hollow in a surface; a dent.

IDIOMS – **by dint of** by means of.

diocese /**dī**əsiss/ > *noun* (pl. **dioceses** /**dī**əseez, **dī**əseeziz/) a district under the pastoral care of a bishop in the Christian Church.

DERIVATIVES – **diocesan** /dīˈossisˈn/ *adjective*.

ORIGIN – Latin *dioecesis* 'governor's jurisdiction, diocese' from Greek *dioikein* 'keep house, administer'.

diode /**dī**ōd/ > *noun* Electronics **1** a semiconductor device with two terminals, typically allowing the flow of current in one direction only. **2** a thermionic valve with two electrodes.

dioecious /dīˈeeshəss/ > *adjective* Biology (of a species of plant or invertebrate animal) having male and female reproductive organs in separate individuals. Compare with **MONOECIOUS**.

ORIGIN – from **DI-** + Greek *-oikos* 'house'.

Dionysiac /dīəˈnissiak/ (also **Dionysian** /dīəˈnissiən/) > *adjective* **1** Greek Mythology relating to Dionysus, the god of fertility in nature and later of wine, associated with ecstatic religious rites. **2** uninhibited and emotional; frenzied.

dioptre /dīˈoptə/ (US **diopter**) > *noun* a unit of refractive power, equal to the reciprocal of the focal length (in metres) of a given lens.

ORIGIN – from Greek *di-* 'through' + *optos* 'visible'.

dioptric > *adjective* of or relating to the refraction of light.

DERIVATIVES – **dioptrics** *plural noun*.

diorama /dīəˈraamə/ > *noun* a model representing a scene with three-dimensional figures against a painted background.

diorite /**dī**ərīt/ > *noun* Geology a speckled, coarse-grained igneous rock.

ORIGIN – French, from Greek *diorizein* 'distinguish'.

dioxide /dīˈoksīd/ > *noun* Chemistry an oxide containing two atoms of oxygen.

dioxin /dīˈoksin/ > *noun* a highly toxic organic compound produced as a by-product in some industrial processes.

Dip. > *abbreviation* diploma.

dip > *verb* (**dipped, dipping**) **1** (**dip in** or **into**) put or lower briefly in or into. **2** sink, drop, or slope downwards. **3** (of a level or amount) temporarily become lower or smaller. **4** lower or move downwards. **5** (**dip into**) put a hand or implement into (a bag or container) in order to take something out. **6** (**dip into**) spend from (one's financial resources). **7** Brit. lower the beam of (a vehicle's headlights). **8** (**dip out**) Austral./NZ informal fail. > *noun* **1** an act of dipping. **2** a thick sauce in which pieces of food are dipped before being eaten. **3** a brief swim. **4** a brief downward slope followed by an upward one.

SYNONYMS – *verb* **1** duck, dunk, immerse, plunge, submerge.

diphtheria* /difˈtheeriə/ > *noun* a serious bacterial disease causing inflammation of the mucous membranes, especially in the throat.

*SPELLING – do not omit the first *h*: dip*h*theria.

ORIGIN – Greek *diphthera* 'skin, hide' (referring to a false membrane that forms in the throat).

diphthong* /**dif**thong/ > *noun* a sound formed by the combination of two vowels in a single syllable (as in *coin*).

*SPELLING – do not omit the first *h*: dip*h*thong.

ORIGIN – Greek *diphthongos*, from *di-* 'twice' + *phthongos* 'sound'.

diplodocus /di**plodd**əkəss/ > *noun* a huge herbivorous dinosaur of the late Jurassic period, with a long slender neck and tail.

ORIGIN – from Greek *diplous* 'double' + *dokos* 'wooden beam'.

diploid /**dip**loyd/ > *adjective* Genetics (of a cell or nucleus) containing two complete sets of chromosomes, one from each parent. Compare with **HAPLOID**.

ORIGIN – from Greek *diplous* 'double'.

diploma > *noun* a certificate awarded by an educational establishment for passing an examination or completing a course.

wordpower facts

Diploma

The words **diploma**, **diplomacy**, **diplomat**, and **diplomatic** all derive ultimately from Greek *diplōma* 'folded paper', from *diplous* 'double'. The original sense of **diploma** was 'state paper', and that of **diplomatic** 'relating to official documents'. **Diplomatic** acquired its modern sense 'relating to the management of international affairs' in the 18th century, from its use in the titles of two collections of important public documents, many of which dealt with international affairs.

diplomacy > *noun* 1 the profession, activity, or skill of managing international relations. 2 skill and tact in dealing with people.

SYNONYMS – 2 discretion, sensitivity, tact, tactfulness.

diplomat > *noun* an official representing a country abroad.

diplomatic > *adjective* 1 concerning diplomacy. 2 able to deal with people in a sensitive and effective way.

DERIVATIVES – **diplomatically** *adverb*.

SYNONYMS – 2 sensitive, tactful.

COMBINATIONS – **diplomatic bag** chiefly Brit. a container in which official mail is sent to or from an embassy, which is not subject to customs inspection. **diplomatic corps** the body of diplomats representing other countries in a particular state. **diplomatic**

immunity the exemption from certain laws granted to diplomats by the state in which they are working.

dipole /**dī**pōl/ > *noun* 1 Physics a pair of equal and oppositely charged or magnetised poles separated by a distance. 2 an aerial consisting of a horizontal metal rod with a connecting wire at its centre.

DERIVATIVES – **dipolar** *adjective*.

dipper > *noun* 1 a short-tailed songbird living by fast-flowing streams and able to enter the water to feed. 2 a ladle.

dippy > *adjective* (**dippier**, **dippiest**) informal foolish or eccentric.

dipsomania /dipsə**may**niə/ > *noun* alcoholism.

DERIVATIVES – **dipsomaniac** *noun*.

ORIGIN – Greek *dipsa* 'thirst'.

dipstick > *noun* 1 a graduated rod for measuring the depth of a liquid, especially oil in an engine. 2 informal a stupid or inept person.

dipteran /**dip**tərən/ > *noun* Entomology an insect of the order that comprises the two-winged or true flies. > *adjective* relating to this order of insects.

DERIVATIVES – **dipterous** *adjective*.

ORIGIN – from Greek *dipteros* 'two-winged'.

diptych /**dip**tik/ > *noun* a painting on two hinged wooden panels, typically forming an altarpiece.

ORIGIN – Greek *diptukha* 'pair of writing tablets', from *diptukhos* 'folded in two'.

dire > *adjective* 1 extremely serious or urgent. 2 informal of a very poor quality.

DERIVATIVES – **direly** *adverb* **direness** *noun*.

SYNONYMS – 1 critical, desperate, parlous. 2 appalling, atrocious, deplorable, dreadful, horrendous, terrible.

ORIGIN – Latin *dirus* 'fearful, threatening'.

direct /di**rekt**, dī**rekt**/ > *adjective* 1 going from one place to another without changing direction or stopping. 2 without intervening factors or intermediaries. 3 straightforward and frank. 4 clear and unambiguous. 5 (of descent) proceeding in continuous succession from parent to child. > *adverb* in a direct way or by a direct route. > *verb* 1 control the operations of. 2 aim (something) in a particular direction. 3 tell or show (someone) the way. 4 supervise and control (a film, play, etc.). 5 give an official or authoritative instruction to.

DERIVATIVES – **directness** *noun*.

SYNONYMS – *adjective* 1 straight, undeviating, unswerving. 3 candid, forthright, frank, open, straightforward. 4 categorical, clear, positive, unambiguous, unequivocal. *verb* 1 administer, control, manage, run, supervise. 2 aim, level, point, target. 5 charge, command, enjoin, order.

COMBINATIONS – **direct action** the use of

public forms of protest rather than negotiation to achieve one's aims. **direct current** an electric current flowing in one direct only. Compare with *alternating current*. **direct debit** Brit. an arrangement made with a bank that allows a third party to transfer money from a person's account. **direct mail** unsolicited commercial literature mailed to prospective customers. **direct object** a noun phrase denoting a person or thing that is the recipient of the action of a transitive verb. **direct speech** the reporting of speech by repeating the actual words of a speaker, for example *'I'm going', she said*. Contrasted with *reported speech*. **direct tax** a tax, such as income tax, which is levied on the income or profits of the person who pays it.

ORIGIN – Latin *directus*, from *dirigere*, from *di-* 'distinctly' or *de-* 'down' + *regere* 'put straight'.

direction /di**rek**sh'n, dī**rek**sh'n/ > *noun* 1 a course along which someone or something moves, or which leads to a destination. 2 a point to or from which a person or thing moves or faces. 3 the action of directing or managing people. 4 (**directions**) instructions on how to reach a destination or how to do something.

DERIVATIVES – **directional** *adjective*.

SYNONYMS – 1 course, path, route, way. 3 management, supervision.

directionless > *adjective* lacking in general aim or purpose.

directive > *noun* an official or authoritative instruction. > *adjective* involving the direction of operations.

SYNONYMS – *noun* command, decree, dictate, diktat, order, regulation.

directly > *adverb* 1 in a direct manner. 2 exactly in a specified position. 3 immediately. > *conjunction* Brit. as soon as.

director > *noun* 1 a person who is in charge of a group of people or an activity. 2 a member of the managing board of a business. 3 a person who directs a film, play, etc.

DERIVATIVES – **directorial** *adjective* **directorship** *noun*.

SYNONYMS – 1 controller, manager, overseer, supervisor.

COMBINATIONS – **director-general** (pl. **directors-general**) chiefly Brit. the chief executive of a large organisation.

directorate > *noun* 1 the board of directors of a company. 2 a section of a government department in charge of a particular activity.

directory > *noun* (pl. **directories**) a book listing individuals or organisations with details such as addresses and telephone numbers.

SYNONYMS – catalogue, index, listing, register, roll.

COMBINATIONS – **directory enquiries** a telephone service used to find out someone's telephone number.

dirge /durj/ > *noun* **1** a lament for the dead, especially one forming part of a funeral rite. **2** a mournful song, piece of music, or sound.

ORIGIN – from Latin *dirige!* 'direct!', the first word of a psalm used in the Latin Office for the Dead.

dirham /**deer**əm/ > *noun* the basic monetary unit of Morocco and the United Arab Emirates.

ORIGIN – from Arabic, from Greek *drakhmē* 'drachma'.

dirigible /**dirr**ijib'l/ > *noun* a steerable airship.

ORIGIN – from Latin *dirigere* 'to direct'.

dirigisme /**dirr**izhiz'm/ > *noun* state control of economic and social matters.

DERIVATIVES – **dirigiste** *adjective*.

ORIGIN – French, from *diriger* 'to direct'.

dirk /durk/ > *noun* a short dagger of a kind formerly carried by Scottish Highlanders.

dirndl /**durn**d'l/ > *noun* **1** (also **dirndl skirt**) a full, wide skirt gathered into a tight waistband. **2** a woman's dress with a dirndl skirt and a close-fitting bodice.

ORIGIN – German dialect, 'little girl'.

dirt > *noun* **1** a substance that causes uncleanliness. **2** loose soil or earth. **3** informal excrement. **4** informal scandalous or sordid information or material.

SYNONYMS – **1** filth, grime, muck.

COMBINATIONS – **dirt bike** a motorcycle designed for use on rough terrain, especially in scrambling. **dirt cheap** extremely cheap. **dirt poor** extremely poor. **dirt track** a racing track made of earth or rolled cinders.

ORIGIN – Old Norse *drit* 'excrement'.

dirty > *adjective* (**dirtier**, **dirtiest**) **1** covered or marked with dirt; not clean. **2** lewd; obscene. **3** dishonest; dishonourable. **4** (of weather) rough and unpleasant. > *adverb* Brit. informal used for emphasis: *a dirty great slab of stone.* > *verb* (**dirties**, **dirtied**) make dirty.

IDIOMS – **do the dirty on** Brit. informal cheat on or betray. **get one's hands dirty** (or **dirty one's hands**) do manual, menial, or other hard work. **play dirty** informal act in a dishonest or unfair way.

DERIVATIVES – **dirtily** *adverb* **dirtiness** *noun*.

SYNONYMS – *adjective* **1** filthy, grimy, grubby, mucky.

COMBINATIONS – **dirty look** informal a look expressing disapproval, disgust, or anger. **dirty old man** informal an older man who is sexually interested in younger women or girls. **dirty weekend** Brit. informal a weekend spent away with a lover, especially in secret. **dirty word 1** an offensive or indecent word. **2** a reference to something regarded

with dislike or disapproval. **dirty work** unpleasant or dishonest activities that are delegated to someone else.

dis (also **diss**) > *verb* (**dissed, dissing**) US informal speak disrespectfully to or of.

dis- /diss/ > *prefix* **1** expressing negation: *disadvantage*. **2** denoting reversal or absence of an action or state: *discharge*. **3** denoting removal, separation, or expulsion: *disbar*. **4** expressing completeness or intensification of an action: *disgruntled*.

ORIGIN – Latin.

disability > *noun* (pl. **disabilities**) **1** a physical or mental condition that limits a person's movements, senses, or activities. **2** a disadvantage or handicap.

disable > *verb* **1** (of a disease, injury, or accident) limit (someone) in their movements, senses, or activities. **2** put out of action.

DERIVATIVES – **disablement** *noun*.

SYNONYMS – **2** cripple, debilitate, handicap, immobilise, incapacitate.

disabled > *adjective* having a physical or mental disability.

USAGE – **disabled** is the standard term for people with physical or mental disabilities, and should be used instead of outmoded, sometimes offensive terms such as **crippled**, **defective**, or **handicapped**.

disabuse /dissəbyōōz/ > *verb* persuade (someone) that an idea or belief is mistaken.

disaccharide /dīsakkərīd/ > *noun* Chemistry a sugar whose molecule can be broken down to give two simple sugar molecules.

disadvantage > *noun* an unfavourable circumstance or condition. > *verb* **1** put in an unfavourable position. **2** (**disadvantaged**) living in conditions of social or economic deprivation.

DERIVATIVES – **disadvantageous** *adjective*.

SYNONYMS – *noun* drawback, hindrance, impediment, pitfall, snag. *verb* **2** (**disadvantaged**) deprived, . needy, underprivileged.

disaffected > *adjective* discontented through having lost one's feelings of loyalty or commitment.

DERIVATIVES – **disaffection** *noun*.

SYNONYMS – discontented, disgruntled, malcontent, restive.

ANTONYMS – contented.

disafforest > *verb* another term for DEFOREST.

disagree > *verb* (**disagrees, disagreed, disagreeing**) **1** have a different opinion. **2** (usu. **disagree with**) be inconsistent. **3** (**disagree with**) make slightly unwell.

DERIVATIVES – **disagreement** *noun*.

SYNONYMS – **1** differ, dispute, dissent.

disagreeable > *adjective* **1** unpleasant. **2** unfriendly and bad-tempered.

DERIVATIVES – **disagreeably** *adverb*.

SYNONYMS – objectionable, unpleasant, unwelcome.

disallow > *verb* declare invalid.

DERIVATIVES – **disallowance** *noun*.

disambiguate > *verb* remove uncertainty of meaning from.

DERIVATIVES – **disambiguation** *noun*.

disappear* > *verb* **1** cease to be visible. **2** cease to exist or be in use. **3** go missing or be killed.

DERIVATIVES – **disappearance** *noun*.

*SPELLING – one *s*, two *p*s: disappear.

SYNONYMS – **1** vanish; literary evanesce.

disappoint* > *verb* **1** fail to fulfil the hopes or expectations of. **2** prevent (hopes or expectations) from being realised.

DERIVATIVES – **disappointing** *adjective* **disappointingly** *adverb* **disappointment** *noun*.

*SPELLING – one *s*, two *p*s: disappoint.

SYNONYMS – fail, frustrate, let down, thwart.

ORIGIN – first used in the sense 'deprive of a position'; from Old French *desappointer*.

disappointed > *adjective* sad or displeased because one's hopes or expectations have not been fulfilled.

DERIVATIVES – **disappointedly** *adverb*.

SYNONYMS – disheartened, disillusioned, downcast, frustrated, thwarted.

ANTONYMS – pleased, satisfied.

disapprobation /dissaprəbaysh'n/ > *noun* strong disapproval.

disapprove > *verb* (often **disapprove of**) have or express an unfavourable opinion.

DERIVATIVES – **disapproval** *noun* **disapproving** *adjective* **disapprovingly** *adverb*.

SYNONYMS – (**disapprove of**) be against, frown on, look askance at, object to, take a dim view of.

disarm > *verb* **1** take a weapon or weapons away from. **2** (of a country or force) give up or reduce its armed forces or weapons. **3** remove the fuse from (a bomb). **4** allay the hostility or suspicions of; win over.

DERIVATIVES – **disarmer** *noun*.

SYNONYMS – **4** charm, mollify, soften, win over.

disarmament /disaarməmənt/ > *noun* the reduction or withdrawal of military forces and weapons.

disarming > *adjective* **1** allaying suspicion or hostility. **2** captivating; charming.

DERIVATIVES – **disarmingly** *adverb*.

disarrange > *verb* make untidy or disordered.

disarray > *noun* a state of disorganisation or untidiness. > *verb* throw into a state of disarray.

SYNONYMS – chaos, confusion, disorder, mess, turmoil.

disassemble > *verb* take to pieces.

DERIVATIVES – **disassembly** *noun*.

disassociate > *verb* another term for DISSOCIATE.

DERIVATIVES – **disassociation** *noun*.

disaster > *noun* **1** a sudden accident or a natural catastrophe that causes great damage or loss of life. **2** an event or fact leading to ruin or failure.

SYNONYMS – calamity, cataclysm, catastrophe, tragedy.

ORIGIN – Italian *disastro* 'ill-starred event', from Latin *astrum* 'star'.

disastrous* > *adjective* **1** causing great damage. **2** informal highly unsuccessful.

DERIVATIVES – **disastrously** *adverb*.

***SPELLING** – no *e*: disa*str*ous, not *-erous*.

SYNONYMS – **1** calamitous, cataclysmic, catastrophic, devastating, ruinous.

disavow > *verb* deny any responsibility or support for.

DERIVATIVES – **disavowal** *noun*.

disband > *verb* (with reference to an organised group) break up or cause to break up.

ORIGIN – obsolete French *desbander*.

disbar > *verb* (**disbarred, disbarring**) **1** expel (a barrister) from the Bar. **2** exclude.

DERIVATIVES – **disbarment** *noun*.

disbelief > *noun* **1** inability or refusal to accept that something is true or real. **2** lack of faith.

SYNONYMS – **1** doubt, incredulity, scepticism, suspicion.

ANTONYMS – belief, faith.

disbelieve > *verb* **1** be unable to believe. **2** have no religious faith.

DERIVATIVES – **disbeliever** *noun* **disbelieving** *adjective* **disbelievingly** *adverb*.

SYNONYMS – **1** distrust, doubt, mistrust, reject.

ANTONYMS – believe.

disbenefit > *noun* Brit. a disadvantage.

disburden > *verb* relieve of a burden or responsibility.

disburse > /dis**burss**/ > *verb* pay out (money from a fund).

DERIVATIVES – **disbursal** *noun* **disbursement** *noun*.

ORIGIN – Old French *desbourser*, from *des-* (expressing removal) + *bourse* 'purse'.

disc (US also **disk**) > *noun* **1** a flat, thin, round object. **2** (**disk**) an information storage device for a computer, on which data is stored either magnetically or optically. **3** a layer of cartilage separating vertebrae in the spine. **4** dated a gramophone record.

USAGE – generally speaking, the British spelling is **disc** and the US spelling is **disk**. However, the spelling for senses relating to computers is nearly always **disk**.

COMBINATIONS – **disc brake** a type of vehicle brake employing the friction of pads against a disc attached to the wheel.

ORIGIN – Latin *discus*.

discard > *verb* /dis**kaard**/ get rid of as no longer useful or desirable. > *noun* /**dis**kaard/ a discarded item.

DERIVATIVES – **discardable** *adjective*.

SYNONYMS – *verb* abandon, dispense with, jettison, shed, throw away.

ORIGIN – first used in the sense 'reject (a playing card)'; from DIS- + CARD[1].

discern > /di**sern**/ > *verb* **1** come to see or notice (something that is not readily perceptible). **2** recognise or find out.

DERIVATIVES – **discernible** *adjective*.

SYNONYMS – detect, make out, notice, perceive.

ORIGIN – Latin *discernere*, from *dis-* 'apart' + *cernere* 'to separate'.

discerning > *adjective* having or showing good judgement.

DERIVATIVES – **discerningly** *adverb* **discernment** *noun*.

SYNONYMS – cultivated, discriminating, judicious, perspicacious, refined.

discharge > *verb* /dis**chaarj**/ **1** emit or send out (a liquid, gas, or other substance). **2** fire (a gun or missile). **3** do all that is required to fulfil (a responsibility). **4** dismiss or allow to leave. **5** release from a contract or obligation. **6** Physics release or neutralise the electric charge of. > *noun* /**dis**chaarj, dis**chaarj**/ **1** the action of discharging. **2** a substance that has been discharged. **3** a flow of electricity through the air or other gas.

DERIVATIVES – **discharger** *noun*.

SYNONYMS – *verb* **1** emanate, emit, exude, release, secrete.

ORIGIN – Old French *descharger*, from Latin *discarricare* 'unload'.

disciple > /di**sīp**'l/ > *noun* **1** a personal follower of Christ during his life, especially one of the twelve Apostles. **2** a follower or pupil of a teacher, leader, or philosophy.

DERIVATIVES – **discipleship** *noun*.

SYNONYMS – **2** acolyte, adherent, devotee, follower, pupil.

ORIGIN – Latin *discipulus* 'learner', from *discere* 'learn'.

disciplinarian > *noun* a person who enforces firm discipline.

discipline > /**dissi**plin/ > *noun* **1** the practice of training people to obey rules or a code of behaviour. **2** controlled behaviour resulting from such training. **3** a branch of knowledge, especially one studied in higher education. > *verb* **1** train in obedience or self-control by punishment or imposing rules. **2** punish or rebuke formally for an offence. **3** (**disciplined**) behaving in a controlled way.

DERIVATIVES – **disciplinary** *adjective*.

SYNONYMS – *noun* **2** docility, obedience, restraint, self-mastery. *verb* **1** drill, mould, school, tame, train. **2** censure, chastise, penalise, punish, rebuke, reprimand. **3** (**disciplined**) abstemious, moderate, restrained, self-controlled, temperate.

ORIGIN – Latin *disciplina* 'instruction, knowledge'.

disc jockey > *noun* a person who introduces and plays recorded popular music, especially on radio or at a disco.

disclaim > *verb* **1** refuse to acknowledge. **2** Law renounce a legal claim to (a property or title).

disclaimer > *noun* a statement disclaiming something, especially responsibility.

disclose > *verb* **1** make (secret or new information) known. **2** expose to view.

DERIVATIVES – **disclosure** *noun*.

SYNONYMS – **1** divulge, impart, publish, reveal.

disco > *noun* (pl. **discos**) informal **1** a club or party at which people dance to pop music. **2** (also **disco music**) melodic pop music with a regular bass beat, influenced by soul music.

discography > /dis**kog**rəfi/ > *noun* (pl. **discographies**) a descriptive catalogue of musical recordings, particularly those of a particular performer or composer.

DERIVATIVES – **discographer** *noun*.

discoid > /**dis**koyd/ > *adjective* shaped like a disc.

DERIVATIVES – **discoidal** *adjective*.

discolour (US **discolor**) > *verb* become or cause to become stained, yellowed, or otherwise changed in colour.

DERIVATIVES – **discoloration** (also **discolouration**) *noun*.

SYNONYMS – blemish, mark, stain, tarnish.

discombobulate > /diskəm**bob**yoolayt/ > *verb* humorous, chiefly N. Amer. disconcert or confuse.

discomfit > /dis**kum**fit/ > *verb* (**discomfited, discomfiting**) make uneasy or embarrassed.

DERIVATIVES – **discomfiture** *noun*.

ORIGIN – first meaning 'defeat in battle': from Old French *desconfire*, from Latin *dis-* (expressing reversal) + *conficere* 'put together'.

discomfort > *noun* **1** slight pain. **2** slight anxiety or embarrassment. > *verb* cause discomfort to.

discommode > /diskə**mōd**/ > *verb* formal cause trouble or inconvenience to.

DERIVATIVES – **discommodious** *adjective*.

ORIGIN – obsolete French *discommoder*, variant of *incommoder* 'incommode'.

discompose > *verb* disturb or agitate.

DERIVATIVES – **discomposure** *noun*.

disconcert > /diskən**sert**/ > *verb* disturb the composure of.

DERIVATIVES – **disconcerted** *adjective* **disconcerting** *adjective*.

SYNONYMS – agitate, alarm, perturb, ruffle, unnerve, unsettle.

ORIGIN – obsolete French *desconcerter*, from

des- (expressing reversal) + *concerter* 'bring together'.

disconnect > *verb* **1** break the connection of or between. **2** detach (an electrical device) from a power supply.

DERIVATIVES – **disconnection** *noun*.

disconnected > *adjective* (of speech, writing, or thought) lacking a logical sequence.

disconsolate /dis**kon**sələt/ > *adjective* unable to be comforted or consoled; very unhappy.

DERIVATIVES – **disconsolately** *adverb*.

SYNONYMS – dejected, desolate, despairing, downcast, heart-broken, inconsolable.

discontent > *noun* lack of contentment or satisfaction.

DERIVATIVES – **discontentment** *noun*.

discontented > *adjective* dissatisfied with one's circumstances.

DERIVATIVES – **discontentedly** *adverb*.

SYNONYMS – aggrieved, disaffected, dissatisfied, fed up, unhappy.

discontinue > *verb* (**discontinues**, **discontinued**, **discontinuing**) stop doing, providing, or making.

DERIVATIVES – **discontinuation** *noun*.

discontinuous > *adjective* having intervals or gaps; not continuous.

DERIVATIVES – **discontinuity** *noun*.

discord > *noun* /**dis**kord/ **1** lack of agreement or harmony. **2** Music lack of harmony between notes sounding together. **3** Music a chord which is regarded as displeasing or requiring resolution by another.

SYNONYMS – **1** conflict, disagreement, friction, hostility, strife.

ORIGIN – Latin *discors* 'discordant', from *dis-* (expressing negation) + *cor* 'heart'.

discordant > *adjective* **1** disagreeing or incongruous. **2** (of sounds) harsh and jarring because of a lack of harmony.

DERIVATIVES – **discordance** *noun* **discordancy** *noun* **discordantly** *adverb*.

SYNONYMS – **1** conflicting, disagreeing, dissimilar, incompatible, incongruous. **2** cacophonous, clashing, dissonant, jarring, unmusical.

discotheque /**dis**kətek/ > *noun* another term for DISCO (in sense 1).

ORIGIN – French *discothèque*, originally 'record library', on the pattern of *bibliothèque* 'library'.

discount > *noun* /**dis**kownt/ a deduction from the usual cost of something. > *verb* /dis**kownt**/ **1** deduct an amount from (the usual price of something). **2** disregard as lacking credibility or significance. **3** Finance buy or sell (a bill of exchange) before its due date at a discount.

DERIVATIVES – **discounter** /dis**kown**tər/ *noun*.

SYNONYMS – *noun* concession, deduction, markdown, reduction. *verb* **2** dismiss, disregard, ignore, overlook.

COMBINATIONS – **discount house** Brit. a company that discounts bills of exchange. **discount rate** Finance **1** a minimum interest rate set by the US Federal Reserve for lending to other banks. **2** a rate used for discounting bills of exchange.

discountenance > *verb* **1** refuse to approve of. **2** disturb the composure of.

SYNONYMS – **2** disconcert, perturb, rattle, ruffle, unsettle.

discourage > *verb* **1** cause a loss of confidence or enthusiasm in. **2** prevent or seek to prevent by showing disapproval or creating difficulties. **3** (**discourage from**) persuade (someone) against (an action).

DERIVATIVES – **discouragement** *noun* **discouraging** *adjective* **discouragingly** *adverb*.

SYNONYMS – **1** cast down, demoralise, dishearten. **2** hinder, inhibit, prevent. **3** (**discourage from**) advise against, deter from, dissuade from, put off, talk out of.

ANTONYMS – encourage.

ORIGIN – Old French *descouragier*, from *corage* 'courage'.

discourse > *noun* /**dis**korss/ **1** written or spoken communication or debate. **2** a formal discussion of a topic in speech or writing. > *verb* /dis**korss**/ **1** speak or write authoritatively about a topic. **2** engage in conversation.

SYNONYMS – *noun* **1** communication, debate, dialogue, discussion, talk. **2** dissertation, essay, thesis, treatise.

ORIGIN – Latin *discursus* 'running to and fro', from *discurrere* 'run away'.

discourteous > *adjective* rude and lacking consideration for others.

DERIVATIVES – **discourteously** *adverb* **discourteousness** *noun* **discourtesy** (pl. **discourtesies**) *noun*.

SYNONYMS – bad-mannered, disrespectful, impolite, rude, uncivil.

ANTONYMS – courteous, polite.

discover > *verb* **1** find unexpectedly or in the course of a search. **2** become aware of (a fact or situation). **3** be the first to find or observe (a place, substance, or scientific phenomenon).

DERIVATIVES – **discoverer** *noun*.

SYNONYMS – **1** come across, find, uncover, unearth. **2** discern, find out, learn, realise. **3** devise, find, invent, originate, pioneer.

discovery > *noun* (pl. **discoveries**) **1** the action or process of discovering or being discovered. **2** a person or thing discovered. **3** Law the compulsory disclosure of documents relevant to an action.

SYNONYMS – **1** detection, disclosure, realisation, revelation, uncovering, unearthing. **2** breakthrough, innovation, invention.

discredit > *verb* (**discredited**, **discrediting**) **1** harm the good reputation of. **2** cause (an idea or piece of evidence) to seem false or unreliable. > *noun* loss or lack of reputation.

DERIVATIVES – **discreditable** *adjective*.

SYNONYMS – *verb* **1** compromise, demean, disgrace, dishonour. **2** disprove, invalidate.

discreet /dis**kreet**/ > *adjective* (**discreeter**, **discreetest**) **1** careful not to attract attention or give offence. **2** intentionally unobtrusive.

DERIVATIVES – **discreetly** *adverb*.

USAGE – do not confuse **discreet** with **discrete**, which means 'separate, distinct'.

SYNONYMS – **1** careful, cautious, circumspect, politic, prudent. **2** restrained, subtle, understated, unobtrusive.

ANTONYMS – **1** careless, indiscreet. **2** obtrusive, showy.

ORIGIN – Latin *discretus* 'separate'; the sense arises from Latin *discretio* 'separation', in late Latin 'discernment'.

discrepancy /dis**krepp**ənsi/ > *noun* (pl. **discrepancies**) an illogical or surprising lack of compatibility between facts.

DERIVATIVES – **discrepant** *adjective*.

SYNONYMS – disparity, divergence, incompatibility, inconsistency.

ANTONYMS – agreement, correspondence.

ORIGIN – Latin *discrepantia*, from *discrepare* 'be discordant'.

discrete /dis**kreet**/ > *adjective* individually separate and distinct.

DERIVATIVES – **discretely** *adverb* **discreteness** *noun*.

USAGE – do not confuse **discrete** with **discreet**, which means 'not attracting attention, unobtrusive'.

ORIGIN – Latin *discretus* 'separate'.

discretion > *noun* **1** the quality of being discreet. **2** the freedom to decide what should be done in a particular situation.

IDIOMS – **discretion is the better part of valour** *proverb* it's better to avoid a dangerous situation than to confront it.

DERIVATIVES – **discretionary** *adjective*.

SYNONYMS – **1** care, circumspection, discernment, prudence. **2** judgement, volition, will.

ANTONYMS – **1** carelessness, indiscretion.

COMBINATIONS – **discretionary income** income left after deduction of taxes, social security charges, and basic living costs.

discriminable > *adjective* able to be discriminated; distinguishable.

DERIVATIVES – **discriminably** *adverb*.

discriminate /dis**krimm**inayt/ > *verb* **1** recognise a distinction. **2** make an unjust distinction in the treatment of different categories of people, especially on the grounds of race, sex, or age.

DERIVATIVES – **discriminative** *adjective*.

SYNONYMS – **1** differentiate, distinguish.

ORIGIN – Latin *discriminare* 'distinguish between'.

discriminating > *adjective* having or showing good taste or judgement.

SYNONYMS – discerning, judicious.

discrimination > *noun* 1 the action of discriminating against people. 2 recognition of the difference between one thing and another. 3 good judgement or taste.

SYNONYMS – 1 bigotry, intolerance, prejudice. 2 differentiation, discernment, selectivity, shrewdness. 3 discernment, judgement, taste.

discriminatory > *adjective* showing discrimination or prejudice.

SYNONYMS – biased, partial, preferential, prejudiced.

discursive /dis**kur**siv/ > *adjective* 1 digressing from subject to subject. 2 fluent and expansive rather than formulaic or abbreviated. 3 relating to discourse or modes of discourse.

DERIVATIVES – **discursively** *adverb* **discursiveness** *noun*.

ORIGIN – Latin *discursivus*, from *discurrere* (see DISCOURSE).

discus > *noun* (pl. **discuses**) a heavy thick-centred disc thrown by an athlete, in ancient Greek games or in modern field events.

wordpower facts

Discus

The Latin word *discus*, derived from Greek *diskos*, is the root of several seemingly unrelated English words. Its main classical meanings were 'disc or dish', but it was used in medieval Latin to mean 'table'. As well as **discus** itself and **disc**, *discus* gave rise to **dish** and **desk**. The most radical development of meaning occurs with **dais**, a raised platform for a speaker: in the Middle Ages **dais** meant a raised table for an honoured guest, a 'high table'. The term died out in about 1600 but was revived by historical writers in the 19th century.

discuss > *verb* 1 talk about so as to reach a decision. 2 talk or write about (a topic) in detail.

DERIVATIVES – **discussable** *adjective* **discussion** *noun*.

SYNONYMS – 1 consider, debate, deliberate on, talk over. 2 analyse, examine, explore, review.

ORIGIN – Latin *discutere* 'dash to pieces', later 'investigate'.

discussant > *noun* a person who takes part in a discussion.

disdain > *noun* the feeling that someone or something is unworthy of one's consideration or respect. > *verb* consider with disdain.

DERIVATIVES – **disdainful** *adjective* **disdainfully** *adverb*.

SYNONYMS – *noun* contempt, disrespect, scorn. *verb* belittle, deride, disparage, dismiss, scorn.

ANTONYMS – respect.

ORIGIN – Old French *desdeignier*, from Latin *dedignari* 'consider unworthy'.

disease > *noun* a disorder of structure or function in a human, animal, or plant, especially one that produces specific symptoms.

WORDFINDER – aetiology (*study of the causes of disease*), communicable, infectious (*denoting disease which can be passed to others*), contagious (*denoting disease spread by contact*), epidemic (*widespread occurrence of a disease*), epidemiology (*study of the spread of disease*), hypochondriac (*person abnormally anxious about their health*), nosology (*medical science concerned with classification of diseases*), pandemic (*large-scale epidemic*), pathogen (*micro-organism that can cause disease*), pathology (*branch of medicine concerned with specific diseases*).

DERIVATIVES – **diseased** *adjective*.

SYNONYMS – illness, malady, sickness.

ORIGIN – Old French *desaise* 'lack of ease'.

diseconomy > *noun* (pl. **diseconomies**) an economic disadvantage arising from an increase in the size of an organisation.

disembark > *verb* leave a ship, aircraft, or train.

DERIVATIVES – **disembarkation** *noun*.

disembarrass > *verb* (**disembarrass oneself of** or **from**) free oneself of (a burden or nuisance).

disembodied > *adjective* 1 separated from or existing without the body. 2 (of a sound) lacking any obvious physical source.

DERIVATIVES – **disembodiment** *noun* **disembody** *verb*.

SYNONYMS – 1 bodiless, incorporeal, insubstantial, spectral.

disembowel > *verb* (**disembowelled**, **disembowelling**; US **disemboweled**, **disemboweling**) cut open and remove the internal organs of.

DERIVATIVES – **disembowelment** *noun*.

disempower > *verb* make less powerful or confident.

DERIVATIVES – **disempowerment** *noun*.

disenchant > *verb* make disillusioned.

DERIVATIVES – **disenchanting** *adjective* **disenchantment** *noun*.

disencumber > *verb* free from an encumbrance.

disenfranchise* > *verb* 1 deprive of the right to vote. 2 deprive of a right or privilege.

DERIVATIVES – **disenfranchisement** *noun*.

*SPELLING – **disenfranchise** cannot be spelled with an *-ize* ending.

disengage > *verb* 1 separate, release, or detach. 2 remove (troops) from an area of conflict. 3 (**disengaged**) emotionally detached; uninvolved.

DERIVATIVES – **disengagement** *noun*.

disentangle > *verb* free from entanglement; untwist.

SYNONYMS – extricate, free, unsnarl, untwist.

disequilibrium > *noun* a loss or lack of equilibrium, especially in relation to supply, demand, and prices.

disestablish > *verb* deprive (an organisation, especially a national Church) of its official status.

DERIVATIVES – **disestablishment** *noun*.

disfavour (US **disfavor**) > *noun* 1 disapproval or dislike. 2 the state of being disliked. > *verb* regard with disfavour.

disfigure > *verb* spoil the appearance of.

DERIVATIVES – **disfiguration** *noun* **disfigurement** *noun*.

SYNONYMS – blemish, deface, mar, scar.

ORIGIN – Old French *desfigurer*, from Latin *figura* 'figure'.

disgorge > *verb* 1 discharge; cause to pour out. 2 bring up or vomit (food). 3 yield or give up (funds, especially when dishonestly acquired).

ORIGIN – from Old French, from *des-* (expressing removal) + *gorge* 'throat'.

disgrace > *noun* 1 loss of reputation as the result of a dishonourable action. 2 a person or thing regarded as shameful and unacceptable. > *verb* bring disgrace on.

SYNONYMS – *noun* 1 discredit, dishonour, ignominy, shame.

ANTONYMS – 1 honour.

ORIGIN – Italian *disgrazia*, from *dis-* (expressing reversal) + Latin *gratia* 'grace'.

disgraceful > *adjective* shockingly unacceptable.

DERIVATIVES – **disgracefully** *adverb*.

SYNONYMS – contemptible, deplorable, scandalous, shameful.

disgruntled > *adjective* angry or dissatisfied.

DERIVATIVES – **disgruntlement** *noun*.

ORIGIN – from dialect *gruntle* 'utter little grunts'.

disguise > *verb* 1 alter the appearance, sound, taste, or smell of (something) so as to conceal its identity. 2 conceal the nature or existence of (a feeling or situation). > *noun* a means of disguising one's identity.

SYNONYMS – *verb* 1 alter, falsify, misrepresent. 2 camouflage, conceal, hide, mask.

ORIGIN – first meaning 'change one's usual style of dress': from Old French *desguisier*.

disgust > *noun* strong revulsion or profound indignation. > *verb* cause disgust in.

DERIVATIVES – **disgusted** *adjective* **disgustedly** *adverb* **disgusting** *adjective* **disgustingly** *adverb*.

SYNONYMS – *noun* abhorrence, aversion, distaste, repugnance, revulsion. *verb* nauseate, repulse, revolt, sicken.

ORIGIN – Latin *dis-* (expressing reversal) + *gustus* 'taste'.

dish > *noun* **1** a shallow container for cooking or serving food. **2** (**the dishes**) all the items that have been used in the preparation, serving, and eating of a meal: *she's washed the dishes*. **3** a particular variety of food served as part of a meal. **4** *informal* a sexually attractive person. **5** a shallow, concave receptacle. > *verb* **1** (**dish out** or **up**) put (food) on to a plate or plates before a meal. **2** (**dish out**) dispense in a casual or indiscriminate way. **3** N. Amer. *informal* gossip.

IDIOMS – **dish the dirt** *informal* reveal or spread scandal or gossip.

COMBINATIONS – **dishwasher 1** a machine for washing dishes automatically. **2** a person employed to wash dishes.

ORIGIN – Latin *discus* (see **DISCUS**).

disharmony > *noun* lack of harmony.

DERIVATIVES – **disharmonious** *adjective* **disharmoniously** *adverb*.

SYNONYMS – conflict, discord, friction.

dishearten > *verb* cause to lose determination or confidence.

DERIVATIVES – **disheartening** *adjective* **dishearteningly** *adverb*.

SYNONYMS – demoralise, deter, discourage, dismay.

dishevelled /diˈshevv'ld/ (US **disheveled**) > *adjective* (of a person's hair, clothes, or appearance) untidy; disordered.

DERIVATIVES – **dishevelment** *noun*.

SYNONYMS – bedraggled, messy, scruffy, unkempt, untidy.

ORIGIN – first meaning 'having the hair uncovered': from Old French *deschevele*, from Latin *capillus* 'hair'.

dishonest > *adjective* not honest, trustworthy, or sincere.

DERIVATIVES – **dishonestly** *adverb* **dishonesty** *noun*.

SYNONYMS – deceitful, devious, fraudulent, mendacious, untruthful.

dishonour (US **dishonor**) > *noun* a state of shame or disgrace. > *verb* **1** bring dishonour to. **2** fail to honour (an agreement, cheque, etc.).

SYNONYMS – *noun* discredit, disgrace, ignominy, shame.

dishonourable (US **dishonorable**) > *adjective* bringing shame or disgrace.

DERIVATIVES – **dishonourably** *adverb*.

SYNONYMS – discreditable, disgraceful, ignominious, shameful.

COMBINATIONS – **dishonourable discharge** dismissal from the armed forces as a result of criminal or morally unacceptable actions.

dishy > *adjective* (**dishier**, **dishiest**) *informal*, chiefly Brit. sexually attractive.

disillusion > *noun* the disappointing loss of a belief or an ideal. > *verb* cause to experience disillusion.

DERIVATIVES – **disillusioned** *adjective* **disillusionment** *noun*.

SYNONYMS – *noun* disabuse, disappointment, disenchantment. *verb* disabuse, disappoint, disenchant.

disincentive > *noun* a factor that discourages a particular action.

SYNONYMS – curb, deterrent, impediment, obstacle.

disinclination > *noun* a reluctance to do something.

disinclined > *adjective* reluctant; unwilling.

disinfect > *verb* make clean and free from infection, especially with a chemical disinfectant.

DERIVATIVES – **disinfection** *noun*.

SYNONYMS – decontaminate, purify, sanitise, sterilise.

disinfectant > *noun* a chemical liquid that destroys bacteria. > *adjective* causing disinfection.

disinflation > *noun* Economics reduction in the rate of inflation.

DERIVATIVES – **disinflationary** *adjective*.

disinformation > *noun* information which is intended to mislead.

disingenuous /dissinˈjenyooəss/ > *adjective* not candid or sincere, especially in feigning ignorance.

DERIVATIVES – **disingenuously** *adverb* **disingenuousness** *noun*.

SYNONYMS – dissembling, duplicitous, insincere.

ANTONYMS – candid, ingenuous.

disinherit > *verb* (**disinherited**, **disinheriting**) dispossess of or bar from an inheritance.

DERIVATIVES – **disinheritance** *noun*.

disintegrate > *verb* **1** break up into small parts as a result of impact or decay. **2** lose strength or cohesion.

DERIVATIVES – **disintegrator** *noun*.

SYNONYMS – **1** break up, crumble, decompose, fragment, shatter. **2** collapse, fail, founder, weaken.

disintegration > *noun* **1** the process of disintegrating. **2** Physics a process in which a subatomic particle emits a smaller particle or divides into smaller particles.

disinter /dissinˈter/ > *verb* (**disinterred**, **disinterring**) dig up (something that has been buried).

DERIVATIVES – **disinterment** *noun*.

SYNONYMS – exhume, unearth.

disinterest > *noun* **1** impartiality. **2** lack of interest.

SYNONYMS – **1** impartiality, neutrality, objectivity. **2** detachment, indifference.

disinterested > *adjective* **1** not influenced by considerations of personal advantage; impartial. **2** having or feeling no interest.

DERIVATIVES – **disinterestedly** *adverb* **disinterestedness** *noun*.

USAGE – be aware of the difference between **disinterested** and **uninterested**: **disinterested** primarily means 'impartial', while **uninterested** means 'not interested' (although the earliest recorded use of **disinterested** is in the sense 'not interested').

disintermediation > *noun* Economics reduction in the use of intermediaries between producers and consumers.

disinvest > *verb* withdraw or reduce an investment.

DERIVATIVES – **disinvestment** *noun*.

disjoint > *verb* disturb the cohesion or organisation of.

disjointed > *adjective* lacking a coherent sequence or connection.

DERIVATIVES – **disjointedness** *noun*.

SYNONYMS – disconnected, discontinuous, erratic, fragmented, incoherent.

disjunction > *noun* a lack of correspondence or consistency.

disjunctive > *adjective* **1** lacking connection. **2** Grammar (of a conjunction) expressing a choice between two mutually exclusive possibilities, for example *or* in *she asked if he was going or staying*.

disk > *noun* variant spelling in the US and in computing contexts of **DISC**.

COMBINATIONS – **disk drive** a device which allows a computer to read from and write on to computer disks.

diskette > *noun* Computing a floppy disk.

dislike > *verb* feel distaste for or hostility towards. > *noun* **1** a feeling of distaste for or hostility towards someone or something. **2** a thing that is disliked.

DERIVATIVES – **dislikable** (also **dislikeable**) *adjective*.

SYNONYMS – *noun* **1** antipathy, aversion, disfavour, distaste.

dislocate > *verb* **1** disturb the normal arrangement or position of (a joint in the body). **2** disrupt.

dislocation > *noun* the process or state of dislocating or being dislocated.

dislodge > *verb* remove from a fixed position.

DERIVATIVES – **dislodgement** *noun*.

disloyal > *adjective* not loyal or faithful.

DERIVATIVES – **disloyally** *adverb* **disloyalty** *noun*.

SYNONYMS – false, inconstant, perfidious, unfaithful.

dismal > *adjective* **1** causing or demonstrating a mood of gloom or depression. **2** *informal* pitifully or disgracefully bad.

IDIOMS – **the dismal science** humorous economics.

DERIVATIVES – **dismally** adverb.

SYNONYMS – **1** bleak, cheerless, depressing, dreary, gloomy, melancholy.

ORIGIN – from *dismals*, the two days in each month which in medieval times were believed to be unlucky, from Old French *dis mal*, from Latin *dies mali* 'evil days'.

dismantle > *verb* take to pieces.

DERIVATIVES – **dismantler** noun.

SYNONYMS – disassemble, take apart.

ORIGIN – Old French *desmanteler*, from *des-* (expressing reversal) + *manteler* 'fortify'.

dismast > *verb* break or force down the mast or masts of (a ship).

dismay > *noun* discouragement and distress. > *verb* cause to feel dismay.

SYNONYMS – *noun* apprehension, consternation, discouragement, distress. *verb* disconcert, discourage, dishearten, distress.

ORIGIN – Old French.

dismember > *verb* **1** tear or cut the limbs from. **2** divide up (a territory or organisation).

DERIVATIVES – **dismembered** adjective **dismemberment** noun.

ORIGIN – from Latin *dis-* 'apart' + *membrum* 'limb'.

dismiss > *verb* **1** order or allow to leave; send away. **2** discharge from employment. **3** Law refuse further hearing to (a case). **4** Cricket end the innings of (a batsman or side). **5** regard as unworthy of consideration.

DERIVATIVES – **dismissal** noun **dismissible** adjective.

SYNONYMS – **1** disband, discharge, send away, set free. **2** expel, oust, sack. **5** discount, disregard.

ORIGIN – Latin, from *dimittere* 'send away'.

dismissive > *adjective* feeling or showing that something is unworthy of serious consideration; disdainful.

DERIVATIVES – **dismissively** adverb **dismissiveness** noun.

SYNONYMS – contemptuous, disdainful, disparaging, scornful.

dismount > *verb* **1** alight from a horse or bicycle. **2** remove (something) from its support.

disobedient > *adjective* failing or refusing to be obedient.

DERIVATIVES – **disobedience** noun **disobediently** adverb.

SYNONYMS – insubordinate, naughty, rebellious, uncooperative.

ANTONYMS – cooperative, obedient.

disobey > *verb* fail or refuse to obey.

DERIVATIVES – **disobeyer** noun.

SYNONYMS – contravene, defy, flout, resist.

disoblige > *verb* offend (someone) by not acting in accordance with their wishes.

DERIVATIVES – **disobliging** adjective.

disorder > *noun* **1** lack of order; confusion.

2 the disruption of peaceful and law-abiding behaviour. **3** Medicine a disruption of normal physical or mental functions. > *verb* bring disorder to.

SYNONYMS – *noun* **1** chaos, confusion, disarray, disorganisation, mayhem. **2** disruption, disturbance, fracas, lawlessness, unrest. **3** ailment, illness.

ORIGIN – Old French *desordener*, from Latin *ordinare* 'ordain'.

disorderly > *adjective* **1** lacking organisation; untidy. **2** involving a breakdown of peaceful and law-abiding behaviour.

DERIVATIVES – **disorderliness** noun.

SYNONYMS – **1** chaotic, confused, disorganised, muddled, untidy. **2** antisocial, disruptive, lawless, unruly.

COMBINATIONS – **disorderly conduct** Law unruly behaviour constituting a minor offence.

disorganised (also **disorganized**) > *adjective* **1** not properly planned and controlled. **2** (of a person) inefficient.

DERIVATIVES – **disorganisation** noun.

SYNONYMS – **1** confused, disorderly, inefficient, muddled.

disorient > *verb* chiefly N. Amer. another term for **DISORIENTATE**.

disorientate > *verb* cause (someone) to lose their sense of direction or feel confused.

DERIVATIVES – **disorientated** adjective **disorientation** noun.

disown > *verb* refuse to acknowledge any connection with.

SYNONYMS – forsake, renounce, repudiate.

disparage /dɪsparrɪj/ > *verb* represent as being of little worth; scorn.

DERIVATIVES – **disparagement** noun **disparaging** adjective **disparagingly** adverb.

SYNONYMS – belittle, denigrate, discredit, scorn.

ORIGIN – Old French *desparagier* 'marry someone of unequal rank', from Latin *par* 'equal'.

disparate /dɪspərət/ > *adjective* essentially different in kind; not able to be compared.

DERIVATIVES – **disparately** adverb **disparateness** noun.

SYNONYMS – contrasting, different, dissimilar, unalike.

ORIGIN – from Latin *disparare* 'separate'.

disparity > *noun* (pl. **disparities**) a lack of parity or equivalence; a difference.

SYNONYMS – difference, discrepancy, dissimilarity, inconsistency, variance.

ORIGIN – Latin *disparitas*, from *paritas* 'parity'.

dispassionate > *adjective* not influenced by strong emotion; rational and impartial.

DERIVATIVES – **dispassion** noun **dispassionately** adverb.

SYNONYMS – impartial, rational, sober, unemotional, unsentimental.

dispatch (also **despatch**) > *verb* **1** send off to a destination or for a purpose. **2** deal with (a task or problem) quickly and efficiently. **3** kill. > *noun* **1** an instance of dispatching. **2** an official report on the latest situation in state or military affairs. **3** a report sent from abroad by a journalist. **4** promptness and efficiency.

DERIVATIVES – **dispatcher** noun.

SYNONYMS – *verb* **1** convey, remit, send, transmit. **2** deal with, discharge, execute. *noun* **2,3** bulletin, communiqué, report, statement.

COMBINATIONS – **dispatch box 1** (also **dispatch case**) a container for state or military dispatches. **2** (**the Dispatch Box**) a box in the House of Commons next to which ministers stand when speaking. **dispatch rider** a messenger who delivers urgent business documents or military dispatches.

ORIGIN – Italian *dispacciare* or Spanish *despachar* 'expedite'.

dispel > *verb* (**dispelled**, **dispelling**) make (a doubt, feeling, or belief) disappear.

SYNONYMS – allay, banish, dismiss, eliminate.

ORIGIN – Latin *dispellere* 'drive apart'.

dispensable > *adjective* able to be replaced or done without.

SYNONYMS – disposable, expendable, non-essential, replaceable, superfluous.

ANTONYMS – essential, indispensable.

dispensary > *noun* (pl. **dispensaries**) **1** a room in a hospital, school, etc. where medicines are prepared and provided. **2** a place where patients are treated; a clinic.

dispensation > *noun* **1** the action of dispensing. **2** exemption from a usual requirement. **3** a religious or political system prevailing at a particular time. **4** archaic an act of divine providence.

DERIVATIVES – **dispensational** adjective.

dispense > *verb* **1** distribute to a number of people. **2** (of a chemist) supply (medicine) according to a doctor's prescription. **3** (of a machine or container) supply or release (a product). **4** (**dispense with**) get rid of or manage without.

DERIVATIVES – **dispenser** noun.

SYNONYMS – **1** bestow, distribute, hand out, supply.

ORIGIN – Latin *dispensare* 'continue to weigh out or disburse', from *pendere* 'weigh'.

dispersant > *noun* a liquid or gas used to disperse small particles in a medium.

disperse > *verb* **1** go or spread over a wide area. **2** thin out and eventually disappear. **3** Physics divide (light) into constituents of different wavelengths.

DERIVATIVES – **dispersal** noun **disperser** noun **dispersible** adjective **dispersive** adjective.

SYNONYMS – **1** break up, disband, scatter, split up.

ORIGIN – Latin *dispergere* 'scatter widely'.

dispersion > *noun* **1** the action, process, or state of dispersing or being dispersed. **2** (**the dispersion**) the spread of the Jews beyond Israel; the diaspora.

dispirit > *verb* (usu. **be dispirited**) cause to lose enthusiasm or hope.

DERIVATIVES – **dispiritedly** *adverb* **dispiritedness** *noun* **dispiriting** *adjective* **dispiritingly** *adverb*.

displace > *verb* **1** shift (something) from its proper or usual position. **2** take the place, position, or role of. **3** (especially of war or natural disaster) force (someone) to leave their home.

SYNONYMS – **1** dislodge, move, shift.

displacement > *noun* **1** the action or process of displacing. **2** the amount by which a thing is moved from a position. **3** the volume or weight of water displaced by a floating ship, used as a measure of the ship's size.

display > *verb* **1** place (something) prominently so that it may readily be seen. **2** show (data or an image) on a screen. **3** give a conspicuous demonstration of (a quality, emotion, or skill). **4** (of a male animal) engage in behaviour intended to attract a mate. > *noun* **1** the action or an instance of displaying. **2** a collection of objects being displayed. **3** an electronic device for the visual presentation of data. **4** a performance, show, or event for public entertainment.

SYNONYMS – *verb* **1** demonstrate, exhibit, present, show. **3** flaunt, flourish, parade, reveal. *noun* **2** arrangement, exhibition, exposition, presentation.

ANTONYMS – *verb* conceal, hide.

ORIGIN – Old French *despleier*, from Latin *displicare* 'scatter, disperse'.

displease > *verb* annoy or upset.

DERIVATIVES – **displeased** *adjective* **displeasing** *adjective*.

displeasure > *noun* a feeling of annoyance or dissatisfaction.

disport > *verb* (**disport oneself**) enjoy oneself unrestrainedly; frolic.

ORIGIN – Old French *desporter* 'carry away'.

disposable > *adjective* **1** (of an article) intended to be used once and then thrown away. **2** (of financial assets) readily available for the owner's use as required. > *noun* a disposable article.

DERIVATIVES – **disposability** *noun*.

SYNONYMS – *adjective* **1** expendable, replaceable, throwaway. **2** accessible, available, spendable, usable.

COMBINATIONS – **disposable income** income remaining after deduction of taxes

and national insurance, available to be spent or saved as one wishes.

disposal > *noun* the action or process of disposing.

IDIOMS – **at one's disposal** available for one to use whenever or however one wishes.

dispose > *verb* **1** (**dispose of**) get rid of. **2** arrange in a particular position. **3** incline (someone) towards a particular activity or frame of mind.

DERIVATIVES – **disposer** *noun*.

SYNONYMS – **1** (**dispose of**) discard, jettison, throw away, throw out. **2** arrange, order, place, position, range. **3** encourage, incline, persuade, prompt.

ORIGIN – Latin *disponere* 'arrange'.

disposed > *adjective* **1** inclined to do or feel something. **2** having a specified attitude to or towards: *he is well disposed towards journalists.*

disposition > *noun* **1** a person's inherent qualities of character. **2** an inclination or tendency. **3** the action or result of arranging people or things in a particular way.

SYNONYMS – **1** character, make-up, nature, temperament.

dispossess > *verb* **1** deprive of land or property. **2** (**the dispossessed**) people who have been deprived of land or property. **3** (in sport) deprive (a player) of the ball.

DERIVATIVES – **dispossession** *noun*.

disproof > *noun* evidence that something is untrue.

disproportion > *noun* a lack of proportion.

DERIVATIVES – **disproportional** *adjective* **disproportionally** *adverb*.

disproportionate > *adjective* too large or too small in comparison with something else.

DERIVATIVES – **disproportionately** *adverb*.

disprove > *verb* prove to be false.

DERIVATIVES – **disprovable** *adjective*.

SYNONYMS – falsify, invalidate, negate, refute.

disputable > *adjective* open to debate.

disputation > *noun* debate or argument.

DERIVATIVES – **disputative** *adjective*.

disputatious > *adjective* **1** fond of argument. **2** (of an argument or situation) motivated by or causing strong opinions.

DERIVATIVES – **disputatiously** *adverb* **disputatiousness** *noun*.

dispute > *verb* /di**spyoot**/ **1** argue about. **2** compete for; aim to acquire. **3** question whether (a statement) is true or valid. **4** resist (a military landing or advance). > *noun* /di**spyoot**, **dis**pyoot/ **1** an argument. **2** a disagreement between management and employees that leads to industrial action.

DERIVATIVES – **disputant** *noun*.

SYNONYMS – *verb* **1** argue about, debate,

quarrel over. **3** challenge, contest, question, take issue with. *noun* **1** altercation, argument, disagreement, quarrel.

ORIGIN – Latin *disputare* 'to estimate'.

disqualify > *verb* (**disqualifies**, **disqualified**) **1** pronounce (someone) ineligible for an office or activity. **2** (of a feature or characteristic) make (someone) unsuitable for an office or activity.

DERIVATIVES – **disqualification** *noun*.

disquiet > *noun* a feeling of anxiety. > *verb* make (someone) anxious.

DERIVATIVES – **disquieting** *adjective* **disquietingly** *adverb* **disquietude** *noun*.

SYNONYMS – *noun* agitation, anxiety, concern, unease. *verb* agitate, concern, disconcert, disturb, perturb, unsettle.

ANTONYMS – calm.

disquisition /diskwi**zish**'n/ > *noun* a piece of long or complex discourse.

ORIGIN – Latin, 'investigation', based on *quaerere* 'seek'.

disrate > *verb* reduce (a sailor) to a lower rank.

disregard > *verb* pay no attention to. > *noun* lack of attention or care.

SYNONYMS – *verb* discount, ignore, overlook.

disrepair > *noun* a poor condition due to neglect.

disreputable > *adjective* not respectable in appearance or character.

SYNONYMS – discreditable, down at heel, dubious, raffish, reprehensible, shoddy.

disrepute > *noun* the state of being discredited.

disrespect > *noun* lack of respect or courtesy. > *verb* informal, chiefly N. Amer. show a lack of respect for.

DERIVATIVES – **disrespectful** *adjective* **disrespectfully** *adverb*.

SYNONYMS – *noun* contempt, discourtesy, disdain, insolence, scorn.

disrobe > *verb* **1** undress. **2** take off official regalia or vestments.

disrupt > *verb* disturb or interrupt.

DERIVATIVES – **disrupter** (also **disruptor**) *noun* **disruption** *noun* **disruptive** *adjective*.

SYNONYMS – disturb, hinder, interrupt, obstruct, upset.

ORIGIN – Latin *disrumpere* 'break apart'.

diss > *verb* variant spelling of **DIS**.

dissatisfied > *adjective* not content or happy.

USAGE – the words **dissatisfied** and **unsatisfied** have different meanings: if you are **dissatisfied** you are unhappy because what you have is not what you want; if you are **unsatisfied** you lack or do not have enough of something you want or need.

SYNONYMS – aggrieved, discontented, disgruntled, displeased, unhappy.

dissatisfy > *verb* (**dissatisfies**, **dissatisfied**) fail to satisfy or give pleasure to.
DERIVATIVES – **dissatisfaction** *noun*.

dissect* /dɪˈsekt, dʌɪˈsekt/ > *verb* **1** methodically cut up (a body, part, or plant) in order to study its internal parts. **2** analyse in great detail. **3** (**dissected**) technical divided into separate parts.
DERIVATIVES – **dissection** *noun* **dissector** *noun*.
***SPELLING** – unlike **bisect**, with which it is sometimes confused, **dissect** is spelled with a double *s*.
ORIGIN – Latin *dissecare* 'cut up'.

dissemble > *verb* hide or disguise one's true motives or feelings.
DERIVATIVES – **dissembler** *noun*.
SYNONYMS – bluff, dissimulate, pretend, sham.
ORIGIN – Latin *dissimulare* 'disguise, conceal'.

disseminate > *verb* spread widely.
DERIVATIVES – **dissemination** *noun* **disseminator** *noun*.
SYNONYMS – circulate, distribute, promulgate, publish, spread.
ORIGIN – Latin *disseminare* 'scatter', from *dis-* 'abroad' + *semen* 'seed'.

dissension > *noun* disagreement that leads to discord.
SYNONYMS – antagonism, disagreement, discord, disputation, variance.
ORIGIN – Latin, from *dissentire* 'differ in sentiment'.

dissent > *verb* **1** express disagreement with a prevailing or official view. **2** disagree with the doctrine of an established or orthodox Church. > *noun* the holding or expression of a dissenting view.
SYNONYMS – *verb* demur, differ, disagree.
ANTONYMS – *verb* agree, assent.
ORIGIN – Latin *dissentire* 'differ in sentiment'.

dissenter > *noun* **1** a person who dissents. **2** (**Dissenter**) Brit. historical a member of a non-established Church; a Nonconformist.

dissentient /dɪˈsenʃ'nt/ > *adjective* in opposition to a majority or official opinion. > *noun* a dissentient person.
ORIGIN – Latin, from *dissentire* 'differ in opinion'.

dissertation > *noun* a long essay, especially one written for a university degree or diploma.
SYNONYMS – essay, paper, thesis, treatise.
ORIGIN – Latin, from *dissertare* 'continue to discuss'.

disservice > *noun* a harmful action.

dissident > *noun* a person who opposes official policy. > *adjective* in opposition to official policy.
DERIVATIVES – **dissidence** *noun*.

SYNONYMS – *noun* dissenter, objector, rebel.
ORIGIN – Latin, from *dissidere* 'sit apart, disagree'.

dissimilar > *adjective* not similar; different.
DERIVATIVES – **dissimilarity** *noun* **dissimilarly** *adverb*.

dissimulate > *verb* hide or disguise one's thoughts or feelings.
DERIVATIVES – **dissimulation** *noun* **dissimulator** *noun*.
SYNONYMS – bluff, dissemble, pretend, sham.
ORIGIN – Latin *dissimulare* 'to conceal'.

dissipate* > *verb* **1** be or cause to be dispelled or dispersed. **2** waste (money, energy, or resources).
DERIVATIVES – **dissipative** *adjective* **dissipator** (also **dissipater**) *noun*.
***SPELLING** – two *ss*, one *p*: di*ss*i*p*ate.
SYNONYMS – **1** disappear, dispel, disperse, evaporate, vanish. **2** fritter, squander, waste.
ORIGIN – Latin *dissipare* 'scatter'.

dissipated > *adjective* overindulgent in sensual pleasures.

dissipation > *noun* **1** dissipated living. **2** the action of dissipating something.

dissociate > *verb* **1** disconnect or separate. **2** (**dissociate oneself from**) declare that one is not connected with.
DERIVATIVES – **dissociation** *noun* **dissociative** *adjective*.
ORIGIN – Latin *dissociare* 'separate'.

dissoluble > *adjective* able to be dissolved, loosened, or disconnected.
ORIGIN – Latin *dissolubilis*, from *dissolvere* (see **DISSOLVE**).

dissolute /ˈdɪsəluːt/ > *adjective* overindulgent in sensual pleasures.
SYNONYMS – debauched, decadent, licentious, libertine, wanton.
ORIGIN – Latin *dissolutus* 'disconnected, loose', from *dissolvere* (see **DISSOLVE**).

dissolution > *noun* **1** the closing down of an assembly, partnership, or official body. **2** the action or process of dissolving. **3** disintegration; decomposition. **4** archaic death. **5** debauched living; dissipation.

dissolve > *verb* **1** (with reference to a solid) become or cause to become incorporated into a liquid so as to form a solution. **2** gradually disappear. **3** close down, dismiss, or annul (an assembly, partnership, etc.). **4** (**dissolve into** or **in**) subside uncontrollably into (an expression of strong feelings).
DERIVATIVES – **dissolvable** *adjective*.
SYNONYMS – **2** disappear, dissipate, evaporate, vanish.
ORIGIN – Latin *dissolvere*, from *dis-* 'apart' + *solvere* 'loosen or solve'.

dissonant > *adjective* **1** Music sounding harsh or discordant. **2** unsuitable in combination; clashing.
DERIVATIVES – **dissonance** *noun* **dissonantly** *adverb*.
ORIGIN – Latin, from *dissonare* 'be discordant', from *dis-* 'apart' + *sonare* 'to sound'.

dissuade /dɪˈsweɪd/ > *verb* (**dissuade from**) persuade or advise not to do.
DERIVATIVES – **dissuasion** *noun* **dissuasive** *adjective*.
SYNONYMS – deter, discourage, put off.
ANTONYMS – encourage, persuade.
ORIGIN – Latin *dissuadere*, from *dis-* (expressing reversal) + *suadere* 'advise, persuade'.

distaff > *noun* **1** a stick or spindle on to which wool or flax is wound for spinning. **2** (before another noun) denoting the female side of a family. Compare with **SPEAR**.

distal > *adjective* chiefly Anatomy situated away from the centre of the body or an area or from the point of attachment. The opposite of **PROXIMAL**.
DERIVATIVES – **distally** *adverb*.

distance > *noun* **1** the length of the space between two points. **2** the condition of being far off; remoteness. **3** a far-off point or place. **4** the full length or time of a race or other contest. **5** an interval of time or relation. **6** aloofness. **7** Brit. Horse Racing a space of more than twenty lengths between two finishers in a race. > *verb* **1** make distant. **2** (**distance oneself from**) dissociate or separate oneself from.
IDIOMS – **go the distance** continue to participate until the scheduled end of a contest.
SYNONYMS – *noun* **1** gap, interval, range, reach, space, span.
COMBINATIONS – **distance learning** a method of studying in which lectures are broadcast and lessons are conducted by correspondence.
ORIGIN – Latin *distantia*, from *distare* 'stand apart'.

distant > *adjective* **1** far away in space or time. **2** at a specified distance. **3** remote or far apart in resemblance or relationship. **4** (of a person) cool or reserved. **5** thinking about something else; remote.
DERIVATIVES – **distantly** *adverb*.
SYNONYMS – **1** far, far-flung, outlying, remote.
ANTONYMS – **1** near.

distaste > *noun* dislike or aversion.
DERIVATIVES – **distasteful** *adjective* **distastefully** *adverb*.

distemper[1] > *noun* a kind of paint having a base of glue or size, used on walls. > *verb* paint with distemper.

wordpower facts

Distemper

The two meanings of **distemper**, a kind of paint and a disease of animals, both have the same ultimate root, Latin *distemperare* 'soak'. **Distemper** meaning 'paint' was originally a verb in the senses 'dilute' and 'steep'; it took on its modern noun sense from the idea of mixing powdered colours with a glutinous substance dissolved in water. **Distemper** in the sense 'disease' originally had the meanings 'bad temper', 'ailment or illness', and 'disturbance of the bodily humours'; it too was originally a verb, meaning 'mix elements in the wrong proportions, disturb the due proportion of', later 'upset, derange'.

distemper² > *noun* a disease of some animals, especially dogs, spread by a virus and causing fever.

distend > *verb* swell because of internal pressure.
DERIVATIVES – **distended** *adjective* **distensibility** *noun* **distensible** *adjective* **distension** *noun*.
SYNONYMS – bloat, bulge, inflate, swell.
ORIGIN – Latin *distendere*, from *dis-* 'apart' + *tendere* 'to stretch'.

distil (US **distill**) > *verb* (**distilled**, **distilling**) **1** purify (a liquid) by heating it so that it vaporises, then cooling and condensing the vapour and collecting the resulting liquid. **2** make (spirits) in this way. **3** extract the essential meaning of.
DERIVATIVES – **distillate** *noun* **distillation** *noun*.
ORIGIN – Latin *distillare*, from *de-* 'down, away' + *stillare* (from *stilla* 'a drop').

distiller > *noun* a person or company that manufactures spirits.

distillery > *noun* (pl. **distilleries**) a place where spirits are manufactured.

distinct > *adjective* **1** recognisably different or individual. **2** readily distinguishable by the senses.
DERIVATIVES – **distinctly** *adverb* **distinctness** *noun*.
SYNONYMS – **1** different, discrete, distinctive, individual, separate. **2** clear, evident, palpable, perceptible, obvious, well defined.
ANTONYMS – **2** indistinct.
ORIGIN – Latin *distinctus* 'separated, distinguished', from *distinguere* (see **DISTINGUISH**).

distinction > *noun* **1** a marked difference or contrast. **2** the action of distinguishing. **3** excellence that serves to mark someone or something out from others. **4** special honour or recognition.
SYNONYMS – **1** contrast, difference, dissimilarity. **3** excellence, illustriousness, importance, significance.

distinctive > *adjective* individually characteristic; distinct from others of its kind.
DERIVATIVES – **distinctively** *adverb* **distinctiveness** *noun*.
SYNONYMS – characteristic, distinct, individual, particular.

distinguish > *verb* **1** recognise, show, or treat as different. **2** manage to discern (something barely perceptible). **3** (**distinguish oneself**) make oneself worthy of respect. **4** be an identifying characteristic of.
DERIVATIVES – **distinguishable** *adjective*.
SYNONYMS – **1** differentiate, discriminate. **2** discern, make out, perceive.
ORIGIN – Latin *distinguere*, from *dis-* 'apart' + *stinguere* 'put out'.

distinguished > *adjective* **1** dignified in appearance. **2** successful and commanding great respect.
SYNONYMS – **1** dignified, noble, patrician. **2** august, eminent, esteemed, illustrious.

distort > *verb* **1** pull or twist out of shape. **2** give a misrepresentative account of. **3** change the form of (an electrical signal or sound wave) during transmission or amplification.
DERIVATIVES – **distorted** *adjective* **distortedly** *adverb* **distortion** *noun*.
SYNONYMS – **1** buckle, contort, twist, warp. **2** manipulate, misrepresent, skew, twist.
ORIGIN – Latin *distorquere* 'twist apart'.

distract > *verb* **1** prevent (someone) from giving their full attention to something. **2** divert (attention) from something.
DERIVATIVES – **distracted** *adjective* **distractedly** *adverb* **distracting** *adjective* **distractingly** *adverb*.
SYNONYMS – **1** disturb, divert, sidetrack.
ORIGIN – Latin *distrahere* 'draw apart'.

distraction > *noun* **1** a thing that diverts attention. **2** a thing offering entertainment. **3** an agitated mental state.
IDIOMS – **to distraction** almost to a state of madness.
SYNONYMS – **1** disturbance, diversion, interference, interruption. **2** amusement, diversion, entertainment. **3** agitation, confusion, derangement.

distrain > *verb* Law impose distraint on.
ORIGIN – Old French *destreindre*, from Latin *distringere* 'stretch apart'.

distraint /dɪstraynt/ > *noun* Law the seizure of someone's property in order to obtain payment of rent or other money owed.

distrait /dɪstray/ > *adjective* (fem. **distraite** /dɪstrayt/) distracted; absent-minded.

ORIGIN – French, from Old French *destrait* 'distracted'.

distraught > *adjective* very worried and upset.
SYNONYMS – distressed, frantic, overwrought, worked up.
ORIGIN – Latin *distractus* 'pulled apart'.

distress > *noun* **1** anxiety or suffering. **2** the state of a ship or aircraft when in danger or difficulty. **3** Medicine a state of physical strain. **4** Law another term for **DISTRAINT**. > *verb* **1** cause distress to. **2** give (furniture, leather, etc.) simulated marks of age and wear.
DERIVATIVES – **distressed** *adjective* **distressful** *adjective* **distressing** *adjective* **distressingly** *adverb*.
SYNONYMS – *noun* **1** anguish, anxiety, dismay, pain, suffering, torment. *verb* **1** disturb, torment, trouble, upset, worry.
ANTONYMS – *noun* & *verb* **1** calm, comfort.
ORIGIN – Latin *distringere* 'stretch apart'.

distribute > *verb* **1** hand or share out to a number of recipients. **2** (**be distributed**) be spread over an area. **3** supply (goods) to retailers.
DERIVATIVES – **distributable** *adjective* **distribution** *noun* **distributional** *adjective*.
NOTE – **distribute** is pronounced either with the stress on the **-stri-** or with the stress on the **dis-**. Until recently the second was considered incorrect, but now both pronunciations are accepted.
SYNONYMS – **1** allocate, allot, apportion, dispense, hand out, share out.
COMBINATIONS – **distributed system** Computing a number of independent computers linked by a network.
ORIGIN – Latin *distribuere* 'divide up'.

distributive > *adjective* **1** relating to the processes of distribution or things that are distributed. **2** Grammar (of a determiner or pronoun) referring to each individual of a class, not to the class collectively, e.g. *each*, *either*.
DERIVATIVES – **distributively** *adverb*.

distributor > *noun* **1** an agent who supplies goods to retailers. **2** a device in a petrol engine for passing electric current to each spark plug in turn.

district > *noun* **1** a part of a town or region having a particular character or quality. **2** a locality or neighbourhood. **3** Brit. a division of a county or region that elects its own councillors.
SYNONYMS – **1,2** area, locality, neighbourhood, quarter, region.
COMBINATIONS – **district attorney** (in the US) a public official who acts as prosecutor in a particular district. **district nurse** (in the UK) a nurse who treats patients in their homes, operating within a particular district.

ORIGIN – Latin *districtus* 'territory of jurisdiction', from *distringere* 'draw apart'.

distrust > *noun* lack of trust. > *verb* have little trust in; regard with suspicion.

DERIVATIVES – **distrustful** *adjective* **distrustfully** *adverb*.

SYNONYMS – *noun* disbelief, doubt, mistrust, scepticism, suspicion. *verb* disbelieve, mistrust, question, suspect.

disturb > *verb* **1** interfere with the normal arrangement or functioning of. **2** interrupt the sleep, relaxation, or privacy of. **3** cause to feel anxious.

DERIVATIVES – **disturbing** *adjective* **disturbingly** *adverb*.

SYNONYMS – **1** disrupt, interfere with, interrupt. **2** bother, distract, interrupt, trouble. **3** concern, perturb, trouble, unsettle, worry.

ORIGIN – Latin *disturbare*, from *dis-* 'utterly' + *turbare* 'disturb'.

disturbance > *noun* **1** the action of disturbing or the process of being disturbed. **2** a breakdown of peaceful behaviour.

SYNONYMS – **1** disruption, interference, interruption, upheaval. **2** commotion, disorder, fracas, riot.

disturbed > *adjective* suffering from emotional or psychological problems.

SYNONYMS – disordered, distressed, troubled, unbalanced, upset.

disunion > *noun* the breaking of or a lack of union; separation.

disunited > *adjective* lacking unity.

DERIVATIVES – **disunity** *noun*.

disuse > *noun* the state of not being used; neglect.

DERIVATIVES – **disused** *adjective*.

SYNONYMS – abandonment, dereliction, discontinuance, neglect, obsolescence.

disyllable /dīˈsilləb'l, disˈiləb'l/ > *noun* **Poetry** a word or metrical foot consisting of two syllables.

DERIVATIVES – **disyllabic** *adjective*.

ORIGIN – from Greek *disullabos* 'of two syllables'.

ditch > *noun* a narrow channel dug to hold or carry water. > *verb* **1** provide with a ditch. **2** (with reference to an aircraft) bring or come down in a forced landing on the sea. **3** informal get rid of; give up.

DERIVATIVES – **ditcher** *noun* **ditching** *noun*.

dither > *verb* be indecisive. > *noun* informal **1** a state of dithering. **2** a state of agitation.

DERIVATIVES – **ditherer** *noun* **dithery** *adjective*.

SYNONYMS – *verb* falter, hesitate, vacillate, waver.

dithyramb /ˈdithiram/ > *noun* **1** a wildly ecstatic choral hymn of ancient Greece, especially one dedicated to the god Dionysus. **2** a passionate or inflated speech or text.

DERIVATIVES – **dithyrambic** *adjective*.
ORIGIN – Greek *dithurambos*.

ditsy > *adjective* variant spelling of DITZY.

ditto > *noun* **1** the same thing again (used in lists and often indicated by a ditto mark). **2** (also **ditto mark**) a symbol consisting of two apostrophes („) indicating that the item above is to be repeated.

ORIGIN – first used to mean 'in the aforesaid month': from Italian *detto* 'said'.

ditty > *noun* (pl. **ditties**) a short simple song.

ORIGIN – Old French *dite* 'composition', from Latin *dictatum* 'something dictated', from *dictare* 'to dictate'.

ditz > *noun* N. Amer. informal a scatterbrained person.

ditzy (also **ditsy**) > *adjective* N. Amer. informal silly or scatterbrained.

DERIVATIVES – **ditziness** *noun*.

diuretic /dīyooˈrettik/ Medicine > *adjective* causing increased passing of urine. > *noun* a diuretic drug.

ORIGIN – Greek *diourētikos*, from *diourein* 'urinate'.

diurnal /dīˈurn'l/ > *adjective* **1** of or during the daytime. **2** daily; of each day.

DERIVATIVES – **diurnally** *adverb*.

ORIGIN – Latin *diurnalis*, from *dies* 'day'.

diva /ˈdeevə/ > *noun* a celebrated female opera singer.

ORIGIN – Latin, 'goddess'.

Divali > *noun* variant spelling of DIWALI.

divan /diˈvan/ > *noun* **1** a bed consisting of a base and mattress but no footboard or headboard. **2** a long, low sofa without a back or arms.

---

wordpower facts

Divan

When it first entered English in the 16th century the word **divan**, which was adopted via French or Italian from Persian, denoted a council chamber or court of justice in the Ottoman Empire. The original Persian word had a range of meanings, from 'bundle of papers' to 'anthology', 'register', 'custom house', 'court', and 'bench'. By the early 18th century the use to mean 'bench' had also been absorbed into English: a **divan** was a low step, bench, or raised section of floor, furnished with cushions and used as a long seat against the wall of a room, an arrangement commonly found in Middle Eastern countries. By the late 19th century the word was in use for the European equivalent of this type of furnishing, the low, flat sofa or bed.

---

dive > *verb* (past and past participle **dived**; US also **dove** /dōv/) **1** plunge head first and with arms outstretched into water. **2** go to a deeper level in water. **3** swim under water using breathing equipment. **4** plunge steeply downwards through the air. **5** move quickly or suddenly in a downward direction or under cover. **6** Soccer deliberately fall as if fouled in order to deceive the referee. > *noun* **1** an act or instance of diving. **2** informal a disreputable nightclub or bar.

DERIVATIVES – **diving** *noun*.

SYNONYMS – *verb* **1,4,5** lunge, pitch, plummet, plunge, swoop.

COMBINATIONS – **diving bell** an open-bottomed chamber supplied with air, in which a person can be let down under water. **diving board** a board projecting over a swimming pool or other body of water, from which people dive or jump in. **diving suit** a watertight suit, typically with a helmet and an air supply, worn for working or exploring deep under water.

dive-bomb > *verb* bomb (a target) while diving steeply in an aircraft.

DERIVATIVES – **dive-bomber** *noun*.

diver > *noun* **1** a person who dives under water as a sport or as part of their work. **2** a large diving waterbird with a straight pointed bill.

diverge > *verb* **1** (of a road, route, or line) separate and go in a different direction. **2** (of an opinion or approach) differ. **3** (**diverge from**) depart from (a set course or standard).

SYNONYMS – **1** divide, fork, separate, split.
ANTONYMS – **1** converge, meet.

ORIGIN – Latin *divergere*, from *dis-* 'in two ways' + *vergere* 'to turn or incline'.

divergent > *adjective* **1** going in different directions. **2** differing.

DERIVATIVES – **divergence** *noun*.

SYNONYMS – **2** differing, disparate, dissimilar, varying.

divers /ˈdīvərz/ > *adjective* archaic or literary of varying types; several.

ORIGIN – Latin *diversus* 'diverse', from *divertere* (see DIVERT).

diverse /dīˈverss/ > *adjective* widely varied.

DERIVATIVES – **diversely** *adverb*.

SYNONYMS – assorted, dissimilar, divergent, varied.

ANTONYMS – uniform, unvaried.

ORIGIN – Latin *diversus* 'diverse', from *divertere* (see DIVERT).

diversify > *verb* (**diversifies, diversified**) **1** make or become more diverse. **2** (of a company) enlarge or vary its range of products or field of operation.

DERIVATIVES – **diversification** *noun*.

SYNONYMS – expand, extend, vary, widen.

diversion > *noun* **1** an instance of diverting. **2** Brit. an alternative route for use when the usual road is closed. **3** something intended to distract someone's attention. **4** a recreation or pastime.

DERIVATIVES – **diversionary** adjective.

SYNONYMS – **1** deflection, deviation, digression, divergence. **2** detour, redirection, re-routing. **3** disturbance, distraction. **4** amusement, entertainment, pastime, recreation.

diversity > noun (pl. **diversities**) **1** the state of being varied. **2** a varied range; a variety.

ANTONYMS – uniformity.

divert /dīvert, divert/ > verb **1** cause to change course or take a different route. **2** reallocate (a resource) to a different purpose. **3** draw the attention of; distract or entertain.

DERIVATIVES – **diverting** adjective.

SYNONYMS – **1** deflect, redirect, re-route. **2** channel, reallocate, transfer. **3** amuse, distract, entertain, interest.

ORIGIN – Latin divertere, from di- 'aside' + vertere 'to turn'.

diverticula plural of **DIVERTICULUM**.

diverticulitis /dīvertikyoolītiss/ > noun Medicine inflammation of a diverticulum, causing pain and disturbance of bowel function.

diverticulum /dīvertikyoolǝm/ > noun (pl. **diverticula** /dīvertikyoolǝ/) Anatomy & Zoology **1** a blind tube leading from a cavity or passage. **2** Medicine an abnormal sac or pouch formed in the wall of the alimentary tract.

ORIGIN – Latin deverticulum 'byway', from devertere 'turn down or aside'.

divertimento /divertimentō, divairtimentō/ > noun (pl. **divertimenti** /-menti/ or **divertimentos**) Music a light and entertaining composition.

ORIGIN – Italian, 'diversion'.

divertissement /divertissmǝnt, divairteesmoN/ > noun **1** a minor entertainment. **2** Ballet a short separate dance within a ballet.

ORIGIN – from French divertir, from Latin divertere 'turn in separate ways'.

divest /dīvest/ > verb (**divest of**) **1** deprive or dispossess (someone or something) of. **2** free or rid of.

ORIGIN – Old French desvestir, from des- (expressing removal) + Latin vestire (from vestis 'garment').

divestiture (also **divesture**) > noun another term for **DIVESTMENT**.

divestment > noun the action or process of selling off subsidiary business interests or investments.

divi > noun (pl. **divis**) variant spelling of **DIVVY**.

divide > verb **1** separate into parts. **2** distribute or share out. **3** disagree or cause to disagree. **4** form a boundary between. **5** Mathematics find how many times (a number) contains another. **6** (of a number) be susceptible of division without a remainder.

7 (of a legislative body) separate into two groups for voting. > noun an instance of dividing.

IDIOMS – **divide and rule** (or **conquer**) maintain control over opponents by encouraging a disunity that makes their opposition less effective.

DERIVATIVES – **divided** adjective.

SYNONYMS – verb **1** branch, break up, diverge, separate, split. **2** apportion, distribute, share out.

ANTONYMS – verb **1** unite.

ORIGIN – Latin dividere 'force apart, remove'.

dividend > noun **1** a sum of money that is divided among a number of people, such as the part of a company's profits paid to its shareholders or the winnings from a football pool. **2** (**dividends**) a benefit from an action or policy. **3** Mathematics a number to be divided by another number.

ORIGIN – Latin dividendum 'something to be divided', from dividere (see **DIVIDE**).

divider > noun **1** (also **room divider**) a screen or piece of furniture that divides a room into two parts. **2** (**dividers**) a measuring compass, especially one with a screw for making fine adjustments.

divination > noun the practice of divining or seeking knowledge by supernatural means.

WORDFINDER – methods of divination: cartomancy (from playing cards), chiromancy (reading palms), geomancy (by handfuls of earth), necromancy (by communicating with the dead), oneiromancy (by interpreting dreams), sortes (by a random passage from a text).

DERIVATIVES – **divinatory** adjective.

divine[1] > adjective **1** of, from, or like God or a god. **2** informal excellent. > noun **1** dated a cleric or theologian. **2** (**the Divine**) providence or God.

WORDFINDER – apotheosis (elevation to divine status), numinous (suggesting the presence of the divine).

DERIVATIVES – **divinely** adverb.

SYNONYMS – adjective **1** celestial, godly, holy, sacred.

ANTONYMS – mortal.

ORIGIN – Latin divinus, from divus 'godlike'.

divine[2] > verb **1** discover by guesswork or intuition. **2** have supernatural insight into (the future). **3** discover (water) by dowsing.

DERIVATIVES – **diviner** noun.

SYNONYMS – **1** guess, intuit, perceive, surmise. **2** foresee, foretell, predict, prophesy.

COMBINATIONS – **divining rod** a stick or rod used for dowsing.

ORIGIN – Old French deviner 'predict', from Latin divinare, from divinus (see **DIVINE**[1]).

divinity > noun (pl. **divinities**) **1** the state or quality of being divine. **2** a divine being. **3** (**the Divinity**) God. **4** the study of religion; theology.

divisible > adjective **1** capable of being divided. **2** Mathematics (of a number) containing another number a number of times without a remainder.

DERIVATIVES – **divisibility** noun.

division > noun **1** the action or process of dividing. **2** each of the parts into which something is divided. **3** a major unit or section of an organisation. **4** a number of teams or competitors grouped together in a sport for competitive purposes. **5** a partition that divides two groups or things.

IDIOMS – **division of labour** the assignment of different parts of a process or task to different people.

DERIVATIVES – **divisional** adjective.

SYNONYMS – **2** component, part, portion, segment, unit. **3** branch, department, section, unit.

COMBINATIONS – **division bell** a bell rung in the British parliament to announce an imminent vote. **division sign** the sign ÷, placed between two numbers showing that the first is to be divided by the second, as in $6 ÷ 3 = 2$.

division bell > noun a bell rung in the British parliament to announce an imminent division.

divisive /divīsiv/ > adjective causing disagreement or hostility.

DERIVATIVES – **divisiveness** noun.

divisor > noun Mathematics a number by which another number is to be divided.

divorce > noun the legal dissolution of a marriage. > verb **1** legally dissolve one's marriage with. **2** detach or dissociate.

ORIGIN – Latin divortium, from divertere (see **DIVERT**).

divorcee /divorsee/ > noun (US masc. **divorcé**, fem. **divorcée** /divorsay/) a divorced person.

ORIGIN – French divorcé 'divorced man' or divorcée 'divorced woman'.

divot /divvǝt/ > noun a piece of turf cut out of the ground by a golf club in making a stroke.

divulge /dīvulj, divulj/ > verb make known.

SYNONYMS – communicate, disclose, impart, reveal.

ANTONYMS – conceal.

ORIGIN – Latin divulgare, from di- 'widely' + vulgare 'publish' (from vulgus 'common people').

divvy informal > noun (also **divi**) (pl. **divvies**) Brit. a dividend or share, especially of profits earned by a cooperative. > verb (**divvies**, **divvied**) share out.

Diwali /diwaali/ (also **Divali**) > noun a Hindu festival marked by the lighting of

lamps, held in October and November to celebrate the end of the monsoon.
ORIGIN – Sanskrit 'row of lights'.

Dixie > *noun* an informal name for the Southern states of the US.
COMBINATIONS – **Dixieland** a kind of jazz with a strong two-beat rhythm and collective improvisation.

dixie > *noun* (pl. **dixies**) a large iron cooking pot used especially by campers or soldiers.
ORIGIN – Persian *degča* 'small pot'.

DIY > *noun* chiefly Brit. the activity of decorating and making repairs in the home oneself rather than employing a professional.
DERIVATIVES – **DIY'er** noun.
ORIGIN – abbreviation of **DO-IT-YOURSELF**.

dizygotic /dīzīgottik/ > *adjective* (of twins) derived from two separate ova, and so not identical.

dizzy > *adjective* (**dizzier**, **dizziest**) **1** having a sensation of spinning around and losing one's balance. **2** informal (of a woman) silly but attractive. > *verb* (**dizzies**, **dizzied**) make (someone) feel unsteady, confused, or amazed.
IDIOMS – **the dizzy heights** informal a position of great importance in a particular field.
DERIVATIVES – **dizzily** adverb **dizziness** noun.
SYNONYMS – *adjective* **1** giddy, reeling, spinning, wheeling.
ORIGIN – Old English, 'foolish'.

DJ¹ > *noun* **1** a disc jockey. **2** a person who uses samples of recorded music to make techno or rap music.

DJ² > *abbreviation* Brit. dinner jacket.

djellaba /jelləbə/ (also **djellabah** or **jellaba**) > *noun* a loose woollen cloak of a kind traditionally worn by Arabs.
ORIGIN – Arabic.

Djiboutian /jibōōtiən/ > *noun* a person from Djibouti, a country on the north-east coast of Africa. > *adjective* relating to Djibouti.

djinn > *noun* variant spelling of **JINN**.

dl > *abbreviation* decilitre(s).

DLitt > *abbreviation* Doctor of Letters.
ORIGIN – Latin *Doctor Litterarum*.

DM (also **D-mark**) > *abbreviation* Deutschmark.

dm > *abbreviation* decimetre(s).

DMA > *abbreviation* Computing direct memory access.

DMs > *abbreviation* Dr Martens (shoes or boots).

DMus > *abbreviation* Doctor of Music.

DNA > *noun* deoxyribonucleic acid, a substance which is present in the cell nuclei of nearly all living organisms and is the carrier of genetic information.
COMBINATIONS – **DNA fingerprinting**

(also **DNA profiling**) genetic fingerprinting.

do¹ > *verb* (**does**; past **did**; past participle **done**) **1** perform or carry out (an action). **2** achieve or complete (a specified target). **3** act or progress in a specified way. **4** work on (something) to bring it to a required state. **5** have a specified result or effect on: *the walk will do me good.* **6** work at for a living or take as one's subject of study: *what does she do?* **7** make or provide. **8** be suitable or acceptable: *he'll do.* **9** (**be** or **have done with**) give up concern for; have finished with. **10** informal regularly take (a narcotic drug). > *auxiliary verb* **1** used before a verb in questions and negative statements. **2** used to refer back to a verb already mentioned: *he looks better than he did before.* **3** used in negative or positive commands, or to give emphasis to a positive verb: *do sit down.* > *noun* (pl. **dos** or **do's**) informal, chiefly Brit. a party or other social event.
IDIOMS – **be done up** be dressed elaborately. **do away with** informal put an end to; kill. **do for 1** informal defeat, ruin, or kill. **2** suffice for. **do one's head in** Brit. informal make one extremely angry or agitated. **do in** informal **1** kill. **2** tire out. **do or die** persist, even if death is the result. **do out of** deprive of (something) in an unfair way. **dos and don'ts** rules of behaviour. **do time** informal spend a period of time in prison. **do up 1** fasten, wrap, or arrange. **2** informal renovate or redecorate (a room or building). **do with** informal **1** (**can** or **could do with**) would find useful or would like: *I could do with a cup of tea.* **2** (**can't** or **won't be doing with**) Brit. be unwilling to tolerate.
DERIVATIVES – **doable** adjective (informal) **doer** noun.
COMBINATIONS – **do-or-die** showing or requiring a determination not to be deterred.

do² > *noun* variant spelling of **DOH**.

do. > *abbreviation* ditto.

DOA > *abbreviation* dead on arrival.

dob > *verb* (**dobbed**, **dobbing**) Austral./NZ informal inform against.
ORIGIN – a use of dialect *dob* 'put down abruptly', later 'throw something at a target'.

Dobermann /dōbərmən/ (also **Dobermann pinscher** /pinshər/, chiefly N. Amer. also **Doberman**) > *noun* a large breed of dog with powerful jaws, typically black with tan markings.
ORIGIN – named after the 19th-century German dog-breeder Ludwig *Dobermann* (+ German *Pinscher* 'terrier').

dobra /dobrə/ > *noun* the basic monetary unit of São Tomé and Principe, equal to 100 centavos.
ORIGIN – Portuguese *dóbra* 'doubloon'.

dobro /dobrō/ > *noun* (pl. **dobros**) trademark a type of acoustic guitar with steel resonating discs inside the body under the bridge.
ORIGIN – from *Do(bra) Bro(thers)*, the Czech-American inventors of the instrument.

doc > *abbreviation* informal doctor.

docent /dōsənt/ > *noun* **1** (in certain US and European universities) a member of the teaching staff immediately below professor in rank. **2** N. Amer. a person who acts as a guide in a museum, art gallery, or zoo.
ORIGIN – from Latin *docere* 'teach'.

docile > *adjective* ready to accept control or instruction; submissive.
DERIVATIVES – **docilely** adverb **docility** noun.
SYNONYMS – amenable, compliant, meek, submissive.
ANTONYMS – wilful.
ORIGIN – Latin *docilis*, from *docere* 'teach'.

dock¹ > *noun* **1** an enclosed area of water in a port for the loading, unloading, and repair of ships. **2** (also **loading dock**) a platform for loading trucks or goods trains. > *verb* **1** (with reference to a ship) come or bring into a dock. **2** (of a spacecraft) join with a space station or another spacecraft in space. **3** attach (a piece of equipment) to another.
COMBINATIONS – **docking station** a device to which a portable computer is connected so that it can be used like a desktop computer. **dockland** (also **docklands**) the area containing a city's docks. **dockyard** an area with docks and equipment for repairing and maintaining ships.

dock² > *noun* the enclosure in a criminal court where a defendant stands or sits.

dock³ > *noun* a plant with inconspicuous greenish or reddish flowers and broad leaves often used to relieve nettle stings.

dock⁴ > *verb* **1** deduct (money or a point in a score). **2** cut short (an animal's tail).

docker > *noun* a person employed in a port to load and unload ships.

docket > *noun* **1** Brit. a document accompanying a consignment of goods that lists its contents, certifies payment of duty, or entitles the holder to delivery. **2** N. Amer. a list of pending legal cases. > *verb* (**docketed**, **docketing**) identify with or assign to a docket.

doctor > *noun* **1** a person who is qualified to practise medicine. **2** (**Doctor**) a person who holds the highest university degree. **3** Austral./NZ informal a cook on board a ship or in a camp or station. > *verb* **1** change in order to deceive; falsify. **2** adulterate (a food or drink) with an undesired ingredient. **3** Brit. remove the sexual organs of (an animal) so that it cannot reproduce.
WORDFINDER – *doctors and their specialties:*

cardiologist (*disorders of the heart*), dermatologist (*disorders of the skin*), epidemiologist (*incidence and distribution of disease*), geriatrician (*care and health of old people*), gynaecologist (*female reproductive system*), haematologist (*physiology of the blood*), obstetrician (*childbirth*), oncologist (*tumours*), ophthalmologist (*disorders of the eye*), paediatrician (*childhood disorders*), pathologist (*causes and effects of diseases*).

IDIOMS – **go for the doctor** Austral./NZ informal make an all-out effort. **what the doctor ordered** informal something beneficial or desirable.

DERIVATIVES – **doctoring** noun.

ORIGIN – Latin, 'teacher', from *docere* 'teach'.

doctoral > *adjective* relating to a doctorate.

doctorate > *noun* the highest degree awarded by a university faculty.

doctrinaire /doktri**nair**/ > *adjective* seeking to impose a doctrine without compromise.

SYNONYMS – authoritarian, dictatorial, dogmatic.

ORIGIN – French.

doctrine /**dok**trin/ > *noun* a set of beliefs or principles held and taught by a Church, political party, or other group.

DERIVATIVES – **doctrinal** /dok**trī**n'l, **dok**trin'l/ *adjective* **doctrinally** *adverb*.

SYNONYMS – belief, creed, dogma, ideology, teaching.

ORIGIN – Old French, from Latin *doctrina* 'teaching, learning', from *doctor* 'teacher'.

docudrama > *noun* a dramatised film based on real events and incorporating documentary features.

document > *noun* /**dok**yoomənt/ a piece of written, printed, or electronic matter that provides information or evidence. > *verb* /**dok**yooment/ record in written or other form.

WORDFINDER – archive (*collection of historical documents*), manuscript (*handwritten document*), notary (*person authorised to draw up legal documents*), pro forma (*standard document*), recto (*front of a loose document*), rubric (*heading on a document*), scribe (*person who copied out documents*), verso (*back of a loose document*).

SYNONYMS – chronicle, log, record.

ORIGIN – Latin *documentum* 'lesson, proof', from *docere* 'teach'.

documentary > *adjective* **1** consisting of documents and other material providing a factual account. **2** using film, photographs, and sound recordings of real events. > *noun* (pl. **documentaries**) a documentary film or television or radio programme.

documentation > *noun* **1** the documents required in the provision of information or evidence. **2** written specifications or instructions.

docusoap > *noun* a documentary following

people in a particular occupation or location over a period of time (in the manner of a soap opera).

DOD > *abbreviation* (in the US) Department of Defense.

dodder[1] > *verb* be slow and unsteady.

DERIVATIVES – **dodderer** noun **doddering** *adjective* **doddery** *adjective*.

SYNONYMS – shuffle, teeter, totter.

dodder[2] > *noun* a parasitic climbing plant with leafless stems that are attached to the host plant by means of suckers.

doddle > *noun* Brit. informal a very easy task.

dodecagon /dō**dekk**əgən/ > *noun* a plane figure with twelve straight sides and angles.

dodecahedron /dōdekkə**hee**drən/ > *noun* (pl. **dodecahedra** /dōdekkə**hee**drə/ or **dodecahedrons**) a three-dimensional shape having twelve plane faces.

ORIGIN – Greek *dōdekaedron*, from *dōdekaedros* 'twelve-faced'.

dodge > *verb* **1** avoid by a sudden quick movement. **2** cunningly avoid doing or paying. > *noun* **1** an act or instance of dodging. **2** informal a cunning trick, especially one used to avoid something.

SYNONYMS – *verb* avoid, circumvent, duck, elude, evade, sidestep.

dodgem > *noun* a small electrically powered car driven within an enclosure at a funfair, with the aim of bumping other such cars.

ORIGIN – US proprietary name (as *Dodg'em*), from the phrase *dodge them*.

dodger > *noun* informal a person who evades something that is required of them: *a tax dodger*.

dodgy > *adjective* (**dodgier**, **dodgiest**) Brit. informal **1** dishonest. **2** risky. **3** not good or reliable.

dodo /**dō**dō/ > *noun* (pl. **dodos** or **dodoes**) a large extinct flightless bird found on Mauritius until the end of the 17th century.

IDIOMS – **as dead as a dodo** utterly dead or finished.

ORIGIN – Portuguese *doudo* 'simpleton' (because the birds were tame and easy to catch).

DoE > *abbreviation* (in the UK) Department of the Environment.

doe > *noun* **1** a female roe or fallow deer or reindeer. **2** a female hare, rabbit, rat, ferret, or kangaroo.

COMBINATIONS – **doe-eyed** having large gentle dark eyes.

does third person singular present of DO[1].

doesn't > *contraction* does not.

doff > *verb* remove (an item of clothing, especially a hat).

ORIGIN – contraction of *do off*.

dog > *noun* **1** a domesticated carnivorous

mammal with a barking or howling voice and an acute sense of smell. **2** a wild animal resembling this, in particular any member of the dog family (Canidae), which includes the wolf, fox, coyote, jackal, and other species. **3** the male of such an animal. **4** (**the dogs**) Brit. informal greyhound racing. **5** informal, derogatory an unattractive woman. **6** informal, dated a contemptible man. **7** dated a person of a specified kind: *you lucky dog!* > *verb* (**dogged**, **dogging**) **1** follow closely and persistently. **2** (of a problem) cause continual trouble for.

WORDFINDER – canine (*relating to or resembling a dog*); Canis Major (*constellation, the Great Dog*), Canis Minor (*constellation, the Little Dog*).

IDIOMS – **a dog in the manger** a person who prevents others from having things that they do not need themselves. [ORIGIN – alluding to the fable of the dog that lay in a manger to prevent the ox and horse from eating the hay.] **a dog's dinner** (or **breakfast**) Brit. informal a mess. **every dog has his** (or **its**) **day** proverb everyone will have good luck or success at some point in their lives. **go to the dogs** informal deteriorate badly. **you can't teach an old dog new tricks** proverb you cannot make people change their ways. **why keep a dog and bark yourself?** proverb why pay someone to work for you and then do the work yourself?

DERIVATIVES – **dogdom** noun **doggish** *adjective*.

COMBINATIONS – **dog cart** a two-wheeled cart for driving in, with cross seats back to back. **dog collar 1** a collar for a dog. **2** informal a clerical collar. **dog days** chiefly literary the hottest period of the year (reckoned in ancient times on the time when Sirius, the Dog Star, rises at the same time as the sun). **dog-leg** a sharp bend. **dog rose** a delicately scented wild rose with pink or white flowers. **Dog Star** Sirius, the brightest star in the sky. [ORIGIN – so named as it appears to follow at the heels of Orion (the hunter).] **dog tag** informal, chiefly N. Amer. a soldier's metal identity tag. **dog-tired** extremely tired. **dog-tooth 1** Architecture a small pointed moulding forming one of a series radiating from a raised centre. **2** (also **dogstooth**) a small check pattern with notched corners.

doge /dōj/ > *noun* historical the chief magistrate of Venice or Genoa.

ORIGIN – Italian *doze*, from Latin *dux* 'leader'.

dog-eared > *adjective* having worn or battered corners.

dog-end > *noun* informal **1** a cigarette end. **2** the last and least pleasing part of something.

dogfight > *noun* **1** a close combat between military aircraft. **2** a ferocious struggle or fight.
DERIVATIVES – **dogfighting** *noun*.

dogfish > *noun* a small bottom-dwelling shark with a long tail.

dogged /**dogg**id/ > *adjective* very persistent.
DERIVATIVES – **doggedly** *adverb* **doggedness** *noun*.

doggerel /**dogg**ərəl/ > *noun* **1** comic verse composed in irregular rhythm. **2** badly written verse.

doggo > *adverb* (in phrase **lie doggo**) Brit. informal, dated remain motionless and quiet to escape detection.

doggone /**dogg**on/ N. Amer. informal > *adjective* damned. > *verb* damn (used to express surprise or irritation).
ORIGIN – probably from *dog on it*, euphemism for *God damn it*.

doggy > *adjective* **1** of or like a dog. **2** fond of dogs. > *noun* (also **doggie**) (pl. **doggies**) a child's word for a dog.
COMBINATIONS – **doggy bag** a bag used to take home leftover food from a restaurant, supposedly for one's dog.

doggy-paddle > *noun* an elementary swimming stroke resembling that of a dog. > *verb* swim using this stroke.

doghouse > *noun* N. Amer. a dog's kennel.
IDIOMS – **in the doghouse** informal in disgrace or disfavour.

dogma > *noun* an inflexible principle or set of principles laid down by an authority.
SYNONYMS – doctrine, ideology, orthodoxy, teaching.
ORIGIN – Greek *dogma* 'opinion', from *dokein* 'seem good, think'.

dogmatic > *adjective* inclined to impose dogma; firmly asserting personal opinions as true.
DERIVATIVES – **dogmatically** *adverb* **dogmatism** *noun* **dogmatist** *noun*.
SYNONYMS – dictatorial, domineering, emphatic, insistent, pontifical.

do-gooder > *noun* a well-meaning but unrealistic or interfering person.
DERIVATIVES – **do-goodery** *noun* **do-goodism** *noun*.

dogsbody > *noun* (pl. **dogsbodies**) Brit. informal a person who is given boring, menial tasks.

dogwatch > *noun* either of two short watches on a ship (4–6 or 6–8 p.m.).

dogwood > *noun* a flowering shrub or small tree with red stems, colourful berries, and hard wood.
ORIGIN – so named because the wood was used to make 'dogs' (i.e. skewers).

DoH > *abbreviation* (in the UK) Department of Health.

doh /dō/ (also **do**) > *noun* Music the first note of a major scale, coming before 'ray'.

doily > *noun* (pl. **doilies**) a small ornamental mat made of lace or paper.
ORIGIN – named after a 17th-century London draper.

doing > *noun* **1** (also **doings**) the activities in which someone engages. **2** (treated as sing. or pl.) informal, chiefly Brit. things whose name one has forgotten. **3** (**doings**) informal excrement.

do-it-yourself > *noun* full form of **DIY**.

dojo /**dō**jō/ > *noun* (pl. **dojos**) a place in which judo and other martial arts are practised.
ORIGIN – Japanese, from *dō* 'way, pursuit' + *jō* 'a place'.

Dolby /**dol**bi/ > *noun* trademark **1** a noise-reduction system used in tape recording. **2** an electronic system providing stereophonic sound for cinemas and televisions.
ORIGIN – named after the American engineer Ray M. *Dolby* (born 1933).

dolce far niente /dolchay faar ni**en**tay/ > *noun* pleasant idleness.
ORIGIN – Italian, 'sweet doing nothing'.

Dolcelatte /dolchə**laa**tay/ > *noun* trademark a kind of soft creamy blue-veined cheese from Italy.
ORIGIN – Italian, 'sweet milk'.

doldrums /**dol**drəmz/ > *plural noun* (**the doldrums**) **1** a state of stagnation or depression. **2** a region of the Atlantic Ocean with calms, sudden storms, and light unpredictable winds.

dole > *noun* (often in phrase **on the dole**) Brit. informal benefit paid by the state to the unemployed. > *verb* (**dole out**) distribute (something).
ORIGIN – Old English, 'division, portion, or share'.

doleful > *adjective* **1** sorrowful. **2** causing grief or misfortune.
DERIVATIVES – **dolefully** *adverb*.
ORIGIN – from obsolete *dole* 'sorrow or mourning', from Latin *dolere* 'grieve'.

dolerite /**doll**ərīt/ > *noun* Geology a dark igneous rock typically occurring in dykes and sills.
ORIGIN – from Greek *doleros* 'deceptive' (because it resembles diorite).

doll > *noun* **1** a small model of a human figure, used as a child's toy. **2** informal an attractive young woman. > *verb* (**doll up**) informal dress (someone) smartly and attractively.
COMBINATIONS – **doll's house** (N. Amer. also **dollhouse**) a miniature toy house.
ORIGIN – first used to denote a mistress: from the given name *Dorothy*.

dollar > *noun* the basic monetary unit of the US, Canada, Australia, and certain countries in the Pacific, Caribbean, SE Asia, Africa, and South America.
COMBINATIONS – **dollar sign** (also **dollar mark**) the sign $, representing a dollar.

wordpower facts

Dollar

The word **dollar** is associated primarily with the United States, but it has its origins far away, in central Europe. It comes from German *Thaler*, short for *Joachimsthaler*, a coin from the silver-mine of Joachimsthal ('Joachim's valley'), now *Jáchymov* in the Czech Republic. The term was later applied to a coin used in the Spanish-American colonies, which was also widely used in the British North American colonies at the time of the American War of Independence. It was adopted as the name of the US monetary unit in the late 18th century.

dollop informal > *noun* a shapeless mass or lump, especially of soft food. > *verb* (**dolloped**, **dolloping**) add or serve out in large shapeless quantities.

dolly > *noun* (pl. **dollies**) **1** a child's word for a doll. **2** informal, dated an attractive young woman. **3** a small platform on wheels for holding heavy objects, typically film cameras. > *verb* (**dollies**, **dollied**) (of a film camera) be moved on a dolly.
COMBINATIONS – **dolly bird** Brit. informal, dated an attractive but unintelligent young woman.

dolma /**dol**mə/ > *noun* (pl. **dolmas** or **dolmades** /dol**maa**thez/) a Greek and Turkish dish of spiced rice and meat wrapped in vine or cabbage leaves.
ORIGIN – Turkish, from *dolmak* 'fill, be filled'.

dolman /**dol**mən/ > *noun* **1** a long Turkish robe open in front. **2** a woman's loose cloak with cape-like sleeves.
COMBINATIONS – **dolman sleeve** a loose sleeve cut in one piece with the body of a garment.
ORIGIN – Turkish.

dolmen /**dol**men/ > *noun* a megalithic tomb with a large flat stone laid on upright ones.
ORIGIN – Cornish, 'hole of a stone'.

dolomite /**doll**əmīt/ > *noun* a mineral or sedimentary rock consisting chiefly of a carbonate of calcium and magnesium.
DERIVATIVES – **dolomitic** *adjective*.
ORIGIN – named after the French geologist *Dolomieu* (1750–1801).

dolorous /**doll**ərəss/ > *adjective* literary feeling great sorrow or distress.
DERIVATIVES – **dolorously** *adverb*.
ORIGIN – Latin *dolorosus*, from *dolor* 'pain, grief'.

dolour /**doll**ər/ (US **dolor**) > *noun* literary a state of great sorrow or distress.
ORIGIN – Latin *dolor* 'pain, grief'.

dolphin > *noun* a small gregarious toothed whale with a beak-like snout and a curved fin on the back.
ORIGIN – Old French *dauphin*, from Greek *delphin*.

dolphinarium /dolfi**nair**iəm/ > *noun* (pl. **dolphinariums** or **dolphinaria**) an aquarium in which dolphins are kept and trained for public entertainment.

dolt /dōlt/ > *noun* a stupid person.
DERIVATIVES – **doltish** *adjective*.
SYNONYMS – blockhead, dope, dunce, fool, idiot, numbskull.

Dom /dom/ > *noun* a title prefixed to the names of some Roman Catholic dignitaries and Benedictine and Carthusian monks.
ORIGIN – Latin *dominus* 'master'.

-dom > *suffix* forming nouns: **1** denoting a state or condition: *freedom*. **2** denoting status: *earldom*. **3** denoting a domain: *fiefdom*. **4** denoting a class of people: *officialdom*.
ORIGIN – Old English 'decree, judgement'.

domain /də**mayn**/ > *noun* **1** an area controlled by a ruler or government. **2** a sphere of activity or knowledge. **3** Computing a distinct subset of the Internet with addresses sharing a common suffix.
SYNONYMS – **1** dominion, empire, province, realm, territory. **2** arena, field, sphere.
ORIGIN – French *domaine*, from *demeine* (see DEMESNE).

dome > *noun* **1** a rounded vault forming the roof of a building. **2** a sports stadium or other building with a domed roof. **3** a natural vault or canopy. **4** informal the top of the head.
WORDFINDER – cupola (*dome forming a roof or ceiling*), drum (*a circular vertical wall supporting a dome*), geodesic (*denoting a dome made from struts that follow geodesic lines*), squinch (*structure lying across the internal angle of a square tower to support a dome*).
DERIVATIVES – **domed** *adjective* **domical** *adjective*.
ORIGIN – Italian *duomo* 'cathedral, dome', from Latin *domus* 'house'.

domestic > *adjective* **1** relating to a home or family affairs or relations. **2** of or for use in the home. **3** (of a person) fond of family life and running a home. **4** (of an animal) tame and kept by humans. **5** existing or occurring within a country. > *noun* **1** (also **domestic worker** or **domestic help**) a person who is employed to do domestic tasks. **2** informal a violent quarrel between family members.
DERIVATIVES – **domestically** *adverb*.
COMBINATIONS – **domestic science** dated home economics.
ORIGIN – Latin *domesticus*, from *domus* 'house'.

domesticate > *verb* **1** tame (an animal) and keep it as a pet or for farm produce. **2** cultivate (a plant) for food.
DERIVATIVES – **domestication** *noun*.

domesticity > *noun* home or family life.

domicile /**domm**isīl, **domm**issil/ > *noun* formal or Law **1** the country in which a person has permanent residence. **2** chiefly N. Amer. a person's home. > *verb* (**be domiciled**) formal or Law **1** treat a specified country as a permanent home. **2** chiefly N. Amer. reside; be based.
ORIGIN – Latin *domicilium* 'dwelling', from *domus* 'home'.

domiciliary /dommi**silli**əri/ > *adjective* concerned with or occurring in someone's home.

dominant > *adjective* **1** most important, powerful, or influential. **2** (of a high place or object) overlooking others. **3** Genetics (of a heritable characteristic) controlled by a gene that is expressed in offspring even when inherited from only one parent. Compare with RECESSIVE. > *noun* Genetics a dominant trait or gene.
DERIVATIVES – **dominance** *noun* **dominantly** *adverb*.
SYNONYMS – *adjective* **1** authoritative, commanding, controlling, forceful, influential, powerful.

dominate > *verb* **1** have a commanding or controlling influence over. **2** (of something tall or high) overlook.
DERIVATIVES – **domination** *noun* **dominator** *noun*.
SYNONYMS – **1** control, govern, master, subjugate.
ORIGIN – Latin *dominari* 'rule, govern', from *dominus* 'lord, master'.

dominatrix /dommi**nay**triks/ > *noun* (pl. **dominatrices** /dommi**nay**triseez/ or **dominatrixes**) a dominating woman, especially in sadomasochistic practices.
ORIGIN – Latin, feminine of *dominator*, from *dominari* 'rule, govern'.

domineering > *adjective* asserting one's will in an unwelcome manner.
DERIVATIVES – **domineeringly** *adverb*.
SYNONYMS – bossy, controlling, imperious, overbearing.
ORIGIN – from the verb *domineer*, from Dutch *domineren*, from Latin *dominari* 'rule, govern'.

Dominican[1] /də**minni**kən/ > *noun* a member of the order of preaching friars founded by St Dominic, or of a similar religious order for women. > *adjective* relating to St Dominic or the Dominicans.

Dominican[2] /də**minni**kən/ > *noun* a person from the Dominican Republic in the Caribbean. > *adjective* relating to the Dominican Republic.

Dominican[3] /dommi**nee**kən, də**minni**kən/ > *noun* a person from the Caribbean island of Dominica. > *adjective* relating to the island of Dominica.

dominion > *noun* **1** sovereignty; control. **2** the territory of a sovereign or government. **3** (**Dominion**) historical a self-governing territory of the British Commonwealth.
ORIGIN – Latin *dominium*, from *dominus* 'lord, master'.

domino > *noun* (pl. **dominoes**) **1** any of 28 small oblong pieces marked with 0–6 pips in each half. **2** (**dominoes**) (treated as sing.) the game played with such pieces. **3** historical a loose cloak worn with a mask for the upper part of the face at masquerades.
COMBINATIONS – **domino effect** the hypothetical influence of political events in one country upon its neighbours.
ORIGIN – probably from Latin *dominus* 'lord, master'.

don[1] > *noun* **1** a university teacher, especially a senior member of a college at Oxford or Cambridge. **2** (**Don**) a Spanish title prefixed to a male forename. **3** N. Amer. informal a high-ranking member of the Mafia.
ORIGIN – Spanish, from Latin *dominus* 'lord, master'.

don[2] > *verb* (**donned, donning**) put on (an item of clothing).
ORIGIN – contraction of *do on*.

donate > *verb* **1** give (money or goods) for a good cause. **2** allow the removal of (blood or an organ) from one's body for transfusion or transplantation.
SYNONYMS – bestow, contribute, give, pledge.

donation > *noun* something that is given to a good cause.
SYNONYMS – benefaction, contribution, endowment, gift.
ORIGIN – Latin, from *donare* 'give', from *donum* 'gift'.

done past participle of DO[1]. > *adjective* **1** (of food) cooked thoroughly. **2** no longer happening or existing. **3** informal socially acceptable: *the done thing*. > *exclamation* (in response to an offer) accepted.
IDIOMS – **done for** informal in serious trouble.

donee /dō**nee**/ > *noun* a person who receives a gift.

doner kebab /**donn**ə, **dō**nə/ > *noun* a Turkish dish consisting of spiced lamb cooked on a spit and served in slices.
ORIGIN – Turkish *döner kebap*, from *döner* 'rotating' and *kebap* 'roast meat'.

dong[1] > *verb* (of a bell) make a deep resonant sound. > *noun* a deep resonant sound.

dong[2] > *noun* the basic monetary unit of Vietnam, equal to 100 xu.
ORIGIN – Vietnamese, 'coin'.

donga /**dong**gə/ > *noun* **1** S. African a dry watercourse. **2** Austral. a makeshift shelter.
ORIGIN – Xhosa and Zulu.

donjon /**don**jən, **dun**jən/ > *noun* **1** the great tower or innermost keep of a castle. **2** archaic a dungeon.

ORIGIN – from **DUNGEON**.

Don Juan /don jōoən, waan/ > *noun* a seducer of women.

ORIGIN – from the name of a legendary Spanish nobleman.

donkey > *noun* (pl. **donkeys**) **1** a domesticated hoofed mammal of the horse family with long ears and a braying call. **2** informal a stupid or foolish person.

WORDFINDER – asinine (*relating to a donkey*), hinny (*offspring of female donkey and male horse*), jackass (*male donkey*), jenny (*female donkey*), mule (*offspring of male donkey and female horse*).

IDIOMS – **donkey's years** informal a very long time. **talk the hind leg off a donkey** Brit. informal talk incessantly.

COMBINATIONS – **donkey engine** a small auxiliary engine. **donkey jacket** Brit. a heavy jacket with a patch of waterproof material across the shoulders. **donkey work** informal the laborious part of a job.

donna /**don**nə/ > *noun* **1** an Italian, Spanish, or Portuguese lady. **2** (**Donna**) a courtesy title prefixed to the forename of such a lady.

ORIGIN – Latin *domina* 'mistress', feminine of *dominus* 'lord, master'.

donnish > *adjective* resembling a college don, particularly in having a pedantic manner.

donor > *noun* **1** someone who donates. **2** a substance, molecule, etc. which provides electrons for a physical or chemical process.

COMBINATIONS – **donor card** a card consenting to the use of one's organs for transplant surgery in the event of one's death.

ORIGIN – Old French *doneur*, from Latin *donare* 'give'.

don't > *contraction* do not.

donut > *noun* US spelling of **DOUGHNUT**.

doodah /**dōo**daa/ (N. Amer. **doodad** /**dōo**dad/) > *noun* informal an object that the speaker cannot name precisely.

ORIGIN – perhaps from the refrain of the song *Camptown Races*.

doodle > *verb* scribble absent-mindedly. > *noun* a drawing made absent-mindedly.

DERIVATIVES – **doodler** *noun*.

ORIGIN – first meaning 'simpleton', later 'make a fool of': from German *dudeldopp*.

doodlebug > *noun* Brit. informal (in the Second World War) a German flying bomb.

ORIGIN – used earlier in various senses (chiefly US), such as 'insect larva', 'prospecting device', 'small vehicle', etc.

doo-doo > *noun* a child's word for excrement.

doofus /**dōo**fəss/ (also **dufus**) > *noun* (pl. **doofuses**) N. Amer. informal a stupid person.

doolally /dōo**lal**i/ > *adjective* informal temporarily insane.

ORIGIN – from *doolally tap*, Indian army slang, from *Deolali* (a town near Bombay) + Urdu *tap* 'fever'.

doom > *noun* death, destruction, or another terrible fate. > *verb* condemn to certain destruction or failure.

DERIVATIVES – **doomy** adjective.

SYNONYMS – *noun* death, destruction, downfall, ruination.

ORIGIN – Old English, 'statute, judgement'.

doomsayer > *noun* a person who predicts disaster.

DERIVATIVES – **doomsaying** noun.

doomsday > *noun* **1** the last day of the world's existence. **2** (in Christian and some other religious traditions) the day of the Last Judgement.

doomster > *noun* a doomsayer.

doona /**dōo**nə/ > *noun* Austral. trademark a quilt or duvet.

door > *noun* **1** a movable barrier at the entrance to a building, room, or vehicle, or in the framework of a cupboard. **2** used to refer to a house: *he lived two doors away.*

WORDFINDER – architrave (*moulded frame around a doorway*), escutcheon (*flat piece of metal around a keyhole or door handle*), fanlight (*small window over a door*), jamb (*side post of a doorway*), lintel (*horizontal support across the top of a door*), portière (*curtain hung over a door or doorway*), scuncheon (*inside face of a jamb*).

IDIOMS – **as one door closes, another opens** proverb you shouldn't be discouraged by failure, as other opportunities will soon present themselves. **lay at someone's door** blame someone for (something). **out of doors** in or into the open air.

DERIVATIVES – **doored** adjective.

COMBINATIONS – **doorbell** a bell in a building which can be rung by visitors outside. **door furniture** the handles, lock, and other fixtures on a door. **doorkeeper** a person on duty at the entrance to a building. **doorman** a man who is on duty at the entrance to a large building. **doormat 1** a mat placed in a doorway for wiping the shoes. **2** informal a submissive person. **doornail** (in phrase **dead as a doornail**) quite dead. **doorpost** an upright part of a door frame. **doorstop** (also **doorstopper**) an object that keeps a door open or in place.

doorpost > *noun* an upright part of a door frame.

doorstep > *noun* **1** a step leading up to the outer door of a house. **2** Brit. informal a thick sandwich or slice. > *verb* (**doorstepped, doorstepping**) Brit. informal **1** (of a journalist) wait uninvited outside the home of (someone) for an interview or photograph.

2 go from door to door selling or canvassing.

doo-wop /**dōo**wop/ > *noun* a style of pop music involving close harmony vocals and nonsense phrases.

dopamine /**dō**pəmeen/ > *noun* Biochemistry a compound which exists in the body as a neurotransmitter and as a precursor of other substances, including adrenalin.

ORIGIN – from *dopa* (a related substance) + **AMINE**; *dopa* is an acronym of *dihydroxyphenylalanine*.

dope informal > *noun* **1** an illegal drug, especially cannabis or (US) heroin. **2** a drug used to enhance the performance of an athlete, racehorse, or greyhound. **3** a stupid person. **4** information. **5** a thick liquid varnish, lubricant, or other preparation. > *verb* **1** administer dope to (a racehorse, greyhound, or athlete). **2** (**be doped up**) informal be heavily under the influence of drugs.

DERIVATIVES – **doper** *noun*.

ORIGIN – Dutch *doop* 'sauce', from *doopen* 'to dip, mix'.

dopey (also **dopy**) > *adjective* (**dopier, dopiest**) informal **1** stupefied by sleep or a drug. **2** idiotic.

DERIVATIVES – **dopily** adverb.

doppelgänger /**dopp**'lgengər/ > *noun* an apparition or double of a living person.

ORIGIN – German, 'double-goer'.

Doppler effect /**dop**lər/ (also **Doppler shift**) > *noun* Physics an increase (or decrease) in the apparent frequency of sound, light, or other waves as the source and the observer move towards (or away from) each other.

ORIGIN – named after the Austrian physicist Johann Christian *Doppler* (1803–53).

dorado /də**raa**dō/ > *noun* (pl. **dorados**) a large edible fish of warm seas, with bright coloration.

ORIGIN – Spanish, 'gilded'.

Dorian /**dor**iən/ > *noun* a member of a people speaking the Doric dialect of Greek, thought to have entered Greece from the north *c.*1100 BC. > *adjective* relating to the Dorians or to Doris in central Greece.

Doric /**dor**ik/ > *adjective* **1** referring to a classical order of architecture characterised by a plain column and a square abacus. **2** referring to the ancient Greek dialect of the Dorians.

dork > *noun* informal a socially inept person.

dorm > *noun* informal a dormitory.

dormant > *adjective* **1** in or as if in a deep sleep; inactive. **2** (of a plant or bud) alive but not growing.

DERIVATIVES – **dormancy** noun.

ORIGIN – Old French, 'sleeping', from Latin *dormire* 'to sleep'.

dormer (also **dormer window**) > *noun* a window set vertically into a sloping roof.

ORIGIN – first used in reference to a dormitory or bedroom window: from Old French *dormir* 'to sleep'.

dormitory > *noun* (pl. **dormitories**) **1** a bedroom for a number of people in an institution. **2** (before another noun) denoting a small town or suburb from which people travel to work in a nearby city.

ORIGIN – Latin *dormitorium*, from *dormire* 'to sleep'.

dormouse > *noun* (pl. **dormice**) an agile mouse-like rodent with a bushy tail.

dormy > *adjective* Golf (of a player) ahead by as many holes as there are holes left to play.

dorsal > *adjective* Anatomy, Zoology, & Botany on or relating to the upper side or back. Compare with VENTRAL.

DERIVATIVES – **dorsally** *adverb*.

ORIGIN – Latin *dorsalis*, from *dorsum* 'back'.

dory /ˈdori/ > *noun* (pl. **dories**) a narrow marine fish with a large mouth.

ORIGIN – French *dorée* 'gilded', from Latin *aurum* 'gold'.

DOS > *abbreviation* Computing disk operating system.

dosage > *noun* the size of a dose of medicine or radiation.

dose > *noun* **1** a quantity of a medicine or drug taken at one time. **2** an amount of ionising radiation received or absorbed at one time. **3** informal a venereal infection. > *verb* administer a dose to.

IDIOMS – **like a dose of salts** Brit. informal very fast and efficiently. [ORIGIN – from the use of Epsom salts as a laxative.]

ORIGIN – Greek *dosis* 'gift', from *didonai* 'give'.

dosh > *noun* Brit. informal money.

do-si-do /ˌdoʊziˈdoʊ, ˌdoʊsiˈdoʊ/ (also **do-se-do**) > *noun* (pl. **do-si-dos**) (in country dancing) a figure in which two dancers pass round each other back to back.

ORIGIN – French *dos-à-dos* 'back to back'.

dosimeter /doʊˈsɪmɪtər/ > *noun* a device used to measure an absorbed dose of ionising radiation.

DERIVATIVES – **dosimetry** *noun*.

doss Brit. informal > *verb* **1** sleep in rough or improvised conditions. **2** spend time idly. > *noun* **1** archaic a bed in a cheap lodging house. **2** an easy task giving time for idling.

DERIVATIVES – **dosser** *noun*.

COMBINATIONS – **dosshouse** Brit. informal a cheap lodging house for homeless people.

dossier /ˈdossiər, ˈdossiay/ > *noun* a collection of documents about a person or subject.

---

dost /dust/ archaic second person singular present of DO¹.

DoT > *abbreviation* (in the UK and Canada) Department of Transport.

dot > *noun* **1** a small round mark or spot. **2** a dot written as part of an *i* or *j*, as one of a series to signify omission, or as a full stop. **3** Music a dot used to denote the lengthening of a note or rest by half, or to indicate staccato. **4** the shorter signal of the two used in Morse code. > *verb* (**dotted**, **dotting**) **1** mark with a dot or dots. **2** scatter over (an area).

IDIOMS – **on the dot** informal exactly on time. **the year dot** Brit. informal a very long time ago.

SYNONYMS – *noun* **1** fleck, mark, speck, spot.

COMBINATIONS – **dot matrix** a grid of dots which are filled selectively to produce an image.

ORIGIN – Old English, 'head of a boil'.

dotage /ˈdoʊtɪdʒ/ > *noun* the period of life in which a person is old and weak.

ORIGIN – from *dote* 'be silly or feeble-minded'.

dotard /ˈdoʊtəd/ > *noun* an old person, especially one who is weak or senile.

dot-com > *noun* a company that conducts its business on the Internet.

ORIGIN – from '.com' in an Internet address, indicating a commercial site.

dote > *verb* (**dote on**) be extremely and uncritically fond of.

DERIVATIVES – **doting** *adjective*.

SYNONYMS – (**dote on**) adore, cherish, prize, treasure.

ORIGIN – related to Dutch *doten* 'be silly'.

doth /duth/ archaic third person singular present of DO¹.

dotterel /ˈdottərəl/ > *noun* a small migratory plover.

ORIGIN – from DOTE (with reference to the bird's tameness).

dottle > *noun* a remnant of tobacco left in a pipe after smoking.

ORIGIN – first denoting a plug for a barrel: from DOT.

> ### wordpower facts
> #### Dossier
> The word **dossier** is related to **dorsal** 'on or relating to the back' and to some other rather unexpected words. Its root is Latin *dorsum* 'back': it came into English from French, and originally had the meaning (found also in French) 'bundle of papers with a label on the back'. Other words from *dorsum* include **endorse**, which originally meant 'write on the back of', and possibly **doss**.

---

dotty > *adjective* (**dottier**, **dottiest**) informal, chiefly Brit. slightly mad or eccentric.

DERIVATIVES – **dottiness** *noun*.

double > *adjective* **1** consisting of two equal, identical, or similar parts or things. **2** having twice the usual size, quantity, or strength: *a double brandy*. **3** designed to be used by two people. **4** having two different roles or interpretations: *she began a double life*. **5** (of a flower) having more than one circle of petals. > *predeterminer* twice as much or as many. > *adverb* at or to twice the amount or extent. > *noun* **1** a thing which is twice as large as usual or is made up of two parts. **2** a person who looks exactly like another. **3** (**doubles**) a game involving sides made up of two players. **4** Brit. (**the double**) the winning of two sporting trophies in the same season. **5** Darts a hit on the ring enclosed by the two outer circles of a dartboard, scoring double. > *pronoun* an amount twice as large as usual. > *verb* **1** make or become double. **2** fold or bend over on itself. **3** (**double up**) bend over or curl up with pain or laughter. **4** (**double as** or **double up as**) be used in or play another, different role. **5** (**double back**) go back in the direction one has come.

WORDFINDER – doppelgänger (*a double of a living person*).

IDIOMS – **at the double** very fast.

DERIVATIVES – **doubleness** *noun* **doubler** *noun* **doubly** *adverb*.

COMBINATIONS – **double act** a performance involving two people. **double agent** an agent who pretends to act as a spy for one country while in fact acting for its enemy. **double-barrelled 1** (of a gun) having two barrels. **2** Brit. (of a surname) having two parts joined by a hyphen. **double bass** the largest and lowest-pitched instrument of the violin family. **double bill** a programme of entertainment with two main items. **double bind** a dilemma. **double bluff** an action or statement intended to appear as a bluff, but which is in fact genuine. **double boiler** a saucepan with an upper compartment heated by boiling water in the lower one. **double bond** a chemical bond in which two pairs of electrons are shared between two atoms. **double-book** inadvertently reserve (something) for two different customers at the same time. **double-breasted** (of a jacket or coat) having a large overlap at the front and two rows of buttons. **double cream** Brit. thick cream containing a high proportion of milk fat. **double Dutch** Brit. informal incomprehensible language. **double-entry** relating to a system of bookkeeping in which each transaction is entered as a debit in one account and a credit in another. **double exposure** the repeated exposure of a photographic plate or film.

double figures a number between 10 and 99. **double first** Brit. a university degree with first-class honours in two subjects or examinations. **Double Gloucester** a hard cheese originally made in Gloucestershire. [ORIGIN – so named because the curd is processed twice.] **double helix** a pair of parallel helices intertwined about a common axis, especially that in the structure of DNA. **double jeopardy** Law the prosecution of a person twice for the same offence. **double-jointed** (of a person) having unusually flexible joints. **double negative** Grammar 1 a negative statement containing two negative elements (e.g. *didn't say nothing*), regarded as incorrect in standard English. 2 a positive statement in which two negative elements are used to produce the positive force, e.g. *there is not nothing to worry about!* **double-park** park (a vehicle) alongside one that is already parked. **double pneumonia** pneumonia affecting both lungs. **double standard** a rule or principle applied unfairly in different ways to different people. **double take** a delayed reaction to something unexpected. **double time** a rate of pay equal to double the standard rate. **double vision** the perception of two overlapping images of a single scene. **double whammy** informal a twofold blow or setback.

ORIGIN – Latin *duplus*, from *duo* 'two'.

double-bank > *verb* chiefly Brit. arrange in two similar or parallel lines.

double-blind > *adjective* (of a test or trial) in which information which may influence the behaviour of the tester or subject is withheld.

double-check > *verb* check again.

double chin > *noun* a roll of flesh below a person's chin.

DERIVATIVES – **double-chinned** *adjective*.

double-cross > *verb* betray (a person one is supposedly helping). > *noun* an act of double-crossing.

double-dealing > *noun* deceitful behaviour. > *adjective* acting deceitfully.

double-decker > *noun* something, especially a bus, with two levels.

double-edged > *adjective* 1 (of a blade) having two cutting edges. 2 having two contradictory aspects or possible outcomes.

double entendre /doob'l ontondrə/ > *noun* (pl. **double entendres** pronunc. same) a word or phrase open to two interpretations, one of which is usually indecent.

ORIGIN – from obsolete French, 'double understanding'.

double fault > *noun* Tennis an instance of two consecutive faults in serving, forfeiting a point. > *verb* (**double-fault**) serve a double fault.

double glazing > *noun* windows having two layers of glass with a space between them, designed to reduce heat loss and exclude noise.

DERIVATIVES – **double-glaze** verb.

double-header > *noun* 1 a train pulled by two locomotives. 2 chiefly N. Amer. a sporting event in which two games are played in succession at the same venue.

DERIVATIVES – **double-headed** *adjective*.

doublespeak > *noun* deliberately ambiguous or obscure language.

ORIGIN – coined by George Orwell in his novel *Nineteen Eighty-Four* (1949).

double-stopping > *noun* the sounding of two strings at once on a violin or similar instrument.

DERIVATIVES – **double stop** noun.

doublet > *noun* 1 a man's short close-fitting padded jacket, commonly worn from the 14th to the 17th century. 2 a pair of similar things.

ORIGIN – Old French, 'something folded', from *double* 'double'.

doubletalk > *noun* chiefly N. Amer. doublespeak.

doublethink > *noun* the acceptance of contrary opinions or beliefs at the same time.

ORIGIN – coined by George Orwell in his novel *Nineteen Eighty-Four* (1949).

doubloon /dubloon/ > *noun* historical a Spanish gold coin.

ORIGIN – Spanish *doblón*, from *doble* 'double' (because the coin was worth double the value of another former Spanish coin, the pistole).

doubt > *noun* a feeling of uncertainty. > *verb* 1 feel uncertain about. 2 question the truth of.

IDIOMS – **no doubt** 1 certainly. 2 probably.

DERIVATIVES – **doubter** noun **doubting** *adjective*.

SYNONYMS – *noun* hesitation, scepticism, uncertainty, wariness. *verb* disbelieve, mistrust, query, question.

ANTONYMS – *noun* certainty, trust. *verb* trust.

COMBINATIONS – **doubting Thomas** a person who refuses to believe something without proof. [ORIGIN – with reference to the apostle Thomas in the Bible (the Gospel of John, chapter 20).]

ORIGIN – Old French *douter*, from Latin *dubitare* 'hesitate', from *dubius* 'doubtful'.

doubtful > *adjective* 1 uncertain. 2 not known with certainty. 3 improbable.

DERIVATIVES – **doubtfully** adverb **doubtfulness** noun.

doubtless > *adverb* very probably.

DERIVATIVES – **doubtlessly** adverb.

douceur /dōsör/ > *noun* a bribe.

ORIGIN – French, 'sweetness'.

douche /doosh/ > *noun* 1 a shower of water. 2 a jet of liquid applied to part of the body for cleansing or medicinal purposes. 3 a device for washing out the vagina as a contraceptive measure. > *verb* 1 spray or shower with water. 2 use a contraceptive douche.

ORIGIN – French, from Italian *doccia* 'conduit pipe'.

dough > *noun* 1 a thick mixture of flour and liquid, for baking into bread or pastry. 2 informal money.

DERIVATIVES – **doughy** (**doughier**, **doughiest**) *adjective*.

ORIGIN – Old English; related to DAIRY, LADY.

doughnut (also US **donut**) > *noun* a small fried cake or ring of sweetened dough.

doughty /dowti/ > *adjective* (**doughtier**, **doughtiest**) archaic or humorous brave and resolute.

Douglas fir > *noun* a tall, slender conifer valued for its wood.

ORIGIN – named after the Scottish botanist and explorer David *Douglas* (1798–1834).

dour /dooər, dowər/ > *adjective* relentlessly stern or gloomy.

DERIVATIVES – **dourly** adverb **dourness** *noun*.

SYNONYMS – forbidding, grim, stern, unsmiling.

ANTONYMS – cheerful.

ORIGIN – probably from Scottish Gaelic, 'dull, obstinate, stupid'.

douse /dowz/ (also **dowse**) > *verb* 1 drench with liquid. 2 extinguish (a fire or light).

dove[1] /duv/ > *noun* 1 a stocky bird with a small head, short legs, and a cooing voice, very similar to but generally smaller than a pigeon. 2 a person who advocates conciliatory policies, especially in foreign affairs. Contrasted with HAWK[1].

DERIVATIVES – **dovish** *adjective*.

dove[2] /dōv/ US past of DIVE.

dovecote /duvkot/ (also **dovecot**) > *noun* a shelter with nest holes for domesticated pigeons.

Dover sole > *noun* a marine flatfish which is highly valued as food.

dovetail > *noun* a joint formed by interlocking tenons and mortises. > *verb* 1 join by means of a dovetail. 2 fit together easily or conveniently.

dowager /dowəjər/ > *noun* 1 a widow with a title or property derived from her late husband. 2 informal a dignified elderly woman.

ORIGIN – from Old French *douer* 'endow', from Latin *dos* 'dowry'.

dowdy > *adjective* (**dowdier**, **dowdiest**) (especially of a woman) unfashionable and dull in appearance.

SYNONYMS – drab, frumpy, unfashionable.

dowel > *noun* a headless peg used for holding

together components. > *verb* (**dowelled,
dowelling**; US **doweled, doweling**) fasten
with a dowel.

dowelling (US **doweling**) > *noun* cylindrical
rods for cutting into dowels.

dower > *noun* **1** a widow's share for life of
her husband's estate. **2** archaic a dowry.
COMBINATIONS – **dower house** Brit. a
house intended for a widow, typically one
on her late husband's estate.
ORIGIN – Old French *douaire*, from Latin
dotare 'endow', from *dos* 'dowry'.

Dow Jones index /dowjōnz/ > *noun* an
index of figures indicating the relative price
of shares on the New York Stock
Exchange.
ORIGIN – named after the American
financial news agency *Dow Jones & Co, Inc.*

down¹ > *adverb* **1** towards or in a lower place
or position. **2** to or at a lower level or value.
3 so as to lie flush or flat. **4** in or into a
weaker or worse position, mood, or
condition. **5** to a smaller amount or size, or
a simpler or more basic state. **6** in or into
writing. **7** from an earlier to a later point in
time or order. **8** (of a computer system) out
of action. **9** away from a central place or the
north. **10** (**down with ——**) expressing
strong dislike. **11** (with reference to partial
payment of a sum) made initially. **12** (of
sailing) with the current or the wind.
> *preposition* **1** from a higher to a lower
point of. **2** at a point further along the
course of. **3** throughout (a period of time).
4 along the course or extent of. **5** informal at
or to a place: *they're going down the pub.*
> *adjective* **1** directed or moving towards a
lower place or position. **2** unhappy. **3** (of a
computer system) out of action. > *verb*
informal **1** knock or bring to the ground. **2**
consume (a drink).
IDIOMS – **be** (or **have a**) **down on** informal
feel hostile towards. **be down to 1** be
attributable to (a factor). **2** be left with only
(the specified amount). **down at heel** chiefly
Brit. **1** (of a shoe) with the heel worn down.
2 shabby or impoverished. **down in the
mouth** informal unhappy. **down on one's
luck** informal having a period of bad luck.
down-to-earth practical and realistic.
down tools Brit. informal stop work.
COMBINATIONS – **downlink** a
telecommunications link for signals coming
to the earth from a satellite, spacecraft, or
aircraft. **down payment** an initial payment
made when buying on credit. **downpipe**
(N. Amer. **downspout**) a pipe to carry
rainwater from a roof to a drain or to
ground level. **down time** time during
which a computer or other machine is out
of action.

down² > *noun* **1** soft fine feathers used for
stuffing cushions and quilts. **2** fine soft
hairs.

down³ > *noun* **1** a gently rolling hill. **2** (**the
Downs**) ridges of undulating chalk and
limestone hills in southern England.
COMBINATIONS – **downland** gently rolling
hill country.

down and out > *adjective* destitute. > *noun*
(**down-and-out**) a destitute person.

downbeat > *adjective* **1** pessimistic; gloomy.
2 understated. > *noun* Music an accented
beat, usually the first of the bar.

downcast > *adjective* **1** (of eyes) looking
downwards. **2** (of a person) feeling
despondent.

downer > *noun* informal **1** a depressant or
tranquillising drug. **2** something dispiriting
or depressing.

downfall > *noun* a loss of power, prosperity,
or status.

downgrade > *verb* /downgrayd/ reduce to
a lower grade, rank, or level of importance.
> *noun* /downgrayd/ an instance of
downgrading.

downhearted > *adjective* discouraged;
dejected.

downhill > *adverb & adjective* /downhil/ **1**
towards the bottom of a slope. **2** into a
steadily worsening situation. > *noun*
/downhil/ **1** a downward slope. **2** Skiing a
downhill race.

download Computing > *verb* /downlōd/ copy
(data) from one computer system to
another or to a disk. > *noun* /downlōd/ the
act or process of downloading.
DERIVATIVES – **downloadable** *adjective*.

downmarket > *adjective & adverb* chiefly Brit.
towards or relating to the cheaper or less
prestigious sector of the market.

downplay > *verb* make (something) appear
less important than it really is.

downpour > *noun* a heavy fall of rain.

downright > *adjective* utter; complete.
> *adverb* to an extreme degree; thoroughly.

downriver > *adverb & adjective* towards or
situated at a point nearer the mouth of a
river.

downscale N. Amer. > *verb* reduce in size or
extent. > *adjective* at the lower end of a
scale; downmarket.

downshift chiefly N. Amer. > *verb* /downshift/ **1**
change to a lower gear. **2** change to a less
stressful lifestyle. > *noun* /downshift/ an
instance of downshifting.

downside > *noun* the negative aspect of
something.

downsize > *verb* chiefly N. Amer. **1** make smaller.
2 (of a company) shed staff.

downspout > *noun* North American term
for DOWNPIPE.

Down's syndrome > *noun* Medicine a
congenital disorder causing intellectual
impairment and physical abnormalities.
USAGE – **Down's syndrome** is the
accepted modern term for this condition.
Avoid older words such as **mongol** and

mongolism, which are likely to cause
offence.
ORIGIN – named after the English physician
John L. H. *Down* (1828–96).

downstage > *adjective & adverb* at or towards
the front of a stage.

downstairs > *adverb & adjective* down a
flight of stairs; on or to a lower floor.
> *noun* the ground floor or lower floors of a
building.

downstream > *adverb & adjective* situated or
moving in the direction in which a stream
or river flows.

downtown chiefly N. Amer. > *adjective & adverb*
of, in, or towards the central area of a city.
> *noun* the central area of a city.
DERIVATIVES – **downtowner** *noun*.

downtrodden > *adjective* oppressed or
treated badly by people in power.

downturn > *noun* a decline in economic or
other activity.

down under informal > *adverb* in or to
Australia or New Zealand. > *noun* Australia
and New Zealand.

downward > *adverb* (also **downwards**)
towards a lower point or level. > *adjective*
moving towards a lower point or level.
DERIVATIVES – **downwardly** *adverb*.

downwind > *adverb & adjective* in the
direction in which the wind is blowing.

downy > *adjective* (**downier, downiest**)
covered with fine soft hair or feathers.

dowry /dowri/ > *noun* (pl. **dowries**)
property or money brought by a bride to
her husband on their marriage.
ORIGIN – Old French *dowarie*, from Latin
dotarium: related to DOWER.

dowse¹ /dowz/ > *verb* search for
underground water or minerals with a
pointer which is supposedly moved by their
unseen influence.
DERIVATIVES – **dowser** *noun*.

dowse² > *verb* variant spelling of DOUSE.

doxology /doksollaji/ > *noun* (pl.
doxologies) a liturgical formula of praise
to God.
ORIGIN – Greek *doxologia*, from *doxa*
'appearance, glory'.

doxy > *noun* (pl. **doxies**) archaic **1** a lover or
mistress. **2** a prostitute.

doyen /doyən, dwaayaN/ > *noun* (fem.
doyenne /doyen, dwaayen/) the most
respected or prominent person in a
particular field.
ORIGIN – Old French *deien* (see DEAN).

doze > *verb* sleep lightly. > *noun* a short light
sleep.
SYNONYMS – *verb* catnap, nap, snooze. *noun*
nap, snooze, zizz.

dozen > *noun* (pl. same) a group or set of
twelve.
IDIOMS – **talk nineteen to the dozen** Brit.
talk quickly and incessantly.
DERIVATIVES – **dozenth** *adjective*.

ORIGIN – Old French *dozeine*, from Latin *duodecim* 'twelve'.

dozer > *noun* informal short for BULLDOZER.

dozy > *adjective* (**dozier**, **doziest**) 1 feeling drowsy and lazy. 2 Brit. informal not alert; stupid.

SYNONYMS – 1 dopey, drowsy, enervated, lazy, sleepy.

DP > *abbreviation* data processing.

dpc > *abbreviation* damp-proof course.

DPhil > *abbreviation* Doctor of Philosophy.

DPP > *abbreviation* (in the UK) Director of Public Prosecutions.

Dr > *abbreviation* 1 debit. [ORIGIN – formerly representing *debtor*.] 2 (as a title) Doctor.

dr. > *abbreviation* 1 drachma(s). 2 dram(s).

drab[1] > *adjective* (**drabber**, **drabbest**) drearily dull. > *noun* a dull light brown colour.

DERIVATIVES – **drably** adverb **drabness** noun.

SYNONYMS – *adjective* colourless, dismal, dreary, dull, grey.

ORIGIN – probably from Old French *drap* 'cloth'.

drab[2] > *noun* archaic a slovenly woman or a prostitute.

drachm /dram/ > *noun* historical 1 a unit of weight equivalent to 60 grains or one eighth of an ounce. 2 (also **fluid drachm**) a liquid measure equivalent to 60 minims or one eighth of a fluid ounce.

ORIGIN – from the same source as DRACHMA (its original meaning).

drachma /drakmə/ > *noun* (pl. **drachmas** or **drachmae** /drakmee/) 1 the basic monetary unit of Greece. 2 a silver coin of ancient Greece.

ORIGIN – Greek *drakhmē*, an Attic weight and coin.

draconian /drəkōniən, draykōniən/ > *adjective* (of laws) excessively harsh.

ORIGIN – named after the Athenian legislator *Draco* (7th century BC), notorious for the severity of his laws.

draft > *noun* 1 a preliminary version of a piece of writing. 2 a plan or sketch. 3 a written order to pay a specified sum. 4 (**the draft**) chiefly US compulsory recruitment for military service. 5 US spelling of DRAUGHT. > *verb* 1 prepare a preliminary version of (a text). 2 (often **draft in**) select (a person or group) and bring them somewhere for a certain purpose. 3 US conscript for military service.

DERIVATIVES – **drafter** noun.

USAGE – make sure that you distinguish correctly between the related words **draft** and **draught**. In British English **draft** means 'a preliminary version' or 'an order to pay a sum', whereas a **draught** is a current of air or an act of drinking; in American English the spelling **draft** is used

for all senses. The verb is usually spelled **draft**.

draftee > *noun* chiefly US a person conscripted for military service.

draftsman > *noun* 1 a person who drafts legal documents. 2 chiefly N. Amer. variant spelling of DRAUGHTSMAN.

drafty > *adjective* US spelling of DRAUGHTY.

drag > *verb* (**dragged**, **dragging**) 1 pull along forcefully, roughly, or with difficulty. 2 trail along the ground. 3 take (someone) somewhere, despite their reluctance. 4 (of time) pass slowly. 5 (**drag out**) protract (something) unnecessarily. 6 (**drag up**) informal deliberately mention (something unwelcome). 7 move (an image) across a computer screen using a mouse. 8 search the bottom of (a body of water) with grapnels or nets. 9 (**drag on**) informal inhale the smoke from (a cigarette). > *noun* 1 the action of dragging. 2 the longitudinal retarding force exerted by air or other fluid surrounding a moving object. 3 informal a boring or tiresome person or thing. 4 informal women's clothing worn by a man. 5 informal an act of inhaling smoke from a cigarette. 6 a strong-smelling lure drawn before hounds as a substitute for a fox.

IDIOMS – **drag one's feet** 1 walk wearily or with difficulty. 2 be slow or reluctant to act.

SYNONYMS – *verb* 1 haul, heave, lug, pull, tug. 5 (**drag out**) draw out, prolong, protract, spin out.

COMBINATIONS – **dragline** a large excavator with a bucket pulled in by a wire cable. **dragnet** 1 a net drawn through water or across ground to trap fish or game. 2 a systematic search for criminals. **drag queen** informal a man who ostentatiously dresses up in women's clothes.

dragée /draazhay/ > *noun* 1 a sweet consisting of a centre covered with a coating, such as a sugared almond. 2 a small silver ball for decorating a cake.

ORIGIN – French, from Old French *dragie* (see DREDGE[2]).

dragger > *noun* N. Amer. a fishing boat that uses a dragnet.

draggle > *verb* 1 make dirty or wet. 2 hang untidily. 3 archaic trail behind others.

dragoman /draggəmən/ > *noun* (pl. **dragomans** or **dragomen**) an interpreter or guide in a country speaking Arabic, Turkish, or Persian.

ORIGIN – Arabic, 'interpreter'.

dragon > *noun* 1 a mythical monster like a giant reptile, typically able to breathe out fire. 2 derogatory a fierce and intimidating woman.

WORDFINDER – Draco (*constellation, the Dragon*).

ORIGIN – Greek *drakōn* 'serpent'.

dragonfly > *noun* (pl. **dragonflies**) a fast-

flying long-bodied insect with two pairs of large transparent wings.

dragoon /drəgoon/ > *noun* 1 a member of any of several British cavalry regiments. 2 historical a mounted infantryman armed with a carbine. > *verb* coerce into doing something.

ORIGIN – first used in reference to a kind of carbine or musket, thought of as breathing fire: from French *dragon* 'dragon'.

drag race > *noun* a short race between two cars as a test of acceleration.

DERIVATIVES – **drag racer** noun **drag racing** noun.

dragster > *noun* a car used in drag races.

drain > *verb* 1 cause the liquid in (something) to run out. 2 (of liquid) run off or out. 3 become dry as liquid runs off. 4 deprive of strength or resources. 5 drink the entire contents of. > *noun* 1 a channel or pipe for carrying off surplus liquid. 2 a thing that uses up a resource or one's strength.

IDIOMS – **go down the drain** informal be totally wasted. **laugh like a drain** Brit. informal laugh raucously.

SYNONYMS – verb 1 empty, void. 2 filter, flow, percolate, pour, seep. 4 deplete, empty, exhaust, sap, use up.

COMBINATIONS – **draining board** Brit. a sloping grooved surface on which crockery is left to drain into an adjacent sink. **drainpipe** 1 a pipe for carrying off rainwater from a building. 2 (**drainpipes** or **drainpipe trousers**) trousers with very narrow legs.

drainage > *noun* 1 the action or process of draining something. 2 a system of drains.

drainer > *noun* 1 a rack used to hold draining crockery. 2 a draining board.

drake > *noun* a male duck.

Dralon /draylon/ > *noun* trademark, chiefly Brit. a synthetic textile made from acrylic fibre.

DRAM > *abbreviation* Computing dynamic random-access memory.

dram[1] > *noun* 1 chiefly Scottish a small drink of spirits. 2 another term for DRACHM.

ORIGIN – from the same source as DRACHM (its original sense).

dram[2] /draam/ > *noun* the basic monetary unit of Armenia, equal to 100 luma.

drama > *noun* 1 a play. 2 plays as a genre. 3 an exciting series of events.

ORIGIN – Greek, from *dran* 'do, act'.

dramatic > *adjective* 1 of or relating to drama. 2 sudden and striking: *a dramatic increase*. 3 exciting or impressive. 4 intended to create an effect; theatrical.

DERIVATIVES – **dramatically** adverb.

SYNONYMS – 1 theatrical, thespian. 2 conspicuous, remarkable, striking, sudden. 4 exaggerated, histrionic, ostentatious, showy, theatrical.

dramatics > *plural noun* 1 the study or

practice of acting in and producing plays. **2** theatrically exaggerated behaviour.

dramatise (also **dramatize**) > *verb* **1** adapt or present (a novel, event, etc.) as a play. **2** exaggerate the excitement or seriousness of.

DERIVATIVES – **dramatisation** *noun*.

SYNONYMS – **2** embellish, exaggerate, overplay.

ANTONYMS – **2** underplay.

dramatis personae /drammətiss pərsōnī/ > *plural noun* the characters of a play, novel, or narrative.

ORIGIN – Latin, 'persons of the drama'.

dramatist > *noun* a person who writes plays.

dramaturgy /dramməturji/ > *noun* the theory and practice of dramatic composition.

DERIVATIVES – **dramaturgic** *adjective* **dramaturgical** *adjective*.

Drambuie /drambyōoi/ > *noun* trademark a sweet Scotch whisky liqueur.

ORIGIN – from Scottish Gaelic *dram buidheach* 'satisfying drink'.

drank past of DRINK.

drape > *verb* arrange (cloth or clothing) loosely on or round something. > *noun* **1** (**drapes**) long curtains. **2** the way in which a garment or fabric hangs.

SYNONYMS – *verb* envelop, festoon, swathe, wrap.

draper > *noun* Brit. dated a person who sells textile fabrics.

drapery > *noun* (pl. **draperies**) cloth, curtains, or clothing hanging in loose folds.

ORIGIN – Old French *draperie*, from *drap* 'cloth'.

drastic > *adjective* having a strong or far-reaching effect.

DERIVATIVES – **drastically** *adverb*.

SYNONYMS – desperate, dire, extreme, far-reaching, radical.

ORIGIN – Greek *drastikos*, from *dran* 'do'.

drat > *exclamation* used to express mild annoyance.

DERIVATIVES – **dratted** *adjective*.

ORIGIN – shortening of *od rat*, a euphemism for *God rot*.

draught (US **draft**) > *noun* **1** a current of cool air in a room or confined space. **2** a single act of drinking or inhaling. **3** literary or archaic a quantity of a liquid with medicinal properties: *a sleeping draught*. **4** the depth of water needed to float a particular ship. **5** the drawing in of a fishing net. > *verb* variant spelling of DRAFT. > *adjective* **1** (of beer) served from a cask rather than from a bottle or can. **2** (of an animal) used for pulling heavy loads.

USAGE – on the difference between **draft** and **draught**, see the note at DRAFT.

ORIGIN – first used in the sense 'drawing, pulling': from Old Norse *dráttr*.

draughtboard > *noun* Brit. a square chequered board of sixty-four squares, used for playing draughts.

draughtproof > *adjective* sealed so as to keep out draughts. > *verb* make (a building, window, etc.) draughtproof.

draughts > *noun* Brit. a game played on a chequered board by two players with pieces which are moved diagonally.

ORIGIN – related to obsolete *draught* in the sense 'move' (in chess).

draughtsman (or **draughtswoman**) > *noun* **1** a person who makes detailed technical plans or drawings. **2** an artist skilled in drawing. **3** variant spelling of DRAFTSMAN.

DERIVATIVES – **draughtsmanship** *noun*.

draughty (US **drafty**) > *adjective* (**draughtier**, **draughtiest**) uncomfortable because of draughts of cold air.

Dravidian /drəviddiən/ > *noun* **1** a family of languages spoken in southern India and Sri Lanka, including Tamil and Kannada. **2** a member of any of the peoples speaking these languages. > *adjective* relating to Dravidian or Dravidians.

ORIGIN – Sanskrit, 'relating to the Tamils'.

draw > *verb* (past **drew**; past participle **drawn**) **1** produce (a picture or diagram) by making lines and marks on paper. **2** produce (a line) on a surface. **3** pull or drag (a vehicle) so as to make it follow behind. **4** pull or move (something) in a specified direction. **5** pull (curtains) shut or open. **6** arrive at a point in time: *the campaign drew to a close*. **7** extract from a container or receptacle: *he drew his gun*. **8** take in (a breath). **9** be the cause of (a specified response). **10** attract to a place or an event. **11** induce to reveal or do something. **12** reach (a conclusion) by deduction or inference. **13** (**draw on**) suck smoke from (a cigarette or pipe). **14** finish (a contest or game) with an even score. > *noun* **1** an act of selecting names randomly, for prizes, sporting fixtures, etc. **2** a game or match that ends with the scores even. **3** a person or thing that is very attractive or interesting. **4** an act of inhaling smoke from a cigarette. **5** Cricket a game which is left incomplete for lack of time. Compare with TIE.

IDIOMS – **draw someone's fire** attract hostile criticism away from a more important target. **draw the line at** set (a limit) of what one is willing to do or accept. **draw in** (of successive days) become shorter because of the changing seasons. **draw on** (of a period of time) pass by and approach its end. **draw out 1** make (something) last longer. **2** induce (someone) to be more talkative. **draw up 1** come to a

halt. **2** prepare (a plan or document) in detail.

USAGE – do not confuse **draw**, which is primarily a verb, with **drawer** meaning 'sliding storage compartment'.

SYNONYMS – *verb* **1** delineate, mark out, pencil, sketch. **3,4** drag, pull, tug. **7** extract, pull out, withdraw. **10** attract, bring in, capture, win.

COMBINATIONS – **drawbridge** a bridge which is hinged at one end so that it can be raised. **drawstring** (also **drawcord**) a string in the seam of a garment or bag, which can be pulled to tighten or close it.

ORIGIN – Old English, related to DRAUGHT.

drawback > *noun* a disadvantage or problem.

drawee /drawee/ > *noun* the person or organisation who has to pay a draft or bill.

drawer > *noun* **1** /draw/ a lidless storage compartment made to slide horizontally in and out of a desk or chest. **2** (**drawers**) /drawz/ dated or humorous knickers or underpants. **3** /drawər/ a person who draws something. **4** /drawər/ the person who writes a cheque.

USAGE – **drawer** rather than **draw** is the correct spelling in the sense 'sliding storage compartment'.

drawing > *noun* **1** a monochrome picture or diagram made with a pencil, pen, or crayon rather than paint. **2** the art or skill of making such pictures.

COMBINATIONS – **drawing pin** Brit. a short flat-headed pin for fastening paper to a surface. **drawing room** a room in a large private house in which guests can be received. [ORIGIN – abbreviation of *withdrawing-room* 'a room to withdraw to'.]

drawing board > *noun* a board on which paper can be spread for artists or designers to work on.

IDIOMS – **back to the drawing board** a plan has failed and a new one is needed.

drawl > *verb* speak in a slow, lazy way with prolonged vowel sounds. > *noun* a drawling accent.

drawn past participle of DRAW. > *adjective* looking strained from illness or exhaustion.

COMBINATIONS – **drawn-out** lasting longer than is necessary.

dray > *noun* a low truck or cart without sides, for delivering barrels or other heavy loads.

ORIGIN – first used to denote a sledge: perhaps from Old English *dræge* 'dragnet', related to DRAW.

dread > *verb* anticipate with great apprehension or fear. > *noun* great fear or apprehension. > *adjective* greatly feared; dreadful.

DERIVATIVES – **dreaded** *adjective*.

SYNONYMS – *verb* cower at, fear, shrink from. *noun* apprehension, fear, foreboding, trepidation. *adjective* alarming, dreadful, feared, frightful.

dreadful > *adjective* **1** extremely bad or serious. **2** used for emphasis: *a dreadful flirt.*

DERIVATIVES – **dreadfully** *adverb.*

SYNONYMS – **1** awful, dire, frightful, ghastly, harrowing, shocking, terrible.

dreadlocks > *plural noun* a Rastafarian hairstyle in which the hair is twisted into tight braids or ringlets.

DERIVATIVES – **dreadlocked** *adjective.*

dreadnought > *noun* historical a type of battleship of the early 20th century, equipped entirely with large-calibre guns. [ORIGIN – named after Britain's HMS *Dreadnought*, completed 1906.]

dream > *noun* **1** a series of thoughts, images, and sensations occurring in a person's mind during sleep. **2** a state of mind in which someone is unaware of their immediate surroundings. **3** a cherished aspiration, ambition or ideal; a fantasy. **4** informal someone or something perceived as wonderful or perfect. > *verb* (**past and past participle dreamed** /dreemd/ or **dreamt** /dremt/) **1** experience dreams during sleep. **2** indulge in daydreams or fantasies. **3** contemplate the possibility of: *I never dreamed she'd take offence.* **4** (**dream up**) imagine or invent.

WORDFINDER – oneiric *(relating to dreams or dreaming).*

IDIOMS – **like a dream** informal very easily or successfully.

DERIVATIVES – **dreamer** *noun* **dreamless** *adjective* **dreamlike** *adjective.*

SYNONYMS – *noun* **2** daydream, hallucination, reverie, trance. **3** ambition, aspiration, fantasy, ideal, illusion. *verb* **2** daydream, fantasise, muse.

COMBINATIONS – **dreamboat** informal a very attractive person, especially a man. **dreamland 1** sleep regarded as a world of dreams. **2** an unrealistically ideal world.

dreamscape > *noun* a scene with the strangeness or mystery characteristic of dreams.

dreamy > *adjective* (**dreamier, dreamiest**) **1** dreamlike; pleasantly distracting or unreal. **2** given to daydreaming.

DERIVATIVES – **dreamily** *adverb* **dreaminess** *noun.*

drear > *adjective* literary dreary.

dreary > *adjective* (**drearier, dreariest**) dull and depressing.

DERIVATIVES – **drearily** *adverb* **dreariness** *noun.*

SYNONYMS – bleak, cheerless, depressing, desolate, dismal, drab, dull.

ANTONYMS – bright, cheerful.

ORIGIN – Old English, 'gory, cruel, melancholy'.

dreck /drek/ > *noun* informal rubbish.

ORIGIN – Yiddish, 'filth, dregs'.

dredge¹ > *verb* **1** clean out the bed of (a harbour, river, etc.) with a dredge. **2** bring up or remove with a dredge. **3** (**dredge up**) bring (something unwelcome and forgotten) to people's attention. > *noun* an apparatus for bringing up objects or mud from a river or seabed by scooping or dragging.

DERIVATIVES – **dredger** *noun.*

dredge² > *verb* sprinkle (food) with sugar or other powdered substance.

ORIGIN – from obsolete *dredge* 'sweet confection, mixture of spices', from Old French *dragie*, perhaps from Greek *tragēmata* 'spices'.

dregs > *noun* **1** the remnants of a liquid left in a container, together with any sediment. **2** the most worthless parts: *the dregs of society.*

SYNONYMS – **1** grounds, lees, residue, remains, sediment.

ORIGIN – probably Scandinavian.

drench > *verb* **1** wet thoroughly; soak. **2** cover liberally with something. **3** forcibly give a liquid medicine to (an animal). > *noun* a dose of medicine administered to an animal.

SYNONYMS – **1** douse, drown, saturate, soak, swamp.

ORIGIN – Old English, related to DRINK.

dress > *verb* **1** (also **get dressed**) put on one's clothes. **2** (also **be dressed**) wear clothes in a particular way or of a particular type. **3** put clothes on (someone). **4** decorate or arrange in an artistic or attractive way. **5** clean, treat, or apply a dressing to (a wound). **6** clean and prepare (food) for cooking or eating. **7** add a dressing to (a salad). **8** apply fertiliser to. **9** treat or smooth the surface of (leather, fabric, or stone). > *noun* **1** a one-piece garment for a woman or girl that covers the body and extends down over the legs. **2** clothing of a specified kind. **3** (before another noun) (of clothing) formal or ceremonial: *a dress suit.*

IDIOMS – **dress down** informal **1** reprimand (someone). **2** wear informal clothes. **dressed to kill** informal wearing glamorous clothes intended to create a striking impression. **dress up** dress in smart or formal clothes, or in a special costume.

SYNONYMS – *verb* **2** (**be dressed in**) be attired in, be clothed in, be garbed in, be wearing.

COMBINATIONS – **dress circle** the first level of seats above the ground floor in a theatre. **dressing-down** informal a severe reprimand. **dressing gown** a long, loose robe worn after getting out of bed or bathing. **dressing room 1** a room in which actors or other performers change clothes. **2** a small room attached to a bedroom for storing clothes. **dressing table** a table with a mirror and drawers, used while dressing or applying make-up. **dressmaker** a person who makes women's clothes. **dress rehearsal** a final rehearsal in which everything is done as it would be in a real performance. **dress sense** instinct for selecting clothes. **dress shirt 1** a man's white shirt worn with a bow tie and a dinner jacket on formal occasions. **2** N. Amer. a shirt suitable for wearing with a tie.

ORIGIN – Old French *dresser* 'arrange, prepare', from Latin *directus* 'direct, straight'.

dressage /**dress**aazh/ > *noun* the art of riding and training horses so as to develop obedience, flexibility, and balance.

dresser¹ > *noun* **1** a sideboard with shelves above for storing and displaying crockery. **2** N. Amer. a dressing table or chest of drawers.

dresser² > *noun* **1** a person who dresses in a specified way: *a snappy dresser.* **2** a person who looks after theatrical costumes.

dressing > *noun* **1** a sauce for salads, usually consisting of oil and vinegar with herbs or other flavourings. **2** N. Amer. stuffing. **3** a piece of material placed on a wound to protect it. **4** size or stiffening used in the finishing of fabrics. **5** a fertiliser spread over land.

dressy > *adjective* (**dressier, dressiest**) (of clothes) suitable for a smart or formal occasion.

drew past of DRAW.

drey /dray/ > *noun* (pl. **dreys**) a squirrel's nest of twigs in a tree.

dribble > *verb* **1** (of a liquid) fall slowly in drops or a thin stream. **2** allow saliva to run from the mouth. **3** (in sport) take (the ball) forward with slight touches or (in basketball) by continuous bouncing. > *noun* **1** a thin stream of liquid. **2** (in sport) an act of dribbling.

DERIVATIVES – **dribbler** *noun* **dribbly** *adjective.*

SYNONYMS – *verb* **2** drool, salivate, slaver, slobber.

ORIGIN – first used in sense 'shoot an arrow short or wide of its target': from obsolete *drib*, variant of DRIP.

driblet > *noun* **1** a thin stream or small drop of liquid. **2** a small or insignificant amount.

dribs and drabs > *plural noun* (in phrase **in dribs and drabs**) informal in small scattered or sporadic amounts.

dried past and past participle of DRY.

drier > *noun* variant spelling of DRYER.

drift > *verb* **1** be carried slowly by a current of air or water. **2** walk or move slowly or casually. **3** (of snow, leaves, etc.) be blown into heaps by the wind. > *noun* **1** a continuous slow movement from one place to another. **2** the general intention or meaning of someone's remarks: *he got her drift*. **3** a large mass of snow, leaves, etc. piled up by the wind. **4** deviation from a course because of currents or winds. **5** Geology deposits left by retreating ice sheets. **6** S. African a ford.

SYNONYMS – *verb* **1** be borne, be carried, float, waft. *noun* **1** flow, gravitation, shift. **2** essence, gist, import, tenor, thrust.

COMBINATIONS – **drift net** a large fishing net kept upright by weights at the bottom and floats at the top and allowed to drift in the sea. **driftwood** pieces of wood floating on the sea or washed ashore.

ORIGIN – Old Norse, 'snowdrift, something driven'; related to **DRIVE**.

drifter > *noun* **1** a person who is continually moving from place to place, without any fixed home or job. **2** a fishing boat equipped with a drift net.

drill¹ > *noun* **1** a tool or machine used for boring holes. **2** training in military exercises. **3** instruction by means of repeated exercises. **4** (**the drill**) informal the correct or recognised procedure. > *verb* **1** bore (a hole) in something with a drill. **2** subject to military training or other intensive instruction. **3** informal hit (something) so that it travels fast in a straight line.

DERIVATIVES – **driller** noun.

SYNONYMS – *noun* **2** coaching, exercises, instruction, training. *verb* **2** coach, discipline, exercise, instruct, train.

ORIGIN – Dutch *drillen* 'bore, turn in a circle'.

drill² > *noun* **1** a machine which makes small furrows, sows seed in them, and then covers the sown seed. **2** a small furrow made by such a machine. > *verb* sow with a drill.

drill³ > *noun* a West African baboon with a naked blue or purple rump.

ORIGIN – probably a local word; compare with **MANDRILL**.

drill⁴ > *noun* a coarse twilled cotton or linen fabric.

ORIGIN – abbreviation of earlier *drilling*, from Latin *trilix* 'triple-twilled'.

drily /drīli/ (also **dryly**) > *adverb* **1** in a matter-of-fact or ironically humorous way. **2** in a dry way or condition.

drink > *verb* (past **drank**; past participle **drunk**) **1** take (a liquid) into the mouth and swallow. **2** consume alcohol, especially to excess. **3** (**drink in**) watch or listen eagerly to (something). > *noun* **1** a liquid consumed as refreshment or nourishment. **2** a quantity of liquid swallowed at one go. **3** alcohol, or the habitual or excessive consumption of alcohol. **4** (**the drink**) informal the sea.

IDIOMS – **drink someone's health** (or **drink to someone**) express good wishes for someone by raising one's glass and

drinking a small amount. **in drink** when intoxicated.

DERIVATIVES – **drinkable** adjective.

SYNONYMS – *verb* **1** imbibe, quaff, swallow, swig. *noun* **1** beverage, liquid; archaic or humorous libation, potation. **2** gulp, mouthful, swallow, swig. **3** alcohol, liquor.

COMBINATIONS – **drink-driving** Brit. the crime of driving a vehicle with an excess of alcohol in the blood. **drinking chocolate** a mixture of cocoa powder, milk solids, and sugar added to hot water to make a chocolate drink. **drinking fountain** a device producing a small jet of water for drinking.

drinker > *noun* **1** a person who drinks. **2** a container from which an animal can drink.

drip > *verb* (**dripped**, **dripping**) fall or let fall in small drops of liquid. > *noun* **1** a small drop of a liquid. **2** an apparatus which slowly passes fluid, nutrients, or drugs into a patient's body intravenously. **3** informal a weak and ineffectual person. **4** Architecture a projection which is channelled to prevent rain from running down the wall below.

SYNONYMS – *verb* dribble, drop, leak, splash, trickle. *noun* **1** bead, dribble, drop, splash.

COMBINATIONS – **dripstone 1** Architecture a moulding over a door or window which deflects rain. **2** Geology rock formed from dripping water, e.g. as stalactites and stalagmites.

ORIGIN – Old English, related to **DROP**.

drip-dry > *verb* (of fabric or a garment) become dry without forming creases when hung up after washing. > *adjective* capable of drip-drying.

drip feed > *noun* a device for introducing fluid drop by drop into a system. > *verb* (**drip-feed**) introduce (fluid) drop by drop.

dripping > *noun* Brit. fat that has melted and dripped from roasting meat. > *adjective* extremely wet.

drippy > *adjective* (**drippier**, **drippiest**) **1** informal weak, ineffectual, or sloppily sentimental. **2** tending to drip.

DERIVATIVES – **drippily** adverb **drippiness** noun.

drive > *verb* (past **drove**; past participle **driven**) **1** operate and control (a motor vehicle). **2** convey in a motor vehicle. **3** propel or carry along in a specified direction. **4** urge (animals or people) to move in a specified direction. **5** compel to act in a particular way. **6** provide the energy to keep (an engine or machine) in motion. > *noun* **1** a trip or journey in a car. **2** (also **driveway**) a short private road leading to a house. **3** an innate, biologically determined urge. **4** an organised effort to achieve a particular purpose. **5** determination and ambition to achieve something. **6** the transmission of

power to machinery or to the wheels of a vehicle. **7** (in ball games) a forceful stroke. **8** Golf a shot from the tee. **9** Brit. a large organised gathering for playing a game: *a whist drive*.

IDIOMS – **what someone is driving at** the point that someone is attempting to make.

DERIVATIVES – **drivable** (also **driveable**) *adjective*.

SYNONYMS – *verb* **3** carry, impel, propel, sweep, urge. **4** herd, impel, propel, shepherd, urge. **5** compel, force, goad, impel, spur. *noun* **1** excursion, jaunt, journey, outing, run, spin, trip. **3** appetite, impulse, instinct, urge. **4** campaign, crusade, effort, movement, push. **5** ambition, determination, enterprise, vigour, vim.

COMBINATIONS – **driveshaft** a rotating shaft which transmits torque in an engine. **drivetrain** the system in a motor vehicle which connects the transmission to the drive axles. **driving range** an area where golfers can practise drives.

drive-by > *adjective* chiefly N. Amer. (of a shooting) carried out from a passing vehicle.

drive-in > *adjective* chiefly N. Amer. (of a cinema, restaurant, etc.) that one can visit without leaving one's car.

drivel /drivv'l/ > *noun* nonsense. > *verb* (**drivelled**, **drivelling**; US **driveled**, **driveling**) **1** talk nonsense. **2** archaic let saliva or mucus flow from the mouth or nose.

driven past participle of **DRIVE**.

driver > *noun* **1** a person or thing that drives something. **2** a flat-faced golf club used for driving.

IDIOMS – **in the driver's seat** in control.

DERIVATIVES – **driverless** adjective.

driving > *adjective* **1** having a controlling influence: *the driving force behind the plan*. **2** being blown by the wind with great force: *driving rain*.

IDIOMS – **in the driving seat** in control.

drizzle > *noun* light rain falling in very fine drops. > *verb* **1** (**it drizzles**, **it is drizzling**, etc.) rain lightly. **2** Cookery pour a thin stream of (a liquid ingredient) over a dish.

DERIVATIVES – **drizzly** adjective.

ORIGIN – probably from Old English *drēosan* 'to fall', related to **DREARY**.

drogue /drōg/ > *noun* a device towed behind a boat or aircraft to reduce speed or improve stability, or as an aerial target for gunnery practice.

COMBINATIONS – **drogue parachute** a small parachute used as a brake or to pull out a larger parachute.

ORIGIN – a whaling term for a board attached to a harpoon line, used to slow down or mark the position of a whale: perhaps related to **DRAG**.

droid /droyd/ > *noun* (in science fiction) an android; a robot.

droit de seigneur /drwaa də senyör/ > *noun* the alleged right of a medieval feudal lord to have sexual intercourse with a vassal's bride on her wedding night.
ORIGIN – French, 'lord's right'.

droll /drōl/ > *adjective* amusing in a strange or quaint way.
DERIVATIVES – **drollery** *noun* **drollness** *noun* **drolly** /drōl-li/ *adverb*.
ORIGIN – French, perhaps from Dutch *drolle* 'imp, goblin'.

dromaeosaur /drōmiəsawr/ > *noun* a carnivorous bipedal dinosaur of a group including the velociraptors.
ORIGIN – from Greek *dromaios* 'swift-running' + *sauros* 'lizard'.

-drome > *combining form* 1 denoting a place for running or racing: *velodrome*. 2 denoting something that proceeds in a certain way: *palindrome*.
ORIGIN – from Greek *dromos* 'running'.

dromedary /drommidəri/ > *noun* (pl. **dromedaries**) an Arabian camel, with one hump.
ORIGIN – from Latin *dromedarius camelus* 'swift camel', from Greek *dromas* 'runner'.

drone > *verb* 1 make a continuous low humming sound. 2 (often **drone on**) speak tediously and at length. > *noun* 1 a low continuous humming sound. 2 a pipe (especially in a set of bagpipes) or string used to sound a continuous low note. 3 a male bee which does no work in a colony but can fertilise a queen. 4 an idler. 5 a remote-controlled pilotless aircraft.
SYNONYMS – *verb* 1 buzz, hum, murmur, purr, whirr.
ORIGIN – Old English, 'male bee'.

drongo /dronggō/ > *noun* (pl. **drongos** or **drongoes**) 1 a long-tailed, crested songbird with glossy black plumage, found in Africa, southern Asia, and Australia. 2 informal, chiefly Austral./NZ a stupid or incompetent person.
ORIGIN – Malagasy; sense 2 is said to be from the name of a very unsuccessful Australian racehorse of the 1920s.

drool > *verb* 1 drop saliva uncontrollably from the mouth. 2 (often **drool over**) informal show excessive pleasure or desire. > *noun* saliva falling from the mouth.
SYNONYMS – *verb* 1 dribble, salivate, slaver, slobber.
ORIGIN – contraction of DRIVEL.

droop > *verb* 1 bend or hang downwards limply. 2 sag down from weariness or dejection. > *noun* an act or instance of drooping.
SYNONYMS – *verb* dangle, flop, hang, sag, wilt.
ORIGIN – Old Norse *drúpa* 'hang the head'; related to DRIP and DROP.

droopy > *adjective* (**droopier**, **droopiest**) 1 hanging down limply; drooping. 2 lacking strength or spirit.
DERIVATIVES – **droopily** *adverb* **droopiness** *noun*.

drop > *verb* (**dropped**, **dropping**) 1 fall or cause to fall. 2 sink to the ground. 3 make or become lower, weaker, or less. 4 abandon, discontinue, or discard. 5 (often **drop off**) set down or unload (a passenger or goods). 6 place or leave (something) without ceremony. 7 informal collapse from exhaustion. 8 lose (a point, a match, etc.). 9 mention casually. 10 (of an animal) give birth to. > *noun* 1 a small round or pear-shaped portion of liquid. 2 an instance of falling or dropping. 3 a small drink, especially of alcohol. 4 an abrupt fall or slope. 5 informal a delivery. 6 a sweet or lozenge.
IDIOMS – **at the drop of a hat** informal without delay or good reason. **drop back** (or **behind**) fall back or get left behind. **drop by** (or **in**) visit informally and briefly. **drop a clanger** Brit. informal make an embarrassing or foolish mistake. **drop a curtsy** Brit. make a curtsy. **drop dead** die suddenly and unexpectedly. **drop one's guard** abandon a previously watchful attitude. **a drop in the ocean** a very small amount compared with what is needed. **drop a line** informal send (someone) a note or letter. **drop off** fall asleep, especially without intending to. **drop out** 1 cease to participate. 2 pursue an alternative lifestyle.
SYNONYMS – *noun* 1 bead, dribble, drip, splash, tear.
COMBINATIONS – **drop cloth** 1 (also **drop curtain**) a curtain or painted cloth lowered vertically on to a theatre stage. 2 N. Amer. a dust sheet. **drop goal** Rugby a goal scored by drop-kicking the ball over the crossbar. **drop handlebars** handlebars with the handles bent below the rest of the bar, used especially on racing cycles. **drop kick** a kick made by dropping the ball and kicking it as it bounces. **drop scone** a small, thick pancake made by dropping batter on to a heated surface. **drop shot** (in tennis or squash) a softly hit shot which drops abruptly to the ground. **drop shoulder** a style of shoulder on a garment cut with the seam positioned on the upper arm rather than the shoulder. **drop tank** an external fuel tank on an aircraft which can be jettisoned when empty. **drop waist** a style of waistline with the seam positioned at the hips rather than the waist. **drop zone** a designated area into which troops or supplies are dropped by parachute.

drop-dead > *adjective* informal used to emphasise attractiveness: *drop-dead gorgeous*.

drophead > *noun* Brit. a convertible car.

droplet > *noun* a very small drop of a liquid.

drop-off > *noun* 1 a decline or decrease. 2 chiefly N. Amer. a sheer downward slope.

dropout > *noun* 1 a person who has dropped out of society or a course of study. 2 Rugby the restarting of play with a drop kick.

dropper > *noun* a short glass tube with a rubber bulb at one end, for measuring out drops of liquid.

droppings > *plural noun* the excrement of animals.

dropsy /dropsi/ > *noun* old-fashioned or less technical term for OEDEMA.
DERIVATIVES – **dropsical** *adjective*.
ORIGIN – shortening of obsolete *hydropsy*, from Greek *hudrōps*, from *hudōr* 'water'.

droshky /droshki/ > *noun* (pl. **droshkies**) a low four-wheeled open carriage of a kind formerly used in Russia.
ORIGIN – Russian *drozhki* 'little wagon'.

drosophila /drəsoffilə/ > *noun* a fruit fly of a kind used extensively in genetic research.
ORIGIN – from Greek *drosos* 'dew, moisture' + *philos* 'loving'.

dross > *noun* 1 rubbish. 2 scum on the surface of molten metal.

drought /drowt/ > *noun* a prolonged period of abnormally low rainfall, or a resultant shortage of water.
ORIGIN – Old English, 'dryness'.

drove[1] past of DRIVE.

drove[2] > *noun* 1 a flock of animals being driven. 2 a large number of people doing the same thing: *tourists arrived in droves*. > *verb* historical drive (livestock) to market.
DERIVATIVES – **drover** *noun*.

drown > *verb* 1 die or kill through submersion in water. 2 submerge or flood (an area). 3 (usu. **drown out**) make inaudible by being much louder.
IDIOMS – **drown one's sorrows** forget one's problems by getting drunk.
SYNONYMS – *verb* 2 deluge, engulf, flood, inundate, submerge, swamp. 3 bury, deaden, muffle, overpower, overwhelm.

drowse /drowz/ > *verb* be half asleep; doze. > *noun* an instance or state of drowsing.

drowsy > *adjective* (**drowsier**, **drowsiest**) sleepy and lethargic.
DERIVATIVES – **drowsily** *adverb* **drowsiness** *noun*.
SYNONYMS – dozy, lethargic, sleepy, sluggish, somnolent.
ORIGIN – probably from Old English *drūsian* 'be languid or slow'; related to DREARY.

drub > *verb* (**drubbed**, **drubbing**) 1 hit or beat repeatedly. 2 informal defeat thoroughly.
DERIVATIVES – **drubbing** *noun*.
ORIGIN – first used with reference to the punishment of bastinado: probably from Arabic.

drudge > *noun* a person made to do hard, menial, or dull work.

SYNONYMS – lackey, menial, skivvy, slave.

drudgery > *noun* hard, menial, or dull work.

SYNONYMS – chores, donkey work, grind, labour, slog.

drug > *noun* 1 a medicine or other substance which has a marked effect when taken into the body. 2 a substance taken for its narcotic or stimulant effects. > *verb* (**drugged, drugging**) make (someone) unconscious or stupefied by administering a drug.

WORDFINDER – *recreational drugs:* alcohol, amphetamines, barbiturates, cannabis, cocaine, ecstasy, heroin, LSD, mescaline, nicotine, opium.

SYNONYMS – *noun* 1 elixir, medicament, medicine, potion, remedy.

COMBINATIONS – **drugstore** N. Amer. a pharmacy which also sells toiletries and other articles.

ORIGIN – Old French *drogue*, perhaps from Dutch *droge vate* 'dry vats'.

drugget /**drugg**it/ > *noun* a floor covering made of a coarse woven fabric.

ORIGIN – French *droguet*, from *drogue* in the sense 'poor-quality article'.

druggist > *noun* chiefly N. Amer. a pharmacist or retailer of medicinal drugs.

druggy informal > *adjective* caused by or involving drugs. > *noun* (also **druggie**) (pl. **druggies**) a drug addict.

Druid /**droo**id/ > *noun* a priest, magician, or soothsayer in the ancient Celtic religion.

DERIVATIVES – **Druidic** adjective **Druidical** adjective **Druidism** noun.

ORIGIN – Gaulish; related to Irish *draoidh* 'magician, sorcerer'.

drum > *noun* 1 a percussion instrument with a skin stretched across a rounded frame, sounded by being struck with sticks or the hands. 2 a cylindrical object or part, especially a container. 3 a sound made by or resembling that of a drum. 4 Austral./NZ informal a piece of reliable inside information. > *verb* (**drummed, drumming**) 1 play on a drum. 2 make a continuous rhythmic noise. 3 (**drum into**) instruct (someone) in (something) by prolonged repetition. 4 (**drum out**) expel (someone) from somewhere in disgrace. 5 (**drum up**) attempt to obtain (something) by canvassing or soliciting.

WORDFINDER – *types of drum:* bodhrán, bongo, conga, hi-hat, kettledrum, snare drum, tabla, tabor, tambour, timpani, tom-tom.

SYNONYMS – *verb* 2 beat, knock, pound, rap, tap. 3 (**drum into**) drive into, din into, hammer in, inculcate in, instil in.

COMBINATIONS – **drum and bass** a type of dance music consisting largely of electronic drums and bass. **drumbeat** a stroke or pattern of strokes on a drum. **drum kit** a set of drums, cymbals, and other percussion instruments. **drum major** 1 a non-commissioned officer in command of regimental drummers. 2 the male leader of a marching band. **drum majorette** 1 the female leader of a marching band. 2 a female member of such a band. **drum roll** a rapid succession of drumbeats. **drumstick** 1 a stick used for beating a drum. 2 the lower joint of the leg of a cooked fowl.

drumfire > *noun* heavy, continuous, rapid artillery fire.

drumhead > *noun* 1 the membrane or skin of a drum. 2 (before another noun) summary, as carried out by an army in the field: *a drumhead court martial.*

drumlin /**drum**lin/ > *noun* Geology a mound or small hill consisting of compacted boulder clay shaped by glacial action.

ORIGIN – from *drum* 'long narrow hill', from Scottish Gaelic and Irish *druim* 'ridge'.

drummer > *noun* a person who plays a drum or drums.

drunk past participle of **DRINK**. > *adjective* affected by alcohol to the extent of losing control of one's faculties or behaviour. > *noun* a person who is drunk or who habitually drinks to excess.

IDIOMS – **drunk and disorderly** creating a public disturbance under the influence of alcohol.

USAGE – strictly speaking, **drunk** should be used after a noun (*the man was drunk*) and **drunken** before a noun (*a drunken man*).

SYNONYMS – *adjective* drunken, inebriated, intoxicated, tipsy; literary bibulous, crapulent. *noun* alcoholic, drinker, drunkard, imbiber, inebriate, sot, tippler.

ANTONYMS – *adjective* sober.

drunkard > *noun* a person who is habitually drunk.

drunken > *adjective* 1 drunk, especially habitually or frequently. 2 caused by or showing the effects of drink.

DERIVATIVES – **drunkenly** adverb **drunkenness** noun.

USAGE – see the note at **DRUNK**.

drupe /droop/ > *noun* Botany a fleshy fruit with thin skin and a central stone, e.g. a plum or olive.

ORIGIN – Latin *drupa* 'overripe olive'.

drupel /**droo**p'l/ (also **drupelet** /**droo**plit/) > *noun* Botany any of the small individual drupes forming a fleshy aggregate fruit such as a raspberry.

dry > *adjective* (**drier, driest**) 1 free from moisture or liquid. 2 not yielding water, oil, or milk. 3 without grease or other moisturiser or lubricator. 4 dully factual. 5 unemotional or undemonstrative. 6 (of humour) subtle and expressed in a matter-of-fact way. 7 (of wine) not sweet. 8 prohibiting the sale or consumption of alcoholic drink. > *verb* (**dries, dried**) 1 make or become dry. 2 preserve by evaporating the moisture from. 3 (**dry up**) (of a supply or flow) decrease and stop. 4 (**dry up**) informal cease talking. 5 theatrical slang forget one's lines. 6 (**dry out**) informal overcome alcoholism. > *noun* (pl. **dries** or **drys**) 1 (**the dry**) a dry place. 2 Brit. a Conservative politician (especially in the 1980s) in favour of strict monetarist policies.

DERIVATIVES – **dryness** noun.

SYNONYMS – *adjective* 1 arid, dehydrated, desiccated, parched, waterless. 4 arid, dreary, dull, flat, unexciting, uninspiring. *verb* 1 dehydrate, desiccate, parch.

ANTONYMS – *adjective* 1 wet. 4 interesting, lively. *verb* 1 moisten, wet.

COMBINATIONS – **dry cell** (also **dry battery**) an electric cell (or battery) in which the electrolyte is absorbed in a solid to form a paste. **dry-clean** clean (a garment) with an organic solvent. **dry dock** a dock which can be drained of water to allow a ship's hull to be repaired. **dry fly** an artificial fishing fly which floats lightly on the water. **dry goods** 1 solid commodities traded in bulk, e.g. tea or sugar. 2 chiefly N. Amer. drapery and haberdashery. **dry ice** 1 solid carbon dioxide. 2 white mist produced with this as a theatrical effect. **dry measure** a measure of volume for dry goods. **dry rot** a fungus causing decay of wood in poorly ventilated conditions. **dry run** informal a rehearsal of a performance or procedure. **dry-shod** without wetting one's shoes. **dry slope** (also **dry ski slope**) an artificial ski slope. **drystone** Brit. (of a stone wall) built without using mortar. **drysuit** a waterproof rubber suit for water sports, under which warm clothes can be worn. **drywall** N. Amer. plasterboard.

dryad /**dri**ad/ > *noun* (in folklore and Greek mythology) a nymph inhabiting a tree or wood.

ORIGIN – Greek *druas*, from *drus* 'tree'.

dryer (also **drier**) > *noun* a machine or device for drying something, especially the hair or laundry.

dryly > *adverb* variant spelling of **DRILY**.

DSC > *abbreviation* (in the UK) Distinguished Service Cross.

DSc > *abbreviation* Doctor of Science.

DSM > *abbreviation* (in the UK) Distinguished Service Medal.

DSO > *abbreviation* (in the UK) Distinguished Service Order.

DSP > *abbreviation* digital signal processor or processing.

DSS > *abbreviation* (in the UK) Department of Social Security.

DTI > *abbreviation* (in the UK) Department of Trade and Industry.

DTP > *abbreviation* desktop publishing.

DTp > *abbreviation* (in the UK) Department of Transport.

DTs > *plural noun* informal delirium tremens.

dual > *adjective* consisting of two parts, elements, or aspects. > *verb* (**dualled**, **dualling**) Brit. convert (a road) into a dual carriageway.

DERIVATIVES – **dualise** (also **dualize**) *verb* **dually** *adverb*.

SYNONYMS – *adjective* binary, coupled, double, duplicate, paired, twin.

COMBINATIONS – **dual carriageway** Brit. a road consisting of two or more lanes in each direction, with a dividing strip separating the two directions.

ORIGIN – Latin *dualis*, from *duo* 'two'.

dualism > *noun* 1 division into two opposed or contrasted aspects, such as good and evil or mind and matter. 2 duality.

DERIVATIVES – **dualist** noun & adjective **dualistic** *adjective*.

duality > *noun* (pl. **dualities**) 1 the quality or condition of being dual. 2 an opposition or contrast between two concepts or aspects.

dub¹ > *verb* (**dubbed**, **dubbing**) 1 give an unofficial name or nickname to. 2 knight (someone) by the ritual touching of the shoulder with a sword. 3 smear (leather) with grease.

ORIGIN – Old French *adober* 'equip with armour'.

dub² > *verb* (**dubbed**, **dubbing**) 1 provide (a film) with a soundtrack in a different language from the original. 2 add (sound effects or music) to a film or a recording. 3 make a copy of (a recording). > *noun* 1 an instance of dubbing sound effects or music. 2 a style of popular music originating from the remixing of recorded music (especially reggae).

ORIGIN – abbreviation of **DOUBLE**.

dubbin /**dub**bin/ Brit. > *noun* prepared grease used for softening and waterproofing leather. > *verb* (**dubbined**, **dubbining**) apply dubbin to (leather).

ORIGIN – from **DUB¹** (sense 3).

dubiety /dyoo**bī**əti/ > *noun* formal the state of being doubtful; uncertainty.

dubious /**dyoo**biəss/ > *adjective* 1 hesitating or doubting. 2 not to be relied upon. 3 of questionable value; suspect.

DERIVATIVES – **dubiously** *adverb* **dubiousness** *noun*.

SYNONYMS – 1 doubtful, hesitant, sceptical, uncertain, unsure. 2,3 questionable, suspect, suspicious, unreliable, untrustworthy.

ANTONYMS – 1 certain, definite. 2,3 reliable, trustworthy.

ORIGIN – Latin *dubiosus*, from *dubium* 'a doubt'.

dubnium /**dub**niəm/ > *noun* a very unstable chemical element made by high-energy atomic collisions.

ORIGIN – named after *Dubna* in Russia, site of the laboratory in which it was made.

Dubonnet /dyoo**bonn**ay/ > *noun* trademark a sweet French red wine.

ORIGIN – from the name of a family of French wine merchants.

ducal /**dyoo**k'l/ > *adjective* relating to a duke or dukedom.

ducat /**dukk**ət/ > *noun* 1 a gold coin formerly used in most European countries. 2 (**ducats**) informal money.

ORIGIN – Italian *ducato*, originally referring to a silver coin minted by the Duke of Apulia in 1190.

duchess > *noun* 1 the wife or widow of a duke. 2 a woman holding a rank equivalent to duke.

ORIGIN – Old French, from Latin *ducissa* from *dux* 'duke'.

duchesse /doo**shess**, **duch**iss/ > *noun* 1 (also **duchesse satin**) a soft, heavy, glossy kind of satin. 2 a chaise longue resembling two armchairs linked by a stool. 3 a dressing table with a pivoting mirror.

COMBINATIONS – **duchesse potatoes** mashed potatoes mixed with egg yolk, piped into small shapes and baked.

ORIGIN – French, 'duchess'.

duchy /**duch**i/ > *noun* (pl. **duchies**) the territory of a duke or duchess.

duck¹ > *noun* (pl. same or **ducks**) 1 a waterbird with a broad, blunt bill, short legs, webbed feet, and a waddling gait. 2 the female of such a bird. Contrasted with **DRAKE¹**. 3 (also **ducks**) Brit. informal an affectionate form of address.

IDIOMS – **like water off a duck's back** (of a critical remark) having no effect.

COMBINATIONS – **duckbill** an animal with jaws resembling a duck's bill, especially a platypus. **ducks and drakes** a game of throwing flat stones so that they skim along the surface of water. **duck soup** N. Amer. informal an easy task. **duckwalk** walk in a squatting posture. **duckweed** a tiny aquatic flowering plant that floats in large quantities on still water.

ORIGIN – Old English, related to **DUCK²** (expressing the notion of 'diving bird').

duck² > *verb* 1 lower the head or body quickly to avoid a blow or missile or so as not to be seen. 2 push (someone) under water. 3 informal evade (an unwelcome duty). > *noun* a quick lowering of the head.

IDIOMS – **duck and dive** informal use one's ingenuity to deal with or evade a situation.

DERIVATIVES – **ducker** *noun*.

SYNONYMS – *verb* 1 bend, bow down, crouch, dodge. 2 dip, dunk, immerse, plunge, submerge.

duck³ > *noun* Cricket a batsman's score of nought.

IDIOMS – **break one's duck** score the first run of one's innings.

ORIGIN – short for *duck's egg*, used for the figure 0.

duck⁴ > *noun* 1 a strong untwilled linen or cotton fabric, used for work clothes and sails. 2 (**ducks**) trousers made from such a fabric.

ORIGIN – Dutch *doek* 'linen'.

duckboards > *plural noun* wooden slats joined together to form a path over muddy ground.

duckling > *noun* a young duck.

ducky informal > *noun* Brit. a friendly form of address. > *adjective* chiefly N. Amer. delightful.

duct > *noun* 1 a tube or passageway for air, cables, etc. 2 a vessel in the body for conveying lymph or glandular secretions. > *verb* convey through a duct.

DERIVATIVES – **ducting** noun **ductless** *adjective*.

COMBINATIONS – **duct tape** N. Amer. strong cloth-backed waterproof adhesive tape.

ORIGIN – Latin *ductus* 'leading, aqueduct', from *ducere* 'to lead'.

ductile /**duk**tīl/ > *adjective* 1 (of a metal) able to be drawn out into a thin wire. 2 able to be deformed without losing toughness.

DERIVATIVES – **ductility** *noun*.

dud informal > *noun* 1 a thing that fails to work properly. 2 (**duds**) clothes. > *adjective* failing to work or meet a standard.

dude /dyood, dood/ > *noun* N. Amer. informal 1 a man. 2 a dandy.

COMBINATIONS – **dude ranch** (in the western US) a cattle ranch converted to a holiday centre for tourists.

ORIGIN – probably from German dialect *Dude* 'fool'.

dudgeon /**du**jən/ > *noun* (often in phrase **in high dudgeon**) deep resentment.

due > *adjective* 1 owing or payable. 2 expected at or planned for a certain time. 3 (often **due to**) merited; fitting. 4 (also **due for**) (of a person) having reached a point where (something) is owed or merited. 5 proper; appropriate: *due process of law*. > *noun* 1 (**one's due** or **dues**) one's right. 2 (**dues**) fees. > *adverb* (with reference to a point of the compass) directly.

IDIOMS – **due to 1** caused by. **2** because of; owing to. **give someone their due** be fair to someone. **in due course** at the appropriate time. **pay one's dues** fulfil one's obligations.

USAGE – the use of **due to** as a prepositional phrase equivalent to **owing to** has been condemned on the grounds that **due** is an adjective. However, this use is widespread and increasingly accepted.

SYNONYMS – *adjective* 1 outstanding, owed, owing, payable, unpaid. 2 anticipated, awaited, expected, scheduled. **4** entitled to, owed.

ORIGIN – Old French *deu* 'owed', from Latin *debere* 'owe'.

duel > *noun* **1** historical a pre-arranged contest with deadly weapons between two people to settle a point of honour. **2** a contest between two parties. > *verb* (**duelled, duelling**; US **dueled, dueling**) fight a duel.

DERIVATIVES – **dueller** (US **dueler**) *noun* **duellist** (US **duelist**) *noun*.

ORIGIN – Latin *duellum*, literary form of *bellum* 'war'.

duenna /dooennə/ > *noun* an older woman acting as a governess and chaperone to girls in a Spanish family.

ORIGIN – Spanish, from Latin *domina* 'lady, mistress'.

duet > *noun* **1** a performance by two singers, instrumentalists, or dancers. **2** a musical composition for two performers. > *verb* (**duetted, duetting**) perform a duet.

ORIGIN – Italian *duetto*, from *duo* 'duet'.

duff¹ > *noun* a flour pudding boiled or steamed in a cloth bag.

ORIGIN – northern English form of **DOUGH**.

duff² > *adjective* Brit. informal worthless or false.

duff³ > *verb* informal **1** (**duff up**) Brit. beat (someone) up. **2** Austral. steal and alter brands on (cattle). **3** Golf mishit (a shot).

duff⁴ > *noun* N. Amer. informal a person's buttocks.

duff⁵ > *noun* (in phrase **up the duff**) Brit. informal pregnant.

duffel (also **duffle**) > *noun* **1** a coarse woollen cloth with a thick nap. **2** N. Amer. sporting or camping equipment.

COMBINATIONS – **duffel bag** a cylindrical canvas bag closed by a drawstring. **duffel coat** a hooded coat made of duffel, typically fastened with toggles.

ORIGIN – from *Duffel*, the name of a town in Belgium where the cloth was originally made.

duffer¹ > *noun* informal an incompetent or stupid person.

ORIGIN – from Scots *dowfart* 'stupid person'.

duffer² > *noun* Austral. informal a person who steals cattle and alters the brands on them.

dug¹ past and past participle of **DIG**.

dug² > *noun* the udder, teat, or nipple of a female animal.

dugong /doogong/ > *noun* a sea cow found in the Indian Ocean.

ORIGIN – Malay.

dugout > *noun* **1** a trench that is roofed over as a shelter for troops. **2** an underground air-raid or nuclear shelter. **3** a low shelter at the side of a sports field for a team's coaches and substitutes. **4** (also **dugout canoe**) a canoe made from a hollowed tree trunk.

duiker /dīkər/ > *noun* (pl. same or **duikers**) a small African antelope.

ORIGIN – Dutch, literally 'diver', from the antelope's habit of plunging through bushes when pursued.

du jour /doo zhooər/ > *adjective* informal enjoying great but probably short-lived popularity: *black comedy is the genre du jour.*

ORIGIN – French, 'of the day'.

duke > *noun* **1** a male holding the highest hereditary title in the British and certain other peerages. **2** chiefly historical (in parts of Europe) a male ruler of a small independent state. **3** (**dukes**) informal fists.

IDIOMS – **duke it out** N. Amer. informal fight it out.

DERIVATIVES – **dukedom** *noun*.

ORIGIN – Old French *duc*, from Latin *dux* 'leader'; sense 3 is from rhyming slang *Duke of Yorks* 'forks' (= fingers).

DUKW /duk/ > *noun* an amphibious transport vehicle used by the Allies during the Second World War.

ORIGIN – a combination of factory-applied letters referring to features of the vehicle.

dulcet /dulsit/ > *adjective* often ironic (of a sound) sweet and soothing.

ORIGIN – Old French *doucet*, from Latin *dulcis* 'sweet'.

dulcimer /dulsimər/ > *noun* a musical instrument with strings of graduated length struck with hand-held hammers.

ORIGIN – Old French *doulcemer*, probably from Latin *dulce melos* 'sweet melody'.

dull > *adjective* **1** lacking interest or excitement. **2** lacking brightness or sheen. **3** (of the weather) overcast. **4** indistinctly felt or heard. **5** slow to understand; rather unintelligent. > *verb* make or become dull.

DERIVATIVES – **dullness** (also **dulness**) *noun* **dully** /dul-li/ *adverb*.

SYNONYMS – *adjective* **1** boring, dry, flat, monotonous, tedious, uninteresting. **2** drab, muted, sombre, subdued. **3** cloudy, gloomy, grey, overcast. **4** faint, indistinct, muffled. **5** obtuse, slow, unintelligent. *verb* dampen, diminish, muffle, mute, suppress.

ANTONYMS – *adjective* **1** interesting. **2** bright. **3** bright, sunny. **4** clear, sharp. **5** clever, intelligent. *verb* brighten.

ORIGIN – Old English, 'stupid'.

dullard /dullərd/ > *noun* a slow or stupid person.

duly > *adverb* in accordance with what is required, appropriate, or expected.

dumb > *adjective* **1** unable to speak; lacking the power of speech. **2** temporarily unable or unwilling to speak. **3** informal, chiefly N. Amer. stupid. **4** (of a computer terminal) having no independent processing capability. > *verb* **1** (**dumb down**) informal, chiefly N. Amer. make or become less intellectually challenging. **2** literary make dumb or silent.

DERIVATIVES – **dumbly** *adverb* **dumbness** *noun*.

USAGE – avoid **dumb** in the sense meaning 'not able to speak', as it likely to cause offence; use alternatives such as **speech-impaired**.

SYNONYMS – *adjective* **2** mute, silent, speechless, tongue-tied.

COMBINATIONS – **dumbshow 1** gestures used to convey something without speech. **2** (especially in English drama of the 16th and 17th centuries) a part of a play acted in mime. **dumb waiter 1** a small lift for carrying food and crockery between floors. **2** Brit. a movable table, typically with revolving shelves, used in a dining room.

dumb-bell > *noun* **1** a short bar with a weight at each end, used for exercise or muscle-building. **2** informal a stupid person.

ORIGIN – first used to denote an object similar to that used to ring a church bell (but without the bell, so 'dumb').

dumbfound (also **dumfound**) > *verb* astonish greatly.

ORIGIN – blend of **DUMB** and **CONFOUND**.

dumbo > *noun* (pl. **dumbos**) informal a stupid person.

ORIGIN – from **DUMB**: originally US, popularised by the cartoon film *Dumbo*.

dumbstruck > *adjective* so shocked or surprised as to be unable to speak.

dumdum (also **dumdum bullet**) > *noun* a kind of soft-nosed bullet that expands on impact and inflicts laceration.

ORIGIN – from *Dum Dum*, the name of a town and arsenal near Calcutta, India, where the bullets were first produced.

dum-dum > *noun* informal a stupid person.

dummy > *noun* (pl. **dummies**) **1** a model or replica of a human being. **2** an object designed to resemble and serve as a substitute for the real one. **3** Brit. a rubber or plastic teat for a baby to suck on. **4** (in sport) a feigned pass or kick. **5** informal, chiefly N. Amer. a stupid person. > *verb* (**dummies, dummied**) feign a pass or kick.

IDIOMS – **sell a dummy** deceive (an opponent) by feigning a pass or kick.

SYNONYMS – *noun* **1** lay figure, manikin, mannequin. **2** fake, imitation, likeness, mock-up, model.

COMBINATIONS – **dummy run** a practice or trial.

ORIGIN – first used in the sense 'a person who cannot speak', later 'an imaginary fourth player in whist' and then 'a substitute for the real thing': from **DUMB**.

dump > *noun* **1** a site for depositing rubbish or waste. **2** a heap of rubbish left at a dump. **3** informal an unpleasant or dreary place. **4** Computing an act of dumping stored data. **5** Military a temporary store of weaponry or provisions. > *verb* **1** deposit or dispose of (rubbish or something unwanted). **2** put down (something) firmly and carelessly. **3** informal abandon (someone). **4** send (goods) to a foreign market for sale at a low price. **5** Computing copy (stored data) to a different location.

SYNONYMS – *noun* **1** dumping ground, rubbish heap, tip. *verb* **1** deposit, dispose of, scrap, throw away, throw out.

COMBINATIONS – **dump truck** a dumper truck.

dumper > *noun* **1** a person or thing that dumps something. **2** (also **dumper truck**) Brit. a truck with a body that tilts or opens at the back for unloading.

dumpling > *noun* **1** a small savoury ball of dough boiled in water or in a stew. **2** a pudding consisting of fruit enclosed in a sweet dough and baked.

ORIGIN – apparently from the rare adjective *dump* 'of the consistency of dough'.

dumps > *plural noun* (in phrase (**down**) **in the dumps**) informal depressed or unhappy.

ORIGIN – first used as *dump* in the sense 'a dazed or puzzled state': probably a figurative use of Dutch *domp* 'haze, mist'.

dumpster > *noun* N. Amer. a rubbish skip.

dumpy > *adjective* (**dumpier**, **dumpiest**) short and stout.

dun[1] > *adjective* of a dull greyish-brown colour. > *noun* **1** a dull greyish-brown colour. **2** a horse with a sandy coat and a dark side stripe.

ORIGIN – Old English, probably related to DUSK.

dun[2] > *verb* (**dunned**, **dunning**) make persistent demands on (someone) for payment of a debt.

ORIGIN – perhaps from obsolete *Dunkirk privateer* (with connotations of piratical demands), or from the name of a Joe *Dun*, a well-known bailiff.

dunce > *noun* a person who is slow at learning.

SYNONYMS – dimwit, dolt, dullard, ignoramus, simpleton.

ANTONYMS – genius.

COMBINATIONS – **dunce's cap** a paper cone formerly put on the head of a dunce at school as a mark of disgrace.

Dundee cake > *noun* a rich fruit cake decorated with almonds.

dunderhead > *noun* informal a stupid person.

DERIVATIVES – **dunderheaded** adjective.

ORIGIN – perhaps from obsolete Scots *dunder, dunner* 'resounding noise'.

dune > *noun* a mound or ridge of sand formed by the wind, especially on the sea coast or in a desert.

ORIGIN – Dutch, related to DOWN[3].

dung > *noun* manure.

WORDFINDER – coprolite (*fossilised dung*), stercoraceous (*consisting of or resembling dung*).

COMBINATIONS – **dung beetle** a beetle whose larvae feed on dung, especially a scarab. **dunghill** a heap of dung or refuse, especially in a farmyard. **dungworm** an earthworm found in dung or compost, used by anglers as bait.

wordpower facts
Dunce

Dunce was originally a name for a follower of the 13th-century Scottish theologian John *Duns* Scotus. He was a leading exponent of *scholasticism*, the system of theology and philosophy taught in medieval European universities, based on Aristotelian logic and the writings of the early Christian Fathers and having a strong emphasis on tradition and dogma. The followers of Duns Scotus, known as *Duns* men, *dunce* men, or *dunces*, were ridiculed by 16th-century humanists and reformers as hair-splitting pedants and enemies of learning, and thus the word **dunce** acquired its negative connotations.

dungaree /dunggəree/ > *noun* **1** (**dungarees**) a garment consisting of trousers with a bib held up by straps over the shoulders. **2** a kind of coarse Indian calico.

ORIGIN – Hindi.

dungeon > *noun* a strong underground prison cell, especially in a castle.

ORIGIN – Old French, probably originally with the sense 'lord's tower', based on Latin *dominus* 'lord'.

dunk > *verb* **1** dip (bread or other food) into a drink or soup before eating it. **2** immerse in water. **3** Basketball score a field goal by shooting the ball down through the basket with the hands above the rim. > *noun* Basketball a goal scored by dunking.

SYNONYMS – *verb* **2** dip, duck, immerse, plunge, submerge.

ORIGIN – German *tunken* 'dip or plunge'.

dunlin /dunlin/ > *noun* a sandpiper with a downcurved bill and (in winter) greyish-brown upper parts.

ORIGIN – probably from DUN[1] + -LING.

dunnage /dunnij/ > *noun* **1** loose wood, matting, or similar material used to keep a cargo in position in a ship's hold. **2** informal baggage.

dunnart /dunnaart/ > *noun* a mouse-like marsupial with a pointed snout and prominent eyes, found in Australia and New Guinea.

ORIGIN – Nyungar (an Aboriginal language).

dunnock /dunnək/ > *noun* a small songbird with a dark grey head and a reddish-brown back.

ORIGIN – apparently from DUN[1].

dunny /dunni/ > *noun* (pl. **dunnies**) Austral./NZ informal a toilet.

ORIGIN – probably from DUNG (the original sense) + archaic slang *ken* 'house'.

duo > *noun* (pl. **duos**) **1** a pair of people or things, especially in music or entertainment. **2** Music a duet.

ORIGIN – Latin, 'two'.

duodecimal /dyoo-ōdessim'l/ > *adjective* relating to or denoting a system of counting or numbers based on twelve.

ORIGIN – Latin *duodecimus* 'twelfth'.

duodecimo /dyoo-ōdessimō/ > *noun* (pl. **duodecimos**) a size of book page that results from folding each printed sheet into twelve leaves (twenty-four pages).

duodenum /dyooədeenəm/ > *noun* (pl. **duodenums** or **duodena** /dyooədeenə/) the first part of the small intestine immediately beyond the stomach.

DERIVATIVES – **duodenal** adjective.

ORIGIN – Latin, from *duodeni* 'in twelves', its length being equivalent to the breadth of approximately twelve fingers.

duologue /dyooəlog/ > *noun* a play or part of a play with speaking roles for only two actors.

duopoly /dyoo-oppəli/ > *noun* (pl. **duopolies**) a situation in which two suppliers dominate a market.

dupe > *verb* deceive or trick. > *noun* a victim of deception.

DERIVATIVES – **duper** noun.

SYNONYMS – *verb* deceive, hoax, hoodwink, take in, trick. *noun* gull, victim.

ORIGIN – from French dialect *dupe* 'hoopoe', from the bird's supposedly stupid appearance.

dupion /dyoopiən/ > *noun* a rough silk fabric woven from the threads of double cocoons.

ORIGIN – French *doupion*, from Italian *doppio* 'double'.

duple /dyoop'l/ > *adjective* Music (of rhythm) based on two main beats to the bar.

duplex > *noun* **1** N. Amer. a residential building divided into two apartments. **2** chiefly N. Amer. & Austral. a semi-detached house. > *adjective* having two parts.

ORIGIN – Latin, from *duplicare* 'double'.

duplicate > *adjective* /dyooplikət/ **1** exactly like something else. **2** having two corresponding parts. **3** twice the number or quantity. > *noun* /dyooplikət/ one of two or more identical things. > *verb* /dyooplikayt/ **1** make or be an exact copy of. **2** multiply by two. **3** do (something) again unnecessarily.

DERIVATIVES – **duplication** noun.

SYNONYMS – *noun* copy, double, match,

twin. *verb* **1** copy, replicate. **3** redo, repeat, replicate.

ORIGIN – Latin *duplicare*, from *duo* 'two' + *plicare* 'to fold'.

duplicator > *noun* a machine for copying something.

duplicitous > *adjective* deceitful.

duplicity > *noun* deceitfulness.

duppy /dupp*i*/ > *noun* (pl. **duppies**) W. Indian a malevolent spirit or ghost.

ORIGIN – probably West African.

durable > *adjective* **1** able to withstand wear, pressure, or damage; hard-wearing. **2** (of goods) able to be kept for a period of time.

DERIVATIVES – **durability** *noun* **durably** *adverb*.

SYNONYMS – **1** hard-wearing, long-lasting, strong, sturdy, tough.

ORIGIN – Latin *durabilis*, from *durare* 'to last'.

dura mater /dyoorə **may**tər/ > *noun* Anatomy the tough outermost membrane enveloping the brain and spinal cord.

ORIGIN – Latin, 'hard mother', translation of an Arabic term.

durance > *noun* archaic imprisonment.

duration > *noun* the time during which something continues.

IDIOMS – **for the duration** informal for a very long time.

DERIVATIVES – **durational** *adjective*.

ORIGIN – Latin, from *durare* 'to last', from *durus* 'hard'.

durbar /**dur**baar/ > *noun* historical **1** the court of an Indian ruler. **2** a public reception held by an Indian prince or a British governor or viceroy in India.

ORIGIN – Persian, 'court'.

duress /dyoo**ress**/ > *noun* threats, violence, etc. used to coerce a person into doing something: *confessions extracted under duress*.

ORIGIN – first used in the sense 'harshness, cruel treatment': from Latin *durus* 'hard'.

Durex > *noun* (pl. same) Brit. trademark a contraceptive sheath.

durian /**doo**riən/ > *noun* a tropical fruit containing a creamy pulp with a foul smell but agreeable taste.

ORIGIN – Malay.

during > *preposition* **1** throughout the course or duration of. **2** at a particular point in the course of.

ORIGIN – from the obsolete verb *dure* 'last, endure, extend', from Latin *durare* 'to last'.

durum wheat /**dyoo**rəm/ > *noun* a kind of hard wheat grown in arid regions, yielding flour that is used to make pasta.

ORIGIN – Latin, from *durus* 'hard'.

dusk > *noun* the darker stage of twilight.

ORIGIN – Old English, 'dark, swarthy'.

dusky > *adjective* (**duskier**, **duskiest**) darkish in colour.

DERIVATIVES – **duskily** *adverb* **duskiness** *noun*.

dust > *noun* **1** fine, dry powder consisting of tiny particles of earth or waste matter. **2** any material in the form of tiny particles: *coal dust*. **3** an act of dusting. > *verb* **1** remove dust from the surface of. **2** cover lightly with a powdered substance. **3** (**dust down** or **off**) bring (something) out for use again after a long period of neglect.

IDIOMS – **not see someone for dust** find that a person has made a hasty departure. **when the dust settles** when things quieten down.

COMBINATIONS – **dust bowl** an area where vegetation has been lost and soil reduced to dust and eroded. **dustcart** Brit. a vehicle for collecting household refuse. **dust cover** a dust jacket or dust sheet. **dust devil** a whirlwind visible as a column of dust and debris. **dust jacket** a removable paper cover on a book. **dustman** Brit. a man employed to remove household refuse from dustbins. **dustpan** a flat hand-held receptacle into which dust and waste can be swept. **dust sheet** Brit. a large sheet for covering furniture to protect it from dust or while decorating. **dust storm** a strong wind carrying clouds of fine dust and sand.

dustbin > *noun* Brit. a large container for household refuse.

duster > *noun* Brit. a cloth for dusting furniture.

dust-up > *noun* informal a fight or quarrel.

dusty > *adjective* (**dustier**, **dustiest**) **1** covered with or resembling dust. **2** staid and uninteresting.

DERIVATIVES – **dustily** *adverb* **dustiness** *noun*.

COMBINATIONS – **dusty answer** Brit. a curt and unhelpful reply.

Dutch > *adjective* relating to the Netherlands or its language. > *noun* the Germanic language of the Netherlands.

IDIOMS – **go Dutch** share the cost of a meal equally.

COMBINATIONS – **Dutch auction** a method of selling in which the price is reduced until a buyer is found. **Dutch barn** Brit. a farm building comprising a curved roof set on an open frame, used to cover hay. **Dutch cap 1** a woman's lace cap with triangular flaps on each side, worn as part of Dutch traditional dress. **2** see CAP (sense 7). **Dutch courage** confidence gained from drinking alcohol. **Dutch elm disease** a disease of elm trees, caused by a fungus and spread by bark beetles. **Dutch hoe** a hoe used with a pushing action just under the surface of the soil. **Dutch oven 1** a covered container of earthenware or cast iron, for cooking casseroles. **2** chiefly historical a large metal box serving as a simple oven, heated by being placed under or next to hot coals. **Dutch uncle** informal, chiefly N. Amer. a person giving firm but benevolent advice.

ORIGIN – Dutch *dutsch* 'Dutch, Netherlandish, German'.

dutch > *noun* (usu. **one's old dutch**) Brit. informal (among cockneys) one's wife.

ORIGIN – abbreviation of DUCHESS.

dutiable /**dyoo**tiəb'l/ > *adjective* liable to customs or other duties.

dutiful > *adjective* conscientiously fulfilling one's duty.

DERIVATIVES – **dutifully** *adverb*.

SYNONYMS – conscientious, dedicated, faithful, responsible.

duty > *noun* (pl. **duties**) **1** moral or legal obligation. **2** a task required as part of one's job. **3** a payment levied on the import, export, manufacture, or sale of goods. **4** Brit. a payment levied on the transfer of property, for licences, and for the legal recognition of documents.

IDIOMS – **on** (or **off**) **duty** engaged (or not engaged) in one's regular work.

SYNONYMS – **1** commitment, obligation, responsibility. **2** assignment, function, job, role, task.

COMBINATIONS – **duty-bound** morally or legally obliged. **duty-free** exempt from payment of duty.

ORIGIN – Old French *duete*, from *deu* 'owed, due'.

duvet /**doo**vay/ > *noun* chiefly Brit. a soft, thick quilt used instead of an upper sheet and blankets.

ORIGIN – French, 'down'.

DVD > *abbreviation* digital versatile disc (formerly digital videodisc).

dwarf > *noun* (pl. **dwarfs** or **dwarves**) **1** a member of a mythical race of short, stocky human-like creatures. **2** an abnormally small person. **3** (before another noun) (of an animal or plant) much smaller than is usual for its type or species. **4** (also **dwarf star**) Astronomy a star of relatively small size and low luminosity. > *verb* cause to seem small in comparison.

DERIVATIVES – **dwarfish** *adjective*.

USAGE – in the sense 'an abnormally small person', **dwarf** is normally considered offensive; however, there is no accepted alternative, since terms such as **person of restricted growth** have gained little currency.

dwarfism > *noun* unusually low stature or small size.

dweeb > *noun* N. Amer. informal a boring, studious, or socially inept person.

dwell > *verb* (past and past participle **dwelt** or **dwelled**) **1** formal live in or at a place. **2** (**dwell on**) think, speak, or write at length about.

DERIVATIVES – **dweller** *noun*.

SYNONYMS – **1** live, lodge, reside. **2** (**dwell on**) brood about, linger over, mull over, muse on.

dwelling (also **dwelling place**) > *noun* a house or other place of residence.

dwindle > *verb* diminish gradually.
SYNONYMS – contract, decrease, diminish, lessen, reduce.
ORIGIN – from Scots and dialect *dwine* 'fade away'.

Dy > *symbol* the chemical element dysprosium.

dyad /**dī**ad/ > *noun* technical something consisting of two elements or parts.
ORIGIN – from Latin *dyas*, from Greek *duo* 'two'.

Dyak > *noun* variant spelling of **DAYAK**.

dye > *noun* a natural or synthetic substance used to colour something. > *verb* (**dyed**, **dyeing**) make (something) a specified colour with dye.
IDIOMS – **dyed in the wool** unchanging in a particular belief.
DERIVATIVES – **dyer** *noun*.
COMBINATIONS – **dyestuff** a substance used as or yielding a dye.

dying present participle of **DIE**[1].

dyke[1] (also **dike**) > *noun* **1** an embankment built to prevent flooding from the sea. **2** a ditch or watercourse. **3** an earthwork serving as a boundary or defence: *Offa's Dyke.* **4** Geology an intrusion of igneous rock cutting across existing strata. Compare with **SILL**. > *verb* provide (land) with a dyke to prevent flooding.
ORIGIN – Old Norse *dík*, related to **DITCH**.

dyke[2] (also **dike**) > *noun* informal a lesbian.

dynamic > *adjective* **1** (of a process or system) characterised by constant change or activity. **2** full of energy and new ideas. **3** Physics relating to forces producing motion. Contrasted with **STATIC**. **4** Music relating to the volume of sound produced by an instrument or voice. > *noun* **1** an energising or motive force. **2** Music another term for **DYNAMICS** (in sense 3).
DERIVATIVES – **dynamical** *adjective* **dynamically** *adverb*.
SYNONYMS – **2** energetic, enterprising, high-powered, lively, spirited, vigorous.
COMBINATIONS – **dynamic equilibrium** a state of balance between continuing processes. **dynamic range** the range of sound intensity that occurs in a piece of music or that can be satisfactorily handled by a piece of equipment.
ORIGIN – Greek *dunamikos*, from *dunamis* 'power'.

dynamics > *plural noun* **1** (treated as sing.) the branch of mechanics concerned with the motion of bodies under the action of forces. **2** the forces which stimulate development or change within a system or process. **3** Music the varying levels of volume of sound in a musical performance.

dynamism > *noun* **1** the quality of being dynamic. **2** Philosophy, chiefly historical the theory that phenomena can be explained by the action of forces.
DERIVATIVES – **dynamist** *noun*.

dynamite > *noun* **1** a high explosive consisting of nitroglycerine mixed with an absorbent material. **2** informal an extremely impressive or potentially dangerous person or thing. > *verb* blow up with dynamite.
ORIGIN – from Greek *dunamis* 'power'.

dynamo /**dī**nəmō/ > *noun* (pl. **dynamos**) a machine for converting mechanical energy into electrical energy by rotating conducting coils in a magnetic field.
ORIGIN – abbreviation of *dynamo-electric machine.*

dynamometer /dīnə**mommi**tər/ > *noun* an instrument which measures the power output of an engine.

dynast /**dinn**ast, **dīnn**ast/ > *noun* a member of a dynasty, especially a hereditary ruler.

dynasty /**dinn**əsti/ > *noun* (pl. **dynasties**) **1** a line of hereditary rulers. **2** a succession of prominent people from the same family.
DERIVATIVES – **dynastic** *adjective* **dynastically** *adverb*.
ORIGIN – Greek *dunasteia* 'lordship', from *dunasthai* 'be able'.

dyne /**dīn**/ > *noun* Physics a unit of force that, acting on a mass of one gram, increases its velocity by one centimetre per second every second along the direction in which it acts.
ORIGIN – from Greek *dunamis* 'power'.

dys- /diss/ > *combining form* bad; difficult: *dyspepsia.*
ORIGIN – from Greek *dus-*.

dysentery /**diss**əntri/ > *noun* a disease in which the intestines are infected, resulting in severe diarrhoea with blood and mucus in the faeces.
ORIGIN – Greek *dusenteria*, from *dusenteros* 'afflicted in the bowels'.

dysfunctional > *adjective* **1** not operating normally or properly. **2** unable to deal adequately with normal social relations.
DERIVATIVES – **dysfunction** *noun* **dysfunctionally** *adverb*.

dyskinesia /diski**nee**ziə, diskī**nee**ziə/ > *noun* Medicine abnormality or impairment of voluntary movement.
ORIGIN – from Greek *dys-* 'bad, difficult' + *kinēsis* 'motion'.

dyslexia /dis**lek**siə/ > *noun* a disorder involving difficulty in learning to read or interpret words, letters, and other symbols.
DERIVATIVES – **dyslexic** *adjective & noun*.
ORIGIN – from Greek *dys-* 'bad, difficult' + *lexis* 'speech' (apparently by confusion of Greek *legein* 'to speak' and Latin *legere* 'to read').

dysmenorrhoea /dismenə**ree**ə/ (US **dysmenorrhea**) > *noun* Medicine painful menstruation.

dyspepsia /dis**pep**siə/ > *noun* indigestion.
ORIGIN – Greek *duspepsia*, from *duspeptos* 'difficult to digest'.

dyspeptic > *adjective* **1** relating to or suffering from dyspepsia. **2** irritable.

dysphasia /dis**fay**ziə/ > *noun* difficulty in using language coherently, due to brain disease or damage.
DERIVATIVES – **dysphasic** *adjective*.
ORIGIN – from Greek *dus-* 'bad, difficult' + *phatos* 'spoken'.

dysphoria /dis**for**iə/ > *noun* a state of unease or general dissatisfaction.
DERIVATIVES – **dysphoric** *adjective*.
ORIGIN – Greek *dusphoria*, from *dusphoros* 'hard to bear'.

dysplasia /dis**play**ziə/ > *noun* Medicine the enlargement of an organ or tissue by the proliferation of abnormal cells.
ORIGIN – from Greek *dys-* 'bad, difficult' + *plasis* 'formation'.

dyspnoea /disp**nee**ə/ (US **dyspnea**) > *noun* Medicine laboured breathing.
ORIGIN – Greek *duspnoia*, from *dus-* 'difficult' + *pnoē* 'breathing'.

dyspraxia /dis**prak**siə/ > *noun* a disorder of the brain in childhood causing difficulty in activities requiring coordination and movement.
ORIGIN – from Greek *dus-* 'bad or difficult' + *praxis* 'action'.

dysprosium /dis**prō**ziəm/ > *noun* a soft silvery-white metallic chemical element of the lanthanide series.
ORIGIN – from Greek *dusprositos* 'hard to get at'.

dysthymia /dis**thī**miə/ > *noun* persistent mild depression.
DERIVATIVES – **dysthymic** *adjective*.
ORIGIN – Greek *dusthumia*.

dystopia /dis**tō**piə/ > *noun* an imaginary place or society in which everything is bad.
DERIVATIVES – **dystopian** *adjective*.
ORIGIN – from **DYS-** + **UTOPIA**.

dystrophy /**dis**trəfi/ > *noun* Medicine a disorder in which an organ or tissue of the body wastes away. See also *muscular dystrophy*.
DERIVATIVES – **dystrophic** *adjective*.
ORIGIN – from Greek *dus-* 'bad' + *-trophia* 'nourishment'.

e

E¹ (also **e**) > *noun* (pl. **Es** or **E's**) **1** the fifth letter of the alphabet. **2** denoting the fifth in a set. **3** Music the third note of the diatonic scale of C major.

E² > *abbreviation* **1** East or Eastern. **2** informal the drug Ecstasy. **3** Physics energy. **4** denoting products, in particular food additives, which comply with EU regulations.

each > *determiner* & *pronoun* every one of two or more people or things, regarded and identified separately. > *adverb* to, for, or by every one of a group.

IDIOMS – **each and every** every single. **each other** the other one or ones.

COMBINATIONS – **each-way** Brit. (of a bet) backing a horse or other competitor either to win or to finish in the first three.

eager > *adjective* **1** (usu. **eager for** or **to do**) strongly wanting to do or have something. **2** keenly expectant or interested.

DERIVATIVES – **eagerly** *adverb* **eagerness** *noun*.

SYNONYMS – avid, enthusiastic, keen.

ANTONYMS – apathetic, unenthusiastic.

ORIGIN – Old French *aigre* 'keen', from Latin *acer* 'sharp, pungent'.

eagle > *noun* a large keen-sighted bird of prey with a massive hooked bill and long broad wings.

WORDFINDER – Aquila (*constellation, the Eagle*), aquiline (*like an eagle*), eyrie (*eagle's nest*).

DERIVATIVES – **eaglet** *noun*.

COMBINATIONS – **eagle-eyed** sharp-sighted and keenly observant. **eagle owl** a very large owl with ear tufts and a deep hoot.

ORIGIN – Old French *aigle*, from Latin *aquila*.

ear¹ > *noun* **1** the organ of hearing and balance in humans and other vertebrates. **2** the fleshy external part of this organ. **3** (in other animals) an organ sensitive to sound. **4** an ability to recognise and appreciate music or language. **5** (usu. **one's ear**) willingness to listen and pay attention.

WORDFINDER – aural, auricular, otic (*of or relating to the ear*), auditory (*of hearing*), otology (*study of the ear*); *parts of the ear:*

auricle or pinna, cochlea, eardrum or tympanum, semicircular canals; *ear defects:* glue ear, labyrinthitis, otalgia (*earache*), otitis, tinnitus.

IDIOMS – **be all ears** informal be listening attentively. **one's ears are burning** one is subconsciously aware of being talked about. **have someone's ear** have access to and power to persuade or influence someone. **have** (or **keep**) **an ear to the ground** be well informed about events and trends. **be out on one's ear** informal be dismissed ignominiously. **up to one's ears in** informal very busy with.

DERIVATIVES – **eared** *adjective*.

COMBINATIONS – **earache** pain inside the ear. **earbashing** informal a lengthy and reproachful speech. **earhole** the external opening of the ear. **ear lobe** the soft, rounded fleshy part at the lower edge of the external ear. **earmuffs** a pair of soft fabric coverings, connected by a band, worn over the ears to protect them from cold or noise. **earpiece** the part of a telephone, radio receiver, or other aural device that is applied to the ear during use. **earplug** a piece of wax, cotton wool, etc., placed in the ear as protection against noise or water. **ear-splitting** extremely loud. **ear trumpet** a trumpet-shaped device formerly used as a hearing aid. **earwax** the protective yellow waxy substance secreted in the passage of the outer ear.

ear² > *noun* the seed-bearing head or spike of a cereal plant.

eardrum > *noun* the membrane of the middle ear, which vibrates in response to sound waves.

earful > *noun* informal a prolonged reprimand.

earl > *noun* a British nobleman ranking above a viscount and below a marquess.

DERIVATIVES – **earldom** *noun*.

Earl Grey > *noun* a kind of China tea flavoured with bergamot.

ORIGIN – probably named after the 2nd *Earl Grey* (1764–1845), said to have been given the recipe by a Chinese mandarin.

early > *adjective* (**earlier**, **earliest**) & *adverb* **1** before the usual or expected time. **2** of or at the beginning of a particular time, period, or sequence.

IDIOMS – **at the earliest** not before the time or date specified. **early bird** humorous a person who rises or arrives early. **the early bird catches the worm** proverb the person who takes the earliest opportunity to do something will gain the advantage over others. **early on** at an early stage.

DERIVATIVES – **earliness** *noun*.

SYNONYMS – *adjective* **1** advance, forward, premature, untimely. **2** ancient, first, initial, old, primitive.

ANTONYMS – late.

COMBINATIONS – **Early English** denoting

a style of English Gothic architecture typical of the late 12th and 13th centuries, characterised by pointed arches and narrow pointed windows. **early music** medieval, Renaissance, and early baroque music, especially as revived and played on period instruments.

ORIGIN – Old English, related to ERE.

earmark > *noun* **1** a mark on the ear of a domesticated animal indicating ownership or identity. **2** an identifying feature. > *verb* **1** apply an earmark to. **2** designate for a particular purpose.

SYNONYMS – *verb* **2** allocate, assign, commit, designate, reserve, set aside.

earn > *verb* **1** obtain (money) in return for labour or services. **2** gain as the reward for hard work or merit. **3** (of capital invested) gain (money) as interest or profit.

DERIVATIVES – **earner** *noun*.

SYNONYMS – **1** get, make, be paid, receive, take home. **2** attain, deserve, gain, merit, warrant.

COMBINATIONS – **earned income** money derived from paid work as opposed to profit from investments.

earnest¹ /**er**nist/ > *adjective* intensely serious.

IDIOMS – **in earnest** with sincere and serious intention.

DERIVATIVES – **earnestly** *adverb* **earnestness** *noun*.

SYNONYMS – committed, intense, serious, sincere, sober.

ANTONYMS – casual, frivolous.

earnest² /**er**nist/ > *noun* a sign or promise of what is to come.

ORIGIN – first occurring as *ernes*, meaning 'instalment paid to confirm a contract', from Old French *erres*, from Latin *arrabo* 'a pledge'.

earnings > *plural noun* money or income earned.

SYNONYMS – income, pay, profit, revenue, salary, wages.

earphone > *noun* an electrical device worn on the ear to receive radio or telephone communications or to listen to a radio or tape recorder.

ear-piercing > *adjective* loud and shrill.

earring > *noun* a piece of jewellery worn on the lobe or edge of the ear.

earshot > *noun* the range or distance over which one can hear or be heard.

earth > *noun* **1** (also **Earth**) the planet on which we live. **2** the substance of the land surface; soil. **3** Brit. electrical connection to the ground, regarded as having zero electrical potential. **4** the underground lair of a badger or fox. **5** one of the four elements (air, earth, fire, and water) in ancient and medieval philosophy and in astrology. > *verb* **1** Brit. connect (an electrical device) to earth. **2** Hunting (of a fox) run to its earth.

WORDFINDER – circumnavigate (*travel around the earth*), Gaia (*earth viewed as self-regulating organism*), geocentric (*having the earth at the centre*), geomancy (*divination from handfuls of earth*), terrestrial, telluric (*of the earth*).

IDIOMS – **come back** (or **down**) **to earth** return to reality. **the earth** chiefly Brit. a very large amount: *her hat cost the earth*. **go to earth** go into hiding. **on earth** used for emphasis: *what on earth are you doing?*

DERIVATIVES – **earthward** *adjective & adverb* **earthwards** *adverb*.

SYNONYMS – *noun* **2** clay, dirt, ground, loam, soil.

COMBINATIONS – **earth closet** Brit. a basic type of toilet with dry earth used to cover excrement. **earth sciences** the various branches of science concerned with the physical constitution of the earth and its atmosphere.

earthbound > *adjective* **1** confined to the earth or earthly things. **2** moving towards the earth.

earthen > *adjective* **1** made of compressed earth. **2** (of a pot) made of baked or fired clay.

COMBINATIONS – **earthenware** pottery made of fired clay.

earthling > *noun* (in science fiction) an inhabitant of the earth.

earthly > *adjective* **1** relating to the earth or human life on the earth. **2** material; worldly. **3** informal used for emphasis: *there was no earthly reason to rush.*

DERIVATIVES – **earthliness** *noun*.

earthquake > *noun* a sudden violent shaking of the ground as a result of movements within the earth's crust.

WORDFINDER – seismic (*of earthquakes*), seismograph, seismometer (*instruments for detecting or measuring earthquakes*), seismology (*study of earthquakes*); focus (*point of origin of earthquake*), epicentre (*point on surface directly above focus*), Richter scale (*of earthquake intensity*), tsunami (*sea wave caused by earthquake*).

earth-shattering > *adjective* informal very important or shocking.

earthwork > *noun* a large artificial bank of soil, especially one made as a defence in ancient times.

earthworm > *noun* a burrowing segmented worm that lives in the soil.

earthy > *adjective* (**earthier**, **earthiest**) **1** resembling or suggestive of soil. **2** direct and uninhibited, especially about sexual subjects or bodily functions.

DERIVATIVES – **earthily** *adverb* **earthiness** *noun*.

SYNONYMS – **2** bawdy, crude, robust, rough, uninhibited.

earwig > *noun* a small elongated insect with a pair of appendages on its tail, resembling pincers. > *verb* (**earwigged**, **earwigging**) informal eavesdrop.

ORIGIN – Old English, from *ēare* 'ear' + *wicga* 'earwig' (probably related to *wiggle*); the insect was once thought to crawl into the human ear.

ease > *noun* **1** absence of difficulty or effort. **2** freedom from worries or problems. > *verb* **1** make or become less serious or severe. **2** move carefully or gradually. **3** (**ease off** or **up**) do something with more moderation. **4** (of share prices, interest rates, etc.) decrease in value or amount.

IDIOMS – **at ease 1** (also **at one's ease**) relaxed. **2** Military in a relaxed attitude with the feet apart and the hands behind the back.

DERIVATIVES – **easeful** *adjective* (literary).

SYNONYMS – *noun* **1** dexterity, easiness, effortlessness, facility, simplicity. **2** calm, comfort, peace, relaxation, tranquillity. *verb* **1** alleviate, mitigate, relieve, soften, soothe.

ANTONYMS – *noun* **1** difficulty, effort. **2** hardship, trouble. *verb* **1** aggravate.

ORIGIN – Old French *aise*, from Latin *adjacere* 'lie close by'.

easel /eez'l/ > *noun* a wooden frame on legs for holding an artist's work in progress.

ORIGIN – Dutch *ezel* 'ass'.

easement /eezmənt/ > *noun* **1** Law a right to cross or otherwise use another's land for a specified purpose. **2** literary comfort or peace.

easily > *adverb* **1** without difficulty or effort. **2** without doubt. **3** very probably.

east > *noun* (**the east**) **1** the direction towards the point of the horizon where the sun rises at the equinoxes. **2** the eastern part of a country, region, or town. **3** (**the East**) the regions or countries lying to the east of Europe, especially China, Japan, and India. **4** (**the East**) historical the former communist states of eastern Europe. > *adjective* **1** lying towards, near, or facing the east. **2** (of a wind) blowing from the east. > *adverb* to or towards the east.

WORDFINDER – oriental (*of the Far East*).

DERIVATIVES – **eastbound** *adjective & adverb*.

COMBINATIONS – **east-north-east** (or **east-south-east**) the direction or compass point midway between east and north-east (or south-east).

Easter (also **Easter Day** or **Easter Sunday**) > *noun* the festival of the Christian Church celebrating the resurrection of Christ, held (in the Western Church) on the first Sunday after the first full moon following the northern spring equinox.

WORDFINDER – paschal (*relating to Easter*).

COMBINATIONS – **Easter egg** an artificial chocolate egg or decorated hard-boiled egg given as a gift at Easter.

ORIGIN – Old English, related to **EAST**.

easterly > *adjective & adverb* **1** in an eastward position or direction. **2** (of a wind) blowing from the east. > *noun* a wind blowing from the east.

eastern > *adjective* **1** situated in, directed towards, or facing the east. **2** (usu. **Eastern**) coming from or characteristic of the regions to the east of Europe.

DERIVATIVES – **easternmost** *adjective*.

COMBINATIONS – **Eastern Church** (also **Eastern Orthodox Church**) **1** the Orthodox Church. **2** any of the Christian Churches originating in eastern Europe and the Middle East.

easterner > *noun* a person from the east of a particular region or country.

Eastertide > *noun* the Easter period.

East Indian > *adjective* **1** relating to the islands of SE Asia. **2** archaic relating to the whole of SE Asia to the east of and including India.

easting > *noun* **1** distance travelled or measured eastward. **2** a figure or line representing eastward distance on a map.

eastward > *adjective* in an easterly direction. > *adverb* (also **eastwards**) towards the east.

easy > *adjective* (**easier**, **easiest**) **1** achieved without great effort; presenting few difficulties. **2** free from worry or problems. **3** lacking anxiety or awkwardness. **4** informal, derogatory willingly responsive to sexual advances. > *exclamation* be careful!

IDIOMS – **easy on the eye** (or **ear**) informal pleasant to look at (or listen to). **go** (or **be**) **easy on** informal refrain from being harsh with or critical of. **take it easy 1** proceed calmly. **2** make no unnecessary effort.

DERIVATIVES – **easiness** *noun*.

SYNONYMS – *adjective* **1** effortless, simple, straightforward, undemanding.

ANTONYMS – *adjective* **1** demanding, difficult, hard.

COMBINATIONS – **easy chair** a large, comfortable chair, especially an armchair. **easy listening** popular music that is tuneful and undemanding. **easy street** informal a state of financial comfort or security.

ORIGIN – Old French *aisie*, from Latin *adjacere* 'lie close by'.

easy-going > *adjective* relaxed and open-minded.

eat > *verb* (past **ate** /et, ayt/; past participle **eaten**) **1** put (food) into the mouth and chew and swallow it. **2** (**eat out** or **in**) have a meal in a restaurant (or at home). **3** (**eat away** or **into**) gradually erode or destroy. **4** (**eat up**) use (resources) in very large quantities. > *noun* (**eats**) informal light food or snacks.

WORDFINDER – anorexia (*disorder in which sufferer refuses to eat*), bulimia (*disorder in which sufferer engages in bouts of overeating*).

IDIOMS – **eat one's heart out** suffer from longing for something unattainable. **eat one's words** retract what one has said. **what's eating you?** informal what is worrying or annoying you?

DERIVATIVES – **eater** noun.

SYNONYMS – verb **1** consume, feed on, ingest, partake of.

eatable > adjective fit to be consumed as food. > noun (**eatables**) items of food.

eatery > noun (pl. **eateries**) informal a restaurant or cafe.

eau de cologne /ō də kəlōn/ > noun (pl. **eaux de cologne** pronunc. same) a toilet water with a strong, characteristic scent.

ORIGIN – French, 'water of Cologne'.

eau de Nil /ō də **neel**/ > noun a pale greenish colour.

ORIGIN – French, 'water of the Nile'.

eau de toilette /ō də twaa**let**/ > noun (pl. **eaux de toilette** pronunc. same) a dilute form of perfume.

ORIGIN – French, 'toilet water'.

eau de vie /ō də **vee**/ > noun (pl. **eaux de vie** pronunc. same) brandy.

ORIGIN – French, 'water of life'.

eaves > plural noun the part of a roof that meets or overhangs the walls of a building.

eavesdrop > verb (**eavesdropped**, **eavesdropping**) secretly listen to a conversation.

DERIVATIVES – **eavesdropper** noun.

SYNONYMS – listen in, overhear, snoop, spy.

ORIGIN – from the obsolete noun eavesdrop 'the ground on to which water drips from the eaves'.

ebb > noun the movement of the tide out to sea. > verb **1** (of tidewater) move away from the land; recede. The opposite of **EBB**. **2** (often **ebb away**) (of an emotion or quality) gradually become smaller or less intense.

IDIOMS – **at a low ebb** in a poor state.

SYNONYMS – verb **2** diminish, dwindle, fade, lessen, wane.

E-boat > noun a German torpedo boat used in the Second World War.

ORIGIN – from E- for enemy.

Ebola fever /eebōlə/ > noun an infectious and generally fatal disease spread by a virus and marked by fever and severe internal bleeding.

ORIGIN – named after a river in Zaire (Democratic Republic of Congo).

ebonise (also **ebonize**) > verb make (wood or furniture) look like ebony.

ebonite > noun another term for **VULCANITE**.

ebony /**ebb**əni/ > noun **1** heavy blackish or very dark brown wood from a tree of tropical and warm regions. **2** a very dark brown or black colour.

ORIGIN – Greek ebenos 'ebony tree'.

ebullient /i**bull**iənt/ > adjective **1** cheerful and full of energy. **2** archaic or literary boiling or agitated as if boiling.

DERIVATIVES – **ebullience** noun **ebulliently** adverb.

ORIGIN – Latin, from ebullire 'boil up'.

EC > abbreviation **1** East Central (London postal district). **2** European Commission. **3** European Community.

eccentric /ik**sen**trik/ > adjective **1** unconventional and slightly strange. **2** technical not placed centrally or not having its axis placed centrally. **3** technical (of an orbit) not circular, especially to a marked degree. > noun **1** an eccentric person. **2** a cam or other part mounted eccentrically on a revolving shaft in order to transform rotation into motion back and forth.

DERIVATIVES – **eccentrically** adverb **eccentricity** noun.

SYNONYMS – adjective **1** idiosyncratic, odd, quirky, strange, unconventional.

ORIGIN – Greek ekkentros, from ek 'out of' + kentron 'centre'.

Eccles cake /**ekk**'lz/ > noun Brit. a round, flat cake of sweetened pastry filled with currants.

ORIGIN – named after the town of Eccles near Manchester.

ecclesiastic /ikleezi**a**stik/ formal > noun a priest or clergyman. > adjective another term for **ECCLESIASTICAL**.

ecclesiastical > adjective of or relating to the Christian Church or its clergy.

DERIVATIVES – **ecclesiastically** adverb.

ORIGIN – Greek ekklēsiastikos, from ekklēsiastēs 'member of an assembly', from ekklēsia 'assembly, church'.

ecclesiology /ikleezi**oll**əji/ > noun **1** the study of churches. **2** theology as applied to the nature and structure of the Christian Church.

DERIVATIVES – **ecclesiological** adjective **ecclesiologist** noun.

ecdysis /ek**dī**siss/ > noun Zoology the process of shedding the old skin (in reptiles) or casting off the outer cuticle (in insects and other arthropods).

DERIVATIVES – **ecdysial** /ek**dizz**iəl/ adjective.

ORIGIN – Greek ekdusis, from ekduein 'put off'.

ECG > abbreviation electrocardiogram or electrocardiograph.

echelon /**esh**əlon/ > noun **1** a level or rank in an organisation, profession, or society. **2** Military a formation of troops, ships, etc. in parallel rows with the end of each row projecting further than the one in front. > verb Military arrange in an echelon formation.

ORIGIN – French, from échelle 'ladder'.

echidna /i**kid**nə/ > noun a spiny egg-laying mammal with a long snout and claws, native to Australia and New Guinea.

ORIGIN – Greek ekhidna 'viper'.

echinoderm /i**kī**nəderm, **ekk**inəderm/ > noun Zoology a marine invertebrate of a large group (the phylum Echinodermata) including starfishes, sea urchins, and sea cucumbers.

ORIGIN – from Greek ekhinos 'hedgehog, sea urchin' + derma 'skin'.

echo > noun (pl. **echoes**) **1** a sound caused by the reflection of sound waves from a surface back to the listener. **2** a reflected radio or radar beam. **3** something suggestive of, parallel to, or remaining from something else. > verb (**echoes**, **echoed**) **1** (of a sound) reverberate or be repeated after the original sound has stopped. **2** have a continued significance or influence. **3** repeat (someone's words or opinions).

DERIVATIVES – **echoey** adjective.

SYNONYMS – noun **1** repeat, repetition, reverberation. **3** copy, duplicate, reiteration, trace, vestige. verb **1** ring, resonate, resound, reverberate. **3** copy, imitate, parrot, reiterate, repeat.

COMBINATIONS – **echo chamber** an enclosed space for producing reverberation of sound. **echogram** a recording of depth or distance under water made by an echo sounder. **echograph** an instrument for recording echograms. **echo sounder** a device for determining the depth of the seabed or detecting objects in water by measuring the time taken for echoes to return to the listener.

ORIGIN – Greek ēkhō.

echocardiography /ekkōkaardi**og**rəfi/ > noun the use of ultrasound waves to investigate the action of the heart.

DERIVATIVES – **echocardiogram** noun **echocardiograph** noun **echocardiographic** adjective.

echoic /e**kō**ik/ > adjective **1** of or like an echo. **2** representing a sound by imitation; onomatopoeic.

DERIVATIVES – **echoically** adverb.

echolocation /ekkōlōkaysh'n/ > noun the location of objects by reflected sound, in particular as used by animals such as dolphins and bats.

echt /ekht/ > adjective authentic and typical.

ORIGIN – German.

eclair /i**klayr**/ > noun a small, soft cake of choux pastry filled with cream and typically topped with chocolate icing.

ORIGIN – French, 'lightning'.

eclampsia /i**klamp**siə/ > noun Medicine a condition in which one or more convulsions occur in a pregnant woman suffering from high blood pressure, often followed by coma.

DERIVATIVES – **eclamptic** adjective.

ORIGIN – Greek *eklampsis* 'sudden development'.

éclat /ayklaa/ > *noun* a conspicuously brilliant or successful effect.
ORIGIN – French, from *éclater* 'burst out'.

eclectic /iklektik/ > *adjective* deriving ideas or style from a broad and varied range of sources. > *noun* an eclectic person.
DERIVATIVES – **eclectically** *adverb* **eclecticism** *noun*.
ORIGIN – Greek *eklektikos*, from *eklegein* 'pick out'.

eclipse /iklips/ > *noun* **1** an obscuring of the light from one celestial body by the passage of another between it and the observer or between it and its source of illumination. **2** a sudden loss of significance, power, or prominence in relation to another person or thing. > *verb* **1** (of a celestial body) obscure the light from or to (another body). **2** deprive of significance, power, or prominence.
SYNONYMS – *noun* **2** decline, deterioration, overshadowing, surpassing. *verb* **2** outdo, outshine, overshadow, surpass, transcend.
COMBINATIONS – **eclipse plumage** a male duck's plumage during a moult, with distinctive markings obscured.
ORIGIN – Greek *ekleipsis*, from *ekleipein* 'fail to appear, be eclipsed'.

ecliptic /ikliptik/ Astronomy > *noun* the great circle on the celestial sphere which represents the sun's apparent path during the year, so called because lunar and solar eclipses can only occur when the moon crosses it. > *adjective* of eclipses or the ecliptic.

eclogue /eklog/ > *noun* a short pastoral poem, especially one in the form of a dialogue.
ORIGIN – Greek *eklogē* 'selection'.

ECM > *abbreviation* electronic counter-measures.

eco- /eekō/ > *combining form* ecological; environmental.

eco-friendly > *adjective* not harmful to the environment.

eco-labelling > *noun* the use of labels to identify products conforming to recognised environmental standards.
DERIVATIVES – **eco-label** *noun*.

E. coli /kōlī/ > *noun* the bacterium *Escherichia coli*, commonly found in the intestines of humans and other animals, some strains of which can cause severe food poisoning.

ecology /ikolləji/ > *noun* the branch of biology concerned with the relations of organisms to one another and to their physical surroundings.
DERIVATIVES – **ecological** *adjective* **ecologically** *adverb* **ecologist** *noun*.
ORIGIN – from Greek *oikos* 'house'.

e-commerce > *noun* business and financial transactions conducted electronically on the Internet.

econometrics /ikonnəmetriks/ > *plural noun* (treated as sing.) the branch of economics concerned with the use of mathematical methods (especially statistics) in describing economic systems.
DERIVATIVES – **econometric** *adjective* **econometrical** *adjective* **econometrician** *noun* **econometrist** *noun*.

economic /eekənommik, ekənommik/ > *adjective* **1** relating to economics or the economy. **2** justified in terms of profitability.
SYNONYMS – **1** budgetary, financial, fiscal, monetary. **2** cost-effective, money-making, profitable, viable.

economical > *adjective* **1** giving good value or return in relation to the resources used or money spent. **2** sparing in the use of resources or money.
IDIOMS – **economical with the truth** euphemistic lying or deliberately withholding information.
SYNONYMS – **1** cheap, inexpensive, reasonable. **2** careful, frugal, parsimonious, prudent, sensible, sparing.
ANTONYMS – **1** expensive. **2** extravagant, spendthrift.

economically > *adverb* **1** in a way that relates to economics or finance. **2** in an economical way.

economics > *plural noun* (often treated as sing.) the branch of knowledge concerned with the production, consumption, and transfer of wealth.

economise (also **economize**) > *verb* spend less; be economical.
DERIVATIVES – **economiser** *noun*.
SYNONYMS – budget, cut back, retrench.

economist > *noun* an expert in economics.

economy > *noun* (pl. **economies**) **1** the state of a country or region in terms of the production and consumption of goods and services and the supply of money. **2** careful management of available resources. **3** a financial saving. **4** (also **economy class**) the cheapest class of air or rail travel. **5** (before another noun) offering good value for money: *an economy pack of soap flakes*.
IDIOMS – **economy of scale** a proportionate saving in costs gained by an increased level of production.
SYNONYMS – **2** carefulness, frugality, prudence, restraint, thrift, thriftiness.
ANTONYMS – **2** extravagance.
ORIGIN – Greek *oikonomia* 'household management'.

ecosphere > *noun* a region in which life exists or could exist; the biosphere.

ecosystem > *noun* a biological community of interacting organisms and their physical environment.

ecotourism > *noun* tourism directed towards unspoiled natural environments and intended to support conservation efforts.
DERIVATIVES – **ecotour** *noun* & *verb* **ecotourist** *noun*.

ecotype > *noun* Botany & Zoology a distinct form or race of a plant or animal species occupying a particular habitat.

eco-warrior > *noun* a person actively involved in protecting the environment from damage.

ecru /aykrōō/ > *noun* the light cream or beige colour of unbleached linen.
ORIGIN – French, 'unbleached'.

ecstasy* /ekstəsi/ > *noun* (pl. **ecstasies**) **1** an overwhelming feeling of great happiness or joyful excitement. **2** an emotional or religious frenzy or trance-like state. **3** (**Ecstasy**) an illegal amphetamine-based synthetic drug with euphoric effects.
***SPELLING** – no *x*: there is a *cs* at the beginning and an *s* at the end: ec*s*tasy.
SYNONYMS – **1** bliss, elation, euphoria, joy.

wordpower facts
Ecstasy
The idea at the root of the word **ecstasy** is of 'standing outside oneself'. It entered English via Old French *extasie* from Greek *ekstasis*, which is based on *ek-* 'out' + *histanai* 'to place, stand, or set up'. This Greek verb is the source of English words such as **stand**, **static**, and **system**. At first **ecstasy** referred to a state of frenzy or stupor caused by strong emotion, of being 'beside oneself'. Later it came to denote a state of unconsciousness, or of religious frenzy or trance; the modern idea of 'overwhelming joy' arose by way of the sense 'a state of heightened feeling', which survives today in such phrases as *an ecstasy of grief*.

ecstatic /ikstattik/ > *adjective* feeling or characterised by ecstasy. > *noun* a person who is subject to mystical experiences.
DERIVATIVES – **ecstatically** *adverb*.
SYNONYMS – *adjective* blissful, delirious, elated, euphoric, joyful, joyous.

ECT > *abbreviation* electroconvulsive therapy.

ecto- > *combining form* outer; external: *ectoderm*.
ORIGIN – from Greek *ektos* 'outside'.

ectomorph /ektōmorf/ > *noun* Physiology a person with a lean and delicate build of body. Compare with **ENDOMORPH** and **MESOMORPH**.
DERIVATIVES – **ectomorphic** *adjective*.
ORIGIN – from *ectodermal* (the ectoderm

being the layer of the embryo giving rise to these physical characteristics).

-ectomy > *combining form* denoting surgical removal of a specified part of the body: *appendectomy*.

ORIGIN – from Greek *ektomē* 'excision'.

ectopic /ek**to**pik/ > *adjective* Medicine in an abnormal place or position.

COMBINATIONS – **ectopic pregnancy** a pregnancy in which the fetus develops outside the womb, typically in a Fallopian tube.

ORIGIN – Greek *ektopos* 'out of place'.

ectoplasm /**ek**tōplaz'm/ > *noun* a viscous substance that supposedly exudes from the body of a medium during a spiritualistic trance and forms the material for the manifestation of spirits.

DERIVATIVES – **ectoplasmic** *adjective*.

ecu /e**kyoo**, **ay**kyoo/ (also **ECU**) > *noun* (pl. same or **ecus**) former term for EURO.

ORIGIN – acronym from *European currency unit*.

Ecuadorean /ekwə**dor**iən/ (also **Ecuadorian**) > *noun* a person from Ecuador. > *adjective* relating to Ecuador.

ecumenical /eekyoo**menn**ik'l, ekyoo-/ > *adjective* **1** representing a number of different Christian Churches. **2** promoting or relating to unity among the world's Christian Churches.

DERIVATIVES – **ecumenically** *adverb*.

ORIGIN – Greek *oikoumenikos*, from *oikoumenē* 'the inhabited earth'.

ecumenism /i**kyoo**məniz'm/ > *noun* the principle or aim of promoting unity among the world's Christian Churches.

eczema /**eks**imə/ > *noun* a condition in which patches of skin become rough and inflamed, causing itching and bleeding.

DERIVATIVES – **eczematous** /ek**see**mətəss/ *adjective*.

ORIGIN – Greek *ekzema*, from *ekzein* 'boil over, break out'.

-ed¹ > *suffix* forming adjectives: **1** (added to nouns) having; possessing; affected by: *talented*. **2** from phrases consisting of adjective and noun: *bad-tempered*.

-ed² > *suffix* forming: **1** the past tense and past participle of weak verbs: *landed*. **2** participial adjectives: *wounded*.

Edam /**ee**dam/ > *noun* a round pale yellow cheese with a red wax coating.

ORIGIN – from *Edam* in the Netherlands, where it is made.

eddo /**edd**ō/ > *noun* (pl. **eddoes**) a cultivated West Indian plant, a variety of taro, with many small, edible corms.

ORIGIN – West African.

eddy > *noun* (pl. **eddies**) a circular movement of water causing a small whirlpool. > *verb* (**eddies**, **eddied**) (of water, air, smoke, etc.) move in a circular way.

SYNONYMS – *verb* churn, flow, surge, swirl.

edelweiss /**ay**d'lvīss/ > *noun* a European mountain plant which has woolly white bracts around its small flowers and downy grey-green leaves.

ORIGIN – German, from *edel* 'noble' + *weiss* 'white'.

edema > *noun* US spelling of OEDEMA.

Eden /**ee**d'n/ > *noun* **1** (also **Garden of Eden**) the place where Adam and Eve lived in the biblical account of the Creation. **2** a place or state of unspoilt happiness or beauty.

ORIGIN – Hebrew, probably from a word meaning 'delight'.

edentate /**ee**dentayt/ > *noun* Zoology a mammal of a group having no incisor or canine teeth, including the anteaters, sloths, and armadillos.

ORIGIN – from Latin *edentatus* 'toothless'.

edge > *noun* **1** the outside limit of an object, area, or surface. **2** the line along which two surfaces of a solid meet. **3** the sharpened side of a blade. **4** an intense or striking quality. **5** a quality or factor which gives superiority over close rivals. > *verb* **1** provide with an edge or border. **2** move carefully or furtively.

IDIOMS – **on edge** tense, nervous, or irritable. **set someone's teeth on edge** (of a sound or taste) cause intense discomfort or irritation to someone.

DERIVATIVES – **edged** *adjective* **edger** *noun*.

SYNONYMS – *noun* **1** border, boundary, fringe, margin, perimeter, periphery. **4** acerbity, asperity, bite, pointedness, sharpness.

ORIGIN – Old English, 'sharpened side of a blade'.

edgeways (also **edgewise**) > *adverb* with the edge uppermost or towards the viewer.

IDIOMS – **get a word in edgeways** manage to break into a lively conversation.

edging > *noun* something forming an edge or border.

edgy > *adjective* (**edgier**, **edgiest**) tense, nervous, or irritable.

DERIVATIVES – **edgily** *adverb* **edginess** *noun*.

EDI > *abbreviation* electronic data interchange.

edible > *adjective* fit to be eaten. > *noun* (**edibles**) items of food.

DERIVATIVES – **edibility** *noun*.

SYNONYMS – *adjective* consumable, digestible, eatable, palatable, wholesome.

ORIGIN – Latin *edibilis*, from *edere* 'eat'.

edict /**ee**dikt/ > *noun* an official order or proclamation.

SYNONYMS – declaration, decree, dictate, order, proclamation.

ORIGIN – Latin *edictum* 'something proclaimed', from *dicere* 'say, tell'.

edifice /**edd**ifiss/ > *noun* **1** a large, imposing building. **2** a complex abstract or conceptual system.

edify /**edd**ifī/ > *verb* (**edifies**, **edified**) formal instruct or improve morally or intellectually.

DERIVATIVES – **edification** *noun* **edifying** *adjective*.

wordpower facts
Edify
The words **edifice** and **edify** share the root concept of 'build'. **Edifice** comes from *aedificium* 'building' and **edify** from *aedificare* 'build', both of these Latin words being based on *aedis* 'dwelling' + *facere* 'make'. In English **edify** originally meant 'construct a building', also 'strengthen', hence 'build up' morally or spiritually.

edit > *verb* (**edited**, **editing**) **1** prepare (written material) for publication by correcting, condensing, or otherwise modifying it. **2** prepare and arrange material for (a recording or broadcast). **3** (**edit out**) remove (material) in preparing a recording or broadcast. **4** be editor of (a newspaper or magazine). > *noun* a change or correction made as a result of editing.

DERIVATIVES – **editable** *adjective*.

SYNONYMS – *verb* **1** abridge, check, copy-edit, correct, polish, revise.

ORIGIN – from EDITOR, reinforced by French *éditer* 'to edit'.

edition > *noun* **1** a particular form or version of a published text. **2** the total number of copies of a book, newspaper, etc. issued at one time. **3** a particular version or instance of a regular programme or broadcast.

editor > *noun* **1** a person who is in charge of a newspaper, magazine, or multi-author book. **2** a person who commissions written texts for publication. **3** a person who prepares texts or recorded material for publication or broadcasting.

DERIVATIVES – **editorship** *noun*.

ORIGIN – Latin, from *edere* 'put out'.

editorial > *adjective* relating to the commissioning or preparing of material for publication. > *noun* a newspaper article giving an opinion on a topical issue.

DERIVATIVES – **editorialist** *noun* **editorially** *adverb*.

editorialise (also **editorialize**) > *verb* (of a newspaper or editor) express opinions rather than just report news.

editress (also **editrix**) > *noun* dated or humorous a female editor.

EDT > *abbreviation* Eastern Daylight Time.

educate /**ed**yookayt/ > *verb* **1** give intellectual, moral, and social instruction to.

2 train or give information on a particular subject.

DERIVATIVES – **educable** *adjective* **educative** *adjective* **educator** *noun*.

SYNONYMS – **1** guide, inform, instruct, school, train, tutor.

COMBINATIONS – **educated guess** a guess based on knowledge and experience.

ORIGIN – Latin *educare* 'lead out'.

education > *noun* **1** the process of educating or being educated. **2** the theory and practice of teaching. **3** information about or training in a particular subject. **4** (**an education**) informal an enlightening experience.

DERIVATIVES – **educational** *adjective* **educationalist** *noun* **educationally** *adverb* **educationist** *noun*.

SYNONYMS – **1** guidance, instruction, schooling, training, tuition.

educe /iˈdyooss/ > *verb* formal **1** bring out or develop (something latent or potential). **2** infer from data.

DERIVATIVES – **eduction** *noun*.

ORIGIN – Latin *educere* 'lead out'.

Edwardian /edˈwawrdiən/ > *adjective* relating to the reign of King Edward VII (1901–10). > *noun* a person who lived during this period.

-ee > *suffix* forming nouns: **1** denoting the person affected directly or indirectly by the action of a verb: *employee*. **2** denoting a person described as or concerned with: *absentee*. **3** denoting an object of relatively smaller size: *bootee*.

ORIGIN – Old French *-é*, from Latin *-atus*; some forms are anglicised modern French nouns (e.g. *refugee* from *réfugié*).

EEC > *abbreviation* European Economic Community.

EEG > *abbreviation* electroencephalogram or electroencephalograph.

eejit /ˈeejit/ > *noun* informal Irish and Scottish form of **IDIOT**.

eel > *noun* a snake-like fish with a slender elongated body and poorly developed fins.

WORDFINDER – anguilliform (*eel-like*), elver (*young eel*).

DERIVATIVES – **eel-like** *adjective* **eely** *adjective*.

COMBINATIONS – **eelgrass 1** a marine plant with long ribbon-like leaves. **2** a submerged aquatic plant with narrow, grass-like leaves. **eelworm** a small soil nematode that can become a serious pest of crops and ornamental plants.

e'er /air/ > *adverb* literary form of **EVER**.

-eer > *suffix* **1** denoting a person concerned with or engaged in an activity: *auctioneer*. **2** denoting concern or involvement with an activity: *electioneer*.

ORIGIN – French *-ier*, from Latin *-arius*.

eerie /ˈeeri/ > *adjective* (**eerier**, **eeriest**) strange and frightening.

DERIVATIVES – **eerily** *adverb* **eeriness** *noun*.

SYNONYMS – ghostly, sinister, supernatural, uncanny, weird.

ORIGIN – first in northern English and Scots use, meaning 'fearful': probably from Old English *earg* 'cowardly'.

EFA > *abbreviation* essential fatty acid.

eff > *noun & verb* Brit. used as a euphemism for 'fuck'.

IDIOMS – **eff and blind** informal use swear words.

DERIVATIVES – **effing** *adjective & adverb*.

efface /iˈfayss/ > *verb* **1** erase (a mark) from a surface. **2** (**efface oneself**) make oneself appear insignificant or inconspicuous.

DERIVATIVES – **effacement** *noun*.

ORIGIN – first used in the sense 'pardon or be absolved from (an offence)': from French *effacer*, from *e-* 'away from' + *face* 'face'.

effect > *noun* **1** a change which is a result or consequence of an action or other cause. **2** the state of being or becoming operative. **3** the extent to which something succeeds or is operative: *wind power can be used to great effect*. **4** (**effects**) the lighting, sound, or scenery used in a play or film. **5** (**effects**) personal belongings. **6** Physics a physical phenomenon, typically named after its discoverer: *the Renner effect*. > *verb* cause to happen; bring about.

IDIOMS – **for effect** in order to impress people. **in effect** in practice, even if not formally acknowledged. **to that effect** having that general result, purpose, or meaning.

USAGE – do not confuse **effect** and **affect**. **Affect** means 'make a difference to', whereas **effect** means 'a result' or 'bring about (a result)'.

SYNONYMS – *noun* **1** consequence, impact, result. *verb* **1** bring about, carry out, cause, do, implement.

ORIGIN – Latin *effectus*, from *efficere* 'accomplish'.

effective > *adjective* **1** producing a desired or intended result. **2** (of a law or policy) operative. **3** existing in fact, though not formally acknowledged as such.

DERIVATIVES – **effectively** *adverb* **effectiveness** *noun* **effectivity** *noun*.

SYNONYMS – **1** effectual, efficacious, efficient, powerful, successful.

ANTONYMS – **1** ineffective, unsuccessful.

effectual /iˈfektyooəl/ > *adjective* **1** effective. **2** Law (of a legal document) valid or binding.

DERIVATIVES – **effectuality** *noun* **effectually** *adverb* **effectualness** *noun*.

effeminate /iˈfemminət/ > *adjective* (of a man) having characteristics regarded as typical of a woman.

DERIVATIVES – **effeminacy** *noun* **effeminately** *adverb*.

SYNONYMS – effete, unmanly, womanly.

ANTONYMS – manly, virile.

ORIGIN – from Latin *effeminare* 'make feminine'.

effendi /eˈfendi/ > *noun* (pl. **effendis**) a man of high education or social standing in an eastern Mediterranean or Arab country.

ORIGIN – Turkish *efendi*, from Greek *authentēs* 'lord, master'.

efferent /ˈeffərənt/ Physiology > *adjective* relating to the conduction of nerve impulses or blood outwards or away from something. The opposite of **AFFERENT**. > *noun* an efferent nerve fibre or blood vessel.

ORIGIN – from Latin *efferre* 'carry out'.

effervescent > *adjective* **1** (of a liquid) giving off bubbles; fizzy. **2** vivacious and enthusiastic.

DERIVATIVES – **effervesce** *verb* **effervescence** *noun*.

ORIGIN – Latin, from *effervescere* 'boil up'.

effete /iˈfeet/ > *adjective* **1** affected, over-refined, and ineffectual. **2** having lost vitality; worn out.

DERIVATIVES – **effetely** *adverb* **effeteness** *noun*.

ORIGIN – Latin *effetus* 'worn out by bearing young'; related to **FETUS**.

efficacious /effiˈkayshəss/ > *adjective* formal effective.

DERIVATIVES – **efficaciously** *adverb* **efficaciousness** *noun* **efficacy** /ˈeffikəsi/ *noun*.

ORIGIN – from Latin *efficere* 'accomplish'.

efficiency > *noun* (pl. **efficiencies**) the state or quality of being efficient.

SYNONYMS – competence, orderliness, organisation.

ANTONYMS – inefficiency.

efficient > *adjective* **1** (of a system or machine) working productively with minimum wasted effort or expense. **2** (of a person) well organised and competent.

DERIVATIVES – **efficiently** *adverb*.

SYNONYMS – **1** methodical, productive, streamlined, systematic. **2** able, capable, competent, organised, professional.

ANTONYMS – inefficient.

ORIGIN – Latin, from *efficere* 'accomplish'.

effigy /ˈeffiji/ > *noun* (pl. **effigies**) a sculpture or model of a person.

ORIGIN – Latin *effigies*, from *effingere* 'to fashion'.

effloresce /efloˈress/ > *verb* **1** (of a substance) lose moisture and turn to a fine powder on exposure to air. **2** (of salts) come to the surface of brickwork or other material and crystallise. **3** reach an optimum stage of development.

DERIVATIVES – **efflorescence** *noun* **efflorescent** *adjective*.

ORIGIN – Latin *efflorescere*, from *e-* 'out' + *florescere* 'begin to bloom'.

effluence /**eff**loo‍ənss/ > *noun* **1** a substance that flows out. **2** the action of flowing out.

ORIGIN – from Latin *effluere* 'flow out'.

effluent > *noun* liquid waste or sewage discharged into a river or the sea.

effluvium /i**floo**viəm/ > *noun* (pl. **effluvia** /i**floo**viə/) an unpleasant or harmful odour or discharge.

ORIGIN – Latin, from *effluere* 'flow out'.

effort > *noun* **1** a vigorous or determined attempt. **2** strenuous physical or mental exertion.

DERIVATIVES – **effortful** *adjective*.

SYNONYMS – **1** attempt, endeavour, try. **2** application, endeavour, exertion, labour, sweat, toil.

ORIGIN – Old French *esforcier*, from Latin *ex-* 'out' + *fortis* 'strong'.

effortless > *adjective* done or achieved without effort; natural and easy.

DERIVATIVES – **effortlessly** *adverb* **effortlessness** *noun*.

SYNONYMS – easy, painless, simple, straightforward.

ANTONYMS – awkward, difficult.

effrontery /i**frun**təri/ > *noun* insolence or impertinence.

ORIGIN – French *effronterie*, from Latin *effrons* 'shameless, barefaced', from *ex-* 'out' + *frons* 'forehead'.

effulgent /i**ful**jənt/ > *adjective* literary shining brightly.

DERIVATIVES – **effulgence** *noun* **effulgently** *adverb*.

ORIGIN – Latin, from *effulgere* 'shine brightly'.

effusion > *noun* **1** an instance of giving off a liquid, light, or smell. **2** Medicine an escape of fluid into a body cavity. **3** an instance of unrestrained speech or writing.

DERIVATIVES – **effuse** *verb*.

ORIGIN – Latin, from *effundere* 'pour out'.

effusive > *adjective* expressing gratitude, pleasure, or approval in an unrestrained manner.

DERIVATIVES – **effusively** *adverb* **effusiveness** *noun*.

SYNONYMS – extravagant, fulsome, gushing, unreserved, unrestrained.

ANTONYMS – reserved, restrained.

EFL > *abbreviation* English as a foreign language.

eft /eft/ > *noun* **1** dialect a newt. **2** Zoology the juvenile stage of a newt.

EFTA > *abbreviation* European Free Trade Association.

e.g. > *abbreviation* for example.

ORIGIN – from Latin *exempli gratia* 'for the sake of example'.

egalitarian /igali**tair**iən/ > *adjective* in accordance with the principle that all people are equal and deserve equal rights and opportunities. > *noun* an egalitarian person.

DERIVATIVES – **egalitarianism** *noun*.

ORIGIN – French *égalitaire*, from *égal* 'equal', from Latin *aequalis*.

egg[1] > *noun* **1** an oval or round object laid by a female bird, reptile, fish, or invertebrate and containing an ovum which if fertilised can develop into a new organism. **2** an infertile egg of the domestic hen, used for food. **3** Biology the female reproductive cell in animals and plants; an ovum. **4** informal, dated a person of a specified kind: *a good egg*.

WORDFINDER – albumen (*egg white*), clutch (*set of eggs laid together*), incubate (*keep eggs warm for hatching*), oology (*study of birds' eggs*), ovate, oviform, ovoid (*egg-shaped*), oviparous (*egg-laying*), spawn (*fish or amphibian eggs*).

IDIOMS – **don't put all your eggs in one basket** proverb don't risk everything on the success of one venture. **kill the goose that lays the golden eggs** destroy a reliable and valuable source of income. [ORIGIN – with allusion to one of Aesop's fables.] **with egg on one's face** informal appearing foolish or ridiculous.

DERIVATIVES – **eggy** *adjective*.

COMBINATIONS – **egg custard** a custard made with milk and eggs, typically sweetened and baked. **egg-nog** (Brit. also **egg-flip**) a drink consisting of wine or other alcohol mixed with beaten egg and milk. **eggshell 1** the thin, hard, fragile outer layer of an egg. **2** (of china) extremely thin and delicate. **3** denoting an oil-based paint that dries with a slight sheen. **egg white** the clear, viscous substance round the yolk of an egg that turns white when cooked or beaten.

egg[2] > *verb* (**egg on**) urge or encourage (someone) to do something foolish or risky.

ORIGIN – Old Norse *eggja* 'incite'.

egghead > *noun* informal a very academic or studious person.

eggplant > *noun* chiefly N. Amer. another term for **AUBERGINE**.

eglantine /**eg**lantīn/ > *noun* another term for **SWEETBRIAR**.

ORIGIN – Old French, from Provençal *aiglentina*, from Latin *acus* 'needle' or *aculeus* 'prickle'.

EGM > *abbreviation* extraordinary general meeting.

ego /**ee**gō, **eg**ō/ > *noun* (pl. **egos**) **1** a person's sense of self-esteem or self-importance. **2** Psychoanalysis the part of the mind that is responsible for the interpretation of reality and the development of a sense of self. Compare with **ID** and **SUPEREGO**.

COMBINATIONS – **ego trip** informal something done as a result of an undue sense of self-importance.

ORIGIN – Latin, 'I'.

egocentric > *adjective* **1** self-centred. **2** centred in or arising from a person's own individual existence or perspective. > *noun* an egocentric person.

DERIVATIVES – **egocentrically** *adverb* **egocentricity** *noun* **egocentrism** *noun*.

egoism > *noun* an ethical theory that treats self-interest as the foundation of morality.

DERIVATIVES – **egoist** *noun* **egoistic** *adjective* **egoistical** *adjective*.

USAGE – Although they are often confused, **egoism** and **egotism** do not mean the same thing. It is **egotism**, not **egoism**, that means 'excessive conceit or self-absorption'; **egoism** is a less common and more technical word.

egomania > *noun* obsessive egotism.

DERIVATIVES – **egomaniac** *noun* **egomaniacal** *adjective*.

egotism > *noun* the quality of being excessively conceited or absorbed in oneself.

DERIVATIVES – **egotist** *noun* **egotistic** *adjective*.

egotistical > *adjective* excessively conceited or self-absorbed.

DERIVATIVES – **egotistically** *adverb*.

SYNONYMS – conceited, egocentric, self-absorbed, self-centred, selfish.

SYNONYMS – modest, unassuming.

egregious /i**gree**jəss/ > *adjective* **1** outstandingly bad; shocking. **2** archaic remarkably good.

DERIVATIVES – **egregiously** *adverb* **egregiousness** *noun*.

ORIGIN – Latin *egregius* 'illustrious', literally 'standing out from the flock', from *ex-* 'out' + *grex* 'flock'.

egress /**ee**gress/ > *noun* formal **1** the action of going out of or leaving a place. **2** a way out. > *verb* chiefly US go out of or leave (a place).

DERIVATIVES – **egression** *noun*.

ORIGIN – Latin, from *egredi* 'go out'.

egret /**ee**grit/ > *noun* a heron with mainly white plumage, having long plumes in the breeding season.

ORIGIN – Old French *aigrette*, from the base of **HERON**.

Egyptian /i**jip**sh'n/ > *noun* **1** a person from Egypt. **2** the Afro-Asiatic language used in ancient Egypt, represented in its oldest stages by hieroglyphic inscriptions. > *adjective* relating to Egypt.

Egyptology /eejip**toll**əji/ > *noun* the study of the language, history, and culture of ancient Egypt.

DERIVATIVES – **Egyptological** *adjective* **Egyptologist** *noun*.

Eid /eed/ (also **Id**) > *noun* **1** (in full **Eid ul-Fitr** /eed oʻol **fee**trə/) the Muslim festival marking the end of the fast of

Ramadan. **2** (in full **Eid ul-Adha** /eed ŏŏl **aa**də/) the festival marking the culmination of the annual pilgrimage to Mecca.
ORIGIN – Arabic, 'feast'.

eider /**ī**də/ > *noun* (pl. same or **eiders**) **1** (also **eider duck**) a northern sea duck. **2** (also **eider down**) small, soft feathers from the breast of the female eider duck.
ORIGIN – Old Norse *æthr*.

eiderdown > *noun* chiefly Brit. a quilt filled with down (originally from the eider) or some other soft material.

eidetic /ī**dett**ik/ > *adjective* Psychology relating to mental images having unusual vividness and detail.
DERIVATIVES – **eidetically** *adverb*.
ORIGIN – Greek *eidētikos*, from *eidos* 'form'.

eight > *cardinal number* **1** one more than seven; 8. (Roman numeral: **viii** or **VIII**.) **2** an eight-oared rowing boat or its crew.
WORDFINDER – octad (*group or set of eight*), octagon (*plane figure with eight straight sides and angles*), octahedron (*three-dimensional shape with eight faces*), octennial (*lasting for or recurring every eight years*), octet (*group of eight musicians*).
IDIOMS – **figure of eight** (N. Amer. **figure eight**) an object or movement having the shape of the number eight. **have one over the eight** Brit. informal have one drink too many. **pieces of eight** historical Spanish dollars, equivalent to eight reals.

eighteen > *cardinal number* one more than seventeen; 18. (Roman numeral: **xviii** or **XVIII**.)
DERIVATIVES – **eighteenth** *ordinal number*.

eighth* > *ordinal number* **1** constituting number eight in a sequence; 8th. **2** (**an eighth** or **one eighth**) each of eight equal parts into which something is divided.
DERIVATIVES – **eighthly** *adverb*.
*SPELLING – there are two *h*s: eig*h*th.
COMBINATIONS – **eighth note** Music, chiefly N. Amer. a quaver.

eights > *plural noun* a race for eight-oared rowing boats.

eightsome reel > *noun* a lively Scottish dance for eight people.

eighty > *cardinal number* (pl. **eighties**) ten less than ninety; 80. (Roman numeral: **lxxx** or **LXXX**.)
WORDFINDER – octogenarian (*person aged 80–89*).
DERIVATIVES – **eightieth** *ordinal number*.

Einstein /**īn**stīn/ > *noun* informal a genius.
ORIGIN – from the name of the German-born physicist Albert *Einstein* (1879–1955), originator of the theory of relativity.

einsteinium /īn**stīn**iəm/ > *noun* an unstable radioactive chemical element made by high-energy atomic collisions.

eisteddfod /ī**steth**vod/ > *noun* (pl. **eisteddfods** or **eisteddfodau** /īsteth-

vədī/) a competitive festival of music and poetry in Wales.
ORIGIN – Welsh, 'session'.

either /**ī**thər, **ee**thər/ > *conjunction & adverb* **1** used before the first of two (or occasionally more) alternatives specified (the other being introduced by 'or'). **2** (adverb) used to indicate a similarity or link with a statement just made: *You don't like him, do you? I don't either.* **3** (adverb) for that matter; moreover. > *determiner & pronoun* **1** one or the other of two people or things. **2** each of two.

ejaculate > *verb* /i**jak**yoolayt/ **1** (of a man or male animal) eject semen from the body at the moment of sexual climax. **2** dated say something quickly and suddenly. > *noun* /i**jak**yoolət/ semen that has been ejaculated.
DERIVATIVES – **ejaculation** *noun* **ejaculator** *noun* **ejaculatory** /ijak-**yool**ətəri/ *adjective*.

eject > *verb* **1** force or throw out violently or suddenly. **2** compel (someone) to leave a place. **3** (of a pilot) escape from an aircraft by means of an ejection seat.
DERIVATIVES – **ejection** *noun* **ejector** *noun*.
SYNONYMS – **1** emit, expel, force out, throw out. **2** evict, expel, throw out.
COMBINATIONS – **ejection seat** (also **ejector seat**) an aircraft seat that can propel its occupant from the craft in an emergency.

---

wordpower facts

Eject

Eject is one of a number of words based on Latin *jacere* 'to throw'. This Latin verb is the source of the *-ject-* part of many words with a core idea of throwing or movement, for example **inject, interject, object, project, reject, subject,** and **trajectory; ejaculate** and **jet** are also ultimately from *jacere*, as are **abject** (literally 'rejected') and **dejected** (literally 'thrown down'). There is also another Latin verb *jacere*, which means 'to lie down' and is the source of **adjacent** and **joist**.

---

eke¹ /eek/ > *verb* (**eke out**) **1** use or consume frugally. **2** make (a living) with difficulty.
SYNONYMS – (**eke out**) **1** economise on, skimp on, be thrifty with.
ORIGIN – Old English, 'increase'.

eke² /eek/ > *adverb* archaic term for ALSO.

elaborate > *adjective* /i**labb**ərət/ involving many carefully arranged parts; detailed and complicated. > *verb* /i**labb**ərayt/ **1** develop or present in detail. **2** (**elaborate on**) add more detail to (something already said).

DERIVATIVES – **elaborately** *adverb* **elaborateness** *noun* **elaboration** *noun*.
SYNONYMS – *adjective* complex, complicated, detailed, intricate, involved, ornate. *verb* **2** (**elaborate on**) amplify, enlarge on, expand on, expatiate on, flesh out.
ANTONYMS – *adjective* simple.
ORIGIN – from Latin *elaborare* 'work out'.

elan /i**lan**/ > *noun* energy and flair.
ORIGIN – French, from *élancer* 'to dart'.

eland /**ee**lənd/ > *noun* a spiral-horned African antelope, the largest of the antelopes.
ORIGIN – Dutch, 'elk'.

elapse > *verb* (of time) pass.
SYNONYMS – go by, pass, slip by.
ORIGIN – Latin *elabi* 'slip away'.

elastane /i**last**ayn/ > *noun* an elastic polyurethane material, used for close-fitting clothing.

elastic /i**last**ik/ > *adjective* **1** able to resume normal shape spontaneously after being stretched or squeezed. **2** flexible and adaptable. > *noun* cord, tape, or fabric which returns to its original length or shape after being stretched.
DERIVATIVES – **elastically** *adverb* **elasticise** (also **elasticize**) *verb* **elasticity** /illas**tiss**iti/ *noun*.
SYNONYMS – *adjective* **1** flexible, pliable, pliant, resilient, springy, stretchy, supple.
ANTONYMS – *adjective* rigid.
COMBINATIONS – **elastic band** a rubber band.
ORIGIN – Greek *elastikos* 'propulsive'.

elasticated > *adjective* chiefly Brit. (of a garment or material) made elastic by the insertion of rubber thread or tape.

elastin /i**last**in/ > *noun* Biochemistry an elastic, fibrous protein found in connective tissue.

elastomer /i**last**əmər/ > *noun* a natural or synthetic polymer having elastic properties, e.g. rubber.
DERIVATIVES – **elastomeric** *adjective*.

Elastoplast > *noun* trademark sticking plaster for covering cuts and wounds.

elated /i**layt**id/ > *adjective* extremely happy and excited.
DERIVATIVES – **elatedly** *adverb* **elation** *noun*.
SYNONYMS – ecstatic, euphoric, exultant, joyful, jubilant, overjoyed.
ORIGIN – Latin *elatus* 'raised', from *efferre* 'to raise'.

elbow > *noun* **1** the joint between the forearm and the upper arm. **2** a piece of piping or something similar bent through an angle. > *verb* **1** strike with one's elbow. **2** shove roughly in a particular direction: *she elbowed him out of the way.* **3** (often **elbow one's way**) move by pushing past people with one's elbows.
IDIOMS – **give someone the elbow** informal

summarily reject or dismiss someone. **up to one's elbows in** informal deeply involved in.

COMBINATIONS – **elbow grease** informal hard physical work, especially vigorous polishing or cleaning. **elbow room** informal adequate space to move or work in.

ORIGIN – Old English, related to ELL, BOW[1].

eld > noun literary 1 old age. 2 former times; the past.

ORIGIN – Old English, related to ELDER[1] and OLD.

elder[1] > adjective (of one or more out of a group of people) of a greater age. > noun 1 (one's elder) a person of greater age than oneself. 2 a leader or senior figure in a tribe. 3 an official or minister in certain Churches.

COMBINATIONS – **elder statesman** an experienced and respected politician or other public figure.

elder[2] > noun a small tree or shrub with white flowers and bluish-black or red berries.

COMBINATIONS – **elderberry** the berry of the elder, used for making jelly or wine. **elderflower** the blossom of the elder, used to make wines and cordials.

elderly > adjective old or ageing.

DERIVATIVES – **elderliness** noun.

SYNONYMS – aged, ageing, old; technical senescent.

eldest > adjective (of one out of a group of people) oldest.

El Dorado /el dəraadō/ (also **eldorado**) > noun (pl. **El Dorados**) a place of great abundance and wealth.

ORIGIN – Spanish, 'the gilded one', the name of a country or city formerly believed to exist in South America.

eldritch /**el**drich/ > adjective weird and sinister or ghostly.

ORIGIN – Scots: perhaps related to ELF.

elect > verb 1 choose (someone) to hold a position, especially public office, by voting. 2 opt for or choose to do something. > adjective 1 chosen or singled out. 2 elected to a position but not yet in office: the President Elect.

DERIVATIVES – **electable** adjective.

SYNONYMS – verb 1 appoint, return, vote in. adjective 2 designate, future, to be.

ORIGIN – Latin eligere 'pick out'.

election > noun 1 a formal procedure whereby a person is elected, especially to a political office. 2 the action or fact of electing or being elected.

WORDFINDER – psephology (statistical study of elections and voting).

SYNONYMS – 1 ballot, plebiscite, poll, referendum, vote.

electioneer > verb campaign to be elected

to public office. > noun a campaigning politician during an election.

elective > adjective 1 relating to or appointed by election. 2 (of a course of study, treatment, etc.) selected by the person concerned; not compulsory. > noun chiefly N. Amer. an optional course of study.

DERIVATIVES – **electively** adverb.

elector > noun 1 a person who has the right to vote in an election. 2 (in the US) a member of the electoral college. 3 historical a German prince entitled to take part in the election of the Holy Roman Emperor.

DERIVATIVES – **electorship** noun.

electoral > adjective of or relating to elections or electors.

DERIVATIVES – **electorally** adverb.

COMBINATIONS – **electoral college 1** a body of electors chosen or appointed by a larger group. 2 (in the US) a body of people representing the states of the US, who formally cast votes for the election of the President and Vice-President. **electoral roll** (also **electoral register**) an official list of the people in a district who are entitled to vote in an election.

electorate /i**lek**tərət/ > noun 1 the body of people in a country or area who are entitled to vote in an election. 2 Austral./NZ the area represented by one Member of Parliament. 3 historical the office or territories of a German elector.

electric > adjective 1 of, worked by, or producing electricity. 2 thrillingly exciting. > noun 1 (**electrics**) Brit. the system of electric wiring and parts in a house or vehicle. 2 an electric train or other vehicle.

DERIVATIVES – **electrically** adverb.

COMBINATIONS – **electric blanket** an electrically wired blanket used for heating a bed. **electric blue** a steely or brilliant light blue. **electric chair** a chair in which convicted criminals are executed by electrocution. **electric eel** a large eel-like freshwater fish of South America, which uses pulses of electricity to kill prey, assist in navigation, and for defence. **electric eye** informal a photoelectric cell operating a relay when the beam of light illuminating it is obscured. **electric fence** a fence through which an electric current can be passed, giving an electric shock to any person or animal touching it. **electric guitar** a guitar with a built-in pickup which converts sound vibrations into electrical signals for amplification. **electric shock** a sudden discharge of electricity through a part of the body. **electric storm** a thunderstorm or other violent disturbance of the electrical condition of the atmosphere.

ORIGIN – from Latin electrum 'amber', from Greek ēlektron (because rubbing amber causes electrostatic phenomena).

electrical > adjective concerned with, operating by, or producing electricity. > noun (**electricals**) electrical equipment or circuitry.

electrician > noun a person who installs and maintains electrical equipment.

electricity > noun 1 a form of energy resulting from the existence of charged particles (such as electrons or protons), either statically as an accumulation of charge or dynamically as a current. 2 the supply of electric current to a building for heating, lighting, etc. 3 thrilling excitement.

electrify > verb (**electrifies, electrified**) 1 charge with electricity. 2 convert to the use of electrical power.

DERIVATIVES – **electrification** noun **electrifier** noun.

electrifying > adverb causing thrilling excitement or admiration.

electrocardiography /ilektrōkaardi-**og**rəfi/ > noun the measurement and recording of activity in the heart using electrodes placed on the skin.

DERIVATIVES – **electrocardiogram** noun **electrocardiograph** noun **electrocardiographic** adjective.

electroconvulsive > adjective relating to or denoting the treatment of mental illness by applying electric shocks to the brain.

electrocute > verb injure or kill by electric shock.

DERIVATIVES – **electrocution** noun.

electrode /i**lek**trōd/ > noun a conductor through which electricity enters or leaves something.

ORIGIN – from Greek hodos 'way', on the pattern of anode and cathode.

electrodynamics > plural noun (usu. treated as sing.) the branch of mechanics concerned with the interaction of electric currents with magnetic or electric fields.

DERIVATIVES – **electrodynamic** adjective.

electroencephalography /ilektrō-ensef**alog**rəfi, -keff-/ > noun the measurement and recording of electrical activity in the brain.

DERIVATIVES – **electroencephalogram** noun **electroencephalograph** noun.

electrolyse /i**lek**trəliz/ (US **electrolyze**) > verb subject to electrolysis.

DERIVATIVES – **electrolyser** noun.

electrolysis /ilek**troll**isiss/ > noun 1 chemical decomposition produced by passing an electric current through a conducting liquid. 2 the breaking up and removal of hair roots or small blemishes on the skin by means of an electric current.

DERIVATIVES – **electrolytic** /ilektrə**litt**ik/ adjective.

electrolyte /i**lek**trəlīt/ > noun 1 a liquid or gel which contains ions and can be decomposed by electrolysis (as found in a

307

battery, for example). **2** *Physiology* the ionic constituents of cells, blood, etc.

ORIGIN – from Greek *lutos* 'released'.

electromagnet > *noun* a metal core made into a magnet by the passage of electric current through a surrounding coil.

electromagnetic > *adjective* relating to the interrelation of electric currents or fields and magnetic fields.

DERIVATIVES – **electromagnetically** *adverb* **electromagnetism** *noun*.

COMBINATIONS – **electromagnetic radiation** a kind of radiation including visible light, radio waves, gamma rays, and X-rays, in which electric and magnetic fields vary simultaneously.

electrometer /illek**tromm**itər/ > *noun* an instrument for measuring electrical potential without drawing any current from the circuit.

electromotive /ilektrə**mō**tiv/ > *adjective* tending to produce an electric current.

COMBINATIONS – **electromotive force** a difference in potential that tends to give rise to an electric current.

electromyography /ilektrōmī**og**rəfi/ > *noun* the measurement and recording of the electrical activity of muscles by means of electrodes.

DERIVATIVES – **electromyogram** *noun* **electromyograph** *noun* **electromyographic** *adjective*.

electron > *noun* Physics a stable negatively charged subatomic particle with a mass 1,836 times less than that of the proton, found in all atoms and acting as the major carrier of electricity in solids.

COMBINATIONS – **electron gun** a device for producing a narrow stream of electrons from a heated cathode. **electron microscope** a microscope with high magnification and resolution, employing electron beams in place of light.

electronic > *adjective* **1** having components such as microchips and transistors that control and direct electric currents. **2** relating to electrons or electronics. **3** relating to or carried out by means of a computer or other electronic device: *electronic shopping*.

DERIVATIVES – **electronically** *adverb*.

COMBINATIONS – **electronic mail** email. **electronic publishing** the issuing of texts in machine-readable form rather than on paper.

electronics > *plural noun* **1** (usu. treated as sing.) the branch of physics and technology concerned with the behaviour and movement of electrons, especially in semiconductors and gases. **2** (treated as pl.) circuits or devices using transistors, microchips, etc.

electronvolt > *noun* Physics a unit of energy equal to the work done on an electron in

accelerating it through a potential difference of one volt.

electrophoresis /ilektrōfə**ree**siss/ > *noun* Physics & Chemistry the movement of charged particles in a fluid or gel under the influence of an electric field.

DERIVATIVES – **electrophoretic** *adjective*.

ORIGIN – from Greek *phorēsis* 'being carried'.

electroplate /i**lek**trəplayt/ > *verb* coat (a metal object) with a layer of another metal by means of electrolysis. > *noun* electroplated articles.

DERIVATIVES – **electroplater** *noun* **electroplating** *noun*.

electroscope > *noun* an instrument for detecting and measuring electric charge.

electroshock > *adjective* another term for **ELECTROCONVULSIVE**.

electrostatic > *adjective* relating to stationary electric charges or fields as opposed to electric currents.

DERIVATIVES – **electrostatics** *plural noun*.

electrosurgery > *noun* surgery using a high-frequency electric current to cut tissue.

DERIVATIVES – **electrosurgical** *adjective*.

electrotechnology > *noun* the technological application of electricity.

DERIVATIVES – **electrotechnical** *adjective*.

electrotherapy > *noun* the use of electric currents passed through the body to treat paralysis and other disorders.

electrum /i**lek**trəm/ > *noun* an alloy of gold with at least 20 per cent of silver, used for jewellery.

ORIGIN – Greek *ēlektron* 'amber, electrum'.

eleemosynary /elli-ee**moss**inəri/ > *adjective* formal charitable.

ORIGIN – first used as a noun denoting a place where alms were distributed: from Latin *eleemosyna*, from Greek *eleēmosunē* 'compassion'; compare with **ALMS**.

elegant > *adjective* **1** graceful and stylish. **2** pleasingly ingenious and simple.

DERIVATIVES – **elegance** *noun* **elegantly** *adverb*.

SYNONYMS – **1** chic, graceful, refined, stylish, suave.

ANTONYMS – **1** inelegant.

ORIGIN – Latin *elegans* 'discriminating', related to *eligere* 'choose, select'.

elegiac /elli**ji**ək/ > *adjective* **1** relating to or characteristic of an elegy. **2** wistfully mournful.

DERIVATIVES – **elegiacally** *adverb*.

elegise /**elli**jīz/ (also **elegize**) > *verb* write in a wistfully mournful way.

elegy /**ell**iji/ > *noun* (pl. **elegies**) a mournful poem, typically a lament for the dead.

ORIGIN – Greek *elegos* 'mournful poem'.

element > *noun* **1** a basic constituent part: *there are four elements to the proposal*. **2** (also **chemical element**) each of more than one

hundred substances that cannot be chemically interconverted or broken down. **3** any of the four substances (earth, water, air, and fire) regarded as the fundamental constituents of the world in ancient and medieval philosophy. **4** a trace: *an element of danger*. **5** a distinct group within a larger group: *right-wing elements in the army*. **6** (**the elements**) the weather, especially bad weather. **7** (**one's element**) one's natural or preferred environment: *he was in his element working around the house*. **8** a part in an electric device consisting of a wire through which an electric current is passed to provide heat.

WORDFINDER – allotrope (*different form of a chemical element*), isotope (*form of the same element having different atomic mass*), periodic table (*tabulation of chemical elements*), transmutation (*change of one element into another, in particle physics or supposedly in alchemy*), valency (*combining power of an element*).

SYNONYMS – **1** component, constituent, ingredient, part.

ORIGIN – Latin *elementum* 'principle, rudiment'.

elemental /elli**ment**'l/ > *adjective* **1** fundamental. **2** of or resembling the powerful and primitive forces of nature: *elemental hatred*. **3** relating to or of the nature of a chemical element.

elementary > *adjective* **1** of or relating to the most rudimentary aspects of a subject. **2** straightforward and uncomplicated. **3** not decomposable into elements or other primary constituents.

DERIVATIVES – **elementarily** *adverb*.

COMBINATIONS – **elementary school** a primary school, especially (N. Amer.) for the first six or eight grades.

elephant > *noun* (pl. same or **elephants**) a very large plant-eating mammal with a trunk, long curved tusks, and large ears, native to Africa and southern Asia.

WORDFINDER – howdah (*seat on elephant's back*), mahout (*elephant driver*), pachyderm (*elephant or other large thick-skinned mammal*).

DERIVATIVES – **elephantoid** /elli**fan**toyd/ *adjective*.

COMBINATIONS – **elephant grass** a very tall tropical African grass.

ORIGIN – Greek *elephas* 'ivory, elephant'.

elephantiasis /ellifən**tī**əsiss/ > *noun* Medicine a condition in which a limb becomes greatly swollen due to obstruction of the lymphatic vessels, especially by nematode parasites.

elephantine /elli**fan**tīn/ > *adjective* resembling or characteristic of an elephant, especially in being large or clumsy.

elevate /**ell**ivayt/ > *verb* **1** lift to a higher position. **2** raise to a higher level or status.
ORIGIN – Latin *elevare* 'to raise'.

elevated > *adjective* of a high intellectual or moral level.

elevation > *noun* **1** the action of elevating or the fact of being elevated. **2** height above a given level, especially sea level. **3** the angle of something with the horizontal. **4** a particular side of a building. **5** a scale drawing showing the vertical projection of one side of a building.
DERIVATIVES – **elevational** *adjective*.

elevator > *noun* **1** North American term for **LIFT** (in sense 1). **2** a machine consisting of an endless belt with scoops attached, used for raising grain. **3** N. Amer. a tall building used for storing grain.

eleven > *cardinal number* **1** one more than ten; 11. (Roman numeral: **xi** or **XI**.) **2** a sports team of eleven players.
DERIVATIVES – **elevenfold** *adjective* & *adverb*.
COMBINATIONS – **eleven-plus** (in the UK, especially formerly) an examination taken at the age of 11–12 to determine the type of secondary school a child should enter.
ORIGIN – Old English, from the base of **ONE** + a second element occurring also in **TWELVE**.

elevenses > *plural noun* Brit. informal a break for light refreshments taken at about eleven o'clock in the morning.

eleventh > *ordinal number* constituting number eleven in a sequence; 11th.
IDIOMS – **the eleventh hour** the latest possible moment.

elf > *noun* (pl. **elves**) a supernatural creature of folk tales, represented as a small, delicate human figure with pointed ears and a capricious nature.
DERIVATIVES – **elfish** *adjective* **elven** *adjective* (literary) **elvish** *adjective*.

elfin > *adjective* of or resembling an elf, especially in being small and delicate.

elicit /i**liss**it/ > *verb* (**elicited**, **eliciting**) **1** evoke or draw out (a response or reaction). **2** archaic draw forth into existence.
DERIVATIVES – **elicitation** *noun* **elicitor** *noun*.
SYNONYMS – **1** evoke, extract, generate, induce, prompt.
ORIGIN – Latin *elicere* 'to draw out by trickery'.

elide /i**līd**/ > *verb* **1** omit (a sound or syllable) when speaking. **2** join together; merge.
ORIGIN – Latin *elidere* 'crush out'.

eligible /**ell**ijib'l/ > *adjective* **1** satisfying the conditions to do or receive something: *you may be eligible for a refund.* **2** desirable or suitable as a spouse.
DERIVATIVES – **eligibility** *noun*.
ORIGIN – Latin *eligibilis*, from *eligere* 'choose, select'.

eliminate /i**limm**inayt/ > *verb* **1** completely remove or get rid of. **2** reject or exclude from consideration or further participation.
DERIVATIVES – **elimination** *noun* **eliminator** *noun*.
SYNONYMS – **1** eradicate, exterminate, remove, stamp out.
ORIGIN – Latin *eliminare* 'turn out of doors'.

elision /i**lizh**'n/ > *noun* **1** the omission of a sound or syllable in speech. **2** joining or merging.
ORIGIN – Latin, from *elidere* 'crush out'.

elite /i**leet**/ > *noun* **1** a group of people regarded as the best in a particular society or organisation. **2** a size of letter in typewriting, with 12 characters to the inch (about 4.7 to the centimetre).
SYNONYMS – **1** best, cream, crème de la crème, pick.
ORIGIN – French, 'selection, choice'.

elitism > *noun* **1** the belief that a society or system should be run by an elite. **2** the superior attitude or behaviour associated with an elite.
DERIVATIVES – **elitist** *adjective* & *noun*.

elixir /i**lik**seer/ > *noun* a magical or medicinal potion, especially (in former times) one supposedly able to change metals into gold or (the **elixir of life**) one able to prolong life indefinitely.
ORIGIN – Arabic, from Greek *xērion* 'powder for drying wounds'.

Elizabethan /ilizzə**bee**thən/ > *adjective* relating to or characteristic of the reign of Queen Elizabeth I. > *noun* a person, especially a writer, of the Elizabethan age.

elk /elk/ > *noun* (pl. same or **elks**) **1** a large northern deer with palmate antlers and a growth of skin hanging from the neck. **2** North American term for **WAPITI**.

ell > *noun* a former measure of length used mainly for textiles, normally 45 inches in England and 37 inches in Scotland.
ORIGIN – Old English, related to Latin *ulna* (see **ULNA**); the measure was originally linked to the length of the human arm or forearm. Compare with **CUBIT**.

ellipse /i**lips**/ > *noun* a regular oval shape, resulting when a cone is cut by a slanted plane which does not intersect the base or traced by a point moving in a plane so that the sum of its distances from two other points is constant.
ORIGIN – Greek *elleipsis* (see **ELLIPSIS**).

ellipsis /i**lip**siss/ > *noun* (pl. **ellipses** /i**lip**seez/) **1** the omission of words from speech or writing. **2** a set of dots indicating such an omission.
ORIGIN – Greek *elleipsis*, from *elleipein* 'leave out'.

ellipsoid /i**lip**soyd/ > *noun* a symmetrical three-dimensional figure with a circular cross-section when viewed along one axis and elliptical cross-sections when viewed along the other axes.
DERIVATIVES – **ellipsoidal** *adjective*.

elliptic > *adjective* relating to or having the form of an ellipse.
DERIVATIVES – **ellipticity** *noun*.

elliptical > *adjective* **1** another term for **ELLIPTIC**. **2** (of speech or text) using or involving ellipsis, especially so as to be difficult to understand.
DERIVATIVES – **elliptically** *adverb*.

elm > *noun* a tall deciduous tree with rough serrated leaves.

El Niño /el **nee**njō/ > *noun* (pl. **El Niños**) an irregularly occurring cycle of changes to ocean currents, atmospheric circulation, and weather patterns, affecting the Pacific region and other parts of the world.

wordpower facts

El Niño

El Niño in Spanish means 'the child' and is short for *El Niño de Navidad* 'the Christmas child'. Fishermen in South America used this name to refer ironically to an unwelcome warm ocean current which affected the Pacific Ocean off Peru and Ecuador annually, beginning usually in late December. Every few years **El Niño**, which temporarily displaced the cold, nutrient-rich Peruvian current, was much stronger than usual and had a damaging effect on fisheries. In recent decades the warm current has been recognised as part of a far-reaching climatic phenomenon extending across the entire Pacific region and beyond, and the name **El Niño** is used for the whole system. A reverse effect involving a cold current is referred to as **La Niña**, the female counterpart of El Niño.

elocution /ellə**kyoo**sh'n/ > *noun* **1** the skill of clear and expressive speech, especially of distinct pronunciation and articulation. **2** a particular style of speaking.
DERIVATIVES – **elocutionist** *noun*.
ORIGIN – Latin, from *eloqui* 'speak out'.

elongate /**ee**longgayt/ > *verb* make or become longer.
DERIVATIVES – **elongation** *noun*.
ORIGIN – first used in the sense 'move away': from Latin *elongare* 'place at a distance'.

elongated > *adjective* unusually long in relation to its width.

elope > *verb* run away secretly in order to get married.
DERIVATIVES – **elopement** *noun*.
ORIGIN – Old French *aloper*.

eloquence /**ell**əkwənss/ > *noun* fluent or persuasive speaking or writing.
ORIGIN – Latin *eloquentia*, from *eloqui* 'speak out'.

eloquent > *adjective* **1** fluent or persuasive in speech or writing. **2** clearly indicative or expressive: *his silence was eloquent of all he could have said.*
DERIVATIVES – **eloquently** *adverb*.
SYNONYMS – **1** articulate, fluent, lucid, silver-tongued.
ANTONYMS – **1** inarticulate.

else > *adverb* **1** in addition; besides. **2** different; instead.
IDIOMS – **or else 1** used to introduce the second of two alternatives. **2** in circumstances different from those mentioned; otherwise.

elsewhere > *adverb* in, at, or to some other place or other places. > *pronoun* some other place.

ELT > *abbreviation* English language teaching.

elucidate /iˈlōōsidayt, iˈlyōōsidayt/ > *verb* make clear; explain.
DERIVATIVES – **elucidation** *noun* **elucidatory** *adjective*.
ORIGIN – Latin *elucidare* 'to make clear'.

elude /iˈlōōd, iˈlyōōd/ > *verb* **1** evade or escape adroitly from. **2** fail to be attained or understood by: *the logic of this eluded her.*
SYNONYMS – **1** avoid, dodge, escape, evade.
ORIGIN – Latin *eludere*, from *ludere* 'to play'.

elusive > *adjective* **1** difficult to find, catch, or achieve. **2** difficult to remember.
DERIVATIVES – **elusively** *adverb* **elusiveness** *noun*.
ORIGIN – from Latin *eludere* 'elude'.

elver /**el**vər/ > *noun* a young eel.
ORIGIN – variant of dialect *eel-fare* 'the passage of young eels up a river', from FARE in its original sense 'a journey'.

elves plural of ELF.

Elysian /iˈlizziən/ > *adjective* **1** relating to Elysium or the Elysian Fields, the place in Greek mythology where heroes were conveyed after death. **2** of or like paradise.

em > *noun* Printing **1** a unit for measuring the width of printed matter, equal to the height of the type size being used. **2** a unit of measurement equal to twelve points.
COMBINATIONS – **em rule** Brit. a long dash used in punctuation, roughly the width of the letter *M*.

em- /im, em/ > *prefix* variant spelling of EN-¹, EN-² assimilated before *b*, *p* (as in *emblazon*, *emplacement*).

emaciated /iˈmay*siaytid/ > *adjective* abnormally thin and weak.
DERIVATIVES – **emaciation** *noun*.
SYNONYMS – atrophied, cadaverous, skeletal, wasted.
ORIGIN – from Latin *emaciare* 'make thin'.

email > *noun* the sending of messages by electronic means from one computer user to one or more recipients via a network. > *verb* mail or send using email.
WORDFINDER – flaming (*sending abusive or vitriolic emails*), spam (*irrelevant messages sent to many users*); *common email acronyms:* btw (*by the way*), FAQ (*frequently asked questions*), FWIW (*for what it's worth*), IMHO (*in my humble opinion*), OTOH (*on the other hand*), RTFM (*read the fucking manual*).
DERIVATIVES – **emailer** *noun*.
ORIGIN – abbreviation of *electronic mail*.

emalangeni plural of LILANGENI.

emanate /**emm**ənayt/ > *verb* **1** (**emanate from**) issue or spread out from (a source). **2** give out or emit: *he emanated a brooding air.*
ORIGIN – Latin *emanare* 'flow out'.

emanation > *noun* **1** something which emanates from a source. **2** (in various mystical traditions) a being or force which is a manifestation of God. **3** the action or process of emanating.

emancipate /iˈman*sipayt/ > *verb* **1** set free, especially from legal, social, or political restrictions. **2** free from slavery.
DERIVATIVES – **emancipation** *noun* **emancipator** *noun* **emancipatory** *adjective*.
SYNONYMS – **2** deliver, free, liberate, release; historical manumit.
ANTONYMS – **2** enslave.
ORIGIN – Latin *emancipare* 'transfer as property', from *mancipium* 'slave'.

emasculate /iˈmas*kyoolayt/ > *verb* **1** make weaker or less effective. **2** deprive (a man) of his male role or identity.
DERIVATIVES – **emasculation** *noun*.
ORIGIN – Latin *emasculare* 'castrate'.

embalm /imˈbaam/ > *verb* preserve (a corpse) from decay, originally with spices and now usually by injection of a preservative.
DERIVATIVES – **embalmer** *noun*.
ORIGIN – Old French *embaumer*, from *baume* 'balm'.

embankment > *noun* **1** a wall or bank built to prevent flooding by a river. **2** a bank of earth or stone built to carry a road or railway over an area of low ground.

embargo /emˈbaargō/ > *noun* (pl. **embargoes**) **1** an official ban, especially on trade or other commercial activity with a particular country. **2** historical an order of a state forbidding foreign ships to enter, or any ships to leave, its ports. > *verb* (**embargoes**, **embargoed**) impose an embargo on.
ORIGIN – Spanish, from *embargar* 'to arrest'.

embark > *verb* **1** go on board a ship or aircraft. **2** (**embark on**) begin (a new project or course of action).
DERIVATIVES – **embarkation** *noun*.

ORIGIN – French *embarquer*, from *barque* 'bark, ship'.

embarras de richesses /oNbaraa də reeˈshess/ (also **embarras de choix** /oNbaraa də ˈshwaa/) > *noun* a situation of having more options or resources than one knows what to do with.
ORIGIN – French, 'embarrassment of riches (or choice)'.

embarrass* /imˈbarrəss/ > *verb* **1** cause to feel awkward, self-conscious, or ashamed. **2** (**be embarrassed**) be caused financial difficulties.
DERIVATIVES – **embarrassed** *adjective* **embarrassedly** *adverb* **embarrassing** *adjective* **embarrassingly** *adverb* **embarrassment** *noun*.
*SPELLING – two *r*s, two *ss*: emba*rr*a*ss*.
SYNONYMS – **1** abash, humiliate, mortify, shame.
ORIGIN – Spanish *embarazar*, probably from Portuguese *embaraçar*, from *baraço* 'halter'.

embassy > *noun* (pl. **embassies**) **1** the official residence or offices of an ambassador. **2** chiefly historical a deputation sent by one state to another.
ORIGIN – Old French *ambasse*, from Latin *ambactus* 'servant' (related to AMBASSADOR).

embattled > *adjective* **1** prepared for battle, especially because surrounded by enemy forces. **2** beset by difficulties: *the embattled Chancellor.* **3** fortified; having battlements.

embed (also **imbed**) > *verb* (**embedded**, **embedding**) **1** fix firmly and deeply in a surrounding mass. **2** implant (an idea or feeling).
DERIVATIVES – **embedment** *noun*.

embellish > *verb* **1** make more attractive; decorate. **2** add extra details to (a story or account) for interest.
DERIVATIVES – **embellisher** *noun* **embellishment** *noun*.
SYNONYMS – **1** adorn, beautify, decorate, ornament. **2** elaborate, embroider, exaggerate.
ORIGIN – Old French *embellir*, from *bel* 'handsome'.

ember /**em**bər/ > *noun* a small piece of burning wood or coal in a dying fire.

Ember day > *noun* any of a number of days reserved for fasting and prayer in the Western Christian Church.
ORIGIN – Old English, perhaps from *ymbryne* 'period'.

embezzle /imˈbezz'l/ > *verb* steal or misappropriate (money placed in one's trust or under one's control).
DERIVATIVES – **embezzlement** *noun* **embezzler** *noun*.
ORIGIN – Old French *embesiler*, from *besiler* 'destroy, maltreat'.

embitter > *verb* make bitter or resentful.
DERIVATIVES – **embittered** *adjective*.

emblazon /imˈblayzˈn/ > verb 1 (usu. **be emblazoned**) conspicuously display (a design) on something. 2 depict (a heraldic device) on something.

emblem /ˈemblǝm/ > noun 1 a heraldic device or symbolic object as a distinctive badge of a nation, organisation, or family. 2 a symbol or symbolic representation.
DERIVATIVES – **emblematic** adjective.
SYNONYMS – **1** badge, crest, insignia, logo. **2** image, mark, sign, symbol.
ORIGIN – Greek emblēma 'insertion'.

emblematise /imˈblemmǝtīz/ (also **emblematize**) > verb formal serve as an emblem of.

embody > verb (**embodies, embodied**) 1 give a tangible or visible form to (an idea or quality). 2 include or contain as a constituent part.
DERIVATIVES – **embodiment** noun.

embolden > verb give courage or confidence to.

embolism /ˈembǝlizˈm/ > noun Medicine obstruction of an artery, typically by a clot of blood or an air bubble.
ORIGIN – Greek embolismos, from emballein 'insert'.

embolus /ˈembǝlǝss/ > noun (pl. **emboli** /ˈembǝlī/) a blood clot, air bubble, fatty deposit, or other object obstructing a blood vessel.
DERIVATIVES – **embolic** adjective.
ORIGIN – Greek embolos 'peg, stopper'.

embonpoint /ˈoNboNˈpwaN/ > noun plumpness or fleshiness, especially with reference to a woman's bosom.
ORIGIN – from French en bon point 'in good condition'.

emboss > verb carve a design in relief on.
DERIVATIVES – **embossed** adjective **embosser** noun.
ORIGIN – obsolete French embosser, from boce 'protuberance'.

embouchure /ˈombooshoor/ > noun 1 Music the way in which a player applies the mouth and tongue in playing a brass or wind instrument. 2 archaic the mouth of a river.
ORIGIN – French, from emboucher 'put in or to the mouth'.

embrace > verb 1 hold closely in one's arms, especially as a sign of affection. 2 include or contain. 3 accept or support (a belief or change) willingly. > noun an act of embracing.
DERIVATIVES – **embraceable** adjective.
SYNONYMS – verb **1** clasp, cuddle, enfold, hug.
ORIGIN – Old French embracer, from Latin bracchium 'arm'.

embrasure /imˈbrayzhǝr/ > noun 1 an opening in a wall or parapet, used for shooting through. 2 an opening or recess around a window or door forming an enlargement of the area from the inside.
ORIGIN – French, from obsolete embraser 'widen an opening'.

embrocation /ˈembrǝkayshˈn/ > noun a liquid medication rubbed on the body to relieve pain from sprains and strains.
ORIGIN – from Greek embrokhē 'lotion'.

embroider > verb 1 sew decorative needlework patterns on. 2 add fictitious or exaggerated details to.
DERIVATIVES – **embroiderer** noun.
ORIGIN – Old French enbrouder.

embroidery > noun (pl. **embroideries**) 1 the art or pastime of embroidering. 2 embroidered cloth.

embroil > verb involve deeply in a conflict or difficult situation.
DERIVATIVES – **embroilment** noun.
ORIGIN – French embrouiller 'to muddle'.

embryo /ˈembriō/ > noun (pl. **embryos**) 1 an unborn or unhatched offspring in the process of development, especially an unborn human in the first eight weeks from conception. Compare with FETUS. 2 the part of a seed which develops into a new plant.
IDIOMS – **in embryo** at a rudimentary stage.
DERIVATIVES – **embryonal** /ˈembriǝnˈl/ adjective.
ORIGIN – Greek embruon 'fetus'.

embryology /ˈembriollǝji/ > noun the branch of biology and medicine concerned with the study of embryos.
DERIVATIVES – **embryological** adjective **embryologist** noun.

embryonic /ˈembrionnik/ > adjective 1 relating to an embryo. 2 in or at a rudimentary stage.

emcee /ˈemsee/ N. Amer. informal > noun a master of ceremonies. > verb (**emcees, emceed, emceeing**) act as a master of ceremonies for or at.
ORIGIN – representing the pronunciation of **MC**.

emend /iˈmend/ > verb correct and revise (a text).
DERIVATIVES – **emendation** noun.
USAGE – **emend** and **amend** have similar, but not identical, meanings: **emend** means 'correct and revise (a text)', while **amend** means 'make minor improvements to (a document, rule, or proposal)'.
ORIGIN – Latin emendare, from menda 'a fault'.

emerald > noun 1 a bright green gem variety of beryl. 2 a bright green colour.
ORIGIN – Old French esmeraud, from Greek smaragdos.

emerge > verb 1 become gradually visible or apparent. 2 (of facts) become known. 3 recover from or survive a difficult period.
DERIVATIVES – **emergence** noun.
ORIGIN – Latin emergere, from mergere 'to dip'.

emergency > noun (pl. **emergencies**) 1 a serious, unexpected, and potentially dangerous situation requiring immediate action. 2 (before another noun) arising from or used in an emergency: an emergency exit. 3 N. Amer. the casualty department in a hospital.
SYNONYMS – **1** crisis, danger, predicament.
ORIGIN – Latin emergentia, from emergere 'emerge'.

emergent > adjective in the process of coming into being.

emeritus /iˈmerritǝss/ > adjective having retired but allowed to retain a title as an honour: an emeritus professor.
ORIGIN – Latin, from emereri 'earn one's discharge by service'.

emery /ˈemmǝri/ > noun a greyish-black form of corundum, used in powdered form as an abrasive.
COMBINATIONS – **emery board** a strip of thin wood or card coated with emery or another abrasive and used as a nail file.
ORIGIN – Old French esmeri, from Greek smuris 'polishing powder'.

emetic /iˈmettik/ > adjective (of a substance) causing vomiting. > noun an emetic substance.
ORIGIN – Greek emetikos, from emein 'to vomit'.

EMF > abbreviation 1 electromagnetic field(s). 2 (emf) electromotive force.

-emia > combining form US spelling of **-AEMIA**.

emigrant > noun a person who emigrates.

emigrate /ˈemmigrayt/ > verb leave one's own country in order to settle permanently in another.
DERIVATIVES – **emigration** noun.
ORIGIN – Latin emigrare, from migrare 'migrate'.

émigré /ˈemmigray/ > noun a person who has emigrated, especially for political reasons.
ORIGIN – French, from émigrer 'emigrate'.

eminence /ˈemminǝnss/ > noun 1 acknowledged superiority within a particular sphere. 2 an important or distinguished person. 3 (**His** or **Your Eminence**) a title given to a Roman Catholic cardinal. 4 formal or literary a piece of higher ground; a small hill.
ORIGIN – Latin eminentia, from eminere 'jut, project'.

éminence grise /ˈayminoNs ˈgreez/ > noun (pl. **éminences grises** pronunc. same) a person who exercises power or influence without holding an official position.
ORIGIN – French, 'grey eminence'; the term was originally applied to Cardinal Richelieu's grey-cloaked private secretary, Père Joseph (1577–1638).

eminent > *adjective* **1** famous and respected within a particular sphere or profession. **2** outstanding or conspicuous: *the eminent reasonableness of their claim.*
DERIVATIVES – **eminently** *adverb.*
SYNONYMS – **1** distinguished, esteemed, illustrious, renowned, respected.

emir /em**eer**/ (also **amir**) > *noun* a title of various Muslim (mainly Arab) rulers.
ORIGIN – Arabic, 'commander': originally denoting a male descendant of Muhammad.

emirate /**emm**irət/ > *noun* the rank, lands, or reign of an emir.

emissary /**emm**isəri/ > *noun* (pl. **emissaries**) a person sent as a diplomatic representative on a special mission.
ORIGIN – Latin *emissarius* 'scout, spy', from *emittere* 'emit'.

emission /i**mi**sh'n/ > *noun* **1** the action of emitting something, especially heat, light, gas, or radiation. **2** a substance which is emitted.
ORIGIN – Latin, from *emittere* 'emit'.

emit > *verb* (**emitted**, **emitting**) **1** discharge; send forth or give out. **2** make (a sound).
DERIVATIVES – **emitter** *noun.*
SYNONYMS – **1** discharge, exude, issue, release, secrete.
ORIGIN – Latin *emittere*, from *mittere* 'send'.

Emmental /**emm**əntaal/ (also **Emmenthal**) > *noun* a kind of hard Swiss cheese with holes in it, similar to Gruyère.
ORIGIN – the name of a valley in Switzerland where the cheese was originally made.

Emmy > *noun* (pl. **Emmys**) (in the US) a statuette awarded annually to an outstanding television programme or performer.
ORIGIN – said to be from *Immy*, short for *image orthicon tube* (a kind of television camera tube).

emollient /i**moll**iənt/ > *adjective* **1** having the quality of softening or soothing the skin. **2** attempting to avoid confrontation or anger; calming. > *noun* an emollient substance.
DERIVATIVES – **emollience** *noun.*
ORIGIN – from Latin *emollire* 'make soft'.

emolument /i**mol**joomənt/ > *noun* formal a salary, fee, or benefit from employment or office.
ORIGIN – Latin *emolumentum* (originally probably meaning 'payment for grinding corn'), from *molere* 'grind'.

emote /i**mōt**/ > *verb* portray emotion in an exaggerated way.

emoticon /i**mōt**ikon/ > *noun* a representation of a facial expression such as a smile :-), formed with keyboard characters and used in electronic communications to convey the writer's feelings.
ORIGIN – blend of **EMOTION** and **ICON**.

emotion > *noun* **1** a strong feeling, such as joy or anger. **2** instinctive feeling as distinguished from reasoning or knowledge.
DERIVATIVES – **emotionless** *adjective.*
SYNONYMS – **1** feeling, passion, sentiment. **2** instinct, intuition, sentiment.

wordpower facts

Emotion

The word **emotion** comes from Latin *emovere* 'disturb', which is from *e-* 'out' + *movere* 'to move'. At first sight it seems to be the odd one out among the set of *-motion* words derived from *movere*: **commotion**, **locomotion**, **motion**, and **promotion** all express or at least imply movement. When **emotion** entered English in the 16th century it denoted a public disturbance or commotion: the sense 'mental agitation' arose in the mid 17th century, and the current general sense in the early 19th century.

emotional > *adjective* **1** relating to the emotions. **2** characterised by or arousing emotion. **3** easily affected by or readily displaying emotion.
DERIVATIVES – **emotionalise** (also **emotionalize**) *verb* **emotionalism** *noun* **emotionality** *noun* **emotionally** *adverb.*
SYNONYMS – **2** affecting, moving, stirring, touching. **3** demonstrative, excitable, fiery, intense, passionate.

emotive > *adjective* arousing intense feeling.
DERIVATIVES – **emotively** *adverb* **emotivity** /eemō**tiv**viti/ *noun.*
USAGE – **emotive** and **emotional** do not mean the same thing: **emotive** means 'arousing intense feeling', while **emotional** tends to mean 'characterised by intense feeling'. Thus an *emotive issue* is one which is likely to arouse people's passions, while an *emotional response* is one which is itself full of passion.
SYNONYMS – contentious, controversial, inflammatory, sensitive.

empanada /empə**naa**də/ > *noun* a South American pastry turnover filled with savoury ingredients and baked or fried.
ORIGIN – Spanish, from *empanar* 'roll in pastry'.

empanel > *verb* variant spelling of **IMPANEL**.

empathise (also **empathize**) > *verb* understand and share the feelings of another.

empathy /**em**pəthi/ > *noun* the ability to empathise.
DERIVATIVES – **empathetic** *adjective* **empathic** /em**path**ik/ *adjective.*
USAGE – strictly, **empathy** does not mean the same thing as **sympathy**: if you have **empathy** for someone you understand and share their feelings, whereas if you have **sympathy** for them you feel sorry for them because they are suffering some misfortune.
ORIGIN – Greek *empatheia*, from *pathos* 'feeling'.

emperor > *noun* the ruler of an empire.
COMBINATIONS – **emperor penguin** the largest kind of penguin, which breeds in the Antarctic and has a yellow patch on each side of the head.
ORIGIN – Old French *emperere*, from Latin *imperator* 'military commander'.

emphasis /**em**fəsiss/ > *noun* (pl. **emphases** /**em**fəseez/) **1** special importance, value, or prominence given to something. **2** stress laid on a word or words in speaking.
SYNONYMS – **1** attention, importance, prominence, stress, weight. **2** accent, stress, weight.
ORIGIN – Greek, originally in the sense 'appearance, show', later denoting a figure of speech in which more is implied than said.

emphasise (also **emphasize**) > *verb* give special importance or prominence to.
SYNONYMS – accentuate, highlight, spotlight, stress, underline.

emphatic > *adjective* **1** showing or giving emphasis. **2** definite and clear: *an emphatic win.*
DERIVATIVES – **emphatically** *adverb.*
SYNONYMS – **1** firm, insistent, vehement. **2** conclusive, decisive.

emphysema /emfi**see**mə/ (also **pulmonary emphysema**) > *noun* Medicine a condition in which the air sacs of the lungs are damaged and enlarged, causing breathlessness.
ORIGIN – Greek *emphusēma*, from *emphusan* 'puff up'.

empire > *noun* **1** an extensive group of states ruled over by a single monarch or ruling authority. **2** supreme political power. **3** a large commercial organisation under the control of one person or group. > *adjective* (**Empire**) denoting a neoclassical style of furniture and dress fashionable chiefly during the First Empire (1804–15) in France.
COMBINATIONS – **empire line** a style of women's clothing characterised by a waistline cut just under the bust and a low neckline, popular during the First Empire.
ORIGIN – Old French, from Latin *imperium*.

empirical (also **empiric**) > *adjective* based

on observation or experience rather than theory or pure logic.

DERIVATIVES – **empirically** adverb.

ORIGIN – from Greek *empeirikos*, from *empeiria* 'experience'.

empiricism /em**pirr**isiz'm/ > noun Philosophy the theory that all knowledge is derived from experience and observation.

DERIVATIVES – **empiricist** noun & adjective.

emplacement > noun a structure or platform where a gun is placed for firing.

employ > verb **1** give work to (someone) and pay them for it. **2** make use of. **3** keep occupied.

IDIOMS – **in the employ of** employed by.

DERIVATIVES – **employability** noun **employable** adjective.

SYNONYMS – **1** engage, hire, recruit. **2** apply, use, utilise. **3** absorb, engage, occupy.

ORIGIN – Old French *employer*, from Latin *implicari* 'be involved in', from *implicare* 'entwine, involve, imply'.

employee > noun a person employed for wages or salary.

employer > noun a person or organisation that employs people.

employment > noun **1** the action of employing or the state of being employed. **2** a person's work or profession.

emporium /em**por**iəm/ > noun (pl. **emporia** /em**por**iə/ or **emporiums**) a large store selling a wide variety of goods.

ORIGIN – Greek *emporion*, from *emporos* 'merchant'.

empower > verb **1** give authority or power to; authorise. **2** give strength and confidence to.

DERIVATIVES – **empowerment** noun.

empress /**em**priss/ > noun **1** a female emperor. **2** the wife or widow of an emperor.

empty > adjective (**emptier**, **emptiest**) **1** containing nothing; not filled or occupied. **2** having no meaning or likelihood of fulfilment: *an empty threat.* **3** having no value or purpose. > verb (**empties**, **emptied**) **1** make or become empty. **2** discharge (the contents) from a container. **3** (of a river) flow into the sea or a lake. > noun (pl. **empties**) informal a bottle or glass left empty of its contents.

IDIOMS – **empty vessels make most noise** (or **sound**) proverb those with least wisdom or knowledge are always the most talkative. **be running on empty** have exhausted all of one's resources.

DERIVATIVES – **emptily** adverb **emptiness** noun.

SYNONYMS – adjective **1** unfilled, uninhabited, unoccupied, vacant. **2** idle, meaningless, vain. **3** futile, hollow, meaningless, worthless. verb **1** clear,

evacuate, unload, unpack. **2** discharge, drain.

ANTONYMS – adjective **1** full. verb **1** fill.

COMBINATIONS – **empty-handed** having failed to obtain or achieve what one wanted. **empty-headed** unintelligent and foolish. **empty-nester** informal, chiefly N. Amer. a parent whose children have grown up and left home.

ORIGIN – Old English, 'at leisure, empty'.

empyrean /empī**ree**ən, em**pirr**iən/ literary > noun (**the empyrean**) heaven or the sky. > adjective relating to heaven.

ORIGIN – Greek *empurios* (used by the ancients to refer to the highest part of heaven, thought to be the realm of pure fire), from *pur* 'fire'.

EMS > abbreviation European Monetary System.

EMU > abbreviation Economic and Monetary Union.

emu > noun a large fast-running flightless Australian bird similar to an ostrich.

ORIGIN – Portuguese *ema*.

emulate /**em**yoolayt/ > verb try to equal or surpass, typically by imitation.

DERIVATIVES – **emulation** noun **emulative** adjective **emulator** noun.

ORIGIN – Latin *aemulari* 'to rival or equal'.

emulsifier > noun a substance that stabilises an emulsion, especially an additive used to stabilise processed foods.

emulsify /i**mul**sifī/ > verb (**emulsifies**, **emulsified**) make into or become an emulsion.

DERIVATIVES – **emulsifiable** adjective **emulsification** noun.

emulsion > noun **1** a fine dispersion of minute droplets of one liquid in another in which it does not dissolve or form a homogeneous mixture. **2** a type of paint consisting of pigment bound in a synthetic resin which forms an emulsion with water. **3** a light-sensitive coating for photographic films and plates, containing crystals of a silver compound dispersed in a medium such as gelatin.

ORIGIN – first denoting a milky liquid made by crushing almonds in water: from Latin, from *mulgere* 'to milk'.

en > noun Printing a unit of measurement equal to half an em.

ORIGIN – from the letter *N*, since it is approximately this width.

en-¹ (also **em-**) > prefix forming verbs: **1** (added to nouns) meaning 'put into or on': *engulf.* **2** (added to nouns and adjectives) meaning 'bring into the condition of': *enliven.* **3** (added to verbs) meaning 'in, into, or on' or as an intensifier: *ensnare.*

ORIGIN – French, from Latin *in-*.

en-² (also **em-**) > prefix within; inside: *enthusiasm.*

ORIGIN – Greek.

-en¹ > suffix forming verbs from adjectives or nouns denoting the development or intensification of a state or quality: *widen | strengthen.*

-en² > suffix (also **-n**) forming adjectives from nouns: **1** made or consisting of: *earthen.* **2** resembling: *golden.*

-en³ (also **-n**) > suffix forming past participles of strong verbs: **1** as a regular inflection: *spoken.* **2** as an adjective: *mistaken.*

enable > verb **1** provide with the ability or means to do something. **2** make possible.

DERIVATIVES – **enablement** noun **enabler** noun.

enact > verb **1** make (a bill or other proposal) law. **2** act out (a role or play).

DERIVATIVES – **enactor** noun.

enactment > noun **1** the process of enacting. **2** a law that has been passed.

enamel > noun **1** a coloured opaque glassy substance applied to metal, glass, or pottery for decorative or protective purposes. **2** the hard glossy substance that covers the crown of a tooth. **3** a paint that dries to give a smooth, hard coat. > verb (**enamelled**, **enamelling**; US **enameled**, **enameling**) coat or decorate with enamel.

WORDFINDER – champlevé (*decorative enamel inlay*), cloisonné (*decorative enamels separated by wire*).

DERIVATIVES – **enamelled** adjective **enameller** noun.

ORIGIN – Old French *enamailler*, from *amail* 'enamel'.

enamour /i**namm**ər/ (US **enamor**) > verb (**be enamoured of** or **with** or **by**) be filled with love or admiration for.

ORIGIN – Old French *enamourer*, from *amour* 'love'.

enantiomer /i**nan**tiəmər/ > noun Chemistry each of a pair of molecules that are mirror images of each other.

DERIVATIVES – **enantiomeric** adjective.

ORIGIN – from Greek *enantios* 'opposite'.

en bloc /oN **blok**/ > adverb all together or all at once.

ORIGIN – French.

encamp > verb settle in or establish a camp.

encampment > noun **1** a place where a camp is set up. **2** a prehistoric enclosed or fortified site, especially an Iron Age hill fort.

encapsulate /in**kap**syoolayt/ > verb **1** enclose in or as if in a capsule. **2** express concisely and succinctly.

DERIVATIVES – **encapsulation** noun.

encase (also **incase**) > verb enclose or cover in a case or close-fitting surround.

DERIVATIVES – **encasement** noun.

encash > verb Brit. convert (a cheque, bond, etc.) into money.

DERIVATIVES – **encashment** noun.

encaustic /en**kaw**stik/ > adjective (in painting and ceramics) decorated with coloured clays or pigments mixed with hot wax, which are burnt in as an inlay. > *noun* the art or process of encaustic painting.

ORIGIN – Greek *enkaustikos*, from *enkaiein* 'burn in'; related to INK.

-ence > *suffix* forming nouns: **1** denoting a quality: *impertinence*. **2** denoting an action or its result: *reference*.

ORIGIN – from Latin *-entia, -antia*.

encephalitis /enseffə**lī**tiss, enkeffə**lī**tiss/ > *noun* inflammation of the brain.

DERIVATIVES – **encephalitic** *adjective*.

ORIGIN – from Greek *enkephalos* 'brain'.

encephalography /enseffə**log**rəfi, enkef-fə**log**rəfi/ > *noun* any of various techniques for recording the structure or electrical activity of the brain.

DERIVATIVES – **encephalogram** *noun* **encephalograph** *noun*.

encephalomyelitis /enseffəlōmīə**lī**tiss, enkeffəlōmīə**lī**tiss/ > *noun* Medicine inflammation of the brain and spinal cord, typically due to acute infection with a virus.

encephalopathy /enseffə**lopp**əthi, enkef-fə**lopp**əthi/ > *noun* a disease in which the functioning of the brain is affected, especially by infection with a virus or toxins in the blood.

enchant > *verb* **1** fill (someone) with great delight; charm. **2** put under a spell.

DERIVATIVES – **enchanted** *adjective* **enchanter** *noun* **enchantment** *noun* **enchantress** *noun*.

SYNONYMS – **1** bewitch, captivate, charm, delight, enrapture, entrance.

ORIGIN – French *enchanter*, from Latin *incantare*, from *cantare* 'sing'.

enchanting > *adjective* delightfully charming or attractive.

DERIVATIVES – **enchantingly** *adverb*.

SYNONYMS – captivating, charming, delightful, entrancing, spellbinding.

enchilada /enchi**laa**də/ > *noun* a tortilla filled with meat or cheese and served with chilli sauce.

ORIGIN – Latin American Spanish, from *enchilar* 'season with chilli'.

encipher > *verb* convert into a coded form.

DERIVATIVES – **encipherment** *noun*.

encircle > *verb* form a circle around; surround.

DERIVATIVES – **encirclement** *noun*.

enclave /en**klayv**/ > *noun* **1** a portion of territory surrounded by a larger territory whose inhabitants are culturally or ethnically distinct. **2** a group that is different in character from those surrounding it: *a male enclave*.

ORIGIN – French, from Old French *enclaver* 'enclose', from Latin *clavis* 'key'.

enclose (also **inclose**) > *verb* **1** surround or close off on all sides. **2** place in an envelope together with a letter.

ORIGIN – from Old French *enclore*, from Latin *includere* 'shut in'.

enclosure /in**klō**zhər/ (also **inclosure**) > *noun* **1** an area that is enclosed by a fence, wall, or other barrier. **2** a document or object placed in an envelope together with a letter.

encode > *verb* convert into a coded form.

DERIVATIVES – **encoder** *noun*.

encomium /en**kō**miəm/ > *noun* (pl. **encomiums** or **encomia**) formal a speech or piece of writing expressing praise.

ORIGIN – Greek *enkōmion* 'eulogy'.

encompass /in**kum**pəss/ > *verb* **1** surround and have or hold within. **2** include comprehensively.

encore /**ong**kor/ > *noun* a repeated or additional performance of an item at the end of a concert, as called for by an audience. > *exclamation* again! (as called by an audience at the end of a concert) > *verb* perform an encore or as an encore.

ORIGIN – French, 'still, again'.

encounter > *verb* unexpectedly meet or be faced with. > *noun* **1** an unexpected or casual meeting. **2** a confrontation or difficult struggle.

ORIGIN – Old French *encontrer*, from Latin *contra* 'against'.

encourage > *verb* **1** give support, confidence, or hope to. **2** help or stimulate the development of.

DERIVATIVES – **encouragement** *noun* **encourager** *noun*.

SYNONYMS – **1** cheer, fortify, hearten, inspire, rally. **2** advance, assist, foster, help.

ANTONYMS – **1** discourage.

ORIGIN – French *encourager*, from *corage* 'courage'.

encroach > *verb* **1** (**encroach on**) gradually intrude on (a person's territory, rights, etc.). **2** advance gradually beyond expected or acceptable limits: *the sea has encroached all round the coast*.

DERIVATIVES – **encroachment** *noun*.

ORIGIN – Old French *encrochier* 'seize' (the original meaning in English).

en croute /on **kroot**/ > *adjective & adverb* in a pastry crust.

ORIGIN – French.

encrust (also **incrust**) > *verb* cover with a hard crust.

DERIVATIVES – **encrusted** *adjective* **encrustation** *noun*.

ORIGIN – Latin *incrustare*, from *crusta* 'a crust'.

encrypt /en**kript**/ > *verb* convert into code.

DERIVATIVES – **encryption** *noun*.

ORIGIN – from Greek *kruptos* 'hidden'.

encumber /in**kum**bər/ > *verb* be a burden or impediment to.

ORIGIN – Old French *encombrer* 'block up', from *combre* 'river barrage'.

encumbrance > *noun* **1** a burden or impediment. **2** Law a mortgage or other charge on property or assets.

-ency > *suffix* forming nouns denoting a quality or state: *efficiency* | *presidency*.

ORIGIN – from Latin *-entia*.

encyclical /en**sik**lik'l/ > *noun* a letter sent by the pope to all bishops of the Roman Catholic Church.

ORIGIN – from Greek *enkuklios* 'circular, general'.

encyclopedia* /ensīklə**pee**diə/ (also **encyclopaedia**) > *noun* a book or set of books giving information on many subjects or on many aspects of one subject, typically arranged alphabetically.

***SPELLING** – as with other words of similar form, such as **medieval**, the simpler *-e*-spelling is now commoner than the *-ae-*: *encyclopedia*.

ORIGIN – pseudo-Greek *enkuklopaideia*, for *enkuklios paideia* 'all-round education'.

encyclopedic /ensīklə**pee**dik/ (also **encyclopaedic**) > *adjective* **1** comprehensive: *an encyclopedic knowledge of food*. **2** relating to encyclopedias or information suitable for an encyclopedia.

encyclopedist (also **encyclopaedist**) > *noun* a person who writes, edits, or contributes to an encyclopedia.

end > *noun* **1** the final part of something. **2** the furthest or most extreme part. **3** a termination of a state or situation: *they called for an end to violence*. **4** a person's death or downfall. **5** a goal or desired result. **6** a small piece that is left after use. **7** a part or share of an activity: *your end of the deal*. **8** the part of a sports field or court defended by one team or player. > *verb* **1** come or bring to an end; finish. **2** (**end in**) have as its result. **3** (**end up**) eventually reach or come to a particular state or place.

WORDFINDER – apocalypse (*the end of the world*), eschatology (*part of theology concerned with the end of the world*).

IDIOMS – **at the end of the day** informal, chiefly Brit. when everything is taken into consideration. **at the end of one's tether** having no patience or energy left. **be the end** informal be the limit of what one can tolerate. **end it all** commit suicide. **the end of the road** (or **line**) the point beyond which progress or survival cannot continue. **end on** situated on or viewed from the end. **in the end** eventually. **keep** (or **hold**) **one's end up** informal perform well in a difficult or competitive situation. **make** (**both**) **ends meet** earn just enough money to live on. **no end** informal very much. **no end of** informal a vast number or amount of. **on end 1** continuously. **2** upright. **the sharp end** informal the most challenging and risky part of an activity. **the —— to end all ——s** informal the most impressive or successful of its kind: *the party to end all parties.*

SYNONYMS – *noun* **1** close, conclusion, ending, finish. **2** edge, extremity, limit, tip. **4** death, demise, downfall, ruin. **5** aim, goal, object, objective, target. **6** butt, remnant, stub. *verb* **1** conclude, close, finish, terminate.

ANTONYMS – *noun* **1,2** beginning, start. *verb* **1** begin, start.

COMBINATIONS – **end-user** the person who uses a particular product.

endanger > *verb* put in danger.
DERIVATIVES – **endangerment** *noun.*
SYNONYMS – imperil, jeopardise, put at risk, threaten.

endangered > *adjective* (of a species) in danger of extinction.

endear /in**deer**/ > *verb* (often **endear to**) cause to be loved or liked.

endearing > *adjective* inspiring love or affection.
DERIVATIVES – **endearingly** *adverb.*
SYNONYMS – adorable, lovable, sweet, winning.

endearment > *noun* **1** love or affection. **2** a word or phrase expressing this.

endeavour /in**devv**ər/ (US **endeavor**) > *verb* try hard to do or achieve something. > *noun* **1** an earnest attempt to achieve something. **2** earnest and industrious effort.
SYNONYMS – *verb* attempt, strive, try, venture. *noun* **1** attempt, bid, effort. **2** effort, exertion, industry, labour.
ORIGIN – from the phrase *put oneself in devoir* 'do one's utmost' (from the archaic word *devoir* 'one's duty').

endemic /en**demm**ik/ > *adjective* **1** (of a disease or condition) regularly found among particular people or in a certain area. **2** (of a plant or animal) native or restricted to a certain area.
DERIVATIVES – **endemicity** /endi**miss**iti/ *noun* **endemism** /**en**dimiz'm/ *noun.*
ORIGIN – Greek *endēmios* 'native', from *dēmos* 'people'.

endgame > *noun* the final stage of a game such as chess or bridge, when few pieces or cards remain.

ending > *noun* an end or final part.

endive /**en**dīv, **en**div/ > *noun* **1** a plant with bitter curly or smooth leaves, eaten in salads. **2** (also **Belgian endive**) N. Amer. a chicory crown.
ORIGIN – Old French, from Greek *entubon.*

endless > *adjective* **1** having or seeming to have no end or limit. **2** innumerable. **3** (of a belt, chain, or tape) having the ends joined to allow for continuous action.
DERIVATIVES – **endlessly** *adverb* **endlessness** *noun.*
SYNONYMS – **1** boundless, infinite, limitless, unlimited.
ANTONYMS – **1** limited.

endmost > *adjective* nearest to the end.

endo- > *combining form* internal; within: *endoderm.*
ORIGIN – from Greek *endon* 'within'.

endocarditis /endōkaar**dī**tiss/ > *noun* Medicine inflammation of the membrane lining the interior of the heart.
ORIGIN – from Greek *kardia* 'heart'.

endocrine /**en**dōkrīn, **en**dōkrin/ > *adjective* (of a gland) secreting hormones or other products directly into the blood.
ORIGIN – from Greek *krinein* 'sift'.

endocrinology /endōkri**noll**əji/ > *noun* the branch of physiology and medicine concerned with endocrine glands and hormones.
DERIVATIVES – **endocrinologist** *noun.*

endogenous /en**doj**inəss/ > *adjective* technical relating to an internal cause or origin. Contrasted with EXOGENOUS.
DERIVATIVES – **endogenously** *adverb.*

endometriosis /endōmeetri**ō**siss/ > *noun* Medicine a condition in which endometrial tissue proliferates in other parts of the body, causing pelvic pain.

endometrium /endō**mee**triəm/ > *noun* the mucous membrane lining the womb.
DERIVATIVES – **endometrial** *adjective.*
ORIGIN – from Greek *mētra* 'womb'.

endomorph /**en**dōmorf/ > *noun* a person with a soft, round build of body and a high proportion of fat tissue. Compare with ECTOMORPH and MESOMORPH.
DERIVATIVES – **endomorphic** *adjective.*
ORIGIN – from *endodermal* (the endoderm being the layer of the embryo giving rise to these physical characteristics).

endorphin /en**dor**fin/ > *noun* any of a group of hormones secreted within the brain and nervous system and having the effect of relieving pain.
ORIGIN – blend of ENDOGENOUS and MORPHINE.

endorse /in**dorss**/ (US & Law also **indorse**) > *verb* **1** publicly declare one's approval of. **2** sign (a cheque or bill of exchange) on the back to specify another as the payee or to accept responsibility for paying it. **3** Brit. enter an endorsement on (a driving licence).
DERIVATIVES – **endorsable** *adjective* **endorsee** *noun* **endorser** *noun.*
SYNONYMS – **1** advocate, back, sanction, support.
ANTONYMS – **1** oppose.
ORIGIN – Latin *indorsare*, from *dorsum* 'back'.

endorsement (chiefly US also **indorsement**) > *noun* **1** an act or the action of endorsing. **2** (in the UK) a note on a driving licence recording the penalty points incurred for a driving offence. **3** a clause in an insurance policy detailing an exemption from or change in cover.

endoscope /**en**dəskōp/ > *noun* an instrument which can be introduced into the body to view its internal parts.
DERIVATIVES – **endoscopic** *adjective* **endoscopically** *adverb* **endoscopist** *noun* **endoscopy** *noun.*

endoskeleton > *noun* an internal skeleton, such as that of vertebrates, as opposed to an exoskeleton.

endosperm > *noun* Botany the part of a seed which acts as a food store for the developing plant embryo.

endothelium /endō**thee**liəm/ > *noun* the layer of cells lining the blood vessels, heart, and other organs and cavities of the body.
ORIGIN – Latin, from Greek *thēlē* 'teat'.

endothermic /endō**ther**mic/ > *adjective* **1** Chemistry (of a reaction) accompanied by the absorption of heat. The opposite of EXOTHERMIC. **2** Zoology (of an animal) dependent on the internal generation of heat.

endow /in**dow**/ > *verb* **1** (**endow with**) give or bequeath an income or property to. **2** (usu. **be endowed with**) provide with a quality, ability, or asset. **3** establish (a university post, annual prize, etc.) by donating funds.
DERIVATIVES – **endower** *noun.*
ORIGIN – Old French *endouer*, from *douer* 'give as a gift', from Latin *dotare* 'endow'.

endowment > *noun* **1** the action of endowing. **2** a quality or ability with which a person is endowed. **3** an income or form of property endowed. **4** (before another noun) denoting a form of life insurance involving payment of a fixed sum to the insured person on a specified date, or to their estate should they die before this date.
COMBINATIONS – **endowment mortgage** Brit. a mortgage linked to an endowment insurance policy which is intended to repay the capital sum on maturity.

endpaper > *noun* a leaf of paper at the beginning or end of a book, fixed to the inside of the cover.

endue /in**dyoo**/ (also **indue**) > *verb* (**endues**, **endued**, **enduing**) literary (usu. **be endued with**) endow with a quality or ability.
ORIGIN – Old French *enduire*, partly from Latin *inducere* 'lead in', reinforced by the sense of Latin *induere* 'put on clothes'.

endurance > *noun* **1** the fact or power of enduring something painful and prolonged. **2** the capacity of something to last or to withstand wear and tear.
SYNONYMS – **1** forbearance, fortitude. **2** stamina, staying power, tolerance.

endure /in**dyoor**/ > *verb* **1** suffer (something painful and prolonged) patiently. **2** tolerate. **3** remain in existence.
DERIVATIVES – **endurable** *adjective.*

SYNONYMS – **1** bear, brave, weather, withstand. **2** abide, bear, brook, countenance. **3** abide, last, persist, survive.

ORIGIN – Latin *indurare* 'harden'.

enduro /in**dyoo**rō/ > *noun* (pl. **enduros**) a long-distance race for motor vehicles or bicycles over rough terrain, designed to test endurance.

endways (also **endwise**) > *adverb* **1** with its end facing upwards, forwards, or towards the viewer. **2** end to end.

ENE > *abbreviation* east-north-east.

-ene > *suffix* **1** denoting an inhabitant: *Nazarene.* **2** Chemistry forming names of unsaturated hydrocarbons containing a double bond: *benzene.*

ORIGIN – from Greek *-ēnos.*

enema /**enn**imə/ > *noun* (pl. **enemas** or **enemata** /i**nemm**ətə/) a procedure in which fluid is injected into the rectum, typically to expel its contents.

ORIGIN – Greek, from *enienai* 'send or put in'.

enemy > *noun* (pl. **enemies**) **1** a person who is actively opposed or hostile to someone or something. **2** (**the enemy**) a hostile nation or its armed forces in time of war. **3** a thing that damages or opposes something: *routine is the enemy of art.*

SYNONYMS – **1** adversary, antagonist, foe, opponent, rival.

ANTONYMS – **1** ally, friend.

ORIGIN – Old French *enemi*, from Latin *inimicus*, from *in-* 'not' + *amicus* 'friend'.

energetic > *adjective* **1** showing or involving great energy or activity. **2** Physics relating to energy.

DERIVATIVES – **energetically** *adverb.*

SYNONYMS – **1** animated, dynamic, lively, spirited, vigorous.

ANTONYMS – **1** lethargic.

energy > *noun* (pl. **energies**) **1** the strength and vitality required for sustained activity. **2** (**energies**) a person's physical and mental powers as applied to a particular activity. **3** power derived from physical or chemical resources to provide light and heat or to work machines. **4** Physics the property of matter and radiation which is manifest as a capacity to perform work.

WORDFINDER – calorie, erg, joule (*units of energy*), kinetic energy (*energy of a moving body*), potential energy (*energy possessed by a body by virtue of its position*), quantum (*tiny fixed quantity of energy*).

DERIVATIVES – **energise** (also **energize**) *verb.*

SYNONYMS – **1** liveliness, vigour, vitality, zest.

ORIGIN – Greek *energeia*, from *ergon* 'work'.

enervate /**enn**ərvayt/ > *verb* cause to feel drained of energy.

DERIVATIVES – **enervation** *noun.*

ORIGIN – Latin *enervare* 'weaken (by extraction of the sinews)', from *nervus* 'sinew'.

en famille /oN fa**meey**/ > *adverb* **1** with one's family. **2** as or like a family; informally.

ORIGIN – French, 'in family'.

enfant terrible /oNfoN te**reeb**lə/ > *noun* (pl. **enfants terribles** pronunc. same) a person who behaves in an unconventional or controversial way.

ORIGIN – French, 'terrible child'.

enfeeble > *verb* weaken.

DERIVATIVES – **enfeeblement** *noun.*

enfilade /enfi**layd**/ > *noun* **1** a volley of gunfire directed along a line from end to end. **2** a suite of rooms with doorways in line with each other. > *verb* direct an enfilade at.

ORIGIN – first meaning 'a military post commanding the length of a line': from French, from *enfiler* 'thread on a string'.

enfold > *verb* surround; envelop.

enforce > *verb* **1** compel people to comply with (a law, rule, or obligation). **2** cause to happen by necessity or force.

DERIVATIVES – **enforceable** *adjective* **enforcement** *noun* **enforcer** *noun.*

SYNONYMS – **1** administer, implement, impose, insist on. **2** compel, demand, force.

enfranchise* /in**fran**chīz/ > *verb* **1** give the right to vote to. **2** historical free (a slave).

DERIVATIVES – **enfranchisement** *noun.*

*SPELLING – **enfranchise** cannot be spelled with an *-ize* ending.

ORIGIN – Old French *enfranchir*, from *franc*, *franche* 'free'.

engage > *verb* **1** attract or involve (someone's interest or attention). **2** (**engage in** or **with**) participate or become involved in. **3** chiefly Brit. employ or hire. **4** enter into a contract to do. **5** enter into combat with. **6** (with reference to a part of a machine or engine) move into position so as to come into operation.

SYNONYMS – **1** attract, captivate, catch, grip, hold.

wordpower facts

Engage

The word **engage** comes ultimately from the base of **gage**, an archaic term for a valued object deposited as a guarantee of good faith. **Engage** originally meant 'to pawn or pledge something', later 'pledge oneself to do something', hence 'enter into a contract' or 'involve oneself in an activity'.

engagé /oNga**zhay**/ > *adjective* (of a writer or artist) morally committed to a particular cause.

ORIGIN – French, 'engaged'.

engaged > *adjective* **1** busy; occupied. **2** Brit. (of a telephone line) unavailable because already in use. **3** having formally agreed to marry.

engagement > *noun* **1** a formal agreement to get married. **2** an appointment. **3** the action of engaging or being engaged. **4** a fight or battle between armed forces.

engaging > *adjective* charming and attractive.

DERIVATIVES – **engagingly** *adverb.*

SYNONYMS – appealing, charming, fetching, winning.

engender /in**jen**dər/ > *verb* give rise to.

ORIGIN – Old French *engendrer*, from Latin *ingenerare*, from *generare* 'beget'.

engine > *noun* **1** a machine with moving parts that converts power into motion. **2** (also **railway engine**) a locomotive. **3** historical a mechanical device or instrument, especially one used in warfare: *a siege engine.*

DERIVATIVES – **engined** *adjective.*

wordpower facts

Engine

The word **engine** comes from Old French *engin*, from Latin *ingenium* 'talent, device', which is the root also of **ingenious**. The original sense was 'ingenuity, cunning' (which survives in Scots as *ingine*), hence 'the product of ingenuity, a plot or snare', also 'tool, weapon'; the latter use came to apply specifically to a large mechanical weapon, from which arose the idea of a machine in the mid 17th century.

engineer > *noun* **1** a person qualified in engineering. **2** a person who maintains or controls an engine or machine. **3** a person who skilfully originates something. > *verb* **1** design and build. **2** contrive to bring about.

SYNONYMS – *verb* **2** choreograph, contrive, orchestrate, stage-manage.

engineering > *noun* the branch of science and technology concerned with the design, building, and use of engines, machines, and structures.

English > *noun* the language of England, now used in many varieties throughout the world. > *adjective* relating to England.

WORDFINDER – anglophone (*English-speaking*).

DERIVATIVES – **Englishness** *noun.*

COMBINATIONS – **English breakfast** a substantial cooked breakfast typically including bacon and eggs. **English muffin**

North American term for **muffin** (in sense 1). **English rose** an attractive English girl with a delicate, fair-skinned complexion.

ORIGIN – Old English, related to **Angle**.

Englishman (or **Englishwoman**) > *noun* a person from England, or a person of English descent.

IDIOMS – **an Englishman's home is his castle** Brit. *proverb* an English person's home is a place where they may do as they please.

engorge /inˈgorj/ > *verb* (often **be engorged**) swell or cause to swell with blood, water, etc.

DERIVATIVES – **engorgement** *noun*.

ORIGIN – first meaning 'gorge oneself': from Old French *engorgier* 'feed to excess'.

engraft (also **ingraft**) > *verb* another term for **graft**[1].

DERIVATIVES – **engraftment** *noun*.

engrain > *verb* variant spelling of **ingrain**.

engrained > *adjective* variant spelling of **ingrained**.

engrave > *verb* **1** cut or carve (a text or design) on a hard surface. **2** cut or carve a text or design on. **3** (**be engraved on** or **in**) be permanently fixed in (one's mind).

DERIVATIVES – **engraver** *noun*.

ORIGIN – from **en-**[1] + **grave**[3].

engraving > *noun* **1** a print made from an engraved plate, block, or other surface. **2** the process or art of cutting or carving a design on a hard surface, especially on a metal plate so as to make a print.

engross /inˈgrōss/ > *verb* **1** (often **be engrossed in**) absorb all the attention of. **2** Law produce (a legal document) in its final or definitive form.

SYNONYMS – **1** absorb, enthral, grip, preoccupy, rivet.

wordpower facts

Engross

As one would imagine from its form if not its meaning, the word **engross** is related to **gross**. Both derive ultimately from Latin *grossus* 'large'. **Engross** comes from the Latin phrase *in grosso* 'wholesale', and originally meant 'buy up the whole of (a commodity) in order to sell it at a monopoly price'. It is also linked to **grocer**: a grocer was originally a person who sold things 'in the gross', i.e. in large quantities.

engrossment > *noun* Law the final version of a legal document, eventually becoming the original deed.

engulf > *verb* (of a natural force) sweep over so as to completely surround or cover.

DERIVATIVES – **engulfment** *noun*.

enhance /inˈhaans/ > *verb* improve the quality, value, or extent of.

DERIVATIVES – **enhancement** *noun* **enhancer** *noun*.

SYNONYMS – augment, boost, improve, increase.

ORIGIN – first meaning 'elevate': from Old French *enhauncer*, from Latin *altus* 'high'.

enharmonic /enhaarˈmonnik/ > *adjective* Music **1** relating to notes which are the same in pitch though bearing different names (e.g. F sharp and G flat). **2** of or having intervals smaller than a semitone.

ORIGIN – Greek *enarmonikos*, from *harmonia* 'harmony'.

enigma /iˈnigmə/ > *noun* a mysterious or puzzling person or thing.

DERIVATIVES – **enigmatic** *adjective* **enigmatical** *adjective* **enigmatically** *adverb*.

SYNONYMS – conundrum, mystery, puzzle, riddle.

ORIGIN – Greek *ainigma* 'riddle'.

enjoin > *verb* **1** instruct or urge to do. **2** (**enjoin from**) Law prohibit (someone) from performing (an action) by an injunction.

ORIGIN – Old French *enjoindre*, from Latin *injungere* 'join, attach, impose'.

enjoy > *verb* **1** take pleasure in. **2** (**enjoy oneself**) have a pleasant time. **3** possess and benefit from: *these professions enjoy high status.*

DERIVATIVES – **enjoyment** *noun*.

SYNONYMS – **1** appreciate, like, love, relish, savour.

ORIGIN – Old French *enjoier* 'give joy to' or *enjoïr* 'enjoy'.

enjoyable > *adjective* giving delight or pleasure.

DERIVATIVES – **enjoyability** *noun* **enjoyably** *adverb*.

SYNONYMS – agreeable, diverting, entertaining, pleasant, pleasurable.

enlarge > *verb* **1** make or become bigger. **2** (**enlarge on**) speak or write about in greater detail.

DERIVATIVES – **enlarger** *noun*.

enlargement > *noun* **1** the action of enlarging or state of being enlarged. **2** a photograph that is larger than the original negative or than an earlier print.

enlighten > *verb* **1** give greater knowledge and understanding to. **2** (**enlightened**) rational, tolerant, and well-informed.

SYNONYMS – **1** edify, illuminate, inform, teach.

enlightenment > *noun* **1** the action of enlightening or the state of being enlightened. **2** (**the Enlightenment**) a European intellectual movement of the late 17th and 18th centuries emphasising reason and individualism rather than tradition.

WORDFINDER – nirvana (*Buddhist state of enlightenment*).

enlist > *verb* **1** enrol or be enrolled in the armed services. **2** engage (a person or their help).

DERIVATIVES – **enlistment** *noun*.

COMBINATIONS – **enlisted man** US a member of the armed forces below the rank of officer.

enliven /enˈlīvˈn/ > *verb* **1** make more interesting or appealing. **2** make more cheerful or animated.

en masse /oN ˈmass/ > *adverb* all together.

ORIGIN – French, 'in a mass'.

enmesh > *verb* (usu. **be enmeshed in**) entangle.

DERIVATIVES – **enmeshment** *noun*.

enmity /ˈenmiti/ > *noun* (pl. **enmities**) the state of being an enemy; hostility.

SYNONYMS – animosity, antagonism, antipathy, discord, hostility.

ORIGIN – Old French *enemistie*, from Latin *inimicus* 'enemy'.

ennoble > *verb* **1** give a noble rank or title to. **2** give greater dignity to; elevate.

DERIVATIVES – **ennoblement** *noun*.

ennui /onˈwee/ > *noun* listlessness and dissatisfaction arising from boredom.

ORIGIN – French, from the same Latin base as **annoy**.

enology > *noun* US spelling of **oenology**.

enormity > *noun* (pl. **enormities**) **1** (**the enormity of**) the extreme seriousness or extent of (something bad). **2** great size or scale. **3** a grave crime or sin.

USAGE – **enormity** originally meant 'a crime'; for this reason some people object to its being used as a synonym for **hugeness**.

ORIGIN – first meaning 'deviation from rectitude, transgression, crime': from Latin *enormitas*, from *norma* 'pattern, standard'.

enormous > *adjective* very large.

DERIVATIVES – **enormously** *adverb* **enormousness** *noun*.

SYNONYMS – colossal, gigantic, huge, immense, massive, vast.

ANTONYMS – tiny.

ORIGIN – Latin *enormis* 'unusual, huge'.

enough > *determiner & pronoun* as much or as many as is necessary or desirable. > *adverb* **1** to the required degree or extent. **2** to a moderate degree.

IDIOMS – **enough is as good as a feast** *proverb* moderation is more satisfying than excess. **enough is enough** no more will be tolerated. **enough said** all is understood and there is no need to say more.

en passant /oN paˈsoN/ > *adverb* in passing.

ORIGIN – French.

enquire > *verb* **1** ask for information. **2** (**enquire after**) ask about the health and well-being of. **3** (**enquire into**) investigate.

DERIVATIVES – **enquirer** *noun* **enquiring** *adjective*.

USAGE – traditionally, in British English, **enquire** means 'ask', while **inquire** is used more specifically to mean 'make a formal investigation'.

ORIGIN – Latin *inquirere*, from *quaerere* 'seek'.

enquiry > *noun* (pl. **enquiries**) **1** an act of asking for information. **2** an official investigation.

enrage > *verb* make very angry.

DERIVATIVES – **enraged** *adjective*.

SYNONYMS – anger, incense, infuriate, madden.

enrapture > *verb* give intense pleasure to.

DERIVATIVES – **enrapt** *adjective*.

enrich > *verb* **1** improve the quality or value of. **2** make wealthy or wealthier.

DERIVATIVES – **enrichment** *noun*.

COMBINATIONS – **enriched uranium** uranium containing an increased proportion of the fissile isotope U-235.

enrobe > *verb* formal dress in a robe or vestment.

enrol /inrōl/ (US **enroll**) > *verb* (**enrolled**, **enrolling**) officially register or recruit as a member or student.

ORIGIN – Old French *enroller*, from *rolle* 'a roll': names were originally written on a roll of parchment.

enrolment (US **enrollment**) > *noun* **1** the action of enrolling or being enrolled. **2** N. Amer. the number of people enrolled at a school or college.

en route /on rōot/ > *adverb* on the way.

ORIGIN – French.

en rule /en rōol/ > *noun* Brit. a short dash, the width of an en, used in punctuation.

ensconce /inskonss/ > *verb* establish in a comfortable, safe, or secret place.

ORIGIN – first used in the senses 'fortify' and 'shelter within or behind a fortification': from archaic *sconce*, 'a small defensive fort or earthwork'.

ensemble /onsomb'l/ > *noun* **1** a group of musicians, actors, or dancers who perform together. **2** a passage for a whole choir or group of instruments. **3** a group of items viewed as a whole, in particular a set of clothes worn together.

ORIGIN – French, from Latin *simul* 'at the same time'.

enshrine > *verb* **1** place (a revered or precious object) in an appropriate receptacle. **2** preserve (a right, tradition, or idea) in a form that ensures it will be respected.

DERIVATIVES – **enshrinement** *noun*.

enshroud /inshrowd/ > *verb* literary envelop completely and hide from view.

ensign /ensīn/ > *noun* **1** a flag, especially a military or naval one indicating nationality. **2** the lowest rank of commissioned officer in the US and some other navies, above chief warrant officer and below lieutenant. **3** historical a standard-bearer.

ORIGIN – Old French *enseigne*, from Latin *insignia* (see INSIGNIA).

enslave > *verb* **1** make (someone) a slave. **2** cause (someone) to lose freedom of choice or action.

DERIVATIVES – **enslavement** *noun* **enslaver** *noun*.

SYNONYMS – **1** disenfranchise, subjugate.

ANTONYMS – **1** emancipate.

ensnare > *verb* catch in or as in a trap.

DERIVATIVES – **ensnarement** *noun*.

ensue > *verb* (**ensues**, **ensued**, **ensuing**) happen or occur afterwards or as a result.

ORIGIN – Old French *ensivre*, from Latin *sequi* 'follow'.

en suite /on sweet/ > *adjective & adverb* Brit. (of a bathroom) immediately adjoining and with access directly from a bedroom.

ORIGIN – first used in the sense 'in agreement': from French, 'in sequence'.

ensure /inshoor/ > *verb* **1** make certain that (something) will occur or be so. **2** (**ensure against**) make sure that (a problem) does not occur.

USAGE – **ensure** does not mean 'provide compensation in the event of damage to property'; however in more general senses **ensure** and **insure** mean the same thing.

ORIGIN – Old French *enseurer*, earlier form of *assurer* 'assure'.

ENT > *abbreviation* ear, nose, and throat (as a department in a hospital).

-ent > *suffix* **1** (forming adjectives) denoting a state or an occurrence of action: *convenient*. **2** (forming nouns) denoting an agent: *coefficient*.

ORIGIN – from the Latin present participial verb stem *-ent-*.

entablature /intabləchər/ > *noun* Architecture the upper part of a classical building supported by columns or a colonnade, comprising the architrave, frieze, and cornice.

ORIGIN – Italian *intavolatura* 'boarding'.

entail > *verb* **1** involve (something) as an inevitable part or consequence. **2** Law settle the inheritance of (property) over a number of generations so it remains within a family. > *noun* Law an instance of entailing property.

DERIVATIVES – **entailment** *noun*.

ORIGIN – from Old French *taille* (see TAIL[2]).

entangle > *verb* (usu. **be entangled in** or **with**) **1** cause to become tangled. **2** involve in complicated circumstances.

DERIVATIVES – **entanglement** *noun*.

entente /oNtoNt/ (also **entente cordiale** /kordiaal/) > *noun* a friendly understanding or informal alliance between states or factions.

ORIGIN – French *entente cordiale* 'friendly understanding'.

enter > *verb* **1** come or go into. **2** (often **enter into** or **on**) begin to be involved in or do. **3** join (an institution or profession). **4** register as a competitor or participant in. **5** (**enter into**) undertake to bind oneself by (an agreement). **6** record (information) in a book, computer, etc.

ORIGIN – Old French *entrer*, from Latin *intrare*, from *intra* 'within'.

enteric /enterrik/ > *adjective* relating to or occurring in the intestines.

COMBINATIONS – **enteric fever** typhoid or paratyphoid.

ORIGIN – Greek *enterikos*, from *enteron* 'intestine'.

enteritis /entərītiss/ > *noun* Medicine inflammation of the intestine, especially the small intestine, usually accompanied by diarrhoea.

enterprise* > *noun* **1** a project or undertaking, especially a bold one. **2** bold resourcefulness. **3** a business or company.

*****SPELLING** – *-ise* not *-ize*: enterprise.

SYNONYMS – **1** endeavour, project, pursuit, undertaking, venture. **2** initiative, inventiveness, resourcefulness; informal gumption.

ORIGIN – Old French, 'something undertaken', from Latin *prehendere* 'to take'.

enterprising > *adjective* showing initiative and resourcefulness.

DERIVATIVES – **enterprisingly** *adverb*.

SYNONYMS – imaginative, inventive, resourceful.

entertain > *verb* **1** provide with amusement or enjoyment. **2** show hospitality to. **3** give attention or consideration to (an idea, suggestion, or feeling).

SYNONYMS – **1** amuse, divert, engage, interest. **2** accommodate, receive, welcome. **3** consider, contemplate.

---

wordpower facts

Entertain

The word **entertain** comes through Old French *entretenir* from Latin *inter* 'among' + *tenere* 'to hold'. *Tenere* is also the root of words such as **contain**, **maintain**, **sustain**, **tenacious**, and **tenant**. In medieval times **entertain** meant 'maintain or continue'; later it came to mean 'treat in a certain way, maintain in a certain condition' and so 'show hospitality'.

---

entertainer > *noun* a person, such as a singer or comedian, whose job is to entertain others.

entertaining > *adjective* providing amusement or enjoyment.

DERIVATIVES – **entertainingly** *adverb*.

entertainment > *noun* **1** the action of entertaining or being entertained. **2** an event, performance, or activity designed to entertain others.

enthral* /inˈthrawl/ (US **enthrall**) > *verb* (**enthralled**, **enthralling**) **1** fascinate (someone) and hold their attention. **2** (also **inthrall**) archaic enslave.

DERIVATIVES – **enthralment** (US **enthrallment**) *noun*.

*SPELLING – one *l* in **enthral** and **enthrals**, two in **enthralled** and **enthralling**.

ORIGIN – from EN-¹ + THRALL.

enthrone > *verb* ceremonially install (a monarch or bishop) on a throne.

DERIVATIVES – **enthronement** *noun*.

enthuse /inˈthyooz/ > *verb* **1** (often **enthuse over**) express one's great enthusiasm for something: *they both enthused over my new look.* **2** make (someone) enthusiastic about something.

enthusiasm > *noun* **1** intense enjoyment, interest, or approval. **2** an object of such feelings. **3** archaic, derogatory religious fervour supposedly resulting directly from divine inspiration.

SYNONYMS – **1** ardour, eagerness, fervour, gusto, keenness, zeal.

ORIGIN – Greek *enthousiasmos*, from *enthous* 'possessed by a god'.

enthusiast > *noun* **1** a person who is full of enthusiasm for something. **2** archaic, derogatory a person with intense and visionary Christian views.

enthusiastic > *adjective* having or showing great enthusiasm.

DERIVATIVES – **enthusiastically** *adverb*.

SYNONYMS – ardent, eager, fervent, keen, zealous.

ANTONYMS – indifferent, unenthusiastic.

entice /inˈtiss/ > *verb* attract by offering pleasure or advantage.

DERIVATIVES – **enticement** *noun* **enticer** *noun* **enticing** *adjective* **enticingly** *adverb*.

SYNONYMS – attract, lure, tempt.

ORIGIN – Old French *enticier*, probably from a base meaning 'set on fire'.

entire /inˈtir/ > *adjective* **1** with no part left out; whole. **2** not broken, damaged, or decayed. **3** without qualification; absolute.

SYNONYMS – **1** complete, total, whole. **3** absolute, total, utter.

ANTONYMS – **1,3** partial.

ORIGIN – Old French *entier*, from Latin *integer* 'untouched, whole'.

entirely > *adverb* **1** wholly; completely. **2** solely.

entirety /inˈtirəti/ > *noun* (**the entirety**) the whole.

IDIOMS – **in its entirety** as a whole.

entitle > *verb* **1** give (someone) a right to receive or do something. **2** give a title to (a book, play, etc.).

DERIVATIVES – **entitlement** *noun*.

entity /ˈentiti/ > *noun* (pl. **entities**) a thing with distinct and independent existence.

SYNONYMS – article, being, object, organism, thing.

ORIGIN – French *entité*, from Latin *ens* 'being'.

entomb > *verb* **1** place in a tomb. **2** (**entomb in** or **under**) bury in or under.

DERIVATIVES – **entombment** *noun*.

entomology /entəˈmolləji/ > *noun* the branch of zoology concerned with the study of insects.

DERIVATIVES – **entomological** *adjective* **entomologist** *noun*.

ORIGIN – from Greek *entomon* 'insect', from *entomos* 'cut up, segmented'.

entourage /ˈontooraazh/ > *noun* a group of people attending or surrounding an important person.

ORIGIN – French, from *entourer* 'to surround'.

entr'acte /ˈontrakt/ > *noun* **1** an interval between two acts of a play or opera. **2** a piece of music or a dance performed during such an interval.

ORIGIN – French, from *entre* 'between' + *acte* 'act'.

entrails /ˈentraylz/ > *plural noun* a person's or animal's intestines or internal organs.

ORIGIN – Latin *intralia* 'internal things'.

entrain¹ > *verb* board or put on board a train.

entrain² > *verb* **1** (of a current or fluid) incorporate and sweep along in its flow. **2** bring about as a consequence.

DERIVATIVES – **entrainment** *noun*.

ORIGIN – French *entraîner*, from *en-* 'in' + *traîner* 'to drag'.

entrammel /inˈtramm'l/ > *verb* (**entrammelled**, **entrammelling**; US **entrammeled**, **entrammeling**) literary entangle or trap.

entrance¹ /ˈentrənss/ > *noun* **1** an opening that allows access to a place. **2** an act of entering. **3** the right, means, or opportunity to enter.

entrance² /inˈtraanss/ > *verb* **1** fill (someone) with wonder and delight. **2** cast a spell on.

DERIVATIVES – **entrancement** *noun* **entrancing** *adjective* **entrancingly** *adverb*.

SYNONYMS – **1** bewitch, captivate, charm, delight, enchant. **2** hypnotise, mesmerise.

entrant > *noun* a person who enters, joins, or takes part in something.

entrap > *verb* (**entrapped**, **entrapping**) **1** catch in a trap. **2** (of a police officer) deceive (someone) into committing a crime in order to secure their prosecution.

DERIVATIVES – **entrapment** *noun*.

en travesti /ON travəˈstee/ > *adverb & adjective* dressed as a member of the opposite sex, especially for a theatrical role.

ORIGIN – French, 'in disguise'.

entreat > *verb* **1** ask (someone) earnestly or anxiously. **2** ask earnestly or anxiously for (something).

ORIGIN – Old French *entraitier*, from Latin *tractare* 'to handle'.

entreaty > *noun* (pl. **entreaties**) an earnest or humble request.

SYNONYMS – appeal, petition, plea, request.

entrechat /ˈontrəshaa/ > *noun* Ballet a vertical jump during which the dancer repeatedly crosses the feet and beats them together.

ORIGIN – from Italian *capriola intrecciata* 'complicated caper'.

entrecôte /ˈontrəkōt/ > *noun* a boned steak cut off the sirloin.

ORIGIN – French, from *entre* 'between' + *côte* 'rib'.

entrée /ˈontray/ > *noun* **1** the main course of a meal. **2** Brit. a savoury dish served before the main course at a formal dinner. **3** right of entry.

ORIGIN – French, from *entrer* 'enter'.

entrench > *verb* **1** establish (something) so firmly that change is difficult. **2** establish (a military force, camp, etc.) in trenches or other fortified positions.

DERIVATIVES – **entrenchment** *noun*.

entre nous /ontrə ˈnoo/ > *adverb* between ourselves.

ORIGIN – French.

entrepôt /ˈontrəpō/ > *noun* a port or other place which acts as a centre for import and export.

ORIGIN – French, from *entreposer* 'to store'.

entrepreneur /ontrəprəˈnör/ > *noun* a person who sets up a business or businesses.

DERIVATIVES – **entrepreneurial** /ontrəprəˈnörial, ontrəprəˈnyoorial/ *adjective* **entrepreneurialism** *noun* **entrepreneurially** *adverb* **entrepreneurism** *noun*.

ORIGIN – French, from *entreprendre* 'undertake'.

entropy /ˈentrəpi/ > *noun* Physics a thermodynamic quantity expressing the unavailability of a system's thermal energy for conversion into mechanical work, often interpreted as the degree of disorder or randomness in the system.

DERIVATIVES – **entropic** /enˈtroppik/ *adjective*.

ORIGIN – from Greek *tropē* 'transformation'.

entrust > *verb* **1** (**entrust with**) assign a responsibility to (someone). **2** (**entrust to**) put (something) into someone's care.

entry > *noun* (pl. **entries**) **1** an act or the action of entering. **2** an opening through which one may enter, e.g. a door, gate, etc. **3** dialect a passage between buildings. **4** the right, means, or opportunity to enter. **5** an item entered in a list, account book, reference book, etc. **6** a person who enters a competition.

COMBINATIONS – **entry-level** suitable for a beginner or first-time user. **entryphone** Brit. trademark a type of intercom at the entrance to a building by which visitors may identify themselves.

entryism > *noun* the infiltration of a political party by members of another group, to subvert its policies or objectives.

DERIVATIVES – **entryist** noun.

entwine > *verb* wind or twist together.

E-number > *noun* Brit. a code number preceded by the letter E, given to food additives numbered in accordance with EU directives.

enumerate /inˈyoomərayt/ > *verb* **1** mention one by one. **2** formal establish the number of.

DERIVATIVES – **enumerable** *adjective* **enumeration** noun **enumerative** *adjective*.

ORIGIN – Latin *enumerare* 'count out'.

enumerator > *noun* a person employed in taking a census of the population.

enunciate /inˈunsiayt/ > *verb* **1** say or pronounce clearly. **2** set out precisely or definitely.

DERIVATIVES – **enunciation** noun **enunciator** noun.

ORIGIN – Latin *enuntiare* 'announce clearly'.

enuresis /enyooˈreesiss/ > *noun* involuntary urination, especially by children at night.

DERIVATIVES – **enuretic** *adjective*.

ORIGIN – Latin, from Greek *enourein* 'urinate in'.

envelop* /inˈveləp/ > *verb* (**enveloped**, **enveloping**) wrap up, cover, or surround completely.

DERIVATIVES – **envelopment** noun.

*SPELLING – unlike the noun *envelope*, the verb **envelop** has no final e. An e is added for the past tense (*enveloped*) but not the present (*envelop*, *envelops*).

SYNONYMS – cover, enfold, engulf, shroud, surround.

ORIGIN – Old French *envoluper*, related to **DEVELOP**.

envelope /ˈenvəlōp, ˈonvəlōp/ > *noun* **1** a flat paper container with a sealable flap, used to enclose a letter or document. **2** a covering or containing structure or layer. **3** the outer housing of a vacuum tube, electric light, etc. **4** the structure within a balloon or non-rigid airship containing the gas.

IDIOMS – **push the (edge of the) envelope** informal approach or extend the limits of what is possible. [ORIGIN – aviation slang, relating to graphs of aerodynamic performance.]

ORIGIN – first used in the sense 'enveloping layer': from French *envelopper* 'envelop'.

envenom > *verb* poison by biting or stinging.

enviable /ˈenviəb'l/ > *adjective* arousing or likely to arouse envy.

DERIVATIVES – **enviably** adverb.

envious > *adjective* feeling or showing envy.

DERIVATIVES – **enviously** adverb.

SYNONYMS – covetous, jealous.

environment* > *noun* **1** the surroundings or conditions in which a person, animal, or plant lives or operates. **2** (**the environment**) the natural world, especially as affected by human activity. **3** Computing the overall structure within which a user, computer, or program operates.

WORDFINDER – conservationist (*person who is dedicated to protecting the environment*), eco-friendly (*not harmful to the environment*), ecology (*study of the interaction of organisms and the environment*), habitat (*natural environment of an organism*), milieu (*social environment*).

DERIVATIVES – **environmental** *adjective* **environmentally** adverb.

*SPELLING – remember the n before -ment: environment.

SYNONYMS – domain, habitat, territory.

environmentalist > *noun* **1** a person who is concerned with the protection of the environment. **2** a person who considers that environment has the primary influence on the development of a person or group.

DERIVATIVES – **environmentalism** noun.

environs > *plural noun* the surrounding area or district.

ORIGIN – French, plural of *environ* 'surroundings'.

envisage /inˈvizzij/ > *verb* **1** regard or conceive of as a possibility. **2** form a mental picture of.

SYNONYMS – **1** anticipate, envision, expect, foresee. **2** imagine, picture, visualise.

ORIGIN – French *envisager*, from *visage* 'face'.

envision > *verb* visualise; envisage.

envoi /ˈenvoy/ (also **envoy**) > *noun* archaic an author's concluding words.

ORIGIN – Old French, from *envoyer* 'send'.

envoy /ˈenvoy/ > *noun* **1** a messenger or representative, especially one on a diplomatic mission. **2** (also **envoy extraordinary**) a minister plenipotentiary, ranking below ambassador and above chargé d'affaires.

ORIGIN – French *envoyé* 'sent', from *en voie* 'on the way', from Latin *via* 'way'.

envy > *noun* (pl. **envies**) **1** discontented or resentful longing aroused by another's possessions, qualities, or luck. **2** (**the envy of**) a person or thing that inspires such a feeling. > *verb* (**envies**, **envied**) feel envy of: *I envy Jane her happiness.*

SYNONYMS – *noun* **1** covetousness, enviousness, jealousy.

ORIGIN – Old French, from Latin *invidia* 'hostility, ill will', the root also of **INVIDIOUS**.

enwrap > *verb* (**enwrapped**, **enwrapping**) wrap; envelop.

Enzed /enˈzed/ > *noun* Austral./NZ informal New Zealand or a New Zealander.

DERIVATIVES – **Enzedder** noun.

ORIGIN – representing a pronunciation of the initials *NZ*.

enzyme /ˈenzīm/ > *noun* a substance produced by a living organism and acting as a catalyst to promote a specific biochemical reaction.

DERIVATIVES – **enzymatic** *adjective* **enzymic** *adjective*.

ORIGIN – from modern Greek *enzumos* 'leavened'.

EOC > *abbreviation* (in the UK) Equal Opportunities Commission.

Eocene /ˈeeəseen/ > *adjective* Geology relating to the second epoch of the Tertiary period (between the Palaeocene and Oligocene epochs, 56.5 to 35.4 million years ago), a time when the first horses, bats, and whales appeared.

ORIGIN – from Greek *ēōs* 'dawn' + *kainos* 'new'.

eolian > *adjective* US spelling of **AEOLIAN**.

eon > *noun* US and technical spelling of **AEON**.

EP > *abbreviation* **1** extended-play (of a record or compact disc). **2** European Parliament.

ep- > *prefix* variant spelling of **EPI-**, shortened before a vowel or h.

épater /aypatˈtay/ > *verb* (in phrase **épater les bourgeois**) deliberately shock or displease people regarded as conventional or complacent.

ORIGIN – French.

epaulette /ˈeppəlet/ (US also **epaulet**) > *noun* an ornamental shoulder piece on a coat or jacket, especially as part of military uniform.

ORIGIN – French, 'little shoulder'.

épée /ˈaypay, ˈeppay/ > *noun* a sharp-pointed duelling sword, used, with the end blunted, in fencing.

ORIGIN – French, 'sword'.

ephedrine /ˈeffədrin/ > *noun* a drug which causes constriction of the blood vessels and widening of the bronchial passages and is used to relieve asthma and hay fever.

ORIGIN – from *ephedra*, an evergreen plant which is the source of the drug.

ephemera /iˈfemmərə/ > *plural noun* items of short-lived interest or usefulness.

ORIGIN – Greek, 'things lasting only a day': originally as singular *ephemeron*, denoting a plant said to last only one day, or an insect with a short lifespan.

ephemeral > *adjective* lasting or living for a very short time.

DERIVATIVES – **ephemerality** *noun* **ephemerally** *adverb*.

SYNONYMS – fleeting, impermanent, short-lived, transient, transitory.

ANTONYMS – long-lived, permanent.

epi- (also **ep-**) > *prefix* **1** upon: *epigraph*. **2** above: *epicotyl*. **3** in addition: *epiphenomenon*.

ORIGIN – from Greek *epi* 'upon, near to, in addition'.

epic > *noun* **1** a long poem describing the deeds of heroic or legendary figures or the past history of a nation. **2** a long film, book, etc. portraying heroic deeds or covering an extended period of time. > *adjective* **1** relating to or characteristic of an epic. **2** heroic or grand in scale or character.

DERIVATIVES – **epical** *adjective* **epically** *adverb*.

ORIGIN – from Greek *epikos*, from *epos* 'word, song'.

epicanthic fold /eppi**kan**thik/ > *noun* a fold of skin from the upper eyelid covering the inner angle of the eye, typical in many peoples of eastern Asia.

epicene /**epp**iseen/ > *adjective* **1** having characteristics of both sexes or no characteristics of either sex. **2** effete.

ORIGIN – Greek *epikoinos*, from *koinos* 'common'.

epicentre (US **epicenter**) > *noun* the point on the earth's surface vertically above the focus of an earthquake.

ORIGIN – from Greek *epikentros* 'situated on a centre'.

epicure /**epp**ikyoor/ > *noun* a person who takes particular pleasure in fine food and drink.

ORIGIN – from *Epicurus* (see **EPICUREAN**).

Epicurean /eppikyoo**ree**ən/ > *noun* **1** a follower of the Greek philosopher Epicurus (341–270 BC), who taught that pleasure, particularly mental pleasure, was the highest good. **2** (**epicurean**) an epicure. > *adjective* **1** relating to Epicurus or his ideas. **2** (**epicurean**) relating to or suitable for an epicure.

DERIVATIVES – **Epicureanism** *noun*.

epidemic > *noun* **1** a widespread occurrence of an infectious disease in a community at a particular time. **2** a sudden, widespread occurrence of something undesirable. > *adjective* relating to or of the nature of an epidemic.

ORIGIN – Greek *epidēmia*, from *epi* 'upon' + *dēmos* 'the people'.

epidemiology /eppideemi**oll**əji/ > *noun* the study of the incidence and distribution of diseases and other factors relating to health.

DERIVATIVES – **epidemiological** *adjective* **epidemiologist** *noun*.

epidermis /eppi**der**miss/ > *noun* **1** the surface layer of an animal's skin, overlying the dermis. **2** the outer layer of tissue in a plant.

DERIVATIVES – **epidermal** *adjective*.

ORIGIN – Greek, from *epi* 'upon' + *derma* 'skin'.

epidiascope /eppi**dī**əskōp/ > *noun* an optical projector capable of giving images of both opaque and transparent objects.

ORIGIN – from **EPI-** + **DIA-** **-SCOPE**.

epididymis /eppi**didd**imiss/ > *noun* (pl. **epididymides** /eppidi**dimm**ideez/) Anatomy a duct behind the testis, along which sperm passes to the vas deferens.

ORIGIN – Greek *epididumis*, from *epi* 'upon' + *didumos* 'testicle'.

epidural /eppi**dyoor**əl/ > *adjective* on or around the dura mater of the spinal cord. > *noun* an anaesthetic introduced into the space around the dura mater, used especially in childbirth.

epigenetic /eppiji**nett**ik/ > *adjective* Biology resulting from external rather than genetic influences.

epiglottis /eppi**glott**iss/ > *noun* a flap of cartilage at the root of the tongue, which is depressed during swallowing to cover the opening of the windpipe.

ORIGIN – Greek, from *epi* 'upon, near to' + *glōtta* 'tongue'.

epigone /**epp**igōn/ > *noun* (pl. **epigones** or **epigoni** /i**pigg**ənī/) a less distinguished follower or imitator.

ORIGIN – from Greek *epigonoi* 'those born afterwards'.

epigram /**epp**igram/ > *noun* **1** a concise and witty saying or remark. **2** a short witty poem.

DERIVATIVES – **epigrammatic** *adjective*.

ORIGIN – Greek *epigramma*, from *epi* 'upon, in addition' + *gramma* 'writing'.

epigraph /**epp**igraaf/ > *noun* **1** an inscription on a building, statue, or coin. **2** a short quotation or saying introducing a book or chapter.

epigraphy /i**pi**grəfi/ > *noun* the study of ancient inscriptions.

DERIVATIVES – **epigraphic** *adjective*.

epilation /eppi**lay**sh'n/ > *noun* the removal of hair by the roots.

ORIGIN – from French *épiler*, from Latin *pilus* 'strand of hair'.

epilepsy /**epp**ilepsi/ > *noun* a disorder marked by sudden recurrent episodes of sensory disturbance, loss of consciousness, or convulsions.

DERIVATIVES – **epileptic** *adjective & noun*.

ORIGIN – Greek *epilēpsia*, from *epilambanein* 'seize, attack'.

epilogue /**epp**ilog/ (US also **epilog**) > *noun* a section or speech at the end of a book or play serving as a comment on or conclusion to what has happened.

ORIGIN – Greek *epilogos*, from *epi* 'in addition' + *logos* 'speech'.

epiphany /i**piff**əni/ > *noun* (pl. **epiphanies**) **1** (**Epiphany**) (in Christian belief) the manifestation of Christ to the Magi (the Gospel of Matthew, chapter 2). **2** (**Epiphany**) the festival commemorating this, on 6 January. **3** a moment of sudden and great revelation.

DERIVATIVES – **epiphanic** /eppi**fann**ik/ *adjective*.

ORIGIN – from Greek *epiphainein* 'reveal'.

epiphenomenon /eppifi**nomm**inən/ > *noun* (pl. **epiphenomena**) **1** Medicine a secondary symptom, occurring simultaneously with a disease or condition but not directly related to it. **2** a mental state regarded as a by-product of brain activity.

DERIVATIVES – **epiphenomenal** *adjective*.

epiphyte /**epp**ifīt/ > *noun* a plant that grows on a tree or other plant but is not a parasite.

DERIVATIVES – **epiphytic** /eppi**fitt**ik/ *adjective*.

ORIGIN – from Greek *epi* 'upon' + *phuton* 'plant'.

episcopacy /i**pisk**əpəsi/ > *noun* (pl. **episcopacies**) **1** government of a Church by bishops. **2** (**the episcopacy**) the bishops of a region or church collectively.

episcopal /i**pisk**əp'l/ > *adjective* **1** of a bishop or bishops. **2** (of a Church) governed by or having bishops.

DERIVATIVES – **episcopally** *adverb*.

COMBINATIONS – **Episcopal Church** the Anglican Church in Scotland and the US, with elected bishops.

ORIGIN – Latin *episcopus* 'bishop', from Greek *episkopos* 'overseer'.

episcopalian /ipiskə**payl**iən/ > *adjective* **1** of or advocating government of a Church by bishops. **2** of or belonging to an episcopal Church. > *noun* **1** an advocate of government of a Church by bishops. **2** (**Episcopalian**) a member of the Episcopal Church.

DERIVATIVES – **episcopalianism** *noun*.

episcopate /i**pisk**əpət/ > *noun* **1** the office or term of office of a bishop. **2** (**the episcopate**) the bishops of a church or region collectively.

episiotomy /ipisi**ott**əmi/ > *noun* (pl. **episiotomies**) a surgical cut made at the opening of the vagina during childbirth, to prevent a tear during delivery.

ORIGIN – from Greek *epision* 'pubic region'.

episode > *noun* **1** an event or a group of events occurring as part of a sequence. **2** each of the separate instalments into which a serialised story or programme is divided.

ORIGIN – Greek *epeisodion*, from *epeisodios* 'coming in besides'.

episodic /eppi**sodd**ik/ > *adjective* **1** occurring as or presented in episodes. **2** occurring at irregular intervals.

DERIVATIVES – **episodically** *adverb*.

epistemology /ipisti**moll**əji/ > *noun* the branch of philosophy that deals with knowledge, especially with regard to its methods, validity, and scope.

DERIVATIVES – **epistemic** *adjective* **epistemological** *adjective* **epistemologist** *noun*.

ORIGIN – from Greek *epistēmē* 'knowledge'.

epistle /i**piss**'l/ > *noun* **1** formal or humorous a letter. **2** (**Epistle**) a book of the New Testament in the form of a letter from an Apostle.

ORIGIN – Greek *epistolē*, from *epistellein* 'send news'.

epistolary /i**pist**ələri/ > *adjective* **1** relating to the writing of letters. **2** (of a literary work) in the form of letters.

epistyle /**epp**istīl/ > *noun* Architecture an architrave.

ORIGIN – Greek *epistulion*, from *epi* 'upon' + *stulos* 'pillar'.

epitaph /**epp**itaaf/ > *noun* words written in memory of a person who has died, especially as an inscription on a tombstone.

ORIGIN – Greek *epitaphion* 'funeral oration', from *ephitaphios* 'over or at a tomb'.

epithalamium /eppithə**laym**iəm/ > *noun* (pl. **epithalamiums** or **epithalamia**) a song or poem celebrating a marriage.

ORIGIN – Latin, from Greek *epi* 'upon' + *thalamos* 'bridal chamber'.

epithelium /eppi**theel**iəm/ > *noun* (pl. **epithelia** /eppi**theel**iə/) Anatomy the thin tissue forming the outer layer of the body's surface and lining the alimentary canal and other hollow structures.

DERIVATIVES – **epithelial** *adjective*.

ORIGIN – Latin, from Greek *thēlē* 'teat'.

epithet /**epp**ithet/ > *noun* a word or phrase expressing a quality or attribute of the person or thing mentioned.

ORIGIN – Greek *epitheton*, from *epitithenai* 'add'.

epitome /i**pitt**əmi/ > *noun* **1** (**the epitome of**) a perfect example of a quality or type. **2** a summary of a written work.

ORIGIN – Greek, from *epitemnein* 'abridge'.

epitomise (also **epitomize**) > *verb* **1** be a perfect example of. **2** archaic summarise (a written work).

SYNONYMS – **1** embody, exemplify, personify, typify.

e pluribus unum /ay ploori**booss** **yōō**noōm/ > *noun* one out of many (the motto of the US).

ORIGIN – Latin.

epoch /**ee**pok/ > *noun* **1** a period of time marked by particular events or characteristics. **2** the beginning of a period of history. **3** Geology a division of time that is a subdivision of a period and is itself subdivided into ages.

DERIVATIVES – **epochal** *adjective*.

COMBINATIONS – **epoch-making** significant; historic.

ORIGIN – Greek *epokhē* 'stoppage, fixed point of time'.

eponym /**epp**ənim/ > *noun* **1** a word or name derived from the name of a person. **2** a person after whom a discovery, invention, place, etc. is named.

ORIGIN – from Greek *epōnumos* 'given as a name, giving one's name', from *epi* 'upon' + *onoma* 'name'.

---

wordpower facts

Eponym

Many familiar English words are eponyms, that is they are derived from the name of a person. Some fall into categories: food and drink (**pavlova**, **sandwich**, **stroganoff**), clothing (**bowler**, **cardigan**, **wellington**), plants and animals (**begonia**, **buddleia**, **dahlia**, **guppy**), and scientific units (**ampere**, **joule**, **ohm**, **volt**, **watt**). Some rather surprising words are eponyms: the **biro** is named after its Hungarian inventor László József Biró (1899–1985), while the **sequoia** or redwood tree of California takes its name from *Sequoya*, the Cherokee Indian who invented the written characters for the Cherokee language.

---

eponymous /i**ponn**iməss/ > *adjective* **1** (of a person) giving their name to something. **2** (of a thing) named after a particular person.

epoxide /i**poks**īd/ > *noun* Chemistry an organic compound whose molecule contains a three-membered ring involving an oxygen atom and two carbon atoms.

epoxy /i**poks**i/ (also **epoxy resin**) > *noun* (pl. **epoxies**) an adhesive, plastic, paint, etc. made from synthetic polymers containing epoxide groups.

EPROM /**ee**prom/ > *noun* Computing a read-only memory whose contents can be erased and reprogrammed using special means.

ORIGIN – from *erasable programmable ROM*.

epsilon /**ep**silon, ep**sī**lon/ > *noun* the fifth letter of the Greek alphabet (E, ε), transliterated as 'e'.

ORIGIN – Greek, 'bare or simple E', from *psilos* 'bare'.

Epsom salts > *plural noun* crystals of hydrated magnesium sulphate used as a laxative.

ORIGIN – named after the town of *Epsom* in Surrey, where the salts were first found occurring naturally.

equable /**ek**wəb'l/ > *adjective* **1** calm and even-tempered. **2** not varying or fluctuating greatly.

DERIVATIVES – **equability** *noun* **equably** *adverb*.

ORIGIN – Latin *aequabilis*, from *aequare* 'make equal'.

equal > *adjective* **1** being the same in quantity, size, degree, value, or status. **2** evenly or fairly balanced. **3** (**equal to**) having the ability or resources to meet (a challenge). > *noun* a person or thing that is equal to another. > *verb* (**equalled, equalling; US equaled, equaling**) **1** be equal or equivalent to. **2** match or rival.

WORDFINDER – ceteris paribus (*'other things being equal'*), egalitarianism (*the belief that all people deserve equal rights*).

DERIVATIVES – **equality** *noun*.

USAGE – on the use of **equal** with *more*, *very*, etc. see the note at UNIQUE.

SYNONYMS – *adjective* **1** equivalent, identical, uniform. **2** balanced, even, level.

ANTONYMS – *adjective* unequal.

COMBINATIONS – **equals sign** (also **equal sign**) the symbol =.

ORIGIN – Latin *aequalis*, from *aequus* 'even, level, equal'.

equalise (also **equalize**) > *verb* **1** make or become equal. **2** level the score in a match by scoring a goal.

DERIVATIVES – **equalisation** *noun*.

equaliser (also **equalizer**) > *noun* **1** a thing that has an equalising effect. **2** a goal that levels the score in a match.

equally > *adverb* **1** in an equal manner. **2** in amounts or parts that are equal. **3** to an equal degree.

USAGE – avoid the construction **equally as**, as in *follow-up discussion is equally as important*: just use either **equally** or **as** alone.

equanimity /ekwə**nimm**iti, eekwə**nimm**iti/ > *noun* calmness; composure.

DERIVATIVES – **equanimous** /i**kwann**iməss/ *adjective*.

ORIGIN – Latin *aequanimitas*, from *aequus* 'equal' + *animus* 'mind'.

equate /i**kwayt**/ > *verb* (often **equate to** or **with**) **1** consider (one thing) as equal or equivalent to another. **2** be or cause to be the same as or equivalent to.

equation /i**kwayzh**'n/ > *noun* **1** the process of equating one thing with another. **2** Mathematics a statement that the values of two mathematical expressions are equal (indicated by the sign =). **3** Chemistry a symbolic representation of the changes which occur in a chemical reaction.

equator /i**kwayt**ər/ > *noun* **1** a notional line around the earth equidistant from the poles, dividing the earth into northern and southern hemispheres. **2** Astronomy short for *celestial equator*.

ORIGIN – Latin *aequator*, in the phrase *circulus aequator diei et noctis* 'circle equalising day and night'.

equatorial /ekwətoriəl/ > *adjective* of, at, or near the equator.

DERIVATIVES – **equatorially** adverb.

equerry /ekwəri, ikwerri/ > *noun* (pl. **equerries**) **1** an officer of the British royal household who attends members of the royal family. **2** historical an officer of the household of a prince or noble who had charge over the stables.

ORIGIN – Old French *esquierie* 'company of squires, prince's stables', perhaps associated with Latin *equus* 'horse'.

equestrian /ikwestriən/ > *adjective* **1** relating to horse riding. **2** depicting or representing a person on horseback. > *noun* (fem. **equestrienne** /ikwestrien/) a person on horseback.

ORIGIN – Latin *equester*, from *eques* 'horseman, knight', from *equus* 'horse'.

equestrianism > *noun* the skill or sport of horse riding.

equi- /eekwi, ekwi/ > *combining form* equal; equally: *equidistant*.

ORIGIN – from Latin *aequus* 'equal'.

equiangular > *adjective* having equal angles.

equidistant > *adjective* at equal distances.

DERIVATIVES – **equidistance** noun **equidistantly** adverb.

equilateral /eekwilattərəl, ekwilattərəl/ > *adjective* having all its sides of the same length.

equilibrate /ikwillibrayt, eekwilībrayt/ > *verb* bring into or maintain a state of equilibrium.

DERIVATIVES – **equilibration** noun.

equilibrist /ikwillibrist/ > *noun* chiefly archaic an acrobat, especially a tightrope walker.

equilibrium /eekwilibriəm, ekwilibriəm/ > *noun* (pl. **equilibria** /eekwilibriə, ekwilibriə/) **1** a state in which opposing forces or influences are balanced. **2** the state of being physically balanced. **3** a calm state of mind.

ORIGIN – Latin *aequilibrium*, from *libra* 'balance'.

equine /ekwīn/ > *adjective* **1** relating to horses or other members of the horse family. **2** resembling a horse. > *noun* a horse or other member of the horse family.

ORIGIN – Latin *equinus*, from *equus* 'horse'.

equinoctial /eekwinoksh'l, ekwinoksh'l/ > *adjective* **1** relating to or at the time of the equinox. **2** at or near the equator. > *noun* (also **equinoctial line**) the celestial equator.

COMBINATIONS – **equinoctial point** either of two points at which the ecliptic cuts the celestial equator. **equinoctial year** another term for *solar year*.

equinox /ekwinoks, eekwinoks/ > *noun* **1** the time or date (twice each year, about 20 March and 22 September) at which the sun crosses the celestial equator, when day and night are of equal length. **2** Astronomy another term for EQUINOCTIAL POINT.

WORDFINDER – precession (*progressively earlier occurrence of equinoxes*).

ORIGIN – Latin *aequinoctium*, from *aequus* 'equal' + *nox* 'night'.

equip > *verb* (**equipped**, **equipping**) **1** supply with the items needed for a particular purpose. **2** prepare (someone) mentally for a particular situation or task.

SYNONYMS – **1** furnish, issue, provide, supply.

ORIGIN – French *équiper*, probably from Old Norse *skipa* 'to man a ship'.

equipage /ekwipij/ > *noun* **1** archaic equipment. **2** historical a carriage and horses with attendants.

equipment > *noun* **1** the items needed for a particular purpose. **2** the process of supplying these items.

SYNONYMS – **1** apparatus, gadgetry, impedimenta, kit, paraphernalia.

equipoise /ekwipoyz/ > *noun* **1** balance of forces or interests. **2** a counterbalance or balancing force.

equitable /ekwitəb'l/ > *adjective* **1** fair and impartial. **2** Law valid in equity as distinct from law.

DERIVATIVES – **equitably** adverb.

equitation /ekwitaysh'n/ > *noun* formal the art and practice of horse riding.

ORIGIN – Latin, from *equitare* 'ride a horse'.

equity /ekwiti/ > *noun* (pl. **equities**) **1** the quality of being fair and impartial. **2** Law a branch of law that developed alongside common law in order to remedy some of its defects in fairness and justice. **3** the value of a mortgaged property after deduction of charges against it. **4** the value of the shares issued by a company. **5** (**equities**) stocks and shares that carry no fixed interest.

ORIGIN – Latin *aequitas*, from *aequus* 'equal'.

equivalent /ikwivvələnt/ > *adjective* (often **equivalent to**) **1** equal in value, amount, function, meaning, etc. **2** having the same or a similar effect. > *noun* a person or thing that is equivalent to another.

DERIVATIVES – **equivalence** noun **equivalency** noun **equivalently** adverb.

SYNONYMS – *adjective* analogous, comparable, equal, parallel.

ORIGIN – from Latin *aequivalere* 'be of equal worth'.

equivocal /ikwivvək'l/ > *adjective* unclear in meaning or intention; ambiguous.

DERIVATIVES – **equivocally** adverb.

SYNONYMS – ambiguous, imprecise, indefinite, vague.

ORIGIN – from Latin *aequus* 'equal' + *vocare* 'to call'.

equivocate /ikwivvəkayt/ > *verb* use ambiguous or evasive language.

DERIVATIVES – **equivocation** noun.

ER > *abbreviation* **1** Queen Elizabeth. [ORIGIN – from Latin *Elizabetha Regina* ('queen').] **2** N. Amer. emergency room.

Er > *symbol* the chemical element erbium.

-er¹ > *suffix* **1** denoting a person or thing that performs a specified action or activity: *farmer*. **2** denoting a person or thing that has a specified attribute or form: *two-wheeler*. **3** denoting a person concerned with a specified thing: *milliner*. **4** denoting a person belonging to a specified place or group: *city-dweller*.

-er² > *suffix* forming the comparative of adjectives (as in *bigger*) and adverbs (as in *faster*).

-er³ > *suffix* forming nouns used informally, usually by distortion of the root word: *footer*.

ORIGIN – Rugby School slang, later adopted at Oxford University.

era /eerə/ > *noun* **1** a long and distinct period of history. **2** Geology a major division of time that is a subdivision of an aeon and is itself subdivided into periods.

SYNONYMS – **1** age, epoch, period.

ORIGIN – Latin *aera*, denoting a number used as a basis of reckoning, plural of *aes* 'money, counter'.

eradicate /iraddikayt/ > *verb* remove or destroy completely.

DERIVATIVES – **eradication** noun **eradicator** noun.

SYNONYMS – annihilate, destroy, eliminate, exterminate, extirpate, obliterate.

ORIGIN – Latin *eradicare* 'tear up by the roots', from *radix* 'root'.

erase /irayz/ > *verb* rub out or obliterate; remove all traces of.

DERIVATIVES – **erasable** adjective **erasure** noun.

SYNONYMS – delete, excise, obliterate, remove, rub out.

ORIGIN – Latin *eradere* 'scrape away'.

eraser > *noun* a piece of rubber or plastic used to rub out something written.

erbium /erbiəm/ > *noun* a soft silvery-white metallic chemical element of the lanthanide series.

ORIGIN – named after *Ytterby* in Sweden (see YTTERBIUM).

ere /air/ > *preposition & conjunction* literary or archaic before (in time).

erect > *adjective* **1** rigidly upright or straight. **2** (of a body part) enlarged and rigid, especially in sexual excitement. > *verb* **1** construct (a building, wall, etc.). **2** create or establish (a theory or system).

DERIVATIVES – **erectly** *adverb* **erectness** *noun* **erector** *noun*.

SYNONYMS – *adjective* **1** perpendicular, straight, upright. *verb* **1** assemble, build, construct, put up.

ORIGIN – Latin *erigere* 'set up'.

erectile /irekt**ī**l/ > *adjective* able to become erect.

erection > *noun* **1** the action of erecting. **2** a building or other upright structure. **3** an erect state of the penis.

eremite /err**imīt**/ > *noun* a Christian hermit.

DERIVATIVES – **eremitic** *adjective* **eremitical** *adjective*.

ORIGIN – Latin *eremita* 'hermit'.

erg /erg/ > *noun* Physics a unit of work or energy, equal to the work done by a force of one dyne when its point of application moves one centimetre in the direction of action of the force.

ORIGIN – Greek *ergon* 'work'.

ergo /erg**ō**/ > *adverb* therefore.

ORIGIN – Latin.

ergocalciferol /ergōkalsiffərol/ > *noun* another term for CALCIFEROL.

ORIGIN – blend of **ERGOT** and **CALCIFEROL**.

ergonomic /ergənommik/ > *adjective* **1** relating to ergonomics. **2** designed to be conducive to efficient use.

DERIVATIVES – **ergonomist** *noun*.

ergonomics > *plural noun* (treated as sing.) the study of people's efficiency in their working environment.

ORIGIN – from Greek *ergon* 'work', on the pattern of *economics*.

ergot /ergət/ > *noun* a disease of rye and other cereals, caused by a fungus.

ORIGIN – French, from Old French *argot* 'cock's spur' (because of the appearance produced by the disease).

ergotism /ergətiz'm/ > *noun* poisoning caused by eating food affected by ergot, which produces a number of toxic compounds.

erica /errikə/ > *noun* a plant of a large genus including the heaths.

ORIGIN – Greek *ereikē*.

ericaceous /errikaysh**ə**ss/ > *adjective* Botany **1** relating to plants of the heather family (Ericaceae). **2** (of compost) suitable for heathers and other lime-hating plants.

Erin /errin, eerin/ > *noun* archaic or literary Ireland.

Erinys /erinnis/ > *noun* (pl. **Erinyes** /erinieez/) (in Greek mythology) a Fury.

Eritrean /erritrayən/ > *noun* a person from the independent state of Eritrea in NE Africa. > *adjective* relating to Eritrea.

erk /erk/ > *noun* Brit. informal a male member of the RAF of the lowest rank.

erl-king /erl king/ > *noun* (in Germanic mythology) a bearded giant or goblin believed to lure little children to the land of death.

ORIGIN – German *Erlkönig* 'alder-king', a mistranslation of Danish *ellerkonge* 'king of the elves'.

ERM > *abbreviation* Exchange Rate Mechanism.

ermine /ermin/ > *noun* (pl. same or **ermines**) **1** a stoat. **2** the white winter fur of the stoat, used for trimming the ceremonial robes of judges or peers.

ORIGIN – Old French *hermine*, probably from Latin *mus Armenius* 'Armenian mouse'.

Ernie /erni/ > *noun* (in the UK) the computer that randomly selects the prize-winning numbers of Premium Bonds.

ORIGIN – from *electronic random number indicator equipment*.

erode /ir**ō**d/ > *verb* **1** gradually wear or be worn away. **2** gradually destroy (an abstract quality or state).

DERIVATIVES – **erodible** *adjective*.

SYNONYMS – **1** abrade, corrode, wear.

ORIGIN – Latin *erodere*, from *rodere* 'gnaw'.

erogenous zone /iroj**i**nəss/ > *noun* a part of the body sensitive to sexual stimulation.

Eros /eeross/ > *noun* sexual love or desire.

ORIGIN – Greek, 'sexual love' (also the name of the god of love in Greek mythology).

erosion /ir**ō**zh'n/ > *noun* the process or result of wearing away or of being worn away.

DERIVATIVES – **erosional** *adjective* **erosive** *adjective*.

erotic /irottik/ > *adjective* relating to or tending to arouse sexual desire or excitement.

DERIVATIVES – **erotically** *adverb*.

SYNONYMS – amatory, arousing, sensual, sexy.

ORIGIN – French *érotique*, from Greek *erōtikos*, from *erōs* 'sexual love'.

erotica /irottikə/ > *plural noun* (treated as sing. or pl.) erotic literature or art.

eroticise (also **eroticize**) > *verb* give erotic qualities to.

DERIVATIVES – **eroticisation** *noun*.

eroticism > *noun* **1** the quality or character or being erotic. **2** sexual desire or excitement.

erotism /errətiz'm/ > *noun* sexual desire or excitement.

erotogenic /irottəjennik/ > *adjective* another term for EROGENOUS.

erotomania /irottōmayniə/ > *noun* **1** excessive sexual desire. **2** a delusion in which a person believes that another person is in love with them.

DERIVATIVES – **erotomaniac** *noun*.

err /er/ > *verb* **1** be mistaken or incorrect. **2** do wrong.

IDIOMS – **err on the side of** display more rather than less of (a specified quality) in one's actions. **to err is human, to forgive divine** proverb it is human nature to make mistakes oneself while finding it hard to forgive others.

ORIGIN – Latin *errare* 'to stray'.

errand > *noun* a short journey made to deliver or collect something, especially on someone else's behalf.

IDIOMS – **errand of mercy** a journey or mission carried out to help someone in difficulty or danger.

ORIGIN – Old English, 'message, mission'.

errant /errənt/ > *adjective* **1** chiefly formal or humorous straying from the accepted course or standards. **2** archaic or literary travelling in search of adventure.

DERIVATIVES – **errancy** *noun* **errantry** *noun*.

erratic /irattik/ > *adjective* not even or regular in pattern or movement.

DERIVATIVES – **erratically** *adverb* **erraticism** *noun*.

SYNONYMS – changeable, fluctuating, irregular, unstable.

erratum /eraatəm/ > *noun* (pl. **errata**) **1** an error in printing or writing. **2** (**errata**) a list of corrected errors added to a publication.

ORIGIN – Latin, 'error'.

erroneous /ir**ō**niəss/ > *adjective* wrong; incorrect.

DERIVATIVES – **erroneously** *adverb*.

ORIGIN – Latin *erroneus*, from *errare* 'to stray, err'.

error > *noun* **1** a mistake. **2** the state of being wrong in conduct or judgement. **3** technical a measure of the estimated difference between the observed or calculated value of a quantity and its true value.

IDIOMS – **see the error of one's ways** acknowledge one's wrongdoing.

SYNONYMS – **1** blunder, fault, flaw, inaccuracy, mistake, slip.

ORIGIN – Latin, from *errare* 'to stray, err'.

ersatz /ersats, airsats/ > *adjective* **1** (of a product) made or used as an inferior substitute for something else. **2** not real or genuine: *ersatz emotion*.

ORIGIN – German, 'replacement'.

Erse /erss/ > *noun* the Scottish or Irish Gaelic language.

ORIGIN – early Scots form of IRISH.

erst /erst/ > *adverb* archaic long ago; formerly.

erstwhile > *adjective* former. > *adverb* archaic formerly.

eructation /eeruktaysh'n/ > *noun* formal a belch.

ORIGIN – Latin, from *ructare* 'belch'.

erudite /err**oo**d**ī**t/ > *adjective* having or showing knowledge or learning.

DERIVATIVES – **eruditely** *adverb* **erudition** *noun*.

SYNONYMS – knowledgeable, learned, scholarly.

ORIGIN – Latin *eruditus*, from *erudire* 'instruct, train'.

erupt > *verb* **1** (of a volcano) forcefully eject lava, rocks, ash, or gases. **2** break out suddenly. **3** give vent to feelings in a sudden and noisy way. **4** (of a spot, rash, etc.) suddenly appear on the skin. **5** (of a tooth) break through the gums.

DERIVATIVES – **eruptive** *adjective*.

ORIGIN – Latin *erumpere* 'break out'.

eruption > *noun* an act or instance of erupting.

-ery (also **-ry**) > *suffix* forming nouns: **1** denoting a class or kind: *greenery*. **2** denoting an occupation, a state or condition, or behaviour: *archery | bravery*. **3** denoting a place set aside for an activity or a grouping of things, animals, etc.: *rookery*.

ORIGIN – from Latin *-arius* and *-ator*.

erysipelas /erri**sipp**iləss/ > *noun* a skin disease caused by a streptococcus and characterised by large raised red patches on the face and legs.

ORIGIN – Greek *erusipelas*; perhaps related to *eruthros* 'red' and *pella* 'skin'.

erythema /erri**thee**mə/ > *noun* superficial reddening of the skin caused by dilation of the blood capillaries.

ORIGIN – Greek *eruthēma*, from *eruthros* 'red'.

erythrocyte /i**rith**rōsīt/ > *noun* a red blood cell, containing the pigment haemoglobin and transporting oxygen to the tissues.

ORIGIN – from Greek *eruthros* 'red' + *kutos* 'vessel'.

Es > *symbol* the chemical element einsteinium.

ESA > *abbreviation* **1** (in the UK) Environmentally Sensitive Area. **2** European Space Agency.

escalade /eskə**layd**/ > *noun* historical the scaling of fortified walls using ladders, as a form of military attack.

ORIGIN – French, from Latin *scalare* 'to scale, climb', from *scala* 'ladder'.

escalate /**es**kəlayt/ > *verb* **1** increase rapidly. **2** become more intense or serious.

DERIVATIVES – **escalation** *noun*.

ORIGIN – first meaning 'travel on an escalator': from **ESCALATOR**.

escalator > *noun* a moving staircase consisting of a circulating belt of steps driven by a motor.

ORIGIN – from **ESCALADE**, on the pattern of *elevator*.

escallonia /eskə**lō**niə/ > *noun* an evergreen South American shrub with pink or white flowers.

ORIGIN – named after the 18th-century Spanish traveller *Escallon*, who discovered the plants.

escalope /i**skal**əp/ (also **escallop**) > *noun* a thin slice of coated and fried meat, especially veal.

ORIGIN – Old French, 'shell'.

escapade /**es**kəpayd/ > *noun* an incident involving daring and adventure.

SYNONYMS – adventure, caper, exploit, stunt.

escape > *verb* **1** break free from confinement or control. **2** elude or get free from (someone). **3** succeed in eluding (something dangerous or undesirable). **4** fail to be noticed or remembered by (someone). > *noun* **1** an act of escaping. **2** a means of escaping. **3** (also **escape key**) Computing a key which interrupts the current operation or converts subsequent characters to a control sequence.

DERIVATIVES – **escapable** *adjective* **escapee** *noun* **escaper** *noun*.

COMBINATIONS – **escape clause** a clause in a contract which specifies the conditions under which one party can be freed from an obligation. **escape wheel** a toothed wheel in the escapement of a watch or clock.

ORIGIN – Old French *eschaper*, from Latin *ex-* 'out' + *cappa* 'cloak'.

escapement /i**skayp**mənt/ > *noun* **1** a mechanism in a clock or watch that connects and regulates the motive power. **2** a mechanism in a typewriter that shifts the carriage a small fixed amount to the left after a key is pressed and released. **3** the part of the mechanism in a piano that enables the hammer to fall back as soon as it has struck the string.

escapism > *noun* the seeking of distraction from reality by engaging in entertainment or fantasy.

DERIVATIVES – **escapist** *noun* & *adjective*.

escapologist /eskə**poll**əjist/ > *noun* an entertainer who specialises in breaking free from ropes, handcuffs, and chains.

DERIVATIVES – **escapology** *noun*.

escargot /e**skaar**gō/ > *noun* an edible snail.

ORIGIN – French.

escarpment /i**skaarp**mənt/ > *noun* a long, steep slope at the edge of a plateau or separating areas of land at different heights.

ORIGIN – French, from Italian *scarpa* 'slope'.

eschatology /eskə**toll**əji/ > *noun* the part of theology concerned with death, judgement, and destiny.

DERIVATIVES – **eschatological** *adjective* **eschatologist** *noun*.

ORIGIN – from Greek *eskhatos* 'last'.

escheat /iss**cheet**/ > *noun* chiefly historical the reversion of property to the state, or (in feudal law) to a lord, on the owner's dying without legal heirs.

ORIGIN – Old French *eschete*, from Latin *excidere* 'fall away'.

eschew /iss**choo**/ > *verb* abstain from.

DERIVATIVES – **eschewal** *noun*.

ORIGIN – Old French *eschiver*, related to **SHY**[1].

escort > *noun* /**es**kort/ **1** a person, vehicle, or group accompanying another to provide protection or as a mark of rank. **2** a person who accompanies a member of the opposite sex to a social event. > *verb* /i**skort**/ accompany as an escort.

WORDFINDER – chaperone, duenna (*female escort for young woman*), gigolo (*male escort of older woman*).

SYNONYMS – *verb* accompany, conduct, guide, shepherd, usher.

ORIGIN – French *escorte*, from Italian *scorta* 'conducted, guided'.

escritoire /eskrit**waar**/ > *noun* a small writing desk with drawers and compartments.

ORIGIN – French, from Latin *scriptorium* 'room for writing'.

escrow /**es**krō/ > *noun* Law **1** a bond, deed, or deposit kept by a third party until a specified condition has been fulfilled. **2** the state of being kept in this way.

ORIGIN – Old French *escroe* 'scrap, scroll', related to **SHRED**.

escudo /e**skyoo**dō/ > *noun* (pl. **escudos**) the basic monetary unit of Portugal and Cape Verde, equal to 100 centavos.

ORIGIN – Portuguese, from Latin *scutum* 'shield'.

esculent /**es**kyoolənt/ > *adjective* formal fit to be eaten.

ORIGIN – Latin *esculentus*, from *esca* 'food'.

escutcheon /i**sku**chən/ > *noun* **1** a shield or emblem bearing a coat of arms. **2** a flat piece of metal framing a keyhole, door handle, or light switch.

IDIOMS – **a blot on one's escutcheon** a stain on one's reputation or character.

ORIGIN – Old French *escuchon*, from Latin *scutum* 'shield'.

ESE > *abbreviation* east-south-east.

-ese > *suffix* forming adjectives and nouns: **1** denoting an inhabitant or language of a country or city: *Chinese*. **2** often derogatory (especially with reference to language) denoting character or style: *journalese*.

ORIGIN – from Latin *-ensis*.

esker /**es**kər/ > *noun* Geology a long winding ridge of sediment deposited by meltwater from a retreating glacier or ice sheet.

ORIGIN – Irish *eiscir*.

Eskimo > *noun* (pl. same or **Eskimos**) **1** a member of a people inhabiting northern Canada, Alaska, Greenland, and eastern Siberia. **2** either of the two main languages of this people (Inuit and Yupik). > *adjective* relating to the Eskimos or their languages.

USAGE – the word **Eskimo** is regarded by some as offensive, but it is the only term that covers both the Inuit and the Yupik, and is still widely used.

ORIGIN – an Algonquian word, perhaps in the sense 'people speaking a different language'.

ESL > *abbreviation* English as a second language.

ESN > *abbreviation* electronic serial number.

ESOL > *abbreviation* English for speakers of other languages.

esophagus etc. US spelling of **OESOPHAGUS** etc.

esoteric /essəˈterrik, eesəˈterrik/ > *adjective* intended for or understood by only a small number of people with a specialised knowledge.

DERIVATIVES – **esoterically** *adverb* **esotericism** *noun*.

SYNONYMS – abstruse, obscure, recherché, recondite, specialised.

ORIGIN – Greek *esōterikos*, from *esō* 'within'.

esoterica /essəˈterrikə, eesə-/ > *plural noun* esoteric subjects or publications.

ESP > *abbreviation* extrasensory perception.

espadrille /ˈespədril/ > *noun* a light canvas shoe with a plaited fibre sole.

ORIGIN – Provençal *espardilhos*, from *espart* 'esparto', from Greek *sparton* 'rope'.

espalier /iˈspaliər/ > *noun* a fruit tree or ornamental shrub whose branches are trained to grow flat against a wall. > *verb* train (a tree or shrub) in such a way.

ORIGIN – Italian *spalliera*, from Latin *spatula* 'small spathe'.

esparto /eˈspaartō/ (also **esparto grass**) > *noun* (pl. **espartos**) a coarse grass native to Spain and North Africa, used to make ropes, wickerwork, and paper.

ORIGIN – Greek *sparton* 'rope'.

especial > *adjective* 1 notable; special. 2 for or belonging chiefly to one person or thing.

ORIGIN – Latin *specialis* 'special', from *species* (see **SPECIES**).

especially > *adverb* 1 in particular. 2 to a great extent; very much. 3 particularly.

USAGE – **especially** and **specially** are not interchangeable, although both can mean 'particularly'. Only **especially** means 'in particular', as in *he despised them all, especially Thomas*, and only **specially** means 'for a special purpose', as in *the car was specially made for the occasion*.

Esperanto /espəˈrantō/ > *noun* an artificial language devised in 1887 as an international medium of communication.

DERIVATIVES – **Esperantist** *noun*.

ORIGIN – from *Dr Esperanto*, a pen name of the inventor of the language, Polish physician Ludwik L. Zamenhof; the literal sense is 'one who hopes'.

espionage /ˈespiənaazh/ > *noun* the practice of spying or of using spies.

ORIGIN – from French *espion* 'a spy'.

esplanade /espləˈnayd/ > *noun* a long, open, level area, typically beside the sea, along which people may promenade.

ORIGIN – from Latin *explanatus* 'levelled', from *explanare* (see **EXPLAIN**).

espousal /iˈspowz'l/ > *noun* the action of espousing.

espouse /iˈspowz/ > *verb* adopt or support (a cause, belief, or way of life).

ORIGIN – Old French *espouser*, from Latin *spondere* 'betroth'.

espresso* /eˈspressō/ (also **expresso**) > *noun* (pl. **espressos**) strong black coffee made by forcing steam through ground coffee beans.

*SPELLING – strictly, the correct spelling is **espresso**, as in Italian.

ORIGIN – from Italian *caffè espresso* 'pressed out coffee'.

esprit /eˈspree/ > *noun* liveliness.

ORIGIN – French, from Latin *spiritus* 'spirit'.

esprit de corps /espree də ˈkor/ > *noun* a feeling of pride and loyalty uniting the members of a group.

ORIGIN – French, 'spirit of the body'.

espy /iˈspī/ > *verb* (**espies**, **espied**) literary catch sight of.

ORIGIN – Old French *espier*.

Esq. > *abbreviation* Esquire.

-esque > *suffix* (forming adjectives) in the style of: *Kafkaesque*.

ORIGIN – French, from Latin *-iscus*.

Esquimau > *noun* (pl. **Esquimaux**) archaic spelling of **ESKIMO**.

esquire /iˈskwīr/ > *noun* 1 (**Esquire**) Brit. a polite title appended to a man's name when no other title is used. 2 historical a young nobleman who acted as an attendant to a knight.

ORIGIN – Old French *esquier*, from Latin *scutarius* 'shield bearer', from *scutum* 'shield'.

-ess > *suffix* forming nouns denoting female gender: *abbess*.

USAGE – feminine forms such as **poetess** and **authoress** are now likely to be regarded as old-fashioned or sexist: avoid them in favour of the 'neutral' base form (e.g. **poet**, **author**).

ORIGIN – French *-esse*, from Greek *-issa*.

essay > *noun* /ˈessay/ 1 a piece of writing on a particular subject. 2 formal an attempt or effort. > *verb* /eˈsay/ formal attempt.

DERIVATIVES – **essayist** *noun* **essayistic** *adjective*.

ORIGIN – first meaning 'test the quality of': an alteration of **ASSAY**. The noun is from Old French *essai* 'trial'.

essence > *noun* 1 the intrinsic nature of something; the quality which determines something's character. 2 an extract or concentrate obtained from a plant or other substance and used for flavouring or scent.

IDIOMS – **in essence** basically; fundamentally. **of the essence** critically important.

SYNONYMS – 1 character, core, heart, nature, quintessence, substance.

ORIGIN – Latin *essentia*, from *esse* 'be'.

essential > *adjective* 1 constituting the essence; fundamental. 2 absolutely necessary. > *noun* (**essentials**) 1 the fundamental elements. 2 things that are absolutely necessary.

DERIVATIVES – **essentially** *adverb*.

SYNONYMS – *adjective* 1 basic, central, fundamental, intrinsic, quintessential. 2 crucial, imperative, indispensable, key, vital.

ANTONYMS – 1 peripheral, secondary. 2 inessential.

COMBINATIONS – **essential oil** a natural oil extracted from a plant.

EST > *abbreviation* Eastern Standard Time.

est. > *abbreviation* 1 established. 2 estimated.

-est > *suffix* forming the superlative of adjectives (such as *shortest*) and of adverbs (such as *soonest*).

establish > *verb* 1 set up on a firm or permanent basis. 2 initiate or bring about. 3 (**be established**) be settled or accepted in a particular place or role. 4 show to be true or certain by determining the facts. 5 (of a plant) take root and grow. 6 (**established**) recognised by the state as the national Church or religion.

SYNONYMS – 1 create, form, found, institute, set up. 4 confirm, demonstrate, determine, prove, show.

ORIGIN – Old French *establir*, from Latin *stabilire* 'make firm'.

establishment > *noun* 1 the action of setting something up on a firm or permanent basis. 2 a business organisation, public institution, or household. 3 (**the Establishment**) a group in a society exercising power and influence over matters of policy or opinion, and seen as resisting change.

SYNONYMS – 1 creation, formation, founding, institution, setting up. 2 concern, institution, operation, organisation, premises.

establishmentarian
/istablishmənˈtairiən/ > *adjective* advocating or relating to the principle of an established Church. > *noun* a person advocating this.

DERIVATIVES – **establishmentarianism** *noun*.

estate > *noun* 1 a property consisting of a large house and extensive grounds. 2 Brit. an area of land and modern buildings developed for residential, industrial, or commercial purposes. 3 a property where crops such as coffee or rubber are cultivated or where wine is produced. **4** a person's money and property in its entirety at the time of their death. **5** (also **estate of the realm**) (in Britain) one of the three groups constituting Parliament, now the Lords spiritual (the heads of the Church), the Lords temporal (the peerage), and the Commons. **6** archaic or literary a particular state, period, or condition in life. **7** Brit. short for **estate car**.

COMBINATIONS – **estate car** Brit. a car incorporating a large carrying area behind the seats. **estate duty** Brit. a former death duty levied on property.

ORIGIN – Old French *estat*, from Latin *status* 'state, condition'.

estate agency > *noun* chiefly Brit. a business that sells and rents out buildings and land for clients.

DERIVATIVES – **estate agent** noun.

esteem > *noun* respect and admiration. > *verb* **1** respect and admire. **2** formal consider; deem.

SYNONYMS – *noun* admiration, high opinion, honour, regard, respect. *verb* **1** admire, hold in high regard, respect, think highly of.

ANTONYMS – *noun* disrespect, low opinion. *verb* **1** disparage, scorn.

ORIGIN – Latin *aestimare* 'to estimate'.

ester /*est*ər/ > *noun* Chemistry an organic compound made by replacing the hydrogen of an acid by an alkyl or other organic group.

ORIGIN – German, probably from a blend of *Essig* 'vinegar' and *Äther* 'ether'.

esthetic etc. US spelling of AESTHETIC etc.

estimable > *adjective* worthy of great respect.

estimate > *noun* /*est*imət/ **1** an approximate calculation or judgement. **2** a written statement indicating the likely price that will be charged for specified work. **3** a judgement or appraisal. > *verb* /*est*imayt/ form an estimate of.

DERIVATIVES – **estimation** noun **estimator** noun.

SYNONYMS – *noun* **1** approximation, assessment, estimation, guess. *verb* assess, gauge, guess, judge, reckon.

ORIGIN – Latin *aestimare* 'determine, appraise'.

Estonian /istōniən/ > *noun* a person from Estonia. > *adjective* relating to Estonia.

estop /istop/ > *verb* (**estopped, estopping**) Law bar or preclude by estoppel.

estoppel /istopp'l/ > *noun* Law the principle by which a person cannot assert something contrary to their previous statements or to a relevant judicial determination.

ORIGIN – Old French *estouppail* 'bung', from *estopper* 'stop up, impede'.

estradiol > *noun* US spelling of OESTRADIOL.

estrange /istraynj/ > *verb* **1** cause to feel less close or friendly. **2** (**estranged**) (of a husband or wife) no longer living with their spouse.

DERIVATIVES – **estrangement** noun.

SYNONYMS – **1** alienate, antagonise, drive away.

ORIGIN – Old French *estranger*, from Latin *extraneare* 'treat as a stranger'.

estrogen etc. US spelling of OESTROGEN etc.

estrus > *noun* US spelling of OESTRUS.

estuary /*est*yoori/ > *noun* (pl. **estuaries**) the tidal mouth of a large river.

DERIVATIVES – **estuarine** /*est*yoorīn/ *adjective*.

COMBINATIONS – **Estuary English** (in the UK) a type of accent containing features of both received pronunciation and London speech.

ORIGIN – Latin *aestuarium* 'tidal part of a shore', from *aestus* 'tide'.

esurient /isyooriənt/ > *adjective* archaic or humorous hungry or greedy.

ORIGIN – from Latin *esurire* 'be hungry'.

ET > *abbreviation* **1** (in North America) Eastern time. **2** extraterrestrial.

ETA > *abbreviation* estimated time of arrival.

eta /*eet*ə/ > *noun* the seventh letter of the Greek alphabet (**H, η**), transliterated as 'e' or 'ē'.

ORIGIN – Greek *ēta*.

e-tailer > *noun* a retailer who sells goods via electronic transactions on the Internet.

et al. /et **al**/ > *abbreviation* and others.

ORIGIN – Latin *et alii*.

etc. > *abbreviation* et cetera.

et cetera /etsettrə/ (also **etcetera**) > *adverb* and other similar things; and so on. > *noun* (**et ceteras**) unspecified extra items.

NOTE – avoid the mistake of pronouncing **et cetera** as **ek-** rather than **et-**.

ORIGIN – Latin, from *et* 'and' and *cetera* 'the rest' (from *ceterus* 'left over').

etch > *verb* **1** engrave (metal, glass, or stone) by drawing on a protective layer with a needle, and then covering it with acid to attack the exposed parts. **2** (of an acid or other solvent) corrode the surface of. **3** cut (a text or design) on a surface. **4** cause to be clearly defined: *the incident was etched in her memory*.

DERIVATIVES – **etcher** noun.

ORIGIN – Dutch *etsen*, from German *ätzen*.

etching > *noun* **1** the art or process of etching. **2** a print produced by the process of etching.

eternal > *adjective* **1** lasting or existing forever. **2** valid for all time: *eternal truths*. **3** informal tediously lengthy or persistent.

IDIOMS – **the Eternal City** the city of Rome. **eternal triangle** a relationship

between three people involving sexual rivalry.

DERIVATIVES – **eternally** adverb.

SYNONYMS – **1** endless, everlasting, never-ending, permanent, perpetual; rare sempiternal.

ANTONYMS – **1** temporary, transient.

ORIGIN – Latin *aeternalis*, from *aevum* 'age'.

eternity > *noun* (pl. **eternities**) **1** infinite or unending time. **2** Theology endless life after death. **3** (**an eternity**) informal an undesirably long period of time.

SYNONYMS – **1** all time, perpetuity. **3** (**an eternity**) aeons, ages, an age, a lifetime.

COMBINATIONS – **eternity ring** a ring given as a symbol of lasting affection, typically set with an unbroken circle of gems.

eth /eth/ > *noun* an Old English letter, ð or Ð, eventually superseded by *th*.

ORIGIN – Danish *edh*, perhaps representing the sound of the letter.

ethane /*eeth*ayn/ > *noun* Chemistry a flammable hydrocarbon gas of the alkane series, present in petroleum and natural gas.

ORIGIN – from ETHER.

ethanol /*eth*ənol/ > *noun* systematic chemical name for ALCOHOL (in sense 1).

ether /*eeth*ər/ > *noun* **1** (also **diethyl ether**) a volatile, highly flammable liquid used as an anaesthetic and as a solvent. **2** Chemistry any organic compound with an oxygen atom linking two alkyl groups. **3** (also **aether**) chiefly literary the clear sky; the upper regions of air. **4** (also **aether**) Physics, historical a substance formerly thought to permeate all space and to transmit light.

DERIVATIVES – **etheric** /eetherrik/ *adjective*.

ORIGIN – Greek *aithēr* 'upper air', from *aithein* 'burn, shine'.

ethereal /itheeriəl/ (also **etherial**) > *adjective* **1** extremely delicate and light. **2** heavenly or spiritual.

DERIVATIVES – **ethereality** noun **ethereally** adverb.

SYNONYMS – **1** dainty, delicate, exquisite, fragile, insubstantial.

ORIGIN – Greek *aitherios*, from *aithēr* 'ether, upper air'.

Ethernet /*eeth*ərnet/ > *noun* Computing a system for connecting a number of computer systems to form a local area network.

ORIGIN – blend of ETHER and NETWORK.

ethic /*eth*ik/ > *noun* a set of moral principles.

ORIGIN – Latin *ethice*, from Greek *hē ēthikē tekhnē* 'the science of morals', from *ēthos* 'nature, disposition'.

ethical > *adjective* **1** relating to moral principles or the branch of knowledge concerned with these. **2** morally correct. **3**

(of a medicine) available only on prescription.

DERIVATIVES – **ethically** adverb.

SYNONYMS – **2** good, just, moral, principled, right, righteous.

ANTONYMS – **2** immoral, unethical.

ethics > plural noun **1** the moral principles governing or influencing conduct. **2** the branch of knowledge concerned with moral principles.

DERIVATIVES – **ethicist** noun.

Ethiopian > noun a person from Ethiopia. > adjective relating to Ethiopia.

ethnic > adjective **1** relating to a group of people having a common national or cultural tradition. **2** referring to origin by birth rather than by present nationality: ethnic Albanians. **3** relating to a non-Western cultural tradition: ethnic dresses.

DERIVATIVES – **ethnically** adverb **ethnicity** noun.

SYNONYMS – **1** cultural, national, racial, tribal.

COMBINATIONS – **ethnic minority** a group within a community which differs ethnically from the main population.

ORIGIN – Greek ethnikos 'heathen', from ethnos 'nation'.

ethnic cleansing > noun the mass expulsion or killing of members of an ethnic or religious group.

ethnocentric /ethnōsentrik/ > adjective evaluating other cultures according to the preconceptions of one's own.

DERIVATIVES – **ethnocentrically** adverb **ethnocentricity** noun **ethnocentrism** noun.

ethnography /ethnogrəfi/ > noun the scientific description of peoples and cultures.

DERIVATIVES – **ethnographer** noun **ethnographic** adjective.

ethnology /ethnolləji/ > noun the study of the characteristics of different peoples and the differences and relationships between them.

DERIVATIVES – **ethnologic** adjective **ethnological** adjective **ethnologist** noun.

ethology /eetholləji/ > noun **1** the science of animal behaviour. **2** the study of human behaviour from a biological perspective.

DERIVATIVES – **ethological** adjective **ethologist** noun.

ORIGIN – Greek ēthologia, from ēthos 'nature, disposition'.

ethos /eethoss/ > noun the characteristic spirit of a culture, era, or community.

SYNONYMS – character, code, mood, philosophy, spirit, tone.

ORIGIN – Greek ēthos 'nature, disposition', (plural) 'customs'.

ethyl /ethīl/ > noun Chemistry the alkyl radical −C₂H₅, derived from ethane.

COMBINATIONS – **ethyl alcohol** another term for ALCOHOL (in sense 1).

ethylene /ethileen/ > noun Chemistry a flammable hydrocarbon gas of the alkene series, present in natural gas and coal gas.

COMBINATIONS – **ethylene glycol** a colourless viscous liquid used in antifreeze and in wood preservatives.

etiolated /eetiəlaytid/ > adjective (of a plant) pale and weak due to a lack of light.

ORIGIN – from French étieuler 'grow into a stalk'.

etiology > noun US spelling of AETIOLOGY.

etiquette /ettiket/ > noun the code of polite behaviour in a society.

SYNONYMS – convention, decorum, form, manners, politeness, protocol.

ORIGIN – French étiquette 'list of ceremonial observances of a court', also 'label, etiquette', from Old French estiquette 'ticket'.

Etruscan /itruskən/ > noun **1** a person from Etruria, an ancient Italian state that was at its height c.500 BC. **2** the language of Etruria. > adjective relating to Etruria or Etruscan.

ORIGIN – Latin Etruscus.

et seq. > adverb and what follows (used in page references).

ORIGIN – Latin et sequens 'and the following'.

-ette > suffix forming nouns: **1** denoting small size: kitchenette. **2** denoting an imitation or substitute: leatherette. **3** denoting female gender: suffragette.

ORIGIN – Old French.

étude /aytyōod/ > noun a short musical composition or exercise.

ORIGIN – French, 'study'.

etymology /ettimolləji/ > noun (pl. **etymologies**) an account of the origins and the developments in meaning of a word.

DERIVATIVES – **etymological** adjective **etymologically** adverb **etymologist** noun.

ORIGIN – Greek etumologia, from etumologos 'student of etymology', from etumos 'true'.

etymon /ettimon/ > noun (pl. **etymons** or **etyma**) a word or morpheme from which a later word is derived.

ORIGIN – Greek etumon, from etumos 'true'.

EU > abbreviation European Union.

Eu > symbol the chemical element europium.

eucalyptus /yōokəliptəss/ (also **eucalypt**) > noun (pl. **eucalyptuses** or **eucalypti** /yōokəliptī/) **1** an evergreen Australasian tree valued for its wood, oil, gum, and resin. **2** the oil from eucalyptus leaves, used for its medicinal properties.

ORIGIN – from Greek eu 'well' + kaluptos 'covered', because the unopened flower is protected by a cap.

Eucharist /yōokərist/ > noun **1** the Christian ceremony commemorating the Last Supper, in which consecrated bread and wine are consumed. **2** the consecrated elements, especially the bread.

DERIVATIVES – **Eucharistic** adjective.

ORIGIN – Greek eukharistia 'thanksgiving', from eu 'well' + kharizesthai 'offer graciously' (from kharis 'grace').

euchre /yōokər/ > noun a card game played with the thirty-two highest cards, the aim being to win at least three of the five tricks played. > verb **1** (in euchre) prevent (another player) from taking three tricks. **2** N. Amer. informal deceive or outwit.

ORIGIN – German Juckerspiel.

Euclidean /yōokliddiən/ > adjective (of systems of geometry) obeying the postulates of the ancient Greek mathematician Euclid, in particular that only one line through a given point can be parallel to a given line.

eugenics /yōojenniks/ > plural noun the practice of using controlled breeding to increase the occurrence of favoured heritable characteristics in a population.

DERIVATIVES – **eugenic** adjective **eugenicist** noun & adjective.

ORIGIN – from Greek eu 'well' + genēs 'born'.

eukaryote /yōokariōt/ > noun Biology an organism consisting of a cell or cells in which the genetic material is DNA in the form of chromosomes contained within a distinct nucleus (that is, all living organisms other than the bacteria and archaea). Compare with PROKARYOTE.

DERIVATIVES – **eukaryotic** adjective.

ORIGIN – from Greek eu 'well' + karuon 'kernel'.

eulogise /yōoləjīz/ (also **eulogize**) > verb praise highly.

DERIVATIVES – **eulogist** noun **eulogistic** adjective.

eulogy /yōoləji/ > noun (pl. **eulogies**) a speech or piece of writing that praises someone highly.

SYNONYMS – accolade, paean, panegyric, testimonial, tribute.

ORIGIN – Greek eulogia 'praise'.

eunuch /yōonək/ > noun a man who has been castrated.

ORIGIN – Greek eunoukhos 'bedroom guard', from eunē 'bed' + ekhein 'to hold'.

euonymus /yōoonniməss/ > noun a shrub or small tree noted for its autumn colours and bright fruit.

ORIGIN – Greek euōnumos 'having an auspicious or honoured name', from eus 'good' + onoma 'name'.

euphemism /yōofəmiz'm/ > noun a mild or less direct word substituted for one that is harsh or blunt when referring to something unpleasant or embarrassing.

DERIVATIVES – **euphemistic** adjective **euphemistically** adverb.

ORIGIN – from Greek *euphēmizein* 'use auspicious words', from *eu* 'well' + *phēmē* 'speaking'.

euphonious /yoofṓniəss/ > *adjective* sounding pleasant.

DERIVATIVES – **euphoniously** *adverb*.

euphonium /yoofṓniəm/ > *noun* a brass musical instrument resembling a small tuba.

ORIGIN – from Greek *euphōnos* 'having a pleasing sound'.

euphony /yoofəni/ > *noun* (pl. **euphonies**) **1** the quality of being pleasing to the ear. **2** the tendency to make a change in a sound in speech for ease of pronunciation.

DERIVATIVES – **euphonic** *adjective*.

ORIGIN – Greek *euphōnia*, from *euphōnos* 'well sounding' (based on *phōnē* 'sound').

euphorbia /yoofórbiə/ > *noun* a plant of a genus that comprises the spurges.

ORIGIN – named after *Euphorbus*, Greek physician to the reputed discoverer of the plant, Juba II of Mauretania (1st century BC).

euphoria /yoofóriə/ > *noun* a feeling of intense happiness.

DERIVATIVES – **euphoric** *adjective* **euphorically** *adverb*.

SYNONYMS – ecstasy, elation, exhilaration, joy, rapture.

ORIGIN – Greek, from *euphoros* 'borne well, healthy'.

Eurasian /yoorayzh'n/ > *adjective* **1** of mixed European (or European-American) and Asian parentage. **2** relating to Eurasia (the continental land mass of Europe and Asia combined). > *noun* a person of Eurasian parentage.

USAGE – the word **Eurasian** was formerly used to refer to a person of mixed British and Indian parentage, but today it more often denotes a person of mixed white American and SE Asian parentage.

eureka /yooreekə/ > *exclamation* a cry of joy or satisfaction when one finds or discovers something. > *noun* an alloy of copper and nickel used for electrical filament and resistance wire.

ORIGIN – Greek *heurēka* 'I have found it', said to have been uttered by Archimedes (died 212 BC) when he hit upon a method of determining the purity of gold.

Euro > *adjective* informal European, especially concerned with the European Union. > *noun* (**euro**) the single European currency, introduced in the European Union in 1999.

Eurobond > *noun* an international bond issued in Europe or elsewhere outside the country in whose currency its value is stated.

Eurocentric > *adjective* implicitly regarding European culture as pre-eminent.

DERIVATIVES – **Eurocentrism** *noun*.

Eurocrat > *noun* informal, chiefly derogatory a bureaucrat in the administration of the European Union.

Eurodollar > *noun* a US dollar held in Europe or elsewhere outside the US.

European > *noun* **1** a person from Europe. **2** a person who is white or of European parentage. > *adjective* relating to Europe or the European Union.

DERIVATIVES – **Europeanisation** (also **Europeanization**) *noun* **Europeanise** (also **Europeanize**) *verb* **Europeanism** *noun*.

European Union > *noun* an economic and political association of certain European countries as a unit with internal free trade and common external tariffs.

europium /yoorópiəm/ > *noun* a soft silvery-white metallic chemical element of the lanthanide series.

ORIGIN – from *Europe*.

Euro-sceptic > *noun* a person who is opposed to increasing the powers of the European Union.

DERIVATIVES – **Euro-scepticism** *noun*.

Eurotrash > *noun* informal rich European socialites, especially those living in the United States.

Eustachian tube /yoostaysh'n/ > *noun* Anatomy a narrow passage leading from the pharynx to the middle ear, enabling pressure to be equalised on each side of the eardrum.

ORIGIN – named after the Italian anatomist Bartolomeo *Eustachio* (died 1574).

eutectic /yootektik/ > *adjective* Chemistry (of a mixture of two substances) having a distinct melting point which is lower than the melting points of the separate constituents.

ORIGIN – Greek *eutēktos* 'easily melting'.

euthanasia /yoothənayziə/ > *noun* the painless killing of a patient suffering from an incurable disease or in an irreversible coma.

ORIGIN – from Greek *eu* 'well' + *thanatos* 'death'.

eutrophic /yootrṓfik, yootroffik/ > *adjective* Ecology (of a body of water) rich in nutrients and so supporting a dense plant population.

DERIVATIVES – **eutrophication** *noun*.

ORIGIN – from Greek *eutrophia*, from *eu* 'well' + *trephein* 'nourish'.

EVA > *abbreviation* ethyl vinyl acetate.

evacuate > *verb* **1** remove from a place of danger to a safer place. **2** leave (a dangerous place). **3** technical remove air, water, or other contents from (a container). **4** empty (the bowels or another bodily organ).

DERIVATIVES – **evacuation** *noun*.

ORIGIN – Latin *evacuare*, from *e-* 'out of' + *vacuus* 'empty'.

evacuee > *noun* a person evacuated from a place of danger.

evade /ivayd/ > *verb* **1** escape or avoid, especially by guile or trickery. **2** avoid giving a direct answer to (a question). **3** escape paying (tax or duty), especially by illegitimate presentation of one's finances.

DERIVATIVES – **evader** *noun*.

SYNONYMS – **1** avoid, elude, escape. **2** avoid, dodge, parry, sidestep.

ORIGIN – Latin *evadere*, from *e-* 'out of' + *vadere* 'go'.

evaluate > *verb* **1** form an idea of the amount or value of; assess. **2** Mathematics find a numerical expression or equivalent for (a formula, function, etc.).

DERIVATIVES – **evaluation** *noun* **evaluative** *adjective* **evaluator** *noun*.

SYNONYMS – **1** assess, estimate, gauge, judge, rate.

ORIGIN – French *évaluer*, from *es-* 'out, from' + Old French *value* 'value'.

evanescent /evvəness'nt/ > *adjective* chiefly literary quickly fading from sight, memory, or existence.

DERIVATIVES – **evanesce** *verb* **evanescence** *noun*.

ORIGIN – from Latin *evanescere* 'disappear'.

evangelical /eevanjellik'l/ > *adjective* **1** of or according to the teaching of the gospel or the Christian religion. **2** relating to a tradition within Protestant Christianity emphasising Biblical authority and personal conversion. **3** fervent in advocating something. > *noun* a member of the evangelical tradition in the Christian Church.

DERIVATIVES – **evangelicalism** *noun* **evangelically** *adverb*.

ORIGIN – from Greek *euangelion* 'good news', from *eu-* 'well' + *angelein* 'announce'.

evangelise /ivanjəliz/ > *verb* (also **evangelize**) **1** convert or seek to convert (someone) to Christianity. **2** preach the gospel.

DERIVATIVES – **evangelisation** *noun*.

evangelist /ivanjəlist/ > *noun* **1** a person who seeks to convert others to the Christian faith. **2** the writer of one of the four Gospels. **3** a passionate advocate of something.

DERIVATIVES – **evangelism** *noun* **evangelistic** *adjective*.

evaporate /ivappərayt/ > *verb* **1** turn from liquid into vapour. **2** (of something abstract) cease to exist: *my goodwill evaporated*.

DERIVATIVES – **evaporation** *noun* **evaporative** *adjective* **evaporator** *noun*.

SYNONYMS – **2** disappear, dissolve, melt away, vanish.

COMBINATIONS – **evaporated milk** thick milk that has had some of the liquid removed by evaporation.

ORIGIN – Latin *evaporare*, from *e-* 'out of' + *vapor* 'steam, vapour'.

evasion > *noun* the action or an instance of evading.

evasive > *adjective* **1** tending to avoid speaking openly or making revelations about oneself. **2** directed towards avoidance or escape: *evasive action*.
DERIVATIVES – **evasively** *adverb* **evasiveness** *noun*.
SYNONYMS – **1** disingenuous, equivocal, non-committal, prevaricating, vague.
ANTONYMS – **1** frank, open.

eve > *noun* **1** the day or period of time immediately before an event or occasion. **2** chiefly literary evening.
ORIGIN – short form of EVEN².

even¹ > *adjective* **1** flat and smooth; level. **2** equal in number, amount, or value. **3** having little variation in quality, extent, or intensity; regular. **4** equally balanced: *the match was even*. **5** (of a person's temper or disposition) placid; calm. **6** (of a number) divisible by two without a remainder. > *verb* (often **even out** or **up**) make or become even. > *adverb* used to emphasise something surprising or extreme, or in comparisons.
IDIOMS – **even as** at the very same time as. **even if** despite the possibility that. **even now** (or **then**) **1** now (or then) as well as before. **2** in spite of what has (or had) happened. **3** at this (or that) very moment. **even so** nevertheless. **even though** despite the fact that. **on an even keel** not listing or tilting to one side.
DERIVATIVES – **evenly** *adverb* **evenness** *noun*.
SYNONYMS – *adjective* **1** flat, level, regular, smooth. **3** constant, regular, stable, steady, uniform.
COMBINATIONS – **even money** (in betting) odds offering an equal chance of winning or losing.

even² > *noun* archaic or literary evening.

even-handed > *adjective* fair and impartial.
DERIVATIVES – **even-handedly** *adverb* **even-handedness** *noun*.

evening > *noun* the period of time at the end of the day. > *adverb* (**evenings**) informal in the evening; every evening.
COMBINATIONS – **evening primrose** a plant with pale yellow flowers that open in the evening, used for a medicinal oil. **evening star** the planet Venus, seen shining in the western sky after sunset.

evens > *plural noun* Brit. another term for *even money*.

evensong > *noun* (especially in the Anglican Church) a service of evening prayers, psalms, and canticles.

event > *noun* **1** a thing that happens or takes place. **2** each of several contests making up a sports competition. **3** a public or social occasion.
IDIOMS – **in any event** (or **at all events**) whatever happens or may have happened. **in the event 1** as it turned out. **2** (**in the event of** or **that**) if the specified thing happens.
SYNONYMS – **1** affair, episode, happening, incident, occasion, occurrence. **3** function, gathering, occasion.
COMBINATIONS – **event horizon** Astronomy a notional boundary around a black hole from within which no light or other radiation can escape.
ORIGIN – Latin *eventus*, from *evenire* 'result, happen'.

eventer > *noun* Brit. a horse or rider that takes part in eventing.

eventful > *adjective* marked by interesting or exciting events.
DERIVATIVES – **eventfully** *adverb*.
SYNONYMS – busy, exciting, hectic, interesting, lively.
ANTONYMS – quiet, uneventful.

eventide > *noun* archaic or literary evening.

eventing > *noun* an equestrian sport in which competitors take part in each of several contests, usually cross-country, dressage, and showjumping.

eventual > *adjective* occurring at the end of or resulting from a process or period of time.
DERIVATIVES – **eventually** *adverb*.
SYNONYMS – concluding, ensuing, final, ultimate.

eventuality > *noun* (pl. **eventualities**) a possible event or outcome.

eventuate > *verb* formal **1** occur as a result. **2** (**eventuate in**) lead to as a result.

ever > *adverb* **1** at any time. **2** used in comparisons for emphasis: *better than ever*. **3** always. **4** increasingly; constantly: *ever larger sums*. **5** used for emphasis in questions expressing astonishment: *why ever did you do it?*
IDIOMS – **ever and anon** archaic occasionally.

evergreen > *adjective* **1** (of a plant) retaining green leaves throughout the year. Contrasted with DECIDUOUS. **2** having an enduring freshness or success. > *noun* an evergreen plant.

everlasting > *adjective* lasting forever or a very long time. > *noun* a flower that retains its shape and colour after being dried.
DERIVATIVES – **everlastingly** *adverb*.
SYNONYMS – endless, eternal, never-ending, permanent, perpetual; rare sempiternal.
ANTONYMS – temporary, transient.

evermore > *adverb* archaic or literary always; forever.

evert /ivert/ > *verb* technical turn inside out.
DERIVATIVES – **eversion** *noun*.

ORIGIN – Latin *evertere*, from *e-* 'out' + *vertere* 'to turn'.

every > *determiner* **1** used to refer to all the individual members of a set without exception. **2** used to indicate something happening at specified intervals: *every thirty minutes*. **3** all possible; the utmost: *every effort was made*.
IDIOMS – **every bit as** (in comparisons) quite as. **every which way** informal **1** in all directions. **2** by all available means.

everybody > *pronoun* every person.

everyday > *adjective* **1** daily. **2** commonplace.

Everyman > *noun* an ordinary or typical human being.

everyone > *pronoun* every person.

every one > *pronoun* each one.

everything > *pronoun* **1** all things, or all the things of a group or class. **2** the most important thing or aspect: *money isn't everything*. **3** the current situation; life in general.

everywhere > *adverb* **1** in or to all places. **2** very common or widely distributed.

evict > *verb* expel (someone) from a property, especially with the support of the law.
DERIVATIVES – **eviction** *noun*.
SYNONYMS – eject, expel, oust, remove, throw out.
ORIGIN – Latin *evincere* 'overcome, defeat'.

evidence > *noun* **1** information indicating whether a proposition is true or valid. **2** Law information used to establish facts in a legal investigation or admissible as testimony in a law court. **3** signs or indications of something. > *verb* be or show evidence of.
IDIOMS – **in evidence** noticeable; conspicuous. **turn Queen's** (or **King's** or US state's) **evidence** Law (of a criminal) give information in court against one's partners in order to receive a less severe punishment.
SYNONYMS – *noun* **1** confirmation, corroboration, proof, substantiation.
ORIGIN – Latin *evidentia*, from *evidens* 'obvious to the mind or eye'.

evident > *adjective* clearly visible or understandable; plain and obvious.
DERIVATIVES – **evidently** *adverb*.
SYNONYMS – apparent, clear, conspicuous, manifest, obvious, plain.
ANTONYMS – obscure, unclear.
ORIGIN – Latin *evidens* 'obvious to the eye or mind', from *e-* 'out' + *videre* 'to see'.

evidential > *adjective* formal of or providing evidence.

evil > *adjective* **1** deeply immoral and malevolent. **2** embodying or associated with the devil. **3** harmful or tending to harm. **4** extremely unpleasant: *an evil smell*. > *noun* **1** profound wickedness and depravity, especially when regarded as a supernatural force. **2** something harmful or undesirable.

IDIOMS – **the evil eye** a gaze superstitiously believed to cause harm. **the Evil One** archaic the Devil. **speak evil of** slander.

DERIVATIVES – **evilly** adverb.

SYNONYMS – adjective **1** bad, immoral, sinful, unholy, wicked, wrong. noun **1** badness, immorality, sin, unholiness, vice, wickedness.

ANTONYMS – good.

COMBINATIONS – **evil-doer** a person who commits evil deeds.

evince > verb formal reveal the presence of; indicate (a quality or feeling).

ORIGIN – Latin *evincere* 'overcome, defeat'.

eviscerate /ivissərayt/ > verb formal disembowel.

DERIVATIVES – **evisceration** noun.

ORIGIN – Latin *eviscerare*, from *e-* 'out' + *viscera* 'internal organs'.

evocative /ivokkətiv/ > adjective (often **evocative of**) evoking strong images, memories, or feelings.

DERIVATIVES – **evocatively** adverb.

SYNONYMS – atmospheric, redolent, reminiscent, resonant, suggestive.

evoke /ivōk/ > verb **1** bring or recall to the conscious mind. **2** elicit (a response). **3** invoke (a spirit or deity).

DERIVATIVES – **evocation** noun.

SYNONYMS – **1** arouse, awaken, call to mind, conjure up, elicit, summon up.

ORIGIN – Latin *evocare*, from *e-* 'out of, from' + *vocare* 'to call'.

evolution > noun **1** the process by which different kinds of living organism are believed to have developed from earlier forms, especially by natural selection. **2** gradual development. **3** Chemistry the giving off of a gaseous product or of heat. **4** a pattern of movements or manoeuvres.

DERIVATIVES – **evolutionarily** adverb **evolutionary** adjective.

SYNONYMS – **2** advance, development, emergence, growth, rise.

evolutionist > noun a person who accepts the theories of evolution and natural selection.

DERIVATIVES – **evolutionism** noun.

evolve > verb **1** develop gradually. **2** (of an organism or biological feature) develop over successive generations by evolution. **3** Chemistry give off (gas or heat).

SYNONYMS – **1** develop, emerge, grow, progress, unfold.

ewe > noun a female sheep.

ewer /yo͞oər/ > noun a large jug with a wide mouth.

ORIGIN – from Old French *aiguiere*, Latin *aquarius* 'of water'.

wordpower facts

Evolution

The words **evolution** and **evolve** entered English in the 17th century from Latin *evolvere* 'roll out, unfold'. Both originally had a more general sense. **Evolve** meant 'make more complex, develop', whereas the early sense of **evolution** related to physical movement, in particular a tactical 'wheeling' manoeuvre in the realignment of troops or ships. Current senses of **evolution** stem from a notion of 'opening out' and 'unfolding', giving rise to a general sense of 'development'. Scientists began to discuss the possible evolution of animals and plants in the 18th century; Charles Darwin, who first described evolution by natural selection in *On the Origin of Species* (1859), was not the first to use the word in this context.

ex¹ > preposition (of goods) sold direct from.

ORIGIN – Latin, 'out of'.

ex² > noun informal a former husband, wife, or partner in a relationship.

ex-¹ (also **e-**; **ef-** before *f*) > prefix **1** out: *exclude*. **2** upward: *extol*. **3** thoroughly: *excruciate*. **4** referring to removal or release: *excommunicate*. **5** forming verbs which indicate inducement of a state: *exasperate*. **6** referring to a former state: *ex-husband*.

ORIGIN – Latin *ex* 'out of'.

ex-² > prefix out: *exodus*.

ORIGIN – Greek *ex* 'out of'.

exa- > combining form denoting a factor of one million million million (10^{18}).

ORIGIN – alteration of **HEXA-**.

exacerbate /igzassərbayt/ > verb make (something bad) worse.

DERIVATIVES – **exacerbation** noun.

SYNONYMS – aggravate, compound, heighten, intensify, worsen.

ANTONYMS – ameliorate, improve.

ORIGIN – Latin *exacerbare* 'make harsh'.

exact > adjective **1** not approximated in any way; precise. **2** tending to be accurate about minor details. > verb **1** demand and obtain (something) from someone. **2** inflict (revenge) on someone.

DERIVATIVES – **exactitude** noun **exactness** noun.

SYNONYMS – adjective **1** accurate, correct, faithful, precise. **2** careful, methodical, meticulous, painstaking, precise, punctilious. verb **1** claim, demand, extract, require.

ANTONYMS – adjective **1** inaccurate, inexact. **2** careless, sloppy.

ORIGIN – from Latin *exigere* 'complete, ascertain, enforce'.

exacting > adjective making great demands on one's endurance or skill.

DERIVATIVES – **exactingly** adverb.

SYNONYMS – challenging, demanding, difficult, hard, testing, tough.

ANTONYMS – easy, undemanding.

exaction > noun formal **1** the action of exacting something, especially a payment. **2** a sum of money exacted.

exactly > adverb **1** in exact terms. **2** used to confirm or agree with what has just been said.

exaggerate > verb **1** represent (something) as being better, greater, worse, etc. than it really is. **2** (**exaggerated**) enlarged or altered beyond normal proportions.

DERIVATIVES – **exaggeratedly** adverb **exaggeration** noun.

SYNONYMS – **1** amplify, embellish, inflate, overemphasise, overstate.

ORIGIN – Latin *exaggerare* 'heap up'.

exalt > verb **1** praise or regard highly. **2** raise to a higher rank or position.

ORIGIN – Latin *exaltare*, from *ex-* 'out, upward' + *altus* 'high'.

exaltation /egzawltaysh'n/ > noun **1** extreme happiness. **2** the action of exalting.

exalted > adjective **1** at a high level. **2** (of an idea) noble; lofty. **3** extremely happy.

exam > noun short for **EXAMINATION** (in sense 2).

examination > noun **1** a detailed inspection or investigation. **2** a formal test of knowledge or proficiency in a subject or skill. **3** the action of examining. **4** Law the formal questioning of a defendant or witness in court.

SYNONYMS – **1** analysis, appraisal, inspection, investigation, scrutiny.

examine > verb **1** inspect closely to determine the nature or condition of; investigate thoroughly. **2** test the knowledge or proficiency of. **3** Law formally question (a defendant or witness) in court.

DERIVATIVES – **examinee** noun **examiner** noun.

SYNONYMS – **1** analyse, appraise, inspect, investigate, look into, scrutinise.

ORIGIN – Latin *examinare* 'weigh, test'.

example > noun **1** a thing characteristic of its kind or illustrating a general rule. **2** a person or thing regarded in terms of their fitness to be imitated: *parents should set an example*.

IDIOMS – **for example** by way of illustration. **make an example of** punish as a warning to others.

SYNONYMS – **1** exemplar, illustration, instance, paradigm, sample, specimen. **2** exemplar, guide, lead, model, precedent.

ORIGIN – Latin *exemplum*, from *eximere* 'take out'.

exasperate /igˈzaaspərayt/ > *verb* irritate intensely.

DERIVATIVES – **exasperated** *adjective* **exasperatedly** *adverb* **exasperating** *adjective* **exasperatingly** *adverb* **exasperation** *noun*.

SYNONYMS – enrage, incense, infuriate, madden.

ORIGIN – Latin *exasperare* 'irritate to anger'.

ex cathedra /eks kəˈtheedrə/ > *adverb & adjective* with the full authority of office (especially that of the Pope).

ORIGIN – Latin, 'from the teacher's chair'.

excavate /ˈekskəvayt/ > *verb* **1** make (a hole or channel) by digging. **2** extract (material) from the ground by digging. **3** carefully remove earth from (an area) in order to find buried remains.

DERIVATIVES – **excavation** *noun* **excavator** *noun*.

ORIGIN – Latin *excavare* 'hollow out'.

exceed* > *verb* **1** be greater in number or size than. **2** go beyond what is stipulated by (a set limit). **3** surpass.

***SPELLING** – double *ee*, not *-ede*: exceed.

SYNONYMS – **1** beat, go over, pass. **2** go beyond, overstep.

ORIGIN – Latin *excedere*, from *ex-* 'out' + *cedere* 'go'.

exceeding archaic or literary > *adjective* very great. > *adverb* exceedingly.

exceedingly > *adverb* **1** extremely. **2** archaic to a great extent.

excel > *verb* (**excelled, excelling**) **1** be exceptionally good at an activity or subject. **2** (**excel oneself**) perform exceptionally well.

SYNONYMS – **1** be very good, shine, stand out.

ORIGIN – Latin *excellere*, from *ex-* 'out, beyond' + *celsus* 'lofty'.

excellence > *noun* the quality of being excellent.

SYNONYMS – distinction, merit, quality.

Excellency > *noun* (pl. **Excellencies**) (**His, Your,** etc. **Excellency**) a title or form of address for certain high officials of state, especially ambassadors, or of the Roman Catholic Church.

excellent > *adjective* extremely good.

DERIVATIVES – **excellently** *adverb*.

SYNONYMS – admirable, exceptional, fine, first-class, superb.

ANTONYMS – inferior, poor.

except > *preposition* not including; other than. > *conjunction* used before a statement that forms an exception to one just made. > *verb* specify as not included: *present company excepted.*

ORIGIN – Latin *excipere* 'take out'.

excepting > *preposition* except for; apart from.

exception > *noun* **1** a person or thing that is not included or that does not follow a rule. **2** the action or state of excluding or being excluded.

IDIOMS – **the exception proves the rule** *proverb* the fact that some cases do not follow a rule proves that the rule applies in all other cases. **take exception to** object strongly to; be offended by.

SYNONYMS – **1** anomaly, departure, deviation, irregularity, special case.

exceptionable > *adjective* formal open to objection; causing disapproval or offence.

USAGE – do not confuse **exceptionable** with **exceptional**.

exceptional > *adjective* **1** unusual; not typical. **2** unusually good.

DERIVATIVES – **exceptionally** *adverb*.

SYNONYMS – **1** abnormal, anomalous, atypical, extraordinary, unusual. **2** matchless, outstanding, peerless, remarkable, unrivalled.

excerpt > *noun* /ˈekserpt/ a short extract from a film or piece of music or writing. > *verb* /ikˈserpt/ take (a short extract) from a text.

SYNONYMS – *noun* extract, part, passage, selection.

ORIGIN – from Latin *excerpere* 'pluck out'.

excess /ikˈsess, ˈeksess/ > *noun* **1** an amount that is more than necessary, permitted, or desirable. **2** the amount by which one quantity or number exceeds another. **3** lack of moderation, especially in eating or drinking. **4** (**excesses**) outrageous or immoderate behaviour. **5** Brit. a part of an insurance claim to be paid by the insured. > *adjective* /usu. ˈeksess/ **1** exceeding a prescribed or desirable amount. **2** Brit. required as extra payment.

SYNONYMS – *noun* **1** overabundance, superfluity, surfeit, surplus. **2** remainder, rest, surplus. **3** debauchery, dissipation, intemperance, overindulgence.

ANTONYMS – *noun* **1** lack, shortage. **3** moderation, restraint.

COMBINATIONS – **excess baggage** luggage weighing more than the limit allowed on an aircraft, liable to an extra charge.

ORIGIN – Latin *excessus*, from *excedere* (see **EXCEED**).

excessive > *adjective* more than is necessary, normal, or desirable.

DERIVATIVES – **excessively** *adverb* **excessiveness** *noun*.

SYNONYMS – immoderate, inordinate, superfluous.

exchange > *verb* give something and receive something else in return. > *noun* **1** an act or the action of exchanging. **2** a short conversation or argument. **3** the giving of money for its equivalent in the currency of another country. **4** a building or institution used for the trading of commodities. **5** a set of equipment that connects telephone lines during a call.

DERIVATIVES – **exchangeable** *adjective* **exchanger** *noun*.

SYNONYMS – *verb* change, interchange, swap, switch, trade. *noun* **1** interchange, swapping, trade.

COMBINATIONS – **exchange rate** the value of one currency for the purpose of conversion to another.

ORIGIN – Old French *eschangier*, from *changer* 'change'.

exchequer /iksˈchekkər/ > *noun* **1** a royal or national treasury. **2** (**Exchequer**) Brit. the account at the Bank of England into which tax receipts and other public monies are paid.

wordpower facts

Exchequer

The word **exchequer** comes via Old French *eschequier* from medieval Latin *scaccarium* 'chessboard', its original sense in English, and ultimately from Persian *šāh* 'king'; it is related to **check**[1], **chess**, and **chequer**. The current senses of **exchequer** derive from the department of state established by the Norman kings to deal with the royal revenues, named *Exchequer* from the chequered tablecloth on which accounts were kept by means of counters.

excise[1] /ˈeksīz/ > *noun* a tax levied on certain goods, commodities, and licences.

COMBINATIONS – **exciseman** Brit. historical an official who collected excise duty and prevented smuggling.

ORIGIN – Dutch *excijs*.

excise[2] /ikˈsīz/ > *verb* **1** cut out surgically. **2** remove (a section) from a text or piece of music.

DERIVATIVES – **excision** *noun*.

ORIGIN – Latin *excidere* 'cut out'.

excitable > *adjective* easily excited.

excite > *verb* **1** cause strong feelings of enthusiasm and eagerness in. **2** arouse (someone) sexually. **3** give rise to (a feeling or reaction). **4** produce a state of increased energy or activity in (a physical or biological system).

DERIVATIVES – **excitation** *noun* **excited** *adjective* **excitedly** *adverb* **exciter** *noun* **exciting** *adjective* **excitingly** *adverb*.

SYNONYMS – **1** animate, enliven, exhilarate, stimulate, thrill. **3** arouse, awaken, elicit, provoke, stimulate, trigger.

ORIGIN – Latin *excitare*, from *exciere* 'call out'.

excitement > *noun* **1** a feeling of great

enthusiasm and eagerness. **2** an exciting incident. **3** sexual arousal.

SYNONYMS – **1** animation, elation, exhilaration, thrill.

exclaim > *verb* cry out suddenly, especially with emotion or in surprise or pain.

DERIVATIVES – **exclamatory** *adjective*.

SYNONYMS – call, cry out, shout; dated ejaculate.

ORIGIN – Latin *exclamare*, from *ex-* 'out' + *clamare* 'to shout'.

exclamation > *noun* a sudden cry or remark, especially one expressing emotion, surprise, or pain.

COMBINATIONS – **exclamation mark** (N. Amer. **exclamation point**) a punctuation mark (!) indicating an exclamation.

exclosure /ikskl**ō**zhər/ > *noun* Forestry an area from which unwanted animals are excluded.

exclude > *verb* **1** deny access to; keep out. **2** remove from consideration; rule out. **3** prevent the occurrence of. **4** not include; be exclusive of. **5** expel (a pupil) from a school.

DERIVATIVES – **excludable** *adjective* **excluder** *noun*.

SYNONYMS – **1** ban, bar, keep out, shut out.

ANTONYMS – include.

ORIGIN – Latin *excludere*, from *ex-* 'out' + *claudere* 'to shut'.

excluding > *preposition* not taking into account; except.

exclusion > *noun* the process or state of excluding or being excluded.

DERIVATIVES – **exclusionary** *adjective*.

exclusive > *adjective* **1** excluding or not admitting other things. **2** restricted to the person, group, or area concerned. **3** (**exclusive of**) not including; excepting. **4** high-class and expensive; select. **5** not published or broadcast elsewhere. > *noun* an exclusive story or broadcast.

DERIVATIVES – **exclusively** *adverb* **exclusiveness** *noun* **exclusivity** *noun*.

SYNONYMS – **4** chic, choice, high-class, select, upmarket.

excommunicate > *verb* /ekskə**myōō**nikayt/ officially exclude (someone) from the sacraments and services of the Christian Church. > *adjective* /ekskə**myōō**nikət/ excommunicated. > *noun* /ekskə**myōō**nikət/ an excommunicated person.

DERIVATIVES – **excommunication** *noun*.

ORIGIN – Latin *excommunicare*, from *ex-* 'out' + *communis* 'common to all'.

ex-con > *noun* informal an ex-convict.

excoriate /iks**kor**iayt/ > *verb* **1** chiefly Medicine damage or remove part of the surface of (the skin). **2** formal censure or criticise severely.

DERIVATIVES – **excoriation** *noun*.

ORIGIN – Latin *excoriare* 'to skin', from *ex-* 'out, from' + *corium* 'skin, hide'.

excrement /**ek**skrimənt/ > *noun* faeces.

DERIVATIVES – **excremental** *adjective*.

ORIGIN – Latin *excrementum*, from *excernere* 'sift out'.

excrescence /iks**kress**'nss/ > *noun* **1** an abnormal outgrowth on a body or plant. **2** an unattractive addition or feature.

ORIGIN – Latin *excrescentia*, from *excrescere* 'grow out'.

excreta /iks**kree**tə/ > *noun* waste discharged from the body, especially faeces and urine.

excrete > *verb* (of a living organism) expel (a substance) from the body as waste.

DERIVATIVES – **excretion** *noun* **excretory** *adjective*.

ORIGIN – Latin *excernere* 'sift out'.

excruciating /iks**krōō**shiayting/ > *adjective* **1** intensely painful. **2** very embarrassing, awkward, or tedious.

DERIVATIVES – **excruciatingly** *adverb*.

SYNONYMS – **1** acute, agonising, intense, racking, torturous.

ORIGIN – from Latin *excruciare* 'torment', from *crux* 'a cross'.

exculpate /**ek**skulpayt/ > *verb* formal show or declare to be not guilty of wrongdoing.

DERIVATIVES – **exculpation** *noun* **exculpatory** *adjective*.

ORIGIN – Latin *exculpare* 'free from blame', from *ex-* 'out, from' + *culpa* 'blame'.

excursion > *noun* a short journey or trip, especially one taken for leisure.

DERIVATIVES – **excursionist** *noun*.

SYNONYMS – expedition, jaunt, journey, outing, trip.

ORIGIN – Latin, from *excurrere* 'run out'.

excursus /iks**kur**səss/ > *noun* (pl. same or **excursuses**) **1** a detailed discussion of a particular point in a book. **2** a digression in a written text.

ORIGIN – Latin, 'excursion', from *excurrere* 'run out'.

excuse > *verb* /iks**kyōōz**/ **1** seek or serve to justify (a fault or offence). **2** release from a duty or requirement. **3** forgive (a fault or a person committing one). **4** allow (someone) to leave a room or gathering (used in polite formulas). **5** (**excuse oneself**) say politely that one is leaving. > *noun* /iks**kyōōss**/ **1** a defence or justification of a fault or offence. **2** something said to conceal the real reason for an action. **3** (**an excuse for**) informal a poor or inadequate example of.

IDIOMS – **excuse me 1** a polite apology. **2** chiefly N. Amer. used to ask someone to repeat what they have just said.

DERIVATIVES – **excusable** *adjective* **excusably** *adverb*.

SYNONYMS – *verb* **1** condone, defend, justify, mitigate. **2** absolve, exempt, exonerate, let off, liberate, release. **3** absolve, forgive, pardon. *noun* **1** apology,

defence, explanation, justification, mitigation. **2** front, pretence, pretext.

ORIGIN – Latin *excusare* 'to free from blame', from *ex-* 'out' + *causa* 'accusation, cause'.

ex-directory > *adjective* Brit. (of a telephone number) not listed in a telephone directory at the wish of the subscriber.

exec > *noun* informal an executive.

execrable /**ek**sikrəb'l/ > *adjective* extremely bad or unpleasant.

DERIVATIVES – **execrably** *adverb*.

ORIGIN – Latin *execrabilis*, from *exsecrari* 'curse'.

execrate /**ek**sikrayt/ > *verb* **1** feel or express great loathing for. **2** archaic curse; swear.

DERIVATIVES – **execration** *noun*.

ORIGIN – Latin *exsecrari* 'curse'.

executable /ig**zek**yoōtəb'l/ Computing > *adjective* able to be run by a computer. > *noun* an executable file or program.

execute > *verb* **1** carry out or put into effect (a plan, order, etc.). **2** perform (an activity or manoeuvre). **3** carry out a sentence of death on (a condemned person). **4** Law make (a legal instrument) valid by signing or sealing it. **5** Law carry out (a judicial sentence, the terms of a will, or other order). **6** Computing run (a file or program).

DERIVATIVES – **execution** *noun*.

SYNONYMS – **1,2** accomplish, carry out, do, implement, perform, put into effect. **3** put to death.

ORIGIN – Latin *executare*, from *exsequi* 'follow up, carry out, punish'.

executioner > *noun* an official who puts condemned criminals to death.

executive /ig**zek**yoōtiv/ > *adjective* having the power to execute plans, actions, or laws. > *noun* **1** a person with senior managerial responsibility in a business organisation. **2** (**the executive**) the branch of a government responsible for executing plans, actions, or laws. **3** an executive committee within an organisation.

executor /ig**zek**yoōtər/ > *noun* Law a person appointed by a person making a will to carry out the instructions in it.

executrix /ig**zek**yoōtriks/ > *noun* (pl. **executrices** /ig**zek**yoōtriseez/ or **executrixes**) Law a female executor.

exegesis /**ek**sijeesiss/ > *noun* (pl. **exegeses** /eksi**jee**seez/) critical explanation or interpretation of a text, especially of scripture.

DERIVATIVES – **exegetic** /eksi**jett**ik/ *adjective* **exegetical** *adjective*.

ORIGIN – Greek *exēgēsis*, from *exēgeisthai* 'interpret'.

exegete /**ek**sijeet/ > *noun* a person who interprets texts, especially scriptures.

ORIGIN – Greek *exēgētēs*, from *exēgeisthai* 'interpret'.

exemplar /igˈzemplər/ > noun a person or thing serving as a typical example or appropriate model.

ORIGIN – Latin exemplarium, from eximere 'take out'.

exemplary > adjective 1 serving as a desirable model; very good. 2 (of a punishment) serving as a warning.

SYNONYMS – 1 faultless, flawless, ideal, outstanding.

exemplify /igˈzemplifī/ > verb (exemplifies, exemplified) be or give a typical example of.

DERIVATIVES – exemplification noun.

SYNONYMS – embody, epitomise, represent, symbolise, typify.

exemplum /igˈzempləm/ > noun (pl. exempla) an example or model, especially a moralising or illustrative story.

ORIGIN – Latin.

exempt /igˈzempt/ > adjective (often exempt from) free from an obligation or liability imposed on others. > verb make exempt.

DERIVATIVES – exemption noun.

SYNONYMS – adjective (exempt from) excused, free of, immune from, not liable to, not subject to. verb excuse, let off, release, spare.

ORIGIN – from Latin eximere 'take out, free'.

exequies /ˈeksikwiz/ > plural noun (sing. exequy) formal funeral rites.

ORIGIN – Latin exsequiae 'funeral ceremonies', from exsequi 'follow after'.

exercise* > noun 1 activity requiring physical effort carried out for the sake of health and fitness. 2 a task set to practise or test a skill. 3 an activity carried out for a specific purpose: a public relations exercise. 4 a military drill or training manoeuvre. 5 the application of a faculty, right, or process: the exercise of authority. > verb 1 use or apply (a faculty, right, or process). 2 take or subject to exercise. 3 worry or perplex.

DERIVATIVES – exercisable adjective exerciser noun.

*SPELLING – unlike most verbs ending in -ise, exercise cannot be spelled with an -ize ending.

SYNONYMS – noun 1 drill, exertion, training, working out; informal physical jerks. verb 2 drill, exert oneself, train, work out.

COMBINATIONS – exercise bike a stationary piece of exercise equipment resembling an ordinary bicycle. exercise book Brit. a booklet with blank pages for students to write in.

ORIGIN – Latin exercitium, from exercere 'keep busy, practise'.

exert /igˈzert/ > verb 1 apply or bring to bear (a force, influence, or quality). 2 (exert oneself) make a physical or mental effort.

SYNONYMS – 2 (exert oneself) apply oneself, do one's utmost, endeavour, strive, sweat.

ORIGIN – Latin exserere 'put forth'.

exertion > noun 1 physical or mental effort. 2 the application of a force, influence, or quality.

SYNONYMS – 1 effort, endeavour, strain, sweat, toil.

exeunt /ˈeksiunt/ > verb (as a stage direction) (actors) leave the stage.

ORIGIN – Latin, 'they go out'.

exfoliant /eksˈfōliənt/ > noun a cosmetic for exfoliating the skin.

exfoliate /eksˈfōliayt/ > verb 1 shed or be shed from a surface in scales or layers. 2 wash or rub (the skin) with a granular substance to remove dead cells.

DERIVATIVES – exfoliation noun exfoliative adjective exfoliator noun.

ORIGIN – Latin exfoliare 'strip of leaves', from ex- 'out, from' + folium 'leaf'.

ex gratia /eks ˈgraysha/ > adverb & adjective (with reference to payment) done from a sense of moral obligation rather than because of any legal requirement.

ORIGIN – Latin, 'from favour'.

exhale > verb 1 breathe out. 2 give off (vapour or fumes).

DERIVATIVES – exhalation noun.

ORIGIN – Latin exhalare, from ex- 'out' + halare 'breathe'.

exhaust > verb 1 tire out completely. 2 use up (resources or reserves) completely. 3 expel (gas or steam) from an engine or other machine. 4 explore (a subject) thoroughly. > noun 1 waste gases or air expelled from an engine or other machine. 2 the system through which such gases are expelled.

DERIVATIVES – exhauster noun exhaustible adjective exhausting adjective exhaustingly adverb.

SYNONYMS – verb 1 drain, fatigue, tire out, wear out. 2 consume, finish, use up.

ORIGIN – Latin exhaurire 'drain out'.

exhaustion > noun 1 the action of using something up or state of being used up. 2 extreme tiredness.

SYNONYMS – 1 consumption, depletion, using up. 2 debility, fatigue, lassitude, tiredness, weariness.

exhaustive > adjective including or considering all elements; very thorough.

DERIVATIVES – exhaustively adverb exhaustiveness noun.

SYNONYMS – all-encompassing, complete, comprehensive, thorough.

ANTONYMS – perfunctory.

exhibit > verb 1 publicly display (an item) in an art gallery or museum. 2 manifest one's possession of (a quality). 3 show as a sign or symptom. > noun 1 an object or collection of objects on display in an art gallery or museum. 2 Law a document or other object produced in a court as evidence. 3 N. Amer. an exhibition.

DERIVATIVES – exhibitor noun.

SYNONYMS – verb 1 display, put on show, show. 2 betray, evince, manifest, reveal, show.

ORIGIN – Latin exhibere 'hold out'.

exhibition > noun 1 a public display of items in an art gallery or museum. 2 a display or demonstration of a skill or quality.

IDIOMS – make an exhibition of oneself behave very foolishly in public.

exhibitionism > noun 1 extravagant behaviour that is intended to attract attention to oneself. 2 Psychiatry a mental condition characterised by the compulsion to display one's genitals in public.

DERIVATIVES – exhibitionist noun exhibitionistic adjective.

exhilarate* > verb cause to feel very happy or animated.

DERIVATIVES – exhilarated adjective exhilarating adjective exhilaratingly adverb exhilaration noun.

*SPELLING – remember the h: exhilarate.

SYNONYMS – delight, elate, intoxicate, thrill.

ORIGIN – Latin exhilarare 'make cheerful', from ex- + hilaris 'cheerful'.

exhort /igˈzort/ > verb strongly encourage or urge (someone) to do something.

DERIVATIVES – exhortation noun exhortatory /igˈzortətri/ adjective.

SYNONYMS – call on, encourage, entreat, press, urge.

ORIGIN – Latin exhortari, from ex- 'thoroughly' + hortari 'encourage'.

exhume /igˈzyoom/ > verb dig out (something buried, especially a corpse) from the ground.

DERIVATIVES – exhumation noun.

ORIGIN – Latin exhumare, from ex- 'out of' + humus 'ground'.

exigency /ˈeksijənsi/ (also exigence) > noun (pl. exigencies) urgent need or demand.

ORIGIN – Latin exigentia, from exigere 'complete, ascertain, enforce'.

exigent /ˈeksijənt/ > adjective formal pressing; demanding.

exiguous /igˈzigyooəss/ > adjective formal very small.

ORIGIN – Latin exiguus 'scanty', from exigere 'weigh exactly'.

exile > noun 1 the state of being barred from one's native country. 2 a person who lives in exile. > verb expel and bar (someone) from their native country.

SYNONYMS – noun 1 banishment, deportation, expatriation, expulsion. 2 displaced person, émigré, expatriate, outcast, refugee. verb banish, deport, displace, expel.

ORIGIN – Latin exilium 'banishment'.

exilic /ek**zill**ik/ > *adjective* relating to a period of exile.

exist > *verb* **1** have objective reality or being. **2** live, especially under adverse conditions. **3** be found: *two conflicting stereotypes exist.*
SYNONYMS – **1** be, be in existence, be extant, have being, live. **2** eke out a living, live, manage, scrape by, subsist. **3** be found, obtain, occur, prevail.

existence* > *noun* **1** the fact or state of existing. **2** a way of living.
*SPELLING – -*ence*, not -*ance*: exist*ence*.
SYNONYMS – **1** actuality, being, continuation, living, survival. **2** life, lifestyle, situation, way of life.
ORIGIN – Latin *existentia*, from *exsistere* 'come into being'.

existent > *adjective* existing.

existential /egzi**sten**sh'l/ > *adjective* **1** relating to existence. **2** Philosophy concerned with existentialism.
DERIVATIVES – **existentially** *adverb*.

existentialism > *noun* a philosophical theory which emphasises the existence of the individual person as a free and responsible agent.
DERIVATIVES – **existentialist** *noun* & *adjective*.

exit > *noun* **1** a way out of a building, room, or passenger vehicle. **2** an act of leaving. **3** a place for traffic to leave a major road or roundabout. **4** a departure of an actor from the stage. > *verb* (**exited, exiting**) **1** go out of or leave a place. **2** (of an actor) leave the stage. **3** Computing terminate a process or program.
SYNONYMS – *noun* **1** door, egress, way out. **2** departure, going, leaving, withdrawal.
COMBINATIONS – **exit poll** a poll of people leaving a polling station, asking how they voted. **exit strategy** a means of extricating oneself from a difficult situation.
ORIGIN – Latin *exit* 'he or she goes out', from *ex-* 'out' + *ire* 'go'.

exlamation > *noun* a sudden cry or remark, especially expressing surprise, emotion, or pain.

ex libris /eks **lee**briss/ > *adverb* used as an inscription on a bookplate to show the name of the book's owner.
ORIGIN – Latin, 'out of the books or library (of someone)'.

ex nihilo /eks **nī**hilō/ > *adverb* formal out of nothing.
ORIGIN – Latin.

exo- > *prefix* external; from outside.
ORIGIN – Greek *exō* 'outside'.

exobiology > *noun* the branch of science concerned with the possibility and likely nature of life on other planets or in space.
DERIVATIVES – **exobiologist** *noun*.

exocrine /**ek**sōkrīn, **ek**sōkrin/ > *adjective* (of a gland) secreting hormones or other products through ducts rather than directly into the blood.
ORIGIN – from Greek *krinein* 'sift'.

exodus > *noun* a mass departure of people, especially emigrants.
ORIGIN – Greek *exodos*, from *ex-* 'out of' + *hodos* 'way'.

ex officio /eks ə**fish**iō/ > *adverb* & *adjective* by virtue of one's position or status.
ORIGIN – from Latin *ex* 'out of, from' + *officium* 'duty'.

exogenous /ek**so**jinəss/ > *adjective* technical relating to external factors. Contrasted with ENDOGENOUS.
DERIVATIVES – **exogenously** *adverb*.

exonerate /ig**zonn**ərayt/ > *verb* **1** officially absolve from blame. **2** (**exonerate from**) release (someone) from (a duty or obligation).
DERIVATIVES – **exoneration** *noun*.
SYNONYMS – **1** absolve, acquit, clear, vindicate.
ORIGIN – Latin *exonerare* 'free from a burden', from *onus* 'a burden'.

exophthalmic /eksof**thal**mik/ > *adjective* Medicine having abnormally protruding eyeballs.
ORIGIN – Greek *exophthalmos* 'having prominent eyes'.

exoplanet /**ek**sōplannit/ > *noun* a planet which orbits a star outside the solar system.

exorbitant* /ig**zor**bitənt/ > *adjective* (of a price or amount charged) unreasonably high.
DERIVATIVES – **exorbitance** *noun* **exorbitantly** *adverb*.
*SPELLING – no *h*: ex*or*bitant.
SYNONYMS – extortionate, inflated, outrageous, prohibitive.
ANTONYMS – cheap, reasonable.
ORIGIN – from Latin *exorbitare* 'go off the track'.

exorcise /**ek**sorsīz/ (also **exorcize**) > *verb* drive out (a supposed evil spirit) from a person or place.
DERIVATIVES – **exorcism** *noun* **exorcist** *noun*.
ORIGIN – Greek *exorkizein*, from *ex-* 'out' + *horkos* 'oath'.

exoskeleton > *noun* Zoology the rigid external covering of the body in insects and some other invertebrate animals.

exothermic /eksō**ther**mik/ > *adjective* Chemistry (of a reaction) accompanied by the release of heat. The opposite of ENDOTHERMIC.

exotic /ig**zott**ik/ > *adjective* **1** originating in or characteristic of a distant foreign country. **2** strikingly colourful or unusual. > *noun* an exotic plant or animal.
DERIVATIVES – **exotically** *adverb* **exoticism** *noun*.

SYNONYMS – *adjective* **1** faraway, foreign. **2** novel, strange, striking.
ANTONYMS – *adjective* **1** familiar, nearby. **2** conventional, unremarkable.
ORIGIN – Greek *exōtikos* 'foreign', from *exō* 'outside'.

exotica /ig**zott**ikə/ > *plural noun* objects considered exotic.

expand /ik**spand**/ > *verb* **1** make or become larger or more extensive. **2** (**expand on**) give a fuller version or account of. **3** become less reserved.
DERIVATIVES – **expandable** *adjective* **expander** *noun* **expansible** *adjective*.
SYNONYMS – **1** broaden, develop, enlarge, increase, widen. **2** (**expand on**) elaborate on, enlarge on, explain, flesh out.
ANTONYMS – **1** contract.
ORIGIN – Latin *expandere* 'to spread out'.

expanded > *adjective* **1** denoting materials which have a light cellular structure. **2** denoting sheet metal slit and stretched into a mesh, used to reinforce concrete and other brittle materials. **3** relatively broad in shape.

expanse > *noun* **1** a wide continuous area of something, typically land or sea. **2** the distance to which something expands or can be expanded.
SYNONYMS – **1** area, spread, stretch, sweep, tract.

expansion > *noun* **1** the action or an instance of expanding. **2** extension of a state's territory by encroachment on that of other nations.
DERIVATIVES – **expansionary** *adjective*.
COMBINATIONS – **expansion joint** a joint that makes allowance for thermal expansion.

expansionism > *noun* the policy of territorial expansion.
DERIVATIVES – **expansionist** *noun* & *adjective*.

expansive > *adjective* **1** covering a wide area; extensive. **2** relaxed, genial, and communicative. **3** tending towards territorial expansion.
DERIVATIVES – **expansively** *adverb* **expansiveness** *noun*.
SYNONYMS – **2** affable, communicative, forthcoming, friendly, genial, open.
ANTONYMS – **2** reserved, taciturn, uncommunicative.

expansivity > *noun* the amount a material expands or contracts per unit length due to a one-degree change in temperature.

ex parte /eks **paar**tay/ > *adjective* & *adverb* Law with respect to or in the interests of one side only.
ORIGIN – Latin, 'from a side'.

expat > *noun* & *adjective* informal short for EXPATRIATE.

expatiate /ik**spay**shiayt/ > *verb* speak or write at length or in detail.

expatriate–expert

DERIVATIVES – **expatiation** noun.
ORIGIN – Latin exspatiari 'move beyond one's usual bounds', from spatium 'space'.

expatriate > noun /eks**pa**triət/ a person who lives outside their native country. > adjective living outside one's native country. > verb /eks**pa**triayt/ settle abroad.
DERIVATIVES – **expatriation** noun.
ORIGIN – from Latin ex- 'out' + patria 'native country'.

expect > verb 1 regard as likely to happen. 2 regard (someone) as likely to do or be something. 3 require as appropriate or rightfully due. 4 believe that (someone) will arrive or (something) will happen soon. 5 (**be expecting**) informal be pregnant.
DERIVATIVES – **expectable** adjective.
SYNONYMS – 1 anticipate, envisage, forecast, presume, suppose. 3 ask for, demand, look for, require. 4 anticipate, await, look for.
ORIGIN – Latin exspectare 'look out for'.

expectancy > noun (pl. **expectancies**) 1 hope or anticipation that something will happen. 2 something expected; an expectation: life expectancy is reduced.

expectant > adjective 1 hoping or anticipating that something is about to happen. 2 (of a woman) pregnant.
DERIVATIVES – **expectantly** adverb.
SYNONYMS – 1 anticipatory, eager, hopeful.

expectation > noun 1 belief that something will happen or be the case. 2 a thing that is expected to happen.

expectorant > noun a medicine which promotes the secretion of sputum, used to treat coughs.

expectorate /ik**spek**tərayt/ > verb cough or spit out (phlegm) from the throat or lungs.
DERIVATIVES – **expectoration** noun.
ORIGIN – Latin expectorare 'expel from the chest', from pectus 'chest, breast'.

expedient /ik**spee**diənt/ > adjective 1 advantageous. 2 advisable on practical rather than moral grounds. > noun a means of attaining an end.
DERIVATIVES – **expedience** noun **expediency** noun **expediently** adverb.
SYNONYMS – noun device, manoeuvre, means, measure, ploy, tactic.

expedite /**ek**spidīt/ > verb cause to happen sooner or be accomplished more quickly.
DERIVATIVES – **expediter** (also **expeditor**) noun.

expedition > noun 1 a journey undertaken by a group of people with a particular purpose. 2 formal promptness or speed in doing something.
DERIVATIVES – **expeditionary** adjective.
SYNONYMS – 1 journey, mission, trek, trip.

wordpower facts

Expedition

What connects **expedition** with **pedal**? The words **expedient**, **expedite**, **expedition**, and **expeditious** all derive from Latin expedire 'extricate (originally by freeing the feet), put in order', from ex- 'out' + pes 'foot', which is the root of **pedal**, **quadruped**, and many other English words. **Expedite** originally meant 'perform quickly', while early senses of **expedition** included 'prompt supply of something' and 'setting out with aggressive intent'; the notions of 'speed' and 'purpose' are retained in current senses.

expeditious /ekspi**di**shəss/ > adjective quick and efficient.
DERIVATIVES – **expeditiously** adverb **expeditiousness** noun.

expel > verb (**expelled, expelling**) 1 force or drive out. 2 force (a pupil) to leave a school.
DERIVATIVES – **expellable** adjective **expellee** noun **expeller** noun.
SYNONYMS – 1 banish, drive out, eject, force out, oust, throw out.
ORIGIN – Latin expellere, from ex- 'out' + pellere 'to drive'.

expend > verb spend or use up (a resource).
SYNONYMS – consume, disburse, pay out, spend, use up.
ORIGIN – Latin expendere, from ex- 'out' + pendere 'weigh, pay'.

expendable > adjective 1 able to be used rather than preserved. 2 of little significance when compared to an overall purpose; able to be sacrificed or abandoned.
DERIVATIVES – **expendability** noun **expendably** adverb.
SYNONYMS – dispensable, disposable, replaceable, throwaway.
ANTONYMS – indispensable.

expenditure /ik**spen**dichər/ > noun 1 the action of spending funds. 2 the amount of money spent.
SYNONYMS – 1 disbursement, outlay, spending. 2 expenses, outgoings, outlay, spending.
ANTONYMS – 2 income.

expense > noun 1 cost incurred in or required for something. 2 (**expenses**) specific costs incurred in the performance of a job or task. 3 something on which money must be spent.
IDIOMS – **at the expense of 1** paid for by. 2 to the detriment of.
SYNONYMS – 1 cost, outlay, price. 2 (**expenses**) expenditure, outgoings, overheads.

COMBINATIONS – **expense account** an arrangement under which money spent in the course of business is later reimbursed by one's employer.

expensive > adjective costing a lot of money.
DERIVATIVES – **expensively** adverb **expensiveness** noun.
SYNONYMS – costly, dear, lavish, luxurious, valuable.
ANTONYMS – cheap, inexpensive.

experience > noun 1 practical contact with and observation of facts or events. 2 knowledge or skill acquired over time. 3 an event or occurrence which leaves an impression on one. > verb 1 encounter or undergo (an event or occurrence). 2 feel (an emotion).
SYNONYMS – noun 1 background, familiarity, involvement, participation. 2 expertise, know-how, knowledge, savoir faire, understanding. 3 adventure, episode. verb encounter, endure, face, go through, meet, suffer, undergo.
ORIGIN – Latin experientia, from experiri 'try'.

experienced > adjective having knowledge or skill in a particular field gained over time.
SYNONYMS – accomplished, expert, knowledgeable, seasoned, well-versed.
ANTONYMS – inexperienced.

experiential /ikspeeri**en**sh'l/ > adjective involving or based on experience and observation.
DERIVATIVES – **experientially** adverb.

experiment > noun 1 a scientific procedure undertaken to make a discovery, test a hypothesis, or demonstrate a known fact. 2 a course of action tentatively adopted without being sure of the eventual outcome. > verb 1 perform a scientific experiment. 2 try out new things.
DERIVATIVES – **experimentation** noun **experimenter** noun.
SYNONYMS – noun 1 demonstration, enquiry, investigation, procedure, test, trial. verb 1 investigate, probe, research.
ORIGIN – Latin experimentum, from experiri 'try'.

experimental > adjective 1 based on untested ideas or techniques and not yet established or finalised. 2 relating to scientific experiments. 3 (of art, music, etc.) radically new and innovative.
DERIVATIVES – **experimentalism** noun **experimentalist** noun **experimentally** adverb.
SYNONYMS – 1 exploratory, provisional, untested. 3 alternative, avant-garde, innovative, radical.

expert > noun a person who is very knowledgeable about or skilful in a particular area. > *adjective* having or involving such knowledge or skill.

DERIVATIVES – **expertly** *adverb* **expertness** *noun*.

SYNONYMS – *noun* authority, master, professional, specialist. *adjective* accomplished, adept, knowledgeable, practised, skilled, specialised.

ANTONYMS – *noun* novice. *adjective* incompetent, inexpert.

ORIGIN – Latin *expertus*, from *experiri* 'try'.

expertise /eksperteez/ > *noun* great skill or knowledge in a particular field.

SYNONYMS – know-how, knowledge, mastery, proficiency, prowess, skill, virtuosity.

ANTONYMS – incompetence.

expiate /ekspiayt/ > *verb* atone for (guilt or sin).

DERIVATIVES – **expiable** *adjective* **expiation** *noun* **expiator** *noun* **expiatory** /ekspiətri/ *adjective*.

ORIGIN – Latin *expiare* 'appease by sacrifice', from *pius* 'pious'.

expire /ikspīr/ > *verb* 1 (of a document or agreement) come to the end of the period of validity. 2 (of a period of time) come to an end. 3 (of a person) die. 4 technical exhale (air) from the lungs.

DERIVATIVES – **expiration** *noun* **expiratory** *adjective*.

SYNONYMS – 1 become void, end, lapse, terminate.

ORIGIN – Latin *exspirare* 'breathe out'.

expiry > *noun* 1 the time when something expires. 2 archaic death.

explain > *verb* 1 make (something) clear by describing it in more detail. 2 give a reason or justification for. 3 (**explain oneself**) excuse or justify one's motives or conduct. 4 (**explain away**) minimise the significance of (something awkward) by giving an excuse or justification.

DERIVATIVES – **explainable** *adjective* **explainer** *noun* **explanation** *noun*.

SYNONYMS – 1 clarify, describe, elucidate, expound. 2 account for, justify.

ORIGIN – Latin *explanare*, from *planus* 'plain'.

explanatory /iksplannətri/ > *adjective* serving to explain something.

DERIVATIVES – **explanatorily** *adverb*.

expletive /ikspleetiv/ > *noun* an oath or swear word.

ORIGIN – first meaning 'word used merely to fill out a sentence': from Latin *explere* 'fill out'.

explicable /iksplikkəb'l, eksplikəb'l/ > *adjective* able to be explained or accounted for.

ORIGIN – from Latin *explicare* 'unfold'.

explicate /eksplikayt/ > *verb* 1 analyse and develop (an idea or principle) in detail. 2 analyse (a literary work) in order to reveal its meaning.

DERIVATIVES – **explication** *noun* **explicative** /eksplikkətiv, eksplikətiv/ *adjective* **explicator** *noun* **explicatory** /eksplikkətri/ *adjective*.

ORIGIN – Latin *explicare* 'unfold'.

explicit /iksplissit/ > *adjective* 1 clear and detailed, with no room for confusion or doubt. 2 graphically describing or representing sexual activity.

DERIVATIVES – **explicitly** *adverb* **explicitness** *noun*.

SYNONYMS – 1 candid, clear, plain, precise, unambiguous, unequivocal. 2 graphic, obscene, uncensored.

ANTONYMS – 1 implicit, vague.

ORIGIN – from Latin *explicare* 'unfold'.

explode > *verb* 1 burst or shatter violently as a result of rapid combustion or excessive internal pressure. 2 cause to burst or shatter in this way. 3 suddenly give expression to violent emotion. 4 show (a belief or theory) to be false or unfounded. 5 increase suddenly in number or extent. 6 (**exploded**) (of a diagram) showing parts or components of something in the normal relative positions but slightly separated from each other.

DERIVATIVES – **exploder** *noun*.

SYNONYMS – 1 burst, erupt, shatter. 2 blow up, detonate. 4 debunk, discredit, disprove, refute.

wordpower facts

Explode

Explode is related to **applaud** (and also to **plaudits** and **plausible**) through its root word, Latin *plaudere* 'to clap'. It entered English from Latin *explodere* 'drive out by clapping, hiss off the stage', and originally meant 'reject scornfully, discard', an idea that is retained in the modern sense 4. The meaning 'burst or shatter violently' evolved via an old sense 'expel with violence and sudden noise', perhaps influenced by obsolete *displode* 'burst with a noise'.

exploit > *verb* /iksployt/ 1 make use of and derive benefit from (a resource). 2 make use of unfairly; benefit unjustly from the work or actions of. > *noun* /eksployt/ a bold or daring feat.

DERIVATIVES – **exploitable** *adjective* **exploitation** *noun* **exploitative** *adjective* **exploiter** *noun* **exploitive** *adjective*.

SYNONYMS – *verb* 1 benefit from, capitalise on, make use of, use, utilise. 2 abuse, ill-treat, prey on, take advantage of, use.

ORIGIN – first used in the sense 'success, progress': from Latin *explicare* 'unfold'.

exploratory > *adjective* relating to or involving exploration or investigation.

explore > *verb* 1 travel through (an unfamiliar area) in order to learn about it. 2 inquire into or discuss in detail. 3 evaluate (a new option or possibility). 4 examine or scrutinise by searching through or touching.

DERIVATIVES – **exploration** *noun* **explorative** *adjective* **explorer** *noun*.

SYNONYMS – 1 investigate, reconnoitre, scout, tour, traverse. 2,3 consider, inquire into, investigate, look into, research, survey.

ORIGIN – Latin *explorare* 'search out', from *ex-* 'out' + *plorare* 'utter a cry'.

explosion > *noun* an act or instance of exploding.

SYNONYMS – blast, burst, detonation, discharge, report.

explosive > *adjective* 1 able or likely to explode. 2 likely to cause an eruption of anger or controversy. 3 (of an increase) sudden and dramatic. 4 Phonetics (of a vocal sound) produced with a sharp release of air. > *noun* a substance which can be made to explode.

DERIVATIVES – **explosively** *adverb* **explosiveness** *noun*.

SYNONYMS – 1 combustible, incendiary. 2 controversial, fiery, highly charged, tense, unstable, volatile.

exponent /ikspōnənt/ > *noun* 1 a promoter of an idea or theory. 2 a person who does a particular thing skilfully. 3 Mathematics the power to which a given quantity is raised (e.g. 3 in $2^3 = 2 \times 2 \times 2$).

SYNONYMS – 1 advocate, champion, promoter, proponent, supporter. 2 performer, practitioner.

ORIGIN – Latin, from *exponere* 'present, explain'.

exponential /ekspənensh'l/ > *adjective* 1 (of an increase) becoming more and more rapid. 2 Mathematics of or expressed by a mathematical exponent.

DERIVATIVES – **exponentially** *adverb*.

export > *verb* /iksport/ 1 send (goods or services) to another country for sale. 2 spread or introduce (ideas or customs) to another country. > *noun* /eksport/ 1 the exporting of goods or services. 2 an exported commodity, article, or service.

DERIVATIVES – **exportable** *adjective* **exportation** *noun* **exporter** *noun*.

ORIGIN – Latin *exportare*, from *ex-* 'out' + *portare* 'carry'.

expose > *verb* 1 uncover and make visible. 2 reveal the true nature of. 3 (**expose to**) make vulnerable to. 4 subject (photographic film) to light. 5 (**expose oneself**) publicly and indecently display one's genitals.

DERIVATIVES – **exposer** noun.

SYNONYMS – **1** bare, reveal, uncover. **2** make public, manifest, reveal, uncover, unmask.

ORIGIN – Latin exponere 'present, explain', influenced by expositus 'put or set out' and Old French poser 'to place'.

exposé /ik**spō**zay/ > noun a report in the media that reveals something discreditable.

ORIGIN – French, 'shown, set out'.

exposed > adjective unprotected from the weather.

SYNONYMS – bare, barren, unprotected, unsheltered, windswept.

ANTONYMS – sheltered.

exposition > noun **1** a comprehensive description and explanation of a theory. **2** a large public exhibition of art or trade goods. **3** Music the part of a movement in which the principal themes are first presented.

DERIVATIVES – **expositional** adjective.

ORIGIN – Latin, from exponere 'present, explain'.

expositor /ik**spozz**itər/ > noun a person or thing that explains complicated ideas or theories.

DERIVATIVES – **expository** adjective.

ex post facto /eks pōst **fakt**ō/ > adjective & adverb with retrospective action or force.

ORIGIN – Latin ex postfacto 'in the light of subsequent events'.

expostulate /ik**sposs**tyoolayt/ > verb express strong disapproval or disagreement.

DERIVATIVES – **expostulation** noun **expostulatory** /ik**sposs**tyoolətri/ adjective.

ORIGIN – Latin expostulare 'demand'.

exposure > noun **1** the state of being exposed to something harmful. **2** a physical condition resulting from being exposed to severe weather conditions. **3** the action of exposing a photographic film. **4** the quantity of light reaching a photographic film, as determined by shutter speed and lens aperture. **5** the revelation of something secret. **6** the publicising of information or an event.

expound > verb present and explain (a theory or idea) systematically.

DERIVATIVES – **expounder** noun.

ORIGIN – Latin exponere 'present, explain', from ex- 'out' + ponere 'put'.

express¹ /ik**spress**/ > verb **1** convey (a thought or feeling) in words or by gestures and conduct. **2** (**express oneself**) say what one thinks or means. **3** squeeze out (liquid or air).

DERIVATIVES – **expresser** noun **expressible** adjective.

SYNONYMS – **1** articulate, communicate, convey, demonstrate, indicate, voice.

express² /ik**spress**/ > adjective **1** operating at high speed. **2** (of a delivery) made by a special messenger. > adverb by express train

or delivery service. > noun **1** (also **express train**) a train that travels quickly and stops at few stations. **2** a special delivery service. > verb send by express messenger or delivery.

wordpower facts

Express

The three words **express** are related to each other, despite their dissimilarity in meaning. **Express** meaning 'convey a thought or feeling' and **express** meaning 'stated explicitly' are from Latin ex- 'out' and the connected verbs pressare and primere, both of which have the stem press- and mean 'press'. **Express** as in express train is an extended use: express trains were so named because they served a particular destination without intermediate stops, reflecting another sense of **express**, 'done or made for a special purpose', later interpreted in the sense 'rapid'.

express³ /ik**spress**, **ek**spress/ > adjective **1** stated explicitly. **2** specific.

DERIVATIVES – **expressly** adverb.

expression > noun **1** the action of expressing something. **2** the look on someone's face. **3** a word or phrase expressing an idea. **4** Mathematics a collection of symbols expressing a quantity.

DERIVATIVES – **expressional** adjective **expressionless** adjective.

SYNONYMS – **1** articulation, declaration, statement, utterance, voicing. **2** air, aspect, countenance, look, mien. **3** adage, formula, idiom, phrase, saying.

expressionism > noun a style in art, music, or drama in which the artist or writer seeks to express the inner world of emotion rather than external reality.

DERIVATIVES – **expressionist** noun & adjective **expressionistic** adjective.

expressive > adjective **1** effectively conveying thought or feeling. **2** (**expressive of**) conveying (a specified quality or idea).

DERIVATIVES – **expressively** adverb **expressiveness** noun

SYNONYMS – **1** eloquent, meaningful, revealing, telling.

ANTONYMS – **1** deadpan, inexpressive.

expresso > noun variant spelling of **ESPRESSO**.

expressway > noun chiefly N. Amer. an urban motorway.

expropriate /ek**sprō**priayt/ > verb (of the state) take (property) from its owner for public use or benefit.

DERIVATIVES – **expropriation** noun **expropriator** noun.

ORIGIN – Latin expropriare 'take from the owner', from ex- 'out, from' + proprium 'property'.

expulsion > noun the action of expelling.

DERIVATIVES – **expulsive** adjective.

expunge /ik**spunj**/ > verb obliterate or remove completely.

DERIVATIVES – **expungement** noun **expunger** noun.

ORIGIN – Latin expungere 'mark for deletion by means of points', from ex- 'out' + pungere 'to prick'.

expurgate /**ek**spergayt/ > verb remove matter regarded as obscene or unsuitable from (a text or account).

DERIVATIVES – **expurgation** noun **expurgator** noun **expurgatory** /ek**sper**gətri/ adjective.

ORIGIN – Latin expurgare 'cleanse thoroughly'.

exquisite /ek**skwi**zit, **ek**skwizit/ > adjective **1** of great beauty and delicacy. **2** highly refined: exquisite taste. **3** intensely felt; acute.

DERIVATIVES – **exquisitely** adverb **exquisiteness** noun.

SYNONYMS – **1** beautiful, delicate, elegant, graceful, lovely, perfect. **2** consummate, cultured, fastidious, impeccable, refined.

ORIGIN – first meaning 'carefully ascertained, precise': from Latin exquirere 'seek out'.

ex-serviceman (or **ex-servicewoman**) > noun chiefly Brit. a former member of the armed forces.

extant /**ek**stant/ > adjective still in existence.

ORIGIN – Latin, from exstare 'be visible or prominent'.

extemporaneous /ikstempə**ray**niəss/ > adjective another term for **EXTEMPORARY**.

DERIVATIVES – **extemporaneously** adverb **extemporaneousness** noun.

extemporary /ik**stem**pərəri/ > adjective spoken or done without preparation.

DERIVATIVES – **extemporarily** adverb **extemporariness** noun.

ORIGIN – from **EXTEMPORE**.

extempore /ik**stem**pəri/ > adjective & adverb spoken or done without preparation.

ORIGIN – Latin ex tempore 'on the spur of the moment', literally 'out of the time'.

extemporise /ik**stem**pərīz/ (also **extemporize**) > verb improvise.

DERIVATIVES – **extemporisation** noun.

extend > verb **1** make larger in area or extent. **2** cause to last longer. **3** occupy a specified area or continue for a specified distance. **4** hold or stretch out (a part of the body). **5** offer; make available.

DERIVATIVES – **extendable** adjective **extendible** adjective **extensible** adjective.

SYNONYMS – **1** enlarge, expand, increase, lengthen, stretch, widen. **2** increase, lengthen, prolong. **3** continue, reach, spread, stretch.

COMBINATIONS – **extended family** a family which extends beyond the nuclear family to include relatives living close by.

ORIGIN – Latin *extendere* 'stretch out'.

extender > *noun* **1** a person or thing that extends something. **2** a substance added to a liquid or soft product to increase its bulk.

extensile /ik**sten**sīl/ > *adjective* capable of being extended.

extension > *noun* **1** the action or process of enlarging or extending something. **2** a part added to a structure or building to enlarge it. **3** an additional period of time. **4** (also **extension lead** or **cable**) an additional length of electric cable which can be plugged into a fixed socket and terminates in a further socket. **5** a subsidiary telephone, especially one with its own additional number on a line leading from a main switchboard. **6** the extending of a limb from a bent to a straight position.

DERIVATIVES – **extensional** *adjective*.

ORIGIN – Latin, from *extendere* 'stretch out'.

extensive > *adjective* **1** covering a large area. **2** large in amount or scale.

DERIVATIVES – **extensively** *adverb* **extensiveness** *noun*.

SYNONYMS – **1** broad, expansive, large, sizeable. **2** comprehensive, considerable, large, profound, significant, substantial.

ANTONYMS – small.

extensor /ik**sten**sər/ > *noun* Anatomy a muscle whose contraction extends a limb or other part of the body.

extent > *noun* **1** the area covered by something. **2** the size or scale of something. **3** the particular degree to which something is the case.

SYNONYMS – **1** area, dimensions, expanse, proportions, size. **2** degree, level, magnitude, scale, size.

ORIGIN – first used in the sense 'valuation of property': from Latin *extendere* 'stretch out'.

extenuate /ik**sten**yooayt/ > **1** *verb* lessen the seriousness of (guilt or an offence) by referring to a mitigating factor. **2** (**extenuated**) literary thin.

DERIVATIVES – **extenuating** *adjective* **extenuation** *noun* **extenuatory** /ik**sten**yooətri/ *adjective*.

ORIGIN – Latin *extenuare* 'make thin', from *tenuis* 'thin'.

exterior > *adjective* forming, situated on, or relating to the outside. > *noun* the outer surface or structure of something.

DERIVATIVES – **exteriorly** *adverb*.

SYNONYMS – *adjective* external, outer, outward. *noun* outside, surface.

ANTONYMS – *adjective & noun* interior.

ORIGIN – Latin, from *exter* 'outer'.

exterminate /ik**ster**minayt/ > *verb* destroy completely; eradicate.

DERIVATIVES – **extermination** *noun* **exterminator** *noun* **exterminatory** /ik**ster**minətri/ *adjective*.

ORIGIN – first used in the sense 'drive out': from Latin *exterminare*, from *ex-* 'out' + *terminus* 'boundary'.

external > *adjective* **1** belonging to, situated on, or forming the outside. **2** coming or derived from a source outside the subject affected. **3** coming from or relating to another country or institution. > *noun* (**externals**) outward features.

DERIVATIVES – **externally** *adverb*.

SYNONYMS – *adjective* **1** exterior, outer, outward.

ANTONYMS – *adjective* **1** internal.

ORIGIN – Latin, from *exter* 'outer'.

external ear > *noun* the parts of the ear outside the eardrum, especially the pinna.

externalise (also **externalize**) > *verb* **1** give external existence or concrete form to. **2** express (a thought or feeling) in words or actions.

DERIVATIVES – **externalisation** *noun*.

extinct > *adjective* **1** (of a species or other large group) having no living members. **2** no longer in existence. **3** (of a volcano) not having erupted in recorded history.

ORIGIN – first meaning 'no longer alight': Latin, from *exstinguere* 'extinguish'.

extinction > *noun* the state or process of being or becoming extinct.

extinguish > *verb* **1** put out (a fire or light). **2** put an end to. **3** cancel (a debt) by full payment. **4** Law render (a right or obligation) void.

DERIVATIVES – **extinguishable** *adjective* **extinguisher** *noun*.

SYNONYMS – **1** douse, put out, quench.

ORIGIN – Latin *exstinguere*, from *ex-* 'out' + *stinguere* 'quench'.

extirpate /**ek**stərpayt/ > *verb* search out and destroy completely.

DERIVATIVES – **extirpation** *noun* **extirpator** *noun*.

ORIGIN – Latin *exstirpare*, from *ex-* 'out' + *stirps* 'a stem'.

extol /ik**stōl**/ > *verb* (**extolled**, **extolling**) praise enthusiastically.

DERIVATIVES – **extoller** *noun*.

SYNONYMS – acclaim, eulogise, hymn, laud, praise.

ORIGIN – Latin *extollere*, from *ex-* 'out, upward' + *tollere* 'raise'.

extort /ik**stort**/ > *verb* obtain by force, threats, or other unfair means.

DERIVATIVES – **extorter** *noun* **extortion** *noun* **extortionist** *noun*.

ORIGIN – Latin *extorquere*, from *ex-* 'out' + *torquere* 'twist'.

extortionate /ik**stor**shənət/ > *adjective* **1** (of a price) much too high. **2** using or given to extortion.

DERIVATIVES – **extortionately** *adverb*.

SYNONYMS – **1** exorbitant, inflated, prohibitive.

ANTONYMS – **1** cheap, reasonable.

extra > *adjective* added to an existing or usual amount or number. > *adverb* **1** to a greater extent than usual. **2** in addition. > *noun* **1** an item for which an extra charge is made. **2** an extra item. **3** a person engaged temporarily to take part in a crowd scene in a film or play.

SYNONYMS – *adjective* additional, auxiliary, further, supplementary.

COMBINATIONS – **extra cover** Cricket a fielding position between cover point and mid-off but further from the wicket. **extra time** chiefly Brit. (in sport) a further period of play added on to a game if the scores are equal. **extra virgin** denoting a superior grade of olive oil made from the first pressing of the olives.

ORIGIN – probably a shortening of **EXTRAORDINARY**.

extra- > *prefix* **1** outside; beyond: *extramarital*. **2** beyond the scope of: *extra-curricular*.

ORIGIN – Latin *extra* 'outside'.

extract > *verb* /ik**strakt**/ **1** remove with care or effort. **2** obtain (money, information, etc.) from someone unwilling to give it. **3** obtain (a substance or resource) from something by a special method. **4** select (a passage from a text, film, or piece of music) for performance or reproduction. > *noun* /**ek**strakt/ **1** a short passage taken from a text, film, or piece of music. **2** a preparation containing the active ingredient of a substance in concentrated form.

DERIVATIVES – **extractable** *adjective* **extractive** *adjective*.

SYNONYMS – *verb* **1** remove, take out, withdraw. **2** exact, extort, wring out. **4** abstract, choose, excerpt, quote, select. *noun* **1** citation, excerpt, passage, quotation, selection.

ORIGIN – Latin *extrahere* 'draw out'.

extraction > *noun* **1** the action of extracting. **2** the ethnic origin of someone's family.

extractor > *noun* **1** a machine or device used to extract something. **2** (before another noun) denoting a fan or other device for extracting odours and stale air.

extra-curricular > *adjective* (of an activity at a school or college) pursued in addition to the normal curriculum.

extradite /**ek**strədīt/ > *verb* hand over (a person accused or convicted of committing a crime in a foreign state) to the jurisdiction of that state.

DERIVATIVES – **extraditable** *adjective* **extradition** *noun*.

ORIGIN – first as *extradition*, from French, from *ex-* 'out, from' + *tradition* 'delivery'.

extramarital /ekstrəˈmarrɪtˈl/ > *adjective* (especially of sexual relations) occurring outside marriage.

DERIVATIVES – **extramaritally** *adverb*.

extramural /ekstrəˈmyoorəl/ > *adjective* **1** Brit. (of a course of study) arranged for people who are not full-time members of a university or other educational establishment. **2** outside the walls or boundaries of a town or city.

DERIVATIVES – **extramurally** *adverb*.

ORIGIN – from Latin *extra muros* 'outside the walls'.

extraneous /ikˈstraynɪəss/ > *adjective* **1** irrelevant or unrelated to the subject. **2** of external origin.

DERIVATIVES – **extraneously** *adverb* **extraneousness** *noun*.

ORIGIN – Latin *extraneus*.

extraordinaire /ikstrordɪˈnair/ > *adjective* outstanding in a particular capacity: *a gardener extraordinaire*.

ORIGIN – French, 'extraordinary'.

extraordinary /ikˈstrordɪnəri/ > *adjective* **1** very unusual or remarkable. **2** (of a meeting) specially convened rather than being one of a regular series. **3** (of an official) specially employed: *Ambassador Extraordinary*.

DERIVATIVES – **extraordinarily** *adverb* **extraordinariness** *noun*.

SYNONYMS – **1** astonishing, astounding, phenomenal, remarkable, unbelievable.

ORIGIN – Latin *extraordinarius*, from *extra ordinem* 'outside the normal course of events'.

extrapolate /ikˈstrappəlayt/ > *verb* **1** extend (a graph) by inferring unknown values from trends in the known data. **2** extend the application of (a method, conclusion, etc.) to different or larger groups.

DERIVATIVES – **extrapolation** *noun* **extrapolative** *adjective* **extrapolator** *noun*.

ORIGIN – from **EXTRA-** + a shortened form of **INTERPOLATE**.

extrasensory perception /ekstrəˈsensəri/ > *noun* the supposed faculty of perceiving things by means other than the known senses, e.g. by telepathy.

extraterrestrial /ekstrətəˈrestriəl/ > *adjective* of or from outside the earth or its atmosphere. > *noun* a hypothetical or fictional being from outer space.

extravagant /ikˈstravvəgənt/ > *adjective* **1** lacking restraint in spending money or using resources. **2** resulting from or showing this. **3** exceeding what is reasonable or appropriate: *extravagant claims*.

DERIVATIVES – **extravagance** *noun* **extravagantly** *adverb*.

SYNONYMS – **1** immoderate, improvident, lavish, prodigal, profligate, spendthrift. **2** costly, lavish, luxurious, valuable. **3** exaggerated, excessive, grandiose, immoderate, lavish, unrestrained.

ANTONYMS – **1** thrifty. **2** cheap, economical. **3** moderate, restrained.

---

wordpower facts

Extravagant

The word **extravagant** originally had the sense 'unusual, unsuitable'. It comes from Latin *extravagari* 'diverge greatly', from *extra-* 'outside' + *vagari* 'wander'. Its derivation from *vagari* links it with words such as **astray** (which comes from *extravagari* via Old French *estraier*), **vagabond**, **vagary**, and **vagrant**.

---

extravaganza /ikstravvəˈganzə/ > *noun* an elaborate and spectacular entertainment.

ORIGIN – Italian *estravaganza* 'extravagance'.

extreme > *adjective* **1** reaching a high or the highest degree; very great. **2** highly unusual; exceptional. **3** very severe or serious. **4** not moderate, especially politically. **5** furthest from the centre or a given point. > *noun* **1** either of two abstract things that are as different from each other as possible. **2** the most extreme degree of something.

DERIVATIVES – **extremely** *adverb* **extremeness** *noun*.

SYNONYMS – *adjective* **1** exceptional, extraordinary, maximum, supreme, ultimate. **3** desperate, drastic, far-reaching, forceful, radical, serious. **4** extremist, fanatical, immoderate, militant, radical.

ANTONYMS – *adjective* **1** mild, slight. **3** mild, moderate. **4** moderate.

COMBINATIONS – **extreme unction** (in the Roman Catholic Church) a former name for the sacrament of the anointing of the sick, especially when administered to the dying.

ORIGIN – Latin *extremus* 'outermost, utmost', from *exterus* 'outer'.

extremist > *noun* a person who holds extreme political or religious views.

DERIVATIVES – **extremism** *noun*.

extremity /ikˈstremmiti/ > *noun* (pl. **extremities**) **1** the furthest point or limit. **2** (**extremities**) the hands and feet. **3** severity or seriousness. **4** extreme adversity.

extricate /ˈekstrikayt/ > *verb* free from a constraint or difficulty.

DERIVATIVES – **extrication** *noun*.

ORIGIN – Latin *extricare* 'unravel', from *ex-* 'out' + *tricae* 'perplexities'.

extrinsic /ikˈstrinsik/ > *adjective* not essential or inherent.

DERIVATIVES – **extrinsically** *adverb*.

ORIGIN – Latin *extrinsecus* 'outward', from *exter* 'outer'.

extrovert* /ˈekstrəvert/ > *noun* **1** an outgoing, socially confident person. **2** Psychology a person predominantly concerned with external things or objective considerations. > *adjective* of or characteristic of an extrovert.

DERIVATIVES – **extroversion** *noun* **extroverted** *adjective*.

*****SPELLING** – *extro-*, not *extra-*: extrovert. The variant spelling *extravert* is sometimes used in psychology.

SYNONYMS – *adjective* gregarious, lively, outgoing, sociable.

ANTONYMS – *noun* introvert. *adjective* introverted.

ORIGIN – from *extro-* (variant of **EXTRA-**) + Latin *vertere* 'to turn'.

extrude /ikˈstrood/ > *verb* **1** thrust or force out. **2** shape (a material such as metal or plastic) by forcing it through a die.

DERIVATIVES – **extrudable** *adjective* **extrusion** *noun*.

ORIGIN – Latin *extrudere*, from *ex-* 'out' + *trudere* 'to thrust'.

extrusive > *adjective* Geology referring to rock that has been extruded at the earth's surface as lava or other volcanic deposits.

exuberant /igˈzyoobərənt/ > *adjective* **1** lively and cheerful. **2** growing profusely.

DERIVATIVES – **exuberance** *noun* **exuberantly** *adverb*.

SYNONYMS – **1** animated, buoyant, ebullient, effervescent, lively.

ORIGIN – Latin, from *exuberare* 'be abundantly fruitful', from *uber* 'fertile'.

exude /igˈzyood/ > *verb* **1** discharge or be discharged slowly and steadily. **2** display (an emotion or quality) strongly and openly.

DERIVATIVES – **exudation** *noun*.

SYNONYMS – **1** discharge, emit, give off, secrete.

ORIGIN – Latin *exsudare*, from *ex-* 'out' + *sudare* 'to sweat'.

exult /igˈzult/ > *verb* show or feel triumphant elation.

DERIVATIVES – **exultation** *noun* **exulting** *adjective* **exultingly** *adverb*.

SYNONYMS – glory, rejoice, triumph.

ORIGIN – Latin *exsultare*, from *exsilire* 'leap up'.

exultant > *adjective* triumphantly happy.

DERIVATIVES – **exultancy** *noun* **exultantly** *adverb*.

SYNONYMS – elated, jubilant, rejoicing, triumphant.

exurb /eksurb/ > *noun* N. Amer. a prosperous area beyond a city's suburbs.

DERIVATIVES – **exurban** *adjective*.

ex-voto /eks vōtō/ > *noun* (pl. **ex-votos**) an offering given in order to fulfil a vow.

ORIGIN – Latin *ex voto* 'from a vow'.

eye > *noun* **1** the organ of sight in humans and animals. **2** a rounded eye-like marking on an animal or bird. **3** a round, dark spot on a potato from which a new shoot grows. **4** the small hole in a needle through which the thread is passed. **5** a small metal loop into which a hook is fitted as a fastener on a garment. **6** Nautical a loop at the top end of a shroud or stay rope. **7** the calm region at the centre of a storm. **8** used to refer to a person's attitude or feelings: *to European eyes, it may seem that the city is overcrowded.* > *verb* (**eyed**, **eyeing** or **eying**) **1** look at closely or with interest. **2** (**eye up**) informal look at (someone) in a way that reveals a sexual interest.

WORDFINDER – ocular (*of or relating to the eye*), oculist, ophthalmologist (*specialist in eye diseases*), ophthalmic optician, optometrist (*person qualified to prescribe glasses*), ophthalmoscope (*instrument for inspecting eyes*), orbit (*eye socket*); exophthalmic (*having bulging eyes*); *parts of the eye*: aqueous humour, conjunctiva, cornea, crystalline lens, iris, optic nerve, pupil, retina, sclera, vitreous humour; *eye defects or diseases*: astigmatism, cataract, colour blindness, conjunctivitis, glaucoma, hypermetropia (*long-sightedness*), keratitis, myopia (*short-sightedness*), ophthalmia, retinitis, scleritis.

IDIOMS – **be all eyes** be watching eagerly and attentively. **close one's eyes to** refuse to acknowledge (something unpleasant). **an eye for an eye and a tooth for a tooth** retaliation in kind is the appropriate way to deal with an offence or crime. [ORIGIN – with reference to the Book of Exodus, chapter 21 (in the Bible).] **give someone the eye** informal look at someone with sexual interest. **have an eye for** be able to recognise and judge wisely. **have** (or **keep**) **one's eye on 1** keep under careful observation. **2** (**have one's eye on**) aim to acquire. **have** (or **with**) **an eye to** have (or having) as one's objective. **only have eyes for** be exclusively interested in. **have eyes in the back of one's head** know what is going on around one even when one cannot see it. **keep an eye on** keep under careful observation. **keep an eye out** (or **open**) look out for something. **keep one's eyes open** (or **peeled** or Brit. **skinned**) watch out for something. **make eyes at** look at in a way that indicates sexual interest. **one in the eye for** a disappointment or setback for. **open someone's eyes** cause someone to realise something. **see eye to eye** be in full agreement. **a twinkle** (or **gleam**) **in someone's eye** something that is as yet no more than an attractive idea or dream. **up to one's eyes** informal extremely busy. **what the eye doesn't see, the heart doesn't grieve over** proverb if someone is unaware of an unpleasant fact or situation they can't be troubled by it. **with one's eyes open** fully aware of possible difficulties.

DERIVATIVES – **eyed** *adjective*.

COMBINATIONS – **eyebath** chiefly Brit. a small container used for applying cleansing solutions to the eye. **eye-catching** immediately appealing or noticeable. **eyeglass 1** a single lens for correcting or assisting defective eyesight, especially a monocle. **2** (**eyeglasses**) chiefly N. Amer. another term for GLASSES. **eyelash** each of the short hairs growing on the edges of the eyelids. **eyelid** each of the upper and lower folds of skin which cover the eye when closed. **eyeliner** a cosmetic applied as a line round the eyes. **eye-opener** informal an unexpected revelation. **eyepatch** a patch worn to protect an injured eye. **eye-popping** informal astonishingly large or blatant. **eyeshade** a translucent visor used to protect the eyes from strong light. **eyeshadow** a coloured cosmetic applied to the eyelids or to the skin around the eyes. **eyesight** a person's ability to see. **eye socket** the cavity in the skull which encloses an eyeball with its surrounding muscles.

eyeball > *noun* the round part of the eye of a vertebrate, within the eyelids and socket. > *verb* informal, chiefly N. Amer. stare at closely.

IDIOMS – **eyeball to eyeball** face to face with someone, especially in an aggressive way.

eyebright > *noun* a small white-flowered plant, traditionally used as a remedy for eye problems.

eyebrow > *noun* the strip of hair growing on the ridge above a person's eye socket.

IDIOMS – **raise one's eyebrows** (or **an eyebrow**) show surprise or mild disapproval.

eyeful > *noun* informal **1** a long steady look. **2** an eye-catching person or thing.

eyelet > *noun* **1** a small round hole made in leather or cloth, used for threading a lace, string, or rope through. **2** a metal ring reinforcing such a hole.

eyepiece > *noun* the lens that is closest to the eye in a microscope or other optical instrument.

eyesore > *noun* a thing that is very ugly.

eye tooth > *noun* a canine tooth, especially one in the upper jaw.

IDIOMS – **give one's eye teeth for** (or **to be** or **to do**) do anything in order to have or to be or do.

eyewash > *noun* **1** cleansing lotion for a person's eye. **2** informal nonsense.

eyewitness > *noun* a person who has seen something happen and so can give a first-hand description of it.

eyrie /eeri, īri/ (US also **aerie**) > *noun* a large nest of an eagle or other bird of prey, typically built high in a tree or on a cliff.

ORIGIN – probably from Old French *aire*, from Latin *area* 'level piece of ground', in late Latin 'nest of a bird of prey'.

eyrir /īreer/ > *noun* (pl. **aurar** /awraar/) a monetary unit of Iceland, equal to one hundredth of a krona.

ORIGIN – Icelandic, probably from Latin *aureus* 'golden, a gold coin'.

F¹ (also **f**) > *noun* (pl. **Fs** or **F's**) **1** the sixth letter of the alphabet. **2** denoting the next item after E in a set. **3** Music the fourth note of the diatonic scale of C major.

COMBINATIONS – **F-word** euphemistic the word 'fuck'.

F² > *abbreviation* **1** Fahrenheit. **2** farad(s). **3** (in racing results) favourite. **4** female. **5** Brit. fine (used in describing grades of pencil lead). **6** Franc(s). > *symbol* the chemical element fluorine.

f > *abbreviation* **1** Grammar feminine. **2** focal length. **3** (in textual references) folio. **4** Music forte. **5** (in racing results) furlong(s).

COMBINATIONS – **f-stop** Photography a camera setting corresponding to a particular f-number.

FA > *abbreviation* (in the UK) Football Association.

fa > *noun* variant spelling of FAH.

fab > *adjective* informal fabulous; wonderful.

Fabian /**fay**biən/ > *noun* a member or supporter of the Fabian Society, an organisation of socialists aiming to achieve socialism gradually rather than by revolution. > *adjective* **1** relating to the Fabians. **2** employing cautious delaying tactics to wear out an enemy.

DERIVATIVES – **Fabianism** *noun* **Fabianist** *noun*.

ORIGIN – from the name of the Roman general Quintus *Fabius* Maximus Verrucosus (died 203 BC), known for his delaying tactics.

fable > *noun* **1** a short story with a moral, typically featuring animals as characters. **2** a supernatural story incorporating elements of myth and legend. **3** myth and legend.

ORIGIN – Old French, from Latin *fabula* 'story', from *fari* 'speak'.

fabled > *adjective* **1** famous. **2** mythical or imaginary.

fabric > *noun* **1** material produced by weaving or knitting textile fibres; cloth. **2** the essential structure or framework of something: *the fabric of the building*.

SYNONYMS – **1** cloth, material, stuff, textile. **3** constitution, framework, make-up, structure, substance.

ORIGIN – first denoting a building or machine, i.e. 'something made': from Latin *fabrica* 'something skilfully produced'.

fabricate > *verb* **1** invent, typically with deceitful intent. **2** construct or manufacture (an industrial product).

DERIVATIVES – **fabrication** *noun* **fabricator** *noun*.

SYNONYMS – **1** counterfeit, fake, forge, invent, make up. **2** create, construct, make, manufacture, put together.

ORIGIN – Latin *fabricare* 'manufacture'.

fabulate /**fab**yoolayt/ > *verb* tell invented stories.

DERIVATIVES – **fabulation** *noun*.

ORIGIN – Latin *fabulari* 'narrate as a fable'.

fabulist > *noun* **1** a person who composes fables. **2** a liar.

fabulous > *adjective* **1** extraordinary, especially in being very large. **2** informal very good; wonderful. **3** mythical.

DERIVATIVES – **fabulously** *adverb* **fabulousness** *noun*.

SYNONYMS – **1** extraordinary, phenomenal, prodigious, remarkable, stupendous, tremendous.

ORIGIN – Latin *fabulosus* 'celebrated in fable', from *fabula* 'story'.

facade /fə**saad**/ > *noun* **1** the face of a building, especially the front. **2** a deceptive outward appearance.

SYNONYMS – **2** appearance, front, guise, show.

ORIGIN – French *façade*, from *face* 'face'.

face > *noun* **1** the front part of a person's head from the forehead to the chin, or the corresponding part in an animal. **2** an expression on someone's face. **3** the surface of a thing, especially one that is presented to the view or has a particular function. **4** a vertical or sloping side of a mountain or cliff. **5** an aspect of something: *the unacceptable face of social drinking*. > *verb* **1** be positioned with the face or front towards or in a specified direction. **2** confront and deal with. **3** have (a difficult event or situation) in prospect. **4** cover the surface of (something) with a layer of a different material. **5** (**face off**) chiefly N. Amer. take up an attitude of confrontation.

IDIOMS – **one's face fits** Brit. one has the necessary qualities for something. **face the music** be confronted with the unpleasant consequences of one's actions. **face to face** close together and looking directly at one another. **in the face of** when confronted with. **lose** (or **save**) **face** incur (or avoid) humiliation. **on the face of it** apparently. **set one's face against** resist with determination. **to one's face** openly in one's presence.

DERIVATIVES – **faced** *adjective*.

SYNONYMS – *noun* **1** countenance, features, physiognomy, visage. *verb* **1** front on to,

look towards, overlook. **2** confront, cope with, deal with, get to grips with. **3** be confronted by, be up against, encounter, experience.

COMBINATIONS – **facecloth 1** (Brit. also **face flannel**) a small towelling cloth for washing one's face. **2** smooth-surfaced woollen cloth. **face mask 1** a protective mask covering the face or part of the face. **2** (also **face pack**) a cream or gel spread over the face to cleanse and tone the skin. **face paint** bold-coloured paint used to decorate the face. **face-saving** preserving one's reputation or dignity. **face value 1** the value printed or depicted on a coin, postage stamp, etc. **2** the apparent value or nature of something. **faceworker** a miner who works at the coalface.

ORIGIN – Old French, from Latin *facies* 'form, appearance, face'.

faceless > *adjective* remote and impersonal.

DERIVATIVES – **facelessness** *noun*.

facelift > *noun* a cosmetic surgical operation to remove unwanted wrinkles by tightening the skin of the face.

facet /**fass**it/ > *noun* **1** one side of something many-sided, especially of a cut gem. **2** a particular aspect of something.

DERIVATIVES – **faceted** *adjective*.

ORIGIN – French *facette*, from Old French *face* 'face'.

facetious /fə**see**shəss/ > *adjective* trivially or inappropriately humorous.

DERIVATIVES – **facetiously** *adverb* **facetiousness** *noun*.

ORIGIN – French *facétieux*, from Latin *facetia* 'jest'.

facia > *noun* chiefly Brit. variant spelling of FASCIA.

facial /**fay**sh'l/ > *adjective* of or affecting the face. > *noun* a beauty treatment for the face.

DERIVATIVES – **facially** *adverb*.

facile /**fass**īl/ > *adjective* ignoring the complexities of an issue; superficial.

DERIVATIVES – **facilely** *adverb* **facileness** *noun*.

ORIGIN – Latin *facilis* 'easy'.

facilitate /fə**sill**itayt/ > *verb* make easy or easier.

DERIVATIVES – **facilitation** *noun* **facilitative** *adjective* **facilitator** *noun* **facilitatory** *adjective*.

SYNONYMS – aid, assist, ease, expedite, help, smooth.

ANTONYMS – hinder, impede.

facility > *noun* (pl. **facilities**) **1** a building, service, or piece of equipment provided for a particular purpose. **2** a natural aptitude. **3** absence of difficulty or effort; ease.

SYNONYMS – **1** amenity, installation, provision, resource, service, site.

facing > *noun* **1** a piece of material attached to the edge of a garment at the neck, armhole, etc. and turned inside, used to strengthen the edge. **2** an outer layer covering the surface of a wall. > *adjective* positioned so as to face.

facsimile /fak**simm**ili/ > *noun* an exact copy. > *verb* (**facsimiled**, **facsimileing**) make a copy of.
ORIGIN – from Latin *fac!* (imperative of *facere* 'make') and *simile* (from *similis* 'like').

fact > *noun* **1** a thing that is indisputably the case. **2** (**facts**) information used as evidence or as part of a report.
IDIOMS – **before** (or **after**) **the fact** Law before (or after) the committing of a crime. **a fact of life** something that must be accepted, even if unpalatable. **the facts of life** information about sexual matters. **in** (**point of**) **fact** in reality.
SYNONYMS – **1** certainty, reality, truth.
ORIGIN – from Latin *factum*, from *facere* 'do': first meaning 'an act', later 'a crime'.

faction¹ > *noun* a small dissenting group within a larger one.
DERIVATIVES – **factional** *adjective* **factionalism** *noun*.
SYNONYMS – cabal, camp, clique, coterie.
ORIGIN – first denoting the action of doing or making: from Latin *facere* 'do, make'.

faction² > *noun* the use of real events as a basis for a fictional narrative or dramatisation.
ORIGIN – blend of FACT and FICTION.

factious /fak**sh**əss/ > *adjective* relating or inclined to dissension.
DERIVATIVES – **factiously** *adverb* **factiousness** *noun*.

factitious /fak**ti**shəss/ > *adjective* artificial; contrived.
DERIVATIVES – **factitiously** *adverb* **factitiousness** *noun*.
ORIGIN – first meaning 'made by human skill': from Latin *facticius* 'made by art'.

factoid > *noun* **1** an item of unreliable information that is repeated so often that it becomes accepted as fact. **2** N. Amer. a brief or trivial item of information.

factor > *noun* **1** a circumstance, fact, or influence that contributes to a result. **2** Mathematics a number or quantity that when multiplied with another produces a given number or expression. **3** Physiology any of a number of substances in the blood which are involved in coagulation. **4** Biology a gene that determines a hereditary characteristic. **5** a commercial agent buying or selling on commission. **6** chiefly Scottish a land agent. > *verb* (**factor in** or **out**) include (or exclude) as relevant when making a decision.
SYNONYMS – **1** aspect, consideration, facet, element, point.
COMBINATIONS – **factor VIII** (also **factor eight**) Physiology a blood protein involved in

clotting, a deficiency of which causes one of the main forms of haemophilia.
ORIGIN – Latin, 'doer, agent', from *facere* 'do'.

factorial > *adjective* of or relating to factors. > *noun* Mathematics the product of a whole number and all the numbers below it, e.g. $4 \times 3 \times 2 \times 1$ (*factorial 4*, written *4!* and equal to 24).
DERIVATIVES – **factorially** *adverb*.

factorise (also **factorize**) > *verb* Mathematics resolve or be resolvable into factors.
DERIVATIVES – **factorisation** *noun*.

factory > *noun* (pl. **factories**) a place where goods are manufactured or assembled chiefly by machine.
SYNONYMS – mill, plant, works, workshop; archaic manufactory.
COMBINATIONS – **factory farming** a system of rearing poultry, pigs, or cattle indoors intensively and under strictly controlled conditions. **factory floor** the workers in a company or industry, rather than the management.
ORIGIN – Latin *factorium* 'oil press'.

factotum /fak**tō**təm/ > *noun* (pl. **factotums**) an employee who does all kinds of work.
ORIGIN – from Latin *fac!* 'do!' + *totum* 'the whole thing'.

factual /fak**t**yooəl/ > *adjective* based on or concerned with fact or facts.
DERIVATIVES – **factuality** *noun* **factually** *adverb*.
SYNONYMS – accurate, correct, faithful, true, unbiased.
ANTONYMS – fictitious.

facultative /fak**k**əltətiv/ chiefly Biology > *adjective* **1** occurring optionally according to circumstances. **2** capable of but not restricted to a particular behaviour: *a facultative parasite*.
DERIVATIVES – **facultatively** *adverb*.

faculty > *noun* (pl. **faculties**) **1** an inherent mental or physical power. **2** an aptitude or talent. **3** chiefly Brit. a group of university departments. **4** N. Amer. the teaching or research staff of a university or college.
SYNONYMS – **1** capability, capacity, facility, power.
ORIGIN – Latin *facultas*, from *facilis* 'easy', from *facere* 'make, do'.

fad > *noun* **1** a craze. **2** an idiosyncrasy or arbitrary like or dislike.
DERIVATIVES – **faddish** *adjective* **faddism** *noun* **faddist** *noun*.
ORIGIN – probably from FIDDLE-FADDLE.

faddy > *adjective* (**faddier**, **faddiest**) Brit. having many likes and dislikes about food; fussy.
DERIVATIVES – **faddily** *adverb* **faddiness** *noun*.

fade > *verb* **1** gradually grow faint and disappear. **2** lose or cause to lose colour. **3**

(with reference to a film or video image or recorded sound) increase or decrease in clarity or volume. > *noun* an act or instance of fading.
SYNONYMS – *verb* **1** die away, dim, dwindle, fail, wane. **2** bleach, discolour, dull, pale, wash out.
ORIGIN – Old French *fader*, from *fade* 'dull, insipid'.

fader > *noun* a device for varying the volume of sound, the intensity of light, or the gain on a video or audio signal.

fado /faa**dō**/ > *noun* (pl. **fados**) a type of popular Portuguese song, usually with a melancholy theme.
ORIGIN – Portuguese, 'fate'.

faeces /**fee**seez/ (US **feces**) > *plural noun* waste matter remaining after food has been digested, discharged from the bowels.
DERIVATIVES – **faecal** /**fee**k'l/ *adjective*.
ORIGIN – Latin, plural of *faex* 'dregs'.

faerie /**fai**ri/ (also **faery**) > *noun* archaic or literary fairyland.
ORIGIN – introduced as a pseudo-archaic variant of *fairy* by the English poet Edmund Spenser in his allegorical romance *The Faerie Queene* (1590).

Faeroese > *noun & adjective* variant spelling of FAROESE.

faff Brit. informal > *verb* bustle ineffectually. > *noun* ineffectual activity.
ORIGIN – first used in dialect in the sense 'blow in puffs', describing the wind.

fag¹ > *noun* **1** informal, chiefly Brit. a tiring or unwelcome task. **2** Brit. a junior pupil at a public school who does minor chores for a senior pupil. > *verb* (**fagged**, **fagging**) **1** informal work hard. **2** Brit. (of a public-school pupil) act as a fag. **3** (**fagged out**) informal exhausted.

fag² > *noun* N. Amer. informal, derogatory a male homosexual.
DERIVATIVES – **faggy** *adjective*.
ORIGIN – short for FAGGOT (in sense 3).

fag³ > *noun* Brit. informal a cigarette.
COMBINATIONS – **fag end 1** a cigarette end. **2** a useless remnant.
ORIGIN – from *fag end*, from 15th-century *fag* 'a flap'.

faggot /**fagg**ət/ > *noun* **1** Brit. a ball of seasoned chopped liver, baked or fried. **2** (US **fagot**) a bundle of sticks bound together as fuel. **3** N. Amer. informal, derogatory a male homosexual. > *verb* (**faggoted**, **faggoting**; US **fagoted**, **fagoting**) (in embroidery) join by faggoting.
DERIVATIVES – **faggoty** *adjective*.
ORIGIN – Old French *fagot*, from Greek *phakelos* 'bundle'.

faggoting (US **fagoting**) > *noun* embroidery in which threads are fastened together in bundles.

fah (also **fa**) > *noun* Music the fourth note of a major scale, coming between 'me' and 'soh'.

Fahr. > *abbreviation* Fahrenheit.

Fahrenheit /farrənhīt/ > *adjective* of or denoting a scale of temperature on which water freezes at 32° and boils at 212°.

ORIGIN – named after the German physicist Gabriel Daniel *Fahrenheit* (1686–1736).

faience /fīONss/ > *noun* decorated tin-glazed earthenware of the type which includes delftware.

ORIGIN – French, named after the city of *Faenza* in Italy, where such pottery was first made.

fail > *verb* **1** be unsuccessful in an undertaking. **2** be unable to meet the standards set by (a test). **3** judge (a candidate in an examination or test) not to have passed. **4** neglect to do something. **5** disappoint expectations: *it has failed to materialise.* **6** stop working properly. **7** become weaker or less good. **8** go out of business. **9** desert or let down. > *noun* a mark which is not high enough to pass an examination or test.

IDIOMS – **without fail** whatever happens.

SYNONYMS – *verb* **1** be unsuccessful, collapse, founder, misfire, not succeed. **4** forget, neglect, omit. **6** break, break down, give out, go wrong, malfunction. **7** decline, degenerate, deteriorate, give out, wane. **8** collapse, fold, go bankrupt, go bust.

ORIGIN – Old French *faillir*, from Latin *fallere* 'deceive'.

failing > *noun* a weakness in someone's character. > *preposition* if not.

SYNONYMS – *noun* fault, flaw, imperfection, shortcoming, weakness.

ANTONYMS – *noun* strength.

fail-safe > *adjective* **1** causing a piece of machinery to revert to a safe condition in the event of a breakdown. **2** unlikely or unable to fail.

failure > *noun* **1** lack of success. **2** an unsuccessful person or thing. **3** the omission of expected or required action. **4** the action or state of not functioning.

SYNONYMS – **1** collapse, foundering, misfiring. **2** debacle, fiasco, flop. **3** dereliction, neglect, negligence, omission, oversight.

ANTONYMS – success.

fain archaic > *adjective* **1** pleased or willing under the circumstances. **2** obliged. > *adverb* gladly.

faint > *adjective* **1** (of a sight, smell, or sound) barely perceptible. **2** (of a hope, chance, or idea) slight. **3** close to losing consciousness. > *verb* briefly lose consciousness because of an insufficient supply of oxygen to the brain. > *noun* a sudden loss of consciousness.

DERIVATIVES – **faintly** *adverb* **faintness** *noun*.

SYNONYMS – *adjective* **1** dim, ill-defined, indistinct, unclear, unobtrusive. **2** distant, outside, remote, slight, slim. **3** dizzy, giddy, light-headed, muzzy, unsteady, weak. *verb* black out, collapse, lose consciousness, pass out, swoon.

ANTONYMS – *adjective* **1,2** clear, strong.

ORIGIN – Old French, from Latin *fingere* 'mould, contrive'; related to FEIGN.

faint heart > *noun* a person who has a timid or reserved nature.

IDIOMS – **faint heart never won fair lady** *proverb* timidity will prevent you from achieving your objective.

DERIVATIVES – **faint-hearted** *adjective*.

fair¹ > *adjective* **1** just or appropriate in the circumstances. **2** treating people equally. **3** (of hair or complexion) light; blonde. **4** considerable or moderately good. **5** (of weather) fine and dry. **6** archaic beautiful. > *adverb* **1** in a fair manner. **2** dialect to a high degree.

IDIOMS – **all's fair in love and war** *proverb* in certain highly charged situations, any method of achieving your objective is justifiable. **fair and square 1** with absolute accuracy. **2** honestly and straightforwardly. **the fair sex** (also **the fairer sex**) dated or humorous women. **it's a fair cop** informal an admission that the speaker has been caught doing wrong and deserves punishment.

DERIVATIVES – **fairness** *noun*.

SYNONYMS – *adjective* **1** equitable, honest, impartial, just, right. **2** equitable, even-handed, impartial, just, unbiased. **4** acceptable, decent, moderate, reasonable, respectable.

ANTONYMS – *adjective* **1,2** unfair, unjust.

COMBINATIONS – **fair copy** written or printed matter transcribed or reproduced after final correction. **fair game** a person or thing that is considered a reasonable target for criticism or exploitation. **fair-minded** impartial; just. **fair play** respect for the rules or equal treatment of all concerned. **fair trade** trade in which fair payments are made to producers and workers in developing countries. **fair-weather friend** a person who stops being a friend in times of difficulty.

fair² > *noun* **1** a gathering of stalls and amusements for public entertainment. **2** a periodic gathering for the sale of goods. **3** an exhibition to promote particular products.

ORIGIN – Latin *feria*, from *feriae* 'holy days' (on which fairs were often held).

fairground > *noun* an outdoor area where a fair is held.

Fair Isle > *noun* a traditional multicoloured geometric design used in woollen knitwear.

ORIGIN – named after *Fair Isle* in the Shetlands, where the design was first devised.

fairly > *adverb* **1** with justice. **2** moderately. **3** actually; positively.

IDIOMS – **fairly and squarely** another term for *fair and square*.

fairway > *noun* **1** the part of a golf course between a tee and a green. **2** a navigable channel in a river or harbour.

fairy > *noun* (pl. **fairies**) **1** a small imaginary being with wings and a human form, that has magical powers. **2** informal, derogatory a male homosexual.

COMBINATIONS – **fairy cake** Brit. a small iced sponge cake. **fairy floss** Austral. candyfloss. **fairy godmother** a female character in some fairy stories who brings unexpected good fortune to the hero or heroine. **fairyland** the imaginary home of fairies. **fairy lights** chiefly Brit. small coloured electric lights used for decoration, especially on a Christmas tree. **fairy ring** a ring of grass that is darker in colour than the surrounding grass due to the growth of certain fungi, popularly believed to have been caused by fairies dancing. **fairy story 1** a children's tale about magical and imaginary beings and lands. **2** an untrue account. **fairy tale 1** a fairy story. **2** (**fairy-tale**) resembling a fairy story in being magical or idealised: *a fairy-tale romance.*

ORIGIN – first denoting fairyland: from Old French *faerie*, from *fae* 'a fairy', from Latin *fata* 'the Fates' (see FATE).

fait accompli /fayt əkompli/ > *noun* a thing that has been done or decided and cannot now be altered.

ORIGIN – French, 'accomplished fact'.

faith > *noun* **1** complete trust or confidence. **2** strong belief in a religion. **3** a system of religious belief.

SYNONYMS – **1** belief, confidence, credence, trust. **3** church, creed, denomination, doctrine, religion, sect.

ANTONYMS – **1** distrust, mistrust.

COMBINATIONS – **faith healing** healing achieved by religious faith and prayer, rather than by medical treatment.

ORIGIN – Old French *feid*, from Latin *fides*.

faithful > *adjective* **1** remaining loyal and steadfast. **2** remaining sexually loyal to a lover or spouse. **3** true to the facts or the original. > *noun* (**the faithful**) the believers in a particular religion.

DERIVATIVES – **faithfulness** *noun*.

SYNONYMS – *adjective* **1,2** constant, devoted, loyal, staunch, steadfast, true. **3** accurate, close, exact, strict, true.

ANTONYMS – *adjective* **1,2** disloyal, unfaithful. **3** inaccurate.

faithfully > *adverb* in a faithful manner.

IDIOMS – **yours faithfully** chiefly Brit. a formula for ending a formal letter in which the recipient is not addressed by their personal name.

faithless > *adjective* **1** disloyal, especially to a spouse or lover. **2** without religious faith.

DERIVATIVES – **faithlessly** *adverb* **faithlessness** *noun*.

fajitas /fəheetəz/ > *plural noun* a dish of Mexican origin consisting of strips of spiced meat with vegetables and cheese, wrapped in a soft tortilla.

ORIGIN – Mexican Spanish, 'little strips'.

fake > *adjective* not genuine; counterfeit. > *noun* a person or thing that is not genuine. > *verb* **1** forge or counterfeit. **2** pretend to feel or suffer from (an emotion or illness).

DERIVATIVES – **faker** *noun* **fakery** *noun*.

SYNONYMS – *adjective* bogus, counterfeit, false, forged, imitation, simulated. *noun* counterfeit, dummy, forgery, imitation, sham, simulation. *verb* **1** counterfeit, doctor, falsify, forge. **2** affect, feign, pretend, put on, sham.

ANTONYMS – *adjective* genuine, real.

fakir /**fay**keer, fə**keer**/ > *noun* a Muslim (or, loosely, a Hindu) religious ascetic who lives solely on alms.

ORIGIN – from an Arabic word meaning 'needy man'.

falafel /fə**laff**'l/ (also **felafel**) > *noun* a Middle Eastern dish of spiced mashed chickpeas formed into balls and deep-fried.

ORIGIN – from an Arabic word meaning 'pepper'.

falciparum /fal**sipp**ərəm/ > *noun* the most severe form of malaria, caused by the parasitic protozoan *Plasmodium falciparum*.

ORIGIN – from Latin *falx* 'sickle' + -*parum* 'bearing'.

falcon /**fawl**kən/ > *noun* **1** a fast-flying bird of prey with long pointed wings. **2** Falconry the female of such a bird, especially a peregrine. Compare with TERCEL.

ORIGIN – Old French *faucon*, from Latin *falx* 'scythe'.

falconer > *noun* a person who takes part in falconry.

falconry > *noun* the keeping and training of falcons or other birds of prey and the use of them for hunting.

falderal /**fal**dəral/ > *noun* variant spelling of FOLDEROL.

fall > *verb* (past **fell**; past participle **fallen**) **1** move rapidly and without control from a higher to a lower level. **2** (often **fall down** or **over**) lose one's balance and tumble to the ground. **3** decrease in number, amount, intensity, or quality. **4** hang down. **5** (of someone's face) show sudden dismay or disappointment. **6** be captured or defeated. **7** be killed in battle. **8** pass into a specified state. **9** occur. **10** be classified in the way specified: *canals fall within the Minister's brief.*

> *noun* **1** an act of falling. **2** a downward difference in height between parts of a surface. **3** a thing which falls or has fallen. **4** a decrease in size, rate, or level. **5** a defeat or downfall. **6** a waterfall or cascade. **7** N. Amer. autumn.

IDIOMS – **fall about** Brit. informal laugh uncontrollably. **fall apart** (or **to pieces**) informal lose one's capacity to cope. **fall back** retreat. **fall back on** have recourse to when in difficulty. **fall for** informal **1** fall in love with. **2** be deceived by. **fall foul** (or chiefly N. Amer. **afoul**) **of** come into conflict with. **fall in** (or **into**) **line** conform. **fall into place** begin to make sense. **fall in with 1** meet by chance and become involved with. **2** agree to. **fall on 1** attack fiercely or unexpectedly. **2** (of someone's eyes or gaze) be directed towards. **3** (of a burden or duty) be borne or incurred by. **fall out** have an argument. **fall over oneself to do something** informal be excessively eager to do something. **fall short 1** (of a missile) fail to reach its target. **2** be deficient or inadequate. **fall through** fail. **fall to** become the duty of.

SYNONYMS – *verb* **1** descend, drop, plummet, plunge, tumble. **2** pitch forward, stumble, trip, tumble. **3** decrease, decline, diminish, drop, dwindle, lessen. *noun* **1** drop, slip, stumble, trip, tumble. **4** decline, decrease, dip, drop, lessening, reduction. **5** collapse, defeat, demise, downfall, ruin.

COMBINATIONS – **fall guy** informal a scapegoat. **falling-out** a quarrel. **falling star** a meteor or shooting star.

fallacious /fə**lay**shəss/ > *adjective* of the nature of a fallacy; false or mistaken.

DERIVATIVES – **fallaciously** *adverb*.

SYNONYMS – erroneous, false, mistaken, untrue, wrong.

fallacy /**fal**əsi/ > *noun* (pl. **fallacies**) **1** a mistaken belief. **2** a failure in reasoning which renders an argument invalid.

SYNONYMS – **1** delusion, error, illusion, misapprehension, misconception, myth.

ORIGIN – Latin *fallacia*, from *fallax* 'deceiving'.

fallback > *noun* **1** an alternative plan for use in an emergency. **2** a reduction.

fallen past participle of FALL. > *adjective* **1** dated (of a woman) regarded as having lost her honour through engaging in an extramarital sexual relationship. **2** killed in battle.

COMBINATIONS – **fallen angel** (in Christian, Jewish, and Muslim tradition) an angel who rebelled against God and was cast out of heaven.

faller > *noun* **1** Brit. a person or thing that falls, especially a horse that falls during a race. **2** N. Amer. a person who fells trees for a living.

fallible /**fal**ib'l/ > *adjective* capable of making mistakes or being wrong.

DERIVATIVES – **fallibility** *noun* **fallibly** *adverb*.

SYNONYMS – flawed, human, imperfect.

ANTONYMS – infallible, perfect.

ORIGIN – Latin *fallibilis*, from *fallere* 'deceive'.

fall-off (also **falling-off**) > *noun* a decrease.

Fallopian tube /fə**lō**piən/ > *noun* Anatomy (in a female mammal) either of a pair of tubes along which eggs travel from the ovaries to the uterus.

ORIGIN – from the name of Gabriello *Fallopio*, the 16th-century Italian anatomist who first described them.

fallout > *noun* **1** radioactive particles released over a wide area by a nuclear explosion or accident. **2** the adverse results of a situation.

fallow[1] > *adjective* **1** (of farmland) ploughed and harrowed but left for a period without being sown. **2** characterised by inactivity. **3** (of a sow) not pregnant. > *noun* a piece of fallow land. > *verb* leave (land) fallow.

DERIVATIVES – **fallowness** *noun*.

COMBINATIONS – **fallow deer** a deer with branched antlers, having a white-spotted reddish-brown coat in summer.

fallow[2] > *noun* a pale brown or reddish yellow colour.

false > *adjective* **1** not in accordance with the truth or facts. **2** made as a copy of something real; artificial. **3** deliberately intended to deceive. **4** not actually so; illusory: *a false sense of security.* **5** treacherous or disloyal. **6** invalid or illegal: *false imprisonment.*

DERIVATIVES – **falsely** *adverb* **falseness** *noun* **falsity** *noun*.

SYNONYMS – **1** erroneous, fallacious, inaccurate, incorrect, untrue, wrong. **2** artificial, fake, imitation, simulated.

ANTONYMS – **1** true. **2** genuine, real.

COMBINATIONS – **false alarm** a warning given about something that fails to take place. **false dawn** a transient light which precedes the rising of the sun by about an hour, commonly seen in Eastern countries. **false economy** an apparent financial saving that in fact leads to greater expenditure. **false memory syndrome** the apparent recollection during psychoanalysis of an event which did not actually occur, especially childhood sexual abuse. **false move** an unwise action with potentially dangerous consequences. **false pretences** behaviour intended to deceive. **false start** an invalid start to a race. **false step 1** a slip or stumble. **2** a mistake.

ORIGIN – from Latin *falsum* 'fraud', from *fallere* 'deceive'.

falsehood > *noun* **1** the state of being untrue. **2** a lie.

falsetto /fawlsettō/ > *noun* (pl. **falsettos**) a method of voice production used by male singers, especially tenors, to sing notes higher than their normal range.
ORIGIN – Italian, from *falso* 'false'.

falsies > *plural noun* informal **1** pads of material used to increase the apparent size of the breasts. **2** false eyelashes.

falsify /fawlsifī/ > *verb* (**falsifies, falsified**) **1** alter (information or evidence) so as to mislead. **2** prove (a statement or theory) to be false.
DERIVATIVES – **falsifiable** *adjective* **falsification** *noun*.
ORIGIN – from Latin *falsificus* 'making false', from *falsus* 'false' + *facere* 'make'.

Falstaffian /fawlstaafiən/ > *adjective* of or resembling Shakespeare's character Sir John Falstaff in being fat, jolly, and debauched.

falter /fawltər/ > *verb* **1** lose strength or momentum. **2** move or speak hesitantly.
DERIVATIVES – **faltering** *adjective* **falteringly** *adverb*.
SYNONYMS – **1** hesitate, oscillate, vacillate, waver. **2** hesitate, stammer, stumble, stutter.
ORIGIN – perhaps from FOLD¹ (which was occasionally used of the faltering of the legs or tongue).

fame > *noun* the state of being famous.
SYNONYMS – celebrity, eminence, note, prominence, renown.
ANTONYMS – obscurity.
ORIGIN – first used also in the sense 'reputation', which survives in the phrase *house of ill fame*: from Latin *fama*.

famed > *adjective* famous; well known.

familiar > *adjective* **1** (often **familiar to**) well known through long or close association. **2** frequently encountered; common. **3** (**familiar with**) having a good knowledge of. **4** in close friendship. **5** inappropriately intimate or informal. > *noun* **1** (also **familiar spirit**) a spirit supposedly attending and obeying a witch. **2** a close friend or associate.
IDIOMS – **familiarity breeds contempt** proverb extensive knowledge of or close association with someone or something leads to a loss of respect for them or it.
DERIVATIVES – **familiarity** (pl. **familiarities**) *noun* **familiarly** *adverb*.
SYNONYMS – *adjective* **2** common, commonplace, everyday, routine, standard, usual. **4** close, friendly, intimate, near. **5** bold, forward, impertinent, overfamiliar, presumptuous.
ANTONYMS – *adjective* **2** unfamiliar, unusual. **4** distant, formal.
ORIGIN – Latin *familiaris*, from *familia* 'household servants, family'.

familiarise (also **familiarize**) > *verb* (**familiarise with**) make (someone) familiar with.
DERIVATIVES – **familiarisation** *noun*.

family > *noun* (pl. **families**) **1** a group consisting of two parents (or a single parent) and their children living together as a unit. **2** a group of people related by blood or marriage. **3** the children of a person or couple. **4** all the descendants of a common ancestor. **5** a group united by a significant shared characteristic. **6** Biology a principal taxonomic category ranking above genus and below order. > *adjective* designed to be suitable for children as well as adults: *a family newspaper*.
IDIOMS – **in the family way** informal pregnant.
DERIVATIVES – **familial** *adjective*.
SYNONYMS – *noun* **1** household. **2** clan, kin, tribe.
COMBINATIONS – **family credit** (in the UK) a regular payment by the state to a family with an income below a certain level. **family name** a surname. **family planning** the practice of controlling the number of children in a family and the intervals between their births, particularly by means of contraception. **family tree** a diagram showing the relationship between people in several generations of a family.
ORIGIN – Latin *familia* 'household servants, family', from *famulus* 'servant'.

famine /fammin/ > *noun* **1** extreme scarcity of food. **2** archaic hunger.
SYNONYMS – **1** deprivation, want.
ORIGIN – Old French, from *faim* 'hunger', from Latin *fames*.

famish /fammish/ > *verb* archaic reduce or be reduced to extreme hunger.
ORIGIN – Old French *afamer*, from Latin *fames* 'hunger'.

famished > *adjective* informal extremely hungry.

famous > *adjective* **1** known about by many people. **2** informal magnificent.
DERIVATIVES – **famously** *adverb* **famousness** *noun*.
SYNONYMS – celebrated, eminent, illustrious, renowned.
ORIGIN – Latin *famosus* 'famed', from *fama* 'fame'.

fan¹ > *noun* **1** an apparatus with rotating blades that creates a current of air for cooling or ventilation. **2** a hand-held device, typically folding and circular, that is waved so as to move the air and so cool the user. > *verb* (**fanned, fanning**) **1** cool by waving something to create a current of air. **2** (of an air current) increase the strength of (a fire). **3** cause (a belief or emotion) to become stronger. **4** (**fan out**) spread out from a central point to cover a wide area.
COMBINATIONS – **fan belt** (in a motor-vehicle engine) a belt that drives the radiator fan and usually also the dynamo or alternator.
ORIGIN – Latin *vannus* 'winnowing fan'.

fan² > *noun* a person who has a strong interest in or admiration for a particular sport, art form, or famous person.
DERIVATIVES – **fandom** *noun*.
SYNONYMS – admirer, aficionado, devotee, enthusiast, follower, supporter.
COMBINATIONS – **fan club** an organised group of fans.
ORIGIN – abbreviation of FANATIC.

fanatic > *noun* **1** a person filled with excessive zeal, especially for an extreme cause. **2** informal a person with an obsessive enthusiasm for a pastime or hobby. > *adjective* filled with or expressing excessive zeal.
DERIVATIVES – **fanaticism** *noun*.
SYNONYMS – *noun* **1** extremist, radical, zealot. **2** addict, buff, devotee.

wordpower facts
Fanatic
The word **fanatic** derives from Latin *fanaticus*, meaning 'of a temple' or 'inspired by a god', from *fanum* 'temple'. The adjective originally described behaviour that might result from possession by a god or demon, hence the earliest sense of the noun 'a religious maniac'. **Profane** comes from Latin *profanus*, meaning 'outside the temple'.

fanatical > *adjective* filled with excessive and single-minded zeal.
DERIVATIVES – **fanatically** *adverb*.
SYNONYMS – extreme, extremist, maniacal, rabid, radical, zealous.

fancier > *noun* a person who has a special interest in or breeds a particular animal.

fanciful > *adjective* **1** over-imaginative and unrealistic. **2** existing only in the imagination. **3** highly ornamental or imaginative in design.
DERIVATIVES – **fancifully** *adverb* **fancifulness** *noun*.
SYNONYMS – **1** dreamy, imaginative, unrealistic, whimsical. **2** extravagant, fantastic, far-fetched, imaginary, romantic, unlikely, unrealistic.
ANTONYMS – **1,2** down to earth, realistic.

fancy > *verb* (**fancies, fancied**) **1** Brit. informal feel a desire for. **2** Brit. informal find sexually attractive. **3** regard as a likely winner. **4** imagine. **5** used to express surprise: *fancy that!* > *adjective* (**fancier, fanciest**) elaborate or highly decorated. > *noun* (pl. **fancies**) **1** a superficial or transient feeling of attraction. **2** the faculty of imagination. **3** (also **fancy cake**) a small iced cake or biscuit. **4** an unfounded or tentative belief or idea.

IDIOMS – **take someone's fancy** appeal to someone. **take a fancy to** become fond of, especially without an obvious reason.

DERIVATIVES – **fanciable** *adjective* (informal) **fancily** *adverb* **fanciness** *noun*.

SYNONYMS – *adjective* decorated, elaborate, ornate, ostentatious, showy.

ANTONYMS – *adjective* plain.

COMBINATIONS – **fancy dress** a costume worn to make someone look like a famous person, fictional character, or an animal. **fancy-free** without any emotional commitments. **fancy man** informal, derogatory a woman's lover. **fancy woman** informal, derogatory a married man's mistress.

ORIGIN – contraction of **FANTASY**.

fandango /fan**dang**gō/ > *noun* (pl. **fandangoes** or **fandangos**) a lively Spanish dance for two people, typically accompanied by castanets or tambourine.

ORIGIN – Spanish.

fanfare > *noun* **1** a short ceremonial tune or flourish played on brass instruments. **2** an elaborate welcome or introduction.

ORIGIN – French.

fang > *noun* **1** a large sharp tooth, especially a canine tooth of a dog or wolf. **2** a tooth with which a snake injects poison. **3** the biting mouthpart of a spider.

DERIVATIVES – **fanged** *adjective*.

ORIGIN – Old Norse, 'capture, grasp'.

fankle /**fang**k'l/ > *verb* Scottish entangle.

ORIGIN – from Scots *fank* 'coil of rope'.

fanlight > *noun* a small window, typically semicircular, over a door or another window.

fanny > *noun* (pl. **fannies**) **1** Brit. vulgar slang a woman's genitals. **2** informal, chiefly N. Amer. a person's buttocks.

Fanny Adams (also **sweet Fanny Adams**) > *noun* Brit. informal nothing at all.

ORIGIN – a nautical term for canned meat or stew (a reference to the name of a murder victim *c.*1870).

fantabulous /fan**tab**yooləss/ > *adjective* informal excellent; wonderful.

ORIGIN – blend of **FANTASTIC** and **FABULOUS**.

fantail > *noun* **1** a fan-shaped tail or end. **2** chiefly N. Amer. the overhanging part of the stern of a warship. **3** a domestic pigeon of a broad-tailed variety.

DERIVATIVES – **fan-tailed** *adjective*.

fantasia /fan**tay**ziə, fantə**zee**ə/ > *noun* **1** a musical composition with a free form and often an improvisatory style. **2** a musical composition based on several familiar tunes.

ORIGIN – Italian, 'fantasy'.

fantasise (also **fantasize**) > *verb* indulge in daydreaming or speculation about something desired.

DERIVATIVES – **fantasist** *noun*.

fantastic > *adjective* **1** derived from fantasy or imagination; remote from reality. **2** bizarre or grotesque. **3** informal extraordinarily good or attractive.

DERIVATIVES – **fantastical** *adjective* **fantastically** *adverb*.

SYNONYMS – **1** extravagant, fanciful, far-fetched, imaginative, romantic, unlikely, unrealistic.

ORIGIN – Greek *phantastikos*, from *phantazein* 'make visible', from *phantos* 'visible'.

fantasy > *noun* (pl. **fantasies**) **1** the imagining of improbable or impossible things. **2** an idea with no basis in reality. **3** a fanciful mental image on which a person dwells. **4** a genre of imaginative fiction involving magic and adventure.

NOTE – **fantasy** is sometimes spelled with a *ph*, **phantasy**, reflecting the original Greek form. This spelling chiefly occurs in archaic uses or in psychology and psychiatry.

SYNONYMS – **2** daydream, delusion, dream, fancy, illusion, pipe dream.

ORIGIN – Greek *phantasia* 'imagination, appearance', from *phantazein* (see **FANTASTIC**).

fanzine /**fan**zeen/ > *noun* a magazine for fans of a particular team, performer etc.

FAO > *abbreviation* for the attention of.

FAQ > *abbreviation* Computing frequently asked questions.

far > *adverb* (**further**, **furthest** or **farther**, **farthest**) **1** at, to, or by a great distance. **2** over a large expanse of time or space. **3** by a great deal. > *adjective* **1** situated at a great distance in space or time. **2** distant from the centre; extreme. **3** more distant than another object of the same kind: *the far corner*.

IDIOMS – **as far as 1** for as great a distance as. **2** to the extent that. **be a far cry from** be very different to. **by far** by a great amount. **far and away** by a very large amount. **far and wide** over a large area. **far be it from** (or **for**) **me to** used to express reluctance. **far gone 1** in a bad or worsening state. **2** advanced in time. **far out 1** unconventional or avant-garde. **2** informal, dated excellent. **go far 1** achieve a great deal. **2** be worth or amount to much. **go too far** exceed the limits of what is reasonable or acceptable. (**in**) **so far as** (or **that**) to the extent that.

farad /**farr**ad/ > *noun* the unit of electrical capacitance in the SI system.

ORIGIN – from the name of the English physicist Michael *Faraday* (1791–1867).

faraway > *adjective* **1** distant in space or time. **2** seeming remote; dreamy: *a faraway look*.

farce > *noun* **1** a comic drama or genre using buffoonery and horseplay and typically including ludicrously improbable situations. **2** an absurd or chaotic event or situation.

SYNONYMS – **2** absurdity, charade, mockery, shambles, travesty.

wordpower facts
Farce

In the 1796 edition of her book *The Art of Cookery*, the English cookery writer Hannah Glasse instructs her readers to 'make a farce with the livers minced small'. **Farce**, meaning 'stuffing' or 'forcemeat', came into English in the 15th century, from the French word meaning 'to stuff', *farcir* (ultimately from Latin *farcire*). This sense became used metaphorically for comic interludes 'stuffed' into the texts of religious plays, and from this the current meaning developed. The word **forcemeat** comes from the same root, its spelling showing the influence of the verb *force*.

farceur /faar**sör**/ > *noun* a writer of or performer in farces.

ORIGIN – French.

farcical /**faar**sik'l/ > *adjective* resembling farce; absurd or ridiculous.

DERIVATIVES – **farcically** *adverb*.

SYNONYMS – absurd, ludicrous, nonsensical, preposterous, ridiculous.

fardel /**faar**d'l/ > *noun* archaic a bundle.

ORIGIN – Old French.

fare > *noun* **1** the money a passenger on public transport has to pay. **2** a range of food. > *verb* **1** perform in a specified way in a particular situation or period. **2** archaic travel.

SYNONYMS – *noun* **2** cooking, cuisine, food. *verb* **1** get on, manage, make out, progress.

ORIGIN – Old English, 'travelling, a journey or expedition'.

Far East > *noun* China, Japan, and other countries of east Asia.

DERIVATIVES – **Far Eastern** *adjective*.

farewell > *exclamation* used to express good wishes on parting. > *noun* an act of parting or of marking someone's departure.

farfalle /faar**fal**ay/ > *plural noun* small pieces of pasta shaped like bows or butterflies' wings.

ORIGIN – Italian, 'butterflies'.

far-fetched > *adjective* unconvincing; implausible.

far-flung > *adjective* distant or remote.

farina /fə**ree**nə/ > *noun* flour or meal made of cereal grains, nuts, or starchy roots.

DERIVATIVES – **farinaceous** /farri**nay**shəss/ *adjective*.

ORIGIN – Latin, from *far* 'corn'.

farl > *noun* a thin Scottish cake of oatmeal or flour.

ORIGIN – obsolete *fardel* 'quarter', contraction of *fourth deal*.

farm > *noun* **1** an area of land and its buildings used for growing crops and rearing animals. **2** a farmhouse. **3** an establishment for breeding or growing something, or devoted to a particular thing: *a fish farm*. > *verb* **1** make one's living by growing crops or keeping livestock. **2** use (land) for this purpose. **3** (**farm out**) send out or subcontract (work) to others. **4** breed or grow (a type of livestock or crop) commercially.

DERIVATIVES – **farming** *noun*.

COMBINATIONS – **farmhand** a worker on a farm. **farmhouse** a house attached to a farm. **farmyard** a yard or enclosure attached to a farmhouse.

ORIGIN – Old French *ferme*, from Latin *firma* 'fixed payment', from *firmus* 'constant, firm'; first meaning 'a fixed annual amount payable as rent or tax', later 'a lease', 'land leased for cultivation'. Compare with **FIRM**².

farmer > *noun* a person who owns or manages a farm.

SYNONYMS – archaic husbandman, yeoman.

farmstead > *noun* a farm and its buildings.

Faroese /fairōeez/ (also **Faeroese**) > *noun* (pl. same) **1** a person from the Faroe Islands. **2** the language of the Faroe Islands.

farouche /fərōosh/ > *adjective* sullen or shy in company.

ORIGIN – Old French *forache*, from Latin *foras* 'out of doors'.

farrago /fəraagō/ > *noun* (pl. **farragos** or US **farragoes**) a confused mixture.

ORIGIN – Latin, 'mixed fodder', from *far* 'corn'.

far-reaching > *adjective* having important and extensive effects or implications.

farrier /farriər/ > *noun* a smith who shoes horses.

DERIVATIVES – **farriery** *noun*.

ORIGIN – Old French *ferrier*, from Latin *ferrum* 'iron, horseshoe'.

farrow > *noun* a litter of pigs. > *verb* (of a sow) give birth to (piglets).

ORIGIN – Old English 'young pig'.

far-seeing > *adjective* having shrewd judgement and foresight.

Farsi /faarsee/ > *noun* the modern form of the Persian language, spoken in Iran.

ORIGIN – from the Persian word for 'Persia'.

far-sighted > *adjective* **1** far-seeing. **2** N. Amer. long-sighted.

fart informal > *verb* **1** emit wind from the anus. **2** (**fart about** or **around**) waste time on silly or trivial things. > *noun* **1** an emission of wind from the anus. **2** a boring or contemptible person: *an old fart*.

farther > *adverb* & *adjective* variant form of **FURTHER**.

USAGE – on the difference in use between **farther** and **further**, see the note at **FURTHER**.

farthermost > *adjective* variant form of **FURTHERMOST**.

farthest > *adjective* & *adverb* variant form of **FURTHEST**.

farthing > *noun* **1** a former monetary unit and coin of the UK, equal to a quarter of an old penny. **2** the least possible amount: *she didn't care a farthing*.

ORIGIN – Old English, 'fourth'.

farthingale /farrthinggayl/ > *noun* historical a hooped petticoat formerly worn under women's skirts to extend and shape them.

ORIGIN – from Spanish *verdugo* 'rod, stick'.

fartlek /faartlek/ > *noun* Athletics a system of training for distance runners in which the terrain and pace are continually varied.

ORIGIN – from Swedish *fart* 'speed' + *lek* 'play'.

fasces /fasseez/ > *plural noun* historical a bundle of rods with a projecting axe blade, a symbol of a magistrate's power in ancient Rome.

ORIGIN – Latin, from *fascis* 'bundle'.

fascia (chiefly Brit. also **facia** except in sense 5) > *noun* **1** /fayshə/ a board covering the ends of rafters or other fittings. **2** a signboard on a shopfront. **3** chiefly Brit. the dashboard of a motor vehicle. **4** (in classical architecture) a long flat surface between mouldings on an architrave. **5** /fashə/ (pl. **fasciae** /fashi-ee/) Anatomy a thin sheath of fibrous tissue enclosing a muscle or other organ.

ORIGIN – Latin, 'band, door frame'.

fascicle /fassik'l/ > *noun* a separately published instalment of a book.

ORIGIN – Latin *fasciculus* 'little bundle', from *fascis* 'bundle'.

fascinate > *verb* irresistibly attract the interest of.

DERIVATIVES – **fascinating** *adjective* **fascinatingly** *adverb*.

SYNONYMS – absorb, captivate, compel, enchant, engross, enthral.

ORIGIN – Latin *fascinare* 'bewitch', from *fascinum* 'spell, witchcraft'.

fascination > *noun* **1** the power to fascinate; irresistible attractiveness. **2** (**fascination for** or **with**) a powerful feeling of attraction or interest.

SYNONYMS – **1** allure, appeal, attraction, charm, compulsion, interest.

fascism* /fashiz'm/ > *noun* **1** an authoritarian and nationalistic right-wing system of government. **2** extreme right-wing, authoritarian, or intolerant views or practice.

DERIVATIVES – **fascist** *noun* & *adjective* **fascistic** *adjective*.

*SPELLING – only one *s* before *c*: fascism.

wordpower facts

Fascism

The word **fascism** derives from Latin *fascis*, meaning 'a bundle'. The plural form, *fasces*, referred to the bundle of rods bound together, with an axe projecting from its centre, carried in ancient Rome by officers attending a consul or magistrate. From the mid 17th century the **fasces** came to be regarded as an emblem of authority. However, the term **fascism** itself entered English much later, in the 20th century, coming directly from Italian; it was first used of the totalitarian regime of Benito Mussolini in Italy (1922–43).

fash > *verb* (**fash oneself**) Scottish feel upset or worried.

ORIGIN – French *fascher*, from Latin *fastus* 'disdain, contempt'.

fashion > *noun* **1** a popular trend, especially in dress. **2** the production and marketing of new styles of clothing and cosmetics. **3** a manner of doing something. > *verb* make into a particular form or article.

IDIOMS – **after a fashion** to a certain extent but not perfectly. **in** (or **out of**) **fashion** fashionable (or unfashionable).

SYNONYMS – *noun* **1** craze, rage, style, trend, vogue. **3** manner, method, mode, style, system. *verb* construct, contrive, fabricate, form, shape.

COMBINATIONS – **fashion victim** a person who follows popular fashions slavishly.

ORIGIN – Old French *façon*, from Latin *facere* 'do, make'.

fashionable > *adjective* characteristic of or influenced by a current popular trend or style.

DERIVATIVES – **fashionability** *noun* **fashionably** *adverb*.

SYNONYMS – chic, in fashion, in vogue, trendy, voguish.

ANTONYMS – old-fashioned, passé, unfashionable.

fashionista /fashənisstə/ > *noun* informal **1** a designer of haute couture. **2** a devoted follower of fashion.

fast¹ > *adjective* **1** moving or capable of moving at high speed. **2** taking place or acting rapidly. **3** (of a clock or watch) ahead of the correct time. **4** firmly fixed or attached. **5** (of a dye) not fading in light or when washed. **6** Photography needing only a short exposure. **7** involving exciting or shocking activities. > *adverb* **1** at high speed. **2** within a short time. **3** so as to be hard to move; firmly or securely.

IDIOMS – **fast asleep** sleeping deeply. **pull**

a fast one informal try to gain an unfair advantage.

SYNONYMS – *adjective* **1** quick, rapid, speedy, swift. **4** firm, fixed, secure, stuck, tight.

ANTONYMS – *adjective* **1** slow. **4** loose.

COMBINATIONS – **fast breeder** a breeder reactor in which the neutrons causing fission are not slowed by any moderator. **fast food** cooked food sold in snack bars and restaurants as a quick meal.

ORIGIN – Old English, 'firmly fixed, steadfast'.

fast² > *verb* abstain from food or drink, especially as a religious observance. > *noun* an act or period of fasting.

fastback > *noun* a car with a rear that slopes continuously down to the bumper.

fasten > *verb* **1** close or do up securely. **2** fix or hold in place. **3** (**fasten on**) single out (something) and concentrate on it obsessively. **4** (**fasten off**) secure the end of (a thread) with stitches or a knot.

DERIVATIVES – **fastener** *noun* **fastening** *noun*.

SYNONYMS – **1** bolt, chain, lock, make fast, secure. **2** affix, attach, fix, join.

ORIGIN – Old English, 'make sure, confirm'.

fast forward > *noun* a control on a tape or video player for advancing the tape rapidly. > *verb* (**fast-forward**) advance (a tape) with such a control.

fastidious /faˈstɪdɪəss/ > *adjective* **1** very attentive to accuracy and detail. **2** very concerned about matters of cleanliness.

DERIVATIVES – **fastidiously** *adverb* **fastidiousness** *noun*.

SYNONYMS – fussy, meticulous, painstaking, punctilious, scrupulous.

ANTONYMS – easy-going, sloppy.

ORIGIN – first meaning 'disgusting, unpleasant', later 'easily disgusted' and 'difficult to please': from Latin *fastidiosus*, from *fastidium* 'loathing'.

fastigiate /faˈstɪdʒɪət/ > *adjective* Botany (of a tree) having the branches more or less parallel to the main stem.

ORIGIN – from Latin *fastigium* 'tapering point, gable'.

fastness > *noun* **1** a secure place well protected by natural features. **2** the ability of a dye to maintain its colour.

fast track > *noun* a rapid route or method. > *verb* (**fast-track**) accelerate the development or progress of.

fat > *noun* **1** a natural oily substance in animal bodies, deposited under the skin or around certain organs. **2** such a substance, or a similar one made from plants, used in cooking. **3** Chemistry any of a group of solid natural esters of glycerol and various fatty acids, the main constituents of animal and vegetable fat. Compare with OIL. > *adjective*

(**fatter**, **fattest**) **1** (of a person or animal) having much excess fat. **2** (of food) containing much fat. **3** informal substantial: *fat profits*. **4** informal very little: *fat chance*.

IDIOMS – **kill the fatted calf** produce one's best food to celebrate, especially at a prodigal's return. [ORIGIN – with biblical allusion to the Gospel of Luke, chapter 15.] **live off the fat of the land** have the best of everything.

DERIVATIVES – **fatness** *noun* **fattish** *adjective*.

SYNONYMS – *adjective* **1** heavy, obese, overweight, plump, portly, stout.

ANTONYMS – *adjective* **1** lean, thin.

COMBINATIONS – **fat cat** derogatory a wealthy and powerful businessman or politician.

fatal > *adjective* **1** causing death. **2** leading to failure or disaster.

DERIVATIVES – **fatally** *adverb*.

SYNONYMS – **1** deadly, lethal, mortal. **2** calamitous, catastrophic, devastating, dire, disastrous.

ORIGIN – Latin *fatalis*, from *fatum* (see FATE).

fatalism > *noun* **1** the belief that events are predetermined and inevitable. **2** a submissive attitude to events.

DERIVATIVES – **fatalist** *noun* **fatalistic** *adjective*.

fatality > *noun* (pl. **fatalities**) **1** an occurrence of death by accident, in war, or from disease. **2** the condition of being determined by.

fate > *noun* **1** the development of events outside a person's control, regarded as predetermined. **2** the outcome of a particular situation, especially the end of a person's life. **3** (**the Fates**) Greek & Roman Mythology the three goddesses (Clotho, Lachesis, and Atropos) who preside over the birth and life of humans. > *verb* (**be fated**) be destined to happen or act in a particular way.

IDIOMS – **seal someone's fate** make it inevitable that something unpleasant will happen to someone.

SYNONYMS – *noun* **1** chance, destiny, fortune, kismet, providence, the stars. **2** destiny, end, future, lot, outcome. *verb* (**be fated**) be bound, be doomed, be guaranteed, be predestined, be preordained.

ORIGIN – Latin *fatum* 'that which has been spoken', from *fari* 'speak'.

fateful > *adjective* having far-reaching, especially disastrous consequences.

DERIVATIVES – **fatefully** *adverb*.

SYNONYMS – critical, crucial, decisive, key, pivotal.

fathead > *noun* informal a stupid person.

father > *noun* **1** a man in relation to his natural child or children. **2** an important figure in the origin and early history of

something: *Pasteur, the father of microbiology.* **3** a male animal in relation to its offspring. **4** (often as a title or form of address) a priest. **5** (**the Father**) (in Christian belief) the first person of the Trinity; God. **6** literary a male ancestor. > *verb* **1** be the father of. **2** be the source or originator of.

WORDFINDER – paternal (*relating to a father*), patricide (*the killing of one's father*), patrimony (*things inherited from one's father*).

IDIOMS – **how's your father** Brit. informal sexual intercourse. **like father, like son** proverb a son's character or behaviour can be expected to resemble that of his father.

DERIVATIVES – **fatherhood** *noun* **fatherless** *adjective*.

COMBINATIONS – **Father Christmas** an imaginary being said to bring presents for children on the night before Christmas Day. **father-in-law** (pl. **fathers-in-law**) the father of one's husband or wife. **Father's Day** a day of the year on which fathers are honoured with gifts and greetings cards (in the US and Britain usually the third Sunday in June).

fatherland > *noun* a person's native country.

fatherly > *adjective* of or characteristic of a father, especially in being protective and affectionate.

fathom > *noun* a unit of length equal to six feet (1.8 metres), chiefly used in reference to the depth of water. > *verb* **1** understand (something) after much thought: *I can't fathom it.* **2** measure the depth of.

wordpower facts

Fathom

The original sense of the word **fathom**, in Old English, was 'the enclosure formed by the breast and arms'; **fathoms** were 'arms extended in an embrace', or 'outstretched arms'. From this the word came to represent a unit of measurement, based on the span of the outstretched arms to the tips of the fingers, later standardised to six feet. Other early units of measurement, such as the **ell** and the **cubit**, were similarly based on the length of the arm or forearm.

fathomless > *adjective* **1** of immeasurable depth. **2** incomprehensible.

fatigue > *noun* **1** extreme tiredness, especially resulting from mental or physical exertion or illness. **2** brittleness in metal or other materials caused by repeated stress. **3** (**fatigues**) loose-fitting clothing of a sort worn by soldiers. **4** (**fatigues**) menial non-military tasks performed by a soldier. > *verb* (**fatigues**, **fatigued**, **fatiguing**) cause (someone) to suffer fatigue.

DERIVATIVES – **fatigued** adjective.

SYNONYMS – noun **1** exhaustion, lassitude, tiredness, weariness. verb exhaust, tire, wear out, weary.

ORIGIN – Latin fatigare 'tire out', from ad fatim 'to satiety or surfeit, to bursting'.

fatso > noun (pl. **fatsoes**) informal, derogatory a fat person.

fatten > verb make or become fat or fatter.

fatty > adjective (**fattier**, **fattiest**) **1** containing a large amount of fat. **2** Medicine involving abnormal deposition of fat. > noun (pl. **fatties**) informal a fat person.

COMBINATIONS – **fatty acid** Chemistry an organic acid whose molecule contains a hydrocarbon chain.

fatuous /**fat**yooəss/ > adjective silly and pointless.

DERIVATIVES – **fatuity** (pl. **fatuities**) noun **fatuously** adverb **fatuousness** noun.

SYNONYMS – asinine, foolish, idiotic, inane, silly, stupid.

ORIGIN – Latin fatuus 'foolish'.

fatwa /**fat**waa/ > noun an authoritative ruling on a point of Islamic law.

wordpower facts

Fatwa

The word **fatwa**, a direct borrowing from Arabic, has been in use in English (in the forms fetwa or fetfa) since the 17th century. It was an obscure and unfamiliar word until 1989, when it suddenly gained new and widespread currency. In this year Iran's Ayatollah Khomeini issued a **fatwa** sentencing the British writer Salman Rushdie to death for publishing *The Satanic Verses* (1988), a book regarded by many Muslims as blasphemous. **Fatwa** is a generic term for any legal decision made by an Islamic religious authority, but, because of the particular context in which the English-speaking world became familiar with the word, it is sometimes wrongly thought to denote a death sentence.

faucet /**faw**sit/ > noun chiefly N. Amer. a tap.

ORIGIN – Provençal falset, from falsar 'to bore'.

fault > noun **1** an unattractive or unsatisfactory feature; a flaw. **2** a defect in a device or piece of machinery. **3** responsibility for an accident or misfortune. **4** (in tennis) a service that infringes the rules. **5** Geology an extended break in a rock formation, marked by the displacement and discontinuity of layers on either side. > verb **1** criticise for inadequacy or mistakes. **2** (**be**

faulted) Geology be broken by a fault or faults.

IDIOMS – **find fault** make an adverse criticism or objection, especially unfairly. ——— **to a fault** displaying the specified quality to an excessive extent.

SYNONYMS – noun **1** blemish, defect, flaw, imperfection, shortcoming, weakness. **3** culpability, liability, guilt, responsibility.

ORIGIN – Old French faute, from Latin fallere 'deceive'.

faultless > adjective free from defect or error; perfect.

DERIVATIVES – **faultlessly** adverb.

faulty > adjective (**faultier**, **faultiest**) (of a thing) having or displaying faults.

SYNONYMS – broken, defective, inoperative, malfunctioning.

faun /fawn/ > noun Roman Mythology a lustful rural god represented as a man with a goat's horns, ears, legs, and tail.

USAGE – on the difference between a **faun** and a **fawn**, see the note at **FAWN**[1].

ORIGIN – from the name of the pastoral god Faunus.

fauna /**faw**nə/ > noun the animals of a particular region, habitat, or geological period. Compare with **FLORA**.

DERIVATIVES – **faunal** adjective.

ORIGIN – Latin, from the name Fauna, a rural goddess, sister of Faunus (see **FAUN**).

Faustian /**fow**stiən/ > adjective relating to the German astronomer and necromancer Johann Faust (died c.1540), reputed to have sold his soul to the Devil.

faute de mieux /fōt də **myö**/ > adverb for want of a better alternative.

ORIGIN – French.

Fauve /fōv/ > noun a member of a group of early 20th-century French painters who favoured a vivid, expressionistic use of colour.

DERIVATIVES – **Fauvism** noun **Fauvist** noun & adjective.

ORIGIN – French, 'wild beast', with reference to a remark by the art critic Louis Vauxcelles.

faux /fō/ > adjective made in imitation; artificial.

ORIGIN – French, 'false'.

faux pas /fō **paa**/ > noun (pl. same) a social blunder.

ORIGIN – French, 'false step'.

fava bean /**faa**və/ > noun North American term for **broad bean**.

ORIGIN – from Latin faba 'bean'.

favela /fa**vell**ə/ > noun (in Brazil) a shack or shanty town.

ORIGIN – Portuguese.

favour (US **favor**) > noun **1** approval or liking. **2** overgenerous preferential treatment. **3** an act of kindness beyond what is due or usual. **4** (**one's favours**) dated a woman's consent to a man having sexual intercourse with

her. **5** archaic a badge, ribbon, etc. worn as a mark of favour or support. > verb **1** regard or treat with favour. **2** work to the advantage of. **3** (**favour with**) give or grant (something) to. **4** informal resemble (a relative) in facial features.

IDIOMS – **in favour of 1** to be replaced by. **2** in support or to the advantage of.

SYNONYMS – noun **1** approbation, approval, goodwill, liking, support. **2** bias, favouritism, partiality, prejudice. **3** courtesy, good turn, kindness, service. verb **1** advocate, approve of, back, prefer, support. **2** assist, benefit, help.

ANTONYMS – noun **1** disapproval, disfavour. **2** impartiality. verb **1** oppose. **2** hinder.

ORIGIN – Latin favor, from favere 'show kindness to'.

favourable (US **favorable**) > adjective **1** expressing approval or consent. **2** to the advantage of someone or something. **3** auspicious.

DERIVATIVES – **favourably** adverb.

SYNONYMS – **1** appreciative, approving, commendatory, complimentary, positive. **2** advantageous, beneficial, good, helpful, suitable.

favourite (US **favorite**) > adjective preferred to all others of the same kind. > noun **1** a favourite person or thing. **2** the competitor thought most likely to win.

SYNONYMS – adjective chosen, favoured, ideal, preferred.

COMBINATIONS – **favourite son** a famous man who is particularly popular in his native area.

ORIGIN – Italian favorito 'favoured', from favorire 'to favour'.

favouritism (US **favoritism**) > noun the unfair favouring of one person or group at the expense of another.

fawn[1] > noun **1** a young deer in its first year. **2** a light brown colour. > verb (of a deer) produce young.

USAGE – do not confuse **fawn** with **faun**: a **fawn** is a young deer, and a light brown colour; a **faun** is a Roman deity that is part man, part goat.

ORIGIN – Old French faon, from Latin fetus 'offspring'.

fawn[2] > verb (often **fawn on** or **over**) **1** give a servile display of exaggerated flattery or affection. **2** (of an animal, especially a dog) show slavish devotion.

DERIVATIVES – **fawning** adjective.

ORIGIN – Old English, 'make or be glad'.

fax > noun **1** an exact copy of a document made by electronic scanning and transmitted by telecommunications links. **2** the production or transmission of documents in this way. **3** (also **fax machine**) a machine for transmitting and receiving such documents. > *verb* **1** send (a document) by fax. **2** contact by fax.

ORIGIN – abbreviation of **FACSIMILE**.

fay > *noun* literary a fairy.

ORIGIN – Old French *fae*, from Latin *fatum* (see **FATE**).

fayre > *noun* pseudo-archaic spelling of **FAIR²**.

faze /fayz/ > *verb* informal disturb or disconcert.

ORIGIN – from dialect *feeze* 'drive off'.

FBI > *abbreviation* (in the US) Federal Bureau of Investigation.

FC > *abbreviation* Football Club.

FCO > *abbreviation* (in the UK) Foreign and Commonwealth Office.

FDA > *abbreviation* (in the US) Food and Drug Administration.

FE > *abbreviation* (in the UK) further education.

Fe > *symbol* the chemical element iron.

ORIGIN – Latin *ferrum*.

fealty /feeəlti/ > *noun* historical a feudal tenant's or vassal's sworn loyalty to a lord.

ORIGIN – Old French *feaulte* from Latin *fidelitas* (see **FIDELITY**).

fear > *noun* **1** an unpleasant emotion caused by the threat of danger, pain, or harm. **2** (**fear for**) a feeling of anxiety concerning the outcome of something or the safety of someone. **3** the likelihood of something unwelcome happening. > *verb* **1** be afraid of. **2** (**fear for**) feel anxiety on behalf of. **3** archaic regard (God) with reverence and awe.

IDIOMS – **no fear** Brit. informal used as an emphatic expression of denial or refusal. **put the fear of God in** (or **into**) cause (someone) to be very frightened. **without fear or favour** impartially.

SYNONYMS – *noun* **1** apprehension, dread, fright, terror, trepidation. *verb* **1** be afraid of, dread, quail at, shrink from.

ORIGIN – Old English, 'danger'.

fearful > *adjective* **1** showing or causing fear. **2** informal very great.

DERIVATIVES – **fearfully** *adverb* **fearfulness** *noun*.

SYNONYMS – **1** afraid, apprehensive, frightened, nervous, scared.

fearless > *adjective* showing a lack of fear; brave.

DERIVATIVES – **fearlessly** *adverb* **fearlessness** *noun*.

fearsome > *adjective* frightening, especially in appearance.

DERIVATIVES – **fearsomely** *adverb*.

SYNONYMS – alarming, daunting, formidable, frightening.

feart > *adjective* Scottish afraid.

feasible > *adjective* **1** possible and practical to achieve easily or conveniently. **2** informal likely.

DERIVATIVES – **feasibility** *noun* **feasibly** *adverb*.

USAGE – In formal contexts, avoid using **feasible** to mean 'likely' or 'probable'.

SYNONYMS – **1** practicable, practical, manageable, viable, workable.

ANTONYMS – impractical, unfeasible.

ORIGIN – Old French *faisible*, from *faire* 'do, make', from Latin *facere*.

feast > *noun* **1** a large meal, especially a celebratory one. **2** an annual religious celebration. **3** a day dedicated to a particular saint. > *verb* **1** eat and drink sumptuously. **2** (**feast on**) eat large quantities of.

IDIOMS – **ghost** (or **skeleton**) **at the feast** a person or thing that brings gloom to an otherwise pleasant occasion. **feast one's eyes on** gaze at with pleasure.

SYNONYMS – *noun* **1** banquet. *verb* **1** banquet, dine, gourmandise. **2** gorge.

COMBINATIONS – **feast day** a day on which an annual Christian celebration is held.

ORIGIN – Latin *festa*, from *festus* 'joyous'.

feat > *noun* an achievement requiring great courage, skill, or strength.

SYNONYMS – accomplishment, achievement, attainment, exploit.

ORIGIN – Old French *fait*, from Latin *factum* (see **FACT**).

feather > *noun* any of the flat appendages growing from a bird's skin, consisting of a partly hollow horny shaft fringed with vanes of barbs. > *verb* **1** rotate the blades of (a propeller) to lessen the air or water resistance. **2** (**feathered**) covered or decorated with feathers.

WORDFINDER – covert (*feather covering the base of a main feather*), fledge (*develop flight feathers*), pinnate (*shaped like or resembling a feather*), plumage (*a bird's feathers*), plumy (*resembling or decorated with feathers*), quill (*main wing or tail feather of a bird*), rectrices (*larger feathers in a bird's tail, used for steering*), remiges (*bird's flight feathers*).

IDIOMS – **a feather in one's cap** an achievement to be proud of. **feather one's nest** make money illicitly and at someone else's expense.

DERIVATIVES – **feathery** *adjective*.

COMBINATIONS – **feather-brained** silly or absent-minded.

feather bed > *noun* a bed with a mattress stuffed with feathers. > *verb* (**feather-bed**) provide with excessively favourable economic or working conditions.

feathering > *noun* **1** a bird's plumage. **2** the feathers or vanes of an arrow. **3** feather-like markings or structure.

featherweight > *noun* **1** a weight in boxing intermediate between bantamweight and lightweight. **2** a person or thing not worth serious consideration.

feature > *noun* **1** a distinctive attribute or aspect of something. **2** a part of the face, such as the mouth, making a significant contribution to its overall appearance. **3** a newspaper or magazine article or a broadcast programme devoted to a particular topic. **4** (also **feature film**) a full-length film intended as the main item in a cinema programme. > *verb* **1** have as a feature. **2** have as an important actor or participant. **3** be a feature of or take an important part in.

DERIVATIVES – **featured** *adjective* **featureless** *adjective*.

SYNONYMS – *noun* **1** aspect, attribute, characteristic, facet, property, quality.

ORIGIN – Old French *faiture* 'form', from Latin *factura*, from *frangere* 'to break'.

Feb. > *abbreviation* February.

febrifuge /febrifyōōj/ > *noun* a medicine used to reduce fever.

ORIGIN – from Latin *febris* 'fever' + *fugare* 'drive away'.

febrile /feebrīl/ > *adjective* **1** having or showing the symptoms of a fever. **2** having or showing a great deal of nervous excitement.

ORIGIN – Latin *febrilis*, from *febris* 'fever'.

February* /febrooəri, febyooəri/ > *noun* (pl. **Februaries**) the second month of the year.

*SPELLING – *ruary*, not *uary*: February. Because it is difficult to pronounce **February** in the way it is spelled, an easier pronunciation, **Feb-yoo** rather than **Feb-roo**, is often used.

ORIGIN – Latin *februarius*, from *februa*, the name of a Roman purification feast held in this month.

feces > *noun* US spelling of **FAECES**.

feckless > *adjective* **1** (of a person) lacking in vigour and efficiency. **2** unthinking and irresponsible.

DERIVATIVES – **fecklessly** *adverb* **fecklessness** *noun*.

SYNONYMS – **1** feeble, idle, ineffectual, shiftless, useless.

ORIGIN – from Scots and northern English dialect *feck* (from *effeck*, variant of **EFFECT**).

feculent /fekyoolənt/ > *adjective* of or containing dirt, sediment, or waste matter.

ORIGIN – Latin *faeculentus*, from *faex* 'dregs'.

fecund /fekənd, feekənd/ > *adjective* highly fertile; able to produce offspring.

DERIVATIVES – **fecundity** *noun*.

ORIGIN – Latin *fecundus*.

Fed > *noun* US informal **1** a member of the FBI or other federal agent or official. **2** the Federal Reserve.

fed past and past participle of **FEED**.

federal > *adjective* **1** of, relating to, or constituting a federation. **2** referring to the central government as distinguished from the separate units constituting a federation. **3** (**Federal**) US historical of the Northern States in the Civil War.
DERIVATIVES – **federalism** *noun* **federalist** *noun* & *adjective* **federally** *adverb*.
COMBINATIONS – **Federal Reserve** (in the US) the banking authority that performs the functions of a central bank.
ORIGIN – from Latin *foedus* 'league, covenant'.

federate > *verb* /**fedd**ərayt/ (of a number of states or organisations) organise or be organised on a federal basis. > *adjective* /**fedd**ərət/ belonging to a federation.
ORIGIN – Latin *foederatus*, based on *foedus* 'league, covenant'.

federation > *noun* **1** a group of states which form a unity but remain independent in internal affairs. **2** an organisation within which smaller divisions have some internal autonomy. **3** the action of federating.

fedora /fi**dor**ə/ > *noun* a soft felt hat with a curled brim and the crown creased lengthways.
ORIGIN – from *Fédora* (1882), the title of a play by the French dramatist Victorien Sardou.

fed up > *adjective* informal annoyed or bored.

fee > *noun* **1** a payment made in exchange for advice or services. **2** a charge made for a privilege such as admission.
SYNONYMS – charge, cost, payment, price, rate, tariff.
COMBINATIONS – **fee simple** (pl. **fees simple**) Law a permanent and absolute tenure of an estate in land with freedom to dispose of it at will.

wordpower facts
Fee
Coming via Old French *feu* or *fief* from Latin *feodum*, the word **fee** is closely related to **fief** and **feudal**, which have the same root. Historically **fee** was used as a variant of **fief**, denoting an estate of land held on condition of military service to the Crown or a lord. The social system based on such relations is called **feudalism** or the **feudal** system. The word **feud**, however, is unrelated to **feudal**; it comes from Old French *feide*, meaning 'hostility', from a Germanic root which is the source also of **foe**.

feeble > *adjective* (**feebler**, **feeblest**) **1** lacking physical or mental strength. **2** failing to convince or impress: *a feeble excuse*.

DERIVATIVES – **feebleness** *noun* **feebly** *adverb*.
SYNONYMS – **1** frail, puny, weak. **2** ineffective, poor, unconvincing, weak.
ANTONYMS – **1** strong. **2** convincing.
COMBINATIONS – **feeble-minded** **1** foolish; stupid. **2** dated having less than average intelligence.
ORIGIN – Old French *fieble*, from Latin *flebilis* 'lamentable', from *flere* 'weep'.

feed > *verb* (past and past participle **fed**) **1** give food to. **2** provide an adequate supply of food for. **3** take food; eat something. **4** (**feed on** or **off**) derive regular nourishment from (a particular substance). **5** supply with material, power, water, etc. **6** pass gradually through a confined space. **7** prompt (an actor) with (a line). > *noun* **1** an act of feeding or of being fed. **2** food for domestic animals. **3** a device or pipe for supplying material to a machine. **4** the supply of raw material to a machine or device. **5** a prompt given to an actor on stage.
SYNONYMS – *verb* **1** nourish, sustain; archaic victual. **4** (**feed on or off**) eat, live on, subsist on.
COMBINATIONS – **feeding frenzy** **1** a competitive group attack on prey by sharks or piranhas. **2** an episode of frantic competition for something. **feedstock** raw material to supply a machine or industrial process.
ORIGIN – Old English, related to FOOD.

feedback > *noun* **1** information given in response to a product, performance etc., used as a basis for improvement. **2** the modification or control of a process or system by its results or effects. **3** the return of a fraction of the output of an amplifier, microphone, or other device to the input, causing distortion or a whistling sound.
COMBINATIONS – **positive** (or **negative**) **feedback** feedback that tends to increase (or reduce) the effect by which it is produced.

feeder > *noun* **1** a person or animal that eats a particular food or in a particular manner. **2** a container filled with food for birds or mammals. **3** Brit. a child's feeding bottle. **4** a thing that supplies something. **5** a road or rail route linking outlying districts with a main system.

feel > *verb* (past and past participle **felt**) **1** perceive, examine, or search by touch. **2** be aware of through physical sensation. **3** give a sensation of a particular physical quality when touched: *the wool feels soft*. **4** experience (an emotion or sensation). **5** have a belief or impression, especially without an identifiable reason. **6** have a specified reaction to or attitude towards something. **7** consider oneself to be. **8** be emotionally affected by. > *noun* **1** an act of

feeling. **2** a sensation given by something when touched. **3** the impression given by something. **4** the sense of touch.
IDIOMS – **feel up to** have the strength and energy to. **get a feel for** become accustomed to. **have a feel for** have a sensitive appreciation or understanding of. **make oneself** (or **one's presence**) **felt** have a noticeable effect.
SYNONYMS – *verb* **1** caress, finger, fondle, handle. **2** detect, experience, have a sensation of, perceive, sense. **4** experience, go through, suffer, undergo. **5** believe, consider, hold, judge, maintain, think.

feeler > *noun* **1** an animal organ such as an antenna that is used for testing things by touch. **2** a tentative proposal intended to ascertain someone's attitude or opinion.
COMBINATIONS – **feeler gauge** a gauge consisting of a number of thin blades for measuring narrow gaps or clearances.

feel-good > *adjective* informal causing a feeling of happiness and well-being: *a feel-good movie*.

feeling > *noun* **1** a physical or emotional state or reaction. **2** a belief or opinion, especially a vague or irrational one. **3** the capacity to feel. **4** the sensation of touching or being touched. **5** (**feelings**) emotional responses or tendencies to respond. **6** strong emotion. **7** (**feeling for**) a sensitivity to or intuitive understanding of. > *adjective* showing emotion or sensitivity.
IDIOMS – **one's better feelings** one's conscience.
DERIVATIVES – **feelingly** *adverb*.
SYNONYMS – *noun* **1** awareness, consciousness, perception, sensation. **2** fancy, idea, impression, inkling, notion. **5** (**feelings**) ego, emotions, passions, sensibilities, sensitivities. *adjective* caring, compassionate, sensitive, sympathetic, understanding.

feet plural of FOOT.

feign /fayn/ > *verb* pretend to be affected by (a feeling, state, or injury).
SYNONYMS – fake, pretend, put on, simulate.
ORIGIN – Old French *feindre*, from Latin *fingere* 'mould, contrive'.

feint[1] /faynt/ > *noun* a deceptive or pretended attacking movement, especially in boxing or fencing. > *verb* make a feint.
ORIGIN – French *feinte*, from *feindre* 'feign'.

feint[2] /faynt/ > *adjective* denoting paper printed with faint lines as a guide for handwriting.
ORIGIN – variant of FAINT.

feisty /**fī**sti/ > *adjective* (**feistier**, **feistiest**) informal **1** spirited and exuberant. **2** touchy and aggressive.
DERIVATIVES – **feistiness** *noun*.

wordpower facts

Feisty

The word **feisty** is rooted in the amusing notion of a little farting dog. It comes from the earlier and now obsolete word **feist**, or **fist**, meaning 'small dog', from **fisting cur** or **fisting hound**. This was a derogatory term for a lapdog, deriving from the old (Middle English) verb **fist**, meaning 'to break wind'. *Fist*, a word of Germanic origin, may also be the source of **fizzle**, which in the 16th century meant 'to break wind quietly' (or **fizzle** may have arisen simply as an imitative word, related to **fizz**).

felafel > *noun* variant spelling of FALAFEL.

feldspar /**feld**spaar/ (also **felspar**) > *noun* a pale rock-forming silicate mineral.
ORIGIN – German *Feldspat* 'field spar'.

felicitations > *plural noun* congratulations.

felicitous /fə**liss**itəss/ > *adjective* well chosen or appropriate.
DERIVATIVES – **felicitously** *adverb*.

felicity > *noun* (pl. **felicities**) 1 complete happiness. 2 the ability to express oneself appropriately. 3 a felicitous feature of a work of literature or art.
ORIGIN – Latin *felicitas*, from *felix* 'happy'.

feline /**fee**līn/ > *adjective* of or relating to a cat or cats. > *noun* an animal of the cat family.
ORIGIN – Latin *felinus*, from *feles* 'cat'.

fell¹ past of FALL.

fell² > *verb* 1 cut down (a tree). 2 knock down. 3 stitch down (the edge of a seam) to lie flat.
DERIVATIVES – **feller** *noun*.

fell³ > *noun* a hill or stretch of high moorland, especially in northern England.
ORIGIN – Old Norse, 'hill'.

fell⁴ > *adjective* literary of terrible evil or ferocity.
IDIOMS – **in** (or **at**) **one fell swoop** all in one go. [ORIGIN – from Shakespeare's *Macbeth* (IV. iii. 219).]
ORIGIN – Old French *fel*, from *felon* 'wicked, a wicked person'.

fellatio /fə**lay**shiō/ > *noun* oral stimulation of a man's penis.
DERIVATIVES – **fellate** *verb*.
ORIGIN – from Latin *fellare* 'to suck'.

felloes /**fell**ōz/ (also **fellies** /**fell**iz/) > *plural noun* the outer rim of a wheel, to which the spokes are fixed.

fellow > *noun* 1 informal a man or boy. 2 a person in the same position or otherwise associated with another. 3 a thing of the same kind as another. 4 a member of a learned society. 5 Brit. an incorporated senior member of a college. > *adjective* sharing a particular activity, quality, or condition: *a fellow sufferer*.
SYNONYMS – 1 character, guy, individual, man, person; Brit. bloke, chap. 2 associate, companion, peer.
COMBINATIONS – **fellow feeling** sympathy based on shared experiences.
ORIGIN – Old English 'one who lays down money in a joint enterprise', from an Old Norse word meaning 'property, money'.

fellowship > *noun* 1 friendliness and companionship based on shared interests. 2 a group of people meeting to pursue a shared interest or aim. 3 the status of a fellow of a college or society.

fellow-traveller > *noun* a person who is sympathetic to communism but it not a member of the Communist Party.
DERIVATIVES – **fellow-travelling** *adjective*.

felon /**fell**ən/ > *noun* a person who has committed a felony.
ORIGIN – Old French, 'wicked, a wicked person', from Latin *fello*.

felony > *noun* (pl. **felonies**) a crime, typically one involving violence, regarded in the US and other judicial systems as more serious than a misdemeanour.
DERIVATIVES – **felonious** *adjective* **feloniously** *adverb*.

felspar > *noun* variant spelling of FELDSPAR.

felt¹ > *noun* cloth made by rolling and pressing wool or another suitable textile accompanied by the application of moisture or heat, which causes the fibres to mat together. > *verb* 1 mat together or become matted. 2 cover with felt.
COMBINATIONS – **felt-tip pen** (also **felt-tipped pen**) a pen with a writing point made of felt or tightly packed fibres.

felt² past and past participle of FEEL.

felucca /fe**lukk**ə/ > *noun* a small boat propelled by oars or sails, used on the Nile and formerly more widely in the Mediterranean region.
ORIGIN – Italian, from Arabic.

fem > *noun* variant spelling of FEMME.

female > *adjective* 1 referring to the sex that can bear offspring or produce eggs. 2 relating to or characteristic of women or female animals. 3 (of a plant or flower) having a pistil but no stamens. 4 (of a fitting) manufactured hollow so that a corresponding male part can be inserted. > *noun* a female person, animal, or plant.
DERIVATIVES – **femaleness** *noun*.
ORIGIN – Latin *femella*, from *femina* 'a woman'.

feminine > *adjective* 1 having qualities traditionally associated with women, especially delicacy and prettiness. 2 female. 3 Grammar referring to a gender of nouns and adjectives conventionally regarded as female. > *noun* (**the feminine**) the female sex or gender.
DERIVATIVES – **femininely** *adverb* **femininity** *noun*.
SYNONYMS – 1 female, girlish, womanly.
ANTONYMS – masculine.
ORIGIN – Latin *femininus*, from *femina* 'woman'.

feminise (also **feminize**) > *verb* make more feminine or female.
DERIVATIVES – **feminisation** *noun*.

feminism > *noun* the advocacy of women's rights on the grounds of sexual equality.
DERIVATIVES – **feminist** *noun* & *adjective*.
ORIGIN – French *féminisme*.

femme /fem/ (also **fem**) > *noun* informal a lesbian who takes a traditionally feminine sexual role.
ORIGIN – French, 'woman'.

femme fatale /fam fə**taal**/ > *noun* (pl. **femmes fatales** pronunc. same) an attractive and seductive woman.
ORIGIN – French, 'disastrous woman'.

femto- > *combining form* denoting a factor of one thousand million millionth (10^{-15}).
ORIGIN – from Danish or Norwegian *femten* 'fifteen'.

femur /**fee**mər/ > *noun* (pl. **femurs** or **femora** /**femm**ərə/) Anatomy the bone of the thigh or upper hindlimb.
DERIVATIVES – **femoral** *adjective*.
ORIGIN – Latin, 'thigh'.

fen¹ > *noun* 1 a low and marshy or frequently flooded area of land. 2 (**the Fens**) flat low-lying areas of eastern England, formerly marshland but now largely drained.
DERIVATIVES – **fenny** *adjective*.

fen² > *noun* (pl. same) a monetary unit of China, equal to one hundredth of a yuan.
ORIGIN – Chinese, 'a hundredth part'.

fence > *noun* 1 a barrier enclosing an area, typically consisting of posts connected by wire, wood, etc. 2 a large upright obstacle in steeplechasing, showjumping, or cross-country. 3 informal a dealer in stolen goods. 4 a guard or guide on a plane or other tool. > *verb* 1 surround or protect with a fence. 2 informal deal in (stolen goods). 3 practise the sport of fencing.
IDIOMS – **sit on the fence** avoid making a decision or commitment.
DERIVATIVES – **fencer** *noun*.
ORIGIN – shortening of DEFENCE.

fencing > *noun* 1 the sport of fighting with blunted swords in order to score points. 2 a series of fences. 3 material for making fences.

fend > *verb* 1 (**fend for oneself**) look after and provide for oneself. 2 (**fend off**) defend oneself from (an attack or attacker).
SYNONYMS – 2 (**fend off**) fight off, foil, hold off, repel, resist.
ORIGIN – shortening of DEFEND.

fender > *noun* **1** a low frame bordering a fireplace to keep in falling coals. **2** a cushioning device hung over a ship's side to protect it against impact. **3** N. Amer. the mudguard or area around the wheel well of a vehicle.

fenestration /fennistraysh'n/ > *noun* **1** Architecture the arrangement of windows in a building. **2** Medicine a surgical operation in which a new opening is formed, especially in the labyrinth of the inner ear to improve hearing.
ORIGIN – from Latin *fenestra* 'window'.

feng shui /fəN shway/ > *noun* (in Chinese thought) a system of laws considered to govern spatial arrangement in relation to the flow of energy, and whose effects are taken into account when designing buildings.
ORIGIN – Chinese, from *fēng* 'wind' + *shuǐ* 'water'.

Fenian /feeniən/ > *noun* **1** a member of the Irish Republican Brotherhood, a 19th-century Irish revolutionary nationalist organisation. **2** informal, offensive (chiefly in Northern Ireland) a Protestant name for a Catholic.
ORIGIN – from an Old Irish name of an ancient Irish people.

fennel /fenn'l/ > *noun* an aromatic yellow-flowered plant, with feathery leaves used as culinary herbs or eaten as a vegetable.
ORIGIN – Latin *faeniculum*, from *faenum* 'hay'.

fenugreek /fenyoogreek/ > *noun* a white-flowered plant with aromatic seeds that are used as a spice.
ORIGIN – from Latin *faenum graecum* 'Greek hay' (the Romans used the dried plant as fodder).

feral /feerəl, ferrəl/ > *adjective* **1** (of an animal or plant) in a wild state, especially after having been domesticated. **2** resembling a wild animal.
ORIGIN – from Latin *fera* 'wild animal'.

Fermat's last theorem /fermaaz/ > *noun* Mathematics the theorem that if *n* is a whole number greater than 2, the equation $x^n + y^n = z^n$ has no solutions in which *x*, *y*, and *z* are positive whole numbers.

ferment > *verb* /fərment/ **1** undergo or cause to undergo fermentation. **2** stir up (disorder). > *noun* /ferment/ **1** agitation and social unrest. **2** dated a fermenting agent or enzyme.
DERIVATIVES – **fermentable** *adjective* **fermenter** *noun*.
ORIGIN – from Latin *fermentum* 'yeast', from *fervere* 'to boil'.

fermentation > *noun* the chemical breakdown of a substance by bacteria, yeasts, or other micro-organisms, especially that involved in the making of beers, wines, and spirits.

DERIVATIVES – **fermentative** *adjective*.

wordpower facts
Fermat's last theorem
The French mathematician Pierre de Fermat (1601–65) originated a number of mathematical theorems. His last theorem became famous, or notorious, because on his copy of a mathematics text Fermat wrote that he had 'a truly wonderful proof', but that 'the margin was too small to contain it'. He never returned to the subject, and whether he actually had proved it (and if so, how) remains a mystery. For over three hundred years proving Fermat's last theorem was a challenge which many mathematicians tried and failed to achieve, until in 1995 a general proof was published by the Princeton-based British mathematician Andrew Wiles.

fermion /fermion/ > *noun* Physics a subatomic particle, such as a nucleon, which has a spin of a half integer.
ORIGIN – named after the Italian physicist Enrico *Fermi* (1901–54).

fermium /fermiəm/ > *noun* an unstable radioactive chemical element made by high-energy atomic collisions.

fern > *noun* (pl. same or **ferns**) a flowerless plant which has feathery or leafy fronds and reproduces by spores released from the undersides of the fronds.
WORDFINDER – pteridology (*study of ferns*).
DERIVATIVES – **fernery** (pl. **ferneries**) *noun* **ferny** *adjective*.

ferocious > *adjective* **1** savagely fierce, cruel, or violent. **2** informal very great; extreme.
DERIVATIVES – **ferociously** *adverb* **ferocity** *noun*.
SYNONYMS – **1** fierce, savage, vicious, wild.
ORIGIN – Latin *ferox* 'fierce'.

-ferous (usu. **-iferous**) > *combining form* having, bearing, or containing (a specified thing): *Carboniferous*.
ORIGIN – from Latin *-fer* 'producing', from *ferre* 'to bear'.

ferret /ferrit/ > *noun* **1** a domesticated albino or brown polecat, used for catching rabbits. **2** an assiduous search. > *verb* (**ferreted**, **ferreting**) **1** hunt with ferrets. **2** search for something in a place or container. **3** (**ferret out**) investigate (something) assiduously.
DERIVATIVES – **ferreter** *noun* **ferrety** *adjective*.
ORIGIN – Old French *fuiret*, from Latin *furo* 'thief, ferret', from *fur* 'thief'.

ferric /ferrik/ > *adjective* Chemistry of iron with a valency of three.
ORIGIN – from Latin *ferrum* 'iron'.

Ferris wheel > *noun* a fairground ride consisting of a giant vertical revolving wheel with passenger cars suspended on its outer edge.
ORIGIN – named after the American engineer George W. G. *Ferris* (1859–96).

ferrite /ferrīt/ > *noun* a magnetic oxide of iron and one or more other metals.

ferroconcrete > *noun* concrete reinforced with steel.

ferromagnetism > *noun* Physics strong, persistent magnetism of the kind possessed by iron.
DERIVATIVES – **ferromagnetic** *adjective*.

ferrous /ferrəss/ > *adjective* **1** (chiefly of metals) containing iron. **2** Chemistry of iron with a valency of two.
ORIGIN – from Latin *ferrum* 'iron'.

ferruginous /fərōojinəss/ > *adjective* **1** containing iron oxides or rust. **2** rust-coloured.
ORIGIN – from Latin *ferrugo* 'rust, dark red'.

ferrule /ferrōol/ > *noun* **1** a ring or cap which strengthens the end of a handle, stick, or tube. **2** a metal band strengthening or forming a joint.
ORIGIN – from Old French *virelle*, from Latin *viriae* 'bracelets'.

ferry > *noun* (pl. **ferries**) a boat or ship for conveying passengers and goods, especially as a regular service. > *verb* (**ferries**, **ferried**) convey by ferry or other transport, especially on short, regular trips.
DERIVATIVES – **ferryman** *noun*.

fertile > *adjective* **1** (of soil or land) producing or capable of producing abundant vegetation or crops. **2** (of a person, animal, or plant) able to conceive young or produce seed. **3** productive in generating new ideas.
DERIVATIVES – **fertility** *noun*.
SYNONYMS – **1,2** fecund, fruitful, productive.
ANTONYMS – **1,2** barren, infertile.
ORIGIN – Latin *fertilis*, from *ferre* 'to bear'.

fertilise (also **fertilize**) > *verb* **1** cause (an egg, female animal, or plant) to develop a new individual by introducing male reproductive material. **2** add fertiliser to.
DERIVATIVES – **fertilisation** *noun*.

fertiliser (also **fertilizer**) > *noun* a chemical or natural substance added to soil to increase its fertility.

fervent /ferv'nt/ > *adjective* intensely passionate.
DERIVATIVES – **fervently** *adverb*.
SYNONYMS – ardent, impassioned, intense, vehement, zealous.
ANTONYMS – apathetic.
ORIGIN – Latin, from *fervere* 'boil'.

fervid /**fer**vid/ > *adjective* intensely enthusiastic, especially to an excessive degree.

fervour (US **fervor**) > *noun* intense and passionate feeling.

SYNONYMS – ardour, intensity, passion, vehemence, zeal.

ANTONYMS – apathy.

fescue /**fes**kyoo/ > *noun* a narrow-leaved grass, some kinds of which are valuable for pasture and fodder.

ORIGIN – Old French *festu*, from Latin *festuca* 'stalk, straw'.

festal /**fes**t'l/ > *adjective* relating to a festival; festive.

ORIGIN – Latin *festalis*, from *festa* 'feast'.

fester > *verb* 1 (of a wound or sore) become septic. 2 (of food or rubbish) become rotten. 3 (of a negative feeling or a problem) intensify, especially through neglect.

ORIGIN – from Old French *festre*, from Latin *fistula* 'reed, fistula'.

festival > *noun* 1 a day or period of celebration, typically for religious reasons. 2 an organised series of concerts, films, etc.

SYNONYMS – 1 fair, fête, fiesta, gala, holiday.

ORIGIN – Latin *festivalis*, from *festa* 'feast'.

festive > *adjective* 1 relating to a festival. 2 jovially celebratory.

DERIVATIVES – **festively** *adverb*.

SYNONYMS – 2 celebratory, convivial, jolly, merry.

festivity > *noun* (pl. **festivities**) 1 joyful and exuberant celebration. 2 (**festivities**) celebratory activities or events.

SYNONYMS – 1 celebration, conviviality, gaiety, jollity, merriment, revelry. 2 (**festivities**) carousing, celebrations, jollification, merrymaking, revelry.

festoon /fe**stoon**/ > *noun* 1 an ornamental chain or garland of flowers, leaves, or ribbons, hung in a curve. 2 a carved or moulded ornament representing this. > *verb* adorn with festoons or other decorations.

ORIGIN – Italian *festone* 'festal ornament'.

Festschrift /**fest**shrift/ > *noun* (pl. **Festschriften** or **Festschrifts**) a collection of writings published in honour of a scholar.

ORIGIN – German, from *Fest* 'celebration' + *Schrift* 'writing'.

feta /**fet**ə/ > *noun* a white salty Greek cheese made from the milk of ewes or goats.

ORIGIN – modern Greek *pheta*.

fetal /**fee**t'l/ (Brit. (in non-technical use) also **foetal**) > *adjective* 1 relating to a fetus. 2 referring to a posture characteristic of a fetus, with the limbs folded in front of the body.

fetch > *verb* 1 go for and bring back. 2 cause to come to a place. 3 achieve (a particular price) when sold. 4 informal inflict (a blow) on (someone). 5 (**fetch up**) informal arrive or come to rest. 6 archaic bring forth (blood or tears).

SYNONYMS – 1 collect, get, go for, pick up, summon. 3 bring in, raise, sell for, realise, yield.

fetching > *adjective* attractive.

DERIVATIVES – **fetchingly** *adverb*.

fête /fayt/ > *noun* 1 Brit. an outdoor public function to raise funds for a charity or institution, typically involving entertainment and the sale of goods. 2 chiefly N. Amer. a celebration or festival. > *verb* honour or entertain lavishly.

ORIGIN – French, from Latin *festus* 'joyous'.

fetid /**fett**id, **fee**tid/ (also **foetid**) > *adjective* smelling unpleasant.

SYNONYMS – acrid, foul, rank, smelly, stinking.

ANTONYMS – fragrant.

ORIGIN – Latin *fetidus*, from *fetere* 'to stink'.

fetish > *noun* 1 an inanimate object worshipped for its supposed magical powers. 2 an abnormal form of sexual desire in which gratification is linked to a particular object, part of the body, or activity. 3 a course of action to which one has an excessive and irrational commitment.

DERIVATIVES – **fetishism** *noun* **fetishist** *noun* **fetishistic** *adjective*.

ORIGIN – Portuguese *feitiço* 'charm, sorcery'.

fetishise (also **fetishize**) > *verb* worship or treat (something) as a fetish.

DERIVATIVES – **fetishisation** *noun*.

fetlock > *noun* a joint of a horse's leg between the knee and the hoof.

fetter > *noun* 1 a chain or shackle placed around a prisoner's ankles. 2 a restraint or check. > *verb* 1 restrain with fetters. 2 (**be fettered**) be restricted.

fettle > *noun* condition: *in fine fettle*.

fettuccine /fettoo**chee**ni/ (also **fettucini**) > *plural noun* pasta made in ribbons.

ORIGIN – Italian, 'little ribbons', from *fetta* 'ribbon'.

fetus /**fee**təss/ (Brit. (in non-technical use) also **foetus**) > *noun* (pl. **fetuses**) an unborn or unhatched offspring of a mammal, in particular an unborn human more than eight weeks after conception.

WORDFINDER – amniocentesis (*procedure to check for abnormalities in the fetus*), amniotic fluid (*fluid surrounding a fetus*), caul (*membrane enclosing a fetus*), fetal (*relating to a fetus*), placenta (*organ that nourishes the fetus*), umbilical cord (*cord attaching the fetus to the placenta*).

NOTE – the spelling **foetus** has no etymological basis but is recorded from the 16th century and until recently was the standard British spelling; in technical usage **fetus** is the standard spelling throughout the English-speaking world.

ORIGIN – Latin, 'pregnancy, childbirth, offspring'.

feud /fyood/ > *noun* 1 a prolonged and bitter quarrel or dispute. 2 a state of prolonged mutual hostility. > *verb* take part in a feud.

SYNONYMS – *noun* conflict, dispute, quarrel, vendetta.

ORIGIN – Old French *feide* 'hostility'.

feudal > *adjective* of or relating to the system of feudalism.

ORIGIN – Latin *feudalis*, from *feodum* 'fee'.

feudalism > *noun* the dominant social system in medieval Europe, in which the nobility held lands from the Crown in exchange for military service, and vassals were tenants of and protected by the nobles.

feuilleton /**fö**itoN/ > *noun* a part of a newspaper or magazine devoted to fiction, criticism, or light literature.

ORIGIN – French, from *feuillet* 'small leaf'.

fever > *noun* 1 an abnormally high body temperature, usually accompanied by shivering, headache, and in severe instances delirium. 2 a state of nervous excitement or agitation.

WORDFINDER – antipyretic (*used to prevent or reduce fever*), febrifuge (*medicine used to reduce fever*), febrile (*having or showing the symptoms of fever*).

COMBINATIONS – **fever pitch** a state of extreme excitement.

ORIGIN – Latin *febris*.

fevered > *adjective* 1 having or showing the symptoms of fever. 2 nervously excited or agitated.

feverfew > *noun* an aromatic plant with feathery leaves and daisy-like flowers, used as a herbal remedy for headaches.

ORIGIN – Latin *febrifuga*, from *febris* 'fever' + *fugare* 'drive away'.

feverish > *adjective* 1 having or showing the symptoms of a fever. 2 displaying a frenetic excitement or energy.

DERIVATIVES – **feverishly** *adverb*.

SYNONYMS – 2 frantic, frenetic, frenzied, manic, wild.

few > *determiner, pronoun, & adjective* 1 (**a few**) a small number of. 2 not many. > *plural noun* (**the few**) a select minority.

IDIOMS – **few and far between** scarce.

USAGE – use the comparative form **fewer** with plural nouns, as in *there are fewer people here today*; use **less** with nouns denoting things that cannot be counted, as in *there is less blossom on this tree*. The use of **less** with a plural noun (*less people*) is incorrect in standard English.

fey /fay/ > *adjective* 1 unworldly and vague. 2 having clairvoyant powers.

fez > *noun* (pl. **fezzes**) a flat-topped conical red hat, worn by men in some Muslim countries.
ORIGIN – Turkish, named after the city of *Fez* in Morocco.

ff > *abbreviation* Music fortissimo.

ff. > *abbreviation* **1** folios. **2** following pages.

fiancé /fionsay/ > *noun* (fem. **fiancée** pronunc. same) a person to whom another is engaged to be married.
ORIGIN – French, from *fiancer* 'betroth'.

fiasco /fiaskō/ > *noun* (pl. **fiascos**) a ludicrous or humiliating failure.

wordpower facts

Fiasco

Fiasco is an Italian word, meaning 'bottle' or 'flask', and it was briefly used in English in this sense (**flagon** and **flask** come from the same root, Latin *flaska*). However, **fiasco** was taken up more readily in English in the sense 'ludicrous or humiliating failure'; this came from the Italian phrase *far fiasco*, literally 'make a bottle', a phrase used figuratively in Italian theatre to mean 'fail in a performance'.

fiat /fīat/ > *noun* an official order or authorisation.
ORIGIN – Latin, 'let it be done', from *fieri* 'be done or made'.

fib > *noun* a trivial lie. > *verb* (**fibbed**, **fibbing**) tell a fib.
DERIVATIVES – **fibber** *noun*.
ORIGIN – perhaps from obsolete *fible-fable* 'nonsense', a reduplication of FABLE.

fiber etc. US spelling of FIBRE etc.

fibre (US **fiber**) > *noun* **1** a thread or filament from which a plant or animal tissue, mineral substance, or textile is formed. **2** a substance formed of fibres. **3** dietary material containing substances, especially cellulose, that are resistant to digestive enzymes. **4** strength of character: *moral fibre*.
COMBINATIONS – **fibreboard** a building material made of wood or other plant fibres compressed into boards. **fibrescope** a fibre-optic device for viewing inaccessible internal structures, especially in the human body.
ORIGIN – Latin *fibra* 'fibre, entrails'.

fibreglass (US **fiberglass**) > *noun* **1** a reinforced plastic material composed of glass fibres embedded in a resin matrix. **2** a textile fabric made from woven glass filaments.

fibre optics > *plural noun* (treated as sing.) the use of thin flexible transparent fibres to transmit light signals, chiefly for telecommunications or for internal inspection of the body.
DERIVATIVES – **fibre-optic** *adjective*.

fibril /fībril/ > *noun* technical a small or slender fibre.
DERIVATIVES – **fibrillar** *adjective* **fibrillary** *adjective*.
ORIGIN – Latin *fibrilla*, from *fibra* 'fibre, entrails'.

fibrillate /fibrilayt, fī-/ > *verb* (of a muscle, especially in the heart) make a quivering movement due to uncoordinated contraction of the individual fibrils.
DERIVATIVES – **fibrillation** *noun*.

fibrin /fībrin/ > *noun* Biochemistry an insoluble protein formed as a mesh of fibres during the clotting of blood.
DERIVATIVES – **fibrinoid** *adjective* **fibrinous** *adjective*.

fibroblast /fībrōblast/ > *noun* Physiology a cell in connective tissue which produces collagen and other fibres.

fibroid > *adjective* referring to fibres or fibrous tissue. > *noun* Medicine a benign tumour of muscular and fibrous tissues, typically developing in the wall of the womb.

fibrosis /fībrōsiss/ > *noun* Medicine the thickening and scarring of connective tissue, usually as a result of injury.
DERIVATIVES – **fibrotic** *adjective*.

fibrous /fībrəss/ > *adjective* consisting of or characterised by fibres.

fibula /fibyoolə/ > *noun* (pl. **fibulae** /fibyoolee/ or **fibulas**) Anatomy the outer and usually smaller of the two bones between the knee and the ankle, parallel with the tibia.
ORIGIN – Latin, 'brooch', because the shape it makes with the tibia resembles a clasp.

-fic (usu. as **-ific**) > *suffix* (forming adjectives) producing; making: *prolific*.
DERIVATIVES – **-fically** *suffix*.
ORIGIN – Latin *-ficus*, from *facere* 'do, make'.

fickle > *adjective* changeable, especially as regards one's loyalties.
DERIVATIVES – **fickleness** *noun*.
SYNONYMS – capricious, changeable, mercurial, unreliable, variable, volatile.
ANTONYMS – constant, steady.
ORIGIN – Old English, 'deceitful'.

fiction > *noun* **1** prose literature, especially novels, describing imaginary events and people. **2** invention as opposed to fact. **3** a false belief or statement, accepted as true as an expedient.
DERIVATIVES – **fictional** *adjective* **fictionalise** (also **fictionalize**) *verb* **fictionality** *noun* **fictionally** *adverb*
SYNONYMS – **2** fabrication, falsehood, invention, lies, untruth.
ANTONYMS – **2** fact, truth.

wordpower facts

Fiction

The word **fiction** comes from the Latin verb *fingere*, meaning 'to form' or 'to contrive'. This Latin word is the root from which a number of other words are derived, including **effigy**, **faint**, **feign**, and **figment**.

fictitious /fiktishəss/ > *adjective* **1** not real or true, being imaginary or invented. **2** (of characters and events) found in fiction.
SYNONYMS – fabricated, fictional, imaginary, invented, made up.
ANTONYMS – factual, genuine, real.

fictive > *adjective* creating or created by imagination.

ficus /feekəss/ > *noun* (pl. same) a tropical tree, shrub, or climber belonging to a genus that includes the figs and the rubber plant.
ORIGIN – Latin, 'fig, fig tree'.

fiddle > *noun* informal **1** a violin. **2** chiefly Brit. an act of fraud or cheating. **3** an excessively intricate or awkward task. > *verb* **1** touch or fidget with something restlessly or nervously. **2** informal, chiefly Brit. falsify (figures, data, or records).
IDIOMS – **fiddle while Rome burns** be concerned with trivial matters while ignoring the serious events going on around one. [ORIGIN – with reference to the story of the Emperor Nero fiddling during the great fire in Rome in 64 AD; in contemporary accounts, he sang an aria in full costume, celebrating the beauty of the flames.] **fit as a fiddle** in very good health. **play second fiddle to** take a subordinate role to.
DERIVATIVES – **fiddler** *noun*.
SYNONYMS – *verb* **1** fidget, mess about, play, toy.
ORIGIN – from Latin *vitulari* 'celebrate a festival'.

fiddle-de-dee > *noun* dated nonsense.

fiddle-faddle > *noun* trivial matters; nonsense.

fiddlesticks > *exclamation* informal nonsense!

fiddling > *adjective* informal annoyingly trivial.

fiddly > *adjective* (**fiddlier**, **fiddliest**) Brit. informal complicated and awkward to do or use.

fideism /fīdi-iz'm/ > *noun* the doctrine that knowledge depends on faith or revelation.
ORIGIN – from Latin *fides* 'faith'.

fidelity /fidelliti/ > *noun* **1** continuing faithfulness to a person, cause, or belief. **2** the degree of exactness with which something is copied or reproduced.
SYNONYMS – **1** constancy, commitment, devotion, faithfulness, loyalty.
ANTONYMS – **1** infidelity, unfaithfulness.

wordpower facts
Fidelity
The words **faith** and **fidelity** come from the Latin word meaning 'faith', *fides. Fides* is the root of a number of related words: **fiancé** (which comes via Old French *fiance* 'a promise', from Latin *fidere* 'to trust'), **infidel**, and **perfidy** (in which *per-* means 'to ill effect').

fidget /ˈfijit/ > *verb* (**fidgeted, fidgeting**) make many small movements through nervousness or impatience. > *noun* 1 a person who fidgets. 2 (**fidgets**) mental or physical restlessness.
DERIVATIVES – **fidgety** *adjective*.
SYNONYMS – *verb* fiddle, jiggle, squirm, twitch, wriggle.
ORIGIN – from obsolete or dialect *fidge* 'to twitch'.

fiducial /fiˈdyo͞osh'l/ > *adjective* technical (of a point or line) used as a fixed basis of comparison.
ORIGIN – from Latin *fiducia* 'trust, confidence'.

fiduciary /fiˈdyo͞oshəri/ > *adjective* Law involving trust, especially with regard to the relationship between a trustee and a beneficiary. > *noun* (pl. **fiduciaries**) a trustee.

fie /fī/ > *exclamation* archaic used to express disgust or outrage.

fief /feef/ > *noun* 1 historical an estate of land held on condition of feudal service. 2 a person's sphere of operation or control.
DERIVATIVES – **fiefdom** *noun*.
ORIGIN – Old French, variant of *feu* 'fee'.

field > *noun* 1 an area of open land, especially one planted with crops or pasture. 2 a piece of land used for a sport or game. 3 a subject of study or sphere of activity. 4 a region or space with a particular property: *a magnetic field.* 5 (**the field**) all the participants in a contest or sport. 6 archaic a battle: *Bosworth Field.* > *verb* 1 chiefly Cricket & Baseball attempt to catch or stop the ball and return it after it has been hit. 2 select (someone) to play in a game or to stand in an election. 3 try to deal with (a question, problem, etc.). > *adjective* 1 carried out or working in the natural environment, rather than in a laboratory or office. 2 (of military equipment) light and mobile for use on campaign.
IDIOMS – **in the field** 1 engaged in combat or manoeuvres. 2 engaged in fieldwork. **play the field** informal indulge in a series of casual sexual relationships. **take the field** go on to a field to begin a game.
SYNONYMS – *noun* 1 meadow, pasture. 2 arena, ground, pitch, stadium. 3 area, department, domain, province, sphere.
COMBINATIONS – **fieldcraft** the techniques involved in living in or making military or scientific observations in the field. **field day** an opportunity for action or success, especially at the expense of others. **field events** athletic sports other than races, such as throwing and jumping events. **field glasses** binoculars for outdoor use. **field hockey** hockey played on grass or a hard pitch, as opposed to ice hockey. **field hospital** a temporary hospital set up near a battlefield. **field marshal** the highest rank of officer in the British army. **field mouse** a common dark brown mouse with a long tail and large eyes. **field mushroom** the common edible mushroom. **field officer** a major, lieutenant colonel, or colonel. **field sports** outdoor sports, especially hunting, shooting, and fishing. **fieldstone** stone used in its natural form.

fielder > *noun* chiefly Cricket & Baseball a player on the fielding team, especially one other than the bowler or pitcher.

fieldfare > *noun* a large grey-headed northern thrush.
ORIGIN – probably from *fare* 'to travel'.

field test > *noun* (also **field trial**) a test carried out in the environment in which a product is to be used. > *verb* (**field-test**) test in such a way.

fieldwork > *noun* practical work conducted by a researcher in the field.

fiend /feend/ > *noun* 1 an evil spirit or demon. 2 a very wicked or cruel person. 3 informal an enthusiast or devotee: *an exercise fiend.*
ORIGIN – Old English, 'an enemy, the devil'.

fiendish > *adjective* 1 extremely cruel or unpleasant. 2 extremely difficult.
DERIVATIVES – **fiendishly** *adverb* **fiendishness** *noun.*
SYNONYMS – 1 cruel, diabolical, evil, wicked. 2 complex, devilish, thorny, ticklish.

fierce > *adjective* 1 intensely aggressive and uncontrolled; ferocious. 2 intense: *fierce opposition.* 3 (of a mechanism) having a powerful abruptness of action.
DERIVATIVES – **fiercely** *adverb* **fierceness** *noun.*
SYNONYMS – 1 ferocious, savage, vicious, wild.
ANTONYMS – 1 gentle, mild.
ORIGIN – Latin *ferus* 'untamed'.

fiery > *adjective* (**fierier, fieriest**) 1 resembling or consisting of fire. 2 quick-tempered or passionate.
DERIVATIVES – **fierily** *adverb* **fieriness** *noun.*
SYNONYMS – 1 blazing, burning, flaming, incandescent, red-hot. 2 ardent, fervent, passionate, spirited, volatile.

fiesta /fiˈestə/ > *noun* 1 (in Spanish-speaking countries) a religious festival. 2 a festive occasion.
ORIGIN – Spanish, from Latin *festum* 'feast'.

FIFA /ˈfeefə/ > *abbreviation* Fédération Internationale de Football Association, the international governing body of soccer.

fife > *noun* a small, shrill flute used with the drum in military bands.
ORIGIN – German *Pfeife* 'pipe'.

fifteen > *cardinal number* 1 one more than fourteen; 15. (Roman numeral: **xv** or **XV**.) 2 a team of fifteen players, especially in rugby union.
DERIVATIVES – **fifteenth** *ordinal number.*

fifth > *ordinal number* 1 constituting number five in a sequence; 5th. 2 (**a fifth** or **one fifth**) each of five equal parts into which something is or may be divided. 3 Music an interval spanning five consecutive notes in a diatonic scale, in particular (also **perfect fifth**) an interval of three tones and a semitone.
IDIOMS – **take the fifth** informal (in the US) exercise the right guaranteed by the Fifth Amendment to the Constitution to refuse to answer questions in order to avoid incriminating oneself.
DERIVATIVES – **fifthly** *adverb.*

fifth column > *noun* a group within a country at war who are working for its enemies.
DERIVATIVES – **fifth columnist** *noun.*
ORIGIN – from a reported incident in the Spanish Civil War, when General Mola, leading four columns of troops towards Madrid, declared that he had a fifth column inside the city.

fifty > *cardinal number* (pl. **fifties**) ten less than sixty; 50. (Roman numeral: **l** or **L**.)
WORDFINDER – quinquagenarian (*person aged 50–59*).
DERIVATIVES – **fiftieth** *ordinal number.*
COMBINATIONS – **fifty-fifty** with equal shares or chances.

fig[1] > *noun* 1 a soft pear-shaped fruit with sweet, dark flesh and many small seeds. 2 the tree or shrub which produces this fruit.
IDIOMS – **not give** (or **care**) **a fig** not care at all.
COMBINATIONS – **fig leaf** a leaf of a fig tree used to conceal the genitals in paintings and sculpture. [ORIGIN – with reference to the story of Adam and Eve in the Bible, who made clothes out of fig leaves after becoming aware of their nakedness.]
ORIGIN – Old French *figue*, from Latin *ficus.*

fig[2] > *noun* (in phrase **full fig**) informal the complete set of clothes appropriate to a particular occasion or profession.

ORIGIN – from the obsolete verb *feague* 'liven up', literally 'whip'.

fight > *verb* (past and past participle **fought**) **1** take part in a violent struggle involving physical force or weapons. **2** engage in (a war or contest). **3** quarrel or argue. **4** (**fight off**) defend oneself against an attack by. **5** struggle to overcome, eliminate, or prevent. **6** (**fight for**) try very hard to obtain or do. > *noun* an act of fighting.

IDIOMS – **fight fire with fire** use the weapons or tactics of one's opponent, even if one finds them distasteful. **fight one's way** move forward with difficulty. **fight or flight** the instinctive physiological response to a threatening situation, which readies one either to resist forcibly or to run away. **fight shy of** avoid through unwillingness.

SYNONYMS – *verb* **1** battle, contend, engage, struggle. **2** conduct, engage in, prosecute, pursue, wage. **5** challenge, combat, contest, dispute, oppose. *noun* altercation, battle, clash, fracas, struggle, tussle.

COMBINATIONS – **fighting chance** a possibility of success if great effort is made. **fighting fit** in excellent health.

fightback > *noun* Brit. a rally or recovery.

fighter > *noun* **1** a person or animal that fights. **2** a fast military aircraft designed for attacking other aircraft.

figment /**fig**mənt/ > *noun* a thing believed to be real but existing only in the imagination.

ORIGIN – Latin *figmentum*, related to *fingere* 'form, contrive'.

figural /**fig**yoorəl/ > *adjective* another term for FIGURATIVE.

figuration /figgə**ray**shʹn/ > *noun* **1** ornamentation using figures. **2** Music use of elaborate counterpoint. **3** representation by allegory.

figurative > *adjective* **1** not using words literally; metaphorical. **2** Art representing forms that are recognisably derived from life.

DERIVATIVES – **figuratively** *adverb* **figurativeness** *noun*.

figure > *noun* **1** a number or numerical symbol. **2** an amount of money. **3** a person's bodily shape, especially that of a woman. **4** a person seen indistinctly. **5** an artistic representation of a human or animal form. **6** a shape defined by one or more lines. **7** a diagram or illustrative drawing. **8** Music a short succession of notes producing a single impression. > *verb* **1** be a significant part of or contributor to something. **2** calculate arithmetically. **3** (**figure out**) informal reach an understanding of. **4** informal, chiefly N. Amer. be perfectly understandable: *that figures!* **4** (**figure on**) N. Amer. informal count or rely on something happening or being the case. **5** informal, chiefly N. Amer. think; consider. **6** represent in a diagram or picture.

WORDFINDER – *plane figures:* triangle (*three sides*), quadrilateral (*four*), pentagon (*five*), hexagon (*six*), heptagon (*seven*), octagon (*eight*), nonagon (*nine*), decagon (*ten*), hendecagon (*eleven*), dodecagon (*twelve*).

SYNONYMS – *noun* **1** digit, integer, number, numeral; dated cipher. **2** amount, cost, price, quantity, value. **3** body, build, form, frame, physique, shape. **4** form, outline, shape, silhouette.

COMBINATIONS – **figure skating** the sport of skating in prescribed patterns from a stationary position.

ORIGIN – Latin *figura* 'figure, form'.

figurehead > *noun* **1** a carved bust or full-length figure set at the prow of an old-fashioned sailing ship. **2** a nominal leader without real power.

figure of speech > *noun* a word or phrase used in a non-literal sense for rhetorical or vivid effect.

WORDFINDER – hysteron proton, oxymoron, simile, syllepsis, synecdoche, zeugma (*figures of speech*).

figurine /**fig**yooreen/ > *noun* a small statue of a human form.

Fijian /fee**jee**ən/ > *noun* a person from Fiji, a country in the South Pacific consisting of some 840 islands. > *adjective* relating to Fiji.

filagree > *noun* variant spelling of FILIGREE.

filament /**fill**əmənt/ > *noun* **1** a slender thread-like object or fibre. **2** a metal wire in an electric light bulb, which glows white-hot when an electric current is passed through it. **3** Botany the slender part of a stamen that supports the anther.

DERIVATIVES – **filamentary** *adjective* **filamentous** *adjective*.

wordpower facts

Filament

The word **filament** comes from the Latin verb *filare*, meaning 'to spin', from *filum* 'a thread'. *Filum* is the common root from which a number of English words are derived, including **file**, **filigree**, **fillet**, and **profile**.

filariasis /filairi**ay**siss, fillə**rī**əsiss/ > *noun* a disease caused by infestation with parasitic nematode worms, transmitted by biting flies and mosquitoes in the tropics.

ORIGIN – from Latin *Filaria*, former name of a genus of nematodes, from *filum* 'thread'.

filbert > *noun* a cultivated oval hazelnut.

ORIGIN – from French *noix de filbert* (so named because it is ripe about 20 August, the feast day of St *Philibert*).

filch > *verb* informal pilfer; steal.

file¹ > *noun* **1** a folder or box for keeping loose papers together and in order. **2** Computing a collection of data or programs stored under a single identifying name. **3** a line of people or things one behind another. **4** Military a small detachment of men. **5** Chess a row of squares on a chessboard running away from the player toward the opponent. Compare with RANK¹. > *verb* **1** place (a document) in a file for preservation and easy reference. **2** submit (a legal document, application, or charge) to be officially placed on record. **3** walk one behind the other.

DERIVATIVES – **filing** *noun*.

COMBINATIONS – **filing cabinet** a large piece of office furniture with deep drawers for storing files.

ORIGIN – French *fil* 'a thread', from Latin *filum*.

file² > *noun* a tool with a roughened surface or surfaces, used for smoothing or shaping a hard material. > *verb* smooth or shape with a file.

filet mignon /feelay **meen**yoN/ > *noun* a small, tender piece of beef from the end of the undercut.

ORIGIN – French, 'dainty fillet'.

filial /**fill**iəl/ > *adjective* relating to or due from a son or daughter.

DERIVATIVES – **filially** *adverb*.

ORIGIN – Latin *filialis*, from *filius* 'son', *filia* 'daughter'.

filibuster /**fill**ibustər/ > *noun* prolonged speaking which obstructs progress in a legislative assembly. > *verb* obstruct legislation with a filibuster.

wordpower facts

Filibuster

The word **filibuster** entered English from French in the 18th century, in the form *flibustier*. It came ultimately from the Dutch *vrijbuiter* 'freebooter', and referred specifically to pirates who pillaged the Spanish colonies in the West Indies. In the middle of the 19th century, influenced by Spanish *filibustero*, it was applied to a number of American adventurers who travelled from the US to incite revolution in Latin America. It then broadened in sense, coming to mean someone who engages in unauthorised warfare against foreign states, and then someone who obstructs progress in a legislative assembly, hence the modern meaning.

filicide /**fill**isīd/ > *noun* **1** the killing of one's son or daughter. **2** a person who does this.

ORIGIN – from Latin *filius* 'son', *filia* 'daughter'.

filigree /filligree/ (also **filagree**) > *noun* delicate ornamental work of fine gold, silver, or copper wire.

DERIVATIVES – **filigreed** *adjective*.

ORIGIN – from Latin *filum* 'thread' + *granum* 'seed'.

filings > *plural noun* small particles rubbed off by a file.

Filipino /fillipeenō/ > *noun* (pl. **Filipinos**; fem. **Filipina**, pl. **Filipinas**) 1 a person from the Philippines. 2 the national language of the Philippines. > *adjective* relating to the Philippines or their language.

ORIGIN – Spanish, from *las Islas Filipinas* 'the Philippine Islands'.

fill > *verb* 1 make or become full. 2 block up (a hole, gap, etc.). 3 appoint a person to hold (a vacant post). 4 hold and perform the duties of (a position or role). 5 occupy (time). > *noun* (**one's fill**) as much as one wants or can bear.

IDIOMS – **fill in** 1 make (a hole) completely full of material. 2 complete (a form) by adding information. 3 inform (someone) more fully of a matter. 4 act as a substitute. **fill out** 1 put on weight. 2 chiefly N. Amer. fill in (a form). **fill someone's shoes** (or **boots**) informal take over someone's role and fulfil it satisfactorily.

SYNONYMS – *verb* 1 charge, load, pack, top up. 2 block up, close, plug, seal, stop. 4 hold, occupy.

ANTONYMS – *verb* 1 empty.

COMBINATIONS – **filling station** a petrol station.

filler[1] > *noun* 1 something used to fill a gap or cavity, or to increase bulk. 2 an item serving only to fill space or time.

COMBINATIONS – **filler cap** a cap closing the pipe leading to the petrol tank of a motor vehicle.

filler[2] /filör/ > *noun* (pl. same) a monetary unit of Hungary, equal to one hundredth of a forint.

ORIGIN – Hungarian.

fillet > *noun* 1 a fleshy boneless piece of meat from near the loins or the ribs of an animal. 2 a boned side of a fish. 3 a band or ribbon binding the hair. 4 Architecture a narrow flat band separating two mouldings. > *verb* (**filleted**, **filleting**) 1 remove the bones from (a fish). 2 cut into fillets.

ORIGIN – Old French *filet* 'thread', from Latin *filum*.

filling > *noun* 1 a quantity or piece of material that fills or is used to fill something. 2 a piece of material used to fill a cavity in a tooth. > *adjective* (of food) leaving one with a pleasantly satiated feeling.

fillip /fillip/ > *noun* a stimulus or boost.

ORIGIN – from an archaic sense of the word meaning 'a flick with the fingers'.

filly > *noun* (pl. **fillies**) 1 a young female horse, especially one less than four years old. 2 humorous a lively girl or young woman.

ORIGIN – Old Norse, related to FOAL.

film > *noun* 1 a thin flexible strip of plastic or other material coated with light-sensitive emulsion for exposure in a camera. 2 a story or event recorded by a camera as a series of moving images and shown in a cinema or on television. 3 motion pictures considered as an art or industry. 4 material in the form of a very thin flexible sheet. 5 a thin layer covering a surface. > *verb* 1 make a film of; record on film. 2 become covered with a thin film.

SYNONYMS – *noun* 2 movie, picture, programme. 5 blanket, coat, dusting, layer, patina, skin. *verb* 1 photograph, record, shoot.

COMBINATIONS – **film star** a well-known film actor or actress. **filmstrip** a series of transparencies in a strip for projection.

ORIGIN – Old English, 'membrane'.

filmic > *adjective* of or relating to films or cinematography.

film noir /film **nwaar**/ > *noun* a style of film marked by a mood of pessimism, fatalism, and menace.

ORIGIN – French, 'black film'.

filmography > *noun* (pl. **filmographies**) a list of films by one director or actor, or on one subject.

filmy > *adjective* (**filmier**, **filmiest**) 1 thin and translucent. 2 covered with a thin film.

DERIVATIVES – **filminess** *noun*.

filo /feelō/ (also **phyllo**) > *noun* a kind of flaky pastry stretched into very thin sheets, used in eastern Mediterranean cookery.

ORIGIN – Modern Greek *phullo* 'leaf'.

Filofax /fīlōfaks/ > *noun* trademark a loose-leaf notebook for recording appointments, addresses, and notes.

fils[1] /feess/ > *noun* used after a surname to distinguish a son from a father of the same name.

ORIGIN – French, 'son'.

fils[2] /filss/ > *noun* (pl. same) a monetary unit of Iraq, Bahrain, Jordan, Kuwait, and Yemen, equal to one hundredth of a riyal in Yemen and one thousandth of a dinar elsewhere.

ORIGIN – from an Arabic word denoting a small copper coin.

filter > *noun* 1 a porous device for removing solid particles from a liquid or gas passed through it. 2 a screen, plate, or layer which absorbs some of the light passing through it. 3 Brit. an arrangement at a junction whereby vehicles may turn while traffic waiting to go straight ahead is stopped by a red light. > *verb* 1 pass through a filter. 2 (often **filter in** or **out** or **through**) move gradually through something or in a specified direction. 3 (of information) gradually become known.

DERIVATIVES – **filterable** *adjective* **filtration** *noun*.

SYNONYMS – *verb* 1 clarify, purify, sieve, sift, strain.

COMBINATIONS – **filter-feeder** an aquatic animal which feeds by filtering out plankton or nutrients suspended in the water. **filter tip** a filter attached to a cigarette for removing impurities from the inhaled smoke.

ORIGIN – Latin *filtrum* 'felt used as a filter'.

filth > *noun* 1 disgusting dirt. 2 obscene and offensive language or printed material. 3 (**the filth**) Brit. informal, derogatory the police.

SYNONYMS – 1 dirt, grime, muck, mud, ordure. 2 pornography, smut, vice.

ORIGIN – Old English, related to FOUL.

filthy > *adjective* (**filthier**, **filthiest**) 1 disgustingly dirty. 2 obscene and offensive. 3 informal very unpleasant or disagreeable: *filthy weather*. > *adverb* informal extremely: *filthy rich*.

DERIVATIVES – **filthily** *adverb* **filthiness** *noun*.

SYNONYMS – *adjective* 1 dirty, foul, grimy, mucky, squalid. 2 dirty, indecent, mucky, obscene, pornographic, rude.

ANTONYMS – clean; spotless, wholesome.

filtrate > *noun* a liquid which has passed through a filter.

fin > *noun* 1 an external organ on the body of a fish or other aquatic animal, used for propelling, steering, and balancing. 2 an underwater swimmer's flipper. 3 a projection on an aircraft, rocket, or car, for providing aerodynamic stability.

WORDFINDER – *types of fish fins:* adipose, anal, dorsal, pectoral, pelvic or ventral, tail or caudal, vertical.

DERIVATIVES – **finned** *adjective*.

finagle /finayg'l/ > *verb* N. Amer. informal obtain or act dishonestly or deviously.

ORIGIN – from dialect *fainaigue* 'cheat'.

final > *adjective* 1 coming at the end of a series. 2 reached as the outcome of a process. 3 allowing no further doubt or dispute. > *noun* 1 the last game in a tournament, which will decide the overall winner. 2 (**finals**) a series of games in the last stage of a competition. 3 (**finals**) Brit. a series of examinations at the end of a degree course.

SYNONYMS – *adjective* 1 closing, concluding, culminating, eventual, last, ultimate. 3 absolute, binding, conclusive, definitive, irrevocable, settled.

ANTONYMS – *adjective* 1 first, initial. 3 provisional.

COMBINATIONS – **final solution** the Nazi policy (1941–5) of exterminating Jews.

ORIGIN – Latin *finalis*, from *finis* 'end'.

finale /finaali/ > *noun* the last part of a piece of music, an entertainment, or a public event.

SYNONYMS – climax, culmination, ending, finish.

ORIGIN – Italian.

finalise (also **finalize**) > *verb* **1** complete (a transaction) after discussion of the terms. **2** produce or agree on a finished version of.

DERIVATIVES – **finalisation** *noun*.

finalist > *noun* **1** a participant in a final or finals. **2** a student taking finals.

finality > *noun* **1** the fact or quality of being complete or conclusive. **2** a tone or manner which indicates that no further comment or argument is possible.

finally > *adverb* **1** after a long time and much difficulty or delay. **2** as a final point or reason.

finance /fīnanss, fīnans/ > *noun* **1** the management of large amounts of money, especially by governments or large companies. **2** monetary support for an enterprise. **3** (**finances**) monetary resources. > *verb* provide funding for.

SYNONYMS – *noun* **3** (**finances**) assets, capital, funds, money, resources. *verb* back, fund, pay for, sponsor, underwrite.

COMBINATIONS – **finance company** (also **finance house**) a company concerned primarily with providing money, e.g. for hire-purchase transactions.

ORIGIN – Old French, from *finer* 'settle a debt'.

financial > *adjective* **1** relating to finance. **2** Austral./NZ informal possessing money.

DERIVATIVES – **financially** *adverb*.

COMBINATIONS – **financial year** a year as reckoned for taxing or accounting purposes, especially the British tax year reckoned from 6 April.

financier /fīnansiər/ > *noun* a person engaged in managing the finances of governments or other large organisations.

finch > *noun* a seed-eating songbird of a large group including the chaffinch, goldfinch, linnet, etc.

find > *verb* (past and past participle **found**) **1** discover by chance or deliberately. **2** (often **be found**) recognise or discover to be present or to be the case. **3** ascertain by research or calculation. **4** Law (of a court) officially declare to be the case. **5** (**find against** or **for**) Law (of a court) make a decision against (or in favour of). **6** reach or arrive at by a natural or normal process. > *noun* a valuable or interesting discovery.

IDIOMS – **find out 1** discover (information, a fact, etc). **2** detect (someone) in a crime or lie. **find one's feet** establish oneself in a particular field.

SYNONYMS – *verb* **1** come across, discover, happen on, light on, unearth. **2** (**be found**) appear, exist, occur, be present.

finder > *noun* **1** a person that finds someone or something. **2** a small telescope attached to a large one to locate an object for observation. **3** a viewfinder.

IDIOMS – **finders keepers** (**losers weepers**) informal whoever finds something is entitled to keep it.

fin de siècle /faN də syeklə/ > *adjective* relating to or characteristic of the end of a century, especially the 19th century.

ORIGIN – French, 'end of century'.

finding > *noun* a conclusion reached as a result of an inquiry, investigation, or trial.

fine¹ > *adjective* **1** of very high quality. **2** satisfactory. **3** in good health and feeling well. **4** (of the weather) bright and clear. **5** (of threads, particles, material, etc.) very thin, small, or light. **6** of delicate or intricate workmanship. **7** (of speech or writing) impressive but ultimately insincere: *fine words.* **8** subtle and hard to grasp: *fine distinctions.* > *adverb* informal in a satisfactory or pleasing manner. > *verb* **1** clarify (beer or wine) by causing the precipitation of sediment. **2** (usu. **fine down**) make thinner.

IDIOMS – **cut it fine** allow a very small margin of time. **fine feathers make fine birds** proverb beautiful clothes or an eye-catching appearance make a person appear similarly beautiful or impressive. **one's finest hour** the time of one's greatest success. **fine words butter no parsnips** proverb nothing is achieved by empty promises or flattery. **have something down to a fine art** achieve a high level of skill in something through experience. **not to put too fine a point on it** to speak bluntly. **one fine day** at some unspecified time.

DERIVATIVES – **finely** *adverb* **fineness** *noun.*

SYNONYMS – *adjective* **1** excellent, exceptional, first-class, outstanding, select, superior. **4** bright, clement, dry, fair, sunny. **6** delicate, detailed, dainty, intricate, ornate. **8** abstruse, minute, nice, subtle.

ANTONYMS – *adjective* **1** poor. **4** inclement, wet. **6** coarse.

COMBINATIONS – **fine art** art intended to be appreciated primarily or solely for its aesthetic content. **fine print** small print. **fine-spun** (especially of fabric) fine or delicate in texture.

ORIGIN – Old French *fin*, from Latin *finire* 'finish'.

fine² > *noun* a sum of money exacted as a penalty by a court of law or other authority. > *verb* punish by a fine.

ORIGIN – Latin *finis* 'end'.

finery /fīnəri/ > *noun* showy clothes or decoration.

fines herbes /feenz airb/ > *plural noun* mixed herbs used in cooking.

ORIGIN – French, 'fine herbs'.

finesse /finess/ > *noun* **1** refinement and delicacy. **2** subtle skill in handling or manipulating people or situations. **3** (in bridge and whist) an attempt to win a trick with a card that is not a certain winner. > *verb* **1** do in a subtle and delicate manner. **2** slyly attempt to avoid blame when dealing with (a situation). **3** play (a card) as a finesse.

SYNONYMS – *noun* **1** flair, refinement, skill, subtlety. **2** delicacy, discretion, subtlety, tact.

ORIGIN – French.

fine-tooth comb (also **fine-toothed comb**) > *noun* (in phrase **with a fine-tooth comb**) with a very thorough search or analysis. Compare with TOOTHCOMB.

fine-tune > *verb* make small adjustments to (something) in order to achieve the best performance.

finger > *noun* **1** each of the four slender jointed parts attached to either hand (or five, if the thumb is included). **2** a measure of liquor in a glass, based on the breadth of a finger. **3** an object with the long, narrow shape of a finger. > *verb* **1** touch or feel with the fingers. **2** Music play (a passage) with a particular sequence of positions of the fingers. **3** informal, chiefly N. Amer. inform on (someone).

WORDFINDER – digital (*relating to a finger or fingers*), lunula (*white area at the base of a fingernail*), polydactyly (*condition of having more than five fingers on one, or each, hand*).

IDIOMS – **be all fingers and thumbs** Brit. informal be clumsy. **burn one's fingers** suffer unpleasant consequences as a result of one's actions. **have a finger in the pie** be involved in a matter. **have one's finger on the pulse** be aware of the latest trends. **lay a finger on** touch (someone), especially with the intention of harming them. **pull one's finger out** Brit. informal cease prevaricating and start to act. **put one's finger on** identify exactly. **snap** (or **click**) **one's fingers** make a sharp clicking sound by bending the middle finger against the thumb and suddenly releasing it.

COMBINATIONS – **fingerboard** a flat strip on the neck of a stringed instrument, against which the strings are pressed in order to vary the pitch. **finger bowl** a small bowl holding water for rinsing the fingers at a meal. **finger food** food that can conveniently be eaten with the fingers. **fingernail** the nail on the upper surface of the tip of each finger. **finger paint** thick paint applied with the fingers, used by young children. **fingerpick** play (a guitar or similar instrument) using the fingernails or plectrums worn on the fingertips. **fingerplate** a piece of metal or porcelain fixed to a door above the handle to prevent fingermarks on the door itself. **fingerpost** a post at a road junction from which signs project in the direction of the place indicated. **fingerstall** a cover to protect a finger.

fingering > *noun* a manner or technique of using the fingers to play a musical instrument.

fingerprint > *noun* a mark made on a surface by a person's fingertip, useful for purposes of identification. > *verb* record the fingerprints of.

fingertip > *adjective* using or operated by the fingers.

IDIOMS – **at one's fingertips** (especially of information) readily available.

finial /finnial/ > **1** *noun* a distinctive section or ornament at the highest point of a roof, pinnacle, or similar structure in a building. **2** an ornament at the top, end, or corner of an object.

ORIGIN – from Latin *finis* 'end'.

finical /finnik'l/ > *adjective* another term for FINICKY.

DERIVATIVES – **finically** *adverb*.

finicky > *adjective* **1** fussy. **2** excessively detailed or elaborate.

DERIVATIVES – **finickiness** *noun*.

fining > *noun* a substance used for clarifying beer or wine.

finis /feeniss/ > *noun* the end (printed at the end of a book or shown at the end of a film).

ORIGIN – Latin.

finish > *verb* **1** bring or come to an end. **2** consume or get through the whole or the remainder of (food or drink). **3** (**finish with**) have nothing more to do with. **4** reach the end of a race or other sporting competition. **5** (**finish up**) end by doing something or being in a particular position. **6** (**finish off**) kill or comprehensively defeat. **7** complete the manufacture or decoration of (something) by giving it an attractive surface appearance. > *noun* **1** an end or final stage. **2** the place at which a race or competition ends. **3** the manner in which a manufactured article is finished.

IDIOMS – **fight to the finish** a contest which ends only with the complete defeat of one of the participants.

DERIVATIVES – **finisher** *noun*.

SYNONYMS – *verb* **1** complete, conclude, end, terminate. *noun* **1** close, completion, conclusion, end, termination. **3** appearance, gloss, patina, surface, texture.

COMBINATIONS – **finishing school** a private college where girls are prepared for entry into fashionable society. **finishing touch** a final detail completing and enhancing a piece of work.

ORIGIN – Latin *finis* 'end'.

finite /fīnīt/ > *adjective* limited in size or extent.

DERIVATIVES – **finitely** *adverb* **finiteness** *noun*.

SYNONYMS – determinate, fixed, limited, restricted.

ANTONYMS – infinite.

finito /fineetō/ > *adjective* informal finished.

ORIGIN – Italian.

fink N. Amer. informal > *noun* **1** an unpleasant or contemptible person. **2** an informer. > *verb* **1** (**fink on**) inform on. **2** (**fink out**) back out of a responsibility.

Finn > *noun* a person from Finland.

finnan haddock /finnən/ > *noun* haddock cured with the smoke of green wood, turf, or peat.

ORIGIN – from the fishing village *Findon* near Aberdeen, but sometimes confused with the Scottish river and village of *Findhorn*.

Finnish > *noun* the language of the Finns. > *adjective* relating to the Finns or their language.

fino /feenō/ > *noun* (pl. **finos**) a light-coloured dry sherry.

ORIGIN – Spanish, 'fine'.

fiord > *noun* variant spelling of FJORD.

fir > *noun* an evergreen coniferous tree with upright cones and flat needle-shaped leaves.

fire > *noun* **1** the state of burning, in which substances combine chemically with oxygen from the air and give out bright light, heat, and smoke. **2** an instance of destructive burning. **3** a collection of fuel burnt in a hearth or stove for heating or cooking. **4** (also **electric fire** or **gas fire**) Brit. a domestic heating appliance that uses electricity (or gas) as fuel. **5** one of the four elements (air, earth, fire, and water) in ancient and medieval philosophy and in astrology. **6** a burning sensation. **7** passionate emotion or enthusiasm. **8** the firing of guns. **9** strong criticism. > *verb* **1** propel (a bullet or projectile) from a gun or other weapon. **2** direct a rapid succession of (questions or statements) towards someone. **3** informal dismiss from a job. **4** supply (a furnace, power station, etc.) with fuel. **5** set fire to. **6** stimulate (the imagination or an emotion). **7** (**fire up**) fill with enthusiasm. **8** bake or dry (pottery, bricks, etc.) in a kiln.

WORDFINDER – arson (*act of deliberately setting fire to property*), pyrogenic (*resulting from combustion or strong heat*), pyromania (*the obsessive desire to set fire to things*), pyrophoric (*liable to catch fire spontaneously*).

IDIOMS – **catch fire** begin to burn. **fire and brimstone** the supposed torments of hell. **fire away** informal go ahead. **firing on all cylinders** functioning at a peak level. **go through fire** (**and water**) face any peril. **on fire 1** burning. **2** very excited. **set fire to** (or **set on fire**) cause to burn. **set the world on fire** do something

remarkable or sensational. **under fire 1** being shot at. **2** being rigorously criticised.

SYNONYMS – *noun* **1** burning, combustion, flames. **2** blaze, conflagration, holocaust, inferno. **7** animation, dynamism, energy, passion, vigour. *verb* **1** discharge, launch, let off, shoot.

COMBINATIONS – **fire alarm** a device that makes a loud noise to give warning of a fire. **fire blanket** a sheet of flexible material used to smother a fire. **fireblight** a serious disease of fruit trees and other plants, which gives leaves a scorched appearance. **firebreak** an obstacle to the spread of fire, e.g. a strip of open space in a forest. **firebrick** a brick capable of withstanding intense heat, used especially to line furnaces and fireplaces. **fire brigade** chiefly Brit. an organised body of people trained and employed to extinguish fires. **firebug** informal an arsonist. **fireclay** clay capable of withstanding high temperatures, used for making firebricks. **firedamp** methane, especially as forming an explosive mixture with air in coal mines. **firedog** each of a pair of decorative metal supports for wood burning in a fireplace. **fire door** a fire-resistant door to prevent the spread of fire. **fire drill** a practice of the emergency procedures to be used in case of fire. **fire-eater** an entertainer who appears to eat fire. **fire engine** a vehicle carrying firefighters and their equipment. **fire escape** a staircase or other apparatus used for escaping from a building where there is a fire. **fire extinguisher** a portable device that discharges a jet of liquid, foam, or gas to extinguish a fire. **fireguard** a protective screen or grid placed in front of an open fire. **firehouse** N. Amer. a fire station. **fire irons** tongs, a poker, and a shovel for tending a domestic fire. **firelighter** Brit. a piece of flammable material used to help start a fire. **fireman** a male firefighter. **fireplace** a partially enclosed space at the base of a chimney for a domestic fire. **fire practice** Brit. a fire drill. **fire-raiser** Brit. an arsonist. **fire sale 1** a sale of goods remaining after a fire. **2** a sale of goods or assets at a very low price. **fire screen 1** a fireguard. **2** an ornamental screen placed in front of a fireplace when the fire is unlit. **fire station** the headquarters of a fire brigade. **firestorm** a very intense and destructive fire fanned by strong currents of air drawn in from the surrounding area. **firetrap** a building without proper provision for escape in case of fire. **firewater** informal strong alcoholic liquor. **fireweed** rosebay willowherb. [ORIGIN – so called from its tendency to grow on burnt land.] **firewood** wood that is burnt as fuel. **firing line 1** the front line of troops in a battle. **2** a position where one is subject to criticism or blame. **firing squad** a group of soldiers detailed to shoot a condemned person.

firearm > *noun* a rifle, pistol, or other portable gun.

fireball > *noun* **1** a ball of flame or fire. **2** a large, bright meteor. **3** an energetic or hot-tempered person.

firebomb > *noun* a bomb designed to cause a fire. > *verb* attack with a firebomb.

firebrand > *noun* a fervent supporter of a particular cause, especially one who incites unrest.

firecracker > *noun* chiefly N. Amer. a loud, explosive firework.

firefight > *noun* a battle using guns rather than bombs or other weapons.

firefighter > *noun* a person whose job is to extinguish fires.

DERIVATIVES – **firefighting** noun.

firefly > *noun* a soft-bodied beetle which glows in the dark.

firepower > *noun* the destructive capacity of guns, missiles, or a military force.

fireproof > *adjective* able to withstand fire or great heat. > *verb* make fireproof.

fireside > *noun* the area round a fireplace, especially as considered to be the focus of domestic life.

COMBINATIONS – **fireside chat** an informal and intimate conversation.

firewall > *noun* **1** a wall or partition designed to stop the spread of fire. **2** Computing a part of a computer system or network which is designed to block unauthorised access while permitting outward communication.

firework > *noun* **1** a device containing combustible chemicals which causes spectacular effects and explosions when ignited. **2** (**fireworks**) an outburst of anger or a display of brilliance.

WORDFINDER – pyrotechnic (*relating to fireworks*).

firkin /**fur**kin/ > *noun* chiefly historical a small cask used for liquids, butter, or fish.

ORIGIN – probably from Dutch *vierde* 'fourth' (a firkin originally contained a quarter of a barrel).

firm¹ > *adjective* **1** having an unyielding surface or structure. **2** solidly in place and stable. **3** having steady power or strength: *a firm grip.* **4** showing resolute determination. **5** fixed or definite. > *verb* **1** make stable or unyielding. **2** (often **firm up**) make (an agreement or plan) explicit and definite. > *adverb* in a resolute and determined manner.

IDIOMS – **be on firm ground** be sure of one's facts or secure in one's position. **a firm hand** strict discipline or control.

DERIVATIVES – **firmly** adverb **firmness** noun.

SYNONYMS – *adjective* **1** hard, resistant, rigid, solid, unyielding. **2** fixed, secure,

stable, steady, unshakeable. **3** powerful, robust, strong. **4** determined, decided, resolute, resolved, steadfast.

ANTONYMS – *adjective* **1** soft, yielding. **2** unstable. **3** feeble, limp. **4** irresolute.

firm² > *noun* a company or business partnership.

SYNONYMS – business, company, concern, corporation.

wordpower facts

Firm

The two English words **firm** are related to each other, and also to **farm**, by virtue of their shared root, Latin *firmus* 'firm, strong, immovable'. **Firm** meaning 'unyielding' or 'solid' developed in a straightforward way by way of Old French *ferme*, but the progress of **firm** in the sense 'company or business partnership' was more convoluted. It entered English via Spanish and Italian *firma* from Latin *firmare* 'fix, settle', which by the late Latin period had come to mean 'confirm by signature'. In English **firm** originally denoted an autograph or signature, later the name under which the business of a firm was transacted, and so eventually the firm itself. See also **FARM**.

firmament /**fur**məmənt/ > *noun* literary the heavens; the sky.

ORIGIN – Latin *firmamentum*, from *firmare* 'fix, settle'.

firmware > *noun* Computing permanent software programmed into a read-only memory.

first > *ordinal number* **1** coming before all others in time or order; earliest; 1st. **2** before doing something else specified or implied. **3** foremost in position, rank, or importance. **4** informal something never previously achieved or occurring. **5** Brit. a place in the top grade in an examination for a degree.

IDIOMS – **at first** at the beginning. **first and foremost** most importantly; more than anything else. **first and last** fundamentally; on the whole. **first of all 1** before doing anything else; at the beginning. **2** most importantly. **first off** informal, chiefly N. Amer. as a first point; first of all. **first past the post** Brit. (of an electoral system) in which a candidate or party is selected by achievement of a simple majority. **first thing** early in the morning; before anything else. **first things first** important matters should be dealt with before other things. **first up** informal first of all. **in the first place 1** as the first consideration or point. **2** at the beginning;

to begin with. **of the first order** (or **magnitude**) excellent or considerable of its kind.

SYNONYMS – *ordinal number* **1** earliest, introductory, initial, opening, original. **3** chief, foremost, principal, paramount, prime.

COMBINATIONS – **first aid** help given to a sick or injured person until full medical treatment is available. **first-day cover** an envelope bearing one or more stamps postmarked on their day of issue. **first fruits 1** the first agricultural produce of a season. **2** the initial results of an enterprise or endeavour. **first lady** the wife of the President of the US or other head of state. **first lieutenant** a rank of officer in the US army or air force, above second lieutenant and below captain. **first mate** the officer second in command to the master of a merchant ship. **first night** the first public performance of a play or show. **first officer 1** the first mate on a merchant ship. **2** the second in command to the captain on an aircraft. **first person** the form of a pronoun or verb used to refer to oneself, or to a group including oneself. **first principles** the fundamental concepts or assumptions on which a theory, system, or method is based. **first reading** the first presentation of a bill to a legislative assembly, to permit its introduction. **first refusal** the privilege of deciding whether to accept or reject something before it is offered to others. **first school** Brit. a school for children from five to nine years old. **first strike** an opening attack with nuclear weapons. **First World** the industrialised capitalist countries of western Europe, North America, Japan, Australia, and New Zealand.

firstborn > *noun* the first child to be born to someone.

first class > *noun* **1** a set of people or things grouped together as the best. **2** the best accommodation in an aircraft, train, or ship. **3** Brit. the highest division in the results of the examinations for a university degree. > *adjective & adverb* of the best quality or in the first class.

first-degree > *adjective* **1** (of burns) affecting only the surface of the skin and causing reddening. **2** Law, chiefly N. Amer. (of crime, especially murder) in the most serious category.

IDIOMS – **first-degree relative** a person's parent, sibling, or child.

first-foot > *verb* be the first person to cross someone's threshold in the New Year. > *noun* the first person to cross a threshold in such a way.

DERIVATIVES – **first-footer** noun.

first-hand > *adjective & adverb* from the original source or personal experience; direct: *first-hand knowledge.*

IDIOMS – **at first hand** directly or from personal experience.

firstly > *adverb* in the first place; first.

first name > *noun* a personal name given to someone at birth or baptism and used before a family name.

IDIOMS – **on first-name terms** having a friendly and informal relationship.

first-rate > *adjective* of the best class, quality, or condition; excellent.

firth /furth/ > *noun* a narrow inlet of the sea.

ORIGIN – Old Norse *fjqrthr*; compare with **FJORD**.

fiscal /**fis**k'l/ > *adjective* **1** relating to government revenue, especially taxes. **2** chiefly N. Amer. relating to financial matters.

DERIVATIVES – **fiscally** adverb.

COMBINATIONS – **fiscal year** N. Amer. a financial year.

ORIGIN – Latin *fiscalis*, from *fiscus* 'rush basket, purse, treasury'; compare with **CONFISCATE**.

fish¹ > *noun* (pl. same or **fishes**) **1** a limbless cold-blooded animal with a backbone, gills, and fins, living wholly in water. **2** the flesh of fish as food. **3** informal a person who is strange in a specified way: *he's a cold fish.* > *verb* **1** catch fish with a net or hook and line. **2** (**fish out**) pull or take (something) out of water or a receptacle. **3** grope or feel for something concealed. **4** try subtly or deviously to elicit a response or information.

WORDFINDER – cartilaginous fishes (*having a skeleton of cartilage rather than bone*), demersal (*denoting fishes living close to the seabed*), ichthyology (*scientific study of fishes*), pelagic (*denoting fishes inhabiting the upper layers of the open sea*), piscine (*relating to fish*), teleost (*bony fish*); Pisces (*constellation and zodiac sign, the Fish or Fishes*).

IDIOMS – **all's fish that comes to the net** proverb you can or should take advantage of anything that comes your way. **a big fish in a small pond** a person who is important only within a small community. **a fish out of water** a person who is in surroundings in which they feel out of place. **have other** (or **bigger**) **fish to fry** have more important matters to attend to.

DERIVATIVES – **fishing** noun.

USAGE – the normal plural of **fish** is **fish**, as in *a shoal of fish* and *he caught two huge fish*; however the older form **fishes** is still used when referring to different kinds of fish: *freshwater fishes of the British Isles*.

SYNONYMS – *verb* **1** angle, cast, go fishing, trawl. **3** delve, feel, grope, hunt, rummage. **4** angle, cast about.

COMBINATIONS – **fishbowl** a round glass bowl for keeping pet fish in. **fishcake** a patty of shredded fish and mashed potato. **fish finger** Brit. a small oblong piece of flaked or minced fish coated in batter or breadcrumbs. **fishing line** a long thread of silk or nylon attached to a baited hook and used for catching fish. **fishing rod** a long, tapering rod to which a fishing line is attached. **fish kettle** an oval pan for boiling fish. **fish knife** a blunt knife with a broad blade used for eating or serving fish. **fishmeal** ground dried fish used as fertiliser or animal feed. **fish slice** Brit. a kitchen utensil with a broad flat blade for lifting fish and fried foods. **fishwife** a coarse-mannered woman who is prone to shouting.

fish² > *noun* **1** (also **fishplate**) a flat connecting or strengthening piece fixed across a joint, e.g. in railway track. **2** a long curved piece of wood lashed to a ship's damaged mast or spar as a temporary repair. > *verb* join, strengthen, or repair with a fish.

ORIGIN – probably from French *fiche*, from *ficher* 'to fix'.

fisher > *noun* **1** a large brown marten found in North American woodland. **2** archaic a fisherman.

fisherfolk > *plural noun* people who catch fish for a living.

fisherman > *noun* a person who catches fish for a living or for sport.

fishery > *noun* (pl. **fisheries**) **1** a place where fish are reared, or caught in numbers. **2** the occupation or industry of catching or rearing fish.

fisheye > *noun* a very wide-angle lens with a field of vision covering up to 180°, the scale being reduced towards the edges.

fishmonger > *noun* a person or shop that sells fish for food.

fishnet > *noun* an open mesh fabric resembling a fishing net.

fishtail > *noun* a thing resembling a fish's tail in shape or movement. > *verb* travel with a side-to-side motion.

fishy > *adjective* (**fishier**, **fishiest**) **1** relating to or resembling a fish or fish. **2** informal arousing feelings of doubt or suspicion.

fissile /**fis**īl/ > *adjective* **1** (of an atom or element) able to undergo nuclear fission. **2** (chiefly of rock) easily split.

ORIGIN – Latin *fissilis*, from *findere* 'split, crack'.

fission /**fis**h'n/ > *noun* **1** the action of splitting or being split into two or more parts. **2** a reaction in which an atomic nucleus splits in two, releasing much energy. **3** Biology reproduction by means of cell division. > *verb* undergo fission.

DERIVATIVES – **fissionable** adjective.

COMBINATIONS – **fission bomb** an atom bomb.

fissiparous /fi**sipp**ərəss/ > *adjective* inclined to cause or undergo fission.

DERIVATIVES – **fissiparousness** noun.

ORIGIN – from Latin *fissus* 'split', on the pattern of *viviparous*.

fissure /**fis**hər/ > *noun* a long, narrow crack. > *verb* split; crack.

ORIGIN – Latin *fissura*, from *findere* 'to split'.

fist > *noun* a person's hand when the fingers are bent in towards the palm and held there tightly.

IDIOMS – **make a —— fist of** informal do something to the specified degree of success.

DERIVATIVES – **fistful** noun.

fisticuffs > *plural noun* fighting with the fists.

fistula /**fis**tyoolə/ > *noun* (pl. **fistulas** or **fistulae** /**fis**tyoolee/) Medicine an abnormal or surgically made passage between an organ and the body surface, or between two organs.

ORIGIN – Latin, 'pipe, flute, fistula'.

fit¹ > *adjective* (**fitter**, **fittest**) **1** of a suitable quality, standard, or type. **2** in good health, especially through regular physical exercise. **3** (**fit to do**) informal on the point of doing the extreme thing specified: *they were fit to kill him.* **4** Brit. informal sexually attractive. > *verb* (**fitted** (US also **fit**), **fitting**) **1** be of the right shape and size for. **2** be or make able to occupy a particular position, place, or period of time. **3** fix into place. **4** (often **be fitted with**) provide with a particular component or article. **5** join together to form a whole. **6** be or make suitable for. **7** (usu. **be fitted for**) try clothing on (someone) in order to make or alter it to the correct size. > *noun* the particular way in which something fits.

IDIOMS – **fit in 1** be compatible or in harmony. **2** (also **fit into**) constitute part of a particular situation or larger structure. **fit out** (or **up**) provide with necessary items. **fit to be tied** informal very angry. **fit up** Brit. informal incriminate (someone) by falsifying evidence against them. **see** (or **think**) **fit** consider it correct or acceptable.

DERIVATIVES – **fitness** noun **fitter** noun **fitly** adverb.

SYNONYMS – *adjective* **1** appropriate, apt, fitting, proper, suitable. **2** exercised, healthy, in good shape, trim, toned. verb **3** fix, insert, install, lay, put in. **4** endow, equip, furnish, provide, supply. **5** connect, join, link. **6** accord with, correspond to, suit, tally with.

ANTONYMS – *adjective* **1** inappropriate, unfit. **2** unfit.

fit² > *noun* **1** a sudden attack of convulsions. **2** a sudden attack of coughing, fainting, etc. **3** a sudden burst of intense feeling or activity.

IDIOMS – **in** (or **by**) **fits and starts** with irregular bursts of activity.

SYNONYMS – **1** attack, convulsion, paroxysm, seizure, spasm. **2** attack, bout, burst, outbreak.

ORIGIN – Old English, 'conflict'.

fitful > *adjective* active or occurring intermittently; not regular or steady.

DERIVATIVES – **fitfully** *adverb*.

fitment > *noun* chiefly Brit. a fixed item of furniture or piece of equipment.

fitted > *adjective* **1** made to fill a space or to cover something closely. **2** chiefly Brit. (of a room) equipped with matching units of furniture. **3** attached to or provided with a particular component or article. **4** (**fitted for** or **to do**) being fit for or to do.

fitting > *noun* **1** an attachment. **2** (**fittings**) items which are fixed in a building but can be removed when the owner moves. **3** the action of fitting or being fitted. > *adjective* appropriate; right or proper.

DERIVATIVES – **fittingly** *adverb*.

COMBINATIONS – **fitting room** a room in a shop where one can try on clothes before purchase.

five > *cardinal number* one more than four; 5. (Roman numeral: **v** or **V**.)

WORDFINDER – pentad (*group or set of five*), pentagon (*plane figure with five straight sides and angles*), pentagram (*five-pointed star drawn using a continuous line*), pentathlon (*athletic event comprising five different events*), quinquennial (*lasting for or recurring every five years*), quintet (*group of five musicians*).

DERIVATIVES – **fivefold** *adjective & adverb*.

COMBINATIONS – **five-and-dime** (also **five-and-ten**) N. Amer. a shop selling a wide variety of inexpensive goods. **five-a-side** a form of soccer with five players in each team. **five o'clock shadow** a slight growth of beard visible on a man's chin several hours after he has shaved. **five-spice** a blend of five powdered spices, typically fennel seeds, cinnamon, cloves, star anise, and peppercorns, used in Chinese cuisine.

fiver > *noun* informal **1** Brit. a five-pound note. **2** N. Amer. a five-dollar bill.

fives > *plural noun* (treated as sing.) a game in which a ball is hit with a gloved hand or a bat against a wall.

fix > *verb* **1** attach or position securely. **2** repair or restore. **3** decide or settle on. **4** (often **fix up**) make arrangements for; organise. **5** make unchanging, constant, or permanent. **6** (**fix on**) direct or be directed unwaveringly toward. **7** informal, chiefly N. Amer. prepare (food or drink). **8** informal deviously influence the outcome of. **9** informal take an injection of a narcotic drug. > *noun* **1** an act of fixing. **2** informal a difficult or awkward situation. **3** informal a dose of a narcotic drug to which one is addicted.

IDIOMS – **get a fix on 1** determine the position of. **2** informal determine the nature or facts of.

DERIVATIVES – **fixable** *adjective* **fixer** *noun*.

SYNONYMS – *verb* **1** affix, attach, implant, install, join, secure. **2** mend, repair, restore. **3** arrange, decide, determine, establish, settle on. **4** arrange, contrive, engineer, manage, organise.

ORIGIN – Latin *figere* 'fix, fasten'.

fixate /fiksayt/ > *verb* **1** (**fixate on** or **be fixated on**) be or cause to be obsessively interested in. **2** technical direct one's eyes towards.

fixation > *noun* **1** the action or condition of fixating or being fixated. **2** an obsessive interest in or feeling about someone or something. **3** the process of chemically stabilising or preserving something. **4** the assimilation of a gas, especially nitrogen, into organic compounds in plants or bacteria.

fixative /fiksətiv/ > *noun* a substance used to fix, protect, or stabilise something.

fixed > *adjective* **1** fastened securely in position. **2** predetermined or inflexibly established. **3** (**fixed for**) informal situated with regard to: *how are you fixed for money?*

DERIVATIVES – **fixedly** *adverb* **fixedness** *noun*.

SYNONYMS – **1** anchored, fastened, fast, firm, secure. **2** agreed, definite, established, predetermined, set.

ANTONYMS – **1** loose. **2** flexible, provisional.

COMBINATIONS – **fixed assets** assets which are purchased for long-term use and are not likely to be converted quickly into cash, such as land, buildings, and equipment (as opposed to *current assets*). **fixed odds** betting odds that are predetermined, as opposed to a pool system or a starting price. **fixed-wing** (of aircraft) of the conventional type as opposed to those with rotating wings, such as helicopters.

fixings > *plural noun* Brit. screws, bolts, etc. used to fix or assemble building material, furniture, or equipment.

fixity > *noun* the state of being unchanging or permanent.

fixture /fikschər/ > *noun* **1** a piece of equipment or furniture which is fixed in position in a building or vehicle. **2** (**fixtures**) articles attached to a house or land and considered legally part of it so that they normally remain in place when an owner moves. **3** informal a person or thing that has become established in a particular place. **4** Brit. a sporting event which takes place on a particular date.

fizz > *verb* **1** (of a liquid) produce bubbles of gas and make a hissing sound. **2** make a buzzing or crackling sound. > *noun* **1** the action or sound of fizzing. **2** informal an effervescent drink, especially sparkling wine. **3** exuberance.

SYNONYMS – *verb* **1** bubble, effervesce, froth, sparkle.

fizzle > *verb* **1** make a feeble hissing or spluttering sound. **2** (**fizzle out**) end or fail in a weak or disappointing way. > *noun* an instance of fizzling.

fizzog > *noun* variant of PHIZ.

fizzy > *adjective* (**fizzier, fizziest**) **1** (of a drink) effervescent; sparkling. **2** exuberant.

DERIVATIVES – **fizzily** *adverb* **fizziness** *noun*.

fjord /fyord/ (also **fiord**) > *noun* a long, narrow, deep inlet of the sea between high cliffs, found predominantly in Norway.

ORIGIN – Norwegian, from Old Norse *fjqrthr*. Compare with FIRTH.

FL > *abbreviation* Florida.

fl. > *abbreviation* **1** floruit. **2** fluid.

flab > *noun* informal soft, loose flesh on a person's body; fat.

flabbergast /flabbərgaast/ > *verb* informal surprise greatly.

DERIVATIVES – **flabbergasted** *adjective*.

flabby > *adjective* (**flabbier, flabbiest**) **1** (of a person's body) soft, loose, and fleshy. **2** not tightly controlled and therefore ineffective.

DERIVATIVES – **flabbily** *adverb* **flabbiness** *noun*.

SYNONYMS – **1** fat, flaccid, fleshy, soft.

ANTONYMS – **1** lean, taut.

flaccid /flassid/ > *adjective* soft and limp.

ORIGIN – Latin *flaccus* 'flabby'.

flack¹ N. Amer. informal > *noun* a publicity agent. > *verb* publicise or promote.

flack² > *noun* variant spelling of FLAK.

flag¹ > *noun* **1** a piece of cloth that is raised on a pole and used as an emblem. **2** a device or symbol resembling a flag, used as a marker. **3** a small paper badge given to people who donate to a charity appeal. > *verb* (**flagged, flagging**) **1** mark (an item) for attention. **2** direct or alert (someone) by waving a flag or using hand signals. **3** (**flag down**) signal to (a driver) to stop.

IDIOMS – **fly the flag 1** (of a ship) be registered in a particular country and sail under its flag. **2** represent one's country or demonstrate one's affiliation with a party or organisation. **put the flags out** celebrate.

SYNONYMS – *noun* **1** banner, ensign, pennant, standard.

COMBINATIONS – **flag day** Brit. a day on which money is collected in the street for a charity and contributors are given flags to wear. **flagpole** (also **flagstaff**) a pole used for flying a flag.

flag² > *noun* a flat rectangular or square stone slab, used for paving.

DERIVATIVES – **flagged** *adjective*.

ORIGIN – probably Scandinavian.

flag³ > *noun* a plant with long sword-shaped leaves, especially an iris.

flag⁴ > *verb* (**flagged, flagging**) **1** become

tired or less enthusiastic. **2** become weaker or less dynamic.

flagellant /ˈflajələnt/ > *noun* a person who subjects themselves to flagellation.

flagellate¹ /ˈflajəlayt/ > *verb* flog (someone), either as a religious discipline or for sexual gratification.

DERIVATIVES – **flagellation** *noun*.

ORIGIN – Latin *flagellare* 'to whip'.

flagellate² /ˈflajələt/ *Zoology* > *noun* any of a large group of protozoans that have one or more flagella used for swimming. > *adjective* having one or more flagella.

flagellum /fləˈjelləm/ > *noun* (pl. **flagella**) *Biology* a microscopic whip-like appendage which enables many protozoans, bacteria, and spermatozoa to swim.

ORIGIN – Latin, 'little whip'.

flageolet¹ /ˈflajəlet/ > *noun* **1** a very small flute-like instrument resembling a recorder. **2** a tin whistle.

ORIGIN – French, from Provençal *flaujol*.

flageolet² /ˈflajəlay/ > *noun* a small variety of French kidney bean.

ORIGIN – French, from Latin *phaseolus* 'bean'.

flagitious /fləˈjishəs/ > *adjective* formal extremely and criminally wicked.

ORIGIN – Latin *flagitiosus*, from *flagitium* 'importunity, shameful crime'.

flagon /ˈflaggən/ > *noun* **1** a large container for drinks. **2** a large bottle in which wine or cider is sold, typically holding 1.13 litres (about 2 pints).

ORIGIN – Old French *flacon*, from Latin *flasco*.

flagrant /ˈflaygrənt/ > *adjective* (of an action) conspicuously or obviously wrong; blatant.

DERIVATIVES – **flagrancy** *noun* **flagrantly** *adverb*.

SYNONYMS – barefaced, blatant, glaring, overt, shameless.

ORIGIN – Latin, from *flagrare* 'blaze'.

flagship > *noun* **1** the ship in a fleet which carries the commanding admiral. **2** the best or most important thing owned or produced by an organisation.

flagstone > *noun* a flat square or rectangular stone slab, used for paving.

DERIVATIVES – **flagstoned** *adjective*.

flail /flayl/ > *noun* a tool or machine with a swinging action, used for threshing. > *verb* **1** swing wildly. **2** (**flail around** or **about**) flounder; struggle.

SYNONYMS – *verb* **1** flap, swing, thrash about, wave, windmill.

ORIGIN – Latin *flagellum* 'little whip'.

flair > *noun* **1** a natural ability or talent. **2** stylishness.

SYNONYMS – **1** ability, aptitude, bent, inclination, talent. **2** dash, elan, panache, style, verve.

ORIGIN – French, from *flairer* 'to smell'.

flak (also **flack**) > *noun* **1** anti-aircraft fire. **2** strong criticism.

COMBINATIONS – **flak jacket** a sleeveless jacket made of heavy fabric reinforced with metal, worn as protection against bullets and shrapnel.

ORIGIN – abbreviation of German *Fliegerabwehrkanone* 'aviator-defence gun'.

flake¹ > *noun* **1** a small, flat, very thin piece of something. **2** N. Amer. informal a crazy or eccentric person. > *verb* **1** come away from a surface in flakes. **2** split into flakes.

flake² > *verb* (**flake out**) informal fall asleep or drop from exhaustion.

ORIGIN – first used in the senses 'become languid' and (of a garment) 'fall in folds': variant of obsolete *flack* and **FLAG⁴**.

flaky > *adjective* (**flakier**, **flakiest**) **1** breaking or separating easily into flakes. **2** N. Amer. informal crazy or eccentric.

DERIVATIVES – **flakiness** *noun*.

COMBINATIONS – **flaky pastry** pastry consisting of a number of thin layers.

flambé /ˈflombay/ > *adjective* (after a noun) (of food) covered with spirits and set alight briefly. > *verb* (**flambés**, **flambéed**, **flambéing**) cover (food) with spirits and set it alight briefly.

ORIGIN – French, 'singed'.

flambeau /ˈflambō/ > *noun* (pl. **flambeaus** or **flambeaux** /ˈflambōz/) **1** a flaming torch. **2** a branched candlestick.

ORIGIN – French, from *flambe* 'a flame'.

flamboyant /flamˈboyənt/ > *adjective* **1** conspicuously and confidently exuberant. **2** brightly coloured and showy.

DERIVATIVES – **flamboyance** *noun* **flamboyantly** *adverb*.

SYNONYMS – **1** exuberant, lively, showy, theatrical, vibrant, vivacious. **2** bright, colourful, gaudy, ostentatious, vivid.

ANTONYMS – **1** quiet, restrained. **2** dull, restrained.

ORIGIN – French, 'flaming, blazing'.

flame > *noun* **1** a hot glowing body of ignited gas produced by something on fire. **2** something thought of as burning fiercely or being extinguished: *the flame of hope*. **3** a brilliant orange-red colour. > *verb* **1** give off flames. **2** apply a flame to; set alight. **3** (of an intense emotion) appear suddenly and fiercely. **4** (of a person's face) become red with embarrassment or anger. **5** Computing, informal send (someone) abusive or vitriolic email messages.

COMBINATIONS – **flame-thrower** a weapon that sprays out burning fuel. **old flame** informal a former lover.

ORIGIN – Latin *flamma*.

flamenco /fləˈmengkō/ > *noun* **1** a style of Spanish music played especially on the guitar and accompanied by singing and dancing. **2** a style of spirited, rhythmical dance performed to such music.

flameproof > *adjective* **1** (of fabric) treated so as to be non-flammable. **2** (of cookware) able to be used either in an oven or on a hob. > *verb* make flameproof.

flaming > *adjective* **1** emitting flames. **2** very hot. **3** of a brilliant orange-red colour. **4** (of an argument) passionate. **5** informal expressing annoyance: *that flaming dog*.

flamingo /fləˈminggō/ > *noun* (pl. **flamingos** or **flamingoes**) a tall wading bird with mainly pink or scarlet plumage, long legs and neck, and a crooked bill.

wordpower facts

Flamingo

The **flamingo** and the **flamenco** are undoubtedly connected, although exactly how is uncertain. Both words came into English from the Spanish word *flamenco*, which means both 'flamingo' and 'flamenco', and also 'like a gypsy', 'strong and healthy-looking', and 'Flemish'. How 'Flemish' is related to the other meanings is not clear: it may be from the pink cheeks of northern Europeans, or because of an apparent reputation that the people of Flanders had in the Middle Ages for flamboyant clothing! The name of the bird might have been influenced by Latin *flamma* 'flame', on account of its bright pink colour.

flammable /ˈflamməb'l/ > *adjective* easily set on fire.

DERIVATIVES – **flammability** *noun*.

USAGE – the words **flammable** and **inflammable** have the same meaning. However, to avoid ambiguity it is safer to use **flammable**, as the *in-* in **inflammable** can give the impression that the word means 'non-flammable'.

flan > *noun* a baked dish consisting of an open-topped pastry case with a savoury or sweet filling.

ORIGIN – Old French *flaon*, from Latin *flado*.

flâneur /flanˈör/ > *noun* (pl. **flâneurs** pronunc. same) a man about town who strolls around and observes society.

ORIGIN – French, from *flâner* 'saunter, lounge'.

flange /flanj/ > *noun* a projecting rim or piece.

DERIVATIVES – **flanged** *adjective*.

ORIGIN – perhaps from Old French *flanchir* 'to bend'.

flank > *noun* **1** the side of a person's or animal's body between the ribs and the hip. **2** the side of something such as a building or mountain. **3** the left or right side of a body of people. > *verb* be situated on each or on one side of.

ORIGIN – Old French *flanc*.

flanker > *noun* 1 Rugby a wing forward. 2 American Football an offensive back who is positioned to the outside of an end. 3 Military a fortification to the side of a force or position.

flannel > *noun* 1 a kind of soft-woven woollen or cotton fabric. 2 (**flannels**) men's trousers made of woollen flannel. 3 Brit. a small piece of towelling for washing oneself. 4 Brit. informal empty or flattering talk used to avoid dealing with a difficult subject. > *verb* (**flannelled, flannelling**; US also **flanneled, flanneling**) informal, chiefly Brit. use empty or flattering talk to avoid dealing with a difficult subject.

ORIGIN – probably from Welsh *gwlanen* 'woollen article'.

flannelette /flannəlet/ > *noun* a napped cotton fabric resembling flannel.

flap > *verb* (**flapped, flapping**) 1 move up and down or from side to side. 2 (**flap at**) strike at with a light blow, a cloth, etc. 3 informal be agitated. > *noun* 1 a piece of something attached on one side only, that covers an opening. 2 a hinged or sliding section of an aircraft wing used to control lift. 3 a single flapping movement. 4 informal a panic.

DERIVATIVES – **flappy** *adjective*.

flapjack > *noun* 1 Brit. a soft, thick biscuit made from oats and butter. 2 N. Amer. a pancake.

ORIGIN – from **FLAP** (in the dialect sense 'toss a pancake') + **JACK**.

flapper > *noun* informal a fashionable and unconventional young woman of the 1920s.

flare > *noun* 1 a sudden brief burst of flame or light. 2 a device producing a very bright flame as a signal or marker. 3 a gradual widening towards the hem of a garment. 4 (**flares**) trousers of which the legs widen from the knees down. > *verb* 1 burn, shine, or be revealed with a sudden intensity. 2 (**flare up**) suddenly become intense, angry, or violent. 3 gradually become wider at one end.

SYNONYMS – *noun* 1 blaze, flash, flicker. *verb* blaze, flame.

COMBINATIONS – **flarepath** an area illuminated to enable an aircraft to land or take off.

flash > *verb* 1 shine with a bright but brief or intermittent light. 2 move, pass, or send swiftly in a particular direction: *the scenery flashed by.* 3 display or be displayed briefly or repeatedly. 4 informal display conspicuously so as to impress: *they flash their money about.* 5 informal (of a man) briefly show one's genitals in public. > *noun* 1 a sudden brief burst of bright light. 2 a camera attachment

that produces a flash of light, for taking photographs in poor light. 3 a sudden or brief manifestation or occurrence: *a flash of inspiration.* 4 a bright patch of colour. 5 Brit. a coloured patch of cloth worn on a uniform as a distinguishing emblem. > *adjective* informal ostentatiously stylish or expensive.

IDIOMS – **flash in the pan** a sudden but brief success. [ORIGIN – with allusion to the priming of a firearm, the flash arising from an explosion of gunpowder within the lock.] **in a flash** very quickly.

DERIVATIVES – **flasher** *noun*.

SYNONYMS – *verb* 1 blaze, flash, sparkle. 2 bolt, dart, dash, zoom. 3 flaunt, flourish, show off. *noun* blaze, burst, flare, sparkle.

COMBINATIONS – **flashboard** a board used for sending more water from a mill dam into a mill race. **flashbulb** a bulb for a flashgun. **flashcard** a card containing a clear display of a word or words, used in teaching reading. **flash flood** a sudden local flood resulting from extreme rainfall. **flashgun** a device which gives a brief flash of intense light, used for taking photographs in poor light. **flashlight** 1 an electric torch with a strong beam. 2 a flashgun. **flash memory** Computing memory that retains data in the absence of a power supply.

flashback > *noun* 1 a scene in a film or novel set in a time earlier than the main story. 2 a sudden vivid memory of a past event.

flashing > *noun* a strip of metal used to seal the junction of a roof with another surface.

flashover > *noun* 1 a high-voltage electric short circuit. 2 the rapid spread of a fire through the air because of intense heat.

flashpoint > *noun* 1 a point or place at which anger or violence flares up. 2 Chemistry the temperature at which a flammable compound gives off sufficient vapour to ignite in air.

flashy > *adjective* (**flashier, flashiest**) ostentatiously stylish; showy.

DERIVATIVES – **flashily** *adverb* **flashiness** *noun*.

flask > *noun* 1 a narrow-necked conical or spherical bottle. 2 Brit. a vacuum flask. 3 a hip flask. 4 a lead-lined container for radioactive nuclear waste.

ORIGIN – Latin *flasca* 'cask or bottle'.

flat¹ > *adjective* (**flatter, flattest**) 1 having a level and even surface. 2 not sloping. 3 with a level surface and little height or depth: *a flat cap.* 4 lacking vitality or interest: *a flat voice.* 5 (of a sparkling drink) having lost its effervescence. 6 (of something kept inflated) having lost some or all of its air. 7 Brit. (of a battery) having exhausted its charge. 8 (of a fee, charge, or price) unvarying; fixed. 9 (of a negative statement)

definite and firm: *a flat denial.* 10 (of musical sound) below true or normal pitch. 11 (after a noun) (of a note or key) lower by a semitone than a specified note or key. > *adverb* 1 in or to a horizontal position. 2 so as to become level and even. 3 informal completely; absolutely: *she turned him down flat.* 4 emphasising the speed of an action: *in ten minutes flat.* 5 below the true or normal pitch of musical sound. > *noun* 1 the flat part of something. 2 an upright section of stage scenery. 3 informal a flat tyre. 4 (**flats**) an area of low level ground, especially near water. 5 (**the Flat**) Brit. flat racing. 6 a musical note lowered a semitone below natural pitch. 7 the sign (♭) indicating this.

IDIOMS – **fall flat** fail to produce the intended effect. **flat out** as fast or as hard as possible. **on the flat 1** on level ground as opposed to uphill. **2** (**on the Flat**) (of a horse race) on a course without jumps.

DERIVATIVES – **flatly** *adverb* **flatness** *noun* **flattish** *adjective*.

SYNONYMS – *adjective* 2 horizontal, level. 5 boring, dull, monotonous, tedious.

COMBINATIONS – **flat feet** feet with arches that are lower than usual. **flat file** Computing a file having no internal hierarchy. **flat-footed 1** having flat feet. 2 informal clumsy. **flat iron** historical an iron heated on a hotplate or fire. **flat-pack** (of furniture or other equipment) sold in pieces and assembled by the buyer. **flat race** a horse race over a course with no jumps, as opposed to a steeplechase or hurdles. **flatware 1** items of crockery such as plates and saucers. 2 N. Amer. domestic cutlery.

ORIGIN – Old Norse *flatr*.

flat² > *noun* chiefly Brit. a set of rooms comprising an individual place of residence within a larger building. > *verb* (**flatted, flatting**) Austral./NZ live in or share a flat.

DERIVATIVES – **flatlet** *noun*.

COMBINATIONS – **flatmate** Brit. a person with whom one shares a flat.

ORIGIN – alteration of obsolete *flet* 'floor, dwelling'; related to **FLAT¹**.

flatbed > *noun* 1 (before another noun) denoting a vehicle with a flat load-carrying area. 2 Computing a scanner, plotter, or other device which keeps paper flat during use.

flatfish > *noun* a marine fish, such as a plaice or sole, that swims on its side with both eyes on the upper side of its flattened body.

flatline > *verb* informal die.

DERIVATIVES – **flatliner** *noun*.

ORIGIN – with reference to the continuous straight line displayed on a heart monitor when a person dies.

flatten > *verb* 1 make or become flat or flatter. 2 informal knock down.

DERIVATIVES – **flattener** *noun*.

flatter > *verb* 1 praise or compliment

insincerely, especially to further one's own interests. **2** (usu. **be flattered**) cause to feel honoured and pleased. **3** (**flatter oneself**) believe something favourable about oneself, especially something unfounded. **4** (of clothing or a colour) make (someone) look attractive. **5** give an unrealistically favourable impression of.
DERIVATIVES – **flatterer** noun **flattering** adjective **flatteringly** adverb.

flattery > noun (pl. **flatteries**) excessive and insincere praise.
SYNONYMS – blandishments, puffery.
ORIGIN – Old French flaterie, from flater 'stroke, flatter'.

flattie (also **flatty**) > noun (pl. **flatties**) informal a low-heeled shoe.

flatulent /**flat**yoolənt/ > adjective suffering from or marked by an accumulation of gas in the alimentary canal.
DERIVATIVES – **flatulence** noun.
ORIGIN – Latin flatulentus, from flatus 'blowing'.

flatus /**flay**təss/ > noun formal gas in or from the stomach or intestines.
ORIGIN – Latin, 'blowing', from flare 'to blow'.

flatworm > noun a worm of a large group (the phylum Platyhelminthes) which includes the parasitic flukes and tapeworms, distinguished by a simple flat body without blood vessels.

flaunt > verb display ostentatiously.
USAGE – do not confuse **flaunt** with **flout**; **flaunt** means 'display ostentatiously', while **flout** means 'openly disregard (a rule)'.
SYNONYMS – exhibit, parade, show off.

flautist /**flaw**tist/ > noun a flute player.
ORIGIN – Italian flautista, from flauto 'flute'.

flavonoid /**flay**vənoyd/ > noun Chemistry any of a class of compounds including several white or yellow plant pigments.
ORIGIN – from Latin flavus 'yellow'.

flavour (US **flavor**) > noun **1** the distinctive taste of a food or drink. **2** a quality reminiscent of something specified: balconies gave the building a Spanish flavour. **3** chiefly N. Amer. a flavouring. **4** Physics a property of quarks with values designated up, down, charmed, strange, top, and bottom. > verb give flavour to.
IDIOMS – **flavour of the month** a person or thing that is currently popular.
DERIVATIVES – **flavourful** adjective **flavourless** adjective **flavoursome** adjective.
SYNONYMS – noun **1** savour, tang, taste. **2** character, quality, spirit.
ORIGIN – Old French flaor 'a smell', perhaps from a blend of Latin flatus 'blowing' and foetor 'stench'.

flavouring (US **flavoring**) > noun a substance used to enhance the flavour of a food or drink.

flaw > noun **1** something which mars a substance or object. **2** a fundamental weakness or error. > verb (usu. **be flawed**) mar or weaken.
SYNONYMS – **1** blemish, deficiency, fault, imperfection.
ORIGIN – first occurring in the sense 'a snowflake', later 'a fragment': perhaps from Old Norse flaga 'stone slab'.

flawless > adjective without any blemishes or imperfections; perfect.
DERIVATIVES – **flawlessly** adverb.

flax > noun **1** a blue-flowered herbaceous plant that is cultivated for its seed (linseed) and for textile fibre made from its stalks. **2** textile fibre obtained from this plant.

flaxen > adjective **1** literary (of hair) of the pale yellow colour of dressed flax. **2** of flax.

flaxseed > noun another term for LINSEED.

flay > verb **1** strip the skin from (a body or carcass). **2** whip or beat harshly. **3** criticise harshly.
DERIVATIVES – **flayer** noun.

flea > noun a small wingless jumping insect which feeds on the blood of mammals and birds.
IDIOMS – (**as**) **fit as a flea** in very good health. **a flea in one's ear** a sharp reproof.
COMBINATIONS – **flea-bitten 1** bitten by or infested with fleas. **2** dilapidated or disreputable. **flea collar** a collar for a cat or dog that is impregnated with insecticide to kill or deter fleas. **flea market** a street market selling second-hand goods. **fleapit** chiefly Brit. a dingy, dirty place, especially a run-down cinema.

fleadh /flaa/ > noun a festival of Irish or Celtic music, dancing, and culture.
ORIGIN – from Irish fleadh ceoil 'music festival'.

fleck > noun **1** a very small patch of colour or light. **2** a small particle. > verb (usu. **be flecked**) mark or dot with flecks.
ORIGIN – perhaps from Old Norse flekkr, or from Low German, Dutch vlecke.

fled past and past participle of FLEE.

fledge /flej/ > verb **1** (of a young bird) develop wing feathers that are large enough for flight. **2** bring up (a young bird) until its wing feathers are developed enough for flight.
ORIGIN – from the obsolete adjective fledge 'ready to fly'; related to FLY¹.

fledged > adjective having just taken on the role specified: a newly fledged Detective Inspector.

fledgling (also **fledgeling**) > noun **1** a young bird that has just fledged. **2** (before another noun) new and inexperienced: the fledgling democracies of eastern Europe.

flee > verb (**flees**, **fleeing**; past and past participle **fled**) run away from danger or trouble.
SYNONYMS – abscond, bolt, take to one's heels.

fleece > noun **1** the wool coat of a sheep. **2** a soft, warm fabric with a pile, or a garment made from this. > verb informal defraud, especially by overcharging.
DERIVATIVES – **fleeced** adjective **fleecy** adjective.

fleer /**flee**ər/ > verb literary laugh impudently or jeeringly. > noun archaic an impudent or jeering look or speech.
ORIGIN – probably Scandinavian.

fleet¹ > noun **1** a group of ships sailing together. **2** a country's navy. **3** a number of vehicles or aircraft operating together.
ORIGIN – Old English, 'ship, shipping'.

fleet² > adjective fast and nimble.
DERIVATIVES – **fleetly** adverb **fleetness** noun.
ORIGIN – probably from Old Norse fljótr and related to FLEETING.

fleeting > adjective lasting for a very short time.
DERIVATIVES – **fleetingly** adverb.
SYNONYMS – brief, cursory, ephemeral, transitory.
ORIGIN – from the archaic verb fleet 'move or pass quickly'; related to FLIT and FLOAT.

Fleming /**flemm**ing/ > noun **1** a Flemish person. **2** a member of the Flemish-speaking people inhabiting northern and western Belgium. Compare with WALLOON.

Flemish /**flemm**ish/ > noun the Dutch language as spoken in Flanders, a region divided between Belgium, France, and the Netherlands. > adjective relating to the people or language of Flanders.
ORIGIN – Dutch Vlāmisch.

flense /flenz/ > verb slice the skin or fat from (a carcass, especially that of a whale).
DERIVATIVES – **flenser** noun.
ORIGIN – Danish flensa.

flesh > noun **1** the soft substance in the body consisting of muscle tissue and fat. **2** the edible pulpy part of a fruit or vegetable. **3** the surface of the human body (with reference to its appearance or sensory properties). **4** (**the flesh**) the physicality of the human body as contrasted with the mind or the soul: the pleasures of the flesh. > verb (**flesh out**) make more substantial.
WORDFINDER – carnal (relating to flesh or the physical).
IDIOMS – **go the way of all flesh** die or come to an end. **in the flesh** in person or (of a thing) in its actual state. **make someone's flesh creep** (or **crawl**) cause someone to feel fear, horror, or disgust.
DERIVATIVES – **fleshless** adjective.
COMBINATIONS – **flesh wound** a wound that breaks the skin but does not damage bones or vital organs.

fleshly > *adjective* relating to the body; sensual.

fleshpots > *plural noun* places providing a self-indulgently luxurious or sensual experience.

ORIGIN – with biblical allusion to the *fleshpots of Egypt* mentioned in the Book of Exodus.

fleshy > *adjective* (**fleshier, fleshiest**) **1** having a substantial amount of flesh; plump. **2** (of plant or fruit tissue) soft and thick. **3** resembling flesh.

DERIVATIVES – **fleshiness** *noun*.

fleur-de-lis /flör də lee/ (also **fleur-de-lys**) > *noun* (pl. **fleurs-de-lis** pronunc. same) Art & Heraldry a stylised lily composed of three petals bound together near their bases.

ORIGIN – Old French *flour de lys* 'flower of the lily'.

flew past of **FLY**[1].

flex[1] > *verb* **1** bend (a limb or joint). **2** contract or tense (a muscle). **3** warp or bend and then revert to shape.

---

wordpower facts

Flex

The root of **flex**, the Latin verb *flectere*, meaning 'to bend', is shared by a number of related words, including **circumflex, flexible, genuflect**, and **reflect**.

---

flex[2] > *noun* chiefly Brit. a flexible insulated cable used for carrying electric current to an appliance.

flexible > *adjective* **1** capable of bending easily without breaking. **2** able to change or be changed to respond to different circumstances.

DERIVATIVES – **flexibility** *noun* **flexibly** *adverb*.

SYNONYMS – **1** elastic, pliable, supple. **2** accommodating, adaptable, malleable.

ANTONYMS – rigid.

flexion /fleksh'n/ (also **flection**) > *noun* the action of bending or the condition of being bent.

flexitime (N. Amer. also **flextime**) > *noun* a system allowing some flexibility as to when staff work their allotted hours.

flexor /fleksər/ > *noun* a muscle whose contraction bends a limb or other part of the body.

flexuous /fleksyooəss/ > *adjective* full of bends and curves.

flibbertigibbet /flibbərtijibbət/ > *noun* a frivolous and restless person.

flick > *noun* **1** a sudden sharp movement up and down or from side to side. **2** the sudden release of a finger or thumb held bent against another finger. **3** informal a cinema film. **4** (**the flicks**) informal the cinema.

> *verb* **1** make or cause to make a sudden sharp movement. **2** propel with a flick of the fingers. **3** (**flick through**) look quickly through (a book or a collection of papers).

SYNONYMS – *noun* **1** flip, jerk, snap.

COMBINATIONS – **flick knife** Brit. a knife with a blade that springs out from the handle when a button is pressed.

flicker > *verb* **1** shine or burn unsteadily and intermittently. **2** (of a feeling) be briefly perceptible. **3** make small, quick movements. > *noun* **1** a flickering movement or light. **2** a brief and transient occurrence of a feeling.

SYNONYMS – *verb* **1** glimmer, glisten, sparkle, twinkle.

flier > *noun* variant spelling of **FLYER**.

flight > *noun* **1** the action or process of flying. **2** a journey made in an aircraft or in space. **3** the path of a projectile through the air. **4** a series of steps between floors or levels. **5** the action or an act of fleeing: *the enemy were in flight.* **6** an uninhibited mental journey: *a flight of fancy.* **7** a flock of birds flying together. **8** a unit of about six military aircraft operating together. **9** the tail of an arrow or dart.

IDIOMS – **in full flight** having gained optimum momentum. **take flight 1** (of a bird) take off and fly. **2** flee.

SYNONYMS – **3** course, path, trajectory. **5** escape, getaway.

COMBINATIONS – **flight deck 1** the cockpit of a large aircraft. **2** the deck of an aircraft carrier, used as a runway. **flight feather** any of the large primary or secondary feathers in a bird's wing, supporting it in flight. **flight lieutenant** a rank of officer in the RAF, above flying officer and below squadron leader. **flight path** the course of an aircraft or spacecraft. **flight recorder** an electronic device in an aircraft that records technical details during a flight, used in the event of an accident to discover its cause. **flight sergeant** a rank of non-commissioned officer in the RAF, above sergeant and below warrant officer.

ORIGIN – Old English; related to **FLY**[1].

flightless > *adjective* (of a bird or insect) naturally unable to fly.

DERIVATIVES – **flightlessness** *noun*.

flighty > *adjective* (**flightier, flightiest**) frivolous and fickle.

SYNONYMS – changeable, erratic, fickle, frivolous, inconstant.

ANTONYMS – steady, responsible.

flimflam informal > *noun* **1** insincere and unconvincing talk. **2** a confidence trick. > *verb* (**flimflammed, flimflamming**) swindle (someone) with a confidence trick.

flimsy > *adjective* (**flimsier, flimsiest**) **1** weak and insubstantial. **2** (of clothing) light and thin. **3** (of a pretext or account) weak;

unconvincing. > *noun* (pl. **flimsies**) Brit. a document, especially a copy, made on very thin paper.

DERIVATIVES – **flimsily** *adverb* **flimsiness** *noun*.

SYNONYMS – *adjective* **1** frail, insubstantial, light, slight, weak. **3** feeble, implausible, thin, unconvincing, weak.

ANTONYMS – *adjective* **1** sturdy. **3** solid.

ORIGIN – probably from **FLIMFLAM**.

flinch > *verb* **1** make a quick, nervous movement as an instinctive reaction to fear or pain. **2** (**flinch from**) avoid through fear or anxiety. > *noun* an act of flinching.

SYNONYMS – *verb* **1** recoil, shrink, wince.

ORIGIN – Old French *flenchir* 'turn aside'.

flinders > *plural noun* small fragments or splinters.

ORIGIN – probably Scandinavian.

fling > *verb* (past and past participle **flung**) **1** throw forcefully; hurl. **2** (**fling oneself into**) wholeheartedly engage in (an activity or enterprise). **3** move with speed: *he flung away to his study.* **4** (**fling on** or **off**) put on or take off (clothes) carelessly and rapidly. > *noun* **1** a short period of enjoyment or wild behaviour. **2** a short sexual relationship. **3** a Highland fling.

DERIVATIVES – **flinger** *noun*.

SYNONYMS – *verb* **1** hurl, pitch, sling, throw, toss. *noun* **1** binge, spree. **2** dalliance, entanglement, liaison.

ORIGIN – perhaps related to Old Norse *flengja* 'flog'.

flint > *noun* **1** a hard grey rock consisting of nearly pure silica, occurring chiefly as nodules in chalk. **2** a piece of this rock. **3** a piece of flint or an alloy used with steel to produce an igniting spark, especially in a cigarette lighter.

flintlock > *noun* an old-fashioned type of gun fired by a spark from a flint.

flinty > *adjective* (**flintier, flintiest**) **1** of, containing, or resembling flint. **2** grim and unyielding: *a flinty stare.*

DERIVATIVES – **flintily** *adverb* **flintiness** *noun*.

flip > *verb* (**flipped, flipping**) **1** turn over with a quick, smooth movement. **2** move, push, or throw with a sudden sharp movement: *he flipped a switch.* **3** toss (something, especially a coin) so it turns over in the air. **4** informal suddenly become deranged or very angry. > *noun* an action or movement in which something is flipped. > *adjective* flippant; glib: *a flip remark.* > *exclamation* informal used to express mild annoyance.

IDIOMS – **flip one's lid** informal suddenly become deranged or lose one's self-control.

COMBINATIONS – **flip chart** a very large pad of paper bound so that pages can be turned over at the top, used on a stand at presentations. **flip side** informal **1** the B-side of a pop single. **2** the reverse or unwelcome aspect of a situation.

ORIGIN – probably a contraction of **FILLIP**.

flip-flop > noun **1** a light sandal with a thong that passes between the big and second toes. **2** Electronics a switching circuit which works by changing between two stable states. > verb move with a flapping sound or motion.

flippant > adjective not showing the proper seriousness or respect.

DERIVATIVES – **flippancy** noun **flippantly** adverb.

SYNONYMS – disrespectful, frivolous, glib, impertinent, irreverent.

ANTONYMS – respectful, serious.

ORIGIN – from **FLIP**: originally in the senses 'nimble' and 'talkative', then 'playful'.

flipper > noun **1** a broad, flat limb without fingers, used for swimming by sea animals such as seals and turtles. **2** a flat rubber attachment worn on the foot for underwater swimming. **3** a pivoted arm in a pinball machine.

flipping > adjective informal, chiefly Brit. used for emphasis or to express mild annoyance.

flirt > verb **1** behave playfully in a sexually enticing manner. **2** (**flirt with**) experiment casually with (an idea or activity). **3** (**flirt with**) deliberately risk (danger or death). > noun a person who habitually flirts.

DERIVATIVES – **flirtation** noun **flirtatious** adjective **flirty** (**flirtier, flirtiest**) adjective.

SYNONYMS – verb **2** (**flirt with**) dabble with, toy with, trifle with.

wordpower facts
Flirt

Like words such as *biff, bounce, flick, gloop, loll, plod,* and *spurt,* **flirt** is apparently of symbolic origin: that is, it arose because it somehow 'sounded right' to convey the idea it represented. In the case of **flirt** the elements *fl-* and *-irt* are thought to suggest sudden movement: the original verb senses were 'give someone a sharp blow', 'move or propel suddenly', and 'sneer at'. As a noun it first meant 'joke, gibe' and 'flighty girl' (defined by Dr Johnson in his *Dictionary of the English Language* (1755) as 'a pert young hussey'), with a notion originally of cheekiness rather than of playfully amorous behaviour.

flit > verb (**flitted, flitting**) **1** move swiftly and lightly. **2** chiefly Scottish & N. English move house or leave one's home, especially in secrecy. > noun Brit. informal an act of leaving one's home in secrecy.

ORIGIN – Old Norse *flytja*; related to **FLEETING**.

flitch /flich/ > noun **1** a slab of wood cut from a tree trunk. **2** chiefly dialect a side of bacon.

flitter > verb move quickly in a random manner.

float > verb **1** rest on the surface of a liquid without sinking. **2** move slowly, hover, or be suspended in a liquid or the air. **3** put forward (an idea) as a suggestion or test of reactions. **4** remain unsettled in one's opinions, where one lives, etc. **5** offer the shares of (a company) for sale on the stock market for the first time. **6** (of a currency) fluctuate in value. > noun **1** any hollow or lightweight object or device designed to float on water. **2** a small floating object attached to a fishing line to indicate when a fish bites. **3** a floating device which forms part of a valve apparatus controlling a flow of water. **4** Brit. a small vehicle powered by electricity: *a milk float.* **5** a platform mounted on a truck and carrying a display in a procession. **6** Brit. a sum of money available for minor expenses or to provide change. **7** a hand tool with a rectangular blade used for smoothing plaster.

DERIVATIVES – **floater** noun.

COMBINATIONS – **floating-point** Computing denoting a mode of representing numbers as two sequences of bits, one representing the digits in the number and the other representing the position of the radix point. **floating rib** any of the lower ribs which are not attached directly to the breastbone. **floating voter** a person who does not consistently vote for the same party. **floatplane** a seaplane. **float valve** a ball valve.

ORIGIN – Old English, related to **FLEETING**.

floatation > noun variant spelling of **FLOTATION**.

floaty > adjective chiefly Brit. (especially of a woman's garment or a fabric) light and flimsy.

floccinaucinihilipilification /floksi-nawsinihilpillifi**kay**sh'n/ > noun the action of rating something as worthless.

ORIGIN – from Latin *flocci, nauci, nihili, pili* (words meaning 'of little or no value').

flocculate /**flok**yoolayt/ > verb technical form into small clumps or masses.

DERIVATIVES – **flocculation** noun.

ORIGIN – from Latin *flocculus* 'small tuft of wool'.

flocculent /**flok**yoolənt/ > adjective **1** having or resembling tufts of wool. **2** having a loosely clumped texture.

flock¹ > noun **1** a number of birds moving or resting together. **2** a number of domestic animals, especially sheep, that are kept together. **3** (**a flock** or **flocks**) a large number or crowd. **4** a Christian congregation under the charge of a particular minister. > verb congregate or move in a flock.

SYNONYMS – noun **3** (**a flock** or **flocks**) assembly, gathering, mass, throng. verb assemble, collect, converge, foregather, gather.

flock² > noun **1** a soft material for stuffing cushions and quilts, made of wool refuse or torn-up cloth. **2** powdered wool or cloth, used in making flock wallpaper. **3** a lock or tuft of wool or cotton.

COMBINATIONS – **flock wallpaper** wallpaper with a raised flock pattern.

ORIGIN – Latin *floccus* 'lock or tuft of wool'.

floe /flō/ > noun a sheet of floating ice.

ORIGIN – probably from Norwegian *flo* 'layer'.

flog > verb (**flogged, flogging**) **1** beat with a whip or stick as a punishment. **2** Brit. informal sell or offer for sale. **3** informal focus on or promote to excess: *beware of flogging this issue too hard.*

IDIOMS – **flog a dead horse** waste energy on a lost cause or unalterable situation.

DERIVATIVES – **flogger** noun.

SYNONYMS – **1** flagellate, lash, thrash.

ORIGIN – perhaps imitative, or from Latin *flagellare* 'to whip'.

flokati /flo**kaa**ti/ > noun (pl. **flokatis**) a Greek woven woollen rug with a thick, loose pile.

ORIGIN – modern Greek *phlokatē* 'peasant's blanket'.

flood > noun **1** an overflow of a large amount of water over dry land. **2** (**the Flood**) the biblical flood brought by God upon the earth because of the wickedness of the human race. **3** an overwhelming quantity of things or people appearing at once. **4** an outpouring of tears or emotion. **5** the inflow of the tide. **6** a floodlight. > verb **1** cover or become covered with water in a flood. **2** (of a river) become swollen and overflow its banks. **3** arrive in or overwhelm with very large numbers. **4** fill or suffuse completely: *she flooded the room with light.* **5** overfill the carburettor of (an engine) with petrol.

WORDFINDER – alluvium (*fertile deposit left by floodwater*), antediluvian (*occurring before the Biblical flood*), diluvial (*relating to a flood*), levee (*embankment built to prevent a river flooding*), spate (*sudden flood in a river*).

SYNONYMS – noun **3** cascade, deluge, tide, torrent. verb **1** deluge, inundate, swamp. **3** glut, saturate, swamp.

COMBINATIONS – **flood plain** an area of low-lying ground adjacent to a river that is subject to flooding. **flood tide** an incoming tide.

ORIGIN – Old English, related to **FLOW**.

floodgate > *noun* 1 a gate that can be opened or closed to admit or exclude water, especially the lower gate of a lock. 2 (**the floodgates**) the last restraints holding back something powerful or substantial.

floodlight > *noun* a large, powerful light used to illuminate a stage, sports ground, etc. > *verb* (past and past participle **floodlit**) illuminate with floodlights.

floor > *noun* 1 the lower surface of a room. 2 a storey of a building. 3 the bottom of the sea, a cave, etc. 4 (**the floor**) the part of a legislative assembly in which members sit and from which they speak. 5 (**the floor**) the right to speak in an assembly: *other speakers have the floor.* 6 a minimum level of prices or wages. > *verb* 1 provide with a floor. 2 informal knock to the ground. 3 informal baffle completely.
DERIVATIVES – **flooring** *noun.*
COMBINATIONS – **floorboard** a long plank making up part of a wooden floor. **floor manager** 1 the stage manager of a television production. 2 a supervisor of shop assistants in a large store. **floor show** an entertainment presented on the floor of a nightclub or restaurant.

floozy (also **floozie**) > *noun* (pl. **floozies**) informal a girl or woman who dresses or behaves in a sexually provocative way.
ORIGIN – perhaps related to **FLOSSY** or to dialect *floosy* 'fluffy'.

flop > *verb* (**flopped, flopping**) 1 hang or swing loosely: *her hair flopped over her face.* 2 sit or lie down heavily and clumsily. 3 informal fail totally. > *noun* 1 a heavy and clumsy fall. 2 informal a total failure.
SYNONYMS – *verb* 1 dangle, droop, drop.
ORIGIN – variant of **FLAP**.

flophouse > *noun* informal, chiefly N. Amer. a cheap lodging house.

floppy > *adjective* (**floppier, floppiest**) tending to flop; not firm or rigid. > *noun* (pl. **floppies**) (also **floppy disk**) Computing a flexible removable magnetic disk used for storing data.
DERIVATIVES – **floppily** *adverb* **floppiness** *noun.*

flora > *noun* (pl. **floras** or **florae**) 1 the plants of a particular region, habitat, or geological period. Compare with **FAUNA**. 2 the symbiotic bacteria occurring naturally in the intestines.
ORIGIN – from Latin *flos* 'flower'.

floral > *adjective* 1 of or decorated with flowers. 2 Botany of flora or floras.
DERIVATIVES – **florally** *adverb.*

Florentine /**florr**əntīn/ > *adjective* 1 relating to the city of Florence in Italy. 2 (**florentine** /**florr**ənteen/) (after a noun) (of a dish) served on a bed of spinach: *eggs florentine.* > *noun* 1 a person from Florence. 2 a biscuit consisting mainly of nuts and preserved fruit, coated on one side with chocolate.

florescence /flo**ress**'nss/ > *noun* the process of flowering.
ORIGIN – Latin *florescentia*, from *florescere* 'begin to flower'.

floret /**florr**it/ > *noun* 1 each of the small flowers making up a composite flower head. 2 each of the flowering stems making up a head of cauliflower or broccoli.
ORIGIN – from Latin *flos* 'flower'.

floribunda /florri**bun**də/ > *noun* a plant, especially a rose, which bears dense clusters of flowers.
ORIGIN – Latin, from *floribundus* 'freely flowering'.

floriculture /**flor**ikulchər/ > *noun* the cultivation of flowers.
DERIVATIVES – **floriculturist** *noun.*

florid /**florr**id/ > *adjective* 1 having a red or flushed complexion. 2 elaborately or excessively ornate or intricate: *florid prose.*
DERIVATIVES – **floridity** *noun* **floridly** *adverb* **floridness** *noun.*
SYNONYMS – 1 red-faced, rubicund, ruddy. 2 flowery, ornate, over-elaborate.
ANTONYMS – 2 plain.
ORIGIN – Latin *floridus*, from *flos* 'flower'.

floriferous /flo**riff**ərəss/ > *adjective* producing many flowers.

florin /**florr**in/ > *noun* 1 a former British coin worth two shillings. 2 an English gold coin of the 14th century, worth six shillings and eight old pence. 3 a Dutch guilder.
ORIGIN – Italian *fiorino* 'little flower' (originally referring to a Florentine coin bearing a fleur-de-lis).

florist > *noun* a person who sells and arranges cut flowers.
DERIVATIVES – **floristry** *noun.*

floruit /**florr**oo-it/ > *verb* used to indicate when a historical figure lived, worked, or was most active.
ORIGIN – Latin, 'he or she flourished'.

floss > *noun* 1 the rough silk enveloping a silkworm's cocoon. 2 untwisted silk fibres used in embroidery. 3 (also **dental floss**) a soft thread used to clean between the teeth. > *verb* clean between (one's teeth) with dental floss.
ORIGIN – Old French *flosche* 'down, nap of velvet'.

flossy > *adjective* (**flossier, flossiest**) 1 of or like floss. 2 N. Amer. informal excessively showy.

flotation* /flō**tay**sh'n/ (also **floatation**) > *noun* 1 the action of floating or capacity to float. 2 the process of offering a company's shares for sale on the stock market for the first time.
*SPELLING – strictly *flotation* rather than *floatation*, although the latter is also accepted.
COMBINATIONS – **flotation tank** a lightproof, soundproof tank of salt water in which a person floats as a form of deep relaxation.

flotilla /flə**till**ə/ > *noun* a small fleet of ships or boats.
ORIGIN – Spanish, 'small fleet'.

flotsam /**flot**səm/ > *noun* wreckage found floating on or washed up by the sea. Compare with **JETSAM**.
IDIOMS – **flotsam and jetsam** useless or discarded objects.
ORIGIN – Old French *floteson*, from *floter* 'to float'.

flounce¹ > *verb* move in an exaggeratedly impatient or angry manner. > *noun* an exaggerated action expressing annoyance or impatience.
ORIGIN – perhaps related to Norwegian *flunsa* 'hurry', or perhaps symbolic, like *bounce*.

flounce² > *noun* a wide ornamental strip of material gathered and sewn to a skirt or dress; a frill.
DERIVATIVES – **flounced** *adjective* **flouncy** *adjective.*
ORIGIN – from an alteration of obsolete *frounce* 'a fold or pleat', from Old French *fronce*.

flounder¹ > *verb* 1 stagger clumsily in mud or water. 2 have trouble doing or understanding something.
USAGE – do not confuse **flounder** with **founder**: **flounder**, in its general use, means 'have trouble doing or understanding something, be confused', while **founder** means 'fail or come to nothing'.
SYNONYMS – 1 blunder, struggle, stumble, thrash.
ORIGIN – perhaps a blend of **FOUNDER³** and **BLUNDER**.

flounder² > *noun* a small flatfish of shallow coastal waters.
ORIGIN – Old French *flondre*.

flour > *noun* a powder obtained by grinding grain, used to make bread, cakes, and pastry. > *verb* sprinkle with flour.
WORDFINDER – farinaceous (*made of or like flour*).
ORIGIN – a specific use of **FLOWER** in the sense 'the best part', used originally to mean 'the finest quality of ground wheat'.

flourish > *verb* 1 grow or develop in a healthy or vigorous way. 2 be working or at the height of one's career during a specified period. 3 wave about dramatically. > *noun* 1 a bold or extravagant gesture or action. 2 an ornamental flowing curve in handwriting or scrollwork. 3 an ornate musical passage. 4 a fanfare played by brass instruments.
SYNONYMS – *verb* 1 bloom, blossom, burgeon, thrive. 3 brandish, twirl, wave, wield.
ANTONYMS – *verb* 1 wither.

ORIGIN – Old French *florir*, from Latin *florere*, from *flos* 'a flower'.

floury > *adjective* **1** covered with flour. **2** (of a potato) having a soft, fluffy texture when cooked.

flout /flowt/ > *verb* **1** openly disregard (a rule, law, or convention). **2** archaic mock; scoff.

USAGE – do not confuse **flaunt** with **flout**: **flout** means 'openly disregard', whereas **flaunt** means 'display ostentatiously'.

ORIGIN – perhaps from Dutch *fluiten* 'whistle, play the flute, hiss derisively'.

flow > *verb* **1** move steadily and continuously in a current or stream. **2** move or issue forth steadily and freely: *people flowed into the courtyard*. **3** hang loosely and elegantly. **4** (of tidewater) move towards the land; rise. The opposite of EBB. > *noun* **1** the action or process of flowing. **2** a steady, continuous stream. **3** the rise of a tide or a river.

IDIOMS – **go with the flow** informal be relaxed and accept a situation. **in full flow** talking or performing fluently and enthusiastically.

DERIVATIVES – **flowing** *adjective*.

SYNONYMS – *verb* **1,2** course, ripple, run, stream, sweep.

COMBINATIONS – **flow chart** (also **flow diagram**) a diagram of a sequence of operations or functions making up a complex process or computer program.

ORIGIN – Old English, related to FLOOD.

flower > *noun* **1** the seed-bearing part of a plant, consisting of reproductive organs typically surrounded by brightly coloured petals and green sepals. **2** (often in phrase **in flower**) the state or period in which a plant's flowers have developed and opened. **3** (**the flower of**) the best of a group. > *verb* **1** produce flowers. **2** be in or reach a peak of development.

WORDFINDER – *parts of a flower:* anther, bract, calyx, carpel, corolla, filament, pistil, sepal, stamen, stigma, style; inflorescence (*complete flower head*).

DERIVATIVES – **flowerer** *noun* **flowerless** *adjective*.

COMBINATIONS – **flower head** a compact mass of flowers at the top of a stem, especially a dense flat cluster of florets. **flowerpot** an earthenware or plastic container in which to grow a plant. **flower power** the promotion by hippies of peace and love as means of changing the world. **flowers of sulphur** Chemistry a fine yellow powdered form of sulphur.

ORIGIN – Old French *flour*, *flor*, from Latin *flos*.

flowered > *adjective* **1** having a floral design. **2** bearing flowers of a specified kind: *yellow-flowered japonica*.

flowery > *adjective* **1** full of, decorated with,

or resembling flowers. **2** (of speech or writing) elaborate.

SYNONYMS – **1** elaborate, fancy, high-flown, ornate.

flown past participle of FLY[1].

flowsheet > *noun* a flow chart.

flu > *noun* influenza or any similar, milder infection.

flub N. Amer. informal > *verb* (**flubbed**, **flubbing**) botch or bungle. > *noun* a blunder.

fluctuate /fluktyooayt/ > *verb* rise and fall irregularly in number or amount.

DERIVATIVES – **fluctuation** *noun*.

ORIGIN – Latin *fluctuare* 'undulate', from *fluere* 'to flow'.

flue /floo/ > *noun* **1** a duct in a chimney for smoke and waste gases. **2** a pipe or passage for conveying heat.

fluence /flooanss/ > *noun* Brit. informal magical or hypnotic power.

ORIGIN – shortening of INFLUENCE.

fluent /flooant/ > *adjective* **1** speaking or writing in an articulate and natural manner. **2** (often **fluent in**) able to speak a particular foreign language well. **3** smoothly graceful and easy: *a runner in fluent motion*. **4** able to flow freely; fluid.

DERIVATIVES – **fluency** *noun* **fluently** *adverb*.

SYNONYMS – **1** articulate, eloquent, expressive.

ORIGIN – from Latin *fluere* 'to flow'.

fluff > *noun* **1** soft fibres accumulated in small, light clumps. **2** the soft fur or feathers of a young mammal or bird. **3** trivial or superficial entertainment or writing. **4** informal a mistake, especially in speech, sport, or music. > *verb* **1** (usu. **fluff up**) make (something) fuller and softer by shaking or patting it. **2** informal fail to accomplish properly: *he fluffed his only line*.

ORIGIN – probably a dialect alteration of *flue* 'down, nap, fluff'.

fluffy > *adjective* (**fluffier**, **fluffiest**) **1** of, like, or covered with fluff. **2** (of food) light in texture. **3** informal frivolous, silly, or vague.

DERIVATIVES – **fluffily** *adverb* **fluffiness** *noun*.

flugelhorn /floog'lhorn/ > *noun* a valved brass musical instrument like a cornet but with a broader tone.

ORIGIN – from German *Flügel* 'wing' + *Horn* 'horn'.

fluid > *noun* a substance, such as a liquid or gas, that has no fixed shape and yields easily to external pressure. > *adjective* **1** able to flow easily. **2** not settled or stable. **3** smoothly elegant or graceful.

DERIVATIVES – **fluidity** *noun* **fluidly** *adverb*.

COMBINATIONS – **fluid mechanics** the study of forces and flow within fluids. **fluid ounce 1** Brit. a unit of capacity equal to one twentieth of a pint (approximately 0.028

litre). **2** (also **fluidounce**) US a unit of capacity equal to one sixteenth of a US pint (approximately 0.03 litre).

ORIGIN – Latin *fluidus*, from *fluere* 'to flow'.

fluke[1] > *noun* a lucky chance occurrence. > *verb* achieve by luck rather than skill.

DERIVATIVES – **fluky** (also **flukey**) *adjective*.

fluke[2] > *noun* **1** a parasitic flatworm which typically has suckers and hooks for attaching itself to the host. **2** chiefly dialect or N. Amer. a flounder or other flatfish.

fluke[3] > *noun* **1** a broad triangular plate on the arm of an anchor. **2** either of the lobes of a whale's tail.

ORIGIN – perhaps from FLUKE[2] (because of the shape).

flume /floom/ > *noun* **1** an artificial channel conveying water, typically used for transporting logs. **2** a water slide or chute at a swimming pool or amusement park.

ORIGIN – first denoting a river or stream: from Old French *flum*, from Latin *flumen* 'river'.

flummery > *noun* (pl. **flummeries**) **1** empty talk or compliments. **2** a sweet dish made with beaten eggs and sugar.

ORIGIN – Welsh *llymru*.

flummox /flumməks/ > *verb* (usu. **be flummoxed**) informal perplex; bewilder.

flump > *verb* fall, sit, or throw down heavily. > *noun* a heavy fall.

flung past and past participle of FLING.

flunk > *verb* informal, chiefly N. Amer. **1** fail to reach the required standard in (an examination). **2** (**flunk out**) fail utterly and leave or be dismissed from school or college.

ORIGIN – perhaps related to FUNK[1] or to US *flink* 'be a coward'.

flunkey (also **flunky**) > *noun* (pl. **flunkeys** or **flunkies**) chiefly derogatory **1** a liveried manservant or footman. **2** a person who performs menial tasks.

ORIGIN – perhaps from FLANK in the sense 'a person who stands at one's flank'.

fluoresce /flooress/ > *verb* shine or glow brightly due to fluorescence.

fluorescence > *noun* **1** light emitted by a substance when it is exposed to radiation such as ultraviolet light or X-rays. **2** the property of emitting light in this way.

ORIGIN – from FLUORSPAR (which fluoresces), on the pattern of *opalescence*.

fluorescent* > *adjective* **1** having or showing fluorescence. **2** (of lighting) based on fluorescence from a substance illuminated by ultraviolet light. **3** vividly colourful.

*SPELLING – *fluor-*, not *flour-*: *fluorescent*.

COMBINATIONS – **fluorescent screen** a transparent screen coated with fluorescent material to show images from X-rays.

fluoridate /**floor**idayt/ > *verb* add traces of fluorides to (something, especially a water supply).
DERIVATIVES – **fluoridation** *noun*.

fluoride /**floor**īd/ > *noun* 1 Chemistry a compound of fluorine with another element or group. 2 sodium fluoride or another fluorine-containing salt added to water supplies or toothpaste in order to reduce tooth decay.

fluorinate /**floo**rinayt/ > *verb* 1 Chemistry introduce fluorine into (a compound). 2 another term for FLUORIDATE.
DERIVATIVES – **fluorination** *noun*.

fluorine /**floo**rin/ > *noun* a poisonous, extremely reactive, pale yellow gaseous chemical element.
ORIGIN – from *fluor* (see FLUORSPAR).

fluorite > *noun* a mineral form of calcium fluoride.

fluorocarbon > *noun* Chemistry a compound formed by replacing one or more of the hydrogen atoms in a hydrocarbon with fluorine atoms.

fluoroscope > *noun* an instrument with a fluorescent screen used for viewing X-ray images without taking and developing X-ray photographs.
DERIVATIVES – **fluoroscopic** *adjective* **fluoroscopy** *noun*.

fluorspar /**floor**spaar/ > *noun* another term for FLUORITE.
ORIGIN – from Latin *fluor* 'a flow' (formerly used in English to mean 'fluorspar, a flow, a flux') + SPAR³.

flurried > *adjective* agitated, nervous, or anxious.

flurry > *noun* (pl. **flurries**) 1 a small swirling mass of snow, leaves, etc. moved by a sudden gust of wind. 2 a sudden short spell of commotion or excitement. 3 a number of things arriving suddenly and simultaneously. > *verb* (**flurries**, **flurried**) move in an agitated or excited way.
ORIGIN – from obsolete *flurr* 'fly up, flutter', probably influenced by HURRY.

flush¹ > *verb* 1 (of a person's skin or face) become red and hot, typically through illness or emotion. 2 glow or cause to glow with warm colour or light. 3 (**be flushed with**) be excited or elated by. 4 cleanse (something, especially a toilet) by passing large quantities of water through it. 5 remove or dispose of by flushing with water. 6 drive (a bird or animal, especially a game bird) from cover. 7 (often **flush out**) force into the open: *their task was to flush out the rebels*. > *noun* 1 a reddening of the face or skin. 2 a sudden rush of intense emotion. 3 a period of freshness and vigour: *the first flush of youth*. 4 an act of flushing.
DERIVATIVES – **flusher** *noun*.
SYNONYMS – *verb* 1 blush, colour, redden.
ORIGIN – first used in the sense 'spring or

fly up': symbolic; perhaps influenced by FLASH and BLUSH.

flush² > *adjective* 1 completely level or even with another surface. 2 informal having plenty of money. > *verb* fill in (a joint) level with a surface.
ORIGIN – first used in the sense 'perfect, lacking nothing': probably related to FLUSH¹.

flush³ > *noun* (in poker or brag) a hand of cards all of the same suit.
ORIGIN – French *flux* (formerly *flus*), from Latin *fluxus* 'flux'.

fluster > *verb* make (someone) agitated or confused. > *noun* a flustered state.
DERIVATIVES – **flustered** *adjective*.
SYNONYMS – *verb* agitate, bother, disconcert, ruffle, unsettle.
ORIGIN – first used in the sense 'make slightly drunk': perhaps related to Icelandic *flaustra* 'hurry, bustle'.

flute > *noun* 1 a high-pitched wind instrument consisting of a tube with holes along it, usually held horizontally so that the breath can be directed against a fixed edge. 2 Architecture an ornamental vertical groove in a column. 3 a tall, narrow wine glass. > *verb* 1 speak in a melodious way. 2 make grooves in.
WORDFINDER – flautist (*flute player*).
DERIVATIVES – **fluted** *adjective* **fluting** *noun* **fluty** (also **flutey**) *adjective*.
ORIGIN – Old French *flahute*, probably from Provençal *flaüt*, perhaps a blend of *flaujol* 'flageolet' + *laüt* 'lute'.

flutist > *noun* US term for FLAUTIST.

flutter > *verb* 1 fly unsteadily by flapping the wings quickly and lightly. 2 move or fall with a light irregular motion. 3 (of a pulse or heartbeat) beat feebly or irregularly. > *noun* 1 an act or instance of fluttering. 2 a state of tremulous excitement. 3 Brit. informal a small bet. 4 Electronics rapid variation in the pitch or amplitude of a signal, especially of recorded sound. Compare with WOW².
DERIVATIVES – **fluttery** *adjective*.
ORIGIN – Old English, related to FLIT and FLOAT.

fluvial /**floo**viəl/ > *adjective* chiefly Geology of or found in a river.
ORIGIN – Latin *fluvialis*, from *fluvius* 'river'.

flux /fluks/ > *noun* 1 continuous change. 2 the action or an instance of flowing. 3 Medicine an abnormal discharge of blood or other matter from or within the body. 4 Physics the total amount of radiation, or of electric or magnetic field lines, passing through an area. 5 a substance mixed with a solid to lower the melting point, especially in soldering or smelting.
ORIGIN – Latin *fluxus*, from *fluere* 'to flow'.

fly¹ > *verb* (**flies**; past **flew**; past participle **flown**) 1 (of a winged creature or aircraft) move through the air under control. 2 control the

flight of or convey in (an aircraft). 3 move or be hurled quickly through the air. 4 go or move quickly. 5 wave or flutter in the wind. 6 (of a flag) be displayed on a flagpole. 7 (**fly into**) suddenly go into (a rage or other strong emotion). 8 (**fly at**) attack verbally or physically. 9 archaic flee. > *noun* (pl. **flies**) 1 (Brit. also **flies**) an opening at the crotch of a pair of trousers, closed with a zip or buttons. 2 a flap of material covering the opening of a tent. 3 (**the flies**) the space over the stage in a theatre.
IDIOMS – **fly in the face of** be openly at variance with (what is usual or expected). **fly a kite** informal try something out to test public opinion. **fly off the handle** informal lose one's temper suddenly.
DERIVATIVES – **flyable** *adjective*.
SYNONYMS – *verb* 4 race, rush, speed, tear.
COMBINATIONS – **flyaway** (of hair) fine and difficult to control. **fly-by-night** unreliable or untrustworthy, especially in business or financial matters. **fly-by-wire** a semi-automatic, computer-regulated system for controlling an aircraft or spacecraft. **fly half** Rugby a stand-off half. **fly-past** Brit. a ceremonial flight of aircraft past a person or a place. **fly-tip** Brit. illegally dump waste.
ORIGIN – Old English, related to FLY².

fly² > *noun* (pl. **flies**) 1 a flying insect of a large order characterised by a single pair of transparent wings and sucking or piercing mouthparts. 2 used in names of other flying insects, e.g. **dragonfly**. 3 a fishing bait consisting of a mayfly or other natural or artificial flying insect.
IDIOMS – **a fly in the ointment** a minor irritation that spoils the enjoyment of something. **fly on the wall** an unnoticed observer. **there are no flies on ——** the person specified is quick and astute.
COMBINATIONS – **fly agaric** a poisonous toadstool which has a red cap with fluffy white spots. **fly-fishing** the sport of fishing using a rod and an artificial fly as bait. **flypaper** sticky, poison-treated strips of paper that are hung indoors to catch and kill flies. **flyspeck** 1 a tiny stain made by the excrement of an insect. 2 something contemptibly small or insignificant.
ORIGIN – Old English, related to FLY¹.

fly³ > *adjective* (**flyer**, **flyest**) informal 1 Brit. knowing and clever; worldly-wise. 2 N. Amer. stylish and fashionable.

flyblown > *adjective* contaminated by contact with flies and their eggs and larvae.

flycatcher > *noun* a songbird that catches flying insects in short flights from a perch.

flyer (also **flier**) > *noun* 1 a person or thing that flies. 2 informal a fast-moving person or thing. 3 a small handbill advertising an event or product. 4 a flying start.

flying > *adjective* 1 moving through or

fluttering in the air. **2** hasty; brief: *a flying visit*.

IDIOMS – **with flying colours** with distinction.

COMBINATIONS – **flying boat** a large seaplane that lands with its fuselage in the water. **flying bomb** a small pilotless aircraft with an explosive warhead. **flying buttress** Architecture a buttress slanting from a separate column, typically forming an arch with the wall it supports. **flying doctor** (in Australia) a doctor who travels by aircraft to visit patients in remote areas. **flying fish** a fish of warm seas which leaps out of the water and uses its wing-like pectoral fins to glide for some distance. **flying fox** a large fruit bat with a foxlike face, found in Madagascar, SE Asia, and northern Australia. **flying officer** a rank of commissioned officer in the RAF, above pilot officer and below flight lieutenant. **flying saucer** a disc-shaped flying craft supposedly piloted by aliens. **flying squad** Brit. a division of a police force which is capable of reaching an incident quickly. **flying start 1** a start of a race in which the competitors are already moving at speed as they pass the starting point. **2** a good beginning giving an advantage over competitors.

flyleaf > *noun* (pl. **flyleaves**) a blank page at the beginning or end of a book.

flyover > *noun* chiefly Brit. a bridge carrying one road or railway line over another.

fly-post > *verb* Brit. put up (advertising posters) in unauthorised places.

DERIVATIVES – **fly-poster** *noun*.

flysheet > *noun* **1** Brit. a fabric cover pitched over a tent to give extra protection against bad weather. **2** a tract or circular of two or four pages.

flyweight > *noun* a weight in boxing and other sports intermediate between light flyweight and bantamweight.

flywheel > *noun* a heavy revolving wheel in a machine, used to increase momentum and thereby provide greater stability or a reserve of available power.

FM > *abbreviation* **1** Field Marshal. **2** frequency modulation.

Fm > *symbol* the chemical element fermium.

fm > *abbreviation* fathom(s).

f-number > *noun* the ratio of the focal length of a camera lens to the diameter of the aperture being used.

FO > *abbreviation* Foreign Office.

foal > *noun* a young horse or related animal. > *verb* (of a mare) give birth to a foal.

ORIGIN – Old English, related to FILLY.

foam > *noun* **1** a mass of small bubbles formed on or in liquid. **2** a liquid preparation containing many small bubbles: *shaving foam*. **3** a lightweight form of rubber or plastic made by solidifying foam. > *verb* form or produce foam.

IDIOMS – **foam at the mouth** informal be overcome with anger.

DERIVATIVES – **foamy** *adjective*.

SYNONYMS – *noun* **1** bubbles, froth, spume. *verb* bubble, effervesce, froth.

fob¹ > *noun* **1** a chain attached to a watch for carrying in a waistcoat or waistband pocket. **2** (also **fob pocket**) a small pocket for carrying a watch. **3** a tab on a key ring.

COMBINATIONS – **fob watch** a pocket watch.

ORIGIN – probably related to German dialect *Fuppe* 'pocket'.

fob² > *verb* (**fobbed**, **fobbing**) **1** (**fob off**) try to deceive (someone) into accepting an excuse or an inferior thing. **2** (**fob off on**) give (something inferior) to.

ORIGIN – perhaps related to German *foppen* 'deceive, banter', or to FOP.

focaccia /fəˈkachə/ > *noun* a type of flat Italian bread made with olive oil and flavoured with herbs.

ORIGIN – Italian.

focal /ˈfōkʼl/ > *adjective* relating to a focus, especially the focus of a lens.

COMBINATIONS – **focal length** the distance between the centre of a lens or curved mirror and its focus. **focal point 1** the point at which rays or waves meet after reflection or refraction, or from which diverging rays or waves appear to proceed. **2** the centre of interest or activity.

fo'c'sle /ˈfōksʼl/ > *noun* variant spelling of FORECASTLE.

focus* /ˈfōkəss/ > *noun* (pl. **focuses** or **foci** /ˈfōsī/) **1** the centre of interest or activity. **2** the state or quality of having or producing clear visual definition: *his face is out of focus*. **3** the point at which an object must be situated with respect to a lens or mirror for an image of the object to be well defined. **4** a focal point. **5** an act of focusing on something. **6** the point of origin of an earthquake. Compare with EPICENTRE. **7** Geometry one of the points from which the distances to any point of an ellipse, parabola, or other curve are connected by a linear relation. > *verb* (**focused**, **focusing** or **focussed**, **focussing**) **1** adapt to the prevailing level of light and become able to see clearly. **2** adjust the focus of (a telescope, camera, etc.). **3** (with reference to rays or waves) meet or cause to meet at a single point. **4** (**focus on**) pay particular attention to.

DERIVATIVES – **focuser** *noun*.

***SPELLING** – do not double the *s* when forming the plural of the noun **focus**: focuses. A single *s* is also usual in inflected forms of the verb: focused, focusing.

COMBINATIONS – **focus group** a group of people assembled to assess a new product, political campaign, television series, etc.

ORIGIN – Latin, 'domestic hearth'.

fodder > *noun* **1** food for cattle and other livestock. **2** a person or thing regarded only as material to satisfy a need: *young people ending up as factory fodder*.

ORIGIN – Old English, related to FOOD.

foe > *noun* formal or literary an enemy or opponent.

ORIGIN – Old English, 'hostile'; related to FEUD.

foehn > *noun* variant spelling of FÖHN.

foetid > *adjective* variant spelling of FETID.

foetus > *noun* variant spelling of FETUS (chiefly in British non-technical use).

DERIVATIVES – **foetal** *adjective*.

fog > *noun* **1** a thick cloud of tiny water droplets suspended in the atmosphere at or near the earth's surface which obscures or restricts visibility. **2** a state or cause of perplexity or confusion. **3** Photography cloudiness obscuring the image on a developed negative or print. > *verb* (**fogged**, **fogging**) **1** cover or become covered with steam. **2** bewilder or confuse. **3** Photography make (a film, negative, or print) obscure or cloudy.

COMBINATIONS – **foghorn** a device making a loud, deep sound as a warning to ships in fog.

ORIGIN – perhaps from FOGGY.

fogey /ˈfōgi/ (also **fogy**) > *noun* (pl. **fogeys** or **fogies**) a very old-fashioned or conservative person.

DERIVATIVES – **fogeyish** *adjective* **fogeyism** *noun*.

foggy > *adjective* (**foggier**, **foggiest**) **1** full of or accompanied by fog. **2** confused or obscure.

IDIOMS – **not have the foggiest (idea)** informal, chiefly Brit. have no idea at all.

SYNONYMS – **1** hazy, misty, murky.

ORIGIN – perhaps from *fog* 'grass growing after a crop of hay has been cut'.

föhn /fön/ (also **foehn**) > *noun* a hot southerly wind on the northern slopes of the Alps.

ORIGIN – German, from Latin *ventus Favonius* 'mild west wind', *Favonius* being the Roman personification of the west or west wind.

foible /ˈfoybʼl/ > *noun* a minor weakness or eccentricity.

SYNONYMS – eccentricity, idiosyncrasy, peculiarity, quirk.

ORIGIN – French, obsolete form of Old French *fieble* 'feeble'.

foie gras /fwaa ˈgraa/ > *noun* short for PÂTÉ DE FOIE GRAS.

foil¹ > *verb* prevent the success of.

SYNONYMS – baulk, frustrate, thwart.

ORIGIN – first used in the sense 'trample down': perhaps from Old French *fouler* 'to full cloth, trample'.

foil² > *noun* **1** metal hammered or rolled into a thin flexible sheet. **2** a person or thing that contrasts with and so enhances the qualities of another.

ORIGIN – Latin *folium* 'leaf'; sense 2 arose from a use denoting a thin leaf of metal placed under a precious stone to increase its brilliance.

foil³ > *noun* a light, blunt-edged fencing sword with a button on its point.

foist /foyst/ > *verb* (**foist on**) impose (an unwelcome person or thing) on.

SYNONYMS – (**foist on**) force on, offload on, palm off on, thrust on.

ORIGIN – first occurring in the sense 'dishonestly manipulate a dice': from Dutch dialect *vuisten* 'take in the hand'.

folate /fōlayt/ > *noun* Biochemistry a salt or ester of folic acid.

fold¹ > *verb* **1** bend (something) over on itself so that one part of it covers another. **2** be able to be folded into a flatter shape. **3** use (a soft or flexible material) to cover or wrap something in. **4** affectionately clasp in one's arms. **5** informal (of a company) cease trading as a result of financial problems. **6** (**fold in** or **into**) mix (an ingredient) gently with (another ingredient). > *noun* **1** a folded part or thing. **2** a line or crease produced by folding. **3** chiefly Brit. a slight hill or hollow. **4** Geology a bend or curvature of strata.

IDIOMS – **fold one's arms** bring one's arms together and cross them over one's chest.

DERIVATIVES – **foldable** *adjective*.

SYNONYMS – *verb* **1** crease, double, double over, tuck.

fold² > *noun* **1** a pen or enclosure for livestock, especially sheep. **2** (**the fold**) a group or community with shared aims and values.

-fold > *suffix* forming adjectives and adverbs from cardinal numbers: **1** in an amount multiplied by: *threefold*. **2** consisting of so many parts or facets: *twofold*.

ORIGIN – Old English, related to **FOLD¹**.

folder > *noun* **1** a folding cover or wallet for storing loose papers. **2** Computing a directory containing related files or documents.

folderol /foldərol/ (also **falderal**) > *noun* **1** trivial or nonsensical fuss. **2** a showy but useless item.

ORIGIN – from a meaningless refrain in old songs.

foley > *noun* (before another noun) chiefly US the addition of sound effects after the shooting of a film: *a foley artist*.

ORIGIN – named after the inventor of the editing process.

foliage /fōli-ij/ > *noun* leaves of plants collectively.

ORIGIN – Old French *feuillage*, from Latin *folium* 'leaf'.

foliar /fōliər/ > *adjective* technical relating to leaves.

foliate > *adjective* /fōliət/ decorated with leaves or a leaf-like pattern. > *verb* /fōliayt/ **1** decorate with leaves or a leaf-like pattern. **2** (**foliated**) chiefly Geology consisting of thin sheets or laminae.

folic acid /fōlik/ > *noun* a vitamin of the B complex found especially in leafy green vegetables, liver, and kidney.

ORIGIN – from Latin *folium* 'leaf'.

folie à deux /folli a dö/ > *noun* (pl. **folies à deux**) a delusion or mental illness shared by two people in close association.

ORIGIN – French, 'shared madness'.

folie de grandeur /folli də gronˈdör/ > *noun* delusions of grandeur.

ORIGIN – French.

folio /fōliō/ > *noun* (pl. **folios**) **1** a sheet of paper folded once to form two leaves (four pages) of a book. **2** a book made up of such sheets. **3** an individual leaf of paper numbered on the front side only. **4** the page number in a printed book.

ORIGIN – Latin, used to mean 'on leaf (as specified)', from *folium* 'leaf'.

folk /fōk/ > *plural noun* **1** (also **folks**) informal people in general. **2** (**one's folks**) informal one's family, especially one's parents. **3** (also **folk music**) traditional music of unknown authorship, transmitted orally. **4** (before another noun) originating from the beliefs, culture, and customs of ordinary people: *folk wisdom*.

COMBINATIONS – **folk dance** a traditional dance associated with a particular people or area. **folk etymology 1** a well-known but mistaken account of the origin of a word or phrase. **2** the process by which the form of an unfamiliar or foreign word is adapted to a more familiar form through popular usage. **folk memory** a body of recollections or legends that persists among a people. **folk tale** a traditional story originally transmitted orally.

folkie > *noun* informal a singer, player, or fan of folk music.

folkish > *adjective* **1** characteristic of ordinary people or traditional culture. **2** resembling folk music.

folklore > *noun* the traditional beliefs, stories, and customs of a community, passed on by word of mouth.

DERIVATIVES – **folkloric** *adjective* **folklorist** *noun*.

SYNONYMS – fable, legend, lore, mythology.

folksy > *adjective* (**folksier**, **folksiest**) traditional and homely, especially in an artificial way.

DERIVATIVES – **folksiness** *noun*.

folky > *adjective* (**folkier**, **folkiest**) resembling or characteristic of folk music.

follicle /follik'l/ > *noun* a small glandular cavity or pouch, especially that in which the root of a hair develops.

DERIVATIVES – **follicular** /folikyoolər/ *adjective*.

ORIGIN – Latin *folliculus* 'little bag'.

follow > *verb* **1** move or travel behind. **2** go after (someone) so as to observe or monitor them. **3** go along (a route or path). **4** come after in time or order. **5** be a logical consequence. **6** (also **follow on from**) occur as a result of. **7** act according to (an instruction or precept). **8** act according to the lead or example of. **9** take an interest in or pay close attention to. **10** understand the meaning of. **11** practise or undertake (a career or course of action). **12** (**follow through**) continue (an action or task) to its conclusion. **13** (**follow up**) pursue or investigate further.

IDIOMS – **follow one's nose 1** trust to one's instincts. **2** go straight ahead. **follow on** (of a cricket team) be required to bat again immediately after failing to reach a certain score in their first innings. **follow suit 1** conform to another's actions. **2** (in bridge, whist, and other card games) play a card of the suit led.

SYNONYMS – **2** shadow, stalk, trail. **7** abide by, adhere to, obey, observe. **8** copy, emulate, mimic.

COMBINATIONS – **follow-the-leader** (also **follow-my-leader**) a children's game in which the participants must copy the actions and words of a person acting as leader.

follower > *noun* **1** a person who follows. **2** a supporter, fan, or disciple.

SYNONYMS – **2** acolyte, apostle, devotee, votary.

following > *preposition* coming after or as a result of. > *noun* a body of supporters or admirers. > *adjective* **1** next in time or order. **2** about to be mentioned: *the following information*.

follow-through > *noun* the continuing of an action or task to its conclusion.

follow-up > *noun* **1** an activity carried out to monitor or further develop earlier work. **2** a work that follows or builds on an earlier work.

folly > *noun* (pl. **follies**) **1** foolishness. **2** a foolish act or idea. **3** an ornamental building with no practical purpose, especially a tower or mock-Gothic ruin.

SYNONYMS – **1** foolhardiness, idiocy, insanity, lunacy, madness, stupidity.

ANTONYMS – **1** wisdom.

ORIGIN – Old French *folie* 'madness'.

foment /fōment/ > *verb* **1** instigate or stir up (revolution or strife). **2** archaic bathe (a part of the body) with warm or medicated lotions.

DERIVATIVES – **fomentation** noun.

SYNONYMS – **1** incite, instigate, provoke, stir up.

ORIGIN – Latin fomentare, from fomentum 'poultice, lotion'.

fond > adjective **1** (**fond of**) having an affection or liking for. **2** affectionate; loving: fond memories. **3** (of a hope or belief) foolishly optimistic; naive.

DERIVATIVES – **fondly** adverb **fondness** noun.

SYNONYMS – **1** (**fond of**) attached to, keen on, partial to.

ORIGIN – first used in the sense 'infatuated, foolish': from obsolete fon 'a fool, be foolish'.

fondant /fondənt/ > noun **1** a thick paste made of sugar and water, used in making sweets and icing cakes. **2** a sweet made of fondant.

ORIGIN – French, 'melting'.

fondle > verb stroke or caress lovingly or erotically. > noun an act of fondling.

DERIVATIVES – **fondler** noun.

ORIGIN – from obsolete fondling 'much-loved or petted person'.

fondue /fondyōō/ > noun a dish in which small pieces of food are dipped into melted cheese, a hot sauce, or a hot cooking medium such as oil.

ORIGIN – French, 'melted'.

fons et origo /fonz et orrigō/ > noun the source and origin of something.

ORIGIN – Latin, originally as fons et origo mali 'the source and origin of evil'.

font[1] > noun a receptacle in a church for the water used in baptism.

ORIGIN – Latin fons 'spring, fountain'.

font[2] (Brit. also **fount**) > noun Printing a set of type of a particular face and size.

ORIGIN – first used with reference to casting or founding: from French fonte, from fondre 'to melt'.

fontanelle /fontənel/ (US **fontanel**) > noun a soft area between the bones of the cranium in an infant or fetus, where the sutures are not yet fully formed.

ORIGIN – Old French, 'little fountain'.

fontina /fonteenə/ > noun a pale yellow Italian cheese.

ORIGIN – Italian.

food > noun any nutritious substance that people or animals eat or drink or that plants absorb to maintain life and growth.

IDIOMS – **food for thought** something that warrants serious consideration.

SYNONYMS – nourishment, nutriment, sustenance; formal comestibles; archaic viands, victuals.

COMBINATIONS – **food chain** a series of organisms each dependent on the next as a source of food. **food poisoning** illness

caused by bacteria or other toxins in food, typically with vomiting and diarrhoea.

ORIGIN – Old English, related to FODDER.

foodie (also **foody**) > noun (pl. **foodies**) informal a person with a strong interest in food; a gourmet.

foodstuff > noun a substance suitable for consumption as food.

fool[1] > noun **1** a person who acts unwisely. **2** historical a jester or clown. > verb **1** trick or deceive. **2** (**fool about** or **around**) act in a joking or frivolous way. **3** (**fool around**) N. Amer. engage in casual or extramarital sexual activity. > adjective N. Amer. informal foolish or silly.

IDIOMS – **be no** (or **nobody's**) **fool** be shrewd or prudent. **a fool and his money are soon parted** proverb a foolish person spends money carelessly and will soon be penniless. **fools rush in where angels fear to tread** proverb people without good sense or judgement will have no hesitation in tackling a situation that even the wisest would avoid. **make a fool of 1** trick or deceive (someone) so that they look foolish. **2** (**make a fool of oneself**) appear foolish through incompetent or inappropriate behaviour. **more fool ——** used to express the view that the specified person is behaving unwisely. **there's no fool like an old fool** proverb the foolish behaviour of an older person seems especially foolish as they are expected to think and act more sensibly than a younger one.

DERIVATIVES – **foolery** noun.

SYNONYMS – noun **1** idiot, lunatic, moron.

COMBINATIONS – **fool's errand** a task or activity that has no hope of success. **fool's gold** a brassy yellow mineral that can be mistaken for gold, especially pyrite. **fool's paradise** a state of happiness based on not knowing about or ignoring potential trouble.

ORIGIN – Old French fol 'fool, foolish', from Latin follis 'bellows, windbag', by extension 'empty-headed person'.

fool[2] > noun chiefly Brit. a cold dessert made of puréed fruit mixed or served with cream or custard.

foolhardy > adjective recklessly bold or rash.

DERIVATIVES – **foolhardily** adverb **foolhardiness** noun.

SYNONYMS – impetuous, rash, reckless.

ORIGIN – Old French folhardi, from fol 'foolish' + hardi 'emboldened'.

foolish > adjective lacking good sense or judgement; silly or unwise.

DERIVATIVES – **foolishly** adverb **foolishness** noun.

SYNONYMS – idiotic, senseless, silly, unwise.

foolproof > adjective incapable of going wrong or being misused.

foolscap /fōōlskap/ > noun Brit. a size of paper, about 330 × 200 (or 400) mm.

ORIGIN – said to be named from a former watermark representing a fool's cap.

foot > noun (pl. **feet**) **1** the lower extremity of the leg below the ankle, on which a person walks. **2** the lowest part of something vertical; the base or bottom. **3** the end of a bed where the occupant's feet normally rest. **4** a unit of linear measure equal to 12 inches (30.48 cm). **5** Poetry a group of syllables constituting a metrical unit. > verb **1** informal pay (a bill). **2** (**foot it**) cover a distance on foot.

WORDFINDER – chiropody, podiatry (medical treatment of the feet), metatarsus (bones of the foot), pedal (of or relating to the feet), pedicure (cosmetic treatment of the feet), plantar (of the sole of the foot), verruca (wart on the sole of the foot).

IDIOMS – **feet of clay** a flaw or weakness in a person otherwise revered. **fleet of foot** able to walk or move swiftly. **get** (or **start**) **off on the right** (or **wrong**) **foot** make a good (or bad) start at something. **have** (or **keep**) **one's feet on the ground** be (or remain) practical and sensible. **have** (or **get**) **a foot in the door** have (or gain) a first introduction to a profession or organisation. **have one foot in the grave** humorous be very old or ill. **land** (or **fall**) **on one's feet** have good luck or success. **on** (or **by**) **foot** walking rather than using a car or other transport. **put one's best foot forward** start doing something with as much effort and determination as possible. **put one's foot down** informal **1** adopt a firm policy when faced with opposition or disobedience. **2** Brit. accelerate a motor vehicle by pressing the accelerator pedal. **put one's foot in it** informal say or do something tactless or embarrassing. **put a foot wrong** make a mistake: he never put a foot wrong with his hosts. **under one's feet** in one's way. **under foot** on the ground.

DERIVATIVES – **footless** adjective.

COMBINATIONS – **foot-and-mouth disease** a contagious disease of cattle and sheep, spread by a virus and causing ulceration of the hoofs and around the mouth. **footbrake** a foot-operated brake lever in a motor vehicle. **footbridge** a bridge for pedestrians. **foot fault** (in tennis, squash, etc.) an infringement of the rules made by overstepping the baseline when serving. **footlights** a row of spotlights along the front of a stage at the level of the actors' feet. **footmark** a footprint. **footpath** a path for people to walk along, especially a right of way in the countryside. **footplate** chiefly Brit. the platform for the crew in the cab of a locomotive. **footprint** the impression left by a foot or shoe on the ground. **foot soldier 1** a soldier who fights on foot. **2** a low-ranking person who nevertheless does valuable work. **footstool** a low stool for resting the feet on when sitting. **footwear** shoes, boots, and other coverings for the feet. **footwell** a space for the feet in front of a seat in a vehicle. **footwork** the manner in which one moves one's feet in dancing and sport.

footage > *noun* **1** a length of film made for cinema or television. **2** size or length measured in feet.

football > *noun* **1** any of a number of forms of team game involving kicking a ball, in particular (in the UK) soccer or (in the US) American football. **2** a ball used in such a game.

DERIVATIVES – **footballer** *noun*.

footer¹ /foŏtər/ > *noun* **1** a person or thing of a specified number of feet in length or height: *a six-footer*. **2** a kick of a football performed with a specified foot: *a low left-footer*. **3** variant of FOOTY. **4** a line of text appearing at the foot of each page of a book or document.

footer² /foŏtər/ > *verb* Scottish fiddle about.

ORIGIN – variant of obsolete *foutre* 'valueless thing, contemptible person', from Old French *foutre* 'have sexual intercourse with'.

footfall > *noun* **1** the sound of a footstep or footsteps. **2** the number of people entering a shop or shopping area in a given time.

foothill > *noun* a low hill at the base of a mountain or mountain range.

foothold > *noun* **1** a place where one can lodge a foot to give secure support while climbing. **2** a secure position from which further progress may be made.

footie > *noun* variant spelling of FOOTY.

footing > *noun* **1** (**one's footing**) a secure grip with one's feet. **2** the basis on which something is established or operates. **3** the foundations of a wall, usually with a course of brickwork wider than the base of the wall.

footle /foŏt'l/ > *verb* chiefly Brit. engage in fruitless activity; mess about.

ORIGIN – perhaps from FOOTER².

footling /foŏtling/ > *adjective* trivial and irritating.

SYNONYMS – piffling, silly, trifling.

footloose > *adjective* free to go where one likes and do as one pleases.

footman > *noun* a liveried servant whose duties include admitting visitors and waiting at table.

footnote > *noun* an additional piece of information printed at the bottom of a page.

footpad > *noun* historical a highwayman operating on foot rather than riding a horse.

footsie /foŏtsi/ > *noun* (usu. in phrase **play footsie**) informal the action of touching someone's feet lightly with one's own as a playful expression of romantic interest.

footslog > *verb* (**footslogged, footslogging**) laboriously walk or march for a long distance. > *noun* a long and exhausting walk or march.

DERIVATIVES – **footslogger** *noun*.

footsore > *adjective* having sore feet from much walking.

footstep > *noun* a step taken in walking, especially as heard by another person.

IDIOMS – **follow** (or **tread**) **in someone's footsteps** do as another person did before.

footy (also **footie** or **footer**) > *noun* Brit. informal football; soccer.

foo yong > *noun* a Chinese dish or sauce made with egg as a main ingredient.

ORIGIN – Chinese, 'hibiscus'.

fop > *noun* a man who is excessively concerned with his clothes and appearance.

DERIVATIVES – **foppery** *noun* **foppish** *adjective* **foppishly** *adverb* **foppishness** *noun*.

ORIGIN – first used in the sense 'fool'.

for > *preposition* **1** in favour of. **2** affecting or with regard to. **3** on behalf of or to the benefit of. **4** having as a purpose or function. **5** having as a reason or cause. **6** having as a destination. **7** representing. **8** in exchange for. **9** in relation to the expected norm of. **10** indicating the extent of (a distance) or the length of (a period of time). **11** indicating an occasion in a series. > *conjunction* literary because; since.

IDIOMS – **be for it** Brit. informal be about to be punished or get into trouble.

for- > *prefix* **1** denoting prohibition: *forbid*. **2** denoting abstention, neglect, or renunciation: *forgive*. **3** used as an intensifier: *forlorn*.

fora plural of FORUM (in sense 3).

forage /forrij/ > *verb* **1** search for food or provisions. **2** obtain (food) by searching. > *noun* **1** food for horses and cattle. **2** an act of foraging.

DERIVATIVES – **forager** *noun*.

COMBINATIONS – **forage cap** a soldier's peaked cap.

ORIGIN – Old French *fourrager*, from *fuerre* 'straw'.

foramen /fəraymen/ > *noun* (pl. **foramina** /fərammīnə/) Anatomy an opening, hole, or passage, especially in a bone.

ORIGIN – Latin.

foraminifera /forrəminnifərə/ > *plural noun* (sing. **foraminifer**) Zoology single-celled planktonic animals with a perforated chalky shell.

ORIGIN – from Latin *foramen* 'foramen' + *-fer* 'bearing'.

forasmuch as > *conjunction* archaic because; since.

foray /forray/ > *noun* **1** a sudden attack or incursion into enemy territory. **2** a brief but spirited attempt to become involved in a new activity. > *verb* make or go on a foray.

DERIVATIVES – **forayer** *noun*.

ORIGIN – from Old French *forrier* 'forager'.

forbade (also **forbad**) past of FORBID.

forbear¹ /forbair/ > *verb* (past **forbore**; past participle **forborne**) refrain from doing something.

USAGE – **forbear** means 'refrain from doing something'; it is also a less common spelling for **forebear**, 'an ancestor'.

forbear² /forbair/ > *noun* variant spelling of FOREBEAR.

forbearance > *noun* **1** patient self-control and restraint. **2** tolerance.

forbearing > *adjective* patient and restrained.

forbid /forbid/ > *verb* (**forbidding**; past **forbade** /forbad, forbayd/ or **forbad**; past participle **forbidden**) **1** refuse to allow. **2** order (someone) not to do.

IDIOMS – **the forbidden degrees** the number of steps of descent from the same ancestor that bar two related people from marrying. **forbidden fruit** a thing that is desired all the more because it is not allowed. [ORIGIN – with biblical allusion to the Book of Genesis, chapter 2.] **God** (or **Heaven**) **forbid** expressing a fervent wish that something does not happen.

SYNONYMS – ban, bar, prohibit, proscribe.

ANTONYMS – allow, permit.

forbidding > *adjective* unfriendly or threatening.

DERIVATIVES – **forbiddingly** *adverb*.

forbore past of FORBEAR¹.

forborne past participle of FORBEAR¹.

force > *noun* **1** physical strength or energy as an attribute of action or movement. **2** Physics an influence tending to change the motion of a body or produce motion or stress in a stationary body. **3** coercion backed by the use or threat of violence. **4** mental or moral strength or power. **5** a person or thing regarded as exerting power or influence. **6** an organised body of military personnel, police, or workers. **7** (**the forces**) Brit. informal the army, navy, and air force. > *verb* **1** make a way through or into by force. **2** push into a specified position using force. **3** achieve or bring about by effort. **4** make (someone) do something against their will. **5** (**force on**) impose (something) on (someone). **6** artificially hasten the development or maturity of (a plant).

IDIOMS – **force someone's hand** make someone do something. **force the issue** compel the making of a decision. **in force 1** in great strength or numbers. **2** (**in** or **into force**) in or into effect.

DERIVATIVES – **forceable** *adjective* **forcer** *noun*.

SYNONYMS – *verb* **4** coerce, compel, constrain, pressure.

COMBINATIONS – **forced march** a fast march by soldiers over a long distance. **force field** (chiefly in science fiction) an invisible barrier of force.

ORIGIN – Old French *force*, from Latin *fortis* 'strong'.

forced landing > *noun* the abrupt landing of an aircraft in an emergency.

DERIVATIVES – **force-land** *verb*.

force-feed > *verb* force to eat food.

forceful > *adjective* powerful and assertive or vigorous.

DERIVATIVES – **forcefully** *adverb* **forcefulness** *noun*.

SYNONYMS – assertive, authoritative, commanding, powerful, strong, vigorous.

force majeure /forss ma**zhör**/ > *noun* **1** Law unforeseeable circumstances that prevent someone from fulfilling a contract. **2** superior strength.

ORIGIN – French, 'superior strength'.

forcemeat > *noun* a mixture of meat or vegetables chopped and seasoned for use as a stuffing or garnish.

forceps /**for**seps/ > *plural noun* **1** a pair of pincers used in surgery or in a laboratory. **2** a large instrument of such a type with broad blades, used in delivering a baby.

ORIGIN – Latin, 'tongs, pincers'.

forcible > *adjective* done by force.

DERIVATIVES – **forcibly** *adverb*.

ford > *noun* a shallow place in a river or stream where it can be crossed. > *verb* cross at a ford.

DERIVATIVES – **fordable** *adjective*.

fore > *adjective* situated or placed in front. > *noun* the front part of something, especially a ship. > *exclamation* called out as a warning to people in the path of a golf ball.

IDIOMS – **to the fore** in or to a conspicuous or leading position.

fore- > *combining form* **1** (added to verbs) in front: *foreshorten*. **2** in advance: *forebode*. **3** (added to nouns) situated in front of: *forecourt*. **4** the front part of: *forebrain*. **5** preceding: *forefather*.

fore and aft > *adverb* **1** at the front and rear. **2** backwards and forwards. > *adjective* **1** backwards and forwards. **2** (of a sail or rigging) set lengthwise, not on the yards.

forearm[1] /**for**aarm/ > *noun* the part of a person's arm extending from the elbow to the wrist or the fingertips.

forearm[2] /for**aarm**/ > *verb* (**be forearmed**) be prepared in advance for danger or attack.

forebear (also **forbear**) > *noun* an ancestor or predecessor.

USAGE – **forebear**, 'an ancestor', can also be spelled **forbear**; **forbear** is the usual

spelling for the verb meaning 'refrain from doing something'.

ORIGIN – from **FORE** + *bear*, variant of obsolete *beer* 'someone who exists'.

forebode /for**bōd**/ > *verb* archaic or literary act as an advance warning of (something bad).

foreboding > *noun* fearful apprehension. > *adjective* ominous.

DERIVATIVES – **forebodingly** *adverb*.

SYNONYMS – *noun* disquiet, trepidation, unease.

forebrain > *noun* Anatomy the front part of the brain.

forecast > *verb* (past and past participle **forecast** or **forecasted**) predict or estimate (a future event or trend). > *noun* a prediction or estimate, especially of the weather or a financial trend.

DERIVATIVES – **forecaster** *noun*.

SYNONYMS – *verb* prognosticate, prophesy. *noun* prognosis, projection, prophecy.

forecastle /**fōk**s'l/ (also **fo'c's'le**) > *noun* the forward part of a ship below the deck, traditionally used as the crew's living quarters.

foreclose > *verb* **1** take possession of a mortgaged property as a result of defaults in mortgage payments. **2** rule out or prevent.

DERIVATIVES – **foreclosure** *noun*.

ORIGIN – first used in the sense 'bar from escaping', 'shut out': from Old French *forclore*, from *for-* 'out' + *clore* 'to close'.

forecourt > *noun* **1** an open area in front of a large building or petrol station. **2** Tennis the part of the court between the service line and the net.

foredoom > *verb* (**be foredoomed**) be condemned beforehand to certain failure.

forefather (or **foremother**) > *noun* an ancestor.

forefinger > *noun* the finger next to the thumb.

forefoot > *noun* (pl. **forefeet**) each of the two front feet of a four-footed animal.

forefront > *noun* the leading position or place.

foregather (also **forgather**) > *verb* formal assemble or gather together.

forego[1] > *verb* variant spelling of **FORGO**.

forego[2] > *verb* (**foregoes**; past **forewent**; past participle **foregone**) archaic precede in place or time.

USAGE – do not confuse **forego** and **forgo**: **forego** means 'precede', but is also a less common spelling for **forgo**, 'go without'.

foregoing > *adjective* previously mentioned.

foregone past participle of **FOREGO**[2]. > *adjective* archaic past.

IDIOMS – **a foregone conclusion** an easily predictable result.

foreground > *noun* **1** the part of a view or image nearest to the observer. **2** the most prominent or important position.

forehand > *noun* (in tennis and other racket sports) a stroke played with the palm of the hand facing in the direction of the stroke.

DERIVATIVES – **forehanded** *adjective*.

forehead /**for**hed, **forr**id/ > *noun* the part of the face above the eyebrows.

foreign /**forr**in/ > *adjective* **1** of, from, in, or characteristic of a country or language other than one's own. **2** dealing with or relating to other countries. **3** coming or introduced from outside. **4** strange and unfamiliar. **5** (**foreign to**) not belonging to or characteristic of.

DERIVATIVES – **foreignness** *noun*.

SYNONYMS – **1** alien, non-native, overseas. **4** alien, exotic, outlandish, strange.

ANTONYMS – **1** domestic, native. **4** familiar.

COMBINATIONS – **Foreign and Commonwealth Office** (also **Foreign Office**) the British government department dealing with foreign affairs. **foreign body** a piece of matter that has entered a substance or the body from outside. **foreign exchange** the currency of other countries. **Foreign Legion** a military formation of the French army composed chiefly of non-Frenchmen and originally founded to fight France's colonial wars. **Foreign Secretary** (in the UK) the government minister who heads the Foreign and Commonwealth Office.

ORIGIN – Old French *forein, forain*, from Latin *foras, foris* 'outside', from *fores* 'door'.

foreigner > *noun* **1** a person from a foreign country. **2** informal a stranger or outsider.

WORDFINDER – xenophobia (*fear or dislike of foreigners*).

foreknowledge > *noun* awareness of something before it happens or exists.

foreland > *noun* **1** an area of land in front of a particular feature. **2** a cape or promontory.

forelock > *noun* a lock of hair growing just above the forehead.

IDIOMS – **touch** (or **tug**) **one's forelock** raise a hand to one's forehead in deference to a person of higher social rank.

foreman (or **forewoman**) > *noun* **1** a worker who supervises other workers. **2** (in a law court) a person who presides over a jury and speaks on its behalf.

SYNONYMS – **1** manager, overseer, superintendent, supervisor.

foremast > *noun* the mast of a ship nearest the bow.

foremost > *adjective* the most prominent in rank, importance, or position. > *adverb* in the first place.

SYNONYMS – *adjective* elite, leading, pre-eminent.

377

forename > *noun* another term for FIRST NAME.

forenoon > *noun* N. Amer. or Nautical the morning.

forensic /fərensik/ > *adjective* 1 relating to or denoting the application of scientific methods to the investigation of crime. 2 of or relating to courts of law. > *noun* (**forensics**) forensic tests or techniques.
DERIVATIVES – **forensically** *adverb*.
COMBINATIONS – **forensic medicine** the application of medical knowledge to the investigation of crime, particularly in establishing the causes of injury or death.
ORIGIN – Latin *forensis* 'in open court, public', from *forum* 'what is out of doors'.

foreordain /forordayn/ > *verb* (of God or fate) appoint or decree beforehand.

foreplay > *noun* sexual activity that precedes intercourse.

forequarters > *plural noun* the front legs and adjoining parts of a four-legged animal.

forerun > *verb* (**forerunning**; past **foreran**; past participle **forerun**) literary go before or indicate the coming of.

forerunner > *noun* 1 a person or thing that comes before another of the same kind. 2 archaic an advance messenger.
SYNONYMS – 1 antecedent, precursor, predecessor. 2 harbinger, herald.

foresail /forsayl, fors'l/ > *noun* the principal sail on a foremast.

foresee > *verb* (**foresees**, **foreseeing**; past **foresaw**; past participle **foreseen**) be aware of beforehand; predict.
DERIVATIVES – **foreseeable** *adjective* **foreseeably** *adverb* **foreseer** *noun*.
SYNONYMS – anticipate, forecast, prophesy.

foreshadow > *verb* be a warning or indication of.
SYNONYMS – augur, herald, portend, presage.

foresheet > *noun* Nautical 1 a rope by which the lee corner of a foresail is kept in place. 2 (**foresheets**) the inner part of the bows.

foreshore > *noun* the part of a shore between high- and low-water marks, or between the water and cultivated or developed land.

foreshorten > *verb* 1 represent (something) as having less depth or distance than in reality, so as to convey an effect of perspective. 2 shorten or reduce in time or scale.

foresight > *noun* 1 ability to predict the future. 2 the application of care and attention to the likely outcome of something or to future needs. 3 the front sight of a gun.
DERIVATIVES – **foresighted** *adjective*.

SYNONYMS – 2 anticipation, forethought, preparedness.

foreskin > *noun* the retractable roll of skin covering the end of the penis.

forest > *noun* 1 a large area covered with trees and undergrowth. 2 historical an area, typically owned by the sovereign and partly wooded, kept for hunting and having its own laws. 3 a mass of vertical or tangled objects.
DERIVATIVES – **forestation** *noun* **forested** *adjective*.
ORIGIN – from Latin *forestis silva* 'outside wood', from *foris* 'outside'.

forestall /forstawl/ > *verb* 1 prevent or obstruct (something anticipated) by taking advance action. 2 anticipate and prevent the action of.
DERIVATIVES – **forestaller** *noun* **forestalment** *noun*.
SYNONYMS – anticipate, pre-empt.
ORIGIN – Old English, 'an ambush'.

forestay /forstay/ > *noun* a rope supporting a ship's foremast, running from its top to the deck at the bow.

forester > *noun* 1 a person in charge of a forest or skilled in forestry. 2 chiefly archaic a person or animal living in a forest.

forestry > *noun* the science or practice of planting, managing, and caring for forests.

foretaste > *noun* a sample or suggestion of something that lies ahead.

foretell > *verb* (past and past participle **foretold**) predict.
DERIVATIVES – **foreteller** *noun*.
SYNONYMS – forecast, foresee, prophesy.

forethought > *noun* careful consideration of what will be necessary or may happen in the future.

foretoken literary > *verb* /fortōkən/ be a sign of. > *noun* /fortōkən/ a sign of something to come.

foretop > *noun* a platform around the head of the lower section of a sailing ship's foremast.

forever > *adverb* 1 (also **for ever**) for all future time. 2 for a very long time. 3 continually.
SYNONYMS – 1 always, eternally, evermore, perpetually.

forewarn > *verb* warn in advance.
IDIOMS – **forewarned is forearmed** proverb prior knowledge of possible dangers or problems gives one a tactical advantage.

forewent past of FOREGO¹, FOREGO².

foreword > *noun* a short introduction to a book.

forex > *abbreviation* foreign exchange.

forfeit /forfit/ > *verb* (**forfeited**, **forfeiting**) 1 lose or be deprived of (property or a right

or privilege) as a penalty for wrongdoing. 2 lose or give up (something) as a necessary consequence. > *noun* 1 a fine or penalty for wrongdoing. 2 Law a forfeited right, privilege, or item of property. 3 (**forfeits**) a game in which trivial penalties are exacted for minor misdemeanours. > *adjective* lost or surrendered as a forfeit.
DERIVATIVES – **forfeitable** *adjective* **forfeiter** *noun* **forfeiture** *noun*.
SYNONYMS – *verb* 1 relinquish, sacrifice, surrender.
ORIGIN – first used to denote a crime or transgression: from Old French *forfet*, *forfait*, from *forfaire* 'transgress'.

forfend /forfend/ > *verb* 1 archaic prevent or ward off (something evil or unpleasant). 2 US protect by precautionary measures.
IDIOMS – **God** (or **Heaven**) **forfend** archaic or humorous used to express dismay at the thought of something.

forgather > *verb* variant spelling of FOREGATHER.

forgave past of FORGIVE.

forge¹ > *verb* 1 make or shape (a metal object) by heating and hammering the metal. 2 create. 3 produce a fraudulent copy or imitation of (a banknote, work of art, signature, etc.). > *noun* 1 a blacksmith's workshop. 2 a furnace or hearth for melting or refining metal.
DERIVATIVES – **forgeable** *adjective* **forger** *noun*.
SYNONYMS – *verb* 3 copy, counterfeit, fake, simulate.
ORIGIN – Old French *forger*, from Latin *fabricare* 'fabricate'.

forge² > *verb* 1 move forward gradually or steadily. 2 (**forge ahead**) make progress.

forgery /forjəri/ > *noun* 1 the action of forging a banknote, work of art, signature, etc. 2 a forged or copied item.
SYNONYMS – 2 copy, counterfeit, dummy, fraud.

forget > *verb* (**forgetting**; past **forgot**; past participle **forgotten** or chiefly US **forgot**) 1 fail to remember. 2 inadvertently neglect to do something. 3 cease to think of. 4 (**forget oneself**) neglect to behave appropriately.
DERIVATIVES – **forgettable** *adjective* **forgetter** *noun*.

forgetful > *adjective* apt or likely to forget things.
DERIVATIVES – **forgetfully** *adverb* **forgetfulness** *noun*.
SYNONYMS – absent-minded, amnesiac, scatter-brained, vague.

forget-me-not > *noun* a low-growing plant with small, typically bright blue flowers.
ORIGIN – translating the Old French name *ne m'oubliez mye*; it was said that the wearer

of the flower would never be forgotten by a lover.

forgive > *verb* (past **forgave**; past participle **forgiven**) **1** stop feeling angry or resentful towards (someone) for an offence or mistake. **2** excuse (an offence, flaw, or mistake).
DERIVATIVES – **forgivable** *adjective* **forgiveness** *noun* **forgiver** *noun* **forgiving** *adjective*.
SYNONYMS – absolve, exonerate, pardon.

forgo (also **forego**) > *verb* (**forgoes**; past **forwent**; past participle **forgone**) go without (something desirable).
USAGE – do not confuse **forgo** and **forego**: **forgo** means 'go without', **forego** means 'precede'; however, **forego** is also an alternative spelling of **forgo**.
SYNONYMS – go without, renounce, sacrifice, waive.

forgot past of **FORGET**.

forgotten past participle of **FORGET**.

forint /**forr**int/ > *noun* the basic monetary unit of Hungary, equal to 100 filler.
ORIGIN – Hungarian, from Italian *fiorino* (see **FLORIN**).

fork > *noun* **1** an implement with two or more prongs used for lifting or holding food. **2** a farm or garden tool of larger but similar form used for digging or lifting. **3** each of a pair of supports in which a bicycle or motorcycle wheel revolves. **4** the point where a road, path, or river divides into two parts. **5** either of two such parts. > *verb* **1** (of a road, path, etc.) divide into two parts. **2** take one route or the other at a fork. **3** dig or lift with a fork. **4** (**fork out** or N. Amer. **over**) informal pay money for something, especially reluctantly.
SYNONYMS – *verb* **1** bifurcate, branch, diverge.
ORIGIN – Latin *furca* 'pitchfork, forked stick'.

forked > *adjective* having a divided or pronged end.
COMBINATIONS – **forked lightning** lightning that is visible in the form of a zigzag or branching line across the sky.

forklift truck > *noun* a vehicle with a pronged device in front for lifting and carrying heavy loads.

forlorn /fə**lorn**/ > *adjective* **1** pitifully sad and lonely. **2** unlikely to succeed or be fulfilled.
DERIVATIVES – **forlornly** *adverb* **forlornness** *noun*.
SYNONYMS – **1** pathetic, pitiful, wretched.
ORIGIN – Old English, 'depraved, lost'.

forlorn hope > *noun* a persistent or desperate hope that is unlikely to be fulfilled.

wordpower facts
Forlorn hope
The phrase **forlorn hope** is not derived from the English words **forlorn** and **hope**. It actually comes from Dutch *verloren hoop* 'lost troop', from *verloren* (past participle of *verliezen* 'lose') and *hoop* 'company' (related to **heap**). The phrase originally denoted a band of soldiers picked to begin an attack, many of whom would not survive; the current sense arose from a misunderstanding of the etymology.

form > *noun* **1** visible shape or configuration. **2** a way in which a thing exists or appears. **3** a type or variety of something. **4** the customary or correct method or procedure. **5** a printed document with blank spaces for information to be inserted. **6** chiefly Brit. a class or year in a school. **7** the state of a sports player with regard to their current standard of play. **8** details of previous performances by a racehorse or greyhound. **9** a person's mood and state of health. **10** Brit. a long bench without a back. > *verb* **1** bring together parts to create. **2** go to make up. **3** establish or develop. **4** make or be made into a certain form.
IDIOMS – **in** (or chiefly Brit. **on**) **form** playing or performing well. **off** (or chiefly Brit. **out of**) **form** not playing or performing well.
DERIVATIVES – **formable** *adjective*.
SYNONYMS – *verb* **1** assemble, build, construct. **3** devise, found, institute, organise.
ORIGIN – Latin *forma* 'a mould or form'.

formal > *adjective* **1** done in accordance with rules of convention or etiquette. **2** (of a person or their manner) prim or stiff. **3** of or concerned with outward form rather than content. **4** (of language) characterised by the use of studied grammatical structure and conservative vocabulary. **5** (especially of a garden) arranged in a precise or symmetrical manner. **6** officially recognised: *a formal complaint*. > *noun* N. Amer. **1** an evening dress. **2** an occasion on which evening dress is worn.
DERIVATIVES – **formally** *adverb*.
SYNONYMS – *adjective* **1** ceremonial, conventional, dignified, official, prescribed, solemn.
ANTONYMS – casual, informal.

formaldehyde /for**mald**ihīd/ > *noun* Chemistry a colourless pungent gas derived from methanol, used in solution as a preservative for biological specimens.
ORIGIN – blend of **FORMIC ACID** and **ALDEHYDE**.

formalin /**for**məlin/ > *noun* a solution of formaldehyde in water.

formalise (also **formalize**) > *verb* **1** give legal or official status to. **2** give a definite form to.
DERIVATIVES – **formalisation** *noun*.

formalism > *noun* **1** excessive adherence to prescribed forms. **2** concern with form rather than content in artistic creation. **3** a description in formal mathematical or logical terms.
DERIVATIVES – **formalist** *noun*.

formality > *noun* (pl. **formalities**) **1** the rigid observance of rules or convention. **2** a thing that is done simply to comply with convention or regulations. **3** (**a formality**) something done or occurring as a matter of course.

format > *noun* **1** the way in which something is arranged or presented. **2** the shape, size, and presentation of a book, document, etc. **3** the medium in which a recording is made available. **4** Computing a defined structure for the processing, storage, or display of data. > *verb* (**formatted**, **formatting**) (especially in computing) arrange or put into a format.
ORIGIN – from Latin *formatus liber* 'shaped book'.

formation > *noun* **1** the action of forming or the process of being formed. **2** a structure or arrangement. **3** a formal arrangement of aircraft in flight or troops.
DERIVATIVES – **formational** *adjective*.

formative > *adjective* serving to form something, in particular having a profound influence on a person's development.
DERIVATIVES – **formatively** *adverb*.

former[1] > *adjective* **1** having been previously: *her former boyfriend*. **2** of or occurring in the past. **3** (**the former**) denoting the first of two things mentioned.

former[2] > *noun* **1** a person or thing that forms something. **2** Brit. a person in a particular school year: *a fifth-former*. **3** a transverse strengthening part in an aircraft wing or fuselage.

formerly > *adverb* in the past.

Formica /for**mī**kə/ > *noun* trademark a hard durable plastic laminate used for worktops and other surfaces.

formic acid /**for**mik/ > *noun* an irritant organic acid present in the fluid emitted by some ants.
ORIGIN – *formic* from Latin *formica* 'ant'.

formication /formi**kay**sh'n/ > *noun* a sensation like that of insects crawling over the skin.
ORIGIN – Latin, from *formicare* 'crawl like an ant'.

formidable /**for**midəb'l, for**midd**əb'l/ > *adjective* inspiring fear or respect through being impressively large, powerful, or capable.
DERIVATIVES – **formidably** *adverb*.

NOTE – The traditional pronunciation of **formidable** places the stress on the first syllable, **for-**, but a stress on **-mid-** is now common in British English. Both pronunciations are acceptable.

SYNONYMS – daunting, impressive, intimidating, redoubtable.

ORIGIN – Latin *formidabilis*, from *formidare* 'to fear'.

formless > *adjective* without a clear or definite shape or structure.

DERIVATIVES – **formlessness** *noun*.

formula /formyoolə/ > *noun* (pl. **formulae** /formyoolee/ (in senses 1 and 2) or **formulas**) 1 a mathematical relationship or rule expressed in symbols. 2 (also **chemical formula**) a set of chemical symbols showing the elements present in a compound and their relative proportions. 3 a fixed form of words, as used conventionally or in particular contexts. 4 a method or procedure for achieving something. 5 (before another noun) denoting a rule or style followed without originality: *a formula fantasy film*. 6 a list of ingredients with which something is made. 7 an infant's liquid food preparation based on cow's milk or soya protein. 8 (usually followed by a numeral) a classification of racing car.

SYNONYMS – 4 blueprint, recipe.

ORIGIN – Latin, 'small shape or mould'.

formulaic /formyoo**lay**ik/ > *adjective* 1 constituting or containing a verbal formula or set form of words. 2 produced in accordance with a slavishly followed rule or style.

formulary /**for**myoolǝri/ > *noun* (pl. **formularies**) 1 a collection of set forms, especially for use in religious ceremonies. 2 an official list giving details of prescribable medicines.

formulate /**for**myoolayt/ > *verb* 1 create or prepare methodically. 2 express (an idea) in a concise or systematic way.

DERIVATIVES – **formulator** *noun*.

formulation > *noun* 1 the action of formulating. 2 a material or mixture prepared according to a formula.

fornicate /**for**nikayt/ > *verb* formal or humorous have sexual intercourse with someone one is not married to.

DERIVATIVES – **fornication** *noun* **fornicator** *noun*.

ORIGIN – Latin, from *fornicari* 'to arch', from *fornix* 'vaulted chamber', later 'brothel'.

forsake > *verb* (past **forsook**; past participle **forsaken**) chiefly literary 1 abandon. 2 renounce or give up (something valued or pleasant).

forsooth /fǝr**sooth**/ > *adverb* archaic or humorous indeed.

forswear > *verb* (past **forswore**; past participle **forsworn**) formal 1 agree to give up or do

without. 2 (**forswear oneself** or **be forsworn**) commit perjury.

forsythia /for**sī**thiǝ/ > *noun* an ornamental shrub whose bright yellow flowers appear in early spring before its leaves.

ORIGIN – named after the 18th-century Scottish botanist William *Forsyth*.

fort > *noun* a fortified building or strategic position.

IDIOMS – **hold the fort** take responsibility for something temporarily.

ORIGIN – Old French, from Latin *fortis* 'strong'.

forte[1] /**for**tay/ > *noun* a thing at which someone excels.

ORIGIN – French, from *fort* 'strong'.

forte[2] /**for**tay/ > *adverb* & *adjective* Music loud or loudly.

ORIGIN – Italian, 'strong, loud'.

Fortean /**for**tiǝn/ > *adjective* relating to or denoting paranormal phenomena.

ORIGIN – from the name of the American student of paranormal phenomena Charles H. *Fort* (1874–1932).

fortepiano /fortaypiannō/ > *noun* (pl. **fortepianos**) Music a piano, especially of the kind made in the 18th and early 19th centuries.

forth > *adverb* chiefly archaic 1 out from a starting point and forwards or into view. 2 onwards in time.

IDIOMS – **and so forth** and so on.

forthcoming > *adjective* 1 about to happen or appear. 2 ready or made available when required: *help was not forthcoming*. 3 willing to divulge information.

DERIVATIVES – **forthcomingness** *noun*.

SYNONYMS – 1 approaching, future, imminent. 3 communicative, informative, open.

ANTONYMS – 3 reticent.

forthright > *adjective* direct and outspoken.

DERIVATIVES – **forthrightly** *adverb* **forthrightness** *noun*.

SYNONYMS – blunt, direct, plain-speaking, straightforward.

forthwith > *adverb* at once; immediately.

fortify /**for**tifī/ > *verb* (**fortifies**, **fortified**) 1 provide with defensive works as protection against attack. 2 invigorate or encourage. 3 add spirits to (wine) to make port, sherry, etc. 4 increase the nutritional value of (food) by adding vitamins.

DERIVATIVES – **fortifiable** *adjective* **fortification** *noun* **fortifier** *noun*.

ORIGIN – Latin *fortificare*, from *fortis* 'strong'.

fortissimo /for**tiss**imō/ > *adverb* & *adjective* Music very loud or loudly.

ORIGIN – Italian, from Latin *fortissimus* 'very strong'.

fortitude /**for**tityōōd/ > *noun* courage and strength in bearing pain or trouble.

ORIGIN – Latin *fortitudo*, from *fortis* 'strong'.

fortnight > *noun* chiefly Brit. a period of two weeks.

ORIGIN – Old English, 'fourteen nights'.

fortnightly chiefly Brit. > *adjective* happening or produced every two weeks. > *adverb* every two weeks.

fortress > *noun* a military stronghold, especially a strongly fortified town fit for a large garrison.

ORIGIN – Old French *forteresse* 'strong place', from Latin *fortis* 'strong'.

fortuitous /for**tyōō**itǝss/ > *adjective* 1 happening by chance rather than design. 2 fortunate; lucky.

DERIVATIVES – **fortuitously** *adverb* **fortuitousness** *noun* **fortuity** *noun*.

USAGE – strictly speaking, **fortuitous** means 'happening by chance' (whether good or bad), although it is commonly used to mean 'fortunate' or 'lucky'.

ORIGIN – Latin *fortuitus*, from *forte* 'by chance'.

fortunate > *adjective* 1 favoured by or involving good luck. 2 auspicious or favourable.

fortunately > *adverb* it is fortunate that.

fortune > *noun* 1 chance as an arbitrary force affecting human affairs. 2 luck, especially good luck. 3 (**fortunes**) the success or failure of a person or enterprise. 4 a large amount of money or assets.

IDIOMS – **fortune favours the brave** proverb a successful person is often one who is willing to take risks. **a small fortune** informal a large amount of money. **tell someone's fortune** make predictions about a person's future by palmistry or similar divining methods.

SYNONYMS – 1 accident, chance, fortuity.

COMBINATIONS – **fortune-teller** a person who tells people's fortunes.

ORIGIN – Latin *Fortuna*, the name of a goddess personifying luck or chance.

forty* > *cardinal number* (pl. **forties**) 1 ten less than fifty; 40. (Roman numeral: **xl** or **XL**.) 2 (**the Forties**) the central North Sea between Scotland and southern Norway, having a prevailing depth of forty fathoms. See also **the roaring forties**.

WORDFINDER – quadragenarian (*person aged 40–49*).

IDIOMS – **forty winks** informal a short daytime sleep.

DERIVATIVES – **fortieth** ordinal number.

*SPELLING – for-, not four-: *forty*.

COMBINATIONS – **forty-five** a gramophone record played at 45 rpm and usually having only one song on each side; a single.

forum /**for**ǝm/ > *noun* (pl. **forums**) 1 a meeting or medium for an exchange of views. 2 chiefly N. Amer. a court or tribunal. 3 (pl. **fora**) (in ancient Rome) a public square or marketplace used for judicial and other business.

ORIGIN – Latin, 'what is out of doors'.

forward > *adverb* (also **forwards**) **1** in the direction that one is facing or travelling. **2** onward so as to make progress. **3** ahead in time. **4** in or near the front of a ship or aircraft. > *adjective* **1** towards the direction that one is facing or travelling. **2** relating to the future. **3** bold or over-familiar in manner. **4** further advanced than expected or required. **5** situated in or near the front of a ship or aircraft. > *noun* an attacking player in football, hockey, or other sports. > *verb* **1** send (a letter) on to a further destination. **2** dispatch; send. **3** promote.

DERIVATIVES – **forwarder** *noun* **forwardly** *adverb* **forwardness** *noun*.

COMBINATIONS – **forward-looking** favouring innovation; progressive.

forwent past of FORGO.

fosse /foss/ > *noun* Archaeology a long trench or ditch.

ORIGIN – Latin *fossa*.

fossick /**foss**ik/ > *verb* Austral./NZ informal **1** rummage; search. **2** search for gold in abandoned workings.

DERIVATIVES – **fossicker** *noun*.

ORIGIN – probably from the English dialect sense 'obtain by asking'.

fossil /**foss**'l/ > *noun* **1** the remains or impression of a prehistoric plant or animal embedded in rock and preserved in petrified form. **2** humorous an antiquated person or thing.

WORDFINDER – palaeontology (*the scientific study of fossils*).

COMBINATIONS – **fossil fuel** a natural fuel such as coal or gas, formed in the geological past from the remains of living organisms.

ORIGIN – from Latin *fossilis* 'dug up'.

fossiliferous /fossi**liff**ərəss/ > *adjective* (of a rock or rock layer) containing fossils.

fossilise (also **fossilize**) > *verb* (usu. **be fossilised**) preserve (an animal or plant) so that it becomes a fossil.

DERIVATIVES – **fossilisation** *noun*.

foster > *verb* **1** promote the development of. **2** bring up (a child that is not one's own by birth). **3** Brit. assign (a child) to be fostered.

DERIVATIVES – **fosterage** *noun* **fosterer** *noun*.

SYNONYMS – **1** advance, encourage, further, promote.

ORIGIN – Old English, 'feed, nourish'; related to FOOD.

fought past and past participle of FIGHT.

foul > *adjective* **1** having an offensive smell or taste; causing disgust. **2** informal very disagreeable or unpleasant: *a foul mood*. **3** (of the weather) wet and stormy. **4** morally offensive; wicked or obscene. **5** done contrary to the rules of a sport. **6** polluted or contaminated. **7** (**foul with**) clogged or

choked with. **8** Nautical (of a rope or anchor) entangled. > *noun* **1** (in sport) an unfair or invalid piece of play. **2** a collision or entanglement in riding, rowing, or running. > *verb* **1** make foul; pollute. **2** (of an animal) dirty with excrement. **3** (in sport) commit a foul against. **4** (**foul up**) make a mistake with; spoil. **5** (of a ship) collide with or interfere with the passage of (another). **6** cause (a cable, anchor, etc.) to become entangled or jammed.

DERIVATIVES – **foully** *adverb* **foulness** *noun*.

SYNONYMS – *adjective* **1** disgusting, repulsive, revolting. *verb* **1** besmirch, dirty, soil, stain.

COMBINATIONS – **foul-mouthed** using bad language habitually. **foul play 1** unfair play in a game or sport. **2** criminal or violent activity, especially murder.

foulard /**foo**laard/ > *noun* a thin, soft material of silk or silk and cotton.

ORIGIN – French.

found¹ past and past participle of FIND.

found² > *verb* **1** establish (an institution or organisation). **2** (**be founded on** or **upon**) be based on a particular principle or concept.

SYNONYMS – **1** inaugurate, institute, set up.

COMBINATIONS – **founding father 1** a founder. **2** (**Founding Father**) a member of the convention that drew up the constitution of the US in 1787.

ORIGIN – Old French *fonder*, from Latin *fundare*, from *fundus* 'bottom, base'.

found³ > *verb* **1** melt and mould (metal). **2** fuse (materials) to make glass. **3** make by founding.

ORIGIN – French *fondre*, from Latin *fundere* 'melt, pour'.

foundation > *noun* **1** the lowest load-bearing part of a building, typically below ground level. **2** an underlying basis or principle. **3** justification or reason: *there was no foundation for the claim*. **4** the action of founding an institution or organisation. **5** an institution so established. **6** a cream or powder applied to the face as a base for other make-up.

DERIVATIVES – **foundational** *adjective*.

COMBINATIONS – **foundation course** Brit. a preparatory course taken at some colleges and universities, either in a wide range of subjects or in one subject at a basic level. **foundation garment** a woman's supportive undergarment, such as a corset. **foundation stone** a stone laid with ceremony to celebrate the founding of a building.

founder¹ > *noun* a person who founds an institution or settlement.

founder² > *noun* the owner or operator of a foundry.

founder³ > *verb* **1** (of a ship) fill with water and sink. **2** (of a plan or undertaking) fail. **3** (of a horse) stumble or fall.

USAGE – do not confuse **founder** with **flounder**; **founder**, in its general use, means 'fail or come to nothing', while **flounder** means 'struggle; be in a state of confusion'.

ORIGIN – Old French *fondrer* 'submerge, collapse', from Latin *fundus* 'bottom, base'.

foundling > *noun* an infant that has been abandoned by its parents and is discovered and cared for by others.

foundry > *noun* (pl. **foundries**) a workshop or factory for casting metal.

fount¹ > *noun* **1** a source of a desirable quality. **2** literary a spring or fountain.

fount² > *noun* Brit. variant spelling of FONT².

fountain > *noun* **1** a spring of water, especially an ornamental jet of water pumped into the air artificially. **2** a source of something desirable. > *verb* spurt or cascade like a fountain.

COMBINATIONS – **fountainhead** an original source. **fountain pen** a pen with a reservoir or cartridge from which ink flows continuously to the nib.

ORIGIN – Old French *fontaine*, from Latin *fons* 'a spring'.

four > *cardinal number* **1** one more than three; 4. (Roman numeral: **iv** or **IV**.) **2** Cricket a hit that reaches the boundary after first striking the ground, scoring four runs. **3** a four-oared rowing boat or its crew.

WORDFINDER – quadrennial (*lasting for or recurring every four years*), quadrilateral (*four-sided figure*), quadruped (*animal with four feet*), quartet (*group or set of four; group of four musicians*), tetrad (*group or set of four*), tetralogy (*group of four related literary or operatic works*).

COMBINATIONS – **four-dimensional** having the three dimensions of space (length, breadth, and depth) plus time. **four-leaf clover** a clover leaf with four lobes, thought to bring good luck. **four-letter word** any of several short words regarded as coarse or offensive. **four-poster** a canopied bed with a post at each corner. **four-stroke** denoting an internal-combustion engine having a cycle of four strokes (intake, compression, combustion, and exhaust). **four-wheel drive** a transmission system which provides power directly to all four wheels of a vehicle.

fourscore > *cardinal number* archaic eighty.

foursome > *noun* a group of four people.

four-square > *adjective* **1** (of a building) having a square shape and solid appearance. **2** firm and resolute. > *adverb* **1** squarely and solidly. **2** firmly and resolutely.

fourteen > *cardinal number* one more than thirteen; 14. (Roman numeral: **xiv** or **XIV**.)

DERIVATIVES – **fourteenth** *ordinal number*.

fourth* > *ordinal number* **1** constituting number four in a sequence; 4th. **2** (**a fourth** or **one fourth**) *chiefly N. Amer.* a quarter. **3** *Music* an interval spanning four consecutive notes in a diatonic scale, in particular an interval of two tones and a semitone.

DERIVATIVES – **fourthly** *adverb*.

***SPELLING** – *four-*, not *for-*: *fourth*.

COMBINATIONS – **fourth dimension** time regarded as a dimension analogous to the three linear dimensions. **the fourth estate** the press; journalism. [ORIGIN – so called because it was considered to have as much power as the three original 'estates' of the British Parliament: Crown, Lords, and Commons.] **Fourth World** those countries and areas considered to be the poorest and most underdeveloped of the Third World.

fowl > *noun* (pl. same or **fowls**) **1** (also **domestic fowl**) a domesticated bird, derived from a junglefowl, kept for its eggs or flesh; a cock or hen. **2** any domesticated bird, e.g. a turkey or duck. **3** birds collectively, especially as the quarry of hunters.

DERIVATIVES – **fowler** *noun* **fowling** *noun*.

ORIGIN – Old English, related to **FLY**[1].

fox > *noun* **1** an animal of the dog family with a pointed muzzle, bushy tail, and reddish coat. **2** *informal* a cunning or sly person. **3** *N. Amer. informal* a sexually attractive woman. > *verb informal* baffle or deceive.

WORDFINDER – vixen (*female fox*), vulpine (*relating to foxes*).

COMBINATIONS – **foxhound** a breed of dog with smooth hair and drooping ears, trained to hunt foxes in packs. **fox-hunting** the sport of hunting a fox across country with a pack of hounds, carried out by a group of people on foot and horseback. **foxtail** a common meadow grass with soft brush-like flowering spikes. **fox terrier** a short- or wire-haired breed of terrier originally used for unearthing foxes.

foxed > *adjective* (of the paper of old books or prints) discoloured with brown spots.

DERIVATIVES – **foxing** *noun*.

foxglove > *noun* a tall plant having erect spikes of typically pinkish-purple flowers shaped like the fingers of gloves.

foxhole > *noun* a hole in the ground used by troops as a shelter against enemy fire or as a firing point.

foxtrot > *noun* a ballroom dance having an uneven rhythm with alternation of slow and quick steps. > *verb* (**foxtrotted**, **foxtrotting**) dance the foxtrot.

foxy > *adjective* (**foxier**, **foxiest**) **1** resembling or characteristic of a fox. **2** *informal* cunning;

sly. **3** *informal* (of a woman) sexually attractive.

DERIVATIVES – **foxily** *adverb* **foxiness** *noun*.

foyer /**foy**ay/ > *noun* a large entrance hall in a hotel or theatre.

ORIGIN – first used to denote the centre of attention or activity: from French, 'hearth, home'.

Fr > *abbreviation* Father (as a courtesy title of priests). [ORIGIN – from French *frère* 'brother'.] > *symbol* the chemical element francium.

fr. > *abbreviation* franc(s).

Fra /fraa/ > *noun* a prefixed title given to an Italian monk or friar.

ORIGIN – Italian, from *frate* 'brother'.

fracas /**frak**aa/ > *noun* (pl. same /**frak**aaz/ or US **fracases** /**frak**əsiz/) a noisy disturbance or quarrel.

SYNONYMS – altercation, row, rumpus.

ORIGIN – French, from Italian *fracassare* 'make an uproar'.

fractal /**frakt**'l/ *Mathematics* > *noun* a curve or geometrical figure of which each part has the same statistical character as the whole. > *adjective* relating to or of the nature of a fractal or fractals.

ORIGIN – French, from Latin *frangere* 'break'.

fraction /**frak**sh'n/ > *noun* **1** a numerical quantity that is not a whole number (e.g. ½, 0.5). **2** a small or tiny part, amount, or proportion. **3** *Chemistry* each of the portions into which a mixture may be separated according to a physical property such as boiling point or solubility.

WORDFINDER – decimal fraction (*fraction with numbers either side of a decimal point*), denominator (*number below the line in a vulgar fraction*), improper fraction (*in which numerator is greater than denominator*), numerator (*number above the line in a vulgar fraction*), proper fraction (*fraction less than one, with numerator less than denominator*), vulgar fraction (*fraction expressed by numerator and denominator*).

ORIGIN – Latin, from *frangere* 'to break'.

fractional > *adjective* **1** relating to or expressed as a fraction. **2** small or tiny in amount. **3** *Chemistry* relating to or denoting the separation of a mixture into fractions.

DERIVATIVES – **fractionally** *adverb*.

fractionalise (also **fractionalize**) > *verb* divide into separate groups or parts.

DERIVATIVES – **fractionalisation** *noun*.

fractionate > *verb chiefly Chemistry* divide into fractions or components.

DERIVATIVES – **fractionation** *noun*.

fractious /**frak**shəss/ > *adjective* **1** easily irritated. **2** difficult to control.

DERIVATIVES – **fractiously** *adverb* **fractiousness** *noun*.

SYNONYMS – **1** irascible, irritable, petulant.

ORIGIN – from **FRACTION**, probably on the pattern of the pair *faction*, *factious*.

fracture > *noun* **1** the cracking or breaking of a hard object or material. **2** a crack or break, especially in a bone or layer of rock. > *verb* **1** break sharply or suddenly. **2** (of a group or organisation) break up or fragment.

wordpower facts

Fracture

The root of the word **fracture**, the Latin verb *frangere* 'to break', is shared by a number of apparently unrelated words, including **fraction**, **fragile**, **frail**, and **fragment**. The name of the plant **saxifrage** is from *frangere* and *saxum* 'rock', through which the plant appears to 'break'. This was translated by English herbalists into **breakstone**, a name which has fallen into disuse. Similarly formed from *frangere* was the name of the bone-breaking bird of prey the **ossifrage** (see box at **OSPREY**).

fragile > *adjective* **1** easily broken or damaged. **2** delicate and vulnerable.

DERIVATIVES – **fragilely** *adverb* **fragility** *noun*.

SYNONYMS – **1** breakable, brittle, delicate, frangible.

ANTONYMS – **1** durable, tough.

ORIGIN – Latin *fragilis*, from *frangere* 'to break'.

fragment > *noun* /**frag**mənt/ **1** a small part broken off or detached. **2** an isolated or incomplete part: *a fragment of conversation.* > *verb* /frag**ment**/ break into fragments.

DERIVATIVES – **fragmentary** *adjective*.

SYNONYMS – *noun* **1** chip, piece, shard, shred.

ORIGIN – Latin *fragmentum*, from *frangere* 'to break'.

fragmentation > *noun* the process or state of breaking or being broken into small or separate parts.

COMBINATIONS – **fragmentation bomb** (or **grenade**) a bomb (or grenade) designed to break into small fragments as it explodes.

fragrance /**fray**grənss/ > *noun* **1** a pleasant, sweet smell. **2** a perfume or aftershave.

DERIVATIVES – **fragranced** *adjective*.

SYNONYMS – **1** aroma, bouquet, perfume, scent.

fragrant > *adjective* having a pleasant, sweet smell.

DERIVATIVES – **fragrantly** *adverb*.

SYNONYMS – aromatic, perfumed, scented.

ANTONYMS – malodorous.

ORIGIN – Latin, from *fragrare* 'smell sweet'.

frail > *adjective* **1** (of a person) weak and delicate. **2** easily damaged or broken.

DERIVATIVES – **frailly** *adverb* **frailness** *noun*.

SYNONYMS – delicate, flimsy, fragile, weak.

ANTONYMS – robust.

ORIGIN – Old French *fraile*, from Latin *fragilis*; related to **FRAGILE**.

frailty > *noun* (pl. **frailties**) **1** the condition of being frail. **2** weakness in character or morals.

frame > *noun* **1** a rigid structure surrounding a picture, door, etc. **2** (**frames**) a metal or plastic structure holding the lenses of a pair of glasses. **3** the rigid supporting structure of a vehicle, piece of furniture, or other object. **4** a person's body with reference to its size or build. **5** the underlying structure of a system, concept, or text. **6** a single complete picture in a series forming a cinema or video film. **7** the triangular structure for positioning the red balls in snooker. **8** a single game of snooker. > *verb* **1** place (a picture or photograph) in a frame. **2** surround so as to create a sharp or attractive image. **3** formulate or construct. **4** informal produce false incriminating evidence against (an innocent person).

IDIOMS – **be in** (or **out of**) **the frame 1** be (or not be) eligible. **2** be wanted (or not wanted) by the police. **frame of mind** a particular mood.

DERIVATIVES – **framed** *adjective* **frameless** *adjective* **framer** *noun* **framing** *noun*.

COMBINATIONS – **frame house** chiefly N. Amer. a house constructed from a wooden frame covered with timber boards. **frame of reference 1** a set of criteria in relation to which judgements can be made. **2** a system of geometrical axes in relation to which size, position, or motion can be defined. **frame saw** a saw with a thin blade kept rigid by being stretched in a frame. **frame tent** chiefly Brit. a tent supported by a tall frame, giving it nearly perpendicular sides and standing headroom throughout.

ORIGIN – Old English 'be useful', later 'prepare timber for building' and 'make the wooden parts of a building'.

frame-up > *noun* informal a conspiracy to incriminate someone falsely.

framework > *noun* a supporting or underlying structure.

franc /frangk/ > *noun* the basic monetary unit of France, Belgium, Switzerland, Luxembourg, and several other countries, equal to 100 centimes.

ORIGIN – Old French, from Latin *Francorum Rex* 'king of the Franks', the legend on gold coins struck in the 14th century

franchise /franchīz/ > *noun* **1** an authorisation granted by a government or company to an individual or group enabling them to carry out specified commercial activities. **2** a business or service granted such authorisation. **3** the right to vote in public elections. **4** N. Amer. an authorisation given by a professional league to own a sports team. **5** N. Amer. informal a team granted such authorisation. > *verb* **1** grant a franchise to. **2** grant a franchise for the sale of (goods) or the operation of (a service).

DERIVATIVES – **franchisee** *noun* **franchiser** (also **franchisor**) *noun*.

ORIGIN – first used to denote a grant of legal immunity: from Old French, from *franc* 'free'.

Franciscan /fransiskən/ > *noun* a monk or nun of a Christian religious order following the rule of the Italian monk St Francis of Assisi (*c*.1181–1226). > *adjective* of St Francis or the Franciscans.

francium /fransiəm/ > *noun* an unstable radioactive chemical element of the alkali-metal group.

ORIGIN – from *France*, native country of the discoverer, Marguerite Perey (1909–75).

Franco- (also **franco-**) > *combining form* **1** French; French and …: *francophone* | *Franco-German*. **2** relating to France.

ORIGIN – from Latin *Francus* 'Frank'.

Francoist /frangkōist/ > *noun* a supporter of the Spanish dictator General Francisco Franco (1892–1975) or his policies. > *adjective* relating to Franco's regime or policies.

DERIVATIVES – **Francoism** *noun*.

francolin /frangkōlin/ > *noun* a large game bird resembling a partridge, found in Africa and South Asia.

ORIGIN – Italian *francolino*.

Francophile /frangkəfīl/ > *noun* a person who is fond of or greatly admires France or the French.

francophone /frangkəfōn/ > *adjective* French-speaking. > *noun* a French-speaking person.

frangible /franjib'l/ > *adjective* fragile; brittle.

ORIGIN – Latin *frangibilis*, from *frangere* 'to break'.

frangipane /franjipayn/ > *noun* an almond-flavoured cream or paste.

ORIGIN – from the *frangipani* plant, which was used to flavour frangipane.

frangipani /franjipaani/ > *noun* (pl. **frangipanis**) **1** a tropical American tree or shrub with clusters of fragrant white, pink, or yellow flowers. **2** perfume obtained from this plant.

ORIGIN – named after the Marquis Muzio *Frangipani*, a 16th-century Italian nobleman who invented a perfume for scenting gloves.

franglais /froNglay/ > *noun* a blend of French and English, either French that makes excessive use of English expressions, or unidiomatic French spoken by an English person.

ORIGIN – coined in French, from a blend of *français* 'French' and *anglais* 'English'.

Frank > *noun* a member of a Germanic people that conquered Gaul in the 6th century.

DERIVATIVES – **Frankish** *adjective* & *noun*.

frank¹ > *adjective* **1** honest and direct, especially when dealing with unpleasant matters. **2** open or undisguised: *frank admiration*.

DERIVATIVES – **frankness** *noun*.

SYNONYMS – candid, direct, forthright.

ANTONYMS – evasive, insincere.

wordpower facts

Frank

Early use in English of the adjective **frank** was in the senses 'free' and 'generous': the obsolete phrase **frank and free** meant 'not in serfdom or slavery'. The word entered English from Old French, ultimately from Latin *francus* 'free'. The Latin word was coined in reference to the Franks, as only they had full freedom in Frankish Gaul. The name of the Franks is likely to have come from a weapon associated with them, a type of javelin known in Old English as a *franca*.

frank² > *verb* **1** stamp an official mark on (a letter or parcel) to indicate that postage has been paid or does not need to be paid. **2** historical sign (a letter or parcel) to ensure delivery free of charge. > *noun* a franking mark or signature on a letter or parcel.

DERIVATIVES – **franker** *noun* **franking** *noun*.

ORIGIN – from **FRANK¹**.

Frankenstein /frangkənstīn/ (also **Frankenstein's monster**) > *noun* a thing that becomes terrifying or destructive to its maker.

frankfurter /frangkfurtər/ > *noun* a seasoned smoked sausage made of beef and pork.

ORIGIN – from German *Frankfurter Wurst* 'Frankfurt sausage'.

frankincense /frangkinsenss/ > *noun* an aromatic gum resin obtained from an African tree and burnt as incense.

ORIGIN – Old French *franc encens* 'high-quality incense', from *franc* 'free, generous', also 'of high quality' + *encens* 'incense'.

franklin–free

wordpower facts

Frankenstein

The name **Frankenstein** comes from a novel written in 1818 by Mary Shelley, in which a scientist by the name of Victor *Frankenstein* attempts to restore life in the body of a dead man; his experiment results in the creation of a terrifying monster, who eventually destroys his maker. Note that in the original story **Frankenstein** is the name of the scientist, not the monster. In the 1990s the element *Franken-* came to be used as a derogatory prefix to mean 'genetically modified', as in **Frankenfood** and **Frankenplants**.

---

franklin > *noun* a landowner of free but not noble birth in the 14th and 15th centuries in England.
ORIGIN – Latin *francalanus*, from *francalis* 'held without dues', from *francus* 'free'.

frankly > *adverb* 1 in a frank manner. 2 to be frank.

frantic > *adjective* 1 distraught with fear, anxiety, etc. 2 conducted in a hurried and chaotic way.
DERIVATIVES – **frantically** *adverb* **franticness** *noun*.
SYNONYMS – 1 beside oneself, distraught, overwrought. 2 frenetic, frenzied.
ORIGIN – Old French *frenetique*, ultimately from Greek *phrenitis* 'delirium'; related to **FRENETIC**.

frappé /frappay/ > *adjective* (of a drink) iced or chilled. > *noun* a drink served with ice or frozen to a slushy consistency.
ORIGIN – French.

Frascati /fraskaati/ > *noun* a white wine produced in the region of Frascati, Italy.

frass /frass/ > *noun* 1 powdery refuse produced by wood-boring insects. 2 the excrement of insect larvae.
ORIGIN – German, from *fressen* 'devour'.

fraternal /fraətern'l/ > *adjective* 1 of or like a brother; brotherly. 2 of or denoting a fraternity. 3 (of twins) developed from separate ova and therefore not identical.
DERIVATIVES – **fraternalism** *noun* **fraternally** *adverb*.
ORIGIN – Latin *fraternus*, from *frater* 'brother'.

fraternise /frattərnīz/ (also **fraternize**) > *verb* (usu. **fraternise with**) be on friendly terms.
DERIVATIVES – **fraternisation** *noun*.

fraternity /frəterniti/ > *noun* (pl. **fraternities**) 1 a group of people sharing a common profession or interests. 2 N. Amer. a male students' society in a university or college. 3 a religious or masonic society or

guild. 4 friendship and mutual support within a group.

fratricide /fratrisīd/ > *noun* 1 the killing of one's brother or sister. 2 the accidental killing of one's own forces in war.
DERIVATIVES – **fratricidal** *adjective*.
ORIGIN – from Latin *frater* 'brother'.

Frau /frow/ > *noun* (pl. **Frauen** /frowən/) a title or form of address for a married or widowed German woman.
ORIGIN – German.

fraud /frawd/ > *noun* 1 wrongful or criminal deception intended to result in financial or personal gain. 2 a person intending or thing intended to deceive.
DERIVATIVES – **fraudster** *noun*.
SYNONYMS – 1 deception, hoax, swindling, trickery. 2 charlatan, cheat, impostor, sham.
ORIGIN – Latin *fraus* 'deceit, injury'.

fraudulent /frawdyoolənt/ > *adjective* 1 done by or involving fraud. 2 deceitful or dishonest.
DERIVATIVES – **fraudulence** *noun* **fraudulently** *adverb*.
SYNONYMS – cheating, deceitful, dishonest, duplicitous, swindling.

fraught /frawt/ > *adjective* 1 (**fraught with**) filled with (something undesirable). 2 causing or affected by anxiety or stress.
ORIGIN – from obsolete *fraught* 'load with cargo', from Dutch *vrachten*, from *vracht* 'ship's cargo'; related to **FREIGHT**.

Fräulein /froylīn/ > *noun* a title or form of address for a young German woman.
ORIGIN – German, from **FRAU**.

fray[1] > *verb* 1 (of a fabric, rope, or cord) unravel or become worn at the edge. 2 (of a person's nerves or temper) show the effects of strain.
ORIGIN – Old French *freiier*, from Latin *fricare* 'to rub'.

fray[2] > *noun* (**the fray**) 1 a situation of intense competitive activity. 2 a battle or fight.
ORIGIN – from archaic *fray* 'to quarrel', from Old French *afrayer* 'disturb, startle'; related to **AFFRAY**.

frazzle informal > *verb* 1 cause to shrivel up with burning. 2 (**frazzled**) completely exhausted. > *noun* (**a frazzle**) 1 an exhausted state. 2 a charred or burnt state.

freak > *noun* 1 (also **freak of nature**) a person, animal, or plant which is abnormal or deformed. 2 (before another noun) unusual and unexpected: *a freak storm*. 3 informal a person who is obsessed with a particular activity or interest. > *verb* (usu. **freak out**) informal behave or cause to behave in a wild and irrational way.
DERIVATIVES – **freakish** *adjective*.
SYNONYMS – *noun* 1 aberration, abnormality, mutant, oddity.

freaky > *adjective* (**freakier**, **freakiest**) informal very odd or strange.

DERIVATIVES – **freakily** *adverb* **freakiness** *noun*.

freckle > *noun* a small light brown spot on the skin, caused and accentuated by exposure to the sun. > *verb* cover or become covered with freckles.
DERIVATIVES – **freckly** *adjective*.
ORIGIN – Old Norse *freknur* 'freckles'.

free > *adjective* (**freer**, **freest**) 1 not under the control or in the power of another. 2 permitted to take a specified action. 3 not or no longer confined, obstructed, or fixed. 4 not subject to engagements or obligations. 5 not occupied or in use. 6 (**free of** or **from**) not subject to or affected by. 7 available without charge. 8 generous or lavish. 9 frank and unrestrained. 10 not subject to the normal conventions; improvised. 11 (of a translation or interpretation) conveying only the broad sense; not literal. > *adverb* without cost or payment. > *verb* (**frees**, **freed**, **freeing**) 1 make free; release. 2 make available.
IDIOMS – **free and easy** informal and relaxed. **a free hand** freedom to act completely at one's own discretion. **a free ride** a situation in which someone benefits without having to make a fair contribution. **the free world** the non-communist countries of the world, as formerly opposed to the Soviet bloc. **make free with** treat without ceremony or proper respect.
SYNONYMS – *adjective* 7 complimentary, gratis. *verb* 1 let go, liberate, release.
COMBINATIONS – **freeborn** not born in slavery. **Free Church** a Christian Church which has dissented or seceded from an established Church. **free enterprise** an economic system in which private business operates in competition and largely free of state control. **free-form** not conforming to a regular or formal structure. **freehand** done manually without the aid of instruments such as rulers. **free-handed** generous, especially with money. **free house** Brit. a public house not controlled by a brewery and therefore not restricted to selling particular brands of beer or liquor. **free kick** (in soccer and rugby) an unimpeded kick of the stationary ball awarded for a foul or infringement by the opposing team. **free love** the practice of having sexual relations without fidelity to one partner. **freeman** 1 a person who has been given the freedom of a city or borough. 2 historical a person who is not a slave or serf. **free market** an economic system in which prices are determined by unrestricted competition between privately owned businesses. **free pardon** an unconditional remission of the legal consequences of an offence or conviction. **free port** 1 a port open to all traders. 2 a port area where goods in transit are exempt

from customs duty. **free radical** Chemistry a molecule (typically highly reactive) with an unpaired electron. **free-range** (of livestock or their produce) kept or produced in natural conditions, where the animals have freedom of movement. **free-standing** not attached to or supported by another structure. **free state** historical any of the states of the US in which slavery did not exist. **freestyle** (of a contest, race, or type of sport) in which there are few restrictions on the style or technique that competitors employ. **free trade** international trade left to its natural course without tariffs, quotas, or other restrictions. **free verse** poetry that does not rhyme or have a regular rhythm. **free vote** chiefly Brit. a parliamentary division in which members vote independently of party policy. **free will** the power to act without the constraints of necessity or fate; the ability to act at one's own discretion.
ORIGIN − Old English; related to FRIEND.

freebase > noun cocaine that has been purified by heating with ether, taken by inhaling the fumes or smoking the residue. > verb take (cocaine) in such a way.

freebie > noun informal a thing given free of charge.

freeboard > noun the height of a ship's side between the waterline and the deck.

freebooter > noun a pirate or lawless adventurer.
DERIVATIVES − **freeboot** verb.
ORIGIN − Dutch vrijbuiter, from vrij 'free' + buit 'booty'.

freedom > noun 1 the power or right to act, speak, or think freely. 2 the state of being free. 3 (**freedom from**) exemption or immunity from. 4 unrestricted use of something. 5 a special privilege or right of access, especially that of full citizenship of a particular city given to a public figure as an honour: the freedom of the City of Glasgow.
COMBINATIONS − **freedom fighter** a person who takes part in a revolutionary struggle.

free fall > noun 1 downward movement under the force of gravity. 2 rapid descent or decline without means of stopping. > verb (**free-fall**) move under the force of gravity; fall rapidly.

free-for-all > noun a disorganised or unrestricted situation or event in which everyone may take part, especially a fight or discussion.

freehold > noun 1 permanent and absolute tenure of land or property with freedom to dispose of it at will. 2 chiefly Brit. a piece of land or property held by such tenure.
DERIVATIVES − **freeholder** noun.

freelance /freelaanss/ > adjective self-employed and hired to work for different companies on particular assignments. > adverb earning one's living in such a way.

> noun (also **freelancer**) a freelance worker. > verb earn one's living as a freelance.
ORIGIN − from FREE + LANCE: originally denoting a mercenary in medieval Europe.

freeloader > noun informal a person who takes advantage of others' generosity without giving anything in return.
DERIVATIVES − **freeload** verb.

freely > adverb 1 not under the control of another. 2 without restriction or interference. 3 in copious or generous amounts. 4 openly and honestly. 5 willingly and readily.

Freemason > noun a member of an international order established for mutual help and fellowship, which holds elaborate secret ceremonies.
DERIVATIVES − **Freemasonry** noun.

freesia /freeziə/ > noun a small plant with fragrant, colourful tubular flowers, native to southern Africa.
ORIGIN − named after the 19th-century German physician Friedrich H. T. Freese.

freethinker > noun a person who questions or rejects accepted opinions, especially those concerning religious belief.

freeway > noun N. Amer. 1 a dual-carriageway main road. 2 a toll-free highway.

freewheel > noun a bicycle wheel which is able to revolve freely when no power is being applied to the pedals. > verb 1 coast on a bicycle without using the pedals. 2 (**freewheeling**) cheerily unconcerned.
DERIVATIVES − **freewheeler** noun.

freeze > verb (past **froze**; past participle **frozen**) 1 (with reference to a liquid) turn or be turned into ice or another solid as a result of extreme cold. 2 become or cause to become blocked or rigid with ice. 3 be or cause to be very cold. 4 store at a very low temperature as a means of preservation. 5 become suddenly motionless or paralysed with fear or shock. 6 (of a computer screen) suddenly become locked. 7 keep or stop at a fixed level or in a fixed state. 8 (**freeze out**) informal cause (someone) to feel excluded by being hostile or obstructive towards them. > noun 1 an act of freezing. 2 informal a period of very cold weather.
DERIVATIVES − **freezable** adjective.
COMBINATIONS − **freeze-frame** 1 a single frame forming a motionless image from a film or videotape. 2 the facility or process of stopping a film or videotape to obtain such a frame.

freeze-dry > verb preserve by rapid freezing followed by subjection to a high vacuum which removes ice by sublimation.

freezer > noun a refrigerated cabinet or room for preserving food at very low temperatures.

freezing > adjective 1 having a temperature below 0°C. 2 informal very cold. 3 (of fog or rain) consisting of droplets which freeze

rapidly on contact with a surface. > noun the freezing point of water (0°C).
COMBINATIONS − **freezing point** the temperature at which a liquid turns into a solid when cooled.

freight /frayt/ > noun 1 transport of goods in bulk, especially by truck, train, or ship. 2 goods transported by freight. 3 a charge for such transport. > verb 1 transport by freight. 2 (**be freighted with**) be laden or burdened with.
ORIGIN − Dutch and Low German vrecht, from vracht 'ship's cargo'.

freightage > noun 1 the carrying of goods in bulk. 2 goods carried in bulk; freight.

freighter > noun 1 a large ship or aircraft designed to carry freight. 2 a person who loads, receives, or forwards goods for transport.

French > adjective relating to France or its people or language. > noun the language of France, also used in parts of Belgium, Switzerland, and Canada, in certain countries in Africa and the Caribbean, and elsewhere.
WORDFINDER − Francophile (person who admires France or the French), francophone (French-speaking), Gallic (relating to France or the French).
IDIOMS − **excuse** (or **pardon**) **my French** informal used to apologise for swearing.
DERIVATIVES − **Frenchness** noun.
COMBINATIONS − **French bean** Brit. a bean plant of which many varieties are commercially cultivated for food. **French bread** white bread in a long, crisp loaf. **French chalk** a kind of steatite used for marking cloth and removing grease and as a dry lubricant. **French cricket** an informal game resembling cricket, in which a soft ball is bowled at the batter's legs. **French dressing** a salad dressing of vinegar, oil, and seasonings. **French fries** chiefly N. Amer. potatoes deep-fried in thin strips; chips. **French horn** a brass instrument with a coiled tube, valves, and a wide bell. **French kiss** a kiss with contact between tongues. **French knickers** women's loose-fitting, wide-legged underpants. **French leave** informal, dated absence from work or duty without permission. [ORIGIN − said to derive from the French custom of leaving a function without saying goodbye to the host.] **French letter** Brit. informal, dated a condom. **Frenchman** a man who is French by birth or descent. **French stick** a loaf of French bread. **French toast** 1 bread coated in egg and milk and fried. 2 Brit. bread buttered on one side and toasted on the other. **French windows** a pair of glazed doors in an outside wall. **Frenchwoman** a woman who is French by birth or descent.
ORIGIN − from the root of FRANK.

wordpower facts
French

French is a Romance language which developed from the Latin spoken in Gaul. In Britain, the Norman Conquest of 1066 and the arrival of the French-speaking ruling classes resulted in French becoming the language of the aristocracy, the law courts, and the Church hierarchy. Large numbers of French words were adopted into English, including words connected with law and government, such as **council**, **justice**, and **tax**, and a number of abstract words such as **charity**, **conflict**, and **liberty**. Some eventually replaced their Old English equivalents: for example **victory**, from Old French *victorie*, replaced the Old English word *sige*. Often new and old words existed side by side, producing pairs of words which survive in English today: **shut** (Old English) and **close** (from Old French); **buy** (Old English) and **purchase** (from Old French).

Frenchify /frenchifī/ > *verb* (**Frenchifies, Frenchified**) *often derogatory* make French in form or character.

French polish > *noun* shellac polish that produces a high gloss on wood. > *verb* (**french-polish**) treat with French polish.

Frenchy (also **Frenchie**) *informal, chiefly derogatory* > *adjective* French in character. > *noun* (pl. **Frenchies**) a French person.

frenetic /frənettik/ > *adjective* fast and energetic in a rather wild and uncontrolled way; frantic.
DERIVATIVES – **frenetically** *adverb*.
ORIGIN – Greek *phrenitikos*, from *phrenitis* 'delirium'.

frenzied > *adjective* wildly excited or uncontrolled.
DERIVATIVES – **frenziedly** *adverb*.
SYNONYMS – crazed, frantic, frenetic, mad, manic, wild.

frenzy > *noun* (pl. **frenzies**) a state or period of uncontrolled excitement or wild behaviour.
ORIGIN – Latin *phrenesia*, from Greek *phrēn* 'mind'.

frequency > *noun* (pl. **frequencies**) 1 the rate at which something occurs over a particular period or in a given sample. 2 the fact or state of being frequent. 3 the rate per second of a vibration constituting a wave, e.g. sound, light, or radio waves. 4 the particular waveband at which radio signals are broadcast or transmitted.
COMBINATIONS – **frequency modulation** the modulation of a wave by varying its frequency, used as a means of broadcasting an audio signal by radio.

frequent > *adjective* /freekwənt/ 1 occurring or done many times at short intervals. 2 habitual. > *verb* /frikwent/ visit (a place) often or habitually.
DERIVATIVES – **frequenter** *noun* **frequently** *adverb*.
SYNONYMS – *adjective* 1 persistent, recurrent, regular, repeated.
ANTONYMS – *adjective* 1 infrequent, rare.
ORIGIN – Latin *frequens* 'crowded, frequent'.

fresco /freskō/ > *noun* (pl. **frescoes** or **frescos**) a painting done on wet plaster on a wall or ceiling, in which the colours become fixed as the plaster dries.
DERIVATIVES – **frescoed** *adjective*.

wordpower facts
Fresco

The word **fresco** derives from the Italian adjective *fresco*, meaning 'cool, fresh'. It is first recorded in English at the end of the 16th century, in the phrase **in fresco**, meaning 'while the plaster is still fresh'; hence a painting done on wet plaster became known as a **fresco**. In the 17th and 18th centuries **fresco** was also used as a noun meaning 'cool, fresh air' (the English poet Thomas Gray wrote in a letter of 1740: 'they...walk about the city, or upon the sea-shore...to enjoy the fresco'). The noun in this sense is now obsolete, but the meaning survives in the word **alfresco**.

fresh > *adjective* 1 not previously known or used; new or different. 2 (of food) recently made or obtained; not preserved. 3 recently created and not faded or impaired. 4 full of energy and vigour. 5 (of water) not salty. 6 (of the wind) cool and fairly strong. 7 pleasantly clean, invigorating, and cool: *fresh air.* 8 (of a colour or a person's complexion) bright or healthy in appearance. 9 *informal* presumptuous or impudent. > *adverb* newly; recently.
DERIVATIVES – **freshly** *adverb* **freshness** *noun*.
ORIGIN – Old English, 'not salt, fit for drinking'.

freshen > *verb* 1 make or become fresh. 2 (of wind) become stronger and colder. 3 *chiefly N. Amer.* top up (a drink).

fresher > *noun* Brit. *informal* a first-year student at college or university.

freshet > *noun* 1 the flood of a river from heavy rain or melted snow. 2 a rush of fresh water flowing into the sea.

ORIGIN – probably from Old French *freschete*, from *freis* 'fresh'.

freshman > *noun* a first-year student at university or (N. Amer.) at high school.

fret¹ > *verb* (**fretted, fretting**) 1 be constantly or visibly anxious. 2 gradually wear away by rubbing or gnawing. > *noun* chiefly Brit. a state of anxiety.
SYNONYMS – *verb* 1 agonise, brood, lose sleep, worry.
ORIGIN – Old English, 'devour, consume'.

fret² > *noun* Art & Architecture an ornamental design of vertical and horizontal lines. > *verb* (**fretted, fretting**) decorate with fretwork.
COMBINATIONS – **fretsaw** a saw with a narrow blade for cutting designs in thin wood or metal. **fretwork** ornamental design done with a fretsaw.
ORIGIN – Old French *frete* 'trellis-work'.

fret³ > *noun* each of a sequence of ridges on the fingerboard of some stringed instruments, used for fixing the positions of the fingers. > *verb* (**fretted, fretting**) 1 provide with frets. 2 play (a note) while pressing against a fret.
DERIVATIVES – **fretless** *adjective*.

fretful > *adjective* anxious or irritated.
DERIVATIVES – **fretfully** *adverb*.

Freudian /froydiən/ > *adjective* 1 relating to or influenced by the Austrian neurologist Sigmund Freud (1856–1939) and his methods of psychoanalysis. 2 susceptible to analysis in terms of unconscious thoughts or desires: *a Freudian slip.* > *noun* a follower of Freud or his methods.
DERIVATIVES – **Freudianism** *noun*.

Fri. > *abbreviation* Friday.

friable /frīəb'l/ > *adjective* easily crumbled.
DERIVATIVES – **friability** *noun*.
ORIGIN – Latin *friabilis*, from *friare* 'to crumble'.

friar > *noun* a member of any of certain religious orders of men, especially the four mendicant orders (Augustinians, Carmelites, Dominicans, and Franciscans).
ORIGIN – Old French *frere*, from Latin *frater* 'brother'.

friary > *noun* (pl. **friaries**) a building or community occupied by friars.

fricassée /frikəsee/ > *noun* a dish of stewed or fried pieces of meat served in a thick white sauce.
DERIVATIVES – **fricasséed** *adjective*.
ORIGIN – French, from *fricasser* 'cut up and cook in a sauce'.

fricative /frikətiv/ Phonetics > *adjective* referring to a type of consonant (e.g. *f* and *th*) made by the friction of breath in a narrow opening. > *noun* a fricative consonant.
ORIGIN – Latin *fricativus*, from *fricare* 'to rub'.

friction > *noun* 1 the resistance that one

surface or object encounters when moving over another. **2** the action of one surface or object rubbing against another. **3** conflict or disagreement.

DERIVATIVES – **frictional** *adjective* **frictionless** *adjective*.

ORIGIN – Latin, from *fricare* 'to rub'.

Friday > *noun* the day of the week before Saturday and following Thursday.

COMBINATIONS – **man Friday** a male helper or follower. [ORIGIN – a character in Daniel Defoe's novel *Robinson Crusoe* (1719).]

ORIGIN – Old English, from the name of the Germanic goddess *Frigga*; translation of Latin *Veneris dies* 'day of the planet Venus'.

fridge > *noun* short for **REFRIGERATOR**.

COMBINATIONS – **fridge-freezer** chiefly Brit. an upright unit comprising a separate refrigerator and freezer.

fried past and past participle of **FRY**[1].

friend* > *noun* **1** a person with whom one has a bond of mutual affection, typically one exclusive of sexual or family relations. **2** a familiar or helpful thing. **3** a person who supports a particular cause or organisation. **4** (**Friend**) a Quaker.

IDIOMS – **a friend in need is a friend indeed** proverb a person who helps at a difficult time is a person to be relied upon.

DERIVATIVES – **friendless** *adjective* **friendship** *noun*.

*SPELLING – note it is *ie*, not *ei*: fr**ie**nd.

friendly > *adjective* (**friendlier**, **friendliest**) **1** kind and pleasant; of or like a friend. **2** Military of or allied with one's own forces. **3** favourable or serviceable. **4** (in combination) not harmful to a specified thing: *environment-friendly*. > *noun* (pl. **friendlies**) Brit. a game or match not forming part of a serious competition.

DERIVATIVES – **friendlily** *adverb* **friendliness** *noun*.

SYNONYMS – *adjective* **1** affable, amiable, amicable, convivial, good-natured.

COMBINATIONS – **friendly fire** Military weapon fire coming from one's own side that causes accidental injury or death to one's own forces. **friendly society** (in the UK) a mutual association providing sickness benefits, life assurance, and pensions.

Friesian* /**free**zhən/ > *noun* Brit. a breed of a black-and-white dairy cattle originally from Friesland in the Netherlands.

*SPELLING – *Fries*-, not *Fris*-: *Fries*ian; contrast with the name of the people and language, **Frisian**.

frieze /freez/ > *noun* **1** a broad horizontal band of sculpted or painted decoration. **2** Architecture the part of an entablature between the architrave and the cornice.

ORIGIN – Latin *frisium*, from *Phrygium opus* 'work of Phrygia'.

frig > *verb* (**frigged**, **frigging**) vulgar slang **1** have sexual intercourse with. **2** masturbate.

frigate /**frig**ət/ > *noun* **1** a warship carrying mixed weapons, generally lighter than a destroyer. **2** historical a sailing warship of a size just below that of a ship of the line.

COMBINATIONS – **frigate bird** a predatory tropical seabird with a deeply forked tail and a long hooked bill.

ORIGIN – Italian *fregata*.

fright > *noun* **1** a sudden intense feeling of fear. **2** an experience causing fright; a shock.

IDIOMS – **look a fright** informal look ridiculous or grotesque. **take fright** suddenly become frightened.

SYNONYMS – **1** dread, horror, terror.

COMBINATIONS – **fright wig** a wig with the hair arranged sticking out, as worn by a clown.

frighten > *verb* **1** cause to be afraid. **2** (**frighten off**) drive (someone) away by making them afraid.

DERIVATIVES – **frightened** *adjective* **frightening** *adjective* **frighteningly** *adverb*.

SYNONYMS – **1** petrify, scare, terrify.

frightener > *noun* a frightening person or thing.

IDIOMS – **put the frighteners on** Brit. informal threaten or intimidate (someone).

frightful > *adjective* **1** very unpleasant, serious, or shocking. **2** informal very bad; terrible.

DERIVATIVES – **frightfully** *adverb*.

SYNONYMS – **1** dreadful, ghastly, hideous, horrible, terrible.

frigid /**frig**id/ > *adjective* **1** very cold. **2** (of a woman) unable to be sexually aroused. **3** stiff or formal in style.

DERIVATIVES – **frigidity** *noun* **frigidly** *adverb*.

ORIGIN – Latin *frigidus*, from *frigere* 'be cold'.

frill > *noun* **1** a strip of gathered or pleated material used as a decorative edging. **2** a frill-like fringe of feathers, hair, skin, etc. on a bird, reptile, or other animal. **3** (**frills**) inessential extra features or embellishments.

DERIVATIVES – **frilled** *adjective* **frilly** *adjective*.

ORIGIN – from or related to Flemish *frul*.

fringe > *noun* **1** a border of threads, tassels, or twists, used to edge clothing or material. **2** chiefly Brit. the front part of someone's hair, cut so as to hang over the forehead. **3** a natural border of hair or fibres in an animal or plant. **4** the outer or marginal part of something. **5** (before another noun) not part of the mainstream; unconventional: *fringe theatre*. > *verb* provide with or form a fringe.

DERIVATIVES – **fringing** *noun* **fringy** *adjective*.

COMBINATIONS – **fringe benefit** a benefit, such as a car or health insurance, given to an employee in addition to their salary or wages.

ORIGIN – Old French *frenge*, from Latin *fimbria* 'fibres, shreds'.

frippery > *noun* (pl. **fripperies**) **1** showy or unnecessary ornament. **2** a frivolous thing.

ORIGIN – Old French *freperie* 'second-hand clothes', from *frepe* 'rag'.

frisbee /**friz**bi/ > *noun* trademark a plastic disc designed for skimming through the air as an outdoor game.

ORIGIN – said to be named after the pie tins of the *Frisbie* bakery in Connecticut.

frisée /**free**zay/ > *noun* a kind of endive with curled leaves.

ORIGIN – French, from *chicorée frisée* 'curly endive'.

Frisian* /**free**zhən, **friz**hən/ > *noun* **1** a person from Frisia or Friesland in the Netherlands. **2** the Germanic language spoken in northern parts of the Netherlands and adjacent islands. > *adjective* relating to Frisia or Friesland.

*SPELLING – no *e*: see the note at **FRIESIAN**.

frisk > *verb* **1** (of a police officer or official) pass the hands over (someone) in a search for hidden weapons or drugs. **2** (of an animal or person) skip or move playfully; frolic. > *noun* **1** a search by frisking. **2** a playful skip or leap.

ORIGIN – Old French *frisque* 'alert, lively'.

frisky > *adjective* (**friskier**, **friskiest**) playful and full of energy.

SYNONYMS – coltish, frolicsome, lively.

frisson /**free**sson/ > *noun* a strong feeling of excitement or fear; a thrill.

ORIGIN – French.

fritillary /**fri**tilləri/ > *noun* **1** a plant with hanging bell-like flowers. **2** a butterfly with orange-brown wings chequered with black.

ORIGIN – from Latin *fritillus* 'dice-box'.

frittata /fri**taat**ə/ > *noun* an Italian dish made with fried beaten eggs, resembling a Spanish omelette.

ORIGIN – Italian, from *friggere* 'to fry'.

fritter[1] > *verb* (**fritter away**) waste (time, money, or energy) on trifling matters.

ORIGIN – from obsolete *fitter* 'break into fragments'.

fritter[2] > *noun* a piece of fruit, vegetable, or meat coated in batter and deep-fried.

ORIGIN – Old French *friture*, from Latin *frigere* 'fry'.

fritto misto /**fritt**ō **mist**ō/ > *noun* a dish of various foods deep-fried in batter.

ORIGIN – Italian, 'mixed fry'.

frivolous > *adjective* **1** not having any serious purpose or value. **2** (of a person) carefree and superficial.
DERIVATIVES – **frivolity** *noun* **frivolously** *adverb*.
SYNONYMS – **1** shallow, superficial, trifling, trivial. **2** flighty, shallow, silly.
ANTONYMS – important, serious.
ORIGIN – from Latin *frivolus* 'silly, trifling'.

frizz > *verb* (of hair) form into a mass of tight curls. > *noun* a mass of tightly curled hair.
ORIGIN – French *friser*.

frizzle¹ > *verb* fry until crisp or burnt.
ORIGIN – from **FRY¹**, probably influenced by **SIZZLE**.

frizzle² > *verb* form (hair) into tight curls. > *noun* a tight curl in hair.

frizzy > *adjective* (**frizzier**, **frizziest**) formed of a mass of small, tight, wiry curls.

fro > *adverb* see **to and fro**.

frock > *noun* **1** chiefly Brit. a woman's or girl's dress. **2** a loose outer garment, in particular a long gown with flowing sleeves worn by monks, priests, or clergy.
COMBINATIONS – **frock coat** a man's double-breasted, long-skirted coat, now worn chiefly on formal occasions.
ORIGIN – Old French *froc*.

frog¹ > *noun* **1** a tailless amphibian with a short squat body and very long hind legs for leaping. **2** (**Frog**) derogatory a French person. [ORIGIN – partly from alliteration with *French*, partly from the reputation of the French for eating frogs' legs.]
WORDFINDER – batrachian (*relating to frogs and toads*).
IDIOMS – **have a frog in one's throat** informal lose one's voice or find it hard to speak because of hoarseness.
DERIVATIVES – **froggy** *adjective* **froglet** *noun*.
COMBINATIONS – **froghopper** a jumping, plant-sucking bug, the larva of which produces cuckoo spit. **frogspawn** a mass of frogs' eggs surrounded by transparent jelly.

frog² > *noun* **1** a thing used to hold or fasten something. **2** an ornamental coat fastener.

frog³ > *noun* an elastic horny pad in the sole of a horse's hoof.

frogman > *noun* a diver equipped with a rubber suit, flippers, and breathing equipment.

frogmarch > *verb* force (someone) to walk forward by pinning their arms from behind.

froideur /frwadör/ > *noun* coolness or reserve between people.
ORIGIN – French, from *froid* 'cold'.

frolic > *verb* (**frolicked**, **frolicking**) play or move about in a cheerful and lively way. > *noun* a playful action or movement.
SYNONYMS – *verb* caper, cavort, frisk, gambol.
ORIGIN – Dutch *vrolijk* 'merry, cheerful'.

frolicsome > *adjective* lively and playful.
SYNONYMS – frisky, sportive.

from > *preposition* **1** indicating the point in space or time at which a journey, process, or action starts. **2** indicating source or provenance. **3** indicating the starting point of a specified range. **4** indicating separation, removal, or prevention. **5** indicating a cause. **6** indicating a difference.

fromage frais /frommaazh fray/ > *noun* a type of smooth soft fresh cheese.
ORIGIN – French, 'fresh cheese'.

frond > *noun* the leaf or leaf-like part of a palm, fern, or similar plant.
ORIGIN – Latin *frons* 'leaf'.

front > *noun* **1** the side or part of an object that presents itself to view or that is normally seen first. **2** the position directly ahead. **3** the forward-facing part of a person's body. **4** the face of a building in which the main entrance is situated. **5** the furthest position that an army has reached and where the enemy is or may be engaged. **6** Meteorology the boundary of an advancing mass of air. **7** a particular situation or sphere of operation. **8** a deceptive appearance or mode of behaviour. **9** a person or organisation serving as a cover for subversive activities. **10** boldness and confidence of manner. > *adjective* of or at the front. > *verb* **1** have the front facing towards. **2** place or be placed at the front of. **3** provide with a front or facing. **4** lead or be at the forefront of. **5** present or host (a television or radio programme). **6** act as a front for.
WORDFINDER – anterior (*further forward in position*), prone (*lying down on one's front*).
IDIOMS – **front of house 1** the parts of a theatre in front of the proscenium arch. **2** the business of a theatre that concerns the audience, such as ticket sales. **in front of** in the presence of.
COMBINATIONS – **front line** the military line or part of an army that is closest to the enemy. **frontman** a person who acts as a front, in particular the leader of a band or the representative of an illegal organisation. **front-runner** the contestant that is leading in a race or other competition. **front-wheel drive** a transmission system that provides power to the front wheels of a motor vehicle.
ORIGIN – Latin *frons* 'forehead, front'.

frontage > *noun* **1** the facade of a building. **2** a strip or extent of land abutting on a street or waterway.

frontal > *adjective* **1** of or at the front. **2** relating to the forehead or front part of the skull.
DERIVATIVES – **frontally** *adverb*.
COMBINATIONS – **frontal lobe** each of the paired lobes of the brain lying immediately behind the forehead.

front bench > *noun* (in the UK) the foremost seats in the House of Commons, occupied by the members of the cabinet and shadow cabinet.
DERIVATIVES – **frontbencher** *noun*.

front-end > *adjective* **1** relating to the front, especially of a vehicle. **2** informal (of money) paid or charged at the beginning of a transaction. **3** Computing (of a device or program) directly accessed by the user and allowing access to further devices or programs. > *noun* Computing the front-end part of a computer or program.

frontier > *noun* **1** a border separating two countries. **2** the extreme limit of settled land beyond which lies wilderness. **3** the limit of advanced understanding or achievement in a particular area.
COMBINATIONS – **frontiersman** (or **frontierswoman**) a man (or woman) living in the region of a frontier.
ORIGIN – Latin *frons* 'front'.

frontispiece /fruntispeess/ > *noun* an illustration facing the title page of a book.
ORIGIN – Latin *frontispicium* 'facade', from *frons* 'front' + *specere* 'to look'.

frost > *noun* **1** a deposit of white ice crystals formed on surfaces when the temperature falls below freezing. **2** a period of cold weather when frost forms. > *verb* **1** cover or be covered with or as if with frost; freeze. **2** N. Amer. decorate with icing.

frostbite > *noun* injury to body tissues, especially the nose, fingers, or toes, caused by exposure to extreme cold.

frosted > *adjective* **1** covered with or as if with frost. **2** (of glass) having a translucent textured surface so that it is difficult to see through.

frosting > *noun* **1** N. Amer. icing. **2** a roughened matt finish on otherwise shiny material.

frosty > *adjective* (**frostier**, **frostiest**) **1** (of the weather) very cold with frost forming on surfaces. **2** cold and unfriendly.
DERIVATIVES – **frostily** *adverb* **frostiness** *noun*.
SYNONYMS – **2** cool, frigid, glacial, icy.

froth > *noun* **1** a mass of small bubbles in liquid caused by agitation, fermentation, or salivating. **2** worthless or insubstantial talk, ideas, or activities. **3** impure matter that rises to the surface of liquid. > *verb* form, produce, or contain froth.
DERIVATIVES – **frothily** *adverb* **frothy** *adjective*.
SYNONYMS – *noun* **1** foam, spume. *verb* bubble, effervesce, foam.

frottage /frotaazh/ > *noun* **1** Art the technique or process of taking a rubbing from an uneven surface to form the basis of a work of art. **2** the practice of rubbing against the clothed body of another person to obtain sexual gratification.

ORIGIN – French, 'rubbing, friction', from *frotter* 'to rub'.

frou-frou /froofroo/ > *noun* **1** a rustling noise made by a long skirt. **2** frills or other ornamentation.

ORIGIN – French.

frown > *verb* **1** furrow one's brows in an expression indicating disapproval, displeasure, or concentration. **2** (**frown on**) disapprove of. > *noun* a facial expression of this type.

DERIVATIVES – **frowning** *adjective*.

SYNONYMS – *verb* **1** glower, scowl.

ORIGIN – Old French *froignier*, from *froigne* 'surly look'.

frowst /frowst/ informal, chiefly Brit. > *noun* a warm stuffy atmosphere in a room. > *verb* lounge about in such an atmosphere.

frowsty > *adjective* (**frowstier, frowstiest**) Brit. having a stale, warm, and stuffy atmosphere.

frowzy /frowzy/ (also **frowsy**) > *adjective* (**frowzier, frowziest**) scruffy, dingy, and neglected in appearance.

froze past of FREEZE.

frozen past participle of FREEZE.

FRS > *abbreviation* (in the UK) Fellow of the Royal Society.

fructify /fruktifī/ > *verb* (**fructifies, fructified**) **1** formal make or become fruitful. **2** bear fruit.

ORIGIN – Latin *fructificare*, from *fructus* 'fruit'.

fructose /fruktōz/ > *noun* Chemistry a simple sugar found chiefly in honey and fruit.

ORIGIN – from Latin *fructus* 'fruit'.

frugal /froog'l/ > *adjective* sparing or economical with regard to money or food.

DERIVATIVES – **frugality** *noun* **frugally** *adverb*.

SYNONYMS – economical, prudent, sparing, thrifty.

ANTONYMS – extravagant, spendthrift.

ORIGIN – Latin *frugalis*, from *frugi* 'economical, thrifty', from *frux* 'fruit'.

frugivore /froojivor/ > *noun* Zoology an animal that feeds on fruit.

DERIVATIVES – **frugivorous** *adjective*.

ORIGIN – from Latin *frux* 'fruit' + *vorare* 'devour'.

fruit > *noun* **1** the sweet and fleshy product of a tree or other plant that contains seed and can be eaten as food. **2** Botany the seed-bearing structure of a plant, e.g. an acorn. **3** the result or reward of work or activity. **4** informal, derogatory, chiefly N. Amer. a male homosexual. > *verb* produce fruit.

IDIOMS – **bear fruit** have good results.

COMBINATIONS – **fruit bat** a large bat which feeds chiefly on fruit or nectar. **fruit cocktail** a finely chopped fruit salad, commercially produced in tins. **fruit fly** a small fly which feeds on fruit in both its adult and larval stages. **fruiting body** Botany the spore-producing organ of a fungus, often seen as a toadstool. **fruit machine** Brit. a coin-operated gambling machine that generates combinations of symbols (typically representing fruit), certain combinations winning money for the player. **fruit salad** a mixture of different types of chopped fruit served in syrup or juice. **fruit sugar** fructose.

ORIGIN – Latin *fructus* 'enjoyment of produce, harvest', from *frui* 'enjoy'.

fruitarian > *noun* a person who eats only fruit.

DERIVATIVES – **fruitarianism** *noun*.

fruitcake > *noun* **1** a cake containing dried fruit and nuts. **2** informal an eccentric or insane person.

fruiterer > *noun* chiefly Brit. a retailer of fruit.

fruitful > *adjective* **1** producing much fruit; fertile. **2** producing good results.

DERIVATIVES – **fruitfully** *adverb* **fruitfulness** *noun*.

SYNONYMS – **2** beneficial, productive, profitable, successful.

ANTONYMS – **2** fruitless, futile.

fruition /frooish'n/ > *noun* **1** the realisation or fulfilment of a plan. **2** literary the state or action of producing fruit.

ORIGIN – Latin, from *frui* 'enjoy'.

fruitless > *adjective* **1** failing to achieve the desired results; unproductive. **2** not producing fruit.

DERIVATIVES – **fruitlessly** *adverb*.

SYNONYMS – **1** futile, ineffectual, pointless, unproductive.

ANTONYMS – beneficial, fruitful.

fruitlet > *noun* an immature or small fruit.

fruity > *adjective* (**fruitier, fruitiest**) **1** of, resembling, or containing fruit. **2** (of a voice) mellow, deep, and rich. **3** Brit. informal sexually suggestive.

DERIVATIVES – **fruitiness** *noun*.

frump > *noun* informal an unattractive woman who wears dowdy old-fashioned clothes.

DERIVATIVES – **frumpy** *adjective*.

ORIGIN – probably from Dutch *verrompelen* 'wrinkle'.

frustrate > *verb* **1** prevent (a plan or action) from progressing or succeeding. **2** prevent (someone) from doing or achieving something. **3** cause to feel dissatisfied or unfulfilled.

DERIVATIVES – **frustrated** *adjective* **frustrating** *adjective* **frustratingly** *adverb* **frustration** *noun*.

SYNONYMS – **1,2** baulk, foil, thwart. **3** discourage, dissatisfy, exasperate, irk.

ORIGIN – Latin *frustrare* 'disappoint', from *frustra* 'in vain'.

fry¹ > *verb* (**fries, fried**) **1** cook or be cooked in hot fat or oil. **2** informal (of a person) burn or overheat in the sun. > *noun* (pl. **fries**) **1** a fried dish or meal. **2** (**fries**) N. Amer. short for *French fries*.

ORIGIN – Old French *frire*, from Latin *frigere*.

fry² > *plural noun* young fish, especially when newly hatched.

fryer > *noun* a large, deep container for frying food.

frying pan (also **frypan**) > *noun* a shallow pan with a long handle, used for frying food.

IDIOMS – **out of the frying pan into the fire** from a bad situation to one that is worse.

fry-up > *noun* Brit. informal a dish or meal of fried food.

ft > *abbreviation* foot or feet.

FTP > *abbreviation* Computing file transfer protocol, a standard for the exchange of program and data files across a network.

FTSE index /footsi/ (also **FT index**) > *noun* a figure (published by the *Financial Times*) indicating the relative prices of shares on the London Stock Exchange.

fuchsia /fyoosha/ > *noun* **1** an ornamental shrub with drooping tubular flowers that are typically of two contrasting colours. **2** a vivid purplish-red colour.

ORIGIN – named after the German botanist Leonhard *Fuchs* (1501–66).

fuck vulgar slang > *verb* **1** have sexual intercourse with. **2** damage or ruin. > *noun* an act of sexual intercourse. > *exclamation* a strong expression of annoyance or contempt.

IDIOMS – **fuck about** (or **around**) spend time doing unimportant or trivial things. **fuck all** Brit. absolutely nothing. **fuck off** go away. **fuck up 1** damage or confuse (someone) emotionally. **2** do (something) badly or ineptly.

DERIVATIVES – **fucker** *noun*.

ORIGIN – Germanic (compare with Swedish dialect *focka* and Dutch dialect *fokkelen*); possibly from an Indo-European root meaning 'strike', shared by Latin *pugnus* 'fist'.

fucus /fyookass/ > *noun* (pl. **fuci** /fyoosī/) a seaweed of a large genus of brown algae having flat leathery fronds.

DERIVATIVES – **fucoid** *adjective & noun*.

ORIGIN – Latin, from Greek *phukos* 'seaweed'.

fuddle > *verb* (usu. **fuddled**) confuse or stupefy, especially with alcohol.

SYNONYMS – (**fuddled**) addled, muddled, muzzy.

fuddy-duddy > *noun* (pl. **fuddy-duddies**) informal a person who is very old-fashioned and pompous.

fudge > *noun* **1** a soft crumbly or chewy sweet made from sugar, butter, and milk or cream. **2** (before another noun) chiefly N. Amer. rich chocolate, used as a sauce or a filling for cakes. **3** an attempt to fudge an issue. > *verb* **1** present in a vague way, especially to mislead. 2 manipulate (facts or figures) so as to present a desired picture.

---

wordpower facts

Fudge

The word **fudge** is probably from the obsolete *fadge*, which meant 'to fit'. Early use of **fudge** was as a verb in the sense 'turn out as expected' and also 'merge together' (this probably gave rise, later, to the name of the sweet). In the 17th century the verb came to mean 'fit together in a clumsy or underhand manner', or 'cobble (facts and figures) together in a superficially convincing way'. This led, in the 18th century, to the exclamation **fudge!**, an expression of disgust equivalent to 'stuff and nonsense!'.

Fuehrer > *noun* variant spelling of **Führer**.

fuehrer > *noun* variant spelling of **Führer**.

fuel > *noun* **1** material such as coal, gas, or oil that is burned to produce heat or power. **2** food, drink, or drugs as a source of energy. **3** something that acts to inflame argument or intense emotion. > *verb* (**fuelled**, **fuelling**; US **fueled**, **fueling**) **1** supply or power with fuel. **2** sustain or inflame.
COMBINATIONS – **fuel cell** a cell producing an electric current direct from a chemical reaction.
ORIGIN – Old French *fouaille*, from Latin *focus* 'hearth'.

fuel injection > *noun* the direct introduction of fuel under pressure into the combustion units of an internal-combustion engine.
DERIVATIVES – **fuel-injected** *adjective*.

fug > *noun* Brit. informal a warm, stuffy atmosphere.
DERIVATIVES – **fuggy** *adjective*.

fugal /fyoog'l/ > *adjective* relating to a fugue.

fugitive /fyoojitiv/ > *noun* a person who has escaped from captivity or is in hiding. > *adjective* quick to disappear; fleeting.
SYNONYMS – *noun* escapee, runaway.
ORIGIN – Latin *fugitivus*, from *fugere* 'flee'.

fugu /foogoo/ > *noun* a pufferfish that is eaten as a Japanese delicacy, after some highly poisonous parts have been removed.
ORIGIN – Japanese.

fugue /fyoog/ > *noun* **1** Music a composition in which a short melody or phrase is successively taken up by different parts in counterpoint. **2** Psychiatry loss of awareness of one's identity.
ORIGIN – Latin *fuga* 'flight'.

Führer /fyoorer/ (also **Fuehrer**) > *noun* the title assumed by Hitler as leader of Germany.
ORIGIN – German, 'leader'.

führer /fyoorer/ (also **fuehrer**) > *noun* the title assumed by Hitler as leader of Germany.
ORIGIN – German *Führer* 'leader'.

-ful > *suffix* **1** (forming adjectives from nouns) full of; having the qualities of: *sorrowful*. **2** forming adjectives from adjectives or from Latin stems with little change of sense: *grateful*. **3** (forming adjectives from verbs) apt to; able to; accustomed to: *forgetful*. **4** (pl. **-fuls**) forming nouns denoting the amount needed to fill the specified container: *bucketful*.

fulcrum /foolkrəm/ > *noun* (pl. **fulcra** /foolkrə/ or **fulcrums**) the point against which a lever is placed to get a purchase, or on which it turns or is supported.
ORIGIN – Latin, 'post of a couch', from *fulcire* 'to prop up'.

fulfil* (US **fulfill**) > *verb* (**fulfilled**, **fulfilling**) **1** achieve or realise (something desired, promised, or predicted). **2** satisfy or meet (a requirement or condition). **3** (**fulfil oneself**) gain happiness or satisfaction by fully achieving one's potential.
DERIVATIVES – **fulfilled** *adjective* **fulfilling** *adjective* **fulfilment** (US **fulfillment**) *noun*.
*SPELLING – in British English this is spelled with one *l* at the end: fulfil.
SYNONYMS – **1** accomplish, achieve, discharge, perform, realise. **2** comply with, conform to, meet, satisfy.
ORIGIN – Old English, 'fill up, make full'.

full¹ > *adjective* **1** containing or holding as much or as many as possible; having no empty space. **2** (**full of**) having a large number or quantity of. **3** not lacking or omitting anything; complete. **4** plump or rounded. **5** (**full of**) unable to stop talking or thinking about. **6** (of flavour, sound, or colour) strong, rich, or intense. > *adverb* **1** straight; directly. **2** very.
IDIOMS – **full of oneself** very self-satisfied and with an exaggerated sense of self-worth. **full on 1** running at or providing maximum power or capacity. **2** so as to make a direct or significant impact. **full out** with maximum effort or power. **full steam** (or **speed**) **ahead** proceeding with as much speed or energy as possible. **full up** filled to capacity. **to the full** to the greatest possible extent.
COMBINATIONS – **full-blooded 1** of unmixed ancestry. **2** vigorous and whole-hearted. **full board** Brit. provision of accommodation and all meals at a hotel or guest house. **full-bodied** rich and satisfying in flavour or sound. **full-fledged** N. Amer. fully fledged. **full-frontal** with full exposure of the front of the body. **full house 1** a theatre or meeting that is filled to capacity. **2** a poker hand with three of a kind and a pair. **3** a winning card at bingo. **full marks** the maximum award in an examination or assessment. **full moon** the phase of the moon in which its whole disc is illuminated. **full-scale 1** (of a model or representation) of the same size as the thing represented. **2** unrestricted in extent or intensity: *a full-scale invasion*. **full stop** a punctuation mark (.) used at the end of a sentence or an abbreviation. **full toss** Cricket a ball pitched right up to the batsman.

full² > *verb* clean, shrink, and felt (cloth) by heat, pressure, and moisture.
ORIGIN – probably a back-formation from *fuller*, influenced by Old French *fouler* 'press hard upon' or medieval Latin *fullare*.

fullback > *noun* a player in a defensive position near the goal in a ball game such as soccer.

full-blown > *adjective* fully developed; complete.

full bore chiefly N. Amer. > *adverb* at full speed or maximum capacity. > *adjective* **1** denoting firearms of relatively large calibre. **2** complete; thoroughgoing.

full dress > *noun* clothes worn on very formal occasions. > *adjective* formal and serious.

fuller > *noun* a person whose occupation is fulling cloth.
COMBINATIONS – **fuller's earth** a type of clay used in fulling cloth and as an adsorbent.
ORIGIN – Old English *fullere*, from Latin *fullo*.

full face > *adverb* with all the face visible; facing directly at someone or something. > *adjective* **1** showing all of the face. **2** covering all of the face.

fullness (also **fulness**) > *noun* **1** the state of being full. **2** richness or abundance.
IDIOMS – **in the fullness of time** after a due length of time has elapsed.

full-time > *adjective* occupying the whole of the time available. > *adverb* on a full-time basis. > *noun* (**full time**) the end of a sports match.
DERIVATIVES – **full-timer** *noun*.

fully > *adverb* **1** completely or entirely. **2** no less or fewer than: *fully 65 per cent*.
SYNONYMS – **1** completely, entirely, totally, utterly, wholly.
COMBINATIONS – **fully fashioned** (of women's clothing) shaped and seamed to fit the body. **fully fledged 1** with fully developed wing feathers and able to fly. **2** Brit. completely developed or established; of full status.

-fully > *suffix* forming adverbs corresponding to adjectives ending in *-ful* (such as *sorrowfully* corresponding to *sorrowful*).

fulmar /foolmər/ > *noun* a grey and white northern seabird of the petrel family.

ORIGIN – from Old Norse *fúll* 'stinking, foul' + *már* 'gull' (because of its habit of regurgitating its stomach contents when disturbed).

fulminant /**ful**minənt/ > *adjective* Medicine (of a disease or symptom) severe and sudden in onset.

ORIGIN – from Latin *fulminare* 'strike with lightning', from *fulmen* 'lightning'.

fulminate > *verb* **1** express vehement protest. **2** literary explode violently or flash like lightning. **3** (of a disease or symptom) develop suddenly and severely.

DERIVATIVES – **fulmination** *noun*.

SYNONYMS – **1** (**fulminate against**) inveigh against, rail against.

ORIGIN – Latin *fulminare* 'strike with lightning', from *fulmen* 'lightning'.

fulmination > *noun* an expression of vehement protest.

fulness > *noun* variant spelling of FULLNESS.

fulsome > *adjective* having or showing a quality to a great or excessive degree.

DERIVATIVES – **fulsomely** *adverb*.

USAGE – although it is increasingly used simply to mean 'plentiful, generous', **fulsome** has usually carried a derogatory connotation of excess. An expression like *fulsome praise*, therefore, can be ambiguous: to some it means 'generous praise', but to others 'flattering or insincere praise'.

fumarole /**fyoo**mərōl/ > *noun* an opening in or near a volcano, through which hot sulphurous gases emerge.

ORIGIN – Latin *fumariolum* 'hole for smoke'.

fumble > *verb* **1** use the hands clumsily while doing or handling something. **2** (of the hands) do or handle something clumsily. **3** (**fumble about** or **around**) move about clumsily using the hands to find one's way. **4** express oneself or deal with something clumsily or nervously. **5** (in ball games) fail to catch or field (the ball) cleanly. > *noun* an act of fumbling.

DERIVATIVES – **fumbler** *noun* **fumbling** *adjective*.

SYNONYMS – *verb* **1,2** grope, scrabble. **3** (**fumble about** or **around**) blunder, grope one's way, stumble.

ORIGIN – Low German *fommeln* or Dutch *fommelen*.

fume > *noun* a gas or vapour that smells strongly or is dangerous to inhale. > *verb* **1** emit fumes. **2** expose (something, especially wood) to ammonia fumes in order to produce dark tints. **3** feel great anger.

DERIVATIVES – **fuming** *adjective* **fumy** *adjective*.

SYNONYMS – *verb* **3** boil, rage, seethe.

ORIGIN – Latin *fumare* 'to smoke'.

fumigate > *verb* disinfect or purify with the fumes of certain chemicals.

DERIVATIVES – **fumigant** *noun* **fumigation** *noun* **fumigator** *noun*.

ORIGIN – Latin *fumigare*, from *fumus* 'smoke'.

fun > *noun* **1** light-hearted pleasure or amusement. **2** a source of this. **3** playfulness or good humour. > *adjective* informal enjoyable.

IDIOMS – **make fun of** tease or laugh at in a mocking way.

SYNONYMS – *noun* **1,2** amusement, diversion, entertainment, recreation. **3** gaiety, jollity, merriment, playfulness.

COMBINATIONS – **fun run** informal an uncompetitive run for sponsored runners, held in support of a charity.

ORIGIN – first used as a verb meaning 'to cheat or hoax': related to FOND.

function > *noun* **1** an activity that is natural to or the purpose of a person or thing. **2** a large or formal social event or ceremony. **3** a computer operation corresponding to a single instruction from the user. **4** Mathematics a relation or expression involving one or more variables. **5** a variable quantity regarded as depending on another variable; a consequence: *depreciation is a function of time.* > *verb* **1** work or operate in a proper or particular way. **2** (**function as**) fulfil the purpose or task of (a specified thing).

DERIVATIVES – **functionless** *adjective*.

SYNONYMS – *verb* **1** go, operate, run, work. **2** act, operate, serve.

COMBINATIONS – **function key** Computing a key on a computer keyboard to which software can assign a particular function.

ORIGIN – French *fonction*, from Latin *fungi* 'perform'.

functional > *adjective* **1** of, relating to, or having a function. **2** designed to be practical and useful, rather than attractive. **3** working or operating. **4** (of a disease) affecting the operation rather than the structure of an organ.

DERIVATIVES – **functionality** *noun* **functionally** *adverb*.

SYNONYMS – **2** serviceable, utilitarian. **3** going, operating, operative, running, working.

COMBINATIONS – **functional food** a food containing health-giving additives.

functionalism > *noun* the theory that the design of an object should be governed by function rather than aesthetics.

DERIVATIVES – **functionalist** *noun* & *adjective*.

functionary > *noun* (pl. **functionaries**) an official.

fund > *noun* **1** a sum of money saved or made available for a particular purpose. **2** (**funds**) financial resources. **3** a large stock. > *verb* provide with a fund.

DERIVATIVES – **funding** *noun*.

ORIGIN – Latin *fundus* 'bottom, piece of landed property'.

fundament > *noun* **1** the foundation or basis of something. **2** humorous a person's buttocks or anus.

ORIGIN – Latin *fundamentum*, from *fundare* 'to found'.

fundamental > *adjective* of or serving as a foundation or core; of central importance. > *noun* a central or primary rule or principle.

DERIVATIVES – **fundamentally** *adverb*.

SYNONYMS – *adjective* basic, central, elemental, primary, underlying.

ANTONYMS – secondary, superficial.

COMBINATIONS – **fundamental note** Music the lowest note of a chord.

fundamentalism > *noun* **1** a form of Protestant Christianity which upholds belief in the strict and literal interpretation of the Bible. **2** the strict maintenance of the ancient or fundamental doctrines of any religion or ideology.

DERIVATIVES – **fundamentalist** *noun* & *adjective*.

fundholding > *noun* (in the UK) a former system of state funding in which a general practitioner controls their own budget for the purchase of hospital services.

DERIVATIVES – **fundholder** *noun*.

fundie /**fun**di/ (also **fundi**) > *noun* (pl. **fundies** or **fundis**) informal a Christian fundamentalist.

funeral > *noun* a ceremony in which a dead person is buried or cremated.

WORDFINDER – cortège (*funeral procession*), dirge (*lament for the dead*), hearse (*vehicle for conveying the coffin*), inter (*place (a corpse) in a grave or tomb*), knell (*sound of a funeral bell*), obsequies (*funeral rites*), pall (*cloth spread over a coffin, hearse, or tomb*), wake (*party held after a funeral*).

IDIOMS – **it's your funeral** informal it is your own responsibility (used to imply that an undesirable outcome is possible).

COMBINATIONS – **funeral director** an undertaker. **funeral parlour** (also **funeral home**) an establishment where the dead are prepared for burial or cremation.

ORIGIN – Latin *funeralia*, from *funus* 'funeral, death, corpse'.

funerary /**fyoo**nərəri, **fyoo**nəri/ > *adjective* relating to a funeral or the commemoration of the dead.

funereal /fyoo**neer**iəl/ > *adjective* having the sombre character appropriate to a funeral.

SYNONYMS – drab, gloomy, grave, solemn.

funfair > *noun* chiefly Brit. a fair consisting of rides, sideshows, and other amusements.

fungi plural of FUNGUS.

fungible /**fun**jib'l/ > *adjective* Law (of goods contracted for without an individual specimen being specified) interchangeable with other identical items.

ORIGIN – Latin *fungibilis*, from *fungi* 'perform, enjoy'.

fungicide /**fun**jisīd/ > *noun* a chemical that destroys fungus.

DERIVATIVES – **fungicidal** *adjective*.

fungus /**fung**gəss/ > *noun* (pl. **fungi** /**fung**gī/) any of a large group of spore-producing organisms which feed on organic matter and include moulds, yeast, mushrooms, and toadstools.

WORDFINDER – mycology (*scientific study of fungi*).

DERIVATIVES – **fungal** *adjective* **fungoid** *adjective*.

ORIGIN – Latin, perhaps from Greek *spongos* 'sponge'.

funicular /fyoo**nik**yələr/ > *adjective* (of a railway on a steep slope) operated by cable with ascending and descending cars counterbalanced. > *noun* a funicular railway.

ORIGIN – from Latin *funiculus* 'little rope', from *funis* 'rope'.

funk¹ informal > *noun* (also **blue funk**) a state of panic or depression. > *verb* avoid out of fear.

ORIGIN – perhaps from **FUNK**² in the informal sense 'tobacco smoke', or from obsolete Flemish *fonck* 'disturbance, agitation'.

funk² > *noun* a style of popular dance music of US black origin, having a strong rhythm that typically accentuates the first beat in the bar.

ORIGIN – perhaps from French dialect *funkier* 'blow smoke on'.

funky > *adjective* (**funkier**, **funkiest**) informal **1** (of music) having a strong dance rhythm. **2** unconventionally modern and stylish.

DERIVATIVES – **funkily** *adverb* **funkiness** *noun*.

funnel > *noun* **1** a tubular utensil that is wide at the top and narrow at the bottom, used for guiding liquid or powder into a small opening. **2** a metal chimney on a ship or steam engine. > *verb* (**funnelled**, **funnelling**; US **funneled**, **funneling**) **1** guide or move through or as if through a funnel. **2** assume the shape of a funnel: *the crevice funnelled out.*

COMBINATIONS – **funnel-web spider** a dangerously poisonous Australian spider that builds a funnel-shaped web.

ORIGIN – Latin *fundibulum*, from *infundere* 'pour into'.

funny > *adjective* (**funnier**, **funniest**) **1** causing laughter or amusement. **2** strange; peculiar. **3** arousing suspicion. **4** informal slightly unwell; out of sorts. > *noun* (**funnies**) informal **1** amusing jokes. **2** N. Amer. the comic strips in newspapers.

IDIOMS – **funny ha-ha** (or **funny peculiar**) funny meaning 'amusing' rather than 'strange' (or vice versa). [ORIGIN –

coined by Ian Hay in his novel *Housemaster* (1936).]

DERIVATIVES – **funnily** *adverb*.

SYNONYMS – *adjective* **1** amusing, comical, droll, humorous. **2** bizarre, odd, peculiar, strange, weird. **3** dubious, suspicious.

COMBINATIONS – **funny bone** informal the part of the elbow over which the ulnar nerve passes, which may cause numbness, tingling, and pain if knocked. **funny farm** informal a psychiatric hospital. **funny man** a professional clown or comedian.

funster > *noun* informal a joker.

fur > *noun* **1** the short, soft hair of certain animals. **2** the skin of an animal with fur on it, used in making garments. **3** a coat made from fur. **4** Brit. a coating of limescale deposited by hard water on the inside surface of a pipe, kettle, etc. **5** a coating formed on the tongue as a symptom of sickness. > *verb* (**furred**, **furring**) Brit. coat or clog with a deposit.

DERIVATIVES – **furred** *adjective*.

ORIGIN – Old French *forrer* 'to line, sheathe', from *forre* 'sheath'.

furbelow > *noun* **1** a flounce on a skirt or petticoat. **2** (**furbelows**) showy trimmings.

ORIGIN – French *falbala* 'trimming, flounce'.

furbish > *verb* archaic **1** give a fresh look to; renovate. **2** polish (a weapon).

ORIGIN – Old French *forbir*.

furious > *adjective* **1** extremely angry. **2** full of energy or intensity.

DERIVATIVES – **furiously** *adverb*.

SYNONYMS – **1** enraged, fuming, infuriated. **2** fierce, violent.

ORIGIN – Latin *furiosus*, from *furia* 'fury'.

furl > *verb* roll or fold up neatly and securely.

DERIVATIVES – **furled** *adjective*.

ORIGIN – French *ferler*, from *ferm* 'firm' + *lier* 'bind', from Latin *ligare*.

furlong > *noun* an eighth of a mile, 220 yards.

ORIGIN – from the Old English words for 'furrow' and 'long' (originally referring to the length of a furrow in a common field).

furlough /**fur**lō/ > *noun* leave of absence, especially from military duty. > *verb* US grant furlough to.

ORIGIN – Dutch *verlof*.

furnace > *noun* **1** an enclosed chamber in which material can be heated to very high temperatures. **2** a very hot place.

ORIGIN – Latin *fornax*, from *fornus* 'oven'.

furnish > *verb* **1** provide (a room or building) with furniture and fittings. **2** supply with equipment or information. **3** be a source of; provide.

DERIVATIVES – **furnished** *adjective* **furnisher** *noun*.

SYNONYMS – **2,3** equip, provide, supply.

ORIGIN – Old French *furnir*.

furnishing > *noun* **1** (**furnishings**) furniture and fittings in a room or building. **2** (before another noun) used for curtains or upholstery: *furnishing fabrics.*

furniture > *noun* **1** the movable articles that are used to make a room or building suitable for living or working in, such as tables, chairs, or desks. **2** the small accessories or fittings that are required for a particular task or function: *door furniture.*

COMBINATIONS – **furniture beetle** a small brown beetle, the larva of which (the woodworm) bores holes in dead wood.

ORIGIN – French *fourniture*, from *fournir* 'to furnish'.

furore /fyoo**ror**i/ (US **furor** /fyoo**ror**/) > *noun* an outbreak of public anger or excitement.

SYNONYMS – commotion, tumult, uproar.

ORIGIN – Italian.

furphy /**fur**fi/ > *noun* (pl. **furphies**) Austral. informal a far-fetched rumour.

ORIGIN – from the name painted on water and sanitary carts manufactured by the *Furphy* family of Shepparton, Victoria.

furrier /**furr**iər/ > *noun* a person who prepares or deals in furs.

furrow > *noun* **1** a long, narrow trench made in the ground by a plough. **2** a rut or groove. **3** a deep wrinkle on a person's face. > *verb* **1** make a furrow in. **2** mark or be marked with furrows.

furry > *adjective* (**furrier**, **furriest**) covered with or resembling fur.

further comparative of **FAR**. > *adverb* (also **farther**) **1** at, to, or by a greater distance. **2** over a greater expanse of space or time. **3** beyond the point already reached. **4** at or to a more advanced or desirable stage. **5** in addition; also. > *adjective* **1** (also **farther**) more distant in space. **2** additional. > *verb* help the progress or development of.

IDIOMS – **further to** formal following on from (used especially at the beginning of a letter).

USAGE – are there rules governing the use of **further** and **farther**? In the sense 'at, to, or by a greater distance' they may be used interchangeably: *she moved further down the train* and *she moved farther down the train* are both correct. However **further** is a much commoner word, and in addition it is used in certain abstract contexts in which it would be unusual to substitute **farther**, e.g. *without further delay; have you anything further to say?* The same distinction is made between **farthest** and **furthest**.

COMBINATIONS – **further education** Brit. education below degree level for people above school age.

furtherance > *noun* the advancement of a scheme or interest.

furthermore > *adverb* in addition; besides.

furthermost (also **farthermost**) > *adjective*

at the greatest distance from a central point or implicit standpoint.

furthest (also **farthest**) superlative of FAR. > *adjective* **1** situated at the greatest distance. **2** covering the greatest area or distance. > *adverb* **1** at or by the greatest distance. **2** over the greatest distance or area. **3** to the most extreme or advanced point.

furtive > *adjective* characterised by guilty or evasive secrecy; stealthy.
DERIVATIVES – **furtively** adverb.
SYNONYMS – covert, stealthy, surreptitious.
ORIGIN – Latin *furtivus*, from *furtum* 'theft'.

fury > *noun* (pl. **furies**) **1** extreme anger. **2** extreme strength or violence in an action or a natural phenomenon. **2** (**Fury**) Greek Mythology a supernatural being embodying punishment, often represented as one of three goddesses.
IDIOMS – **like fury** informal with great energy or effort.
SYNONYMS – *noun* **1** ire, rage, wrath.
ORIGIN – Latin *furia*, from *furere* 'be mad, rage'.

furze > *noun* another term for GORSE.

fuse¹ > *verb* **1** join, blend, or coalesce to form a single entity. **2** melt (a material or object) with intense heat, so as to join it with something else. **3** Brit. (with reference to an electrical appliance) stop or cause to stop working when a fuse melts. **4** provide (a circuit or electrical appliance) with a fuse. > *noun* a safety device consisting of a strip of wire that melts and breaks an electric circuit if the current exceeds a safe level.
COMBINATIONS – **fuse box** a box or board housing the fuses for circuits in a building.
ORIGIN – from Latin *fundere* 'pour, melt'.

fuse² (US **fuze**) > *noun* **1** a length of material along which a small flame moves to explode a bomb or firework. **2** a device in a bomb that controls the timing of the explosion. > *verb* fit a fuse to (a bomb).
ORIGIN – Latin *fusus* 'spindle'.

fuselage /fyoozəlaazh/ > *noun* the main body of an aircraft.
ORIGIN – French, from *fuseler* 'shape into a spindle'.

fusible /fyoozib'l/ > *adjective* able to be fused or melted easily.

fusil /fyoozil/ > *noun* historical a light musket.
ORIGIN – French, from Latin *focus* 'fire'.

fusilier /fyoozileer/ > *noun* (**Fusilier**) a member of any of several British regiments formerly armed with fusils.

fusillade /fyoozilayd/ > *noun* a series of shots fired together or in rapid succession.

fusilli /fyoozeeli/ > *plural noun* pasta pieces in the form of short spirals.
ORIGIN – Italian, 'little spindles'.

fusion > *noun* **1** the process or result of fusing. **2** a reaction in which light atomic nuclei fuse to form a heavier nucleus, releasing much energy. **3** music that is a mixture of different styles, especially jazz and rock.
ORIGIN – from Latin *fundere* 'pour, melt'.

fuss > *noun* **1** a display of unnecessary or excessive excitement, activity, or interest. **2** a protest or complaint. > *verb* **1** show unnecessary or excessive concern about something. **2** (usu. **be fussed**) Brit. disturb or bother. **3** treat with excessive attention or affection.
IDIOMS – **not be fussed** Brit. informal not have strong feelings about something.
SYNONYMS – *noun* **1** commotion, flurry, palaver. **2** complaint, grouse, objection, protest.

fusspot > *noun* informal a fussy person.

fussy > *adjective* (**fussier, fussiest**) **1** fastidious about one's requirements and hard to please. **2** full of unnecessary detail or decoration.
DERIVATIVES – **fussily** adverb **fussiness** noun.
SYNONYMS – **1** fastidious, finicky, particular.

fustian /fustiən/ > *noun* a thick, hard-wearing twilled cloth.
ORIGIN – from Latin *pannus fustaneus* 'cloth from *Fostat*', a suburb of Cairo.

fusty > *adjective* (**fustier, fustiest**) **1** smelling stale, damp, or stuffy. **2** old-fashioned.
DERIVATIVES – **fustiness** noun.
ORIGIN – Old French *fuste* 'smelling of the cask'.

futile > *adjective* producing no useful result; pointless.
DERIVATIVES – **futilely** adverb **futility** noun.
SYNONYMS – fruitless, pointless, vain.
ANTONYMS – fruitful.
ORIGIN – Latin *futilis* 'leaky, futile'.

futon /footon/ > *noun* a padded unsprung mattress of a type originating in Japan, that can be rolled up.
ORIGIN – Japanese.

future > *noun* **1** (**the future**) time that is still to come. **2** events or conditions occurring or existing in that time. **3** a prospect of success or happiness: *I might have a future as an artist.* **4** Grammar a tense of verbs expressing events that have not yet

happened. **5** (**futures**) contracts for assets bought at agreed prices but delivered and paid for later. > *adjective* **1** existing or occurring in the future. **2** planned or destined to hold a specified position: *his future wife.* **3** Grammar (of a tense) expressing an event yet to happen.
IDIOMS – **in future** from now onwards.
COMBINATIONS – **future perfect** Grammar a tense of verbs expressing expected completion in the future, in English exemplified by *will have done.*
ORIGIN – Latin *futurus* 'going to be', from *esse* 'be'.

Futurism > *noun* an artistic movement launched in Italy in 1909, which strongly rejected traditional forms and embraced modern technology.

futurist > *noun* **1** (**Futurist**) an adherent of Futurism. **2** a person who studies the future and makes predictions about it.

futuristic > *adjective* **1** having or involving very modern technology or design. **2** (of a film or book) set in the future.

futurity > *noun* (pl. **futurities**) **1** the future time. **2** a future event.

futurology > *noun* systematic forecasting of the future based on present trends.
DERIVATIVES – **futurologist** noun.

fuze > *noun* US spelling of FUSE².

fuzz¹ > *noun* **1** a frizzy mass of hair or fibre. **2** a blurred image. > *verb* make or become fuzzy.
DERIVATIVES – **fuzzed** adjective.

fuzz² > *noun* (**the fuzz**) informal the police.

fuzzy > *adjective* (**fuzzier, fuzziest**) **1** having a frizzy texture or appearance. **2** indistinct or vague.
DERIVATIVES – **fuzzily** adverb **fuzziness** noun.
COMBINATIONS – **fuzzy logic** a form of logic in which statements can be given fractional values rather than simply 'true' or 'false'.

FX > *abbreviation* visual or sound effects.
ORIGIN – from the pronunciation of the two syllables of *effects.*

-fy > *suffix* **1** (added to nouns) forming verbs denoting making or producing: *speechify.* **2** denoting transformation or the process of making into: *petrify.* **3** forming verbs denoting the making of a state defined by an adjective: *falsify.* **4** forming verbs expressing a causative sense: *horrify.*
ORIGIN – Latin *-ficare*, from *facere* 'do, make'.

FYI > *abbreviation* for your information.

g

G¹ (also **g**) > *noun* (pl. **Gs** or **G's**) **1** the seventh letter of the alphabet. **2** denoting the next item after F in a set. **3** Music the fifth note in the diatonic scale of C major.

G² > *abbreviation* **1** giga- (10⁹). **2** N. Amer. informal grand (a thousand dollars). **3** the force exerted by the earth's gravitational field.

g > *abbreviation* gram(s). > *symbol* Physics the acceleration due to gravity (9.81 m s⁻²).

G8 > *abbreviation* Group of Eight (leading industrial nations: the US, Japan, Germany, France, the UK, Italy, Canada, and Russia).

GA > *abbreviation* Georgia.

Ga > *symbol* the chemical element gallium.

gab informal > *verb* (**gabbed**, **gabbing**) talk at length. > *noun* talk; chatter.
IDIOMS – **the gift of the gab** the ability to speak with eloquence and fluency.
DERIVATIVES – **gabby** (**gabbier**, **gabbiest**) *adjective*.
ORIGIN – from GOB¹.

gabardine > *noun* variant spelling of GABERDINE.

gabble > *verb* talk rapidly and unintelligibly. > *noun* rapid, unintelligible talk.
DERIVATIVES – **gabbler** *noun*.
SYNONYMS – *verb* babble, gibber, jabber.
ORIGIN – Dutch *gabbelen*.

gabbro /ˈgabrō/ > *noun* (pl. **gabbros**) a dark, coarse-grained igneous rock.
ORIGIN – from Latin *glaber* 'smooth'.

gaberdine /gabbərˈdeen/ > *noun* **1** a smooth, durable twill-woven worsted or cotton cloth. **2** Brit. a raincoat made of gaberdine.
ORIGIN – Old French *gauvardine*, earlier *gallevardine*, perhaps from German *wallevart* 'pilgrimage' and originally 'a garment worn by a pilgrim'.

gable > *noun* **1** the triangular upper part of a wall at the end of a ridged roof. **2** a gable-shaped canopy over a window or door.
DERIVATIVES – **gabled** *adjective*.
ORIGIN – Old French, from Old Norse *gafl*.

Gabonese /gaabəˈneez/ > *noun* (pl. same) a person from Gabon, a country in West Africa. > *adjective* relating to Gabon.

gad > *verb* (**gadded**, **gadding**) (**gad about** or **around**) informal go around from one place to another seeking pleasure and entertainment.
ORIGIN – from obsolete *gadling* 'wanderer, vagabond'.

gadabout > *noun* informal a person who gads about.

Gadarene /gaddəˈreen/ > *adjective* involving or engaged in a headlong or disastrous rush.
ORIGIN – Greek *Gadarēnos* 'inhabitant of *Gadara*', with reference to the story in the Gospel of Matthew of the swine that rushed down a steep cliff into the sea and drowned.

gadfly > *noun* (pl. **gadflies**) **1** a fly that bites livestock, especially a horsefly, warble fly, or botfly. **2** an annoying and provocative person.
ORIGIN – from GAD, or obsolete *gad* 'goad, spike', from Old Norse *gaddr*.

gadget > *noun* a small mechanical device or tool.
DERIVATIVES – **gadgetry** *noun*.
ORIGIN – probably from French *gâchette* 'lock mechanism' or from the French dialect word *gagée* 'tool'.

gadolinium /gaddəˈlinniəm/ > *noun* a soft silvery-white metallic chemical element of the lanthanide series.
ORIGIN – from *gadolinite* (a rare mineral containing the element), named after the Finnish mineralogist Johan *Gadolin* (1760–1852).

gadroon /gəˈdroon/ > *noun* a decorative curved edging on silverware, wood, etc.
DERIVATIVES – **gadrooned** *adjective* **gadrooning** *noun*.
ORIGIN – French *godron*, probably related to *goder* 'to pucker'.

gadwall /ˈgadwawl/ > *noun* a brownish-grey freshwater duck.

gadzooks > *exclamation* archaic expressing surprise or annoyance.
ORIGIN – alteration of *God's hooks*, i.e. the nails by which Christ was fastened to the cross.

Gael /gayl/ > *noun* a Gaelic-speaking person.
ORIGIN – Scottish Gaelic *Gaidheal*.

Gaelic /ˈgaylik, ˈgalik/ > *noun* **1** (also **Scottish Gaelic**) a Celtic language spoken in western Scotland. **2** (also **Irish Gaelic**) another term for IRISH (the language). > *adjective* relating to the Celtic languages and their speakers.
COMBINATIONS – **Gaelic coffee** coffee served with cream and whisky.

gaff¹ > *noun* **1** a stick with a hook, or a barbed spear, for landing large fish. **2** Sailing a spar to which the head of a fore-and-aft sail is bent. > *verb* seize or impale with a gaff.
ORIGIN – Provençal *gaf* 'hook'; related to GAFFE.

wordpower facts

Gaelic

Scottish Gaelic is descended from the Celtic language of Ireland, having been brought to Scotland from Ireland in the 5th and 6th centuries AD. Scottish Gaelic and Irish have supplied English with numerous words. Many relate to things associated with the Scottish Highlands or Irish countryside, for example **bog, caber, ceilidh, clan, glen, loch, plaid**, and **sporran**. Others are more unexpected. **Pillion** is from a Gaelic word meaning 'small cushion': in English it originally meant 'light saddle'. **Trousers** and **trews** are of Gaelic origin, as is **slogan**: a *slogan* was originally a Scottish Highland war cry.

gaff² > *noun* (in phrase **blow the gaff**) Brit. informal reveal a plot or secret.

gaff³ > *noun* Brit. informal a person's house, flat, or shop.

gaffe /gaf/ (also **gaff**) > *noun* a tactless remark or other embarrassing blunder.
SYNONYMS – faux pas, indiscretion, slip.
ORIGIN – French, 'boathook', in colloquial use 'blunder'.

gaffer > *noun* Brit. **1** informal an old man. **2** informal a boss. **3** the chief electrician in a film or television production unit.
ORIGIN – probably a contraction of GODFATHER.

gaffer tape > *noun* strong cloth-backed waterproof adhesive tape.

gag¹ > *noun* **1** a piece of cloth put in or over a person's mouth to prevent them from speaking. **2** a restriction on free speech. > *verb* (**gagged**, **gagging**) **1** put a gag on. **2** choke or retch.

gag² > *noun* a joke or funny story or act. > *verb* tell jokes.

gaga /ˈgaagaa/ > *adjective* informal rambling in speech or thought; senile or slightly mad.
ORIGIN – French, 'senile, a senile person', from *gâteur*, hospital slang in the sense 'bed-wetter'.

gage¹ /gayj/ archaic > *noun* **1** a valued object deposited as a guarantee of good faith. **2** a glove or other object thrown down as a challenge to fight. > *verb* offer as a gage.
ORIGIN – Old French; related to WAGE and WED.

gage² /gayj/ > *noun* a greengage.

gage³ > *noun & verb* variant spelling of GAUGE.

gaggle > *noun* **1** a flock of geese. **2** informal a disorderly group of people.

Gaia /ˈgīə/ > *noun* the earth viewed as a vast self-regulating organism.
ORIGIN – coined by the English scientist

James Lovelock (born 1919) from the name of the Greek goddess *Gaia*.

gaiety (US also **gayety**) > *noun* (pl. **gaieties**) **1** the state or quality of being light-hearted and cheerful. **2** merrymaking; festivity.

ORIGIN – French *gaieté*.

gaijin /gījin/ > *noun* (pl. same) (in Japan) a foreigner.

ORIGIN – Japanese, from the words meaning 'foreign country' and 'person'.

gaillardia /gaylaardiə/ > *noun* an American plant cultivated for its bright red and yellow flowers.

ORIGIN – Latin, named in memory of *Gaillard* de Marentonneau, 18th-century French amateur botanist.

gaily > *adverb* **1** in a light-hearted and cheerful manner. **2** without thinking of the consequences. **3** with a bright appearance.

gain > *verb* **1** obtain or secure. **2** reach or arrive at. **3** (**gain on**) come closer to (a person or thing pursued). **4** increase the amount or rate of (weight, speed, etc.). **5** increase in value. **6** (**gain in**) improve or advance in a particular respect. **7** (of a clock or watch) become fast. > *noun* **1** a thing that is gained. **2** an increase in wealth or resources.

DERIVATIVES – **gainable** *adjective* **gainer** *noun*.

SYNONYMS – *verb* **1** acquire, attain, get, obtain, secure.

ORIGIN – first used in the sense 'booty': from Old French *gaignier* 'to gain'.

gainful > *adjective* serving to increase wealth or resources.

DERIVATIVES – **gainfully** *adverb* **gainfulness** *noun*.

SYNONYMS – fruitful, lucrative, productive, profitable, remunerative.

gainsay /gaynsay/ > *verb* (past and past participle **gainsaid**) formal deny or contradict; speak against.

DERIVATIVES – **gainsayer** *noun*.

ORIGIN – from obsolete *gain-* 'against' + SAY.

gait /gayt/ > *noun* **1** a person's manner of walking. **2** the paces of a horse or dog.

ORIGIN – from GATE².

gaiter > *noun* **1** a covering of cloth or leather for the ankle and lower leg. **2** chiefly US a shoe or overshoe extending to the ankle or above.

DERIVATIVES – **gaitered** *adjective*.

ORIGIN – French *guêtre*.

gal > *noun* informal, chiefly N. Amer. a girl or young woman.

gal. > *abbreviation* gallon(s).

gala /gaalə, gaylə/ > *noun* **1** a festive entertainment or performance. **2** Brit. a special sports event, especially a swimming competition.

ORIGIN – first used in the sense 'showy dress': from Old French *gale* 'rejoicing'.

galactic /gəlaktik/ > *adjective* **1** relating to a galaxy or galaxies. **2** Astronomy measured relative to the galactic equator.

COMBINATIONS – **galactic equator** Astronomy the great circle of the celestial sphere passing through the densest parts of the Milky Way.

galactose /gəlaktōz/ > *noun* Chemistry a simple sugar which is a constituent of lactose and some other compound sugars.

galago /gəlaygō/ > *noun* (pl. **galagos**) another term for BUSHBABY.

ORIGIN – Latin.

galah /gəlaa/ > *noun* a small grey and pink Australian cockatoo, regarded as a pest.

ORIGIN – from an Aboriginal language.

galangal /galənggʼl/ (also **galingale**) > *noun* an Asian plant of the ginger family, the root of which is used in cookery and herbal medicine.

ORIGIN – Old French *galingale*, from Arabic, perhaps ultimately from Chinese, from a place name.

galant /gəlant/ > *adjective* relating to or denoting a light and elegant style of 18th-century music.

ORIGIN – French and German (see GALLANT).

galantine /galənteen/ > *noun* a dish of cooked meat or fish served cold in aspic.

ORIGIN – Old French.

Galatian /gəlaysh'n/ > *noun* an inhabitant of Galatia, an ancient region of Asia Minor. > *adjective* relating to Galatia.

galaxy > *noun* (pl. **galaxies**) **1** a system of millions or billions of stars, together with gas and dust, held together by gravitational attraction. **2** (**the Galaxy**) the galaxy of which the solar system is a part; the Milky Way. **3** a large and impressive group of people or things.

---

wordpower facts

Galaxy

The **galaxy** originally meant 'the Milky Way'; the word is based on the Greek *galaxias kuklos*, literally 'milky vault', from *gala* **milk**. Later, **galaxy** was applied to the whole star system of which the Milky Way is part, and to other star systems when these were recognised. Astronomers originally called the outer galaxies **nebulae**, a reference to their cloudy appearance, but this term is now only used of gas or dust clouds within the galaxy. The word *gala* is also present in other technical terms related to milk, such as **galactorrhoea** 'excessive production of milk'.

---

gale > *noun* **1** a very strong wind. **2** an outburst of laughter.

galena /gəleenə/ > *noun* a metallic grey or black mineral consisting of lead sulphide.

ORIGIN – Latin, 'lead ore'.

galette /gəlet/ > *noun* a pancake, especially a savoury one incorporating potatoes.

ORIGIN – French.

Galilean¹ /galilayən/ > *adjective* relating to the Italian astronomer and physicist Galileo Galilei (1564–1642) or his methods.

Galilean² /galileeən/ > *noun* a person from Galilee, the region of ancient Palestine associated with the ministry of Jesus and now part of Israel. > *adjective* relating to Galilee.

galingale /galinggayl/ > *noun* **1** (also **English** or **sweet galingale**) a sedge with an aromatic rhizome, formerly used in perfumes. **2** variant spelling of GALANGAL.

ORIGIN – from GALANGAL.

gall¹ /gawl/ > *noun* **1** bold and impudent behaviour. **2** archaic the contents of the gall bladder; bile. **3** an animal's gall bladder. **4** a feeling of bitter resentment.

SYNONYMS – **1** audacity, effrontery, insolence, temerity. **4** acrimony, bitterness, rancour, resentment.

COMBINATIONS – **gall bladder** a small sac-shaped organ beneath the liver, in which bile is stored.

ORIGIN – Old English, 'bile'.

gall² /gawl/ > *noun* **1** annoyance; humiliation. **2** a sore on the skin made by chafing. > *verb* **1** annoy; humiliate. **2** make sore by chafing.

DERIVATIVES – **galling** *adjective*.

ORIGIN – Old English, 'sore on a horse'.

gall³ /gawl/ > *noun* an abnormal growth formed in response to the presence of insect larvae, mites, or fungi on plants and trees.

ORIGIN – Latin *galla*.

gall. > *abbreviation* gallon(s).

gallant /galənt/ > *adjective* **1** brave; heroic. **2** /gəlant/ (of a man) charming; chivalrous. **3** archaic of fine appearance; grand. > *noun* /gəlant/ a man who is charmingly attentive to women.

DERIVATIVES – **gallantly** *adverb*.

SYNONYMS – *verb* **1** bold, brave, courageous, daring, heroic, valiant. **2** charming, chivalrous, courtly, gentlemanly.

ORIGIN – first used in the sense 'finely dressed': from Old French *galant*, from *galer* 'have fun, make a show', from *gale* 'pleasure, rejoicing'.

gallantry > *noun* (pl. **gallantries**) **1** courageous behaviour. **2** polite attention or respect given by men to women.

SYNONYMS – *noun* **1** bravery, courage, daring, heroism, valour.

galleon > *noun* historical a large square-rigged sailing ship with three or more decks and masts.

ORIGIN – French *galion* or Spanish *galeón*.

galleria /galəreeə/ > *noun* an arcade of small shops.

ORIGIN – Italian, 'gallery'.

gallery > *noun* (pl. **galleries**) **1** a room or building for the display or sale of works of art. **2** a balcony or upper floor projecting from a back or side wall inside a hall or church. **3** the highest balcony in a theatre, having the cheapest seats. **4** (**the gallery**) a group of spectators. **5** a long room or passage forming a portico or colonnade. **6** a horizontal underground passage in a mine.

IDIOMS – **play to the gallery** aim to attract popular attention.

DERIVATIVES – **galleried** *adjective*.

ORIGIN – Italian *galleria*: first used in sense 5.

galley > *noun* (pl. **galleys**) **1** historical a low, flat ship with one or more sails and up to three banks of oars, often manned by slaves or criminals. **2** a narrow kitchen in a ship or aircraft. **3** (also **galley proof**) a printer's proof in the form of long single-column strips.

ORIGIN – Greek *galaia*; sense 3 is from French *galée* denoting an oblong tray for holding set-up type.

galliard /galiaard/ > *noun* historical a lively dance in triple time for two people.

ORIGIN – first used as an adjective meaning 'valiant, sturdy' and 'lively, brisk'): from Old French *gaillard* 'valiant'.

Gallic /galik/ > *adjective* **1** of or characteristic of France or the French. **2** of or relating to the Gauls.

DERIVATIVES – **Gallicise** (also **Gallicize**) *verb*.

ORIGIN – Latin *Gallicus*, from *Gallus* 'a Gaul'.

Gallicism /galisiz'm/ > *noun* a French word or idiom adopted in another language.

gallimaufry /galimawfri/ > *noun* a jumble or medley of things.

ORIGIN – archaic French *galimafrée* 'unappetising dish'.

gallimimus /galimīməss/ > *noun* (pl. **gallimimuses**) an ostrich-like dinosaur of the late Cretaceous period.

ORIGIN – from Latin *galli* 'of a cockerel' + *mimus* 'mime, pretence'.

gallinaceous /galinayshəss/ > *adjective* referring to birds of an order which includes domestic poultry and game birds.

ORIGIN – Latin *gallinaceus*.

gallium /galiəm/ > *noun* a soft, silvery-white metallic chemical element which melts just above room temperature.

ORIGIN – from Latin *Gallia* 'France' or *gallus* 'cock'; named by the French chemist Paul-Émile Lecoq de Boisbaudran.

gallivant /galivant/ > *verb* informal go from place to place seeking pleasure and entertainment.

ORIGIN – perhaps from GALLANT.

gallon /galən/ > *noun* **1** a unit of volume for liquid measure equal to eight pints: in Britain (also **imperial gallon**), equivalent to 4.55 litres; in the US, equivalent to 3.79 litres. **2** (**gallons**) informal large quantities.

ORIGIN – Old French *galon*, from Latin *galleta* 'pail, liquid measure'.

gallop > *noun* **1** the fastest pace of a horse or other quadruped, with all the feet off the ground together in each stride. **2** a ride on a horse at a gallop. > *verb* (**galloped**, **galloping**) **1** go or cause to go at the pace of a gallop. **2** proceed at great speed.

DERIVATIVES – **galloper** *noun*.

ORIGIN – Old French *galoper*; related to WALLOP.

gallows > *plural noun* (usu. treated as sing.) **1** a structure consisting of two uprights and a crosspiece, used for hanging a person. **2** (**the gallows**) execution by hanging.

COMBINATIONS – **gallows humour** grim and ironical humour in a desperate or hopeless situation.

gallstone /gawlstōn/ > *noun* a small, hard crystalline mass formed abnormally in the gall bladder or bile ducts from bile pigments, cholesterol, and calcium salts.

Gallup poll /galəp/ > *noun* trademark an assessment of public opinion by the questioning of a representative sample, used in forecasting voting results in an election.

ORIGIN – named after the American statistician George H. *Gallup* (1901–84).

galoot /gəloōt/ > *noun* N. Amer. & Scottish informal a clumsy or stupid person.

ORIGIN – a nautical term meaning 'an inexperienced marine'.

galore > *adjective* in abundance: *there were prizes galore*.

SYNONYMS – aplenty, in abundance, in profusion.

ORIGIN – from Irish *go leor* 'to sufficiency'.

galosh /gəlosh/ > *noun* a waterproof rubber overshoe.

ORIGIN – from Latin *gallica solea* 'Gallic shoe': originally denoting a type of clog.

galumph /gəlumf/ > *verb* informal move in a clumsy, ponderous, or noisy manner.

ORIGIN – first used in the sense 'prance in triumph': coined by Lewis Carroll in *Through the Looking Glass*; perhaps a blend of GALLOP and TRIUMPH.

galvanic /galvannik/ > *adjective* **1** relating to or involving electric currents produced by chemical action. **2** sudden and dramatic.

DERIVATIVES – **galvanically** *adverb*.

galvanise /galvənīz/ (also **galvanize**) > *verb* **1** shock or excite into action. **2** (**galvanised**) (of iron or steel) coated with a protective layer of zinc.

DERIVATIVES – **galvanisation** *noun* **galvaniser** *noun*.

---

wordpower facts

Galvanise

The common element in the group of words named after the Italian anatomist Luigi *Galvani* (1737–98) is electricity. Galvani became famous for experiments in which he made dead frogs' legs twitch violently by subjecting them to an electric field. This showed the involvement of electricity in the workings of the body; the electricity involved was described as **galvanic**, a device to measure it became a **galvanometer**, and the electrified frogs were said to have been **galvanised**. **Galvanise** soon acquired the sense 'shock, excite to action', although a literal electric shock is no longer necessary. The **galvanised iron** shed roof is another story: the process for coating iron with zinc originally involved passing a current through iron immersed in a solution of zinc salts, but nowadays electricity is not involved in the process.

---

galvanometer /galvənommitər/ > *noun* an instrument for detecting and measuring small electric currents.

DERIVATIVES – **galvanometric** *adjective*.

Gamay /gammay/ > *noun* a variety of black wine grape native to the Beaujolais district of France.

ORIGIN – from a French place name.

Gambian /gambiən/ > *noun* a person from Gambia, a country in West Africa. > *adjective* relating to Gambia.

gambit > *noun* **1** an action or remark calculated to gain an advantage. **2** (in chess) an opening move in which a player makes a sacrifice for the sake of some compensating advantage.

SYNONYMS – **1** machination, ruse, stratagem.

ORIGIN – Italian *gambetto* 'tripping up'.

gamble > *verb* **1** play games of chance for money; bet. **2** bet (a sum of money). **3** take risky action in the hope of a desired result. > *noun* **1** an act of gambling. **2** a risky undertaking.

DERIVATIVES – **gambler** *noun*.

SYNONYMS – *verb* bet, speculate, wager.

ORIGIN – from obsolete *gamel* 'play games', or from the verb GAME[1].

gamboge /gambōzh/ > *noun* a gum resin produced by certain East Asian trees, used as a yellow pigment and in medicine as a laxative.

ORIGIN – Latin *gambaugium*, from *Cambodia*.

gambol > *verb* (**gambolled, gambolling**; US **gamboled, gamboling**) run or jump about playfully. > *noun* an act of gambolling.

SYNONYMS – *verb* caper, frisk, frolic, skip.

ORIGIN – Italian *gambata* 'trip up'.

gambrel /**gam**brəl/ > *noun* 1 a roof with two sides, each of which has a shallower slope above a steeper one. 2 Brit. a hipped roof with a small gable forming the upper part of each end.

ORIGIN – Old French *gamberel*, from *gambier* 'forked stick'.

game[1] > *noun* 1 an activity engaged in for amusement. 2 a form of competitive activity or sport played according to rules. 3 a complete episode or period of competitive activity, ending in a final result. 4 a single portion of play, forming a scoring unit within a contest. 5 (**games**) a meeting for sporting contests. 6 (**games**) Brit. athletics or sports as a period of activity and instruction in a school. 7 the equipment used in playing a board game, computer game, etc. 8 a type of activity or business regarded as a game: *this was a game of shuttle diplomacy*. 9 a secret plan or trick. 10 wild mammals or birds hunted for sport or food. > *adjective* eager and willing to do something new or challenging. > *verb* play at games of chance for money.

IDIOMS – **ahead of the game** ahead of one's competitors or peers. **beat someone at their own game** use someone's own methods to outdo them. **the game is up** the deception or crime is revealed or foiled. **on the game** Brit. informal working as a prostitute. **play the game** behave in a fair or honourable way; abide by the rules.

DERIVATIVES – **gamely** *adverb* **gameness** *noun* **gamester** *noun*.

SYNONYMS – *noun* 1 amusement, diversion, entertainment, pastime.

COMBINATIONS – **game bird** 1 a bird shot for sport or food. 2 a bird of a large group that includes pheasants, grouse, quails, guineafowl, etc. **game fish** (pl. same) a fish caught by anglers for sport, especially (in fresh water) salmon and trout and (in the sea) marlins, sharks, bass, and mackerel. Compare with *coarse fish*. **gamekeeper** a person employed to breed and protect game for a large estate. **game plan** a planned strategy in sport, politics, or business. **game point** (in tennis) a point which if won by the player in the lead will also win them the game. **game show** a programme on television in which people compete to win prizes. **game theory** the mathematical study of strategies for dealing with competitive situations where the outcome of a participant's choice of action depends

critically on the actions of other participants.

game[2] > *adjective* (of a person's leg) lame.

gamelan /**gamm**əlan/ > *noun* a traditional Javanese or Balinese instrumental ensemble including many bronze percussion instruments.

ORIGIN – Javanese.

gamer > *noun* 1 a participant in a computer or role-playing game. 2 N. Amer. (especially in sporting contexts) a person known for consistently making a strong effort.

gamesmanship > *noun* the art of winning games by using ploys and tactics to gain a psychological advantage.

DERIVATIVES – **gamesman** *noun*.

gamete /**gamm**eet/ > *noun* Biology a mature haploid male or female germ cell which is able to unite with another of the opposite sex in sexual reproduction to form a zygote.

DERIVATIVES – **gametic** /gəmettik/ *adjective*.

ORIGIN – Greek *gametē* 'wife', *gametēs* 'husband', from *gamos* 'marriage'.

gamey > *adjective* variant spelling of GAMY.

gamine /ga**meen**/ > *noun* a girl with a lively, boyish charm. > *adjective* characteristic of a gamine.

ORIGIN – French.

gamma /**gamm**ə/ > *noun* 1 the third letter of the Greek alphabet (Γ, γ), transliterated as 'g'. 2 Brit. a third-class mark given for a piece of work.

COMBINATIONS – **gamma globulin** Biochemistry a mixture of blood plasma proteins, mainly immunoglobulins, often given to boost immunity. **gamma rays** (also **gamma radiation**) penetrating electromagnetic radiation of shorter wavelength than X-rays.

ORIGIN – Greek.

gammon[1] > *noun* 1 ham which has been cured like bacon. 2 the bottom piece of a side of bacon, including a hind leg.

ORIGIN – Old French *gambon*, from *gambe* 'leg'.

gammon[2] informal, dated > *noun* nonsense; rubbish. > *verb* hoax or deceive.

gammy > *adjective* Brit. informal (especially of a leg) unable to function normally because of injury or chronic pain.

ORIGIN – dialect form of GAME[2].

gamut /**gamm**ət/ > *noun* 1 the complete range or scope of something. 2 Music a complete scale of musical notes; the compass or range of a voice or instrument. 3 a scale consisting of seven overlapping hexachords, containing all the recognised notes used in medieval music. 4 the lowest note in this scale.

IDIOMS – **run the gamut** experience, display, or perform the complete range of something.

ORIGIN – Latin *gamma ut* (in sense 4): the Greek letter Γ (gamma) was used for bass G, with *ut* indicating that it was the first note in the lowest of the hexachords or six-note scales.

gamy (also **gamey**) > *adjective* (**gamier, gamiest**) 1 (of meat) having the strong flavour or smell of game when it is high. 2 chiefly N. Amer. racy or risqué.

DERIVATIVES – **gamily** *adverb* **gaminess** *noun*.

gander /**gan**dər/ > *noun* 1 a male goose. 2 informal a look or glance.

ORIGIN – Old English, related to GANNET.

gang[1] > *noun* 1 an organised group of criminals or disorderly young people. 2 informal a group of people who regularly meet and do things together. 3 an organised group of people doing manual work. 4 a set of switches, sockets, or other devices grouped together. > *verb* 1 (**gang together**) form a group or gang. 2 (**gang up**) join together in opposition to someone. 3 arrange (electrical devices or machines) together to work in coordination.

COMBINATIONS – **gang rape** the rape of one person by a group of other people.

ORIGIN – Old Norse *gangr*, *ganga* 'gait, course, going'; related to GANG[2].

gang[2] > *verb* Scottish go; proceed.

ORIGIN – Old English, related to GO[1].

gang bang > *noun* informal 1 a gang rape. 2 a sexual orgy. 3 N. Amer. an instance of violence involving members of a criminal gang.

DERIVATIVES – **gang-bang** *verb* **gang banger** *noun*.

gangbuster > *noun* informal 1 a police officer engaged in breaking up criminal gangs. 2 (before another noun) N. Amer. very successful.

IDIOMS – **go** (or **like**) **gangbusters** N. Amer. with great vigour or success.

ganger > *noun* Brit. the foreman of a gang of labourers.

gangling (also **gangly**) > *adjective* tall, thin, and awkward.

ORIGIN – from the verb GANG[2].

ganglion /**gang**gliən/ > *noun* (pl. **ganglia** or **ganglions**) Anatomy & Medicine 1 a structure containing a number of nerve cells, often forming a swelling on a nerve fibre. 2 a well-defined mass of grey matter within the central nervous system. 3 an abnormal benign swelling on a tendon sheath.

DERIVATIVES – **ganglionic** *adjective*.

ORIGIN – Greek *ganglion* 'tumour on or near sinews or tendons'.

gangplank > *noun* a movable plank used to board or disembark from a ship or boat.

gangrene /**gang**green/ > *noun* Medicine localised death and decomposition of body tissue, resulting from either obstructed circulation or bacterial infection. > *verb* become affected with gangrene.

DERIVATIVES – **gangrenous** /**gang**grinəss/ *adjective*.

ORIGIN – Greek *gangraina*.

gangsta > *noun* N. Amer. black slang a gang member.

gangster > *noun* a member of an organised gang of violent criminals.

DERIVATIVES – **gangsterism** noun.

gangue /gang/ > *noun* the commercially valueless material in which ore is found.

ORIGIN – German *Gang* 'course, lode'.

gangway > *noun* 1 a raised platform or walkway providing a passage. 2 a movable bridge linking a ship to the shore. 3 Brit. a passage between rows of seats in an auditorium, aircraft, etc. > *exclamation* make way!

ganja /**gan**jə/ > *noun* cannabis.

ORIGIN – Hindi.

gannet /**gann**it/ > *noun* 1 a large, mainly white seabird, catching fish by plunge-diving. 2 Brit. informal a greedy person.

DERIVATIVES – **gannetry** noun.

ORIGIN – Old English, related to GANDER.

gantlet /**gant**lit/ > *noun* US spelling of GAUNTLET[2].

gantry > *noun* (pl. **gantries**) a bridge-like overhead structure supporting equipment such as a crane or railway signals.

ORIGIN – first denoting a wooden stand for barrels: probably from GALLON + TREE.

gaol > *noun* Brit. variant spelling of JAIL.

gap > *noun* 1 a break or hole in an object or between two objects. 2 a space, interval, or break.

DERIVATIVES – **gapped** adjective **gappy** adjective.

SYNONYMS – 1 aperture, breach, cavity, crevice, fissure. 2 blank, break, hiatus, interval, lacuna, space, void.

ORIGIN – Old Norse, 'chasm'; related to GAPE.

gape > *verb* 1 be or become wide open. 2 stare with one's mouth open wide in amazement or wonder. > *noun* 1 a wide opening. 2 an open-mouthed stare. 3 a widely open mouth or beak.

DERIVATIVES – **gaper** noun.

ORIGIN – Old Norse *gapa*; related to GAP.

gap year > *noun* a period, typically an academic year, taken by a student as a break from education between leaving school and starting a university or college course.

gar > *noun* the freshwater garfish of North America.

garage /**garr**aaj, **garr**ij/ > *noun* 1 a building for housing a motor vehicle or vehicles. 2 an establishment which sells fuel or which repairs and sells motor vehicles. > *verb* put or keep (a motor vehicle) in a garage.

COMBINATIONS – **garage sale** chiefly N. Amer. a sale of unwanted goods held in a garage or front garden.

ORIGIN – French, from *garer* 'to shelter'.

garam masala /**gurr**əm mə**saal**ə/ > *noun* a spice mixture used in Indian cookery.

ORIGIN – Urdu, 'pungent spice'.

garb > *noun* clothing or dress of a distinctive kind. > *verb* dress in distinctive clothes.

ORIGIN – French, from Italian *garbo* 'elegance'; related to GEAR.

garbage > *noun* chiefly N. Amer. 1 domestic rubbish or waste. 2 something worthless or meaningless.

ORIGIN – Old French: first used in the sense 'offal'.

garbanzo /gaar**banz**ō/ > *noun* (pl. **garbanzos**) N. Amer. a chickpea.

ORIGIN – Spanish.

garble > *verb* reproduce (a message or transmission) in a confused and distorted way. > *noun* a garbled account or transmission.

DERIVATIVES – **garbler** noun.

SYNONYMS – *verb* confuse, distort, jumble.

ORIGIN – first used in the sense 'sift out, cleanse': from an Arabic word meaning 'sift'.

garçon /**gaar**sON/ > *noun* a waiter in a French restaurant.

ORIGIN – French, 'boy'.

Garda /**gaar**də/ > *noun* (pl. **Gardai** /gaar-di/) 1 the state police force of the Irish Republic. 2 a member of the Irish police force.

ORIGIN – Irish *Garda Síochána* 'Civic Guard'.

garden > *noun* 1 chiefly Brit. a piece of ground adjoining a house, typically cultivated to provide a lawn and flowerbeds. 2 (**gardens**) ornamental grounds laid out for public enjoyment. > *verb* cultivate or work in a garden.

DERIVATIVES – **gardener** noun.

COMBINATIONS – **garden centre** an establishment where plants and gardening equipment are sold. **garden city** a new town built on a plan incorporating open space and greenery. **garden party** a social event held on a lawn in a garden. **garden suburb** Brit. a suburb set in rural surroundings or incorporating much landscaping. **garden-variety** N. Amer. of the usual or ordinary type; commonplace.

ORIGIN – Old French *jardin*; related to YARD[2].

gardenia /gaar**deen**iə/ > *noun* a tree or shrub of warm climates, with large fragrant white or yellow flowers.

ORIGIN – named in honour of the Scottish naturalist Dr Alexander *Garden* (1730–91).

garderobe /**gaard**rōb/ > *noun* 1 a toilet in a medieval building. 2 a wardrobe or storeroom in a medieval building.

ORIGIN – French, from *garder* 'to keep' + *robe* 'robe, dress'; related to WARDROBE.

garfish > *noun* 1 a long, slender marine fish with beak-like jaws and sharp teeth. 2 N. Amer. a similar freshwater fish.

ORIGIN – Old English *gār* 'spear' + FISH[1].

garganey /**gaar**gəni/ > *noun* (pl. same or **garganeys**) a small duck, the male of which has a brown head with a white stripe.

ORIGIN – Italian *garganei*.

gargantuan /gaar**gan**tyooən/ > *adjective* enormous.

SYNONYMS – colossal, enormous, gigantic, immense, vast.

ORIGIN – from *Gargantua*, the name of a voracious giant in Rabelais's book of the same name.

gargle > *verb* wash one's mouth and throat with a liquid that is kept in motion by breathing through it with a gurgling sound. > *noun* 1 an act of gargling. 2 a liquid used for gargling.

ORIGIN – French *gargouiller* 'gurgle, bubble', from Old French *gargouille* (see GARGOYLE).

gargoyle /**gaar**goyl/ > *noun* a grotesque carved human or animal face or figure projecting from the gutter of a building, usually as a spout to carry water clear of a wall.

ORIGIN – Old French *gargouille* 'throat', also 'gargoyle', related to Greek *gargarizein* 'to gargle'.

garibaldi /garri**bawl**di/ > *noun* (pl. **garibaldis**) Brit. a thin biscuit containing a compressed layer of currants.

ORIGIN – named after the Italian patriot Giuseppe *Garibaldi* (1807–82).

garish /**gair**ish/ > *adjective* obtrusively bright and showy; lurid.

DERIVATIVES – **garishly** adverb **garishness** noun.

SYNONYMS – flashy, gaudy, loud, lurid.

ANTONYMS – sober.

garland > *noun* 1 a wreath of flowers and leaves, worn on the head or round the neck or hung as a decoration. 2 a prize or distinction. 3 archaic a literary anthology. > *verb* adorn or crown with a garland.

ORIGIN – Old French *garlande*.

garlic > *noun* the strong-smelling pungent-tasting bulb of a central Asian plant closely related to the onion, used as a flavouring in cookery.

DERIVATIVES – **garlicky** adjective.

ORIGIN – Old English, from *gār* 'spear' (because the shape of a clove resembles the head of a spear) + *lēac* 'leek'.

garment > *noun* an item of clothing.

ORIGIN – Old French *garnement* 'equipment'.

garner > *verb* 1 gather or collect. 2 archaic store; deposit. > *noun* archaic a storehouse for corn; a granary.

SYNONYMS – *verb* 1 accumulate, amass, assemble, collect, gather.

ORIGIN – Old French *gernier*, from Latin *granarium* 'granary'.

garnet /**gaar**nit/ > *noun* a deep red semi-precious stone.

ORIGIN – perhaps from *granatum*, as in *pomum granatum* 'pomegranate' (literally 'apple having many seeds'), because the garnet is similar in colour to the pulp of the fruit.

garnish > *verb* decorate or embellish (something, especially food). > *noun* a decoration or embellishment.

SYNONYMS – *verb* adorn, decorate, embellish, ornament. *noun* adornment, decoration, embellishment, ornament.

ORIGIN – from Old French *garnir*; related to **WARN**: originally in the sense 'equip, arm'.

garniture /**gaar**nichər/ > *noun* a set of decorative vases.

ORIGIN – French, from *garnir* 'to garnish'.

garotte > *verb & noun* variant spelling of **GARROTTE**.

garret > *noun* a top-floor or attic room.

ORIGIN – Old French *garite*, from *garir* 'defend, provide': originally in the sense 'watchtower', and related to **GARRISON**.

garrison > *noun* a body of troops stationed in a fortress or town to defend it. > *verb* provide (a place) with a garrison.

ORIGIN – first used in the sense 'safety, means of protection': from Old French *garison*, from *garir* 'defend, provide'.

garrotte /gərot/ (also **garotte**; US **garrote**) > *verb* kill by strangulation. > *noun* a wire, cord, or apparatus used for garrotting.

ORIGIN – Spanish *garrote* 'cudgel, garrotte'.

garrulous /**garr**ooləss/ > *adjective* excessively talkative.

DERIVATIVES – **garrulity** /gərooliti/ *noun* **garrulously** *adverb* **garrulousness** *noun*.

SYNONYMS – loquacious, prolix, verbose.

ORIGIN – Latin *garrulus*, from *garrire* 'to chatter, prattle'.

garter > *noun* **1** a band worn around the leg to keep up a stocking or sock. **2 N. Amer.** a suspender for a sock or stocking.

DERIVATIVES – **gartered** *adjective*.

COMBINATIONS – **garter snake** a common, harmless North American snake with well-defined longitudinal stripes. **garter stitch** knitting in which all of the rows are knitted in plain stitch, rather than alternating with purl rows.

ORIGIN – Old French *gartier*, from *garet* 'bend of the knee, calf of the leg'.

garth > *noun* **1 Brit.** an open space surrounded by cloisters. **2 archaic** a yard or garden.

ORIGIN – Old Norse *garthr*; related to **YARD²**.

gas* > *noun* (pl. **gases** or chiefly **US gasses**) **1** an air-like fluid substance which expands freely to fill any space available, irrespective of its quantity. **2** a flammable substance of this type used as a fuel. **3** a gaseous anaesthetic such as nitrous oxide, used in dentistry. **4 chiefly N. Amer.** flatulence. **5 Mining** an explosive mixture of firedamp with air. **6 N. Amer. informal** short for **GASOLINE**. **7** (**a gas**) informal an entertaining or amusing person or thing. > *verb* (**gases, gassed, gassing**) **1** attack with, expose to, or kill with gas. **2 N. Amer. informal** fill the tank of (a motor vehicle) with petrol. **3** informal talk idly; chatter.

DERIVATIVES – **gasification** *noun* **gasify** *verb* **gasser** *noun*.

*SPELLING – in British English, the usual spelling of the plural is *gases*: no double *s*.

COMBINATIONS – **gasbag** informal a person who talks idly and excessively. **gas chamber** an airtight room that can be filled with poisonous gas to kill people or animals. **gas mask** a protective mask used to cover the face as a defence against poison gas. **gas-permeable** (of a contact lens) allowing the diffusion of gases into and out of the cornea. **gas turbine** a turbine driven by expanding hot gases produced by burning fuel, as in a jet engine. **gasworks** a place where gas is manufactured and processed.

ORIGIN – coined by the Belgian chemist J. B. van Helmont (1577–1644) to denote an intangible substance which he believed to exist in all matter; suggested by Greek *khaos* 'chaos'.

Gascon /**gas**kən/ > *noun* a person from Gascony, a region in SW France.

ORIGIN – Old French, from Latin *Vasco*; related to **BASQUE**.

gaseous /**gass**iəss, **gay**siəss/ > *adjective* relating to or having the characteristics of a gas.

DERIVATIVES – **gaseousness** *noun*.

gash > *noun* a long, deep slash, cut, or wound. > *verb* make a gash in.

SYNONYMS – *verb* cut, lacerate, slash, slice.

ORIGIN – from Old French *garcer* 'to chap, crack', perhaps based on Greek *kharassein* 'sharpen, scratch, engrave'.

gasket /**gas**kit/ > *noun* **1** a sheet or ring of rubber or other material sealing the junction between two surfaces in an engine or other device. **2 archaic** a cord securing a furled sail to the yard of a sailing ship.

ORIGIN – perhaps from French *garcette* 'thin rope' (originally 'little girl').

gaslight > *noun* light from lamps in which an incandescent mantle is heated by a jet of burning gas.

DERIVATIVES – **gaslit** *adjective*.

gasoline > *noun* North American term for **PETROL**.

gasometer > *noun* a large tank in which gas for use as fuel is stored before being distributed to consumers.

gasp > *verb* **1** catch one's breath with an open mouth, owing to pain or astonishment. **2** (**gasp for**) strain to obtain (air) by gasping. **3** (**be gasping for**) informal be desperate to have; crave. > *noun* a convulsive catching of breath.

IDIOMS – **the last gasp** the point of exhaustion, death, or completion.

ORIGIN – Old Norse *geispa* 'to yawn'.

gasper > *noun* **Brit. informal, dated** a cigarette.

gassy > *adjective* (**gassier, gassiest**) **1** resembling or full of gas. **2** informal verbose; idly chattering.

DERIVATIVES – **gassiness** *noun*.

Gastarbeiter /**gast**aarbītər/ > *noun* (pl. same or **Gastarbeiters**) a person with temporary permission to work in another country, especially in Germany.

ORIGIN – German, 'guest worker'.

gastrectomy /gastrektəmi/ > *noun* (pl. **gastrectomies**) surgical removal of a part or the whole of the stomach.

gastric > *adjective* of the stomach.

COMBINATIONS – **gastric flu** a short-lived stomach disorder of unknown cause, popularly attributed to a virus. **gastric juice** an acid fluid secreted by the stomach glands and active in promoting digestion.

ORIGIN – from Greek *gastēr* 'stomach'.

gastritis /gastrītiss/ > *noun* **Medicine** inflammation of the lining of the stomach.

gastro-enteritis > *noun* inflammation of the stomach and intestines, typically due to infection with bacteria or a virus and causing vomiting and diarrhoea.

gastroenterology > *noun* the branch of medicine concerned with disorders of the stomach and intestines.

DERIVATIVES – **gastroenterological** *adjective* **gastroenterologist** *noun*.

ORIGIN – from Greek *gastēr* 'stomach' and *enteron* 'intestine'.

gastrointestinal > *adjective* of or relating to the stomach and the intestines.

gastronome /**gas**trənōm/ > *noun* a gourmet.

gastronomy /gastronnəmi/ > *noun* the practice or art of choosing, cooking, and eating good food.

DERIVATIVES – **gastronomic** *adjective*.

ORIGIN – Greek *gastronomia*, from *gastēr* 'stomach'.

gastropod /**gas**trəpod/ > *noun* **Zoology** any of a large class of molluscs including snails, slugs, and whelks.

ORIGIN – from Greek *gastēr* 'stomach' + *pous* 'foot'.

gastroscope > *noun* an optical instrument used for inspecting the interior of the stomach.

DERIVATIVES – **gastroscopic** *adjective* **gastroscopy** *noun*.

gat archaic past of **GET**.

gate¹ > *noun* **1** a hinged barrier used to close an opening in a wall, fence, or hedge. **2** an

exit from an airport building to an aircraft. **3** a hinged or sliding barrier for controlling the flow of water. **4** the number of people who pay to enter a sports ground for an event. **5** an electric circuit with an output which depends on the combination of several inputs. > *verb* Brit. confine (a pupil or student) to school or college.
IDIOMS – **get** (or **be given**) **the gate** N. Amer. informal be dismissed from a job.
DERIVATIVES – **gated** *adjective*.
COMBINATIONS – **gatefold** an oversized page in a book or magazine folded to the same size as the other pages, to be opened out for reading. **gatehouse 1** a house standing by the gateway to a country estate. **2** historical a room over a city or palace gate, often used as a prison. **gatekeeper** an attendant at a gate. **gatepost** a post on which a gate is hinged or against which it shuts. **gateway 1** an opening that can be closed by a gate. **2** a frame or arch built around or over a gate. **3** Computing a device used to connect two different networks, especially a connection to the Internet.
gate² > *noun* Brit. (in place names) a street.
ORIGIN – Old Norse *gata*: at first also meaning 'way' in general.
gateau /gattō/ > *noun* (pl. **gateaus** or **gateaux** /gattōz/) chiefly Brit. a rich cake, typically one containing layers of cream or fruit.
ORIGIN – French, 'cake'.
gatecrash > *verb* enter (a party) without an invitation or ticket.
DERIVATIVES – **gatecrasher** *noun*.
gateleg table > *noun* a table with hinged legs that may be swung out from the centre to support folding leaves.
DERIVATIVES – **gatelegged** *adjective*.
gather > *verb* **1** come or bring together; assemble or accumulate. **2** harvest (a crop). **3** collect (plants, fruits, etc.) for food. **4** draw together or towards oneself. **5** develop a higher degree of: *the movement is gathering pace.* **6** infer; understand. **7** pull and hold together (fabric) in a series of folds by drawing thread through it. > *noun* (**gathers**) a series of folds in fabric, formed by gathering.
IDIOMS – **gather way** (of a ship) begin to move.
DERIVATIVES – **gatherer** *noun*.
SYNONYMS – *verb* **1** accumulate, assemble, collect. **6** assume, believe, deduce, infer, understand.
ANTONYMS – *verb* **1** disperse, scatter.
ORIGIN – Old English, related to **TOGETHER**.
gathering > *noun* an assembly of people.
Gatling gun > *noun* an early type of machine gun, with clustered barrels.
ORIGIN – named after the American inventor Richard J. *Gatling* (1818–1903).

gauche /gōsh/ > *adjective* socially awkward or unsophisticated.
DERIVATIVES – **gauchely** *adverb* **gaucheness** *noun*.
SYNONYMS – awkward, clumsy, maladroit.
ORIGIN – French, 'left'.
gaucherie /gōshəri/ > *noun* awkward or unsophisticated ways.
gaucho /gowchō/ > *noun* (pl. **gauchos**) a cowboy from the South American pampas.
ORIGIN – Latin American Spanish, probably from a Tupi-Guarani word meaning 'friend'.
gaudy¹ > *adjective* (**gaudier**, **gaudiest**) extravagantly or tastelessly bright or showy.
DERIVATIVES – **gaudily** *adverb* **gaudiness** *noun*.
SYNONYMS – flashy, garish, ostentatious.
ORIGIN – probably from Old French *gaudir* 'rejoice', from Latin *gaudere*.
gaudy² > *noun* (pl. **gaudies**) Brit. a celebratory dinner or entertainment held by a college for old members.
ORIGIN – from Latin *gaudere* 'rejoice'.
gauge* /gayj/ (chiefly US also **gage**) > *noun* **1** an instrument that measures and gives a visual display of the amount, level, or contents of something. **2** the thickness, size, or capacity of a wire, sheet, tube, bullet, etc., especially as a standard measure. **3** the distance between the rails of a line of railway track. > *verb* **1** estimate or determine the amount or level of. **2** measure the dimensions of with a gauge. **3** (**gauged**) made in standard dimensions. **4** judge or assess (a situation, mood, etc.).
DERIVATIVES – **gaugeable** *adjective* **gauger** *noun*.
***SPELLING** – unlike **guard**, **gauge** has -*au*- in the middle: *gauge*.
SYNONYMS – *verb* **1** assess, estimate, evaluate.
ORIGIN – Old French.
Gaul /gawl/ > *noun* a person from the ancient European region of Gaul.
ORIGIN – Latin *Gallus*, probably of Celtic origin.
Gauleiter /gowlitər/ > *noun* **1** historical an official governing a district under Nazi rule. **2** an overbearing official.
ORIGIN – German, from *Gau* 'administrative district' + *Leiter* 'leader'.
Gaulish > *noun* the Celtic language of the ancient Gauls. > *adjective* relating to the ancient Gauls.
Gaullism /gōliz'm/ > *noun* the principles and policies of the French statesman Charles de Gaulle (1890–1970), characterised by conservatism, nationalism, and advocacy of centralised government.
DERIVATIVES – **Gaullist** *noun & adjective*.
gaunt > *adjective* **1** lean and haggard, especially through suffering, hunger, or age.

2 (of a place) grim or desolate in appearance.
DERIVATIVES – **gauntly** *adverb* **gauntness** *noun*.
SYNONYMS – **1** drawn, emaciated, haggard, lean, skeletal.
gauntlet¹ > *noun* **1** a stout glove with a long loose wrist. **2** a glove worn as part of medieval armour, made of leather with protective steel plates.
IDIOMS – **take up** (or **throw down**) **the gauntlet** accept (or issue) a challenge. [ORIGIN – from the medieval custom of issuing a challenge by throwing one's gauntlet to the ground; whoever picked it up was deemed to have accepted the challenge.]
ORIGIN – Old French *gantelet*, from *gant* 'glove'.
gauntlet² (US also **gantlet**) > *noun* (in phrase **run the gauntlet**) **1** go through an intimidating crowd, place, or experience in order to reach a goal. **2** historical undergo the military punishment of receiving blows while running between two rows of men with sticks.
ORIGIN – alteration of *gantlope* (from Swedish *gata* 'lane' + *lopp* 'course'), associated with **GAUNTLET¹**.
gauss /gowss/ > *noun* (pl. same or **gausses**) a unit of magnetic flux density, equal to one ten-thousandth of a tesla.
ORIGIN – named after the German physicist and mathematician Karl Friedrich *Gauss* (1777–1855).
gauze /gawz/ > *noun* **1** a thin transparent fabric. **2** Medicine thin, loosely woven cloth used for dressing and swabbing wounds. **3** (also **wire gauze**) a very fine wire mesh.
DERIVATIVES – **gauzy** *adjective*.
ORIGIN – French *gaze*.
gave past of **GIVE**.
gavel /gavv'l/ > *noun* a small hammer with which an auctioneer, judge, etc., hits a surface to call for attention or order. > *verb* (**gavelled**, **gavelling**; US **gaveled**, **gaveling**) bring to order by use of a gavel.
ORIGIN – first denoting a stonemason's mallet.
gavial > *noun* variant spelling of **GHARIAL**.
gavotte /gəvot/ > *noun* a medium-paced French dance, popular in the 18th century.
ORIGIN – Provençal *gavoto* 'dance of the mountain people', from *Gavot* 'a native of the Alps'.
gawk > *verb* stare openly and stupidly. > *noun* an awkward or shy person.
DERIVATIVES – **gawker** *noun* **gawkish** *adjective*.
ORIGIN – perhaps related to obsolete *gaw* 'to gaze', from Old Norse *gá* 'heed'.
gawky > *adjective* (**gawkier**, **gawkiest**) nervously awkward and ungainly.

DERIVATIVES – **gawkily** adverb **gawkiness** noun.

gawp > verb Brit. informal stare openly in a stupid or rude manner.

DERIVATIVES – **gawper** noun.

ORIGIN – perhaps an alteration of GAPE.

gay > adjective (**gayer**, **gayest**) **1** (especially of a man) homosexual. **2** relating to homosexuals. **3** dated light-hearted and carefree. **4** dated brightly coloured; showy. > noun a homosexual person, especially a man.

DERIVATIVES – **gayness** noun.

USAGE – **gay** is now a standard term for 'homosexual', and is the term preferred by homosexual men to describe themselves. As a result, it is now very difficult to use **gay** to mean 'carefree' or 'bright and showy' without arousing a sense of double entendre, although these meanings date back to medieval times. **Gay** in its modern sense typically refers to men, **lesbian** being the standard term for homosexual women.

ORIGIN – Old French gai.

gayety > noun US variant spelling of GAIETY.

gaze > verb look steadily and intently. > noun a steady intent look.

DERIVATIVES – **gazer** noun.

ORIGIN – perhaps related to obsolete gaw (see GAWK).

gazebo /gəzeebō/ > noun (pl. **gazebos** or **gazeboes**) a summer house or similar structure offering a wide view of the surrounding area.

ORIGIN – perhaps humorously from GAZE, in imitation of Latin future tenses ending in -ebo.

gazelle > noun a small slender antelope with curved horns and white underparts.

ORIGIN – French, probably from Arabic.

gazette > noun a journal or newspaper, especially the official journal of an organisation or institution. > verb Brit. announce or publish in an official gazette.

wordpower facts
Gazette

Gazette and **gazetteer** are both ultimately from the Italian word gazeta, a Venetian coin of small value. **Gazette** is from Italian gazzetta, which came from Venetian gazeta de la novità 'a halfpennyworth of news', with reference to a news-sheet sold for a gazeta. A **gazetteer** was originally a journalist; the current sense is from a 17th-century publication called The Gazetteer's: or, Newsman's Interpreter: Being a Geographical Index.

gazetteer /gazziteer/ > noun a geographical index or dictionary.

gazillion /gəzillyən/ (also **kazillion**) > cardinal number N. Amer. informal a very large number or quantity.

ORIGIN – fanciful formation on the pattern of billion and million.

gazpacho /gəspachō/ > noun (pl. **gazpachos**) a cold Spanish soup made from tomatoes, peppers, and other salad vegetables.

ORIGIN – Spanish.

gazump /gəzump/ > verb Brit. informal deprive (someone whose offer to purchase a house has already been accepted) from proceeding with the purchase by offering or accepting a higher figure.

DERIVATIVES – **gazumper** noun.

ORIGIN – first used in the sense 'swindle': from Yiddish gezumph 'overcharge'.

GB > abbreviation **1** Great Britain. **2** (also **Gb**) Computing gigabyte(s).

GBE > abbreviation Knight or Dame Grand Cross of the Order of the British Empire.

GBH > abbreviation Brit. grievous bodily harm.

GC > abbreviation George Cross.

GCB > abbreviation Knight or Dame Grand Cross of the Order of the Bath.

GCE > abbreviation General Certificate of Education.

GCHQ > abbreviation Government Communications Headquarters.

GCMG > abbreviation Knight or Dame Grand Cross of the Order of St Michael and St George.

GCSE > abbreviation (in the UK except Scotland) General Certificate of Secondary Education (the lower of the two main levels of the GCE examination).

GCVO > abbreviation Knight or Dame Grand Cross of the Royal Victorian Order.

Gd > symbol the chemical element gadolinium.

GDP > abbreviation gross domestic product.

GDR > abbreviation historical German Democratic Republic.

Ge > symbol the chemical element germanium.

gean /jeen/ > noun a tall woodland cherry tree bearing white blossom; a wild cherry.

ORIGIN – Old French guine.

gear > noun **1** a toothed wheel that works with others to alter the relation between the speed of an engine and the speed of the driven parts (e.g. wheels). **2** a particular setting of engaged gears. **3** informal apparatus, equipment, or clothing. > verb **1** design or adjust gears to give a specified speed or power output. **2** (often **gear up**) make ready; equip or prepare. **3** (**gear down** or **up**) change to a lower (or higher) gear.

WORDFINDER – derailleur (bicycle gear which moves the chain between sprocket wheels), differential (gear allowing vehicle's wheels to revolve at different speeds), overdrive (giving a

higher gear ratio than usual), synchromesh (mechanism causing parts to revolve at the same speed during gear change).

IDIOMS – **in** (or **out of**) **gear** with a gear (or no gear) engaged.

COMBINATIONS – **gearbox** a set of gears with its casing, especially in a motor vehicle; the transmission. **gear lever** (also **gearstick**) Brit. a lever used to engage or change gear in a motor vehicle. **gear shift** chiefly N. Amer. a gear lever. **gearwheel 1** a toothed wheel in a set of gears. **2** (on a bicycle) a cogwheel driven directly by the chain.

ORIGIN – Scandinavian.

gecko /gekkō/ > noun (pl. **geckos** or **geckoes**) a nocturnal lizard with adhesive pads on the feet, found in warm regions.

ORIGIN – Malay (from a word that is imitative of its cry).

gee[1] (also **gee whiz**) > exclamation informal, chiefly N. Amer. a mild expression of surprise, enthusiasm, or sympathy.

gee[2] > exclamation (**gee up**) a command to a horse to go faster. > verb (**gees**, **geed**, **geeing**) (**gee up**) command (a horse) to go faster.

COMBINATIONS – **gee-gee** Brit. informal a child's word for a horse.

geek /geek/ > noun informal, chiefly N. Amer. **1** an unfashionable or socially inept person. **2** an obsessive enthusiast.

DERIVATIVES – **geeky** adjective.

ORIGIN – from the related English dialect word geck 'fool'.

geese plural of GOOSE.

gee-string > noun variant spelling of G-STRING.

Ge'ez /geeez/ > noun an ancient Semitic language of Ethiopia, which survives as the liturgical language of the Ethiopian Orthodox Church.

geezer /geezər/ > noun informal a man.

ORIGIN – representing a dialect pronunciation of earlier guiser 'mummer'.

gefilte fish /gəfiltə/ > noun a dish of stewed or baked stuffed fish, or of fishcakes boiled in a fish or vegetable broth.

ORIGIN – Yiddish, 'stuffed fish'.

Geiger counter /gīgər/ > noun a device for measuring radioactivity by detecting and counting ionising particles.

ORIGIN – named after the German physicist Hans Geiger (1882–1945).

geisha /gayshə/ > noun (pl. same or **geishas**) a Japanese hostess trained to entertain men with conversation, dance, and song.

ORIGIN – Japanese, 'entertainer'.

gel[1] /jel/ > noun **1** a jelly-like substance containing a cosmetic, medicinal, or other preparation. **2** Chemistry a semi-solid colloidal suspension of a solid dispersed in a liquid.

> *verb* (**gelled**, **gelling**) **1** Chemistry form into a gel. **2** smooth (one's hair) with gel.

ORIGIN – from GELATIN.

gel² > *verb* variant spelling of JELL.

gelatin /jellətin/ (also **gelatine** /jelləteen/) > *noun* **1** a virtually colourless and tasteless water-soluble protein made from collagen and used in food preparation, in photographic processing, and for making glue. **2** a high explosive containing a gel of nitroglycerine with added cellulose nitrate.

DERIVATIVES – **gelatinisation** (also **gelatinization**) *noun* **gelatinise** (also **gelatinize**) *verb* **gelatinous** *adjective*.

ORIGIN – French *gélatine*, from Latin *gelata* 'frozen'; related to JELLY.

geld /geld/ > *verb* castrate (a male animal).

ORIGIN – from Old Norse *geldr* 'barren'.

gelding > *noun* a castrated animal, especially a male horse.

gelid /jellid/ > *adjective* icy; extremely cold.

ORIGIN – Latin *gelidus*, from *gelu* 'frost, intense cold'.

gelignite /jellignīt/ > *noun* a high explosive made from a gel of nitroglycerine and nitrocellulose in a base of wood pulp and sodium or potassium nitrate, used particularly for blasting rock.

ORIGIN – probably from GELATIN + Latin *lignis* 'wood'.

gelt /gelt/ > *noun* informal money.

ORIGIN – German *Geld*.

gem > *noun* **1** a precious or semi-precious stone, especially one that has been cut and polished. **2** informal an outstanding person or thing.

WORDFINDER – cabochon (*a polished gem without facets*), intaglio (*a gem with an incised design*), lapidary (*a person who cuts, polishes, or engraves gems*), troy (*system of weights used for gems*).

DERIVATIVES – **gemmed** *adjective*.

COMBINATIONS – **gemstone** a gem used in a piece of jewellery.

ORIGIN – Latin *gemma* 'bud, jewel'.

Gemini /jemminī/ > *noun* **1** Astronomy a northern constellation (the Twins), said to represent the twins Castor and Pollux. **2** Astrology the third sign of the zodiac, which the sun enters about 21 May.

DERIVATIVES – **Geminian** /jemmineeən/ *noun & adjective*.

ORIGIN – Latin, 'twins'.

gemsbok /gemzbok/ > *noun* a large African antelope with distinctive black-and-white head markings and long straight horns.

ORIGIN – Dutch, 'chamois'.

gemütlich /gəmootlikh/ > *adjective* pleasant and cheerful.

ORIGIN – German.

Gemütlichkeit /gəmootlikhkīt/ > *noun* geniality; friendliness.

gen /jen/ Brit. informal > *noun* information.

> *verb* (**genned**, **genning**) (**gen up**) provide with or obtain information.

ORIGIN – first in military use: perhaps from *general information*.

-gen > *combining form* **1** Chemistry denoting a substance that produces something: *allergen*. **2** Botany denoting a substance or plant that is produced.

ORIGIN – from Greek *genēs* '-born, of a specified kind'.

gendarme /zhondaarm/ > *noun* a paramilitary police officer in French-speaking countries.

ORIGIN – French, from *gens d'armes* 'men of arms'.

gender > *noun* **1** Grammar a class (usually masculine, feminine, common, or neuter) into which nouns and pronouns are placed. **2** the state of being male or female. **3** the members of one or other sex.

DERIVATIVES – **gendered** *adjective*.

USAGE – the words **gender** and **sex** both have the sense 'the state of being male or female', but they are typically used in slightly different ways: **sex** tends to refer to biological differences, while **gender** tends to refer to cultural or social ones.

ORIGIN – Old French *gendre*, from Latin *genus* 'birth, family, nation'.

gene /jeen/ > *noun* Biology a distinct sequence of DNA forming part of a chromosome, by which offspring inherit characteristics from a parent.

WORDFINDER – allele (*one of two or more different forms of the same gene*), chimera (*individual containing mixture of genes*), chromosome (*thread-like structure in a cell carrying genetic information*), clone (*genetically identical individual*), dominant (*gene expressed in offspring when inherited from only one parent*), Mendelism (*theory of heredity based on genes*), mutation (*a change in gene structure*), recessive (*gene expressed in offspring only when inherited from both parents*), transcription (*the natural copying of genetic information*).

COMBINATIONS – **gene pool** the stock of different genes in an interbreeding population. **gene therapy** the introduction of normal genes into cells in place of missing or defective ones in order to correct genetic disorders.

ORIGIN – German *Gen*, from *Pangen*, a supposed ultimate unit of heredity (from Greek *pan*- 'all' + *genos* 'stock, race').

genealogy /jeenialəji/ > *noun* (pl. **genealogies**) **1** a line of descent traced continuously from an ancestor. **2** the study of lines of descent.

DERIVATIVES – **genealogical** *adjective* **genealogise** (also **genealogize**) *verb* **genealogist** *noun*.

ORIGIN – Greek *genealogia*, from *genea* 'race, generation' + *logos* 'account'.

genera plural of GENUS.

general > *adjective* **1** affecting or concerning all or most people or things; not specialised or limited. **2** involving only the main features or elements and disregarding exceptions; overall. **3** chief or principal. > *noun* a commander or high-ranking officer of an army, in particular an officer ranking above lieutenant general.

IDIOMS – **in general 1** usually; mainly. **2** as a whole.

SYNONYMS – **1** common, universal, unrestricted. **2** broad, comprehensive, overall.

ANTONYMS – **1** restricted. **2** specific.

COMBINATIONS – **general anaesthetic** an anaesthetic that affects the whole body and causes a loss of consciousness. **general election** the election of representatives to a legislature from constituencies throughout the country. **general meeting** a meeting open to all members of an organisation. **general-purpose** having a range of potential uses or functions. **general staff** the staff assisting a military commander. **general strike** a widespread strike involving workers in all or most industries.

generalise (also **generalize**) > *verb* **1** make a general or broad statement by inferring from specific cases. **2** make more common or more widely applicable. **3** (**generalised**) Medicine (of a disease) affecting much or all of the body; not localised.

DERIVATIVES – **generalisable** *adjective* **generalisation** *noun* **generaliser** *noun*.

generalist > *noun* a person competent in a range of fields or activities.

generality > *noun* (pl. **generalities**) **1** a statement or principle having general rather than specific validity or force. **2** the quality or state of being general. **3** (**the generality**) the majority.

generally > *adverb* **1** in most cases. **2** without regard to particulars or exceptions. **3** widely.

SYNONYMS – **1,2** normally, ordinarily, typically, usually.

general practitioner > *noun* a community doctor who treats patients with minor or chronic illnesses.

DERIVATIVES – **general practice** *noun*.

generate > *verb* **1** cause to arise or come about. **2** produce (energy, especially electricity).

DERIVATIVES – **generable** *adjective*.

SYNONYMS – **1** create, engender, produce.

generation > *noun* **1** all of the people born and living at about the same time, regarded collectively. **2** the average period in which children grow up and have children of their own (usually reckoned as about thirty years). **3** a set of members of a family regarded as a single stage in descent. **4** the action of producing or generating. **5** the propagation of living organisms; pro-creation.

DERIVATIVES – **generational** adjective.

COMBINATIONS – **generation gap** a difference in attitudes between people of different generations, leading to lack of understanding.

Generation X > noun the generation born between the mid 1960s and the mid 1970s, perceived as being disaffected and directionless.

DERIVATIVES – **Generation Xer** noun.

generative > adjective relating to or capable of production or reproduction.

generator > noun 1 a person or thing that generates. 2 a dynamo or similar machine for converting mechanical energy into electricity.

generic /jinerrik/ > adjective 1 referring to a class or group; not specific. 2 (of goods) having no brand name. 3 Biology relating to a genus.

DERIVATIVES – **generically** adverb.

generous > adjective 1 freely giving more of something than is necessary or expected. 2 kind towards others. 3 larger or more plentiful than is usual or expected.

DERIVATIVES – **generosity** noun **generously** adverb.

SYNONYMS – **1** bountiful, liberal, magnanimous, munificent. **2** altruistic, charitable, kind, unselfish. **3** abundant, copious, lavish, liberal.

ANTONYMS – **1,2** mean, selfish.

---

wordpower facts
Generous

The word **generous** is from Latin generosus 'noble, magnanimous', which is from genus 'stock, race', the source of words such as **benign, gender, generate, general, generic** and **genus** itself. The original sense of **generous** was 'of noble birth', hence 'characteristic of noble birth, courageous, magnanimous, not mean'.

---

genesis /jennisiss/ > noun 1 the origin or mode of formation of something. 2 (**Genesis**) the first book of the Bible, which includes the story of the creation of the world.

SYNONYMS – **1** beginning, birth, creation, generation, origin.

ORIGIN – Greek, 'generation, creation', from gignesthai 'be born or produced'.

genet /jennit/ > noun a nocturnal catlike mammal with short legs and a long bushy tail.

ORIGIN – Arabic.

genetic /jinettik/ > adjective 1 relating to

---

genes or heredity. 2 relating to genetics. 3 relating to origin or genesis.

DERIVATIVES – **genetical** adjective **genetically** adverb.

COMBINATIONS – **genetic code** the means by which DNA and RNA molecules carry genetic information. **genetic engineering** the deliberate modification of an organism by manipulating its genetic material. **genetic fingerprinting** (also **genetic profiling**) the analysis of DNA from samples of body tissues or fluids in order to identify individuals. **genetic pollution** the spread of altered genes from genetically engineered organisms to other, non-engineered organisms.

genetically modified > adjective (of an organism) containing genetic material that has been artificially altered so as to produce a desired characteristic.

genetics > plural noun 1 (treated as sing.) the study of heredity and the variation of inherited characteristics. 2 (treated as sing. or pl.) the genetic properties or features of an organism.

DERIVATIVES – **geneticist** noun.

genial > adjective 1 friendly and cheerful. 2 literary (of weather) pleasantly mild and warm.

DERIVATIVES – **geniality** noun **genially** adverb.

SYNONYMS – **1** affable, amiable, benign, cordial, jovial.

ANTONYMS – **1** unfriendly.

ORIGIN – Latin genialis 'nuptial, productive', from genius (see GENIUS).

-genic > combining form 1 producing or produced by: carcinogenic. 2 well suited to: photogenic.

genie /jeeni/ > noun (pl. **genii** /jeeni-ī/ or **genies**) (in Arabian folklore) a jinn or spirit, especially one capable of granting wishes when summoned.

ORIGIN – French, from Latin genius (see GENIUS).

genii plural of GENIE, GENIUS.

genital > adjective referring to the reproductive organs. > noun (**genitals**) a person's or animal's external organs of reproduction.

ORIGIN – Latin genitalis, from gignere 'beget'.

genitalia /jennitayliə/ > plural noun formal or technical the genitals.

genitive /jennitiv/ Grammar > adjective denoting a case indicating possession or close association. > noun a word in the genitive case.

ORIGIN – Latin genitivus casus 'case of production or origin', from gignere 'beget'.

genito-urinary > adjective chiefly Medicine relating to the genital and urinary organs.

genius /jeeniəss/ > noun (pl. **geniuses**) 1 exceptional intellectual or creative power or

---

other natural ability. 2 an exceptionally intelligent or able person. 3 (pl. **genii** /jeeni-ī/) (in some mythologies) a spirit associated with a person, place, or institution. 4 the prevalent character or spirit of a nation, period, etc.

SYNONYMS – **1** brilliance, virtuosity. **2** maestro, mastermind, prodigy, virtuoso.

ANTONYMS – **1** stupidity.

---

wordpower facts
Genius

In Latin genius (from the verb gignere 'beget') meant 'attendant spirit present from one's birth' or 'innate ability or inclination'. The original sense in English was 'spirit attending on a person', which gave rise to the meanings 'a person's characteristic disposition' then 'a person's natural ability', and finally 'exceptional natural ability'. **Genie** is essentially the same word but came from French génie; it was adopted in the current sense by the 18th-century French translators of the Arabian Nights, because of its similarity to Arabic jinnī 'jinn'.

---

genlock /jenlok/ > noun a device for synchronising two different video signals, or a video signal and a computer or audio signal, enabling video images and computer graphics to be mixed.

ORIGIN – from GENERATOR + LOCK[1].

genoa /jennōə/ > noun Sailing a large jib or foresail whose foot extends aft of the mast, used especially on racing yachts.

ORIGIN – from Genoa, a city in Italy.

genocide /jennəsīd/ > noun the deliberate killing of a very large number of people from a particular ethnic group or nation.

DERIVATIVES – **genocidal** adjective.

ORIGIN – from Greek genos 'race' + -CIDE.

genome /jeenōm/ > noun Biology 1 the haploid set of chromosomes of an organism. 2 the complete set of genetic material of an organism.

DERIVATIVES – **genomic** adjective.

ORIGIN – blend of GENE and CHROMOSOME.

genotype /jeenətīp/ > noun Biology the genetic constitution of an individual organism. Contrasted with PHENOTYPE.

DERIVATIVES – **genotypic** adjective.

-genous > combining form 1 producing; inducing: erogenous. 2 originating in: endogenous.

ORIGIN – from -GEN + -OUS.

genre /zhonRə/ > noun 1 a style or category of art or literature. 2 (before another noun) denoting a style of painting depicting scenes from ordinary life.

ORIGIN – French, 'a kind', from Latin *genus* 'birth, family, nation'.

gent > *noun informal* **1** a gentleman. **2** (**the Gents**) Brit. a men's public toilet.

genteel > *adjective* **1** characteristic of the upper social classes; refined. **2** affectedly polite and cultivated.

DERIVATIVES – **genteelly** *adverb*.

SYNONYMS – **1** gentlemanly, ladylike, refined, well-bred. **2** affected, mannered; *informal* posh.

---

wordpower facts
Genteel

The words **genteel**, **Gentile**, and **gentle** share a root word, Latin *gentilis* 'of a family or nation, of the same clan', from *gens* 'family, race'. **Genteel** and **gentle** entered English from French *gentil* 'well-born', and formerly meant the same thing. From the 17th to the 19th centuries **genteel** was used to mean 'of good social position', 'having the manners of a well-born person', 'well-bred'; the ironic or derogatory implication dates from the 19th century. The original sense of **gentle** was 'nobly born', from which came 'courteous, chivalrous' (and thus **gentleman**) and later 'mild, moderate in action or disposition'.

---

gentian /**jen**sh'n/ > *noun* a plant of temperate and mountainous regions with violet or blue trumpet-shaped flowers.

COMBINATIONS – **gentian violet** a synthetic violet dye used as an antiseptic.

ORIGIN – allegedly named after *Gentius*, an ancient king of Illyria who discovered the plant's medicinal properties.

Gentile /**jen**tīl/ > *adjective* not Jewish. > *noun* a person who is not Jewish.

gentility > *noun* socially superior or genteel character or behaviour.

SYNONYMS – courteousness, cultivation, nobility, refinement.

gentle > *adjective* (**gentler**, **gentlest**) **1** mild or kind; not rough or violent. **2** moderate in effect or degree. **3** *archaic* noble or courteous.

DERIVATIVES – **gentleness** *noun* **gently** *adverb*.

SYNONYMS – **1** kind, mild, placid, soft, sweet-tempered. **2** light, mild, moderate.

ANTONYMS – **1** rough. **2** extreme.

COMBINATIONS – **gentlefolk** *archaic* people of noble birth or good social position.

gentleman > *noun* **1** a courteous or honourable man. **2** a man of good social

position, especially one of wealth and leisure. **3** (in polite or formal use) a man.

DERIVATIVES – **gentlemanliness** *noun* **gentlemanly** *adjective*.

COMBINATIONS – **gentleman's agreement** an arrangement which is based on trust rather than being legally binding.

gentlewoman > *noun archaic* a woman of noble birth or good social standing.

gentrify > *verb* (**gentrifies**, **gentrified**) renovate and improve (a house or district) so that it conforms to middle-class taste.

DERIVATIVES – **gentrification** *noun* **gentrifier** *noun*.

gentry > *noun* (**the gentry**) people of good social position, specifically the class next below the nobility.

genuflect /**jen**yooflekt/ > *verb* lower one's body briefly by bending one knee to the ground in worship or as a sign of respect.

DERIVATIVES – **genuflection** *noun*.

genuine > *adjective* **1** truly what it is said to be; authentic. **2** sincere; honest.

DERIVATIVES – **genuinely** *adverb* **genuineness** *noun*.

SYNONYMS – **1** authentic, bona fide, legitimate, real, true. **2** candid, honest, sincere.

ANTONYMS – **1** bogus, fake.

---

wordpower facts
Genuine

The words **genuine** and **genuflect** are rather unexpectedly linked by their shared root word, Latin *genu* 'knee'. **Genuflect** is straightforwardly derived from *genu* 'knee' + *flectere* 'to bend'. **Genuine** is from Latin *genuinus*; its connection with 'knee' comes from the Roman custom of a father acknowledging paternity of a newborn child by placing it on his knee.

---

genus /**jee**nəss/ > *noun* (pl. **genera** /**jenn**ərə/) **1** Biology a principal taxonomic category that ranks above species and below family, denoted by a capitalised Latin name, e.g. *Geranium*. **2** a class of things which have common characteristics.

ORIGIN – Latin, 'birth, race, stock'.

-geny > *combining form* denoting the mode by which something develops or is produced: *ontogeny*.

ORIGIN – Greek *-geneia*, from *gignomai* 'be born, become' and *genos* 'a kind'.

geo- /**jee**ō/ > *combining form* relating to the earth: *geocentric*.

ORIGIN – from Greek *gē* 'earth'.

geocentric > *adjective* **1** having the earth as

the centre, as in former astronomical systems. Compare with **HELIOCENTRIC**. **2** *Astronomy* measured from or considered in relation to the centre of the earth.

geochemistry > *noun* the study of the chemical composition of the earth and its rocks and minerals.

DERIVATIVES – **geochemical** *adjective* **geochemist** *noun*.

geode /**jee**ōd/ > *noun* **1** a small cavity in rock lined with crystals or other mineral matter. **2** a rock containing such a cavity.

ORIGIN – Greek *geōdēs* 'earthy'.

geodesic /jeeō**dee**zik/ > *adjective* **1** referring to the shortest possible line between two points on a sphere or other curved surface. **2** (of a dome) constructed from struts which follow geodesic lines and form an open framework of triangles and polygons.

geodesy /ji**odd**isi/ > *noun* the branch of mathematics concerned with the shape and area of the earth or large portions of it.

DERIVATIVES – **geodesist** *noun*.

ORIGIN – Greek *geōdaisia*, from *gē* 'earth' + *daiein* 'to divide'.

geodetic /jiō**dett**ik/ > *adjective* relating to geodesy, especially as applied to land surveying.

geographical > *adjective* relating to geography.

DERIVATIVES – **geographic** *adjective* **geographically** *adverb*.

COMBINATIONS – **geographical mile** a distance equal to one minute of longitude or latitude at the equator (about 1,850 metres).

geography > *noun* **1** the study of the physical features of the earth and of human activity as it relates to these. **2** the relative arrangement of places and physical features.

DERIVATIVES – **geographer** *noun*.

ORIGIN – Greek *geōgraphia*, from *gē* 'earth' + *-graphia* 'writing'.

geology > *noun* **1** the science which deals with the physical structure and substance of the earth. **2** the geological features of a district.

WORDFINDER – *geological time periods:* Archaean, Cambrian, Carboniferous, Cretaceous, Devonian, Jurassic, Ordovician, Permian, Precambrian, Proterozoic, Quaternary, Silurian, Tertiary, Triassic; *epochs:* Eocene, Holocene, Miocene, Oligocene, Palaeocene, Pleistocene, Pliocene; *eras:* Cenozoic, Mesozoic, Palaeozoic.

DERIVATIVES – **geologic** *adjective* **geological** *adjective* **geologically** *adverb* **geologist** *noun*.

ORIGIN – Latin *geologia*, from Greek *gē* 'earth' + *-logia* (see **-LOGY**).

geomagnetism > *noun* the branch of geology concerned with the magnetic properties of the earth.
DERIVATIVES – **geomagnetic** *adjective*.

geomancy /**jee**ōmansi/ > *noun* **1** the art of siting buildings auspiciously. **2** divination from the configuration of a handful of earth or random dots.
DERIVATIVES – **geomantic** *adjective*.

geometer /jee**omm**itər/ > *noun* a person skilled in geometry.

geometric /jiə**me**trik/ > *adjective* **1** relating to geometry. **2** (of a design) characterised by regular lines and shapes.
DERIVATIVES – **geometrical** *adjective* **geometrically** *adverb*.
COMBINATIONS – **geometric progression** (also **geometric series**) a sequence of numbers with a constant ratio between each number and the one before (e.g. 1, 3, 9, 27, 81).

geometry /ji**omm**itri/ > *noun* (pl. **geometries**) **1** the branch of mathematics concerned with the properties and relations of points, lines, surfaces, and solids. **2** the shape and relative arrangement of the parts of something.
DERIVATIVES – **geometrician** *noun*.
ORIGIN – Greek, from *gē* 'earth' + *metria*, from -*metrēs* 'measurer'.

geomorphology /jeeōmor**foll**əji/ > *noun* the study of the physical features of the surface of the earth and their relation to its geological structures.
DERIVATIVES – **geomorphological** *adjective* **geomorphologist** *noun*.

geophysics > *plural noun* (treated as sing.) the physics of the earth.
DERIVATIVES – **geophysical** *adjective* **geophysicist** *noun*.

geopolitics > *plural noun* (treated as sing. or pl.) politics, especially international relations, as influenced by geographical factors.
DERIVATIVES – **geopolitical** *adjective*.

Geordie > *noun* Brit. informal a person from Tyneside.
ORIGIN – from the given name *George*.

georgette /**jor**jet/ > *noun* a thin silk or crêpe dress material.
ORIGIN – named after the French dressmaker *Georgette de la Plante* (who worked *c.*1900).

Georgian¹ > *adjective* **1** relating to or characteristic of the reigns of the British Kings George I–IV (1714–1830). **2** relating to British neoclassical architecture of this period.

Georgian² > *noun* **1** a person from the country of Georgia. **2** the official language of Georgia. > *adjective* relating to Georgia.

geostationary > *adjective* (of an artificial satellite) orbiting in such a way that it appears to be stationary above a fixed point on the earth's surface.

geosynchronous > *adjective* another term for **SYNCHRONOUS** (in sense 2).

geothermal > *adjective* relating to or produced by the internal heat of the earth.

geranium > *noun* **1** a herbaceous plant or small shrub of a genus that comprises the cranesbills. **2** (in general use) a cultivated pelargonium.
ORIGIN – Greek *geranion*, from *geranos* 'crane'.

gerbera /**jer**bərə/ > *noun* a tropical plant with large brightly coloured flowers.
ORIGIN – Latin, named after the German naturalist Traugott *Gerber* (died 1743).

gerbil > *noun* a burrowing mouse-like desert rodent.
ORIGIN – Latin *gerbillus* 'little jerboa'.

geriatric /jerri**a**trik/ > *adjective* **1** relating to old people. **2** informal decrepit or out of date. > *noun* an old person, especially one receiving special care.
USAGE – **geriatric** is the normal term used in Britain and the US when referring to the health care of old people (*a geriatric ward*; *geriatric patients*). It can be offensive and should be avoided outside these contexts.
ORIGIN – from Greek *gēras* 'old age' + *iatros* 'doctor'.

geriatrics > *plural noun* (treated as sing. or pl.) the branch of medicine or social science concerned with the health and care of old people.
DERIVATIVES – **geriatrician** *noun*.

germ > *noun* **1** a micro-organism, especially one which causes disease. **2** a portion of an organism capable of developing into a new one or part of one. **3** an initial stage from which something may develop: *the germ of an idea*.
SYNONYMS – **1** bacterium, microbe; informal bug. **3** beginning, embryo, root, seed.
COMBINATIONS – **germ cell** Biology a gamete, or an embryonic cell with the potential of developing into one. **germ warfare** the use of disease-spreading micro-organisms as a military weapon.
ORIGIN – Latin *germen* 'seed, sprout'.

German > *noun* **1** a person from Germany. **2** the language of Germany, Austria, and parts of Switzerland. > *adjective* relating to Germany or German.
DERIVATIVES – **Germanise** (also **Germanize**) *verb*.
COMBINATIONS – **German measles** rubella. **German shepherd** a large breed of dog often used as guard dogs or for police work; an Alsatian. **German silver** a white alloy of nickel, zinc, and copper.

germane /jer**mayn**/ > *adjective* relevant to a subject under consideration.
ORIGIN – Latin *germanus* 'genuine, of the same parents'.

Germanic /jer**mann**ik/ > *adjective* **1** referring to the branch of the Indo-European language family that includes English, German, Dutch, Frisian, and the Scandinavian languages. **2** referring to the peoples of ancient northern and western Europe speaking such languages. **3** characteristic of Germans or Germany. > *noun* **1** the Germanic languages collectively. **2** the unrecorded ancient language from which these developed.

germanium /jer**may**niəm/ > *noun* a grey crystalline chemical element with semiconducting properties, resembling silicon.
ORIGIN – from Latin *Germanus* 'German'.

germicide > *noun* a substance which destroys harmful micro-organisms.
DERIVATIVES – **germicidal** *adjective*.

germinal > *adjective* **1** relating to a germ cell or embryo. **2** in the earliest stage of development. **3** providing material for future development.

germinate > *verb* (of a seed or spore) begin to grow and put out shoots after a period of dormancy.
DERIVATIVES – **germination** *noun*.
ORIGIN – Latin *germinare* 'sprout forth, bud', from *germen* 'sprout, seed'.

Geronimo /jə**ronn**imō/ > *exclamation* used to express exhilaration when leaping or moving quickly.
ORIGIN – adopted as a slogan by American paratroopers, by association with the Apache chief *Geronimo* (*c.*1829–1909).

gerontic /jə**ron**tik/ > *adjective* technical relating to old age.
ORIGIN – from Greek *gerōn* 'old man'.

gerontocracy /jerrən**tok**rəsi/ > *noun* **1** a state, society, or group governed by old people. **2** government based on rule by old people.
DERIVATIVES – **gerontocrat** *noun* **gerontocratic** *adjective*.

gerontology /jerrən**toll**əji/ > *noun* the scientific study of old age and old people.
DERIVATIVES – **gerontological** *adjective* **gerontologist** *noun*.

gerrymander > *verb* manipulate the boundaries of (an electoral constituency) so as to favour one party or class.
ORIGIN – from the name of Governor Elbridge *Gerry* of Massachusetts + **SALAMANDER**, from the supposed similarity between a salamander and the shape of a new voting district created when he was in office, which was felt to favour his party.

gerund /**jerr**ənd/ > *noun* Grammar a verb form which functions as a noun, in English ending in *-ing* (e.g. *asking* in *do you mind my asking you?*).

ORIGIN – Latin *gerundum*, from *gerere* 'do'.

gesso /**jess**ō/ > *noun* (pl. **gessoes**) a hard compound of plaster of Paris or whiting in glue, used in sculpture.

ORIGIN – Italian, from Greek *gupsos* 'gypsum'.

gestalt /gə**staalt**/ > *noun* Psychology an organised whole that is perceived as more than the sum of its parts.

COMBINATIONS – **gestalt psychology** a movement in psychology seeking to explain perceptions as gestalts rather than analysing their constituents.

ORIGIN – German, 'form, shape'.

Gestapo /gə**staa**pō/ > *noun* the German secret police under Nazi rule.

ORIGIN – German, from *Geheime Staatspolizei* 'secret state police'.

gestation /je**stay**sh'n/ > *noun* 1 the process of carrying or being carried in the womb between conception and birth. 2 the development of a plan or idea over a period of time.

DERIVATIVES – **gestate** verb.

ORIGIN – Latin, from *gestare* 'carry, carry in the womb'.

gesticulate /je**stik**yoolayt/ > *verb* gesture dramatically in place of or to emphasise speech.

DERIVATIVES – **gesticulation** noun.

ORIGIN – Latin *gesticulari*, from *gestus* 'action'.

gesture > *noun* 1 a movement of part of the body to express an idea or meaning. 2 an action performed to convey one's feelings or intentions. 3 an action performed for show in the knowledge that it will have no effect. > *verb* make a gesture.

DERIVATIVES – **gestural** adjective.

SYNONYMS – *noun* 1 indication, motion, sign, signal. 2 act, action, deed. *verb* gesticulate, indicate, motion, signal.

ORIGIN – Latin *gestura*, from *gerere* 'bear, wield, perform'.

gesundheit /gə**zoo**ondhīt/ > *exclamation* used to wish good health to a person who has just sneezed.

ORIGIN – German, 'health'.

get > *verb* (**getting**; past **got**; past participle **got**, N. Amer. or archaic **gotten**) 1 come to have or hold; receive. 2 succeed in attaining, achieving, or experiencing; obtain. 3 experience, suffer, or be afflicted with. 4 move in order to pick up, deal with, or bring. 5 bring or come into a specified state or condition. 6 catch, apprehend, or thwart. 7 come or go eventually or with some difficulty. 8 move or come into a

specified position or state. 9 tend to meet with or find. 10 travel by or catch (a form of transport). 11 begin to be or do something, especially gradually or by chance. 12 strike or wound. 13 informal punish, injure, or kill. 14 used with past participle to form the passive mood.

IDIOMS – **get across** manage to communicate (an idea) clearly. **get at 1** reach or gain access to. **2** informal imply. **3** Brit. informal criticise subtly and repeatedly. **get away** escape. **get away with** escape blame or punishment for. **get back at** take revenge on. **get by** manage with difficulty to live or accomplish something. **get down** N. Amer. informal dance energetically. **get down to** begin to do or give serious attention to. **get off 1** informal escape a punishment. **2** go to sleep. **3** (**get off with**) Brit. informal have a sexual encounter with. **get on 1** manage or make progress with a task. **2** chiefly Brit. have a friendly relationship. **3** (**be getting on**) informal be old or comparatively old. **get out of** contrive to avoid or escape. **get over 1** recover from (an ailment or an unpleasant experience). **2** manage to communicate (an idea or theory). **3** promptly complete (an unpleasant but necessary task). **4** overcome (a difficulty). **get one's own back** informal have one's revenge. **get round** chiefly Brit. **1** coax or persuade (someone) to do or allow something. **2** deal successfully with (a problem). **get round to** chiefly Brit. deal with (a task) in due course. **get through 1** pass or endure (a difficult experience or period). **2** chiefly Brit. use up (a large amount or number of something). **3** make contact by telephone. **4** succeed in communicating with someone. **getting on for** chiefly Brit. almost (a specified time, age, or amount). **get to** informal annoy or upset by persistent action. **get together** gather or assemble socially or to cooperate. **get up 1** rise from bed after sleeping. **2** (of wind or the sea) become strong or agitated. **get up to** Brit. informal be involved in (something illicit or surprising).

USAGE – despite its high frequency of use and many meanings, there is still a feeling that **get** is always somewhat informal. In formal writing it should only be used with caution.

SYNONYMS – **1,2** acquire, attain, gain, obtain, receive, secure. **4** collect, fetch, retrieve. **6** apprehend, arrest, capture, catch.

COMBINATIONS – **getaway** an escape or quick departure, especially after committing a crime. **get-together** an informal gathering. **get-up** informal a style or arrangement of dress, especially an elaborate or unusual one.

ORIGIN – Old Norse, 'obtain, beget, guess'.

gewgaw /**gyoo**gaw/ > *noun* a showy thing, especially one that is useless or worthless.

Gewürztraminer /gə**voorts**tramminər/ > *noun* a variety of white wine grape grown mainly in Alsace, Austria, and the Rhine valley.

ORIGIN – German, from *Gewürz* 'spice' + *Traminer*, a white wine grape grown in Germany and Alsace.

geyser /**gee**zər/ > *noun* 1 /also **gī**zər/ a hot spring in which water intermittently boils, sending a tall column of water and steam into the air. 2 Brit. a gas-fired water heater.

ORIGIN – from the name of a particular spring in Iceland.

Ghanaian /gaa**nay**ən/ > *noun* a person from Ghana. > *adjective* relating to Ghana.

gharial /**gair**iəl/ (also **gavial** /**gay**viəl/) > *noun* a large fish-eating crocodile with a long, narrow snout.

ORIGIN – Hindi.

ghastly > *adjective* (**ghastlier**, **ghastliest**) 1 causing great horror or fear. 2 deathly white or pallid. 3 informal very unpleasant.

SYNONYMS – 1 awful, dreadful, frightful, horrible, horrid. 2 ashen, pallid, wan.

ORIGIN – from obsolete *gast* 'terrify'; related to **GHOST** and **AGHAST**.

ghat /gaat/ > *noun* 1 (in the Indian subcontinent) a flight of steps leading down to a river. 2 (in the Indian subcontinent) a mountain pass.

ORIGIN – Hindi.

GHB > *abbreviation* (sodium) gamma-hydroxybutyrate, a designer drug with anaesthetic properties.

ghee /gee/ > *noun* clarified butter used in Indian cooking.

ORIGIN – Hindi, from a Sanskrit word meaning 'sprinkled'.

Gheg /geg/ > *noun* (pl. same or **Ghegs**) 1 a member of one of the two main ethnic groups of Albania, living mainly in the north of the country. Compare with **TOSK**. 2 the dialect of Albanian spoken by this people.

gherkin /**ger**kin/ > *noun* a small variety of cucumber, or a young green cucumber, used for pickling.

ORIGIN – Dutch *gurkje*, from Greek *angourion* 'cucumber'.

ghetto /**gett**ō/ > *noun* (pl. **ghettos** or **ghettoes**) 1 a part of a city, especially a slum area, occupied by a minority group. 2 historical the Jewish quarter in a city.

DERIVATIVES – **ghettoisation** (also **ghettoization**) noun **ghettoise** (also **ghettoize**) verb.

COMBINATIONS – **ghetto blaster** informal a large portable radio and cassette or CD player.

wordpower facts

Ghetto

The word **ghetto** was first used in reference to the Jewish quarter of a city, which in the past would have been enclosed within walls, with gates that were locked at night. Although similar enclosed quarters had previously existed elsewhere, the first one to be called a *ghetto* was founded in Venice in 1516. The word is perhaps from Italian *getto* 'foundry', because this first ghetto was established on the site of a foundry, or it may derive from *borghetto* 'small borough'.

Ghibelline /gibbilīn/ > *noun* a member of one of the two great political factions in Italian medieval politics, traditionally supporting the Holy Roman emperor against the Pope and his supporters, the Guelphs.

ORIGIN – Italian *Ghibellino*, perhaps from German *Waiblingen*, an estate belonging to Hohenstaufen emperors.

ghillie > *noun* variant spelling of GILLIE.

ghost > *noun* 1 an apparition of a dead person which is believed to appear to the living. 2 a faint trace. 3 archaic a spirit or soul. 4 a faint secondary image produced by a fault in an optical system or on a cathode ray screen. > *verb* act as ghostwriter of.

WORDFINDER – spectral (*of or like a ghost*).

IDIOMS – **give up the ghost** die or stop functioning.

SYNONYMS – *noun* 1 apparition, phantom, spectre, wraith; informal spook. 2 glimmer, hint, suggestion, trace.

COMBINATIONS – **ghost town** a town with few or no remaining inhabitants. **ghost train** a miniature train at a funfair that travels through a dark tunnel in which there are eerie effects.

ghosting > *noun* the appearance of a secondary image on a television or other display screen.

ghostly > *adjective* (**ghostlier, ghostliest**) of or like a ghost; eerie and unnatural.

SYNONYMS – eerie, phantasmal, spectral, wraithlike; informal spooky.

ghostwriter > *noun* a person employed to write material for another person, who is the named author.

DERIVATIVES – **ghostwrite** *verb*.

ghoul /gool/ > *noun* 1 an evil spirit or phantom, especially one supposed to rob graves and feed on dead bodies. 2 a person morbidly interested in death or disaster.

DERIVATIVES – **ghoulish** *adjective* **ghoulishly** *adverb* **ghoulishness** *noun*.

ORIGIN – from the Arabic word for a desert demon believed to rob graves and devour corpses.

GHQ > *abbreviation* General Headquarters.

GI > *noun* (pl. **GIs**) a private soldier in the US army.

ORIGIN – abbreviation of *government* (or *general*) *issue*: originally denoting equipment supplied to US forces.

giant > *noun* 1 an imaginary or mythical being of human form but superhuman size. 2 an abnormally tall or large person, animal, or plant. 3 Astronomy a star of relatively great size and luminosity. > *adjective* of very great size or force; gigantic.

WORDFINDER – *races of giants:* Brobdingnagians, Cyclops, Titans.

DERIVATIVES – **giantess** *noun*.

SYNONYMS – *noun* 1 behemoth, colossus, ogre, Titan. *adjective* colossal, enormous, gargantuan, gigantic, monstrous.

ORIGIN – from Greek *gigas*.

giantism > *noun* a tendency towards abnormally large size; gigantism.

giant-killer > *noun* a person or team that defeats a seemingly much more powerful opponent.

DERIVATIVES – **giant-killing** *noun*.

gibber /jibbər/ > *verb* speak rapidly and unintelligibly, typically through fear or shock.

DERIVATIVES – **gibbering** *adjective*.

gibberish /jibbərish/ > *noun* unintelligible or meaningless speech or writing.

gibbet /jibbit/ historical > *noun* 1 a gallows. 2 an upright post with an arm on which the bodies of executed criminals were left hanging as a warning to others. > *verb* (**gibbeted, gibbeting**) hang up on a gibbet or execute by hanging.

ORIGIN – Old French *gibet* 'staff, cudgel, gallows', from *gibe* 'club, staff'.

gibbon /gibbən/ > *noun* a small tree-dwelling ape with long, powerful arms, native to the forests of SE Asia.

ORIGIN – French, from an Indian dialect word.

gibbous /gibbəss/ > *adjective* (of the moon) having the illuminated part greater than a semicircle and less than a circle.

ORIGIN – Latin *gibbosus*, from *gibbus* 'hump'.

gibe /jīb/ > *noun & verb* variant spelling of JIBE¹.

giblets /jiblits/ > *plural noun* the liver, heart, gizzard, and neck of a chicken or other fowl, removed before the bird is cooked and sometimes used in making stuffing, soup, etc.

ORIGIN – Old French *gibelet* 'game bird stew', probably from *gibier* 'birds or mammals hunted for sport'.

Gibraltarian /jibrawltairiən/ > *noun* a person from Gibraltar. > *adjective* relating to Gibraltar.

giddy > *adjective* (**giddier, giddiest**) 1 having or causing a sensation of whirling and a tendency to fall or stagger; dizzy. 2 excitable and frivolous. > *verb* (**giddies, giddied**) make (someone) feel excited to the point of disorientation.

DERIVATIVES – **giddily** *adverb* **giddiness** *noun*.

SYNONYMS – *adjective* 1 dizzy, light-headed, unsteady, vertiginous. 2 capricious, flighty, skittish.

ORIGIN – Old English, 'insane', literally 'possessed by a god'.

giddy-up > *exclamation* said to induce a horse to start moving or go faster.

ORIGIN – reproducing a pronunciation of *get up*.

GIF > *abbreviation* Computing graphic interchange format, a popular format for image files, with built-in data compression.

gift > *noun* 1 a thing given willingly to someone without payment; a present. 2 a natural ability or talent. 3 informal a very easy task or unmissable opportunity. > *verb* 1 give as a gift, especially formally. 2 (**gift with**) endow (someone) with (an ability or talent). 3 (**gifted**) having exceptional talent or ability.

IDIOMS – **don't look a gift horse in the mouth** proverb don't reject something that you have been given.

DERIVATIVES – **giftedness** *adjective*.

SYNONYMS – *noun* 1 donation, offering, present. 2 ability, aptitude, flair, talent.

COMBINATIONS – **gift token** (also **gift voucher**) Brit. a voucher given as a gift which is exchangeable for goods.

gift wrap > *noun* decorative paper for wrapping gifts. > *verb* (**gift-wrap**) wrap (a gift) in decorative paper.

gig¹ /gig/ > *noun* 1 chiefly historical a light two-wheeled carriage pulled by one horse. 2 a light, fast, narrow boat adapted for rowing or sailing.

ORIGIN – apparently from obsolete *gig* 'a flighty girl'.

gig² /gig/ informal > *noun* a live performance by a musician or other performer. > *verb* (**gigged, gigging**) perform a gig or gigs.

giga- /gigə, jigə/ > *combining form* 1 denoting a factor of one thousand million (10^9). 2 Computing denoting a factor of 2^{30}.

ORIGIN – from Greek *gigas* 'giant'.

gigabyte /gigəbīt, jigəbīt/ > *noun* Computing a unit of information equal to one thousand million (10^9) or (strictly) 2^{30} bytes.

gigaflop > *noun* Computing a unit of computing speed equal to one thousand million floating-point operations per second.

gigantic > *adjective* of very great size or extent.

DERIVATIVES – **gigantically** *adverb*.

SYNONYMS – colossal, enormous, gargantuan, giant, immense, vast.

ANTONYMS – tiny.

ORIGIN – from Latin *gigas* 'giant'.

gigantism > *noun* chiefly Biology unusual or abnormal largeness.

giggle > *verb* laugh lightly in a nervous, affected, or silly manner. > *noun* **1** a laugh of such a kind. **2** informal an amusing person or thing.

DERIVATIVES – **giggler** *noun* **giggly** (**gigglier**, **giggliest**) *adjective*.

SYNONYMS – *verb* chuckle, snicker, snigger, titter.

GIGO /ˈgīgō/ > *abbreviation* chiefly Computing garbage in, garbage out.

gigolo /ˈjiggəlō/ > *noun* (pl. **gigolos**) a young man paid by an older woman to be her escort or lover.

ORIGIN – French, from colloquial *gigue* 'leg': first meaning 'professional male dancing partner'.

gigot /ˈjiggət/ > *noun* a leg of mutton or lamb.

ORIGIN – French, from colloquial *gigue* 'leg'.

gild > *verb* **1** cover thinly with gold. **2** (**gilded**) wealthy and privileged: *gilded youth*.

IDIOMS – **gild the lily** try to improve what is already beautiful or excellent. [ORIGIN – misquotation from Shakespeare's *King John* (VI. ii. 11): 'To gild refined gold, to paint the lily; to throw perfume on the violet, … is wasteful, and ridiculous excess'.]

DERIVATIVES – **gilding** *noun*.

gilet /ˈjilay/ > *noun* (pl. **gilets** pronunc. same) a light sleeveless padded jacket.

ORIGIN – French, 'waistcoat', from Turkish.

gill¹ /gil/ > *noun* **1** the paired respiratory organ of fishes and some amphibians. **2** the vertical plates on the underside of mushrooms and many toadstools. **3** (**gills**) the wattles or dewlap of a fowl. > *verb* gut or clean (a fish).

IDIOMS – **green about the gills** sickly-looking. **to the gills** until completely full.

DERIVATIVES – **gilled** *adjective*.

gill² /jil/ > *noun* a unit of liquid measure, equal to a quarter of a pint.

ORIGIN – Old French *gille* 'measure or container for wine', from Latin *gillo* 'water pot'.

gill³ /gil/ > *noun* chiefly N. English **1** a deep ravine, especially a wooded one. **2** a narrow mountain stream.

gillie /ˈgilli/ (also **ghillie**) > *noun* (in Scotland) an attendant on a hunting or fishing expedition.

ORIGIN – Scottish Gaelic *gille* 'lad, servant'.

gillyflower /ˈjilliflowr/ (also **gilliflower**) > *noun* any of a number of fragrant flowers, such as the wallflower or white stock.

ORIGIN – from Greek *karuophullon* (from *karuon* 'nut' + *phullon* 'leaf').

gilt¹ > *adjective* covered thinly with gold leaf or gold paint. > *noun* **1** gold leaf or gold paint applied in a thin layer to a surface. **2** (**gilts**) fixed-interest loan securities issued by the UK government.

COMBINATIONS – **gilt-edged** referring to stocks or securities (such as gilts) that are regarded as extremely reliable investments.

ORIGIN – archaic past participle of **GILD**.

gilt² > *noun* a young sow.

gimbal /ˈjimb'l/ (also **gimbals**) > *noun* a device for keeping an instrument horizontal in a moving vessel or aircraft.

DERIVATIVES – **gimballed** *adjective*.

ORIGIN – obsolete *gemel* 'twin, hinge', from Old French *gemel* 'twin'.

gimcrack /ˈjimkrak/ > *adjective* showy but flimsy or poorly made. > *noun* a cheap and showy ornament.

DERIVATIVES – **gimcrackery** *noun*.

gimlet /ˈgimlit/ > *noun* a small T-shaped tool with a screw-tip for boring holes.

ORIGIN – Old French *guimbelet*, from *guimble* 'drill'.

gimmick > *noun* a trick or device intended to attract attention rather than fulfil a useful purpose.

DERIVATIVES – **gimmickry** *noun* **gimmicky** *adjective*.

gimp¹ /gimp/ > *noun* **1** twisted, reinforced material used as upholstery trimming. **2** (in lacemaking) coarser thread forming the outline of the design. **3** fishing line made of silk bound with wire.

ORIGIN – Dutch.

gimp² /gimp/ N. Amer. informal, derogatory > *noun* **1** a physically handicapped or lame person. **2** a feeble or contemptible person. > *verb* limp; hobble.

DERIVATIVES – **gimpy** *adjective*.

gin¹ > *noun* **1** a clear alcoholic spirit distilled from grain or malt and flavoured with juniper berries. **2** (also **gin rummy**) a form of the card game rummy.

ORIGIN – abbreviation of *genever*, a kind of Dutch gin, from Latin *juniperus* 'juniper' (gin being flavoured with juniper berries).

gin² > *noun* **1** a machine for separating cotton from its seeds. **2** a machine for raising and moving heavy weights. **3** a trap for catching small game. > *verb* (**ginned**, **ginning**) treat (cotton) in a gin.

ORIGIN – Old French *engin* 'engine'.

ginger > *noun* **1** a hot, fragrant spice made from the rhizome of a SE Asian plant resembling bamboo. **2** a light reddish-yellow colour. **3** spirit; mettle. > *verb* **1** flavour with ginger. **2** (**ginger up**) stimulate or enliven (someone or something).

DERIVATIVES – **gingery** *adjective*.

COMBINATIONS – **ginger ale** (also **ginger beer**) an effervescent, sometimes alcoholic drink flavoured with ginger. **gingerbread** cake made with treacle or syrup and flavoured with ginger. **ginger group** chiefly Brit. a highly active faction within a party or movement that presses for stronger action on a particular issue.

ORIGIN – Latin *gingiber*, from Greek *zingiberis*, from a Dravidian word.

gingerly > *adverb* in a careful or cautious manner. > *adjective* showing great care or caution.

SYNONYMS – *adverb* carefully, cautiously, hesitantly, timidly, warily.

ORIGIN – perhaps from Old French *gensor* 'delicate', from Latin *genitus* 'well-born'.

gingham /ˈgingəm/ > *noun* lightweight plain-woven cotton cloth, typically checked.

ORIGIN – from a Malay word meaning 'striped'.

gingival /ˈjinjīv'l/ > *adjective* Medicine concerned with the gums.

ORIGIN – from Latin *gingiva* 'gum'.

gingivitis /jinjivītiss/ > *noun* Medicine inflammation of the gums.

ORIGIN – from Latin *gingiva* 'gum'.

ginkgo /ˈginkgō/ (also **gingko** /ˈgingkō/) > *noun* (pl. **ginkgos** or **ginkgoes**) a deciduous Chinese tree with fan-shaped leaves and yellow flowers.

ORIGIN – Chinese.

ginormous > *adjective* Brit. informal extremely large.

ORIGIN – blend of *giant* and *enormous*.

ginseng /ˈjinseng/ > *noun* a plant tuber credited with various tonic and medicinal properties.

ORIGIN – from Chinese words meaning 'man' and denoting a kind of herb (because of the supposed resemblance of the forked root to a person).

gip > *noun* variant spelling of **GYP¹**.

gipsy > *noun* variant spelling of **GYPSY**.

giraffe > *noun* (pl. same or **giraffes**) a large mammal with a very long neck and forelegs, the tallest living animal.

ORIGIN – French *girafe*, from Arabic.

gird > *verb* (past and past participle **girded** or **girt**) literary **1** encircle or secure with a belt or band. **2** (in phrase **gird one's loins**) prepare and strengthen oneself for what is to come.

girder > *noun* a large metal beam used in building bridges and large buildings.

ORIGIN – from **GIRD** in the archaic sense 'brace, strengthen'.

girdle¹ > *noun* **1** a belt or cord worn round the waist. **2** a woman's elasticated corset extending from waist to thigh. > *verb* encircle with a girdle or belt.

girdle² > *noun* Scottish and northern English term for **GRIDDLE** (in sense 1).

girl > *noun* **1** a female child. **2** a young or

relatively young woman. **3** a person's girlfriend. **4** dated a female servant.

DERIVATIVES – **girlhood** noun **girlish** adjective **girlishly** adverb.

COMBINATIONS – **girlfriend 1** a person's regular female companion in a romantic or sexual relationship. **2** chiefly N. Amer. a woman's female friend. **Girl Guide** a member of the Guides Association. **Girl Scout** a girl belonging to the Scout Association.

girlie > noun (also **girly**) (pl. **girlies**) informal a girl or young woman. > adjective **1** (usu. **girly**) often derogatory like or characteristic of a girl. **2** depicting nude or partially nude young women in erotic poses: *girlie magazines*.

giro > noun (pl. **giros**) **1** a system of electronic credit transfer involving banks, post offices, and public utilities. **2** a cheque or payment by giro, especially a social security payment.

ORIGIN – Italian, 'circulation (of money)'.

girt past participle of **GIRD**.

girth > noun **1** the measurement around the middle of something, especially a person's waist. **2** a band attached to a saddle and fastened around a horse's belly.

gist /jist/ > noun the substance or essence of a speech or text.

ORIGIN – from Old French *gesir* 'to lie'.

git > noun Brit. informal an unpleasant or contemptible person.

ORIGIN – from dialect *get* 'stupid or unpleasant person'.

gîte /zheet/ > noun a small furnished holiday house in France.

ORIGIN – French, 'home'.

give > verb (past **gave**; past participle **given**) **1** freely transfer the possession of; cause to receive or have. **2** yield as a product or result. **3** carry out (an action). **4** cause to experience or suffer. **5** state or put forward (information or argument). **6** present (an appearance or impression). **7** alter in shape under pressure rather than resist or break. **8** (**give off** or **out**) emit (odour, vapour, etc). **9** produce (a sound). **10** concede or yield (something) as valid or deserved in respect of (someone). > noun capacity to bend or alter in shape under pressure.

IDIOMS – **give oneself airs** act pretentiously or snobbishly. **give and take** mutual concessions and compromises. **give away 1** reveal (something secret or concealed). **2** (in sport) concede (a goal or advantage) to the opposition. **give the game** (or **show**) **away** inadvertently reveal something secret. **give in** cease fighting or arguing; yield. **give or take** —— informal to within a specified amount. **give out** be completely used up or broken. **give rise to** cause or induce to happen. **give up 1** cease making an effort; resign oneself to failure. **2**

stop the habitual doing or consuming of (something). **3** deliver (a wanted person) to authority.

DERIVATIVES – **giver** noun.

SYNONYMS – **1** bestow, confer, donate, hand over, present. **2** afford, produce, yield. **5** announce, communicate, impart. **9** emit, issue, produce, utter.

ANTONYMS – **1** receive, take.

COMBINATIONS – **giveaway** informal **1** something given free, especially for promotional purposes. **2** something that makes an inadvertent revelation.

given past participle of **GIVE**. > adjective **1** specified or stated. **2** (**given to**) inclined or disposed to. > preposition taking into account. > noun an established fact or situation.

COMBINATIONS – **given name** a person's first name.

gizmo > noun (pl. **gizmos**) informal a gadget, especially one the speaker cannot name.

gizzard > noun **1** a muscular, thick-walled part of a bird's stomach for grinding food, typically with grit. **2** a muscular stomach of some fish, insects, molluscs, etc.

ORIGIN – Latin *gigeria* 'cooked entrails of fowl'.

GLA > abbreviation gamma linolenic acid.

glabrous /glaybrəss/ > adjective technical free from hair or down; smooth.

ORIGIN – from Latin *glaber* 'hairless, smooth'.

glacé /glassay/ > adjective **1** (of fruit) having a glossy surface due to preservation in sugar. **2** (of cloth or leather) smooth and highly polished.

COMBINATIONS – **glacé icing** icing made with icing sugar and water.

ORIGIN – French, 'iced', from *glace* 'ice'.

glacial /glaysh'l, glaysiəl/ > adjective **1** relating to ice, especially in the form of glaciers. **2** extremely cold or unfriendly; icy.

DERIVATIVES – **glacially** adverb.

COMBINATIONS – **glacial period** a period in the earth's history when ice sheets were unusually extensive; an ice age.

ORIGIN – Latin *glacialis* 'icy'.

glaciated /glaysiaytid/ > adjective covered or having been covered by glaciers or ice sheets.

ORIGIN – from Latin *glaciare* 'freeze'.

glaciation > noun Geology **1** the condition or result of being glaciated. **2** a glacial period.

glacier /glassiər, glaysiər/ > noun a slowly moving mass of ice formed by the accumulation of snow on mountains or near the poles.

WORDFINDER – crevasse (*an open crack in a glacier*), moraine (*deposit left by glacier*), serac (*an ice ridge on a glacier*).

ORIGIN – French, from *glace* 'ice'.

glaciology > noun the study of glaciers.

DERIVATIVES – **glaciologist** noun.

glad > adjective (**gladder**, **gladdest**) **1** pleased; delighted. **2** (often **glad of**) grateful. **3** causing happiness.

DERIVATIVES – **gladly** adverb **gladness** noun.

SYNONYMS – **1** delighted, gratified, happy, pleased, thrilled.

COMBINATIONS – **glad rags** informal clothes for a party or special occasion.

ORIGIN – Old English, 'bright, shining'.

gladden > verb make glad.

glade > noun an open space in a wood or forest.

glad-hand chiefly N. Amer. > verb (especially of a politician) greet or welcome warmly. > noun (**glad hand**) a warm and hearty greeting or welcome.

DERIVATIVES – **glad-hander** noun.

gladiator > noun (in ancient Rome) a man trained to fight with weapons against other men or wild animals in an arena.

DERIVATIVES – **gladiatorial** adjective.

ORIGIN – Latin, from *gladius* 'sword'.

gladiolus /gladdiōləss/ > noun (pl. **gladioli** /gladdiōlī/ or **gladioluses**) a plant with sword-shaped leaves and spikes of brightly coloured flowers.

ORIGIN – Latin, from *gladius* 'sword'.

Gladstone bag > noun a bag like a briefcase having two equal compartments joined by a hinge.

ORIGIN – named after the British Liberal statesman W. E. *Gladstone* (1809–98).

Glagolitic /glaggəlittik/ > adjective referring to an alphabet based on Greek minuscules, formerly used in some Slavic languages.

ORIGIN – from an Old Church Slavonic word meaning 'word'.

Glam. > abbreviation Glamorgan.

glam informal > adjective glamorous. > noun glamour. > verb (**glammed**, **glamming**) (**glam up**) make oneself look glamorous.

COMBINATIONS – **glam rock** a style of rock music characterised by male performers wearing exaggerated flamboyant clothes and make-up.

glamorise (also **glamorize**) > verb make (something) seem glamorous or desirable, especially spuriously so.

glamorous* > adjective having glamour.

DERIVATIVES – **glamorously** adverb.

*SPELLING – **glamorous** drops the *u* of **glamour**: glamorous.

SYNONYMS – attractive, chic, elegant, glittering, stylish.

glamour (US also **glamor**) > noun an attractive and exciting quality.

SYNONYMS – allure, appeal, attraction, charm, magic.

wordpower facts

Glamour

Although the two concepts are not often associated with each other, **glamour** and **grammar** are linked. **Glamour** was originally a Scots word meaning 'enchantment, magic', and is an alteration of **grammar**. Although **grammar** itself was not used in this sense, the Latin word *grammatica* (from which it derives) was often used in the Middle Ages to mean 'scholarship, learning', including occult practices then associated with learning, such as magic and astrology. Similarly, **grimoire** 'book of spells' is formed from French *grammaire* 'grammar'.

glance > *verb* **1** take a brief or hurried look. **2** strike at an angle and bounce off obliquely. > *noun* a brief or hurried look.
DERIVATIVES – **glancing** *adjective* **glancingly** *adverb*.
ORIGIN – Old French *glacier* 'to slip', from *glace* 'ice'.

gland > *noun* **1** an organ of the body which secretes particular chemical substances. **2** a lymph node.
WORDFINDER – *examples of glands:* adrenal, pancreas, parathyroid, pineal, pituitary, prostate, thymus, thyroid; endocrinology (*study of glands and hormones*).
ORIGIN – Latin *glandulae* 'throat glands'.

glanders /**gland**ərz/ > *plural noun* (usu. treated as sing.) a contagious disease of horses, characterised by swellings below the jaw and mucous discharge from the nostrils.
ORIGIN – Old French *glandre*, from Latin *glandulae* 'throat glands'.

glandular > *adjective* relating to or affecting a gland or glands.
COMBINATIONS – **glandular fever** an infectious disease caused by a virus and characterised by swelling of the lymph glands and prolonged lassitude.

glans /glanz/ > *noun* (pl. **glandes** /**glan**deez/) Anatomy the rounded part forming the end of the penis or clitoris.
ORIGIN – Latin, 'acorn'.

glare > *verb* **1** stare in an angry or fierce way. **2** shine with a strong or dazzling light. **3** (**glaring**) highly obvious or conspicuous. > *noun* **1** a fierce or angry stare. **2** strong and dazzling light.
DERIVATIVES – **glaringly** *adverb* **glary** *adjective*.
SYNONYMS – *verb & noun* **1** glower, lour, scowl. **2** blaze, dazzle.
ORIGIN – Dutch and Low German *glaren* 'to gleam or glare'.

glasnost /**glaz**nost/ > *noun* (in the former Soviet Union) the policy or practice of more open government.
ORIGIN – Russian *glasnost'* 'the fact of being public, openness'.

glass > *noun* **1** a hard, brittle, usually transparent or translucent substance made by fusing sand with soda and lime. **2** a drinking container made of glass. **3** a lens or optical instrument, in particular a monocle or a magnifying lens. **4** chiefly Brit. a mirror. > *verb* (usu. **glass in** or **over**) enclose or cover with glass.
WORDFINDER – vitreous (*of or like glass*), vitrify (*turn into glass*), obsidian (*natural volcanic glass*).
IDIOMS – **people (who live) in glass houses shouldn't throw stones** proverb you shouldn't criticise others when you have similar faults of your own.
DERIVATIVES – **glassful** *noun* **glassware** *noun*.
COMBINATIONS – **glass-blowing** the craft of making glassware by blowing semi-molten glass through a long tube. **glass ceiling** an unacknowledged barrier to advancement in a profession, especially affecting women and members of minorities. **glass fibre** chiefly Brit. a strong plastic or other material containing embedded glass filaments for reinforcement. **glasshouse 1** Brit. a greenhouse. **2** Brit. military slang a place of detention. **glasspaper** paper covered with powdered glass, used for smoothing and polishing. **glass wool** glass in the form of fine fibres used for packing and insulation.

glasses > *plural noun* a pair of lenses set in a frame that rests on the nose and ears, used to correct defective eyesight.

glassy > *adjective* (**glassier**, **glassiest**) **1** of or resembling glass. **2** (of a person's eyes or expression) showing no interest or animation; unfocused.
DERIVATIVES – **glassily** *adverb*.

Glaswegian /glaz**wee**jən/ > *noun* a native of Glasgow. > *adjective* relating to Glasgow.

glaucoma /glaw**kō**mə/ > *noun* Medicine a condition of increased pressure within the eyeball, causing gradual loss of sight.
ORIGIN – Greek *glaukōma*, from *glaukos* 'bluish green or grey' (because of the grey-green haze in the pupil).

glaucous /**glaw**kəss/ > *adjective* technical or literary **1** of a dull greyish-green or blue colour. **2** covered with a powdery bloom like that on grapes.
ORIGIN – Greek *glaukos*.

glaze > *verb* **1** fit panes of glass into (a window frame or similar structure). **2** enclose or cover with glass. **3** cover with a glaze. **4** (of the eyes) lose brightness and animation. > *noun* **1** a glass-like substance fused on to the surface of pottery to form an impervious decorative coating. **2** a thin topcoat of transparent paint used to modify the tone of an underlying colour. **3** a liquid such as milk or beaten egg, used to form a smooth shiny coating on food.
DERIVATIVES – **glazer** *noun* **glazing** *noun*.

glazier /**glay**ziər/ > *noun* a person whose trade is fitting glass in windows and doors.

gleam > *verb* **1** shine with reflected light. **2** (of the eyes) be bright with emotion. > *noun* **1** a faint or brief light. **2** a brief or faint show of a quality or emotion.
IDIOMS – **a gleam in someone's eye** see EYE.
DERIVATIVES – **gleaming** *adjective* **gleamingly** *adverb*.
SYNONYMS – *verb* flash, glint, glisten, shimmer. *noun* flash, flicker, glimmer, glint, shimmer.
ORIGIN – Old English, 'brilliant light'.

glean > *verb* **1** collect gradually from various sources. **2** historical gather (leftover grain) after a harvest.
DERIVATIVES – **gleaner** *noun*.
ORIGIN – Latin *glennare*.

gleanings > *plural noun* things collected from various sources rather than together.

glebe /gleeb/ > *noun* historical a piece of land serving as part of a clergyman's benefice and providing income.
ORIGIN – Latin *gleba* 'clod, land, soil'.

glee > *noun* **1** great delight. **2** a song for men's voices in three or more parts.
SYNONYMS – **1** delight, elation, exhilaration, joy, mirth.
COMBINATIONS – **glee club** a society for singing part songs.
ORIGIN – Old English, 'entertainment, music, fun'.

gleeful > *adjective* exuberantly or triumphantly joyful.
DERIVATIVES – **gleefully** *adverb*.
SYNONYMS – cock-a-hoop, elated, exhilarated, high-spirited, overjoyed.

glen > *noun* a narrow valley, especially in Scotland or Ireland.
ORIGIN – from Scottish Gaelic and Irish.

glib > *adjective* (**glibber**, **glibbest**) articulate and voluble but insincere and shallow.
DERIVATIVES – **glibly** *adverb* **glibness** *noun*.

glide > *verb* **1** move with a smooth, quiet, continuous motion. **2** fly without power or in a glider. > *noun* an instance of gliding.
DERIVATIVES – **gliding** *noun*.
SYNONYMS – *verb* **1** sail, skim, slide, slip.
COMBINATIONS – **glide path** an aircraft's line of descent to land.

glider > *noun* **1** a light aircraft designed to fly without using an engine. **2** a person or thing that glides.

glimmer > *verb* shine faintly with a wavering light. > *noun* **1** a faint or wavering light. **2** a faint sign of a feeling or quality: *a glimmer of hope*.

DERIVATIVES – **glimmering** adjective & noun.

SYNONYMS – verb flicker, gleam, twinkle. noun **1** flicker, gleam, glint, twinkle. **2** flicker, gleam, trace.

glimpse > noun a momentary or partial view. > verb see briefly or partially.

glint > verb give out or reflect small flashes of light. > noun a small flash of light, especially a reflected one.

glissade /glisaad, glisayd/ > noun **1** a slide down a steep slope of snow or ice, typically on the feet with the support of an ice axe. **2** Ballet a gliding movement. > verb perform or move by means of a glissade.
ORIGIN – French, from glisser 'to slip, slide'.

glissando /glisandō/ > noun (pl. **glissandi** /glisandi/ or **glissandos**) Music a continuous slide upwards or downwards between two notes.
ORIGIN – from French glisser 'to slip, slide'.

glisten > verb (especially of something wet or greasy) shine or sparkle. > noun a sparkling light, especially one reflected from something wet.
SYNONYMS – verb gleam, shimmer, shine, sparkle.

glitch > noun informal **1** a sudden malfunction or irregularity of equipment. **2** an unexpected setback in a plan.

glitter > verb **1** shine with a bright, shimmering reflected light. **2** (**glittering**) impressively successful or glamorous: a glittering career. > noun **1** bright, shimmering reflected light. **2** tiny pieces of sparkling material used for decoration. **3** an attractive but superficial quality.
IDIOMS – **all that glitters is not gold** proverb the attractive external appearance of something is not a reliable indication of its true nature.
DERIVATIVES – **glittery** adjective.
SYNONYMS – verb **1** gleam, shimmer, sparkle, twinkle.

glitterati /glittəraati/ > plural noun informal fashionable people involved in show business or some other glamorous activity.
ORIGIN – blend of **GLITTER** and **LITERATI**.

glitz > noun informal extravagant but superficial display.
DERIVATIVES – **glitzy** adjective.
ORIGIN – blend of **GLITTER** and **RITZ**.

gloaming > noun (**the gloaming**) literary twilight; dusk.

gloat > verb contemplate one's own success or another's misfortune with smugness or malignant pleasure. > noun an act of gloating.
DERIVATIVES – **gloater** noun **gloating** adjective & noun.

glob > noun informal a lump of a semi-liquid substance.

ORIGIN – perhaps a blend of **BLOB** and **GOB²**.

global > adjective **1** relating to the whole world; worldwide. **2** relating to or embracing the whole of something, or of a group of things. **3** Computing operating or applying through the whole of a file or program.
DERIVATIVES – **globalist** noun **globally** adverb.
SYNONYMS – **1** international, universal, worldwide. **2** all-encompassing, all-inclusive, comprehensive.
COMBINATIONS – **global village** the world considered as a single community linked by telecommunications. **global warming** the gradual increase in the overall temperature of the earth's atmosphere due to the greenhouse effect caused by carbon dioxide, CFCs, and other pollutants.

globalise (also **globalize**) > verb develop (business, society, etc.) so as to make international influence or action possible.
DERIVATIVES – **globalisation** noun.

globe > noun **1** a spherical or rounded object. **2** (**the globe**) the earth. **3** a spherical representation of the earth with a map on the surface.
DERIVATIVES – **globose** adjective.
ORIGIN – Latin globus.

globetrotter > noun informal a person who travels widely.
DERIVATIVES – **globetrotting** noun & adjective.

globular > adjective **1** globe-shaped; spherical. **2** composed of globules.

globule > noun a small round particle of a substance; a drop.
ORIGIN – Latin globulus, from globus 'spherical object, globe'.

globulin /globyoolin/ > noun Biochemistry any of a group of simple proteins found in blood serum and soluble in salt solution.

glockenspiel /glokkənspeel, -shpeel/ > noun a musical percussion instrument incorporating tuned metal pieces which are struck with small hammers.
ORIGIN – German Glockenspiel 'bell play'.

gloom > noun **1** partial darkness. **2** a state of depression or despondency.
SYNONYMS – **1** dimness, gloominess, murkiness. **2** dejection, depression, despondency, melancholy, unhappiness.

gloomy > adjective (**gloomier**, **gloomiest**) **1** poorly lit, especially so as to cause fear or depression. **2** causing or feeling depression or despondency.
DERIVATIVES – **gloomily** adverb **gloominess** noun.
SYNONYMS – **1** dark, dim, dingy, dull, murky. **2** despondent, glum, melancholy, miserable, morose, unhappy.

gloop > noun informal sloppy or sticky semi-fluid matter.
DERIVATIVES – **gloopy** adjective.

glorify > verb (**glorifies**, **glorified**) **1** praise and worship (God). **2** describe or represent as admirable, especially unjustifiably or undeservedly. **3** reveal the glory of (God) through one's actions. **4** (**glorified**) represented as or appearing more elevated or special than is the case: a glorified courier.
DERIVATIVES – **glorification** noun.
SYNONYMS – **1** exalt, honour, venerate. **2** aggrandise, dignify, ennoble, magnify.

glorious > adjective **1** having or bringing glory. **2** strikingly beautiful or impressive.
DERIVATIVES – **gloriously** adverb.
SYNONYMS – **1** celebrated, distinguished, illustrious, noble, renowned. **2** beautiful, brilliant, splendid, wonderful.

glory > noun (pl. **glories**) **1** high renown or honour won by notable achievements. **2** worship and thanksgiving offered to God. **3** magnificence; great beauty. > verb (**glory in**) **1** take great pride or pleasure in. **2** exult in unpleasantly or boastfully.
IDIOMS – **in one's glory** informal in a state of extreme joy or exaltation.
SYNONYMS – noun **1** acclaim, distinction, honour, prestige, renown. **2** adoration, honour, veneration. **3** grandeur, magnificence, majesty, splendour.
COMBINATIONS – **glory box** Austral./NZ a box in which a woman stores clothes and household items in preparation for marriage. **glory hole** informal an untidy room or cupboard used for storage.
ORIGIN – Latin gloria.

Glos. > abbreviation Gloucestershire.

gloss¹ > noun **1** the shine on a smooth surface. **2** (also **gloss paint**) a type of paint which dries to a bright shiny surface. **3** a superficially attractive appearance or impression. > verb **1** give a glossy appearance to. **2** (**gloss over**) try to conceal or pass over by mentioning briefly or misleadingly.
SYNONYMS – noun **1** finish, lustre, sheen, shine.

gloss² > noun a translation or explanation of a word, phrase, or passage. > verb provide a gloss for.
SYNONYMS – noun annotation, commentary, explanation, footnote, translation. verb annotate, comment on, explain, translate.
ORIGIN – alteration of **GLOZE**, suggested by Latin glossa 'explanation of a difficult word'.

glossary > noun (pl. **glossaries**) an alphabetical list of words relating to a specific subject, text, or dialect, with explanations.
ORIGIN – Latin glossarium, from glossa 'explanation of a difficult word'.

glossolalia /glossəˈlayliə/ > *noun* (in Christian belief) the phenomenon of the gift of tongues.

DERIVATIVES – **glossolalic** *adjective*.

ORIGIN – from Greek *glōssa* 'language, tongue' + *lalia* 'speech'.

glossy > *adjective* (**glossier, glossiest**) **1** shiny and smooth. **2** superficially attractive and stylish. > *noun* (pl. **glossies**) informal a magazine printed on glossy paper with colour photographs.

DERIVATIVES – **glossily** *adverb* **glossiness** *noun*.

glottal > *adjective* of or produced by the glottis.

COMBINATIONS – **glottal stop** a consonant sounded by the audible release of the airstream after complete closure of the glottis.

glottis /ˈglottiss/ > *noun* the part of the larynx consisting of the vocal cords and the slit-like opening between them.

ORIGIN – Greek, from *glōtta*, variant of *glōssa* 'tongue'.

glove > *noun* **1** a covering for the hand having separate parts for each finger and the thumb. **2** a padded protective covering for the hand used in boxing and other sports.

IDIOMS – **fit like a glove** (of clothes) fit exactly.

DERIVATIVES – **gloved** *adjective*.

COMBINATIONS – **glovebox 1** a glove compartment. **2** a closed chamber with sealed-in gloves for handling radioactive or other hazardous material. **glove compartment** a small recess for storage in the dashboard of a motor vehicle. **glove puppet** chiefly Brit. a cloth puppet fitted on the hand and worked by the fingers.

glover > *noun* a maker of gloves.

glow > *verb* **1** give out steady light without flame. **2** have an intense colour and a slight radiance. **3** convey deep pleasure through one's expression and bearing. > *noun* **1** a steady radiance of light or heat. **2** a feeling or appearance of warmth. **3** a strong feeling of pleasure or well-being.

SYNONYMS – *verb* **1** gleam, shine, smoulder. *noun* **1** incandescence, phosphorescence, radiance.

COMBINATIONS – **glow-worm** a soft-bodied beetle whose larva-like wingless female emits light to attract males.

glower /ˈglowr/ > *verb* have an angry or sullen look on one's face; scowl. > *noun* an angry or sullen look.

SYNONYMS – *verb* & *noun* frown, glare, lour, scowl.

ORIGIN – perhaps a Scots variant of dialect *glore*, or from obsolete *glow* 'to stare', both possibly Scandinavian.

glowing > *adjective* expressing great praise: *a glowing report*.

DERIVATIVES – **glowingly** *adverb*.

gloxinia /gloksˈinniə/ > *noun* a tropical American plant with large, velvety, bell-shaped flowers.

ORIGIN – Latin, named after the 18th-century German botanist Benjamin P. *Gloxin.*

gloze /glōz/ > *verb* archaic **1** (often **gloze over**) conceal or pass over; explain away. **2** use ingratiating or fawning language.

ORIGIN – from Old French *glose* 'a gloss, comment', from Latin *glossa* 'explanation of a difficult word'.

glucose /ˈglōōkōz/ > *noun* a simple sugar which is an important energy source in living organisms and is a component of many carbohydrates.

ORIGIN – from Greek *gleukos* 'sweet wine'.

glue > *noun* an adhesive substance used for sticking objects or materials together. > *verb* (**glues, glued, gluing** or **glueing**) **1** fasten or join with glue. **2** (**be glued to**) informal be paying very close attention to.

DERIVATIVES – **gluey** *adjective*.

COMBINATIONS – **glue ear** blocking of the Eustachian tube by mucus, occurring especially in children and causing impaired hearing. **glue-sniffing** the practice of inhaling intoxicating fumes from the solvents in adhesives.

ORIGIN – Latin *glus*, from *gluten*.

glug informal > *verb* (**glugged, glugging**) pour or drink (liquid) with a hollow gurgling sound. > *noun* a hollow gurgling sound.

DERIVATIVES – **gluggable** *adjective*.

ORIGIN – imitative.

Glühwein /ˈglōōvīn/ > *noun* mulled wine.

ORIGIN – German, from *glühen* 'to mull' + *Wein* 'wine'.

glum > *adjective* (**glummer, glummest**) dejected; morose.

DERIVATIVES – **glumly** *adverb*.

SYNONYMS – dejected, despondent, downcast, lugubrious, miserable, morose.

ORIGIN – related to dialect *glum* 'to frown', variant of **GLOOM**.

gluon /ˈglōōon/ > *noun* Physics a hypothetical massless particle believed to transmit the force binding quarks together.

ORIGIN – from **GLUE**.

glut > *noun* an excessively abundant supply. > *verb* (**glutted, glutting**) supply or fill to excess.

SYNONYMS – *noun* excess, superabundance, surfeit, surplus. *verb* flood, inundate, saturate.

ORIGIN – probably from Latin *gluttire* 'to swallow'; related to **GLUTTON**.

glutamate /ˈglōōtəmayt/ > *noun* Biochemistry a salt or ester of an amino acid (**glutamic acid**) which is a constituent of many proteins.

ORIGIN – from **GLUTEN** + **AMINE**.

glutamine /ˈglōōtəmeen/ > *noun* Biochemistry an amino acid which is a constituent of most proteins.

gluten /ˈglōōt'n/ > *noun* a protein present in cereal grains, especially wheat, which is responsible for the elastic texture of dough.

ORIGIN – Latin, 'glue'.

gluteus /ˈglōōtiəss/ > *noun* (pl. **glutei** /ˈglōōti-ī/) any of three muscles in each buttock which move the thigh.

DERIVATIVES – **gluteal** *adjective*.

ORIGIN – Greek *gloutos* 'buttock'.

glutinous /ˈglōōtinəss/ > *adjective* like glue in texture; sticky.

DERIVATIVES – **glutinously** *adverb*.

ORIGIN – Latin *glutinosus*, from *gluten* 'glue'.

glutton > *noun* **1** an excessively greedy eater. **2** a person with a great eagerness or capacity for something: *a glutton for adventure*.

IDIOMS – **a glutton for punishment** a person who is eager to undertake difficult or unpleasant tasks.

DERIVATIVES – **gluttonous** *adjective*.

SYNONYMS – **1** gourmand, gorger, guzzler.

ORIGIN – Latin *glutto*, related to *gluttire* 'to swallow' and *gluttus* 'greedy'.

gluttony > *noun* habitual greed or excess in eating.

glycerine /ˈglissəreen/ (US **glycerin** /ˈglissərin/) > *noun* another term for **GLYCEROL**.

ORIGIN – from Greek *glukeros* 'sweet'.

glycerol /ˈglissərol/ > *noun* a colourless, sweet, viscous liquid, formed as a by-product in soap manufacture and used as an emollient and laxative.

glycine /ˈglīseen/ > *noun* Biochemistry the simplest naturally occurring amino acid, a constituent of most proteins.

ORIGIN – from Greek *glukus* 'sweet' + **–INE**[4].

glycogen /ˈglīkəjən/ > *noun* a substance deposited in bodily tissues as a store of carbohydrates.

glycol /ˈglīkol/ > *noun* short for *ethylene glycol*.

glycoprotein /ˈglīkōprōteen/ > *noun* any of a class of proteins which have carbohydrate groups attached to the polypeptide chain.

glycoside /ˈglīkəsīd/ > *noun* Biochemistry a compound formed from a simple sugar and another compound by replacement of a hydroxyl group in the sugar molecule.

glyph /glif/ > *noun* **1** a hieroglyphic character; a pictograph or sculptured symbol. **2** Architecture an ornamental carved groove or channel, as on a Greek frieze. **3** Computing a small graphic symbol.

ORIGIN – Greek *gluphē* 'carving'.

glyphosate /ˈglīfəsayt/ > *noun* a synthetic compound which is a non-selective systemic herbicide.

glyptic /gliptik/ > *adjective* of or concerning carving or engraving.

ORIGIN – from Greek *gluptēs* 'carver'.

GM > *abbreviation* **1** general manager. **2** genetically modified. **3** George Medal. **4** (of a school) grant-maintained.

gm > *abbreviation* gram(s).

G-man > *noun* informal **1** US an FBI agent. **2** Irish a political detective.

ORIGIN – probably an abbreviation of *Government man*.

GMO > *abbreviation* genetically modified organism.

GMT > *abbreviation* Greenwich Mean Time.

gn > *abbreviation* guinea(s).

gnarled /naarld/ > *adjective* knobbly, rough, and twisted, especially with age.

ORIGIN – variant of *knarled*, from obsolete *knarre* 'rugged rock or stone'.

gnarly > *adjective* (**gnarlier**, **gnarliest**) **1** gnarled. **2** N. Amer. informal dangerous, challenging, or unpleasant.

gnash /nash/ > *verb* grind (one's teeth) together, especially as a sign of anger.

ORIGIN – perhaps related to an Old Norse word meaning 'a gnashing of teeth'.

gnashers > *plural noun* Brit. informal teeth.

gnat /nat/ > *noun* a small two-winged fly resembling a mosquito.

gnaw /naw/ > *verb* **1** bite at or nibble persistently. **2** (often as adj. **gnawing**) cause persistent anxiety or pain.

DERIVATIVES – **gnawingly** adverb.

SYNONYMS – **1** bite, chew, masticate, nibble, worry.

ORIGIN – ultimately imitative.

gneiss /nīss/ > *noun* a metamorphic rock with a banded or foliated structure, typically consisting of feldspar, quartz, and mica.

ORIGIN – German, from High German *gneisto* 'spark' (because of the rock's sheen).

gnocchi /**nyokk**i/ > *plural noun* (in Italian cooking) small dumplings made from potato, semolina, or flour.

ORIGIN – Italian, plural of *gnocco*, alteration of *nocchio* 'knot in wood'.

gnome > *noun* **1** a legendary dwarfish creature supposed to guard the earth's treasures underground. **2** a small garden ornament in the form of a bearded man with a pointed hat. **3** informal a person having secret or sinister influence, especially in financial matters: *the gnomes of Zurich*.

DERIVATIVES – **gnomish** adjective.

ORIGIN – Latin *gnomus*, a word used by the Swiss physician Paracelsus (*c.*1493–1541) as a synonym of *Pygmaeus* 'pygmy'.

gnomic /nōmik/ > *adjective* **1** in the form of short, pithy maxims or aphorisms. **2** enigmatic; ambiguous.

DERIVATIVES – **gnomically** adverb.

ORIGIN – from Greek *gnōmē* 'thought, opinion'.

gnomon /nōmon/ > *noun* the projecting piece on a sundial that shows the time by its shadow.

ORIGIN – Greek *gnōmōn* 'indicator, carpenter's square'.

gnosis /nōsiss/ > *noun* knowledge of spiritual mysteries.

ORIGIN – Greek, 'knowledge'.

gnostic /nostik/ > *adjective* **1** relating to knowledge, especially esoteric mystical knowledge. **2** (**Gnostic**) relating to Gnosticism. > *noun* (**Gnostic**) an adherent of Gnosticism.

ORIGIN – Greek *gnōstikos*, from *gnōstos* 'known'.

Gnosticism /nostisiz'm/ > *noun* a heretical movement of the 2nd-century Christian Church, teaching that esoteric knowledge (gnosis) of the deity enabled the redemption of the human spirit.

GNP > *abbreviation* gross national product.

gnu /noo/ > *noun* a large African antelope with a long head and a beard and mane.

ORIGIN – from Khoikhoi and San, perhaps imitative of the sound made by the animal when alarmed.

GNVQ > *abbreviation* General National Vocational Qualification.

go¹ > *verb* (**goes**, **going**; past **went**; past participle **gone**) **1** move to or from a place. **2** pass into or be in a specified state: *her mind went blank*. **3** (**go to** or **into**) enter into a specified state or course of action: *go to sleep*. **4** lie or extend in a certain direction. **5** come to an end; cease to exist. **6** disappear or be used up. **7** (of time) pass. **8** pass time in a particular way: *they went for months without talking*. **9** engage in a specified activity. **10** have a particular outcome. **11** (**be going to be** or **do**) used to express a future tense. **12** function or operate. **13** be harmonious or matching. **14** be acceptable or permitted: *anything goes*. **15** fit into or be regularly kept in a particular place. **16** make a specified sound. **17** informal say. **18** (**go by** or **under**) be known or called by (a specified name). > *noun* (pl. **goes**) informal **1** an attempt: *give it a go*. **2** a turn to do or use something. **3** Brit. informal a single item, action, or spell of activity: *it costs ten quid a go*. **4** spirit or energy. **5** Brit. vigorous activity.

IDIOMS – **go about** begin or carry on work at. **go along with** agree to. **go at** energetically attack or tackle. **go back on** fail to keep (a promise). **go down 1** be defeated in a contest. **2** be recorded or remembered in a particular way. **3** elicit a specified reaction. **go for 1** decide on. **2** attempt to gain. **3** attack. **4** apply to. **go halves** (or **shares**) share something equally. **go in for 1** enter (a contest) as a competitor. **2** like or habitually take part in. **going!**, **gone!** an auctioneer's announcement that bidding is closing or closed. **go into 1** investigate or enquire into. **2** (of a whole number) be capable of dividing another, typically without a remainder. **go off 1** (of a gun or bomb) explode or fire. **2** chiefly Brit. (of food) begin to decompose. **3** informal, chiefly Brit. begin to dislike. **go on 1** continue or persevere. **2** take place. **3** proceed to do. **go out 1** be extinguished. **2** (of the tide) ebb. **3** carry on a regular romantic relationship with someone. **go over 1** examine or check the details of. **2** be received in a specified way. **go round** Brit. (N. Amer. **go around**) be sufficient to supply everybody present. **go through 1** undergo (a difficult experience). **2** examine carefully. **3** informal use up or spend. **go under** become bankrupt. **go with 1** give one's consent or agreement to. **2** have a romantic or sexual relationship with. **go without** suffer lack or deprivation. **have a go at** chiefly Brit. attack or criticise. **have a lot** (or **a little**) **going for one** informal have a lot (or a little) in one's favour or to one's advantage. **make a go of** informal be successful in. **no go** informal impossible, hopeless, or forbidden. **on the go** informal very active or busy. **to go** chiefly N. Amer. (of food or drink from a restaurant or cafe) to be eaten or drunk off the premises. **what goes around comes around** proverb the consequences of one's actions will have to be dealt with eventually.

SYNONYMS – *verb* **1** move, pass, proceed, progress. **7** elapse, fly, lapse, pass. **12** function, operate, work. **13** blend, harmonise, match. *noun* **1** attempt, try; informal shot, stab.

ANTONYMS – *verb* **1** come.

COMBINATIONS – **go-between** an intermediary or negotiator. **go-go 1** denoting an unrestrained and erotic style of dancing to popular music. **2** assertively dynamic. **go-slow** chiefly Brit. a form of industrial action in which work is delayed or slowed down.

go² > *noun* a Japanese board game of territorial possession and capture.

goad /gōd/ > *noun* **1** a spiked stick used for driving cattle. **2** a thing that stimulates someone into action. > *verb* **1** provoke to action. **2** urge on with a goad.

SYNONYMS – *verb* **1** badger, chivvy, prompt, spur.

go-ahead informal > *noun* (**the go-ahead**) permission to proceed. > *adjective* enterprising and ambitious.

goal > *noun* **1** (in soccer, rugby, etc.) a pair of posts linked by a crossbar and forming a space into or over which the ball has to be sent to score. **2** an instance of sending the ball into or over a goal. **3** an aim or desired result.

DERIVATIVES – **goalless** adjective.

SYNONYMS – **3** aim, end, objective, purpose, target.

COMBINATIONS – **goal average** Soccer the ratio of the numbers of goals scored for and against a team in a series of matches. **goal difference** Soccer the difference between the number of goals scored for and against a team in a series of matches. **goalkeeper** a player in soccer or field hockey whose special role is to stop the ball from entering the goal. **goal kick 1** Soccer a free kick taken by the defending side after attackers send the ball over the byline. **2** Rugby an attempt to kick a goal. **goal line** a line across a football or hockey field on which the goal is placed or which acts as the boundary beyond which a try or touchdown is scored.

goalie > noun informal a goalkeeper.

goalpost > noun either of the two upright posts of a goal.

IDIOMS – **move the goalposts** unfairly alter the conditions or rules of a procedure during its course.

goanna /gōannə/ > noun Austral. a monitor lizard.

ORIGIN – alteration of **IGUANA**.

goat > noun **1** a hardy domesticated mammal that has backward-curving horns and (in the male) a beard. **2** a wild mammal related to this, such as the ibex. **3** informal a lecherous man. **4** Brit. informal a stupid person.

WORDFINDER – caprine, hircine (*of or like a goat*), billy goat (*male goat*), kid (*young goat*), nanny (*female goat*); Capricorn (*zodiac sign, the Goat*), Capricornus (*constellation, the Goat*).

IDIOMS – **get someone's goat** informal irritate someone.

DERIVATIVES – **goatish** adjective **goaty** adjective.

COMBINATIONS – **goat-antelope** a mammal of a group including the chamois and musk ox, with characteristics of both goats and antelopes. **goatherd** a person who tends goats.

goatee /gōtee/ > noun a small pointed beard like that of a goat.

DERIVATIVES – **goateed** adjective.

gob[1] > noun informal, chiefly Brit. a person's mouth.

COMBINATIONS – **gobstopper** chiefly Brit. a large, hard, spherical sweet.

ORIGIN – perhaps from Scottish Gaelic.

gob[2] informal > noun **1** a lump or clot of a slimy or viscous substance. **2** (**gobs of**) N. Amer. a lot of. > verb (**gobbed, gobbing**) Brit. spit.

ORIGIN – Old French gobe 'mouthful, lump', from gober 'to swallow, gulp'.

gobbet /gobbit/ > noun a piece or lump of flesh, food, or other matter.

ORIGIN – Old French gobet 'little lump or mouthful'.

gobble[1] > verb (often **gobble up**) **1** eat hurriedly and noisily. **2** use a large amount of (something) very quickly.

DERIVATIVES – **gobbler** noun.

SYNONYMS – **1** bolt, devour, guzzle, wolf; informal scoff.

ORIGIN – probably from **GOB**[2].

gobble[2] > verb (of a turkeycock) make a characteristic swallowing sound.

DERIVATIVES – **gobbler** noun.

ORIGIN – imitative, perhaps influenced by **GOBBLE**[1].

gobbledegook /gobb'ldigōōk/ (also **gobbledygook**) > noun informal pompous or unintelligible jargon.

ORIGIN – probably imitating a turkey's gobble.

goblet > noun a drinking glass with a foot and a stem.

ORIGIN – Old French gobelet 'little cup'.

goblin > noun a mischievous, ugly, dwarf-like creature of folklore.

ORIGIN – Old French gobelin, possibly related to German Kobold (denoting a spirit who haunts houses or lives underground) or to Greek kobalos 'mischievous goblin'.

gobshite /gobshīt/ > noun vulgar slang, chiefly Irish a stupid or incompetent person.

gobsmacked > adjective Brit. informal utterly astonished.

DERIVATIVES – **gobsmacking** adjective.

goby /gōbi/ > noun (pl. **gobies**) a small marine fish, typically with a sucker on the underside.

ORIGIN – Greek kōbios.

go-cart > noun **1** variant spelling of **GO-KART**. **2** a handcart. **3** a pushchair.

God > noun **1** (in Christianity and other monotheistic religions) the creator and supreme ruler of the universe. **2** (**god**) a superhuman being or spirit worshipped as having power over nature and human fortunes. **3** (**god**) a greatly admired or influential person. **4** (**the gods**) informal the gallery in a theatre. > exclamation used to express surprise, anger, etc. or for emphasis.

WORDFINDER – atheism (*disbelief in a god or gods*), ditheism (*belief in two gods as independent principles of good and evil*), henotheism (*adherence to one god out of several*), pantheism (*belief that God is in everything*), polytheism (*belief in more than one god*), tritheism (*belief in the three persons of the Christian Trinity as three distinct gods*).

IDIOMS – **God the Father, Son, and Holy Ghost** (in Christian doctrine) the persons of the Trinity. **God Save the Queen** (or **King**) the British national anthem.

DERIVATIVES – **godhood** noun **godlike** adjective **godward** adjective & adverb.

SYNONYMS – **2** (**god**) deity, divinity, numen.

COMBINATIONS – **God-awful** informal extremely bad or unpleasant. **God-fearing** earnestly religious. **godforsaken** lacking any merit or attraction. **godhead 1** (**the Godhead**) God. **2** divine nature. **godsend** something very helpful or opportune. **God's gift** chiefly ironic the best possible person or thing. **Godspeed** dated an expression of good wishes to a person starting a journey.

godchild > noun (pl. **godchildren**) a person in relation to a godparent.

god-daughter > noun a female godchild.

goddess > noun **1** a female deity. **2** a woman who is adored, especially for her beauty.

godet /gōday/ > noun a triangular piece of material inserted in a garment to make it flared or for ornamentation.

ORIGIN – French.

godetia /gōdeeshə/ > noun a North American plant with showy lilac to red flowers.

ORIGIN – Latin, named after the Swiss botanist Charles H. Godet (1797–1879).

godfather > noun **1** a male godparent. **2** the male head of an illegal organisation, especially a leader of the American Mafia.

godless > adjective **1** not believing in a god or God. **2** profane; wicked.

DERIVATIVES – **godlessness** noun.

SYNONYMS – **1** agnostic, atheistic, faithless. **2** impious, irreligious, profane, wicked.

godly > adjective (**godlier, godliest**) devoutly religious; pious.

DERIVATIVES – **godliness** noun.

SYNONYMS – devout, God-fearing, holy, pious.

godmother > noun a female godparent.

godown /gōdown/ > noun (in east Asia, especially India) a warehouse.

ORIGIN – Portuguese gudão, from Tamil.

godparent > noun a person who presents a child at baptism and promises to take responsibility for their education as a Christian.

godson > noun a male godchild.

godwit > noun a large, long-legged wader with a long bill.

goer > noun **1** a person who regularly attends a specified place or event: a theatre-goer. **2** informal a person or thing that goes. **3** informal a sexually unrestrained woman.

goes third person singular present of **GO**[1].

gofer /gōfər/ (also **gopher**) > noun informal, chiefly N. Amer. a person who runs errands; a dogsbody.

ORIGIN – from go for (i.e. go and fetch).

goffer /goffər/ > verb crimp or flute (a lace edge or frill) with heated irons. > noun an iron used for goffering.

ORIGIN – French *gaufre* 'honeycomb', from Low German *wāfel* 'waffle'; compare with **WAFER**.

go-getter > *noun informal* an energetically enterprising person.

DERIVATIVES – **go-getting** *adjective*.

goggle > *verb* 1 look with wide open eyes. 2 (of the eyes) protrude or open wide. > *noun* (**goggles**) close-fitting protective glasses with side shields.

COMBINATIONS – **goggle-box** Brit. informal a television. **goggle-eyed** having wide-open eyes, especially through astonishment.

ORIGIN – probably from a base symbolic of oscillating movement.

going > *noun* 1 the condition of the ground viewed in terms of suitability for horse racing or walking. 2 conditions for, or progress in, an endeavour. > *adjective* 1 chiefly Brit. existing or available: *any jobs going?* 2 (of a price) acceptable or current.

COMBINATIONS – **going concern** a thriving business. **going-over** informal 1 a thorough cleaning or inspection. 2 a beating. **goings-on** activities of a suspect or unusual nature.

goitre /goytər/ (US **goiter**) > *noun* a swelling of the neck resulting from enlargement of the thyroid gland.

DERIVATIVES – **goitrous** *adjective*.

ORIGIN – French, or from Old French *goitron* 'gullet', both from Latin *guttur* 'throat'.

go-kart (also **go-cart**) > *noun* a small racing car with a lightweight or skeleton body.

gold > *noun* 1 a yellow precious metal, used in jewellery and decoration and as a monetary medium. 2 a deep lustrous yellow or yellow-brown colour. 3 coins or articles made of gold. 4 wealth.

WORDFINDER – auriferous (*containing gold*), carat (*measure of purity for gold*), El Dorado (*fabulous place full of gold*), electrum (*alloy of gold and silver*), gild (*cover with gold*), Midas touch (*power of turning everything into gold*), ormolu, pinchbeck (*gold-like alloys*).

IDIOMS – **pot** (or **crock**) **of gold** a large but distant or imaginary reward. [ORIGIN – with allusion to the story of a pot of gold supposedly to be found at the end of a rainbow.]

COMBINATIONS – **goldcrest** a very small songbird with a yellow or orange crest. **gold-digger** informal a woman who forms relationships with men purely for financial gain. **gold disc** a framed golden disc awarded to a recording artist or group for sales exceeding a specified figure. **gold dust** 1 fine particles of gold. 2 something rare and very valuable. **goldfield** a district in which gold is found as a mineral. **goldfinch** a brightly coloured finch with a yellow patch on each wing. **gold leaf** gold beaten into a very thin sheet, used in gilding. **gold medal** a medal made of or coloured gold, awarded for first place in a race or competition. **gold mine** 1 a place where gold is mined. 2 a source of great wealth or valuable resources. **gold reserve** a quantity of gold held by a central bank. **gold rush** a rapid movement of people to a newly discovered goldfield. **goldsmith** a person who makes gold articles. **gold standard** historical the system by which the value of a currency was defined in terms of gold.

golden > *adjective* 1 made of or resembling gold. 2 precious or excellent.

COMBINATIONS – **golden age** 1 an idyllic, often imaginary past time of peace, prosperity, and happiness. 2 the period when a specified art or activity is at its peak. **golden boy** (or **golden girl**) informal a very popular or successful young man or woman. **Golden Delicious** a variety of dessert apple with a greenish-yellow skin. **golden eagle** a large eagle with yellow-tipped head feathers. **golden goose** a continuing source of wealth or profit that may be exhausted if it is misused. **golden handcuffs** informal benefits provided by an employer to discourage an employee from working elsewhere. **golden handshake** informal a payment given to someone who is made redundant or retires early. **golden jubilee** the fiftieth anniversary of a significant event. **golden mean** the ideal moderate position between two extremes. **golden oldie** informal 1 an old song of enduring popularity. 2 a person who is no longer young but is still successful. **golden parachute** informal a payment guaranteed to a company executive should they be dismissed as a result of a merger or takeover. **golden retriever** a breed of retriever with a thick golden-coloured coat. **goldenrod** a plant with tall spikes of small bright yellow flowers. **golden rule** a basic principle which should always be followed. **golden section** the division of a line so that the ratio of the whole to the larger part is the same as the ratio of the larger part to the smaller part, a proportion considered to be particularly pleasing to the eye. **golden share** Brit. a share in a company that gives control of at least 51 per cent of the voting rights. **golden syrup** Brit. a pale treacle. **golden wedding** the fiftieth anniversary of a wedding.

goldeneye > *noun* a northern diving duck, the male of which has a dark head with a white cheek patch and yellow eyes.

goldfish > *noun* a small reddish-golden carp popular in ponds and aquaria.

COMBINATIONS – **goldfish bowl** chiefly Brit. 1 a spherical glass container for goldfish. 2 a place or situation lacking privacy or creating a feeling of claustrophobia.

gold plate > *noun* 1 a thin layer of gold applied as a coating to another metal. 2 plates, dishes, etc. made of or plated with gold. > *verb* (**gold-plate**) cover with gold plate.

golem /gōləm/ > *noun* 1 (in Jewish legend) a clay figure brought to life by magic. 2 an automaton or robot.

ORIGIN – Hebrew, 'shapeless mass'.

golf > *noun* a game played on an outdoor course, the aim of which is to strike a small, hard ball with a club into a series of small holes with the fewest possible strokes. > *verb* (usu. as noun **golfing**) play golf.

WORDFINDER – caddie (*golfer's assistant*); par (*standard number of strokes required for hole or course*), birdie (*hole played in one stroke less than par*), eagle (*two less than par*), albatross (*three less than par*), bogey (*one stroke more than par*); *golf clubs:* driver, iron, putter, wedge, wood; (*informal or dated*) brassie, mashie, niblick.

DERIVATIVES – **golfer** *noun*.

COMBINATIONS – **golf ball** 1 a ball used in golf. 2 (**golfball**) a small metal globe used in some typewriters to carry the type.

ORIGIN – perhaps related to Dutch *kolf* 'club, bat'.

golliwog > *noun* a soft doll with a black face and fuzzy hair.

ORIGIN – from *Golliwogg*, the name of a doll character in books by the US writer Bertha Upton (died 1912).

golly[1] > *exclamation* informal used to express surprise or delight.

ORIGIN – euphemism for **GOD**.

golly[2] > *noun* (pl. **gollies**) Brit. informal a golliwog.

-gon > *combining form* in nouns denoting plane figures with a specified number of angles and sides: *hexagon*.

ORIGIN – from Greek *-gōnos* '-angled'.

gonad /gōnad/ > *noun* a bodily organ that produces gametes; a testis or ovary.

DERIVATIVES – **gonadal** *adjective*.

ORIGIN – from Greek *gonē* 'generation, seed'.

gonadotrophin /gōnadōtrōfin/ (also **gonadotropin** /gōnadōtrōpin/) > *noun* any of a group of hormones secreted by the pituitary gland which stimulate the activity of the gonads.

gondola /gondələ/ > *noun* 1 a light flat-bottomed boat used on Venetian canals, having a high point at each end and worked by one oar at the stern. 2 a cabin on a ski lift, or suspended from an airship or balloon.

ORIGIN – Venetian Italian.

gondolier /gondəleer/ > *noun* a person who propels and steers a gondola.

gone past participle of **GO**[1]. > *adjective* 1 no longer present or in existence. 2 informal in a trance or stupor, especially through alcohol or drugs. **3** informal having reached a specified time in a pregnancy: *four months gone.* > *preposition* Brit. **1** (of time) past. **2** (of age) older than.

IDIOMS – **be gone on** informal be infatuated with.

goner /gonnər/ > *noun* informal a person or thing that is doomed or cannot be saved.

gong > *noun* **1** a metal disc with a turned rim, giving a resonant note when struck. **2** Brit. informal a medal or decoration. > *verb* sound a gong or make a sound like that of a gong.
ORIGIN – Malay.

gonna > *contraction* informal going to.

gonorrhoea /gonnəreeə/ (US **gonorrhea**) > *noun* a sexually transmitted disease involving inflammatory discharge from the urethra or vagina.
ORIGIN – Greek *gonorrhoia*, from *gonos* 'semen' + *rhoia* 'flux'.

gonzo > *adjective* informal, chiefly N. Amer. **1** of or associated with journalism of an exaggerated, subjective, and fictionalised style. **2** bizarre or crazy.
ORIGIN – perhaps from Italian *gonzo* 'foolish' or Spanish *ganso* 'goose, fool'.

goo > *noun* informal a sticky or slimy substance.
ORIGIN – perhaps from *burgoo*, a nautical slang term for porridge, from a Persian word meaning 'bruised grain'.

good > *adjective* (**better**, **best**) **1** to be desired or approved of. **2** having the required qualities; of a high standard. **3** morally right; virtuous. **4** well behaved. **5** enjoyable or satisfying. **6** appropriate. **7** (**good for**) beneficial to. **8** thorough. **9** at least: *she's a good twenty years younger.* > *noun* **1** that which is morally right or beneficial. **2** (**goods**) merchandise or possessions. **3** (**goods**) Brit. freight.
IDIOMS – **as good as** —— very nearly ——. **be** —— **to the good** have a specified net profit or advantage. **come up with** (or **deliver**) **the goods** informal do what is expected or required. **do good 1** act virtuously, especially by helping others. **2** be helpful or beneficial. **for good** forever. **the Good Book** the Bible. **good for** (or **on**) **you!** well done! **a good word** words in recommendation or defence of a person. **in good time 1** with no risk of being late. **2** (also **all in good time**) in due course but without haste. **make good 1** compensate for (loss, damage, or expense). **2** fulfil (a promise or claim). **3** be successful. **take something in good part** not be offended.
SYNONYMS – *adjective* **1** beneficial, desirable, valuable. **2** acceptable, adequate, fine, satisfactory. **3** ethical, moral, righteous, virtuous. **5** agreeable, enjoyable, pleasing,

pleasurable, satisfying. **6** appropriate, fitting, suitable. *noun* **1** goodness, morality, virtue.
ANTONYMS – *adjective* bad. *noun* **1** evil.
COMBINATIONS – **good faith** honesty or sincerity of intention. **good form** behaviour complying with social conventions. **Good Friday** (in the Christian Church) the Friday before Easter Sunday, on which the Crucifixion of Christ is commemorated. **good-hearted** kind and well meaning. **good-humoured** genial or cheerful. **good-looking** attractive. **good-natured** kind and unselfish. **goodnight** expressing good wishes on parting at night or before going to bed. **goods and chattels** all kinds of personal possessions. **good-tempered** not easily irritated or made angry. **good-time** recklessly pursuing pleasure. **goodwill 1** friendly or helpful feelings or attitude. **2** the established reputation of a business regarded as a quantifiable asset. **good works** charitable acts.

goodbye (US also **goodby**) > *exclamation* used to express good wishes when parting or ending a conversation. > *noun* (pl. **goodbyes**; US also **goodbys**) an instance of saying 'goodbye'; a parting.
ORIGIN – contraction of *God be with you!*

good-for-nothing > *adjective* worthless. > *noun* a worthless person.

goodie > *noun* variant spelling of GOODY.

goodish > *adjective* **1** fairly good. **2** fairly large.

goodly > *adjective* (**goodlier**, **goodliest**) **1** considerable in size or quantity. **2** archaic attractive, excellent, or virtuous.

goodness > *noun* **1** the quality of being good. **2** the nutritious element of food. > *exclamation* (as a substitution for 'God') expressing surprise, anger, etc.

goody > *noun* (also **goodie**) (pl. **goodies**) informal **1** Brit. a good or favoured person, especially a hero in a story or film. **2** (**goodies**) tasty things to eat. > *exclamation* expressing childish delight.

goody-goody informal > *noun* a smugly virtuous person. > *adjective* smugly virtuous.

gooey > *adjective* (**gooier**, **gooiest**) informal **1** soft and sticky. **2** mawkishly sentimental.
DERIVATIVES – **gooeyness** noun.

goof informal, chiefly N. Amer. > *noun* **1** a mistake. **2** a foolish or stupid person. > *verb* **1** fool around. **2** make a mistake.

goofy > *adjective* (**goofier**, **goofiest**) informal **1** chiefly N. Amer. foolish; harmlessly eccentric. **2** having protruding or crooked front teeth.
DERIVATIVES – **goofily** adverb **goofiness** noun.

goog > *noun* Austral./NZ informal an egg.
IDIOMS – (**as**) **full as a goog** very drunk.

ORIGIN – from Scottish dialect *goggie*, a child's word for an egg.

googly > *noun* (pl. **googlies**) Cricket an off break bowled with an apparent leg-break action.

gook[1] /gook/ > *noun* N. Amer. informal, offensive a person of SE Asian descent.

gook[2] /gook/ (also N. Amer. **guck**) > *noun* informal a sloppy wet or viscous substance.

goolie (also **gooly**) > *noun* (pl. **goolies**) Brit. informal a testicle.
ORIGIN – perhaps related to a Hindi word meaning 'bullet, ball, pill'.

goon > *noun* informal **1** a foolish or eccentric person. **2** chiefly N. Amer. a ruffian or thug.
ORIGIN – perhaps from dialect *gooney* 'stupid person'; later influenced by the American cartoon character 'Alice the *Goon*'.

goosander /goosandər/ > *noun* (pl. same or **goosanders**) a large merganser (diving duck), the male of which has a dark green head and whitish underparts.
ORIGIN – probably from GOOSE + *-ander* as in dialect *bergander* 'shelduck'.

goose > *noun* (pl. **geese**) **1** a large waterbird with a long neck, short legs, webbed feet, and a short, broad bill. **2** the female of such a bird. **3** informal a foolish person. > *verb* informal poke (someone) in the bottom.
WORDFINDER – anserine (*of or like a goose*), gaggle (*flock of geese*), gander (*male goose*), gosling (*young goose*), skein (*line of flying geese*).
COMBINATIONS – **goose egg** N. Amer. informal a zero score in a game. **gooseflesh** (also chiefly N. Amer. **goosebumps**) a pimply state of the skin with the hairs erect, produced by cold or fright. **goosefoot** (pl. **goosefoots**) a plant with divided leaves which are said to resemble the foot of a goose. **goosegrass** a widely distributed scrambling plant with hooked bristles on the stem, leaves, and seeds. **goose pimples** gooseflesh.

gooseberry > *noun* (pl. **gooseberries**) **1** a round edible yellowish-green berry with a hairy skin, growing on a thorny shrub. **2** Brit. informal a third person in the company of two lovers, who would prefer to be alone.
ORIGIN – the first element is perhaps from GOOSE, or is perhaps based on Old French *groseille*. Sense 2 may be from *gooseberry-picking*, with reference to such an activity as a pretext for lovers to be together.

goose step > *noun* a military marching step in which the legs are not bent at the knee. > *verb* (**goose-step**) march with such a step.

GOP > *abbreviation* informal Grand Old Party (a name for the US Republican Party).

gopher /gōfər/ > *noun* **1** (also **pocket gopher**) a burrowing American rodent with pouches on its cheeks. **2** N. Amer. informal a ground squirrel. **3** variant spelling of **GOFER**.

ORIGIN – perhaps from Canadian French *gaufre* 'honeycomb' (because the gopher 'honeycombs' the ground with its burrows).

gopik /gōpik/ > *noun* (pl. same or **gopiks**) a monetary unit of Azerbaijan, equal to one hundredth of a manat.

gorblimey > *exclamation* Brit. informal an expression of surprise or indignation.

ORIGIN – alteration of *God blind me*.

Gordian knot /gordiən/ > *noun* (in phrase **cut the Gordian knot**) solve a difficult problem in a direct or forceful way.

ORIGIN – from the legendary knot tied by *Gordius*, king of Gordium, and cut through by Alexander the Great in response to the prophecy that whoever untied it would rule Asia.

Gordon Bennett > *exclamation* expressing surprise, incredulity, or exasperation.

ORIGIN – probably an alteration of **GORBLIMEY**, after the American publisher and sports sponsor James *Gordon Bennett* (1841–1918).

gore¹ > *noun* blood that has been shed, especially as a result of violence.

ORIGIN – Old English, 'dung, dirt'.

gore² > *verb* (of an animal such as a bull) pierce or stab with a horn or tusk.

gore³ > *noun* a triangular or tapering piece of material used in making a garment, sail, or umbrella. > *verb* shape with a gore or gores.

ORIGIN – Old English, 'triangular piece of land'.

Gore-tex /gorteks/ > *noun* trademark a breathable waterproof fabric used in outdoor clothing.

gorge > *noun* **1** a steep, narrow valley or ravine. **2** archaic the contents of the stomach. > *verb* eat a large amount greedily.

IDIOMS – **one's gorge rises** one is sickened or disgusted.

DERIVATIVES – **gorger** *noun*.

ORIGIN – Old French, 'throat', from Latin *gurges* 'whirlpool'.

gorgeous > *adjective* **1** very attractive. **2** informal very pleasant.

DERIVATIVES – **gorgeously** *adverb* **gorgeousness** *noun*.

SYNONYMS – **1** beautiful, dazzling, lovely, stunning.

ORIGIN – Old French *gorgias* 'fine, elegant'.

gorget /gorjit/ > *noun* **1** historical an article of clothing or piece of armour covering the throat. **2** a patch of colour on the throat of a bird or other animal.

ORIGIN – Old French *gorgete*, from *gorge* 'throat'.

gorgio /gorjiō/ > *noun* (pl. **gorgios**) the gypsy name for a non-gypsy.

ORIGIN – Romany.

gorgon /gorgən/ > *noun* **1** Greek Mythology each of three sisters with snakes for hair, who had the power to turn anyone who looked at them to stone. **2** a fierce, frightening, or repulsive woman.

ORIGIN – Greek *Gorgō*, from *gorgos* 'terrible'.

Gorgonzola /gorgənzōlə/ > *noun* a rich, strong-flavoured Italian cheese with bluish-green veins.

ORIGIN – named after the Italian village of *Gorgonzola*.

gorilla > *noun* **1** a powerfully built great ape of central Africa, the largest living primate. **2** informal a heavily built aggressive-looking man.

ORIGIN – Greek, representing an alleged African word for a wild or hairy person.

gormless > *adjective* Brit. informal stupid or slow-witted.

DERIVATIVES – **gormlessly** *adverb* **gormlessness** *noun*.

ORIGIN – from dialect *gaum* 'understanding', from Old Norse *gaumr* 'care, heed'.

gorse > *noun* a yellow-flowered shrub, the leaves of which have the form of spines.

gory > *adjective* (**gorier**, **goriest**) **1** involving violence and bloodshed. **2** covered in blood.

IDIOMS – **the gory details** humorous explicit details.

DERIVATIVES – **goriness** *noun*.

SYNONYMS – **1** bloody, brutal, sanguinary, violent.

gosh > *exclamation* informal used to express surprise or give emphasis.

ORIGIN – euphemism for **GOD**.

goshawk /goss-hawk/ > *noun* a short-winged hawk resembling a large sparrowhawk.

ORIGIN – Old English 'goose hawk'.

gosling > *noun* a young goose.

ORIGIN – Old Norse, from *gás* 'goose'.

gospel > *noun* **1** the teachings of Christ. **2** (**Gospel**) the record of Christ's life and teaching in the first four books of the New Testament. **3** (**Gospel**) each of these books. **4** (also **gospel truth**) something absolutely true. **5** (also **gospel music**) a fervent style of black American evangelical religious singing.

ORIGIN – Old English, 'good news'.

gospeller (US **gospeler**) > *noun* **1** a zealous preacher. **2** the reader of the Gospel in a Communion service.

gossamer > *noun* a fine, filmy substance consisting of cobwebs spun by small spiders. > *adjective* very fine and insubstantial.

wordpower facts
Gossamer

The word **gossamer** is apparently formed from **GOOSE** and **SUMMER**. The connection is uncertain, but it may be a reference to the time of year (early November) when geese were traditionally eaten and gossamer is often seen. The time around St Martin's day (11 November) was known as 'St Martin's summer' because the weather was often fine then, and gossamer is most easily seen in sunny conditions.

gossip > *noun* **1** casual conversation or unsubstantiated reports about other people. **2** chiefly derogatory a person who likes talking about other people's private lives. > *verb* (**gossiped**, **gossiping**) engage in gossip.

DERIVATIVES – **gossiper** *noun* **gossipy** *adjective*.

SYNONYMS – *noun* **1** hearsay, rumour, tittle-tattle. **2** busybody; archaic quidnunc. *verb* chat, chatter, prattle.

COMBINATIONS – **gossip column** a section of a newspaper devoted to gossip about well-known people.

wordpower facts
Gossip

A **gossip** was originally a rather more serious and worthy person than one might imagine. In Old English the word was spelled *godsibb* and meant 'godfather, godmother, baptismal sponsor', literally 'a person related to one in God'; it came from *sibb* 'a relative', the source of **sibling**. In medieval times the sense was 'a close friend, a person with whom one gossips', hence 'a person who gossips', later (early 19th century) 'idle talk'.

got past and past participle of **GET**.

Goth /goth/ > *noun* **1** a member of a Germanic people that invaded the Roman Empire between the 3rd and 5th centuries. **2** (**goth**) a style of rock music typically having apocalyptic or mystical lyrics. **3** a member of a subculture favouring black clothing and goth music.

ORIGIN – Greek *Gothoi*, from Gothic.

Gothic > *adjective* **1** relating to the ancient Goths or their language. **2** of the style of architecture prevalent in western Europe in the 12th–16th centuries, with pointed arches. **3** portentously gloomy or horrifying. **4** (of lettering) derived from the angular style of handwriting with broad vertical downstrokes used in medieval western Europe. > *noun* **1** the language of the Goths. **2** Gothic architecture. **3** Gothic type.

DERIVATIVES – **Gothicism** *noun*.

COMBINATIONS – **gothic novel** an English genre of fiction popular in the 18th to early 19th centuries, characterised by an atmosphere of mystery and horror.

gotten N. Amer. past participle of **GET**.

gouache /goōaash/ > *noun* **1** a method of painting using opaque pigments ground in water and thickened with a glue-like substance. **2** paint of this kind.

ORIGIN – French, from Italian *guazzo*.

Gouda /gowdə/ > *noun* a flat, round Dutch cheese with a yellow rind.

ORIGIN – from *Gouda* in the Netherlands, where it was originally made.

gouge /gowj/ > *verb* **1** make (a rough hole or indentation) in a surface. **2** (**gouge out**) cut or force out roughly or brutally. > *noun* **1** a chisel with a concave blade. **2** an indentation or groove made by gouging.

DERIVATIVES – **gouger** *noun*.

ORIGIN – Old French, from Latin *gubia*, *gulbia*.

goujons /goōjənz/ > *plural noun* Brit. deep-fried strips of chicken or fish.

ORIGIN – French *goujon* 'gudgeon'.

goulash /goōlash/ > *noun* a rich Hungarian stew of meat and vegetables, flavoured with paprika.

ORIGIN – from Hungarian *gulyás* 'herdsman' + *hús* 'meat'.

gourami /gooraami/ > *noun* (pl. **gouramis**) an Asian fish of a large group including many kinds popular in aquaria.

ORIGIN – Malay.

gourd /goord/ > *noun* **1** the large hard-skinned fleshy fruit of a climbing or trailing plant. **2** a container made from the hollowed and dried skin of a gourd.

ORIGIN – Old French *gourde*, from Latin *cucurbita*.

gourde > *noun* the basic monetary unit of Haiti, equal to 100 centimes.

ORIGIN – formerly the Franco-American name for a dollar: from French *gourde* 'stupid, dull, heavy'.

gourmand /goormand/ > *noun* **1** a person who enjoys eating, sometimes to excess. **2** a connoisseur of good food; a gourmet.

USAGE – the words **gourmand** and **gourmet** overlap in meaning but are not identical: both can be used to mean 'a connoisseur of good food', but a **gourmand** is more usually 'a person who enjoys eating and sometimes eats too much'.

ORIGIN – Old French.

gourmandise (also **gourmandize**) > *verb* indulge in good eating; eat greedily. > *noun* appreciation or consumption of good food.

gourmet /goormay/ > *noun* **1** a connoisseur of good food. **2** (before another noun) suitable for a gourmet: *a gourmet meal*.

SYNONYMS – **1** epicure, gastronome.

ORIGIN – French, originally 'wine taster', influenced by **GOURMAND**.

gout /gowt/ > *noun* **1** a disease in which defective metabolism of uric acid causes arthritis, especially in the smaller bones of the feet. **2** literary a drop or spot.

DERIVATIVES – **gouty** *adjective*.

ORIGIN – Latin *gutta* 'drop' (because gout was believed to be caused by diseased matter dropped from the blood into the joints).

govern > *verb* **1** manage the policy and affairs of (a state, organisation, or people). **2** control or influence. **3** constitute a rule, standard, or principle for. **4** Grammar (of a word) require that (another word or group of words) be in a particular case.

DERIVATIVES – **governability** *noun* **governable** *adjective*.

SYNONYMS – **1** administer, command, control, direct, manage, rule, run. **2** control, determine, influence, sway.

COMBINATIONS – **governing body** a group of people who govern an institution in partnership with the managers.

ORIGIN – Old French *governer*, from Greek *kubernan* 'to steer'.

governance > *noun* the action or manner of governing.

governess > *noun* a woman employed to teach children in a private household.

DERIVATIVES – **governessy** *adjective*.

government > *noun* **1** the governing body of a state. **2** the system by which a state or community is governed. **3** the action or manner of governing a state, organisation, or people.

DERIVATIVES – **governmental** *adjective*.

SYNONYMS – **1** administration, regime. **3** administration, command, direction, guidance, management.

COMBINATIONS – **Government House** Brit. the official residence of a governor. **government securities** bonds or other promissory certificates issued by the government.

governor > *noun* **1** an official appointed to govern a town or region. **2** the elected executive head of a US state. **3** the representative of the British Crown in a colony or in a Commonwealth state that regards the monarch as head of state. **4** the head of a public institution. **5** a member of a governing body. **6** Brit. informal the person in authority in a particular place or situation. **7** a device automatically regulating the supply of fuel, steam, or water to a machine.

DERIVATIVES – **governorate** *noun* **governorship** *noun*.

COMBINATIONS – **Governor-General** (pl. **Governors-General**) the chief representative of the Crown in a Commonwealth country of which the British monarch is head of state.

gown > *noun* **1** a long dress worn on formal occasions. **2** a protective garment worn in hospital by surgical staff or patients. **3** a loose cloak indicating one's profession or status, worn by a lawyer, teacher, academic, or university student. **4** the members of a university as distinct from the residents of a town. Contrasted with **TOWN**. > *verb* (**be gowned**) be dressed in a gown.

ORIGIN – Old French *goune*, from Latin *gunna* 'fur garment'.

goy /goy/ > *noun* (pl. **goyim** /goyim/ or **goys**) informal, offensive a Jewish name for a non-Jew.

DERIVATIVES – **goyish** *adjective*.

ORIGIN – Hebrew, 'people, nation'.

GP > *abbreviation* **1** general practitioner. **2** Grand Prix.

gr. > *abbreviation* **1** grain(s). **2** gram(s). **3** gross.

grab > *verb* (**grabbed**, **grabbing**) **1** seize suddenly and roughly. **2** informal obtain quickly or opportunistically. **3** informal impress: *how does that grab you?* > *noun* **1** a quick sudden attempt to seize. **2** a mechanical device for gripping, lifting, and moving loads.

IDIOMS – **up for grabs** informal available.

DERIVATIVES – **grabber** *noun*.

SYNONYMS – *verb* **1** grasp, pluck, seize, snatch.

COMBINATIONS – **grab bag** N. Amer. **1** a lucky dip in which wrapped items are chosen blindly from a bag. **2** an assortment of items in a sealed bag which one buys or is given without knowing what the contents are.

ORIGIN – Low German and Dutch *grabben*.

grace > *noun* **1** elegance of movement. **2** courteous good will: *she had the grace to look sheepish*. **3** (**graces**) attractive qualities or behaviour: *a horrible character with no saving graces*. **4** (in Christian belief) the free and unearned favour of God. **5** a person's favour. **6** a period officially allowed for fulfilment of an obligation. **7** a short prayer of thanks said before or after a meal. **8** (**His**, **Her**, or **Your Grace**) used as forms of description or address for a duke, duchess, or archbishop. > *verb* **1** honour by one's presence. **2** be an attractive presence in or on.

IDIOMS – **be in someone's good** (or **bad**) **graces** be regarded by someone with favour (or disfavour). **the (Three) Graces** Greek Mythology three beautiful goddesses, daughters of Zeus, believed to personify and bestow charm, grace, and beauty. **with**

good (or **bad**) **grace** in a willing (or reluctant) manner.
SYNONYMS – *noun* **1** ease, elegance, fluidity, poise. **2** courtesy, graciousness. *verb* **1** dignify, distinguish, honour.
COMBINATIONS – **grace and favour** Brit. (of accommodation) occupied by permission of a sovereign or government. **grace note** Music an extra note added as an embellishment and not essential to the harmony or melody.
ORIGIN – Latin *gratia*, from *gratus* 'pleasing, thankful'.

graceful > *adjective* having or showing grace or elegance.
DERIVATIVES – **gracefully** *adverb* **gracefulness** *noun*.
SYNONYMS – elegant, fluid, lissom, lithe, refined.
ANTONYMS – graceless.

graceless > *adjective* lacking grace, elegance, or charm.
DERIVATIVES – **gracelessly** *adverb* **gracelessness** *noun*.
SYNONYMS – awkward, clumsy, gauche, inelegant, uncouth.
ANTONYMS – graceful.

gracious > *adjective* **1** courteous, kind, and pleasant. **2** showing the elegance and comfort associated with high social status or wealth. **3** (in Christian belief) showing divine grace. > *exclamation* expressing polite surprise.
DERIVATIVES – **graciously** *adverb* **graciousness** *noun*.
SYNONYMS – *adjective* **1** charitable, considerate, courteous, kind, polite.

grackle > *noun* **1** a songbird of the American blackbird family, the male of which is shiny black with a blue-green sheen. **2** an Asian mynah or starling with mainly black plumage.
ORIGIN – Latin *graculus* 'jackdaw'.

gradation > *noun* **1** a scale of successive changes, stages, or degrees. **2** a stage in a such a scale.
DERIVATIVES – **gradational** *adjective*.

grade > *noun* **1** a specified level of rank, quality, proficiency, or value. **2** a mark indicating the quality of a student's work. **3** N. Amer. those pupils in a school who are grouped by age or ability for teaching at a particular level for a year: *first grade*. > *verb* **1** arrange in or allocate to grades. **2** pass gradually from one level to another. **3** N. Amer. give a grade to (a student or their work). **4** reduce (a road) to an easy gradient.
IDIOMS – **make the grade** informal succeed.
SYNONYMS – *noun* **1** class, degree, echelon, level, rank. *verb* **1** classify, rank, rate.
COMBINATIONS – **grade crossing** N. Amer. a

level crossing. **grade school** N. Amer. elementary school.

wordpower facts
Grade
The word **grade** is from Latin *gradus* 'step', which, with the related verb *gradi* 'walk, step, proceed', is the ancestor of many English words. Words from *gradus* include **centigrade**, **degrade**, **degree**, **gradation**, **gradual**, and **retrograde**, while *gradi* (stem gress-) gave rise to **aggression**, **congress**, **ingredient**, and **progress**.

grader > *noun* **1** a person or thing that grades. **2** N. Amer. a pupil of a specified grade in a school: *a first-grader*.

gradient /**gray**diənt/ > *noun* **1** a sloping part of a road or railway. **2** the degree of a slope, expressed as change of height divided by distance travelled. **3** Physics a change in the magnitude of a property (e.g. temperature) observed in passing from one point or moment to another.
SYNONYMS – **1** acclivity, declivity, incline, slope.

gradual > *adjective* **1** taking place in stages over an extended period. **2** (of a slope) not steep or abrupt.
DERIVATIVES – **gradually** *adverb* **gradualness** *noun*.

gradualism > *noun* a policy or theory of gradual rather than sudden change.
DERIVATIVES – **gradualist** *noun*.

graduand /**grad**yooand/ > *noun* Brit. a person about to receive an academic degree.

graduate > *noun* /**grad**yooət/ a person who has been awarded a first academic degree, or (N. Amer.) a high-school diploma. > *verb* /**grad**yooayt/ **1** successfully complete a degree, course, or (N. Amer.) high school. **2** (**graduate to**) move up to (something more advanced). **3** arrange or mark out in gradations. **4** change gradually.
DERIVATIVES – **graduation** *noun*.
COMBINATIONS – **graduate school** N. Amer. a department of a university for advanced work by graduates.
ORIGIN – from Latin *graduare* 'take a degree', from *gradus* 'degree, step'.

Graeco- /**gree**kō/ (also **Greco-**) > *combining form* Greek; Greek and …: *Graeco-Roman*.
ORIGIN – from Latin *Graecus* 'Greek'.

graffiti /grəfeeti/ > *plural noun* (sing. **graffito** /grəfeetō/) (treated as sing. or pl.) unauthorised writing or drawings on a surface in a public place. > *verb* write or draw graffiti on.
DERIVATIVES – **graffitist** *noun*.
USAGE – in Italian the word **graffiti** is a

plural noun, but in modern English it is generally treated as a singular, similar to a word like **writing**.
ORIGIN – Italian, from *graffio* 'a scratch'.

graft¹ > *noun* **1** a shoot from one plant inserted into a slit cut into another to form a new growth. **2** a piece of living bodily tissue that is transplanted surgically to replace diseased or damaged tissue. **3** an operation in which tissue is transplanted. > *verb* **1** insert or transplant as a graft. **2** (often **graft on**) incorporate in or attach to something else, especially inappropriately.
WORDFINDER – rootstock (*plant on to which another is grafted*), scion (*plant shoot cut for grafting on to rootstock*).

wordpower facts
Graft
Graft is linked to a range of words apparently unrelated to it. It comes from Greek *graphion* 'writing implement', with reference to the tapered tip of a plant shoot. Its ultimate root, *graphein* 'write', is the source of words such as **diagram**, **geography**, **graphic**, **paragraph**, **pornography**, and **programme**. The slang use of **graft** to mean 'hard work' possibly arose from the phrase *spade's graft* 'the amount of earth that one stroke of a spade will move'; *graft* in this case is from an unrelated Old Norse word meaning 'digging'.

graft² Brit. informal > *noun* hard work. > *verb* work hard.
DERIVATIVES – **grafter** *noun*.

graft³ informal > *noun* bribery and other corrupt measures pursued for gain in politics or business. > *verb* make money by graft.
DERIVATIVES – **grafter** *noun*.

graham > *adjective* N. Amer. denoting wholewheat flour, or biscuits or bread made from it.
ORIGIN – named after the American advocate of dietary reform Sylvester *Graham* (1794–1851).

Grail (also **Holy Grail**) > *noun* (in medieval legend) the cup or platter used by Christ at the Last Supper and in which Joseph of Arimathea received Christ's blood, especially as the object of quests by knights.
ORIGIN – Old French *graal*, from Latin *gradalis* 'dish'.

grain > *noun* **1** wheat or other cultivated cereal used as food. **2** a single seed or fruit of a cereal. **3** a small, hard particle of a substance such as sand. **4** the smallest unit of weight in the troy and avoirdupois systems, equal to ⅟₅₇₆₀ of a pound troy and ⅟₇₀₀₀ of a pound avoirdupois (approximately 0.0648 grams). **5** the smallest possible amount: *there wasn't a grain of truth in it.* **6** the longitudinal arrangement of fibres, particles, or layers in wood, paper, rock, etc. **7** the texture resulting from the grain of wood, rock, etc. **8** a grainy appearance of a photograph or negative. > *verb* **1** give a rough surface or texture to. **2** form into grains.

WORDFINDER – glean (*gather leftover grain*), granivorous (*eating grain*), grist (*grain for milling*), thresh (*separate grain from chaff by beating*), winnow (*separate grain from chaff by the wind*).

IDIOMS – **against the grain** contrary to one's nature or instinct.

DERIVATIVES – **grainer** noun **grainless** *adjective.*

ORIGIN – Old French, from Latin *granum*; sense 4 arose because the weight was originally equivalent to that of a grain of wheat.

grainy > *adjective* (**grainier**, **grainiest**) **1** granular. **2** (of a photograph) showing visible grains of emulsion. **3** (of wood) having prominent grain.

DERIVATIVES – **graininess** noun.

gram (Brit. also **gramme**) > *noun* a metric unit of mass equal to one thousandth of a kilogram.

ORIGIN – French *gramme*, from Latin *gramma* 'a small weight'.

-gram > *combining form* forming nouns denoting something written or recorded: *anagram.*

ORIGIN – from Greek *gramma* 'thing written, letter of the alphabet'.

graminivorous /grammi**nivv**ərəss/ > *adjective* (of an animal) feeding on grass.

ORIGIN – from Latin *gramen* 'grass'.

grammar* > *noun* **1** the whole system and structure of a language or of languages in general, usually taken as consisting of syntax and morphology. **2** knowledge and use of the rules or principles of grammar: *bad grammar.* **3** a book on grammar. **4** the basic elements of an area of knowledge or skill.

WORDFINDER – solecism (*a grammatical mistake*).

***SPELLING** – -ar, not -er: gramm*ar*.

COMBINATIONS – **grammar school 1** (in the UK) a state secondary school to which pupils are admitted on the basis of ability. **2** US an elementary school.

ORIGIN – from Greek *grammatikē tekhnē* 'art of letters', from *gramma* 'letter of the alphabet'.

grammarian /grəmairiən/ > *noun* a person who studies and writes about grammar.

grammatical /grəmattik'l/ > *adjective* **1** relating to grammar. **2** in accordance with the rules of grammar.

DERIVATIVES – **grammaticality** noun **grammatically** adverb.

gramme > *noun* variant spelling of GRAM.

Grammy > *noun* (pl. **Grammys** or **Grammies**) an annual award given by the American National Academy of Recording Arts and Sciences for achievement in the record industry.

ORIGIN – blend of GRAMOPHONE and EMMY.

gramophone > *noun* dated, chiefly Brit. a record player.

COMBINATIONS – **gramophone record** fuller form of RECORD (in sense 3).

ORIGIN – formed by inversion of elements of *phonogram* 'sound recording'.

grampa (also **gramps**, **grampy**) > *noun* dialect or informal one's grandfather.

grampus /**gram**pəss/ > *noun* (pl. **grampuses**) a killer whale or other cetacean of the dolphin family.

ORIGIN – alteration (by association with GRAND) of Old French *grapois*, from Latin *crassus piscis* 'fat fish'.

gran > *noun* informal, chiefly Brit. one's grandmother.

granadilla /grannə**dill**ə/ (also **grenadilla** /grennə**dill**ə/) > *noun* a passion fruit.

ORIGIN – Spanish, 'little pomegranate'.

granary > *noun* (pl. **granaries**) **1** a storehouse for threshed grain. **2** a region supplying large quantities of corn.

COMBINATIONS – **granary bread** Brit. trademark a type of brown bread containing whole grains of wheat.

ORIGIN – Latin *granarium*, from *granum* 'grain'.

grand > *adjective* **1** magnificent and imposing. **2** large, ambitious, or impressive in scope or scale. **3** of the highest importance or rank. **4** dignified, noble, or proud. **5** informal excellent. **6** Law (of a crime) serious. Compare with PETTY. **7** (in names of family relationships) denoting one generation removed in ascent or descent. > *noun* **1** (pl. same) informal a thousand dollars or pounds. **2** a grand piano.

DERIVATIVES – **grandly** adverb **grandness** noun.

SYNONYMS – *adjective* **1** imposing, impressive, magnificent, majestic, splendid, stately. **2** ambitious, imperious, impressive, ostentatious. **3** chief, main, principal.

COMBINATIONS – **grand duchess 1** the wife or widow of a grand duke. **2** a woman holding the rank of grand duke in her own right. **grand duchy** a territory ruled by a grand duke or duchess. **grand duke 1** a prince or nobleman ruling over a territory in certain European countries. **2** historical a son (or son's son) of a Russian tsar. **grand jury** US Law a jury selected to examine the validity of an accusation prior to trial. **grand larceny** Law (in many US states and

formerly in Britain) theft of personal property having a value above a specified amount. **grand master 1** a chess player of the highest class. **2** (**Grand Master**) the head of an order of chivalry or of Freemasons. **Grand National** an annual steeplechase held at Aintree, Liverpool. **grand opera** an opera on a serious theme in which the entire libretto is sung. **grand piano** a large, full-toned piano which has the body, strings, and soundboard arranged horizontally and is supported by three legs. **grand slam 1** the winning of each of a group of major championships or matches in a particular sport in the same year. **2** Bridge the bidding and winning of all thirteen tricks. **grand total** the final amount after everything is added up. **grand tour** a cultural tour of Europe formerly undertaken by upper-class young men.

ORIGIN – Latin *grandis* 'full-grown, great'.

grandad (also **granddad**) > *noun* **1** informal one's grandfather. **2** (before another noun) (of a shirt) having a collar in the form of a narrow upright band.

grandam /**gran**dam/ (also **grandame**) > *noun* archaic term for GRANDMOTHER.

grandchild > *noun* a child of one's son or daughter.

granddaughter > *noun* a daughter of one's son or daughter.

grande dame /groND **daam**/ > *noun* a woman who is influential within a particular sphere.

ORIGIN – French, 'grand lady'.

grandee /gran**dee**/ > *noun* **1** a Spanish or Portuguese nobleman of the highest rank. **2** a high-ranking or eminent man.

grandeur /**gran**dyər/ > *noun* **1** splendid and impressive appearance. **2** high rank or social importance.

SYNONYMS – **1** magnificence, majesty, splendour. **2** eminence, illustriousness, nobility.

grandfather > *noun* **1** the father of one's father or mother. **2** the founder or originator of something.

COMBINATIONS – **grandfather clock** a clock in a tall free-standing wooden case, driven by weights.

Grand Guignol /groN gee**nyol**/ > *noun* a dramatic entertainment of a sensational or horrific nature, originally as performed at the Grand Guignol theatre in Paris.

ORIGIN – *Guignol* was the bloodthirsty chief character in a French puppet show resembling Punch and Judy.

grandiflora /grandi**flor**ə/ > *adjective* (of a cultivated plant) bearing large flowers.

ORIGIN – from Latin *grandis* 'great' + *flos* 'flower'.

grandiloquent /gran**dill**əkwənt/ > *adjective* pompous or extravagant in language, style, or manner.

DERIVATIVES – **grandiloquence** *noun* **grandiloquently** *adverb*.

SYNONYMS – high-flown, ostentatious, pompous, pretentious.

ORIGIN – Latin *grandiloquus* 'grand-speaking'.

grandiose /**gran**diōss/ > *adjective* **1** impressive or magnificent, especially pretentiously so. **2** conceived on a very ambitious scale.

DERIVATIVES – **grandiosely** *adverb* **grandiosity** *noun*.

grandma > *noun* informal one's grandmother.

grand mal /groN **mal**/ > *noun* a serious form of epilepsy with muscle spasms and prolonged loss of consciousness. Compare with PETIT MAL.

ORIGIN – French, 'great sickness'.

Grand Marnier /groN **maar**niay/ > *noun* trademark an orange-flavoured cognac-based liqueur.

ORIGIN – French.

grandmother > *noun* the mother of one's father or mother.

IDIOMS – **teach one's grandmother to suck eggs** presume to advise a more experienced person.

COMBINATIONS – **grandmother clock** a clock similar to a grandfather clock but about two thirds the size.

grandpa > *noun* informal one's grandfather.

grandparent > *noun* a grandmother or grandfather.

Grand Prix /groN **pree**/ > *noun* (pl. **Grands Prix** pronunc. same) a race forming part of a motor-racing or motorcycling world championship.

ORIGIN – French, 'great or chief prize'.

grandsire > *noun* archaic term for GRANDFATHER.

grandson > *noun* the son of one's son or daughter.

grandstand > *noun* the main stand at a racecourse or sports ground.

COMBINATIONS – **grandstand finish** a close or exciting finish to a race or competition.

grange > *noun* Brit. **1** a country house with farm buildings attached. **2** archaic a barn.

ORIGIN – Old French, from Latin *granica villa* 'grain house or farm', from *granum* 'grain'.

graniferous /grəniffərəss/ > *adjective* Botany producing grain or a grain-like seed.

granita /grəneetə/ > *noun* (pl. **granite** /grəneetay/) a coarse Italian-style water ice.

ORIGIN – Italian.

granite /**grann**it/ > *noun* a very hard crystalline igneous rock consisting mainly of quartz, mica, and feldspar.

DERIVATIVES – **granitic** /grənittik/ *adjective*.

ORIGIN – from Italian *granito* 'grained'.

granivorous /grənivvərəss/ > *adjective* (of an animal) feeding on grain.

DERIVATIVES – **granivore** *noun*.

granny (also **grannie**) > *noun* (pl. **grannies**) informal one's grandmother.

COMBINATIONS – **granny bond** Brit. informal a form of index-linked National Savings certificate, originally available only to old-age pensioners. **granny flat** informal a part of a house made into self-contained accommodation suitable for an elderly relative. **granny glasses** informal round metal-rimmed glasses. **granny knot** a reef knot with the ends crossed the wrong way and therefore liable to slip. **Granny Smith** a bright green variety of apple with crisp flesh, originating in Australia. [ORIGIN – named after Maria Ann (*Granny*) *Smith* (c.1801–70).]

granola /grənōlə/ > *noun* N. Amer. a kind of breakfast cereal resembling muesli.

grant > *verb* **1** agree to give or allow (something requested) to (someone). **2** give (something) formally or legally to (someone). **3** agree or admit to (someone) that (something) is true. > *noun* **1** a sum of money given by a government or public body for a particular purpose. **2** formal the action of granting something. **3** Law a legal conveyance or formal conferment.

IDIOMS – **take for granted** **1** fail to appreciate through over-familiarity. **2** assume that (something) is true.

DERIVATIVES – **grantee** *noun* **granter** *noun* **grantor** *noun*.

SYNONYMS – *verb* **1** assent to, consent to, permit. **2** award, bestow, confer, present. **3** admit, acknowledge, concede. *noun* **1** award, endowment, subsidy.

COMBINATIONS – **grant aid** Brit. financial assistance granted by central government to local government or an institution. **grant-in-aid** (pl. **grants-in-aid**) a grant given to local government, an institution, or a particular scholar. **grant-maintained** Brit. (of a school) funded by central rather than local government, and self-governing.

ORIGIN – Old French *granter* 'consent to support', from Latin *credere* 'entrust'.

granted > *adverb* admittedly; it is true. > *conjunction* (**granted that**) even assuming that.

gran turismo /gran toorizmō/ > *noun* (pl. **gran turismos**) a high-performance model of car.

ORIGIN – Italian, 'great touring'.

granular > *adjective* **1** resembling or consisting of granules. **2** having a roughened surface or structure.

DERIVATIVES – **granularity** *noun*.

granulated > *adjective* **1** in the form of granules. **2** chiefly Biology having a roughened surface.

DERIVATIVES – **granulation** *noun*.

granule /**gran**yōōl/ > *noun* a small compact particle.

ORIGIN – Latin *granulum* 'little grain'.

grape > *noun* **1** a green, purple, or black berry growing in clusters on a vine, eaten as fruit and used in making wine. **2** (**the grape**) informal wine.

WORDFINDER – botrytis (*fungus cultivated on grapes*), marc (*grape skins after pressing*), must (*grape juice for fermentation*), phylloxera (*pest of grapes*), vintage (*grape harvest*), viticulture (*cultivation of grapes*); *common grape varieties:* Cabernet Sauvignon, Gamay, Grenache, Merlot, Pinot noir, Shiraz, Zinfandel (*black*); Chardonnay, Gewürztraminer, Muscadelle, Pinot blanc, Riesling, Sauvignon Blanc, Semillon (*white*).

DERIVATIVES – **grapey** *adjective*.

COMBINATIONS – **grape hyacinth** a small plant with clusters of small globular blue flowers. **grapeshot** historical ammunition consisting of a number of small iron balls fired together from a cannon.

ORIGIN – Old French, 'bunch of grapes', probably from *grap* 'hook' (used in harvesting grapes).

grapefruit > *noun* (pl. same) a large round yellow citrus fruit with an acid juicy pulp.

ORIGIN – from GRAPE + FRUIT, probably because the fruits grow in clusters.

grapevine > *noun* **1** a vine bearing grapes. **2** (**the grapevine**) informal the circulation of rumours and unofficial information.

graph > *noun* a diagram showing the relation between variable quantities, typically of two variables measured along a pair of lines at right angles. > *verb* plot or trace on a graph.

WORDFINDER – abscissa (*distance of a point from the vertical or y axis*), ordinate (*distance of point from horizontal or x axis*); coordinates (*numbers indicating position on a graph*); Cartesian coordinates (*system of coordinates using perpendicular axes*), extrapolation (*extension of graph to unknown values*), intercept (*point at which line cuts axis*).

COMBINATIONS – **graph paper** paper printed with a network of small squares to assist the drawing of graphs or other diagrams.

ORIGIN – abbreviation of *graphic formula*.

-graph > *combining form* **1** in nouns denoting something written or drawn in a specified way: *autograph*. **2** in nouns denoting an instrument that records: *seismograph*.

ORIGIN – from Greek *graphos* 'written, writing'.

graphic > *adjective* **1** relating to visual art, especially involving drawing, engraving, or lettering. **2** giving vividly explicit detail. **3** of or in the form of a graph. > *noun* Computing a visual image displayed on a screen or stored as data.

DERIVATIVES – **graphically** *adverb*.

COMBINATIONS – **graphic arts** visual arts based on the use of line and tone rather than three-dimensional work or the use of colour. **graphic design** the art or profession of combining text and pictures in advertisements, magazines, or books. **graphic equaliser** a device for controlling the strength and quality of selected frequency bands. **graphic novel** a novel in comic-strip format.

ORIGIN – Greek *graphikos*, from *graphē* 'writing, drawing'.

graphical > *adjective* **1** of or in the form of a graph. **2** relating to visual art or computer graphics.

DERIVATIVES – **graphically** *adverb*.

COMBINATIONS – **graphical user interface** Computing a visual way of interacting with a computer using items such as windows and icons.

graphics > *plural noun* (usu. treated as sing.) **1** products of the graphic arts, especially commercial design or illustration. **2** the use of diagrams in calculation and design. **3** (also **computer graphics**) (treated as pl.) visual images produced or manipulated by computer processing.

graphite > *noun* a grey form of carbon used as a solid lubricant and as pencil lead.

DERIVATIVES – **graphitic** *adjective*.

ORIGIN – from Greek *graphein* 'write' (because of its use in pencils).

graphology > *noun* **1** the study of handwriting, especially as used to infer a person's character. **2** Linguistics the study of written and printed symbols and of writing systems.

DERIVATIVES – **graphological** *adjective* **graphologist** *noun*.

-graphy > *combining form* in nouns denoting: **1** a descriptive science: *geography*. **2** a technique of producing images: *radiography*. **3** a style or method of writing or drawing: *calligraphy*. **4** writing about (a specified subject): *hagiography*. **5** a written or printed list: *filmography*.

DERIVATIVES – **-graphic** *combining form*.

grapnel /ˈgrapnəl/ > *noun* **1** a grappling hook. **2** a small anchor with several flukes.

ORIGIN – Old French *grapon*, related to **GRAPE**.

grappa /ˈgrappə/ > *noun* a brandy distilled from the fermented residue of grapes after they have been pressed in winemaking.

ORIGIN – Italian, 'grape stalk'.

grapple > *verb* **1** engage in a close fight or struggle without weapons. **2** (**grapple with**) struggle to deal with or understand. **3** archaic seize with a grapnel. > *noun* **1** an act of grappling. **2** a grapnel.

DERIVATIVES – **grappler** *noun*.

SYNONYMS – *verb* **1** struggle, tussle, wrestle.

COMBINATIONS – **grappling hook** (also

grappling iron) a device with iron claws, attached to a rope and used for dragging or grasping.

ORIGIN – Old French *grapil* 'small hook', related to **GRAPE**.

graptolite /ˈgraptəlʌɪt/ > *noun* an extinct planktonic invertebrate animal of the Palaeozoic era.

ORIGIN – from Greek *graptos* 'marked with letters' + **-LITE**: so named because impressions left on hard shales resemble slate pencil marks.

grasp /grɑːsp/ > *verb* **1** seize and hold firmly. **2** comprehend fully. > *noun* **1** a firm grip. **2** a person's capacity to attain or understand something.

DERIVATIVES – **graspable** *adjective* **grasper** *noun*.

SYNONYMS – *verb* **1** clasp, clutch, grip. *noun* **1** clasp, clutch, grip, hold. **2** apprehension, comprehension.

ORIGIN – perhaps related to **GROPE**.

grasping > *adjective* avaricious; greedy.

grass > *noun* **1** vegetation consisting of short plants with long, narrow leaves, growing wild or cultivated on lawns and pasture. **2** ground covered with grass. **3** informal cannabis. **4** Brit. informal a police informer. > *verb* **1** cover with grass. **2** (often **grass on**) Brit. informal inform the police of someone's criminal activity or plans.

WORDFINDER – *grasses*: bent, couch, esparto, fescue, marram, ryegrass, spinifex, timothy; *grasslands*: pampas, prairie, savannah, steppe, veld; graminaceous (*of the grass family*), graminivorous (*eating grass*), sward (*area of short grass*), tussock (*clump of grass*).

IDIOMS – **at grass** grazing. **the grass is always greener on the other side of the fence** proverb other people's lives or situations always seem better than your own. **not let the grass grow under one's feet** not delay in taking action. **put out to grass 1** put (an animal) out to graze. **2** informal force (someone) to retire.

COMBINATIONS – **grasshopper** a plant-eating insect with long hind legs which are used for jumping and for producing a chirping sound. **grass roots** the most basic level of an activity or organisation. **grass skirt** a skirt made of long grass and leaves, worn by female dancers from some Pacific islands. **grass snake** a harmless grey-green snake with a yellowish band around the neck. **grass tree** an Australian tree or erect shrub with long, stiff grass-like leaves. **grass widow** a woman whose husband is away often or for a prolonged period. [ORIGIN – first meaning an unmarried woman with a child: perhaps from the idea of a couple having lain on grass instead of in bed.]

ORIGIN – Old English, related to **GREEN**

and **GROW**. The sense 'police informer' is perhaps related to 19th-century rhyming slang *grasshopper* 'copper'.

grassy > *adjective* (**grassier**, **grassiest**) covered with or resembling grass.

grate¹ > *verb* **1** reduce (food) to small shreds by rubbing it on a grater. **2** make an unpleasant rasping sound. **3** (often **grate on**) have an irritating effect.

SYNONYMS – **2** jar, rasp, scrape.

ORIGIN – Old French *grater*.

grate² > *noun* **1** the recess of a fireplace or furnace. **2** a metal frame confining fuel in a fireplace or furnace.

ORIGIN – Old French, from Latin *cratis* 'hurdle'.

grateful > *adjective* feeling or showing gratitude.

DERIVATIVES – **gratefully** *adverb*.

SYNONYMS – appreciative, obliged, thankful.

ORIGIN – from obsolete *grate* 'pleasing, thankful', from Latin *gratus*.

grater > *noun* a device having a surface covered with sharp-edged holes, used for grating food.

graticule /ˈgratɪkjuːl/ > *noun* a network of fine lines for use as a measuring scale or an aid in locating objects, e.g. in an eyepiece or on an oscilloscope screen.

ORIGIN – Latin *graticula* 'a little grating'.

gratify > *verb* (**gratifies**, **gratified**) **1** give pleasure or satisfaction. **2** indulge or satisfy (a desire).

DERIVATIVES – **gratification** *noun* **gratifier** *noun* **gratifying** *adjective* **gratifyingly** *adverb*.

SYNONYMS – **1** delight, gladden, please.

ORIGIN – Latin *gratificari* 'give or do as a favour', from *gratus* 'pleasing, thankful'.

gratin /ˈgrataN/ > *noun* a dish cooked au gratin.

gratiné /ˈgratɪnay/ > *adjective* (after a noun) another term for **AU GRATIN**.

grating¹ > *adjective* **1** sounding harsh and unpleasant. **2** irritating or jarring.

DERIVATIVES – **gratingly** *adverb*.

SYNONYMS – **1** discordant, jarring, rasping.

grating² > *noun* **1** a framework of parallel or crossed bars that prevents access through an opening. **2** Optics a set of equally spaced parallel wires or ruled lines, used to produce spectra by diffraction.

gratis /ˈgrɑːtɪs/ > *adverb* & *adjective* free of charge.

ORIGIN – Latin, from *gratia* 'grace, kindness'.

gratitude > *noun* thankfulness; appreciation of kindness.

ORIGIN – Latin *gratitudo*, from *gratus* 'pleasing, thankful'.

gratuitous /grətyoͦoitəss/ > *adjective* **1** (of something bad) done without good reason. **2** free of charge.

DERIVATIVES – **gratuitously** *adverb* **gratuitousness** *noun*.

SYNONYMS – **1** needless, uncalled for, unjustified, unwarranted.

ORIGIN – Latin *gratuitus* 'given freely, spontaneous'.

gratuity /grətyoͦoiti/ > *noun* (pl. **gratuities**) **1** formal a tip given to a waiter, porter, etc. **2** Brit. a sum of money paid to an employee at the end of a period of employment.

ORIGIN – Latin *gratuitas* 'gift'.

gravadlax > *noun* variant spelling of **GRAVLAX**.

gravamen /grəvaymen/ > *noun* (pl. **gravamina** /grəvaymɪnə/) chiefly Law the essence or most serious part of a complaint or accusation.

ORIGIN – Latin, 'physical inconvenience'.

grave[1] > *noun* **1** a hole dug in the ground to receive a coffin or corpse. **2** (**the grave**) death.

IDIOMS – **dig one's own grave** do something foolish which causes one's downfall. **turn in one's grave** (of a dead person) be likely to have been angry or distressed about something had they been alive.

COMBINATIONS – **gravestone** an inscribed headstone marking a grave. **graveyard** a burial ground beside a church. **graveyard shift** informal, chiefly N. Amer. a work shift that runs from midnight to 8 a.m.

grave[2] > *adjective* **1** giving cause for alarm. **2** serious or solemn in manner or appearance.

DERIVATIVES – **gravely** *adverb* **graveness** *noun*.

SYNONYMS – **1** critical, crucial, pressing, serious, urgent. **2** earnest, serious, solemn, sombre.

ORIGIN – Old French, from Latin *gravis* 'heavy, serious'.

grave[3] > *verb* (past participle **graven** or **graved**) **1** archaic engrave on a surface. **2** literary fix indelibly in the mind.

COMBINATIONS – **graven image** a carved figure of a god used as an idol. [ORIGIN – with biblical allusion to the Book of Exodus, chapter 20.]

ORIGIN – Old English, related to **GRAVE**[1] and **GROOVE**.

grave accent /graav/ > *noun* a mark (`) placed over a vowel in some languages to indicate altered sound quality.

ORIGIN – French *grave* 'heavy, serious'.

gravel > *noun* a loose mixture of small stones and coarse sand, used for paths and roads.

> *verb* (**gravelled**, **gravelling**; US **graveled**, **graveling**) cover with gravel.

ORIGIN – Old French, from *grave* 'shore'.

gravelly > *adjective* **1** resembling, containing, or consisting of gravel. **2** (of a voice) deep and rough-sounding.

graver > *noun* **1** a burin or other engraving tool. **2** archaic an engraver.

Graves /graav/ > *noun* a red or white wine from Graves, a district of SW France.

gravid /gravvid/ > *adjective* **1** technical pregnant. **2** literary full of meaning or a specified quality.

ORIGIN – Latin *gravidus* 'laden, pregnant'.

gravimeter /grəvimmɪtər/ > *noun* an instrument for measuring the force of gravity at different places.

gravimetric /gravvimetrik/ > *adjective* relating to the measurement of weight, or of gravity.

DERIVATIVES – **gravimetry** /grəvimmɪtri/ *noun*.

graving dock > *noun* a dry dock.

ORIGIN – from *grave* 'clean a ship's bottom by burning and tarring'.

gravitas /gravvitass/ > *noun* dignity or solemnity of manner.

ORIGIN – Latin, from *gravis* 'serious'.

gravitate /gravvitayt/ > *verb* **1** be drawn towards a place, person, or thing. **2** Physics move, or tend to move, towards a centre of gravity.

gravitation > *noun* **1** movement, or a tendency to move, towards a centre of gravity. **2** Physics gravity.

DERIVATIVES – **gravitational** *adjective* **gravitationally** *adverb*.

gravity > *noun* **1** the force that attracts a body towards the centre of the earth, or towards any other physical body having mass. **2** extreme importance or seriousness. **3** solemnity of manner.

ORIGIN – Latin *gravitas* 'weight, seriousness'.

gravlax (also **gravadlax**) > *noun* a Scandinavian dish of dry-cured salmon marinated in herbs.

ORIGIN – Swedish, from *grav* 'trench' + *lax* 'salmon' (from the former practice of burying the salmon in salt in a hole in the ground).

gravure /grəvyoor/ > *noun* short for **PHOTOGRAVURE**.

gravy > *noun* (pl. **gravies**) **1** the fat and juices that come out of meat during cooking. **2** a sauce made from these juices together with stock and other ingredients. **3** informal unearned or unexpected money.

COMBINATIONS – **gravy boat** a long, narrow jug used for serving gravy. **gravy train** informal a situation in which someone can easily make a lot of money.

wordpower facts

Gravy

In medieval times **gravy** was a sauce for white meat, fish, and vegetables made from broth, milk of almonds, spices, and usually wine or beer. Medieval English recipes for *gravy* are very similar to French ones, in which the sauce is called *grané*: it seems likely that *gravy* arose from a misreading of this word. The Old French word *grané* probably comes from *grain* 'spice', from Latin *granum* 'grain', the source of **garner**, **grain**, **grange**, **granite** ('grained' rock), **granule**, and **pomegranate**.

gray[1] > *noun* Physics the unit of the absorbed dose of ionising radiation in the SI system, corresponding to one joule per kilogram.

ORIGIN – named after the English physicist Louis H. *Gray* (1905–65).

gray[2] > *adjective* US spelling of **GREY**.

grayling > *noun* an edible silvery-grey freshwater fish with horizontal violet stripes.

graze[1] > *verb* **1** (of cattle, sheep, etc.) eat grass in a field. **2** informal eat frequent snacks at irregular intervals.

DERIVATIVES – **grazer** *noun*.

ORIGIN – Old English, related to **GRASS**.

graze[2] > *verb* **1** scrape and break the skin on (part of the body). **2** touch or scrape (something) lightly in passing. > *noun* a superficial injury caused by grazing the skin.

grazier /grayziər/ > *noun* a person who rears or fattens cattle or sheep for market.

grazing > *noun* grassland suitable for use as pasture.

grease > *noun* **1** a thick oily substance, especially one used as a lubricant. **2** animal fat used or produced in cooking. > *verb* smear or lubricate with grease.

IDIOMS – **grease the palm of** informal bribe. **like greased lightning** informal extremely rapidly.

COMBINATIONS – **grease gun** a device for pumping grease under pressure to a particular point. **grease monkey** informal a mechanic. **greasepaint** a waxy substance used as make-up by actors. **greaseproof** impermeable to grease.

ORIGIN – Old French *graisse*, from Latin *crassus* 'thick, fat'.

greaser > *noun* **1** a motor mechanic or unskilled engineer on a ship. **2** informal a long-haired young man belonging to a motorcycle gang. **3** US informal, offensive a Hispanic American, especially a Mexican.

greasy > *adjective* (**greasier**, **greasiest**) **1** covered with or resembling grease. **2**

effusively polite in a repellently insincere way.

DERIVATIVES – **greasily** adverb **greasiness** noun.

SYNONYMS – oily, oleaginous.

COMBINATIONS – **greasy pole** informal the difficult route to the top of a profession.

great > adjective **1** of an extent, amount, or intensity considerably above average. **2** of ability, quality, or eminence considerably above average. **3** informal excellent; very good. **4** most important: *the great thing is the challenge.* **5** particularly deserving a specified description: *I was a great fan of Hank's.* **6** (**Greater**) (of a city) including adjacent urban areas. **7** (in names of family relationships) referring to one degree further removed upwards or downwards: *a great-great-grandfather.* > noun **1** a distinguished person. **2** (**Greats**) the honours course in classics, philosophy, and ancient history at Oxford University. > adverb informal very well.

DERIVATIVES – **greatness** noun.

SYNONYMS – *adjective* **1** enormous, immense, large, vast.

COMBINATIONS – **great ape** a large ape of a family closely related to humans, including the gorilla and chimpanzees. **great-aunt** an aunt of one's father or mother. **great circle** a circle on the surface of a sphere which lies in a plane passing through the sphere's centre, especially as representing the shortest path between two given points on the sphere. **greatcoat** a long, heavy overcoat. **Great Dane** a very large, powerful, short-haired breed of dog. **great-nephew** a son of one's nephew or niece. **great-niece** a daughter of one's nephew or niece. **Great Scott!** expressing surprise or amazement. [ORIGIN – euphemism for *Great God!*] **great-uncle** an uncle of one's mother or father. **Great War** the First World War.

greatly > adverb very much.

SYNONYMS – considerably, extremely, tremendously, very much.

greave > noun historical a piece of armour for the shin.

ORIGIN – Old French *greve* 'shin, greave'.

grebe /greeb/ > noun a diving waterbird with a long neck, lobed toes, and a very short tail.

ORIGIN – French.

Grecian /greesh'n/ > adjective relating to ancient Greece, especially its architecture.

COMBINATIONS – **Grecian nose** a straight nose that continues the line of the forehead without a dip.

greed > noun intense and selfish desire for food, wealth, or power.

SYNONYMS – avarice, cupidity, gluttony, rapacity, voracity.

greedy > adjective (**greedier**, **greediest**) having or showing greed.

DERIVATIVES – **greedily** adverb **greediness** noun.

SYNONYMS – acquisitive, avaricious, covetous, gluttonous, rapacious, voracious.

Greek > noun **1** a person from Greece. **2** the ancient or modern language of Greece. > adjective relating to Greece or its language.

WORDFINDER – *related adjective:* Hellenic; philhellene (*lover of Greece and Greek culture*); *principal Greek gods:* Zeus (*supreme god*), Ares (*war*), Eros (*love*), Hephaestus (*fire*), Hermes (*messenger of the gods*), Pluto or Hades (*the underworld*), Poseidon (*the sea*); *goddesses:* Hera (*queen of heaven*), Aphrodite (*beauty*), Artemis (*hunting*), Athene (*wisdom*), Demeter (*crops*), Eirene (*peace*), Eos (*dawn*).

IDIOMS – **beware** (or **fear**) **the Greeks bearing gifts** proverb if a rival or enemy shows one generosity or kindness, one should be suspicious of their motives. [ORIGIN – with allusion to the warning given by Laocoön to the Trojans in Virgil's *Aeneid*, against admitting the wooden horse to Troy.] **it's all Greek to me** informal I can't understand it at all.

COMBINATIONS – **Greek coffee** very strong black coffee served with the fine grounds in it. **Greek cross** a cross of which all four arms are of equal length. **Greek Orthodox Church** the Eastern Orthodox Church which uses the Byzantine rite in Greek, in particular the national Church of Greece.

green > adjective **1** of the colour between blue and yellow in the spectrum; coloured like grass. **2** covered with grass or other vegetation. **3** (**Green**) concerned with or supporting protection of the environment. **4** (of a plant or fruit) young or unripe. **5** in an untreated or original state; not cured, seasoned, fired, etc. **6** inexperienced or naive. **7** pale and sickly-looking. > noun **1** green colour, pigment, or material. **2** a piece of common grassy land, especially in the centre of a village. **3** an area of smooth, very short grass immediately surrounding a hole on a golf course. **4** (**greens**) green vegetables. **5** (**Green**) a member or supporter of an environmentalist group or party. > verb **1** make or become green. **2** make less harmful to the environment.

WORDFINDER – *shades of green:* aquamarine, emerald, jade, olive, verdant; chlorophyll (*green pigment in leaves*), chlorosis (*loss of green colour in leaves*), patina, verdigris (*green sheen or film*), verdure (*lush green vegetation*), virescent (*turning green*).

DERIVATIVES – **greenish** adjective **greenness** noun.

COMBINATIONS – **greenback** US informal a dollar bill. **green belt** an area of open land around a city, on which building is restricted. **Green Beret** informal a British commando or a member of the US Army Special Forces. **green card 1** (in the UK) an international insurance document for motorists. **2** (in the US) a permit allowing a foreign national to live and work permanently in the US. **the green-eyed monster** jealousy personified. [ORIGIN – from Shakespeare's *Othello* (III. 3. 166).] **greenfield** (of a site for building) previously undeveloped. **greenfinch** a large finch with green and yellow plumage. **green fingers** Brit. informal natural ability in growing plants. **greenfly** chiefly Brit. a green aphid. **greenhorn** informal, chiefly N. Amer. an inexperienced or naive person. **green light 1** a green traffic light giving permission to proceed. **2** permission to go ahead with a project. **green man** historical a man dressed up in greenery to represent a wild man of the woods or seasonal fertility. **Green Paper** (in the UK) a preliminary report of government proposals published to stimulate discussion. **green pepper** the mild-flavoured unripe fruit of a sweet pepper. **green plover** Brit. the lapwing. **green pound** the exchange rate for the pound applied to payments for agricultural produce in the EU. **green revolution** a large increase in crop production in developing countries achieved by the use of artificial fertilisers, pesticides, and high-yield crop varieties. **green room** a room in a theatre or studio in which performers can relax when they are not performing. **greensand** Geology a greenish kind of sandstone. **greenstick fracture** a fracture of the bone, occurring typically in children, in which one side of the bone is broken and the other only bent. **greenstone 1** Geology a greenish igneous rock containing feldspar and hornblende. **2** chiefly NZ a variety of jade. **green tea** tea made from unfermented leaves, produced mainly in China and Japan. **green thumb** North American term for *green fingers*. **greenware** unfired pottery. **greenwood** archaic a wood or forest in leaf, especially as a refuge for outlaws.

ORIGIN – Old English, related to GRASS and GROW.

greenery > noun green foliage or vegetation.

greengage > noun a sweet greenish fruit resembling a small plum.

ORIGIN – named after the English botanist Sir William *Gage* (1657–1727).

greengrocer > noun Brit. a retailer of fruit and vegetables.

DERIVATIVES – **greengrocery** noun.

greenhouse > noun a glass building in which plants that need protection from cold weather are grown.

COMBINATIONS – **greenhouse effect** the

trapping of the sun's warmth in a planet's lower atmosphere, due to the greater transparency of the atmosphere to visible radiation from the sun than to infrared radiation emitted from the planet's surface. **greenhouse gas** a gas, such as carbon dioxide, that contributes to the greenhouse effect by absorbing infrared.

Greenlander > *noun* a person from Greenland.

greenshank > *noun* a large grey and white sandpiper with long greenish legs.

greensward /**green**swawrd/ > *noun* archaic or literary grass-covered ground.

Greenwich Mean Time > *noun* the mean solar time at the Greenwich meridian, used as the standard time in a zone that includes the British Isles.

Greenwich meridian > *noun* the meridian of zero longitude, passing through Greenwich in London, the former site of the Royal Observatory.

greet¹ > *verb* **1** give a word or sign of welcome when meeting (someone). **2** receive or acknowledge in a specified way. **3** (of a sight or sound) become apparent to (a person arriving somewhere).
DERIVATIVES – **greeter** *noun*.

greet² > *verb* Scottish weep; cry.

greeting > *noun* **1** a word or sign of welcome or recognition. **2** (usu. **greetings**) a formal expression of goodwill.
COMBINATIONS – **greetings card** (N. Amer. **greeting card**) a decorative card sent to convey good wishes.

gregarious /gri**gair**iəss/ > *adjective* **1** fond of company; sociable. **2** (of animals) living in flocks or colonies.
DERIVATIVES – **gregariously** *adverb* **gregariousness** *noun*.
SYNONYMS – **1** companionable, convivial, friendly, sociable.
ANTONYMS – **1** reserved, unsociable.
ORIGIN – Latin *gregarius*, from *grex* 'a flock'.

Gregorian calendar /gri**gor**iən/ > *noun* the modified form of the Julian calendar introduced in 1582 by Pope Gregory XIII, and still used today.

Gregorian chant > *noun* medieval church plainsong.
ORIGIN – named after St *Gregory* the Great (*c*.540–604).

gremlin > *noun* a mischievous sprite regarded as responsible for unexplained mechanical or electrical faults.
ORIGIN – a Second World War term: perhaps suggested by **GOBLIN**.

Grenache /grə**nash**/ > *noun* a variety of black wine grape native to the Languedoc-Roussillon region of France.
ORIGIN – French.

grenade /grə**nayd**/ > *noun* a small bomb thrown by hand or launched mechanically.

ORIGIN – first used in the sense 'pomegranate', because of a supposed resemblance in shape: from Old French *pome grenate* 'pomegranate'.

Grenadian /grə**nay**diən/ > *noun* a person from the Caribbean country of Grenada. > *adjective* relating to Grenada.

grenadier /grennə**deer**/ > *noun* **1** historical a soldier armed with grenades. **2** (**Grenadiers** or **Grenadier Guards**) the first regiment of the royal household infantry.

grenadilla > *noun* variant spelling of **GRANADILLA**.

grenadine /**grenn**ədeen/ > *noun* a sweet cordial made from pomegranates.
ORIGIN – French.

grew past of **GROW**.

grey (US **gray**) > *adjective* **1** of a colour intermediate between black and white, as of ashes or lead. **2** (of hair) turning grey or white with age. **3** (of the weather) cloudy and dull; without sun. **4** dull and nondescript: *grey, faceless men*. **5** not accounted for in official statistics: *the grey economy*. > *noun* grey colour or pigment. > *verb* (especially of hair) become grey with age.
WORDFINDER – *shades of grey:* charcoal, gunmetal, lead, slate, taupe.
DERIVATIVES – **greyish** *adjective* **greyly** *adverb* **greyness** *noun*.
COMBINATIONS – **grey area** an ill-defined area of activity that does not readily conform to an existing category or set of rules. **greybeard** humorous or derogatory an old man. **Grey Friar** a friar of the Franciscan order (who wear grey habits). **grey matter 1** the darker tissue of the brain and spinal cord. **2** informal intelligence. **grey seal** a large North Atlantic seal with a spotted greyish coat. **grey squirrel** a tree squirrel with mainly grey fur, native to eastern North America and introduced to Britain and elsewhere.

greyhound > *noun* a swift, slender breed of dog used in racing and coursing.
ORIGIN – Old English, related to Old Norse *grey* 'bitch'.

greylag > *noun* a large goose with mainly grey plumage, the ancestor of the domestic goose.
ORIGIN – probably from dialect *lag* 'goose'.

gricer /**grī**sər/ > *noun* Brit. informal a trainspotter.
ORIGIN – perhaps a humorous representation of an upper-class pronunciation of *grouser* 'grouse-shooter'.

grid > *noun* **1** a framework of spaced bars that are parallel to or cross each other. **2** a network of lines that cross each other to form a series of squares or rectangles. **3** a network of cables or pipes for distributing power, especially high-voltage electricity. **4**

a pattern of lines marking the starting places on a motor-racing track. > *verb* put into or set out as a grid.
ORIGIN – from **GRIDIRON**.

griddle > *noun* a circular iron plate that is heated and used for cooking food. > *verb* cook on a griddle.
ORIGIN – Old French *gredil*, from Latin *craticula* 'small hurdle'.

gridiron /**gridd**īən/ > *noun* **1** a frame of parallel metal bars used for grilling meat or fish over an open fire. **2** a grid pattern, especially of streets. **3** a field for American football, marked with regularly spaced parallel lines. **4** N. Amer. American football.
ORIGIN – alteration of *gredile* 'griddle'.

gridlock > *noun* a traffic jam affecting a whole network of intersecting streets.
DERIVATIVES – **gridlocked** *adjective*.

grief > *noun* **1** intense sorrow, especially caused by someone's death. **2** informal trouble or annoyance.
IDIOMS – **come to grief** have an accident; meet with disaster. **good grief!** an exclamation of surprise or alarm.
SYNONYMS – **1** anguish, desolation, heartbreak, misery, mourning, sorrow.
ORIGIN – Old French, from *grever* 'grieve'.

grievance > *noun* a real or imagined cause for complaint.

grieve > *verb* **1** suffer grief. **2** cause great distress to.
DERIVATIVES – **griever** *noun*.
SYNONYMS – **1** mourn, sorrow, suffer. **2** distress, hurt, pain, wound.
ORIGIN – Old French *grever* 'grieve, burden, encumber', from Latin *gravis* 'heavy, serious'.

grievous > *adjective* formal (of something bad) very severe or serious.
DERIVATIVES – **grievously** *adverb* **grievousness** *noun*.
COMBINATIONS – **grievous bodily harm** Law serious physical injury inflicted on a person by the deliberate action of another, considered more serious than actual bodily harm.

griffin (also **gryphon** or **griffon**) > *noun* a mythical creature with the head and wings of an eagle and the body of a lion.
ORIGIN – Greek *grups*.

griffon > *noun* **1** a small terrier-like breed of dog. **2** a large vulture with predominantly pale brown plumage. **3** variant spelling of **GRIFFIN**.

grig > *noun* dialect **1** a small eel. **2** a grasshopper or cricket.

grill > *noun* Brit. **1** a device on a cooker that radiates heat downwards for cooking food. **2** a gridiron used for cooking food on an open fire. **3** a dish of food cooked using a grill. **4** a restaurant serving grilled food. **5** variant form of **GRILLE**. > *verb* **1** cook with a grill. **2** informal subject to intense questioning or interrogation.

ORIGIN – Old French *graille* 'grille', from Latin *craticula* 'small hurdle'; related to **CRATE**, **GRATE**², and **GRIDDLE**.

grille (also **grill**) > *noun* a grating or screen of metal bars or wires.

grilse /grilss/ > *noun* a salmon that has returned to fresh water after a single winter at sea.

grim > *adjective* (**grimmer**, **grimmest**) **1** very serious or gloomy; forbidding. **2** horrifying, depressing, or unappealing.

IDIOMS – **like** (or **for**) **grim death** with great determination.

DERIVATIVES – **grimly** *adverb* **grimness** *noun*.

SYNONYMS – **1** forbidding, menacing, sombre, stern.

grimace /grimməss/ > *noun* an ugly, twisted expression on a person's face, expressing disgust, pain, or wry amusement. > *verb* make a grimace.

ORIGIN – French, from Spanish *grima* 'fright'.

grimalkin /grimalkin/ > *noun* archaic **1** a cat. **2** a spiteful old woman.

ORIGIN – from **GREY** + *Malkin* (familiar form of the given name *Matilda*).

grime > *noun* dirt ingrained on a surface. > *verb* blacken or make dirty with grime.

ORIGIN – Low German and Dutch.

grimoire /grimwaar/ > *noun* a book of magic spells and invocations.

ORIGIN – French, alteration of *grammaire* 'grammar'.

grimy > *adjective* (**grimier**, **grimiest**) covered with or characterised by grime.

DERIVATIVES – **grimily** *adverb* **griminess** *noun*.

grin > *verb* (**grinned**, **grinning**) **1** smile broadly. **2** grimace grotesquely in a way that reveals the teeth. > *noun* a smile or grimace produced by grinning.

IDIOMS – **grin and bear it** suffer pain or misfortune in a stoical manner.

grind > *verb* (past and past participle **ground**) **1** reduce to small particles or powder by crushing. **2** sharpen, smooth, or produce by crushing or friction. **3** rub together or move gratingly. **4** (**grind down**) wear (someone) down with harsh treatment. **5** (**grind out**) produce (something) slowly and laboriously. **6** (**grinding**) oppressive and seemingly endless: *grinding poverty*. **7** (often **grind away**) work or study hard. **8** informal (of a dancer) rotate the hips. > *noun* **1** an act or process of grinding. **2** hard, dull work: *the daily grind*.

IDIOMS – **grind to a halt** (or **come to a grinding halt**) stop laboriously and noisily.

DERIVATIVES – **grinder** *noun* **grindingly** *adverb*.

SYNONYMS – *verb* **1** crush, mill, pound, pulverise. **7** labour, slave, toil.

grindstone > *noun* **1** a thick revolving disc of abrasive material used for sharpening or polishing metal objects. **2** a millstone.

IDIOMS – **keep one's nose to the grindstone** work hard and continuously.

gringo /gringgō/ > *noun* (pl. **gringos**) informal (in Latin America) a white English-speaking person.

ORIGIN – Spanish, 'foreign, foreigner, or gibberish'.

griot /greeō/ > *noun* a West African travelling poet, musician, and storyteller.

ORIGIN – French, perhaps from Portuguese *criado*.

grip > *verb* (**gripped**, **gripping**) **1** take and keep a firm hold of; grasp tightly. **2** deeply affect or afflict. **3** compel the attention or interest of. > *noun* **1** a firm hold; a tight grasp or clasp. **2** intellectual understanding. **3** a part or attachment by which something is held in the hand. **4** a travelling bag. **5** a stage hand in a theatre. **6** a member of a camera crew responsible for moving and setting up equipment.

IDIOMS – **come** (or **get**) **to grips with 1** engage in combat with. **2** begin to deal with or understand. **lose one's grip** become unable to understand or control one's situation.

DERIVATIVES – **gripper** *noun* **gripping** *adjective*.

SYNONYMS – *verb* **1** clasp, clench, clutch, grab, grasp. **3** absorb, engross, rivet, spellbind. *noun* **1** clasp, clutch, grasp, hold. **2** apprehension, comprehension, understanding.

gripe > *verb* **1** informal express a trivial complaint; grumble. **2** affect with gastric or intestinal pain. > *noun* **1** informal a trivial complaint. **2** gastric or intestinal pain; colic.

grisaille /grizīl/ > *noun* a method of painting in grey monochrome, typically to imitate sculpture.

ORIGIN – French, from *gris* 'grey'.

gris-gris /greegree/ > *noun* (pl. same) **1** an African or Caribbean charm or amulet. **2** the use of such charms, especially in voodoo.

ORIGIN – West African.

grisly /grizli/ > *adjective* (**grislier**, **grisliest**) **1** causing horror and revulsion. **2** informal very bad or unappealing.

DERIVATIVES – **grisliness** *noun*.

USAGE – do not confuse **grisly** with **grizzly**, as in *grizzly bear*. **Grisly** means 'causing horror or revulsion', whereas **grizzly** is from the same root as **grizzled** and refers to the bear's white-tipped fur.

SYNONYMS – **1** ghastly, gruesome, horrifying.

ORIGIN – Old English, 'terrifying'.

grissini /griseeni/ > *plural noun* thin, crisp Italian breadsticks.

ORIGIN – Italian.

grist > *noun* **1** corn that is ground to make flour. **2** malt crushed to make mash for brewing.

IDIOMS – **grist to the mill** useful experience or knowledge.

ORIGIN – Old English, 'grinding'.

gristle /griss'l/ > *noun* cartilage, especially when found as tough inedible tissue in meat.

DERIVATIVES – **gristly** *adjective*.

grit > *noun* **1** small loose particles of stone or sand. **2** (also **gritstone**) a coarse sandstone. **3** courage and resolve. > *verb* (**gritted**, **gritting**) **1** clench (one's teeth), especially in order to keep one's resolve. **2** spread grit on (an icy road).

DERIVATIVES – **gritter** *noun*.

SYNONYMS – *noun* **3** backbone, mettle, pluck.

grits > *plural noun* US coarsely ground maize kernels, served boiled with water or milk.

gritty > *adjective* (**grittier**, **grittiest**) **1** containing or covered with grit. **2** showing courage and resolve. **3** tough and uncompromising: *a gritty look at urban life*.

DERIVATIVES – **grittily** *adverb* **grittiness** *noun*.

grizzle > *verb* informal, chiefly Brit. (of a child) cry or whimper fretfully.

grizzled > *adjective* having grey or grey-streaked hair.

ORIGIN – from Old French *gris* 'grey'.

grizzly bear > *noun* a large variety of brown bear often having white-tipped fur, native to western North America.

USAGE – do not confuse **grizzly** with **grisly**. **Grisly** means 'causing horror or revulsion', whereas **grizzly** is from the same root as **grizzled** and refers to the bear's white-tipped fur.

groan > *verb* **1** make a deep inarticulate sound in response to pain or despair. **2** make a low creaking sound when pressure or weight is applied. **3** (**groan beneath** or **under**) be oppressed by. > *noun* a groaning sound.

DERIVATIVES – **groaner** *noun*.

SYNONYMS – *verb* **1** moan, sigh, whimper.

groat > *noun* historical an English silver coin worth four old pence.

ORIGIN – from Dutch *groot* or Low German *grōte* 'great, thick', hence 'thick penny'.

groats > *plural noun* hulled or crushed grain, especially oats.

ORIGIN – Old English, related to **GRIT** and **GRITS**.

grocer > *noun* a person who sells food and small household goods.

ORIGIN – from Latin *grossus* 'gross': originally 'a person who sold things by the gross'.

grocery > *noun* (pl. **groceries**) **1** a grocer's shop or business. **2** (**groceries**) items of food sold in a grocer's shop or supermarket.

grockle > *noun* Brit. informal, derogatory a holidaymaker, especially one in the West Country.

ORIGIN – an invented word, originally a fantastic creature in a children's comic, popularised by the film *The System* (1962).

grog > *noun* **1** spirits (originally rum) mixed with water. **2** informal alcoholic drink.

---

wordpower facts

Grog

Grog was the term in the Royal Navy for the rum mixed with water which was formerly served to sailors as part of their daily rations. The name is said to be from *Old Grog*, the reputed nickname (because of his grogram cloak) of Admiral Edward Vernon (1684–1757). In 1740, concerned at the drunkenness resulting from men rapidly downing half a pint of neat rum each, Vernon ordered diluted rum to be served, in two portions. The rum ration continued until 1970.

---

groggy > *adjective* (**groggier**, **groggiest**) dazed and unsteady after intoxication, sleep, a blow, etc.

DERIVATIVES – **groggily** *adverb* **grogginess** *noun*.

SYNONYMS – befuddled, dizzy, muddled.

grogram /grógrəm/ > *noun* a coarse fabric made of silk, often combined with mohair or wool and stiffened with gum.

ORIGIN – from French *gros grain* 'coarse grain'.

groin[1] > *noun* **1** the area between the abdomen and the thigh on either side of the body. **2** (in non-technical use) the region of the genitals. **3** Architecture a curved edge formed by two intersecting vaults.

WORDFINDER – inguinal (*of the groin*).

groin[2] > *noun* US spelling of **GROYNE**.

grommet /grómmit/ > *noun* **1** a protective eyelet in a hole that a rope or cable passes through. **2** a tube surgically implanted in the eardrum to drain fluid from the middle ear.

ORIGIN – first used to mean 'circle of rope used as a fastening': from obsolete French *gourmer* 'to curb'.

groom > *verb* **1** brush and clean the coat of (a horse or dog). **2** give a neat and tidy appearance to. **3** prepare or train for a particular purpose or activity. > *noun* **1** a person employed to take care of horses. **2** a bridegroom. **3** Brit. any of various officials of the royal household.

SYNONYMS – *verb* **3** coach, prepare, prime, train.

groove > *noun* **1** a long, narrow cut or depression in a hard material. **2** a spiral track cut in a gramophone record, into which the stylus fits. **3** an established routine or habit. **4** informal a rhythmic pattern in popular or jazz music. > *verb* **1** make a groove or grooves in. **2** informal dance to or play popular or jazz music.

WORDFINDER – bezel (*groove holding gem or glass in position*), glyph (*ornamental carved groove*), rifling (*spiral groove in gun barrel*), sulcate (*marked with grooves*).

IDIOMS – **in the groove** informal **1** performing confidently. **2** enjoying oneself, especially by dancing.

DERIVATIVES – **grooved** *adjective*.

ORIGIN – Dutch *groeve* 'furrow, pit'; related to **GRAVE**[1].

groovy > *adjective* (**groovier**, **grooviest**) informal, dated or humorous fashionable and exciting.

DERIVATIVES – **groovily** *adverb* **grooviness** *noun*.

grope > *verb* **1** feel about or search blindly or uncertainly with the hands. **2** informal feel or fondle (someone) for sexual pleasure, especially against their will. > *noun* informal an act of groping someone.

SYNONYMS – *verb* **1** feel, fumble, scrabble.

groper[1] > *noun* a person who gropes.

groper[2] > *noun* chiefly Austral./NZ variant spelling of **GROUPER**.

grosbeak /grósbeek/ > *noun* a finch or related songbird with a large conical bill and brightly coloured plumage.

ORIGIN – from French *gros* 'big, fat' + *bec* 'beak'.

groschen /gróshən/ > *noun* (pl. same) a monetary unit of Austria, equal to one hundredth of a schilling.

ORIGIN – German, from Latin *denarius grossus* 'thick penny'; compare with **GROAT**.

grosgrain /grógrayn/ > *noun* a heavy ribbed fabric, typically of silk or rayon.

ORIGIN – French, 'coarse grain'.

gros point /grō pwaN/ > *noun* a type of needlepoint embroidery consisting of stitches crossing two or more threads of the canvas in each direction.

ORIGIN – French, 'large stitch'.

gross > *adjective* **1** unattractively large or bloated. **2** very vulgar or unrefined. **3** informal very unpleasant; repulsive. **4** complete; blatant: *a gross exaggeration*. **5** (of income, profit, or interest) without deduction of tax or other contributions; total. Contrasted with **NET**[2]. **6** (of weight) including contents or other variable items; overall. > *adverb* without tax or other contributions having been deducted. > *verb* **1** produce or earn (an amount of money) as gross profit or income. **2** (**gross up**) add deductions such as tax to (a net amount). **3** (**gross out**) informal, chiefly N. Amer. disgust (someone) with repulsive behaviour or appearance. > *noun* **1** (pl. same) an amount equal to twelve dozen; 144. **2** (pl. **grosses**) a gross profit or income.

DERIVATIVES – **grossly** *adverb* **grossness** *noun*.

SYNONYMS – *adjective* **2** coarse, crude, indelicate, unrefined, vulgar.

ANTONYMS – *adjective* **2** delicate, refined.

COMBINATIONS – **gross domestic product** the total value of goods produced and services provided within a country during one year. **gross national product** the total value of goods produced and services provided by a country during one year, equal to the gross domestic product plus the net income from foreign investments.

ORIGIN – Old French *gros* 'large', from Latin *grossus*; sense 1 of the noun is from French *grosse douzaine* 'large dozen'.

grosz /grawss/ > *noun* (pl. **groszy** or **grosze**) a monetary unit of Poland, equal to one hundredth of a zloty.

ORIGIN – Polish.

grot[1] > *noun* Brit. informal something unpleasant, dirty, or of poor quality; rubbish.

grot[2] > *noun* literary a grotto.

grotesque /grōtesk/ > *adjective* **1** comically or repulsively ugly or distorted. **2** shockingly incongruous or inappropriate. > *noun* **1** a grotesque figure or image. **2** a style of decorative painting or sculpture consisting of the interweaving of human and animal forms with flowers and foliage.

DERIVATIVES – **grotesquely** *adverb* **grotesqueness** *noun*.

SYNONYMS – *adjective* **1** freakish, misshapen. **2** bizarre, incongruous, weird.

ORIGIN – French *crotesque*, from Italian *grottesca*, from *opera* or *pittura grottesca* 'work or painting resembling that found in a grotto': probably with reference to excavated Roman buildings decorated with murals.

grotesquerie /grōteskəri/ > *noun* (pl. **grotesqueries**) grotesque quality or things.

grotto > *noun* (pl. **grottoes** or **grottos**) a small picturesque cave, especially an artificial one in a park or garden.

ORIGIN – Italian *grotta*, from Greek *kruptē* 'vault'.

grotty > *adjective* (**grottier**, **grottiest**) Brit. informal **1** unpleasant and of poor quality. **2** unwell.

DERIVATIVES – **grottiness** *noun*.

ORIGIN – from **GROTESQUE**.

grouch /growch/ informal > *noun* **1** a habitually grumpy person. **2** a complaint or grumble. > *verb* complain ill-temperedly; grumble.

ORIGIN – variant of obsolete *grutch*, from Old French *grouchier* 'to grumble, murmur'.

grouchy > *adjective* (**grouchier**, **grouchiest**) irritable and bad-tempered; grumpy.

DERIVATIVES – **grouchily** *adverb* **grouchiness** *noun*.

ground¹ > *noun* **1** the solid surface of the earth or (Brit.) the floor of a room. **2** land of a specified kind: *marshy ground*. **3** an area of land or sea with a specified use: *fishing grounds*. **4** (**grounds**) an area of enclosed land surrounding a large house. **5** (**grounds**) factors forming a basis for action or the justification for a belief. **6** a prepared surface to which paint or other decoration is applied. **7** (**grounds**) solid particles, especially of coffee, which form a residue. **8** N. Amer. electrical connection to the earth. > *verb* **1** prohibit or prevent (a pilot or aircraft) from flying. **2** run (a ship) aground. **3** (usu. **be grounded in** or **on**) give a firm theoretical or practical basis to. **4** place on the ground or touch the ground with. **5** informal, chiefly N. Amer. (of a parent) refuse to allow (a child) to go out socially, as a punishment. **6** N. Amer. connect (an electrical device) with the ground.

IDIOMS – **break new ground** be innovative. **gain ground 1** become more popular or accepted. **2** (usu. **gain ground on**) get closer to someone being pursued. **get off the ground** start happening or functioning successfully. **give** (or **lose**) **ground** retreat or lose one's advantage. **go to ground** (of a fox or other animal) enter its earth or burrow. **hold** (or **stand**) **one's ground** not retreat or lose one's advantage. **on the ground** in a place where real, practical work is done. **on one's own ground** in one's own territory or area of knowledge. **be thick** (or **thin**) **on the ground** exist in large (or small) numbers or amounts. **work** (or **run**) **oneself into the ground** exhaust oneself by working or running very hard.

COMBINATIONS – **groundbait** Brit. bait thrown into the water while fishing. **ground-breaking** innovative; pioneering. **ground control** the personnel and equipment that monitor and direct the flight and landing of aircraft or spacecraft. **ground elder** a common weed with leaves that resemble those of the elder and spreading underground stems. **ground floor** Brit. the floor of a building at ground level. **ground frost** Brit. frost formed on the surface of the ground or in the top layer of soil. **ground glass 1** glass with a smooth ground surface that makes it non-transparent. **2** glass ground into an abrasive powder. **ground ivy** a creeping plant with bluish-purple flowers. **groundnut** a peanut. **ground rent** Brit. rent paid by the owner of a building to the owner of the land on which it is built. **ground rule** a basic principle established to govern action or procedure. **groundsheet** a waterproof sheet spread on the ground inside a tent. **groundsman** (N. Amer. **groundskeeper**) Brit. a person who maintains a sports ground or the grounds of a large building. **ground speed** an aircraft's speed relative to the ground. **ground squirrel** a burrowing squirrel of a large group including the chipmunks. **groundwater** water held underground in the soil or in pores and crevices in rock. **groundwork** preliminary or basic work. **ground zero** the point on the earth's surface directly below an exploding nuclear bomb.

ground² past and past participle of GRIND.

groundhog > *noun* North American term for WOODCHUCK.

COMBINATIONS – **Groundhog Day** (in the US) 2 February. [ORIGIN – commemorating the traditional belief that if the groundhog sees its shadow on emerging from hibernation (i.e. the weather is sunny) there will be six weeks more of winter weather.]

grounding > *noun* basic training or instruction in a subject.

groundless > *adjective* not based on any good reason.

SYNONYMS – baseless, unfounded.

groundling > *noun* a spectator or reader of inferior taste.

ORIGIN – with reference to Shakespeare's *Hamlet* III. ii. 11: a *groundling* was originally a member of the part of a theatre audience that stood in the pit beneath the stage.

groundmass > *noun* Geology the compact, finer-grained material of a crystalline rock, in which larger crystals are embedded.

groundsel /**grown**s'l/ > *noun* a plant of the daisy family with small yellow flowers.

ORIGIN – Old English, probably from *gund* 'pus' + *swelgan* 'to swallow' (with reference to its use in poultices).

groundswell > *noun* **1** a large swell in the sea. **2** a build-up of opinion in a large section of the population.

group > *noun* **1** a number of people or things located, gathered, or classed together. **2** a number of musicians who play popular music together. **3** a division of an air force. **4** Chemistry a combination of atoms having a recognisable identity in a number of compounds. > *verb* place in or form a group or groups.

DERIVATIVES – **grouping** *noun*.

SYNONYMS – *noun* **1** category, class, set. *verb* categorise, class, classify.

COMBINATIONS – **group captain** a rank of officer in the RAF, above wing commander and below air commodore. **group therapy** a form of psychiatric therapy in which patients meet to discuss their problems. **groupware** Computing software designed to facilitate collective working by a number of different users.

ORIGIN – Italian *gruppo*; related to CROP.

grouper (chiefly Austral./NZ also **groper**) > *noun* a large heavy-bodied fish found in warm seas.

ORIGIN – Portuguese *garoupa*, probably from a local term in South America.

groupie > *noun* informal **1** a young woman who follows a pop group or celebrity, especially in the hope of having sex with them. **2** derogatory an enthusiastic or uncritical follower.

grouse¹ > *noun* (pl. same) a medium-sized game bird with a plump body and feathered legs.

ORIGIN – perhaps related to Latin *gruta* or to Old French *grue* 'crane'.

grouse² > *verb* complain pettily; grumble. > *noun* a grumble or complaint.

SYNONYMS – grumble, moan, whinge.

grout /growt/ > *noun* a mortar or paste for filling crevices, especially the gaps between wall or floor tiles. > *verb* fill in with grout.

grouts /growts/ > *plural noun* archaic sediment; dregs; grounds.

grove > *noun* a small wood, orchard, or group of trees.

grovel > *verb* (**grovelled**, **grovelling**; US **groveled**, **groveling**) **1** crouch or crawl abjectly on the ground. **2** act obsequiously to obtain forgiveness or favour.

DERIVATIVES – **groveller** *noun*.

SYNONYMS – *verb* **2** abase oneself, bow and scrape, kowtow.

ORIGIN – from obsolete *groof*, *grufe* 'the face or front', from Old Norse *á grúfu* 'face downwards'.

grow > *verb* (past **grew**; past participle **grown**) **1** (of a living thing) undergo natural development by increasing in size and changing physically. **2** (of a plant) germinate and develop. **3** become larger or greater over a period of time; increase. **4** become gradually or increasingly: *we grew braver*. **5** (**grow up**) advance to maturity; become an adult. **6** (**grow out of** or **into**) become too large (or large enough) to wear. **7** (**grow on**) become gradually more appealing to.

DERIVATIVES – **grower** *noun*.

SYNONYMS – *verb* **3** enlarge, expand, increase, multiply.

ANTONYMS – *verb* **3** decrease, shrink.

COMBINATIONS – **growbag** Brit. a bag containing potting compost, in which plants such as tomatoes can be grown. **growing pains 1** pains occurring in the limbs of young children. **2** difficulties experienced in the early stages of an enterprise.

ORIGIN – Old English, related to **GRASS** and **GREEN**.

growl > *verb* **1** (especially of a dog) make a low guttural sound of hostility in the throat. **2** say something in a low grating voice. **3** make a low or harsh rumbling sound. > *noun* a growling sound.

growler > *noun* **1** a person or thing that growls. **2** a small iceberg.

grown past participle of **GROW**.

grown-up > *adjective* adult. > *noun* informal an adult.

growth > *noun* **1** the process of growing. **2** something that has grown or is growing. **3** a tumour or other abnormal formation.

WORDFINDER – acromegaly (*abnormal growth of hands and feet*), neoteny (*retention of juvenile features in an adult animal*), pituitary gland, thyroid gland (*glands regulating growth*), somatotrophin, thyroxine (*growth hormones*).

COMBINATIONS – **growth hormone** a hormone which stimulates growth in animal or plant cells. **growth industry** an industry that is developing particularly rapidly. **growth ring** a concentric layer of wood, shell, or bone developed during a regular period of growth. **growth stock** a company stock that tends to increase in capital value rather than yield high income.

groyne (US **groin**) > *noun* a low wall or barrier built out into the sea from a beach to prevent erosion and drifting.

ORIGIN – from dialect *groin* 'snout', from Latin *grunium* 'pig's snout'.

GRP > *abbreviation* glass-reinforced plastic.

grub > *noun* **1** the larva of an insect, especially a beetle. **2** informal food. > *verb* (**grubbed**, **grubbing**) **1** dig shallowly in soil. **2** (**grub up**) dig (something) up. **3** (often **grub about** or **around**) search or work clumsily and unmethodically.

DERIVATIVES – **grubber** noun.

SYNONYMS – *verb* **3** dig, ferret, root around, rummage.

COMBINATIONS – **grub screw** Brit. a small headless screw. **Grub Street** the world or class of impoverished journalists and writers. [ORIGIN – the name of a street (later Milton Street) in London inhabited by such authors in the 17th century.]

grubby > *adjective* (**grubbier**, **grubbiest**) **1** dirty; grimy. **2** disreputable; sordid.

DERIVATIVES – **grubbily** adverb **grubbiness** noun.

grudge > *noun* a persistent feeling of ill will or resentment resulting from a past insult or injury. > *verb* **1** be resentfully unwilling to grant or allow (something). **2** feel resentful that (someone) has achieved (something).

DERIVATIVES – **grudging** adjective **grudgingly** adverb.

ORIGIN – variant of the obsolete verb *grutch*

'complain, murmur, grumble': see **GROUCH**.

gruel > *noun* a thin liquid food of oatmeal or other meal boiled in milk or water.

ORIGIN – Old French.

gruelling (US **grueling**) > *adjective* extremely tiring and demanding.

DERIVATIVES – **gruellingly** adverb.

SYNONYMS – arduous, exhausting, fatiguing, wearying.

ORIGIN – from *gruel* 'exhaust, punish', from an old phrase *get one's gruel* 'receive one's punishment'.

gruesome > *adjective* **1** causing repulsion or horror. **2** informal extremely unpleasant.

DERIVATIVES – **gruesomely** adverb **gruesomeness** noun.

SYNONYMS – **1** ghastly, grisly.

ORIGIN – from Scottish *grue* 'to feel horror, shudder'; rare before the late 18th century, the word was popularised by Sir Walter Scott.

gruff > *adjective* **1** (of a voice) rough and low in pitch. **2** abrupt or taciturn in manner.

DERIVATIVES – **gruffly** adverb **gruffness** noun.

SYNONYMS – **1** hoarse, husky, rasping. **2** brusque, curt, surly.

ORIGIN – from Flemish and Dutch *grof* 'coarse, rude'.

grumble > *verb* **1** complain or protest in a bad-tempered but muted way. **2** make a low rumbling sound. **3** (**grumbling**) (of an internal organ) giving intermittent discomfort. > *noun* an instance of grumbling; a complaint.

DERIVATIVES – **grumbler** noun.

grump informal > *noun* **1** a grumpy person. **2** a fit of sulking. > *verb* act in a sulky, grumbling manner.

grumpy > *adjective* (**grumpier**, **grumpiest**) bad-tempered and sulky.

DERIVATIVES – **grumpily** adverb **grumpiness** noun.

SYNONYMS – churlish, cross, crotchety, surly, tetchy.

grunge > *noun* **1** chiefly N. Amer. grime; dirt. **2** a style of rock music characterised by a raucous guitar sound and lazy vocal delivery. **3** a casual style of fashion including loose, layered clothing and ripped jeans.

DERIVATIVES – **grungy** adjective.

ORIGIN – first occurring as *grungy*: perhaps suggested by **GRUBBY** and **DINGY**.

grunt[1] > *verb* **1** (of an animal, especially a pig) make a low, short guttural sound. **2** make a low inarticulate sound to express effort or indicate assent. > *noun* a grunting sound.

DERIVATIVES – **grunter** noun.

grunt[2] > *noun* informal, chiefly N. Amer. a low-ranking or unskilled soldier or other worker.

ORIGIN – alteration of *ground*, from *ground*

man (with reference to unskilled railway work before progressing to lineman).

Gruyère /**groo**yair/ > *noun* a firm, tangy Swiss cheese.

ORIGIN – named after *Gruyère*, a district in Switzerland.

gryphon > *noun* variant spelling of **GRIFFIN**.

GSM > *abbreviation* Global System (or Standard) for Mobile.

gsm > *abbreviation* grams per square metre.

GSOH > *abbreviation* good sense of humour.

G-spot > *noun* a sensitive area of the front wall of the vagina believed by some to be highly erogenous.

ORIGIN – short for *Gräfenberg spot*, named after the German-born US gynaecologist Ernst *Gräfenberg* (1881–1957).

GST > *abbreviation* (in New Zealand and Canada) Goods and Services Tax.

G-string > *noun* a skimpy undergarment covering the genitals, consisting of a narrow strip of cloth attached to a waistband.

G-suit > *noun* a garment with inflatable pressurised pouches, worn by fighter pilots and astronauts to enable them to withstand high gravitational forces.

GT > *noun* a high-performance car.

ORIGIN – abbreviation of **GRAN TURISMO**.

GTi > *noun* a GT car with a fuel-injected engine.

guacamole /gwakkə**mō**lay/ > *noun* a dish of mashed avocado mixed with chilli peppers, tomatoes, etc.

ORIGIN – Nahuatl, 'avocado sauce'.

Guadeloupian /gwaadə**loo**piən/ > *noun* a person from Guadeloupe, a group of islands in the Lesser Antilles. > *adjective* relating to Guadeloupe.

guanaco /gwə**naa**kō/ > *noun* (pl. **guanacos**) a wild mammal native to the Andes of South America, similar to the domestic llama.

ORIGIN – Quechua.

guanine /**gwaa**neen/ > *noun* Biochemistry a compound that occurs in guano and fish scales, and is one of the four constituent bases of nucleic acids.

guano /**gwaa**nō/ > *noun* (pl. **guanos**) **1** the excrement of seabirds. **2** an artificial fertiliser resembling natural guano.

ORIGIN – Quechua, 'dung'.

Guarani /gwaarə**nee**/ > *noun* (pl. same) **1** a member of an American Indian people of Paraguay and adjacent regions. **2** (**guarani**) the basic monetary unit of Paraguay, equal to 100 centimos.

ORIGIN – Spanish.

guarantee* > *noun* **1** a formal assurance that certain conditions will be fulfilled, especially that a product will be of a specified quality. **2** something that makes an outcome certain. **3** variant spelling of

GUARANTY. 4 a guarantor. > *verb*
(**guarantees, guaranteed, guaranteeing**)
1 provide a guarantee for something. **2**
promise with certainty. **3** provide financial
security for; underwrite.

*SPELLING – unlike **gauge, guarantee** has
-*ua*- in the middle: gu*a*rantee.

SYNONYMS – *noun* **1** assurance, pledge,
promise.

ORIGIN – perhaps from Spanish *garante*;
related to WARRANT.

guarantor /garrən**tor**/ > *noun* a person or
organisation that gives or acts as a
guarantee.

guaranty /**garr**ənti/ (also **guarantee**)
> *noun* (pl. **guaranties**) **1** an undertaking to
answer for the payment of a debt or for the
performance of an obligation by another
person liable in the first instance. **2** a thing
serving as security for such an
undertaking.

guard* > *verb* **1** watch over in order to
protect or control. **2** (**guard against**) take
precautions against. > *noun* **1** a person,
especially a soldier, who guards or keeps
watch. **2** a body of soldiers serving to
protect a place or person. **3** a device worn
or fitted to prevent injury or damage. **4**
(often in phrase **on** (or **off**) **guard**) a state
of vigilance or readiness to fight. **5** Brit. an
official who rides on and is in general
charge of a train. **6** (**Guards**) the household
troops of the British army. **7** N. Amer. a prison
warder.

IDIOMS – **guard of honour** a group of
soldiers ceremonially welcoming an
important visitor.

*SPELLING – unlike **gauge, guard** has -*ua*-
in the middle: gu*a*rd.

SYNONYMS – *verb* **1** defend, protect,
shield.

COMBINATIONS – **guard hair** long, coarse
hair forming an animal's outer fur.
guardhouse (or **guardroom**) a building
(or room) used to accommodate a military
guard or to detain military prisoners.
guard's van Brit. a carriage or wagon
occupied by the guard on a train.

ORIGIN – Old French *garder*; related to
WARD.

guarded > *adjective* cautious and having
possible reservations.

DERIVATIVES – **guardedly** *adverb*.

guardian > *noun* **1** a defender, protector, or
keeper. **2** a person legally responsible for
someone unable to manage their own
affairs, especially a child whose parents have
died.

DERIVATIVES – **guardianship** *noun*.

COMBINATIONS – **guardian angel** a spirit
believed to watch over and protect a person
or place.

guardsman > *noun* **1** (in the UK) a soldier

of a regiment of Guards. **2** (in the US) a
member of the National Guard.

guar gum /gwaar/ > *noun* a gum used in
the food and paper industries, obtained
from the seeds of an African and Asian bean
plant.

ORIGIN – Hindi.

Guatemalan /gwaatə**maal**ən/ > *noun* a
person from Guatemala in Central
America. > *adjective* relating to Guatemala.

guava /**gwaa**və/ > *noun* a tropical American
fruit with pink juicy flesh.

ORIGIN – probably from Taino (an extinct
Caribbean language).

gubbins > *plural noun* Brit. informal **1** (treated
as sing. or pl.) miscellaneous items;
paraphernalia. **2** (treated as sing.) a gadget.

ORIGIN – first used in the sense 'fragments':
from obsolete *gobbon* 'piece, slice, gob',
probably related to GOBBET.

gubernatorial /go͞obərnə**tor**iəl/ > *adjective*
relating to a governor, particularly of a US
state.

ORIGIN – from Latin *gubernator* 'governor'.

gudgeon[1] /**gu**jən/ > *noun* a small freshwater
fish often used as bait by anglers.

ORIGIN – Old French *goujon*, from Latin
gobius 'goby'.

gudgeon[2] /**gu**jən/ > *noun* **1** a pivot or
spindle on which something swings or
rotates. **2** the tubular part of a hinge into
which the pin fits. **3** a socket at the stern of
a boat, into which the rudder is fitted. **4** a
pin holding two blocks of stone together.

COMBINATIONS – **gudgeon pin** a pin
holding a piston rod and a connecting rod
together.

ORIGIN – Old French *goujon*, from *gouge*
'chisel'.

guelder rose /**gel**dər/ > *noun* a shrub with
flattened heads of fragrant creamy-white
flowers followed by translucent red berries.

ORIGIN – from Dutch *geldersche roos* 'rose of
Gelderland' (a province of the
Netherlands).

Guelph /gwelf/ > *noun* **1** a member of one
of two great factions in Italian medieval
politics, traditionally supporting the Pope
against the Holy Roman emperor and his
supporters, the Ghibellines. **2** a member of
a German princely family from which the
British royal house is descended.

ORIGIN – Italian *Guelfo*, from *Welf*, the
name of the founder of the Guelph faction
in the Holy Roman Empire.

guerdon /**ger**d'n/ archaic > *noun* a reward or
recompense. > *verb* give a reward to.

ORIGIN – Old French, related to Latin
donum 'gift'.

Guernsey /**gern**zi/ > *noun* (pl. **Guernseys**)
1 a breed of dairy cattle from Guernsey in
the Channel Islands, noted for producing
rich, creamy milk. **2** (**guernsey**) a thick

sweater made from oiled wool. **3**
(**guernsey**) Austral. a football shirt.

guerrilla /gə**rill**ə/ (also **guerilla**) > *noun* a
soldier in a small independent group
fighting against the government or regular
forces.

ORIGIN – Spanish, 'little war'.

guess > *verb* **1** estimate or suppose
(something) without sufficient information
to be sure of being correct. **2** correctly
estimate or conjecture. **3** (**I guess**) informal,
chiefly N. Amer. I suppose. > *noun* an estimate
or conjecture.

DERIVATIVES – **guesser** *noun*.

SYNONYMS – *verb* **1** conjecture, reckon,
speculate, surmise.

COMBINATIONS – **guesswork** the process
or results of guessing.

ORIGIN – perhaps from Dutch *gissen*;
probably related to GET.

guesstimate (also **guestimate**) informal
> *noun* /**ges**timət/ an estimate based on a
mixture of guesswork and calculation.
> *verb* /**ges**timayt/ estimate in such a way.

guest > *noun* **1** a person invited to visit
someone's home or take part in a function.
2 a visiting performer invited to take part in
an entertainment. **3** a person staying at a
hotel or boarding house. > *verb* informal
appear as a guest.

IDIOMS – **be my guest** informal please do!
guest of honour the most important guest
at an occasion.

COMBINATIONS – **guest beer** Brit. a draught
beer offered temporarily or in addition to
those produced by the parent brewery.
guest house a private house offering
accommodation to paying guests. **guest
worker** a person with temporary
permission to work in another country.

ORIGIN – Old Norse *gestr*; related to Latin
hostis 'enemy', originally 'stranger'.

guff > *noun* **1** informal trivial or worthless talk
or ideas. **2** Scottish an unpleasant smell.

guffaw /gə**faw**/ > *noun* a loud and boisterous
laugh. > *verb* laugh in such a way.

GUI > *abbreviation* Computing graphical user
interface.

guidance > *noun* **1** advice or information
aimed at resolving a problem or difficulty. **2**
the directing of the motion or position of
something.

SYNONYMS – **1** advice, counselling,
counsel, help. **2** direction, management.

guide > *noun* **1** a person who advises or
shows the way to others. **2** a directing
principle or standard. **3** a book providing
information on a subject. **4** a structure or
marking which directs the motion or
positioning of something. **5** (**Guide**) a
member of the Guides Association, a girls'
organisation corresponding to the Scouts.
> *verb* **1** show or indicate the way to. **2**
direct the motion, positioning, or course

of. **3** (**guided**) directed by remote control or internal equipment: *a guided missile.*

SYNONYMS – *noun* **1** conductor, director, escort, leader, navigator. **2** criterion, model, pattern. *verb* **1** conduct, escort, lead, shepherd.

COMBINATIONS – **guidebook** a book of information about a place for visitors or tourists. **guide dog** a dog that has been trained to lead a blind person.

ORIGIN – Old French, related to **WIT²**.

guideline > *noun* a general rule, principle, or piece of advice.

Guider > *noun* an adult leader in the Guides Association.

guild > *noun* **1** a medieval association of craftsmen or merchants. **2** an association of people for a common purpose.

ORIGIN – Old English, related to **YIELD**.

guilder /gildər/ > *noun* (pl. same or **guilders**) **1** the basic monetary unit of the Netherlands, equal to 100 cents. **2** historical a gold or silver coin formerly used in the Netherlands, Germany, and Austria.

ORIGIN – Dutch, from *gulden* 'golden'.

guildhall > *noun* **1** the meeting place of a guild or corporation. **2** Brit. a town hall. **3** (**the Guildhall**) the hall of the Corporation of the City of London.

guile /gīl/ > *noun* sly or cunning intelligence.

DERIVATIVES – **guileful** *adjective.*

SYNONYMS – craftiness, cunning, wiliness.

ORIGIN – Old French, related to **WILE**.

guileless > *adjective* lacking guile; innocent and without deception.

DERIVATIVES – **guilelessly** *adverb.*

SYNONYMS – artless, ingenuous, open, sincere.

guillemot /gillimot/ > *noun* an auk with a narrow pointed bill, typically nesting on cliff ledges.

ORIGIN – French, from *Guillaume* 'William'.

guillotine /gilləteen/ > *noun* **1** a machine with a heavy blade sliding vertically in grooves, used for beheading people. **2** a device with a descending or sliding blade used for cutting paper or sheet metal. **3** Brit. (in Parliament) a procedure used to limit discussion of a legislative bill by fixing times at which various parts of it must be voted on. > *verb* **1** execute by guillotine. **2** Brit. (in Parliament) apply a guillotine to (a bill or debate).

WORDFINDER – tricoteuse (*woman knitting next to the guillotine*), tumbril (*cart carrying prisoners to the guillotine*).

ORIGIN – named after the French physician Joseph-Ignace *Guillotin* (1738–1814), who recommended its use for executions in 1789.

guilt > *noun* **1** the fact of having committed an offence or crime. **2** a troubling feeling of having done something wrong or failed in an obligation.

SYNONYMS – **1** blameworthiness, culpability, responsibility. **2** contrition, regret, remorse.

ANTONYMS – **1** innocence.

COMBINATIONS – **guilt trip** informal a feeling of guilt, especially when self-indulgent or unjustified.

guiltless > *adjective* **1** having no guilt; innocent. **2** (**guiltless of**) lacking.

DERIVATIVES – **guiltlessly** *adverb.*

guilty > *adjective* (**guiltier, guiltiest**) **1** (often **guilty of**) responsible for a specified wrongdoing, fault, or error. **2** having or showing a feeling of guilt.

DERIVATIVES – **guiltily** *adverb.*

SYNONYMS – **1** at fault, blameworthy, culpable, responsible.

guinea /ginni/ > *noun* Brit. **1** the sum of £1.05 (21 shillings in pre-decimal currency), used mainly for determining professional fees and auction prices. **2** a former British gold coin with a value of 21 shillings.

ORIGIN – named after *Guinea* in West Africa, the source of the gold from which the first guineas were minted.

guineafowl > *noun* (pl. same) a large African game bird with slate-coloured, white-spotted plumage.

Guinean /ginniən/ > *noun* a person from Guinea, a country on the west coast of Africa. > *adjective* relating to Guinea.

guinea pig > *noun* **1** a tailless South American cavy, domesticated as a pet or laboratory animal. **2** a person or thing used as a subject for experiment.

guipure /gipyoor/ > *noun* heavy lace consisting of embroidered motifs held together by large connecting stitches.

ORIGIN – French, from *guiper* 'cover with silk'.

guise /gīz/ > *noun* an external form, appearance, or manner of presentation.

ORIGIN – Old French, related to **WISE²**.

guitar > *noun* a stringed musical instrument with six (or occasionally twelve) strings, played by plucking or strumming with the fingers or a plectrum.

DERIVATIVES – **guitarist** *noun.*

ORIGIN – Spanish *guitarra*, from Greek *kithara*, denoting an instrument similar to the lyre.

Gujarati /goojəraati/ (also **Gujerati**) > *noun* (pl. **Gujaratis**) **1** a person from the Indian state of Gujarat. **2** the language of the Gujaratis. > *adjective* relating to the Gujaratis or their language.

Gulag /goolag/ > *noun* (**the Gulag**) a system of harsh labour camps maintained in the Soviet Union 1930–55.

ORIGIN – Russian, from *G(lavnoe) u(pravlenie ispravitel' no-trudovykh) lag(ereĭ)*

'Chief Administration for Corrective Labour Camps'.

gulch /gulch/ > *noun* N. Amer. a narrow, steep-sided ravine.

ORIGIN – perhaps from dialect *gulch* 'to swallow'.

gulden > *noun* (pl. same or **guldens**) another term for **GUILDER**.

ORIGIN – Dutch and German, 'golden'.

gules /gyoolz/ > *noun* red, as a conventional heraldic colour.

ORIGIN – Old French *goles* 'throats', from Latin *gula*, used to denote pieces of red-dyed fur used as a neck ornament.

gulf > *noun* **1** a deep inlet of the sea almost surrounded by land, with a narrow mouth. **2** a deep ravine, chasm, or abyss. **3** a substantial difference between two people, concepts, or situations.

ORIGIN – Italian *golfo*, from Greek *kolpos* 'bosom, gulf'.

Gulf War syndrome > *noun* an unexplained medical condition affecting some veterans of the 1991 Gulf War, causing fatigue, chronic headaches, and skin and respiratory disorders.

gull¹ > *noun* a long-winged seabird having white plumage with a grey or black back.

COMBINATIONS – **gull-wing** (of a door on a car or aircraft) opening upwards.

ORIGIN – Celtic.

gull² > *verb* fool or deceive (someone). > *noun* a person who is fooled or deceived.

gullet > *noun* the passage by which food passes from the mouth to the stomach; the oesophagus.

ORIGIN – Old French *goulet* 'little throat'.

gullible > *adjective* easily persuaded to believe something; credulous.

DERIVATIVES – **gullibility** *noun* **gullibly** *adverb.*

SYNONYMS – credulous, naive, trustful.

ANTONYMS – sceptical.

ORIGIN – from **GULL²**.

gully > *noun* (pl. **gullies**) **1** (also **gulley**) a ravine worn by running water. **2** (also **gulley**) a gutter or drain. **3** Cricket a fielding position on the off side between point and the slips.

ORIGIN – first used in the sense 'gullet': from French *goulet* (see **GULLET**).

gulp > *verb* **1** swallow (drink or food) quickly or in large mouthfuls. **2** swallow with difficulty in response to strong emotion. > *noun* **1** an act of gulping. **2** a large mouthful of liquid hastily drunk.

gum¹ > *noun* **1** a viscous substance secreted by some trees and shrubs. **2** glue used for sticking paper or other light materials together. **3** chewing gum or bubble gum. **4** a firm, jelly-like sweet made with gelatin or gum arabic. > *verb* (**gummed, gumming**) **1** cover or fasten with gum or glue. **2** (**gum**

up) clog up (a mechanism) and prevent it from working properly.

COMBINATIONS – **gum arabic** a gum exuded by acacia trees, used as glue and in incense. **gumboot** a long rubber boot; a wellington. **gumdrop** a firm, jelly-like sweet. **gum resin** a plant secretion consisting of resin mixed with gum.

ORIGIN – Greek *kommi*, from Egyptian.

gum² > *noun* the firm area of flesh around the roots of the teeth in the upper or lower jaw.

WORDFINDER – gingival (*of the gums*), gingivitis (*inflamed gums*).

COMBINATIONS – **gumshield** a pad or plate used by a sports player to protect the teeth and gums.

gum³ > *noun* (in phrase **by gum!**) chiefly N. English an exclamation used for emphasis.

ORIGIN – euphemistic alteration of *God*.

gumbo /**gum**bō/ > *noun* (pl. **gumbos**) N. Amer. 1 okra, especially the gelatinous pods used in cooking. 2 (in Cajun cooking) a spicy chicken or seafood soup thickened with okra or rice.

ORIGIN – Angolan.

gumboil > *noun* a swelling of the gum over an abscess at the root of a tooth.

gummy¹ > *adjective* (**gummier**, **gummiest**) viscous; sticky.

DERIVATIVES – **gumminess** noun.

gummy² > *adjective* (**gummier**, **gummiest**) toothless: *a gummy grin*.

DERIVATIVES – **gummily** adverb.

gumption > *noun* informal shrewd or spirited initiative and resourcefulness.

gumshoe > *noun* N. Amer. informal a detective.

ORIGIN – from *gumshoes* in the sense 'sneakers', suggesting stealth.

gum tree > *noun* a tree that exudes gum, especially a eucalyptus.

IDIOMS – **up a gum tree** Brit. informal in a predicament.

gun > *noun* 1 a weapon incorporating a metal tube from which bullets or shells are propelled by explosive force. 2 a device for discharging something such as grease in a required direction. 3 N. Amer. a gunman: *a hired gun*. > *verb* (**gunned**, **gunning**) 1 (**gun down**) shoot (someone) with a gun. 2 (**gun for**) aggressively pursue or act against. 3 informal cause (an engine) to race.

IDIOMS – **at gunpoint** while threatening or being threatened with a gun. **go great guns** informal proceed forcefully or successfully. **jump the gun** informal act before the proper or appropriate time. **stick to one's guns** informal refuse to compromise or change.

COMBINATIONS – **gun carriage** a wheeled support for a piece of artillery. **guncotton** an explosive made by steeping cotton or wood pulp in a mixture of nitric and sulphuric acids. **gun dog** a dog trained to retrieve game that has been shot. **gunfire** the repeated firing of a gun or guns. **gunmetal 1** a grey corrosion-resistant form of bronze containing zinc. **2** a dull bluish-grey colour. **gunplay** the use of guns. **gunrunner** a person engaged in the illegal sale or importing of firearms. **gunship** a heavily armed helicopter. **gunshot** a shot fired from a gun. **gunsight** a device on a gun enabling it to be aimed accurately. **gunslinger** informal a man who carries a gun. **gunsmith** a person who makes and sells small firearms.

ORIGIN – perhaps from a familiar form of the Scandinavian female forename *Gunnhildr*, from *gunnr* and *hildr*, both meaning 'war': originally applied to siege engines as well as to cannons and firearms.

gunboat > *noun* a small ship armed with guns.

COMBINATIONS – **gunboat diplomacy** foreign policy supported by the use or threat of military force.

gunfight > *noun* a fight involving an exchange of fire with guns.

DERIVATIVES – **gunfighter** noun.

gunge Brit. informal > *noun* sticky, viscous, and unpleasantly messy material. > *verb* (**gunged**, **gungeing**) (**gunge up**) clog or obstruct with gunge.

DERIVATIVES – **gungy** adjective.

gung-ho /gung**hō**/ > *adjective* unthinkingly enthusiastic and eager, especially about taking part in fighting or warfare.

ORIGIN – from a Chinese word taken to mean 'work together' and adopted as a slogan by US Marines.

gunk > *noun* informal unpleasantly sticky or messy matter.

gunman > *noun* a man who uses a gun to commit a crime or terrorist act.

gunnel¹ /**gunn**'l/ > *noun* an elongated marine fish with a dorsal fin running along most of the back.

gunnel² /**gunn**'l/ > *noun* variant spelling of GUNWALE.

gunner > *noun* 1 a person who operates a gun. 2 a British artillery soldier (used especially as an official term for a private).

gunnery > *noun* the design, manufacture, or firing of heavy guns.

gunpowder > *noun* 1 an explosive consisting of a powdered mixture of saltpetre, sulphur, and charcoal. 2 a fine green China tea, the leaves of which are rolled up into pellets.

gunwale /**gunn**'l/ (also **gunnel**) > *noun* the upper edge or planking of the side of a boat.

ORIGIN – from GUN + WALE (because it was formerly used to support guns).

gunyah /**gun**yə/ > *noun* Austral. an Aboriginal bush hut.

ORIGIN – Dharuk (an Aboriginal language).

guppy /**guppi**/ > *noun* (pl. **guppies**) a small freshwater fish native to tropical America, widely kept in aquaria.

ORIGIN – named after the Trinidadian clergyman R. J. Lechmere *Guppy* (1836–1916), who sent the first specimen to the British Museum.

gurdwara /gur**dwaa**rə/ > *noun* a Sikh place of worship.

ORIGIN – from Sanskrit words meaning 'teacher' and 'door'.

gurgle > *verb* make a hollow bubbling sound. > *noun* a gurgling sound.

Gurkha /**gur**kə/ > *noun* 1 a member of any of several Nepalese peoples noted for their military prowess. 2 a member of a regiment in the British army for Nepalese recruits.

ORIGIN – a Nepalese place name.

gurn /gurn/ (also **girn**) > *verb* Brit. pull a grotesque face.

ORIGIN – dialect variant of GRIN.

gurnard /**gur**nərd/ > *noun* a small fish with three finger-like pectoral rays with which it searches for food and walks on the seabed.

ORIGIN – Old French *gornart* 'grunter'.

gurney > *noun* (pl. **gurneys**) N. Amer. a wheeled stretcher for transporting hospital patients.

ORIGIN – apparently named after J. T. *Gurney*, the patentee of a new cab design in 1883.

guru /**goo**roo/ > *noun* 1 a Hindu spiritual teacher. 2 each of the ten first leaders of the Sikh religion. 3 an influential teacher: *a management guru*.

SYNONYMS – 3 mentor, sage, tutor.

ORIGIN – Sanskrit, 'weighty, grave'.

gush > *verb* 1 send out or flow in a rapid and plentiful stream. 2 speak or write effusively. > *noun* 1 a rapid and plentiful stream. 2 effusiveness.

DERIVATIVES – **gusher** noun **gushing** adjective **gushingly** adverb.

SYNONYMS – *verb* 1 jet, spout, spurt, stream.

gushy > *adjective* (**gushier**, **gushiest**) excessively effusive.

gusset /**guss**it/ > *noun* 1 a piece of material sewn into a garment to strengthen or enlarge a part of it, e.g. the crotch of an undergarment. 2 a bracket strengthening an angle of a structure.

ORIGIN – Old French *gousset* 'small pod or shell'.

gust > *noun* 1 a brief, strong rush of wind. 2 a burst of rain, sound, emotion, etc. > *verb* blow in gusts.

ORIGIN – Old Norse *gustr*.

gustation /gu**stay**sh'n/ > *noun* formal the action or faculty of tasting.

DERIVATIVES – **gustatory** adjective.

ORIGIN – Latin, from *gustare* 'to taste'.

gusto > *noun* enjoyment or vigour in doing something.

SYNONYMS – enthusiasm, relish, zest.

ORIGIN – Italian, from Latin *gustus* 'taste'.

gusty > *adjective* (**gustier, gustiest**) **1** characterised by or blowing in gusts. **2** showing gusto.

DERIVATIVES – **gustily** *adverb*.

gut > *noun* **1** the stomach or belly. **2** Medicine & Biology the intestine. **3** (**guts**) entrails that have been removed or exposed. **4** (**guts**) the internal parts or essence of something. **5** (**guts**) informal courage and determination. **6** (before another noun) informal instinctive: *a gut feeling*. **7** fibre from the intestines of animals, used for violin or racket strings. > *verb* (**gutted, gutting**) **1** take out the internal organs of (a fish) before cooking. **2** remove or destroy the internal parts of.

IDIOMS – **bust a gut** informal make a strenuous effort. **hate someone's guts** informal dislike someone intensely. **have someone's guts for garters** informal, humorous used as a threat of punishment.

gutless > *adjective* informal lacking courage or determination.

gutsy > *adjective* (**gutsier, gutsiest**) informal **1** showing courage and determination. **2** strongly flavoured. **3** greedy.

DERIVATIVES – **gutsiness** *noun*.

gutta-percha /guttəˈperchə/ > *noun* the hard, tough coagulated latex of certain Malaysian trees, resembling rubber.

ORIGIN – Malay.

gutted > *adjective* Brit. informal bitterly disappointed or upset.

gutter > *noun* **1** a shallow trough beneath the edge of a roof, or a channel at the side of a street, for carrying off rainwater. **2** (**the gutter**) a poor or squalid environment. **3** technical a groove or channel for flowing liquid. **4** the blank space between facing pages of a book or between adjacent columns of type or stamps in a sheet. > *verb* (of a flame) flicker and burn unsteadily.

COMBINATIONS – **gutter press** chiefly Brit. newspapers engaging in sensational journalism.

ORIGIN – Old French *gotiere*, from Latin *gutta* 'a drop'.

guttering > *noun* chiefly Brit. the gutters of a building.

guttersnipe > *noun* a street urchin.

guttural* /ˈguttərəl/ > *adjective* **1** (of a speech sound) produced in the throat. **2** (of speech) characterised by guttural sounds. > *noun* a guttural consonant (e.g. *k, g*).

DERIVATIVES – **gutturally** *adverb*.

***SPELLING** – -*tur*-, not -*ter*-: gut*tur*al.

ORIGIN – Latin *gutturalis*, from *guttur* 'throat'.

guv (also **guv'nor**) > *noun* Brit. informal (as a form of address) sir.

guy¹ > *noun* **1** informal a man. **2** (**guys**) N. Amer. informal people of either sex. **3** Brit. a figure representing the Catholic conspirator Guy Fawkes, burnt on a bonfire on 5 November to commemorate the foiling of a plot to blow up Parliament in 1605. > *verb* make fun of; ridicule.

guy² > *noun* a line fixed to the ground to secure a tent. > *verb* secure with a guy or guys.

Guyanese /gīəˈneez/ > *noun* (pl. same) a person from Guyana, a country in South America. > *adjective* relating to Guyana.

Guy Fawkes Night > *noun* another term for *Bonfire Night*.

guzzle > *verb* eat or drink greedily.

DERIVATIVES – **guzzler** *noun*.

ORIGIN – perhaps from Old French *gosillier* 'chatter, vomit'.

GWR > *abbreviation* historical (in the UK) Great Western Railway.

Gy > *abbreviation* Physics gray(s).

gybe /jīb/ (US **jibe**) Sailing > *verb* **1** change course by swinging the sail across a following wind. **2** (of a sail or boom) swing across the wind. > *noun* an act of gybing.

ORIGIN – obsolete Dutch *gijben*.

gym > *noun* informal **1** a gymnasium. **2** gymnastics.

gymkhana /jimˈkaanə/ > *noun* an event comprising competitions on horseback, typically for children.

ORIGIN – Urdu, 'racket court'.

gymnasium /jimˈnayziəm/ > *noun* (pl. **gymnasiums** or **gymnasia** /jimˈnayziə/) a hall or building equipped for gymnastics and other physical exercise.

ORIGIN – Latin, from Greek *gumnasion*, from *gumnazein* 'exercise naked'.

gymnast > *noun* a person trained in gymnastics.

gymnastics > *plural noun* (also treated as sing.) **1** exercises involving physical agility, flexibility, and coordination, especially tumbling and acrobatic feats. **2** physical or mental agility or skill: *vocal gymnastics*.

DERIVATIVES – **gymnastic** *adjective*.

gymnosperm /ˈjimnōsperm/ > *noun* Botany a plant with seeds unprotected by an ovary or fruit, such as a conifer or cycad. Compare with **ANGIOSPERM**.

ORIGIN – from Greek *gumnos* 'naked' + *sperma* 'seed'.

gymslip > *noun* Brit. dated a sleeveless belted tunic reaching from the shoulder to the knee, worn by schoolgirls doing physical education.

gynaecology* /gīniˈkolləji/ (US **gynecology**) > *noun* the branch of physiology and medicine concerned with the functions and diseases specific to women and girls, especially those affecting the reproductive system.

DERIVATIVES – **gynaecological** *adjective* **gynaecologically** *adverb* **gynaecologist** *noun*.

***SPELLING** – in British English there is -*ae*- in the middle, not -*e*-: gyn*ae*cology.

ORIGIN – from Greek *gunē* 'woman'.

gynophobia /gīnəˈfōbiə/ > *noun* extreme or irrational fear of women.

DERIVATIVES – **gynophobic** *adjective*.

gyp¹ /jip/ (also **gip**) > *noun* Brit. informal pain or discomfort.

gyp² /jip/ > *verb* (**gypped, gypping**) informal cheat or swindle (someone).

gypsum /ˈjipsəm/ > *noun* a soft white or grey mineral used to make plaster of Paris and in the building industry.

ORIGIN – Latin, from Greek *gupsos* 'chalk'.

gypsy (also **gipsy**) > *noun* (pl. **gypsies**) a member of a travelling people with dark skin and hair, speaking the Romany language.

ORIGIN – first occurring as *gipcyan*, short for **EGYPTIAN** (because gypsies were believed to have come from Egypt).

gyrate /jīˈrayt/ > *verb* **1** move in a circle or spiral. **2** dance wildly or suggestively.

DERIVATIVES – **gyration** *noun*.

ORIGIN – Latin *gyrare* 'revolve', from Greek *guros* 'a ring'.

gyratory /jīˈraytəri/ > *adjective* involving circular or spiral motion. > *noun* (pl. **gyratories**) a traffic system requiring the circular movement of traffic.

gyre /jīr/ > *verb* literary whirl; gyrate. > *noun* a spiral or vortex.

gyrfalcon /ˈjurfawlkən/ > *noun* a large, mainly grey or white arctic falcon.

ORIGIN – probably related to High German *gēr* 'spear'.

gyro /ˈjīrō/ > *noun* (pl. **gyros**) a gyroscope or gyrocompass.

gyrocompass > *noun* a compass in which the direction of true north is maintained by a gyroscope rather than magnetism.

ORIGIN – from Greek *guros* 'a ring'.

gyroscope > *noun* a device used to provide stability or maintain a fixed orientation, consisting of a wheel or disc spinning rapidly about an axis which is itself free to alter in direction.

DERIVATIVES – **gyroscopic** *adjective*.

gyve /jīv, gīv/ > *noun* archaic a fetter or shackle.

H¹ (also **h**) > *noun* (pl. **Hs** or **H's**) **1** the eighth letter of the alphabet. **2** denoting the next after G in a set.

H² > *abbreviation* **1** (of a pencil lead) hard. **2** height. **3** Physics henry(s). > *symbol* the chemical element hydrogen.

h > *abbreviation* **1** (in measuring the height of horses) hand(s). **2** hour(s). **3** Brit. (with reference to sporting fixtures) home.

ha > *abbreviation* hectare(s).

habdabs > *plural noun* variant spelling of ABDABS.

habeas corpus /haybiəss **kor**pəss/ > *noun* Law a writ requiring a person to be brought before a judge or into court, especially to investigate the lawfulness of their detention.
ORIGIN – Latin, 'you shall have the body (in court)'.

haberdasher /**habb**ərdashər/ > *noun* **1** Brit. a dealer in dressmaking and sewing goods. **2** N. Amer. a dealer in men's clothing.
DERIVATIVES – **haberdashery** noun.
ORIGIN – probably from Old French *hapertas*, perhaps the name of a fabric.

habergeon /**habb**ərjən/ > *noun* historical a sleeveless coat of mail or scale armour.
ORIGIN – Old French *haubergeon*, from *hauberc* 'hauberk'.

habiliment /hə**bill**imənt/ > *noun* archaic clothing.
ORIGIN – Old French *habillement*, from Latin *habilis* 'able'.

habit > *noun* **1** a settled or regular tendency or practice. **2** informal an addiction to drugs. **3** general shape or mode of growth, especially of a plant or mineral. **4** a long, loose garment worn by a member of a religious order. > *verb* archaic dress.
SYNONYMS – *noun* **1** custom, pattern, practice, routine, tendency.
COMBINATIONS – **habit-forming** (of a drug) addictive.
ORIGIN – Latin *habitus* 'condition, appearance', from *habere* 'have, consist of'.

habitable > *adjective* suitable to live in.
DERIVATIVES – **habitability** noun.
ORIGIN – Latin *habitabilis*, from *habitare* 'possess, inhabit'.

habitant > *noun* **1** /abbi**ton**/ an early French settler in Canada or Louisiana. **2** /**habb**it'nt/ archaic an inhabitant.

habitat > *noun* the natural home or environment of an organism.
ORIGIN – Latin, 'it inhabits'.

habitation > *noun* **1** the state or process of inhabiting. **2** formal a house or home.

habitual /hə**bi**tyooəl/ > *adjective* **1** done constantly or as a habit. **2** regular; usual.
DERIVATIVES – **habitually** adverb.
SYNONYMS – **1** compulsive, constant, continual, inveterate, perpetual, persistent.

habituate > *verb* chiefly Zoology make or become accustomed to something.
DERIVATIVES – **habituation** noun.

habitué /hə**bi**tyoo-ay/ > *noun* a resident of or frequent visitor to a place.
ORIGIN – French, 'accustomed'.

haboob /hə**boob**/ > *noun* (especially in Sudan) a violent and oppressive summer wind bringing sand from the desert.
ORIGIN – Arabic, 'blowing furiously'.

háček /**ha**check/ > *noun* a diacritic mark (ˇ) placed over a letter to modify the sound in Slavic and other languages.
ORIGIN – Czech, 'little hook'.

hachures /ha**shyoorz**/ > *plural noun* parallel lines used on maps to shade in hills, their closeness indicating steepness of gradient.
DERIVATIVES – **hachured** adjective.
ORIGIN – French, from *hacher* (see HATCH³).

hacienda /hassi**en**də/ > *noun* (in Spanish-speaking countries) a large estate with a house.
ORIGIN – Spanish, from Latin *facienda* 'things to be done'.

hack¹ > *verb* **1** cut with rough or heavy blows. **2** kick wildly or roughly. **3** use a computer to gain unauthorised access to data. **4** (**hack it**) informal manage; cope. **5** (**hack off**) informal annoy (someone). > *noun* **1** a rough cut or blow. **2** a tool for rough striking or cutting.
DERIVATIVES – **hacker** noun.
SYNONYMS – *verb* **1** chop, hew, slash.
COMBINATIONS – **hacking cough** a dry, frequent cough.

hack² > *noun* **1** a writer producing dull, unoriginal work. **2** a horse for ordinary riding, or one that is inferior or let out for hire. **3** a ride on a horse. **4** N. Amer. a taxi. > *verb* ride a horse.
DERIVATIVES – **hackery** noun.
COMBINATIONS – **hacking jacket** a riding jacket with slits at the side or back.
ORIGIN – abbreviation of HACKNEY.

hackle > *noun* **1** (**hackles**) hairs along an animal's back which rise when it is angry or alarmed. **2** a long, narrow feather on the neck or saddle of a domestic cock or other bird. **3** a steel comb for dressing flax.

IDIOMS – **make someone's hackles rise** make someone angry or indignant.

hackney > *noun* (pl. **hackneys**) chiefly historical **1** a light horse with a high-stepping trot, used in harness. **2** a horse-drawn vehicle kept for hire.
COMBINATIONS – **hackney carriage** Brit. the official term for a taxi.

hackneyed > *adjective* (of a phrase or idea) unoriginal and trite.
SYNONYMS – banal, clichéd, overused, stereotyped, trite, unoriginal.

wordpower facts

Hackneyed

The word **hackneyed** comes ultimately from the noun **hackney**. A **hackney** was originally an ordinary riding horse, as opposed to a war horse or draught horse, especially one available for hire. This gave rise to the term **hackney carriage**, and the obsolete verb *hackney*, meaning 'to make a hackney of; to use (a horse) for general riding purposes'. From there developed the sense 'make commonplace by overuse', which led to the formation of the adjective **hackneyed**. The use of **hackney** for the horse probably derives from the name of the district of *Hackney*, now in East London, where horses were pastured.

hacksaw > *noun* a saw with a narrow blade set in a frame, used for cutting metal.

had past and past participle of HAVE.

haddock > *noun* (pl. same) a silvery-grey fish of North Atlantic coastal waters, popular as a food fish.
ORIGIN – Old French *hadoc*.

Hades /**hay**deez/ > *noun* **1** Greek Mythology the underworld; the abode of the spirits of the dead. **2** informal hell.

Hadith /ha**deeth**/ > *noun* (pl. same or **Hadiths**) a collection of Islamic traditions containing sayings of the prophet Muhammad.
ORIGIN – Arabic, 'tradition'.

hadn't > *contraction* had not.

hadron /**had**ron/ > *noun* Physics a subatomic particle that can take part in the strong interaction, such as a baryon or meson.
ORIGIN – from Greek *hadros* 'bulky'.

hadrosaur /**had**rəsor/ > *noun* a large herbivorous dinosaur with jaws flattened like a duck's bill.
ORIGIN – from Greek *hadros* 'thick, stout' + *sauros* 'lizard'.

hadst archaic second person singular past of HAVE.

haemal /**hee**m'l/ (US **hemal**) > *adjective* **1** Physiology relating to the blood. **2** Zoology situated on the same side of the body as the heart and major blood vessels.

ORIGIN – from Greek *haima* 'blood'.

haematite /heeмətīt/ (US **hematite**) > *noun* a reddish-black mineral consisting of ferric oxide.

ORIGIN – from Greek *haimatitēs lithos* 'blood-like stone'.

haematology* /heeмətolləji/ (US **hematology**) > *noun* the study of the physiology of the blood.

DERIVATIVES – **haematological** *adjective* **haematologist** *noun*.

*****SPELLING – in British English the spelling is *-ae-*, not *-e-*: haematology.

wordpower facts

Haematology

The root of several of the words on this page lies in the Greek word for blood, *haima*. Similarly formed from *haima*, often via modern Latin forms, are a number of words ending in *-aemia* which refer to abnormal conditions of the blood, such as **anaemia**, **leukaemia**, and **septicaemia**.

haematoma /heeмətōмə/ (US **hematoma**) > *noun* (pl. **haematomas** or **haematomata** /heeмətōмətə/) Medicine a solid swelling of clotted blood within the tissues.

haemodialysis /heeмōdīalisiss/ (US **hemodialysis**) > *noun* (pl. **haemodialyses** /heeмōdīaliseez/) Medicine kidney dialysis.

haemoglobin /heeмəglōbin/ (US **hemoglobin**) > *noun* a red protein containing iron, responsible for transporting oxygen in the blood of vertebrates.

ORIGIN – shortening of *haematoglobulin*, from GLOBULE in the archaic sense 'blood corpuscle'.

haemophilia /heeмəfilliə/ (US **hemophilia**) > *noun* a medical condition in which the ability of the blood to clot is severely reduced, causing severe bleeding from even a slight injury.

DERIVATIVES – **haemophilic** *adjective*.

haemophiliac (US **hemophiliac**) > *noun* a person suffering from haemophilia.

haemorrhage /hemмərij/ (US **hemorrhage**) > *noun* 1 an escape of blood from a ruptured blood vessel. 2 a damaging loss of something valuable. > *verb* 1 suffer a haemorrhage. 2 expend in large amounts, seemingly uncontrollably.

ORIGIN – Greek *haimorrhagia*, from *haima* 'blood' + *rhēgnunai* 'burst'.

haemorrhoid /hemмəroyd/ (US **hemorrhoid**) > *noun* a swollen vein or group of veins (piles) at the side of the anus.

ORIGIN – from Greek *haimorrhoides phlebes* 'bleeding veins'.

haemostasis /heeмōstaysiss/ (US **hemostasis**) > *noun* Medicine the stopping of a flow of blood.

DERIVATIVES – **haemostatic** *adjective*.

haere mai /hīrə mī/ > *exclamation* a Maori greeting.

ORIGIN – Maori, 'come hither'.

hafiz /haafeez/ > *noun* a Muslim who knows the Koran by heart.

ORIGIN – Arabic, 'guardian'.

hafnium /hafniəm/ > *noun* a hard silver-grey metal resembling zirconium.

ORIGIN – from *Hafnia*, the Latin form of *Havn*, a former name of Copenhagen.

haft /haaft/ > *noun* the handle of a knife, axe, or spear. > *verb* provide with a haft.

ORIGIN – Old English, related to HEAVE.

hag¹ > *noun* 1 an ugly old woman. 2 a witch.

DERIVATIVES – **haggish** *adjective*.

COMBINATIONS – **hag-ridden** afflicted by nightmares or anxieties.

hag² > *noun* Scottish & N. English a soft place on a moor or a firm place in a bog.

ORIGIN – Old Norse, 'gap'.

haggard > *adjective* 1 looking exhausted and unwell. 2 (of a hawk) caught and trained as an adult.

SYNONYMS – 1 careworn, drawn, gaunt, pinched.

ORIGIN – first used in sense 2: from French *hagard*, perhaps related to HEDGE.

haggis > *noun* (pl. same) a Scottish dish consisting of seasoned sheep's or calf's offal mixed with suet and oatmeal, boiled in a bag traditionally made from the animal's stomach.

ORIGIN – probably from earlier *hag* 'hack, hew'.

haggle > *verb* dispute or bargain persistently, especially over a price. > *noun* a period of haggling.

DERIVATIVES – **haggler** *noun*.

ORIGIN – first used in the sense 'hack, mangle': from Old Norse *hǫggva*.

hagiographer /haggiogrəfər/ > *noun* 1 a writer of the lives of the saints. 2 a writer of a biography that idealises its subject.

ORIGIN – from Greek *hagios* 'holy'.

hagiography /haggiogrəfi/ > *noun* 1 the writing of the lives of saints. 2 a biography idealising its subject.

DERIVATIVES – **hagiographic** *adjective* **hagiographical** *adjective*.

hagiolatry /haggiollətri/ > *noun* the worship of saints.

hagiology /haggiolləji/ > *noun* literature concerned with the lives and legends of saints.

DERIVATIVES – **hagiological** *adjective* **hagiologist** *noun*.

ha-ha > *noun* a ditch with a wall on its inner side below ground level, forming a boundary to a park or garden without interrupting the view.

ORIGIN – said to be from the cry of surprise uttered on encountering such an obstacle.

haiku /hīkōō/ > *noun* (pl. same or **haikus**) a Japanese poem of seventeen syllables, in three lines of five, seven, and five.

ORIGIN – Japanese, contraction of a phrase meaning 'light verse'.

hail¹ > *noun* 1 pellets of frozen rain falling in showers from cumulonimbus clouds. 2 a large number of things hurled forcefully through the air. > *verb* (**it hails**, **it is hailing**, etc.) hail falls.

COMBINATIONS – **hailstone** a pellet of hail.

hail² > *verb* 1 call out to (someone) to attract attention. 2 acclaim enthusiastically: *he has been hailed as the new James Dean.* 3 (**hail from**) have one's home or origins in. > *exclamation* archaic expressing greeting or acclaim. > *noun* a call to attract attention.

IDIOMS – **within hail** within earshot.

COMBINATIONS – **hail-fellow-well-met** showing excessive familiarity.

ORIGIN – from obsolete *hail* 'healthy', related to HALE¹, WHOLE, and WASSAIL.

Hail Mary > *noun* (pl. **Hail Marys**) a prayer to the Virgin Mary used chiefly by Roman Catholics.

hair > *noun* 1 any of the fine thread-like strands growing from the skin of mammals and other animals, or from the epidermis of a plant. 2 strands of hair collectively, especially on a person's head. 3 a very small quantity or extent.

WORDFINDER – alopecia (*abnormal hair loss*), depilate (*remove hair from*), follicle (*sheath surrounding the root of a hair*), glabrous (*hairless*), hirsute (*hairy*), trichology (*branch of medicine and cosmetics concerned with the hair and scalp*).

IDIOMS – **hair of the dog** informal an alcoholic drink taken to cure a hangover. [ORIGIN – from *hair of the dog that bit you*, formerly recommended as a remedy for the bite of a mad dog.] **a hair's breadth** a very small margin. **in** (or **out of**) **someone's hair** informal burdening (or ceasing to burden) someone. **keep your hair on!** Brit. informal stay calm. **let one's hair down** informal behave wildly or uninhibitedly. **make someone's hair stand on end** alarm someone. **not turn a hair** remain apparently unmoved. **split hairs** make overfine distinctions.

DERIVATIVES – **haired** *adjective* **hairless** *adjective*.

COMBINATIONS – **hairball** a ball of hair which collects in the stomach of an animal as a result of the animal licking its coat. **hairband** a band for securing or tying back one's hair. **hairbrush** a brush for smoothing one's hair. **hairdryer** (also **hairdrier**) an electrical device for drying the hair with warm air. **hairgrip** Brit. a flat hairpin with the ends close together. **hairnet** a fine mesh for confining the hair. **hairpiece** a patch or bunch of false hair used to augment a person's natural hair. **hair-raising** alarming, astonishing, or terrifying. **hair shirt** a shirt made of stiff cloth woven from horsehair, formerly worn by penitents and ascetics. **hairslide** Brit. a clip for keeping a woman's hair in position. **hair-splitting** the making of overfine distinctions. **hairspray** a solution sprayed on to hair to keep it in place. **hairspring** a slender flat coiled spring regulating the movement of the balance wheel in a watch. **hair trigger** a firearm trigger set for release at the slightest pressure.

haircut > *noun* **1** the style in which someone's hair is cut. **2** an act of cutting someone's hair.

hairdo > *noun* (pl. **hairdos**) informal the style of a woman's hair.

hairdresser > *noun* a person who cuts and styles hair.
WORDFINDER – tonsorial (*of or related to hairdressing*).
DERIVATIVES – **hairdressing** noun.

hairline > *noun* **1** the edge of a person's hair. **2** (before another noun) very thin or fine: *a hairline fracture.*

hairpin > *noun* a U-shaped pin for fastening the hair.

hairpin bend > *noun* Brit. a sharp U-shaped bend in a road.

hairstyle > *noun* a way in which someone's hair is cut or arranged.
DERIVATIVES – **hairstyling** noun **hairstylist** noun.

hairy > *adjective* (**hairier, hairiest**) **1** covered with or resembling hair. **2** informal alarming and difficult.
DERIVATIVES – **hairiness** noun.

Haitian /haysh'n/ > *noun* a person from Haiti. > *adjective* relating to Haiti.

haji /haji/ (also **hajji**) > *noun* (pl. **hajis**) a Muslim who has been to Mecca as a pilgrim.
ORIGIN – Persian and Turkish, from the Arabic root of **HAJJ**.

hajj /haj/ (also **haj**) > *noun* the pilgrimage to Mecca which all Muslims are expected to make at least once.
ORIGIN – Arabic, 'great pilgrimage'.

haka /haakə/ > *noun* a Maori ceremonial war dance involving chanting.
ORIGIN – Maori.

hake > *noun* a large-headed elongated food fish with long jaws and strong teeth.

halal /həlaal/ > *adjective* (of meat) prepared as prescribed by Muslim law.
ORIGIN – Arabic, 'according to religious law'.

halala /həlaalə/ > *noun* (pl. same or **halalas**) a monetary unit of Saudi Arabia, equal to one hundredth of a rial.
ORIGIN – Arabic.

halberd /halbərd/ (also **halbert**) > *noun* historical a combined spear and battleaxe.
ORIGIN – High German *helmbarde*, from *helm* 'handle' + *barde* 'hatchet'.

halberdier /halbərdeer/ > *noun* historical a man armed with a halberd.

halcyon /halsiən/ > *adjective* (of a past time) idyllically happy and peaceful.

---

wordpower facts
Halcyon
The word **halcyon** comes from Greek *alkuōn*, from *hals* 'sea' and *kuōn* 'conceiving'. The Greek word referred to a mythical bird that was said to breed in the middle of winter in a nest floating on the sea; this **halcyon** was able to charm the winter wind and waves into a state of calm. The mythical bird became identified with a species of kingfisher, and by the late 18th century **halcyon** had come to be used as a genus name and a poetic term for the kingfisher. The adjective first arose in the phrase **halcyon days**, the fourteen days of calm weather when the mythical halcyon was sitting on its eggs.

---

hale¹ > *adjective* (of an old person) strong and healthy.
ORIGIN – Old English, 'whole'.

hale² > *verb* archaic haul.
ORIGIN – Old French *haler*.

haler /haalər/ > *noun* (pl. same or **haleru** /haalərōō/) a monetary unit of the Czech Republic and Slovakia, equal to one hundredth of a koruna.
ORIGIN – Czech, from *Schwäbisch Hall*, a German town where coins were minted.

half > *noun* (pl. **halves**) **1** either of two equal or corresponding parts into which something is or can be divided. **2** either of two equal periods into which a match or performance is divided. **3** Brit. informal half a pint of beer. **4** informal a half-price fare or ticket. **5** a halfback. > *adverb* **1** to the extent of half. **2** partly: *half-cooked.*
WORDFINDER – bisect (*cut in half*).
IDIOMS – **at half mast 1** (of a flag) flown halfway down its mast, as a mark of respect for a person who has died. **2** humorous (of clothing) in a lower position than normal. **half a chance** informal the slightest opportunity. **half past one** (**two**, etc.) thirty minutes after one (two, etc.) o'clock. **not do things by halves** do things thoroughly or extravagantly. **not half 1** not nearly. **2** informal not at all. **3** Brit. informal to an

extreme degree. **one's better half** informal one's husband, wife, or partner. **too ——by half** excessively ——.
COMBINATIONS – **half-and-half** in equal parts. **half-arsed** vulgar slang incompetent or inadequate. **halfback** a player in a ball game such as rugby whose position is between the forwards and fullbacks. **half-baked** incompetently planned or considered. **half binding** a type of bookbinding in which the spine and corners are bound in a different material to the rest of the cover. **half blood 1** the relationship between people having one parent in common. **2** a person related to another in this way. **3** offensive another term for *half-breed.* **half board** Brit. provision of bed, breakfast, and a main meal at a hotel or guest house. **half-breed** offensive a person of mixed race. **half-brother** (or **half-sister**) a brother (or sister) with whom one has only one parent in common. **half-caste** offensive a person of mixed race. **half-century 1** a period of fifty years. **2** a score of fifty in cricket. **half-crown** (also **half a crown**) a former British coin and monetary unit equal to two shillings and sixpence (12½p). **half-cut** Brit. informal drunk. **half-dozen** (also **half a dozen**) a group of six. **half-hardy** (of a plant) able to grow outdoors except in severe frost. **half-hearted** without enthusiasm or energy. **half hitch** a knot formed by passing the end of a rope round its standing part and then through the loop. **half holiday** a half day taken as a holiday, especially at school. **half-hour 1** (also **half an hour**) a period of thirty minutes. **2** a point in time thirty minutes after a full hour of the clock. **half-hunter** a pocket watch with a small opening in the cover allowing one to read the approximate time. **half-inch** Brit. informal steal. [ORIGIN – rhyming slang for 'pinch'.] **half landing** Brit. a landing where a flight of stairs turns through 180 degrees. **half-life** the time taken for something to decrease by half, in particular the radioactivity of an isotope. **half-light** dim light, as at dusk. **half measure** an inadequate action or policy. **half-moon 1** the moon when only half its surface is visible from the earth. **2** a semicircular or crescent-shaped object. **half nelson** see **NELSON**. **half note** Music, chiefly N. Amer. a minim. **half relief** a method of moulding, carving, or stamping a design in which figures project to half their true proportions. **half-term** Brit. a short holiday halfway through a school term. **half-timbered** having walls with a timber frame and a brick or plaster filling. **half-time** (in sport) a short interval between two halves of a match. **half-title** the title of a book, printed on the right-hand page before the title page. **half-track** a vehicle with wheels

at the front and caterpillar tracks at the rear.
half-truth a statement conveying only part of the truth. **half-volley** (in sport) a strike or kick of the ball immediately after it bounces.

half-cock > *noun* the partly raised position of the cock of a gun.
IDIOMS – **at half-cock 1** (of a gun) with the cock partly raised. **2** when only partly ready.
DERIVATIVES – **half-cocked** *adjective*.

halfpenny /**hayp**ni/ (also **ha'penny**) > *noun* (pl. **halfpennies** (for separate coins); **halfpence** /**hayp**'nss/ (for a sum of money)) a former British coin equal to half an old or new penny.

halfpennyworth /**hayp**əth, **hayp**niwəth/ (also **ha'p'orth**) > *noun* Brit. **1** as much as could be bought for a halfpenny. **2** (**ha'p'orth**) informal a negligible amount: *he's never been a ha'p'orth of bother.*
IDIOMS – **don't spoil the ship for a ha'p'orth of tar** *proverb* don't risk the failure of a large project by trying to economise on trivial things. [ORIGIN – referring to the use of tar to keep flies off sores on sheep (from dialect pronunciation of *sheep* as *ship*).]

half-pie > *adjective* NZ informal imperfect; mediocre.

half-tone > *noun* **1** a reproduction of an image in which the tones of grey or colour are produced by variously sized dots. **2** Music, chiefly N. Amer. a semitone.

halfway > *adverb & adjective* **1** at or to a point equidistant between two others. **2** (as adverb) to some extent: *halfway decent.*
COMBINATIONS – **halfway house 1** the halfway point in a progression. **2** a compromise. **3** a centre for rehabilitating former prisoners or psychiatric patients.

halfwit > *noun* informal a stupid person.
DERIVATIVES – **half-witted** *adjective*.

halibut /**hal**ibət/ > *noun* (pl. same) a large marine flatfish, used as food.
ORIGIN – from *haly* 'holy' + obsolete *butt* 'flatfish' (because it was often eaten on holy days).

halide /**hay**līd/ > *noun* Chemistry a binary compound of a halogen with another element or group: *silver halide.*

halite /**hal**īt/ > *noun* sodium chloride as a mineral; rock salt.
ORIGIN – from Greek *hals* 'salt'.

halitosis /halit**ō**siss/ > *noun* unpleasant-smelling breath.
ORIGIN – from Latin *halitus* 'breath'.

hall > *noun* **1** (also **hallway**) the room or space just inside the front entrance of a house. **2** a large room for meetings, concerts, etc. **3** (also **hall of residence**) chiefly Brit. a university building in which students live. **4** Brit. a large country house. **5** N. Amer. a corridor or passage in a building. **6** the dining room of a college, university, or school. **7** the principal living room of a medieval house.
COMBINATIONS – **Hall of Fame** chiefly N. Amer. the group of people who have excelled in a particular sphere.

hallelujah /halil**oo**yə/ (also **alleluia**) > *exclamation* God be praised! > *noun* an utterance of the word 'hallelujah'.
ORIGIN – Hebrew, 'praise ye the Lord'.

hallmark > *noun* **1** a mark stamped on articles of gold, silver, or platinum by the British assay offices, certifying purity. **2** a distinctive feature, especially of excellence. > *verb* stamp with a hallmark.
ORIGIN – from *Goldsmiths' Hall* in London, where articles were tested and stamped.

hallo > *exclamation* variant spelling of **HELLO**.

halloo > *exclamation* used to incite dogs to the chase during a hunt.
ORIGIN – probably from the rare verb *hallow* 'pursue or urge on with shouts'.

hallow /**hal**ō/ > *verb* **1** make holy; consecrate. **2** honour as holy. **3** (**hallowed**) greatly revered.

Halloween (also **Hallowe'en**) > *noun* the night of 31 October, the eve of All Saints' Day.
ORIGIN – contraction of *All Hallows Even*, the night before All Hallows or All Saints' Day.

hallucinate /hə**loo**sinayt/ > *verb* experience a seemingly real perception of something not actually present.
DERIVATIVES – **hallucination** *noun* **hallucinator** *noun* **hallucinatory** *adjective*.
ORIGIN – Latin *hallucinari* 'go astray in thought', from Greek *alussein* 'be uneasy or distraught'.

hallucinogen /hə**loo**sinnəjən/ > *noun* a drug causing hallucinations.
DERIVATIVES – **hallucinogenic** *adjective*.

halo /**hay**lō/ > *noun* (pl. **haloes** or **halos**) **1** (in a painting) a circle of light surrounding the head of a holy person. **2** a circle of light round the sun or moon. > *verb* (**haloes**, **haloed**) surround with or as if with a halo.
ORIGIN – Greek *halōs* 'disc of the sun or moon'.

halogen /**hal**əjən/ > *noun* **1** Chemistry any of the group of reactive, non-metallic elements fluorine, chlorine, bromine, iodine, and astatine. **2** (before another noun) using a filament surrounded by halogen vapour: *a halogen bulb.*
ORIGIN – from Greek *hals* 'salt'.

halon /**hay**lon/ > *noun* any of a number of unreactive gaseous compounds of carbon with halogens, used in fire extinguishers.

halt¹ > *verb* bring or come to an abrupt stop. > *noun* **1** a suspension of movement or activity. **2** Brit. a minor stopping place on a railway line.
IDIOMS – **call a halt** order a stop.
SYNONYMS – *verb* stop, terminate. *noun* **1** break, cessation, stoppage, suspension.
ORIGIN – German *halten* 'to hold'.

halt² archaic > *adjective* lame. > *verb* walk with a limp.

halter > *noun* **1** a rope or strap placed around the head of an animal and used to lead or tether it. **2** archaic a noose for hanging a person. **3** a strap passing behind the neck by which the bodice of a sleeveless dress or top is held in place. > *verb* put a halter on (an animal).
COMBINATIONS – **halter neck** a style of neckline incorporating a halter.

halting > *adjective* slow and hesitant.
DERIVATIVES – **haltingly** *adverb*.

halva /**hal**və/ (also **halvah**) > *noun* a Middle Eastern sweet made of sesame flour and honey.
ORIGIN – Arabic and Persian, 'sweetmeat'.

halve > *verb* **1** divide into two parts of equal size. **2** reduce or be reduced by half.

halves plural of **HALF**.

halyard /**hal**yərd/ > *noun* a rope used for raising and lowering a sail, yard, or flag on a ship.
ORIGIN – from **HALE²**.

ham¹ > *noun* **1** meat from the upper part of a pig's leg salted and dried or smoked. **2** (**hams**) the back of the thigh or the thighs and buttocks.
COMBINATIONS – **ham-fisted** (also **ham-handed**) clumsy and unskilful.

---

wordpower facts

Ham

The Germanic root of the word **ham** was a verb meaning 'be crooked'. In Old English **ham**, or **hom**, referred to the angle or the back of the knee; by the late 15th century it had come to denote the back of the thigh, and subsequently the thigh or hock of an animal. Specific use in reference to the thigh of a hog used for food, especially when salted and smoked, dates from the early 17th century. A **hamburger** has nothing to do with **ham**: Hamburger is a German word denoting a person or a thing from the city of Hamburg in northern Germany. Although a **hamburger** is made from beef the erroneous assumption that it is made from ham led to the formation of the word **beefburger**.

---

ham² > *noun* **1** an inexpert or unsubtle actor or piece of acting. **2** (also **radio ham**) informal an amateur radio operator. > *verb* (**hammed**, **hamming**) (often in phrase **ham it up**) informal overact.

ORIGIN – perhaps from the first syllable of AMATEUR.

hamadryad /hamməˈdrīad/ > *noun* Greek & Roman Mythology a nymph who lives in a tree and dies when it dies.

ORIGIN – Greek *Hamadruas*, from *hama* 'together' + *drus* 'tree'.

hamburger > *noun* a small flat cake of minced beef, fried or grilled and typically served in a bread roll.

hamlet > *noun* a small village, especially (in Britain) one without a church.

ORIGIN – Old French *hamelet*, from *hamel* 'little village'.

hammer > *noun* **1** a tool consisting of a heavy metal head mounted at the end of a handle, used for breaking things and driving in nails. **2** an auctioneer's mallet tapped sharply against a table to indicate that an article is sold. **3** a part of a mechanism that hits another, e.g. one exploding the charge in a gun. **4** a heavy metal ball attached to a wire for throwing in an athletic contest. > *verb* **1** hit or beat repeatedly with or as with a hammer. **2** (**hammer away**) work hard and persistently. **3** (**hammer in** or **into**) instil (information or opinions) forcefully or repeatedly. **4** (**hammer out**) laboriously work out (the details of a plan or agreement). **5** (**hammer out**) play (a tune) loudly and unskilfully, especially on the piano. **6** informal utterly defeat.

WORDFINDER – malleable (*able to be hammered into shape*); types of hammer: claw hammer, gavel, jackhammer, mallet, plexor, sledgehammer, trip hammer.

IDIOMS – **come** (or **go**) **under the hammer** be sold at an auction. **hammer and tongs** informal enthusiastically or vehemently.

COMBINATIONS – **hammer and sickle** the symbols of the industrial worker and the peasant used as the emblem of the former USSR and of international communism. **hammer beam** a short wooden beam projecting from a wall to support a principal rafter or one end of an arch. **hammer drill** a power drill that delivers a rapid succession of blows. **hammerhead** a shark with flattened blade-like extensions on either side of the head. **hammerlock** an armlock in which a person's arm is bent up behind their back. **hammer toe** a toe that is bent permanently downwards, typically as a result of pressure from footwear.

hammock > *noun* a wide strip of canvas or rope mesh suspended by two ends, used as a bed.

ORIGIN – Taino (an extinct Caribbean language).

Hammond organ > *noun* trademark a type of electronic organ.

ORIGIN – named after the American mechanical engineer Laurens *Hammond* (1895–1973).

hammy > *adjective* (**hammier**, **hammiest**) informal (of acting or an actor) exaggerated or over-theatrical.

hamper[1] > *noun* **1** a basket with a carrying handle and a hinged lid, used for food, cutlery, etc. on a picnic. **2** Brit. a box containing food and drink for a special occasion.

ORIGIN – Old French *hanaper* 'case for a goblet', from *hanap* 'goblet'.

hamper[2] > *verb* hinder or impede the movement or progress of.

SYNONYMS – hinder, impede, inhibit, obstruct, retard.

hamster* > *noun* a burrowing rodent with a short tail and large cheek pouches, native to Europe and North Asia.

*SPELLING – no *p*: hamster, not hamp-.

ORIGIN – Old High German *hamustro* 'corn weevil'.

hamstring > *noun* **1** any of five tendons at the back of a person's knee. **2** the great tendon at the back of a quadruped's hock. > *verb* (past and past participle **hamstrung**) **1** cripple by cutting the hamstrings. **2** severely restrict; thwart.

Han /han/ > *noun* **1** the Chinese dynasty that ruled almost continuously from 206 BC until AD 220. **2** the dominant ethnic group in China.

hand > *noun* **1** the end part of the arm beyond the wrist. **2** (before another noun) operated by or held in the hand: *hand luggage*. **3** (before another noun or in combination) done or made manually: *hand-stitched*. **4** a pointer on a clock or watch indicating the passing of units of time. **5** (**hands**) a person's power or control: *taking the law into their own hands*. **6** an active role: *he had a big hand in organising the event*. **7** (**a hand**) help in doing something. **8** a person engaging in manual labour. **9** informal a round of applause. **10** the set of cards dealt to a player in a card game. **11** a person's handwriting. **12** a unit of measurement of a horse's height, equal to 4 inches (10.16 cm). [ORIGIN – denoting the breadth of a hand.] **13** a pledge of marriage by a woman. > *verb* **1** give to (someone). **2** hold the hand of, in order to assist.

WORDFINDER – ambidextrous (*able to use right or left hands equally well*), dexterity (*skill with the hands*), manual (*involving the hands*), manicure (*cosmetic treatment of the hands*), metacarpus (*bones of the hand*), palmate (*shaped like an open hand*).

IDIOMS – **at hand** near; readily accessible. **by hand** by a person and not a machine. **get** (or **keep**) **one's hand in** become (or remain) practised in something. **hand down 1** pass on to a successor. **2** announce (something) formally or publicly. **hand in glove** in close association. **hand out** distribute (something) among a group. (**from**) **hand to mouth** satisfying only one's immediate needs because of lack of money. **hands down** easily and decisively. **have to hand it to someone** informal used to acknowledge the merit or achievement of someone. **in hand 1** in progress; requiring immediate attention. **2** ready for use if required; in reserve. **in safe hands** protected by someone trustworthy. **many hands make light work** proverb a task is soon accomplished if several people help. **on hand 1** present and available. **2** needing to be dealt with. **on someone's hands 1** under the responsibility of the person specified. **2** at someone's disposal. **on the one** (or **the other**) **hand** used to present factors for (and against). **out of hand 1** not under control. **2** without taking time to think. **to hand** within easy reach. **turn one's hand to** undertake (an activity different from one's usual occupation). **wait on hand and foot** attend to (someone's) needs or requests, especially when excessive.

COMBINATIONS – **handbag** Brit. a small bag used by a woman to carry everyday personal items. **handball 1** a game similar to fives, in which the ball is hit with the hand in a walled court. **2** Soccer illegal touching of the ball with the hand or arm. **handbill** a small printed advertisement or other notice distributed by hand. **handbrake** a brake operated by hand, used to hold an already stationary vehicle. **handcart** a small cart pushed or drawn by hand. **hand grenade** a hand-thrown grenade. **handgun** a gun designed for use by one hand, chiefly either a pistol or a revolver. **handhold** something for a hand to grip on. **handmade** made by hand rather than machine. **hand-pick** select carefully. **handprint** the mark left by the impression of a hand. **handset 1** the part of a telephone that is held up to speak into and listen to. **2** a hand-held control device for a piece of electronic equipment. **handspring** a jump through the air on to one's hands followed by another on to one's feet. **handstand** an act of balancing upside down on one's hands. **hand-to-hand** (of fighting) at close quarters.

handbook > *noun* a book giving brief information such as facts on a particular subject or instructions for operating a machine.

h & c > *abbreviation* Brit. hot and cold (water).

handcraft > *verb* make skilfully by hand. > *noun* another term for HANDICRAFT.

handcuff > *noun* (**handcuffs**) a pair of

lockable linked metal rings for securing a prisoner's wrists. > *verb* put handcuffs on.

handful > *noun* **1** a quantity that fills the hand. **2** a small number or amount. **3** *informal* a person who is difficult to deal with or control.

handicap > *noun* **1** a condition that markedly restricts a person's ability to function physically, mentally, or socially. **2** a disadvantage imposed on a superior competitor in sports such as golf and horse racing in order to make the chances more equal. **3** the number of strokes by which a golfer normally exceeds par for a course. > *verb* (**handicapped**, **handicapping**) act as a handicap to; place at a disadvantage.

wordpower facts
Handicap

The word **handicap** derives from the phrase *hand in cap*. This was the name given to an old pastime in which one person claimed an article belonging to another and offered something in exchange, any difference in value being decided by an umpire. All three deposited forfeit money in a cap; the two opponents showed their agreement or disagreement with the valuation by bringing out their hands either full or empty. If both were the same, the umpire took the forfeit money; if not it went to the person who accepted the valuation. This game had a long history, being mentioned (by a different name) in Langland's *Piers Plowman* in the middle of the 14th century and again in 1660 in Samuel Pepys's diary. The term *handicap race* was applied in the late 18th century to a horse race in which an umpire decided the weight to be carried by each horse, the owners showing acceptance or dissent in a similar way: hence in the late 19th century *handicap* came to mean the extra weight given to the superior horse.

handicapped > *adjective* having a handicap. USAGE – in the middle of the 20th century **handicapped** was the standard term used in reference to people with physical and mental disabilities. However, by the 1980s it had been superseded in British English by **disabled**. It is now regarded as dated, if not actually offensive.

handicraft > *noun* **1** a particular skill of making decorative domestic or other objects by hand. **2** an object made using a skill of this kind. ORIGIN – alteration of **HANDCRAFT**, on the pattern of *handiwork*.

handiwork > *noun* **1** (**one's handiwork**) something that one has made or done. **2** the making of things by hand. ORIGIN – Old English, from **HAND** + a word meaning 'something made'.

handkerchief /**hang**kərchif/ > *noun* (pl. **handkerchiefs** or **handkerchieves**) a square of cotton or other material for wiping one's nose.

handle > *verb* **1** feel or manipulate with the hands. **2** manage or cope with (a situation, person, or problem). **3** deal with. **4** control or manage commercially. **5** (**handle oneself**) conduct oneself. **6** (of a vehicle) respond in a specified way when being driven. > *noun* **1** the part by which a thing is held, carried, or controlled. **2** a means of understanding, controlling, or approaching a person or situation. **3** *informal* the name of a person or place. DERIVATIVES – **handled** *adjective* **handling** *noun*. SYNONYMS – *verb* **1** feel, finger, hold, manipulate, paw, touch. ORIGIN – Old English, from **HAND**.

handlebar (also **handlebars**) > *noun* the steering bar of a bicycle, motorbike, or other similar vehicle. COMBINATIONS – **handlebar moustache** a wide, thick moustache with the ends curving slightly upwards.

handler > *noun* **1** a person who handles a particular type of article or commodity. **2** a person who trains or has charge of an animal. **3** a person who trains or manages another person.

handmaid (also **handmaiden**) > *noun* **1** *archaic* a female servant. **2** a subservient partner or element.

hand-me-down > *noun* a garment or other item that has been passed on from another person.

handout > *noun* **1** an amount of money or other aid given to a needy person or organisation. **2** a piece of printed information provided free of charge, especially to accompany a lecture.

handover > *noun* *chiefly Brit.* an act of handing something over.

handshake > *noun* an act of shaking a person's hand. DERIVATIVES – **handshaking** *noun*.

handsome > *adjective* (**handsomer**, **handsomest**) **1** (of a man) good-looking. **2** (of a woman) striking and imposing rather than conventionally pretty. **3** (of a thing) well made, imposing, and of obvious quality. **4** (of an amount) substantial; sizeable. IDIOMS – **handsome is as handsome does** *proverb* character and behaviour are more important than appearance. DERIVATIVES – **handsomely** *adverb* **handsomeness** *noun*.

SYNONYMS – **1** attractive, good-looking, personable, striking; *informal* dishy. ANTONYMS – **1** ugly. ORIGIN – from **HAND** + **-SOME**[1]; the original sense was 'easy to handle or use', hence 'apt, clever'.

handwriting > *noun* **1** writing with a pen or pencil rather than by typing or printing. **2** a person's particular style of writing. WORDFINDER – calligraphy (*decorative handwriting*), chirography (*handwriting as opposed to typography*), copperplate (*an elaborate looped style of handwriting*), cursive (*written with the characters joined*), graphology (*study of handwriting*). DERIVATIVES – **handwritten** *adjective*.

handy > *adjective* (**handier**, **handiest**) **1** convenient to handle or use. **2** ready to hand; nearby. **3** placed or occurring conveniently. **4** skilful or adept. IDIOMS – **come in handy** *informal* turn out to be useful. DERIVATIVES – **handily** *adverb*. SYNONYMS – **1** convenient, helpful, practical, useful.

handyman > *noun* a person employed to do general decorating or domestic repairs.

hang > *verb* (past and past participle **hung** except in sense 2) **1** suspend or be suspended from above with the lower part not attached. **2** (past and past participle **hanged**) kill or be killed by tying a rope attached from above around the neck and removing the support from beneath the feet (used as a form of capital punishment). **3** attach so as to allow free movement about the point of attachment: *hanging a door*. **4** (of fabric or a garment) fall or drape in a specified way. **5** attach (meat or game) to a hook and leave it until dry, tender, or high. **6** remain static in the air. **7** be present or imminent, especially oppressively or threateningly. **8** paste (wallpaper) to a wall. > *noun* the way in which something hangs or is hung. > *exclamation* *dated* used in expressions as a mild oath. IDIOMS – **get the hang of** *informal* learn how to operate or do. **hang around 1** loiter; wait around. **2** (**hang around with**) associate with. **hang back** remain behind. **hang fire** delay or be delayed in taking action. **hanging valley** a valley which is cut across by a deeper valley or a cliff. **hang on 1** hold tightly. **2** *informal* wait for a short time. **3** be contingent or dependent on. **4** listen closely to. **hang out** *informal* spend time relaxing or enjoying oneself. **hang up** end a telephone conversation by cutting the connection. **let it all hang out** *informal* be very relaxed or uninhibited. USAGE – **hang** has two past tense and past participle forms, **hanged** and **hung**. Use **hung** in general contexts, as in *they hung out the washing*: **hanged** is restricted to the context of execution by hanging, as in *the prisoner was hanged*.

COMBINATIONS – **hang-out** informal a place one lives in or frequently visits. **hang-up** informal an emotional problem or inhibition.

hangar* /**hang**ər/ > *noun* a large building with extensive floor area, typically for housing aircraft.

***SPELLING** – *-ar*, not *-er*: hang*ar*.

ORIGIN – French, probably from Germanic words meaning 'hamlet' and 'enclosure'.

hangdog > *adjective* having a dejected or guilty appearance; shamefaced.

hanger > *noun* **1** a person who hangs something. **2** (also **coat hanger**) a shaped piece of wood, plastic, or metal with a hook at the top, for hanging clothes from a rail.

COMBINATIONS – **hanger-on** (pl. **hangers-on**) a person who associates sycophantically with another person.

hang-glider > *noun* an unpowered flying apparatus for a single person, consisting of a frame with a fabric aerofoil stretched over it from which the operator is suspended.

DERIVATIVES – **hang-glide** *verb* **hang-gliding** *noun*.

hangi /**hang**i, **haang**i/ > *noun* NZ **1** a pit in which food is cooked on heated stones. **2** the food or meal cooked in such a pit.

ORIGIN – Maori.

hanging > *noun* **1** the practice of hanging condemned people as a form of capital punishment. **2** a decorative piece of fabric hung on the wall of a room or around a bed. > *adjective* suspended in the air.

hangman > *noun* an executioner who hangs condemned people.

hangnail > *noun* a piece of torn skin at the root of a fingernail.

ORIGIN – alteration of *agnail* 'painful swelling around a nail', influenced by HANG.

hangover > *noun* **1** a severe headache or other after-effects caused by drinking too much alcohol. **2** a thing that has survived from the past.

hank > *noun* a coil or skein of wool, hair, or other material.

hanker > *verb* (**hanker after, for,** or **to do**) feel a strong desire for or to do (something).

DERIVATIVES – **hankering** *noun*.

SYNONYMS – (**hanker after, for, or to do**) crave, desire, long for, yearn for.

hanky (also **hankie**) > *noun* (pl. **hankies**) informal a handkerchief.

hanky-panky > *noun* informal, humorous behaviour considered improper but not seriously so.

Hanoverian /hannə**veer**iən/ > *adjective* relating to the royal house of Hanover, who ruled as monarchs in Britain from 1714 to 1901.

Hansard /**han**saard/ > *noun* the official

verbatim record of debates in the British, Canadian, Australian, or New Zealand parliament.

ORIGIN – named after the English printer Thomas C. *Hansard* (1776–1833).

Hansen's disease > *noun* another term for LEPROSY.

ORIGIN – named after the Norwegian physician Gerhard *Hansen* (1841–1912).

hansom /**han**səm/ (also **hansom cab**) > *noun* historical a two-wheeled horse-drawn cab having space for two inside, with the driver seated behind.

ORIGIN – named after the English architect Joseph A. *Hansom* (1803–82), who patented such a cab.

hantavirus /**han**təvīrəss/ > *noun* a virus of a kind carried by rodents and causing various diseases characterised by fever and haemorrhaging.

ORIGIN – from *Hantaan*, a river in Korea where the virus was first isolated.

Hants > *abbreviation* Hampshire.

Hanukkah /**hann**əkə/ (also **Chanukkah**) > *noun* an eight-day Jewish festival of lights held in December, commemorating the rededication of the Jewish Temple in Jerusalem.

ORIGIN – Hebrew, 'consecration'.

hap > *noun* archaic luck; fortune.

ORIGIN – Old Norse *happ*.

hapax legomenon /happaks li**gomm**inon/ > *noun* (pl. **hapax legomena** /li**gomm**inə/) a term of which only one instance of use is recorded.

ORIGIN – Greek, 'a thing said once', from *hapax* 'once' and *legein* 'to say'.

ha'penny > *noun* variant spelling of HALFPENNY.

haphazard > *adjective* lacking order or organisation.

DERIVATIVES – **haphazardly** *adverb*.

SYNONYMS – chaotic, disorderly, disorganised, higgledy-piggledy, random.

ORIGIN – from HAP + HAZARD.

hapless > *adjective* unlucky; unfortunate.

DERIVATIVES – **haplessly** *adverb*.

ORIGIN – from HAP.

haplography /hap**log**rəfi/ > *noun* the inadvertent omission of a repeated letter or letters in writing (e.g. writing *philogy* for *philology*).

ORIGIN – from Greek *haploos* 'single'.

haploid /**hap**loyd/ > *adjective* Genetics (of a cell or nucleus) having a single set of unpaired chromosomes. Compare with DIPLOID.

happen > *verb* **1** take place; occur. **2** come about by chance. **3** (**happen to**) be experienced by; befall. **4** (**happen to do**) chance to do something or come about. **5** (**happen to**) become of. **6** come across by chance.

IDIOMS – **as it happens** actually; as a matter of fact.

ORIGIN – from HAP.

happening > *noun* **1** an event or occurrence. **2** a partly improvised or spontaneous performance. > *adjective* informal fashionable; trendy.

happenstance /**happ**ənstanss/ > *noun* chiefly N. Amer. coincidence.

ORIGIN – blend of HAPPEN and CIRCUMSTANCE.

happy > *adjective* (**happier**, **happiest**) **1** feeling or showing pleasure or contentment. **2** willing to do or accept something. **3** fortunate and convenient: *a happy coincidence*. **4** informal inclined to use a specified thing excessively or at random: *trigger-happy*.

DERIVATIVES – **happily** *adverb* **happiness** *noun*.

SYNONYMS – **1** cheerful, contented, joyful, merry, pleased. **2** glad, pleased, satisfied, willing. **3** fortunate, lucky, opportune.

ANTONYMS – **1** sad, unhappy.

COMBINATIONS – **happy hour** a period of the day when drinks are sold at reduced prices in a bar or other establishment. **happy hunting ground** a place where success or enjoyment is obtained. [ORIGIN – referring to the hope of American Indians for good hunting grounds in the afterlife.]

ORIGIN – first used in the sense 'lucky': from HAP.

happy-go-lucky > *adjective* cheerfully unconcerned about the future.

SYNONYMS – carefree, devil-may-care, light-hearted.

hara-kiri /harrə**kirr**i/ > *noun* ritual suicide by disembowelment with a sword, formerly practised in Japan by samurai.

ORIGIN – Japanese, 'belly cutting'.

haram /haa**raam**/ > *adjective* forbidden or proscribed by Islamic law.

ORIGIN – Arabic.

harangue /hə**rang**/ > *verb* criticise at length in an aggressive and hectoring manner. > *noun* a forceful and aggressive speech.

SYNONYMS – *verb* lecture, sermonise. *noun* diatribe, lecture, tirade.

ORIGIN – Old French *arenge*, from Latin *harenga*.

harass* /**harr**əss, hə**rass**/ > *verb* **1** torment (someone) by subjecting them to constant interference or intimidation. **2** make repeated small-scale attacks on (an enemy) in order to wear down resistance.

DERIVATIVES – **harasser** *noun* **harassment** *noun*.

NOTE – the word **harass** is pronounced either with the stress on the **har-** or on the **-rass**; the first pronunciation, which is the older one, is considered by some people to be the only correct one.

*SPELLING – note that there is only one *r*: ha**r**ass.

SYNONYMS – **1** bother, hound, pester.

ORIGIN – French *harasser*, from *harer* 'set a dog on'.

harbinger /**haar**binjer/ > *noun* a person or thing that announces or signals the approach of something.

SYNONYMS – augur, forerunner, herald, omen, portent, precursor, sign.

---

wordpower facts

Harbinger

The word **harbinger** came into English via Old French from a Germanic root. The Old German word *heriberga* meant 'shelter or lodging for an army'. In Old French *herberge*, 'lodging', gave rise to the verb *herbergier*, 'to provide lodgings', and the noun *herbergere*, 'one who provides lodging'. This entered Middle English as **herberger**, or **herbenger**, with the meanings 'one who provides lodgings' and 'a host or entertainer'. Later it came to denote a person sent ahead to find lodgings for troops, or, more generally, a pioneer who prepares the way for others. By the end of the 16th century the modern sense, with its broad figurative use, had become established.

---

harbour (US **harbor**) > *noun* a place on the coast where ships may moor in shelter. > *verb* **1** keep (a thought or feeling) secretly in one's mind. **2** give a refuge or shelter to. **3** carry the germs of (a disease).

SYNONYMS – *verb* **1** entertain, nurse. **2** conceal, hide, shelter.

ORIGIN – Old English, 'shelter'.

hard > *adjective* **1** solid, firm, and rigid; not easily broken, bent, or pierced. **2** requiring or demonstrating a great deal of endurance or effort; difficult. **3** (of a person) not showing any signs of weakness; tough. **4** (of information or a subject of study) concerned with precise and verifiable facts. **5** harsh or unpleasant to the senses. **6** done with a great deal of force or strength. **7** very potent, strong, or intense. **8** (of a drug) potent and addictive. **9** (of pornography) highly obscene and explicit. **10** denoting an extreme faction within a political party. **11** (of water) containing mineral salts. > *adverb* **1** with a great deal of effort or force. **2** so as to be solid or firm. **3** to the fullest extent possible.

IDIOMS – **be hard put** (**to it**) find it very difficult. **hard and fast** (of a rule or distinction) fixed and definitive. **hard at it** informal busily working. **hard done by** Brit. harshly or unfairly treated. **hard feelings** feelings of resentment. **hard going** difficult to understand or enjoy. **hard luck** (or **lines**) Brit. informal used to express sympathy or commiserations. **hard of hearing** not able to hear well. **hard up** informal short of money. **play hard to get** informal deliberately adopt an uninterested attitude. **put the hard word on** Austral./NZ informal ask a favour of.

DERIVATIVES – **hardness** *noun*.

SYNONYMS – *adjective* **1** firm, inflexible, rigid, solid, unyielding. **2** arduous, complicated, difficult, formidable, strenuous, tough. **6** forceful, heavy, powerful, strong.

ANTONYMS – *adjective* **1** soft. **2** easy.

COMBINATIONS – **hardback** a book bound in stiff covers. **hardball** N. Amer. **1** baseball, especially as contrasted with softball. **2** informal uncompromising and ruthless methods or dealings. **hardboard** stiff board made of compressed and treated wood pulp. **hard-boiled 1** (of an egg) boiled until solid. **2** (of a person) tough and cynical. **hard cash** negotiable coins and banknotes as opposed to other forms of payment. **hard copy** a printed version on paper of data held in a computer. **hard core 1** the most committed or doctrinaire members of a group. **2** popular music that is experimental in nature and typically characterised by high volume and aggressive presentation. **3** pornography of a very explicit kind. **4** Brit. broken bricks and rubble used as a filling or foundation in building. **hardcover** chiefly N. Amer. a hardback. **hard disk** (also **hard drive**) Computing a rigid non-removable magnetic disk with a large data storage capacity. **hard hat** a rigid protective helmet, as worn by factory and building workers. **hard labour** heavy manual work as a punishment. **hard-nosed** informal realistic and tough-minded. **hard-on** vulgar slang an erection of the penis. **hard palate** the bony front part of the palate. **hard-pressed 1** closely pursued. **2** in difficulties. **hard rock** highly amplified rock music with a heavy beat. **hard sell** a policy or technique of aggressive selling or advertising. **hard shoulder** Brit. a hardened strip alongside a motorway for use in an emergency. **hardstanding** Brit. ground surfaced with a hard material for parking vehicles on. **hard tack** archaic hard dry bread or biscuit, especially as rations for sailors or soldiers. **hardtop** a motor vehicle with a rigid roof which in some cases is detachable. **hard-wired** Electronics involving permanently connected circuits rather than software. **hardwood** the wood from a broadleaved tree as distinguished from that of conifers.

hardbitten > *adjective* tough and cynical.

harden > *verb* make or become hard or harder.

DERIVATIVES – **hardener** *noun*.

SYNONYMS – solidify, stiffen, strengthen, toughen.

hard-headed > *adjective* tough and realistic.

DERIVATIVES – **hard-headedly** *adverb* **hard-headedness** *noun*.

hard-hearted > *adjective* incapable of being moved to pity or tenderness; unfeeling.

DERIVATIVES – **hard-heartedly** *adverb* **hard-heartedness** *noun*.

hardihood > *noun* dated boldness; daring.

hard line > *noun* an uncompromising adherence to a firm policy.

DERIVATIVES – **hardliner** *noun*.

hardly > *adverb* **1** scarcely; barely. **2** only with great difficulty. **3** no or not (suggesting surprise at or disagreement with a statement).

USAGE – avoid using **hardly** in a negative construction, such as *I can't hardly wait*; the correct construction is *I can hardly wait*.

hardship > *noun* severe suffering or privation.

SYNONYMS – adversity, deprivation, privation, suffering, tribulation.

ANTONYMS – comfort, ease.

hardware > *noun* **1** heavy military equipment such as tanks and missiles. **2** the machines, wiring, and other physical components of a computer. Compare with **SOFTWARE**. **3** tools, implements, and other items used in the home and in activities such as gardening.

hardy > *adjective* (**hardier, hardiest**) **1** capable of enduring difficult conditions; robust. **2** (of a plant) able to survive outside during winter.

DERIVATIVES – **hardily** *adverb* **hardiness** *noun*.

SYNONYMS – **1** healthy, robust, strong, sturdy, tough.

ORIGIN – Old French *hardi*, from *hardir* 'become bold'.

hare > *noun* a fast-running, long-eared mammal resembling a large rabbit, with very long hind legs. > *verb* run with great speed.

WORDFINDER – leporine (*relating to hares*); buck (*male hare*), doe (*female hare*), leveret (*young hare*).

IDIOMS – **run with the hare and hunt with the hounds** Brit. try to remain on good terms with both sides in a conflict.

harebell > *noun* a plant with slender stems and pale blue bell-shaped flowers.

hare-brained > *adjective* rash; ill-judged.

Hare Krishna /haari **krish**nə/ > *noun* a member of the International Society for Krishna Consciousness, a religious sect based on the worship of the Hindu god Krishna.

ORIGIN – Sanskrit, 'O Vishnu Krishna'.

harelip > *noun* another term for *cleft lip*.

DERIVATIVES – **harelipped** *adjective*.

USAGE – avoid using the word **harelip**, as it may cause offence; use **cleft lip** instead.

ORIGIN – from a perceived resemblance to the mouth of a hare.

harem /**haa**reem, haa**reem**/ > *noun* **1** the separate part of a Muslim household reserved for women. **2** the wives and concubines collectively of a polygamous man. **3** a group of female animals sharing a single mate.

ORIGIN – Arabic, 'prohibited place'.

haricot /**harr**ikō/ > *noun* a variety of French bean with small white seeds, which can be dried and used as a vegetable.

ORIGIN – French, perhaps from Aztec.

harissa /**arr**issə, hə**riss**ə/ > *noun* a hot sauce or paste used in North African cuisine, made from chilli peppers, paprika, and olive oil.

ORIGIN – Arabic.

hark > *verb* **1** literary listen. **2** (**hark at**) informal used to draw attention to an ill-advised or foolish remark or action. **3** (**hark back**) recall an earlier period.

harken > *verb* variant spelling of **HEARKEN**.

harlequin /**haar**likwin/ > *noun* (**Harlequin**) a mute character in traditional pantomime, typically masked and dressed in a diamond-patterned costume. > *adjective* in varied colours; variegated.

ORIGIN – French, from earlier *Herlequin*, the leader of a legendary troop of demon horsemen.

harlequinade /haarlikwi**nayd**/ > *noun* **1** historical the section of a traditional pantomime in which Harlequin played a leading role. **2** dated a piece of buffoonery.

harlot > *noun* archaic a prostitute or promiscuous woman.

ORIGIN – first meaning 'vagabond or beggar', later 'lecherous person': from Old French 'young man, knave'.

harm > *noun* **1** physical injury, especially that which is deliberately inflicted. **2** material damage. **3** actual or potential ill effect. > *verb* **1** physically injure. **2** have an adverse effect on.

IDIOMS – **out of harm's way** in a safe place.

SYNONYMS – noun **1** damage, hurt, injury, pain, suffering. verb **1** damage, hurt, injure, wound. **2** damage, mar, spoil.

ANTONYMS – verb **2** benefit.

harmattan /haar**matt**'n/ > *noun* a very dry, dusty easterly or north-easterly wind on the West African coast.

ORIGIN – Akan.

harmful > *adjective* causing or likely to cause harm.

DERIVATIVES – **harmfully** adverb.

SYNONYMS – dangerous, detrimental, injurious, pernicious.

ANTONYMS – benign, harmless.

harmless > *adjective* not able or likely to cause harm.

DERIVATIVES – **harmlessly** adverb **harmlessness** noun.

SYNONYMS – benign, innocuous, safe.

ANTONYMS – harmful, unsafe.

harmonic /haar**monn**ik/ > *adjective* **1** relating to or characterised by harmony. **2** Music relating to or denoting a harmonic or harmonics. > *noun* Music an overtone accompanying a fundamental tone at a fixed interval.

DERIVATIVES – **harmonically** adverb.

COMBINATIONS – **harmonic progression 1** Music a series of chord changes forming the underlying harmony of a piece of music. **2** Mathematics a sequence of quantities whose reciprocals are in arithmetical progression (e.g. 1, ⅓, ⅕, ⅟₇, etc.).

harmonica > *noun* a small rectangular wind instrument with a row of metal reeds capable of producing different notes.

ORIGIN – Greek *harmonikos*, from *harmonia* (see **HARMONY**).

harmonious /haar**mō**niəss/ > *adjective* **1** tuneful; not discordant. **2** forming a pleasing or consistent whole. **3** free from conflict.

DERIVATIVES – **harmoniously** adverb.

SYNONYMS – **1** euphonious, melodious, tuneful. **3** amicable, congenial, friendly, peaceful.

harmonise (also **harmonize**) > *verb* **1** Music provide harmony for. **2** make or be harmonious. **3** make consistent.

DERIVATIVES – **harmonisation** noun.

harmonium > *noun* a keyboard instrument in which the notes are produced by air driven through metal reeds by foot-operated bellows.

harmony > *noun* (pl. **harmonies**) **1** the combination of simultaneously sounded musical notes to produce chords and chord progressions having a pleasing effect. **2** the quality of forming a pleasing and consistent whole. **3** agreement or concord.

ORIGIN – Latin *harmonia* 'joining, concord', from Greek *harmos* 'joint'.

harness > *noun* **1** a set of straps and fittings by which a horse or other draught animal is fastened to a cart, plough, etc. and is controlled by its driver. **2** a similar arrangement of straps, as for fastening a parachute to a person's body or for restraining a young child. > *verb* **1** fit with a harness. **2** control and make use of (resources).

IDIOMS – **in harness 1** (of an animal) used for draught work. **2** in the routine of daily work.

ORIGIN – Old French *harneis* 'military equipment'.

harp > *noun* a musical instrument consisting of a frame supporting a graduated series of parallel strings, played by plucking with the fingers. > *verb* (**harp on**) talk or write persistently and tediously on a particular topic.

DERIVATIVES – **harper** noun **harpist** noun.

harpoon > *noun* a barbed spear-like missile attached to a long rope and thrown by hand or fired from a gun, used for catching whales. > *verb* spear with a harpoon.

DERIVATIVES – **harpooner** noun.

ORIGIN – French *harpon*, from *harpe* 'dog's claw, clamp'.

harpsichord /**haarp**sikord/ > *noun* a keyboard instrument similar in shape to a grand piano, with horizontal strings plucked by points operated by depressing the keys.

DERIVATIVES – **harpsichordist** noun.

ORIGIN – from Latin *harpa* 'harp' + *chorda* 'string'.

harpy > *noun* (pl. **harpies**) **1** Greek & Roman Mythology a rapacious monster usually depicted with a woman's head and body and a bird's wings and claws. **2** a grasping, unscrupulous woman.

COMBINATIONS – **harpy eagle** a very large crested eagle of tropical rainforests.

ORIGIN – Greek *harpuiai* 'snatchers'.

harpy eagle > *noun* a very large crested eagle of tropical rainforests.

harquebus /**haark**wibəss/ (also **arquebus**) > *noun* historical an early type of portable gun supported on a tripod or a forked rest.

ORIGIN – Low German *hakebusse*, from *hake* 'hook' + *busse* 'gun'.

harridan /**harr**idən/ > *noun* a strict, bossy, or belligerent old woman.

ORIGIN – perhaps from French *haridelle* 'old horse'.

harrier¹ > *noun* a person who harries others.

harrier² > *noun* a hound of a breed used for hunting hares.

ORIGIN – from **HARE**.

harrier³ > *noun* a long-winged, slender-bodied bird of prey with low hunting flight.

ORIGIN – from obsolete *harrow* 'harry, rob'.

Harris tweed > *noun* trademark handwoven tweed made traditionally on the island of Lewis and Harris in Scotland.

harrow > *noun* an implement consisting of a heavy frame set with teeth which is dragged over ploughed land to break up or spread the soil. > *verb* **1** draw a harrow over. **2** (**harrowing**) very distressing.

harrumph > *verb* **1** clear the throat noisily. **2** grumpily express dissatisfaction.

harry > *verb* (**harries**, **harried**) **1** persistently carry out attacks on (an enemy). **2** persistently harass.

harsh > *adjective* **1** unpleasantly rough or jarring to the senses. **2** cruel or severe.

DERIVATIVES – **harshly** *adverb* **harshness** *noun*.

SYNONYMS – **1** grating, jarring, rough, strident.

ORIGIN – Low German *harsch* 'rough', from *haer* 'hair'.

hart > *noun* an adult male deer, especially a red deer over five years old.

COMBINATIONS – **hart's tongue** a fern whose long, narrow fronds are said to resemble the tongues of deer.

hartebeest /**haar**tibeest/ > *noun* a large African antelope with a long head and sloping back.

ORIGIN – from Dutch *hert* 'hart' + *beest* 'beast'.

harum-scarum /hairəm**skair**əm/ > *adjective* reckless; impetuous.

ORIGIN – from **HARE** and **SCARE**.

harvest > *noun* **1** the process or period of gathering in crops. **2** the season's yield or crop. > *verb* gather as a harvest.

DERIVATIVES – **harvestable** *adjective* **harvester** *noun*.

COMBINATIONS – **harvest home 1** the gathering in of the final part of the year's harvest. **2** a festival marking the end of the harvest period. **harvest moon** the full moon that is seen closest to the time of the autumn equinox. **harvest mouse** a small mouse with a prehensile tail, nesting among the stalks of growing cereals.

ORIGIN – Old English, 'autumn'.

harvestman > *noun* a spider-like creature (arachnid) with a globular body and very long, thin legs.

Harvey Wallbanger > *noun* a cocktail made from vodka or gin, orange juice, and Galliano.

has third person singular present of **HAVE**.

has-been > *noun* informal a person or thing that is outmoded or no longer significant.

hash¹ > *noun* **1** a dish of diced cooked meat reheated with potatoes. **2** a jumble; a mess. > *verb* make or chop into a hash.

IDIOMS – **make a hash of** informal make a mess of.

COMBINATIONS – **hash browns** chiefly N. Amer. a dish of chopped and fried cooked potatoes.

ORIGIN – French *hacher*, from *hache* 'axe'.

hash² > *noun* informal short for **HASHISH**.

hash³ > *noun* the symbol #.

ORIGIN – probably an alteration of **HATCH³**.

hashish /ha**sheesh**/ > *noun* cannabis.

ORIGIN – Arabic, 'dry herb, powdered hemp leaves'.

Hasid /**hass**id/ (also **Chasid, Chassid** /**khass**id/ or **Hassid**) > *noun* (pl. **Hasidim**) an adherent of Hasidism.

DERIVATIVES – **Hasidic** /ha**sidd**ik/ *adjective*.

ORIGIN – Hebrew, 'pious'.

Hasidism /**hass**idiz'm/ (also **Chasidism, Chassidism** /**khass**idiz'm/ or **Hassidism**) > *noun* a mystical Jewish movement founded in Poland in the 18th century.

haslet /**haz**lit/ > *noun* chiefly Brit. a cold meat consisting of chopped and compressed pork offal.

ORIGIN – Old French *hastelet*, from *haste* 'roast meat, spit'.

hasn't > *contraction* has not.

hasp > *noun* a slotted hinged metal plate that forms part of a fastening for a door or lid and is fitted over a metal loop and secured by a pin or padlock.

Hassid > *noun* variant spelling of **HASID**.

Hassidism > *noun* variant spelling of **HASIDISM**.

hassium /**hass**iəm/ > *noun* a very unstable chemical element made by high-energy atomic collisions.

ORIGIN – from *Hassias*, Latin name for the German state of *Hesse*.

hassle informal > *noun* **1** irritating inconvenience. **2** deliberate harassment. > *verb* harass; pester.

ORIGIN – perhaps a blend of **HAGGLE** and **TUSSLE**: originally a dialect word meaning 'hack or saw at'.

hassock > *noun* chiefly Brit. a cushion for kneeling on in church.

hast archaic second person singular present of **HAVE**.

haste > *noun* excessive speed or urgency of action.

IDIOMS – **more haste, less speed** proverb you make better progress with a task if you don't try to do it too quickly.

SYNONYMS – hastiness, hurry, impetuosity.

hasten > *verb* **1** be quick to do something; move quickly. **2** cause (something) to happen sooner than anticipated.

SYNONYMS – **1** dash, hurry, rush. **2** accelerate, precipitate, quicken.

hasty > *adjective* (**hastier, hastiest**) done or acting with haste; hurried.

DERIVATIVES – **hastily** *adverb*.

SYNONYMS – hurried, impetuous, rash, rushed.

ANTONYMS – considered, leisurely.

hat > *noun* a shaped covering for the head, typically with a brim and a crown.

WORDFINDER – hatter (*person who makes or sells hats*), milliner (*person who makes or sells women's hats*).

IDIOMS – **keep under one's hat** keep (something) a secret. **pick out of a hat** select (something) at random. **take one's hat off to** used to express admiration or

praise for. **throw one's hat into the ring** express willingness to take up a challenge.

DERIVATIVES – **hatful** *noun* **hatless** *adjective* **hatted** *adjective*.

COMBINATIONS – **hatband** a decorative ribbon encircling a hat, held in position above the brim.

ORIGIN – Old English, related to **HOOD¹**.

hatch¹ > *noun* **1** a small opening in a floor, wall, or roof allowing access from one area to another. **2** a door in an aircraft, spacecraft, or submarine.

IDIOMS – **down the hatch** informal used as a toast before drinking.

COMBINATIONS – **hatchback** a car with a door across the full width at the back end that opens upwards to provide easy access for loading. **hatchway** an opening or hatch, especially in a ship's deck.

ORIGIN – Old English *hæcc*, denoting the lower half of a divided door.

hatch² > *verb* **1** (of a young bird, fish, or reptile) emerge from its egg. **2** (of an egg) open and produce a young animal. **3** cause (a young animal) to emerge from its egg. **4** conspire to devise (a plot or plan). > *noun* a newly hatched brood.

hatch³ > *verb* (in technical drawing) shade with closely drawn parallel lines.

DERIVATIVES – **hatching** *noun*.

ORIGIN – Old French *hacher*, from *hache* 'axe'.

hatchery > *noun* (pl. **hatcheries**) an establishment where fish or poultry eggs are hatched.

hatchet > *noun* a small axe with a short handle for use in one hand.

IDIOMS – **bury the hatchet** end a quarrel or conflict. [ORIGIN – in allusion to an American Indian custom.]

COMBINATIONS – **hatchet-faced** informal sharp-featured and grim-looking. **hatchet job** informal a fierce verbal or written attack. **hatchet man** informal **1** a person employed to carry out controversial or disagreeable tasks. **2** a harsh critic.

ORIGIN – Old French *hachette* 'little axe', from *hache* 'axe'.

hatchling > *noun* a newly hatched young animal.

hate > *verb* feel intense dislike for or a strong aversion towards. > *noun* **1** intense dislike; strong aversion. **2** informal a disliked person or thing. **3** (before a noun) denoting hostile actions motivated by intense dislike or prejudice: *a hate campaign*.

DERIVATIVES – **hater** *noun*.

SYNONYMS – *verb* abhor, despise, detest, execrate, loathe. *noun* **1** abhorrence, detestation, execration, loathing.

ANTONYMS – *verb* like, love. *noun* love.

hateful > *adjective* arousing or deserving of hatred.

DERIVATIVES – **hatefully** adverb **hate-fulness** noun.

SYNONYMS – abhorrent, despicable, detestable, execrable, odious.

hath archaic third person singular present of **HAVE**.

hatha yoga /hathə yōgə/ > noun a system of physical exercises and breathing control used in yoga.

ORIGIN – hatha from a Sanskrit word meaning 'force'.

hatred > noun intense dislike.

SYNONYMS – abhorrence, detestation, execration, hate, loathing.

hatter > noun a person who makes and sells hats.

IDIOMS – **(as) mad as a hatter** informal completely insane. [ORIGIN – with allusion to the effects of mercury poisoning from the former use of mercurous nitrate in the manufacture of felt hats.]

hat-trick > noun three successes of the same kind, especially (in soccer) a player scoring three goals in a game or (in cricket) a bowler taking three wickets with successive balls.

ORIGIN – referring originally to the club presentation of a new hat to a bowler taking a hat-trick.

hauberk /hawberk/ > noun historical a full-length coat of mail.

ORIGIN – Old French hauberc.

haughty > adjective (**haughtier, haughtiest**) arrogantly superior and disdainful.

DERIVATIVES – **haughtily** adverb **haughtiness** noun.

SYNONYMS – arrogant, lofty, proud, supercilious, superior; informal snooty; literary orgulous.

ANTONYMS – humble, modest.

ORIGIN – Old French haut 'high', from Latin altus 'high'.

haul > verb **1** pull or drag with effort or force. **2** transport in a truck or cart. > noun **1** a quantity of something obtained, especially illegally. **2** a number of fish caught at one time. **3** a distance to be travelled.

IDIOMS – **haul over the coals** see COAL.

DERIVATIVES – **hauler** noun.

SYNONYMS – verb **1** drag, draw, heave, lug, pull, tug.

ORIGIN – variant of HALE²: originally in the nautical sense 'trim sails for sailing closer to the wind'.

haulage > noun the commercial transport of goods.

haulier > noun Brit. a person or company employed in the commercial transport of goods by road.

haulm /hawm/ > noun **1** a stalk or stem. **2** the stalks or stems of peas, beans, or potatoes collectively.

haunch > noun **1** the buttock and thigh considered together, in a human or animal. **2** the leg and loin of an animal, as food.

haunt > verb **1** (of a ghost) manifest itself regularly at (a place). **2** (of a person) frequent (a place). **3** be persistently and disturbingly present in: the sight haunted me for years. > noun a place frequented by a specified person.

DERIVATIVES – **haunter** noun.

ORIGIN – Old French hanter.

haunted > adjective **1** (of a place) frequented by a ghost. **2** having or showing signs of mental anguish.

haunting > adjective poignant; evocative.

DERIVATIVES – **hauntingly** adverb.

hausfrau /howssfrow/ > noun a German housewife, especially with reference to orderliness and efficiency.

ORIGIN – German, from Haus 'house' + Frau 'woman, wife'.

hautboy /ōboy, hōboy/ > noun archaic form of OBOE.

ORIGIN – French hautbois, from haut 'high' + bois 'wood'.

haute couture /ōt kootyoor/ > noun the designing and making of high-quality clothes by leading fashion houses.

ORIGIN – French, 'high dressmaking'.

haute cuisine /ōt kwizeen/ > noun high-quality cooking following the style of traditional French cuisine.

ORIGIN – French, 'high cookery'.

hauteur /ōtör/ > noun proud haughtiness of manner.

ORIGIN – French, from haut 'high'.

Havana > noun a cigar made in Cuba or from Cuban tobacco.

ORIGIN – named after Havana, the capital of Cuba.

have > verb (**has**; past and past participle **had**) **1** possess, own, or hold. **2** experience; undergo: have difficulty. **3** be able to make use of. **4** (**have to**) be obliged to; must. **5** perform the action indicated by the noun specified: he had a look round. **6** demonstrate (a personal attribute). **7** suffer from (an illness or disability). **8** cause to be in a particular state. **9** cause to be done for one by someone else. **10** place, hold, or keep in a particular position. **11** be the recipient or host of. **12** eat or drink. **13** (**not have**) refuse to tolerate. **14** (**be had**) informal be cheated or deceived. > auxiliary verb used with a past participle to form the perfect, pluperfect, and future perfect tenses, and the conditional mood. > noun (**the haves**) (usu. in phrase **the haves and the have-nots**) informal people with plenty of money.

IDIOMS – **have had it** informal **1** be beyond repair or revival. **2** be unable to tolerate any longer. **have it in for** informal dislike (someone) greatly and behave in a hostile way towards them. **have it out** informal attempt to resolve a dispute by confrontation. **have on** Brit. informal try to make (someone) believe something untrue, especially as a joke. **have up** Brit. informal bring (someone) before a court to answer for an alleged offence.

haven > noun **1** a place of safety or refuge. **2** a harbour or small port.

SYNONYMS – **1** refuge, sanctuary, shelter.

haven't > contraction have not.

haver /hayvər/ > verb **1** Scottish talk foolishly; babble. **2** Brit. act in an indecisive manner.

haversack > noun a small, stout bag carried on the back or over the shoulder.

ORIGIN – obsolete German Habersack, denoting a bag used to carry oats as horse feed, from Haber 'oats' + Sack 'sack, bag'.

havoc > noun **1** widespread destruction. **2** great confusion or disorder.

IDIOMS – **play havoc with** completely disrupt.

SYNONYMS – **1** desolation, devastation, ruin. **2** chaos, confusion, disorder, mayhem.

wordpower facts
Havoc

The root of the word **havoc** lies in an Old French phrase crier havot, which in English became cry havoc. To **cry havoc** was to instruct your army, with the signal '**havoc!**', to start pillaging and plundering enemy property or land. Shakespeare used the phrase in Julius Caesar (1616): 'And Caesar's spirit…Shall…with a monarch's voice Cry 'Havoc!' and let slip the dogs of war', and after this it came to be used figuratively to mean 'predict imminent disaster'. Thus **havoc** broadened to mean 'destruction' or 'disaster', and from this the weakened sense 'confusion, disorder' naturally arose.

haw¹ > noun the red fruit of the hawthorn.

haw² > verb see **hum and haw**.

Hawaiian > noun **1** a person from Hawaii, a US state comprising an island group in the North Pacific. **2** the language of Hawaii. > adjective relating to Hawaii or its people or language.

COMBINATIONS – **Hawaiian guitar** a steel-stringed guitar in which a characteristic glissando effect is produced by sliding a metal bar along the strings as they are plucked.

hawfinch > noun a large finch with a massive bill for cracking open cherry stones and other hard seeds.

hawk¹ > noun **1** a fast-flying bird of prey with broad rounded wings and a long tail. **2** any bird used in falconry. **3** a person who advocates an aggressive policy, especially in foreign affairs. Compare with **DOVE**[1]. > *verb* hunt game with a trained hawk.

WORDFINDER – accipitrine (*hawk-like*), haggard (*hawk caught and trained when an adult*), jess (*strap fastened to each of a hawk's legs*), lure (*device to attract a hawk back to the falconer*), mew (*cage for trained hawks*), tercel (*male hawk*).

DERIVATIVES – **hawkish** *adjective*.

hawk[2] > *verb* carry about and offer (goods) for sale in the street.
ORIGIN – probably from **HAWKER**.

hawk[3] > *verb* **1** clear the throat noisily. **2** bring (phlegm) up from the throat.

hawker > *noun* a person who travels about selling goods.
ORIGIN – probably from Low German or Dutch and related to **HUCKSTER**.

hawkmoth > *noun* a large swift-flying moth with a stout body and narrow forewings.

hawksbeard > *noun* a plant which resembles a dandelion but has a branched stem with several flowers.

hawkweed > *noun* a plant with yellow dandelion-like flower heads.

hawser /ˈhawzər/ > *noun* a thick rope or cable for mooring or towing a ship.
ORIGIN – from Old French *haucier* 'to hoist', from Latin *altus* 'high'.

hawthorn > *noun* a thorny shrub or tree with white, pink, or red blossom and small dark red fruits (haws).
ORIGIN – Old English, probably with the literal meaning 'hedge thorn'.

hay > *noun* grass that has been mown and dried for use as fodder.
IDIOMS – **hit the hay** informal go to bed. **make hay** (**while the sun shines**) make good use of an opportunity while it lasts.
DERIVATIVES – **haying** *noun*.
COMBINATIONS – **hay fever** an allergy caused by pollen or dust in which the mucous membranes of the eyes and nose are inflamed, causing sneezing and watery eyes. **hayloft** a loft over a stable used for storing hay or straw. **hayride** chiefly N. Amer. a ride taken for pleasure in a wagon carrying hay. **haystack** (also **hayrick**) a large packed pile of hay.
ORIGIN – Old English, related to **HEW**.

haycock > *noun* a conical heap of hay left in the field to dry.

haymaker > *noun* **1** a person occupied in making hay. **2** an apparatus for shaking and drying hay. **3** informal a forceful blow.
DERIVATIVES – **haymaking** *noun*.

hayseed > *noun* **1** grass seed obtained from hay. **2** informal, chiefly N. Amer. a simple, unsophisticated country person.

haywire > *adjective* informal very erratic; out of control.
ORIGIN – from **HAY** + **WIRE**, with reference to the use of hay-baling wire in makeshift repairs.

hazard > *noun* **1** a danger or risk. **2** a permanent feature of a golf course which presents an obstruction. **3** literary chance; probability. **4** a gambling game using two dice. > *verb* **1** venture to say. **2** put (something) at risk of being lost; chance.
SYNONYMS – *noun* **1** danger, menace, peril, risk, threat. *verb* **1** proffer, venture, volunteer.
COMBINATIONS – **hazard lights** flashing indicator lights on a vehicle, used to warn that the vehicle is stationary or unexpectedly slow.
ORIGIN – Old French *hasard*, from Persian or Turkish words meaning 'dice'.

hazardous > *adjective* risky; dangerous.
DERIVATIVES – **hazardously** *adverb*.

haze[1] > *noun* **1** a slight obscuration of the lower atmosphere, typically caused by fine particles of dust, pollutants, etc. **2** a state of obscurity or confusion.

haze[2] > *verb* N. Amer. torment or harass (a new student or recruit) by subjection to strenuous, humiliating, or dangerous tasks.
ORIGIN – Scots and dialect in the sense 'frighten, scold, or beat'.

hazel > *noun* **1** a shrub or small tree bearing prominent catkins in spring and edible nuts (**hazelnuts**) in autumn. **2** a rich reddish-brown colour.

hazy > *adjective* (**hazier**, **haziest**) **1** covered by a haze. **2** vague, indistinct, or ill-defined.
DERIVATIVES – **hazily** *adverb* **haziness** *noun*.

HB > *abbreviation* **1** half board. **2** (also **hb**) hardback. **3** hard black (as a medium grade of pencil lead).

H-bomb > *noun* short for *hydrogen bomb*.

HC > *abbreviation* **1** (in the UK) House of Commons. **2** hydrocarbon.

HDTV > *abbreviation* high-definition television.

HE > *abbreviation* high explosive.

He > *symbol* the chemical element helium.

he > *pronoun* (third person sing.) **1** used to refer to a man, boy, or male animal previously mentioned or easily identified. **2** used to refer to a person or animal of unspecified sex (in modern use, now largely replaced by 'he or she' or 'they'). **3** any person (in modern use, now largely replaced by 'anyone' or 'the person'). > *noun* a male; a man.
USAGE – until recently, **he** was used uncontroversially to refer to a person of unspecified sex; however, this use is now regarded as a hallmark of dated, sexist language. A solution has been to use **he or she**, but this can be tiresomely long-winded if used repeatedly. Use of **they** as an alternative to **he** (as in *everyone needs to feel that they matter*) is now increasingly accepted: see the note at **THEY**.

head > *noun* **1** the upper part of the human body, or the front or upper part of the body of an animal, containing the brain, mouth, and sense organs. **2** the front, forward, or upper part or end of something. **3** a person in charge; a director or leader. **4** the cutting or operational end of a tool or mechanism. **5** a compact mass of leaves or flowers at the top of a stem. **6** a person considered as a numerical unit. **7** (treated as pl.) a number of cattle or game as specified: *seventy head of cattle.* **8** a component in an audio, video, or information system by which information is transferred from an electrical signal to the recording medium, or vice versa. **9** the flattened or knobbed end of a nail, pin, screw, or match. **10** the source of a river or stream. **11** the foam on top of a glass of beer. **12** (**heads**) the side of a coin bearing the image of a head. **13** pressure of water or steam in an engine or other confined space. > *adjective* chief; principal. > *verb* **1** be or act as the head of. **2** give a title or heading to. **3** move in a specified direction. **4** (**head off**) intercept and turn aside (someone or something); forestall. **5** Soccer shoot or pass (the ball) with the head.
WORDFINDER – cephalic (*relating to the head*), decapitate (*cut off the head of*), occiput (*back of the head*); brachycephalic (*having a broad, short skull*), dolichocephalic (*having a long skull*), leptocephalic (*having a narrow skull*), macrocephalic (*having a large head*), mesocephalic (*having a head of medium proportions*).
IDIOMS – **be banging one's head against a brick wall** be doggedly attempting the impossible. **come to a head** reach a crisis. **get one's head down** Brit. informal **1** sleep. **2** concentrate on the task in hand. **give someone his** (or **her**) **head** allow someone complete freedom of action. **go to someone's head 1** (of alcohol) make someone slightly drunk. **2** (of success) make someone conceited. **head first 1** with the head in front of the rest of the body. **2** without sufficient forethought. **a head for** an aptitude for or tolerance of. —— **one's head off** informal talk, laugh, shout, etc. unrestrainedly. **head over heels 1** turning over completely in forward motion, as in a somersault. **2** madly in love. **keep one's head** remain calm. **keep one's head above water** avoid succumbing to difficulties. **lose one's head** lose self-control; panic. **over someone's head 1** (also **above someone's head**) beyond someone's ability to understand. **2** without consulting or involving the specified person. **turn someone's head** make someone conceited. **be unable to make**

head or tail of be unable to understand at all.

DERIVATIVES – **headed** adjective **headless** adjective.

SYNONYMS – noun **3** chief, commander, director, leader.

COMBINATIONS – **headband** a band of fabric worn around the head as a decoration or to keep the hair off the face. **headbanger** informal a fan or performer of heavy metal music. **headbanging** violent rhythmic shaking of the head by fans of heavy metal music. **headboard** an upright panel at the head of a bed. **head case** informal a person who is mentally ill or unstable. **headcount** a count of the number of people present or available. **headdress** an ornamental covering for the head. **headgear** hats, helmets, and other items worn on the head. **headlight** (also **headlamp**) a powerful light at the front of a motor vehicle or railway engine. **headlock** a method of restraining someone by holding an arm firmly around their head. **head louse** a louse which infests the hair of the human head. **headman** the chief or leader of a tribe. **head of state** the chief public representative of a country, who may also be the head of government. **head-on 1** with or involving the front of a vehicle. **2** with or involving direct confrontation. **headphones** a pair of earphones joined by a band placed over the head. **headpiece** a device worn on the head. **headrest** a padded support for the head on the back of a seat or chair. **headroom** the space between the top of a person's head and the ceiling or other structure above. **headscarf** (pl. **headscarves**) a square of fabric worn as a covering for the head. **headset** a set of headphones with a microphone attached. **headshrinker** informal, chiefly N. Amer. a psychiatrist. **head start** an advantage granted or gained at the beginning. **headstone** an inscribed stone slab set up at the head of a grave. **head teacher** the teacher in charge of a school. **head-to-head** involving two parties confronting each other. **head-turning** extremely noticeable or attractive. **headwater** a tributary stream of a river close to or forming part of its source. **headwind** a wind blowing from directly in front. **headword** a word which begins a separate entry in a reference work. **headwork** mental effort.

headache > noun **1** a continuous pain in the head. **2** informal something that causes worry or trouble.

DERIVATIVES – **headachy** adjective.

headage > noun the number of animals held as stock on a farm.

headbutt > verb attack (someone) using a forceful thrust with the head. > noun an act of headbutting.

header > noun **1** Soccer a shot or pass made with the head. **2** informal a headlong fall or dive. **3** a brick or stone laid at right angles to the face of a wall. Compare with **STRETCHER** (in sense 3). **4** (also **header tank**) a raised tank of water maintaining pressure in a plumbing system. **5** a line or block of text appearing at the top of each page of a book or document.

headhunt > verb **1** (**headhunting**) the practice among some peoples of collecting the heads of dead enemies as trophies. **2** identify and approach (someone employed elsewhere) to fill a business position.

DERIVATIVES – **headhunter** noun.

heading > noun **1** a title at the head of a page or section of a book. **2** a direction or bearing. **3** the top of a curtain extending above the hooks or wire by which it is suspended. **4** a horizontal passage made in preparation for building a tunnel.

headland > noun a narrow piece of land projecting into the sea.

headline > noun **1** a heading at the top of an article or page in a newspaper or magazine. **2** (**the headlines**) a summary of the most important items of news. > verb **1** provide with a headline. **2** appear as the star performer at (a concert).

headliner > noun the performer or act promoted as the star attraction on a bill.

headlong > adverb & adjective **1** with the head foremost. **2** in a rush; with reckless haste.

headmaster > noun chiefly Brit. a male head teacher.

headmistress > noun chiefly Brit. a female head teacher.

headquarter > verb (**be headquartered**) have headquarters at a specified place.

headquarters > noun **1** the managerial and administrative centre of an organisation. **2** the premises of a military commander and their staff.

headship > noun **1** the position of leader or chief. **2** chiefly Brit. the position of head teacher in a school.

headstrong > adjective obstinate and determined.

headway > noun forward movement or progress.

heady > adjective (**headier**, **headiest**) **1** (of alcohol) potent; intoxicating. **2** having a strong or exhilarating effect.

DERIVATIVES – **headily** adverb.

heal > verb **1** make or become sound or healthy again. **2** put right (an undesirable situation).

DERIVATIVES – **healer** noun.

ORIGIN – Old English, related to **WHOLE**.

heal-all > noun **1** a universal remedy; a panacea. **2** any of a number of medicinal plants, especially roseroot and self-heal.

health > noun **1** the state of being free from illness or injury. **2** a person's mental or physical condition.

WORDFINDER – convalesce (gradually recover one's health after illness), hypochondriac (person abnormally anxious about their health), salubrious (health-giving or healthy), sanitary (relating to conditions affecting health), valetudinarian (person in poor health or overly concerned about their health).

SYNONYMS – **1** fitness, healthiness, soundness, well-being. **2** condition, constitution.

COMBINATIONS – **health centre** an establishment housing local medical services or the practice of a group of doctors. **health farm** a residential establishment where people seek improved health by dieting, exercise, and treatment. **health food** natural food that is thought to have health-giving qualities. **health service** a public service providing medical care. **health visitor** Brit. a nurse who visits the homes of the chronically ill or parents with very young children.

healthful > adjective having or conducive to good health.

DERIVATIVES – **healthfully** adverb **healthfulness** noun.

healthy > adjective (**healthier**, **healthiest**) **1** having or promoting good health. **2** normal, sensible, or desirable: a healthy balance. **3** of a very satisfactory size or amount: a healthy profit.

DERIVATIVES – **healthily** adverb **healthiness** noun.

SYNONYMS – **1** fit, hale, hearty, salubrious.

ANTONYMS – **1** ill, unhealthy, unwell.

heap > noun **1** a mound or pile of a substance or collection of objects. **2** informal a large amount or number: heaps of room. **3** informal an untidy or dilapidated place or vehicle. > verb **1** put in or form a heap. **2** (**heap with**) load copiously with. **3** (**heap on**) bestow liberally on: the press heaped abuse on him.

SYNONYMS – noun **1** mass, mound, pile, stack. verb **1** mound, stack.

hear > verb (past and past participle **heard**) **1** perceive (a sound) with the ear. **2** be told or informed of. **3** (**have heard of**) be aware of the existence of. **4** (**hear from**) receive a letter or phone call from. **5** listen or pay attention to. **6** Law listen to and judge (a case or plaintiff).

IDIOMS – **hear! hear!** used to express wholehearted agreement with something said in a speech. **will** (or **would**) **not hear of** will (or would) not allow or agree to.

DERIVATIVES – **hearable** adjective **hearer** noun.

hearing > *noun* **1** the faculty of perceiving sounds. **2** the range within which sounds may be heard; earshot. **3** an opportunity to state one's case: *a fair hearing.* **4** an act of listening to evidence, especially a trial before a judge without a jury.

WORDFINDER – acoustic (*relating to sound or hearing*), audiology (*the branch of medicine concerned with hearing*), audiometry (*the measurement of the range and sensitivity of a person's hearing*), auditory (*relating to the sense of hearing*), aural (*relating to the ear or sense of hearing*).

COMBINATIONS – **hearing aid** a small amplifying device worn on the ear by a partially deaf person.

hearken /haarkən/ (also **harken**) > *verb* (usu. **hearken to**) archaic listen.

hearsay > *noun* information which cannot be adequately substantiated; rumour.

SYNONYMS – gossip, rumour, tittle-tattle.

hearse /herss/ > *noun* a vehicle for conveying the coffin at a funeral.

---

wordpower facts

Hearse

The modern meaning of the word **hearse** is far removed from that of its ancient roots. It derives ultimately from a word in an extinct language spoken in southern Italy, denoting the teeth of a wolf. This word was absorbed into Latin as *hirpex*, denoting, with reference to the teeth-like form, a large rake. This entered Old French in the form *herce*, meaning 'harrow'. In English a **hearse** was originally a triangular frame similar in shape to an ancient harrow, designed to hold candles. From this it became an elaborate framework or canopy, again holding candles, which was constructed over the bier or coffin of an important person prior to their funeral. By the middle of the 17th century the word referred to a carriage built to carry a coffin, from which evolved the modern **hearse**, or funeral car.

---

heart > *noun* **1** a hollow muscular organ that pumps the blood through the circulatory system by rhythmic contraction and dilation. **2** the central, innermost, or vital part: *the heart of the city.* **3** a person's feeling of or capacity for love or compassion. **4** mood or feeling: *a change of heart.* **5** courage or enthusiasm. **6** a symbolic representation of a heart with two equal curves meeting at a point at the bottom and a cusp at the top. **7** (**hearts**) one of the four suits in a pack of playing cards, denoted by a red symbol of a heart.

WORDFINDER – cardiac (*relating to the heart*), cardiology (*branch of medicine concerned with the heart*), cordate (*heart-shaped*), coronary (*relating to the arteries that supply the heart*); *parts of the heart:* aorta, atrium, mitral valve, vena cava, ventricle.

IDIOMS – **after one's own heart** sharing one's tastes. **at heart** in one's real nature, in contrast to how one may appear. **break someone's heart** overwhelm someone with sadness. **by heart** from memory. **close** (or **dear**) **to one's heart** of deep interest and concern to one. **from the** (or **the bottom of one's**) **heart** with sincere feeling. **have a heart!** be merciful. **have a heart of gold** have a generous or compassionate nature. **have one's heart in one's mouth** be greatly alarmed or apprehensive. **have one's heart in the right place** be sincere or well intentioned. **one's heart's desire** something that one greatly wishes for. **one's heartstrings** used in reference to one's deepest feelings of love or compassion. **in one's heart of hearts** in one's innermost feelings. **take to heart** take (criticism) seriously and be affected by it. **wear one's heart on one's sleeve** make one's feelings apparent.

SYNONYMS – **2** centre, core, crux, middle, hub, nucleus.

COMBINATIONS – **heartache** emotional anguish or grief. **heart attack** a sudden occurrence of coronary thrombosis. **heartburn** a form of indigestion felt as a burning sensation in the chest, caused by acid regurgitation into the oesophagus. **heart failure** severe failure of the heart to function properly, especially as a cause of death. **heartland** the central or most important part of a country or area. **heart-lung machine** a machine that temporarily takes over the functions of the heart and lungs, especially during heart surgery. **heart-rending** very sad or distressing. **heart-searching** thorough examination of one's feelings and motives. **heartsick** (also **heartsore**) chiefly literary despondent from grief or loss of love. **heart-stopping** very exciting. **heart-throb** informal a man whom women find very attractive. **heart-to-heart** (of a conversation) intimate and personal. **heart-warming** emotionally rewarding or uplifting. **heartwood** the dense inner part of a tree trunk, yielding the hardest wood.

heartbeat > *noun* **1** a pulsation of the heart. **2** an animating force or influence: *conflict is the heartbeat of fiction.* **3** a very brief moment of time: *I'd go back there in a heartbeat.*

WORDFINDER – arrhythmia (*an irregular heartbeat*), bradycardia (*an abnormally slow heartbeat*), diastole (*the phase when the heart muscle relaxes*), palpitation (*rapid, strong, or irregular heartbeat*), systole (*the phase when the heart muscle contracts*), tachycardia (*an abnormally rapid heart rate*).

IDIOMS – **a heartbeat away** very close.

heartbreak > *noun* overwhelming distress.

DERIVATIVES – **heartbreaker** *noun* **heartbreaking** *adjective* **heartbroken** *adjective.*

hearten > *verb* make more cheerful or confident.

DERIVATIVES – **heartening** *adjective.*

SYNONYMS – cheer, encourage, uplift.

heartfelt > *adjective* deeply and strongly felt.

SYNONYMS – earnest, profound, sincere, wholehearted.

hearth /haarth/ > *noun* **1** the floor or surround of a fireplace (often used as a symbol of domestic comfort). **2** the base or lower part of a furnace, where molten metal collects.

COMBINATIONS – **hearthrug** a rug laid in front of a fireplace. **hearthstone** a flat stone forming a hearth.

heartily > *adverb* **1** in a hearty manner. **2** very: *she was heartily sick of them.*

heartless > *adjective* completely lacking in feeling or consideration.

DERIVATIVES – **heartlessly** *adverb* **heartlessness** *noun.*

SYNONYMS – callous, cold, hard-hearted, ruthless, unfeeling.

heartsease /haartseez/ > *noun* a wild pansy with purple and yellow flowers, source of most garden varieties.

hearty > *adjective* (**heartier**, **heartiest**) **1** enthusiastic and friendly. **2** strong and healthy. **3** (of a feeling or opinion) heartfelt. **4** (of a meal) wholesome and substantial.

DERIVATIVES – **heartiness** *noun.*

SYNONYMS – **1** ebullient, unreserved, warm. **2** hardy, robust, sound, sturdy, vigorous. **4** filling, nourishing, substantial, wholesome.

heat > *noun* **1** the quality of being hot; high temperature. **2** heat seen as a form of energy arising from the random motion of molecules. **3** a source or level of heat for cooking. **4** intensity of feeling, especially of anger or excitement. **5** (**the heat**) informal intensive and unwelcome pressure: *the heat is on.* **6** a preliminary round in a race or contest. > *verb* **1** make or become hot or warm. **2** (**heat up**) become more intense and exciting. **3** (**heated**) inflamed with passion or conviction: *a heated argument.*

WORDFINDER – *methods of transmitting heat:* conduction, convection, radiation; adiabatic (*impassable to heat*), calorimeter (*apparatus for measuring heat given off*), diathermy (*medical and surgical use of heat*), homeotherm (*animal* dependent on internal generation of heat), poikilotherm (animal dependent on external sources of heat), refractory (heat-resistant), therm (unit of heat), thermal (relating to heat), thermodynamics (science of heat and other forms of energy).

IDIOMS – **if you can't stand the heat, get out of the kitchen** proverb if you can't cope with the pressures of a situation, you should leave others to deal with it rather than complaining. **in the heat of the moment** while temporarily angry or excited and without stopping for thought. **on heat** (of a female mammal) in the receptive period of the sexual cycle; in oestrus.

DERIVATIVES – **heatedly** adverb.

COMBINATIONS – **heat-seeking** (of a missile) able to detect and home in on infrared radiation emitted by a target. **heatstroke** a feverish condition caused by failure of the body's temperature-regulating mechanism when exposed to excessively high temperatures. **heat treatment** the use of heat for therapeutic purposes in medicine or to modify the properties of a material. **heatwave** a prolonged period of abnormally hot weather.

ORIGIN – Old English, related to **HOT**.

heater > noun 1 a device for heating something. 2 N. Amer. informal, dated a gun.

heath > noun 1 chiefly Brit. an area of open uncultivated land, typically on sandy soil and covered with heather, gorse, and coarse grasses. 2 a dwarf shrub with small leathery leaves and small pink or purple flowers, characteristic of heaths and moors.

DERIVATIVES – **heathy** adjective.

heathen /heethən/ > noun derogatory a person who does not belong to a widely held religion (especially Christianity, Judaism, or Islam) as regarded by those who do. > adjective relating to heathens.

DERIVATIVES – **heathendom** noun **heathenish** adjective **heathenism** noun.

ORIGIN – Old English, probably from a Germanic word meaning 'inhabiting open country, savage', from the base of **HEATH**.

heather > noun a purple-flowered heath typical of moorland and heathland.

DERIVATIVES – **heathery** adjective.

Heath Robinson > adjective Brit. ingeniously or ridiculously over-complicated in design or construction.

ORIGIN – named after the English cartoonist William Heath Robinson (1872–1944).

heating > noun equipment or devices used to provide heat, especially to a building.

heave > verb (past and past participle **heaved** or chiefly Nautical **hove**) 1 lift or haul with great effort. 2 produce (a sigh) noisily. 3 informal throw (something heavy). 4 rise and fall rhythmically or spasmodically. 5 try to

vomit; retch. 6 (**heave to**) Nautical come to a stop. > noun an act of heaving.

IDIOMS – **heave in sight** (or **into view**) Nautical come into view.

DERIVATIVES – **heaver** noun.

SYNONYMS – verb 1 haul, hoist, lift, pull, tug.

heave-ho > exclamation a cry emitted when performing an action that requires physical effort. > noun (**the heave-ho**) informal dismissal.

heaven > noun 1 a place regarded in various religions as the abode of God or the gods and of the good after death, often depicted as being above the sky. 2 (**the heavens**) literary the sky. 3 informal a place or state of supreme bliss. 4 (also **heavens**) used in exclamations as a substitute for 'God'.

IDIOMS – **the heavens open** it suddenly starts to rain very heavily. **in seventh heaven** in a state of ecstasy. **move heaven and earth** make extraordinary efforts to do something.

DERIVATIVES – **heavenward** adjective & adverb **heavenwards** adverb.

COMBINATIONS – **heaven-sent** occurring at a very favourable time.

heavenly > adjective 1 of heaven; divine. 2 relating to the sky. 3 informal very pleasing; wonderful.

SYNONYMS – 1 celestial, divine, ethereal, paradisiacal; literary empyrean. 2 celestial.

COMBINATIONS – **heavenly body** a planet, star, or other celestial body. **heavenly host** a literary or biblical term for the angels.

heaving > adjective Brit. informal extremely crowded.

heavy > adjective (**heavier**, **heaviest**) 1 of great weight; difficult to lift or move. 2 of great density; thick or substantial. 3 of more than the usual size, amount, or force. 4 striking or falling with force: a heavy blow. 5 doing something to excess: a heavy smoker. 6 not delicate or graceful; coarse or slow. 7 needing much physical effort. 8 hard to endure. 9 very important or serious. 10 informal strict, harsh, or difficult to deal with: things were getting heavy. 11 (of music, especially rock) having a strong bass component and a forceful rhythm. 12 (of ground) muddy or full of clay. > noun (pl. **heavies**) 1 something large or heavy of its kind. 2 informal a large, strong man, especially one hired for protection. 3 informal an important person.

IDIOMS – **heavy going** a person or situation that is difficult or boring to deal with.

DERIVATIVES – **heavily** adverb **heaviness** noun **heavyish** adjective.

SYNONYMS – adjective 1 burdensome, heavy, weighty. 4 forceful, hard, strong. 7 arduous, demanding, difficult, hard, laborious. 8

burdensome, onerous, oppressive. 9 deep, profound, serious, weighty.

ANTONYMS – adjective light.

COMBINATIONS – **heavy cream** N. Amer. double cream. **heavy-duty** 1 designed to withstand demanding use or wear. 2 informal intense, important, or abundant. **heavy-handed** clumsy, insensitive, or overly forceful. **heavy-hearted** depressed or melancholy. **heavy horse** a large, strong horse of a type used for draught work. **heavy hydrogen** deuterium. **heavy industry** the manufacture of large, heavy articles and materials in bulk. **heavy metal** 1 a metal of relatively high density, or of high relative atomic weight. 2 a type of highly amplified harsh-sounding rock music with a strong beat. **heavy petting** erotic contact between two people involving stimulation of the genitals but stopping short of intercourse. **heavy water** water in which the hydrogen in the molecules is partly or wholly replaced by the isotope deuterium, used especially in nuclear reactors.

ORIGIN – Old English, related to **HEAVE**.

heavyweight > noun 1 a weight in boxing and other sports, typically the heaviest category. 2 informal an important or influential person. > adjective 1 of above-average weight. 2 informal serious, important, or influential.

hebdomadal /hebdomməd'l/ > adjective formal weekly.

ORIGIN – from Greek hebdomas 'the number seven, seven days'.

hebe /heebi/ > noun an evergreen flowering shrub with spikes of mauve, pink, or white flowers, native to New Zealand.

ORIGIN – named after the Greek goddess Hebe, cup-bearer of the gods.

hebetude /hebbityood/ > noun literary the state of being dull or lethargic.

ORIGIN – Latin hebetudo, from hebes 'blunt'.

Hebraic /hibrayik/ > adjective of Hebrew or the Hebrews.

Hebraist /heebrayist/ > noun a scholar of the Hebrew language.

Hebrew /heebroo/ > noun 1 a member of an ancient people living in what is now Israel and Palestine, who established the kingdoms of Israel and Judaea. 2 the Semitic language of the Hebrews, in its ancient or modern form. 3 dated, offensive a Jewish person.

COMBINATIONS – **Hebrew Bible** the sacred writings of Judaism, called by Christians the Old Testament.

ORIGIN – Greek Hebraios, from a Hebrew word understood to mean 'one from the other side (of the river)'.

Hebridean /hebrideeən/ > noun a person from the Hebrides off the NW coast of

Scotland. > *adjective* relating to the Hebrides.

hecatomb /hekkətoōm/ > *noun* (in ancient Greece or Rome) a great public sacrifice, originally of a hundred oxen.
ORIGIN – Greek *hekatombē*, from *hekaton* 'hundred' + *bous* 'ox'.

heck > *exclamation* used for emphasis, or to express surprise, annoyance, etc.
ORIGIN – euphemistic alteration of **HELL**.

heckle > *verb* interrupt (a public speaker) with derisive comments or abuse. > *noun* an instance of heckling.
DERIVATIVES – **heckler** *noun*.

wordpower facts

Heckle

In medieval times a **heckle**, or **hackle**, was a comb used to split and straighten the fibres of flax or hemp. To **heckle**, therefore, was to comb or dress flax. From this developed the figurative sense 'to question (a person) severely, in order to discover their weak points' and then 'to scold or chastise', from which the modern sense developed. A similar development is seen in the modern sense of **tease**, which originally meant 'to comb (wool)'; for this task a prickly **teasel** was a useful tool.

hectare /hektair/ > *noun* a metric unit of square measure, equal to 10,000 square metres (2.471 acres).
DERIVATIVES – **hectarage** *noun*.
ORIGIN – from Greek *hekaton* 'hundred' + **ARE²**.

hectic > *adjective* full of incessant or frantic activity.
DERIVATIVES – **hectically** *adverb*.
SYNONYMS – busy, chaotic, frantic, frenetic, hurried.
ORIGIN – Greek *hektikos* 'habitual'.

hecto- > *combining form* a hundred: *hectometre*.
ORIGIN – French, formed from Greek *hekaton* 'hundred'.

hectogram (also **hectogramme**) > *noun* a metric unit of mass equal to one hundred grams.

hectolitre /hektōleetər/ (US **hectoliter**) > *noun* a metric unit of capacity equal to one hundred litres.

hectometre /hektōmeetər/ (US **hecto-meter**) > *noun* a metric unit of length equal to one hundred metres.

hector /hektər/ > *verb* talk to in a bullying or intimidating way.
DERIVATIVES – **hectoring** *adjective*.

wordpower facts

Hector

The origins of the word **hector** lie in Greek mythology, in the name of the Trojan warrior *Hector*, killed by Achilles. Hector was regarded as a great hero, and it was in this sense, 'a hero', that the word **hector** entered English in the 14th century. By the 17th century, however, it had acquired pejorative connotations, being applied specifically to a group of swaggering young men who were notorious in London. The *Oxford English Dictionary* includes this quotation from 1693: 'On Sunday night last three hectors came out of a tavern in Holborn, with their swords drawn, and began to break windows'. The verb, meaning 'to brag or bully', then 'to intimidate by bluster or threats', was also first recorded in the 17th century.

he'd > *contraction* **1** he had. **2** he would.

hedge > *noun* **1** a fence or boundary formed by closely growing bushes or shrubs. **2** a contract entered into or asset held as a protection against possible financial loss. **3** a word or phrase, for example *etc.*, used to allow for additional possibilities or to avoid over-precise commitment. > *verb* **1** surround with a hedge. **2** limit or qualify by conditions or exceptions. **3** avoid making a definite statement or commitment. **3** protect (an investor or investment) against loss by making compensating contracts or transactions.
WORDFINDER – topiary (*art of clipping hedges into ornamental shapes*).
IDIOMS – **hedge one's bets** avoid committing oneself when faced with a difficult choice.
DERIVATIVES – **hedger** *noun*.
COMBINATIONS – **hedge-hop** fly an aircraft at a very low altitude. **hedge sparrow** the dunnock.

hedgehog > *noun* a small nocturnal insectivorous mammal with a spiny coat, able to roll itself into a ball for defence.

hedgerow > *noun* a hedge of wild shrubs and occasional trees bordering a field.

hedging > *noun* **1** the planting or trimming of hedges. **2** bushes and shrubs planted to form hedges.

hedonism /heedəniz'm, hedəniz'm/ > *noun* **1** the pursuit of pleasure; sensual self-indulgence. **2** Philosophy the theory that pleasure (in the sense of the satisfaction of desires) is the highest good and proper aim of human life.
DERIVATIVES – **hedonist** *noun* **hedonistic** *adjective*.
ORIGIN – from Greek *hēdonē* 'pleasure'.

-hedron > *combining form* (pl. **-hedra** or **-hedrons**) forming nouns denoting geometrical solids having faces of various numbers or shapes: *decahedron*.
DERIVATIVES – **-hedral** *combining form*.
ORIGIN – from Greek *hedra* 'seat, base'.

heebie-jeebies > *plural noun* (**the heebie-jeebies**) informal a state of nervous fear or anxiety.

heed > *verb* pay attention to. > *noun* (usually **pay** (or **take**) **heed**) careful attention.
DERIVATIVES – **heedful** *adjective*.
SYNONYMS – *verb* mark, mind, notice, take notice of.

heedless > *adjective* showing a reckless lack of care or attention.
DERIVATIVES – **heedlessly** *adverb* **heedlessness** *noun*.
SYNONYMS – careless, neglectful, negligent, reckless, thoughtless.

hee-haw > *noun* the loud, harsh cry of a donkey or mule. > *verb* make such a cry.

heel¹ > *noun* **1** the back part of the foot below the ankle. **2** the part of a shoe or boot supporting the heel. **3** the part of the palm of the hand next to the wrist. **4** informal, dated a contemptible person. > *exclamation* a command to a dog to walk close behind its owner. > *verb* fit or renew a heel on (a shoe or boot).
IDIOMS – **at** (or **on**) **the heels of** following closely after. **bring to heel** bring under control. **cool** (or Brit. **kick**) **one's heels** be kept waiting. **take to one's heels** run away. **turn** (**on one's**) **heel** turn sharply.
DERIVATIVES – **heeled** *adjective* **heelless** *adjective*.

heel² > *verb* (of a ship) lean over owing to the pressure of wind or an uneven load. > *noun* an instance of heeling, or the amount that a ship heels.
ORIGIN – from obsolete *heeld*, *hield* 'incline'.

heel³ > *verb* (**heel in**) set (a plant) in the ground and cover its roots; plant temporarily.
ORIGIN – Old English, 'cover, hide'.

heelball > *noun* a mixture of hard wax and lampblack used by shoemakers for polishing or in brass rubbing.

heft > *verb* **1** lift or carry (something heavy). **2** lift or hold (something) to test its weight.
ORIGIN – probably from **HEAVE**, on the pattern of words such as *cleft*.

hefty > *adjective* (**heftier**, **heftiest**) **1** large, heavy, and powerful. **2** (of a number or amount) considerable.
DERIVATIVES – **heftily** *adverb*.

Hegelian /haygeeliən, higayliən/ > *adjective* relating to the German philosopher Georg Hegel (1770–1831) or his philosophy. > *noun* a follower of Hegel.
DERIVATIVES – **Hegelianism** *noun*.

449

hegemony /hi**jemm**əni, hi**gemm**əni/ > *noun* dominance, especially by one state or social group over others.

DERIVATIVES – **hegemonic** adjective.

ORIGIN – Greek *hēgemonia*, from *hēgemōn* 'leader'.

Hegira /he**jir**ə/ (also **Hejira** or **Hijra** /**hij**rə/) > *noun* **1** Muhammad's departure from Mecca to Medina in AD 622, which marked the consolidation of the first Muslim community. **2** the Muslim era reckoned from this date. See also **AH**.

ORIGIN – Arabic, 'departure'.

heifer /**heff**ər/ > *noun* a cow that has not borne a calf, or has borne only one calf.

heigh-ho /hay**hō**/ > *exclamation* informal expressing boredom, resignation, or jollity.

height > *noun* **1** the measurement of someone or something from head to foot or from base to top. **2** the distance of something above ground or sea level. **3** the quality of being tall or high. **4** a high place or area. **5** the most intense part or period: *at the height of the attack.* **6** an extreme instance or example: *the height of folly.*

WORDFINDER – acrophobia (*fear of heights*), vertigo (*sensation of loss of balance caused by heights*).

SYNONYMS – **2** altitude, elevation. **5** climax, peak, zenith.

ORIGIN – Old English, related to **HIGH**.

heighten > *verb* **1** make higher. **2** make or become more intense.

SYNONYMS – **1** elevate, lift, raise. **2** build up, intensify.

heinous /**hay**nəs, **hee**nəs/ > *adjective* utterly abhorrent and wicked: *a heinous crime.*

DERIVATIVES – **heinously** adverb **heinousness** noun.

SYNONYMS – abominable, atrocious, despicable, loathsome, monstrous.

ORIGIN – Old French *haineus*, from *hair* 'to hate'.

heir /air/ > *noun* **1** a person legally entitled to the property or rank of another on that person's death. **2** a person who continues the work of a predecessor.

DERIVATIVES – **heirship** noun.

COMBINATIONS – **heir apparent** (pl. **heirs apparent**) **1** an heir whose claim cannot be set aside by the birth of another heir. **2** a person who is most likely to succeed to the place of another. **heir presumptive** (pl. **heirs presumptive**) an heir whose claim may be set aside by the birth of another heir.

ORIGIN – Old French, from Latin *heres*.

heiress > *noun* a female heir, especially to vast wealth.

heirloom > *noun* a valuable object that has belonged to a family for several generations. [ORIGIN – from **HEIR** + **LOOM**¹ (in the former senses 'tool, heirloom').]

heist /hīst/ informal, chiefly N. Amer. > *noun* a robbery. > *verb* steal.

ORIGIN – from a local pronunciation of **HOIST**.

Hejira > *noun* variant spelling of **HEGIRA**.

held past and past participle of **HOLD**¹.

Heldentenor /**held**əntennor/ > *noun* a powerful tenor voice suitable for heroic roles in opera.

ORIGIN – German, 'hero tenor'.

helical /**hell**ik'l/ > *adjective* having the shape or form of a helix; spiral.

DERIVATIVES – **helically** adverb.

helices plural of **HELIX**.

helichrysum /helli**krī**səm/ > *noun* a plant of the daisy family, with flowers retaining their shape and colour when dried.

ORIGIN – Greek *helikhrusos*, from *helix* 'spiral' + *khrusos* 'gold'.

helicopter > *noun* a type of aircraft deriving both lift and propulsion from one or two sets of horizontally revolving rotors.

ORIGIN – from Greek *helix* 'spiral' + *pteron* 'wing'.

heliocentric /heeliō**sen**trik/ > *adjective* based on or representing the sun as the centre.

ORIGIN – from Greek *hēlios* 'sun'.

heliograph /**hee**liəgraaf/ > *noun* **1** a signalling device by which sunlight is reflected in flashes from a movable mirror. **2** a message sent by heliograph. **3** a telescopic apparatus for photographing the sun.

DERIVATIVES – **heliographic** adjective.

heliotrope /**hee**liətrōp/ > *noun* a plant of the borage family, grown for its fragrant purple or blue flowers.

ORIGIN – Greek *hēliotropion* (denoting a plant whose flowers turn towards the sun or a sundial), from *hēlios* 'sun' + *trepein* 'to turn'.

helipad > *noun* a landing and take-off area for helicopters.

heliport > *noun* an airport or landing place for helicopters.

heli-skiing > *noun* skiing in which the skier is taken up the mountain by helicopter.

helium /**hee**liəm/ > *noun* an inert gaseous chemical element, the lightest member of the noble gas series.

ORIGIN – from Greek *hēlios* 'sun', because before it was discovered on the earth its existence had been proposed to explain lines in the sun's spectrum.

helix /**hee**liks/ > *noun* (pl. **helices** /**hee**liseez/) an object with a three-dimensional spiral shape like that of a wire wound uniformly in a single layer around a cylinder or cone.

ORIGIN – Greek.

hell > *noun* **1** a place regarded in various religions as a spiritual realm of evil and suffering, often depicted as a place of perpetual fire beneath the earth to which the wicked are sent after death. **2** a state or place of great suffering. > *exclamation* used to express annoyance or surprise or for emphasis.

IDIOMS – **all hell breaks** (or **is let**) **loose** informal suddenly there is pandemonium. **come hell or high water** whatever difficulties may occur. **for the hell of it** informal just for fun. **give someone hell** informal severely reprimand or harass someone. **hell for leather** as fast as possible. **hell hath no fury like a woman scorned** proverb a woman rejected by a man can be ferociously angry and vindictive. **hell's bells** informal an exclamation of annoyance or anger. **like hell** informal very fast, much, hard, etc. **not a hope in hell** informal no chance at all. **play hell** (or **merry hell**) informal create havoc or cause damage. **the road to hell is paved with good intentions** proverb promises and plans must be put into action, otherwise they are useless. **there will be hell to pay** informal serious trouble will result. **until hell freezes over** forever.

COMBINATIONS – **hell-bent** determined to achieve something at all costs. **hellcat** a spiteful, violent woman. **hellfire** the fire regarded as existing in hell. **hellhole** an oppressive or unbearable place. **hellhound** a demon in the form of a dog. **hellraiser** a person who causes trouble by violent, drunken, or outrageous behaviour. **Hell's Angel** a member of a gang of male motorcycle enthusiasts notorious for lawless behaviour.

he'll > *contraction* he shall or he will.

hellebore /**hell**ibor/ > *noun* a poisonous winter-flowering plant with large white, green, or purplish flowers.

ORIGIN – Greek *helleboros*.

helleborine /**hell**ibəreen/ > *noun* an orchid with greenish, white, or pink flowers, growing chiefly in woodland.

ORIGIN – Greek.

Hellene /**hell**een/ > *noun* a Greek.

ORIGIN – named after *Hellen*, son of Deucalion, who was held in Greek mythology to be the ancestor of all the Greeks.

Hellenic /he**lenn**ik, he**leen**ik/ > *adjective* **1** Greek. **2** relating to Iron Age and Classical Greek culture. > *noun* the Greek language.

Hellenism /**hell**əniz'm/ > *noun* **1** the national character or culture of Greece, especially ancient Greece. **2** the study or imitation of ancient Greek culture.

DERIVATIVES – **Hellenise** (also **Hellenize**) verb **Hellenist** noun.

Hellenistic > *adjective* relating to Greek culture from the death of Alexander the Great (323 BC) to the defeat of Cleopatra and Mark Antony by Octavian in 31 BC.

hellish > *adjective* **1** of or like hell. **2** informal extremely difficult or unpleasant. > *adverb* **Brit.** *informal* very; extremely.

DERIVATIVES – **hellishly** *adverb* **hellishness** *noun*.

hello (also **hallo** or **hullo**) > *exclamation* **1** used as a greeting or to begin a telephone conversation. **2 Brit.** used to express surprise or to attract someone's attention.

helm¹ > *noun* **1** a tiller or wheel for steering a ship or boat. **2** (**the helm**) a position of leadership. > *verb* **1** steer (a boat or ship). **2** manage the running of.

ORIGIN – Old English, probably related to **HELVE**.

helm² > *noun archaic* a helmet.

ORIGIN – Old English, related to **HELMET**.

helmet > *noun* a hard or padded protective hat.

DERIVATIVES – **helmeted** *adjective*.

ORIGIN – Old French, 'little helmet'; related to **HELM²**.

helmsman > *noun* a person who steers a boat.

helot /**hell**ət/ > *noun* **1** a member of a class of serfs in ancient Sparta, intermediate in status between slaves and citizens. **2** a serf or slave.

ORIGIN – Greek *Heilōtes*, traditionally taken to mean 'inhabitants of *Helos*', an ancient Greek town whose people were enslaved.

help > *verb* **1** make it easier for (someone) to do something. **2** improve (a situation or problem). **3** (**help to**) serve (someone) with (food or drink). **4** (**help oneself**) take something without permission. **5** (**can or could not help**) cannot or could not refrain from. > *noun* **1** assistance or a source of assistance. **2** a domestic servant or employee.

IDIOMS – **so help me** (**God**) used to emphasise that one means what one is saying. **there is no help for it** there is no way of avoiding a situation.

DERIVATIVES – **helper** *noun*.

SYNONYMS – *verb* **1** aid, assist, succour, support. **2** alleviate, ameliorate, ease, improve, relieve, soothe. *noun* **1** aid, assistance, support.

COMBINATIONS – **helpline** a telephone service providing help with problems. **helpmate** (also **helpmeet**) a helpful companion or partner. [ORIGIN – from an erroneous reading of a passage in the Book of Genesis (chapter 2), where Adam's future wife is described as 'an help meet for him' (i.e. a suitable helper for him).]

helpful > *adjective* **1** giving or ready to give help. **2** useful.

DERIVATIVES – **helpfully** *adverb* **helpfulness** *noun*.

SYNONYMS – **1** accommodating, kind, obliging, supportive.

helping > *noun* a portion of food served to one person at one time.

helpless > *adjective* **1** unable to defend oneself or to act without help. **2** uncontrollable.

DERIVATIVES – **helplessly** *adverb* **helplessness** *noun*.

SYNONYMS – **1** defenceless, impotent, powerless, vulnerable.

helter-skelter > *adjective & adverb* in disorderly haste or confusion. > *noun* **Brit.** a tall spiral slide winding around a tower at a fair.

ORIGIN – perhaps symbolic of running feet or from obsolete *skelte* 'hasten'.

helve /helv/ > *noun* the handle of a weapon or tool.

ORIGIN – Old English, related to **HALTER**.

Helvetian /hel**veesh**'n/ (also **Helvetic** /hel**vett**ik/) > *adjective* Swiss. > *noun* a person from Switzerland.

ORIGIN – from Latin *Helvetia* 'Switzerland'.

hem¹ > *noun* the edge of a piece of cloth or clothing which has been turned under and sewn. > *verb* (**hemmed**, **hemming**) **1** turn under and sew the edge of. **2** (**hem in**) surround and restrict the space or movement of.

COMBINATIONS – **hemline** the level of the lower edge of a garment such as a skirt or coat.

hem² > *exclamation* expressing the sound made when coughing or clearing the throat to attract someone's attention or show hesitation.

IDIOMS – **hem and haw** be indecisive; hum and haw.

hemal etc. US spelling of **HAEMAL** etc.

he-man > *noun informal* a very well-built, masculine man.

hemi- > *prefix* half.

ORIGIN – Greek.

-hemia > *combining form* US spelling of **-AEMIA**.

hemidemisemiquaver > *noun* Music a note with the time value of half a demisemiquaver.

hemiparesis /hemmipə**ree**siss/ > *noun* another term for **HEMIPLEGIA**.

hemiplegia /hemmi**plee**jə/ > *noun* paralysis of one side of the body.

DERIVATIVES – **hemiplegic** *noun* & *adjective*.

ORIGIN – from Greek *plēgē* 'blow, stroke'.

hemisphere > *noun* **1** a half of a sphere. **2** a half of the earth, usually as divided into northern and southern halves by the equator, or into western and eastern halves by an imaginary line passing through the poles.

DERIVATIVES – **hemispheric** *adjective* **hemispherical** *adjective*.

hemlock > *noun* **1** a highly poisonous plant of the parsley family, with fern-like leaves and small white flowers. **2** a sedative or poison obtained from this plant.

hemp > *noun* **1** (also **Indian hemp**) the cannabis plant. **2** the fibre of this plant, extracted from the stem and used to make rope, strong fabrics, paper, etc. **3** the drug cannabis.

hen > *noun* **1** a female bird, especially of a domestic fowl. **2** (**hens**) domestic fowls of either sex.

IDIOMS – **as rare** (or **scarce**) **as hen's teeth** extremely rare.

COMBINATIONS – **hen night** Brit. *informal* a celebration held for a woman who is about to get married, attended only by women. **hen party** informal a social gathering of women.

henbane /**hen**bayn/ > *noun* a poisonous plant with sticky, hairy leaves and an unpleasant smell.

hence > *adverb* **1** as a consequence; for this reason. **2** from now; in the future. **3** (also **from hence**) archaic from here.

henceforth (also **henceforward**) > *adverb* from this or that time on.

henchman > *noun* **1** chiefly derogatory a faithful supporter or aide, especially one prepared to engage in underhand practices. **2** historical a squire or page attending a prince or noble.

wordpower facts

Henchman

The word **henchman** comes from Old English *hengest* 'male horse' and *man*: the original sense was probably 'a groom', from which developed the meaning 'a squire, or page of honour' (who rode alongside his prince or nobleman). In the 18th century the sense 'principal attendant of a Highland chief' was popularised in the historical novels of Sir Walter Scott, and from this the modern use 'faithful supporter' developed.

hendeca- > *combining form* eleven; having eleven: *hendecagon*.

ORIGIN – from Greek *hendeka* 'eleven'.

hendecagon /hen**dekk**əgən/ > *noun* a plane figure with eleven straight sides and angles.

hendiadys /hen**dī**ədiss/ > *noun* the expression of a single idea by two words connected with 'and', e.g. *nice and warm*, when one could be used to modify the other, as in *nicely warm*.

ORIGIN – from Greek *hen dia duoin* 'one thing by two'.

henge /henj/ > *noun* a prehistoric monument consisting of a circle of stone or wooden uprights.

ORIGIN – from *Stonehenge*, such a monument in Wiltshire, from two Old English words meaning 'stone' + 'to hang'.

henna > *noun* the powdered leaves of a tropical shrub, used as a reddish-brown dye to colour the hair and decorate the body. > *verb* (**hennas**, **hennaed**, **hennaing**) dye with henna.

ORIGIN – Arabic.

henpeck > *verb* (of a woman) continually criticise and order about (her husband).

DERIVATIVES – **henpecked** *adjective*.

henry > *noun* (pl. **henries** or **henrys**) Physics the unit of inductance in the SI system.

ORIGIN – named after the American physicist Joseph *Henry* (1797–1878).

heparin /**hepp**ərin/ > *noun* a compound occurring in the liver and other tissues which prevents blood coagulation, used as an anticoagulant in the treatment of thrombosis.

ORIGIN – from Greek *hēpar* 'liver'.

hepatic /hi**patt**ik/ > *adjective* relating to the liver.

ORIGIN – Greek *hēpatikos*, from *hēpar* 'liver'.

hepatitis /heppə**tī**tiss/ > *noun* a disease in which the liver becomes inflamed and there is jaundice and other symptoms, mainly spread by a series of viruses (**hepatitis A**, **B**, and **C**) transmitted in blood or food.

hepcat > *noun* informal, dated a stylish or fashionable person.

ORIGIN – from *hep* (variant of **HIP³**) + *cat* (informal term for a man, especially among jazz enthusiasts).

hepta- > *combining form* seven; having seven: *heptathlon*.

ORIGIN – from Greek *hepta* 'seven'.

heptagon /**hep**təgən/ > *noun* a plane figure with seven straight sides and angles.

DERIVATIVES – **heptagonal** *adjective*.

heptahedron /heptə**hee**drən/ > *noun* (pl. **heptahedra** or **heptahedrons**) a solid figure with seven plane faces.

heptane > *noun* Chemistry a colourless liquid hydrocarbon of the alkane series, present in petroleum spirit.

ORIGIN – from **HEPTA-** 'seven' (denoting seven carbon atoms) + **-ANE**.

heptathlon /hep**tath**lən/ > *noun* an athletic contest for women that consists of seven separate events: 100 metres hurdles, high jump, shot-put, 200 metres, long jump, javelin, and 800 metres.

DERIVATIVES – **heptathlete** *noun*.

ORIGIN – from Greek *hepta* 'seven' + *athlon* 'contest'.

her > *pronoun* (third person sing.) **1** used as the object of a verb or preposition to refer to a female person or animal previously mentioned. **2** referring to a ship, country, or other inanimate thing regarded as female. > *possessive determiner* **1** belonging to or associated with a female person or animal previously mentioned. **2** (**Her**) used in titles.

IDIOMS – **her indoors** Brit. informal, humorous one's wife.

herald > *noun* **1** historical a person who carried official messages, made proclamations, and oversaw tournaments. **2** a person or thing viewed as a sign that something is about to happen. **3** an official employed to oversee state ceremonial, precedence, and the use of armorial bearings. **4** (in the UK) an official of the College of Arms ranking above a pursuivant. > *verb* **1** signal that (something) is about to happen. **2** acclaim.

SYNONYMS – *noun* **2** harbinger, omen, portent, sign. *verb* **1** augur, foreshadow, portend, presage.

ORIGIN – Old French *herault*.

heraldic /he**ral**dik/ > *adjective* relating to heraldry.

DERIVATIVES – **heraldically** *adverb*.

heraldry > *noun* **1** the system by which coats of arms and other armorial bearings are devised, described, and regulated. **2** armorial bearings or other heraldic symbols.

WORDFINDER – *colours used in heraldry:* argent (*silver*), azure (*blue*), gules (*red*), or (*gold or yellow*), purpure (*purple*), sable (*black*), sanguine (*blood red*), tenné (*orange-brown*), vert (*green*).

DERIVATIVES – **heraldist** *noun*.

herb > *noun* **1** any plant with leaves, seeds, or flowers used for flavouring, food, medicine, or perfume. **2** Botany any seed-bearing plant which does not have a woody stem and dies down to the ground after flowering.

WORDFINDER – *herbs:* basil, bay leaf, bergamot, chervil, chives, dill, fennel, lemon balm, marjoram, mint, oregano, parsley, rosemary, sage, savory, spearmint, tarragon, thyme, yerba buena.

DERIVATIVES – **herby** (**herbier**, **herbiest**) *adjective*.

ORIGIN – Latin *herba* 'grass, green crops, herb'.

herbaceous /her**bay**shəss/ > *adjective* relating to herbs (in the botanical sense).

COMBINATIONS – **herbaceous border** a garden border containing mainly perennial flowering plants.

herbage > *noun* herbaceous plants, especially grass used for grazing.

herbal > *adjective* relating to or made from herbs, especially those used in cooking and medicine. > *noun* a book that describes herbs and their culinary and medicinal properties.

herbalism > *noun* the study or practice of the medicinal and therapeutic use of plants.

herbalist > *noun* **1** a practitioner of herbalism. **2** a dealer in medicinal herbs.

herbarium /her**bair**iəm/ > *noun* (pl. **herbaria**) a systematically arranged collection of dried plants.

herbed > *adjective* cooked or flavoured with herbs.

herbicide /**her**bisīd/ > *noun* a toxic substance used to destroy unwanted vegetation.

herbivore /**her**bivor/ > *noun* an animal that feeds on plants.

herbivorous /her**bivv**ərəss/ > *adjective* (of an animal) feeding on plants.

Herculean /herkyoo**lee**ən, her**kyoo**liən/ > *adjective* requiring or having great strength or effort.

ORIGIN – named after the Roman and Greek mythological hero *Hercules* (famed for his strength).

herd > *noun* **1** a large group of animals, especially hoofed mammals, that live or are kept together. **2** derogatory a large group or class of people. > *verb* **1** move in a large group. **2** keep or look after (livestock).

DERIVATIVES – **herder** *noun*.

COMBINATIONS – **herd instinct** an inclination to behave or think like the majority.

herdsman > *noun* the owner or keeper of a herd of domesticated animals.

WORDFINDER – Boötes (*constellation, the Herdsman*).

here > *adverb* **1** in, at, or to this place or position. **2** (usu. **here is** or **are**) used when introducing or handing over something or someone. **3** used when indicating a time, point, or situation that has arrived or is happening. > *exclamation* used to attract someone's attention.

IDIOMS – **here and now** at the present time. **here and there** in various places. **here goes** said to indicate that one is about to start something difficult or exciting. **here's to** used to wish health or success to (someone) before drinking. **neither here nor there** of no importance or relevance.

hereabouts (also **hereabout**) > *adverb* near this place.

hereafter > *adverb* formal **1** from now on or at some time in the future. **2** after death. > *noun* (**the hereafter**) life after death.

hereby > *adverb* formal as a result of this.

hereditary /hi**redd**itri/ > *adjective* **1** conferred by, based on, or relating to inheritance. **2** (of a disease or characteristic) able to be passed on genetically from parents to their offspring.

DERIVATIVES – **hereditarily** *adverb*.

heredity /hi**redd**iti/ > *noun* **1** the passing on of physical or mental characteristics genetically from one generation to another. **2** inheritance of title, office, or right.

ORIGIN – Latin *hereditas* 'heirship', from *heres* 'heir'.

Hereford /**herr**ifərd/ > *noun* a breed of red and white beef cattle.

ORIGIN – from *Hereford* in west central England.

herein > *adverb* formal in this document, book, or matter.

hereinafter > *adverb* formal further on in this document.

hereof > *adverb* formal of this document.

heresiarch /he**ree**ziaark/ > *noun* the founder of a heresy or the leader of a heretical sect.

ORIGIN – Greek *hairesiarkhēs*, from *hairesis* 'heretical sect, heresy' + *arkhēs* 'ruler'.

heresy /**herr**isi/ > *noun* (pl. **heresies**) 1 belief or opinion contrary to orthodox religious (especially Christian) doctrine. 2 opinion profoundly at odds with what is generally accepted.

SYNONYMS – dissent, heterodoxy, nonconformity, unorthodoxy.

ORIGIN – Greek *hairesis* 'choice, sect'.

heretic /**herr**itik/ > *noun* a person believing in or practising heresy.

DERIVATIVES – **heretical** /hi**rett**ik'l/ *adjective* **heretically** *adverb*.

hereto > *adverb* formal to this matter or document.

heretofore > *adverb* formal before now.

hereunder > *adverb* formal 1 as provided for under the terms of this document. 2 further on in this document.

hereupon > *adverb* archaic after or as a result of this.

herewith > *adverb* formal with this letter.

heritable > *adjective* able to be inherited.

DERIVATIVES – **heritability** *noun* **heritably** *adverb*.

heritage > *noun* 1 property that is or may be inherited; an inheritance. 2 valued things such as historic buildings that have been passed down from previous generations. 3 (before another noun) relating to things of historic or cultural value that are worthy of preservation.

heritor > *noun* a person who inherits.

hermaphrodite /her**maf**rədīt/ > *noun* 1 a person or animal having both male and female sex organs or other sexual characteristics. 2 Botany a plant having stamens and pistils in the same flower.

DERIVATIVES – **hermaphroditic** *adjective* **hermaphroditism** *noun*.

ORIGIN – Greek *hermaphroditos*, originally the name of the son of Hermes and Aphrodite who became joined in one body with the nymph Salmacis.

hermeneutic /hermi**nyoo**tik/ > *adjective* concerning interpretation, especially of the Bible or literary texts.

DERIVATIVES – **hermeneutical** *adjective*.

ORIGIN – Greek *hermēneutikos*, from *hermēneuein* 'interpret'.

hermeneutics > *plural noun* (usu. treated as sing.) the branch of knowledge concerned with interpretation, especially of the Bible or literary texts.

hermetic /her**mett**ik/ > *adjective* 1 (of a seal or closure) complete and airtight. 2 insulated or protected from outside influences. 3 esoteric or cryptic: *hermetic poems*.

DERIVATIVES – **hermetically** *adverb* **hermeticism** *noun*.

ORIGIN – from Latin *Hermes Trismegistus* 'thrice-greatest Hermes', the legendary founder of alchemy and astrology identified with the Greek god Hermes.

hermit > *noun* 1 a person living in solitude as a religious discipline. 2 a reclusive or solitary person.

WORDFINDER – anchorite (*religious recluse*), eremitic (*relating to a hermit*), marabout (*a Muslim hermit*).

DERIVATIVES – **hermitic** *adjective*.

COMBINATIONS – **hermit crab** a crab with a soft abdomen, which lives in a cast-off mollusc shell for protection.

ORIGIN – Greek *erēmitēs*, from *erēmos* 'solitary'.

hermitage > *noun* the home of a hermit, especially when small and remote.

hernia /**her**niə/ > *noun* (pl. **hernias** or **herniae** /**her**ni-ee/) a condition in which part of an organ (typically the intestine) is displaced and protrudes through the wall of the cavity containing it.

DERIVATIVES – **herniated** *adjective* **herniation** *noun*.

ORIGIN – Latin.

hero > *noun* (pl. **heroes**) 1 a person, typically a man, who is admired for their courage or outstanding achievements. 2 the chief male character in a book, play, or film. 3 (in mythology and folklore) a person of superhuman qualities.

ORIGIN – Greek *hērōs*.

heroic > *adjective* 1 of or like a hero or heroine; very brave. 2 grand or grandiose in scale or intention: *pyramids on a heroic scale*. > *noun* (**heroics**) behaviour or talk that is bold or dramatic.

DERIVATIVES – **heroically** *adverb*.

SYNONYMS – 1 brave, courageous, fearless, intrepid, valiant, valorous.

COMBINATIONS – **heroic couplet** (in verse) a pair of rhyming iambic pentameters.

heroin* > *noun* a highly addictive painkilling drug derived from morphine, often used illicitly as a narcotic.

*SPELLING – no final e: heroin.

ORIGIN – German, from Latin *heros* 'hero' (because of its effects on the user's self-esteem).

heroine > *noun* 1 a woman admired for her courage or outstanding achievements. 2 the chief female character in a book, play, or film.

heroism > *noun* great bravery.

SYNONYMS – bravery, courage, daring, fearlessness, intrepidity, valour.

heron > *noun* a large fish-eating wading bird with long legs, a long neck, and a long pointed bill.

ORIGIN – Old French.

heronry > *noun* (pl. **heronries**) a breeding colony of herons, typically in a group of trees.

hero worship > *noun* excessive admiration for someone. > *verb* (**hero-worship**) admire excessively.

herpes /**her**peez/ > *noun* a disease caused by a virus, affecting the skin (often with blisters) or the nervous system.

DERIVATIVES – **herpetic** *adjective*.

COMBINATIONS – **herpes simplex** a form of herpes which can produce cold sores, genital inflammation, or conjunctivitis. **herpes zoster** medical name for SHINGLES. [ORIGIN – Greek *zōstēr* 'girdle, shingles'.]

ORIGIN – Greek, 'shingles, creeping', from *herpein* 'to creep'.

herpetology /herpi**toll**əji/ > *noun* the branch of zoology concerned with reptiles and amphibians.

DERIVATIVES – **herpetological** *adjective* **herpetologist** *noun*.

ORIGIN – from Greek *herpeton* 'creeping thing', from *herpein* 'to creep'.

Herr /hair/ > *noun* (pl. **Herren** /**herr**ən/) a title or form of address for a German-speaking man, corresponding to *Mr* and also used before a rank or occupation.

ORIGIN – from High German *hērro* 'more exalted'.

Herrenvolk /**herr**ənfolk/ > *noun* the German nation as considered by the Nazis to be innately superior to others.

ORIGIN – German, 'master race'.

herring > *noun* a silvery fish which is most abundant in coastal waters and is an important food fish.

COMBINATIONS – **herring gull** a common northern gull with grey black-tipped wings.

herringbone > *noun* a zigzag pattern consisting of columns of short parallel lines, with all the lines in one column sloping one way and all the lines in the next column sloping the other way.

hers* > *possessive pronoun* used to refer to a thing or things belonging to or associated with a female person or animal previously mentioned.

*SPELLING – no apostrophe: hers.

herself > *pronoun* (third person sing.) 1 (reflexive) used as the object of a verb or preposition to refer to a female person or animal previously mentioned as the subject of the clause. **2** (emphatic) she or her personally.

Herts. /haarts/ > *abbreviation* Hertfordshire.

hertz /herts/ > *noun* (pl. same) the unit of frequency in the SI system, equal to one cycle per second.
ORIGIN – named after the German physicist H. R. *Hertz* (1857–94).

Herzegovinian /hertsəgovvinyən/ > *noun* a person from Herzegovina, the southern part of Bosnia–Herzegovina. > *adjective* relating to Herzegovina.

he's > *contraction* **1** he is. **2** he has.

hesitant > *adjective* slow to act or speak through indecision or reluctance.
DERIVATIVES – **hesitance** *noun* **hesitancy** *noun* **hesitantly** *adverb*.
SYNONYMS – faltering, indecisive, reluctant, tentative.

hesitate > *verb* **1** pause in indecision. **2** be reluctant to do something.
IDIOMS – **he who hesitates is lost** *proverb* delay or vacillation may have unfortunate consequences.
DERIVATIVES – **hesitation** *noun*.
SYNONYMS – **1** delay, dither, falter, pause.
ORIGIN – Latin *haesitare* 'stick fast, leave undecided'.

hessian > *noun* a strong, coarse fabric made from hemp or jute, used especially for sacks and in upholstery.
ORIGIN – from *Hesse*, a state of western Germany.

hetero- /hettərō/ > *combining form* other; different: *heterosexual*.
ORIGIN – from Greek *heteros* 'other'.

heterodox /hettərədoks/ > *adjective* not conforming with orthodox standards or beliefs.
DERIVATIVES – **heterodoxy** *noun*.
ORIGIN – from Greek *heteros* 'other' + *doxa* 'opinion'.

heterodyne /hettərədīn/ > *noun* (usu. before another noun) Electronics a radio receiver or other circuit which produces a lower frequency signal by combining two almost equal high frequencies: *a heterodyne receiver*.
DERIVATIVES – **heterodyning** *noun*.
ORIGIN – from HETERO- + *-dyne*, from Greek *dunamis* 'power'.

heterogeneous* /hettərəjeeniəss/ > *adjective* diverse in character or content: *a heterogeneous collection of animals*.
DERIVATIVES – **heterogeneity** /hettərə-jəneeəti/ *noun* **heterogeneously** *adverb*.
*SPELLING – note that the ending is *-eous*, with an *e*, not *-ous*: heterogeneous.
ORIGIN – from Greek *heteros* 'other' + *genos* 'a kind'.

heterosexism > *noun* discrimination or prejudice against homosexuals on the assumption that heterosexuality is normal.
DERIVATIVES – **heterosexist** *adjective*.

heterosexual > *adjective* **1** sexually attracted to the opposite sex. **2** involving or characterised by such sexual attraction. > *noun* a heterosexual person.
DERIVATIVES – **heterosexuality** *noun* **heterosexually** *adverb*.

het up > *adjective* informal angry and agitated.
ORIGIN – from dialect *het* 'heated, hot'.

heuristic /hyooristik/ > *adjective* **1** enabling a person to discover or learn something for themselves. **2** Computing proceeding to a solution by trial and error or by rules that are only loosely defined. > *noun* **1** (**heuristics**) (usu. treated as sing.) the study and use of heuristic techniques. **2** a heuristic process or method.
DERIVATIVES – **heuristically** *adverb*.
ORIGIN – from Greek *heuriskein* 'to find'.

hew /hyoo/ > *verb* (past participle **hewn** or **hewed**) **1** chop or cut (wood, coal, etc.) with an axe, pick, or other tool. **2** (usu. **be hewn**) make or shape by hewing a hard material.

hewer > *noun* dated a person who hews something, especially a miner who cuts coal from a seam.
IDIOMS – **hewers of wood and drawers of water** menial drudges. [ORIGIN – with biblical allusion to the Book of Joshua, chapter 9.]

hex chiefly N. Amer. > *verb* cast a spell on. > *noun* **1** a magic spell. **2** a witch.
ORIGIN – German *hexen*.

hexa- (also **hex-** before a vowel) > *combining form* six; having six: *hexagon*.
ORIGIN – from Greek *hex* 'six'.

hexadecimal /heksədessim'l/ > *adjective* Computing relating to or using a system of numerical notation that has 16 rather than 10 as its base.

hexagon /heksəgən/ > *noun* a plane figure with six straight sides and angles.
DERIVATIVES – **hexagonal** *adjective*.

hexagram > *noun* a six-pointed star formed by two intersecting equilateral triangles.

hexahedron /heksəheedrən/ > *noun* (pl. **hexahedra** or **hexahedrons**) a solid figure with six plane faces.
DERIVATIVES – **hexahedral** *adjective*.

hexameter /heksammitər/ > *noun* a line of verse consisting of six metrical feet.

hexane > *noun* Chemistry a colourless liquid hydrocarbon of the alkane series, present in petroleum spirit.
ORIGIN – from HEXA- 'six' (denoting six carbon atoms) + -ANE.

hey > *exclamation* used to attract attention or to express surprise, interest, etc.

heyday > *noun* (**one's heyday**) the period of one's greatest success, activity, or vigour.
ORIGIN – first used as an exclamation of joy or surprise.

HF > *abbreviation* Physics high frequency.

Hf > *symbol* the chemical element hafnium.

HFC > *abbreviation* hydrofluorocarbon.

Hg > *symbol* the chemical element mercury.
ORIGIN – from Latin *hydrargyrum*.

hg > *abbreviation* hectogram(s).

HGV > *abbreviation* Brit. heavy goods vehicle.

HH > *abbreviation* extra hard (as a grade of pencil lead).

H-hour > *noun* the time of day at which an attack or other military operation is scheduled to begin.
ORIGIN – from *H* (for hour) + HOUR.

HI > *abbreviation* Hawaii.

hi > *exclamation* informal used as a friendly greeting.

hiatus /hīaytəss/ > *noun* (pl. **hiatuses**) a pause or gap in continuity.
COMBINATIONS – **hiatus hernia** (also **hiatal hernia**) the protrusion of an organ (usually the stomach) through the oesophageal opening in the diaphragm.
ORIGIN – Latin, 'gaping'.

Hib > *noun* a bacterium that causes infant meningitis.
ORIGIN – acronym from *Haemophilus influenzae type B*.

hibachi /hibachi/ > *noun* (pl. **hibachis**) **1** a portable cooking apparatus similar to a small barbecue. **2** (in Japan) a large earthenware pan or brazier in which charcoal is burnt to provide indoor heating.
ORIGIN – Japanese, from *hi* 'fire' + *hachi* 'bowl, pot'.

hibernate > *verb* (of an animal or plant) spend the winter in a dormant state.
DERIVATIVES – **hibernation** *noun* **hibernator** *noun*.
ORIGIN – Latin *hibernare*, from *hiberna* 'winter quarters'.

Hibernian /hīberniən/ > *adjective* Irish (now chiefly used in names).
ORIGIN – from Latin *Hibernia*, from Celtic.

hibiscus /hibiskəss/ > *noun* a plant of the mallow family with large brightly coloured flowers.
ORIGIN – Greek *hibiskos* 'marsh mallow'.

hiccup (also **hiccough** (pronounced same)) > *noun* **1** an involuntary spasm of the diaphragm and respiratory organs, with a sudden closure of the glottis and a characteristic gulping sound. **2** a minor difficulty or setback. > *verb* (**hiccuped**, **hiccuping**) make the sound of a hiccup or series of hiccups.
DERIVATIVES – **hiccupy** *adjective*.

hick > *noun* informal, chiefly N. Amer. an unsophisticated country-dweller.
ORIGIN – familiar form of the given name *Richard*.

hickey > *noun* (pl. **hickeys**) N. Amer. informal **1** a gadget. **2** a love bite.

hickory > *noun* **1** a chiefly North American tree which yields tough, heavy wood and bears edible nuts. **2** a stick made of hickory wood.

ORIGIN – from *pohickery*, the local Virginian name, from Algonquian.

hidden past participle of HIDE¹.

DERIVATIVES – **hiddenness** *noun*.

COMBINATIONS – **hidden agenda** an ulterior motive or undivulged plan. **hidden reserves** a company's funds that are not declared on its balance sheet.

hide¹ > *verb* (past **hid**; past participle **hidden**) **1** put or keep out of sight. **2** conceal oneself. **3** keep secret. > *noun* Brit. a camouflaged shelter used to observe wildlife at close quarters.

IDIOMS – **hide one's light under a bushel** keep quiet about one's talents or accomplishments. [ORIGIN – with biblical allusion to the Gospel of Matthew, chapter 15.]

DERIVATIVES – **hider** *noun*.

SYNONYMS – *verb* **1** camouflage, cloak, conceal, secrete, shroud.

COMBINATIONS – **hide-and-seek** a children's game in which one or more players hide and the other or others have to look for them.

hide² > *noun* the skin of an animal, especially when tanned or dressed.

IDIOMS – **neither hide nor hair of** not the slightest trace of. **save one's hide** escape from difficulty. **tan** (or **whip**) **someone's hide** beat or flog someone.

hideaway > *noun* a place where one may hide or find seclusion.

hidebound > *adjective* constrained by tradition or convention; narrow-minded.

---

wordpower facts

Hidebound

The word **hidebound** originally denoted a condition of malnourished cattle, in which the hide clings closely to the back and ribs. It was later applied to people who were so thin that their skin was tightly stretched over their bones. From this developed the sense 'restricted', leading to the current sense 'narrow in outlook'.

---

hideous > *adjective* **1** extremely ugly. **2** extremely unpleasant.

DERIVATIVES – **hideously** *adverb* **hideousness** *noun*.

SYNONYMS – **1** grotesque, monstrous, repulsive, revolting.

ORIGIN – Old French *hidos*, *hideus*, from *hide* 'fear'.

hideout > *noun* a hiding place, especially one used by someone who has broken the law.

hidey-hole (also **hidy-hole**) > *noun* informal a hiding place.

hiding¹ > *noun* **1** a physical beating. **2** informal a severe defeat.

IDIOMS – **be on a hiding to nothing** Brit. be unlikely to succeed.

ORIGIN – from HIDE².

hiding² > *noun* the action of hiding or the state of being hidden.

hie /hī/ > *verb* (**hies**, **hied**, **hieing** or **hying**) archaic go quickly.

ORIGIN – Old English, 'strive, pant'.

hierarch /ˈhīəraark/ > *noun* a chief priest, archbishop, or other leader.

ORIGIN – Greek *hierarkhēs*, from *hieros* 'sacred' + *arkhēs* 'ruler'.

hierarchy* /ˈhīəraarki/ > *noun* (pl. **hierarchies**) **1** a ranking system ordered according to status or authority. **2** an arrangement or classification according to relative importance or inclusiveness. **3** (**the hierarchy**) the clergy of the Catholic Church or of an episcopal Church. **4** Theology the traditional system of orders of angels and other heavenly beings.

DERIVATIVES – **hierarchic** *adjective* **hierarchical** *adjective* **hierarchise** (also **hierarchize**) *verb*.

*SPELLING – *ie* not *ei*, and remember the second *r*: hierarchy.

ORIGIN – Greek *hierarkhia*, from *hieros* 'sacred' + *arkhēs* 'ruler'.

hieratic /ˌhīəˈrattik/ > *adjective* of or concerning priests.

DERIVATIVES – **hieratically** *adverb*.

ORIGIN – Greek *hieratikos*, from *hierasthai* 'be a priest'.

hieroglyph /ˈhīərəglif/ > *noun* a stylised picture of an object representing a word, syllable, or sound, as found in ancient Egyptian and some other writing systems.

hieroglyphic* > *noun* (**hieroglyphics**) writing consisting of hieroglyphs. > *adjective* of or written in hieroglyphs.

DERIVATIVES – **hieroglyphical** *adjective*.

*SPELLING – *ie* not *ei*: hieroglyphic.

ORIGIN – Greek *hierogluphikos*, from *hieros* 'sacred' + *gluphē* 'carving'.

hierophant /ˈhīərəfant/ > *noun* a person, especially a priest, who interprets sacred or esoteric mysteries.

ORIGIN – Greek *hierophantēs*, from *hieros* 'sacred' + *phainein* 'show'.

hi-fi informal > *adjective* relating to the reproduction of high fidelity sound. > *noun* (pl. **hi-fis**) a set of equipment for high-fidelity sound reproduction.

higgledy-piggledy > *adverb* & *adjective* in confusion or disorder.

ORIGIN – probably with reference to the irregular herding together of pigs.

high > *adjective* **1** of great vertical extent. **2** of a specified height. **3** far above ground or sea level. **4** extending above the normal level. **5** great in amount, value, size, or intensity. **6** (of a period or movement) at its peak. **7** great in rank or status. **8** morally or culturally superior. **9** (of a sound or note) having a frequency at the upper end of the auditory range. **10** informal euphoric, especially from the effects of drugs or alcohol. **11** (of food) strong-smelling because beginning to go bad. **12** (of game) slightly decomposed and so ready to cook. > *noun* **1** a high point, level, or figure. **2** an anticyclone. **3** informal a state of euphoria. **4** informal, chiefly N. Amer. high school. > *adverb* **1** at or to a high or specified level or position. **2** at a high price. **3** (of a sound) at or to a high pitch.

IDIOMS – **from on high** from heaven or another remote authority. **high and dry 1** stranded by the sea as it retreats. **2** without resources. **high and low** in many different places. **high and mighty** informal arrogant. **the high ground** a position of superiority. **a high old time** informal a most enjoyable time. **it is high time that ——** it is past the time when something should have happened or been done. **on one's high horse** informal behaving arrogantly or pompously. **run high 1** (of a river) be full and close to overflowing, with a strong current. **2** (of feelings) be intense.

SYNONYMS – *adjective* **1** elevated, lofty, towering. **8** lofty, noble, virtuous.

COMBINATIONS – **high altar** the chief altar of a church. **highboy** N. Amer. a tall chest of drawers on legs. **high chair** a small chair with long legs for a baby or small child, fitted with a tray and used at mealtimes. **High Church** a tradition within the Anglican Church emphasising ritual, priestly authority, sacraments, and historical continuity with Catholic Christianity. **high colour** a flushed complexion. **high command** the commander-in-chief and associated senior staff of an army, navy, or air force. **highest common factor** the highest number that can be divided exactly into each of two or more numbers. **high explosive** a powerful chemical explosive of the kind used in shells and bombs. **high fashion** haute couture. **high fidelity** the reproduction of sound with little distortion. **high finance** financial transactions involving large sums. **high five** a gesture of celebration or greeting in which two people slap each other's palms with their arms raised. **high-flown** (especially of language) extravagant or grandiose. **high-flyer** (also **high-flier**) a very successful person. **high frequency** (in radio) a frequency of 3–30 megahertz. **high gear** a gear that causes a wheeled vehicle to move fast. **High German** the standard literary and spoken form of German, originally used in the highlands in the south of Germany. **high-handed** domineering or inconsiderate. **high-impact 1** (of plastic or a similar substance) able to withstand great impact without breaking. **2** (of aerobic exercises) extremely strenuous. **high jinks** boisterous fun. **high-level 1** of relatively high importance. **2** Computing denoting a programming language that has instructions resembling an existing language such as English. **high life** an extravagant social life as enjoyed by the wealthy. **High Mass** a Roman Catholic or Anglo-Catholic mass with full ceremonial, including music and incense. **high-minded** having strong moral principles. **high-octane 1** (of petrol) having a high octane number and thus good anti-knock properties. **2** powerful or dynamic. **high-powered** informal (of a person) dynamic and forceful. **high priest 1** a chief priest of a non-Christian religion, especially of historic Judaism. **2** (also **high priestess**) the leader of a cult or movement. **high relief** see RELIEF (sense 8). **high-rise** (of a building) having many storeys. **high road 1** a main road. **2** N. Amer. a morally superior approach. **high roller** informal, chiefly N. Amer. a person who gambles or spends large sums of money. **high school 1** N. Amer. a secondary school. **2** (in the UK) used chiefly in names of grammar schools or independent fee-paying secondary schools. **the high seas** the open ocean, especially that not within any country's jurisdiction. **high season** Brit. the most popular time of year for a holiday, when prices are highest. **high sheriff** see SHERIFF. **high sign** N. Amer. informal a surreptitious gesture indicating a warning or that all is well. **high street** Brit. **1** the main street of a town. **2** (**high-street**) (of retail goods) catering to the needs of the ordinary public: high-street fashion. **high table** Brit. a table in a dining hall at which high-ranking people, such as the fellows of a college, sit. **high tea** Brit. a meal eaten in the late afternoon or early evening, typically consisting of a cooked dish and tea. **high technology** advanced technological development, especially in electronics. **high-tensile** (of metal) very strong under tension. **high tide** the state of the tide when at its highest level. **high treason** see TREASON. **high water** high tide. **high-water mark** the level reached by the sea at high tide, or by a lake or river in time of flood. **high wire** a high tightrope.

highball N. Amer. > *noun* **1** a long drink consisting of a spirit and a mixer such as soda, served with ice. **2** informal a railway signal to proceed. > *verb* informal travel fast.

highbrow > *adjective* often derogatory intellectual or rarefied in taste.

high commission > *noun* an embassy of one Commonwealth country in another.
DERIVATIVES – **high commissioner** noun.

high court > *noun* **1** a supreme court of justice. **2** (in full **High Court of Justice**) (in England and Wales) the court of unlimited civil jurisdiction forming part of the Supreme Court. **3** (in full **High Court of Justiciary**) the supreme criminal court of Scotland.

high day > *noun* Brit. the day of a religious festival.
IDIOMS – **high days and holidays** informal special occasions.

higher > *adjective* comparative of HIGH. > *noun* (**Higher**) (in Scotland) the more advanced of the two main levels of the Scottish Certificate of Education. Compare with *ordinary grade*.
COMBINATIONS – **higher animals** mammals and other vertebrates, regarded as having relatively advanced characteristics. **higher court** Law a court that can overrule the decision of another. **higher education** education provided at universities or similar educational establishments, to degree level or equivalent. **higher mathematics** the more advanced aspects of mathematics, such as number theory and topology. **higher plants** vascular plants, regarded as having relatively advanced characteristics.

highfalutin /hīfəloŏtin/ (also **highfaluting**) > *adjective* informal pompous or pretentious.
ORIGIN – perhaps from HIGH + *fluting*.

high hat > *noun* **1** a top hat. **2** N. Amer. informal a snobbish or supercilious person.

high jump > *noun* (**the high jump**) an athletic event in which competitors jump as high as possible over a bar of adjustable height.
IDIOMS – **be for the high jump** Brit. informal be about to be severely reprimanded.
DERIVATIVES – **high jumper** noun.

highland > *noun* (also **highlands**) **1** an area of high or mountainous land. **2** (**the Highlands**) the mountainous northern part of Scotland.
DERIVATIVES – **highlander** noun.
COMBINATIONS – **Highland cattle** a shaggy-haired breed of cattle with long, curved, widely spaced horns. **Highland dress** the kilt and other clothing in the traditional style of the Scottish Highlands. **Highland fling** a vigorous solo Scottish dance consisting of a series of complex steps.

highlight > *noun* **1** an outstanding part of an event or period of time. **2** a bright or reflective area in a painting, picture, or design. **3** (**highlights**) bright tints in the hair, produced by bleaching or dyeing.
> *verb* **1** draw attention to. **2** mark with a highlighter. **3** create highlights in (hair).

highlighter > *noun* **1** a broad marker pen used to overlay transparent fluorescent colour on a part of a text or plan. **2** a cosmetic used to emphasise the cheekbones or other features.

highly > *adverb* **1** to a high degree or level. **2** favourably.
COMBINATIONS – **highly strung** Brit. very nervous and easily upset.

highness > *noun* **1** (**His, Your**, etc. **Highness**) a title given to a person of royal rank, or used in addressing them. **2** the state of being high.

high spirits > *plural noun* lively and cheerful behaviour or mood.
DERIVATIVES – **high-spirited** adjective.
SYNONYMS – animation, exuberance, liveliness, vivacity.

high spot > *noun* the most enjoyable or significant part of an experience or period of time.
IDIOMS – **hit the high spots** informal visit the most exciting places in town.

hight /hīt/ > *adjective* archaic or literary named.

hightail > *verb* informal, chiefly N. Amer. move or travel fast.

high-tech (also **hi-tech**) > *adjective* **1** employing, requiring, or involved in high technology. **2** (of architecture and interior design) employing a functional style and industrial materials, such as steel and plastic.

high-top > *adjective* denoting a soft-soled sports shoe with a laced upper that extends above the ankle. > *noun* (**high-tops**) a pair of such shoes.

highway > *noun* **1** chiefly N. Amer. a main road. **2** (chiefly in official use) a public road.

highwayman > *noun* historical a man, typically on horseback, who held up and robbed travellers.

hi-hat (also **high-hat**) > *noun* a pair of foot-operated cymbals forming part of a drum kit.

hijack > *verb* **1** illegally seize control of (an aircraft, ship, etc.) while it is in transit. **2** take over (something) and use it for a different purpose. > *noun* an instance of hijacking.
DERIVATIVES – **hijacker** noun.

Hijra > *noun* variant spelling of HEGIRA.

hijra /hijrə/ > *noun* Indian a transvestite or eunuch.
ORIGIN – Hindi.

hike > *noun* **1** a long walk or walking tour. **2** a sharp increase, especially in price. > *verb* **1** go on a hike. **2** pull or lift up (clothing). **3** increase (a price) sharply.

IDIOMS – **take a hike** informal, chiefly N. Amer. go away.

DERIVATIVES – **hiker** noun.

hilarious /hɪlairɪəss/ > adjective extremely funny.

DERIVATIVES – **hilariously** adverb **hilarity** noun.

SYNONYMS – comical, hysterical, riotous, uproarious; informal side-splitting.

ORIGIN – Greek hilaros 'cheerful'.

hill > noun a naturally raised area of land, not as high or craggy as a mountain.

IDIOMS – **over the hill** informal old and past one's best.

COMBINATIONS – **hill fort** a fort built on a hill, in particular an Iron Age system of defensive banks and ditches. **hill station** a town in the low mountains of the Indian subcontinent, popular as a holiday resort during the hot season. **hillwalking** the pastime of walking in hilly country.

hillbilly > noun (pl. **hillbillies**) N. Amer. informal, chiefly derogatory an unsophisticated country person, originally one from the Appalachian mountains.

ORIGIN – from **HILL** + Billy (familiar form of the given name William).

hillock > noun a small hill or mound.

DERIVATIVES – **hillocky** adjective.

hilly > adjective (**hillier**, **hilliest**) having many hills.

DERIVATIVES – **hilliness** noun.

hilt > noun the handle of a sword, dagger, or knife.

IDIOMS – **to the hilt** completely.

him > pronoun (third person sing.) used as the object of a verb or preposition to refer to a male person or animal previously mentioned.

Himalayan /himməlayən/ > adjective relating to the Himalayas, a mountain system in southern Asia.

himself > pronoun (third person sing.) **1** (reflexive) used as the object of a verb or preposition to refer to a male person or animal previously mentioned as the subject of the clause. **2** (emphatic) he or him personally.

hind[1] /hīnd/ > adjective situated at the back.

hind[2] /hīnd/ > noun an adult female deer.

hind- > combining form (added to nouns) posterior; back: hindlimb.

hinder /hindər/ > verb cause delay or obstruction to (someone or something).

SYNONYMS – delay, hamper, hold back, impede, obstruct.

ORIGIN – Old English, 'damage'; related to **BEHIND**.

Hindi /hindi/ > noun a language of northern India derived from Sanskrit. > adjective relating to Hindi.

ORIGIN – Urdu, from Hind 'India'.

wordpower facts

Hindi

English has been enriched by numerous words derived from Hindi. These include words relating to Indian cuisine or culture, such as **basmati**, **chapatti**, **chutney**, and **dhurrie**; but there are also a number of words which have been familiar in English long enough for the Hindi origin to be less apparent, many of them dating from the 17th century, when British trading with India started, or from the period of British rule in India (1765–1947). These include **bungalow**, **dinghy**, **dungarees**, **jodhpurs**, **shampoo**, and **thug**.

hindmost > adjective furthest back.

hindquarters > plural noun the hind legs and adjoining parts of a four-legged animal.

hindrance /hindrənss/ > noun a thing that hinders.

SYNONYMS – handicap, impediment, obstacle, obstruction.

hindsight > noun understanding of a situation or event after it has happened.

Hindu /hindōō/ > noun (pl. **Hindus**) a follower of Hinduism. > adjective relating to Hinduism.

WORDFINDER – Hindu festivals: Diwali, Dussehra, Holi, Kumbh Mela, Navaratri.

ORIGIN – Urdu, from Hind 'India'.

Hinduism > noun a major religious and cultural tradition of the Indian subcontinent, which includes belief in reincarnation and the worship of a large number of gods and goddesses.

Hindustani /hindōōstaani/ > noun **1** a group of mutually intelligible languages and dialects spoken in NW India, principally Hindi and Urdu. **2** the Delhi dialect of Hindi, widely used throughout India as a lingua franca. > adjective relating to the culture of NW India.

USAGE – **Hindustani** was the usual term in the 18th and 19th centuries for the native language of NW India. The usual modern terms are **Hindi** or **Urdu**, although **Hindustani** is still used to refer to the dialect of Delhi (see sense 2).

hinge > noun a movable joint or mechanism by which a door, gate, or lid opens and closes or which connects linked objects. > verb (**hinged**, **hingeing** or **hinging**) **1** attach or join with a hinge. **2** (**hinge on**) depend entirely on.

ORIGIN – related to **HANG**.

hinky > adjective (**hinkier**, **hinkiest**) US informal dishonest or suspect.

hinny > noun (pl. **hinnies**) the offspring of a female donkey and a male horse.

ORIGIN – Latin hinnus.

hint > noun **1** a slight or indirect indication. **2** a very small trace. **3** a small piece of practical information. > verb **1** indicate indirectly. **2** (**hint at**) be a slight indication of.

SYNONYMS – noun **1** allusion, clue, implication, indication, suggestion. **3** pointer, tip.

ORIGIN – apparently from obsolete hent 'grasp'; related to **HUNT**.

hinterland /hintərland/ > noun **1** the remote areas of a country, away from the coast and major rivers. **2** the area around or beyond a major town or port.

ORIGIN – German, from hinter 'behind' + Land 'land'.

hip[1] > noun **1** a projection of the pelvis and upper thigh bone on each side of the body. **2** (**hips**) the circumference of the body at the buttocks. **3** the edge formed where two sloping sides of a roof meet.

DERIVATIVES – **hipped** adjective.

COMBINATIONS – **hip bath** a bath for sitting rather than lying down in. **hip bone** a large bone forming the main part of the pelvis on each side of the body. **hip flask** a small flask for spirits, carried in a hip pocket.

ORIGIN – Old English, related to **HOP**[1].

hip[2] > noun the fruit of a rose.

hip[3] > adjective (**hipper**, **hippest**) informal **1** fashionable. **2** (**hip to**) aware of or informed about.

DERIVATIVES – **hipness** noun.

hip[4] > exclamation introducing a communal cheer.

hip hop > noun a style of popular music of US black and Hispanic origin, featuring rap with an electronic backing.

hippie > noun & adjective variant spelling of **HIPPY**[1].

hippo > noun (pl. same or **hippos**) informal term for **HIPPOPOTAMUS**.

hippocampus /hippəkampəss/ > noun (pl. **hippocampi** /hippəkampī/) Anatomy the system of elongated ridges on the floor of the lateral ventricles of the brain, thought to be the centre of emotion, memory, and the autonomic nervous system.

ORIGIN – Greek hippokampos, from hippos 'horse' + kampos 'sea monster'.

Hippocratic oath /hippəkrattik/ > noun a former oath taken by those beginning medical practice to observe a code of professional behaviour (parts of which are still used in some medical schools).

ORIGIN – with reference to Hippocrates, a Greek physician of the 5th century BC.

hippodrome /hippədrōm/ > noun **1** a theatre or concert hall. **2** (in ancient Greece or Rome) a course for chariot or horse races.

ORIGIN – Greek *hippodromos*, from *hippos* 'horse' + *dromos* 'race, course'.

hippopotamus /hippəpottəməss/ > *noun* (pl. **hippopotamuses** or **hippopotami** /hippəpottəmī/) a large African mammal with a thick skin and massive jaws, living partly on land and partly in water.

ORIGIN – Greek *hippopotamos*, from *hippos ho potamios* 'river horse'.

hippy[1] (also **hippie**) > *noun* (pl. **hippies**) (especially in the 1960s) a young person associated with a subculture which advocated peace and free love and adopted an unconventional appearance.

DERIVATIVES – **hippiedom** *noun* **hippiness** *noun* **hippyish** *adjective*.

ORIGIN – from **HIP**[3].

hippy[2] > *adjective* (of a woman) having large hips.

hipster[1] Brit. > *adjective* (of a garment) having the waistline at the hips rather than the waist. > *noun* (**hipsters**) trousers with such a waistline.

hipster[2] > *noun* informal a person who follows the latest trends and fashions.

ORIGIN – from **HIP**[3].

hire > *verb* 1 chiefly Brit. obtain the temporary use of (something) in return for payment. 2 (**hire out**) grant the temporary use of (something) in return for payment. 3 employ (someone) to do a job. > *noun* 1 the action of hiring. 2 N. Amer. a recently recruited employee.

IDIOMS – **for** (or **on**) **hire** available to be hired.

DERIVATIVES – **hireable** (US also **hirable**) *adjective* **hirer** *noun*.

SYNONYMS – *verb* 1 charter, lease, rent. 3 appoint, employ, engage, take on.

COMBINATIONS – **hired gun** N. Amer. informal 1 a mercenary or hired assassin. 2 a bodyguard. 3 an expert brought in to resolve legal or financial problems or disputes. 4 a lobbyist on behalf of others. **hire purchase** Brit. a system by which someone pays for a thing in regular instalments while having the use of it.

hireling > *noun* chiefly derogatory a person who is hired, especially for morally dubious or illegal work.

hirsute /hursyoot/ > *adjective* having abundant hair on the face or body; hairy.

DERIVATIVES – **hirsuteness** *noun*.

ORIGIN – Latin *hirsutus*.

hirsutism > *noun* Medicine abnormal growth of hair on a woman's face and body.

his > *possessive determiner* 1 belonging to or associated with a male person or animal previously mentioned. 2 (**His**) used in titles. > *possessive pronoun* used to refer to a thing belonging to or associated with a

male person or animal previously mentioned.

Hispanic /hispannik/ > *adjective* relating to Spain or the Spanish-speaking countries of Central and South America. > *noun* a Spanish-speaking person, especially one of Latin American descent.

DERIVATIVES – **Hispanicise** (also **Hispanicize**) *verb*.

ORIGIN – Latin *Hispanicus*, from *Hispania* 'Spain'.

Hispanist /hispənist/ (also **Hispanicist** /hispannisist/) > *noun* an expert in Hispanic language and culture.

hiss > *verb* 1 make a sharp sibilant sound as of the letter *s*, often as a sign of disapproval or derision. 2 whisper something in an urgent or angry way. > *noun* 1 a hissing sound. 2 electrical interference at audio frequencies.

histamine /histəmeen/ > *noun* a compound which is released by cells in response to injury and in allergic and inflammatory reactions, causing muscle contraction and capillary dilation.

DERIVATIVES – **histaminic** *adjective*.

ORIGIN – from Greek *histos* 'web, tissue' and **AMINE**.

histidine /histideen/ > *noun* Biochemistry an amino acid which is a constituent of most proteins and is essential in the human diet.

histogram /histəgram/ > *noun* Statistics a diagram consisting of rectangles whose positions and dimensions represent the values of a variable quantity.

ORIGIN – from Greek *histos* 'mast, web'.

histology /histolləji/ > *noun* the branch of biology concerned with the microscopic structure of tissues.

DERIVATIVES – **histological** *adjective* **histologist** *noun*.

histopathology > *noun* the branch of medicine concerned with the changes in tissues caused by disease.

DERIVATIVES – **histopathological** *adjective* **histopathologist** *noun*.

historian > *noun* an expert in history.

historic > *adjective* 1 famous or important in history, or potentially so. 2 Grammar (of a tense) used in relating past events.

USAGE – on the use of *an historic moment* or *a historic moment*, see the note at **AN**.

COMBINATIONS – **historic present** Grammar the present tense used instead of the past in vivid narrative.

historical > *adjective* 1 of or concerning history. 2 belonging to or set in the past. 3 (of the study of a subject) based on an analysis of its development over a period.

DERIVATIVES – **historically** *adverb*.

USAGE – **historic** generally means 'famous or important in history', as in *a historic battle*, whereas the chief meanings of **historical** are 'concerning history' and

'belonging to or set in the past' (*a historical novel*; *of purely historical interest*).

historicism > *noun* 1 the theory that social and cultural phenomena are determined by history. 2 (in art and architecture) excessive regard for past styles.

DERIVATIVES – **historicise** (also **historicize**) *verb* **historicist** *noun*.

historicity /histərissiti/ > *noun* historical authenticity.

historiography /historiogrəfi/ > *noun* 1 the study of the writing of history and of written histories. 2 the writing of history.

DERIVATIVES – **historiographer** *noun* **historiographic** *adjective* **historiographical** *adjective*.

history > *noun* (pl. **histories**) 1 the study of past events. 2 the past considered as a whole. 3 the past events connected with someone or something. 4 a continuous record of past events or trends.

IDIOMS – **be history** informal be dismissed or dead; be finished. **the rest is history** the events succeeding those already related are so well known that they need not be recounted again.

ORIGIN – Greek *historia* 'narrative, history', from *histōr* 'learned, wise man'.

histrionic /histrionnik/ > *adjective* 1 overly theatrical or melodramatic. 2 formal of or concerning actors or acting. > *noun* (**histrionics**) dramatised behaviour designed to attract attention.

DERIVATIVES – **histrionically** *adverb*.

ORIGIN – Latin *histrionicus*, from *histrio* 'actor'.

hit > *verb* (**hitting**; past and past participle **hit**) 1 direct a blow at (someone or something) with one's hand or a tool or weapon. 2 propel (a ball) with a bat, racket, etc. 3 accidentally strike (part of one's body) against something. 4 (of a moving object or body) come into contact with (someone or something stationary) quickly and forcefully. 5 strike (a target). 6 cause harm or distress to. 7 (**hit out**) make a strongly worded criticism or attack. 8 informal reach or arrive at. 9 be suddenly and vividly realised by: *it hit me that I was successful*. 10 (**hit on**) suddenly discover or think of. 11 (**hit on**) N. Amer. informal make sexual advances towards. > *noun* 1 an instance of hitting or being hit. 2 informal, chiefly N. Amer. a murder carried out by a criminal organisation. 3 a successful and popular film, pop record, person, etc. 4 Computing an instance of identifying an item of data which matches the requirements of a search. 5 informal a dose of a narcotic drug.

IDIOMS – **hit-and-miss** done or occurring at random. **hit-and-run** denoting a road accident from which the driver responsible escapes rapidly without lending assistance. **hit below the belt** 1 Boxing give (one's

opponent) an illegal low blow. **2** behave unfairly towards (someone). **hit for six** Brit. affect (someone) very severely. [ORIGIN – with allusion to a forceful hit that scores six runs in cricket.] **hit the ground running** informal start something new at a fast pace and with enthusiasm. **hit it off** informal be naturally friendly or well suited. **hit the nail on the head** find exactly the right answer. **hit-or-miss** as likely to be unsuccessful as successful. **hit the road** (or **N. Amer. trail**) informal set out on a journey.
DERIVATIVES – **hitter** noun.
SYNONYMS – verb **1** beat, punch, smack, strike, thump. noun **1** blow, impact, strike, thump.
COMBINATIONS – **hit list** informal a list of people to be killed for criminal or political reasons. **hit man** informal a hired assassin. **hit parade** dated a weekly listing of the current best-selling pop records.
ORIGIN – Old Norse *hitta* 'come upon, meet with'.

hitch > verb **1** move (something) into a different position with a jerk. **2** fasten or tether with a rope. **3** informal travel or obtain (a lift) by hitch-hiking. > noun **1** a temporary difficulty. **2** a knot of a kind used to fasten one thing temporarily to another. **3** informal an act of hitch-hiking.
IDIOMS – **get hitched** informal get married. **hitch one's wagon to a star** try to succeed by forming a relationship with a successful person.

hitcher > noun a hitch-hiker.

hitch-hike > verb travel by getting free lifts in passing vehicles. > noun a journey made by hitch-hiking.
DERIVATIVES – **hitch-hiker** noun.

hither > adverb archaic or literary to or towards this place.

hitherto > adverb until the point in time under discussion.

Hitlerian /hit**leer**iən/ > adjective relating to or characteristic of the Austrian-born Nazi leader Adolf Hitler (1889–1945), Chancellor of Germany 1933–45.

Hittite /**hitt**īt/ > noun **1** a member of an ancient people who maintained an empire in Asia Minor and Syria c.1700–1200 BC. **2** the language of the Hittites, the oldest Indo-European language. > adjective relating to the Hittites or their language.

HIV > abbreviation human immunodeficiency virus, a retrovirus which causes Aids.
COMBINATIONS – **HIV-positive** having had a positive result in a blood test for HIV.

hive > noun **1** a beehive. **2** a place filled with busily occupied people: *a hive of activity*. > verb place (bees) in a hive.
IDIOMS – **hive off** chiefly Brit. separate from a larger group or organisation.

hives > plural noun (treated as sing. or pl.) another term for **URTICARIA**.

HK > abbreviation Hong Kong.

HL > abbreviation (in the UK) House of Lords.

hl > abbreviation hectolitre or hectolitres.

HM > abbreviation (in the UK) Her (or His) Majesty or Majesty's.

hm > abbreviation hectometre or hectometres.

HMG > abbreviation (in the UK) Her or His Majesty's Government.

HMI > abbreviation historical (in the UK) Her or His Majesty's Inspector (of Schools).

HMS > abbreviation Her or His Majesty's Ship.

HMSO > abbreviation (in the UK) Her or His Majesty's Stationery Office, which publishes government documents and legislation.

HNC > abbreviation (in the UK) Higher National Certificate.

HND > abbreviation (in the UK) Higher National Diploma.

Ho > symbol the chemical element holmium.

hoagie /**hō**gi/ > noun (pl. **hoagies**) chiefly N. Amer. a sandwich made of a long roll filled with meat, cheese, and salad.

hoar /hor/ archaic or literary > adjective grey or grey-haired. > noun hoar frost.

hoard > noun **1** a store of money or valued objects. **2** an amassed store of useful information. > verb amass and hide or store away.
DERIVATIVES – **hoarder** noun.
USAGE – do not confuse **hoard** with **horde**: a **hoard** is a store of something valuable; **horde** is a disparaging term for a large group of people.
SYNONYMS – noun **1** cache, reserve, stockpile, supply.

hoarding > noun Brit. **1** a large board used to display advertisements. **2** a temporary board fence around a building site.

hoar frost > noun a greyish-white feathery deposit of frost.

hoarse > adjective (of a voice) rough and harsh.
DERIVATIVES – **hoarsely** adverb **hoarsen** verb **hoarseness** noun.
SYNONYMS – gravelly, husky, rasping.

hoary > adjective (**hoarier**, **hoariest**) **1** greyish-white. **2** having grey hair; aged. **3** (of a phrase, idea, etc.) old and trite.
DERIVATIVES – **hoarily** adverb **hoariness** noun.

hoax > noun a humorous or malicious deception. > verb deceive with a hoax.
DERIVATIVES – **hoaxer** noun.
ORIGIN – probably a contraction of *hocus*, from **HOCUS-POCUS**.

hob > noun Brit. **1** the flat top part of a cooker, with hotplates or burners. **2** a flat metal shelf at the side of a fireplace, used for

heating pans. **3** a machine tool for cutting gears or screw threads.
ORIGIN – first used in sense 3: alteration of **HUB**.

hobbit > noun a member of an imaginary race similar to humans, of small size and with hairy feet.
ORIGIN – invented by the British writer J. R. R. Tolkien (1892–1973) in his book *The Hobbit*, and said by him to mean 'hole-dweller'.

hobble > verb **1** walk awkwardly, typically because of pain. **2** strap together the legs of (a horse) to prevent it straying. **3** be or cause a problem for. > noun **1** an awkward way of walking. **2** a rope or strap for hobbling a horse.
DERIVATIVES – **hobbler** noun.
COMBINATIONS – **hobble skirt** a skirt so narrow at the hem as to impede walking, popular in the 1910s.
ORIGIN – Dutch or Low German.

hobbledehoy /**hobb**'ldihoy/ > noun informal, dated a clumsy or awkward youth.

hobby[1] > noun (pl. **hobbies**) **1** an activity followed regularly for pleasure. **2** archaic a small horse or pony. **3** historical a very early type of bicycle propelled by the pressure of the rider's feet against the ground.
SYNONYMS – **1** pastime, recreation.
ORIGIN – first used in the sense 'small horse', later 'toy horse or hobby horse', from a familiar form of the given name *Robin*.

hobby[2] > noun (pl. **hobbies**) a small migratory falcon which hunts birds and insects on the wing.
ORIGIN – Old French *hobet*, from *hobe* 'falcon'.

hobby horse > noun **1** a child's toy consisting of a stick with a model of a horse's head at one end. **2** a rocking horse. **3** a favourite topic.

hobbyist > noun a person with a particular hobby.

hobgoblin > noun a mischievous imp.
ORIGIN – from *hob*, familiar form of the names *Robin* and *Robert*, used in the sense 'country fellow', + **GOBLIN**.

hobnail > noun **1** a short heavy-headed nail used to reinforce the soles of boots. **2** a blunt projection, especially in cut or moulded glassware.
DERIVATIVES – **hobnailed** adjective.

hobnob > verb (**hobnobbed**, **hobnobbing**) informal mix socially, especially with those of higher social status.
ORIGIN – first used in the sense 'drink together, drink each other's health': from archaic *hob or nob*, or *hob and nob*, probably meaning 'give and take'.

hobo /**hō**bō/ > noun (pl. **hoboes** or **hobos**) N. Amer. a vagrant.

Hobson's choice > *noun* a choice of taking what is offered or nothing at all.

ORIGIN – named after Thomas *Hobson* (1554–1631), a carrier who hired out horses, making the customer take the one nearest the door or none at all.

hock¹ > *noun* **1** the joint in the hind leg of a four-legged animal, between the knee and the fetlock. **2** a knuckle of pork or ham.

hock² > *noun* Brit. a dry white wine from the German Rhineland.

ORIGIN – from German *Hochheimer Wein* 'wine from Hochheim'.

hock³ > *verb informal* pawn (an object).

IDIOMS – **in hock 1** having been pawned. **2** in debt.

ORIGIN – from Dutch *hok* 'hutch, prison, debt'.

hockey¹ /hokki/ > *noun* a game played between two teams of eleven players each, using hooked sticks to drive a small hard ball towards a goal.

hockey² > *noun* variant spelling of OCHE.

hocus-pocus > *noun* **1** meaningless talk used to deceive. **2** a form of words used by a conjuror.

ORIGIN – from *hax pax max Deus adimax*, a pseudo-Latin phrase used as a magic formula by conjurors.

hod > *noun* **1** a builder's V-shaped open trough attached to a short pole, used for carrying bricks. **2** a coal scuttle.

ORIGIN – Old French *hotte* 'pannier'.

hodgepodge > *noun* N. Amer. variant of **HOTCHPOTCH**.

Hodgkin's disease > *noun* a malignant disease of lymphatic tissues typically causing enlargement of the lymph nodes, liver, and spleen.

ORIGIN – named after the English physician Thomas *Hodgkin* (1798–1866).

hoe > *noun* a long-handled gardening tool with a thin metal blade, used mainly for cutting through weeds at their roots. > *verb* (**hoes, hoed, hoeing**) **1** use a hoe to turn (earth) or cut through (weeds). **2** (**hoe in**) Austral./NZ informal eat eagerly. **3** (**hoe into**) Austral./NZ informal attack or criticise.

DERIVATIVES – **hoer** *noun*.

ORIGIN – Old French *houe*; related to HEW.

hoedown > *noun* N. Amer. a lively folk dance.

hog > *noun* **1** a pig, especially a castrated male reared for slaughter. **2** informal a greedy person. > *verb* (**hogged, hogging**) informal take or hoard selfishly.

IDIOMS – **go the whole hog** informal do something completely or thoroughly. **live high on** (or **off**) **the hog** N. Amer. informal have a luxurious lifestyle.

DERIVATIVES – **hogger** *noun* **hoggery** *noun* **hoggish** *adjective*.

---

wordpower facts
Go the whole hog
What is the story behind this familiar but (on close inspection) rather odd phrase? One theory relates it to a fable mentioned by the English poet William Cowper (1731–1800). Certain Muslims, knowing that their religion forbade pork as food, maintained that Muhammad had only one part of the animal in mind; however, they could not agree as to which part, and between them they ate 'the whole hog', each person telling themselves that the part they ate was not the forbidden one. Other possibilities are that the phrase is connected to buying a 'whole hog' from a butcher rather than merely a joint, or to *hog* in the old slang sense 'shilling' or (in America) 'ten cent piece'.

hogback (also **hog's back**) > *noun* a long, steep hill or mountain ridge.

hogget > *noun* **1** Brit. a yearling sheep. **2** NZ a lamb between weaning and first shearing.

Hogmanay /hogmənay, hogmənay/ > *noun* (in Scotland) New Year's Eve.

ORIGIN – perhaps from Norman French *hoguinané*, from *aguillanneuf* 'last day of the year, new year's gift'.

hogshead > *noun* **1** a large cask. **2** a measure of liquid volume equal to 52.5 imperial gallons (63 US gallons, 238.7 litres) for wine or 54 imperial gallons (64 US gallons, 245.5 litres) for beer.

hog-tie > *verb* N. Amer. **1** secure (a person or animal) by fastening the hands and feet or all four feet together. **2** impede.

hogwash > *noun* informal nonsense.

ORIGIN – first meaning 'kitchen swill for pigs'.

hogweed > *noun* a large white-flowered weed of the parsley family, formerly used as forage for pigs.

hoick Brit. informal > *verb* lift or pull with a jerk. > *noun* a jerky pull.

ORIGIN – perhaps from HIKE.

hoi polloi /hoy pəloy/ > *plural noun* derogatory the common people.

USAGE – strictly speaking, use of *the* is not necessary with **hoi polloi**, because in the original Greek phrase *the* is represented by *hoi*. However, the expression has inevitably come to be treated as any other English noun phrase; use of *the* is therefore accepted as standard.

SYNONYMS – the common herd, the masses, the mob, the rabble, the riff-raff.

ORIGIN – Greek, 'the many'.

hoisin sauce /hoyzin/ > *noun* a sweet, spicy, dark red sauce made from soya beans, used in Chinese cooking.

ORIGIN – Cantonese, 'seafood'.

hoist > *verb* **1** raise by means of ropes and pulleys. **2** haul (something) up. > *noun* **1** an act of hoisting. **2** an apparatus for hoisting. **3** the part of a flag nearest the staff. **4** a group of flags raised as a signal.

IDIOMS – **hoist one's flag** (of an admiral) take up command. **hoist the flag** stake one's claim to territory by displaying a flag.

DERIVATIVES – **hoister** *noun*.

ORIGIN – probably from Dutch *hijsen* or Low German *hiesen*.

hoity-toity > *adjective* haughty.

ORIGIN – from obsolete *hoit* 'indulge in riotous mirth': first used in the sense 'frolicsome, flighty'.

hokey > *adjective* (**hokier, hokiest**) N. Amer. informal excessively sentimental or contrived.

DERIVATIVES – **hokeyness** (also **hokiness**) *noun*.

ORIGIN – from HOKUM.

hokey-cokey (US **hokey-pokey**) > *noun* a communal song and dance performed in a circle, involving synchronised shaking of each limb in turn.

ORIGIN – perhaps from HOCUS-POCUS.

hoki /hōki/ > *noun* an edible marine fish found off southern New Zealand.

ORIGIN – Maori.

hokum /hōkəm/ > *noun* informal **1** nonsense. **2** triteness; sentimentality.

hold¹ > *verb* (past and past participle **held**) **1** grasp, carry, or support with one's arms or hands. **2** keep or detain (someone). **3** contain or be capable of containing. **4** have in one's possession. **5** have or occupy (a job or position). **6** have (a belief or opinion). **7** (**hold in**) regard (someone or something) with (a specified feeling). **8** arrange and take part in (a meeting or conversation). **9** continue to follow (a course). **10** (**hold to**) adhere or cause to adhere to (a commitment). **11** stay or cause to stay at a certain value or level. **12** N. Amer. informal refrain from adding or using. > *noun* **1** a grip. **2** a handhold. **3** a degree of power or control.

IDIOMS – **get hold of 1** grasp. **2** informal find or contact. **hold against** allow (a past action) to have a negative influence on one's attitude towards (someone). **hold back** hesitate. **hold down** informal succeed in keeping (a job). **hold fast 1** remain tightly secured. **2** continue to adhere to a principle. **hold forth** talk at length or tediously. **hold good** (or **true**) remain true or valid. **hold it!** informal wait or stop doing something. **hold off 1** resist (an attacker or challenge). **2** postpone (an action or decision). **3** (of bad weather) fail to occur. **hold on 1** wait; stop. **2** keep going in

difficult circumstances. **hold out 1** resist difficult circumstances. **2** continue to be sufficient. **hold out for** continue to demand. **hold over 1** postpone. **2** use (information) to threaten. **hold up 1** delay the progress of. **2** rob (someone) using the threat of violence. **3** present as an example. **4** remain strong or vigorous. **no holds barred 1** (in wrestling) with no restrictions on the kinds of holds that are used. **2** without rules or restrictions. **on hold 1** waiting to be connected by telephone. **2** pending. **take hold** start to have an effect.
DERIVATIVES – **holder** noun.
SYNONYMS – verb **1** bear, carry, clasp, clutch, grasp, grip, support. **2** confine, detain, impound, incarcerate, keep. **3** accommodate, comprise, take. noun **1** grasp, clasp, grip. **3** authority, influence, power.

hold² > noun a storage space in the lower part of a ship or aircraft.
ORIGIN – from **HOLE**; the -d was added by association with **HOLD¹**.

holdall > noun Brit. a large bag with handles and a shoulder strap.

holding > noun **1** an area of land held by lease. **2** (**holdings**) financial assets.
COMBINATIONS – **holding company** a company created to buy shares in other companies, which it then controls. **holding pattern** the flight path maintained by an aircraft awaiting permission to land.

hold-up > noun **1** a cause of delay. **2** a robbery conducted with the threat of violence. **3** a stocking held up by an elasticated top.

hole > noun **1** an empty space in a solid body or surface. **2** informal a small, awkward, or unpleasant place or situation. **3** a cavity on a golf course into which the ball is directed. > verb **1** make a hole or holes in. **2** Golf hit (the ball) into a hole. **3** (**hole up**) informal hide oneself.
IDIOMS – **hole-and-corner** secret. **hole-in-one** (pl. **holes-in-one**) Golf a shot that enters the hole directly from the tee. **make a hole in** use a significant amount of.
DERIVATIVES – **holey** adjective.
SYNONYMS – noun **1** aperture, breach, break, fissure, opening, orifice. verb **1** perforate, pierce, puncture.
COMBINATIONS – **hole in the heart** a congenital defect in the wall between the chambers of the heart, resulting in inadequate circulation of oxygenated blood. **hole in the wall** informal **1** Brit. an automatic cash dispenser installed in an outside wall. **2** a small dingy place.

holiday chiefly Brit. > noun **1** an extended period of recreation, especially away from home. **2** a day of festivity or recreation when no work is done. > verb spend a holiday.
SYNONYMS – noun **1** break, vacation.

COMBINATIONS – **holiday camp** Brit. a residential camp for holidaymakers with entertainment and other facilities. **holidaymaker** Brit. a tourist.
ORIGIN – Old English, 'holy day'.

holiness > noun **1** the state of being holy. **2** (**His** or **Your Holiness**) the title of the Pope, Orthodox patriarchs, and the Dalai Lama.
SYNONYMS – **1** sacredness, saintliness, sanctity.

holism /hōliz'm/ > noun Medicine the treating of the whole person, rather than just the symptoms of a disease.
DERIVATIVES – **holistic** adjective.
ORIGIN – from Greek holos 'whole'.

hollandaise sauce /holləndayz/ > noun a creamy sauce for fish, made of butter, egg yolks, and vinegar.
ORIGIN – French hollandais 'Dutch'.

holler informal > verb give a loud shout. > noun a loud shout.
ORIGIN – from the rare verb hollo; related to **HALLOO**.

hollow > adjective **1** having a hole or empty space inside. **2** concave. **3** (of a sound) echoing. **4** insincere: a hollow promise. > noun **1** a hole or depression. **2** a small valley. > verb (usu. **hollow out**) **1** make hollow. **2** form by hollowing.
IDIOMS – **beat hollow** informal defeat thoroughly.
DERIVATIVES – **hollowly** adverb **hollowness** noun.
SYNONYMS – adjective **1** empty, vacant, void.
ORIGIN – Old English, 'cave'; related to **HOLE**.

holly > noun an evergreen shrub with prickly dark green leaves and red berries.

hollyhock > noun a tall plant of the mallow family, with large showy flowers.
ORIGIN – from **HOLY** + obsolete hock 'mallow'.

holmium /hōlmiəm/ > noun a soft silvery-white metallic chemical element of the lanthanide series.
ORIGIN – from Holmia, Latinised form of Stockholm, capital of Sweden (because holmium was discovered in minerals from near Stockholm).

holm oak > noun an evergreen oak with dark green glossy leaves.
ORIGIN – from dialect hollin, from Old English holen 'holly'.

holo- > combining form whole; complete: holocaust.
ORIGIN – from Greek holos 'whole'.

holocaust /holləkawst/ > noun **1** destruction or slaughter on a mass scale. **2** (**the Holocaust**) the mass murder of Jews under the German Nazi regime in the Second World War.

ORIGIN – Greek holokauston, from holos 'whole' + kaustos 'burnt'.

Holocene /holləseen/ > adjective Geology relating to or denoting the present epoch (from about 10,000 years ago, following the Pleistocene).
ORIGIN – from Greek holos 'whole' + kainos 'new'.

hologram /holləgram/ > noun **1** a three-dimensional image formed by the interference of light beams from a laser or similar light source. **2** a photograph of an interference pattern which, when suitably illuminated, produces a three-dimensional image.
DERIVATIVES – **holographic** adjective **holography** noun.

holograph /holləgraaf/ > noun a manuscript handwritten by its author.

hols > plural noun Brit. informal holidays.

holster /hōlstər/ > noun a holder for carrying a handgun, typically worn on a belt or under the arm. > verb put (a gun) into its holster.

holt /hōlt/ > noun the den of an otter.
ORIGIN – from **HOLD¹**.

holy > adjective (**holier**, **holiest**) **1** dedicated to God or a religious purpose; sacred: I do not lead a holy life. **2** morally and spiritually excellent and to be revered: I do not lead a holy life.
SYNONYMS – **1** blessed, consecrated, hallowed, sacred, sanctified. **2** devout, godly, pious.
ANTONYMS – impious, ungodly.
COMBINATIONS – **holier-than-thou** offensively self-righteous. **holy day** a religious festival. **Holy Father** the Pope. **holy of holies 1** historical the inner chamber of the sanctuary in the Jewish Temple in Jerusalem. **2** a place regarded as most sacred or special. **holy orders** see **ORDER** (in sense 10). **Holy Roman Empire** the western part of the Roman empire, as revived by Charlemagne in 800. **Holy Scripture** the Bible. **Holy See** the papacy or the papal court. **Holy Spirit** (also **Holy Ghost**) (in Christianity) the third person of the Trinity; God as spiritually active in the world. **holy war** a war waged in support of a religious cause. **holy water** water blessed by a priest and used in religious ceremonies. **Holy Week** the week before Easter. **Holy Writ** sacred writings collectively, especially the Bible.
ORIGIN – Old English, related to **WHOLE**.

homage /hommij/ > noun (often in phrase **pay homage to**) **1** honour or respect shown publicly. **2** formal public acknowledgement of feudal allegiance.
ORIGIN – Old French, from Latin homo 'man'.

hombre /ombray/ > *noun* informal, chiefly N. Amer. a man.

ORIGIN – Spanish.

homburg /homburg/ > *noun* a man's felt hat having a narrow curled brim and a lengthwise indentation in the crown.

ORIGIN – named after *Homburg*, a town in western Germany, where such hats were first worn.

home > *noun* 1 the place where one lives. 2 an institution for people needing professional care. 3 a place where something flourishes or from which it originated. 4 the finishing point in a race. 5 (in games) the place where a player is free from attack. > *adjective* 1 relating to one's home. 2 made, done, or intended for use in the home. 3 relating to one's own country. 4 (in sport) at or denoting a team's own ground. > *adverb* 1 to or at one's home. 2 to the end or conclusion of something. 3 to the intended or correct position. > *verb* 1 (of an animal) return by instinct to its territory. 2 (**home in on**) move or be aimed towards.

IDIOMS – **at home** 1 comfortable and at ease. 2 ready to receive visitors. **bring home to** cause to be aware of the significance of. **close to home** (of a remark) uncomfortably accurate. **drive** (or **hammer**) **home** stress forcefully. **hit** (or **strike**) **home** 1 (of words) have the intended effect. 2 (of the significance of a situation) be fully realised. **home and dry** chiefly Brit. having achieved one's objective. **home is where the heart is** proverb your home will always be the place for which you feel the deepest affection, no matter where you are.

DERIVATIVES – **homeless** *adjective* **homelessness** *noun*.

SYNONYMS – *noun* 1 abode, domicile, habitation, residence.

COMBINATIONS – **homebody** informal, chiefly N. Amer. a person who likes to stay at home. **home brew** alcoholic drink, especially beer, brewed at home. **home economics** the study of cookery and household management. **home farm** Brit. a farm on an estate that provides produce for the estate owner. **home-grown** grown or produced in one's own garden or country. **Home Guard** the British volunteer force organised in 1940 to defend the UK against invasion. **home help** Brit. a person employed to help with domestic work. **home-made** made at home. **homemaker** a person who manages a home. **home movie** a film made in the home or in a domestic setting by an amateur. **Home Office** the British government department dealing with law and order, immigration, etc. in England and Wales. **home page** Computing the introductory document of an

organisation or individual on the Internet. **home plate** Baseball the five-sided flat white rubber base which must be touched in scoring a run. **home rule** the government of a place by its own citizens. **home run** Baseball a hit that allows the batter to make a complete circuit of the bases. **Home Secretary** (in the UK) the Secretary of State in charge of the Home Office. **home straight** (also **home stretch**) the concluding stretch of a racecourse. **home truth** an unpleasant fact about oneself. **home unit** Austral./NZ a flat that is one of several in a building. **homeworker** a person who works from home.

homeboy (or **homegirl**) > *noun* US & S. African informal a person from one's own town or neighbourhood.

homecoming > *noun* an instance of returning home.

homeland > *noun* 1 a person's native land. 2 an autonomous state occupied by a particular people. 3 historical (in South Africa) a partially self-governing area designated for an indigenous African people.

homely > *adjective* (**homelier**, **homeliest**) 1 Brit. simple but comfortable. 2 unsophisticated. 3 N. Amer. (of a person) unattractive in appearance.

DERIVATIVES – **homeliness** *noun*.

SYNONYMS – 1 comfortable, cosy, snug.

homeopath /hōmiəpath, hommiəpath/ (also **homoeopath**) > *noun* a person who practises homeopathy.

homeopathy /hōmioppəthi, hommi-/ (also **homoeopathy**) > *noun* a system of complementary medicine in which disease is treated by minute doses of natural substances that in large quantities would produce symptoms of the disease.

DERIVATIVES – **homeopathic** *adjective*.

ORIGIN – from Greek *homoios* 'like' + *patheia* 'suffering, feeling'.

homeostasis /hōmiəstaysiss, homm-/ (also **homoeostasis**) > *noun* (pl. **homeostases** /hōmiəstayseez, hommi-/) the maintenance of a stable equilibrium, especially through physiological processes.

DERIVATIVES – **homeostatic** *adjective*.

ORIGIN – from Greek *homoios* 'like' + *stasis* 'standing'.

homeotherm /hōmiətherm, homm-/ > *noun* Zoology an organism that keeps a constant body temperature by means of its metabolic activity; a warm-blooded organism. Contrasted with **POIKILO-THERM**.

DERIVATIVES – **homeothermic** *adjective*.

ORIGIN – from Greek *homoios* 'like' + *thermē* 'heat'.

Homeric /hōmerrik/ > *adjective* of, or in the style of, the ancient Greek poet Homer (8th century BC) or the epic poems (the *Iliad* and the *Odyssey*) ascribed to him.

homesick > *adjective* feeling upset because one is missing one's home.

homespun > *adjective* 1 simple and unsophisticated. 2 (of cloth or yarn) made or spun at home. > *noun* cloth of this type.

homestead > *noun* 1 a house with surrounding land and outbuildings. 2 N. Amer. historical an area of land (usually 160 acres) granted to a settler as a home. 3 (in South Africa) a hut or cluster of huts occupied by one family or clan.

DERIVATIVES – **homesteader** *noun* **homesteading** *noun*.

homeward > *adverb* (also **homewards**) towards home. > *adjective* going or leading towards home.

homework > *noun* 1 school work that a pupil is required to do at home. 2 preparation done for an event or situation. 3 paid work done in one's own home, especially piecework.

homey (also **homy**) > *adjective* (**homier**, **homiest**) 1 comfortable and cosy. 2 unsophisticated. > *noun* variant of **HOMIE**.

DERIVATIVES – **homeyness** (also **hominess**) *noun*.

homicide /hommisīd/ > *noun* murder.

DERIVATIVES – **homicidal** *adjective*.

ORIGIN – Latin *homicidium*, from *homo* 'man' + *caedere* 'kill'.

homie (also **homey**) > *noun* (pl. **homies** or **homeys**) informal, chiefly US a homeboy or homegirl.

homiletic /hommilettik/ > *adjective* of or like a homily. > *noun* (**homiletics**) (usu. treated as sing.) the art of preaching or writing sermons.

homily /hommili/ > *noun* (pl. **homilies**) 1 a talk on a religious subject, intended to be spiritually uplifting rather than giving doctrinal instruction. 2 a tedious moralising talk.

DERIVATIVES – **homilist** *noun*.

SYNONYMS – 2 lecture, sermon.

ORIGIN – Greek *homilia* 'discourse', from *homilos* 'crowd'.

homing > *adjective* 1 (of a pigeon or other animal) able to find its way back home from a great distance. 2 (of a weapon) able to find and hit a target electronically.

hominid /homminid/ > *noun* Zoology a member of a family of primates (Hominidae) which includes humans and their fossil ancestors.

ORIGIN – from Latin *homo* 'man'.

hominoid > *noun* Zoology a primate of a group (Hominoidea) that includes humans, their fossil ancestors, and the great apes.

hominy /hommini/ > *noun* US coarsely ground maize used to make grits.

ORIGIN – Algonquian.

Homo /hōmō, hommō/ > *noun* the genus of primates of which modern humans

(*Homo sapiens*) are the present-day representatives.

ORIGIN – Latin, 'man'.

homo /hōmō/ *informal, chiefly derogatory* > *noun* (pl. **homos**) a homosexual man. > *adjective* homosexual.

homo- /hommə/ > *combining form* **1** same: *homogeneous*. **2** relating to homosexual love: *homoerotic*.

ORIGIN – from Greek *homos* 'same'.

homoeopath > *noun* variant spelling of HOMEOPATH.

homoeopathy > *noun* variant spelling of HOMEOPATHY.

homoeostasis > *noun* variant spelling of HOMEOSTASIS.

homoerotic /hōmōirottik, hommō-/ > *adjective* concerning or arousing sexual desire centred on a person of the same sex.

DERIVATIVES – **homoeroticism** *noun*.

homogeneous* /homməjeeniəss/ > *adjective* **1** of the same kind. **2** consisting of parts all of the same kind.

DERIVATIVES – **homogeneity** *noun* **homogeneously** *adverb* **homogeneousness** *noun*.

*SPELLING – note that the ending is *-eous*, with an *e*, not *-ous*: homogen*eous*. The word **homogenous**, without the *e*, is now usually a misspelling of **homogeneous**; however, it is used sometimes in biology to mean 'homologous'.

SYNONYMS – **1** comparable, similar. **2** alike, uniform, unvarying.

ORIGIN – Greek *homogenēs*, from *homos* 'same' + *genos* 'race, kind'.

homogenise (also **homogenize**) > *verb* **1** make homogeneous. **2** subject (milk) to a process in which the fat droplets are emulsified and the cream does not separate.

DERIVATIVES – **homogenisation** *noun* **homogeniser** *noun*.

homogenous /həmojinəss/ > *adjective* Biology old-fashioned term for HOMOLOGOUS.

homograph > *noun* each of two or more words having the same spelling but different meanings and origins.

DERIVATIVES – **homographic** *adjective*.

homologate /həmolləgayt/ > *verb* **1** formal agree with or approve of. **2** approve (a vehicle or engine) for sale or for a class of racing.

DERIVATIVES – **homologation** *noun*.

ORIGIN – Latin *homologare* 'agree'.

homologous /həmolləgəss/ > *adjective* **1** having the same relation, relative position, or structure. **2** Biology (of organs) similar in position, structure, and evolutionary origin.

DERIVATIVES – **homologise** (also **homologize**) *verb* **homology** *noun*.

ORIGIN – Greek *homologos* 'agreeing, consistent', from *homos* 'same' + *logos* 'ratio, proportion'.

homologue /homməlog/ (US **homolog**) > *noun* technical a homologous thing.

homomorphic > *adjective* technical of the same or similar form.

DERIVATIVES – **homomorphically** *adverb*.

homonym /hommənim/ > *noun* each of two or more words having the same spelling or pronunciation but different meanings and origins.

DERIVATIVES – **homonymic** *adjective* **homonymous** *adjective* **homonymy** /həmonnimi/ *noun*.

ORIGIN – Greek *homōnumos* 'having the same name', from *homos* 'same' + *onoma* 'name'.

homophobia > *noun* an extreme and irrational aversion to homosexuality and homosexuals.

DERIVATIVES – **homophobe** *noun* **homophobic** *adjective*.

homophone > *noun* each of two or more words having the same pronunciation but different meanings, origins, or spelling (e.g. *new* and *knew*).

ORIGIN – from HOMO- + Greek *phōnē* 'sound, voice'.

homophonic > *adjective* **1** Music characterised by the movement of accompanying parts in the same rhythm as the melody. **2** another term for HOMOPHONOUS.

DERIVATIVES – **homophonically** *adverb*.

homophonous /həmoffənəss/ > *adjective* **1** (of music) homophonic. **2** (of a word or words) having the same pronunciation as another but different meaning, origin, or spelling.

DERIVATIVES – **homophony** *noun*.

Homo sapiens /hōmō sappienz/ > *noun* the primate species to which modern humans belong.

ORIGIN – Latin, 'wise man'.

homosexual > *adjective* feeling or involving sexual attraction to people of one's own sex. > *noun* a homosexual person.

DERIVATIVES – **homosexuality** *noun* **homosexually** *adverb*.

homunculus /həmungkyooləss/ (also **homuncule** /həmungkyool/) > *noun* (pl. **homunculi** /həmungkyoolī/ or **homuncules**) a very small human or human-like creature.

ORIGIN – Latin, 'little man'.

homy > *adjective* variant spelling of HOMEY.

Hon. > *abbreviation* **1** (in official job titles) Honorary. **2** (in titles of the British nobility, MPs, and (in the US) judges) Honourable.

honcho /honchō/ > *noun* (pl. **honchos**) informal a leader or boss.

ORIGIN – Japanese, 'group leader'; the term was brought back to the US by servicemen stationed in Japan.

Honduran /hondyoorən/ > *noun* a person from Honduras, a country in Central America. > *adjective* relating to Honduras.

hone /hōn/ > *verb* **1** sharpen with a whetstone. **2** make sharper or more focused or efficient. > *noun* a whetstone.

ORIGIN – Old English, 'stone'.

honest > *adjective* **1** free of deceit; truthful and sincere. **2** morally correct or virtuous. **3** fairly earned: *an honest living*. **4** simple and unpretentious. > *adverb* informal genuinely; really.

IDIOMS – **make an honest woman of** dated or humorous (of a man) marry (a woman) with whom he is having a sexual relationship.

SYNONYMS – *adjective* **1** candid, frank, genuine, sincere, truthful. **2** ethical, honourable, moral, principled, upright.

ANTONYMS – *adjective* **1** deceitful, dishonest. **2** dishonest, dishonourable.

ORIGIN – Latin *honestus*, from *honor* 'honour'.

honestly > *adverb* **1** in an honest way. **2** really (used for emphasis).

SYNONYMS – **1** fairly, honourably, lawfully.

honest-to-God informal > *adjective* genuine; real. > *adverb* genuinely; really.

honest-to-goodness > *adjective* informal genuine and straightforward.

honesty > *noun* **1** the quality of being honest. **2** a plant with purple or white flowers and round, flat, translucent seed pods. [ORIGIN – so named from its seed pods, translucency symbolising lack of deceit.]

IDIOMS – **honesty is the best policy** proverb there are often practical as well as moral reasons for being honest.

SYNONYMS – candour, honour, sincerity, truthfulness.

honey > *noun* (pl. **honeys**) **1** a sweet, sticky yellowish-brown fluid made by bees from flower nectar. **2** chiefly N. Amer. darling; sweetheart. **3** informal an excellent example of something.

COMBINATIONS – **honeybee** the common bee. **honeypot 1** a container for honey. **2** a place to which many people are attracted. **honeytrap** a stratagem in which an attractive person entices another person into unwittingly revealing information.

honeycomb > *noun* **1** a structure of hexagonal cells of wax, made by bees to store honey and eggs. **2** a structure of linked cavities. > *verb* fill with cavities or tunnels.

honeydew > *noun* a sweet, sticky substance excreted by aphids.

COMBINATIONS – **honeydew melon** a melon of a variety with smooth, pale skin and sweet green flesh.

honeyed > *adjective* **1** containing or coated with honey. **2** having a warm yellow colour. **3** soothing and soft: *honeyed words*.

honeymoon > *noun* **1** a holiday taken by a

newly married couple. **2** an initial period of enthusiasm or goodwill. > *verb* spend a honeymoon.

DERIVATIVES – **honeymooner** *noun*.

wordpower facts

Honeymoon

Earliest uses of the term **honeymoon** make no explicit reference to a period of time; instead they compare the mutual affection of a newly married couple to the waxing of the moon, before, inevitably, it starts to wane. W. Fennor wrote in *Cornucopiae* (1612): 'And now their hony-moone, that late was cleare, Did pale, obscure, and tenebrous appeare.' However, the period of a month is inevitably associated with the moon, and this is seen in later use of the term. Samuel Johnson, in his dictionary published in 1755, defined the **honeymoon** as 'the first month after marriage, when there is nothing but tenderness and pleasure'. In modern life the **honeymoon**, usually not as long as a month, is likely to involve a holiday away from home.

honeysuckle > *noun* a climbing shrub with fragrant yellow and pink flowers.

hongi /**hong**i/ > *noun* **NZ** the traditional Maori greeting, in which people press their noses together.

ORIGIN – Maori.

honk > *noun* **1** the cry of a goose. **2** the sound of a car horn. > *verb* **1** emit or cause to emit a honk.

honky > *noun* (pl. **honkies**) N. Amer. informal, derogatory a white person.

honky-tonk > *noun* informal **1** chiefly N. Amer. a cheap or disreputable bar or club. **2** ragtime piano music.

honor > *noun* & *verb* US spelling of **HONOUR**.

honorable > *adjective* US spelling of **HONOURABLE**.

honorarium /onnə**rair**iəm/ > *noun* (pl. **honorariums** or **honoraria** /onnə**rair**iə/) a payment for professional services which are given nominally without charge.

ORIGIN – Latin, denoting a gift made to someone admitted to public office.

honorary* > *adjective* **1** (of a title or position) conferred as an honour. **2** Brit. (of an office or its holder) unpaid.

***SPELLING** – honor-, not honour-: honorary.

honorific > *adjective* given as a mark of respect.

honour (US **honor**) > *noun* **1** high respect. **2** a feeling of pride and pleasure from being shown respect. **3** a person or thing that brings credit. **4** a clear sense of what is morally right. **5** a thing conferred as a distinction, especially an official award for achievement or bravery. **6** (**honours**) a course of degree studies more specialised than for an ordinary pass. **7** (**His**, **Your**, etc. **Honour**) a title of respect for a circuit judge. **8** dated a woman's chastity. **9** Bridge an ace, king, queen, jack, or ten. > *verb* **1** regard with great respect. **2** pay public respect to. **3** bestow grace or privilege on. **4** fulfil (an obligation) or keep (an agreement).

IDIOMS – **do the honours** informal perform a social duty for others, especially serve food or drink. **in honour of** as an expression of respect for. **on one's honour** under a moral obligation. **there's honour among thieves** proverb dishonest people may have certain standards of behaviour which they will respect.

SYNONYMS – *noun* **1** acclaim, credit, esteem, fame, prestige, renown. **4** ethics, integrity, probity, rectitude.

COMBINATIONS – **honours list** a list of people to be awarded honours. **honour system** a system relying on the honesty of those concerned.

ORIGIN – Latin *honor*.

honourable (US **honorable**) > *adjective* **1** bringing or worthy of honour. **2** (**Honourable**) a title given to certain high officials, members of the nobility, and MPs.

DERIVATIVES – **honourably** *adverb*.

COMBINATIONS – **honourable mention** a commendation for a candidate in an examination or competition not awarded a prize.

hooch /hooch/ (also **hootch**) > *noun* informal alcoholic liquor, especially inferior or illicit whisky.

ORIGIN – abbreviation of *Hoochinoo*, an Alaskan Indian people who made liquor.

hood¹ > *noun* **1** a covering for the head and neck with an opening for the face. **2** Brit. a folding waterproof cover of a vehicle or pram. **3** N. Amer. the bonnet of a vehicle. **4** a protective canopy. > *verb* put a hood on or over.

DERIVATIVES – **hooded** *adjective*.

hood² > *noun* informal, chiefly N. Amer. a gangster or violent criminal.

ORIGIN – abbreviation of **HOODLUM**.

hood³ > *noun* US informal a neighbourhood.

-hood > *suffix* forming nouns: **1** denoting a condition or quality: *falsehood*. **2** denoting a collection or group: *brotherhood*.

ORIGIN – Old English *-hād*, originally an independent noun meaning 'person, condition, quality'.

hoodlum /**hood**ləm/ > *noun* a hooligan or gangster.

hoodoo > *noun* **1** voodoo. **2** a run of bad luck. **3** a cause of bad luck. > *verb* (**hoodoos**, **hoodooed**) bring bad luck to.

ORIGIN – an alternative US word for **VOODOO**.

hoodwink > *verb* deceive or trick.

ORIGIN – from **HOOD¹** + an obsolete sense of **WINK** 'close the eyes': originally meaning 'to blindfold'.

hooey > *noun* informal nonsense.

hoof > *noun* (pl. **hoofs** or **hooves**) the horny part of the foot of a horse, cow, etc. > *verb* informal **1** kick (a ball) powerfully. **2** (**hoof it**) go on foot. **3** (**hoof it**) dance.

WORDFINDER – ungual (*relating to a hoof*), ungulate (*a hoofed mammal*).

IDIOMS – **on the hoof 1** (of livestock) not yet slaughtered. **2** informal without great thought or preparation.

DERIVATIVES – **hoofed** *adjective*.

hoofer > *noun* informal a professional dancer.

hoo-ha > *noun* informal a commotion.

hook > *noun* **1** a piece of curved metal or other material for catching hold of things or hanging things on. **2** a curved cutting instrument. **3** a short swinging punch made with the elbow bent and rigid. **4** a thing designed to catch people's attention. **5** a catchy passage in a song. > *verb* **1** be or become attached or fastened with a hook. **2** (**hook up**) link or be linked to electronic equipment. **3** bend into the shape of a hook. **4** catch with a hook. **5** (**be hooked**) informal be captivated or addicted. **6** (in sport) hit (the ball) in a curving path.

IDIOMS – **by hook or by crook** by any possible means. **get one's hooks into** informal get hold of. **hook, line, and sinker** entirely. **off the hook 1** informal no longer in trouble. **2** (of a telephone receiver) not on its rest. **sling one's hook** Brit. informal leave.

COMBINATIONS – **hook and eye** a small metal hook and loop used to fasten a garment. **hook nose** an aquiline nose. **hook-up** a connection to mains electricity, a communications system, etc.

hookah /**hoo**kə/ > *noun* an oriental tobacco pipe with a long, flexible tube which draws the smoke through water in a bowl.

ORIGIN – Urdu, from Arabic.

hooked > *adjective* having or resembling a hook or hooks.

hooker > *noun* **1** Rugby the player in the middle of the front row of the scrum. **2** informal, chiefly N. Amer. a prostitute.

hookey (also **hooky**) > *noun* (in phrase **play hookey**) N. Amer. informal play truant.

hookworm > *noun* a parasitic worm which inhabits the intestines and feeds by attaching itself with hook-like mouthparts.

hooligan > *noun* a violent young troublemaker.

DERIVATIVES – **hooliganism** *noun*.

SYNONYMS – hoodlum, ruffian, thug.

ORIGIN – possibly from *Hooligan*, the surname of a fictional rowdy Irish family in a music-hall song.

hoon Austral./NZ informal > *noun* a lout. > *verb* behave like a lout.

hoop > *noun* **1** a rigid circular band. **2** a large ring used as a toy or for circus performers to jump through. **3** chiefly Brit. a metal arch through which the balls are hit in croquet. **4** a contrasting horizontal band on a sports shirt or cap. > *verb* bind or encircle with hoops.
IDIOMS – **put someone** (or **go**) **through hoops** make someone undergo (or be made to undergo) a gruelling test.
DERIVATIVES – **hooped** *adjective*.

hoopla /hōoplaa/ > *noun* **1** Brit. a game in which rings are thrown in an attempt to encircle a prize. **2** informal unnecessary fuss.

hoopoe /hōopōo/ > *noun* a salmon-pink bird with a long downcurved bill, a large crest, and black-and-white wings and tail.
ORIGIN – Latin *upupa*, imitative of the bird's call.

hooray > *exclamation* **1** hurrah. **2** Austral./NZ goodbye.
COMBINATIONS – **Hooray Henry** (pl. **Hooray Henrys** or **Hooray Henries**) Brit. informal a lively but ineffectual young upper-class man.

hoot > *noun* **1** a low musical sound made by an owl, or a similar sound made by a horn, siren, etc. **2** a shout expressing scorn or disapproval. **3** an outburst of laughter. **4** (**a hoot**) informal an amusing person or thing. > *verb* make or cause to make a hoot.
IDIOMS – **not care** (or **give**) **a hoot** (or **two hoots**) informal not care at all.

hootch > *noun* variant spelling of HOOCH.

hootenanny /hōot'nanni/ > *noun* (pl. **hootenannies**) informal, chiefly US an informal gathering with folk music.

hooter > *noun* **1** Brit. a siren, steam whistle, or horn. **2** informal a person's nose. **3** (**hooters**) N. Amer. vulgar slang a woman's breasts.

Hoover Brit. > *noun* trademark a vacuum cleaner. > *verb* (**hoover**) clean with a vacuum cleaner.
ORIGIN – named after the American industrialist William H. *Hoover* (1849–1932).

hooves plural of HOOF.

hop¹ > *verb* (**hopped**, **hopping**) **1** move by jumping on one foot. **2** (of a bird or animal) move by jumping with two or all feet at once. **3** jump over or on to. **4** informal move or go quickly. **5** (**hop it**) Brit. go away. > *noun* **1** a hopping movement. **2** a short journey or distance.
IDIOMS – **hopping mad** informal extremely angry. **hop, skip** (or **step**), **and jump 1** old-fashioned term for *triple jump*. **2** informal a short distance. **on the hop** Brit. informal **1** unprepared. **2** busy.

hop² > *noun* **1** a climbing plant whose dried flowers (**hops**) are used in brewing to give a bitter flavour. **2** (**hops**) Austral./NZ informal beer.

> *verb* (**hopped**, **hopping**) flavour with hops.
DERIVATIVES – **hoppy** *adjective*.

hope > *noun* **1** a feeling of expectation and desire. **2** a person or thing that gives cause for hope. > *verb* **1** want something to happen or be the case. **2** intend if possible to do something.
IDIOMS – **hope against hope** cling to a mere possibility. **hope springs eternal in the human breast** proverb it is human nature always to find fresh cause for optimism. **not a** (or **some**) **hope** informal no chance at all.
DERIVATIVES – **hoper** *noun*.
COMBINATIONS – **hope chest** N. Amer. a chest in which household linen is stored by a woman in preparation for marriage.

hopeful > *adjective* feeling or inspiring hope. > *noun* a person likely or hoping to succeed.
DERIVATIVES – **hopefulness** *noun*.
SYNONYMS – *adjective* confident, optimistic, sanguine.
ANTONYMS – *adjective* pessimistic.

hopefully > *adverb* **1** in a hopeful manner. **2** it is to be hoped that.
USAGE – the traditional and long-established sense of **hopefully** is 'in a hopeful manner'. In the 20th century a new use arose, with the meaning 'it is to be hoped that'. Although this newer use is now very much the dominant one, it is regarded by some people as incorrect. Why is this, when a number of other adverbs, such as **fortunately**, **regrettably**, and **sadly**, are used in the same way? Part of the reason is that the others can be phrased in another way, as 'it is fortunate/regrettable/sad that', and this is not possible with **hopefully**. Even if this argument is not strong, it is as well to be aware of it, especially in formal or written contexts.

hopeless > *adjective* **1** feeling or causing despair. **2** totally inadequate or incompetent.
DERIVATIVES – **hopelessly** *adverb* **hopelessness** *noun*.
SYNONYMS – **1** defeatist, disconsolate, pessimistic. **2** feeble, useless, worthless.

Hopi /hōpi/ > *noun* (pl. same or **Hopis**) a member of an American Indian people living chiefly in NE Arizona.
ORIGIN – the Hopis' name for themselves.

hoplite /hoplīt/ > *noun* a heavily armed foot soldier of ancient Greece.
ORIGIN – Greek *hoplitēs*, from *hoplon* 'weapon'.

hopper > *noun* **1** a tapering container that discharges its contents at the bottom. **2** a person or thing that hops.

hopsack > *noun* a coarse clothing fabric of a loose weave.

hopscotch > *noun* a children's game of

hopping into and over squares marked on the ground to retrieve a marker.
ORIGIN – from HOP¹ + SCOTCH in the sense 'put an end to, stop', reflecting the pattern of hopping and stopping characteristic of the game.

horde > *noun* **1** chiefly derogatory a large group of people. **2** an army or tribe of nomadic warriors.
USAGE – do not confuse **horde** with **hoard**: a **horde** is a large group of people, whereas a **hoard** is a store of something valuable.
SYNONYMS – **1** mob, multitude, throng.
ORIGIN – Polish *horda*, from Turkish *ordu* 'royal camp'.

horehound /horhownd/ > *noun* a plant of the mint family, traditionally used as a medicinal herb.
ORIGIN – Old English, from *hār* 'hoar' + *hūne*, the name of the white horehound.

horizon > *noun* **1** the line at which the earth's surface and the sky appear to meet. **2** the limit of a person's mental perception, experience, or interest. **3** Geology & Archaeology a layer or level having particular characteristics or representing a particular period.
IDIOMS – **on the horizon** imminent.
ORIGIN – Latin, from Greek *horizōn kuklos* 'limiting circle'.

horizontal > *adjective* parallel to the plane of the horizon; at right angles to the vertical. > *noun* a horizontal line, plane or structure.
DERIVATIVES – **horizontality** *noun* **horizontally** *adverb*.

hormone > *noun* a substance produced by a living thing and transported in tissue fluids to specific cells or tissues to stimulate them into action.
WORDFINDER – endocrine (*referring to a gland which secretes hormones*); *some important hormones*: adrenalin, cortisone, endorphins, insulin, oestrogen, progesterone, progestogen, testosterone, thyroxine.
DERIVATIVES – **hormonal** *adjective*.
COMBINATIONS – **hormone replacement therapy** treatment with certain hormones to alleviate menopausal symptoms or osteoporosis.
ORIGIN – from Greek *hormōn* 'setting in motion'.

horn > *noun* **1** a hard bony outgrowth, often curved and pointed, found in pairs on the heads of cattle, sheep, and other animals. **2** the substance of which horns are composed. **3** a wind instrument, now usually of brass, conical in shape or wound into a spiral. **4** an instrument sounding a warning or other signal. **5** a pointed projection or extremity. > *verb* **1** butt or gore with the horns. **2** (**horn in**) informal interfere.

WORDFINDER – **corneous** (*horn-like or made of horn*).

IDIOMS – **blow** (or **toot**) **one's own horn** N. Amer. informal boast about oneself or one's achievements. **draw** (or **pull**) **in one's horns** become less assertive or ambitious. **on the horns of a dilemma** faced with a decision involving equally unfavourable alternatives.

DERIVATIVES – **horned** *adjective*.

COMBINATIONS – **horn of plenty** a cornucopia. **hornpipe 1** a lively solo dance traditionally performed by sailors. **2** a piece of music for such a dance. **horn-rimmed** (of glasses) having rims made of horn or a similar substance.

hornbeam > *noun* a deciduous tree with hard, pale wood.

ORIGIN – so named because of the tree's hard wood.

hornbill > *noun* a tropical bird with a horn-like structure on its large curved bill.

hornblende /**horn**blend/ > *noun* a dark brown, black, or green mineral present in many rocks.

ORIGIN – German.

hornet > *noun* a kind of large wasp, typically red and yellow or red and black.

IDIOMS – **stir up a hornets' nest** provoke opposition or difficulties.

hornswoggle /**horn**swogg'l/ > *verb* informal, chiefly N. Amer. outwit by cheating or deception.

hornwort > *noun* a submerged aquatic plant with narrow forked leaves that become translucent and horny as they age.

horny > *adjective* (**hornier**, **horniest**) **1** of or like horn. **2** hard and rough. **3** informal sexually aroused or arousing.

horology /həˈrolləji/ > *noun* **1** the study and measurement of time. **2** the art of making clocks and watches.

ORIGIN – from Greek *hōra* 'time'.

horoscope > *noun* a forecast of a person's future based on the relative positions of the stars and planets at the time of their birth.

ORIGIN – Greek *hōroskopos*, from *hōra* 'time' + *skopos* 'observer'.

horrendous > *adjective* extremely unpleasant or horrifying.

DERIVATIVES – **horrendously** *adverb*.

ORIGIN – Latin *horrendus*, from *horrere* 'tremble, shudder, (of hair) stand on end'.

horrible > *adjective* **1** causing or likely to cause horror. **2** informal very unpleasant.

DERIVATIVES – **horribly** *adverb*.

SYNONYMS – **1** awful, dreadful, frightful, hideous, horrendous.

horrid > *adjective* **1** causing horror. **2** informal very unpleasant.

DERIVATIVES – **horridly** *adverb*.

SYNONYMS – **1** abhorrent, awful, dreadful, ghastly, revolting.

---

wordpower facts

Horrid

Horrid comes from Latin *horridus*, from the verb *horrere*, meaning 'tremble, shudder, bristle'. *Horrere* is the root of a group of related words, including **abhor**, **abhorrence**, **horrendous**, **horrible**, **horrific**, **horror**, and **horrify**. It is also the root of **ordure** (which comes via Old French *ord*, meaning 'foul').

---

horrific > *adjective* causing horror.

DERIVATIVES – **horrifically** *adverb*.

ORIGIN – Latin *horrificus*, from *horrere* 'tremble, shudder, bristle'.

horrify > *verb* (**horrifies**, **horrified**) fill with horror.

DERIVATIVES – **horrified** *adjective* **horrifying** *adjective* **horrifyingly** *adverb*.

SYNONYMS – appal, intimidate, outrage, shock, terrify.

horror > *noun* **1** an intense feeling of fear, shock, or disgust. **2** a thing causing such a feeling. **3** intense dismay. **4** informal a bad or mischievous person, especially a child.

SYNONYMS – **1** abhorrence, alarm, revulsion, terror.

ORIGIN – Latin, from *horrere* 'tremble, shudder, (of hair) stand on end'.

hors de combat /or də koNbaa/ > *adjective* out of action due to injury or damage.

ORIGIN – French, literally 'out of the fight'.

hors d'oeuvre /or dörv/ > *noun* (pl. same or **hors d'oeuvres** pronunc. same or /or dörvz/) a savoury appetiser.

ORIGIN – French, literally 'outside the work'.

horse > *noun* **1** a large four-legged mammal with a flowing mane and tail, used for riding and for pulling heavy loads. **2** an adult male horse, as opposed to a mare or colt. **3** a frame or structure on which something is mounted or supported: *a clothes horse.* > *verb* (**horse around** or **about**) informal fool about.

WORDFINDER – **equine** (*relating to horses*); **colt** (*young uncastrated male horse*), **foal** (*young horse*), **filly** (*young female horse*), **gelding** (*castrated male horse*), **mare** (*female horse*), **stallion** (*uncastrated adult male horse*).

IDIOMS – **don't change horses in midstream** proverb choose a sensible moment to change your mind. **from the horse's mouth** from an authoritative source. **hold one's horses** informal wait a moment. **horses for courses** Brit. proverb different people are suited to different things or situations. **you can lead a horse to water but you can't make him drink**

proverb you can give someone an opportunity, but you can't force them to take it.

COMBINATIONS – **horsebox** Brit. a motorised vehicle or a trailer for transporting one or more horses. **horse chestnut 1** a large deciduous tree producing nuts (conkers) enclosed in a spiny case. **2** a conker. **horseflesh** horses considered collectively. **Horse Guards** the mounted squadrons provided from the Household Cavalry for ceremonial duties. **horsehair** hair from the mane or tail of a horse, used in furniture for padding. **horse laugh** a loud, coarse laugh. **horse sense** informal common sense. **horse-trading** informal hard and shrewd bargaining.

horseback > *noun* (in phrase **on horseback**) & *adjective* mounted on a horse.

horsefly > *noun* a large fly that inflicts painful bites on horses and other large mammals.

horse latitudes > *plural noun* a belt of calm air and sea occurring in both the northern and southern hemispheres between the trade winds and the westerlies.

---

wordpower facts

Horse latitudes

Although the origin of this term remains obscure, some interesting theories have been put forward over the years, as seen in these citations in the *Oxford English Dictionary*: 'The latitudes where these calms chiefly reign are named the horse-latitudes by mariners...because they are fatal to horses and other cattle which are transported' (1777); and 'The Horse Latitudes...from the Spanish *El Golfo de las Yeguas*, the Mares' Sea, from its unruly and boisterous nature...in contradistinction to the Trade-wind zone, *El Golfo de las Damas*, so called from the pleasant weather to be met with there' (1883). Another possibility is that the **horse latitudes** were so called because horses were sometimes thrown overboard to conserve water when ships were becalmed.

---

horseman (or **horsewoman**) > *noun* a rider on horseback, especially a skilled one.

DERIVATIVES – **horsemanship** *noun*.

horseplay > *noun* rough, boisterous play.

horsepower > *noun* (pl. same) an imperial unit of power equal to 550 foot-pounds per second (about 750 watts), especially as a measurement of engine power.

horseradish > *noun* a plant grown for its pungent root, which is made into a sauce.

horseshoe > *noun* an iron shoe for a horse in the form of an extended circular arc.

horsetail > *noun* a flowerless plant with a jointed stem carrying whorls of narrow leaves.

horsewhip > *noun* a long whip used for driving and controlling horses. > *verb* (**horsewhipped**, **horsewhipping**) beat with such a whip.

horsey (also **horsy**) > *adjective* 1 of or resembling a horse. 2 devoted to horses or horse racing.

hortatory /hortətəri/ > *adjective* formal intended to urge someone to do something.
ORIGIN – Latin *hortatorius*, from *hortari* 'exhort'.

horticulture /hortikulchər/ > *noun* the art or practice of garden cultivation and management.
DERIVATIVES – **horticultural** *adjective* **horticulturalist** *noun* **horticulturist** *noun*.
ORIGIN – from Latin *hortus* 'garden'.

hosanna (also **hosannah**) > *noun* & *exclamation* a biblical cry of praise or joy.
ORIGIN – Greek, from a Hebrew phrase meaning 'save, we pray'.

hose (Brit. also **hosepipe**) > *noun* 1 a flexible tube conveying water. 2 (treated as pl.) stockings, socks, and tights. > *verb* water or spray with a hose.

hosel /hōz'l/ > *noun* the socket of a golf club head which the shaft fits into.
ORIGIN – from HOSE, in the dialect sense 'sheathing'.

hosier /hōziər/ > *noun* a manufacturer or seller of hosiery.

hosiery > *noun* stockings, socks, and tights collectively.

hospice > *noun* 1 a home providing care for the sick or terminally ill. 2 archaic a lodging for travellers, especially one run by a religious order.
ORIGIN – Latin *hospitium*, from *hospes* 'host, guest'.

hospitable /hospittəb'l, hosspitəb'l/ > *adjective* 1 showing or inclined to show hospitality. 2 (of an environment) pleasant and favourable for living in.
DERIVATIVES – **hospitably** *adverb*.

hospital > *noun* 1 an institution providing medical and surgical treatment and nursing care for sick or injured people. 2 historical a hospice, especially one run by the Knights Hospitallers.
COMBINATIONS – **hospital corners** overlapping folds used to tuck sheets neatly and securely under the mattress at the corners. **hospital trust** a UK National Health Service hospital which has opted to

withdraw from local authority control and be managed by a trust instead.
ORIGIN – Latin *hospitale*, form of *hospitalis* 'hospitable', from *hospes* 'host, guest'.

hospitalise (also **hospitalize**) > *verb* admit or cause (someone) to be admitted to hospital for treatment.
DERIVATIVES – **hospitalisation** *noun*.

hospitality > *noun* the friendly and generous treatment of guests or strangers.

hospitaller (US **hospitaler**) > *noun* 1 a member of a charitable religious order. 2 (**Hospitaller** or **Knights Hospitaller**) historical a member of the Knights of the Order of the Hospital of St John of Jerusalem, a military and religious order founded in the 11th century.

host¹ > *noun* 1 a person who receives or entertains guests. 2 the presenter of a television or radio programme. 3 a person, place, or organisation that holds and organises an event to which others are invited. 4 Biology an animal or plant on or in which a parasite lives. 5 the recipient of transplanted tissue or a transplanted organ. > *verb* act as host at (an event) or for (a television or radio programme).
ORIGIN – Old French *hoste*, from Latin *hospes* 'host, guest'.

host² > *noun* (**a host** or **hosts of**) a large number of.
ORIGIN – Latin *hostis* 'stranger, enemy', later 'army'.

host³ > *noun* (**the Host**) the bread consecrated in the Eucharist.
ORIGIN – Latin *hostia* 'victim'.

hosta /hostə/ > *noun* a shade-tolerant plant with ornamental foliage.
ORIGIN – Latin, named after the Austrian physician Nicolaus T. *Host* (1761–1834).

hostage > *noun* a person seized or held in order to induce others to comply with a demand or condition.
IDIOMS – **a hostage to fortune** an act or remark regarded as unwise because it invites trouble in the future.
ORIGIN – Old French, from Latin *obses* 'hostage'.

hostel > *noun* an establishment which provides cheap food and lodging for students, workers, travellers, etc.
ORIGIN – Old French, from Latin *hospitale*.

hostelling (US **hosteling**) > *noun* the practice of staying in youth hostels when travelling.
DERIVATIVES – **hosteller** *noun*.

hostelry > *noun* (pl. **hostelries**) archaic or humorous an inn or pub.

hostess > *noun* 1 a female host. 2 a woman employed to welcome and entertain customers at a nightclub or bar. 3 a stewardess on an aircraft, train, etc.

hostile > *adjective* 1 showing or feeling aggressive opposition; antagonistic. 2 of or

belonging to a military enemy. 3 (of a takeover bid) opposed by the company to be bought.
DERIVATIVES – **hostilely** *adverb*.
SYNONYMS – 1 antagonistic, averse, inimical, opposed, unfriendly.
ANTONYMS – 1 friendly.
ORIGIN – Latin *hostilis*, from *hostis* 'stranger, enemy'.

hostility > *noun* (pl. **hostilities**) 1 hostile behaviour; unfriendliness or opposition. 2 (**hostilities**) acts of warfare.

hot > *adjective* (**hotter**, **hottest**) 1 having a high temperature. 2 feeling or producing an uncomfortable sensation of heat. 3 feeling or showing intense excitement, anger, lust, or other emotion. 4 currently popular, fashionable, or interesting. 5 informal (of goods) stolen and difficult to dispose of because easily identifiable. 6 (often **hot on**) informal very knowledgeable or skilful. 7 (**hot on**) informal strict about. > *verb* (**hotted**, **hotting**) (**hot up**) Brit. informal become or make more intense or exciting.
IDIOMS – **go hot and cold** experience a sudden feeling of fear or shock. **have the hots for** informal be sexually attracted to. **hot under the collar** informal angry or resentful. **in hot water** informal in trouble or disgrace. **make it** (or **things**) **hot for** informal stir up trouble for (someone).
DERIVATIVES – **hotly** *adverb* **hotness** *noun*.
SYNONYMS – *verb* 1 boiling, burning, fiery, roasting, searing, sizzling. 2 blistering, boiling, sultry, sweltering. 3 ardent, fervent, passionate.
COMBINATIONS – **hot air** informal empty or boastful talk. **hot-blooded** lustful or passionate. **hot button** N. Amer. informal an issue that is highly charged emotionally or politically. **hot cross bun** a bun marked with a cross, traditionally eaten on Good Friday. **hot-desking** the allocation of desks to office workers when they are required or on a rota system. **hot dog** a hot sausage served in a long, soft roll. **hot flush** (or chiefly N. Amer **hot flash**) a sudden feeling of feverish heat, especially as a symptom of the menopause. **hot key** Computing a key or combination of keys providing quick access to a function within a program. **hotline** a direct telephone line set up for a specific purpose. **hot pants** women's tight, brief shorts. **hotplate** a flat heated metal or ceramic surface on an electric cooker. **hot potato** informal a controversial and awkward issue. **the hot seat** informal 1 the position of a person who carries full responsibility for something. 2 N. Amer. the electric chair. **hot shoe** Photography a socket on a camera with direct electrical contacts for an attached flashgun or other accessory. **hot spot** 1 a small area with a relatively high temperature. 2 a place of significant activity

or danger. **hot stuff 1** informal a person or thing of outstanding talent or interest. **2** a sexually exciting person, book, etc. **hot-tempered** easily angered. **hot ticket** informal a person or thing that is much in demand. **hot tub** a large tub filled with hot aerated water, used for recreation or physical therapy. **hot-water bottle** (US also **hot-water bag**) a flat, oblong rubber container that is filled with hot water and used for warming a bed or part of the body.

hotbed > noun **1** a bed of earth heated by fermenting manure, for raising or forcing plants. **2** an environment promoting the growth of an activity or trend.

hotchpotch (N. Amer. **hodgepodge**) > noun a confused mixture.

SYNONYMS – jumble, melange, mishmash.

ORIGIN – variant of hotchpot, a legal term for the reunion and blending together of properties, from Old French hocher 'to shake' + pot 'pot'.

hotel > noun an establishment providing accommodation and meals for travellers and tourists.

USAGE – the normal pronunciation of **hotel** sounds the h-, which means that the word is preceded by the indefinite article **a** rather than **an**. For more information on this, see the note at AN.

ORIGIN – French, from Old French hostel.

hotelier > noun a person who owns or manages a hotel.

hotfoot > adverb in eager haste. > verb (**hotfoot it**) hurry eagerly.

hothead > noun an impetuous or quick-tempered person.

DERIVATIVES – **hot-headed** adjective.

hothouse > noun **1** a heated greenhouse. **2** an environment that encourages rapid growth or development. > verb educate (a child) to a higher level than is usual for their age.

hotpot (also **Lancashire hotpot**) > noun Brit. a casserole of meat and vegetables with a covering layer of sliced potato.

hot rod > noun a motor vehicle that has been specially modified to give it extra power and speed. > verb (**hot-rod**) **1** modify (a vehicle or other device) to make it faster or more powerful. **2** drive a hot rod.

DERIVATIVES – **hot-rodder** noun.

hotshot > noun informal an important or exceptionally able person.

Hottentot /hott'ntot/ > noun & adjective used to refer to the Khoikhoi peoples of South Africa and Namibia.

USAGE – the word **Hottentot** is now regarded as offensive with reference to people (where **Khoikhoi** or, specifically, **Nama**, are the standard terms) but is still standard when used in the names of some animals and plants.

ORIGIN – Dutch, perhaps a repetitive formula in a Khoikhoi dancing song, transferred by Dutch sailors to the people themselves, or from German hotteren-totteren 'stutter' (with reference to their click language).

hot-wire > verb informal start the engine of (a vehicle) by bypassing the ignition switch.

Houdini /hoōdeeni/ > noun a person skilled at escaping from desperate situations.

ORIGIN – from the name of Harry Houdini (Erik Weisz), American magician and escape artist (1874–1926).

hound > noun **1** a dog of a breed used for hunting. **2** a person keen in pursuit of something: a publicity hound. > verb harass or pursue relentlessly.

SYNONYMS – verb bother, harass, harry, pester, pursue.

houndstooth > noun a large check pattern with notched corners.

hour > noun **1** a period of time equal to a twenty-fourth part of a day and night; 60 minutes. **2** a time of day specified as an exact number of hours from midnight or midday. **3** a period set aside for a particular purpose or activity. **4** a point in time.

IDIOMS – **on the hour 1** at an exact hour, or on each hour, of the day or night. **2** after a period of one hour.

ORIGIN – Greek hōra 'season, hour'.

hourglass > noun a device with two connected glass bulbs containing sand that takes an hour to fall from the upper to the lower bulb. > adjective shaped like an hourglass: her hourglass figure.

houri /hoori/ > noun (pl. **houris**) **1** a beautiful young woman. **2** one of the virgin companions of the faithful in the Muslim Paradise.

ORIGIN – French, from an Arabic word meaning 'having eyes with a marked contrast of black and white'.

hourly > adjective **1** done or occurring every hour. **2** reckoned hour by hour. > adverb **1** every hour. **2** by the hour.

house > noun /howss/ **1** a building for human habitation. **2** a building in which animals live or in which things are kept: a reptile house. **3** a building devoted to a particular activity: a house of prayer. **4** a firm or institution: a fashion house. **5** a religious community occupying a particular building. **6** chiefly Brit. a body of pupils living in the same building at a boarding school. **7** a legislative or deliberative assembly. **8** (**the House**) (in the UK) the House of Commons or Lords; (in the US) the House of Representatives. **9** a dynasty. **10** (also **house music**) a style of fast popular dance music. **11** Astrology a twelfth division of the celestial sphere. > verb /howz/ **1** provide with shelter or accommodation; accommodate. **2** provide space for. **3** enclose or encase.

IDIOMS – **get on like a house on fire** informal have a very good and friendly relationship. **a house divided cannot stand** proverb a group or organisation weakened by internal disagreements will be unable to withstand external pressures. **keep house** run a household. **on the house** at the management's expense. **put one's house in order** make necessary reforms.

DERIVATIVES – **houseful** noun.

COMBINATIONS – **house arrest** the state of being kept as a prisoner in one's own house. **houseboat** a boat which is fitted for use as a dwelling. **houseboy** a boy or man employed to undertake domestic duties. **housecoat** a woman's long, loose robe for informal wear around the house. **housefly** a common small fly occurring in and around human habitation. **house husband** a man who lives with a partner and carries out the household duties traditionally done by a housewife. **houseleek** a succulent plant with rosettes of fleshy leaves and small pink flowers, growing on walls and roofs. **house lights** the lights in the auditorium of a theatre. **houseman 1** Brit. a house officer. **2** N. Amer. a houseboy. **housemaster** (or **housemistress**) a teacher in charge of a house at a boarding school. **house mouse** a common greyish-brown mouse found as a scavenger in human dwellings. **house officer** Brit. a recent medical graduate receiving supervised training in a hospital and acting as an assistant physician or surgeon. **house of God** a place of religious worship. **house plant** a plant which is grown indoors. **house-proud** attentive to, or preoccupied with, the care and appearance of one's home. **house sparrow** a common brown and grey sparrow that nests in the eaves and roofs of houses. **house style** a company's preferred manner of presentation and layout of written material. **house-to-house** performed at or taken to each house in turn. **house-train** chiefly Brit. train (a pet) to excrete outside the house. **house-warming** a party celebrating a move to a new home. **housework** regular work done in housekeeping, such as cleaning and cooking.

housebound > adjective unable to leave one's house, especially due to illness or old age.

housebreaking > noun the action of breaking into a building, especially in daytime, to commit a crime.

DERIVATIVES – **housebreaker** noun.

housefather (or **housemother**) > noun a person in charge of and living in a boarding school house or children's home.

household > noun a house and its occupants regarded as a unit.

DERIVATIVES – **householder** noun.

COMBINATIONS – **household name** (or **household word**) a famous person or thing.

Household Cavalry > *noun* the two cavalry regiments of the British army responsible for guarding the monarch.

household troops > *plural noun* (in the UK) troops nominally employed to guard the sovereign.

house-hunting > *noun* the process of seeking a house to buy or rent.
DERIVATIVES – **house-hunter** noun.

housekeeper > *noun* a person, typically a woman, employed to manage a household.
DERIVATIVES – **housekeeping** noun.

housemaid > *noun* a female domestic employee who cleans rooms.
COMBINATIONS – **housemaid's knee** inflammation of the fluid-filled cavity covering the kneecap, often due to excessive kneeling.

house martin > *noun* a black-and-white bird of the swallow family, nesting on buildings.

House of Commons > *noun* the elected chamber of Parliament in the UK.

House of Keys > *noun* the elected chamber of Tynwald, the parliament of the Isle of Man.

House of Lords > *noun* 1 the chamber of Parliament in the UK composed of peers and bishops. 2 a committee of specially qualified members of this chamber, appointed as the ultimate judicial appeal court of England and Wales.

House of Representatives > *noun* the lower house of the US Congress.

houseroom > *noun* space or accommodation in one's house.
IDIOMS – **not give something houseroom** Brit. be unwilling to have or consider something.

house-sit > *verb* live in and look after a house while its owner is away.
DERIVATIVES – **house-sitter** noun.

Houses of Parliament > *plural noun* the Houses of Lords and Commons in the UK regarded together.

housewife > *noun* (pl. **housewives**) a married woman whose main occupation is caring for her family and running the household.
DERIVATIVES – **housewifely** adjective **housewifery** noun.

housey-housey > *noun* Brit. old-fashioned term for BINGO.

housing > *noun* 1 houses and flats considered collectively. 2 the provision of a house or living quarters. 3 a rigid casing for a piece of equipment. 4 a groove cut in a piece of wood to allow another piece to be attached to it.
COMBINATIONS – **housing estate** Brit. a residential area planned and built as a unit.

hove chiefly Nautical past tense of HEAVE.

hovel > *noun* a small squalid or poorly constructed dwelling.
SYNONYMS – shack, shanty.

hover > *verb* 1 remain in one place in the air. 2 linger close at hand in an uncertain manner. 3 remain at or near a particular level. > *noun* an act of hovering.
COMBINATIONS – **hoverfly** a fly which hovers in the air and feeds on the nectar of flowers. **hoverport** a terminal for hovercraft.

hovercraft > *noun* (pl. same) a vehicle or craft that travels over land or water on a cushion of air.

how¹ > *adverb* 1 in what way or by what means. 2 in what condition or health. 3 to what extent or degree. 4 the way in which.
IDIOMS – **and how!** informal very much so. **how about?** would you like? **the how and why** the methods and reasons for doing something. **how do you do?** a formal greeting. **how many** what number. **how much** what amount or price. **how's that?** Cricket is the batsman out? (said to an umpire).

how² > *exclamation* a greeting attributed to North American Indians.
ORIGIN – perhaps from Sioux or Omaha.

howbeit > *adverb* archaic nevertheless.

howdah /**how**də/ > *noun* a seat for riding on the back of an elephant, usually having a canopy.
ORIGIN – Arabic, 'litter'.

howdy > *exclamation* N. Amer. an informal friendly greeting.
ORIGIN – alteration of how d'ye.

how-d'ye-do (also **how-de-do**) > *noun* informal an awkward or annoying situation.

however > *adverb* 1 used to introduce a statement contrasting with a previous one. 2 in whatever way. 3 to whatever extent.

howitzer /**how**itsər/ > *noun* a short gun for firing shells at a high angle.
ORIGIN – Dutch houwitser, from Czech houfnice 'catapult'.

howk /howk/ > *verb* chiefly Scottish dig out or up.

howl > *noun* 1 a long doleful cry uttered by an animal. 2 a loud cry of pain, amusement, etc. > *verb* make a howling sound.
SYNONYMS – *noun* 1 bay, yelp. 2 bellow, wail, yell. verb cry, wail, yelp.

howler > *noun* informal a ludicrous mistake.

howling > *adjective* informal great: *a howling success.*

howsoever formal or archaic > *adverb* to whatever extent. > *conjunction* in whatever way.

howzat > *exclamation* Cricket shortened form of *how's that*.

hoy > *exclamation* used to attract someone's attention. > *noun* Austral. a game resembling bingo, using playing cards.

hoya /**hoy**ə/ > *noun* a evergreen climbing shrub with ornamental foliage and waxy flowers, native to SE Asia and the Pacific.
ORIGIN – named after the English gardener Thomas *Hoy* (c.1750–c.1821).

hoyden /**hoy**d'n/ > *noun* dated a boisterous girl.
DERIVATIVES – **hoydenish** adjective.
ORIGIN – probably from Dutch heiden, denoting a rude man.

h.p. (also **HP**) > *abbreviation* 1 high pressure. 2 Brit. hire purchase. 3 horsepower.

HQ > *abbreviation* headquarters.

hr > *abbreviation* hour.

HRH > *abbreviation* Brit. Her (or His) Royal Highness.

HRT > *abbreviation* hormone replacement therapy.

Hs > *symbol* the chemical element hassium.

HT > *abbreviation* (electrical) high tension.

HTML > *noun* Computing Hypertext Mark-up Language.

HTTP > *abbreviation* Computing Hypertext Transport (or Transfer) Protocol.

hub > *noun* 1 the central part of a wheel, rotating on or with the axle. 2 the centre of an activity, region, or network.
COMBINATIONS – **hubcap** a cover for the hub of a motor vehicle's wheel.
ORIGIN – related to HOB.

hubbub > 1 *noun* a chaotic din caused by a crowd. 2 a busy, noisy situation.

hubby > *noun* (pl. **hubbies**) informal one's husband.

hubris /**hyoo**briss/ > *noun* excessive pride or self-confidence.
DERIVATIVES – **hubristic** adjective.
ORIGIN – Greek, originally denoting presumption towards or defiance of the gods, leading to nemesis.

huckleberry > *noun* the soft edible blue-black fruit of a low-growing North American plant of the heath family.
ORIGIN – probably originally a dialect name for the bilberry, from huckle 'hip, haunch' (because of the plant's jointed stems).

huckster > *noun* 1 a person who sells small items, either door-to-door or from a stall. 2 N. Amer. a person who uses aggressive selling techniques. > *verb* chiefly N. Amer. 1 promote or sell aggressively. 2 bargain.
DERIVATIVES – **hucksterism** noun.

huddle > *verb* 1 crowd together. 2 curl one's body into a small space. > *noun* a number of people or things crowded together.
SYNONYMS – *verb* 1 flock, herd, throng. noun cluster, crowd, mass.

hue > *noun* 1 a colour or shade. 2 technical the attribute of a colour, dependent on its dominant wavelength, by virtue of which it is seen as red, green, etc. 3 character; aspect.

ORIGIN – Old English, 'form', 'appearance'.

hue and cry > *noun* a loud clamour or public outcry.

SYNONYMS – commotion, furore, uproar.

ORIGIN – from an Old French legal phrase *hu e cri*, literally 'outcry and cry'.

huff > *verb* (often **huff and puff**) **1** exhale noisily. **2** show one's annoyance in an obvious way. > *noun* a fit of petty annoyance.

huffy > *adjective* (**huffier**, **huffiest**) easily offended.

DERIVATIVES – **huffily** *adverb*.

hug > *verb* (**hugged**, **hugging**) **1** squeeze or hold tightly in one's arms. **2** keep close to: *a few craft hugged the shore.* > *noun* an act of hugging.

DERIVATIVES – **huggable** *adjective*.

SYNONYMS – *verb* **1** clasp, cuddle, embrace. *noun* cuddle, embrace, squeeze.

huge > *adjective* (**huger**, **hugest**) extremely large.

DERIVATIVES – **hugely** *noun* **hugeness** *noun*.

SYNONYMS – colossal, enormous, gigantic, immense, massive.

ANTONYMS – diminutive, tiny.

hugger-mugger > *adjective* **1** confused. **2** secret. > *noun* **1** confusion. **2** secrecy.

ORIGIN – probably related to **HUDDLE** and to dialect *mucker* 'hoard money, conceal'.

Huguenot /**hyoo**gənō/ > *noun* a French Protestant of the 16th–17th centuries.

wordpower facts

Huguenot

The origin of the French name **Huguenot** was the Swiss German word *Eidgenoss*, meaning 'confederate' (from *Eid* 'oath' + *Genoss* 'associate'). In French this became *eiguenot*, and it was then further altered by association with the name of a mayor of Geneva, Besançon *Hugues*. Largely Calvinist, the Huguenots suffered severe persecution at the hands of the Catholic majority in France. They were granted freedom of worship by the Edict of Nantes of 1598, but this was only a temporary reprieve. Persecution intensified under both Cardinal Richelieu and Louis XIV, who revoked the Edict of Nantes, and many thousands of Huguenots were forced to flee from France, settling permanently elsewhere.

hui /**hoo**i/ > *noun* (pl. **huis** or **huies**) NZ a large social or ceremonial gathering.

ORIGIN – Maori.

hula /**hoo**lə/ (also **hula-hula**) > *noun* a dance performed by Hawaiian women, characterised by undulating hips and symbolic gestures.

COMBINATIONS – **hula hoop** (also US trademark **Hula-Hoop**) a large hoop spun round the body by gyrating the hips.

ORIGIN – Hawaiian.

hulk > *noun* **1** an old ship stripped of fittings and permanently moored. **2** a large or clumsy boat, object, or person.

ORIGIN – Old English *hulc* 'fast ship', related to Greek *holkas* 'cargo ship'.

hulking > *adjective* informal very large or clumsy.

hull[1] > *noun* the main body of a ship or other vessel, including the bottom, sides, and deck but not the superstructure, engines, and other fittings.

hull[2] > *noun* **1** the outer covering of a fruit or seed. **2** the green calyx of a strawberry or raspberry. > *verb* remove the hulls from.

hullabaloo > *noun* informal a commotion or uproar.

hullo > *exclamation* variant spelling of **HELLO**.

hum > *verb* (**hummed**, **humming**) **1** make a low, steady continuous sound like that of a bee. **2** sing with closed lips. **3** informal be in a state of great activity. **4** Brit. informal smell unpleasant. > *noun* a low, steady continuous sound.

IDIOMS – **hum and haw** (or **ha**) Brit. be indecisive; vacillate.

DERIVATIVES – **hummable** *adjective* **hummer** *noun*.

human > *adjective* **1** of, relating to, or characteristic of humankind. **2** showing the better qualities of humankind, such as sensitivity. > *noun* a human being.

WORDFINDER – anthropology (*the study of humankind*), anthropomorphism (*attributing human characteristics to something*); *early humans:* Australopithecus, Cro-Magnon, Homo erectus, Homo habilis, Neanderthal.

DERIVATIVES – **humanly** *adjective* **humanness** *noun*.

COMBINATIONS – **human interest** the aspect of a news story concerned with the experiences or emotions of individuals. **human nature** the general characteristics, feelings, and traits of people. **human rights** rights which are believed to belong justifiably to every person.

ORIGIN – Latin *humanus*, from *homo* 'man, human being'.

human being > *noun* a man, woman, or child of the species Homo sapiens.

humane /**hyoo**mayn/ > *adjective* **1** having or showing compassion or benevolence. **2** formal (of a branch of learning) intended to civilise.

DERIVATIVES – **humanely** *adverb* **humaneness** *noun*.

SYNONYMS – **1** benevolent, benign, compassionate, kind, magnanimous.

ANTONYMS – **1** brutal, cruel.

ORIGIN – the earlier form of **HUMAN**, restricted to the senses above in the 18th century.

humanise (also **humanize**) > *verb* **1** make more humane. **2** give (something) a human character.

DERIVATIVES – **humanisation** *noun*.

humanism > *noun* **1** a system of thought which attaches prime importance to human rather than divine or supernatural matters. **2** a Renaissance cultural movement which turned away from medieval scholasticism and revived interest in ancient Greek and Roman thought.

DERIVATIVES – **humanist** *noun & adjective* **humanistic** *adjective*.

humanitarian /hyoomanni**tair**iən/ > *adjective* concerned with or seeking to promote human welfare. > *noun* a humanitarian person.

DERIVATIVES – **humanitarianism** *noun*.

USAGE – in sentences such as *this is the worst humanitarian disaster this country has seen*, **humanitarian** is used loosely to mean 'human'. This use is quite common, especially in journalism, but is not generally considered good style.

humanity > *noun* (pl. **humanities**) **1** humankind. **2** the condition of being human. **3** compassion or benevolence. **4** (**humanities**) learning or literature concerned with human culture.

humankind > *noun* human beings considered collectively.

humanoid /**hyoo**mənoyd/ > *adjective* having human characteristics. > *noun* a humanoid being.

humble > *adjective* (**humbler**, **humblest**) **1** having or showing a modest or low estimate of one's own importance. **2** of low rank. **3** of modest pretensions or dimensions: *humble beginnings.* > *verb* lower in dignity or importance.

IDIOMS – **eat humble pie** make a humble apology and accept humiliation. [ORIGIN – *humble pie* is from a pun based on *umbles* 'offal', considered inferior food.]

DERIVATIVES – **humbly** *adverb*.

SYNONYMS – *adjective* **1** meek, modest, self-effacing. **2** common, ordinary.

ANTONYMS – *adjective* **1** arrogant, proud.

ORIGIN – Latin *humilis* 'low, lowly', from *humus* 'ground'.

humblebee > *noun* dated a bumblebee.

humbug > *noun* **1** deceptive or false talk or behaviour. **2** a hypocrite. **3** Brit. a boiled peppermint sweet. > *verb* (**humbugged**, **humbugging**) deceive; trick.

DERIVATIVES – **humbuggery** *noun*.

humdinger /hum**ding**ər/ > *noun* informal a

remarkable or outstanding person or thing of its kind.

humdrum > *adjective* dull or monotonous. > *noun* monotonous routine.

humectant /hyoo**mek**tənt/ > *adjective* retaining or preserving moisture. > *noun* a substance used to reduce the loss of moisture.

ORIGIN – from Latin *humectare* 'moisten'.

humerus /**hyoo**mərəss/ > *noun* (pl. **humeri** /**hyoo**mərī/) Anatomy the bone of the upper arm or forelimb, between the shoulder and the elbow.

DERIVATIVES – **humeral** *adjective*.

ORIGIN – Latin, 'shoulder'.

humid /**hyoo**mid/ > *adjective* marked by a high level of water vapour in the atmosphere.

WORDFINDER – hygrometer (*instrument for measuring humidity*), hygroscope (*instrument which indicates humidity*).

DERIVATIVES – **humidity** noun **humidly** *adverb*.

SYNONYMS – clammy, muggy, steamy, sticky, sultry.

ORIGIN – Latin *humidus*, from *humere* 'be moist'.

humidify > *verb* (**humidifies, humidified**) increase the level of moisture in (the air).

DERIVATIVES – **humidification** noun **humidifier** noun.

humidor /**hyoo**midor/ > *noun* an airtight container for keeping cigars or tobacco moist.

humiliate > *verb* injure the dignity and self-respect of (someone).

DERIVATIVES – **humiliating** adjective **humiliatingly** adverb **humiliation** noun **humiliator** noun.

SYNONYMS – degrade, humble, shame.

humility > *noun* a humble view of one's own importance.

SYNONYMS – meekness, modesty, self-effacement.

ANTONYMS – arrogance.

ORIGIN – Latin *humilitas*, from *humilis* 'low, lowly'.

hummingbird > *noun* a small long-billed American bird able to hover by beating its wings extremely fast.

hummock > *noun* a hillock or mound.

DERIVATIVES – **hummocky** *adjective*.

hummus* /**hoo**məss/ > *noun* a thick Middle Eastern dip made from ground chickpeas and sesame seeds.

*SPELLING – because there are several ways in which the original Arabic word is transliterated into English, there are several different English spellings: **hummus, houmous, hoummos,** and **humous** are all commonly used, and all are acceptable. **Hummus** is, however, more common than the others.

ORIGIN – Arabic.

humongous /hyoo**mung**gəss/ (also **humungous**) > *adjective* informal enormous.

ORIGIN – perhaps based on **HUGE** and **MONSTROUS**, influenced by the stress pattern of *stupendous*.

humor > *noun* US spelling of **HUMOUR**.

humoral /**hyoo**mərəl/ > *adjective* Medicine of or relating to the body fluids.

ORIGIN – Latin *humoralis*, from *humor* 'moisture'.

humoresque /hyoomə**resk**/ > *noun* a short, lively piece of music.

ORIGIN – German *Humoreske*, from *Humor* 'humour'.

humorist > *noun* a humorous writer, performer, or artist.

humorous* > *adjective* **1** funny; causing amusement. **2** having or showing a sense of humour.

DERIVATIVES – **humorously** *adverb*.

*SPELLING – *-or-* not *-our-*: hum*or*ous.

SYNONYMS – **1** amusing, comical, droll, funny, hilarious. **2** amusing, funny, jocular, witty.

---

wordpower facts

Humour

The word **humour** entered English from Old French in the 14th century. Ultimately it comes from the Latin word *humor*, meaning 'moisture', from *humere* 'be moist' (**humid** is from the same root). The original sense in English was 'bodily fluid', surviving still today in the medical terms **aqueous humour** and **vitreous humour**, fluids present in the eyeball. In the Middle Ages it was believed that the relative proportions of the four bodily fluids known as the **cardinal humours**, blood, phlegm, choler, and melancholy, affected a person's general physical and mental health. This idea led, in the 16th century, to the use of **humour** in the senses 'state of mind, mood' and 'whim, fancy'. Use of the verb, in the sense 'to indulge the whim of', followed, and by the end of the 16th century the current core sense, 'the quality of being amusing or comic', had become established.

---

humour (US **humor**) > *noun* **1** the quality of being amusing or comic. **2** a state of mind. **3** (also **cardinal humour**) historical each of four fluids of the body (blood, phlegm, yellow bile or choler, and black bile or melancholy), formerly believed to control a person's physical and mental qualities. > *verb* comply with the wishes or whims of (someone).

IDIOMS – **out of humour** in a bad mood.

DERIVATIVES – **humourless** *adjective*.

hump > *noun* **1** a rounded protuberance found on the back of a camel or other animal or as an abnormality on a person's back. **2** a rounded raised mass of earth or land. > *verb* **1** informal lift or carry with difficulty. **2** make hump-shaped. **3** vulgar slang have sexual intercourse with.

IDIOMS – **get the hump** Brit. informal become annoyed or sulky. **over the hump** informal past the most difficult part of something.

DERIVATIVES – **humped** adjective **humpless** adjective **humpy** adjective.

humpback > *noun* another term for **HUNCHBACK**.

DERIVATIVES – **humpbacked** *adjective*.

COMBINATIONS – **humpback bridge** Brit. a small road bridge with a steep ascent and descent.

humpback whale > *noun* a baleen whale which has a hump (instead of a dorsal fin) and long white flippers.

humungous > *adjective* variant spelling of **HUMONGOUS**.

humus /**hyoo**məss/ > *noun* the organic component of soil, formed by the decomposition of leaves and other plant material.

DERIVATIVES – **humic** *adjective*.

ORIGIN – Latin, 'soil'.

Hun > *noun* **1** a member of an Asiatic people who invaded Europe in the 4th–5th centuries. **2** informal, derogatory a German (especially in military contexts during the First and Second World Wars).

ORIGIN – Greek *Hounnoi*.

hunch > *verb* raise (one's shoulders) and bend the top of one's body forward. > *noun* a feeling or guess based on intuition.

SYNONYMS – *noun* feeling, inkling, intuition, premonition, presentiment.

hunchback > *noun* **1** a deformed back in the shape of a hump, often caused by collapse of a vertebra. **2** often offensive a person with such a deformity.

DERIVATIVES – **hunchbacked** *adjective*.

hundred > *cardinal number* (pl. **hundreds** or (with numeral or quantifying word) same) **1** ten more than ninety; 100. (Roman numeral: **c** or **C**.) **2** (**hundreds**) informal an unspecified large number. **3** used to express whole hours in the twenty-four-hour system. > *noun* Brit. historical a subdivision of a county or shire, having its own court.

WORDFINDER – centenarian (*a person one hundred or more years old*), centenary (*hundredth anniversary*), centennial (*relating to a hundredth anniversary*).

IDIOMS – **a** (or **one**) **hundred per cent 1** entirely. **2** informal completely fit and healthy: *she didn't feel one hundred per cent.* **3** informal maximum effort and commitment.

DERIVATIVES – **hundredfold** adjective & adverb **hundredth** ordinal number.

COMBINATIONS – **hundreds and thousands** Brit. tiny sugar beads of varying colours used for decorating cakes and desserts.

hundredweight > *noun* **1** (also **long hundredweight**) Brit. a unit of weight equal to 112 lb (about 50.8 kg). **2** (also **short hundredweight**) US a unit of weight equal to 100 lb (about 45.4 kg). **3** (also **metric hundredweight**) a unit of weight equal to 50 kg.

hung past and past participle of HANG. > *adjective* **1** having no political party with an overall majority: *a hung parliament.* **2** unable to agree on a verdict: *a hung jury.* **3** (**hung up**) informal emotionally confused or disturbed. **4** (**hung over**) suffering from a hangover.

Hungarian /hungˈgairiən/ > *noun* **1** a person from Hungary. **2** the official language of Hungary. > *adjective* relating to Hungary or Hungarians.

hunger > *noun* **1** a feeling of discomfort or weakness caused by lack of food, coupled with the desire to eat. **2** a strong desire. > *verb* (**hunger after** or **for**) have a strong desire for.

COMBINATIONS – **hunger strike** a prolonged refusal to eat, carried out as a protest by a prisoner.

hungry > *adjective* (**hungrier, hungriest**) **1** feeling or showing hunger. **2** (often **hungry for**) having a strong desire.

DERIVATIVES – **hungrily** adverb.

hunk > *noun* **1** a large piece cut or broken from something larger. **2** informal a sexually attractive man.

DERIVATIVES – **hunky** adjective.

hunker > *verb* **1** squat or crouch down low. **2** (**hunker down**) apply oneself seriously to a task.

hunkers > *plural noun* informal haunches.

hunky-dory > *adjective* informal excellent.

ORIGIN – *hunky* from Dutch *honk* 'home' (in games); the origin of *dory* is unknown.

hunt > *verb* **1** pursue and kill (a wild animal) for sport or food. **2** (also **hunt for** or **after**) try to find by diligent searching. **3** (**hunt down**) pursue and capture (someone). **4** (**hunted**) appearing alarmed or harassed as if being hunted. **5** (of a device) undergo a cyclic variation in its working speed. > *noun* **1** an act or the process of hunting. **2** an association of people who meet regularly to hunt animals as a sport.

DERIVATIVES – **hunting** noun.

COMBINATIONS – **hunting crop** a short, rigid riding whip with a handle at right angles to the stock and a long leather thong. **hunting ground** a place likely to be a fruitful source of something desired or sought. **hunt saboteur** a person who attempts to disrupt a hunt.

hunter > *noun* **1** a person or animal that hunts. **2** a watch with a hinged cover protecting the glass.

WORDFINDER – Orion (*constellation, the Hunter*).

DERIVATIVES – **huntress** noun.

COMBINATIONS – **hunter-gatherer** a member of a nomadic people who live chiefly by hunting and fishing, and harvesting wild food. **hunter's moon** the first full moon after a harvest moon.

Huntington's disease > *noun* a hereditary disease marked by degeneration of brain cells, causing chorea and progressive dementia.

ORIGIN – named after the US neurologist George *Huntington* (1851–1916).

huntsman > *noun* **1** a man who hunts. **2** a hunt official in charge of hounds.

hurdle > *noun* **1** each of a series of upright frames which athletes in a race must jump over. **2** (**hurdles**) a hurdle race. **3** an obstacle or difficulty. **4** a portable rectangular frame used as a temporary fence. > *verb* **1** run in a hurdle race. **2** jump over (a hurdle or other obstacle) while running. **3** enclose or fence off with hurdles.

DERIVATIVES – **hurdler** noun.

hurdy-gurdy /ˈhurdiɡurdi/ > *noun* (pl. **hurdy-gurdies**) **1** a musical instrument with a droning sound played by turning a handle, with keys worked by the other hand. **2** informal a barrel organ.

ORIGIN – probably imitative of the instrument's sound.

hurl > *verb* **1** throw or impel with great force. **2** utter (abuse) vehemently. > *noun* Scottish informal a ride in a vehicle.

SYNONYMS – *verb* **1** fling, pitch, toss.

hurley > *noun* **1** a stick used in the game of hurling. **2** another term for HURLING.

ORIGIN – from HURL.

hurling > *noun* an Irish game resembling hockey, played with a shorter stick with a broader oval blade.

hurly-burly > *noun* busy, boisterous activity.

Huron /ˈhyooron/ > *noun* (pl. same or **Hurons**) a member of a confederation of native North American peoples formerly living in the region east of Lake Huron on the US–Canadian border.

ORIGIN – French, literally 'having hair standing in bristles on the head'.

hurrah (also **hooray, hurray**) > *exclamation* used to express joy or approval.

ORIGIN – alteration of HUZZA; perhaps originally a sailors' cry when hauling.

hurricane > *noun* a storm with a violent wind, in particular a tropical cyclone in the Caribbean.

COMBINATIONS – **hurricane lamp** an oil lamp with a glass chimney, designed to protect the flame even in high winds.

ORIGIN – Spanish *huracán*, probably from a word in Taino (an extinct Caribbean language) meaning 'god of the storm'.

hurry > *verb* (**hurries, hurried**) move or act quickly or more quickly. > *noun* great haste; urgency.

IDIOMS – **in a hurry 1** rushed; in a rushed manner. **2** informal easily; readily: *an experience you won't forget in a hurry.*

DERIVATIVES – **hurried** adjective **hurriedly** adverb.

SYNONYMS – *verb* hasten, make haste, rush. *noun* bustle, haste, rush, urgency.

hurt > *verb* (past and past participle **hurt**) **1** cause or feel physical pain or injury. **2** cause or feel mental pain or distress. > *noun* injury or pain; harm.

SYNONYMS – *verb* **1** injure, pain, smart, wound. **2** distress, upset, wound.

ORIGIN – Old French *hurter*.

hurtful > *adjective* causing mental pain or distress.

DERIVATIVES – **hurtfully** adverb.

SYNONYMS – cruel, distressing, upsetting, wounding.

hurtle > *verb* move at great speed, especially in a wildly uncontrolled manner.

husband > *noun* a married man considered in relation to his wife. > *verb* use (resources) economically.

WORDFINDER – cuckold (*husband of an adulteress*), polyandry (*having more than one husband*).

ORIGIN – Old Norse *húsbóndi* 'master of a house'; early senses in English were 'manager of a household, steward' and 'farmer'.

husbandman > *noun* archaic a farmer.

husbandry > *noun* **1** the care, cultivation, and breeding of crops and animals. **2** management and conservation of resources.

hush > *verb* **1** make or become quiet. **2** (**hush up**) suppress public mention of (something). > *noun* a silence.

COMBINATIONS – **hush–hush** informal highly secret or confidential. **hush money** informal money paid to someone to prevent them from disclosing information.

ORIGIN – from obsolete *husht* 'silent', from an interjection *husht* 'quiet!'

husk > *noun* **1** the dry outer covering of some fruits or seeds. **2** a dry or rough discarded outer layer. > *verb* remove the husk from.

husky¹ > *adjective* (**huskier, huskiest**) **1** sounding low-pitched and slightly hoarse. **2** chiefly N. Amer. strong; hefty.

DERIVATIVES – **huskily** adverb **huskiness** noun.

husky² > *noun* (pl. **huskies**) a powerful breed of dog with a thick double coat, used in the Arctic for pulling sledges.

ORIGIN – first used to denote the Eskimo

language or an Eskimo: from a North American dialect.

huss /huss/ > *noun* Brit. a dogfish.

hussar /hoozaar/ > *noun* historical (except in titles) a soldier in a light cavalry regiment which adopted a dress uniform modelled on that of the Hungarian light horsemen of the 15th century.
ORIGIN – Hungarian *huszár*, from Italian *corsaro* 'corsair'.

hussy > *noun* (pl. **hussies**) dated or humorous a promiscuous or immoral girl or woman.
ORIGIN – contraction of HOUSEWIFE.

hustings > *noun* (treated as pl. or sing.) **1** a meeting at which candidates in an election address potential voters. **2** (**the hustings**) political campaigning; electioneering.

wordpower facts

Hustings

In Old English the word *husting* denoted an assembly or council, especially one summoned by a king. It came from Old Norse *hústhing*, meaning 'household assembly held by a leader', from *hús* 'house' + *thing* 'assembly, parliament'. The term **hustings** was applied in Middle English to the highest court of the City of London, presided over by the Recorder of London. Subsequently it denoted the platform in the Guildhall where the Lord Mayor and aldermen presided, and then, by the 18th century, a temporary platform on which parliamentary candidates were nominated. From this the modern uses developed.

hustle > *verb* **1** push roughly; jostle. **2** informal, chiefly N. Amer. obtain illicitly or by forceful action or persuasion. **3** (**hustle into**) coerce or pressure into doing something. **4** N. Amer. informal engage in prostitution. > *noun* **1** busy movement and activity. **2** N. Amer. informal a fraud or swindle.
DERIVATIVES – **hustler** noun.
ORIGIN – Dutch *hutselen*.

hut > *noun* a small single-storey building of simple or crude construction.
ORIGIN – French *hutte*.

hutch > *noun* a box or cage for keeping rabbits or other small domesticated animals.
ORIGIN – first used in the sense 'storage chest': from Latin *hutica*.

Hutu /hootoo/ > *noun* (pl. same or **Hutus** or **Bahutu** /bəhootoo/) a member of a people forming the majority population in Rwanda and Burundi.
ORIGIN – a local name.

huzza /həzaa/ (also **huzzah**) > *exclamation* archaic used to express approval or delight.

hwyl /hooil/ > *noun* (in Welsh use) a stirring, emotional feeling.
ORIGIN – Welsh.

hyacinth /hīəsinth/ > *noun* **1** a plant with a spike of bell-shaped fragrant flowers. **2** another term for JACINTH.
ORIGIN – named after *Hyacinthus* in Greek mythology: Hyacinthus was a youth loved by the god Apollo but accidentally killed by him, from whose blood Apollo caused a flower to grow.

hyaena > *noun* variant spelling of HYENA.

hyalite /hīəlīt/ > *noun* a translucent, colourless variety of opal.
ORIGIN – from Greek *hualos* 'glass'.

hyaluronic acid /hīəlyooronnik/ > *noun* a viscous fluid carbohydrate present in connective tissue, synovial fluid, and the humours of the eye.
ORIGIN – from a blend of *hyaloid* 'glassy' and *uronic acid*.

hybrid /hībrid/ > *noun* **1** the offspring of two plants or animals of different species or varieties, such as a mule. **2** a thing made by combining two different elements.
WORDFINDER – *hybrid fruits:* loganberry, minneola, tangelo, ugli fruit; *hybrid animals:* liger (*offspring of male lion and tigress*), mule (*male donkey and mare*), tigon (*male tiger and lioness*).
COMBINATIONS – **hybrid vigour** the tendency of a cross-bred individual to show qualities superior to those of both parents.
ORIGIN – Latin *hybrida* 'offspring of a tame sow and wild boar, child of a freeman and slave, etc.'

hybridise (also **hybridize**) > *verb* cross-breed to produce hybrids.
DERIVATIVES – **hybridisation** noun.

hydra /hīdrə/ > *noun* a minute freshwater animal with a stalk-like tubular body and a ring of tentacles around the mouth.
ORIGIN – named after the *Hydra* of Greek mythology, a many-headed snake whose heads regrew as they were cut off: the hydra is so named because, if cut into pieces, each section can grow into a whole animal.

hydrangea /hīdraynjə/ > *noun* a shrub with large white, blue, or pink flowers, native to Asia and America.
ORIGIN – from Greek *hudro-* 'water' + *angeion* 'vessel' (from the cup shape of its seed capsule).

hydrant /hīdrənt/ > *noun* a water pipe with a nozzle to which a fire hose can be attached.

hydrate > *noun* /hīdrayt/ Chemistry a compound in which water molecules are chemically bound to another compound or an element. > *verb* /hīdrayt/ cause to absorb or combine with water.
DERIVATIVES – **hydration** noun.

hydraulic /hīdrollik/ > *adjective* **1** relating to a liquid moving in a confined space under pressure. **2** relating to the science of hydraulics. **3** (of cement) hardening under water.
DERIVATIVES – **hydraulically** adverb.
ORIGIN – Greek *hudraulikos*, from *hudro-* 'water' + *aulos* 'pipe'.

hydraulics > *plural noun* (usu. treated as sing.) the branch of science and technology concerned with the conveyance of liquids through pipes and channels.

hydride /hīdrīd/ > *noun* Chemistry a binary compound of hydrogen with a metal.

hydro > *noun* (pl. **hydros**) **1** Brit. a hotel or clinic originally providing hydropathic treatment. **2** a hydroelectric power plant.

hydro- (also **hydr-**) > *combining form* **1** water; relating to water: *hydraulic*. **2** Medicine affected with an accumulation of serous fluid: *hydrocephalus*. **3** Chemistry combined with hydrogen: *hydrocarbon*.
ORIGIN – from Greek *hudōr* 'water'.

hydrocarbon > *noun* a compound of hydrogen and carbon, such as any of those which are the chief components of petroleum and natural gas.

hydrocephalus /hīdrəseffələss, hīdrəkeffələss/ > *noun* a condition in which fluid accumulates in the brain.
DERIVATIVES – **hydrocephalic** adjective **hydrocephaly** noun.
ORIGIN – from Greek *hudro-* 'water' + *kephalē* 'head'.

hydrochloric acid > *noun* a strongly acidic solution of the gas hydrogen chloride.

hydrochloride > *noun* a compound of an organic base with hydrochloric acid.

hydrocortisone > *noun* a steroid hormone produced by the adrenal glands, used medicinally to treat inflammation and rheumatism.

hydrocyanic acid /hīdrōsīannik/ > *noun* a highly poisonous acidic solution of hydrogen cyanide.

hydrodynamics > *plural noun* (treated as sing.) the science of the forces acting on or exerted by fluids (especially liquids).
DERIVATIVES – **hydrodynamic** adjective.

hydroelectric > *adjective* relating to or denoting the generation of electricity using flowing water to drive a turbine which powers a generator.
DERIVATIVES – **hydroelectricity** noun.

hydrofoil > *noun* **1** a boat fitted with structures (known as foils) which lift the hull clear of the water at speed. **2** each of the foils of such a craft.

hydrogen /hīdrəjən/ > *noun* a colourless, odourless, highly flammable gas which is the lightest of the chemical elements.
COMBINATIONS – **hydrogen bomb** a nuclear bomb which derives its destructive power from the fusion of isotopes of hydrogen (deuterium and tritium). **hydrogen cyanide** a highly poisonous gas

or volatile liquid with an odour of bitter almonds, made by the action of acids on cyanides. **hydrogen peroxide** a colourless viscous liquid used in some disinfectants and bleaches. **hydrogen sulphide** a colourless poisonous gas with a smell of bad eggs, made by the action of acids on sulphides.

hydrogenate /hīdrojinayt/ > verb charge with or cause to combine with hydrogen.
DERIVATIVES – **hydrogenation** noun.

hydrogeology > noun the branch of geology concerned with underground or surface water.
DERIVATIVES – **hydrogeological** adjective **hydrogeologist** noun.

hydrography /hīdrogrəfi/ > noun the science of surveying and charting bodies of water.
DERIVATIVES – **hydrographer** noun **hydrographic** adjective.

hydroid /hīdroyd/ > noun Zoology an aquatic invertebrate animal of an order which includes the hydras and many corals.

hydrology /hīdrolləji/ > noun the science of the properties and distribution of water on the earth's surface.
DERIVATIVES – **hydrologic** adjective **hydrological** adjective **hydrologist** noun.

hydrolyse /hīdrəlīz/ (also **hydrolyze**) > verb Chemistry break down (a compound) by chemical reaction with water.

hydrolysis /hīdrollisiss/ > noun Chemistry the chemical breakdown of a compound due to reaction with water.
DERIVATIVES – **hydrolytic** adjective.

hydromassage > noun massage using jets of water.

hydromechanics > plural noun (treated as sing.) the mechanics of liquids; hydrodynamics.
DERIVATIVES – **hydromechanical** adjective.

hydrometer /hīdrommitər/ > noun an instrument for measuring the density of liquids.
DERIVATIVES – **hydrometric** adjective **hydrometry** noun.

hydropathy /hīdroppəthi/ > noun the treatment of illness through the use of water, either internally or externally.
DERIVATIVES – **hydropathic** adjective **hydropathist** noun.

hydrophilic /hīdrəfillik/ > adjective having a tendency to mix with, dissolve in, or be wetted by water.

hydrophobia > noun 1 extreme or irrational fear of water, especially as a symptom of rabies. 2 rabies.

hydrophobic > adjective 1 tending to repel or fail to mix with water. 2 of or suffering from hydrophobia.

hydrophone > noun a microphone which detects sound waves under water.

hydroplane > noun 1 a light, fast motor boat. 2 a fin-like attachment which enables a moving submarine to rise or fall in the water. 3 US a seaplane. > verb chiefly N. Amer. another term for AQUAPLANE.

hydroponics /hīdrəponniks/ > plural noun (treated as sing.) the growing of plants in sand, gravel, or liquid, with added nutrients but without soil.
DERIVATIVES – **hydroponic** adjective **hydroponically** adverb.
ORIGIN – from Greek hudōr 'water' + ponos 'labour'.

hydrosphere > noun the seas, lakes, and other waters of the earth's surface, considered collectively.

hydrostatic > adjective relating to the equilibrium of liquids and the pressure exerted by liquid at rest.
DERIVATIVES – **hydrostatics** plural noun.

hydrotherapy > noun 1 the therapeutic use of exercises in a pool. 2 another term for HYDROPATHY.
DERIVATIVES – **hydrotherapist** noun.

hydrothermal > adjective relating to the action of heated water in the earth's crust.
DERIVATIVES – **hydrothermally** adverb.
COMBINATIONS – **hydrothermal vent** an opening in the sea floor out of which very hot mineral-rich water flows.

hydrous > adjective containing water.

hydroxide > noun a compound containing the hydroxide ion OH⁻ or the group —OH.

hydroxyl /hīdroksīl/ > noun Chemistry the radical —OH, present in alcohols and many other organic compounds.

hyena /hīeenə/ (also **hyaena**) > noun a doglike carnivorous African mammal with long forelimbs and an erect mane.
ORIGIN – Greek huaina 'female pig' (probably because of the resemblance of the mane to a hog's bristles).

hygiene > noun conditions or practices that help to maintain health and prevent disease, especially cleanliness.
SYNONYMS – cleanliness, sanitation.
ORIGIN – from Greek hugieinē tekhnē 'art of health', from hugiēs 'healthy'.

hygienic* > adjective promoting or conducive to hygiene; sanitary.
DERIVATIVES – **hygienically** adverb.
*SPELLING – remember, i before e except after c: hygienic.
SYNONYMS – clean, sanitary, sterile.
ANTONYMS – unhygienic.

hygienist > noun a specialist in the promotion of hygiene.

hygrometer /hīgrommitər/ > noun an instrument for measuring humidity.

DERIVATIVES – **hygrometric** adjective **hygrometry** noun.
ORIGIN – from Greek hugros 'wet'.

hygroscope /hīgrəskōp/ > noun an instrument which indicates (though does not necessarily measure) the humidity of the air.

hygroscopic > adjective tending to absorb moisture from the air.
DERIVATIVES – **hygroscopically** adverb.

hying present participle of HIE.

hymen /hīmən/ > noun a membrane which partially closes the opening of the vagina and whose presence is traditionally taken to indicate virginity.
ORIGIN – Greek humēn 'membrane'.

hymeneal /hīmineeəl/ > adjective literary of or concerning marriage.
ORIGIN – from Hymen, the Greek god of marriage.

hymenopteran /hīmənoptərən/ > noun an insect of a large group (the order Hymenoptera) including the bees, wasps, and ants, having four transparent wings.
DERIVATIVES – **hymenopterous** adjective.
ORIGIN – from Greek humenopteros 'membrane-winged'.

hymn > noun a religious song of praise, especially a Christian song in praise of God. > verb 1 sing hymns. 2 praise or celebrate.
ORIGIN – Greek humnos 'ode or song in praise'.

hymnal /himn'l/ > noun a book of hymns. > adjective relating to hymns.

hymnary /himnəri/ > noun (pl. **hymnaries**) another term for HYMNAL.

hymnody /himnədi/ > noun the singing or composition of hymns.
ORIGIN – Greek humnōidia, from humnos 'hymn' + ōidē 'song'.

hyoscine /hīəseen/ > noun a poisonous substance found in plants and used to prevent motion sickness and as a preoperative medication for examination of the eye.
ORIGIN – from Greek huoskamos 'henbane'.

hype¹ informal > noun 1 extravagant or intensive publicity or promotion. 2 a deception or hoax. > verb promote or publicise intensively or extravagantly.

hype² > verb (**be hyped up**) informal be stimulated or excited.
ORIGIN – abbreviation of HYPODERMIC: first used in sense 'hypodermic needle, drug addict'.

hyper > adjective informal hyperactive or unusually energetic.

hyper- > prefix 1 over; beyond; above: hypersonic. 2 excessively; above normal: hyperthyroidism.

wordpower facts

Hyper- and hypo-

The prefix **hyper-** 'over, above' (from Greek *huper*) looks and sounds very similar to its opposite, **hypo-** 'under, below' (from Greek *hupo*). Both have been used to form many technical terms, often with the same suffixes, resulting in potential confusion. For example, someone with **hypertension**, 'high blood pressure', has the opposite problem from someone with **hypotension** 'low blood pressure'. Similar confusable pairs include **hyperthermia** and **hypothermia**, **hyperglycaemia** and **hypoglycaemia**. **Hypocritical** 'showing hypocrisy' should not be confused with **hypercritical** 'excessively critical'. **Hypocrisy** has come via French and Latin from Greek *hupokrisis* 'acting a theatrical part', from *hupo* and *krinein* 'decide, judge'.

hyperactive > *adjective* abnormally or extremely active.
DERIVATIVES – **hyperactivity** *noun*.

hyperaemia /hīpəreemiə/ (US **hyperemia**) > *noun* Medicine an excess of blood in an organ or other part of the body.

hyperbaric /hīpərbarrik/ > *adjective* (of gas) at a pressure greater than normal.
ORIGIN – from HYPER- + Greek *baros* 'heavy'.

hyperbola /hīperbələ/ > *noun* (pl. **hyperbolas** or **hyperbolae** /hīperbəlee/) a symmetrical open curve such as results when a cone is intersected by a plane that makes a smaller angle with the axis of the cone than does the side of the cone.
ORIGIN – Latin, from Greek *huperbolē* (see HYPERBOLE).

hyperbole /hīperbəli/ > *noun* deliberate exaggeration, not meant to be taken literally.
DERIVATIVES – **hyperbolical** *adjective* **hyperbolically** *adverb*.
ORIGIN – Greek *huperbolē* 'excess', from *ballein* 'to throw'.

hyperbolic /hīpərbollik/ > *adjective* 1 (of language) deliberately exaggerated. 2 relating to a hyperbola.

hyperborean /hīpərboreeən/ > *noun* 1 literary an inhabitant of the extreme north. 2 (**Hyperborean**) Greek Mythology a member of a race living in a land of sunshine beyond the north wind. > *adjective* literary relating to the extreme north.
ORIGIN – from Greek *huper* 'beyond' + *boreas* 'north wind'.

hypercorrection > *noun* the use of an erroneous word form or pronunciation based on a false analogy with a correct or prestigious form, such as the use of *I* in *he invited my husband and I to lunch*.
DERIVATIVES – **hypercorrect** *adjective*.

hypercritical > *adjective* excessively and unreasonably critical.

hyperdrive > *noun* (in science fiction) a supposed propulsion system for travel in hyperspace.

hyperglycaemia /hīpərglīseemiə/ (US **hyperglycemia**) > *noun* an excess of glucose in the bloodstream, often associated with diabetes mellitus.
DERIVATIVES – **hyperglycaemic** *adjective*.

hypericum /hīperrikəm/ > *noun* a yellow-flowered plant of a family that includes St John's wort and rose of Sharon.
ORIGIN – Greek *hupereikon*, from *huper* 'over' + *ereikē* 'heath'.

hyperinflation > *noun* monetary inflation occurring at a very high rate.

hyperkinesis /hīpərkineesiss, hīpərkīneesiss/ (also **hyperkinesia**) > *noun* 1 Medicine muscle spasm. 2 Psychiatry a disorder of children marked by hyperactivity and inability to concentrate.
DERIVATIVES – **hyperkinetic** *adjective*.

hyperlink > *noun* Computing a link from a hypertext document to another location, activated by clicking on a highlighted word or image.

hyperlipaemia /hīpərlipeemiə/ (US **hyperlipemia**) > *noun* Medicine an abnormally high concentration of fats or lipids in the blood.

hypermarket > *noun* chiefly Brit. a very large supermarket.

hypermedia > *noun* Computing an extension to hypertext providing multimedia facilities, such as sound and video.

hyperreal > *adjective* 1 exaggerated in comparison to reality. 2 (of art) extremely realistic in detail.

hypersensitive > *adjective* abnormally or excessively sensitive.

hypersonic > *adjective* 1 relating to speeds of more than five times the speed of sound (Mach 5). 2 relating to sound frequencies above about a thousand million hertz.

hyperspace > *noun* 1 space of more than three dimensions. 2 (in science fiction) a notional space–time continuum in which it is possible to travel faster than light.

hypertension > *noun* abnormally high blood pressure.
DERIVATIVES – **hypertensive** *adjective*.

hypertext > *noun* Computing a software system for text files allowing extensive links to be made between sections of a file or with other files.

hyperthermia /hīpərthermiə/ > *noun* the condition of having a body temperature greatly above normal.

hyperthyroidism /hīpərthīroydiz'm/ > *noun* overactivity of the thyroid gland, resulting in a rapid heartbeat and an increased rate of metabolism.
DERIVATIVES – **hyperthyroid** *adjective*.

hypertonic /hīpərtonnik/ > *adjective* 1 having a higher osmotic pressure than a particular fluid. 2 having abnormally high muscle tone.
DERIVATIVES – **hypertonia** *noun*.

hypertrophy /hīpertrəfi/ > *noun* enlargement of an organ or tissue resulting from an increase in size of its cells.
DERIVATIVES – **hypertrophic** *adjective* **hypertrophied** *adjective*.
ORIGIN – from HYPER- + Greek *-trophia* 'nourishment'.

hyperventilate > *verb* 1 breathe at an abnormally rapid rate. 2 be or become overexcited.
DERIVATIVES – **hyperventilation** *noun*.

hypha /hīfə/ > *noun* (pl. **hyphae** /hīfee/) Botany each of the branching filaments that make up the mycelium of a fungus.
ORIGIN – Greek *huphē* 'web'.

hyphen /hīfən/ > *noun* the sign (-) used to join words to indicate that they have a combined meaning or that they are grammatically linked, or to indicate word division at the end of a line.
ORIGIN – from Greek *huphen* 'together'.

hyphenate > *verb* write or separate with a hyphen.
DERIVATIVES – **hyphenation** *noun*.

hypnagogic /hipnəgojik/ (also **hypnogogic**) > *adjective* relating to the state immediately before falling asleep.
ORIGIN – from Greek *hupnos* 'sleep' + *agōgos* 'leading'.

hypnosis > *noun* the induction of a state of consciousness in which a person loses the power of voluntary action and is highly responsive to suggestion or direction.
ORIGIN – from Greek *hupnos* 'sleep'.

hypnotherapy > *noun* the use of hypnosis as a therapeutic technique.
DERIVATIVES – **hypnotherapist** *noun*.

hypnotic > *adjective* 1 of, producing, or relating to hypnosis. 2 having a compelling or soporific effect. 3 (of a drug) sleep-inducing. > *noun* a sleep-inducing drug.
DERIVATIVES – **hypnotically** *adverb*.
SYNONYMS – *adjective* 2 magnetic, mesmeric, soporific, spellbinding.

hypnotise (also **hypnotize**) > *verb* produce a state of hypnosis in (someone).

hypnotism > *noun* the study or practice of hypnosis.
DERIVATIVES – **hypnotist** *noun*.

hypo¹ > *noun* Photography the chemical sodium thiosulphate (formerly called hyposulphite) used as a photographic fixer.

hypo² > *noun* (pl. **hypos**) informal a hypodermic.

hypo³ > *noun* (pl. **hypos**) informal an attack of hypoglycaemia.

hypo- (also **hyp-**) > *prefix* **1** under: *hypodermic*. **2** below normal: *hypoglycaemia*. **3** slightly: *hypomanic*.
NOTE – the prefix **hypo-** 'under, below' looks and sounds very similar to its opposite, **hyper-** 'over, above': **hypothermia** implies 'not enough heat' while **hyperthermia** implies 'too much heat'.
ORIGIN – from Greek *hupo* 'under'.

hypo-allergenic > *adjective* unlikely to cause an allergic reaction.

hypocaust /hīpəkawst/ > *noun* an ancient Roman heating system, comprising a hollow space under the floor into which hot air was directed.
ORIGIN – Greek *hupokauston* 'place heated from below'.

hypochlorite /hīpəklorīt/ > *noun* a salt of a weak acid (**hypochlorous acid**) formed when chlorine dissolves in cold water.

hypochondria /hīpəkondriə/ > *noun* abnormal chronic anxiety about one's health.
ORIGIN – Greek *hupokhondria*, denoting the soft body area below the ribs, thought to be the seat of melancholy.

hypochondriac > *noun* a person who is abnormally anxious about their health. > *adjective* (also **hypochondriacal**) related to or affected by hypochondria.
SYNONYMS – valetudinarian.

hypocoristic /hīpəkəristik/ > *adjective* used as a pet name or diminutive form of a name.
ORIGIN – from Greek *hupokorisma*, from *hupokorizesthai* 'play the child'.

hypocotyl /hīpəkottil/ > *noun* Botany the part of the stem of an embryo plant between the stalks of the cotyledons and the root.
ORIGIN – from **HYPO-** + **COTYLEDON**.

hypocrisy > *noun* (pl. **hypocrisies**) the practice of claiming to have higher standards or beliefs than is the case.
SYNONYMS – cant, falsity, humbug, sanctimoniousness.
ORIGIN – Greek *hupokrisis* 'acting of a theatrical part'.

hypocrite* > *noun* a person who is given to hypocrisy.
DERIVATIVES – **hypocritical** *adjective* **hypocritically** *adverb*.
*SPELLING – hypo- not hyper-: hypocrite.
SYNONYMS – humbug, whited sepulchre; **Brit.** informal creeping Jesus.

hypodermic > *adjective* **1** relating to the region immediately beneath the skin. **2** used to inject beneath the skin. > *noun* a hypodermic needle, syringe, or injection.
DERIVATIVES – **hypodermically** *adverb*.
ORIGIN – from Greek *derma* 'skin'.

hypoglycaemia /hīpōglīseemiə/ (US **hypoglycemia**) > *noun* an abnormally low concentration of glucose in the blood.
DERIVATIVES – **hypoglycaemic** *adjective*.
NOTE – the prefix **hypo-** 'under, below' looks and sounds very similar to its opposite, **hyper-** 'over, above'. **hypoglycaemia** means 'not enough blood sugar' while **hyperglycaemia** means 'too much blood sugar'.

hypomania > *noun* a mild form of mania, marked by elation and hyperactivity.
DERIVATIVES – **hypomanic** *adjective*.

hypostasise (also **hypostasize**) > *verb* formal treat or represent as concrete reality.

hypostyle /hīpōstīl/ > *adjective* having a roof supported by pillars. > *noun* a building having such a roof.
ORIGIN – from Greek *hupo* 'under' + *stulos* 'column'.

hypotension > *noun* abnormally low blood pressure.
DERIVATIVES – **hypotensive** *adjective*.

hypotenuse /hīpottənyōōz/ > *noun* the longest side of a right-angled triangle, opposite the right angle.
ORIGIN – from Greek *hupoteinousa grammē* 'subtending line'.

hypothalamus /hīpəthaləməss/ > *noun* (pl. **hypothalami** /hīpəthaləmī/) a region of the forebrain below the thalamus, controlling body temperature, thirst, and hunger, and involved in sleep and emotional activity.
DERIVATIVES – **hypothalamic** *adjective*.

hypothecate /hīpothikayt/ > *verb* pledge (money) by law to a specific purpose.
DERIVATIVES – **hypothecation** *noun*.
ORIGIN – Latin *hypothecare* 'give as a pledge'.

hypothermia /hīpəthermiə/ > *noun* the condition of having an abnormally low body temperature.
ORIGIN – from Greek *thermē* 'heat'.

hypothesis /hīpothisiss/ > *noun* (pl. **hypotheses** /hīpothiseez/) a supposition made on the basis of limited evidence as a starting point for the investigation or explanation of a set of facts or phenomena.
SYNONYMS – **1** assumption, conjecture, supposition.
ORIGIN – Greek *hupothesis* 'foundation'.

hypothesise (also **hypothesize**) > *verb* put forward as a hypothesis.

hypothetical /hīpəthettik'l/ > *adjective* **1** of, based on, or serving as a hypothesis. **2** supposed but not necessarily real or true.
DERIVATIVES – **hypothetically** *adverb*.
SYNONYMS – assumed, conjectured, presumed, speculative, supposed.

hypothyroidism > *noun* abnormally low activity of the thyroid gland, resulting in retarded growth and mental development.
DERIVATIVES – **hypothyroid** *adjective*.

hypoventilation > *noun* breathing at an abnormally slow rate.

hypoxia /hīpoksiə/ > *noun* deficiency in the amount of oxygen reaching the tissues.
DERIVATIVES – **hypoxic** *adjective*.

hypsilophodont /hipsəloffədont/ > *noun* a small swift-running bipedal dinosaur of the late Jurassic and Cretaceous periods.
ORIGIN – from Greek *hupsilophos* 'high-crested' + *odous* 'tooth'.

hyrax /hīraks/ > *noun* a small short-tailed herbivorous mammal, found in Africa and Arabia.
ORIGIN – Greek *hurax* 'shrew-mouse'.

hyssop /hissəp/ > *noun* **1** a small bushy aromatic plant whose leaves are used in cookery and herbal medicine. **2** (in biblical use) a wild shrub whose twigs were used in ancient Jewish rites of purification.
ORIGIN – Greek *hyssōpos*, of Semitic origin.

hysterectomy /histərektəmi/ > *noun* (pl. **hysterectomies**) a surgical operation to remove all or part of the womb.
ORIGIN – from Greek *hustera* 'womb'.

hysteresis /histəreesiss/ > *noun* Physics the phenomenon by which the value of a physical property lags behind changes in the effect causing it, especially that involving magnetic induction and a magnetising force.
ORIGIN – Greek *husterēsis* 'shortcoming'.

hysteria > *noun* **1** a psychological disorder whose symptoms include volatile emotions and attention-seeking behaviour. **2** exaggerated or uncontrollable emotion or excitement.

hysteric > *noun* **1** (**hysterics**) wildly emotional behaviour. **2** (**hysterics**) informal uncontrollable laughter. **3** a person suffering from hysteria. > *adjective* hysterical.
ORIGIN – Greek *husterikos* 'of the womb', from *hustera* 'womb' (hysteria being thought to be associated with the womb).

hysterical > *adjective* **1** associated with or suffering from hysteria. **2** informal extremely funny.
DERIVATIVES – **hysterically** *adverb*.
SYNONYMS – **2** crazed, delirious, frenzied.

Hz > *abbreviation* hertz.

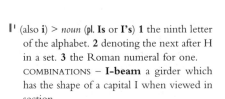

I¹ (also **i**) > *noun* (pl. **Is** or **I's**) **1** the ninth letter of the alphabet. **2** denoting the next after H in a set. **3** the Roman numeral for one.

COMBINATIONS – **I-beam** a girder which has the shape of a capital I when viewed in section.

I² > *pronoun* (**first person sing.**) used by a speaker to refer to himself or herself.

I³ > *abbreviation* (**I.**) Island(s) or Isle(s). > *symbol* the chemical element iodine.

IA > *abbreviation* Iowa.

IAEA > *abbreviation* International Atomic Energy Agency.

iambic Poetry > *adjective* of or using iambuses. > *noun* (**iambics**) verse using iambuses.

iambus /ˈīambəss/ (also **iamb**) > *noun* (pl. **iambuses** or **iambi** /ˈīambī/) Poetry a metrical foot consisting of one short (or unstressed) syllable followed by one long (or stressed) syllable.

ORIGIN – Greek *iambos* 'iambus, lampoon' (because the iambic meter was first used by Greek satirists).

-ian > *suffix* forming adjectives and nouns such as *antediluvian* and *Bostonian*.

ORIGIN – from French *-ien* or Latin *-ianus*.

-iasis > *suffix* variant form of **–ASIS**.

IATA /ˈīaatə/ > *abbreviation* International Air Transport Association.

iatrogenic /ˌīatrəˈjennik/ > *adjective* (of illness) caused by medical treatment.

ORIGIN – from Greek *iatros* 'physician'.

IB > *abbreviation* International Baccalaureate.

IBA > *abbreviation* Independent Broadcasting Authority.

Iberian /īˈbeeriən/ > *adjective* relating to Iberia (the peninsula containing Spain and Portugal). > *noun* a person from Iberia.

ibex /ˈībeks/ > *noun* (pl. **ibexes**) a wild mountain goat with long, thick, ridged horns.

ORIGIN – Latin.

IBF > *abbreviation* International Boxing Federation.

ibid. /ˈibid/ > *adverb* in the same source (referring to a previously cited work).

ORIGIN – abbreviation of Latin *ibidem* 'in the same place'.

ibis /ˈībiss/ > *noun* (pl. **ibises**) a large wading bird with a long downcurved bill, long neck, and long legs.

ORIGIN – Greek.

Ibizan /iˈbeethən/ > *noun* a person from Ibiza, the westernmost of the Balearic Islands. > *adjective* relating to Ibiza.

-ible > *suffix* forming adjectives: **1** able to be: *defensible*. **2** suitable for being: *edible*. **3** causing: *horrible*.

DERIVATIVES – **-ibility** *suffix* **-ibly** *suffix*.

IBM > *abbreviation* International Business Machines.

IBS > *abbreviation* irritable bowel syndrome.

ibuprofen /ˌībyooˈprōfen/ > *noun* a synthetic compound used as a painkiller and anti-inflammatory drug.

IC > *abbreviation* integrated circuit.

i/c > *abbreviation* **1** in charge of. **2** in command.

-ic > *suffix* **1** forming adjectives such as *Islamic*, *terrific*. **2** forming nouns such as *lyric*, *mechanic*. **3** Chemistry of an element in a higher valency: *ferric*. Compare with **–OUS**.

ORIGIN – from Latin *-icus* or Greek *-ikos*.

-ical > *suffix* forming adjectives: **1** corresponding to nouns or adjectives usually ending in *-ic* (such as *comical* corresponding to *comic*). **2** corresponding to nouns ending in *-y* (such as *pathological* corresponding to *pathology*).

DERIVATIVES – **-ically** *suffix*.

ICBM > *abbreviation* intercontinental ballistic missile.

ICC > *abbreviation* International Cricket Council.

ice > *noun* **1** frozen water, a brittle transparent crystalline solid. **2** chiefly Brit. an ice cream or water ice. **3** informal diamonds. > *verb* **1** decorate with icing. **2** (usu. **ice up** or **over**) become covered or blocked with ice. **3** N. Amer. informal kill.

WORDFINDER – floe, pack ice (*floating ice on the sea*), glacial (*of or relating to ice; icy*), glissade (*slide down an icy slope*); frappé (*drink served with crushed ice*), sorbet (*water ice made with fruit*).

IDIOMS – **break the ice** start conversation at the beginning of a social gathering or between strangers. **on thin ice** in a precarious or risky situation.

DERIVATIVES – **iced** *adjective*.

COMBINATIONS – **ice age** a period when ice sheets were unusually extensive across the earth's surface, in particular during the Pleistocene period. **ice axe** a small axe used by climbers for cutting footholds in ice. **icebox 1** a chilled container for keeping food cold. **2** Brit. a compartment in a refrigerator for making and storing ice. **3** US dated a refrigerator. **ice-breaker** a ship designed for breaking a channel through ice. **ice cap** a permanent covering of ice over a large area, especially on the polar region of a planet. **ice cream** a semi-soft frozen dessert made with sweetened and flavoured milk fat. **ice dancing** a form of ice skating incorporating choreographed dance moves based on ballroom dances. **ice field** a large permanent expanse of ice, especially in polar regions. **ice hockey** a form of hockey played on an ice rink between two teams of six skaters. **ice house** a building for storing ice. **ice lolly** (also **iced lolly**) Brit. a piece of flavoured water ice or ice cream on a stick. **ice pack** a bag filled with ice and applied to the body to reduce swelling or lower temperature. **ice pick** a small pick used by climbers or for breaking ice. **ice shelf** a floating sheet of ice attached to a land mass.

-ice > *suffix* forming nouns such as *service*, *police*, and abstract nouns such as *justice*.

ORIGIN – from Latin *-itia*, *-itius*, *-itium*.

iceberg > *noun* a large mass of ice floating in the sea.

WORDFINDER – calve (*split off from an iceberg*), growler (*small iceberg*).

IDIOMS – **the tip of the iceberg** the small perceptible part of a much larger situation or problem.

COMBINATIONS – **iceberg lettuce** a kind of lettuce having a dense round head of crisp pale leaves.

ORIGIN – Dutch *ijsberg* 'ice hill'.

Icelander > *noun* a person from Iceland.

Icelandic /īsˈlandik/ > *noun* the language of Iceland. > *adjective* relating to Iceland or its language.

Iceni /īˈseenī, -ni/ > *plural noun* a tribe of ancient Britons inhabiting an area of SE England, whose queen was Boudicca (Boadicea).

ice skate > *noun* a boot with a blade attached to the sole, used for skating on ice. > *verb* (**ice-skate**) skate on ice as a sport or pastime.

DERIVATIVES – **ice skater** *noun* **ice skating** *noun*.

I Ching /ee ˈching/ > *noun* an ancient Chinese manual of divination based on eight symbolic trigrams and sixty-four hexagrams, interpreted in terms of the principles of yin and yang.

ORIGIN – Chinese, 'book of changes'.

ichneumon /ikˈnyoomən/ > *noun* **1** a slender parasitic wasp which deposits its eggs in or on the larvae of other insects. **2** the Egyptian mongoose.

ORIGIN – Greek *ikhneumōn* 'tracker'.

ichor /ˈīkor/ > *noun* **1** Greek Mythology the fluid said to flow like blood in the veins of the gods. **2** archaic a watery discharge from a wound.

ORIGIN – Greek *ikhōr*.

ichthyology /ˌikthiˈolləji/ > *noun* the branch of zoology concerned with fishes.

DERIVATIVES – **ichthyological** *adjective* **ichthyologist** *noun*.

ORIGIN – from Greek *ikhthus* 'fish'.

ichthyosaur /ˈikthiəsɔːr/ (also **ichthyosaurus** /ikthiəˈsɔːrəss/) > *noun* a fossil marine reptile with a long pointed head, four flippers, and an upright tail.

ICI > *abbreviation* Imperial Chemical Industries.

-ician > *suffix* (forming nouns) denoting a person involved in a particular subject: *statistician*.

ORIGIN – from French *-icien*.

icicle > *noun* a hanging, tapering piece of ice formed by the freezing of dripping water.

icing > *noun* a mixture of sugar with liquid or fat, used as a coating for cakes or biscuits.

IDIOMS – **the icing on the cake** an attractive but inessential addition or enhancement.

COMBINATIONS – **icing sugar** chiefly Brit. finely powdered sugar used to make icing.

icky > *adjective* informal, chiefly N. Amer. **1** unpleasantly sticky. **2** distastefully sentimental.

icon /ˈīkon/ > *noun* **1** (also **ikon**) a devotional painting of Christ or another holy figure, typically on wood, venerated in the Byzantine and other Eastern Churches. **2** a person regarded with particular admiration or as a representative symbol. **3** Computing a symbol or graphic representation on a VDU screen of a program, window, etc.

ORIGIN – Greek *eikōn* 'image'.

iconic > *adjective* relating to or of the nature of an icon.

DERIVATIVES – **iconically** *adverb*.

iconify /ˈīkonnifī/ > *verb* (**iconifies**, **iconified**) Computing reduce (a window on a VDU screen) to an icon.

iconoclast /ˈīkonnəklast/ > *noun* **1** a person who attacks cherished beliefs or institutions. **2** a person who destroys images used in religious worship, especially one belonging to a movement opposing the veneration of icons in the Byzantine Church during the 8th and 9th century.

DERIVATIVES – **iconoclasm** *noun* **iconoclastic** *adjective*.

ORIGIN – Greek *eikonoklastēs*, from *eikōn* 'image, likeness' + *klan* 'to break'.

iconography /ˈīkənogrəfi/ > *noun* **1** the use or study of images or symbols in visual arts. **2** the visual images associated with a person or movement. **3** the illustration of a subject by drawings or figures.

DERIVATIVES – **iconographer** *noun* **iconographic** *adjective*.

iconostasis /ˈīkonostəsiss/ > *noun* (pl. **iconostases** /ˈīkonostəseez/) a screen bearing icons, separating the sanctuary of many Eastern churches from the nave.

ORIGIN – from Greek *eikōn* 'image' + *stasis* 'standing'.

icosahedron /ˈīkossəheedrən/ > *noun* (pl. **icosahedra** or **icosahedrons**) a three-dimensional shape having twenty plane faces, in particular a regular solid figure with twenty equal triangular faces.

DERIVATIVES – **icosahedral** *adjective*.

ORIGIN – from Greek *eikosaedros* 'twenty-faced'.

-ics > *suffix* (forming nouns) denoting a subject of study or branch of knowledge, or a field of activity: *politics*.

ORIGIN – from Latin *-ica* or Greek *-ika* (plural forms).

icy > *adjective* (**icier**, **iciest**) **1** covered with or consisting of ice. **2** very cold. **3** very unfriendly or hostile.

DERIVATIVES – **icily** *adverb* **iciness** *noun*.

ID > *abbreviation* **1** identification or identity. **2** Idaho.

Id > *noun* variant spelling of EID.

I'd > *contraction* **1** I had. **2** I should; I would.

id /id/ > *noun* Psychoanalysis the part of the mind in which innate instinctive impulses and primary processes are manifest. Compare with EGO and SUPEREGO.

ORIGIN – Latin, 'that'.

id. > *abbreviation* idem.

-ide > *suffix* Chemistry forming nouns: **1** denoting binary compounds: *chloride*. **2** denoting groups of elements: *lanthanide*.

idea > *noun* **1** a thought or suggestion about a possible course of action. **2** a mental impression. **3** a belief. **4** (**the idea**) the aim or purpose.

WORDFINDER – abstract (*of ideas rather than objects*), caprice, conceit, whim (*fanciful idea*), ideology, theory (*a system of ideas*), plagiarism (*stealing someone else's idea*), sacred cow (*an idea held to be above criticism*), stereotype (*a widely held fixed idea of something*).

SYNONYMS – **2** concept, impression, inkling, notion. **3** belief, opinion, view.

ORIGIN – Greek, 'form, pattern'.

ideal > *adjective* **1** most suitable; perfect. **2** desirable or perfect but existing only in the imagination. > *noun* **1** a person or thing regarded as perfect. **2** a principle to be aimed for; a standard of perfection.

DERIVATIVES – **ideality** *noun* **ideally** *adverb*.

SYNONYMS – *adjective* **1** exemplary, model, perfect. *noun* **1** nonpareil, paragon. **2** archetype, exemplar, model, standard.

idealise (also **idealize**) > *verb* regard or represent as perfect or better than in reality.

DERIVATIVES – **idealisation** *noun*.

idealism > *noun* **1** the practice of forming or pursuing ideals, especially unrealistically. **2** (in art or literature) the representation of things in ideal form.

DERIVATIVES – **idealist** *noun* **idealistic** *adjective* **idealistically** *adverb*.

SYNONYMS – **1** utopianism.

idée fixe /ˈeeday ˈfeeks/ > *noun* (pl. **idées fixes** pronunc. same) an obsession.

ORIGIN – French, 'fixed idea'.

idem /ˈiddem, ˈīdem/ > *adverb* used in citations to indicate an author or word that has just been mentioned.

ORIGIN – Latin, 'the same'.

identical > *adjective* **1** exactly alike or the same. **2** (of twins) developed from a single fertilised ovum, and therefore of the same sex and usually very similar in appearance.

WORDFINDER – clones (*genetically identical individuals*), monozygotic twins (*identical*), dizygotic (*not identical*).

DERIVATIVES – **identically** *adverb*.

ORIGIN – Latin *identicus*, from *identitas* (see IDENTITY).

identification > *noun* **1** the action or process of identifying or the fact of being identified. **2** an official document or other proof of one's identity.

identify > *verb* (**identifies**, **identified**) **1** establish the identity of. **2** recognise or select by analysis. **3** (**identify with**) regard oneself as sharing the same characteristics or thinking as (someone else). **4** (**identify with**) associate (someone or something) closely with.

DERIVATIVES – **identifiable** *adjective* **identifiably** *adverb* **identifier** *noun*.

SYNONYMS – **2** diagnose, establish, pinpoint, recognise, select.

identikit > *noun* trademark a picture of a person sought by the police, reconstructed from typical facial features according to witnesses' descriptions. > *adjective* often derogatory typical and ordinary; nondescript.

identity > *noun* (pl. **identities**) **1** the fact of being who or what a person or thing is. **2** the characteristics determining this. **3** a close similarity or affinity. **4** Mathematics an equation expressing the equality of two expressions for all values of the variables, e.g. $(x + 1)^2 = x^2 + 2x + 1$.

SYNONYMS – **2** character, individuality, personality, selfhood.

COMBINATIONS – **identity operation** Mathematics a transformation that leaves an object unchanged. **identity parade** Brit. a group of people assembled so that an eyewitness may identify a suspect for a crime from among them.

ORIGIN – Latin *identitas*, from *idem* 'same'.

ideogram /ˈiddiəgram, ˈīdiəgram/ > *noun* a character symbolising the idea of a thing without indicating the sounds used to say it (e.g. a numeral).

ideograph /ˈiddiəgraaf, ˈīdiəgraaf/ > *noun* another term for IDEOGRAM.
DERIVATIVES – **ideographic** *adjective*.

ideologue /ˈiddiəlog, ˈīdiəlog/ > *noun* a person who follows an ideology in a dogmatic or uncompromising way.

ideology /īdiˈolləji/ > *noun* (pl. **ideologies**) 1 a system of ideas and ideals forming the basis of an economic or political theory. 2 the set of beliefs characteristic of a social group or individual.
DERIVATIVES – **ideological** *adjective* **ideologically** *adverb* **ideologist** *noun*.
SYNONYMS – **1,2** creed, doctrine, dogma, theory.

ides /īdz/ > *plural noun* (in the ancient Roman calendar) a day falling roughly in the middle of each month, from which other dates were calculated.
ORIGIN – Old French, from Latin *idus* (plural).

idiocy > *noun* (pl. **idiocies**) extremely stupid behaviour.
SYNONYMS – asininity, foolishness, imbecility, stupidity.

idiom > *noun* 1 a group of words whose meaning cannot be deduced from those of the individual words (e.g. *over the moon*). 2 a form of expression natural to a language, person, or group. 3 a characteristic mode of expression in music or art.
ORIGIN – Greek *idiōma* 'private property'.

idiomatic > *adjective* 1 using or relating to expressions that are natural to a native speaker. 2 appropriate to a particular style of art or music.
DERIVATIVES – **idiomatically** *adverb*.

idiosyncrasy* /iddiəˈsingkrəsi/ > *noun* (pl. **idiosyncrasies**) 1 a way of behaving or thinking peculiar to an individual. 2 a distinctive characteristic of a thing.
*SPELLING – note the ending is *-asy*, not *-acy*: idiosyncr*asy*.
SYNONYMS – characteristic, eccentricity, quirk.
ORIGIN – Greek *idiosunkrasia*, from *idios* 'own' + *sun* 'with' + *krasis* 'mixture'.

idiosyncratic /iddiəsingˈkrattik/ > *adjective* characterised by idiosyncrasy; peculiar or individual.
DERIVATIVES – **idiosyncratically** *adverb*.

idiot > *noun* 1 informal a stupid person. 2 Medicine, archaic a mentally handicapped person.
ORIGIN – Greek *idiōtēs* 'layman, ignorant person', from *idios* 'own'.

idiotic > *adjective* very stupid or foolish.
DERIVATIVES – **idiotically** *adverb*.
SYNONYMS – asinine, foolish, moronic, stupid.

idiot savant /iddiō saˈvon/ > *noun* (pl. **idiot savants** or **idiots savants** pronunc. same) a mentally handicapped person who displays brilliance in a specific area, especially one involving memory.
ORIGIN – French, 'knowledgeable idiot'.

idle > *adjective* (**idler, idlest**) 1 avoiding work; lazy. 2 not working or in use. 3 having no purpose or basis: *idle threats*. > *verb* 1 spend time doing nothing. 2 (of an engine) run slowly while disconnected from a load or out of gear.
DERIVATIVES – **idleness** *noun* **idler** *noun* **idly** *adverb*.
SYNONYMS – *adjective* 1 indolent, lazy, slothful. 2 inactive, unemployed. *verb* 1 laze, loaf.

idol > *noun* 1 an image or representation of a god used as an object of worship. 2 a person who is greatly admired: *a soccer idol*.
SYNONYMS – 1 effigy, graven image, icon.
ORIGIN – Greek *eidōlon*, from *eidos* 'form'.

idolatry /īˈdollətri/ > *noun* 1 worship of idols. 2 adulation.
DERIVATIVES – **idolater** *noun* **idolatrous** *adjective*.
ORIGIN – from Greek *eidōlon* 'idol' + *-latreia* 'worship'.

idolise (also **idolize**) > *verb* revere or love greatly or excessively.
DERIVATIVES – **idolisation** *noun*.
SYNONYMS – adulate, hero-worship.

idyll /ˈiddil/ > *noun* 1 a blissful or peaceful period or situation. 2 a short description in verse or prose of a picturesque pastoral scene or incident.
ORIGIN – Greek *eidullion* 'little form'.

idyllic /iˈdillik/ > *adjective* extremely happy, peaceful, or picturesque.
DERIVATIVES – **idyllically** *adverb*.
SYNONYMS – blissful, heavenly.

i.e. > *abbreviation* that is to say.
ORIGIN – from Latin *id est* 'that is'.

IF > *abbreviation* intermediate frequency.

if > *conjunction* 1 introducing a conditional clause; on the condition or supposition that. 2 despite the possibility or fact that. 3 whether. 4 every time that; whenever. 5 expressing a polite request or tentative opinion. 6 expressing surprise or regret. > *noun* a condition or supposition.
IDIOMS – **if anything** used to suggest tentatively that something may be the case. **if only** even if for no other reason than. **if so** if that is the case.
USAGE – **if** and **whether** are more or less interchangeable in sentences like *I'll see if he left an address* and *I'll see whether he left an address*, although **whether** is more formal and more suitable for written use.

iffy > *adjective* (**iffier, iffiest**) informal 1 full of uncertainty; doubtful. 2 of questionable quality or legality.

igloo > *noun* a dome-shaped Eskimo house, typically built from blocks of solid snow.
ORIGIN – Inuit, 'house'.

igneous /ˈigniəss/ > *adjective* Geology (of rock) having solidified from lava or magma.
ORIGIN – from Latin *ignis* 'fire'.

ignite /igˈnīt/ > *verb* 1 catch fire or set on fire. 2 provoke or inflame (an emotion or situation).
ORIGIN – Latin *ignire*, from *ignis* 'fire'.

igniter > *noun* 1 a device for igniting a fuel mixture in an engine. 2 a device for causing an electric arc.

ignition > *noun* 1 the action of igniting or the state of being ignited. 2 the process of starting the burning of fuel in an internal-combustion engine.

ignoble > *adjective* (**ignobler, ignoblest**) 1 not honourable. 2 of humble origin or social status.
DERIVATIVES – **ignobly** *adverb*.
ORIGIN – Latin *ignobilis*, from *in-* 'not' + *gnobilis* 'noble'.

ignominious /ignəˈminniəss/ > *adjective* deserving or causing public disgrace or shame.
DERIVATIVES – **ignominiously** *adverb*.
SYNONYMS – dishonourable, humiliating, shameful, undignified.
ORIGIN – Latin *ignominiosus*, from *in-* 'not' + a variant of *nomen* 'name'.

ignominy /ˈignəmini/ > *noun* public shame or disgrace.
SYNONYMS – disgrace, dishonour, humiliation, opprobrium, shame.

ignoramus /ignəˈrayməss/ > *noun* (pl. **ignoramuses**) an ignorant or stupid person.

wordpower facts

Ignoramus

Ignoramus was originally a formula uttered by a grand jury on an indictment that it considered not to be backed by sufficient evidence to bring before a petty jury: the word is Latin for 'we do not know' (in legal use 'we take no notice of it'). The modern sense may derive from the name of a character in George Ruggle's *Ignoramus* (1615), a comedy satirising lawyers.

ignorance > *noun* lack of knowledge or information.
SYNONYMS – incomprehension, unawareness; literary nescience.
ANTONYMS – knowledge.

ignorant > *adjective* 1 lacking knowledge or awareness in general. 2 (often **ignorant of**) uninformed about or unaware of a specific subject or fact. 3 informal rude; discourteous.
DERIVATIVES – **ignorantly** *adverb*.

SYNONYMS – **1** benighted, unenlightened, uninformed.

ORIGIN – from Latin *ignorare* 'not know'.

ignore > *verb* **1** disregard intentionally. **2** fail to consider (something significant).

SYNONYMS – **1** disregard, pass over, push aside. **2** neglect, overlook.

ORIGIN – Latin *ignorare* 'not know'.

iguana /i**gwaa**nə/ > *noun* a large lizard with a spiny crest along the back.

ORIGIN – Arawak.

iguanodon /i**gwaa**nədon/ > *noun* a large plant-eating dinosaur with a broad stiff tail and the thumb developed into a spike.

ORIGIN – from **IGUANA** + Greek *odous* 'tooth' (because its teeth resemble those of the iguana).

IHS > *abbreviation* Jesus.

ORIGIN – from Greek IHΣ as an abbreviation of *Iēsous* 'Jesus'.

ikat /**i**kat/ > *noun* fabric made using an Indonesian decorative technique in which warp or weft threads, or both, are tie-dyed before weaving.

ORIGIN – Malay, 'fasten, tie'.

ikebana /ikki**baa**nə/ > *noun* the art of Japanese flower arrangement.

ORIGIN – Japanese, 'living flowers'.

ikon > *noun* variant spelling of **ICON** (in sense 1).

IL > *abbreviation* Illinois.

il- > *prefix* variant spelling of **IN-¹**, **IN-²** before *l*.

-il (also **-ile**) > *suffix* forming adjectives and nouns such as *civil*.

ORIGIN – from Latin *-ilis*.

ileum /**ill**iəm/ > *noun* (pl. **ilea**) Anatomy the third portion of the small intestine, between the jejunum and the caecum.

ORIGIN – Latin, variant of **ILIUM**.

ilex /**ī**leks/ > *noun* **1** the holm oak. **2** a tree or shrub of a family that includes holly.

ORIGIN – Latin.

iliac /**ill**iak/ > *adjective* relating to the ilium or the nearby regions of the lower body.

ilium /**ill**iəm/ > *noun* (pl. **ilia**) the large broad bone forming the upper part of each half of the pelvis.

ORIGIN – Latin, singular of *ilia* 'flanks, entrails'.

ilk > *noun* **1** a type: *fascists, racists, and others of that ilk*. **2** (**of that ilk**) Scottish, chiefly archaic of the place or estate of the same name.

ORIGIN – Old English, related to **ALIKE**.

I'll > *contraction* I shall; I will.

ill > *adjective* **1** not in full health; unwell. **2** poor in quality. **3** harmful, hostile, or unfavourable. > *adverb* **1** badly, wrongly, or imperfectly: *ill-chosen*. **2** only with difficulty. > *noun* **1** a problem or misfortune. **2** evil or harm.

IDIOMS – **house of ill fame** (or **repute**) archaic or humorous a brothel. **ill at ease** uncomfortable or embarrassed.

USAGE – **ill** meaning 'unwell' should not be used before a noun: say *a person who is ill* but not *an ill person* (better, *a sick person*). On the differences in meaning between **ill** and **sick**, see the note at **SICK¹**.

SYNONYMS – *adjective* **1** indisposed, infirm, poorly, sick, unwell. **2** deficient, poor. *noun* **1** affliction, misfortune, pain, problem, woe. **2** evil, harm, injury, mischief, trouble.

ANTONYMS – *adjective* **1** healthy, well.

COMBINATIONS – **ill-advised** unwise or badly thought out. **ill-assorted** not well matched. **ill-bred** badly brought up or rude. **ill-disposed** unfriendly or unsympathetic. **ill fame** dated disrepute. **ill-fated** destined to fail or have bad luck. **ill-favoured** unattractive or offensive. **ill-gotten** acquired by illegal or unfair means. **ill humour** irritability or bad temper. **ill-natured** bad-tempered and churlish. **ill-omened** accompanied by bad omens. **ill-starred** unlucky. **ill-tempered** irritable or morose. **ill-treat** (also **ill-use**) act cruelly towards. **ill will** animosity.

ORIGIN – Old Norse, 'evil, difficult'.

illegal > *adjective* contrary to or forbidden by law.

DERIVATIVES – **illegality** *noun* **illegally** *adverb*.

USAGE – what is the difference between **illegal** and **unlawful**? Both can mean 'contrary to or forbidden by law', but **unlawful** has a broader meaning 'not permitted by rules': thus handball in soccer is **unlawful**, but not **illegal**.

SYNONYMS – criminal, felonious, illicit, unlawful.

ANTONYMS – legal, lawful.

illegible /i**lej**ib'l/ > *adjective* not clear enough to be read.

DERIVATIVES – **illegibility** *noun* **illegibly** *adverb*.

SYNONYMS – indecipherable, unintelligible, unreadable.

ANTONYMS – legible.

illegitimate /illi**jitt**imət/ > *adjective* **1** not in accordance with the law or accepted standards. **2** (of a child) born of parents not lawfully married to each other.

DERIVATIVES – **illegitimacy** *noun* **illegitimately** *adverb*.

illiberal > *adjective* opposed to liberal principles.

DERIVATIVES – **illiberality** *noun* **illiberally** *adverb*.

illicit /i**liss**it/ > *adjective* forbidden by law, rules, or custom.

DERIVATIVES – **illicitly** *adverb*.

SYNONYMS – criminal, illegal, illegitimate, prohibited, unlawful.

ORIGIN – Latin *illicitus*, from *in-* 'not' + *licitus* 'allowed'.

illimitable > *adjective* limitless.

DERIVATIVES – **illimitably** *adverb*.

illiquid /i**lik**wid/ > *adjective* **1** (of assets) not easily converted into cash. **2** (of a market) with a low volume of activity.

DERIVATIVES – **illiquidity** *noun*.

illiterate /i**litt**ərət/ > *adjective* **1** unable to read or write. **2** ignorant in a particular subject or activity: *politically illiterate*.

DERIVATIVES – **illiteracy** *noun* **illiterately** *adverb*.

SYNONYMS – **1** unlettered.

ANTONYMS – literate.

illness > *noun* a disease or period of sickness.

SYNONYMS – affliction, ailment, disease, malady, sickness.

illogical > *adjective* contrary to logic; lacking sense or sound reasoning.

DERIVATIVES – **illogicality** (pl. **illogicalities**) *noun* **illogically** *adverb*.

SYNONYMS – absurd, irrational, unreasoning, unsound.

ANTONYMS – logical.

illuminance /i**loo**minənss/ > *noun* Physics the amount of luminous flux per unit area.

illuminate /i**loo**minayt/ > *verb* **1** light up. **2** help to clarify or explain. **3** decorate (a page or initial letter in a manuscript) with gold, silver, or coloured designs.

DERIVATIVES – **illuminative** *adjective* **illuminator** *noun*.

SYNONYMS – **1** brighten, lighten; literary illumine. **2** clarify, elucidate, enlighten, shed light on.

ORIGIN – Latin *illuminare*, from *lumen* 'light'.

illuminati /i**loo**mi**naa**ti/ > *plural noun* people claiming to possess special enlightenment or knowledge.

ORIGIN – plural of Italian *illuminato* or Latin *illuminatus* 'enlightened'.

illumination > *noun* **1** lighting or light. **2** (**illuminations**) lights used in decorating a building or other structure. **3** the action or process of illuminating.

illumine > *verb* literary light up; illuminate.

illusion /i**loo**zh'n/ > *noun* **1** a false or unreal perception or belief. **2** a deceptive appearance or impression.

WORDFINDER – hallucination (*an illusion experienced as real*), mirage (*atmospheric optical illusion*), trompe l'oeil (*method of painting which creates an illusion*).

SYNONYMS – **1** delusion, fallacy, misapprehension, misconception.

wordpower facts

Illusion

The word **illusion** comes via Old French from Latin *illudere* 'to mock', which is based on *ludere* 'to play'.

Illusion originally meant 'deceiving, deception', and thus shares with most of the other English words formed from *ludere* (such as **allude**, **collude**, **delude**, and **elude**) an implication of subtle or surreptitious behaviour. The only members of the group that retain the idea of 'play' are **prelude**, which first meant 'a short play performed before the main play', and **ludic**, a formal word meaning 'playful'.

illusionism > *noun* the use of perspective in art to give a three-dimensional appearance.

illusionist > *noun* a magician or conjuror.

illusive /il$\overline{oo}$siv/ > *adjective* chiefly literary deceptive; illusory.

illusory /il$\overline{oo}$səri/ > *adjective* apparently real but not actually so; deceptive.
DERIVATIVES – **illusorily** *adverb*.

illustrate > *verb* **1** provide (a book or periodical) with pictures. **2** make clear by using examples, charts, etc. **3** serve as an example of.
DERIVATIVES – **illustrator** *noun*.
ORIGIN – Latin *illustrare* 'light up'.

illustration > *noun* **1** a picture illustrating a book or periodical. **2** the action or fact of illustrating. **3** an illustrative example.
DERIVATIVES – **illustrational** *adjective*.

illustrative > *adjective* serving as an example or explanation.
DERIVATIVES – **illustratively** *adverb*.

illustrious /ilustriəss/ > *adjective* famous and admired for past achievements.
DERIVATIVES – **illustriousness** *noun*.
SYNONYMS – acclaimed, celebrated, distinguished, esteemed, renowned.
ORIGIN – from Latin *illustris* 'clear, bright'.

illywhacker /illiwakkər/ > *noun* Austral. informal a small-time confidence trickster.

I'm > *contraction* I am.

im- > *prefix* variant spelling of IN-[1], IN-[2] assimilated before *b, m, p* (as in *imbibe, immediate, impart*).

image > *noun* **1** a representation of the external form of a person or thing in art. **2** a visible impression obtained by a camera, displayed on a video screen, or produced by reflection or refraction. **3** the general impression that a person, organisation, or product presents to the public. **4** a picture in the mind. **5** a simile or metaphor. **6** a person or thing closely resembling another. **7** likeness. **8** (in biblical use) an idol. > *verb* make or form an image of.
WORDFINDER – anamorphosis (*a distorted image which appears normal when viewed in a particular way*), eidetic (*relating to vivid mental images*), hologram (*three-dimensional image*), iconography (*use or study of images*), iconolatry (*worship of images*).
DERIVATIVES – **imageless** *adjective*.
SYNONYMS – *noun* **1** likeness, portrait, representation. **4** concept, idea, impression.
ORIGIN – Latin *imago*; related to IMITATE.

imager > *noun* an electronic or other device which records images.

imagery > *noun* **1** figurative language, especially in a literary work. **2** visual symbolism. **3** visual images collectively.

imaginable > *adjective* possible to be thought of or believed.
DERIVATIVES – **imaginably** *adverb*.

imaginary > *adjective* **1** existing only in the imagination. **2** Mathematics (of a number or quantity) expressed in terms of the square root of −1 (represented by *i* or *j*).
DERIVATIVES – **imaginarily** *adverb*.
SYNONYMS – **1** fanciful, fictitious, insubstantial, mythical, unreal.
ANTONYMS – real.

imagination > *noun* **1** the faculty or action of forming ideas or images in the mind. **2** the ability of the mind to be creative or resourceful.

imaginative > *adjective* having or showing creativity or inventiveness.
DERIVATIVES – **imaginatively** *adverb* **imaginativeness** *noun*.
SYNONYMS – creative, innovative, inventive, original, visionary.

imagine > *verb* **1** form a mental image or concept of. **2** (often as adj. **imagined**) believe (something unreal) to exist. **3** suppose or assume.
DERIVATIVES – **imaginer** *noun*.
SYNONYMS – **1** conceive, envisage, envision, picture, visualise. **3** assume, fancy, presume, reckon, suppose.
ORIGIN – from Latin *imaginare* 'form an image of' and *imaginari* 'picture to oneself', both from *imago* 'image'.

imaginings > *plural noun* thoughts or fantasies.

imagism /immijiz'm/ > *noun* a movement in early 20th-century English and American poetry which sought clarity of expression by means of precise images.
DERIVATIVES – **imagist** *noun* **imagistic** *adjective*.

imago /imayg$\overline{o}$/ > *noun* (pl. **imagos** or **imagines** /imayjineez/) the final and fully developed adult stage of an insect.
ORIGIN – Latin, 'image'.

imam /imaam/ > *noun* **1** the person who leads prayers in a mosque. **2** (**Imam**) a title of various Muslim leaders, especially of one succeeding Muhammad as leader of Shiite Islam.
DERIVATIVES – **imamate** *noun*.
ORIGIN – Arabic, 'leader'.

IMAX /īmaks/ > *noun* trademark a cinematographic technique which produces an image approximately ten times larger than that from standard 35 mm film.

imbalance > *noun* a lack of proportion or balance.

imbecile /imbiseel/ > *noun* informal a stupid person. > *adjective* stupid.
DERIVATIVES – **imbecilic** *adjective* **imbecility** (pl. **imbecilities**) *noun*.
ORIGIN – Latin *imbecillus* 'without a supporting staff': originally in the sense 'physically weak'.

imbed > *verb* variant spelling of EMBED.

imbibe /imbīb/ > *verb* **1** formal or humorous drink (alcohol). **2** absorb (ideas or knowledge).
DERIVATIVES – **imbiber** *noun*.
ORIGIN – Latin *imbibere*, from *bibere* 'to drink'.

imbricate /imbrikət/ (also **imbricated**) > *adjective* technical arranged in an overlapping manner like roof tiles.
DERIVATIVES – **imbrication** *noun*.
ORIGIN – from Latin *imbricare* 'cover with roof tiles'.

imbroglio /imbr$\overline{o}$liō/ > *noun* (pl. **imbroglios**) a very confused or complicated situation.
ORIGIN – Italian.

imbue /imbyoo/ > *verb* (**imbues, imbued, imbuing**) (often **be imbued with**) fill with a feeling or quality.
ORIGIN – first in the sense 'saturate': from Latin *imbuere* 'moisten'.

IMF > *abbreviation* International Monetary Fund.

IMHO > *abbreviation* in my humble opinion.

imitate > *verb* **1** follow as a model. **2** copy (a person's speech or mannerisms), especially for comic effect. **3** reproduce; simulate: *synthetic fabrics that imitate silk*.
DERIVATIVES – **imitable** *adjective* **imitator** *noun*.
SYNONYMS – **1** copy, emulate. **2** ape, copy, impersonate, mimic.
ORIGIN – Latin *imitari*, related to *imago* 'image'.

imitation > *noun* **1** the action of imitating. **2** a copy.
WORDFINDER – burlesque (*comical imitation*), ersatz (*denoting an inferior imitation of something*), mimetic (*of mimicry or imitation*), parody (*mocking imitation*), pastiche (*imitation of artistic style*), travesty (*distorted imitation*).
IDIOMS – **imitation is the sincerest form of flattery** proverb copying someone or something is an implicit way of paying them a compliment.
SYNONYMS – **1** emulation, impersonation, mimicry. **2** copy, forgery, reproduction.

imitative /immitətiv/ > *adjective* **1** following a model. **2** (of a word) reproducing a natural sound (e.g. *fizz*) or pronounced in a way that suggests the appearance or character of something (e.g. *blob*).
DERIVATIVES – **imitatively** *adverb*.

immaculate > *adjective* **1** perfectly clean, neat, or tidy. **2** free from flaws or mistakes. **3** Catholic Theology free from sin.
DERIVATIVES – **immaculacy** *noun* **immaculately** *adverb*.
SYNONYMS – **1** pristine, spotless. **2** faultless, flawless, unblemished.
COMBINATIONS – **Immaculate Conception 1** (in the Roman Catholic Church) the doctrine that God preserved the Virgin Mary from the taint of original sin from the moment she was conceived. **2** the feast commemorating the Immaculate Conception on December 8th.
ORIGIN – Latin *immaculatus*, from *in-* 'not' + *maculatus* 'stained'.

immanent /immənənt/ > *adjective* **1** present within; inherent. **2** (of God) permanently pervading the universe.
DERIVATIVES – **immanence** *noun*.
ORIGIN – from Latin *immanere* 'remain within'.

immaterial > *adjective* **1** unimportant under the circumstances; irrelevant. **2** having no physical substance.
DERIVATIVES – **immateriality** *noun*.

immature > *adjective* **1** not fully developed. **2** having or showing emotional or intellectual development appropriate to someone younger.
DERIVATIVES – **immaturely** *adverb* **immaturity** *noun*.
SYNONYMS – **1** unfinished, unripe. **2** callow, childish, infantile, juvenile.
ANTONYMS – mature.

immeasurable > *adjective* too large or extreme to measure.
DERIVATIVES – **immeasurably** *adverb*.

immediate > *adjective* **1** occurring or done at once. **2** nearest in time, space, or relationship. **3** most urgent; current. **4** without an intervening medium or agency; direct: *a coronary was the immediate cause of death*.
DERIVATIVES – **immediacy** *noun*.
SYNONYMS – **1** instant, instantaneous. **2** adjacent, closest, nearest, proximate.
ORIGIN – Latin *immediatus*, from *in-* 'not' + *mediatus* 'intervening'.

immediately > *adverb* **1** at once. **2** very close in time, space, or relationship. > *conjunction* chiefly Brit. as soon as.

immemorial > *adjective* existing from before what can be remembered or found in records: *from time immemorial*.
DERIVATIVES – **immemorially** *adverb*.

immense > *adjective* extremely large or great.
DERIVATIVES – **immensity** *noun*.
SYNONYMS – enormous, gigantic, huge, massive, vast.
ORIGIN – Latin *immensus* 'immeasurable'.

immensely > *adverb* to a great extent; extremely.

immerse > *verb* **1** dip or submerge in a liquid. **2** (**immerse oneself** or **be immersed**) involve oneself deeply in an activity or interest.
ORIGIN – Latin *immergere* 'dip into'.

immersion > *noun* **1** the action of immersing or the state of being immersed. **2** deep involvement.
COMBINATIONS – **immersion heater** an electric heating element that is positioned in the liquid to be heated, typically in a domestic hot-water tank.

immersive > *adjective* (of a computer display) generating a three-dimensional image which appears to surround the user.

immigrant > *noun* a person who comes to live permanently in a foreign country.
WORDFINDER – Gastarbeiter (*immigrant worker, especially in Germany*).

immigrate > *verb* come to live permanently in a foreign country.
DERIVATIVES – **immigration** *noun*.
ORIGIN – Latin *immigrare*.

imminent > *adjective* about to happen.
DERIVATIVES – **imminence** *noun* **imminently** *adverb*.
SYNONYMS – forthcoming, impending, looming.
ORIGIN – from Latin *imminere* 'overhang, impend'.

immiscible /imissib'l/ > *adjective* (of liquids) not forming a homogeneous mixture when added together.

immobile > *adjective* **1** not moving. **2** incapable of moving or being moved.
DERIVATIVES – **immobility** *noun*.

immobilise (also **immobilize**) > *verb* **1** prevent from moving or operating as normal. **2** restrict the movements of (a limb or patient) to allow healing.
DERIVATIVES – **immobilisation** *noun* **immobiliser** *noun*.

immoderate > *adjective* lacking moderation; excessive.
DERIVATIVES – **immoderately** *adverb* **immoderation** *noun*.

immodest > *adjective* not humble, decent, or decorous.
DERIVATIVES – **immodestly** *adverb* **immodesty** *noun*.

immolate /imməlayt/ > *verb* kill or offer as a sacrifice, especially by burning.

DERIVATIVES – **immolation** *noun*.

wordpower facts
Immolate
The word **immolate** comes from the Latin verb *immolare* 'to sacrifice', literally 'sprinkle with meal', which is based on *mola* 'meal', the root of **mill** and **molar**. The meaning developed from one of the stages in a Roman ritual sacrifice, whereby the priest poured wine over the head of the victim and sprinkled salted flour on its back before it was killed.

immoral > *adjective* not conforming to accepted standards of morality.
DERIVATIVES – **immorality** *noun* **immorally** *adverb*.
USAGE – do not confuse **immoral** with **amoral**: **amoral** means 'not concerned with morality', while **immoral** means 'not conforming to accepted standards of morality'.
SYNONYMS – base, corrupt, dissolute, unethical.
ANTONYMS – moral.
COMBINATIONS – **immoral earnings** earnings from prostitution.

immortal /imort'l/ > *adjective* **1** living forever. **2** deserving to be remembered forever. > *noun* **1** an immortal being, especially a god of ancient Greece or Rome. **2** a person of enduring fame.
DERIVATIVES – **immortalise** (also **immortalize**) *verb* **immortality** *noun*.
SYNONYMS – *adjective* **1** deathless, eternal, everlasting, undying.
ANTONYMS – mortal.

immortelle /immortel/ > *noun* another term for EVERLASTING.
ORIGIN – French, 'immortal'.

immovable (also **immoveable**) > *adjective* **1** not able to be moved or changed. **2** Law (of property) consisting of land, buildings, or other permanent items.
DERIVATIVES – **immovability** *noun* **immovably** *adverb*.

immune > *adjective* **1** resistant to a particular infection owing to the presence of specific antibodies or sensitised white blood cells. **2** relating to such resistance: *the immune system*. **3** exempt from an obligation or penalty. **4** (often **immune to**) not susceptible.
WORDFINDER – vaccine (*a preparation providing immunity*), inoculation, vaccination (*treatment with vaccine*).
COMBINATIONS – **immune response** the reaction of the cells and fluids of the body to the presence of an antigen.
ORIGIN – Latin *immunis* 'exempt from

public service or charge', from *in-* 'not' + *munis* 'ready for service'.

immunise (also **immunize**) > *verb* make immune to infection, typically by inoculation.
DERIVATIVES – **immunisation** *noun*.

immunity > *noun* (pl. **immunities**) **1** the ability of an organism to resist a particular infection: *immunity to malaria*. **2** exemption from an obligation or penalty: *the rebels were given immunity from prosecution*.

immunoblotting > *noun* a technique for analyzing or identifying proteins in a mixture, involving separation by electrophoresis followed by staining with antibodies.

immunodeficiency > *noun* reduced ability of the immune system to protect the body from infection.

immunoglobulin /imyoonō**glob**yoolin/ > *noun* any of a class of blood proteins which function as antibodies.

immunology > *noun* the branch of medicine and biology concerned with immunity.
DERIVATIVES – **immunological** (US also **immunologic**) *adjective* **immunologically** *adverb* **immunologist** *noun*.

immunosuppression > *noun* suppression of an individual's immune response, especially as induced to help the survival of an organ after a transplant operation.
DERIVATIVES – **immunosuppressant** *noun* **immunosuppressed** *adjective*.

immunosuppressive > *adjective* (chiefly of drugs) partially or completely suppressing the immune response of an individual. > *noun* an immunosuppressive drug.

immunotherapy > *noun* the prevention or treatment of disease with substances that stimulate the immune response.

immure /i**myoor**/ > *verb* (usu. **be immured**) confine or imprison.
DERIVATIVES – **immurement** *noun*.
ORIGIN – Latin *immurare*, from *murus* 'wall'.

immutable /i**myoo**təb'l/ > *adjective* unchanging or unchangeable.
DERIVATIVES – **immutability** *noun* **immutably** *adverb*.

imp > *noun* **1** a small, mischievous devil or sprite. **2** a mischievous child.

impact > *noun* /**im**pakt/ **1** the action of one object coming forcibly into contact with another. **2** a marked effect or influence. > *verb* /im**pakt**/ **1** come into forcible contact with another object. **2** (often **impact on**) have a strong effect on. **3** press firmly.
DERIVATIVES – **impactor** *noun*.
ORIGIN – from Latin *impingere* 'drive something in or at'.

wordpower facts
Imp
In Old English an **imp** was a young shoot, or a child or young person. In medieval times the word denoted a descendant, especially of a noble family; later it came to mean a child of the devil or a person regarded as such, hence a 'little devil' or mischievous child. Its ultimate derivation is from the Greek *phuein*, meaning 'come into being', 'generate', and also 'to plant': this word is the source of **neophyte** and of various botanical and biological terms beginning or ending with *phyto-* or *-phyte*.

impacted > *adjective* **1** (of a tooth) wedged between another tooth and the jaw. **2** (of a fractured bone) having the parts crushed together.
DERIVATIVES – **impaction** *noun*.

impair > *verb* weaken or damage.
DERIVATIVES – **impairment** *noun*.
ORIGIN – Old French *empeirier*, from Latin *pejorare* 'make worse'.

impaired > *adjective* having a disability of a specified kind: *hearing-impaired*.

impala /im**paa**lə/ > *noun* (pl. same) a graceful antelope of southern and East Africa, with lyre-shaped horns.
ORIGIN – Zulu.

impale > *verb* transfix or pierce with a sharp instrument.
DERIVATIVES – **impalement** *noun* **impaler** *noun*.
ORIGIN – Latin *impalare*, from *palus* 'a stake'.

impalpable /im**pal**pəb'l/ > *adjective* **1** unable to be felt by touch. **2** not easily comprehended.
DERIVATIVES – **impalpably** *adverb*.

impanel (also **empanel**) > *verb* (**impanelled, impanelling**; US **impaneled, impaneling**) enrol (a jury) or enrol (someone) on to a jury.
DERIVATIVES – **impanelment** *noun*.
ORIGIN – Old French *empaneller*, from *panel* 'panel'.

impart > *verb* **1** communicate (information). **2** give (a quality).
ORIGIN – first meaning 'give a share of': from Latin *impartire*, from *pars* 'part'.

impartial /im**paar**sh'l/ > *adjective* treating all rivals or disputants equally.
DERIVATIVES – **impartiality** *noun* **impartially** *adverb*.
SYNONYMS – disinterested, equitable, even-handed, neutral, unbiased.

impassable > *adjective* impossible to travel along or over.
DERIVATIVES – **impassability** *noun*.

impasse /**am**paas/ > *noun* a deadlock.
ORIGIN – French, from *passer* 'to pass'.

impassioned > *adjective* filled with or showing great emotion.

impassive > *adjective* not feeling or showing emotion.
DERIVATIVES – **impassively** *adverb* **impassiveness** *noun* **impassivity** *noun*.

impasto /im**pas**tō/ > *noun* Art the process or technique of laying on paint or pigment thickly so that it stands out from a surface.
ORIGIN – Italian, from *pasta* 'a paste'.

impatiens /im**pat**ienz/ > *noun* a plant of a genus that includes busy Lizzie and its many hybrids.
ORIGIN – Latin, 'impatient' (because the capsules of the plant readily burst open when touched).

impatient > *adjective* **1** lacking patience or tolerance. **2** restlessly eager: *impatient for change*.
DERIVATIVES – **impatience** *noun* **impatiently** *adverb*.

impeach > *verb* **1** call into question the integrity or validity of (a practice). **2** Brit. charge with treason or another crime against the state. **3** chiefly US charge (a public official) with misconduct.
DERIVATIVES – **impeachable** *adjective* **impeachment** *noun*.
ORIGIN – Old French *empecher* 'impede', from Latin *impedicare* 'entangle', from *pes* 'foot'.

impeccable /im**pekk**əb'l/ > *adjective* in accordance with the highest standards; faultless.
DERIVATIVES – **impeccability** *noun* **impeccably** *adverb*.
SYNONYMS – exemplary, faultless, flawless, perfect.
ORIGIN – first used in the sense 'not liable to sin': from Latin *impeccabilis*, from *peccare* 'to sin'.

impecunious /impi**kyoo**niəss/ > *adjective* having little or no money.
DERIVATIVES – **impecuniosity** *noun* **impecuniousness** *noun*.
ORIGIN – from IN-¹ + Latin *pecuniosus* 'wealthy'.

impedance /im**peed**'nss/ > *noun* the total effective opposition to the flow of an alternating electric current, arising from the combined effects of resistance and reactance.

impede /im**peed**/ > *verb* delay or block the progress or action of.
SYNONYMS – block, check, delay, hamper, hinder, obstruct.
ORIGIN – Latin *impedire* 'shackle the feet of', from *pes* 'foot'.

impediment /im**pedd**imənt/ > *noun* **1** a hindrance or obstruction. **2** (also **speech impediment**) a defect in a person's speech, such as a lisp or stammer.

impedimenta /impeddi**men**tə/ > *plural noun* equipment for an activity or expedition, especially when regarded as an encumbrance.
ORIGIN – Latin, plural of *impedimentum* 'impediment'.

impel /im**pel**/ > *verb* (**impelled, impelling**) **1** drive, force, or urge to do. **2** drive forward.
DERIVATIVES – **impeller** *noun*.
ORIGIN – Latin *impellere*, from *in-* 'towards' + *pellere* 'to drive'.

impending /im**pen**ding/ > *adjective* (especially of something bad or momentous) about to happen.
ORIGIN – from Latin *impendere* 'overhang'.

impenetrable /im**penn**itrəb'l/ > *adjective* **1** impossible to get through or into. **2** impossible to understand. **3** impervious to new ideas or influences.
DERIVATIVES – **impenetrability** *noun* **impenetrably** *adverb*.
SYNONYMS – **1** impassable, impermeable, impervious. **2** incomprehensible, inscrutable, unintelligible.

impenitent > *adjective* not feeling shame or regret.
DERIVATIVES – **impenitence** *noun* **impenitently** *adverb*.

imperative > *adjective* **1** of vital importance. **2** giving an authoritative command. **3** Grammar denoting the mood of a verb that expresses a command or exhortation, as in *come here!* > *noun* an essential or urgent thing.
DERIVATIVES – **imperatively** *adverb* **imperativeness** *noun*.
SYNONYMS – **1** critical, crucial, essential, vital.
ORIGIN – Latin *imperativus* 'specially ordered', from *imperare* 'to command'.

imperceptible > *adjective* so slight, gradual, or subtle as not to be perceived.
DERIVATIVES – **imperceptibly** *adverb*.

imperfect > *adjective* **1** faulty or incomplete. **2** Grammar (of a tense) denoting a past action in progress but not completed at the time in question.
DERIVATIVES – **imperfection** *noun* **imperfectly** *adverb*.
SYNONYMS – **1** defective, deficient, faulty, flawed, incomplete.
ANTONYMS – **1** flawless, perfect.

imperial > *adjective* **1** relating to an empire or an emperor. **2** characteristic of an emperor; majestic or magnificent. **3** of or relating to the system of non-metric units formerly used for all weights and measures in the UK, and still used for some.
DERIVATIVES – **imperially** *adverb*.
ORIGIN – Latin *imperialis*, from *imperium* 'command, empire'.

imperialism > *noun* a policy of extending a country's power and influence through colonisation, use of military force, or other means.
DERIVATIVES – **imperialist** *noun* & *adjective* **imperialistic** *adjective*.

imperil > *verb* (**imperilled, imperilling**; US **imperiled, imperiling**) put into danger.

imperious /im**peer**iəss/ > *adjective* arrogant and domineering.
DERIVATIVES – **imperiously** *adverb* **imperiousness** *noun*.
ORIGIN – Latin *imperiosus*, from *imperium* 'command, empire'.

imperishable > *adjective* enduring forever.
DERIVATIVES – **imperishably** *adverb*.

impermanent > *adjective* not permanent.
DERIVATIVES – **impermanence** *noun* **impermanently** *adverb*.

impermeable /im**per**miəb'l/ > *adjective* not allowing fluid to pass through.
DERIVATIVES – **impermeability** *noun*.

impersonal > *adjective* **1** not influenced by or involving personal feelings. **2** featureless and anonymous. **3** not existing as a person. **4** Grammar (of a verb) used only with a formal subject (in English usually *it*) and expressing an action not attributable to a definite subject (as in *it is snowing*).
DERIVATIVES – **impersonality** *noun* **impersonally** *adverb*.
SYNONYMS – **1** detached, disinterested, neutral, objective, unprejudiced.
COMBINATIONS – **impersonal pronoun** the pronoun *it* when used without definite reference or antecedent, as in *it was snowing*.

impersonate > *verb* pretend to be (another person) for entertainment or fraud.
DERIVATIVES – **impersonation** *noun* **impersonator** *noun*.
ORIGIN – from IN-² + Latin *persona* 'person'.

impertinent > *adjective* **1** not showing proper respect. **2** formal not pertinent; irrelevant.
DERIVATIVES – **impertinence** *noun* **impertinently** *adverb*.
SYNONYMS – **1** cheeky, disrespectful, forward, impolite, impudent, insolent.

imperturbable /impər**tur**bəb'l/ > *adjective* unable to be upset or excited.
DERIVATIVES – **imperturbability** *noun* **imperturbably** *adverb*.

impervious /im**per**viəss/ > *adjective* **1** not allowing fluid to pass through. **2** (**impervious to**) unable to be affected by.
DERIVATIVES – **imperviously** *adverb* **imperviousness** *noun*.

impetigo /impi**tī**gō/ > *noun* a contagious bacterial skin infection forming pustules and yellow crusty sores.
ORIGIN – Latin, from *impetere* 'to attack'.

impetuous /im**pet**yooəss/ > *adjective* **1** acting or done quickly and rashly. **2** moving forcefully or rapidly.
DERIVATIVES – **impetuosity** *noun* **impetuously** *adverb* **impetuousness** *noun*.
SYNONYMS – **1** hasty, impulsive, precipitate, rash.
ORIGIN – Latin *impetuosus*, from *impetere* 'to attack'.

impetus /**im**pitəss/ > *noun* **1** the force or energy with which a body moves. **2** a driving force.
SYNONYMS – **1** momentum. **2** incentive, motivation, stimulus.
ORIGIN – Latin, 'assault, force'.

impi /**im**pi/ > *noun* (pl. **impis**) **1** a group of Zulu warriors. **2** an armed band of Zulus involved in urban or rural conflict.
ORIGIN – Zulu.

impiety /im**pī**əti/ > *noun* lack of piety or reverence.

impinge /im**pinj**/ > *verb* (**impinge, impinging**) (usu. **impinge on**) **1** have an effect or impact. **2** come into contact; encroach.
DERIVATIVES – **impingement** *noun*.
ORIGIN – Latin *impingere* 'drive something in or at'.

impious /**im**piəss/ > *adjective* not showing respect or reverence.
DERIVATIVES – **impiously** *adverb*.

impish > *adjective* mischievous.
DERIVATIVES – **impishly** *adverb* **impishness** *noun*.

implacable > *adjective* **1** unable to be appeased. **2** relentless; unstoppable.
DERIVATIVES – **implacability** *noun* **implacably** *adverb*.

implant > *verb* /im**plaant**/ **1** insert or fix (tissue or an artificial object) into the body. **2** establish (an idea) in the mind. > *noun* /**im**plaant/ a thing implanted.
DERIVATIVES – **implantation** *noun*.

implausible /im**plaw**zib'l/ > *adjective* not seeming reasonable or probable.
DERIVATIVES – **implausibility** *noun* **implausibly** *adverb*.
SYNONYMS – doubtful, dubious, improbable, unconvincing, unlikely.

implement > *noun* /**im**plimənt/ a tool, utensil, or other piece of equipment, used for a particular purpose. > *verb* /**im**pliment/ put into effect.
DERIVATIVES – **implementation** *noun* **implementer** *noun*.
SYNONYMS – *verb* carry out, effect, execute, fulfil, perform.
ORIGIN – from Latin *implere* 'fill up' (later 'employ').

implicate > *verb* /**im**plikayt/ **1** show to be involved in a crime. **2** (**be implicated in**) bear some of the responsibility for. **3** convey (a meaning or intention) indirectly; imply.
DERIVATIVES – **implicative** /im**plikk**ətiv/ *adjective*.

wordpower facts

Implicate

Employ, implicate, and imply form a small set of words derived from the Latin verb *implicare* 'enfold, entangle, involve, imply' and originally had very similar meanings. Each entered English in medieval times and formerly meant 'enfold, entangle, entwine'. Furthermore, in the 16th and 17th centuries **employ** also meant 'imply', and **imply** meant 'employ'! **Implicit** is also from *implicare*.

implication > *noun* **1** the implicit conclusion that can be drawn from something. **2** a likely consequence. **3** the action of implicating or the state of being implicated.
DERIVATIVES – **implicational** *adjective*.

implicit /imˈplissit/ > *adjective* **1** implied though not directly expressed. **2** (**implicit in**) contained in as a basic principle. **3** with no qualification or question: *implicit faith*.
DERIVATIVES – **implicitly** *adverb* **implicitness** *noun*.
SYNONYMS – **1** implied, indirect, inferred, tacit.
ANTONYMS – **1** explicit.

implode /imˈplōd/ > *verb* collapse or cause to collapse violently inwards.
DERIVATIVES – **implosion** *noun* **implosive** *adjective*.

implore > *verb* beg earnestly or desperately.
ORIGIN – Latin *implorare* 'invoke with tears'.

imply /imˈplī/ > *verb* (**implies, implied**) **1** indicate by suggestion rather than explicit reference. **2** (of a fact or occurrence) suggest as a logical consequence.
USAGE – do not confuse **imply** and **infer**. **Imply** is used with a speaker as its subject, as in *he implied that the General was a traitor*, and indicates that the speaker is suggesting something though not making an explicit statement. **Infer** is used in sentences such as *we inferred from his words that the General was a traitor*, and indicates that something in the speaker's words enabled the listeners to deduce that the man was a traitor.
SYNONYMS – **1** hint, insinuate, intimate, suggest.

impolite > *adjective* not having or showing good manners.
DERIVATIVES – **impolitely** *adverb* **impoliteness** *noun*.
SYNONYMS – discourteous, ill-mannered, impudent, insolent, rude, uncivil.
ANTONYMS – polite, well-mannered.

impolitic > *adjective* failing to possess or display prudence.

imponderable > *adjective* difficult or impossible to assess. > *noun* an imponderable factor.

import > *verb* /imˈport/ **1** bring (goods or services) into a country from abroad. **2** Computing transfer (data) into a file or document. **3** archaic indicate or signify. > *noun* /ˈimport/ **1** an imported article or service. **2** the action or process of importing. **3** the implied meaning of something. **4** importance.
DERIVATIVES – **importable** *adjective* **importation** *noun* **importer** *noun*.
ORIGIN – Latin *importare* 'bring in'.

important > *adjective* **1** of great significance or value. **2** having high rank or social status.
DERIVATIVES – **importance** *noun* **importantly** *adverb*.
SYNONYMS – **1** consequential, noteworthy, salient, significant, valuable. **2** distinguished, high-ranking, notable, influential.
ANTONYMS – insignificant, unimportant.

importunate /imˈportyoonət/ > *adjective* persistent or pressing.
DERIVATIVES – **importunately** *adverb* **importunity** (pl. **importunities**) *noun*.

wordpower facts

Importunate

The words **importunate** and **importune** come from the Latin adjective *importunus* 'inconvenient, unseasonable', which is based on *Portunus*, the name of the Roman god who protected harbours; the root word is *portus* 'harbour'. Conversely, **opportune** is derived from Latin *opportunus*, from *ob-* 'in the direction of' + *portus* 'harbour'; the Latin word originally referred to a wind blowing towards the harbour, and thus came to mean 'seasonable'.

importune /imˈportyoon/ > *verb* **1** harass with persistent requests. **2** approach (someone) to offer one's services as a prostitute.

impose > *verb* **1** force to be accepted, undertaken, or complied with. **2** (often **impose on**) take unfair advantage of someone.
ORIGIN – French *imposer*, from Latin *imponere* 'inflict, deceive'.

imposing > *adjective* grand and impressive.
DERIVATIVES – **imposingly** *adverb*.

imposition > *noun* **1** the action or process of imposing or being imposed. **2** something imposed, especially an unfair or resented demand or burden.

impossible > *adjective* **1** not able to occur, exist, or be done. **2** very difficult to deal with: *an impossible situation*.
DERIVATIVES – **impossibility** (pl. **impossibilities**) *noun* **impossibly** *adverb*.

impost /ˈimpōst/ > *noun* **1** a tax or similar compulsory payment. **2** Horse Racing the weight carried by a horse as a handicap.
ORIGIN – from Latin *impostus* 'imposed'.

impostor (also **imposter**) > *noun* a person who assumes a false identity in order to deceive or defraud.
ORIGIN – Latin, contraction of *impositor*, from *imponere* (see **IMPOSE**).

imposture > *noun* an instance of assuming a false identity.

impotent /ˈimpətənt/ > *adjective* **1** helpless or powerless. **2** (of a man) abnormally unable to achieve an erection or orgasm.
DERIVATIVES – **impotence** *noun* **impotency** *noun* **impotently** *adverb*.

impound > *verb* **1** seize and take legal custody of. **2** shut up (domestic animals) in a pound. **3** (of a dam) hold back or confine (water).
DERIVATIVES – **impoundment** *noun*.

impoverish > *verb* **1** make poor. **2** exhaust the strength or natural fertility of.
DERIVATIVES – **impoverishment** *noun*.
ORIGIN – Old French *empoverir*, from *povre* 'poor'.

impracticable > *adjective* impossible in practice to do or carry out.
DERIVATIVES – **impracticability** *noun* **impracticably** *adverb*.
USAGE – although there is considerable overlap between them, **impracticable** and **impractical** do not mean exactly the same thing. **Impracticable** means 'impossible to carry out' and is normally used of a specific procedure or course of action; **impractical**, on the other hand, is used in more general senses, often to mean simply 'unrealistic' or 'not sensible'.

impractical > *adjective* **1** not adapted for use or action; not sensible or practical. **2** chiefly N. Amer. impracticable.
DERIVATIVES – **impracticality** *noun* **impractically** *adverb*.

imprecation /imprikāshˈn/ > *noun* formal a spoken curse.
ORIGIN – Latin, from *imprecari* 'invoke (evil)'.

imprecise > *adjective* lacking exactness.
DERIVATIVES – **imprecisely** *adverb* **imprecision** *noun*.
SYNONYMS – approximate, inexact, rough, vague.

impregnable > *adjective* **1** unable to be captured or broken into. **2** unable to be overcome.
DERIVATIVES – **impregnability** *noun* **impregnably** *adverb*.
ORIGIN – Old French *imprenable*, from *in-* 'not' + *prendre* 'take'.

impregnate /ˈimpregnayt/ > *verb* **1** (usu. **be impregnated with**) soak or saturate with a substance. **2** fill with a feeling or quality. **3** make pregnant.

DERIVATIVES – **impregnation** noun.

ORIGIN – Latin impregnare 'make pregnant'.

impresario* /imprisaariō/ > noun (pl. **impresarios**) a person who organises and often finances theatrical or musical productions.

***SPELLING** – just one s: impresario.

ORIGIN – Italian, from impresa 'undertaking'.

impress¹ > verb **1** make (someone) feel admiration and respect. **2** make a mark or design on using a stamp or seal. **3** (**impress on**) emphasise (an idea) in the mind of. > noun **1** an act of impressing a mark. **2** an impressed mark. **3** a person's characteristic mark or quality.

ORIGIN – Old French empresser 'press in'.

impress² > verb historical force (someone) to serve in an army or navy.

DERIVATIVES – **impressment** noun.

ORIGIN – from IN-² + PRESS².

impression > noun **1** an idea, feeling, or opinion. **2** an effect produced on someone. **3** an imitation of a person or thing, done to entertain. **4** a mark impressed on a surface. **5** the printing of a number of copies of a publication for issue at one time. **6** chiefly Brit. a particular printed version of a book, especially one reprinted with no or only minor alteration.

impressionable > adjective (of a person) easily influenced.

DERIVATIVES – **impressionability** noun.

Impressionism > noun **1** a late 19th-century style or movement in painting concerned with depicting the visual impression of the moment, especially the shifting effects of light. **2** a literary style that seeks to capture a feeling or experience rather than to achieve accurate depiction. **3** Music a style of composition in which clarity of structure and theme is subordinate to harmonic effects.

DERIVATIVES – **Impressionist** noun & adjective.

ORIGIN – from French impressionniste, originally applied unfavourably with reference to Monet's painting Impression: soleil levant (1872).

impressionist > noun an entertainer who impersonates famous people.

impressionistic > adjective **1** based on subjective impressions presented in an unsystematic way. **2** (**Impressionistic**) in the style of Impressionism.

DERIVATIVES – **impressionistically** adverb.

impressive > adjective evoking admiration through size, quality, or skill.

DERIVATIVES – **impressively** adverb **impressiveness** noun.

imprimatur /imprimaytər/ > noun **1** a person's approval or endorsement of an

action, publication, etc. **2** an official licence issued by the Roman Catholic Church to print an ecclesiastical or religious book.

ORIGIN – Latin, 'let it be printed'.

imprint > verb /imprint/ **1** (usu. **be imprinted**) make (a mark) on an object by pressure. **2** make an impression or mark on. **3** (**imprint on**) (of a young animal) come to recognise as a parent. > noun /imprint/ **1** an impressed mark. **2** a printer's or publisher's name and other details in a publication. **3** a brand name under which books are published, typically the name of a former publishing house now part of a larger group.

ORIGIN – Latin imprimere 'impress, imprint'.

imprison > verb put or keep in prison.

DERIVATIVES – **imprisonment** noun.

ORIGIN – Old French emprisoner.

improbable > adjective not likely to be true or to happen.

DERIVATIVES – **improbability** (pl. **improbabilities**) noun **improbably** adverb.

SYNONYMS – doubtful, dubious, implausible, questionable, unlikely.

impromptu /impromptyōō/ > adjective & adverb unplanned or unrehearsed. > noun (pl. **impromptus**) a short piece of instrumental music, especially a solo, reminiscent of an improvisation.

ORIGIN – from Latin in promptu 'in readiness'.

improper > adjective **1** not conforming with accepted standards of behaviour. **2** unseemly or indecent.

DERIVATIVES – **improperly** adverb.

SYNONYMS – **1** impolite, inappropriate, incorrect. **2** indecent, indecorous, indelicate, unseemly.

COMBINATIONS – **improper fraction** a fraction in which the numerator is greater than the denominator, such as $\frac{5}{4}$.

impropriety /imprəprīəti/ > noun (pl. **improprieties**) improper behaviour or character.

improve > verb **1** make or become better. **2** (**improve on** or **upon**) achieve or produce something better than. **3** (**improving**) giving moral or intellectual benefit.

DERIVATIVES – **improvable** adjective **improver** noun.

SYNONYMS – **1** advance, ameliorate, better, develop.

ANTONYMS – **1** deteriorate, exacerbate.

ORIGIN – Old French emprower, from prou 'profit'.

improvement > noun **1** an instance of improving or being improved. **2** the action of improving or being improved. **3** a thing that makes something better or is better than something else.

improvident > adjective failing to take proper care for the future.

DERIVATIVES – **improvidence** noun **improvidently** adverb.

SYNONYMS – profligate, spendthrift, thoughtless.

improvise* > verb **1** create and perform (music, drama, or verse) spontaneously or without preparation. **2** make from whatever is available.

DERIVATIVES – **improvisation** noun **improvisational** adjective **improvisatory** adjective **improviser** noun.

***SPELLING** – unlike most verbs ending in -ise, **improvise** cannot be spelled with an -ize ending.

ORIGIN – from Latin improvisus 'unforeseen'.

imprudent > adjective not showing care for the consequences of an action; rash.

DERIVATIVES – **imprudence** noun **imprudently** adverb.

impudent /impyoodənt/ > adjective not showing due respect for another person; impertinent.

DERIVATIVES – **impudence** noun **impudently** adverb.

ORIGIN – Latin impudens 'shameless': originally in the sense 'immodest'.

impugn /impyōōn/ > verb dispute the truth, validity, or honesty of.

ORIGIN – Latin impugnare 'assail'.

impulse > noun **1** a sudden strong and unreflective urge to act. **2** a driving force; an impetus. **3** a pulse of electrical energy; a brief current. **4** Physics a force acting briefly on a body and producing a change of momentum.

SYNONYMS – **1** caprice, desire, urge, whim. **2** drive, force, impetus.

ORIGIN – Latin impulsus 'a push', from impellere 'impel'.

impulsion > noun **1** a strong urge to do something. **2** the force or motive behind an action or process.

impulsive > adjective **1** acting or done without forethought. **2** Physics acting as an impulse.

DERIVATIVES – **impulsively** adverb **impulsiveness** noun **impulsivity** noun.

SYNONYMS – **1** hasty, impetuous, rash, spontaneous.

impunity /impyōōniti/ > noun (usu. in phrase **with impunity**) exemption from punishment or from the harmful consequences of an action.

ORIGIN – Latin impunitas, from impunis 'unpunished'.

impure > adjective **1** (of a substance) mixed with undesirable extraneous matter. **2** morally wrong, especially in sexual matters. **3** requiring purification by religious ceremonial.

SYNONYMS – **1** adulterated, contaminated,

defiled, polluted, tainted. **2** corrupt, depraved, dissolute, immoral.

ANTONYMS – pure, uncontaminated.

impurity > *noun* (pl. **impurities**) **1** the quality or condition of being impure. **2** a thing which makes something impure.

impute /im**pyoot**/ > *verb* (usu. **impute to**) attribute (something, especially something bad) to someone.

DERIVATIVES – **imputable** *adjective* **imputation** *noun*.

ORIGIN – Latin *imputare* 'enter in the account'.

IN > *abbreviation* Indiana.

In > *symbol* the chemical element indium.

in > *preposition* **1** expressing the situation of being enclosed or surrounded. **2** expressing motion that results in being within or surrounded by something. **3** expressing a period of time during which an event takes place or a situation remains the case. **4** expressing the length of time before a future event is expected to take place. **5** expressing a state, condition, or quality. **6** expressing inclusion or involvement. **7** indicating a person's occupation or profession. **8** indicating the language or medium used. **9** expressing a value as a proportion of (a whole). > *adverb* **1** expressing movement that results in being enclosed or surrounded. **2** expressing the situation of being enclosed or surrounded. **3** present at one's home or office. **4** expressing arrival at a destination. **5** (of the tide) rising or at its highest level. > *adjective* informal fashionable.

IDIOMS – **be in for** have good reason to expect (something, typically something unpleasant). **in on** privy to (a secret). **in that** for the reason that. **in with** informal enjoying friendly relations with. **the ins and outs** informal all the details.

in. > *abbreviation* inch(es).

in-¹ (also **il-** before *l*; **im-** before *b, m, p*; **ir-** before *r*) > *prefix* **1** (added to adjectives) not: *infertile*. **2** (added to nouns) without; a lack of: *inattention*.

ORIGIN – Latin.

in-² (also **il-** before *l*; **im-** before *b, m, p*; **ir-** before *r*) > *prefix* in; into; towards; within: *influx*.

inability > *noun* the state of being unable to do something.

in absentia /in ab**sen**tiə/ > *adverb* while not present.

ORIGIN – Latin, 'in absence'.

inaccessible > *adjective* **1** unable to be reached or used. **2** difficult to understand or appreciate. **3** not open to advances or influence; unapproachable.

DERIVATIVES – **inaccessibility** *noun* **inaccessibly** *adverb*.

inaccurate > *adjective* not accurate.

DERIVATIVES – **inaccuracy** *noun* **inaccurately** *adverb*.

inaction > *noun* lack of action where some is expected or appropriate.

inactivate > *verb* make inactive or inoperative.

DERIVATIVES – **inactivation** *noun* **inactivator** *noun*.

inactive > *adjective* not active, working, or energetic.

DERIVATIVES – **inactivity** *noun*.

SYNONYMS – dormant, idle, inert, quiescent, torpid.

inadequate > *adjective* **1** insufficient for a purpose. **2** unable to deal with a situation or with life.

DERIVATIVES – **inadequacy** (pl. **inadequacies**) *noun* **inadequately** *adverb*.

inadmissible > *adjective* **1** (especially of evidence in court) not accepted as valid. **2** not to be allowed.

DERIVATIVES – **inadmissibility** *noun*.

inadvertent* > *adjective* not resulting from or achieved through deliberate planning.

DERIVATIVES – **inadvertence** *noun* **inadvertently** *adverb*.

*SPELLING – -*ent*, not -*ant*: inadvert*ent*.

ORIGIN – from **IN-¹** + Latin *advertere* 'turn the mind to'.

inadvisable > *adjective* likely to have unfortunate consequences; unwise.

DERIVATIVES – **inadvisability** *noun*.

inalienable > *adjective* unable to be taken away from or given away by the possessor.

DERIVATIVES – **inalienability** *noun* **inalienably** *adverb*.

inamorato /inammə**raa**tō/ > *noun* (pl. **inamoratos**; fem. **inamorata**, pl. **inamoratas**) a person's lover.

ORIGIN – Italian, 'enamoured'.

inane /i**nayn**/ > *adjective* lacking sense or meaning; silly.

DERIVATIVES – **inanely** *adverb* **inanity** (pl. **inanities**) *noun*.

SYNONYMS – fatuous, foolish, mindless, silly, vacuous.

ORIGIN – Latin *inanis* 'empty, vain'.

inanimate > *adjective* **1** not alive, especially not in the manner of animals and humans. **2** showing no sign of life; lifeless.

inanition /innə**nish**'n/ > *noun* exhaustion caused by lack of nourishment.

ORIGIN – Latin, from *inanire* 'make empty'.

inapplicable > *adjective* not relevant or appropriate.

DERIVATIVES – **inapplicability** *noun*.

inapposite /in**app**əzit/ > *adjective* out of place; inappropriate.

inappropriate > *adjective* not suitable or appropriate.

DERIVATIVES – **inappropriately** *adverb* **inappropriateness** *noun*.

inapt > *adjective* not suitable or appropriate.

DERIVATIVES – **inaptly** *adverb*.

inarguable > *adjective* another term for UNARGUABLE.

DERIVATIVES – **inarguably** *adverb*.

inarticulate /innaar**tik**yoolət/ > *adjective* **1** unable to speak distinctly or express oneself clearly. **2** unspoken or not expressed in words. **3** without joints or articulations.

DERIVATIVES – **inarticulacy** *noun* **inarticulately** *adverb* **inarticulateness** *noun*.

SYNONYMS – **1** faltering, halting, incoherent. **2** silent, unspoken, wordless.

ANTONYMS – **1** articulate, eloquent.

inasmuch > *adverb* (**inasmuch as**) **1** to the extent that. **2** considering that; since.

inattentive > *adjective* not paying attention.

DERIVATIVES – **inattention** *noun* **inattentively** *adverb* **inattentiveness** *noun*.

inaudible > *adjective* unable to be heard.

DERIVATIVES – **inaudibility** *noun* **inaudibly** *adverb*.

inaugurate /in**aw**gyoorayt/ > *verb* **1** begin or introduce (a system, project, etc.). **2** admit formally to office. **3** officially mark the beginning or first public use of (a building, service, etc).

DERIVATIVES – **inaugural** *adjective* **inauguration** *noun* **inaugurator** *noun*.

ORIGIN – from Latin *inauguratus* 'consecrated after interpreting omens', from *augurare* 'to augur'.

inauspicious > *adjective* not conducive to success; unpromising.

DERIVATIVES – **inauspiciously** *adverb* **inauspiciousness** *noun*.

inauthentic > *noun* not authentic, genuine, or sincere.

DERIVATIVES – **inauthenticity** *noun*.

inboard > *adverb* & *adjective* within or towards the centre of a ship, aircraft, or vehicle.

inborn > *adjective* existing from birth.

inbound > *adjective* & *adverb* travelling towards a place, especially when returning to the original point of departure.

inbred > *adjective* **1** produced by inbreeding. **2** existing from birth; congenital.

inbreed > *verb* (past and past participle **inbred**) breed from closely related people or animals, especially over many generations.

DERIVATIVES – **inbreeding** *noun*.

inbuilt > *adjective* existing as an original or essential part.

Inc. > *abbreviation* N. Amer. Incorporated.

Inca /**ing**kə/ > *noun* **1** a member of a South American Indian people living in the central Andes before the Spanish conquest in the early 1530s. **2** the supreme ruler of this people.

DERIVATIVES – **Incan** *adjective*.

ORIGIN – Quechua, 'lord, royal person'.

incalculable > *adjective* **1** too great to be calculated or estimated. **2** not able to be calculated, estimated, or predicted.

DERIVATIVES – **incalculability** *noun* **incalculably** *adverb*.

in camera > *adverb* see CAMERA.

incandescent /inkan**dess**'nt/ > *adjective* **1** glowing as a result of being heated. **2** (of an electric light) containing a filament which glows white-hot when heated by a current passed through it. **3** *informal* extremely angry.

DERIVATIVES – **incandescence** *noun* **incandescently** *adverb*.

ORIGIN – from Latin *incandescere* 'glow'.

incant /in**kant**/ > *verb* chant or intone.

incantation > *noun* words said as a magic spell or charm.

DERIVATIVES – **incantatory** *adjective*.

ORIGIN – Latin, from *incantare* 'chant, bewitch'.

incapable > *adjective* **1** (**incapable of**) lacking the ability or required quality to do. **2** unable to behave rationally.

DERIVATIVES – **incapability** *noun*.

incapacitate /inkə**pass**itayt/ > *verb* prevent from functioning in a normal way.

DERIVATIVES – **incapacitant** *noun* **incapacitation** *noun*.

incapacity > *noun* (pl. **incapacities**) **1** inability to do something or to manage one's affairs. **2** *legal* disqualification.

incarcerate /in**kaar**sərayt/ > *verb* imprison or confine.

DERIVATIVES – **incarceration** *noun*.

ORIGIN – Latin *incarcerare*, from *carcer* 'prison'.

incarnadine /in**kaar**nədīn/ *literary* > *noun* a bright crimson or pinkish-red colour. > *verb* make (something) this colour.

ORIGIN – Italian *incarnatino* 'flesh colour'.

incarnate > *adjective* /in**kaar**nət/ (often after a noun) **1** (of a deity or spirit) embodied in flesh; in human form. **2** represented in the ultimate or most typical form: *capitalism incarnate*. > *verb* /in**kaar**nayt/ **1** embody or represent (a deity or spirit) in human form. **2** be the living embodiment of (a quality).

ORIGIN – from Latin *incarnare* 'make flesh', from *caro* 'flesh'.

incarnation > *noun* **1** a living embodiment of a deity, spirit, or abstract quality. **2** (**the Incarnation**) (in Christian theology) the embodiment of God the Son in human flesh as Jesus Christ. **3** (with reference to reincarnation) each of a series of earthly lifetimes or forms.

incase > *verb* variant spelling of ENCASE.

incautious > *adjective* heedless of potential problems or risks.

DERIVATIVES – **incaution** *noun* **incautiously** *adverb*.

SYNONYMS – heedless, imprudent, reckless, unwary.

incendiary /in**sen**diəri/ > *adjective* **1** (of a bomb or other device) designed to cause fires. **2** tending to stir up conflict or controversy. > *noun* (pl. **incendiaries**) an incendiary device.

DERIVATIVES – **incendiarism** *noun*.

ORIGIN – Latin *incendiarius*, from *incendium* 'conflagration'.

incense¹ /**in**senss/ > *noun* a gum, spice, or other substance that is burned for the sweet smell it produces. > *verb* perfume with incense or a similar fragrance.

ORIGIN – Latin *incensum* 'something burnt, incense'.

incense² /in**senss**/ > *verb* make very angry.

ORIGIN – Latin *incendere* 'set fire to'.

incentive > *noun* a thing that motivates or encourages someone to action or increased effort.

DERIVATIVES – **incentivise** (also **incentivize**) *verb*.

SYNONYMS – encouragement, enticement, impetus, inducement, motivation.

wordpower facts
Incentive

The word **incentive** is from Latin *incentivum* 'something that sets the tune or incites', from *incantare* 'to chant or charm'. Through *incantare* **incentive** is thus linked to **enchant** and **incantation**, while the root word *cantare* 'sing' connects it to **cantata**, **chant**, and **recant**.

inception > *noun* the establishment or starting point of an institution or activity.

ORIGIN – Latin, from *incipere* 'begin'.

incertitude > *noun* a state of uncertainty or hesitation.

incessant > *adjective* continuing without pause or interruption.

DERIVATIVES – **incessantly** *adverb*.

SYNONYMS – ceaseless, constant, endless, interminable, relentless.

ORIGIN – Latin, from *in-* 'not' + *cessare* 'cease'.

incest > *noun* sexual relations between people classed as being too closely related to marry each other.

ORIGIN – from Latin *in-* 'not' + *castus* 'chaste'.

incestuous /in**sest**yooəss/ > *adjective* **1** involving or guilty of incest. **2** (of a relationship or community) excessively close and resistant to outside influence.

DERIVATIVES – **incestuously** *adverb*.

inch > *noun* **1** a unit of linear measure equal to one twelfth of a foot (2.54 cm). **2** a very small amount or distance: *don't yield an inch*. > *verb* move along slowly and carefully.

IDIOMS – **every inch 1** the whole area or distance. **2** entirely; very much so. **give someone an inch and they will take a mile** *proverb* once concessions have been made to someone they will demand a great deal. (**to**) **within an inch of one's life** almost to the point of death.

ORIGIN – Latin *uncia* 'twelfth part': compare with OUNCE.

inchoate > *adjective* /in**kō**ayt/ **1** not fully formed or developed; rudimentary. **2** confused or incoherent.

DERIVATIVES – **inchoately** *adverb*.

ORIGIN – from Latin *inchoare*, variant of *incohare* 'begin'.

incidence > *noun* **1** the occurrence, rate, or frequency of a disease, crime, or other undesirable thing. **2** *Physics* the intersection of a line or ray with a surface.

incident > *noun* **1** an event or occurrence. **2** a violent event, such as an attack. **3** the occurrence of dangerous or exciting events: *the plane landed without incident*. > *adjective* **1** (**incident to**) resulting from. **2** (of light or other radiation) falling on or striking something. **3** *Physics* relating to incidence.

ORIGIN – from Latin *incidere* 'fall upon, happen to'.

incidental > *adjective* **1** occurring as a minor accompaniment or by chance in connection with something else. **2** (**incidental to**) liable to happen as a consequence of. > *noun* an incidental detail, expense, etc.

COMBINATIONS – **incidental music** music used in a film or play as a background.

incidentally > *adverb* **1** by the way. **2** in an incidental manner.

incinerate /in**sinn**ərayt/ > *verb* destroy by burning.

DERIVATIVES – **incineration** *noun*.

ORIGIN – Latin *incinerare* 'burn to ashes'.

incinerator > *noun* an apparatus for incinerating waste material.

incipient /in**sipp**iənt/ > *adjective* beginning to happen or develop.

DERIVATIVES – **incipiently** *adverb*.

ORIGIN – from Latin *incipere* 'undertake, begin'.

incise* /in**sīz**/ > *verb* **1** make a cut or cuts in (a surface). **2** cut (a mark or decoration) into a surface.

***SPELLING** – **incise** cannot be spelled with an *-ize* ending.

ORIGIN – Latin *incidere* 'cut into'.

incision > *noun* **1** a surgical cut in skin or flesh. **2** the action or process of incising.

incisive > *adjective* **1** (of an action) quick and direct. **2** intelligently analytical and concise.

DERIVATIVES – **incisively** *adverb* **incisiveness** *noun*.

incisor > *noun* a narrow-edged tooth at the front of the mouth, adapted for cutting.

incite > *verb* **1** encourage or stir up (violent

or unlawful behaviour). **2** urge or persuade to act in a violent or unlawful way.

DERIVATIVES – **incitement** noun **inciter** noun.

ORIGIN – Latin *incitare*, from *citare* 'rouse'.

incivility > noun (pl. **incivilities**) rude or unsociable speech or behaviour.

inclement /inklemmənt/ > adjective (of the weather) unpleasantly cold or wet.

DERIVATIVES – **inclemency** noun.

inclination > noun **1** a natural tendency to act or feel in a particular way. **2** an interest in or liking for doing something. **3** a slope or slant. **4** the angle at which a straight line or plane is inclined to another.

SYNONYMS – **1** predisposition, proclivity, propensity, tendency. **2** liking, penchant, predilection.

incline > verb /inklīn/ **1** (usu. **be inclined to** or **towards** or **to do**) be favourably disposed towards or willing to do something. **2** (usu. **be inclined to** or **to do**) have a specified tendency or talent. **3** lean or turn away from a given plane or direction, especially the vertical or horizontal. **4** bend (one's head) forwards and downwards. > noun /inklīn/ an inclined surface or slope.

COMBINATIONS – **inclined plane** a plane inclined at an angle to the horizontal, especially as a means of reducing the force needed to raise a load.

ORIGIN – Latin *inclinare* 'to bend towards'.

inclose > verb variant spelling of ENCLOSE.

inclosure > noun variant spelling of ENCLOSURE.

include > verb **1** comprise or contain as part of a whole. **2** make or treat as part of a whole or set.

SYNONYMS – **1** comprise, contain, embrace, encompass, incorporate. **2** add, enter, insert, introduce.

ANTONYMS – exclude, omit.

ORIGIN – Latin *includere* 'shut in'.

including > preposition containing as part of the whole being considered.

inclusion > noun **1** the action of including or the state of being included. **2** a person or thing that is included.

inclusive > adjective **1** including all the expected or required services or items. **2** (**inclusive of**) containing (a specified element) as part of a whole. **3** (after a noun) between and including the limits stated: *from 55 to 59 inclusive.* **4** not excluding any section of society or any party.

DERIVATIVES – **inclusively** adverb **inclusiveness** noun.

ANTONYMS – exclusive.

incognito /inkogneetō/ > adjective & adverb having one's true identity concealed. > noun (pl. **incognitos**) an assumed or false identity.

ORIGIN – Italian, 'unknown'.

incoherent > adjective **1** incomprehensible or confusing in speech or writing. **2** internally inconsistent; illogical. **3** Physics (of light or other waves) having no fixed phase relationship.

DERIVATIVES – **incoherence** noun **incoherency** noun **incoherently** adverb.

SYNONYMS – **1** confusing, disconnected, disjointed, incomprehensible, muddled.

incombustible > adjective (especially of a building material) not inflammable.

income > noun money received, especially on a regular basis, for work or through investments.

COMBINATIONS – **income support** (in the UK and Canada) payment made by the state to people on a low income. **income tax** tax levied directly on personal income.

incomer > noun chiefly Brit. a person who has come to live in an area in which they have not grown up.

incoming > adjective **1** coming in. **2** (of an official or administration) having just been elected or appointed to succeed another. > noun (**incomings**) revenue; income.

incommensurable /inkəmensherəb'l/ > adjective **1** not able to be judged or measured by the same standards. **2** Mathematics (of numbers) in a ratio that cannot be expressed by means of whole numbers.

DERIVATIVES – **incommensurability** noun.

incommensurate > adjective **1** (**incommensurate with**) out of keeping or proportion with. **2** another term for INCOMMENSURABLE (in sense 1).

DERIVATIVES – **incommensurateness** noun.

incommode > verb formal cause inconvenience to.

ORIGIN – Latin *incommodare*, from *in-* 'not' + *commodus* 'convenient'.

incommodious > adjective formal or dated causing inconvenience or discomfort.

incommunicable > adjective not able to be communicated to others.

incommunicado /inkəmyōōnikaadō/ > adjective & adverb not able to communicate with other people.

ORIGIN – Spanish *incomunicado*, from *incomunicar* 'deprive of communication'.

incomparable /inkompərəb'l/ > adjective **1** without an equal in quality or extent. **2** unable to be compared; totally different.

DERIVATIVES – **incomparably** adverb.

incompatible > adjective **1** (of two things) not able to exist or be used together. **2** (of two people) unable to have a harmonious relationship.

DERIVATIVES – **incompatibility** noun.

incompetent > adjective **1** not sufficiently skilful to do something successfully. **2** Law not qualified to act in a particular capacity. > noun an incompetent person.

DERIVATIVES – **incompetence** noun **incompetency** noun **incompetently** adverb.

SYNONYMS – adjective **1** hopeless, incapable, ineffectual, inept.

incomplete > adjective not complete.

DERIVATIVES – **incompletely** adverb **incompleteness** noun **incompletion** noun.

SYNONYMS – partial, unfinished.

incomprehensible > adjective not able to be understood.

DERIVATIVES – **incomprehensibility** noun **incomprehensibly** adverb **incomprehension** noun.

SYNONYMS – impenetrable, mysterious, unfathomable, unintelligible.

ANTONYMS – comprehensible, understandable.

incompressible > adjective not able to be compressed.

inconceivable > adjective not capable of being imagined or grasped mentally.

DERIVATIVES – **inconceivably** adverb.

inconclusive > adjective not conclusive.

DERIVATIVES – **inconclusively** adverb **inconclusiveness** noun.

incongruous /inkonggrooəss/ > adjective out of place.

DERIVATIVES – **incongruity** (pl. **incongruities**) noun **incongruously** adverb.

inconsequent > adjective **1** not connected or following logically. **2** inconsequential.

DERIVATIVES – **inconsequence** noun **inconsequently** adverb.

inconsequential > adjective not important or significant.

DERIVATIVES – **inconsequentiality** noun **inconsequentially** adverb.

inconsiderable > adjective small in size, amount, extent, etc.: *a not inconsiderable number.*

inconsiderate > adjective thoughtlessly causing hurt or inconvenience to others.

DERIVATIVES – **inconsiderately** adverb **inconsiderateness** noun.

SYNONYMS – insensitive, tactless, thoughtless, unthinking.

inconsistent > adjective not consistent.

DERIVATIVES – **inconsistency** noun **inconsistently** adverb.

inconsolable > adjective not able to be comforted or consoled.

DERIVATIVES – **inconsolably** adverb.

inconspicuous > adjective not clearly visible or attracting attention.

DERIVATIVES – **inconspicuously** adverb **inconspicuousness** noun.

SYNONYMS – discreet, unobtrusive.

inconstant > adjective frequently changing; variable or irregular.

DERIVATIVES – **inconstancy** *noun*.

SYNONYMS – changeable, irregular, mutable, unstable, variable.

ANTONYMS – constant, unchanging.

incontestable > *adjective* not able to be disputed.

DERIVATIVES – **incontestably** *adverb*.

incontinent > *adjective* **1** lacking voluntary control over urination or defecation. **2** lacking self-restraint; uncontrolled.

DERIVATIVES – **incontinence** *noun* **incontinently** *adverb*.

incontrovertible > *adjective* not able to be denied or disputed.

DERIVATIVES – **incontrovertibly** *adverb*.

inconvenience > *noun* the state or fact of being slightly troublesome or difficult. > *verb* cause inconvenience to.

DERIVATIVES – **inconvenient** *adjective* **inconveniently** *adverb*.

incorporate > *verb* **1** take in or include as part of a whole. **2** constitute (a company, city, or other organisation) as a legal corporation. > *adjective* constituted as a legal corporation; incorporated.

DERIVATIVES – **incorporation** *noun* **incorporative** *adjective* **incorporator** *noun*.

ORIGIN – Latin *incorporare* 'embody', from *corpus* 'body'.

incorporeal /inkor**por**iəl/ > *adjective* not composed of matter; having no material existence.

incorrect > *adjective* not in accordance with fact or standards; wrong.

DERIVATIVES – **incorrectly** *adverb* **incorrectness** *noun*.

SYNONYMS – erroneous, inaccurate, mistaken, untrue, wrong.

ANTONYMS – correct, right.

incorrigible > *adjective* not able to be corrected or reformed.

DERIVATIVES – **incorrigibility** *noun* **incorrigibly** *adverb*.

ORIGIN – Latin *incorrigibilis*, from *in-* 'not' + *corrigibilis* 'able to be corrected'.

incorruptible > *adjective* **1** not susceptible to corruption, especially by bribery. **2** not subject to death or decay.

DERIVATIVES – **incorruptibility** *noun*.

increase > *verb* make or become greater in size, amount, or degree. > *noun* an instance or the action of increasing.

DERIVATIVES – **increasing** *adjective* **increasingly** *adverb*.

SYNONYMS – *verb* expand, extend, multiply. *noun* expansion, extension, growth.

ANTONYMS – *verb* decrease, reduce.

ORIGIN – Latin *increscere*, from *crescere* 'grow'.

incredible > *adjective* **1** impossible or hard to believe. **2** informal extraordinarily good.

DERIVATIVES – **incredibility** *noun* **incredibly** *adverb*.

SYNONYMS – **1** far-fetched, implausible, improbable, unbelievable, unlikely.

incredulous > *adjective* unwilling or unable to believe.

DERIVATIVES – **incredulity** *noun* **incredulously** *adverb*.

USAGE – something that cannot be believed is **incredible**; someone who cannot believe it is **incredulous**.

SYNONYMS – disbelieving, doubtful, dubious, sceptical.

increment /**ing**krimənt/ > *noun* an increase or addition, especially one of a series on a fixed scale.

DERIVATIVES – **incremental** *adjective* **incrementally** *adverb*.

ORIGIN – Latin *incrementum*, from *increscere* 'increase'.

incrementalism > *noun* belief in or advocacy of change by degrees.

DERIVATIVES – **incrementalist** *noun* & *adjective*.

incriminate /in**krimm**inayt/ > *verb* make (someone) appear guilty of a crime or wrongdoing.

DERIVATIVES – **incrimination** *noun* **incriminatory** *adjective*.

ORIGIN – Latin *incriminare* 'accuse', from *crimen* 'crime'.

in-crowd > *noun* (**the in-crowd**) informal a small group of people that are particularly fashionable or popular.

incrust > *verb* variant spelling of ENCRUST.

incubate /**ing**kyoobayt/ > *verb* **1** (of a bird) sit on (eggs) to keep them warm and bring them to hatching. **2** keep (bacteria, cells, etc.) at a suitable temperature so that they develop. **3** (with reference to an infectious disease) develop slowly without outward or perceptible signs.

DERIVATIVES – **incubation** *noun*.

ORIGIN – Latin *incubare* 'lie on'.

incubator > *noun* **1** an apparatus used to hatch eggs or grow micro-organisms under controlled conditions. **2** an enclosed apparatus providing a controlled and protective environment for the care of premature babies.

incubus /**ing**kyoobəss/ > *noun* (pl. **incubi** /**ing**kyoobī/) **1** a male demon believed to have sexual intercourse with sleeping women. **2** archaic a nightmare.

ORIGIN – Latin *incubo* 'nightmare', from *incubare* 'lie on'.

inculcate /in**kul**kayt/ > *verb* instil (an idea or habit) by persistent instruction.

DERIVATIVES – **inculcation** *noun*.

ORIGIN – Latin *inculcare* 'press in'.

incumbency > *noun* (pl. **incumbencies**) the period during which someone holds a particular office or post.

incumbent /in**kum**b'nt/ > *adjective* **1** (**incumbent on** or **upon**) required of (someone) as a duty. **2** currently holding office. > *noun* the holder of an office or post.

ORIGIN – Latin *incumbens*, from *incumbere* 'lie or lean on'.

incunabulum /inkyoo**nab**yooləm/ > *noun* (pl. **incunabula**) an early printed book, especially one printed before 1501.

ORIGIN – from Latin *incunabula* 'swaddling clothes, cradle'.

incur* > *verb* (**incurred**, **incurring**) become subject to (something unpleasant) as a result of one's actions.

*****SPELLING – one *r* in *incur* and *incurs*, two in *incurred* and *incurring*.

ORIGIN – Latin *incurrere* 'run into or towards'.

incurable > *adjective* not able to be cured. > *noun* an incurable person.

DERIVATIVES – **incurability** *noun* **incurably** *adverb*.

incurious > *adjective* not eager to know something; lacking curiosity.

DERIVATIVES – **incuriosity** *noun* **incuriously** *adverb*.

incursion > *noun* an invasion or attack, especially a sudden or brief one.

ORIGIN – Latin, from *incurrere* 'run into or towards'.

indebted > *adjective* owing money or gratitude.

DERIVATIVES – **indebtedness** *noun*.

indecent > *adjective* **1** not conforming with accepted standards of behaviour or morality. **2** not appropriate; unseemly: *indecent haste.*

DERIVATIVES – **indecency** *noun* **indecently** *adverb*.

SYNONYMS – **1** crude, immodest, improper, obscene, vulgar.

ANTONYMS – **1** decent, proper.

COMBINATIONS – **indecent assault** sexual assault that does not involve rape. **indecent exposure** the crime of intentionally showing one's genitals in public.

indecipherable /indi**sī**fərəb'l/ > *adjective* not able to be read or understood.

indecisive > *adjective* **1** not able to make decisions quickly and effectively. **2** not settling an issue: *indecisive results.*

DERIVATIVES – **indecision** *noun* **indecisively** *adverb* **indecisiveness** *noun*.

indecorous /in**dekk**ərəss/ > *adjective* not in keeping with good taste and propriety; improper.

DERIVATIVES – **indecorously** *adverb*.

indeed > *adverb* **1** used to emphasise a statement, description, or response. **2** used to introduce a further and stronger or more surprising point. **3** used in a response to express interest, incredulity, or contempt.

ORIGIN – at first as *in deed*.

indefatigable /indi**fatt**igəb'l/ > *adjective* never tiring or stopping.

DERIVATIVES – **indefatigably** *adverb*.

ORIGIN – Latin *indefatigabilis*, from *fatigare* 'wear out'.

indefensible > *adjective* for which no reasonable justification can be given.

DERIVATIVES – **indefensibly** *adverb*.

indefinable > *adjective* not able to be defined or described exactly.

DERIVATIVES – **indefinably** *adverb*.

indefinite > *adjective* 1 not clearly expressed or defined; vague. 2 lasting for an unknown or unstated length of time. 3 Grammar (of a word, inflection, etc.) not determining the person or thing referred to.

DERIVATIVES – **indefinitely** *adverb* **indefiniteness** *noun*.

SYNONYMS – 1 imprecise, uncertain, undecided, vague. 2 indeterminate, unspecified.

COMBINATIONS – **indefinite article** Grammar a determiner (*a* and *an* in English) that introduces a noun phrase and implies that the thing referred to is non-specific. **indefinite pronoun** Grammar a pronoun that does not refer to any person or thing in particular, e.g. *anything, everyone*.

indelible /inˈdellib'l/ > *adjective* 1 (of ink or a mark) unable to be removed. 2 unable to be forgotten.

DERIVATIVES – **indelibly** *adverb*.

ORIGIN – Latin *indelebilis*, from *in-* 'not' + *delere* 'delete'.

indelicate > *adjective* 1 lacking sensitive understanding or tact. 2 slightly indecent.

DERIVATIVES – **indelicacy** *noun* **indelicately** *adverb*.

indemnify /inˈdemnifī/ > *verb* (**indemnifies, indemnified**) 1 compensate (someone) for harm or loss. 2 exempt (someone) from legal responsibility for their actions.

DERIVATIVES – **indemnification** *noun* **indemnifier** *noun*.

indemnity /inˈdemniti/ > *noun* (pl. **indemnities**) 1 security or protection against a loss or other financial burden. 2 security against or exemption from legal responsibility for one's actions. 3 a sum of money paid as compensation, especially by a country defeated in war.

ORIGIN – Latin *indemnitas*, from *indemnis* 'unhurt, free from loss'.

indent[1] > *verb* /inˈdent/ 1 form deep recesses or notches in. 2 position or begin (a line or block of text) further from the margin than the main part of the text. 3 make a requisition or written order for something. > *noun* /ˈindent/ 1 Brit. an official order or requisition for goods or stores. 2 a space left by indenting text. 3 an indentation.

ORIGIN – Latin *indentare*, from *dens* 'tooth'.

indent[2] /inˈdent/ > *verb* make a dent or depression in.

indentation > *noun* 1 the action of indenting or the state of being indented. 2 a deep recess or notch.

indenture /inˈdenchər/ > *noun* 1 a formal agreement, contract, or list, originally one of which copies with indented edges were made for the contracting parties. 2 an agreement binding an apprentice to a master. 3 historical a contract by which a person agreed to work for a set period for a colonial landowner in exchange for passage to the colony. > *verb* chiefly historical bind by an indenture.

DERIVATIVES – **indentureship** *noun*.

independence > *noun* the fact or state of being independent.

SYNONYMS – autonomy, freedom, individualism, self-reliance, self-sufficiency.

independent* > *adjective* 1 free from outside control or influence. 2 (of a country) self governing. 3 not depending on another for livelihood or subsistence. 4 not connected with another; separate. 5 (of broadcasting, a school, etc.) not supported by public funds. > *noun* an independent person or body.

DERIVATIVES – **independency** *noun* **independently** *adverb*.

*SPELLING – *-ent*, not *-ant*: independ*ent*.

SYNONYMS – 2 autonomous, self-determining, self-governing, sovereign. 3 self-reliant, self-sufficient. 4 individual, separate.

ANTONYMS – dependent, subservient.

in-depth > *adjective* comprehensive and thorough.

indescribable > *adjective* too unusual, extreme, or indefinite to be adequately described.

DERIVATIVES – **indescribably** *adverb*.

indestructible > *adjective* not able to be destroyed.

DERIVATIVES – **indestructibility** *noun* **indestructibly** *adverb*.

indeterminable > *adjective* not able to be determined.

indeterminate /indiˈterminət/ > *adjective* 1 not exactly known, established, or defined. 2 Mathematics (of a quantity) having no definite or definable value.

DERIVATIVES – **indeterminacy** *noun* **indeterminately** *adverb*.

index /ˈindeks/ > *noun* (pl. **indexes** or especially in technical use **indices** /ˈindiseez/) 1 an alphabetical list of names, subjects, etc., with references to the places in a book where they occur. 2 an alphabetical list or catalogue of books or documents. 3 an indicator, sign, or measure of something: *national security was no longer an index of weaponry*. 4 a number representing the relative value or magnitude of something in terms of a standard. 5 Mathematics an exponent or other superscript or subscript number appended to a quantity. > *verb* 1 record in or provide with an index. 2 link the value of (prices, wages, etc.) automatically to the value of a price index.

DERIVATIVES – **indexable** *adjective* **indexation** *noun* **indexer** *noun*.

COMBINATIONS – **index finger** the forefinger. **index-linked** Brit. adjusted according to the value of a retail price index.

ORIGIN – Latin, 'forefinger, informer, sign'.

India ink > *noun* North American term for *Indian ink*.

Indiaman > *noun* historical a ship engaged in trade between Europe and India or the East or West Indies.

Indian > *noun* 1 a person from India. 2 an American Indian. > *adjective* 1 relating to India. 2 relating to American Indians.

WORDFINDER – *Indian languages:* Sanskrit (*ancient language of India*), Bengali, Gujarati, Hindi, Hindustani, Marathi, Tamil, Urdu; *Indian food:* biriani, chapatti, curry, jalfrezi, kedgeree, korma, nan, pilaf, poppadom, tikka, vindaloo.

DERIVATIVES – **Indianise** (also **Indianize**) *verb* **Indianism** *noun* **Indianness** *noun*.

USAGE – **American Indian** should be used in preference to **Indian** or **Red Indian** for the indigenous inhabitants of North America: the latter terms are old-fashioned and recall the stereotypical images of the Wild West. In the US, **Native American** is often preferred.

COMBINATIONS – **Indian clubs** a pair of bottle-shaped clubs swung to exercise the arms in gymnastics. **Indian corn** maize. **Indian file** single file. **Indian ink** a deep black ink, used especially in drawing and technical graphics. **Indian summer** a period of dry, warm weather occurring in late autumn.

wordpower facts

Indian

India is a Greek word that comes from Persian *Hind* (the root of **Hindi** and **Hindu**) and ultimately from Sanskrit *sindhu* 'river', specifically 'the Indus'. Both the Greeks and the Persians extended the name to include all the country east of the Indus. American native peoples were called 'Indian' as a result of Christopher Columbus and other early voyagers believing that, when they reached the east coast of America, they had reached the Indies by a new route.

India rubber > *noun* natural rubber.

indicate > *verb* **1** point out; show. **2** be a sign or symptom of. **3** state briefly or indirectly. **4** suggest as a desirable or necessary course of action. **5** chiefly Brit. (of a driver) use an indicator to signal an intention to change lanes or turn.

DERIVATIVES – **indication** *noun*.

SYNONYMS – **1** demonstrate, display, reveal, show. **2** betoken, denote, signal.

ORIGIN – Latin *indicare*, from *dicare* 'make known'.

indicative /in**dikk**ətiv/ > *adjective* **1** serving as a sign or indication. **2** Grammar (of a form of a verb) expressing a simple statement of fact, rather than something imagined, wished, or commanded. > *noun* Grammar an indicative verb.

DERIVATIVES – **indicatively** *adverb*.

indicator > *noun* **1** a thing that indicates a state or level. **2** a gauge or meter of a specified kind. **3** a flashing light on a vehicle to show that it is about to change lanes or turn. **4** Brit. an information board or screen in a railway station, airport, etc. **5** Chemistry a compound which changes colour at a specific pH value or in the presence of a particular substance, and can be used to monitor a chemical change.

indices plural of INDEX.

indict /in**dīt**/ > *verb* formally accuse or charge with a serious crime.

DERIVATIVES – **indictee** *noun* **indicter** *noun*.

ORIGIN – Latin *indicere* 'proclaim, appoint'.

indictable > *adjective* (of an offence) chargeable as a serious crime and warranting a trial by jury.

indictment > *noun* **1** Law a formal charge or accusation of a serious crime. **2** an indication that a system or situation is bad and deserves to be condemned.

indie informal > *adjective* (of a pop group or record label) not belonging or affiliated to a major record company. > *noun* **1** an indie pop group or record label. **2** an independent film company.

indifferent > *adjective* **1** having no particular interest or sympathy; unconcerned. **2** not particularly good; mediocre.

DERIVATIVES – **indifference** *noun* **indifferently** *adverb*.

SYNONYMS – **1** apathetic, blasé, unconcerned, uninterested. **2** average, commonplace, mediocre, undistinguished.

ANTONYMS – **1** enthusiastic.

ORIGIN – Latin, 'making no difference'.

indigenise /in**di**jinīz/ (also **indigenize**) > *verb* bring under the control of native people.

DERIVATIVES – **indigenisation** *noun*.

indigenous > *adjective* originating or occurring naturally in a particular place; native.

DERIVATIVES – **indigenously** *adverb* **indigenousness** *noun*.

ORIGIN – from Latin *indigena* 'a native'.

indigent /in**di**jənt/ > *adjective* poor; needy. > *noun* a needy person.

DERIVATIVES – **indigence** *noun*.

ORIGIN – Latin, from *indigere* 'to lack'.

indigestible > *adjective* **1** difficult or impossible to digest. **2** difficult to read or understand.

DERIVATIVES – **indigestibility** *noun* **indigestibly** *adverb*.

indigestion > *noun* pain or discomfort in the stomach caused by difficulty in digesting food.

DERIVATIVES – **indigestive** *adjective*.

indignation > *noun* annoyance provoked by what is perceived as unfair treatment.

DERIVATIVES – **indignant** *adjective* **indignantly** *adverb*.

ORIGIN – Latin, from *indignari* 'regard as unworthy'.

indignity > *noun* (pl. **indignities**) treatment or circumstances causing one to feel shame or to lose one's dignity.

indigo /in**di**gō/ > *noun* (pl. **indigos** or **indigoes**) **1** a dark blue dye obtained from a tropical plant. **2** a colour between blue and violet in the spectrum.

ORIGIN – Greek *indikos* 'Indian'.

indirect > *adjective* **1** not direct. **2** (of costs) deriving from overhead charges or subsidiary work. **3** (of taxation) levied on goods and services rather than income or profits.

DERIVATIVES – **indirection** *noun* **indirectly** *adverb* **indirectness** *noun*.

SYNONYMS – **1** circuitous, meandering, oblique, roundabout.

COMBINATIONS – **indirect object** Grammar a noun phrase referring to a person or thing that is affected by the action of a transitive verb but is not the primary object (e.g. *him* in *give him the book*). **indirect question** Grammar a question in reported speech (e.g. *they asked who I was*). **indirect speech** reported speech.

indiscernible /indi**ser**nib'l/ > *adjective* impossible to see or clearly distinguish.

DERIVATIVES – **indiscernibility** *noun* **indiscernibly** *adverb*.

indiscipline > *noun* lack of discipline.

indiscreet > *adjective* too ready to reveal things that should remain secret or private.

DERIVATIVES – **indiscreetly** *adverb*.

indiscretion > *noun* behaviour or an act or statement that is indiscreet.

indiscriminate /indi**skrimm**inət/ > *adjective* done or acting at random or without careful judgement.

DERIVATIVES – **indiscriminately** *adverb* **indiscriminateness** *noun*.

SYNONYMS – arbitrary, haphazard, random, unselective.

indispensable* > *adjective* that cannot be dispensed with; essential.

DERIVATIVES – **indispensability** *noun* **indispensableness** *noun* **indispensably** *adverb*.

*****SPELLING** – *-able*, not *-ible*: indispens*able*.

SYNONYMS – crucial, essential, fundamental, vital.

indisposed > *adjective* **1** slightly unwell. **2** (**indisposed to**) unwilling to do something.

indisposition > *noun* **1** a slight illness. **2** unwillingness.

indisputable > *adjective* unable to be challenged or denied.

DERIVATIVES – **indisputability** *noun* **indisputably** *adverb*.

indissoluble /indi**sol**yoob'l/ > *adjective* unable to be destroyed; lasting.

DERIVATIVES – **indissolubility** *noun* **indissolubly** *adverb*.

indistinct > *adjective* not clear or sharply defined.

DERIVATIVES – **indistinctly** *adverb* **indistinctness** *noun*.

indistinguishable > *adjective* not able to be identified as different or distinct.

DERIVATIVES – **indistinguishably** *adverb*.

indium /in**di**əm/ > *noun* a soft, silvery-white metallic chemical element resembling zinc, used in some alloys and semiconductor devices.

ORIGIN – from INDIGO (because of two indigo lines in its spectrum).

individual > *adjective* **1** single; separate. **2** of or for one particular person. **3** striking or unusual; original. > *noun* **1** a single human being or item as distinct from a group. **2** a distinctive or original person.

DERIVATIVES – **individualisation** (also **individualization**) *noun* **individualise** (also **individualize**) *verb* **individually** *adverb*.

ORIGIN – from Latin *individuus*, from *in-* 'not' + *dividere* 'to divide'; originally meaning 'indivisible'.

individualism > *noun* **1** independence and self-reliance. **2** a social theory favouring freedom of action for individuals.

DERIVATIVES – **individualist** *noun* & *adjective* **individualistic** *adjective*.

individuality > *noun* **1** distinctive quality or character. **2** separate existence.

individuate > *verb* distinguish from others of the same kind; single out.

DERIVATIVES – **individuation** *noun*.

indivisible > *adjective* **1** unable to be divided or separated. **2** (of a number) unable to be divided by another number exactly without leaving a remainder.

DERIVATIVES – **indivisibility** *noun* **indivisibly** *adverb*.

Indo-Chinese > *adjective* relating to the peninsula of Indo-China, which contains

Burma (Myanmar), Thailand, Malaya, Laos, Cambodia, and Vietnam.

indoctrinate /in**dok**trinayt/ > *verb* cause to accept a set of beliefs uncritically through repeated instruction.

DERIVATIVES – **indoctrination** *noun* **indoctrinator** *noun*.

ORIGIN – from DOCTRINE: originally in the sense 'teach or instruct'.

Indo-European > *noun* **1** the family of languages spoken over the greater part of Europe and Asia as far as northern India. **2** a speaker of an Indo-European language. > *adjective* of or relating to this family of languages.

indolent /in**də**lənt/ > *adjective* wanting to avoid activity or exertion; lazy.

DERIVATIVES – **indolence** *noun* **indolently** *adverb*.

ORIGIN – Latin, from *in-* 'not' + *dolere* 'suffer or give pain'.

indomitable /in**domm**itəb'l/ > *adjective* impossible to subdue or defeat.

DERIVATIVES – **indomitability** *noun* **indomitableness** *noun* **indomitably** *adverb*.

ORIGIN – Latin *indomitabilis*, from *in-* 'not' + *domitare* 'to tame'.

Indonesian /ind**ə**neezyən/ > *noun* **1** a person from Indonesia. **2** the group of languages spoken in Indonesia. > *adjective* relating to Indonesia.

indoor > *adjective* situated, conducted, or used within a building or under cover.

indoors > *adverb* into or within a building. > *noun* the area or space inside a building.

indorse > *verb* US & Law variant spelling of ENDORSE.

indorsement > *noun* US & Law variant spelling of ENDORSEMENT.

indrawn > *adjective* **1** (of breath) taken in. **2** (of a person) shy and introspective.

indubitable /in**dyoo**bitəb'l/ > *adjective* impossible to doubt; unquestionable.

DERIVATIVES – **indubitably** *adverb*.

ORIGIN – Latin *indubitabilis*, from *in-* 'not' + *dubitare* 'to doubt'.

induce /in**dyooss**/ > *verb* **1** succeed in persuading or leading (someone) to do something. **2** bring about or give rise to. **3** produce (an electric charge or current or a magnetic state) by induction. **4** Medicine bring on (childbirth or abortion) artificially.

DERIVATIVES – **inducer** *noun* **inducible** *adjective*.

ORIGIN – Latin *inducere* 'lead in'.

inducement > *noun* **1** a thing that persuades or leads someone to do something. **2** a bribe.

induct > *verb* **1** admit (someone) formally to a post or organisation. **2** US enlist (someone) for military service.

DERIVATIVES – **inductee** *noun*.

ORIGIN – Latin *inducere* 'lead in'.

inductance > *noun* Physics the property of an electric conductor or circuit that causes an electromotive force to be generated by a change in the current flowing.

induction > *noun* **1** the action or process of inducting someone to a post, organisation, etc. **2** the action or process of inducing something. **3** Philosophy the inference of a general law from particular instances. Contrasted with DEDUCTION. **4** the production of an electric or magnetic state by the proximity (without contact) of an electrified or magnetised body. **5** the drawing of the fuel mixture into the cylinders of an internal-combustion engine.

COMBINATIONS – **induction coil** a coil for generating intermittent high voltage from a direct current. **induction loop** a sound system in which a loop of wire around an area in a building produces an electromagnetic signal received directly by hearing aids.

inductive > *adjective* **1** Philosophy characterised by the inference of general laws from particular instances. **2** of or relating to electric or magnetic induction. **3** possessing inductance.

DERIVATIVES – **inductively** *adverb* **inductiveness** *noun* **inductivism** *noun* **inductivist** *noun* & *adjective*.

inductor > *noun* a circuit component which possesses inductance.

indue > *verb* variant spelling of ENDUE.

indulge > *verb* **1** (**indulge in**) allow oneself to enjoy the pleasure of. **2** satisfy or yield freely to (a desire or interest). **3** allow (someone) to do or have something.

DERIVATIVES – **indulger** *noun*.

SYNONYMS – **1** (**indulge in**) luxuriate in, wallow in. **2** appease, fulfil, gratify, satisfy. **3** humour, pamper, pander to.

ORIGIN – Latin *indulgere* 'give free rein to'.

indulgence > *noun* **1** the action or fact of indulging. **2** a thing that is indulged in; a luxury. **3** the state or attitude of being indulgent or tolerant. **4** an extension of the time in which a bill or debt has to be paid. **5** chiefly historical (in the Roman Catholic Church) the setting aside or cancellation by the Pope of the punishment still due for sins after absolution.

indulgent > *adjective* **1** readily indulging someone or overlooking their faults; tolerant or lenient. **2** self-indulgent.

DERIVATIVES – **indulgently** *adverb*.

indurate /in**dyoo**rayt/ > *verb* technical make hard or harder.

DERIVATIVES – **induration** *noun*.

ORIGIN – Latin *indurare*, from *durus* 'hard'.

industrial > *adjective* of, relating to, or used in industry.

DERIVATIVES – **industrially** *adverb*.

COMBINATIONS – **industrial action** Brit. action taken by employees of a company as a protest, especially striking or working to rule. **industrial archaeology** the study of equipment and buildings formerly used in industry. **industrial estate** (N. Amer. **industrial park**) an area of land developed as a site for factories and other industrial use. **industrial relations** the relations between management and workers in industry. **industrial-strength** very strong or powerful.

industrialise (also **industrialize**) > *verb* develop industries in (a country or region) on a wide scale.

DERIVATIVES – **industrialisation** *noun*.

industrialism > *noun* a social or economic system in which manufacturing industries are prevalent.

industrialist > *noun* a person involved in the ownership and management of industry.

industrious > *adjective* diligent and hard-working.

DERIVATIVES – **industriously** *adverb* **industriousness** *noun*.

SYNONYMS – assiduous, diligent, hard-working, sedulous.

industry > *noun* (pl. **industries**) **1** economic activity concerned with the processing of raw materials and manufacture of goods in factories. **2** a particular branch of economic or commercial activity: *the leisure industry*. **3** hard work; diligence.

ORIGIN – Latin *industria*.

-ine¹ > *suffix* (forming adjectives) belonging to; resembling: *canine*.

-ine² > *suffix* forming adjectives from the names of minerals, plants, etc.: *crystalline*.

-ine³ > *suffix* forming feminine nouns such as *heroine*.

-ine⁴ > *suffix* **1** forming chiefly abstract nouns and diminutives such as *doctrine*, *medicine*. **2** Chemistry forming names of alkaloids, halogens, amino acids, and other substances: *cocaine*.

inebriate > *verb* /in**ee**briayt/ make drunk; intoxicate. > *adjective* /in**ee**briət/ drunk.

DERIVATIVES – **inebriation** *noun* **inebriety** *noun*.

ORIGIN – Latin *inebriare*, from *ebrius* 'drunk'.

inedible > *adjective* not fit to be eaten.

ineducable /in**ed**yookəb'l/ > *adjective* considered incapable of being educated.

ineffable /in**eff**əb'l/ > *adjective* **1** too great or extreme to be expressed in words. **2** too sacred to be uttered.

DERIVATIVES – **ineffability** *noun* **ineffably** *adverb*.

ORIGIN – Latin *ineffabilis*, from *in-* 'not' + *effari* 'utter'.

ineffective > *adjective* not producing any or the desired effect.

DERIVATIVES – **ineffectively** *adverb* **ineffectiveness** *noun*.

SYNONYMS – fruitless, futile, ineffectual, unavailing, unsuccessful, vain.

ineffectual > *adjective* **1** not producing any or the desired effect. **2** lacking adequate forcefulness in a role or situation.

DERIVATIVES – **ineffectuality** *noun* **ineffectually** *adverb* **ineffectualness** *noun*.

inefficient > *adjective* not achieving maximum efficiency or productivity; not making the best use of time or resources.

DERIVATIVES – **inefficiency** *noun* **inefficiently** *adverb*.

SYNONYMS – uneconomical, wasteful.

inelastic > *adjective* (of a material) not elastic.

inelegant > *adjective* lacking elegance or refinement.

DERIVATIVES – **inelegance** *noun* **inelegantly** *adverb*.

ineligible > *adjective* not eligible.

DERIVATIVES – **ineligibility** *noun* **ineligibly** *adverb*.

ineluctable /inil**uk**təb'l/ > *adjective* unable to be resisted or avoided; inescapable.

DERIVATIVES – **ineluctability** *noun* **ineluctably** *adverb*.

ORIGIN – Latin *ineluctabilis*, from *in-* 'not' + *eluctari* 'struggle out'.

inept > *adjective* having or showing no skill or expertise.

DERIVATIVES – **ineptitude** *noun* **ineptly** *adverb* **ineptness** *noun*.

SYNONYMS – awkward, bungling, clumsy, incompetent, maladroit, unskilful.

ORIGIN – Latin *ineptus* 'unsuitable', from *in-* 'not' + *aptus* 'apt, fitted'.

inequality > *noun* (pl. **inequalities**) lack of equality.

inequitable > *adjective* unfair; unjust.

DERIVATIVES – **inequitably** *adverb*.

inequity > *noun* (pl. **inequities**) lack of fairness or justice.

ineradicable /inni**rad**dikəb'l/ > *adjective* unable to be removed or destroyed.

DERIVATIVES – **ineradicably** *adverb*.

inert > *adjective* **1** lacking the ability or strength to move. **2** chemically inactive.

DERIVATIVES – **inertly** *adverb* **inertness** *noun*.

SYNONYMS – **1** immobile, inactive, inanimate, static, stationary. **2** unreactive.

COMBINATIONS – **inert gas** Chemistry a noble gas.

ORIGIN – Latin, 'unskilled, inactive', from *in-* 'not' + *ars* 'skill, art'.

inertia /i**ner**shə/ > *noun* **1** a tendency to do nothing or to remain unchanged. **2** Physics a property of matter by which it continues in its existing state of rest or uniform motion in a straight line, unless changed by an external force.

DERIVATIVES – **inertial** *adjective*.

COMBINATIONS – **inertia reel** a reel device which allows a vehicle seat belt to unwind freely but which locks under the force of an impact or rapid deceleration.

inescapable > *adjective* unable to be avoided or denied.

DERIVATIVES – **inescapability** *noun* **inescapably** *adverb*.

inessential > *adjective* not absolutely necessary. > *noun* an inessential thing.

inestimable > *adjective* too great to be calculated or measured.

DERIVATIVES – **inestimably** *adverb*.

inevitable > *adjective* certain to happen; unavoidable. > *noun* (**the inevitable**) an unavoidable turn of events.

DERIVATIVES – **inevitability** *noun* **inevitably** *adverb*.

SYNONYMS – *adjective* fixed, inescapable, inexorable, irrevocable, unavoidable.

ORIGIN – Latin *inevitabilis*, from *in-* 'not' + *evitare* 'avoid'.

inexact > *adjective* not exact; imprecise.

DERIVATIVES – **inexactitude** *noun* **inexactly** *adverb* **inexactness** *noun*.

inexcusable > *adjective* too bad to be justified or tolerated.

DERIVATIVES – **inexcusably** *adverb*.

SYNONYMS – indefensible, unforgivable, unjustifiable, unpardonable.

inexhaustible > *adjective* **1** (of a supply) never ending; incapable of being used up. **2** tireless.

DERIVATIVES – **inexhaustibility** *noun* **inexhaustibly** *adverb*.

inexorable /inek**sə**rəb'l/ > *adjective* **1** impossible to stop or prevent. **2** impossible to persuade by request or entreaty.

DERIVATIVES – **inexorability** *noun* **inexorably** *adverb*.

ORIGIN – Latin *inexorabilis*, from *in-* 'not' + *exorare* 'entreat'.

inexpensive > *adjective* not costing a great deal; cheap.

DERIVATIVES – **inexpensively** *adverb* **inexpensiveness** *noun*.

SYNONYMS – affordable, cheap, economical.

inexperience > *noun* lack of experience.

DERIVATIVES – **inexperienced** *adjective*.

inexpert > *adjective* lacking skill or knowledge in a particular field.

DERIVATIVES – **inexpertly** *adverb*.

inexplicable /inni**splik**kəb'l/ > *adjective* unable to be explained or accounted for.

DERIVATIVES – **inexplicability** *noun* **inexplicably** *adverb*.

SYNONYMS – baffling, mysterious, perplexing, unfathomable.

inexpressible > *adjective* not able to be expressed.

DERIVATIVES – **inexpressibly** *adverb*.

inexpressive > *adjective* showing no expression.

DERIVATIVES – **inexpressively** *adverb* **inexpressiveness** *noun*.

inextinguishable > *adjective* unable to be extinguished.

in extremis /in ek**stree**miss/ > *adverb* **1** in an extremely difficult situation. **2** at the point of death.

ORIGIN – Latin, from *extremus* 'outermost'.

inextricable /inek**strik**kəb'l/ > *adjective* **1** impossible to disentangle or separate. **2** impossible to escape from.

DERIVATIVES – **inextricability** *noun* **inextricably** *adverb*.

infallible /in**fal**ib'l/ > *adjective* **1** incapable of making mistakes or being wrong. **2** never failing; always effective.

DERIVATIVES – **infallibility** *noun* **infallibly** *adverb*.

SYNONYMS – **1** faultless, perfect, unerring. **2** foolproof, reliable, sure.

infamous /**in**fəməss/ > *adjective* **1** well known for some bad quality or deed. **2** morally bad; shocking.

DERIVATIVES – **infamously** *adverb* **infamy** (pl. **infamies**) *noun*.

SYNONYMS – **1** notorious.

infancy > *noun* **1** the state or period of early childhood or babyhood. **2** the early stage in the development or growth of something.

infant > *noun* **1** a very young child or baby. **2** Brit. a schoolchild between the ages of five and seven.

ORIGIN – Old French *enfant*, from Latin *in-* 'not' + *fari* 'to speak'.

infanta /in**fan**tə/ > *noun* historical a daughter of the ruling monarch of Spain or Portugal, especially the eldest daughter who was not heir to the throne.

infanticide /in**fan**tisīd/ > *noun* the killing of an infant.

DERIVATIVES – **infanticidal** *adjective*.

infantile /**in**fəntīl/ > *adjective* **1** of or occurring among infants. **2** derogatory childish.

DERIVATIVES – **infantility** *noun*.

infantilism /in**fan**tiliz'm/ > *noun* **1** childish behaviour. **2** Psychology the persistence of infantile characteristics or behaviour in adult life.

infantry > *noun* foot soldiers collectively.

DERIVATIVES – **infantryman** *noun*.

ORIGIN – Italian *infanteria*, from *infante* 'youth, infantryman'.

infarct /**in**faarkt/ > *noun* Medicine a small localised area of dead tissue resulting from failure of blood supply.

ORIGIN – Latin *infarctus*, from *infarcire* 'stuff into or with'.

infarction /in**faark**sh'n/ > *noun* Medicine the formation of a infarct.

infatuate /in**fat**yooayt/ > *verb* (**be infatuated with**) be inspired with an intense passion for.

DERIVATIVES − **infatuation** noun.

ORIGIN − Latin *infatuare* 'make foolish'.

infect > verb **1** affect with a disease-causing organism. **2** contaminate; affect adversely.

DERIVATIVES − **infector** noun.

ORIGIN − Latin *inficere* 'taint', from *in-* 'into' + *facere* 'put'.

infection > noun **1** the process of infecting or the state of being infected. **2** an infectious disease.

infectious > adjective **1** (of a disease or disease-causing organism) liable to be transmitted through the environment. **2** liable to spread infection. **3** likely to spread to or influence others.

DERIVATIVES − **infectiously** adverb **infectiousness** noun.

SYNONYMS − **1** catching, communicable, contagious, transmittable.

infective > adjective capable of causing infection.

infelicitous > adjective unfortunate; inappropriate.

DERIVATIVES − **infelicitously** adverb.

infelicity > noun (pl. **infelicities**) **1** an inappropriate remark or action. **2** archaic unhappiness; misfortune.

infer > verb (**inferred**, **inferring**) deduce from evidence and reasoning rather than from explicit statements.

DERIVATIVES − **inferable** (also **inferrable**) adjective.

USAGE − on the difference between **infer** and **imply**, see the note at **IMPLY**.

SYNONYMS − conclude, deduce, gather, reason, surmise.

ORIGIN − first meaning 'bring about, inflict': from Latin *inferre* 'bring in, bring about'.

inference /ˈinfərənss/ > noun **1** a conclusion reached on the basis of evidence and reasoning. **2** the process of reaching a conclusion by inferring.

DERIVATIVES − **inferential** adjective.

inferior > adjective **1** lower in rank, status, or quality. **2** of low standard or quality. **3** chiefly Anatomy low or lower in position. **4** (of a letter or symbol) written or printed below the line. > noun a person lower than another in rank, status, or ability.

DERIVATIVES − **inferiority** noun.

SYNONYMS − adjective **1** lesser, lower, subordinate. **2** second-rate, substandard.

ANTONYMS − adjective superior.

COMBINATIONS − **inferiority complex** a feeling of general inadequacy caused by actual or supposed inferiority, marked by aggressive behaviour or withdrawal.

ORIGIN − Latin, from *inferus* 'low'.

infernal > adjective **1** of or relating to hell or the underworld. **2** informal terrible; awful.

DERIVATIVES − **infernally** adverb.

ORIGIN − Latin *infernus* 'below, underground'.

inferno > noun (pl. **infernos**) **1** a large uncontrollable fire. **2** (**Inferno**) hell.

ORIGIN − from Latin *infernus* 'below, underground'; sense 2 is with reference to *The Divine Comedy* (*c.*1309−20) by the Italian poet Dante.

infertile > adjective **1** unable to reproduce. **2** (of land) unable to sustain crops or vegetation.

DERIVATIVES − **infertility** noun.

SYNONYMS − **1** barren, childless, infecund, sterile. **2** arid, fruitless, sterile, unproductive.

infest > verb (of insects or organisms) be present in large numbers, typically so as to cause damage or disease.

DERIVATIVES − **infestation** noun.

ORIGIN − Latin *infestare* 'assail', from *infestus* 'hostile'.

infibulation /infibyooˈlaysh'n/ > noun the practice in some societies of removing the clitoris and labia of a girl or woman and stitching together the edges of the vulva to prevent sexual intercourse.

DERIVATIVES − **infibulate** verb.

ORIGIN − from Latin *infibulare* 'fasten with a clasp'.

infidel /ˈinfid'l/ > noun chiefly archaic a person who has no religion or whose religion is not that of the majority.

ORIGIN − Latin *infidelis*, from *in-* 'not' + *fidelis* 'faithful'.

infidelity > noun (pl. **infidelities**) **1** the action or state of being sexually unfaithful. **2** the state of being an infidel.

infield > noun the inner part of a cricket or baseball field.

DERIVATIVES − **infielder** noun.

infighting > noun conflict within a group or organisation.

DERIVATIVES − **infighter** noun.

infill > noun (also **infilling**) material or buildings used to fill a space or hole. > verb fill or block up (a space or hole).

infiltrate /ˈinfiltrayt/ > verb **1** surreptitiously and gradually enter or gain access to (an organisation or place). **2** permeate or cause to permeate by filtration.

DERIVATIVES − **infiltration** noun **infiltrator** noun.

infinite /ˈinfinit/ > adjective **1** limitless in space, extent, or size. **2** very great in amount or degree.

DERIVATIVES − **infinitely** adverb **infiniteness** noun **infinitude** noun.

USAGE − on the use of **infinite** with *more*, *very*, etc., see the note at **UNIQUE**.

SYNONYMS − **1** boundless, endless, limitless, never-ending. **2** countless, incalculable, innumerable.

ORIGIN − Latin *infinitus*, from *in-* 'not' + *finitus* 'finished, finite'.

infinitesimal /infiniˈtessim'l/ > adjective extremely or indefinitely small.

DERIVATIVES − **infinitesimally** adverb.

COMBINATIONS − **infinitesimal calculus** see **CALCULUS**.

infinitive /inˈfinnitiv/ > noun the basic form of a verb, without an inflection binding it to a particular subject or tense (normally occurring in English with the word *to*, as in *to see, to ask*).

ORIGIN − from Latin *infinitus*, from *in-* 'not' + *finitus* 'finished, finite'.

infinity > noun (pl. **infinities**) **1** the state or quality of being infinite. **2** a very great number or amount. **3** Mathematics a number greater than any assignable quantity or countable number (symbol ∞). **4** a point in space or time that is or seems infinitely distant.

infirm > adjective (of a person) physically weak.

SYNONYMS − decrepit, feeble, frail, weak.

ORIGIN − Latin *infirmus*, from *in-* 'not' + *firmus* 'firm'.

infirmary > noun (pl. **infirmaries**) a hospital or place set aside for the care of the sick or injured.

infirmity > noun (pl. **infirmities**) physical or mental weakness.

in flagrante delicto /in fləˈgrantay diˈliktō/ > adverb in the very act of wrongdoing, especially illicit sexual intercourse.

ORIGIN − Latin, 'in the heat of the crime' (literally 'in blazing crime').

inflame > verb **1** intensify or aggravate. **2** provoke (someone) to strong feelings. **3** cause inflammation in.

inflammable > adjective easily set on fire. > noun a flammable substance.

DERIVATIVES − **inflammability** noun **inflammableness** noun **inflammably** adverb.

USAGE − the words **flammable** and **inflammable** have the same meaning. It is, however, safer to use **flammable** in order to avoid ambiguity, as the *in-* prefix of **inflammable** can give the impression that the word means 'non-flammable'.

inflammation > noun a condition in which an area of the skin or body becomes reddened, swollen, hot, and often painful, especially as a reaction to injury or infection.

inflammatory > adjective **1** relating to or causing inflammation. **2** arousing or intended to arouse angry or violent feelings.

inflatable > adjective capable of being inflated. > noun a plastic or rubber object that is inflated before use.

inflate > verb **1** expand by filling with air or gas. **2** increase by a large or excessive amount. **3** exaggerate. **4** bring about inflation of (a currency).

ORIGIN − Latin *inflare* 'blow into'.

inflation > *noun* **1** the action of inflating or the condition of being inflated. **2** Economics a general increase in prices and fall in the purchasing value of money.
DERIVATIVES – **inflationary** *adjective* **inflationism** *noun* **inflationist** *noun* & *adjective*.

inflect > *verb* **1** Grammar change or be changed by inflection. **2** vary the intonation or pitch of (the voice). **3** technical bend or deflect inwards.
DERIVATIVES – **inflective** *adjective*.
ORIGIN – Latin *inflectere*, from *in-* 'into' + *flectere* 'to bend'.

inflection /inˈfleksh'n/ (chiefly Brit. also **inflexion**) > *noun* **1** Grammar a change in the form of a word (typically the ending) to express a grammatical function or attribute such as tense, mood, person, number, case, and gender. **2** a variation in intonation or pitch of the voice. **3** Mathematics a change of curvature from convex to concave.
DERIVATIVES – **inflectional** *adjective* **inflectionally** *adverb* **inflectionless** *adjective*.

inflexible > *adjective* **1** not able to be altered or adapted. **2** unwilling to change or compromise. **3** not able to be bent; stiff.
DERIVATIVES – **inflexibility** *noun* **inflexibly** *adverb*.

inflict > *verb* (**inflict on**) **1** cause (something unpleasant or painful) to be suffered by. **2** impose (something unwelcome) on.
DERIVATIVES – **infliction** *noun*.
ORIGIN – Latin *infligere* 'strike against'.

in-flight > *adjective* occurring or provided during an aircraft flight.

inflorescence /inflərˈess'nss/ > *noun* Botany **1** the complete flower head of a plant, including stems, stalks, bracts, and flowers. **2** the process of flowering.
ORIGIN – from Latin *inflorescere* 'come into flower'.

inflow > *noun* **1** the action of flowing or moving in; influx. **2** something, such as water or money, that flows or moves in.

influence > *noun* **1** the power or ability to affect someone's beliefs or actions. **2** a person or thing with such ability or power. **3** power arising out of status, contacts, or wealth. **4** the power to produce a physical change. > *verb* have an influence on.
IDIOMS – **under the influence** informal affected by alcoholic drink.
DERIVATIVES – **influencer** *noun*.
ORIGIN – first used in the sense 'influx': from Latin *influere* 'flow in'.

influential > *adjective* having great influence.
DERIVATIVES – **influentially** *adverb*.
SYNONYMS – authoritative, dominant, powerful, significant.

influenza > *noun* a highly contagious infection of the respiratory passages, spread by a virus and causing fever, aching, and often catarrh.
DERIVATIVES – **influenzal** *adjective*.

---

wordpower facts

Influenza

Influenza is an Italian word that simply means 'influence'. In Italian it also has the sense 'an outbreak of an epidemic', hence 'epidemic'. It was applied specifically to an influenza epidemic which began in Italy in 1743, and was later adopted in English as the name of the disease. The poet Robert Southey complained in a letter in 1839: 'I have had a pretty fair share of the Flue'. This was the first recorded instance of the informal shortening **flu**, a term often applied loosely to other ill-defined and short-lived infections. Real **influenza**, however, is serious: the so-called **Spanish influenza** epidemic in 1918–19 may have caused more deaths (up to 30 million) than the First World War.

---

influx > *noun* **1** the arrival or entry of large numbers of people or things. **2** an inflow of water into a river, lake, or the sea.
ORIGIN – Latin *influxus*, from *influere* 'flow in'.

infomercial > *noun* chiefly N. Amer. an advertising film which promotes a commercial product in an informative and supposedly objective style.

inform > *verb* **1** give facts or information to. **2** (**inform on**) give incriminating information about (someone) to the police or other authority. **3** give an essential or formative principle or quality to.
SYNONYMS – **1** advise, apprise, brief, notify, tell.
ORIGIN – Latin *informare* 'shape, describe'.

informal > *adjective* **1** relaxed and unofficial; not formal. **2** denoting the language of everyday speech and writing, rather than that used in official and formal contexts.
DERIVATIVES – **informality** *noun* **informally** *adverb*.
SYNONYMS – **1** casual, relaxed, unceremonious, unofficial. **2** colloquial.
COMBINATIONS – **informal vote** Austral./NZ an invalid vote or voting paper.

informant > *noun* **1** a person who gives information to another. **2** another term for **INFORMER**.

information > *noun* **1** facts or knowledge provided or learned. **2** what is conveyed or represented by a particular sequence of symbols, impulses, etc.
DERIVATIVES – **informational** *adjective*.
COMBINATIONS – **information super-highway** an extensive electronic network such as the Internet, used for the rapid transfer of information in digital form. **information technology** the study or use of systems such as computers and telecommunications for storing, retrieving, and sending information. **information theory** the mathematical study of the coding and transmission of information in the form of sequences of symbols, impulses, etc.

informative > *adjective* providing useful information.
DERIVATIVES – **informatively** *adverb* **informativeness** *noun*.

informed > *adjective* **1** having or showing knowledge. **2** (of a judgement) based on a sound understanding of the facts.

informer > *noun* a person who informs on another person to the police or another authority.

infotainment > *noun* broadcast material which is intended both to entertain and to inform.

infotech > *noun* short for **information technology**.

infra- > *prefix* below: *infrasonic*.
ORIGIN – Latin *infra* 'below'.

infraction > *noun* chiefly Law a violation or infringement of a law or agreement.
DERIVATIVES – **infractor** *noun*.
ORIGIN – Latin, from *infringere*, from *in-* 'into' + *frangere* 'break'.

infra dig /infrə ˈdig/ > *adjective* informal beneath one's dignity; demeaning.
ORIGIN – Latin *infra dignitatem* 'beneath dignity'.

infrared > *noun* electromagnetic radiation having a wavelength just greater than that of red light but less than that of microwaves, emitted particularly by heated objects. > *adjective* of or relating to such radiation.

infrasonic > *adjective* relating to or denoting sound waves with a frequency below the lower limit of human audibility.

infrasound > *noun* infrasonic sound waves.

infrastructure > *noun* the basic physical and organisational structures (e.g. buildings, roads, power supplies) needed for the operation of a society or enterprise.
DERIVATIVES – **infrastructural** *adjective*.

infrequent > *adjective* occurring only rarely.
DERIVATIVES – **infrequency** *noun* **infrequently** *adverb*.
SYNONYMS – occasional, rare, sporadic, uncommon.

infringe > *verb* **1** violate (a law, agreement, etc.). **2** encroach on (a right or privilege).
DERIVATIVES – **infringement** *noun* **infringer** *noun*.
ORIGIN – Latin *infringere*, from *in-* 'into' + *frangere* 'to break'.

infuriate > *verb* /inˈfyooriayt/ make irritated or angry.

DERIVATIVES – **infuriating** *adjective*.

SYNONYMS – anger, enrage, exasperate, incense, irritate, madden, rile.

ORIGIN – Latin *infuriare*.

infuse > *verb* **1** pervade; fill. **2** instil (a quality) in someone or something. **3** soak (tea, herbs, etc.) to extract the flavour or healing properties. **4** Medicine allow (a liquid) to flow into the bloodstream or a part of the body.

DERIVATIVES – **infuser** *noun*.

ORIGIN – Latin *infundere* 'pour in'.

infusible > *adjective* not able to be melted or fused.

DERIVATIVES – **infusibility** *noun*.

infusion > *noun* **1** a drink, remedy, or extract prepared by infusing. **2** the action or process of infusing.

-ing¹ > *suffix* **1** denoting a verbal action, activity, or result: *building*. **2** denoting material used for or associated with a process: *piping*. **3** forming the gerund of verbs (such as *painting* as in *I love painting*).

-ing² > *suffix* **1** forming the present participle of verbs: *calling*. **2** forming adjectives from nouns: *hulking*.

ingenious /inˈjeeniəss/ > *adjective* clever, original, and inventive.

DERIVATIVES – **ingeniously** *adverb* **ingeniousness** *noun*.

SYNONYMS – artful, crafty, creative, cunning, imaginative.

ORIGIN – from Latin *ingenium* 'mind, intellect'; related to ENGINE.

ingénue /ˈanzhaynyōo/ > *noun* an innocent or unsophisticated young woman.

ORIGIN – French, from *ingénu* 'ingenuous'.

ingenuity /injiˈnyōoiti/ > *noun* the quality of being clever, original, and inventive.

ingenuous /inˈjenyooəss/ > *adjective* innocent and unsuspecting.

DERIVATIVES – **ingenuously** *adverb* **ingenuousness** *noun*.

SYNONYMS – artless, guileless, innocent, trusting.

ANTONYMS – artful, devious.

wordpower facts

Ingenuous

The word **ingenuous** is from Latin *ingenuus*, literally 'native, inborn'. The original English use was 'noble, generous', which gave rise to 'honourably straightforward, frank', hence 'innocent and unsuspecting'. **Ingenuous** is often confused with **ingenious** 'clever and inventive': it is interesting to note that **ingenuity**, now the standard noun from **ingenious**, is actually derived from *ingenuus* and took on its current meaning by confusion of **ingenuous** with **ingenious**.

ingest /inˈjest/ > *verb* take (food or drink) into the body by swallowing or absorbing it.

DERIVATIVES – **ingestion** *noun* **ingestive** *adjective*.

ORIGIN – Latin *ingerere* 'bring in'.

inglenook > *noun* a chimney corner on either side of a large fireplace.

ORIGIN – from dialect *ingle* 'fire, fireplace', perhaps from Irish *aingeal* 'live ember', + NOOK.

inglorious > *adjective* **1** not worthy of honour. **2** not famous or renowned.

DERIVATIVES – **ingloriously** *adverb* **ingloriousness** *noun*.

ingoing > *adjective* going towards or into.

ingot /ˈinggət/ > *noun* a rectangular block of steel, gold, or other metal.

ORIGIN – first meaning a mould: perhaps from Old English *geotan* 'pour, cast'.

ingraft > *verb* variant spelling of ENGRAFT.

ingrain > *verb* (also **engrain**) firmly fix or establish (a habit, belief, or attitude) in a person.

ORIGIN – first used in the sense 'dye with cochineal', from the old use of *grain* meaning 'kermes, cochineal'.

ingrained > *adjective* (also **engrained**) **1** (of a habit or attitude) firmly established. **2** (of dirt) deeply embedded.

ingrate /ˈingrayt/ formal or literary > *noun* an ungrateful person. > *adjective* ungrateful.

ORIGIN – Latin *ingratus*, from *in-* 'not' + *gratus* 'grateful'.

ingratiate /inˈgrayshiayt/ > *verb* (**ingratiate oneself**) bring oneself into favour with someone by flattering or trying to please them.

DERIVATIVES – **ingratiating** *adjective* **ingratiation** *noun*.

ORIGIN – from Latin *in gratiam* 'into favour'.

ingratitude > *noun* a discreditable lack of gratitude.

ingredient > *noun* **1** any of the substances that are combined to make a particular dish. **2** a component part or element.

ORIGIN – from Latin *ingredi* 'enter'.

ingress /ˈingress/ > *noun* **1** the action or fact of entering or coming in. **2** a place or means of access.

DERIVATIVES – **ingression** *noun*.

ORIGIN – from Latin *ingredi* 'enter'.

in-group > *noun* an exclusive group of people with a shared interest or identity.

ingrown > *adjective* **1** growing or having grown within; innate. **2** inward-looking. **3** (of a toenail) having grown into the flesh.

DERIVATIVES – **ingrowing** *adjective* **ingrowth** *noun*.

inguinal /ˈinggwinəl/ > *adjective* Anatomy of the groin.

ORIGIN – Latin *inguinalis*, from *inguen* 'groin'.

inhabit > *verb* (**inhabited**, **inhabiting**) live in or occupy.

DERIVATIVES – **inhabitable** *adjective* **inhabitation** *noun*.

ORIGIN – from Latin *in-* 'in' + *habitare* 'dwell'.

inhabitant > *noun* a person or animal that lives in or occupies a place.

WORDFINDER – aboriginal, autochthon (*indigenous inhabitant*).

inhalant > *noun* **1** a medicinal preparation for inhaling. **2** a solvent or other material producing vapour that is inhaled by drug abusers.

inhale /inˈhayl/ > *verb* breathe in (air, gas, smoke, etc.).

DERIVATIVES – **inhalation** *noun*.

ORIGIN – Latin *inhalare*.

inhaler > *noun* a portable device for administering a drug which is to be inhaled.

inhere /inˈheer/ > *verb* (**inhere in** or **within**) formal exist or be vested in.

ORIGIN – Latin *inhaerere* 'stick to'.

inherent /inˈherrənt, inˈheerənt/ > *adjective* existing in something as a permanent or essential feature or quality.

DERIVATIVES – **inherently** *adverb*.

SYNONYMS – built-in, immanent, innate, intrinsic.

inherit > *verb* (**inherited**, **inheriting**) **1** receive (money, property, or a title) as an heir at the death of the previous holder. **2** derive (a quality or characteristic) from one's parents or ancestors. **3** receive or be left with (a situation, object, etc.) from a predecessor or former owner.

WORDFINDER – disinherit (*prevent from inheriting*), entail (*property inheritance settled over succeeding generations*), heirloom (*valuable inherited article*), hereditary (*gained by inheritance*), primogeniture (*eldest son's right of inheritance*).

DERIVATIVES – **inheritable** *adjective* **inheritor** *noun*.

ORIGIN – Latin *inhereditare* 'appoint as heir'.

inheritance > *noun* **1** a thing that is inherited. **2** the action of inheriting.

COMBINATIONS – **inheritance tax** (in the UK) tax levied on property and money acquired by gift or inheritance.

inhibit > *verb* (**inhibited**, **inhibiting**) **1** hinder or restrain (an action or process). **2** make (someone) unable to act in a relaxed and natural way.

DERIVATIVES – **inhibited** *adjective* **inhibitive** *adjective*.

SYNONYMS – **1** hamper, hinder, impede, obstruct, restrain.

ORIGIN – Latin *inhibere*.

inhibition > *noun* **1** the action or process of inhibiting or being inhibited. **2** a feeling that makes one unable to act in a relaxed and natural way.

inhibitor > *noun* a substance which slows down or prevents a particular chemical reaction or other process.
DERIVATIVES – **inhibitory** *adjective*.

inhospitable > *adjective* **1** (of an environment) harsh and difficult to live in. **2** unwelcoming.
DERIVATIVES – **inhospitableness** *noun* **inhospitably** *adverb* **inhospitality** *noun*.
SYNONYMS – **1** bleak, forbidding, harsh, uninviting. **2** discourteous, uncongenial, unfriendly, unwelcoming.

in-house > *adjective & adverb* within an organisation.

inhuman > *adjective* **1** lacking positive human qualities; cruel and barbaric. **2** not human in nature or character.
DERIVATIVES – **inhumanly** *adverb*.

inhumane > *adjective* without compassion for misery or suffering; cruel.
DERIVATIVES – **inhumanely** *adverb*.
SYNONYMS – cold-blooded, cruel, heartless, inhuman, savage, unkind.

inhumanity > *noun* (pl. **inhumanities**) cruel and brutal behaviour.

inhumation /inhyoomaysh'n/ > *noun* chiefly Archaeology **1** the action or practice of burying the dead. **2** a burial or buried corpse.
ORIGIN – from Latin *inhumare* 'bury', from *humus* 'ground'.

inimical /inimmik'l/ > *adjective* tending to obstruct or harm; hostile.
DERIVATIVES – **inimically** *adverb*.
ORIGIN – from Latin *inimicus*, from *in-* 'not' + *amicus* 'friend'.

inimitable /inimmitəb'l/ > *adjective* impossible to imitate; unique.
DERIVATIVES – **inimitability** *noun* **inimitably** *adverb*.

iniquity /inikwiti/ > *noun* (pl. **iniquities**) injustice or immoral behaviour.
DERIVATIVES – **iniquitous** *adjective* **iniquitously** *adverb* **iniquitousness** *noun*.
ORIGIN – from Latin *iniquus*, from *in-* 'not' + *aequus* 'equal, just'.

initial > *adjective* existing or occurring at the beginning. > *noun* the first letter of a name or word, especially that of a person's given name. > *verb* (**initialled, initialling**; N. Amer. **initialed, initialing**) mark with one's initials as a sign of approval or endorsement.
DERIVATIVES – **initially** *adverb*.
ORIGIN – from Latin *initium* 'beginning'.

initialism > *noun* an abbreviation consisting of initial letters pronounced separately (e.g. *BBC*).

initiate > *verb* /inishiayt/ **1** cause (a process or action) to begin. **2** admit with formal ceremony or ritual into a society or group. **3** (**initiate into**) introduce to (a new

activity or skill). > *noun* /inishiət/ a person who has been initiated.
DERIVATIVES – **initiation** *noun* **initiatory** *adjective*.
SYNONYMS – **1** begin, instigate, launch, originate, set in motion. **2** admit, induct.
ORIGIN – Latin *initiare* 'begin'.

initiative > *noun* **1** the ability to act independently and with a fresh approach. **2** the power or opportunity to act before others do. **3** a new development or fresh approach to a problem.
IDIOMS – **on one's own initiative** without being prompted by others.

initiator > *noun* **1** a person or thing that initiates. **2** Chemistry a substance which starts a chain reaction. **3** an explosive or device used to detonate a main charge.

inject > *verb* **1** introduce into the body with a syringe. **2** administer a drug or medicine to (a person or animal) with a syringe. **3** introduce or feed under pressure into. **4** introduce (a new or different element).
DERIVATIVES – **injectable** *adjective & noun* **injector** *noun*.
ORIGIN – Latin *inicere* 'throw in'.

injection > *noun* **1** an act of injecting or being injected. **2** a substance that is injected. **3** short for **FUEL INJECTION**.
WORDFINDER – ampoule (*a glass capsule of liquid for injecting*), hypodermic (*a needle for injection beneath the skin*), intramuscular (*denoting injection into muscle tissue*), intravenous (*denoting injection into a vein*), subcutaneous (*denoting injection beneath the skin*), syringe (*an instrument for making injections*).
COMBINATIONS – **injection moulding** the shaping of rubber or plastic articles by injecting heated material into a mould.

in-joke > *noun* a joke that is shared exclusively by a small group.

injudicious > *adjective* showing poor judgement; unwise.
DERIVATIVES – **injudiciously** *adverb* **injudiciousness** *noun*.

injunction > *noun* **1** Law a judicial order restraining a person from an action, or compelling a person to carry out a certain act. **2** an authoritative warning.
DERIVATIVES – **injunctive** *adjective*.
ORIGIN – from Latin *injungere* 'join, attach, impose'.

injure > *verb* **1** do physical harm to; wound. **2** offend or hurt.
SYNONYMS – **1** damage, hurt, wound. **2** harm, hurt, ill-treat, offend, wrong.

injured > *adjective* **1** harmed or wounded. **2** offended; wronged.

injurious /injooriəss/ > *adjective* **1** causing or likely to cause injury. **2** (of language) maliciously insulting; libellous.
DERIVATIVES – **injuriously** *adverb* **injuriousness** *noun*.

injury > *noun* (pl. **injuries**) **1** an instance of being injured. **2** the fact of being injured; harm or damage.
WORDFINDER – lesion (*an injured or diseased part of body*), trauma (*severe physical injury*), traumatic (*relating to injury*).
COMBINATIONS – **injury time** Brit. (in soccer and other sports) extra playing time to make up for time lost as a result of injuries.
ORIGIN – Latin *injuria* 'a wrong'.

injustice > *noun* **1** lack of justice. **2** an unjust act or occurrence.
SYNONYMS – inequity, iniquity, unfairness, wrong.

ink > *noun* **1** a coloured fluid used for writing, drawing, or printing. **2** Zoology a black liquid ejected by a cuttlefish, octopus, or squid to confuse a predator. > *verb* **1** write or mark with ink. **2** cover (type or a stamp) with ink before printing.
WORDFINDER – indelible (*denoting ink that cannot be removed*), sepia (*cuttlefish ink*).
COMBINATIONS – **ink cap** a mushroom with a tall, narrow cap and slender white stem, that turns into a black liquid after the spores are shed. **ink-jet printer** a printer in which the characters are formed by minute jets of ink. **inkstand** a stand for ink bottles, pens, and other stationery items. **inkwell** a container for ink, normally housed in a hole in a desk.
ORIGIN – Greek *enkauston*, denoting the purple ink used by Roman emperors for signatures, from *enkaiein* 'burn in'; related to **ENCAUSTIC**.

inkling > *noun* a slight suspicion; a hint.
ORIGIN – from the rare verb *inkle* 'utter in an undertone'.

inky > *adjective* (**inkier, inkiest**) **1** as dark as ink. **2** stained with ink.
DERIVATIVES – **inkiness** *noun*.

INLA > *abbreviation* Irish National Liberation Army.

inlaid past and past participle of **INLAY**.

inland > *adjective & adverb* **1** in or into the interior of a country. **2** (before another noun) chiefly Brit. carried on within the limits of a country; domestic: *inland trade*. > *noun* the interior of a country or region.
DERIVATIVES – **inlander** *noun*.
COMBINATIONS – **inland revenue** Brit. public revenue consisting of income tax and some other direct taxes.

in-law > *noun* a relative by marriage. > *combining form* related by marriage.

inlay > *verb* (past and past participle **inlaid**) ornament by embedding pieces of a different material in a surface. > *noun* **1** inlaid decoration. **2** a material or substance used for inlaying. **3** a filling shaped to fit a tooth cavity.
DERIVATIVES – **inlayer** *noun*.

inlet > *noun* **1** a small arm of the sea, a lake,

or a river. **2** a place or means of entry. **3** (in tailoring and dressmaking) an inserted piece of material.

in-line ▷ *adjective* **1** having parts arranged in a line. **2** constituting an integral part of a continuous sequence of operations or machines.

in loco parentis /in lōkō pərentiss/ ▷ *adverb & adjective* acting in the capacity of a parent.
ORIGIN – Latin, 'in the place of a parent'.

inlying /inlī-ing/ ▷ *adjective* within or near a centre.

inmate ▷ *noun* a person living in an institution such as a prison or hospital.

in medias res /in meediass rayz/ ▷ *adverb* into the middle of things; without preamble.
ORIGIN – Latin.

in memoriam /in mimoriam/ ▷ *preposition* in memory of (a dead person).
ORIGIN – Latin.

inmost ▷ *adjective* innermost.

inn ▷ *noun* a public house, traditionally an establishment also providing food and lodging.
COMBINATIONS – **innkeeper** chiefly archaic a person who runs an inn. **Inn of Court** (in the UK) each of the four legal societies having the exclusive right of admitting people to the English bar.

innards /innərdz/ ▷ *plural noun* informal **1** internal organs; entrails. **2** the internal workings of a device or machine.
ORIGIN – representing a dialect pronunciation of INWARDS.

innate /inayt/ ▷ *adjective* inborn; natural.
DERIVATIVES – **innately** *adverb* **innateness** *noun*.
ORIGIN – Latin *innatus*, from *innasci* 'be born into'.

inner ▷ *adjective* **1** situated inside; close to the centre. **2** mental or spiritual; not visible. **3** private; not expressed. ▷ *noun* an inner part.
COMBINATIONS – **inner bar** (in the UK) Queen's or King's Counsel collectively. **inner city** an area in or near the centre of a city, especially when associated with social and economic problems. **inner ear** the part of the ear embedded in the temporal bone, consisting of the semicircular canals and cochlea. **inner tube** a separate inflatable tube inside a pneumatic tyre casing.

innermost ▷ *adjective* **1** furthest in; closest to the centre. **2** (of thoughts) most private and deeply felt.

inning ▷ *noun* Baseball each division of a game during which both sides have a turn at batting.

innings ▷ *noun* (pl. same) (treated as sing.) Cricket each of the divisions of a game during which one side has a turn at batting.

IDIOMS – **a good innings** Brit. informal a long and fulfilling life or career.

innocent ▷ *adjective* **1** not guilty of a crime or offence. **2** free from moral wrong; not corrupted. **3** not intended to cause offence; harmless. **4** (**innocent of**) without experience or knowledge of. ▷ *noun* an innocent person.
WORDFINDER – acquit, exculpate, exonerate (*find someone innocent*).
DERIVATIVES – **innocence** *noun* **innocently** *adverb*.
SYNONYMS – *adjective* **1** blameless, guiltless. **2** pure, righteous, sinless, uncorrupted, virtuous. **3** harmless, innocuous, playful.
ANTONYMS – *adjective* **1** guilty.
ORIGIN – Latin, 'not harming', from *in-* 'not' + *nocere* 'to hurt'.

innocuous /inokyooəss/ ▷ *adjective* not harmful or offensive.
DERIVATIVES – **innocuously** *adverb* **innocuousness** *noun*.
ORIGIN – Latin *innocuus*, from *in-* 'not' + *nocere* 'to hurt'.

innominate /inomminət/ ▷ *adjective* not named or classified.
ORIGIN – Latin *innominatus*, from *in-* 'not' + *nominatus* 'named'.

innovate /innəvayt/ ▷ *verb* introduce new methods, ideas, or products.
DERIVATIVES – **innovation** *noun* **innovational** *adjective* **innovative** *adjective* **innovator** *noun* **innovatory** *adjective*.
ORIGIN – Latin *innovare* 'renew, alter', from *novus* 'new'.

innuendo /inyooendō/ ▷ *noun* (pl. **innuendoes** or **innuendos**) an allusive or oblique remark, typically a suggestive or disparaging one.

wordpower facts

Innuendo

The word **innuendo** was first used as an adverb in legal documents, introducing explanations and meaning 'that is to say'. It is a Latin word that means literally 'by nodding at, by pointing to', and is based on *nuere* 'to nod'. As a noun it first referred to the explanation of a word or expression given as an aside, as in 'he (*innuendo* the Plaintiff) is a thief'; in particular it served as a pointer to the libellous or slanderous meaning alleged to be conveyed by a word or expression that was not in itself actionable.

innumerable ▷ *adjective* too many to be counted.
DERIVATIVES – **innumerability** *noun* **innumerably** *adverb*.

innumerate ▷ *adjective* without a basic knowledge of mathematics and arithmetic. ▷ *noun* an innumerate person.
DERIVATIVES – **innumeracy** *noun*.

inoculate* /inokyoolayt/ ▷ *verb* **1** another term for VACCINATE. **2** introduce (cells or organisms) into a culture medium.
DERIVATIVES – **inoculable** *adjective* **inoculation** *noun* **inoculator** *noun*.
*SPELLING – one *n*, one *c*: inoculate.
ORIGIN – first used in the sense 'graft a bud or shoot': from Latin *inoculare* 'engraft', from *oculus* 'eye, bud'.

inoffensive ▷ *adjective* not objectionable or harmful.
DERIVATIVES – **inoffensively** *adverb* **inoffensiveness** *noun*.

inoperable ▷ *adjective* **1** Medicine not able to be operated on to beneficial effect. **2** not able to be used or operated. **3** impractical; unworkable.
DERIVATIVES – **inoperability** *noun* **inoperably** *adverb*.

inoperative ▷ *adjective* not working or taking effect.

inopportune ▷ *adjective* occurring at an inconvenient time.
DERIVATIVES – **inopportunely** *adverb* **inopportuneness** *noun*.

inordinate /inordinət/ ▷ *adjective* unusually large; excessive.
DERIVATIVES – **inordinately** *adverb*.
ORIGIN – first meaning 'not controlled or restrained; disorderly': from Latin *inordinatus*, from *in-* 'not' + *ordinatus* 'set in order'.

inorganic ▷ *adjective* **1** not arising from natural growth. **2** Chemistry relating to or denoting compounds which are not organic (broadly, compounds not containing carbon).
DERIVATIVES – **inorganically** *adverb*.

inpatient ▷ *noun* a patient who is staying day and night in a hospital while receiving treatment.

in propria persona /in prōpriə persōnə/ ▷ *adverb* in his or her own person.
ORIGIN – Latin.

input ▷ *noun* **1** what is put or taken in or operated on by any process or system. **2** the action or process of putting or feeding something in. **3** energy supplied to a device or system; an electrical signal. **4** Electronics a place or device from which energy or information enters a system. **5** a person's contribution. ▷ *verb* (**inputting**; past and past participle **input** or **inputted**) put (data) into a computer.
DERIVATIVES – **inputter** *noun*.

inquest ▷ *noun* **1** a judicial inquiry to ascertain the facts relating to an incident. **2** Brit. an inquiry by a coroner's court into the cause of a death.
ORIGIN – Old French *enqueste*, from Latin *inquirere*, from *quaerere* 'speak'.

inquire > *verb* **1** make a formal investigation. **2** another term for ENQUIRE.

DERIVATIVES – **inquirer** *noun*.

inquiry > *noun* (pl. **inquiries**) **1** a formal investigation. **2** another term for ENQUIRY.

inquisition > *noun* **1** a period of prolonged and intensive questioning or investigation. **2** the verdict of a coroner's jury.

DERIVATIVES – **inquisitional** *adjective*.

ORIGIN – Latin 'examination', from *inquirere*, from *quaerere* 'seek'.

inquisitive > *adjective* **1** eagerly seeking knowledge. **2** prying.

DERIVATIVES – **inquisitively** *adverb* **inquisitiveness** *noun*.

inquisitor /in**kwizz**itər/ > *noun* a person making an inquiry or conducting an inquisition, especially when regarded as harsh or very searching.

DERIVATIVES – **inquisitorial** *adjective*.

inquorate /in**kwor**ayt/ > *adjective* Brit. (of an assembly) not having a quorum.

in re /in **ree**, in **ray**/ > *preposition* in the legal case of; with regard to.

ORIGIN – Latin, 'in the matter of'.

inroad > *noun* **1** an instance of something being encroached or intruded upon. **2** a hostile attack.

inrush > *noun* a sudden inward rush or flow.

DERIVATIVES – **inrushing** *adjective & noun*.

INS > *abbreviation* (in the US) Immigration and Naturalisation Service.

insalubrious /insə**loo**briəss/ > *adjective* seedy; unwholesome.

insane > *adjective* **1** in an unsound state of mind; seriously mentally ill. **2** extremely foolish; irrational.

DERIVATIVES – **insanely** *adverb* **insanity** *noun*.

SYNONYMS – **1** crazy, demented, deranged, mad, unhinged. **2** absurd, crazy, idiotic, irrational, nonsensical.

ORIGIN – Latin *insanus*, from *in-* 'not' + *sanus* 'healthy'.

insanitary > *adjective* so dirty or germ-ridden as to be a danger to health.

insatiable /in**say**shəb'l/ > *adjective* impossible to satisfy.

DERIVATIVES – **insatiability** *noun* **insatiably** *adverb*.

inscribe > *verb* **1** write or carve (words or symbols) on a surface. **2** write a dedication to someone in (a book). **3** Geometry draw (a figure) within another so that their boundaries touch but do not intersect.

DERIVATIVES – **inscribable** *adjective* **inscriber** *noun*.

ORIGIN – Latin *inscribere*, from *in-* 'into' + *scribere* 'write'.

inscription > *noun* **1** words or symbols inscribed on a monument, in a book, etc. **2** the action of inscribing.

WORDFINDER – graffito (*scratched inscription*), epigraphy (*the study of ancient inscriptions*), epitaph (*inscription on a tombstone*).

DERIVATIVES – **inscriptional** *adjective* **inscriptive** *adjective*.

inscrutable /in**skroo**təb'l/ > *adjective* giving no indication of true feelings or meaning; impossible to interpret.

DERIVATIVES – **inscrutability** *noun* **inscrutably** *adverb*.

ORIGIN – Latin *inscrutabilis*, from *in-* 'not' + *scrutari* 'to search'.

insect > *noun* a small invertebrate animal with a head, thorax, and abdomen, six legs, two antennae, and usually one or two pairs of wings.

WORDFINDER – arthropod (*animal of group including insects, spiders, and crustaceans*), entomologist (*person who studies insects*), insectivorous (*insect-eating*); *the main insect orders:* Coleoptera (*beetles*), Diptera (*flies*), Hemiptera (*bugs*), Hymenoptera (*ants, bees, and wasps*), Lepidoptera (*butterflies and moths*), Odonata (*dragonflies*), Orthoptera (*grasshoppers and crickets*).

ORIGIN – from Latin *animal insectum* 'segmented animal' (translating Greek *zōion entomon*), from *insecare* 'cut up or into'.

insectarium /insek**tair**iəm/ (also **insectary** /in**sek**təri/) > *noun* (pl. **insectariums**, **insectaries**) a place where insects are kept, exhibited, and studied.

insecticide /in**sek**tisīd/ > *noun* a substance used for killing insects.

DERIVATIVES – **insecticidal** *adjective*.

insectile /in**sek**tīl/ > *adjective* resembling an insect.

insectivore /in**sek**tivor/ > *noun* an animal that eats insects and other invertebrates, especially a mammal of an order (Insectivora) including the shrews, moles, and hedgehogs.

DERIVATIVES – **insectivorous** *adjective*.

insecure > *adjective* **1** not confident or assured. **2** not firm or firmly fixed. **3** (of a place) easily broken into; not protected.

DERIVATIVES – **insecurely** *adverb* **insecurity** *noun*.

inseminate /in**semm**inayt/ > *verb* introduce semen into (a woman or a female animal).

DERIVATIVES – **insemination** *noun* **inseminator** *noun*.

ORIGIN – Latin *inseminare* 'sow'.

insensate /in**sen**sayt/ > *adjective* **1** lacking physical sensation. **2** lacking sympathy; unfeeling. **3** completely lacking sense or reason.

DERIVATIVES – **insensately** *adverb*.

insensible > *adjective* **1** without one's mental faculties; unconscious. **2** numb; without feeling. **3** (**insensible of** or **to**) unaware of; indifferent to. **4** too small or gradual to be perceived.

DERIVATIVES – **insensibly** *adverb* **insensibility** *noun*.

insensitive > *adjective* **1** showing or feeling no concern for the feelings of others. **2** not sensitive to physical sensation. **3** not appreciative of or able to respond to something.

DERIVATIVES – **insensitively** *adverb* **insensitiveness** *noun* **insensitivity** *noun*.

SYNONYMS – **1** callous, heartless, unfeeling, unsympathetic.

insentient /in**sen**sh'nt/ > *adjective* incapable of feeling; inanimate.

DERIVATIVES – **insentience** *noun*.

inseparable > *adjective* unable to be separated or treated separately.

DERIVATIVES – **inseparability** *noun* **inseparably** *adverb*.

insert > *verb* /in**sert**/ place, fit, or incorporate into. > *noun* /**in**sert/ **1** a loose page or section in a magazine. **2** an ornamental section of cloth inserted into a garment. **3** a shot inserted in a film or video.

DERIVATIVES – **insertable** *adjective* **inserter** *noun*.

ORIGIN – Latin *inserere* 'put in'.

insertion > *noun* **1** the action of inserting. **2** an amendment or addition inserted in a text. **3** each appearance of an advertisement in a newspaper or periodical. **4** an insert in a garment.

in-service > *adjective* taking place during the course of employment.

inset > *noun* /**in**set/ **1** a thing inserted; an insert. **2** a small picture or map inserted within the border of a larger one. > *verb* /in**set**/ (**insetting**; past and past participle **inset** or **insetted**) **1** put in as an inset. **2** decorate with an inset.

DERIVATIVES – **insetter** *noun*.

inshore > *adjective* at sea but close to the shore; operating near the coast. > *adverb* towards or closer to the shore.

inside > *noun* **1** the inner side or surface of a thing. **2** the inner part; the interior. **3** (**one's insides**) informal one's stomach and bowels. **4** (**the inside**) informal a position affording private information. **5** the part of a road furthest from the centre. **6** the side of a bend where the edge is shorter. > *adjective* **1** situated on or in, or derived from, the inside. **2** (in some sports) denoting positions nearer to the centre of the field. > *preposition & adverb* **1** situated or moving within. **2** within (the body or mind of a person). **3** informal in prison. **4** (in some sports) closer to the centre of the field than. **5** in less than (the period of time specified).

COMBINATIONS – **inside job** informal a crime committed by or with the assistance of a person associated with the premises where it occurred. **inside leg** the length of a person's leg or trouser leg from crotch to ankle.

inside out > *adverb* with the inner surface turned outwards.

IDIOMS – **know something inside out** know something very thoroughly.

insider > *noun* a person within an organisation, especially someone privy to information unavailable to others.

COMBINATIONS – **insider dealing** (also **insider trading**) the illegal practice of trading on the stock exchange to one's own advantage through having access to confidential information.

insidious /inˈsiddiəss/ > *adjective* proceeding in a gradual, subtle way, with harmful effect.

DERIVATIVES – **insidiously** *adverb* **insidiousness** *noun*.

ORIGIN – Latin *insidiosus* 'cunning'.

insight > *noun* **1** the capacity to gain an accurate and intuitive understanding of something. **2** understanding of this kind.

DERIVATIVES – **insightful** *adjective*.

insignia /inˈsigniə/ > *noun* (pl. same or **insignias**) **1** a badge or distinguishing mark of authority, office, or membership. **2** a token of something.

USAGE – in Latin **insignia** is a plural noun, but in English it is treated as singular, with the plural **insignia** or, occasionally, **insignias**.

ORIGIN – Latin, plural of *insigne* 'sign, badge', from *insignis* 'distinguished'.

insignificant > *adjective* having little or no importance or value.

DERIVATIVES – **insignificance** *noun* **insignificantly** *adverb*.

SYNONYMS – inconsequential, negligible, trifling, trivial, unimportant.

insincere > *adjective* not expressing genuine feelings.

DERIVATIVES – **insincerely** *adverb* **insincerity** (pl. **insincerities**) *noun*.

SYNONYMS – dishonest, disingenuous, dissembling, false, two-faced.

insinuate /inˈsinyooayt/ > *verb* **1** suggest or hint (something bad) in an indirect and unpleasant way. **2** (**insinuate oneself into**) manoeuvre oneself gradually into (a favourable position).

DERIVATIVES – **insinuating** *adjective* **insinuator** *noun*.

ORIGIN – first used in the sense 'enter (a document) on the official register': from Latin *insinuare* 'introduce tortuously', from *in-* 'in' + *sinuare* 'to curve'.

insinuation > *noun* an unpleasant hint or suggestion.

insipid /inˈsippid/ > *adjective* **1** lacking flavour. **2** lacking vigour or interest.

DERIVATIVES – **insipidity** *noun* **insipidly** *adverb* **insipidness** *noun*.

SYNONYMS – **1** bland, flavourless, tasteless.

2 bland, dull, tedious, unimaginative, vapid.

ORIGIN – Latin *insipidus*, from *in-* 'not' + *sapidus* 'tasty, savoury'.

insist > *verb* **1** demand or state forcefully, without accepting refusal or contradiction. **2** (**insist on**) persist in (doing).

ORIGIN – Latin *insistere* 'persist', from *in-* 'upon' + *sistere* 'stand'.

insistent* > *adjective* **1** insisting or very demanding. **2** repeated and demanding attention.

DERIVATIVES – **insistence** *noun* **insistency** *noun* **insistently** *adverb*.

*SPELLING – *-ent*, not *-ant*: insist*ent*.

SYNONYMS – **1** determined, emphatic, firm, forceful, resolute.

in situ /in ˈsityoo/ > *adverb* & *adjective* in the original or appropriate position.

ORIGIN – Latin.

insobriety /insəˈbrīəti/ > *noun* formal drunkenness.

insofar > *adverb* variant spelling of **in so far**.

insolation /insəˈlaysh'n/ > *noun* technical exposure to the sun's rays.

ORIGIN – Latin, from *insolare*, from *in-* 'towards' + *sol* 'sun'.

insole > *noun* **1** a removable sole worn inside a shoe for warmth or to improve the fit. **2** the fixed inner sole of a boot or shoe.

insolent > *adjective* rude and disrespectful.

DERIVATIVES – **insolence** *noun* **insolently** *adverb*.

ORIGIN – Latin, 'immoderate, arrogant'.

insoluble > *adjective* **1** impossible to solve. **2** (of a substance) incapable of being dissolved.

DERIVATIVES – **insolubility** *noun* **insolubly** *adverb*.

insolvent > *adjective* **1** having insufficient money to pay debts owed. **2** relating to bankruptcy. > *noun* an insolvent person.

DERIVATIVES – **insolvency** *noun*.

insomnia > *noun* habitual sleeplessness.

DERIVATIVES – **insomniac** *noun* & *adjective*.

ORIGIN – Latin, from *insomnis* 'sleepless'.

insomuch > *adverb* (**insomuch that** or **as**) to the extent that.

insouciant /inˈsoosiənt/ > *adjective* casually unconcerned.

DERIVATIVES – **insouciance** *noun* **insouciantly** *adverb*.

ORIGIN – French, from *in-* 'not' + *souciant* 'worrying'.

inspect > *verb* **1** look at closely. **2** examine officially.

DERIVATIVES – **inspection** *noun*.

SYNONYMS – check, examine, scrutinise, study.

ORIGIN – Latin *inspicere* 'look into, examine'.

inspector > *noun* **1** an official who ensures

that regulations are obeyed. **2** a police officer ranking below a chief inspector.

DERIVATIVES – **inspectorate** *noun* **inspectorial** *adjective* **inspectorship** *noun*.

inspiration > *noun* **1** the process or quality of being inspired. **2** a person or thing that inspires. **3** a sudden clever or timely idea. **4** the process of inhalation.

DERIVATIVES – **inspirational** *adjective*.

inspiratory /inˈspīrətri/ > *adjective* Physiology relating to inhalation.

inspire > *verb* **1** fill with the urge or ability to do or feel something. **2** create (a feeling) in a person. **3** give rise to. **4** inhale.

DERIVATIVES – **inspirer** *noun* **inspiring** *adjective*.

SYNONYMS – **1** motivate, stimulate. **2** arouse, awaken, kindle, rouse.

ORIGIN – Latin *inspirare* 'breathe or blow into'.

inspired > *adjective* **1** showing or characterised by inspiration. **2** (of air or another substance) having been inhaled.

inspirit > *verb* (**inspirited, inspiriting**) (usu. as adj. **inspiriting**) encourage and enliven.

DERIVATIVES – **inspiritingly** *adverb*.

inspissate /inˈspissayt/ > *verb* thicken or congeal.

ORIGIN – Latin *inspissare*, from *spissus* 'thick, dense'.

instability > *noun* (pl. **instabilities**) the state of being unstable; lack of stability.

install* (US also **instal**) > *verb* (**installed, installing**) **1** place or fix (equipment) in position ready for use. **2** establish in a new place, condition, or role.

DERIVATIVES – **installer** *noun*.

*SPELLING – in British English **install** is spelled with two *l*s, while **instalment** is spelt with only one.

ORIGIN – Latin *installare*, from *in-* 'into' + *stallum* 'place, stall'.

installation > *noun* **1** the action or process of installing or being installed. **2** a large piece of equipment installed for use. **3** a military or industrial establishment. **4** an art exhibit constructed within a gallery.

instalment (US also **installment**) > *noun* **1** a sum of money due as one of several payments made over a period of time. **2** one of several parts of something published or broadcast at intervals.

ORIGIN – from Old French *estaler* 'to fix'.

instance > *noun* **1** an example or single occurrence of something. **2** a particular case. > *verb* cite as an example.

IDIOMS – **for instance** as an example. **in the first** (or **second** etc.) **instance** in the first (or second etc.) place or stage of a proceeding.

ORIGIN – first used in the sense 'urgent entreaty', later 'example to the contrary': from Latin *instantia* 'presence, urgency', from *instare* 'be present, press upon'.

instant > *adjective* 1 immediate. 2 urgent; pressing. 3 (of food) processed to allow quick preparation. > *noun* 1 a precise moment of time. 2 a very short time.

DERIVATIVES – **instantly** *adverb*.

SYNONYMS – *adjective* 1 immediate, instantaneous, on-the-spot. *noun* 1 juncture, moment, point. 2 flash, minute, moment, second, trice.

ORIGIN – Latin, from *instare* 'be at hand', from *in-* 'in, at' + *stare* 'to stand'.

instantaneous /instəntayniəss/ > *adjective* 1 occurring or done instantly. 2 Physics existing or measured at a particular instant.

DERIVATIVES – **instantaneity** *noun* **instantaneously** *adverb* **instantaneousness** *noun*.

instantiate /instanshiayt/ > *verb* represent as or by a particular instance or example.

DERIVATIVES – **instantiation** *noun*.

instate > *verb* install or establish.

instead > *adverb* 1 as an alternative or substitute. 2 (**instead of**) in place of.

instep > *noun* the part of a person's foot between the ball and the ankle.

instigate /instigayt/ > *verb* bring about or initiate; foment.

DERIVATIVES – **instigation** *noun* **instigator** *noun*.

ORIGIN – Latin *instigare*, from *stigare* 'prick, incite.'

instil /instil/ (also **instill**) > *verb* (**instilled**, **instilling**) 1 gradually but firmly establish (an idea or attitude) in someone's mind. 2 put (a liquid) into something in drops.

DERIVATIVES – **instillation** *noun*.

ORIGIN – Latin *instillare* 'put in by drops'.

instinct > *noun* 1 an inborn tendency or impulse to behave in a certain way. 2 a natural ability or skill. > *adjective* (**instinct with**) literary imbued or filled with (a quality).

DERIVATIVES – **instinctual** *adjective*.

ORIGIN – Latin *instinctus* 'impulse'.

instinctive > *adjective* relating to or prompted by instinct; apparently natural or automatic.

DERIVATIVES – **instinctively** *adverb*.

SYNONYMS – automatic, intuitive, involuntary, natural, reflex.

institute > *noun* an organisation for the promotion of science, education, etc. > *verb* 1 begin or establish. 2 appoint to a position, especially as a cleric.

ORIGIN – from Latin *instituere* 'establish'.

institution > *noun* 1 an important organisation or public body, such as a university, bank, hospital, or Church. 2 an organisation providing residential care for people with special needs. 3 an established law or custom. 4 informal a well-established and familiar person or thing. 5 the action of instituting something.

institutional > *adjective* 1 of, in, or like an institution. 2 typical of an institution, especially in being regimented or unimaginative.

DERIVATIVES – **institutionally** *adverb*.

institutionalise (also **institutionalize**) > *verb* 1 establish as a convention or norm in an organisation or culture. 2 place in a residential institution. 3 (**be** or **become institutionalised**) suffer the adverse effects of long-term residence in a residential institution.

DERIVATIVES – **institutionalisation** *noun*.

instruct > *verb* 1 direct or command. 2 teach. 3 inform of a fact or situation. 4 chiefly Brit. authorise (a solicitor or barrister) to act on one's behalf.

SYNONYMS – 1 command, direct, order, tell. 2 educate, school, teach, tutor. 3 advise, inform, notify, tell.

ORIGIN – Latin *instruere* 'construct, equip, teach'.

instruction > *noun* 1 a direction or order. 2 teaching or education. 3 a code in a computer program which defines and carries out an operation.

DERIVATIVES – **instructional** *adjective*.

instructive > *adjective* useful and informative.

DERIVATIVES – **instructively** *adverb*.

instructor (or **instructress**) > *noun* 1 a teacher. 2 N. Amer. a university teacher ranking below assistant professor.

DERIVATIVES – **instructorship** *noun*.

instrument > *noun* 1 a tool or implement, especially for very precise work. 2 a measuring device, especially in a vehicle or aircraft. 3 (also **musical instrument**) a device for producing musical sounds. 4 a means of pursuing an aim. 5 a person who is made use of. 6 a formal or legal document.

ORIGIN – Latin *instrumentum* 'equipment, implement'.

instrumental > *adjective* 1 (usu. **be instrumental in**) serving as a means of pursuing an aim. 2 (of music) performed on instruments. 3 relating to an implement or measuring device. > *noun* a piece of music performed on instruments, with no vocals.

DERIVATIVES – **instrumentality** *noun* **instrumentally** *adverb*.

instrumentalist > *noun* a player of a musical instrument.

instrumentation > *noun* 1 the instruments used in a piece of music. 2 the arrangement of a piece of music for particular instruments. 3 measuring instruments collectively.

insubordinate > *adjective* disobedient.

DERIVATIVES – **insubordination** *noun*.

insubstantial > *adjective* 1 lacking strength and solidity. 2 imaginary.

DERIVATIVES – **insubstantiality** *noun* **insubstantially** *adverb*.

SYNONYMS – 1 feeble, flimsy, slight, weak. 2 fanciful, illusory, imaginary, unreal.

insufferable > *adjective* 1 too extreme to bear; intolerable. 2 unbearably arrogant or conceited.

DERIVATIVES – **insufferableness** *noun* **insufferably** *adverb*.

ORIGIN – from Latin *sufferre* (see **SUFFER**).

insufficient > *adjective* not enough.

DERIVATIVES – **insufficiency** *noun* **insufficiently** *adverb*.

insulant > *noun* an insulating material.

insular /insyoolər/ > *adjective* 1 isolated from outside influences, and often narrow-minded as a result. 2 of or relating to an island.

DERIVATIVES – **insularity** *noun*.

wordpower facts

Insular

The words **insular**, **insulate**, and **insulin** are all based on Latin *insula* 'island', which is also the root of **isle**, **isolated**, and **peninsula**. 'Insulin' and 'island' are related through the *islets of Langerhans*, groups of cells in the pancreas that secrete insulin. The word **island** itself is from the unrelated Old English word *īegland*, from a base meaning 'watery, watered': the change in the spelling of the first syllable was due to association with **isle**.

insulate > *verb* 1 protect by interposing material to prevent loss of heat or intrusion of sound. 2 cover with non-conducting material to prevent the passage of electricity. 3 protect from something unpleasant.

DERIVATIVES – **insulator** *noun*.

COMBINATIONS – **insulating tape** adhesive tape used to cover exposed electric wires.

insulation > *noun* 1 the action of insulating or state of being insulated. 2 material used to insulate something.

insulin /insyoolin/ > *noun* a hormone produced in the pancreas, which regulates glucose levels in the blood, and the lack of which causes diabetes.

insult > *verb* /insult/ speak to or treat with disrespect or abuse. > *noun* /insult/ 1 an insulting remark or action. 2 a thing so worthless or contemptible as to be offensive: *the pay offer is an absolute insult*.

SYNONYMS – *verb* 1 abuse, disparage, revile, slight. *noun* 1 affront, slight, slur.

ORIGIN – Latin *insultare* 'jump or trample on'.

insuperable /insooperəb'l/ > *adjective* impossible to overcome.

DERIVATIVES – **insuperably** *adverb*.

ORIGIN – Latin *insuperabilis*, from *superare* 'overcome'.

insupportable > *adjective* **1** unable to be supported or justified. **2** intolerable.

DERIVATIVES – **insupportably** *adverb*.

insurance > *noun* **1** the action of insuring someone or something. **2** the business of providing insurance. **3** money paid for insurance, or as compensation under an insurance policy. **4** a thing providing protection against a possible eventuality.

NOTE – in the context of life insurance, **insurance** and **assurance** do not mean the same thing. **Assurance** is used of policies under whose terms a payment is guaranteed, either after a fixed term or on the death of the insured person; **insurance** is the general term, and is used in particular of policies under whose terms a payment is made only in certain circumstances (e.g. accident or death within a limited period).

insure > *verb* **1** arrange for compensation in the event of damage to or loss of (property, life, or a person), in exchange for regular payments to a company. **2** secure the payment of (a sum) in this way. **3** (**insure against**) protect against (a possible contingency). **4** another term for ENSURE.

DERIVATIVES – **insurable** *adjective* **insurer** *noun*.

USAGE – **insure** and **ensure** mean the same thing in the general sense 'make certain that (something) will occur or be so', but only **insure** is used in relation to the provision of compensation for loss or damage.

ORIGIN – alteration of ENSURE.

insurgent /insurjənt/ > *adjective* rising in active revolt. > *noun* a rebel or revolutionary.

DERIVATIVES – **insurgence** *noun* **insurgency** (pl. **insurgencies**) *noun*.

ORIGIN – from Latin *insurgere* 'arise'.

insurmountable > *adjective* too great to be overcome.

DERIVATIVES – **insurmountably** *adverb*.

insurrection /insəreksh'n/ > *noun* a violent uprising against authority.

DERIVATIVES – **insurrectionary** *adjective* **insurrectionist** *noun & adjective*.

ORIGIN – Latin, from *insurgere* 'rise up'.

insusceptible > *adjective* not susceptible.

DERIVATIVES – **insusceptibility** *noun*.

intact > *adjective* not damaged or impaired.

DERIVATIVES – **intactness** *noun*.

SYNONYMS – complete, entire, sound, unbroken, whole.

ORIGIN – Latin *intactus* 'untouched'.

intaglio /intaaliō/ > *noun* (pl. **intaglios**) **1** an incised or engraved design. **2** a gem with an incised design.

ORIGIN – Italian, from *intagliare* 'engrave'.

intake > *noun* **1** an amount or quantity taken in. **2** an act of taking in. **3** a structure through which air, fuel, or other material is taken in.

intangible /intanjib'l/ > *adjective* **1** unable to be touched; not solid or real. **2** vague and abstract. > *noun* an intangible thing.

DERIVATIVES – **intangibility** *noun* **intangibly** *adverb*.

intarsia /intaarsiə/ > *noun* **1** a method of knitting in which a separate length or ball of yarn is used for each area of colour. **2** elaborate marquetry or inlaid work.

ORIGIN – Italian *intarsio*; superseding earlier *tarsia* 'marquetry'.

integer /intijər/ > *noun* a whole number.

ORIGIN – Latin, 'intact, whole', from *tangere* 'to touch'; compare with ENTIRE.

integral > *adjective* /intigrəl, integrəl/ **1** necessary to make a whole complete; fundamental. **2** included as part of a whole. **3** forming a whole; complete. **4** Mathematics of or denoted by an integer or integers. > *noun* /intigrəl/ Mathematics a function of which a given function is the derivative, and which may express the area under the curve of a graph of the function.

DERIVATIVES – **integrally** *adverb*.

NOTE – there are two possible ways of pronouncing **integral**: one with the stress on **in-** and the other with the stress on **-teg-**. In British English, the second pronunciation is sometimes frowned on, but both are broadly accepted as standard.

SYNONYMS – **1** basic, essential, fundamental, necessary, requisite. **3** complete, entire, integrated, unified.

COMBINATIONS – **integral calculus** Mathematics the part of calculus concerned with the integrals of functions.

integrate > *verb* /intigrayt/ **1** combine or be combined to form a whole. **2** bring or come into equal participation in an institution or body. **3** Mathematics find the integral of.

DERIVATIVES – **integrable** /intigrəb'l/ *adjective* **integrative** /intigrətiv/ *adjective* **integrator** *noun*.

COMBINATIONS – **integrated circuit** an electronic circuit on a small piece of semiconducting material, performing the same function as a larger circuit of discrete components. **integrated services digital network** a telecommunications network through which sound, images, and data can be transmitted as digitised signals.

ORIGIN – Latin *integrare* 'make whole', from *integer* 'whole, intact'.

integration > *noun* **1** the action or process of integrating. **2** the intermixing of peoples or groups previously segregated.

DERIVATIVES – **integrationist** *noun*.

integrity /integriti/ > *noun* **1** the quality of being honest and morally upright. **2** the state of being whole or unified. **3** soundness of construction.

SYNONYMS – **1** decency, honesty, probity, uprightness. **2** completeness, unity.

ORIGIN – Latin *integritas*, from *integer* 'intact, whole'.

integument /integyoomənt/ > *noun* a tough outer protective layer, especially of an animal or plant.

ORIGIN – Latin *integumentum*, from *integere* 'to cover'.

intellect > *noun* **1** the faculty of reasoning and understanding objectively. **2** a person's mental powers. **3** a clever person.

SYNONYMS – **1** intelligence, reason, understanding.

ORIGIN – Latin *intellectus* 'understanding'.

intellectual /intəlektyooəl/ > *adjective* **1** relating or appealing to the intellect. **2** having a highly developed intellect. > *noun* a person with a highly developed intellect.

DERIVATIVES – **intellectuality** *noun* **intellectually** *adverb*.

SYNONYMS – *adjective* **1** academic, cerebral, mental. **2** erudite, intelligent, learned.

COMBINATIONS – **intellectual property** Law intangible property that is the result of creativity, e.g. patents or copyrights.

intellectualise (also **intellectualize**) > *verb* **1** give an intellectual character to. **2** talk or write intellectually.

intellectualism > *noun* the exercise of the intellect at the expense of the emotions.

DERIVATIVES – **intellectualist** *noun*.

intelligence > *noun* **1** the ability to acquire and apply knowledge and skills. **2** the gathering of information of military or political value. **3** information gathered in this way.

SYNONYMS – **1** acumen, brainpower, cleverness, intellect.

COMBINATIONS – **intelligence quotient** a number representing a person's reasoning ability compared to the statistical norm, 100 being average.

ORIGIN – Latin *intelligentia*, from *intelligere* 'understand'.

intelligent > *adjective* **1** having intelligence, especially of a high level. **2** (of a device) able to vary its state or action in response to varying situations and past experience. **3** (of a computer terminal) having its own processing capability.

DERIVATIVES – **intelligently** *adverb*.

SYNONYMS – **1** bright, clever, quick, smart; informal brainy.

ANTONYMS – **1** stupid, unintelligent.

intelligentsia /intellijentsiə/ > *noun* (treated as sing. or pl.) intellectuals or highly educated people, regarded as having cultural and political influence.

intelligible /intellijib'l/ > *adjective* able to be understood.

DERIVATIVES – **intelligibility** *noun* **intelligibly** *adverb*.

ORIGIN – Latin *intelligibilis*, from *intelligere* 'understand'.

intemperate > *adjective* **1** lacking self-control. **2** characterised by excessive indulgence, especially in alcohol.

DERIVATIVES – **intemperance** *noun* **intemperately** *adverb*.

intend > *verb* **1** have as one's aim or plan. **2** plan that (something) should be, do, or mean something: *the book was intended as a satire*. **3** (**intend for** or **to do**) design or destine for a particular purpose. **4** (**be intended for**) be meant for the use of.

DERIVATIVES – **intender** *noun*.

SYNONYMS – **1** aim, mean, plan; formal purpose.

ORIGIN – Latin *intendere* 'intend, extend, direct'.

intended > *adjective* planned or meant. > *noun* (**one's intended**) informal one's fiancé(e).

intense > *adjective* (**intenser, intensest**) **1** of extreme force, degree, or strength. **2** extremely earnest or serious.

DERIVATIVES – **intensely** *adverb* **intenseness** *noun*.

USAGE – **intense** and **intensive** are similar in meaning, but they differ in emphasis: **intense** tends to relate to subjective responses, while **intensive** relates to objective descriptions. Thus, *an intensive course* is a course designed to cover a lot of ground in a short time; on the other hand, in *the course was intense*, **intense** describes how someone felt about the course.

SYNONYMS – **1** acute, extreme, fierce, severe.

ORIGIN – Latin *intensus* 'stretched tightly, strained', from *intendere* 'intend, extend'.

intensifier > *noun* **1** a thing that intensifies. **2** Grammar an adverb or prefix used to give force or emphasis.

intensify > *verb* (**intensifies, intensified**) make or become more intense.

DERIVATIVES – **intensification** *noun*.

SYNONYMS – deepen, heighten, magnify, strengthen.

intensity > *noun* (pl. **intensities**) **1** the quality of being intense. **2** chiefly Physics the measurable amount of a property, such as force or brightness.

intensive > *adjective* **1** very thorough or vigorous. **2** (of agriculture) aiming to achieve maximum production within a limited area. **3** (in combination) concentrating on or making much use of something: *labour-intensive methods*.

DERIVATIVES – **intensively** *adverb* **intensiveness** *noun*.

COMBINATIONS – **intensive care** special medical treatment of a dangerously ill or hurt patient.

intent > *noun* intention or purpose. > *adjective* **1** (**intent on** or **upon**) determined to do. **2** (**intent on** or **upon**) attentively occupied with. **3** showing earnest and eager attention.

IDIOMS – **to all intents and purposes** in all important respects. **with intent** Law with the intention of committing a crime.

DERIVATIVES – **intently** *adverb* **intentness** *noun*.

ORIGIN – Old French *entent, entente*, from Latin *intendere* 'intend'.

intention > *noun* **1** an aim or plan. **2** the action or fact of intending. **3** (**one's intentions**) a man's plans in respect to marriage.

DERIVATIVES – **intentioned** *adjective*.

SYNONYMS – **1** aim, goal, objective, plan, purpose. **2** design, premeditation.

intentional > *adjective* deliberate.

DERIVATIVES – **intentionality** *noun* **intentionally** *adverb*.

SYNONYMS – calculated, conscious, deliberate, planned, purposeful.

ANTONYMS – accidental, unintentional.

inter /inter/ > *verb* (**interred, interring**) place (a corpse) in a grave or tomb.

USAGE – someone who is **interred** is buried; someone who is **interned** is imprisoned.

ORIGIN – Old French *enterrer*, from Latin *in-* 'into' + *terra* 'earth'.

inter- > *prefix* **1** between; among: *interbreed*. **2** mutually; reciprocally: *interaction*.

ORIGIN – Latin *inter* 'between, among'.

interact > *verb* (of two people or things) act in such a way that they have an effect on each other.

DERIVATIVES – **interactant** *adjective & noun* **interaction** *noun*.

interactive > *adjective* **1** influencing each other. **2** (of a computer or other electronic device) allowing a two-way flow of information between it and a user, responding to the user's input.

DERIVATIVES – **interactively** *adverb* **interactivity** *noun*.

inter alia /inter aylia, inter aalia/ > *adverb* among other things.

ORIGIN – Latin.

interbreed > *verb* (past and past participle **interbred**) breed or cause to breed with an animal of a different race or species.

intercalary /interkaləri, intakaləri/ > *adjective* (of a day or month) inserted in the calendar to harmonise it with the solar year, e.g. 29 February.

ORIGIN – Latin *intercalarius*, from *intercalare* 'proclaim as inserted in the calendar'.

intercalate /interkəlayt/ > *verb* insert (an additional item or items) into a sequence or series.

DERIVATIVES – **intercalation** *noun*.

intercede /interseed/ > *verb* intervene on behalf of another.

ORIGIN – Latin *intercedere* 'intervene'.

intercellular > *adjective* located or occurring between cells.

intercept > *verb* /intersept/ obstruct and prevent from continuing to a destination. > *noun* /intersept/ **1** an act of intercepting. **2** Mathematics the point at which a line cuts the axis of a graph.

DERIVATIVES – **interception** *noun* **interceptor** *noun*.

ORIGIN – Latin *intercipere* 'catch between'.

intercession /intersesh'n/ > *noun* **1** the action of interceding. **2** the saying of a prayer on behalf of another person.

DERIVATIVES – **intercessor** *noun* **intercessory** *adjective*.

ORIGIN – Latin, from *intercedere* 'intervene'.

interchange > *verb* /interchaynj/ **1** exchange (things) with each other. **2** put each of (two things) in the other's place. > *noun* /interchaynj/ **1** the action of interchanging. **2** an exchange of words. **3** a road junction constructed on several levels so that traffic streams do not intersect.

DERIVATIVES – **interchangeability** *noun* **interchangeable** *adjective* **interchangeably** *adverb*.

intercity > *adjective* existing or travelling between cities.

intercom > *noun* an electrical device allowing one-way or two-way communication.

intercommunicate > *verb* **1** engage in two-way communication. **2** (of rooms) have a common connecting door.

DERIVATIVES – **intercommunication** *noun*.

interconnect > *verb* connect with each other.

DERIVATIVES – **interconnection** *noun*.

intercontinental > *adjective* relating to or travelling between continents.

interconvert > *verb* (**be interconverted**) be converted into each other.

DERIVATIVES – **interconversion** *noun* **interconvertible** *adjective*.

intercooler > *noun* an apparatus for cooling gas between successive compressions, especially in a supercharged engine.

DERIVATIVES – **intercool** *verb*.

intercostal /interkost'l/ Anatomy > *adjective* situated between the ribs. > *noun* an intercostal muscle.

intercourse > *noun* **1** (also **sexual intercourse**) sexual contact between individuals involving penetration, especially the insertion of a man's erect penis into a woman's vagina culminating in orgasm and the ejaculation of semen. **2** formal communication or dealings between people.

ORIGIN – Latin *intercursus*, from *intercurrere* 'intervene'.

intercrop > *verb* (**intercropped, intercropping**) grow (a crop) among plants of a different kind.

intercut > *verb* (**intercutting**; past and past participle **intercut**) alternate (scenes) with contrasting scenes in a film.

interdenominational > *adjective* relating to more than one religious denomination.

interdepartmental > *adjective* relating to more than one department.

interdependent > *adjective* dependent on each other.
DERIVATIVES – **interdependence** *noun* **interdependency** *noun*.

interdict > *noun* /**in**tərdikt/ **1** an authoritative prohibition. **2** (in the Roman Catholic Church) a sentence debarring a person or place from ecclesiastical functions and privileges. > *verb* /intər**dikt**/ chiefly N. Amer. prohibit or forbid.
DERIVATIVES – **interdiction** *noun*.
ORIGIN – Latin *interdictum*, from *interdicere* 'interpose, forbid by decree'.

interdisciplinary > *adjective* relating to more than one branch of knowledge.

interest > *noun* **1** the state of wanting to know about something or someone. **2** the quality of exciting curiosity or holding the attention. **3** a subject about which one is concerned or enthusiastic. **4** money paid for the use of money lent. **5** a person's advantage or benefit. **6** a share, right, or stake in property or a financial undertaking. **7** a group having a common concern, especially in politics or business. > *verb* **1** excite the curiosity or attention of. **2** (**interest in**) persuade (someone) to undertake or acquire. **3** (**interested**) not impartial: *interested parties*.
IDIOMS – **at interest** (of money borrowed) on the condition that interest is payable.
DERIVATIVES – **interestedly** *adverb*.
SYNONYMS – *noun* **1** attention, attentiveness, curiosity. **2** appeal, attraction. *verb* **1** absorb, engross, intrigue.
ORIGIN – Latin *interesse* 'differ, be important'.

interesting > *adjective* arousing curiosity or interest.
DERIVATIVES – **interestingly** *adverb* **interestingness** *noun*.
SYNONYMS – absorbing, appealing, engrossing, fascinating, intriguing.

interface > *noun* **1** a point where two things meet and interact. **2** technical a surface forming a boundary between two portions of matter or space. **3** a device or program enabling a user to communicate with a computer, or for connecting two items of hardware or software. > *verb* (**interface with**) **1** interact with. **2** Computing connect with (something) by an interface.

interfacing > *noun* an extra layer of material or an adhesive stiffener, applied to the facing of a garment to add support.

interfaith > *adjective* relating to or between different religions.

interfere > *verb* **1** (**interfere with**) prevent from continuing or being carried out properly. **2** (**interfere with**) handle or adjust without permission. **3** intervene without invitation or necessity. **4** (**interfere with**) Brit. euphemistic sexually molest. **5** Physics interact to produce interference.
DERIVATIVES – **interferer** *noun*.
ORIGIN – Old French *s'entreferir* 'strike each other'.

interference > *noun* **1** the action of interfering or process of being interfered with. **2** disturbance to radio or television signals caused by unwanted signals from other sources. **3** Physics the combination of two or more waveforms with the effect that the wave motions are either reinforced or cancelled (e.g. the combination of beams of light to form a pattern of light and dark bands).
DERIVATIVES – **interferential** *adjective*.

interferometer /intəfə**romm**itər/ > *noun* Physics an instrument in which interference between beams of light or radiation is used to make precise measurements in terms of the wavelength.
DERIVATIVES – **interferometric** *adjective* **interferometry** *noun*.

interferon /intər**feer**on/ > *noun* a protein released by animal cells which inhibits virus replication.

interfuse > *verb* literary join or mix together.
DERIVATIVES – **interfusion** *noun*.

intergalactic > *adjective* relating to or situated between galaxies.

intergovernmental > *adjective* relating to or conducted between governments.

interim /**in**tərim/ > *noun* (**the interim**) the intervening time. > *adjective* in or for the intervening time; provisional.
ORIGIN – Latin, 'meanwhile'.

interior > *adjective* **1** situated within or inside; inner. **2** remote from the coast or frontier; inland. **3** relating to a country's internal affairs. **4** existing or occurring in the mind or soul. > *noun* **1** the interior part. **2** the internal affairs of a country.
DERIVATIVES – **interiorise** (also **interiorize**) *verb* **interiorly** *adverb*.
SYNONYMS – *adjective* **1** inner, inside, internal, inward.
ANTONYMS – *adjective* **1** exterior.
COMBINATIONS – **interior decoration** the decoration of the interior of a building or room, especially with regard for colour combination and artistic effect. **interior design** the design or decoration of the interior of a room or building. **interior monologue** a piece of writing expressing a character's thoughts.
ORIGIN – Latin, 'inner'.

interiority > *noun* the quality of being interior or inward.

interject /intər**jekt**/ > *verb* say abruptly, especially as an interruption.
ORIGIN – Latin *interjicere* 'interpose'.

interjection > *noun* an exclamation (e.g. *ah!*, *good grief!*).

interlace > *verb* **1** interweave. **2** (**interlace with**) mingle or intersperse with.

interlard > *verb* (**interlard with**) intersperse (speech or writing) with (contrasting words and phrases).

interleave > *verb* **1** insert blank leaves between the pages of (a book). **2** place something between the layers of.

interline > *verb* put an extra lining in (a garment, curtain, etc.).

interlinear > *adjective* written between the lines of a text.

interlining > *noun* material used to interline a garment, curtain, etc.

interlink > *verb* join or connect together.
DERIVATIVES – **interlinkage** *noun*.

interlock > *verb* engage with each other by overlapping or fitting together. > *noun* **1** a device or mechanism for connecting or coordinating the function of components. **2** (also **interlock fabric**) a fabric with closely interlocking stitches allowing it to stretch.

interlocutor /intər**lok**yootər/ > *noun* formal a person who takes part in a conversation.
DERIVATIVES – **interlocution** *noun*.
ORIGIN – from Latin *interloqui* 'interrupt (with speech)'.

interlocutory /intər**lok**yootəri/ > *adjective* **1** Law (of a decree or judgement) given provisionally during the course of a legal action. **2** relating to dialogue.

interloper /**in**tərlōpər/ > *noun* a person who becomes involved in a place or situation where they are not wanted or do not belong; an intruder.
DERIVATIVES – **interlope** *verb*.
ORIGIN – from **INTER-** + *-loper* as in archaic *landloper* 'vagabond' (from Dutch *landlooper*).

interlude > *noun* **1** an intervening period of time or activity that contrasts with what goes before or after: *a romantic interlude*. **2** a pause between the acts of a play. **3** a piece of music played between other pieces or between the verses of a hymn.
ORIGIN – Latin *interludium*, from *inter-* 'between' + *ludus* 'play'.

intermarriage > *noun* **1** marriage between people of different races, castes, or religions. **2** marriage between close relations.
DERIVATIVES – **intermarry** *verb*.

intermediary /intər**mee**diəri/ > *noun* (pl. **intermediaries**) a person who acts as a link or helps to make an agreement between two or more others. > *adjective* intermediate.

intermediate /intər**mee**diət/ > *adjective* **1** coming between two things in time, place, character, etc. **2** having more than basic knowledge or skills but not yet advanced. > *noun* an intermediate person or thing. > *verb* /inter**mee**diayt/ act as an intermediary.

DERIVATIVES – **intermediacy** *noun* **intermediation** *noun*.

ORIGIN – from Latin *inter*- 'between' + *medius* 'middle'.

interment /inter**ment**/ > *noun* the burial of a corpse in a grave or tomb.

intermezzo /intər**met**sō/ > *noun* (pl. **intermezzi** /intər**met**see/ or **intermezzos**) **1** a short connecting instrumental movement in an opera or other musical work. **2** a short piece for a solo instrument. **3** a light dramatic or other performance between the acts of a play.

ORIGIN – Italian, from Latin *intermedium* 'interval'.

interminable /inter**min**əb'l/ > *adjective* endless.

DERIVATIVES – **interminably** *adverb*.

intermingle > *verb* mix or mingle together.

intermission > *noun* **1** a pause or break. **2** an interval between parts of a play or film.

ORIGIN – Latin, from *intermittere* 'discontinue, stop'.

intermittent > *adjective* occurring at irregular intervals.

DERIVATIVES – **intermittency** *noun* **intermittently** *adverb*.

SYNONYMS – irregular, occasional, periodic, sporadic.

ORIGIN – Latin, 'ceasing', from *intermittere* (see INTERMISSION).

intermix > *verb* mix together.

DERIVATIVES – **intermixable** *adjective* **intermixture** *noun*.

intermodal > *adjective* involving two or more different modes of transport.

intermolecular > *adjective* existing or occurring between molecules.

intern > *noun* /**in**tern/ (also **interne**) **1** chiefly N. Amer. a recent medical graduate receiving supervised training in a hospital and acting as an assistant physician or surgeon. **2** a student or trainee who does a job to gain work experience or for a qualification. > *verb* **1** /in**tern**/ confine as a prisoner. **2** /**in**tern/ chiefly N. Amer. serve as an intern.

DERIVATIVES – **internment** *noun* **internship** *noun*.

USAGE – someone who is **interned** is a prisoner; someone who is **interred** is a corpse.

ORIGIN – from Latin *internus* 'inward, internal'.

internal > *adjective* **1** of or situated on the inside. **2** inside the body. **3** relating to affairs and activities within a country. **4** existing or used within an organisation. **5** in or of one's mind or soul. > *noun* (**internals**) inner parts or features.

DERIVATIVES – **internality** *noun* **internally** *adverb*.

SYNONYMS – *adjective* **1** inner, inside, interior, inward.

ANTONYMS – *adjective* **1** external.

COMBINATIONS – **internal-combustion engine** an engine in which power is generated by the expansion of hot gases from the burning of fuel with air inside the engine. **internal exile** penal banishment from a part of one's own country. **internal market 1** a single market. **2** (in the UK) a system in the National Health Service whereby hospital departments purchase each other's services contractually.

ORIGIN – Latin *internalis*, from *internus* 'inward, internal'.

internalise (also **internalize**) > *verb* make (attitudes or behaviour) part of one's nature by learning or unconscious assimilation.

DERIVATIVES – **internalisation** *noun*.

international > *adjective* **1** existing or occurring between nations. **2** agreed on or used by all or many nations. > *noun* **1** Brit. a game or contest between teams representing different countries. **2** a player who has taken part in such a contest. **3** (**International**) any of four associations founded (1864–1936) to promote socialist or communist action.

DERIVATIVES – **internationality** *noun* **internationally** *adverb*.

SYNONYMS – *adjective* cosmopolitan, global, universal, worldwide.

COMBINATIONS – **International Date Line** an imaginary North–South line through the Pacific Ocean, chiefly along the meridian furthest from Greenwich, to the east of which the date is a day earlier than it is to the west. **international law** a body of rules established by custom or treaty and recognised by nations as binding in their relations with one another.

Internationale /intərnashyə**naal**/ > *noun* (**the Internationale**) a revolutionary song composed in France, adopted as an international anthem by socialists.

internationalise (also **internationalize**) > *verb* make international.

DERIVATIVES – **internationalisation** *noun*.

internationalism > *noun* **1** the advocacy of cooperation and understanding between nations. **2** the state or process of being international.

DERIVATIVES – **internationalist** *noun*.

interne > *noun* variant spelling of INTERN noun.

internecine /intər**nee**sīn/ > *adjective* **1** destructive to both sides in a conflict. **2** relating to conflict within a group: *internecine rivalries.*

ORIGIN – from Latin *inter*- 'among' + *necare* 'to kill'.

internee > *noun* a prisoner.

Internet > *noun* an international information network linking computers, accessible to the public via modem links.

WORDFINDER – bulletin board, chat room, newsgroup (*Internet forums for exchange of views or information*), webcam (*video camera connected to the Internet*), webcast (*broadcast over Internet*).

internist > *noun* N. Amer. a specialist in internal diseases.

interoperable > *adjective* (of computer systems or software) able to operate in conjunction.

DERIVATIVES – **interoperability** *noun*.

interpenetrate > *verb* mix or merge together.

DERIVATIVES – **interpenetration** *noun* **interpenetrative** *adjective*.

interpersonal > *adjective* relating to relationships or communication between people.

DERIVATIVES – **interpersonally** *adverb*.

interplanetary > *adjective* situated or travelling between planets.

interplant > *verb* plant (a crop or plant) together with another.

interplay > *noun* the way in which things affect each other; interaction.

Interpol /**in**tərpol/ > *noun* an international organisation that coordinates investigations made by the police forces of member countries into international crimes.

interpolate /inter**pə**layt/ > *verb* **1** insert (words) in a book, especially to give a false impression as to its date. **2** insert or introduce (something different or additional). **3** interject (a remark) in a conversation. **4** Mathematics insert (an intermediate term) into a series by estimating or calculating it from surrounding known values.

DERIVATIVES – **interpolation** *noun* **interpolator** *noun*.

ORIGIN – Latin *interpolare* 'refurbish, alter'.

interpose > *verb* **1** insert between one thing and another. **2** intervene between parties. **3** say as an interruption. **4** exercise or advance (a veto or objection).

DERIVATIVES – **interposition** *noun*.

ORIGIN – French *interposer*, from Latin *interponere* 'put in'.

interpret > *verb* (**interpreted**, **interpreting**) **1** explain the meaning of. **2** translate orally the words of a person speaking a different language. **3** understand as having a particular meaning or significance. **4** perform (a creative work) in a way that conveys one's understanding of the creator's ideas.

DERIVATIVES – **interpretable** *adjective* **interpretive** (also **interpretative**) *adjective*.

SYNONYMS – **1** elucidate, explain, explicate. **3** construe, read, take, understand.

ORIGIN – Latin *interpretari* 'explain, translate'.

interpretation > *noun* **1** the action of explaining the meaning of something. **2** an explanation or way of explaining. **3** a performer's representation of a creative work.

DERIVATIVES – **interpretational** *adjective*.

interpreter > *noun* a person who interprets foreign speech orally.

interracial > *adjective* existing between or involving different races.

DERIVATIVES – **interracially** *adverb*.

interregnum /intəregnəm/ > *noun* (pl. **interregnums** or **interregna** /intəregnə/) a period when normal government is suspended, especially between successive reigns or regimes.

ORIGIN – Latin, from *inter-* 'between' + *regnum* 'reign'.

interrelate > *verb* relate or connect to one other.

DERIVATIVES – **interrelatedness** *noun* **interrelation** *noun* **interrelationship** *noun*.

interrogate > *verb* **1** ask questions of (someone) closely, aggressively, or formally. **2** obtain data or information automatically from (a device, database, etc.).

DERIVATIVES – **interrogation** *noun* **interrogator** *noun*.

SYNONYMS – **1** cross-examine, grill, quiz.

ORIGIN – Latin *interrogare* 'question'.

interrogative /intəroggətiv/ > *adjective* **1** having the force of a question. **2** Grammar used in questions. > *noun* an interrogative word, e.g. *how* or *what*.

DERIVATIVES – **interrogatively** *adverb*.

interrogatory /intəroggətri/ > *adjective* questioning.

interrupt > *verb* **1** stop the continuous progress of. **2** stop (a person who is speaking) by saying or doing something. **3** break the continuity of (a line, view, etc.).

DERIVATIVES – **interrupter** (also **interruptor**) *noun* **interruptible** *adjective* **interruption** *noun* **interruptive** *adjective*.

SYNONYMS – **1** discontinue, disrupt, disturb, hold up, suspend. **2** butt in on, cut in on, heckle.

ORIGIN – Latin *interrumpere* 'break, interrupt'.

intersect /intərsekt/ > *verb* **1** divide (something) by passing or lying across it. **2** (of lines, roads, etc.) cut or cross each other.

ORIGIN – Latin *intersecare* 'cut, intersect'.

intersection > *noun* **1** a point or line common to lines or surfaces that intersect. **2** a point at which two roads intersect.

DERIVATIVES – **intersectional** *adjective*.

intersex > *noun* **1** hermaphroditism. **2** a hermaphrodite.

intersexual > *adjective* **1** existing or occurring between the sexes. **2** hermaphroditic.

DERIVATIVES – **intersexuality** *noun*.

interspace > *noun* a space between objects. > *verb* (usu. **be interspaced**) put or occupy a space between.

intersperse > *verb* (usu. **be interspersed**) **1** scatter among or between other things. **2** diversify with other things at intervals.

DERIVATIVES – **interspersion** *noun*.

ORIGIN – Latin *interspergere* 'scatter between'.

interstate > *adjective* existing or carried on between states, especially of the US. > *noun* one of a system of motorways running between US states. > *adverb* Austral. from one state to another.

interstellar /intərstellər/ > *adjective* occurring or situated between stars.

interstice /intərstiss/ > *noun* a small gap or crack.

ORIGIN – Latin *interstitium*, from *intersistere* 'stand between'.

interstitial /intərstish'l/ > *adjective* of, forming, or occupying interstices.

DERIVATIVES – **interstitially** *adverb*.

intertextuality > *noun* the relationship between texts.

DERIVATIVES – **intertextual** *adjective*.

intertribal > *adjective* existing or occurring between different tribes.

intertwine > *verb* twist or twine together.

interval > *noun* **1** an intervening time or space. **2** a pause or break. **3** Brit. a pause between parts of a theatrical or musical performance or a sports match. **4** Music the difference in pitch between two notes.

ORIGIN – Latin *intervallum* 'space between ramparts, interval'.

intervene > *verb* **1** come between so as to prevent or alter the result or course of events. **2** (usu. as adj. **intervening**) occur or be between or among.

DERIVATIVES – **intervener** (also **intervenor**) *noun*.

SYNONYMS – **1** intercede, interpose, mediate, step in.

ORIGIN – Latin *intervenire* 'come between'.

intervention > *noun* **1** the action or process of intervening. **2** interference by a state in another's affairs. **3** action taken to improve a medical disorder.

DERIVATIVES – **interventional** *adjective*.

interventionist > *adjective* favouring intervention, especially by a government in its domestic economy or by one state in the affairs of another. > *noun* an interventionist person.

DERIVATIVES – **interventionism** *noun*.

interview > *noun* **1** a conversation between a journalist or broadcaster and a person of public interest. **2** an oral examination of an applicant for a job or college place. **3** a session of formal questioning of a person by the police. > *verb* hold an interview with.

DERIVATIVES – **interviewee** *noun* **interviewer** *noun*.

ORIGIN – French *entrevue*, from *s'entrevoir* 'see each other'.

inter vivos /intər veevōs/ > *adverb* & *adjective* (especially of a gift as opposed to a legacy) between living people.

ORIGIN – Latin.

interwar > *adjective* existing in the period between wars, especially the two world wars.

interweave > *verb* (past **interwove**; past participle **interwoven**) weave or become woven together.

intestate /intestət/ > *adjective* not having made a will before one dies. > *noun* a person who has died intestate.

DERIVATIVES – **intestacy** /intestəsi/ *noun*.

intestine (also **intestines**) > *noun* the lower part of the alimentary canal from the end of the stomach to the anus.

WORDFINDER – enteric (*of the intestines*), peristalsis (*muscular motion of the intestines*); *parts of the intestine:* caecum, colon, duodenum, jejunum, ileum, rectum.

DERIVATIVES – **intestinal** *adjective*.

ORIGIN – Latin *intestinum*, from *intus* 'within'.

intifada /intifaadə/ > *noun* the Palestinian uprising against Israeli occupation of the West Bank and Gaza Strip, beginning in 1987.

ORIGIN – Arabic.

intimacy > *noun* (pl. **intimacies**) **1** close familiarity or friendship. **2** an intimate act or remark.

intimate¹ /intimət/ > *adjective* **1** closely acquainted; familiar. **2** private and personal. **3** euphemistic having a sexual relationship. **4** involving very close connection: *an intimate involvement*. **5** (of knowledge) detailed. **6** having an informal friendly atmosphere. > *noun* a very close friend.

DERIVATIVES – **intimately** *adverb*.

SYNONYMS – **1** close, familiar, friendly. **2** confidential, personal, private, secret. **5** detailed, in-depth, thorough.

ORIGIN – from Latin *intimare* 'impress, make familiar', from *intimus* 'inmost'.

intimate² /intimayt/ > *verb* **1** state or make known. **2** imply or hint.

DERIVATIVES – **intimation** *noun*.

ORIGIN – Latin *intimare* (see **INTIMATE¹**).

intimidate > *verb* frighten or overawe, especially so as to coerce into doing something.

DERIVATIVES – **intimidation** *noun* **intimidator** *noun* **intimidatory** *adjective*.

SYNONYMS – browbeat, bully, cow, daunt, frighten, overawe.

ORIGIN – Latin *intimidare* 'make timid'.

into > *preposition* **1** expressing motion or direction to a point on or within. **2** expressing a change of state or the result of an action. **3** indicating the direction towards which someone or something is turned. **4** indicating an object of interest. **5** expressing division. **6** informal taking a lively and active interest in.

intolerable > *adjective* unable to be endured.

DERIVATIVES – **intolerably** *adverb*.

SYNONYMS – insufferable, insupportable, unbearable, unendurable.

intolerant > *adjective* not accepting of opinions, behaviour, etc. that differ from one's own.

DERIVATIVES – **intolerance** *noun* **intolerantly** *adverb*.

intonation > *noun* **1** the rise and fall of the voice in speaking. **2** the action of intoning. **3** accuracy of musical pitch.

DERIVATIVES – **intonational** *adjective*.

intone /intōn/ > *verb* say or recite with little rise and fall of the pitch of the voice.

ORIGIN – Latin *intonare*, from *tonus* 'tone'.

in toto /in tōtō/ > *adverb* as a whole.

ORIGIN – Latin.

intoxicant > *noun* an intoxicating substance.

intoxicate > *verb* (usu. as adj. **intoxicated**) **1** (of alcoholic drink or a drug) cause (someone) to lose control of their faculties. **2** excite or exhilarate. **3** technical poison.

DERIVATIVES – **intoxication** *noun*.

ORIGIN – Latin *intoxicare*, from *toxicum* 'poison'.

intra- /intrə/ > *prefix* (added to adjectives) on the inside; within: *intramural*.

ORIGIN – Latin, 'inside'.

intractable /intraktəb'l/ > *adjective* **1** hard to solve or deal with. **2** stubborn.

DERIVATIVES – **intractability** *noun* **intractably** *adverb*.

intramural /intrəmyoorəl/ > *adjective* **1** situated or done within a building. **2** forming part of normal university or college studies.

ORIGIN – from INTRA- + Latin *murus* 'wall'.

intramuscular > *adjective* situated or taking place within, or administered into, a muscle.

DERIVATIVES – **intramuscularly** *adverb*.

Intranet /intrənet/ > *noun* Computing a private communications network created with Internet software.

intransigent /intransijənt/ > *adjective* refusing to change one's views. > *noun* an intransigent person.

DERIVATIVES – **intransigence** *noun* **intransigency** *noun* **intransigently** *adverb*.

ORIGIN – from Spanish *los intransigentes* (a name adopted by extreme republicans); ultimately from Latin *transigere* 'come to an understanding'.

intransitive /intransitiv/ > *adjective* (of a verb) not taking a direct object, e.g. *look* in *he looked at the sky*. The opposite of **TRANSITIVE**.

DERIVATIVES – **intransitively** *adverb* **intransitivity** *noun*.

intrauterine /intrəyōōtərīn/ > *adjective* within the uterus.

COMBINATIONS – **intrauterine device** a contraceptive device fitted inside the uterus and physically preventing the implantation of fertilised ova.

intravenous /intrəveenəss/ > *adjective* within or into a vein or veins.

DERIVATIVES – **intravenously** *adverb*.

in tray > *noun* chiefly Brit. a tray on a desk for incoming letters and documents.

intrepid > *adjective* fearless; adventurous.

DERIVATIVES – **intrepidity** *noun* **intrepidly** *adverb*.

ORIGIN – Latin *intrepidus* 'not alarmed'.

intricacy /intrikəsi/ > *noun* (pl. **intricacies**) **1** the quality of being intricate. **2** (**intricacies**) details.

intricate > *adjective* very complicated or detailed.

DERIVATIVES – **intricately** *adverb*.

SYNONYMS – complex, complicated, convoluted, elaborate.

ORIGIN – from Latin *intricare* 'entangle', from *tricae* 'tricks, puzzles'.

intrigue > *verb* /intreeg/ (**intrigues**, **intrigued**, **intriguing**) **1** arouse the curiosity or interest of. **2** plot something illicit or harmful. > *noun* /intreeg/ **1** the plotting of something illicit or harmful. **2** a secret love affair.

DERIVATIVES – **intriguer** *noun* **intriguing** *adjective*.

SYNONYMS – *verb* **1** absorb, interest. **2** connive, conspire, plot, scheme. *noun* **1** conspiracy, plot, scheme.

ORIGIN – French *intriguer* 'tangle, plot', from Latin *intricare* 'entangle'.

intrinsic /intrinsik/ > *adjective* belonging to the basic nature of someone or something; essential.

DERIVATIVES – **intrinsically** *adverb*.

ORIGIN – Latin *intrinsecus* 'inwardly, inwards': originally used in the sense 'interior, inner'.

intro > *noun* (pl. **intros**) informal an introduction.

intro- > *prefix* into; inwards: *introvert*.

ORIGIN – Latin *intro* 'to the inside'.

introduce > *verb* **1** bring into use or operation for the first time. **2** present (someone) by name to another. **3** (**introduce to**) bring (a subject) to the attention of (someone) for the first time. **4** insert or bring into. **5** occur at the start of. **6** provide an opening announcement for. **7** present (new legislation) for debate in a legislative assembly.

DERIVATIVES – **introducer** *noun*.

SYNONYMS – **1** establish, institute, launch. **2** announce, present. **4** infuse, inject, insert.

ORIGIN – Latin *introducere*, from *ducere* 'to lead'.

introduction > *noun* **1** the action of introducing or being introduced. **2** an act of introducing one person to another. **3** a preliminary thing, such as an explanatory section at the beginning of a book. **4** a thing newly brought in. **5** a book or course of study intended to introduce a subject to a person. **6** a person's first experience of a subject or activity.

introductory > *adjective* serving as an introduction; basic or preliminary.

introit /introyt/ > *noun* a psalm or antiphon sung or said while the priest approaches the altar for the Eucharist.

ORIGIN – Latin *introitus*, from *introire* 'enter'.

intromission > *noun* technical the inserting of the penis into the vagina in sexual intercourse.

introspection > *noun* the examination of one's own thoughts or feelings.

DERIVATIVES – **introspective** *adjective* **introspectively** *adverb*.

ORIGIN – from Latin *introspicere* 'look into', or from *introspectare* 'keep looking into'.

introvert /intrəvert/ > *noun* **1** a shy, reticent person. **2** Psychology a person predominantly concerned with their own thoughts and feelings. > *adjective* (also **introverted**) of or characteristic of an introvert.

DERIVATIVES – **introversion** *noun*.

ORIGIN – from Latin *intro-* 'to the inside' + *vertere* 'to turn'.

intrude > *verb* **1** come into a place or situation where one is unwelcome or uninvited. **2** introduce into or enter with adverse effect. **3** Geology (of igneous rock) be forced or thrust into (a pre-existing formation).

SYNONYMS – **1** barge in, break in, encroach, interfere, trespass.

ORIGIN – Latin *intrudere*, from *trudere* 'to thrust'.

intruder > *noun* a person who intrudes, especially into a building with criminal intent.

intrusion > *noun* **1** the action or an act of intruding. **2** a thing that intrudes.

intrusive > *adjective* **1** intruding or tending to intrude. **2** (of igneous rock) that has been forced when molten into cracks in neighbouring strata.

DERIVATIVES – **intrusively** *adverb* **intrusiveness** *noun*.

SYNONYMS − **1** interfering, invasive, meddlesome, obtrusive.

intuit /in**tyoo**it/ > *verb* understand or work out by intuition.
ORIGIN − Latin *intueri* 'contemplate'.

intuition > *noun* the ability to understand or know something, without conscious reasoning.

intuitive > *adjective* **1** able to understand or know something without conscious reasoning. **2** (chiefly of computer software) easy to use and understand.
DERIVATIVES − **intuitively** *adverb* **intuitiveness** *noun*.

Inuit /**in**yoo-it/ > *noun* **1** (pl. same or **Inuits**) a member of an indigenous people of northern Canada and parts of Greenland and Alaska. **2** the language of this people.
USAGE − the term **Inuit** is sometimes used as a synonym for **Eskimo** in general. However, this use, in including people from Siberia who are not Inupiaq-speakers, is not accurate; **Eskimo** is the only word that covers both groups, and is still widely used.
ORIGIN − Inuit, 'people'.

inundate /**in**undayt/ > *verb* (usu. **be inundated**) **1** flood. **2** overwhelm with things to be dealt with.
DERIVATIVES − **inundation** *noun*.
ORIGIN − Latin *inundare* 'flood', from *unda* 'a wave'.

Inupiaq /in**oo**piak/ (also **Inupiat** /in**oo**piat/, **Inupik** /in**oo**pik/) > *noun* (pl. same) **1** a member of a group of Inuit people inhabiting northern Alaska. **2** the Inuit language.
ORIGIN − Inuit, 'genuine person'.

inure /in**yoor**/ > *verb* (usu. **be inured to**) accustom to something, especially something unpleasant.
ORIGIN − from an Old French phrase meaning 'in use or practice', from *en* 'in' + *euvre* 'work', from Latin *opera*.

in utero /in yootərō/ > *adverb & adjective* in a woman's uterus; before birth.
ORIGIN − Latin.

in vacuo /in **vak**yoo-ō/ > *adverb* in a vacuum.
ORIGIN − Latin.

invade > *verb* **1** enter (a country) as or with an army so as to subjugate or occupy it. **2** enter in large numbers, especially intrusively. **3** (of a parasite or disease) attack and spread into (an organism or bodily part). **4** encroach on: *his privacy was being invaded*.
DERIVATIVES − **invader** *noun*.
SYNONYMS − **1** occupy, overrun. **2** assail, attack, permeate, pervade. **4** encroach on, intrude on, trespass on, violate.
ORIGIN − Latin *invadere*, from *vadere* 'go'.

invagination > *noun* chiefly Anatomy & Biology **1** the action or process of being turned inside out or folded back on itself to form a cavity or pouch. **2** a cavity or pouch so formed.
DERIVATIVES − **invaginate** *verb*.
ORIGIN − Latin, from *vagina* 'sheath'.

invalid¹ /**in**vəlid/ > *noun* a person made weak or disabled by illness or injury. > *verb* (**invalided**, **invaliding**) (usu. **be invalided**) remove from active military service because of injury or illness.
DERIVATIVES − **invalidism** *noun*.
ORIGIN − a special sense of **INVALID²**, with a change of pronunciation.

invalid² /in**val**id/ > *adjective* **1** not legally recognised because contravening a regulation or law. **2** not true because based on incorrect information or unsound reasoning.
DERIVATIVES − **invalidate** *verb* **invalidation** *noun* **invalidly** *adverb*.
SYNONYMS − **1** null, void. **2** false, groundless, unfounded, unsound, unsubstantiated, untenable.
ANTONYMS − valid.
ORIGIN − Latin *invalidus* 'not strong'.

invalidity > *noun* **1** Brit. the condition of being an invalid. **2** the fact of being invalid.

invaluable > *adjective* extremely useful.
DERIVATIVES − **invaluably** *adverb*.

invariable > *adjective* **1** never changing. **2** Mathematics (of a quantity) constant.
DERIVATIVES − **invariability** *noun*.

invariably > *adverb* always.

invariant > *adjective* not changing.
DERIVATIVES − **invariance** *noun*.

invasion > *noun* **1** an instance of invading. **2** the action or process of being invaded.

invasive > *adjective* **1** tending to invade or intrude: *invasive weeds*. **2** (of medical procedures) involving the introduction of instruments or other objects into the body.

invective > *noun* strongly abusive or critical language.
ORIGIN − from Latin *invectivus* 'attacking', from *invehere* (see **INVEIGH**).

inveigh /in**vay**/ > *verb* (**inveigh against**) speak or write about with great hostility.
ORIGIN − first used in the sense 'introduce': from Latin *invehere* 'carry in' or *invehi* 'be carried into, attack'.

inveigle /in**vayg**'l/ > *verb* (**inveigle into**) persuade (someone) by deception or flattery into (taking certain action).
DERIVATIVES − **inveiglement** *noun*.
ORIGIN − Old French *aveugler* 'to blind'.

invent > *verb* **1** create or design (a new device, process, etc.). **2** make up (a false story, name, etc.).
DERIVATIVES − **inventor** *noun*.
SYNONYMS − **1** coin, create, design, devise, formulate, innovate. **2** concoct, fabricate.
ORIGIN − Latin *invenire* 'contrive, discover'.

invention > *noun* **1** the action of inventing. **2** something invented. **3** a false story. **4** creative ability.

inventive > *adjective* having or showing creativity or original thought.
DERIVATIVES − **inventively** *adverb* **inventiveness** *noun*.

inventory /**in**vəntri/ > *noun* (pl. **inventories**) **1** a complete list of items such as goods in stock or the contents of a building. **2** a quantity of goods in stock. > *verb* (**inventories**, **inventoried**) make an inventory of.
ORIGIN − Latin *inventarium* 'a list of what is found', from *invenire* 'discover'.

inverse /**in**verss, in**verss**/ > *adjective* opposite in position, direction, order, or effect. > *noun* **1** a thing that is the opposite or reverse of another. **2** Mathematics a reciprocal quantity.
DERIVATIVES − **inversely** *adverb*.
COMBINATIONS − **inverse proportion** (also **inverse ratio**) a relation between two quantities such that one increases in proportion as the other decreases. **inverse square law** Physics a law stating that the intensity of an effect changes in inverse proportion to the square of the distance from the source.
ORIGIN − Latin *inversus*, from *invertere* 'turn inside out'.

inversion > *noun* **1** the action of inverting or the state of being inverted. **2** (also **temperature** or **thermal inversion**) a reversal of the normal decrease of air temperature with altitude, or of water temperature with depth.
DERIVATIVES − **inversive** *adjective*.

invert /in**vert**/ > *verb* put upside down or in the opposite position, order, or arrangement.
DERIVATIVES − **inverter** *noun* **invertible** *adjective*.
COMBINATIONS − **inverted comma** chiefly Brit. a quotation mark. **inverted snobbery** the attitude of disdaining anything associated with wealth or high social status, while elevating those things associated with lack of wealth and social position.
ORIGIN − Latin *invertere* 'turn inside out'.

invertebrate /in**vert**ibrət/ > *noun* an animal having no backbone, such as an arthropod, mollusc, etc. > *adjective* relating to such animals.

invest > *verb* **1** put money into financial schemes, shares, or property with the expectation of achieving a profit. **2** devote (time or energy) to an undertaking with the expectation of a worthwhile result. **3** (**invest in**) informal buy (something) whose usefulness will repay the cost. **4** (**invest with**) endow (someone or something) with (a quality or attribute). **5** confer (a rank or office) on.

DERIVATIVES – **investable** (also **investible**) *adjective* **investor** *noun*.

ORIGIN – Latin *investire*, from *vestire* 'clothe' (its original sense in English).

investigate > *verb* **1** carry out a systematic or formal inquiry into (an incident or allegation) so as to establish the truth. **2** carry out research into (a subject). **3** make a search or systematic inquiry.

DERIVATIVES – **investigable** *adjective* **investigation** *noun* **investigator** *noun* **investigatory** *adjective*.

SYNONYMS – **2** consider, examine, explore, research, study.

ORIGIN – Latin *investigare* 'trace out'.

investigative /investigətiv/ > *adjective* **1** of or concerned with investigating. **2** (of journalism or a journalist) investigating and seeking to expose malpractice or the miscarriage of justice.

investiture /investityoor/ > *noun* **1** the action of formally investing a person with honours or rank. **2** a ceremony at which this takes place.

investment > *noun* **1** the action or process of investing. **2** a thing worth buying because it may be profitable or useful in the future.

COMBINATIONS – **investment trust** a limited company which buys and sells shares in selected companies to make a profit for its members.

inveterate /invettərət/ > *adjective* **1** having a long-standing and firmly established habit or activity: *an inveterate gambler.* **1** (of a feeling or habit) firmly established.

DERIVATIVES – **inveteracy** *noun* **inveterately** *adverb*.

ORIGIN – Latin *inveteratus* 'made old'.

invidious /inviddiəss/ > *adjective* unacceptable, unfair, and likely to arouse resentment or anger in others.

DERIVATIVES – **invidiously** *adverb* **invidiousness** *noun*.

ORIGIN – Latin *invidiosus*, from *invidia* 'hostility'.

invigilate /invijilayt/ > *verb* Brit. supervise candidates during an examination.

DERIVATIVES – **invigilation** *noun* **invigilator** *noun*.

ORIGIN – Latin *invigilare* 'watch over'.

invigorate /invviggərayt/ > *verb* give strength or energy to.

DERIVATIVES – **invigorating** *adjective* **invigoration** *noun*.

SYNONYMS – energise, enliven, rejuvenate, revitalise, stimulate.

ORIGIN – Latin *invigorare* 'make strong'.

invincible /invinsib'l/ > *adjective* too powerful to be defeated or overcome.

DERIVATIVES – **invincibility** *noun* **invincibly** *adverb*.

SYNONYMS – indomitable, invulnerable, unassailable, unbeatable, unconquerable.

ORIGIN – from Latin *in-* 'not' + *vincibilis* 'able to be overcome'.

in vino veritas /in veenō verritaas/ > *exclamation* people speak the truth when drunk.

ORIGIN – Latin, 'truth in wine'.

inviolable /invīələb'l/ > *adjective* never to be infringed or dishonoured.

DERIVATIVES – **inviolability** *noun* **inviolably** *adverb*.

inviolate /invīələt/ > *adjective* free from harm or violation.

ORIGIN – from Latin *in-* 'not' + *violare* 'violate'.

invisible > *adjective* **1** unable to be seen, either by nature or because concealed. **2** treated as if unable to be seen; ignored. **3** relating to or denoting earnings which a country makes from the sale of services rather than tangible commodities.

DERIVATIVES – **invisibility** *noun* **invisibly** *adverb*.

SYNONYMS – **1** concealed, hidden, imperceptible, undetectable.

invitation > *noun* **1** a written or verbal request inviting someone to go somewhere or to do something. **2** the action of inviting. **3** a situation or action inviting a particular outcome or response: *his tactics were an invitation to disaster.*

invite > *verb* **1** ask in a friendly or formal way to go somewhere or to do something. **2** request (something) formally or politely. **3** tend to provoke (a particular outcome or response). > *noun* informal an invitation.

DERIVATIVES – **invitee** *noun* **inviter** *noun*.

SYNONYMS – *verb* **1** ask, bid, summon. **2** petition, request, solicit. **3** cause, induce, provoke.

ORIGIN – Latin *invitare*.

inviting > *adjective* tempting or attractive.

DERIVATIVES – **invitingly** *adverb*.

in vitro /in veetrō/ > *adjective & adverb* (of biological processes) taking place in a test tube, culture dish, or elsewhere outside a living organism.

ORIGIN – Latin, 'in glass'.

in vivo /in veevō/ > *adverb & adjective* (of biological processes) taking place in a living organism.

ORIGIN – Latin, 'in a living thing'.

invocation /invəkaysh'n/ > *noun* **1** the action of invoking. **2** an appeal to a deity or the supernatural.

DERIVATIVES – **invocatory** /invokkətri/ *adjective*.

invoice > *noun* a list of goods or services provided, with a statement of the sum due. > *verb* **1** send an invoice to. **2** send an invoice for (goods or services).

ORIGIN – from 'French' *envoyer* 'send' (originally the plural of obsolete *invoy*).

invoke /invōk/ > *verb* **1** appeal to as an authority or in support of an argument. **2** call on (a deity or spirit) in prayer or as a witness. **3** call earnestly for. **4** summon (a spirit) by charms or incantation. **5** give rise to; evoke.

DERIVATIVES – **invoker** *noun*.

SYNONYMS – **1,2** appeal to, entreat, petition, solicit.

ORIGIN – Latin *invocare*, from *vocare* 'to call'.

involuntary > *adjective* **1** done without conscious control. **2** (especially of muscles or nerves) concerned in bodily processes that are not under the control of the will. **3** done against someone's will.

DERIVATIVES – **involuntarily** *adverb* **involuntariness** *noun*.

involute /invəloot/ > *adjective* **1** (also **involuted**) formal complicated. **2** technical curled spirally.

ORIGIN – Latin *involutus* 'wrapped up'.

involve > *verb* **1** (of a situation or event) include as a necessary part or result. **2** cause to experience or participate in an activity or situation.

DERIVATIVES – **involvement** *noun*.

SYNONYMS – **1** entail, necessitate, require. **2** include, incorporate.

ORIGIN – first used in the senses 'enfold' and 'entangle': from Latin *involvere*, from *volvere* 'to roll'.

involved > *adjective* **1** connected, typically on an emotional or personal level. **2** difficult to comprehend; complicated.

invulnerable > *adjective* impossible to harm or damage.

DERIVATIVES – **invulnerability** *noun* **invulnerably** *adverb*.

inward > *adjective* **1** directed or proceeding towards the inside. **2** mental or spiritual. > *adverb* variant of **INWARDS**.

DERIVATIVES – **inwardly** *adverb* **inwardness** *noun*.

COMBINATIONS – **inward investment** investment made within a country from outside. **inward-looking** self-absorbed or insular.

inwards (also **inward**) > *adverb* **1** towards the inside. **2** into or towards the mind, spirit, or soul.

in-your-face > *adjective* informal blatantly aggressive or provocative.

I/O > *abbreviation* Electronics input-output.

iodide > *noun* a compound of iodine with another element or group.

iodine /īədeen/ > *noun* **1** a black, crystalline, non-metallic chemical element of the halogen group. **2** an antiseptic solution of iodine in alcohol.

ORIGIN – from Greek *iōdēs* 'violet-coloured' (the colour of iodine vapour).

IOM > *abbreviation* Isle of Man.

ion /īən/ > *noun* an atom or molecule with a net electric charge through loss or gain of electrons, either positive (a **cation**) or negative (an **anion**).

COMBINATIONS – **ion exchange** the exchange of ions of the same charge between an insoluble solid and a solution in contact with it, used in purification and separation processes.

ORIGIN – Greek, 'going'.

-ion > *suffix* **1** forming nouns denoting verbal action or an instance of this: *communion*. **2** denoting a resulting state or product: *oblivion*.

ORIGIN – Latin.

Ionian /īōniən/ > *noun* **1** a member of an ancient people inhabiting Ionia (a part of western Asia Minor), Attica, and the Aegean islands in pre-classical times. **2** a person from the Ionian Islands, a chain of islands off the western coast of mainland Greece. > *adjective* relating to the Ionians, Ionia, or the Ionian Islands.

Ionic /īonnik/ > *adjective* relating to a classical order of architecture characterised by a column with scroll shapes on either side of the capital.

ORIGIN – Greek *Iōnikos*, from *Iōnia* 'Ionia' (an ancient region of Asia Minor).

ionic /īonnik/ > *adjective* **1** relating to ions. **2** (of a chemical bond) formed by the electrostatic attraction of oppositely charged ions. Contrasted with **COVALENT**.

DERIVATIVES – **ionically** *adverb*.

ionise /īənīz/ (also **ionize**) > *verb* convert (an atom, molecule, or substance) into an ion or ions, typically by removing one or more electrons.

DERIVATIVES – **ionisable** *adjective* **ionisation** *noun*.

COMBINATIONS – **ionising radiation** radiation consisting of particles, X-rays, or gamma rays which produce ions in the medium through which it passes.

ioniser (also **ionizer**) > *noun* a device which produces ions, especially one used to improve the quality of the air in a room.

ionosphere /īonnəsfeer/ > *noun* the layer of the atmosphere above the mesosphere, which contains a high concentration of ions and electrons and is able to reflect radio waves.

DERIVATIVES – **ionospheric** *adjective*.

iota /īōtə/ > *noun* **1** the ninth letter of the Greek alphabet (Ι, ι), transliterated as 'i'. **2** an extremely small amount: *it wouldn't make one iota of difference*.

ORIGIN – Greek; sense 2 derives from *iota* being the smallest letter of the Greek alphabet (compare with **JOT**).

IOU > *noun* a signed document acknowledging a debt.

ORIGIN – representing the pronunciation of *I owe you*.

IOW > *abbreviation* Isle of Wight.

IP > *abbreviation* Computing Internet Protocol.

IPA > *abbreviation* International Phonetic Alphabet.

ipecacuanha /ippikakyooaanə/ > *noun* the dried root of a South American shrub, used as an emetic and expectorant drug.

ORIGIN – Tupi-Guarani, 'emetic creeper'.

IPO > *abbreviation* chiefly US initial public offering.

ipsilateral /ipsilattərəl/ > *adjective* belonging to or occurring on the same side of the body.

ORIGIN – formed irregularly from Latin *ipse* 'self' + **LATERAL**.

ipso facto /ipsō faktō/ > *adverb* by that very fact or act.

ORIGIN – Latin.

IQ > *abbreviation* intelligence quotient.

Ir > *symbol* the chemical element iridium.

IRA > *abbreviation* Irish Republican Army.

Iranian /irayniən/ > *noun* a person from Iran. > *adjective* relating to Iran or Iranians.

Iraqi /iraaki/ > *noun* (pl. **Iraqis**) **1** a person from Iraq. **2** the form of Arabic spoken in Iraq. > *adjective* relating to Iraq or Iraqis.

irascible /irassib'l/ > *adjective* hot-tempered; irritable.

DERIVATIVES – **irascibility** *noun* **irascibly** *adverb*.

SYNONYMS – fractious, hot-tempered, irritable, quick-tempered, testy.

ORIGIN – Latin *irascibilis*, from *ira* 'anger'.

irate /īrayt/ > *adjective* extremely angry.

DERIVATIVES – **irately** *adverb*.

SYNONYMS – enraged, furious, incensed.

ORIGIN – Latin *iratus*, from *ira* 'anger'.

IRC > *abbreviation* Computing Internet Relay Chat.

ire /īr/ > *noun* chiefly literary anger.

ORIGIN – Latin *ira*.

iridaceous /irridayshəss/ > *adjective* Botany relating to or denoting plants of the iris family (Iridaceae).

iridescent* /irridess'nt/ > *adjective* showing luminous colours that seem to change when seen from different angles.

DERIVATIVES – **iridescence** *noun* **iridescently** *adverb*.

***SPELLING** – just one *r*: iridescent.

ORIGIN – from Latin *iris* 'rainbow'.

iridium /iriddiəm/ > *noun* a hard, dense silvery-white metallic chemical element.

ORIGIN – from Latin *iris* 'rainbow' (so named because it forms compounds of various colours).

iridology /irridolləji/ > *noun* (in alternative medicine) diagnosis by examination of the iris of the eye.

DERIVATIVES – **iridologist** *noun*.

iris > *noun* **1** a flat, coloured, ring-shaped membrane behind the cornea of the eye, with an adjustable circular opening (pupil) in the centre. **2** a plant with sword-shaped leaves and purple or yellow flowers.

ORIGIN – Greek, 'rainbow, iris'.

Irish > *noun* (also **Irish Gaelic**) the Celtic language of Ireland. > *adjective* **1** relating to Ireland. **2** offensive illogical.

WORDFINDER – Dáil (*the lower House of Parliament in the Irish Republic*), Garda (*the police force of the Irish Republic*), Hibernian (*of Ireland*), Taoiseach (*the Prime Minister of the Irish Republic*).

DERIVATIVES – **Irishman** *noun* **Irishness** *noun* **Irishwoman** *noun*.

COMBINATIONS – **Irish coffee** coffee mixed with a dash of Irish whiskey and served with cream on top. **Irish moss** carrageen. **Irish setter** a breed of setter with a long, silky dark red coat and a long feathered tail. **Irish stew** a stew made with mutton, potatoes, and onions. **Irish wolfhound** a large, greyish, rough-coated breed of hound.

irk /urk/ > *verb* irritate; annoy.

DERIVATIVES – **irksome** *adjective* **irksomely** *adverb*.

SYNONYMS – anger, annoy, irritate, nettle, vex.

iron > *noun* **1** a strong, hard magnetic silvery-grey metal, used in construction and manufacturing. **2** a tool or implement made of iron. **3** a hand-held implement with a flat heated steel base, used to smooth clothes and linen. **4** a golf club used for lofting the ball. **5** (**irons**) fetters or handcuffs. > *verb* **1** smooth (clothes) with an iron. **2** (**iron out**) settle (a difficulty or problem).

WORDFINDER – ferric, ferrous (*of iron*); chalybeate (*of springs containing iron salts*); *iron-containing minerals:* haematite, magnetite, pyrites.

IDIOMS – **have many** (or **other**) **irons in the fire** have a range of options or interests available to one. **an iron hand** (or **fist**) **in a velvet glove** firmness or ruthlessness cloaked in outward gentleness.

COMBINATIONS – **Iron Age** a period that followed the Bronze Age, when weapons and tools came to be made of iron. **ironbark** an Australian eucalyptus with thick, solid bark and hard, dense wood. **ironclad 1** covered or protected with iron. **2** impossible to weaken or change. **the Iron Curtain** historical a notional barrier separating the communist states of the former Soviet bloc from the West. **iron lung** a rigid case fitted over a patient's body, used for administering prolonged artificial respiration by means of mechanical pumps. **iron maiden** a former instrument of torture consisting of a coffin-shaped box lined with iron spikes. **iron man 1** an exceptionally strong or robust man. **2** a multi-event sporting contest demanding stamina. **iron rations** a small emergency supply of food. **ironstone 1** sedimentary rock containing iron compounds. **2** a kind of dense, opaque stoneware. **ironworks** a place where iron is smelted or iron goods are made.

ironbark > *noun* an Australian eucalyptus with thick, solid bark and hard, dense wood.

ironic /ī**ronn**ik/ > *adjective* **1** using or characterised by irony. **2** happening in the opposite way to what is expected.
DERIVATIVES – **ironical** *adjective* **ironically** *adverb*.

ironing > *noun* clothes and linen that need to be or have just been ironed.
COMBINATIONS – **ironing board** a long, narrow board with folding legs, on which clothes are ironed.

ironist > *noun* a person who uses irony.
DERIVATIVES – **ironise** (also **ironize**) *verb*.

ironmonger > *noun* Brit. a retailer of tools and other hardware.
DERIVATIVES – **ironmongery** *noun*.

irony /ī**ran**i/ > *noun* (pl. **ironies**) **1** the expression of meaning through the use of language which normally signifies the opposite, typically for humorous effect. **2** a state of affairs that appears perversely contrary to what one expects: *the irony is that I thought he could help me.*
USAGE – **irony** and **sarcasm** do not mean exactly the same thing. **Irony** is generally used in a gentle or humorous way, whereas **sarcasm** tends to be used to mock someone or convey contempt.
ORIGIN – Greek *eirōneia* 'simulated ignorance'.

Iroquois /**irr**əkwoy/ > *noun* (pl. same) a member of a former confederacy of six American Indian peoples (Mohawk, Oneida, Seneca, Onondaga, Cayuga, and Tuscarora) who lived mainly in southern Ontario and Quebec and northern New York State.
ORIGIN – French, from an Algonquian language.

irradiant > *adjective* literary shining brightly.
DERIVATIVES – **irradiance** *noun*.

irradiate > *verb* **1** (often **be irradiated**) expose to radiation. **2** shine light on.
DERIVATIVES – **irradiation** *noun*.
ORIGIN – Latin *irradiare* 'shine upon'.

irrational > *adjective* **1** not logical or reasonable. **2** Mathematics (of a number or quantity) not expressible as a ratio of two integers (e.g. π).
DERIVATIVES – **irrationality** *noun* **irrationally** *adverb*.
SYNONYMS – **1** groundless, illogical, senseless, unreasoned.

irrationalism > *noun* a system of belief or action that disregards rational principles.
DERIVATIVES – **irrationalist** *noun* & *adjective*.

irreconcilable > *adjective* **1** incompatible: *the two points of view were irreconcilable.* **2** mutually and implacably hostile.

SYNONYMS – **1** at odds, at variance, conflicting, incompatible.

irrecoverable > *adjective* not able to be recovered or remedied.
DERIVATIVES – **irrecoverably** *adverb*.

irredeemable > *adjective* not able to be saved, improved, or corrected.
DERIVATIVES – **irredeemably** *adverb*.

irredentist /irri**den**tist/ > *noun* a person advocating the restoration to their country of any territory formerly belonging to it.
DERIVATIVES – **irredentism** *noun*.
ORIGIN – Italian *irredentista*, from *irredenta* 'unredeemed'.

irreducible > *adjective* not able to be reduced or simplified.
DERIVATIVES – **irreducibly** *adverb*.

irrefutable /irri**fyōo**təb'l, i**reff**yōotəb'l/ > *adjective* impossible to deny or disprove.
DERIVATIVES – **irrefutably** *adverb*.
SYNONYMS – conclusive, incontestable, undeniable.

irregular > *adjective* **1** not regular in shape, arrangement, or occurrence. **2** contrary to a rule, standard, or convention. **3** not belonging to regular army units. **4** Grammar (of a word) having inflections that do not conform to the usual rules. > *noun* a member of an irregular military force.
DERIVATIVES – **irregularity** (pl. **irregularities**) *noun* **irregularly** *adverb*.

irrelevant > *adjective* not relevant.
DERIVATIVES – **irrelevance** *noun* **irrelevancy** (pl. **irrelevancies**) *noun* **irrelevantly** *adverb*.
SYNONYMS – beside the point, immaterial.

irreligious > *adjective* indifferent or hostile to religion.
DERIVATIVES – **irreligion** *noun*.
SYNONYMS – atheistic, impious, unbelieving, ungodly.

irremediable /irri**mee**diəb'l/ > *adjective* impossible to remedy.
DERIVATIVES – **irremediably** *adverb*.

irremovable > *adjective* incapable of being removed.

irreparable /i**repp**ərəb'l/ > *adjective* impossible to rectify or repair.
DERIVATIVES – **irreparably** *adverb*.

irreplaceable > *adjective* impossible to replace if lost or damaged.
DERIVATIVES – **irreplaceably** *adverb*.

irrepressible > *adjective* not able to be restrained.
DERIVATIVES – **irrepressibly** *adverb*.

irreproachable > *adjective* beyond criticism.
DERIVATIVES – **irreproachably** *adverb*.

irresistible* > *adjective* too tempting or powerful to be resisted.
DERIVATIVES – **irresistibly** *adverb*.
*SPELLING – *-ible*, not *-able*: irresistible.

irresolute > *adjective* uncertain.

DERIVATIVES – **irresolutely** *adverb* **irresolution** *noun*.
SYNONYMS – doubtful, hesitant, uncertain, undecided.

irresolvable > *adjective* impossible to solve: *an irresolvable problem.*

irrespective > *adjective* (**irrespective of**) regardless of.
DERIVATIVES – **irrespectively** *adverb*.

irresponsible > *adjective* not showing a proper sense of responsibility.
DERIVATIVES – **irresponsibility** *noun* **irresponsibly** *adverb*.
SYNONYMS – careless, rash, reckless, thoughtless, unreliable.

irretrievable > *adjective* not able to be retrieved.
DERIVATIVES – **irretrievably** *adverb*.

irreverent > *adjective* disrespectful.
DERIVATIVES – **irreverence** *noun* **irreverently** *adverb*.
SYNONYMS – disrespectful, impertinent, insolent.

irreversible > *adjective* impossible to be reversed or altered.
DERIVATIVES – **irreversibility** *noun* **irreversibly** *adverb*.

irrevocable /i**revv**əkəb'l/ > *adjective* not able to be changed or reversed.
DERIVATIVES – **irrevocability** *noun* **irrevocably** *adverb*.
ORIGIN – Latin *irrevocabilis*.

irrigate /**irr**igayt/ > *verb* **1** supply water to (land or crops) by means of channels. **2** Medicine apply a flow of water or medication to (an organ or wound).
DERIVATIVES – **irrigable** *adjective* **irrigation** *noun* **irrigator** *noun*.
ORIGIN – Latin *irrigare* 'moisten'.

irritable* > *adjective* **1** easily annoyed or angered. **2** Medicine abnormally sensitive.
DERIVATIVES – **irritability** *noun* **irritableness** *noun* **irritably** *adverb*.
*SPELLING – *-able*, not *-ible*: irritable.
SYNONYMS – **1** bad-tempered, irascible, testy.
ANTONYMS – **1** good-humoured.
COMBINATIONS – **irritable bowel syndrome** a condition involving recurrent abdominal pain and diarrhoea or constipation.

irritant > *noun* **1** a substance that irritates a part of the body. **2** a source of continual annoyance. > *adjective* causing irritation to the body.

irritate > *verb* **1** make annoyed or angry. **2** cause inflammation in.
DERIVATIVES – **irritating** *adjective* **irritatingly** *adverb* **irritation** *noun*.
SYNONYMS – **1** annoy, irk, nettle, vex.
ORIGIN – Latin *irritare*.

irrupt /i**rupt**/ > *verb* **1** enter forcibly or suddenly. **2** (chiefly of a bird) migrate into an area in abnormally large numbers.

DERIVATIVES – **irruption** *noun* **irruptive** *adjective.*

ORIGIN – Latin *irrumpere* 'break into'.

IRS > *abbreviation* Internal Revenue Service.

is third person singular present of **BE**.

ISA > *abbreviation* **1** /īsə/ individual savings account. **2** Computing industry standard architecture.

ISBN > *abbreviation* international standard book number.

ischaemia /iskeemiə/ (US **ischemia**) > *noun* Medicine an inadequate blood supply to a part of the body, especially the heart muscles.

DERIVATIVES – **ischaemic** *adjective.*

ORIGIN – from Greek *iskhaimos* 'stopping blood'.

ISDN > *abbreviation* integrated services digital network.

-ise (also **-ize**) > *suffix* forming verbs meaning: **1** make or become: *privatise.* **2** cause to resemble: *Americanise.* **3** treat in a specified way: *pasteurise.* **4** treat or cause to combine with a specified substance: *carbonise.* **5** perform or subject (someone) to a specified practice: *agonise, hospitalise.*

USAGE – the forms **-ise** and **-ize** are, in many cases, straightforward spelling variants. However, the **-ise** spelling is obligatory in certain cases: first, where it forms part of a larger word element, such as *-mise* in **compromise**; and second, in verbs corresponding to nouns with **-s-** in the stem, such as **advertise** and **televise**.

ORIGIN – Latin *-izare*, from Greek *-izein.*

-ish > *suffix* forming adjectives: **1** having the qualities or characteristics of: *girlish.* **2** of the nationality of: *Swedish.* **3** somewhat: *yellowish.* **4** informal denoting an approximate age or time of day: *sixish.*

Ishmaelite /ishməlīt/ > *noun* a descendant of Ishmael, a son of Abraham and Hagar, and in Islamic belief the traditional ancestor of Muhammad and of the Arab peoples.

isinglass /īzingglaass/ > *noun* **1** a kind of gelatin obtained from fish. **2** chiefly US mica in thin transparent sheets.

ORIGIN – from obsolete Dutch *huysenblas* 'sturgeon's bladder', altered by association with *glass.*

Islam /izlaam/ > *noun* **1** the religion of the Muslims, regarded by them to have been revealed through Muhammad as the Prophet of Allah. **2** the Muslim world.

WORDFINDER – ayatollah (*Shiite religious leader*), hajj (*pilgrimage to Mecca*), imam (*leader of prayers in a mosque*), mosque (*Muslim place of worship*), muezzin (*man who calls Muslims to prayer*), Ramadan (*month of fasting*), Shia, Sunni (*main branches of Islam*).

DERIVATIVES – **Islamise** (also **Islamize**) *verb* **Islamist** *noun.*

ORIGIN – Arabic, 'submission', from a verb meaning 'submit (to God)'.

Islamic /izlammik/ > *adjective* relating to Islam.

island > *noun* **1** a piece of land surrounded by water. **2** a thing that is isolated, detached, or surrounded.

WORDFINDER – archipelago (*large group of islands*), insular (*of or like an island*).

DERIVATIVES – **islander** *noun.*

isle > *noun* literary (except in place names) an island.

ORIGIN – Old French *ile*, from Latin *insula.*

islet /īlit/ > *noun* a small island.

COMBINATIONS – **islets of Langerhans** groups of cells in the pancreas secreting insulin and glucagon. [ORIGIN – named after the German anatomist Paul *Langerhans* (1847–88).]

ism /izz'm/ > *noun* informal, chiefly derogatory an unspecified system, philosophy, or ideological movement.

-ism > *suffix* forming nouns: **1** denoting an action or its result: *baptism.* **2** denoting a state or quality: *barbarism.* **3** denoting a system, principle, or ideological movement: *Anglicanism.* **4** denoting a basis for prejudice or discrimination: *racism.* **5** denoting a peculiarity in language: *colloquialism.* **6** denoting a diseased condition: *alcoholism.*

ORIGIN – Greek *-ismos.*

Ismaili /izmīeeli/ > *noun* (pl. **Ismailis**) a member of a Shiite Muslim sect believing that Ismail, son of the sixth Shiite imam, should have become the seventh imam.

isn't > *contraction* is not.

ISO > *abbreviation* International Organisation for Standardisation.

isobar /īsəbaar/ > *noun* Meteorology a line on a map connecting points having the same atmospheric pressure.

ORIGIN – from Greek *isobaros* 'of equal weight'.

isochronous /īsokrənəss/ > *adjective* **1** occurring at the same time. **2** occupying equal time.

isolate > *verb* **1** place apart or alone; cut off. **2** Chemistry & Biology obtain or extract (a compound, micro-organism, etc.) in a pure form. **3** cut off the electrical or other connection to (something). > *noun* a person or thing that has become isolated.

DERIVATIVES – **isolator** *noun.*

ORIGIN – from **ISOLATED**.

isolated > *adjective* **1** remote; lonely. **2** single; exceptional.

ORIGIN – Latin *insulatus* 'made into an island', from *insula* 'island'.

isolation > *noun* the process or fact of isolating or being isolated.

IDIOMS – **in isolation** without relation to others; separately.

isolationism > *noun* a policy of remaining apart from the political affairs of other countries.

DERIVATIVES – **isolationist** *noun.*

isomer /īsəmər/ > *noun* **1** Chemistry each of two or more compounds with the same formula but a different arrangement of atoms and different properties. **2** Physics each of two or more atomic nuclei with the same atomic number and mass number but different energy states.

DERIVATIVES – **isomeric** *adjective* **isomerise** (also **isomerize**) *verb* **isomerism** *noun.*

ORIGIN – from Greek *isomerēs* 'sharing equally', from *isos* 'equal' + *meros* 'a share'.

isometric /īsəmetrik/ > *adjective* **1** having equal dimensions. **2** Physiology involving an increase in muscle tension without contraction. **3** (of perspective drawing) in which the three principal dimensions are represented by axes 120° apart.

DERIVATIVES – **isometrically** *adverb.*

ORIGIN – from Greek *isometria* 'equality of measure'.

isometrics > *plural noun* a system of physical exercises in which muscles are caused to act against each other or against a fixed object.

isomorphic /īsəmorfik/ > *adjective* corresponding in form and relations.

DERIVATIVES – **isomorphism** *noun* **isomorphous** *adjective.*

isosceles /īsossəleez/ > *adjective* (of a triangle) having two sides of equal length.

ORIGIN – Greek *isoskelēs*, from *isos* 'equal' + *skelos* 'leg'.

isotherm /īsətherm/ > *noun* a line on a map or diagram connecting points having the same temperature.

DERIVATIVES – **isothermal** *adjective.*

isotonic /īsətonnik/ > *adjective* **1** Physiology (of a muscle action) taking place with normal contraction. **2** containing essential salts and minerals in the same concentration as in the body.

ORIGIN – from Greek *isotonos*, from *isos* 'equal' + *tonos* 'tone'.

isotope /īsətōp/ > *noun* Chemistry each of two or more forms of the same element that contain equal numbers of protons but different numbers of neutrons in their nuclei.

DERIVATIVES – **isotopic** *adjective.*

ORIGIN – from Greek *isos* 'equal' + *topos* 'place', because the isotopes occupy the same place in the periodic table.

isotropic /īsətroppik/ > *adjective* Physics having the same magnitude or properties when measured in different directions.

ISP > *abbreviation* Internet service provider.

Israeli /izrayli/ > *noun* (pl. **Israelis**) a person from Israel. > *adjective* relating to the modern country of Israel.

Israelite /ˈizrəlīt/ > *noun* a member of the ancient Hebrew nation. > *adjective* relating to the Israelites.

ISSN > *abbreviation* international standard serial number.

issue > *noun* **1** an important topic for debate or resolution. **2** the action of issuing. **3** each of a regular series of publications. **4** formal or Law children of one's own. > *verb* (**issues**, **issued**, **issuing**) **1** supply or distribute (something). **2** formally send out or make known: *issue a statement*. **3** (**issue from**) come, go, or flow out from.
IDIOMS – **at issue** under discussion. **make an issue of** treat too seriously or as a problem. **take issue with** challenge.
SYNONYMS – *noun* **1** matter, subject, topic.
ORIGIN – Old French, based on Latin *exire* 'go out'.

-ist > *suffix* forming personal nouns and some related adjectives: **1** denoting a person who subscribes to a system of beliefs or prejudice or who practises discrimination, expressed by nouns ending in *-ism*: *hedonist* | *sexist*. **2** denoting a member of a profession or business activity: *dentist*. **3** denoting a person who uses something: *flautist*. **4** denoting a person who does something expressed by a verb ending in *-ize*: *plagiarist*.

isthmus /ˈissməss/ > *noun* (pl. **isthmuses**) a narrow strip of land with sea on either side, linking two larger areas of land.
ORIGIN – Greek *isthmos*.

IT > *abbreviation* information technology.

it > *pronoun* (third person sing.) **1** used to refer to a thing previously mentioned or easily identified. **2** referring to an animal or child of unspecified sex. **3** used to identify a person: *it's me*. **4** used in the normal subject position in statements about time, distance, or weather: *it is raining*. **5** used to refer to something specified later in the sentence: *it is impossible to get there today*. **6** used to emphasise a following part of a sentence: *it is the child who is the victim*. **7** the situation or circumstances. **8** exactly what is needed or desired.

Italian > *noun* **1** a person from Italy. **2** the language of Italy, descended from Latin. > *adjective* relating to Italy.
WORDFINDER – autostrada (*an Italian motorway*), carabinieri (*Italian paramilitary police*), pensione (*small Italian hotel*), trattoria (*Italian restaurant*); *Italian food*: antipasto, ciabatta, focaccia, gnocchi, lasagne, minestrone, pizza, prosciutto, ravioli, salami, tiramisu, zabaglione.

Italianate > *adjective* Italian in character or appearance.

italic /iˈtalik/ > *adjective* Printing **1** denoting the sloping typeface used especially for emphasis and in foreign words. **2** denoting a style of handwriting, sloping and with pointed letters, resembling 16th-century Italian handwriting. > *noun* (also **italics**) an italic typeface or letter.
DERIVATIVES – **italicise** (also **italicize**) *verb*.
ORIGIN – Greek *Italikos* 'Italian'.

ITC > *abbreviation* Independent Television Commission.

itch > *noun* **1** an uncomfortable sensation that causes a desire to scratch the skin. **2** informal an impatient desire. > *verb* **1** be the site of or experience an itch. **2** informal feel an impatient desire to do something.

itchy > *adjective* (**itchier**, **itchiest**) having or causing an itch.
IDIOMS – **have itchy feet** informal have a strong urge to travel.
DERIVATIVES – **itchiness** noun.

it'd > *contraction* **1** it had. **2** it would.

-ite > *suffix* **1** forming names denoting people from a country: *Israelite*. **2** often derogatory denoting followers of a movement: *Luddite*. **3** forming names of minerals, rocks, or fossil organisms: *ammonite*. **4** forming names of anatomical or other structures: *dendrite*. **5** forming names of explosives and other commercial products: *dynamite*. **6** Chemistry forming names of salts or esters of acids ending in *-ous*: *sulphite*.
ORIGIN – from Greek *ītes*.

item > *noun* an individual article or unit. > *adverb* archaic (used to introduce each item in a list) also.
IDIOMS – **be an item** informal (of a couple) be in a romantic or sexual relationship.
ORIGIN – Latin, 'in like manner, also'.

itemise (also **itemize**) > *verb* present as a list of individual items or parts.

iterate /ˈittərayt/ > *verb* **1** perform or utter repeatedly. **2** make repeated use of a mathematical or computational procedure, applying it each time to the result of the previous application.
DERIVATIVES – **iteration** noun **iterative** adjective.
ORIGIN – Latin *iterare* 'repeat'.

-itic > *suffix* forming adjectives and nouns: **1** corresponding to nouns ending in *-ite*: *Semitic*. **2** corresponding to nouns ending in *-itis*: *arthritic*. **3** from other bases: *syphilitic*.

itinerant /īˈtinnərənt/ > *adjective* travelling from place to place. > *noun* an itinerant person.
ORIGIN – from Latin *itinerari* 'travel', from *iter* 'journey, road'.

itinerary* /īˈtinnərəri/ > *noun* (pl. **itineraries**) a planned route or journey.
*SPELLING – itin*erary*, not *-ery*.

-itis > *suffix* forming names of inflammatory diseases: *cystitis*.
ORIGIN – from Greek *-ītes*.

it'll > *contraction* **1** it shall. **2** it will.

its > *possessive determiner* **1** belonging to or associated with a thing previously mentioned or easily identified. **2** belonging to or associated with a child or animal of unspecified sex.
USAGE – do not confuse the possessive **its** (as in *turn the camera on its side*) with the contraction **it's** (short for either **it is** or **it has**, as in *it's my fault; it's been a hot day*).

it's > *contraction* **1** it is. **2** it has.

itself > *pronoun* (third person sing.) **1** (reflexive) used to refer to something previously mentioned as the subject of the clause: *his horse hurt itself*. **2** (emphatic) used to emphasise a particular thing or animal mentioned: *the toy mouse was as big as the kitten itself*.
IDIOMS – **in itself** viewed in its essential qualities.

itsy-bitsy (also **itty-bitty**) > *adjective* informal very small.

ITV > *abbreviation* Independent Television.

-ity > *suffix* forming nouns denoting quality or condition: *humility*.
ORIGIN – Latin *-itas*.

IUD > *abbreviation* intrauterine device.

IV > *abbreviation* intravenous or intravenously.

I've > *contraction* I have.

-ive > *suffix* (forming adjectives and nouns derived from them) tending to; having the nature of: *talkative*.

IVF > *abbreviation* in vitro fertilisation.

ivied > *adjective* covered in ivy.

Ivorian /īˈvoriən/ > *noun* a person from the Ivory Coast, a country in West Africa. > *adjective* relating to the Ivory Coast.

ivory > *noun* (pl. **ivories**) **1** a hard creamy-white substance composing the main part of the tusks of an elephant, walrus, or narwhal. **2** the creamy-white colour of ivory. **3** (**the ivories**) informal the keys of a piano. **4** (**ivories**) informal a person's teeth.
COMBINATIONS – **an ivory tower** a state of privileged seclusion or separation from the harsh realities of life.
ORIGIN – Old French *ivurie*, from Latin *ebur*.

ivy > *noun* a woody evergreen climbing plant, typically with shiny five-pointed leaves.
COMBINATIONS – **Ivy League** a group of long-established and prestigious universities in the eastern US. [ORIGIN – with reference to ivy growing over their walls.]

iwi /ˈeewee/ > *noun* (pl. same) NZ a community or people.
ORIGIN – Maori.

-ize > *suffix* variant spelling of **-ISE**.

J[1] (also **j**) > *noun* (pl. **Js** or **J's**) **1** the tenth letter of the alphabet. **2** denoting the next after I in a set. **3** archaic a Roman numeral used instead of an I when in a final position.

J[2] > *abbreviation* **1** jack. **2** Physics joule(s).

jab > *verb* (**jabbed**, **jabbing**) poke roughly or quickly with something sharp or pointed. > *noun* **1** a quick, sharp poke or blow. **2** Brit. informal a hypodermic injection, especially a vaccination.

jabber > *verb* talk rapidly and excitedly but with little sense. > *noun* such talk.
SYNONYMS – *verb* babble, gibber, prattle.

jabiru /**jabb**iroo/ > *noun* a large black-necked stork with an upturned bill.
ORIGIN – Tupi-Guarani.

jabot /**zhabb**ō/ > *noun* an ornamental ruffle on the front of a shirt or blouse.
ORIGIN – French, originally 'crop of a bird'.

jacaranda /**jakk**ə**ran**də/ > *noun* a tropical American tree which has blue trumpet-shaped flowers, fern-like leaves, and fragrant wood.
ORIGIN – Portuguese.

jacinth /**jass**inth, **jay**sinth/ > *noun* a reddish-orange gem variety of zircon.
ORIGIN – Old French *iacinte*, from Latin *hyacinthus* (see **HYACINTH**).

jack > *noun* **1** a device for lifting heavy objects. **2** a playing card bearing a representation of a soldier, page, or knave, normally ranking next below a queen. **3** (also **jack socket**) a socket designed to receive a jack plug. **4** the small white ball at which bowls players aim. **5** a small playing-piece used in tossing and catching games. **6** (**jacks**) a game played by tossing and catching jacks. **7** a small national flag flown at the bow of a vessel in harbour. **8** the male of various animals, e.g. the donkey. **9** a perch-like marine fish, typically having a row of large spiky scales along each side. > *verb* **1** (**jack up**) raise with a jack. **2** (**jack up**) informal increase by a considerable amount. **3** (**jack in** or **into**) log into or connect up (a computer or electronic device). **4** (**jack in**) Brit. informal give up. **5**

(**jack up**) Austral. give up or refuse to participate.
IDIOMS – **every man jack** informal every single person. **jack of all trades** (**and master of none**) a person who can do many different types of work (but has special skill in none).
COMBINATIONS – **Jack Frost** a personification of frost. **jack-in-the-box** a toy consisting of a box containing a figure on a spring which pops up when the lid is opened. **jack-o'-lantern 1** a lantern made from a hollowed-out pumpkin or turnip in which holes are cut to represent facial features. **2** archaic a will-o'-the wisp. **jack pine** a small, hardy North American pine with short needles. **jack plug** a plug consisting of a single shaft used to make a connection which transmits a signal, typically used in sound equipment. **jackrabbit** a North American prairie hare. **Jack tar** Brit. informal, dated a sailor. **Jack the Lad** informal a brash, cocky young man. [ORIGIN – nickname of *Jack* Sheppard, an 18th-century thief.]

wordpower facts

Jack

The noun **jack** is from the name *Jack*, a familiar form of *John*. It was used in medieval times to refer to an ordinary man or a youth, hence the 'knave' in cards, and 'male animal'. The word also denoted various devices that saved human labour (as in sense 1) as though one had a helper, and occurred in compounds such as **jackhammer** and **jackknife**; the general sense 'labourer' arose in the early 18th century and survives in **cheapjack**, **lumberjack**, **steeplejack**, etc. Since the mid 16th century a notion of 'smallness' has arisen, hence senses 4, 5, and 7 and names of animals and plants (such as **jack pine**) that are smaller than the usual kind.

jackal /**jakk**'l/ > *noun* a slender, long-legged wild dog that often hunts or scavenges in packs, found in Africa and southern Asia.
ORIGIN – Turkish *çakal*.

jackanapes /**jakk**ənayps/ > *noun* **1** dated an impertinent person. **2** archaic a tame monkey.
ORIGIN – in early use written as *Jack Napes*, perhaps a name for a pet ape.

jackaroo /**jakk**əroo/ Austral. informal > *noun* a young, inexperienced worker on a sheep or cattle station. > *verb* work as a jackaroo.
ORIGIN – alteration of an Aboriginal term meaning 'wandering white man'.

jackass > *noun* **1** a stupid person. **2** a male ass or donkey.

jackboot > *noun* a large leather military boot reaching to the knee.
DERIVATIVES – **jackbooted** *adjective*.

jackdaw > *noun* a small grey-headed crow, noted for its inquisitiveness.

jackeen /**ja**keen/ > *noun* Irish, chiefly derogatory a city-dweller, especially a Dubliner.

jacket > *noun* **1** an outer garment extending to the waist or hips, with sleeves. **2** an outer covering placed around something for protection or insulation. **3** the skin of a potato. > *verb* (**jacketed**, **jacketing**) cover with a jacket.
ORIGIN – Old French *jaquet*.

jackfruit > *noun* the very large edible fruit of an Asian tree, resembling a breadfruit.
ORIGIN – from Portuguese *jaca* + **FRUIT**.

jackhammer chiefly N. Amer. > *noun* a portable pneumatic hammer or drill. > *verb* beat or hammer heavily or loudly and repeatedly.

jackknife > *noun* (pl. **jackknives**) **1** a large knife with a folding blade. **2** a dive in which the body is bent at the waist and then straightened. > *verb* (**jackknifed**, **jackknifing**) **1** move (one's body) into a bent or doubled-up position. **2** (of an articulated vehicle) bend into a V-shape in an uncontrolled skidding movement. **3** (of a diver) perform a jackknife.

jackpot > *noun* a large cash prize in a game or lottery.
IDIOMS – **hit the jackpot** informal **1** win a jackpot. **2** have great or unexpected success.

Jack Russell (also **Jack Russell terrier**) > *noun* a small breed of terrier with short legs.
ORIGIN – named after the English clergyman Revd John (*Jack*) *Russell*, a breeder of such terriers.

jacksie (also **jacksy**) > *noun* Brit. informal a person's bottom.

Jacobean /**jakk**əbeeən/ > *adjective* relating to or characteristic of the reign of James I of England (1603–1625). > *noun* a person who lived in the Jacobean period.
ORIGIN – from Latin *Jacobus* 'James'.

Jacobin /**jakk**əbin/ > *noun* **1** historical a member of a radical democratic club established in Paris in 1789, in the wake of the French Revolution. **2** an extreme political radical. **3** chiefly historical a Dominican friar.
ORIGIN – Old French, from Latin *Jacobus* 'James': originally denoting the Dominican friars, after the church in Paris, St Jacques, near which they built their first convent, later the headquarters of the French revolutionary group.

Jacobite /**jakk**əbīt/ > *noun* a supporter of the deposed James II and his descendants in their claim to the British throne after the Revolution of 1688.

Jacob's ladder > *noun* a herbaceous plant with blue or white flowers and slender pointed leaves formed in ladder-like rows.

ORIGIN – with biblical allusion to Jacob's dream of a ladder reaching to heaven.

jacquard /jakkaard/ > *noun* **1** a device incorporating perforated cards, fitted to a loom for the weaving of figured and brocaded fabrics. **2** a fabric woven using such a device

ORIGIN – named after the French weaver Joseph M. *Jacquard* (1787–1834).

jacquerie /jaykəri/ > *noun* a communal uprising or revolt.

ORIGIN – Old French, literally 'villeins, feudal tenants', from *Jacques*, a given name used in the sense 'peasant'.

jacuzzi /jəkōozi/ > *noun* (pl. **jacuzzis**) trademark a large bath incorporating jets of water to massage the body.

ORIGIN – named after the Italian-born American inventor Candido *Jacuzzi* (c.1903–86).

jade¹ > *noun* **1** a hard stone used for ornaments and jewellery. **2** the light bluish green colour of jade.

ORIGIN – from French *le jade* (earlier *l'ejade*), from Spanish *piedra de ijada* 'stone of the flank' (i.e. stone for colic, which it was believed to cure).

jade² > *noun* archaic **1** a bad-tempered or disreputable woman. **2** an inferior or worn-out horse.

jaded > *adjective* tired out or lacking enthusiasm after having had too much of something.

ORIGIN – first in the sense 'disreputable': from JADE².

jadeite /jaydīt/ > *noun* a green, blue, or white form of jade.

jaeger /jaygər/ > *noun* N. Amer. a skua.

ORIGIN – German *Jäger* 'hunter'.

Jaffa /jaffə/ > *noun* Brit. a large thick-skinned variety of orange.

ORIGIN – from the city of *Jaffa* in Israel.

jag¹ > *verb* (**jagged**, **jagging**) stab, pierce, or prick. > *noun* **1** a sharp projection. **2** chiefly Scottish a prick or injection.

jag² > *noun* informal, chiefly N. Amer. a bout of unrestrained activity: *a crying jag.*

jagged /jaggid/ > *adjective* with rough, sharp points protruding.

jaggery /jaggəri/ > *noun* a coarse brown sugar made in India from the sap of palm trees.

ORIGIN – Portuguese *xagara, jag(a)ra* 'sugar', from Sanskrit.

jaggy > *adjective* (**jaggier**, **jaggiest**) **1** jagged. **2** (also **jaggie**) Scottish prickly.

jaguar /jagyooər/ > *noun* a large, heavily built cat that has a yellowish-brown coat

with black spots, found mainly in Central and South America.

ORIGIN – Portuguese.

Jah /jaa/ > *noun* the Rastafarian name for God.

ORIGIN – representing Hebrew *Yāh*, abbreviation of YAHWEH.

jail (Brit. also **gaol**) > *noun* a place for the confinement of people accused or convicted of a crime. > *verb* put (someone) in jail.

DERIVATIVES – **jailer** (also **gaoler**) *noun*.

SYNONYMS – *verb* detain, imprison, incarcerate.

COMBINATIONS – **jailbait** informal a sexually mature young woman under the age of consent, or such young women collectively. **jailbird** informal a person who is or has repeatedly been in prison. **jailbreak** an escape from jail. **jailhouse** chiefly N. Amer. a prison.

ORIGIN – based on Latin *cavea* (see CAGE); the word came into English in two forms, *jaiole* and *gayole*, (surviving in the spelling *gaol*), both from Old French.

Jain /jayn/ > *noun* an adherent of Jainism. > *adjective* relating to Jainism.

ORIGIN – Sanskrit, 'relating to a *jina* or great teacher'.

Jainism > *noun* an Indian religion founded in the 6th century BC, characterised by non-violence and asceticism.

DERIVATIVES – **Jainist** *noun*.

jake > *adjective* N. Amer. & Austral./NZ informal all right; satisfactory.

jalapeño /haləpaynyō/ > *noun* (pl. **jalapeños**) a very hot green chilli pepper.

ORIGIN – Spanish, from the name of the Mexican city *Jalapa*.

jalfrezi /jalfrayzi/ > *noun* a medium-hot Indian dish consisting of chicken or lamb with fresh chillies, tomatoes, and onions.

ORIGIN – Bengali.

jalopy /jəloppi/ > *noun* (pl. **jalopies**) informal an old car in a dilapidated condition.

jalousie /zhaloozee/ > *noun* a blind or shutter made of a row of angled slats.

ORIGIN – French, literally 'jealousy', from Italian *geloso* 'jealous', also (by extension) 'screen', associated with the screening of women from view in the Middle East.

jam¹ > *verb* (**jammed**, **jamming**) **1** squeeze or pack tightly into a space. **2** push roughly and forcibly into a position. **3** block (something such as a road) through crowding. **4** become or make unable to function due to a part becoming stuck. **5** (**jam on**) apply forcibly: *he jammed on the brakes.* **6** make a radio transmission unintelligible by causing interference. **7** informal improvise with other musicians. > *noun* **1** an instance of jamming. **2** informal an awkward situation or predicament. **3**

informal an improvised performance by a group of musicians.

SYNONYMS – *verb* **1** cram, pack, squeeze, stuff, wedge. **3** clog, congest, obstruct.

COMBINATIONS – **jam-packed** informal extremely crowded or full to capacity.

jam² > *noun* chiefly Brit. a conserve and spread made from fruit and sugar. > *verb* (**jammed**, **jamming**) make (fruit) into jam.

Jamaican /jəmaykən/ > *noun* a person from Jamaica. > *adjective* relating to Jamaica.

jamb /jam/ > *noun* a side post of a doorway, window, or fireplace.

ORIGIN – Old French *jambe* 'leg, vertical support', from Greek *kampē* 'joint'.

jambalaya /jambəlīə/ > *noun* a Cajun dish of rice with shrimps, chicken, and vegetables.

ORIGIN – Provençal *jambalaia*.

jamboree /jambəree/ > *noun* **1** a lavish or boisterous celebration or party. **2** a large rally of Scouts or Guides.

jammy > *adjective* (**jammier**, **jammiest**) **1** covered, filled with, or resembling jam. **2** Brit. informal lucky.

Jan. > *abbreviation* January.

Jane Doe > *noun* female counterpart of JOHN DOE.

jangle > *verb* **1** make or cause to make a ringing metallic sound. **2** (of one's nerves) be set on edge. > *noun* an instance of jangling.

DERIVATIVES – **jangly** *adjective*.

ORIGIN – Old French *jangler*.

janissary /jannisəri/ (also **janizary** /jannizəri/) > *noun* (pl. **janissaries**) historical a Turkish infantryman in the Sultan's guard.

ORIGIN – French *janissaire*, from Turkish *yeniçeri*, from *yeni* 'new' + *çeri* 'troops'.

janitor /jannitər/ > *noun* chiefly N. Amer. a caretaker of a building.

DERIVATIVES – **janitorial** *adjective*.

ORIGIN – Latin, from *janua* 'door'.

jankers /jangkərz/ > *noun* Brit. military slang punishment for committing a military offence.

Jansenism /jansəniz'm/ > *noun* a strict Christian movement of the 17th and 18th centuries, based on the writings of the Catholic theologian Cornelius Jansen (1585–1638).

DERIVATIVES – **Jansenist** *noun*.

January > *noun* (pl. **Januaries**) the first month of the year.

ORIGIN – from Latin *Januarius mensis* 'month of *Janus*' (the Roman god who presided over doors and beginnings).

Jap > *noun & adjective* informal, offensive short for JAPANESE.

japan > *noun* a black glossy varnish of a type originating in Japan. > *verb* (**japanned**, **japanning**) cover with japan.

Japanese > *noun* (pl. same) **1** a person from Japan. **2** the language of Japan. > *adjective* relating to Japan or Japanese.

WORDFINDER – *Japanese culture:* bonsai (*art of growing miniature trees*), futon (*padded mattress*), geisha (*hostess*), haiku (*poem of 17 syllables*), kabuki (*drama performed by men*), kaizen (*business philosophy of continuous improvement*), kimono (*loose robe*), manga (*fantasy cartoons and animation*), Noh (*traditional masked drama*), Shinto (*religion of spirit worship*), shogun (*feudal commander*), sumo (*traditional wrestling*), yakuza (*criminal organisation*).

ORIGIN – from *Japan*, via Chinese *Riben* from Japanese *Ni-pon*, literally 'sunrise' or 'orient'.

jape > *noun* a practical joke. > *verb* say or do something in jest or mockery.

ORIGIN – apparently combining the form of Old French *japer* 'to yelp, yap' with the sense of Old French *gaber* 'to mock'.

japonica /jəˈponnikə/ > *noun* an Asian shrub of the rose family, with bright red flowers followed by edible fruits.

ORIGIN – Latin, 'Japanese'.

jar¹ > *noun* **1** a wide-mouthed cylindrical container made of glass or pottery. **2** Brit. informal a glass of beer.

ORIGIN – French *jarre*, from Arabic.

jar² > *verb* (**jarred**, **jarring**) **1** send a painful or uncomfortable shock through (a part of the body). **2** strike against something with an unpleasant vibration or jolt. **3** have an unpleasant or incongruous effect. > *noun* an instance of jarring.

DERIVATIVES – **jarring** adjective **jarringly** adverb.

SYNONYMS – *verb* **1** jerk, jolt.

jardinière /ˌzhaardinˈyair/ > *noun* **1** an ornamental pot or stand for displaying plants. **2** a garnish of mixed vegetables.

ORIGIN – French, literally 'female gardener'.

jargon > *noun* words or expressions used by a particular group that are difficult for others to understand.

ORIGIN – Old French *jargon*: originally used in the sense 'twittering, chattering', later 'gibberish'.

jarrah /ˈjarrə/ > *noun* a eucalyptus tree native to western Australia.

ORIGIN – from Nyungar (an extinct Aboriginal language).

jasmine (also **jessamine**) > *noun* a shrub or climbing plant with fragrant, often yellow, flowers.

ORIGIN – French *jasmin*.

jasper > *noun* an opaque reddish-brown variety of chalcedony.

ORIGIN – Old French *jasp(r)e*, from Latin *iaspis*.

jaundice /ˈjawndiss/ > *noun* **1** Medicine yellowing of the skin due to a bile disorder. **2** bitterness or resentment.

DERIVATIVES – **jaundiced** adjective.

ORIGIN – Old French *jaunice* 'yellowness'.

jaunt > *noun* a short excursion for pleasure. > *verb* go on a jaunt.

SYNONYMS – *noun* outing, trip.

jaunty > *adjective* (**jauntier**, **jauntiest**) having a lively and self-confident manner.

DERIVATIVES – **jauntily** adverb **jauntiness** noun.

SYNONYMS – breezy, buoyant, perky.

Java /ˈjaavə/ > *noun* trademark a computer programming language designed to work across different computer systems.

java /ˈjaavə/ > *noun* N. Amer. informal coffee.

Javan > *noun* a person from Java. > *adjective* Javanese.

Javanese > *noun* (pl. same) **1** a person from the Indonesian island of Java. **2** the language of central Java. > *adjective* relating to Java.

javelin /ˈjavvəlin/ > *noun* a long, light spear thrown in a competitive sport or as a weapon.

ORIGIN – Old French *javeline*, of Celtic origin.

javelina /ˌhavvəˈleenə/ > *noun* North American term for PECCARY.

ORIGIN – Spanish *jabalina* 'wild boar'.

jaw > *noun* **1** each of the upper and lower bony structures in vertebrates forming the framework of the mouth and containing the teeth. **2** (**jaws**) the grasping, biting, or crushing mouthparts of an invertebrate. **3** (**jaws**) the gripping parts of a wrench, vice, etc. **4** (**jaws**) the grasping or destructive power of something: *the jaws of death*. > *verb* informal talk or gossip at length.

WORDFINDER – gnathic (*relating to the jaw*), mandible, maxilla (*bones of the jaw*), prognathous (*having a projecting jaw*).

DERIVATIVES – **jawed** adjective.

COMBINATIONS – **jawbone** a bone of the jaw, especially that of the lower jaw (the mandible). **jaw-dropping** informal amazing. **jawline** the contour of the lower edge of a person's jaw.

ORIGIN – Old French *joe* 'cheek, jaw'.

jay > *noun* a noisy bird of the crow family with boldly patterned plumage.

ORIGIN – Latin *gaius*, perhaps from the Latin given name *Gaius*.

jaywalk > *verb* chiefly N. Amer. walk in or across a road without regard for approaching traffic.

DERIVATIVES – **jaywalker** noun.

jazz > *noun* a type of music of black American origin which is characterised by improvisation, syncopation, and a regular rhythm. > *verb* (**jazz up**) make more lively.

WORDFINDER – *types of jazz:* bebop, big band, cool, Dixieland, swing, trad.

IDIOMS – **and all that jazz** informal and such similar things.

SYNONYMS – *verb* (**jazz up**) animate, brighten up, enliven.

COMBINATIONS – **jazz age** the 1920s in the US, characterised as a period of hedonism, freedom, and exuberance.

wordpower facts

Jazz

The word **jazz** was first recorded in 1909 in the musical sense, and in 1913 with the meaning 'energy, animation'. The origin of the word is unknown, although it is thought by many to be African and to have been brought to the US by slaves. Some people believe it to be derived from the American dialect word *jasm*, meaning 'energy, enthusiasm'. Another theory links the word to the name of a *Jasbo* or *Jazzbo* Brown, an itinerant black musician who played along the Mississippi and later in Chicago cabarets, but like all the other suggestions this has not been confirmed.

jazzy > *adjective* (**jazzier**, **jazziest**) **1** of or in the style of jazz. **2** bright, colourful, and showy.

SYNONYMS – **2** fancy, flashy, gaudy.

JCB > *noun* Brit. trademark a type of mechanical excavator with a shovel at the front and a digging arm at the rear.

ORIGIN – the initials of *J. C. Bamford*, the makers.

J-cloth > *noun* trademark (in the UK) a type of cloth used for household cleaning.

ORIGIN – *J* from *Johnson and Johnson*, the original makers.

JCR > *abbreviation* Brit. Junior Common (or Combination) Room.

jealous > *adjective* **1** envious of someone else's achievements or advantages. **2** resentful of a perceived sexual rival. **3** fiercely protective of one's rights or possessions: *they kept a jealous eye over their interests*. **4** (of God) demanding faithfulness and exclusive worship.

DERIVATIVES – **jealously** adverb **jealousy** noun.

SYNONYMS – **1** covetous, envious. **2** doubting, possessive, suspicious. **3** possessive, proprietorial, protective.

ORIGIN – Old French *gelos*, from Latin *zelosus* 'zealous'.

jean > *noun* **1** heavy twilled cotton cloth, especially denim. **2** (**jeans**) hard-wearing trousers made of denim or a similar fabric.

ORIGIN – Old French *Janne* (now *Gênes*), from Latin *Janua* 'Genoa', the place of original production.

jebel /jebb'l/ > *noun* (in the Middle East and North Africa) a mountain or hill, or a range of hills.

ORIGIN – Arabic.

jeep > *noun* trademark a small, sturdy motor vehicle with four-wheel drive.

ORIGIN – from the initials *GP* 'general purpose', used in the US military in the Second World War: influenced by 'Eugene the Jeep', a creature of great resourcefulness and power in the *Popeye* comic strip.

jeepers (also **jeepers creepers**) > *exclamation* informal, chiefly N. Amer. expressing surprise or alarm.

ORIGIN – alteration of JESUS.

jeer > *verb* make rude and mocking remarks at someone. > *noun* a rude and mocking remark.

DERIVATIVES – **jeering** *adjective* & *noun* **jeeringly** *adverb*.

SYNONYMS – *verb* deride, mock, ridicule, taunt.

Jeez (also **Jeeze** or **Geez**) > *exclamation* informal expressing surprise or annoyance.

ORIGIN – abbreviation of JESUS.

jehad > *noun* variant spelling of JIHAD.

Jehovah /jihōvə/ > *noun* a form of the Hebrew name of God used in some translations of the Bible.

COMBINATIONS – **Jehovah's Witness** a member of a fundamentalist Christian sect that denies many traditional Christian doctrines and preaches the Second Coming.

ORIGIN – Latin *Iehouah*, from Hebrew.

jejune /jijoon/ > *adjective* 1 naive and simplistic. 2 (of ideas or writings) dull.

SYNONYMS – 2 arid, banal, dull, insipid.

wordpower facts

Jejune

The word **jejune** comes from the Latin adjective *jejunus* 'fasting, barren'. The first senses in English were 'without food, fasting or hungry' and 'meagre, unsatisfying, not nourishing, barren'. The subsequent sense 'dull, lacking in substance or interest' was the prevailing one until the late 19th century, when a new sense, 'naive and simplistic', arose: it is first recorded as being used by George Bernard Shaw in the play *Arms and the Man*. This use may have arisen from the mistaken belief that the word is connected to Latin *juvenis* or French *jeune* 'young'.

jejunum /jijoonəm/ > *noun* Anatomy the part of the small intestine between the duodenum and ileum.

ORIGIN – Latin, 'fasting' (because it is usually found to be empty after death).

Jekyll /jekk'l/ > *noun* (in phrase **a Jekyll and Hyde**) a person displaying alternately good and evil personalities.

ORIGIN – after the central character in Robert Louis Stevenson's story *The Strange Case of Dr Jekyll and Mr Hyde* (1886).

jell (also **gel**) > *verb* (**jelled**, **jelling**) 1 (of jelly or a similar substance) set or become firmer. 2 take definite form or begin to work well.

jellaba > *noun* variant spelling of DJELLABA.

jello (also trademark **Jell-O**) > *noun* N. Amer. a fruit-flavoured gelatin dessert made up from a powder.

jelly > *noun* (pl. **jellies**) 1 chiefly Brit. a dessert consisting of a sweet, fruit-flavoured liquid set with gelatin to form a semi-solid mass. 2 a small sweet made with gelatin. 3 a similar preparation or a substance of a similar semi-solid consistency. 4 Brit. informal term for GELIGNITE. > *verb* (**jellies**, **jellied**) set (food) in a jelly.

WORDFINDER – gelatinous (*jelly-like*).

COMBINATIONS – **jelly baby** Brit. a jelly sweet in the stylised shape of a baby. **jelly bean** a jelly sweet in the shape of a bean. **jelly shoe** (also **jelly sandal**) a sandal made from translucent moulded plastic.

ORIGIN – Old French *gelee* 'frost, jelly', from Latin *gelata* 'frozen'.

jellyfish > *noun* a free-swimming marine animal with a soft bell- or saucer-shaped body that has stinging tentacles around the edge.

jemmy (N. Amer. **jimmy**) > *noun* (pl. **jemmies**) a short crowbar. > *verb* (**jemmies**, **jemmied**) informal force open (a window or door) with a jemmy.

ORIGIN – familiar form of the given name *James*.

je ne sais quoi /zhə nə say kwaa/ > *noun* a quality that cannot be easily identified.

ORIGIN – French, 'I do not know what'.

jenny > *noun* (pl. **jennies**) a female donkey or ass.

ORIGIN – familiar form of the given name *Janet*.

jeon /jun/ > *noun* (pl. same) a monetary unit of South Korea, equal to one hundredth of a won.

jeopardise /jeppərdīz/ (also **jeopardize**) > *verb* put into a situation in which there is a danger of loss, harm, or failure.

SYNONYMS – endanger, imperil, risk.

jeopardy /jeppərdi/ > *noun* danger of loss, harm, or failure.

SYNONYMS – danger, hazard, peril, risk.

ORIGIN – from Old French *ieu parti* 'evenly divided game', originally used in chess to denote a position in which the chances of winning or losing were evenly balanced.

jerboa /jerbōə/ > *noun* a desert-dwelling rodent with very long hind legs, found from North Africa to central Asia.

ORIGIN – Latin, from Arabic.

jeremiad /jerrimīad/ > *noun* a long complaint or lamentation; a list of woes.

ORIGIN – French *jérémiade*, with reference to the Lamentations of Jeremiah in the Old Testament.

Jeremiah /jerrimīə/ > *noun* a person who complains continually or foretells disaster.

jerk¹ > *noun* 1 a quick, sharp, sudden movement. 2 Weightlifting the raising of a barbell above the head from shoulder level by an abrupt straightening of the arms and legs. 3 informal, chiefly N. Amer. a contemptibly foolish person. > *verb* 1 move with a jerk. 2 Weightlifting raise with a jerk. 3 (**jerk around**) N. Amer. informal deal with (someone) dishonestly or unfairly. 4 (**jerk off**) vulgar slang, chiefly N. Amer masturbate.

SYNONYMS – *noun* & *verb* 1 pull, tug, wrench.

jerk² > *verb* cure (meat) by cutting it into strips and drying it (originally in the sun). > *noun* jerked meat.

ORIGIN – Spanish *charquear*, from a word in Quechua meaning 'dried flesh'.

jerkin > *noun* a sleeveless jacket.

jerky¹ > *adjective* (**jerkier**, **jerkiest**) characterised by abrupt stops and starts.

DERIVATIVES – **jerkily** *adverb* **jerkiness** *noun*.

SYNONYMS – fitful, irregular, shaky, spasmodic.

jerky² > *noun* strips of meat that has been cured by drying.

jeroboam /jerrəbōəm/ > *noun* a wine bottle with a capacity four times larger than that of an ordinary bottle.

ORIGIN – named after *Jeroboam*, a king of Israel.

Jerry > *noun* (pl. **Jerries**) Brit. informal, dated a German or Germans collectively.

ORIGIN – probably an alteration of GERMAN.

jerry-built > *adjective* badly or hastily built.

DERIVATIVES – **jerry-builder** *noun*.

jerrycan (also **jerrican**) > *noun* a large flat-sided metal container for storing or transporting liquids.

ORIGIN – from JERRY, because such containers were first used in Germany.

jersey > *noun* (pl. **jerseys**) 1 a knitted garment with long sleeves. 2 a distinctive shirt worn by a participant in certain sports. 3 a soft knitted fabric. 4 (**Jersey**) a breed of light brown dairy cattle from Jersey.

ORIGIN – from *Jersey* in the Channel Islands, where the fabric was made.

wordpower facts

Jerry-built

The origin of the term **jerry-built** is uncertain, but two theories in particular have been advanced. It may be a biblical allusion, in which an insubstantial jerry-built house is likened to the walls of Jericho, which fell down at the sound of Joshua's trumpets (Book of Joshua, chapter 6). The second theory is that it derives from the name of a firm of builders in Liverpool, as was claimed in a letter to a newspaper in 1884. **Jerry-built** was first recorded in 1869.

Jerusalem artichoke > *noun* a knobbly tuber with white flesh, eaten as a vegetable.

ORIGIN – *Jerusalem* is an alteration of Italian *girasole* 'sunflower' (to which the plant is related).

jess > *noun* Falconry a short leather strap that is fastened round each leg of a hawk, to which a leash may be attached.

ORIGIN – Old French *ges*, from Latin *jactus* 'a throw'.

jessamine /jessəmin/ > *noun* variant spelling of JASMINE.

jessie (also **jessy**) > *noun* (pl. **jessies**) Brit. informal, derogatory an effeminate, weak, or over-sensitive man.

ORIGIN – from the female given name *Jessie*.

jest > *noun* a joke. > *verb* speak or act in a joking manner.

SYNONYMS – *noun* gag, jape, joke, quip, witticism. *verb* banter, joke, quip, tease.

ORIGIN – Old French *geste*, from Latin *gesta* 'actions, exploits': at first spelled *gest* and meaning 'exploit, heroic deed', later 'heroic narrative', 'idle tale', and 'joke'.

jester > *noun* historical a professional joker or 'fool' at a medieval court.

Jesuit /jezyoo-it/ > *noun* a member of a Roman Catholic order of priests founded by St Ignatius Loyola and others in 1534.

Jesuitical > *adjective* 1 of or concerning the Jesuits. 2 secretive or equivocating, in a manner once associated with Jesuits.

Jesus (also **Jesus Christ**) > *noun* the central figure of the Christian religion, considered by Christians to be the Christ or Messiah and the Son of God. > *exclamation* informal expressing irritation, dismay, or surprise.

jet¹ > *noun* 1 a rapid stream of liquid or gas forced out of a small opening. 2 an aircraft powered by jet engines. > *verb* (**jetted**, **jetting**) 1 spurt out in a jet. 2 travel by jet aircraft.

SYNONYMS – *noun & verb* 1 gush, spout, spurt, squirt.

COMBINATIONS – **jet engine** an aircraft engine which provides thrust by ejecting a high-speed jet of gas obtained by burning fuel in air. **jetliner** a large jet aircraft carrying passengers. **jet stream** any of several narrow variable bands of very strong predominantly westerly air currents encircling the globe several miles above the earth.

ORIGIN – from French *jeter* 'to throw', based on Latin *jacere*.

jet² > *noun* 1 a hard black semi-precious variety of lignite. 2 (also **jet black**) a glossy black colour.

ORIGIN – Old French *jaiet*, from Greek *gagatēs* 'from *Gagai*', a town in Asia Minor.

jeté /zhetay/ > *noun* Ballet a spring from one foot to the other, with the following leg extended backwards while in the air.

ORIGIN – French, from *jeter* 'to throw'.

jet lag > *noun* extreme tiredness and other effects felt by a person after a long flight across different time zones.

DERIVATIVES – **jet-lagged** *adjective*.

jetsam /jetsəm/ > *noun* unwanted material or goods that have been thrown overboard from a ship and washed ashore. Compare with FLOTSAM.

ORIGIN – first as *jetson*; contraction of JETTISON.

jet set > *noun* (**the jet set**) informal wealthy people who travel widely and frequently for pleasure.

DERIVATIVES – **jet-setter** *noun* **jet-setting** *adjective*.

jet ski > *noun* trademark a small jet-propelled vehicle which skims across the surface of water and is ridden like a motorcycle. > *verb* (**jet-ski**) ride on a jet ski.

DERIVATIVES – **jet-skier** *noun* **jet-skiing** *noun*.

jettison /jettis'n/ > *verb* 1 throw or drop from an aircraft or ship. 2 abandon or discard.

SYNONYMS – 2 abandon, discard, dump, scrap, throw out.

ORIGIN – Old French *getaison*, from Latin *jacere* 'to throw'.

jetty > *noun* (pl. **jetties**) 1 a landing stage or small pier. 2 a construction built out into the water to protect a harbour, riverbank, etc.

ORIGIN – Old French *jetee*, from *jeter* 'to throw'.

jeu d'esprit /zhö despree/ > *noun* (pl. **jeux d'esprit** pronunc. same) a light-hearted display of wit.

ORIGIN – French, 'game of the mind'.

jeunesse dorée /zhöness doray/ > *noun* young people of wealth, fashion, and flair.

ORIGIN – French, 'gilded youth'.

Jew > *noun* a member of the people whose traditional religion is Judaism and who trace their origins to the ancient Hebrew people of Israel.

WORDFINDER – *Jewish festivals:* Hanukkah, Purim, Rosh Hashana (*Jewish New Year*), Shavuoth, Succoth, Yom Kippur; Ashkenazi (*a Jew of central or eastern European descent*), Sephardi (*a Jew of Spanish or Portuguese descent*).

COMBINATIONS – **Jew's harp** a small lyre-shaped musical instrument held between the teeth and struck with a finger.

ORIGIN – from the Hebrew form of the name 'Judah'.

jewel > *noun* 1 a precious stone, especially a single crystal or a cut and polished piece of a lustrous or translucent mineral. 2 (**jewels**) pieces of jewellery. 3 a hard precious stone used as a bearing in a watch, compass, etc. 4 a highly valued person or thing.

IDIOMS – **the jewel in the crown** the most valuable or successful part of something.

DERIVATIVES – **jewelled** (US **jeweled**) *adjective*.

ORIGIN – Old French *joel*, from *jeu* 'game, play', from Latin *jocus* 'jest'.

jeweller (US **jeweler**) > *noun* a person who makes or sells jewellery.

COMBINATIONS – **jeweller's rouge** finely ground ferric oxide, used as a polish for metal and optical glass.

jewellery (US also **jewelry**) > *noun* personal ornaments, such as necklaces, rings, or bracelets, that are made from or contain jewels and precious metal.

Jewess > *noun* a Jewish woman or girl.

Jewish > *adjective* relating to, associated with, or denoting Jews or Judaism.

DERIVATIVES – **Jewishness** *noun*.

Jewry /joori/ > *noun* (pl. **Jewries**) 1 Jews collectively. 2 historical a Jewish quarter in a town or city.

Jezebel /jezzəbel/ > *noun* a shameless or immoral woman.

ORIGIN – the name of the wife of Ahab in the Bible.

jiao /jow/ > *noun* (pl. same) a monetary unit of China, equal to one tenth of a yuan.

ORIGIN – Chinese.

jib¹ > *noun* 1 Sailing a triangular staysail set forward of the mast. 2 the projecting arm of a crane.

jib² > *verb* (**jibbed**, **jibbing**) 1 (usu. **jib at**) be unwilling to do or accept something. 2 (of a horse) stop and refuse to go on.

DERIVATIVES – **jibber** *noun*.

SYNONYMS – 1 baulk at, refuse.

ORIGIN – perhaps related to French *regimber* (earlier *regiber*) 'buck or rear; baulk'; related to JIBE¹.

jibe¹ (also **gibe**) > *noun* an insulting or mocking remark. > *verb* make jibes.

ORIGIN – perhaps from Old French *giber* 'handle roughly'; related to JIB².

jibe² > *verb & noun* US variant of GYBE.

jibe³ > *verb* N. Amer. informal be in accordance; agree.

jiffy (also **jiff**) > *noun informal* a moment.

jig > *noun* **1** a lively dance with leaping movements and music in compound time. **2** a device that guides tools and holds materials or parts securely. > *verb* (**jigged**, **jigging**) **1** dance a jig. **2** move up and down with a quick jerky motion.

jigger¹ > *noun* **1** a machine or vehicle with a part that rocks or moves to and fro. **2** a person who dances a jig. **3** a small sail set at the stern of a ship. **4** a small tackle consisting of a double and single block with a rope. **5** a measure of spirits or wine. > *verb* Brit. informal **1** rearrange or tamper with. **2** (**jiggered**) damaged, broken, or exhausted.
IDIOMS – **I'll be jiggered** Brit. informal, dated expressing astonishment.

jigger² > *noun* variant spelling of CHIGGER.

jiggery-pokery > *noun informal, chiefly* Brit. deceitful or dishonest behaviour.
ORIGIN – probably a variant of Scots *joukery-pawkery*, from *jouk* 'dodge, skulk'.

jiggle > *verb* move lightly and quickly from side to side or up and down. > *noun* an instance of jiggling.
DERIVATIVES – **jiggly** *adjective*.

jigsaw > *noun* **1** a puzzle consisting of a picture printed on cardboard or wood and cut into numerous interlocking shapes that have to be fitted together. **2** a machine saw with a fine blade enabling it to cut curved lines in a sheet of wood, metal, etc.

jihad /jiˈhad/ (also **jehad**) > *noun* a holy war undertaken by Muslims against unbelievers.
ORIGIN – Arabic, 'effort'.

jilt > *verb* abruptly break a relationship with (a lover).
ORIGIN – first meaning 'deceive, trick'.

Jim Crow > *noun* US **1** the former practice of segregating black people in the US. **2** offensive a black person.
DERIVATIVES – **Jim Crowism** *noun*.
ORIGIN – the name of a black character in a plantation song.

jim-jams > *plural noun informal* **1** (**the jim-jams**) a fit of depression or nervousness. **2** Brit. pyjamas.

jimmy > *noun & verb* US spelling of JEMMY.

jingle > *noun* **1** a light, loose ringing sound such as that made by metal objects being shaken together. **2** a short easily remembered slogan, verse, or tune. > *verb* make or cause to make a jingle.
DERIVATIVES – **jingler** *noun* **jingly** *adjective*.

jingo /ˈjɪŋɡoʊ/ > *noun* (pl. **jingoes**) dated, chiefly derogatory a vociferous supporter of a patriotic war policy.
IDIOMS – **by jingo!** an exclamation of surprise.

---

wordpower facts

Jingo

First recorded in 1670, the word **jingo** was originally used by conjurors in phrases such as *hey* or *high jingo!*, by which the magician called for something to appear. The exclamation **by jingo**, and the noun sense with its related words **jingoism**, **jingoist**, and **jingoistic**, come from a popular song supporting the sending of a British fleet into Turkish waters to resist Russia in 1878. The chorus ran: 'We don't want to fight, yet by Jingo! if we do, We've got the ships, we've got the men, and got the money too'.

---

jingoism > *noun* chiefly derogatory extreme patriotism, especially in the form of aggressive foreign policy.
DERIVATIVES – **jingoist** *noun* **jingoistic** *adjective*.

jink > *verb* change direction suddenly and nimbly. > *noun* a sudden quick change of direction.
ORIGIN – in early Scottish use as *high jinks*, denoting antics at drinking parties.

jinn /jin/ (also **djinn**) > *noun* (pl. same or **jinns**) (in Arabian and Muslim mythology) an intelligent spirit able to appear in human or animal form.
ORIGIN – Arabic.

jinx > *noun* a person or thing that brings bad luck. > *verb* bring bad luck to.
ORIGIN – probably a variant of the rare word *jynx* 'wryneck' (from modern Latin), because the bird was used in witchcraft.

jitter informal > *noun* **1** (**the jitters**) a feeling of raw nervousness. **2** slight, irregular variation in an electrical signal. > *verb* **1** act nervously. **2** suffer from jitter.
DERIVATIVES – **jitteriness** *noun* **jittery** *adjective*.

jitterbug > *noun* a fast dance performed to swing music, popular in the 1940s. > *verb* (**jitterbugged**, **jitterbugging**) dance the jitterbug.

jiu-jitsu > *noun* variant spelling of JU-JITSU.

jive > *noun* **1** a style of lively dance popular in the 1940s and 1950s, performed to swing music or rock and roll. **2** informal, chiefly N. Amer. exaggerated or misleading talk. > *verb* **1** dance the jive. **2** informal, chiefly N. Amer. talk in an exaggerated or misleading way.
DERIVATIVES – **jiver** *noun*.
ORIGIN – first (in the US) denoting meaningless or misleading speech, later the slang associated with black American jazz musicians, giving rise in the 1940s to the sense 'dance performed to jazz'.

joanna > *noun* Brit. rhyming slang a piano.

job > *noun* **1** a paid position of regular employment. **2** a task or piece of work. **3** informal a crime, especially a robbery. **4** informal a procedure to improve the appearance of something: *a nose job*. > *verb* (**jobbed**, **jobbing**) **1** (usu. as adj. **jobbing**) do casual or occasional work. **2** buy and sell (stocks) on a small scale as a broker-dealer. **3** N. Amer. informal cheat; betray.
IDIOMS – **a good job** informal, chiefly Brit. a fortunate fact or circumstance. **jobs for the boys** Brit. the practice of giving paid employment to one's friends, supporters, or relations. **just the job** Brit. informal exactly what is needed. **on the job 1** while working; at work. **2** Brit. informal engaged in sexual intercourse.
SYNONYMS – *noun* **1** occupation, profession, trade. **2** assignment, chore, task, undertaking.
COMBINATIONS – **jobcentre** (in the UK) a government office in a local area, giving information about available jobs and administering benefits to unemployed people. **job lot** a batch of articles sold or bought at one time, especially at a discount. **jobsworth** Brit. informal an official who mindlessly upholds petty rules. [ORIGIN – from 'it's more than my *job's worth* (not) to…'.]

jobber > *noun* **1** historical (in the UK) a dealer on the Stock Exchange who dealt only with brokers, not directly with the public. **2** N. Amer. a wholesaler. **3** a person who does casual or occasional work.
NOTE – the term **jobber** was officially replaced in the UK Stock Exchange by **broker-dealer** in 1986.

jobbery > *noun* the practice of using a public office or position of trust for one's own gain or advantage.

jobless > *adjective* without a paid job; unemployed.
DERIVATIVES – **joblessness** *noun*.

Job's comforter /joʊbz/ > *noun* a person who aggravates someone's distress while appearing to offer them comfort.
ORIGIN – alluding to the biblical story of the patriarch *Job*.

job-share > *verb* (of two part-time employees) share a single full-time job. > *noun* an arrangement of such a kind.
DERIVATIVES – **job-sharer** *noun*.

Jock > *noun* informal, often offensive a Scotsman.
ORIGIN – Scottish form of the given name *Jack*.

jock¹ > *noun* informal **1** a disc jockey. **2** N. Amer. an enthusiast or participant in a specified activity: *a computer jock*.

jock² > *noun* N. Amer. informal **1** another term for JOCKSTRAP. **2** an enthusiastic male athlete or sports fan.
DERIVATIVES – **jockish** *adjective*.

jockey > *noun* (pl. **jockeys**) a professional rider in horse races. > *verb* (**jockeys**,

jockeyed) 1 struggle to gain or achieve something. **2** handle or manipulate in a skilful manner.

COMBINATIONS – **jockey cap** a strengthened cap with a long peak of a kind worn by jockeys.

wordpower facts
Jockey

The word **jockey** is a diminutive of **Jock** and, like **jack**, ultimately derives from the name *Jack*. Originally the name for an ordinary man, lad, or underling, the word came to mean 'mounted courier', hence the current sense. Another early use, 'horse-dealer' (long a byword for dishonesty), probably gave rise to the verb sense 'manipulate', whereas the first verb sense probably relates to the behaviour of jockeys manoeuvring for an advantageous position during a race.

jockstrap > *noun* a support or protection for the male genitals, worn especially by sportsmen.

ORIGIN – from slang *jock* 'genitals'.

jocose /jəkōss/ > *adjective* formal playful or humorous.

DERIVATIVES – **jocosely** *adverb* **jocoseness** *noun* **jocosity** (pl. **jocosities**) *noun*.

ORIGIN – Latin *jocosus*, from *jocus* 'jest, joke'.

jocular /jokyoolər/ > *adjective* fond of or characterised by joking; humorous.

DERIVATIVES – **jocularity** *noun* **jocularly** *adverb*.

SYNONYMS – comic, funny, humorous.

ANTONYMS – serious, solemn.

ORIGIN – Latin *jocularis*, from *joculus*, from *jocus* 'jest, joke'.

jocund /jokkənd/ > *adjective* formal cheerful and light-hearted.

DERIVATIVES – **jocundity** (pl. **jocundities**) *noun*. **jocundly** *adverb*.

ORIGIN – Latin *jocundus*, from *jucundus* 'pleasant, agreeable' (influenced by *jocus* 'joke').

jodhpurs /jodpərz/ > *plural noun* trousers worn for horse riding that are close-fitting below the knee and have reinforced patches on the inside of the leg.

ORIGIN – named after the Indian city of *Jodhpur*.

joe > *noun* **1** an ordinary man. [ORIGIN – familiar form of the given name *Joseph*.] **2** N. Amer. informal coffee.

joey > *noun* (pl. **joeys**) Austral. **1** a young kangaroo, wallaby, or possum. **2** informal a baby or young child.

ORIGIN – Aboriginal.

jog > *verb* (**jogged**, **jogging**) **1** run at a steady, gentle pace, especially as a form of exercise. **2** (of a horse) move at a slow trot. **3** (**jog along** or **on**) continue in a steady, uneventful way. **4** nudge or knock slightly. **5** trigger; stimulate. > *noun* **1** a spell of jogging. **2** a gentle running pace. **3** a slight push or nudge.

COMBINATIONS – **jogtrot** a slow trot.

ORIGIN – first used in the sense 'stab, pierce': from JAG¹.

jogger > *noun* **1** a person who jogs. **2** (**joggers**) tracksuit trousers worn for jogging.

joggle > *verb* move with repeated small bobs or jerks. > *noun* a joggling movement.

ORIGIN – from JOG.

john > *noun* informal **1** chiefly N. Amer. a toilet. **2** a prostitute's client.

John Bull > *noun* a personification of England or the typical Englishman.

ORIGIN – from the name of a character in John Arbuthnot's satire *Law is a Bottomless Pit; or, the History of John Bull* (1712).

John Doe > *noun* chiefly US **1** (in legal and official contexts) a male whose name is unknown or undisclosed. **2** informal an average or ordinary man.

NOTE – the equivalent female name is **Jane Doe**.

ORIGIN – first used in law as a name of a fictitious plaintiff, corresponding to *Richard Roe*, a fictitious defendant.

John Dory > *noun* (pl. **John Dories**) an edible dory (fish) of the eastern Atlantic and Mediterranean, with a black oval mark on each side.

johnny > *noun* (pl. **johnnies**) Brit. informal **1** a man. **2** a condom.

johnny-come-lately > *noun* informal a newcomer or late starter.

joie de vivre /zhwaa də veevrə/ > *noun* exuberant enjoyment of life.

ORIGIN – French.

join > *verb* **1** link or become linked or connected to. **2** unite. **3** become a member or employee of. **4** (**join up**) become a member of the armed forces. **5** take part in (an activity). **6** come into the company of. > *noun* a place where two or more things are joined.

IDIOMS – **join forces** combine efforts.

DERIVATIVES – **joinable** *adjective*.

SYNONYMS – *verb* **1** attach, bind, connect, couple, fasten. **2** amalgamate, combine, merge, unify, unite.

ORIGIN – Old French *joindre*, from Latin *jungere* 'to join'.

joiner > *noun* **1** a person who constructs the wooden components of a building. **2** informal a person who readily joins groups.

joinery > *noun* **1** the wooden components of a building collectively. **2** the work of a joiner.

joint > *noun* **1** a point at which parts are joined. **2** a structure in a body by which two bones are fitted together. **3** the part of a plant stem from which a leaf or branch grows. **4** Brit. a large piece of meat. **5** informal an establishment of a specified kind: *a burger joint*. **6** informal a cannabis cigarette. > *adjective* **1** shared, held, or made by two or more people. **2** sharing in an achievement or activity. > *verb* **1** provide or fasten with joints. **2** prepare (a board) to be joined to another by planing its edge. **3** point (masonry or brickwork). **4** cut (the body of an animal) into joints.

WORDFINDER – arthritis (*inflammation and stiffness of a joint of the body*), articulation (*the state of being jointed*), chiropractic (*manipulative treatment of joints*), dislocation (*injury in which a joint is disturbed*); *types of mechanical joint*: ball-and-socket, dovetail, mitre, universal joint.

IDIOMS – **out of joint 1** dislocated. **2** in a state of disorder or disorientation.

DERIVATIVES – **jointless** *adjective* **jointly** *adverb*.

COMBINATIONS – **joint and several** (of a legal obligation) undertaken by two or more people, each having liability for the whole. **joint-stock company** Finance a company whose stock is owned jointly by the shareholders.

jointer > *noun* **1** a plane for preparing a wooden edge for joining to another. **2** a tool for pointing masonry and brickwork. **3** a person who joints pipes or wires.

joist /joyst/ > *noun* a length of timber or steel supporting part of the structure of a building.

DERIVATIVES – **joisted** *adjective*.

ORIGIN – Old French *giste* 'beam supporting a bridge', from Latin *jacere* 'lie down'.

jojoba /həhōbə/ > *noun* an oil extracted from the seeds of a North American shrub, widely used in cosmetics.

ORIGIN – Mexican Spanish.

joke > *noun* **1** a statement made or short story told in order to cause amusement. **2** a trick played for fun. **3** informal a ridiculously inadequate or inappropriate thing. > *verb* make jokes.

DERIVATIVES – **jokey** (also **joky**) *adjective* **jokingly** *adverb*.

SYNONYMS – *noun* **1** gag, jest, pun, quip, witticism. **2** hoax, jape, prank. *verb* banter, jest, tease.

ORIGIN – perhaps from Latin *jocus* 'jest, wordplay'.

joker > *noun* **1** a person who is fond of joking. **2** informal a foolish or inept person. **3** a playing card with the figure of a jester, used as a wild card. **4** US a clause in a bill or document affecting its operation in a way that is not immediately apparent.

IDIOMS − **the joker in the pack** an unpredictable person or factor.

jollification > *noun* merrymaking.

jollity > *noun* **1** lively and cheerful activity. **2** the quality of being jolly.

jolly > *adjective* (**jollier, jolliest**) **1** happy and cheerful. **2** informal lively and entertaining. > *verb* (**jollies, jollied**) informal encourage in a friendly way: *he jollied her along.* > *adverb* Brit. informal very. > *noun* (pl. **jollies**) Brit. informal a party or celebration.

DERIVATIVES − **jollily** *adverb* **jolliness** *noun*.

SYNONYMS − *adjective* **1** cheerful, happy, jovial, merry.

ANTONYMS − *adjective* **1** lugubrious, miserable.

COMBINATIONS − **Jolly Roger** a pirate's flag with a white skull and crossbones on a black background.

ORIGIN − from Old French *joli* 'pretty', perhaps from Old Norse *jól* (see **Yule**).

jolt > *verb* **1** push or shake abruptly and roughly. **2** shock (someone) into taking certain action. > *noun* **1** an act of jolting. **2** a surprise or shock.

jonquil /**jong**kwil/ > *noun* a narcissus with small fragrant yellow flowers and cylindrical leaves.

ORIGIN − Spanish *junquillo*, from Latin *juncus* 'rush, reed'.

Jordanian > *noun* a person from Jordan. > *adjective* relating to Jordan.

josh informal > *verb* tease playfully; banter. > *noun* N. Amer. good-natured banter.

DERIVATIVES − **josher** *noun*.

Joshua tree > *noun* a tall branching yucca of SW North America, with clusters of spiky leaves.

ORIGIN − apparently from *Joshua* in the Bible, the plant being likened to a man with a spear.

joss stick > *noun* a thin stick of a fragrant substance, burnt as incense.

ORIGIN − from *joss*, denoting a Chinese religious statue or idol, in front of which the incense is traditionally burned; from a Javanese word derived from Latin *deus* 'god'.

jostle > *verb* **1** push or bump against roughly. **2** (**jostle for**) struggle or compete energetically for. > *noun* the action of jostling.

ORIGIN − from **joust**.

jot > *verb* (**jotted, jotting**) write quickly. > *noun* a very small amount: *it made not a jot of difference.*

ORIGIN − Greek *iōta*, the smallest letter of the Greek alphabet (see **iota**).

jotter > *noun* Brit. a small notebook.

jotting > *noun* a brief note.

joule /jool/ > *noun* the unit of work or energy in the SI system, equal to the work done by a force of one newton when its point of application moves one metre in the direction of action of the force.

ORIGIN − named after the English physicist James P. *Joule* (1818–89).

jounce /jownss/ > *verb* jolt or bounce.

journal > *noun* **1** a newspaper or magazine dealing with a particular subject. **2** a diary or daily record. **3** the part of a shaft or axle that rests on bearings.

ORIGIN − Old French *jurnal*, from Latin *diurnalis*, from *diurnus* 'daily'.

journalese > *noun* informal a hackneyed writing style supposedly characteristic of journalists.

journalism > *noun* the activity or profession of being a journalist.

journalist > *noun* a person who writes for newspapers or magazines or prepares news or features to be broadcast on radio or television.

DERIVATIVES − **journalistic** *adjective*.

journey > *noun* (pl. **journeys**) an act of travelling from one place to another. > *verb* (**journeys, journeyed**) travel.

DERIVATIVES − **journeyer** *noun*.

ORIGIN − Old French *jornee* 'day, a day's travel, a day's work', from Latin *diurnum* 'daily portion', from *diurnus* 'daily'.

journeyman > *noun* **1** a skilled worker who is employed by another. **2** a worker who is reliable but not outstanding.

ORIGIN − from **journey** (in the obsolete sense 'day's work'); so named because the journeyman was paid by the day.

journo > *noun* (pl. **journos**) informal a journalist.

joust /jowst/ > *verb* **1** (of a medieval knight) engage in a contest in which two opponents on horseback fight with lances. **2** compete for superiority. > *noun* a jousting contest.

DERIVATIVES − **jouster** *noun*.

ORIGIN − Old French *jouster* 'bring together', from Latin *juxta* 'near'.

Jove /jōv/ > *noun* (in phrase **by Jove**) dated used for emphasis or to indicate surprise.

ORIGIN − from *Jove*, the chief of the Roman gods, equivalent to Jupiter.

jovial /jōviəl/ > *adjective* cheerful and friendly.

DERIVATIVES − **joviality** *noun* **jovially** *adverb*.

SYNONYMS − cheerful, jolly, merry.

ANTONYMS − miserable, morose.

ORIGIN − Latin *jovialis* 'of Jupiter', with reference to the supposed influence of the planet Jupiter on those born under it.

Jovian /jōviən/ > *adjective* **1** (in Roman mythology) of or like the god Jove (or Jupiter). **2** of or relating to the planet Jupiter.

jowl > *noun* **1** the lower part of a cheek, especially when fleshy or drooping. **2** N. Amer. the cheek of a pig as meat. **3** the dewlap of cattle or wattle of birds.

DERIVATIVES − **jowled** *adjective* **jowly** *adjective*.

ORIGIN − Old English, related to **jaw**.

joy > *noun* **1** a feeling of great pleasure and happiness. **2** a cause of joy. **3** Brit. informal success or satisfaction.

DERIVATIVES − **joyless** *adjective*.

SYNONYMS − **1** bliss, delight, ecstasy, euphoria, rapture.

ANTONYMS − **1** misery.

COMBINATIONS − **joypad** a device for a computer games console which uses buttons to control an image on the screen. **joystick** informal **1** the control column of an aircraft. **2** a lever which controls the movement of an image on a screen, especially in computer games.

ORIGIN − Old French *joie*, from Latin *gaudium*, from *gaudere* 'rejoice'.

joyful > *adjective* feeling or causing joy.

DERIVATIVES − **joyfully** *adverb* **joyfulness** *noun*.

joyous > *adjective* chiefly literary full of happiness and joy.

DERIVATIVES − **joyously** *adverb* **joyousness** *noun*.

joyride > *noun* informal **1** a fast ride in a stolen vehicle. **2** a ride for enjoyment.

DERIVATIVES − **joyrider** *noun* **joyriding** *noun*.

JP > *abbreviation* Justice of the Peace.

JPEG /**jay**peg/ > *abbreviation* Computing a popular format for image files, with built-in data compression.

ORIGIN − acronym from *Joint Photographic Experts Group*.

jubilant > *adjective* happy and triumphant.

DERIVATIVES − **jubilance** *noun* **jubilantly** *adverb*.

SYNONYMS − exultant, rejoicing,

jubilation /jōobilaysh'n/ > *noun* a feeling of great happiness and triumph.

SYNONYMS − elation, exultation, rapture.

ORIGIN − from Latin *jubilare* 'shout for joy'.

jubilee > *noun* **1** a special anniversary, especially one celebrating twenty-five or fifty years of something. **2** Jewish History a year of emancipation and restoration, kept every fifty years.

COMBINATIONS − **Jubilee clip** trademark an adjustable steel band secured with a screw.

ORIGIN − from Latin *jubilaeus annus* 'year of jubilee', from a Hebrew word meaning 'ram's-horn trumpet', with which the jubilee year was proclaimed.

Judaean /jōodeeən/ > *noun* a person from Judaea, the southern part of ancient Palestine. > *adjective* relating to Judaea.

Judaeo- /jōodeeō/ (US **Judeo-**) > *combining*

form **1** Jewish; Jewish and …: *Judaeo-Christian*. **2** relating to Judaea.

ORIGIN – from Latin *Judaeus* 'Jewish'.

Judaic /jŏŏ**day**ik/ > *adjective* of or relating to Judaism or the ancient Jews.

Judaism /jŏŏ**day**iz'm/ > *noun* **1** the religion of the Jews, based on the Old Testament and the Talmud. **2** Jews collectively.

DERIVATIVES – **Judaist** *noun*.

ORIGIN – Greek *Ioudaïsmos*, from the Hebrew form of the name 'Judah'.

Judas /jŏŏ**d**əss/ > *noun* a person who betrays a friend.

COMBINATIONS – **Judas tree** a Mediterranean tree with purple flowers that appear before the rounded leaves. [ORIGIN – from a popular notion that Judas Iscariot hanged himself from a tree of this kind.]

ORIGIN – from the name of *Judas* Iscariot, the disciple who betrayed Christ.

judder > *verb* chiefly Brit. shake and vibrate rapidly and forcefully. > *noun* an instance of juddering.

DERIVATIVES – **juddery** *adjective*.

Judeo- > *combining form* US spelling of **JUDAEO-**.

judge > *noun* **1** a public officer appointed to decide cases in a law court. **2** a person who decides the results of a competition. **3** a person able or qualified to give an opinion. > *verb* **1** form an opinion about. **2** give a verdict on in a law court. **3** decide the results of (a competition).

WORDFINDER – judicial (*relating to a judge or law court*).

SYNONYMS – *verb* **1** appraise, assess, evaluate.

ORIGIN – Old French *juge*, from Latin *judex*, from *jus* 'law'.

judgement* (also **judgment**) > *noun* **1** the ability to make considered decisions or form sensible opinions. **2** an opinion or conclusion. **3** a decision of a law court or judge.

IDIOMS – **against one's better judgement** contrary to what one feels to be wise.

*SPELLING – in British English, usually spelled *judge*ment; the spelling *judg*ment is conventional in legal contexts, and in North American English.

SYNONYMS – **1** acumen, discernment, perspicacity. **2** adjudication, ruling, verdict.

COMBINATIONS – **Judgement Day** the time of the Last Judgement.

judgemental (also **judgmental**) > *adjective* **1** of or concerning the use of judgement. **2** having an excessively critical point of view.

DERIVATIVES – **judgementally** *adverb*.

judicature /jŏŏ**dikk**əchər, jŏŏ**dikk**əchər/ > *noun* **1** the administration of justice. **2** (**the judicature**) the judiciary.

DERIVATIVES – **judicatory** *adjective*.

ORIGIN – from Latin *judicare* 'to judge'.

judicial /jŏŏ**dish**'l/ > *adjective* of, by, or appropriate to a law court or judge.

DERIVATIVES – **judicially** *adverb*.

COMBINATIONS – **judicial review 1** (in the UK) a procedure by which a court can pronounce on an administrative action by a public body. **2** (in the US) review by the Supreme Court of the constitutional validity of a legislative act. **judicial separation** a legal separation.

ORIGIN – from Latin *judicium* 'judgement'.

judiciary /jŏŏ**dish**əri/ > *noun* (pl. **judiciaries**) (usu. **the judiciary**) the judicial authorities of a country.

judicious /jŏŏ**dish**əss/ > *adjective* having or done with good judgement.

DERIVATIVES – **judiciously** *adverb* **judiciousness** *noun*.

SYNONYMS – astute, politic, prudent, shrewd.

ANTONYMS – foolish, injudicious.

judo > *noun* a sport of unarmed combat derived from ju-jitsu, using holds and leverage to unbalance the opponent.

WORDFINDER – dan (*advanced grade in judo*), dojo (*place where judo is practised*), gi (*white jacket worn in judo*), judoka (*a person who practises judo*).

ORIGIN – Japanese, 'gentle way'.

jug > *noun* **1** Brit. a container with a handle and a lip, for holding and pouring liquids. **2** N. Amer. a large container for liquids, with a narrow mouth. **3** (**the jug**) informal prison. **4** (**jugs**) vulgar slang a woman's breasts. > *verb* (**jugged**, **jugging**) stew or boil (a hare or rabbit) in a covered container.

COMBINATIONS – **jug band** a group of jazz, blues, or folk musicians using simple or improvised instruments such as jugs and washboards.

juggernaut /**jugg**ərnawt/ > *noun* Brit. a large heavy vehicle, especially an articulated truck.

ORIGIN – Hindi, from a Sanskrit word meaning 'Lord of the world', in reference to an image of the Hindu god Krishna carried in procession on a heavy chariot.

juggle > *verb* **1** continuously toss into the air and catch a number of objects so as to keep at least one in the air at any time. **2** cope with by adroitly balancing (several activities). **3** misrepresent (facts). > *noun* an act of juggling.

DERIVATIVES – **juggler** *noun* **jugglery** *noun*.

ORIGIN – Latin *joculari* 'to jest': originally in the sense 'entertain with jesting, tricks, etc.'

Jugoslav > *noun* & *adjective* old-fashioned spelling of **YUGOSLAV**.

jugular /**jug**yoolər/ > *adjective* of the neck or throat. > *noun* a jugular vein.

COMBINATIONS – **jugular vein** any of several large veins in the neck, carrying blood from the head.

ORIGIN – from Latin *jugulum* 'collarbone, throat', from *jugum* 'yoke'.

juice > *noun* **1** the liquid present in fruit or vegetables. **2** a drink made from this. **3** (**juices**) fluid secreted by the stomach. **4** (**juices**) liquid coming from meat or other food in cooking. **5** informal electrical energy. **6** informal petrol. **7** (**juices**) informal one's vitality or creative faculties. **8** N. Amer. informal alcoholic drink. > *verb* **1** extract the juice from. **2** (**juice up**) informal, chiefly N. Amer. enliven. **3** (**juiced**) N. Amer. informal drunk.

ORIGIN – Latin *jus* 'broth, vegetable juice'.

juicer > *noun* an appliance for extracting juice from fruit and vegetables.

juicy > *adjective* (**juicier**, **juiciest**) **1** full of juice. **2** informal interestingly scandalous. **3** informal tempting: *a juicy profit*.

DERIVATIVES – **juicily** *adverb* **juiciness** *noun*.

ju-jitsu /jŏŏ**jit**sŏŏ/ (also **jiu-jitsu** or **ju-jutsu** /jŏŏ**jut**sŏŏ/) > *noun* a Japanese system of unarmed combat and physical training.

ORIGIN – Japanese, 'gentle skill'.

juju¹ /**jŏŏ**jŏŏ/ > *noun* a style of Nigerian music characterised by the use of guitars and variable-pitch drums.

ORIGIN – perhaps from a Yoruba word meaning 'dance'.

juju² /**jŏŏ**jŏŏ/ > *noun* **1** a charm or fetish. **2** supernatural power.

ORIGIN – of West African origin, perhaps from French *joujou* 'toy'.

jujube /**jŏŏ**jŏŏb/ > *noun* **1** an edible berry-like fruit of a shrub, formerly taken as a cough cure. **2** chiefly N. Amer. a jujube-flavoured lozenge or sweet.

ORIGIN – Latin *jujuba*, from Greek *zizuphos*.

juke N. Amer. informal > *noun* (also **juke joint**) a roadhouse, nightclub, or bar providing food, drinks, and music for dancing. > *verb* **1** dance. **2** (in sport) make a sham move to confuse or mislead an opponent. **3** move in a zigzag fashion.

COMBINATIONS – **jukebox** a machine that plays a selected musical recording when a coin is inserted.

ORIGIN – Creole, 'disorderly'.

Jul. > *abbreviation* July.

julep /**jŏŏ**lep/ > *noun* a sweet drink made from sugar syrup.

ORIGIN – Latin *julapium*, from a Persian word meaning 'rose water'.

Julian calendar > *noun* a calendar introduced by the Roman general Julius Caesar (100–44 BC), in which the year consisted of 365 days, every fourth year having 366 (replaced by the Gregorian calendar).

julienne /jŏoliˈen/ > *noun* a portion of food cut into short, thin strips.

ORIGIN – French.

July > *noun* (pl. **Julys**) the seventh month of the year.

ORIGIN – from Latin *Julius mensis* 'month of July', named after the Roman general Julius Caesar.

jumble > *noun* **1** an untidy collection of things. **2** Brit. articles collected for a jumble sale. > *verb* mix up in a confused way.

SYNONYMS – *noun* **1** clutter, mishmash, muddle. *verb* disarrange, disorder, muddle.

COMBINATIONS – **jumble sale** Brit. a sale of miscellaneous second-hand goods, typically for charity.

jumbo informal > *noun* (pl. **jumbos**) **1** a very large person or thing. **2** a jumbo jet. > *adjective* very large.

COMBINATIONS – **jumbo jet** a very large airliner carrying several hundred passengers.

jumbuck /jumˈbuk/ > *noun* Austral. informal a sheep.

ORIGIN – perhaps Australian pidgin for *jump up*.

jump > *verb* **1** push oneself off the ground using the muscles in one's legs and feet. **2** move over, onto, or down from by jumping. **3** move suddenly and quickly. **4** make a sudden involuntary movement in surprise. **5** (**jump at** or **on**) accept eagerly. **6** (**jump on**) informal attack or criticise suddenly. **7** informal leap out at and attack suddenly and unexpectedly. **8** pass abruptly from one subject or state to another. **9** rise or increase suddenly. **10** informal (of a place) be very lively. **11** vulgar slang, chiefly N. Amer. have sexual intercourse with. > *noun* **1** an act of jumping. **2** a large or sudden change. **3** a sudden dramatic increase. **4** an obstacle to be jumped by a horse. **5** vulgar slang, chiefly N. Amer. an act of sexual intercourse.

IDIOMS – **jump down someone's throat** informal respond in a sudden and angry way. **jump out of one's skin** informal be startled. **jump the queue** (or N. Amer. **jump in line**) **1** move ahead of one's proper place in a queue of people. **2** take unfair precedence over others. **jump ship** (of a sailor) leave a ship without permission. **jump through hoops** be made to go through a complicated procedure.

DERIVATIVES – **jumpable** adjective.

SYNONYMS – *verb* **1** bound, leap, spring. **4** flinch, recoil, start. *noun* **1** bound, leap, spring.

COMBINATIONS – **jumped-up** informal considering oneself to be more important than one really is. **jump jet** a jet aircraft that can take off and land vertically. **jump lead** Brit. each of a pair of cables for recharging a battery in a motor vehicle by connecting it to the battery in another.

jump-off a deciding round in a showjumping competition. **jump rope** N. Amer. a skipping rope. **jumpstation** another term for **PORTAL** (in sense 2). **jumpsuit** a garment incorporating trousers and a sleeved top in one piece. [ORIGIN – first denoting a garment worn when parachuting.]

jumper¹ > *noun* **1** Brit. a pullover or sweater. **2** N. Amer. a pinafore dress.

ORIGIN – probably from dialect *jump* 'short coat', perhaps from Scottish *jupe* 'loose jacket or tunic', via Old French from an Arabic root.

jumper² > *noun* a person or animal that jumps.

COMBINATIONS – **jumper cable** N. Amer. a jump lead.

jump-start > *verb* start (a car with a flat battery) with jump leads or by a sudden release of the clutch while it is being pushed. > *noun* an act of jump-starting a car.

jumpy > *adjective* (**jumpier**, **jumpiest**) informal **1** anxious and uneasy. **2** stopping and starting abruptly.

DERIVATIVES – **jumpily** adverb **jumpiness** *noun*.

Jun. > *abbreviation* June.

jun /jun/ > *noun* (pl. same) a monetary unit of North Korea, equal to one hundredth of a won.

junction > *noun* **1** a point where two or more things meet or are joined. **2** a place where two or more roads or railway lines meet. **3** the action of joining or being joined.

COMBINATIONS – **junction box** a box containing a junction of electric wires or cables.

ORIGIN – Latin, from *jungere* 'to join'.

juncture /junkˈchər/ > *noun* **1** a particular point in time. **2** a place where things join.

ORIGIN – Latin *junctura* 'joint', from *jungere* 'to join'.

June > *noun* the sixth month of the year.

COMBINATIONS – **June bug** chiefly N. Amer. a chafer or similar beetle which often flies in June.

ORIGIN – from Latin *Junius mensis* 'month of June', from *Junonius* 'sacred to the goddess Juno'.

Jungian /yŏongˈiən/ > *adjective* of or relating to the Swiss psychologist Carl Jung (1875–1961) or his work. > *noun* a follower of Jung or his work.

jungle > *noun* **1** an area of land with dense forest and tangled vegetation, typically in the tropics. **2** a very bewildering or competitive place. **3** (also **jungle music**) a style of dance music with very fast electronic drum tracks and slower synthesised bass lines.

IDIOMS – **the law of the jungle** the principle that those who are strongest and most selfish will be the most successful.

DERIVATIVES – **junglist** noun & *adjective* **jungly** adjective.

COMBINATIONS – **jungle fever** a severe form of malaria. **junglefowl** a southern Asian game bird related to the domestic fowl.

ORIGIN – Sanskrit, 'rough and arid terrain'.

junior > *adjective* **1** of or relating to young or younger people. **2** Brit. of, for, or denoting schoolchildren aged 7–11. **3** N. Amer. of or for students in the third year of a four-year course at college or high school. **4** (after a name) denoting the younger of two with the same name in a family. **5** low or lower in rank or status. > *noun* **1** a person who is a specified number of years younger than someone else: *he's five years her junior.* **2** Brit. a child at a junior school. **3** N. Amer. a student in the third year at college or high school. **4** (in sport) a young competitor, typically under 16 or 18. **5** N. Amer. informal a nickname for one's son. **6** a person with low rank or status.

DERIVATIVES – **juniority** noun.

SYNONYMS – *adjective* **5** inferior, lesser, subordinate.

COMBINATIONS – **junior college** (in the US) a college offering courses for two years beyond high school. **junior common room** Brit. a room used for social purposes by the undergraduates of a college. **junior high school** (in the US and Canada) a school intermediate between an elementary school and a high school. **junior school** a school for young children, especially (in England and Wales) for those aged 7–11. **junior technician** a rank in the RAF, above senior aircraftman or aircraftwoman and below corporal.

ORIGIN – Latin, from *juvenis* 'young'.

juniper /jŏoˈnipər/ > *noun* an evergreen shrub or small tree bearing aromatic berry-like cones.

ORIGIN – Latin *juniperus*.

junk¹ > informal *noun* **1** useless or worthless articles; rubbish. **2** the drug heroin. > *verb* discard unceremoniously.

COMBINATIONS – **junk bond** a high-yielding high-risk security, typically issued to finance a takeover. **junk food** food with little nutritional value. **junk mail** unsolicited advertising material sent by post. **junk shop** a shop selling second-hand goods or inexpensive antiques. **junkyard** N. Amer. a scrapyard.

ORIGIN – first used to denote an old or inferior rope.

junk² > *noun* a flat-bottomed sailing boat with a prominent stem, used in China and the East Indies.

ORIGIN – Malay.

junket /**jung**kit/ > noun **1** a dish of sweetened curds of milk. **2** informal an extravagant trip or party. > verb (**junketed**, **junketing**) informal take part in an extravagant trip or party.

ORIGIN – Old French *jonquette* 'rush basket': the first sense in English was 'cream cheese made in a rush basket'.

junkie (also **junky**) > noun informal a drug addict.

ORIGIN – from JUNK¹.

junky informal > adjective regarded as junk.

Junoesque /jōōnōesk/ > adjective (of a woman) tall and shapely.

ORIGIN – from the name of *Juno*, the most important ancient Roman goddess.

junta /**jun**tə/ > noun a military or political group ruling a country after taking power by force.

ORIGIN – Spanish and Portuguese (denoting a council), from Latin *juncta*, from *jungere* 'to join'.

Jurassic /joo**rass**ik/ > adjective Geology relating to the second period of the Mesozoic era (between the Triassic and Cretaceous periods, about 208 to 146 million years ago), a time when large reptiles were dominant and the first birds appeared.

ORIGIN – named after the *Jura* Mountains on the border of France and Switzerland.

juridical /joo**ridd**ik'l/ > adjective Law relating to judicial proceedings and the law.

DERIVATIVES – **juridically** adverb.

ORIGIN – Latin *juridicus*, from *jus* 'law' + *dicere* 'say'.

jurisdiction /joorisdiksh'n/ > noun **1** the official power to make legal decisions and judgements. **2** the territory or sphere over which the legal authority of a court or other institution extends. **3** a system of law courts.

DERIVATIVES – **jurisdictional** adjective.

ORIGIN – Latin, from *jus* 'law' + *dicere* 'say'.

jurisprudence /joorisprōōd'nss/ > noun **1** the theory or philosophy of law. **2** a legal system.

DERIVATIVES – **jurisprudential** adjective.

ORIGIN – from Latin *jus* 'law' + *prudentia* 'knowledge'.

jurist /**joo**rist/ > noun **1** an expert in law. **2** N. Amer. a lawyer or a judge.

DERIVATIVES – **juristic** adjective.

juror > noun **1** a member of a jury. **2** historical a person taking an oath.

jury¹ > noun (pl. **juries**) **1** a body of people (typically twelve) sworn to give a verdict on the basis of evidence submitted in court. **2** a body of people judging a competition. > verb (**juries**, **juried**) chiefly N. Amer. judge (an art or craft exhibit).

IDIOMS – **the jury is out** a decision has not yet been reached.

ORIGIN – Old French *juree* 'oath, enquiry', from Latin *jurare* 'swear', from *jus* 'law'.

jury² > adjective Nautical (of fittings) improvised or temporary.

COMBINATIONS – **jury-rigged 1** (of a ship) having makeshift rigging. **2** chiefly N. Amer. makeshift; improvised.

ORIGIN – perhaps from Old French *ajurie* 'aid'.

jus /zhōō/ > noun (especially in French cuisine) a sauce.

ORIGIN – French, 'juice'.

just > adjective **1** morally right and fair. **2** (of treatment) appropriate or deserved in the circumstances. **3** (of an opinion or appraisal) well founded. > adverb **1** exactly. **2** exactly or nearly at this or that moment. **3** very recently. **4** barely; by a little. **5** simply; only.

IDIOMS – **just in case** as a precaution. **just so 1** arranged or done very carefully. **2** formal expressing agreement.

DERIVATIVES – **justly** adverb **justness** noun.

SYNONYMS – adjective **1** ethical, fair, honest, honourable, principled, right. **2** equitable, fair, reasonable. **3** sound, valid, warranted.

ORIGIN – Latin *justus*, from *jus* 'law, right'.

justice > noun **1** just behaviour or treatment. **2** the quality of being just. **3** the administration of law or some other authority according to the principles of just behaviour and treatment. **4** a judge or magistrate.

IDIOMS – **bring to justice** arrest and try (someone) in court for a crime. **do oneself justice** perform as well as one is able. **do justice to** treat or represent (someone or something) with due fairness.

COMBINATIONS – **Justice of the Peace** (in the UK) a lay magistrate appointed to hear minor cases, grant licences, etc., in a town or county.

ORIGIN – Old English, 'administration of the law', from Latin *jus* 'law, right'.

justifiable > adjective able to be justified.

DERIVATIVES – **justifiability** noun **justifiableness** noun **justifiably** adverb.

SYNONYMS – defensible, excusable, justified, reasonable, warranted.

justify > verb (**justifies**, **justified**) **1** prove to be right or reasonable. **2** be a good reason for. **3** Printing adjust (text) so that the lines of type fill a given width exactly, forming a straight right edge.

DERIVATIVES – **justification** noun **justificatory** adjective **justifier** noun.

ORIGIN – Latin *justificare* 'do justice to'.

jut > verb (**jutted**, **jutting**) extend out, over, or beyond the main body or line of something. > noun a point that sticks out.

SYNONYMS – verb project, protrude, stick out.

ORIGIN – from JET¹.

Jute /jōōt/ > noun a member of a Germanic people that settled in southern Britain in the 5th century.

DERIVATIVES – **Jutish** adjective.

jute /jōōt/ > noun rough fibre made from the stems of a tropical plant, used for making rope or woven into sacking.

ORIGIN – Bengali.

juvenile /**jōō**vənīl/ > adjective **1** relating to young people, birds, or animals. **2** childish. > noun **1** a young person, bird, or animal. **2** Law a person below the age at which ordinary criminal prosecution is possible (18 in most countries).

DERIVATIVES – **juvenility** noun.

COMBINATIONS – **juvenile court** a court for the trial or legal supervision of juveniles.

ORIGIN – Latin *juvenilis*, from *juvenis* 'young, a young person'.

juvenile delinquency > noun the habitual committing of criminal acts by a juvenile.

DERIVATIVES – **juvenile deliquent** noun.

juvenilia /jōōvə**nill**iə/ > plural noun works produced by an author or artist when young.

ORIGIN – Latin, neuter plural of *juvenilis* 'juvenile'.

juxtapose /jukstə**pōz**/ > verb place (two or more things) close together.

DERIVATIVES – **juxtaposition** noun.

ORIGIN – French *juxtaposer*, from Latin *juxta* 'next' + French *poser* 'to place'.

K¹ (also **k**) > *noun* (pl. **Ks** or **K's**) **1** the eleventh letter of the alphabet. **2** denoting the next item after J in a set.

K² > *abbreviation* **1** kelvin(s). **2** Computing kilobyte(s). **3** kilometre(s). **4** (in card games and chess) king. **5** Köchel (catalogue of Mozart's works). **6** informal thousand. [ORIGIN – from **KILO-**.] > *symbol* the chemical element potassium. [ORIGIN – from Latin *kalium*.]

k > *abbreviation* **1** kilo-. **2** used to represent a constant in a formula or equation.

Kabbalah /kəbaalə, kabbələ/ (also **Kabbala, Cabbala, Cabala,** or **Qabalah**) > *noun* the ancient Jewish tradition of mystical interpretation of the Bible.
DERIVATIVES – **Kabbalism** *noun* **Kabbalist** *noun* **Kabbalistic** *adjective*.
ORIGIN – from a Hebrew word meaning 'receive, accept'.

kabob > *noun* US spelling of **KEBAB**.

kabuki /kəbooki/ > *noun* a form of traditional Japanese drama performed by men, with stylised song, mime, and dance.
ORIGIN – Japanese, interpreted originally as a verb meaning 'act dissolutely', later as a combination of 'song', 'dance', and 'art'.

Kaddish /kaddish/ > *noun* **1** an ancient Jewish prayer sequence recited in the synagogue service. **2** a form of this recited for the dead.
ORIGIN – Aramaic, 'holy'.

Kaffir /kaffər/ > *noun* offensive, chiefly S. African a black African.
USAGE – the word **Kaffir** was originally simply a descriptive term for a particular ethnic group; now, however, it is a racially abusive and offensive term, and in South Africa its use is actionable.
ORIGIN – Arabic, 'infidel'.

Kaffir lily > *noun* a South African plant with strap-like leaves and star-shaped flowers.

kaffiyeh > *noun* variant spelling of **KEFFIYEH**.

kafir /kafeer/ > *noun* (among Muslims) a person who is not a Muslim.
ORIGIN – Arabic, 'infidel'; related to **KAFFIR**.

Kafkaesque /kafkəesk/ > *adjective* relating to the Czech novelist Franz Kafka (1883–1924) or his nightmarish fictional world.

kaftan /kaftan/ (also **caftan**) > *noun* **1** a man's long belted tunic, worn in the Near East. **2** a woman's long, loose dress. **3** a loose shirt or top.
ORIGIN – Persian, influenced by French *cafetan*.

kagoul > *noun* variant spelling of **CAGOULE**.

kai /kī/ > *noun* NZ informal food.
ORIGIN – Maori.

kaiser /kīzər/ > *noun* historical the German Emperor, the Emperor of Austria, or the head of the Holy Roman Empire.
ORIGIN – German, from Latin *Caesar*.

kaizen /kīzen/ > *noun* a Japanese business philosophy of continuous improvement.
ORIGIN – Japanese, 'improvement'.

kaka /kaakaa/ > *noun* a large New Zealand parrot having olive-brown and green plumage with reddish underparts.
ORIGIN – Maori.

kakapo /kaakəpō/ > *noun* (pl. **kakapos**) a flightless New Zealand parrot with greenish plumage.
ORIGIN – Maori.

Kalashnikov /kəlashnikof/ > *noun* a type of rifle or sub-machine gun made in Russia.
ORIGIN – named after the Russian designer Mikhail T. *Kalashnikov* (born 1919).

kale /kayl/ > *noun* a variety of hardy cabbage producing erect stems with large leaves and no compact head.
ORIGIN – northern English form of **COLE**.

kaleidoscope /kəlīdəskōp/ > *noun* **1** a toy consisting of a tube containing mirrors and pieces of coloured glass or paper, whose reflections produce changing patterns when the tube is rotated. **2** a constantly changing pattern or sequence.
DERIVATIVES – **kaleidoscopic** *adjective*.
ORIGIN – from Greek *kalos* 'beautiful' + *eidos* 'form' + **-SCOPE**.

kalends > *plural noun* variant spelling of **CALENDS**.

Kama Sutra /kaamə sootrə/ > *noun* an ancient Sanskrit text on the art of love and sexual technique.
ORIGIN – Sanskrit, 'love thread'.

kameez /kəmeez/ > *noun* (pl. same or **kameezes**) a long tunic worn by people from the Indian subcontinent.
ORIGIN – Arabic, perhaps from Latin *camisia* 'chemise, shirt'.

kamikaze /kammikaazi/ > *noun* (in the Second World War) a Japanese warplane making a deliberate suicidal crash on an enemy target. > *adjective* reckless or potentially self-destructive.
ORIGIN – Japanese, 'divine wind', originally referring to the gale that, in Japanese tradition, destroyed the fleet of invading Mongols in 1281.

kampong /kampong/ > *noun* a Malaysian enclosure or village.
ORIGIN – Malay; related to **COMPOUND²**.

Kampuchean /kampoocheeən/ > *noun* & *adjective* another term for **CAMBODIAN**.

kangaroo > *noun* a large Australian marsupial with a long, powerful tail and strongly developed hindlimbs that enable it to travel by leaping.
WORDFINDER – buck (*male kangaroo*), doe (*female kangaroo*), joey (*young kangaroo*); macropod (*kangaroo or wallaby*), marsupium (*kangaroo's pouch*).
COMBINATIONS – **kangaroo court** an unofficial court formed by a group of people to settle disputes among themselves. **kangaroo paw** an Australian plant with strap-like leaves and tubular flowers with woolly outer surfaces. **kangaroo rat** a North American hopping rodent with large cheek pouches and long hind legs.

wordpower facts

Kangaroo

Kangaroo is first recorded as an English word in 1770, in the journals of Captain James Cook and the botanist Joseph Banks, who encountered the animal on their expedition to Australia. They believed it to be the name used by the Aborigines living along the Endeavour River, Queensland; later writers cast doubt on the word, as they found no evidence for it, but it is now thought to be based on *gangurru*, a word in the extinct Aboriginal language Guugu Yimidhirr for a particular type of large kangaroo, believed to have been the type first seen by the English explorers. The appealing theory that **kangaroo** really means 'I don't understand' (the supposed reply of an Aborigine to his questioner) seems to be of recent origin and lacks confirmation.

kaolin /kayəlin/ > *noun* a fine, soft white clay, used for making china and in medicine as an absorbent substance.
DERIVATIVES – **kaolinise** (also **kaolinize**) *verb*.
ORIGIN – French, from the Chinese name of a mountain in Jiangxi province where the clay is found.

kapellmeister /kəpelmīstər/ > *noun* (in German-speaking countries) the leader or conductor of an orchestra or choir.
ORIGIN – German, from *Kapelle* 'court orchestra' + *Meister* 'master'.

kapok /kaypok/ > *noun* a fine fibrous substance which grows around the seeds of a tropical tree, used as stuffing for cushions, soft toys, etc.

ORIGIN – Malay.

Kaposi's sarcoma /kəpōsiz/ > *noun* a form of cancer involving multiple tumours of the lymph nodes or skin, occurring chiefly as a result of Aids.

ORIGIN – named after the Hungarian dermatologist M. K. *Kaposi* (1837–1902).

kappa /kappə/ > *noun* the tenth letter of the Greek alphabet (Κ, κ), transliterated as 'k'.

ORIGIN – Greek.

kaput /kəpoŏt/ > *adjective* informal broken and useless.

ORIGIN – German *kaputt*, from French *être capot* 'be without tricks in a card game'.

karabiner /karrəbeenər/ (also **carabiner**) > *noun* a coupling link with a safety closure, used by rock climbers.

ORIGIN – from German *Karabiner-haken* 'spring hook'.

karakul /karrəkoŏl/ (also **caracul**) > *noun* **1** a breed of Asian sheep having a dark curled fleece when young. **2** cloth or fur made from or resembling this fleece.

ORIGIN – Russian.

karaoke /karriōki/ > *noun* a form of entertainment in which people sing popular songs over pre-recorded backing tracks.

ORIGIN – Japanese, 'empty orchestra'.

karat > *noun* US spelling of **CARAT** (in sense 2).

karate /kəraati/ > *noun* an oriental system of unarmed combat using the hands and feet to deliver and block blows.

ORIGIN – Japanese, 'empty hand'.

karma /kaarmə/ > *noun* (in Hinduism and Buddhism) the sum of a person's actions in this and previous states of existence, viewed as affecting their future fate.

DERIVATIVES – **karmic** *adjective*.

ORIGIN – Sanskrit, 'action, effect, fate'.

karri /karri/ > *noun* (pl. **karris**) a tall Australian eucalyptus with hard red wood.

ORIGIN – Nyungar (an Aboriginal language).

karst /kaarst/ > *noun* Geology landscape underlain by limestone which has been eroded by dissolution, producing towers, fissures, sinkholes, etc.

ORIGIN – from the name of a limestone region in Slovenia.

kart > *noun* a small unsprung motor-racing vehicle with a tubular frame and a rear-mounted engine.

DERIVATIVES – **karting** *noun*.

ORIGIN – shortening of **GO-KART**.

kasbah /kazbaa/ (also **casbah**) > *noun* **1** a North African citadel. **2** the area of old, narrow streets surrounding a citadel.

ORIGIN – Arabic.

katharevousa /kathərevoŏsə/ > *noun* a

form of modern Greek used in traditional literary writing. Compare with **DEMOTIC**.

ORIGIN – modern Greek, 'purified'.

katydid /kaytidid/ > *noun* a large bush cricket native to North America, the male of which makes a characteristic sound which resembles the name.

kauri /kowri/ > *noun* (pl. **kauris**) a tall coniferous forest tree native to New Zealand, producing valuable wood and resin.

ORIGIN – Maori.

kava /kaavə/ > *noun* a narcotic drink made in Polynesia from the crushed roots of a plant of the pepper family.

ORIGIN – Tongan.

kayak /kīak/ > *noun* a canoe of a type used originally by the Inuit, made of a light frame with a watertight covering. > *verb* (**kayaked**, **kayaking**) travel in a kayak.

ORIGIN – Inuit.

kayo /kayō/ informal > *noun* (pl. **kayos**) a knockout. > *verb* (**kayoes**, **kayoed**) knock (someone) out.

ORIGIN – representing the pronunciation of *KO*.

Kazakh /kəzak/ > *noun* a member of a traditionally nomadic people living chiefly in the central Asian republic of Kazakhstan.

ORIGIN – Turkic, related to **COSSACK**.

kazillion /kəzilyən/ > *cardinal number* another term for **GAZILLION**.

kazoo /kəzoŏ/ > *noun* a simple musical instrument consisting of a pipe with a hole in it, producing a buzzing sound when the player hums into it.

KB (also **Kb**) > *abbreviation* kilobyte(s).

KBE > *abbreviation* (in the UK) Knight Commander of the Order of the British Empire.

KC > *abbreviation* King's Counsel.

kcal > *abbreviation* kilocalorie(s).

KCB > *abbreviation* (in the UK) Knight Commander of the Order of the Bath.

KCMG > *abbreviation* (in the UK) Knight Commander of the Order of St Michael and St George.

KCVO > *abbreviation* (in the UK) Knight Commander of the Royal Victorian Order.

kea /keeə/ > *noun* a New Zealand mountain parrot with a long, narrow bill and mainly olive-green plumage.

ORIGIN – Maori.

kebab /kibab/ (N. Amer. also **kabob**) > *noun* a dish of pieces of meat, fish, or vegetables roasted or grilled on a skewer or spit.

ORIGIN – Arabic.

ked > *noun* a wingless bloodsucking insect that is a parasite of sheep.

kedge /kej/ > *verb* move (a boat) by hauling in a hawser attached at a distance to an

anchor. > *noun* a small anchor used for such a purpose.

kedgeree /kejəree/ > *noun* **1** an Indian dish containing rice, split pulses, onions, and eggs. **2** a European dish containing smoked fish, rice, and hard-boiled eggs.

ORIGIN – Hindi.

keel > *noun* a lengthwise structure along the base of a ship, in some vessels extended downwards as a ridge to increase stability. > *verb* (**keel over**) **1** (of a boat or ship) turn over on its side; capsize. **2** informal fall over; collapse.

COMBINATIONS – **keelboat 1** a yacht built with a permanent keel rather than a centreboard. **2** a large, flat freight boat used on American rivers. **keelhaul 1** historical punish (someone) by dragging them through the water from one side of a boat to the other, under the keel. **2** humorous punish or reprimand severely.

ORIGIN – Old Norse *kjǫlr*.

keelson /keels'n/ (also **kelson** /kels'n/) > *noun* a structure running the length of a ship, that fastens the timbers or plates of the floor to the keel.

ORIGIN – from Low German *kiel* 'keel' + *swīn* 'swine' (used as the name of a timber).

keen[1] > *adjective* **1** having or showing eagerness and enthusiasm. **2** (**keen on**) interested in or attracted by. **3** (of a blade) sharp. **4** mentally acute or quick. **5** Brit. (of prices) very low; competitive.

DERIVATIVES – **keenly** *adverb* **keenness** *noun*.

SYNONYMS – **1** ardent, assiduous, avid, eager, enthusiastic.

ANTONYMS – **1** indifferent, reluctant.

ORIGIN – Old English, 'wise, clever', also 'brave, daring'.

keen[2] > *verb* **1** wail in grief for a dead person. **2** make an eerie wailing sound. > *noun* an Irish funeral song accompanied with wailing in lamentation for the dead.

SYNONYMS – *verb* **1** moan, weep, wail.

ORIGIN – Irish *caoinim* 'I wail'.

keep > *verb* (past and past participle **kept**) **1** have or retain possession of. **2** retain or reserve for use in the future. **3** put or store in a regular place. **4** (of a perishable commodity) remain in good condition. **5** continue in a specified condition, position, or activity: *she kept quiet about it.* **6** provide accommodation and food for; support. **7** delay or detain; cause to be late. **8** honour, fulfil, or observe (a commitment or undertaking). **9** record or regularly maintain (a note or diary). **10** (**kept**) supported financially in return for sexual favours. > *noun* **1** food, clothes, and other essentials for living. **2** the strongest or central tower of a castle. **3** archaic charge; control.

IDIOMS – **for keeps** informal permanently; indefinitely. **keep from 1** cause to stay out of. **2** cause (something) to remain a secret from. **3** avoid doing something. **4** guard or protect (someone) from. **keep on 1** continue to do something. **2** continue to use or employ. **keep to 1** avoid leaving (a path, road, or place). **2** adhere to (a schedule). **3** observe (a promise). **4** confine or restrict oneself to. **keep up 1** move or progress at the same rate as someone or something else. **2** continue (a course of action). **keep up with 1** learn about or be aware of (current events or developments). **2** continue to be in contact with (someone). **keep up with the Joneses** strive not to be outdone by one's neighbours or peers.

SYNONYMS – *verb* **1** hold on to, retain. **2** keep in reserve, reserve, save, save up, store up.

COMBINATIONS – **keep-fit** chiefly Brit. regular exercises to improve personal fitness and health. **keepnet** a fishing net secured in the water and used to keep alive fish that have been caught.

keeper > *noun* **1** a person who manages or looks after something or someone. **2** a goalkeeper or wicketkeeper. **3** an object which protects or secures another. **4** a bar of soft iron placed across the poles of a horseshoe magnet to maintain its strength.

SYNONYMS – **1** curator, guardian, steward, superintendent.

keeping > *noun* the action of keeping something.

IDIOMS – **in** (or **out of**) **keeping with** in (or out of) harmony or conformity with.

keepsake > *noun* a small item kept in memory of the person who gave or originally owned it.

kef > *noun & adjective* variant spelling of **KIF**.

keffiyeh /keˈfeeyə/ (also **kaffiyeh**) > *noun* a Bedouin Arab's headdress.

ORIGIN – Arabic.

keg > *noun* **1** a small barrel, especially one of less than 10 gallons or (in the US) 30 gallons. **2** (before another noun) Brit. (of beer) supplied in a keg, to which carbon dioxide has been added.

ORIGIN – variant of Scots and US dialect *cag*.

keister /ˈkeestər/ > *noun* N. Amer. informal **1** a person's buttocks. **2** dated a suitcase, bag, or box for carrying possessions or merchandise.

kelim > *noun* variant spelling of **KILIM**.

keloid /ˈkeeloyd/ > *noun* Medicine an area of irregular fibrous tissue formed at the site of a scar or injury.

ORIGIN – from Greek *khēlē* 'crab's claw'.

kelp > *noun* **1** a brown seaweed having very long, broad fronds. **2** the ashes of seaweed used as a source of minerals.

kelpie /ˈkelpi/ > *noun* **1** a water spirit of Scottish folklore, typically appearing as a horse. **2** an Australian breed of sheepdog originally bred from a Scottish collie.

ORIGIN – perhaps from Scottish Gaelic *cailpeach, colpach* 'bullock, colt'.

kelson > *noun* variant spelling of **KEELSON**.

kelt > *noun* a salmon or sea trout after spawning and before returning to the sea.

kelvin > *noun* the unit of temperature in the SI system, equivalent to a degree Celsius.

COMBINATIONS – **Kelvin scale** the scale of temperature with absolute zero as zero and the freezing point of water as 273.15 kelvins.

ORIGIN – named after the British physicist William T. *Kelvin* (1824–1907).

kempt > *adjective* in a neat and clean condition.

ORIGIN – from Old English *cemban* 'to comb'.

ken > *noun* (**one's ken**) one's range of knowledge or sight. > *verb* (**kenning**; past and past participle **kenned** or **kent**) Scottish & N. English **1** know. **2** recognise; identify.

kendo /ˈkendō/ > *noun* a Japanese form of fencing with two-handed bamboo swords.

ORIGIN – Japanese, 'sword way'.

kennel > *noun* **1** a small shelter for a dog. **2** (**kennels**) (treated as sing. or pl.) a boarding or breeding establishment for dogs. > *verb* (**kennelled, kennelling**; US **kenneled, kenneling**) put or keep (a dog) in a kennel or kennels.

ORIGIN – Old French *chenil*, from Latin *canis* 'dog'.

kenning > *noun* a compound expression in Old English and Old Norse poetry with metaphorical meaning, e.g. *oar-steed* 'ship'.

ORIGIN – Old Norse, from *kenna* 'know, perceive'; related to **KEN**.

kent past and past participle of **KEN**.

Kenyan /ˈkenyən, ˈkeenyən/ > *noun* a person from Kenya. > *adjective* relating to Kenya.

kepi /ˈkeppi/ > *noun* (pl. **kepis**) a French military cap with a horizontal peak.

ORIGIN – French, from Swiss German *Käppi* 'little cap'.

kept past and past participle of **KEEP**.

keratin /ˈkerrətin/ > *noun* a fibrous protein forming the main constituent of hair, feathers, hoofs, claws, and horns.

ORIGIN – from Greek *keras* 'horn'.

keratitis /kerrəˈtītiss/ > *noun* Medicine inflammation of the cornea of the eye.

keratotomy /kerrəˈtottəmi/ > *noun* a surgical operation involving cutting into the cornea of the eye, in particular one (**radial keratotomy**) performed to correct myopia.

kerb (US **curb**) > *noun* a stone edging to a pavement or raised path.

COMBINATIONS – **kerb-crawling** Brit. the action of driving slowly along the edge of the road in search of a prostitute or to harass female pedestrians. **kerb drill** Brit. a set of precautions taken before crossing the road, as taught to children. **kerbstone** a long, narrow stone or concrete block, laid end to end with others to form a kerb. **kerb weight** the weight of a motor car without occupants or baggage.

ORIGIN – variant of **CURB**.

kerbing > *noun* **1** the stones of a kerb. **2** the action of hitting a kerb with a car tyre.

kerchief /ˈkercheef/ > *noun* **1** a piece of fabric used to cover the head. **2** a handkerchief.

ORIGIN – Old French *cuevrechief*, from *couvrir* 'to cover' + *chief* 'head'.

kerf /kerf/ > *noun* **1** a slit made by cutting with a saw. **2** the cut end of a felled tree.

ORIGIN – Old English, related to **CARVE**.

kerfuffle /kəˈfuff'l/ > *noun* informal, chiefly Brit. a commotion or fuss.

ORIGIN – perhaps from Scots *curfuffle* (from *fuffle* 'to disorder'), or related to Irish *cior thual* 'confusion, disorder'.

kermes /ˈkermeez/ > *noun* a red dye made from the dried bodies of insects which cause galls on the kermes oak.

COMBINATIONS – **kermes oak** a very small evergreen Mediterranean oak with prickly, holly-like leaves.

ORIGIN – Arabic: see box at **VERMILION**.

kern[1] Printing > *noun* a part of a metal type projecting beyond the body or shank, or a part of a printed character that overlaps its neighbours. > *verb* **1** provide (metal type or a printed character) with a kern. **2** adjust the spacing between (characters).

ORIGIN – perhaps from French *carne* 'corner'.

kern[2] > *noun* **1** historical a light-armed Irish foot soldier. **2** archaic a peasant; a rustic.

ORIGIN – from Old Irish *ceithern* 'band of foot soldiers'.

kernel* /ˈkern'l/ > *noun* **1** a softer part of a nut, seed, or fruit stone contained within its hard shell. **2** the seed and hard husk of a cereal, especially wheat. **3** the central or most important part of something.

*SPELLING – *-el*, not *-al*: kernel.

SYNONYMS – **3** core, essence, heart.

ORIGIN – Old English, 'small corn'.

kerosene /ˈkerrəseen/ (also **kerosine**) > *noun* a light fuel oil obtained by distilling petroleum, used especially in jet engines and domestic heating boilers; paraffin oil.

ORIGIN – from Greek *kēros* 'wax'.

kerria /ˈkerriə/ > *noun* an Asian shrub cultivated for its yellow flowers.

ORIGIN – named after the English botanical collector William *Ker(r)* (died 1814).

kersey /ˈkerzi/ > *noun* a kind of coarse, ribbed woollen cloth with a short nap.

ORIGIN – probably from *Kersey*, a town in Suffolk where woollen cloth was made.

kestrel > *noun* a small falcon that hunts by hovering with rapidly beating wings.
ORIGIN – from Old French *crecerelle*.

ketamine /**kee**təmeen/ > *noun* a synthetic compound used as an anaesthetic and pain-killing drug and also illicitly as a hallucinogen.
ORIGIN – blend of **KETONE** and **AMINE**.

ketch > *noun* a two-masted sailing boat with a mizzenmast stepped forward of the rudder and smaller than its foremast.
ORIGIN – probably from **CATCH**.

ketchup (US also **catsup**) > *noun* a spicy sauce made from tomatoes and vinegar.
ORIGIN – perhaps from a Chinese word meaning 'tomato juice'.

ketone /**kee**tōn/ > *noun* Chemistry an organic compound containing the group =C=O bonded to two alkyl groups, e.g. acetone.
ORIGIN – from German *Aketon* 'acetone'.

kettle > *noun* a metal or plastic container with a lid, spout, and handle, used for boiling water.
IDIOMS – **a different kettle of fish** informal something altogether different from the one just mentioned. **the pot calling the kettle black** used to convey that the criticisms a person is aiming at someone could equally well apply to themselves. **a pretty** (or **fine**) **kettle of fish** informal an awkward state of affairs.
ORIGIN – Latin *catillus* 'little pot'.

kettledrum > *noun* a large drum shaped like a bowl, with adjustable pitch.

kewpie /**kyoo**pi/ > *noun* (trademark in the US) a type of doll with a large head, big eyes, chubby cheeks, and a curl or topknot on top of its head.
ORIGIN – from **CUPID**.

key¹ > *noun* (pl. **keys**) **1** a small piece of shaped metal which is inserted into a lock and rotated to open or close it. **2** an instrument for grasping and turning a screw, peg, or nut. **3** a lever depressed by the finger in playing an instrument such as the organ, piano, or flute. **4** each of several buttons on a panel for operating a typewriter or computer terminal. **5** a lever operating a mechanical device for making or breaking an electric circuit. **6** a thing that provides access to or understanding of something: *a key to success*. **7** an explanatory list of symbols used in a map or table. **8** a word or system for solving a cipher or code. **9** Music a group of notes based on a particular note and comprising a scale. **10** roughness on a surface, provided to assist adhesion of plaster or other material. **11** the dry winged fruit of an ash, maple, or sycamore. > *adjective* of crucial importance: *a key figure*. > *verb* (**keys**, **keyed**) **1** enter or operate on (data) by means of a computer keyboard. **2** (**be keyed up**) be nervous,

tense, or excited. **3** (**key into** or **in with**) be connected or in harmony with.
DERIVATIVES – **keyed** adjective.
SYNONYMS – *adjective* critical, crucial, decisive, vital.
COMBINATIONS – **key grip** the person in a film crew who is in charge of the camera equipment. **keypad** a miniature keyboard or set of buttons for operating a portable electronic device or telephone. **keypunch** a device for transferring data by means of punched holes or notches on a series of cards or paper tape. **key ring** a metal ring for holding keys together in a bunch. **key signature** Music a combination of sharps or flats after the clef at the beginning of each stave, indicating the key of a composition. **keystroke** a single depression of a key on a keyboard.

key² > *noun* a low-lying island or reef, especially in the Caribbean.
ORIGIN – Spanish *cayo* 'reef'.

keyboard > *noun* **1** a panel of keys for use with a computer or typewriter. **2** a set of keys on a piano or similar musical instrument. **3** an electronic instrument with keys arranged as on a piano. > *verb* enter (data) by means of a keyboard.
DERIVATIVES – **keyboarder** noun.

keyhole > *noun* a hole in a lock into which the key is inserted.
COMBINATIONS – **keyhole surgery** surgery carried out through a very small incision.

Keynesian /**kayn**ziən/ > *adjective* relating to the theories of the English economist John Maynard Keynes (1883–1946), who advocated government spending on public works to stimulate the economy and provide employment.
DERIVATIVES – **Keynesianism** noun.

keynote > *noun* **1** Music the note on which a key is based. **2** a prevailing tone or central theme. **3** (before another noun) setting out the central theme of a conference: *a keynote speech*.

keystone > *noun* **1** a central stone in an arch, locking the arch together. **2** the central principle or part of a policy or system.

keyword > *noun* **1** a word which acts as the key to a cipher or code. **2** a word or concept of great significance. **3** a significant word mentioned in an index. **4** a word used in an information-retrieval system to indicate the content of a document.

KG > *abbreviation* (in the UK) Knight of the Order of the Garter.

kg > *abbreviation* kilogram(s).

khaki /**kaa**ki/ > *noun* (pl. **khakis**) **1** a cotton or wool fabric of a dull brownish-yellow colour, used especially in military clothing. **2** a dull brownish-yellow colour.
ORIGIN – Urdu, 'dust-coloured'.

Khalsa /**kul**sə/ > *noun* the company of fully

initiated Sikhs to which devout orthodox Sikhs are ritually admitted at puberty.
ORIGIN – from an Arabic word meaning 'pure, belonging to'.

khamsin /**kam**sin/ > *noun* an oppressive, hot southerly or south-easterly wind blowing in Egypt in spring.
ORIGIN – from an Arabic word meaning 'fifty' (the approximate duration in days).

khan /kaan/ > *noun* a title given to rulers and officials in central Asia, Afghanistan, and certain other Muslim countries.
DERIVATIVES – **khanate** noun.
ORIGIN – Turkic, 'lord, prince': originally denoting any of the successors of Genghis Khan.

khat /kaat/ > *noun* the leaves of an Arabian shrub, which are chewed (or drunk as an infusion) as a stimulant.
ORIGIN – Arabic.

khazi /**kaa**zi/ > *noun* (pl. **khazies**) Brit. informal a toilet.
ORIGIN – from Italian *casa* 'house'.

Khmer /kmair/ > *noun* **1** a native of the ancient kingdom of Khmer in SE Asia. **2** a person from Cambodia. **3** the language of the Khmers, the official language of Cambodia.

Khoikhoi /**koy**koy/ (also **Khoi**) > *noun* (pl. same) a member of a group of indigenous peoples of South Africa and Namibia, including the Nama.
USAGE – **Khoikhoi** or **Nama** are the standard accepted terms in this context. The older word **Hottentot** is obsolete, and may now cause offence.
ORIGIN – Nama (a Khoikhoi language), 'men of men'.

khoum /kōōm/ > *noun* a monetary unit of Mauritania, one fifth of an ouguiya.
ORIGIN – Arabic, 'one fifth'.

kHz > *abbreviation* kilohertz.

kia ora /kiə **awr**ə/ > *exclamation* (in New Zealand) a greeting wishing good health.
ORIGIN – Maori.

kibble > *verb* grind or chop (beans, grain, etc.) coarsely. > *noun* N. Amer. ground meal shaped into pellets, especially for pet food.

kibbutz /ki**bōōts**/ > *noun* (pl. **kibbutzim** /ki**bōōt**sim/) a communal farming settlement in Israel.
ORIGIN – modern Hebrew, 'gathering'.

kibbutznik > *noun* a member of a kibbutz.

kibitz /**kibb**its/ > *verb* N. Amer. informal **1** look on and offer unwelcome advice, especially at a card game. **2** speak informally; chat.
DERIVATIVES – **kibitzer** noun.
ORIGIN – Yiddish.

kibosh /**kī**bosh/ (also **kybosh**) > *noun* (in phrase **put the kibosh on**) informal put a decisive end to.

kick > *verb* **1** strike or propel forcibly with the foot. **2** strike out with the foot or feet. **3** informal succeed in giving up (a habit or addiction). **4** (of a gun) recoil when fired. > *noun* **1** an instance of kicking. **2** informal a sharp stimulant effect. **3** informal a thrill of pleasurable excitement.

IDIOMS – **kick against** express disagreement or frustration with (an institution or restriction). **kick around** (or **about**) **1** lie unwanted or unexploited. **2** treat (someone) roughly or without respect. **3** discuss (an idea) casually or experimentally. **kick the bucket** informal die. **kick in** become activated; come into effect. **a kick in the teeth** informal a grave setback or disappointment. **kick off** (of a football match) be started or resumed by a player kicking the ball from the centre spot. **kick oneself** be annoyed with oneself. **kick out** informal expel or dismiss. **kick upstairs** informal remove (someone) from an influential position by giving them an ostensible promotion.

DERIVATIVES – **kicker** *noun.*

COMBINATIONS – **kick-ass** N. Amer. informal forceful and aggressive. **kickback 1** a sudden forceful recoil. **2** informal an illicit payment made to someone who has facilitated a transaction or appointment. **kick-boxing** a martial art combining boxing with elements of karate, in particular kicking with bare feet. **kick-down** Brit. a device for changing gear in a motor vehicle with automatic transmission by full depression of the accelerator. **kick drum** informal a bass drum played using a pedal. **kick-off** the start or resumption of a football match, in which a player kicks the ball from the centre spot. **kick-pleat** an inverted pleat in a narrow skirt to allow freedom of movement. **kickstand** a metal rod attached to a bicycle or motorcycle that may be kicked into a vertical position to support the vehicle when it is stationary.

kicking > *adjective* informal (especially of music) lively and exciting.

kickshaw > *noun* **1** archaic a fancy but insubstantial cooked dish. **2** chiefly N. Amer. an elegant but insubstantial trinket.

ORIGIN – from French *quelque chose* 'something'.

kick-start > *verb* **1** start (an engine on a motorcycle) with a downward thrust of a pedal. **2** provide an impetus to start or restart (a process). > *noun* **1** an act of kick-starting. **2** a device to kick-start an engine.

kid[1] > *noun* **1** a young goat. **2** informal a child or young person. > *verb* (**kidded, kidding**) (of a goat) give birth.

IDIOMS – **handle** (or **treat**) **with kid gloves** deal with very carefully. **kids' stuff** informal something very easy to do.

COMBINATIONS – **kid brother** (or **kid sister**) informal a younger brother or sister.

ORIGIN – Old Norse *kith.*

kid[2] > *verb* (**kidded, kidding**) informal **1**

deceive (someone) playfully; tease. **2** fool into believing something.

ORIGIN – perhaps from **KID**[1], expressing the notion 'make a child or goat of'.

kiddie (also **kiddy**) > *noun* (pl. **kiddies**) informal a young child.

kiddiewink > *noun* Brit. humorous a small child.

kidnap > *verb* (**kidnapped, kidnapping**; US also **kidnaped, kidnaping**) abduct and hold (someone) captive, typically to obtain a ransom. > *noun* an act of kidnapping.

DERIVATIVES – **kidnapper** *noun.*

ORIGIN – from **KID**[1] + slang *nap* 'nab, seize'.

kidney > *noun* (pl. **kidneys**) **1** each of a pair of organs in the abdominal cavity, with one concave and one convex side, that purify the blood and excrete urine. **2** the kidney of a sheep, ox, or pig as food. **3** archaic nature or temperament.

WORDFINDER – dialysis, haemodialysis (*artificial purification of the blood*), nephritis (*inflammation of a kidney*), nephrosis (*kidney disease*), renal (*relating to the kidneys*).

COMBINATIONS – **kidney bean** a kidney-shaped bean, especially a dark red one from a dwarf French bean plant. **kidney dish** a kidney-shaped receptacle used in medicine. **kidney machine** an artificial kidney or dialysis machine. **kidney stone** a hard crystalline mass formed in the kidneys.

kidology /kiˈdollaji/ > *noun* Brit. informal deliberate deception or teasing.

kieselguhr /ˈkeezˈlgoor/ > *noun* a soft, crumbly sedimentary material, used as a filter, filler, and insulator.

ORIGIN – German, from *Kiesel* 'gravel' + *Guhr* 'yeast'.

kif /kif/ (also **kef** /kef/) > *noun* a substance, especially cannabis, smoked to produce a drowsy state.

ORIGIN – Arabic, 'enjoyment, well-being'.

Kikuyu /kiˈkooyoo/ > *noun* (pl. same or **Kikuyus**) a member of a people forming the largest ethnic group in Kenya.

COMBINATIONS – **kikuyu grass** a creeping grass which is native to Kenya and cultivated elsewhere as a lawn and fodder grass.

ORIGIN – the name in Kikuyu.

kilim /kiˈleem/ (also **kelim**) > *noun* a carpet or rug woven without a pile, made in Turkey, Kurdistan, and neighbouring areas.

ORIGIN – Persian.

kill > *verb* **1** cause the death of. **2** put an end to. **3** informal overwhelm with an emotion. **4** informal cause pain or anguish to. **5** pass (time). **6** stop (a computing process). **7** (in sport) make (the ball) stop. > *noun* **1** an act of killing, especially of one animal by another. **2** an animal or animals killed by a hunter or another animal. **3** informal an act of destroying an enemy aircraft or vessel.

WORDFINDER – euthanasia (*mercy killing*), manslaughter (*unintentional killing*); deicide (*killing of a god*), filicide (*killing of a son or daughter*), fratricide (*of a brother or sister*), genocide (*of a whole people*), homicide (*of another person, murder*), infanticide (*of a child*), matricide (*of one's mother*), parricide (*of a close relative*), patricide (*of one's father*), regicide (*of a king*), suicide (*of oneself*), uxoricide (*of one's wife*).

IDIOMS – **kill two birds with one stone** proverb achieve two aims at once. **kill with kindness** spoil (someone) by overindulging them.

killdeer /ˈkildeer/ > *noun* an American plover with a plaintive call that resembles its name.

killer > *noun* **1** a person or thing that kills. **2** informal a formidable person or thing. **3** informal a hilarious joke.

SYNONYMS – **1** assassin, butcher, murderer.

COMBINATIONS – **killer cell** a white blood cell which destroys infected or cancerous cells. **killer instinct** a ruthless determination to succeed or win. **killer whale** a black-and-white toothed whale with a prominent dorsal fin.

killifish > *noun* a small, brightly coloured fish of fresh or brackish water.

killing > *noun* an act of causing death. > *adjective* informal overwhelming or unbearable.

IDIOMS – **make a killing** have a great financial success.

COMBINATIONS – **killing bottle** a bottle containing poisonous vapour to kill insects collected as specimens. **killing field** a place where many people have been killed.

killjoy > *noun* a person who spoils the enjoyment of others through resentful or overly sober behaviour.

kiln > *noun* a furnace or oven for burning, baking, or drying, especially one for firing pottery.

ORIGIN – Latin *culina* 'kitchen, cooking stove'.

Kilner jar /ˈkilnər/ > *noun* trademark a glass jar with a lid which forms an airtight seal, used to bottle fruit and vegetables.

ORIGIN – from the maker's name.

kilo /ˈkeelō/ > *noun* (pl. **kilos**) a kilogram.

kilo- /ˈkeelō, ˈkillō/ > *combining form* denoting a factor of one thousand (10^3): *kilolitre.*

ORIGIN – from Greek *khilioi* 'thousand'.

kilobyte > *noun* Computing a unit of memory or data equal to 1,024 bytes.

kilocalorie > *noun* a unit of energy of one thousand calories (equal to one large calorie).

kilogram (also **kilogramme**) > *noun* the unit of mass in the SI system, equal to 1,000 grams (approximately 2.205 lb).

kilohertz > *noun* a measure of frequency equivalent to 1,000 cycles per second.

kilojoule > *noun* 1,000 joules, especially as a measure of the energy value of foods.

kilolitre (US **kiloliter**) > *noun* 1,000 litres (equivalent to 220 imperial gallons).

kilometre /**kill**əmeetər, ki**lomm**itər/ (US **kilometer**) > *noun* a metric unit of measurement equal to 1,000 metres (approximately 0.62 miles).

NOTE – the second pronunciation, with the stress on the **-lom-**, is regarded as incorrect by some people.

kiloton (also **kilotonne**) > *noun* a unit of explosive power equivalent to 1,000 tons (or tonnes) of TNT.

kilovolt > *noun* 1,000 volts.

kilowatt > *noun* 1,000 watts.

COMBINATIONS – **kilowatt-hour** a unit of electrical energy equivalent to a power consumption of one thousand watts for one hour.

kilt > *noun* a knee-length skirt of pleated tartan cloth, traditionally worn by men as part of Scottish Highland dress. > *verb* **1** arrange (a garment or material) in vertical pleats. **2** (**kilt up**) hoist or tuck up (one's skirt or coat).

DERIVATIVES – **kilted** *adjective*.

ORIGIN – Scandinavian, originally in the sense 'tuck up around the body'.

kilter > *noun* (in phrase **out of kilter**) out of harmony or balance; awry.

kimberlite /**kim**bərlīt/ > *noun* a rare blue-tinged igneous rock sometimes containing diamonds.

ORIGIN – from *Kimberley*, a South African city and diamond-mining centre.

kimchi /**kim**chhi/ > *noun* spicy pickled cabbage, the national dish of Korea.

ORIGIN – Korean.

kimono /ki**mō**nō/ > *noun* (pl. **kimonos**) a long, loose Japanese robe having wide sleeves and tied with a sash.

ORIGIN – Japanese, 'wearing thing'.

kin > *noun* (treated as pl.) one's family and relations. > *adjective* (of a person) related.

-kin > *suffix* forming diminutive nouns such as *catkin*.

ORIGIN – from Dutch *-kijn*, *-ken*, Low German *-kīn*.

kina¹ /**kee**nə/ > *noun* (pl. same) the basic monetary unit of Papua New Guinea, equal to 100 toea.

ORIGIN – Papuan.

kina² /**kee**nə/ > *noun* (pl. same) an edible sea urchin occurring on New Zealand coasts.

ORIGIN – Maori.

kinaesthesia /kinnəss**thee**ziə/ (US **kin-esthesia**) > *noun* awareness of the position and movement of the parts of the body by means of sensory receptors in the muscles and joints.

DERIVATIVES – **kinaesthetic** *adjective*.

ORIGIN – from Greek *kinein* 'to move' + *aisthēsis* 'sensation'.

kind¹ > *noun* **1** a class or type of people or things having similar characteristics. **2** character; nature. **3** each of the elements (bread and wine) of the Eucharist.

IDIOMS – **in kind 1** in the same way. **2** (of payment) in goods or services as opposed to money. **kind of** informal rather. **of a kind** hardly or only partly deserving the name. **one of a kind** unique. **two** (or **three, four**, etc.) **of a kind 1** the same or very similar. **2** (of cards) having the same face value but of a different suit.

USAGE – when using **kind** to refer to a plural noun, avoid the ungrammatical construction *these kind*: say *these kinds of questions are not relevant* rather than *these kind of questions are not relevant*.

SYNONYMS – **1** category, class, form, type, variety.

wordpower facts

Kind

The two words **kind** are both of Old English origin, and both have had an interesting sense development. The noun **kind** is related to **kin** and originally meant 'nature, the natural order', also 'innate character, form, or condition', hence 'a class or race distinguished by innate characteristics'. **Kind** as an adjective first meant 'natural, native'; in the Middle Ages the earliest sense was 'well born or well bred', from which came 'well disposed by nature, courteous, gentle, benevolent'.

kind² > *adjective* **1** considerate and generous. **2** archaic affectionate; loving.

SYNONYMS – **1** benevolent, caring, considerate, generous, warm-hearted.

ANTONYMS – cruel.

kindergarten /**kin**dərgaart'n/ > *noun* a nursery school.

ORIGIN – German, 'children's garden'.

kindle¹ /**kin**d'l/ > *verb* **1** light (a flame); set on fire. **2** arouse (an emotion).

SYNONYMS – **1** ignite, light, set light to, spark. **2** arouse, awaken, inspire, stimulate.

ORIGIN – from Old Norse *kindill* 'candle, torch'.

kindle² /**kin**d'l/ > *verb* (of a hare or rabbit) give birth.

ORIGIN – probably from **KIND¹**.

kindling /**kind**ling/ > *noun* small sticks or twigs used for lighting fires.

kindly > *adverb* **1** in a kind manner. **2** please (used in a polite request). > *adjective* (**kindlier, kindliest**) kind; warm-hearted.

IDIOMS – **not take kindly to** not welcome or be pleased by. **take kindly** like or be pleased by.

DERIVATIVES – **kindliness** *noun*.

kindness > *noun* **1** the quality of being kind. **2** a kind act.

SYNONYMS – **1** benevolence, generosity, tenderness, warm-heartedness.

ANTONYMS – **1** cruelty.

kindred /**kin**drid/ > *noun* **1** (treated as pl.) one's family and relations. **2** relationship by blood. > *adjective* similar in kind.

SYNONYMS – *adjective* alike, allied, related, similar.

COMBINATIONS – **kindred spirit** a person whose interests or attitudes are similar to one's own.

kine /kīn/ > *plural noun* archaic cows collectively.

kinematics /kinni**matt**iks, kīni-/ > *plural noun* (treated as sing.) the branch of mechanics concerned with the motion of objects without reference to the forces which cause the motion.

DERIVATIVES – **kinematic** *adjective*.

ORIGIN – from Greek *kinēma* 'motion'.

kinesiology /kineesi**oll**əji/ > *noun* the study of the mechanics of body movements.

kinesis /ki**nee**siss, kī**nee**siss/ > *noun* (pl. **kineses**) technical movement; motion.

ORIGIN – Greek.

kinetic /ki**nett**ik, kī-/ > *adjective* **1** relating to or resulting from motion. **2** (of a work of art) depending on movement for its effect.

DERIVATIVES – **kinetically** *adverb*.

COMBINATIONS – **kinetic energy** Physics energy which a body possesses by virtue of being in motion. **kinetic theory** the theory which explains the physical properties of matter in terms of the motions of atoms and molecules.

kinetics > *plural noun* (treated as sing.) **1** the branch of chemistry concerned with the rates of chemical reactions. **2** Physics another term for **DYNAMICS** (in sense 1).

kinetoscope /ki**nee**təskōp, kī-/ > *noun* an early motion-picture device in which the images were viewed through a peephole.

kinfolk > *plural noun* variant form of **KINSFOLK**.

king > *noun* **1** the male ruler of an independent state, especially one who inherits the position by birth. **2** the best or most important person or thing in a sphere or group. **3** a playing card bearing a representation of a king, ranking next below an ace. **4** the most important chess piece, which the opponent has to checkmate in order to win.

WORDFINDER – regal (*of or relating to a king*), regent (*ruler replacing king during childhood, illness, etc.*), regicide (*killing of a king*).

DERIVATIVES – **kingly** *adjective* **kingship** *noun*.

COMBINATIONS – **kingbolt** a kingpin. **King Charles spaniel** a small breed of spaniel with a white, black, and tan coat. [ORIGIN – named after King Charles II.] **kingcup** Brit. a marsh marigold. **King Edward** an variety of potato having a white skin mottled with red. [ORIGIN – named after King Edward VII.] **King James Bible** the Authorised Version. **King of Arms** (in the UK) a chief official of the College of Arms. **king of beasts** the lion. **king of birds** the eagle. **King of Kings** a name for God. **king post** an upright post extending from the tie beam to the apex of a roof truss. **king prawn** a large edible prawn. **King's Bench** (in the reign of a king) the Queen's Bench. **King's Counsel** (in the reign of a king) a Queen's Counsel. **King's evidence** (in the reign of a king) the term for *Queen's evidence*. **king's evil** historical scrofula, formerly believed to be curable by the royal touch. **king-sized** (also **king-size**) of a larger size than the standard; very large. **King's speech** (in the reign of a king) the Queen's Speech.

ORIGIN – Old English, related to KIN.

kingdom > *noun* **1** a country, state, or territory ruled by a king or queen. **2** a realm associated with a particular person or thing. **3** the spiritual reign or authority of God. **4** each of the three divisions (animal, vegetable, and mineral) in which natural objects are classified.

IDIOMS – **till kingdom come** informal forever. **to kingdom come** informal into the next world.

kingfisher > *noun* a colourful bird with a large head and long sharp beak which dives to catch fish in rivers and ponds.

kinglet > *noun* **1** chiefly derogatory a minor king. **2** chiefly N. Amer. a very small warbler of a group that includes the goldcrest.

kingmaker > *noun* a person who brings leaders to power through the exercise of political influence.

ORIGIN – used originally with reference to the Earl of Warwick (1428–71), influential in the Wars of the Roses.

kingpin > *noun* **1** a main or large bolt in a central position. **2** a vertical bolt used as a pivot. **3** a person or thing that is essential to the success of an organisation or operation.

kink > *noun* **1** a sharp twist or curve in something long and narrow. **2** a flaw or obstacle in a plan or operation. **3** a quirk of character or behaviour. > *verb* form a kink.

SYNONYMS – *noun* **3** eccentricity, foible, idiosyncrasy.

ORIGIN – Low German *kinke*, probably from Dutch *kinken* 'to kink'.

kinkajou /kingkəjoo/ > *noun* a fruit-eating mammal with a prehensile tail, found in Central and South America.

ORIGIN – French *quincajou*, from *carcajou* 'wolverine', from Algonquian.

kinky > *adjective* (**kinkier**, **kinkiest**) **1** having kinks or twists. **2** informal involving or given to unusual sexual behaviour.

DERIVATIVES – **kinkily** *adverb* **kinkiness** *noun*.

-kins > *suffix* equivalent to -KIN.

kinsfolk (also **kinfolk**) > *plural noun* (in anthropological or formal use) a person's blood relations, regarded collectively.

kinship > *noun* **1** blood relationship. **2** a sharing of characteristics or origins.

SYNONYMS – **2** affinity, rapport, sympathy.

kinsman (also **kinswoman**) > *noun* (in anthropological or formal use) one of a person's blood relations.

kiosk /keeosk/ > *noun* **1** a small open-fronted hut or cubicle from which newspapers, refreshments, tickets, etc. are sold. **2** Brit. a public telephone booth.

ORIGIN – Turkish *köşk* 'pavilion'.

kip¹ informal > *noun* **1** Brit. a sleep; a nap. **2** a bed or cheap lodging house. **3** Irish a dirty or sordid place. > *verb* (**kipped**, **kipping**) Brit. sleep.

kip² > *noun* (in Australia) a small piece of wood from which coins are spun in the game of two-up.

kip³ > *noun* (pl. same or **kips**) the basic monetary unit of Laos, equal to 100 ats.

ORIGIN – Thai.

kipper > *noun* a herring that has been split open, salted, and dried or smoked. > *verb* cure (a herring) in such a way.

COMBINATIONS – **kipper tie** a brightly coloured and very wide tie.

Kir /keer/ > *noun* trademark a drink made from dry white wine and crème de cassis.

ORIGIN – named after Canon Félix *Kir*, a mayor of Dijon, said to have invented the recipe.

kirby grip (also trademark **Kirbigrip**) > *noun* Brit. a hairgrip consisting of a thin folded and sprung metal strip.

ORIGIN – named after *Kirby*, Beard, & Co. Ltd, the original manufacturers.

Kirghiz > *noun* variant spelling of KYRGYZ.

kirk > *noun* Scottish & N. English **1** a church. **2** (**the Kirk** or **the Kirk of Scotland**) the Church of Scotland.

COMBINATIONS – **Kirk session** the lowest court in the Church of Scotland.

ORIGIN – Old Norse *kirkja*; related to CHURCH.

kirsch /keersh/ > *noun* brandy distilled from the fermented juice of cherries.

ORIGIN – German, from *Kirschenwasser* 'cherry water'.

kirtle /kurt'l/ > *noun* archaic **1** a woman's gown or outer petticoat. **2** a man's tunic or coat.

ORIGIN – from Latin *curtus* 'short'.

kismet /kizmet/ > *noun* destiny; fate.

ORIGIN – Arabic, 'division, portion, lot'.

kiss > *verb* **1** touch or caress with the lips as a sign of love, affection, or greeting. **2** Billiards & Snooker (of a ball) lightly touch (another ball). > *noun* **1** a touch or caress with the lips. **2** Billiards & Snooker a slight touch of a ball against another ball. **3** N. Amer. a small cake, biscuit, or sweet.

WORDFINDER – osculation (*the action of kissing*).

IDIOMS – **kiss someone's arse** (or N. Amer. **ass**) vulgar slang behave obsequiously towards someone. **kiss of death** an action that ensures the failure of an enterprise. **kiss off** N. Amer. informal dismiss (someone) rudely or abruptly. **kiss of life 1** mouth-to-mouth resuscitation. **2** something that revives a failing enterprise. **kiss of peace** a ceremonial kiss signifying unity, especially during the Eucharist.

DERIVATIVES – **kissable** *adjective*.

COMBINATIONS – **kiss curl** a small curl of hair on the forehead, at the nape of the neck, or in front of the ear. **kissing cousin** a relative known well enough to greet with a kiss. **kissing gate** Brit. a small gate hung in a U- or V-shaped enclosure, letting one person through at a time. **kiss-off** N. Amer. informal a rude or abrupt dismissal.

kisser > *noun* **1** a person who kisses someone. **2** informal a person's mouth.

kissogram > *noun* a novelty greeting delivered by a man or woman who accompanies it with a kiss.

kist > *noun* Scottish & S. African a storage chest.

ORIGIN – variant of CHEST.

Kiswahili /keeswaaheeli/ > *noun* another term for SWAHILI (the language).

kit¹ > *noun* **1** a set of articles or equipment for a specific purpose. **2** Brit. the clothing and other items needed for an activity or belonging to a soldier. **3** a set of all the parts needed to assemble something. **4** Brit. a large basket or box, especially for fish. > *verb* (**kit out**) provide with appropriate clothing or equipment.

IDIOMS – **get one's kit off** Brit. informal take off one's clothes.

SYNONYMS – *noun* **1** appliances, implements, instruments, tools, utensils.

COMBINATIONS – **kitbag** a long, cylindrical canvas bag for a soldier's belongings.

wordpower facts

Kit

Kit is from the Dutch word *kitte*, meaning 'wooden vessel', and entered English in the Middle Ages. The original sense, 'wooden tub', was later applied to other containers, and survives in the modern sense 4. Use to denote a soldier's equipment (late 18th century), and thus the first three modern senses, probably arose from the idea of a set of articles packed in a container.

kit² > *noun* the young of certain animals, e.g. the beaver, ferret, and mink.

kit³ > *noun* historical a small violin, especially one used by a dancing master.
ORIGIN – perhaps from Latin *cithara*, denoting a kind of harp.

kit-cat > *noun* a canvas of a standard size (typically 36 × 28 in., 91.5 × 71 cm), especially as used for a portrait showing the sitter's head, shoulders, and hands.
ORIGIN – named after portraits of members of the *Kit-Cat* Club, an 18th-century association of Whigs and literary figures.

kitchen > *noun* 1 a room where food is prepared and cooked. 2 a set of fitments and units installed in a kitchen.
COMBINATIONS – **kitchen cabinet** informal a group of unofficial advisers considered to be unduly influential. **kitchen garden** a garden where vegetables and fruit are grown for domestic use. **kitchen paper** absorbent paper used for drying and cleaning in a kitchen. **kitchen-sink** (of drama) realistic in the depiction of drab or sordid subjects. **kitchen tea** Austral./NZ a party before a wedding to which female guests bring kitchen equipment for the bride-to-be.
ORIGIN – Old English, from Latin *coquere* 'to cook'.

kitchenette > *noun* a small kitchen or part of a room equipped as a kitchen.

kitchenware > *noun* kitchen utensils.

kite > *noun* 1 a toy consisting of a light frame with thin material stretched over it, flown in the wind at the end of a long string. 2 Brit. informal, dated an aircraft. 3 a long-winged bird of prey with a forked tail, frequently seen soaring. 4 Geometry a quadrilateral figure having two pairs of equal adjacent sides, symmetrical only about one diagonal. 5 informal a fraudulent cheque, bill, or receipt. > *verb* 1 fly a kite. 2 informal, chiefly N. Amer. write or use (a fraudulent cheque, bill, or receipt).
IDIOMS – (as) **high as a kite** informal intoxicated with drugs or alcohol. **fly a kite** informal try something out to test public opinion.

COMBINATIONS – **Kitemark** trademark a kite-shaped official mark on goods approved by the British Standards Institution.

kith /kith/ > *noun* (in phrase **kith and kin**) one's relations.
ORIGIN – Old English, at first meaning 'knowledge', 'one's native land', and 'friends and neighbours'. The phrase *kith and kin* originally denoted one's country and relatives, later one's friends and relations.

kitsch /kich/ > *noun* art, objects, or design considered to be excessively garish or sentimental, but appreciated in an ironic or knowing way.
DERIVATIVES – **kitschiness** noun **kitschy** adjective.
ORIGIN – German.

kitten > *noun* 1 a young cat. 2 the young of certain other animals, such as the rabbit and beaver. > *verb* give birth to kittens.
IDIOMS – **have kittens** Brit. informal be extremely nervous or upset.
COMBINATIONS – **kitten heel** a type of low stiletto heel.
ORIGIN – Old French *chitoun*, from *chat* 'cat'.

kittenish > *adjective* playful, lively, or flirtatious.
DERIVATIVES – **kittenishly** adverb **kittenishness** noun.

kittiwake /kittiwayk/ > *noun* a small gull that nests in colonies on sea cliffs and has a loud call that resembles its name.

kitty¹ > *noun* (pl. **kitties**) 1 a fund of money for communal use. 2 a pool of money in some card games. 3 (in bowls) the jack.

kitty² > *noun* (pl. **kitties**) a pet name for a cat.

kitty-corner > *adjective* & *adverb* another term for **CATER-CORNERED**.

kiwi > *noun* (pl. **kiwis**) 1 a flightless, tailless New Zealand bird with hair-like feathers and a long downcurved bill. 2 (**Kiwi**) informal a New Zealander.
COMBINATIONS – **kiwi fruit** the fruit of an Asian climbing plant, with a thin hairy skin, green flesh, and black seeds.
ORIGIN – Maori.

kJ > *abbreviation* kilojoule(s).

KKK > *abbreviation* Ku Klux Klan.

kl > *abbreviation* kilolitre(s).

Klansman (or **Klanswoman**) > *noun* a member of the Ku Klux Klan, an extremist right-wing secret society in the US.

klaxon /klaks'n/ > *noun* trademark a vehicle horn or warning hooter.
ORIGIN – the name of the manufacturers.

Kleenex > *noun* (pl. same or **Kleenexes**) trademark a paper tissue.

kleptomania /kleptəmayniə/ > *noun* a recurrent urge to steal.
DERIVATIVES – **kleptomaniac** noun & adjective.
ORIGIN – from Greek *kleptēs* 'thief'.

klieg light /kleeg/ > *noun* a powerful electric lamp used in filming.
ORIGIN – named after the American brothers, Anton T. *Kliegl* and John H. *Kliegl*, who invented it.

Klondike /klondīk/ > *noun* a source of valuable material.
ORIGIN – from *Klondike* in Yukon, Canada, where gold was found in 1896.

kludge /kluj/ > *noun* informal something hastily or badly put together.

klutz /kluts/ > *noun* informal, chiefly N. Amer. a clumsy, awkward, or foolish person.
DERIVATIVES – **klutzy** adjective.
ORIGIN – Yiddish *klots* 'wooden block'.

km > *abbreviation* kilometre(s).

knack > *noun* 1 an acquired or natural skill at performing a task. 2 a tendency to do something.
SYNONYMS – 1 flair, gift, method, talent.
ORIGIN – probably related to obsolete *knack* 'sharp blow or sound'.

knacker Brit. > *noun* 1 a person who disposes of dead or unwanted animals. 2 (**knackers**) vulgar slang testicles. > *verb* informal exhaust; wear out.
DERIVATIVES – **knackered** adjective.
ORIGIN – first denoting a harness-maker: possibly from obsolete *knack* 'trinket'; sense 2 may be from dialect *knacker* 'castanet'.

knacker's yard > *noun* Brit. a place where old or injured animals are slaughtered.

knackwurst /nakwurst/ > *noun* a type of highly seasoned German sausage.
ORIGIN – German, from *knacken* 'make a cracking noise' + *Wurst* 'sausage'.

knap¹ /nap/ > *noun* archaic the crest of a hill.

knap² /nap/ > *verb* (**knapped, knapping**) shape (a stone) by striking it, so as to make a tool or a flat stone for building walls.

knapsack > *noun* a soldier's or hiker's bag with shoulder straps, carried on the back.
ORIGIN – Dutch *knapzack*, probably from German *knappen* 'to bite' + *zak* 'sack'.

knapweed > *noun* a tough-stemmed plant with purple thistle-like flower heads.
ORIGIN – from *knop* 'knob' (because of its rounded flower heads).

knave > *noun* 1 archaic a dishonest or unscrupulous man. 2 (in cards) a jack.
DERIVATIVES – **knavery** noun **knavish** adjective.
ORIGIN – Old English, 'boy, servant'.

knead > *verb* 1 work (dough or clay) with the hands. 2 massage as if kneading.

knee > *noun* **1** the joint between the thigh and the lower leg. **2** a person's lap. **3** something resembling a knee in shape or position, e.g. an angled piece of wood or metal or a sharp turn in a graph. > *verb* (**knees**, **kneed**, **kneeing**) hit with the knee.

WORDFINDER – *genuflect (lower one's body by bending one knee to the ground), patella (the bone of the kneecap), popliteal (situated in the hollow behind the knee).*

IDIOMS – **at one's mother's knee** at an early age. **bend** (or **bow**) **one's knee** submit. **bring someone to their knees** reduce (someone) to a state of weakness or submission.

COMBINATIONS – **knee-jerk 1** an involuntary reflex kick caused by a blow on the tendon just below the knee. **2** automatic and unthinking: *a knee-jerk reaction.* **knees-up** Brit. informal a lively party. **knee-trembler** vulgar slang an act of sexual intercourse between people in a standing position.

kneecap > *noun* the convex bone in front of the knee joint; the patella. > *verb* shoot in the knee or leg as a punishment.

knee-high > *adjective & adverb* so high as to reach the knees.

IDIOMS – **knee-high to a grasshopper** informal very small or young.

kneel > *verb* (past and past participle **knelt** or chiefly N. Amer. also **kneeled**) fall or rest on a knee or the knees.

kneeler > *noun* **1** a person who kneels. **2** a cushion or bench for kneeling on.

knee-pan > *noun* dated a kneecap.

knell /nel/ literary > *noun* the sound of a bell, especially when rung solemnly for a death or funeral. > *verb* (of a bell) ring solemnly.

knelt past and past participle of KNEEL.

Knesset /knessit/ > *noun* the parliament of modern Israel.

ORIGIN – Hebrew, 'gathering'.

knew past of KNOW.

knickerbocker > *noun* **1** (**knickerbockers**) loose-fitting breeches gathered at the knee or calf. **2** (**Knickerbocker**) informal a New Yorker.

COMBINATIONS – **Knickerbocker Glory** Brit. a dessert consisting of ice cream, fruit, and cream in a tall glass.

knickers > *plural noun* Brit. **1** a woman's or girl's undergarment covering the body from the waist or hips to the top of the thighs and having two holes for the legs. **2** N. Amer. knickerbockers.

IDIOMS – **get one's knickers in a twist** Brit. informal become upset or angry.

knick-knack (also **nick-nack**) > *noun* a small object, especially an ornament of little value.

wordpower facts
Knickerbocker

The word **knickerbocker** was first used in the mid 19th century to mean 'New Yorker'. It derives from the name of Diedrich *Knickerbocker*, pretended author of Washington Irving's *History of New York* (1809). Sense 1 is said to have arisen from the resemblance of knickerbockers to the breeches worn by Dutch men in the illustrations for Irving's book by George Cruikshank. The word **knickers** is an abbreviation of **knickerbockers**.

knife > *noun* (pl. **knives**) **1** a cutting instrument consisting of a blade fixed into a handle. **2** a cutting blade on a machine. > *verb* **1** stab with a knife. **2** cut like a knife.

WORDFINDER – *kinds of knife:* dagger, jackknife, kris, kukri, lancet, machete, penknife, scalpel, switchblade.

IDIOMS – **at knifepoint** under threat of injury from a knife. **stick the knife into** informal treat in a hostile or aggressive manner. **that one could cut with a knife** (of an accent or atmosphere) very obvious.

COMBINATIONS – **knife pleat** a sharp, narrow pleat on a skirt.

knife-edge > *noun* **1** the cutting edge of a knife. **2** a very tense or dangerous situation. **3** (before another noun) (of creases or pleats) very fine. **4** a steel wedge on which a pendulum or other device oscillates or is balanced. **5** a sharp mountain ridge.

knight > *noun* **1** (in the Middle Ages) a man raised to honourable military rank after service as a page and squire. **2** (in the UK) a man awarded a non-hereditary title by the sovereign and entitled to use 'Sir' in front of his name. **3** a chess piece, typically shaped like a horse's head, that moves by jumping to the opposite corner of a rectangle two squares by three. **4** (also **knight of the shire**) historical a gentleman representing a shire or county in Parliament. > *verb* give (a man) the title of knight.

WORDFINDER – *chivalry (medieval knights' code), dub (make someone a knight by touching their shoulder with a sword), esquire, squire (knight's attendant), joust, tilt (knights' mock combat), paladin (brave, chivalrous knight), quest (knight's expedition).*

IDIOMS – **knight in shining armour** an idealised chivalrous man.

DERIVATIVES – **knighthood** noun **knightly** adjective.

COMBINATIONS – **knight bachelor** (pl. **knights bachelor**) a knight not belonging to a particular order. **knight commander** a very high class in some orders of knighthood. **knight errant** a medieval knight wandering in search of chivalrous adventures. **knight marshal** historical an officer of the royal household with judicial functions.

ORIGIN – Old English, 'boy, youth, servant'.

kniphofia /nifōfiə/ > *noun* a plant of a genus comprising the red-hot pokers.

ORIGIN – named after the 18th-century German botanist Johann H. *Kniphof*.

knit > *verb* (**knitting**; past and past participle **knitted** or (especially in sense 3) **knit**) **1** make by interlocking loops of yarn with knitting needles or on a machine. **2** make (a plain stitch) in knitting. **3** unite or join together. **4** tighten (one's eyebrows) in a frown. > *noun* (**knits**) knitted garments.

DERIVATIVES – **knitter** noun **knitting** noun.

COMBINATIONS – **knitting needle** a long, thin, pointed rod used in pairs for hand knitting. **knitwear** knitted garments.

ORIGIN – Old English, related to KNOT[1].

knives plural of KNIFE.

knob > *noun* **1** a rounded lump or ball at the end or on the surface of something. **2** a ball-shaped handle on a door or drawer. **3** a round button on a machine. **4** a small lump of something. **5** chiefly N. Amer. a prominent round hill. **6** vulgar slang a man's penis.

IDIOMS – **with knobs on** Brit. informal and something more.

DERIVATIVES – **knobbed** adjective **knobby** adjective.

SYNONYMS – **1** bulge, bump, lump, protuberance.

knobble > *noun* Brit. a small lump on something.

DERIVATIVES – **knobbly** (**knobblier**, **knobbliest**) adjective.

knobkerrie /nobkerri/ > *noun* a short stick with a knobbed head, used as a weapon by indigenous peoples of South Africa.

ORIGIN – from KNOB + Nama *kieri* 'knobkerrie'.

knock > *verb* **1** strike a surface noisily to attract attention. **2** collide forcefully with. **3** force to move or fall with a collision or blow. **4** make (a hole, dent, etc.) in something by striking it. **5** informal criticise. **6** (of a motor) make a thumping or rattling noise. > *noun* **1** a sudden short sound caused by a blow. **2** a blow or collision. **3** a setback. **4** Cricket, informal an innings.

IDIOMS – **knock about** (or **around**) informal **1** travel or spend time without a specific purpose. **2** happen to be present. **knock back** informal consume (a drink) quickly. **knock down 1** (at an auction) confirm (a sale) by a knock with a hammer. **2** informal reduce the price of (an article). **knock it off** informal stop doing something. **knock off** informal **1** stop work. **2** produce (a piece of work) quickly and easily. **3** Brit. informal steal. **4** kill someone. **be knocking on** informal be ageing. **knock on the head 1** euphemistic kill. **2** Brit. informal put an end to. **knock out 1** make (someone) unconscious. **2** informal astonish or greatly impress. **3** eliminate from a knockout competition. **4** informal produce (work) at a steady fast rate. **knock spots off** Brit. informal easily outdo. **knock together** assemble (something) roughly and hastily. **knock up 1** informal, chiefly N. Amer. make (a woman) pregnant. **2** Brit. make (something) hurriedly. **the school of hard knocks** painful or difficult but useful life experiences.

SYNONYMS – *verb* **1** bang, pound, rap, thump. **2** bang, bump, crack.

COMBINATIONS – **knock-back** informal a refusal or setback. **knocking shop** Brit. informal a brothel. **knock-kneed** having legs that curve inwards at the knee. **knock-off** informal a copy or imitation. **knock-on effect** a secondary, indirect, or cumulative effect. **knock-up** Brit. (in racket sports) a period of practice play before a game.

knockabout > *adjective* **1** (of comedy) rough and slapstick. **2** (of clothes) suitable for rough use. > *noun* **1** US & Austral. a tramp. **2** Austral./NZ a farm or station handyman.

knock-down > *adjective* **1** informal (of a price) very low. **2** (of furniture) easily dismantled. > *noun* Austral./NZ informal an introduction.

knocker > *noun* **1** an object hinged to a door and rapped by visitors to attract attention. **2** informal a person who buys or sells from door to door. **3** informal a person who continually finds fault. **4** (**knockers**) informal a woman's breasts.

IDIOMS – **on the knocker** informal **1** Brit. going from door to door. **2** Austral./NZ (of payment) on demand.

knockout > *noun* **1** an act of knocking someone out. **2** Brit. a tournament in which the loser in each round is eliminated. **3** informal an extremely attractive or impressive person or thing.

COMBINATIONS – **knockout drops** a liquid drug added to a drink to cause unconsciousness.

knoll /nōl/ > *noun* a small hill or mound.

knot¹ > *noun* **1** a fastening made by looping a piece of string, rope, etc. on itself and tightening it. **2** a tangled mass in hair, wool, etc. **3** a protuberance in a stem, branch, or root. **4** a hard mass in wood at the intersection of a trunk with a branch. **5** a hard lump of bodily tissue. **6** a small group of people. **7** a unit of speed equivalent to one nautical mile per hour, used of ships, aircraft, or winds. > *verb* (**knotted, knotting**) **1** fasten with a knot. **2** tangle. **3** cause (a muscle) to become tense and hard. **4** (of the stomach) tighten as a result of tension.

WORDFINDER – *kinds of knot:* bend, bowline, clove hitch, granny, half hitch, reef knot, sheepshank, slip knot.

IDIOMS – **at a rate of knots** Brit. informal very fast. **get knotted!** Brit. informal go away. **tie (up) in knots** informal confuse (someone) completely. **tie the knot** informal get married.

SYNONYMS – *noun* **6** band, bunch, cluster, huddle. *verb* **1** bind, fasten, tie.

COMBINATIONS – **knot garden** an intricately designed formal garden. **knotgrass** a common plant with jointed creeping stems and small pink flowers. **knothole** a hole in a piece of wood where a knot has fallen out. **knotweed** knotgrass or a related plant.

wordpower facts

Knot

The senses of **knot** 'fastening in string or rope' and 'unit of a ship's speed' are connected through the knotted line of the nautical device called a *log* (see box at **LOG**). The number of **knots**, or length of line, that was run out in a certain time gave an estimate of the vessel's speed. The name of the shorebird, the **knot**, is unrelated to this, and there is also no foundation for the attractive story that relates it to King Canute (Danish *Knut*), who tried to stop the tide coming in. Like many old bird names it was originally descriptive, in this case representing the knot's grunting call.

knot² > *noun* a short-billed northern sandpiper.

knotty > *adjective* (**knottier, knottiest**) **1** full of knots. **2** extremely difficult or intricate.

SYNONYMS – **2** complex, convoluted, tangled.

knout /nowt/ > *noun* (in imperial Russia) a whip used for punishment.

ORIGIN – Russian *knut*, from Old Norse *knútr*; related to **KNOT¹**.

know > *verb* (past **knew**; past participle **known**) **1** have knowledge of through observation, inquiry, or information. **2** be absolutely sure of something. **3** be familiar or friendly with. **4** have a good command of (a subject or language). **5** have personal experience of. **6** (usu. **be known as**) regard as having a specified characteristic or title. **7** archaic have sexual intercourse with.

WORDFINDER – gnostic (*of or relating to knowledge, especially mystical knowledge*), omniscient (*knowing everything*), philosophy (*study of nature of knowledge*), prescient (*knowing in advance*).

IDIOMS – **be in the know** be aware of

something known only to a few people. **God** (or **goodness** or **heaven**) **knows** I have no idea. **know better than** be wise enough to avoid doing something. **know no bounds** have no limits. **know one's own mind** be decisive and certain. **know the ropes** informal have experience of the appropriate procedures. **know what's what** informal be experienced and competent in a particular area.

COMBINATIONS – **know-all** (also **know-it-all**) informal a person who behaves as if they know everything. **know-how** practical knowledge or skill; expertise. **know-nothing** an ignorant person.

ORIGIN – Old English, 'recognise, identify'; related to **CAN¹** and **KEN**.

knowing > *adjective* **1** suggesting that one has secret knowledge: *a knowing smile.* **2** chiefly derogatory experienced or shrewd, especially excessively or prematurely so. > *noun* the state of being aware or informed.

IDIOMS – **there is no knowing** no one can tell.

DERIVATIVES – **knowingly** adverb **knowingness** noun.

knowledge > *noun* **1** information and skills acquired through experience or education. **2** the sum of what is known. **3** awareness or familiarity gained by experience of a fact or situation: *he denied all knowledge of the incident.*

IDIOMS – **come to one's knowledge** become known to one. **to** (**the best of**) **my knowledge 1** so far as I know. **2** as I know for certain.

COMBINATIONS – **knowledge worker** a person whose job involves handling or using information.

knowledgeable (also **knowledgable**) > *adjective* intelligent and well informed.

DERIVATIVES – **knowledgeably** adverb.

SYNONYMS – erudite, informed, learned.

ANTONYMS – ignorant.

known past participle of **KNOW**. > *adjective* **1** recognised, familiar, or within the scope of knowledge. **2** publicly acknowledged to be: *a known criminal.* **3** Mathematics (of a quantity or variable) having a value that can be stated.

knuckle > *noun* **1** a part of a finger at a joint where the bone is near the surface. **2** a projection of the carpal or tarsal joint of a quadruped. **3** this projection as a joint of meat. > *verb* rub or press with the knuckles.

IDIOMS – **knuckle down 1** apply oneself seriously to a task. **2** (also **knuckle under**) submit. **near the knuckle** Brit. informal verging on the indecent or offensive. **rap on** (or **over**) **the knuckles** rebuke or criticise.

COMBINATIONS – **knuckleduster** a metal guard worn over the knuckles in fighting to increase the effect of blows. **knucklehead** informal a stupid person. **knuckle sandwich** informal a punch in the mouth.

ORIGIN – Low German, Dutch *knökel* 'little bone'. The phrase *knuckle down* derives from the idea of setting the knuckles down to start a game of marbles.

knurl /nurl/ > *noun* a small projecting knob or ridge.

DERIVATIVES – **knurled** adjective.

KO[1] > *abbreviation* kick-off.

KO[2] Boxing > *noun* a knockout in a boxing match. > *verb* (**KO's**, **KO'd**, **KO'ing**) knock out in a boxing match.

koala /kōaalə/ > *noun* a bear-like tree-dwelling Australian marsupial that has thick grey fur and feeds on eucalyptus leaves.

NOTE – the form **koala bear** is strictly incorrect as koalas are completely unrelated to bears.

ORIGIN – from Dharuk (an Aboriginal language).

koan /kōaan/ > *noun* a paradoxical anecdote or riddle, used in Zen Buddhism to show the inadequacy of logical reasoning and provoke enlightenment.

ORIGIN – Japanese, literally 'matter for public thought'.

kobo /kōbō/ > *noun* (pl. same) a monetary unit of Nigeria, equal to one hundredth of a naira.

ORIGIN – corruption of COPPER[1].

kofta /koftə/ > *noun* (pl. same or **koftas**) (in Middle Eastern and Indian cookery) a savoury ball of minced meat or vegetables.

ORIGIN – Urdu and Persian, 'pounded meat'.

kohanga reo /kəhəngə rayō/ > *noun* NZ a kindergarten where lessons are conducted in Maori.

ORIGIN – Maori, 'language nest'.

kohl /kōl/ > *noun* a black powder used as eye make-up.

ORIGIN – Arabic.

kohlrabi /kōlraabi/ > *noun* (pl. **kohlrabies**) a cabbage of a variety with an edible turnip-like swollen stem.

ORIGIN – German, from Latin *caulorapa*, from *caulis* 'cabbage' + *rapum* 'turnip'.

koi /koy/ > *noun* (pl. same) a large ornamental variety of carp.

ORIGIN – Japanese, 'carp'.

kola > *noun* variant spelling of COLA (in sense 2).

kolkhoz /kolkoz/ > *noun* (pl. same or **kolkhozes** or **kolkhozy**) a collective farm in the former USSR.

ORIGIN – Russian, from *kollektivnoe khozyaĭstvo* 'collective farm'.

Komodo dragon /kəmōdō/ > *noun* a very large lizard native to Komodo and neighbouring Indonesian islands.

Komsomol /komsəmol/ > *noun* an organisation for communist youth in the former Soviet Union.

ORIGIN – Russian, from *Kommunisticheskiĭ Soyuz Molodëzhi* 'Communist League of Youth'.

kook > *noun* N. Amer. informal a mad or eccentric person.

DERIVATIVES – **kooky** adjective.

ORIGIN – probably from CUCKOO.

kookaburra /kookəburrə/ > *noun* a very large, noisy Australasian kingfisher that feeds on reptiles and birds.

ORIGIN – from Wiradhuri (an Aboriginal language).

kop > *noun* Brit. a high bank of terracing at a soccer ground.

ORIGIN – Afrikaans, from Dutch, 'head'; the term entered English from *Spion Kop* in South Africa, site of a Boer War battle.

kopek /kōpek/ (also **copeck** or **kopeck**) > *noun* a monetary unit of Russia and some other countries of the former USSR, equal to one hundredth of a rouble.

ORIGIN – from Russian *kopeĭka* 'small lance' (from the figure on the coin (1535) of Tsar Ivan IV, bearing a lance).

kora /korə/ > *noun* a West African musical instrument shaped like a lute and played like a harp.

ORIGIN – a local word.

Koran /koraan/ (also **Quran** or **Qur'an** /kooraan/) > *noun* the Islamic sacred book, believed to be the word of God as dictated to Muhammad and written down in Arabic.

DERIVATIVES – **Koranic** /kərannik/ adjective.

ORIGIN – Arabic 'recitation'.

Korean /kəreeən/ > *noun* 1 a person from Korea. 2 the language of Korea. > *adjective* relating to Korea or its language.

korma /kormə/ > *noun* a mild Indian curry of meat or fish marinaded in yogurt or curds.

ORIGIN – Urdu, from Turkish *kavurma*.

koruna > *noun* the basic monetary unit of the Czech Republic and Slovakia, equal to 100 haleru.

ORIGIN – Czech, 'crown'.

kosher /kōshər/ > *adjective* 1 satisfying the requirements of Jewish law with regards to the preparation of food. 2 informal genuine and legitimate. > *verb* prepare (food) according to Jewish law.

ORIGIN – Hebrew, 'proper'.

Kosovar /kossəvaar/ > *noun* a person from Kosovo, a province of Serbia whose population is largely of Albanian descent.

DERIVATIVES – **Kosovan** noun & adjective.

koto /kōtō/ > *noun* (pl. **kotos**) a large Japanese zither, with thirteen strings.

ORIGIN – Japanese.

koumiss /koomiss/ > *noun* a fermented liquor prepared from mare's milk, used as a drink and medicine by Asian nomads.

ORIGIN – Tartar.

kowhai /kōwī/ > *noun* a tree native to New Zealand and Chile, with hanging clusters of yellow flowers.

ORIGIN – Maori.

kowtow /kowtow/ > *verb* 1 historical kneel and touch the ground with the forehead in submission as part of Chinese custom. 2 be excessively subservient towards someone.

SYNONYMS – 2 abase oneself, bow and scrape, creep, fawn, grovel.

ORIGIN – Chinese.

kph > *abbreviation* kilometres per hour.

Kr > *symbol* the chemical element krypton.

kraal /kraal/ S. African > *noun* 1 a traditional African village of huts. 2 an animal enclosure. > *verb* drive (animals) into a kraal.

ORIGIN – Dutch, from Portuguese *curral*; related to CORRAL.

kraft /kraaft/ > *noun* a kind of strong, smooth brown wrapping paper.

ORIGIN – Swedish, literally 'strength'.

kraken /kraakən/ > *noun* a mythical sea monster said to appear off the coast of Norway.

ORIGIN – Norwegian.

Kraut /krowt/ > *noun* informal, offensive a German.

ORIGIN – shortening of SAUERKRAUT.

kremlin /kremlin/ > *noun* 1 a citadel within a Russian town. 2 (**the Kremlin**) the citadel in Moscow, housing the Russian government.

ORIGIN – Russian *kreml'* 'citadel'.

krill > *plural noun* small shrimp-like planktonic crustaceans which are the principal food of baleen whales.

ORIGIN – Norwegian *kril* 'small fish fry'.

kris /kreess/ > *noun* a Malay or Indonesian dagger with a wavy-edged blade.

ORIGIN – Malay.

krona /krōnə/ > *noun* 1 (pl. **kronor** pronunc. same) the basic monetary unit of Sweden. 2 (pl. **kronur** pronunc. same) the basic monetary unit of Iceland.

ORIGIN – Swedish and Icelandic, 'crown'.

krone /krōnə/ > *noun* (pl. **kroner** pronunc. same) the basic monetary unit of Denmark and Norway.

ORIGIN – Danish and Norwegian, 'crown'.

kroon > *noun* (pl. **kroons** or **krooni**) the basic monetary unit of Estonia, equal to 100 sents.

ORIGIN – Estonian, 'crown'.

krugerrand /kroogərand/ > *noun* a South African gold coin with a portrait of President Kruger on the obverse.

ORIGIN – named after Paul *Kruger*, President of Transvaal 1883–99.

krummhorn /krumhorn/ (also **crumhorn**) > *noun* a medieval wind instrument with an enclosed double reed and an upward-curving end.

ORIGIN – German, 'crooked horn'.

krypton /**krip**ton/ > *noun* an inert gaseous chemical element, present in trace amounts in the air and used in some kinds of electric light.

ORIGIN – from Greek *krupton* 'hidden'.

KS > *abbreviation* **1** Kansas. **2** Kaposi's sarcoma.

Kshatriya /**kshat**riə/ > *noun* a member of the second-highest Hindu caste, that of the military.

ORIGIN – Sanskrit, 'rule, authority'.

KStJ > *abbreviation* Knight of the Order of St John.

KT > *abbreviation* (in the UK) Knight of the Order of the Thistle.

kt > *abbreviation* knot(s).

kudos /**kyoo**dos/ > *noun* praise and honour.

USAGE – despite appearances, **kudos** is not a plural form: there is no singular form **kudo**, and use as a plural is incorrect.

SYNONYMS – cachet, glory, honour, prestige.

ORIGIN – Greek.

kudu /**koo**doo/ > *noun* (pl. same or **kudus**) a striped African antelope, the male of which has long spirally curved horns.

ORIGIN – Afrikaans.

Kufic /**kyoo**fik/ > *noun* an early form of the Arabic alphabet found chiefly in decorative inscriptions. > *adjective* of or in this type of script.

ORIGIN – from the name *Kufa*, a city south of Baghdad, Iraq (because it was attributed to the city's scholars).

Ku Klux Klan > *noun* an extreme white supremacist secret society in the US.

ORIGIN – perhaps from Greek *kuklos* 'circle' and CLAN.

kukri /**koo**kri/ > *noun* (pl. **kukris**) a curved knife broadening towards the point, used by Gurkhas.

ORIGIN – Nepalese.

kulak /**koo**lak/ > *noun* historical a peasant in Russia wealthy enough to own a farm and hire labour.

ORIGIN – Russian, literally 'fist, tight-fisted person'.

kumara /**koo**mərə/ > *noun* (pl. same) NZ a sweet potato.

ORIGIN – Maori.

kumkum /**koo**mkoom/ > *noun* a red pigment used by Hindu women to make a ceremonial mark on the forehead.

ORIGIN – Sanskrit, 'saffron'.

kümmel /**koo**mm'l/ > *noun* a sweet liqueur flavoured with caraway and cumin seeds.

ORIGIN – German, from High German *kumil*, variant of *kumín* 'cumin'.

kumquat /**koo**mkwot/ (also **cumquat**) > *noun* a citrus-like East Asian fruit with an edible sweet rind and acid pulp.

ORIGIN – Chinese, 'little orange'.

kuna /**koo**nə/ > *noun* (pl. **kune**) the basic monetary unit of Croatia, equal to 100 lipa.

ORIGIN – Serbo-Croat, 'marten': marten fur was formerly a medium of exchange.

kundalini /**koo**ndəleeni/ > *noun* (in yoga) latent female energy believed to lie coiled at the base of the spine.

ORIGIN – Sanskrit, literally 'snake'.

kung fu /kung **foo**/ > *noun* a Chinese martial art resembling karate.

ORIGIN – Chinese, from words meaning 'merit' and 'master'.

Kurd /kurd/ > *noun* a member of a mainly pastoral Islamic people living in Kurdistan, a region of the Middle East including parts of Turkey, Iraq, and Iran.

kurdaitcha /kə**dī**chə/ > *noun* the use among Australian Aboriginals of a bone in spells intended to cause sickness or death.

ORIGIN – probably from Aranda (an Aboriginal language).

Kurdish /**kur**dish/ > *noun* the Iranian language of the Kurds. > *adjective* relating to the Kurds or their language.

kurgan /koor**gaan**/ > *noun* Archaeology **1** a prehistoric burial mound of a type found in southern Russia and the Ukraine. **2** (**Kurgan**) a member of the ancient people who built such mounds.

ORIGIN – Russian.

kurrajong /**kurr**əjong/ > *noun* an Australian plant which produces useful tough fibre.

ORIGIN – Dharuk (an Aboriginal language), 'fibre fishing line'.

kurta /**kur**tə/ > *noun* a loose collarless shirt worn by people from the Indian subcontinent.

ORIGIN – Urdu and Persian.

kuru /**koo**roo/ > *noun* Medicine a fatal brain disease occurring in New Guinea, spread by cannibalism.

ORIGIN – a local word.

kurus /kə**roosh**/ > *noun* (pl. same) a monetary unit of Turkey, equal to one hundredth of a lira.

ORIGIN – Turkish *kuruş*.

Kuwaiti /koo**way**ti/ > *noun* a person from Kuwait. > *adjective* relating to Kuwait.

kV > *abbreviation* kilovolt(s).

kvell /kvel/ > *verb* N. Amer. informal feel happy and proud.

ORIGIN – Yiddish *kveln*, from High German, literally 'well up'.

kvetch /kvech/ N. Amer. informal > *noun* **1** a person who complains a great deal. **2** a complaint. > *verb* complain.

ORIGIN – Yiddish *kvetsh*, from High German *quetschen* 'crush'.

kW > *abbreviation* kilowatt(s).

kwacha /**kwaa**chə/ > *noun* the basic monetary unit of Zambia and Malawi, equal to 100 ngwee in Zambia and 100 tambala in Malawi.

ORIGIN – from a Bantu word meaning 'dawn', used as a Zambian nationalist slogan calling for a new 'dawn' of freedom.

kwanza > *noun* the basic monetary unit of Angola, equal to 100 lwei.

ORIGIN – perhaps from a Kiswahili word meaning 'first'.

Kwanzaa /**kwan**zaa/ > *noun* (in the US) a festival observed by many African Americans from 26 December to 1 January as a celebration of their cultural heritage.

ORIGIN – Kiswahili, 'first fruits'.

kwashiorkor /kwoshi**or**kor/ > *noun* malnutrition caused by protein deficiency.

ORIGIN – a local word in Ghana.

kwela /**kway**lə/ > *noun* a style of African popular music resembling jazz.

ORIGIN – Afrikaans, perhaps from Zulu *khwela* 'mount, climb'.

kWh > *abbreviation* kilowatt-hour(s).

KY > *abbreviation* Kentucky.

kyat > *noun* the basic monetary unit of Burma (Myanmar), equal to 100 pyas.

ORIGIN – Burmese.

kybosh > *noun* variant spelling of KIBOSH.

kyle > *noun* Scottish a narrow sea channel.

ORIGIN – Scottish Gaelic *caol* 'strait'.

kylie /**kī**li/ > *noun* Austral. a boomerang.

ORIGIN – Nyungar (an Aboriginal language).

kyphosis /kī**fō**siss/ > *noun* Medicine excessive forward curvature of the spine, causing a hunched back. Compare with LORDOSIS.

ORIGIN – Greek *kuphōsis*, from *kuphos* 'bent, hunchbacked'.

Kyrgyz /**ker**giz/ (also **Kirghiz**) > *noun* (pl. same) **1** a member of a people of central Asia, living chiefly in Kyrgyzstan. **2** the language of this people.

Kyrie /**kirr**iay/ (also **Kyrie eleison** /kirriay i**lay**izon/) > *noun* a short repeated invocation used in Christian liturgies.

ORIGIN – Greek *Kurie eleēson* 'Lord, have mercy'.

L¹ (also **l**) > *noun* (pl. **Ls** or **L's**) **1** the twelfth letter of the alphabet. **2** denoting the next after K in a set. **3** the Roman numeral for 50. [ORIGIN – a symbol identified with the letter *L*, because of coincidence of form; in ancient Roman notation, *L* with a stroke above denoted 50,000.]

L² > *abbreviation* **1** (**L.**) Lake, Loch, or Lough. **2** large (as a clothes size). **3** Brit. learner driver. **4** lire. **5** (in tables of sports results) lost.

l > *abbreviation* **1** left. **2** length(s). **3** (**l.**) line. **4** litre(s). **5** (**l.**) archaic pound(s).

£ > *abbreviation* pound(s).
ORIGIN – the initial letter of Latin *libra* 'pound, balance'.

LA > *abbreviation* **1** Los Angeles. **2** Louisiana.

La > *symbol* the chemical element lanthanum.

la > *noun* Music variant spelling of **LAH**.

laager /**laa**gər/ S. African > *noun* **1** historical an encampment formed by a circle of wagons. **2** an entrenched position or viewpoint. > *verb* historical form or enclose with a laager.
ORIGIN – South African Dutch, from Dutch *lager* 'camp'.

lab > *noun* informal a laboratory.

label* > *noun* **1** a small piece of paper, fabric, etc. attached to an object and giving information about it. **2** the name or trademark of a fashion company. **3** a company that produces recorded music. **4** a classifying name applied to a person or thing. **5** Biology & Chemistry a radioactive isotope, fluorescent dye, or enzyme used to make something identifiable. > *verb* (**labelled, labelling**; US **labeled, labeling**) **1** attach a label to. **2** assign to a category. **3** Biology & Chemistry make (a substance, cell, etc.) identifiable using a label.
*SPELLING – *-el*, not *-le*: label.
ORIGIN – Old French, 'ribbon'.

labia /**lay**biə/ > *plural noun* Anatomy the smaller inner folds (**labia minora**) or larger outer folds (**labia majora**) of the vulva.
ORIGIN – Latin, plural of *labium* 'lip'.

labial > *adjective* chiefly Anatomy & Biology relating to the lips or a labium.

labiate > *adjective* Botany relating to plants of the mint family (Labiatae), having distinctive two-lobed flowers.
ORIGIN – Latin *labiatus*, from *labium* 'lip'.

labile /**lay**bīl/ > *adjective* **1** technical liable to change; easily altered. **2** Chemistry easily broken down or displaced.
ORIGIN – Latin *labilis*, from *labi* 'to fall'.

labium /**lay**biəm/ > *noun* (pl. **labia** /**lay**biə/) Entomology a fused mouthpart forming the floor of the mouth of an insect.
ORIGIN – Latin, 'lip'.

labor etc. US and Australian spelling of **LABOUR** etc.

laboratory /lə**borr**ətri/ > *noun* (pl. **laboratories**) a room or building equipped for scientific experiments, research, or teaching, or for the manufacture of drugs or chemicals.
ORIGIN – Latin *laboratorium*, from *laborare* 'to labour'.

laborious /lə**bor**iəss/ > *adjective* **1** requiring considerable time and effort. **2** showing obvious signs of effort.
DERIVATIVES – **laboriously** adverb.
SYNONYMS – **1** arduous, gruelling, hard, strenuous. **2** laboured, ponderous, strained.
ANTONYMS – effortless.

labour (US & Austral. **labor**) > *noun* **1** work, especially hard physical work. **2** workers collectively. **3** (**Labour**) the Labour Party. **4** the process of childbirth. > *verb* **1** work hard. **2** work at an unskilled manual job. **3** have difficulty despite working hard. **4** move with difficulty. **5** (**labour under**) be misled by (a mistaken belief).
IDIOMS – **a labour of love** a task done for pleasure, not reward. **labour the point** elaborate something at excessive length.
SYNONYMS – *noun* **1** drudgery, industry, toil, work. *verb* **1** slave, struggle, toil, work.
COMBINATIONS – **labour camp** a prison camp with a regime of hard labour. **Labour Day** a public holiday held in honour of working people in some countries on 1 May, or (in the US and Canada) on the first Monday in September. **labour exchange** former term for *jobcentre*. **labour force** the members of a population who are able to work. **labour-intensive** needing a large workforce or a large amount of work in relation to output. **Labour Party** a left-of-centre political party formed to represent the interests of ordinary working people. **labour-saving** designed to reduce or eliminate work. **labour union** chiefly N. Amer. a trade union.
ORIGIN – Latin *labor* 'toil, trouble'.

laboured (US **labored**) > *adjective* **1** done with great difficulty. **2** not spontaneous or fluent.

SYNONYMS – **1** forced, laborious, strained. **2** contrived, mannered, stilted.
ANTONYMS – **1** easy. **2** natural.

labourer (US **laborer**) > *noun* a person doing unskilled manual work.

Labourite (US **Laborite**) > *noun* a member or supporter of a Labour Party.

Labrador /**labr**ədor/ (also **Labrador retriever**) > *noun* a breed of retriever with a black or yellow coat, used as a gun dog or guide dog.
ORIGIN – named after the *Labrador* Peninsula of eastern Canada, where the breed was developed.

Labrador tea > *noun* a northern shrub with fragrant evergreen leaves, sometimes used in Canada to make tea.

labrum /**lay**brəm/ > *noun* (pl. **labra** /**lay**brə/) Zoology a structure corresponding to a lip, especially the upper border of the mouthparts of a crustacean or insect.
ORIGIN – Latin, 'lip'.

laburnum /lə**burn**əm/ > *noun* a small hardwood tree with hanging clusters of yellow flowers followed by pods of poisonous seeds.
ORIGIN – Latin.

labyrinth /**labb**ərinth/ > *noun* **1** a complicated irregular network of passages or paths. **2** an intricate and confusing arrangement. **3** Anatomy the complex fluid-filled bony structure in the inner ear containing the organs of hearing and balance.
SYNONYMS – **1** maze, warren.
ORIGIN – Greek *laburinthos*, referring to the maze constructed by Daedalus in Greek mythology to house the Minotaur.

labyrinthine /labb**ərinth**īn/ > *adjective* like a labyrinth, especially in being complicated or twisted.

labyrinthitis /labbərinth**ī**tiss/ > *noun* Medicine inflammation of the labyrinth or inner ear.

lac¹ > *noun* a resinous substance secreted by an Asian insect (the **lac insect**), used to make varnish, shellac, etc.
ORIGIN – Hindi or Persian.

lac² > *noun* variant spelling of **LAKH**.

lace > *noun* **1** a fine open fabric of cotton or silk made by looping, twisting, or knitting thread in patterns. **2** a cord or leather strip used to fasten a shoe or garment. > *verb* **1** fasten with a lace or laces. **2** entwine. **3** (often **be laced with**) add an ingredient, especially alcohol, to (a drink or dish) to enhance its flavour or strength.
ORIGIN – Old French *laz*, from Latin *laqueus* 'noose'.

lacerate /**lass**ərayt/ > *verb* tear or deeply cut (the flesh or skin).
DERIVATIVES – **laceration** noun.
SYNONYMS – gash, rip, slash.
ORIGIN – Latin *lacerare*, from *lacer* 'torn'.

lacewing > *noun* a delicate, slender insect with large, clear membranous wings.

lachrymal /lakrim'l/ (also **lacrimal** or **lacrymal**) > *adjective* **1** formal or literary connected with weeping or tears. **2** Physiology & Anatomy concerned with the secretion of tears.
ORIGIN – Latin *lachrymalis*, from *lacrima* 'tear'.

lachrymatory /lakrimətəri/ (also **lacrimatory**) > *adjective* technical or literary relating to, causing, or containing tears.

lachrymose /lakrimōss/ > *adjective* formal or literary **1** tearful. **2** inducing tears; sad.

lacing > *noun* **1** a laced fastening of a shoe or garment. **2** a dash of spirits added to a drink.

lack > *noun* absence or deficiency of something. > *verb* (also **lack for**) be without or deficient in.
SYNONYMS – *noun* absence, dearth, deficiency, paucity, shortage.
ANTONYMS – *noun* abundance.

lackadaisical /lakkədayzik'l/ > *adjective* lacking enthusiasm and thoroughness.
DERIVATIVES – **lackadaisically** adverb.
SYNONYMS – apathetic, lethargic, listless, sluggish.
ORIGIN – from the archaic interjection *lackaday, lackadaisy*.

lackey > *noun* (pl. **lackeys**) **1** a servant. **2** a servile or obsequious person.
ORIGIN – French *laquais*.

lacking > *adjective* absent or deficient.

lacklustre (US **lackluster**) > *adjective* **1** lacking in vitality, force, or conviction. **2** not shining; dull.
SYNONYMS – **1** bland, dull, flat, insipid.

laconic /ləkonnik/ > *adjective* using very few words; terse.
DERIVATIVES – **laconically** adverb.
SYNONYMS – crisp, pithy, succinct, terse.
ANTONYMS – verbose.
ORIGIN – Greek *Lakōnikos*, from *Lakōn* 'Laconia, Sparta', the Spartans being known for their terse speech.

lacquer /lakkər/ > *noun* **1** a varnish made of shellac or of synthetic substances. **2** the sap of an East Asian tree (the **lacquer tree**) used as a varnish. **3** decorative wooden ware coated with lacquer. **4** Brit. a chemical substance sprayed on hair to keep it in place. > *verb* coat with lacquer.
ORIGIN – obsolete French *lacre* 'sealing wax', from Portuguese *laca* LAC¹.

lacrimal > *adjective* & *noun* variant spelling of LACHRYMAL.

lacrimatory > *adjective* variant spelling of LACHRYMATORY.

lacrosse /ləkross/ > *noun* a team game in which a ball is thrown, carried, and caught with a long-handled stick bearing a net at one end.

ORIGIN – French *la crosse* 'the hooked stick'.

lacrymal > *adjective* & *noun* variant spelling of LACHRYMAL.

lactate¹ /laktayt/ > *verb* (of a female mammal) secrete milk.
ORIGIN – Latin *lactare* 'suckle', from *lac* 'milk'.

lactate² /laktayt/ > *noun* Chemistry a salt or ester of lactic acid.

lactation > *noun* **1** the secretion of milk by the mammary glands. **2** the suckling of young.

lacteal /laktiəl/ > *adjective* conveying milk or milky fluid. > *noun* (**lacteals**) Anatomy the lymphatic vessels of the small intestine which absorb digested fats.

lactic /laktik/ > *adjective* relating to or obtained from milk.
COMBINATIONS – **lactic acid** an organic acid present in sour milk, and produced in the muscles during strenuous exercise.

lactose /laktōz/ > *noun* Chemistry a compound sugar present in milk.

lacto-vegetarian > *noun* a person who eats dairy products and vegetables but no meat or eggs.

lacuna /ləkyōonə/ > *noun* (pl. **lacunae** /ləkyōonee/ or **lacunas**) **1** a gap or missing portion. **2** Anatomy a cavity or depression, especially in bone.
DERIVATIVES – **lacunar** adjective.
ORIGIN – Latin, 'pool'.

lacustrine /ləkustrīn/ > *adjective* technical or literary relating to lakes.
ORIGIN – from Latin *lacus* 'lake'.

lacy > *adjective* (**lacier**, **laciest**) made of, resembling, or trimmed with lace.

lad > *noun* informal **1** a boy or young man. **2** (**lads**) chiefly Brit. a group of men sharing recreational or working interests. **3** Brit. a boisterously macho or high-spirited man.
DERIVATIVES – **laddish** adjective.

ladder > *noun* **1** a structure consisting of a series of bars or steps between two uprights, used for climbing up or down. **2** a hierarchical structure. **3** Brit. a vertical strip of unravelled fabric in tights or stockings. > *verb* Brit. develop or cause to develop a ladder in tights or stockings.
COMBINATIONS – **ladder-back** an upright chair with a back resembling a ladder. **ladder stitch** a stitch in embroidery consisting of transverse bars.

laddie > *noun* chiefly Scottish a boy or young man.

lade /layd/ > *verb* (past participle **laden**) archaic put cargo on board (a ship).

laden > *adjective* heavily loaded or weighed down.

SYNONYMS – burdened, encumbered, overloaded.

la-di-da (also **lah-di-dah**) > *adjective* informal pretentious or snobbish.
ORIGIN – imitative of an affected manner of speech.

ladies plural of LADY.
COMBINATIONS – **ladies' fingers** Brit. okra. **ladies' man** (also **lady's man**) informal a man who enjoys spending time and flirting with women. **ladies' night** a function at a men's institution or club to which women are invited. **ladies' room** chiefly N. Amer. a women's toilet in a public or institutional building.

Ladino /lədeenō/ > *noun* (pl. **Ladinos**) **1** the language of some Sephardic Jews, based on medieval Spanish with some Hebrew, Greek, and Turkish words. **2** a mestizo or Spanish-speaking white person in Central America.
ORIGIN – Spanish, from Latin *Latinus* (see LATIN).

ladle > *noun* a large long-handled spoon with a cup-shaped bowl. > *verb* **1** serve or transfer with a ladle. **2** (**ladle out**) distribute in large amounts.
DERIVATIVES – **ladleful** noun.

lady > *noun* (pl. **ladies**) **1** (in polite or formal use) a woman. **2** a woman of superior social position. **3** (**Lady**) a title used by peeresses, female relatives of peers, the wives and widows of knights, etc. **4** a courteous or genteel woman. **5** (**the Ladies**) Brit. a women's public toilet.
IDIOMS – **it isn't over till the fat lady sings** there is still time for a situation to change. [ORIGIN – by association with the final aria in tragic opera.] **My Lady** a polite form of address to female judges and certain noblewomen.
COMBINATIONS – **Lady chapel** a chapel dedicated to the Virgin Mary in a church or cathedral. **Lady Day** the feast of the Annunciation, 25 March. **lady-in-waiting** (pl. **ladies-in-waiting**) a woman who attends a queen or princess. **ladykiller** informal a charming man who habitually seduces women. **lady of the night** euphemistic a prostitute. **lady's bedstraw** a yellow-flowered bedstraw which smells of hay when dried and was formerly used to make mattresses. **lady's finger** Brit. a finger-shaped sponge cake with a sugar topping. **lady's maid** chiefly historical a maid who attended to the personal needs of her mistress. **lady's man** variant spelling of *ladies' man*. **lady's mantle** a plant with inconspicuous greenish flowers, formerly valued in herbal medicine. **lady's slipper** an orchid whose flower has a pouch- or slipper-shaped lip.

wordpower facts

Lady

The word **lady** has a long and interesting history. In Old English *hlǣfdīge* (the forerunner of the modern form) meant the female head of a household, or a woman to whom homage or obedience was due, such as the wife of a lord or specifically the Virgin Mary. The Old English word came from *hlāf* 'loaf' and a Germanic base meaning 'knead', which is related to **dough** and **dairy**; thus a *lady* was a 'loaf-kneader'. The word **lord** developed in a similar way; in Old English it literally meant 'bread-keeper'.

ladybird > *noun* a small beetle with a domed back, typically red or yellow with black spots.

ladybug > *noun* North American term for **LADYBIRD**.

ladylike > *adjective* appropriate for or typical of a well-mannered woman or girl.

ladyship > *noun* (**Her** or **Your Ladyship**) a respectful form of reference or address to a Lady.

laevulose /leevyōōlōz/ (US **levulose**) > *noun* Chemistry a naturally occurring form of the sugar fructose.
ORIGIN – from Latin *laevus* 'left', because solutions of laevulose rotate the plane of polarised light to the left (i.e. anticlockwise).

lag¹ > *verb* (**lagged**, **lagging**) fall behind; follow after a delay. > *noun* (also **time lag**) a period of time between two events; a delay.
SYNONYMS – *verb* dawdle, fall behind, hang back, straggle.

lag² > *verb* (**lagged**, **lagging**) enclose or cover (a boiler, pipes, etc.) with insulating material.

lag³ > *noun* Brit. informal a habitual convict.

lager > *noun* a light effervescent beer.
COMBINATIONS – **lager lout** Brit. informal a young man who behaves offensively as a result of excessive drinking.
ORIGIN – from German *Lagerbier* 'beer brewed for keeping', from *Lager* 'storehouse'.

laggard /laggərd/ > *noun* a person who falls behind others. > *adjective* slower than desired or expected.

lagging > *noun* material providing heat insulation for a boiler, pipes, etc.

lagniappe /lanyap/ > *noun* N. Amer. something given as a bonus or gratuity.
ORIGIN – Louisiana French, from Spanish *la ñapa*.

lagoon > *noun* 1 a stretch of salt water separated from the sea by a low sandbank or coral reef. 2 N. Amer. & Austral./NZ a small freshwater lake near a larger lake or river.
ORIGIN – Italian and Spanish *laguna*, from Latin *lacuna* 'pool'.

lah (also **la**) > *noun* Music the sixth note of a major scale, coming between 'soh' and 'te'.

lah-di-dah > *noun* variant spelling of **LA-DI-DA**.

laicise /layisīz/ (also **laicize**) > *verb* formal withdraw clerical character, control, or status from.
DERIVATIVES – **laicisation** noun **laicism** noun.

laid past and past participle of **LAY¹**.
COMBINATIONS – **laid-back** informal relaxed and easy-going.

lain past participle of **LIE¹**.

lair¹ > *noun* 1 a wild animal's resting place. 2 a person's hiding place or den.

lair² Austral./NZ informal > *noun* a flashily dressed man who enjoys showing off. > *verb* dress or behave in a flashy manner.
DERIVATIVES – **lairy** adjective.
ORIGIN – from *lairy* (earlier as Cockney slang in the sense 'knowing, conceited'), variant of **LEERY**.

laird /laird/ > *noun* (in Scotland) a person who owns a large estate.
DERIVATIVES – **lairdship** noun.
ORIGIN – Scots form of **LORD**.

laissez-faire /lessayfair/ > *noun* a policy of non-interference, especially avoidance by governments of interfering in the workings of the free market.
ORIGIN – French, literally 'allow to do'.

laity /layiti/ > *noun* (**the laity**) lay people.

lake¹ > *noun* 1 a large area of water surrounded by land. 2 (**the Lakes**) the *Lake District*.
WORDFINDER – lacustrine (*relating to lakes*), littoral (*relating to the shore of a lake*).
DERIVATIVES – **lakelet** noun.
COMBINATIONS – **Lake District** a region of lakes and mountains in Cumbria.
ORIGIN – Latin *lacus* 'pool, lake'.

lake² > *noun* 1 an insoluble pigment made by combining an organic dye and a mordant. 2 a purplish-red pigment of this kind, originally made with lac.

lakh /lak/ (also **lac**) > *noun* Indian a hundred thousand.
ORIGIN – Hindi.

la-la land > *noun* N. Amer. informal 1 Los Angeles or Hollywood, especially with regard to the film and television industry. 2 a dreamworld.
ORIGIN – reduplication of *LA* (i.e. Los Angeles).

lalapalooza > *noun* variant spelling of **LOLLAPALOOZA**.

laldy /laldi/ > *noun* Scottish informal a beating.
IDIOMS – **give it laldy** do something vigorously or enthusiastically.

Lallans /lalənz/ > *noun* a distinctive Scottish literary form of English, based on standard older Scots.
ORIGIN – Scots variant of *Lowlands*.

lallygag > *verb* variant spelling of **LOLLYGAG**.

lam¹ > *verb* (**lammed**, **lamming**) (often **lam into**) informal hit hard or repeatedly.

lam² N. Amer. informal > *noun* (in phrase **on the lam**) in flight, especially from the police. > *verb* (**lammed**, **lamming**) flee.

lama /laamə/ > *noun* 1 an honorific title applied to a spiritual leader in Tibetan Buddhism. 2 a Tibetan or Mongolian Buddhist monk.
ORIGIN – Tibetan, 'superior one'.

Lamarckism /lamaarkiz'm/ > *noun* the theory of evolution based on the supposed inheritance of acquired characteristics, devised by the French naturalist Jean Baptiste de Lamarck (1744–1829).
DERIVATIVES – **Lamarckian** noun & adjective.

lamasery /laaməsəri/ > *noun* (pl. **lamaseries**) a monastery of lamas.

lamb > *noun* 1 a young sheep. 2 a mild-mannered, gentle, or innocent person. > *verb* 1 (of a ewe) give birth to lambs. 2 tend (ewes) at lambing time.
DERIVATIVES – **lambing** noun.
COMBINATIONS – **Lamb of God** a title of Jesus Christ. **lamb's fry** Brit. lamb's testicles or other offal as food. **lamb's lettuce** a small blue-flowered herbaceous plant, used in salad. **lamb's-tails** Brit. catkins from the hazel tree.

lambada /lambaadə/ > *noun* a fast Brazilian dance which couples perform in close physical contact.
ORIGIN – Portuguese, literally 'a beating'.

lambaste /lambayst/ (also **lambast** /lambast/) > *verb* criticise harshly.
DERIVATIVES – **lambasting** noun.
SYNONYMS – berate, castigate, upbraid.

lambda /lamdə/ > *noun* the eleventh letter of the Greek alphabet (Λ, λ), transliterated as 'l'.
ORIGIN – Greek.

lambent /lambənt/ > *adjective* literary glowing or flickering with a soft radiance.
ORIGIN – from Latin *lambere* 'to lick'.

Lambrusco /lambrōōskō/ > *noun* 1 a variety of wine grape grown in the Emilia-Romagna region of North Italy. 2 a sparkling red or white wine made from this grape.
ORIGIN – Italian, 'grape of the wild vine'.

lame > *adjective* 1 disabled in the leg or foot. 2 (of an explanation or excuse) unconvincingly feeble. 3 dull and uninspiring. > *verb* make lame.
DERIVATIVES – **lamely** adverb **lameness** noun.
SYNONYMS – noun 2 flimsy, implausible, unconvincing.

ANTONYMS – *noun* **2** convincing.

COMBINATIONS – **lamebrained** informal stupid; dull-witted. **lame duck 1** an ineffectual or unsuccessful person or thing. **2** N. Amer. a president or administration in the final period of office, after the election of a successor.

lamé /**laa**may/ > *noun* fabric with interwoven gold or silver threads.

ORIGIN – French, from Latin *lamina* 'thin plate'.

lamella /ləˈmellə/ > *noun* (pl. **lamellae** /ləˈmellee/) **1** a thin layer, membrane, or plate of tissue, especially in bone. **2** Botany a membranous fold in a chloroplast.

ORIGIN – Latin, 'small, thin plate'.

lamellibranch /ləˈmellibrangk/ > *noun* another term for BIVALVE.

ORIGIN – from Latin *lamella* + Greek *brankhia* 'gills'.

lament > *noun* **1** a passionate expression of grief. **2** a song, piece of music, or poem expressing grief or regret. > *verb* **1** mourn (a person's death). **2** (**lamented** or **late lamented**) a conventional way of referring to a dead person. **3** express regret or disappointment about.

DERIVATIVES – **lamentation** *noun*.

SYNONYMS – *noun* **1** dirge, elegy, requiem. *verb* **1** grieve, mourn, weep for.

ORIGIN – Latin *lamenta* (plural) 'weeping'.

lamentable /ˈlamməntəb'l/ > *adjective* deplorable or regrettable.

DERIVATIVES – **lamentably** *adverb*.

lamina /ˈlamminə/ > *noun* (pl. **laminae** /ˈlamminee/) technical a thin layer, plate, or scale of sedimentary rock, organic tissue, or other material.

ORIGIN – Latin.

laminar /ˈlamminər/ > *adjective* **1** consisting of laminae. **2** Physics (of fluid flow) taking place along unchanging lines, without turbulence.

laminate > *verb* /ˈlamminayt/ **1** overlay (a flat surface) with a layer of protective material. **2** manufacture by placing layer on layer. **3** split into layers or laminae. **4** beat or roll (metal) into thin plates. > *noun* /ˈlamminət/ a laminated structure or material. > *adjective* in the form of a lamina or laminae.

DERIVATIVES – **lamination** *noun* **laminator** *noun*.

lamington /ˈlammingtən/ > *noun* Austral./NZ a square of sponge cake dipped in melted chocolate and grated coconut.

ORIGIN – apparently from the name of Lord *Lamington*, Governor of Queensland 1895–1901.

laminitis /lamminˈītiss/ > *noun* the inflammation of sensitive layers of tissue inside the hoof in horses and other animals, often causing lameness.

Lammas /ˈlamməss/ (also **Lammas Day**) > *noun* the first day of August, formerly observed as harvest festival.

ORIGIN – Old English 'loaf mass'.

lammergeier /ˈlammərgīər/ (also **lammergeyer**) > *noun* a long-winged, long-tailed vulture, noted for dropping bones in order to break them and gain access to the marrow.

ORIGIN – German, from *Lämmer* 'lambs' + *Geier* 'vulture'.

lamp > *noun* **1** an electric, oil, or gas device for giving light. **2** an electrical device producing ultraviolet or other radiation, especially for therapeutic purposes.

COMBINATIONS – **lampblack** a black pigment made from soot.

ORIGIN – Latin *lampas* 'torch'.

lampoon /lamˈpoon/ > *verb* publicly satirise or ridicule. > *noun* a satirical attack.

SYNONYMS – *verb* caricature, mock, parody. *noun* burlesque, caricature, parody, skit.

ORIGIN – French *lampon*, said to be from *lampons* 'let us drink'.

lamprey /ˈlampri/ > *noun* (pl. **lampreys**) an eel-like jawless fish that has a sucker mouth with horny teeth and a rasping tongue.

ORIGIN – Latin *lampreda*, probably from *lambere* 'to lick' + *petra* 'stone' (because the lamprey attaches itself to stones by its mouth).

LAN > *abbreviation* local area network.

lanai /ləˈnī/ > *noun* (pl. **lanais**) a porch or veranda.

ORIGIN – Hawaiian.

Lancashire hotpot > *noun* a stew of meat and vegetables, covered with a layer of sliced potato.

Lancastrian /langˈkastriən/ > *noun* **1** a person from Lancashire or Lancaster. **2** a follower of the House of Lancaster in the Wars of the Roses. > *adjective* relating to Lancashire or Lancaster, or the House of Lancaster.

lance > *noun* **1** a long weapon with a wooden shaft and a pointed steel head, formerly used by a horseman in charging. **2** a metal pipe supplying a jet of oxygen to a furnace or to make a very hot flame for cutting. > *verb* **1** Medicine prick or cut open with a lancet or other sharp instrument. **2** pierce with a lance.

COMBINATIONS – **lance corporal** a rank of non-commissioned officer in the British army, above private and below corporal. [ORIGIN – on the analogy of obsolete *lancepesade*, the lowest grade of non-commissioned officer, based on Italian *lancia spezzata* 'broken lance'.]

ORIGIN – Old French, from Latin *lancea*.

lancelet /ˈlaanslit/ > *noun* a jawless fish-like marine animal that possesses a notochord and typically burrows in sand.

lanceolate /ˈlaansiələt/ > *adjective* technical of a narrow oval shape tapering to a point at each end.

ORIGIN – Latin *lanceolatus*, from *lanceola* 'a small lance'.

lancer > *noun* **1** a soldier of a cavalry regiment armed with lances. **2** (**lancers**) (treated as sing.) a quadrille (dance) for eight or sixteen pairs.

lancet /ˈlaansit/ > *noun* a small, broad two-edged surgical knife with a sharp point.

ORIGIN – Old French *lancette* 'a small lance'.

lancet window > *noun* a narrow window with an acutely pointed head.

Lancs. > *abbreviation* Lancashire.

land > *noun* **1** the part of the earth's surface that is not covered by water. **2** an area of ground in terms of its ownership or use. **3** ground or soil as a basis for agriculture. **4** a country or state. > *verb* **1** put or go ashore. **2** come or bring down to the ground. **3** bring (a fish) to land with a net or rod. **4** informal succeed in obtaining or achieving (something desirable). **5** (**land up**) reach a place or destination. **6** (**land up with**) end up with (an unwelcome situation). **7** (**land in**) informal cause (someone) to be in (a difficult situation). **8** (**land with**) inflict (something unwelcome or difficult) on (someone). **9** informal inflict (a blow) on someone.

IDIOMS – **how the land lies** what the state of affairs is. **in the land of the living** humorous alive or awake. **the land of Nod** humorous a state of sleep. [ORIGIN – punningly, with biblical allusion to the place name *Nod*.]

COMBINATIONS – **land agent** Brit. **1** a person employed to manage an estate on behalf of its owners. **2** a person who deals with the sale of land. **land bank 1** a large body of land held in trust for future development or disposal. **2** a bank providing loans for land purchase. **land breeze** a breeze blowing towards the sea from the land. **land bridge** an area of land formerly connecting two land masses which are now separate. **land crab** a crab that lives in burrows on land and migrates to the sea to breed. **landfill 1** the disposal of waste material by burying it. **2** waste material used in this way. **landform** a natural feature of the earth's surface, such as a mountain or valley. **land girl** (in the UK) a woman doing farm work during the Second World War. **landline** a conventional telecommunications connection by cable laid across land. **land mass** a continent or other large body of land. **landmine** an explosive mine laid on or just under the surface of the ground. **landslide 1** (chiefly Brit. also **landslip**) the sliding down of a mass of earth or rock from a mountain or cliff. **2** an overwhelming majority of votes for one party in an election.

landau /**lan**daw/ > *noun* a four-wheeled enclosed horse-drawn carriage with adjustable covers.

ORIGIN – named after *Landau* in Germany, where it was first made.

landed > *adjective* **1** owning much land, especially through inheritance. **2** consisting of or relating to such land.

lander > *noun* a spacecraft designed to land on the surface of a planet or moon.

landfall > *noun* **1** an arrival at land on a sea or air journey. **2** a collapse of a mass of land.

landgrave /**land**grayv/ > *noun* historical the title of certain German princes.

ORIGIN – Low German, from *land* 'land' + *grave* 'count'.

landing > *noun* **1** the process of coming to or bringing something to land. **2** a place where people and goods can be landed from a boat. **3** a level area at the top of a staircase or between flights of stairs.

COMBINATIONS – **landing craft** a boat specially designed for putting troops and military equipment ashore on a beach. **landing gear** the undercarriage of an aircraft. **landing stage** a platform on to which passengers or cargo can be landed from a boat.

landlady > *noun* **1** a woman who leases land or property. **2** a woman who keeps lodgings, a boarding house, or (Brit.) a public house.

landlocked > *adjective* almost or entirely surrounded by land.

landlord > *noun* **1** a man (in legal use also a woman) who leases land or property. **2** a man who keeps lodgings, a boarding house, or (Brit.) a public house.

landlordism > *noun* the system whereby land or property is owned by landlords to whom tenants pay a fixed rent.

landlubber > *noun* informal a person unfamiliar with the sea or sailing.

ORIGIN – from LAND + archaic LUBBER 'clumsy person'.

landmark > *noun* **1** an object or feature of a landscape or town that is easily seen and recognised from a distance. **2** an event, discovery, or change marking an important stage or turning point.

SYNONYMS – **2** milestone, watershed.

landowner > *noun* a person who owns land.

DERIVATIVES – **landownership** *noun* **landowning** *adjective & noun*.

landrace > *noun* a pig of a large white breed, originally developed in Denmark.

ORIGIN – Danish.

landrail > *noun* a corncrake (bird).

landscape > *noun* **1** all the visible features of an area of land. **2** a picture representing an area of countryside. **3** the distinctive features of a sphere of intellectual activity. **4** (before another noun) denoting a format of printed matter which is wider than it is high. Compare with PORTRAIT. > *verb* improve the appearance of (a piece of land) by changing its contours, planting trees and shrubs, etc.

DERIVATIVES – **landscaper** *noun* **landscapist** *noun*.

COMBINATIONS – **landscape architecture** the art and practice of designing the outdoor environment, especially designing parks or gardens to harmonise with buildings or roads. **landscape gardening** the art and practice of laying out grounds in a way which is ornamental or which imitates natural scenery.

ORIGIN – Dutch *lantscap*, from *land* 'land' + *scap* (equivalent of -SHIP).

landsman > *noun* a person unfamiliar with the sea or sailing.

landward > *adverb* (also **landwards**) towards land. > *adjective* facing towards land as opposed to sea.

lane > *noun* **1** a narrow road, especially in a rural area. **2** a division of a road intended to separate single lines of traffic according to speed or direction. **3** each of a number of parallel strips of track or water for competitors in a race. **4** a path or course prescribed for or regularly followed by ships or aircraft.

IDIOMS – **it's a long lane that has no turning** proverb nothing goes on forever; change is inevitable.

langlauf /**lang**lowf/ > *noun* cross-country skiing.

ORIGIN – German, 'long run'.

langouste /long**goost**/ > *noun* a spiny lobster, especially when prepared and cooked.

ORIGIN – French, from Latin *locusta* 'locust, crustacean'.

langoustine /long**goos**teen/ > *noun* a Norway lobster.

ORIGIN – French.

language > *noun* **1** the method of human communication, either spoken or written, consisting of the use of words in a structured and conventional way. **2** the system of communication used by a particular community or country. **3** the phraseology and vocabulary of a particular group. **4** the manner or style of a piece of writing or speech. **5** Computing a system of symbols and rules for writing programs or algorithms.

WORDFINDER – linguist (*person who studies language or languages*), monolingual (*speaking or expressed in only one language*), multilingual (*in or using several languages*), polyglot (*person who knows several languages*), vernacular (*spoken by ordinary people*).

IDIOMS – **speak the same language** understand one another as a result of shared opinions or values.

COMBINATIONS – **language engineering** the use of computers to process language for purposes such as speech recognition, speech synthesis, and machine translation. **language laboratory** a room equipped with audio and visual equipment for learning a foreign language. **language of flowers** a set of symbolic meanings attached to different flowers.

> **wordpower facts**
>
> ### Language
>
> The word **language** is based on Latin *lingua* 'tongue', which, like the English word **tongue**, can also mean 'speech or language'. *Lingua* is the source of words such as **bilingual**, **linguist**, and **lingo**, and also **linguine**, narrow ribbons of pasta that were originally thought of as 'little tongues'.

langue de chat /lon də **shaa**/ > *noun* a very thin finger-shaped crisp biscuit or piece of chocolate.

ORIGIN – French, 'cat's tongue'.

langue d'oc /long **dok**/ > *noun* the form of medieval French spoken south of the Loire, characterised by the use of *oc* to mean 'yes' and forming the basis of modern Provençal.

ORIGIN – Old French, 'language of *oc*'.

langue d'oïl /long **doyl**/ > *noun* the form of medieval French spoken north of the Loire, characterised by the use of *oïl* to mean 'yes' and forming the basis of modern French.

ORIGIN – Old French, 'language of *oïl*'.

languid > *adjective* **1** disinclined to exert oneself physically. **2** weak or faint from illness or fatigue.

DERIVATIVES – **languidly** *adverb*.

SYNONYMS – **1** indolent, languorous, lethargic.

languish > *verb* **1** grow weak or feeble. **2** archaic pine with love or grief. **3** be kept in an unpleasant place or situation.

SYNONYMS – **1** droop, flag, wilt.

ORIGIN – Old French *languir*, from Latin *languere*, related to *laxus* 'lax'.

languor /**lang**gə/ > *noun* **1** tiredness or inactivity, especially when pleasurable. **2** an oppressive stillness of the air.

DERIVATIVES – **languorous** *adjective* **languorously** *adverb*.

langur /**lang**gə/ > *noun* a long-tailed Asian monkey with a characteristic loud call.

ORIGIN – Hindi.

laniard > *noun* variant spelling of LANYARD.

La Niña /laa **nee**njə/ > *noun* an irregularly occurring movement of colder water in the central Pacific Ocean, opposite in effect to El Niño.
ORIGIN – Spanish, 'the girl child': see box at **EL NIÑO**.

lank > *adjective* **1** (of hair) long, limp, and straight. **2** lanky.
ORIGIN – Old English, 'thin'.

lanky > *adjective* (**lankier**, **lankiest**) (of a person) ungracefully thin and tall.
DERIVATIVES – **lankily** *adverb* **lankiness** *noun*.
SYNONYMS – gangling, gangly, gawky, lank, rangy.

lanolin /**lann**əlin/ > *noun* a fatty substance found naturally on sheep's wool and used as a base for ointments.
ORIGIN – from Latin *lana* 'wool' + *oleum* 'oil'.

lantern > *noun* **1** a lamp with a transparent case protecting the flame or electric bulb. **2** the light chamber at the top of a lighthouse. **3** a square, curved, or polygonal structure on the top of a dome or a room, with glazed or open sides.
COMBINATIONS – **lanternfish** a deep-sea fish with light-emitting organs on its body. **lantern-jawed** having long, thin jaws that give a drawn look to the face. **lantern slide** *historical* a mounted photographic transparency suitable for projection by a magic lantern.
ORIGIN – Latin *lanterna*, from Greek *lamptēr* 'lamp'.

lanthanide /**lan**thənīd/ > *noun* any of the series of fifteen similar elements from lanthanum to lutetium in the periodic table. Compare with *rare earth*.

lanthanum /**lan**thənəm/ > *noun* a silvery-white metallic chemical element.
ORIGIN – from Greek *lanthanein* 'escape notice' (because it was long undetected in cerium oxide).

lanyard /**lan**yərd/ (also **laniard**) > *noun* **1** a rope used to secure or raise and lower something such as a ship's sails. **2** a cord passed round the neck, shoulder, or wrist for holding a whistle or similar object.
ORIGIN – Old French *laniere*, altered by association with **YARD**[1].

Laodicean /layōdi**see**ən/ > *adjective* *archaic* half-hearted or indifferent, especially with respect to religion or politics.
ORIGIN – from *Laodicea* in Asia Minor, with reference to the early Christians there (Book of Revelation, chapter 3).

Laotian /**low**sh'n/ > *noun* a person from the country of Laos in SE Asia. > *adjective* relating to Laos.

lap[1] > *noun* the flat area between the waist and knees of a seated person.

IDIOMS – **fall** (or **drop**) **into someone's lap** be acquired by or happen to someone without any effort. **in someone's lap** as someone's responsibility. **in the lap of the gods** open to chance. **in the lap of luxury** in conditions of great comfort and wealth.
COMBINATIONS – **lap dancing** erotic dancing in which the dancer performs a striptease near to or on the lap of a person watching. **lapdog 1** a small pampered pet dog. **2** a person who is completely under the influence of another. **laptop** a portable microcomputer suitable for use while travelling.
ORIGIN – Old English, 'fold, flap', later denoting the front of a skirt when held up to carry something.

lap[2] > *noun* **1** one circuit of a track or racetrack. **2** a part of a journey: *the last lap*. **3** an overlapping or projecting part. **4** a single turn of rope, thread, or cable round a drum or reel. > *verb* (**lapped**, **lapping**) **1** overtake (a competitor in a race) to become one or more laps ahead. **2** (**lap in**) *literary* enfold (someone or something) protectively in. **3** project beyond or overlap something.
COMBINATIONS – **lap joint** a joint made by halving the thickness of each member at the joint and fitting them together. **lap of honour** *Brit.* a celebratory circuit of a sports field or track by the victorious person or team.
ORIGIN – from **LAP**[1]: originally as a verb in the sense 'fold or wrap'.

lap[3] > *verb* (**lapped**, **lapping**) **1** (of an animal) take up (liquid) with the tongue. **2** (**lap up**) accept with obvious pleasure. **3** (of water) wash against with a gentle rippling sound. > *noun* the action of water lapping.

laparoscopy /lappə**rosk**əpi/ > *noun* (pl. **laparoscopies**) a surgical procedure in which a fibre-optic instrument is inserted through the abdominal wall to view the organs in the abdomen or permit small-scale surgery.
DERIVATIVES – **laparoscope** *noun* **laparoscopic** *adjective*.
ORIGIN – from Greek *lapara* 'flank'.

laparotomy /lappə**rott**əmi/ > *noun* (pl. **laparotomies**) a surgical incision into the abdominal cavity, for diagnosis or in preparation for major surgery.

lapel > *noun* the part on each side of a coat or jacket immediately below the collar which is folded back against the front opening.
ORIGIN – diminutive of **LAP**[1].

lapidary /**lapp**idəri/ > *adjective* **1** relating to the engraving, cutting, or polishing of stones and gems. **2** (of language) elegant and concise. > *noun* (pl. **lapidaries**) a person who cuts, polishes, or engraves stones and gems.

ORIGIN – Latin *lapidarius*, from *lapis* 'stone'.

lapis lazuli /**lapp**iss **laz**yooli/ (also **lapis**) > *noun* **1** a bright blue metamorphic rock used in jewellery. **2** ultramarine, originally made by crushing this rock.
ORIGIN – Latin, from *lapis* 'stone' and a Persian word for the rock, related to **AZURE**.

Laplander /**lap**landər/ > *noun* a person from Lapland in northern Europe.

Lapp > *noun* **1** a member of an indigenous people of the extreme north of Scandinavia. **2** the language of this people.
DERIVATIVES – **Lappish** *adjective* & *noun*.
USAGE – although the term **Lapp** is still widely used and is the most familiar term to many people, the people themselves prefer to be called **Sami**.
ORIGIN – Swedish, perhaps originally a term of contempt and related to High German *lappe* 'simpleton'.

lappet /**lapp**it/ > *noun* **1** a fold or hanging piece of flesh in some animals. **2** a loose or overlapping part of a garment.
ORIGIN – diminutive of **LAP**[1].

lapse > *noun* **1** a brief failure of concentration, memory, or judgement. **2** a decline from previously high standards. **3** an interval of time. **4** *Law* the termination of a right or privilege through disuse or failure to follow appropriate procedures. > *verb* **1** (of a right, privilege, or agreement) become invalid because it is not used, claimed, or renewed. **2** cease to follow the rules and practices of a religion or doctrine. **3** (**lapse into**) pass gradually into (a different, often worse, state or condition).
SYNONYMS – *noun* **1** failure, slip. **2** decline, drop, slide, slump. **3** break, gap, interval, pause.
ORIGIN – Latin *lapsus*, from *labi* 'to slip or fall'.

lapwing > *noun* a large crested plover with a dark green back, black-and-white head and underparts, and a loud call.
ORIGIN – Old English, from a word meaning 'to leap' and a base meaning 'move from side to side' (because of the way it flies).

larboard /**laa**bord, **laa**bərd/ > *noun* *Nautical, archaic* port (side of a ship).
ORIGIN – first spelled *ladebord* (see **LADE**, **BOARD**), referring to the side on which cargo was loaded; the change to *lar*- was due to association with **STARBOARD**. See also **PORT**[3].

larceny /**laar**səni/ > *noun* (pl. **larcenies**) theft of personal property (in English law replaced as a statutory crime by theft in 1968).
DERIVATIVES – **larcenist** *noun* **larcenous** *adjective*.

ORIGIN – Old French *larcin*, from Latin *latro* 'robber'.

larch > *noun* a northern coniferous tree with bunches of deciduous bright green needles and tough wood.

ORIGIN – High German *larche*, from Latin *larix*.

lard > *noun* fat from the abdomen of a pig, rendered and clarified for use in cooking. > *verb* **1** insert strips of fat or bacon in (meat) before cooking. **2** (usu. **be larded with**) embellish (talk or writing) excessively with esoteric or technical expressions.

DERIVATIVES – **lardy** *adjective*.

ORIGIN – Latin *lardum*.

larder > *noun* a room or large cupboard for storing food.

ORIGIN – Latin *lardarium*, from *lardum* 'lard': originally denoting a store of meat.

lardon /laard'n/ (also **lardoon** /laardoon/) > *noun* a chunk or strip of bacon used to lard meat.

ORIGIN – French.

lardy cake > *noun* Brit. a cake made with bread dough, lard, and currants.

large > *adjective* **1** of considerable or relatively great size, extent, or capacity. **2** pursuing an occupation or activity on a significant scale. **3** of wide range or scope. > *verb* (**large it**) Brit. informal go out and have a good time.

IDIOMS – **at large 1** escaped or not yet captured. **2** as a whole.

DERIVATIVES – **largeness** *noun* **largish** *adjective*.

SYNONYMS – *adjective* **1** big, considerable, grand, great, sizeable, substantial.

ANTONYMS – *adjective* **1** little, small.

COMBINATIONS – **large intestine** Anatomy the caecum, colon, and rectum collectively. **large-scale 1** extensive. **2** (of a map or model) large enough to show much detail.

ORIGIN – Latin *largus* 'copious'.

largely > *adverb* on the whole; mostly.

largesse /laarzhess/ (also **largess**) > *noun* **1** generosity in giving to others. **2** money or gifts given generously.

SYNONYMS – **1** bountifulness, generosity, liberality, magnanimity, munificence.

ORIGIN – Old French, from Latin *largus* 'copious'.

largo /laargō/ > *adverb & adjective* Music with a slow tempo and dignified style.

ORIGIN – Italian, from Latin *largus* 'copious'.

lari /laari/ > *noun* (pl. same or **laris**) a monetary unit of the Maldives, equal to one hundredth of a rufiyaa.

ORIGIN – Persian.

lariat /larriət/ > *noun* a rope used as a lasso or for tethering.

ORIGIN – Spanish *la reata*, from *la* 'the' and *reatar* 'tie again'.

lark¹ > *noun* a songbird with brown streaky plumage and a song that is delivered on the wing.

IDIOMS – **be up with the lark** be out of bed very early in the morning.

lark² informal > *noun* **1** an amusing adventure or escapade. **2** Brit. an activity regarded as foolish or a waste of time: *he's serious about this music lark*. > *verb* behave in a playful and mischievous way.

DERIVATIVES – **larky** *adjective*.

ORIGIN – perhaps from dialect *lake* 'play', but compare with **SKYLARK** in the same sense, which is recorded earlier.

larkspur > *noun* a Mediterranean plant resembling a delphinium, with spikes of spurred flowers.

larrikin /larrikin/ > *noun* Austral./NZ **1** dated a hooligan. **2** a person who disregards convention.

ORIGIN – English dialect, perhaps from the name *Larry* + **-KIN**, or from a pronunciation of *larking*.

larva /laarvə/ > *noun* (pl. **larvae** /laarvee/) an active immature form of an insect or other animal that later undergoes metamorphosis into the adult form, such as a caterpillar or tadpole.

DERIVATIVES – **larval** *adjective*.

ORIGIN – Latin, 'ghost, mask': originally denoting a disembodied spirit.

laryngeal /lərinjiəl/ > *adjective* relating to the larynx.

laryngitis /larrinjītiss/ > *noun* inflammation of the larynx.

larynx /larrinks/ > *noun* (pl. **larynges** /lərinjeez/) the hollow muscular organ forming an air passage to the lungs and containing the vocal cords.

ORIGIN – Greek *larunx*.

lasagne /ləzanjə/ > *noun* **1** pasta in the form of sheets or wide strips. **2** an Italian dish consisting of this baked with meat or vegetables and a cheese sauce.

ORIGIN – Italian, from Latin *lasanum* 'chamber pot'.

Lascar /laskər/ > *noun* dated a sailor from India or SE Asia.

ORIGIN – Urdu and Persian 'soldier'.

lascivious /ləsivviəss/ > *adjective* feeling or showing an overt or offensive sexual desire.

DERIVATIVES – **lasciviously** *adverb* **lasciviousness** *noun*.

SYNONYMS – lecherous, libidinous, lustful, salacious.

ORIGIN – from Latin *lascivia* 'lustfulness'.

laser /layzər/ > *noun* a device that generates an intense narrow beam of light of a single wavelength by stimulating the emission of photons from excited atoms or molecules.

COMBINATIONS – **laserdisc** a disc resembling a large compact disc, used for high-quality video and for interactive multimedia. **laser printer** a computer printer in which a laser is used to form a pattern of electrically charged dots on a light-sensitive drum, which attracts toner.

ORIGIN – acronym from *light amplification by stimulated emission of radiation*.

lash > *verb* **1** beat with a whip or stick. **2** beat forcefully against. **3** (**lash out**) launch a verbal or physical attack. **4** (of an animal) move (a part of the body, especially the tail) quickly and violently. **5** fasten securely with a cord or rope. **6** (**lash out**) Brit. spend money extravagantly. > *noun* **1** a sharp blow or stroke with a whip or stick. **2** the flexible leather part of a whip. **3** an eyelash.

DERIVATIVES – **lashless** *adjective*.

SYNONYMS – *verb* **1** flail, flog, scourge, thrash, whip. **2** batter, buffet, pound.

COMBINATIONS – **lash-up** informal, chiefly Brit. a makeshift, improvised structure or arrangement.

lashing > *noun* **1** a whipping or beating. **2** a cord used to fasten something securely.

lashings > *plural noun* Brit. informal a copious amount of something, especially food or drink.

lass (also **lassie**) > *noun* chiefly Scottish & N. English a girl or young woman.

ORIGIN – from Old Norse *laskura* 'unmarried'.

Lassa fever /lassə/ > *noun* an acute and often fatal disease caused by a virus and occurring chiefly in West Africa.

ORIGIN – named after the village of *Lassa* in Nigeria, where it was first reported.

lassi /lassi/ > *noun* a sweet or savoury Indian drink made from a yogurt or buttermilk base with water.

ORIGIN – Hindi.

lassitude /lassityood/ > *noun* physical or mental weariness; lack of energy.

ORIGIN – Latin *lassitudo*, from *lassus* 'tired'.

lasso /lasoo/ > *noun* (pl. **lassos** or **lassoes**) a rope with a noose at one end, used especially in North America for catching cattle. > *verb* (**lassoes**, **lassoed**) catch with a lasso.

DERIVATIVES – **lassoer** *noun*.

ORIGIN – Spanish *lazo*, from Latin *laqueus* 'noose'.

last¹ > *adjective* **1** coming after all others in time or order. **2** most recent in time. **3** immediately preceding in order. **4** lowest in importance or rank. **5** (**the last**) the least likely or suitable. **6** only remaining: *our last hope*. > *adverb* **1** on the last occasion before the present. **2** after all others in order: *the last-named film*. **3** (in enumerating points) lastly. > *noun* (pl. same) **1** the last person or thing. **2** (**the last of**) the only remaining part. **3** (**the last**) the end or last moment, especially death.

IDIOMS – **at last** (or **at long last**) in the end; after much delay. **last thing** late in the evening, especially just before going to bed.

SYNONYMS – *adjective* **1** endmost, final, furthest, rearmost, ultimate.

ANTONYMS – *adjective* first.

COMBINATIONS – **last-ditch** denoting a final desperate attempt to do or achieve something. **last-gasp** informal done at the last possible moment. **Last Judgement** the judgement of humankind expected in some religious traditions to take place at the end of the world. **last minute** (also **last moment**) the latest possible time before an event. **last name** one's surname. **last post** (in the British armed forces) the second of two bugle calls giving notice of the hour of retiring at night, played also at military funerals and acts of remembrance. **last rites** (in the Christian Church) rites administered to a person who is about to die. **Last Supper** the supper eaten by Jesus and his disciples on the night before the Crucifixion. **last trump** the trumpet blast that in some religious beliefs is thought will wake the dead on Judgement Day. **last word 1** a final or definitive pronouncement on a matter. **2** the most modern or advanced example of something: *the last word in luxury*.

ORIGIN – Old English, related to **LATE**.

last² > *verb* **1** continue for a specified period of time. **2** remain operating or usable for a considerable or specified length of time. **3** (of provisions or resources) be sufficient for (someone) for a specified length of time. **4** (often **last out**) manage to survive or endure.

SYNONYMS – **1** continue, endure, persist, proceed. **2** endure, survive.

ORIGIN – Old English, related to **LAST³**.

last³ > *noun* a shoemaker's model for shaping or repairing a shoe or boot.

ORIGIN – Old English, from a base meaning 'follow'.

lasting > *adjective* enduring or able to endure for a long time.

DERIVATIVES – **lastingly** *adverb* **lastingness** *noun*.

lastly > *adverb* in the last place; last.

lat /lat/ > *noun* (pl. **lati** /latti/ or **lats**) the basic monetary unit of Latvia, equal to 100 santims.

ORIGIN – from the first syllable of *Latvija* 'Latvia'.

lat. > *abbreviation* latitude.

latch > *noun* **1** a bar with a catch and lever used for fastening a door or gate. **2** a spring lock for an outer door, which catches when the door is closed and can only be opened from the outside with a key. > *verb* **1** fasten with a latch. **2** (**latch on**) understand. **3** (**latch on to**) enthusiastically associate oneself with.

IDIOMS – **on the latch** (of a door or gate) closed but not locked.

ORIGIN – Old English, 'take hold of, grasp'.

latchkey > *noun* (pl. **latchkeys**) a key of an outer door of a house.

COMBINATIONS – **latchkey child** a child who is alone at home after school until a parent returns from work.

late > *adjective* **1** acting, arriving, or happening after the proper or usual time. **2** belonging or taking place far on in a particular time or period. **3** far on in the day or night. **4** (**the** or **one's late**) (of a person) no longer alive. **5** (**the** or **one's late**) no longer having the specified status; former. **6** (**latest**) of most recent date or origin. > *adverb* **1** after the proper or usual time. **2** towards the end of a period. **3** far on in the day or night. **4** (**later**) at a time in the near future; afterwards. **5** (**late of**) formerly but not now living or working in (a place). > *noun* (**the latest**) the most recent news or fashion.

IDIOMS – **at the latest** no later than the time specified. **of late** recently.

DERIVATIVES – **lateness** *noun*.

SYNONYMS – *adjective* **1** belated, delayed, overdue, tardy, unpunctual.

ANTONYMS – *adjective* **1** early, punctual.

COMBINATIONS – **latecomer** a person who arrives late.

lateen sail /lateen/ > *noun* a triangular sail on a long yard at an angle of 45° to the mast.

ORIGIN – from French *voile Latine* 'Latin sail', so named because it was common in the Mediterranean.

lately > *adverb* recently; not long ago.

latent > *adjective* existing but not yet developed, manifest, or active.

DERIVATIVES – **latency** *noun* **latently** *adverb*.

SYNONYMS – dormant, hidden, potential, undeveloped, undiscovered.

COMBINATIONS – **latent heat** the heat required to convert a solid into a liquid or vapour, or a liquid into a vapour, without change of temperature. **latent image** an image on film that has not yet been made visible by developing. **latent period** Medicine the period between infection and the onset of symptoms.

ORIGIN – from Latin *latere* 'be hidden'.

lateral /lattərəl/ > *adjective* of, at, towards, or from the side or sides. > *noun* a lateral part, especially a shoot or branch growing out from the side of a stem.

DERIVATIVES – **laterally** *adverb*.

COMBINATIONS – **lateral thinking** chiefly Brit. the solving of problems by an indirect and creative approach.

ORIGIN – Latin *lateralis*, from *latus* 'side'.

laterite /lattərīt/ > *noun* a reddish clayey topsoil, hard when dry, found in tropical regions and sometimes used to make roads.

ORIGIN – from Latin *later* 'brick'.

latex /layteks/ > *noun* (pl. **latexes** or **latices** /laytiseez/) **1** a milky fluid found in many plants, notably the rubber tree, which coagulates on exposure to the air. **2** a synthetic product resembling this, used to make paints, coatings, etc.

ORIGIN – Latin, 'liquid, fluid'.

lath /laath/ > *noun* (pl. **laths** /laaths/) a thin, flat strip of wood, especially each of a series forming a foundation for the plaster of a wall.

ORIGIN – Old English, related to **LATTICE**.

lathe /layth/ > *noun* a machine for shaping wood or metal by means of a rotating drive which turns the piece being worked on against changeable cutting tools.

ORIGIN – probably from Old Danish *lad* 'structure, frame'.

lather /laathər/ > *noun* **1** a frothy white mass of bubbles produced by soap when mixed with water. **2** heavy sweat visible on a horse's coat as a white foam. **3** (**a lather**) informal a state of agitation or nervous excitement. > *verb* **1** form or cause to form a lather. **2** rub with soap until a lather is produced. **3** cover or spread liberally with (a substance). **4** informal thrash.

lathi /laatee/ > *noun* (pl. **lathis**) (in the Indian subcontinent) a long metal-bound bamboo stick used as a weapon, especially by police.

ORIGIN – Hindi.

latices plural of **LATEX**.

Latin > *noun* **1** the language of ancient Rome and its empire. **2** a person from a country whose language developed from Latin, e.g. a Latin American. > *adjective* **1** relating to the Latin language. **2** relating to countries using languages that developed from Latin, especially Latin America. **3** relating to the Western or Roman Catholic Church.

DERIVATIVES – **Latinism** *noun* **Latinist** *noun* **Latinity** *noun*.

COMBINATIONS – **Latin Church** the Roman Catholic Church as distinguished from Orthodox and Uniate Churches. **Latin cross** a plain cross in which the vertical part below the horizontal is longer than the other three parts.

wordpower facts

Latin

The word **Latin** derives from the name of the ancient region of *Latium* in central Italy, which is roughly equivalent to the modern *Lazio*. The *Latins* were an ancient Italian people who from the 4th century BC were dominated by Rome. Latin was the language of Rome and its empire, and after the decline of the Roman Empire it continued to be used for communication among educated people throughout the Middle Ages in Europe and elsewhere. It remained the liturgical language of the Roman Catholic Church until the reforms of the second Vatican Council (1962–5), and it is still used for scientific names in biology and astronomy. The Romance languages (e.g. French, Italian, Portuguese, and Spanish) are derived from it.

Latin American > *adjective* relating to Latin America, the parts of the American continent where Spanish or Portuguese is the main national language. > *noun* a person from Latin America.

Latinate /**latt**inayt/ > *adjective* (of language) having the character of Latin.

Latinise (also **Latinize**) > *verb* **1** give a Latin or Latinate form to (a word). **2** cause to conform to the ideas and customs of the ancient Romans, the Latin Church, or Latin peoples.
DERIVATIVES – **Latinisation** *noun*.

Latino /**lateen**ō/ > *noun* (pl. **Latinos**; fem. **Latina**, pl. **Latinas**) N. Amer. a Latin American inhabitant of the United States.
ORIGIN – Latin American Spanish.

latitude /**latt**ityōod/ > *noun* **1** the angular distance of a place north or south of the equator. **2** (**latitudes**) regions with reference to their temperature and distance from the equator: *northern latitudes*. **3** scope for freedom of action or thought.
DERIVATIVES – **latitudinal** *adjective* **latitudinally** *adverb*.
SYNONYMS – **3** freedom, leeway, scope.
ORIGIN – Latin *latitudo* 'breadth'.

latitudinarian /lattityōodi**nair**iən/ > *adjective* liberal, especially in religious views. > *noun* a latitudinarian person.
DERIVATIVES – **latitudinarianism** *noun*.

latke /**lut**kə/ > *noun* (in Jewish cookery) a pancake, especially one made with grated potato.
ORIGIN – Yiddish.

latrine /lə**treen**/ > *noun* a toilet, especially a communal one in a camp or barracks.
ORIGIN – Latin *latrina*, from *lavare* 'to wash'.

latte /**laa**tay/ > *noun* a drink of frothy steamed milk to which a shot of espresso coffee is added.
ORIGIN – Italian, short for *caffè latte* 'milk coffee'.

latter > *adjective* **1** nearer to the end than to the beginning. **2** recent: *in latter years*. **3** (**the latter**) denoting the second or second-mentioned of two people or things.
COMBINATIONS – **Latter-Day Saints** the Mormons' name for themselves.
ORIGIN – Old English, 'slower'; related to **LATE**.

latter-day > *adjective* contemporary or modern, especially when resembling some person or thing of the past: *a latter-day Noah*.

latterly > *adverb* **1** recently. **2** in the later stages of a period of time.

lattice > *noun* **1** a structure or pattern consisting of strips crossing each other with square or diamond-shaped spaces left between. **2** a regular repeated three-dimensional arrangement of atoms or molecules in a crystalline solid.
DERIVATIVES – **latticed** *adjective* **latticework** *noun*.
COMBINATIONS – **lattice window** a window with small panes set in diagonally crossing strips of lead.
ORIGIN – Old French *lattis*, from *latte* 'lath'.

Latvian /**lat**viən/ > *noun* **1** a person from Latvia. **2** the language of Latvia. > *adjective* relating to Latvia.

laud /lawd/ > *verb* formal praise highly.
DERIVATIVES – **laudation** *noun*.
SYNONYMS – acclaim, exalt, extol, hail, praise.
ORIGIN – Latin *laudare*, from *laus* 'praise'.

laudable > *adjective* deserving praise and commendation.
DERIVATIVES – **laudably** *adverb*.
SYNONYMS – admirable, commendable, meritorious, praiseworthy, worthy.

laudanum /**law**dənəm/ > *noun* a solution prepared from opium and formerly used as a narcotic painkiller.
ORIGIN – Latin, perhaps a variant of *ladanum*, a kind of gum resin.

laudatory /**law**dətri/ > *adjective* expressing praise and commendation.
SYNONYMS – adulatory, celebratory, commendatory, extolling, praising.

lauds /lawdz/ > *noun* a service of morning prayer in the Divine Office of the Western Christian Church, traditionally said or chanted at daybreak.
ORIGIN – from the use, in Psalms 148–150, of Latin *laudate!* 'praise!'

laugh > *verb* **1** make the sounds and movements that express lively amusement and sometimes also derision. **2** (**laugh at**) make fun of; ridicule. **3** (**laugh off**) dismiss (something) by treating it light-heartedly. **4** (**be laughing**) informal be in a fortunate or successful position. > *noun* **1** an act of laughing. **2** (**a laugh**) informal a source of laughter or amusement.
IDIOMS – **have the last laugh** be finally vindicated. **he who laughs last laughs longest** proverb don't rejoice too soon, in case your delight at your own good fortune is premature. **laugh on the other side of one's face** be discomfited after feeling confident or triumphant. **laugh out of court** dismiss with contempt as being obviously ridiculous. **laugh up one's sleeve** be secretly or inwardly amused.
DERIVATIVES – **laugher** *noun*.
SYNONYMS – *verb* & *noun* **1** chortle, chuckle, giggle, guffaw, snicker, snigger, titter.
COMBINATIONS – **laughing gas** nitrous oxide. **laughing hyena** a southern African hyena with a loud laughing call. **laughing jackass** Austral. the kookaburra. **laughing stock** a person or group subjected to general ridicule.

laughable > *adjective* so ludicrous as to be amusing.
DERIVATIVES – **laughably** *adverb*.
SYNONYMS – absurd, ludicrous, preposterous, ridiculous, risible.

laughter > *noun* the action or sound of laughing.

launch[1] > *verb* **1** move (a boat or ship) from land into the water. **2** send out or hurl (a rocket or other missile). **3** begin (an enterprise) or introduce (a new product). **4** (**launch into**) begin energetically and enthusiastically. > *noun* an act or instance of launching.
SYNONYMS – *verb* **1** float. **2** catapult, dispatch, fire, propel. **3** begin, establish, initiate, instigate, introduce.
ORIGIN – Old French *launcher*, variant of *lancier* 'to lance'.

launch[2] > *noun* **1** a large motor boat. **2** historical the largest boat carried on a man-of-war.
ORIGIN – Spanish *lancha* 'pinnace', perhaps from a Malay word meaning 'swift'.

launcher > *noun* a structure that holds a rocket or missile during launching.

launder > *verb* **1** wash and iron (clothes or linen). **2** informal pass (illegally obtained money) through legitimate businesses or foreign banks to conceal its origins.
DERIVATIVES – **launderer** *noun*.
ORIGIN – from Old French *lavandier*, denoting a person who washes linen, from Latin *lavare* 'to wash'.

launderette (also **laundrette**) > *noun* an establishment with coin-operated washing machines and dryers for public use.

laundress > *noun* a woman employed to launder clothes and linen.

laundromat > *noun* chiefly N. Amer. (trademark in the US) a launderette.

laundry > *noun* (pl. **laundries**) **1** clothes and linen that need to be washed or that have been newly washed. **2** a room or building where clothes and linen are washed and ironed.

laureate /lorriət/ > *noun* **1** a person given an award for outstanding creative or intellectual achievement. **2** a poet laureate. > *adjective* literary wreathed with laurel as a mark of honour.

DERIVATIVES – **laureateship** *noun*.

ORIGIN – from Latin *laurea* 'laurel wreath'.

laurel > *noun* **1** an aromatic evergreen shrub or small tree with dark green glossy leaves. **2** historical a bay tree. **3** (**laurels**) a crown woven from bay leaves, awarded as an emblem of victory or mark of honour in classical times. **4** (**laurels**) honour or praise.

IDIOMS – **look to one's laurels** be careful not to lose one's superior position to a rival. **rest on one's laurels** be so satisfied with what one has already achieved that one makes no further effort.

ORIGIN – Latin *laurus*.

lava > *noun* hot molten or semi-fluid rock erupted from a volcano or fissure, or solid rock resulting from cooling of this.

WORDFINDER – igneous (*denoting rock formed from solidified lava or magma*), magma (*molten rock in the earth's crust, erupted as lava*).

COMBINATIONS – **lava lamp** a transparent electric lamp containing a viscous liquid in which a suspended waxy substance rises and falls in constantly changing shapes.

wordpower facts

Lava

The Latin word *lavare* 'to wash' is the unexpected link between **lava** and **lavatory**. **Lava** entered English from Italian, in which language it originally referred to a stream caused by sudden rain. Other words based on *lavare* include **lavish**, **launder**, and **lotion**. The Hawaiians distinguished two main forms of solid lava: rough, jagged clinkers or **aa** (pronounced aa-aa) and smooth, undulating masses or **pahoehoe** (pronounced pəhōihōi). Another rare kind was slender threads of glass formed when lava spray cooled in the air. This was known as **Pele's hair**, in Hawaiian *lauohu o Pele*, Pele being the goddess of the volcanoes. All of these terms have become standard in volcanology.

lavage /lavvij/ > *noun* Medicine washing out of a body cavity, such as the colon or stomach, with water or a medicated solution.

lavatorial > *adjective* **1** relating to or resembling lavatories. **2** (of conversation or humour) characterised by undue reference to lavatories and excretion.

lavatory > *noun* (pl. **lavatories**) a toilet.

ORIGIN – Latin *lavatorium* 'place for washing', from *lavare* 'to wash'.

lave /layv/ > *verb* literary wash or wash over.

ORIGIN – Latin *lavare* 'to wash'.

lavender > *noun* **1** a small aromatic evergreen shrub of the mint family, with narrow leaves and bluish-purple flowers. **2** a pale blue colour with a trace of mauve.

COMBINATIONS – **lavender water** a perfume made from distilled lavender.

ORIGIN – Latin *lavandula*.

laver /laavər/ (also **purple laver**) > *noun* an edible seaweed with thin reddish-purple and green sheet-like fronds.

COMBINATIONS – **laver bread** a Welsh dish of laver which is boiled, dipped in oatmeal, and fried.

ORIGIN – Latin.

lavish > *adjective* **1** sumptuously rich, elaborate, or luxurious. **2** giving or given in profusion. > *verb* (usu. **lavish on**) give or spend in abundant or extravagant quantities.

DERIVATIVES – **lavishly** *adverb* **lavishness** *noun*.

SYNONYMS – **1** elaborate, grand, luxurious, opulent, rich, sumptuous. **2** abundant, bountiful, generous, liberal.

ANTONYMS – **1** austere.

ORIGIN – first used as a noun meaning 'profusion': from Old French *lavasse* 'deluge of rain', from Latin *lavare* 'to wash'.

law > *noun* **1** a rule or system of rules recognised by a country or community as regulating the actions of its members and enforced by the imposition of penalties. **2** such rules as a subject of study or as the basis of the legal profession. **3** statute law and the common law. **4** a statement of fact to the effect that a particular natural or scientific phenomenon always occurs if certain conditions are present. **5** a rule defining correct procedure or behaviour in a sport. **6** something having binding force or effect: *his word was law*. **7** (**the law**) informal the police.

IDIOMS – **be a law unto oneself** behave in a very unconventional or unpredictable manner. **lay down the law** issue instructions in an authoritative or dogmatic way. **take the law into one's own hands** illegally or violently punish someone according to one's own ideas of justice.

COMBINATIONS – **law-abiding** obedient to the laws of society. **law agent** (in Scotland) a solicitor. **lawbreaker** a person who breaks the law. **law centre** (in the UK) an independent publicly funded advisory service on legal matters. **law clerk** N. Amer. **1** a judge's research assistant. **2** an articled clerk. **law court** a court of law. **lawgiver** a person who draws up and enacts laws. **law lord** a member of the House of Lords qualified to perform its legal work. **lawmaker** a legislator. **law of averages** the supposed principle that future events are likely to turn out so that they balance any past deviation from a presumed average. **law of nature 1** a natural law. **2** informal a regularly occurring phenomenon observable in society. **lawsuit** a claim or dispute brought to a law court for adjudication.

ORIGIN – Old Norse *lag* 'something laid down or fixed'; related to **LAY¹**.

lawful > *adjective* conforming to, permitted by, or recognised by law or rules.

DERIVATIVES – **lawfully** *adverb* **lawfulness** *noun*.

USAGE – what is the difference between **lawful** and **legal**? **Lawful** refers to the law but also to the rules applying to an activity, whereas **legal** refers only to law: thus there might be some debate as to whether a goal scored in soccer is **lawful**, but not whether it is **legal**.

SYNONYMS – just, legitimate, licit, permissible.

ANTONYMS – unlawful.

lawless > *adjective* not governed by or obedient to laws.

DERIVATIVES – **lawlessly** *adverb* **lawlessness** *noun*.

SYNONYMS – anarchic, disorderly, lawbreaking, rebellious, unruly.

lawman > *noun* (in the US) a law-enforcement officer, especially a sheriff.

lawn¹ > *noun* an area of mown grass in a garden or park.

DERIVATIVES – **lawned** *adjective*.

COMBINATIONS – **lawnmower** a machine for cutting the grass on a lawn. **lawn tennis dated** or formal tennis.

ORIGIN – Old French *launde* 'wooded district, heath'.

lawn² > *noun* a fine linen or cotton fabric.

ORIGIN – probably from *Laon*, a city in France important for linen manufacture.

lawrencium /lərensiəm/ > *noun* a very unstable chemical element made by high-energy collisions.

ORIGIN – named after the American physicist Ernest O. *Lawrence* (1901–58).

lawyer > *noun* a person who practises or studies law, especially (in the UK) a solicitor or a barrister or (in the US) an attorney.

DERIVATIVES – **lawyerly** *adjective*.

lax > *adjective* **1** not sufficiently strict, severe, or careful. **2** (of limbs or muscles) relaxed.

DERIVATIVES – **laxity** *noun* **laxly** *adverb* **laxness** *noun*.

SYNONYMS – **1** careless, casual, neglectful, remiss, slack, slipshod.

ORIGIN – Latin *laxus* 'loose': first used with reference to the bowels.

laxative > *adjective* tending to stimulate or facilitate evacuation of the bowels. > *noun* a laxative drug or medicine.

lay¹ > *verb* (past and past participle **laid**) **1** put down, especially gently or carefully. **2** put down and set in position for use. **3** assign or place: *lay the blame*. **4** (**lay before**) present (material) for consideration and action to. **5** (of a female bird, reptile, etc.) produce (an egg) from inside the body. **6** stake (an amount of money) in a wager. **7** cause (a ghost) to stop appearing; exorcise. **8** vulgar slang have sexual intercourse with. > *noun* **1** the general appearance of an area of land. **2** the position or direction in which something lies. **3** vulgar slang a sexual partner or act of sexual intercourse.

IDIOMS – **lay about one** strike out wildly. **lay claim to** assert one's right to or possession of. **lay down 1** formulate and enact (a rule or principle). **2** build up a deposit of (a substance). **3** store (wine) in a cellar. **4** pay or wager (money). **lay in/up** build up (a stock) in case of need. **lay into** informal attack violently. **lay off 1** discharge (a worker) temporarily or permanently because of a shortage of work. **2** informal give up. **lay on** chiefly Brit. provide (a service or amenity). **lay on thick** (or **with a trowel**) informal grossly exaggerate or overemphasise (something). **lay open to** expose (someone) to the risk of. **lay out 1** construct or arrange (buildings or gardens) according to a plan. **2** arrange and present (material) for printing and publication. **3** prepare (someone) for burial after death. **4** informal spend (a sum of money). **lay to rest 1** bury (a body) in a grave. **2** soothe and dispel (fear, anxiety, etc.). **lay up 1** put out of action through illness or injury. **2** see *lay in*. **3** take (a ship or other vehicle) out of service.

USAGE – make sure that you use **lay** and **lie** correctly. You *lay* something, as in *they are going to lay the carpet*, but you *lie* down on a bed or other flat surface. The past tense and past participle of **lay** is **laid**, as in *they laid the groundwork* or *she had laid careful plans*; the past tense of **lie** is **lay** (*he lay on the floor*) and the past participle is **lain** (*she had lain on the bed for hours*).

SYNONYMS – *verb* **1** deposit, place, rest, set. **2** arrange, fix, position. **3** ascribe, assign, attach, fix, place.

ORIGIN – Old English, related to LIE¹.

lay² > *adjective* **1** not ordained into or belonging to the clergy. **2** not having professional qualifications or expert knowledge.

COMBINATIONS – **lay brother** (or **lay sister**) a person who has taken the vows of a religious order but is not ordained and is employed in ancillary or manual work. **lay reader** (in the Anglican Church) a layperson licensed to preach and to conduct some services but not to celebrate the Eucharist.

ORIGIN – from Greek *laos* 'people'.

lay³ > *noun* **1** a short lyric or narrative poem intended to be sung. **2** literary a song.

ORIGIN – Old French *lai*.

lay⁴ past of LIE¹.

layabout > *noun* derogatory a person who habitually does little or no work.

lay-by > *noun* (pl. **lay-bys**) **1** Brit. an area at the side of a road where vehicles may pull off the road and stop. **2** Austral./NZ & S. African a system of paying a deposit to secure an article for later purchase.

layer > *noun* **1** a sheet or thickness of material, typically one of several, covering a surface. **2** a person or thing that lays something: *a cable-layer*. **3** a shoot fastened down to take root while attached to the parent plant. > *verb* **1** arrange or cut in a layer or layers. **2** propagate (a plant) as a layer.

DERIVATIVES – **layered** *adjective*.

wordpower facts

Layer

In medieval times a **layer** was 'a person who lays stones, a mason'. The sense 'stratum of material covering a surface' (early 17th century) may represent a respelling of an obsolete agricultural use of LAIR¹, which referred to quality of soil.

layette > *noun* a set of clothing and bedclothes for a newborn child.

ORIGIN – French, originally in the sense 'little drawer'.

lay figure > *noun* a jointed model of the human body used by artists.

ORIGIN – from obsolete *layman*, from Dutch *leeman*, from *lid* 'joint'.

layman (or **layperson**) > *noun* **1** a non-ordained member of a Church. **2** a person who has no professional or specialised knowledge.

lay-off > *noun* **1** a temporary or permanent discharge of a worker or workers. **2** a temporary break from an activity.

layout > *noun* **1** the way in which something, especially a page, is laid out. **2** a thing set out in a particular way.

layover > *noun* chiefly N. Amer. a period of rest or waiting before a further stage in a journey.

layshaft > *noun* Brit. a second or intermediate transmission shaft in a machine.

laywoman > *noun* a non-ordained female member of a Church.

laze > *verb* spend time relaxing or doing very little. > *noun* a spell of lazing.

SYNONYMS – *verb* idle, loaf, lounge, relax.

lazy > *adjective* (**lazier**, **laziest**) **1** unwilling to work or use energy. **2** showing or characterised by a lack of effort or care.

DERIVATIVES – **lazily** adverb **laziness** noun.

SYNONYMS – **1** idle, inactive, indolent, languid, slothful, work-shy.

ANTONYMS – **1** energetic, hard-working.

COMBINATIONS – **lazybones** (pl. same) informal a lazy person. **lazy eye** an eye with poor vision due to underuse, especially the unused eye in a squint.

ORIGIN – perhaps related to Low German *lasich* 'languid, idle'.

lb > *abbreviation* pound(s) (in weight).

ORIGIN – from Latin *libra*.

lbw > *abbreviation* Cricket leg before wicket.

l.c. > *abbreviation* **1** in the passage cited. [ORIGIN – from Latin *loco citato*.] **2** lower case.

LCD > *abbreviation* **1** Electronics & Computing liquid crystal display. **2** Mathematics lowest (or least) common denominator.

LCM > *abbreviation* Mathematics lowest (or least) common multiple.

L-driver > *noun* Brit. a learner driver.

LEA > *abbreviation* Local Education Authority.

lea > *noun* literary an open area of grassy or arable land.

leach > *verb* remove (a soluble substance) from soil or other material by the action of rainwater or other liquid seeping or flowing through it.

ORIGIN – Old English, 'to water'.

lead¹ /leed/ > *verb* (past and past participle **led** /led/) **1** cause (a person or animal) to go with one, especially by drawing them along or by preceding them to a destination. **2** be a route or means of access: *the street led into the square*. **3** (**lead to**) result in. **4** influence to do or believe something: *that may lead them to reconsider*. **5** be in charge of. **6** have the advantage in a race or game. **7** be superior to (a competitor). **8** have or experience (a particular way of life). **9** (often **lead with** or **off with**) begin with a particular action or item. **10** (**lead up to**) precede or result in. **11** (**lead on**) deceive (someone) into believing that one is attracted to them. **12** (in card games) play (the first card) in a trick or round of play. > *noun* **1** the initiative in an action: *other companies followed our lead*. **2** (**the lead**) a position of advantage in a contest; first place. **3** an amount by which a competitor is ahead of the others: *a one-goal lead*. **4** the chief part in a play or film. **5** (before another noun) playing the chief part in a musical group: *the lead singer*. **6** (before another noun) denoting the principal item in a report or text: *the lead article.* **7** a clue to be followed in the resolution of a problem. **8** Brit. a strap or cord for restraining and guiding a dog. **9** a wire conveying electric current from a source to an appliance, or connecting two points of a circuit together. **10** (in card games) an act or the right of playing first in a trick or round of play.

IDIOMS – **lead astray** cause (someone) to act or think foolishly or wrongly. **lead up the garden path** informal give misleading clues or signals to. **lead with one's chin** informal **1** (of a boxer) leave one's chin unprotected. **2** behave or speak incautiously.

SYNONYMS – *verb* **1** conduct, guide, pilot, usher. **5** command, control, direct, head. **8** experience, have, live, pass, spend. *noun* **1** example, initiative, precedent.

COMBINATIONS – **lead-in** an introduction or preamble. **lead time** the time between the initiation and completion of a production process. **lead-up** an event or sequence that leads up to something else.

ORIGIN – Old English, related to **LOAD** and **LODE**.

lead² /led/ > *noun* **1** a heavy, soft, ductile bluish-grey metallic chemical element. **2** graphite used as the part of a pencil that makes a mark. **3** Printing a blank space between lines of print (originally created by a metal strip). **4** Nautical a lump of lead suspended on a line to determine the depth of water. **5** (**leads**) Brit. sheets or strips of lead covering a roof. **6** (**leads**) lead frames holding the glass of a lattice or stained-glass window.

WORDFINDER – plumbism (*lead poisoning*).

IDIOMS – **go down like a lead balloon** (of a speech, proposal, or joke) be poorly received.

COMBINATIONS – **lead crystal** (also **lead glass**) glass containing lead oxide, making it more refractive.

leaded > *adjective* **1** framed, covered, or weighted with lead. **2** (of petrol) containing tetraethyl lead.

leaden > *adjective* **1** dull, heavy, or slow. **2** of the dull grey colour of lead. **3** archaic made of lead.

DERIVATIVES – **leadenly** *adverb.*

leader > *noun* **1** a person or thing that leads. **2** a person or thing that is the most successful or advanced in a particular area. **3** the principal player in a music group. **4** Brit. a leading article in a newspaper. **5** (also **Leader of the House**) Brit. a member of the government officially responsible for initiating business in Parliament. **6** a short strip of non-functioning material at each end of a reel of film or recording tape for connection to the spool.

DERIVATIVES – **leaderless** *adjective.*

SYNONYMS – **1** captain, chief, commander, director, guide, head, ruler.

ANTONYMS – **1** follower.

COMBINATIONS – **leader board** a scoreboard showing the names and current scores of the leading competitors, especially in a golf match.

leadership > *noun* **1** the action of leading a group or organisation. **2** the state or position of being a leader. **3** the leaders of an organisation, country, etc.

leading /leeding/ > *adjective* most important or in first place.

COMBINATIONS – **leading aircraftman** (or **leading aircraftwoman**) a rank in the RAF immediately above aircraftman (or aircraftwoman). **leading article** Brit. a newspaper article giving the editorial opinion. **leading edge 1** the foremost edge of an aerofoil, especially a wing or propeller blade. **2** the forefront or vanguard, especially of technological development. **leading light** a person who is prominent or influential in a particular field or organisation. **leading man** (or **leading lady**) the actor playing the principal part in a play, film, or television show. **leading question** a question that prompts or encourages the answer wanted. **leading seaman** a rank in the Royal Navy immediately above able seaman.

leaf > *noun* (pl. **leaves**) **1** a flattened, typically green structure of a plant, that is attached to a stem and is the chief site of photosynthesis and transpiration. **2** the state of having leaves: *the trees were in leaf.* **3** a single thickness of paper, especially in a book. **4** gold, silver, or other metal in the form of very thin foil. **5** a hinged or detachable part, especially of a table. > *verb* **1** (of a plant) put out new leaves. **2** (**leaf through**) turn over (pages or papers), reading them quickly or casually.

WORDFINDER – foliaceous (*of or resembling leaves*), foliate (*decorated with leaves*); deciduous (*shedding its leaves annually*), evergreen (*retaining green leaves throughout the year*), frond (*leaf of a palm or fern*), petiole (*the stalk that joins a leaf to a stem*), phyllophagous (*leaf-eating*), pinnate (*having leaflets arranged either side of a stem*).

IDIOMS – **turn over a new leaf** start to act or behave in a better way.

DERIVATIVES – **leafage** *noun* **leafed** (also **leaved**) *adjective* **leafless** *adjective.*

COMBINATIONS – **leaf mould** soil consisting chiefly of decayed leaves. **leaf spring** a spring made of a number of strips of metal curved slightly upwards and clamped together one above the other.

leaflet > *noun* **1** a printed sheet of paper containing information or advertising and usually distributed free. **2** a small leaf, especially a component of a compound leaf.

> *verb* (**leafleted**, **leafleting**) distribute leaflets to.

leafy > *adjective* (**leafier**, **leafiest**) **1** having many leaves. **2** full of trees and shrubs: *a leafy avenue.*

DERIVATIVES – **leafiness** *noun.*

league¹ > *noun* **1** a collection of people, countries, or groups that combine for mutual protection or cooperation. **2** a group of sports clubs which play each other over a period for a championship. **3** a class of quality or excellence: *the two men were not in the same league.* > *verb* (**leagues**, **leagued**, **leaguing**) join in a league or alliance.

IDIOMS – **in league** conspiring with another or others.

SYNONYMS – *noun* **1** alliance, association, coalition, confederation, federation.

COMBINATIONS – **league table** Brit. **1** a list of the competitors in a league ranked according to performance. **2** a list in order of merit or achievement.

ORIGIN – Italian *lega*, from Latin *ligare* 'to bind'.

league² > *noun* a former measure of distance by land, usually about three miles.

ORIGIN – Latin *leuga, leuca.*

leaguer > *noun* chiefly N. Amer. a member of a particular league, especially a sports player.

leak > *verb* **1** accidentally allow contents to escape or enter through a hole or crack. **2** (of liquid, gas, etc.) escape or enter accidentally through a hole or crack. **3** intentionally disclose (secret information). **4** (of secret information) become known. > *noun* **1** a hole or crack through which contents leak. **2** an instance of leaking.

IDIOMS – **have** (or **take**) **a leak** informal urinate.

DERIVATIVES – **leakage** *noun* **leaker** *noun* **leakiness** *noun* **leaky** *adjective.*

SYNONYMS – *verb* **1** discharge, exude, ooze, secrete. **2** emanate, escape, ooze, seep. **3** disclose, divulge, reveal.

ORIGIN – probably from Low German or Dutch and related to **LACK**.

lean¹ > *verb* (past and past participle **leaned** or chiefly Brit. **leant**) **1** be in or move into a sloping position. **2** (**lean against** or **on**) incline from the perpendicular and rest against. **3** (**lean on**) rely on for support. **4** (**lean to** or **towards**) incline or be partial to (a view or position). **5** (**lean on**) informal intimidate into doing something. > *noun* a deviation from the perpendicular; an inclination.

SYNONYMS – *verb* **1** incline, slant, slope, tilt.

COMBINATIONS – **lean-to** (pl. **lean-tos**) a building sharing a wall with a larger building and having a roof that leans against that wall.

lean² > *adjective* **1** (of a person) having no superfluous fat; thin. **2** (of meat) containing little fat. **3** offering little reward, substance, or nourishment: *the lean years.* **4** informal (of an industry or company) efficient and with no wastage. **5** (of a vaporised fuel mixture) having a high proportion of air. > *noun* the lean part of meat.

DERIVATIVES – **leanly** *adverb* **leanness** *noun.*

SYNONYMS – *adjective* **1** slender, slim, spare, thin. **3** barren, hard, unfruitful.

ANTONYMS – *adjective* **1** fat, fleshy. **3** fruitful, productive. **5** rich.

COMBINATIONS – **lean-burn** (of an internal-combustion engine) designed to run on a lean mixture to reduce pollution.

leaning > *noun* a tendency or preference: *communist leanings.*

leap > *verb* (past or past participle **leaped** or **leapt**) **1** jump or spring a long way. **2** jump across. **3** move quickly and suddenly. **4** (**leap at**) accept eagerly. **5** increase dramatically. > *noun* **1** an instance of leaping. **2** a sudden abrupt change or increase.

IDIOMS – **by** (or **in**) **leaps and bounds** with startlingly rapid progress. **a leap in the dark** a daring step or enterprise whose consequences are unpredictable. **leap to the eye** (or **leap out**) be immediately apparent.

DERIVATIVES – **leaper** *noun.*

SYNONYMS – *verb* **1** bound, hop, jump, spring. **2** hop over, hurdle, jump, vault. **3** hasten, hurtle, rush. **5** rocket, skyrocket, soar.

COMBINATIONS – **leap year** a year, occurring once every four years, which has 366 days including 29 February as an intercalary day. [ORIGIN – probably from the fact that feast days after February in a leap year fell two days later than in the previous year, rather than one day later as in other years, and could be said to have 'leaped' a day.]

ORIGIN – Old English, related to LOPE.

leapfrog > *noun* a game in which players take turns to vault with parted legs over others who are bending down. > *verb* (**leapfrogged**, **leapfrogging**) **1** perform such a vault. **2** progress by overtaking others to move into a leading position.

learn > *verb* (past and past participle **learned** or chiefly Brit. **learnt**) **1** acquire knowledge of or skill in (something) through study or experience or by being taught. **2** become aware of (something) by information or from observation. **3** memorise. **4** archaic or informal teach.

DERIVATIVES – **learnable** *adjective* **learner** *noun.*

SYNONYMS – **1** assimilate, grasp, master, pick up, study.

ORIGIN – Old English, related to LORE[1].

wordpower facts
Learn

In modern standard English, it is incorrect to use **learn** to mean **teach**, as in *that'll learn you*. However, this use has been recorded since the 13th century, and for a long time was not considered incorrect. Over the centuries it was used by writers such as Edmund Spenser, John Bunyan, and Samuel Johnson, and did not fall into disfavour until the early 19th century. It is now found only in non-standard and dialect use.

learned /lernid/ > *adjective* having or characterised by much knowledge acquired by study.

DERIVATIVES – **learnedly** *adverb* **learnedness** *noun.*

learning > *noun* knowledge or skills acquired through study or by being taught.

WORDFINDER – heuristic (*enabling a person to learn for themselves*), rote (*learning by mechanical repetition*).

COMBINATIONS – **learning curve** the rate of a person's progress in gaining experience or new skills. **learning difficulties** difficulties in acquiring knowledge and skills to the normal level expected of those of the same age, especially because of mental handicap or cognitive disorder. **learning disability** a condition giving rise to learning difficulties, especially when not associated with physical handicap.

lease > *noun* a contract by which one party conveys land, property, services, etc. to another for a specified time, in return for payment. > *verb* let or rent on lease.

IDIOMS – **a new lease of life** a substantially improved prospect of life or use after recovery or repair.

DERIVATIVES – **leasable** *adjective.*

COMBINATIONS – **leaseback** the leasing of a property back to the party that sold it.

ORIGIN – from Old French *lesser, laissier* 'let, leave', from Latin *laxus* 'loose, lax'.

leasehold > *noun* **1** the holding of property by lease. **2** a piece of land or property held by lease.

DERIVATIVES – **leaseholder** *noun.*

leash > *noun* a dog's lead. > *verb* put a leash on (a dog).

ORIGIN – from Old French *laissier* (see LEASE) in the specific sense 'let run on a slack lead'.

least > *determiner & pronoun* (usu. **the least**) smallest in amount, extent, or significance. > *adjective* used in names of very small animals and plants: *least shrew.* > *adverb* to the smallest extent or degree.

IDIOMS – **at least 1** not less than. **2** if

nothing else. **3** anyway. **at the least** (or **very least**) **1** not less than. **2** taking the most pessimistic or unfavourable view. **least said, soonest mended** *proverb* a difficult situation will be resolved more quickly if there is no more discussion of it. **not in the least** not at all. **not least** in particular. **to say the least** to put it mildly.

COMBINATIONS – **least significant bit** Computing the bit in a binary number which is of the lowest numerical value.

ORIGIN – Old English, related to LESS.

leastways (also **leastwise**) > *adverb* dialect or informal at least.

leat /leet/ > *noun* Brit. an open watercourse conducting water to a mill.

leather > *noun* **1** a material made from the skin of an animal by tanning or a similar process. **2** a piece of leather as a polishing cloth. **3** (**leathers**) leather clothes worn by a motorcyclist. > *verb* **1** cover with leather. **2** informal beat or thrash.

WORDFINDER – *kinds of leather:* buff, chamois, mocha, morocco, nubuck, shagreen, suede.

DERIVATIVES – **leathered** *adjective.*

COMBINATIONS – **leatherjacket** Brit. the tough-skinned larva of a large crane fly.

leatherette > *noun* imitation leather.

leathern > *adjective* archaic made of leather.

leathery > *adjective* having a tough, hard texture like leather.

DERIVATIVES – **leatheriness** *noun.*

leave[1] > *verb* (past and past participle **left**) **1** go away from. **2** cease living at, attending, or working for: *he left home at 16.* **3** allow or cause to remain; go away without taking. **4** (**be left** (**over**)) remain to be used or dealt with. **5** cause to be in a particular state or position: *leave the door open.* **6** let (someone) do something without assistance or interference. **7** (**leave to**) entrust (a decision, choice, or action) to. **8** deposit (something) to be collected or attended to. **9** have as (a surviving relative) after one's death. **10** bequeath.

IDIOMS – **leave be** informal refrain from disturbing or interfering with (someone). **leave go** informal remove one's hold or grip. **leave hold of** cease holding. **leave much** (or **a lot**) **to be desired** be highly unsatisfactory. **leave off 1** discontinue or stop. **2** cease to wear. **leave out** fail to include.

DERIVATIVES – **leaver** *noun.*

SYNONYMS – **1** depart from, quit, retire from, withdraw from. **3** abandon, desert, forsake.

leave[2] > *noun* **1** (also **leave of absence**) time when one has permission to be absent from work or duty. **2** formal permission: *seeking leave to appeal.*

IDIOMS – **take one's leave** formal say

goodbye. **take leave to do** formal venture or presume to do.

COMBINATIONS – **leave-taking** an act of saying goodbye.

ORIGIN – Old English, 'permission', related to LIEF and LOVE.

leaven /**levv**'n/ > *noun* **1** a substance, typically yeast, added to dough to make it ferment and rise. **2** an influence or quality that modifies or improves something. > *verb* **1** cause (dough or bread) to ferment and rise by adding leaven. **2** permeate and improve (something): *the proceedings should be leavened with humour.*

ORIGIN – Latin *levamen* 'relief', from *levare* 'to lift'.

leaves plural of LEAF.

leavings > *plural noun* things that have been left as worthless.

Lebanese /lebbə**neez**/ > *noun* (pl. same) a person from Lebanon. > *adjective* relating to Lebanon.

Lebensraum /**lay**bənzrowm/ > *noun* territory which a state or nation believes is needed for its natural development.

ORIGIN – German, 'living space'.

lech /lech/ informal, derogatory > *noun* **1** a lecher. **2** a lecherous urge or desire. > *verb* act in a lecherous manner.

lecher > *noun* a lecherous man.

DERIVATIVES – **lechery** noun.

lecherous > *adjective* having or showing excessive or offensive sexual desire.

DERIVATIVES – **lecherously** adverb **lecherousness** noun.

SYNONYMS – lascivious, libidinous, lustful, salacious.

ORIGIN – Old French *lecheros*, from *lechier* 'live in debauchery or gluttony'; related to LICK.

lecithin /**less**ithin/ > *noun* a substance found in egg yolk and other animal and plant tissues, often used as an emulsifier in food processing.

ORIGIN – from Greek *lekithos* 'egg yolk'.

lectern /**lek**tərn/ > *noun* a tall stand with a sloping top from which a speaker can read while standing up.

ORIGIN – Latin *lectrum*, from *legere* 'to read'.

lecture > *noun* **1** an educational talk to an audience, especially one of students in a university. **2** a lengthy reprimand or warning. > *verb* **1** deliver an educational lecture or lectures. **2** give (someone) a reprimand or serious talk.

ORIGIN – Latin *lectura*, from *legere* 'read, choose'.

lecturer > *noun* a person who gives lectures, especially as a teacher in higher education.

lectureship > *noun* a post as a lecturer.

LED > *abbreviation* light-emitting diode, a semiconductor diode which glows when a voltage is applied.

led past and past participle of LEAD[1].

lederhosen /**lay**dərhōz'n/ > *plural noun* leather shorts with braces, traditionally worn by men in Alpine regions.

ORIGIN – German, from *Leder* 'leather' + *Hosen* 'trousers'.

ledge > *noun* **1** a narrow horizontal surface projecting from a wall, cliff, etc. **2** an underwater ridge, especially one of rocks near the seashore.

ORIGIN – perhaps from an early form of LAY[1]: originally denoting a strip of wood or other material fixed across a door or gate.

ledger > *noun* a book or other collection of financial accounts.

ORIGIN – probably from variants of LAY[1] and LIE[1].

ledger line (also **leger line**) > *noun* Music a short line added for notes above or below the range of a stave.

lee > *noun* **1** shelter from wind or weather given by an object. **2** (also **lee side**) the sheltered side; the side away from the wind. Contrasted with WEATHER.

COMBINATIONS – **lee shore** a shore lying on the leeward side of a ship (and on to which the ship could be blown).

leech[1] > *noun* **1** a parasitic or predatory worm with suckers at both ends, formerly used in medicine for bloodletting. **2** a person who extorts profit from or lives off others. > *verb* (**leech on** or **off**) habitually exploit or rely on.

leech[2] > *noun* archaic a doctor or healer.

leek > *noun* a plant related to the onion, with flat overlapping leaves forming an elongated cylindrical bulb which together with the leaf bases is eaten as a vegetable.

leer > *verb* look or gaze in a lustful or unpleasant way. > *noun* a lustful or unpleasant look.

ORIGIN – first meaning 'look sideways or askance': perhaps from obsolete *leer* 'cheek'.

leery > *adjective* (**leerier, leeriest**) cautious or wary.

DERIVATIVES – **leeriness** noun.

ORIGIN – from obsolete *leer* 'looking askance', from LEER.

lees > *plural noun* the sediment of wine in the barrel; dregs.

ORIGIN – Latin *liae*.

leeward /**lee**wərd, **loo**ərd/ > *adjective* & *adverb* on or towards the side sheltered from the wind or towards which the wind is blowing. Contrasted with WINDWARD. > *noun* the leeward side.

leeway > *noun* **1** the amount of freedom to move or act that is available. **2** the sideways drift of a ship to leeward of the desired course.

IDIOMS – **make up (the) leeway** Brit. struggle out of a bad position, especially by recovering lost time.

left[1] > *adjective* **1** on, towards, or relating to the side of a human body or of a thing which is to the west when the person or thing is facing north. **2** relating to a left-wing person or group. > *adverb* on or to the left side. > *noun* **1** (**the left**) the left-hand part, side, or direction. **2** a left turn. **3** a person's left fist, or a blow given with it. **4** (often **the Left**) (treated as sing. or pl.) a group or party favouring radical, reforming, or socialist views.

WORDFINDER – sinistral (*relating to the left hand or left side*).

IDIOMS – **have two left feet** be clumsy or awkward. **left, right, and centre** on all sides.

DERIVATIVES – **leftish** adjective **leftmost** adjective **leftward** adjective & adverb **leftwards** adverb.

COMBINATIONS – **left back** a defender in soccer or field hockey who plays primarily on the left of the field. **left bank** the bank of a river on the left as one faces downstream. **left-field** unconventional or experimental.

ORIGIN – Old English, 'weak'.

left[2] past and past participle of LEAVE[1].

COMBINATIONS – **left luggage** Brit. travellers' luggage left in temporary storage at a railway station, bus station, or airport.

left hand > *noun* **1** the hand of a person's left side. **2** the region or direction on the left side. > *adjective* **1** on or towards the left side. **2** done with or using the left hand.

COMBINATIONS – **left-hand drive** a motor-vehicle steering system with the steering wheel fitted on the left side, for use in countries where vehicles drive on the right. **left-handed 1** using or done with the left hand. **2** turning to the left; towards the left. **3** (of a screw) advanced by turning anticlockwise. **4** ambiguous. **left-hander 1** a left-handed person. **2** a blow struck with a person's left hand.

leftism > *noun* left-wing political views or policies.

DERIVATIVES – **leftist** noun & adjective.

leftover > *noun* (usu. **leftovers**) something, especially food, remaining after the rest has been used. > *adjective* remaining; surplus.

left wing > *noun* **1** the radical, reforming, or socialist section of a political party or system. [ORIGIN – with reference to the National Assembly in France (1789–91), where the nobles sat to the president's right and the commons to the left.] **2** the left side of a sports team on the field or of an army.

DERIVATIVES – **left-winger** noun.

lefty (also **leftie**) > *noun* (pl. **lefties**) informal **1** a left-wing person. **2** a left-handed person.

leg > *noun* **1** each of the limbs on which a person or animal moves and stands. **2** a long, thin support or prop, especially of a chair or table. **3** a section of a journey, process, or race. **4** (in sport) each of two or more games or stages constituting a round or match. **5** (**legs**) informal sustained momentum or success. **6** (also **leg side**) Cricket the half of the field away from which the batsman's feet are pointed when standing to receive the ball. The opposite of **OFF**.

WORDFINDER – crural (*relating to the leg or thigh*); bones of the leg: femur, fibula, patella, tibia.

IDIOMS – **get one's leg over** vulgar slang (of a man) have sexual intercourse. **have the legs of** Brit. be able to go faster or further than (a rival). **leg before wicket** Cricket (of a batsman) adjudged to be out through obstructing the ball with the leg (or other part of the body) when the ball would otherwise have hit the wicket. **leg it** informal **1** travel by foot; walk. **2** run away. **not have a leg to stand on** have no sound justification for one's arguments or actions. **on one's last legs** near the end of life, usefulness, or existence.

DERIVATIVES – **legged** adjective.

COMBINATIONS – **leg break** Cricket a ball which spins from the leg side towards the off side after pitching. **leg bye** Cricket a run scored from a ball that has touched the batsman's body without touching the bat. **leg iron** a metal band or chain placed around a prisoner's ankle as a restraint. **leg-of-mutton sleeve** a sleeve which is full on the upper arm but close-fitting on the forearm and wrist. **legroom** space in which a seated person can put their legs. **leg-up 1** an act of helping someone to mount a horse or high object. **2** an act of helping someone to improve their position. **leg warmers** a pair of tubular knitted garments covering the legs from ankle to knee or thigh. **legwork** work that involves tiring or tedious movement from place to place.

ORIGIN – Old Norse *leggr*.

legacy > *noun* (pl. **legacies**) **1** an amount of money or property left to someone in a will. **2** something handed down by a predecessor.

ORIGIN – Old French *legacie*, from Latin *legare* 'delegate, bequeath.'

legal > *adjective* **1** of, based on, or required by the law. **2** permitted by law.

DERIVATIVES – **legally** adverb.

USAGE – on the difference between **legal** and **lawful**, see the note at **LAWFUL**.

SYNONYMS – **2** legitimate, licit, permissible.

ANTONYMS – **2** unlawful.

COMBINATIONS – **legal aid** payment from public funds allowed, in cases of need, to help pay for legal advice or proceedings. **legal eagle** (also **legal beagle**) informal a

lawyer. **legal fiction** an assumption of the truth of something, though unproven or unfounded, for legal purposes. **legal separation 1** an arrangement by which a husband or wife remain married but live apart, following a court order. **2** an arrangement by which a child lives apart from a natural parent and with another natural or foster-parent of their choice, following a court decree. **legal tender** coins or banknotes that must be accepted if offered in payment of a debt.

ORIGIN – Latin *legalis*, from *lex* 'law'.

legalese /leegəleez/ > *noun* informal the formal and technical language of legal documents.

legalise (also **legalize**) > *verb* make legal.

DERIVATIVES – **legalisation** noun.

SYNONYMS – authorise, decriminalise, legitimise, license.

legalism > *noun* excessive adherence to the details of law.

DERIVATIVES – **legalist** noun & adjective **legalistic** adjective.

legality > *noun* (pl. **legalities**) **1** the quality or state of being legal. **2** (**legalities**) obligations imposed by law.

legate /leggət/ > *noun* **1** a member of the clergy who represents the Pope. **2** a general or governor of an ancient Roman province, or their deputy.

ORIGIN – Latin *legatus*, from *legare* 'depute, delegate, bequeath'.

legatee /leggətee/ > *noun* a person who receives a legacy.

legation > *noun* **1** a diplomatic minister and their staff. **2** the official residence of a diplomat. **3** archaic the sending of a papal legate on a mission.

legato /ligaatō/ > *adverb & adjective* Music in a smooth, flowing manner.

ORIGIN – Italian, 'bound'.

legator /ligaytər/ > *noun* rare a person leaving a legacy.

legend > *noun* **1** a traditional story which is popularly regarded as historical but is not authenticated. **2** an extremely famous or notorious person: *a screen legend.* **3** an inscription, caption, or key. > *adjective* very well known.

SYNONYMS – **1** epic, fable, folk tale, myth, saga, tale.

ORIGIN – from Latin *legenda* 'things to be read', from *legere* 'read'.

legendary > *adjective* **1** of, described in, or based on legends. **2** remarkable enough to be famous.

DERIVATIVES – **legendarily** adverb.

SYNONYMS – **1** fabled, mythical, traditional.

legerdemain /lejərdəmayn/ > *noun* **1** skilful use of one's hands when performing conjuring tricks. **2** deception; trickery.

ORIGIN – from French *léger de main* 'dexterous' (literally 'light of hand').

leger line > *noun* variant spelling of **LEDGER LINE**.

leggings > *plural noun* **1** a woman's tight-fitting stretchy garment covering the legs, hips, and bottom. **2** stout protective overgarments for the legs from knee to ankle.

leggy > *adjective* (**leggier**, **leggiest**) **1** long-legged. **2** (of a plant) having a long and straggly stem or stems.

legible > *adjective* (of handwriting or print) clear enough to read.

DERIVATIVES – **legibility** noun **legibly** adverb.

SYNONYMS – clear, decipherable, neat, readable.

ANTONYMS – illegible.

ORIGIN – Latin *legibilis*, from *legere* 'to read'.

legion > *noun* **1** a division of 3,000–6,000 men in the ancient Roman army. **2** (**a legion** or **legions of**) a vast number of people or things. > *adjective* great in number: *her fans are legion.*

ORIGIN – Latin, from *legere* 'choose, levy (an army)'.

legionary* > *noun* (pl. **legionaries**) a soldier in an ancient Roman legion. > *adjective* of an ancient Roman legion.

*SPELLING – single *n*: legionary.

legionella /leejənellə/ > *noun* (pl. **legionellae** /leejənellee/) the bacterium responsible for legionnaires' disease.

legionnaire* /leejənair/ > *noun* **1** a member of the Foreign Legion. **2** a member of a national association for former servicemen and servicewomen, such as the Royal British Legion.

*SPELLING – *legionnaire* is a French word and has a double *n*: legionnaire.

COMBINATIONS – **legionnaires' disease** a form of bacterial pneumonia spread chiefly in water droplets through air conditioning and similar systems. [ORIGIN – so named because it was identified after an outbreak at an American Legion meeting in 1976.]

legislate /lejislayt/ > *verb* **1** make or enact laws. **2** (**legislate for** or **against**) make provision or preparation for (an occurrence).

legislation > *noun* laws collectively.

ORIGIN – Latin, 'proposing of a law', from *lex* 'law'.

legislative /lejislətiv/ > *adjective* **1** having the power to make laws. **2** relating to laws or a legislature.

DERIVATIVES – **legislatively** adverb.

legislator > *noun* a person who makes laws; a member of a legislative body.

legislature /lejisləchər/ > *noun* the law-making body of a state.

legit > *adjective* informal legitimate.

legitimate* > *adjective* /liˈjittimət/ **1** conforming to the law or to rules. **2** able to be defended with logic or justification: *a legitimate excuse.* **3** (of a child) born of parents lawfully married to each other. **4** (of a sovereign) having a title based on strict hereditary right. > *verb* /liˈjittimayt/ make legitimate.
DERIVATIVES – **legitimacy** *noun* **legitimately** *adverb* **legitimation** *noun*.
*SPELLING – *leg* not *lig*: legitimate.
SYNONYMS – *adjective* **1** authorised, lawful, legal, licit, permissible. **2** justifiable, reasonable, sound, valid.
ANTONYMS – *adjective* illegitimate.
ORIGIN – from Latin *legitimare* 'make legal'.

legitimise (also **legitimize** or **legitimatise**) > *verb* make legitimate.
DERIVATIVES – **legitimisation** *noun*.

legless > *adjective* **1** having no legs. **2** Brit. informal extremely drunk.

Lego > *noun* trademark a toy consisting of interlocking plastic building blocks.
ORIGIN – from Danish *leg godt* 'play well'.

legume /ˈleɡyoom/ > *noun* **1** a leguminous plant grown as a crop. **2** a seed, pod, or other edible part of a leguminous plant, used as food.
ORIGIN – Latin *legumen*, from *legere* 'to pick'.

leguminous /liˈɡyoominəss/ > *adjective* relating to plants of the pea family (Leguminosae), typically having seeds in pods and root nodules containing nitrogen-fixing bacteria.

lei /lay/ > *noun* a Polynesian garland of flowers.
ORIGIN – Hawaiian.

Leicester > (also **Red Leicester**) *noun* a kind of mild, firm orange-coloured cheese originally made in Leicestershire.

Leics. > *abbreviation* Leicestershire.

leisure > *noun* time spent in or free for relaxation or enjoyment.
IDIOMS – **at leisure 1** not occupied; free. **2** in an unhurried manner. **at one's leisure** at one's convenience.
DERIVATIVES – **leisured** *adjective*.
SYNONYMS – recreation, relaxation, rest, spare time, time off.
COMBINATIONS – **leisure centre** a public building or complex offering facilities for sport and recreation. **leisurewear** casual clothes worn for leisure activities.
ORIGIN – Old French *leisir*, from Latin *licere* 'be allowed'.

leisurely > *adjective* relaxed and unhurried. > *adverb* without hurry.
DERIVATIVES – **leisureliness** *noun*.
SYNONYMS – *adjective* easy, relaxed, sedate, slow, unhurried.
ANTONYMS – brisk, hurried, rushed.

leitmotif /ˈlitmoteef/ (also **leitmotiv**) > *noun* a recurring theme in a musical or literary composition.
ORIGIN – German *Leitmotiv*, from *leit-* 'leading' + *Motiv* 'motive'.

lek¹ > *noun* the basic monetary unit of Albania, equal to 100 qintars.
ORIGIN – Albanian.

lek² > *noun* a patch of ground used for communal display in the breeding season by the males of certain birds and mammals.
DERIVATIVES – **lekking** *noun*.
ORIGIN – perhaps from Swedish *leka* 'to play'.

leman /ˈlemmən, ˈleemən/ > *noun* (pl. **lemans**) archaic a lover or sweetheart.

lemme > *contraction* informal let me.

lemming > *noun* **1** a short-tailed Arctic rodent, noted for fluctuating populations and periodic mass migrations. **2** a person who unthinkingly joins a mass movement, especially a headlong rush to destruction.
ORIGIN – Norwegian and Danish.

lemon > *noun* **1** a pale yellow oval citrus fruit with thick skin and fragrant, acidic juice. **2** a drink made from or flavoured with lemon juice. **3** a pale yellow colour. **4** informal a feeble or unsatisfactory person or thing.
DERIVATIVES – **lemony** *adjective*.
COMBINATIONS – **lemon balm** a bushy lemon-scented herb of the mint family. **lemon curd** a conserve made from lemons, butter, eggs, and sugar. **lemon grass** a fragrant tropical grass which yields an oil that smells of lemon, used in Asian cooking and in perfumery and medicine. **lemon verbena** a shrub with lemon-scented leaves, used as flavouring and to make a sedative tea.
ORIGIN – Old French *limon*, from Arabic.

lemonade > *noun* a sweetened drink made from lemon juice or lemon flavouring and still or carbonated water.

lemon sole > *noun* a common flatfish of the plaice family.
ORIGIN – from French *limande*.

lempira /lemˈpeerə/ > *noun* the basic monetary unit of Honduras, equal to 100 centavos.
ORIGIN – named after *Lempira*, a 16th-century Indian chieftain who opposed the Spanish conquest of Honduras.

lemur /ˈleemər/ > *noun* a tree-dwelling primate with a pointed snout and typically a long tail, found only in Madagascar.
ORIGIN – from Latin *lemures* 'spirits of the dead' (from their spectre-like faces).

lend > *verb* (past and past participle **lent**) **1** grant to (someone) the use of (something) on the understanding that it shall be returned. **2** allow (a person) the use of (a sum of money) under an agreement to pay it back later, typically with interest. **3** contribute or add (a quality) to. **4** (**lend oneself to**) accommodate or adapt oneself to. **5** (**lend itself to**) (of a thing) be suitable for.
DERIVATIVES – **lender** *noun*.
COMBINATIONS – **lending library** a public library from which books may be borrowed for a limited time.
ORIGIN – Old English, related to LOAN.

length > *noun* **1** the measurement or extent of something from end to end; the greater or greatest of two or more dimensions of a body. **2** the amount of time occupied by something. **3** the quality of being long. **4** the full distance that a thing extends for. **5** the extent of a garment in a vertical direction when worn. **6** the length of a horse, boat, etc., as a measure of the lead in a race. **7** a stretch or piece of something. **8** a degree to which a course of action is taken.
IDIOMS – **at length 1** in detail; fully. **2** after a long time. **the length and breadth of** the whole extent of.
ORIGIN – Old English, related to LONG¹.

lengthen > *verb* make or become longer.

lengthways > *adverb* in a direction parallel with a thing's length.

lengthwise > *adverb* lengthways. > *adjective* lying or moving lengthways.

lengthy > *adjective* (**lengthier**, **lengthiest**) (especially in reference to time) of considerable or unusual length.
DERIVATIVES – **lengthily** *adverb*.
SYNONYMS – extended, long, long-lasting, prolonged, protracted.

lenient /ˈleeniənt/ > *adjective* merciful or tolerant.
DERIVATIVES – **leniency** *noun* **leniently** *adverb*.
SYNONYMS – charitable, forbearing, indulgent, merciful, mild, tolerant.
ORIGIN – Latin, from *lenire* 'soothe', from *lenis* 'mild, gentle'.

Leninism > *noun* Marxism as interpreted and applied by the Soviet premier Lenin (1870–1924).
DERIVATIVES – **Leninist** *noun* & *adjective*.

lens > *noun* **1** a piece of transparent material with one or both sides curved for concentrating or dispersing light rays. **2** the light-gathering device of a camera, containing a group of compound lenses. **3** Anatomy the transparent elastic structure behind the iris by which light is focused on to the retina of the eye. **4** a contact lens.
DERIVATIVES – **lensed** *adjective*.
ORIGIN – Latin, 'lentil' (because of the similarity in shape).

lensman > *noun* a professional photographer or cameraman.

Lent > *noun* (in the Christian Church) the period preceding Easter, which is devoted to fasting, abstinence, and penitence in commemoration of Christ's fasting in the wilderness.

ORIGIN – abbreviation of **LENTEN**.

lent past and past participle of **LEND**.

Lenten > *adjective* relating to or appropriate to Lent.

ORIGIN – Old English, 'spring, Lent'; related to **LONG**¹ (perhaps with reference to the lengthening of the day in spring).

lenticular /lentikyoolər/ > *adjective* **1** shaped like a lens or a lentil. **2** relating to the lens of the eye.

lentil > *noun* a high-protein pulse which is dried and then soaked and cooked prior to eating.

ORIGIN – Latin *lenticula*, from *lens* 'lentil'.

lento > *adverb & adjective* Music slow or slowly.

ORIGIN – Italian.

Leo > *noun* **1** Astronomy a large constellation (the Lion), said to represent the lion killed by Hercules. **2** Astrology the fifth sign of the zodiac, which the sun enters about 23 July.

DERIVATIVES – **Leonian** *noun & adjective*.

ORIGIN – Latin.

leone /liōn/ > *noun* the basic monetary unit of Sierra Leone, equal to 100 cents.

leonine /leeənīn/ > *adjective* of or resembling a lion or lions.

ORIGIN – Latin *leoninus*, from *leo* 'lion'.

leopard > *noun* **1** (fem. **leopardess**) a large solitary cat that has a fawn or brown coat with black spots, found in the forests of Africa and southern Asia. **2** (before another noun) spotted like a leopard: *a leopard-print bikini*.

IDIOMS – **a leopard can't change his spots** proverb people can't change their basic nature.

ORIGIN – Greek *leopardos*, from *leōn* 'lion' + *pardos* 'panther'.

leotard /leeətaard/ > *noun* a close-fitting, stretchy one-piece garment covering the body to the top of the thighs, worn for dance, gymnastics, and exercise.

ORIGIN – named after the French trapeze artist Jules *Léotard* (1839–70).

leper > *noun* **1** a person suffering from leprosy. **2** a person who is shunned by others.

ORIGIN – first in the sense 'leprosy', from Greek *lepra, lepros* 'scaly', from *lepos* 'scale'.

lepidopteran /leppidoptərən/ > *noun* an insect of the order Lepidoptera, comprising the butterflies and moths.

DERIVATIVES – **lepidopterist** *noun* **lepidopterous** *adjective*.

ORIGIN – from Greek *lepis* 'scale' + *pteron* 'wing'.

leprechaun /leprəkawn/ > *noun* (in Irish folklore) a small, mischievous sprite.

ORIGIN – Irish *leipreachán*, from Old Irish *lu* 'small' + *corp* 'body'.

leprosy > *noun* a contagious bacterial disease that affects the skin, mucous membranes, and nerves, causing discoloration and lumps on the skin and, in severe cases, disfigurement and deformities.

leprous > *adjective* referring to or suffering from leprosy.

lepta plural of **LEPTON**¹.

leptin /leptin/ > *noun* Biochemistry a protein produced by fatty tissue which is believed to regulate fat storage in the body.

ORIGIN – from Greek *leptos* 'fine, thin'.

lepton /lepton/ > *noun* Physics a subatomic particle that does not take part in the strong interaction, such as an electron or neutrino.

ORIGIN – from Greek *leptos* 'small'.

lesbian > *noun* a homosexual woman. > *adjective* referring to lesbians or lesbianism.

DERIVATIVES – **lesbianism** *noun*.

ORIGIN – from Greek *Lesbios*, from *Lesbos*, Greek island and home of Sappho (early 7th century BC), who expressed affection for women in her poetry.

lese-majesty /leez majisti/ (also **lèse-majesté** /layz/) > *noun* the insulting of a sovereign; treason.

ORIGIN – from French *lèse-majesté*, from Latin *laesa majestas* 'injured sovereignty'.

lesion /leezh'n/ > *noun* chiefly Medicine a region in an organ or tissue which has suffered damage through injury or disease.

ORIGIN – from Latin *laedere* 'injure'.

less > *determiner & pronoun* **1** a smaller amount of; not as much. **2** fewer in number. > *adverb* to a smaller extent; not so much. > *preposition* minus.

USAGE – be careful to use **less** and **few** correctly. The use of **less** with a plural noun (*less people*) is incorrect in standard English: use **fewer** instead, as in *there are fewer people here today*. Use **less** with nouns denoting things that cannot be counted, as in *there is less blossom on this tree*.

-less > *suffix* forming adjectives and adverbs: **1** (from nouns) not having; without; free from: *flavourless*. **2** (from verbs) not affected by or not carrying out the action of the verb: *tireless*.

DERIVATIVES – **-lessly** *suffix* **-lessness** *suffix*.

ORIGIN – Old English, 'devoid of'.

lessee > *noun* a person who holds the lease of a property.

ORIGIN – Old French *lesse*, from *lesser* 'to let, leave'.

lessen > *verb* make or become less.

SYNONYMS – assuage, diminish, minimise, reduce, weaken.

lesser > *adjective* not so great or important as the other or the rest.

lesson > *noun* **1** a period of learning or teaching. **2** a thing learned. **3** a thing that serves as a warning or encouragement. **4** a passage from the Bible read aloud during a church service.

ORIGIN – Old French *leçon*, from Latin *legere* 'read'.

lessor > *noun* a person who leases or lets a property to another.

ORIGIN – from Old French *lesser* 'let, leave'.

lest > *conjunction* formal **1** with the intention of preventing; to avoid the risk of. **2** because of the possibility of.

USAGE – if you use the rather formal word **lest**, note that the correct constructions are *she was worrying lest he be attacked* (not *lest he was …*) or *she is using headphones lest she disturb anyone* (not *… lest she disturbs anyone*). The reason is that **lest** takes the *subjunctive* mood.

ORIGIN – Old English, 'whereby less that'.

let¹ > *verb* (**letting**; past and past participle **let**) **1** not prevent or forbid; allow. **2** used in the imperative to express an intention, proposal, or instruction. **3** used to express an assumption on which a theory or calculation is to be based: *let v = velocity*. **4** allow someone to have the use of (a room or property) in return for payment. > *noun* Brit. a period for which a room or property is rented.

IDIOMS – **let alone** not to mention. **let down** fail to support or help. **let fly** attack physically or verbally. **let go 1** allow to go free. **2** dismiss (an employee). **3** relinquish one's grip on. **let into** set (something) back into (a surface). **let off 1** cause (a gun, firework, or bomb) to fire or explode. **2** refrain from punishing. **3** excuse (someone) from a task or obligation. **let on** informal divulge information. **let oneself go 1** act in an uninhibited way. **2** become careless or untidy in one's habits or appearance. **let out 1** utter (a sound or cry). **2** make (a garment) looser or larger. **let up** informal become less intense. **to let** available for rent.

DERIVATIVES – **letting** *noun*.

COMBINATIONS – **let-down** a disappointment. **let-off** informal an instance of unexpectedly escaping or avoiding something. **let-up** informal a pause or reduction in the intensity of something dangerous, difficult, or tiring.

ORIGIN – Old English, 'leave behind, leave out'; related to **LATE**.

let² > *noun* (in racket sports) a circumstance under which a service is nullified and has to be retaken, especially (in tennis) when the ball clips the top of the net and falls within bounds.

IDIOMS – **play a let** (in racket sports) play a point again because the ball or one of the players has been obstructed. **without let or hindrance** formal with no obstruction or impediment.

ORIGIN – Old English 'hinder'; related to **LATE**.

-let > *suffix* **1** (forming nouns) denoting a smaller or lesser kind: *booklet*. **2** denoting articles of ornament or dress: *anklet*.

ORIGIN – corresponding to French *-ette*, added to words ending in *-l*.

lethal /leeth'l/ > *adjective* **1** sufficient to cause death. **2** very harmful or destructive.

DERIVATIVES – **lethality** *noun* **lethally** *adverb*.

SYNONYMS – **1** deadly, fatal, mortal.

ORIGIN – Latin *lethalis*, from *letum* 'death'.

lethargy /letharji/ > *noun* **1** a lack of energy and enthusiasm. **2** Medicine a pathological state of sleepiness or extreme unresponsiveness.

DERIVATIVES – **lethargic** *adjective* **lethargically** *adverb*.

SYNONYMS – **1** apathy, inertia, listlessness, sluggishness, torpor.

ANTONYMS – **1** animation.

ORIGIN – Greek *lēthargia*, from *lēthargos* 'forgetful'.

let's > *contraction* let us.

letter > *noun* **1** a character representing one or more of the sounds used in speech; any of the symbols of an alphabet. **2** a written, typed, or printed communication, sent by post or messenger. **3** the strict verbal interpretation of a statement or requirement, especially as opposed to its spirit or purpose. **4** (**letters**) literature. > *verb* inscribe or provide with letters.

WORDFINDER – epistolary (*relating to the writing of letters*).

IDIOMS – **to the letter** with adherence to every detail.

DERIVATIVES – **lettering** *noun*.

COMBINATIONS – **letter bomb** an explosive device hidden in a small package and detonated when the package is opened. **letterbox 1** chiefly Brit. a slot in a door through which mail is delivered. **2** a format for presenting widescreen films on a standard television screen, in which the image fills the width but not the height of the screen. **letterhead** a printed heading on stationery, stating the sender's name and address. **letter of credit** a letter issued by one bank to another to serve as a guarantee for payments made to a specified person. **letterpress** printing from a hard, raised image under pressure, using viscous ink. **letters of administration** Law authority to

administer the estate of someone who has died without making a will.

ORIGIN – Latin *littera* 'letter of the alphabet', (plural) 'epistle, literature, culture'.

letters patent > *plural noun* an open document issued by a monarch or government conferring a patent or other right.

ORIGIN – from Latin *litterae patentes* 'letters lying open'.

lettuce > *noun* **1** a cultivated plant with edible leaves that are eaten in salads. **2** used in names of other plants with edible green leaves, e.g. **lamb's lettuce**.

WORDFINDER – *varieties of lettuce:* cos, iceberg, lollo rosso.

ORIGIN – Old French *letues*, from Latin *lactuca*, from *lac* 'milk' (because of its milky juice).

leu /layoo/ > *noun* (pl. **lei** /lay/) the basic monetary unit of Romania, equal to 100 bani.

ORIGIN – Romanian, 'lion'.

leucine /looseen/ > *noun* Biochemistry an amino acid which is an essential nutrient in the diet.

ORIGIN – from Greek *leukos* 'white'.

leucocyte /lookəsīt/ (also **leukocyte**) > *noun* Physiology a white blood cell, a colourless cell which circulates in the blood and body fluids and is involved in counteracting infection.

ORIGIN – from Greek *leukos* 'white' + *kutos* 'vessel'.

leukaemia* /lookeemiə/ (US **leukemia**) > *noun* a malignant progressive disease in which the bone marrow and other blood-forming organs produce increased numbers of immature or abnormal white cells, suppressing the production of normal blood cells.

DERIVATIVES – **leukaemic** *adjective*.

*SPELLING – in British English there is *-ae-*, not *-e-* (or *-ea-*), in the middle: leuk*ae*mia.

ORIGIN – from Greek *leukos* 'white' + *haima* 'blood'.

lev /lev/ (also **leva** /levvə/) > *noun* (pl. **leva** or **levas** or **levs**) the basic monetary unit of Bulgaria, equal to 100 stotinki.

ORIGIN – Bulgarian, 'lion'.

Levant /livant/ > *noun* (**the Levant**) historical the eastern part of the Mediterranean.

DERIVATIVES – **Levantine** *noun & adjective*.

ORIGIN – French, 'rising', from *lever* 'lift, rise', used as a noun in the sense 'point of sunrise, east'.

levanter > *noun* a strong easterly wind in the Mediterranean region.

levee[1] /levvi, levvay/ > *noun* a reception or assembly of people.

ORIGIN – French *levé* 'rising', from *lever* 'lift'

(because such receptions were formerly held by a monarch on rising from bed).

levee[2] /levvi, livee/ > *noun* **1** an embankment built to prevent the overflow of a river. **2** a ridge of sediment deposited naturally alongside a river. **3** chiefly N. Amer. a landing place; a quay.

ORIGIN – French *levée*, from *lever* 'lift, rise'.

level > *noun* **1** a horizontal plane or line with respect to the distance above or below a given point. **2** a height or distance from the ground or another base. **3** a position or stage on a scale of quantity, extent, rank, or quality. **4** a floor within a multi-storey building. **5** a flat area of land. **6** an instrument giving a line parallel to the plane of the horizon for testing whether things are horizontal. > *adjective* **1** having a flat, horizontal surface. **2** at the same height as someone or something else. **3** having the same relative position; not in front or behind. **4** calm and steady. > *verb* (**levelled**, **levelling**; US **leveled**, **leveling**) **1** make or become level. **2** aim or direct (a weapon, criticism, or accusation). **3** (**level with**) informal be frank or honest with.

IDIOMS – **be level pegging** Brit. be equal in score or achievement during a contest. **a level playing field** a situation in which everyone has an equal chance of succeeding. **on the level** informal truthful.

DERIVATIVES – **levelly** *adverb* **levelness** *noun*.

SYNONYMS – *noun* **3** degree, grade, position, rank, stage. *adjective* **1** even, flat, flush.

COMBINATIONS – **level crossing** Brit. a place where a railway and a road cross at the same level.

ORIGIN – Old French *livel*, from Latin *libra* 'scales, balance'.

level-headed > *adjective* calm and sensible.

DERIVATIVES – **level-headedly** *adverb* **level-headedness** *noun*.

leveller (US **leveler**) > *noun* **1** a person or thing that levels something. **2** (**Leveller**) a member of a group of radical egalitarian dissenters in the English Civil War (1642–9).

lever > *noun* **1** a rigid bar resting on a pivot, used to move a load with one end when pressure is applied to the other. **2** a projecting arm or handle that is moved to operate a mechanism. > *verb* **1** lift or move with a lever. **2** cause to move with a concerted physical effort.

ORIGIN – Old French *levier*, from *lever* 'lift, rise'.

leverage > *noun* **1** the exertion of force by means of a lever. **2** the power to influence.

leveraged buyout > *noun* the purchase of a controlling share in a company by its management using outside capital.

leveret /**levv**ərit/ > *noun* a young hare in its first year.
ORIGIN – Old French, from Latin *lepus* 'hare'.

leviathan /livvī**ə**thən/ > *noun* **1** (in biblical use) a sea monster. **2** something very large or powerful.
ORIGIN – Hebrew.

levitate /**levv**itayt/ > *verb* rise or cause to rise and hover in the air.
DERIVATIVES – **levitation** *noun*.
ORIGIN – from Latin *levis* 'light'.

levity > *noun* the treatment of a serious matter with humour or lack of respect.
SYNONYMS – flippancy, frivolity, irreverence, light-heartedness.
ORIGIN – Latin *levitas*, from *levis* 'light'.

levy > *noun* (pl. **levies**) **1** the imposition of a tax, fee, fine, or subscription. **2** a sum of money raised by a levy. **3** archaic a body of enlisted troops. > *verb* (**levies**, **levied**) **1** impose or seize as a levy. **2** archaic enlist for military service. **3** archaic begin to wage (war).
ORIGIN – from Old French *lever* 'raise', from Latin *levis* 'light'.

lewd > *adjective* crude and offensive in a sexual way.
DERIVATIVES – **lewdly** *adverb* **lewdness** *noun*.
SYNONYMS – crude, indecent, obscene, rude, smutty, vulgar.

wordpower facts

Lewd

Lewd was originally an Old English word meaning 'not in holy orders, belonging to the laity'. From this it came to mean 'uneducated, unlettered', 'ignorant, unskilled', and 'belonging to the common people, vulgar'. A little later the sense 'worthless, bad', or simply 'naughty' arose: in 1709 one could speak of 'the lewd boy...[who] set his mother's house on fire because she had corrected him'. The current sense, the only one still in use, was first recorded in the 14th-century writings of Geoffrey Chaucer.

lexical /**lek**sikk'l/ > *adjective* **1** relating to the words or vocabulary of a language. **2** relating to a lexicon or dictionary.
DERIVATIVES – **lexically** *adverb*.
ORIGIN – from Greek *lexikos* 'of words'.

lexicography /leksi**kog**rəfi/ > *noun* the practice of compiling dictionaries.
DERIVATIVES – **lexicographer** *noun* **lexicographic** *adjective* **lexicographical** *adjective*.

lexicon /**lek**sikən/ > *noun* **1** the vocabulary of a person, language, or branch of knowledge. **2** a dictionary.
ORIGIN – from Greek *lexikon biblion* 'book of words', from *lexis* 'word'.

lexis /**lek**siss/ > *noun* the total stock of words in a language.
ORIGIN – Greek, 'word'.

ley[1] /lay/ > *noun* a piece of land temporarily put down to grass, clover, etc.
ORIGIN – Old English, 'fallow'; related to **LAY**[1] and **LIE**[1].

ley[2] /lay/ (also **ley line**) > *noun* a supposed straight line connecting three or more ancient sites, associated by some with lines of energy and other paranormal phenomena.
ORIGIN – variant of **LEA**.

leylandii /laylan**di**-ī/ > *noun* (pl. same) a fast-growing conifer, widely grown as a screening plant or for shelter.
ORIGIN – Latin, from the name of the British horticulturist Christopher *Leyland* (1849–1926).

LF > *abbreviation* low frequency.

LGV > *abbreviation* Brit. large goods vehicle.

Li > *symbol* the chemical element lithium.

liability > *noun* (pl. **liabilities**) **1** the state of being liable. **2** a thing for which someone is liable, especially a financial obligation. **3** a person or thing likely to cause one embarrassment or put one at a disadvantage.

liable > *adjective* **1** responsible by law; legally answerable. **2** (**liable to do**) likely to do (something). **3** (**liable to**) likely to experience (something undesirable).
SYNONYMS – **1** accountable, answerable, responsible. **3** (**liable to**) apt to, inclined to, likely to, prone to.
ORIGIN – perhaps from French *lier* 'to bind', from Latin *ligare*.

liaise > *verb* **1** cooperate on a matter of mutual concern. **2** (**liaise between**) act as a link to assist communication between.

liaison* > *noun* **1** communication or cooperation between people or organisations. **2** a sexual relationship, especially one that is secret. **3** the binding or thickening agent of a sauce, often based on egg yolks.
*SPELLING – remember the second *i*: li*ai*son.
ORIGIN – French, from *lier* 'to bind'.

liana /li**aa**nə/ (also **liane** /li**aan**/) > *noun* a woody climbing plant that hangs from trees, especially in tropical rainforests.
ORIGIN – French *liane* 'clematis, liana'.

liar > *noun* a person who tells lies.

lias /**lī**əss/ > *noun* (also **blue lias**) a blue-grey clayey limestone deposited in the Jurassic period, chiefly in SW England.
ORIGIN – Old French *liais* 'hard limestone'.

lib > *noun* informal (in the names of political movements) the liberation of a specified group: *women's lib*.
DERIVATIVES – **libber** *noun*.

libation /lī**bay**sh'n/ > *noun* **1** the pouring out of a drink as an offering to a deity. **2** such a drink. **3** humorous an alcoholic drink.
ORIGIN – from Latin *libare* 'pour as an offering'.

Lib Dem > *noun* informal (in the UK) Liberal Democrat.

libel /**lī**b'l/ > *noun* **1** Law the publication of a false statement that is damaging to a person's reputation. Compare with **SLANDER**. **2** such a statement; a written defamation. > *verb* (**libelled**, **libelling**; US **libeled**, **libeling**) Law defame by libel.
DERIVATIVES – **libellous** (US also **libelous**) *adjective*.
ORIGIN – from Latin *libellus* 'little book', from *liber* 'book'.

liberal > *adjective* **1** respectful and accepting of behaviour or opinions different from one's own. **2** (of a society, law, etc.) favourable to individual rights and freedoms. **3** (in a political context) favouring individual liberty, free trade, and moderate reform. **4** (**Liberal**) (in the UK) relating to the Liberal Democrat party. **5** (especially of an interpretation of a law) not strictly literal. **6** given, used, or occurring in generous amounts. **7** giving generously. **8** (of education) concerned with broadening general knowledge and experience. > *noun* **1** a person of liberal views. **2** (**Liberal**) (in the UK) a Liberal Democrat.
DERIVATIVES – **liberalism** *noun* **liberality** *noun* **liberally** *adverb*.
SYNONYMS – **1** broad-minded, enlightened, open-minded, tolerant, unprejudiced. **3** progressive, reformist. **6** abundant, copious, lavish, plentiful. **7** bountiful, generous, unsparing.
ANTONYMS – **1** bigoted, intolerant.
COMBINATIONS – **liberal arts** chiefly N. Amer. arts subjects such as literature and history, as distinct from science and technology. **Liberal Democrat** (in the UK) a member of a party formed from the Liberal Party and the Social Democratic Party.
ORIGIN – from Latin *liberalis*, from *liber* 'free man'.

liberalise (also **liberalize**) > *verb* remove or loosen restrictions on (something, typically an economic or political system).
DERIVATIVES – **liberalisation** *noun*.

liberate > *verb* **1** set free, especially from imprisonment or oppression. **2** (**liberated**) free from social conventions, especially with regard to issues associated with gender.
DERIVATIVES – **liberated** *adjective*

liberating *adjective* **liberation** *noun* **liberationist** *noun* **liberator** *noun*.

SYNONYMS – **1** deliver, emancipate, free, release.

COMBINATIONS – **liberation theology** a Christian movement which attempts to address the problems of poverty and social injustice, especially in Latin America.

ORIGIN – Latin *liberare* 'to free', from *liber* 'free'.

Liberian /lībeerɪən/ > *noun* a person from Liberia, a country in West Africa. > *adjective* relating to Liberia.

libertarian > *noun* **1** an adherent of libertarianism. **2** a person who advocates civil liberty.

libertarianism > *noun* an extreme laissez-faire political philosophy advocating only minimal state intervention in the lives of citizens.

libertine /libbərteen/ > *noun* a person who is freely indulgent in sensual pleasures. > *adjective* characterised by such indulgence.

DERIVATIVES – **libertinism** *noun*.

ORIGIN – Latin *libertinus* 'freedman', from *liber* 'free'.

liberty > *noun* (pl. **liberties**) **1** the state of being free from oppression or imprisonment. **2** a right or privilege. **3** the power or scope to act as one pleases. **4** *informal* a presumptuous remark or action.

IDIOMS – **take liberties 1** behave in an unduly familiar manner towards a person. **2** treat something freely, without strict faithfulness to the facts or to an original. **take the liberty** do something without first asking permission.

SYNONYMS – **1** autonomy, freedom, independence. **3** freedom, latitude, leave, licence.

ANTONYMS – **1** bondage.

COMBINATIONS – **liberty bodice** Brit. trademark a girl's or woman's bodice made from thick or quilted cotton, formerly worn as an undergarment. **Liberty Hall** a place where one may do as one likes.

ORIGIN – Latin *libertas*, from *liber* 'free'.

libidinous /libiddinəss/ > *adjective* having or showing excessive sexual drive.

ORIGIN – Latin *libidinosus*, from *libido* 'desire, lust'.

libido /libeedō/ > *noun* (pl. **libidos**) the urge to seek sexual gratification.

DERIVATIVES – **libidinal** *adjective*.

ORIGIN – Latin, 'desire, lust'.

Libra /leebrə/ > *noun* **1** Astronomy a small constellation (the Scales or Balance), said to represent a pair of scales symbolising justice. **2** Astrology the seventh sign of the zodiac, which the sun enters at the northern autumnal equinox (about 23 September).

DERIVATIVES – **Libran** *noun & adjective*.

---

wordpower facts

Libra

The name of the constellation **Libra** is from the Latin word *libra* 'pound, balance', which is also the source of **deliberate**, **equilibrium**, **level**, and **lira** (the Italian unit of currency). In ancient Rome a *libra* was a standard unit of weight equivalent to twelve ounces. The English word **pound** comes from Latin *libra pondo* 'pound weight', and *libra* is used for *pound* in the abbreviation l.s.d: the *l* stands for *librae* (the plural form), while the *s* and *d* are short for *solidi* and *denarii*, two Roman coins. Similarly, the pound sign £ is formed from the initial letter of *libra* written in copperplate with one or two crossbars (crossbars were formerly used to indicate an abbreviation).

---

librarian > *noun* a person in charge of or assisting in a library.

DERIVATIVES – **librarianship** *noun*.

ORIGIN – from Latin *librarius* 'relating to books'.

library > *noun* (pl. **libraries**) **1** a building or room containing a collection of books and periodicals for use by the public or the members of an institution. **2** a private collection of books. **3** a collection of films, recorded music, etc., kept for research or borrowing.

WORDFINDER – carrel (*small cubicle with a desk in a library*), Dewey (*decimal system of library classification*).

ORIGIN – Latin *libraria* 'bookshop', from *liber* 'book'.

libretto /librettō/ > *noun* (pl. **libretti** /libretti/ or **librettos**) the text of an opera or other long vocal work.

DERIVATIVES – **librettist** *noun*.

ORIGIN – Italian 'small book', from *libro* 'book'.

Libyan /libbiən/ > *noun* a person from Libya. > *adjective* relating to Libya.

lice plural of LOUSE.

licence* (US **license**) > *noun* **1** a permit from an authority to own or use something, do a particular thing, or carry on a trade. **2** a writer's or artist's conventional freedom to deviate from facts or accepted rules. **3** freedom to behave without restraint.

*SPELLING – in British English, lic*ence* is the spelling for the noun, and lic*ense* for the verb; American English favours the *-ense* spelling for both.

COMBINATIONS – **license plate** North American term for **number plate**.

ORIGIN – Latin *licentia* 'freedom, licentiousness', from *licere* 'be lawful or permitted'.

license > *verb* **1** grant a licence to. **2** authorise.

DERIVATIVES – **licensed** *adjective* **licensing** *adjective* **licensor** *noun*.

SYNONYMS – **2** allow, authorise, permit, sanction.

licensee > *noun* the holder of a licence, especially to sell alcoholic drinks.

licentiate /līsenshiət/ > *noun* the holder of a certificate of competence to practise a particular profession.

ORIGIN – from Latin *licentiatus* 'having freedom', based on *licentia* 'freedom'.

licentious /līsenshəss/ > *adjective* promiscuous and unprincipled in sexual matters.

DERIVATIVES – **licentiously** *adverb* **licentiousness** *noun*.

SYNONYMS – debauched, dissolute, immoral, promiscuous, wanton.

ORIGIN – Latin *licentiosus*, from *licentia* 'freedom'.

lichen /līkən, lichən/ > *noun* a simple plant consisting of a fungus living in close association with an alga, typically growing as a soft crust on rocks, walls, and trees.

DERIVATIVES – **lichened** *adjective* **lichenous** *adjective*.

NOTE – the first pronunciation, with the first syllable *like*, is sometimes thought more correct because it is closer to that of the original Greek.

ORIGIN – Greek *leikhēn*.

licit /lissit/ > *adjective* not forbidden; lawful.

SYNONYMS – allowed, lawful, legal, legitimate, permitted.

ANTONYMS – illicit.

ORIGIN – Latin *licitus* 'allowed', from *licere* 'allow'.

lick > *verb* **1** pass the tongue over (something), typically in order to taste, moisten, or clean it. **2** move lightly and quickly like a tongue. **3** *informal* defeat comprehensively. > *noun* **1** an act of licking. **2** *informal* a small amount or quick application of something. **3** *informal* a short phrase or solo in jazz or popular music.

IDIOMS – **at a lick** *informal* at a fast pace. **lick someone's boots** (or *vulgar slang* **arse**) be excessively obsequious towards someone.

DERIVATIVES – **licking** *noun*.

COMBINATIONS – **lickspittle** a person who behaves obsequiously to those in power.

lickerish > *adjective* lecherous.

DERIVATIVES – **lickerishly** *adverb*.

ORIGIN – Old French *lecheros* (see LECHEROUS).

lickety-split > *adverb* N. Amer. informal at full speed.

ORIGIN – first used in the phrase *as fast as lickety* 'at full speed': from LICK + SPLIT.

licorice > *noun* US spelling of LIQUORICE.

lid > *noun* **1** a removable or hinged cover for the top of a container. **2** an eyelid.

DERIVATIVES – **lidded** *adjective* **lidless** *adjective*.

ORIGIN – Old English, from a word meaning 'cover'.

lido /**lee**dō/ > *noun* (pl. **lidos**) a public open-air swimming pool or bathing beach.

ORIGIN – from Italian *Lido*, the name of a bathing beach near Venice, from *lido* 'shore'.

lie¹ > *verb* (**lying**; past **lay**; past participle **lain**) **1** (often **lie down**) be in or assume a horizontal or resting position on a supporting surface. **2** be or remain in a specified state. **3** reside or be found. **4** be situated in a particular place. > *noun* **1** the way, direction, or position in which something lies or comes to rest. **2** the place of cover of an animal or a bird.

IDIOMS – **let lie** take no action regarding (a sensitive matter). **lie in state** (of the corpse of a person of national importance) be laid in a public place of honour before burial. **lie low** keep out of sight; avoid attention. **the lie** (N. Amer. **lay**) **of the land 1** the features or characteristics of an area. **2** the current situation or state of affairs. **take lying down** accept (an insult, setback, or rebuke) without protest.

USAGE – make sure that you use **lay** and **lie** correctly. You *lay* something, as in *they are going to lay the carpet*, but you *lie* down on a bed or other flat surface. The past tense and past participle of **lay** is **laid**, as in *they laid the groundwork* or *she had laid careful plans*; the past tense of **lie** is **lay** (*he lay on the floor*) and the past participle is **lain** (*she had lain on the bed for hours*).

SYNONYMS – *verb* **1** (**lie down**) be prone, be prostrate, be recumbent, be supine, recline.

COMBINATIONS – **lie-down** chiefly Brit. a short rest on a bed or sofa. **lie-in** chiefly Brit. a prolonged stay in bed in the morning.

lie² > *noun* **1** an intentionally false statement. **2** a situation involving deception or founded on a mistaken impression. > *verb* (**lies**, **lied**, **lying**) **1** tell a lie or lies. **2** (of a thing) present a false impression.

IDIOMS – **give the lie to** serve to show that (something assumed to be true) is not true.

SYNONYMS – *noun* **1** fabrication, falsehood, fib, fiction, untruth. *verb* **1** bear false witness, bluff, fib.

COMBINATIONS – **lie detector** an instrument for determining whether a person is telling the truth by testing for physiological changes considered to be associated with lying.

Liebfraumilch /**leeb**frowmilsh/ > *noun* a light white wine from the Rhine region.

ORIGIN – from German *lieb* 'dear' + *Frau* 'lady' (referring to the Virgin Mary,

patroness of the convent where it was first made) + *Milch* 'milk'.

Liechtensteiner /**likt**ənstīnər/ > *noun* a person from Liechtenstein, a small independent principality in the Alps.

lied /leed/ > *noun* (pl. **lieder** /**lee**dər/) a type of German song, typically for solo voice with piano accompaniment.

ORIGIN – German.

lief /leef/ > *adverb* (**as lief**) archaic as happily; as gladly.

ORIGIN – Old English, 'dear, pleasant': related to LEAVE² and LOVE.

liege /leej/ historical > *adjective* referring to the relationship between a feudal superior and a vassal. > *noun* **1** (also **liege lord**) a feudal superior or sovereign. **2** a vassal or subject.

ORIGIN – Old French, from Latin *laeticus*.

lien /**lee**ən/ > *noun* Law a right to keep the property of another person until a debt owed by that person is discharged.

ORIGIN – Old French *loien* from Latin *ligamen* 'bond'.

lierne /lee-**ern**/ > *noun* Architecture (in vaulting) a short rib connecting the bosses and intersections of the principal ribs.

ORIGIN – French, perhaps from dialect *lierne* 'clematis'.

lieu /lyōo/ > *noun* (in phrase **in lieu** or **in lieu of**) instead (of).

ORIGIN – French, from Latin *locus* 'place'.

lieutenant /lef**tenn**ənt, US loo**tenn**ənt/ > *noun* **1** a deputy or substitute acting for a superior. **2** a rank of officer in the British army, above second lieutenant and below captain. **3** a rank of officer in the navy, above sub lieutenant and below lieutenant commander.

DERIVATIVES – **lieutenancy** (pl. **lieutenancies**) *noun*.

COMBINATIONS – **lieutenant colonel** a rank of officer in the army and the US air force, above major and below colonel. **lieutenant commander** a rank of officer in the navy, above lieutenant and below commander. **lieutenant general** a high rank of officer in the army, above major general and below general.

ORIGIN – Old French, 'place-holding' (see LIEU, TENANT).

life > *noun* (pl. **lives**) **1** the condition that distinguishes animals and plants from inorganic matter, and includes the capacity for growth and functional activity. **2** the existence of an individual human being or animal. **3** a particular type or aspect of people's existence: *school life*. **4** living things and their activity. **5** a biography. **6** vitality, vigour, or energy. **7** informal a sentence of life imprisonment. **8** (in various games) each of a specified number of chances each player has before being put out. **9** (before another noun) (in art) based on a living rather than an imagined form.

IDIOMS – **for the life of me** informal however hard I try. **as large as** (or **larger than**) **life** informal conspicuously present. **take one's life in one's hands** risk being killed.

SYNONYMS – **2** being, existence.

COMBINATIONS – **life assurance** chiefly Brit. another term for *life insurance*. **lifebelt** chiefly Brit. a ring of buoyant or inflatable material used to help a person who has fallen into water to stay afloat. **lifeblood 1** literary blood, as being necessary to life. **2** an indispensable factor or force giving something its vitality. **lifeboat 1** a specially constructed boat launched from land to rescue people in distress at sea. **2** a small boat kept on a ship for use in an emergency. **lifebuoy** chiefly Brit. a buoyant support such as a lifebelt for keeping a person afloat in water. **life cycle** the series of changes in the life of an organism including reproduction. **life expectancy** the period that a person may expect to live. **life force** the force that gives something its life, vitality, or strength. **life form** any living thing. **lifeguard** a person employed to rescue bathers who get into difficulty at a beach or swimming pool. **Life Guards** (in the UK) a regiment of the Household Cavalry. **life imprisonment** a long term of imprisonment (rarely the whole of a person's life), which (in the UK) is now the only sentence for murder and the maximum for any crime. **life insurance** insurance that pays out a sum of money either on the death of the insured person or after a set period. **life jacket** a sleeveless buoyant or inflatable jacket for keeping a person afloat in water. **lifelike** accurate in its representation of a living person or thing. **lifeline 1** a rope or line used for life-saving, typically one thrown to rescue someone in difficulties in water or one used by sailors to secure themselves to a boat. **2** a thing which is essential for the continued existence of someone or something or which provides a means of escape from a difficult situation. **3** (in palmistry) a line on the palm of a person's hand, regarded as indicating how long they will live. **lifelong** lasting or remaining in a particular state throughout a person's life. **life peer** (or **peeress**) (in the UK) a peer (or peeress) whose title cannot be inherited. **life preserver** a life jacket or lifebelt. **life raft** an inflatable raft for use in an emergency at sea. **lifesaver 1** informal a thing that saves one from serious difficulty. **2** Austral./NZ a lifeguard on a beach. **life sciences** the sciences concerned with the study of living organisms, including biology, botany, and zoology. **life sentence** a punishment of life imprisonment. **life-size** (also **life-sized**) of the same size as the person or thing represented. **lifespan** the length of time for which a person or animal lives or a thing functions. **lifestyle** the way in which one lives. **life support** Medicine maintenance of vital functions following disablement or in an adverse environment. **life-threatening** potentially fatal. **lifetime 1** the duration of a person's life. **2** the duration of a thing or its usefulness.

ORIGIN – Old English, related to LIVE[1].

lifeless > *adjective* **1** dead or apparently dead. **2** devoid of living things. **3** lacking vigour, vitality, or excitement.

DERIVATIVES – **lifelessly** *adverb* **lifelessness** *noun*.

lifer > *noun* informal a person serving a life sentence.

lift > *verb* **1** raise or be raised to a higher position or level. **2** pick up and move to a different position. **3** formally remove or end (a legal restriction, decision, etc.). **4** (**lift off**) (of an aircraft, spacecraft, etc.) take off, especially vertically. **5** carry off or win (a prize or event). **6** informal steal. > *noun* **1** Brit. a platform or compartment housed in a shaft for raising and lowering people or things. **2** an act or instance of lifting. **3** a free ride in another person's vehicle. **4** a device for carrying people up or down a mountain. **5** a feeling of increased cheerfulness. **6** upward force exerted by the air on an aerofoil or other structure.

IDIOMS – **lift a finger** (or **hand**) make the slightest effort: *they wouldn't lift a finger to help.*

DERIVATIVES – **lifter** *noun*.

COMBINATIONS – **lift-off** the vertical take-off of a spacecraft, rocket, etc.

ORIGIN – Old Norse; related to LOFT.

lig Brit. informal > *verb* (**ligged**, **ligging**) take advantage of free parties, shows, or travel offered by companies for publicity purposes. > *noun* a free party or show of this type.

DERIVATIVES – **ligger** *noun*.

ORIGIN – from a dialect variant of LIE[1] meaning 'lie about, loaf'.

ligament /liggəmənt/ > *noun* Anatomy **1** a short band of tough, flexible, fibrous tissue which connects two bones or cartilages or holds together a joint. **2** a membranous fold that supports an organ and keeps it in position.

DERIVATIVES – **ligamentous** *adjective*.

ORIGIN – Latin *ligamentum* 'bond', from *ligare* 'to bind'.

ligand /liggənd/ > *noun* Chemistry an ion or molecule that forms a bond to a particular atom or substance.

ORIGIN – Latin *ligandus* 'that can be tied'.

ligate /ligayt/ > *verb* Surgery tie up (an artery or vessel).

ORIGIN – from Latin *ligare* 'to tie'.

ligature /liggəchər/ > *noun* **1** a thing used for tying something tightly. **2** a cord used in surgery, especially to tie up a bleeding artery. **3** Music a slur or tie. **4** Printing a character consisting of two or more joined letters, e.g. æ. > *verb* bind or connect with a ligature.

ORIGIN – Latin *ligatura* from *ligare* 'to tie'.

light[1] > *noun* **1** the natural agent that stimulates sight and makes things visible; electromagnetic radiation from about 390 to 740 nanometers in wavelength. **2** a source of illumination. **3** a device producing a flame or spark. **4** (**lights**) traffic lights. **5** an expression in someone's eyes. **6** an area that is brighter or paler than its surroundings. **7** enlightenment. **8** (**lights**) a person's opinions, standards, and abilities. **9** a window or opening to let light in. > *verb* (past **lit**; past participle **lit** or **lighted**) **1** provide with light. **2** (**light up**) become illuminated. **3** ignite or be ignited. **4** (**light up**) ignite a cigarette, cigar, or pipe and begin to smoke it. > *adjective* **1** having a considerable or sufficient amount of light. **2** (of a colour or object) reflecting a lot of light; pale.

WORDFINDER – photic (*relating to light*), photon (*a quantum or 'particle' of light*), superluminal (*faster than the speed of light*), tachyon (*hypothetical faster-than-light particle*).

IDIOMS – **bring** (or **come**) **to light** make (or become) widely known or evident. **in a —— light** in the way specified. **in (the) light of** taking (something) into consideration. **light at the end of the tunnel** an indication that a period of difficulty is ending. **see the light 1** understand or realise something. **2** undergo religious conversion. **throw** (or **cast** or **shed**) **light on** help to explain by providing further information.

DERIVATIVES – **lightless** *adjective* **lightness** *noun*.

COMBINATIONS – **light box** a box with a translucent top and containing an electric light, providing an evenly lighted flat surface for viewing transparencies. **light bulb** a glass bulb containing inert gas, fitted into a lamp or ceiling socket, which provides light when an electric current is passed through it. **lighthouse** a tower or other structure containing a beacon light to warn ships at sea. **light meter** an instrument measuring the intensity of light, used when taking photographs. **light pen 1** Computing a hand-held pen-like photosensitive device used for passing information to a computer. **2** a hand-held device for reading bar codes. **light pollution** excessive brightening of the night sky by street lights and other man-made sources. **lightship** an anchored boat with a beacon light to warn ships at sea. **light year** Astronomy a unit of distance equivalent to the distance that light travels in one year, 9.4607×10^{12} km (nearly 6 million million miles).

light[2] > *adjective* **1** of little weight. **2** deficient in weight. **3** not strongly or heavily built. **4** relatively low in density, amount, or intensity. **5** carrying or suitable for small loads. **6** gentle or delicate. **7** not profound or serious. **8** (of sleep or a sleeper) easily disturbed. **9** easily borne or done. **10** free from worry.

IDIOMS – **make light of** treat as unimportant. **make light work of** accomplish quickly and easily. **travel light** travel with little luggage.

DERIVATIVES – **lightish** *adjective* **lightly** *adverb* **lightness** *noun*.

SYNONYMS – **1** insubstantial, lightweight. **2** underweight. **3** flimsy, insubstantial. **6** delicate, faint, gentle, soft.

ANTONYMS – heavy.

COMBINATIONS – **light-fingered** prone to steal. **light flyweight** the lowest weight in amateur boxing. **light-footed** fast, nimble, or stealthy on one's feet. **light-headed** dizzy and slightly faint. **light heavyweight** a weight in boxing and other sports intermediate between middleweight and heavyweight. **light industry** the manufacture of small or light articles. **light middleweight** a weight in amateur boxing intermediate between welterweight and middleweight. **light welterweight** a weight in amateur boxing intermediate between lightweight and welterweight.

light[3] > *verb* (past and past participle **lit** or **lighted**) (**light on** or **upon**) come upon or discover by chance.

lighten[1] > *verb* **1** make or become lighter in weight. **2** make or become less serious.

SYNONYMS – **1** decrease, lessen, reduce. **2** brighten, gladden, sweeten.

lighten[2] > *verb* make or become brighter.

SYNONYMS – brighten, illuminate.

lighter[1] > *noun* a device producing a small flame, used to light cigarettes.

lighter[2] > *noun* a flat-bottomed barge used to transfer goods to and from ships in harbour.

ORIGIN – from LIGHT[2] (in the sense 'unload'), or from Low German *luchter*.

lightfast > *adjective* (of a pigment) not prone to discolour when exposed to light.

DERIVATIVES – **lightfastness** *noun*.

light-hearted > *adjective* **1** amusing and entertaining. **2** happy and carefree.

DERIVATIVES – **light-heartedly** *adverb*.

SYNONYMS – **1** playful, sportive, unserious; formal jocund. **2** blithe, carefree, cheerful, happy.

lighting > *noun* **1** equipment for producing light. **2** the arrangement or effect of lights.

COMBINATIONS – **lighting-up time** Brit. the time at which motorists are required by law to switch their vehicles' lights on.

lightning–limbo

lightning* > *noun* **1** the occurrence of a high-voltage electrical discharge between a cloud and the ground or within a cloud, accompanied by a bright flash and typically thunder. **2** (before another noun) very quick: *lightning reflexes.*

WORDFINDER – *types of lightning:* ball lightning, forked lightning, sheet lightning.

*SPELLING – although the word developed from **LIGHTEN²**, the modern spelling is **lightning**, not -ten-.

COMBINATIONS – **lightning conductor** (also chiefly N. Amer. **lightning rod**) Brit. a metal rod or wire fixed in a high and exposed place to divert lightning into the ground.

lights > *plural noun* the lungs of sheep, pigs, or bullocks as food for pets.

ORIGIN – from **LIGHT²** (so named because of their lightness).

lightweight > *noun* **1** a weight in boxing and other sports intermediate between featherweight and welterweight. **2** informal a person of little importance. > *adjective* **1** of thin material or build. **2** informal having little importance.

ligneous /ligniəss/ > *adjective* consisting of or resembling wood.

ORIGIN – from Latin *ligneus* 'relating to wood'.

lignin /lignin/ > *noun* Botany a complex organic polymer deposited in the cell walls of many plants, making them rigid and woody.

ORIGIN – from Latin *lignum* 'wood'.

lignite > *noun* soft brownish coal, intermediate between bituminous coal and peat.

ORIGIN – from Latin *lignum* 'wood'.

lignocaine /lignōkayn/ > *noun* Medicine a synthetic compound used as a local anaesthetic and in treating abnormal heart rhythms.

ORIGIN – from Latin *lignum* 'wood' + -caine (from **COCAINE**).

likable > *adjective* variant spelling of **LIKEABLE**.

like¹ > *preposition* **1** similar to. **2** in the manner of. **3** in a way appropriate to. **4** in this manner. **5** such as. **6** used to ask about someone's or something's characteristics. > *conjunction* informal **1** in the same way that. **2** as though. > *noun* **1** a similar person or thing. **2** (the like) things of the same kind. > *adjective* having similar characteristics to another. > *adverb* informal used in speech as a meaningless filler.

IDIOMS – **and the like** et cetera. (as) **like as not** probably. **like so** informal in this manner.

USAGE – it is unacceptable in formal English to use **like** as a conjunction to mean 'as if', as in *he's behaving like he owns the place,*

although it has been used in this way by many respected writers over the years.

COMBINATIONS – **like-minded** having similar tastes or opinions.

ORIGIN – Old Norse; related to **ALIKE**.

like² > *verb* **1** find agreeable or satisfactory. **2** wish for; want. > *noun* (**likes**) the things one likes.

SYNONYMS – *verb* **1** admire, appreciate, be fond of, be keen on, be partial to, enjoy.

ORIGIN – Old English, 'be pleasing'.

-like > *combining form* (added to nouns) similar to; characteristic of: *crust-like.*

likeable (also **likable**) > *adjective* pleasant; easy to like.

DERIVATIVES – **likeably** *adverb.*

SYNONYMS – attractive, congenial, personable, pleasant.

likelihood > *noun* the state or fact of being likely.

likely > *adjective* (**likelier**, **likeliest**) **1** such as well might be the case; probable. **2** promising. > *adverb* probably.

IDIOMS – **a likely story!** used to express disbelief. **as likely as not** probably. **not likely!** informal certainly not.

USAGE – when using **likely** as an adverb, you should precede it with a word such as **very**, **most**, or **more**, as in *we will most likely see him later*; sentences such as *we will likely see him later* are acceptable only in informal US English.

SYNONYMS – *adjective* **1** convincing, plausible, probable, reasonable.

liken > *verb* (**liken to**) point out the resemblance (of someone or something) to.

likeness > *noun* **1** resemblance. **2** the semblance or outward appearance of. **3** a portrait or representation.

SYNONYMS – **1** correspondence, resemblance, similarity. **2** guise, semblance, shape.

likewise > *adverb* **1** also; moreover. **2** similarly.

ORIGIN – from the phrase *in like wise.*

liking > *noun* **1** a regard or fondness for something. **2** one's taste.

SYNONYMS – **1** affection, fondness, penchant, soft spot.

likuta /likōotə/ > *noun* (pl. **makuta** /məkōotə/) a monetary unit of Zaire (Democratic Republic of Congo), equal to one hundredth of a zaire.

ORIGIN – from Kikongo, a Bantu language.

lilac > *noun* **1** a shrub or small tree with fragrant violet, pink, or white blossom. **2** a pale pinkish-violet colour.

ORIGIN – from a Persian word for 'bluish'.

lilangeni /leelanggayni/ > *noun* (pl. **emalangeni** /imalanggayni/) the basic monetary unit of Swaziland, equal to 100 cents.

ORIGIN – from a Bantu prefix *li-* used to denote a singular + *-langeni* 'member of a royal family'.

Lilliputian /lillipyōosh'n/ > *adjective* trivial or very small. > *noun* a Lilliputian person or thing.

ORIGIN – from the imaginary country of *Lilliput* in Jonathan Swift's *Gulliver's Travels* (1726), inhabited by 6-inch high people.

lilo /līlō/ (also trademark **Li-lo**) > *noun* (pl. **lilos**) an inflatable mattress used as a bed or for floating on water.

lilt > *noun* **1** a pleasant gentle accent. **2** a gentle rhythm in a tune. > *verb* speak, sing, or sound with a lilt.

ORIGIN – from earlier *lulte*, meaning 'sound (an alarm)' or 'lift up (the voice)'.

lily > *noun* a plant with large trumpet-shaped flowers on a tall, slender stem.

COMBINATIONS – **lily-livered** cowardly. **lily of the valley** a plant of the lily family, with broad leaves and spikes of tiny white bell-shaped flowers. **lily pad** a leaf of a water lily. **lily-white 1** pure white. **2** totally innocent or pure.

ORIGIN – Greek *leirion.*

lima bean /leemə/ > *noun* an edible flat whitish bean.

ORIGIN – from *Lima*, the capital of Peru.

limb¹ > *noun* **1** an arm, leg, or wing. **2** a large branch of a tree. **3** a branch of a cross.

IDIOMS – **life and limb** life and bodily faculties. **out on a limb** isolated.

limb² > *noun* Astronomy a specified edge of the disc of the sun, moon, or other celestial object.

ORIGIN – Latin *limbus* 'hem, border'.

limber¹ > *adjective* supple; flexible. > *verb* (**limber up**) warm up in preparation for exercise or activity.

ORIGIN – perhaps from **LIMBER²** in the dialect sense 'cart shaft', with allusion to the to-and-fro motion.

limber² > *noun* the detachable front part of a gun carriage. > *verb* attach a limber to (a gun).

ORIGIN – apparently related to Latin *limonarius* from *limo* 'shaft'.

limbic system > *noun* a complex system of nerves and networks in the brain, controlling the basic emotions and drives.

ORIGIN – from Latin *limbus* 'edge, border'.

limbo¹ > *noun* **1** (in some Christian beliefs) the supposed abode of the souls of unbaptised infants, and of good people who died before Christ. **2** an uncertain period of awaiting a decision or resolution.

ORIGIN – Latin *limbus* 'border, limbo'.

limbo² > *noun* (pl. **limbos**) a West Indian dance in which the dancer bends backwards to pass under a horizontal bar which is progressively lowered towards the ground. > *verb* dance the limbo.

ORIGIN – from **LIMBER¹**.

lime¹ > *noun* **1** quicklime, slaked lime, or any salt or alkali containing calcium. **2** archaic birdlime. > *verb* treat with lime.

DERIVATIVES – **limy** (**limier**, **limiest**) *adjective*.

COMBINATIONS – **limekiln** a kiln in which quicklime is produced.

ORIGIN – Old English, related to LOAM.

lime² > *noun* **1** a rounded green citrus fruit similar to a lemon. **2** a bright light green colour. **3** a drink made from lime juice.

ORIGIN – French, from Arabic.

lime³ (also **lime tree**) > *noun* a deciduous tree with heart-shaped leaves and yellowish blossom.

limeade > *noun* a drink made from lime juice sweetened with sugar.

limelight > *noun* **1** (**the limelight**) the focus of public attention. **2** an intense white light produced by heating lime in a very hot flame, formerly used in theatres.

limerick > *noun* a humorous five-line poem with a rhyme scheme *aabba*.

ORIGIN – said to be from the chorus 'will you come up to Limerick?', sung between improvised verses at a gathering.

limescale > *noun* a crust-like deposit of minerals which forms on a surface when hard water is heated and then cooled.

limestone > *noun* a hard sedimentary rock composed mainly of calcium carbonate.

limewash > *noun* a mixture of lime and water for coating walls. > *verb* apply limewash to.

Limey > *noun* (pl. **Limeys**) N. Amer. & Austral., chiefly derogatory a British person.

ORIGIN – from LIME², because of the former enforced consumption of lime juice in the British navy.

liminal /limmin'l/ > *adjective* technical **1** relating to a transitional or initial stage. **2** at a boundary or threshold.

DERIVATIVES – **liminality** *noun*.

ORIGIN – from Latin *limen* 'threshold'.

limit > *noun* **1** a point beyond which something does not or may not pass. **2** a restriction on the size or amount of something. **3** the furthest extent of one's endurance. > *verb* (**limited**, **limiting**) set or serve as a limit to.

IDIOMS – **off limits** out of bounds. **within limits** up to a point.

DERIVATIVES – **limiter** *noun* **limitless** *adjective* **limitlessly** *adverb*.

SYNONYMS – *noun* **1** boundary, edge, margin, threshold. **3** breaking point, extremity. *verb* confine, curb, regulate, restrict.

ORIGIN – Latin *limes* 'boundary'.

limitation > *noun* **1** a restriction. **2** a defect or failing. **3** (also **limitation period**) Law a legally specified period beyond which an action may be defeated or a property right is not to continue.

SYNONYMS – **1** check, curb, restraint, restriction. **2** defect, deficiency, failing, inadequacy, shortcoming.

limited > *adjective* **1** restricted in size, amount, or extent. **2** not great in ability. **3** (of a monarchy or government) exercised under limitations of power prescribed by a constitution. **4** (**Limited**) Brit. denoting a limited company.

COMBINATIONS – **limited company** Brit. a private company whose owners are legally responsible for its debts only to the extent of the amount of capital they invested. **limited liability** Brit. the condition of being legally responsible for the debts of a company only to the extent of the nominal value of one's shares.

limn /lim/ > *verb* literary depict or describe in painting or words.

DERIVATIVES – **limner** *noun*.

ORIGIN – from obsolete *lumine* 'illuminate', from Latin *luminare* 'make light'.

limo > *noun* (pl. **limos**) informal a limousine.

limonene /limmoneen/ > *noun* Chemistry a colourless liquid hydrocarbon with a lemon-like scent, present in lemon oil, orange oil, etc.

ORIGIN – from German *Limone* 'lemon'.

Limousin /limoozaN/ > *noun* a French breed of beef cattle.

limousine > *noun* a large, luxurious car.

wordpower facts

Limousine

The word **limousine** is derived from the name of *Limousin*, a region around Limoges in central France that also gave its name to the **Limousin** breed of beef cattle. The car acquired its name from a caped cloak worn by cart drivers in Limousin: original limousines had an outside driving seat and an enclosed passenger compartment, the roof of which was likened to the cart driver's cloak.

limp¹ > *verb* walk with difficulty because of an injured leg or foot. > *noun* a limping gait.

limp² > *adjective* **1** not stiff or firm. **2** without energy or will.

DERIVATIVES – **limply** *adverb*.

SYNONYMS – **1** drooping, flaccid, floppy, soft.

COMBINATIONS – **limp-wristed** informal effeminate.

ORIGIN – perhaps related to LIMP¹.

limpet > *noun* a marine mollusc with a shallow conical shell and a muscular foot for clinging tightly to rocks.

COMBINATIONS – **limpet mine** a mine that attaches magnetically to a ship's hull and explodes after a certain time.

ORIGIN – Latin *lampreda* 'limpet, lamprey'.

limpid > *adjective* **1** (of a liquid or the eyes) clear. **2** (especially of writing or music) clear or melodious.

DERIVATIVES – **limpidity** *noun* **limpidly** *adverb*.

ORIGIN – Latin *limpidus*.

linage > *noun* the number of lines in printed or written matter.

linchpin (also **lynchpin**) > *noun* **1** a pin through the end of an axle keeping a wheel in position. **2** an indispensable person or thing.

ORIGIN – from Old English *lynis* 'linchpin'.

Lincs. > *abbreviation* Lincolnshire.

linctus > *noun* Brit. thick liquid medicine, especially cough mixture.

ORIGIN – Latin, from *lingere* 'to lick'.

lindane > *noun* a synthetic insecticide, now restricted in use owing to its persistence in the environment.

ORIGIN – named after the 20th-century Dutch chemist Teunis van der *Linden*.

linden > *noun* a lime tree.

line¹ > *noun* **1** a long, narrow mark or band. **2** a length of cord, wire, etc. serving a purpose. **3** a row or connected series of people or things. **4** a row of written or printed words. **5** a direction, course, or channel. **6** a telephone connection. **7** a railway track or route. **8** a connected series of military defences facing an enemy force. **9** a line of battle. **10** a wrinkle in the skin. **11** a contour or outline considered as a feature of design or composition. **12** a range of commercial goods. **13** a sphere of activity. **14** (**lines**) a way of doing something: *thinking along the same lines*. **15** (**lines**) the words of an actor's part. **16** (**lines**) a number of repetitions of a sentence written out as a school punishment. > *verb* **1** stand or be positioned at intervals along. **2** (**line up**) arrange (people or things) in a row. **3** (**line up**) have (someone or something) prepared. **4** (**lined**) marked or covered with lines.

WORDFINDER – asymptote (*straight line approaching a curve on a graph but never meeting it*), collinear (*lying in the same straight line*), linear (*arranged in or consisting of a line*), tangent (*straight line that touches a curve at a point but does not cross it*).

IDIOMS – **the end of the line** the point at which one can go no further. **hold the line 1** not yield to pressure. **2** maintain a telephone connection. **in line** under control. **in line for** likely to receive. **in (or out of) line with** in (or not in) alignment or accordance with. **lay (or put) it on the line** speak frankly. **line of fire** the expected path of gunfire or a missile. **on the line** at serious risk. **out of line** informal behaving inappropriately or incorrectly.

COMBINATIONS – **line drawing** a drawing based on the use of line rather than shading. **line-up 1** a group of people or things assembled for a particular purpose. **2** an identity parade.

ORIGIN – Old English, 'rope, series', from Latin *linum* 'flax'.

line² > *verb* cover the inner surface of (something) with a layer of different material.

ORIGIN – from obsolete *line* 'flax', with reference to the use of linen for linings.

lineage /**linn**i-ij/ > *noun* **1** ancestry or pedigree. **2** Biology a sequence of species each of which evolved from its predecessor.

lineal /**linn**iəl/ > *adjective* **1** in a direct line of descent or ancestry. **2** linear.

DERIVATIVES – **lineally** *adverb*.

lineament /**linn**iəmənt/ > *noun* **1** literary a distinctive feature, especially of the face. **2** Geology a linear feature on the earth's surface.

linear /**linn**iər/ > *adjective* **1** arranged in or extending along a straight line. **2** consisting of lines or outlines. **3** involving one dimension only. **4** sequential. **5** Mathematics able to be represented by a straight line on a graph.

DERIVATIVES – **linearise** (also **linearize**) *verb* **linearity** *noun* **linearly** *adverb*.

COMBINATIONS – **linear equation** an equation between two variables that gives a straight line when plotted on a graph.

lineation /**linn**iaysh'n/ > *noun* **1** a line or linear marking. **2** the action of drawing lines or marking with lines.

line dancing > *noun* a type of country and western dancing in which a line of dancers follow a choreographed pattern of steps.

DERIVATIVES – **line-dance** *verb* **line dancer** *noun*.

lineman > *noun* **1** a person who lays and maintains railway tracks. **2** North American term for LINESMAN (in sense 2).

line manager > *noun* chiefly Brit. a manager to whom an employee is directly responsible.

DERIVATIVES – **line management** *noun*.

linen > *noun* **1** cloth woven from flax. **2** articles such as sheets or clothes made, or originally made, of linen.

COMBINATIONS – **linen basket** chiefly Brit. a basket for soiled clothing.

ORIGIN – Old English, as an adjective in the sense 'made of flax'; from obsolete *line* 'flax'.

line-out > *noun* Rugby Union a formation of parallel lines of opposing forwards at right angles to the touchline when the ball is thrown in.

liner¹ > *noun* **1** a large passenger ship. [ORIGIN – so-called because such a ship

originally belonged to a line, or company, providing passenger ships on particular routes.] **2** a fine paintbrush. **3** a cosmetic for outlining or accentuating a facial feature. **4** a boat engaged in sea fishing with lines.

liner² > *noun* a lining of a garment, container, etc.

linesman > *noun* **1** (in games played on a field or court) an official who assists the referee or umpire in deciding whether the ball is out of play. **2** Brit. a person who repairs and maintains telephone or electricity power lines.

ling¹ > *noun* a long-bodied edible marine fish of the cod family.

COMBINATIONS – **lingcod** a large slender greenish-brown fish with golden spots, of the Pacific coast of North America.

ORIGIN – probably from Dutch; related to LONG¹.

ling² > *noun* the common heather.

ORIGIN – Old Norse.

-ling > *suffix* **1** forming nouns from nouns: *sapling*. **2** forming nouns from adjectives and adverbs: *darling* | *underling*. **3** forming diminutive nouns: *gosling*.

lingam /**ling**gam/ (also **linga** /**ling**gə/) > *noun* Hinduism a phallus or phallic object as a symbol of Shiva, the god of reproduction.

ORIGIN – from a Sanskrit word meaning 'mark, sexual characteristic'.

linger > *verb* **1** be slow or reluctant to leave. **2** (**linger over**) spend a long time over. **3** be slow to fade, disappear, or die.

DERIVATIVES – **lingerer** *noun* **lingering** *adjective*.

SYNONYMS – **1** delay, hover, loiter. **3** endure, persist, remain, survive.

ORIGIN – from obsolete *leng* 'prolong'; related to LONG¹.

lingerie /**la**Nzhəri/ > *noun* women's underwear and nightclothes.

ORIGIN – French, from *linge* 'linen'.

lingo > *noun* (pl. **lingos** or **lingoes**) informal, often humorous **1** a foreign language. **2** the jargon of a particular subject or group.

ORIGIN – probably from Portuguese *lingoa*, from Latin *lingua* 'tongue'.

lingua franca /**ling**gwə **frang**kə/ > *noun* (pl. **lingua francas**) a language used as a common language between speakers whose native languages are different.

ORIGIN – Italian, 'Frankish tongue', in reference to a language formerly used in the eastern Mediterranean, consisting of Italian mixed with French, Greek, Arabic, and Spanish.

lingual /**ling**gwəl/ > *adjective* technical **1** relating to the tongue. **2** relating to speech or language.

DERIVATIVES – **lingually** *adverb*.

ORIGIN – Latin *lingualis*, from *lingua* 'tongue, language'.

linguine /**ling**gweeni/ > *plural noun* small ribbons of pasta.

ORIGIN – Italian, plural of *linguina* 'little tongue'.

linguist > *noun* **1** a person skilled in foreign languages. **2** a person who studies linguistics.

ORIGIN – from Latin *lingua* 'language'.

linguistic > *adjective* of or relating to language or linguistics.

DERIVATIVES – **linguistically** *adverb*.

linguistics > *plural noun* (treated as sing.) the scientific study of language and its structures.

DERIVATIVES – **linguistician** *noun*.

liniment > *noun* an ointment rubbed on the body to relieve pain or bruising.

ORIGIN – Latin *linimentum*, from *linire* 'to smear'.

lining > *noun* a layer of different material covering or attached to the inside of something.

link > *noun* **1** a relationship or connection between people or things. **2** something that facilitates communication between people. **3** a means of contact or transport between two places. **4** a loop in a chain. > *verb* make, form, or suggest a link with or between.

DERIVATIVES – **linker** *noun*.

SYNONYMS – *noun* **1** association, attachment, connection, relationship. *verb* associate, attach, connect, join, twin.

COMBINATIONS – **link-up 1** an instance of two or more people or things linking. **2** a connection enabling people or machines to communicate with each other.

ORIGIN – Old Norse.

linkage > *noun* **1** the action of linking or the state of being linked. **2** a system of links.

linkman > *noun* Brit. **1** a person serving as a connection between others. **2** a person providing continuity between items on radio or television.

links > *plural noun* **1** (also **golf links**) (treated as sing. or pl.) a golf course, especially on grassland near the sea. **2** sandy ground near the sea, covered by coarse grass.

ORIGIN – Old English, 'rising ground'.

Linnaean /**li**neeən/ (also **Linnean**) > *adjective* relating to the Swedish botanist Linnaeus (Latinised name of Carl von Linné) (1707–78) or his use of names in the classification of animals and plants. > *noun* a follower of Linnaeus.

linnet > *noun* a mainly brown and grey finch with a reddish breast and forehead.

ORIGIN – Old French *linette*, from *lin* 'flax' (because the bird feeds on flaxseed).

lino > *noun* (pl. **linos**) informal, chiefly Brit. linoleum.

COMBINATIONS – **linocut** a design carved on a block of linoleum, used for printing.

linoleic acid /linnəlayik/ > *noun* Chemistry a polyunsaturated fatty acid present in linseed and other oils and essential in the diet.

DERIVATIVES – **linoleate** *noun*.

linoleum /linōliəm/ > *noun* a material consisting of a canvas backing thickly coated with a preparation of linseed oil and powdered cork, used as a floor covering.

ORIGIN – from Latin *linum* 'flax' + *oleum* 'oil'.

linseed > *noun* the seeds of the flax plant.

COMBINATIONS – **linseed cake** pressed linseed used as cattle food. **linseed oil** oil extracted from linseed, used especially in paint and varnish.

ORIGIN – Old English, from *līn* 'flax'.

linsey-woolsey /linzi**woo**lzi/ > *noun* a strong, coarse fabric with a linen or cotton warp and a woollen weft.

ORIGIN – from *linsey*, originally denoting a coarse linen fabric (probably from *Lindsey*, a village in Suffolk) + **WOOL** + -*sey* as a rhyming suffix.

lint > *noun* 1 short, fine fibres which separate from cloth or yarn during processing. 2 Scottish flax fibres prepared for spinning. 3 the fibrous material of a cotton boll. 4 Brit. a fabric with a raised nap on one side, used for dressing wounds.

DERIVATIVES – **linty** *adjective*.

ORIGIN – first as *lynnet* 'flax prepared for spinning', perhaps from Old French *linette* 'linseed', from *lin* 'flax'.

lintel > *noun* a horizontal support across the top of a door or window.

DERIVATIVES – **lintelled** (US **linteled**) *adjective*.

ORIGIN – Old French, from Latin *limen* 'threshold'.

lion > *noun* (fem. **lioness**) 1 a large tawny-coloured cat of Africa and NW India, of which the male has a shaggy mane. 2 a brave, strong, or fierce person. 3 a celebrity: *a literary lion*.

WORDFINDER – Leo (*constellation and zodiac sign, the Lion*), leonine (*of or resembling a lion or lions*), pride (*group of lions*).

IDIOMS – **the lion's den** an intimidating or unpleasant place. **the lion's share** the largest part of something.

COMBINATIONS – **lion-hearted** brave and determined.

ORIGIN – Old French *liun*, from Latin *leo*, from Greek *leōn*.

lionise (also **lionize**) > *verb* treat as a celebrity.

DERIVATIVES – **lionisation** *noun*.

lip > *noun* 1 either of the two fleshy parts forming the edges of the mouth opening. 2 informal impudent talk. 3 the edge of a hollow container or an opening. 4 another term for **LABIUM**. > *verb* (of water) lap against.

WORDFINDER – labial (*relating to the lips*).

IDIOMS – **bite one's lip** stifle laughter or a retort. **curl one's lip** sneer. **pass one's lips** be eaten, drunk, or spoken. **pay lip service to** express superficial or insincere respect or support for.

DERIVATIVES – **lipless** *adjective* **lipped** *adjective*.

COMBINATIONS – **lip gloss** a glossy cosmetic applied to the lips. **lip salve** Brit. a preparation to prevent or relieve sore or chapped lips. **lipstick** coloured cosmetic applied to the lips from a small solid stick.

ORIGIN – Old English *lippa*, of Germanic origin; from an Indo-European root shared by Latin *labia* 'lips'.

lipa /leepə/ > *noun* (pl. same or **lipas**) a monetary unit of Croatia, equal to one hundredth of a kuna.

ORIGIN – Serbo-Croat, 'lime tree'.

lipase /lippayz, līpayz/ > *noun* Biochemistry an enzyme secreted by the pancreas that promotes the breakdown of fats.

ORIGIN – from Greek *lipos* 'fat'.

lipid /lippid/ > *noun* Chemistry any of a class of fats that are insoluble in water and include many natural oils, waxes, and steroids.

liposome /lippəsōm, līpəsōm/ > *noun* Biochemistry a tiny artificial sac of insoluble fat enclosing a water droplet, used to carry medicinal drugs into the tissues.

ORIGIN – from Greek *lipos* 'fat' + *sōma* 'body'.

liposuction /lippəsuksh'n, līpə-/ > *noun* a technique in cosmetic surgery for removing excess fat from under the skin by suction.

ORIGIN – from Greek *lipos* 'fat'.

lippy informal > *adjective* (**lippier**, **lippiest**) impertinent. > *noun* (also **lippie**) lipstick.

lip-read > *verb* understand speech from observing a speaker's lip movements.

DERIVATIVES – **lip-reader** *noun*.

lip-sync (also **lip-synch**) > *noun* the movement of a performer's lips in synchronisation with a pre-recorded soundtrack. > *verb* perform (a song or speech) in this way.

DERIVATIVES – **lip-syncer** *noun*.

liquefy* /likwifī/ (also **liquify**) > *verb* (**liquefies**, **liquefied**) make or become liquid.

DERIVATIVES – **liquefaction** *noun* **liquefactive** *adjective* **liquefiable** *adjective* **liquefier** *noun*.

*SPELLING – the standard spelling is liqu*e*fy, although liqu*i*fy is very common.

ORIGIN – French *liquéfier*, from Latin *liquefacere* 'make liquid'.

liquescent /likwess'nt/ > *adjective* becoming or apt to become liquid.

liqueur /likyoor/ > *noun* a strong, sweet-flavoured alcoholic spirit.

WORDFINDER – *types of liqueur:* absinthe, advocaat, amaretto, Benedictine, cassis, chartreuse, cherry brandy, Cointreau, crème de menthe, curaçao, Drambuie, Grand Marnier, kümmel, maraschino, mirabelle, ratafia, sambuca, sloe gin, Strega, Tia Maria.

ORIGIN – French.

liquid > *adjective* 1 having a consistency like that of water or oil, i.e. flowing freely but of constant volume. 2 having the translucence of water. 3 (of a sound) clear and flowing. 4 not fixed or stable. 5 (of assets) held in or easily converted into cash. 6 having ready cash or liquid assets. > *noun* a liquid substance.

DERIVATIVES – **liquidly** *adverb* **liquidness** *noun*.

COMBINATIONS – **liquid crystal** a liquid with some degree of ordering in the arrangement of its molecules. **liquid crystal display** an electronic visual display in which the application of an electric current to a liquid crystal layer makes it opaque. **liquid measure** a unit for measuring the volume of liquids. **liquid paraffin** chiefly Brit. a colourless, odourless oily liquid obtained from petroleum, used as a laxative.

ORIGIN – Latin *liquidus*, from *liquere* 'be liquid'.

liquidate > *verb* 1 wind up the affairs of (a company) by ascertaining liabilities and apportioning assets. 2 convert (assets) into cash. 3 pay off (a debt). 4 informal eliminate; kill.

DERIVATIVES – **liquidation** *noun* **liquidator** *noun*.

ORIGIN – Latin *liquidare* 'make clear': originally used in the sense 'set out (accounts) clearly'.

liquidise (also **liquidize**) > *verb* Brit. convert (solid food) into a liquid or purée.

liquidiser (also **liquidizer**) > *noun* Brit. a machine for liquidising.

liquidity /likwidditi/ > *noun* Finance 1 the availability of liquid assets to a market or company. 2 liquid assets.

liquify > *verb* variant spelling of **LIQUEFY**.

liquor /likkər/ > *noun* 1 alcoholic drink, especially spirits. 2 water used in brewing. 3 liquid that has been produced in or used for cooking. 4 the liquid from which a substance has been crystallised or extracted.

ORIGIN – Latin *liquor*; related to *liquere* 'be fluid'.

liquorice /likkəriss, likkərish/ (US **licorice**) > *noun* a sweet, chewy, aromatic black substance made from the juice of a root and used as a sweet and in medicine.
ORIGIN – Old French *licoresse*, from Latin *liquiritia*, from Greek *glukurrhiza*, from *glukus* 'sweet' + *rhiza* 'root'.

lira /leerə/ > *noun* (pl. **lire** /leerə, leeray/) 1 the basic monetary unit of Italy, notionally equal to 100 centesimos. 2 the basic monetary unit of Turkey, equal to 100 kurus.
ORIGIN – Italian, from Provençal *liura*, from Latin *libra* 'pound'.

lisle /līl/ > *noun* a fine, smooth cotton thread formerly used for stockings, gloves, etc.
ORIGIN – from *Lisle*, former spelling of *Lille*, a city in northern France where lisle was made.

lisp > *noun* a speech defect in which *s* is pronounced like *th* in *thick* and *z* is pronounced like *th* in *this*. > *verb* speak with a lisp.
DERIVATIVES – **lisper** *noun* **lisping** *noun* & *adjective*.

lissom (also **lissome**) > *adjective* slim, supple, and graceful.
DERIVATIVES – **lissomness** *noun*.
SYNONYMS – agile, limber, lithe, supple.
ORIGIN – from **LITHE** + **-SOME**[1].

list[1] > *noun* 1 a number of connected items or names written consecutively. 2 (**lists**) historical palisades enclosing an area for a tournament 3 a selvedge or strip of cloth forming the edge of a piece of fabric. > *verb* 1 make a list of. 2 include in a list. 3 archaic enlist for military service.
IDIOMS – **enter the lists** issue or accept a challenge.
SYNONYMS – *noun* 1 catalogue, directory, index, inventory, roll. *verb* 1 catalogue, index, itemise, register.
COMBINATIONS – **list price** the price of an article as listed by the manufacturer.
ORIGIN – sense 1 is from French *liste*, from an obsolete use of sense 3 denoting a strip of paper; sense 3 itself is from an Old English word meaning 'a border or edging'; sense 2 is from Old French *lisse*.

list[2] > *verb* (of a ship) lean over to one side. > *noun* an instance of listing.
SYNONYMS – *verb* cant, careen, lean, tilt.

listed > *adjective* 1 (of a building in the UK) officially designated as being of historical importance and so protected. 2 denoting companies whose shares are quoted on the main market of the London Stock Exchange.

listen > *verb* 1 give one's attention to a sound. 2 make an effort to hear something. 3 (**listen in**) listen to a private conversation. 4 (**listen in**) listen to a radio broadcast. 5 respond to advice or a request. > *noun* an act of listening.
DERIVATIVES – **listener** *noun*.
SYNONYMS – *verb* 1,2 attend, hear, lend an ear; literary hark.
COMBINATIONS – **listening post** a station for detecting and monitoring electronic communications by others.
ORIGIN – Old English, 'pay attention to'.

listenable > *adjective* easy or pleasant to listen to.
DERIVATIVES – **listenability** *noun*.

listeria /listeeriə/ > *noun* a type of bacterium which infects humans and other animals through contaminated food.
ORIGIN – named after the English surgeon Joseph *Lister* (1827–1912).

listeriosis /listeeriōsiss/ > *noun* disease caused by infection with listeria, which can resemble influenza or meningitis and may cause miscarriage.

listing > *noun* 1 a list or catalogue. 2 an entry in a list.

listless > *adjective* lacking energy or enthusiasm.
DERIVATIVES – **listlessly** *adverb* **listlessness** *noun*.
SYNONYMS – enervated, lackadaisical, lethargic, spiritless, unenthusiastic.
ORIGIN – from archaic *list* 'desire'.

lit past and past participle of **LIGHT**[1], **LIGHT**[3].

litany /littəni/ > *noun* (pl. **litanies**) 1 a series of appeals to God made in church services, usually recited by the clergy and responded to by the people. 2 a tedious recital.
ORIGIN – Greek *litaneia* 'prayer', from *litē* 'supplication'.

litas /leetass/ > *noun* (pl. same) the basic monetary unit of Lithuania, equal to 100 centas.
ORIGIN – Lithuanian.

litchi > *noun* variant spelling of **LYCHEE**.

-lite > *suffix* forming names of rocks, minerals, and fossils.
ORIGIN – Greek *lithos* 'stone'.

liter > *noun* US spelling of **LITRE**.

literacy > *noun* the ability to read and write.

literal > *adjective* 1 using or interpreting words in their usual or most basic sense without metaphor or allegory. 2 (of a translation) representing the exact words of the original text. 3 free from distortion. 4 informal absolute. 5 relating to a letter or letters of the alphabet. > *noun* Brit. Printing a misprint of a letter.
DERIVATIVES – **literalise** (also **literalize**) *verb* **literality** *noun* **literalness** *noun*.
SYNONYMS – *adjective* 2 faithful, strict, verbatim, word-for-word.

wordpower facts
Literal
The words **literal**, **literary**, **literate**, and **literature** are all from Latin *littera* or *litera*, which means 'letter of the alphabet' or in the plural 'literature, culture'. In fact, *littera* behaves very like the English word **letter**, which is derived from it and can also mean 'literature, culture' when used in the plural. Other words deriving from *littera* are **alliteration**, **obliterate**, and **transliterate**.

literalism > *noun* the literal interpretation of words.
DERIVATIVES – **literalist** *noun* **literalistic** *adjective*.

literally > *adverb* 1 with the exact literal meaning of the words used. 2 informal used for emphasis (rather than to suggest literal truth): *we were literally killing ourselves laughing*.

literary > *adjective* 1 concerning the writing, study, or content of literature, especially of the kind valued for quality of form. 2 associated with literary works or formal writing.
DERIVATIVES – **literarily** *adverb* **literariness** *noun*.
COMBINATIONS – **literary criticism** the art or practice of judging the qualities and character of literary works. **literary executor** a person entrusted with a dead writer's papers and works. **literary history** the history of the treatment of a subject in literature.

literate > *adjective* 1 able to read and write. 2 knowledgeable in a particular field: *computer literate*. > *noun* a literate person.
DERIVATIVES – **literately** *adverb*.

literati /littəraati/ > *plural noun* educated people who are interested in literature.

literature > *noun* 1 written works, especially those regarded as having artistic merit. 2 books and writings on a particular subject. 3 leaflets and other material used to give information or advice.

lithe /līth/ > *adjective* slim, supple, and graceful.
DERIVATIVES – **lithely** *adverb* **litheness** *noun*.
SYNONYMS – agile, limber, lissom, supple.
ORIGIN – Old English, 'gentle, meek, mellow'.

lithium /lithiəm/ > *noun* 1 a light, soft, silver-white reactive metallic chemical element. 2 a lithium salt used as a mood-stabilising drug.

lithograph /lithəgraaf/ > *noun* a print made by lithography. > *verb* print by lithography.
DERIVATIVES – **lithographic** *adjective*.

lithography /lithogrəfi/ > *noun* the process of printing from a flat metal, formerly stone, surface treated so as to repel the ink except where it is required for printing.
DERIVATIVES – **lithographer** *noun*.
ORIGIN – from Greek *lithos* 'stone'.

lithology /lithollǝji/ > *noun* the study of the physical characteristics of rocks.
DERIVATIVES – **lithological** *adjective*.

lithosphere /lithəsfeer/ > *noun* Geology the rigid outer part of the earth, consisting of the crust and upper mantle.
DERIVATIVES – **lithospheric** *adjective*.

lithotomy /lithottəmi/ > *noun* surgical removal of a calculus (stone) from the bladder, kidney, or urinary tract.
DERIVATIVES – **lithotomist** *noun*.
ORIGIN – from Greek *lithos* 'stone' + *-tomia* 'cutting'.

Lithuanian /lithyooaynian/ > *noun* 1 a person from Lithuania. 2 the Baltic language of Lithuania. > *adjective* relating to Lithuania.

litigant > *noun* a person involved in litigation.

litigate /littigayt/ > *verb* 1 go to law; be a party to a lawsuit. 2 take (a dispute) to a law court.
DERIVATIVES – **litigation** *noun* **litigator** *noun*.
ORIGIN – Latin *litigare*, from *lis* 'lawsuit'.

litigious /litijəss/ > *adjective* 1 concerned with lawsuits or litigation. 2 having a tendency to go to law to settle disputes.
DERIVATIVES – **litigiously** *adverb* **litigiousness** *noun*.
ORIGIN – from Latin *litigium* 'litigation', from *lis* 'lawsuit'.

litmus /litməss/ > *noun* a dye obtained from certain lichens that is red under acid conditions and blue under alkaline conditions.
COMBINATIONS – **litmus paper** paper stained with litmus, used as a test for acids or alkalis. **litmus test 1** a test using litmus. **2** a decisively indicative test.
ORIGIN – Old Norse *lit-mosi*, from *litr* 'dye' + *mosi* 'moss'.

litotes /lītōteez/ > *noun* ironical understatement in which an affirmative is expressed by the negative of its contrary (e.g. *I shan't be sorry* for *I shall be glad*).
ORIGIN – Greek, from *litos* 'plain, meagre'.

litre (US **liter**) > *noun* a metric unit of capacity, formerly the volume of one kilogram of water under standard conditions, now equal to 1,000 cubic centimetres (about 1.75 pints).
DERIVATIVES – **litreage** *noun*.
ORIGIN – French, from *litron* (an obsolete measure of capacity), from Greek *litra*, a Sicilian monetary unit.

LittD > *abbreviation* Doctor of Letters.
ORIGIN – from Latin *Litterarum Doctor*.

litter > *noun* 1 rubbish left in an open or public place. 2 an untidy collection of things. 3 a number of young born to an animal at one time. 4 (also **cat litter**) granular absorbent material lining a tray for a cat to urinate and defecate in indoors. 5 straw or other plant matter used as animal bedding. 6 (also **leaf litter**) decomposing leaves and other matter forming a layer on top of soil. 7 historical a vehicle containing a bed or seat enclosed by curtains and carried by men or animals. 8 stretcher for transporting the sick or wounded. > *verb* make untidy with discarded articles.
COMBINATIONS – **litterbug** (Brit. also **litter lout**) informal a person who carelessly drops rubbish on the ground and leaves it.
ORIGIN – Old French *litiere*, from Latin *lectus* 'bed': originally used in sense 7 of the noun.

little > *adjective* 1 small in size, amount, or degree. 2 (of a person) young or younger. 3 of short distance or duration. 4 trivial, unimportant, or humble. > *determiner* & *pronoun* 1 (**a little**) a small amount of. 2 (**a little**) a short time or distance. 3 not much. > *adverb* (**less**, **least**) 1 (**a little**) to a small extent. 2 hardly or not at all.
IDIOMS – **little by little** gradually. **little or nothing** hardly anything.
DERIVATIVES – **littleness** *noun*.
SYNONYMS – *adjective* 1 diminutive, short, small, tiny; informal pint-sized. 4 inconsequential, insignificant, minor, trivial, unimportant.
ANTONYMS – *adjective* 1 big, large.
COMBINATIONS – **little end** (in a piston engine) the smaller end of a connecting rod, attached to the piston. **little people 1** the ordinary people of a country or organisation. 2 fairies or leprechauns.

little finger > *noun* the smallest finger, at the outer side of the hand.
IDIOMS – **twist** (or **wind** or **wrap**) **someone around one's little finger** make someone do whatever one wants.

littoral /littərəl/ > *adjective* relating to the shore of the sea or a lake. > *noun* a littoral region.
ORIGIN – Latin *littoralis*, from *litus* 'shore'.

liturgical /liturjik'l/ > *adjective* of or related to liturgy or public worship.
DERIVATIVES – **liturgically** *adverb* **liturgist** /littərjist/ *noun*.

liturgy /littərji/ > *noun* (pl. **liturgies**) a prescribed form of public worship used in the Christian Church.
ORIGIN – Greek *leitourgia* 'public service, worship of the gods'.

livable > *adjective* variant spelling of LIVEABLE.

live¹ /liv/ > *verb* 1 remain alive. 2 be alive at a specified time. 3 spend one's life in a particular way or under particular circumstances: *they are living in fear.* 4 make one's home in a particular place or with a particular person. 5 (**live in** or **out**) reside at (or away from) the place where one works or studies. 6 supply oneself with the means of subsistence: *they live by hunting and fishing.* 7 (**live for**) regard as the most important aspect of one's life. 8 survive in someone's mind.
IDIOMS – **live and breathe something** be devoted to a subject or activity. **live and let live** proverb you should tolerate the opinions and behaviour of others so that they will similarly tolerate your own. **live down** succeed in making others forget (something regrettable or embarrassing): *we'll never live down the shame.* **live in the past** have outdated ideas and attitudes. **live it up** informal lead a life of extravagance and exciting social activity. **live off** (or **on**) 1 depend on or have available as a source of income or support. 2 eat as a major part of one's diet. **live rough** live outdoors as a result of being homeless. **live up to** fulfil. **live with 1** share a home and have a sexual relationship with (someone to whom one is not married). 2 accept or tolerate (something unpleasant).
SYNONYMS – 1 breathe, draw breath, exist, survive. 4 reside; formal dwell.
ANTONYMS – 1 die.
COMBINATIONS – **lived-in 1** (of a room or building) showing comforting signs of wear and habitation. 2 informal (of a person's face) marked by experience.
ORIGIN – Old English, related to LIFE and LEAVE¹.

live² /līv/ > *adjective* 1 living. 2 (of a musical performance) given in concert; not recorded. 3 (of a broadcast) transmitted at the time of occurrence; not recorded. 4 of current or continuing interest and importance. 5 (of a wire or device) connected to a source of electric current. 6 of, containing, or using undetonated explosive. 7 (of coals) burning. 8 (of yogurt) containing the living micro-organisms by which it is formed. > *adverb* as or at an actual event or performance.
IDIOMS – **go live** Computing (of a system) become operational.
COMBINATIONS – **live action** action in films involving real people or animals, as contrasted with animation or computer-generated effects. **live bait** small living fish or worms used as bait. **livestock** farm animals regarded as an asset. **live wire** informal an energetic and lively person.

liveable (US also **livable**) > *adjective* 1 worth living. 2 fit to live in. 3 (**liveable with**) informal easy to live with.
DERIVATIVES – **liveability** *noun*.

live-bearing > *adjective* bearing live young rather than laying eggs.

DERIVATIVES – **livebearer** *noun*.

live-in > *adjective* **1** (of a domestic employee) resident in an employer's house. **2** living with another in a sexual relationship: *his live-in girlfriend.* **3** (of a course of study, treatment, etc.) residential.

livelihood > *noun* a means of securing the necessities of life.

SYNONYMS – bread and butter, income, means, sustenance.

ORIGIN – Old English, 'way of life'.

livelong /**liv**long/ > *adjective* literary (of a period of time) entire: *all this livelong day.*

lively > *adjective* (**livelier**, **liveliest**) **1** full of life and energy. **2** (of a place) full of activity. **3** intellectually stimulating or perceptive.

IDIOMS – **look lively** informal move more quickly and energetically.

DERIVATIVES – **livelily** *adverb* **liveliness** *noun*.

SYNONYMS – **1** animated, dynamic, energetic, exuberant, high-spirited, vivacious. **2** bustling, hectic, teeming.

liven > *verb* (**liven up**) make or become more lively or interesting.

liver[1] > *noun* **1** a large organ in the abdomen that secretes bile and neutralises toxins. **2** the flesh of an animal's liver as food.

WORDFINDER – hepatic (*of the liver*), hepatitis (*inflammation of the liver*).

COMBINATIONS – **liver fluke** a fluke of which the adult lives in the liver of a vertebrate and the larva in a secondary host such as a snail or fish. **liver sausage** chiefly Brit. a savoury meat paste in the form of a sausage containing cooked liver, or a mixture of liver and pork. **liver spot** a small brown spot on the skin.

liver[2] > *noun* a person who lives in a specified way: *a clean liver.*

liverish > *adjective* **1** slightly ill, as though having a disordered liver. **2** unhappy and bad-tempered.

DERIVATIVES – **liverishly** *adverb* **liverishness** *noun*.

Liverpudlian /livvər**pud**liən/ > *noun* **1** a person from Liverpool. **2** the dialect or accent of people from Liverpool. > *adjective* relating to Liverpool.

ORIGIN – humorous formation from *Liverpool* + PUDDLE.

liverwort /**livv**ərwurt/ > *noun* a small flowerless green plant with leaf-like stems or lobed leaves, lacking true roots and reproducing by spores.

ORIGIN – from LIVER[1] + WORT, translating the Latin taxonomic name *hepatica*.

livery /**livv**əri/ > *noun* (pl. **liveries**) **1** an official uniform. **2** a distinctive design and colour scheme used on the vehicles or products of a company. **3** the members of a livery company collectively.

IDIOMS – **at livery** (of a horse) kept for the owner and cared for at a fixed charge.

DERIVATIVES – **liveried** *adjective*.

COMBINATIONS – **livery company** (in the UK) any of a number of Companies of the City of London descended from the medieval trade guilds. **livery stable** (also **livery yard**) a stable where horses are kept at livery or let out for hire.

wordpower facts
Livery
The word **livery** comes from Old French *livree* 'delivered', which is ultimately from Latin *liberare*, meaning 'liberate' or in medieval Latin 'hand over'. The original sense was 'the dispensing of food, provisions, or clothing to servants', also 'allowance of food for horses', which survives in the phrase **at livery** and in **livery stable**. Sense 1 arose because medieval nobles provided matching clothes to distinguish their servants from others'.

liveryman > *noun* (in the UK) a member of a livery company.

lives plural of LIFE.

livid > *adjective* **1** informal furiously angry. **2** having a dark inflamed appearance.

DERIVATIVES – **lividity** *noun* **lividly** *adverb* **lividness** *noun*.

ORIGIN – Latin *lividus*, from *livere* 'be bluish'.

living > *noun* **1** the action of leading one's life; being alive. **2** an income sufficient to live on, or the means of earning it. > *adjective* **1** alive. **2** (of a language) still spoken and used.

IDIOMS – **in** (or **within**) **living memory** within or during a time that is remembered by people still alive. **the living image of** an exact copy or likeness of.

COMBINATIONS – **living room** a room in a house used for relaxation. **living wage** a wage which is high enough to maintain a normal standard of living. **living will** a written statement detailing a person's desires regarding their medical treatment in circumstances in which they are no longer able to express informed consent.

lizard > *noun* a four-legged reptile with a long body and tail, movable eyelids, and a rough, scaly, or spiny skin.

WORDFINDER – saurian (*relating to lizards*).

ORIGIN – Old French *lesard*, from Latin *lacertus* 'lizard, sea fish', also 'muscle'.

LJ > *abbreviation* (pl. **L JJ**) (in the UK) Lord Justice.

ll. > *abbreviation* (in textual references) lines.

'll > *contraction* shall; will.

llama /**laa**mə/ > *noun* a domesticated animal of the camel family found in the Andes, used for carrying loads and valued for its soft woolly fleece.

ORIGIN – Spanish, probably from Quechua.

llano /**laa**nō, **lyaa**nō/ > *noun* (pl. **llanos**) (in South America) a treeless grassy plain.

ORIGIN – Spanish, from Latin *planum* 'plain'.

LLB > *abbreviation* Bachelor of Laws.

ORIGIN – Latin *legum baccalaureus*.

LLD > *abbreviation* Doctor of Laws.

ORIGIN – Latin *legum doctor*.

LLM > *abbreviation* Master of Laws.

ORIGIN – Latin *legum magister*.

lm > *abbreviation* lumen or lumens.

LMS > *abbreviation* **1** (in the UK) local management of schools. **2** historical (in the UK) London Midland and Scottish (Railway).

ln > *abbreviation* Mathematics natural logarithm.

ORIGIN – Latin *logarithmus naturalis*.

LNB > *abbreviation* low noise blocker.

LNER > *abbreviation* historical (in the UK) London and North Eastern Railway.

LNG > *abbreviation* liquefied natural gas.

lo > *exclamation* archaic used to draw attention to an interesting event.

IDIOMS – **lo and behold** used to present a new scene or situation.

loach /lōch/ > *noun* a slender freshwater fish with several barbels near the mouth.

ORIGIN – Old French *loche*.

load > *noun* **1** a heavy or bulky thing being carried. **2** a weight or source of pressure. **3** the total number or amount carried in a vehicle or container. **4** (**a load** or **loads of**) informal a lot of. **5** the amount of work to be done by a person or machine. **6** the amount of power supplied by a source. **7** a burden of responsibility, worry, or grief. > *verb* **1** put a load on or in. **2** place (a load) on or in a vehicle, container, etc. **3** insert (something) into a device so that it will operate. **4** charge (a firearm) with ammunition. **5** bias towards a particular outcome.

IDIOMS – **get a load of** informal take a look at (used to draw attention to someone or something). **load the dice against** (or **in favour of**) put at a disadvantage (or advantage).

DERIVATIVES – **loader** *noun*.

SYNONYMS – *verb* **1** fill, pack. **2** pack, pile, stack, stow.

COMBINATIONS – **load factor** the ratio of the average or actual amount of some quantity and the maximum possible or permissible. **load line** a ship's Plimsoll line. **loadmaster** the member of an aircraft's crew responsible for the cargo. **loadstone** variant spelling of *lodestone*.

ORIGIN – Old English, 'journey, conveyance'; related to LEAD[1] and LODE.

loaded > *adjective* **1** carrying or bearing a load. **2** weighted or biased towards a particular outcome. **3** charged with an underlying meaning. **4** informal wealthy. **5** N. Amer. informal drunk.

loading > *noun* **1** the application of a load to something. **2** the amount of load applied. **3** an increase in an insurance premium due to an extra factor of risk. **4** Austral. an increment added to a basic wage for special skills or qualifications.

loaf[1] > *noun* (pl. **loaves**) a quantity of bread that is shaped and baked in one piece.
IDIOMS – **half a loaf is better than no bread** proverb it is better to accept less than one wants or expects than to have nothing at all. **use one's loaf** Brit. informal use one's common sense. [ORIGIN – probably from *loaf of bread*, rhyming slang for 'head'.]

loaf[2] > *verb* idle one's time away.
SYNONYMS – idle, laze, lounge, take it easy.
ORIGIN – probably from **LOAFER**.

loafer > *noun* **1** a person who idles their time away. **2** trademark a leather shoe with a flat heel, shaped like a moccasin.
SYNONYMS – **1** idler, layabout.
ORIGIN – perhaps from German *Landläufer* 'tramp'.

loam > *noun* **1** a fertile soil of clay and sand containing humus. **2** a paste of clay and water with sand and chopped straw, used in making bricks and plastering walls.
DERIVATIVES – **loaminess** *noun* **loamy** *adjective*.
ORIGIN – Old English, 'clay': related to **LIME**[1].

loan > *noun* **1** a thing that is borrowed, especially a sum of money that is expected to be paid back with interest. **2** the action of lending. > *verb* give as a loan; lend.
IDIOMS – **on loan** being borrowed.
DERIVATIVES – **loanable** *adjective* **loanee** *noun* **loaner** *noun*.
COMBINATIONS – **loan shark** informal a moneylender who charges exorbitant rates of interest. **loanword** a word adopted from a foreign language with little or no modification.
ORIGIN – Old Norse; related to **LEND**.

loath /lōth/ (also **loth**) > *adjective* reluctant; unwilling.
USAGE – do not confuse with **loathe**, which is a verb meaning 'dislike greatly'.
ORIGIN – Old English, 'hostile'.

loathe /lōth/ > *verb* feel hatred or disgust for.
DERIVATIVES – **loather** *noun*.
SYNONYMS – abhor, despise, detest, hate, scorn.
ORIGIN – Old English, related to **LOATH**.

loathsome > *adjective* causing hatred or disgust.

DERIVATIVES – **loathsomely** *adverb* **loathsomeness** *noun*.
SYNONYMS – abhorrent, abominable, hateful, odious, repulsive.
ORIGIN – from archaic *loath* 'disgust'.

loaves plural of **LOAF**[1].

lob > *verb* (**lobbed**, **lobbing**) throw or hit in a high arc. > *noun* **1** (in soccer or tennis) a ball lobbed over an opponent or a stroke producing this result. **2** (in cricket) a ball bowled with a slow underarm action.

wordpower facts
Lob
The word **lob** has a long history and a wide range of former meanings. Probably entering English from Low German or Dutch, in the Middle Ages it meant 'country bumpkin or lout' or 'pollack or saithe' (kinds of fishes). It later took on the meanings 'pendulous object' (from which **lobworm** was derived) and 'lump or large piece', and also functioned as an adjective meaning 'loutish, clumsy, rustic'. As a verb **lob** meant 'cause or allow to hang heavily' and 'behave like a lout' before taking on its current sporting sense in the 19th century.

lobby > *noun* (pl. **lobbies**) **1** a room out of which one or more other rooms or corridors lead, typically forming a small entrance hall. **2** any of several large halls in the Houses of Parliament in which MPs meet members of the public. **3** (also **division lobby**) each of two corridors in the Houses of Parliament to which MPs retire to vote. **4** a group of people seeking to influence legislators on a particular issue. **5** an organised attempt by members of the public to influence legislators. > *verb* (**lobbies**, **lobbied**) seek to influence (a legislator).
DERIVATIVES – **lobbyist** *noun*.
ORIGIN – Latin *lobia* 'covered walk': first used in the sense 'monastic cloister'.

lobe > *noun* **1** a roundish and flattish projecting or hanging part of something, often one of two or more such parts divided by a fissure. **2** an ear lobe.
DERIVATIVES – **lobar** *adjective* **lobed** *adjective*.
ORIGIN – Greek *lobos* 'lobe, pod'.

lobelia /ləbeeliə/ > *noun* a plant of the bellflower family, with blue or scarlet flowers.
ORIGIN – named after the Flemish botanist Matthias de *Lobel* (1538–1616).

lobotomise (also **lobotomize**) > *verb* Surgery perform a lobotomy on.
DERIVATIVES – **lobotomisation** *noun*.

lobotomy /ləbottəmi/ > *noun* (pl. **lobotomies**) a surgical operation involving incision into the prefrontal lobe of the brain, formerly used to treat mental illness.

lobster > *noun* **1** a large marine crustacean with stalked eyes and large pincers. **2** the flesh of this animal as food. > *verb* catch lobsters.
COMBINATIONS – **lobster pot** a basket-like trap in which lobsters are caught. **lobster thermidor** a dish of lobster cooked in a cream sauce, returned to its shell, sprinkled with cheese, and browned under the grill. [ORIGIN – from *Thermidor*, the eleventh month of the French Republican calendar.]
ORIGIN – Old English: see box at **LOCUST**.

lobworm > *noun* a large earthworm used as fishing bait.

local > *adjective* **1** relating to a particular area. **2** relating or belonging to one's neighbourhood. **3** (in technical use) relating to a particular region or part: *a local infection.* > *noun* **1** a local person or thing. **2** Brit. informal a pub convenient to a person's home.
DERIVATIVES – **locally** *adverb* **localness** *noun*.
COMBINATIONS – **local anaesthetic** an anaesthetic that affects a restricted area of the body. **local area network** a computer network that links devices within a building or group of adjacent buildings. **local authority** Brit. an administrative body in local government. **local derby** see **DERBY**. **local government** the administration of a particular county or district, with representatives elected by those who live there. **local time** time as reckoned in a particular time zone.
ORIGIN – Latin *localis*, from *locus* 'place'.

locale /lōkaal/ > *noun* a place associated with particular events.

localise (also **localize**) > *verb* **1** restrict or assign to a particular place. **2** make local in character.
DERIVATIVES – **localisation** *noun* **localised** *adjective*.

locality > *noun* (pl. **localities**) **1** an area or neighbourhood. **2** the position or site of something.
SYNONYMS – **1** area, community, district, neighbourhood, region, vicinity. **2** location, place, position, site, situation.

locate > *verb* **1** discover the exact place or position of. **2** (**be located**) be situated in a particular place. **3** N. Amer. establish oneself or one's business in a specified place.
DERIVATIVES – **locatable** *adjective* **locator** *noun*.
SYNONYMS – **1** discover, find, identify, pinpoint, track down.
ORIGIN – Latin *locare* 'to place': first used as a legal term meaning 'let out on hire'.

location > *noun* **1** the action or process of locating. **2** a particular place or position. **3** an actual place in which a film or broadcast is made, as distinct from a simulation in a studio.
DERIVATIVES – **locational** *adjective*.
SYNONYMS – **2** locality, place, position, site, situation, whereabouts.

locative /lokkətiv/ > *adjective* Grammar relating to or denoting a case in some languages of nouns, pronouns, and adjectives, expressing location.

loc. cit. > *abbreviation* in the passage already cited.
ORIGIN – Latin *loco citato*.

loch /lok, lokh/ > *noun* Scottish **1** a lake. **2** a long, narrow arm of the sea.
ORIGIN – Scottish Gaelic.

loci plural of LOCUS.

loci classici plural of LOCUS CLASSICUS.

lock¹ > *noun* **1** a mechanism for keeping a door or container fastened, typically operated by a key. **2** a similar device used to prevent the operation of a vehicle or other machine. **3** a short section of a canal or river with gates and sluices at each end which can be opened or closed to change the water level, used for raising and lowering boats. **4** the turning of the front wheels of a vehicle to change its direction of motion. **5** (in wrestling and martial arts) a hold that prevents an opponent from moving a limb. **6** Rugby a lock forward. **7** archaic a mechanism for exploding the charge of a gun. > *verb* **1** fasten or be fastened with a lock. **2** enclose or secure by locking a door. **3** (**lock up** or **away**) imprison. **4** make or become rigidly fixed or immovable. **5** (**lock in**) engage or entangle in: *they were locked in a legal battle*. **6** (**lock on to**) locate and then track (a target) by radar or similar means. **7** go through a lock on a canal.
WORDFINDER – *types of lock:* combination, deadlock, mortise, padlock, Yale.
IDIOMS – **lock horns** engage in conflict. **lock, stock, and barrel** including everything. [ORIGIN – referring to the complete mechanism of a firearm.]
DERIVATIVES – **lockable** *adjective*.
COMBINATIONS – **lockdown** N. Amer. the confining of prisoners to their cells. **lock forward** Rugby a player in the second row of the scrum. **lock-in 1** an arrangement which obliges a person or company to negotiate or trade only with a specific company. **2** a period during which some customers are permitted by the landlord to remain in a bar or pub after the doors are locked at closing time. **locknut 1** a nut screwed down on another to keep it tight. **2** a nut designed so that, once tightened, it cannot be accidentally loosened. **lockout** the exclusion of employees by their

employer from their place of work until certain terms are agreed to. **locksmith** a person who makes and repairs locks. **lock-up 1** a makeshift jail. **2** Brit. non-residential premises, such as a garage, that can be locked. **3** an investment in assets which cannot readily be realised or sold on in the short term.

lock² > *noun* **1** a section of a person's hair that coils or hangs in a piece. **2** (**locks**) chiefly literary a person's hair. **3** a tuft of wool or cotton.
DERIVATIVES – **locked** *adjective*.

locker > *noun* a small lockable cupboard or compartment, typically one in a row of several.
COMBINATIONS – **locker room 1** a sports changing room containing rows of lockers. **2** (**locker-room**) coarse or ribald: *locker-room humour*.

locket > *noun* a small ornamental case worn on a chain round a person's neck, used to hold an item of sentimental value such as a photograph or a lock of hair.
ORIGIN – Old French *locquet*, from *loc* 'latch, lock'; related to LOCK¹.

lockjaw > *noun* spasm of the jaw muscles, causing the mouth to remain tightly closed, typically as a symptom of tetanus.

loco¹ > *noun* (pl. **locos**) informal a locomotive.

loco² > *adjective* informal crazy.
ORIGIN – Spanish, 'insane'.

locomotion > *noun* movement or the ability to move from one place to another.
DERIVATIVES – **locomotory** *adjective*.
ORIGIN – from Latin *loco* 'from a place' + *motio* 'motion'.

locomotive > *noun* a powered railway vehicle used for pulling trains. > *adjective* relating to locomotion.

locomotor (also **locomotory**) > *adjective* chiefly Biology relating to locomotion.

locum /lōkəm/ > *noun* a doctor or cleric standing in for another who is temporarily away.
ORIGIN – from Latin *locum tenens* 'one holding a place'.

locus /lōkəss/ > *noun* (pl. **loci** /lōsī/) **1** technical a particular position, point, or place. **2** Mathematics a curve or other figure formed by all the points satisfying a particular condition.
ORIGIN – Latin, 'place'.

locus classicus /lōkəss klassikəss/ > *noun* (pl. **loci classici** /lōsī klassisī/) the best known or most authoritative passage on a subject.
ORIGIN – Latin, 'classical place'.

locus standi /lōkəss standī/ > *noun* (pl. **loci standi** /lōsī standī/) Law the right or capacity to bring an action or to appear in a court.
ORIGIN – Latin, 'place of standing'.

locust > *noun* **1** a large tropical grasshopper

which migrates in vast swarms and is very destructive to vegetation. **2** (also **locust tree**) a carob tree or similar pod-bearing tree.

wordpower facts
Locust and lobster
The ultimate source of both **locust** and **lobster** is the Latin word *locusta*, originally denoting a lobster or other crustacean and later extended to the insect. **Lobster** comes from Old English *lopustre*, which is an alteration of *locusta*. The word **locust** for the insect entered English, via Old French *locuste*, in the Middle Ages, and represents a second importation of *locusta*. The Old French word *languste* 'lobster' also came from *locusta* and is the source of the English words **langouste** and **langoustine**.

locution /ləkyōōsh'n/ > *noun* **1** a word or phrase. **2** a person's style of speech.
DERIVATIVES – **locutionary** *adjective*.
ORIGIN – Latin, from *loqui* 'speak'.

lode /lōd/ > *noun* a vein of metal ore in the earth.
COMBINATIONS – **lodestar** a star that is used to guide the course of a ship, especially the pole star. **lodestone** (also **loadstone**) a piece of magnetite or other mineral able to be used as a magnet.
ORIGIN – Old English, 'way, course'; related to LOAD.

loden /lōd'n/ > *noun* **1** a thick waterproof woollen cloth. **2** the dark green colour in which such cloth is often made.
ORIGIN – German *Loden*.

lodge > *noun* **1** a small house at the gates of a large house with grounds, occupied by a gatekeeper or other employee. **2** a small country house occupied in season for sports such as hunting and shooting. **3** a porter's quarters at the entrance of a college or other large building. **4** an American Indian tent or other dwelling. **5** a beaver's den. **6** a branch or meeting place of an organisation such as the Freemasons. > *verb* **1** formally present (a complaint, appeal, etc.). **2** make or become firmly fixed in a place. **3** rent accommodation in another person's house. **4** provide with such accommodation. **5** (**lodge in** or **with**) leave (money or a valuable item) for safekeeping in or with.
SYNONYMS – *verb* **1** file, record, register, submit. **2** catch, wedge. **3** board.
ORIGIN – Old French *loge* 'arbour, hut', from Latin *lobia* 'covered walk'; related to LOBBY.

lodgement > *noun* **1** chiefly literary a place in

which a person or thing is lodged. 2 the depositing of money in a bank.

lodger > *noun* a person who pays rent to live in a property with the owner.

lodging > *noun* 1 a temporary place of residence. 2 (**lodgings**) rented accommodation in another person's house.
COMBINATIONS – **lodging house** a private house providing rented accommodation.

loess /lōiss/ > *noun* Geology a loosely compacted yellowish-grey deposit of wind-blown sediment.
ORIGIN – from Swiss German *lösch* 'loose'.

lo-fi (also **low-fi**) > *adjective* of or employing sound reproduction of a lower quality than hi-fi.

loft > *noun* 1 a room or storage space directly under the roof of a house or other building. 2 a large, open area in a warehouse or other large building, that has been converted into living space. 3 a gallery in a church or hall. 4 a shelter with nest holes for pigeons. 5 Golf upward inclination given to the ball in a stroke. 6 the thickness of an insulating material such as that in a sleeping bag. > *verb* kick, hit, or throw (a ball or missile) high up.
ORIGIN – Old Norse, 'air, upper room'.

lofty > *adjective* (**loftier**, **loftiest**) 1 of imposing height. 2 noble; elevated. 3 haughty and aloof. 4 (of wool and other textiles) thick and resilient.
DERIVATIVES – **loftily** adverb **loftiness** noun.
SYNONYMS – 1 high, soaring, tall, towering. 2 elevated, exalted, grand, noble. 3 aloof, arrogant, disdainful, haughty, proud.

log¹ > *noun* 1 a part of the trunk or a large branch of a tree that has fallen or been cut off. 2 an official record of events during the voyage of a ship or aircraft. 3 an apparatus for determining the speed of a ship, originally one consisting of a float attached to a knotted line. > *verb* (**logged**, **logging**) 1 enter in a log. 2 achieve (a certain distance, speed, or time). 3 (**log in** or **on** or **out** or **off**) go through the procedures to begin (or conclude) use of a computer system. 4 cut down (an area of forest) to exploit the wood commercially.
DERIVATIVES – **logger** noun **logging** noun.
COMBINATIONS – **logbook** a book containing an official or systematic record of events. **logjam** 1 a crowded mass of logs blocking a river. 2 a deadlock. 3 a backlog. **logrolling** N. Amer. informal the exchange of favours between politicians by reciprocal voting for each other's proposed legislation. [ORIGIN – from the phrase *you roll my log and I'll roll yours*.]

wordpower facts
Log
What is the connection between **log** as a noun meaning 'a section of a fallen tree' and as a verb with the sense 'record particulars of events'? The link is to be found in sense 3 of the noun, 'an apparatus for determining the speed of a ship'. This originally consisted of a 'log' or wooden float attached to a very long knotted line; the log was tossed overboard and the length of line run out in a certain time was used as an estimate of the vessel's speed. From here came the notion of a ship's journal or **logbook**, in which a detailed daily record of a voyage was entered, and thus the verb. See also **KNOT¹**.

log² > *noun* short for **LOGARITHM**.

loganberry > *noun* an edible soft fruit, considered to be a hybrid of a raspberry and an American dewberry.
ORIGIN – from the name of the American horticulturalist John H. *Logan* (1841–1928).

logarithm /loggərithəm/ > *noun* a quantity representing the power to which a fixed number (the base) must be raised to produce a given number.
WORDFINDER – common logarithms (*to base ten*), Napierian or natural logarithms (*to base* e, *equal to approximately 2.71828*).
DERIVATIVES – **logarithmic** adjective.
ORIGIN – from Greek *logos* 'reckoning, ratio' + *arithmos* 'number'.

loge /lōzh/ > *noun* a private box or enclosure in a theatre.
ORIGIN – French.

loggerhead > *noun* 1 (also **loggerhead turtle**) a large-headed reddish-brown turtle of warm seas. 2 archaic a foolish person.
IDIOMS – **at loggerheads** in irreconcilable dispute or disagreement.
ORIGIN – from dialect *logger* 'block of wood for hobbling a horse' + **HEAD**; the phrase perhaps represents a use of *loggerhead* in a 17th-century sense 'long-handled iron instrument for heating liquids' (when wielded as a weapon).

loggia /lōjə/ > *noun* a gallery or room with one or more open sides, especially one having one side open to a garden.
ORIGIN – Italian, 'lodge'.

logic > *noun* 1 reasoning conducted or assessed according to strict principles of validity. 2 the ability to reason correctly. 3 (**the logic of**) the course of action following as a necessary consequence of. 4 a system or set of principles underlying the arrangements of elements in a computer or

electronic device so as to perform a specified task.
DERIVATIVES – **logician** noun.
COMBINATIONS – **logic bomb** Computing a set of instructions secretly incorporated into a program so that if a particular condition is satisfied they will be carried out, usually with harmful effects.
ORIGIN – from Greek *logikē tekhnē* 'art of reason'.

logical > *adjective* 1 of or according to the rules of logic. 2 capable of or showing rational thought. 3 expected or reasonable under the circumstances.
DERIVATIVES – **logicality** noun **logically** adverb.
SYNONYMS – 1,2 cogent, rational, reasonable.
ANTONYMS – illogical.
COMBINATIONS – **logical positivism** (also **logical empiricism**) a form of positivism which considers that the only meaningful philosophical problems are those which can be solved by logical analysis.

-logical (also **-logic**) > *combining form* in adjectives corresponding chiefly to nouns ending in *-logy* (such as *pharmacological* corresponding to *pharmacology*).

-logist > *combining form* indicating a person skilled or involved in a branch of study denoted by a noun ending in *-logy* (such as *biologist* corresponding to *biology*).

logistic > *adjective* of or relating to logistics.
DERIVATIVES – **logistical** adjective.

logistics /ləjistiks/ > *plural noun* (**treated as sing. or pl.**) the detailed coordination of a large and complex operation.
ORIGIN – first meaning 'movement and supply of troops and equipment': from French *logistique*, from *loger* 'lodge'.

logo /lōgō/ > *noun* (pl. **logos**) an emblematic design adopted by an organisation to identify its products.
ORIGIN – abbreviation of **LOGOGRAM** or **LOGOTYPE**.

logocentric > *adjective* regarding words and language as a fundamental expression of an external reality.
DERIVATIVES – **logocentrism** noun.

logogram /loggəgram/ > *noun* a sign or character representing a word or phrase, as used in shorthand and some ancient writing systems.
ORIGIN – from Greek *logos* 'word'.

logorrhoea /loggəreeə/ (US **logorrhea**) > *noun* a tendency to produce too many words; extreme talkativeness or prolixity.
ORIGIN – from Greek *logos* 'word' + *rhoia* 'flow'.

logotype > *noun* Printing a single piece of type that prints a word, a group of separate letters, or a logo.

-logy > *combining form* 1 (usu. as **-ology**) denoting a subject of study or interest:

psychology. **2** denoting a characteristic of speech or language: *eulogy.* **3** denoting a type of discourse: *trilogy.*

loin > *noun* **1** the part of the body on both sides of the spine between the lowest ribs and the hip bones. **2** (**loins**) literary the region of the sexual organs, regarded as the source of erotic or procreative power. **3** a joint of meat that includes the vertebrae of the loins.
COMBINATIONS – **loincloth** a garment consisting of a piece of cloth wrapped between the legs and round the hips.
ORIGIN – Old French *loigne*, from Latin *lumbus.*

loiter > *verb* stand around or move without apparent purpose.
IDIOMS – **loiter with intent** English Law, dated stand around with the intention of committing an offence.
DERIVATIVES – **loiterer** *noun.*
SYNONYMS – hang around, hover, linger.
ORIGIN – perhaps from Dutch *loteren* 'wiggle around'.

Lolita /lōleetə/ > *noun* a sexually precocious young girl.
ORIGIN – the name of a character in the novel *Lolita* (1958) by Vladimir Nabokov.

loll > *verb* **1** sit, lie, or stand in a lazy, relaxed way. **2** hang loosely.
SYNONYMS – **1** flop, lounge, slouch, sprawl.

lollapalooza /lolləpalōōzə/ (also **lala-palooza**) > *noun* N. Amer. informal a particularly impressive or attractive person or thing.

Lollard /lollərd/ > *noun* a follower of the English religious reformer John Wyclif (c.1330–84).
ORIGIN – from a Dutch word meaning 'mumbler', from *lollen* 'to mumble': originally a derogatory term.

lollipop > *noun* **1** a large, flat, rounded boiled sweet on the end of a stick. **2** British term for ICE LOLLY.
COMBINATIONS – **lollipop lady** (or **lollipop man**) Brit. informal a person employed to help children cross the road safely near a school by holding up a circular sign on a pole to stop the traffic.
ORIGIN – perhaps from dialect *lolly* 'tongue' + POP¹.

lollop > *verb* (**lolloped, lolloping**) move in an ungainly way in a series of clumsy bounds.
ORIGIN – probably from LOLL, associated with TROLLOP.

lollo rosso /lollō rossō/ > *noun* a variety of lettuce with deeply divided red-edged leaves.
ORIGIN – Italian, from *lolla* 'husk, chaff' + *rosso* 'red'.

lolly > *noun* (pl. **lollies**) informal **1** chiefly Brit. a lollipop. **2** Austral./NZ a boiled sweet. **3** Brit. money.

lollygag (also **lallygag**) > *verb* (**lollygagged, lollygagging**) N. Amer. informal spend time or move aimlessly.

Lombard /lombaard/ > *noun* **1** a member of a Germanic people who invaded Italy in the 6th century. **2** a person from Lombardy in northern Italy. **3** the Italian dialect of Lombardy.
DERIVATIVES – **Lombardic** *adjective.*
ORIGIN – Italian *lombardo*, from Latin *Langobardus*, from the base of LONG¹ + the ethnic name *Bardi.*

Lombardy poplar /lombərdi/ > *noun* a variety of poplar from Italy with a distinctive tall, slender columnar form.

Londoner > *noun* a person from London.

London pride > *noun* a saxifrage with rosettes of fleshy leaves and stems of pink starlike flowers.

lone > *adjective* **1** having no companions; solitary. **2** literary unfrequented and remote.
SYNONYMS – **1** single, solitary, solo, unaccompanied.
COMBINATIONS – **lone wolf** a person who prefers to act alone.
ORIGIN – shortening of ALONE.

lonely > *adjective* (**lonelier, loneliest**) **1** sad because one has no companions. **2** solitary. **3** unfrequented and remote.
DERIVATIVES – **loneliness** *noun.*
SYNONYMS – **1** forlorn, lonesome. **3** deserted, isolated, out of the way, remote, unfrequented.
COMBINATIONS – **lonely hearts** people looking for a lover or friend through the personal columns of a newspaper.

loner > *noun* a person who prefers not to associate with others.

lonesome > *adjective* chiefly N. Amer. lonely.
IDIOMS – **by** (or Brit. **on**) **one's lonesome** informal all alone.
DERIVATIVES – **lonesomeness** *noun.*

long¹ > *adjective* (**longer, longest**) **1** of a great distance or duration. **2** relatively great in extent. **3** having a specified length, distance, or duration. **4** (of a ball in sport) travelling a great distance, or further than expected. **5** Phonetics (of a vowel) categorised as long with regard to quality and length (e.g. in standard British English the vowel /ōō/ in *food*). **6** (of odds or a chance) reflecting or representing a low level of probability. **7** (of a drink) large and refreshing, and in which alcohol, if present, is not concentrated. **8** (**long on**) informal well supplied with. > *noun* a long time. > *adverb* (**longer, longest**) **1** for a long time. **2** at a distant time: *long ago.* **3** throughout a specified period of time: *all day long.* **4** (with reference to the ball in sport) at, to, or over a great distance.
IDIOMS – **as** (or **so**) **long as 1** during the whole time that. **2** provided that. **be long**

take a long time. **in the long run** (or **term**) eventually. **the long and the short of it** all that can or need be said. **long in the tooth** rather old. [ORIGIN – first used of horses, from the recession of the gums with age.]
DERIVATIVES – **longish** *adjective.*
SYNONYMS – *adjective* **2** extended, extensive, lengthy.
ANTONYMS – *adjective* short.
COMBINATIONS – **longboat 1** historical a sizeable boat which could be launched from a large sailing ship. **2** a longship. **longbow** a large bow drawn by hand and shooting a long feathered arrow. **long division** division of numbers with details of intermediate calculations written down. **long-drawn** (also **long-drawn-out**) prolonged, especially unduly. **long face** an unhappy or disappointed expression. **longhand** ordinary handwriting (as opposed to shorthand or typing). **long haul 1** a long distance (with reference to the transport of goods or passengers). **2** a lengthy and difficult task. **long hop** Cricket a short-pitched, easily hit ball. **longhorn** a breed of cattle with long horns. **longhouse** a large communal house in parts of Malaysia and Indonesia or among some North American Indians. **long johns** informal underpants with closely fitted legs extending to the wearer's ankles. **long leg** Cricket a fielding position far behind the batsman on the leg side. **long-life** (of perishable goods) treated so as to stay fresh for longer than usual. **longline** a deep-sea fishing line with a large number of hooks attached to it. **long off** Cricket a fielding position far behind the bowler and towards the off side. **long on** Cricket a fielding position far behind the bowler and towards the on side. **long pig** a translation of a term formerly used in some Pacific Islands for human flesh as food. **long-playing** (of a record) 12 inches (about 30 cm) in diameter and designed to rotate at 33⅓ revolutions per minute. **long-range 1** able to be used or be effective over long distances. **2** relating to a period of time far into the future. **longship** a long, narrow warship with oars and a sail, used by the Vikings. **long-sighted** having an abnormal inability to see things clearly if they are relatively close to the eyes. **long-standing** having existed for a long time. **long-suffering** bearing problems or provocation with patience. **long suit 1** (in bridge or whist) a holding of several cards of one suit in a hand. **2** an outstanding personal quality or achievement: *insight was her long suit.* **long vacation** Brit. the summer break of three months taken by universities and (formerly) law courts. **long-waisted** (of a dress or a person's body) having a low waist. **long**

wave 1 a radio wave of a wavelength above one kilometre (and a frequency below 300 kilohertz). **2** broadcasting using radio waves of 1 to 10 km wavelength.

long² > *verb* (**long for** or **to do**) have a strong wish for or to do.

SYNONYMS – (**long for** or **to do**) crave, hanker for, hunger for, pine for, yearn for.
ORIGIN – Old English, 'grow long', also 'yearn'.

long. > *abbreviation* longitude.

long distance > *adjective* **1** travelling or operating between distant places. **2** Athletics denoting a race distance of 6 miles or 10,000 metres (6 miles 376 yds), or longer. > *adverb* between distant places.

longe > *noun* variant of LUNGE².

longevity /lonjevviti/ > *noun* long life.
ORIGIN – Latin *longaevitas*, from *longus* 'long' + *aevum* 'age'.

long-headed > *adjective* dated having or showing foresight and good judgement.
DERIVATIVES – **long-headedness** noun.

longing > *noun* a yearning desire. > *adjective* having or showing a yearning desire.
DERIVATIVES – **longingly** adverb.
SYNONYMS – *noun* ache, craving, desire, hunger, thirst, yearning.

longitude /longgityōod/ > *noun* the distance of a place east or west of a standard meridian, especially the Greenwich meridian, measured in degrees.

longitudinal /longgityōodin'l/ > *adjective* **1** running lengthwise. **2** relating to longitude.
DERIVATIVES – **longitudinally** adverb.

long jump > *noun* (**the long jump**) an athletic event in which competitors jump as far as possible along the ground in one leap.
DERIVATIVES – **long jumper** noun.

long-lived > *adjective* living or lasting a long time.

longshore > *adjective* relating to or moving along the seashore.
COMBINATIONS – **longshore drift** the movement of material along a coast by waves which approach at an angle to the shore but recede directly away from it. **longshoreman** N. Amer. a docker.
ORIGIN – from *along shore*.

long shot > *noun* a venture or guess that has only the slightest chance of succeeding or being accurate.
IDIOMS – (**not**) **by a long shot** informal (not) by far or at all.

long-term > *adjective* occurring over or relating to a long period of time: *long-term unemployment.*

longueur /longör/ > *noun* a tedious passage or period.
ORIGIN – French, 'length'.

longways (also **longwise**) > *adverb* lengthways.

long-winded > *adjective* **1** tediously lengthy. **2** archaic capable of doing something for a long time without becoming breathless.
SYNONYMS – **1** diffuse, prolix, rambling, verbose; formal sesquipedalian.
ANTONYMS – **1** brief, concise.

lonicera /lonissərə/ > *noun* a plant of a genus which comprises the honeysuckles.
ORIGIN – Latin, from the name of the 16th-century German botanist Adam *Lonitzer*.

Lonsdale belt > *noun* an ornate belt awarded to a professional boxer winning a British title fight.
ORIGIN – named after the fifth Earl of *Lonsdale*, Hugh Cecil Lowther (1857–1944), who presented the first one.

loo¹ > *noun* Brit. informal a toilet.

wordpower facts

Loo

Loo meaning 'toilet' was first recorded in the early 1930s; the origin of the word is uncertain, although various theories have been put forward. One suggests that the source is *Waterloo*, a trade name for iron cisterns in the early 20th century. Another idea is that it is from French *lieux d'aisances* 'water closet', an expression which could have been picked up by British troops in France during the First World War. Yet another theory traces the term back to the cry *gardy loo!* (from French *gardez l'eau* 'beware of the water'), formerly uttered by people who were about to throw the contents of their chamber pots out of their windows.

loo² > *noun* a gambling card game in which a player who fails to win a trick must pay a sum to a pool.
ORIGIN – abbreviation of *lanterloo*, a meaningless refrain in old songs.

loofah /lōofə/ > *noun* a fibrous cylindrical object used like a bath sponge, consisting of the dried inner parts of a marrow-like tropical fruit.
ORIGIN – Egyptian Arabic.

look > *verb* **1** direct one's gaze in a particular direction. **2** have an outlook in a specified direction. **3** have the appearance or give the impression of being. > *noun* **1** an act of looking. **2** an expression of a feeling or thought by looking at someone. **3** the appearance of someone or something. **4** (**looks**) a person's facial appearance considered aesthetically. **5** a style or fashion. > *exclamation* (also **look here!**) used to call attention to what one is going to say.
IDIOMS – **look after** take care of. **look at 1** regard in a specified way. **2** examine (a matter) and consider what action to take.

look before you leap proverb one shouldn't act without first considering the possible consequences or dangers. **look down on** (also **look down one's nose at**) regard with a feeling of superiority. **look for** attempt to find. **look in** make a short visit or call. **look into** investigate. **look like** informal show a likelihood of. **look lively** (or **sharp**) informal be quick; get moving. **look on** watch without getting involved. **look out 1** be vigilant and take notice. **2** Brit. search for and produce (something). **look over** inspect (something) to establish its merits. **look to 1** rely on (someone) to do something. **2** hope or expect to do. **3** archaic make sure. **look up 1** get better; improve. **2** search for and find (a piece of information) in a reference work. **3** informal make social contact with. **look up to** have a great deal of respect for.
SYNONYMS – *verb* **1** gaze, glance, peek, peer, stare. **3** appear, seem. *noun* **1** glance, peek. **3** air, appearance, aspect.
COMBINATIONS – **look-in** informal a chance of participation or success. **looking glass** a mirror. **look-see** informal a brief look or inspection.

lookalike > *noun* a person or thing that closely resembles another.

looker > *noun* informal a very attractive person.

lookism > *noun* prejudice or discrimination on the grounds of appearance.
DERIVATIVES – **lookist** noun & *adjective*.

lookout > *noun* **1** a place from which to keep watch or view landscape. **2** a person stationed to keep watch. **3** informal, chiefly Brit. a good or bad prospect or outcome. **4** (**one's lookout**) Brit. informal one's own concern.
IDIOMS – **be on the lookout for 1** be alert to. **2** keep searching for.

look-up > *noun* the action of or a facility for looking something up in a database, file, etc.

loom¹ > *noun* an apparatus for making fabric by weaving yarn or thread.
ORIGIN – Old English, 'tool'.

loom² > *verb* **1** appear as a vague form, especially one that is threatening. **2** (of an event regarded as threatening) seem about to happen.
ORIGIN – probably from Low German or Dutch.

loon¹ > *noun* informal a silly or foolish person. > *verb* Brit. informal act in a foolish or desultory way.
ORIGIN – from LOON² (referring to the bird's wailing calls), perhaps influenced by LOONY.

loon² > *noun* North American term for DIVER (in sense 2).
ORIGIN – probably from Shetland dialect *loom*.

loons (also **loon pants**) > plural noun Brit. dated close-fitting casual trousers widely flared from the knees downwards.

loony informal > noun (pl. **loonies**) a mad or silly person. > adjective (**loonier**, **looniest**) mad or silly.
DERIVATIVES – **looniness** noun.
COMBINATIONS – **loony bin** informal, derogatory an institution for people with mental illnesses.
ORIGIN – abbreviation of LUNATIC.

loop > noun 1 a shape produced by a curve that bends round and crosses itself. 2 (also **loop line**) a length of railway track which is connected at either end to the main line. 3 (also **loop-the-loop**) a manoeuvre in which an aircraft describes a vertical circle in the air. 4 an endless strip of tape or film allowing continuous repetition. 5 a complete circuit for an electric current. 6 Computing a programmed sequence of instructions that is repeated until or while a particular condition is satisfied. > verb 1 form into a loop or loops; encircle. 2 follow a course that forms a loop or loops. 3 put into or execute a loop of tape, film, or computing instructions. 4 (also **loop the loop**) circle an aircraft vertically in the air.
IDIOMS – **in** (or **out of**) **the loop** informal, chiefly N. Amer. aware (or unaware) of information known to only a privileged few.

looper > noun a kind of moth caterpillar which moves forward by arching itself into loops.

loophole > noun 1 an ambiguity or inadequacy in the law or a set of rules. 2 an arrow slit in a wall.
ORIGIN – from obsolete loop 'embrasure'.

loopy > adjective (**loopier**, **loopiest**) informal mad or silly.
DERIVATIVES – **loopiness** noun.

loose /lōōss/ > adjective 1 not firmly or tightly fixed in place. 2 not held, tied, or packaged together. 3 not bound or tethered. 4 not fitting tightly or closely. 5 not dense or compact. 6 relaxed or slack. 7 (of the ball in a game) in play but not in any player's possession. 8 careless and indiscreet: loose talk. 9 dated promiscuous or immoral. > verb 1 unfasten or set free. 2 relax (one's grip). 3 (usu. **loose off**) discharge; fire.
IDIOMS – **hang** (or **stay**) **loose** informal, chiefly N. Amer. be relaxed. **on the loose** having escaped from confinement.
DERIVATIVES – **loosely** adverb **looseness** noun.
USAGE – do not confuse **loose** with **lose**: as a verb **loose** means 'unfasten or set free', while **lose** means 'cease to have' or 'become unable to find'.
SYNONYMS – adjective 1 detached, insecure, slack, unattached, unfastened. 2 unbound, untied. 3 at large, free, unbound, untethered.
COMBINATIONS – **loose box** Brit. a stable or stall in which a horse is kept without a tether. **loose cannon** an unpredictable person who is liable to cause unintentional damage. **loose cover** Brit. a removable fitted cloth cover for a chair or sofa. **loose forward** Rugby a forward who plays at the back of the scrum. **loose-leaf** (of a notebook or folder) having each sheet of paper separate and removable. **loose scrum** Rugby a scrum formed by the players round the ball during play, not ordered by the referee.
ORIGIN – Old Norse.

loose end > noun a detail that is not yet settled or explained.
IDIOMS – **be at a loose end** (or N. Amer. **at loose ends**) have nothing specific to do.

loosen > verb 1 make or become loose. 2 (**loosen up**) warm up in preparation for an activity.
IDIOMS – **loosen someone's tongue** make someone talk freely.
DERIVATIVES – **loosener** noun.
SYNONYMS – 1 slacken, undo, unfasten.

loosestrife /lōōss-strīf/ > noun a waterside plant with a tall upright spike of purple or yellow flowers.
ORIGIN – from the plant's Greek name lusimakheion, actually from Lusimakhos, the name of its discoverer, but interpreted as being from luein 'undo, loose' + makhē 'battle'.

loot > noun 1 private property taken from an enemy in war or stolen by thieves. 2 informal money. > verb steal (goods) from somewhere, especially during a war or riot.
DERIVATIVES – **looter** noun.
SYNONYMS – noun 1 booty, plunder, spoils. verb despoil, pillage, plunder, raid, rob.
ORIGIN – Sanskrit, 'rob'.

lop > verb (**lopped**, **lopping**) 1 cut off (a branch or limb) from a tree or body. 2 informal remove (something unnecessary or burdensome). > noun (also **lop and top**) branches and twigs lopped off trees.
DERIVATIVES – **lopper** noun.

lope > verb run with a long bounding stride. > noun a long bounding stride.
ORIGIN – Old Norse.

lop-eared > adjective (of an animal) having drooping ears.
DERIVATIVES – **lop ears** plural noun.
ORIGIN – from archaic lop 'hang loosely or limply'.

lopsided > adjective with one side lower or smaller than the other.
DERIVATIVES – **lopsidedly** adverb **lopsidedness** noun.
SYNONYMS – asymmetrical, uneven.

loquacious /lokwayshəss/ > adjective talkative.
DERIVATIVES – **loquaciously** adverb **loquaciousness** noun **loquacity** noun.
SYNONYMS – chatty, garrulous, talkative, voluble.
ANTONYMS – taciturn.
ORIGIN – from Latin loquax, from loqui 'to talk'.

loquat /lōkwot/ > noun a small egg-shaped yellow fruit from an East Asian tree.
ORIGIN – Chinese dialect, 'rush orange'.

loquitur /lokwitər/ > verb he or she speaks (as a stage direction).
ORIGIN – Latin, from loqui 'talk, speak'.

lord > noun 1 a man of noble rank or high office. 2 (**Lord**) a title given formally to a baron, less formally to a marquess, earl, or viscount, and as a courtesy title to a younger son of a duke or marquess. 3 (**the Lords**) the House of Lords, or its members collectively. 4 a master or ruler. 5 (**Lord**) a name for God or Christ. > exclamation (**Lord**) used in exclamations expressing surprise or worry, or for emphasis. > verb (**lord it over**) act in a superior and domineering manner towards.
IDIOMS – **the Lord's Day** Sunday. **the Lord's Prayer** the prayer taught by Christ to his disciples, beginning 'Our Father.'
COMBINATIONS – **Lord Advocate** the principal Law Officer of the Crown in Scotland. **Lord Chamberlain** (also **Lord Chamberlain of the Household**) (in the UK) the official in charge of the royal household, formerly the licenser of plays. **Lord Chancellor** the highest officer of the British Crown, presiding in the House of Lords. **Lord Chief Justice** the officer presiding over the Queen's Bench Division and the Court of Appeal. **Lord Justice** (pl. **Lords Justices**) a judge in the Court of Appeal. **Lord Lieutenant** (in the UK) the chief executive authority and head of magistrates in each county. **Lord of Appeal** (in full **Lord of Appeal in Ordinary**) formal term for law lord. **Lord President of the Council** the cabinet minister presiding at the Privy Council. **Lord Privy Seal** (in the UK) a senior cabinet minister without specified official duties. **Lord Provost** the head of a municipal corporation or borough in certain Scottish cities. **lords and ladies** cuckoo pint. **Lords spiritual** the bishops in the House of Lords. **Lords temporal** the members of the House of Lords other than the bishops.
ORIGIN – Old English, 'bread-keeper'; compare with LADY.

lordly > adjective (**lordlier**, **lordliest**) of, characteristic of, or suitable for a lord.
DERIVATIVES – **lordliness** noun.

Lord Mayor > noun the title of the mayor in London and some other large cities.

lordosis /lordōsiss/ > noun Medicine excessive

backward curvature of the spine, causing concavity of the back. Compare with **KYPHOSIS**.
ORIGIN – Greek, from *lordos* 'bent backwards'.

lordship > *noun* **1** supreme power or rule. **2** (**His** or **Your** etc. **Lordship**) a form of address to a judge, bishop, or titled man. **3** archaic the authority or state of being a lord.

lore¹ > *noun* a body of traditions and knowledge on a subject: *farming lore.*
ORIGIN – Old English, 'instruction'; related to **LEARN**.

lore² > *noun* Zoology the surface on each side of a bird's head between the eye and the upper base of the beak, or between the eye and nostril in snakes.
ORIGIN – Latin *lorum* 'strap'.

lorgnette /lornyet/ (also **lorgnettes**) > *noun* a pair of glasses or opera glasses held by a long handle at one side.
ORIGIN – French, from *lorgner* 'to squint'.

lorikeet /lorrikeet/ > *noun* a small bird of the lory family, found chiefly in New Guinea.

loris /loriss/ > *noun* (pl. **lorises**) a small, slow-moving nocturnal primate living in dense vegetation in South Asia.
ORIGIN – French, perhaps from obsolete Dutch *loeris* 'clown'.

lorry > *noun* (pl. **lorries**) Brit. a large, heavy motor vehicle for transporting goods.
IDIOMS – **fall off the back of a lorry** informal (of goods) be stolen or acquired in dubious circumstances.
ORIGIN – perhaps from the given name *Laurie.*

lory /lori/ > *noun* (pl. **lories**) a small Australasian or SE Asian parrot.
ORIGIN – Malay.

lose /looz/ > *verb* (past and past participle **lost**) **1** be deprived of or cease to have or retain. **2** become unable to find. **3** fail to win. **4** earn less (money) than one is spending. **5** waste or fail to take advantage of. **6** (**be lost**) be destroyed or killed. **7** evade or shake off (a pursuer). **8** (**lose oneself in** or **be lost in**) be or become deeply absorbed in. **9** (of a watch or clock) become slow.
IDIOMS – **lose face** lose one's credibility. **lose heart** become discouraged. **lose it** informal lose control of one's temper or emotions. **lose one's mind** (or **marbles**) informal go insane. **lose out** be disadvantaged. **lose one's** (or **the**) **way** become lost. **losing battle** a struggle in which failure seems certain.
SYNONYMS – **2** mislay, misplace. **3** be beaten, be conquered, suffer defeat. **7** dodge, elude, evade, shake off.
ANTONYMS – **2** find. **3** win.
ORIGIN – Old English, 'perish, destroy', also 'become unable to find'.

loser > *noun* **1** a person or thing that loses or has lost. **2** informal a person who fails frequently.

loss > *noun* **1** the fact or process of losing something or someone. **2** the feeling of grief after losing a valued person or thing. **3** a person or thing that is badly missed when lost. **4** a defeat in sport.
IDIOMS – **at a loss 1** uncertain or puzzled. **2** making less money than is spent in operation or production.
COMBINATIONS – **loss adjuster** an insurance agent who assesses the amount of compensation that should be paid to a claimant. **loss-leader** a product sold at a loss to attract customers.
ORIGIN – Old English, 'destruction'.

lost past and past participle of **LOSE**.
IDIOMS – **be lost for words** be so surprised or upset that one cannot think what to say. **be lost on** fail to be noticed or appreciated by. **get lost!** informal go away!
COMBINATIONS – **lost cause** a person or thing that can no longer hope to succeed or be changed for the better. **lost generation 1** a generation with many of its men killed in war, especially the First World War. **2** an unfulfilled generation maturing during a period of instability.

lot* > *pronoun* informal **1** (**a lot** or **lots**) a large number or amount; a great deal. **2** (**the lot**) chiefly Brit. the whole number or quantity. > *adverb* (**a lot** or **lots**) informal a great deal. > *noun* **1** informal a particular group or set of people or things. **2** an item or set of items for sale at an auction. **3** a method of deciding something by random selection, especially of one from a number of pieces of paper. **4** a person's destiny, luck, or condition in life. **5** chiefly N. Amer. a plot of land. **6** (also **parking lot**) N. Amer. a car park. > *verb* (**lotted**, **lotting**) divide into lots for sale at an auction.
IDIOMS – **draw** (or **cast**) **lots** decide by lot. **fall to someone's lot** become someone's task or responsibility. **throw in one's lot with** decide to share the fate of.
*SPELLING – **a lot** is a two-word phrase, not one word.

loth > *adjective* variant spelling of **LOATH**.

Lothario /lǝthaariō/ > *noun* (pl. **Lotharios**) a womaniser.
ORIGIN – from a character in Nicholas Rowe's tragedy *The Fair Penitent* (1703).

loti > *noun* (pl. **maloti**) the basic monetary unit of Lesotho, equal to 100 lisente.
ORIGIN – Sesotho (a Bantu language).

lotion > *noun* a thick liquid preparation applied to the skin as a medicine or cosmetic.
ORIGIN – Latin, from *lavare* 'wash'.

lottery > *noun* (pl. **lotteries**) **1** a means of raising money by selling numbered tickets and giving prizes to the holders of numbers drawn at random. **2** something whose success is governed by chance.
ORIGIN – probably from Dutch *loterij*, from *lot* 'lot'.

lotto > *noun* **1** a children's game similar to bingo, using illustrated counters or cards. **2** chiefly N. Amer. a lottery.
ORIGIN – Italian.

lotus > *noun* **1** a large water lily. **2** (in Greek mythology) a legendary plant whose fruit induces a dreamy forgetfulness and an unwillingness to leave.
COMBINATIONS – **lotus-eater** a person given to indulgence in pleasure and luxury. **lotus position** a cross-legged position for meditation, with the feet resting on the thighs.
ORIGIN – Greek *lōtos*, of Semitic origin.

louche /loosh/ > *adjective* disreputable or dubious in a rakish way; shifty.
ORIGIN – French, 'squinting'.

loud > *adjective* **1** producing or capable of producing much noise. **2** strong in expression: *loud protests.* **3** obtrusive or gaudy. > *adverb* with a great deal of volume.
IDIOMS – **out loud** audibly.
DERIVATIVES – **louden** *verb* **loudly** *adverb* **loudness** *noun*.
SYNONYMS – *adjective* **1** booming, deafening, noisy, thunderous. **3** bold, garish, gaudy, lurid.
ANTONYMS – *adjective* quiet.
COMBINATIONS – **loudhailer** chiefly Brit. a megaphone. **loudmouth** informal a person who talks too much, especially tactlessly.
ORIGIN – Old English, from a root meaning 'hear'.

loudspeaker > *noun* an apparatus that converts electrical impulses into sound.
WORDFINDER – tweeter (*loudspeaker designed to reproduce high frequencies*), woofer (*designed for low frequencies*).

lough /lok, lokh/ > *noun* Anglo-Irish spelling of **LOCH**.

lounge > *verb* recline or stand in a relaxed or lazy way. > *noun* **1** Brit. a sitting room. **2** a public sitting room in a hotel or theatre. **3** a seating area in an airport for waiting passengers.
SYNONYMS – *verb* laze, loll, slump, sprawl.
COMBINATIONS – **lounge bar** Brit. a bar in a pub or hotel offering comfortable seating. **lounge lizard** informal an idle, pleasure-seeking man who spends his time in fashionable society. **lounge suit** Brit. a man's suit for ordinary day wear.

lounger > *noun* **1** a comfortable chair, especially an outdoor chair that reclines. **2** a person spending their time lazily or in a relaxed way.

lour /lowr/ (also **lower**) > *verb* **1** scowl. **2** (of the sky) look dark and threatening. > *noun* **1** a scowl. **2** a louring appearance of the sky.

louse > *noun* **1** (pl. **lice**) a small wingless parasitic insect which infests human skin and hair. **2** a related insect which lives on the skin of mammals or birds. **3** (pl. **louses**) informal a contemptible person. > *verb* **1** (**louse up**) informal spoil (something). **2** archaic remove lice from.

WORDFINDER – nit (*louse egg*), pediculosis (*infestation with lice*).

lousy > *adjective* (**lousier**, **lousiest**) **1** informal very poor or bad. **2** infested with lice. **3** (**lousy with**) informal teeming with (something undesirable).

DERIVATIVES – **lousily** *adverb* **lousiness** *noun*.

lout > *noun* an uncouth or aggressive man or boy.

DERIVATIVES – **loutish** *adjective* **loutishly** *adverb* **loutishness** *noun*.

SYNONYMS – boor, oaf, ruffian, thug; Brit. informal yob.

ORIGIN – perhaps from archaic *lout* 'to bow down'.

louvre /loōvər/ (US also **louver**) > *noun* **1** each of a set of angled slats fixed at regular intervals in a door, shutter, or cover to allow air or light through. **2** a domed structure on a roof, with side openings for ventilation.

DERIVATIVES – **louvred** *adjective*.

ORIGIN – Old French *lover*, *lovier* 'skylight'.

lovable (also **loveable**) > *adjective* inspiring love or affection.

DERIVATIVES – **lovableness** *noun* **lovably** *adverb*.

SYNONYMS – adorable, dear, endearing, winning, winsome.

lovage /luvvij/ > *noun* a large edible white-flowered plant of the parsley family.

ORIGIN – Old French *luvesche*, from Latin *ligusticus* 'of Liguria (in NW Italy)'.

lovat /luvvət/ > *noun* a muted green used especially in tweed and woollen garments.

ORIGIN – from *Lovat*, a place in Highland Scotland.

love > *noun* **1** an intense feeling of deep affection. **2** a deep romantic or sexual attachment to someone. **3** a great interest and pleasure in something. **4** a person or thing that one loves. **5** (in tennis, squash, etc.) a score of zero. [ORIGIN – apparently from the phrase *play for love* (i.e. the love of the game, not for money).] > *verb* **1** feel love for. **2** like very much. **3** (**loving**) showing love or great care.

IDIOMS – **love me, love my dog** proverb if you love someone, you must accept everything about them, even their faults or weaknesses. **make love 1** have sexual intercourse. **2** (**make love to**) dated pay attention to in a romantic or flirtatious way. **there's no love lost between** there is mutual dislike between.

DERIVATIVES – **loveless** *adjective* **lovingly** *adverb*.

SYNONYMS – *noun* **1** adoration, devotion. **2** infatuation, passion. **4** beloved, darling, sweetheart. *verb* **1** adore, cherish, treasure, worship. **2** delight in, enjoy, like, be partial to.

ANTONYMS – hate.

COMBINATIONS – **love affair 1** a romantic or sexual relationship, especially outside marriage. **2** an intense enthusiasm for something. **love apple** archaic a tomato. **lovebird 1** a very small African or Madagascan parrot, noted for the affectionate behaviour of mated birds. **2** (**lovebirds**) informal an affectionate couple. **love bite** a temporary red mark on the skin caused by biting or sucking during sexual play. **love child** a child born to parents who are not married to each other. **love handles** informal deposits of excess fat at the waistline. **love-in** informal (especially among hippies in the 1960s) a gathering at which people are encouraged to express friendship and physical attraction. **love-in-a-mist** a plant whose blue flowers are surrounded by thread-like green bracts, giving them a hazy appearance. **love interest** an actor whose main role in a story or film is that of a lover of the central character. **love-lies-bleeding** a South American plant with long drooping tassels of crimson flowers. **love life** the part of one's life concerning relationships with lovers. **love nest** informal a secluded place where two lovers spend time together. **love seat** a sofa designed in an S-shape so that two people can face each other. **loving cup** a two-handled cup passed round at banquets. **loving kindness** tenderness and consideration.

ORIGIN – Old English, related to LEAVE[2] and LIEF.

loveable > *adjective* variant spelling of LOVABLE.

lovelorn > *adjective* unhappy because of unrequited love.

ORIGIN – from LOVE + past participle of obsolete *lese* 'lose'.

lovely > *adjective* (**lovelier**, **loveliest**) **1** exquisitely beautiful. **2** informal very pleasant. > *noun* (pl. **lovelies**) informal a beautiful woman or girl.

DERIVATIVES – **loveliness** *noun*.

SYNONYMS – *adjective* **1** beautiful, comely, exquisite, gorgeous, stunning.

lover > *noun* **1** a person having a sexual or romantic relationship with another. **2** a person who enjoys a specified thing: *a music lover*.

lovesick > *adjective* pining or feeling weak due to being in love.

DERIVATIVES – **lovesickness** *noun*.

lovey-dovey > *adjective* informal very affectionate or romantic.

low[1] > *adjective* **1** of less than average height. **2** situated not far above the ground, horizon, etc. **3** below average in amount, extent, or intensity. **4** lacking importance, prestige, or quality. **5** (of a sound) deep. **6** (of a sound) not loud. **7** unfavourable: *a low opinion*. **8** depressed or lacking energy. **9** unscrupulous or dishonest. > *noun* **1** a low point, level, or figure. **2** an area of low barometric pressure. > *adverb* **1** in or into a low position or state. **2** quietly or at a low pitch.

DERIVATIVES – **lowish** *adjective* **lowness** *noun*.

SYNONYMS – *adjective* **1** short, squat. **4** inferior, poor, substandard. **6** faint, hushed, muted, quiet. **7** negative, poor, unfavourable.

COMBINATIONS – **lowboy** N. Amer. a low chest or table with drawers. **Low Church** a tradition within the Anglican Church giving relatively little emphasis to ritual and sacraments. **low comedy** comedy bordering on farce. **lowest common denominator 1** Mathematics the lowest common multiple of the denominators of several vulgar fractions. **2** the least desirable common feature of members of a group. **lowest common multiple** Mathematics the lowest quantity that is a multiple of two or more given quantities. **low frequency** (in radio) 30–300 kilohertz. **low gear** a gear that causes a wheeled vehicle to move slowly. **Low German** a German dialect spoken in much of northern Germany. **low-impact 1** (of exercises) putting little stress on the body. **2** affecting or altering the environment as little as possible. **low-level 1** of relatively little importance. **2** Computing denoting a programming language that is close to machine code in form. **low life 1** disreputable or criminal people or activities. **2** (**lowlife**) informal a disreputable or criminal person. **lowlight 1** (**lowlights**) darker dyed streaks in the hair. **2** informal a disappointing or dull event or feature. **low-loader** Brit. a truck with a low floor and no sides, for heavy loads. **low-lying** at low altitude above sea level. **low-minded** vulgar or sordid. **low-rider** US a vehicle with a chassis that can be lowered nearly to the road. **low-rise** (of a building) having few storeys. **low season** Brit. the least popular time of year for a holiday, when prices are lowest. **low spirits** sadness and despondency. **Low Sunday** the Sunday after Easter. **low technology** less advanced technological development or equipment. **low tide** the state of the tide when at its lowest level. **low water** low tide. **low-**

water mark 1 the level reached by the sea at low tide. **2** a minimum recorded level or value.
ORIGIN – Old Norse, related to LIE¹.

low² > *verb* (of a cow) moo. > *noun* a moo.

lowbrow > *adjective* informal, chiefly derogatory not highly intellectual or cultured.

low-down informal > *adjective* mean and unfair. > *noun* (**the low-down**) the relevant information.

lower¹ > *adjective* comparative of LOW¹. **1** less high. **2** (in place names) situated to the south. **3** Geology & Archaeology older (and hence forming more deeply buried strata): *the Lower Cretaceous.*
COMBINATIONS – **lower animals** invertebrate animals, regarded as having relatively primitive characteristics. **lower case** small or non-capital letters. **lower class** the working class. **lower house** (also **lower chamber**) **1** the larger, typically elected, body of a parliament with two chambers. **2** (**the Lower House**) the House of Commons. **lower plants** plants without vascular systems, e.g. algae, mosses, and liverworts. **lower regions** archaic hell.

lower² > *verb* **1** cause to move downward or be less high. **2** make or become less in amount, extent, or value. **3** (**lower oneself**) demean oneself.
SYNONYMS – **1** drop, let down. **2** cut, decrease, lessen, reduce.
ANTONYMS – **1,2** raise.

lower³ > *verb & noun* variant spelling of LOUR.

low-fi > *adjective* variant spelling of LO-FI.

low-key > *adjective* modest or restrained.
SYNONYMS – discreet, downbeat, modest, muted, restrained, understated.

lowland /lōlənd/ > *noun* **1** (also **lowlands**) low-lying country. **2** (**the Lowlands**) the part of Scotland lying south and east of the Highlands.
DERIVATIVES – **lowlander** noun.

lowly > *adjective* (**lowlier, lowliest**) **1** low in status or importance. **2** (of an organism) primitive or simple. > *adverb* to a low degree.
DERIVATIVES – **lowliness** noun.

lox /loks/ > *noun* N. Amer. smoked salmon.
ORIGIN – Yiddish *laks.*

loyal > *adjective* showing firm and constant support or allegiance to a person or institution.
DERIVATIVES – **loyally** adverb.
SYNONYMS – constant, faithful, staunch, steadfast, true.
ANTONYMS – disloyal, treacherous.
COMBINATIONS – **loyal toast** a toast to one's sovereign.
ORIGIN – French, from Latin *legalis* 'legal'.

loyalist > *noun* **1** a person who remains loyal to the established ruler or government. **2**

(**Loyalist**) a supporter of union between Great Britain and Northern Ireland.
DERIVATIVES – **loyalism** noun.

loyalty > *noun* (pl. **loyalties**) **1** the state of being loyal. **2** a strong feeling of support or allegiance.
SYNONYMS – **1** constancy, faithfulness, fidelity, steadfastness.
COMBINATIONS – **loyalty card** Brit. a card issued by a retailer to its customers, on which credits are accumulated for future discounts.

lozenge /lozinj/ > *noun* **1** a rhombus or diamond shape. **2** a small medicinal sweet for dissolving in the mouth.
ORIGIN – Old French *losenge*, probably from Latin *lausiae lapides* 'stone slabs'.

LP > *abbreviation* long-playing (gramophone record).

LPG > *abbreviation* liquefied petroleum gas.

L-plate > *noun* Brit. a sign bearing the letter L, attached to a vehicle to indicate that the driver is a learner.

Lr > *symbol* the chemical element lawrencium.

LSD > *noun* a synthetic crystalline compound, lysergic acid diethylamide, which is a powerful hallucinogenic drug.

LSE > *abbreviation* London School of Economics.

LSO > *abbreviation* London Symphony Orchestra.

Lt > *abbreviation* Lieutenant.

Ltd > *abbreviation* Brit. (after a company name) Limited.

Lu > *symbol* the chemical element lutetium.

lubber > *noun* **1** archaic or dialect a big, clumsy person. **2** short for LANDLUBBER.
DERIVATIVES – **lubberly** adjective & adverb.
COMBINATIONS – **lubber line** a line on a compass, showing the direction straight ahead.
ORIGIN – perhaps from Old French *lobeor* 'swindler, parasite', from *lober* 'deceive'.

lube /loob/ informal, chiefly N. Amer. & Austral./NZ > *noun* a lubricant. > *verb* lubricate.

lubricant > *noun* a substance, e.g. oil or grease, for lubricating an engine or component. > *adjective* lubricating.

lubricate /loobrikayt/ > *verb* apply oil or grease to (an engine or component) to minimise friction.
DERIVATIVES – **lubrication** noun **lubricator** noun.
ORIGIN – Latin *lubricare* 'make slippery', from *lubricus* 'slippery'.

lubricious /loobrishəss/ (also **lubricous** /loobrikəss/) > *adjective* **1** lewd. **2** smooth and slippery with oil or grease.
DERIVATIVES – **lubriciously** adverb **lubricity** noun.

luce /looss/ > *noun* (pl. same) a pike (fish), especially when full-grown.
ORIGIN – Old French, from Latin *lucius.*

lucent /looss'nt/ > *adjective* literary shining.
DERIVATIVES – **lucency** noun.
ORIGIN – Latin, from *lucere* 'shine'.

lucerne /loosern/ > *noun* another term for ALFALFA.
ORIGIN – modern Provençal *luzerno* 'glow-worm' (with reference to its shiny seeds).

lucid /loossid/ > *adjective* **1** clear; easy to understand. **2** showing an ability to think clearly. **3** literary bright or luminous.
DERIVATIVES – **lucidity** noun **lucidly** adverb.
SYNONYMS – **1** clear, coherent, fluent, perspicuous, straightforward.
ORIGIN – Latin *lucidus*, from *lux* 'light'.

Lucifer /loosifər/ > *noun* **1** the Devil. **2** literary the planet Venus in the morning. **3** (**lucifer**) archaic a match.
ORIGIN – Latin, 'light-bringing, morning star'.

luck > *noun* **1** success or failure apparently brought by chance. **2** chance considered as a force causing success or failure. **3** good fortune. > *verb* informal **1** (**luck into** or **upon**) chance to find or acquire. **2** (**luck out**) N. Amer. succeed due to good luck.
IDIOMS – **one's luck is in** one is fortunate. **no such luck** informal unfortunately not. **try one's luck** attempt something risky. **worse luck** informal unfortunately.
SYNONYMS – *noun* **2** chance, destiny, fate, fortune. **3** serendipity.
ORIGIN – Low German *lucke.*

luckily > *adverb* it is fortunate that.

luckless > *adjective* unfortunate.

lucky > *adjective* (**luckier, luckiest**) having, bringing, or resulting from good luck.
SYNONYMS – fortunate, providential.
ANTONYMS – unfortunate, unlucky.
COMBINATIONS – **lucky bag** Brit. a grab bag. **lucky dip** Brit. a game in which small prizes are concealed in a tub, traditionally filled with sawdust, and chosen at random by participants.

lucky bag > *noun* Brit. another term for *grab bag.*

lucrative /lookrətiv/ > *adjective* profitable.
DERIVATIVES – **lucratively** adverb.
ORIGIN – Latin *lucrativus*, from *lucrari* 'to gain'.

lucre /lookər/ > *noun* literary money, especially when gained dishonourably.
ORIGIN – Latin *lucrum*; the phrase *filthy lucre* is with biblical allusion to the Epistle to Titus, chapter 1.

lucubrate /lookyoobrayt/ > *verb* archaic discourse learnedly in writing.
ORIGIN – Latin *lucubrare* 'work by lamplight'.

lucubration > *noun* formal **1** study; meditation. **2** a piece of writing, especially a pedantic or over-elaborate one.

Lucullan /lookullən/ > *adjective* (especially of food) luxurious.

ORIGIN – from the name of Licinius *Lucullus*, a Roman general famous for his lavish banquets.

lud > *noun* (**m'lud** or **my lud**) Brit. used to address a judge in court.

ORIGIN – alteration of LORD.

Luddite /**ludd**īt/ > *noun* **1** a member of any of the bands of English workers who opposed mechanisation and destroyed machinery in the early 19th century. **2** a person opposed to new industrial processes or new technology.

DERIVATIVES – **Luddism** noun **Ludditism** noun.

ORIGIN – perhaps named after Ned *Lud*, a member of an early Luddite band.

ludic /**loo**dik/ > *adjective* formal spontaneous; playful.

ORIGIN – French *ludique*, from Latin *ludere* 'to play'.

ludicrous /**loo**dikrəss/ > *adjective* absurd; ridiculous.

DERIVATIVES – **ludicrously** adverb **ludicrousness** noun.

SYNONYMS – absurd, farcical, laughable, preposterous, ridiculous, risible.

ORIGIN – Latin *ludicrus*, probably from *ludicrum* 'stage play'.

ludo > *noun* Brit. a board game in which players move counters according to throws of a dice.

ORIGIN – Latin, 'I play'.

luff > *noun* Sailing the edge of a fore-and-aft sail next to the mast or stay. > *verb* **1** Sailing steer (a yacht) nearer the wind. **2** raise or lower (the jib of a crane).

ORIGIN – Old French *lof*.

Luftwaffe /**loo**ftvaffə/ > *noun* the German air force until the end of the Second World War.

ORIGIN – German, from *Luft* 'air' + *Waffe* 'weapon'.

lug[1] > *verb* (**lugged, lugging**) carry or drag with great effort. > *noun* a box for transporting fruit.

ORIGIN – probably Scandinavian.

lug[2] > *noun* **1** Scottish & N. English or informal an ear. **2** a projection on an object by which it may be carried or fixed in place. **3** informal, chiefly N. Amer. a lout.

ORIGIN – probably Scandinavian.

luge /**loo**zh/ > *noun* a light toboggan ridden in a sitting or lying position. > *verb* ride on a luge.

ORIGIN – Swiss French.

Luger /**loo**gər/ > *noun* (trademark in the US) a type of German automatic pistol.

ORIGIN – named after the German firearms expert George *Luger* (1849–1923).

luggage > *noun* suitcases or other bags used when travelling.

ORIGIN – from LUG[1].

lugger > *noun* a small ship with two or three masts and a lugsail on each.

lughole > *noun* Brit. informal an ear.

lugsail /**lug**sayl, **lug**s'l/ > *noun* an asymmetrical four-sided sail, bent on and hoisted from a steeply inclined yard.

ORIGIN – probably from LUG[2].

lugubrious /loo**goo**briəss/ > *adjective* mournful; sad and dismal.

DERIVATIVES – **lugubriously** adverb **lugubriousness** noun.

ORIGIN – Latin *lugubris*, from *lugere* 'mourn'.

lugworm > *noun* a bristle worm living in muddy sand and leaving characteristic worm casts, used as fishing bait.

lukewarm > *adjective* **1** only moderately warm. **2** unenthusiastic.

SYNONYMS – **1** tepid, warmish. **2** apathetic, half-hearted, indifferent, unenthusiastic.

ORIGIN – from dialect *luke*, related to LEE.

lull > *verb* **1** calm or send to sleep with soothing sounds or movements. **2** cause to feel deceptively secure. **3** allay (doubts, fears, etc.), typically by deception. **4** (of noise or a storm) abate. > *noun* a temporary period of quiet or inactivity.

SYNONYMS – *noun* calm, hush, respite.

lullaby > *noun* (pl. **lullabies**) a soothing song sung to send a child to sleep.

lulu > *noun* informal an outstanding person or thing.

lum /lum/ > *noun* Scottish & N. English a chimney.

ORIGIN – perhaps from Old French *lum* 'light'.

luma /**loo**mə/ > *noun* (pl. same or **lumas**) a monetary unit of Armenia, equal to one hundredth of a dram.

ORIGIN – Armenian.

lumbago /lum**bay**gō/ > *noun* pain in the lower back.

ORIGIN – Latin, from *lumbus* 'loin'.

lumbar /**lum**bər/ > *adjective* relating to the lower back.

COMBINATIONS – **lumbar puncture** Medicine the withdrawal of spinal fluid from the lower back through a hollow needle, usually for diagnosis.

ORIGIN – Latin *lumbaris*, from *lumbus* 'loin'.

lumber[1] > *verb* move in a slow, heavy, awkward way.

lumber[2] > *noun* **1** chiefly Brit. disused articles of furniture that inconveniently take up space. **2** chiefly N. Amer. partly prepared timber. > *verb* **1** (usu. **be lumbered with**) Brit. informal burden with an unwanted responsibility. **2** chiefly N. Amer. cut and prepare forest timber for transport and sale.

COMBINATIONS – **lumberjack** (also **lumberman**) a person who fells trees, cuts them into logs, or transports them. **lumberjacket** a thick jacket, typically with a bright check pattern, of the kind worn by lumberjacks. **lumber room** Brit. a room for storing disused or bulky things.

lumen /**loo**men/ > *noun* Physics the unit of luminous flux in the SI system, equal to the amount of light emitted per second in a unit solid angle of one steradian from a uniform source of one candela.

ORIGIN – Latin, 'light'.

luminaire /**loo**minair/ > *noun* a complete electric light unit.

ORIGIN – French.

luminance /**loo**minənss/ > *noun* **1** Physics the intensity of light emitted from a surface per unit area in a given direction. **2** the component of a television signal which specifies the brightness of the image.

luminary /**loo**minəri/ > *noun* (pl. **luminaries**) **1** a person who inspires or influences others. **2** literary a natural light-giving body, especially the sun or moon.

luminesce /**loo**mi**ness**/ > *verb* emit light by luminescence.

luminescence /**loo**mi**ness**'nss/ > *noun* the emission of light by a substance that has not been heated, as in fluorescence and phosphorescence.

DERIVATIVES – **luminescent** adjective.

luminosity > *noun* luminous quality.

luminous /**loo**minəss/ > *adjective* **1** bright or shining, especially in the dark. **2** Physics relating to visible light.

DERIVATIVES – **luminously** adverb.

SYNONYMS – **1** bright, brilliant, glowing, radiant, shining.

ORIGIN – Latin *luminosus*, from *lumen* 'light'.

lumme /**lumm**i/ > *exclamation* Brit. informal, dated an expression of surprise.

ORIGIN – from *Lord love me*.

lummox /**lumm**əks/ > *noun* informal, chiefly N. Amer. a clumsy, stupid person.

lump[1] > *noun* **1** a compact mass, especially one without a definite or regular shape. **2** a swelling under the skin. **3** informal a heavy, ungainly, or slow-witted person. **4** (**the lump**) Brit. informal casual employment in the building trade. > *verb* **1** (often **lump together**) put in an indiscriminate mass or group. **2** Brit. carry (a heavy load) somewhere with difficulty.

IDIOMS – **a lump in the throat** a feeling of tightness in the throat caused by strong emotion.

SYNONYMS – *noun* **1** blob, chunk, clod, dollop, mass.

COMBINATIONS – **lump sum** a single payment made at one time, as opposed to many instalments.

lump[2] > *verb* (**lump it**) informal accept or tolerate something whether one likes it or not.

lumpectomy > *noun* (pl. **lumpectomies**) a surgical operation in which a lump, typically a tumour, is removed from the breast.

lumpen > *adjective* **1** (in Marxist contexts) belonging to or characteristic of the lumpenproletariat. **2** boorish and stupid. **3** lumpy and misshapen.

lumpenproletariat /lumpənprōli**tair**iət/ > *noun* (in Marxist terminology) the lower orders of society who are indifferent to politics and uninterested in revolutionary advancement.
ORIGIN – German, from *Lumpen* 'rag, rogue' + **PROLETARIAT**.

lumpfish > *noun* a North Atlantic lumpsucker with edible roe.
ORIGIN – from Low German *lumpen*, Dutch *lompe*, possibly related to **LUMP¹**.

lumpish > *adjective* **1** roughly or clumsily formed. **2** stupid and lethargic.
DERIVATIVES – **lumpishly** *adverb* **lumpishness** *noun*.

lumpsucker > *noun* a round-bodied northern coastal fish with an abdominal sucker and spiny fins.

lumpy > *adjective* (**lumpier, lumpiest**) full of or covered with lumps.
DERIVATIVES – **lumpily** *adverb* **lumpiness** *noun*.

lunacy > *noun* (pl. **lunacies**) **1** insanity (not in technical use). **2** extreme folly.
SYNONYMS – derangement, folly, idiocy, imbecility, insanity, madness.

lunar /**loo**nər/ > *adjective* of, determined by, or resembling the moon.
COMBINATIONS – **lunar day** the interval between two successive crossings of the meridian by the moon (roughly 24 hours and 50 minutes). **lunar eclipse** an eclipse in which the moon passes into the earth's shadow. **lunar month 1** a month measured between successive new moons (roughly 29½ days). **2** (in general use) four weeks. **lunar year** a period of twelve lunar months (approximately 354 days).
ORIGIN – Latin *lunaris*, from *luna* 'moon'.

lunate /**loo**nayt/ > *adjective* crescent-shaped.

lunatic > *noun* **1** a person who is mentally ill (not in technical use). **2** an extremely foolish person.
SYNONYMS – madman, maniac; informal crackpot, nutcase.
COMBINATIONS – **lunatic fringe** an extreme or eccentric minority.
ORIGIN – Latin *lunaticus*, from *luna* 'moon' (from the belief that changes of the moon caused intermittent insanity).

lunation /**loo**naysh'n/ > *noun* Astronomy a lunar month.

lunch > *noun* a meal eaten in the middle of the day. > *verb* eat lunch.
IDIOMS – **out to lunch** informal unbalanced or stupid. **there's no such thing as a free**

lunch proverb it isn't possible to get something for nothing.
DERIVATIVES – **luncher** *noun*.
COMBINATIONS – **lunch box 1** a container for a packed meal. **2** humorous a man's genitals.
ORIGIN – abbreviation of **LUNCHEON**.

luncheon > *noun* formal lunch.
COMBINATIONS – **luncheon meat** finely minced cooked pork mixed with cereal, sold in a tin. **luncheon voucher** Brit. a voucher exchangeable for food at restaurants and shops, given by some companies to employees.
ORIGIN – possibly from Spanish *lonja* 'slice': originally in the sense 'thick piece, hunk'.

luncheonette > *noun* N. Amer. a small restaurant serving light lunches.

lunette /loo**net**/ > *noun* **1** an arched aperture or window in a domed ceiling. **2** a crescent-shaped or semicircular alcove containing a painting or statue. **3** a fortification with two faces forming a projecting angle. **4** (in the Roman Catholic Church) a holder for the consecrated host in a monstrance. **5** a ring on a vehicle, by which it can be towed.
ORIGIN – French, 'little moon'.

lung > *noun* each of the pair of organs within the ribcage into which air is drawn in breathing, so that oxygen can pass into the blood and carbon dioxide be removed.
WORDFINDER – pulmonary (*relating to the lungs*); alveoli (*tiny air sacs in the lungs*), bronchi (*air passages of the lungs*), pleura (*membranes enclosing the lungs*), pneumonia (*lung infection in which pus collects in the lungs*).
DERIVATIVES – **lunged** *adjective* **lungful** *noun*.
COMBINATIONS – **lungfish** an elongated freshwater fish with one or two sacs which function as lungs, enabling it to breath air and live dormant in mud to survive drought. **lungwort 1** a bristly pink-flowered plant with white-spotted leaves said to resemble a diseased lung. **2** a large lichen which grows on trees, formerly used to treat lung disease.
ORIGIN – Old English, related to **LIGHT²** and **LIGHTS**.

lunge¹ > *noun* **1** a sudden forward movement of the body. **2** a thrust in fencing, in which the leading leg is bent while the back leg remains straightened. > *verb* (**lunged, lunging** or **lungeing**) make a lunge.
ORIGIN – from French *allonger* 'lengthen'.

lunge² (also **longe**) > *noun* a long rein on which a horse is made to move in a circle round its trainer.
ORIGIN – French *longe*, from *allonge* 'lengthening out'.

lungi /**loong**gee/ > *noun* (pl. **lungis**) a length

of cotton cloth worn as a loincloth in India or as a skirt in Burma (Myanmar).
ORIGIN – Urdu.

lunk (also **lunkhead**) > *noun* informal a slow-witted person.
ORIGIN – probably from an alteration of **LUMP¹**.

lupin /**loo**pin/ (also **lupine** pronunc. same) > *noun* a plant with deeply divided leaves and tall colourful tapering spikes of flowers.
ORIGIN – Latin *lupinus*.

lupine /**loo**pīn/ > *adjective* of or like a wolf or wolves.
ORIGIN – Latin *lupinus*, from *lupus* 'wolf'.

lupus /**loo**pəss/ > *noun* an ulcerous skin condition, especially one due to direct infection with tuberculosis.
COMBINATIONS – **lupus erythematosus** /erritheemə**tō**səss/ an inflammatory disease causing scaly red patches on the skin.
ORIGIN – Latin, 'wolf'; *erythematosus* is from Greek *eruthēma* 'reddening'.

lurch¹ > *noun* a sudden unsteady movement. > *verb* make such a movement; stagger.
SYNONYMS – *verb* reel, stagger, stumble.

lurch² > *noun* (in phrase **leave in the lurch**) leave (someone) in a difficult situation without assistance or support.
ORIGIN – French *lourche*, the name of a game resembling backgammon, used in the phrase *demeurer lourche* 'be discomfited'.

lurcher > *noun* Brit. a cross-bred dog, typically a retriever, collie, or sheepdog crossed with a greyhound, originally used for hunting and by poachers.
ORIGIN – from obsolete *lurch*, variant of **LURK**.

lure /loor/ > *verb* tempt to do something or to go somewhere. > *noun* **1** a thing that lures a person or animal to do something. **2** the attractive qualities of a person or thing. **3** a type of bait used in fishing or hunting. **4** Falconry a bunch of feathers with a piece of meat attached to a card, swung around the head of a falconer to recall a hawk.
SYNONYMS – *verb* draw, entice, tempt. *noun* **1** bait, decoy. **2** appeal, attraction, draw, pull.
ORIGIN – Old French *luere*.

lurex /**loor**eks/ > *noun* trademark yarn or fabric incorporating a glittering metallic thread.

lurgy /**lur**gi/ > *noun* (pl. **lurgies**) Brit. humorous an unspecified illness.
ORIGIN – of unknown origin; frequently used in the British radio series *The Goon Show*, of the 1950s and 1960s.

lurid /**lyoor**id/ > *adjective* **1** unpleasantly vivid in colour. **2** (of a description) shocking or sensational.
DERIVATIVES – **luridly** *adverb* **luridness** *noun*.
SYNONYMS – **1** garish, gaudy, loud.

ORIGIN – Latin *luridus*, related to *luror* 'wan or yellow colour': originally in the sense 'pale and dismal'.

lurk > *verb* **1** be or remain hidden so as to wait in ambush. **2** be present in a latent or barely discernible state. > *noun* Austral./NZ informal a dodge or scheme.

DERIVATIVES – **lurker** *noun*.

SYNONYMS – *verb* **1** lie in wait, prowl, skulk.

ORIGIN – perhaps from LOUR.

luscious > *adjective* **1** having a pleasingly rich, sweet taste. **2** richly verdant or opulent. **3** (of a woman) sexually attractive.

DERIVATIVES – **lusciously** *adverb* **lusciousness** *noun*.

ORIGIN – perhaps an alteration of obsolete *licious*, shortened form of DELICIOUS.

lush¹ > *adjective* **1** (of vegetation) luxuriant. **2** rich or luxurious. **3** informal sexually attractive.

DERIVATIVES – **lushly** *adverb* **lushness** *noun*.

ORIGIN – perhaps an alteration of obsolete *lash* 'soft, lax'.

lush² > *noun* informal, chiefly N. Amer. a drunkard.

ORIGIN – perhaps a humorous use of LUSH¹.

lusophone /loosəfōn/ > *adjective* Portuguese-speaking.

ORIGIN – from *luso-* (representing *Lusitania*, an ancient Roman province corresponding to modern Portugal) + -PHONE.

lust > *noun* **1** strong sexual desire. **2** a passionate desire for something. **3** Theology a sensuous appetite regarded as sinful. > *verb* (usu. **lust for** or **after**) feel lust for someone or something.

SYNONYMS – *noun* **1** desire, passion; formal concupiscence. **2** appetite, craving, hunger, longing. **3** lechery.

lustful > *adjective* filled with lust; lecherous.

DERIVATIVES – **lustfully** *adverb* **lustfulness** *noun*.

SYNONYMS – lascivious, lecherous, libidinous.

lustra plural of LUSTRUM.

lustral /lustrəl/ > *adjective* relating to or used in ceremonial purification.

ORIGIN – Latin *lustralis*, from *lustrum*.

lustre (US **luster**) > *noun* **1** a gentle sheen or soft glow. **2** glory or distinction. **3** a thin metallic coating giving an iridescent glaze to ceramics. **4** (also **lustreware**) ceramics with an iridescent metallic glaze. **5** a fabric or yarn with a sheen.

DERIVATIVES – **lustred** *adjective*.

SYNONYMS – **1** gloss, glow, sheen, shine.

ORIGIN – Italian *lustro*, from Latin *lustrare* 'illuminate'.

lustrous > *adjective* having lustre; shining.

DERIVATIVES – **lustrously** *adverb* **lustrousness** *noun*.

SYNONYMS – gleaming, glossy, glowing, radiant, shining, shiny.

lustrum /lustrəm/ > *noun* (pl. **lustra** /lustrə/ or **lustrums**) chiefly literary or historical a period of five years.

ORIGIN – Latin, originally denoting a purificatory sacrifice after a five-yearly census.

lusty > *adjective* (**lustier**, **lustiest**) healthy and strong; vigorous.

DERIVATIVES – **lustily** *adverb* **lustiness** *noun*.

lute¹ > *noun* a stringed instrument with a long neck and a rounded body with a flat front, played by plucking.

ORIGIN – Old French *lut*, *leut*, probably from Arabic.

lute² > *noun* **1** liquid clay or cement used to seal a joint, protect a graft, etc. **2** a rubber seal for a jar. > *verb* seal, join, or coat with lute.

ORIGIN – Latin *lutum* 'potter's clay'.

lutenist /lootənist/ (also **lutanist**) > *noun* a lute player.

lutetium /lootteeshəm/ > *noun* a rare silvery-white metallic chemical element of the lanthanide series.

ORIGIN – from Latin *Lutetia*, the ancient name of Paris, where its discoverer Georges Urbain (1872–1938) lived.

Lutheran /loothərən/ > *noun* **1** a follower of the German Protestant theologian Martin Luther (1483–1546). **2** a member of the Lutheran Church. > *adjective* **1** of or characterised by the theology of Martin Luther. **2** relating to the Lutheran Church.

DERIVATIVES – **Lutheranism** *noun*.

COMBINATIONS – **Lutheran Church** the Protestant Church founded on the doctrines of Martin Luther, with justification by faith alone as a cardinal doctrine.

luthier /lootiər/ > *noun* a maker of stringed instruments.

ORIGIN – French, from *luth* 'lute'.

lutist > *noun* **1** a lute player. **2** a lute maker.

lutz /loots/ > *noun* a jump in skating from the backward outside edge of one skate to the backward outside edge of the other, with a full turn in the air.

ORIGIN – named after the Austrian skater Alois *Lutz* (1899–1918).

luvvy (also **luvvie**) > *noun* (pl. **luvvies**) Brit. informal an effusive or affected actor or actress.

lux /luks/ > *noun* (pl. same) the unit of illuminance in the SI system, equal to one lumen per square metre.

ORIGIN – Latin, 'light'.

luxe /luks, looks/ > *noun* luxury.

ORIGIN – French.

Luxembourger /luksəmbergər/ > *noun* a person from Luxembourg.

Luxemburgish /luksəmburgish/ > *noun* a form of German spoken in Luxembourg.

luxuriant /lugzyooriənt/ > *adjective* **1** (of vegetation) rich and profuse in growth. **2** (of hair) thick and healthy.

DERIVATIVES – **luxuriance** *noun* **luxuriantly** *adverb*.

USAGE – do not confuse **luxuriant** with **luxurious**, which means 'characterised by luxury; very comfortable and extravagant'.

SYNONYMS – **1** abundant, dense, lush, profuse, prolific, rich.

luxuriate /lugzyooriayt/ > *verb* (**luxuriate in** or **over**) enjoy as a luxury.

luxurious > *adjective* **1** characterised by luxury. **2** giving self-indulgent pleasure.

DERIVATIVES – **luxuriously** *adverb* **luxuriousness** *noun*.

SYNONYMS – **1** lavish, opulent, sumptuous. **2** extravagant, hedonistic, self-indulgent.

ANTONYMS – **1** spartan.

luxury > *noun* (pl. **luxuries**) **1** a state of living extravagantly and in great comfort. **2** an inessential but desirable item. > *adjective* of the nature of a luxury.

SYNONYMS – *noun* **1** comfort, grandeur, luxuriousness, opulence, sumptuousness. **2** extravagance, indulgence, treat.

wordpower facts

Luxury

A surprising shift of meaning has taken place in the development of the words **luxury** and **luxurious** since their first entry into English from Old French. Ultimately they come from Latin *luxuria*, from *luxus*, which means 'excess'. The original sense of **luxury** was 'lechery', or 'lust', while **luxurious** meant 'lecherous, lascivious', or 'outrageous, excessive'. The words did not acquire their modern meanings until the 17th century. The word **luxuriant**, with which **luxurious** is often confused, comes from the same source, via the Latin verb *luxuriare*, meaning 'grow rankly'.

LVO > *abbreviation* Lieutenant of the Royal Victorian Order.

lwei /ləway/ > *noun* (pl. same) a monetary unit of Angola, equal to one hundredth of a kwanza.

ORIGIN – a local word.

lx > *abbreviation* Physics lux.

-ly¹ > *suffix* forming adjectives meaning: **1** having the qualities of: *brotherly*. **2** recurring at intervals of: *hourly*.

ORIGIN – Old English, related to LIKE¹.

-ly² > *suffix* forming adverbs from adjectives: *greatly*.

lycanthrope /lī̆kənthrŏp/ > *noun* a werewolf.

lycanthropy /līkanthrəpi/ > *noun* the mythical transformation of a person into a wolf.
DERIVATIVES – **lycanthropic** *adjective*.
ORIGIN – Greek *lukanthrōpia*, from *lukos* 'wolf' + *anthrōpos* 'man'.

lycée /leesay/ > *noun* (pl. pronunc. same) a French secondary school funded by the state.
ORIGIN – French, from Latin *lyceum*.

Lyceum /līseeəm/ > *noun* **1** the garden at Athens in which Aristotle taught philosophy. **2** (**lyceum**) US archaic a literary institution, lecture hall, or teaching place.
ORIGIN – Latin, from Greek *Lukeios*, a name for the god Apollo (from whose neighbouring temple the Lyceum was named).

lychee /līchee/ (also **litchi**) > *noun* a small rounded fruit with sweet white scented flesh, a large stone, and thin rough skin.
ORIGIN – Chinese.

lychgate /lichgayt/ > *noun* a roofed gateway to a churchyard, formerly used at burials for sheltering a coffin until the clergyman's arrival.
ORIGIN – from Old English *līc* 'body'.

Lycra /līkrə/ > *noun* trademark an elastic polyurethane fibre or fabric used to provide stretch in clothing.

Lydian /liddiən/ > *noun* a person from the ancient region of Lydia in western Asia Minor. > *adjective* relating to Lydia.

lye > *noun* a strongly alkaline solution, especially of potassium hydroxide, used for washing or cleansing.
ORIGIN – Old English, related to LATHER.

lying¹ present participle of LIE¹.

lying² present participle of LIE².

lyke wake /līk/ > *noun* Brit. a night spent watching over a dead body.
ORIGIN – from Old English *līc* 'body'.

Lyme disease /līm/ > *noun* a form of arthritis caused by bacteria that are transmitted by ticks.
ORIGIN – named after *Lyme*, a town in Connecticut, US, where an outbreak occurred.

lymph /limf/ > *noun* **1** a colourless fluid containing white blood cells, which bathes the tissues and drains through the lymphatic system into the bloodstream. **2** fluid exuding from a sore or inflamed tissue.
ORIGIN – Latin *lympha*, *limpa* 'water'.

lymphatic /limfattik/ > *adjective* **1** relating to lymph or its secretion. **2** archaic (of a person) pale, flabby, or sluggish. > *noun* a vein-like vessel conveying lymph in the body.
COMBINATIONS – **lymphatic system** the network of vessels through which lymph drains from the tissues into the blood.

lymph node (also **lymph gland**) > *noun* each of a number of small swellings in the lymphatic system where lymph is filtered and lymphocytes are formed.

lymphocyte /limfəsīt/ > *noun* a form of small leucocyte (white blood cell) with a single round nucleus, occurring especially in the lymphatic system.

lymphoid /limfoyd/ > *adjective* relating to tissue responsible for producing lymphocytes and antibodies.

lymphoma /limfōmə/ > *noun* (pl. **lymphomas** or **lymphomata** /limfōmətə/) cancer of the lymph nodes.

lynch > *verb* (of a group) kill (someone) as punishment for an alleged offence without a legal trial.
DERIVATIVES – **lyncher** *noun*.
ORIGIN – from *Lynch's law*, named after Captain William *Lynch*, head of a self-constituted judicial tribunal in Virginia *c*.1780.

lynchet /linchit/ > *noun* a ridge or ledge formed along the downhill side of a plot by ploughing in ancient times.
ORIGIN – probably from dialect *linch* 'rising ground'; related to LINKS.

lynchpin > *noun* variant spelling of LINCHPIN.

lynx > *noun* a wild cat with a short tail and tufted ears.
COMBINATIONS – **lynx-eyed** having very keen eyesight.
ORIGIN – Greek *lunx*.

lyonnaise /liənayz/ > *adjective* (of sliced potatoes) cooked with onions or with a white wine and onion sauce.
ORIGIN – French, 'characteristic of the city of Lyons'.

lyrate /līrayt/ > *adjective* Biology lyre-shaped.

lyre > *noun* a stringed instrument like a small U-shaped harp with strings fixed to a crossbar, used especially in ancient Greece.
COMBINATIONS – **lyrebird** a large Australian songbird, the male of which has a long lyre-shaped tail.
ORIGIN – Latin *lyra* from Greek *lura*.

lyric /lirrik/ > *noun* **1** (also **lyrics**) the words of a song. **2** a lyric poem or verse. > *adjective* **1** (of poetry) expressing the writer's emotions, usually briefly and in stanzas or recognised forms. **2** (of a singing voice) using a light register.
ORIGIN – Greek *lurikos*, from *lura* 'lyre'.

lyrical > *adjective* **1** (of literature, art, or music) expressing emotion in an imaginative and eloquent way. **2** (of poetry) lyric. **3** relating to the words of a popular song.
IDIOMS – **wax lyrical** talk in a highly enthusiastic and effusive way.
DERIVATIVES – **lyrically** *adverb*.

lyricism > *noun* the imaginative and eloquent expression of emotion in literature, art, or music.

lyricist > *noun* a person who writes the words to popular songs.

lyrist > *noun* **1** /līrist/ a person who plays the lyre. **2** /lirrist/ a lyric poet.

lysergic acid /līserjik/ > *noun* a crystalline compound prepared from natural ergot alkaloids or synthetically, from which the drug LSD (**lysergic acid diethylamide**) can be made.
ORIGIN – from *hydrolysis* + *ergot*.

lysine /līseen/ > *noun* Biochemistry an amino acid which is a constituent of most proteins and is an essential nutrient in the diet.
ORIGIN – German *Lysin*, based on LYSIS.

lysis /līsiss/ > *noun* Biology the disintegration of a cell by rupture of the cell wall or membrane.
ORIGIN – Greek *lusis* 'loosening'.

lytic /littik/ > *adjective* Biology relating to or causing lysis.

M¹ (also **m**) > *noun* (pl. **Ms** or **M's**) **1** the thirteenth letter of the alphabet. **2** the Roman numeral for 1,000. [ORIGIN – from Latin *mille*.]

M² > *abbreviation* **1** male. **2** medium. **3** mega-. **4** Monsieur. **5** motorway.

m > *abbreviation* **1** married. **2** masculine. **3** Physics mass. **4** Chemistry meta-. **5** metre(s). **6** mile(s). **7** milli-. **8** million(s). **9** minute(s).

MA > *abbreviation* **1** Massachusetts. **2** Master of Arts.

ma > *noun* informal one's mother.

ma'am /mam, maam/ > *noun* a respectful form of address for a woman; madam.

mac > *noun* Brit. informal a mackintosh.

macabre /məkaabrə, məkaabər/ > *adjective* disturbing or horrifying because concerned with death and injury.
SYNONYMS – grisly, gruesome.

---

wordpower facts

Macabre

Macabre entered English from French in the late 19th century, originally in the phrase *Danse Macabre* or 'dance of death' (a medieval allegory in which Death leads people to the grave). The French word perhaps comes from Old French *Macabé* 'a Maccabee' (a member of a Jewish sect of the 2nd century BC led by Judas Maccabaeus), with reference to a miracle play depicting the slaughter of the Maccabees.

---

macadam /məkaddəm/ > *noun* broken stone used with tar or bitumen for surfacing roads and paths.
ORIGIN – named after the British surveyor John L. *McAdam* (1756–1836).

macadamia /makkədaymiə/ > *noun* an Australian rainforest tree that bears round edible nuts.
ORIGIN – named after the Australian chemist John *Macadam* (1827–65).

macaque /məkak/ > *noun* a medium-sized monkey with a long face and cheek pouches for holding food.

ORIGIN – from Bantu *makaku* 'some monkeys'.

macaroni /makkərōni/ > *noun* **1** pasta in the form of narrow tubes. **2** (pl. **macaronies**) an 18th-century British dandy affecting Continental fashions.
ORIGIN – Italian *maccaroni*, from Greek *makaria* 'food made from barley'.

macaronic /makəronnik/ > *adjective* (of language, especially verse) containing a mixture of words from two or more languages.

macaroon /makkərōon/ > *noun* a light biscuit made with egg white and ground almonds or coconut.
ORIGIN – French *macaron*, from Italian *maccarone* 'macaroni'.

Macassar /məkassər/ > *noun* a kind of hair oil formerly used by men.
ORIGIN – from *Makassar* (now Ujung Pandang) in Indonesia.

macaw /məkaw/ > *noun* a large long-tailed parrot with brightly coloured plumage, native to Central and South America.
ORIGIN – Portuguese *macau*.

McCarthyism > *noun* a campaign against alleged communists in the US government and other institutions carried out under Senator Joseph McCarthy from 1950 to 1954.
DERIVATIVES – **McCarthyite** adjective & noun.

McCoy > *noun* (in phrase **the real McCoy**) informal the real thing; the genuine article.
ORIGIN – perhaps from *the real Mackay*, an advertising slogan used by the whisky distillers G. Mackay and Co.; the form *McCoy* may come from the name of the American inventor Elijah *McCoy*.

mace¹ > *noun* **1** historical a heavy club with a spiked metal head. **2** a staff of office, especially the symbol of the Speaker's authority in the House of Commons. **3** (**Mace**) trademark an irritant chemical used in an aerosol to disable attackers.
ORIGIN – Old French *masse* 'large hammer'.

mace² > *noun* the reddish outer covering of the nutmeg, dried as a spice.
ORIGIN – Latin *macir*.

macédoine /massidwaan/ > *noun* a mixture of vegetables or fruit cut into small pieces.
ORIGIN – French, 'Macedonia', with reference to the mixture of peoples in the Macedonian Empire of Alexander the Great.

Macedonian /massidōniən/ > *noun* a person from the republic of Macedonia (formerly part of Yugoslavia), ancient Macedonia, or the modern Greek region of Macedonia. > *adjective* relating to Macedonia.

macerate /massərayt/ > *verb* soften or break up (food) by soaking in a liquid.
DERIVATIVES – **maceration** noun.
ORIGIN – Latin *macerare*.

McGuffin > *noun* an object or device in a film or a book which serves as a trigger for the plot.
ORIGIN – a Scottish surname, said to have been borrowed by the English film director Alfred Hitchcock from a humorous story involving such a pivotal factor.

Mach /maak, mak/ > *noun* used with a numeral (as **Mach 1**, **Mach 2**, etc.) to indicate the speed of sound, twice the speed of sound, etc.
ORIGIN – named after the Austrian physicist Ernst *Mach* (1838–1916).

machair /makkər/ > *noun* (in Scotland) low-lying coastal land formed from sand and shell fragments deposited by the wind.
ORIGIN – Scottish Gaelic.

machete /məshetti/ > *noun* a broad, heavy knife used as a tool or weapon.
ORIGIN – Spanish, from *macho* 'large hammer'.

Machiavellian /makiəvelliən/ > *adjective* cunning, scheming, and unscrupulous.
ORIGIN – from the name of the Italian statesman and writer Niccolò *Machiavelli* (1469–1527), whose work *The Prince* (1532) advises that acquiring and exercising power may require unethical methods.

machicolation /məchikkəlaysh'n/ > *noun* (in medieval fortifications) an opening between the supports of a projecting structure, through which stones or burning objects could be dropped on attackers.
DERIVATIVES – **machicolated** adjective.
ORIGIN – from Provençal *machacol*, from *macar* 'to crush' + *col* 'neck'.

machinations /mashinaysh'nz/ > *plural noun* plots and intrigues; scheming.
ORIGIN – from Latin *machinari* 'contrive', from *machina*, from Greek *mēkhanē* 'machine'.

machine > *noun* **1** an apparatus using mechanical power and having several parts, for performing a particular task. **2** an efficient and well-organised group of powerful people. > *verb* make or operate on with a machine.
SYNONYMS – **1** appliance, contraption, device.
COMBINATIONS – **machine code** (also **machine language**) a computer programming language consisting of instructions which a computer can respond to directly. **machine-readable** in a form that a computer can process. **machine tool** a fixed powered tool for cutting or shaping metal, wood, etc. **machine translation** translation carried out by a computer.
ORIGIN – Greek *mēkhanē*, from *mēkhos* 'contrivance'.

machine gun > *noun* an automatic gun that fires bullets in rapid succession for as long as the trigger is pressed. > *verb* (**machine-gun**) shoot with a machine gun.

DERIVATIVES – **machine-gunner** *noun*.

machinery > *noun* **1** machines collectively, or the components of a machine. **2** the organisation or structure of something.

machinist > *noun* a person who operates a machine or who makes machinery.

machismo /məchizmō, məkizmō/ > *noun* strong or aggressive masculine pride.

macho /machō/ > *adjective* aggressively masculine.

ORIGIN – Mexican Spanish.

mackerel > *noun* a fast-swimming sea fish with a greenish-blue back, important as a food fish.

COMBINATIONS – **mackerel sky** a sky dappled with rows of small white clouds, like the pattern on a mackerel's back.

ORIGIN – Old French *maquerel*.

mackintosh (also **macintosh**) > *noun* Brit. a full-length waterproof coat.

ORIGIN – named after the Scottish inventor Charles *Macintosh* (1766–1843).

macramé /məkraami/ > *noun* the craft of knotting cord or string in patterns to make decorative articles.

ORIGIN – French, from Turkish *makrama* 'tablecloth or towel'.

macro > *noun* (pl. **macros**) Computing a single instruction that expands automatically into a set of instructions to perform a particular task. > *adjective* large-scale; overall.

macro- > *combining form* **1** long; over a long period: *macroevolution*. **2** large or large-scale: *macrocosm*.

ORIGIN – from Greek *makros* 'long, large'.

macrobiotic /makrōbīottik/ > *adjective* (of diet) consisting of pure wholefoods, based on Buddhist principles of the balance of yin and yang.

macrocarpa /makrōkaarpə/ > *noun* a Californian cypress tree with a large spreading crown of horizontal branches.

macrocosm /makrōkoz'm/ > *noun* the whole of a complex structure, especially the world or the universe, contrasted with a small or representative part of it. Contrasted with MICROCOSM.

DERIVATIVES – **macrocosmic** *adjective*.

macroeconomics > *plural noun* (treated as sing.) the branch of economics concerned with large-scale or general economic factors, such as interest rates.

macro lens > *noun* Photography a lens suitable for taking photographs unusually close to the subject.

macromolecule > *noun* Chemistry a molecule containing a very large number of atoms, such as a protein, nucleic acid, or synthetic polymer.

DERIVATIVES – **macromolecular** *adjective*.

macron /makron/ > *noun* a written or printed mark (ˉ) used to indicate a long vowel in some languages, or a stressed vowel in verse.

macroscopic > *adjective* **1** visible to the naked eye; not microscopic. **2** relating to large-scale or general analysis.

macula /makyoolə/ > *noun* (pl. **maculae** /makyoolee/) **1** (also **macule**) a dark permanent spot on the skin. **2** an oval yellowish area near the centre of the retina in the eye, which is the region of keenest vision.

DERIVATIVES – **macular** *adjective*.

ORIGIN – Latin; related to IMMACULATE.

macumba /məkumbə/ > *noun* a religious cult practised by black people in Brazil, using sorcery, ritual dance, and fetishes.

ORIGIN – Portuguese.

mad > *adjective* (**madder, maddest**) **1** mentally ill. **2** extremely foolish or ill-advised. **3** showing impulsiveness, confusion, or frenzy. **4** informal very enthusiastic about something. **5** informal very angry. **6** (of a dog) rabid.

DERIVATIVES – **madly** *adverb* **madness** *noun*.

SYNONYMS – **1** demented, deranged, insane. **2** absurd, idiotic, ridiculous, senseless.

ANTONYMS – **1** sane.

COMBINATIONS – **madhouse 1** historical a mental institution. **2** informal a scene of extreme confusion or uproar. **madman 1** a man who is mentally ill. **2** a foolish or reckless person.

Madagascan /maddəgaskən/ > *noun* a person from Madagascar. > *adjective* relating to Madagascar.

madam /maddəm/ > *noun* **1** a polite form of address for a woman. **2** Brit. informal a conceited or precocious girl. **3** a female brothel-keeper.

ORIGIN – French *ma dame* 'my lady'.

Madame /mədaam/ > *noun* (pl. **Mesdames**) /maydaam/ a title or form of address for a French-speaking woman.

madcap > *adjective* impulsive or reckless.

mad cow disease > *noun* informal term for BSE.

madden > *verb* **1** drive insane. **2** irritate or annoy greatly.

SYNONYMS – **2** enrage, exasperate, incense, infuriate.

madder > *noun* a red dye or pigment obtained from the roots of a plant.

madding > *adjective* literary **1** acting madly; frenzied. **2** maddening.

made past and past participle of MAKE.

Madeira /mədeerə/ > *noun* a fortified white wine from the island of Madeira.

COMBINATIONS – **Madeira cake** Brit. a close-textured, rich kind of sponge cake.

Madeiran > *noun* a person from Madeira, an island in the Atlantic Ocean off NW Africa. > *adjective* relating to Madeira.

madeleine /maddəlen/ > *noun* a small rich sponge cake, often decorated with coconut and jam.

ORIGIN – probably named after *Madeleine Paulmier*, 19th-century French pastry cook.

Mademoiselle /maddəmwəzel/ > *noun* (pl. **Mesdemoiselles**) /maydamwəzel/ a title or form of address for an unmarried French-speaking woman.

made-up > *adjective* **1** wearing make-up. **2** invented; untrue.

Madonna > *noun* (**the Madonna**) the Virgin Mary.

ORIGIN – Italian, from *ma* 'my' + *donna* 'lady'.

madras /mədrass/ > *noun* **1** a strong cotton fabric, typically patterned with colourful stripes or checks. **2** a hot spiced curry dish.

ORIGIN – named after the Indian city of *Madras*.

madrigal /maddrigg'l/ > *noun* a 16th or 17th-century part song for several voices, typically unaccompanied.

ORIGIN – Italian *madrigale*, from Latin *carmen matricale* 'simple song'.

maelstrom /maylstrəm/ > *noun* **1** a powerful whirlpool. **2** a scene of confused movement or upheaval.

SYNONYMS – **2** commotion, melee, tumult.

ORIGIN – Dutch, from *maalen* 'grind, whirl' + *stroom* 'stream'.

maenad /meenad/ > *noun* (in ancient Greece) a female follower of the god Bacchus, traditionally associated with frenzied rites.

ORIGIN – Greek *Mainas*, from *mainesthai* 'to rave'.

maestro /mīstrō/ > *noun* (pl. **maestri** /mīstri/ or **maestros**) **1** a distinguished male conductor or performer of classical music. **2** a distinguished man in any sphere.

ORIGIN – Italian, 'master'.

Mae West > *noun* informal, dated an inflatable life jacket.

ORIGIN – named (by RAF personnel during the Second World War) after the American film actress *Mae West* (1892–1980), noted for her large bust.

MAFF > *abbreviation* (in the UK) Ministry of Agriculture, Fisheries, and Food.

Mafia > *noun* **1** (**the Mafia**) an international criminal organisation originating in Sicily. **2** (**mafia**) a group exerting a hidden sinister influence.

WORDFINDER – Camorra (*Neapolitan Mafia*); Cosa Nostra (*US Mafia*); capo, godfather (*leader of US Mafia*), goodfella

(*US informal term for a Mafia gangster*), omertà (*Mafia code of silence*).

ORIGIN – Italian, originally meaning 'bragging'.

Mafioso /maffiōsō/ > *noun* (pl. **Mafiosi** /maffiōsi/) a member of the Mafia.

magazine > *noun* **1** a periodical publication containing articles and illustrations. **2** a regular television or radio programme comprising a variety of items. **3** a chamber holding a supply of cartridges to be fed automatically to the breech of a gun. **4** a store for arms, ammunition, and explosives.

---

wordpower facts

Magazine

The term **magazine** comes from the French word *magasin*, which derives from an Arabic word meaning 'storehouse'. In the 16th century **magazine** in English meant 'store' and was often used in the title of books providing information for particular groups of people, giving rise to sense 1. The sense 'a store for arms, ammunition, and explosives' was a specialised 16th-century use of sense 1, and gave rise to sense 3 during the 18th century.

---

magdalen /**mag**dəlin/ > *noun* archaic a reformed prostitute.

ORIGIN – from the name of St Mary *Magdalene* (to whom Jesus appeared after his resurrection), who is commonly identified (probably wrongly) with the sinner who washed and anointed Christ's feet (Gospel of Luke, chapter 7).

magenta /məˈjentə/ > *noun* **1** a light mauvish crimson. **2** the dye fuchsin.

ORIGIN – named after *Magenta* in Italy, site of a battle (1859) fought shortly before the dye was discovered.

maggot > *noun* a soft-bodied legless larva, especially one of a fly or other insect and found in decaying matter.

magi plural of MAGUS.

magic > *noun* **1** the power of apparently influencing events by using mysterious or supernatural forces. **2** conjuring tricks performed to entertain. **3** a mysterious and enchanting quality. **4** informal exceptional skill or talent. > *adjective* **1** having or apparently having supernatural powers. **2** informal very exciting or good. > *verb* (**magicked**, **magicking**) move, change, or create by or as if by magic.

WORDFINDER – abracadabra, incantation, rune, wand (*used in casting magic spells*), amulet, fetish, juju, talisman (*objects thought to have magical powers*), black magic, devilry,

necromancy, satanism, voodoo, white magic (*types of magic*), grimoire (*book of magic spells*), hex, mojo (*magic spells or charms*).

SYNONYMS – **1** enchantment, sorcery, witchcraft, wizardry. **2** legerdemain, prestidigitation. **3** allure, charm, enchantment, fascination, glamour.

COMBINATIONS – **magic bullet** informal a medicine or other remedy with advanced and highly specific properties. **magic carpet** a mythical carpet that is able to transport people through the air. **magic lantern** a simple form of projector formerly used for showing photographic slides. **magic mushroom** informal a toadstool with hallucinogenic properties if eaten. **magic realism** a literary genre in which realistic narrative is combined with surreal elements of dream or fantasy.

ORIGIN – from Greek *magikē tekhnē* 'art of a magus': magi were regarded as magicians.

magical > *adjective* **1** relating to, using, or resembling magic. **2** beautiful or delightful in a way that seems removed from everyday life.

DERIVATIVES – **magically** adverb.

magician > *noun* **1** a person with magical powers. **2** a conjuror.

SYNONYMS – **1** magus, sorcerer, warlock, witch, wizard.

magick > *noun* archaic spelling of MAGIC.

magisterial /majiˈsteeriəl/ > *adjective* **1** very authoritative. **2** domineering; dictatorial. **3** relating to a magistrate.

DERIVATIVES – **magisterially** adverb.

SYNONYMS – **1** masterful, lordly.

ORIGIN – from Latin *magister* 'master'.

magistracy /**ma**jistrəsi/ > *noun* (pl. **magistracies**) **1** the office or authority of a magistrate. **2** magistrates collectively.

magistrate > *noun* a civil officer who administers the law, especially one who conducts a court concerned with minor offences and holds preliminary hearings for more serious ones.

WORDFINDER – *types of magistrate:* archon (*in ancient Athens*), consul (*in ancient Rome*), doge (*formerly in Venice or Genoa*), jurat (*in the Channel Islands*), reeve (*in Anglo-Saxon England*), sharif (*in an Islamic country*).

ORIGIN – Latin *magistratus* 'administrator', from *magister* 'master'.

maglev /**mag**lev/ > *noun* a transport system in which trains glide above a track, supported by magnetic repulsion and propelled by a linear motor.

ORIGIN – short for *magnetic levitation*.

magma /**mag**mə/ > *noun* hot fluid or semi-fluid material within the earth's crust, from which lava and other igneous rock is formed by cooling.

ORIGIN – Greek, from *massein* 'knead'.

Magna Carta /magnə **kaar**tə/ > *noun* a

charter of liberty and political rights granted by King John of England in 1215.

ORIGIN – Latin, 'great charter'.

magna cum laude /magnə ko͝om **low**day/ > *adverb* & *adjective* chiefly N. Amer. with great distinction.

ORIGIN – Latin, 'with great praise'.

magnanimous /magˈnannimᵊss/ > *adjective* generous or forgiving, especially towards a rival or less powerful person.

DERIVATIVES – **magnanimity** /magnəˈnimmiti/ *noun* **magnanimously** adverb.

SYNONYMS – benevolent, charitable, generous.

ANTONYMS – mean-spirited, vindictive.

ORIGIN – from Latin *magnus* 'great' + *animus* 'soul'.

magnate /**mag**nayt/ > *noun* a wealthy and influential person, especially in business.

SYNONYMS – baron, mogul, tycoon.

ORIGIN – Latin *magnas* 'great man'.

magnesia /magˈneezhə, magˈneeziə/ > *noun* **1** magnesium oxide. **2** hydrated magnesium carbonate used as an antacid and laxative.

ORIGIN – Greek, denoting a mineral from Magnesia in Asia Minor.

magnesium /magˈneeziəm/ > *noun* a silvery-white metallic chemical element which burns with a brilliant white flame.

magnet > *noun* **1** a piece of iron or other material that has the property of attracting similar objects or aligning itself in an external magnetic field. **2** a person or thing that has a powerful attraction: *the white sand is a magnet for sun worshippers.*

ORIGIN – from Greek *magnēs lithos* 'lodestone'.

magnetic > *adjective* **1** having the property of magnetism. **2** very attractive or alluring.

DERIVATIVES – **magnetically** adverb.

SYNONYMS – **2** captivating, entrancing, hypnotic, mesmeric.

COMBINATIONS – **magnetic equator** the irregular imaginary line, passing round the earth near the equator, on which a magnetic needle has no dip. **magnetic field** a region around a magnet within which the force of magnetism acts. **magnetic north** the direction in which the north end of a compass needle will point in response to the earth's magnetic field. **magnetic pole 1** each of the points near the extremities of the axis of rotation of the earth where a magnetic needle dips vertically. **2** each of the two points of a magnet to and from which the lines of magnetic force are directed. **magnetic resonance imaging** a technique for producing images of bodily organs by measuring the properties of atomic nuclei in a strong magnetic field. **magnetic storm** a disturbance of the magnetic field of the earth. **magnetic tape** tape used to record sound, pictures, or computer data.

magnetise (also **magnetize**) > *verb* make magnetic.

magnetism > *noun* **1** the property displayed by magnets and produced by the motion of electric charges, which results in attraction or repulsion between objects. **2** the ability to attract and charm people.
SYNONYMS – **2** allure, charm, seductiveness.

magnetite > *noun* a grey-black, naturally magnetic mineral which is an important form of iron ore.

magneto /magˈneetō/ > *noun* (pl. **magnetos**) a small electric generator containing a permanent magnet and used to provide high-voltage pulses, especially (formerly) in the ignition systems of internal-combustion engines.

magnetohydrodynamics /magneetō-hīdrōdīˈnammiks/ > *plural noun* (treated as sing.) the branch of physics concerned with the behaviour of an electrically conducting fluid in a magnetic field.
DERIVATIVES – **magnetohydrodynamic** *adjective*.

magnetometer /magniˈtommitər/ > *noun* an instrument used for measuring magnetic forces, especially the earth's magnetism.

magnetosphere /magˈneetəsfeer/ > *noun* the region surrounding the earth or another body in which its magnetic field is predominant.

magnetron /ˈmagnitron/ > *noun* an electron tube for amplifying or generating microwaves, with the flow of electrons controlled by an external magnetic field.

Magnificat /magˈniffikat/ > *noun* (in the Christian Church) the hymn of the Virgin Mary (Gospel of Luke, chapter 1) used as a canticle, especially at vespers and evensong.
ORIGIN – Latin, 'magnifies', from the opening words, which translate as 'my soul magnifies the Lord'.

magnificent > *adjective* **1** impressively beautiful, elaborate, or extravagant. **2** very good; excellent.
DERIVATIVES – **magnificence** *noun* **magnificently** *adverb*.
SYNONYMS – **1** excellent, glorious, majestic, superb, very good.
ORIGIN – Latin *magnificus*, from *magnus* 'great'.

magnify > *verb* (**magnifies**, **magnified**) **1** make (something) appear larger than it is, especially with a lens or microscope. **2** intensify or exaggerate. **3** archaic extol; glorify.
DERIVATIVES – **magnification** *noun* **magnifier** *noun*.
COMBINATIONS – **magnifying glass** a lens that produces an enlarged image, used to examine small or finely detailed things.

magniloquent /magˈnilləkwənt/ > *adjective* formal using high-flown language.

magnitude > *noun* **1** great size, extent, or importance. **2** size. **3 Astronomy** the brightness of a star, as represented by a number on a logarithmic scale.
SYNONYMS – **1** immensity, significance, weight.

magnolia > *noun* **1** a tree or shrub with large waxy flowers. **2** a pale creamy-white colour like that of magnolia flowers.
ORIGIN – named after the French botanist Pierre *Magnol* (1638–1715).

magnox > *noun* a magnesium-based alloy used to enclose uranium fuel elements in some nuclear reactors.

magnum > *noun* (pl. **magnums**) **1** a wine bottle of twice the standard size, normally 1.5 litres. **2** (trademark in the US) a gun designed to fire cartridges that are more powerful than its calibre would suggest.
ORIGIN – Latin, 'great thing'.

magnum opus /ˈmagnəm ˈōpəss/ > *noun* (pl. **magnum opuses** or **magna opera**) a large and important work of art, music, or literature, especially a person's most important work.
ORIGIN – Latin, 'great work'.

magpie > *noun* **1** a long-tailed bird of the crow family with pied plumage and a raucous voice. **2** a black-and-white Australian butcher bird with musical calls. **3** a person who obsessively collects things or who chatters idly.
ORIGIN – probably a shortening of dialect *maggot the pie*, *maggoty-pie*, from *Magot*, a former familiar form of the name *Marguerite*, + obsolete *pie* 'magpie', from Latin *pica* 'magpie'.

magsman > *noun* Austral. informal a confidence trickster.
ORIGIN – from English dialect *mag* 'prattle'.

maguey /ˈmagway/ > *noun* an agave plant, especially one whose sap can be made into the drink pulque.
ORIGIN – Taino (an extinct Caribbean language).

magus /ˈmaygəss/ > *noun* (pl. **magi** /ˈmayjī/) **1** a member of a priestly class of ancient Persia. **2** a sorcerer. **3** (**the Magi**) the three wise men from the East who brought gifts to the infant Jesus.
ORIGIN – Latin, from Old Persian.

Magyar /ˈmagyaar/ > *noun* **1** a member of the predominant ethnic group in Hungary. **2** the Hungarian language.
ORIGIN – the name in Hungarian.

maharaja /maahəˈraajə/ (also **maharajah**) > *noun* historical an Indian prince.
ORIGIN – Hindi, from Sanskrit, 'great raja'.

maharani /maahəˈraani/ > *noun* a maharaja's wife or widow.

ORIGIN – Hindi, from Sanskrit, 'great queen'.

maharishi /maahəˈrishi/ > *noun* a great Hindu sage or spiritual leader.
ORIGIN – Sanskrit, 'great sage or saint'.

mahatma /məˈhatmə/ > *noun* (in the Indian subcontinent) a holy person or sage.
ORIGIN – Sanskrit, 'great soul'.

Mahayana /maahəˈyaanə/ > *noun* one of the two major traditions of Buddhism (the other being Theravada), practised especially in China, Tibet, Japan, and Korea.
ORIGIN – Sanskrit, 'great vehicle'.

Mahdi /ˈmaadi/ > *noun* (pl. **Mahdis**) (in popular Muslim belief) a leader who will rule before the end of the world and restore religion and justice.
ORIGIN – Arabic, 'he who is guided in the right way'.

Mahican /məˈhikən/ > *noun* a member of an American Indian people formerly inhabiting the Upper Hudson Valley. See box at **MOHICAN²**. > *adjective* relating to the Mahicans.
ORIGIN – the name in the extinct Mahican language, said to mean 'wolf'.

mah-jong /maaˈjong/ (also **mah-jongg**) > *noun* a Chinese game played with 136 or 144 rectangular tiles.
ORIGIN – Chinese dialect, 'sparrows'.

mahogany /məˈhoggəni/ > *noun* **1** hard reddish-brown wood from a tropical tree, used for furniture. **2** a rich reddish-brown colour.

mahonia /məˈhōniə/ > *noun* an evergreen shrub with clusters of small fragrant yellow flowers.
ORIGIN – named after the American botanist Bernard McMahon (c.1775–1816).

mahout /məˈhowt/ > *noun* (in the Indian subcontinent and SE Asia) a person who works with and rides an elephant.
ORIGIN – Hindi.

maid > *noun* **1** a female domestic servant. **2** archaic or literary a girl or young woman.
COMBINATIONS – **maid of honour 1** an unmarried noblewoman attending a queen or princess. **2** N. Amer. a principal bridesmaid. **maidservant** dated a female domestic servant.

maiden > *noun* **1** archaic or literary a girl or young woman. **2** archaic or literary a virgin. **3** (also **maiden over**) Cricket an over in which no runs are scored. > *adjective* **1** (of an older woman) unmarried. **2** first of its kind: *a maiden voyage*.
COMBINATIONS – **maiden name** the surname of a married woman before her marriage.

maidenhair fern > *noun* a fern of delicate appearance with slender-stalked fronds and rounded divided lobes.

maidenhead > *noun* archaic **1** a girl's or woman's virginity. **2** the hymen.

mail¹ > *noun* **1** letters and parcels sent by post. **2** the postal system. **3** email. > *verb* **1** send by post. **2** send post or email to.

COMBINATIONS – **mailbag** a large sack or bag for carrying mail. **mailbox 1** chiefly N. Amer. a box on a post at the entrance to a person's property, into which mail is delivered. **2** chiefly N. Amer. a post box. **3** a computer file in which email messages are stored. **mailman** N. Amer. a postman. **mail order** the ordering of goods by post.

ORIGIN – first meaning 'travelling bag': from Old French *male* 'wallet'.

mail² > *noun* historical flexible armour made of metal rings or plates.

ORIGIN – Old French *maille*, from Latin *macula* 'spot or mesh'.

mailer > *noun* **1** chiefly N. Amer. the sender of a letter or package by post. **2** Computing a program that sends email messages.

mailing > *noun* something sent by mail, especially a piece of mass advertising.

COMBINATIONS – **mailing list** a list of the names and addresses of people to whom advertising matter or information may be mailed regularly.

maillot /mīyō/ > *noun* (pl. pronunc. same) **1** a pair of tights worn for dancing or gymnastics. **2** a jersey or top worn in cycling. **3** chiefly N. Amer. a woman's one-piece swimsuit.

ORIGIN – French.

mailshot > *noun* Brit. a piece of advertising material, sent to a large number of addresses.

maim > *verb* wound or injure (someone) so that part of the body is permanently damaged.

SYNONYMS – cripple, disable, incapacitate.
ORIGIN – Old French *mahaignier*.

main > *adjective* chief in size or importance. > *noun* **1** a principal water or gas pipe or electricity cable. **2** (**the mains**) Brit. public water, gas, or electricity supply through pipes or cables. **3** (**the main**) archaic or literary the open ocean.

IDIOMS – **by main force** through sheer strength. **in the main** on the whole.

SYNONYMS – *adjective* chief, foremost, key, principal.

ANTONYMS – *adjective* minor, subsidiary.

COMBINATIONS – **main brace** the rope attached to the main yard of a sailing ship. **main drag** informal, chiefly N. Amer. the main street of a town. **main man** N. Amer. informal a close and trusted friend.

mainframe > *noun* **1** a large high-speed computer, especially one supporting numerous workstations. **2** the central processing unit and primary memory of a computer.

mainland > *noun* a large continuous extent of land as opposed to offshore islands and detached territories.

DERIVATIVES – **mainlander** *noun*.

main line > *noun* **1** a chief railway line. **2** informal a principal vein as a site for a drug injection. > *verb* (**mainline**) informal inject (a drug) intravenously.

DERIVATIVES – **mainliner** *noun*.

mainly > *adverb* more than anything else; for the most part.

SYNONYMS – largely, predominantly, principally.

mainmast > *noun* the principal mast of a ship.

mainspring > *noun* **1** the principal spring in a watch, clock, etc. **2** a prime source of motivation or support.

mainstay > *noun* **1** a stay which extends from the maintop to the foot of the foremast of a sailing ship. **2** the chief support or main part.

SYNONYMS – **2** backbone, bulwark, centrepiece, linchpin.

mainstream > *noun* (**the mainstream**) normal or conventional ideas, attitudes, or activities. > *adjective* belonging to or characteristic of the mainstream.

maintain > *verb* **1** cause or enable (a condition or state of affairs) to continue. **2** keep (a building, machine, etc.) in good condition by checking or repairing it regularly. **3** provide with necessities for life or existence. **4** assert to be the case.

SYNONYMS – **1** keep up, preserve, sustain. **3** keep, nurture, support, sustain. **4** declare, pronounce, state.

COMBINATIONS – **maintained school** Brit. a school financed with public money.

ORIGIN – Old French *maintenir*, from Latin *manu tenere* 'hold in the hand'.

maintenance > *noun* **1** the process of maintaining or being maintained. **2** provision for one's former husband or wife after divorce.

maintop > *noun* a platform around the head of the lower section of a sailing ship's mainmast.

maintopmast /mayntopməst/ > *noun* the second section of a sailing ship's mainmast.

maiolica /məyollikə/ > *noun* fine Italian earthenware with coloured decoration on an opaque white glaze.

ORIGIN – Italian, from *Maiolica* 'Majorca' (from or via where such earthenware was shipped).

maisonette /mayzənet/ > *noun* a set of rooms for living in, typically on two storeys of a larger building.

ORIGIN – French *maisonnette* 'small house'.

maître d'hôtel /maytrə dōtel/ (also **maître d'** /maytrə dee/) > *noun* (pl. **maîtres d'hôtel** pronunc. same, **maître d's**) **1** the head waiter of a restaurant. **2** the manager of a hotel.

ORIGIN – French, 'master of the house'.

maize > *noun* chiefly Brit. a cereal plant yielding large grains (corn or sweetcorn) set in rows on a cob.

ORIGIN – Spanish *maíz*, from Taino (an extinct Caribbean language).

majestic > *adjective* impressively beautiful or dignified.

DERIVATIVES – **majestically** *adverb*.

SYNONYMS – grand, imposing, magnificent, stately.

majesty > *noun* (pl. **majesties**) **1** impressive dignity or beauty. **2** royal power. **3** (**His, Your,** etc. **Majesty**) a title given to a sovereign or a sovereign's wife or widow.

SYNONYMS – **1** grandeur, magnificence, splendour.

ORIGIN – Latin *majestas*, from *major* 'major'.

majolica /məjollikə/ > *noun* a kind of earthenware made in imitation of Italian maiolica, especially in England during the 19th century.

major > *adjective* **1** important, serious, or significant. **2** greater or more important; main. **3** Music based on intervals of a semitone between the third and fourth, and seventh and eighth degrees. Contrasted with MINOR. > *noun* **1** a rank of officer in the army and the US air force, above captain and below lieutenant colonel. **2** an officer in charge of a section of band instruments. **3** Music a major key, interval, or scale. **4** N. Amer. a student's principal subject or course. **5** N. Amer. a student specialising in a specified subject. > *verb* (**major in**) N. Amer. & Austral./NZ specialise in (a particular subject) at college or university.

COMBINATIONS – **major general** a rank of officer in the army and the US air force, above brigadier or brigadier general and below lieutenant general. **major league** N. Amer. the highest-ranking league in a particular professional sport, especially baseball. **major planet** any of the nine principal planets of the solar system, as distinct from an asteroid or moon. **major prophet** any of the prophets after whom the longer prophetic books of the Bible are named: Isaiah, Jeremiah, and Ezekiel.

ORIGIN – Latin, comparative of *magnus* 'great'.

Majorcan /məyorkən/ > *noun* a person from Majorca in the Balearic Islands. > *adjective* relating to Majorca.

major-domo /mayjərdōmō/ > *noun* (pl. **major-domos**) the chief steward of a large household.

ORIGIN – Spanish and Italian, from Latin *major domus* 'highest official of the household'.

majoritarian > *adjective* governed by or believing in decision by a majority.

majority > *noun* (pl. **majorities**) **1** the greater number. **2** Brit. the number by which the votes cast for one party or candidate exceed those for the next. **3** the age when a person is legally considered a full adult, usually 18 or 21.

USAGE – strictly speaking, **majority** should be used with plural nouns to mean 'the greater number', as in *the majority of cases*. Use with nouns that do not take a plural, to mean 'the greatest part', as in *she ate the majority of the meal*, is not considered good English.

ANTONYMS – **1** minority.

COMBINATIONS – **majority rule** the principle that the greater number should exercise greater power. **majority verdict** English Law a verdict agreed by all but one or two of the members of a jury.

majuscule /**maj**əskyōol/ > *noun* a large letter, either capital or uncial.

ORIGIN – from Latin *majuscula littera* 'somewhat greater letter'.

make > *verb* (past and past participle **made**) **1** form by putting parts together or combining substances. **2** cause to be or come about. **3** force to do something. **4** (**make into**) alter (something) so that it forms (something else). **5** constitute, amount to, or serve as. **6** estimate as or decide on. **7** gain or earn (money or profit). **8** arrive at or achieve. **9** (**make it**) become successful. **10** prepare to go in a particular direction or do a particular thing: *he made towards the car.* **11** arrange bedclothes tidily on (a bed) ready for use. > *noun* the manufacturer or trade name of a product.

IDIOMS – **have** (**got**) **it made** informal be in a position where success is certain. **make after** pursue. **make away with 1** another way of saying *make off with.* **2** kill furtively and illicitly. **make do** manage with the limited means available. **make for 1** move towards. **2** tend to result in or be received as. **3** (**be made for**) be eminently suited for. **make it up to** compensate for unfair treatment. **make of 1** ascribe (a specified amount of attention or importance) to. **2** gain (understanding) of: *they stared at the stone but could make nothing of it.* **make off** leave hurriedly. **make off with** carry away illicitly. **make or break** be the factor which decides whether (something) will succeed or fail. **make out 1** manage with difficulty to see, hear, or understand. **2** represent as or pretend. **3** draw up (a list or document). **4** informal make progress; fare. **make over 1** transfer the possession of. **2** give (someone) a new image with cosmetics, hairstyling, and clothes. **make sail** spread a sail or sails, especially to begin a voyage. **make time** find an occasion when time is available to do something. **make up 1** put together or prepare from parts or ingredients. **2** concoct or invent (a story). **3** (also **make up for**) compensate for. **4** be reconciled after a quarrel. **5** apply cosmetics to. **make up one's mind** make a decision. **make way** allow room for someone or something else. **on the make** informal **1** intent on gain. **2** looking for a sexual partner.

SYNONYMS – **1** build, construct, manufacture, produce. **2** bring about, cause, generate. **3** coerce, compel, impel.

make-believe > *noun* a state of fantasy or pretence. > *adjective* imitating something real; pretend. > *verb* (**make believe**) pretend; imagine.

makeover > *noun* a complete transformation of a person's appearance with cosmetics, hairstyling, etc.

maker > *noun* **1** a person or thing that makes something. **2** (**our**, **the**, etc. **Maker**) God.

IDIOMS – **meet one's Maker** chiefly humorous die.

makeshift > *adjective* interim and temporary. > *noun* a temporary substitute or device.

make-up > *noun* **1** cosmetics applied to the face. **2** composition or constitution. **3** Printing the arrangement of type, illustrations, etc. on a printed page.

makeweight > *noun* **1** something put on a scale to make up the required weight. **2** an extra person or thing needed to complete something.

making > *noun* **1** the process of making something. **2** (**makings**) the necessary qualities.

IDIOMS – **be the making of** bring about the success or favourable development of.

mako /**maa**kō/ > *noun* (pl. **makos**) a large shark with a deep blue back and white underparts.

ORIGIN – Maori.

makuta plural of **LIKUTA**.

makutu /məkōōtōō/ > *noun* NZ a magic spell.

ORIGIN – Maori.

mal- > *combining form* **1** to an unpleasant degree: *malodorous.* **2** in a faulty or improper manner: *malfunction.* **3** not: *maladroit.*

ORIGIN – from Latin *male* 'badly'.

malacca /məlakkə/ > *noun* a walking stick made of cane obtained from a Malaysian palm.

ORIGIN – from the name *Malacca* (or Melaka), a state of Malaysia.

malachite /**mal**əkīt/ > *noun* a bright green copper-containing mineral.

ORIGIN – Old French *melochite*, from Greek *malakhē* 'mallow'.

maladjusted > *adjective* failing to cope with the demands of a normal social environment.

maladminister > *verb* formal manage or administer badly or dishonestly.

DERIVATIVES – **maladministration** *noun.*

maladroit /maləcroyt/ > *adjective* clumsy and inept.

SYNONYMS – clumsy, incompetent, inept, unskilful.

ANTONYMS – adroit, skilful.

ORIGIN – French.

malady /**mal**ədi/ > *noun* (pl. **maladies**) a disease or ailment.

ORIGIN – from Old French *malade* 'ill'.

Malagasy /maləgassi/ > *noun* (pl. same or **Malagasies**) **1** a person from Madagascar. **2** the language of Madagascar.

malaise /məlayz/ > *noun* a general feeling of unease, ill health, or low spirits.

ORIGIN – French.

malapert /**mal**əpert/ > *adjective* archaic presumptuous and impudent.

ORIGIN – from **MAL-** + archaic *apert* 'insolent'.

malapropism /**mal**əproppiz'm/ (US also **malaprop**) > *noun* the mistaken use of a word in place of a similar-sounding one (e.g. 'dance a *flamingo*' instead of *flamenco*).

ORIGIN – from the name of the character Mrs *Malaprop* in Richard Sheridan's play *The Rivals* (1775).

malaria > *noun* a disease characterised by recurrent attacks of fever, caused by a blood parasite transmitted by mosquitoes in tropical and subtropical regions.

DERIVATIVES – **malarial** *adjective.*

ORIGIN – from Italian *mala aria* 'bad air' (the disease was formerly attributed to unhealthy vapours given off by marshes).

malarkey /məlaarki/ > *noun* informal nonsense; silliness.

malathion /maləthīən/ > *noun* a synthetic insecticide containing phosphorus, relatively harmless to plants and other animals.

ORIGIN – from elements of its chemical name.

Malawian /məlaawiən/ > *noun* a person from Malawi in south central Africa. > *adjective* relating to Malawi.

Malay /məlay/ > *noun* **1** a member of a people inhabiting Malaysia and Indonesia. **2** the Austronesian language of the Malays.

Malayan > *noun* another term for **MALAY**. > *adjective* relating to Malays or Malaya (now part of Malaysia).

Malaysian > *noun* a person from Malaysia. > *adjective* relating to Malaysia.

malcontent /**mal**kəntent/ > *noun* a discontented person.

mal de mer /mal də **mair**/ > *noun* seasickness.

ORIGIN – French.

Maldivian /mawl**div**viən/ > *noun* a person from the Maldives, a country consisting of a chain of islands in the Indian Ocean. > *adjective* relating to the Maldives.

male > *adjective* **1** relating to the sex that can fertilise or inseminate the female to give rise to offspring. **2** relating to or characteristic of men. **3** (of a plant or flower) bearing stamens but lacking functional pistils. **4** (of a fitting) manufactured to fit inside a corresponding female part. > *noun* a male person, animal, or plant.
DERIVATIVES – **maleness** *noun*.
ORIGIN – Old French *masle*, from Latin *masculus*, from *mas* 'a male'.

malediction /malidiksh'n/ > *noun* a curse.
ORIGIN – from Latin *maledicere* 'speak evil of'.

malefactor /malifaktər/ > *noun* formal a person who commits a crime or other misdeed.
ORIGIN – from Latin *malefacere* 'do wrong'.

malevolent /məlevvələnt/ > *adjective* wishing evil to others.
DERIVATIVES – **malevolence** *noun* **malevolently** *adverb*.
SYNONYMS – baleful, malicious, malign.
ANTONYMS – benevolent.
ORIGIN – Latin, from *male* 'ill' + *velle* 'to wish'.

malfeasance /malfeez'nss/ > *noun* Law wrongdoing, especially (US) by a public official.
ORIGIN – Old French *malfaisance*.

malformation > *noun* abnormality of shape or form in a part of the body.
DERIVATIVES – **malformed** *adjective*.

malfunction > *verb* (of a piece of equipment or machinery) fail to function normally. > *noun* a failure of this type.

Malian /maaliən/ > *noun* a person from Mali, a country in West Africa. > *adjective* relating to Mali.

malice > *noun* the desire to do harm to someone; ill will.
SYNONYMS – animosity, hostility, ill will, spite.
COMBINATIONS – **malice aforethought** Law the intention to kill or harm, held to distinguish murder from unlawful killing.
ORIGIN – Old French, from Latin *malus* 'bad'.

malicious > *adjective* characterised by malice; intending or intended to do harm.
DERIVATIVES – **maliciously** *adverb* **maliciousness** *noun*.
SYNONYMS – malevolent, nasty, spiteful, vicious.

malign /məlīn/ > *adjective* harmful or evil. > *verb* speak ill of.
DERIVATIVES – **malignity** /məligniti/ *noun* **malignly** *adverb*.

SYNONYMS – *verb* denigrate, disparage, vilify.
ORIGIN – Latin *malignus* 'tending to evil'.

malignancy > *noun* (pl. **malignancies**) **1** the presence of a malignant tumour; cancer. **2** a cancerous growth. **3** the quality of being malign or malevolent.

malignant > *adjective* **1** harmful; malevolent. **2** (of a tumour) tending to invade normal tissue or to recur after removal; cancerous. Contrasted with **BENIGN**.
SYNONYMS – **1** harmful, malevolent, malicious, malign, spiteful.
ORIGIN – from Latin *malignare* 'contrive maliciously'; the word was first used in English to mean 'likely to rebel against God or authority' and during the English Civil War (1642–9) was used to describe royalist sympathisers.

malinger /məlinggər/ > *verb* exaggerate or feign illness in order to escape duty or work.
DERIVATIVES – **malingerer** *noun*.
ORIGIN – from French *malingre* 'weak, sickly'.

mall /mal, mawl/ > *noun* **1** a large enclosed shopping area from which traffic is excluded. **2** a sheltered walk or promenade.
ORIGIN – probably a shortening of **PALL-MALL**: the modern uses derive from *The Mall*, a walkway in St James's Park, London, formerly the site of an alley where the game of pall-mall was played.

mallard > *noun* a common duck, the male of which has a dark green head and white collar.
ORIGIN – Old French, 'wild drake', from *masle* 'male'.

malleable /maliəb'l/ > *adjective* **1** able to be hammered or pressed into shape without breaking or cracking. **2** (of a person) easily influenced.
DERIVATIVES – **malleability** *noun*.
SYNONYMS – **2** biddable, impressionable, suggestible, tractable.
ORIGIN – from Latin *malleus* 'a hammer'.

mallee /mali/ > *noun* a low-growing bushy Australian eucalyptus.
ORIGIN – from an Aboriginal language.

mallet > *noun* **1** a hammer with a large wooden head. **2** a long-handled wooden stick with a head like a hammer, for hitting a croquet or polo ball.
ORIGIN – Old French *maillet*, from Latin *malleus* 'hammer'.

mallow > *noun* a herbaceous plant with pink or purple flowers.
ORIGIN – Latin *malva*; related to **MAUVE**.

malmsey /maamzi/ > *noun* a sweet fortified Madeira wine.
ORIGIN – first denoting a strong, sweet

white wine imported from Greece: from *Monemvasia*, a port in Greece .

malnourished > *adjective* suffering from malnutrition.
DERIVATIVES – **malnourishment** *noun*.

malnutrition > *noun* lack of proper nutrition.

malocclusion > *noun* Dentistry imperfect positioning of the teeth when the jaws are closed.

malodorous > *adjective* smelling very unpleasant.
SYNONYMS – fetid, foul-smelling, rank.
ANTONYMS – fragrant.

malpractice > *noun* improper, illegal, or negligent action or dealings by a lawyer, doctor, public official, etc.

malt > *noun* barley or other grain that has been steeped, germinated, and dried, used for brewing or distilling. > *verb* **1** convert (grain) into malt. **2** (**malted**) mixed with malt or a malt extract.
COMBINATIONS – **malt liquor** alcoholic liquor made from malt by fermentation rather than distillation, for example beer. **malt whisky** whisky made only from malted barley and not blended with grain whisky.

Maltese /mawlteez/ > *noun* (pl. same) a person from Malta. > *adjective* relating to Malta.
COMBINATIONS – **Maltese cross** a cross with arms of equal length which broaden from the centre and have their ends indented in a shallow V-shape.

Malthusian /malthyoozian/ > *adjective* relating to the theory of the English economist Thomas Malthus (1766–1834) that the population, if not controlled, tends to increase more rapidly than its means of subsistence. > *noun* an adherent of Malthus's theory.

maltose > *noun* a sugar produced by the breakdown of starch, e.g. by enzymes found in malt and saliva.

maltreat > *verb* treat badly or brutally.
DERIVATIVES – **maltreatment** *noun*.
SYNONYMS – abuse, exploit, mistreat.

maltster > *noun* a person who makes malt.

malversation /malvərsaysh'n/ > *noun* formal corrupt behaviour by a person in public office or a position of trust.

mama (also **mamma**) > *noun* dated or N. Amer. one's mother.

mamba > *noun* a large, agile, highly poisonous African snake.
ORIGIN – Zulu.

mambo > *noun* (pl. **mambos**) a Latin American dance similar to the rumba.
ORIGIN – American Spanish.

mammal > *noun* a warm-blooded vertebrate animal that has hair or fur, secretes milk, and (typically) gives birth to live young.
WORDFINDER – marsupials, insectivores, bats, primates, carnivores, cetaceans, ungulates, rodents (*the main groups of mammals*).
DERIVATIVES – **mammalian** *adjective*.
ORIGIN – from Latin *mamma* 'breast'.

mammary /**mamm**əri/ > *adjective* of or relating to the human female breasts or the milk-secreting organs of other mammals. > *noun* (**mammaries**) humorous breasts.

mammogram /**mamm**əgram/ > *noun* an image obtained by mammography.

mammography /ma**mog**rəfi/ > *noun* a technique using X-rays to diagnose and locate tumours of the breasts.

Mammon > *noun* wealth regarded as an evil influence or false object of worship.
ORIGIN – New Testament Greek *mamōnas*, from an Aramaic word meaning 'riches'; see the Gospels of Matthew, chapter 6, and Luke, chapter 16.

mammoth > *noun* a large extinct form of elephant with a hairy coat and long curved tusks. > *adjective* huge; enormous.
ORIGIN – Russian.

mammy > *noun* (pl. **mammies**) informal **1** a child's name for their mother. **2** offensive (formerly in the US) a black nursemaid or nanny in charge of white children.

man > *noun* (pl. **men**) **1** an adult human male. **2** a male member of a workforce, team, etc. **3** a husband or lover. **4** a person. **5** human beings in general. **6** a figure or token used in a board game. > *verb* (**manned**, **manning**) provide (a place or machine) with the personnel to run, operate, or defend it. > *exclamation* informal, chiefly N. Amer. used for emphasis or to express surprise, admiration, or delight.
IDIOMS – **man about town** a fashionable and sociable man. **every man for himself and the devil take the hindmost** proverb everyone should (or does) look after their own interests rather than considering those of others. **man and boy** from childhood. **the man in the street** the average man. **man of the cloth** a clergyman. **man of God** a clergyman. **man of letters** a male scholar or author. **man of straw** (also **straw man**) **1** a person who is a sham. **2** a person undertaking a financial commitment without adequate means. **to a man** without exception.
COMBINATIONS – **man-at-arms** archaic a soldier. **manhole** a covered opening allowing access to a sewer or other underground structure. **man-made** made or caused by human beings. **manservant** a

male servant. **mantrap** a trap for catching people. **men's room** chiefly N. Amer. a men's toilet in a public or institutional building.

wordpower facts

Man

Traditionally the word **man** has been used to refer not only to adult males but also to human beings in general. There is a historical explanation for this: in Old English the principal sense of **man** was 'a human being', and the words **wer** and **wif** were used to refer specifically to 'a male person' and 'a female person' respectively. Subsequently, **man** replaced **wer** as the normal term for 'a male person', but at the same time the older sense 'a human being' remained in use. The generic use of **man** to refer to 'human beings in general' is now often regarded as old-fashioned or sexist. Acceptable alternatives include the **the human race** or **humankind**.

-man > *combining form* **1** in nouns denoting a man of a specified nationality or origin: *Frenchman*. **2** in nouns denoting a person belonging to a specified group or having a specified occupation or role: *chairman*. **3** a ship of a specified kind: *merchantman*.
USAGE – traditional occupational terms ending in **-man**, such as **fireman**, **chairman**, and **sportsman**, are now often challenged as sexist and out of date. As a result, there has been a shift away from **-man** words except where it is known that they refer to a man rather than a woman. Alternative neutral terms are used, for example **firefighter**, and compounds of **-person** such as **chairperson** (alternatively, **chair**) and **sportsperson**.

mana /**maa**nə/ > *noun* (in Polynesian, Melanesian, and Maori belief) pervasive supernatural or magical power.
ORIGIN – Maori.

manacle > *noun* a metal band or chain fastened around a person's hands or ankles to restrict their movement. > *verb* fetter with a manacle or manacles.
ORIGIN – Old French *manicle* 'handcuff', from Latin *manus* 'hand'.

manage > *verb* **1** be in charge of; run. **2** supervise (staff). **3** administer and regulate (resources). **4** succeed in doing or dealing with. **5** succeed despite difficulties; cope. **6** be free to attend (an appointment).
DERIVATIVES – **managing** *adjective* & *noun*.
SYNONYMS – **1** administer, control, direct, run. **4** accomplish, achieve, perform.

wordpower facts

Manage

In the 16th century **manage** meant 'put (a horse) through the paces of the **manège**', the arena in which horses are trained. Both **manage** and **manège** come from Italian *maneggiare* 'handle', which derives from Latin *manus* 'hand', the source of many words such as **manacle**, **mandate**, **manicure**, **manner**, **manoeuvre**, **manual**, and **manuscript**.

manageable > *adjective* able to be managed, controlled, or accomplished without great difficulty.
DERIVATIVES – **manageability** *noun* **manageably** *adverb*.

management > *noun* **1** the process of managing. **2** the managers of an organisation.

manager > *noun* **1** a person who manages an organisation, group of staff, or sports team. **2** a person in charge of the business affairs of a sports player, actor, or performer.
DERIVATIVES – **managerial** *adjective* **managership** *noun*.

manageress > *noun* a female manager.

mañana /man**yaa**nə/ > *adverb* tomorrow, or at some time in the future.
ORIGIN – Spanish.

manat /**mann**at/ > *noun* (pl. same) the basic monetary unit of Azerbaijan and Turkmenistan.

manatee /**mann**ətee/ > *noun* a sea cow of tropical Atlantic coasts, with a rounded tail flipper.
ORIGIN – Carib.

manchester > *noun* Austral./NZ cotton textiles; household linen.
ORIGIN – from the name of the English city of *Manchester*, historically a centre of cotton manufacture.

manciple /**man**sip'l/ > *noun* chiefly historical a person responsible for the supply of provisions in a monastery, college, or Inn of Court.
ORIGIN – Latin *manceps* 'buyer'.

Mancunian /man**kyoo**niən/ > *noun* a person from Manchester. > *adjective* relating to Manchester.
ORIGIN – from *Mancunium*, the Latin name for Manchester.

mandala /**mand**ələ/ > *noun* an intricate circular motif symbolising the universe in Hinduism and Buddhism.
ORIGIN – Sanskrit, 'disc, circle'.

mandarin > *noun* **1** (**Mandarin**) the standard literary and official form of Chinese. **2** a high-ranking official in the former imperial Chinese civil service. **3** a powerful official or senior bureaucrat. **4** (also **mandarine**) a small citrus fruit with a loose yellow-orange skin.

COMBINATIONS – **mandarin collar** a close-fitting upright collar.

ORIGIN – Hindi *mantrī* 'counsellor'; sense 4 perhaps derives from the colour of the fruit being likened to the official's yellow robes.

mandate > *noun* /**man**dayt/ **1** an official order or authorisation. **2** the authority to carry out a policy, regarded as given by the electorate to a party or candidate that wins an election. **3** historical a commission from the League of Nations to a member state to administer a territory. > *verb* /man**dayt**/ **1** give (someone) authority to act in a certain way. **2** make compulsory.

ORIGIN – Latin *mandatum* 'something commanded'.

mandatory /**man**dətri/ > *adjective* required by law or mandate; compulsory.

DERIVATIVES – **mandatorily** *adverb*.

SYNONYMS – compulsory, obligatory.

Mandelbrot set /**man**d'lbrot/ > *noun* Mathematics a particular set of complex numbers which has a very complicated fractal pattern when plotted.

ORIGIN – named after the Polish-born French mathematician Benoit B. *Mandelbrot* (born 1924).

mandible /**man**dib'l/ > *noun* **1** the lower jawbone. **2** either of the upper and lower parts of a bird's beak. **3** either half of the crushing organ in an insect's mouthparts.

ORIGIN – from Latin *mandere* 'to chew'.

mandolin > *noun* **1** a musical instrument resembling a lute, having paired metal strings plucked with a plectrum. **2** (also **mandoline**) a kitchen utensil consisting of a frame with adjustable blades, for slicing vegetables.

DERIVATIVES – **mandolinist** *noun*.

ORIGIN – Italian *mandolino* 'little mandola' (a *mandola* being an early form of mandolin).

mandragora /man**dragg**ərə/ > *noun* literary the mandrake, especially when used as a narcotic.

mandrake > *noun* a plant with a forked fleshy root supposedly resembling a human, used in herbal medicine and magic.

ORIGIN – Latin *mandragora*; the form *mandrake* developed by association with *man*, because of the root (which was believed to shriek when pulled up), and with *drake* in its Old English sense 'dragon'.

mandrel /**man**drəl/ > *noun* **1** a shaft or spindle in a lathe, to which work is fixed while being turned. **2** a rod round which metal or other material is forged or shaped.

mandrill /**man**dril/ > *noun* a large West African baboon with a red and blue face, the male having a blue rump.

ORIGIN – probably from **MAN** + **DRILL**[3].

mane > *noun* **1** a growth of long hair on the neck of a horse, lion, or other mammal. **2** a person's long flowing hair.

manège /ma**nezh**/ > *noun* **1** a riding school. **2** the movements in which a horse is trained in a riding school.

ORIGIN – see **MANAGE**.

manes /**maa**nayz/ > *plural noun* (in Roman mythology) the souls of dead ancestors, worshipped as gods.

ORIGIN – Latin.

maneuver > *noun* & *verb* US spelling of **MANOEUVRE**.

manful > *adjective* brave and resolute.

DERIVATIVES – **manfully** *adverb*.

manga /**mang**gə/ > *noun* Japanese cartoons, comic books, and animated films with a science-fiction or fantasy theme.

ORIGIN – Japanese, from *man* 'indiscriminate' + *ga* 'picture'.

mangabey /**mang**gəbay/ > *noun* a long-tailed monkey from West and central Africa.

ORIGIN – by erroneous association with *Mangabey*, a region of Madagascar.

manganese /**mang**gəneez/ > *noun* a hard grey metallic chemical element used in special steels and magnetic alloys.

ORIGIN – Italian, alteration of *magnesia*.

mange /maynj/ > *noun* a skin disease in some animals (occasionally communicable to humans), caused by mites and characterised by severe itching and hair loss.

ORIGIN – from Old French *mangier* 'eat'.

mangel /**mang**g'l/ (also **mangel-wurzel**) > *noun* another term for **MANGOLD**.

manger /**mayn**jər/ > *noun* a long trough from which horses or cattle feed.

wordpower facts

Manger

The words **mange**, **manger**, and **mangetout** all have connections with the French verb *manger*, meaning 'to eat'. *Manger* comes from Latin *manducare* 'to chew', a root which also gave rise to the English word **mandible**, denoting part of the jaw.

mangetout /**mo**nzhtoo/ > *noun* (pl. same or **mangetouts** pronunc. same) chiefly Brit. a variety of pea with an edible pod.

ORIGIN – French 'eat all'.

mangey > *adjective* variant spelling of **MANGY**.

mangle[1] > *noun* chiefly Brit. a machine having two or more cylinders turned by a handle, between which wet laundry is squeezed to remove excess moisture.

ORIGIN – Dutch *mangel*, ultimately from Greek *manganon* 'axis, engine of war'.

mangle[2] > *verb* destroy or severely damage by tearing or crushing.

ORIGIN – Old French *mahaignier* 'maim'.

mango > *noun* (pl. **mangoes** or **mangos**) a fleshy, oval, yellowish-red tropical fruit.

ORIGIN – Portuguese *manga*.

mangold > *noun* a variety of beet with a large root, grown as feed for farm animals.

ORIGIN – German *Mangoldwurzel*, from *Mangold* 'beet' + *Wurzel* 'root'.

mangonel /**mang**gən'l/ > *noun* historical a military device for throwing stones.

ORIGIN – Old French, ultimately from Greek *manganon* 'axis, engine of war'.

mangosteen /**mang**gəsteen/ > *noun* a tropical fruit with juicy white segments of flesh inside a thick reddish-brown rind.

ORIGIN – Malay.

mangrove > *noun* a tree or shrub which grows in tropical coastal swamps and has tangled roots that grow above ground and form dense thickets.

ORIGIN – probably from Taino (an extinct Caribbean language); later associated with **GROVE**.

mangy /**mayn**ji/ (also **mangey**) > *adjective* (**mangier**, **mangiest**) **1** having mange. **2** in poor condition; shabby.

manhandle > *verb* **1** move (a heavy object) by hand with great effort. **2** handle roughly by dragging or pushing.

manhood > *noun* **1** the state or period of being a man rather than a child. **2** the men of a country or society. **3** the qualities traditionally associated with men, such as strength and sexual potency.

mania > *noun* **1** mental illness marked by periods of excitement, delusions, and overactivity. **2** an obsession.

ORIGIN – Greek, 'madness'.

-mania > *combining form* **1** referring to a specified type of mental abnormality or obsession. **2** denoting extreme enthusiasm or admiration.

WORDFINDER – bibliomania (*a passion for books*), dipsomania (*alcoholism*), egomania (*obsessive self-centredness*), kleptomania (*an uncontrollable need to steal*), megalomania (*obsession with power*), monomania (*obsession with one thing*), mythomania (*compulsion to tell lies*), nymphomania (*uncontrollable sexual desire in a woman*), pyromania (*obsession with setting things on fire*).

DERIVATIVES – **-maniac** combining form.

maniac /**may**niak/ > *noun* **1** a person exhibiting extremely wild or violent behaviour. **2** informal an obsessive enthusiast.

DERIVATIVES – **maniacal** /mənīək'l/ *adjective* **maniacally** *adverb*.

SYNONYMS – **1** lunatic, madman.

manic /**mann**ik/ > *adjective* **1** relating to or affected by mania. **2** showing wild excitement and energy.

DERIVATIVES – **manically** *adverb*.

SYNONYMS – **2** feverish, frenetic, frenzied.

ANTONYMS – **2** calm.

COMBINATIONS – **manic depression** a mental disorder marked by alternating periods of elation and depression.

manicure > *noun* a cosmetic treatment of the hands and nails. > *verb* **1** give a manicure to. **2** (**manicured**) (of a lawn or garden) neatly trimmed and maintained.

DERIVATIVES – **manicurist** *noun*.

ORIGIN – French, from Latin *manus* 'hand' + *cura* 'care'.

manifest¹ > *adjective* clear and obvious. > *verb* **1** show or demonstrate. **2** become apparent. **3** (of a ghost) appear.

DERIVATIVES – **manifestly** *adverb*.

SYNONYMS – *adjective* conspicuous, explicit, plain. *verb* **1** demonstrate, display, exhibit, present, show.

---

wordpower facts
Manifest

The words **manifest**, **manifestation**, and **manifesto** are linked through their common root, Latin *manifestus* 'caught in the act, flagrant', literally 'struck with the hand', from *manus* 'hand' and *festus* 'struck'. **Manifest** probably entered English via French, and was originally an adjective meaning, besides 'flagrant', 'clearly revealed; evident, unmistakable'; the verb, 'show or demonstrate', comes from Latin *manifestare*. **Manifest** meaning 'a list' came from the Italian word **manifesto**, which itself later entered English in a different sense.

---

manifest² > *noun* **1** a document listing a ship's contents, cargo, crew, and passengers. **2** a list of passengers or cargo in an aircraft. **3** a list of the wagons forming a freight train. > *verb* record in a manifest.

manifestation > *noun* **1** a sign or embodiment of something. **2** the materialisation of a god or spirit.

SYNONYMS – **1** demonstration, display, indication.

manifesto > *noun* (pl. **manifestos**) a public declaration of policy and aims.

manifold > *adjective* formal or literary **1** many and various. **2** having many different forms. > *noun* **1** a pipe or chamber branching into several openings. **2** (in an internal-

combustion engine) the part conveying air and fuel from the carburettor to the cylinders or leading from the cylinders to the exhaust pipe.

manikin (also **mannikin**) > *noun* **1** a very small person. **2** a jointed model of the human body.

ORIGIN – Dutch *manneken* 'little man'.

Manila /mənillə/ (also **Manilla**) > *noun* **1** (also **Manila hemp**) a plant fibre used for rope, matting, paper, etc. **2** strong brown paper, originally made from Manila hemp. **3** a cigar or cheroot made in Manila.

ORIGIN – from *Manila*, the capital of the Philippines; the plant yielding the fibre is native to the Philippines.

manioc /**mann**iok/ > *noun* another term for CASSAVA.

ORIGIN – Tupi.

maniple /**mann**ip'l/ > *noun* a subdivision of a Roman legion, consisting of either 120 or 60 men.

manipulate /mə**nip**yoolayt/ > *verb* **1** handle or control with dexterity. **2** examine or treat (a part of the body) by feeling or moving it with the hand. **3** control or influence cleverly or unscrupulously. **4** alter or present (data) so as to mislead.

DERIVATIVES – **manipulable** *adjective* **manipulation** *noun* **manipulator** *noun*.

SYNONYMS – **1** control, handle, manoeuvre, operate, work. **3** engineer, manoeuvre, orchestrate. **4** doctor, fudge, massage.

ORIGIN – from Latin *manipulus* 'handful'.

manipulative > *adjective* **1** tending to manipulate other people cleverly or unscrupulously. **2** relating to manipulation.

DERIVATIVES – **manipulatively** *adverb* **manipulativeness** *noun*.

SYNONYMS – **1** calculating, conniving, scheming.

manitou /**mann**itoō/ > *noun* (among certain North American Indians) a good or evil spirit.

ORIGIN – Algonquian.

mankind > *noun* human beings collectively; the human race.

manky > *adjective* (**mankier**, **mankiest**) Brit. informal **1** inferior; worthless. **2** grimy; dirty.

ORIGIN – probably from obsolete *mank* 'mutilated, defective'.

manly > *adjective* (**manlier**, **manliest**) **1** possessing qualities traditionally associated with men, such as courage and strength. **2** befitting a man.

DERIVATIVES – **manliness** *noun*.

SYNONYMS – **1** masculine, virile.

manna > *noun* **1** (in the Bible) the substance miraculously supplied as food to the Israelites in the wilderness (Book of Exodus, chapter 16). **2** an unexpected and

freely given benefit. **3** a sweet edible laxative gum obtained from a tree.

ORIGIN – Aramaic, from Hebrew.

manned > *adjective* having a human crew.

mannequin /**mann**ikin/ > *noun* a dummy used to display clothes in a shop window.

ORIGIN – French, from Dutch *manneken* 'little man'; related to MANIKIN.

manner > *noun* **1** a way in which something is done or happens. **2** a person's outward bearing or way of behaving towards others. **3** (**manners**) polite social behaviour. **4** a style in literature or art. **5** literary a kind or sort.

IDIOMS – **all manner of** many different kinds of. **in a manner of speaking** in some sense. **to the manner born** naturally at ease in a specified job or situation. [ORIGIN – with allusion to Shakespeare's *Hamlet* (I. iv. 17).]

SYNONYMS – **1** fashion, mode, style. **2** bearing, behaviour, demeanour, mien. **3** (**manners**) decorum, politeness.

ORIGIN – from Latin *manuarius* 'of the hand', from *manus* 'hand'.

mannered > *adjective* **1** behaving in a specified way: *well-mannered*. **2** (of an artistic style) marked by highly distinctive or exaggerated features.

mannerism > *noun* **1** a habitual gesture or way of speaking or behaving. **2** the use of a highly distinctive style in art, literature, or music. **3** (**Mannerism**) a style of 16th-century Italian art characterised by distortions in scale and perspective.

DERIVATIVES – **mannerist** *noun* & *adjective*.

mannerly > *adjective* well-mannered; polite.

mannikin > *noun* variant spelling of MANIKIN.

mannish > *adjective* (of a woman) having an appearance and characteristics that are associated with men.

manoeuvrable (US **maneuverable**) > *adjective* (of a craft or vessel) able to be manoeuvred easily while in motion.

DERIVATIVES – **manoeuvrability** *noun*.

manoeuvre* /mənoōvər/ (US **maneuver**) > *noun* **1** a physical movement or series of moves requiring skill and care. **2** a carefully planned scheme or action. **3** (**manoeuvres**) a large-scale military exercise. > *verb* (**manoeuvred**, **manoeuvring**) **1** perform a manoeuvre. **2** carefully manipulate in order to achieve an end.

*SPELLING – the standard British spelling has *oeu* in the middle and *re* at the end: man*oeu*vre. In the past the *oe* was usually printed as a ligature (*œ*), but this is old-fashioned.

SYNONYMS – *noun* **2** machination, ruse, stratagem. *verb* **2** contrive, engineer, manipulate, orchestrate.

ORIGIN – French *manœuvrer*, from Latin *manus* 'hand' + *operari* 'to work'.

man-of-war (also **man-o'-war**) > *noun* (pl. **men-of-war** or **men-o'-war**) historical an armed sailing ship.

COMBINATIONS – **Portuguese man-of-war** a floating jellyfish-like marine animal with a translucent body, often blue, and long stinging tentacles.

manometer /mənommitər/ > *noun* an instrument for measuring the pressure acting on a column of fluid.

ORIGIN – from Greek *manos* 'thin, rare, rarefied'.

manor > *noun* 1 a large country house with lands. 2 chiefly historical a body of land consisting of a lord's demesne and lands rented to tenants.

DERIVATIVES – **manorial** *adjective*.

ORIGIN – Old French *maner* 'dwelling', from Latin *manere* 'remain'.

manpower > *noun* the number of people working or available for work or service.

manqué /mongkay/ > *adjective* that might have been; unfulfilled: *an actor manqué*.

ORIGIN – French, from *manquer* 'to lack'.

mansard /mansaard/ > *noun* 1 a roof having four sides, in each of which the lower part of the slope is steeper than the upper part. 2 Brit. a gambrel roof.

ORIGIN – named after the 17th-century French architect François *Mansart*.

manse > *noun* a house provided for the minister in the Presbyterian and some other churches.

ORIGIN – Latin *mansus* 'house, dwelling'.

mansion > *noun* a large, impressive house.

COMBINATIONS – **mansion block** Brit. a large block of flats.

ORIGIN – Latin, 'place where someone stays', from *manere* 'remain'.

manslaughter > *noun* the crime of killing a person without intending to do so.

manta > *noun* a very large ray of tropical seas.

ORIGIN – Latin American Spanish, 'large blanket'.

mantel (also **mantle**) > *noun* a mantelpiece or mantelshelf.

COMBINATIONS – **mantelpiece** 1 a structure surrounding a fireplace. 2 a mantelshelf. **mantelshelf** 1 a shelf forming the top of a mantelpiece. 2 Climbing a projecting ledge of rock.

manticore /mantikor/ > *noun* a mythical beast having the body of a lion, the face of a man, and the sting of a scorpion.

ORIGIN – Greek *mantikhōras*, from an Old Persian word meaning 'man-eating creature'.

mantilla /mantillə/ > *noun* (in Spain) a lace or silk scarf worn by women over the hair and shoulders.

ORIGIN – Spanish, 'little mantle or shawl'.

mantis (also **praying mantis**) > *noun* (pl. same or **mantises**) a slender predatory insect with a triangular head, typically waiting motionless for prey with its forelegs folded like hands in prayer.

ORIGIN – Greek, 'prophet'.

mantle > *noun* 1 a woman's loose sleeveless cloak or shawl. 2 a close covering, such as a layer of snow. 3 (also **gas mantle**) a mesh cover fixed round a gas jet to give an incandescent light when heated. 4 an important role or responsibility that passes from one person to another. [ORIGIN – with biblical allusion to the passing of Elijah's cloak to Elisha (2 Kings, chapter 2).] 5 Geology the region of the earth's interior between the crust and the core, consisting of hot, dense silicate rocks. > *verb* literary cloak, envelop, or suffuse.

ORIGIN – Latin *mantellum* 'cloak'.

mantra /mantrə/ > *noun* 1 (originally in Hinduism and Buddhism) a word or sound repeated to aid concentration in meditation. 2 a Vedic hymn.

ORIGIN – Sanskrit, 'instrument of thought'.

manual /manyooəl/ > *adjective* 1 made or worked with the hands. 2 using or working with the hands: *a manual worker*. > *noun* 1 a book giving instructions or information. 2 an organ keyboard played with the hands not the feet.

DERIVATIVES – **manually** *adverb*.

ORIGIN – Latin *manualis*, from *manus* 'hand'.

manufactory > *noun* (pl. **manufactories**) archaic a factory.

manufacture > *verb* 1 make (something), especially on a large scale using machinery. 2 (**manufactured**) made or produced in a merely mechanical way. 3 invent or fabricate (evidence or a story). > *noun* the process of manufacturing.

DERIVATIVES – **manufacturable** *adjective* **manufacturer** *noun*.

SYNONYMS – *verb* 1 assemble, construct, fabricate. 3 concoct, contrive, fabricate, invent. *noun* assembly, construction, fabrication.

ORIGIN – French, from Italian *manifattura*, influenced by Latin *manu factum* 'made by hand'.

manuka /maanōokə, manōokə/ > *noun* a small tree with aromatic leaves, native to New Zealand and Tasmania.

ORIGIN – Maori.

manumit /manyoomit/ > *verb* (**manumitted**, **manumitting**) historical release from slavery; set free.

DERIVATIVES – **manumission** *noun*.

ORIGIN – Latin *manumittere* 'send forth from the hand'.

manure > *noun* animal dung used for fertilising land. > *verb* apply manure to.

---

wordpower facts

Manure

Surprisingly, the words **manure** and **manoeuvre** are closely related.

Manure entered Middle English as a verb in the sense 'work or till land', coming from the Old French *manouvrer*, which derives from Latin *manus* 'hand' and *operari* 'to work'. **Manoeuvre** comes directly from the same root.

---

manuscript > *noun* 1 a handwritten book, document, or piece of music. 2 a text submitted for printing and publication.

ORIGIN – from Latin *manu* 'by hand' + *scriptus* 'written'.

Manx > *noun* the Celtic language formerly spoken in the Isle of Man, still used for ceremonial purposes. > *adjective* relating to the Isle of Man.

COMBINATIONS – **Manx cat** a breed of cat that has no tail.

ORIGIN – from Old Irish *Manu* 'Isle of Man' + -*skr* (equivalent of –ISH).

many > *determiner, pronoun, & adjective* (**more**, **most**) a large number of. > *noun* (**the many**) the majority of people.

IDIOMS – **a good** (or **great**) **many** a large number.

SYNONYMS – *determiner, pronoun, & adjective* countless, diverse, innumerable, a lot of, lots of, numerous.

manzanilla /manzənillə/ > *noun* a pale, very dry Spanish sherry.

ORIGIN – Spanish, 'chamomile' (because the flavour is said to suggest chamomile).

Maoism /mowiz'm/ > *noun* the communist doctrines of Mao Zedong (1893–1976), chairman of the Chinese Communist Party 1949–76.

DERIVATIVES – **Maoist** *noun & adjective*.

Maori /mowri/ > *noun* (pl. same or **Maoris**) 1 a member of the aboriginal people of New Zealand. 2 the Polynesian language of this people.

map > *noun* 1 a flat diagram of an area of land or sea showing physical features, cities, roads, etc. 2 a diagram or collection of data showing the arrangement, distribution, or sequence of something. > *verb* (**mapped**, **mapping**) 1 represent or record on a map. 2 (**map out**) plan in detail.

WORDFINDER – cartography (*the science of map-making*), Ordnance Survey (*official UK map-making organisation*), projection (*a way of representing the earth's surface on a map*), relief map (*a map showing contours by shading*), topography (*the natural features of an area*).

IDIOMS – **put on the map** bring (a place) to prominence. **wipe off the map** obliterate totally.

ORIGIN – Latin *mappa* 'sheet, napkin'.

maple > *noun* a tree or shrub with lobed leaves, winged fruits, and syrupy sap.

COMBINATIONS – **maple leaf** the leaf of the maple, used as the Canadian national emblem. **maple syrup** sugary syrup produced from the sap of a maple tree.

maquette /ma**ket**/ > *noun* a sculptor's small preliminary model or sketch.

ORIGIN – French, from Italian *machietta* 'little spot'.

maquis /ma**kee**/ > *noun* (pl. same) **1** (**the Maquis**) the French resistance movement during the German occupation of France in the Second World War. **2** dense evergreen scrub characteristic of coastal regions in the Mediterranean.

ORIGIN – French, 'brushwood'.

Mar. > *abbreviation* March.

mar > *verb* (**marred, marring**) harm the appearance or quality of.

SYNONYMS – blemish, disfigure, tarnish.

ANTONYMS – enhance.

marabou /**marr**əbōō/ > *noun* **1** an African stork with a massive bill and large neck pouch. **2** down feathers from the marabou used as trimming for hats or clothing.

ORIGIN – French, from Arabic, 'holy man'.

maraca /mə**rakk**ə/ > *noun* a hollow gourd or gourd-shaped container filled with small beans, stones, etc., shaken as a percussion instrument.

ORIGIN – Portuguese, from Tupi.

marae /**mə**rī/ > *noun* (pl. same) the courtyard of a Maori meeting house, especially as a social or ceremonial forum.

ORIGIN – Polynesian, denoting a sacrificial altar or sacred enclosure.

maraschino /marrə**shee**nō/ > *noun* (pl. **maraschinos**) a strong, sweet liqueur made from small black Dalmatian cherries.

COMBINATIONS – **maraschino cherry** a cherry preserved in maraschino.

ORIGIN – Italian, from *marasca* (the name of the cherry), from *amaro* 'bitter'.

marathon > *noun* **1** a long-distance running race, strictly one of 26 miles 385 yards (42.195 km). **2** a long-lasting and arduous task.

maraud /mə**rawd**/ > *verb* go about in search of people or places to attack or rob.

DERIVATIVES – **marauder** *noun* **marauding** *adjective*.

ORIGIN – French *marauder*, from *maraud* 'rogue'.

---

wordpower facts

Marathon

The modern race is named after *Marathon* in Greece, the scene of a battle in which the Athenians defeated the Persians in 490 BC. The race is based on the tradition that a messenger ran from Marathon to Athens (22 miles) with news of the victory, falling dead on arrival. However, the original account by the historian Herodotus told of the messenger Pheidippides running 150 miles from Athens to Sparta before the battle, seeking help.

---

marble > *noun* **1** a hard form of limestone, typically variegated or mottled, which can be polished and is used in sculpture and building. **2** a small ball of coloured glass used as a toy. **3** (**marbles**) (treated as sing.) a game in which marbles are rolled along the ground. **4** (**one's marbles**) informal one's mental faculties. > *verb* give (something) the appearance of marble.

WORDFINDER – marmoreal (*made of or likened to marble*); agate, ally, glassy, peewee, taw (*types of toy marble*).

DERIVATIVES – **marbled** *adjective*.

ORIGIN – from Greek *marmaros* 'shining stone'.

marbling > *noun* **1** colouring or marking that resembles marble. **2** streaks of fat in lean meat.

marc > *noun* **1** the skins and other remains from grapes that have been pressed for winemaking. **2** an alcoholic spirit distilled from this.

ORIGIN – French, from *marcher* in the early sense 'to tread or trample'.

marcasite /**maar**kəsīt, **maar**kəzeet/ > *noun* **1** a semi-precious stone consisting of iron pyrites. **2** a piece of polished metal cut as a gem.

ORIGIN – Latin *marcasita*, from Arabic.

March > *noun* the third month of the year.

COMBINATIONS – **March hare** informal a brown hare in the breeding season, noted for its leaping, boxing, and chasing in circles.

ORIGIN – from Latin *Martius mensis* 'month of Mars'.

march¹ > *verb* **1** walk in a military manner with a regular measured tread. **2** proceed quickly and with determination. **3** force (someone) to walk somewhere quickly. **4** take part in an organised procession to make a protest. > *noun* **1** an act of marching. **2** a procession organised as a protest. **3** a piece of music written to accompany marching.

IDIOMS – **on the march 1** engaged in marching. **2** making progress.

DERIVATIVES – **marcher** *noun*.

SYNONYMS – *verb* **1** parade, process, troop.

COMBINATIONS – **marching orders 1** instructions for troops to depart. **2** (**one's marching orders**) informal one's dismissal.

ORIGIN – French *marcher* 'to walk'.

march² > *noun* (**Marches**) an area of land on the border between two countries or territories. > *verb* (**march with**) literary have a common frontier with.

marchioness /maarshə**ness**/ > *noun* **1** the wife or widow of a marquess. **2** a woman holding the rank of marquess in her own right.

marchpane > *noun* archaic marzipan.

Mardi Gras /maardi **graa**/ > *noun* a carnival held in some countries on Shrove Tuesday.

ORIGIN – French, 'fat Tuesday', alluding to the last day of feasting before the fast and penitence of Lent.

mare¹ /mair/ > *noun* the female of a horse or other equine animal.

COMBINATIONS – **mare's nest 1** a muddle. **2** an illusory discovery. **mare's tail 1** a water plant with whorls of narrow leaves around a tall stout stem. **2** (**mare's tails**) long straight streaks of cirrus cloud.

mare² /**maa**ray/ > *noun* (pl. **maria** /**maa**riə/) Astronomy a large basalt plain on the surface of the moon.

ORIGIN – Latin *mare* 'sea'; these areas were once thought to be seas, as they appear dark by contrast with mountainous areas.

margarine /maarjə**reen**/ > *noun* a butter substitute made from vegetable oils or animal fats.

NOTE – the usual British pronunciation is with a soft g, as in the informal shortening **marge**. Pronunciation with a hard g, although to be expected from the *marga-* spelling and the etymology, is now rare. In American English the stress has shifted to the first syllable and the last syllable is short: **maar**jərin.

ORIGIN – French, from Greek *margaron* 'pearl' (because of the shiny crystals of esters from which it was first made).

margarita > *noun* a cocktail made with tequila and citrus fruit juice.

marge > *noun* Brit. informal short for **MARGARINE**.

margin > *noun* **1** an edge or border. **2** the blank border on each side of the print on a page. **3** the furthest reach or limit. **4** an amount above or below a given level.

IDIOMS – **margin of error** a small amount allowed for in case of miscalculation or change of circumstances.

SYNONYMS – **1** border, edge, fringe, perimeter, verge. **3** boundary, extremity, limit.

COMBINATIONS – **margin call** Stock Exchange a demand by a broker that an investor deposit further cash or securities to cover possible losses.

ORIGIN – Latin *margo* 'edge'.

marginal > *adjective* **1** relating to or situated at or in a margin. **2** of minor importance. **3** (of a decision or distinction) very narrow. **4** chiefly Brit. (of a parliamentary seat) having a small majority. > *noun* chiefly Brit. a marginal parliamentary seat.

DERIVATIVES – **marginality** *noun*.

SYNONYMS – **2** insignificant, negligible, slight.

ANTONYMS – primary.

marginalia /maarji**nay**liə/ > *plural noun* notes written or printed in the margin of a book or manuscript.

marginalise (also **marginalize**) > *verb* treat as marginal or peripheral.

DERIVATIVES – **marginalisation** *noun*.

marginally > *adverb* to only a limited extent; slightly.

margrave /**maar**grayv/ > *noun* historical the hereditary title of some princes of the Holy Roman Empire.

ORIGIN – Dutch, from *marke* 'boundary' + *grave* 'count'.

marguerite /maargə**reet**/ > *noun* another term for *ox-eye daisy*.

maria plural of **MARE**[2].

mariachi /mari**aa**chi/ > *noun* (pl. **mariachis**) (in Mexico) a musician performing traditional folk music.

ORIGIN – Mexican Spanish, 'street singer'.

mariculture /**marr**ikulchər/ > *noun* the cultivation of fish or other marine life for food.

ORIGIN – from Latin *mare* 'sea'.

Marie Rose > *noun* a cold sauce made from mayonnaise and tomato purée and served with seafood.

marigold > *noun* a plant of the daisy family with yellow or orange flowers.

marijuana /marri**hwaa**nə/ > *noun* the drug cannabis.

ORIGIN – Latin American Spanish.

marimba /mə**rim**bə/ > *noun* a deep-toned xylophone of African origin.

ORIGIN – from Kimbundu (a Bantu language of western Angola).

marina > *noun* a purpose-built harbour with moorings for yachts and small boats.

marinade > *noun* /mari**nayd**/ a mixture of ingredients such as oil, vinegar, and herbs, in which food is soaked before cooking in order to flavour or soften it. > *verb* /**ma**rinayd/ another term for **MARINATE**.

ORIGIN – French, from Spanish *marinar* 'pickle in brine', ultimately from Latin *mare* 'sea'.

marinara /maari**naa**rə/ > *noun* (in Italian cooking) a sauce made from tomatoes, onions, and herbs.

ORIGIN – from Italian *alla marinara* 'sailor-style'.

marinate > *verb* soak in a marinade.

DERIVATIVES – **marination** *noun*.

marine > *adjective* **1** relating to the sea. **2** relating to shipping or naval matters. > *noun* a member of a body of troops trained to serve on land or sea, in particular (in the UK) a member of the Royal Marines or (in the US) a member of the Marine Corps.

IDIOMS – **tell that to the marines** a scornful expression of disbelief. [ORIGIN – referring to the *horse marines*, an imaginary corps of cavalrymen employed to serve at sea (thus out of their element).]

SYNONYMS – *adjective* **2** maritime, nautical.

ORIGIN – Latin *marinus*, from *mare* 'sea'.

mariner > *noun* formal or literary a sailor.

Mariolatry /mairi**oll**ətri/ > *noun* idolatrous worship of the Virgin Mary.

marionette > *noun* a puppet worked by strings.

ORIGIN – French, from the given name *Marion*.

marital > *adjective* relating to marriage or the relations between husband and wife.

DERIVATIVES – **maritally** *adverb*.

USAGE – do not confuse **marital**, 'of marriage', with **martial**, 'of war'.

ORIGIN – from Latin *maritus* 'husband'.

maritime > *adjective* **1** relating to shipping or other activity taking place at sea. **2** living or found in or near the sea. **3** (of a climate) moist and temperate owing to the influence of the sea.

ORIGIN – Latin *maritimus*, from *mare* 'sea'.

marjoram /**maar**jərəm/ > *noun* **1** (also **sweet marjoram**) an aromatic plant of the mint family, used as a herb in cooking. **2** (also **wild marjoram**) oregano.

ORIGIN – Latin *majorana*, of unknown ultimate origin.

mark[1] > *noun* **1** a small area on a surface having a different colour from its surroundings. **2** something that indicates position or acts as a pointer. **3** a line, figure, or symbol made to identify or record something. **4** a sign or indication of a quality or feeling. **5** a characteristic feature or property of something. **6** a level or stage. **7** a point awarded for a correct answer or for proficiency in an examination. **8** a particular model or type of a vehicle or machine. > *verb* **1** make a mark on. **2** write a word or symbol on (an object) in order to identify it. **3** indicate the position of. **4** (**mark out**) distinguish or separate off. **5** indicate or acknowledge (a significant event). **6** (**mark up** or **down**) increase or reduce the indicated price of. **7** assess and give a mark to (written work). **8** notice or pay careful attention to. **9** Brit. (in team games) stay close to (an opponent) in order to prevent them getting or passing the ball.

IDIOMS – **be quick off the mark** be fast in responding. **make a mark** have a lasting or significant effect. **mark time 1** (of troops) march on the spot without moving forward. **2** engage temporarily in routine activities. **near** (or **close**) **to the mark** almost accurate. **off** (or **wide of**) **the mark** incorrect; inaccurate. **on the mark** correct; accurate. **on your marks** be ready to start (used to instruct competitors in a race). **up to the mark** up to the required standard or normal level.

SYNONYMS – *noun* **1** fleck, speck, spot, stain. **3** emblem, insignia, seal, stamp. **4** evidence, hint, symptom. **5** attribute, hallmark, trait.

mark[2] > *noun* the basic monetary unit of Germany, equal to 100 pfennig.

markdown > *noun* a reduction in price.

marked > *adjective* **1** having a visible mark or other identifying feature. **2** clearly noticeable: *a marked increase*. **3** singled out as a target for attack: *a marked man*.

DERIVATIVES – **markedly** *adverb* **markedness** *noun*.

SYNONYMS – **2** clear, conspicuous, distinct, pronounced.

ANTONYMS – **2** imperceptible.

marker > *noun* **1** an object used to indicate a position, place, or route. **2** a felt-tip pen with a broad tip. **3** (in team games) a player who marks an opponent. **4** a person who marks a test or examination.

market > *noun* **1** a regular gathering for the purchase and sale of food, livestock, or other commodities. **2** an outdoor space or large hall where vendors sell their goods. **3** a particular area of commercial or competitive activity. **4** demand for a particular commodity or service. > *verb* (**marketed**, **marketing**) **1** offer (goods) for sale. **2** advertise or promote.

WORDFINDER – monopoly (*a market dominated by a single supplier*), duopoly (*by two suppliers*), oligopoly (*by a few suppliers*); monopsony (*a market dominated by a single purchaser*), oligopsony (*by a few purchasers*); perfect competition (*a market that no individual can control*).

IDIOMS – **on the market** available for sale.

DERIVATIVES – **marketable** *adjective* **marketer** *noun*.

COMBINATIONS – **market garden** a place where vegetables and fruit are grown for sale. **market-maker** Stock Exchange a dealer in securities or other assets who undertakes to buy or sell at specified prices at all times. **market research** the activity of gathering information about customers' needs and preferences. **market town** a town of moderate size where a regular market is held. **market value** the amount for which something can be sold in an open market. Contrasted with **book value**.

ORIGIN – Latin *mercatus*, from *mercari* 'buy'.

marketeer > *noun* a person who sells goods or services in a market.

marketing > *noun* the promotion and selling of products or services.

marketplace > *noun* **1** an open space where a market is held. **2** a competitive or commercial arena.

marking > *noun* **1** an identification mark. **2** (also **markings**) a pattern of marks on an animal's fur, feathers, or skin.

markka /**maar**kə/ > *noun* the basic monetary unit of Finland, equal to 100 penniä.

marksman > *noun* a person skilled in shooting.

DERIVATIVES – **marksmanship** noun.

mark-up > *noun* **1** the amount added to the cost price of goods to cover overheads and profit. **2** the annotation and correction of text in preparation for printing. **3** Computing a set of codes assigned to different elements of a text.

marl¹ > *noun* an unconsolidated sedimentary rock or soil consisting of clay and lime, formerly used as fertiliser.

ORIGIN – Old French *marle*, from Latin *marga*, of Celtic origin.

marl² > *noun* a mottled yarn or fabric.

ORIGIN – shortening of *marbled*.

marlin > *noun* a large, edible, fast-swimming fish of warm seas, with a pointed snout.

ORIGIN – from **MARLINSPIKE** (because of its snout).

marlinspike (also **marlinespike**) > *noun* a pointed metal tool used by sailors to separate strands of rope or wire.

ORIGIN – from *marl* 'fasten with marline' (light rope made of two strands).

marmalade > *noun* a preserve made from citrus fruit, especially bitter oranges.

ORIGIN – Portuguese *marmelada* 'quince jam', from *marmelo* 'quince'.

Marmite > *noun* trademark a dark savoury spread made from yeast extract and vegetable extract.

marmite /**maar**mīt, maar**meet**/ > *noun* a cooking pot.

ORIGIN – Old French, 'hypocritical' (with reference to the hidden contents of the lidded pot), from *marmotter* 'to mutter' + *mite* 'cat'.

marmoreal /maar**mor**iəl/ > *adjective* literary made of or resembling marble.

ORIGIN – from Latin *marmoreus*, from *marmor* 'marble'.

marmoset /**maar**məzet/ > *noun* a small tropical American monkey with a silky coat and a long tail.

ORIGIN – Old French *marmouset* 'grotesque image'.

marmot /**maar**mət/ > *noun* a heavily built burrowing rodent.

ORIGIN – French *marmotte*, from Latin *mus montanus* 'mountain mouse'.

Maronite /**marr**ənīt/ > *noun* a member of a Christian sect living chiefly in Lebanon and in communion with the Roman Catholic Church.

ORIGIN – from the name of John *Maro*, a 5th-century Syrian religious leader.

maroon¹ > *noun* **1** a dark brownish-red colour. **2** chiefly Brit. a firework that makes a loud bang, used as a signal or warning.

ORIGIN – French *marron* 'chestnut'; sense 2 was so named because the firework sounded like a chestnut bursting in a fire.

maroon² > *verb* (**be marooned**) be abandoned alone in an inaccessible place.

---

wordpower facts

Maroon

The verb **maroon** entered the language in the 18th century. It derives from the name used for a group of runaway slaves living as fugitives in the mountains and forests of Suriname and the West Indies. These people were called **Maroons**, the name deriving from the French *marron* 'wild, fugitive', which came from the Spanish *cimarrón*. The name **Maroon** is still in occasional use in reference to descendants of these people.

---

marque > *noun* a make of car, as distinct from a specific model.

ORIGIN – French, from *marquer* 'to brand'.

marquee > *noun* **1** chiefly Brit. a large tent used for social or commercial functions. **2** N. Amer. a roof-like projection over the entrance to a theatre, hotel, or other building. **3** (before another noun) N. Amer. leading; pre-eminent: *a marquee player*.

ORIGIN – from **MARQUISE** (formerly a synonym for *marquee*), taken as a plural; sense 3 is with allusion to the practice of billing the name of an entertainer over the entrance to a theatre.

marquess > *noun* a British nobleman ranking above an earl and below a duke. Compare with **MARQUIS**.

marquetry /**maar**kitri/ > *noun* inlaid work made from small pieces of variously coloured wood, used for the decoration of furniture.

ORIGIN – from French *marqueter* 'become different colours'.

marquis /**maar**kwiss/ > *noun* **1** (in some European countries) a nobleman ranking above a count and below a duke. Compare with **MARQUESS**. **2** variant spelling of **MARQUESS**.

ORIGIN – Old French *marchis*, from the base of **MARCH²**.

marquise /maar**keez**/ > *noun* **1** the wife or widow of a marquis, or a woman holding the rank of marquis in her own right. **2** a ring set with a pointed oval gem or cluster of gems.

marram grass > *noun* a coarse grass of coastal sand dunes.

ORIGIN – Old Norse.

marriage > *noun* **1** the formal union of a man and a woman, by which they become husband and wife. **2** a combination of two or more elements.

WORDFINDER – bridal, conjugal, connubial, marital, matrimonial, nuptial (*related adjectives*); nubile (*old enough for marriage*), spouse (*husband or wife*), monogamy (*practice of having only one spouse at at a time*), bigamy (*crime of having more than one spouse at one time*), polygamy (*custom of having several spouses at one time*), polygyny (*custom of a husband taking several wives*), monandry (*custom of a wife taking one husband only*), polyandry (*custom of a wife having several husbands*); epithalamium, prothalamium (*poem celebrating a marriage*).

IDIOMS – **marriage of convenience** a marriage concluded primarily to achieve a practical purpose.

ORIGIN – Old French *mariage*, from *marier* 'marry'.

marriageable > *adjective* fit or suitable for marriage.

married > *adjective* united by marriage. > *noun* (**marrieds**) married people.

marron /**marr**ən/ > *noun* a large Australian freshwater crayfish.

ORIGIN – from an Aboriginal language.

marron glacé /marrɒn **glass**ay/ > *noun* (pl. **marrons glacés** pronunc. same) a chestnut preserved in and coated with sugar.

ORIGIN – French, 'iced chestnut'.

marrow > *noun* **1** Brit. a long gourd with a thin green skin and white flesh, eaten as a vegetable. **2** (also **bone marrow**) a soft fatty substance in the cavities of bones, in which blood cells are produced.

IDIOMS – **to the marrow** to one's innermost being.

COMBINATIONS – **marrowbone** a bone containing edible marrow. **marrowfat pea** a pea of a large variety which is processed and sold in cans.

marry¹ > *verb* (**marries, married**) **1** take as one's wife or husband in marriage. **2** join (two people) in marriage. **3** (**marry into**) become a member of (a family) by marriage. **4** join together; combine harmoniously.

IDIOMS – **marry in haste, repent at leisure** proverb those who rush impetuously into marriage may spend a long time regretting doing so.

ORIGIN – Old French *marier*, from Latin *maritus* 'married, husband'.

marry² > *exclamation* archaic expressing surprise, indignation, or emphatic assertion.

ORIGIN – variant of *Mary* (mother of Jesus).

Marsala /maar**saal**ə/ > *noun* a dark, sweet fortified dessert wine produced in Sicily.

ORIGIN – named after *Marsala*, a town in Sicily.

marsh > *noun* an area of low-lying land which is flooded in wet seasons or at high tide and typically remains waterlogged.

DERIVATIVES – **marshy** *adjective*.

SYNONYMS – bog, mire, quagmire, swamp.

COMBINATIONS – **marsh gas** methane generated by decaying matter in marshes. **marsh mallow** a tall pink-flowered plant growing in marshes, whose roots were formerly used to make marshmallow. **marsh marigold** a plant with large yellow flowers which grows in damp ground and shallow water.

marshal > *noun* **1** an officer of the highest rank in the armed forces of some countries. **2** chiefly historical a high-ranking officer of state. **3** (in the US) a federal or municipal law officer. **4** an official responsible for supervising public events. **5** (in the UK) an official accompanying a judge on circuit. > *verb* (**marshalled**, **marshalling**; US **marshaled**, **marshaling**) **1** assemble (a group of people, especially soldiers) in order. **2** bring together (facts, information, etc.) in an organised way. **3** direct the movement of (an aircraft) on the ground at an airport.

COMBINATIONS – **marshalling yard** a large railway yard in which freight wagons are organised into trains. **Marshal of the Royal Air Force** the highest rank of officer in the RAF.

ORIGIN – Old French *mareschal* 'farrier, commander', from Latin *mariscalcus*.

marshmallow > *noun* a spongy sweet made from a mixture of sugar, egg white, and gelatin.

marsupial /maar**soo**piəl/ > *noun* a mammal whose young are born incompletely developed and are carried and suckled in a pouch on the mother's belly.

WORDFINDER – *kinds of marsupial:* bandicoot, kangaroo, koala, opossum, phalanger, possum, Tasmanian devil, wallaby, wombat.

ORIGIN – from Greek *marsupion* 'little purse' (the pouch being likened to a purse).

mart > *noun* a trade centre or market.

Martello tower /maar**tell**ō/ > *noun* any of a number of small circular defensive forts erected along the coasts of Britain during the Napoleonic Wars.

ORIGIN – alteration of Cape *Mortella* in Corsica, site of a tower which proved difficult for the English to capture in 1794.

marten > *noun* a weasel-like forest mammal, hunted for fur in some northern countries.

ORIGIN – from Old French *peau martrine* 'marten fur', from *martre*.

martial /**maar**sh'l/ > *adjective* of or appropriate to war; warlike.

DERIVATIVES – **martially** *adverb*.

USAGE – do not confuse **martial**, 'of war', with **marital**, 'of marriage'.

COMBINATIONS – **martial arts** various sports or skills, mainly of Japanese origin, which originated as forms of self-defence or attack, such as aikido, judo, karate, kung fu, and kendo. **martial law** military government, involving the suspension of ordinary law.

ORIGIN – Latin *martialis*, from *Mars*, the name of the Roman god of war.

Martian > *adjective* of or relating to the planet Mars. > *noun* a supposed inhabitant of Mars.

martin > *noun* used in names of small short-tailed swallows, e.g. **house martin**.

ORIGIN – probably from the name of St *Martin* of Tours.

martinet /maarti**net**/ > *noun* a strict disciplinarian.

ORIGIN – named after Jean *Martinet*, 17th-century French drill master.

martingale /**maar**tinggayl/ > *noun* **1** a strap or set of straps running from the noseband or reins to the girth of a horse, used to prevent the horse from raising its head too high. **2** a gambling system that involves a continual doubling of the stakes.

ORIGIN – French, from an Arabic word meaning 'the fastening'.

Martini > *noun* **1** trademark a type of vermouth produced in Italy. **2** a cocktail made from gin and dry vermouth.

ORIGIN – named after *Martini* and *Rossi*, an Italian company.

Martiniquan /maarti**neek**'n/ (also **Martinican**) > *noun* a person from Martinique, a French island in the Lesser Antilles. > *adjective* relating to Martinique.

martlet > *noun* a kind of bird depicted in heraldry, resembling a swallow without feet.

ORIGIN – Old French *merlet* 'a swift'.

martyr > *noun* **1** a person who is killed because of their religious or other beliefs. **2** a person who exaggerates their difficulties in order to obtain sympathy or admiration. > *verb* make a martyr of.

DERIVATIVES – **martyrdom** *noun*.

ORIGIN – Greek *martur* 'witness'.

martyrology > *noun* (pl. **martyrologies**) **1** the study of the lives of martyrs. **2** a list of martyrs.

marvel > *verb* (**marvelled**, **marvelling**; US **marveled**, **marveling**) be filled with wonder. > *noun* a person or thing that causes a feeling of wonder.

SYNONYMS – *verb* be amazed, wonder. *noun* miracle, sensation, wonder.

ORIGIN – Old French *merveille*, from Latin *mirabilis* 'wonderful', from *mirari* 'to wonder at'.

marvellous (US **marvelous**) > *adjective* **1** causing great wonder; extraordinary. **2** extremely good or pleasing.

DERIVATIVES – **marvellously** *adverb*.

SYNONYMS – **1** amazing, astonishing, extraordinary, remarkable, sensational. **2** excellent, magnificent, wonderful.

Marxism > *noun* the political and economic theories of Karl Marx (1818–83) and Friedrich Engels (1820–95), later developed by their followers to form the basis for the theory and practice of communism.

DERIVATIVES – **Marxist** *noun* & *adjective*.

COMBINATIONS – **Marxism–Leninism** the doctrines of Marx as interpreted and put into effect by Lenin in the Soviet Union.

marzipan > *noun* a sweet paste of ground almonds, sugar, and egg whites, used to coat cakes or to make confectionery.

wordpower facts

Marzipan

The word **marzipan** entered English in the 15th century in the form *marchpane*, derived from Italian *marzapane*, possibly from an Arabic root. This early form of the word was influenced by the name of the month *March* and the word for bread *pain* (now obsolete in English, but then in use as a borrowing from French). The form *marchpane* was displaced in the 19th century by **marzipan**, under the influence of the German form, which has the same spelling.

Masai /**maa**sī/ (also **Maasai**) > *noun* (pl. same or **Masais**) a member of a pastoral people living in Tanzania and Kenya.

masala /mə**saal**ə/ > *noun* a mixture of spices ground into a paste or powder and used in Indian cookery.

ORIGIN – Urdu, from Arabic, 'ingredients, materials'.

mascara /mas**kaar**ə/ > *noun* a cosmetic for darkening and thickening the eyelashes.

ORIGIN – Italian, 'mask'.

mascarpone /maskə**pō**nay/ > *noun* a soft, mild Italian cream cheese.

mascot > *noun* a person, animal, or object that is identified with a person, group, team, etc. and supposed to bring good luck.

ORIGIN – French *mascotte*, from Provençal *masco* 'witch'.

masculine > *adjective* 1 relating to men; male. 2 having the qualities or appearance traditionally associated with men. 3 Grammar referring to a gender of nouns and adjectives conventionally regarded as male.
DERIVATIVES – **masculinity** noun.
SYNONYMS – 2 male, manly, virile.
ANTONYMS – feminine.
ORIGIN – from Latin *masculus* 'male'.

maser /**may**zər/ > *noun* a form of laser generating a beam of microwaves.
ORIGIN – acronym from *microwave amplification by stimulated emission of radiation*.

mash > *noun* 1 a soft mass made by crushing a substance into a pulp. 2 bran mixed with hot water, given as a warm food to horses. 3 Brit. informal boiled and mashed potatoes. 4 (in brewing) a mixture of powdered malt and hot water, in which the sugars dissolve to form the wort. > *verb* 1 reduce or beat to a mash. 2 (in brewing) mix (powdered malt) with hot water to form wort. 3 Brit. informal (with reference to tea) brew or infuse.
SYNONYMS – *verb* 1 crush, pulp, purée.

mask > *noun* 1 a covering for all or part of the face, worn as a disguise, for protection or hygiene, or for theatrical effect. 2 a respirator used to filter inhaled air or to supply gas for inhalation. 3 a likeness of a person's face moulded or sculpted in clay or wax. 4 a face pack. > *verb* 1 cover (an object or surface) with a mask. 2 conceal or disguise. 3 cover (an object or surface) so as to protect it during painting.
DERIVATIVES – **masked** adjective.
SYNONYMS – *verb* 2 camouflage, cloak, conceal, disguise, hide.
COMBINATIONS – **masked ball** a ball at which participants wear masks to conceal their faces. **masking tape** adhesive tape used in painting to cover areas on which paint is not wanted.
ORIGIN – French *masque*, from Italian *maschera* or *mascara*, probably from Latin *masca* 'witch, spectre', but influenced by an Arabic word meaning 'buffoon'.

masochism /**mass**əkiz'm/ > *noun* the tendency to derive pleasure from one's own pain or humiliation.
DERIVATIVES – **masochist** noun **masochistic** adjective.
ORIGIN – named after Leopold von Sacher-Masoch (1835–95), the Austrian novelist who described it.

mason > *noun* 1 a builder and worker in stone. 2 (**Mason**) a Freemason.
Masonic > *adjective* relating to Freemasons.
masonry > *noun* 1 stonework. 2 (**Masonry**) Freemasonry.
masque /maask/ > *noun* a form of dramatic entertainment popular in the 16th and 17th centuries, consisting of dancing and acting performed by masked players.

masquerade > *noun* 1 a false show or pretence. 2 a masked ball. > *verb* 1 pretend to be someone that one is not. 2 be disguised or passed off as something else.
SYNONYMS – *noun* 1 act, facade, pose, pretence.

Mass > *noun* 1 the Christian ceremony of Eucharist or Holy Communion, especially in the Roman Catholic Church. 2 a musical setting of parts of the liturgy used in the Mass.
ORIGIN – Latin *missa*, from *mittere* 'dismiss', perhaps from the last words of the service, *Ite, missa est* 'Go, it is the dismissal'.

mass > *noun* 1 a body of matter with no definite shape. 2 a large number of people or objects gathered together. 3 (before another noun) done by or affecting large numbers: *a mass exodus*. 4 (**the masses**) the ordinary people. 5 (**the mass of**) the majority of. 6 (**a mass of**) a large amount of. 7 Physics the quantity of matter which a body contains, as measured by its acceleration under a given force or by the force exerted on it by a gravitational field. Compare with **WEIGHT**. > *verb* assemble into a single body or mass.
SYNONYMS – *noun* 2 crowd, host, multitude. *verb* accumulate, collect, congregate.
COMBINATIONS – **mass market** the arena of commercial activity in which goods are produced in large quantities for the broad population. **mass number** Physics the total number of protons and neutrons in an atomic nucleus. **mass noun** Grammar a noun denoting something which cannot be counted, in English usually a noun which has no plural in ordinary usage and is not used with the indefinite article, e.g. *luggage*, *happiness*. Contrasted with **count noun**. **mass-produced** produced in large quantities by an automated mechanical process. **mass spectrometer** Physics an apparatus for separating atoms or molecules according to their mass by ionising them and making them move in different paths by means of electric and magnetic fields.
ORIGIN – Latin *massa*, from Greek *maza* 'barley cake'.

massacre > *noun* 1 a brutal slaughter of a large number of people. 2 informal a very heavy defeat. > *verb* 1 brutally kill (a large number of people). 2 informal inflict a heavy defeat on.
ORIGIN – French.

massage > *noun* the rubbing and kneading of parts of the body with the hands to relieve tension or pain. > *verb* 1 give a massage to. 2 manipulate (figures) to give a more acceptable result. 3 gently flatter (someone's ego).

COMBINATIONS – **massage parlour** 1 an establishment in which massage is provided for payment. 2 euphemistic a brothel.
ORIGIN – French, probably from Portuguese *amassar* 'knead', from *massa* 'dough'.

masseur > *noun* (fem. **masseuse**) a person who provides massage professionally.
massif /**mass**if, ma**seef**/ > *noun* a compact group of mountains.
ORIGIN – French, 'massive'.
massive > *adjective* 1 large and heavy or solid. 2 exceptionally large, intense, or severe. 3 forming a solid or continuous mass.
DERIVATIVES – **massively** adverb **massiveness** noun.
SYNONYMS – 1 colossal, gigantic, huge, immense, vast.

mast¹ > *noun* 1 a tall upright post or spar on a boat, generally carrying a sail or sails. 2 any tall upright post, especially a flagpole or a television or radio transmitter.
WORDFINDER – foremast, fore-topgallant-mast, foretopmast, mainmast, mizzen, royal, topgallant, topmast (*types of mast*); crosstrees (*horizontal struts that spread the rigging*), sprit (*a small spar reaching from a mast to a corner of a sail*), stay (*a support for a mast*), step (*to set up a mast*), yard (*a spar fixed to a mast to support a sail*).
IDIOMS – **before the mast** historical serving as an ordinary seaman (who lived in the forecastle, in the forward part of the ship). **nail one's colours to the mast** declare openly and firmly what one believes.

mast² > *noun* the fruit of beech and other forest trees, especially as food for pigs.

mastectomy /ma**stek**təmi/ > *noun* (pl. **mastectomies**) a surgical operation to remove a breast.
ORIGIN – from Greek *mastos* 'breast'.

master > *noun* 1 a man in a position of authority, control, or ownership. 2 a skilled practitioner of a particular art or activity. 3 the head of a college or school. 4 chiefly Brit. a male schoolteacher. 5 a person who holds a second or further degree. 6 an original film, recording, or document from which copies can be made. 7 a title prefixed to the name of a boy. > *adjective* 1 (of an artist) having great skill or proficiency: *a master painter*. 2 skilled in a particular trade and able to teach others: *a master builder*. 3 main; principal. > *verb* 1 acquire complete knowledge or skill in. 2 gain control of; overcome. 3 make a master copy of (a film or record).
COMBINATIONS – **master-at-arms** a warrant officer responsible for police duties on board a ship. **masterclass** a class given to students by a musician regarded as a master. **master key** a key that opens several locks, each of which also has its own key. **master of ceremonies** a person in charge of procedure at a state occasion, formal

event, or entertainment, who introduces the speakers or performers. **Master of the Rolls** (in England and Wales) the judge who presides over the Court of Appeal.
ORIGIN – Latin *magister*.

masterful > *adjective* **1** powerful and able to control others. **2** performed or performing very skilfully.
DERIVATIVES – **masterfully** *adverb*.
SYNONYMS – **1** authoritative, commanding, magisterial. **2** accomplished, adept, consummate, expert, masterly.

masterly > *adjective* performed or performing very skilfully.
USAGE – strictly, there is a distinction between **masterful** and **masterly**: both mean 'very skilful', but only **masterful** means 'powerful and able to control others'.

mastermind > *noun* **1** a person who plans and directs a complex scheme or enterprise. **2** a person with outstanding intellect. > *verb* be the mastermind of.

masterpiece > *noun* **1** a work of outstanding skill. **2** historical a piece of work by a craftsman accepted as qualification for membership of a guild as an acknowledged master.

mastery > *noun* **1** comprehensive knowledge or command of a subject or skill. **2** control or superiority.

masthead > *noun* **1** the highest part of a ship's mast. **2** the name of a newspaper or magazine printed at the top of the first or editorial page. > *verb* send or raise to the masthead.

mastic > *noun* **1** an aromatic gum from the bark of a Mediterranean tree, used in making varnish and chewing gum and as a flavouring. **2** a putty-like waterproof filler and sealant used in building.
ORIGIN – Greek *mastikhē*, from *mastikhan* 'grind the teeth'.

masticate /**mas**tikayt/ > *verb* chew (food).
DERIVATIVES – **mastication** *noun*.
ORIGIN – Latin *masticare*, from Greek *mastikhan* 'grind the teeth'.

mastiff > *noun* a dog of a large, strong breed with drooping ears and pendulous lips.
ORIGIN – Old French *mastin*, based on Latin *mansuetus* 'tame'.

mastitis /ma**stī**tiss/ > *noun* inflammation of the mammary gland in the breast or udder.
ORIGIN – from Greek *mastos* 'breast'.

mastodon /**mas**tədon/ > *noun* a large extinct elephant-like mammal of the Miocene to Pleistocene epochs.
ORIGIN – from Greek *mastos* 'breast' + *odous* 'tooth' (with reference to nipple-shaped projections on its molar teeth).

mastoid > *noun* **1** (also **mastoid process**) Anatomy a conical projection of the temporal bone behind the ear, to which neck muscles are attached, and which has air spaces linked to the middle ear. **2** (**mastoids**) (treated as sing.) informal mastoiditis.

mastoiditis > *noun* Medicine inflammation of the mastoid.

masturbate > *verb* stimulate one's genitals with one's hand for sexual pleasure.
DERIVATIVES – **masturbation** *noun* **masturbator** *noun* **masturbatory** *adjective*.
ORIGIN – Latin *masturbari*.

mat > *noun* **1** a thick piece of material placed on the floor and used as protection from dirt or as a decorative rug. **2** a piece of resilient material for landing on in gymnastics or similar sports. **3** a small piece of material placed on a surface to protect it from the heat or moisture of an object placed on it. **4** a thick, untidy layer of hairy or woolly material.
IDIOMS – **on the mat** informal being reprimanded by someone in authority.

Matabele /mattə**bee**li/ > *noun* the Ndebele people collectively, particularly those of Zimbabwe.
ORIGIN – Sotho (a Bantu language).

matador > *noun* a bullfighter whose task is to kill the bull.
ORIGIN – Spanish, 'killer'.

match¹ > *noun* **1** a contest in which people or teams compete against each other. **2** an equal contender. **3** an exact equivalent. **4** a corresponding pair. **5** a potential husband or wife. **6** a marriage. > *verb* **1** correspond or cause to correspond; make or be harmonious. **2** be equal to. **3** place in competition with another.
DERIVATIVES – **matching** *adjective*.
SYNONYMS – *noun* **2** counterpart, rival. **3** double, duplicate, facsimile.
COMBINATIONS – **matchboard** interlocking boards joined together by tongue and groove. **match play** golf in which the score is reckoned by holes won. **match point** (in tennis) a point which if won by the player in the lead will also win them the match.
ORIGIN – Old English, 'mate, companion'.

match² > *noun* **1** a short, thin stick tipped with a mixture that ignites when rubbed against a rough surface, used to light a fire. **2** historical a piece of wick or cord which burned uniformly, used for lighting gunpowder.
COMBINATIONS – **matchwood** very small pieces or splinters of wood.
ORIGIN – Old French *meche*.

matchbox > *noun* **1** a small box in which matches are sold. **2** (before another noun) very small: *her matchbox apartment*.

matchless > *adjective* unequalled; incomparable.

matchlock > *noun* historical a type of gun with a lock containing a piece of match.

matchmaker > *noun* a person who tries to bring about marriages or relationships between other people.
DERIVATIVES – **matchmaking** *noun*.

matchstick > *noun* **1** the stem of a match. **2** (before another noun) drawn using thin straight lines: *matchstick men*.

mate¹ > *noun* **1** Brit. informal a friend or companion. **2** (in combination) a fellow member or occupant: *his teammates*. **3** the sexual partner of an animal. **4** an assistant. **5** an officer on a merchant ship subordinate to the master. > *verb* **1** (of animals or birds) come together for breeding. **2** join or connect mechanically.
SYNONYMS – *noun* **1** buddy, chum, crony, pal. *verb* **1** breed, couple, copulate, pair.

mate² > *noun & verb* Chess short for CHECKMATE.

mate /**ma**tay/ (also **yerba maté**) > *noun* a bitter tea-like infusion made in South America from the leaves of a shrub.
ORIGIN – Quechua: *yerba* is Spanish, 'herb'.

matelassé /matə**lass**ay/ > *noun* a fabric having a raised design like quilting.
ORIGIN – French, from *matelas* 'mattress'.

matelot /**mat**lō/ > *noun* Brit. informal a sailor.
ORIGIN – French, from Dutch *mattenoot* 'bed companion' (because sailors had to share hammocks).

mater /**may**tə/ > *noun* Brit. informal, dated mother.
ORIGIN – Latin.

materfamilias /maytərfə**mill**iass/ > *noun* (pl. **matresfamilias**) /maytreezfə**mill**iass/ the female head of a family or household.

material > *noun* **1** the matter from which something is or can be made. **2** (also **materials**) items needed for doing or creating something. **3** cloth or fabric. > *adjective* **1** consisting of or referring to physical objects rather than ideas or spirit. **2** of importance or relevance.
DERIVATIVES – **materiality** *noun* **materially** *adverb*.
SYNONYMS – *noun* **1** matter, stuff, substance. *adjective* **1** concrete, corporeal, physical, real, solid, substantial, tangible. **2** important, pertinent, relevant, significant.
ANTONYMS – *adjective* **1** abstract, intellectual, spiritual.
ORIGIN – Latin *materia* 'matter', from *mater* 'mother'.

materialise (also **materialize**) > *verb* **1** become actual fact; happen. **2** appear in bodily form.
DERIVATIVES – **materialisation** *noun*.

materialism > *noun* **1** a tendency to

consider material possessions and physical comfort as more important than spiritual values. **2** Philosophy the doctrine that nothing exists except matter and its movements and modifications.

DERIVATIVES – **materialist** noun & adjective **materialistic** adjective.

materiel /məteeriel/ > noun military materials and equipment.

ORIGIN – French.

maternal > adjective **1** relating to or characteristic of a mother. **2** related through the mother's side of the family.

DERIVATIVES – **maternally** adverb.

---

wordpower facts
Maternal

The word **maternal** derives from Latin *mater* 'mother', which is the source of a great many English words. *Mater* comes from an Indo-European root shared by **mother** (which is an Old English word), and gave rise to the related words **matron** and **matrimony**, as well as **material** and **matter**. The English word **matrix** also comes from *mater*: it means 'womb' in Latin, and is the source of **madrigal** ('simple song', from the notion 'maternal or primitive') and **matriculate**.

---

maternity > noun **1** motherhood. **2** (before another noun) relating to the period during pregnancy and shortly after childbirth: *maternity clothes*.

mateship > noun Austral./NZ informal companionship or friendship.

matey > adjective (**matier, matiest**) Brit. informal familiar and friendly.

DERIVATIVES – **mateyness** (also **matiness**) noun **matily** adverb.

mathematics > plural noun (usu. treated as sing.) the field of knowledge concerned with number, quantity, and space, either as abstract ideas (**pure mathematics**) or as applied to physics, engineering, and other subjects (**applied mathematics**).

WORDFINDER – algebra, arithmetic, calculus, geometry, group theory, mechanics, number theory, statistics, trigonometry (*branches of mathematics*).

DERIVATIVES – **mathematical** adjective **mathematically** adverb **mathematician** noun.

ORIGIN – from Greek *mathēma* 'science', from *manthanein* 'learn'.

maths (N. Amer. **math**) > noun short for MATHEMATICS.

Matilda > noun Austral./NZ informal, archaic a bushman's bundle.

---

wordpower facts
Matilda

The Australian phrase **waltzing Matilda**, which dates from the 19th century, means 'travelling carrying a bundle of rolled-up bedding and clothes'. It probably derives from a German expression involving the name *Mathilde*, used to refer to a camp follower or prostitute, and it is famous as the title of a song written by the Australian poet A.B. 'Banjo' Paterson in 1903.

---

matinee /mattinay/ > noun an afternoon performance in a theatre or cinema.

COMBINATIONS – **matinee coat** Brit. a baby's short coat. **matinee idol** informal, dated a handsome actor admired chiefly by women.

ORIGIN – French: originally referring to performances in the morning, later extended to any performance earlier than the evening.

matins > noun a service of morning prayer, especially in the Anglican Church.

ORIGIN – Old French *matines*, plural of *matin* 'morning', from Latin *matutinus* 'early in the morning', from *Matuta*, the name of the dawn goddess.

matriarch /maytriaark/ > noun **1** a woman who is the head of a family or tribe. **2** a powerful older woman.

DERIVATIVES – **matriarchal** adjective **matriarchy** noun.

matrices plural of MATRIX.

matricide /maytrisīd/ > noun **1** the killing of one's mother. **2** a person who kills their mother.

DERIVATIVES – **matricidal** adjective.

matriculate /mətrikyoolayt/ > verb enrol or be enrolled at a college or university.

DERIVATIVES – **matriculation** noun.

ORIGIN – Latin *matriculare*, from *matricula* 'register', from *matrix* 'womb'.

matrilineal /matrilinniəl/ > adjective based on kinship with the mother or the female line.

DERIVATIVES – **matrilineally** adverb.

matrimony > noun the state or ceremony of being married.

DERIVATIVES – **matrimonial** adjective.

SYNONYMS – marriage, union, wedlock.

ORIGIN – Latin *matrimonium*, based on *mater* 'mother'.

matrix /maytriks/ > noun (pl. **matrices** /maytriseez/ or **matrixes**) **1** an environment or material in which something develops. **2** a mould in which something is cast or shaped. **3** Mathematics a rectangular array of quantities in rows and columns that is manipulated according to particular rules. **4** a grid-like array of elements; a lattice. **5** a mass of fine-grained rock in which gems, crystals, or fossils are embedded.

ORIGIN – Latin, 'womb', from *mater* 'mother'.

matron > noun **1** a woman in charge of domestic and medical arrangements at a boarding school. **2** a dignified or staid married woman. **3** Brit. dated a woman in charge of nursing in a hospital. **4** chiefly US a female prison officer.

DERIVATIVES – **matronly** adjective.

NOTE – in sense 3, the official term is now **senior nursing officer**.

COMBINATIONS – **matron of honour** a married woman attending the bride at a wedding.

ORIGIN – Latin *matrona*, from *mater* 'mother'.

matt (also **matte**) > adjective not shiny; dull and flat. > noun **1** a matt colour, paint, or finish. **2** a sheet of cardboard placed on the back of a picture, as a mount or border.

ORIGIN – French *mat*.

matte > noun **1** a mask used to obscure part of an image in a film and allow another image to be substituted. **2** an impure product of the smelting of sulphide ores.

matted > adjective (of hair or fur) tangled into a thick mass.

SYNONYMS – dishevelled, knotted, tangled, tousled, unkempt.

matter > noun **1** physical substance or material in general, as distinct from mind and spirit; (in physics) that which occupies space and possesses mass. **2** an affair or situation under consideration. **3** (**the matter**) the reason for a problem. **4** written or printed material. **5** Logic the particular content of a proposition, as distinct from its form. **6** Law something to be tried or proved in court; a case. > verb be important or significant.

IDIOMS – **for that matter** and indeed also. **in the matter of** as regards. **a matter of 1** no more than (a specified period). **2** a question of. **a matter of course** the natural or expected thing. **no matter 1** regardless of. **2** it is of no importance.

SYNONYMS – noun **1** material, stuff, substance. **2** affair, business, point, situation, subject, topic. verb count, signify.

ORIGIN – Latin *materia*, from *mater* 'mother'.

matter of fact > noun a fact as distinct from an opinion or conjecture. > adjective (**matter-of-fact**) **1** concerned only with factual content. **2** unemotional and practical.

IDIOMS – **as a matter of fact** in reality; in fact.

DERIVATIVES – **matter-of-factly** adverb **matter-of-factness** noun.

matting > *noun* material used for mats, especially coarse fabric woven from a natural fibre.

mattock > *noun* an agricultural tool similar to a pickaxe, but with one arm of the head shaped like an adze and the other having a chisel edge.

mattress > *noun* a fabric case filled with soft, firm, or springy material used for sleeping on.
ORIGIN – Arabic, 'carpet or cushion'.

maturation > *noun* 1 the action or process of maturing. 2 the formation of pus in a boil, abscess, etc.

mature > *adjective* 1 fully grown or physically developed; adult. 2 like an adult in mental or emotional development. 3 (of thought or planning) careful and thorough. 4 (of certain foodstuffs or drinks) ready for consumption; full-flavoured. 5 (of a bill) due for payment. > *verb* 1 become mature. 2 (of an insurance policy, security, etc.) become payable at the end of its term.
DERIVATIVES – **maturely** *adverb*.
SYNONYMS – *adjective* 2 adult, grown-up, level-headed, responsible, sensible. 3 careful, considered, thoughtful.
ANTONYMS – childish, immature, juvenile.
ORIGIN – Latin *maturus* 'timely, ripe'.

maturity > *noun* 1 the state, fact, or period of being mature. 2 the time when an insurance policy, security, etc. matures.

matutinal /matyootīnəl/ > *adjective* formal of or occurring in the morning.
ORIGIN – from Latin *matutinus*: see **MATINS**.

matzo /matsō/ (also **matzoh**) > *noun* (pl. **matzos** or **matzoth** /matsōt/) a crisp biscuit of unleavened bread, traditionally eaten by Jews during Passover.
ORIGIN – Yiddish, from Hebrew.

maudlin > *adjective* self-pityingly or tearfully sentimental.
ORIGIN – from the name of Mary *Magdalen* in the Bible, typically depicted weeping.

maul > *verb* 1 wound by scratching and tearing. 2 handle or treat savagely or roughly. > *noun* 1 Rugby Union a loose scrum formed around a player with the ball off the ground. 2 a very heavy mallet.
ORIGIN – from Latin *malleus* 'hammer'.

maulstick > *noun* a light stick with a padded leather ball at one end, held by a painter to support and steady the brush hand.
ORIGIN – Dutch *maalstok* 'paint stick'.

maunder > *verb* move, talk, or act in a rambling or aimless manner.

Maundy > *noun* a public ceremony on the Thursday before Easter (**Maundy Thursday**) at which the British monarch distributes specially minted coins (**Maundy money**) to a group of people.

---

wordpower facts
Maundy
The Maundy ceremony originally involved washing the feet of poor people as well as distributing alms: it commemorated Christ's washing of the apostles' feet at the Last Supper. The word **Maundy** comes, via Old French *mandé*, from Latin *mandatum* 'mandate, commandment', and refers to Christ's words in the Gospel of John (chapter 13), said after washing the apostles' feet: 'I give you a new commandment: love one another'. This verse was traditionally sung at the Maundy ceremony.

Mauritanian /morritaynian/ > *noun* a person from Mauritania, a country in West Africa. > *adjective* relating to Mauritania.

Mauritian /mərish'n/ > *noun* a person from the island of Mauritius in the Indian Ocean. > *adjective* relating to Mauritius.

mausoleum /mawsəleeəm/ > *noun* (pl. **mausolea** /mawsəleeə/ or **mausoleums**) a building housing a tomb or tombs.
ORIGIN – Greek *Mausōleion*, from *Mausōlos*, the name of a king of the 4th century BC to whose tomb in Halicarnassus the name was originally applied.

mauve /mōv/ > *noun* a pale purple colour.
ORIGIN – French, 'mallow', from Latin *malva*.

maven /mayv'n/ > *noun* N. Amer. informal an expert or connoisseur.
ORIGIN – Yiddish.

maverick > *noun* 1 an unorthodox or independent-minded person. 2 N. Amer. an unbranded calf or yearling.
ORIGIN – from the name of Samuel A. *Maverick*, a Texas rancher who did not brand his cattle.

maw > *noun* the jaws or throat, especially of a voracious animal.

mawkish > *adjective* 1 sentimental in a feeble or sickly way. 2 archaic or dialect having a faint sickly flavour.
ORIGIN – from obsolete *mawk* 'maggot'.

max > *abbreviation* maximum.

maxi > *noun* (pl. **maxis**) a skirt or coat reaching to the ankle.

maxilla /maksillə/ > *noun* (pl. **maxillae** /maksillee/) 1 Anatomy the bone of the upper jaw. 2 Zoology (in arthropods) each of a pair of chewing mouthparts.
DERIVATIVES – **maxillary** *adjective*.
ORIGIN – Latin, 'jaw'.

maxim > *noun* a short statement expressing a general truth or rule of conduct.
SYNONYMS – adage, aphorism, axiom, dictum, epigram, precept, saying.

ORIGIN – from Latin *propositio maxima* 'most important proposition'.

maximise (also **maximize**) > *verb* 1 make as great or large as possible. 2 make the best use of.
DERIVATIVES – **maximisation** *noun* **maximiser** *noun*.

maximum > *noun* (pl. **maxima** or **maximums**) the greatest amount, size, or intensity possible or attained. > *adjective* greatest in amount, size, or intensity.
DERIVATIVES – **maximal** *adjective*.
SYNONYMS – *noun* apex, height, limit, peak, pinnacle, summit, utmost. *adjective* highest, largest, supreme, topmost, utmost.
ORIGIN – Latin, 'greatest thing'.

May > *noun* 1 the fifth month of the year. 2 (**may**) the hawthorn or its blossom.
COMBINATIONS – **May Day** 1 May, celebrated as a springtime festival or as a day honouring workers. **maypole** a decorated pole with long ribbons attached to the top, traditionally used for dancing round on May Day. **mayweed** a wild chamomile found as a weed of waste ground. [ORIGIN – from *maythe(n)*, an earlier name for this plant.]
ORIGIN – from Latin *Maius mensis* 'month of the goddess *Maia*'.

may > *modal verb* (3rd sing. present **may**; past **might**) 1 expressing possibility. 2 expressing permission. 3 expressing a wish or hope.
IDIOMS – **be that as it may** nevertheless.
USAGE – when expressing or asking for permission, it is regarded as more formal (and possibly more polite) to use **may** rather than **can** in more formal contexts: it is better to say *May we leave now?* than *Can we leave now?* The verb **can** is generally used to express ability or capability (*can he move?* = is he physically able to move?; *may he move?* = is he allowed to move?).

Maya /mīyə/ > *noun* (pl. same or **Mayas**) a member of a Central American people whose civilisation died out AD *c.*900.
DERIVATIVES – **Mayan** *adjective* & *noun*.

maybe > *adverb* perhaps; possibly.

Mayday > *noun* an international radio distress signal used by ships and aircraft.
ORIGIN – from the pronunciation of French *m'aider* 'help me'.

mayfly > *noun* a slender insect with transparent wings which lives as an adult for only a very short time.

mayhem > *noun* violent disorder; chaos.
ORIGIN – Old French, related to **MAIM**: first denoting the crime of injuring someone maliciously.

mayn't > *contraction* may not.

mayonnaise /mayənayz/ > *noun* a thick creamy dressing made from egg yolks, oil, and vinegar.

ORIGIN – French, meaning 'from Port *Mahon*' (on the island of Minorca).

mayor > *noun* the elected head of a city or borough council.

DERIVATIVES – **mayoral** *adjective* **mayorship** *noun*.

ORIGIN – from Latin *major* 'greater'.

mayoralty > *noun* (pl. **mayoralties**) the period or term of office of a mayor.

mayoress > *noun* **1** the wife of a mayor. **2** a woman elected as mayor.

maze > *noun* **1** a puzzle consisting of a network of paths and walls or hedges through which one has to find a way. **2** a confusing mass of information.

SYNONYMS – **1** labyrinth.

ORIGIN – related to AMAZE: first meaning 'delirium, delusion'.

mazel tov /**mazz**'l tov/ > *exclamation* (among Jews) congratulations; good luck.

ORIGIN – modern Hebrew, 'good star'.

mazurka /mǝzurkǝ/ > *noun* a lively Polish dance in triple time.

ORIGIN – Polish, referring to a woman from the province of Mazovia.

MB > *abbreviation* **1** Bachelor of Medicine. [ORIGIN – Latin *Medicinae Baccalaureus*.] **2** Manitoba. **3** (also **Mb**) Computing megabyte(s).

MBA > *abbreviation* Master of Business Administration.

MBE > *abbreviation* Member of the Order of the British Empire.

MBO > *abbreviation* management buyout.

MC > *abbreviation* **1** Master of Ceremonies. **2** (in the US) Member of Congress. **3** Military Cross.

MCC > *abbreviation* Marylebone Cricket Club.

MCR > *abbreviation* Brit. Middle Common Room.

MD > *abbreviation* **1** Doctor of Medicine. [ORIGIN – Latin *Medicinae Doctor*.] **2** Brit. Managing Director. **3** Maryland. **4** musical director.

Md > *symbol* the chemical element mendelevium.

MDF > *abbreviation* medium density fibreboard.

MDMA > *abbreviation* methylenedioxy-methamphetamine, the drug Ecstasy.

ME > *abbreviation* **1** Maine. **2** myalgic encephalomyelitis.

me¹ > *pronoun* (first person sing.) **1** used as the object of a verb or preposition or after 'than', 'as', or the verb 'to be', to refer to the speaker himself or herself. **2** N. Amer. informal to or for myself.

USAGE – **me** should be used as the object of a verb or preposition, as in *John hates me*, *Come with me!*, or *He gave it to John and me*. It is not correct to use **me** as the subject of a verb, as in *John and me went to the shops*; in this case use **I** instead: *John and I went to the shops*. Strictly speaking, after *it is*, *it was*, *it may be*, etc., *I* should be used, but in practice phrases such as *it's me!* are widely used, and *it is I* can sound rather over-formal.

me² (also **mi**) > *noun* Music the third note of a major scale, coming between 'ray' and 'fah'.

mea culpa /mayǝ kulpǝ/ > *noun* an acknowledgement that one is at fault.

ORIGIN – Latin, 'by my fault'.

mead¹ > *noun* an alcoholic drink of fermented honey and water.

mead² > *noun* literary a meadow.

meadow > *noun* **1** an area of grassland, especially one used for hay. **2** a piece of low ground near a river.

SYNONYMS – field, paddock, pasture; archaic lea.

COMBINATIONS – **meadowlark** an American songbird, brown with yellow and black underparts. **meadow saffron** a poisonous lilac-flowered autumn crocus.

meadowsweet > *noun* a tall plant with heads of creamy-white fragrant flowers.

meagre (US **meager**) > *adjective* **1** lacking in quantity or quality. **2** lean; thin.

DERIVATIVES – **meagrely** *adverb* **meagreness** *noun*.

SYNONYMS – **1** inadequate, insufficient, limited, modest, paltry, scant, scanty, sparse.

ANTONYMS – ample, plentiful.

ORIGIN – Old French *maigre*, from Latin *macer*.

meal¹ > *noun* **1** any of the regular daily occasions when food is eaten. **2** the food eaten on such an occasion.

WORDFINDER – prandial (*relating to a meal or meals*); banquet, barbecue, breakfast, brunch, buffet, dinner, feast, lunch, luncheon, picnic, snack, supper, tea (*meals*).

IDIOMS – **make a meal of** Brit. informal perform (an action) with unnecessary effort or fuss.

COMBINATIONS – **meal ticket** a person or thing exploited as a source of income.

meal² > *noun* **1** the edible part of any grain or pulse ground to powder; flour. **2** any powdery substance made by grinding.

COMBINATIONS – **meal beetle** a dark brown beetle which is a pest of stored grain and cereal products.

mealie > *noun* chiefly S. African a maize plant or cob.

ORIGIN – Afrikaans *mielie*, from Portuguese *milho* 'maize, millet'.

mealworm > *noun* the larva of the meal beetle.

mealy > *adjective* (**mealier**, **mealiest**) **1** of, like, or containing meal. **2** pale in colour.

COMBINATIONS – **mealy bug** a small sap-sucking scale insect which is coated with a white powdery wax resembling meal and which can be a serious pest. **mealy-mouthed** reluctant to speak frankly. [ORIGIN – perhaps from German *Mehl im Maule behalten* 'carry meal in the mouth' (i.e. be unstraightforward in speech), or related to Latin *mel* 'honey'.]

mean¹ > *verb* (past and past participle **meant**) **1** intend to express or refer to. **2** (of a word) have as its explanation in the same language or its equivalent in another language. **3** intend (something) to occur or be the case. **4** have as a consequence. **5** intend or design for a particular purpose. **6** be of specified importance.

IDIOMS – **mean business** be in earnest. **mean well** have good intentions, but not always carry them out.

SYNONYMS – **1,2** denote, designate, express, signify. **3** aim, intend, plan. **4** entail, involve, necessitate, produce. **5** destine, fate, ordain, predestine.

mean² > *adjective* **1** unwilling to give or share; not generous. **2** unkind or unfair. **3** vicious or aggressive. **4** poor in quality and appearance; inferior. **5** dated of low birth or social class. **6** informal excellent.

DERIVATIVES – **meanly** *adverb* **meanness** *noun*.

SYNONYMS – **1** miserly, niggardly, parsimonious, penny-pinching. **2** callous, malicious, nasty, spiteful, unfair, unkind. **4** shabby, squalid.

ANTONYMS – **1** generous.

mean³ > *noun* **1** the average or central value of a set of quantities. **2** something in the middle of two extremes. > *adjective* **1** calculated as a mean. **2** equally far from two extremes.

WORDFINDER – arithmetic mean (*calculated by adding quantities together and dividing*), geometric mean (*calculated by multiplying quantities together and finding the root*), median (*middle value or term*), mode (*most common value*).

ORIGIN – Latin *medianus* 'middle'.

meander /miandǝr/ > *verb* **1** follow a winding course. **2** wander in a leisurely or aimless way. > *noun* a winding bend of a river or road.

SYNONYMS – **1** twist, wind, zigzag. **2** amble, ramble, saunter, stroll, wander.

ORIGIN – Greek, from the name of the winding river *Maeander* in SW Turkey.

meaning > *noun* **1** what is meant by a word, idea, or action. **2** worthwhile quality; purpose. > *adjective* expressive.

WORDFINDER – antonym, synonym, denotation, connotation, nuance (*types of meaning*); semantics (*the study of meaning*).

meaningful > *adjective* **1** having meaning. **2** worthwhile. **3** expressive.

DERIVATIVES – **meaningfully** *adverb* **meaningfulness** *noun*.

meaningless > *adjective* having no meaning or significance.

DERIVATIVES – **meaninglessly** *adverb* **meaninglessness** *noun*.

means > *plural noun* (also treated as sing.) **1** an action or system for achieving a result. **2** financial resources or income. **3** substantial resources; wealth.

IDIOMS – **by all means** of course. **by means of** by using. **by no means** certainly not. **a means to an end** a thing that is not valued in itself but is useful in achieving an aim.

SYNONYMS – **1** manner, measure, mechanism, method, procedure, way.

ORIGIN – plural of MEAN³, the early sense being 'intermediary'.

means test > *noun* an official investigation of a person's finances to determine whether they qualify for state assistance. > *verb* (**means-test**) subject to or base on a means test.

meant past and past participle of MEAN¹.

meantime > *adverb* (also **in the meantime**) meanwhile.

meanwhile > *adverb* **1** (also **in the meanwhile**) in the intervening period of time. **2** at the same time.

measles > *plural noun* (treated as sing.) an infectious disease spread by a virus, causing fever and a red rash.

ORIGIN – probably from Dutch *masel* 'spot'.

measly > *adjective* (**measlier**, **measliest**) informal ridiculously small or few.

measure > *verb* **1** determine the size, amount, or degree of (something) by comparison with a standard unit. **2** be of (a specified size). **3** (**measure out**) take an exact quantity of. **4** (**measure up**) reach the required or expected standard. > *noun* **1** a means adopted to achieve a purpose. **2** a legislative bill. **3** a standard unit used to express size, amount, or degree. **4** a measuring device marked with such units. **5** (**a measure of**) a certain amount or degree of. **6** (**a measure of**) an indication of the extent or quality of. **7** (**measures**) a group of rock strata. **8** a metrical unit or group in poetry.

WORDFINDER – gauge, meter, rule, ruler, scale, tape measure, yardstick (*measuring devices*).

IDIOMS – **for good measure** as an amount or item beyond that which is strictly required. **have the measure of** understand the character or abilities of.

DERIVATIVES – **measurable** *adjective* **measurably** *adverb*.

SYNONYMS – *verb* **1** assess, determine, evaluate, gauge, meter, survey. *noun* **1** action, course, expedient, means, procedure. **2** act, bill, law.

ORIGIN – Latin *mensura*, from *metiri* 'to measure'.

measured > *adjective* **1** slow and regular in rhythm. **2** carefully considered and restrained.

measureless > *adjective* literary having no limits.

measurement > *noun* **1** the action of measuring. **2** an amount, size, or extent found by measuring. **3** a standard unit used in measuring.

meat > *noun* **1** the flesh of an animal as food. **2** the main substance or chief part: *let's get to the meat of the matter.*

WORDFINDER – carnivore (*an animal that eats meat*); bacon, beef, brawn, chicken, duck, game, gammon, ham, lamb, mutton, offal, pork, poultry, turkey, veal, venison (*kinds of meat*).

IDIOMS – **easy meat** informal a person who is easily overcome or outwitted. **one man's meat is another man's poison** proverb things liked or enjoyed by one person may be distasteful to another.

COMBINATIONS – **meatball** a ball of minced or chopped meat. **meat loaf** minced or chopped meat baked in the shape of a loaf. **meatspace** the physical world as opposed to cyberspace or another virtual environment.

ORIGIN – Old English, 'food', 'article of food'.

meaty > *adjective* (**meatier**, **meatiest**) **1** resembling or full of meat. **2** fleshy or muscular. **3** substantial.

DERIVATIVES – **meatiness** *noun*.

Mecca > *noun* a place which attracts many people of a particular group or with a particular interest.

ORIGIN – from the holy city of *Mecca* in Saudi Arabia, centre of pilgrimage for Muslims.

mechanic > *noun* a skilled worker who repairs and maintains machinery.

ORIGIN – Greek, from *mēkhanē* 'machine'.

mechanical > *adjective* **1** relating to or operated by a machine or machinery. **2** lacking thought or spontaneity. **3** relating to physical forces or motion.

DERIVATIVES – **mechanically** *adverb*.

SYNONYMS – **2** automatic, habitual, instinctive, involuntary, reflex, routine, unthinking.

COMBINATIONS – **mechanical advantage** the ratio of the force produced by a machine to the force applied to it. **mechanical drawing** a scale drawing done with precision instruments. **mechanical engineering** the branch of engineering concerned with the design, construction, and use of machines.

mechanics > *plural noun* **1** (treated as sing.) the branch of study concerned with motion and forces producing motion. **2** machinery or working parts. **3** the physical or practical aspects of something.

mechanise (also **mechanize**) > *verb* equip with or make reliant on machines or automatic devices.

DERIVATIVES – **mechanisation** *noun*.

mechanism > *noun* **1** a piece of machinery. **2** the way in which something works or is brought about.

SYNONYMS – **1** apparatus, appliance, contraption, instrument.

mechanistic > *adjective* Philosophy relating to the idea that all natural processes can be explained in purely physical or deterministic terms.

meconium /miˈkōniəm/ > *noun* Medicine a dark green substance forming the first faeces of a newborn infant.

ORIGIN – Latin, 'poppy juice'.

med. > *abbreviation* **1** medium. **2** informal medical.

medal > *noun* a metal disc with an inscription or design, awarded for achievement or to commemorate an event.

WORDFINDER – Air Force Cross, British Empire Medal, Distinguished Conduct Medal, Distinguished Flying Cross, Distinguished Service Cross, Distinguished Service Order, George Cross, George Medal, iron cross, Military Cross, Military Medal, purple heart, Victoria Cross (*medals and decorations*).

SYNONYMS – decoration, honour; informal gong.

ORIGIN – Latin *medalia* 'half a denarius' (a Roman coin).

medallion > *noun* **1** a piece of jewellery in the shape of a medal, worn as a pendant. **2** a decorative oval or circular painting, panel, or design.

medallist (US **medalist**) > *noun* a person awarded a medal.

meddle > *verb* interfere in something that is not one's concern.

DERIVATIVES – **meddler** *noun* **meddlesome** *adjective*.

SYNONYMS – interfere, intrude, pry.

ORIGIN – Old French, from Latin *miscere* 'to mix'.

Mede /meed/ > *noun* a member of a people who inhabited ancient Media (present-day Azerbaijan, NW Iran, and NE Iraq).

media > *noun* **1** the means of mass communication, especially television, radio, and newspapers collectively. **2** plural of MEDIUM.

USAGE – the word **media** comes from the Latin plural of **medium**. In the normal sense 'television, radio, and the press collectively', it often behaves as a collective noun (like **staff** or **clergy**, for example), and can be used with either a singular or a plural verb. Although some people regard the singular use as incorrect, it is now generally accepted in standard English.

mediaeval > *adjective* variant spelling of MEDIEVAL.

medial /**mee**diəl/ > *adjective* situated in the middle.
DERIVATIVES – **medially** *adverb*.

median > *adjective* 1 technical situated in the middle. 2 referring to the middle term (or mean of the middle two terms) of a series of values arranged in order of magnitude. > *noun* 1 a median value. 2 Geometry a straight line drawn from one of the angles of a triangle to the middle of the opposite side.

mediate > *verb* 1 try to settle a dispute between two other parties. 2 technical be a medium for (a process or effect).
DERIVATIVES – **mediation** *noun* **mediator** *noun*.
SYNONYMS – 1 arbitrate, conciliate, intercede, intervene, moderate, negotiate.

medic > *noun* informal a medical practitioner or student.

medical > *adjective* of or relating to medicine. > *noun* an examination to assess a person's physical health.
DERIVATIVES – **medically** *adverb*.
COMBINATIONS – **medical officer** a doctor in charge of the health services of a local authority or other organisation.

medicament /miˈdikkəmənt/ > *noun* a medicine.

medicate > *verb* 1 administer medicine or a drug to. 2 (**medicated**) containing a medicinal substance.

medication > *noun* 1 a medicine or drug. 2 treatment with medicines.
WORDFINDER – anaesthetic, analgesic, anodyne, antacid, antibiotic, antidote, antihistamine, decongestant, emetic, expectorant, laxative, narcotic, painkiller, sedative, stimulant, tonic, tranquilliser (*types of medication*).

Medicean /meddiˈcheeən, meˈdeechiən/ > *adjective* relating to the Medici, a powerful Italian family of bankers and merchants in Florence in the 15th century.

medicinal > *adjective* 1 having healing properties. 2 relating to medicines.
DERIVATIVES – **medicinally** *adverb*.

medicine > *noun* 1 the science or practice of the treatment and prevention of disease. 2 a drug or other preparation taken by mouth in order to treat or prevent disease.
WORDFINDER – *areas of medicine:* cardiology, dermatology, geriatrics, gynaecology, neurology, obstetrics, oncology, orthopaedics, paediatrics, pathology, pharmacology, psychiatry, surgery, therapy.
IDIOMS – **give someone a dose of their own medicine** treat someone in the same unpleasant way that they treated others.
SYNONYMS – 2 drug, medicament, medication, remedy; archaic elixir, physic.
COMBINATIONS – **medicine ball** a large, heavy solid ball thrown and caught for exercise. **medicine man** (among North American Indians) a shaman.
ORIGIN – from Latin *medicus* 'physician'.

medico > *noun* (pl. **medicos**) informal a medical practitioner or student.

medieval (also **mediaeval**) > *adjective* 1 relating to the Middle Ages. 2 informal very old-fashioned or outdated.
*SPELLING – the simpler -e- spelling is now more usual than -ae-: medieval.
ORIGIN – from Latin *medium aevum* 'middle age'.

medievalist (also **mediaevalist**) > *noun* a scholar of medieval history or literature.

medina /məˈdeenə/ > *noun* the old quarter of a North African town.
ORIGIN – Arabic, 'town'.

mediocracy > *noun* (pl. **mediocracies**) a dominant class consisting of mediocre people.

mediocre /meediˈōkər/ > *adjective* of only average or fairly low quality.
SYNONYMS – indifferent, middling, passable, second-rate, undistinguished.
ANTONYMS – excellent, exceptional.
ORIGIN – Latin *mediocris* 'of middle height or degree' (literally 'somewhat rugged or mountainous'), from *medius* 'middle' + *ocris* 'rugged mountain'.

mediocrity > *noun* (pl. **mediocrities**) 1 the quality or state of being mediocre. 2 a person of mediocre ability.
SYNONYMS – 1 averageness, indifference, ordinariness. 2 nobody, nonentity, nothing, second-rater.

meditate > *verb* 1 focus one's mind for a time for spiritual purposes or for relaxation. 2 (**meditate on** or **about**) think carefully about.
SYNONYMS – 2 (**meditate on** or **about**) consider, contemplate, deliberate on, mull over, ponder.
ORIGIN – Latin *meditari* 'contemplate'; related to METE.

meditation > *noun* 1 the action or practice of meditating. 2 a discourse expressing considered thoughts on a subject.
WORDFINDER – dhyana (*profound meditation in Hindu and Buddhist practice*), lotus position (*used for meditation*), mantra (*repeated to aid concentration in meditation*), samadhi (*intense concentration achieved through meditation*), vipassana (*meditation involving concentration on the body*), yantra (*a diagram or object used as an aid to meditation*), zazen (*Zen meditation*).

meditative > *adjective* involving or absorbed in meditation.
DERIVATIVES – **meditatively** *adverb*.
SYNONYMS – pensive, reflective, speculative, thoughtful.

Mediterranean* > *adjective* relating to the Mediterranean Sea or the surrounding countries.
*SPELLING – one d, one t, double r: Mediterranean.
ORIGIN – from Latin *mediterraneus* 'inland', from *medius* 'middle' + *terra* 'land'.

medium > *noun* (pl. **media** or **mediums**) 1 a means by which something is expressed, communicated, or achieved. 2 a substance through which a force or other influence is transmitted. 3 a form of storage for computer software, such as magnetic tape or disks. 4 a liquid with which pigments are mixed to make paint. 5 (pl. **mediums**) a person claiming to be able to communicate between the dead and the living. 6 the middle quality or state between two extremes. > *adjective* between two extremes; average.
SYNONYMS – *noun* 1 agency, channel, instrument, method, vehicle, way. *adjective* middling, moderate, normal, ordinary, standard.
COMBINATIONS – **medium frequency** a radio frequency between 300 kilohertz and 3 megahertz. **medium wave** chiefly Brit. 1 a radio wave of medium frequency. 2 broadcasting using such radio waves.
ORIGIN – Latin, 'middle'.

medlar > *noun* a small brown apple-like fruit.
ORIGIN – Old French *medler*, from Greek *mespilē*.

medley > *noun* (pl. **medleys**) 1 a varied mixture. 2 a collection of songs or other musical items performed as a continuous piece.
SYNONYMS – 1 assortment, combination, melange, miscellany, mix.

wordpower facts

Medley

In its earliest senses in English the word **medley** referred both to the 'mingling' of people in hand-to-hand combat and to a type of multicoloured woollen cloth. It came via Old French from Latin *miscere* 'to mix', a root shared by a number of other words, such as **meddle**, **melee**, **miscellaneous**, **promiscuous**, and **mix** itself.

Medoc /**may**dok/ > *noun* a red wine from the Médoc area of SW France.

medulla /mi**dull**ə/ > *noun* **1** Anatomy a distinct inner region of an organ or tissue. **2** Botany the soft internal tissue of a plant.
COMBINATIONS – **medulla oblongata** /mi**dull**ə oblong**gaat**ə/ the part of the spinal cord extending into the brain.
ORIGIN – Latin, 'pith or marrow'.

medusa /mi**dyōō**zə/ > *noun* (pl. **medusae** /mi**dyōō**zee/ or **medusas**) Zoology the free-swimming stage in the life cycle of a jellyfish or related organism.
ORIGIN – from *Medusa*, a gorgon in Greek mythology with snakes in her hair.

meed > *noun* archaic a deserved share or reward.

meek > *adjective* gentle, quiet, and submissive.
DERIVATIVES – **meekly** *adverb* **meekness** *noun*.
SYNONYMS – biddable, compliant, docile, humble, self-effacing, shy.
ANTONYMS – assertive, overbearing.

meerkat /**meer**kat/ > *noun* a small southern African mongoose.
ORIGIN – Dutch, 'sea cat': the name originally applied to a kind of monkey, perhaps with the notion 'from overseas'.

meerschaum /**meer**shəm/ > *noun* **1** a soft white clay-like material. **2** a tobacco pipe with a bowl made from meerschaum.
ORIGIN – German, 'sea foam'.

meet¹ > *verb* (past and past participle **met**) **1** come together at the same place and moment. **2** see or be introduced to for the first time. **3** come into contact with; touch or join. **4** encounter (a situation). **5** (**meet with**) receive (a reaction). **6** fulfil or satisfy (a requirement). > *noun* a gathering or meeting, especially for races or foxhunting.
SYNONYMS – *verb* **1** assemble, come across, congregate, encounter, gather. **3** connect, join, link up, reach, touch. **6** answer, comply with, fulfil, measure up to, satisfy.

meet² > *adjective* archaic suitable or proper.
ORIGIN – first meaning 'made to fit': related to METE.

meeting > *noun* **1** an organised gathering of people for a discussion or other purpose. **2** a coming together of two or more people.
SYNONYMS – **1** assembly, conference, congregation, convention. **2** appointment, contact, encounter, rendezvous.

mega > *adjective* informal **1** very large. **2** excellent.

mega- > *combining form* **1** large. **2** denoting a factor of one million (10⁶).

megabucks > *plural noun* informal a huge sum of money.

megabyte > *noun* Computing a unit of information equal to one million or (strictly) 1,048,576 bytes.

wordpower facts
Mega-
The prefix **mega-** (from Greek *megas*) forms words with the meaning 'great', as in **megalith** and **megastar**, but it is also used in units of measurement to mean 'one million' (**megahertz**, **megawatt**). Mega- in this case is one of a series of similar prefixes: other familiar ones are **kilo-** (one thousand) and **giga-** (one billion). In computing contexts (e.g. in **megabyte**), mega- strictly means a factor of 2 raised to the power 20, or 1,048,576, rather than exactly one million. The combining form **micro-** is used for factors of one millionth, as in **microgram**.

megaflop > *noun* Computing a unit of computing speed equal to one million or (strictly) 1,048,576 floating-point operations per second.

megahertz > *noun* (pl. same) a unit of frequency equal to one million hertz.

megalith > *noun* a large stone that forms a prehistoric monument or is part of one.
DERIVATIVES – **megalithic** *adjective*.

megalomania > *noun* **1** obsession with the exercise of power. **2** the delusion that one has great power or importance.
DERIVATIVES – **megalomaniac** *noun* & *adjective*.

megaphone > *noun* a large cone-shaped device for amplifying and directing the voice.

megapode /**megg**əpōd/ > *noun* a large ground-dwelling Australasian or SE Asian bird that builds a large mound of plant debris to incubate its eggs.
ORIGIN – from Greek *pous* 'foot'.

megastar > *noun* informal a very famous entertainer or sports player.

megaton > *noun* a unit of explosive power equivalent to one million tons of TNT.

megawatt > *noun* a unit of electrical or other power equal to one million watts.

meiosis /mī**ō**siss/ > *noun* (pl. **meioses** /mī**ō**seez/) **1** Biology a type of cell division that results in daughter cells each with half the number of chromosomes of the parent cell. Compare with MITOSIS. **2** another term for LITOTES.
DERIVATIVES – **meiotic** *adjective*.
ORIGIN – Greek, 'lessening'.

Meistersinger /**mī**stərsingər/ > *noun* (pl. same) a member of one of the guilds of German lyric poets and musicians which flourished from the 12th to 17th century.
ORIGIN – German, 'master singer'.

meitnerium /mīt**neer**iəm/ > *noun* a very unstable chemical element made by high-energy atomic collisions.
ORIGIN – named after the Swedish physicist Lise *Meitner* (1878–1968).

melaleuca /mellə**lōō**kə/ > *noun* an Australian shrub or tree which bears spikes of bottlebrush-like flowers.
ORIGIN – from Greek *melas* 'black' + *leukos* 'white' (because of the fire-blackened white bark of some species).

melamine /**mell**əmeen/ > *noun* a hard plastic used chiefly for laminated coatings.

melancholia /mellən**kōl**iə/ > *noun* severe depression.

melancholy > *noun* **1** deep and long-lasting sadness. **2** (in medieval medicine) black bile, one of the four bodily humours, an excess of which was believed to cause depression. > *adjective* sad or depressed.
DERIVATIVES – **melancholic** *adjective*.
SYNONYMS – *noun* **1** depression, despondency, gloom, misery, unhappiness. *adjective* dejected, depressed, despondent, miserable, sad, unhappy.
ANTONYMS – *adjective* cheerful, happy.
ORIGIN – Greek *melankholia*, from *melas* 'black' and *kholē* 'bile'.

Melanesian > *adjective* relating to Melanesia in the western Pacific. > *noun* a person from Melanesia.

melange /may**lonzh**/ > *noun* a varied mixture.
ORIGIN – French, from *mêler* 'to mix'.

melanin /**mell**ənin/ > *noun* a dark pigment in the hair and skin, responsible for tanning of skin exposed to sunlight.
ORIGIN – from Greek *melas* 'black'.

melanoma /mellə**nō**mə/ > *noun* a form of skin cancer which develops in the cells that produce melanin.

Melba sauce > *noun* a sauce made from puréed raspberries thickened with icing sugar.
ORIGIN – named after the Australian opera singer Dame Nellie *Melba* (1861–1931).

Melba toast > *noun* very thin crisp toast.

meld > *verb* blend; combine.
ORIGIN – perhaps a blend of MELT and WELD.

melee /**mell**ay/ > *noun* **1** a confused fight. **2** a disorderly mass.
ORIGIN – French; related to MEDLEY.

meliorate /**mee**liərayt/ > *verb* formal another term for AMELIORATE.
ORIGIN – Latin *meliorare* 'improve'.

mellifluous /mə**lif**lōōəss/ > *adjective* pleasingly smooth and musical to hear.
DERIVATIVES – **mellifluously** *adverb* **mellifluousness** *noun*.
SYNONYMS – dulcet, euphonious, harmonious, honeyed, sweet.
ANTONYMS – discordant.
ORIGIN – from Latin *mel* 'honey' + *fluere* 'to flow'.

mellotron /**mell**ətron/ > *noun* an electronic keyboard instrument in which the keys control the playback of pre-recorded musical sounds.

ORIGIN – from **MELLOW** + *-tron*, element of **ELECTRONIC**.

mellow > *adjective* **1** pleasantly smooth or soft in sound, taste, or colour. **2** relaxed and good-humoured. > *verb* make or become mellow.

SYNONYMS – *adjective* **1** mellifluous, rich, warm. **2** affable, cheerful, genial, jovial.

melodeon > *noun* **1** a small accordion. **2** a small organ similar to the harmonium.

melodic > *adjective* **1** relating to melody. **2** melodious.

DERIVATIVES – **melodically** *adverb*.

melodious > *adjective* pleasant-sounding; tuneful.

DERIVATIVES – **melodiously** *adverb*.

SYNONYMS – dulcet, euphonious, harmonious, mellifluous, melodic, sweet.

ANTONYMS – discordant.

melodrama > *noun* **1** a sensational play with exaggerated characters and exciting events. **2** behaviour or events resembling melodrama.

ORIGIN – from Greek *melos* 'music' + French *drame* 'drama'; a melodrama was originally a musical, especially of a romantic or sensational nature.

melodramatic > *adjective* like a melodrama; sensationalised or excessively dramatic.

DERIVATIVES – **melodramatically** *adverb*.

SYNONYMS – exaggerated, extravagant, overdramatic, overemotional, sensational.

melody > *noun* (pl. **melodies**) **1** a sequence of notes that is musically satisfying; a tune. **2** the main part in harmonised music.

SYNONYMS – **1** air, song, strain, theme, tune.

ORIGIN – Greek *melōidia*, from *melos* 'song'.

melon > *noun* a large round fruit with sweet pulpy flesh and many seeds.

ORIGIN – Latin *melo*, from Greek *mēlopepōn*, from *mēlon* 'apple' + *pepōn* 'gourd'.

melt > *verb* **1** make or become liquid by heating. **2** (often **melt away**) gradually disappear or disperse. **3** become or make more tender or loving.

SYNONYMS – **2** dissipate, evanesce, evaporate, fade away, vanish.

COMBINATIONS – **melting point** the temperature at which a solid will melt. **melting pot 1** a place where different peoples, styles, etc., are mixed together and influence each other. **2** a changing and uncertain situation.

meltdown > *noun* **1** an accident in a nuclear reactor in which the fuel overheats and melts the reactor core. **2** a disastrous collapse or breakdown.

member > *noun* **1** a person or organisation belonging to a group or society. **2** a part of

a complex structure. **3** archaic a part of the body, especially a limb.

SYNONYMS – **1** adherent, associate, fellow, follower, supporter. **2** component, constituent, element, part, unit.

ORIGIN – Latin *membrum* 'limb'.

membership > *noun* **1** the fact of being a member of a group. **2** the body of members of a group.

membrane > *noun* **1** a skin-like covering or sheet in an organism or cell. **2** a thin skin-like sheet of material.

DERIVATIVES – **membranous** *adjective*.

ORIGIN – Latin, from *membrum* 'limb'.

meme /meem/ > *noun* Biology an element of behaviour or culture passed on by imitation or other non-genetic means.

DERIVATIVES – **memetic** *adjective*.

ORIGIN – from Greek *mimēma* 'that which is imitated', on the pattern of *gene*.

memento* > *noun* (pl. **mementos** or **mementoes**) an object kept as a reminder or souvenir.

***SPELLING** – *memento*, not *mom-*.

SYNONYMS – keepsake, remembrance, reminder, souvenir, token.

ORIGIN – Latin, 'remember!'

memento mori /mimentō **mo**ri/ > *noun* (pl. same) an object kept as a reminder that death is inevitable.

ORIGIN – Latin, 'remember (that you have) to die'.

memo > *noun* (pl. **memos**) informal a memorandum.

memoir > *noun* **1** a historical account or biography written from personal knowledge. **2** (**memoirs**) an account written by a public figure of their life and experiences.

ORIGIN – French *mémoire* 'memory'.

memorabilia > *plural noun* objects kept or collected because of their associations with memorable people or events.

memorable > *adjective* worth remembering or easily remembered.

DERIVATIVES – **memorably** *adverb*.

SYNONYMS – impressive, momentous, notable, remarkable, significant, unforgettable.

ANTONYMS – forgettable, unmemorable.

memorandum > *noun* (pl. **memoranda** or **memorandums**) **1** a written message in business or diplomacy. **2** a note recording something.

ORIGIN – Latin, 'something to be brought to mind'.

memorial > *noun* an object or structure established in memory of a person or event. > *adjective* in memory of someone.

memorise (also **memorize**) > *verb* learn by heart.

memory > *noun* (pl. **memories**) **1** the faculty by which the mind stores and remembers information. **2** a person or

thing remembered. **3** the length of time over which people's memory extends. **4** a computer's equipment or capacity for storing data or instructions for retrieval.

WORDFINDER – amnesia (*loss of memory*), memento (*an item kept as a reminder*), mnemonic (*an aid to memory*), paramnesia (*distorted memory*).

IDIOMS – **in memory of** so as to commemorate.

ORIGIN – Old French *memorie*, from Latin *memoria*.

memsahib /**mem**saab/ > *noun* Indian, dated a respectful form of address for a married white woman.

ORIGIN – from an Indian pronunciation of *ma'am* + **SAHIB**.

men plural of **MAN**.

menace > *noun* **1** a threatening quality. **2** a dangerous or troublesome person or thing. > *verb* put at risk; threaten.

DERIVATIVES – **menacing** *adjective* **menacingly** *adverb*.

SYNONYMS – *noun* **2** danger, hazard, peril, risk, threat. *verb* endanger, intimidate, jeopardise, threaten.

ORIGIN – from Latin *minax* 'threatening'.

ménage à trois /maynaazh aa **trwaa**/ > *noun* an arrangement in which a married couple and the lover of one of them live together.

ORIGIN – French, 'household of three'.

menagerie /mə**naj**əri/ > *noun* a collection of wild animals kept in captivity for showing to the public.

menaquinone /mennə**kwinn**ōn/ > *noun* vitamin K_2, a compound produced by intestinal bacteria and essential for the blood-clotting process.

ORIGIN – from the chemical name *methyl-naphthoquinone*.

menarche /me**naar**ki/ > *noun* the first occurrence of menstruation.

ORIGIN – from Greek *mēn* 'month' + *arkhē* 'beginning'.

mend > *verb* **1** restore to the correct or working condition. **2** improve or settle (an unpleasant situation). > *noun* a repair in a material.

IDIOMS – **mend (one's) fences** make peace with a person. **on the mend** improving in health or condition.

DERIVATIVES – **mendable** *adjective* **mender** *noun*.

SYNONYMS – *verb* **1** fix, repair.

ORIGIN – shortening of **AMEND**.

mendacious > *adjective* untruthful; lying.

DERIVATIVES – **mendaciously** *adverb* **mendacity** *noun*.

ORIGIN – from Latin *mendax* 'lying'.

mendelevium /mendə**lee**viəm/ > *noun* a very unstable radioactive chemical element made by high-energy collisions.

ORIGIN – named after the Russian chemist Dimitri *Mendeleev* (1834–1907).

Mendelism /**men**dəliz'm/ > *noun* the theory of heredity based on characteristics transmitted as genes, as developed by the Austrian botanist G. J. Mendel (1822–84).

DERIVATIVES – **Mendelian** *adjective*.

mendicant /**men**dikənt/ > *adjective* **1** habitually engaged in begging. **2** (of a religious order) originally dependent on alms. > *noun* **1** a beggar. **2** a member of a mendicant order.

ORIGIN – from Latin *mendicus* 'beggar'.

menfolk > *plural noun* the men of a family or community considered collectively.

menhir /**men**heer/ > *noun* a tall upright prehistoric stone erected as a monument.

ORIGIN – from Breton *men* 'stone' + *hir* 'long'.

menial > *adjective* (of work) requiring little skill and lacking prestige. > *noun* a person with a menial job.

DERIVATIVES – **menially** *adverb*.

SYNONYMS – *adjective* humdrum, low-grade, lowly, routine, unskilled.

ORIGIN – Old French, from *mesnée* 'household'.

meninges /mi**nin**jeez/ > *plural noun* (sing. **meninx**) the three membranes that enclose the brain and spinal cord.

ORIGIN – from Greek *mēninx* 'membrane'.

meningitis /menninj**ī**tiss/ > *noun* a disease in which the meninges become inflamed owing to infection with a bacterium or virus.

meniscus /mi**nis**kəss/ > *noun* (pl. **menisci** /mi**nis**sī/) **1** Physics the curved upper surface of a liquid in a tube. **2** a thin lens convex on one side and concave on the other.

menopause > *noun* the ceasing of menstruation or the period in a woman's life (typically between 45 and 50) when this occurs.

DERIVATIVES – **menopausal** *adjective*.

ORIGIN – from Greek *mēn* 'month' + **PAUSE**.

menorah /mi**nōr**ə/ > *noun* a candelabrum used in Jewish worship, typically with eight branches.

ORIGIN – Hebrew.

menses /**men**seez/ > *plural noun* blood discharged from a woman's uterus at menstruation.

ORIGIN – Latin, plural of *mensis* 'month'.

menstrual > *adjective* of or relating to menstruation.

menstruate > *verb* (of a non-pregnant woman) discharge blood from the lining of the womb at intervals of about one lunar month.

DERIVATIVES – **menstruation** *noun*.

ORIGIN – Latin *menstruare*, from *menstrua* 'menses'.

mensuration > *noun* **1** measurement. **2** the part of geometry that is concerned with ascertaining lengths, areas, and volumes.

ORIGIN – Latin, from *mensurare* 'to measure'.

-ment > *suffix* **1** forming nouns expressing the means or result of an action: *treatment*. **2** forming nouns from adjectives: *merriment*.

ORIGIN – from French or Latin.

mental > *adjective* **1** of, done by, or occurring in the mind. **2** relating to disorders or illnesses of the mind. **3** informal insane; crazy.

DERIVATIVES – **mentally** *adverb*.

USAGE – the use of **mental** in sense 2 (as in **mental hospital**) is now regarded as old-fashioned, even offensive, and has largely been replaced by **psychiatric**. The terms **mental handicap** and **mentally handicapped** have fallen out of favour and been replaced in official contexts by terms such as **learning difficulties**.

SYNONYMS – **1** cerebral, cognitive, intellectual, psychological.

COMBINATIONS – **mental age** a person's mental ability expressed as the age at which an average person reaches the same ability. **mental block** an inability to recall something or to perform a mental action. **mental handicap** intellectual capacity that is underdeveloped to an extent which prevents normal function in society.

ORIGIN – from Latin *mens* 'mind'.

mentality > *noun* (pl. **mentalities**) **1** a characteristic way of thinking. **2** the capacity for intelligent thought.

menthol > *noun* a mint-tasting substance found chiefly in peppermint oil, used as a flavouring and in decongestants.

DERIVATIVES – **mentholated** *adjective*.

ORIGIN – from Latin *mentha* 'mint'.

mention > *verb* **1** refer to (something) briefly. **2** refer to (someone) by name as being noteworthy. > *noun* **1** a reference to someone or something. **2** a formal acknowledgement of something noteworthy.

IDIOMS – **be mentioned in dispatches** Brit. be commended for one's actions by name in an official military report. **mention in one's will** leave a legacy to (someone).

SYNONYMS – *verb* **1** allude to, bring up, hint at, raise, touch on. *noun* **1** allusion, comment, remark.

ORIGIN – Latin, related to **MIND**.

mentor > *noun* **1** an experienced and trusted adviser. **2** an experienced person in an organisation or institution who trains and counsels new employees or students.

SYNONYMS – **1** adviser, guide, guru.

ORIGIN – from the name of *Mentor*, the adviser of the young Telemachus in Homer's *Odyssey*.

menu > *noun* **1** a list of dishes available in a restaurant. **2** the food available or to be served in a restaurant or at a meal. **3** Computing a list of commands or facilities displayed on screen.

ORIGIN – French, 'detailed list'.

meow > *noun & verb* variant spelling of **MIAOW**.

MEP > *abbreviation* Member of the European Parliament.

Mephistophelian /meffistə**feel**iən/ (also **Mephistophelean**) > *adjective* wicked or evil.

ORIGIN – from *Mephistopheles*, an evil spirit to whom Faust, in the German legend, sold his soul.

mephitic /mi**fitt**ik/ > *adjective* literary foul-smelling; noxious.

ORIGIN – from Latin *mephitis* 'noxious exhalation'.

mercantile > *adjective* relating to trade or commerce.

ORIGIN – from Italian *mercante* 'merchant'.

mercantilism /**mer**kəntiliz'm/ > *noun* chiefly historical the economic theory that trade generates wealth and is stimulated by the accumulation of bullion, which the government should encourage by means of protectionism.

DERIVATIVES – **mercantilist** *noun* & *adjective*.

Mercator projection /mer**kay**tər/ > *noun* a world map projection made on to a cylinder in such a way that all parallels of latitude have the same length as the equator.

ORIGIN – from *Mercator*, Latinised name of the Flemish geographer Gerhard Kremer (1512–94).

mercenary > *adjective* motivated chiefly by the desire for gain. > *noun* (pl. **mercenaries**) a professional soldier hired to serve in a foreign army.

SYNONYMS – *adjective* avaricious, grasping, greedy, materialistic, venal.

ORIGIN – from Latin *mercenarius* 'hireling', from *merces* 'reward'.

mercer > *noun* chiefly historical a dealer in textile fabrics, especially silk and other fine materials.

ORIGIN – Old French *mercier*, from Latin *merx* 'goods'.

mercerised (also **mercerized**) > *adjective* (of cotton) treated with caustic alkali to give strength and lustre.

ORIGIN – named after John *Mercer* (1791–1866), who is said to have invented the process.

merchandise > *noun* /**mer**chəndīss/ goods for sale. > *verb* /**mer**chəndīz/ (also **merchandize**) promote the sale of.

DERIVATIVES – **merchandiser** *noun*.

SYNONYMS – *noun* goods, stock, wares.

ORIGIN – from Old French *marchand* 'merchant'.

merchant > *noun* **1** a wholesale trader. **2** N. Amer. & Scottish a retail trader. **3** *informal, chiefly derogatory* a person fond of a particular activity: *a speed merchant*. > *adjective* (of ships, sailors, or shipping activity) involved with commerce.

COMBINATIONS – **merchant bank** chiefly Brit. a bank dealing in commercial loans and investment. **merchant navy** (US **merchant marine**) a country's commercial shipping. **merchant prince** a person who has acquired sufficient wealth from trading to wield political influence.

wordpower facts
Merchant
The Latin word *merx*, meaning 'merchandise', forms the base of a number of words in English, such as **commerce**, **market**, and **merchant**. It is also the origin of the name of *Mercury*, the Roman messenger of the gods, who was originally the god of commerce.

merchantable > *adjective* saleable.

merchantman > *noun* a ship conveying merchandise.

merciful > *adjective* **1** showing mercy. **2** giving relief from suffering.
SYNONYMS – **1** compassionate, forgiving, lenient, tolerant.
ANTONYMS – **1** cruel, merciless.

mercifully > *adverb* **1** in a merciful manner. **2** to one's great relief.
SYNONYMS – **2** fortunately, happily, luckily, thankfully.

merciless > *adjective* showing no mercy.
DERIVATIVES – **mercilessly** *adverb* **mercilessness** *noun*.
SYNONYMS – cruel, implacable, pitiless, ruthless.
ANTONYMS – merciful.

mercurial /mer**kyoor**iəl/ > *adjective* **1** subject to sudden changes of mood. **2** of or containing the element mercury.
SYNONYMS – **1** capricious, fickle, temperamental, unpredictable, volatile.
ANTONYMS – **1** constant, stable, steady.

Mercurian > *adjective* relating to the planet Mercury.

mercury > *noun* a heavy silvery-white liquid metallic chemical element used in some thermometers and barometers.
DERIVATIVES – **mercuric** *adjective* **mercurous** *adjective*.
ORIGIN – from the name of *Mercury*, the Roman messenger of the gods.

mercy > *noun* (pl. **mercies**) **1** compassion or forgiveness shown towards an enemy or offender in one's power. **2** something to be grateful for. **3** (before another noun) motivated by compassion: *a mercy killing*. > *exclamation* dated used to express surprise or fear.
IDIOMS – **at the mercy of** in the power of; defenceless against.
SYNONYMS – **1** clemency, compassion, forgiveness, leniency, pity. **2** blessing, boon, godsend.
ANTONYMS – **1** ruthlessness.
ORIGIN – Old French *merci* 'pity, thanks', from Latin *merces* 'reward, pity'.

mere[1] > *adjective* **1** that is nothing more than what is specified. **2** (**the merest**) the smallest or slightest.
ORIGIN – Latin *merus* 'pure, undiluted'.

mere[2] > *noun chiefly literary* a lake or pond.

merely > *adverb* just; only.

meretricious /meri**trish**əss/ > *adjective* showily but falsely attractive.
SYNONYMS – cheap, flashy, tawdry.
ORIGIN – from Latin *meretrix* 'prostitute', from *mereri* 'earn, deserve, be hired'.

merganser /mə**gan**zər/ > *noun* a fish-eating diving duck with a long, thin serrated and hooked bill.
ORIGIN – from Latin *mergus* 'diver' + *anser* 'goose'.

merge > *verb* **1** combine or be combined into a whole. **2** blend gradually into something else.
SYNONYMS – **1** amalgamate, combine, conflate, incorporate, integrate, unite.
ORIGIN – Latin *mergere* 'to dip, plunge' (the first meaning in English was 'immerse oneself in an activity').

merger > *noun* a merging of two things, especially companies, into one.

meridian /mə**ridd**iən/ > *noun* **1** a circle of constant longitude passing through a given place on the earth's surface and the poles. **2** Astronomy a circle passing through the celestial poles and the zenith of a given place on the earth's surface. **3** any of twelve pathways in the body, believed by practitioners of Chinese medicine to be channels for vital energy.
ORIGIN – from Latin *meridianum* 'noon' (because the sun crosses a meridian at noon).

meridional /mə**ridd**iən'l/ > *adjective* **1** of or relating to the south, especially southern Europe. **2** of or relating to a meridian.

meringue /mə**rang**/ > *noun* **1** beaten egg whites and sugar baked until crisp. **2** a small cake made of meringue.
ORIGIN – French.

merino /mə**ree**nō/ > *noun* (pl. **merinos**) **1** a breed of sheep with long, fine wool. **2** a soft woollen or wool-and-cotton material, originally of merino wool.
ORIGIN – Spanish.

meristem /**merr**istem/ > *noun* Botany a region of plant tissue consisting of actively dividing cells.
ORIGIN – from Greek *meristos* 'divisible'.

merit > *noun* **1** superior quality; excellence. **2** a good point or quality. > *verb* (**merited**, **meriting**) be worthy of; deserve.
SYNONYMS – *noun* **1** excellence, distinction, quality, virtue, worth. **2** advantage, asset, benefit. *verb* deserve, rate, warrant.
ORIGIN – Latin *meritum* 'due reward', from *mereri* 'earn, deserve'.

meritocracy > *noun* (pl. **meritocracies**) **1** government or leadership by people of great merit. **2** a society governed by meritocracy.
DERIVATIVES – **meritocratic** *adjective*.

meritorious > *adjective* deserving reward or praise.
SYNONYMS – estimable, commendable, laudable, praiseworthy.

merlin > *noun* a small dark falcon.
ORIGIN – Old French *merilun*.

Merlot /**mer**lō/ > *noun* a variety of black wine grape originally from the Bordeaux region of France.
ORIGIN – French.

mermaid > *noun* a mythical sea creature with the head and trunk of a woman and a fish's tail.
COMBINATIONS – **mermaid's purse** the horny egg case of a skate, ray, or small shark.
ORIGIN – from **MERE**[2] (in the obsolete sense 'sea') + **MAID**.

merman > *noun* the male equivalent of a mermaid.

merriment > *noun* gaiety and fun.
SYNONYMS – fun, gaiety, high spirits, jollity, mirth.

merry > *adjective* (**merrier**, **merriest**) **1** cheerful and lively. **2** Brit. informal slightly drunk.
IDIOMS – **make merry** indulge in merriment; have a good time.
DERIVATIVES – **merrily** *adjective* **merriness** *noun*.
SYNONYMS – **1** cheerful, happy, high-spirited, jolly, light-hearted.
ANTONYMS – **1** gloomy, miserable, sad.
ORIGIN – Old English, 'pleasing, delightful'.

merry-go-round > *noun* **1** a revolving machine with model horses or cars on which people ride for amusement. **2** a continuous cycle of activities or events.

merrymaking > *noun* enjoyable activities; fun.
DERIVATIVES – **merrymaker** *noun*.

mesa /**may**sə/ > *noun* an isolated flat-topped hill with steep sides.
ORIGIN – Spanish, 'table'.

mésalliance /me**zal**iənss/ > *noun* a marriage to a person of a lower social class.
ORIGIN – French, 'misalliance'.

mescal > *noun* **1** alcoholic liquor distilled from a type of agave. **2** a peyote cactus.
ORIGIN – Nahuatl.

mescaline /**mes**kəlin/ (also **mescalin**) > *noun* a hallucinogenic drug made from the peyote cactus.

Mesdames plural of MADAME.

Mesdemoiselles plural of MADE-MOISELLE.

mesembryanthemum
/mizembri**an**thiməm/ > *noun* a succulent plant with brightly coloured daisy-like flowers, native to southern Africa.
ORIGIN – from Greek *mesēmbria* 'noon' + *anthemon* 'flower'.

mesh > *noun* **1** material made of a network of wire or thread. **2** the spacing of the strands of a net. **3** a complex or constricting situation. > *verb* **1** make or become entangled or entwined. **2** (**mesh with**) be in harmony with. **3** (of a gearwheel) lock together with another.
SYNONYMS – *noun* **1** net, netting, reticulation, web, webbing.

mesmeric /mez**merr**ik/ > *adjective* causing one to become transfixed and unaware of one's surroundings; hypnotic.
DERIVATIVES – **mesmerically** *adverb*.

mesmerise /**mez**mərīz/ (also **mesmerize**) > *verb* capture the whole attention of; fascinate.
DERIVATIVES – **mesmerising** *adjective*.
SYNONYMS – captivate, enthral, entrance, fascinate, spellbind, transfix.

mesmerism > *noun* **1** historical a therapeutic technique that involved hypnotism. **2** hypnotism.
DERIVATIVES – **mesmerist** *noun*.
ORIGIN – named after the Austrian physician Franz *Mesmer* (1734–1815).

meso- /**mess**ō/ > *combining form* middle; intermediate: *mesomorph*.
ORIGIN – from Greek *mesos* 'middle'.

Mesolithic > *adjective* relating to the middle part of the Stone Age, between the end of the glacial period and the beginnings of agriculture.
ORIGIN – from Greek *mesos* 'middle' + *lithos* 'stone'.

mesomorph > *noun* a person with a compact and muscular body. Compare with ECTOMORPH, ENDOMORPH.
DERIVATIVES – **mesomorphic** *adjective*.
ORIGIN – from *mesodermal* (the mesoderm being the layer of the embryo giving rise to these physical characteristics).

meson /**mee**zon/ > *noun* Physics a subatomic particle, intermediate in mass between an electron and a proton, that transmits the strong interaction which binds nucleons together.

Mesopotamian /messəpə**taym**iən/ > *adjective* relating to Mesopotamia, an ancient region of what is now Iraq. > *noun* a person from Mesopotamia.

mesosphere > *noun* the region of the earth's atmosphere above the stratosphere and below the thermosphere.

Mesozoic /messō**zō**ic/ > *adjective* Geology relating to the era between the Palaeozoic and Cenozoic eras, about 245 to 65 million years ago, with evidence of the first mammals, birds, and flowering plants.
ORIGIN – from Greek *mesos* 'middle' + *zōion* 'animal'.

mesquite /mess**keet**/ > *noun* a spiny tree of the south-western US and Mexico, yielding wood, medicinal products, and edible pods.
ORIGIN – Mexican Spanish *mezquite*.

mess > *noun* **1** a dirty or untidy state. **2** a state of confusion or difficulty. **3** a portion of semi-solid food. **4** euphemistic a domestic animal's excrement. **5** a place providing meals and recreational facilities for members of the armed forces. > *verb* **1** make untidy or dirty. **2** (**mess about** or **around**) behave or treat in a silly or playful way; fool about, play around. **3** (**mess with**) informal meddle with. **4** eat communally in an armed forces' mess. **5** (of a domestic animal) defecate.
SYNONYMS – *noun* **1** disarray, disorder, jumble, muddle, shambles, untidiness. **2** dilemma, imbroglio, plight, predicament, tight spot. *verb* **1** befoul, disarrange, jumble, litter, pollute.
COMBINATIONS – **mess tin** Brit. a rectangular metal food dish forming part of a soldier's kit.

wordpower facts

Mess

The word **mess** can be traced back through Old French *mes* 'portion of food' to Latin *missum* 'something put on the table', which is from *mittere* 'send, put'. One of the original senses of **mess**, 'a serving of semi-liquid food', gave rise in the early 19th century to the senses 'an unappetising mixture' and 'a predicament', on which sense 1 is based. Sense 5 derives from another Middle English use of the word, to refer to any of the small groups into which the company at a banquet was divided: hence 'a group who eat regularly together' (recorded in military use from the 16th century).

message > *noun* **1** a verbal or written communication. **2** a significant point or central theme. > *verb* send a message to, especially by email.
IDIOMS – **get the message** informal understand what is meant. **on** (or **off**) **message** (of a politician) stating (or deviating from) the official party line.
SYNONYMS – *noun* **1** bulletin, communication, dispatch, note, report.
ORIGIN – Old French, from Latin *mittere* 'send'.

Messeigneurs plural of MONSEIGNEUR.

messenger > *noun* a person who carries a message.
SYNONYMS – courier, emissary, envoy, go-between, herald, legate.
COMBINATIONS – **messenger RNA** the form of RNA in which genetic information transcribed from DNA is transferred to a ribosome.

messiah > *noun* **1** (**the Messiah**) the promised liberator of the Jewish nation prophesied in the Hebrew Bible. **2** (**the Messiah**) Jesus regarded by Christians as the Messiah of these prophecies. **3** a leader or saviour.
ORIGIN – Hebrew, 'anointed'.

messianic /messi**ann**ik/ > *adjective* **1** relating to the Messiah. **2** inspired by belief in a messiah.
DERIVATIVES – **messianism** *noun*.

Messieurs plural of MONSIEUR.

Messrs plural of MR.

messy > *adjective* (**messier**, **messiest**) **1** untidy or dirty. **2** confused and difficult to deal with.
DERIVATIVES – **messily** *adverb* **messiness** *noun*.
SYNONYMS – **1** cluttered, dirty, disorderly, scruffy, untidy. **2** complicated, confused, involved, knotty, taxing.
ANTONYMS – **1** clean, orderly, tidy.

mestizo /me**stee**zō/ > *noun* (pl. **mestizos**; fem. **mestiza**, pl. **mestizas**) a Latin American of mixed race, especially the offspring of a Spaniard and an American Indian.
ORIGIN – Spanish, 'mixed'.

Met > *abbreviation* informal **1** meteorological. **2** (**the Met**) the Metropolitan Police in London.

met past and past participle of MEET[1].

meta- (also **met-** before a vowel or h) > *combining form* forming words referring to: **1** a change of position or condition: *metamorphosis*. **2** position behind, after, or beyond: *metacarpus*. **3** something of a higher or second-order kind: *metalanguage*.
ORIGIN – from Greek *meta* 'with, across, or after'.

metabolise (also **metabolize**) > *verb* process or be processed by metabolism.

metabolism /mi**tabb**əliz'm/ > *noun* the chemical processes in a living organism by which food is used for tissue growth or energy production.
DERIVATIVES – **metabolic** *adjective*.
ORIGIN – from Greek *metabolē* 'change'.

metabolite > *noun* a substance formed in or necessary for metabolism.

metacarpus /mettə**kaar**pəss/ > *noun* (pl. **metacarpi**) the group of five bones of the hand between the wrist and the fingers.

DERIVATIVES – **metacarpal** *adjective & noun*.

metal > *noun* **1** a solid material which is typically hard, shiny, malleable, fusible, and ductile, with good electrical and thermal conductivity. **2** (also **road metal**) broken stone used in road-making.

WORDFINDER – aluminium, chromium, cobalt, copper, gold, iron, lead, magnesium, nickel, platinum, silver, tin, tungsten, zinc (*some common metals*).

COMBINATIONS – **metal detector** an electronic device that gives an audible signal when it is close to metal. **metalwork 1** the art of making things from metal. **2** metal objects collectively.

ORIGIN – Greek *metallon* 'mine, quarry, or metal'.

metalanguage > *noun* a form of language used for the description or analysis of another language.

metalled > *adjective* **1** made from or coated with metal. **2** surfaced with road metal.

metallic > *adjective* **1** of or resembling metal. **2** (of sound) sharp and ringing.

DERIVATIVES – **metallically** *adverb*.

metalliferous /mettə**liff**ərəss/ > *adjective* containing or producing metal.

metallise (also **metallize**, US also **metalise**) > *verb* **1** coat with metal. **2** make metallic.

metallography /mettə**log**rəfi/ > *noun* the descriptive science of the structure and properties of metals.

DERIVATIVES – **metallographic** *adjective*.

metallurgy /mi**tal**ərji, **mett**əlerji/ > *noun* the science concerned with the properties, production, and purification of metals.

DERIVATIVES – **metallurgical** *adjective* **metallurgist** *noun*.

metamorphic > *adjective* Geology (of rock) having undergone transformation by heat, pressure, or other natural agencies.

DERIVATIVES – **metamorphism** *noun*.

metamorphose /mettə**morf**ōz/ > *verb* **1** change completely in form or nature. **2** (of an insect or amphibian) undergo metamorphosis. **3** Geology subject (rock) to metamorphism.

SYNONYMS – **1** change, convert, mutate, transfigure, transform.

metamorphosis /mettə**morf**əsiss/ > *noun* (pl. **metamorphoses** /mettə**morf**əseez/) **1** the transformation of an insect or amphibian from an immature form or larva to an adult form in distinct stages. **2** a change in form or nature.

SYNONYMS – **2** change, conversion, mutation, transfiguration, transformation.

ORIGIN – Greek, from *metamorphoun* 'transform, change shape'.

metaphor > *noun* **1** a figure of speech in which a word or phrase is applied to something to which it is not literally applicable (e.g. *food for thought*). **2** a thing symbolic of something else.

ORIGIN – Greek *metaphora*, from *metapherein* 'to transfer'.

metaphorical (also **metaphoric**) > *adjective* of the nature of or relating to metaphor.

DERIVATIVES – **metaphorically** *adverb*.

SYNONYMS – allegorical, emblematic, figurative, non-literal, symbolic.

metaphysic > *noun* a system of metaphysics.

metaphysical > *adjective* **1** relating to metaphysics. **2** transcending physical matter. **3** referring to a group of 17th century English poets (in particular John Donne, George Herbert, Andrew Marvell, and Henry Vaughan) known for their subtlety of thought and complex imagery.

DERIVATIVES – **metaphysically** *adverb*.

metaphysics > *plural noun* (usu. treated as sing.) **1** philosophy concerned with abstract concepts such as the nature of existence or of truth and knowledge. **2** informal abstract talk; mere theory.

DERIVATIVES – **metaphysician** *noun*.

ORIGIN – from Greek *ta meta ta phusika* 'the things after the Physics', referring to the sequence of Aristotle's works.

metastable /mettə**stay**b'l/ > *adjective* Physics **1** (of a state of equilibrium) stable provided it is only subjected to small forces. **2** theoretically unstable but so long-lived as to be stable for practical purposes.

metastasis /mi**tast**əsiss/ > *noun* (pl. **metastases** /mi**tast**əseez/) Medicine the development of secondary tumours at a distance from a primary site of cancer.

metatarsus /mettə**taar**səss/ > *noun* (pl. **metatarsi**) /mettə**taar**sī/ the bones of the foot, between the ankle and the toes.

DERIVATIVES – **metatarsal** *adjective & noun*.

metathesis /mi**tath**isiss/ > *noun* (pl. **metatheses** /mi**tath**iseez/) Grammar the transposition of sounds or letters in a word.

ORIGIN – Greek, 'transposition'.

metazoan /mettə**zō**ən/ > *noun* Zoology an animal other than a protozoan or sponge.

mete > *verb* (**mete out**) deal out or inflict (justice, punishment, etc.).

SYNONYMS – (**mete out**) allot, deal out, dispense, inflict.

metempsychosis /mettempsī**kō**siss/ > *noun* (pl. **metempsychoses** /-psī**kō**seez/) the supposed transmigration at death of the soul into a new body.

ORIGIN – Greek *metempsukhōsis*, from *psukhē* 'soul'.

meteor > *noun* a small body of matter from outer space that becomes incandescent as a result of friction with the earth's atmosphere and appears as a shooting star.

ORIGIN – Greek *meteōron*, from *meteōros* 'lofty'.

meteoric > *adjective* **1** relating to meteors or meteorites. **2** (of progress or development) very rapid.

meteorite > *noun* a piece of rock or metal that has fallen to the earth from space.

meteoroid > *noun* a small body in space that would become a meteor if it entered the earth's atmosphere.

meteorology /meetiə**roll**əji/ > *noun* the study of atmospheric processes and phenomena, especially for weather forecasting.

DERIVATIVES – **meteorological** *adjective* **meteorologist** *noun*.

meter[1] > *noun* a device that measures and records the quantity, degree, or rate of something. > *verb* measure with a meter.

ORIGIN – from METE (originally in the sense 'person who measures').

meter[2] > *noun* US spelling of METRE[1], METRE[2].

-meter > *combining form* **1** in names of measuring instruments: *thermometer*. **2** in nouns referring to lines of poetry with a specified number of measures: *hexameter*.

ORIGIN – from Greek *metron* 'measure'.

methadone /**meth**ədōn/ > *noun* a powerful synthetic painkiller, used as a substitute for morphine and heroin in the treatment of addiction.

methamphetamine /metham**fett**əmeen, -min/ > *noun* a synthetic drug related to amphetamine, used illegally as a stimulant.

methane /**mee**thayn/ > *noun* a colourless, odourless flammable gas which is the main constituent of natural gas.

ORIGIN – from METHYL.

methanol > *noun* a poisonous flammable alcohol, used to make methylated spirit.

methedrine /**meth**ədrin/ > *noun* (trademark in the UK) methamphetamine.

methinks > *verb* (past **methought**) archaic or humorous it seems to me.

methionine /mi**thī**əneen/ > *noun* Biochemistry a sulphur-containing amino acid which is a constituent of most proteins and is essential in the diet.

ORIGIN – from METHYL + Greek *theion* 'sulphur'.

method > *noun* **1** a way of doing something. **2** orderliness of thought or behaviour.

SYNONYMS – **1** approach, procedure, strategy, system, technique. **2** logic, order, organisation, planning, purpose, structure.

ANTONYMS – **2** chaos, disorder.

607

COMBINATIONS – **method acting** an acting technique in which an actor tries to identify completely with a character's emotions.

wordpower facts
Method

In medieval times, **method** meant 'prescribed medical treatment for a disease', a sense derived from the **Methodist** school of medicine in ancient Greece and Rome. Ancient Methodist doctors believed that diseases resulted from differing states of the body's internal 'pores', and that each condition had an appropriate set of remedies. The word **method** comes ultimately from the Greek noun *methodos* 'pursuit of knowledge', which is based on *hodos* 'way', the source of such English words as **episode**, **exodus**, and **period**. Also from *hodos* are **electrode** and the various kinds of electrode such as **anode** and **cathode**.

methodical (also **methodic**) > *adjective* characterised by method or order.
DERIVATIVES – **methodically** *adverb*.
SYNONYMS – logical, meticulous, orderly, organised, structured, systematic.
ANTONYMS – chaotic, disorganised.

Methodist > *noun* a member of a Christian Protestant denomination originating in the 18th-century evangelistic movement of Charles and John Wesley. > *adjective* relating to Methodists or Methodism.
DERIVATIVES – **Methodism** *noun*.
ORIGIN – probably from the notion of following a specified 'method' of Bible study.

methodology > *noun* (pl. **methodologies**) a system of methods used in a particular field.
DERIVATIVES – **methodological** *adjective* **methodologist** *noun*.

methought past of **METHINKS**.

meths > *noun* Brit. informal methylated spirit.

Methuselah /mithyōōzələ/ > *noun* **1** humorous a very old person. **2** (**methuselah**) a wine bottle of eight times the standard size.
ORIGIN – named after the biblical patriarch *Methuselah*, said to have lived for 969 years (Book of Genesis, chapter 5).

methyl /meethīl/ > *noun* Chemistry the radical −CH₃, derived from methane.
COMBINATIONS – **methyl alcohol** methanol.
ORIGIN – from Greek *methu* 'wine' + *hulē* 'wood'.

methylate > *verb* **1** mix with methanol or methylated spirit. **2** Chemistry introduce a methyl radical into (a molecule).
DERIVATIVES – **methylation** *noun*.

methylated spirit (also **methylated spirits**) > *noun* alcohol for use as a solvent or fuel, made unfit for drinking by the addition of methanol and a violet dye.

metical /mettikal/ > *noun* (pl. **meticais**) /mettikīsh/ the basic monetary unit of Mozambique, equal to 100 centavos.
ORIGIN – Portuguese, from an Arabic word meaning 'to weigh'.

meticulous > *adjective* very careful and precise.
DERIVATIVES – **meticulously** *adverb* **meticulousness** *noun*.
SYNONYMS – fastidious, painstaking, precise, punctilious, scrupulous.
ANTONYMS – careless, haphazard.
ORIGIN – first meaning 'fearful or timid', later 'overcareful about detail': from Latin *meticulosus* 'fearful'.

métier /metyay/ > *noun* **1** a trade, profession, or occupation. **2** a person's strength or special ability.
SYNONYMS – **2** forte, strength, strong point, talent.
ORIGIN – French, from Latin *ministerium* 'service'.

metonym /mettənim/ > *noun* a word or expression used as a substitute for something with which it is closely associated, e.g. *Washington* for the US government.
DERIVATIVES – **metonymic** *adjective* **metonymy** *noun*.
ORIGIN – from Greek *metōnumia* 'change of name'.

metope /mettəpi/ > *noun* Architecture a square space between triglyphs in a Doric frieze.
ORIGIN – Greek, from *meta* 'between' + *opē* 'hole for a beam end'.

metre¹ (US **meter**) > *noun* the fundamental unit of length in the metric system, equal to 100 centimetres (approx. 39.37 inches).

metre² (US **meter**) > *noun* **1** the rhythm of a piece of poetry, determined by the number and length of feet in a line. **2** the basic rhythmic pattern of a piece of music.

metric > *adjective* relating to or using the metric system.
COMBINATIONS – **metric system** the decimal measuring system based on the metre, litre, and gram as units of length, capacity, and weight or mass. **metric ton** (also **metric tonne**) a unit of weight equal to 1,000 kilograms (2,205 lb).

metrical > *adjective* **1** of or composed in poetic metre. **2** of or involving measurement.
DERIVATIVES – **metrically** *adverb*.

wordpower facts
Metre

Introduced in France in 1791 in the aftermath of the French Revolution, the metric system was intended to be a rational and practical alternative to former measuring systems. The word **metre** comes from Greek *metron* 'measure', a root shared by **metre** in poetry or music. As the basic unit of length used in science under the Système Internationale d'Unites (SI), the metre has to be defined very precisely. It was originally made equivalent to one ten-millionth of the length of a quadrant of the meridian, and was for a long time represented by a standard length of metal kept in Paris. However, it has several times become necessary to be more precise: the current definition (adopted in 1983) makes the metre equal to the distance travelled by light in a vacuum in a time of $^1/_{299\,792\,458}$ of a second.

metricate > *verb* convert to a metric system of measurement.
DERIVATIVES – **metrication** *noun*.

metro > *noun* (pl. **metros**) an underground railway system in a city, especially Paris.

metronome > *noun* a musicians' device that marks time at a selected rate by giving a regular tick.
DERIVATIVES – **metronomic** *adjective*.
ORIGIN – from Greek *metron* 'measure' + *nomos* 'law'.

metropolis /mitroppəliss/ > *noun* the principal city of a country or region.
SYNONYMS – capital, city, conurbation, megalopolis.
ORIGIN – Greek, from *mētēr* 'mother' + *polis* 'city'.

metropolitan > *adjective* **1** relating to a metropolis. **2** relating to the parent state of a colony. **3** Christian Church relating to a metropolitan or his see. > *noun* **1** Christian Church a bishop having authority over the bishops of a province. **2** an inhabitant of a metropolis.
COMBINATIONS – **metropolitan county** (in England) each of six units of local government centred on a large urban area (established in 1974; their councils were abolished in 1986).

mettle > *noun* spirit and resilience in the face of difficulty.
IDIOMS – **be on one's mettle** be ready to show one's ability or courage.
SYNONYMS – backbone, fortitude, grit, resolve, spirit, tenacity.
ORIGIN – variant spelling of **METAL**.

meunière /mönyair/ > *adjective* (after a noun)

cooked or served in lightly browned butter with lemon juice and parsley.

ORIGIN – from French *à la meunière* 'in the manner of a miller's wife'.

mew¹ > *verb* (of a cat or gull) make a characteristic high-pitched crying noise. > *noun* a mewing noise.

mew² Falconry > *noun* a cage or building for trained hawks, especially while they are moulting. > *verb* 1 (of a trained hawk) moult. 2 confine (a moulting trained hawk) to a mew. 3 (**mew up**) confine in a restricting place or situation.

ORIGIN – Old French *muer* 'to moult'.

mewl > *verb* 1 cry feebly or querulously. 2 mew.

mews > *noun* (pl. same) Brit. a row of houses or flats converted from stables in a small street or square.

ORIGIN – from **MEW²**: first referring to the royal stables on the site of the hawk mews at Charing Cross, London.

Mexican > *noun* a person from Mexico. > *adjective* relating to Mexico.

COMBINATIONS – **Mexican wave** an effect resembling a moving wave produced by successive sections of a stadium crowd standing, raising their arms, lowering them, and sitting down again. [ORIGIN – because first observed at the 1986 soccer World Cup in Mexico City.]

meze /**may**zay/ (also **mezze**) > *noun* (pl. same or **mezes**) (in Turkish, Greek, and Middle Eastern cookery) a selection of hot and cold hors d'oeuvres.

mezzanine /**mezz**əneen/ > *noun* 1 a low storey between two others, typically between the ground and first floors. 2 N. Amer. the lowest balcony of a theatre or the front rows of the balcony.

ORIGIN – from Italian *mezzano* 'middle'.

mezzo /**met**sō/ (also **mezzo-soprano**) > *noun* (pl. **mezzos**) a female singer with a voice pitched between soprano and contralto.

ORIGIN – Italian, from Latin *medius* 'middle'.

mezzotint /**met**sōtint/ > *noun* a print made from an engraved metal plate, the surface of which has been scraped and polished to give areas of shade and light respectively.

MF > *abbreviation* medium frequency.

Mg > *symbol* the chemical element magnesium.

mg > *abbreviation* milligram(s).

Mgr > *abbreviation* 1 (**mgr**) manager. 2 Monseigneur. 3 Monsignor.

MHR > *abbreviation* (in the US and Australia) Member of the House of Representatives.

MHz > *abbreviation* megahertz.

MI > *abbreviation* Michigan.

mi > *noun* variant spelling of **ME²**.

mi. > *abbreviation* mile(s).

MI5 > *abbreviation* Military Intelligence section 5, the former name for the UK governmental agency responsible for internal security and counter-intelligence on British territory (now officially named the Security Service).

MI6 > *abbreviation* Military Intelligence section 6, the former name for the UK governmental agency responsible for counter-intelligence overseas (now officially named the Secret Intelligence Service).

MIA > *abbreviation* chiefly US missing in action.

mia-mia /**mī**əmīə/ > *noun* Austral. an Aboriginal hut or shelter.

ORIGIN – an Aboriginal word.

miaow (also **meow**) > *noun* the characteristic cry of a cat. > *verb* make a miaow.

miasma /mi**az**mə/ > *noun* literary 1 an unpleasant or unhealthy vapour. 2 an oppressive or unpleasant atmosphere.

ORIGIN – Greek, 'defilement'.

mic > *noun* informal a microphone.

mica /**mī**kə/ > *noun* a silicate mineral found as minute shiny scales in granite and other rocks.

ORIGIN – Latin, 'crumb'.

mice plural of **MOUSE**.

Michaelmas /**mik**əlməss/ > *noun* the day of the Christian festival of St Michael, 29 September.

COMBINATIONS – **Michaelmas daisy** an aster with numerous pinkish-lilac daisy-like flowers which bloom around Michaelmas. **Michaelmas term** (in some British universities) the autumn term.

ORIGIN – Old English, 'Saint Michael's Mass', referring to the Archangel Michael.

mickery (also **mickerie**) > *noun* (pl. **mickeries**) Austral. a waterhole or excavated well, especially in a dry river bed.

ORIGIN – Arabana Wahgahuru (an Aboriginal language).

mickey > *noun* (in phrase **take the mickey**) informal, chiefly Brit. tease or ridicule someone.

DERIVATIVES – **mickey-taking** *noun*.

Mickey Finn > *noun* informal a surreptitiously drugged or doctored drink.

ORIGIN – first recorded in the 1920s: perhaps from the name of a notorious Chicago saloon-keeper.

Mickey Mouse > *adjective* informal ineffective or insignificant.

mickle (also **muckle**) archaic or Scottish & N. English > *noun* a large amount. > *adjective* very large.

IDIOMS – **many a little makes a mickle** (also **many a mickle makes a muckle**) many small amounts accumulate to make a large amount.

NOTE – the forms **mickle** and **muckle** are merely variants of the same word, meaning 'a large amount'. However, the alternative

form of the proverb (originally a misquotation) has led to a misunderstanding that **a mickle** means 'a small amount'.

Micmac /**mik**mak/ > *noun* (pl. same or **Micmacs**) a member of an American Indian people inhabiting the Maritime Provinces of Canada.

ORIGIN – the Micmacs' name for themselves.

micro > *noun* (pl. **micros**) a microcomputer or microprocessor. > *adjective* extremely small or small-scale.

micro- > *combining form* 1 very small or of reduced size: *microbrewery*. 2 denoting a factor of one millionth (10^{-6}): *microfarad*.

ORIGIN – from Greek *mikros* 'small'.

microanalysis > *noun* the analysis of chemical compounds using a sample of a few milligrams.

microbe /**mī**krōb/ > *noun* a micro-organism, especially a bacterium causing disease or fermentation.

DERIVATIVES – **microbial** *adjective*.

ORIGIN – from Greek *mikros* 'small' + *bios* 'life'.

microbiology > *noun* the scientific study of micro-organisms.

microbrewery > *noun* chiefly N. Amer. a brewery producing limited quantities of beer for local consumption.

microchip > *noun* a tiny wafer of semiconducting material used to make an integrated circuit.

microcircuit > *noun* a minute electric circuit, especially an integrated circuit.

microclimate > *noun* the climate of a very small or restricted area.

microcode > *noun* Computing a very low-level instruction set controlling the operation of a computer.

microcomputer > *noun* a small computer with a microprocessor as its central processor.

microcosm /**mī**krōkoz'm/ > *noun* a thing regarded as encapsulating in miniature the characteristics of something much larger. Contrasted with **MACROCOSM**.

DERIVATIVES – **microcosmic** *adjective*.

ORIGIN – from Greek *mikros kosmos* 'little world'.

microdot > *noun* 1 a photograph, especially of a printed document, reduced to a very small size. 2 a tiny tablet of LSD.

microeconomics > *plural noun* (treated as sing.) the part of economics concerned with single factors and the effects of individual decisions.

microelectronics > *plural noun* (usu. treated as sing.) the design, manufacture, and use of microchips and microcircuits.

microfibre > *noun* a very fine synthetic yarn.

microfiche /**mī**krōfeesh/ > *noun* a flat piece of film containing greatly reduced photographs of the pages of a newspaper, book, etc.

ORIGIN – from Greek *mikros* 'small' + French *fiche* 'slip of paper, index card'.

microfilm > *noun* a length of film containing greatly reduced photographs of the pages of a newspaper, book, etc.

microgram > *noun* one millionth of a gram.

micrograph > *noun* a photograph taken using a microscope.

DERIVATIVES – **micrography** *noun*.

microgravity > *noun* very weak gravity, as in an orbiting spacecraft.

microinstruction > *noun* Computing a single instruction in microcode.

microlight > *noun* chiefly Brit. a very small, light, one- or two-seater aircraft.

microlitre (US also **microliter**) > *noun* one millionth of a litre.

micromesh > *noun* a material consisting of a very fine mesh.

micrometer /mīkrommitər/ > *noun* a gauge which measures small distances or thicknesses.

micrometre (US **micrometer**) > *noun* one millionth of a metre.

micron > *noun* one millionth of a metre.

Micronesian > *noun* a person from Micronesia, an island group in the western Pacific. > *adjective* relating to Micronesia.

micronutrient > *noun* a chemical element or substance required in trace amounts by living organisms.

micro-organism > *noun* a microscopic organism, especially a bacterium, virus, or fungus.

microphone > *noun* an instrument for converting sound waves into electrical energy which may then be amplified, transmitted, or recorded.

microphotograph > *noun* a photograph reduced to a very small size.

microprocessor > *noun* an integrated circuit containing all the functions of a central processing unit of a computer.

microprogram > *noun* a microinstruction program.

microscope > *noun* an optical instrument for magnifying very small objects.

microscopic > *adjective* **1** so small as to be visible only with a microscope. **2** informal very small. **3** relating to a microscope.

DERIVATIVES – **microscopically** *adverb*.

microscopy /mīkroskəpi/ > *noun* the use of a microscope.

microsecond > *noun* one millionth of a second.

microstructure > *noun* the fine structure in a material which can be made visible and examined with a microscope.

microsurgery > *noun* intricate surgery performed using miniaturised instruments and a microscope.

microwave > *noun* **1** an electromagnetic wave with a wavelength in the range 0.001–0.3 m, shorter than that of a normal radio wave but longer than those of infrared radiation. **2** (also **microwave oven**) an oven that uses microwaves to cook or heat food. > *verb* cook (food) in a microwave oven.

micturate /miktyoorayt/ > *verb* formal urinate.

DERIVATIVES – **micturition** *noun*.

ORIGIN – Latin *micturire*.

mid > *adjective* of or in the middle part or position of a range. > *preposition* literary in the middle of; amid.

mid- > *combining form* **1** referring to the middle of: *midsection.* **2** in the middle; medium; half: *midway.*

Midas touch /mīdəss/ > *noun* the ability to make a lot of money out of anything one undertakes.

ORIGIN – from *Midas*, king of Phrygia, who in Greek mythology was given by Dionysus the power to turn everything he touched into gold.

midbrain > *noun* Anatomy a small central part of the brainstem, developing from the middle of the primitive or embryonic brain.

midday > *noun* the middle of the day; noon.

midden > *noun* a dunghill or refuse heap.

middle > *adjective* **1** at an equal distance from the extremities of something; central. **2** intermediate in rank, quality, or ability. > *noun* **1** a middle point or position. **2** informal a person's waist and stomach.

SYNONYMS – *noun* **1** centre, heart.

COMBINATIONS – **Middle America** the conservative US middle classes, characterised as inhabiting the Midwest. **middle C** Music the C near the middle of the piano keyboard, written on the first ledger line below the treble stave or the first ledger line above the bass stave. **middle class** the social group between the upper and working classes; professional and business people. **middle distance 1** the part of a real or painted landscape between the foreground and the background. **2** Athletics a race distance between that of a sprint and a long-distance race, in particular between 800 and 1,500 metres. **middle ear** the air-filled central cavity of the ear, behind the eardrum. **Middle England** the conservative middle classes in England outside London. **Middle English** the English language from c.1150 to c.1470. **middle ground** an area of compromise or possible agreement between two extreme positions. **middle name** a person's name placed after the first name and before the surname. **middle of the road 1** moderate. **2** conventional and unadventurous. **middle**

school (in the UK) a school for children from about 9 to 13 years old. **middleweight** a weight in boxing and other sports intermediate between welterweight and light heavyweight.

middle age > *noun* the period between youth and old age, about 45 to 60.

DERIVATIVES – **middle-aged** *adjective*.

Middle Ages > *plural noun* the period of European history from the fall of the Roman Empire in the West (5th century) to the fall of Constantinople (1453), or, more narrowly, from c.1000 to 1453.

middlebrow > *adjective* informal, chiefly derogatory demanding or involving only a moderate degree of intellectual application.

Middle East > *noun* an area of SW Asia and northern Africa stretching from the Mediterranean to Pakistan, in particular Iran, Iraq, Israel, Jordan, Egypt, Lebanon, and Syria.

DERIVATIVES – **Middle Eastern** *adjective*.

middleman > *noun* **1** a person who buys goods from producers and sells them to retailers or consumers. **2** a person who arranges business or political deals between other people.

middling > *adjective* moderate or average. > *adverb* informal fairly or moderately.

Middx > *abbreviation* Middlesex.

midfield > *noun* **1** (chiefly in soccer) the central part of the field. **2** the players who play in a central position between attack and defence.

DERIVATIVES – **midfielder** *noun*.

midge > *noun* **1** a small two-winged fly that forms swarms near water, of which many kinds feed on blood. **2** informal a small person.

midget > *noun* **1** an extremely small person. **2** (before another noun) extremely small: *a midget submarine.*

MIDI > *noun* a device by which electronic musical instruments and computers may be interconnected.

ORIGIN – from *musical instrument digital interface.*

midi > *noun* (pl. **midis**) a woman's calf-length skirt, dress, or coat.

COMBINATIONS – **midi system** Brit. a set of compact stacking hi-fi components.

midi- > *combining form* of medium-size or length.

midland > *noun* **1** the middle part of a country. **2** (**the Midlands**) the inland counties of central England. > *adjective* (also **midlands**) of or in a midland or the Midlands.

DERIVATIVES – **midlander** *noun*.

midlife > *noun* the central period of a person's life, between around 45 and 60 years old.

midnight > *noun* twelve o'clock at night; the middle of the night.

COMBINATIONS – **midnight blue** a very dark blue. **midnight sun** the sun when seen at midnight during the summer within either the Arctic or Antarctic Circle.

mid-off > noun Cricket a fielding position on the off side near the bowler.

mid-on > noun Cricket a fielding position on the on side near the bowler.

midrib > noun a large strengthened vein along the midline of a leaf.

midriff > noun the front of the body between the chest and the waist.

midship > noun the middle part of a ship or boat.

midshipman > noun 1 a rank of officer in the Royal Navy, above naval cadet and below sub lieutenant. 2 a naval cadet in the US navy.

midships > adverb & adjective another term for AMIDSHIPS.

midst archaic or literary > preposition in the middle of. > noun the middle point or part.
IDIOMS – **in our** (or **your**, **their**, etc.) **midst** among us (or you or them).

midstream > noun the middle of a stream or river.
IDIOMS – **in midstream** part-way through an activity, speech, etc.

midsummer > noun 1 the middle part of summer. 2 the summer solstice.
COMBINATIONS – **Midsummer Day** (also **Midsummer's Day**) 24 June.

midterm > noun the middle of a period of office, an academic term, or a pregnancy.

midway > adverb & adjective in or towards the middle.

midweek > noun the middle of the week. > adjective & adverb in the middle of the week.

Midwest > noun the region of the northern US from Ohio west to the Rocky Mountains.
DERIVATIVES – **Midwestern** adjective.

midwicket > noun Cricket a fielding position on the leg side, level with the middle of the pitch.

midwife > noun a nurse who is trained to assist women in childbirth.
DERIVATIVES – **midwifery** /midwifəri/ noun.
ORIGIN – probably from obsolete mid 'with' + WIFE (in the sense 'woman').

midwinter > noun 1 the middle part of winter. 2 the winter solstice.

mien /meen/ > noun a person's look or manner.
ORIGIN – probably from French mine 'expression'.

miffed > adjective informal offended or irritated.

might¹ > modal verb past of MAY. 1 used to express possibility or make a suggestion. 2 used politely or tentatively in questions and requests.

might² > noun great power or strength.
IDIOMS – **with might and main** with all one's strength or power.
SYNONYMS – force, power, strength.
ANTONYMS – weakness.

mightn't > contraction might not.

mighty > adjective (**mightier**, **mightiest**) 1 possessing great power or strength. 2 informal very large. > adverb informal, chiefly N. Amer. extremely.
DERIVATIVES – **mightily** adverb **mightiness** noun.
SYNONYMS – adjective 1 potent, powerful, strong.

mignonette /minyənet/ > noun a plant with spikes of small fragrant greenish flowers.
ORIGIN – French, from mignon 'small and sweet'.

migraine /meegrayn, mīgrayn/ > noun a recurrent throbbing headache, typically affecting one side of the head and often accompanied by nausea and disturbed vision.
NOTE – the standard pronunciation of **migraine** in British English is **mee**grayn, which is closer to the pronunciation of the original word in French. However, many people in Britain say **mī**grayn, and this pronunciation is standard in the US.
ORIGIN – French, from Greek hēmikrania, from hēmi- 'half' + kranion 'skull'.

migrant > noun 1 an animal that migrates. 2 a worker who moves from one place to another to find work. > adjective tending to migrate or having migrated.

migrate > verb 1 (of an animal) move from one habitat to another according to the seasons. 2 move to settle in a new area in order to find work. 3 Computing transfer from one system to another.
DERIVATIVES – **migration** noun **migratory** adjective.
SYNONYMS – 2 emigrate, move, relocate, resettle.
ORIGIN – Latin migrare 'move, shift'.

mihrab /meeraab/ > noun a niche in the wall of a mosque, at the point nearest to Mecca, towards which the congregation faces to pray.
ORIGIN – Arabic, 'place for prayer'.

mikado /mikaadō/ > noun historical a title given to the emperor of Japan.
ORIGIN – Japanese, from mi 'august' + kado 'gate'.

mike noun > informal a microphone.

mil¹ > abbreviation informal millions.

mil² > noun one thousandth of an inch.
ORIGIN – from Latin millesimum 'thousandth'.

milady > noun historical or humorous used to address or refer to an English noblewoman.

milch /milch/ > adjective (of a domestic mammal) giving or kept for milk.
COMBINATIONS – **milch cow** a source of easy profit.
ORIGIN – from Old English -milce in thrimilce 'May' (when cows could be milked three times a day).

mild > adjective 1 gentle and not easily provoked. 2 of moderate severity, intensity, or effect. 3 not sharp or strong in flavour. 4 (of weather) moderately warm; less cold than expected. > noun Brit. a kind of dark beer not strongly flavoured with hops.
DERIVATIVES – **mildish** adjective **mildly** adverb **mildness** noun.
SYNONYMS – adjective 1 placid, unassuming. 2 gentle, light, slight. 4 fine, temperate.
ANTONYMS – adjective 1 harsh. 2 intense.
COMBINATIONS – **mild steel** steel containing a small percentage of carbon, that is strong and tough but not readily tempered.

mildew > noun a coating of minute fungi on plants or damp organic material such as paper or leather. > verb affect with mildew.

mile > noun 1 (also **statute mile**) a unit of linear measure equal to 1,760 yards (approximately 1.609 kilometres). 2 (**miles**) informal a very long way. > adverb (**miles**) informal by a great amount or a long way.
IDIOMS – **be miles away** informal be lost in thought. **go the extra mile** try particularly hard to achieve something. **run a mile** informal run rapidly away; flee. **stand** (or **stick**) **out a mile** informal be very obvious or incongruous.
ORIGIN – from Latin milia, plural of mille 'thousand'; a Roman 'mile' consisted of 1,000 paces (approximately 1,620 yards).

mileage (also **milage**) > noun 1 a number of miles travelled or covered. 2 informal actual or potential benefit or advantage.

mileometer > noun variant spelling of MILOMETER.

milepost > noun chiefly N. Amer. & Austral. 1 a marker indicating the distance to a particular place. 2 a post one mile from the finishing post of a race.

miler > noun informal a person or horse trained to run over races of a mile.

milestone > noun 1 a stone set up beside a road to mark the distance to a particular place. 2 an event marking a significant new development or stage.

milfoil /milfoyl/ > noun 1 the common yarrow, a plant with feathery leaves and heads of small aromatic flowers. 2 (also **water milfoil**) an aquatic plant with whorls of fine submerged leaves.
ORIGIN – from Latin mille 'thousand' + folium 'leaf'.

miliary /**mill**iəri/ > *adjective* Medicine (of a disease) accompanied by a rash with small round lesions resembling millet seed.
ORIGIN – Latin *miliarius*, from *milium* 'millet'.

milieu /**mee**lyö/ > *noun* (pl. **milieux** or **milieus**) a person's social environment.
ORIGIN – French, from *mi* 'mid' + *lieu* 'place'.

militant > *adjective* aggressive and combative in support of a particular cause. > *noun* a militant person.
DERIVATIVES – **militancy** noun **militantly** *adverb*.
SYNONYMS – *adjective* aggressive, confrontational, extreme, extremist.

militaria > *plural noun* military articles of historical interest.

militarise (also **militarize**) > *verb* 1 equip with military resources. 2 give a military character to.
DERIVATIVES – **militarisation** *noun*.

militarism > *noun* the belief that a country should maintain and readily use strong armed forces.
DERIVATIVES – **militarist** noun & *adjective*.

militaristic > *adjective* characterised by militarism.
SYNONYMS – bellicose, belligerent, combative, hawkish, warlike.
ANTONYMS – pacifist, peaceful.

military > *adjective* relating to or characteristic of soldiers or armed forces. > *noun* (**the military**) the armed forces of a country.
WORDFINDER – court martial (*military court*), ordnance (*military stores and materials*), strategy (*long-term military plans*), tactics (*short-term military plans*).
DERIVATIVES – **militarily** *adverb*.
SYNONYMS – armed, martial, soldierly.
ANTONYMS – civil, civilian.
COMBINATIONS – **military attaché** an army officer serving with an embassy or attached as an observer to a foreign army. **Military Cross** (in the UK and the Commonwealth) a decoration awarded for distinguished active service on land (originally for officers). **military honours** ceremonies performed by troops as a mark of respect at the burial of a member of the armed forces. **military-industrial complex** a country's military establishment and arms industries regarded as a powerful vested interest. **Military Medal** (in the UK and the Commonwealth) a decoration awarded for distinguished active service on land (originally for enlisted men). **military police** a body responsible for disciplinary duties in the armed forces.
ORIGIN – Latin *militaris*, from *miles* 'soldier'.

militate > *verb* (**militate against**) be an important factor in preventing.
USAGE – do not confuse **militate** with **mitigate**, which means 'make (something bad) less severe'.
SYNONYMS – (**militate against**) cancel out, counter, counteract, hinder, prevent.

militia /miˈlishə/ > *noun* 1 a military force raised from the civilian population to supplement a regular army in an emergency. 2 a rebel force opposing a regular army.
COMBINATIONS – **militiaman** a member of a militia.

milk > *noun* 1 an opaque white fluid rich in fat and protein, secreted by female mammals for the nourishment of their young. 2 the milk of cows as a food and drink for humans. 3 the milk-like juice of certain plants, such as the coconut. > *verb* 1 draw milk from (a cow or other animal). 2 exploit or defraud over a period of time. 3 get all possible advantage from (a situation).
WORDFINDER – galacto-, lacto- (*combining forms*); dairy, lacteal, lactic (*related adjectives*); albumin, casein, lactoferrin, lactoglobulin (*proteins present in milk*), curds (*soft white substance formed when milk coagulates*), koumiss (*fermented liquor made from mare's milk*), lactate (*secrete milk*), posset (*hot milk curdled with alcohol*), rennet (*curdled milk from the stomach of an unweaned calf*), rennin (*enzyme causing curdling of milk*), whey (*watery part of milk remaining when it has coagulated*).
IDIOMS – **it's no use crying over spilt milk** proverb there is no point regretting something that has already happened. **milk and honey** prosperity and abundance. [ORIGIN – with biblical allusion to the prosperity of the Promised Land (Book of Exodus, chapter 3).] **milk of human kindness** care and compassion for other people. [ORIGIN – from Shakespeare's *Macbeth* i. v. 16.]
DERIVATIVES – **milker** *noun*.
COMBINATIONS – **milk-and-water** feeble; ineffective. **milk bar** Brit. a snack bar selling milk drinks. **milk chocolate** solid chocolate made with added milk to give a creamy taste. **milk fever** 1 an illness in female cows or other animals that have just produced young, caused by calcium deficiency. 2 a fever in women caused by infection after childbirth. **milk float** Brit. an open-sided van used for delivering milk. **milkmaid** chiefly archaic a girl or woman who works in a dairy. **milkman** a man who delivers milk. **milk pudding** Brit. a baked pudding made of milk and rice, sago, or tapioca. **milk round** Brit. 1 a regular milk delivery along a fixed route. 2 a series of

visits to universities and colleges by recruiting staff from large companies. **milk run** a routine, uneventful journey. [ORIGIN – RAF slang in the Second World War for a sortie that was as simple as a milkman's round.] **milk stout** a kind of sweet stout made with lactose. **milk tooth** a temporary tooth in a child or young mammal. **milk vetch** a yellow-flowered plant of the pea family, grown in some regions for fodder.

milkshake > *noun* a cold drink made from milk whisked with ice cream.

milksop > *noun* a timid and indecisive person.

milkweed > *noun* a herbaceous American plant with milky sap.

milkwort > *noun* a small plant with blue, pink, or white flowers, formerly supposed to increase a mother's milk production.

milky > *adjective* 1 containing milk. 2 of a soft white colour or clouded appearance.
DERIVATIVES – **milkiness** *noun*.
SYNONYMS – 2 chalky, cloudy, misty, whitish.

Milky Way > *noun* a faint band of light crossing the night sky, made up of vast numbers of stars forming the bulk of the galaxy of which our solar system is a part.
ORIGIN – translation of Greek *galaxias kuklos* 'milky vault', from *gala* 'milk' and *kuklos* 'circle': see box at **GALAXY**.

mill[1] > *noun* 1 a building equipped with machinery for grinding grain into flour. 2 a device or piece of machinery for grinding grain or other solid substances. 3 a building fitted with machinery for a manufacturing process. > *verb* 1 grind in a mill. 2 cut or shape (metal) with a rotating tool. 3 produce regular ribbed markings on the edge of (a coin). 4 (**mill about** or **around**) move around in a confused mass.
WORDFINDER – flashboard (*board sending water into a mill race*), grist (*corn ground to make flour*), leat (*open watercourse for a watermill*), quern (*hand mill for grinding corn*), tailwater (*water below wheel in a mill race*).
IDIOMS – **go** (or **put**) **through the mill** undergo (or cause to undergo) an unpleasant experience.
DERIVATIVES – **millable** *adjective* **milled** *adjective*.
SYNONYMS – *verb* 1 comminute, crush, grind, kibble, pound, powder, pulverise. 4 (**mill about** or **around**) crowd, seethe, shuffle, swarm, throng.
COMBINATIONS – **millboard** stiff grey pasteboard, used for the covers of books. **mill dam** a dam built across a stream to raise the level of the water so that it will turn a mill wheel. **millpond** 1 the pool created by a mill dam, providing the head of water that powers a watermill. 2 a very

still and calm stretch of water. **mill race** the channel carrying the swift current of water that drives a mill wheel. **millstream** the flowing water that drives a mill wheel. **mill wheel** a wheel used to drive a watermill.

ORIGIN – Latin *mola* 'grindstone, mill'.

mill² > *noun* N. Amer. a monetary unit used only in calculations, worth one thousandth of a dollar.

ORIGIN – from Latin *millesimum* 'thousandth part'; compare with CENT.

millefeuille /meelfö-i/ > *noun* a cake consisting of thin layers of puff pastry filled with jam and cream.

ORIGIN – French, 'thousand-leaf'.

millenarian* /millinairiən/ > *adjective* **1** relating to or believing in Christian millenarianism. **2** seeking rapid and radical change. > *noun* a person who believes in millenarianism.

*SPELLING – the words **millenarian**, **millenarianism**, and **millenary** are spelled with only one *n* in the middle; see the note at MILLENNIUM.

millenarianism > *noun* belief in a future thousand-year age of blessedness, beginning with or culminating in the Second Coming of Christ.

DERIVATIVES – **millenarianist** *noun* & *adjective*.

millenary /milennəri/ > *noun* (pl. **millenaries**) **1** a period of a thousand years. **2** a thousandth anniversary. > *adjective* consisting of a thousand.

millennial > *adjective* relating to a millennium.

millennialism > *noun* another term for MILLENARIANISM.

DERIVATIVES – **millennialist** *noun* & *adjective*.

millennium* /milenniəm/ > *noun* (pl. **millennia** or **millenniums**) **1** a period of a thousand years, especially when calculated from the traditional date of the birth of Christ. **2** an anniversary of a thousand years. **3** (**the millennium**) Christian Theology the prophesied thousand-year reign of Christ at the end of the age, foretold in the Book of Revelation.

*SPELLING – double l, double n: mil*lenn*ium.

millennium bug > *noun* an inability in older computing software to deal correctly with dates of 1 January 2000 or later.

miller > *noun* a person who owns or works in a grain mill.

COMBINATIONS – **miller's thumb** a small freshwater fish with a broad flattened head.

millesimal /milessim'l/ > *adjective* consisting of thousandth parts; thousandth.

---

wordpower facts

Millennium

The correct spelling is **millennium**, with two *n*s. The spelling with one *n* is a common error, formed by confusion with other words such as **millenarian** and **millenary**, which are correctly spelled with only one *n*. The differences in spelling are explained by different origins. **Millennium** was formed from Latin *mille* 'thousand' + *annus* 'year', by analogy with words like **biennium**, while **millenary** and **millenarian** were formed on the Latin *milleni* 'a thousand each'.

---

millet > *noun* a cereal grown in warm countries which bears a large crop of small seeds, used to make flour or alcoholic drinks.

ORIGIN – French, from Latin *milium*.

milli- > *combining form* a thousand, especially a factor of one thousandth (10^{-3}): *milligram*.

ORIGIN – from Latin *mille* 'thousand'.

milliamp > *noun* short for MILLIAMPERE.

milliampere > *noun* one thousandth of an ampere.

milliard > *noun* Brit., dated one thousand million; a billion.

millibar > *noun* one thousandth of a bar, a unit of atmospheric pressure equivalent to 100 pascals.

millieme /milyem/ > *noun* a monetary unit of Egypt, equal to one thousandth of a pound.

ORIGIN – French, 'thousandth'.

milligram (also **milligramme**) > *noun* one thousandth of a gram.

millilitre (US **milliliter**) > *noun* one thousandth of a litre.

millimetre (US **millimeter**) > *noun* one thousandth of a metre.

milliner > *noun* a person who makes or sells women's hats.

DERIVATIVES – **millinery** *noun*.

ORIGIN – from the name of the Italian city *Milan*, originally meaning 'native of Milan', later 'a vendor of fancy goods from Milan'.

million > *cardinal number* **1** the number equivalent to the product of a thousand and a thousand; 1,000,000 or 10^6. **2** (also **millions**) informal a very large number or amount.

DERIVATIVES – **millionth** *ordinal number*.

ORIGIN – Old French, from Italian *mille* 'thousand'.

millionaire* > *noun* (fem. **millionairess**) a person whose assets are worth one million pounds or dollars or more.

*SPELLING – just one *n*: millio*n*aire.

millipede > *noun* a small invertebrate animal

(an arthropod) with an elongated body composed of many segments, most of which bear two pairs of legs.

ORIGIN – from Latin *mille* 'thousand' + *pes* 'foot'.

millisecond > *noun* one thousandth of a second.

millstone > *noun* **1** each of a pair of circular stones used for grinding grain. **2** a burden of responsibility.

COMBINATIONS – **millstone grit** a coarse sandstone occurring in Britain immediately below the coal measures.

milo > *noun* a drought-resistant variety of sorghum which is an important cereal in the central US.

ORIGIN – Sesotho (an African language).

milometer /mīlommitər/ (also **mile-ometer**) > *noun* Brit. an instrument on a vehicle for recording the number of miles travelled.

milord > *noun* historical or humorous used to address or refer to an English nobleman.

Milquetoast /milktōst/ > *noun* chiefly N. Amer. a timid or submissive person.

ORIGIN – from the name of an American cartoon character, Caspar *Milquetoast*, created by H. T. Webster in 1924.

milt > *noun* **1** the semen of a male fish. **2** the reproductive gland of a male fish.

Miltonic /miltonnik/ (also **Miltonian**) > *adjective* relating to the English poet John Milton (1608–74).

mime > *noun* **1** the expression of action, character, or emotion by gesture and movement without words, especially as a form of theatrical performance. **2** (in ancient Greece and Rome) a simple farcical drama including mimicry. **3** (also **mime artist**) a performer of mime. > *verb* **1** perform or convey using mime. **2** pretend to sing or play an instrument as a recording is being played.

ORIGIN – Greek *mimos*.

mimeograph /mimmiəgraaf/ > *noun* a duplicating machine which produces copies from a stencil, now superseded by the photocopier.

ORIGIN – from Greek *mimeomai* 'I imitate'.

mimesis /mimeesiss/ > *noun* **1** imitative representation of the real world in art and literature. **2** Biology mimicry of another animal or plant.

ORIGIN – Greek.

mimetic /mimettik/ > *adjective* relating to or practising mimesis or mimicry.

mimic > *verb* (**mimicked, mimicking**) **1** imitate, especially in order to ridicule. **2** (of an animal or plant) take on the appearance of (another) to deter predators or for camouflage. **3** replicate the effects of. > *noun* **1** a person skilled in mimicking. **2** an animal or plant that mimics.

SYNONYMS – *verb* **1** ape, caricature, imitate, impersonate, lampoon, parody. *noun* **1** imitator, impersonator, impressionist.

mimicry > *noun* **1** imitation of someone or something to entertain or ridicule. **2** Biology the close external resemblance of an animal or plant to another.

mimosa /mimōzə/ > *noun* **1** an acacia tree with delicate fern-like leaves and yellow flowers. **2** a plant of a genus that includes the sensitive plant (*Mimosa pudica*).

ORIGIN – probably from Latin *mimus* 'mime' (because the plant seemingly mimics an animal's sensitivity to touch).

mimsy > *adjective* rather feeble and prim.

ORIGIN – a nonsense word coined by Lewis Carroll from *miserable* and *flimsy*.

min. > *abbreviation* **1** minimum. **2** minute(s).

minaret /minnəret/ > *noun* a slender tower of a mosque, with a balcony from which a muezzin calls Muslims to prayer.

DERIVATIVES – **minareted** *adjective*.

ORIGIN – Arabic, 'lighthouse, minaret'.

minatory /minnətri/ > *adjective* formal threatening.

ORIGIN – from Latin *minari* 'threaten'.

mince > *verb* **1** cut up or shred (meat) into very small pieces. **2** walk in an affected manner with short, quick steps and swinging hips. > *noun* chiefly Brit. minced meat.

IDIOMS – **mince (one's) words** voice one's disapproval delicately or gently.

DERIVATIVES – **mincer** *noun* **mincing** *adjective*.

COMBINATIONS – **mince pie** chiefly Brit. a pie containing mincemeat, typically eaten at Christmas.

ORIGIN – Old French *mincier*, from Latin *minutia* 'smallness'.

mincemeat > *noun* a mixture of currants, raisins, apples, candied peel, sugar, spices, and suet.

IDIOMS – **make mincemeat of** informal defeat decisively.

mind > *noun* **1** the faculty of consciousness and thought. **2** a person's intellect or memory. **3** a person identified with their intellectual faculties: *he was one of the greatest minds of his time.* **4** a person's attention or will. > *verb* **1** be distressed or annoyed by; object to. **2** remember or take care to do. **3** give attention to; watch out for. **4** take care of temporarily. **5** (**be minded**) be inclined to do. **6** (also **mind you**) introducing a qualification to a previous statement.

IDIOMS – **be in** (or **of**) **two minds** be unable to decide between alternatives. **be of one mind** share the same opinion. **give someone a piece of one's mind** rebuke someone. **have a** (or **a good** or **half a**) **mind to do** be inclined to do. **have in mind 1** be thinking of. **2** intend to do. **in one's mind's eye** in one's imagination.

mind one's Ps & Qs be careful to be polite and avoid giving offence. [ORIGIN – perhaps referring to the care that a young pupil must take to differentiate between the tailed letters *p* and *q*.] **never mind 1** do not be concerned or distressed. **2** let alone. **out of one's mind** having lost control of one's mental faculties. **put one in mind of** remind one of. **to my mind** in my opinion.

SYNONYMS – *verb* **1** care about, be concerned by, object to, be troubled by. **4** look after, supervise, tend.

COMBINATIONS – **mind-bending** informal altering one's state of mind. **mind-blowing** (also **mind-boggling**) informal overwhelmingly impressive or great. **mind game** a series of actions planned for its psychological effect on another. **mind-numbing** so extreme or intense as to prevent normal thought. **mindshare** consumer awareness of a product or brand, as opposed to market share.

ORIGIN – Old English, related to Latin *mens*.

minded > *adjective* inclined to think in a particular way.

minder > *noun* **1** a person employed to look after someone or something. **2** informal a bodyguard.

mindful > *adjective* **1** (**mindful of** or **that**) aware of or recognising that. **2** formal inclined or intending to do something.

SYNONYMS – **2** (**mindful of** or **that**) alert to, alive to, aware of, conscious of, recognising that.

mindless > *adjective* **1** acting or done without justification and with no concern for the consequences. **2** (**mindless of**) not thinking of or concerned about. **3** (of an activity) simple and repetitive.

DERIVATIVES – **mindlessly** *adverb* **mindlessness** *noun*.

SYNONYMS – **3** mechanical, robotic.

mindset > *noun* a habitual way of thinking.

mine¹ > *possessive pronoun* referring to a thing or things belonging to or associated with the speaker. > *possessive determiner* archaic (used before a vowel) my.

mine² > *noun* **1** an excavation in the earth for extracting coal or other minerals. **2** an abundant source. **3** a type of bomb placed on or in the ground or water, which detonates on contact. **4** historical a passage tunnelled under the wall of a besieged fortress, in which explosives were placed. > *verb* **1** obtain from a mine. **2** excavate for coal or other minerals. **3** lay a mine or mines on or in (a place or structure).

WORDFINDER – adit, drift, gallery, pithead, shaft, upcast (*passages in a mine*), chokedamp, firedamp (*gases found in mines*), colliery (*coal mine and its equipment*), face, lode, longwall, seam, vein (*strata worked in a mine*), opencast mining, N. Amer. strip-mining (*mining carried out near the ground surface*).

COMBINATIONS – **minefield 1** an area planted with explosive mines. **2** a subject or situation presenting unseen hazards. **mineshaft** a deep, narrow shaft that gives access to a mine. **minesweeper** a warship equipped for detecting and removing or destroying tethered explosive mines.

ORIGIN – Old French.

miner > *noun* a person who works in a mine.

mineral > *noun* **1** a solid inorganic substance of natural occurrence. **2** an inorganic substance needed by the human body for good health. **3** a substance obtained by mining. **4** (**minerals**) Brit. fizzy soft drinks.

WORDFINDER – calcium, fluorine, iodine, iron, magnesium, phosphorus, zinc (*necessary dietary minerals*); boron, chlorine, chromium, cobalt, copper, manganese, molybdenum, selenium, silicon, sulphur, vanadium (*trace elements*).

COMBINATIONS – **mineral oil** petroleum, or a distillation product of petroleum. **mineral water** water having some dissolved salts naturally present.

ORIGIN – Latin *minera* 'ore'.

mineralise (also **mineralize**) > *verb* convert into or impregnate with a mineral substance.

DERIVATIVES – **mineralisation** *noun*.

mineralogy > *noun* the scientific study of minerals.

DERIVATIVES – **mineralogical** *adjective* **mineralogist** *noun*.

minestrone /minnistrōni/ > *noun* an Italian soup containing vegetables and pasta.

ORIGIN – Italian, from *minestrare* 'serve at table'.

Ming > *adjective* (of Chinese porcelain) made during the Ming dynasty (1368–1644) and characterised by elaborate designs and vivid colours.

mingle > *verb* **1** mix together. **2** move around and chat at a social function.

SYNONYMS – **1** blend, combine, merge, mix. **2** circulate, socialise.

ORIGIN – from obsolete *meng* 'mix or blend'.

mingy > *adjective* informal mean; ungenerous.

ORIGIN – perhaps a blend of **MEAN²** and **STINGY**.

mini > *adjective* miniaturised; very small of its kind. > *noun* (pl. **minis**) a very short skirt or dress.

mini- > *combining form* very small or minor of its kind; miniature: *minibus*.

ORIGIN – from **MINIATURE**, reinforced by **MINIMUM**.

miniature* > *adjective* of a much smaller size than normal. > *noun* a thing that is much smaller than normal. **2** a very small and minutely detailed portrait. **3** a picture or decorated letter in an illuminated manuscript.

DERIVATIVES – **miniaturise** (also **miniaturize**) *verb*.

*SPELLING – note the *-ia-* in the middle: min*ia*ture.

SYNONYMS – *adjective* baby, compact, mini, pocket, tiny.

ORIGIN – from Latin *minium* 'red lead, vermilion' (which was used to mark particular words in manuscripts).

miniaturist > *noun* an artist who paints miniatures.

minibar > *noun* a refrigerator in a hotel room containing a selection of drinks.

minibus > *noun* a small bus for about ten to fifteen passengers.

minicab > *noun* Brit. a car that is available for hire as a taxi but must be ordered in advance.

minicam > *noun* a hand-held video camera.

minicomputer > *noun* a computer of medium power, more than a microcomputer but less than a mainframe.

minidisc > *noun* a disc similar to a small CD that is able to record sound or data as well as play it back.

minidress > *noun* a very short dress.

minigolf > *noun* an informal version of golf played on a series of short obstacle courses.

minikin > *adjective* chiefly archaic small; insignificant.

ORIGIN – from Dutch *minne* 'love, friendship' + *-ken* **-KIN**.

minim > *noun* **1** Music, chiefly Brit. a note having the time value of two crotchets or half a semibreve, represented by a ring with a stem. **2** one sixtieth of a fluid drachm, about one drop of liquid.

ORIGIN – from Latin *minimus* 'smallest'.

minima plural of **MINIMUM**.

minimal > *adjective* **1** of a minimum amount, quantity, or degree. **2** Art characterised by the use of simple forms or structures. **3** Music characterised by the repetition and gradual alteration of short phrases.

DERIVATIVES – **minimally** adverb.

minimalist > *noun* **1** an advocate or practitioner of minimal art or music. **2** an advocate of moderate political reform. > *adjective* **1** relating to minimal art or music. **2** advocating moderate political reform.

DERIVATIVES – **minimalism** noun.

minimise (also **minimize**) > *verb* **1** reduce to the smallest possible amount or degree. **2** represent or estimate at less than the true value.

DERIVATIVES – **minimisation** noun **minimiser** noun.

SYNONYMS – **1** cut down, decrease, reduce. **2** play down, underestimate.

minimum > *noun* (pl. **minima** or **minimums**) the least or smallest amount, extent, or intensity possible or recorded. > *adjective* smallest or lowest in amount, extent, or intensity.

COMBINATIONS – **minimum wage** the lowest wage permitted by law or by agreement.

ORIGIN – Latin.

minion > *noun* a servile or unimportant follower of a powerful person.

SYNONYMS – flunkey, lackey, menial, underling.

ORIGIN – from French *mignon* 'pretty, dainty, sweet'; the term was originally used in a derogatory way to refer to a homoerotic relationship between a male minion and his patron.

mini-pill > *noun* a contraceptive pill containing a progestogen and not oestrogen.

miniseries > *noun* a television drama shown in a small number of episodes.

miniskirt > *noun* a very short skirt.

minister > *noun* **1** a head of a government department. **2** a diplomatic agent, usually ranking below an ambassador, representing a state or sovereign in a foreign country. **3** a member of the clergy, especially in the Presbyterian and Nonconformist Churches. **4** archaic a person or thing used to achieve or convey something: *ministers of death*. > *verb* **1** (**minister to**) attend to the needs of. **2** archaic provide.

SYNONYMS – *verb* **1** (**minister to**) look after, nurse, treat.

COMBINATIONS – **Minister of the Crown** (in the UK and Canada) a member of the cabinet. **Minister of State** (in the UK) a government minister ranking below a Secretary of State. **Minister without Portfolio** a government minister with cabinet status but not in charge of a specific department of state.

ORIGIN – Latin, 'servant', from *minus* 'less'.

ministerial > *adjective* relating to a minister or ministers.

DERIVATIVES – **ministerially** adverb.

ministration > *noun* **1** (**ministrations**) chiefly formal or humorous the provision of assistance or care. **2** the services of a minister of religion or of a religious institution. **3** the action of administering the sacrament.

DERIVATIVES – **ministrant** noun.

ministry > *noun* (pl. **ministries**) **1** a government department headed by a minister. **2** a period of government under one Prime Minister. **3** the work or office of a minister of religion.

minivan > *noun* a small van, typically one fitted with seats for passengers.

miniver > *noun* white fur used for lining or trimming clothes.

ORIGIN – from Old French *menu vair* 'little vair' (vair being the fur of a red squirrel, used in medieval times as a trimming or lining for garments).

mink > *noun* a semiaquatic stoat-like carnivore widely farmed for its fur.

ORIGIN – Swedish.

minke /**ming**kə/ > *noun* a small rorqual whale with a dark grey back and white underparts.

ORIGIN – probably from *Meincke*, the name of a Norwegian whaler.

min-min (also **min-min light**) > *noun* Austral. a will-o'-the-wisp.

ORIGIN – probably from an Aboriginal language.

minneola /minniōlə/ > *noun* a thin-skinned deep reddish fruit that is a hybrid of the tangerine and grapefruit.

ORIGIN – named after a town in Florida.

Minnesinger /**minn**əsingər/ > *noun* a German lyric poet and singer of the 12th–14th centuries, who performed songs of courtly love.

ORIGIN – German, 'love singer'.

minnow > *noun* **1** a small freshwater fish of the carp family. **2** a small or unimportant person.

Minoan /minōən/ > *adjective* relating to a Bronze Age civilisation centred on Crete (*c*.3000–1050 BC).

ORIGIN – named after the legendary Cretan king *Minos*, to whom a palace excavated at Knossos was attributed.

minor > *adjective* **1** having little or less importance, seriousness, or significance. **2** Music having or based on intervals of a semitone between the second and third degrees, and (usually) the fifth and sixth, and the seventh and eighth. Contrasted with **MAJOR**. > *noun* **1** a person under the age of full legal responsibility. **2** Music a minor key, interval, or scale. **3** N. Amer. a student's subsidiary subject or course. > *verb* (**minor in**) N. Amer. study or qualify in as a subsidiary subject.

SYNONYMS – *adjective* **1** insignificant, petty, slight, trivial.

COMBINATIONS – **minor canon** a member of the Christian clergy who assists in the daily services of a cathedral but is not a member of the chapter. **minor league** N. Amer. a league below the level of the major league in baseball or American football. **minor planet** an asteroid. **minor prophet** any of the twelve prophets after whom the shorter prophetic books of the Bible, from Hosea to Malachi, are named.

ORIGIN – Latin, 'smaller, less'.

Minorcan > *noun* a person from Minorca. > *adjective* relating to Minorca.

minority > *noun* (pl. **minorities**) **1** the smaller number or part; a number or part representing less than half of the whole. **2** a relatively small group of people differing from the majority in race, religion, language, etc. **3** the state or period of being under the age of full legal responsibility.

Minotaur /ˈmīnətawr/ > *noun* Greek Mythology a creature who was half-man and half-bull, kept in a labyrinth on Crete by King Minos and killed by Theseus.

ORIGIN – Greek *Minōtauros* 'bull of Minos'.

minster > *noun* a large or important church, typically one of cathedral status in the north of England that was built as part of a monastery.

ORIGIN – Old English, from Greek *monastērion* 'monastery'.

minstrel > *noun* a medieval singer or musician.

ORIGIN – Old French *menestral* 'entertainer, servant', from Latin *ministerialis* 'officer'.

minstrelsy > *noun* the practice of performing as a minstrel.

mint¹ > *noun* **1** an aromatic plant, several kinds of which are used as culinary herbs. **2** the flavour of mint, especially peppermint. **3** a peppermint sweet.

DERIVATIVES – **minty** adjective.

COMBINATIONS – **mint julep** a long drink consisting of bourbon, crushed ice, sugar, and fresh mint. **mint sauce** chopped spearmint in vinegar and sugar, traditionally eaten with lamb.

mint² > *noun* **1** a place where money is coined. **2** (**a mint**) informal a large sum of money. > *adjective* in pristine condition; as new. > *verb* **1** make (a coin) by stamping metal. **2** produce for the first time.

wordpower facts
Mint
Mint meaning 'a place where money is coined' derives from Latin *moneta*, which means both 'mint' and 'money' and is the root from which the words **money** and **monetary** are also formed. **Mint** meaning 'an aromatic plant', however, comes ultimately from Greek *minthē*, via Latin *mentha*, which gave us the word **menthol**.

minuet > *noun* a stately ballroom dance in triple time, popular in the 18th century. > *verb* (**minueted**, **minueting**) dance a minuet.

ORIGIN – from French *menuet* 'fine, delicate'.

minus > *preposition* **1** with the subtraction of. **2** (of temperature) falling below zero by: *minus 40° C*. **3** informal lacking: *he was minus*

a finger. > *adjective* **1** (before a number) below zero; negative. **2** (after a grade) slightly below: *C minus*. **3** having a negative electric charge. > *noun* **1** (also **minus sign**) the symbol −, indicating subtraction or a negative value. **2** informal a disadvantage.

ORIGIN – Latin, neuter of *minor* 'less'.

minuscule* > *adjective* **1** extremely small. **2** in lower-case letters, as distinct from capitals or uncials. > *noun* a lower-case letter.

*SPELLING – minus-, not minis-: minuscule.

SYNONYMS – *adjective* **1** infinitesimal, microscopic, minute, tiny.

ORIGIN – from Latin *minuscula littera* 'somewhat smaller letter'.

minute¹ /ˈmɪnɪt/ > *noun* **1** a period of time equal to sixty seconds or a sixtieth of an hour. **2** (**a minute**) informal a very short time. **3** (also **arc minute** or **minute of arc**) a sixtieth of a degree of angular measurement.

IDIOMS – **up to the minute** up to date.

COMBINATIONS – **minute steak** a thin slice of steak cooked very quickly.

wordpower facts
Minute
The three main uses of **minute**, 'period of sixty seconds', 'extremely small', and 'official record of a meeting', all originate from the Latin verb *minuere* 'make small'. The sense 'period of sixty seconds' derives from Latin *pars minuta prima* 'first very small part'; the meaning 'extremely small' comes from a medieval use in the sense 'lesser' (referring to a lesser tithe or tax); while 'official record of a meeting' comes from the notion of a rough copy in 'small writing' (Latin *scriptura minuta*).

minute² /mɪˈnyoot/ > *adjective* (**minutest**) **1** extremely small. **2** precise and meticulous.

DERIVATIVES – **minutely** adverb **minuteness** noun.

SYNONYMS – **1** infinitesimal, microscopic, minuscule, tiny. **2** painstaking, punctilious, scrupulous.

minute³ /ˈmɪnɪt/ > *noun* **1** (**minutes**) a summarised record of the points discussed at a meeting. **2** an official memorandum. > *verb* **1** record or note (the points discussed at a meeting). **2** send an official memorandum to.

minuteman /ˈmɪnɪtman/ > *noun* historical a militiaman of the American revolutionary period who volunteered to be ready for service at a minute's notice.

minutiae /mɪˈnyooshi-ee/ (also **minutia**

/mɪˈnyooshiə/) > *plural noun* small or precise details.

ORIGIN – Latin, from *minutia* 'smallness'.

minx > *noun* humorous or derogatory an impudent, cunning, or boldly flirtatious girl or young woman.

SYNONYMS – coquette, flirt.

Miocene /ˈmīōseen/ > *adjective* Geology relating to the fourth epoch of the Tertiary period (23.3 to 5.2 million years ago), a time when the first apes appeared.

ORIGIN – from Greek *meiōn* 'less' + *kainos* 'new'.

mirabelle > *noun* **1** a sweet yellow plum-like fruit. **2** a liqueur distilled from mirabelles.

ORIGIN – French.

mirabile dictu /mɪraabilay ˈdiktoo/ > *adverb* wonderful to relate.

ORIGIN – Latin.

miracle > *noun* **1** an extraordinary and welcome event attributed to a divine agency. **2** a remarkable and very welcome occurrence. **3** an outstanding example, specimen, or achievement.

SYNONYMS – **1** marvel, mystery, wonder.

COMBINATIONS – **miracle play** a mystery play.

ORIGIN – Latin *miraculum* 'object of wonder', from *mirari* 'to wonder'.

miraculous > *adjective* **1** having the character of a miracle. **2** very surprising and welcome.

DERIVATIVES – **miraculously** adverb.

SYNONYMS – **1** magical, supernatural. **2** amazing, astonishing, astounding, extraordinary, incredible.

mirage /ˈmɪraazh/ > *noun* **1** an optical illusion caused by atmospheric conditions, especially the appearance of a sheet of water in a desert or on a hot road caused by the refraction of light by heated air. **2** something illusory.

SYNONYMS – **2** chimera, delusion, fantasy, illusion.

ORIGIN – French, from Latin *mirare* 'look at'; compare with **MIRROR**.

MIRAS /ˈmīrass/ > *abbreviation* (in the UK) mortgage interest relief at source.

mire > *noun* **1** a stretch of boggy ground. **2** a difficult situation from which it is hard to escape. > *verb* (**be mired**) **1** become stuck in or covered with mud. **2** be in difficulties.

SYNONYMS – *noun* **1** bog, marsh, quagmire, swamp. **2** difficulty, plight, predicament, quandary.

ORIGIN – Old Norse *mýrr*; related to **MOSS**.

miro /ˈmeerō/ > *noun* (pl. **miros**) an evergreen coniferous New Zealand tree which yields useful wood.

ORIGIN – Maori.

mirror > *noun* **1** a surface, typically of glass

coated with a metal amalgam, which reflects a clear image. **2** a thing that accurately represents something else. > *verb* **1** show a reflection of. **2** correspond to.

WORDFINDER – catoptric (*relating to mirrors or reflection*), cheval glass, compact, pier glass, speculum (*kinds of mirror*), chiral (*not able to be superimposed on its mirror image*).

COMBINATIONS – **mirrorball** a revolving ball covered with small mirrored facets, used to provide lighting effects at discos. **mirror image** an image which is identical in form to another but has the structure reversed, as if seen in a mirror. **mirror site** Computing an Internet site which stores contents copied from another site.

ORIGIN – Old French *mirour*, from Latin *mirare* 'look at'; compare with **MIRAGE**.

mirth > *noun* amusement, especially as expressed in laughter.

DERIVATIVES – **mirthful** *adjective*.

SYNONYMS – amusement, humour, jollity, merriment.

mirthless > *adjective* (of a smile or laugh) lacking real amusement and typically expressing irony.

DERIVATIVES – **mirthlessly** *adverb*.

MIRV > *abbreviation* multiple independently targeted re-entry vehicle, an intercontinental nuclear missile with several independent warheads.

miry > *adjective* very muddy or boggy.

MIS > *abbreviation* Computing management information systems.

mis- > *prefix* **1** (added to verbs and their derivatives) wrongly, badly, or unsuitably: *mismanage*. **2** occurring in some nouns expressing a sense with negative force: *misadventure*.

misadventure > *noun* **1** (also **death by misadventure**) Law death caused accidentally during the performance of a legal act without negligence or intent to harm. **2** an unfortunate incident; a mishap.

misalliance > *noun* an unsuitable or unhappy alliance or marriage.

misandry /mɪˈsandri/ > *noun* hatred of men.

ORIGIN – from Greek *miso-* 'hating' + *aner* 'man'.

misanthrope /ˈmɪzənθrəʊp, ˈmɪsənθrəʊp/ (also **misanthropist**) > *noun* a person who dislikes and avoids other people.

DERIVATIVES – **misanthropic** *adjective* **misanthropy** *noun*.

ORIGIN – from Greek *misein* 'to hate' + *anthrōpos* 'human being'.

misapply > *verb* (**misapplies, misapplied**) use for the wrong purpose or in the wrong way.

DERIVATIVES – **misapplication** *noun*.

misapprehension > *noun* a mistaken belief.

misappropriate > *verb* dishonestly or unfairly take for one's own use.

DERIVATIVES – **misappropriation** *noun*.

SYNONYMS – embezzle, expropriate, pocket, steal.

misbegotten > *adjective* **1** badly conceived, designed, or planned. **2** contemptible. **3** archaic (of a child) illegitimate.

misbehave > *verb* behave badly.

DERIVATIVES – **misbehaviour** *noun*.

misbelief > *noun* a wrong or false belief or opinion.

miscalculate > *verb* calculate or assess wrongly.

DERIVATIVES – **miscalculation** *noun*.

miscarriage > *noun* **1** the spontaneous expulsion of a fetus from the womb before it is able to survive independently. **2** an unsuccessful outcome; a failure.

USAGE – a **miscarriage** refers to the expulsion of a fetus before it has survived through the first 28 weeks of pregnancy; a **stillbirth** refers to the birth of an infant that has died in the womb after surviving at least the first 28 weeks.

COMBINATIONS – **miscarriage of justice** a failure of a court or judicial system to fulfil the objective of justice.

miscarry > *verb* (**miscarries, miscarried**) **1** have a miscarriage. **2** (of a plan) fail.

miscast > *verb* (past and past participle **miscast**) (**be miscast**) (of an actor) be given an unsuitable role.

miscegenation /ˌmɪsɪdʒɪˈneɪʃn/ > *noun* the interbreeding of people of different races.

ORIGIN – from Latin *miscere* 'to mix' + *genus* 'race'.

miscellanea /ˌmɪsəˈleɪnɪə/ > *plural noun* miscellaneous items collected together.

miscellaneous > *adjective* **1** of various types. **2** composed of things of different kinds.

DERIVATIVES – **miscellaneously** *adverb*.

SYNONYMS – **1** assorted, multifarious, sundry, varied, various. **2** diverse, heterogeneous, varied.

ORIGIN – Latin *miscellaneus*, from *miscellus* 'mixed'.

miscellany /mɪˈsɛləni/ > *noun* (pl. **miscellanies**) a collection of different things; a mixture.

mischance > *noun* bad luck.

mischief > *noun* **1** playful misbehaviour. **2** harm or injury caused by someone or something.

IDIOMS – **do someone a mischief** informal injure someone.

SYNONYMS – **1** badness, disobedience, misbehaviour, naughtiness.

ORIGIN – Old French *meschief*, from *meschever* 'come to an unfortunate end'.

mischievous* /ˈmɪstʃɪvəs/ > *adjective* **1** causing or disposed to mischief. **2** intended to cause trouble.

DERIVATIVES – **mischievously** *adverb* **mischievousness** *noun*.

*****SPELLING – note that the ending is *-vous*, not *-vious*: mischie**vous**.

SYNONYMS – **1** bad, badly behaved, disobedient, naughty. **2** malevolent, malicious, mean, spiteful.

ANTONYMS – **1** good, obedient.

miscible /ˈmɪsɪb'l/ > *adjective* (of liquids) capable of being mixed together.

ORIGIN – from Latin *miscere* 'to mix'.

misconceive > *verb* **1** fail to understand correctly. **2** (**be misconceived**) be badly judged or planned.

misconception > *noun* a false or mistaken idea or belief.

misconduct > *noun* /mɪsˈkɒndʌkt/ unacceptable or improper behaviour. > *verb* /ˌmɪskənˈdʌkt/ (**misconduct oneself**) behave in an improper manner.

SYNONYMS – *noun* impropriety, malpractice, misbehaviour, mismanagement, negligence, wrongdoing.

misconstruction > *noun* the action of misconstruing something.

misconstrue > *verb* (**misconstrues, misconstrued, misconstruing**) interpret wrongly.

miscreant /ˈmɪskrɪənt/ > *noun* **1** formal a person who behaves badly or unlawfully. **2** archaic a heretic. > *adjective* formal behaving badly or unlawfully.

ORIGIN – Old French *mescreant*, from *mescroire* 'disbelieve'.

miscue > *verb* (**miscues, miscued, miscueing** or **miscuing**) (in billiards and snooker) fail to strike the ball properly. > *noun* an act of miscueing the ball.

misdeed > *noun* a wrongful act.

misdemeanour (US **misdemeanor**) > *noun* **1** a minor wrongdoing. **2** Law a non-indictable offence, regarded in the US (and formerly the UK) as less serious than a felony.

misdiagnose > *verb* diagnose incorrectly.

DERIVATIVES – **misdiagnosis** *noun*.

misdial > *verb* (**misdialled, misdialling; US misdialed, misdialing**) dial a telephone number incorrectly.

misdirect > *verb* direct or instruct wrongly.

DERIVATIVES – **misdirection** *noun*.

misdoing > *noun* a misdeed.

mise en scène /ˌmiːz ɒn ˈsɛn/ > *noun* **1** the arrangement of scenery and stage properties in a play. **2** the setting of an event.

ORIGIN – French, 'putting on stage'.

miser > *noun* a person who hoards wealth and spends as little as possible.

SYNONYMS – hoarder, niggard, penny-pincher, Scrooge, skinflint.

wordpower facts

Miser

The word **miser**, originally used as an adjective in the sense 'parsimonious' and later as a noun meaning 'a miserable person', derives from Latin *miser*, meaning 'wretched, unfortunate'. A number of words connected by the notion of wretchedness share this root, notably **commiserate**, **miserable**, and **misery**, and, offering some prospect of relief, **miserere** and **misericord**.

miserable > *adjective* **1** wretchedly unhappy or depressed. **2** causing unhappiness or discomfort. **3** morose and humourless. **4** pitiably small or inadequate. **5** Austral./NZ & Scottish miserly.

DERIVATIVES – **miserably** *adverb*.

SYNONYMS – **1** depressed, gloomy, melancholy, mournful, sad, unhappy. **2** cheerless, depressing, dismal, dreary, grim.

ANTONYMS – **1** cheerful, happy.

ORIGIN – Latin *miserabilis* 'pitiable', from *miser* 'wretched'.

miserere /mizzə**rair**i/ > *noun* a psalm, prayer, or cry for mercy.

ORIGIN – Latin, 'have mercy!'.

misericord /mi**zerr**ikord/ > *noun* a ledge projecting from the underside of a hinged seat in a choir stall, giving support to someone standing when the seat is folded up.

ORIGIN – Latin *misericordia*, from *misericors* 'compassionate'.

miserly > *adjective* **1** having the characteristics of a miser. **2** (of a quantity) pitiably small.

DERIVATIVES – **miserliness** *noun*.

SYNONYMS – **1** mean, niggardly, parsimonious, penny-pinching. **2** beggarly, meagre, niggardly, paltry, pitiful.

ANTONYMS – generous, lavish.

misery > *noun* (pl. **miseries**) **1** wretched unhappiness. **2** a cause of great unhappiness. **3** Brit. informal a person who is constantly miserable.

SYNONYMS – **1** anguish, grief, sorrow, unhappiness, wretchedness. **2** affliction, hardship, sorrow, tribulation, woe.

ORIGIN – Latin *miseria*, from *miser* 'wretched'.

misfire > *verb* **1** (of a gun) fail to fire properly. **2** (of an internal-combustion engine) fail to ignite the fuel correctly. **3** fail to produce the intended result.

misfit > *noun* a person whose behaviour or attitude sets them apart from others.

misfortune > *noun* **1** bad luck. **2** an unfortunate event.

SYNONYMS – **1** adversity, hardship, ill luck,

mischance. **2** blow, difficulty, problem, setback.

ANTONYMS – **1** good fortune, luck.

misgivings > *plural noun* feelings of doubt or apprehension.

SYNONYMS – doubts, qualms, reservations, scruples, uncertainties.

misgovern > *verb* govern unfairly or poorly.

misguided > *adjective* showing faulty judgement or reasoning.

DERIVATIVES – **misguidedly** *adverb* **misguidedness** *noun*.

SYNONYMS – fallacious, ill-judged, misconceived, misplaced, mistaken.

mishandle > *verb* handle or deal with unwisely or wrongly.

mishap > *noun* an unlucky accident.

SYNONYMS – accident, misfortune, problem, setback.

mishear > *verb* (past and past participle **misheard**) hear incorrectly.

mishit > *verb* (**mishitting**; past and past participle **mishit**) hit or kick (a ball) badly.

mishmash > *noun* a confused mixture.

misidentify > *verb* (**misidentifies**, **misidentified**) identify incorrectly.

DERIVATIVES – **misidentification** *noun*.

misinform > *verb* give false or inaccurate information to.

DERIVATIVES – **misinformation** *noun*.

misinterpret > *verb* (**misinterpreted**, **misinterpreting**) interpret wrongly.

DERIVATIVES – **misinterpretation** *noun*.

misjudge > *verb* **1** form an incorrect opinion of. **2** judge wrongly.

DERIVATIVES – **misjudgement** (also **misjudgment**) *noun*.

mislay > *verb* (past and past participle **mislaid**) lose (an object) by temporarily forgetting where one has left it.

mislead > *verb* (past and past participle **misled**) give the wrong impression to.

misleading > *adjective* giving the wrong idea or impression.

DERIVATIVES – **misleadingly** *adverb*.

mismanage > *verb* manage badly or wrongly.

DERIVATIVES – **mismanagement** *noun*.

mismatch > *noun* **1** a failure to correspond or match. **2** an unequal sporting contest. > *verb* match unsuitably or incorrectly.

misnomer /mis**nō**mər/ > *noun* **1** an inaccurate or misleading name. **2** the wrong use of a name or term.

ORIGIN – from Old French *mesnommer* 'misname', from Latin *nomen* 'name'.

miso /**mee**sō/ > *noun* a paste made from fermented soya beans and barley or rice malt, used in Japanese cookery.

ORIGIN – Japanese.

misogynist /mi**soj**ənist/ > *noun* a man who hates women.

DERIVATIVES – **misogynistic** *adjective*.

misogyny /mi**soj**əni/ > *noun* hatred of women.

ORIGIN – from Greek *misos* 'hatred' + *gunē* 'woman'.

misplace > *verb* put in the wrong place.

misplaced > *adjective* **1** incorrectly placed. **2** unwise or inappropriate.

misprint > *noun* an error in printed text. > *verb* print incorrectly.

mispronounce > *verb* pronounce wrongly.

DERIVATIVES – **mispronunciation** *noun*.

misquote > *verb* quote inaccurately.

DERIVATIVES – **misquotation** *noun*.

misread > *verb* (past and past participle **misread**) read or interpret wrongly.

misrepresent > *verb* give a false or misleading account of.

DERIVATIVES – **misrepresentation** *noun*.

misrule > *noun* **1** unfair or inefficient government. **2** disruption of peace; disorder. > *verb* govern badly.

miss¹ > *verb* **1** fail to hit, reach, or come into contact with. **2** be too late for. **3** fail to notice, hear, or understand. **4** fail to be present. **5** (**miss out**) omit. **6** notice or feel the loss or absence of. > *noun* **1** a failure to hit, catch, or reach something. **2** an unsuccessful record or film.

IDIOMS – **give something a miss** Brit. informal decide not to do or have something. **a miss is as good as a mile** proverb the fact of failure or escape is not affected by the narrowness of the margin. **miss the boat** informal be too slow to take advantage of something.

miss² > *noun* **1** (**Miss**) a title prefixed to the name of an unmarried woman or girl. **2** (**Miss**) used as a form of address to a female teacher. **3** derogatory or humorous a girl or young woman.

ORIGIN – abbreviation of *mistress*.

missal > *noun* a book of the texts used in the Catholic Mass.

ORIGIN – from Latin *missa* 'Mass'.

misshapen > *adjective* not having the normal or natural shape.

SYNONYMS – deformed, distorted, malformed, twisted, warped.

missile > *noun* **1** an object which is forcibly propelled at a target. **2** a weapon that carries explosives and is self-propelled or directed by remote control.

WORDFINDER – ballistic (*denoting guided missile falling on to its target by gravity*), cruise missile (*flying bomb guided by an on-board computer*), MIRV (*nuclear missile with several warheads*), silo (*underground launcher for missile*); air-to-air, air-to-surface, anti-ballistic, surface-to-air (*types of guided missile*).

wordpower facts

Missile

The word **missile** comes from the Latin verb *mittere* (of which the stem is *miss-*), meaning 'to send'. *Mittere* is the root of a great many English words. It gives rise to the -*mit* part of verbs such as **admit**, **commit**, **emit**, **permit**, **submit**, and **transmit**, and is the source, in a more disguised form, of **Mass**, **mess**, **message**, **mission**, **missive**, **premise**, and **promise**.

missing > *adjective* **1** absent and of unknown whereabouts. **2** not present when expected or supposed to be.

COMBINATIONS – **missing link** a hypothetical fossil form intermediate between humans and apes.

mission > *noun* **1** an important assignment, typically involving travel abroad. **2** an organisation or institution involved in a long-term assignment abroad. **3** a military or scientific expedition. **4** the vocation of a religious organisation to spread its faith. **5** a strongly felt aim or calling.

SYNONYMS – **1** assignment, expedition, trip. **5** aim, calling, goal, quest, vocation.

COMBINATIONS – **mission statement** a summary of the aims and values of an organisation.

ORIGIN – Latin, from *mittere* 'send'.

missionary > *noun* (pl. **missionaries**) a person sent on a religious mission. > *adjective* of or characteristic of a missionary or religious mission.

COMBINATIONS – **missionary position** a position for sexual intercourse in which a couple lie face to face with the woman underneath the man. [ORIGIN – said to come from the fact that early missionaries advocated the position as 'proper' to primitive peoples.]

missioner > *noun* a missionary.

missis > *noun* variant spelling of **MISSUS**.

missive > *noun* formal or humorous a letter.

ORIGIN – Latin *missivus*, from *mittere* 'send'.

misspell* > *verb* (past and past participle **misspelt** or **misspelled**) spell wrongly.

*****SPELLING – double *s*: mi**ss**pell.

misspend > *verb* (past and past participle **misspent**) spend (time) foolishly or wastefully.

misstate > *verb* state wrongly or inaccurately.

DERIVATIVES – **misstatement** noun.

misstep > *noun* **1** a badly judged step. **2** a mistake.

missus (also **missis**) > *noun* **1** informal or humorous one's wife. **2** informal a form of address to a woman.

missy > *noun* (pl. **missies**) an affectionate or disparaging form of address to a young girl.

mist > *noun* **1** a cloud of tiny water droplets in the atmosphere, limiting visibility to a lesser extent than fog. **2** a condensed vapour settling on a surface. > *verb* cover or become covered with mist.

mistake > *noun* **1** a thing that is incorrect. **2** an error of judgement. > *verb* (past **mistook**; past participle **mistaken**) **1** be wrong about. **2** (**mistake for**) confuse (someone or something) with.

SYNONYMS – *noun* **1** blunder, error, inaccuracy, oversight, slip.

ORIGIN – from Old Norse *mistaka* 'take in error'.

mistaken > *adjective* **1** wrong in one's opinion or judgement. **2** based on a misunderstanding or faulty judgement.

DERIVATIVES – **mistakenly** adverb.

mister > *noun* **1** variant form of **MR**. **2** informal a form of address to a man.

mistime > *verb* choose an inappropriate moment to do or say (something).

mistle thrush > *noun* a large thrush with a spotted breast and harsh rattling call.

ORIGIN – so named because of its fondness for mistletoe berries.

mistletoe > *noun* an evergreen parasitic plant which grows on broadleaf trees and bears white berries in winter.

ORIGIN – Old English, from *mistel* 'mistletoe' + *tān* 'twig'.

mistook past of **MISTAKE**.

mistral /**miss**traal/ > *noun* a strong, cold north-westerly wind that blows through the Rhône valley and southern France.

ORIGIN – French, from Latin *magistralis ventus* 'master wind'.

mistranslate > *verb* translate incorrectly.

DERIVATIVES – **mistranslation** noun.

mistreat > *verb* treat badly or unfairly.

DERIVATIVES – **mistreatment** noun.

mistress > *noun* **1** a woman in a position of authority, control, or ownership. **2** a woman skilled in a particular subject or activity. **3** a woman (other than a wife) having a sexual relationship with a married man. **4** chiefly Brit. a female schoolteacher. **5** (**Mistress**) archaic Mrs.

ORIGIN – Old French *maistresse*, from *maistre* 'master'.

mistrial > *noun* a trial made invalid through an error in proceedings.

mistrust > *verb* have no trust in. > *noun* lack of trust.

DERIVATIVES – **mistrustful** adjective.

misty > *adjective* (**mistier**, **mistiest**) **1** full of or covered with mist. **2** indistinct or dim in outline.

DERIVATIVES – **mistily** adverb **mistiness** noun.

SYNONYMS – **2** blurred, dim, fuzzy, hazy, indistinct, nebulous.

misunderstand > *verb* (past and past participle **misunderstood**) fail to understand correctly.

SYNONYMS – get wrong, misapprehend, misconstrue, misinterpret.

misunderstanding > *noun* **1** a failure to understand. **2** a slight disagreement or quarrel.

SYNONYMS – **1** misapprehension, misinterpretation, misreading, mistake, mix-up.

misuse > *verb* **1** use wrongly. **2** treat badly or unfairly. > *noun* the action of misusing something.

DERIVATIVES – **misuser** noun.

SYNONYMS – *verb* **2** abuse, exploit, ill-treat, maltreat.

mite¹ > *noun* a minute spider-like creature (arachnid), several kinds of which are parasitic.

mite² > *noun* **1** a small child or animal. **2** a very small amount. > *adverb* (**a mite**) informal slightly.

ORIGIN – Dutch: originally referring to a small Flemish copper coin of low value.

miter > *noun & verb* US spelling of **MITRE**.

mither /**mī**thər/ > *verb* dialect, chiefly N. English **1** make a fuss. **2** pester (someone).

mitigate > *verb* **1** make (something bad) less severe, serious, or painful. **2** (**mitigating**) (of a fact or circumstance) lessening the gravity or culpability of an action.

DERIVATIVES – **mitigation** noun.

USAGE – do not confuse **mitigate** with **militate**: **mitigate** means 'make (something bad) less severe', while **militate** is used in constructions with **against** to mean 'be a powerful factor in preventing'.

SYNONYMS – **1** alleviate, ease, lessen, moderate, soften, temper.

ORIGIN – Latin *mitigare* 'soften, alleviate'.

mitochondrion /mītəkon**dri**ən/ > *noun* (pl. **mitochondria**) Biology a structure found in large numbers in most cells, in which respiration and energy production occur.

DERIVATIVES – **mitochondrial** adjective.

ORIGIN – from Greek *mitos* 'thread' + *khondrion* 'small granule'.

mitosis /mī**tō**siss/ > *noun* (pl. **mitoses**) /mī**tō**seez/ Biology a type of cell division in which daughter cells have the same number and kind of chromosomes as the parent nucleus. Compare with **MEIOSIS**.

ORIGIN – from Greek *mitos* 'thread'.

mitral /**mī**trəl/ > *adjective* Anatomy denoting or relating to the valve between the left atrium and the left ventricle of the heart.

ORIGIN – from Latin *mitra* 'belt or turban' (from the valve's shape).

mitre (US **miter**) > *noun* **1** a tall cleft headdress that tapers to a point at front and back, worn by bishops and senior abbots. **2**

a joint made between two pieces of wood or other material at an angle of 90°, in which the line of the join bisects this angle. > *verb* join by means of a mitre.

ORIGIN – Greek *mitra* 'belt or turban'.

mitt > *noun* **1** a mitten. **2** a fingerless glove. **3** informal a person's hand.

mitten > *noun* a glove having a single section for all four fingers, with a separate section for the thumb.

ORIGIN – Old French *mitaine*, perhaps from *mite*, a pet name for a cat (because mittens were often made of fur).

mix > *verb* **1** combine or be combined to form a whole. **2** make by mixing ingredients. **3** (**mix up**) spoil the order or arrangement of. **4** (**mix up**) confuse (a person or thing) with another. **5** associate with others socially. **6** combine (signals or soundtracks) into one to produce a recording. > *noun* **1** a mixture. **2** the proportion of different people or things constituting a mixture. **3** a version of a recording mixed in a different way from the original.

IDIOMS – **be mixed up in** (or **with**) be involved in or with (dubious actions or people).

SYNONYMS – *verb* **1** amalgamate, blend, combine, incorporate, mingle.

ORIGIN – Latin, *miscere*.

mixed > *adjective* **1** consisting of different kinds, qualities, or elements. **2** of or for members of both sexes.

SYNONYMS – **1** assorted, disparate, diverse, heterogeneous, miscellaneous, varied.

ANTONYMS – **1** homogeneous, uniform.

COMBINATIONS – **mixed bag** a diverse assortment. **mixed blessing** a thing that has both advantages and disadvantages. **mixed economy** an economic system combining private and state enterprise. **mixed farming** farming of both crops and livestock. **mixed grill** a dish of various grilled meats. **mixed marriage** a marriage between people of different races or religions. **mixed metaphor** a combination of incompatible metaphors (e.g. *this tower of strength will forge ahead*).

mixed-up > *adjective* informal suffering from psychological or emotional problems.

mixer > *noun* **1** a machine or device for mixing things. **2** a person considered in terms of their ability to mix socially. **3** a soft drink that can be mixed with alcohol. **4** (in recording and cinematography) a device for merging input signals to produce a combined output.

COMBINATIONS – **mixer tap** a single tap through which both hot and cold water can be drawn simultaneously.

mixture > *noun* **1** a substance made by mixing other substances together. **2** (**a mixture of**) a combination of different things in which the components are individually distinct. **3** the charge of gas or vapour mixed with air admitted to the cylinder of an internal-combustion engine.

SYNONYMS – **1,2** amalgamation, blend, combination, compound, medley, mix.

mix-up > *noun* informal a confusion or misunderstanding.

mizzen (also **mizen**) > *noun* **1** (also **mizzenmast**) the mast to the rear of a ship's mainmast. **2** (also **mizzensail**) a sail on a mizzenmast.

ORIGIN – from Italian *mezzano* 'middle'.

mizzle chiefly dialect > *noun* light rain; drizzle. > *verb* (**it mizzles**, **it is mizzling**, etc.) rain lightly.

ORIGIN – probably from MIST.

Mk > *abbreviation* **1** the German mark. **2** mark (of a vehicle or machine).

ml > *abbreviation* **1** mile or miles. **2** millilitre or millilitres.

MLA > *abbreviation* Member of the Legislative Assembly.

MLitt > *abbreviation* Master of Letters.

ORIGIN – from Latin *Magister Litterarum*.

Mlle > *abbreviation* (pl. **Mlles**) Mademoiselle.

MM > *abbreviation* **1** Messieurs. **2** Military Medal.

mm > *abbreviation* millimetre or millimetres.

Mme > *abbreviation* (pl. **Mmes**) Madame.

MMR > *abbreviation* measles, mumps, and rubella (a vaccination given to children).

MN > *abbreviation* Minnesota.

Mn > *symbol* the chemical element manganese.

mnemonic /niˈmonnik/ > *noun* a pattern of letters or words formulated as an aid to memory. > *adjective* **1** aiding or designed to aid the memory. **2** relating to the power of memory.

ORIGIN – from Greek *mnēmōn* 'mindful'.

MO > *abbreviation* **1** Medical Officer. **2** Missouri. **3** modus operandi. **4** money order.

Mo > *symbol* the chemical element molybdenum.

mo > *noun* informal, chiefly Brit. a moment.

moa /ˈmōə/ > *noun* a large extinct flightless bird resembling the emu, formerly found in New Zealand.

ORIGIN – Maori.

moan > *noun* **1** a low mournful sound, usually expressive of suffering. **2** informal a trivial complaint. > *verb* **1** utter or make a moan. **2** informal complain; grumble.

DERIVATIVES – **moaner** *noun*.

SYNONYMS – *verb* **1** cry, groan, sigh, sob, whimper.

moat > *noun* a deep, wide defensive ditch surrounding a castle or town, typically filled with water.

DERIVATIVES – **moated** *adjective*.

ORIGIN – Old French *mote* 'mound'.

mob > *noun* **1** a disorderly crowd of people. **2** Brit. informal a group of people. **3** (**the Mob**) N. Amer. informal the Mafia. **4** (**the mob**) derogatory the ordinary people. **5** Austral./NZ a flock or herd of animals. > *verb* (**mobbed**, **mobbing**) **1** crowd round or into in an unruly way. **2** (of birds or animals) crowd round so as to harass (a predator).

SYNONYMS – *noun* **1** crowd, gang, horde, pack, rabble, throng. **4** (**the mob**) the common herd, the great unwashed, hoi polloi, the multitude, the plebs, the rabble, the riff-raff. *verb* **1** besiege, harass, jostle, pack, swarm around, throng.

ORIGIN – abbreviation of archaic *mobile*, short for Latin *mobile vulgus* 'excitable crowd'.

mob cap > *noun* a large, soft indoor hat covering the hair, worn by women in the 18th and early 19th centuries.

ORIGIN – variant of obsolete *mab* 'slut'.

mobile > *adjective* **1** able to move or be moved freely or easily. **2** (of a shop, library, etc.) accommodated in a vehicle so as to travel around. **3** able or willing to move between occupations, places of residence, or social classes. **4** (of the features of the face) readily changing expression. > *noun* **1** a decorative structure suspended so as to turn freely in the air. **2** a mobile phone.

IDIOMS – **upwardly** (or **downwardly**) **mobile** moving to a higher (or lower) social class.

SYNONYMS – *adjective* **1** movable, portable, transferable, transportable. **3** adaptable, flexible, itinerant, peripatetic. **4** animated, eloquent, expressive, revealing.

ANTONYMS – **1** immobile, static, stationary. **4** expressionless.

COMBINATIONS – **mobile home** a large caravan used as permanent living accommodation. **mobile phone** a portable telephone using a cellular radio system.

ORIGIN – Latin *mobilis*, from *movere* 'to move'.

mobilise (also **mobilize**) > *verb* **1** prepare and organise (troops) for active service. **2** organise (people or resources) for a particular task. **3** make mobile.

DERIVATIVES – **mobilisation** *noun* **mobiliser** *noun*.

mobility > *noun* the quality of being mobile.

COMBINATIONS – **mobility allowance** Brit. a state travel benefit for people with disabilities.

Möbius strip /ˈmōbiəss/ > *noun* a surface with one continuous side formed by joining the ends of a rectangle after twisting one end through 180°.

ORIGIN – named after the German

mathematician August F. *Möbius* (1790–1868).

mobster > *noun* informal a gangster.

moccasin* > *noun* 1 a soft leather shoe with the sole turned up and sewn to the upper, originally worn by North American Indians. 2 a poisonous American pit viper.
*****SPELLING** – two *c*s one *s*: mo*cca*sin.
ORIGIN – Virginia Algonquian.

mocha /mokkə/ > *noun* 1 a fine-quality coffee. 2 a drink or flavouring made with this, typically with chocolate added. 3 a soft leather made from sheepskin.
ORIGIN – named after *Mocha*, a port on the Red Sea, from where the coffee and leather were first shipped.

mock > *verb* 1 tease scornfully; ridicule. 2 mimic contemptuously. > *adjective* 1 not authentic or real. 2 (of an examination, battle, etc.) arranged for training or practice. > *noun* (**mocks**) Brit. informal examinations taken in school as training for public examinations.
DERIVATIVES – **mocking** *adjective*.
SYNONYMS – *verb* 1 deride, lampoon, make fun of, pillory, ridicule, taunt, tease. 2 ape, caricature, guy, mimic, parody, satirise. *adjective* artificial, fake, false, imitation, sham, simulated, synthetic.
COMBINATIONS – **mock-heroic** (of a literary work) consciously grandiose in style in order to satirise a mundane subject. **mock orange** a bushy shrub (philadelphus) with white flowers whose perfume resembles that of orange blossom. **mock turtle soup** imitation turtle soup made from a calf's head.
ORIGIN – Old French *mocquer* 'deride'.

mocker > *noun* a person who mocks.
IDIOMS – **put the mockers on** Brit. informal 1 put an end to. 2 bring bad luck to.

mockery > *noun* (pl. **mockeries**) 1 ridicule. 2 an absurd representation of something.
IDIOMS – **make a mockery of** cause to appear foolish or absurd.
SYNONYMS – 1 contempt, derision, disdain, ridicule. 2 apology, caricature, charade, excuse, parody, travesty.

mockingbird > *noun* a long-tailed American songbird, noted for its mimicry of the calls of other birds.

mock-up > *noun* a model or replica of a machine or structure for instructional or experimental purposes.

MOD > *abbreviation* (in the UK) Ministry of Defence.

mod > *adjective* informal modern. > *noun* Brit. (especially in the 1960s) a young person of a group characterised by a stylish appearance and the riding of motor scooters.
COMBINATIONS – **mod cons** modern conveniences, i.e. the amenities and appliances characteristic of a well-equipped modern house.

modal > *adjective* 1 relating to mode or form as opposed to substance. 2 Grammar relating to the mood of a verb. 3 Music using melodies or harmonies based on modes other than the ordinary major and minor scales.
DERIVATIVES – **modality** *noun* **modally** *adverb*.
COMBINATIONS – **modal verb** Grammar an auxiliary verb expressing necessity or possibility, e.g. *must, shall, will.*

mode > *noun* 1 a way in which something occurs or is done. 2 a style in clothes, art, etc. 3 Music a set of notes forming a scale and from which melodies and harmonies are constructed. 4 Statistics the value that occurs most frequently in a given data set.

wordpower facts
Mode

The word **mode** entered Middle English in the musical sense and in a grammatical and philosophical sense meaning 'form' (now referred to as a *mood*). The fashion sense (and the related words **modish** and **modiste**) was adopted later from French. Both branches of meaning come from the same Latin word, *modus*, meaning 'measure, manner', which is also at the root of **modest** (from *modestus* 'keeping due measure'), **model**, **modicum**, **modify**, **module**, and **modulus**, and survives in the Latin terms **modus operandi** and **modus vivendi**. The word **mood**, in the familiar sense 'a state of mind or feeling', is unrelated, coming from a different, Germanic, root.

model > *noun* 1 a three-dimensional representation of a person or thing, typically on a smaller scale. 2 (in sculpture) a figure made in clay or wax which is then reproduced in a more durable material. 3 something used as an example. 4 a simplified mathematical description of a system or process, used to assist calculations and predictions. 5 an excellent example of a quality. 6 a person employed to display clothes by wearing them. 7 a person employed to pose for an artist or photographer. 8 a particular design or version of a product. > *verb* (**modelled, modelling**; US **modeled, modeling**) 1 fashion or shape (a figure) in clay, wax, etc. 2 (in drawing, painting, etc.) cause to appear three-dimensional. 3 devise a mathematical model of. 4 (**model on**) use as an example for something else. 5 display (clothes) by wearing them. 6 work as a model.
DERIVATIVES – **modeller** *noun*.
SYNONYMS – *noun* 1 copy, dummy, miniature, mock-up, replica. 3 archetype, blueprint, framework, guide, paradigm, pattern, prototype. *verb* 1 fashion, form, mould, sculpt, shape.
ORIGIN – from Latin *modulus*, from *modus* 'measure'.

modem /mōdem/ > *noun* a device for converting digital to analogue signals and vice versa, especially to enable a computer to be connected to a telephone line.
ORIGIN – blend of *modulator* and *demodulator*.

moderate > *adjective* /moddərət/ 1 average in amount, intensity, or degree. 2 (of a political position) not radical or extreme. > *noun* a person with moderate views. > *verb* /moddərayt/ 1 make or become less extreme or intense. 2 review (examination papers or results) to ensure consistency of marking. 3 preside over (a deliberative body or a debate).
DERIVATIVES – **moderately** *adverb*.
SYNONYMS – *adjective* 1 fair, medium, middling, modest, ordinary. 2 liberal, middle of the road, mild. *verb* 1 check, control, regulate, restrain, temper.
ORIGIN – from Latin *moderare* 'reduce, control'; related to MODEST.

moderation > *noun* 1 the avoidance of extremes in one's actions or opinions. 2 the process of moderating.
SYNONYMS – 1 abstemiousness, restraint, self-control, self-discipline, temperance.

moderator > *noun* 1 an arbitrator or mediator. 2 a chairman of a debate. 3 a person who moderates examination papers.

modern > *adjective* 1 relating to the present or to recent times. 2 characterised by or using the most up-to-date techniques or equipment. 3 (in art, architecture, etc.) marked in style or content by a significant departure from traditional values. > *noun* a person who advocates a departure from traditional styles or values.
DERIVATIVES – **modernity** *noun*.
SYNONYMS – *noun* 1 contemporary, current, present, present-day. 2 advanced, fashionable, new, progressive, voguish.
ORIGIN – Latin *modernus*, from *modo* 'just now'.

modernise (also **modernize**) > *verb* adapt to the requirements of current times; make modern.
DERIVATIVES – **modernisation** *noun* **moderniser** *noun*.

modernism > *noun* **1** modern ideas, methods, or styles. **2** a movement in the arts or religion that aims to break with traditional forms or ideas.
DERIVATIVES – **modernist** *noun* & *adjective* **modernistic** *adjective*.

modest > *adjective* **1** unassuming in the estimation of one's abilities or achievements. **2** relatively moderate, limited, or small. **3** avoiding impropriety or indecency; decorous.
DERIVATIVES – **modestly** *adverb*.
SYNONYMS – **1** humble, self-deprecating, self-effacing, unassuming, unpretentious. **2** mediocre, moderate, ordinary, slight, unexceptional. **3** chaste, coy, demure, proper, seemly, wholesome.
ANTONYMS – **1** boastful, conceited. **2** exceptional. **3** immodest.
ORIGIN – Latin *modestus* 'keeping due measure', related to *modus* 'measure'.

modesty > *noun* the quality or state of being modest.

modicum /**modd**ikəm/ > *noun* a small quantity of something.
SYNONYMS – degree, measure, smattering, sufficiency.
ORIGIN – Latin, from *modicus* 'moderate'.

modification > *noun* **1** the action of modifying. **2** a change made.

modifier > *noun* **1** a person or thing that modifies. **2** Grammar a word that qualifies the sense of a noun (e.g. *good* and *family* in *a good family house*).

modify > *verb* (**modifies, modified**) make partial changes to.
SYNONYMS – adapt, alter, amend, revamp, revise, rework.
ORIGIN – Latin *modificare*, from *modus* 'measure'.

modish /**mō**dish/ > *adjective* fashionable.
DERIVATIVES – **modishly** *adverb*.

modiste /mo**deest**/ > *noun* dated a fashionable milliner or dressmaker.
ORIGIN – French, from *mode* 'fashion'.

modular > *adjective* **1** using or involving modules. **2** Mathematics of or relating to a modulus.
DERIVATIVES – **modularity** *noun*.

modulate > *verb* **1** exert a controlling influence on; regulate. **2** vary the strength, tone, or pitch of (one's voice). **3** adjust the amplitude or frequency of (an oscillation or signal). **4** Music change from one key to another.
DERIVATIVES – **modulation** *noun* **modulator** *noun*.

module /**mod**yool/ > *noun* **1** each of a set of parts or units that can be used to construct a more complex structure. **2** each of a set of independent units of study or training forming part of a course. **3** an independent self-contained unit of a spacecraft.
ORIGIN – Latin *modulus*, from *modus* 'measure'.

modulus /**mod**yooləss/ > *noun* (pl. **moduli** /**mod**yoolī/) **1** Mathematics the magnitude of a number irrespective of whether it is positive or negative. **2** a constant factor relating a physical effect to the force producing it.

modus operandi /mōdəss oppə**ran**di/ > *noun* (pl. **modi operandi** /mōdi oppə**ran**di/) a way of operating or doing something.
ORIGIN – Latin.

modus vivendi /mōdəss vi**ven**di/ > *noun* (pl. **modi vivendi** /mōdi vi**ven**di/) **1** a way of living. **2** an arrangement allowing conflicting parties to coexist peacefully.
ORIGIN – Latin.

moggie (also **moggy**) > *noun* (pl. **moggies**) Brit. informal a cat.
ORIGIN – variant of *Maggie*, familiar form of the given name *Margaret*.

Mogul /**mō**gəl/ (also **Moghul** or **Mughal**) > *noun* **1** a member of the Muslim dynasty of Mongol origin which ruled much of India in the 16th–19th centuries. **2** (**mogul**) informal an important or powerful person.
SYNONYMS – **2** bigwig, grandee, magnate, nabob, potentate, tycoon.
ORIGIN – Persian, 'Mongol'.

MOH > *abbreviation* Ministry of Health.

mohair > *noun* a yarn or fabric made from the hair of the angora goat.
ORIGIN – Arabic, 'cloth made of goat's hair' (literally 'choice, select').

Mohammedan > *noun* variant spelling of MUHAMMADAN.

Mohawk > *noun* (pl. same or **Mohawks**) **1** a member of an American Indian people originally of New York State. **2** chiefly N. Amer. a Mohican haircut.
ORIGIN – Narragansett, literally 'man-eaters'.

Mohegan /mō**hee**gən/ > *noun* a member of an American Indian people formerly inhabiting western parts of Connecticut and Massachusetts. Compare with MAHICAN. > *adjective* relating to the Mohegans.
ORIGIN – Mohegan, 'people of the tidal waters'.

Mohican[1] /mō**hee**kən/ > *noun* a hairstyle in which the sides of the head are shaved and a central strip of hair is made to stand erect.

Mohican[2] /mō**hee**kən/ > *adjective* & *noun* old-fashioned variant of MAHICAN or MOHEGAN.

wordpower facts

Mohican

The term **Mohican** is a blend of the names of the North American Indian peoples the **Mahicans** and **Mohegans**, and is used today chiefly in reference to J. Fenimore Cooper's novel *The Last of the Mohicans* (1826). In the course of the 18th century the remnants of the Mohegan people were scattered around several locations, one group joining the remnants of the Mahicans; Cooper probably had some personal contact with an offshoot of this group in the 1820s. **Mohican** was first recorded in reference to a hairstyle in 1960; the style imitates a topknot traditionally worn by men of some American Indian peoples, which was often featured in illustrations of scenes from *The Last of the Mohicans*.

Moho /**mō**hō/ > *noun* Geology the boundary between the earth's crust and the mantle.
ORIGIN – short for *Mohorovičić discontinuity*, named after the Yugoslav seismologist Andrija *Mohorovičić* (1857–1936).

moiety /**moy**əti/ > *noun* (pl. **moieties**) **1** formal a half. **2** technical each of two parts into which a thing is or can be divided.
ORIGIN – Old French *moité*, from Latin *medius* 'mid, middle'.

moil archaic, dialect, or N. Amer. > *verb* **1** work hard. **2** move around in confusion. > *noun* **1** hard work. **2** confusion.
ORIGIN – Old French *moillier* 'paddle in mud, moisten'.

moire /mwaar/ (also **moiré** /**mwaa**ray/) > *noun* silk fabric treated to give it an appearance like that of rippled water.
ORIGIN – French, 'mohair' (the treatment originally being used on mohair fabric).

moist > *adjective* slightly wet; damp.
DERIVATIVES – **moisten** *verb* **moistly** *adverb* **moistness** *noun*.
SYNONYMS – clammy, damp, dank, soggy.
ORIGIN – Old French *moiste*, from Latin *mucidus* 'mouldy'.

moisture > *noun* water or other liquid diffused in a small quantity as vapour, within a solid, or condensed on a surface.
WORDFINDER – dehydrated, desiccated (*devoid of moisture*), hygroscopic (*tending to absorb moisture*), saturated (*full of moisture*).
SYNONYMS – clamminess, damp, dampness, dankness, wet, wetness.

moisturise (also **moisturize**) > *verb* make (something, especially skin) less dry.

moisturiser (also **moisturizer**) > *noun* a cosmetic preparation for moisturising the skin.

mojo /**mō**jō/ > *noun* (pl. **mojos**) chiefly US **1** a magic charm or spell. **2** supernatural power or luck.

ORIGIN – probably African.

moke > *noun* Brit. informal a donkey.

moko /mōkō/ > *noun* (pl. **mokos**) NZ a traditional Maori tattoo.

ORIGIN – Maori.

mol /mōl/ > *noun* Chemistry short for **MOLE⁴**.

molar¹ > *noun* a grinding tooth at the back of a mammal's mouth.

ORIGIN – from Latin *mola* 'millstone'.

molar² > *adjective* acting on or by means of large masses or units.

ORIGIN – from Latin *moles* 'mass'.

molar³ > *adjective* Chemistry **1** of or relating to one mole of a substance. **2** (of a solution) containing one mole of solute per litre of solvent.

molasses > *noun* **1** a thick, dark brown liquid obtained from raw sugar during the refining process. **2** N. Amer. golden syrup.

ORIGIN – Portuguese *melaço*, from Latin *mellacium* 'must', based on *mel* 'honey'.

mold > *noun & verb* US spelling of **MOULD¹⁻³**.

Moldavian /moldayviən/ > *noun* a person from Moldavia, a former principality of SE Europe. > *adjective* relating to Moldavia.

molder > *verb & noun* US spelling of **MOULDER**.

molding > *noun* US spelling of **MOULDING**.

Moldovan /moldōvən/ > *noun* a person from Moldova, a country in SE Europe. > *adjective* relating to Moldova.

moldy > *adjective* US spelling of **MOULDY**.

mole¹ /mōl/ > *noun* **1** a small burrowing insectivorous mammal with dark velvety fur, a long muzzle, and very small eyes. **2** a spy who manages to achieve an important position within the security defences of a country. **3** someone within an organisation who anonymously betrays confidential information.

COMBINATIONS – **moleskin 1** the skin of a mole used as fur. **2** a thick, strong cotton fabric with a shaved pile surface.

mole² /mōl/ > *noun* a small dark blemish on the skin where there is a high concentration of melanin.

mole³ /mōl/ > *noun* **1** a large solid structure serving as a pier, breakwater, or causeway. **2** a harbour formed by a mole.

ORIGIN – Latin *moles* 'mass'.

mole⁴ /mōl/ > *noun* Chemistry the unit of amount of substance in the SI system, equal to the quantity containing as many elementary units as there are atoms in 0.012 kg of carbon-12.

ORIGIN – German *Mol*, from *Molekul* 'molecule'.

mole⁵ /mōl/ > *noun* Medicine an abnormal mass of tissue in the uterus.

ORIGIN – from Latin *mola* 'millstone' in the sense 'false conception'.

mole⁶ /mōlay/ > *noun* a highly spiced Mexican savoury sauce containing chilli peppers and chocolate.

ORIGIN – Mexican Spanish, from a Nahuatl word meaning 'sauce, stew'.

molecular /məlekyoolər/ > *adjective* relating to or consisting of molecules.

COMBINATIONS – **molecular biology** the branch of biology concerned with the macromolecules (e.g. proteins and DNA) essential to life. **molecular weight** another term for *relative molecular mass*.

molecule /mollikyōol/ > *noun* a group of atoms chemically bonded together, representing the smallest fundamental unit of a compound that can take part in a chemical reaction.

ORIGIN – Latin *molecula* 'small mass', from *moles* 'mass'.

molehill > *noun* a small mound of earth thrown up by a burrowing mole.

IDIOMS – **make a mountain out of a molehill** exaggerate the importance of a minor problem.

molest > *verb* **1** pester or harass in a hostile way. **2** assault or abuse sexually.

DERIVATIVES – **molestation** *noun* **molester** *noun*.

SYNONYMS – **1** beset, harry, persecute, plague, torment. **2** abuse, assault, grope, maul, violate.

ORIGIN – Latin *molestare* 'annoy', from *molestus* 'troublesome'.

moll > *noun* informal **1** a gangster's female companion. **2** a prostitute.

ORIGIN – familiar form of the given name *Mary*.

mollify > *verb* (**mollifies**, **mollified**) **1** appease the anger or anxiety of. **2** reduce the severity of.

DERIVATIVES – **mollification** *noun*.

SYNONYMS – **1** calm, conciliate, pacify, placate, propitiate, soothe. **2** alleviate, blunt, mitigate, moderate, soften, temper.

ORIGIN – from Latin *mollis* 'soft'.

mollusc /molləsk/ (US **mollusk**) > *noun* Zoology an invertebrate animal of a large group including snails, slugs, and mussels, with a soft unsegmented body and often an external shell.

WORDFINDER – malacology (*the study of molluscs*); abalone, argonaut, bivalve, cephalopod, clam, cockle, cuttlefish, gastropod, mussel, nautilus, octopus, ormer, oyster, periwinkle, scallop, sea slug, snail, squid, whelk, winkle (*kinds of mollusc*).

DERIVATIVES – **molluscan** *adjective*.

ORIGIN – Latin *molluscus*, from *mollis* 'soft'.

molly (also **mollie**) > *noun* a small fish which is bred for aquaria in many colours, especially black.

ORIGIN – from the name of the French statesman Count *Mollien* (1758–1850).

mollycoddle > *verb* treat indulgently or

overprotectively. > *noun* an effeminate man or boy.

SYNONYMS – *verb* coddle, cosset, feather-bed, indulge, pamper, spoil.

ORIGIN – from *molly* 'girl' + **CODDLE**.

molly-dooker /molidōokər/ > *noun* Austral. informal a left-handed person.

ORIGIN – from *molly* 'girl' + *-dook* representing a pronunciation of **DUKE** (in sense 3).

mollymawk > *noun* chiefly Austral./NZ an albatross.

ORIGIN – Dutch *mallemok*, from *mal* 'foolish' + *mok* 'gull'.

moloch /mōlok/ > *noun* a spiny lizard of grotesque appearance, found in arid inland Australia.

ORIGIN – Latin, named after a Caananite idol to whom children were sacrificed.

Molotov cocktail /mollətof/ > *noun* a crude incendiary device consisting of a bottle of flammable liquid ignited using a wick.

ORIGIN – named after the Soviet statesman Vyacheslav *Molotov* (1890–1986), who organised the production of similar grenades in the Second World War.

molt > *verb & noun* US spelling of **MOULT**.

molten > *adjective* (especially of metal and glass) liquefied by heat.

ORIGIN – archaic past participle of **MELT**.

molto > *adverb* Music very.

ORIGIN – Italian.

molybdenum /məlibdənəm/ > *noun* a brittle silver-grey metallic chemical element used in some steels and other alloys.

ORIGIN – from Greek *molubdos* 'lead'.

mom > *noun* North American term for **MUM¹**.

moment > *noun* **1** a brief period of time. **2** an exact point in time. **3** formal importance. **4** Physics a turning effect produced by a force on an object, expressed as the product of the force and the distance from its line of action to a given point.

IDIOMS – **have one's** (or **its**) **moments** be very good at times. **moment of truth** a time of crisis or test. [ORIGIN – from a Spanish phrase, referring originally to the final sword thrust in a bullfight.] **of the moment** currently popular, famous, or important.

SYNONYMS – **1** bit, instant, minute, second; informal jiffy; Brit. informal tick.

ORIGIN – Latin *momentum* (see **MOMENTUM**).

momentarily > *adverb* **1** for a very short time. **2** N. Amer. very soon.

momentary > *adjective* very brief or short-lived.

SYNONYMS – fleeting, passing, quick, temporary, transitory.

momentous > *adjective* of great importance or significance.

DERIVATIVES – **momentously** *adverb* **momentousness** *noun*.

SYNONYMS – consequential, crucial, grave, vital, weighty.

momentum > *noun* (pl. **momenta**) **1** impetus gained by movement or progress. **2** Physics the quantity of motion of a moving body, equal to the product of its mass and velocity.

SYNONYMS – **1** force, strength, thrust, velocity.

ORIGIN – Latin, from *movimentum*, from *movere* 'to move'.

mommy > *noun* (pl. **mommies**) North American term for **MUMMY**[1].

Mon. > *abbreviation* Monday.

monad /**monn**ad/ > *noun* technical a single unit; the number one.

ORIGIN – Greek *monas* 'unit', from *monos* 'alone'.

monarch > *noun* **1** a sovereign head of state. **2** a large, migratory, orange and black butterfly found chiefly in North America.

DERIVATIVES – **monarchic** *adjective* **monarchical** *adjective*.

SYNONYMS – **1** emperor, empress, king, potentate, queen, ruler, tsar.

ORIGIN – Greek *monarkhēs*, from *monos* 'alone' + *arkhein* 'to rule'.

monarchism > *noun* support for the principle of monarchy.

DERIVATIVES – **monarchist** *noun* & *adjective*.

monarchy > *noun* (pl. **monarchies**) **1** government by a monarch. **2** a state with a monarch.

monastery > *noun* (pl. **monasteries**) a community of monks living under religious vows.

WORDFINDER – monastic, claustral (*relating to monasteries or monastic life*); *kinds of monastery:* abbey, convent, friary, nunnery, priory; lamasery, vihara (*Buddhist*); ashram (*Indian*); abbot (*head of a monastery*), chapter (*monastery's governing body*), cloister (*covered walk*), refectory (*dining hall*).

ORIGIN – Greek *monastērion*, from *monazein* 'live alone'.

monastic > *adjective* **1** relating to monks or nuns or their communities. **2** resembling monks or their way of life, especially in being austere or reclusive.

DERIVATIVES – **monastically** *adverb* **monasticism** *noun*.

SYNONYMS – **2** ascetic, contemplative, hermitic, secluded, solitary.

monaural /monn**awr**əl/ > *adjective* **1** of or involving one ear. **2** another term for **MONOPHONIC**.

Monday > *noun* the day of the week before Tuesday and following Sunday.

ORIGIN – Old English, 'day of the moon', translation of Latin *lunae dies*.

Monégasque /monnay**gask**/ > *noun* a person from Monaco. > *adjective* relating to Monaco.

monetarism > *noun* the theory that inflation is best controlled by limiting the supply of money circulating in an economy.

DERIVATIVES – **monetarist** *noun* & *adjective*.

monetary > *adjective* relating to money or currency.

DERIVATIVES – **monetarily** *adverb*.

monetise (also **monetize**, **monetarise**) > *verb* **1** convert into or express in the form of currency. **2** (**monetised**) (of a society) adapted to the use of money.

DERIVATIVES – **monetisation** *noun*.

money > *noun* **1** a medium of exchange in the form of coins and banknotes. **2** the assets or resources owned by someone or something. **3** payment or financial gain. **4** (**moneys** or **monies**) formal sums of money.

WORDFINDER – financial, pecuniary, numismatic (*related adjectives*).

IDIOMS – **for my money** informal in my opinion. **money for old rope** (or **money for jam**) Brit. informal money or reward earned for little or no effort. **money talks** proverb wealth gives power and influence to those who possess it. **put one's money where one's mouth is** informal take action to support one's statements.

SYNONYMS – **1** cash, currency, legal tender; informal bread, dough. **2** assets, riches, wealth.

COMBINATIONS – **money-grubbing** informal greedily concerned with making money; grasping. **money market** the trade in short-term loans between banks and other financial institutions. **money order** a printed order for payment of a specified sum, issued by a bank or post office. **money spider** a very small black spider. **money-spinner** chiefly Brit. a thing that brings in a large profit. **money supply** the total amount of money in circulation or in existence in a country.

wordpower facts

Money

The word **money** entered English via Old French *moneie* from Latin *moneta*, which is from the verb *monere* 'to warn or remind'. *Moneta* was originally a title given to the goddess Juno, in whose temple in ancient Rome money was minted; the word *mint* meaning 'a place where money is coined' is also from this source.

moneybags > *plural noun* (treated as sing.) informal a wealthy person.

moneyed > *adjective* having much money; affluent.

-monger > *combining form* **1** referring to a dealer or trader in a specified commodity: *fishmonger*. **2** chiefly derogatory referring to a person engaging in a particular activity: *rumour-monger*.

ORIGIN – from Latin *mango* 'dealer'.

mongo > *noun* (pl. same or **mongos**) a monetary unit of Mongolia, equal to one hundredth of a tugrik.

ORIGIN – Mongolian, 'silver'.

Mongol > *noun* **1** a person from Mongolia. **2** (**mongol**) offensive a person with Down's syndrome.

DERIVATIVES – **mongolism** *noun* (offensive).

USAGE – the term **mongol** was adopted in the late 19th century to refer to a person suffering from **Down's syndrome**, owing to the similarity of some of the physical symptoms of the disorder to the normal facial characteristics of East Asian people. This use is now considered offensive; the term **Down's syndrome** should be used instead.

Mongolian > *noun* **1** a person from Mongolia. **2** the language of Mongolia. > *adjective* relating to Mongolia.

Mongoloid > *adjective* **1** relating to the broad division of humankind including the indigenous peoples of east Asia, SE Asia, and Arctic North America. **2** (**mongoloid**) offensive affected with Down's syndrome. > *noun* a person of a Mongoloid physical type.

USAGE – the term **Mongoloid** belongs to a set of terms introduced by 19th-century anthropologists attempting to categorise human races. Such terms are associated with outdated notions of racial types, and so are now potentially offensive and best avoided.

mongoose > *noun* (pl. **mongooses**) a small carnivorous mammal with a long body and tail, native to Africa and Asia.

ORIGIN – Marathi (a central Indian language).

mongrel > *noun* **1** a dog of no definable breed. **2** offensive a person of mixed descent. **3** something of mixed origin or nature.

monies plural of **MONEY**, as used in financial contexts.

moniker /**monn**ikər/ (also **monicker**) > *noun* informal a name.

DERIVATIVES – **monikered** *adjective*.

monism /**monn**iz'm/ > *noun* Philosophy a theory or doctrine that denies the existence of a distinction or duality, such as that between matter and mind.

DERIVATIVES – **monist** *noun* & *adjective*.

ORIGIN – from Greek *monos* 'single'.

monitor > *noun* **1** a person or device that monitors something. **2** a television used to view a picture from a particular camera or a display from a computer. **3** a loudspeaker used by performers to hear what is being played or recorded. **4** a school pupil with disciplinary or other special duties. **5** (also **monitor lizard**) a large tropical lizard. > *verb* keep under observation, especially so as to regulate, record, or control.

SYNONYMS – *verb* check, keep an eye on, observe, oversee, supervise, watch.

wordpower facts

Monitor

The word **monitor** derives from Latin *monere* 'to warn or remind', which is also the root of **admonish**, **monument**, **premonition**, and **summon**. The English word **monster** also comes from *monere*, via Latin *monstrum* 'divine portent or warning'. The **monitor lizard** is so called because it was formerly believed to warn of the approach of crocodiles.

monk > *noun* a man belonging to a religious community typically living under vows of poverty, chastity, and obedience.

WORDFINDER – Augustinian, Basilian, Benedictine, Carmelite, Carthusian, Cistercian, Cluniac, Culdee, Dominican, Franciscan, Servite (*monastic orders*); cowl (*monk's hood*), habit (*monk's robe*), novice, oblate, postulant (*beginner monk*), scapular (*monk's short cloak*), tonsure (*monk's shaven crown*).

DERIVATIVES – **monkish** *adjective*.

COMBINATIONS – **monk seal** a seal with a dark back and pale underside, found in warm waters of the northern hemisphere.

ORIGIN – from Greek *monakhos* 'solitary'.

monkey > *noun* (pl. **monkeys**) **1** a small to medium-sized primate typically having a long tail and living in trees in tropical countries. **2** informal a mischievous person, especially a child. **3** Brit. informal a sum of £500. > *verb* (**monkeys**, **monkeyed**) **1** (**monkey about** or **around**) behave in a silly or playful way. **2** (**monkey with**) tamper with.

WORDFINDER – baboon, capuchin, colobus. grivet, howler monkey, langur, macaque, marmoset, proboscis monkey, rhesus monkey, vervet (*some common types of monkey*).

IDIOMS – **make a monkey of** (or **out of**) make a fool of. **not give a monkey's** informal not care at all.

COMBINATIONS – **monkey business** informal mischievous or underhand behaviour. **monkey nut** Brit. a peanut. **monkey puzzle** a coniferous tree with branches covered in spirals of tough spiny leaves. **monkey suit** informal a man's evening dress

or formal suit. **monkey tricks** Brit. informal mischievous behaviour. **monkey wrench** a spanner with large adjustable jaws.

monkfish > *noun* **1** an anglerfish, especially when used as food. **2** a bottom-dwelling shark with broad pectoral fins.

monkshood > *noun* an aconite with blue or purple flowers.

mono > *adjective* **1** monophonic. **2** monochrome. > *noun* **1** monophonic reproduction. **2** monochrome reproduction.

mono- /monnō/ (also **mon-** before a vowel) > *combining form* **1** one; alone; single: *monochromatic*. **2** Chemistry (forming names of compounds) containing one atom or group of a specified kind.

ORIGIN – from Greek *monos* 'alone'.

monobasic > *adjective* Chemistry (of an acid) having one replaceable hydrogen atom.

monobloc > *adjective* made as or contained in a single casting.

monochromatic > *adjective* **1** containing only one colour. **2** Physics (of light or other radiation) of a single wavelength or frequency.

monochrome > *noun* representation or reproduction in black and white or in varying tones of one colour. > *adjective* consisting of or displaying images in black and white or in varying tones of one colour.

monocle > *noun* a lens worn to improve sight in one eye.

ORIGIN – from Latin *monoculus* 'one-eyed'.

monoclonal /monnōklōn'l/ > *adjective* Biology relating to a clone or line of clones produced from a single individual or cell.

monocoque /monnəkok/ > *noun* an aircraft or vehicle structure in which the chassis is integral with the body.

ORIGIN – French, from *mono-* 'single' + *coque* 'shell'.

monocotyledon /monōkotileedən/ > *noun* a flowering plant whose seeds have a single cotyledon.

monocular > *adjective* with, for, or using one eye. > *noun* an optical instrument for viewing distant objects with one eye.

ORIGIN – Latin *monoculus* 'having one eye'.

monoculture > *noun* the cultivation of a single crop in a particular area.

monocycle > *noun* a unicycle.

monody /monnədi/ > *noun* (pl. **monodies**) **1** an ode sung by a single actor in a Greek tragedy. **2** music with only one melodic line.

ORIGIN – Greek *monōdia*, from *monōdos* 'singing alone'.

monoecious /məneeshəss/ > *adjective* (of a species of plant or invertebrate animal) having both the male and female reproductive organs in the same individual. Compare with DIOECIOUS.

ORIGIN – from Greek *monos* 'single' + *oikos* 'house'.

monogamy > *noun* the state of having only one husband, wife, or sexual partner at any one time.

DERIVATIVES – **monogamist** *noun* **monogamous** *adjective*.

ORIGIN – from Greek *monos* 'single' + *gamos* 'marriage'.

monoglot > *adjective* using or speaking only one language. > *noun* a monoglot person.

ORIGIN – from Greek *monos* 'single' + *glōtta* 'tongue'.

monogram > *noun* a motif of two or more interwoven letters, typically a person's initials.

DERIVATIVES – **monogrammed** *adjective*.

monograph > *noun* a scholarly written study of a single subject.

DERIVATIVES – **monographic** *adjective*.

monohull > *noun* a boat with only one hull, as opposed to a catamaran or multihull.

monolingual > *adjective* speaking or expressed in only one language.

monolith > *noun* **1** a large single upright block of stone, especially a pillar or monument. **2** a massive and indivisible organisation or institution.

ORIGIN – from Greek *monos* 'single' + *lithos* 'stone'.

monolithic > *adjective* **1** formed of a single large block of stone. **2** massive and uniform or indivisible.

monologue > *noun* **1** a long speech by one actor in a play or film. **2** a long, tedious speech by one person during a conversation.

ORIGIN – from Greek *monologos* 'speaking alone'.

monomania > *noun* an obsessive preoccupation with one thing.

DERIVATIVES – **monomaniac** *noun*.

monomer /monnəmər/ > *noun* Chemistry a molecule that can be linked to other identical molecules to form a polymer.

monomial /mənōmiəl/ Mathematics > *adjective* (of an algebraic expression) consisting of one term. > *noun* a monomial expression.

monophonic > *adjective* (of sound reproduction) using only one transmission channel. Compare with STEREOPHONIC.

monoplane > *noun* an aircraft with one pair of wings.

monopod > *noun* a one-legged support for a camera or fishing rod.

monopole > *noun* **1** Physics a single electric charge or magnetic pole, especially a hypothetical isolated magnetic pole. **2** an aerial or a pylon consisting of a single pole.

monopolise (also **monopolize**) > *verb* take exclusive control or use of.

DERIVATIVES – **monopolisation** *noun*.

monopolist > *noun* a person who has a monopoly.
DERIVATIVES – **monopolistic** *adjective*.

monopoly > *noun* (pl. **monopolies**) **1** the exclusive possession or control of the supply of a commodity or service. **2** an organisation having a monopoly, or a commodity or service controlled by one. **3** exclusive possession or control of something.
ORIGIN – Greek *monopōlion*, from *monos* 'single' + *pōlein* 'sell'.

monopsony /mənopsəni/ > *noun* (pl. **monopsonies**) Economics a market in which there is only one buyer.
ORIGIN – from Greek *opsōnein* 'buy provisions'.

monorail > *noun* a railway in which the track consists of a single rail.

monosaccharide > *noun* a sugar (e.g. glucose) that cannot be broken down to give a simpler sugar.

monoski > *noun* a single broad ski attached to both feet.

monosodium glutamate > *noun* a compound made by the breakdown of vegetable protein and used as a flavour enhancer in food.

monosyllabic > *adjective* **1** consisting of one syllable. **2** using brief words because reluctant to converse.
DERIVATIVES – **monosyllabically** *adverb*.

monosyllable > *noun* a word of one syllable.

monotheism /monnətheeiz'm/ > *noun* the belief that there is a single god.
DERIVATIVES – **monotheist** *noun* & *adjective* **monotheistic** *adjective*.

monotone > *noun* a continuing sound that is unchanging in pitch.

monotonous > *adjective* **1** tedious because of its repetitive or unvarying character. **2** without variation of tone or pitch.
DERIVATIVES – **monotonously** *adverb* **monotony** *noun*.
SYNONYMS – **1** boring, dull, humdrum, repetitious, routine, tedious, unvarying.

monotreme /monnətreem/ > *noun* a mammal which possesses a cloaca and lays eggs, i.e. a platypus or an echidna.
ORIGIN – from Greek *monos* 'single' + *trēma* 'hole'.

monounsaturated > *adjective* referring to fats whose molecules are saturated except for one multiple bond, considered to be less healthy in the diet than polyunsaturated fats.

monoxide > *noun* Chemistry an oxide containing one atom of oxygen.

monozygotic /monnōzīgottik/ > *adjective* (of twins) derived from a single ovum, and so identical.

Monseigneur /monsenyör/ > *noun* (pl. **Messeigneurs** /messenyör/) a title or form of address for a French-speaking prince, cardinal, archbishop, or bishop.
ORIGIN – French, 'my lord'.

Monsieur /məsyör/ > *noun* (pl. **Messieurs** /mesyör/) a title or form of address for a French-speaking man, corresponding to *Mr* or *sir*.
ORIGIN – French, 'my lord'.

Monsignor /monseenyər/ > *noun* (pl. **Monsignori** /monseenyori/) the title of various senior Roman Catholic priests and officials.
ORIGIN – Italian.

monsoon > *noun* **1** a seasonal prevailing wind in the region of the Indian subcontinent and SE Asia, bringing rain when blowing from the south-west. **2** the rainy season (typically May to September) accompanying the south-west monsoon.
DERIVATIVES – **monsoonal** *adjective*.
ORIGIN – Arabic, 'season'.

mons pubis /monz pyōōbiss/ > *noun* the rounded mass of fatty tissue lying over the joint of the pubic bones.
ORIGIN – Latin, 'mount of the pubes'.

monster > *noun* **1** a large, ugly, and frightening imaginary creature. **2** an inhumanly cruel or wicked person. **3** (before another noun) informal extraordinarily large.
WORDFINDER – Abominable Snowman, basilisk, behemoth, bunyip, chimera, cockatrice, dragon, gorgon, harpy, hippogriff, kraken, lamia, leviathan, manticore, troll, yeti (*types of monster*).
SYNONYMS – **2** beast, brute, devil, fiend, savage.
ORIGIN – Latin *monstrum* 'divine portent or warning, monster', from *monere* 'warn'.

monstera /monsteerə/ > *noun* a tropical American climbing plant of a genus including the Swiss cheese plant.
ORIGIN – Latin, probably from *monstrum* 'monster'.

monstrance /monstrənss/ > *noun* (in the Roman Catholic Church) a receptacle in which the consecrated Host is displayed for veneration.
ORIGIN – from Latin *monstrare* 'to show'.

monstrosity > *noun* (pl. **monstrosities**) **1** something outrageously or offensively unsightly or wrong. **2** a grossly malformed animal, plant, or bodily part.
SYNONYMS – **1** carbuncle, excrescence, eyesore, horror.

monstrous > *adjective* **1** very large and ugly or frightening. **2** outrageously evil or wrong.
DERIVATIVES – **monstrously** *adverb* **monstrousness** *noun*.
SYNONYMS – **1** freakish, grotesque, hideous, nightmarish, unnatural. **2** abominable, appalling, heinous, loathsome, vile, wicked.

mons veneris /monz vennəriss/ > *noun* (in women) the mons pubis.
ORIGIN – Latin, 'mount of Venus'.

montage /montaazh/ > *noun* **1** the technique of making a picture or film by putting together pieces from other pictures or films. **2** a picture or film resulting from such a technique.
ORIGIN – French, from *monter* 'to mount'.

montane /montayn/ > *adjective* of or inhabiting mountainous country.

montbretia /monbreeshə/ > *noun* a plant with small orange trumpet-shaped flowers.
ORIGIN – named after the French botanist A. Coquebert de *Montbret* (1780–1801).

Montenegrin /montinegrin/ > *noun* a person from the Yugoslavian republic of Montenegro. > *adjective* of or relating to Montenegro.

Montessori /montisori/ > *noun* a system of education that seeks to develop a child's natural interests and activities rather than use formal teaching methods.
ORIGIN – named after the Italian educationist Maria *Montessori* (1870–1952).

month > *noun* **1** each of the twelve named periods into which a year is divided. **2** a period of time between the same dates in successive calendar months. **3** a period of 28 days or four weeks.
IDIOMS – **a month of Sundays** informal a very long time.
ORIGIN – Old English, related to **MOON** (since in many early civilisations the calendar month was calculated as beginning with the new moon).

monthly > *adjective* done, produced, or occurring once a month. > *adverb* once a month. > *noun* (pl. **monthlies**) **1** a magazine published once a month. **2** (**monthlies**) informal a menstrual period.

monty > *noun* (**the full monty**) Brit. informal the full amount expected, desired, or possible.

wordpower facts
The full monty
Although many suggestions have been put forward, the true origin of the phrase **the full monty** has never been settled. It may be from *the full Montague Burton*, meaning 'Sunday-best three-piece suit' (from the name of a tailor). Another possibility is that it is from the nickname, Monty, of Field Marshal Montgomery (1887–1976), who used to insist on a full cooked English breakfast.

monument > *noun* **1** a statue or structure erected to commemorate a person or event. **2** a structure or site of historical importance. **3** an enduring and memorable example or reminder.

ORIGIN – Latin *monumentum*, from *monere* 'remind'.

monumental > *adjective* **1** very large or impressive: *it's been a monumental effort.* **2** of or serving as a monument.

DERIVATIVES – **monumentality** *noun* **monumentally** *adverb*.

SYNONYMS – **1** enormous, huge, immense, magnificent, massive, prodigious.

COMBINATIONS – **monumental mason Brit.** a person who makes tombstones and similar items.

moo > *verb* (**moos, mooed**) make the characteristic deep vocal sound of cattle. > *noun* (pl. **moos**) such a sound.

mooch > *verb* Brit. informal loiter in a bored or listless way.

ORIGIN – first meaning 'to hoard', later (in English dialect) 'play truant to pick blackberries': probably from Old French *muscher* 'hide, skulk'.

mood > *noun* **1** a temporary state of mind. **2** a fit of bad temper or depression. **3** the atmosphere or tone of something, especially a work of art. **4** Grammar a form or category of a verb expressing fact, command, question, wish, or conditionality.

WORDFINDER – imperative, indicative, interrogative, optative, subjunctive (*moods of a verb*).

SYNONYMS – **1** frame of mind, humour, spirits, temper. **2** rage, sulk, tantrum, temper. **3** ambience, atmosphere, feeling, spirit, tone.

moody > *adjective* (**moodier, moodiest**) **1** given to sudden bouts of gloominess or sullenness. **2** giving a melancholy or mysterious impression.

DERIVATIVES – **moodily** *adverb* **moodiness** *noun*.

SYNONYMS – **1** capricious, mercurial, temperamental, unpredictable, volatile.

moolah > *noun* informal money.

mooli /**moo**li/ > *noun* a variety of large, slender white radish.

ORIGIN – Sanskrit, 'root'.

moon > *noun* **1** (also **Moon**) the natural satellite of the earth, orbiting it every twenty-eight days and shining by reflected light from the sun. **2** a natural satellite of any planet. **3** literary or humorous a month: *many moons ago.* > *verb* **1** (usu. **moon about** or **around**) behave or move in a listless or dreamy manner. **2** informal expose one's buttocks to someone as an insult or joke.

WORDFINDER – apogee (*point in the moon's orbit where it is furthest from the earth*), gibbous (*denoting the phase of the moon between half and full*), lunar (*of the moon*), perigee (*point in the moon's orbit where it is nearest to the earth*), selenographer, selenologist (*person who studies the moon*).

IDIOMS – **over the moon** Brit. informal delighted.

DERIVATIVES – **moonless** *adjective*.

COMBINATIONS – **moon boot** a thickly padded boot with a fabric or plastic outer surface. **moon daisy** an ox-eye daisy. **moon-faced** having a round face. **moonscape** a rocky and barren landscape resembling the moon's surface. **moonstone** a pearly white semi-precious form of feldspar. **moonwalk** move or dance in a way reminiscent of astronauts walking in the moon's reduced gravity.

wordpower facts
Moon
The word **moon** derives ultimately from an Indo-European root shared by Latin *mensis* and Greek *mēn*, both meaning 'month'. This root is the source of English words such as **menstruate** (the menstrual cycle being roughly one lunar month), and, via the Latin verb *metiri*, **measure** (the moon formerly being used to measure time).

mooncalf > *noun* (pl. **mooncalves**) a foolish person.

Moonie > *noun* informal, often derogatory a member of the Unification Church.

ORIGIN – named after its Korean founder and leader, Sun Myung *Moon* (born 1920).

moonlight > *noun* the light of the moon. > *verb* (past and past participle **moonlighted**) informal do a second job, especially at night, without declaring it for tax purposes.

DERIVATIVES – **moonlighter** *noun* **moonlit** *adjective*.

COMBINATIONS – **moonlight flit** Brit. informal a hurried departure by night, especially to avoid paying a debt.

moonshine > *noun* informal **1** foolish talk or ideas. **2** chiefly N. Amer. illicitly distilled or smuggled liquor.

moonstruck > *adjective* slightly deranged, especially because of being in love.

moony > *adjective* (**moonier, mooniest**) dreamy, especially through being in love.

Moor > *noun* a member of a NW African Muslim people of mixed Berber and Arab descent.

DERIVATIVES – **Moorish** *adjective*.

ORIGIN – Greek *Mauros* 'inhabitant of Mauretania' (an ancient region of North Africa).

moor¹ > *noun* a stretch of open uncultivated upland.

moor² > *verb* **1** make fast (a boat) by attaching it by cable or rope to the shore or

to an anchor. **2** be secured somewhere in this way.

moorhen > *noun* an aquatic bird with mainly blackish plumage and a red and yellow bill.

mooring (also **moorings**) > *noun* **1** a place where a boat is moored. **2** the ropes or cables by which a boat is moored.

moose > *noun* (pl. same) North American term for ELK.

ORIGIN – Abnaki (an American Indian language).

moot > *adjective* subject to debate or uncertainty: *a moot point.* > *verb* put forward for discussion. > *noun* **1** (in Anglo-Saxon and medieval England) a legislative or judicial assembly. **2** Law a mock trial set up to examine a hypothetical case as an academic exercise.

SYNONYMS – *adjective* arguable, contentious, disputed, undecided, unresolved.

ORIGIN – from Old English *mōt* 'assembly or meeting' and *mōtian* 'to converse'; related to MEET¹.

mop > *noun* **1** a bundle of thick, loose strings or a sponge attached to a handle, used for wiping floors. **2** a thick mass of disordered hair. > *verb* (**mopped, mopping**) **1** clean or soak up by wiping. **2** (**mop up**) clear up or put an end to.

SYNONYMS – *noun* **2** mane, shock, tangle, thatch. *verb* **1** absorb, blot, dab, sponge.

mope > *verb* be listless and in low spirits.

SYNONYMS – brood, moon, pine, sulk.

moped > *noun* a light motorcycle with an engine capacity below 50 cc.

ORIGIN – from Swedish *motor och pedaler* 'motor and pedals'.

moppet > *noun* informal an endearing small child.

ORIGIN – from obsolete *moppe* 'baby or rag doll'.

moquette /mo**ket**/ > *noun* a thick pile fabric used for carpets and upholstery.

ORIGIN – French.

MOR > *abbreviation* (of music) middle of the road.

moraine /mə**rayn**/ > *noun* a mass of rocks and sediment carried down and deposited by a glacier.

ORIGIN – French, from dialect *morre* 'snout'.

moral > *adjective* **1** concerned with the principles of right and wrong behaviour and the goodness or badness of human character. **2** conforming to accepted standards of behaviour. **3** psychological rather than physical or practical: *moral support.* > *noun* **1** a lesson about right or wrong that can be derived from a story or experience. **2** (**morals**) standards of behaviour, or principles of right and wrong.

DERIVATIVES – **morally** adverb.

SYNONYMS – adjective **1** ethical. **2** honourable, principled, respectable, righteous, upright. noun **1** lesson, message, point, precept.

ANTONYMS – adjective **2** immoral.

COMBINATIONS – **moral majority 1** the part of society favouring strict moral standards. **2** (**Moral Majority**) a right-wing Christian movement in the US. **moral philosophy** the branch of philosophy concerned with ethics. **moral victory** a defeat that can be interpreted as a victory in moral terms.

ORIGIN – Latin moralis, from mos 'custom'.

morale > noun the level of a person's or group's confidence and spirits.

ORIGIN – from French moral, respelled to preserve the final stress in pronunciation.

moralise (also **moralize**) > verb **1** comment on moral issues, especially disapprovingly. **2** improve the morals of. **3** interpret as giving moral lessons.

DERIVATIVES – **moraliser** noun.

moralist > noun **1** a person who teaches or promotes morality. **2** a person who behaves morally.

DERIVATIVES – **moralism** noun **moralistic** adjective.

morality > noun (pl. **moralities**) **1** principles concerning the distinction between right and wrong or good and bad behaviour. **2** moral behaviour. **3** the extent to which an action is right or wrong. **4** a system of values and moral principles.

SYNONYMS – **2** goodness, integrity, probity, propriety, rectitude, virtue.

ANTONYMS – **2** immorality, impropriety.

COMBINATIONS – **morality play** a play presenting a moral lesson and having personified qualities as the main characters, popular in the 15th and 16th centuries.

morass /mə**rass**/ > noun **1** an area of muddy or boggy ground. **2** a complicated or confused situation.

SYNONYMS – **1** marsh, mire, quagmire, swamp. **2** entanglement, imbroglio, mess, mix-up, muddle.

ORIGIN – Dutch moeras, from Latin mariscus.

moratorium /morrə**tōr**iəm/ > noun (pl. **moratoriums** or **moratoria** /morrə**tōr**iə/) **1** a temporary prohibition of an activity. **2** Law a legal authorisation to debtors to postpone payment.

SYNONYMS – **1** ban, embargo, freeze, halt, suspension.

ORIGIN – Latin, from morari 'to delay'.

Moravian /mə**ray**viən/ > noun **1** a person from Moravia in the Czech Republic. **2** a member of a Protestant Church founded by emigrants from Moravia. > adjective relating to Moravia or the Moravian Church.

moray (also **moray eel**) > noun an eel-like predatory fish of warm seas.

ORIGIN – Portuguese moréia, from Greek muraina.

morbid > adjective **1** having or showing an unhealthy interest in unpleasant subjects, especially death and disease. **2** Medicine of the nature of or indicative of disease.

DERIVATIVES – **morbidity** noun **morbidly** adverb.

SYNONYMS – **1** ghoulish, macabre, twisted, unwholesome.

ORIGIN – from Latin morbus 'disease'.

mordant > adjective (especially of humour) sharply sarcastic. > noun **1** a substance that combines with a dye and thereby fixes it in a material. **2** a corrosive liquid used to etch the lines on a printing plate.

SYNONYMS – adjective acerbic, caustic, cutting, incisive, scathing.

ORIGIN – from Latin mordere 'to bite'.

more > determiner & pronoun a greater or additional amount or degree. > adverb **1** forming the comparative of adjectives and adverbs. **2** to a greater extent. **3** again.

IDIOMS – **more and more** at an increasing rate. **more or less** to a certain extent. **more than** extremely. **no more 1** nothing further. **2** no further. **3** (**be no more**) no longer exist.

moreish > adjective Brit. informal so pleasant to eat that one wants more.

morel /mə**rell**/ > noun an edible fungus having a brown oval or pointed cap with an irregular honeycombed surface.

ORIGIN – French morille, from Dutch morilje.

morello > noun (pl. **morellos**) a kind of sour, dark cherry used in cooking.

ORIGIN – Italian, 'blackish'.

moreover > adverb as a further matter; besides.

mores /**mor**ayz/ > plural noun the customs and conventions of a community.

ORIGIN – Latin, plural of mos 'custom'.

morganatic /morgə**natt**ik/ > adjective (of a marriage) between a man of high rank and a woman of low rank who retains her former status, their children having no claim to the father's possessions or title.

ORIGIN – from Latin matrimonium ad morganaticam 'marriage with a morning gift' (because a gift given by a husband on the morning after the marriage was the wife's sole entitlement).

morgue > noun **1** a mortuary. **2** informal a newspaper's files of miscellaneous information kept for reference.

ORIGIN – French, originally the name of a building in Paris where bodies were kept until identified.

moribund > adjective **1** at the point of death. **2** in terminal decline; lacking vigour.

SYNONYMS – **2** atrophying, crumbling, decaying, waning.

ORIGIN – Latin moribundus, from mori 'to die'.

Mormon > noun a member of the Church of Jesus Christ of Latter-Day Saints, a religion founded in the US in 1830 by Joseph Smith Jr (1805–44).

DERIVATIVES – **Mormonism** noun.

ORIGIN – the name of a prophet to whom Smith attributed The Book of Mormon, a collection of supposed revelations.

morn > noun literary morning.

mornay > adjective denoting or served in a cheese-flavoured white sauce.

ORIGIN – named after Mornay, the eldest son of the 19th-century French cook Joseph Voiron, the inventor of the sauce.

morning > noun **1** the period of time between midnight and noon, especially from sunrise to noon. **2** sunrise. > adverb (**mornings**) informal every morning.

COMBINATIONS – **morning-after pill** a contraceptive pill that is effective within about thirty-six hours after intercourse. **morning coat** a man's tailcoat. **morning dress** a man's formal dress of morning coat and striped trousers. **morning glory** a climbing plant of the convolvulus family with trumpet-shaped flowers. **morning sickness** nausea occurring in the mornings during early pregnancy. **morning star** a planet, especially Venus, when visible in the east before sunrise.

Moroccan > noun a person from Morocco in North Africa. > adjective relating to Morocco.

morocco > noun fine flexible leather made (originally in Morocco) from goatskins tanned with sumac.

moron > noun informal a stupid person.

DERIVATIVES – **moronic** adjective.

ORIGIN – from Greek mōros 'foolish'.

morose > adjective sullen and ill-tempered.

DERIVATIVES – **morosely** adverb **moroseness** noun.

SYNONYMS – dour, gloomy, glum, humourless, miserable, sulky.

ANTONYMS – cheerful, jovial.

ORIGIN – Latin morosus 'peevish'.

morph > verb (in computer animation) change smoothly and gradually from one image to another.

ORIGIN – from METAMORPHOSIS.

-morph > combining form denoting something having a specified form or character.

wordpower facts

-morph

The element **-morph** (from Greek *morphē* 'form') gives rise to a number of English words, particularly in technical subjects. Frequently found also as the adjectival endings **-morphic** or **-morphous**, it occurs in words such as **anthropomorphism** 'attribution of human characteristics to an animal or object', **biomorph** 'something resembling a living organism', **metamorphosis** 'complete change', and **zoomorphic** 'having an animal form'. It also forms a small group of words denoting a person's physique: **ectomorph** (lean), **endomorph** (round), and **mesomorph** (compact and muscular).

morpheme /**mor**feem/ > *noun* Linguistics a meaningful morphological unit of a language that cannot be further divided (e.g. *in, come, -ing,* forming *incoming*).
DERIVATIVES – **morphemic** *adjective.*

morphia > *noun* dated morphine.

morphic resonance > *noun* a supposed paranormal influence by which (according to the theory of the British biologist Rupert Sheldrake) a pattern of events or behaviour makes subsequent occurrences of similar patterns more likely.

morphine > *noun* a narcotic drug obtained from opium and used medicinally to relieve pain.
ORIGIN – named after the Roman god of sleep, *Morpheus.*

morphology > *noun* **1** the branch of biology concerned with the forms and structures of living organisms. **2** the study of the forms of words. **3** the study of shape or form.
DERIVATIVES – **morphological** *adjective* **morphologist** *noun.*

morris dancing > *noun* traditional English folk dancing performed outdoors by groups of dancers wearing costumes with small bells attached and carrying handkerchiefs or sticks.
ORIGIN – from a variant of *Moorish*: the association with the Moors remains unexplained.

morrow > *noun* (**the morrow**) archaic or literary the following day.
ORIGIN – from Old English *morgen* 'morning'.

Morse (also **Morse code**) > *noun* a code in which letters are represented by combinations of long and short light or sound signals.
ORIGIN – named after its American inventor Samuel F. B. *Morse* (1791–1872).

morsel > *noun* a small piece of food; a mouthful.
SYNONYMS – bit, bite, mouthful, nibble, titbit.
ORIGIN – Old French, 'little bite'.

mortadella /mortə**dell**ə/ > *noun* a type of smooth-textured Italian sausage containing pieces of fat.
ORIGIN – Italian, from Latin *murtatum* 'sausage seasoned with myrtle berries'.

mortal > *adjective* **1** subject to death. **2** causing death. **3** (of fear, pain, etc.) intense. **4** (of conflict or an enemy) lasting until death; never to be reconciled. **5** without exception; imaginable: *every mortal thing.* **6** Christian Theology (of a sin) regarded as depriving the soul of divine grace. Contrasted with VENIAL. > *noun* a human being.
DERIVATIVES – **mortally** *adverb.*
SYNONYMS – *adjective* **1** corporeal, earthly, temporal. **2** deadly, fatal, lethal, terminal. **5** conceivable, imaginable, possible.
ANTONYMS – *adjective* **1** immortal.
ORIGIN – Latin *mortalis,* from *mors* 'death'.

mortality > *noun* **1** the state of being mortal. **2** death, especially on a large scale. **3** (also **mortality rate**) the number of deaths in a given area or period, or from a particular cause.

mortar > *noun* **1** a mixture of lime with cement, sand, and water, used to bond bricks or stones. **2** a cup-shaped receptacle in which substances are crushed or ground with a pestle. **3** a short cannon for firing shells at high angles. > *verb* **1** fix or bond using mortar. **2** attack with shells fired from a mortar.
COMBINATIONS – **mortar board 1** an academic cap with a stiff, flat square top and a tassel. **2** a small square board held horizontally by a handle on the underside, used for holding mortar.
ORIGIN – Latin *mortarium* 'receptacle in which substances are crushed or ground'; sense 1 of the noun is probably a transferred use of sense 2, the mortar being mixed in a trough or other receptacle.

mortgage > *noun* **1** a legal agreement by which a person takes out a loan using as security real property (usually a house which is being purchased). **2** an amount of money borrowed or lent under such an agreement. > *verb* transfer the title to (a property) to a creditor as security for the payment of a loan.
ORIGIN – Old French, 'dead pledge'.

mortgagee > *noun* the lender in a mortgage.

mortgagor > *noun* the borrower in a mortgage.

mortician > *noun* chiefly N. Amer. an undertaker.

mortify > *verb* (**mortifies, mortified**) **1** cause to feel embarrassed or humiliated. **2** subdue (physical urges) by self-denial or discipline. **3** be affected by gangrene or necrosis.
DERIVATIVES – **mortification** *noun* **mortifying** *adjective.*
SYNONYMS – **1** abash, discomfit, embarrass, humiliate, shame. **2** control, restrain, subjugate, suppress.

mortise /**mor**tiss/ (also **mortice**) > *noun* a hole or recess designed to receive a corresponding projection (a tenon) so that the two are held together. > *verb* **1** join by a mortise and tenon. **2** cut a mortise in.
COMBINATIONS – **mortise lock** a lock set into the framework of a door in a recess or mortise.
ORIGIN – Old French *mortaise.*

mortuary > *noun* (pl. **mortuaries**) a room or building in which dead bodies are kept until burial or cremation. > *adjective* relating to burial or tombs.
ORIGIN – from Latin *mortuus* 'dead': originally denoting a gift claimed by a parish priest from a deceased person's estate, later meaning 'a funeral'.

morwong > *noun* a brightly coloured marine fish of Australian waters.
ORIGIN – probably from an Aboriginal language.

Mosaic > *adjective* of or associated with the biblical Hebrew prophet Moses.

mosaic > *noun* a picture or pattern produced by arranging together small variously coloured pieces of stone, tile, or glass.
DERIVATIVES – **mosaicist** *noun.*
COMBINATIONS – **mosaic disease** a virus disease that causes mottled leaves in tobacco and other plants.
ORIGIN – French *mosaïque,* from Latin *musium* 'decoration with small square stones', perhaps ultimately from Greek *mousa* 'a muse'.

mosasaur /**mō**zəsawr/ > *noun* a large fossil marine reptile with paddle-like limbs and a long flattened tail.
ORIGIN – from *Mosa,* the Latin name for the river Meuse (near which it was first discovered) + Greek *sauros* 'lizard'.

Moselle /mō**zel**/ (also **Mosel**) > *noun* a light medium-dry white wine from the valley of the River Moselle in Germany.

Moses basket > *noun* a carrycot or small portable cot made of wickerwork.
ORIGIN – with allusion to the biblical story of Moses being left in a basket among the bulrushes (Book of Exodus).

mosey informal > *verb* (**moseys, moseyed**) walk or move in a leisurely manner. > *noun* a leisurely walk.

mosh > *verb* informal dance to rock music in a violent manner involving jumping up and down and deliberately colliding with other dancers.

Moslem > *noun & adjective* variant spelling of **Muslim**.

mosque > *noun* a building used by Muslims for worship.
ORIGIN – French, from Arabic.

mosquito > *noun* (pl. **mosquitoes**) a small, slender fly, some kinds of which transmit parasitic diseases through the bite of the bloodsucking female.
WORDFINDER – *kinds of mosquito:* anopheles (*carrying malaria*), culex; dengue, filariasis, malaria, St Louis encephalitis, yellow fever (*diseases transmitted by mosquitoes*).
COMBINATIONS – **mosquito net** a fine net hung across a door or window or around a bed to keep mosquitoes away.
ORIGIN – Spanish and Portuguese, 'little fly'.

moss > *noun* **1** a small flowerless green plant which grows in low carpets or rounded cushions in damp habitats and reproduces by means of spores. **2** Scottish & N. English a peat bog.
DERIVATIVES – **mossy** *adjective*.
COMBINATIONS – **moss agate** agate with moss-like markings. **moss stitch** alternate plain and purl stitches in knitting.

most > *determiner & pronoun* **1** greatest in amount or degree. **2** the majority of. > *adverb* **1** to the greatest extent. **2** forming the superlative of adjectives and adverbs. **3** very. **4** N. Amer. informal almost.
IDIOMS – **at (the) most** not more than. **for the most part** in most cases; usually. **make the most of** use or represent to the best advantage.
COMBINATIONS – **Most Honourable** (in the UK) a title given to marquesses, members of the Privy Council, and holders of the Order of the Bath. **Most Reverend** the title of an Anglican archbishop or an Irish Roman Catholic bishop.

-most > *suffix* forming superlative adjectives and adverbs from prepositions and other words indicating relative position: *innermost*.

mostly > *adverb* **1** on the whole; mainly. **2** usually.
SYNONYMS – **1** chiefly, largely, mainly, predominantly, principally.

MOT > *noun* (in the UK) a compulsory annual test of motor vehicles of more than a specified age.
ORIGIN – abbreviation of *Ministry of Transport*.

mote > *noun* a tiny piece of a substance; a speck.

motel > *noun* a roadside hotel for motorists.

motet /mōtet/ > *noun* a short piece of sacred choral music.
ORIGIN – Old French, 'little word'.

moth > *noun* a chiefly nocturnal insect resembling a butterfly but holding its wings flat when at rest and generally having feathery antennae.
COMBINATIONS – **moth-eaten** damaged or apparently damaged by clothes moths; shabby or threadbare.

mothball > *noun* a small ball of naphthalene or camphor, placed among stored clothes to deter clothes moths. > *verb* **1** store (clothes) among or in mothballs. **2** put into storage or on hold indefinitely.
IDIOMS – **in mothballs** in storage or on hold.

mother > *noun* **1** a female parent. **2** (**Mother**) (especially as a title or form of address) the head of a female religious community. **3** informal an extreme or very large example of: *the mother of all traffic jams*. > *verb* look after kindly and protectively, sometimes excessively so.
DERIVATIVES – **motherhood** *noun* **motherless** *adjective*.
SYNONYMS – *verb* care for, cherish, coddle, nurse, nurture, pamper, spoil.
COMBINATIONS – **motherboard** a printed circuit board containing the main components of a microcomputer. **mother country** a country in relation to its colonies. **Mothering Sunday** Brit. the fourth Sunday in Lent, traditionally a day for honouring one's mother. **mother-in-law** (pl. **mothers-in-law**) the mother of one's husband or wife. **Mother Superior** the head of a female religious community. **mother lode** a principal vein of an ore or mineral. **mother-of-pearl** a smooth pearly substance lining the shells of oysters, abalones, and certain other molluscs. **Mother's Day** a day of the year on which children honour their mothers (in Britain Mothering Sunday, and in North America the second Sunday in May). **mother's ruin** Brit. informal gin. **mother tongue** a person's native language.

motherland > *noun* one's native country.

motherly > *adjective* of or characteristic of a mother, especially in being caring, protective, and kind.
DERIVATIVES – **motherliness** *noun*.

motif /mōteef/ > *noun* **1** a single or repeated image forming a design. **2** a dominant or recurrent theme in an artistic, musical, or literary work. **3** a decorative device applied to a garment or textile.
SYNONYMS – **1** device, emblem, figure, logo. **2** hook, leitmotif, refrain, theme.
ORIGIN – French.

motile /mōtīl/ > *adjective* (of cells, gametes, and single-celled organisms) capable of motion.
DERIVATIVES – **motility** *noun*.

motion > *noun* **1** the action of moving. **2** a movement or gesture. **3** a piece of moving mechanism. **4** a formal proposal put to a legislature or committee. **5** Brit. an emptying of the bowels. **6** Brit. a piece of excrement. > *verb* direct (someone) with a gesture.
WORDFINDER – kinetic (*of or relating to motion*); impetus, momentum (*energy associated with motion*), inertia (*tendency to remain in motion or motionless*).
IDIOMS – **go through the motions** do something in a perfunctory way.
DERIVATIVES – **motional** *adjective* **motionless** *adjective*.
SYNONYMS – *verb* signal, steer, wave.
COMBINATIONS – **motion picture** chiefly N. Amer. a cinema film.
ORIGIN – Latin, from *movere* 'to move'.

motivate > *verb* **1** provide with a motive for doing something: *he was motivated by the desire for profit*. **2** stimulate the interest of.
DERIVATIVES – **motivator** *noun*.
SYNONYMS – **1** drive, influence, inspire, move, prompt. **2** encourage, inspire, stimulate.

motivation > *noun* **1** the reason or reasons behind one's actions or behaviour. **2** desire and willingness to do something.
DERIVATIVES – **motivational** *adjective*.
SYNONYMS – **1** grounds, impulse, incentive, rationale. **2** determination, drive, eagerness, enthusiasm, keenness.

motive > *noun* **1** a factor inducing a person to act in a particular way. **2** a motif. > *adjective* producing physical or mechanical motion.
DERIVATIVES – **motiveless** *adjective*.
SYNONYMS – *noun* **1** cause, impulse, incentive, inspiration, reason, stimulus.
COMBINATIONS – **motive power** the energy used to drive machinery.
ORIGIN – Latin *motivus*, from *movere* 'to move'.

mot juste /mō zhoost/ > *noun* (pl. **mots justes** pronunc. same) (**the mot juste**) the most appropriate word or expression.
ORIGIN – French, 'appropriate word'.

motley > *adjective* incongruously varied in appearance or character. > *noun* a varied mixture.

wordpower facts
Motley
In medieval times **motley** was a noun meaning 'cloth of mixed colours' and an adjective meaning 'multicoloured'. In the 16th century the noun came more specifically to refer to the costume worn by jesters, consisting of differently coloured sections; this sense gave rise to other uses of **motley** such as *a motley crew*.

motocross > *noun* cross-country racing on motorcycles.

motor > *noun* **1** a machine that supplies

motive power for a vehicle or other device. **2** Brit. informal a car. > *adjective* **1** giving or producing motion or action. **2** Physiology relating to muscular movement or the nerves activating it. > *verb* informal, chiefly Brit. travel in a car.

COMBINATIONS – **motorbike** a motorcycle. **motorboat** a boat powered by a motor. **motor car** chiefly Brit. a car. **motor drive** a battery-driven motor in a camera, used to wind the film rapidly between exposures. **motorman** the driver of a train or tram. **motor racing** the sport of racing in specially developed fast cars. **motor vehicle** a road vehicle powered by an internal-combustion engine.

ORIGIN – Latin, 'mover', from *movere* 'to move'.

motorcade > *noun* a procession of motor vehicles.

motorcycle > *noun* a two-wheeled vehicle that is powered by a motor.

WORDFINDER – chopper, dirt bike, moped, quad bike, scooter, trail bike (*types of motorcycle*).

DERIVATIVES – **motorcycling** *noun* **motorcyclist** *noun*.

motorist > *noun* the driver of a car.

motormouth > *noun* informal a person who talks rapidly and incessantly.

DERIVATIVES – **motormouthed** *adjective*.

motor neuron (also **motor neurone**) > *noun* a nerve cell forming part of a pathway along which impulses pass from the brain or spinal cord to a muscle or gland.

COMBINATIONS – **motor neuron disease** a progressive disease involving degeneration of the motor neurons and wasting of the muscles.

motorway > *noun* Brit. a road designed for fast traffic, typically with three lanes in each direction.

motte /mot/ > *noun* historical a mound forming the site of a castle or camp.

ORIGIN – French, 'mound'; related to MOAT.

mottle > *noun* a mottled marking.

mottled > *adjective* marked with patches of a different colour.

SYNONYMS – blotched, dappled, flecked, piebald, pied, speckled, variegated.

ORIGIN – probably from MOTLEY.

motto > *noun* (pl. **mottoes** or **mottos**) a short sentence or phrase encapsulating a belief or ideal.

SYNONYMS – adage, aphorism, epigram, maxim, saying.

ORIGIN – Italian, 'word'.

moue /mo͞o/ > *noun* a pout.

ORIGIN – French.

mouflon /mo͞oflon/ (also **moufflon**)

> *noun* a small wild sheep with chestnut-brown wool, found in mountainous country.

ORIGIN – French, from Italian *muflone*.

mould¹ (US **mold**) > *noun* **1** a hollow container used to give shape to molten or hot liquid material when it cools and hardens. **2** something made in this way, especially a jelly or mousse. **3** a distinctive type, style, or character. > *verb* **1** form (an object) out of a malleable substance. **2** give a shape to (a malleable substance). **3** influence the development of.

IDIOMS – **break the mould** end a restrictive pattern of events or behaviour by doing things differently.

SYNONYMS – *noun* **1** cast, die, matrix. *verb* **1** fashion, form, model, shape. **3** determine, direct, guide, influence, shape.

ORIGIN – probably from Old French *modle*, from Latin *modus* 'measure'.

mould² (US **mold**) > *noun* a furry growth of minute fungi occurring on organic matter in moist, warm conditions typically.

ORIGIN – probably from obsolete *moul* 'grow mouldy'.

mould³ (US **mold**) > *noun* chiefly Brit. soft, loose earth, especially when rich in organic matter.

COMBINATIONS – **mouldboard** the board or plate in a plough that turns the earth over.

ORIGIN – Old English, related to MEAL².

moulder (US **molder**) > *verb* slowly decay.

SYNONYMS – decay, decompose, disintegrate, putrefy, rot, spoil.

moulding (US **molding**) > *noun* a moulded strip of wood, stone, or plaster as a decorative architectural feature.

mouldy (US **moldy**) > *adjective* (**mouldier**, **mouldiest**) **1** covered with or smelling of mould. **2** informal boring or worthless.

DERIVATIVES – **mouldiness** *noun*.

SYNONYMS – **1** fusty, mildewed, musty, putrid.

moules marinière /mo͞ol marinyair/ (also **moules à la marinière**) > *plural noun* mussels served in their shells and cooked in a wine and onion sauce.

ORIGIN – French, 'mussels in the marine style'.

moult (US **molt**) > *verb* shed old feathers, hair, or skin to make way for a new growth. > *noun* a period of moulting.

ORIGIN – from Latin *mutare* 'to change'.

mound > *noun* **1** a raised mass of earth or other compacted material. **2** a small hill. **3** a heap or pile. > *verb* heap up into a mound.

SYNONYMS – *noun* **1** bank, barrow, dune, embankment, tumulus. **2** hillock, hummock, knoll, rise, tor. **3** heap, mountain, pile, stack.

mount¹ > *verb* **1** climb up or on to. **2** get up

on (an animal or bicycle) to ride it. **3** (**be mounted**) be on horseback; be provided with a horse. **4** increase in size, number, or intensity. **5** organise and initiate (something). **6** put or fix in place or on a support. **7** set in or attach (a picture) to a backing. > *noun* **1** (also **mounting**) something on which an object is mounted for support or display. **2** a horse used for riding.

IDIOMS – **mount guard** keep watch.

DERIVATIVES – **mountable** *adjective* **mounted** *adjective*.

SYNONYMS – *verb* **1** ascend, board, go up, scale. **4** escalate, grow, intensify, multiply, rise, soar. **5** arrange, initiate, launch, prepare, stage. **6** erect, install, position, secure, set. *noun* **1** backing, base, fixture, frame, setting, stand.

wordpower facts
Mount
The Latin word *mons*, meaning 'mountain', is the ultimate base of **mount** 'climb up on', **mount** 'mountain', and **mountain**. It is also the direct root of the adjective **montane** 'of or inhabiting mountains' and of the anatomical terms **mons pubis** and **mons veneris**.

mount² > *noun* archaic or in place names a mountain or hill.

mountain > *noun* **1** a mass of land rising abruptly and to a great height from the surrounding level. **2** a large pile or quantity. **3** a surplus stock of a commodity.

WORDFINDER – alpine (*of high mountains*), arête (*sharp mountain ridge*), cirque, corrie, or cwm (*steep-sided valley on mountainside*), col (*high mountain pass*), orogeny (*geological process of mountain building*), sierra or cordillera (*long mountain chain*), tarn (*mountain lake*).

IDIOMS – **if the mountain won't come to Muhammad, Muhammad must go to the mountain** proverb if someone won't do as you wish or a situation can't be arranged to suit you, you must accept it and change your plans accordingly. [ORIGIN – with allusion to a story about Muhammad told by Francis Bacon (*Essays* xii).] **move mountains** achieve spectacular and apparently impossible results.

SYNONYMS – **1** alp, mount, peak; Scottish ben. **2** heap, mass, mound, pile, stack. **3** excess, glut, oversupply, surfeit.

COMBINATIONS – **mountain ash** a rowan tree. **mountain bike** a sturdy bicycle with broad deep-treaded tyres and multiple gears, originally intended for riding on mountainous terrain. **mountain goat** a goat that lives on mountains, proverbial for its agility. **mountain lion** N. Amer. a puma.

mountaineering > *noun* the sport or activity of climbing mountains.

DERIVATIVES – **mountaineer** *noun*.

mountainous > *adjective* **1** having many mountains. **2** huge; enormous.

mountebank /**mown**tibangk/ > *noun* a swindler.

ORIGIN – first meaning 'a person who sold patent medicines in public places': from Italian *monta in banco!* 'climb on the bench!', with allusion to the platform used by mountebanks to attract an audience.

Mountie > *noun* informal a member of the Royal Canadian Mounted Police.

mourn > *verb* feel deep sorrow following the death or loss of.

SYNONYMS – bemoan, bewail, grieve for, lament, regret, rue.

mourner > *noun* a person who attends a funeral as a relative or friend of the dead person.

mournful > *adjective* feeling, showing, or causing sadness or grief.

DERIVATIVES – **mournfully** *adverb* **mournfulness** *noun*.

SYNONYMS – forlorn, melancholy, miserable, sad, sorrowful.

ANTONYMS – cheerful, joyful.

mourning > *noun* **1** the experience or expression of deep sorrow for a person who has died. **2** black clothes conventionally worn in a period of mourning.

mouse > *noun* (pl. **mice**) **1** a small rodent with a pointed snout, relatively large ears and eyes, and a long, thin tail. **2** a timid and quiet person. **3** (pl. also **mouses**) Computing a small hand-held device which controls cursor movements on a computer screen, with a button or buttons which are pressed to control functions. > *verb* hunt for or catch mice.

WORDFINDER – murine (*of or like a mouse*).

DERIVATIVES – **mouser** *noun*.

COMBINATIONS – **mousetrap 1** a trap for catching mice, traditionally baited with cheese. **2** Brit. informal poor-quality cheese.

moussaka /moosaakǝ/ > *noun* a Greek dish of minced lamb layered with aubergines and tomatoes and topped with a cheese sauce.

ORIGIN – Turkish, 'that which is fed liquid' (i.e. a dish to which liquid is added during cooking).

mousse > *noun* **1** a sweet or savoury dish made as a smooth, light mass in which the main ingredient is whipped with cream or egg white. **2** an aerated or light preparation for the skin or hair.

ORIGIN – French, 'moss or froth'.

mousseline /**moo**sleen/ > *noun* **1** a fine, semi-opaque fabric similar to muslin. **2** a soft, light mousse. **3** (also **sauce**

mousseline) hollandaise sauce made frothy with whipped cream or beaten egg white.

ORIGIN – French, related to MUSLIN.

moustache (US also **mustache**) > *noun* a strip of hair left to grow above a man's upper lip.

DERIVATIVES – **moustached** *adjective*.

ORIGIN – French, from Greek *mustax*.

mousy (also **mousey**) > *adjective* (**mousier, mousiest**) **1** of or like a mouse. **2** (of hair) of a dull, light brown colour. **3** timid and ineffectual.

mouth > *noun* **1** the opening in the body of most animals through which food is taken and sounds are emitted. **2** an opening or entrance to a structure that is hollow, concave, or almost completely enclosed. **3** the place where a river enters the sea. **4** informal impudent talk. > *verb* **1** move the lips as if to form (words). **2** say in an insincere or pompous way. **3** (**mouth off**) informal talk in an opinionated or abusive way. **4** take in or touch with the mouth.

WORDFINDER – oral, buccal (*of or relating to the mouth*); stomatology (*the study of the mouth*); epiglottis (*flap at the back of the mouth*), palate (*top of the mouth*), tonsil (*mass of tissue at the back of the mouth*), uvula (*fleshy part at the back of the mouth*).

IDIOMS – **be all mouth (and no trousers)** informal tend to talk boastfully but not to act on one's words. **keep one's mouth shut** informal say nothing, especially to avoid revealing a secret.

COMBINATIONS – **mouthbrooder** a freshwater fish which protects its eggs (and in some cases its young) by carrying them in its mouth. **mouth organ** a harmonica. **mouthpart** any of the appendages surrounding the mouth of an insect or other arthropod and adapted for feeding. **mouth-to-mouth** (of artificial respiration) in which a person breathes into someone's lungs through their mouth. **mouthwash** an antiseptic liquid for rinsing the mouth or gargling. **mouth-watering 1** smelling or looking delicious. **2** very attractive or tempting.

mouthful > *noun* **1** a quantity of food or drink that fills or can be put in the mouth. **2** a long or complicated word or phrase.

IDIOMS – **give someone a mouthful** Brit. informal talk to someone in an angry or abusive way.

SYNONYMS – **1** bite, gulp, morsel, spoonful, swallow.

mouthpiece > *noun* **1** a part of a musical instrument, telephone, etc. that is designed to be put in or against the mouth. **2** a person or publication expressing the views of another person or an organisation.

mouthy > *adjective* (**mouthier, mouthiest**) informal inclined to talk a lot, especially in an impudent way.

movable (also **moveable**) > *adjective* **1** capable of being moved. **2** (of a religious feast day) occurring on a different date each year. **3** Law (of property) of the nature of a chattel, as distinct from land or buildings.

SYNONYMS – **1** ambulatory, mobile, portable, transportable.

move > *verb* **1** go or cause to go in a specified direction or manner. **2** change or cause to change position. **3** change one's place of residence. **4** change from one state, sphere, or activity to another. **5** take or cause to take action. **6** make progress. **7** provoke compassion, affection, or other feelings in. **8** propose for discussion and resolution at a meeting or legislative assembly. **9** empty (the bowels). > *noun* **1** an instance of moving. **2** an action taken towards achieving a purpose. **3** a manoeuvre in a sport or game. **4** a player's turn during a board game.

IDIOMS – **get a move on** informal hurry up. **make a move 1** take action. **2** Brit. set off; leave a place. **make a move on** (or **put the moves on**) informal make a proposition of a sexual nature to. **move in** (or **out**) start (or cease) living or working in a place. **move in/within** be socially active in (a particular sphere) or among (a particular group).

DERIVATIVES – **mover** *noun*.

SYNONYMS – *verb* **1** advance, lead, migrate, proceed, progress, travel. **2** carry, manoeuvre, shift, switch, transfer, transport. **4** alter, convert, modify, shift, vary. **5** act, initiate, instigate, mount, take steps. **7** affect, disturb, shake, stir, touch, upset. **8** advocate, put forward, recommend, submit, suggest. *noun* **1** action, gesture, motion, movement. **2** initiative, measure, step, stratagem, tactic.

wordpower facts

Move

The Latin word *movere*, meaning 'to move', is the source of a wide range of English words, including **emotion**, **mobile**, **momentum**, **motion**, **motive**, **motor**, **promote**, and **move** itself. See box at EMOTION.

movement > *noun* **1** an act of moving. **2** the process of moving or the state of being moved. **3** a group of people working to advance a shared cause. **4** a series of organised actions to advance a shared cause. **5** a trend or development. **6** (**movements**) a person's activities during a particular period of time. **7** Music a principal division of a musical work. **8** the moving parts of a mechanism, especially a clock or watch.

SYNONYMS – **1** action, gesture, manoeuvre, motion, move. **2** conveyance, motion, relocation, transfer, transportation. **3** coalition, faction, front, grouping, organisation, party, wing. **4** campaign, crusade, drive, push. **5** change, drift, growth, progression, swing, tendency.

movie > *noun* chiefly N. Amer. **1** a cinema film. **2** (**the movies**) films generally.

moving > *adjective* **1** in motion. **2** arousing strong emotion.
DERIVATIVES – **movingly** *adverb*.

mow > *verb* (past participle **mowed** or **mown**) **1** cut down or trim (grass or a cereal crop) with a machine or scythe. **2** (**mow down**) kill by gunfire or by knocking down with a motor vehicle.
DERIVATIVES – **mower** *noun*.

moxa > *noun* a downy substance obtained from the dried leaves of an Asian plant, burnt on or near the skin in Eastern medicine as a counterirritant.
ORIGIN – from Japanese *moe kusa* 'burning herb'.

moxibustion /moksi**bus**chən/ > *noun* (in Eastern medicine) the burning of moxa as a counterirritant.

Mozambican /mōzam**bee**kən/ > *noun* a person from Mozambique. > *adjective* relating to Mozambique.

Mozartian /mōt**zaar**tiən/ > *adjective* relating to the Austrian composer Wolfgang Amadeus Mozart (1756–91).

mozzarella /motsə**rell**ə/ > *noun* a firm white Italian cheese made from buffalo's or cow's milk.
ORIGIN – Italian, from *mozzare* 'cut off'.

mozzie (also **mossie**) > *noun* (pl. **mozzies**) informal, chiefly Austral./NZ a mosquito.

MP > *abbreviation* **1** Member of Parliament. **2** military police.

MPD > *abbreviation* multiple personality disorder.

mpg > *abbreviation* miles per gallon.

mph > *abbreviation* miles per hour.

MPhil > *abbreviation* Master of Philosophy.

MPV > *abbreviation* multi-purpose vehicle.

Mr > *noun* **1** a title used before a man's surname or full name. **2** a title used to address the male holder of an office.
ORIGIN – abbreviation of MASTER.

MRI > *abbreviation* magnetic resonance imaging.

Mrs > *noun* a title used before a married woman's surname or full name.
ORIGIN – abbreviation of MISTRESS.

Mrs Grundy > *noun* (pl. **Mrs Grundys**) a person with very conventional standards of propriety.
ORIGIN – a person repeatedly mentioned in T. Morton's comedy *Speed the Plough* (1798).

MS > *abbreviation* **1** manuscript. **2** Mississippi. **3** multiple sclerosis.

Ms > *noun* a title used before the surname or full name of a woman regardless of her marital status (a neutral alternative to **Mrs** or **Miss**).

MSc > *abbreviation* Master of Science.

MS-DOS > *abbreviation* Computing, trademark Microsoft disk operating system.

MSG > *abbreviation* monosodium glutamate.

Msgr > *abbreviation* **1** Monseigneur. **2** Monsignor.

MSP > *abbreviation* Member of the Scottish Parliament.

MT > *abbreviation* Montana.

Mt > *abbreviation* (in place names) Mount. > *symbol* the chemical element meitnerium.

MTB > *abbreviation* **1** Brit. motor torpedo boat. **2** mountain bike.

mu /myoo/ > *noun* the twelfth letter of the Greek alphabet (**M**, **μ**), transliterated as 'm'. > *symbol* (**μ**) 'micro-' in abbreviations for units, e.g. μg for microgram.
ORIGIN – Greek.

much > *determiner & pronoun* (**more**, **most**) **1** a large amount. **2** used to indicate that someone or something is a poor specimen: *I'm not much of a gardener.* > *adverb* **1** to a great extent; a great deal. **2** for a large part of one's time; often.
IDIOMS – **a bit much** informal somewhat excessive or unreasonable. (**as**) **much as** even though. **so much the better** (or **worse**) that is even better (or worse). **too much** too difficult or exhausting to tolerate.

muchness > *noun* (in phrase (**much**) **of a muchness**) very similar.

mucilage /**myoo**silij/ > *noun* **1** a viscous secretion or bodily fluid. **2** a viscous or gelatinous solution extracted from plants, used in medicines and adhesives.
DERIVATIVES – **mucilaginous** /myooossi**laj**inəss/ *adjective*.
ORIGIN – Latin *mucilago* 'musty juice'.

muck > *noun* **1** dirt or rubbish. **2** manure. > *verb* **1** (**muck up**) informal spoil. **2** (**muck about** or **around**) Brit. informal behave in a silly or aimless way. **3** (**muck about** or **around with**) Brit. informal interfere with. **4** (**muck in**) Brit. informal take one's share of the tasks or the accommodation. **5** (**muck out**) chiefly Brit. remove manure and other dirt from (a stable).
IDIOMS – **Lord** (or **Lady**) **Muck** Brit. informal a socially pretentious man (or woman). **where there's muck there's brass** proverb dirty or unpleasant activities are also lucrative.
SYNONYMS – *noun* **1** dirt, filth, grime, mess, mud, rubbish.
COMBINATIONS – **muckraking** the action of searching out and publicising scandal about famous people. [ORIGIN – coined by President Theodore Roosevelt in a speech alluding to the man with the *muck rake* in John Bunyan's *Pilgrim's Progress*.]

mucker > *noun* Brit. informal a friend or companion.

muckle > *noun & adjective* variant form of MICKLE.

mucky > *adjective* (**muckier**, **muckiest**) **1** covered with or consisting of muck; dirty. **2** sordid or indecent.
SYNONYMS – **1** dirty, filthy, foul, grimy, muddy, soiled.

mucosa /myoo**kō**sə/ > *noun* (pl. **mucosae** /myoo**kō**see/) a mucous membrane.

mucous > *adjective* relating to or covered with mucus.
COMBINATIONS – **mucous membrane** a mucus-secreting tissue lining many body cavities and tubular organs, including the respiratory passages.

mucus > *noun* **1** a slimy substance secreted by the mucous membranes and glands of animals for lubrication, protection, etc. **2** mucilage from plants.
ORIGIN – Latin, related to Greek *mussesthai* 'blow the nose', *mukter* 'nose, nostril'.

mud > *noun* **1** soft, sticky matter consisting of mixed earth and water. **2** damaging information or allegations.
IDIOMS – **drag through the mud** slander or criticise publicly. (**here's**) **mud in your eye!** informal used as a toast. **one's name is mud** informal one is in disgrace or unpopular.
COMBINATIONS – **mudbank** a bank of mud on the bed of a river or the bottom of the sea. **mudbath 1** a bath in the mud of mineral springs, taken to relieve rheumatic complaints. **2** a muddy place. **mudflap** a flap hung behind the wheel of a vehicle to protect against mud and stones thrown up from the road. **mudflat** a stretch of muddy land left uncovered at low tide. **mudguard** a curved strip fitted over a wheel of a bicycle or motorcycle to protect against water and dirt thrown up from the road. **mud pack** a paste applied to the face to improve the condition of the skin. **mudslinging** informal the casting of insults and accusations. **mudstone** a dark sedimentary rock formed from consolidated mud.

muddle > *verb* **1** bring into a disordered or confusing state. **2** confuse or perplex (someone). **3** (**muddle up**) confuse (two or more things) with each other. **4** (**muddle along** or **through**) cope more or less satisfactorily. > *noun* a muddled state.
DERIVATIVES – **muddled** *adjective* **muddly** *adjective*.
SYNONYMS – *verb* **1** jumble, scramble, tangle. **2** baffle, bewilder, confuse, perplex. **4** (**muddle along** or **through**) get by, make do, manage. *noun* confusion, disarray, disorder, jumble.
COMBINATIONS – **muddle-headed** disorganised or confused.

ORIGIN – first used in the sense 'wallow in mud', perhaps from Dutch *modden* 'dabble in mud'.

muddy > *adjective* (**muddier**, **muddiest**) **1** covered in or full of mud. **2** clouded; not bright or clear. > *verb* (**muddies**, **muddied**) **1** cause to become muddy. **2** make unclear.
SYNONYMS – *adjective* **1** claggy, dirty, mucky.

mudlark (also **mudlarker**) > *noun* a person who scavenges in river mud for objects of value.

mudskipper > *noun* a small goby of tropical mangrove swamps which is able to move around out of water.

muesli /**myoo̅z**li/ > *noun* (pl. **mueslis**) a mixture of oats and other cereals, dried fruit, and nuts, eaten with milk at breakfast.
ORIGIN – Swiss German.

muezzin /moo̅**ezz**in/ > *noun* a man who calls Muslims to prayer from the minaret of a mosque.
ORIGIN – from an Arabic word meaning 'proclaim'.

muff¹ > *noun* **1** a short tube made of fur or other warm material into which the hands are placed for warmth. **2** vulgar slang a woman's genitals.
ORIGIN – Dutch *mof*.

muff² informal > *verb* handle clumsily; bungle. > *noun* a mistake or failure, especially a failure to catch a ball cleanly.

muffin > *noun* **1** (N. Amer. **English muffin**) a thick, flattened bread roll made from yeast dough and eaten split, toasted, and buttered. **2** chiefly N. Amer. a small domed cake.

muffle > *verb* **1** wrap or cover for warmth. **2** make (a sound) quieter or less distinct by covering its source.
SYNONYMS – **1** cloak, swaddle, swathe. **2** smother, stifle, suppress.
ORIGIN – from Old French *moufle* 'thick glove'.

muffler > *noun* **1** a wrap or scarf worn around the neck and face. **2** a device for deadening the sound of a drum or other instrument. **3** N. Amer. a silencer for a motor vehicle exhaust.

mufti¹ /**muf**ti/ > *noun* (pl. **muftis**) a Muslim legal expert empowered to give rulings on religious matters.
ORIGIN – from an Arabic verb meaning 'decide a point of law'.

mufti² /**muf**ti/ > *noun* civilian clothes when worn by military or police staff.
ORIGIN – perhaps formed humorously from **MUFTI¹**.

mug¹ > *noun* **1** a large cylindrical cup with a handle. **2** informal a person's face. **3** Brit. informal a stupid or gullible person. **4** US informal a hoodlum or thug. > *verb* (**mugged**,

mugging) **1** attack and rob (someone) in a public place. **2** informal make faces before an audience or a camera.
IDIOMS – **a mug's game** informal an activity likely to be unsuccessful or dangerous.
COMBINATIONS – **mugshot** informal a photograph of a person's face made for an official purpose, especially police records.

mug² > *verb* (**mugged**, **mugging**) (**mug up**) Brit. informal learn or study (a subject) quickly and intensively, especially for an exam.

mugger¹ > *noun* a person who attacks and robs another in a public place.

mugger² > *noun* a large short-snouted Indian crocodile, venerated by many Hindus.
ORIGIN – Hindi.

muggins > *noun* (pl. same or **mugginses**) Brit. informal a foolish and gullible person.

muggy > *adjective* (**muggier**, **muggiest**) (of the weather) unpleasantly warm and humid.
SYNONYMS – close, oppressive, sultry.
ORIGIN – from dialect *mug* 'mist, drizzle'.

Mughal > *noun* variant spelling of **MOGUL**.

mugwort > *noun* a plant with aromatic divided leaves that are dark green above and whitish below.
ORIGIN – Old English, from the base of **MIDGE**.

mugwump > *noun* N. Amer. a person who remains aloof or independent, especially from party politics.
ORIGIN – Algonquian, 'great chief'.

Muhammadan /mə**hamm**ədən/ (also **Mohammedan**) > *noun & adjective* archaic term for **MUSLIM** (not favoured by Muslims).
ORIGIN – from the name of the Arab prophet and founder of Islam *Muhammad*.

mujahedin /moo̅jaahi**deen**/ (also **mujaheddin**, **mujahideen**) > *plural noun* Islamic guerrilla fighters.
ORIGIN – Persian and Arabic, 'people who fight a holy war'.

mukluk /**muk**luk/ > *noun* N. Amer. a high, soft sealskin boot worn in the American Arctic.
ORIGIN – Yupik, 'bearded seal'.

mulatto /myoo**latt**ō/ > *noun* (pl. **mulattoes** or **mulattos**) a person with one white and one black parent. > *adjective* relating to such a person.
ORIGIN – Spanish *mulato* 'young mule, mulatto'.

mulberry > *noun* **1** a tree bearing a dark red or white fruit which resembles the loganberry. **2** a dark red or purple colour.
ORIGIN – Latin *morum* 'mulberry'.

mulch > *noun* a mass of leaves, bark, or compost spread around or over a plant for protection or to enrich the soil. > *verb* cover with or apply mulch.

ORIGIN – probably from dialect *mulch* 'soft'.

mulct /mulkt/ formal > *verb* extract money from (someone) by fining or taxing them or by fraudulent means. > *noun* a fine or compulsory payment.
ORIGIN – from Latin *mulcta* 'a fine'.

mule¹ > *noun* **1** the offspring of a male donkey and a female horse, typically sterile. **2** a hybrid plant or animal, especially a sterile one. **3** a stupid or obstinate person. **4** (also **spinning mule**) historical a kind of spinning machine producing yarn on spindles. **5** informal a courier for illegal drugs.
COMBINATIONS – **mule deer** a North American deer with long ears and black markings on the tail.
ORIGIN – Latin *mulus, mula*.

mule² > *noun* a slipper or light shoe without a back.
ORIGIN – French, 'slipper'.

muleteer /myoo̅li**teer**/ > *noun* a person who drives mules.

mulga /**mul**gə/ > *noun* **1** a small Australian acacia tree or shrub, which forms dense scrubby growth and is also grown for its wood. **2** (**the mulga**) Austral. informal the outback.
ORIGIN – from an Aboriginal language.

muliebrity /myoo̅li**ebri**ti/ > *noun* formal womanly qualities; womanhood.
ORIGIN – from Latin *mulier* 'woman'.

mulish > *adjective* stubborn (like a mule).
SYNONYMS – intractable, intransigent, obstinate, recalcitrant, stubborn.

mull¹ > *verb* (**mull over**) think about at length.
SYNONYMS – (**mull over**) cogitate on, ponder, ruminate over.

mull² > *verb* warm (wine or beer) and add sugar and spices to it.

mull³ > *noun* (in Scottish place names) a promontory.

mull⁴ > *noun* humus formed under non-acid conditions.
ORIGIN – Danish *muld* 'soil'.

mull⁵ > *noun* a thin muslin used in bookbinding for joining the spine of a book to its cover.
ORIGIN – Hindi.

mullah /**mull**ə/ > *noun* a Muslim learned in Islamic theology and sacred law.
ORIGIN – Arabic.

mullein /**mull**in/ > *noun* a plant with woolly leaves and tall spikes of yellow flowers.
ORIGIN – Celtic.

muller /**mull**ər/ > *noun* a stone used for grinding materials such as artists' pigments.
ORIGIN – perhaps from Old French *moldre* 'to grind'.

mullet > *noun* any of various chiefly marine fish that are widely caught for food.
ORIGIN – Greek *mullos*.

mulligatawny /mulligə**taw**ni/ > *noun* a spicy meat soup originally made in India.
ORIGIN – Tamil, 'pepper water'.

mullion > *noun* a vertical bar between the panes of glass in a window.
DERIVATIVES – **mullioned** *adjective*.
ORIGIN – probably an altered form of *monial*, from Old French *moinel* 'middle'.

mullock > *noun* **1** Austral./NZ or dialect rubbish or nonsense. **2** Austral./NZ rock which contains no gold or from which gold has been extracted.
ORIGIN – from *mull* 'dust, rubbish', from Dutch.

mulloway > *noun* a large edible predatory fish of Australian coastal waters.
ORIGIN – from an Aboriginal language.

multi- > *combining form* more than one; many: *multicultural*.
ORIGIN – from Latin *multus* 'much, many'.

multicast > *verb* (past and past participle **multicast**) send (data) across a computer network to several users at the same time. > *noun* a set of multicast data.

multicoloured (also **multicolour**; US **multicolored**, **multicolor**) > *adjective* having many colours.

multicultural > *adjective* relating to or constituting several cultural or ethnic groups.
DERIVATIVES – **multiculturalism** *noun* **multiculturalist** *noun & adjective*.

multidisciplinary > *adjective* involving several academic disciplines or professional specialisations.

multifaceted > *adjective* having many facets or aspects.

multifarious /multi**fair**iəss/ > *adjective* having great variety and diversity; many and varied.
SYNONYMS – diverse, eclectic, manifold.
ORIGIN – Latin *multifarius*.

multiform > *adjective* existing in many forms or kinds.

multigym > *noun* an apparatus on which a number of exercises can be performed.

multihull > *noun* a boat with two or more, especially three, hulls.

multilateral > *adjective* involving three or more participants.
DERIVATIVES – **multilateralism** *noun* **multilaterally** *adverb*.

multilingual > *adjective* in or using several languages.

multimedia > *adjective* using more than one medium of expression or communication. > *noun* Computing an extension of hypertext allowing audio and video material to be accessed.

multimillion > *adjective* consisting of several million.

multimillionaire > *noun* a person with assets worth several million pounds or dollars.

multinational > *adjective* **1** including or involving several countries or nationalities. **2** operating in several countries. > *noun* a company operating in several countries.
DERIVATIVES – **multinationally** *adverb*.

multi-occupation > *noun* the occupation of a building by a number of independent individuals or groups, typically tenants.

multiparty > *adjective* of or involving several political parties.

multiphase > *adjective* **1** in or relating to more than one phase. **2** (of an electrical device or circuit) polyphase.

multiple > *adjective* **1** having or involving several parts or elements. **2** numerous and varied. **3** (of a disease or injury) complex in its nature or effect; affecting several parts of the body. > *noun* **1** a number that may be divided by another a certain number of times without a remainder. **2** chiefly Brit. a shop with several branches.
SYNONYMS – *adjective* **1,2** diverse, eclectic, manifold, multifarious.
COMBINATIONS – **multiple-choice** (of a question in an examination) accompanied by several possible answers, from which the candidate must choose the correct one. **multiple sclerosis** see SCLEROSIS. **multiple unit** a passenger train of two or more carriages powered by integral motors.
ORIGIN – Latin *multiplus*.

multiplex > *adjective* **1** consisting of many elements in a complex relationship. **2** (of a cinema) having several separate screens within one building. **3** involving simultaneous transmission of several messages along a single channel of communication. > *noun* **1** a multiplex system or signal. **2** a multiplex cinema.

multiplicand /multipli**kand**/ > *noun* a quantity which is to be multiplied by another (the multiplier).

multiplication > *noun* **1** the process of multiplying. **2** Mathematics the process of combining matrices, vectors, or other quantities under specific rules to obtain their product.
COMBINATIONS – **multiplication sign** the sign ×, used to indicate that one quantity is to be multiplied by another. **multiplication table** a list of multiples of a particular number, typically from 1 to 12.

multiplicative /multi**plikk**ətiv/ > *noun* subject to or of the nature of multiplication.

multiplicity > *noun* (pl. **multiplicities**) a large number or variety.

SYNONYMS – abundance, mass, plurality, profusion.

multiplier > *noun* **1** a quantity by which a given number (the multiplicand) is to be multiplied. **2** a device for increasing the intensity of an electric current, force, etc. to a measurable level.

multiply¹ /**mul**tiplī/ > *verb* (**multiplies**, **multiplied**) **1** obtain from (a number) another which contains the first number a specified number of times. **2** increase in number or quantity. **3** increase in number by reproducing.
SYNONYMS – **2** burgeon, grow, proliferate. **3** breed, procreate, propagate.

multiply² /**mul**tipli/ > *adverb* in different ways or respects.

multipolar > *adjective* **1** having many poles or extremities. **2** polarised in several ways or directions.
DERIVATIVES – **multipolarity** *noun*.

multiprocessing (also **multiprogramming**) > *noun* Computing another term for MULTITASKING.

multiprocessor > *noun* a computer with more than one central processor.

multi-purpose > *adjective* having several purposes.

multiracial > *adjective* consisting of or relating to people of many races.

multi-storey > *adjective* (of a building) having several storeys. > *noun* Brit. informal a multi-storey car park.

multitasking > *noun* Computing the execution of more than one program or task simultaneously.

multi-track > *adjective* relating to or made by the mixing of several separately recorded tracks of sound. > *verb* record using multi-track recording.

multitude > *noun* **1** a large number of people or things. **2** (**the multitude**) the mass of ordinary people.
SYNONYMS – **1** abundance, horde, host. **2** (**the multitude**) hoi polloi, the public, the rank and file.
ORIGIN – Latin *multitudo*, from *multus* 'many'.

multitudinous /multi**tyōō**dinəss/ > *adjective* **1** very numerous. **2** consisting of many individuals or elements.
SYNONYMS – **1** abundant, innumerable, profuse. **2** diverse, eclectic, multifarious.

multivalent /multi**vay**lənt/ > *adjective* having many applications, interpretations, or values.

multum in parvo /**mooltəm** in **paar**vō/ > *noun* a great deal in a small space.
ORIGIN – Latin, 'much in little'.

mum¹ > *noun* Brit. informal one's mother.

mum² > *adjective* (**keep mum**) informal remain silent so as not to reveal a secret.

IDIOMS – **mum's the word** do not reveal the secret.

ORIGIN – imitative of a sound made with closed lips.

mumble > *verb* **1** say something indistinctly and quietly. **2** bite or chew with toothless gums. > *noun* a quiet and indistinct utterance.

SYNONYMS – **1** murmur, mutter.

ORIGIN – from **MUM²**.

mumbo-jumbo > *noun* informal language or ritual causing or intended to cause confusion or bewilderment.

ORIGIN – from *Mumbo Jumbo*, the supposed name of an African idol.

mummer > *noun* **1** an actor in a traditional English folk play typically featuring Saint George and involving miraculous resurrection. **2** archaic or derogatory an actor in the theatre.

DERIVATIVES – **mumming** *noun*.

ORIGIN – Old French *momeur*, from *momer* 'act in a mime'.

mummery > *noun* (pl. **mummeries**) **1** a performance by mummers. **2** ridiculous ceremony.

mummify > *verb* (**mummifies**, **mummified**) **1** (especially in ancient Egypt) preserve (a body) as a mummy. **2** dry up (a body) and so preserve it.

DERIVATIVES – **mummification** *noun*.

mummy¹ > *noun* (pl. **mummies**) Brit. informal one's mother.

mummy² > *noun* (pl. **mummies**) (especially in ancient Egypt) a body that has been preserved for burial by embalming and wrapping in bandages.

ORIGIN – Arabic, 'embalmed body', perhaps from a Persian word meaning 'wax'.

mumps > *plural noun* (treated as sing.) an infectious disease spread by a virus, causing swelling of the salivary glands at the sides of the face.

ORIGIN – from obsolete *mump* 'grimace'.

mumsy Brit. informal > *adjective* (of a woman) homely and unfashionable. > *noun* chiefly humorous one's mother.

munch > *verb* eat steadily and audibly.

SYNONYMS – champ, chomp.

ORIGIN – imitative of the sound of eating.

Munchausen's syndrome /munsh-owz'nz/ > *noun* Psychiatry a mental disorder in which a person pretends to be ill so as to obtain medical attention.

ORIGIN – from the name of Baron *Munchausen*, the hero of a book of fantastic tales written in English by a German, Rudolph Raspe (1785).

munchies > *plural noun* informal **1** snacks or small items of food. **2** (**the munchies**) a sudden strong desire for food.

mundane /mundayn/ > *adjective* **1** lacking interest or excitement. **2** of this earthly world rather than a heavenly or spiritual one.

DERIVATIVES – **mundanely** *adverb* **mundaneness** *noun* **mundanity** *noun*.

SYNONYMS – **1** boring, commonplace, dull, monotonous.

ANTONYMS – **1** exciting, extraordinary.

ORIGIN – from Latin *mundus* 'world'.

mung bean > *noun* a small round green bean grown in the tropics, chiefly as a source of bean sprouts.

ORIGIN – Hindi.

municipal /myoonissip'l, myoonisip'l/ > *adjective* relating to a municipality.

DERIVATIVES – **municipally** *adverb*.

ORIGIN – Latin *municipalis*, from *municipium* 'free city' + *capere* 'take'.

municipality > *noun* (pl. **municipalities**) a town or district that has local government.

munificent /myooniffis'nt/ > *adjective* very generous.

DERIVATIVES – **munificence** *noun* **munificently** *adverb*.

SYNONYMS – bountiful, lavish, unstinting.

ANTONYMS – mean, miserly.

ORIGIN – Latin *munificus*, from *munus* 'gift'.

muniments /myoonimənts/ > *plural noun* chiefly Law title deeds or other documents proving a person's ownership of land.

ORIGIN – Latin *munimentum* 'defence', later 'title deed', from *munire* 'fortify'.

munitions > *plural noun* military weapons, ammunition, equipment, and stores.

ORIGIN – Latin, from *munire* 'fortify'.

Munro > *noun* (pl. **Munros**) any of the 277 mountains in Scotland that are at least 3,000 feet high (approximately 914 metres).

ORIGIN – named after Sir Hugh Thomas *Munro*, who published a list of these mountains in 1891.

muntjac /muntjak/ > *noun* a small SE Asian deer with a doglike bark and small tusks, now naturalised in England.

ORIGIN – Sundanese (a language of Java).

muon /myooon/ > *noun* Physics an unstable meson with a mass around 200 times that of the electron.

ORIGIN – contraction of the earlier name *mu-meson*.

mural > *noun* a painting executed directly on a wall. > *adjective* **1** of or relating to a wall. **2** relating to the painting of murals.

ORIGIN – from Latin *murus* 'wall'.

murder > *noun* **1** the unlawful premeditated killing of one person by another. **2** informal a very difficult or unpleasant situation or experience. > *verb* **1** kill unlawfully and with premeditation. **2** informal spoil by poor performance. **3** informal, chiefly Brit. consume (food or drink) with relish.

IDIOMS – **get away with murder** informal regularly succeed in doing outrageous things without being punished. **murder will out** murder cannot remain undetected. **scream blue murder** informal protest noisily.

DERIVATIVES – **murderer** *noun* **murderess** *noun*.

murderous > *adjective* **1** capable of, intending, or involving murder or extreme violence. **2** informal extremely arduous or unpleasant.

DERIVATIVES – **murderously** *adverb* **murderousness** *noun*.

SYNONYMS – **1** bloodthirsty, brutal, homicidal, savage.

murex /myooreks/ > *noun* (pl. **murices** /myooriseez/ or **murexes**) a predatory tropical marine mollusc with a spiny shell.

ORIGIN – Latin.

murine /myoorin/ > *adjective* Zoology relating to mice or related rodents.

ORIGIN – from Latin *mus* 'mouse'.

murk > *noun* darkness or fog causing poor visibility.

murky > *adjective* (**murkier**, **murkiest**) **1** dark and gloomy. **2** (of water) dirty or cloudy. **3** undisclosed and suspected of being dishonest or morally dubious.

DERIVATIVES – **murkily** *adverb* **murkiness** *noun*.

SYNONYMS – **1** bleak, gloomy, shadowy, sombre. **3** dubious, shadowy, shady.

murmur > *noun* **1** a quietly spoken utterance. **2** a low continuous background noise. **3** a subdued complaint. **4** Medicine a recurring sound heard in the heart through a stethoscope and usually indicating disease or damage. > *verb* **1** say something in a murmur. **2** make a low continuous sound. **3** complain in a subdued way.

SYNONYMS – *noun & verb* **1** mumble, mutter, whisper. **2** buzz, drone, hum.

ORIGIN – Latin.

Murphy's Law > *noun* a supposed law of nature, to the effect that anything that can go wrong will go wrong, and typically at the worst possible moment.

ORIGIN – said to be named after Captain Edward A. *Murphy* of the US Air Force, who noted, in a study of deceleration (1949), that if things could be done wrongly, they would be.

murrain /murrin/ > *noun* **1** an infectious disease affecting cattle, in particular redwater fever. **2** archaic a plague or blight.

ORIGIN – Old French *morine*, from Latin *mori* 'to die'.

Muscadet /**mus**kəday/ > *noun* a dry white wine from the Loire region of France.
ORIGIN – French, from *muscade* 'nutmeg'.

muscat /**mus**kat/ > *noun* **1** a variety of grape with a musky scent. **2** a sweet or fortified white wine made from these grapes.
ORIGIN – from Provençal *musc* 'musk'.

muscatel /muskə**tel**/ > *noun* **1** a muscat grape or a raisin made from such a grape. **2** a sweet wine made from muscat grapes.

muscle > *noun* **1** a band of fibrous tissue in the body that has the ability to contract, producing movement in or maintaining the position of a part of the body. **2** power or strength. > *verb* (**muscle in** or **into**) *informal* interfere forcibly in (another's affairs).
WORDFINDER – *some important muscles:* biceps, deltoid, gastrocnemius, gluteus, psoas, quadriceps, rhomboideus, sartorius, scalenus, soleus, sphincter, splenius, trapezius, triceps.
DERIVATIVES – **muscly** *adjective.*
SYNONYMS – *noun* **2** brawn, force, might.
COMBINATIONS – **muscle-bound** having over-developed muscles. **muscleman** a large, strong man, especially a bodyguard or hired thug.
ORIGIN – Latin *musculus*, diminutive of *mus* 'mouse' (some muscles being thought to be mouse-like in form).

muscovado /muskə**vaa**dō/ > *noun* unrefined sugar made from sugar cane.
ORIGIN – from Portuguese *mascabado açúcar* 'sugar of the lowest quality'.

Muscovite > *noun* **1** a native or citizen of Moscow. **2** (**muscovite**) a silver-grey form of mica. > *adjective* relating to Moscow.

Muscovy /**mus**kəvi/ > *noun* archaic Russia.
COMBINATIONS – **Muscovy duck** a large tropical American duck with glossy greenish-black plumage.
ORIGIN – Russian *Moskva* 'Moscow'.

muscular > *adjective* **1** of or affecting the muscles. **2** having well-developed muscles.
DERIVATIVES – **muscularity** *noun* **muscularly** *adverb.*
SYNONYMS – **2** brawny, burly, sinewy, strapping.
COMBINATIONS – **muscular dystrophy** a hereditary condition marked by progressive weakening and wasting of the muscles.

musculature > *noun* the muscular system or arrangement of a body or an organ.

musculoskeletal > *adjective* relating to the musculature and skeleton together.

muse¹ > *noun* **1** (**Muse**) (in Greek and Roman mythology) each of nine goddesses who preside over the arts and sciences. **2** a woman who is the inspiration for a creative artist.

---

wordpower facts

Muse

The Greek word *mousa*, 'Muse', is at the root of the English words **museum** (from *mouseion* 'place holy to the Muses') and **music** (from *mousikē tekhnē* 'art of the Muses'). It may also be the ultimate origin of **mosaic** (from Latin *musium* 'decoration with small square stones'), as shrines dedicated to the Muses were decorated in such a way. The nine Muses were Calliope (epic poetry), Clio (history), Erato (lyric poetry and hymns), Euterpe (flute playing), Melpomene (tragedy), Polyhymnia (mime), Terpsichore (lyric poetry and dance), Thalia (comedy), Urania (astronomy).

---

muse² > *verb* **1** be absorbed in thought. **2** say to oneself in a thoughtful manner.
SYNONYMS – **1** cogitate, deliberate, ponder, ruminate.
ORIGIN – Old French *muser* 'meditate, waste time'.

museum > *noun* a building in which objects of interest or significance are stored and exhibited.
COMBINATIONS – **museum piece** Brit. an old-fashioned or useless person or object.

mush¹ > *noun* **1** a soft, wet, pulpy mass. **2** cloying sentimentality. > *verb* reduce to mush.
ORIGIN – apparently a variant of MASH.

mush² > *exclamation* a command urging on dogs that pull a sledge.
ORIGIN – probably an alteration of French *marchez!* or *marchons!* 'advance!'.

mush³ > *noun* Brit. informal **1** a person's mouth or face. **2** used as a term of address.
ORIGIN – probably from Romany, 'man'.

mushroom > *noun* **1** a spore-producing body of a fungus, typically having the form of a domed cap at the top of a stalk and often edible. **2** a pale pinkish-brown colour. > *verb* increase or develop rapidly.
WORDFINDER – cep, champignon, chanterelle, field mushroom, morel, oyster mushroom, porcini, portobello mushroom, shiitake (*kinds of mushroom*).
SYNONYMS – *verb* burgeon, explode, snowball.
COMBINATIONS – **mushroom cloud** a mushroom-shaped cloud of dust and debris formed after a nuclear explosion.
ORIGIN – Old French *mousseron*.

mushy > *adjective* (**mushier**, **mushiest**) **1** in the form of mush. **2** cloyingly sentimental.
DERIVATIVES – **mushiness** *noun.*
SYNONYMS – **1** sloppy, slushy.

music > *noun* **1** the art of combining vocal or instrumental sounds in a pleasing way. **2** the

sound so produced. **3** the written or printed signs representing such sound.
WORDFINDER – anthem, aria, ballad, ballet, canticle, carol, chanson, chant, chorale, concerto, duet, étude, fantasia, fugue, hymn, lied, madrigal, march, mass, motet, opera, operetta, oratorio, overture, prelude, quartet, quintet, requiem, rhapsody, rondo, scherzo, serenade, sextet, shanty, sinfonia, solo, sonata, song, spiritual, suite, symphony, toccata, trio (*some musical forms*).
IDIOMS – **music to one's ears** something very pleasant to hear or learn.
COMBINATIONS – **music centre** Brit. a combined radio, cassette player, and record or compact disc player. **music hall 1** a form of entertainment incorporating song, dance, and comedy, popular in Britain *c.*1850–1918. **2** a theatre where such entertainment took place.
ORIGIN – Old French *musique* from Greek *mousikē tekhnē* 'art of the Muses'.

musical > *adjective* **1** relating to or accompanied by music. **2** fond of or skilled in music. **3** pleasant-sounding. > *noun* a play or film in which singing and dancing play an essential part.
DERIVATIVES – **musicality** *noun* **musically** *adverb.*
SYNONYMS – *adjective* **3** euphonious, mellifluous, melodious.
ANTONYMS – *adjective* **3** discordant.
COMBINATIONS – **musical box** Brit. a small box which plays a tune when the lid is opened. **musical chairs 1** a party game in which players compete for a decreasing number of chairs when the accompanying music is stopped. **2** a situation in which people frequently exchange jobs or positions. **musical comedy** a musical.

musician > *noun* a person who plays a musical instrument or is otherwise musically gifted.
WORDFINDER – accompanist, composer, conductor, instrumentalist, minstrel, soloist, (*different types of musician*); maestro, virtuoso (*a distinguished musician*).
DERIVATIVES – **musicianly** *adjective* **musicianship** *noun.*

musicology > *noun* the study of music as an academic subject.
DERIVATIVES – **musicological** *adjective* **musicologist** *noun.*

musique concrète /myoozeek coNkret/ > *noun* music constructed by mixing recorded sounds.
ORIGIN – French, 'concrete music'.

musk > *noun* **1** a strong-smelling substance secreted by the male musk deer, used as an ingredient in perfumery. **2** (also **musk plant**) a musk-scented plant related to the monkey flower.

muskeg-mute

DERIVATIVES – **muskiness** *noun* **musky** (**muskier**, **muskiest**) *adjective*.

COMBINATIONS – **musk deer** a small East Asian deer, the male of which produces musk in an abdominal sac. **musk ox** a large heavily built goat-antelope with a thick shaggy coat, native to the tundra of North America and Greenland.

ORIGIN – Persian, perhaps from a Sanskrit word meaning 'scrotum' (because of the similarity in shape of a musk deer's musk bag).

muskeg /ˈmuskeg/ > *noun* a swamp or bog in northern North America.

ORIGIN – Cree.

musket > *noun* historical a light gun with a long barrel, typically smooth-bored and fired from the shoulder.

ORIGIN – French *mousquet*, from Italian *moschetto* 'crossbow bolt'.

musketeer > *noun* historical **1** a soldier armed with a musket. **2** a member of the household troops of the French king in the 17th and 18th centuries.

musketry > *noun* **1** musket fire. **2** musketeers collectively. **3** the art or technique of handling a musket.

muskrat > *noun* a large semiaquatic North American rodent with a musky smell, valued for its fur.

Muslim (also **Moslem**) > *noun* a follower of Islam. > *adjective* relating to Muslims or Islam.

ORIGIN – Arabic, from a verb meaning 'submit (to God)'.

muslin > *noun* lightweight cotton cloth in a plain weave.

ORIGIN – Italian *mussolina*, from *Mussolo* 'Mosul' (the place in Iraq where it was formerly made).

muso > *noun* (pl. **musos**) Brit. informal a musician or keen music fan.

musquash /ˈmuskwosh/ > *noun* **1** Brit. the fur of the muskrat. **2** archaic a muskrat.

ORIGIN – Abnaki (an American Indian language).

muss informal, chiefly N. Amer. > *verb* make untidy or messy. > *noun* a mess or muddle.

mussel > *noun* **1** a marine mollusc with a dark brown or purplish-black shell. **2** a freshwater mollusc, some kinds of which produce small pearls.

ORIGIN – Latin *musculus* 'muscle'.

Mussulman /ˈmusˈlmən/ > *noun* (pl. **Mussulmans** or **Mussulmen**) & *adjective* archaic term for **Muslim**.

ORIGIN – Persian, from *muslim* (see **Muslim**).

must[1] > *modal verb* (past **had to** or in reported speech **must**) **1** be obliged to; should. **2** expressing insistence. **3** expressing an opinion about something that is very likely. > *noun* informal something that should not be overlooked or missed.

SYNONYMS – *verb* **1** be compelled to, be obliged to, have to, have got to, should.

must[2] > *noun* grape juice before or during fermentation.

ORIGIN – from Latin *mustus* 'new'.

must[3] > *noun* mustiness or mould.

must[4] (also **musth**) > *noun* the frenzied state of a rutting male elephant or camel.

ORIGIN – Urdu, from a Persian word meaning 'intoxicated'.

mustache > *noun* US spelling of **MOUSTACHE**.

mustachios > *plural noun* a long or elaborate moustache.

DERIVATIVES – **mustachioed** *adjective*.

ORIGIN – Spanish *mostacho* from Italian *mostaccio*.

mustang > *noun* a small lightly built feral horse of the south-western US.

ORIGIN – from a blend of Spanish *mestengo* and *mostrenco*, both meaning 'wild or masterless cattle'.

mustard > *noun* **1** a hot-tasting yellow or brown paste made from the crushed seeds of a plant, eaten with meat or used in cooking. **2** a brownish yellow colour.

COMBINATIONS – **mustard gas** a liquid whose vapour causes severe irritation and blistering, used in chemical weapons.

ORIGIN – Old French *moustarde*, from Latin *mustum* 'must' (because mustard was originally prepared with grape must).

mustelid /ˈmustilid/ > *noun* Zoology a mammal of a family including the weasels, martens, skunks, and otters.

ORIGIN – Latin *Mustelidae* (the weasel family), from *mustela* 'weasel'.

muster > *verb* **1** bring (troops) together, especially for inspection or in preparation for battle. **2** (of people) gather together. **3** summon up (a feeling or attitude). **4** Austral./NZ round up (livestock). > *noun* **1** an instance of mustering troops. **2** Austral./NZ a rounding up of livestock.

IDIOMS – **pass muster** be accepted as satisfactory.

SYNONYMS – *verb* **2** assemble, congregate, mass.

ANTONYMS – *verb* **2** disperse.

ORIGIN – Old French *moustrer*, from Latin *monstrare* 'to show'.

musth > *noun* variant spelling of **MUST**[4].

mustn't > *contraction* must not.

musty > *adjective* (**mustier**, **mustiest**) **1** having a stale or mouldy smell or taste. **2** unoriginal or outdated.

DERIVATIVES – **mustiness** noun.

SYNONYMS – **1** dank, fusty, mildewed. **2** clichéd, hackneyed, hoary.

ORIGIN – perhaps an alteration of *moisty* 'moist'.

mutable /ˈmyōōtəbˈl/ > *adjective* liable to change.

DERIVATIVES – **mutability** noun.

SYNONYMS – changeable, variable.

mutagen /ˈmyōōtəjən/ > *noun* a substance which causes genetic mutation.

mutant > *adjective* resulting from or showing the effect of mutation. > *noun* a mutant form.

mutate > *verb* undergo mutation.

SYNONYMS – metamorphose, transmogrify, transmute.

wordpower facts
Mutate

The English words **mutable**, **mutant**, **mutate**, and **mutation** derive from Latin *mutare*, meaning 'to change'. This same root has given rise to a range of English words relating to change or alternation, including **commute**, **permutation**, and **transmutation**. Another word that has come from *mutare* is **moult**, introduced into English (without an *l*) in the 15th century. The *l* is a later addition, presumably by analogy with words like **fault** (in which it was originally silent).

mutation > *noun* **1** the process or an instance of changing. **2** a change in genetic structure which results in a variant form and may be transmitted to subsequent generations. **3** a distinct form resulting from such a change.

DERIVATIVES – **mutational** *adjective*.

mutatis mutandis /myōōˈtaatiss myōōˈtandiss/ > *adverb* (used when comparing two or more cases) making necessary alterations while not affecting the main point.

ORIGIN – Latin, 'things being changed that have to be changed'.

mute > *adjective* **1** refraining from speech or temporarily speechless. **2** dated lacking the power of speech. **3** (of a letter) not pronounced. > *noun* **1** dated a person without the power of speech. **2** historical a professional attendant or mourner at a funeral. **3** a clamp placed over the bridge of a stringed instrument to deaden the resonance of the strings. **4** a pad or cone placed in the opening of a wind instrument to muffle the sound. > *verb* **1** deaden or muffle the sound of. **2** reduce the strength or intensity of. **3** (**muted**) (of colour or lighting) not bright; subdued.

DERIVATIVES – **mutely** *adverb* **muteness** *noun*.

USAGE – avoid describing a person without the power of speech as **mute** (as in **deaf mute**), as today it is likely to cause offence. Since there are no accepted alternative terms in general use, the solution may be to use a longer construction, such as *she is both deaf and unable to speak.*

SYNONYMS – *adjective* **1** silent, taciturn, wordless. *verb* **1** deaden, dull, muffle, stifle. **2** moderate, temper. **3** (**muted**) discreet, low-key, understated.

COMBINATIONS – **mute swan** the common non-migratory Eurasian swan, having an orange-red bill with a black knob at the base.

ORIGIN – Latin *mutus*.

mutilate > *verb* **1** inflict a violent and disfiguring injury on (someone). **2** inflict serious damage on (something).

DERIVATIVES – **mutilation** *noun* **mutilator** *noun*.

SYNONYMS – **1** cripple, maim, mangle. **2** deface, vandalise.

ORIGIN – Latin *mutilare* 'maim'.

mutineer > *noun* a person who mutinies.

mutinous > *adjective* tending to mutiny; rebellious.

DERIVATIVES – **mutinously** *adverb*.

SYNONYMS – insurgent, insurrectionary, rebellious, seditious, subversive.

mutiny > *noun* (pl. **mutinies**) an open rebellion against authority, especially by soldiers or sailors against their officers. > *verb* (**mutinies**, **mutinied**) engage in mutiny; rebel.

SYNONYMS – *noun* insurgency, insurrection, rebellion, uprising.

ORIGIN – from French *mutin* 'mutineer, rebellious'.

mutt > *noun informal* **1** *humorous or derogatory* a dog, especially a mongrel. **2** a stupid or incompetent person.

ORIGIN – abbreviation of *muttonhead*.

mutter > *verb* **1** say in a barely audible voice. **2** talk or grumble in secret or in private. > *noun* a barely audible utterance.

SYNONYMS – *verb* & *noun* **1** mumble, murmur, whisper.

ORIGIN – imitative of the sound of muttering.

mutton > *noun* the flesh of mature sheep used as food.

IDIOMS – **mutton dressed as lamb** Brit. informal, derogatory a middle-aged or old woman dressed in a style suitable for a much younger woman.

COMBINATIONS – **mutton-chop whiskers** whiskers on a man's cheek that are narrow at the top and broad and rounded at the bottom. **muttonhead** informal, dated a dull or stupid person.

ORIGIN – Old French *moton*, from Latin *multo*, probably of Celtic origin.

mutual > *adjective* **1** experienced or done by each of two or more parties towards the other or others. **2** (of two or more parties) having the same specified relationship to each other. **3** held in common by two or more parties. **4** (of a building society or insurance company) owned by its members and dividing its profits between them.

DERIVATIVES – **mutuality** *noun* **mutually** *adverb*.

SYNONYMS – **1** common, joint, reciprocal.

COMBINATIONS – **mutual fund** (in North America) a fund in which contributions from many persons combined are invested in various securities and bonds and in which dividends are paid in proportion to the contributors' holdings.

ORIGIN – Old French *mutuel*, from Latin *mutuus* 'mutual, borrowed'.

muumuu /ˈmo͞omo͞o/ > *noun* a loose, brightly coloured dress as traditionally worn by Hawaiian women.

ORIGIN – Hawaiian, 'cut off'.

muzak > *noun* **trademark** recorded light background music played in public places.

muzzle > *noun* **1** the projecting part of an animal's face, including the nose and mouth. **2** a guard fitted over an animal's nose and mouth to stop it biting or feeding. **3** the open end of the barrel of a firearm. > *verb* **1** put a muzzle on (an animal). **2** prevent (someone) expressing their opinions freely.

SYNONYMS – *verb* **2** censor, gag, silence.

ORIGIN – Latin *musum*.

muzzy > *adjective* (**muzzier**, **muzziest**) **1** dazed or confused. **2** blurred or indistinct.

DERIVATIVES – **muzzily** *adverb* **muzziness** *noun*.

MV > *abbreviation* motor vessel.

MVO > *abbreviation* Member of the Royal Victorian Order.

MVP > *abbreviation* chiefly N. Amer. most valuable player.

MW > *abbreviation* **1** medium wave. **2** megawatt(s).

MY > *abbreviation* motor yacht.

my > *possessive determiner* **1** belonging to or associated with the speaker. **2** used in various expressions of surprise.

IDIOMS – **My Lady** (or **Lord**) a polite form of address to certain titled people.

myalgia /mīˈaljə/ > *noun* pain in a muscle or group of muscles.

DERIVATIVES – **myalgic** *adjective*.

COMBINATIONS – **myalgic encephalomyelitis** another term for *chronic fatigue syndrome*.

ORIGIN – from Greek *mus* 'muscle' + *algos* 'pain'.

myall /ˈmīəl/ > *noun* **1** Austral. an Australian Aboriginal living in a traditional way. **2** an Australian acacia tree with hard scented wood.

ORIGIN – sense 1 is from an Aboriginal word, meaning 'person of another tribe'; sense 2 is perhaps a transferred use of sense 1, with reference to trade in wood between the speakers of two different Aboriginal languages.

myasthenia /mīəsˈtheeniə/ > *noun* a rare chronic autoimmune disease marked by muscular weakness without atrophy.

ORIGIN – from Greek *mus* 'muscle' + *asthenia* 'weakness'.

mycelium /mīˈseeliəm/ > *noun* (pl. **mycelia**) Botany a network of fine white filaments (hyphae) constituting the vegetative part of a fungus.

ORIGIN – from Greek *mukēs* 'fungus'.

Mycenaean /mīsiˈneeən/ (also **Mycenean**) > *adjective* relating to a late Bronze Age civilisation in Greece represented by finds at Mycenae and other ancient cities of the Peloponnese. > *noun* an inhabitant of Mycenae or member of the Mycenaean people.

mycology /mīˈkolləji/ > *noun* the scientific study of fungi.

DERIVATIVES – **mycological** *adjective* **mycologist** *noun*.

ORIGIN – from Greek *mukēs* 'fungus'.

mycoprotein > *noun* protein derived from fungi, especially as produced for human consumption.

myelin /ˈmīəlin/ > *noun* a whitish fatty substance forming a sheath around many nerve fibres.

ORIGIN – from Greek *muelos* 'marrow'.

myelitis /mīəˈlītis/ > *noun* Medicine inflammation of the spinal cord.

myeloid /ˈmīəloyd/ > *adjective* relating to bone marrow or the spinal cord.

myeloma /mīəˈlōmə/ > *noun* (pl. **myelomas** or **myelomata** /mīəˈlōmətə/) Medicine a malignant tumour of the bone marrow.

mynah /ˈmīnə/ (also **mynah bird**) > *noun* a southern Asian or Australasian starling with a loud call, some kinds of which can mimic human speech.

ORIGIN – Hindi.

myocardium /mīəˈkaardiəm/ > *noun* Anatomy the muscular tissue of the heart.

DERIVATIVES – **myocardial** *adjective*.

ORIGIN – from Greek *mus* 'muscle' + *kardia* 'heart'.

myopia /mīˈōpiə/ > *noun* **1** short-sightedness. **2** lack of foresight or intellectual insight.

DERIVATIVES – **myopic** *adjective*.

ORIGIN – from Greek *muein* 'shut' + *ōps* 'eye'.

myositis /mīəˈsītiss/ > *noun* Medicine inflammation and degeneration of muscle tissue.

myosotis /mīəˈsōtis/ > *noun* a plant of a genus which includes the forget-me-nots.

ORIGIN – from Greek *mus* 'mouse' + *ous* 'ear'.

myotonia /mīəˈtōniə/ > *noun* inability to relax voluntary muscle after vigorous effort.

DERIVATIVES – **myotonic** *adjective*.

myriad /**mirr**iəd/ *literary* > *noun* **1** (also **myriads**) an indefinitely great number. **2** (in classical times) a unit of ten thousand. > *adjective* innumerable.

SYNONYMS – *noun* **1** horde, host, legion, throng.

ORIGIN – Greek *murias*, from *murioi* '10,000'.

myriapod /**mirr**iəpod/ > *noun* Zoology a centipede, millipede, or other arthropod having an elongated body with numerous leg-bearing segments.

ORIGIN – from Greek *murioi* '10,000' + *pous* 'foot'.

myrmecology /murmi**koll**əji/ > *noun* the branch of entomology concerned with ants.

ORIGIN – from Greek *murmēx* 'ant'.

myrmidon /**mur**midon/ > *noun* a hired ruffian or unscrupulous subordinate.

ORIGIN – from Greek *Murmidones*, a warlike people of Thessaly who accompanied Achilles to Troy.

myrrh /mur/ > *noun* a fragrant gum resin obtained from certain trees and used in perfumery, medicines, and incense.

ORIGIN – Greek *murra*, of Semitic origin.

myrtle > *noun* an evergreen shrub with glossy aromatic foliage and white flowers followed by purple-black oval berries.

ORIGIN – Greek *murtos*.

myself > *pronoun* (first person sing.) **1** (reflexive) used by a speaker to refer to himself or herself as the object of a verb or preposition when he or she is the subject of the clause. **2** (emphatic) I or me personally. **3** literary term for I[2].

mysterious > *adjective* **1** difficult or impossible to understand, explain, or identify. **2** deliberately enigmatic.

DERIVATIVES – **mysteriously** *adverb* **mysteriousness** *noun*.

SYNONYMS – **1** baffling, impenetrable, inexplicable, unfathomable. **2** enigmatic, inscrutable, secretive.

mystery[1] > *noun* (pl. **mysteries**) **1** something that is difficult or impossible to understand or explain. **2** secrecy or obscurity. **3** a novel, play, or film dealing with a puzzling crime. **4** (**mysteries**) the secret rites of an ancient or tribal religion. **5** chiefly Christian Theology a religious belief based on divine revelation. **6** an incident in the life of Jesus or of a saint as a focus of devotion in the Roman Catholic Church.

SYNONYMS – **1** conundrum, enigma, puzzle.

COMBINATIONS – **mystery play** a popular medieval play based on biblical stories or the lives of the saints. **mystery tour** Brit. a pleasure excursion to an unspecified destination.

---

wordpower facts

Mystery

The word **mystery** comes from the Greek word *mustērion*; like its associated words **mysterious**, **mystic**, and **mystical**, it goes back to Greek *muein* 'close the eyes or lips', also 'initiate'. The connection between the two meanings probably arose from secret religious ceremonies in ancient Greece, which were allowed to be witnessed only by the initiated, who were sworn never to disclose what they had seen. The verb *muein* is also the source of **myopia**, meaning short-sightedness.

---

mystery[2] > *noun* (pl. **mysteries**) archaic a handicraft or trade.

ORIGIN – from Latin *ministerium* 'ministry'.

mystic > *noun* a person who seeks by contemplation and self-surrender to attain unity with the Deity and reach truths beyond human understanding. > *adjective* mystical.

ORIGIN – Greek *mustēs* 'initiated person', from *muein* 'close the eyes or lips', also 'initiate'.

mystical > *adjective* **1** relating to mystics or mysticism. **2** having a spiritual significance that transcends human understanding. **3** inspiring a sense of spiritual mystery, awe, and fascination.

DERIVATIVES – **mystically** *adverb*.

mysticism > *noun* **1** the beliefs or state of mind characteristic of mystics. **2** vague or ill-defined religious or spiritual belief.

mystify > *verb* (**mystifies**, **mystified**) **1** utterly bewilder. **2** make obscure or mysterious.

DERIVATIVES – **mystification** *noun* **mystifying** *adjective*

SYNONYMS – **1** baffle, bewilder, confound, perplex.

mystique > *noun* **1** a fascinating aura of mystery, awe, and power. **2** an air of secrecy surrounding an activity or subject, making it impressive or baffling to the layperson.

SYNONYMS – **1** allure, glamour, magic.

ORIGIN – French.

myth > *noun* **1** a traditional story concerning the early history of a people or explaining a natural or social phenomenon, typically involving the supernatural. **2** a widely held but false belief. **3** a fictitious person or thing.

SYNONYMS – **1** fable, folk tale. **2** fallacy, old wives' tale.

ORIGIN – Greek *muthos*.

mythical > *adjective* **1** occurring in or characteristic of myths or folk tales. **2** fictitious.

DERIVATIVES – **mythic** *adjective* **mythically** *adverb*.

SYNONYMS – **1** fabled, fabulous, fairy-tale. **2** fanciful, fictitious, imaginary, make-believe.

mythological > *adjective* **1** relating to or found in mythology; mythical. **2** fictitious.

DERIVATIVES – **mythologically** *adverb*.

mythologise (also **mythologize**) > *verb* convert into myth or mythology; make the subject of a myth.

mythology > *noun* (pl. **mythologies**) **1** a collection of myths. **2** a set of widely held but exaggerated or fictitious stories or beliefs. **3** the study of myths.

DERIVATIVES – **mythologist** *noun*.

mythomania > *noun* an abnormal or pathological tendency to exaggerate or tell lies.

DERIVATIVES – **mythomaniac** *noun* & *adjective*.

mythopoeia /mithəpeeə/ > *noun* the making of a myth or myths.

DERIVATIVES – **mythopoeic** *adjective* **mythopoetic** *adjective*.

myxomatosis /miksəmətōsiss/ > *noun* a highly infectious and usually fatal disease of rabbits, spread by a virus and causing inflammation and discharge around the eyes.

ORIGIN – from Greek *muxa* 'slime, mucus'.

N¹ (also **n**) > *noun* (pl. **Ns** or **N's**) the fourteenth letter of the alphabet.

N² > *abbreviation* **1** (used in recording moves in chess) knight. [ORIGIN – representing the pronunciation of *kn-*.] **2** (in place names) New. **3** Physics newton(s). **4** North or Northern. > *symbol* the chemical element nitrogen.

n > *abbreviation* **1** nano- (10^{-9}). **2** Grammar neuter. **3** Grammar noun. > *symbol* an unspecified or variable number.

'n (also **'n'**) > *contraction* informal and: *rock 'n roll*.

Na > *symbol* the chemical element sodium.
ORIGIN – from Latin *natrium*.

n/a > *abbreviation* **1** not applicable. **2** not available.

NAAFI /**na**ffi/ > *abbreviation* Navy, Army, and Air Force Institutes. > *noun* a canteen or shop run by the NAAFI.

naan > *noun* variant spelling of **NAN²**.

nab > *verb* (**nabbed**, **nabbing**) informal **1** catch (a wrong-doer). **2** take or grab suddenly.

Nabataean /nabbə**tee**ən/ (also **Nabatean**) > *noun* a member of an ancient Arabian people having a kingdom with its capital at Petra (now in Jordan). > *adjective* relating to the Nabataeans.

nabob /**nay**bob/ > *noun* **1** historical a Muslim official or governor under the Mogul empire. **2** a very wealthy or influential person.
ORIGIN – Urdu; see also **NAWAB**.

nacelle /nə**sel**/ > *noun* the streamlined outer casing of an aircraft engine.
ORIGIN – French, from Latin *navicella* 'small ship'.

nacho /**na**chō/ > *noun* (pl. **nachos**) a small piece of tortilla topped with melted cheese, peppers, etc.
ORIGIN – perhaps from Mexican Spanish *Nacho*, familiar form of *Ignacio*, first name of the chef credited with creating the dish, or from Spanish *nacho* 'flat-nosed'.

nacre /**nay**kər/ > *noun* mother-of-pearl.
DERIVATIVES – **nacreous** *adjective*.
ORIGIN – French.

nada /**naa**də/ > *pronoun* N. Amer. informal nothing.
ORIGIN – Spanish.

nadir /**nay**deer, **nad**eer/ > *noun* **1** Astronomy the point on the celestial sphere directly opposite the zenith and below an observer. **2** the lowest or most unsuccessful point.
ORIGIN – Arabic, 'opposite to the zenith'.

naevus /**nee**vəss/ (US **nevus**) > *noun* (pl. **naevi** /**nee**vī/) a birthmark or a mole on the skin.
ORIGIN – Latin.

naff Brit. informal > *verb* **1** (**naff off**) go away. **2** (**naffing**) used to emphasise annoyance. > *adjective* lacking taste or style.
DERIVATIVES – **naffness** *noun*.
ORIGIN – the verb is a euphemism for **FUCK**; the origin of the adjective is unknown.

NAFTA (also **Nafta**) > *abbreviation* North American Free Trade Agreement.

nag¹ > *verb* (**nagged**, **nagging**) **1** tediously persist in telling (someone) to do something. **2** be persistently worrying or painful to. > *noun* a persistent feeling of anxiety.
SYNONYMS – *verb* **1** badger, chivvy. **2** bother, plague, trouble.

nag² > *noun* informal, often derogatory a horse, especially an old or decrepit one.

Nahuatl /**naa**waat'l, naa**waat**'l/ > *noun* **1** a member of a group of peoples native to southern Mexico and Central America, including the Aztecs. **2** the language of these peoples.
ORIGIN – Nahuatl.

wordpower facts

Nahuatl

A number of English words have their roots in the language of the **Nahuatl** peoples of southern Mexico and Central America, many of them denoting plants and animals, and items of food, coming from that part of the world. They include **avocado, cacao, chilli, chocolate, coyote, guacamole, ocelot, tomato,** and, unexpectedly, **shack.**

naiad /**nī**ad/ > *noun* (pl. **naiads** or **naiades** /**nī**ədeez/) (in classical mythology) a water nymph.
ORIGIN – Greek *Naias*, from *naein* 'to flow'.

naif /**nī**eef/ > *adjective* naive. > *noun* a naive person.
ORIGIN – French.

nail > *noun* **1** a small metal spike with a broadened flat head, hammered in to join things together or to serve as a hook. **2** a horny covering on the upper surface of the tip of the finger and toe in humans and other primates. > *verb* **1** fasten with a nail or nails. **2** informal detect or catch (someone, especially a suspected criminal). **3** (**nail down**) extract a firm commitment from. **4** (**nail down**) identify precisely.
WORDFINDER – cuticle (*dead skin at the base of a nail*), hangnail (*piece of torn skin at the base of a fingernail*), lunula (*white area at the base of a fingernail*), ungual (*relating to a nail*), whitlow (*abscess in soft tissue near a nail*).
IDIOMS – **a nail in the coffin** an action or event likely to have a detrimental or destructive effect. **on the nail** (of payment) without delay.
COMBINATIONS – **nail-biting** causing great anxiety or tension. **nail file** a small file or emery board for smoothing and shaping the fingernails and toenails. **nail polish** (also **nail varnish**) a substance applied to the fingernails or toenails to give them a hard, glossy surface when dry.

naira /**nī**rə/ > *noun* the basic monetary unit of Nigeria, equal to 100 kobo.
ORIGIN – contraction of *Nigeria*.

naive /**nī**eev/ (also **naïve**) > *adjective* **1** lacking experience, wisdom, or judgement. **2** (of art) produced in a simple, childlike style which deliberately rejects sophisticated techniques.
DERIVATIVES – **naively** *adverb*.
SYNONYMS – **1** guileless, ingenuous, innocent, unsophisticated, unworldly.
ANTONYMS – **1** worldly.
ORIGIN – French, from Latin *nativus* 'native, natural'.

naivety /**nī**eevti/ (also **naiveté** /**nī**eevtay/) > *noun* **1** lack of experience, wisdom, or judgement. **2** innocence or unsophistication.

naked > *adjective* **1** without clothes. **2** (of an object) without the usual covering or protection. **3** not concealed; undisguised: *naked aggression*. **4** exposed to harm; vulnerable.
IDIOMS – **the naked eye** vision unassisted by a telescope, microscope, or other optical instrument. **naked of** devoid of.
DERIVATIVES – **nakedly** *adverb* **nakedness** *noun*.
SYNONYMS – **1** bare, nude, unclothed. **3** stark, undisguised. **4** exposed, helpless, undefended, vulnerable.

Nama /**naa**mə/ > *noun* (pl. same or **Namas**) **1** a member of one of the Khoikhoi peoples of South Africa and SW Namibia. **2** the language of this people.
USAGE – **Nama** or **Khoikhoi** are the standard accepted terms in this context.

The older word **Hottentot** may now cause offence.

ORIGIN – Nama.

namby-pamby > *adjective* lacking courage or vigour; feeble. > *noun* (pl. **namby-pambies**) a namby-pamby person.

ORIGIN – fanciful formation from the name of *Ambrose* Philips (1674–1749), an English pastoral poet ridiculed for his insipid verse.

name > *noun* **1** a word or words by which someone or something is known, addressed, or referred to. **2** a famous person. **3** a reputation, especially a good one: *he made a name for himself in the theatre.* **4** (in the UK) an insurance underwriter belonging to a Lloyd's syndicate. > *verb* **1** give a name to. **2** identify or mention by name. **3** specify (a sum, time, or place). **4** appoint or nominate.

WORDFINDER – anonymous (*not identified by name*), nom de plume (*a pen name*), nomenclature (*a body or system of names*), onomastics (*the study of proper names*), patronymic (*name derived from a father*), pen name (*a literary pseudonym*), pseudonym (*a fictitious name*), toponym (*a place name*).

IDIOMS – **call names** insult (someone) verbally. **have to one's name** have in one's possession. **in all but name** existing in practice but not formally recognised as such. **in someone's name 1** formally registered as belonging to or reserved for someone. **2** on behalf of someone. **in the name of** for the sake of. **name the day** arrange the date for a specific occasion, especially a wedding. **name names** mention specific names, especially in accusation. **the name of the game** informal the main purpose or most important aspect of a situation.

DERIVATIVES – **nameable** *adjective*.

SYNONYMS – *noun* **1** designation, title; formal appellation. **2** celebrity. *verb* **1** call, dub, term.

COMBINATIONS – **name day** the feast day of a saint after whom a person is named. **name-dropping** the casual mention of famous people as if one knows them, so as to impress. **nameplate** a plate attached to something and bearing the name of the owner, occupier, or the thing itself.

namecheck > *verb* publicly mention the name of, especially in acknowledgement or for publicity purposes.

nameless > *adjective* **1** having no name. **2** not identified by name; anonymous. **3** too horrific or unpleasant to be described.

SYNONYMS – **1** anonymous, unidentified, unnamed.

namely > *adverb* that is to say.

namesake > *noun* a person or thing with the same name as another.

ORIGIN – from the phrase *for the name's sake.*

Namibian /nəmibiən/ > *noun* a person from Namibia. > *adjective* relating to Namibia.

nan¹ /nan/ > *noun* Brit. informal one's grandmother.

nan² /naan/ (also **naan**) > *noun* a type of leavened Indian bread of a flattened teardrop shape.

ORIGIN – Urdu and Persian.

nana¹ /naanə/ > *noun* Brit. informal a silly person.

ORIGIN – perhaps a shortening of *banana.*

nana² /nannə/ (Brit. also **nanna**) > *noun* informal one's grandmother.

ORIGIN – child's pronunciation of **NANNY** or **GRAN**.

nancy (also **nance**, **nancy boy**) > *noun* (pl. **nancies**) informal, derogatory an effeminate or homosexual man.

ORIGIN – familiar form of the name *Ann.*

nandrolone /nandrəlōn/ > *noun* an anabolic steroid with tissue-building properties, used illegally to enhance performance in sport.

ORIGIN – shortened form of its chemical name *norandrostenolone.*

nankeen /nangkeen/ > *noun* a yellowish cotton cloth.

ORIGIN – named after the city of *Nanking* in China, where it was first made.

nanny > *noun* (pl. **nannies**) **1** a woman employed to look after a child in its own home. **2** (before another noun) interfering and overprotective: *the nanny state.* **3** (also **nanny goat**) a female goat. > *verb* (**nannies**, **nannied**) be overprotective towards.

SYNONYMS – *verb* coddle, cosset, mollycoddle, pamper.

ORIGIN – familiar form of the name *Ann.*

nano- /nannō/ > *combining form* **1** denoting a factor of one thousand millionth (10^{-9}): *nanosecond.* **2** extremely small; submicroscopic: *nanotechnology.*

ORIGIN – via Latin from Greek *nanos* 'dwarf'.

nanobacterium /nannōbakteeriəm/ > *noun* a kind of micro-organism about a tenth the size of the smallest normal bacteria, claimed to exist in various environments.

nanobe /nannōb/ > *noun* another term for **NANOBACTERIUM**.

nanometre /nannōmeetər/ (US **nanometer**) > *noun* one thousand millionth of a metre.

nanosecond > *noun* one thousand millionth of a second.

nanotechnology > *noun* technology on an atomic or molecular scale, concerned with dimensions of less than 100 nanometres.

nap¹ > *noun* a short sleep, especially during the day. > *verb* (**napped**, **napping**) have a nap.

SYNONYMS – catnap, doze.

nap² > *noun* short raised fibres on the surface of certain fabrics, such as velvet.

ORIGIN – Dutch or Low German *noppe.*

nap³ > *noun* **1** a card game resembling whist in which players declare the number of tricks they expect to take, up to five. **2** Brit. a tipster's prediction of the most likely winner. > *verb* (**napped**, **napping**) Brit. name (a horse or greyhound) as a likely winner of a race.

IDIOMS – **go nap 1** try to take all five tricks in nap. **2** score or win five times.

COMBINATIONS – **nap hand** a series of five winning points, victories, etc.

ORIGIN – abbreviation of *napoleon,* the original name of the card game.

napalm /naypaam/ > *noun* a highly flammable jelly-like form of petrol, used in incendiary bombs and flame-throwers.

ORIGIN – from *naphthenic* and *palmitic acids* (compounds used in its manufacture).

nape > *noun* the back of a person's neck.

naphtha* /nafthə/ > *noun* a flammable oil distilled from coal, shale, or petroleum.

*SPELLING – *phth,* not *pth:* n*aphth*a.

ORIGIN – Greek.

naphthalene /nafthəleen/ > *noun* a white crystalline substance distilled from coal tar, used in mothballs and for chemical manufacture.

napkin > *noun* **1** a square piece of cloth or paper used at a meal to wipe the fingers or lips and to protect garments. **2** Brit. dated a baby's nappy.

ORIGIN – Old French *nappe* 'tablecloth', from Latin *mappa* 'map'.

Napoleonic /nəpōlionnik/ > *adjective* relating to or characteristic of the French emperor Napoleon I (1769–1821) or his time.

napper > *noun* Brit. informal a person's head.

nappy > *noun* (pl. **nappies**) Brit. a piece of absorbent material wrapped round a baby's bottom and between its legs to absorb and retain urine and faeces.

narcissism /naarsisiz'm/ > *noun* excessive or erotic interest in oneself and one's physical appearance.

DERIVATIVES – **narcissist** noun **narcissistic** *adjective*.

SYNONYMS – self-love, vanity.

narcissus /naarsissəss/ > *noun* (pl. **narcissi** or **narcissuses**) a daffodil with a flower that has white or pale outer petals and a shallow orange or yellow centre.

wordpower facts
Narcissus
The name of the **narcissus** derives from Greek *narkissos*. The Roman poet Ovid tells us that the flower first sprang up at the place where a beautiful Greek youth, *Narcissus*, fell in love with his own reflection in a pool, pined away, and died. His infatuation with his own beauty links his name with the term **narcissism**, introduced by German psychologists and popularised by Sigmund Freud. It is not clear whether there is any ultimate relation between **narcissus** and the group of words deriving from Greek *narkē* 'numbness', such as **narcotic**.

narcolepsy /naarkəlepsi/ > *noun* a nervous illness characterised by an extreme tendency to fall asleep whenever in relaxing surroundings.
DERIVATIVES – **narcoleptic** *adjective & noun*.

narcosis /naarkōsiss/ > *noun* a state of stupor, drowsiness, or unconsciousness produced by drugs.
ORIGIN – Greek *narkōsis*, from *narkoun* 'make numb'.

narcotic > *noun* **1** an addictive drug, especially an illegal one, affecting mood or behaviour. **2** Medicine a drug which induces drowsiness, stupor, or insensibility and relieves pain. > *adjective* relating to narcotics.

wordpower facts
Narcotic
The word **narcotic** comes from the Greek word *narkōtikos*, from *narkoun* 'make numb', *narkē* 'numbness'. In its early use it denoted an opiate, or a similar drug inducing drowsiness or sleep. Chaucer, in the *Knight's Tale* (c.1385), refers to a preparation made 'of a certeyn wyn With nercotikes and opye'. In the 20th century the use of **narcotic** was extended to any drug which affects mood or behaviour, especially drugs banned by law.
Narcolepsy, meaning an abnormal tendency to fall asleep, is also from *narkē*, on the pattern of **epilepsy**.

nark informal > *noun* **1** chiefly Brit. a police informer. **2** Austral./NZ an annoying person or thing. > *verb* chiefly Brit. annoy.
ORIGIN – Romany *nāk* 'nose'.

narky > *adjective* Brit. informal irritable.

Narragansett /narrəgansət/ (also **Narraganset**) > *noun* (pl. same or **Narragansetts**) a member of an American Indian people originally of Rhode Island.
ORIGIN – the name in Narragansett, literally 'people of the promontory'.

narrate > *verb* **1** give an account of. **2** provide a commentary for (a film, television programme, etc.).
DERIVATIVES – **narration** *noun* **narrator** *noun*.
SYNONYMS – **1** recount, relate, tell.
ORIGIN – Latin *narrare*.

narrative > *noun* **1** an account of connected events; a story. **2** the narrated part of a literary work, as distinct from dialogue. > *adjective* in the form of a narrative or concerned with narration.
DERIVATIVES – **narratively** *adverb*.
SYNONYMS – *noun* **1** account, story, tale.

narrow > *adjective* (**narrower**, **narrowest**) **1** of small width in comparison to length. **2** limited in extent, amount, or scope. **3** barely achieved: *a narrow escape*. > *verb* **1** become or make narrower. **2** (**narrow down**) reduce (the number of possibilities or options). > *noun* (**narrows**) a narrow channel connecting two larger areas of water.
DERIVATIVES – **narrowly** *adverb* **narrowness** *noun*.
ANTONYMS – *adjective* **1,2** broad.
COMBINATIONS – **narrowboat** Brit. a canal boat less than 7 ft (2.1 metres) wide and steered with a tiller rather than a wheel. **narrow gauge** a railway gauge narrower than the standard gauge of 4 ft 8½ inches (1.435 m). **narrow-minded** unwilling to listen to or tolerate the views of others; prejudiced.

narrowcast > (past and past participle **narrowcast** or **narrowcasted**) transmit a television programme, especially by cable, to a comparatively small or specialist audience.

narthex /naartheks/ > *noun* an antechamber or large porch in a church.
ORIGIN – Greek.

narwhal /naarwəl/ > *noun* a small Arctic whale, the male of which has a long spirally twisted tusk.
ORIGIN – Danish *narhval*, perhaps from Old Norse *nár* 'corpse', with reference to the whale's skin colour.

nary /nairi/ > *adjective* informal or dialect form of NOT.
ORIGIN – from *ne'er a* 'never a'.

NASA /nassə/ > *abbreviation* (in the US) National Aeronautics and Space Administration.

nasal > *adjective* **1** relating to the nose. **2** (of a speech sound) pronounced by the breath resonating in the nose, e.g. *m*, *n*, *ng*, or French *en*, *un*. **3** (of speech) characterised by resonance in the nose as well as the mouth.
DERIVATIVES – **nasally** *adverb*.
ORIGIN – from Latin *nasus* 'nose'.

nasalise (also **nasalize**) > *verb* say or speak nasally.
DERIVATIVES – **nasalisation** *noun*.

nascent /nassn't, naysn't/ > *adjective* just coming into existence and beginning to develop.
SYNONYMS – embryonic, fledgling, incipient.
ORIGIN – from Latin *nasci* 'be born'.

nasturtium > *noun* a trailing garden plant with round leaves and bright orange, yellow, or red flowers.
ORIGIN – Latin, apparently from *naris* 'nose' + *torquere* 'to twist' (referring to its pungent scent).

nasty > *adjective* (**nastier**, **nastiest**) **1** causing disgust or repugnance; very unpleasant. **2** spiteful, violent, or bad-tempered. **3** likely to cause or having caused harm; dangerous or serious: *a nasty bang on the head*. > *noun* (pl. **nasties**) informal a nasty person or thing.
DERIVATIVES – **nastily** *adverb* **nastiness** *noun*.
SYNONYMS – *adjective* **1** disgusting, loathsome, repugnant, revolting, unpleasant. **2** bad-tempered, ill-tempered, malicious, spiteful, vicious, violent.
ANTONYMS – *adjective* **1,2** pleasant.

Nat. > *abbreviation* **1** national. **2** nationalist.

natal /nayt'l/ > *adjective* relating to the place or time of one's birth.
ORIGIN – Latin *natalis*, from *nasci* 'be born'.

natch > *adverb* informal naturally.

nation > *noun* a large body of people united by common descent, culture, or language, inhabiting a particular state or territory.
COMBINATIONS – **nation state** a sovereign state of which most of the citizens or subjects are united also by factors which define a nation, such as language or common descent.
ORIGIN – Latin, from *nasci* 'be born'.

national > *adjective* **1** relating to or characteristic of a nation. **2** owned, controlled, or financially supported by the state. > *noun* a citizen of a particular country.
DERIVATIVES – **nationally** *adverb*.
COMBINATIONS – **national curriculum** a curriculum of study laid down to be taught in state schools. **national debt** the total amount of money which a country's government has borrowed. **national grid Brit. 1** the network of high-voltage power lines between major power stations. **2** the metric system of geographical coordinates used in maps of the British Isles. **National Guard** (in the US) the primary reserve military force partly maintained by the

states but also available for federal use. **National Insurance** (in the UK) a system of compulsory payments by employees and employers to provide state assistance for people who are sick, unemployed, or retired. **national park** an area of environmental importance or natural beauty protected by the state and accessible to the public. **national service** a period of compulsory service in the armed forces during peacetime. **National Socialism** historical the political doctrine of the Nazi Party of Germany.

nationalise (also **nationalize**) > *verb* transfer (an industry or business) from private to state ownership or control.
DERIVATIVES – **nationalisation** *noun*.

nationalism > *noun* 1 patriotic feeling, often to an excessive degree. 2 advocacy of political independence for a particular country.
DERIVATIVES – **nationalist** *noun & adjective* **nationalistic** *adjective*.
SYNONYMS – 1 chauvinism, jingoism, patriotism.

nationality > *noun* (pl. **nationalities**) 1 the status of belonging to a particular nation. 2 an ethnic group forming a part of one or more political nations.

nationwide > *adjective & adverb* throughout the whole nation.

native > *noun* 1 a person born in a specified place. 2 a local inhabitant. 3 an indigenous animal or plant. 4 dated, offensive a non-white original inhabitant of a country, as regarded by European colonists or travellers. > *adjective* 1 associated with a person's place of birth. 2 (of a plant or animal) of indigenous origin or growth. 3 of the indigenous inhabitants of a place. 4 in a person's character; innate: *native wit*.
USAGE – in phrases such as *a native of Boston* the use of the noun **native** is quite acceptable. But when used as a noun without qualification, as in *this dance is a favourite with the natives*, it has an old-fashioned and colonial feel and may cause offence.
COMBINATIONS – **native speaker** a person who has spoken the language in question from earliest childhood.
ORIGIN – Latin *nativus*, from *nasci* 'be born'.

Native American > *noun* a member of any of the indigenous peoples of North and South America and the Caribbean Islands. > *adjective* of or relating to these peoples.
USAGE – in the US, **Native American** is now the accepted term in many contexts. See the note at **AMERICAN INDIAN**.

nativity > *noun* (pl. **nativities**) 1 a person's birth. 2 (**the Nativity**) the birth of Jesus Christ.

NATO /**nay**tō/ (also **Nato**) > *abbreviation* North Atlantic Treaty Organisation.

natron /**nay**trən/ > *noun* a mineral salt found in dried lake beds, consisting of hydrated sodium carbonate.
ORIGIN – Spanish *natrón*, via Arabic from Greek *nitron* 'nitre'.

natter informal > *verb* chat casually and at length. > *noun* a lengthy chat.
ORIGIN – imitative (originally dialect, in the sense 'grumble, fret').

natterjack toad > *noun* a small toad with a bright yellow stripe down its back.

natty > *adjective* (**nattier**, **nattiest**) informal smart and fashionable.
DERIVATIVES – **nattily** *adverb* **nattiness** *noun*.
ORIGIN – perhaps related to **NEAT**.

natural > *adjective* 1 existing in or derived from nature; not made, caused by, or processed by humankind. 2 in accordance with nature; normal or to be expected: *a natural death*. 3 born with a particular skill or quality: *a natural leader*. 4 relaxed and unaffected. 5 (of a parent or child) related by blood. 6 archaic illegitimate. 7 Music (of a note) not sharpened or flattened. > *noun* 1 a person with an innate gift or talent. 2 an off-white colour. 3 Music a natural note or a sign (♮) denoting one. 4 archaic a person mentally handicapped from birth.
DERIVATIVES – **naturalness** *noun*.
SYNONYMS – *adjective* 2 normal, ordinary, usual. 4 frank, genuine, spontaneous, unaffected.
ANTONYMS – *adjective* 2 abnormal. 4 affected.
COMBINATIONS – **natural gas** flammable gas, consisting largely of methane, occurring naturally underground and used as fuel. **natural history** the scientific study of animals or plants, especially as concerned with observation rather than experiment. **natural law** 1 a body of unchanging moral principles regarded as inherent in all human beings and forming a basis for human conduct. 2 an observable law relating to natural phenomena. **natural logarithm** a logarithm to the base *e* (equal to approximately 2.71828). **natural numbers** the sequence of whole numbers 1, 2, 3, etc., used for counting. **natural philosophy** archaic natural science, especially physical science. **natural resources** naturally occurring materials which can be exploited for economic gain. **natural science** a branch of science which deals with the physical world, e.g. physics, chemistry, geology, biology. **natural selection** the evolutionary process whereby organisms better adapted to their environment tend to survive and produce more offspring.

naturalise (also **naturalize**) > *verb* 1 admit

(a foreigner) to the citizenship of a country. 2 introduce (a non-native plant or animal) into a region and establish it in the wild. 3 alter (an adopted foreign word) so that it conforms more closely to the adopting language.
DERIVATIVES – **naturalisation** *noun*.

naturalism > *noun* an artistic or literary movement or style based on a detailed and accurate depiction of real life.

naturalist > *noun* 1 an expert in or student of natural history. 2 an exponent or practitioner of naturalism.
USAGE – do not confuse **naturalist** with **naturist**: a **naturist** is a nudist.

naturalistic > *adjective* 1 derived from or imitating real life or nature. 2 based on the theory of naturalism.
DERIVATIVES – **naturalistically** *adverb*.

naturally > *adverb* 1 in a natural manner. 2 of course.

nature > *noun* 1 the physical world, including plants, animals, the landscape, and natural phenomena, as opposed to humans or human creations. 2 the inherent qualities or characteristics of a person or thing. 3 a kind, sort, or class: *topics of a religious nature*. 4 hereditary characteristics as an influence on or determinant of personality. Contrasted with **NURTURE**.
IDIOMS – **in the nature of things** inevitable or inevitably.
COMBINATIONS – **nature reserve** an area of land managed so as to preserve its flora, fauna, and physical features. **nature trail** a signposted path through the countryside designed to draw attention to natural features.
ORIGIN – Latin *natura* 'birth, nature, quality', from *nasci* 'be born'.

naturism > *noun* nudism.
DERIVATIVES – **naturist** *noun & adjective*.
USAGE – do not confuse **naturism** and **naturist** (a nudist) with **naturalism** and **naturalist**: **naturalism** is an artistic or literary approach or style; a **naturalist** is an expert in natural history, or an exponent of naturalism.

naturopathy /naychərə**opp**əthi/ > *noun* a system of alternative medicine involving the treatment or prevention of diseases by diet, exercise, and massage rather than by using drugs.
DERIVATIVES – **naturopath** *noun* **naturopathic** *adjective*.

naught > *pronoun* archaic nothing. > *noun* N. Amer. nought.

naughty > *adjective* (**naughtier**, **naughtiest**) 1 (especially of a child) disobedient; badly behaved. 2 informal mildly rude or indecent.
DERIVATIVES – **naughtily** *adverb* **naughtiness** *noun*.
SYNONYMS – 1 bad, badly behaved, disobedient, misbehaving.

ANTONYMS – **1** good, obedient.

ORIGIN – from **NAUGHT**: the earliest sense was 'possessing nothing'.

nausea /**naw**ziə/ > *noun* **1** a feeling of sickness with an inclination to vomit. **2** disgust or revulsion.

SYNONYMS – **1** biliousness, queasiness.

ORIGIN – Greek *nausia* 'seasickness', from *naus* 'ship'.

nauseate > *verb* cause to feel sick or disgusted.

nauseous > *adjective* **1** affected with nausea. **2** causing nausea.

DERIVATIVES – **nauseously** *adverb*.

nautical > *adjective* of or concerning sailors or navigation; maritime.

DERIVATIVES – **nautically** *adverb*.

COMBINATIONS – **nautical mile** a unit used in measuring distances at sea, equal to 1,852 metres (approximately 2,025 yards).

ORIGIN – Greek *nautikos*, from *nautēs* 'sailor'.

nautilus /**naw**tiləss/ > *noun* (pl. **nautiluses** or **nautili** /**naw**tilī/) a swimming cephalopod mollusc with a spiral shell and numerous short tentacles around the mouth.

ORIGIN – Greek *nautilos* 'sailor'.

Navajo /**navv**əhō/ (also **Navaho**) > *noun* (pl. same or **Navajos**) a member of an American Indian people of New Mexico and Arizona.

ORIGIN – Tewa (an American Indian language), meaning 'fields adjoining a dry gully'.

naval > *adjective* of or relating to a navy or navies.

ORIGIN – Latin *navalis*, from *navis* 'ship'.

navarin /**navv**əraN/ > *noun* a casserole of lamb or mutton with vegetables.

ORIGIN – French.

nave¹ > *noun* the central part of a church apart from the side aisles, chancel, and transepts.

ORIGIN – Latin *navis* 'ship'.

nave² > *noun* the hub of a wheel.

ORIGIN – Old English, related to **NAVEL**.

navel > *noun* the small hollow in the centre of a person's belly caused by the detachment of the umbilical cord.

WORDFINDER – umbilical (*relating to the navel*).

COMBINATIONS – **navel-gazing** absorption in oneself or a single issue. **navel orange** a variety of orange having a navel-like depression at the top containing a small secondary fruit.

navigable > *adjective* of sufficient depth or width to be used by boats and ships.

DERIVATIVES – **navigability** *noun*.

navigate > *verb* **1** plan and direct the route or course of a ship, aircraft, or other form of transport. **2** sail or travel over. **3** guide (a vessel or vehicle) over a specified route.

ORIGIN – Latin *navigare* 'to sail'.

navigation > *noun* **1** the process or activity of navigating. **2** the passage of ships.

DERIVATIVES – **navigational** *adjective*.

COMBINATIONS – **navigation lights** lights shown by a ship or aircraft at night to indicate its position and orientation.

navigator > *noun* **1** a person who navigates a ship, aircraft, etc. **2** historical a person who explores by sea. **3** Computing a browser program for accessing data on the World Wide Web or another information system.

navvy > *noun* (pl. **navvies**) Brit. dated a labourer employed in the excavation and construction of a road or railway.

wordpower facts
Navvy
The word **navvy** is a shortening of **navigator**, which in the 18th century came to denote, as well as a sailor skilled in navigation, a labourer employed in the rapidly expanding enterprise of canal construction (in certain parts of the country a canal was known as a **navigation**). The word **navigate** derives from the Latin word for 'ship', *navis*, which gave rise to **navy** and also, because of its shape, the **nave** of a church or cathedral. Ultimately related to *navis* is the Greek word for 'ship', *naus*, source of **nautical**, **nausea** (originally 'seasickness'), and **noise** (see box at **NOISE**).

navy > *noun* (pl. **navies**) **1** the branch of a state's armed services which conducts military operations at sea. **2** (also **navy blue**) a dark blue colour.

ORIGIN – Old French *navie* 'ship, fleet', from Latin *navis* 'ship'.

nawab /nəwaab/ > *noun* Indian **1** a native governor during the time of the Mogul empire. **2** a Muslim nobleman or person of high status.

ORIGIN – Arabic, 'deputy'; see also **NABOB**.

nay > *adverb* **1** or rather: *it will take months, nay years*. **2** archaic or dialect no. > *noun* a negative answer.

ORIGIN – Old Norse.

Nazarene /nazzəreen/ > *noun* **1** a person from the town of Nazareth in Israel. **2** (**the Nazarene**) Jesus Christ. **3** a member of an early sect of Jewish Christians. > *adjective* relating to Nazareth or Nazarenes.

Nazi /**naat**zi/ > *noun* (pl. **Nazis**) **1** historical a member of the National Socialist German Workers' Party. **2** derogatory a person with extreme racist or authoritarian views.

DERIVATIVES – **Nazism** *noun*.

ORIGIN – German, representing the pronunciation of *Nati-* in *Nationalsozialist*.

NB > *abbreviation* **1** New Brunswick. **2** nota bene.

Nb > *symbol* the chemical element niobium.

nb > *abbreviation* Cricket no-ball.

NC > *abbreviation* **1** network computer. **2** North Carolina.

NCO > *abbreviation* non-commissioned officer.

ND > *abbreviation* North Dakota.

Nd > *symbol* the chemical element neodymium.

Ndebele /əndəbeeli, əndəbayli/ > *noun* (pl. same or **Ndebeles**) a member of a people of Zimbabwe and NE South Africa.

ORIGIN – Nguni (a Bantu language).

NE > *abbreviation* **1** Nebraska. **2** north-east or north-eastern.

Ne > *symbol* the chemical element neon.

Neanderthal /niandərtaal/ > *noun* **1** (also **Neanderthal man**) an extinct human living in ice age Europe between *c.*120,000 and *c.*35,000 years ago. **2** informal an uncivilised or uncouth man.

ORIGIN – from *Neanderthal*, a region in Germany where remains of Neanderthal man were found.

neap /neep/ (also **neap tide**) > *noun* a tide just after the first or third quarters of the moon when there is least difference between high and low water.

Neapolitan /neeəpollit'n/ > *noun* a person from the Italian city of Naples. > *adjective* **1** relating to Naples. **2** (of ice cream) made in layers of different colours and flavours.

near > *adverb* **1** at or to a short distance in space or time. **2** almost. > *preposition* (also **near to**) **1** at or to a short distance in space or time from. **2** close to (a state or in terms of resemblance). > *adjective* **1** at a short distance away in space or time. **2** close to being: *a near disaster*. **3** closely related. **4** located on the nearside of a vehicle. > *verb* approach.

DERIVATIVES – **nearness** *noun*.

SYNONYMS – *adverb & adjective* **1** close, close by, nearby.

ANTONYMS – *adverb* **1** far away. *adjective* **1-3** distant.

COMBINATIONS – **near miss 1** a narrowly avoided collision. **2** a bomb or shot that just misses its target. **near-sighted** short-sighted.

ORIGIN – Old Norse.

nearby > *adjective & adverb* not far away.

Near East > *noun* the countries of SW Asia between the Mediterranean and India (including the Middle East).

DERIVATIVES – **Near Eastern** *adjective*.

nearly > *adverb* very close to; almost.

IDIOMS – **not nearly** nothing like; far from.

SYNONYMS – almost, just about, more or less, practically, very close to.

nearside > *noun* chiefly Brit. **1** the side of a vehicle nearest the kerb. Contrasted with **OFFSIDE**. **2** the left-hand side of a horse.

neat > *adjective* **1** tidy or carefully arranged. **2** done with or demonstrating skill or efficiency. **3** (of a drink of spirits) not diluted or mixed with anything else. **4** N. Amer. informal excellent.

DERIVATIVES – **neatly** *adverb* **neatness** *noun.*

SYNONYMS – **1** orderly, organised, tidy, well ordered.

ANTONYMS – **1** disorderly.

---

wordpower facts
Neat

The word **neat** comes, via French *net*, from Latin *nitidus*, from *nitere*, 'to shine'. It entered English in the late 15th century, in the sense 'free from impurities; clean' (surviving still in sense 3). By the late 16th century it had acquired the sense 'bright' (as in this comment in a work of 1687: 'this stone...is very neat when polished'), but this sense had become obsolete by the end of the 18th century. The current core meaning is recorded from the 17th century.

---

neaten > *verb* make neat.

SYNONYMS – smarten, straighten up, tidy.

neath > *preposition* literary beneath.

neat's-foot oil > *noun* oil obtained by boiling the feet of cattle, used to dress leather.

ORIGIN – from *neat*, an archaic word for a cow or ox.

neb > *noun* Scottish & N. English a nose, snout, or bird's beak.

nebbish > *noun* informal, chiefly N. Amer. a pitifully ineffectual or timid man.

ORIGIN – Yiddish *nebekh* 'poor thing'.

Nebuchadnezzar /nebyookədnezzər/ > *noun* a very large wine bottle, equivalent in capacity to about twenty regular bottles.

ORIGIN – from *Nebuchadnezzar* II, king of Babylon in the 6th century BC.

nebula /nebyoolə/ > *noun* (pl. **nebulae** /nebyoolee/ or **nebulas**) Astronomy a cloud of gas or dust in outer space, visible in the night sky either as a bright patch or as a dark silhouette against other glowing matter.

DERIVATIVES – **nebular** *adjective.*

ORIGIN – Latin, 'mist'.

nebuliser /nebyoolīzər/ (also **nebulizer**) > *noun* a device for producing a fine spray of liquid, used for example for inhaling a medicinal drug.

DERIVATIVES – **nebulise** (also **nebulize**) *verb.*

nebulous > *adjective* **1** in the form of a cloud or haze; hazy. **2** vague or ill-defined: *nebulous concepts.* **3** Astronomy relating to a nebula or nebulae.

DERIVATIVES – **nebulosity** *noun.*

SYNONYMS – **1** cloudy, fuzzy, hazy, indistinct. **2** hazy, ill-defined, imprecise, unclear, vague.

necessarily > *adverb* as a necessary result; inevitably.

necessary* > *adjective* **1** required to be done, achieved, or present; needed. **2** that must be; inevitable: *a necessary result.* > *noun* **1** (**necessaries**) the basic requirements of life, such as food and warmth. **2** (**the necessary**) informal the action, item, or money required.

*SPELLING – one *c*, two *ss*: ne*c*e*ss*ary.

SYNONYMS – *adjective* **1** essential, imperative, indispensable, obligatory, required, requisite. **2** inescapable, inevitable, unavoidable.

ORIGIN – Latin *necessarius*, from *necesse* 'be needful'.

necessitate > *verb* **1** make necessary as a result. **2** force or compel to do something.

SYNONYMS – **1** entail, mean, require.

necessitous > *adjective* lacking the necessities of life; poor.

necessity > *noun* (pl. **necessities**) **1** the state or fact of being required or indispensable. **2** an indispensable thing. **3** a situation enforcing a particular course: *created more by necessity than design.*

IDIOMS – **necessity is the mother of invention** proverb when the need for something becomes imperative, you find ways of getting or achieving it.

neck > *noun* **1** the part of the body connecting the head to the rest of the body. **2** a narrow connecting or end part, such as the part of a bottle near the mouth. **3** the part of a violin, guitar, or other instrument that bears the fingerboard. **4** the length of a horse's head and neck as a measure of its lead in a race. **5** informal impudence or nerve: *he had the neck to charge me full fare.* > *verb* informal **1** kiss and caress amorously. **2** Brit. swallow (a drink).

IDIOMS – **get** (or **catch**) **it in the neck** informal be severely criticised or punished. **neck and neck** level in a race or competition. **neck of the woods** informal a particular locality. **up to one's neck in** informal heavily or busily involved in.

DERIVATIVES – **neckless** *adjective.*

COMBINATIONS – **neckband** a strip of material round the neck of a garment. **neckcloth** a cravat. **necktie** N. Amer. or dated a tie worn around the neck.

ORIGIN – Old English, 'nape of the neck'.

neckerchief > *noun* a square of cloth worn round the neck.

necklace > *noun* an ornamental chain or string of beads, jewels, or links worn round the neck. > *verb* (in South Africa) kill by placing a tyre soaked with petrol round a victim's neck and setting it alight.

necklet > *noun* a close-fitting, typically rigid ornament worn around the neck.

neckline > *noun* the edge of a woman's garment at or below the neck.

necromancy /nekrōmansi/ > *noun* **1** prediction of the future by allegedly communicating with the dead. **2** witchcraft or black magic.

DERIVATIVES – **necromancer** *noun* **necromantic** *adjective.*

---

wordpower facts
Necromancy

The word **necromancy** entered English at the end of the 15th century, in the form *nigromancie*. It came via Old French from medieval Latin *nigromantia*. In this form of Latin the spelling with *i* had developed by association with the Latin word for 'black', *niger*. However, the earlier Latin form of the word was *necromantia*, from Greek *nekros* 'corpse' and *manteia* 'divination', and in the 16th century the spelling in English was changed to conform with this.

---

necrophilia /nekrəfilliə/ > *noun* sexual intercourse with or attraction towards corpses.

DERIVATIVES – **necrophiliac** *noun.*

ORIGIN – from Greek *nekros* 'corpse'.

necrophobia > *noun* extreme or irrational fear of death or dead bodies.

ORIGIN – from Greek *nekros* 'corpse'.

necropolis /nekroppəliss/ > *noun* a cemetery, especially a large ancient one.

ORIGIN – from Greek *nekros* 'corpse' + *polis* 'city'.

necropsy /nekropsi/ > *noun* (pl. **necropsies**) another term for **AUTOPSY**.

necrosis /nekrōsiss/ > *noun* Medicine the death of most or all of the cells in an organ or tissue due to disease, injury, or failure of the blood supply.

DERIVATIVES – **necrotic** *adjective.*

ORIGIN – from Greek *nekros* 'corpse'.

nectar > *noun* **1** a sugary fluid produced by flowers to encourage pollination by insects, made into honey by bees. **2** (in Greek and Roman mythology) the drink of the gods. **3** a delicious drink.

DERIVATIVES – **nectarivorous** *adjective.*

ORIGIN – Greek *nektar*.

nectarine /nektəreen/ > *noun* a variety of

peach with smooth, brightly coloured skin and rich firm flesh.

ORIGIN – from **NECTAR**: first as an adjective meaning 'nectar-like'.

née /nay/ > *adjective* born (used in citing a married woman's maiden name): *Mrs. Hargreaves, née Liddell.*

ORIGIN – French.

need > *verb* **1** require (something) because it is essential or very important. **2** expressing necessity or obligation: *need I say more?* > *noun* **1** circumstances in which a thing or course of action is required. **2** a thing that is wanted or required. **3** a state of poverty, distress, or misfortune.

IDIOMS – **needs must when the Devil drives** proverb sometimes you have to do something you would rather not.

needful > *adjective* **1** formal necessary; requisite. **2** archaic needy. > *noun* (**the needful**) informal what is necessary.

needle > *noun* **1** a very thin pointed piece of metal with a hole or eye for thread at the blunter end, used in sewing. **2** a similar, larger instrument without an eye, used in knitting, crochet, etc. **3** the pointed hollow end of a hypodermic syringe. **4** a stylus used to play records. **5** a thin pointer on a dial, compass, etc. **6** the thin, sharp, stiff leaf of a fir or pine tree. **7** Brit. informal hostility or antagonism provoked by rivalry. > *verb* informal **1** prick or pierce with or as if with a needle. **2** provoke or annoy by continual criticism.

COMBINATIONS – **needlecord** Brit. fine-ribbed corduroy fabric. **needlepoint 1** closely stitched embroidery worked over canvas. **2** (also **needlelace**) lace made by hand using a needle rather than bobbins. **needlewoman** a woman who is skilled in sewing. **needlework** sewing or embroidery.

needless > *adjective* unnecessary; avoidable.

IDIOMS – **needless to say** of course.

DERIVATIVES – **needlessly** adverb.

SYNONYMS – avoidable, gratuitous, inessential, superfluous, unnecessary.

needn't > *contraction* need not.

needy > *adjective* (**needier**, **neediest**) **1** lacking the necessities of life; very poor. **2** needing emotional support; insecure.

DERIVATIVES – **neediness** noun.

neem /neem/ > *noun* a tropical tree which yields wood, oil, medicinal products, and insecticide.

ORIGIN – Sanskrit.

neep > *noun* Scottish & N. English a turnip.

ORIGIN – Latin napus.

ne'er /nair/ > *contraction* literary or dialect never.

ne'er-do-well > *noun* a person who is lazy and irresponsible.

nefarious /nifairiəss/ > *adjective* wicked or criminal.

ORIGIN – from Latin *nefas* 'wrong'.

negate /nigayt/ > *verb* **1** make ineffective; nullify. **2** deny the existence of. **3** Grammar make (a clause, sentence, etc.) negative in meaning.

SYNONYMS – **1** annul, cancel, invalidate, nullify.

ORIGIN – Latin *negare* 'deny'.

negation > *noun* **1** the contradiction or denial of something. **2** the absence or opposite of something actual or positive: *evil is not merely the negation of goodness.* **3** Mathematics the replacement of positive by negative.

negative > *adjective* **1** characterised by the absence rather than the presence of distinguishing features: *a negative test result.* **2** expressing or implying denial, disagreement, or refusal. **3** pessimistic, undesirable, or unwelcome. **4** (of a quantity) less than zero. **5** of, containing, producing, or denoting the kind of electric charge carried by electrons. **6** (of a photographic image) showing light and shade or colours reversed from those of the original. **7** Grammar stating that something is not the case. > *noun* **1** a word or statement expressing denial, refusal, or negation. **2** a negative photographic image from which positive prints may be made. > *verb* **1** reject, veto, or contradict. **2** make ineffective; neutralise.

DERIVATIVES – **negatively** adverb **negativity** noun.

SYNONYMS – *adjective* **3** bleak, defeatist, gloomy, pessimistic.

ANTONYMS – *adjective* positive.

COMBINATIONS – **negative equity** potential indebtedness arising when the market value of a property falls below the outstanding amount of a mortgage secured on it. **negative pole** the south-seeking pole of a magnet. **negative sign** a minus sign.

neglect > *verb* **1** fail to give proper care or attention to. **2** fail to do something: *he neglected to write to her.* > *noun* **1** the state of being neglected. **2** the action of neglecting.

ORIGIN – Latin *neglegere* 'disregard'.

neglectful > *adjective* failing to give proper care or attention.

SYNONYMS – careless, lax, negligent, remiss.

negligee /neglizhay/ > *noun* a woman's light, filmy dressing gown.

ORIGIN – French, 'given little thought or attention'.

negligence > *noun* **1** lack of proper care and attention. **2** Law breach of a duty of care which results in damage.

DERIVATIVES – **negligent** adjective.

SYNONYMS – carelessness, laxity, neglect.

negligible /neglijib'l/ > *adjective* so small or unimportant as to be not worth considering.

DERIVATIVES – **negligibly** adverb.

SYNONYMS – insignificant, trifling, trivial.

ORIGIN – obsolete French, from *négliger* 'to neglect'.

negotiable > *adjective* **1** open to discussion or modification. **2** able to be traversed; passable. **3** (of a document) able to be transferred or assigned to the legal ownership of another person.

DERIVATIVES – **negotiability** noun.

negotiate > *verb* **1** try to reach an agreement or compromise by discussion. **2** obtain or bring about by negotiating. **3** find a way over or through (an obstacle or difficult path). **4** transfer (a cheque, bill, etc.) to the legal ownership of another.

DERIVATIVES – **negotiation** noun **negotiator** noun.

ORIGIN – Latin, from *negotiari* 'do in the course of business'.

Negress /neegris/ > *noun* a woman or girl of black African origin.

USAGE – the term **Negress** is now regarded as old-fashioned or even offensive; **black** is the preferred term.

Negritude /negrityood/ > *noun* the quality, fact, or awareness of being of black African origin.

Negro > *noun* (pl. **Negroes**) a member of a dark-skinned group of peoples originally native to Africa south of the Sahara.

USAGE – the term **Negro** is now regarded as old-fashioned or even offensive; **black** is the preferred term.

ORIGIN – from Latin *niger* 'black'.

Negroid > *adjective* relating to the division of humankind represented by the indigenous peoples of central and southern Africa.

USAGE – the term **Negroid** is associated with outdated notions of racial types; it is potentially offensive and is best avoided.

Negrophobia > *noun* intense or irrational dislike or fear of black people.

DERIVATIVES – **Negrophobe** noun.

neigh > *noun* a characteristic high whinnying sound made by a horse. > *verb* utter a neigh.

neighbour (US **neighbor**) > *noun* **1** a person living next door to or very near to another. **2** a person or place in relation to others next to it. > *verb* be situated next to or very near (another).

DERIVATIVES – **neighbourly** adjective.

neighbourhood (US **neighborhood**) > *noun* **1** a district or community within a town or city. **2** the area surrounding a particular place, person, or object.

IDIOMS – **in the neighbourhood of** approximately.

COMBINATIONS – **neighbourhood watch** a scheme of systematic local vigilance by householders to discourage crime, especially burglary.

neither /**nī**thər, **nee**thər/ > *determiner & pronoun* not the one nor the other of two people or things; not either. > *adverb* **1** used before the first of two (or occasionally more) alternatives (the others being introduced by 'nor') to indicate that they are each untrue or each do not happen. **2** used to introduce a further negative statement.

nelly > *noun* (pl. **nellies**) informal **1** a silly person. **2** derogatory an effeminate homosexual man.

IDIOMS – **not on your nelly** Brit. certainly not. [ORIGIN – first as *not on your Nelly Duff*, rhyming slang for 'puff' (i.e. breath of life).]

ORIGIN – from the given name *Nelly*.

nelson > *noun* a wrestling hold in which one arm is passed under the opponent's arm from behind and the hand is applied to the neck (**half nelson**), or both arms and hands are applied (**full nelson**).

nematode /**nemm**ətōd/ > *noun* Zoology a worm of a group with slender, unsegmented, cylindrical bodies (including the roundworms, threadworms, and eelworms).

ORIGIN – from Greek *nēma* 'thread'.

nem. con. > *adverb* with no one dissenting; unanimously.

ORIGIN – abbreviation of Latin *nemine contradicente*.

nemesis /**nemm**ısiss/ > *noun* (pl. **nemeses** /**nemm**iseez/) **1** an inescapable agent of retribution. **2** retribution caused by such an agent.

ORIGIN – Greek, 'retribution', personified as the goddess of divine punishment.

neo- /**nee**ō/ > *combining form* **1** new: *neonate*. **2** a new or revived form of: *neoclassicism*.

ORIGIN – from Greek *neos* 'new'.

neoclassical (also **neoclassic**) > *adjective* relating to the revival of a classical style in the arts.

DERIVATIVES – **neoclassicism** *noun* **neoclassicist** *noun & adjective*.

neodymium /**nee**ə**dimm**iəm/ > *noun* a silvery-white metallic chemical element of the lanthanide series.

ORIGIN – from **NEO-** + *didymium*, name given to a mixture of the elements praseodymium and neodymium, from Greek *didumos* 'twin'.

neo-Impressionism > *noun* a late 19th-century artistic movement which sought to improve on Impressionism through a systematic approach to form and colour, especially by using pointillist technique.

DERIVATIVES – **neo-Impressionist** *adjective & noun*.

Neolithic /**nee**ə**lith**ik/ > *adjective* relating to the later part of the Stone Age, when ground or polished stone weapons and implements prevailed.

ORIGIN – from **NEO-** + Greek *lithos* 'stone'.

neologism /**nee**ollə*jiz'm/ > *noun* a newly coined word or expression.

ORIGIN – from **NEO-** + Greek *logos* 'word'.

neon > *noun* **1** an inert gaseous chemical element, present in trace amounts in the air, which gives an orange glow when electricity is passed through it and is used in fluorescent lighting. **2** (before another noun) very bright or fluorescent in colour: *bold neon colours*.

COMBINATIONS – **neon tetra** a small brightly coloured tropical freshwater fish, popular in aquaria. [ORIGIN – *tetra* is an abbreviation of Latin *Tetragonopterus* 'tetragonal-finned', a former genus name.]

ORIGIN – Greek, 'something new'.

neonatal /**nee**ə**nayt**'l/ > *adjective* relating to newborn children.

DERIVATIVES – **neonatology** *noun*.

neonate /**nee**ənayt/ > *noun* chiefly Medicine a newborn child or mammal.

ORIGIN – from **NEO-** + Latin *nasci* 'be born'.

neophobia > *noun* extreme or irrational fear or dislike of anything new or unfamiliar.

DERIVATIVES – **neophobic** *adjective*.

neophyte /**nee**əfīt/ > *noun* **1** a person who is new to a subject, skill, or belief. **2** a novice in a religious order, or a newly ordained priest.

ORIGIN – from Greek *neophutos* 'newly planted'.

neoplasm > *noun* a new and abnormal growth of tissue in the body, especially a malignant tumour.

DERIVATIVES – **neoplastic** *adjective*.

ORIGIN – from **NEO-** + Greek *plasma* 'formation'.

Neoplatonism /**nee**ō**playt**əniz'm/ > *noun* a philosophical and religious system dating from the 3rd century, combining Platonic and other Greek thought with oriental mysticism.

DERIVATIVES – **Neoplatonic** *adjective* **Neoplatonist** *noun*.

neoprene /**nee**ōpreen/ > *noun* a synthetic substance resembling rubber.

ORIGIN – from **NEO-** + *prene* (perhaps from **PROPYL** + **-ENE**).

neoteny /**nee**ottəni/ > *noun* Zoology **1** the retention of juvenile features in an adult animal. **2** the sexual maturity of an animal in a larval state, as in the axolotl.

DERIVATIVES – **neotenic** *adjective* **neotenous** *adjective*.

ORIGIN – from Greek *neos* + *teinein* 'extend'.

Nepalese /**nepp**əleez/ > *noun* a person from Nepal. > *adjective* relating to Nepal.

Nepali /ni**paw**li/ > *noun* (pl. same or **Nepalis**) **1** a person from Nepal. **2** the official language of Nepal.

nephew > *noun* a son of one's brother or sister, or of one's brother-in-law or sister-in-law.

ORIGIN – Latin *nepos* 'grandson, nephew'.

nephrite /**nef**rīt/ > *noun* a pale green or white form of jade.

ORIGIN – from Greek *nephros* 'kidney' (with reference to its supposed efficacy in treating kidney disease).

nephritis /ni**frī**tiss/ > *noun* inflammation of the kidneys.

ORIGIN – from Greek *nephros* 'kidney'.

nephrosis /ni**frō**siss/ > *noun* kidney disease.

DERIVATIVES – **nephrotic** *adjective*.

ne plus ultra /nay plooss **ool**traa/ > *noun* (**the ne plus ultra**) the perfect or most extreme example.

ORIGIN – Latin, 'not further beyond', the supposed inscription on the Pillars of Hercules (at the Strait of Gibraltar) prohibiting passage by ships.

nepotism /**nepp**ətiz'm/ > *noun* favouritism shown to relatives or friends, especially by giving them jobs.

ORIGIN – Italian *nepotismo*, from *nipote* 'nephew' (with reference to privileges bestowed on the 'nephews' of popes, often really their illegitimate sons).

Neptunian > *adjective* of or relating to the planet Neptune.

neptunium > *noun* a rare radioactive metallic chemical element produced from uranium by the capture of neutrons.

ORIGIN – from *Neptune*, on the pattern of *uranium* (Neptune being the next planet beyond Uranus).

nerd > *noun* informal a person who lacks social skills or is boringly studious.

DERIVATIVES – **nerdish** *adjective* **nerdy** *adjective*.

Nereid /**neer**i-id/ > *noun* Greek Mythology any of the sea nymphs, daughters of the old sea god Nereus.

neroli /**neer**əli/ (also **neroli oil**) > *noun* an essential oil distilled from the flowers of the Seville orange.

ORIGIN – Italian, said to be the name of a 17th-century Italian princess who discovered the oil.

nerve > *noun* **1** a fibre or bundle of fibres in the body that transmits impulses of sensation between the brain or spinal cord and other parts of the body. **2** (**nerves** or **one's nerve**) steadiness and courage in a demanding situation: *the journey tested her nerves to the full*. **3** (**nerves**) nervousness. **4** informal impudence or audacity. > *verb* (**nerve oneself**) brace oneself for a demanding situation.

WORDFINDER – neural (*relating to a nerve or the nervous system*); axon (*a thread-like part of a nerve cell*), ganglion (*a mass of nerve cells*), synapse (*a gap between nerve cells*).

IDIOMS – **get on someone's nerves** informal irritate someone. **touch** (or **hit**) **a** (**raw**) **nerve** refer to a sensitive topic.

SYNONYMS – *noun* **2** (**nerves** or **one's nerve**) coolness, courage, sangfroid, self-possession. **3** (**nerves**) anxiety, nervousness, tension.

COMBINATIONS – **nerve cell** a neuron. **nerve centre 1** a group of connected nerve cells performing a particular function. **2** the control centre of an organisation or operation. **nerve gas** a poisonous vapour which disrupts the transmission of nerve impulses, causing death or disablement. **nerve-racking** (also **nerve-wracking**) stressful; frightening.

ORIGIN – Latin *nervus*; related to Greek *neuron* 'nerve, sinew, tendon'.

nerveless > *adjective* **1** lacking vigour or feeling. **2** confident. **3** Anatomy & Biology lacking nerves or nervures.

nervous > *adjective* **1** easily agitated or alarmed. **2** apprehensive or anxious. **3** relating to or affecting the nerves.

DERIVATIVES – **nervously** *adverb* **nervousness** *noun*.

SYNONYMS – **1** excitable, highly strung, nervy. **2** anxious, apprehensive, edgy, tense, uneasy, worried.

ANTONYMS – **1** easy-going. **2** calm, relaxed.

COMBINATIONS – **nervous breakdown** a period of mental illness resulting from severe depression or stress. **nervous system** the network of nerve cells and fibres which transmits nerve impulses between parts of the body. **nervous wreck** informal a stressed or emotionally exhausted person.

nervure /**nerv**yoor/ > *noun* **1** Entomology each of the hollow veins forming the framework of an insect's wing. **2** Botany the principal vein of a leaf.

nervy > *adjective* (**nervier**, **nerviest**) **1** chiefly Brit. nervous or tense. **2** N. Amer. informal bold or impudent.

DERIVATIVES – **nervily** *adverb* **nerviness** *noun*.

nescient /**ness**iənt/ > *adjective* literary ignorant.

DERIVATIVES – **nescience** *noun*.

ORIGIN – from Latin *nescire* 'to not know'.

ness > *noun* a headland or promontory.

ORIGIN – Old English, related to 'nose'.

-ness > *suffix* **1** forming nouns denoting a state or condition: *liveliness*. **2** forming nouns denoting something in a certain state: *wilderness*.

nest > *noun* **1** a structure made by a bird for laying eggs and sheltering its young. **2** a place where an animal or insect breeds or shelters. **3** a place filled with undesirable people or things: *a nest of spies*. **4** a set of similar objects of graduated sizes, fitting together for storage. > *verb* **1** use or build a nest. **2** fit (an object or objects) inside a larger one.

WORDFINDER – nidification (*nest-building*).

COMBINATIONS – **nest box** (also **nesting box**) a box provided for a bird to nest in. **nest egg 1** a sum of money saved for the future. **2** a real or artificial egg left in a nest to induce hens to lay there.

nestle > *verb* **1** settle comfortably within or against something. **2** (of a place) lie in a sheltered position.

nestling > *noun* a bird that is too young to leave the nest.

net[1] > *noun* **1** a material with an open mesh, made of twine or cord or plastic filaments. **2** a piece or structure of net for catching fish or insects. **3** a fine fabric with a very open weave. **4** (**the net**) the goal in football. **5** (**nets**) (in cricket) a practice area enclosed by net. **6** a trap or system of selection. **7** a communications or computer network. **8** (**the Net**) the Internet. > *verb* (**netted**, **netting**) **1** catch with a net. **2** (in sport) score (a goal). **3** cover with a net.

WORDFINDER – reticulated (*like a net or network*).

net[2] (Brit. also **nett**) > *adjective* **1** (of an amount, value, or price) remaining after a deduction of tax or other contributions. Contrasted with **GROSS**. **2** (of a price) to be paid in full. **3** (of a weight) excluding that of the packaging. **4** (of an effect or result) overall. > *verb* (**netted**, **netting**) acquire (a sum) as clear profit.

COMBINATIONS – **net profit** the actual profit after working expenses have been paid.

ORIGIN – first meaning 'clean' and 'smart': from French *net* 'neat'.

netball > *noun* a team game in which goals are scored by throwing a ball through a netted hoop.

nether /**neth**ər/ > *adjective* lower in position.

DERIVATIVES – **nethermost** *adjective*.

COMBINATIONS – **nether regions 1** (also **netherworld**) hell; the underworld. **2** euphemistic a person's genitals and bottom.

netsuke /**net**sōoki/ > *noun* (pl. same or **netsukes**) a carved Japanese ornament of wood or ivory, formerly worn tucked into the sash of a kimono.

ORIGIN – Japanese.

nett > *adjective* & *verb* Brit. variant spelling of **NET**[2].

netting > *noun* fabric made of net.

nettle > *noun* a plant having jagged leaves covered with stinging hairs. > *verb* annoy.

IDIOMS – **grasp the nettle** Brit. tackle a difficulty boldly.

COMBINATIONS – **nettlerash** urticaria.

network > *noun* **1** an arrangement of intersecting horizontal and vertical lines. **2** a complex system of railways, roads, etc. **3** a group of broadcasting stations that connect to broadcast a programme simultaneously. **4** a number of interconnected computers, operations, etc. **5** a group of people who interact together. > *verb* **1** connect as or operate with a network. **2** Brit. broadcast on a network. **3** interact with others to exchange information and develop contacts.

DERIVATIVES – **networker** *noun*.

SYNONYMS – *noun* **1** grid, lattice, web. **2** labyrinth, maze, warren.

neural > *adjective* relating to a nerve or the nervous system.

DERIVATIVES – **neurally** *adverb*.

neuralgia /nyoo**ral**jə/ > *noun* intense pain along the course of a nerve, especially in the head or face.

DERIVATIVES – **neuralgic** *adjective*.

neurasthenia /nyoorəss**theen**iə/ > *noun* Medicine, dated a condition of tiredness, headache, and irritability, typically ascribed to emotional disturbance.

DERIVATIVES – **neurasthenic** *adjective* & *noun*.

neuritis /nyoo**rīt**iss/ > *noun* Medicine inflammation of a peripheral nerve or nerves.

neuro- > *combining form* relating to nerves or the nervous system.

ORIGIN – from Greek *neuron* 'nerve, sinew, tendon'.

neurogenic /nyoorō**jenn**ik/ > *adjective* caused by or arising in the nervous system.

neuroleptic /nyoorō**lept**ik/ Medicine > *adjective* tending to reduce nervous tension by depressing nerve functions.

ORIGIN – from **NEURO-** + Greek *lēpsis* 'seizing'.

neurology > *noun* the branch of medicine and biology concerned with the nervous system.

DERIVATIVES – **neurological** *adjective* **neurologist** *noun*.

neuron* (also **neurone**) > *noun* a specialised cell transmitting nerve impulses.

DERIVATIVES – **neuronal** *adjective*.

*SPELLING – in scientific sources the standard spelling is **neuron**. The spelling **neurone** is found only in non-technical sources.

neuropathology > *noun* the pathology of the nervous system.

DERIVATIVES – **neuropathological** *adjective* **neuropathologist** *noun*.

neurophysiology > *noun* the physiology of the nervous system.

DERIVATIVES – **neurophysiological** adjective **neurophysiologist** noun.

neurosis /nyoorōsiss/ > noun (pl. **neuroses** /nyoorōseez/) a relatively mild mental illness not caused by organic disease and involving symptoms such as depression, anxiety, obsessive behaviour, or hypochondria.

neurosurgery > noun surgery performed on the nervous system.

DERIVATIVES – **neurosurgeon** noun **neurosurgical** adjective.

neurotic > adjective 1 having, caused by, or relating to neurosis. 2 informal abnormally sensitive or obsessive. > noun a neurotic person.

DERIVATIVES – **neurotically** adverb **neuroticism** noun.

neurotoxin /nyoorōtoksin/ > noun a poison which acts on the nervous system.

neurotransmitter > noun Physiology a chemical substance released from a nerve fibre and bringing about the transfer of an impulse to another nerve, muscle, etc.

DERIVATIVES – **neurotransmission** noun.

neuter > adjective 1 Grammar (of a noun) not masculine, feminine, or common. 2 (of an animal) lacking developed sexual organs, or having had them removed. 3 (of a plant or flower) having neither functional pistils nor stamens. > noun Grammar a neuter word. > verb 1 castrate or spay. 2 render ineffective.

ORIGIN – Latin, 'neither'.

neutral > adjective 1 not supporting or in favour of either side in a dispute or conflict. 2 having no strongly marked characteristics. 3 Chemistry neither acid nor alkaline; having a pH of about 7. 4 electrically neither positive nor negative. > noun 1 an impartial or unbiased state or person. 2 a neutral colour or shade. 3 a disengaged position of gears. 4 an electrically neutral point, terminal, etc.

DERIVATIVES – **neutrality** noun **neutrally** adverb.

SYNONYMS – adjective 1 disinterested, impartial, non-partisan, objective, open-minded, unbiased.

ANTONYMS – adjective 1 biased, partisan.

ORIGIN – Latin neutralis 'of neuter gender'.

neutralise (also **neutralize**) > verb 1 render ineffective by applying an opposite force or effect. 2 make chemically neutral. 3 disarm (a bomb). 4 euphemistic kill or destroy.

DERIVATIVES – **neutralisation** noun.

SYNONYMS – 1 counteract, counterbalance, negate, nullify, offset.

neutralism > noun a policy of political neutrality.

DERIVATIVES – **neutralist** noun.

neutrino /nyootreenō/ > noun (pl.

neutrinos) a subatomic particle with a mass close to zero and no electric charge.

ORIGIN – Italian, from neutro 'neutral'.

neutron > noun a subatomic particle of about the same mass as a proton but without an electric charge.

COMBINATIONS – **neutron bomb** a nuclear weapon that produces large numbers of neutrons rather than heat or blast, causing harm to life but not property. **neutron star** Astronomy an extremely dense star composed predominantly of neutrons.

névé /nayvay/ > noun uncompressed granular snow, especially at the head of a glacier.

ORIGIN – Swiss French, 'glacier'.

never > adverb 1 not ever. 2 not at all. 3 Brit. informal (expressing surprise) definitely or surely not.

IDIOMS – **never a one** not one. **the never-never** Brit. informal hire purchase. **never-never land** an imaginary perfect place. [ORIGIN – the name of the ideal country in J. M. Barrie's Peter Pan, originally a name for the remote outback of Australia.] **well I never!** informal expressing great surprise.

nevermore > adverb literary never again.

nevertheless > adverb in spite of that.

nevus > noun (pl. **nevi**) US spelling of NAEVUS.

new > adjective 1 not existing before; made, introduced, or discovered recently or now for the first time. 2 not previously used or owned. 3 (often **new to**) seen, experienced, or acquired recently or now for the first time. 4 (**new to** or **at**) inexperienced at or unaccustomed to. 5 reinvigorated, restored, or reformed. 6 (in place names) discovered or founded later than and named after. > adverb newly.

DERIVATIVES – **newness** noun.

SYNONYMS – adjective 1 fresh, novel, recent.

ANTONYMS – adjective old.

COMBINATIONS – **new man** a man who rejects sexist attitudes and the traditional male role. **new maths** (N. Amer. **new math**) a system of teaching mathematics to children, with emphasis on investigation by them and on set theory. **new moon** the phase of the moon when it first appears as a slender crescent. **New Stone Age** the Neolithic period. **New Style** the calculation of dates using the Gregorian calendar. **New Testament** the second part of the Christian Bible, recording the life and teachings of Christ and his earliest followers. **new town** a planned urban centre created in an undeveloped or rural area. **new wave 1** the nouvelle vague (of film directors). **2** a style of rock music popular in the late 1970s, deriving from punk. **New World** North and South

America regarded collectively, in contrast to Europe, Asia, and Africa.

New Age > noun a cultural movement that rejects modern Western values and promotes spiritual and environmental awareness.

newborn > adjective 1 recently born. 2 regenerated. > noun a newborn child or animal.

newcomer > noun 1 a person who has recently arrived. 2 a novice.

newel /nyooəl/ > noun 1 the central supporting pillar of a spiral or winding staircase. 2 the top or bottom supporting post of a stair rail.

ORIGIN – Old French nouel 'knob', from Latin nodus 'knot'.

newfangled > adjective derogatory newly developed and unfamiliar.

ORIGIN – from dialect newfangle 'liking what is new'.

Newfoundland /nyoofowndlənd/ > noun a very large breed of dog, with a thick coarse coat.

ORIGIN – named after Newfoundland in Canada.

New Guinean > noun a person from New Guinea. > adjective relating to New Guinea.

newly > adverb 1 recently. 2 again; afresh. 3 in a new or different manner.

COMBINATIONS – **newly-wed** a recently married person.

news > noun 1 newly received or noteworthy information about recent events. 2 (**the news**) a broadcast or published news report. 3 (**news to**) informal information not previously known to.

IDIOMS – **no news is good news** proverb without information to the contrary you can assume that all is well.

COMBINATIONS – **news agency** an organisation that collects and distributes news items. **newsagent** Brit. a person or shop selling newspapers, magazines, etc. **newsboy** a boy who sells or delivers newspapers. **news conference** a press conference. **newsflash** a single item of important news broadcast separately and often interrupting other programmes. **newsgroup** a group of Internet users who exchange email on a topic of mutual interest. **newsletter** a bulletin issued periodically to those in a particular group. **newsman** a male reporter or journalist. **newsreader** Brit. a person who reads out broadcast news bulletins. **newsreel** a short cinema film of news and current affairs. **newsroom** the area in a newspaper or broadcasting office where news is processed. **news-stand** a stand for the sale of newspapers. **news wire** an Internet news service.

newscast > noun a broadcast news report.

newscaster > *noun* a newsreader.

newspaper > *noun* a daily or weekly publication consisting of folded unstapled sheets and containing news, articles, and advertisements.

WORDFINDER – broadsheet (*newspaper with a large format*), tabloid (*newspaper with pages half the size of a broadsheet, popular in style*).

newspeak > *noun* ambiguous euphemistic language used in political propaganda.

ORIGIN – the name of an artificial official language in George Orwell's *Nineteen Eighty-Four* (1949).

newsprint > *noun* cheap, absorbent printing paper used for newspapers.

newsworthy > *adjective* noteworthy as news.

newsy > *adjective* informal full of news.

newt > *noun* a small slender-bodied amphibian with a well-developed tail.

ORIGIN – from *an ewt* (from Old English *efeta* 'eft'), interpreted (by wrong division) as *a newt*.

newton > *noun* Physics the unit of force in the SI system, equal to the force that would give a mass of one kilogram an acceleration of one metre per second per second.

ORIGIN – named after the English scientist Sir Isaac *Newton* (1642–1727).

Newtonian > *adjective* Physics relating to or arising from the work of Sir Isaac Newton.

new year > *noun* **1** the calendar year just begun or about to begin. **2** the period immediately before and after 31 December.

COMBINATIONS – **New Year's Day** 1 January. **New Year's Eve** 31 December.

New Yorker > *noun* a person from the state or city of New York.

New Zealander > *noun* a person from New Zealand.

next > *adjective* **1** coming immediately after the present one in time, space, or order. **2** (of a day of the week) nearest (or the nearest but one) after the present. > *adverb* **1** immediately afterwards. **2** following in the specified order: *the next oldest.* > *noun* the next person or thing. > *preposition* archaic next to.

IDIOMS – **next of kin** a person's closest living relative or relatives. **next to 1** beside. **2** following in order or importance. **3** almost. **4** in comparison with. **the next world** (in some religious beliefs) the place where one goes after death.

next door > *adverb & adjective* in or to the next house or room.

IDIOMS – **next door to 1** in the next house or room to. **2** almost.

nexus /**nek**səss/ > *noun* (pl. same or **nexuses**) **1** a connection. **2** a connected group or

series. **3** the central and most important point.

ORIGIN – Latin, from *nectere* 'bind'.

Nez Percé /nez **perss**, per**say**/ > *noun* (pl. same or **Nez Percés**) a member of an American Indian people of central Idaho.

ORIGIN – French, 'pierced nose'.

NF > *abbreviation* **1** National Front. **2** Newfoundland.

NFL > *abbreviation* (in the US) National Football League.

ngaio /**nī**ō/ > *noun* (pl. **ngaios**) a small New Zealand tree with edible fruit and light white wood.

ORIGIN – Maori.

NGO > *abbreviation* non-governmental organisation.

ngultrum /əng**goōl**trəm/ > *noun* (pl. same) the basic monetary unit of Bhutan, equal to 100 chetrum.

ORIGIN – from Dzongkha, the official language of Bhutan.

ngwee /əng**gway**/ > *noun* (pl. same) a monetary unit of Zambia, equal to one hundredth of a kwacha.

ORIGIN – a local word.

NH > *abbreviation* New Hampshire.

NHS > *abbreviation* (in the UK) National Health Service.

NI > *abbreviation* **1** (in the UK) National Insurance. **2** Northern Ireland.

Ni > *symbol* the chemical element nickel.

niacin /**nī**əsin/ > *noun* another term for **NICOTINIC ACID**.

nib > *noun* **1** the pointed end part of a pen, which distributes the ink. **2** (**nibs**) shelled and crushed coffee or cocoa beans.

nibble > *verb* **1** take small bites out of. **2** gently bite at. **3** gradually erode. **4** show cautious interest in a project. > *noun* **1** an instance of nibbling. **2** a small piece of food bitten off. **3** (**nibbles**) informal small savoury snacks.

niblet > *noun* a small piece of food.

niblick /**nib**lik/ > *noun* Golf, dated an iron with a heavy, lofted head, used for playing out of bunkers.

nibs > *noun* (**his nibs**) informal a mock title used to refer to a self-important man.

Nicam /**nī**kam/ > *noun* a digital system used in British television to provide video signals with high-quality stereo sound.

ORIGIN – acronym from *near instantaneously companded* (ie. 'compressed and expanded') *audio multiplex*.

Nicaraguan /nikkə**rag**yooən/ > *noun* a person from Nicaragua in Central America. > *adjective* relating to Nicaragua.

nice > *adjective* **1** pleasant; agreeable; satisfactory. **2** (of a person) good-natured; kind. **3** (**nice and ——**) satisfactory in terms of the quality described. **4** fine or subtle. **5** archaic fastidious.

DERIVATIVES – **nicely** *adverb* **niceness** *noun.*

SYNONYMS – **1** acceptable, agreeable, enjoyable, good, pleasant, satisfactory. **2** friendly, good-natured, kind, likeable, pleasant, sympathetic.

ANTONYMS – nasty, unpleasant.

wordpower facts

Nice

The word **nice** entered English in the sense 'stupid', from Latin *nescius*, meaning 'ignorant'. It developed a range of senses, from 'wanton and dissolute' to 'strange or rare' and 'coy, reserved'; it was first used in the sense 'fine or subtle' in the 16th century, and the current main meanings, senses 1 and 2, are recorded in common use from the late 18th century. The development of the word's senses from negative to positive is similar to that of **pretty**.

nicety > *noun* (pl. **niceties**) **1** a fine detail or distinction. **2** accuracy. **3** a detail of etiquette.

IDIOMS – **to a nicety** precisely.

niche /neesh, nitch/ > *noun* **1** a shallow recess, especially one set in a wall. **2** (**one's niche**) a comfortable or suitable position in life. **3** a specialised but profitable corner of the market. **4** Ecology a role taken by a type of organism within its community.

ORIGIN – French, 'recess'.

nick[1] > *noun* **1** a small cut or notch. **2** (**the nick**) Brit. informal prison or a police station. **3** Brit. informal condition: *in good nick.* **4** the junction between the floor and side walls in a squash court. > *verb* **1** make a nick or nicks in. **2** Brit. informal steal. **3** Brit. informal arrest.

IDIOMS – **in the nick of time** only just in time.

nick[2] > *verb* (often **nick off**) Austral./NZ informal go quickly or furtively.

nickel > *noun* **1** a silvery-white metallic chemical element resembling iron, used in alloys. **2** N. Amer. informal a five-cent coin. > *verb* (**nickelled, nickelling; US nickeled, nickeling**) coat with nickel.

COMBINATIONS – **nickel brass** an alloy of copper, zinc, and nickel. **nickel silver** German silver. **nickel steel** stainless steel containing chromium and nickel.

ORIGIN – from German *Kupfernickel*, the copper-coloured ore from which nickel was first obtained, from *Kupfer* 'copper' + *Nickel* 'demon' (with reference to the ore's failure to yield copper).

nickel-and-dime N. Amer. > *verb* spend or charge small amounts of money. > *adjective* unimportant.

ORIGIN – first referring to a store selling articles at five or ten cents.

nickelodeon /nikkəlōdiən/ > *noun* N. Amer. **1** informal, dated a jukebox. **2** historical a cinema charging one nickel.

nicker[1] > *noun* (pl. same) Brit. informal a pound sterling.

nicker[2] > *verb* (of a horse) give a soft breathy whinny. > *noun* a nickering sound.

nick-nack > *noun* variant spelling of KNICK-KNACK.

nickname > *noun* a familiar or humorous name for a person or thing. > *verb* give a nickname to.

SYNONYMS – *noun* byname, sobriquet, pet name, tag.

ORIGIN – from *an eke-name* (*eke* meaning 'addition': see EKE[2]), misinterpreted (by wrong division) as *a neke name*.

Niçois /neeswaa/ (also **Niçoise** /nee-swaaz/) > *adjective* (after a noun) garnished with tomatoes, capers, and anchovies: *salade Niçoise*.

ORIGIN – French, 'relating to the city of Nice'.

nicotiana /nikkotiaanə/ > *noun* an ornamental plant related to tobacco, with tubular flowers that are particularly fragrant at night.

nicotine > *noun* a toxic oily liquid which is the chief active constituent of tobacco.

COMBINATIONS – **nicotine patch** a patch impregnated with nicotine, worn on the skin by a person trying to give up smoking.

ORIGIN – named after Jean *Nicot*, a 16th-century diplomat who introduced tobacco to France.

nicotinic acid > *noun* Biochemistry a vitamin of the B complex which occurs in milk, wheat germ, meat, and other foods.

nictation > *noun* technical blinking.

ORIGIN – Latin, from *nictare* 'to blink'.

nictitating membrane > *noun* Zoology a whitish membrane forming an inner eyelid in birds, reptiles, and some mammals.

nidification /niddifikaysh'n/ > *noun* Zoology nest-building.

ORIGIN – Latin, from *nidus* 'nest'.

nidus /nīdəss/ > *noun* (pl. **nidi** /nīdī/ or **niduses**) **1** a place in which something is formed or deposited. **2** Medicine a place in which bacteria have multiplied or may multiply.

ORIGIN – Latin, 'nest'.

niece* > *noun* a daughter of one's brother or sister, or of one's brother-in-law or sister-in-law.

*****SPELLING – remember *i* before *e* (except after *c*): *niece*.

ORIGIN – Old French, from Latin *neptis* 'granddaughter', feminine of *nepos* 'grandson, nephew'.

niello /niellō/ > *noun* **1** a black compound of sulphur with silver, lead, or copper, used for filling in engraved designs in silver or other metals. **2** objects decorated with this.

ORIGIN – Italian, from Latin *nigellus*, diminutive of *niger* 'black'.

Nietzschean /neechiən/ > *adjective* relating to the German philosopher Friedrich Wilhelm Nietzsche (1844–1900), proponent of the Übermensch.

niff Brit. informal > *noun* an unpleasant smell. > *verb* have an unpleasant smell.

DERIVATIVES – **niffy** *adjective*.

nifty > *adjective* (**niftier**, **niftiest**) informal particularly good, effective, or stylish.

DERIVATIVES – **niftily** *adverb*.

nigella /nījellə/ > *noun* a plant of a genus which includes love-in-a-mist.

ORIGIN – feminine of Latin *nigellus*, diminutive of *niger* 'black'.

Nigerian /nījeeriən/ > *noun* a person from Nigeria. > *adjective* relating to Nigeria.

niggard /niggərd/ > *noun* a mean or ungenerous person.

ORIGIN – from earlier *nigon*, ultimately of Scandinavian origin.

niggardly > *adjective* ungenerous or meagre.

nigger > *noun* offensive a black person.

IDIOMS – **a nigger in the woodpile** dated a hidden cause of trouble.

USAGE – the word **nigger** has had strong offensive connotations since the 17th century. Recently, however, it has started to be used by black people as a mildly disparaging or ironically affectionate way of referring to other black people. Despite this, when used by white people it remains strongly offensive, and should be avoided.

ORIGIN – from Spanish *negro* 'black'.

niggle > *verb* **1** cause (someone) slight but persistent annoyance, discomfort, or anxiety. **2** find fault in a petty way. > *noun* a trifling worry, dispute, or criticism.

DERIVATIVES – **niggling** *adjective* **niggly** *adjective*.

SYNONYMS – *verb* **1** bother, irritate, trouble, worry. **2** carp, cavil, grumble; informal nit-pick. *noun* grumble, quibble; informal gripe.

nigh > *adverb*, *preposition*, & *adjective* archaic near.

night > *noun* **1** the time from sunset to sunrise. **2** the darkness of night. **3** literary nightfall. **4** an evening. > *adverb* (**nights**) informal at night. > *exclamation* informal short for *goodnight*.

WORDFINDER – nocturnal (*done or active at night*), nyctophobia (*fear of the night or darkness*).

COMBINATIONS – **night blindness** nyctalopia. **nightclothes** clothes worn in bed. **nightclub** a club that is open at night, usually having a bar and disco. **nightdress** a light, loose garment worn by a woman or girl in bed. **nightgown 1** a nightdress. **2** archaic a dressing gown. **nightlife** social activities or entertainment available at night. **night light** a lamp or candle providing a dim light during the night. **night owl** (also **night bird**) informal a person who is habitually active or wakeful at night. **night safe** Brit. a safe with access from the outer wall of a bank, used for deposits when the bank is closed. **night school** an institution providing evening classes. **nightshirt** a long loose shirt worn in bed. **nightside** the side of a planet or moon facing away from the sun and therefore in darkness. **night soil** human excrement removed at night from cesspools and privies and disposed of or used as manure. **nightstick** N. Amer. a police officer's truncheon.

nightcap > *noun* **1** historical a cap worn in bed. **2** a hot or alcoholic drink taken at bedtime.

nightfall > *noun* dusk.

nightie > *noun* informal a nightdress.

nightingale > *noun* a small drab brownish bird noted for its rich melodious song, often heard at night.

ORIGIN – Old English, from NIGHT and a base meaning 'sing'.

nightjar > *noun* a nocturnal bird with grey-brown camouflaged plumage, large eyes and gape, and a distinctive call.

nightly > *adjective* **1** happening or done every night. **2** happening, done, or existing in the night. > *adverb* every night.

nightmare > *noun* **1** a frightening or unpleasant dream. **2** a very unpleasant experience or prospect.

DERIVATIVES – **nightmarish** *adjective*.

SYNONYMS – **2** horror, ordeal, torment.

ORIGIN – from NIGHT + Old English *mære* 'incubus': originally denoting a female evil spirit thought to lie upon and suffocate sleepers.

nightspot > *noun* informal a nightclub.

nightwatchman > *noun* **1** a person who guards a building at night. **2** Cricket an inferior batsman sent in to bat near the end of a day's play.

nigrescent /nigress'nt/ > *adjective* rare blackish.

DERIVATIVES – **nigrescence** *noun*.

ORIGIN – Latin, from *nigrescere* 'grow black', from *niger* 'black'.

nigritude /nigrityōod/ > *noun* rare blackness.

nihilism /nīhiliz'm/ > *noun* **1** the rejection of all religious and moral principles. **2** Philosophy extreme scepticism, maintaining that nothing has a real existence.

DERIVATIVES – **nihilist** *noun* **nihilistic** *adjective*.

ORIGIN – from Latin *nihil* 'nothing'.

nihil obstat /nīhil obstat/ > *noun* (in the Roman Catholic Church) a certificate affirming that a book is not open to objection on doctrinal or moral grounds.

ORIGIN – Latin, 'nothing hinders'.

-nik > *suffix* (forming nouns) denoting a person associated with a specified thing or quality: *beatnik*.

ORIGIN – from Russian (on the pattern of *sputnik*) and Yiddish.

Nikkei index /**nikk**ay/ > *noun* a figure indicating the relative price of representative shares on the Tokyo Stock Exchange.

ORIGIN – abbreviation of *Nihon Keizai Shimbun* 'Japanese Economic Journal'.

nil > *noun* nothing; zero. > *adjective* non-existent.

ORIGIN – Latin, contraction of *nihil* 'nothing'.

nil desperandum /nil despə**rand**əm/ > *exclamation* do not despair.

ORIGIN – from Latin *nil desperandum Teucro duce* 'no need to despair with Teucer as your leader', from Horace's *Odes* 1.vii.27.

Nilotic /nī**lott**ik/ > *adjective* **1** relating to the River Nile or to the Nile region of Africa. **2** relating to or belonging to a family of languages spoken in Egypt, Sudan, Kenya, and Tanzania.

ORIGIN – Greek *Neilōtikos*, from *Neilos* 'Nile'.

nimble > *adjective* (**nimbler**, **nimblest**) quick and light in movement or action.

DERIVATIVES – **nimbly** *adverb*.

SYNONYMS – agile, deft, fleet; informal nippy.

ORIGIN – Old English, 'quick to seize or comprehend'.

nimbostratus /nimbō**stray**təss, -**straa**təss/ > *noun* cloud forming a low thick grey layer, from which rain or snow often falls.

nimbus /**nim**bəss/ > *noun* (pl. **nimbi** /**nim**bī/ or **nimbuses**) **1** a large grey rain cloud. **2** a luminous cloud or a halo surrounding a supernatural being or saint.

ORIGIN – Latin, 'cloud, aureole'.

Nimby /**nim**bi/ > *noun* (pl. **Nimbys**) informal a person who objects to the siting of new, especially socially or environmentally undesirable, developments in their neighbourhood.

ORIGIN – acronym from *not in my back yard*.

niminy-piminy > *adjective* affectedly prim or refined.

nimrod /**nim**rod/ > *noun* a skilful hunter.

ORIGIN – from the name of the great-grandson of Noah, known for his skill as a hunter (see Book of Genesis, chapter 10).

nincompoop /**ning**kəmpoop/ > *noun* a stupid person.

ORIGIN – perhaps from the given name *Nicholas*, or from the name of the Pharisee *Nicodemus*, known for his naive questioning of Christ.

nine > *cardinal number* one less than ten; 9. (Roman numeral: **ix** or **IX**.)

WORDFINDER – nonagon (*plane figure with nine straight sides and angles*), nonet (*set of nine; group of nine musicians*).

IDIOMS – **dressed (up) to the nines** dressed very smartly or fancily.

ninepins > *plural noun* (usu. treated as sing.) the traditional form of the game of skittles, using nine pins.

IDIOMS – **go down** (or **drop** or **fall**) **like ninepins** succumb in large numbers.

nineteen > *cardinal number* one more than eighteen; 19. (Roman numeral: **xix** or **XIX**.)

DERIVATIVES – **nineteenth** ordinal number.

COMBINATIONS – **nineteenth hole** informal, humorous the bar in a golf clubhouse, as reached after a round of eighteen holes.

ninety > *cardinal number* (pl. **nineties**) ten less than one hundred; 90. (Roman numeral: **xc** or **XC**.)

WORDFINDER – nonagenarian (*person aged 90–99*).

DERIVATIVES – **ninetieth** ordinal number.

ninja /**nin**jə/ > *noun* a person skilled in ninjutsu.

ORIGIN – Japanese, 'spy'.

ninjutsu /nin**joot**soo/ > *noun* the traditional Japanese technique of espionage, characterised by stealth and camouflage.

ORIGIN – Japanese, from *nin* 'stealth' + *jutsu* 'art, science'.

ninny > *noun* (pl. **ninnies**) informal a foolish and weak person.

ORIGIN – perhaps from **INNOCENT**.

ninth > *ordinal number* **1** constituting number nine in a sequence; 9th. **2** (**a ninth** or **one ninth**) each of nine equal parts into which something is divided. **3** Music an interval spanning nine consecutive notes in a diatonic scale.

DERIVATIVES – **ninthly** *adverb*.

niobium /nī**ō**biəm/ > *noun* a silver-grey metallic chemical element.

ORIGIN – from *Niobe*, daughter of Tantalus in Greek mythology (because the element was first found in the mineral *tantalite*).

Nip > *noun* informal, offensive a Japanese person.

ORIGIN – abbreviation of *Nipponese*, from *Nippon* (the Japanese name for Japan).

nip¹ > *verb* (**nipped**, **nipping**) **1** pinch, squeeze, or bite sharply. **2** (of cold or frost) cause pain or harm to. **3** Brit. informal go quickly. > *noun* **1** an act of nipping. **2** a feeling of biting cold.

IDIOMS – **nip in the bud** suppress or destroy at an early stage.

nip² > *noun* a small quantity or sip of spirits.

ORIGIN – probably an abbreviation of the rare term *nipperkin* 'small measure'.

nip and tuck > *adverb* & *adjective* neck and neck. > *noun* informal a cosmetic surgical operation.

nipper > *noun* **1** informal a child. **2** (**nippers**) pliers, pincers, or a similar tool. **3** the claw of a crab or lobster.

nipple > *noun* **1** the small projection in which the mammary ducts of females terminate and from which milk can be secreted. **2** the corresponding vestigial structure in a male. **3** the teat of a feeding bottle. **4** a small projection on a machine from which oil or other fluid is dispensed. **5** a short section of pipe with a screw thread at each end for coupling.

COMBINATIONS – **nipplewort** a yellow-flowered plant found in woods and on wasteland.

ORIGIN – perhaps a diminutive of **NEB**.

nippy > *adjective* (**nippier**, **nippiest**) informal **1** quick; nimble. **2** chilly.

nirvana /neer**vaa**nə/ > *noun* **1** Buddhism a state in which there is no suffering or desire, and no sense of self. **2** a state of perfect happiness.

ORIGIN – Sanskrit, from a word meaning 'be extinguished'.

Nissen hut /**niss**'n/ > *noun* chiefly Brit. a tunnel-shaped hut of corrugated iron with a cement floor.

ORIGIN – named after the British engineer Peter N. *Nissen* (1871–1930).

nit > *noun* informal **1** the egg or young form of a parasitic insect, especially the egg of a human head louse. **2** Brit. a stupid person.

niterie /**nī**təri/ > *noun* (pl. **niteries**) informal a nightclub.

nit-picking > *noun* informal fussy or pedantic fault-finding.

DERIVATIVES – **nit-pick** *verb* **nit-picker** *noun*.

nitrate /**nī**trayt/ > *noun* a salt or ester of nitric acid. > *verb* treat with nitric acid.

DERIVATIVES – **nitration** *noun*.

nitre /**nī**tər/ (US **niter**) > *noun* potassium nitrate; saltpetre.

ORIGIN – Old French, from Greek *nitron*.

nitric acid > *noun* a colourless or pale yellow acid with strong corrosive and oxidising properties.

nitric oxide > *noun* a colourless toxic gas that reacts with oxygen to form nitrogen dioxide.

nitride /**nī**trīd/ > *noun* a compound of nitrogen with another element or group.

nitrify /**nī**trifī/ > *verb* (**nitrifies**, **nitrified**) convert (ammonia or another nitrogen compound) into nitrites or nitrates.

DERIVATIVES – **nitrification** *noun*.

nitrile /**nī**trīl/ > *noun* an organic compound containing a cyanide group.

nitrite /**nī**trīt/ > *noun* a salt or ester of nitrous acid.

nitro > *noun* short for **NITROGLYCERINE**.

nitro- /**nī**trō/ > *combining form* of or containing nitric acid, nitrates, or nitrogen.

nitrobenzene > *noun* a yellow oily liquid made by nitrating benzene, used in chemical synthesis.

nitrocellulose > *noun* a highly flammable material used to make explosives and celluloid.

nitrogen /ˈnītrəjən/ > *noun* a colourless, odourless, relatively unreactive gaseous chemical element, forming about 78 per cent of the earth's atmosphere.
DERIVATIVES – **nitrogenous** *adjective*.
COMBINATIONS – **nitrogen dioxide** a reddish-brown poisonous gas formed when many metals dissolve in nitric acid. **nitrogen narcosis** Medicine a drowsy state induced by breathing air under pressure, e.g. in deep-sea diving.

nitroglycerine (also **nitroglycerin**) > *noun* an explosive yellow liquid made from glycerol, used in dynamite.

nitrous /ˈnītrəs/ > *adjective* of or containing nitrogen.
COMBINATIONS – **nitrous acid** an unstable, weak acid made by the action of acids on nitrites. **nitrous oxide** a colourless gas with a sweetish odour, used as an anaesthetic.

nitty-gritty > *noun* informal the most important aspects or practical details of a matter.

nitwit > *noun* informal a silly or foolish person.

nix informal > *pronoun* nothing. > *exclamation* **1** expressing denial or refusal. **2** Brit. dated used as a warning that a person in authority is approaching. > *verb* put an end to; cancel.
ORIGIN – German, colloquial variant of *nichts* 'nothing'.

nixie > *noun* a female water sprite.
ORIGIN – German; related to the archaic English word *nicker* 'water demon'.

Nizari /niˈzaːri/ > *noun* a member of an Ismaili Muslim sect led by the Aga Khan.
ORIGIN – named after the 12th-century Egyptian imam *Nizar*.

NJ > *abbreviation* New Jersey.

NM > *abbreviation* New Mexico.

nm > *abbreviation* **1** nanometre. **2** (also **n.m.**) nautical mile.

NMR > *abbreviation* Physics nuclear magnetic resonance.

NNE > *abbreviation* north-north-east.

NNW > *abbreviation* north-north-west.

No¹ > *symbol* the chemical element nobelium.

No² > *noun* variant spelling of **NOH**.

no > *determiner* **1** not any. **2** quite the opposite of. **3** hardly any. > *exclamation* used to give a negative response. > *adverb* **1** (with comparative) not at all. **2** Scottish not. > *noun* (pl. **noes**) a negative answer or decision, especially in voting.
IDIOMS – **no can do** informal I am unable to do it. **no longer** not now as formerly. **no through road** a street where passage is blocked or prohibited. **not take no for an answer** persist in spite of refusals. **no two ways about it** no possible doubt about something. **or no** or not.
COMBINATIONS – **no-account** informal, chiefly N. Amer. unimportant or worthless. **no-ball** Cricket an unlawfully delivered ball. **no-claims bonus** Brit. a reduction in an insurance premium when no claim has been made during an agreed preceding period. **no-go area** Brit. an area to which entry is dangerous, impossible, or forbidden. **no-hitter** Baseball a game in which a pitcher yields no hits to the opposing team. **no-hoper** informal a person who is not expected to be successful. **no place** N. Amer. nowhere. **no way** informal under no circumstances; not at all.

no. > *abbreviation* number.
ORIGIN – from Latin *numero*, ablative of *numerus*.

n.o. > *abbreviation* Cricket not out.

Noachian /nōˈaykiən/ > *adjective* relating to the Hebrew patriarch Noah or the Flood which according to the Bible happened in his time.

nob¹ > *noun* Brit. informal a person of wealth or high social position.
DERIVATIVES – **nobby** *adjective*.

nob² > *noun* informal a person's head.

nobble > *verb* Brit. informal **1** try to influence by underhand or unfair methods. **2** tamper with (a racehorse) to prevent it from winning a race. **3** accost or seize. **4** obtain dishonestly or steal.

Nobelist /ˈnōbellist/ > *noun* chiefly N. Amer. a winner of a Nobel Prize.

nobelium /nōˈbeeliəm/ > *noun* a very unstable chemical element made by high-energy collisions.

Nobel Prize > *noun* any of six international prizes awarded annually for outstanding work in physics, chemistry, physiology or medicine, literature, economics, and the promotion of peace.
ORIGIN – named after the Swedish chemist and engineer Alfred *Nobel* (1833–96), who endowed the prizes.

nobility > *noun* **1** the quality of having fine personal attributes and high moral principles. **2** the aristocracy.
WORDFINDER – *ranks of the British nobility, lowest to highest:* baronet, baron, viscount, earl, marquess, duke.
SYNONYMS – **1** dignity, integrity, nobleness, uprightness, virtue.

noble > *adjective* (**nobler, noblest**) **1** belonging to the aristocracy. **2** having fine personal qualities or high moral principles. **3** imposing; magnificent. > *noun* **1** (especially formerly) a person of noble rank or birth. **2** a former English gold coin.
IDIOMS – **the noble art** (or **science**) (**of self-defence**) chiefly archaic boxing.
DERIVATIVES – **nobly** *adverb*.
SYNONYMS – *adjective* **1** aristocratic, high-born, patrician, titled, upper-class; informal blue-blooded. **2** honourable, righteous, upright, virtuous, worthy. **3** majestic, stately.
ANTONYMS – *adjective* **1** lower-class, plebeian. **2** dishonourable, ignoble.
COMBINATIONS – **noble gas** Chemistry any of the gaseous elements helium, neon, argon, krypton, xenon, and radon, which form compounds with difficulty or not at all. **noble metal** a metal (e.g. gold, silver, or platinum) that resists attack by acids and other reagents and does not corrode. **noble rot** a grey mould cultivated on grapes in order to perfect certain wines. **noble savage** a representative of primitive mankind as idealised in Romantic literature.
ORIGIN – Old French, from Latin *nobilis* 'noted, high-born'.

nobleman (or **noblewoman**) > *noun* a man (or woman) who belongs to the aristocracy; a peer (or peeress).

noblesse /nōˈbless/ > *noun* the nobility of a foreign country.
IDIOMS – **noblesse oblige** /oˈbleezh/ privilege entails responsibility.
ORIGIN – French, 'nobility'.

nobody > *pronoun* no person; no one. > *noun* (pl. **nobodies**) a person of no importance or authority.

nock Archery > *noun* a notch at either end of a bow or at the end of an arrow, for receiving the bowstring. > *verb* fit (an arrow) to the bowstring.
ORIGIN – perhaps from Dutch *nocke* 'point, tip'.

noctambulist /nokˈtambyoolist/ > *noun* rare a sleepwalker.
DERIVATIVES – **noctambulism** *noun*.
ORIGIN – from Latin *nox* 'night' + *ambulare* 'walk'.

noctule /ˈnoktyool/ > *noun* a large golden-brown bat.
ORIGIN – Italian *nottola* 'bat'.

nocturn > *noun* (in the Roman Catholic Church) a part of matins originally said at night.

nocturnal > *adjective* done, occurring, or active at night.
DERIVATIVES – **nocturnally** *adverb*.
COMBINATIONS – **nocturnal emission** an involuntary ejaculation of semen during sleep.
ORIGIN – from Latin *nocturnus*, from *nox* 'night'.

nocturne /ˈnoktern/ > *noun* **1** Music a short composition of a romantic nature. **2** Art a picture of a night scene.
ORIGIN – French.

nod > *verb* (**nodded, nodding**) **1** lower and raise one's head slightly and briefly in

greeting, assent, or understanding, or as a signal. **2** let one's head fall forward when drowsy or asleep. **3** (**nod off**) informal fall asleep. **4** make a mistake due to a momentary lack of attention. **5** Soccer head (the ball) without great force. **6** (**nod through**) informal approve (something) by general agreement and without discussion. > *noun* **1** an act of nodding. **2** a gesture of acknowledgement or concession.
IDIOMS – **be on nodding terms** know someone slightly. **give someone/thing the nod 1** select or approve someone or something. **2** give someone a signal. **a nodding acquaintance** a slight acquaintance. **a nod's as good as a wink to a blind horse** said to convey that a hint or suggestion has been understood without the need of further explanation. **on the nod** Brit. informal **1** by general agreement and without discussion. **2** dated on credit.

noddle > *noun* informal, dated a person's head.

noddy > *noun* (pl. **noddies**) **1** dated a silly or foolish person. **2** a tropical tern with mainly dark-coloured plumage.

node > *noun* technical **1** a point in a network at which lines intersect or branch. **2** a computer or other device attached to a network. **3** Botany the part of a plant stem from which one or more leaves emerge. **4** Anatomy a small mass of distinct tissue. **5** Physics & Mathematics a point at which the amplitude of vibration of a wave is zero.
DERIVATIVES – **nodal** *adjective*.
ORIGIN – Latin *nodus* 'knot'.

nodose /nōdōss/ > *adjective* technical characterised by hard or tight lumps; knotty.
DERIVATIVES – **nodosity** *noun*.

nodule > *noun* **1** a small swelling or aggregation of cells. **2** a swelling on a root of a leguminous plant, containing nitrogen-fixing bacteria. **3** a small rounded lump of matter distinct from its surroundings.
DERIVATIVES – **nodular** *adjective*.
ORIGIN – Latin *nodulus*, diminutive of *nodus* 'knot'.

Noel > *noun* Christmas.
ORIGIN – French *Noël*, based on Latin *natalis* 'relating to birth'.

noetic /nōettik/ > *adjective* relating to mental activity or the intellect.
ORIGIN – from Greek *noētos* 'intellectual'.

nog > *noun* archaic a small block or peg of wood.

noggin > *noun* informal **1** a person's head. **2** a small quantity of alcoholic drink, typically a quarter of a pint.

nogging > *noun* **1** brickwork in a timber frame. **2** a horizontal piece of wood fixed to a framework to strengthen it.

Noh /nō/ (also **No**) > *noun* traditional Japanese masked drama with dance and song.
ORIGIN – Japanese.

nohow > *adverb* informal **1** chiefly US used to emphasise a negative. **2** archaic not well or in good order.

noise > *noun* **1** a sound, especially one that is loud, unpleasant, or disturbing. **2** continuous or repeated loud, confused sounds. **3** (**noises**) conventional remarks expressing some emotion or purpose. **4** technical irregular fluctuations accompanying and tending to obscure an electrical signal. > *verb* **1** (usu. **be noised about**) dated talk about or make known publicly. **2** literary make much noise.
IDIOMS – **noises off 1** sounds made offstage to be heard by the audience of a play. **2** distracting or intrusive background noise.
DERIVATIVES – **noiseless** *adjective*.
SYNONYMS – **2** din, hubbub, racket.

wordpower facts
Noise
The word **noise** comes via Old French from Latin *nausea*, meaning 'seasickness' and also, in literary use, 'discontentment, uneasiness' (ultimately from Greek *naus*, 'ship'). It entered English in the senses 'a loud outcry' and 'a quarrel'. It is related to **nausea**, which comes directly from the same Latin root.

noisette /nwaazet/ > *noun* **1** a small round piece of meat. **2** a chocolate made with hazelnuts.
ORIGIN – French, 'little nut'.

noisome /noysəm/ > *adjective* literary **1** having an offensive smell. **2** disagreeable; unpleasant.
ORIGIN – from obsolete *noy* (shortened form of **ANNOY**).

noisy > *adjective* (**noisier**, **noisiest**) **1** full of or making a lot of noise. **2** technical accompanied by random fluctuations that obscure information.
DERIVATIVES – **noisily** *adverb* **noisiness** *noun*.
SYNONYMS – **1** clamorous, deafening, loud, rowdy.
ANTONYMS – **1** quiet.

nolle prosequi /nolli prossikwī/ > *noun* Law a formal notice that a plaintiff or prosecutor has abandoned a suit.
ORIGIN – Latin, 'refuse to pursue'.

nomad > *noun* **1** a member of a people continually moving to find fresh pasture for its animals and having no permanent home. **2** a wanderer.
DERIVATIVES – **nomadism** *noun*.

ORIGIN – Greek *nomas*, from *nemein* 'to pasture'.

nomadic > *adjective* having the life of a nomad; wandering.
DERIVATIVES – **nomadically** *adverb*.
SYNONYMS – itinerant, peripatetic, roving, wandering, wayfaring.

no-man's-land > *noun* **1** disputed ground between two opposing armies. **2** a piece of wasteland.

nom de guerre /nom də **gair**/ > *noun* (pl. **noms de guerre** pronunc. same) an assumed name under which a person engages in combat.
ORIGIN – French, 'war name'.

nom de plume /nom də **ploom**/ > *noun* (pl. **noms de plume** pronunc. same) a pen name.
ORIGIN – French.

nomen /**nō**men/ > *noun* the second personal name of a citizen of ancient Rome, indicating the name of a group of families to which theirs belongs, e.g. Marcus *Tullius* Cicero.
ORIGIN – Latin, 'name'.

nomenclature /nōmenkləchər, nōmən-klaychər/ > *noun* **1** the selecting of names for things in a particular field. **2** a body or system of names. **3** formal the term or terms applied to someone or something.
DERIVATIVES – **nomenclatural** /nōmən-**kla**chərəl, -klə**choo**rəl/ *adjective*.
ORIGIN – Latin *nomenclatura*, from *nomen* 'name' + *clatura* 'calling, summoning'.

nomenklatura /nomenklə**tyoo**rə/ > *noun* (in the former Soviet Union) a list of influential public positions to be filled by Party appointees.
ORIGIN – Russian, from Latin *nomenclatura*.

nominal > *adjective* **1** existing in name only. **2** relating to or consisting of names. **3** (of a sum of money) very small; far below the real value or cost: *a nominal fee*. **4** informal functioning normally or acceptably. **5** Grammar relating to or functioning as a noun.
DERIVATIVES – **nominally** *adverb*.
SYNONYMS – **1** ceremonial, formal, titular. **3** insignificant, minimal, minor, token.
COMBINATIONS – **nominal value** Economics the face value of a coin, note, etc.
ORIGIN – Latin *nominalis*, from *nomen* 'name'.

nominalise (also **nominalize**) > *verb* Grammar form a noun from (a verb or adjective).
DERIVATIVES – **nominalisation** *noun*.

nominalism > *noun* Philosophy the doctrine that universals or general ideas are mere names without any corresponding reality. Contrasted with **REALISM**.
DERIVATIVES – **nominalist** *noun*.

nominate > *verb* **1** put forward as a candidate for election or for an honour or award. **2** appoint to a job or position. **3** specify formally.
DERIVATIVES – **nomination** *noun* **nominator** *noun*.
SYNONYMS – **1** propose, recommend, suggest. **2** appoint, assign, elect.
ORIGIN – Latin *nominare* 'to name'.

nominative /**nommi**nətiv/ > *adjective* **1** Grammar denoting a case of nouns, pronouns, and adjectives expressing the subject of a verb. **2** /**nommi**naytiv/ of or appointed by nomination as distinct from election. > *noun* Grammar a word in the nominative case.

nominee > *noun* **1** a person who is nominated. **2** a person or company in whose name a company, stock, etc. is registered.

-nomy > *combining form* denoting a specified area of knowledge or its laws: *astronomy*.
ORIGIN – Greek *-nomia*.

non- > *prefix* expressing negation or absence: *non-recognition*.
USAGE – the prefixes **non-** and **un-** both have the meaning 'not', but tend to be used with a difference of emphasis, **non-** being weaker and more neutral than **un-**: for example, **unnatural** implies that something is not natural in a bad way, whereas **non-natural** is neutral.
ORIGIN – Latin, 'not'.

nona- /**nonn**ə, **nōn**ə/ > *combining form* nine; having nine: *nonagon*.
ORIGIN – from Latin *nonus* 'ninth'.

nonage /**nō**nij, **nonn**ij/ > *noun* formal the period of immaturity or youth.
ORIGIN – Old French.

nonagenarian /nonnəjə**nair**iən, nōnəjə**nair**iən/ > *noun* a person between 90 and 99 years old.
ORIGIN – Latin *nonagenarius*, from *nonaginta* 'ninety'.

nonagon /**nonn**əgən/ > *noun* a plane figure with nine straight sides and angles.
DERIVATIVES – **nonagonal** *adjective*.

non-aligned > *adjective* (chiefly during the cold war) neutral towards the superpowers: *non-aligned countries*.
DERIVATIVES – **non-alignment** *noun*.

non-allergenic (also **non-allergic**) > *adjective* not causing an allergic reaction.

non-being > *noun* the state of not being; non-existence.

non-belligerent > *adjective* not engaged in a war or conflict. > *noun* a non-belligerent nation or person.

nonce¹ /nonss/ > *adjective* (of a word or expression) coined for one occasion.
IDIOMS – **for the nonce** for the present; temporarily.
ORIGIN – from *then anes* 'the one (purpose)',

from *then*, obsolete form of **THE**, + *ane* 'one', altered by wrong division.

nonce² /nonss/ > *noun* Brit. informal a sexual deviant, especially a child molester.

nonchalant /**non**shələnt/ > *adjective* casually calm and relaxed.
DERIVATIVES – **nonchalance** *noun* **nonchalantly** *adverb*.
SYNONYMS – blasé, carefree, cool, unconcerned.
ORIGIN – French, 'not being concerned'.

non-com > *noun* military slang a non-commissioned officer.

non-combatant > *noun* a person who is not engaged in fighting during a war, especially a civilian, army chaplain, or army doctor.

non-commissioned > *adjective* (of a military officer) not holding a rank conferred by a commission.

non-committal > *adjective* not displaying commitment to a definite opinion or policy.
DERIVATIVES – **non-committally** *adverb*.
SYNONYMS – equivocal, evasive, guarded, vague; informal cagey.

non compos mentis /non komposs **men**tiss/ > *adjective* not having full control of one's mental faculties.
ORIGIN – Latin.

non-conductor > *noun* a substance that does not conduct heat or electricity.
DERIVATIVES – **non-conducting** *adjective*.

nonconformist > *noun* **1** a person who does not conform to prevailing ideas or established practice. **2** (**Nonconformist**) a member of a Protestant Church which dissents from the established Church of England. > *adjective* not conforming to prevailing ideas or established practice.
DERIVATIVES – **nonconformism** *noun* **nonconformity** *noun*.

non-content > *noun* a member of the House of Lords who votes against a particular motion.

non-contributory > *adjective* **1** (of a pension) funded by regular payments by the employer, not the employee. **2** (of a state benefit) paid irrespective of taxes or other contributions made by recipients.

non-cooperation > *noun* failure to cooperate, especially as a form of protest.

non-delivery > *noun* chiefly Law failure to provide or deliver goods.

non-denominational > *adjective* open or acceptable to people of any Christian denomination.

nondescript > *adjective* lacking distinctive or interesting characteristics.
SYNONYMS – characterless, ordinary, run-of-the-mill, unremarkable.
ANTONYMS – extraordinary.
ORIGIN – from **NON-** + obsolete *descript*

'described, engraved', originally in the sense 'not previously described scientifically'.

non-destructive > *adjective* (of methods of testing) not involving damage to the specimen.

none > *pronoun* **1** not any. **2** no one. > *adverb* (**none the**) (with comparative) by no amount: *none the wiser*.
USAGE – some people say that **none** can only take a singular verb (as in *none of them is coming tonight* rather than *none of them are coming tonight*): however, **none** (which is descended from Old English **nān** meaning 'not one') has been used for around a thousand years with either a singular or a plural verb, depending on the context and the emphasis needed.

nonentity > *noun* (pl. **nonentities**) **1** an unimportant person or thing. **2** non-existence.
SYNONYMS – **1** cipher, lightweight, nobody.

nones /nōnz/ > *plural noun* **1** (in the ancient Roman calendar) the ninth day before the ides. **2** a service forming part of the Divine Office of the Western Christian Church, traditionally said at the ninth hour of the day (3 p.m.).
ORIGIN – Latin *nonas*, from *nonus* 'ninth'.

non-essential > *adjective* not absolutely necessary. > *noun* a non-essential thing.

non est factum /nōn est **fak**təm/ > *noun* Law a plea that a written agreement is invalid because the defendant was mistaken about its character when signing it.
ORIGIN – Latin, 'it was not done'.

nonesuch > *noun* variant spelling of **NONSUCH**.

nonet /nō**net**/ > *noun* **1** a group of nine. **2** a musical composition for nine voices or instruments.
ORIGIN – Italian *nonetto*.

nonetheless (also **none the less**) > *adverb* in spite of that; nevertheless.

non-event > *noun* an unexpectedly insignificant or uninteresting occasion.
SYNONYMS – anticlimax, damp squib, let-down.

non-existent > *adjective* not existing or not real or present.
DERIVATIVES – **non-existence** *noun*.

nonfeasance /non**feez**'nss/ > *noun* Law failure to perform an act required by law.
ORIGIN – from **NON-** + *feasance* (see **MALFEASANCE**).

non-ferrous > *adjective* (of metal) other than iron or steel.

non-fiction > *noun* prose writing that is informative or factual rather than being drawn from the imagination.
DERIVATIVES – **non-fictional** *adjective*.

non-flammable > *adjective* not catching fire easily.

non-fulfilment > *noun* failure to fulfil or carry out something.

non-functional > *adjective* **1** having no function. **2** not in working order.

nong /nong/ > *noun* Austral./NZ informal a foolish or stupid person.

non-governmental > *adjective* not belonging to or associated with any government.

non-inflammable > *adjective* not catching fire easily.

non-interference > *noun* failure or refusal to interfere.

non-intervention > *noun* the policy of not becoming involved in the affairs of others.
DERIVATIVES – **non-interventionist** *adjective & noun.*

non-invasive > *adjective* **1** (of medical procedures) not involving the introduction of instruments into the body. **2** not tending to spread undesirably.

Nonjuror > *noun* historical a member of the clergy who refused to take the oath of allegiance to William and Mary in 1689.

non-linear > *adjective* **1** not linear. **2** Mathematics (of an equation or function) containing a variable raised to a power less than or greater than 1, and hence not able to be represented by a straight line.

non-member > *noun* a person, country, etc. that is not a member of a particular organisation.

non-metal > *noun* an element or substance that is not a metal.
DERIVATIVES – **non-metallic** *adjective.*

non-natural > *adjective* not produced by or involving natural processes.

non-negotiable > *adjective* **1** not open to discussion or modification. **2** not able to be transferred to the legal ownership of another person.

no-no > *noun* (pl. **no-nos**) informal a thing that is not possible or acceptable.

no-nonsense > *adjective* simple and straightforward; sensible.

non-operational > *adjective* **1** not involving active duties. **2** not working or in use.

nonpareil /nonpərayl/ > *adjective* unrivalled. > *noun* an unrivalled person or thing.
ORIGIN – French, 'not equal'.

non-person > *noun* a person regarded as non-existent or insignificant.

nonplussed /nonplusst/ > *adjective* **1** surprised and confused. **2** N. Amer. informal unperturbed.
USAGE – in standard English **nonplussed** means 'surprised and confused'. An opposite meaning, 'not disconcerted; unperturbed', has developed recently in North American English, probably on the assumption that the prefix *non-* must have a

negative meaning; this is not yet accepted as standard usage.
SYNONYMS – **1** baffled, confounded, dumbfounded, perplexed, puzzled.
ORIGIN – from Latin *non plus* 'not more'.

non-productive > *adjective* not producing or able to produce.
DERIVATIVES – **non-productively** *adverb.*

non-profit > *adjective* not making or intended to make a profit.

non-proliferation > *noun* the prevention of an increase or spread of something, especially possession of nuclear weapons.

non-resident > *adjective* not living in a particular country or a place of work. > *noun* a person not living in a particular place.

nonsense > *noun* **1** words that make no sense. **2** foolish or unacceptable behaviour. **3** an absurd or unthinkable scheme, situation, etc.
DERIVATIVES – **nonsensical** *adjective* **nonsensically** *adverb.*
SYNONYMS – **1** balderdash, claptrap, drivel, gibberish; informal gobbledegook, mumbo-jumbo. **2** foolishness, senselessness, silliness, stupidity.

non sequitur /non **sek**witər/ > *noun* a conclusion that does not logically follow from the previous argument or statement.
ORIGIN – Latin, 'it does not follow'.

non-specific > *adjective* not specific; indefinite.
COMBINATIONS – **non-specific urethritis** Medicine urethritis which is not associated with gonorrhoea.

non-standard > *adjective* **1** not average, normal, or usual. **2** (of language) not of the form accepted as standard.

non-starter > *noun* **1** a person or animal that fails to take part in a race. **2** informal something that has no chance of succeeding.

non-stick > *adjective* (of a pan or oven surface) covered with a substance that prevents food sticking to it during cooking.

non-stop > *adjective* **1** continuing without stopping or pausing. **2** having no intermediate stops on the way to a destination. > *adverb* without stopping or pausing.
SYNONYMS – *adjective* **1** ceaseless, continuous, incessant, perpetual, unceasing, uninterrupted.

nonsuch (also **nonesuch**) > *noun* archaic a person or thing regarded as perfect or excellent.

non-U > *adjective* informal, chiefly Brit. (of language or behaviour) not characteristic of the upper social classes.

non-uniform > *adjective* not uniform; varying.

non-verbal > *adjective* not involving or using words or speech.

non-violent > *adjective* not using violence.
DERIVATIVES – **non-violence** *noun.*

non-white > *adjective* relating to a person who is not white or whose origin is not predominantly European. > *noun* a non-white person.

noodle[1] > *noun* (usu. **noodles**) a very thin, long strip of pasta or a similar flour paste.
ORIGIN – German *Nudel*, of unknown origin.

noodle[2] > *noun* informal **1** a stupid or silly person. **2** a person's head.

noodle[3] > *verb* Austral. informal search (an old working) for opals.

nook > *noun* a corner or recess offering seclusion or security.
IDIOMS – **every nook and cranny** every part of something.

nooky (also **nookie**) > *noun* informal sexual activity or intercourse.

noon > *noun* twelve o'clock in the day; midday.
COMBINATIONS – **noonday** the middle of the day. **noontide** (also **noontime**) literary noon.
ORIGIN – from Latin *nona hora* 'ninth hour', originally referring to the ninth hour from sunrise, i.e. approximately 3 p.m.; compare with **NONES**.

no one > *pronoun* no person; not a single person.

noose > *noun* a loop with a running knot which tightens as the rope or wire is pulled, used especially to hang offenders or trap animals. > *verb* catch or hold with a noose.
IDIOMS – **put one's head in a noose** bring about one's own downfall.
ORIGIN – Latin *nodus* 'knot'.

nootropic /nōətrō̄pik, nōətroppik/ > *adjective* (of drugs) used to enhance memory or other mental functions. > *noun* a nootropic drug.
ORIGIN – from Greek *noos* 'mind' + *tropē* 'turning'.

nor > *conjunction & adverb* **1** and not; and not either. **2** archaic or dialect than.
COMBINATIONS – **NOR gate** Electronics a gate circuit which produces an output only when there are no signals on any of the input connections.

nor' > *abbreviation* north: *nor'west.*

Nordic > *adjective* **1** of or relating to Scandinavia, Finland, and Iceland. **2** referring to a tall, blonde physical type associated with northern Europe. > *noun* a native of Scandinavia, Finland, or Iceland.

COMBINATIONS – **Nordic skiing** cross-country skiing and ski jumping.

ORIGIN – French *nordique*, from *nord* 'north'.

Norfolk jacket > *noun* a loose belted jacket with box pleats, typically made of tweed.

norm > *noun* 1 the usual or standard thing. 2 a required or acceptable standard.

SYNONYMS – 1 custom, practice, rule. 2 convention, criterion, standard.

ANTONYMS – 2 exception.

wordpower facts

Norm

The words **norm** and **normal** come from the Latin word for a 'carpenter's square', *norma*. It was in this form, *norma*, that **norm** entered English in the 17th century, in the sense 'a standard or rule; a pattern', its form becoming anglicised to **norm** by the 1820s. **Normal** was originally used to mean 'positioned at right angles', or 'perpendicular', a sense retained today in technical use, in engineering and physics.

normal > *adjective* 1 conforming to a standard; usual, typical, or expected. 2 technical intersecting a given line or surface at right angles. > *noun* 1 the normal state or condition. 2 technical a line at right angles to a given line or surface.

DERIVATIVES – **normalcy** *noun* (chiefly N. Amer.) **normality** *noun* **normally** *adverb*.

SYNONYMS – *adjective* 1 conventional, customary, expected, regular, standard, typical, usual. 2 perpendicular.

ANTONYMS – *adjective* 1 abnormal, unusual.

COMBINATIONS – **normal distribution** Statistics a function that represents the distribution of variables as a symmetrical bell-shaped graph. **normal school** (especially in North America and France) a teacher training college.

normalise (also **normalize**) > *verb* bring to a normal or standard state.

DERIVATIVES – **normalisation** *noun*.

Norman > *noun* 1 a member of a people who settled in Normandy in the 10th century; in particular, any of the Normans who conquered England in 1066 or their descendants. 2 (also **Norman French**) the northern form of Old French spoken by the Normans. 3 a person from modern Normandy. > *adjective* 1 relating to the Normans or Normandy. 2 of the style of Romanesque architecture used in Britain under the Normans.

wordpower facts

Norman

The word **Norman** is a reduced form of **Northman**, first used in Old English in reference to Scandinavians, especially Norwegians (the related form **Norseman** comes from the Dutch word for 'north'). It is recorded in the form **Norman** from the late 13th century; by this time it referred specifically to the people from Normandy, in north-western France, who had conquered England in 1066. The **Normans**, who were of mixed Scandinavian and Frankish origin, had first settled in Normandy in 912 under their chief Rollo, eventually becoming a powerful military force throughout Europe.

normative > *adjective* formal relating to a standard or norm.

normotensive /normōtensiv/ > *adjective* Medicine having normal blood pressure.

Norse historical > *noun* 1 an ancient or medieval form of Norwegian or a related Scandinavian language. 2 (treated as pl.) Norwegians or Scandinavians. > *adjective* of or relating to Norway or Scandinavia, or their inhabitants or language.

DERIVATIVES – **Norseman** *noun*.

ORIGIN – Dutch *noor(d)sch*, from *noord* 'north'.

north > *noun* 1 the direction in which a compass needle normally points, towards the horizon on the left-hand side of a person facing east. 2 the northern part of a country, region, or town. > *adjective* 1 lying towards, near, or facing the north. 2 (of a wind) blowing from the north. > *adverb* to or towards the north.

IDIOMS – **north by east** (or **west**) between north and north-north-east (or north-north-west).

DERIVATIVES – **northbound** *adjective* & *adverb*.

COMBINATIONS – **northland** (also **northlands**) literary the northern part of a country or region. **north light** good natural light without direct sun. **north-north-east** (or **north-north-west**) the compass point or direction midway between north and north-east (or north-west). **North Star** the Pole Star.

North American > *noun* a person from North America, especially a citizen of the US or Canada. > *adjective* of or relating to North America.

Northants > *abbreviation* Northamptonshire.

north-east > *noun* 1 the point of the horizon midway between north and east. 2 the north-eastern part of a country, region, or town. > *adjective* 1 lying towards, near, or facing the north-east. 2 (of a wind) from the north-east. > *adverb* to or towards the north-east.

DERIVATIVES – **north-eastern** *adjective*.

north-easterly > *adjective* & *adverb* in a north-eastward position or direction. > *noun* a wind blowing from the north-east.

north-eastward > *adverb* (also **north-eastwards**) towards the north-east. > *adjective* situated in, directed towards, or facing the north-east.

northerly > *adjective* & *adverb* 1 in a northward position or direction. 2 (of a wind) blowing from the north. > *noun* a wind blowing from the north.

northern > *adjective* 1 situated in, directed towards, or facing the north. 2 (usu. **Northern**) living in, coming from, or characteristic of the north.

DERIVATIVES – **northernmost** *adjective*.

COMBINATIONS – **Northern Lights** the aurora borealis.

northerner > *noun* a person from the north of a particular region or country.

northing > *noun* 1 distance travelled or measured northward. 2 a figure or line representing northward distance on a map.

Northumb. > *abbreviation* Northumberland.

northward > *adjective* in a northerly direction. > *adverb* (also **northwards**) towards the north.

north-west > *noun* 1 the point of the horizon midway between north and west. 2 the north-western part of a country, region, or town. > *adjective* 1 lying towards, near, or facing the north-west. 2 (of a wind) from the north-west. > *adverb* to or towards the north-west.

DERIVATIVES – **north-western** *adjective*.

north-westerly > *adjective* & *adverb* in a north-westward position or direction. > *noun* a wind blowing from the north-west.

north-westward > *adverb* (also **north-westwards**) towards the north-west. > *adjective* situated in, directed towards, or facing the north-west.

Norwegian /norweejən/ > *noun* 1 a person from Norway. 2 the Scandinavian language spoken in Norway. > *adjective* of or relating to Norway or its people or language.

ORIGIN – from Latin *Norvegia* 'Norway'.

nose > *noun* 1 the facial part projecting above the mouth, containing the nostrils and used in breathing and smelling. 2 the sense of smell. 3 the front end of an aircraft, car, or other vehicle. 4 an instinctive talent for detecting something. 5 an act of looking around or prying. 6 the aroma of a wine. > *verb* 1 (of an animal) thrust its nose against or into something. **2** look around or pry into something. **3** make one's way slowly forward. **4** smell or sniff (something).

WORDFINDER – nasal (*relating to the nose*), rhinoplasty (*plastic surgery on the nose*); *types of nose:* aquiline (*curved*), Grecian (*straight and continuing the line of the forehead*), retroussé (*turned up at the tip*), Roman (*having a high bridge*).

IDIOMS – **by a nose** (of a victory) by a very narrow margin. **cut off one's nose to spite one's face** disadvantage oneself through trying to gain an advantage. **get up someone's nose** informal irritate or annoy someone. **keep one's nose clean** informal stay out of trouble. **keep one's nose out of** refrain from interfering in. **nose to tail** (of vehicles) moving or standing close behind one another. **on the nose 1** informal, chiefly N. Amer. precisely. **2** informal (of betting) on a horse to win (as opposed to being placed). **put someone's nose out of joint** informal offend someone or hurt their pride. **turn one's nose up at** informal show distaste or contempt for. **under someone's nose** informal directly in front of someone.

COMBINATIONS – **nosebag** a bag containing fodder, hung from a horse's head and into which it can reach to eat. **noseband** the strap of a bridle that passes over the horse's nose and under its chin. **nosebleed** an instance of bleeding from the nose. **nose job** informal a surgical operation to reshape a person's nose.

nosedive > *noun* **1** a steep downward plunge by an aircraft. **2** a sudden dramatic deterioration. > *verb* make a nosedive.

no-see-um > *noun* N. Amer. a minute biting insect.

nosegay > *noun* a small sweet-scented bunch of flowers.
ORIGIN – from **GAY** in the obsolete sense 'ornament'.

nosey > *adjective & verb* variant spelling of **NOSY**.

nosh informal > *noun* food. > *verb* eat enthusiastically or greedily.
ORIGIN – Yiddish.

no-show > *noun* a person who has made a reservation or appointment but neither keeps nor cancels it.

nosh-up > *noun* Brit. informal a large meal.

nosocomial /nossəkōmiəl/ > *adjective* Medicine (of a disease) originating in a hospital.
ORIGIN – from Greek *nosokomos* 'person who tends the sick'.

nosology /nosolləji/ > *noun* the branch of medical science concerned with the classification of diseases.
ORIGIN – from Greek *nosos* 'disease'.

nostalgia > *noun* sentimental longing or wistful affection for the past.

DERIVATIVES – **nostalgic** *adjective* **nostalgically** *adverb*.

wordpower facts
Nostalgia

Is it true that, as the saying goes, 'Nostalgia isn't what it used to be'? The word **nostalgia** entered English in the late 18th century, in the sense 'acute homesickness'. It had been coined in the late 17th century in modern Latin from the Greek words *nostos* 'return home' and *algos* 'pain', in translation of the German word *Heimweh*, meaning 'homesickness'. The familiar modern meaning, 'longing for the past', became established by the early 20th century. There are a number of medical terms also derived from *algos*, all relating to physical pain, such as **neuralgia** 'pain in a nerve' and **analgesia** 'relief of pain', while **algolagnia**, from Greek *lagneia* 'lust', is another word for sadomasochism.

nostril > *noun* either of two external openings of the nose that admit air to the lungs and smells to the olfactory nerves.
WORDFINDER – narial (*relating to the nostrils*).
ORIGIN – Old English, 'nose hole'.

nostrum > *noun* **1** a quack medicine. **2** a favourite method for bringing about reform.
ORIGIN – Latin, literally 'something of our own making'.

nosy (also **nosey**) > *adjective* (**nosier**, **nosiest**) informal too inquisitive about other people's affairs.
DERIVATIVES – **nosily** *adverb* **nosiness** *noun*.
COMBINATIONS – **nosy parker** an overly inquisitive person. [ORIGIN – from a 1907 picture postcard caption, 'The adventures of Nosey Parker', referring to a peeping Tom in Hyde Park.]

not > *adverb* **1** used to form or express a negative. **2** less than: *not ten feet away*.
USAGE – when used with *be* or another auxiliary verb to form a negative, **not** may be joined to the preceding verb and contracted to **n't**: *she isn't going*.
COMBINATIONS – **NOT gate** Electronics a gate circuit which produces an output only when there is no input signal.

nota bene /nōtə bennay/ > *verb* formal take special note.
ORIGIN – Latin, 'note well!'

notability > *noun* (pl. **notabilities**) a famous or important person.

notable > *adjective* worthy of attention or

notice. > *noun* a famous or important person.
SYNONYMS – *adjective* noteworthy, remarkable, significant, striking.

notably > *adverb* **1** in particular. **2** in a notable way.

notarise (also **notarize**) > *verb* have (a document) legalised by a notary.

notary (in full **notary public**) > *noun* (pl. **notaries** or **notaries public**) a person authorised to perform certain legal formalities, especially to draw up or certify contracts, deeds, etc.
DERIVATIVES – **notarial** *adjective*.
ORIGIN – Latin *notarius* 'secretary'.

notation > *noun* **1** a system of written symbols used to represent numbers, amounts, or elements in a field such as music or mathematics. **2** an annotation.
DERIVATIVES – **notate** *verb* **notational** *adjective*.

notch > *noun* **1** an indentation or incision on an edge or surface. **2** a point or degree in a scale. > *verb* **1** make notches in. **2** score or achieve.
ORIGIN – Old French.

note > *noun* **1** a brief written record of facts, topics, or thoughts, used as an aid to memory. **2** a short written message or document. **3** Brit. a banknote. **4** a single tone of definite pitch made by a musical instrument or voice, or a symbol representing this. **5** a bird's song or call. **6** a particular quality or tone expressing a mood or attitude. **7** a basic component of a fragrance or flavour. > *verb* **1** pay attention to. **2** record in writing.
IDIOMS – **hit the right** (or **wrong**) **note** say or do something in the right (or wrong) way. **of note** important. **take note** pay attention.
SYNONYMS – *verb* **1** heed, mark, mind, notice, observe.
COMBINATIONS – **notepaper** paper for writing letters on.
ORIGIN – Latin *nota* 'a mark', *notare* 'to mark'.

notebook > *noun* **1** a small book for writing notes in. **2** a portable computer smaller than a laptop.

noted > *adjective* well known.

notelet > *noun* a small folded sheet of notepaper with a decorative design on the front.

notepad > *noun* **1** a pad of paper for writing notes on. **2** a pocket-sized personal computer in which text is input using a stylus.

noteworthy > *adjective* interesting or significant.
SYNONYMS – interesting, notable, remarkable, significant, uncommon, unusual.

nothing > *pronoun* **1** not anything. **2** something of no importance or concern. **3** nought. > *adverb* not at all.

IDIOMS – **for nothing 1** without payment or charge. **2** to no purpose. **nothing but** only. **nothing doing** informal **1** there is no prospect of success or agreement. **2** nothing is happening. **sweet nothings** words of affection exchanged by lovers. **think nothing of it** do not apologise or feel bound to show gratitude.

nothingness > *noun* **1** the absence or ending of existence. **2** insignificance.

notice > *noun* **1** the fact or state of noting or observing something or of being noted or observed. **2** advance notification or warning, especially of intention to end an agreement. **3** a displayed sheet or placard giving news or information. **4** a small published announcement or advertisement. **5** a short published review. > *verb* **1** become aware of. **2** (**be noticed**) be recognised as noteworthy. **3** archaic remark on.

IDIOMS – **at short** (or **a moment's**) **notice** with little warning. **put someone on notice** (or **serve notice**) warn someone of something about or likely to occur. **take** (**no**) **notice** (**of**) pay (no) attention (to).

SYNONYMS – *noun* **1** attention, awareness, consciousness, observation, scrutiny. *verb* **1** discern, note, observe, perceive, spot.

ANTONYMS – *verb* **1** overlook.

noticeable > *adjective* easily seen; clear or apparent.

DERIVATIVES – **noticeably** adverb.

SYNONYMS – apparent, clear, conspicuous, marked, obvious, visible.

ANTONYMS – imperceptible, inconspicuous.

notifiable > *adjective* (of an infectious disease) that must be officially reported.

notify > *verb* (**notifies, notified**) inform, typically in a formal or official manner.

DERIVATIVES – **notification** noun.

SYNONYMS – advise, apprise, inform.

ORIGIN – Latin *notificare* 'make known'.

notion > *noun* **1** a concept or belief. **2** an impulse or desire. **3** a vague awareness or understanding. **4** (**notions**) chiefly N. Amer. items used in sewing, such as buttons and pins.

SYNONYMS – **1** belief, concept, idea, impression, opinion, theory. **2** desire, fancy, impulse, inclination, whim.

notional > *adjective* hypothetical or imaginary.

DERIVATIVES – **notionally** adverb.

notochord /nōtəkord/ > *noun* Zoology a skeletal rod of cartilage supporting the body in embryonic and some adult chordate animals.

ORIGIN – from Greek *nōton* 'back' + CHORD².

notorious > *adjective* famous for some bad quality or deed.

DERIVATIVES – **notoriety** noun **notoriously** adverb.

SYNONYMS – infamous.

Notts. > *abbreviation* Nottinghamshire.

notwithstanding > *preposition* in spite of. > *adverb* nevertheless. > *conjunction* although.

nougat /nōōgaa, nuggət/ > *noun* a sweet made from sugar or honey, nuts, and egg white.

ORIGIN – French, from Provençal, from *noga* 'nut'.

nougatine /nōōgəteen/ > *noun* nougat covered with chocolate.

nought > *noun* the digit 0; zero. > *pronoun* variant spelling of NAUGHT.

IDIOMS – **noughts and crosses** a game in which two players seek to complete a row of either three noughts or three crosses drawn alternately in the spaces of a grid of nine squares.

noumenon /nowmənon/ > *noun* (pl. **noumena**) (in Kantian philosophy) a thing as it is in itself, as distinct from what is knowable by the senses.

DERIVATIVES – **noumenal** adjective.

ORIGIN – Greek, 'something conceived'.

noun > *noun* Grammar a word (other than a pronoun) used to identify any of a class of people, places, or things (**common noun**), or to name a particular one of these (**proper noun**).

WORDFINDER – common noun (*noun referring to a class of objects or to a concept*), count noun (*noun that can form plurals and take an indefinite article*), mass noun (*noun that lacks a plural and cannot take an indefinite article*), nominal (*relating to a noun*), proper noun (*name of a person, place, or organisation*).

COMBINATIONS – **noun phrase** Grammar a word or group of words that function in a sentence as subject, object, or prepositional object.

ORIGIN – Old French, from Latin *nomen* 'name'.

nourish > *verb* **1** provide with the food or other substances necessary for growth and health. **2** keep (a feeling or belief) in one's mind for a long time.

DERIVATIVES – **nourishing** adjective **nourishment** noun.

SYNONYMS – **1** feed, maintain, nurture, sustain. **2** cherish, foster, harbour, nurse, nurture.

ORIGIN – Old French *noriss-*, from Latin *nutrire*.

nous /nowss/ > *noun* **1** Brit. informal practical intelligence. **2** Philosophy the mind or intellect.

ORIGIN – Greek, 'mind, intelligence'.

nouveau riche /nōōvō reesh/ > *noun* (pl.

nouveaux riches (pronunc. same) or same) a person who has recently acquired wealth, typically one perceived as lacking good taste.

ORIGIN – French, 'new rich'.

nouvelle cuisine /nōōvel kwizeen/ > *noun* a modern style of cookery with an emphasis on simply cooked, fresh ingredients and stylish presentation.

ORIGIN – French, 'new cookery'.

nouvelle vague /nōōvel vaag/ > *noun* a grouping of stylistically innovative French film directors in the late 1950s and 1960s.

ORIGIN – French, 'new wave'.

Nov. > *abbreviation* November.

nova /nōvə/ > *noun* (pl. **novae** /nōvee/ or **novas**) Astronomy a star which suddenly increases in brightness and then slowly returns to normal.

ORIGIN – Latin, feminine of *novus* 'new' (because such stars were thought to be newly formed).

novation /nōvaysh'n/ > *noun* Law the substitution of a new contract in place of an old one.

ORIGIN – Latin, from *novare* 'make new'.

novel¹ > *noun* a fictional prose narrative of book length.

ORIGIN – Italian *novella storia* 'new story'.

novel² > *adjective* interestingly new or unusual.

SYNONYMS – different, fresh, innovative, new, original, unusual.

ORIGIN – Latin *novellus*, from *novus* 'new'.

novelette > *noun* chiefly derogatory a short novel, typically a light romantic one.

novelise (also **novelize**) > *verb* convert into a novel.

DERIVATIVES – **novelisation** noun.

novelist > *noun* a writer of novels.

DERIVATIVES – **novelistic** adjective.

novella /nəvellə/ > *noun* a short novel or long short story.

ORIGIN – Italian.

novelty > *noun* (pl. **novelties**) **1** the quality of being novel. **2** a new or unfamiliar thing. **3** a small and inexpensive toy or ornament. **4** (before another noun) intended to be amusingly striking or unusual: *a novelty teapot*.

SYNONYMS – **1** freshness, newness, originality, unconventionality, unusualness. **3** bauble, knick-knack, trifle, trinket.

November > *noun* the eleventh month of the year.

ORIGIN – Latin, from *novem* 'nine' (being originally the ninth month of the Roman year).

novena /nəveenə/ > *noun* (in the Roman Catholic Church) a form of worship consisting of special prayers or services on nine successive days.

ORIGIN – from Latin *novem* 'nine'.

novice > *noun* **1** a person new to and inexperienced in a job or situation. **2** a person who has entered a religious order and is under probation, before taking vows. **3** a racehorse that has not yet won a major prize or reached a qualifying level of performance.

SYNONYMS – **1** beginner, initiate, learner, trainee, tyro.

ANTONYMS – **1** expert, veteran.

ORIGIN – Latin *novicius*, from *novus* 'new'.

novitiate /nəvishiət/ (also **noviciate**) > *noun* **1** the period or state of being a novice. **2** a religious novice. **3** a place housing religious novices.

now > *adverb* **1** at the present time. **2** at or from this precise moment. **3** under the present circumstances. > *conjunction* as a consequence of the fact.

IDIOMS – **now and again** (or **then**) from time to time.

nowadays > *adverb* at the present time, in contrast with the past.

nowhere > *adverb* not in or to any place. > *pronoun* **1** no place. **2** a place that is remote or uninteresting.

IDIOMS – **from** (or **out of**) **nowhere** appearing or happening suddenly and unexpectedly. **get** (or **go**) **nowhere** make no progress. **nowhere near** not nearly.

nowise > *adverb* archaic not at all.

nowt > *pronoun & adverb* N. English nothing.

noxious > *adjective* harmful, poisonous, or very unpleasant.

ORIGIN – from Latin *noxa* 'harm'.

nozzle > *noun* a spout used to control a jet of liquid or gas.

ORIGIN – from **NOSE**.

NP > *abbreviation* notary public.

Np > *symbol* the chemical element neptunium.

NS > *abbreviation* **1** (in calculating dates) New Style. **2** Nova Scotia.

ns > *abbreviation* nanosecond.

n/s > *abbreviation* (in personal advertisements) non-smoker; non-smoking.

NSPCC > *abbreviation* (in the UK) National Society for the Prevention of Cruelty to Children.

NSU > *abbreviation* Medicine non-specific urethritis.

NSW > *abbreviation* New South Wales.

NT > *abbreviation* **1** National Trust. **2** New Testament. **3** Northern Territory. **4** Northwest Territories.

-n't > *contraction* not, used with auxiliary verbs (e.g. *can't*).

nth /enth/ > *adjective* **1** Mathematics denoting an unspecified term in a series. **2** denoting the last or latest item in a long series.

nu /nyoo/ > *noun* the thirteenth letter of the Greek alphabet (**N**, **v**), transliterated as 'n'.

ORIGIN – Greek.

nuance /nyooONSS/ > *noun* a subtle difference in or shade of meaning, expression, colour, etc. > *verb* (usu. **be**

nuanced) give nuances to: *a deeply nuanced understanding of human behaviour.*

ORIGIN – French, from *nuer* 'to shade', based on Latin *nubes* 'cloud'.

nub > *noun* **1** (**the nub**) the crux or central point of a matter. **2** a small lump or protuberance.

DERIVATIVES – **nubby** adjective.

nubbin > *noun* a small lump or residual part.

Nubian /nyoobiən/ > *adjective* of or relating to Nubia, an ancient region corresponding to southern Egypt and northern Sudan. > *noun* **1** a person from Nubia. **2** the language spoken by the Nubians.

nubile /nyoobīl/ > *adjective* (of a girl or woman) youthful but sexually mature and attractive.

DERIVATIVES – **nubility** noun.

---

wordpower facts

Nubile

The word **nubile** comes from Latin *nubilis*, meaning 'marriageable', from *nubere* 'veil oneself for a bridegroom'. *Nubere* ultimately derives from the Latin word for a 'cloud', *nubes*, which is the root also of **nuance** 'shade of meaning'.

---

nubuck /nyoobuk/ > *noun* cowhide leather which has been rubbed on the flesh side to give a suede-like effect.

nuchal /nyook'l/ > *adjective* Anatomy of or relating to the nape of the neck.

ORIGIN – from Latin *nucha* 'medulla oblongata'.

nuciferous /nyoosiffərəss/ > *adjective* Botany bearing nuts.

nuclear > *adjective* **1** of or relating to a nucleus. **2** using energy released in the fission or fusion of atomic nuclei. **3** possessing or involving nuclear weapons.

COMBINATIONS – **nuclear family** a couple and their dependent children, regarded as a basic social unit. **nuclear fuel** a substance that will undergo nuclear fission and can be used as a source of nuclear energy. **nuclear medicine** the branch of medicine concerned with the use of radioactive substances in research, diagnosis, and treatment. **nuclear power** power generated by a nuclear reactor. **nuclear waste** radioactive waste material, especially from the use or reprocessing of nuclear fuel. **nuclear winter** a period of abnormal cold and darkness predicted to follow a nuclear war, caused by smoke and dust blocking the sun's rays.

nucleate > *verb* /nyookliayt/ (usu. as adj. **nucleated**) **1** form a nucleus. **2** form

around a central area. > *adjective* /nyookliət/ chiefly Biology having a nucleus.

DERIVATIVES – **nucleation** noun.

nuclei plural of **NUCLEUS**.

nucleic acid /nyooklee-ik, nyooklayik/ > *noun* Biochemistry a complex organic substance, especially DNA or RNA, whose molecules consist of long chains of nucleotides.

nucleon /nyooklion/ > *noun* Physics a proton or neutron.

nucleoside > *noun* Biochemistry an organic compound consisting of a purine or pyrimidine base linked to a sugar, e.g. adenosine.

nucleotide > *noun* Biochemistry a compound consisting of a nucleoside linked to a phosphate group, forming the basic structural unit of nucleic acids.

nucleus /nyooklioss/ > *noun* (pl. **nuclei** /nyookli-ī/) **1** the central and most important part of an object or group. **2** Physics the positively charged central core of an atom, containing nearly all its mass. **3** Biology a structure present in most cells, containing the genetic material.

SYNONYMS – **1** centre, core, heart, kernel.

ORIGIN – Latin, diminutive of *nux* 'nut'.

nude > *adjective* wearing no clothes. > *noun* a naked human figure as a subject in art or photography.

DERIVATIVES – **nudity** noun.

SYNONYMS – *adjective* bare, naked, stripped, unclothed, undressed.

ORIGIN – Latin *nudus* 'plain, explicit'.

nudge > *verb* **1** prod with one's elbow to attract attention. **2** touch or push lightly. **3** give gentle encouragement to. > *noun* a light touch or push.

nudibranch /nyoodibrangk/ > *noun* Zoology a mollusc of an order comprising the sea slugs.

ORIGIN – from Latin *nudus* 'naked' + *branchiae* 'gills'.

nudist > *noun* a person who goes naked wherever possible.

DERIVATIVES – **nudism** noun.

nugatory /nyoogətri/ > *adjective* **1** worthless. **2** useless or invalid.

ORIGIN – Latin *nugatorius*, from *nugari* 'to trifle'.

nugget > *noun* **1** a small lump of gold or other precious metal found ready-formed in the earth. **2** a small but valuable fact.

nuisance > *noun* a person or thing causing inconvenience or annoyance.

SYNONYMS – annoyance, bother, irritant, pest; informal pain.

ORIGIN – Old French, based on Latin *nocere* 'to harm'.

Nuits St George /nwee saN zhorzh/ > *noun* a red burgundy wine produced in the district of Nuits St Georges, in France.

nuke informal > *noun* a nuclear weapon. > *verb* attack or destroy with nuclear weapons.

null > *adjective* **1** (usu. in phrase **null and void**) having no legal force; invalid. **2** having or associated with the value zero. **3** having no positive substance. > *noun* **1** a dummy letter in a cipher. **2** Electronics a condition in which no signal is generated. > *verb* Electronics cancel out.

COMBINATIONS – **null hypothesis** (in a statistical test) the theory that any observed differences between two groups are due to sampling or experimental error.

ORIGIN – Latin *nullus* 'none'.

nulla-nulla /**null**ənullə/ (also **nulla**) > *noun* a hardwood club used as a weapon by Australian Aboriginals.

ORIGIN – Dharuk (an Aboriginal language).

nullify > *verb* (**nullifies**, **nullified**) **1** make null and void. **2** cancel out.

DERIVATIVES – **nullification** *noun*.

SYNONYMS – **1** annul, repeal, revoke, void. **2** negate, neutralise.

nullity > *noun* (pl. **nullities**) **1** the state of being null. **2** a thing that is null.

numb > *adjective* deprived of the power of sensation. > *verb* make numb.

DERIVATIVES – **numbly** *adverb* **numbness** *noun*.

SYNONYMS – *adjective* deadened, frozen, insensitive, senseless. *verb* deaden, desensitise, freeze.

numbat > *noun* a small termite-eating Australian marsupial with a black-and-white-striped back.

ORIGIN – Nyungar (an Aboriginal language).

number > *noun* **1** a quantity or value expressed by a word, symbol, or figure. **2** a quantity or amount of something countable. **3** (**a number of**) several. **4** a single issue of a magazine. **5** a song, dance, or other musical item. **6** informal an item of clothing of a particular type, regarded with approval. **7** a grammatical classification of words that consists typically of singular and plural. > *verb* **1** amount to. **2** assign a number to; count. **3** include as a member of a group.

WORDFINDER – cardinal number (*a number denoting quantity*), numerical (*relating to or expressed as numbers*), numerology (*study of the occult significance of numbers*), ordinal number (*a number defining position in a series*), prime number (*a number divisible only by itself and 1*), root (*a number that when multiplied by itself gives a specified number*), square (*the product of a number multiplied by itself*).

IDIOMS – **by numbers** following simple instructions identified or as if identified by numbers. **have someone's number** informal understand a person's real motives or character. **someone's days are numbered** someone will not survive for much longer. **someone's number is up** informal someone is finished or doomed to die. **without number** too many to count.

DERIVATIVES – **numberless** *adjective*.

COMBINATIONS – **number cruncher** informal **1** a computer for performing complicated calculations. **2** often derogatory a statistician or other person dealing with numerical data. **numbered account** a bank account, especially in a Swiss bank, identified only by a number and not bearing the owner's name. **number one** informal **1** oneself. **2** the foremost person or thing. **3** a first lieutenant in the navy. **number plate** Brit. a sign affixed to the front and rear of a vehicle displaying its registration number. **numbers game 1** often derogatory the manipulation of statistics. **2** N. Amer. a lottery based on the occurrence of unpredictable numbers. **number two** informal a second in command.

ORIGIN – Old French *nombre*, from Latin *numerus*.

numbskull (also **numskull**) > *noun* informal a stupid or foolish person.

numen /**ny**ōōmən/ > *noun* (pl. **numina** /**ny**ōōminə/) a presiding spirit or deity.

ORIGIN – Latin.

numerable > *adjective* able to be counted.

numeral > *noun* a figure, word, or group of figures denoting a number. > *adjective* of or denoting a number.

numerate /**ny**ōōmərət/ > *adjective* having a good basic knowledge of arithmetic.

DERIVATIVES – **numeracy** *noun*.

numeration > *noun* the action or process of numbering or calculating.

numerator > *noun* the number above the line in a vulgar fraction showing how many of the parts indicated by the denominator are taken, e.g. 2 in ⅔.

numerical > *adjective* of, relating to, or expressed as a number or numbers.

DERIVATIVES – **numerically** *adverb*.

numerology > *noun* the branch of knowledge concerned with the occult significance of numbers.

DERIVATIVES – **numerological** *adjective* **numerologist** *noun*.

numerous > *adjective* **1** many. **2** consisting of many members.

SYNONYMS – **1** countless, innumerable, many, multitudinous.

Numidian /nyōō**midd**iən/ > *noun* a person from the ancient region of Numidia in North Africa. > *adjective* relating to Numidia.

numina plural of NUMEN.

numinous /**ny**ōōminəss/ > *adjective* having a strong religious or spiritual quality.

ORIGIN – from Latin NUMEN.

numismatic > *adjective* of or relating to coins or medals.

DERIVATIVES – **numismatically** *adverb*.

ORIGIN – from Greek *nomisma* 'current coin'.

numismatics > *plural noun* (usu. treated as sing.) the study or collection of coins, banknotes, and medals.

DERIVATIVES – **numismatist** *noun*.

numskull > *noun* variant spelling of NUMBSKULL.

nun > *noun* **1** a member of a female religious community, typically one living under vows of poverty, chastity, and obedience. **2** a pigeon of a breed with a crest on its neck.

WORDFINDER – convent (*community of nuns*), nunnery (*religious house of nuns*), wimple (*a nun's headdress*).

ORIGIN – Latin *nonna*, feminine of *nonnus* 'monk'.

nunatak /**nunn**ətak/ > *noun* an isolated peak of rock projecting above a surface of inland ice or snow.

ORIGIN – Eskimo.

Nunc Dimittis /nungk di**mitt**iss/ > *noun* the Song of Simeon (Gospel of Luke, chapter 2) used as a canticle in Christian liturgy.

ORIGIN – Latin, the opening words of the canticle, '(Lord), now you let (your servant) depart'.

nuncio > *noun* (pl. **nuncios**) (in the Roman Catholic Church) a papal ambassador to a foreign government or court.

ORIGIN – Italian, from Latin *nuntius* 'messenger'.

nunnery > *noun* (pl. **nunneries**) a religious house of nuns.

nuptial* /**nup**sh'l/ > *adjective* **1** of or relating to marriage or weddings. **2** Zoology relating to breeding. > *noun* (**nuptials**) a wedding.

*SPELLING – **nuptial** is spelled with an *i*, not a *u*: nuptial.

ORIGIN – Latin *nuptialis*, from *nuptiae* 'wedding'.

nurse¹ > *noun* **1** a person trained to care for the sick or infirm. **2** dated a person employed or trained to take charge of young children. > *verb* **1** give medical and other attention to. **2** feed or be fed at the breast. **3** treat or hold carefully or protectively. **4** harbour (a belief or feeling) for a long time.

COMBINATIONS – **nursing home** a small private institution for the elderly providing residential accommodation with health care.

ORIGIN – Old French *nourice* from Latin *nutrix*, from *nutrire* 'nourish'.

nurse² (also **nurse shark**) > *noun* a slow-moving shark of shallow inshore waters.

ORIGIN – probably from HUSS, by wrong division of *an huss*.

nursemaid > *noun* a woman or girl

employed to look after a young child or children.

nursery > *noun* (pl. **nurseries**) **1** a room in a house for the special use of young children. **2** (also **day nursery**) a nursery school. **3** a place where young plants and trees are grown for sale or for planting elsewhere.
COMBINATIONS – **nurseryman** a worker in or owner of a plant or tree nursery. **nursery nurse** Brit. a person trained to look after young children and babies in nurseries, crèches, etc. **nursery rhyme** a simple traditional song or poem for children. **nursery school** a school for young children, mainly between the ages of three and five. **nursery slope** a gentle ski slope suitable for beginners.

nursling > *noun* dated a baby that is being breastfed.

nurture > *verb* **1** rear and encourage the development of (a child). **2** cherish (a hope, belief, or ambition). > *noun* **1** the action or process of nurturing. **2** upbringing, education, and environment as a factor determining personality. Contrasted with NATURE.

nut > *noun* **1** a fruit consisting of a hard or tough shell around an edible kernel. **2** the hard kernel of such a fruit. **2** a small flat piece of metal or other material, typically square or hexagonal, with a threaded hole through it for screwing on to a bolt. **3** informal a crazy or eccentric person; an obsessive enthusiast. **4** informal a person's head. **5** a small lump of coal or other material. **6** (**nuts**) vulgar slang a man's testicles. > *verb* (**nutted**, **nutting**) informal butt with one's head.
WORDFINDER – *types of nut:* acorn, brazil, cashew, chestnut, filbert, hazelnut, macadamia, pecan, pistachio, walnut.
IDIOMS – **do one's nut** Brit. informal be extremely angry or agitated. **nuts and bolts** informal basic practical details. **a tough** (or **hard**) **nut to crack** informal a problem or an opponent that is hard to solve or overcome.
DERIVATIVES – **nutty** *adjective*.
COMBINATIONS – **nut loaf** a baked vegetarian dish made from ground or chopped nuts, vegetables, and herbs.

nutation /nyōōtaysh'n/ > *noun* a periodic variation in the inclination of an axis of rotation, especially that causing the earth's

precession to follow a wavy rather than a circular path.
ORIGIN – Latin, from *nutare* 'to nod'.

nutcase > *noun* informal a mad or foolish person.

nutcracker > *noun* **1** (**nutcrackers**) a device for cracking nuts. **2** a bird of the crow family that feeds on the seeds of conifers.

nuthatch > *noun* a small grey-backed songbird which climbs up and down tree trunks.
ORIGIN – from obsolete *hatch* (related to HACK[1]).

nutmeg > *noun* a spice made from the seed of a tropical tree native to the Molucca Islands in Indonesia.
ORIGIN – partial translation of Old French *nois muguede* 'musky nut'.

nutria /nyōōtriə/ > *noun* the skin or fur of the coypu.
ORIGIN – Spanish, literally 'otter'.

nutrient > *noun* a substance that provides nourishment essential for life and growth.

nutriment /nyōōtrimənt/ > *noun* nourishment; sustenance.

nutrition > *noun* **1** the process of ingesting and assimilating nutrients. **2** the branch of science concerned with nutrients and their ingestion.
DERIVATIVES – **nutritional** *adjective* **nutritionist** *noun*.
ORIGIN – Latin, from *nutrire* 'nourish'.

nutritious > *adjective* full of nutrients; nourishing.
DERIVATIVES – **nutritiously** *adverb*.
SYNONYMS – alimentary, nourishing, sustaining, wholesome.

nutritive > *adjective* **1** of or relating to nutrition. **2** nutritious.

nuts > *adjective* informal mad.

nutshell > *noun* the hard woody covering around the kernel of a nut.
IDIOMS – **in a nutshell** in the fewest possible words.

nutter > *noun* Brit. informal a mad or eccentric person.

nux vomica /nuks vommikə/ > *noun* a spiny southern Asian tree with berry-like fruit and toxic seeds that contain strychnine.
ORIGIN – Latin, 'nut causing vomiting'.

nuzzle > *verb* rub or push against gently with the nose and mouth.
ORIGIN – from NOSE.

NV > *abbreviation* Nevada.

NVQ > *abbreviation* (in the UK) National Vocational Qualification.

NW > *abbreviation* **1** north-west. **2** north-western.

NY > *abbreviation* New York.

nyala /nyaalə/ > *noun* (pl. same) a southern African antelope with a crest on the neck and back and lyre-shaped horns.
ORIGIN – Zulu.

NYC > *abbreviation* New York City.

nyctalopia /niktəlōpiə/ > *noun* Medicine an abnormal inability to see in very dim light, typically due to vitamin A deficiency.
ORIGIN – from Greek *nux* 'night' + *alaos* 'blind' + *ōps* 'eye'.

nyctophobia /niktəfōbiə/ > *noun* extreme or irrational fear of the night or of darkness.
ORIGIN – from Greek *nux* 'night'.

nylon > *noun* **1** a tough, lightweight, elastic synthetic polymer with a protein-like chemical structure. **2** fabric or yarn made of such polymers. **3** (**nylons**) nylon stockings or tights.
ORIGIN – an invented word.

nymph > *noun* **1** a mythological spirit of nature imagined as a beautiful maiden. **2** literary a beautiful young woman. **3** an immature form of an insect such as a dragonfly.
WORDFINDER – *kinds of nymph in mythology:* dryad (*inhabiting woods*), hamadryad (*inhabiting trees*), naiad (*water nymph*), Nereid (*sea nymph*), oread (*inhabiting mountains*).
DERIVATIVES – **nymphal** *adjective*.
ORIGIN – Greek *numphē* 'nymph, bride'.

nymphet > *noun* an attractive and sexually mature young girl.

nympho > *noun* (pl. **nymphos**) informal a nymphomaniac.

nympholepsy /nimfəlepsi/ > *noun* literary frenzy caused by a desire for the unattainable.
DERIVATIVES – **nympholeptic** *adjective*.

nymphomania > *noun* uncontrollable or excessive sexual desire in a woman.
DERIVATIVES – **nymphomaniac** *noun*.

nystagmus /nistagməss/ > *noun* Medicine rapid involuntary movements of the eyes.
ORIGIN – Greek *nustagmos* 'nodding, drowsiness'.

NZ > *abbreviation* New Zealand.

O

O¹ (also **o**) > *noun* (pl. **Os** or **O's**) **1** the fifteenth letter of the alphabet. **2** (also **oh**) zero, especially when spoken. **3** a human blood type (in the ABO system) lacking both the A and B antigens.
COMBINATIONS – **O level** historical (in the UK except Scotland) the lower of the two main levels of the GCE examination. [ORIGIN – short for *ordinary level*.]

O² > *symbol* the chemical element oxygen.

O³ > *exclamation* **1** archaic spelling of **OH¹**. **2** used before a name in the vocative.

oaf > *noun* a stupid, boorish, or clumsy man.
DERIVATIVES – **oafish** *adjective*.
SYNONYMS – boor, lout, yob.
ORIGIN – Old Norse *álfr* 'elf'.

oak > *noun* **1** a large tree which bears acorns and typically has lobed leaves and hard durable wood. **2** a smoky flavour characteristic of wine aged in oak barrels.
IDIOMS – **great oaks from little acorns grow** *proverb* something of small or modest proportions may grow into something very large or impressive.
DERIVATIVES – **oaken** *adjective* (archaic). **oaky** *adjective*.
COMBINATIONS – **oak apple** a spongy spherical gall which forms on oak trees, caused by wasp larvae.

oakum /ōkəm/ > *noun* chiefly historical loose fibre obtained by untwisting old rope, used especially in caulking wooden ships.
ORIGIN – Old English, 'off-combings'.

OAP > *abbreviation* Brit. old-age pensioner.

oar > *noun* a pole with a flat blade, used to row or steer a boat through the water.
WORDFINDER – catch a crab (*make a faulty stroke with an oar*), feathering (*act of turning an oar to pass through the air edgeways*), rowlock (*fitting serving as the fulcrum of an oar*), sculls (*pair of small oars used by a single rower*), thole (*pin acting as the fulcrum of an oar*).
IDIOMS – **put one's oar in** informal give an opinion without being asked.

oarsman (or **oarswoman**) > *noun* a rower.

OAS > *abbreviation* Organisation of American States.

oasis > *noun* (pl. **oases**) **1** a fertile spot in a desert where water rises to ground level. **2** an area or period of calm in the midst of a difficult or hectic place or situation.
SYNONYMS – **2** haven, refuge, sanctuary.
ORIGIN – Greek, from Egyptian.

oast > *noun* a kiln for drying hops.
COMBINATIONS – **oast house** a building containing an oast, typically conical in shape with a cowl on top.

oat > *noun* a cereal plant with a loose branched cluster of florets, cultivated in cool climates.
WORDFINDER – *dishes made with oats:* brose, farl, flapjack, laver bread, muesli, parkin, porridge.
IDIOMS – **feel one's oats** N. Amer. informal feel lively and energetic. **get one's oats** Brit. informal have sexual intercourse. **sow one's wild oats** go through a period of wild or promiscuous behaviour while young.
DERIVATIVES – **oaty** *adjective*.
COMBINATIONS – **oatcake** a savoury oatmeal biscuit.

oater > *noun* informal, chiefly US a western film.
ORIGIN – with allusion to oats as feed for horses.

oath > *noun* (pl. **oaths**) **1** a solemn promise, especially one that calls on a divine witness. **2** an obscene or blasphemous utterance.
WORDFINDER – affidavit (*statement confirmed by oath*), depose (*give evidence on oath*), perjury (*offence of lying in court under oath*).
IDIOMS – **under** (or **on**) **oath** having sworn to tell the truth, especially in a court of law.
SYNONYMS – **1** avowal, pledge, vow. **2** expletive, profanity, swear word.

oatmeal > *noun* meal made from ground oats, used in making porridge and oatcakes.

ob- (also **oc-** before *c*; **of-** before *f*; **op-** before *p*) > *prefix* forming words meaning: **1** to, towards: *obverse*. **2** against: *opponent*. **3** finality; completeness: *obsolete*.
ORIGIN – Latin *ob* 'towards, against, in the way of'.

obbligato /obligaatō/ (US also **obligato**) > *noun* (pl. **obbligatos** or **obbligati**) an instrumental part integral to a piece of music and not to be omitted in performance.
ORIGIN – Italian, 'obligatory'.

obdurate /obdyoorət/ > *adjective* stubbornly refusing to change one's opinion or course of action.
DERIVATIVES – **obduracy** *noun* **obdurately** *adverb* **obdurateness** *noun*.
SYNONYMS – implacable, intransigent, obstinate.
ORIGIN – Latin *obduratus*, from *ob-* 'in opposition' + *durare* 'harden'.

OBE > *abbreviation* Officer of the Order of the British Empire.

obeah /ōbiə/ (also **obi** /ōbi/) > *noun* a kind of sorcery practised especially in the Caribbean.
ORIGIN – Akan.

obedient > *adjective* willing to obey an order or submit to another's authority.
DERIVATIVES – **obedience** *noun* **obediently** *adverb*.
SYNONYMS – acquiescent, compliant, deferential, docile.
ANTONYMS – disobedient, rebellious.

obeisance /ōbays'nss/ > *noun* **1** deferential respect or homage. **2** a gesture expressing this, such as a bow.
DERIVATIVES – **obeisant** *adjective*.
ORIGIN – Old French *obeissance*, from *obeir* 'obey'.

obelisk > *noun* **1** a tapering stone pillar of square or rectangular cross section, set up as a monument or landmark. **2** an obelus (†).
ORIGIN – Greek *obeliskos* 'small pointed pillar'.

obelus /obbələss/ > *noun* (pl. **obeli** /obbəlī/) **1** a symbol (†) used in printed matter as a reference mark or to indicate that a person is deceased. **2** a mark (– or ÷) used in ancient manuscripts to mark a word or passage as spurious or doubtful.
ORIGIN – Greek *obelos* 'pointed pillar', also 'critical mark'.

obese /ōbeess/ > *adjective* very fat.
DERIVATIVES – **obesity** *noun*.
ORIGIN – Latin *obesus*.

obey > *verb* **1** submit to the authority of. **2** carry out (an order). **3** behave in accordance with (a principle or law).
SYNONYMS – **1** submit to, yield to. **2** discharge, execute, perform. **3** abide by, comply with, observe.
ANTONYMS – defy.

wordpower facts
Obey
The word **obey** comes via Old French *obeir* from Latin *oboedire*. The Latin verb is formed from the elements *ob-* 'in the direction of' and *audire* 'to hear'. Thus **obey** is related to other words which developed from *audire*, such as **audible** and **audience**, and to the exclamation **oyez** 'hear!', which similarly comes via Old French from the same root.

obfuscate /obfuskayt/ > *verb* make unclear or unintelligible.
DERIVATIVES – **obfuscation** *noun* **obfuscatory** *adjective*.
ORIGIN – Latin *obfuscare* 'darken'.

obi¹ > *noun* variant form of **OBEAH**.

obi² /ōbi/ > noun (pl. **obis**) a broad sash worn round the waist of a Japanese kimono.
ORIGIN – Japanese, 'belt'.

obit /obbit, ōbit/ > noun informal an obituary.

obiter dictum /obbitər diktəm/ > noun (pl. **obiter dicta**) **1** Law a judge's expression of opinion uttered in court or when giving judgement, which is not essential to the decision and therefore has no binding authority. **2** an incidental remark.
ORIGIN – Latin, 'something said in passing'.

obituarist > noun a writer of obituaries.

obituary /əbityoori/ > noun (pl. **obituaries**) an announcement that someone has died, especially as published in a newspaper in the form of a brief biography.
ORIGIN – from Latin obitus 'death'.

object > noun /objikt/ **1** a material thing that can be seen and touched. **2** a person or thing to which an action or feeling is directed. **3** a goal or purpose. **4** Grammar a noun or noun phrase governed by a transitive verb or by a preposition. > verb /əbjekt/ express disapproval or opposition.
IDIOMS – **no object** not influencing or restricting choices or decisions: a tycoon for whom money is no object.
DERIVATIVES – **objector** noun.
SYNONYMS – noun **1** article, item, thing. **3** aim, goal, objective, purpose, target. verb disagree, disapprove, protest.
COMBINATIONS – **object lesson** a striking practical example of a principle or ideal.
ORIGIN – Latin objectum, from ob- 'in the way of' + jacere 'to throw'.

objectify > verb (**objectifies**, **objectified**) **1** express (something abstract) in a concrete form. **2** degrade to the status of an object.
DERIVATIVES – **objectification** noun.

objection > noun **1** an expression of disapproval or opposition. **2** the action of challenging or disagreeing.
SYNONYMS – **1** demur, protest, protestation, remonstration.

objectionable > adjective arousing distaste or opposition.
DERIVATIVES – **objectionableness** noun **objectionably** adverb.
SYNONYMS – disagreeable, nasty, offensive, unpleasant.

objective > adjective **1** not influenced by personal feelings or opinions. **2** not dependent on the mind for existence; actual. **3** Grammar relating to a case of nouns and pronouns used for the object of a transitive verb or a preposition. > noun **1** a goal or aim. **2** the lens in a telescope or microscope nearest to the object observed.
DERIVATIVES – **objectively** adverb **objectivise** (also **objectivize**) verb **objectivity** noun.
SYNONYMS – adjective **1** impartial, unbiased,

unprejudiced. **2** actual, real. noun **1** aim, intention, purpose, target.
ANTONYMS – adjective **1** biased, prejudiced. **2** subjective.

objectivism > noun **1** the tendency to emphasise what is external to or independent of the mind. **2** Philosophy the belief that moral truths exist independently of human knowledge or perception.
DERIVATIVES – **objectivist** noun & adjective.

objet d'art /obzhay daar/ > noun (pl. **objets d'art** pronunc. same) a small decorative or artistic object.
ORIGIN – French, 'object of art'.

objet trouvé /obzhay troovay/ > noun (pl. **objets trouvés** pronunc. same) an ordinary object found at random and considered as a work of art.
ORIGIN – French, 'found object'.

oblate¹ /oblayt/ > adjective Geometry (of a spheroid) flattened at the poles. Contrasted with **PROLATE**.
ORIGIN – Latin oblatus, from ob- 'inversely' + -latus 'carried'.

oblate² /oblayt/ > noun a person dedicated to a religious life, but typically not having taken full monastic vows.
ORIGIN – from Latin oblatus 'offered'.

oblation /əblaysh'n/ > noun **1** a thing presented or offered to a god. **2** Christian Church the presentation of bread and wine to God in the Eucharist.
DERIVATIVES – **oblational** adjective **oblatory** adjective.
ORIGIN – Latin, from offerre 'to offer'.

obligate > verb **1** compel legally or morally. **2** US commit (assets) as security. > adjective Biology restricted to a particular function or mode of life: an obligate parasite.
ORIGIN – Latin obligare, from ob- 'towards' + ligare 'to bind'.

obligation > noun **1** an act or course of action to which a person is morally or legally bound. **2** the condition of being so bound. **3** a debt of gratitude for a service or favour.
SYNONYMS – **1** duty, responsibility.

obligato > noun US variant spelling of **OBBLIGATO**.

obligatory > adjective **1** required by a law or rule; compulsory. **2** (of a ruling) having binding force.
SYNONYMS – **1** compulsory, mandatory.
ANTONYMS – **1** voluntary.

oblige > verb **1** compel legally or morally. **2** perform a service or favour for. **3** (**be obliged**) be indebted or grateful.
ORIGIN – Latin obligare, from ob- 'towards' + ligare 'to bind'.

obliging > adjective willing to do a service or kindness; helpful.
DERIVATIVES – **obligingly** adverb.

SYNONYMS – accommodating, cooperative, helpful.

oblique /əbleek/ > adjective **1** neither parallel nor at right angles; slanting. **2** not explicit or direct. **3** Geometry (of a line, plane figure, or surface) inclined at other than a right angle. > noun Brit. a slash (/).
DERIVATIVES – **obliquely** adverb **obliqueness** noun **obliquity** /əblikwiti/ noun.
ORIGIN – Latin obliquus.

obliterate /əblittərayt/ > verb **1** destroy utterly; wipe out. **2** blot out or erase.
DERIVATIVES – **obliteration** noun.
SYNONYMS – eradicate, erase, expunge, wipe out.
ORIGIN – Latin obliterare 'strike out, erase', based on littera 'letter'.

oblivion > noun **1** the state of being unaware of what is happening around one. **2** the state of being forgotten. **3** destruction or extinction.
ORIGIN – Latin, from oblivisci 'forget'.

oblivious > adjective not aware of what is happening around one.
DERIVATIVES – **obliviously** adverb **obliviousness** noun.
SYNONYMS – (**oblivious to or of**) unaware of, unconscious of.

oblong > adjective having a rectangular shape. > noun an oblong object or flat figure.
ORIGIN – Latin oblongus 'longish'.

obloquy /obləkwi/ > noun **1** strong public condemnation. **2** public disgrace.
ORIGIN – Latin obloqui, from ob- 'against' + loqui 'speak'.

obnoxious /əbnokshəss/ > adjective extremely unpleasant.
DERIVATIVES – **obnoxiously** adverb **obnoxiousness** noun.
SYNONYMS – foul, odious, repulsive, vile.
ORIGIN – first meaning 'vulnerable': from Latin obnoxius 'exposed to harm', from ob- 'towards' + noxa 'harm'.

oboe /ōbō/ > noun a woodwind instrument of treble pitch, played with a double reed and having an incisive tone.
DERIVATIVES – **oboist** noun.
ORIGIN – Italian, or from French hautbois, from haut 'high' + bois 'wood'.

obscene > adjective **1** not according with accepted standards of decency; offensive or disgusting. **2** morally repugnant through being excessive: obscene pay rises.
DERIVATIVES – **obscenely** adverb.
SYNONYMS – **1** coarse, crude, disgusting, indecent, offensive.
ORIGIN – French obscène or Latin obscaenus 'ill-omened or abominable'.

obscenity > noun (pl. **obscenities**) **1** the state or quality of being obscene. **2** an obscene action, image, or expression.

obscurantism /obskyoo**ran**tiz'm/ > *noun* the practice of preventing something being fully understood or known.

DERIVATIVES – **obscurantist** *noun* & *adjective*.

ORIGIN – from Latin *obscurare* 'make dark'.

obscure > *adjective* **1** not discovered or known about; uncertain. **2** little known. **3** not clearly expressed or easily understood. **4** hard to make out; indistinct. > *verb* cause to be obscure; conceal or make unclear.

DERIVATIVES – **obscuration** *noun* **obscurely** *adverb* **obscurity** *noun*.

SYNONYMS – *adjective* **1** mysterious, uncertain, unclear. **2** abstruse, arcane, esoteric. **4** blurry, faint, indistinct, vague.

ORIGIN – Latin *obscurus* 'dark'.

obsequies /**ob**sikwiz/ > *plural noun* funeral rites.

ORIGIN – Latin, from *exsequiae* 'funeral rites', influenced by *obsequium* 'dutiful service'.

obsequious /əb**see**kwiəss/ > *adjective* obedient or attentive to an excessive or servile degree.

DERIVATIVES – **obsequiously** *adverb* **obsequiousness** *noun*.

SYNONYMS – fawning, servile, slavish, sycophantic.

ORIGIN – from Latin *obsequium* 'compliance', from *obsequi* 'follow, comply with'.

observance > *noun* **1** compliance with the requirements of law, morality, or ritual. **2** (**observances**) acts performed for religious or ceremonial reasons.

observant > *adjective* **1** quick to notice things. **2** observing the rules of a religion.

SYNONYMS – **1** alert, keen-eyed, sharp-eyed.

observation > *noun* **1** the action or process of closely observing or monitoring. **2** the ability to notice significant details. **3** a comment based on something one has seen, heard, or noticed.

DERIVATIVES – **observational** *adjective* **observationally** *adverb*.

SYNONYMS – **1** inspection, scrutiny, surveillance. **3** remark.

observatory > *noun* (pl. **observatories**) a room or building housing an astronomical telescope or other scientific equipment for the study of natural phenomena.

observe > *verb* **1** become aware of by seeing. **2** watch attentively; monitor. **3** say; remark. **4** fulfil or comply with (a regulation, custom, etc.).

DERIVATIVES – **observable** *adjective* **observer** *noun*.

SYNONYMS – **1** discern, note, notice, perceive, see. **2** inspect, monitor, study, watch.

ORIGIN – Latin *observare* 'to watch'.

obsess > *verb* **1** (usu. **be obsessed**) preoccupy (someone) continually or to a troubling extent. **2** informal, chiefly N. Amer. be preoccupied in this way.

ORIGIN – Latin *obsidere* 'besiege'.

obsession > *noun* **1** the state of being obsessed by someone or something. **2** an idea or thought that continually intrudes on someone's mind.

DERIVATIVES – **obsessional** *adjective*.

obsessive > *adjective* **1** affected by an obsession; prone to obsessions. **2** having the characteristics of an obsession.

DERIVATIVES – **obsessively** *adverb* **obsessiveness** *noun*.

COMBINATIONS – **obsessive–compulsive** Psychiatry (of a disorder) in which a person feels compelled to perform certain actions repeatedly to alleviate persistent fears or intrusive thoughts.

obsidian /əb**sidd**iən/ > *noun* a dark glass-like volcanic rock formed by the rapid solidification of lava.

ORIGIN – Latin *obsidianus*, error for *obsianus*, from *Obsius*, the name (according to the Roman writer Pliny) of the discoverer of a similar stone.

obsolescent /obsə**less**'nt/ > *adjective* becoming obsolete.

DERIVATIVES – **obsolesce** *verb* **obsolescence** *noun*.

ORIGIN – from Latin *obsolescere* 'fall into disuse'.

obsolete /**ob**səleet/ > *adjective* **1** no longer produced or used; out of date. **2** Biology rudimentary or vestigial.

SYNONYMS – **1** defunct, disused, outdated.

ANTONYMS – **1** current.

ORIGIN – Latin *obsoletus* 'grown old, worn out', from *obsolescere* 'fall into disuse'.

obstacle > *noun* a thing that blocks one's way or hinders progress.

SYNONYMS – barrier, impediment, stumbling block.

COMBINATIONS – **obstacle race** a running race in which fences, pits, or similar obstacles have to be negotiated.

ORIGIN – Latin *obstaculum*, from *obstare* 'impede'.

obstetrician /obstə**trish**'n/ > *noun* a physician or surgeon qualified to practise in obstetrics.

obstetrics /əb**stet**riks/ > *plural noun* the branch of medicine and surgery concerned with childbirth.

DERIVATIVES – **obstetric** *adjective*.

ORIGIN – from Latin *obstetrix* 'midwife', from *obstare* 'be present'.

obstinate > *adjective* **1** stubbornly refusing to change one's opinion or chosen course of action. **2** unyielding.

DERIVATIVES – **obstinacy** *noun* **obstinately** *adverb*.

SYNONYMS – **1** intractable, intransigent, stubborn.

ANTONYMS – tractable.

ORIGIN – Latin *obstinatus*, from *obstinare* 'persist'.

obstreperous /əb**strepp**ərəss/ > *adjective* (of a person) noisy and difficult to control.

DERIVATIVES – **obstreperously** *adverb* **obstreperousness** *noun*.

SYNONYMS – rowdy, unmanageable, unruly.

ORIGIN – from Latin *obstrepere*, from *ob-* 'against' + *strepere* 'make a noise'.

obstruct > *verb* **1** block; be in the way of. **2** prevent or hinder.

DERIVATIVES – **obstructive** *adjective* **obstructor** *noun*.

SYNONYMS – **1** block, clog, jam. **2** baulk, hinder, impede, prevent, thwart.

ORIGIN – from Latin *obstruere*.

obstruction > *noun* **1** the action of obstructing or the state of being obstructed. **2** a thing that is in the way of something.

SYNONYMS – **2** barrier, hindrance, obstacle.

obstructionism > *noun* the practice of deliberately blocking or delaying the course of legislative or other procedures.

DERIVATIVES – **obstructionist** *noun* & *adjective*.

obtain > *verb* **1** acquire or secure. **2** formal be prevalent, customary, or established.

DERIVATIVES – **obtainable** *adjective*.

SYNONYMS – **1** acquire, come by, get, procure, secure.

ORIGIN – Latin *obtinere*.

obtrude /əb**trood**/ > *verb* **1** become obtrusive. **2** impose or force on someone.

ORIGIN – Latin *obtrudere*, from *ob-* 'towards' + *trudere* 'to push'.

obtrusive > *adjective* noticeable or prominent in an unwelcome or intrusive way.

DERIVATIVES – **obtrusively** *adverb* **obtrusiveness** *noun*.

obtuse /əb**tyooss**/ > *adjective* **1** annoyingly insensitive or slow to understand. **2** (of an angle) more than 90° and less than 180°. **3** not sharp-pointed or sharp-edged; blunt.

DERIVATIVES – **obtusely** *adverb* **obtuseness** *noun*.

SYNONYMS – **1** dense, slow-witted, stupid.

ORIGIN – Latin *obtusus*, from *obtundere* 'beat against'.

obverse > *noun* **1** the principal side of a coin or medal. **2** the opposite or counterpart of a fact or truth. > *adjective* that is the obverse of something.

DERIVATIVES – **obversely** *adverb*.

ORIGIN – Latin *obversus*, from *obvertere* 'turn towards'.

obviate /**ob**viayt/ > *verb* **1** remove (a need or difficulty). **2** avoid; prevent.

DERIVATIVES – **obviation** *noun*.

ORIGIN – Latin *obviare* 'prevent'.

obvious > *adjective* **1** easily perceived or

understood; clear. **2** derogatory predictable and lacking in subtlety.

DERIVATIVES – **obviously** *adverb* **obviousness** *noun*.

SYNONYMS – **1** clear, conspicuous, manifest, plain, transparent.

ORIGIN – first meaning 'often encountered': from the Latin phrase *ob viam* 'in the way'.

OC > *abbreviation* Officer Commanding.

ocarina /okkəreenə/ > *noun* a small wind instrument with holes for the fingers, typically having the shape of a bird.

ORIGIN – Italian, from *oca* 'goose'.

Occam's razor /okkəmz/ (also **Ockham's razor**) > *noun* the scientific principle that in explaining a thing no more assumptions should be made than are necessary.

ORIGIN – named after the 13th-century English philosopher William of *Occam*.

occasion* > *noun* **1** a particular event, or the time at which it takes place. **2** a suitable or opportune time. **3** a special event or celebration. **4** formal reason or justification: *we have occasion to rejoice.* > *verb* formal cause.

IDIOMS – **on occasion** from time to time. **rise to the occasion** perform well in response to a special situation.

*SPELLING – two *c*s, and one *s*, with no *i* between them: o*cc*a*s*ion.

ORIGIN – Latin, 'juncture, reason', from *occidere* 'go down, set'.

occasional > *adjective* **1** occurring infrequently or irregularly. **2** produced on or intended for particular occasions: *occasional verse.*

DERIVATIVES – **occasionally** *adverb*.

COMBINATIONS – **occasional table** a small table for infrequent and varied use.

Occident /oksidənt/ > *noun* (**the Occident**) formal or literary the countries of the West. Contrasted with *the Orient*.

ORIGIN – from Latin *occidere* 'go down, set', with reference to the setting of the sun.

occidental (also **Occidental**) > *adjective* of or relating to the West or the Occident. > *noun* a person from the Occident.

occiput /oksiput/ > *noun* Anatomy the back of the head.

DERIVATIVES – **occipital** *adjective*.

ORIGIN – Latin, from *ob-* 'against' + *caput* 'head'.

Occitan /oksitən/ > *noun* the medieval or modern language of Languedoc (southern France), including Provençal.

DERIVATIVES – **Occitanian** *noun* & *adjective*.

ORIGIN – French, from Old French *oc* 'yes' (see **LANGUE D'OC**).

occlude /əklood/ > *verb* **1** stop, close up, or obstruct. **2** Chemistry (of a solid) absorb and retain (a gas or impurity). **3** (of a tooth) come into contact with another in the opposite jaw.

COMBINATIONS – **occluded front** a composite weather front produced when a cold front catches up with a warm front, so that the warm air in between them is forced upwards.

ORIGIN – Latin *occludere*.

occlusion > *noun* technical the process of occluding or blocking up.

DERIVATIVES – **occlusive** *adjective*.

occult /okult, okkult/ > *noun* (**the occult**) supernatural beliefs, practices, or phenomena. > *adjective* **1** relating to the occult. **2** esoteric. **3** Medicine present but not readily discernible. > *verb* /okult/ **1** cut off from view by interposing something. **2** Astronomy (of a celestial body) conceal (another body) from view.

DERIVATIVES – **occultation** *noun* **occultism** *noun* **occultist** *noun*.

ORIGIN – from Latin *occulere* 'conceal'.

occupancy > *noun* **1** the action or fact of occupying a place. **2** the proportion of accommodation occupied or used.

occupant > *noun* **1** a person who occupies a place at a given time. **2** the holder of a position or office.

occupation > *noun* **1** the action, state, or period of occupying or being occupied. **2** a job or profession. **3** a way of spending time.

DERIVATIVES – **occupational** *adjective* **occupationally** *adverb*.

COMBINATIONS – **occupational hazard** a risk arising as a consequence of a particular occupation.

occupational therapy > *noun* the use of particular activities as an aid to recuperation from physical or mental illness.

DERIVATIVES – **occupational therapist** *noun*.

occupy > *verb* (**occupies, occupied**) **1** reside or have one's place of business in. **2** take control of (a place) by military conquest or settlement. **3** enter and stay in (a building) without authority. **4** fill or take up (a space, time or position). **5** keep (someone) busy, active, or preoccupied.

DERIVATIVES – **occupier** *noun*.

SYNONYMS – **5** absorb, engage, engross, preoccupy.

ORIGIN – Latin *occupare* 'seize'.

occur* > *verb* (**occurred, occurring**) **1** happen; take place. **2** exist or be found to be present. **3** (**occur to**) come into the mind of.

*SPELLING – note that there is a double *r* in **occurred** and **occurring**.

SYNONYMS – **1** come about, happen, result, take place, transpire.

ORIGIN – Latin *occurrere* 'go to meet, present itself'.

occurrence* > *noun* **1** the fact or frequency of something occurring. **2** a thing that occurs; an incident or event.

*SPELLING – double *r*: occu*rr*ence.

SYNONYMS – **2** affair, event, happening, incident, matter.

ocean > *noun* **1** a very large expanse of sea; in particular, each of the Atlantic, Pacific, Indian, Arctic, and Antarctic Oceans. **2** (**the ocean**) chiefly N. Amer. the sea.

WORDFINDER – abyssal (*relating to the depths of the ocean*), doldrums (*region of the Atlantic Ocean with frequent calms*), hadal (*relating to the deep ocean trenches*), high seas (*the open ocean*), roaring forties (*stormy ocean tracts between latitudes 40° and 50° south*).

wordpower facts
Ocean
The word **ocean** derives from the Greek word *ōkeanos*, meaning 'the great stream encircling the earth's disc'. The ancient Greeks were familiar only with the mass of land comprising the Eastern hemisphere and its islands; the **ocean** denoted the outer sea surrounding this land mass, as opposed to the Mediterranean and other 'inland' seas.

oceanarium /ōshənairiəm/ > *noun* (pl. **oceanariums** or **oceanaria** /ōshənairiə/) a large seawater aquarium.

Oceanian /ōshiaaniəm/ > *adjective* of or relating to Oceania, the islands of the Pacific Ocean and adjacent seas. > *noun* a person from Oceania; a Polynesian.

oceanic /ōshiannik/ > *adjective* **1** of or relating to the ocean. **2** (**Oceanic**) another term for **OCEANIAN**.

oceanography > *noun* the branch of science concerned with the physical and biological properties and phenomena of the oceans and seas.

DERIVATIVES – **oceanographer** *noun* **oceanographic** *adjective*.

oceanology > *noun* **1** another term for **OCEANOGRAPHY**. **2** the branch of technology and economics concerned with human use of the sea.

DERIVATIVES – **oceanological** *adjective* **oceanologist** *noun*.

ocelot /ossəlot/ > *noun* a medium-sized striped and spotted wild cat, native to South and Central America.

ORIGIN – French, from a Nahuatl word meaning 'field tiger'.

och /ok, okh/ > *exclamation* Scottish & Irish expressing surprise, regret, or disbelief.

oche /okki/ (also **hockey**) > *noun* Brit. the line behind which darts players stand when throwing.

ORIGIN – perhaps related to Old French *ocher* 'cut a notch in'.

ochlocracy /oklokrəsi/ > *noun* formal government by the populace; mob rule.
ORIGIN – Greek, from *okhlos* 'mob'.

ochre /ōkər/ (US also **ocher**) > *noun* a pigment containing ferric oxide, varying from light yellow to brown or red.
DERIVATIVES – **ochreous** /ōkriəss/ *adjective* **ochrous** *adjective*.
ORIGIN – Greek *ōkhra*.

ocker /okkər/ Austral. informal > *noun* a boorish or uncultivated Australian.
ORIGIN – alteration of *Oscar*, the name of an Australian TV character.

Ockham's razor > *noun* variant spelling of OCCAM'S RAZOR.

o'clock > *adverb* used to specify the hour when telling the time.
ORIGIN – contraction of *of the clock*.

OCR > *abbreviation* optical character recognition.

Oct. > *abbreviation* October.

octa- (also **oct-** before a vowel) > *combining form* eight; having eight: *octahedron*.
ORIGIN – Greek *oktō* 'eight'.

octad /oktad/ > *noun* a group or set of eight.

octagon > *noun* a plane figure with eight straight sides and eight angles.
DERIVATIVES – **octagonal** *adjective*.

octahedron /oktəheedrən/ > *noun* (pl. **octahedra** or **octahedrons**) a three-dimensional shape having eight plane faces, in particular eight equal triangular faces.
DERIVATIVES – **octahedral** *adjective*.

octal /oktəl/ > *adjective* relating to a system of numerical notation that has 8 rather than 10 as a base.

octane /oktayn/ > *noun* Chemistry a liquid hydrocarbon present in petroleum spirit.
COMBINATIONS – **octane number** (also **octane rating**) a figure indicating the anti-knock properties of a fuel, based on a comparison with a mixture containing octane.
ORIGIN – from OCTO- 'eight' (denoting eight carbon atoms) + -ANE.

octant /oktənt/ > *noun* **1** each of eight equal parts or sectors of a circle. **2** each of eight parts into which a space or object is divided by three intersecting planes.
ORIGIN – Latin, from *octo* 'eight'.

octave /oktiv/ > *noun* **1** Music a series of eight notes occupying the interval between (and including) two notes, one having twice or half the pitch of the other. **2** Music the interval between two such notes, or the notes themselves sounding together. **3** a group or stanza of eight lines.
ORIGIN – from Latin *octava dies* 'eighth day': originally referring to a period of eight days following and including a Church festival.

octavo /oktaavō/ > *noun* (pl. **octavos**) a size of book page that results from folding each printed sheet into eight leaves (sixteen pages).

octennial > *adjective* lasting for or recurring every eight years.

octet > *noun* **1** a group of eight musicians. **2** a musical composition for eight voices or instruments. **3** a group of eight lines of verse.

octo- (also **oct-** before a vowel) > *combining form* eight; having eight: *octosyllabic*.
ORIGIN – Latin *octo* or Greek *oktō* 'eight'.

October > *noun* the tenth month of the year.
ORIGIN – Old English, from Latin *octo* 'eight', being originally the eighth month of the Roman year.

octogenarian /oktəjinairiən/ > *noun* a person between 80 and 89 years old.
ORIGIN – from Latin *octoginta* 'eighty'.

octopus > *noun* (pl. **octopuses**) a cephalopod mollusc with eight sucker-bearing arms, a soft body, beak-like jaws, and no internal shell.
DERIVATIVES – **octopoid** *adjective*.
USAGE – the standard plural in English of **octopus** is **octopuses**. However, since the word comes from Greek, the Greek plural form **octopodes** is still occasionally used. The plural form **octopi**, formed according to rules for Latin plurals, is incorrect.
ORIGIN – Greek, from *oktō* 'eight' + *pous* 'foot'.

octoroon /oktəroon/ > *noun* archaic a person who is one-eighth black by descent.

octuple /oktyoop'l/ > *adjective* **1** consisting of eight parts or things. **2** eight times as many or as much. > *verb* make or become eight times as many or as large.
ORIGIN – Latin *octuplus*.

octuplet > *noun* each of eight children born at one birth.

ocular /okyoolər/ > *adjective* of or connected with the eyes or vision. > *noun* an eyepiece.
ORIGIN – from Latin *oculus* 'eye'.

ocularist > *noun* a person who makes artificial eyes.

oculist /okyoolist/ > *noun* a person who specialises in the medical treatment of diseases or defects of the eye; an ophthalmologist.
ORIGIN – French *oculiste*.

oculus /okyooləss/ > *noun* (pl. **oculi** /okyoolī/) Architecture **1** a circular window. **2** the central boss of a volute. **3** an opening at the apex of a dome.
ORIGIN – Latin, 'eye'.

OD /ōdee/ informal > *verb* (**OD's**, **OD'd**, **OD'ing**) take an overdose of a drug. > *noun* an overdose.

odalisque /ōdəlisk/ > *noun* historical a female slave or concubine in a harem.
ORIGIN – French, from Turkish *odalik*, from *oda* 'chamber' + *lik* 'function'.

odd > *adjective* **1** out of the ordinary. **2** (of whole numbers such as 3 and 5) having one left over as a remainder when divided by two. **3** in the region of: *fifty-odd years*. **4** occasional: *we have the odd drink together*. **5** spare; unoccupied: *an odd five minutes*. **6** detached from a pair or set.
IDIOMS – **odd one out** a person or thing differing in some way from the other members of a group or set. **odds and ends** miscellaneous articles or remnants.
DERIVATIVES – **oddly** *adverb* **oddness** *noun*.
SYNONYMS – **1** abnormal, bizarre, peculiar, strange, unusual.
ANTONYMS – **1** conventional, normal.
COMBINATIONS – **odd-job man** a man who does casual or isolated jobs of work of a routine domestic or manual nature.
ORIGIN – Old Norse *odda-*, found in combinations such as *odda-mathr* 'third or odd man', from *oddi* 'angle'.

oddball informal > *noun* a strange or eccentric person.

oddity > *noun* (pl. **oddities**) **1** the quality of being strange. **2** a strange person or thing.

oddment > *noun* an item or remnant from a larger piece or set.

odds > *plural noun* **1** the ratio between the amounts staked by the parties to a bet, based on the expected probability either way. **2** (**the odds**) the chances of something happening or being the case. **3** (**the odds**) the balance of advantage; superiority in strength, resources, etc.
IDIOMS – **at odds** in conflict or at variance. **it makes no odds** informal, chiefly Brit. it does not matter. **lay** (or **give**) **odds** offer a bet with odds favourable to the other better. **over the odds** Brit. (especially of a price) above what is generally considered acceptable. **take odds** offer a bet with odds unfavourable to the other better.

odds-on > *adjective* **1** (especially of a horse) rated at evens or less to win. **2** very likely to happen or succeed.

ode > *noun* a poem expressing noble feelings, often addressed to a person or celebrating an event.
ORIGIN – Greek *ōidē*, from *aeidein* 'sing'.

odiferous /ōdiffərəss/ > *adjective* another term for ODORIFEROUS.

odious /ōdiəss/ > *adjective* extremely unpleasant; repulsive.
DERIVATIVES – **odiously** *adverb* **odiousness** *noun*.
SYNONYMS – abhorrent, disgusting, repellent, repulsive, revolting.

odium > *noun* general or widespread hatred or disgust.
ORIGIN – Latin.

odometer /ōdommitər/ > *noun* chiefly N. Amer. an instrument for measuring the distance travelled by a wheeled vehicle.

ORIGIN – French *odomètre*, from Greek *hodos* 'way'.

odontology /ōdon**toll**əji/ > *noun* the scientific study of the structure and diseases of teeth.

DERIVATIVES – **odontologist** noun.

ORIGIN – from Greek *odous* 'tooth'.

odor > *noun* US spelling of ODOUR.

odorant > *noun* a substance used to give a scent or odour to a product.

odoriferous /ōdə**riff**ərəss/ > *adjective* having an odour.

ORIGIN – Latin *odorifer* 'odour-bearing'.

odour (US **odor**) > *noun* **1** a distinctive smell. **2** a lingering quality or impression.

IDIOMS – **be in good** (or **bad**) **odour** informal be in (or out of) favour.

DERIVATIVES – **odorous** adjective **odourless** adjective.

SYNONYMS – **1** aroma, fragrance, scent.

ORIGIN – Latin *odor*.

odyssey /**odd**isi/ > *noun* (pl. **odysseys**) a long eventful journey.

DERIVATIVES – **odyssean** /oddi**see**ən/ *adjective*.

ORIGIN – from *Odyssey*, the title of a Greek epic poem attributed to Homer.

OECD > *abbreviation* Organisation for Economic Cooperation and Development.

OED > *abbreviation* Oxford English Dictionary.

oedema /i**dee**mə/ (US **edema**) > *noun* a condition in which there is an abnormal amount of watery fluid in the cavities or tissues of the body; dropsy.

DERIVATIVES – **oedematous** adjective.

ORIGIN – Greek *oidēma*, from *oidein* 'to swell'.

Oedipus complex /**ee**dippəs/ > *noun* (in Freudian theory) the complex of emotions aroused in a child by an unconscious sexual desire for the parent of the opposite sex.

DERIVATIVES – **Oedipal** adjective.

ORIGIN – named after *Oedipus* in Greek mythology, who unwittingly killed his father and married his mother.

OEM > *abbreviation* original equipment manufacturer.

oenology /ee**noll**əji/ (US also **enology**) > *noun* the study of wines.

DERIVATIVES – **oenological** adjective **oenologist** noun.

ORIGIN – from Greek *oinos* 'wine'.

oenophile /**ee**nəfīl/ (US also **enophile**) > *noun* a connoisseur of wines.

DERIVATIVES – **oenophilist** /ee**noff**ilist/ *noun*.

o'er > *adverb & preposition* archaic or literary form of OVER.

oesophagus /ee**soff**əgəss/ (US **esophagus**) > *noun* (pl. **oesophagi** /ee**soff**əjī/ or **oesophaguses**) the part of the alimentary canal which connects the throat to the stomach.

DERIVATIVES – **oesophageal** /eesoffə**jee**əl/ *adjective*.

ORIGIN – Greek *oisophagos*.

oestradiol /eestrə**dī**ol/ (US **estradiol**) > *noun* a major oestrogen produced in the ovaries.

oestrogen /**ee**strəjən/ (US **estrogen**) > *noun* any of a group of steroid hormones which promote the development and maintenance of female characteristics of the body.

ORIGIN – from OESTRUS + -GEN.

oestrus /**ee**strəss/ (US **estrus**) > *noun* a recurring period of sexual receptivity and fertility in many female mammals.

DERIVATIVES – **oestrous** adjective.

ORIGIN – Greek *oistros* 'gadfly, frenzy'.

oeuvre /**ö**vrə/ > *noun* the body of work of an artist, composer, author, etc.

ORIGIN – French, 'work'.

of > *preposition* **1** expressing the relationship between a part and a whole. **2** expressing the relationship between a scale or measure and a value. **3** indicating an association between two things, typically one of belonging. **4** expressing the relationship between a direction and a point of reference. **5** expressing the relationship between a general category and something which belongs to such a category. **6** indicating the material constituting something. **7 N. Amer.** expressing time in relation to the following hour.

USAGE – it is incorrect to write **of** instead of **have** in constructions such as *I could have told you* (not *I could of told you*). This common mistake is made because the unstressed pronunciation of **have** in informal speech is similar to that of **of**, so the two words are confused when it comes to writing them down.

off > *adverb* **1** away from the place in question. **2** so as to be removed or separated. **3** starting a journey or race. **4** so as to bring to an end or be discontinued. **5** (of an electrical appliance or power supply) not functioning or so as to cease to function. **6** having specified material goods or wealth: *badly off*. > *preposition* **1** moving away and often down from. **2** situated or leading in a direction away from. **3** so as to be removed or separated from. **4** informal having a temporary dislike of. > *adjective* **1** unsatisfactory or inadequate. **2** (of food) no longer fresh. **3** located on the offside of a vehicle. **4 Brit.** informal annoying or unfair. **5 Brit.** informal unwell. > *noun* **1** (also **off side**) Cricket the half of the field towards which the batsman's feet are pointed when standing to receive the ball. The opposite of LEG. **2 Brit.** informal the start of a race or journey. > *verb* informal N. Amer. kill; murder.

IDIOMS – **off and on** intermittently.

USAGE – use **off**, not **off of**, in a sentence like *it fell off the table*: the compound

preposition **off of**, although it has always been common in dialect and informal speech, is not regarded as standard English and should be avoided in more formal situations.

COMBINATIONS – **off break** Cricket a ball which spins from the off side towards the leg side after pitching. **off drive** Cricket a drive to the off side. **off-ramp** N. Amer. an exit road from a motorway. **off season** a time of year when a particular activity is not engaged in or a business is quiet.

offal > *noun* **1** the entrails and internal organs of an animal used as food. **2** decaying or waste matter.

ORIGIN – probably from Dutch *afval*, from *af* 'off' + *vallen* 'to fall'.

offbeat > *adjective* **1** Music not coinciding with the beat. **2** informal unconventional; unusual. > *noun* Music any of the normally unaccented beats in a bar.

off-colour > *adjective* **1** Brit. slightly unwell. **2** slightly indecent or obscene.

offcut > *noun* a piece of waste material that is left behind after cutting a larger piece.

offence (US **offense**) > *noun* /ə**fenss**/ **1** an act or instance of offending. **2** resentment or hurt. **3** the action of making a military attack. **4** /**off**enss/ N. Amer. the attacking team in a sport.

SYNONYMS – **1** misdeed, transgression, wrongdoing. **2** affront, injury, insult.

offend > *verb* **1** cause to feel hurt or resentful. **2** be displeasing to. **3** commit an act that is illegal or that goes against an accepted principle.

DERIVATIVES – **offender** noun.

SYNONYMS – **1** affront, displease, distress, upset. **2** be disagreeable to, disgust, repel.

ORIGIN – Latin *offendere* 'strike against'.

offensive > *adjective* **1** causing offence. **2** involved or used in active attack. **3 chiefly N. Amer.** of or relating to the team in possession of the ball in a game. > *noun* a military campaign of attack.

IDIOMS – **be on the offensive** be ready to act aggressively.

DERIVATIVES – **offensively** adverb **offensiveness** noun.

SYNONYMS – **1** abusive, derogatory, insulting, rude.

OFFER > *abbreviation* (in the UK) Office of Electricity Regulation.

offer > *verb* **1** present for acceptance, refusal, or consideration. **2** express willingness to do something for someone. **3** provide (access or opportunity). **4** present (a prayer or sacrifice) to a deity. **5** (**offer up**) place (something) in the desired position for fixing. > *noun* **1** an expression of readiness to do or give something. **2** an amount of money that someone is willing to pay for something. **3** a specially reduced price. **4** a proposal of marriage.

IDIOMS – **on offer 1** available. **2** for sale at a reduced price.

DERIVATIVES – **offerer** noun.

ORIGIN – Latin *offerre* 'bestow, present'.

offering > noun **1** a small gift or donation. **2** a religious sacrifice.

offertory /**off**ərtri/ > noun (pl. **offertories**) Christian Church **1** the offering of the bread and wine at the Eucharist. **2** a collection of money made at a religious service.

ORIGIN – Latin *offertorium*.

offhand > adjective ungraciously casual or cool in manner. > adverb without previous consideration.

office > noun **1** a room, set of rooms, or building used as a place for non-manual work. **2** a position of authority or service. **3** tenure of an official position. **4** (**offices**) service done for others. **5** (also **Divine Office**) Christian Church the services of prayers and psalms said daily by Catholic priests or other clergy. **6** (**offices**) Brit. formal, dated the parts of a large house given over to household work or to storage.

WORDFINDER – depose (*remove from office forcefully*), inaugurate (*admit formally to office*), incumbency (*period during which someone holds an office*), pooh-bah (*person holding many offices simultaneously*).

COMBINATIONS – **office boy** (or **girl**) a young person employed in an office to carry out routine tasks.

ORIGIN – Latin *officium* 'performance of a task', from *opus* 'work' + *facere* 'do'.

officer > noun **1** a person holding a position of authority, especially a member of the armed forces who holds a commission, or a member of the police force. **2** a holder of a public, civil, or ecclesiastical office.

official > adjective **1** relating to an authority or public body and its activities and responsibilities. **2** having the approval or authorisation of such a body. > noun a person holding public office or having official duties.

DERIVATIVES – **officialdom** noun **officialism** noun **officially** adverb.

COMBINATIONS – **official birthday** (in the UK) a day in June chosen for the observance of the sovereign's birthday. **official secret** Brit. a piece of information that is important for national security and is officially classified as confidential.

officialese > noun formal and wordy language considered to be characteristic of official documents.

officiant > noun a priest or minister who performs a religious service or ceremony.

officiate /ə**fish**iayt/ > verb **1** act as an official. **2** perform a religious service or ceremony.

DERIVATIVES – **officiation** noun **officiator** noun.

officious > adjective asserting authority or interfering in an annoyingly domineering way.

DERIVATIVES – **officiously** adverb **officiousness** noun.

USAGE – do not confuse **officious**, which has negative connotations, with **official**, which means 'relating to an authority or public body' and 'having the approval or authorisation of such a body'.

SYNONYMS – bumptious, overbearing, self-important.

offing > noun the more distant part of the sea in view.

IDIOMS – **in the offing** likely to happen or appear soon.

offish > adjective informal aloof or distant in manner.

off-key > adjective & adverb **1** Music not in the correct key or of the correct pitch. **2** inappropriate.

off-licence > noun Brit. a shop selling alcoholic drink for consumption elsewhere.

off-limits > adjective out of bounds.

off-line > adjective not connected to a computer.

offload > verb **1** unload (a cargo). **2** rid oneself of.

off-peak > adjective & adverb at a time when demand is less.

off-piste > adjective & adverb Skiing away from prepared ski runs.

offprint > noun a printed copy of an article that originally appeared as part of a larger publication.

off-putting > adjective unpleasant or disconcerting.

off-road > adverb away from the road; on rough terrain.

offset > noun /**off**set/ **1** a consideration or amount that diminishes or balances the effect of a contrary one. **2** the amount by which something is out of line. **3** a side shoot from a plant serving for propagation. **4** a method of printing in which ink is transferred from a plate or stone to a uniform rubber surface and from that to the paper. > verb /off**set**/ (**offsetting**; past and past participle **offset**) **1** counterbalance; compensate for. **2** place out of line. **3** transfer an impression by means of offset printing.

offshoot > noun **1** a side shoot on a plant. **2** a thing that develops from something else.

offshore > adjective & adverb **1** situated at sea some distance from the shore. **2** (of the wind) blowing towards the sea from the land. **3** relating to the business of extracting oil or gas from the seabed. **4** made, situated, or registered abroad. **5** relating to a foreign country.

offside > adjective & adverb (in games such as football) occupying a position on the field where playing the ball is not allowed. > noun **1** the fact of being offside. **2** chiefly Brit. the side of a vehicle furthest from the kerb. Contrasted with **NEARSIDE**. **3** the right-hand side of a horse.

offspring > noun (pl. same) a person's child or children, or the young of an animal.

offstage > adjective & adverb (in a theatre) not on the stage and so not visible to the audience.

off-white > noun a white colour with a grey or yellowish tinge.

Ofgas > abbreviation (in the UK) Office of Gas Supply.

Ofsted > abbreviation (in the UK) Office for Standards in Education.

OFT > abbreviation (in the UK) Office of Fair Trading.

oft (also **oft-times**) > adverb archaic or literary often.

Oftel > abbreviation (in the UK) Office of Telecommunications.

often (also archaic or N. Amer. **oftentimes**) > adverb (**oftener**, **oftenest**) **1** frequently. **2** in many instances.

USAGE – the comparative and superlative forms **oftener** and **oftenest**, though not incorrect, are rarely used now in British English, in which the constructions **more often** and **most often** are more usual. However **oftener** and **oftenest** do occur more frequently in North American English.

ORIGIN – extended form of **OFT**, probably influenced by *selden* 'seldom'.

Ofwat > abbreviation (in the UK) Office of Water Services.

ogee /**ō**jee/ Architecture > adjective showing in section an S-shaped curve. > noun an S-shaped line or moulding.

COMBINATIONS – **ogee arch** an arch with two ogee curves meeting at the apex.

ORIGIN – apparently from **OGIVE** (with which it was originally synonymous).

ogham /**og**əm/ (also **ogam**) > noun an ancient British and Irish alphabet, consisting of characters formed by strokes across or on either side of a continuous line.

ORIGIN – Irish *ogam*.

ogive /**ō**jīv/ > noun Architecture **1** a pointed or Gothic arch. **2** one of the diagonal groins or ribs of a vault.

DERIVATIVES – **ogival** adjective.

ORIGIN – French.

ogle > verb stare at lecherously. > noun a lecherous look.

DERIVATIVES – **ogler** noun.

ogre > noun (fem. **ogress**) **1** (in folklore) a man-eating giant. **2** a cruel or terrifying person.

DERIVATIVES – **ogreish** (also **ogrish**) adjective.

ORIGIN – French.

OH > abbreviation Ohio.

oh¹ > *exclamation* **1** expressing surprise, disappointment, joy, or other emotion. **2** used to acknowledge something that has just been said.

oh² > *noun* variant spelling of **O¹** (in sense 2).

ohm /ōm/ > *noun* the unit of electrical resistance in the SI system, transmitting a current of one ampere when subjected to a potential difference of one volt.

ORIGIN – named after the German physicist G. S. *Ohm*.

OHMS > *abbreviation* on Her (or His) Majesty's Service.

OHP > *abbreviation* Brit. overhead projector.

-oid > *suffix* forming adjectives and nouns denoting resemblance or relationship: *anthropoid, asteroid*.

DERIVATIVES – **-oidal** suffix.

ORIGIN – Greek *-oeidēs*; related to *eidos* 'form'.

OIEO > *abbreviation* Brit. offers in excess of.

oik (also **oick**) > *noun* informal an uncouth or obnoxious person.

oil > *noun* **1** a viscous liquid obtained from petroleum, used especially as a fuel or lubricant. **2** any of various viscous liquids which are insoluble in water and are obtained from animals or plants. **3** Chemistry any of a group of liquid natural esters of glycerol and various fatty acids. Compare with FAT. **4** (also **oils**) oil paint. > *verb* lubricate, coat, or impregnate with oil.

WORDFINDER – *essential oils:* attar, opopanax, peppermint, petitgrain, vetiver, ylang-ylang.

COMBINATIONS – **oilcake** a mass of compressed linseed or other plant material left after oil has been extracted, used as fodder or fertiliser. **oilcan** a can with a long nozzle used for applying oil to machinery. **oilcloth** cotton fabric treated with oil to make it waterproof. **oil-fired** using oil as fuel. **oil lamp** a lamp using oil as fuel. **oil paint** a paste made with ground pigment and a drying oil such as linseed oil, used by artists. **oil palm** a tropical West African palm which is the chief source of palm oil. **oil platform** (also **oil rig**) a structure designed to stand on the seabed to provide a stable base above water for the drilling and regulation of oil wells. **oilseed** seed from a cultivated crop yielding oil, such as rape, peanuts, or cotton. **oil shale** a fine-grained sedimentary rock from which oil can be extracted. **oil slick** a film or layer of oil floating on an expanse of water. **oilstone** a fine-grained flat stone used with oil for sharpening chisels, planes, or other tools. **oil well** an artificially made well or shaft in rock from which mineral oil is drawn.

ORIGIN – Old French *oile*, from Latin *oleum* 'oil, olive oil', from Greek *elaion*.

oiler > *noun* **1** an oil tanker. **2** an oilcan. **3** N. Amer. informal an oil well. **4** (**oilers**) N. Amer. informal oilskin garments.

oilfield > *noun* an area of land or seabed underlain by strata yielding significant quantities of mineral oil.

oilskin > *noun* **1** heavy cotton cloth waterproofed with oil. **2** (**oilskins**) a set of garments made of oilskin.

oily > *adjective* (**oilier, oiliest**) **1** containing, covered with, or soaked in oil. **2** resembling oil. **3** (of a person) unpleasantly smooth and ingratiating.

DERIVATIVES – **oiliness** noun.

SYNONYMS – **3** obsequious, unctuous.

oink > *noun* the characteristic grunting sound of a pig. > *verb* make such a sound.

ointment > *noun* a smooth substance that is rubbed on the skin for medicinal purposes.

ORIGIN – Old French *oignement*, from Latin *unguentum* (from *unguere* 'anoint'); influenced by obsolete *oint* 'anoint'.

OIRO > *abbreviation* Brit. offers in the region of.

Ojibwa /əjibway/ > *noun* (pl. same or **Ojibwas**) a member of an American Indian people of the area around Lake Superior.

ORIGIN – Ojibwa, said to mean 'puckered', with reference to their moccasins.

OK¹ (also **okay**) informal > *exclamation* **1** expressing agreement, approval, or acquiescence. **2** introducing an utterance. > *adjective* **1** satisfactory, but not especially good. **2** permissible. > *adverb* in a satisfactory manner or to a satisfactory extent. > *noun* an authorisation or approval. > *verb* (**OK's, OK'd, OK'ing**) give approval to.

wordpower facts

OK

The exclamation **OK** entered English in the mid 19th century. It is probably an abbreviation of *orl korrect*, a humorous form of *all correct*, which was popularised as a slogan during President Martin Van Buren's re-election campaign of 1840 in the US. The initials also represented his nickname *Old Kinderhook*, derived from his birthplace, Kinderhook in New York State.

OK² > *abbreviation* Oklahoma.

okapi /ōkaapi/ > *noun* (pl. same or **okapis**) a large mammal of the giraffe family that lives in the rainforests of northern Zaire (Democratic Republic of Congo), having a dark chestnut coat with stripes on the hindquarters and upper legs.

ORIGIN – a local word.

okay > *exclamation, adjective, adverb, noun, & verb* variant spelling of **OK¹**.

okey-dokey (also **okey-doke**) > *exclamation* variant form of **OK¹**.

Okie > *noun* (pl. **Okies**) US informal **1** a person from the state of Oklahoma. **2** derogatory a migrant agricultural worker from Oklahoma who was forced to leave their farm during the depression of the 1930s.

okra /okrə, ōkrə/ > *noun* the long ridged seed pods of a plant of the mallow family, eaten as a vegetable.

ORIGIN – a West African word.

old > *adjective* (**older, oldest**) **1** having lived for a long time; no longer young. **2** made or built long ago. **3** possessed or used for a long time. **4** dating from far back; long-established or known. **5** former; previous. **6** of a specified age. **7** informal expressing affection, familiarity, or contempt: *good old Mum*.

WORDFINDER – dotage (*period of life when one is old and weak*), geriatric (*relating to the health care of old people*), gerontic (*relating to old age*), gerontocracy (*government by old people*), progeria (*disease causing premature ageing*), senescence (*deterioration due to old age*), senile (*weakened through age, especially in mental faculties*).

IDIOMS – **of old 1** in or belonging to the past. **2** for a long time. **the old days** a period in the past. **the old country** the native country of a person who has gone to live abroad. **the old school** the traditional form or type: *a gentleman of the old school*.

DERIVATIVES – **oldish** adjective **oldness** noun.

SYNONYMS – **1** elderly, senior. **2** archaic, antediluvian, antiquated, antique. **5** bygone, former, past, previous.

ANTONYMS – **1** young. **2-4** new.

COMBINATIONS – **old age 1** the later part of normal life. **2** the state of being old. **old-age pensioner** an old person, especially one receiving a retirement pension. **Old English sheepdog** a large sheepdog of a breed with a shaggy blue-grey and white coat. **Old French** the French language up to *c*.1400. **old girl 1** a former female pupil of a school, college, or university. **2** informal an elderly woman. **3** an affectionate term of address to a girl or woman. **Old Glory** US informal the US national flag. **old gold** a dull brownish-gold colour. **old guard** the original or long-standing members of a group, regarded as being unwilling to accept change. **old hand** a person with a lot of experience. **old hat** informal tediously familiar or out of date. **old lady 1** an elderly woman. **2** (**one's old lady**) informal one's mother, wife, or girlfriend. **old maid 1** derogatory a single woman regarded as too old for marriage. **2** a prim and fussy person. **3** a card game in which players collect pairs and try not to be left with an odd penalty card, typically a queen. **old master** a great artist of former times, especially of the 13th–17th century in Europe. **Old Nick** an informal name for the Devil. **Old Norse** the North Germanic language of medieval Norway, Iceland, Denmark, and Sweden, from which the modern Scandinavian languages are derived. **Old Slavonic** Church Slavonic. **old stager** informal a very experienced or long-serving person. **Old Stone Age** the Palaeolithic period. **Old Style** the method of calculating dates using the Julian calendar. **Old Testament** the first part of the Christian Bible, comprising thirty-nine books and corresponding approximately to the Hebrew Bible. **old-time** pleasingly traditional or old-fashioned. **old-timer** informal a very experienced or long-serving person. **old wives' tale** a widely held traditional belief that is now thought to be unscientific or incorrect. **old woman 1** an elderly female person. **2** (**one's old woman**) informal one's mother, wife, or female partner. **3** derogatory a fussy or timid person. **Old World** Europe, Asia, and Africa, regarded collectively as the part of the world known before the discovery of the Americas.

old boy > *noun* **1** a former male pupil of a school. **2** informal an elderly man. **3** an affectionate form of address to a man or boy.

COMBINATIONS – **old boy network** (also **old boys' network**) an informal system through which men use their positions of influence to help others who went to the same school or university, or who share a similar social background.

olde /ōld, ōldi/ (also **olde worlde**) > *adjective* pseudo-archaic old-fashioned in a way intended to be attractively quaint.

olden > *adjective* of a former age.

Old English > *noun* the language of the Anglo-Saxons (up to about 1150), an inflected language with a Germanic vocabulary.

WORDFINDER – *Old English letters:* ash (Æ), eth (ð or Ð), thorn (þ or þ).

old-fashioned > *adjective* **1** relating to styles or views that are no longer current. **2** informal disapproving: *an old-fashioned look.*

oldie > *noun* informal an old person or thing.

old man > *noun* **1** an elderly man. **2** (**one's old man**) informal one's father, husband, or male partner. **3** Brit. informal an affectionate form of address between men or boys.

COMBINATIONS – **old man's beard 1** a wild clematis with grey fluffy hairs around the seeds. **2** a lichen forming shaggy greyish growths on trees.

oldster > *noun* informal, chiefly N. Amer. an older person.

OLE > *abbreviation* Computing object linking and embedding.

ole > *adjective* US informal old.

olé /ōlay/ > *exclamation* bravo!

ORIGIN – Spanish.

oleaginous /ōliajinəss/ > *adjective* **1** oily or greasy. **2** exaggeratedly complimentary; obsequious.

ORIGIN – Latin *oleaginus*, from *oleum* 'oil'.

oleander /ōliandər/ > *noun* a poisonous evergreen shrub grown in warm countries for its clusters of white, pink, or red flowers.

ORIGIN – Latin.

olefin /ōlifin/ (also **olefine**) > *noun* Chemistry another term for ALKENE.

ORIGIN – from French *oléfiant* 'oil-forming'.

oleograph /ōliəgraaf/ > *noun* a print textured to resemble an oil painting.

olfaction /olfaksh'n/ > *noun* the sense of smell.

DERIVATIVES – **olfactive** *adjective*.

olfactory /olfaktəri/ > *adjective* relating to the sense of smell.

ORIGIN – from Latin *olfacere* 'to smell'.

olibanum /olibbənəm/ > *noun* frankincense.

ORIGIN – from Greek *libanos*.

oligarch /olligaark/ > *noun* a ruler in an oligarchy.

oligarchy > *noun* (pl. **oligarchies**) **1** a small group of people having control of a state. **2** a state governed by such a group.

DERIVATIVES – **oligarchic** *adjective* **oligarchical** *adjective* **oligarchically** *adverb*.

ORIGIN – Greek *oligarkhia*, from *oligoi* 'few'.

Oligocene /olligəseen/ > *adjective* Geology relating to the third epoch of the Tertiary period (35.4 to 23.3 million years ago), a time when the first primates appeared.

ORIGIN – from Greek *oligos* 'few' + *kainos* 'new'.

oligopoly /olligoppəli/ > *noun* (pl. **oligopolies**) a state of limited competition, in which a market is shared by a small number of producers or sellers.

oligopsony /olligopsəni/ > *noun* (pl. **oligopsonies**) a state of the market in which only a small number of buyers exists for a product.

ORIGIN – from Greek *oligos* 'small', *oligoi* 'few', on the pattern of *monopsony*.

oligotrophic /olligōtrōfik, -troff-/ > *adjective* Ecology (of a body of water) relatively poor in plant nutrients and containing abundant oxygen in the deeper parts.

DERIVATIVES – **oligotrophy** *noun*.

olivaceous /ollivayshəss/ > *adjective* technical of an olive green colour.

olive > *noun* **1** a small oval fruit with a hard stone and bitter flesh, green when unripe and bluish black when ripe. **2** the small evergreen tree which yields this fruit. **3** (also **olive green**) a greyish-green colour like that of an unripe olive. **4** a slice of beef or veal made into a roll with stuffing inside and stewed. **5** a metal ring or fitting tightened under a threaded nut to form a seal. > *adjective* **1** of the colour olive. **2** (of a person's complexion) yellowish brown; sallow.

COMBINATIONS – **olive branch** an offer of reconciliation. [ORIGIN – in biblical allusion to the story of Noah in Genesis, in which a dove returns with an olive branch after the Flood.] **olive drab** a dull olive-green colour, used in some military uniforms. **olive oil** an oil obtained from olives, used in cookery and salad dressings.

ORIGIN – Latin *oliva*, from Greek *elaia*, from *elaion* 'oil'.

olivine /olliveen/ > *noun* a green or brown silicate mineral found in many igneous rocks.

Olmec /olmek/ > *noun* (pl. same or **Olmecs**) **1** a member of a prehistoric people who lived on the Gulf of Mexico. **2** a native people inhabiting this area during the 15th and 16th centuries.

ORIGIN – Nahuatl, 'inhabitants of the rubber country'.

-ology > *combining form* common form of **-LOGY**.

oloroso /ollərōsō/ > *noun* (pl. **olorosos**) a heavy, dark, medium-sweet sherry.

ORIGIN – Spanish, 'fragrant'.

Olympiad /əlimpiad/ > *noun* **1** a celebration of the ancient or modern Olympic Games. **2** a period of four years between Olympic Games, used by the ancient Greeks in dating events.

Olympian > *adjective* **1** associated with Mount Olympus in NE Greece, traditional home of the Greek gods. **2** superior and aloof like a god. **3** relating to the Olympic Games. > *noun* **1** any of the twelve Greek gods regarded as living on Olympus. **2** a very superior or exalted person. **3** a competitor in the Olympic Games.

Olympic > *adjective* relating to ancient Olympia or the Olympic Games. > *noun* (**the Olympics**) the Olympic Games.

Olympic Games > *plural noun* **1** a sports festival held every four years in different countries, instigated in 1896. **2** an ancient Greek festival with athletic, literary, and musical competitions, held at Olympia every four years.

OM > *abbreviation* (in the UK) Order of Merit.

om /ōm/ > *noun* Hinduism & Tibetan Buddhism a mystic syllable, considered the most sacred mantra.

-oma > *suffix* (forming nouns) denoting tumours and other abnormal growths: *carcinoma*.

ORIGIN – Greek.

Omaha /ōməhaa/ > *noun* (pl. same or **Omahas**) a member of an American Indian people of NE Nebraska.
ORIGIN – Omaha, 'upstream people'.

Omani /ōmaani/ > *noun* a person from Oman in the Arabian peninsula. > *adjective* relating to Oman.

ombré /ombray/ > *adjective* (of a fabric) graduated from light to dark in colour.
ORIGIN – French, 'shaded'.

ombudsman /omboŏdzmən/ > *noun* an official appointed to investigate individuals' complaints against bad or dishonest administration, especially that of public authorities.
ORIGIN – Swedish, 'legal representative'.

omega /ōmigə/ > *noun* **1** the last letter of the Greek alphabet (Ω, ω), transliterated as 'o' or 'ō'. **2** the last of a series; the final development.
ORIGIN – Greek *ō mega* 'the great O'.

omelette (US also **omelet**) > *noun* a dish of beaten eggs cooked in a frying pan and usually served with a savoury topping or filling.
IDIOMS – **one can't make an omelette without breaking eggs** proverb one cannot always accomplish something without risking bad effects elsewhere.
ORIGIN – French, from *lemele* 'knife blade'.

omen > *noun* an event regarded as a portent of good or evil.
SYNONYMS – augury, harbinger, portent, sign.
ORIGIN – Latin.

omertà /ōmairtaa/ > *noun* the Mafia code of silence about criminal activity.
ORIGIN – Italian, 'humility'.

omicron /ōmīkron/ > *noun* the fifteenth letter of the Greek alphabet (O, o), transliterated as 'o'.
ORIGIN – Greek *o mikron* 'small o'.

ominous > *adjective* giving the worrying impression that something bad is going to happen.
DERIVATIVES – **ominously** adverb.
SYNONYMS – menacing, threatening.
ORIGIN – Latin *ominosus*, from *omen* 'omen'.

omission > *noun* **1** the action of leaving something out. **2** a failure to do something. **3** something that has been left out or not done.
WORDFINDER – elision (*omission of a sound or syllable in speech*), ellipsis (*omission of words*), haplography (*inadvertent omission of repeated letter or letters in writing*), syncope (*omission of sounds or letter from within a word*).
SYNONYMS – **1** elimination, excision, exclusion. **2** neglect, negligence, oversight.

omit > *verb* (**omitted**, **omitting**) **1** leave out or exclude. **2** fail to do.

SYNONYMS – **1** delete, erase, exclude, expunge, leave out. **2** neglect, overlook.
ORIGIN – Latin *omittere* 'let go'.

omni- > *combining form* **1** all; of all things: *omnifarious*. **2** in all ways or places: *omnipresent*.
ORIGIN – from Latin *omnis* 'all'.

omnibus > *noun* **1** a volume containing several works previously published separately. **2** a single edition of two or more consecutive programmes previously broadcast separately. **3** dated a bus.
ORIGIN – Latin, 'for all'.

omnicompetent > *adjective* able to deal with all matters or solve all problems.
DERIVATIVES – **omnicompetence** noun.

omnidirectional > *adjective* Telecommunications receiving signals from or transmitting in all directions.

omnifarious /omnifairiəss/ > *adjective* formal comprising or relating to all sorts or varieties.
ORIGIN – Latin *omnifarius*.

omnipotent /omnippət'nt/ > *adjective* having unlimited or very great power.
DERIVATIVES – **omnipotence** noun.

omnipresent > *adjective* **1** (of God) present everywhere at the same time. **2** widely or constantly encountered.
DERIVATIVES – **omnipresence** noun.

omniscient /omnissiənt/ > *adjective* knowing everything.
DERIVATIVES – **omniscience** noun.
ORIGIN – Latin *omnisciens*, from *scire* 'to know'.

omnisexual > *adjective* not restricted in sexual choice with regard to gender or activity.

omnium gatherum /omniəm gathərəm/ > *noun* a miscellaneous collection.
ORIGIN – mock Latin, from Latin *omnium* 'of all' and GATHER.

omnivore /omnivor/ > *noun* an omnivorous animal.

omnivorous /omnivvərəss/ > *adjective* **1** feeding on a variety of food of both plant and animal origin. **2** indiscriminate in taking in or using whatever is available.
DERIVATIVES – **omnivorously** adverb.

omophagy /ōmoffəji/ (also **omophagia**) > *noun* the eating of raw food, especially raw meat.
ORIGIN – Greek, from *ōmos* 'raw' + *-phagia* 'eating'.

omphalos /omfəloss/ > *noun* (pl. **omphaloi** /omfəloy/) **1** (in ancient Greece) a conical stone at Delphi representing the navel of the earth. **2** a boss on an ancient Greek shield.
ORIGIN – Greek, 'navel, boss'.

ON > *abbreviation* Ontario.

on > *preposition* **1** physically in contact with and supported by (a surface). **2** on to. **3** in the personal possession of. **4** forming a

distinctive or marked part of the surface of. **5** about; concerning. **6** as a member of (a committee, jury, etc.). **7** having (the thing mentioned) as a target, aim, or focus. **8** stored in or broadcast by. **9** in the course of or while travelling in. **10** at the time of; during. **11** engaged in. **12** regularly taking (a drug or medicine). **13** informal paid for by. **14** added to. > *adverb* **1** physically in contact with and supported by a surface. **2** (of clothing) being worn by a person. **3** further forward; with continued movement or action. **4** taking place or being presented. **5** in operation; functioning. **6** on duty or on stage. > *noun* (also **on side**) Cricket the leg side.
IDIOMS – **be on about** Brit. informal talk about tediously and at length. **be on at** Brit. informal nag or grumble at. **be on to** informal **1** be close to uncovering an illegal or undesirable activity engaged in by (someone). **2** (**be on to something**) have an idea that is likely to lead to an important discovery. **on and on** continually; at tedious length. **on to** moving to a location on the surface of or aboard.
COMBINATIONS – **on drive** Cricket a drive to the on side.

onager /onnəgər/ > *noun* a wild ass of a race native to northern Iran.
ORIGIN – Greek *onagros* 'wild ass'.

onanism /ōnəniz'm/ > *noun* formal **1** masturbation. **2** coitus interruptus.
DERIVATIVES – **onanist** noun **onanistic** adjective.
ORIGIN – from the name of *Onan* in the Bible, who practised coitus interruptus (Book of Genesis, chapter 38).

once > *adverb* **1** on one occasion or for one time only. **2** at all; on even one occasion: *he never once complained*. **3** formerly; in the past. **4** multiplied by one. > *conjunction* as soon as; when.
IDIOMS – **all at once 1** suddenly. **2** all at the same time. **at once 1** immediately. **2** simultaneously. **for once** (or **this once**) on this occasion only. **once again** (or **more**) one more time. **once and for all** (or **once for all**) now and for the last time; finally. **once** (or **every once**) **in a while** occasionally. **once or twice** a few times. **once upon a time** at some time in the past.

once-over > *noun* informal a rapid inspection, search, or piece of work.

oncer > *noun* Brit. informal (formerly) a one-pound note.

oncogene /ongkəjeen/ > *noun* Medicine a gene which in certain circumstances can transform a cell into a tumour cell.
ORIGIN – from Greek *onkos* 'mass'.

oncogenic /ongkəjennik/ > *adjective* Medicine causing development of a tumour or tumours.

oncology /ongˈkolləji/ > *noun* the study and treatment of tumours.

DERIVATIVES – **oncological** *adjective* **oncologist** *noun*.

oncoming > *adjective* approaching from the front; moving towards one.

oncost > *noun* Brit. an overhead expense.

one > *cardinal number* **1** the lowest cardinal number; 1. (Roman numeral: **i** or **I**.) **2** single, or a single person or thing. **3** (before a person's name) a certain. **4** informal, chiefly N. Amer. a noteworthy example of. **5** identical; the same. > *pronoun* **1** used to refer to a person or thing previously mentioned or easily identified. **2** a person of a specified kind. **3** used to refer to the speaker, or any person, as representing people in general.

IDIOMS – **at one** in agreement or harmony. **one after another** (or **the other**) following one another in quick succession. **one and all** everyone. **one and only** unique; single. **one another** each other. **one by one** separately and in succession. **one day** at a particular but unspecified time in the past or future. **one or another** (or **the other**) a particular but unspecified one out of a set of items. **one or two** informal a few.

COMBINATIONS – **one-armed bandit** informal a fruit machine operated by pulling a long handle at the side. **one-dimensional** lacking depth; superficial. **one-horse race** a contest in which one competitor is clearly superior to all the others. **one-horse town** informal a small town with few and poor facilities. **one-liner** informal a short joke or witty remark. **one-man band 1** a street entertainer who plays many instruments at the same time. **2** a person who runs a business alone. **one-night stand** (also **one-nighter**) **1** informal a sexual relationship lasting only one night. **2** a single performance of a play or show in a particular place. **one-step** a vigorous kind of foxtrot in duple time. **one-time** former. **one-track mind** informal a mind preoccupied with one subject, especially sex. **one-trick pony** informal a person or thing with only one special feature, talent, or area of expertise. **one-two 1** a pair of punches in quick succession with alternate hands. **2** chiefly Soccer a move in which a player plays a short pass to a teammate and moves forward to receive an immediate return pass. **one-way** moving or allowing movement in one direction only.

Oneida /ōˈnīdə/ > *noun* (pl. same or **Oneidas**) a member of an American Indian people formerly inhabiting upper New York State.

ORIGIN – from a local word meaning 'erected stone', the name of successive principal Oneida settlements, near which a large boulder was traditionally erected.

oneiric /əˈnīrik/ > *adjective* formal relating to dreams or dreaming.

ORIGIN – from Greek *oneiros* 'dream'.

oneness > *noun* **1** the state of being unified, whole, or in harmony. **2** the state of being one in number.

one-off informal, chiefly Brit. > *adjective* done, made, or happening only once. > *noun* **1** something done, made, or happening only once. **2** a unique or remarkable person.

onerous /ˈonnərəss, ˈōnərəss/ > *adjective* **1** involving an oppressively burdensome amount of effort and difficulty. **2** Law involving heavy obligations.

SYNONYMS – **1** burdensome, gruelling, strenuous, taxing.

ANTONYMS – effortless.

ORIGIN – Latin *onerosus*, from *onus* 'burden'.

oneself > *pronoun* **1** used as the object of a verb or preposition when this is the same as the subject of the clause and the subject is 'one'. **2** used to emphasise that one does something individually or unaided. **3** in one's normal and individual state of body or mind.

one-sided > *adjective* **1** unfairly biased. **2** (of a contest or conflict) grossly unequal. **3** occurring on or having one side only.

SYNONYMS – **1** partial, partisan, prejudiced.

one-upmanship > *noun* informal the technique of gaining an advantage or feeling of superiority over other people.

ORIGIN – coined by the British writer Stephen Potter (1900–69).

ongoing > *adjective* continuing; still in progress.

onion > *noun* the edible bulb of a plant used as a vegetable, having a pungent taste and smell and composed of several concentric layers.

WORDFINDER – alliaceous (*of onions and related plants such as garlic, leek, and chives*).

IDIOMS – **know one's onions** informal be very knowledgeable.

COMBINATIONS – **onion dome** a dome which bulges in the middle and rises to a point, used in Russian church architecture.

ORIGIN – Old French *oignon*, from Latin *unio*.

online > *adjective* & *adverb* **1** controlled by or connected to a computer. **2** in or into operation or existence.

onlooker > *noun* a non-participating observer; a spectator.

DERIVATIVES – **onlooking** *adjective*.

only > *adverb* **1** and no one or nothing more besides. **2** no longer ago than. **3** not until. **4** with the negative or unfortunate result that. > *adjective* **1** alone of its or their kind; single or solitary. **2** alone deserving consideration. > *conjunction* informal except that.

IDIOMS – **only just 1** by a very small margin. **2** very recently. **only too —— ——** to an extreme or regrettable extent.

o.n.o. > *abbreviation* Brit. or nearest offer.

onomastics /onnəˈmastiks/ > *plural noun* (usu. treated as sing.) the study of the history and origin of proper names, especially personal names.

DERIVATIVES – **onomastic** *adjective*.

ORIGIN – from Greek *onomastikos*, from *onoma* 'name'.

onomatopoeia /onnəmattəˈpeeə/ > *noun* **1** the formation of a word from a sound associated with what is named (e.g. *cuckoo*, *sizzle*). **2** the use of such words for rhetorical effect.

DERIVATIVES – **onomatopoeic** *adjective* **onomatopoeically** *adverb*.

ORIGIN – Greek *onomatopoiia* 'word-making'.

Onondaga /onnənˈdaagə/ > *noun* (pl. same or **Onondagas**) a member of an Iroquois people formerly inhabiting an area near Syracuse, New York.

ORIGIN – from the name of their main settlement, literally 'on the hill'.

onrush > *noun* a surging rush forward.

DERIVATIVES – **onrushing** *adjective*.

onset > *noun* **1** the beginning of something, especially something unpleasant. **2** archaic a military attack.

onshore > *adjective* & *adverb* **1** situated or occurring on land. **2** (of the wind) blowing from the sea towards the land.

onside > *adjective* & *adverb* **1** (in sport) not offside. **2** informal in or into a position of agreement.

onslaught > *noun* **1** a fierce or destructive attack. **2** an overwhelmingly large quantity of people or things.

ORIGIN – Dutch *aenslag*, from *aen* 'on' + *slag* 'blow'.

onstage > *adjective* & *adverb* (in a theatre) on the stage and so visible to the audience.

on-stream > *adverb* & *adjective* in or into industrial production or useful operation.

ontic /ˈontik/ > *adjective* Philosophy relating to entities and the facts about them.

ORIGIN – from Greek *ōn* 'being'.

onto > *preposition* variant form of **on to**.

USAGE – the preposition **onto** written as one word (instead of **on to**) is widely used, but is still not wholly accepted as part of standard British English (unlike **into**). However, it is useful to distinguish meanings, e.g. between *we drove onto the beach* (i.e. in contact with it) and *we drove on to the beach* (i.e. further in that direction). In American English, **onto** is standard.

ontogeny /onˈtojəni/ > *noun* Biology the development of an individual organism or feature from the earliest stage to maturity. Compare with **PHYLOGENY**.

ontology /ontollǝji/ > *noun* Philosophy the branch of metaphysics concerned with the nature of being.

DERIVATIVES – **ontological** *adjective* **ontologically** *adverb* **ontologist** *noun*.

onus /ōnǝss/ > *noun* a burden, duty, or responsibility.

ORIGIN – Latin, 'load or burden'.

onward > *adverb* (also **onwards**) **1** in a continuing forward direction; ahead. **2** so as to make progress or become more successful. > *adjective* moving forward.

-onym > *combining form* forming nouns: **1** denoting a type of name: *pseudonym*. **2** denoting a word having a specified relationship to another: *antonym*.

ORIGIN – from Greek *onoma* 'name'.

onyx /onniks/ > *noun* a semi-precious variety of agate with different colours in layers.

ORIGIN – Greek *onux* 'fingernail, onyx'.

oocyte /ōǝsīt/ > *noun* Biology a cell in an ovary which may divide to form an ovum.

ORIGIN – from Greek *ōion* 'egg' + *kutos* 'vessel'.

oodles > *plural noun* informal a very great number or amount.

oojah /ōōjaa/ (also **oojamaflip** /ōōjǝmǝflip/) > *noun* informal something that one cannot or does not want to name.

oolite /ōǝlīt/ > *noun* Geology limestone consisting of a mass of rounded grains made up of concentric layers.

DERIVATIVES – **oolitic** *adjective*.

oology /ōollǝji/ > *noun* the study or collecting of birds' eggs.

DERIVATIVES – **oologist** *noun*.

oolong /ōōlong/ > *noun* a kind of dark-coloured partly fermented China tea.

ORIGIN – Chinese, 'black dragon'.

oompah > *noun* informal the rhythmical sound of deep-toned brass instruments in a band.

oomph (also **umph**) > *noun* informal the quality of being exciting, energetic, or sexually attractive.

oops > *exclamation* informal used to show recognition of a mistake or minor accident.

ooze > *verb* **1** slowly trickle or seep out. **2** give a powerful impression of: *she oozes sex appeal*. > *noun* **1** the sluggish flow of a fluid. **2** wet mud or slime, especially that found at the bottom of a river, lake, or sea. **3** an infusion of oak bark or other vegetable matter, used in tanning.

DERIVATIVES – **oozy** *adjective*.

SYNONYMS – *verb* **1** exude, leak, seep, trickle. **2** drip, exude. *noun* **1** discharge, dribble, seepage, trickle.

OP > *abbreviation* **1** observation post. **2** (in the Roman Catholic Church) Order of Preachers (Dominican). [ORIGIN – Latin *Ordo Praedicatorum*.] **3** organophosphate(s).

Op. (also **op.**) > *abbreviation* Music (before a number given to each work of a particular composer) opus.

op > *noun* informal **1** a surgical operation. **2** (**ops**) military operations. **3** a radio or telephone operator.

opacify /ōpassifī/ > *verb* (**opacifies**, **opacified**) technical make or become opaque.

opacity /ōpassiti/ > *noun* the condition of being opaque.

opah /ōpǝ/ > *noun* a large deep-bodied fish with a dark blue back and crimson fins, living in deep oceanic waters.

ORIGIN – a West African word.

opal > *noun* a quartz-like gemstone that is typically semi-transparent and shows many small points of shifting colour against a pale or dark ground.

ORIGIN – Latin *opalus*, probably from a Sanskrit word meaning 'precious stone'.

opalescent > *adjective* showing many small points of shifting colour against a pale or dark ground.

DERIVATIVES – **opalescence** *noun*.

opaline /ōpǝleen/ > *adjective* opalescent. > *noun* translucent or semi-translucent glass.

opaque /ōpayk/ > *adjective* **1** not able to be seen through; not transparent. **2** difficult or impossible to understand. > *noun* Photography a substance for producing opaque areas on negatives.

DERIVATIVES – **opaquely** *adverb*.

SYNONYMS – *adjective* **2** impenetrable, obscure, unclear.

ORIGIN – Latin *opacus* 'darkened'.

op art > *noun* a form of abstract art that gives the illusion of movement by its use of pattern and colour.

ORIGIN – abbreviation of *optical art* on the pattern of *pop art*.

op. cit. /op sit/ > *adverb* in the work already cited.

ORIGIN – from Latin *opere citato*.

OPEC /ōpek/ > *abbreviation* Organisation of the Petroleum Exporting Countries.

open > *adjective* **1** allowing access, passage, or view; not closed, fastened, or restricted. **2** exposed to view or attack; not covered or protected. **3** (**open to**) liable, vulnerable, or subject to. **4** spread out, expanded, or unfolded. **5** officially admitting customers or visitors; available for business. **6** (of an offer or opportunity) still available. **7** frank and communicative. **8** not finally settled; still admitting of debate. **9** (often **open to**) accessible, receptive, or available. **10** (**open to**) admitting of; making possible. **11** Music (of a string) allowed to vibrate along its whole length. **12** Phonetics (of a vowel) produced with a relatively wide opening of the mouth and the tongue kept low. **13** (of an electric circuit) having a break in the conducting path. > *verb* **1** cause (a door, container, etc.) to be open. **2** spread out; unfold or be unfolded. **3** make or become officially ready for customers or visitors. **4** formally begin or establish. **5** make available or more widely known. **6** (**open on to** or **into**) give access to. **7** (**open out** or **up**) become more communicative or confiding. **8** break the conducting path of (an electric circuit). > *noun* **1** (**the open**) the open air or open countryside. **2** (**Open**) a championship or competition with no restrictions on who may compete.

IDIOMS – **the open air** a free or unenclosed space outdoors. **in open court** in a court of law, before the judge and the public. **in** (or **into**) **the open** not concealed or secret. **open-and-shut** admitting no doubt or dispute; straightforward. **open up** (or **open fire**) begin shooting.

DERIVATIVES – **openness** *noun*.

COMBINATIONS – **open day** Brit. a day when members of the public may visit a place or institution to which they do not usually have access. **open-ended** having no predetermined limit or boundary. **open-faced 1** having a frank or ingenuous expression. **2** (also **open-face**) chiefly N. Amer. (of a sandwich or pie) without an upper layer of bread or pastry. **open-handed 1** (of a blow) delivered with the palm of the hand. **2** generous. **open-hearted** unrestrainedly warm and kind. **open-hearth process** a steel-making process in which scrap iron or steel, limestone, and pig iron are melted together in a furnace. **open-heart surgery** surgery in which the heart is exposed and the blood made to bypass it. **open house 1** a place or situation in which all visitors are welcome. **2** N. Amer. an open day. **open letter** a letter addressed to a particular person but intended for publication in a newspaper or journal. **open market** an unrestricted market with free access by and competition of buyers and sellers. **open marriage** a marriage in which both partners agree that each may have sexual relations with others. **open-necked** (of a shirt) worn with the collar unbuttoned and without a tie. **open-plan** having large rooms with few or no internal dividing walls. **open prison** Brit. a prison with the minimum of restrictions on prisoners' movements and activities. **open question** a matter that is not yet decided or cannot be decided. **open range** N. Amer. an area of land without fences or other barriers. **open-reel** reel-to-reel. **open sandal** a sandal that does not cover the toes. **open sandwich** a sandwich without a top slice of bread. **open season** the annual period when restrictions on the killing of

opencast–opinion

certain types of wildlife are lifted. **open secret** a supposed secret that is in fact known to many people. **open-toed** (of a shoe) not covering the toes. **open-topped** (also **open-top**) (of a vehicle) having no roof, or having a folding or detachable roof. **open verdict** Law a verdict of a coroner's jury affirming that a suspicious death has occurred but not specifying the cause. **openwork** ornamental work in cloth, leather, etc. with regular patterns of openings and holes.

opencast (N. Amer. **open-pit**) > *adjective* Brit. (of mining) in which coal or ore is extracted from a level near the earth's surface, rather than from shafts.

opener > *noun* 1 a device for opening something. 2 a person or thing that opens or begins, in particular the first goal in a match or a cricketer who opens the batting.
IDIOMS – **for openers** informal to start with; first of all.

opening > *noun* 1 an aperture or gap. 2 a beginning; an initial part. 3 a ceremony at which a building, show, etc. is declared to be open. 4 an opportunity to achieve something. 5 an available job or position. > *adjective* coming at the beginning; initial.
SYNONYMS – *noun* 1 aperture, fissure, gap, hole, orifice.

openly > *adverb* without concealment or deception; frankly or honestly.

open mind > *noun* a mind willing to consider new ideas.
DERIVATIVES – **open-minded** *adjective*.

opera¹ > *noun* 1 a dramatic work set to music for singers and instrumentalists. 2 a building for the performance of opera.
WORDFINDER – aria (*long song for a soloist in an opera*), concert performance (*opera performed without accompanying action*), diva (*a celebrated female opera singer*), libretto (*the text of an opera*), prima donna (*the chief female singer in a company*), recitative (*musical declamation in the narrative and dialogue parts of opera*).
COMBINATIONS – **opera cloak** a cloak of rich material worn over evening clothes, especially by women. **opera glasses** small binoculars for use at the opera or theatre. **opera hat** a collapsible top hat. **opera house** a theatre for the performance of opera. **opera seria** an opera on a serious theme, especially one of the 18th century in Italian. [ORIGIN – Italian, 'serious opera'.] **opera window** chiefly US a small window behind the rear side window of a motor car.
ORIGIN – Italian, from Latin, 'labour, work'.

opera² plural of OPUS.

operable > *adjective* 1 able to be operated. 2 able to be treated by means of a surgical operation.

operand /oppərand/ > *noun* Mathematics the quantity on which an operation is to be done.
ORIGIN – Latin *operandum* 'thing to be operated on'.

operant /oppərənt/ Psychology > *adjective* (of conditioning) involving the modification of behaviour by the effect of the consequences of behaviour. > *noun* an item of behaviour that is spontaneous rather than a response to a stimulus.

operate > *verb* 1 (with reference to a machine, process, etc.) function or control the functioning of. 2 (with reference to an organisation) manage or be managed and run. 3 (of an armed force) conduct military activities. 4 be in effect. 5 perform a surgical operation.
COMBINATIONS – **operating profit** a gross profit before deduction of expenses. **operating system** the low-level software that supports a computer's basic functions. **operating table** a table on which a patient is placed during a surgical operation. **operating theatre** (N. Amer. **operating room**) a room in which surgical operations are performed.
ORIGIN – Latin *operari*, from *opus* 'work'.

operatic > *adjective* 1 relating to or characteristic of opera. 2 extravagantly theatrical.
DERIVATIVES – **operatically** *adverb*.

operatics > *plural noun* (often treated as sing.) the production or performance of operas.

operation > *noun* 1 the action or process of operating. 2 an act of surgery performed on a patient. 3 a concerted action involving a number of people, especially members of the armed forces or the police. 4 a business organisation; a company. 5 Mathematics a process in which a number, expression, etc., is altered or manipulated according to set rules.
WORDFINDER – *operations*: angioplasty (*to repair or unblock a blood vessel*), appendectomy (*to remove the appendix*), Caesarean section (*to deliver a child by cutting through the mother's abdomen*), hysterectomy (*to remove all or part of the womb*), mastectomy (*to remove a breast*), tonsillectomy (*to remove the tonsils*).
SYNONYMS – 1 functioning, performance, working.
COMBINATIONS – **operations room** a room from which military or police operations are directed.

operational > *adjective* 1 in or ready for use. 2 relating to the operation of an organisation.
DERIVATIVES – **operationally** *adverb*.
SYNONYMS – 1 functioning, running, working.

operative > *adjective* 1 functioning; having effect. 2 (of a word) having the most relevance or significance in a phrase. 3 relating to surgery. > *noun* 1 a worker, especially a skilled one. 2 a private detective or secret agent.
SYNONYMS – *adjective* 1 functional, running, working.

operator > *noun* 1 a person who operates equipment or a machine. 2 a person who works at the switchboard of a telephone exchange. 3 a person or company that runs a business or enterprise. 4 informal a person who acts in a specified, especially manipulative, way: *a smooth operator*. 5 Mathematics a symbol or function denoting an operation (e.g. ×, +).

operculum /ōperkyoolǝm/ > *noun* (pl. **opercula** /ōperkyoolǝ/) Zoology 1 a flap of skin protecting a fish's gills, typically stiffened by bony plates. 2 a plate that closes the aperture of a gastropod mollusc's shell.
ORIGIN – Latin, 'lid, covering'.

operetta > *noun* a short opera on a light or humorous theme.
ORIGIN – Italian, 'little opera'.

ophidian /ōfiddiǝn/ > *noun* Zoology an animal of the group which includes the snakes.
ORIGIN – from Greek *ophis*, 'snake'.

ophthalmia /ofthalmiǝ/ > *noun* Medicine inflammation of the eye, especially conjunctivitis.
ORIGIN – Greek, from *ophthalmos* 'eye'.

ophthalmic* /ofthalmik/ > *adjective* relating to the eye and its diseases.
*SPELLING – oph, not opt: ophthalmic.
COMBINATIONS – **ophthalmic optician** Brit. an optician qualified to prescribe and dispense glasses and contact lenses and to detect eye diseases.

ophthalmology* /of-thalmollǝji/ > *noun* the study and treatment of disorders and diseases of the eye.
DERIVATIVES – **ophthalmological** *adjective* **ophthalmologist** *noun*.
*SPELLING – note that it is *oph*, not *opt*: *oph*thalmology.

ophthalmoscope /ofthalmǝskōp/ > *noun* an instrument for inspecting the retina and other parts of the eye.
DERIVATIVES – **ophthalmoscopic** *adjective* **ophthalmoscopy** *noun*.

opiate /ōpiǝt/ > *adjective* relating to, resembling, or containing opium. > *noun* 1 a drug derived from or related to opium. 2 something that induces a false and unrealistic sense of contentment.
DERIVATIVES – **opiated** *adjective*.

opine /ōpīn/ > *verb* formal hold and state as one's opinion.

opinion > *noun* 1 a view or judgement not necessarily based on fact or knowledge. 2 the beliefs or views of people in general: *public opinion*. 3 an estimation of quality or

676

worth. **4** a formal statement of advice by an expert or professional.

IDIOMS – **a matter of opinion** something not capable of being proven either way.

COMBINATIONS – **opinion poll** an assessment of public opinion by questioning of a representative sample.

ORIGIN – Latin, from *opinari* 'think, believe'.

opinionated > *adjective* assertively dogmatic in one's views.

SYNONYMS – doctrinaire, dogmatic, uncompromising.

ANTONYMS – open-minded.

opioid /ōpioyd/ > *noun* a compound resembling opium in its properties or effects. > *adjective* relating to such compounds.

opium > *noun* **1** an addictive drug prepared from the juice of a poppy, used as a narcotic and in medicine as a painkiller. **2** something that induces a false and unrealistic sense of contentment.

ORIGIN – Latin, from Greek *opion* 'poppy juice'.

opossum /əpossəm/ > *noun* **1** an American marsupial with a prehensile tail. **2** Austral./NZ a possum.

ORIGIN – Algonquian, 'white dog'.

oppo > *noun* (pl. **oppos**) Brit. informal a colleague or friend.

ORIGIN – abbreviation of *opposite number*.

opponent > *noun* **1** a person who competes with or fights another in a contest, game, or argument. **2** a person who disagrees with or resists a proposal or practice.

ANTONYMS – **2** ally, supporter.

opportune /oppərtyōōn/ > *adjective* done or occurring at an especially convenient or appropriate time.

DERIVATIVES – **opportunely** *adverb*.

SYNONYMS – auspicious, timely.

wordpower facts

Opportune

The word **opportune** comes from Latin *opportunus*, denoting a wind driving towards the harbour, from *ob-* 'in the direction of' and *portus* 'harbour'. From this developed the senses 'advantageous' and 'seasonable', and the noun **opportunity**. The Romans gave the name *Portunus* to the god who protected their harbours, and this is the root of the related words **importunate** and **importune**.

opportunist > *noun* a person who takes advantage of opportunities as and when they arise, regardless of planning or principle. > *adjective* opportunistic.

DERIVATIVES – **opportunism** *noun*.

opportunistic > *adjective* **1** exploiting immediate opportunities, especially in an unplanned or selfish way. **2** Medicine (of an infection) occurring when the immune system is depressed.

DERIVATIVES – **opportunistically** *adverb*.

opportunity > *noun* (pl. **opportunities**) a favourable time or set of circumstances for doing something.

opposable > *adjective* Zoology (of the thumb of a primate) capable of facing and touching the other digits on the same hand.

oppose > *verb* **1** (also **be opposed to**) disapprove of, resist, or be hostile to. **2** compete with or fight. **3** (**opposed**) (of two or more things) contrasting or conflicting. **4** (**opposing**) opposite.

DERIVATIVES – **opposer** *noun*.

ORIGIN – Old French *opposer*, from Latin *opponere* 'set against'.

opposite > *adjective* **1** situated on the other or further side; facing. **2** completely different. **3** being the other of a contrasted pair. **4** (of angles) between opposite sides of the intersection of two lines. > *noun* an opposite person or thing. > *adverb* in an opposite position. > *preposition* **1** in a position opposite to. **2** co-starring beside.

DERIVATIVES – **oppositely** *adverb*.

COMBINATIONS – **opposite number** a person's counterpart in another organisation or country. **the opposite sex** women in relation to men, or vice versa.

opposition > *noun* **1** resistance or dissent. **2** a group of opponents. **3** (**the Opposition**) Brit. the principal parliamentary party opposed to that in office. **4** a contrast or antithesis. **5** Astronomy the apparent position of two celestial objects that are directly opposite each other in the sky.

DERIVATIVES – **oppositional** *adjective*.

oppress* > *verb* **1** keep in subjection and hardship. **2** cause to feel distressed or anxious.

DERIVATIVES – **oppression** *noun* **oppressor** *noun*.

*SPELLING – double *p*, double *s*: o*ppress*.

SYNONYMS – **1** persecute, tyrannise. **2** depress, lie heavy on, weigh down.

ORIGIN – Old French *oppresser*, from Latin *opprimere* 'press against'.

oppressive > *adjective* **1** harsh and authoritarian. **2** weighing heavily on the mind or spirits. **3** (of weather) close and sultry.

DERIVATIVES – **oppressively** *adverb* **oppressiveness** *noun*.

SYNONYMS – **1** dictatorial, repressive, tyrannical.

opprobrious /əprōbriəss/ > *adjective* highly scornful.

DERIVATIVES – **opprobriously** *adverb*.

opprobrium /əprōbriəm/ > *noun* **1** harsh criticism or scorn. **2** public disgrace arising from shameful conduct.

ORIGIN – Latin, 'infamy'.

oppugn /əpyōōn/ > *verb* archaic dispute the truth or validity of.

ORIGIN – Latin *oppugnare* 'attack, besiege'.

opsimath /opsimath/ > *noun* rare a person who begins to learn or study only late in life.

ORIGIN – Greek, from *opse* 'late' + the stem *math-* 'learn'.

opt > *verb* make a choice.

IDIOMS – **opt out 1** choose not to participate. **2** Brit. (of a school or hospital) decide to withdraw from local authority control.

SYNONYMS – choose, pick, select.

ORIGIN – Latin *optare* 'choose, wish'.

optative /optətiv, optaytiv/ > *adjective* Grammar (of a mood of verbs, especially in Greek) expressing a wish, equivalent in meaning to English *let's* or *if only*.

optic > *adjective* relating to the eye or vision. > *noun* **1** a lens or similar component in an optical instrument. **2** Brit. trademark a device fixed to an inverted bottle for measuring out spirits.

COMBINATIONS – **optic nerves** Anatomy the pair of nerves transmitting impulses from the eyes to the brain.

wordpower facts

Optic

The word **optic** derives from Old French *optique* or Latin *opticus*, from Greek *optikos*, from *optos* 'seen', ultimately from *opsis* 'sight'. The elements *optos* and *opsis* combine with other Greek words or elements to form a number of words, including **autopsy** (from *autos* 'self' and *optos*), **biopsy** (from *bios* 'life' and *opsis*), **optometry** and **optometrist** (from *metron* 'measure' and *optos*), and **synopsis** (from *sun-* 'together' and *opsis*).

optical > *adjective* relating to vision, light, or optics.

DERIVATIVES – **optically** *adverb*.

COMBINATIONS – **optical brightener** a fluorescent substance added to detergents to produce a whitening effect on laundry. **optical fibre** a thin glass fibre through which light can be transmitted. **optical glass** a very pure kind of glass used for lenses. **optical illusion** a thing that deceives the eye by appearing to be other than it is.

optician > *noun* a person qualified to prescribe and dispense glasses and contact lenses, and to detect eye diseases (**ophthalmic optician**), or to make and supply glasses and contact lenses (**dispensing optician**).

optics > *plural noun* (usu. treated as sing.) the branch of science concerned with vision and the behaviour of light.

optimal > *adjective* best or most favourable.
DERIVATIVES – **optimality** *noun* **optimally** *adverb*.
ORIGIN – from Latin *optimus* 'best'.

optimise (also **optimize**) > *verb* make the best or most effective use of (a situation or resource).
DERIVATIVES – **optimisation** *noun*.

optimism* > *noun* **1** hopefulness and confidence about the future or the success of something. **2** Philosophy the doctrine that this world is the best of all possible worlds.
DERIVATIVES – **optimist** *noun* **optimistic** *adjective* **optimistically** *adverb*.
*SPELLING – opti-, not opto-: optimism.
ANTONYMS – **1** pessimism.
ORIGIN – French *optimisme*.

optimum > *adjective* most conducive to a favourable outcome. > *noun* (pl. **optima** or **optimums**) the optimum conditions for growth, reproduction, or success.
ORIGIN – Latin, 'best thing'.

option > *noun* **1** a thing that is or may be chosen. **2** the freedom or right to choose. **3** a right to buy or sell a particular thing at a specified price within a set time.
IDIOMS – **keep** (or **leave**) **one's options open** not commit oneself.
SYNONYMS – **1** alternative, choice, possibility.

optional > *adjective* available to be chosen but not obligatory.
DERIVATIVES – **optionally** *adverb*.
SYNONYMS – discretionary, voluntary.

optometrist /op**tomm**ətrist/ > *noun* chiefly N. Amer. a person who practises optometry; an ophthalmic optician.

optometry /op**tomm**ətri/ > *noun* the occupation of measuring eyesight, prescribing corrective lenses, and detecting eye disease.

opulent /**op**yoolənt/ > *adjective* ostentatiously rich and luxurious.
DERIVATIVES – **opulence** *noun* **opulently** *adverb*.
SYNONYMS – lavish, luxurious, sumptuous.
ORIGIN – Latin *opulens* 'wealthy, splendid'.

opuntia /ə**pun**tiə/ > *noun* a cactus of a genus that comprises the prickly pears.
ORIGIN – Latin, a name given to a plant growing around *Opus*, a city in ancient Greece.

opus /**ō**pəs, **opp**əss/ > *noun* (pl. **opuses** or **opera** /**opp**ərə/) **1** Music a separate composition or set of compositions. **2** an artistic work, especially one on a large scale.
ORIGIN – Latin, 'work'.

opus Dei /**ō**pəss **day**ee, **opp**əss/ > *noun* **1**

Christian Church public worship regarded as humankind's primary duty to God. **2** (**Opus Dei**) a Roman Catholic organisation aiming to re-establish Christian ideals in society.
ORIGIN – Latin, 'work of God'.

OR > *abbreviation* Oregon.

or¹ > *conjunction* **1** used to link alternatives. **2** introducing a synonym or explanation of a preceding word or phrase. **3** otherwise. **4** literary either.
COMBINATIONS – **OR gate** Electronics a gate circuit which produces an output if there is a signal on any of the input connections.

or² > *noun* gold or yellow, as a conventional heraldic colour.
ORIGIN – French, from Latin *aurum* 'gold'.

-or¹ > *suffix* (forming nouns) denoting a person or thing performing the action of a verb: *escalator*.
ORIGIN – Latin.

-or² > *suffix* forming nouns denoting a state or condition: *terror*.
ORIGIN – Latin.

oracle > *noun* **1** (in classical times) a priest or priestess who acted as a medium for divine advice or prophecy. **2** an infallible authority.
IDIOMS – **work the oracle** Brit. informal achieve the desired result.

wordpower facts
Oracle

An **oracle** was originally the agency by which the gods spoke to humans, or the place where their words could be heard (by suitably qualified persons). Later the word came to refer to the message itself (typically ambiguous or mysterious), or (the usual modern sense) the intermediary speaking the divine words. **Oracle** is one of a group of words (including **oral**, **oration**, **oratory**, and **perorate**) having as their root Latin *orare* 'to speak' or its close relative *os* 'mouth'. Other members of this group are **adore** (from *ad-* 'to' and *orare* in the specific sense 'pray') and **orifice** (from *os* and the verb *facere* 'to make').

oracular /o**rak**yoolər/ > *adjective* **1** relating to an oracle. **2** hard to interpret. **3** holding or claiming the authority of an oracle.

oracy /**orr**əsi/ > *noun* Brit. the ability to express oneself fluently and grammatically in speech.

oral > *adjective* **1** spoken rather than written. **2** relating to the mouth. **3** done or taken by the mouth. > *noun* a spoken examination or test.
DERIVATIVES – **orally** *adverb*.

COMBINATIONS – **oral history** the collection and study of historical information from people's personal memories. **oral sex** sexual activity in which the genitals of one partner are stimulated by the mouth of the other.
ORIGIN – Latin *oralis*, from *os* 'mouth'.

oralism > *noun* the teaching of deaf people to communicate by the use of speech and lip-reading rather than sign language.
DERIVATIVES – **oralist** *adjective* & *noun*.

orality > *noun* **1** the quality of being verbally communicated. **2** Psychoanalysis the focusing of sexual energy and feeling on the mouth.

Orange > *adjective* relating to Orangemen or their Order.
COMBINATIONS – **Orangeman** a member of the Orange Order. **Orange Order** a Protestant political society in Northern Ireland.
ORIGIN – named after the Protestant king William of *Orange* (William III).

orange > *noun* **1** a large round citrus fruit with a tough bright reddish-yellow rind. **2** a drink made from or flavoured with the juice of this fruit. **3** a reddish-yellow colour. > *adjective* reddish yellow.
DERIVATIVES – **orangey** (also **orangy**) *adjective*.
COMBINATIONS – **orange flower water** a solution of neroli in water, used in perfumery and as a food flavouring. **orange pekoe** a type of black tea made from young leaves. **orange stick** a thin pointed stick for manicuring the fingernails.
ORIGIN – Old French *orenge*, from Arabic *nāranj*.

orangeade > *noun* Brit. a fizzy soft drink flavoured with orange.

orangery > *noun* (pl. **orangeries**) a building like a large conservatory where orange trees are grown.

orang-utan /ə**rang**ootan/ (also **–utang** /-ootang/) > *noun* a tree-dwelling great ape with long red hair, native to Borneo and Sumatra.
ORIGIN – Malay, 'forest person'.

orate /ə**rayt**/ > *verb* make a long or pompous speech.

oration > *noun* a formal speech, especially one given on a ceremonial occasion.
ORIGIN – Latin, from *orare* 'speak, pray'.

orator > *noun* a proficient public speaker.
DERIVATIVES – **oratorial** *adjective*.

oratorio /orrə**tori**ō/ > *noun* (pl. **oratorios**) a large-scale musical work on a religious theme for orchestra and voices.
ORIGIN – Italian, from the musical services held in the church of the Oratory of St Philip Neri in Rome.

oratory¹ /**orr**ətri/ > *noun* (pl. **oratories**) a small chapel for private worship.

oratory² /**orr**ətri/ > *noun* **1** formal public

speaking. **2** rhetorical or eloquent language.

DERIVATIVES – **oratorical** adjective.

orb > noun **1** a spherical object or shape. **2** a golden globe with a cross on top, forming part of the regalia of a monarch.

ORIGIN – Latin *orbis* 'ring'.

orbicular /orbikyoolər/ > adjective **1** technical having the shape of a flat ring or disc. **2** literary spherical or rounded.

orbit > noun **1** the regularly repeated elliptical course of a celestial object, satellite, or spacecraft around a star or planet. **2** a field of activity or influence. **3** the path of an electron round an atomic nucleus. **4** Anatomy the eye socket. > verb (**orbited**, **orbiting**) move in orbit round (a body).

WORDFINDER – aphelion (*point in a planet's orbit at which it is furthest from the sun*), apogee (*point in a satellite's orbit at which it is furthest from earth*), eccentricity (*extent to which orbit differs from a circle*), geostationary or synchronous (*denoting a satellite orbiting so that it appears stationary above the earth's surface*), perigee (*point in a satellite's orbit at which it is nearest to earth*), perihelion (*point in a planet's orbit at which it is nearest to the sun*).

ORIGIN – Latin *orbita* 'course, track'.

orbital > adjective **1** relating to an orbit or orbits. **2** Brit. (of a road) passing round the outside of a city or town.

COMBINATIONS – **orbital sander** a sander in which the sanding surface has a minute circular motion without rotating relative to the object being worked on.

orbiter > noun a spacecraft designed to go into orbit, especially one that does not subsequently land.

orc > noun a member of an imaginary race of ugly, aggressive human-like creatures.

ORIGIN – perhaps from Latin *orcus* 'hell' or Italian *orco* 'monster'; the word was popularised in the fantasy adventures of J. R. R. Tolkien.

orca /orkə/ > noun a killer whale.

ORIGIN – French *orque* or Latin *orca*.

Orcadian /orkaydiən/ > adjective relating to the Orkney Islands. > noun a person from the Orkney Islands.

ORIGIN – from *Orcades*, the Latin name for the Orkney Islands.

orchard > noun a piece of enclosed land planted with fruit trees.

ORIGIN – Old English, from Latin *hortus* 'garden' + the base of **YARD²**.

orchestra > noun **1** a large group of musicians with string, woodwind, brass, and percussion sections. **2** (also **orchestra pit**) the part of a theatre where the orchestra plays, typically in front of the stage and on a lower level. **3** N. Amer. the stalls in a theatre. **4** the semicircular space in front of an ancient Greek theatre stage where the chorus danced and sang.

DERIVATIVES – **orchestral** adjective **orchestrally** adverb.

ORIGIN – Greek *orkhēstra*, from *orkheisthai* 'to dance'.

orchestrate > verb **1** arrange or score (music) for orchestral performance. **2** direct (a situation) to produce a desired effect.

DERIVATIVES – **orchestration** noun **orchestrator** noun.

SYNONYMS – **2** arrange, manage, organise.

orchid > noun a plant of a large family with complex showy flowers.

DERIVATIVES – **orchidaceous** adjective.

ORIGIN – from Greek *orkhis* 'testicle' (because of the shape of the tuber).

orchitis /orkītiss/ > noun Medicine inflammation of one or both of the testicles.

ordain > verb **1** confer holy orders on. **2** command (something) officially; decree. **3** (of God or fate) decide in advance.

ORIGIN – Latin *ordinare*, from *ordo* 'row, series, order'.

ordeal > noun **1** a prolonged painful or horrific experience. **2** an ancient test of guilt in which the accused was subjected to severe pain, survival of which was taken as divine proof of innocence.

order > noun **1** the arrangement of people or things according to a particular sequence or method. **2** a state in which everything is in its correct place. **3** a state in which the laws and rules regulating public behaviour are observed. **4** an authoritative command or direction. **5** a request for something to be made, supplied, or served. **6** the prescribed procedure followed in a meeting, law court, or religious service. **7** a social class or system. **8** quality or nature: *poetry of the highest order*. **9** a rank in the Christian ministry. **10** (**orders** or **holy orders**) the rank of an ordained minister of the Church. **11** a society of monks, nuns, or friars (or formerly knights) living under the same rule. **12** an institution founded by a monarch to honour good conduct: *the Order of the Garter*. **13** Biology a principal taxonomic category that ranks below class and above family. **14** any of the five classical styles of architecture (Doric, Ionic, Corinthian, Tuscan, and Composite). > verb **1** give an order. **2** request that (something) be made, supplied, or served. **3** arrange methodically.

IDIOMS – **in order 1** in the correct condition for operation or use. **2** appropriate in the circumstances. **in order for** (or **that**) so that. **in order to** with the purpose of doing. **of** (or **in** or **on**) **the order of** approximately. **on order** (of goods) requested but not yet received. **the order of the day 1** the prevailing state of affairs. **2** the day's business to be considered in an meeting or parliament. **out of order 1** not working properly or at all. **2** Brit. informal unacceptable or wrong.

SYNONYMS – noun **2** neatness, orderliness, tidiness. verb **1** command, direct, instruct.

COMBINATIONS – **Order in Council** Brit. a sovereign's order on an administrative matter, given on the advice of the Privy Council. **order of magnitude 1** a class in a system of classification determined by size, typically in powers of ten. **2** size or quantity. **Order Paper** Brit. a paper on which the day's parliamentary business is entered.

ORIGIN – Old French *ordre*, from Latin *ordo* 'row, series, rank'.

orderly > adjective **1** neatly and methodically arranged. **2** well behaved. > noun (pl. **orderlies**) **1** a hospital attendant responsible for cleaning and other non-medical tasks. **2** a soldier who carries orders or performs minor tasks for an officer.

DERIVATIVES – **orderliness** noun.

COMBINATIONS – **orderly officer** Brit. Military the officer in charge of the security and administration of a unit for a particular day. **orderly room** Military the room in a barracks used for regimental or company business.

ordinal > adjective **1** relating to order in a series. **2** Biology relating to a taxonomic order. > noun Christian Church, chiefly historical a book with the forms of service used at ordinations.

COMBINATIONS – **ordinal number** a number defining a thing's position in a series, such as 'first' or 'second'.

ORIGIN – Latin *ordinalis* 'relating to order'.

ordinance /ordinənss/ > noun formal **1** an authoritative order. **2** a religious rite. **3** N. Amer. a by-law.

USAGE – do not confuse **ordinance** with **ordnance**, which means 'guns' or 'munitions'.

ordinand /ordinand/ > noun a person who is training to be ordained as a priest or minister.

ORIGIN – Latin *ordinandus*.

ordinary > adjective **1** with no distinctive features; normal or usual. **2** (of a judge, archbishop, or bishop) exercising authority by virtue of office and not by delegation. > noun (pl. **ordinaries**) **1** (**Ordinary**) those parts of a Roman Catholic service, especially the Mass, which do not vary from day to day. **2** a rule or book laying down the order of divine service. **3** Heraldry any of the simplest principal charges used in coats of arms.

IDIOMS – **out of the ordinary** unusual.

DERIVATIVES – **ordinarily** adverb **ordinariness** noun.

SYNONYMS – *adjective* **1** normal, standard, usual.

COMBINATIONS – **ordinary grade** (in Scotland) the lower of the two main levels of the Scottish Certificate of Education examination. Compare with **HIGHER**. **ordinary level** fuller form of *O level*. **ordinary seaman** the lowest rank of sailor in the Royal Navy, below able seaman. **ordinary share** Brit. a share which entitles the holder to dividends proportionate to the company's profits. Compare with *preference share*.

ORIGIN – Latin *ordinarius* 'orderly', from *ordo* 'row, series, order'.

ordinate /ordinət/ > *noun* Mathematics a straight line from a point on a graph drawn parallel to the vertical axis and meeting the other; the *y*-coordinate.

ORIGIN – from Latin *linea ordinata applicata* 'line applied parallel'.

ordination > *noun* the action of ordaining someone in holy orders.

ordnance /ordnənss/ > *noun* **1** mounted guns; cannon. **2** US munitions. **3** a government department dealing with military stores and materials.

USAGE – do not confuse **ordnance** with **ordinance**, which means 'an authoritative order' or 'a religious rite'.

COMBINATIONS – **ordnance datum** Brit. the mean sea level as defined for Ordnance Survey. **Ordnance Survey** (in the UK) an official survey organisation (originally under the ordnance department) preparing large-scale detailed maps of the country.

Ordovician /ordəvissiən/ > *adjective* Geology relating to the second period of the Palaeozoic era (between the Cambrian and Silurian periods), about 510 to 439 million years ago, a time when the first vertebrates appeared.

ORIGIN – from *Ordovices*, the Latin name of an ancient British tribe in North Wales.

ordure /ordyoor/ > *noun* excrement; dung.

wordpower facts

Ordure

The somewhat formal word **ordure** 'excrement' comes via Old French *ord*, meaning 'foul', from Latin *horridus* 'rough, horrible, shaggy'. *Horridus* comes from the verb *horrere*, meaning 'tremble, shudder, bristle', the root of a group of words including **horrid**, **horror**, and **abhor**.

ore > *noun* a naturally occurring material from which a metal or valuable mineral can be extracted.

ORIGIN – Old English, 'unwrought metal'.

øre /örə/ > *noun* (pl. same) a monetary unit of Denmark and Norway, equal to one hundredth of a krone.

ORIGIN – Danish and Norwegian.

öre /örə/ > *noun* (pl. same) a monetary unit of Sweden, equal to one hundredth of a krona.

ORIGIN – Swedish.

oread /oriad/ > *noun* Greek & Roman Mythology a nymph believed to inhabit mountains.

ORIGIN – from Greek *Oreias*, from *oros* 'mountain'.

oregano /orrigaanō/ > *noun* an aromatic plant with small purple flowers and leaves used as a herb in cookery.

ORIGIN – Spanish, from Greek *origanon*.

orfe /orf/ > *noun* a silvery freshwater fish of the carp family.

ORIGIN – German.

organ > *noun* **1** a distinct part of an animal or plant adapted for a particular purpose, such as the heart or kidneys. **2** a large musical keyboard instrument with rows of pipes supplied with air from bellows. **3** a smaller instrument producing similar sounds electronically. **4** a newspaper or periodical which puts forward the views of a political party or movement. **5** euphemistic a man's penis.

DERIVATIVES – **organist** *noun*.

COMBINATIONS – **organ-grinder** a street musician who plays a barrel organ.

ORIGIN – Greek *organon* 'tool, sense organ'.

organdie /organdi/ (US also **organdy**) > *noun* a fine, translucent, stiff cotton muslin.

ORIGIN – French *organdi*.

organelle /organel/ > *noun* Biology an organised or specialised structure within a cell.

ORIGIN – Latin *organella*.

organic > *adjective* **1** relating to or derived from living matter. **2** not involving or produced with chemical fertilisers or other artificial chemicals. **3** (of the elements of a whole) harmoniously related. **4** characterised by natural development. **5** Chemistry containing carbon and chiefly or ultimately of biological origin. Compare with **INORGANIC**. **6** relating to a bodily organ or organs. **7** (of a disease) affecting the structure of an organ.

DERIVATIVES – **organically** *adverb*.

organisation (also **organization**) > *noun* **1** the action of organising. **2** a systematic arrangement or approach. **3** an organised body of people with a particular purpose, e.g. a business.

DERIVATIVES – **organisational** *adjective* **organisationally** *adverb*.

SYNONYMS – **1** arrangement, management, planning. **2** arrangement, format, structure.

organise (also **organize**) > *verb* **1** arrange systematically; order. **2** Brit. make arrangements or preparations for. **3** form (people) into a trade union or other political group.

DERIVATIVES – **organiser** *noun*.

SYNONYMS – **1** arrange, marshal, order, sort.

ORIGIN – Latin *organizare*, from *organum* 'instrument, tool'.

organism > *noun* **1** an individual animal, plant, or single-celled life form. **2** a whole with interdependent parts.

organo- /organō/ > *combining form* forming names of classes of chemical compounds containing a particular element bonded to organic groups: *organophosphorus compounds*.

organza /organzə/ > *noun* a thin, stiff, transparent dress fabric made of silk or a synthetic yarn.

orgasm > *noun* the climax of sexual excitement, characterised by intensely pleasurable sensations centred in the genitals. > *verb* have an orgasm.

ORIGIN – Greek *orgasmos*, from *organ* 'swell or be excited'.

orgasmic > *adjective* **1** relating to orgasm. **2** informal very enjoyable.

DERIVATIVES – **orgasmically** *adverb*.

orgastic > *adjective* relating to orgasm.

orgiastic > *adjective* relating to or resembling an orgy.

DERIVATIVES – **orgiastically** *adverb*.

orgulous /orgyooləss/ > *adjective* literary haughty.

ORIGIN – Old French *orguillus*, from *orguill* 'pride'.

orgy > *noun* (pl. **orgies**) **1** a wild party with excessive drinking and indiscriminate sexual activity. **2** excessive indulgence in a specified activity.

ORIGIN – Greek *orgia* 'secret rites or revels'.

oriel /oriəl/ > *noun* a large upper-storey bay with a window (an **oriel window**), supported by brackets or on corbels.

ORIGIN – Old French *oriol* 'gallery'.

orient > *noun* /oriənt/ (**the Orient**) literary the countries of the East, especially east Asia. > *adjective* /oriənt/ literary oriental. > *verb* /orient/ **1** align or position relative to the points of a compass or other specified positions. **2** (**orient oneself**) find one's position in relation to unfamiliar surroundings. **3** tailor to specified circumstances.

ORIGIN – from Latin *oriens* 'rising or east', from *oriri* 'to rise'.

oriental (often **Oriental**) > *adjective* of, from, or characteristic of the Far East. > *noun* often offensive a person of Far Eastern descent.

DERIVATIVES – **orientalist** *noun* **orientally** *adverb*.

USAGE – the term **oriental** is now regarded

as old-fashioned and potentially offensive as a term denoting people from the Far East. In US English, **Asian** is the standard modern term; in British English, where **Asian** tends to denote people from the Indian subcontinent, specific terms such as **Chinese** or **Japanese** are more likely to be used.

orientate > *verb* another term for ORIENT.

orientation > *noun* **1** the action of orienting. **2** a relative position. **3** a person's attitude or inclination, especially as regards political or sexual matters.
DERIVATIVES – **orientational** *adjective*.
COMBINATIONS – **orientation course** a course giving information to newcomers to a university or other organisation.

orienteering > *noun* a competitive sport in which runners have to find their way across rough country with the aid of a map and compass.
DERIVATIVES – **orienteer** *noun & verb*.

orifice /**orr**ifiss/ > *noun* an opening, particularly one in the body such as a nostril.
ORIGIN – French, from Latin *os* 'mouth' + *facere* 'make'.

oriflamme /**orr**iflam/ > *noun* literary a scarlet banner or knight's standard.
ORIGIN – Old French, from Latin *aurum* 'gold' + *flamma* 'flame'.

origami /orri**gaa**mi/ > *noun* the Japanese art of folding paper into decorative shapes and figures.
ORIGIN – Japanese, from *oru* 'fold' + *kami* 'paper'.

origin > *noun* **1** the point where something begins or arises. **2** a person's social background or ancestry. **3** Mathematics a fixed point from which coordinates are measured.
WORDFINDER – etymology (*an account of the origin of words*), onomastics (*study of the origin of proper names, especially personal names*).
SYNONYMS – **1** base, basis, beginning, foundation, genesis, root, source. **2** ancestry, background, descent, extraction, heritage, lineage, stock.
ORIGIN – Latin *origo*, from *oriri* 'to rise'.

original > *adjective* **1** used, produced, or existing at the creation or earliest stage of something. **2** produced first-hand; not a copy. **3** inventive or novel. > *noun* the earliest form of something, from which copies can be made.
DERIVATIVES – **originally** *adverb*.
SYNONYMS – *adjective* **1** earliest, first, initial. **2** authentic, bona fide, genuine, real. **3** creative, imaginative, innovative, inspired, inventive, novel, resourceful.
ANTONYMS – *adjective* **2** fake. **3** derivative, unoriginal.
COMBINATIONS – **original sin** (in Christian theology) the tendency to evil of all human beings, held to be a consequence of the Fall.

originality > *noun* **1** the ability to think independently or creatively. **2** the quality of being new or unusual.
SYNONYMS – **1** creativity, ingenuity, inventiveness.

originate > *verb* **1** have a specified beginning. **2** create or initiate.
DERIVATIVES – **origination** *noun* **originator** *noun*.
SYNONYMS – **1** arise, begin, commence, emerge, start, stem. **2** conceive, create, engender, initiate, invent, mastermind.

oriole /**or**iōl/ > *noun* a brightly coloured tree-dwelling bird with a musical call.
ORIGIN – Latin *oriolus*, from *aureus* 'golden'.

orison /**orr**iz'n/ > *noun* literary a prayer.
ORIGIN – Old French *oreison*, from Latin *oratio* 'discourse, prayer'.

Orlon /**or**lon/ > *noun* trademark a synthetic acrylic fibre and fabric used for clothing, knitwear, etc.

ormolu /**or**məlōō/ > *noun* a gold-coloured alloy of copper, zinc, and tin used in decoration.
ORIGIN – French *or moulu* 'powdered gold'.

ornament > *noun* **1** an object designed to add beauty to something. **2** decorative items collectively; decoration. **3** (**ornaments**) Music embellishments made to a melody.
DERIVATIVES – **ornamentation** *noun*.
SYNONYMS – **1** adornment, decoration, embellishment, garnish.
ORIGIN – Latin *ornamentum*, from *ornare* 'adorn'.

ornamental > *adjective* serving or intended as an ornament. > *noun* a plant grown for its attractive appearance.
DERIVATIVES – **ornamentally** *adverb*.

ornate > *adjective* elaborately or highly decorated.
SYNONYMS – baroque, elaborate, fancy, flamboyant, florid, flowery.

ornery /**or**nəri/ > *adjective* N. Amer. informal bad-tempered.
ORIGIN – variant of ORDINARY, representing a dialect pronunciation.

ornithine /**or**nitheen/ > *noun* Biochemistry an amino acid which is produced by the body and is important in protein metabolism.
ORIGIN – from Greek *ornis* 'bird' (because it was first obtained from a constituent of bird droppings) + -INE[4].

ornithischian /ornith**isk**iən/ > *noun* Palaeontology a herbivorous dinosaur of a group with pelvic bones resembling those of birds. Compare with SAURISCHIAN.
ORIGIN – from Greek *ornis* 'bird' + *iskhion* 'hip joint'.

ornithology /ornith**oll**əji/ > *noun* the scientific study of birds.
DERIVATIVES – **ornithological** *adjective* **ornithologist** *noun*.
ORIGIN – from Greek *ornis* 'bird'.

ornithopter > *noun* chiefly historical a flying machine with flapping wings.

orogeny /o**roj**əni/ > *noun* Geology a process in which a section of the earth's crust is folded and deformed by lateral compression to form a mountain range.
DERIVATIVES – **orogenesis** *noun* **orogenic** *adjective*.
ORIGIN – from Greek *oros* 'mountain'.

orotund /**orr**ətund/ > *adjective* **1** (of the voice) resonant and impressive. **2** (of writing or style) pompous.
ORIGIN – from Latin *ore rotundo* 'with rounded mouth'.

orphan > *noun* a child whose parents are dead. > *verb* (usu. **be orphaned**) make (a child) an orphan.
ORIGIN – from Greek *orphanos* 'bereaved'.

orphanage > *noun* a residential institution for the care and education of orphans.

orpiment /**or**pimənt/ > *noun* a bright yellow mineral (arsenic sulphide) formerly used as a dye and artist's pigment.
ORIGIN – Latin *auripigmentum*, from *aurum* 'gold' + *pigmentum* 'pigment'.

orrery /**orr**əri/ > *noun* (pl. **orreries**) a clockwork model of the solar system.
ORIGIN – named after the fourth Earl of *Orrery* (1676–1731), for whom one was made.

orris (also **orris root**) > *noun* a preparation of the fragrant rootstock of an iris, used in perfumery.

ortho- > *combining form* **1** straight; rectangular; upright. **2** correct.
ORIGIN – from Greek *orthos* 'straight, right'.

orthodontics /orthə**don**tiks/ > *plural noun* (treated as sing.) the treatment of irregularities in the teeth and jaws.
DERIVATIVES – **orthodontic** *adjective* **orthodontist** *noun*.
ORIGIN – from ORTHO- + Greek *odous* 'tooth'.

orthodox > *adjective* **1** conforming with traditional or generally accepted beliefs. **2** conventional; normal. **3** (usu. **Orthodox**) of or relating to Orthodox Judaism or the Orthodox Church.
SYNONYMS – **1** conformist, conservative, conventional, mainstream, traditional.
ANTONYMS – **1** heterodox, unconventional, unorthodox.
COMBINATIONS – **Orthodox Church** a Christian Church acknowledging the authority of the patriarch of Constantinople. **Orthodox Judaism** a branch of Judaism which teaches strict

adherence to rabbinical interpretation of Jewish law and its traditional observances.

ORIGIN – from **ORTHO-** + Greek *doxa* 'opinion'.

orthodoxy > *noun* (pl. **orthodoxies**) **1** the state of being orthodox. **2** an orthodox theory, doctrine, or practice. **3** the whole community of Orthodox Jews or Orthodox Christians.

orthoepy /orthōeppi/ > *noun* the study of correct or accepted pronunciation.

DERIVATIVES – **orthoepist** *noun*.

ORIGIN – Greek *orthoepeia* 'correct speech'.

orthogonal /orthoggən'l/ > *adjective* of or involving right angles; at right angles.

orthographic projection > *noun* a method of projection in which an object is depicted using parallel lines to project its outline on to a plane.

orthography /orthogrəfi/ > *noun* (pl. **orthographies**) the conventional spelling system of a language.

DERIVATIVES – **orthographic** *adjective*.

orthopaedics /orthəpeediks/ (US **orthopedics**) > *plural noun* (treated as sing.) the branch of medicine concerned with the correction of deformities of bones or muscles.

DERIVATIVES – **orthopaedic** *adjective* **orthopaedist** *noun*.

ORIGIN – from **ORTHO-** + Greek *paideia* 'rearing of children'.

orthoptics > *plural noun* (treated as sing.) the study or treatment of irregularities of the eyes, especially those of the eye muscles.

DERIVATIVES – **orthoptic** *adjective* **orthoptist** *noun*.

orthotics /orthottiks/ > *plural noun* (treated as sing.) the branch of medicine concerned with the provision and use of artificial supports or braces.

DERIVATIVES – **orthotic** *adjective* & *noun* **orthotist** *noun*.

ortolan /ortələn/ > *noun* a small European bunting formerly eaten as a delicacy.

ORIGIN – Provençal, 'gardener' (because the bird frequents gardens).

Orwellian > *adjective* relating to the work of the British novelist George Orwell (1903–50), especially the totalitarian state depicted in his novel *Nineteen Eighty-four*.

-ory[1] > *suffix* (forming nouns) denoting a place for a particular function: *dormitory*.

-ory[2] > *suffix* forming adjectives relating to or involving a verbal action: *compulsory*.

oryx /orriks/ > *noun* a large long-horned antelope of desert regions of Africa and Arabia.

ORIGIN – Greek *orux* 'stonemason's pickaxe' (because of its pointed horns).

orzo /ortsō/ > *noun* small pieces of pasta, shaped like grains of barley or rice.

ORIGIN – Italian, 'barley'.

OS > *abbreviation* **1** Computing operating system.

2 Ordinary Seaman. **3** (in the UK) Ordnance Survey. **4** (as a size of clothing) outsize.

Os > *symbol* the chemical element osmium.

Oscar > *noun* (trademark in the US) the nickname for a gold statuette given as an Academy award.

ORIGIN – one speculative explanation claims that the statuette reminded an executive director of the Academy of Motion Picture Arts and Sciences of her uncle Oscar.

oscillate /ossilayt/ > *verb* **1** move or swing back and forth at a regular rate. **2** waver between extremes of opinion or emotion.

DERIVATIVES – **oscillation** *noun*.

ORIGIN – Latin *oscillare* 'to swing'.

oscilloscope /əsilləskōp/ > *noun* a device for viewing oscillations by a display on the screen of a cathode ray tube.

osculation /oskyoolaysh'n/ > *noun* humorous kissing.

ORIGIN – from Latin *osculari* 'to kiss'.

osculum /oskyooləm/ > *noun* (pl. **oscula** /oskyoolə/) Zoology a large aperture in a sponge through which water is expelled.

ORIGIN – Latin, 'little mouth'.

-ose[1] > *suffix* (forming adjectives) having a specified quality: *bellicose*.

-ose[2] > *suffix* Chemistry forming names of sugars and other carbohydrates: *cellulose*.

osier /ōziər/ > *noun* a small willow with long flexible shoots used in basketwork.

-osis > *suffix* (pl. **-oses**) denoting a process, condition, or pathological state: *metamorphosis*.

-osity > *suffix* forming nouns from adjectives ending in *-ose* (such as *verbosity* from *verbose*) and from adjectives ending in *-ous* (such as *pomposity* from *pompous*).

osmium /ozmiəm/ > *noun* a hard, dense silvery-white metallic chemical element.

ORIGIN – from Greek *osmē* 'smell' (from the pungent smell of one of its oxides).

osmoregulation > *noun* Biology the maintenance of constant osmotic pressure in the fluids of an organism by the control of water and salt concentrations.

DERIVATIVES – **osmoregulatory** *adjective*.

osmosis /ozmōsiss/ > *noun* **1** Biology & Chemistry a process by which solvent molecules pass through a semipermeable membrane from a less concentrated solution into a more concentrated one. **2** the gradual assimilation of ideas.

DERIVATIVES – **osmotic** *adjective*.

ORIGIN – from Greek *ōsmos* 'a push'.

osmotic pressure /ozmottik/ > *noun* Chemistry the pressure that would have to be applied to a pure solvent to prevent it from passing into a given solution by osmosis.

osprey > *noun* (pl. **ospreys**) a large fish-eating bird of prey with a white underside and crown.

wordpower facts

Osprey

The name **osprey** comes from Old French *ospres*, and has been identified with the Latin word *ossifraga*, a name also represented in English by the archaic term **ossifrage**. The *ossifraga*, literally 'bone-breaker' (from Latin *os* 'bone' and *frangere* 'to break'), was, according to the Roman scholar Pliny, a bird that dropped bones from a great height to break them and eat the marrow. This description exactly fits the **lammergeier**, a kind of vulture, but not the fish-eating osprey. This kind of ornithological confusion is not unknown (see box at **PUFFIN**), but an alternative possibility is that **osprey** may have come from some earlier root (perhaps medieval Latin *avis prede* 'bird of prey'), and may have nothing to do with breaking bones.

osseous /ossiəss/ > *adjective* chiefly Zoology & Medicine consisting of or turned into bone.

ORIGIN – Latin *osseus* 'bony' + **-OUS**.

ossicle > *noun* Anatomy a very small bone, especially one of those which transmit sounds within the middle ear.

ORIGIN – Latin *ossiculum* 'little bone'.

ossify /ossifī/ > *verb* (**ossifies, ossified**) **1** turn into bone or bony tissue. **2** cease developing; become inflexible.

DERIVATIVES – **ossification** *noun*.

ORIGIN – from Latin *os* 'bone'.

ossuary /ossyoori/ > *noun* (pl. **ossuaries**) a container or room for the bones of the dead.

ORIGIN – Latin *ossuarium*, from *os* 'bone'.

ostensible > *adjective* apparently true, but not necessarily so.

DERIVATIVES – **ostensibly** *adverb*.

SYNONYMS – apparent, professed, purported, seeming, supposed.

ORIGIN – from Latin *ostensibilis*, from *ostendere* 'stretch out to view'.

ostentation > *noun* a flamboyant display which is designed to impress.

DERIVATIVES – **ostentatious** *adjective*.

SYNONYMS – affectation, flamboyance, flashiness, pomp, showiness.

ORIGIN – from Latin *ostendere* 'stretch out to view'.

osteo- > *combining form* relating to the bones: *osteoporosis*.

ORIGIN – from Greek *osteon* 'bone'.

osteoarthritis > *noun* Medicine degeneration of joint cartilage, causing pain and stiffness.

osteology /ostiolləji/ > *noun* the study of the skeleton and bone.

DERIVATIVES – **osteological** *adjective* **osteologist** *noun*.

osteomyelitis /ostiōmī-ilītiss/ > *noun* Medicine inflammation of bone or bone marrow.

osteopathy /ostiˈoppəthi/ > *noun* a system of complementary medicine involving the manipulation of the skeleton and musculature.

DERIVATIVES – **osteopath** *noun* **osteopathic** *adjective*.

osteoporosis /ostiōpərōsiss/ > *noun* a medical condition in which the bones become brittle and fragile, typically as a result of hormonal changes, or deficiency of calcium or vitamin D.

DERIVATIVES – **osteoporotic** *adjective*.

ORIGIN – from Greek *osteon* 'bone' + *poros* 'passage, pore' + **-OSIS**.

ostinato /ostinaatō/ > *noun* (pl. **ostinatos** or **ostinati** /ostinaati/) a continually repeated musical phrase or rhythm.

ORIGIN – Italian, 'obstinate'.

ostler /oslər/ (also **hostler**) > *noun* historical a man employed at an inn to look after customers' horses.

ORIGIN – Old French *hostelier* 'innkeeper', from *hostel* (see **HOSTEL**).

Ostpolitik /ostpoliteek/ > *noun* historical the foreign policy of détente of western European countries with reference to the former communist bloc.

ORIGIN – German, from *Ost* 'east' + *Politik* 'politics'.

ostracise /ostrəsīz/ (also **ostracize**) > *verb* exclude from a society or group.

DERIVATIVES – **ostracism** *noun*.

SYNONYMS – banish, blackball, cast out, exclude, reject, shun, spurn.

ORIGIN – Greek *ostrakizein*, from *ostrakon* 'shell or potsherd' (on which names were written in voting to banish unpopular citizens).

ostrich > *noun* 1 a large flightless swift-running African bird with a long neck and long legs. 2 a person who refuses to accept unpleasant truths.

WORDFINDER – struthious (*relating to ostriches*).

ORIGIN – Old French *ostriche*, from Latin *avis* 'bird' + *struthio* (from Greek *strouthos* 'sparrow or ostrich'); sense 2 is from the popular belief that ostriches bury their heads in the sand if pursued.

Ostrogoth /ostrəgoth/ > *noun* a member of the eastern branch of the Goths, who conquered Italy in the 5th–6th centuries AD.

ORIGIN – Latin *Ostrogothi* 'East Goths'. Compare with **VISIGOTH**.

OT > *abbreviation* 1 occupational therapist; occupational therapy. 2 Old Testament.

OTC > *abbreviation* 1 (in the UK) Officers' Training Corps. 2 over the counter.

other > *adjective & pronoun* 1 used to refer to a person or thing that is different from one already mentioned or known. 2 additional. 3 alternative of two. 4 those not already mentioned. 5 (usu. **the Other**) Philosophy & Sociology that which is distinct from, different from, or opposite to something or oneself.

IDIOMS – **no other** archaic nothing else. **the other day** (or **night**, **week**, etc.) a few days (or nights, weeks, etc.) ago.

COMBINATIONS – **other half** Brit. informal one's wife, husband, or partner. **the other place** Brit. humorous 1 hell, as opposed to heaven. 2 the House of Lords as regarded by the House of Commons, and vice versa. **other ranks** Brit. (in the armed forces) all those who are not commissioned officers. **other woman** the mistress of a married man. **other-worldly** 1 of or relating to an imaginary or spiritual world. 2 unworldly.

otherness > *noun* the quality or fact of being different.

otherwise > *adverb* 1 in different circumstances; or else. 2 in other respects. 3 in a different way. 4 alternatively. > *adjective* in a different state or situation.

otic /ōtik/ > *adjective* Anatomy of or relating to the ear.

ORIGIN – Greek *ōtikos*, from *ous* 'ear'.

otiose /ōtiōss, ōshiōss/ > *adjective* serving no practical purpose; pointless.

ORIGIN – Latin *otiosus*, from *otium* 'leisure'.

otitis /ətītiss/ > *noun* Medicine inflammation of part of the ear, especially the middle ear (**otitis media**).

ORIGIN – from Greek *ous* 'ear' + **-ITIS**.

otolaryngology /ōtōlarringgolləji/ > *noun* the study of diseases of the ear and throat.

DERIVATIVES – **otolaryngologist** *noun*.

OTT > *abbreviation* Brit. informal over the top.

otter > *noun* a semiaquatic fish-eating mammal with an elongated body, dense fur, and webbed feet.

WORDFINDER – bitch (*female otter*), dog (*male otter*), holt (*den of an otter*), spraint (*droppings of an otter*).

Ottoman /ottəmən/ > *adjective* historical 1 relating to the Turkish dynasty of Osman I (Othman I), founded in *c*.1300. 2 relating to the Empire ruled by the successors of Osman I. 3 historical Turkish. > *noun* (pl. **Ottomans**) a Turk, especially of the Ottoman period.

ORIGIN – an Arabic form of the name Othman.

ottoman > *noun* (pl. **ottomans**) a low upholstered seat without a back or arms, typically serving also as a box.

OU > *abbreviation* (in the UK) Open University.

oubliette /ōōbliet/ > *noun* a secret dungeon with access only through a trapdoor in its ceiling.

ORIGIN – French, from *oublier* 'forget'.

ouch > *exclamation* used to express pain.

ought > *modal verb* (3rd sing. present and past **ought**) 1 used to indicate duty or correctness. 2 used to indicate something that is probable. 3 used to indicate a desirable or expected state. 4 used to give or ask advice.

USAGE – **ought** is a modal verb and behaves differently from ordinary verbs in certain constructions, such as the formation of a negative. The standard negative is *he ought not to have gone*. The forms *he didn't ought to have gone* and *he hadn't ought to have gone* are found in dialect but are not acceptable in standard English.

oughtn't > *contraction* ought not.

ouguiya /ōōgeeyə/ (also **ougiya**) > *noun* the basic monetary unit of Mauritania, equal to five khoums.

ORIGIN – Arabic, from Latin *uncia* 'ounce'.

Ouija board /weejə/ > *noun* trademark a board with letters, numbers, and other signs around its edge, to which a pointer moves, supposedly in answer to questions at a seance.

ORIGIN – from French *oui* 'yes' + German *ja* 'yes'.

ounce > *noun* 1 a unit of weight equal to one sixteenth of a pound avoirdupois (approximately 28 grams). 2 a unit of one twelfth of a pound troy or apothecaries' measure, equal to 480 grains (approximately 31 grams). 3 a very small amount.

ORIGIN – Latin *uncia* 'twelfth part (of a pound or foot)'; compare with **INCH**.

our > *possessive determiner* 1 belonging to or associated with the speaker and one or more others. 2 belonging to or associated with people in general. 3 used in formal contexts by a royal person to refer to something belonging to himself or herself. 4 informal, chiefly N. English used with a name to refer to a relative or friend of the speaker.

COMBINATIONS – **Our Father** 1 God. 2 the Lord's Prayer. **Our Lady** the Virgin Mary. **Our Lord** God or Jesus.

ours > *possessive pronoun* used to refer to something belonging to or associated with the speaker and one or more others.

ourself > *pronoun* (first person pl.) used instead of 'ourselves' typically when 'we' refers to people in general.

ourselves > *pronoun* (first person pl.) 1 used as the object of a verb or preposition when this is the same as the subject of the clause and the subject is the speaker and one or more other people considered together. 2 (emphatic) we or us personally.

-ous > *suffix* forming adjectives: 1 characterised by: *mountainous*. 2 Chemistry of an element in a lower valency: *ferrous*. Compare with **-IC**.

ORIGIN – from Latin *-osus*.

ousel > *noun* variant spelling of **OUZEL**.

oust /owst/ > *verb* drive out or expel from a position or place.
SYNONYMS – banish, eject, evict, expel, unseat.
ORIGIN – Old French *ouster* 'take away', from Latin *obstare* 'oppose, hinder'.

out > *adverb* 1 moving away from a place, especially from one that is enclosed to one that is open. 2 away from one's usual base or residence. 3 outdoors. 4 to sea, away from the land. 5 (of the tide) falling or at its lowest level. 6 at a specified distance away from the target. 7 so as to be revealed, heard, or known. 8 no longer in prison. 9 at or to an end. > *preposition* non-standard contraction of *out of*. > *adjective* 1 not at home or one's place of work. 2 revealed. 3 no longer existing. 4 not possible or worth considering. 5 unconscious. 6 published. 7 informal open about one's homosexuality. 8 informal in existence or use. 9 mistaken. 10 (of the ball in tennis, squash, etc.) outside the playing area. 11 Cricket & Baseball no longer batting. 12 informal no longer in fashion. > *verb* informal reveal that (someone) is homosexual.
IDIOMS – **out and about** engaging in normal activity. **out and out** 1 in every respect; absolute. 2 completely. **out for** intent on having. **out of** 1 from. 2 not having (something). **out of date** 1 old-fashioned. 2 no longer valid. **out of it** informal 1 not included. 2 unaware of what is happening. **out to do** keenly striving to do something. **out with it!** say what you are thinking.
USAGE – in more formal contexts it is better to use **out of** rather than simply **out** in constructions such as *he threw it out of the window.*

out- > *prefix* 1 to the point of surpassing or exceeding. 2 external; separate; from outside. 3 away from; outward.

outage > *noun* a period when a power supply or other service is not available.

out and out > *adjective* absolute. > *adverb* completely.

outback > *noun* (**the outback**) a remote or sparsely populated inland area, especially in Australia.

outbalance > *verb* be more valuable or important than.

outbid > *verb* (**outbidding**; past and past participle **outbid**) bid more for something than (someone else).

outboard > *adjective & adverb* 1 on, towards, or near the outside of a ship or aircraft. 2 (of a motor) portable and attachable to the outside of the stern of a boat. > *noun* 1 an outboard motor. 2 a boat with such a motor.

outbound > *adjective & adverb* travelling away from a place.

outbreak > *noun* a sudden or violent occurrence of war, disease, etc.
SYNONYMS – eruption, flare-up, upsurge.

outbuilding > *noun* a smaller detached building in the grounds of a main building.

outburst > *noun* a sudden violent occurrence or release of something.
SYNONYMS – effusion, eruption, explosion, outpouring.

outcast > *noun* a person rejected by their society or social group. > *adjective* rejected or cast out.
SYNONYMS – *noun* exile, outsider, pariah, untouchable.

outclass > *verb* be far superior to.

outcome > *noun* a consequence of something.
SYNONYMS – consequence, result, upshot.

outcrop > *noun* a part of a rock formation that is visible on the surface. > *verb* (**outcropped**, **outcropping**) appear as an outcrop.

outcry > *noun* (pl. **outcries**) a strong expression of public disapproval.
SYNONYMS – clamour, complaint, protest, uproar.

outdated > *adjective* out of date; obsolete.

outdistance > *verb* leave (a competitor or pursuer) far behind.

outdo > *verb* (**outdoes**, **outdoing**; past **outdid**; past participle **outdone**) be superior to or more successful than.
SYNONYMS – better, eclipse, outshine, overshadow, surpass.

outdoor > *adjective* 1 done, situated, or used outdoors. 2 (of a person) fond of the open air.

outdoors > *adverb* in or into the open air. > *noun* any area outside buildings or shelter.

outer > *adjective* 1 outside; external. 2 further from the centre or the inside. > *noun* an outer part.
COMBINATIONS – **outer space** the physical universe beyond the earth's atmosphere.

outermost > *adjective* furthest from the centre.

outface > *verb* boldly confront (an opponent) and defeat or disconcert them.

outfall > *noun* the place where a river or drain empties into the sea, a river, etc.

outfield > *noun* the outer part of a cricket or baseball field.

outfit > *noun* 1 a set of clothes worn together. 2 informal a group of people undertaking a particular activity together. > *verb* (**outfitted**, **outfitting**) (usu. **be outfitted**) provide with an outfit of clothes.

outfitter (also **outfitters**) > *noun* Brit. dated a shop selling men's clothing.

outflank > *verb* 1 move round the side of (an enemy) so as to outmanoeuvre them. 2 outwit (someone).

outflow > *noun* 1 the action of flowing or moving out. 2 something, such as water or money, that flows or moves out.

outfox > *verb* informal defeat (someone) with superior cunning.

outgas > *verb* (**outgases**, **outgassing**, **outgassed**) release or give off as a gas or vapour.

outgoing > *adjective* 1 friendly and confident. 2 leaving an office or position. 3 going out or away from a place. > *noun* Brit. (**outgoings**) one's regular expenditure.
SYNONYMS – *adjective* 1 extrovert, forthcoming, sociable, uninhibited.
ANTONYMS – *adjective* 1 introverted, withdrawn.

outgrow > *verb* (past **outgrew**; past participle **outgrown**) 1 grow too big for. 2 leave behind as one matures. 3 grow faster or taller than.

outgrowth > *noun* 1 something that grows out of something else. 2 a natural development or result.

outgun > *verb* (**outgunned**, **outgunning**) have more or better weaponry than.

outhouse > *noun* a smaller building built on to or in the grounds of a house.

outing > *noun* 1 a short trip taken for pleasure. 2 informal a public appearance in something, especially a sporting fixture. 3 informal the practice of revealing someone's homosexuality.
SYNONYMS – 1 excursion, expedition, jaunt, trip.

outlandish > *adjective* looking or sounding bizarre or unfamiliar.
SYNONYMS – bizarre, odd, peculiar, strange, weird.
ORIGIN – Old English, 'not native'.

outlast > *verb* last longer than.

outlaw > *noun* 1 a fugitive from the law. 2 historical a person deprived of the benefit and protection of the law. > *verb* 1 make (something) illegal; ban. 2 historical deprive of the benefit and protection of the law.
DERIVATIVES – **outlawry** *noun*.

outlay > *noun* an amount of money spent.

outlet > *noun* 1 a pipe or hole through which water or gas may escape. 2 a point from which goods are sold or distributed. 3 an output socket in an electrical device. 4 a means of expressing one's talents, energy, or emotions. 5 the mouth of a river.

outlier /owtlīər/ > *noun* 1 a thing detached from a main body or system. 2 Geology a younger rock formation among older rocks.

outline > *noun* 1 a line or lines enclosing or indicating the shape of an object in a sketch or diagram. 2 the contours or bounds of an object. 3 a general plan showing essential features but no detail. > *verb* 1 draw or define the outer edge or shape of. **2** give a summary of.

SYNONYMS – *noun* **2** form, profile, silhouette. **3** framework, plan, skeleton, sketch.

outlive > *verb* live longer than.

outlook > *noun* **1** a person's point of view or attitude to life. **2** a view. **3** the prospect for the future.

SYNONYMS – **1** attitude, perspective, viewpoint. **3** forecast, prognosis, prospect.

outlying > *adjective* situated far from a centre.

outmanoeuvre > *verb* **1** evade by moving faster or more skilfully. **2** use skill and cunning to gain an advantage over.

outmatch > *verb* be superior to.

outmoded > *adjective* old-fashioned.

outnumber > *verb* be more numerous than.

out-of-body experience > *noun* a sensation of being outside one's body, typically of observing oneself from a distance.

out-of-court > *adjective* (of a settlement) made without the intervention of a court.

outpace > *verb* go faster than.

outpatient > *noun* a patient attending a hospital for treatment without staying overnight.

outperform > *verb* perform better than.

outplacement > *noun* assistance given to redundant employees in finding new employment.

outplay > *verb* play better than.

outpost > *noun* **1** a small military camp at a distance from the main army. **2** a remote part of a country or empire.

outpouring > *noun* **1** something that streams out rapidly. **2** an outburst of strong emotion.

SYNONYMS – cascade, deluge, effusion, outflow, torrent.

output > *noun* **1** the amount of something produced. **2** the process of producing something. **3** the power, energy, etc. supplied by a device or system. **4** Electronics a place where power or information leaves a system. > *verb* (**outputting**; past and past participle **output** or **outputted**) (of a computer) produce or supply (data).

SYNONYMS – *noun* **1** crop, harvest, production, yield.

outrage > *noun* **1** an extremely strong reaction of anger or indignation. **2** a cause of outrage. > *verb* **1** arouse outrage in. **2** violate (a law, principle, etc.) flagrantly.

SYNONYMS – *noun* **1** anger, fury, indignation, rage. **2** disgrace, insult, scandal. *verb* **1** anger, enrage, incense, infuriate.

ORIGIN – Old French, based on Latin *ultra* 'beyond'.

outrageous > *adjective* **1** shockingly bad or excessive. **2** very bold and unusual.

DERIVATIVES – **outrageously** *adverb*.

SYNONYMS – **1** appalling, atrocious, disgraceful, scandalous, shocking. **2** adventurous, bold, daring, flamboyant.

outran past of OUTRUN.

outrank > *verb* **1** have a higher rank than. **2** be better or more important than.

outré /ˈoʊtreɪ/ > *adjective* unusual and typically rather shocking.

ORIGIN – French, 'exceeded', past participle of *outrer* 'exceed, exaggerate'.

outreach > *verb* /ˈaʊtriːtʃ/ reach further than. > *noun* /ˈaʊtriːtʃ/ **1** the extent or length of reaching out. **2** an organisation's involvement with the community.

outrider > *noun* a person in a vehicle or on horseback who escorts or guards another vehicle.

outrigger > *noun* **1** a spar or framework projecting from or over a boat's side. **2** a stabilising float fixed parallel to a canoe or small ship. **3** a boat fitted with an outrigger.

outright > *adverb* **1** altogether. **2** openly. **3** immediately. > *adjective* **1** open and direct. **2** complete.

outrun > *verb* (**outrunning**; past **outran**; past participle **outrun**) **1** run or travel faster or further than. **2** exceed.

outsell > *verb* (past and past participle **outsold**) be sold in greater quantities than.

outset > *noun* the start or beginning of something.

outshine > *verb* (past and past participle **outshone**) **1** shine more brightly than. **2** be much better than.

outside > *noun* **1** the external side or surface of something. **2** the external appearance of someone or something. **3** the part of a path nearer to a road. **4** the side of a curve where the edge is longer. > *adjective* **1** situated on or near the outside. **2** not of or belonging to a particular group. **3** (in hockey, soccer, etc.) denoting positions nearer to the sides of the field. > *preposition & adverb* **1** situated or moving beyond the boundaries of. **2** (in hockey, soccer, etc.) closer to the side of the field than. **3** beyond the limits or scope of. **4** not being a member of.

IDIOMS – **at the outside** at the most. **an outside chance** a remote possibility.

COMBINATIONS – **outside broadcast** Brit. a radio or television programme recorded or broadcast live on location. **outside interest** an interest not connected with one's work or studies.

outsider > *noun* **1** a person who does not belong to a particular group. **2** a competitor thought to have little chance of success.

SYNONYMS – **1** alien, foreigner, non-member, stranger, visitor.

outsize > *adjective* (also **outsized**) exceptionally large.

outskirts > *plural noun* the outer parts of a town or city.

SYNONYMS – borders, edges, fringes, periphery, suburbs.

outsmart > *verb* defeat with superior intelligence; outwit.

outsold past and past participle of OUTSELL.

outsole > *noun* the outer sole of a boot or shoe.

outsource > *verb* **1** obtain (something) by contract from an outside supplier. **2** contract (work) out.

outspoken > *adjective* frank in stating one's opinions.

DERIVATIVES – **outspokenly** *adverb* **outspokenness** *noun*.

SYNONYMS – blunt, candid, direct, forthright, frank, unreserved.

outspread > *adjective* fully extended or expanded.

outstanding > *adjective* **1** exceptionally good. **2** clearly noticeable. **3** not yet dealt with.

SYNONYMS – **1** excellent, exceptional, extraordinary, first-class, remarkable.

outstation > *noun* **1** a branch of an organisation situated at a distance from its headquarters. **2** Austral./NZ a part of a farming estate that is separate from the main estate.

outstay > *verb* stay beyond the limit of (one's expected or permitted time).

outstretch > *verb* extend or stretch out.

outstrip > *verb* (**outstripped**, **outstripping**) **1** move faster than and overtake. **2** exceed; surpass.

out-take > *noun* a sequence of a film or recording rejected in editing.

out tray > *noun* a tray on a desk for letters and documents that have been dealt with.

outvote > *verb* defeat by gaining more votes.

outward > *adjective* **1** of, on, or from the outside. **2** going out or away from a place. > *adverb* outwards.

DERIVATIVES – **outwardly** *adverb*.

COMBINATIONS – **Outward Bound** trademark an organisation providing outdoor activities for young people.

outward bound > *adjective* going away from home. > *noun* (**Outward Bound**) trademark an organisation providing outdoor activities for young people.

outwards > *adverb* towards the outside; away from the centre or a place.

outwash > *noun* material carried away from a glacier by meltwater.

outweigh > *verb* be heavier, greater, or more significant than.

outwit > *verb* (**outwitted**, **outwitting**) deceive by greater ingenuity.

SYNONYMS – fool, hoodwink, outmanoeuvre, outsmart, trick.

outwith > *preposition* Scottish outside; beyond.

outwork > *noun* **1** an outer section of a fortification or system of defence. **2** Brit. work done outside the factory or office which provides it.
DERIVATIVES – **outworker** *noun*.

ouzel /ōōz'l/ (also **ousel**) > *noun* used in names of birds resembling the blackbird, e.g. **ring ouzel**.
ORIGIN – Old English, 'blackbird'.

ouzo /ōōzō/ > *noun* (pl. **ouzos**) a Greek aniseed-flavoured spirit.
ORIGIN – modern Greek.

ova plural of OVUM.

oval > *adjective* having a rounded and slightly elongated outline; egg-shaped. > *noun* **1** an oval body, object, or design. **2** an oval sports field or track. **3** a ground for Australian Rules football.
COMBINATIONS – **Oval Office** the office of the US President in the White House.
ORIGIN – Latin *ovalis*, from *ovum* 'egg'.

Oval Office > *noun* the office of the US President in the White House.

ovarian > *adjective* relating to the ovaries.

ovariectomy /ōvariektəmi/ > *noun* (pl. **ovariectomies**) surgical removal of one or both ovaries.

ovariotomy /ōvariottəmi/ > *noun* another term for OVARIECTOMY.

ovary > *noun* (pl. **ovaries**) **1** a female reproductive organ in which ova or eggs are produced. **2** Botany the base of the carpel of a flower, containing one or more ovules.
ORIGIN – Latin *ovarium*, from *ovum* 'egg'.

ovate /ōvayt/ > *adjective* oval; egg-shaped.

ovation > *noun* an enthusiastic display of appreciation from an audience.
ORIGIN – Latin, from *ovare* 'exult'.

oven > *noun* **1** an enclosed chamber or compartment in which things are cooked or heated. **2** a small furnace or kiln.
COMBINATIONS – **oven glove** a padded glove for handling hot dishes from an oven. **oven-ready** (of food) sold as a prepared dish, ready for cooking in an oven. **ovenware** ovenproof dishes.

ovenproof > *adjective* suitable for use in an oven.

over > *preposition* **1** extending upwards from or above. **2** above so as to cover or protect. **3** beyond. **4** expressing movement or a route across. **5** beyond and falling or hanging from. **6** expressing duration. **7** at a higher level or layer than. **8** higher or more than. **9** expressing authority or control. **10** on the subject of. > *adverb* **1** expressing movement or a route across an area. **2** beyond and falling or hanging from a point. **3** in or to the place indicated. **4** expressing action and result. **5** finished. **6** expressing repetition of a process. > *noun* Cricket a sequence of six balls bowled by a bowler from one end of the pitch.
IDIOMS – **be over** be no longer affected by.

over against 1 adjacent to. **2** in contrast with. **over and above** in addition to. **over and out** indicating that a message on a two-way radio has finished.

over- > *prefix* **1** excessively: *overambitious*. **2** completely: *overjoyed*. **3** upper; outer; extra: *overcoat*. **4** over; above: *overcast*.

overact > *verb* act a role in an exaggerated manner.

overactive > *adjective* excessively active.
DERIVATIVES – **overactivity** *noun*.

overall > *adjective* **1** inclusive of everything; total. **2** taking everything into account. > *adverb* taken as a whole. > *noun* (also **overalls**) Brit. a loose-fitting garment worn over ordinary clothes for protection.

overambitious > *adjective* excessively ambitious.

overanxious > *adjective* excessively anxious.
DERIVATIVES – **overanxiety** *noun*.

overarch > *verb* **1** form an arch over. **2** (**overarching**) all-embracing.

overarm > *adjective & adverb* (of a throw, stroke with a racket, etc.) made with the hand brought forward and down from above shoulder level.

overate past of OVEREAT.

overawe > *verb* (usu. **be overawed**) impress (someone) so much that they are silent or inhibited.

overbalance > *verb* **1** fall or cause to fall due to loss of balance. **2** outweigh.

overbearing > *adjective* not heeding other people's wishes or feelings; domineering.
SYNONYMS – dominating, domineering, oppressive, overpowering.

overbite > *noun* the overlapping of the lower teeth by the upper.

overblown > *adjective* **1** excessive or exaggerated. **2** (of a flower) past its prime.

overboard > *adverb* from a ship into the water.
IDIOMS – **go overboard 1** be very enthusiastic. **2** behave immoderately; go too far.

overbook > *verb* accept more reservations for (a flight or hotel) than there is room for.

overburden > *verb* burden excessively.

overcame past of OVERCOME.

overcapacity > *noun* an excess of productive capacity.

overcast > *adjective* **1** cloudy; dull. **2** edged with stitching to prevent fraying. > *verb* (past and past participle **overcast**) stitch over (a raw edge) to prevent fraying.

overcautious > *adjective* excessively cautious.
DERIVATIVES – **overcaution** *noun*

overcharge > *verb* charge too high a price.

overcheck > *noun* a check pattern superimposed on a colour or design.

overcloud > *verb* mar, dim, or obscure.

overcoat > *noun* **1** a long, warm coat. **2** a top, final layer of paint or varnish.

overcome > *verb* (past **overcame**; past participle **overcome**) **1** succeed in dealing with (a problem). **2** defeat. **3** (usu. **be overcome**) (of an emotion) overwhelm (someone).
SYNONYMS – **1** control, curb, deal with, master.

overcompensate > *verb* take excessive measures to compensate for something.
DERIVATIVES – **overcompensation** *noun* **overcompensatory** *adjective*.

overconfident > *adjective* excessively confident.
DERIVATIVES – **overconfidence** *noun*.
SYNONYMS – arrogant, cocksure, cocky, hubristic, smug.

overcook > *verb* cook (something) for too long.

overcrowd > *verb* fill (a place) beyond what is usual or comfortable.

overdetermine > *verb* technical determine, account for, or cause in more than one way or with more conditions than are necessary.
DERIVATIVES – **overdetermination** *noun*.

overdevelop > *verb* (**overdeveloped**, **overdeveloping**) develop (something) to excess.
DERIVATIVES – **overdevelopment** *noun*.

overdo > *verb* (**overdoes**; past **overdid**; past participle **overdone**) **1** do (something) excessively or in an exaggerated manner. **2** (**overdo it** or **things**) exhaust oneself. **3** use or add too much of. **4** overcook.
SYNONYMS – **1** exaggerate, overplay, overstate.
ANTONYMS – **1** play down, understate.

overdose > *noun* an excessive and dangerous dose of a drug. > *verb* take an overdose.
DERIVATIVES – **overdosage** *noun*.

overdraft > *noun* a deficit in a bank account caused by drawing more money than the account holds.

overdramatise (also **overdramatize**) > *verb* react to or portray in an excessively dramatic way.
DERIVATIVES – **overdramatic** *adjective*.

overdrawn > *adjective* **1** (of a bank account) in a state in which the amount of money withdrawn exceeds the amount held. **2** (of a person) having an overdrawn bank account.

overdress > *verb* dress too elaborately or formally.

overdrive > *noun* **1** a gear in a motor vehicle providing a gear ratio higher than that of the usual top gear. **2** a state of high or excessive activity. **3** a mechanism allowing the exceeding of a normal operating level in equipment. > *verb* **1** drive or work to exhaustion. **2** give (an electric guitar) a distorted sound.
DERIVATIVES – **overdriven** *adjective*.

overdub > *verb* (**overdubbed, overdubbing**) record (additional sounds) on an existing recording. > *noun* an instance of overdubbing.

overdue > *adjective* not having arrived, happened, or been done at the expected or desired time.
SYNONYMS – belated, delayed, late, tardy.

overeager > *adjective* excessively eager.

over easy > *adjective* N. Amer. (of an egg) fried on both sides, with the yolk remaining slightly liquid.

overeat > *verb* (past **overate**; past participle **overeaten**) eat too much.
SYNONYMS – binge, gorge, guzzle, overindulge.

over-egg > *verb* (in phrase **over-egg the pudding**) go too far in doing or embellishing something.

overemotional > *adjective* excessively emotional.

overemphasise (also **overemphasize**) > *verb* place excessive emphasis on.
DERIVATIVES – **overemphasis** *noun*.

overenthusiasm > *noun* excessive enthusiasm.
DERIVATIVES – **overenthusiastic** *adjective*.

overestimate > *verb* form too high an estimate of. > *noun* an excessively high estimate.
DERIVATIVES – **overestimation** *noun*.

overexcite > *verb* excite excessively.
DERIVATIVES – **overexcitable** *adjective* **overexcitement** *noun*.

overexert > *verb* (**overexert oneself**) exert oneself excessively.
DERIVATIVES – **overexertion** *noun*.

overexpose > *verb* expose (someone or something) too much, especially to public attention or to risk.
DERIVATIVES – **overexposure** *noun*.

overextend > *verb* (usu. **be overextended**) 1 make too long. 2 impose an excessive burden on.
DERIVATIVES – **overextension** *noun*.

overfall > *noun* 1 a turbulent stretch of open water caused by a strong current or tide over a submarine ridge, or by a meeting of currents. 2 a place where surplus water overflows from a dam, pool, etc.

overfamiliar > *adjective* 1 too well known. 2 inappropriately informal.
DERIVATIVES – **overfamiliarity** *noun*.

overfeed > *verb* (past and past participle **overfed**) feed too much.

overfill > *verb* fill to excess.

overfish > *verb* deplete (a body of water or stock of fish) by too much fishing.

overflow > *verb* 1 flow over the brim of a receptacle. 2 be excessively full or crowded. 3 (**overflow with**) be very full of (an emotion). > *noun* 1 the overflowing of a liquid. 2 the excess not able to be accommodated by a space. 3 (also **overflow pipe**) an outlet for excess water.

overgarment > *noun* a garment worn over others.

overgeneralise (also **overgeneralize**) > *verb* express in a way that is too general.
DERIVATIVES – **overgeneralisation** *noun*.

overgenerous > *adjective* excessively generous.

overglaze > *noun* decoration or a second glaze applied to glazed ceramic. > *adjective* (of decoration) applied on a glazed surface.

overground > *adverb* & *adjective* on or above the ground.

overgrown > *adjective* 1 grown over with vegetation. 2 grown too large.

overgrowth > *noun* excessive growth.

overhand > *adjective* & *adverb* 1 overarm. 2 with the palm downward or inward.

overhang > *verb* (past and past participle **overhung**) jut out or hang over. > *noun* an overhanging part.

overhaul > *verb* 1 examine and repair. 2 Brit. overtake. > *noun* an act of overhauling.
SYNONYMS – *verb* 1 recondition, service.
ORIGIN – from **OVER-** + **HAUL**: originally in nautical use in the sense 'release (rope tackle) by slackening').

overhead > *adverb* above one's head; in the sky. > *adjective* 1 situated overhead. 2 (of a driving mechanism) above the object driven. 3 (of an expense) incurred in the upkeep or running of premises or a business. > *noun* 1 an overhead cost or expense. 2 a transparency for use with an overhead projector.
COMBINATIONS – **overhead projector** a device that projects an enlarged image of a transparency using an overhead mirror.

overhear > *verb* (past and past participle **overheard**) hear accidentally or secretly.

overheat > *verb* 1 make or become too hot. 2 Economics (of an economy) show marked inflation when increased demand results in rising prices.

overindulge > *verb* 1 have too much of something enjoyable. 2 gratify the wishes of (someone) to an excessive extent.
DERIVATIVES – **overindulgence** *noun* **overindulgent** *adjective*.

overinflated > *adjective* 1 filled with too much air. 2 (of a price or value) excessive. 3 exaggerated.

overissue > *verb* (**overissues, overissued, overissuing**) issue (banknotes, shares, etc.) beyond the authorised amount or the issuer's ability to pay. > *noun* the action of overissuing.

overjoyed > *adjective* extremely happy.
SYNONYMS – delighted, ecstatic, elated, euphoric, jubilant, thrilled.

overkill > *noun* 1 the amount by which destruction or destructive capacity exceeds what is necessary. 2 excessive action.

overladen > *adjective* bearing too large a load.

overlaid past and past participle of **OVERLAY**[1].

overlain past participle of **OVERLIE**.

overland > *adjective* & *adverb* by land. > *verb* Austral./NZ historical 1 drive (livestock) over a long distance. 2 travel a long distance by land.

overlander > *noun* 1 Austral./NZ historical a person who overlands livestock. 2 a person who travels a long distance overland.

overlap > *verb* /ōvərlap/ (**overlapped, overlapping**) 1 extend over so as to cover partly. 2 partly coincide. > *noun* /ōvərlap/ an overlapping part or amount.

overlay[1] > *verb* (past and past participle **overlaid**) (often **be overlaid with**) 1 coat the surface of. 2 lie on top of. 3 (of a quality or feeling) become more prominent than (a previous one). > *noun* 1 a covering. 2 a transparent sheet over artwork or a map, giving additional detail. 3 Computing replacement of a block of stored instructions or data with another.

overlay[2] past of **OVERLIE**.

overleaf > *adverb* on the other side of the page.

overlie > *verb* (**overlying**; past **overlay**; past participle **overlain**) lie on top of.

overload > *verb* 1 load excessively. 2 put too great a demand on (an electrical system). > *noun* an excessive amount.
SYNONYMS – *verb* 1 overburden, strain, weigh down.

overlock > *verb* prevent fraying of (an edge of cloth) by oversewing it.

overlook > *verb* 1 fail to notice; miss. 2 ignore or disregard. 3 have a view of from above. > *noun* N. Amer. a commanding position or view.

overlord > *noun* a ruler, especially a feudal lord.

overly > *adverb* excessively.

overlying present participle of **OVERLIE**.

overman > *verb* /ōvərman/ (**overmanned, overmanning**) provide with more people than necessary. > *noun* /ōvəmən/ 1 an overseer in a colliery. 2 Philosophy another term for **SUPERMAN**. [ORIGIN – translation of German *Übermensch*, used by Friedrich Nietzsche.]

overmantel > *noun* an ornamental structure over a mantelpiece.

overmaster > *verb* literary overcome.

overmatch > *verb* chiefly N. Amer. be stronger, better armed, or more skilful than.

overmuch > *adverb, determiner,* & *pronoun* too much.

overnight > *adverb* 1 for the duration of a night. 2 during the course of a night. 3 suddenly. > *adjective* 1 for use overnight. 2 done or happening overnight. 3 sudden.

> *verb* **1** stay overnight. **2** N. Amer. convey (goods) overnight.

overnighter > *noun* **1** a person who stays overnight. **2** N. Amer. an overnight trip or stay. **3** an overnight bag.

overpaint > *verb* cover with paint. > *noun* paint added as a covering layer.

overpass > *noun* a bridge by which a road or railway line passes over another.

overpay > *verb* (past and past participle **overpaid**) pay (someone) too much.

overplay > *verb* overemphasise.

IDIOMS – **overplay one's hand** spoil one's chance of success through excessive confidence.

overpopulate > *verb* populate (an area) with excessively large numbers.

DERIVATIVES – **overpopulation** *noun*.

overpower > *verb* **1** defeat with superior strength. **2** overwhelm.

DERIVATIVES – **overpowering** *adjective*.

SYNONYMS – **1** crush, defeat, overthrow, subdue.

overprice > *verb* charge too high a price for.

overproduce > *verb* **1** produce an excess of. **2** record or produce (a song or film) in an excessively elaborate way.

DERIVATIVES – **overproduction** *noun*.

overproof > *adjective* containing more alcohol than proof spirit does.

overprotective > *adjective* excessively protective.

DERIVATIVES – **overprotect** *verb* **overprotection** *noun*

overqualified > *adjective* too highly qualified for a particular job.

overran past of OVERRUN.

overrate > *verb* rate more highly than is deserved.

DERIVATIVES – **overrated** *adjective*.

overreach > *verb* (**overreach oneself**) fail through being too ambitious or trying too hard.

overreacher > *noun* N. Amer. a fraudster.

overreact > *verb* react more emotionally or forcibly than is justified.

DERIVATIVES – **overreaction** *noun*.

override > *verb* /ˌōvərˈrīd/ (past **overrode**; past participle **overridden**) **1** use one's authority to reject or cancel. **2** interrupt the action of (an automatic function). **3** be more important than. **4** overlap. **5** travel or move over. > *noun* /ˈōvərrīd/ **1** the action or process of overriding. **2** a device on a machine for overriding an automatic function. **3** an excess or increase on a budget, salary, or cost.

overriding > *adjective* **1** more important than any other considerations. **2** extending or moving over.

overripe > *adjective* too ripe.

overrule > *verb* reject or disallow by exercising one's superior authority.

overrun > *verb* (**overrunning**; past **overran**; past participle **overrun**) **1** spread over or occupy in large numbers. **2** move or extend over or beyond. **3** exceed (an expected or allowed time or cost).

oversail > *verb* (of a part of a building) project beyond (a lower part).

ORIGIN – from OVER + French *saillir* 'jut out'.

overseas > *adverb* in or to a foreign country. > *adjective* relating to a foreign country. > *noun* foreign countries regarded collectively.

oversee > *verb* (**oversees**; past **oversaw**; past participle **overseen**) supervise.

DERIVATIVES – **overseer** *noun*.

oversell > *verb* (past and past participle **oversold**) **1** sell more of (something) than exists or can be delivered. **2** exaggerate the merits of.

oversensitive > *adjective* excessively sensitive.

DERIVATIVES – **oversensitivity** *noun*.

oversew > *verb* (past participle **oversewn** or **oversewed**) **1** sew (the edges of two pieces of fabric) together, with the stitches passing over the join. **2** join the sections of (a book) in such a way.

oversexed > *adjective* having unusually strong sexual desires.

overshadow > *verb* **1** tower above and cast a shadow over. **2** cast a gloom over. **3** appear more prominent, important, or successful than.

SYNONYMS – **3** eclipse, outclass, outdo, outshine, upstage.

overshoe > *noun* a protective shoe worn over a normal shoe.

overshoot > *verb* (past and past participle **overshot**) **1** move or travel past unintentionally. **2** exceed (a financial target or limit).

oversight > *noun* an unintentional failure to notice or do something.

oversimplify > *verb* (**oversimplifies**, **oversimplified**) simplify (something) so much that a distorted impression of it is given.

DERIVATIVES – **oversimplification** *noun*.

oversized (also **oversize**) > *adjective* bigger than the usual size.

overskirt > *noun* an outer skirt forming a second layer over a skirt or dress.

oversleep > *verb* (past and past participle **overslept**) sleep longer or later than one has intended.

oversold past and past participle of OVERSELL.

overspend > *verb* (past and past participle **overspent**) spend too much money.

overspill > *noun* Brit. a surplus population moving from an overcrowded area to live elsewhere.

overstaff > *verb* provide with more members of staff than are necessary.

overstate > *verb* exaggerate or state too emphatically.

DERIVATIVES – **overstatement** *noun*.

SYNONYMS – exaggerate, magnify, overemphasise, overstress.

overstay > *verb* stay longer than the duration or limits of.

oversteer > *verb* (of a vehicle) turn more sharply than is desirable.

overstep > *verb* (**overstepped**, **overstepping**) go beyond (a prescribed or generally accepted limit).

IDIOMS – **overstep the mark** go beyond what is intended or acceptable.

overstimulate > *verb* stimulate excessively.

DERIVATIVES – **overstimulation** *noun*.

overstitch > *noun* a stitch made over an edge or over another stitch. > *verb* sew with an overstitch.

overstock > *verb* stock with more than is necessary or sustainable. > *noun* chiefly N. Amer. a supply or quantity in excess of demand.

overstrain > *verb* subject to an excessive demand on strength, resources, or abilities.

overstress > *verb* **1** subject to too much stress. **2** lay too much emphasis on.

overstretch > *verb* **1** stretch too much. **2** make too many demands on.

overstrung > *adjective* (of a piano) with strings in sets crossing each other obliquely.

overstuff > *verb* cover (furniture) completely with a thick layer of stuffing.

overstuffed > *adjective* (of furniture) covered completely with a thick layer of stuffing.

oversubscribed > *adjective* **1** (of something for sale) applied for in greater quantities than are available. **2** (of a course or institution) having more applications than available places.

overt /ˈōvert/ > *adjective* done or shown openly.

DERIVATIVES – **overtly** *adverb* **overtness** *noun*.

SYNONYMS – blatant, clear, evident, open, unconcealed, undisguised.

ANTONYMS – covert, hidden.

ORIGIN – Old French, from *ovrir* 'to open'.

overtake > *verb* (past **overtook**; past participle **overtaken**) **1** catch up with and pass while travelling in the same direction. **2** become greater or more successful than. **3** encounter suddenly or unexpectedly.

overthrow > *verb* (past **overthrew**; past participle **overthrown**) **1** remove forcibly from power. **2** put an end to through force. **3** throw (a ball) further than the intended distance. > *noun* **1** a defeat or removal from power. **2** a throw which sends a ball past its intended recipient or target.

SYNONYMS – *verb* **1** depose, dethrone, oust,

topple, unseat. *noun* **1** defeat, downfall, removal.

overtime > *noun* **1** time worked in addition to one's normal working hours. **2** N. Amer. extra time played at the end of a tie game. > *adverb* in addition to normal working hours.

overtire > *verb* exhaust (someone).
DERIVATIVES – **overtired** *adjective*.

overtone > *noun* **1** a musical tone which is a part of the harmonic series above a fundamental note, and may be heard with it. **2** a subtle or subsidiary quality, implication, or connotation.
SYNONYMS – **2** connotation, echo, hint, implication, intimation, suggestion.

overtop > *verb* (**overtopped, overtopping**) **1** exceed in height. **2** (especially of water) rise over the top of. > *adverb & preposition* chiefly Canadian over.

overtrousers > *plural noun* protective or waterproof trousers worn over other trousers.

overture > *noun* **1** an orchestral piece at the beginning of a musical work. **2** an independent orchestral composition in one movement. **3** an introduction to something more substantial. **4** an approach made with the aim of opening negotiations or establishing a relationship.
SYNONYMS – **3** curtain-raiser, introduction, preliminary, prelude. **4** advance, approach, proposition, tender.
ORIGIN – first used in the sense 'aperture': from Old French, from Latin *apertura* 'aperture'.

overturn > *verb* **1** turn over and come or bring to rest upside down. **2** abolish, invalidate, or reverse (a decision, system, belief, etc.).
SYNONYMS – **1** capsize, flip, invert, tip over.

overuse > *verb* use too much. > *noun* excessive use.

overvalue > *verb* (**overvalues, overvalued, overvaluing**) **1** overestimate the importance of. **2** fix the value of (something, especially a currency) at too high a level.
DERIVATIVES – **overvaluation** *noun*.

overview > *noun* a general review or summary. > *verb* give an overview of.

overweening > *adjective* **1** showing excessive confidence or pride. **2** excessive; immoderate.
ORIGIN – from **OVER** + archaic *ween* 'be of the opinion, think'.

overweight > *adjective* above a normal, desirable, or permitted weight.

overwhelm > *verb* **1** submerge beneath a huge mass. **2** defeat completely; overpower. **3** have a strong emotional effect on.
DERIVATIVES – **overwhelming** *adjective* **overwhelmingly** *adverb*.

SYNONYMS – **1** bury, engulf, submerge, swamp. **2** defeat, overpower, rout, trounce, vanquish.
ORIGIN – from **OVER** + archaic *whelm* 'engulf, submerge, or bury'.

overwind > *verb* (past and past participle **overwound**) wind (a mechanism) beyond the proper stopping point.

overwinter > *verb* **1** spend the winter in a specified place. **2** (of an insect, plant, etc.) live or survive through the winter. **3** maintain through the winter.

overwork > *verb* **1** work or cause to work too hard. **2** use (a word or idea) too much and so make it weaker in effect. > *noun* excessive work.

overwound past and past participle of **OVERWIND**.

overwrite > *verb* (past **overwrote**; past participle **overwritten**) **1** write on top of (other writing). **2** Computing destroy (data) or the data in (a file) by entering new data in its place. **3** write too elaborately or ornately. **4** (in insurance) accept more risk than the premium income limits allow.

overwrought > *adjective* **1** in a state of nervous excitement or anxiety. **2** (of a piece of writing or a work of art) too elaborate or complicated.
SYNONYMS – **1** agitated, distracted, hysterical, keyed up; informal uptight.
ORIGIN – archaic past participle of **OVERWORK**.

overzealous > *adjective* overly enthusiastic or energetic.

oviduct /ōvidukt/ > *noun* Anatomy & Zoology the tube through which an ovum or egg passes from an ovary.
ORIGIN – from Latin *ovum* 'egg' + **DUCT**.

oviform > *adjective* egg-shaped.

ovine /ōvīn/ > *adjective* relating to sheep.
ORIGIN – Latin *ovinus*, from *ovis* 'sheep'.

oviparous /ōvippərəss/ > *adjective* Zoology producing young by means of eggs which are hatched after they have been laid by the parent, as in birds. Compare with **VIVIPAROUS** and **OVOVIVIPAROUS**.
DERIVATIVES – **oviparity** *noun*.

ovipositor /ōvipozzitər/ > *noun* Zoology a tubular organ through which a female insect or fish deposits eggs.

ovoid /ōvoyd/ > *adjective* **1** (of a solid or a three-dimensional surface) more or less egg-shaped. **2** (of a plane figure) oval. > *noun* an ovoid body or surface.

ovoviviparous /ōvōvivippərəss/ > *adjective* Zoology producing young by means of eggs which are hatched within the body of the parent, as in some snakes. Compare with **OVIPAROUS** and **VIVIPAROUS**.
DERIVATIVES – **ovoviviparity** *noun*.

ovulate /ovyoolayt/ > *verb* discharge ova or ovules from the ovary.

DERIVATIVES – **ovulation** *noun* **ovulatory** *adjective*.

ovule > *noun* Botany the part of the ovary of seed plants that contains the female germ cell and after fertilisation becomes the seed.
DERIVATIVES – **ovular** *adjective*.

ovum > *noun* (pl. **ova**) a mature female reproductive cell, which can divide to give rise to an embryo usually only after fertilisation by a male cell.

wordpower facts
Ovum
Ovum is the Latin word for 'egg'. It is the root of a number of words based on the shape or function of an egg, including **oval**, **ovary**, **ovoid**, **ovulate**, and **ovule**.

owe > *verb* **1** have an obligation to pay (money or goods) to (someone) in return for something received. **2** be under a moral obligation to show (gratitude, respect, etc.) or to offer (an explanation) to (someone). **3** be indebted to (someone or something) for (something).

owing > *adjective* yet to be paid or supplied.
IDIOMS – **owing to** because of or on account of.
SYNONYMS – due, outstanding, overdue, owed, unpaid, unsettled.

owl > *noun* a nocturnal bird of prey with large eyes, a hooked beak, and typically a loud hooting call.

owlet > *noun* a young or small owl.

owlish > *adjective* **1** like an owl, especially in being wise or solemn. **2** (of glasses or eyes) resembling the large round eyes of an owl.
DERIVATIVES – **owlishly** *adverb*.

own > *adjective & pronoun* **1** (with a possessive) belonging or relating to the person specified. **2** done or produced by the person specified. **3** particular to the person or thing specified; individual. > *verb* **1** have as a possession. **2** formal admit or acknowledge that something is the case. **3** (**own up**) admit to having done something wrong or embarrassing.
IDIOMS – **be one's own man** (or **woman**) act independently. **come into its** (or **one's**) **own** become fully effective. **hold one's own** retain a position of strength in a challenging situation.
SYNONYMS – *verb* **1** boast, enjoy, have, possess.
COMBINATIONS – **own brand** Brit. a product manufactured specially for a retailer and bearing the retailer's name. **own goal** (in soccer) a goal scored when a player inadvertently strikes or deflects the ball into their own team's goal.

owner > *noun* a person who owns something.

DERIVATIVES – **ownership** *noun*.

SYNONYMS – holder, possessor, proprietor.

COMBINATIONS – **owner-occupier** Brit. a person who owns the house or flat in which they live.

owt /owt/ > *pronoun* N. English anything.

ORIGIN – variant of AUGHT.

ox > *noun* (pl. **oxen**) **1** a domesticated bovine animal kept for milk or meat; a cow or bull. **2** a castrated bull, especially as a draught animal.

COMBINATIONS – **ox-eye daisy** a daisy which has large white flowers with yellow centres. **oxhide** leather made from the hide of an ox.

oxalic acid /oksalik/ > *noun* Chemistry a poisonous crystalline organic acid, present in rhubarb leaves, wood sorrel, and other plants.

DERIVATIVES – **oxalate** /oksəlayt/ *noun*.

ORIGIN – from Greek *oxalis* 'wood sorrel'.

oxalis /oksəliss/ > *noun* a plant of a genus which includes the wood sorrel, typically having three-lobed leaves and white, yellow, or pink flowers.

ORIGIN – Greek, from *oxus* 'sour' (because of its sharp-tasting leaves).

oxbow > *noun* **1** a loop formed by a horseshoe bend in a river. **2** the U-shaped collar of an ox-yoke.

COMBINATIONS – **oxbow lake** a curved lake formed from a horseshoe bend in a river where the main stream has cut across the neck and no longer flows around the loop of the bend.

Oxbridge > *noun* Oxford and Cambridge universities regarded together.

oxen plural of **OX**.

Oxford > *noun* a type of lace-up shoe with a low heel.

ORIGIN – named after the city of *Oxford*.

Oxford bags > *plural noun* Brit. wide baggy trousers.

Oxford blue > *noun* Brit. **1** a dark blue, adopted as the colour of Oxford University. **2** a person who has represented Oxford University in a particular sport.

oxidant > *noun* an oxidising agent.

oxidation > *noun* Chemistry the process or result of oxidising or being oxidised.

DERIVATIVES – **oxidative** *adjective*.

oxide > *noun* Chemistry a compound of oxygen with another element or group.

oxidise (also **oxidize**) > *verb* **1** cause to combine with oxygen. **2** Chemistry cause to undergo a reaction in which electrons are lost to another substance or molecule. The opposite of REDUCE.

DERIVATIVES – **oxidisation** *noun* **oxidiser** *noun*.

COMBINATIONS – **oxidising agent** a substance that tends to bring about oxidation by being reduced and gaining electrons.

oxlip > *noun* a woodland primula with yellow flowers that hang down one side of the stem.

ORIGIN – Old English, from *oxa* 'ox' + *slyppe* 'slime', i.e. ox dung.

Oxon > *abbreviation* **1** Oxfordshire. **2** (in degree titles) of Oxford University.

Oxonian /oksōniən/ > *adjective* relating to Oxford or Oxford University. > *noun* **1** a person from Oxford. **2** a member of Oxford University.

ORIGIN – from *Oxonia* (Latinised name of Oxford, from its old form *Oxenford*).

oxtail > *noun* the tail of an ox (used in making soup).

oxter /okstər/ > *noun* Scottish & N. English a person's armpit.

oxyacetylene > *adjective* denoting welding or cutting techniques using a very hot flame produced by mixing acetylene and oxygen.

oxygen > *noun* a colourless, odourless, gaseous chemical element, forming about 20 per cent of the earth's atmosphere and essential to life.

COMBINATIONS – **oxygen bar** an establishment where people pay to inhale pure oxygen for its reputedly therapeutic effects.

ORIGIN – from French *principe oxygène* 'acidifying constituent' (because at first it was held to be the essential component of acids).

oxygenate > *verb* supply, treat, or enrich with oxygen.

DERIVATIVES – **oxygenated** *adjective* **oxygenation** *noun*.

oxygenator > *noun* Medicine **1** an apparatus for oxygenating the blood. **2** an aquatic plant which enriches the surrounding water with oxygen.

oxyhaemoglobin > *noun* Biochemistry a bright red substance formed by the combination of haemoglobin with oxygen, present in oxygenated blood.

oxymoron /oksimōron/ > *noun* a figure of speech or expressed idea in which apparently contradictory terms appear in conjunction (e.g. *bittersweet*).

DERIVATIVES – **oxymoronic** *adjective*.

ORIGIN – from Greek *oxumōros* 'pointedly foolish', from *oxus* 'sharp' + *mōros* 'foolish'.

oxytocin /oksitōsin/ > *noun* Biochemistry a hormone released by the pituitary gland that causes contraction of the womb during labour and stimulates the flow of milk into the breasts.

ORIGIN – Greek *oxutokia* 'sudden delivery', from *oxus* 'sharp' + *tokos* 'childbirth'.

oyez /ōyez/ (also **oyes**) > *exclamation* a call given by a public crier or a court officer to command silence and attention before an announcement.

ORIGIN – Old French, from *oir* 'hear'.

oyster > *noun* **1** a bivalve marine mollusc with a rough, flattened, irregularly oval shell, several kinds of which are farmed for food or pearls. **2** a shade of greyish white. **3** an oval morsel of meat on each side of the backbone in poultry.

WORDFINDER – angels on horseback (*oysters wrapped in bacon*), cultch (*material of which an oyster bed is formed*), mother-of-pearl (*smooth substance lining an oyster's shell*), spat (*oysters' spawn*), stew (*artificial oyster bed*).

IDIOMS – **the world is one's oyster** one is able to enjoy a very wide range of opportunities. [ORIGIN – from Shakespeare's *Merry Wives of Windsor* (II. ii. 5).]

COMBINATIONS – **oyster mushroom** an edible fungus with a greyish-brown oyster-shaped cap. **oyster sauce** a sauce made with oysters and soy sauce, used especially in oriental cookery.

ORIGIN – Old French *oistre*, from Greek *ostreon*; related to *osteon* 'bone' and *ostrakon* 'shell or tile'.

oystercatcher > *noun* a wading bird with black or black-and-white plumage and a strong orange-red bill, feeding chiefly on shellfish.

oy vey /oy vay/ > *exclamation* indicating dismay or grief (used mainly by Yiddish-speakers).

ORIGIN – Yiddish, 'oh woe'.

Oz > *noun & adjective* informal Australia or Australian.

oz > *abbreviation* ounce(s).

ORIGIN – from Italian *onza* 'ounce'.

ozone > *noun* **1** a pungent, toxic form of oxygen with three atoms in its molecule, formed in electrical discharges or by ultraviolet light. **2** informal invigorating fresh air.

DERIVATIVES – **ozonic** *adjective*.

COMBINATIONS – **ozone-friendly** (of manufactured products) not containing chemicals that are destructive to the ozone layer. **ozone hole** a region of marked thinning of the ozone layer in high latitudes, chiefly in winter, due to CFCs and other atmospheric pollutants. **ozone layer** a layer in the earth's stratosphere at an altitude of about 10 km (6.2 miles) containing a high concentration of ozone, which absorbs most of the ultraviolet radiation reaching the earth from the sun.

ORIGIN – German *Ozon*, from Greek *ozein* 'to smell'.

Ozzie > *noun* variant spelling of AUSSIE.

P¹ (also **p**) > *noun* (pl. **Ps** or **P's**) the sixteenth letter of the alphabet.

P² > *abbreviation* **1** (in tables of sports results) games played. **2** (on road signs and street plans) parking. > *symbol* the chemical element phosphorus.

p > *abbreviation* **1** page. **2** Brit. penny or pence.

PA > *abbreviation* **1** Pennsylvania. **2** Brit. personal assistant. **3** public address.

Pa > *abbreviation* pascal(s). > *symbol* the chemical element protactinium.

pa > *noun* informal father.
ORIGIN – abbreviation of **PAPA**.

p.a. > *abbreviation* per annum.

pa'anga /paaaanggə/ > *noun* (pl. same) the basic monetary unit of Tonga, equal to 100 seniti.
ORIGIN – Tongan.

pabulum /pabyooləm/ (also **pablum** /pabləm/) > *noun* bland intellectual matter or entertainment.
ORIGIN – first used in the sense 'food': Latin, from *pascere* 'to feed'.

paca /pakkə/ > *noun* a large, nocturnal South American rodent that has a reddish-brown coat patterned with white spots.
ORIGIN – Tupi.

pacamac > *noun* variant spelling of **PAKAMAC**.

pace¹ /payss/ > *noun* **1** a single step taken when walking or running. **2** a gait of a horse, especially one of the recognised trained gaits. **3** speed or rate of motion, development, or change. > *verb* **1** measure (a distance) by walking it and counting the number of steps taken. **2** walk at a steady speed, especially without a particular destination and as an expression of anxiety. **3** (of a trained horse) move with a distinctive lateral gait in which both legs on the same side are lifted together. **4** lead (another runner in a race) in order to establish a competitive speed. **5** (**pace oneself**) do something at a restrained and steady rate or speed. **6** move or develop (something) at a particular rate or speed.
IDIOMS – **keep pace with** move or progress at the same speed as. **off the pace** behind the leader in a race or contest. **put someone through their paces** make someone demonstrate their abilities. **stand** (or **stay**) **the pace** be able to keep up with others.
SYNONYMS – *noun* **1** step, stride.
ORIGIN – Latin *passus* 'stretch (of the leg)'.

pace² /paachay, paysi/ > *preposition* with due respect to.
ORIGIN – Latin, 'in peace'.

pacemaker > *noun* **1** (also **pacesetter**) a competitor who sets the pace at the beginning of a race or competition. **2** an artificial device for stimulating and regulating the heart muscle.

pacer > *noun* **1** a pacemaker. **2** chiefly US a horse bred or trained to pace.

pacey > *adjective* variant spelling of **PACY**.

pacha > *noun* variant spelling of **PASHA**.

pachinko /pəchingkō/ > *noun* a Japanese form of pinball.
ORIGIN – Japanese.

pachuco /pəchōōkō/ > *noun* (pl. **pachucos**) chiefly US a member of a gang of young Mexican–Americans.
ORIGIN – Mexican Spanish, meaning 'flashily dressed'.

pachyderm /pakkiderm/ > *noun* a very large mammal with thick skin, especially an elephant, rhinoceros, or hippopotamus.
ORIGIN – Greek *pakhudermos*, from *pakhus* 'thick' + *derma* 'skin'.

pacific > *adjective* **1** peaceful in character or intent. **2** (**Pacific**) relating to the Pacific Ocean. > *noun* (**the Pacific**) the Pacific Ocean.
DERIVATIVES – **pacifically** adverb.
ORIGIN – French *pacifique* or Latin *pacificus* 'peacemaking', from *pax* 'peace'.

pacifier > *noun* **1** a person or thing that pacifies. **2** N. Amer. a baby's dummy.

pacifism > *noun* the belief that disputes should be settled by peaceful means and that war and violence are unjustifiable.
DERIVATIVES – **pacifist** noun & adjective.

pacify > *verb* (**pacifies**, **pacified**) **1** calm the anger or agitation of. **2** bring peace to (a country or warring factions).
DERIVATIVES – **pacification** noun.
SYNONYMS – **1** appease, calm, conciliate, mollify, placate, soothe.
ANTONYMS – **1** provoke.

pack¹ > *noun* **1** a cardboard or paper container and the items inside it. **2** a collection of related documents. **3** Brit. a set of playing cards. **4** a rucksack. **5** a group of animals that live and hunt together. **6** (**Pack**) an organised group of Cub Scouts or Brownies. **7** Rugby a team's forwards considered as a group. **8** (**the pack**) the main body of competitors following the leader in a race or competition. **9** chiefly derogatory a group or set of similar things or people. **10** a hot or cold pad of absorbent material, used for treating an injury. > *verb* **1** fill (a suitcase or bag) with clothes and other items needed for travel. **2** place in a container for transport or storage. **3** be capable of being folded up for transport or storage. **4** informal carry (a gun). **5** cram a large number of things into. **6** cover, surround, or fill. **7** Rugby (of players) form a scrum.
IDIOMS – **pack a punch 1** hit with skill or force. **2** have a powerful effect. **pack in** informal give up (an activity or job). **pack off** informal send (someone) somewhere peremptorily or without much notice. **pack up** Brit. informal (of a machine) break down. **send packing** informal dismiss (someone) in a peremptory way.
DERIVATIVES – **packable** adjective **packer** noun.
SYNONYMS – *verb* **5** cram, jam, press, squeeze, stuff, wedge.
COMBINATIONS – **pack animal 1** an animal used to carry loads. **2** an animal that lives and hunts in a pack. **packed lunch** a cold lunch carried in a bag or box to work or school or on an excursion. **pack ice** (in polar seas) an expanse of large pieces of floating ice driven together into a mass. **packsack** N. Amer. a rucksack. **packsaddle** chiefly N. Amer. a saddle adapted for securing the loads carried by a pack animal.

pack² > *verb* fill (a jury or committee) with people likely to support a particular verdict or decision.
ORIGIN – probably from the obsolete verb *pact* 'enter into an agreement with'.

package > *noun* **1** an object or group of objects wrapped in paper or packed in a box. **2** N. Amer. a packet. **3** (also **package deal**) a set of proposals or terms offered or agreed as a whole. **4** informal a package holiday. **5** Computing a collection of related programs or subroutines. > *verb* **1** put into a box or wrapping. **2** present in an advantageous way. **3** combine (various products) for sale as one unit. **4** commission and produce (a book) to sell as a complete product to publishers.
DERIVATIVES – **packaged** adjective **packager** noun.
COMBINATIONS – **package holiday** (also **package tour**) a holiday organised by a travel agent, with arrangements for transport and accommodation made at an inclusive price.

packaging > *noun* materials used to wrap or protect goods.

pack drill > *noun* a military punishment of marching up and down carrying full equipment.
IDIOMS – **no names, no pack drill** punishment will be prevented if names and details are not mentioned.

packed > *adjective* (of a place) crowded or filled with people.

packet > *noun* **1** a paper or cardboard container. **2** Computing a block of data transmitted across a network. **3** (**a packet**) informal, chiefly Brit. a large sum of money. **4** (also **packet boat**) a boat travelling at regular intervals between two ports, originally carrying mail and later taking passengers. > *verb* (**packeted**, **packeting**) wrap up in a packet.
COMBINATIONS – **packet switching** Computing & Telecommunications data transmission in which a message is broken into parts and reassembled at the destination. **packhorse** a horse used to carry loads.

packetise (also **packetize**) > *verb* Computing separate (data) into units for transmission in a packet-switching network.

packing > *noun* **1** the action or process of packing something. **2** material used to protect fragile goods in transit. **3** material used to seal a join or assist in lubricating an axle.
COMBINATIONS – **packing case** a large, strong box for transportation or storage.

pact > *noun* a formal agreement between individuals or parties.
SYNONYMS – compact, contract, covenant, deal, treaty.
ORIGIN – Latin *pactum* 'something agreed'.

pacy (also **pacey**) > *adjective* (**pacier**, **paciest**) fast-moving.

pad¹ > *noun* **1** a thick piece of soft or absorbent material. **2** the fleshy underpart of an animal's foot or of a human finger. **3** a protective guard worn over a part of the body by a sports player. **4** a number of sheets of blank paper fastened together at one edge. **5** a flat-topped structure or area used for helicopter take-off and landing or for rocket-launching. **6** informal a person's home. > *verb* (**padded**, **padding**) **1** fill or cover with a pad. **2** (**pad up**) (in cricket) put on protective pads. **3** (**pad out**) lengthen (a speech or piece of writing) with unnecessary material. **4** chiefly N. Amer. defraud by adding false items to (an expenses claim or bill).
DERIVATIVES – **padded** *adjective* **padding** *noun*.

pad² > *verb* (**padded**, **padding**) walk with steady steps making a soft, dull sound. > *noun* the sound of such steps.
ORIGIN – Low German *padden* 'tread, go along a path'.

paddle¹ > *noun* **1** a short pole with a broad blade at one or both ends, used to propel a small boat through the water. **2** a short-handled bat such as that used in table tennis. **3** any paddle-shaped instrument used for stirring or mixing. **4** each of the boards fitted round the circumference of a paddle wheel or mill wheel. **5** the fin or flipper of an aquatic mammal or bird. **6** a spell of paddling. > *verb* **1** propel (a boat) with a paddle or paddles. **2** (of a bird or other animal) swim with short fast strokes.
DERIVATIVES – **paddler** *noun*.
COMBINATIONS – **paddle steamer** (also **paddle boat**) a boat propelled by paddle wheels. **paddle wheel** a large steam-driven wheel with paddles round its circumference, attached to the side or stern of a ship and propelling the ship by its rotation.

paddle² > *verb* walk with bare feet in shallow water. > *noun* a spell of paddling.
DERIVATIVES – **paddler** *noun*.
COMBINATIONS – **paddling pool** a shallow artificial pool for children to paddle in.

paddock > *noun* **1** a small field or enclosure for horses. **2** an enclosure adjoining a racecourse or track where horses or cars are gathered and displayed before a race. **3** Austral./NZ a field or plot of land enclosed by fencing or defined by natural boundaries. > *verb* keep or enclose (a horse) in a paddock.

Paddy > *noun* (pl. **Paddies**) informal, often offensive an Irishman.
ORIGIN – familiar form of the Irish given name *Padraig*.

paddy¹ > *noun* (pl. **paddies**) **1** a field where rice is grown. **2** rice still in the husk.
ORIGIN – Malay.

paddy² > *noun* Brit. informal a fit of temper.
ORIGIN – from **Paddy**; associated with obsolete *paddywhack* 'Irishman given to brawling'.

paddy wagon > *noun* N. Amer. informal a police van.

padlock > *noun* a detachable lock hanging by a pivoted hook on the object fastened. > *verb* secure with a padlock.

padre /paadray/ > *noun* informal a chaplain in the armed services.
ORIGIN – Italian, Spanish, and Portuguese, 'father, priest'.

padsaw > *noun* a small saw with a narrow blade, for cutting curves.

paean /peeən/ > *noun* a song of praise or triumph.
ORIGIN – Greek *paian* 'hymn of thanksgiving to the god Apollo' (who was invoked by the name *Paian*, originally the Homeric name for the physician of the gods).

paediatrician /peediətrish'n/ (US **pediatrician**) > *noun* a doctor who specialises in paediatrics.

paediatrics /peediatriks/ (US **pediatrics**) > *plural noun* (treated as sing.) the branch of medicine concerned with children and their diseases.
DERIVATIVES – **paediatric** *adjective*.
ORIGIN – from Greek *pais* 'child' + *iatros* 'physician'.

paedophile /peedəfīl/ (US **pedophile**) > *noun* a person who is sexually attracted to children.
DERIVATIVES – **paedophilia** *noun* **paedophiliac** *adjective & noun*.

paella /pīellə/ > *noun* a Spanish dish of rice, saffron, chicken, seafood, and vegetables, traditionally cooked in a large shallow pan.
ORIGIN – Catalan, from Old French *paele*, from Latin *patella* 'pan'.

paeony > *noun* variant spelling of **PEONY**.

pagan > *noun* a person holding religious beliefs other than those of the main world religions. > *adjective* relating to pagans or their beliefs.
DERIVATIVES – **paganism** *noun*.

wordpower facts
Pagan
The word **pagan** is ultimately from the same root as **peasant**, Latin *pagus* 'country district'. The sense development of **pagan** is a strange and unexpected one. Its source, Latin *paganus* 'rustic, country dweller' was used by Roman soldiers to mean 'civilian'; early Christians called themselves *milites* or 'soldiers' and used *paganus* to mean 'heathen', from the idea of someone who was not enlisted in the 'army' of Christ.

page¹ > *noun* **1** one side of a leaf of a book, magazine, or newspaper, or the material written or printed on it. **2** both sides of such a leaf considered as a single unit. **3** Computing a section of data displayed on a screen at one time. **4** a particular episode considered as part of a longer history. > *verb* **1** (**page through**) leaf through. **2** Computing move through and display (text) one page at a time. **3** paginate (a book).
WORDFINDER – flyleaf (*blank page at the start or end of a book*), gatefold (*large page folded to same size as other pages*), paginate (*number the pages of a book*), recto (*right-hand page of an open book*), verso (*left-hand page*).
COMBINATIONS – **Page Three** Brit. trademark a feature which formerly appeared daily on page three of the *Sun* newspaper, comprising a picture of a topless young woman.
ORIGIN – Latin *pagina*, from *pangere* 'fasten'.

page² > *noun* **1** a boy or young man employed in a hotel or club to run errands,

open doors, etc. **2** a young boy attending a bride at a wedding. **3** *historical* a boy in training for knighthood, ranking next below a squire in the personal service of a knight. **4** *historical* a man or boy employed as the personal attendant of a person of rank. > *verb* **1** summon over a public address system. **2** contact by means of a pager.
ORIGIN – Old French, from Greek *paidion* 'small boy'.

pageant /pajənt/ > *noun* **1** an entertainment consisting of a procession of people in elaborate costumes, or an outdoor performance of a historical scene. **2** (also **beauty pageant**) N. Amer. a beauty contest. **3** *historical* a scene erected on a fixed stage or moving vehicle as a public show.

pageantry > *noun* elaborate display or ceremony.

pageboy > *noun* **1** a page in a hotel or attending a bride at a wedding. **2** a woman's hairstyle consisting of a shoulder-length bob with the ends rolled under.

pager > *noun* a small radio device which bleeps or vibrates to inform the wearer that someone wishes to contact them or that it has received a short text message.

paginate /pajinayt/ > *noun* assign numbers to the pages of a book, journal, etc.
DERIVATIVES – **pagination** noun.

pagoda /pəgōdə/ > *noun* a Hindu or Buddhist temple or sacred building, typically having a many-tiered tower.
ORIGIN – Portuguese *pagode*, perhaps from Persian.

paid past and past participle of **PAY**[1].
IDIOMS – **put paid to** *informal* abruptly stop or destroy.
COMBINATIONS – **paid-up 1** with all subscriptions or charges paid in full. **2** committed to a cause, group, etc.: *a fully paid-up postmodernist*.

pail > *noun* a bucket.

pain > *noun* **1** a strongly unpleasant bodily sensation such as is caused by illness or injury. **2** mental suffering or distress. **3** (also **pain in the neck** or *vulgar slang* **arse**) *informal* an annoying or tedious person or thing. **4** (**pains**) careful effort. > *verb* cause mental or physical pain to.
WORDFINDER – anaesthetic (*a drug making one unable to feel pain*), analgesic, anodyne (*medicine relieving pain*), masochist (*a person who enjoys experiencing pain*), neuralgia (*intense pain along a nerve*), sadist (*a person who enjoys inflicting pain*).
IDIOMS – **on** (or **under**) **pain of** on penalty of.
SYNONYMS – *noun* **1** aching, discomfort, soreness. **2** affliction, anguish, distress, suffering, torment.

wordpower facts
Pain
The word **pain** entered English via Old French *peine* from Latin *poena* 'penalty, punishment, pain'. *Poena* is the source of the English words **impunity, penal, penalty, pine**[2], and **punish**: pain originally had the meaning 'penalty, punishment' as well as its modern senses. This idea survives only in the phrase **on** or **under pain of**.

pained > *adjective* showing or suffering pain, especially mental pain.

painful > *adjective* **1** affected with or causing physical pain. **2** causing distress or trouble.
DERIVATIVES – **painfully** adverb.
SYNONYMS – **1** aching, hurting, sore, tender. **2** distressing, disturbing, traumatic, upsetting.

painkiller > *noun* a medicine for relieving pain.

painless > *adjective* **1** not causing pain. **2** involving little effort or stress.
DERIVATIVES – **painlessly** adverb.

painstaking > *adjective* done with or using great care and thoroughness.
DERIVATIVES – **painstakingly** adverb.
SYNONYMS – careful, diligent, meticulous, scrupulous, thorough.
ANTONYMS – careless, sloppy.

paint > *noun* **1** a substance which is spread over a surface to give a thin decorative or protective coating. **2** an act of painting. > *verb* **1** apply paint to. **2** apply (a liquid) to a surface with a brush. **3** depict or produce with paint. **4** give a description of (something).
IDIOMS – **paint the town red** *informal* go out and enjoy oneself flamboyantly.
COMBINATIONS – **paintball** a combat game in which participants shoot capsules of paint at each other with air guns. **paintbox** a box holding a palette of dry paints for painting pictures. **paintbrush** a brush for applying paint. **painted lady** a butterfly that has predominantly orange-brown wings with darker markings. **paint shop** the part of a factory where goods are painted. **paintwork** *chiefly Brit.* painted surfaces in a building or on a vehicle.
ORIGIN – from Old French *peindre*, from Latin *pingere* 'to paint'.

painter[1] > *noun* **1** an artist who paints pictures. **2** a person who paints buildings.

painter[2] > *noun* a rope attached to the bow of a boat for tying it to a quay.

painterly > *adjective* **1** of or appropriate to a painter; artistic. **2** using paint well.

painting > *noun* **1** the action of painting. **2** a painted picture.
WORDFINDER – *painting techniques and*

media: aquarelle, chiaroscuro, encaustic, fresco, gouache, grisaille, impasto, oils, tempera, watercolour.

pair > *noun* **1** a set of two things used together or regarded as a unit. **2** an article consisting of two joined or corresponding parts. **3** two people or animals related in some way or considered together. **4** two opposing members of a parliament who absent themselves from voting by mutual arrangement. > *verb* **1** join or connect to form a pair. **2** (**pair off** or **up**) form a couple.
DERIVATIVES – **paired** adjective **pairing** noun.
ORIGIN – Old French *paire*, from Latin *paria* 'equal things'.

paisa /pīsaa/ > *noun* (pl. **paise** /pīsay/) a monetary unit of India, Pakistan, and Nepal, equal to one hundredth of a rupee.
ORIGIN – Hindi.

paisley /payzli/ > *noun* a distinctive intricate pattern of curved feather-shaped figures based on an Indian pine cone design.
ORIGIN – named after the town of *Paisley* in Scotland, where a woven woollen cloth with this design was made.

Paiute /pīoot/ > *noun* (pl. same or **Paiutes**) a member of either of two American Indian peoples (the **Southern Paiute** and the **Northern Paiute**) of the western US.
ORIGIN – Spanish *Payuchi, Payuta*.

pajamas > *plural noun* US spelling of **PYJAMAS**.

pakamac /pakkəmak/ (also **pacamac**) > *noun* Brit. a lightweight plastic mackintosh that can be folded up into a small pack when not required.

pak choi /pak **choy**/ (also N. Amer. **bok choy**) > *noun* a Chinese cabbage with smooth-edged tapering leaves.
ORIGIN – Chinese, 'white vegetable'.

Pakeha /paakihaa/ > *noun* NZ a white New Zealander, as opposed to a Maori.
ORIGIN – Maori.

Paki > *noun* (pl. **Pakis**) Brit. informal, offensive a Pakistani.

Pakistani /paakistaani, pakkistanni/ > *noun* a person from Pakistan. > *adjective* relating to Pakistan or Pakistanis.

pakora /pəkorə/ > *noun* (in Indian cookery) a piece of battered and deep-fried vegetable or meat.
ORIGIN – Hindi.

PAL > *abbreviation* phase alternate line (the television broadcasting system used in most of Europe).

pal informal > *noun* a friend. > *verb* (**palled, palling**) (**pal up**) form a friendship.
ORIGIN – Romany, 'brother, mate', from Sanskrit.

palace > *noun* a large, impressive building forming the official residence of a sovereign, president, archbishop, etc.

ORIGIN – Old French *paleis*, from the name of the *Palatine* hill in Rome, where the house of the emperor was situated.

paladin /**pal**ədin/ > *noun* historical **1** any of the twelve bravest knights of Charlemagne's court. **2** a brave, chivalrous knight.

ORIGIN – French, from Latin *palatinus* 'of the palace'.

Palaearctic /paliˈaark̄tik, paylīˈaark̄tik/ (also chiefly US **Palearctic**) > *adjective* Zoology relating to a region comprising Eurasia north of the Himalayas, together with North Africa and part of the Arabian peninsula.

palaeo- /**pal**iō, **pay**liō/ (US **paleo-**) > *combining form* older or ancient: *Palaeolithic*.

ORIGIN – from Greek *palaios* 'ancient'.

Palaeocene /**pal**iōseen, **pay**liōseen/ (US **Paleocene**) > *adjective* Geology relating to the earliest epoch of the Tertiary period (between the Cretaceous period and the Eocene epoch, about 65 to 56.5 million years ago), a time of rapid development of mammals.

ORIGIN – from Greek *palaios* 'ancient' + *kainos* 'new'.

palaeography /paliˈogrəfi, payliˈogrəfi/ (US **paleography**) > *noun* the study of ancient writing systems and manuscripts.

DERIVATIVES – **palaeographer** *noun* **palaeographic** *adjective*.

Palaeolithic /paliəˈlithik, payliəˈlithik/ (US **Paleolithic**) > *adjective* Archaeology relating to the early phase of the Stone Age, up to the end of the glacial period.

ORIGIN – from Greek *palaios* 'ancient' + *lithos* 'stone'.

palaeontology /paliontˈoləji, paylion-ˈtoləji/ (US **paleontology**) > *noun* the branch of science concerned with fossil animals and plants.

DERIVATIVES – **palaeontological** *adjective* **palaeontologist** *noun*.

ORIGIN – from Greek *palaios* 'ancient' + *onta* 'beings'.

Palaeozoic /paliəˈzōik, payliəˈzōik/ (US **Paleozoic**) > *adjective* Geology relating to the era between the Precambrian aeon and the Mesozoic era, about 570 to 245 million years ago, which ended with the rise to dominance of the reptiles.

ORIGIN – from Greek *palaios* 'ancient' + *zōē* 'life'.

palaestra /pəˈleestrə, pəˈlīstrə/ (also **palestra** /pəˈlestrə/) > *noun* (in ancient Greece and Rome) a wrestling school or gymnasium.

ORIGIN – Greek *palaistra*, from *palaiein* 'wrestle'.

palais /**pal**ay/ > *noun* Brit. a public hall for dancing.

ORIGIN – from French *palais de danse* 'dancing hall'.

palanquin /palənˈkeen/ (also **palankeen**) > *noun* (in India and the East) a covered litter for one passenger.

ORIGIN – Portuguese *palanquim*, from a Sanskrit word meaning 'bed, couch'.

palatable /**pal**ətəb'l/ > *adjective* **1** pleasant to taste. **2** (of an action or proposal) acceptable.

DERIVATIVES – **palatability** *noun* **palatably** *adverb*.

SYNONYMS – **1** appetising, edible, tasty.

palatal /**pal**ət'l/ > *adjective* **1** relating to the palate. **2** Phonetics (of a speech sound) made by placing the blade of the tongue against or near the hard palate (e.g. γ in *yes*). > *noun* Phonetics a palatal sound.

DERIVATIVES – **palatalise** (also **palatalize**) *verb*.

palate > *noun* **1** the roof of the mouth, separating the cavities of the mouth and nose in vertebrates. **2** a person's ability to distinguish between and appreciate different flavours. **3** a person's sense of appreciation or discrimination.

USAGE – do not confuse **palate** and **palette**: the **palate** is the roof of the mouth; a **palette**, on the other hand, is an artist's board for mixing colours.

ORIGIN – Latin *palatum*.

palatial > *adjective* resembling a palace, especially in being spacious or grand.

DERIVATIVES – **palatially** *adverb*.

SYNONYMS – grand, majestic, splendid, stately.

palatinate /pəˈlattinət/ > *noun* historical **1** a territory under the jurisdiction of a Count Palatine. **2** (**the Palatinate**) the territory of the German Empire ruled by the Count Palatine of the Rhine.

palatine /**pal**ətīn/ > *adjective* chiefly historical **1** (of an official or feudal lord) having local authority that elsewhere belongs only to a sovereign. **2** (of a territory) subject to such authority.

COMBINATIONS – **Count Palatine** historical **1** a feudal lord having royal authority within part of a kingdom. **2** a high official of the Holy Roman Empire with royal authority within his domain.

ORIGIN – French, from Latin *palatinus* 'of the palace'.

palaver /pəˈlaavər/ informal > *noun* **1** prolonged and tedious fuss or discussion. **2** dated a parley or improvised conference between two sides. > *verb* talk unnecessarily at length.

ORIGIN – Portuguese *palavra* 'word', from Latin *parabola* 'comparison'.

palazzo /pəˈlatsō/ > *noun* (pl. **palazzos** or **palazzi** /pəˈlatsee/) a large, grand building, especially in Italy.

COMBINATIONS – **palazzo pants** women's loose wide-legged trousers.

ORIGIN – Italian, 'palace'.

pale¹ > *adjective* **1** containing little colour; light in colour or shade. **2** (of a person's face) having little colour on account of shock, fear, illness, etc. **3** unimpressive or inferior: *a pale imitation.* > *verb* **1** become pale in one's face. **2** seem or become less important.

DERIVATIVES – **palely** *adverb* **paleness** *noun*.

SYNONYMS – *adjective* **2** ashen, drained, pallid, pasty, wan. *verb* **1** blanch, whiten. **2** dim, diminish, dwindle, fade.

ANTONYMS – *adjective* **1** dark. **2** flushed.

ORIGIN – Old French, from Latin *pallidus*.

pale² > *noun* **1** a wooden stake used with others to form a fence. **2** a boundary. **3** archaic or historical an area that is within set bounds or subject to a particular jurisdiction. **4** Heraldry a broad vertical stripe down the middle of a shield.

IDIOMS – **beyond the pale** outside the bounds of acceptable behaviour.

ORIGIN – Old French *pal*, from Latin *palus* 'stake'.

wordpower facts

Pale

The common phrase **beyond the pale** has an interesting background. A **pale** is a stake used with others to form a fence, and hence also a limit or boundary. Historically the word was applied to various districts or territories, in particular to the area of Ireland under English jurisdiction before the whole island was conquered in the 16th century, and to the territory of Calais in France when it was controlled by the English. The earliest writer to refer to the Pale in Ireland as such (1547) draws the contrast between Ireland's two parts, the English Pale and the 'wyld Irysh': the area *beyond the pale* would have been regarded as dangerous and uncivilised by the English. Although other phrases such as *within* or *outside the pale of* had long been used, **beyond the pale** is first recorded in Charlotte Brontë's *Jane Eyre* (1847): 'I was put beyond the pale of his favour'. An 1885 use, 'Unknown, doubtful Americans…are beyond the pale', has the characteristic modern idea of 'outside the bounds of acceptability'.

Palearctic > *adjective* chiefly US variant spelling of **PALAEARCTIC**.

paleface > *noun* a name supposedly used by North American Indians for a white person.

paleo- > *combining form* US spelling of **PALAEO-**.

Palestinian /paləstinniən/ > *adjective* relating to Palestine. > *noun* a member or descendant of the native Arab population of Palestine.

palestra > *noun* variant spelling of **PALAESTRA**.

palette /palit/ > *noun* **1** a thin board on which an artist lays and mixes colours. **2** the range of colours used by an artist. **3** the range of tonal colour in a musical piece.

COMBINATIONS – **palette knife 1** a thin steel blade with a handle, for mixing colours or applying or removing paint. **2** Brit. a kitchen knife with a long, blunt, flexible round-ended blade.

ORIGIN – French, 'little shovel'.

palfrey /**pawl**fri/ > *noun* (pl. **palfreys**) archaic a docile horse ridden especially by women.

ORIGIN – Old French *palefrei*, from Greek *para* 'beside, extra' + Latin *veredus* 'light horse'.

palimony /palimoni/ > *noun* informal, chiefly N. Amer. compensation made by one member of an unmarried couple to the other after separation.

ORIGIN – from **PAL** + **ALIMONY**.

palimpsest /palimpsest/ > *noun* **1** a parchment or other surface on which writing has been applied over effaced earlier writing. **2** something reused or altered but still bearing traces of its earlier form.

ORIGIN – from Greek *palin* 'again' + *psēstos* 'rubbed smooth'.

palindrome /palindrōm/ > *noun* a word or sequence that reads the same backwards as forwards, e.g. *madam*.

DERIVATIVES – **palindromic** /palindrommik/ *adjective*.

ORIGIN – from Greek *palindromos* 'running back again'.

paling /**pay**ling/ > *noun* **1** a fence made from stakes. **2** a stake used in such a fence.

palinode /palinōd/ > *noun* a poem in which the poet retracts a view or sentiment expressed in a former poem.

ORIGIN – from Greek *palin* 'again' + *ōidē* 'song'.

palisade /palisayd/ > *noun* **1** a fence of stakes or railings forming an enclosure or defence. **2** (**palisades**) US a line of high cliffs.

ORIGIN – French *palissade*, from Provençal *palissa* 'paling'.

pall¹ /pawl/ > *noun* **1** a cloth spread over a coffin, hearse, or tomb. **2** a dark cloud of smoke, dust, etc. **3** an enveloping air of gloom or fear. **4** an ecclesiastical pallium.

COMBINATIONS – **pall-bearer** a person helping to carry or escorting a coffin at a funeral.

ORIGIN – Latin *pallium* 'covering, cloak'.

pall² /pawl/ > *verb* become less appealing or interesting through familiarity.

ORIGIN – shortening of **APPAL**.

Palladian /pəlaydiən/ > *adjective* in the neoclassical style of the 16th-century Italian architect Andrea Palladio, influential also in the 18th century.

DERIVATIVES – **Palladianism** noun.

palladium /pəlaydiəm/ > *noun* a rare silvery-white metallic chemical element resembling platinum.

ORIGIN – from *Pallas*, an asteroid discovered (1803) just before the element.

pallet¹ > *noun* **1** a straw mattress. **2** a crude or makeshift bed.

ORIGIN – Old French *paillete*, from *paille* 'straw'.

pallet² > *noun* **1** a portable platform on which goods can be moved, stacked, and stored. **2** a flat wooden blade with a handle, used to shape clay or plaster. **3** an artist's palette.

DERIVATIVES – **palletise** (also **palletize**) verb.

ORIGIN – French, 'little blade'.

pallia plural of **PALLIUM**.

palliasse /paliass/ > *noun* a straw mattress.

ORIGIN – French *paillasse*, from *paille* 'straw'.

palliate /paliayt/ > *verb* **1** make (the symptoms of a disease) less severe without removing the cause. **2** make (something bad) less severe.

DERIVATIVES – **palliation** noun.

ORIGIN – Latin *palliare* 'to cloak', from *pallium* 'cloak'.

palliative /paliətiv/ > *adjective* relieving pain or alleviating a problem without dealing with the cause. > *noun* a palliative remedy or medicine.

pallid > *adjective* **1** pale, especially because of poor health. **2** feeble or insipid.

SYNONYMS – **1** ashen, pale, pasty, wan.

ORIGIN – Latin *pallidus* 'pale'.

pallium /paliəm/ > *noun* (pl. **pallia** /paliə/ or **palliums**) **1** a clerical garment conferred by the Pope on an archbishop, consisting of a narrow circular band placed round the shoulders. **2** a man's large rectangular cloak worn in antiquity.

ORIGIN – Latin, 'covering, cloak'.

pall-mall /palmal/ > *noun* a 16th- and 17th-century game in which a ball was driven through an iron ring suspended at the end of a long alley.

ORIGIN – from Italian *palla* 'ball' + *maglio* 'mallet'.

pallor > *noun* an unhealthy pale appearance.

ORIGIN – Latin, from *pallere* 'be pale'.

pally > *adjective* (**pallier**, **palliest**) informal having a close, friendly relationship.

palm¹ > *noun* **1** (also **palm tree**) an evergreen tree with a crown of very long feathered or fan-shaped leaves, growing in warm regions. **2** a leaf of a palm awarded as a prize or viewed as a symbol of victory.

WORDFINDER – raffia (*palm fibre*), sago (*starch obtained from a palm*).

COMBINATIONS – **Palm Sunday** the Sunday before Easter, on which Christ's entry into Jerusalem is celebrated by processions in which branches of palms are carried. **palm wine** an alcoholic drink made from fermented palm sap.

ORIGIN – Latin *palma* 'palm (of a hand)', its leaf being likened to a spread hand.

palm² > *noun* the inner surface of the hand between the wrist and fingers. > *verb* **1** conceal (a small object) in the hand, especially as part of a trick. **2** (**palm off**) sell or dispose of by misrepresentation or fraud. **3** (**palm off with**) informal persuade (someone) to accept (something) by deception. **4** deflect (a ball) with the palm of the hand.

IDIOMS – **in the palm of one's hand** under one's control or influence. **read someone's palm** tell someone's fortune by looking at the lines on their palm.

ORIGIN – Latin *palma*.

palmate /palmayt/ > *adjective* chiefly Botany & Zoology shaped like an open hand with a number of lobes resembling fingers.

palmer > *noun* historical a pilgrim, especially one who had returned from the Holy Land with a palm branch or leaf as a sign of having undertaken the pilgrimage.

palmetto /palmettō/ > *noun* (pl. **palmettos**) an American palm with large fan-shaped leaves.

ORIGIN – Spanish *palmito* 'small palm'.

palmier /palmiay/ > *noun* (pl. pronunc. same) a crisp sweet pastry shaped like a palm leaf.

ORIGIN – French, 'palm tree'.

palmistry > *noun* the supposed interpretation of a person's character or prediction of their future by examining the palm of their hand.

DERIVATIVES – **palmist** noun.

palmtop > *noun* a computer small and light enough to be held in one hand.

palmy > *adjective* (**palmier**, **palmiest**) comfortable and prosperous: *the palmy days of the 1970s*.

palomino /paləmeenō/ > *noun* (pl. **palominos**) a pale golden or tan-coloured horse with a white mane and tail.

ORIGIN – Spanish, 'young pigeon'.

palp /palp/ > *noun* Zoology each of a pair of elongated segmented feelers near the mouth of an arthropod.

ORIGIN – Latin *palpus*, from *palpare* 'to feel'.

palpable /palpəb'l/ > *adjective* **1** able to be touched or felt. **2** plain to see or comprehend.

DERIVATIVES – **palpably** adverb.

SYNONYMS – **1** solid, substantial, tangible, touchable. **2** appreciable, discernible, noticeable, perceptible.

ORIGIN – Latin *palpabilis*, from *palpare* 'feel, touch gently'.

palpate /pal**payt**/ > *verb* examine (a part of the body) by touch, especially for medical purposes.

DERIVATIVES – **palpation** *noun*.

palpitate /**pal**pitayt/ > *verb* **1** (of the heart) beat rapidly, strongly, or irregularly. **2** shake; tremble.

SYNONYMS – **1** flutter, pound, pulsate, throb.

ORIGIN – Latin *palpitare* 'touch gently'.

palpitation > *noun* **1** throbbing or trembling. **2** (**palpitations**) a noticeably rapid, strong, or irregular heartbeat.

palpus /**pal**pəss/ > *noun* (pl. **palpi** /**pal**pī/) another term for PALP.

palsy /**pawl**zi/ > *noun* (pl. **palsies**) dated paralysis, especially when accompanied by involuntary tremors. > *verb* (**be palsied**) be affected with palsy.

ORIGIN – Old French *paralisie*, from Latin *paralysis*.

palter /**pawl**tər/ > *verb* archaic **1** speak or act in an evasive way. **2** (**palter with**) trifle with.

paltry > *adjective* (**paltrier**, **paltriest**) **1** (of an amount) very small or meagre. **2** petty; trivial.

DERIVATIVES – **paltriness** *noun*.

SYNONYMS – **1** meagre, scanty, small, trifling.

ORIGIN – probably from dialect *pelt* 'rubbish'.

palynology /pali**noll**əji/ > *noun* the study of pollen grains and other spores, especially as found in archaeological or geological deposits.

DERIVATIVES – **palynological** *adjective* **palynologist** *noun*.

ORIGIN – from Greek *palunein* 'sprinkle'.

pampas /**pam**pəss/ > *noun* (treated as sing. or pl.) extensive treeless plains in South America south of the Amazon.

COMBINATIONS – **pampas grass** a tall South American grass with silky flowering plumes.

ORIGIN – Quechua, 'plain'.

pamper > *verb* indulge (someone) with a great deal of attention and comfort.

SYNONYMS – coddle, cosset, indulge, mollycoddle, spoil.

ORIGIN – first meaning 'cram with food': probably from Low German or Dutch.

pamphlet /**pam**flit/ > *noun* a small booklet or leaflet containing information or arguments about a single subject. > *verb* (**pamphleted**, **pamphleting**) distribute pamphlets to.

ORIGIN – from *Pamphilet*, the familiar name of the 12th-century Latin love poem

Pamphilus, seu de Amore: the poem was so popular that it was widely reproduced, and eventually its title came to refer to any booklet or leaflet.

pamphleteer > *noun* a writer of pamphlets, especially controversial political ones.

DERIVATIVES – **pamphleteering** *noun*.

pan¹ > *noun* **1** a metal container for cooking food in. **2** a bowl fitted at either end of a pair of scales. **3** a shallow bowl in which gravel and mud is shaken and washed by people seeking gold. **4** Brit. the bowl of a toilet. **5** a hollow in the ground in which water collects or in which salt is deposited after evaporation. **6** a part of the lock that held the priming in old types of gun. **7** a steel drum. > *verb* (**panned**, **panning**) **1** informal criticise severely. **2** wash gravel in a pan to separate out (gold). **3** (**pan out**) end up or conclude.

IDIOMS – **go down the pan** informal fail or be totally useless.

COMBINATIONS – **pan-fry** fry in a pan in shallow fat.

pan² > *verb* (**panned**, **panning**) swing (a video or film camera) to give a panoramic effect or follow a subject. > *noun* a panning movement.

ORIGIN – abbreviation of PANORAMA.

pan- > *combining form* including everything or everyone, especially the whole of a continent, people, etc: *pan-African*.

ORIGIN – from Greek *pas* 'all'.

panacea /pannə**see**ə/ > *noun* a solution or remedy for all difficulties or diseases.

ORIGIN – Greek *panakeia*, from *panakēs* 'all-healing'.

panache /pə**nash**/ > *noun* flamboyant confidence of style or manner.

SYNONYMS – dash, elan, flair, style, verve.

ORIGIN – first meaning 'tuft or plume of feathers': from Latin *pinnaculum* 'little feather'.

panama /**pann**əmaa/ > *noun* a man's wide-brimmed hat of straw-like material, originally made from the leaves of a tropical palm tree.

ORIGIN – named after the country of *Panama*.

Panamanian /pannə**may**niən/ > *noun* a person from Panama in Central America. > *adjective* relating to Panama.

panatella /pannə**tell**ə/ > *noun* a long, thin cigar.

ORIGIN – Latin American Spanish *panatela* 'long, thin biscuit'.

pancake > *noun* **1** a thin, flat cake of batter, fried and turned in a pan. **2** theatrical make-up consisting of a flat solid layer of compressed powder. > *verb* **1** (of an aircraft) make a pancake landing. **2** informal flatten or become flattened.

WORDFINDER – *kinds of pancake:* blini, blintze, chapatti, crêpe, crêpe Suzette, galette, latke, tortilla.

IDIOMS – (as) **flat as a pancake** completely flat.

COMBINATIONS – **Pancake Day** Shrove Tuesday, when pancakes are traditionally eaten. **pancake landing** an emergency landing in which an aircraft levels out close to the ground and drops vertically with its undercarriage still retracted. **pancake race** a race in which each competitor must toss a pancake from a pan as they run.

pancetta /pan**chett**ə/ > *noun* Italian cured belly of pork.

ORIGIN – Italian, 'little belly'.

panchromatic > *adjective* (of black-and-white photographic film) sensitive to all visible colours of the spectrum.

pancreas /**pang**kriəss/ > *noun* (pl. **pancreases**) a large gland behind the stomach which secretes digestive enzymes into the duodenum and produces the hormone insulin.

DERIVATIVES – **pancreatic** *adjective*.

ORIGIN – Greek *pankreas*, from *pan* 'all' + *kreas* 'flesh'.

pancreatitis /pangkriə**tī**tiss/ > *noun* Medicine inflammation of the pancreas.

panda > *noun* **1** (also **giant panda**) a large black-and-white bear-like mammal native to bamboo forests in China. **2** (also **red panda**) a raccoon-like Himalayan mammal with reddish-brown fur and a bushy tail.

COMBINATIONS – **panda car** Brit. informal a small police patrol car (originally black and white or blue and white).

ORIGIN – Nepali.

pandanus /pan**day**nəss, pan**dann**əss/ > *noun* a tropical tree or shrub with a twisted stem, long, spiny leaves that yield fibre, and fibrous edible fruit.

ORIGIN – Malay.

pandemic /pan**demm**ik/ > *adjective* (of a disease) prevalent over a whole country or large part of the world. > *noun* an outbreak of such a disease.

ORIGIN – Greek *pandēmos*, from *pan* 'all' + *dēmos* 'people'.

pandemonium /pandi**mō**niəm/ > *noun* wild and noisy disorder or confusion.

SYNONYMS – bedlam, chaos, hullabaloo, mayhem, uproar.

ORIGIN – from Milton's *Paradise Lost*, meaning 'the place of all demons': from Greek *pas* 'all' + *daimōn* 'demon'.

pander > *verb* (**pander to**) gratify or indulge (an immoral or distasteful desire or habit). > *noun* dated a pimp or procurer.

SYNONYMS – *verb* (**pander to**) cater to, gratify, humour, indulge.

wordpower facts
Pander

From medieval times a **pander** was a go-between in clandestine love affairs, and a little later, a pimp or procurer. The word comes from the name of *Pandare*, a character in Chaucer's *Troilus and Criseyde* and (as *Pandarus*) in Shakespeare's *Troilus and Cressida* who acts as a lovers' go-between. Pandarus was a character who fought on the side of the Trojans in Homer's *Iliad*: his role as a go-between was given to him by the Italian writer Boccaccio (14th century). The verb dates from the early 17th century.

pandit (also **pundit**) > *noun* a Hindu scholar learned in Sanskrit and Hindu philosophy and religion.
ORIGIN – Sanskrit, 'learned'.

P. & O. > *abbreviation* Peninsular and Oriental Shipping Company (or Line).

Pandora's box > *noun* a process that once begun generates many complicated problems.
ORIGIN – from *Pandora* in Greek mythology, who was sent to earth with a jar or box of evils which, contrary to instructions, she opened, letting out all the evils to infect the earth; hope alone remained.

p. & p. > *abbreviation* Brit. postage and packing.

pane > *noun* 1 a single sheet of glass in a window or door. 2 a sheet or page of stamps.

wordpower facts
Pane

The word **pane** comes from the same root as **panel**, Latin *pannus* 'piece of cloth'. In the Middle Ages both English words denoted a piece of material forming part of a garment, a sense which **panel** still has; **pane** also meant 'section of a wall or fence', 'side of a face of an object', and 'part, portion, or division' before it acquired the meaning 'sheet of glass'. **Panel**'s early sense 'piece of parchment' was extended to mean 'list', from which came the notion 'advisory group'.

paneer /pəneer/ > *noun* a type of milk curd cheese used in Indian, Iranian, and Afghan cooking.
ORIGIN – Hindi or Persian, 'cheese'.

panegyric /pannijirrik/ > *noun* a speech or text in praise of someone or something.
DERIVATIVES – **panegyrical** *adjective*.
ORIGIN – from Greek *panēgurikos* 'of public assembly'.

panegyrise /pannijirīz/ (also **panegyrize**) > *verb* speak or write in praise of; eulogise.
DERIVATIVES – **panegyrist** *noun*.

panel > *noun* 1 a distinct, usually rectangular section of a door, vehicle, garment, etc. 2 a flat board on which instruments or controls are fixed. 3 a small group of people brought together to investigate or decide on a matter. 4 chiefly N. Amer. a jury, or a list of available jurors.
DERIVATIVES – **panelled** (US **paneled**) *adjective* **panelling** (US **paneling**) *noun*.
COMBINATIONS – **panel beater** Brit. a person whose job is to beat out the bodywork of motor vehicles. **panel game** Brit. a broadcast quiz played by a team of people. **panel pin** Brit. a light, thin nail with a very small head. **panel saw** Brit. a light saw with small teeth, for cutting thin wood. **panel truck** N. Amer. a small enclosed delivery truck.
ORIGIN – Latin *pannus* 'piece of cloth'.

panellist (US **panelist**) > *noun* a member of a panel, especially in a broadcast game or discussion.

panettone /pannitōnay/ > *noun* (pl. **panettoni** /pannitōni/) a rich Italian bread with fruit, eaten at Christmas.
ORIGIN – Italian, from *panetto* 'cake'.

pang > *noun* a sudden sharp pain or painful emotion.
SYNONYMS – ache, spasm, stab, twinge.
ORIGIN – perhaps an alteration of PRONG.

panga /panggə/ > *noun* a bladed African tool like a machete.
ORIGIN – Swahili.

Pangloss /panggloss/ > *noun* a person who remains optimistic regardless of the circumstances.
DERIVATIVES – **Panglossian** *adjective*.
ORIGIN – from the name of the tutor and philosopher in Voltaire's *Candide* (1759).

pangolin /panggōlin/ > *noun* an insectivorous mammal whose body is covered with horny overlapping scales.
ORIGIN – Malay, 'roller' (from the animal's habit of rolling into a ball).

panhandle N. Amer. > *noun* a narrow strip of territory projecting from the main territory of one state into another. > *verb* informal beg in the street.
DERIVATIVES – **panhandler** *noun*.

panic > *noun* 1 sudden uncontrollable fear or anxiety. 2 informal frenzied hurry to do something. > *verb* (**panicked**, **panicking**) be affected by or cause to feel panic.
DERIVATIVES – **panicky** *adjective*.
SYNONYMS – *noun* 1 alarm, consternation, fear, hysteria, terror.
COMBINATIONS – **panic attack** a sudden overwhelming feeling of acute and disabling anxiety. **panic button** a button for summoning help in an emergency. **panic stations** Brit. informal a state of alarm or emergency.
ORIGIN – from the name of the Greek god *Pan*, who was believed to cause sudden terror.

panicle /pannik'l/ > *noun* Botany a loose branching cluster of flowers, as in oats.
ORIGIN – Latin *panicula*, from *panus* 'ear of millet'.

Panjabi > *noun* (pl. **Panjabis**) & *adjective* variant spelling of PUNJABI.

panjandrum /panjandrəm/ > *noun* a person who has or claims to have a great deal of authority or influence.
ORIGIN – from *Grand Panjandrum*, an invented phrase in a nonsense verse (1755) by Samuel Foote.

pannage /pannij/ > *noun* chiefly historical the right of feeding pigs or other animals in a wood.
ORIGIN – Old French *pasnage*, from Latin *pastio* 'pasturing'.

pannier > *noun* 1 a basket, especially each of a pair carried by a beast of burden. 2 a bag or box fitted on either side of the rear wheel of a bicycle or motorcycle. 3 historical part of a skirt looped up round the hips and supported on a frame.
ORIGIN – Old French *panier*, from Latin *panarium* 'bread basket'.

pannikin > *noun* a small metal drinking cup.

panoply /pannəpli/ > *noun* a complete or impressive collection or display.
DERIVATIVES – **panoplied** *adjective*.
SYNONYMS – array, collection, display, range.
ORIGIN – first meaning 'complete protection', later 'complete set of arms or suit of armour': from Greek *pan* 'all' + *hopla* 'arms'.

panoptic /panoptik/ > *adjective* showing or seeing the whole at one view.
ORIGIN – Greek *panoptos* 'seen by all'.

panopticon /panoptikən/ > *noun* historical a circular prison with cells arranged around a central well, from which prisoners could at all times be observed.

panorama /pannəraamə/ > *noun* 1 an unbroken view of a surrounding region. 2 a complete survey of a subject or sequence of events.
DERIVATIVES – **panoramic** *adjective* **panoramically** *adverb*.
ORIGIN – from Greek *pan* 'all' + *horama* 'view'.

pan pipes > *plural noun* a musical instrument made from a row of short pipes fixed together.
ORIGIN – from the name of the Greek god *Pan*.

pansexual > *adjective* another term for **OMNISEXUAL**.

panstick > *noun* a kind of matt cosmetic foundation in stick form, used in theatrical make-up.

ORIGIN – from **PANCAKE** + **STICK¹**.

pansy > *noun* **1** (pl. **pansies**) a plant of the viola family, with flowers in rich colours. **2** informal, derogatory an effeminate or homosexual man.

ORIGIN – French *pensée* 'thought, pansy'.

pant > *verb* **1** breathe with short, quick breaths, typically from exertion or excitement. **2** (usu. **pant for**) long to have or do something. > *noun* a short, quick breath.

SYNONYMS – *verb* **1** gasp, huff, puff, wheeze.

ORIGIN – Old French *pantaisier* 'be agitated, gasp', from Greek *phantasioun* 'cause to imagine', from *phantasia* (see **FANTASY**).

Pantagruelian /pantəgrōōelliən/ > *adjective* rare enormous.

ORIGIN – from *Pantagruel*, the name of a giant in *Gargantua and Pantagruel*, by the French satirist Rabelais (*c.*1494–1553).

pantalettes (chiefly N. Amer. also **pantalets**) > *plural noun* women's long underpants with a frill at the bottom of each leg, worn in the 19th century.

pantaloons > *plural noun* **1** women's baggy trousers gathered at the ankles. **2** historical men's close-fitting breeches fastened below the calf or at the foot.

ORIGIN – from *Pantalone*, a character in Italian commedia dell'arte represented as a foolish old man wearing pantaloons.

pantechnicon /pan**tek**nikən/ > *noun* Brit. a large van for transporting furniture.

ORIGIN – from Greek *pan* 'all' + *tekhnikon* 'piece of art', originally the name of a London bazaar selling artistic work, later converted into a furniture warehouse.

pantheism /**pan**thi-iz'm/ > *noun* **1** the belief that God can be identified with the universe, or that the universe is a manifestation of God. **2** rare worship that admits or tolerates a large number of gods.

DERIVATIVES – **pantheist** *noun* **pantheistic** *adjective* **pantheistically** *adverb*.

pantheon /**pan**thiən/ > *noun* **1** all the gods of a people or religion collectively. **2** an ancient temple dedicated to all the gods. **3** a collection of particularly famous or important people.

ORIGIN – from Greek *pan* 'all' + *theion* 'holy': originally referring especially to a circular temple in Rome.

panther > *noun* **1** a leopard, especially a black one. **2** N. Amer. a puma or a jaguar.

ORIGIN – Latin, *panthera*, from Greek.

panties > *plural noun* legless underpants worn by women and girls; knickers.

pantihose > *plural noun* variant spelling of **PANTYHOSE**.

pantile /**pan**tīl/ > *noun* a roof tile curved to form an S-shaped section, fitted to overlap its neighbour.

panto > *noun* (pl. **pantos**) Brit. informal a pantomime.

panto- > *combining form* all; universal.

ORIGIN – from Greek *pas*, 'all'.

pantograph /**pan**təgraaf/ > *noun* **1** an instrument for copying a plan or drawing on a different scale by a system of hinged and jointed rods. **2** a jointed framework conveying a current to an electric train or tram from overhead wires.

pantomime > *noun* **1** Brit. a theatrical entertainment involving music, topical jokes, and slapstick comedy, usually produced around Christmas. **2** informal a ridiculous or confused action or situation. > *verb* express or represent by extravagant and exaggerated mime.

ORIGIN – Greek *pantomimos* (see **PANTO-, MIME**): originally meaning 'actor using mime', later 'entertainment in which performers mime'.

pantry > *noun* (pl. **pantries**) a small room or cupboard in which food, crockery, and cutlery are kept.

ORIGIN – Old French *panterie*, from *paneter* 'baker', from Latin *panis* 'bread'.

pants > *plural noun* **1** Brit. underpants or knickers. **2** chiefly N. Amer. trousers. **3** Brit. informal rubbish; nonsense.

IDIOMS – **catch someone with their pants** (or **trousers**) **down** informal catch someone in an embarrassingly unprepared state. **fly** (or **drive**) **by the seat of one's pants** informal rely on instinct rather than logic or knowledge. **scare** (or **bore** etc.) **the pants off** informal make (someone) extremely scared, bored, etc.

COMBINATIONS – **pantsuit** (also **pants suit**) chiefly N. Amer. a trouser suit.

ORIGIN – abbreviation of **PANTALOONS**.

panty girdle (also **pantie girdle**) > *noun* a woman's control undergarment with a crotch shaped like pants.

pantyhose (also **pantihose**) > *plural noun* N. Amer. women's thin nylon tights.

pantywaist > *noun* N. Amer. informal a feeble or effeminate person.

ORIGIN – extended use of the literal sense 'child's garment consisting of panties attached to a bodice'.

panzer /**pan**zər/ > *noun* a German armoured unit.

ORIGIN – German, 'coat of mail'.

pap¹ > *noun* **1** bland soft or semi-liquid food suitable for babies or invalids. **2** (in Africa and the Caribbean) maize porridge. **3** worthless or trivial reading matter or entertainment.

ORIGIN – probably from Latin *pappare* 'eat'.

pap² > *noun* archaic or dialect a woman's breast or nipple.

ORIGIN – probably Scandinavian.

papa /pə**paa**/ > *noun* N. Amer. or dated one's father.

ORIGIN – French, from Greek *papas*.

papacy /**pay**pəsi/ > *noun* (pl. **papacies**) the pope's office or tenure.

ORIGIN – from Latin *papa* 'pope'.

papain /pə**pay**in/ > *noun* a protein-digesting enzyme obtained from unripe papaya fruit, used to tenderise meat and as a food supplement.

papal /**pay**p'l/ > *adjective* relating to the pope or the papacy.

DERIVATIVES – **papally** *adverb*.

paparazzo /pappə**rat**sō/ > *noun* (pl. **paparazzi** /pappə**rat**si/) a freelance photographer who pursues celebrities to take photographs of them.

ORIGIN – Italian, from the name of a character in Fellini's film *La Dolce Vita* (1960).

papaw > *noun* variant spelling of **PAWPAW**.

papaya /pə**pī**ə/ > *noun* a tropical fruit like an elongated melon, with edible orange flesh and small black seeds.

ORIGIN – Spanish and Portuguese, from Carib.

paper > *noun* **1** material manufactured in thin sheets from the pulp of wood or other fibrous substances, used for writing or printing on or as wrapping material. **2** (**papers**) sheets of paper covered with writing or printing; documents. **3** (before another noun) officially documented but having no real existence or use: *a paper profit*. **4** a newspaper. **5** a government report or policy document. **6** an essay or dissertation read at a seminar or published in a journal. **7** a set of examination questions. > *verb* **1** cover with wallpaper. **2** (**paper over**) disguise (an awkward problem) instead of resolving it. **3** theatrical slang fill (a theatre) by giving out free tickets.

WORDFINDER – *paper sizes:* demy, foolscap, octavo, quarto; *sides of a sheet of paper:* recto (*front*), verso (*reverse*); origami (*Japanese art of paper-folding*).

IDIOMS – **on paper 1** in writing. **2** in theory rather than in reality.

DERIVATIVES – **papery** *noun*.

COMBINATIONS – **paper boy** (or **paper girl**) a boy (or girl) who delivers newspapers to people's homes. **paper clip** a piece of bent wire or plastic used for holding several sheets of paper together. **paperknife** a blunt knife used for opening envelopes. **paper money** money in the form of banknotes. **paper round** (N. Amer. **paper route**) a job of regularly delivering newspapers. **paper-thin** very thin or insubstantial. **paper tiger** a person or thing that appears threatening but is ineffectual. **paper trail** chiefly N. Amer. the total amount of written evidence of someone's activities.

ORIGIN – Old French *papir*, from Latin *papyrus* (see **PAPYRUS**).

paperback > *noun* a book bound in stiff paper or flexible card.

paperchase > *noun* Brit. a cross-country race in which the runners follow a trail marked by torn-up paper.

paperweight > *noun* a small, heavy object for keeping loose papers in place.

paperwork > *noun* routine work involving written documents.

papier mâché /**pap**yay **ma**shay/ > *noun* a malleable mixture of paper and glue that becomes hard when dry.

ORIGIN – French, 'chewed paper'.

papilla /pə**pill**ə/ > *noun* (pl. **papillae** /pə**pill**ee/) **1** a small rounded protuberance on a part or organ of the body. **2** a small fleshy projection on a plant.

DERIVATIVES – **papillary** *adjective*.

ORIGIN – Latin, 'nipple'.

papilloma /pappi**lō**mə/ > *noun* (pl. **papillomas** or **papillomata** /pappi**lō**mətə/) Medicine a small wart-like growth, usually benign.

papist /**pay**pist/ chiefly derogatory > *noun* **1** a Roman Catholic. **2** a supporter of the papacy. > *adjective* **1** Roman Catholic. **2** supporting the papacy.

DERIVATIVES – **papism** *noun* **papistry** *noun*.

papoose /pə**pōōss**/ > *noun* chiefly offensive a young North American Indian child.

ORIGIN – Algonquian.

pappardelle /papaar**dell**ay/ > *plural noun* pasta in the form of broad flat ribbons.

ORIGIN – Italian, from *pappare* 'eat hungrily'.

pappus /**pap**əss/ > *noun* (pl. **pappi** /**pap**ī/) Botany a tuft of hairs on a seed which helps the seed be carried by the wind.

ORIGIN – Latin, from Greek *pappos*.

pappy¹ > *noun* (pl. **pappies**) a child's name for their father.

pappy² > *adjective* of the nature of pap.

paprika /**pa**prikə, pə**pree**kə/ > *noun* a deep orange-red powdered spice made from certain varieties of sweet pepper.

ORIGIN – Hungarian.

Pap test > *noun* a smear test carried out to detect cancer of the cervix or womb.

ORIGIN – named after the American scientist George N. *Papanicolaou* (1883–1962).

Papuan /**pap**yooən/ > *noun* **1** a person from Papua or Papua New Guinea. **2** a group of languages spoken in Papua New Guinea and neighbouring islands. > *adjective* relating to Papua or its languages.

papule /**pap**yool/ > *noun* Medicine a small pimple or swelling on the skin, often forming part of a rash.

ORIGIN – Latin *papula*.

papyrus /pə**pī**rəss/ > *noun* (pl. **papyri** /pə**pī**rī/ or **papyruses**) **1** a material prepared in ancient Egypt from the pithy stem of a water plant, used for writing or painting on. **2** the tall aquatic sedge from which papyrus was obtained.

ORIGIN – Latin, from Greek *papuros*.

par > *noun* **1** Golf the number of strokes a first-class player should normally require for a particular hole or course. **2** (usu. in phrase **above** or **below** or **under par**, or **on a par with**) the usual or expected level or amount. **3** Stock Exchange the face value of a share or other security. > *verb* (**parred**, **parring**) Golf play (a hole) in par.

IDIOMS – **par for the course** what is normal or expected in any given circumstances.

wordpower facts

Par

Par is a Latin word meaning 'equal' and 'equality'. It is the source of a number of English words, including **apparel**, **compare**, **pair**, **parity**, and **peer**. In English the meanings of **par** appear to develop naturally from the golf sense, but in fact this use was not recorded until comparatively recently (1898). The first use of **par** was in the early 17th century, when, often in the phrase **par of exchange**, it referred to the recognised value of one country's currency in terms of another's. Sense 2 followed a few decades later, and sense 3 in the early 18th century.

para¹ /**parr**ə/ > *noun* informal a paratrooper.

para² /**parr**ə/ > *noun* (pl. same or **paras**) a monetary unit of Bosnia–Herzegovina, Montenegro, and Serbia, equal to one hundredth of a dinar.

ORIGIN – Turkish, from a Persian word meaning 'piece, portion'.

para- /**parr**ə/ (also **par-**) > *prefix* **1** beside; adjacent to: *parathyroid*. **2** beyond or distinct from, but analogous to: *paramilitary*.

ORIGIN – from Greek *para* 'beside, beyond'.

parable > *noun* a simple story used to illustrate a moral or spiritual lesson.

wordpower facts

Parable

Rather surprisingly, the English words **parable** and **parabola** have the same source. They are both from Latin *parabola* 'comparison, allegory, speech', which came from Greek *parabolē* 'placing side by side, application', from *para-* 'beside' + *ballein* 'throw'. In the case of **parabola**, the notion is that of the correspondence between an area and a straight line, involved in the geometric construction of the curve. Other words related to **parable** and **parabola**, all concerned with speech, are **palaver**, **parlance**, **parley**, **parliament**, and **parole**: **parole** acquired its modern sense from its original meaning of a prisoner of war's word of honour not to escape or, if released, not to fight against his former captors.

parabola /pə**rabb**ələ/ > *noun* (pl. **parabolas** or **parabolae** /pə**rabb**əlee/) a symmetrical open plane curve of the kind formed by the intersection of a cone with a plane parallel to its side.

parabolic /parrə**boll**ik/ > *adjective* **1** of or like a parabola or part of one. **2** of or expressed in parables.

paraboloid /pə**rabb**əloyd/ > *noun* a three-dimensional figure generated by rotating a parabola about its axis of symmetry.

paracetamol /parrə**seet**əmol, -**sett**əmol/ > *noun* Brit. a synthetic compound used to relieve pain and reduce fever.

parachute > *noun* a cloth canopy which allows a person or heavy object attached to it to descend slowly when dropped from a high position. > *verb* drop or cause to drop by parachute.

WORDFINDER – drogue (*small parachute used as a brake*), ripcord (*cord pulled to open a parachute*), shrouds (*lines joining a parachute canopy to the harness*).

DERIVATIVES – **parachutist** *noun*.

ORIGIN – from French *para-* 'protection against' + *chute* 'fall'.

Paraclete /**parr**əkleet/ > *noun* (in Christian theology) the Holy Spirit as advocate or counsellor.

ORIGIN – from Greek *paraklētos* 'called in aid'.

parade > *noun* **1** a public procession. **2** a formal march or gathering of troops for inspection or display. **3** a series or succession. **4** a boastful or ostentatious display. **5** Brit. a public square, promenade, or row of shops. > *verb* **1** walk, march, or display in a parade. **2** display (something) publicly in order to impress or attract attention. **3** (**parade as**) masquerade as.

SYNONYMS – *noun* **1** cavalcade, march, pageant, procession. *verb* **1** file, march, process, troop. **2** display, exhibit, flaunt, show off.

COMBINATIONS – **parade ground** a place where troops gather for parade.

ORIGIN – French, 'a showing', from Latin *parare* 'prepare'.

paradiddle /parrədidd'l/ > *noun* Music a simple drum roll consisting of four even strokes.

paradigm /parrədīm/ > *noun* **1** a typical example, pattern, or model of something. **2** a world view underlying the theories and methodology of a scientific subject. **3** Grammar a table of all the inflected forms of a word.

DERIVATIVES – **paradigmatic** /parrədigmatt**ik**/ *adjective.*

COMBINATIONS – **paradigm shift** a fundamental change in approach or underlying assumptions.

ORIGIN – Greek *paradeigma*, from *paradeiknunai* 'show side by side'.

paradise /parrədīss/ > *noun* **1** (in some religions) heaven as the place where the good live after death. **2** the Garden of Eden. **3** an ideal or idyllic place or state.

DERIVATIVES – **paradisal** *adjective* **paradisiacal** /parrədisīak'l/ (also **paradisical** /parrədissik'l/) *adjective.*

ORIGIN – Old French *paradis*, from Greek *paradeisos* 'royal park'.

parador /parrədor/ > *noun* (pl. **paradors** or **paradores** /parrədorayz/) a hotel in Spain owned and run by the government.

ORIGIN – Spanish.

paradox > *noun* **1** a seemingly absurd or self-contradictory statement or proposition that may in fact be true. **2** a person or thing that combines contradictory features or qualities.

DERIVATIVES – **paradoxical** *adjective* **paradoxically** *adverb.*

SYNONYMS – **1** antinomy, oxymoron.

ORIGIN – Greek *paradoxon* 'contrary opinion': the original sense in English was 'statement contrary to accepted opinion'.

paraffin > *noun* **1** (Brit. also **paraffin wax**) a flammable waxy solid obtained from petroleum or shale and used for sealing and waterproofing and in candles. **2** (also **paraffin oil** or **liquid paraffin**) Brit. a liquid fuel made similarly, especially kerosene. **3** Chemistry old-fashioned term for ALKANE.

ORIGIN – from Latin *parum* 'little' + *affinis* 'related' (from its low reactivity).

paragliding > *noun* a sport in which a person glides through the air by means of a wide parachute after jumping from or being hauled to a height.

DERIVATIVES – **paraglide** *verb* **paraglider** *noun.*

paragon > *noun* **1** a model of excellence or of a particular quality. **2** a perfect diamond of 100 carats or more.

SYNONYMS – **1** ideal, nonpareil, shining example.

ORIGIN – Italian *paragone* 'touchstone'.

paragraph > *noun* a distinct section of a piece of writing, beginning on a new line and often indented.

COMBINATIONS – **paragraph mark** a symbol (usually ¶) used to mark a new paragraph or as a reference mark.

ORIGIN – French *paragraphe*, from Greek *paragraphos* 'short stroke marking a break in sense'.

Paraguayan /parrəgwīən/ > *noun* a person from Paraguay. > *adjective* relating to Paraguay.

parakeet /parrəkeet/ (also **parrakeet**) > *noun* a small parrot with predominantly green plumage and a long tail.

ORIGIN – Old French *paroquet*, Italian *parrocchetto*, and Spanish *periquito*, related to **PARROT**.

paralegal /parrəleeg'l/ chiefly N. Amer. > *adjective* relating to auxiliary aspects of the law. > *noun* a person trained in subsidiary legal matters but not fully qualified as a lawyer.

paralipsis /parrəlipsiss/ > *noun* Rhetoric the device of giving emphasis by professing to say little or nothing of a subject, as in *not to mention their unpaid debts.*

ORIGIN – Greek *paraleipsis* 'passing over'.

parallax /parrəlaks/ > *noun* **1** the apparent difference in the position of an object when viewed from different positions, e.g. through the viewfinder and the lens of a camera. **2** Astronomy the angular difference in the apparent positions of a star observed from opposite sides of the earth's orbit.

DERIVATIVES – **parallactic** *adjective.*

ORIGIN – Greek *parallaxis* 'a change'.

parallel > *adjective* **1** (of lines, planes, or surfaces) side by side and having the same distance continuously between them. **2** occurring or existing at the same time or in a similar way; corresponding. **3** Computing involving the simultaneous performance of operations. > *noun* **1** a person or thing that is similar or analogous to another. **2** a similarity or comparison. **3** (also **parallel of latitude**) each of the imaginary parallel circles of constant latitude on the earth's surface. **4** Printing two parallel lines (||) as a reference mark. > *verb* (**paralleled**, **paralleling**) **1** run or lie parallel to. **2** be similar or corresponding to.

WORDFINDER – collimate (*make rays accurately parallel*), hachures (*parallel lines used for shading on maps*), oblique (*neither parallel nor perpendicular*), orthographic (*denoting a projection using parallel lines*), vanishing point (*at which parallel lines appear to converge*).

IDIOMS – **in parallel 1** taking place at the same time and having some connection. **2** (of electrical components or circuits) connected to common points at each end, so that current is divided between them.

SYNONYMS – *adjective* **2** analogous, corresponding, equivalent, similar. *noun* **1** analogue, counterpart, equivalent. **2** analogy, comparison, correspondence, resemblance, similarity.

COMBINATIONS – **parallel bars** a pair of parallel rails on posts, used in gymnastics. **parallel imports** goods imported by unlicensed distributors for sale at less than the manufacturer's official retail price.

ORIGIN – Greek *parallēlos*, from *para-* 'alongside' + *allēlos* 'one another'.

parallelepiped /parrəleleppiped, parrəlellipīped/ > *noun* Geometry a solid body of which each face is a parallelogram.

ORIGIN – from Greek *parallēlos* 'beside another' + *epipedon* 'plane surface'.

parallelogram /parrəlelləgram/ > *noun* a plane figure with four straight sides and opposite sides parallel.

ORIGIN – from Greek *parallēlos* 'alongside another' + *grammē* 'line'.

Paralympics > *plural noun* (usu. treated as sing.) an international athletic competition for disabled athletes.

DERIVATIVES – **Paralympic** *adjective.*

ORIGIN – blend of *paraplegic* and *Olympics*.

paralyse* (US **paralyze**) > *verb* **1** cause (a person or part of the body) to become partly or wholly incapable of movement. **2** bring to a standstill by causing disruption.

*****SPELLING – the ending is *-yse* (in America, *-yze*) not *-ise* or *-ize*: paraly*se*.

SYNONYMS – **1** cripple, disable, immobilise, incapacitate.

paralysis /pəralisiss/ > *noun* (pl. **paralyses** /pəraliseez/) **1** the loss of the ability to move part or most of the body. **2** inability to act or function.

WORDFINDER – hemiplegia (*paralysis of one side of the body*), paraplegia (*of the legs and lower body*), quadriplegia, tetraplegia (*of all four limbs*).

ORIGIN – Greek *paralusis*, from *paraluesthai* 'be disabled at the side'.

paralytic > *adjective* **1** relating to paralysis. **2** informal, chiefly Brit. extremely drunk.

DERIVATIVES – **paralytically** *adverb.*

paramecium /parrəmeesiəm/ > *noun* Zoology a single-celled freshwater animal which has a characteristic slipper-like shape.

ORIGIN – Latin, from Greek *paramēkēs* 'oval'.

paramedic > *noun* a person who is trained

to do medical work, especially emergency first aid, but is not a fully qualified doctor.

DERIVATIVES – **paramedical** adjective.

parameter /pərammitər/ > noun 1 a measurable or quantifiable characteristic of a system. 2 Mathematics a quantity which is fixed for the case in question but may vary in other cases. 3 a limit or boundary which defines the scope of a process or activity.

DERIVATIVES – **parametric** adjective **parametrically** adverb.

ORIGIN – from Greek para- 'beside' + metron 'measure'.

paramilitary > adjective organised on similar lines to a military force. > noun (pl. **paramilitaries**) a member of a paramilitary organisation.

paramotor /parrəmōtər/ > noun (trademark in the US) a motorised and steerable parachute, powered by a motor and propeller strapped to the pilot's back.

DERIVATIVES – **paramotoring** noun.

paramount > adjective 1 more important than anything else; supreme. 2 having supreme power.

DERIVATIVES – **paramountcy** noun.

SYNONYMS – 1 predominant, primary, supreme, uppermost.

ORIGIN – from Old French par 'by' + amont 'above'.

paramour > noun archaic or derogatory a lover, especially the illicit partner of a married person.

ORIGIN – from Old French par amour 'by love'.

paranoia /parrənoyə/ > noun 1 a mental condition characterised by delusions of persecution, unwarranted jealousy, or exaggerated self-importance. 2 unjustified suspicion and mistrust of others.

DERIVATIVES – **paranoiac** /parrənoyik, -nōik/ (also **paranoic**) adjective & noun **paranoiacally** adverb.

ORIGIN – from Greek paranoos 'distracted', from para 'irregular' + noos 'mind'.

paranoid > adjective of, characterised by, or suffering from paranoia. > noun a person who is paranoid.

paranormal > adjective supposedly beyond the scope of normal scientific understanding.

DERIVATIVES – **paranormally** adverb.

parapet /parrəpit/ > noun 1 a low protective wall along the edge of a roof, bridge, or balcony. 2 a protective wall or bank along the top of a military trench.

ORIGIN – French or Italian, 'chest-high wall', from Latin pectus 'chest'.

paraphernalia /parrəfərnayliə/ > noun (treated as sing. or pl.) miscellaneous articles, especially the equipment needed for a particular activity.

SYNONYMS – accessories, equipment, impedimenta, odds and ends, trappings.

wordpower facts
Paraphernalia
Paraphernalia is a Latin word (from Greek parapherna 'property apart from a dowry'), which in ancient Rome referred to the property retained by a woman after her marriage: this excluded her dowry, which passed to her husband. In English and Scottish law, until the Married Women's Property Acts (from 1870), **paraphernalia** was restricted to a wife's personal belongings such as clothing and jewellery, everything else being regarded as the property of the husband. Through association with small personal belongings the word began to take on its modern meaning in the 18th century.

paraphilia /parrəfilliə/ > noun Psychiatry a condition characterised by abnormal sexual desires involving extreme or dangerous activities.

DERIVATIVES – **paraphiliac** adjective & noun.

paraphrase > verb express the meaning of (something) using different words. > noun a rewording of a passage.

SYNONYMS – verb rephrase, reword, rewrite.

paraplegia /parrəpleejə/ > noun paralysis of the legs and lower body.

DERIVATIVES – **paraplegic** adjective & noun.

ORIGIN – Greek, from paraplēssein 'strike at the side'.

parapsychology > noun the study of mental phenomena which are outside the sphere of orthodox psychology (such as hypnosis, telepathy, etc.).

paraquat /parrəkwot/ > noun a toxic fast-acting herbicide.

parasailing > noun the sport of gliding through the air wearing an open parachute while being towed by a motor boat.

DERIVATIVES – **parasail** noun & verb.

parascending > noun Brit. paragliding or parasailing.

DERIVATIVES – **parascend** verb.

parasite > noun 1 an organism which lives in or on another organism and benefits at the other's expense. 2 derogatory a person who lives off or exploits others.

WORDFINDER – ectoparasite (a parasite living on the outside of its host), endoparasite (one living inside its host), facultative (capable of but not restricted to living as a parasite), obligate (living only as a parasite).

DERIVATIVES – **parasitic** adjective **parasitical** adjective **parasitically** adverb **parasitism** noun.

SYNONYMS – 2 informal cadger, freeloader, leech, scrounger, sponger.

ORIGIN – Greek parasitos 'person eating at another's table', from para- 'alongside' + sitos 'food'.

parasitise /parrəsitīz/ (also **parasitize**) > verb infest or exploit as a parasite.

parasitoid /parrəsitoyd/ > noun an insect (e.g. an ichneumon) whose larvae live as parasites which eventually kill their hosts.

parasol > noun 1 a light umbrella used to give shade from the sun. 2 (also **parasol mushroom**) a tall mushroom with a broad, scaly greyish-brown cap.

ORIGIN – Italian parasole, from para- 'protecting against' + sole 'sun'.

parastatal /parrəstayt'l/ > adjective (of an organisation or industry) having some political authority and serving the state indirectly.

parasympathetic > adjective Physiology relating to a system of nerves arising from the brain and the lower end of the spinal cord and supplying the internal organs, blood vessels, and glands.

paratha /pəraatə/ > noun (in Indian cookery) a flat, thick piece of unleavened bread fried on a griddle.

ORIGIN – Hindi.

parathion /parrəthīən/ > noun a highly toxic synthetic insecticide containing phosphorus and sulphur.

parathyroid > noun Anatomy a gland next to the thyroid which secretes a hormone that regulates calcium levels in a person's body.

paratroops > plural noun troops equipped to be dropped by parachute from aircraft.

DERIVATIVES – **paratrooper** noun.

paratyphoid > noun a fever resembling typhoid, caused by related bacteria.

par avion /paar avyoN/ > adverb by airmail.

ORIGIN – French, 'by aeroplane'.

parboil > verb partly cook by boiling.

ORIGIN – Latin perbullire 'boil thoroughly', confused with part-boil.

parcel > noun 1 an object or collection of objects wrapped in paper in order to be carried or sent by post. 2 a quantity or amount of something, in particular land. > verb (**parcelled, parcelling; US parceled, parceling**) 1 make (something) into a parcel by wrapping it. 2 (**parcel out**) divide (something) into portions and then distribute it.

ORIGIN – Old French parcelle, from Latin particula 'small part'.

parch > verb 1 make dry through intense heat. 2 (**parched**) informal extremely thirsty. 3 roast (corn, peas, etc.) lightly.

parchment > noun 1 a stiff material made from the skin of a sheep or goat, formerly used for writing on. 2 (also **parchment paper**) stiff translucent paper treated to resemble parchment. **3** informal a diploma or other formal document.

ORIGIN – Old French *parchemin*, from a blend of Latin *pergamina* 'writing material from Pergamum' and *Parthica pellis* 'Parthian skin' (a kind of scarlet leather).

pard > *noun* archaic or literary a leopard.

pardon > *noun* **1** the action of forgiving or being forgiven for an error or offence. **2** a remission of the legal consequences of an offence or conviction. **3** Christian Church, historical an indulgence. > *verb* **1** forgive or excuse (a person, error, or offence). **2** give (an offender) a pardon. > *exclamation* used to ask a speaker to repeat something because one did not hear or understand it.

WORDFINDER – amnesty (*general pardon*), indulgence (*cancellation by the pope of punishment for sins*).

DERIVATIVES – **pardonable** *adjective*.

SYNONYMS – *noun* **1** absolution, forgiveness. **2** remission, reprieve. *verb* **1** absolve, excuse, exonerate, forgive.

ORIGIN – Old French *pardun*, from Latin *perdonare* 'concede, remit'.

pardoner > *noun* historical a person licensed to sell papal pardons or indulgences.

pare > *verb* **1** trim by cutting away the outer edges of. **2** (often **pare away** or **down**) reduce or diminish in a number of small successive stages.

ORIGIN – Old French *parer*, from Latin *parare* 'prepare'.

paregoric /parri**gorr**ik/ > *noun* a medicine containing opium and camphor, formerly used to treat diarrhoea and coughing in children.

ORIGIN – from Greek *parēgorikos* 'soothing', from *parēgorein* 'speak in the assembly', hence 'soothe, console'.

parenchyma /pə**reng**kimə/ > *noun* **1** Anatomy the functional tissue of an organ as distinguished from the connective and supporting tissue. **2** Botany soft cellular tissue forming the pulp of fruits, pith of stems, etc.

ORIGIN – Greek *parenkhuma* 'something poured in besides', from *para-* 'beside' + *enkhuma* 'infusion'.

parent > *noun* **1** a father or mother. **2** an animal or plant from which younger ones are derived. **3** an organisation or company which owns or controls a number of subsidiaries. **4** archaic a forefather or ancestor. > *verb* be or act as a parent to.

DERIVATIVES – **parental** *adjective* **parentally** *adverb* **parenthood** *noun*.

ORIGIN – Old French, from Latin *parere* 'bring forth'.

parentage > *noun* the identity and origins of one's parents; lineage.

SYNONYMS – ancestry, birth, descent, extraction, lineage.

parenteral /pə**ren**tərəl/ > *adjective* Medicine relating to nutrition involving a part of the body other than the mouth and alimentary canal.

ORIGIN – from **PARA-** + Greek *enteron* 'intestine'.

parenthesis /pə**ren**thisiss/ > *noun* (pl. **parentheses** /pə**ren**thiseez/) **1** a word or phrase inserted as an explanation or afterthought, in writing usually marked off by brackets, dashes, or commas. **2** (**parentheses**) a pair of round brackets ( ) used to include such a word or phrase.

ORIGIN – Greek, from *parentithenai* 'put in beside'.

parenthetic > *adjective* relating to or inserted as a parenthesis.

DERIVATIVES – **parenthetical** *adjective* **parenthetically** *adverb*.

parergon /pə**rer**gən/ > *noun* (pl. **parerga** /pə**rer**gə/) formal a supplementary or subsidiary piece of work.

ORIGIN – Greek, from *para-* 'beside, additional' + *ergon* 'work'.

pareu /**paa**rayōō/ > *noun* a kind of Polynesian sarong.

ORIGIN – Tahitian.

par excellence /paar eksə**lonss**/ > *adjective* (after a noun) better or more than all others of the same kind: *Nash is the Regency architect par excellence.*

ORIGIN – French, 'by excellence'.

parfait /**paar**fay/ > *noun* **1** a rich cold dessert made with whipped cream, eggs, and fruit. **2** a dessert consisting of layers of ice cream, meringue, and fruit, served in a tall glass.

ORIGIN – French, 'perfect'.

pargana /pər**gunn**ə/ > *noun* a group of villages or a subdivision of a district in India.

ORIGIN – Urdu, 'district'.

pargeting /**paar**jiting/ > *noun* patterned or decorative plaster or mortar.

DERIVATIVES – **pargeted** *adjective*.

ORIGIN – from Old French *parjeter*, from *par-* 'all over' + *jeter* 'to throw'.

parhelion /paar**hee**liən/ > *noun* (pl. **parhelia**) a bright spot in the sky on either side of the sun, formed by refraction.

ORIGIN – from Greek *para-* 'beside' + *hēlios* 'sun'.

pariah /pə**rī**ə/ > *noun* **1** an outcast. **2** historical a member of a low caste or of no caste in southern India.

COMBINATIONS – **pariah dog** a half-wild stray mongrel; a pye-dog.

ORIGIN – from a Tamil word meaning 'hereditary drummers' (pariahs were drummers because they were not allowed to join in with religious processions).

Parian /**pair**iən/ > *adjective* relating to the Greek island of Paros, famous as a source of marble.

parietal /pə**rī**it'l/ > *adjective* Anatomy & Biology relating to the wall of the body or of a body cavity.

COMBINATIONS – **parietal bone** a bone forming the central side and upper back part of each side of the skull. **parietal lobe** either of the paired lobes of the brain at the top of the head.

ORIGIN – from Latin *paries* 'wall'.

pari-mutuel /parri**myōō**tyooəl/ > *noun* a form of betting in which those backing the first three places divide the losers' stakes.

ORIGIN – French, 'mutual stake'.

pari passu /parri **pass**ōō/ > *adverb* side by side; equally or equivalently.

ORIGIN – Latin, 'with equal step'.

parish > *noun* **1** (in the Christian Church) a small administrative district with its own church and clergy. **2** (also **civil parish**) Brit. the smallest unit of local government in rural areas.

COMBINATIONS – **parish council** the administrative body in a civil parish. **parish-pump** Brit. of local importance only; parochial. **parish register** a book recording christenings, marriages, and burials at a parish church.

ORIGIN – Old French *paroche*, via Latin *parochia*, from Greek *paroikia* 'staying temporarily'.

parishioner > *noun* a person who lives in a particular Church parish.

Parisian /pə**rizz**iən/ > *adjective* relating to Paris. > *noun* a person from Paris.

Parisienne /pə**rizz**ien/ > *noun* a Parisian girl or woman.

parity[1] /**parr**iti/ > *noun* **1** equality or equivalence. **2** Mathematics the fact of being an even or an odd number.

ORIGIN – Latin *paritas*, from *par* 'equal'.

parity[2] /**parr**iti/ > *noun* Medicine the fact or condition of having borne a specified number of children.

ORIGIN – from Latin *-parus* '-bearing', from *parere* 'bring forth, produce'.

park > *noun* **1** a large public garden in a town, used for recreation. **2** a large area of woodland and pasture attached to a country house. **3** an area devoted to a specified purpose: *a wildlife park.* **4** an area in which vehicles may be parked. **5** (**the park**) Brit. informal a football pitch. > *verb* **1** stop (a vehicle) in a particular spot and keep it there for a time. **2** informal leave (something) in a convenient place until required. **3** (**park oneself**) informal sit down.

COMBINATIONS – **parking meter** a machine next to a parking space in a street, into which coins are inserted to pay for parking a vehicle. **parking ticket** a notice informing a driver of a fine imposed for parking illegally.

wordpower facts

Park

The word **park** entered English from Old French *parc*, which came from medieval Latin *parricus*. It was originally a legal term designating land held by royal grant for keeping game animals: this was enclosed and therefore distinct from a *forest* or *chase*, and (unlike a *forest*) had no special laws or officers. Two military uses, the obsolete verb sense 'lodge (troops) in an encampment' and a noun use meaning 'space occupied by artillery, wagons, stores, etc. in an encampment', are the origins of the verb sense of parking a vehicle (mid 19th century) and of compounds such as *car park*.

parka > *noun* **1** a large windproof hooded jacket. **2** a hooded jacket made of animal skin, worn by Eskimos.
ORIGIN – Russian.

parkin > *noun* Brit. soft, dark gingerbread made with oatmeal and treacle or molasses.
ORIGIN – perhaps from the family name *Parkin*.

Parkinson's disease > *noun* a progressive disease of the brain and nervous system marked by involuntary trembling, muscular rigidity, and slow, imprecise movement.
DERIVATIVES – **Parkinsonism** *noun*.
ORIGIN – named after the English surgeon James *Parkinson* (1755–1824).

Parkinson's law > *noun* the notion that work expands so as to fill the time available for its completion.
ORIGIN – named after the English writer Cyril Northcote *Parkinson* (1909–93).

parkland > *noun* (also **parklands**) land laid out as a park; grassland with scattered groups of trees.

parkway > *noun* **1** N. Amer. an open landscaped highway. **2** Brit. (in names) a railway station with extensive parking facilities.

parky > *adjective* Brit. informal chilly.

parlance /**paar**lənss/ > *noun* a way of using words associated with a particular subject: *medical parlance*.
ORIGIN – Old French, from *parler* 'speak'.

parlay /**paar**lay/ > *verb* (**parlay into**) N. Amer. turn (an initial stake) into (a greater amount) by further gambling.
ORIGIN – from French *paroli*, from Latin *par* 'equal'.

parley /**paar**li/ > *noun* (pl. **parleys**) a meeting between opponents or enemies to discuss terms for an armistice. > *verb* (**parleys, parleyed**) hold a parley.

ORIGIN – perhaps from Old French *parlee* 'spoken'.

parliament* /**paar**ləmənt/ > *noun* **1** (**Parliament**) (in the UK) the highest legislature, consisting of the Sovereign, the House of Lords, and the House of Commons. **2** a similar body in other countries.
WORDFINDER – bicameral (*denoting a parliament with two chambers*), Hansard (*record of UK parliamentary debates*), hung parliament (*with no party having a majority*), prorogue (*discontinue a session of parliament*); *parliaments of various countries:* Bundesrat (*Germany and Austria*), Cortes (*Spain*), Dáil (*Ireland*), Duma (*Russia*), Knesset (*Israel*).
*SPELLING – *lia*-, not *la*-, in the middle: par**lia**ment.
SYNONYMS – **2** assembly, congress, council, legislature, senate.
ORIGIN – Old French *parlement* 'speaking'.

parliamentarian > *noun* **1** a Member of Parliament who is experienced and able in parliamentary procedures and debates. **2** historical a supporter of Parliament in the English Civil War (1642–9); a Roundhead. > *adjective* relating to parliament or parliamentarians.

parliamentary /paarlə**men**tri/ > *adjective* relating to, enacted by, or suitable for a parliament.
COMBINATIONS – **parliamentary private secretary** (in the UK) a Member of Parliament assisting a government minister.

parlour (US **parlor**) > *noun* **1** dated a sitting room. **2** a room in a public building, monastery, etc. for receiving guests or for private conversation. **3** a shop or business providing specified goods or services: *an ice-cream parlour*. **4** a room or building equipped for milking cows.
COMBINATIONS – **parlour game** an indoor game, especially a word game. **parlourmaid** historical a maid employed to wait at table.
ORIGIN – Old French *parlur* 'place for speaking', from Latin *parlare* 'speak'.

parlous /**paar**ləss/ > *adjective* archaic or humorous dangerously uncertain; precarious.
ORIGIN – contraction of **PERILOUS**.

Parma ham /**paar**mə/ > *noun* a strongly flavoured Italian cured ham, eaten uncooked and thinly sliced.
ORIGIN – named after the Italian city of *Parma*.

Parmesan /**paar**mizan/ > *noun* a hard, dry Italian cheese used chiefly in grated form.
ORIGIN – from Italian *Parmigiano* 'of *Parma*'.

parmigiana /paarmi**jaa**nə/ > *adjective* (after a noun) cooked or served with Parmesan cheese: *veal parmigiana*.

parochial /pə**rō**kiəl/ > *adjective* **1** relating to

a parish. **2** having a narrow outlook or scope.
DERIVATIVES – **parochialism** *noun*.
SYNONYMS – **2** insular, limited, narrow-minded, provincial, restricted.
ANTONYMS – **2** broad-minded.
ORIGIN – Latin *parochialis*, from *parochia* 'parish'.

parody /**parr**ədi/ > *noun* (pl. **parodies**) **1** an amusingly exaggerated imitation of the style of a writer, artist, or genre. **2** an imitation or version that falls far short of the real thing; a travesty. > *verb* (**parodies, parodied**) produce a parody of.
DERIVATIVES – **parodic** *adjective* **parodist** *noun*.
SYNONYMS – *noun* **1** burlesque, caricature, lampoon, pastiche, satire. *verb* burlesque, caricature, lampoon, satirise, send up.
ORIGIN – Greek *parōidia* 'burlesque poem or song', from *ōidē* 'ode'.

parole > *noun* **1** the temporary or permanent release of a prisoner before their sentence has been served, on the promise of good behaviour. **2** historical a prisoner of war's word of honour not to escape or, if released, not to fight their former captors. > *verb* release (a prisoner) on parole.
DERIVATIVES – **parolee** *noun*.
ORIGIN – Old French, 'word', from Latin *parabola* 'speech'.

paronomasia /parrənə**mayz**iə/ > *noun* a pun.
ORIGIN – Greek, from *para-* 'beside' + *onomasia* 'naming'.

parotid /pə**rott**id/ > *adjective* relating to or denoting a pair of large salivary glands situated just in front of each ear.
ORIGIN – Greek, from *para-* 'beside' + *ous* 'ear'.

parotitis /parrə**tī**tiss/ > *noun* Medicine inflammation of a parotid gland, especially (**infectious parotitis**) mumps.

paroxysm /**parr**əksiz'm/ > *noun* a sudden attack or outburst: *a paroxysm of weeping*.
DERIVATIVES – **paroxysmal** *adjective*.
SYNONYMS – attack, bout, convulsion, fit, spasm.
ORIGIN – Greek *paroxusmos*, from *paroxunein* 'exasperate'.

parquet /**paar**ki, **paar**kay/ > *noun* flooring composed of wooden blocks arranged in a geometric pattern.
DERIVATIVES – **parquetry** *noun*.
ORIGIN – French, 'small compartment, wooden flooring'.

parr > *noun* (pl. same) a young salmon or trout up to two years old.

parrakeet > *noun* variant spelling of **PARAKEET**.

parricide /**parr**isīd/ > *noun* **1** the killing of a parent or other near relative. **2** a person who commits parricide.
DERIVATIVES – **parricidal** *adjective*.

ORIGIN – Latin *parricidium*, perhaps from *pater* 'father' or *parens* 'parent'.

parrot > *noun* a mainly tropical bird with brightly coloured plumage and a strong downcurved hooked bill, some kinds of which are able to mimic human speech. > *verb* (**parroted**, **parroting**) repeat mechanically.

WORDFINDER – psittacine (*of or like parrots*), psittacosis (*disease of parrots and other birds*); *kinds of parrot:* cockatiel, cockatoo, lory, macaw, parakeet.

COMBINATIONS – **parrotbill** a titmouse-like songbird with brown and grey plumage and a short arched bill. **parrot-fashion** without thought or understanding; mechanically. **parrotfish 1** a brightly coloured sea fish with a parrot-like beak. **2** Austral./NZ a brightly coloured wrasse.

ORIGIN – probably from French dialect *perrot*, diminutive of the male name *Pierre* 'Peter'.

parry > *verb* (**parries**, **parried**) **1** ward off (a weapon or attack) with a countermove. **2** avoid answering (a question) directly. > *noun* (pl. **parries**) an act of parrying.

SYNONYMS – *verb* block, deflect, evade, fend off, ward off.

ORIGIN – probably from French *parer* 'ward off'.

parse /paarz/ > *verb* **1** analyse (a sentence) into its component parts and describe the roles they play in the syntax of the sentence. **2** Computing analyse (text) into logical syntactic components.

DERIVATIVES – **parser** *noun*.

ORIGIN – perhaps from Old French *pars* 'parts'.

parsec > *noun* a unit of astronomical distance equal to about 3.25 light years, corresponding to the distance at which the radius of the earth's orbit subtends an angle of one second of arc.

ORIGIN – blend of **PARALLAX** and **SECOND²**.

Parsee /paarsee/ > *noun* a descendant of a group of Zoroastrian Persians who fled to India during the 7th–8th centuries.

ORIGIN – from a Persian word meaning 'Persian'.

parsimonious /paarsimōniəss/ > *adjective* very unwilling to spend money or use resources.

DERIVATIVES – **parsimoniously** *adverb*.

SYNONYMS – careful, frugal, mean, miserly, niggardly.

parsimony /paarsiməni/ > *noun* extreme unwillingness to spend money or use resources.

ORIGIN – Latin *parsimonia, parcimonia*, from *parcere* 'be sparing'.

parsley > *noun* a herb with crinkly or flat leaves, used for seasoning or garnishing food.

ORIGIN – Greek *petroselinon*, from *petra* 'rock' + *selinon* 'parsley'.

parsnip > *noun* the long, tapering cream-coloured root of a plant of the parsley family, eaten as a vegetable.

ORIGIN – Old French *pasnaie*, from Latin *pastinaca*; ending assimilated to **NEEP**.

parson > *noun* **1** (in the Church of England) a parish priest. **2** informal any clergyman.

COMBINATIONS – **parson's nose** the piece of fatty flesh at the rump of a cooked fowl.

ORIGIN – Old French *persone*, from Latin *persona* 'person', later 'rector'.

parsonage > *noun* a church house provided for a parson.

part > *noun* **1** a piece or segment which is combined with others to make up a whole. **2** some but not all of something. **3** a specified fraction of a whole. **4** a role played by an actor or actress. **5** a person's contribution to an action or situation. **6** (**parts**) informal a region: *he's off to foreign parts.* **7** (**parts**) abilities: *a man of many parts.* **8** Music a melody or other constituent of harmony assigned to a particular voice or instrument. > *verb* **1** move apart or divide to leave a central space. **2** leave or cause to leave someone's company. **3** (**part with**) give up possession of; hand over. > *adverb* partly: *part jazz, part blues.*

IDIOMS – **be part and parcel of** be an essential element of. **for my** (or **his, her,** etc.) **part** as far as I am (or he, she, etc. is) concerned. **in part** to some extent. **on the part of** used to ascribe responsibility for something to someone. **part company** go in different directions. **take part** join in or be involved in an activity. **take the part of** give support and encouragement to.

SYNONYMS – *noun* **1** bit, component, constituent, element, piece, portion, section. *verb* **1** detach, divide, separate, split. **2** break away, break up, separate, split up.

COMBINATIONS – **part exchange** Brit. a transaction in which an article that one already owns is given as part of the payment for a more expensive one, with the balance in money. **part of speech** a category to which a word is assigned in accordance with its syntactic functions, e.g. noun, pronoun, adjective, verb. **part song** a secular song with three or more voice parts, typically unaccompanied.

ORIGIN – Latin *pars*; the verb is from Latin *partire* 'divide, share'.

partake > *verb* (past **partook**; past participle **partaken**) formal **1** (**partake in**) participate in (an activity). **2** (**partake of**) be characterised by. **3** (**partake of**) eat or drink.

ORIGIN – from earlier *partaker* 'person who takes a part'.

parterre /paartair/ > *noun* a group of flower beds laid out in a formal pattern.

ORIGIN – French, from *par terre* 'on the ground'.

parthenogenesis /paarthinōjennisiss/ > *noun* Biology reproduction from an ovum without fertilisation, especially in some invertebrates and lower plants.

DERIVATIVES – **parthenogenetic** *adjective*.

ORIGIN – from Greek *parthenos* 'virgin' + *genesis* 'creation'.

Parthian /paarthiən/ > *noun* a person from Parthia, an ancient kingdom which lay SE of the Caspian Sea. > *adjective* relating to Parthia.

COMBINATIONS – **Parthian shot** a parting shot. [ORIGIN – from the practice among Parthian horsemen of shooting arrows backwards while fleeing.]

partial > *adjective* **1** existing only in part; incomplete. **2** favouring one side in a dispute above the other; biased. **3** (**partial to**) having a liking for.

DERIVATIVES – **partiality** *noun* **partially** *adverb*.

SYNONYMS – **1** incomplete, limited, qualified, restricted, unfinished. **2** biased, one-sided, partisan, prejudiced, slanted.

ANTONYMS – **1** complete, total. **2** impartial, unbiased.

participant > *noun* a person who takes part in something.

participate > *verb* (often **participate in**) join in an activity; take part.

DERIVATIVES – **participation** *noun* **participative** *adjective* **participator** *noun* **participatory** *adjective*.

SYNONYMS – be active, engage, be involved, join, take part.

ORIGIN – Latin *participare* 'share in'.

participle /paartissip'l/ > *noun* Grammar a word formed from a verb (e.g. *going, gone, being, been*) and used as an adjective or noun (as in *burnt toast, good breeding*) or used to make compound verb forms (*is going, has been*).

DERIVATIVES – **participial** /paartisippiəl/ *adjective*.

ORIGIN – Old French, from Latin *participium* 'sharing'.

particle > *noun* **1** a minute portion of matter. **2** Physics a component of the physical world smaller than an atom. **3** Grammar a minor function word that has comparatively little meaning and does not inflect, e.g. *in, up, off,* or *over,* used with verbs to make phrasal verbs.

WORDFINDER – *subatomic particles:* baryon, boson, electron, fermion, gluon, hadron, lepton, meson, muon, neutrino, neutron, photon, pion, positron, proton, quark.

SYNONYMS – **1** atom, bit, fragment, piece, speck.

COMBINATIONS – **particle board**

chipboard. **particle physics** the branch of physics concerned with the properties and interactions of subatomic particles.

ORIGIN – Latin *particula* 'little part'.

particoloured (US **particolored**) > *adjective* partly of one colour, partly of another or others.

particular > *adjective* **1** relating to an individual member of a specified group or class. **2** more than is usual; special: *particular care.* **3** fastidious about something. > *noun* a detail.

IDIOMS – **in particular** especially.

SYNONYMS – *adjective* **1** certain, distinct, individual, separate. **2** especial, exceptional, special, uncommon.

ANTONYMS – *adjective* **1** general. **2** ordinary.

ORIGIN – Latin *particularis*, from *particula* 'small part'.

particularise (also **particularize**) > *verb* formal treat individually or in detail.

DERIVATIVES – **particularisation** *noun.*

particularity > *noun* (pl. **particularities**) **1** the quality of being individual. **2** fullness or minuteness of detail. **3** (**particularities**) small details.

particularly > *adverb* **1** more than is usual; especially or very. **2** in particular; specifically.

particulate /paar**tik**yoolayt/ > *adjective* relating to or in the form of minute particles. > *noun* (**particulates**) matter in such a form.

parting > *noun* **1** the action or an act of parting. **2** Brit. a line of scalp revealed by combing the hair away in opposite directions on either side.

SYNONYMS – **1** break-up, departure, division, leave-taking, separation.

COMBINATIONS – **parting shot** a cutting remark made at the moment of departure. Compare with *Parthian shot.*

parti pris /paarti **pree**/ > *noun* (pl. **partis pris** pronunc. same) a preconceived view; a bias. > *adjective* prejudiced; biased.

ORIGIN – French, 'side taken'.

partisan* /**paar**tizan, paarti**zan**/ > *noun* **1** a strong, often uncritical, supporter of a party, cause, or person. **2** a member of an armed group fighting secretly against an occupying force. > *adjective* prejudiced in favour of a particular cause.

DERIVATIVES – **partisanship** *noun.*

*SPELLING – -*s*-, not -*z*-: partisan.

SYNONYMS – *noun* **1** adherent, devotee, follower, supporter, zealot. *adjective* biased, one-sided, partial, prejudiced, slanted.

ORIGIN – French, from Italian *partigiano*, from *parte* 'part'.

partita /paar**tee**tə/ > *noun* (pl. **partitas** or **partite** /paar**tee**tay/) Music a suite, typically for a solo instrument or chamber ensemble.

ORIGIN – Italian, 'divided off'.

partition > *noun* **1** a structure dividing a space into parts, especially a light interior wall. **2** (especially with reference to a country) division into parts. > *verb* **1** divide into parts. **2** divide or separate (a room or part of a room) with a partition.

DERIVATIVES – **partitionist** *noun.*

SYNONYMS – *noun* **1** barrier, divider, panel, screen, wall. **2** break-up, division, separation.

partitive /**paar**titiv/ Grammar > *adjective* (of a grammatical construction) indicating that only a part of a whole is referred to (e.g. *a slice of bacon, some of the children*). > *noun* a noun or pronoun used as the first term in such a construction.

partly > *adverb* to some extent; not completely.

partner > *noun* **1** a person who takes part in an undertaking with another or others, especially in a business with shared risks and profits. **2** either of two people doing something as a couple or pair. **3** either member of a married couple or of an established unmarried couple. > *verb* be the partner of.

SYNONYMS – **2** associate, collaborator, colleague, confederate. **3** cohabitee, consort, lover, mate, spouse.

ORIGIN – Old French *parcener*, from Latin *partitio* 'partition'.

partnership > *noun* **1** the state of being a partner or partners. **2** an association of two or more people as partners.

partook past of PARTAKE.

partridge > *noun* a short-tailed game bird with mainly brown plumage.

ORIGIN – Old French *perdriz*, from Latin *perdix.*

part-time > *adjective & adverb* for only part of the usual working day or week.

parturient /paar**tyoor**iənt/ > *adjective* technical about to give birth; in labour.

parturition /paartyoor**ish**'n/ > *noun* formal or technical the action of giving birth; childbirth.

ORIGIN – Latin, from *parturire* 'be in labour'.

part-way > *adverb* part of the way.

party > *noun* (pl. **parties**) **1** a social gathering of invited guests. **2** a formally organised political group that puts forward candidates for local or national office. **3** a group of people taking part in an activity or trip. **4** a person or group forming one side in an agreement or dispute. **5** informal, dated a person: *an old party came in to clean.* > *verb* (**parties**, **partied**) informal enjoy oneself at a party or other lively gathering.

IDIOMS – **be party** (or **a party**) **to** be involved in.

SYNONYMS – *noun* **1** ball, celebration, function, gathering, rave, shindig, social. **2** faction, grouping, sect, side. **3** body, company, crowd, group.

COMBINATIONS – **party line 1** a policy or policies officially adopted by a political party. **2** a telephone line shared by two or more subscribers. **party politics** politics that relate to political parties rather than to the public good. **party-pooper** informal a person who throws gloom over social enjoyment. **party wall** a wall common to two adjoining buildings or rooms.

ORIGIN – Old French *partie*, from Latin *partiri* 'divide into parts'.

parvenu /**paar**vənoo/ > *noun* chiefly derogatory a person from a humble background who has recently acquired wealth, influence, or celebrity.

ORIGIN – French, literally 'arrived'.

parvovirus /**paar**vōvīrəss/ > *noun* any of a class of very small viruses causing contagious disease in dogs and other animals.

ORIGIN – from Latin *parvus* 'small'.

pas /paa/ > *noun* (pl. same) a step in classical ballet.

ORIGIN – French.

pascal /**pas**k'l/ > *noun* the unit of pressure in the SI system, equal to one newton per square metre.

ORIGIN – named after the French scientist Blaise *Pascal* (1623–62).

paschal /**pas**k'l/ > *adjective* **1** relating to Easter. **2** relating to the Jewish Passover.

ORIGIN – Latin *paschalis*, from *pascha* 'feast of Passover', from Hebrew.

pas de deux /paa də **dö**/ > *noun* (pl. same) a dance for a couple.

ORIGIN – French, 'step of two'.

pasha /**pash**ə/ (also **pacha**) > *noun* historical the title of a Turkish officer of high rank.

ORIGIN – Turkish.

pashmina /pash**mee**nə/ > *noun* **1** a fine-quality material made from goat's wool. **2** a shawl made from this material.

ORIGIN – Persian, 'wool, down'.

Pashto /**push**tō/ > *noun* the language of the Pathans, spoken in Afghanistan and northern Pakistan.

ORIGIN – the name in Pashto.

paso doble /passō **dō**blay/ > *noun* (pl. **paso dobles**) a fast-paced ballroom dance based on a Latin American marching style.

ORIGIN – Spanish, 'double step'.

pasque flower /pask/ > *noun* a spring-flowering plant with purple flowers and fern-like foliage.

ORIGIN – French *passe-fleur*; later associated with archaic *pasque* 'Easter'.

pass¹ > *verb* **1** move or go onward, through, or across. **2** change from one state or condition to another. **3** transfer (something) to someone. **4** move past; overtake. **5** (in

pass-past

sport) kick, hit, or throw (the ball) to a teammate. **6** (of time) go by. **7** occupy or spend (time). **8** be done or said: *not another word passed between them.* **9** come to an end. **10** be successful in (an examination or test). **11** declare that (something) is satisfactory. **12** approve or put into effect (a proposal or law) by voting. **13** utter (remarks) or pronounce (a judgement or sentence). **14** forgo one's turn or an opportunity to do or have something. **15** discharge (urine or faeces) from the body. > *noun* **1** an act of passing. **2** a success in an examination. **3** a official document authorising the holder to have access to, use, or do something. **4** informal an amorous or sexual advance. **5** a particular state of affairs: *things had come to such a pass that he worried about his safety.*

IDIOMS – **come to a pretty pass** reach a regrettable state of affairs. **pass as** (or **for**) be accepted as. **pass away** euphemistic die. **pass one's eye over** read cursorily. **pass off 1** happen or be carried through in a specified (usually satisfactory) way. **2** evade or lightly dismiss (an awkward remark). **pass off as** falsely represent (something) as. **pass out 1** become unconscious. **2** Brit. complete one's initial training in the armed forces. **pass over 1** ignore the claims of (someone) to advancement. **2** avoid mentioning or considering. **pass up** refrain from taking up (an opportunity). **pass water** urinate.

DERIVATIVES – **passer** noun.

SYNONYMS – *verb* **1** go, move, proceed, progress. **10** gain a pass in, get through, be successful in. **12** approve, carry, enact, endorse, ratify.

ANTONYMS – *verb* **10** fail. **12** reject, turn down.

COMBINATIONS – **pass key 1** a key given only to those who are officially allowed access. **2** a master key.

ORIGIN – Old French *passer*, from Latin *passus* 'pace'.

pass² > *noun* a route over or through mountains.

IDIOMS – **sell the pass** Brit. betray a cause.

ORIGIN – variant of **PACE¹**, influenced by **PASS¹** and French *pas* 'step'.

passable > *adjective* **1** acceptable, but not outstanding. **2** able to be travelled along or on.

DERIVATIVES – **passably** adverb.

SYNONYMS – **1** acceptable, adequate, moderate, reasonable, tolerable. **2** clear, open, negotiable, traversable.

ANTONYMS – **2** impassable.

passage > *noun* **1** the action or process of passing. **2** a way through something; a passageway. **3** a short section from a text, musical composition, etc. **4** a journey by sea or air. **5** the right to pass through somewhere: *a permit for safe passage.*

IDIOMS – **work one's passage** work in return for a free place on a voyage.

SYNONYMS – **2** alley, corridor, hall, passageway, path. **3** citation, excerpt, extract, quotation, selection.

passageway > *noun* a corridor or other narrow passage between buildings or rooms.

passbook > *noun* a book issued by a bank or building society to an account holder, recording transactions.

passé /passay/ > *adjective* no longer fashionable; out of date.

ORIGIN – French, 'gone by'.

passel /pass'l/ > *noun* US informal a large group.

ORIGIN – representing a pronunciation of **PARCEL**.

passenger > *noun* **1** a person other than the driver, pilot, or crew who travels in a vehicle, ship, or aircraft. **2** a member of a team who does very little effective work.

ORIGIN – from Old French *passager* 'passing, transitory'.

passepartout /paspaartoo/ > *noun* a simple picture frame consisting of pieces of glass and card taped together at the edges.

ORIGIN – French, literally 'passes everywhere'.

passer-by > *noun* (pl. **passers-by**) a person who happens to be walking past something or someone.

passerine /passareen/ > *adjective* of or denoting birds of a large group (the order Passeriformes) distinguished by having feet adapted for perching and including all songbirds.

ORIGIN – from Latin *passer* 'sparrow'.

passim /passim/ > *adverb* (of references) at various places throughout the text.

ORIGIN – Latin, 'everywhere'.

passing > *adjective* **1** done quickly and casually. **2** (of a resemblance or similarity) slight. > *noun* **1** the ending of something. **2** euphemistic a person's death.

IDIOMS – **in passing** briefly and casually.

COMBINATIONS – **passing shot** Tennis a shot aiming the ball beyond and out of reach of one's opponent.

passion > *noun* **1** strong and barely controllable emotion. **2** intense sexual love. **3** an intense enthusiasm for something. **4** an outburst of anger. **5** (**the Passion**) the suffering and death of Jesus.

DERIVATIVES – **passionless** adjective.

SYNONYMS – **1** ardour, emotion, fervour, fire, intensity. **2** adoration, ardour, desire, love, lust. **3** fanaticism, fascination, love, mania, obsession. **4** frenzy, fury, paroxysm, rage, temper.

COMBINATIONS – **passion flower** a climbing plant with a flower whose component parts are said to suggest objects associated with the crucifixion of Christ.

passion fruit the edible purple fruit of some species of passion flower. **passion play** a play about Christ's crucifixion.

ORIGIN – Latin, from *pati* 'suffer'.

passionate > *adjective* showing or caused by passion.

DERIVATIVES – **passionately** adverb.

SYNONYMS – ardent, fervent, fiery, impassioned, intense.

ANTONYMS – apathetic, cold, passionless.

passive > *adjective* **1** accepting or allowing what happens or what others do, without active response or resistance. **2** Grammar denoting verbs in which the subject undergoes the action of the verb (e.g. *they were killed* as opposed to the active form *he killed them*). **3** (of a circuit or device) containing no source of energy or electromotive force. **4** Chemistry unreactive because of a thin inert surface layer of oxide.

DERIVATIVES – **passively** adverb **passivity** noun.

SYNONYMS – **1** deferential, docile, submissive, supine, tractable.

ANTONYMS – **1** active, assertive.

COMBINATIONS – **passive resistance** non-violent opposition to authority, especially a refusal to cooperate with legal requirements. **passive smoking** the involuntary inhalation of smoke from other people's cigarettes, cigars, or pipes.

ORIGIN – Latin *passivus*, from *pati* 'suffer'.

Passover > *noun* the major Jewish spring festival, commemorating the liberation of the Israelites from slavery in Egypt.

ORIGIN – from *pass over*, with reference to the exemption of the Israelites from the death of their firstborn (Book of Exodus, chapter 12).

passport > *noun* **1** an official government document certifying the holder's identity and citizenship and entitling them to travel abroad under its protection. **2** a thing that enables someone to do or achieve something: *qualifications are a passport to success.*

password > *noun* a secret word or phrase used to gain admission to a place.

past > *adjective* **1** gone by in time and no longer existing. **2** (of time) that has gone by. **3** Grammar (of a tense) expressing a past action or state. > *noun* **1** (**the past**) the time before the present day or the time referred to. **2** a person's or thing's history or earlier life. **3** Grammar a past tense or form of a verb. > *preposition* **1** beyond in time or space. **2** in front of or from one side to the other of. **3** beyond the scope, limits, or power of. > *adverb* **1** so as to pass from one side to the other. **2** used to indicate the passage of time.

IDIOMS – **not put it past** believe (someone) to be capable of doing something wrong or rash. **past it** informal too old to be good at something any longer.

SYNONYMS – adjective **1** bygone, ended, former, gone, previous.

COMBINATIONS – **past master** a person who is experienced or expert in an activity. **past participle** Grammar the form of a verb, typically ending in -ed in English, which is used in forming perfect and passive tenses and sometimes as an adjective, e.g. looked in have you looked?, lost in lost property.

ORIGIN – variant of passed.

pasta > noun dough formed into various shapes, cooked as part of a dish or boiled and served with a savoury sauce.

WORDFINDER – al dente (denoting pasta cooked so as to be firm when bitten); forms of pasta: cannelloni, capellini, farfalle, fettucine, fusilli, lasagne, linguine, macaroni, pappardelle, penne, ravioli, rigatoni, spaghetti, tagliatelle, tortellini, vermicelli.

ORIGIN – Italian, 'paste'.

paste > noun **1** a thick, soft, moist substance. **2** an adhesive made from water and starch, used especially for sticking paper. **3** a hard glassy substance used in making imitation gems. **4** a mixture of kaolin and water, used for making porcelain. > verb **1** coat or stick with paste. **2** Computing insert (a section of text) into a document. **3** informal beat or defeat severely.

wordpower facts

Paste

The word **paste** originally meant 'dough or pastry' in English, and it is related to the food terms **pasta**, **pastry**, **pâté**, and **patty**. The common root is the late Latin word pasta 'paste', which probably came from Greek pastē 'barley porridge'. Also related to pasta is the word **pastel**, from the Italian form pastello, which was applied to the blue dye woad, obtained by reducing the twigs of the woad plant to a paste. Another seemingly unrelated word, **pastiche**, comes from Italian pasticcio 'pie', a pie being thought of as containing a hotchpotch of different elements in the same way that a literary or musical pastiche can do.

pasteboard > noun thin board made by pasting together sheets of paper.

pastel > noun **1** a crayon made of powdered pigments bound with gum or resin. **2** a picture created using pastels. **3** a pale shade of a colour. > adjective (of a colour) pale, soft, and delicate.

DERIVATIVES – **pastellist** (also **pastelist**) noun.

ORIGIN – Italian pastello, diminutive of pasta 'paste'.

pastern /pastərn/ > noun the part of a horse's or other animal's foot between the fetlock and the hoof.

ORIGIN – Old French pasturon, from pasture 'strap for hobbling a horse'.

pasteurise /paastyərīz/ (also **pasteurize**) > verb make (milk or other food) safe to eat by destroying most of the micro-organisms in it, especially by heating.

DERIVATIVES – **pasteurisation** noun.

ORIGIN – named after the French chemist Louis Pasteur (1822–95).

pastiche /pasteesh/ > noun an artistic work in a style that imitates that of another work, artist, or period.

DERIVATIVES – **pasticheur** /pastishör/ noun.

SYNONYMS – imitation, parody, take-off.

ORIGIN – Italian pasticcio, literally 'pie', from Latin pasta 'paste': see PASTE.

pastie > noun (pl. **pasties**) **1** /paysti/ informal a decorative covering for the nipple worn by a stripper. **2** /pasti/ variant spelling of PASTY¹.

pastille /pastil/ > noun **1** a small sweet or lozenge. **2** a small pellet of aromatic paste burnt as a perfume or deodoriser.

ORIGIN – Latin pastillus 'little loaf, lozenge'.

pastime > noun an activity done regularly for enjoyment; a hobby.

SYNONYMS – hobby, interest, pursuit, recreation.

ORIGIN – from PASS¹ + TIME.

pastis /pastiss, pasteess/ > noun (pl. same) an aniseed-flavoured aperitif.

ORIGIN – French.

pastor /paastər/ > noun a minister in charge of a Christian church or congregation, especially in some non-episcopal churches.

ORIGIN – Latin, 'shepherd'.

pastoral /paastərəl/ > adjective **1** relating to the farming or grazing of sheep or cattle. **2** (of a literary, artistic, or musical work) portraying country life, especially in an idealised form. **3** relating to the giving of spiritual guidance. **4** relating to a teacher's responsibility for the general well-being of pupils or students. > noun a pastoral poem, picture, or piece of music.

DERIVATIVES – **pastoralism** noun.

pastoralist > noun (especially in Australia and New Zealand) a sheep or cattle farmer.

pastrami /pastraami/ > noun highly seasoned smoked beef.

ORIGIN – Yiddish.

pastry > noun (pl. **pastries**) **1** a dough of flour, fat, and water, used as a base and covering in baked dishes such as pies. **2** a cake consisting of sweet pastry with a cream, jam, or fruit filling.

WORDFINDER – kinds of pastry: choux, filo, puff pastry, shortcrust; en croute (in a pastry crust), patisserie (shop selling pastries).

ORIGIN – from PASTE.

pasturage > noun **1** land used for pasture. **2** the pasturing of animals.

pasture > noun **1** land covered with grass, suitable for grazing cattle or sheep. **2** grass growing on such land. > verb put (animals) to graze in a pasture.

IDIOMS – **pastures new** somewhere offering new opportunities. [ORIGIN – suggested by 'Tomorrow to fresh woods and pastures new' (Lycidas by John Milton).] **put out to pasture** force to retire.

ORIGIN – Latin pastura 'grazing', from pascere 'graze'.

pasty¹ /pasti/ (also **pastie**) > noun (pl. **pasties**) chiefly Brit. a folded pastry case filled with seasoned meat and vegetables.

ORIGIN – Old French paste, from Latin pasta 'paste'.

pasty² /paysti/ > adjective (**pastier**, **pastiest**) **1** of or like paste. **2** (of a person's skin) unhealthily pale.

pat¹ > verb (**patted**, **patting**) **1** tap quickly and gently with the flat of the hand. **2** mould or position with gentle taps. > noun **1** an act of patting. **2** a compact mass of butter or another soft substance.

IDIOMS – **a pat on the back** an expression of congratulation or encouragement.

pat² > adjective prompt but glib or unconvincing: a pat answer. > adverb conveniently or opportunely.

IDIOMS – **have off** (or **down**) **pat** have (something) memorised perfectly.

ORIGIN – apparently from the idea 'as if with a pat'.

pataca /pətaakə/ > noun the basic monetary unit of Macao, equivalent to 100 avos.

ORIGIN – Spanish and Portuguese.

Patagonian /pattəgōniən/ > noun a person from the South American region of Patagonia. > adjective relating to Patagonia.

patch > noun **1** a piece of material used to mend a hole or strengthen a weak point. **2** a small area differing in colour, composition, or texture from its surroundings. **3** a small plot of land: a cabbage patch. **4** Brit. informal a brief period of time: a bad patch. **5** Brit. informal an area for which someone is responsible or in which they operate. **6** a shield worn over a sightless or injured eye. **7** an adhesive piece of drug-impregnated material worn on the skin so that the drug may be gradually absorbed. **8** a temporary electrical or telephone connection. **9** Computing a small piece of code inserted to correct or enhance a program. > verb **1** mend, strengthen, or protect by means of a patch. **2** (**patch up**) informal treat (injuries) or repair (something) hastily or temporarily. **3** (**patch up**) informal settle (a quarrel or dispute). **4** (**patch together**) assemble hastily. **5** connect by a temporary electrical, radio, or telephonic connection.

IDIOMS – **not a patch on** Brit. informal greatly inferior to.

DERIVATIVES – **patcher** noun.

SYNONYMS – noun **2** area, blotch, spot.

COMBINATIONS – **patch pocket** a pocket made of a separate piece of cloth sewn on to the outside of a garment. **patch test** an allergy test in which a range of substances are applied to the skin in light scratches or under a plaster.

ORIGIN – perhaps from Old French dialect *pieche* 'piece'.

patchouli /pəchōōli/ > noun an aromatic oil obtained from a SE Asian shrub, used in perfumery, insecticides, and medicine.

ORIGIN – Tamil.

patchwork > noun **1** needlework in which small pieces of cloth in different designs are sewn edge to edge. **2** a thing composed of many different elements: *a patchwork of educational courses.*

patchy > adjective (**patchier**, **patchiest**) **1** existing or happening in small, isolated areas: *patchy fog.* **2** uneven in quality; inconsistent.

DERIVATIVES – **patchily** adverb **patchiness** noun.

pate /payt/ > noun archaic or humorous a person's head.

pâté /pattay/ > noun a rich savoury paste made from finely minced or mashed meat, fish, or other ingredients.

ORIGIN – Old French *paste* 'pie of seasoned meat'; compare with **PASTY**[1].

pâté de foie gras /pattay də fwaa **graa**/ > noun pâté made from fatted goose liver.

patella /pətellə/ > noun (pl. **patellae** /pətellee/) Anatomy the kneecap.

DERIVATIVES – **patellar** adjective.

ORIGIN – Latin, 'small dish'.

paten /patt'n/ > noun a plate for holding the bread during the Eucharist.

ORIGIN – Greek *patanē* 'a plate'.

patent /patt'nt, payt'nt/ > noun a government licence giving an individual or body the sole right to make, use, or sell an invention for a set period. [ORIGIN – from **LETTERS PATENT**.] > adjective /payt'nt/ **1** easily recognisable; obvious. **2** made and marketed under a patent. > verb obtain a patent for.

DERIVATIVES – **patentable** adjective **patently** /paytəntli/ adverb.

COMBINATIONS – **patent leather** glossy varnished leather. **patent medicine** a medicine made and marketed under a patent and available without prescription.

ORIGIN – from Latin *patere* 'lie open'.

patentee /paytəntee/ > noun a person or body that obtains or holds a patent.

pater /paytər/ > noun Brit. informal, dated father.

ORIGIN – Latin.

paterfamilias /paytərfəmilliass/ > noun (pl. **patresfamilias** /paytreezfəmilliass/) the male head of a family or household.

ORIGIN – Latin, 'father of the family'.

paternal > adjective **1** of, like, or appropriate to a father. **2** related through the father.

DERIVATIVES – **paternally** adverb.

paternalism > noun the policy of restricting the freedom and responsibilities of subordinates or dependants in their supposed best interest.

DERIVATIVES – **paternalist** noun & adjective **paternalistic** adjective.

paternity > noun **1** the state of being a father. **2** descent from a father.

COMBINATIONS – **paternity suit** chiefly N. Amer. a court case held to establish the identity of a child's father.

paternoster /pattər**nost**ər/ > noun **1** (in the Roman Catholic Church) the Lord's Prayer, especially in Latin. **2** a lift consisting of a series of linked doorless compartments moving continuously on an endless belt. **3** a fishing line to which hooks or weights are attached at intervals.

ORIGIN – from Latin *pater noster* 'our father', the first words of the Lord's Prayer.

path > noun **1** a way or track laid down for walking or made by continual treading. **2** the direction in which a person or thing moves. **3** a course of action or conduct.

DERIVATIVES – **pathless** adjective.

SYNONYMS – **1** footpath, pathway, track, trail. **2** course, route, way. **3** approach, avenue, course, direction, method.

COMBINATIONS – **path-breaking** pioneering; innovative. **pathname** Computing a description of where an item is to be found in a hierarchy of directories.

-path > combining form **1** denoting a practitioner of curative treatment: *homeopath.* **2** denoting a person who suffers from a disease: *psychopath.*

ORIGIN – from **-PATHY**, or from Greek *-pathēs* '-sufferer'.

Pathan /pətaan/ > noun a member of a Pashto-speaking people inhabiting NW Pakistan and SE Afghanistan.

ORIGIN – Hindi.

pathetic > adjective **1** arousing pity. **2** informal miserably inadequate. **3** archaic relating to the emotions.

DERIVATIVES – **pathetically** adverb.

SYNONYMS – **1** piteous, pitiable, pitiful, plaintive, poignant. **2** awful, feeble, hopeless, terrible, useless.

COMBINATIONS – **pathetic fallacy** the attribution of human feelings to inanimate things or animals.

ORIGIN – Greek *pathētikos* 'sensitive', from *pathos* 'suffering'.

pathfinder > noun a person who goes ahead and discovers or shows others a way.

patho- > combining form relating to disease: *pathology.*

ORIGIN – from Greek *pathos* 'suffering, disease'.

pathogen /pathəjən/ > noun a micro-organism that can cause disease.

DERIVATIVES – **pathogenic** adjective.

pathological (US **pathologic**) > adjective **1** of or caused by a disease. **2** informal compulsive. **3** of or relating to pathology.

DERIVATIVES – **pathologically** adverb.

pathology > noun **1** the branch of medicine concerned with the causes and effects of diseases. **2** the typical behaviour of a disease.

DERIVATIVES – **pathologist** noun.

pathos /paythoss/ > noun a quality that evokes pity or sadness.

SYNONYMS – piteousness, pitiableness, pitifulness, poignancy.

ORIGIN – Greek, 'suffering'.

pathway > noun **1** a path or its course. **2** a sequence of changes or events constituting a progression.

-pathy > combining form **1** denoting feelings: *telepathy.* **2** denoting disorder in a part of the body: *neuropathy.* **3** denoting curative treatment: *hydropathy.*

ORIGIN – from Greek *patheia* 'suffering, feeling'.

patience > noun **1** the capacity to tolerate delay, trouble, or suffering without becoming angry or upset. **2** chiefly Brit. a card game for one player.

IDIOMS – **lose patience** (or **lose one's patience**) become unable to keep one's temper.

SYNONYMS – **1** calm, composure, restraint, self-control, tolerance.

ANTONYMS – **1** impatience.

ORIGIN – Latin *patientia*, from *pati* 'suffer'.

patient > adjective having or showing patience. > noun a person receiving or registered to receive medical treatment.

WORDFINDER – clinical (*relating to the treatment of patients*).

DERIVATIVES – **patiently** adverb.

SYNONYMS – calm, easy-going, forbearing, long-suffering, tolerant.

ANTONYMS – impatient.

patina /pattinə/ > noun **1** a green or brown film on the surface of old bronze. **2** a sheen on wooden furniture produced by age and polishing.

DERIVATIVES – **patinated** adjective **patination** noun.

ORIGIN – Latin, 'shallow dish'.

patio > noun (pl. **patios**) **1** a paved outdoor area adjoining a house. **2** a roofless inner courtyard in a Spanish or Spanish-American house.

COMBINATIONS – **patio door** a large glass

sliding door leading to a patio, garden, or balcony.

ORIGIN – Spanish.

patisserie /pətissəri/ > *noun* **1** a shop where pastries and cakes are sold. **2** pastries and cakes collectively.

ORIGIN – French, from Latin *pasticium* 'pastry'.

patois /patwaa/ > *noun* (pl. same /patwaaz/) the dialect of a region, differing in various respects from the standard language of the country.

ORIGIN – French, 'rough speech'.

patresfamilias plural of PATERFAMILIAS.

patriarch /paytriaark/ > *noun* **1** the male head of a family or tribe. **2** a biblical figure regarded as a father of the human race, especially Abraham, Isaac, and Jacob, and their forefathers, or the sons of Jacob. **3** a powerful or respected older man. **4** a high-ranking bishop in certain Christian churches. **5** the head of an Orthodox Church that is not subject to the authority of an external patriarch or archbishop.

DERIVATIVES – **patriarchal** *adjective* **patriarchate** *noun*.

ORIGIN – Greek *patriarkhēs*, from *patria* 'family' + *arkhēs* 'ruling'.

patriarchy > *noun* (pl. **patriarchies**) **1** a form of social organisation in which the father or eldest male is the head of the family and descent is reckoned through the male line. **2** a system of society in which men hold most or all of the power.

patrician /pətrish'n/ > *noun* **1** an aristocrat. **2** a member of the nobility in ancient Rome. > *adjective* relating to or characteristic of aristocrats; upper-class.

ORIGIN – from Latin *patricius* 'having a noble father', from *pater* 'father'.

patricide /patrisīd/ > *noun* **1** the killing of one's father. **2** a person who kills their father.

ORIGIN – Latin *patricidium*, alteration of *parricidium* 'parricide'.

patrilineal /patrilinniəl/ > *adjective* relating to or based on relationship to the father or descent through the male line.

patrimony /patriməni/ > *noun* (pl. **patrimonies**) **1** property inherited from one's father or male ancestor. **2** heritage.

ORIGIN – Latin *patrimonium*, from *pater* 'father'.

patriot /paytriət, patriət/ > *noun* a person who vigorously supports their country and is prepared to defend it.

DERIVATIVES – **patriotism** *noun*.

SYNONYMS – chauvinist, jingoist, loyalist, nationalist.

ORIGIN – from Greek *patrios* 'of one's fathers', from *patris* 'fatherland'.

patriotic > *adjective* having or expressing devotion to and vigorous support for one's country.

DERIVATIVES – **patriotically** *adverb*.

SYNONYMS – chauvinistic, flag-waving, jingoistic, nationalistic.

patristic /pətristik/ > *adjective* relating to the early Christian theologians or their writings.

patrol > *noun* **1** a person or group sent to keep watch over an area, especially a detachment of guards or police. **2** the action of patrolling an area. **3** a military expedition to carry out reconnaissance. > *verb* (**patrolled**, **patrolling**) keep watch over (an area) by regularly walking or travelling around it.

DERIVATIVES – **patroller** *noun*.

SYNONYMS – *verb* guard, monitor, pound, prowl, roam.

COMBINATIONS – **patrolman** N. Amer. a patrolling police officer.

ORIGIN – from French *patrouiller* 'paddle in mud'.

patron > *noun* **1** a person who gives financial or other support to a person, organisation, cause, etc. **2** a regular customer of a restaurant, hotel, etc.

DERIVATIVES – **patroness** *noun*.

SYNONYMS – **1** backer, philanthropist, sponsor, supporter. **2** client, customer, frequenter, guest.

COMBINATIONS – **patron saint** the protecting or guiding saint of a person or place.

ORIGIN – Latin *patronus* 'protector of clients, defender', from *pater* 'father'; compare with PATTERN.

patronage /patrənij, paytrənij/ > *noun* **1** support given by a patron. **2** the power to control appointments to office or the right to privileges. **3** a patronising manner. **4** the regular custom attracted by a restaurant, hotel, etc.

patronise (also **patronize**) > *verb* **1** treat (someone) condescendingly. **2** be a patron or customer of.

DERIVATIVES – **patronising** *adjective* **patronisingly** *adverb*.

SYNONYMS – **1** condescend to, talk down to. **2** buy from, deal with, frequent, shop at.

patronymic /patrənimik/ > *noun* a name derived from the name of a father or ancestor, e.g. *Johnson, O'Brien, Ivanovich.*

ORIGIN – Greek *patrōnumikos*, from *patēr* 'father' + *onoma* 'name'.

patsy > *noun* (pl. **patsies**) informal, chiefly N. Amer. a person who is taken advantage of, especially by being cheated or blamed for something.

patten /patt'n/ > *noun* historical a shoe or clog having a raised sole or set on an iron ring, worn to raise the feet above wet ground.

ORIGIN – Old French *patin*.

patter¹ > *verb* **1** make a repeated light tapping sound. **2** run with quick, light steps. > *noun* a repeated light tapping sound.

ORIGIN – from PAT¹.

patter² > *noun* **1** rapid continuous talk, such as that used by a comedian or salesman. **2** the jargon of a profession or social group. > *verb* talk trivially and at length.

ORIGIN – from PATERNOSTER; the first sense was 'recite rapidly' (from the rapid and mechanical way in which the prayer was often said).

pattern > *noun* **1** a repeated decorative design. **2** a regular or discernible form or order in which a series of actions, events, or factors occur: *working patterns.* **3** a model, design, or set of instructions for making something. **4** a model from which a mould is made for a casting. **5** an example for others to follow. **6** a sample of cloth or wallpaper. > *verb* **1** decorate with a pattern. **2** give a regular or discernible form to.

SYNONYMS – *noun* **1** decoration, design, device, motif, ornamentation.

wordpower facts

Pattern

Pattern was originally the same word as **patron**. Patron entered English in medieval times via Old French from Latin *patronus* (from *pater* 'father'), which meant 'patron or protector'. The French word acquired the meaning 'pattern, model, or design' from the idea of a patron giving an example to be copied, and this sense also passed into English use. In the 16th century the two distinct spellings *pattern* and *patron* developed; by 1700 *patron* had ceased to be used of things, and the two forms became differentiated in sense.

patty > *noun* (pl. **patties**) **1** N. Amer. a small flat cake of minced food, especially meat. **2** a small pie or pasty.

ORIGIN – alteration of French *pâté*.

paua /powə/ > *noun* **1** a large New Zealand abalone or its shell. **2** a Maori fish hook made from an abalone shell.

ORIGIN – Maori.

paucity /pawsiti/ > *noun* smallness or insufficiency of supply or quantity.

ORIGIN – from Latin *paucus* 'few'.

Pauline /pawlīn/ > *adjective* relating to or characteristic of St Paul.

paunch > *noun* a large or protruding abdomen or stomach. > *verb* disembowel (an animal).

DERIVATIVES – **paunchy** *adjective*.

ORIGIN – Old French, from Latin *pantex* 'intestines'.

pauper > *noun* **1** a very poor person. **2** historical a recipient of public charity.

DERIVATIVES – **pauperise** (also **pauperize**) *verb* **pauperism** *noun*.
ORIGIN – Latin, 'poor'.

pause > *noun* **1** a temporary stop in action or speech. **2** Music a mark (⌢) over a note or rest that is to be lengthened by an unspecified amount. > *verb* stop temporarily.
IDIOMS – **give pause** (or **give pause for thought**) **to** cause to stop and think before doing something.
SYNONYMS – *noun* **1** break, cessation, halt, interruption, stop. *verb* cease, halt, stop.
ORIGIN – Greek *pausis*, from *pausein* 'to stop'.

pavane /pəˈvan/ (also **pavan** /ˈpavv'n/) > *noun* a stately dance in slow duple time, popular in the 16th and 17th centuries.
ORIGIN – perhaps from Italian *pavana* 'Paduan', from the dialect name of the city of *Padua*.

pave > *verb* cover (a piece of ground) with flat stones or bricks.
IDIOMS – **pave the way for** create the circumstances to enable (something) to happen.
DERIVATIVES – **paver** *noun* **paving** *noun*.
ORIGIN – Old French *paver*.

pavement > *noun* **1** Brit. a raised paved or asphalted path for pedestrians at the side of a road. **2** N. Amer. the hard surface of a road or street. **3** Geology a horizontal expanse of bare rock with cracks or joints.
ORIGIN – Old French, from Latin *pavimentum* 'trodden-down floor'.

pavilion > *noun* **1** Brit. a building at a sports ground used for changing and taking refreshments. **2** a summer house or other decorative shelter in a park or large garden. **3** a marquee with a peak and crenellated decorations, used at a show or fair. **4** a temporary display stand or other structure at a trade exhibition.
ORIGIN – Old French *pavillon*, from Latin *papilio* 'butterfly or tent'.

pavlova /pavˈlōvə/ > *noun* a dessert consisting of a meringue base or shell filled with whipped cream and fruit.
ORIGIN – named after the Russian ballerina Anna *Pavlova* (1881–1931).

Pavlovian /pavˈlōviən/ > *adjective* of or relating to conditioned reflexes as described by the Russian physiologist Ivan P. Pavlov (1849–1936), famous for training dogs to respond instantly to various stimuli.

paw > *noun* **1** an animal's foot having claws and pads. **2** informal a person's hand. > *verb* **1** feel or scrape with a paw or hoof. **2** informal touch or handle clumsily or lasciviously.
ORIGIN – Old French *poue*.

pawky > *adjective* (**pawkier**, **pawkiest**) chiefly Scottish & N. English drily humorous; sardonic.
ORIGIN – from Scots and northern English *pawk* 'trick'.

pawl /pawl/ > *noun* **1** a pivoted bar or lever whose free end engages with the teeth of a cogwheel or ratchet, allowing it to move or turn in one direction only. **2** each of a set of short, stout bars used to prevent a capstan, windlass, or winch from recoiling.
ORIGIN – perhaps from Low German and Dutch *pal*.

pawn¹ > *noun* **1** a chess piece of the smallest size and value. **2** a person used by others for their own purposes.
ORIGIN – Old French *poun*, from Latin *pedo* 'foot soldier'.

pawn² > *verb* deposit (an object) with a pawnbroker as security for money lent. > *noun* the state of being pawned: *everything was in pawn.*
COMBINATIONS – **pawnshop** a pawnbroker's shop.
ORIGIN – from Old French *pan* 'pledge, security'.

pawnbroker > *noun* a person licensed to lend money at interest on the security of an article deposited with them.

Pawnee /pawˈnee/ > *noun* (pl. same or **Pawnees**) a member of an American Indian confederacy formerly living in Nebraska, and now mainly in Oklahoma.
ORIGIN – from an American Indian language.

pawpaw /ˈpawpaw/ (also **papaw** /pəˈpaw/) > *noun* **1** a papaya. **2** US the sweet oblong yellow fruit of a North American tree.
ORIGIN – Spanish and Portuguese *papaya*, from Carib.

pax > *noun* **1** (in the Christian Church) the kiss of peace. **2** Brit. informal, dated a call for a truce, used by children when playing.
ORIGIN – Latin, 'peace'.

pay > *verb* (past and past participle **paid**) **1** give (someone) money due for work, goods, or an outstanding debt. **2** give (a sum of money) that is owed. **3** be profitable or advantageous: *crime doesn't pay.* **4** give (attention, respect, or a compliment) to. **5** give what is due or deserved to. **6** suffer a loss or misfortune as a consequence of an action: *someone's got to pay for all that grief.* **7** make (a visit or a call) to. > *noun* money paid for work.
IDIOMS – **he who pays the piper calls the tune** proverb the person providing the money for something has the right to determine how it's spent. **hit** (or **strike**) **pay dirt** N. Amer. informal find or reach a source of profit. [ORIGIN – from *pay dirt* in the sense 'ground containing a profitable amount of ore'.] **pay back** take revenge on. **pay dearly** suffer for a misdemeanour or failure. **pay off 1** dismiss with a final payment. **2** informal yield good results. **pay one's last respects** show respect towards (a dead person) by attending their funeral. **pay one's respects** make a polite visit to someone. **pay out** let out (a rope) by slackening it. **pay through the nose** informal pay much more than a fair price.
DERIVATIVES – **payer** *noun*.
SYNONYMS – *verb* **1** recompense, reimburse, remunerate. **2** disburse, expend, remit, render, spend. *noun* earnings, payment, remuneration, salary, wages.
COMBINATIONS – **paying guest** a lodger. **payphone** a public telephone operated by coins or by a credit or prepaid card. **payroll** a list of a company's employees and the amount of money they are to be paid.

---

wordpower facts

Pay

The English word **pay** comes via Old French *payer* from Latin *pacare* 'appease', from *pax* 'peace'. It is thus related to **pacific**, **pacify**, and **peace**. The notion of 'payment' arose in medieval Latin from the sense of 'pacifying' a creditor; in Middle English **pay** could mean 'pacify', but this sense died out before the end of the 15th century.

---

payable > *adjective* **1** that must be paid. **2** able to be paid.

payback > *noun* **1** profit from an investment equal to the initial outlay. **2** informal an act of revenge.

PAYE > *abbreviation* (in the UK) pay as you earn, a system whereby an employer deducts income tax from an employee's wages.

payee > *noun* a person to whom money is paid or to be paid.

payload > *noun* **1** the part of a vehicle's load which earns revenue; passengers and cargo. **2** an explosive warhead carried by an aircraft or missile. **3** the load carried by a spacecraft.

paymaster > *noun* **1** a person who pays another and therefore controls them. **2** an official who pays troops or workers.

payment > *noun* **1** the action of paying or the process of being paid. **2** an amount paid or payable.

pay-off > *noun* informal **1** a payment, especially a bribe. **2** the return on investment or on a bet. **3** a final outcome.

payola /payˈōlə/ > *noun* chiefly N. Amer. bribery in return for the unofficial promotion of a product in the media.
ORIGIN – from **PAY** + *-ola* as in *Victrola*, the name of a make of gramophone: the term

originally referred to bribery of a disc jockey to promote a record.

Pb > *symbol* the chemical element lead.

ORIGIN – from Latin *plumbum*.

pb > *abbreviation* paperback.

PC > *abbreviation* **1** personal computer. **2** police constable. **3** (also **pc**) politically correct; political correctness.

p.c. > *abbreviation* per cent.

PCB > *abbreviation* **1** Electronics printed circuit board. **2** Chemistry polychlorinated biphenyl.

PCP > *abbreviation* phencyclidine.

PCV > *abbreviation* Brit. passenger-carrying vehicle.

Pd > *symbol* the chemical element palladium.

PDQ > *abbreviation* informal pretty damn quick.

PDSA > *abbreviation* (in the UK) People's Dispensary for Sick Animals.

PDT > *abbreviation* Pacific Daylight Time.

PE > *abbreviation* **1** physical education. **2** Prince Edward Island.

pea > *noun* the spherical green seed of a climbing plant, growing in pods and eaten as a vegetable.

WORDFINDER – leguminous (*denoting plants of the pea family*), mangetout (*pea variety with edible pods*), petits pois (*small, tender peas*).

COMBINATIONS – **pea green** a bright green colour. **pea-shooter** a toy weapon consisting of a small tube out of which dried peas are blown. **pea-souper** Brit. a very thick yellowish fog.

ORIGIN – from **PEASE**, which was interpreted as being plural but in fact meant 'pea' in Old English; ultimately from Greek *pison*.

peace > *noun* **1** freedom from disturbance; tranquillity. **2** freedom from or the ending of war. **3** (**the peace**) Christian Church an action such as a handshake, signifying unity, performed during the Eucharist.

IDIOMS – **at peace 1** free from anxiety or distress. **2** euphemistic dead. **hold one's peace** remain silent. **keep the peace** refrain or prevent others from disturbing civil order. **make (one's) peace** become reconciled.

SYNONYMS – **1** calm, quiet, serenity, tranquillity. **2** accord, concord, harmony, order.

COMBINATIONS – **peace dividend** public money available for other purposes when spending on defence is reduced. **peace offering** a conciliatory gift. **peace sign** a sign of peace made by holding up the hand with palm out-turned and the first two fingers extended in a V-shape. **peacetime** a period when a country is not at war.

ORIGIN – Old French *pais*, from Latin *pax*.

peaceable > *adjective* **1** inclined to avoid argument or conflict. **2** free from conflict; peaceful.

DERIVATIVES – **peaceably** *adverb*.

peaceful > *adjective* **1** free from disturbance; calm. **2** not involving war or violence. **3** inclined to avoid conflict.

DERIVATIVES – **peacefully** *adverb*.

SYNONYMS – **1** calm, serene, still, tranquil, untroubled. **2** amicable, friendly, harmonious, orderly, peaceable.

peacekeeping > *noun* the active maintenance of a truce, especially by an international military force.

DERIVATIVES – **peacekeeper** *noun*.

peacenik > *noun* informal, often derogatory a member of a pacifist movement.

peach[1] > *noun* **1** the round stone fruit of a tree native to China, with juicy yellow flesh and downy yellow skin flushed with red. **2** a pinkish-orange colour. **3** informal an exceptionally good or attractive person or thing.

DERIVATIVES – **peachy** *adjective*.

COMBINATIONS – **peach Melba** ice cream and peaches with Melba sauce.

ORIGIN – Old French *pesche* from Latin *persica*, literally 'Persian'.

peach[2] > *verb* (**peach on**) informal inform on.

ORIGIN – related to **IMPEACH**.

peacock > *noun* a large crested pheasant native to Asia, of which the male has very long tail feathers with eye-like markings that can be fanned out in display.

COMBINATIONS – **peacock blue** a greenish-blue colour. **peacock butterfly** a brightly coloured butterfly with conspicuous eye-like wing spots.

ORIGIN – Old English, from Latin *pavo* 'peacock' + **COCK**.

peafowl > *noun* a peacock or peahen.

peahen > *noun* the female of the peacock, which has drabber colours and a shorter tail than the male.

pea jacket (also **pea coat**) > *noun* a short double-breasted overcoat of coarse woollen cloth, formerly worn by sailors.

ORIGIN – Dutch *pijjakker*, from *pij* 'coat of coarse cloth'.

peak > *noun* **1** the pointed top of a mountain. **2** a mountain with a pointed top. **3** a stiff brim at the front of a cap. **4** the point of highest activity, achievement, intensity, etc. > *verb* reach a highest point or maximum. > *adjective* characterised by maximum activity or demand: *peak hours*.

SYNONYMS – *noun* **4** apex, climax, culmination, pinnacle, summit, zenith. *verb* climax, culminate.

ORIGIN – probably from *peaked*, a variant of *picked*, a dialect word meaning 'pointed'.

peaked[1] > *adjective* (of a cap) having a peak.

peaked[2] > another term for **PEAKY**.

ORIGIN – from an archaic verb *peak* 'to decline in health and spirits'.

peaky > *adjective* (**peakier**, **peakiest**) pale from illness or fatigue.

peal > *noun* **1** a loud or prolonged ringing of a bell or bells. **2** a loud repeated or reverberating sound of thunder or laughter. **3** a set of bells. > *verb* ring or resound in a peal.

ORIGIN – shortening of **APPEAL**.

peanut > *noun* **1** the oval edible seed of a plant native to South America, whose seeds develop in underground pods. **2** (**peanuts**) informal a paltry sum of money.

COMBINATIONS – **peanut butter** a spread made from ground roasted peanuts.

pear > *noun* the yellowish- or brownish-green edible fruit of a tree, narrow at the stalk and wider towards the tip.

WORDFINDER – *varieties of pear:* Bartlett, bergamot, Comice, Conference, Jargonelle, Williams; perry (*drink made from pears*).

IDIOMS – **go pear-shaped** Brit. informal go wrong. [ORIGIN – RAF slang.]

COMBINATIONS – **pear drop** a boiled sweet in the shape of a pear, with a pungently sweet flavour.

ORIGIN – Latin *pirum*.

pearl[1] > *noun* **1** a hard, shiny spherical mass, typically white or bluish-grey, formed within the shell of an oyster or other mollusc and highly prized as a gem. **2** a thing of great worth. **3** a very pale bluish grey or white colour. > *verb* **1** literary form pearl-like drops. **2** (**pearling**) diving or fishing for pearl oysters.

WORDFINDER – mother-of-pearl, nacre (*pearly substance lining oyster shells*).

IDIOMS – **cast pearls before swine** offer valuable things to people who do not appreciate them.

COMBINATIONS – **pearl barley** barley reduced to small round grains by grinding. **pearl onion** a very small onion used for pickling.

ORIGIN – Old French *perle*.

pearl[2] > *noun* Brit. another term for **PICOT**.

ORIGIN – variant of **PURL**[1].

pearled > *adjective* literary adorned with pearls.

pearlescent > *adjective* having a lustre resembling that of mother-of-pearl.

pearly > *adjective* (**pearlier**, **pearliest**) like a pearl in lustre or colour. > *noun* (**pearlies**) Brit. **1** a pearly king's or queen's clothes or pearl buttons. **2** informal a person's teeth.

COMBINATIONS – **Pearly Gates** informal the gates of heaven. [ORIGIN – from a reference in the Book of Revelation to twelve gates, each fashioned from a single pearl.] **pearly king** (or **queen**) a London costermonger

Pearmain-pedal

(or his wife) wearing traditional ceremonial clothes covered with pearl buttons.

Pearmain /**pair**mayn, pər**mayn**/ > *noun* a pear-shaped variety of dessert apple with firm white flesh.
ORIGIN – Old French *parmain*, probably named after the Italian city of *Parma*.

peasant > *noun* **1** a poor smallholder or agricultural labourer of low social status. **2** *informal* an ignorant, rude, or unsophisticated person.
DERIVATIVES – **peasantry** *noun*.
ORIGIN – Old French *paisent*, from *pais* 'country'.

pease > *plural noun* archaic peas.
COMBINATIONS – **pease pudding** chiefly Brit. a dish of split peas boiled with onion and carrot and mashed to a pulp.

peat > *noun* partly decomposed vegetable matter forming a deposit on acidic, boggy ground, dried for use in gardening and as fuel.
DERIVATIVES – **peaty** *adjective*.
COMBINATIONS – **peat moss 1** a large absorbent moss which grows in dense masses on boggy ground. **2** a peat bog.
ORIGIN – Latin *peta*, perhaps of Celtic origin.

peau-de-soie /pōdə**swaa**/ > *noun* a smooth, finely ribbed satin fabric of silk or rayon.
ORIGIN – French, 'skin of silk'.

pebble > *noun* **1** a small stone made smooth and round by the action of water or sand. **2** (before another noun) *informal* with very thick lenses: *pebble glasses.*
DERIVATIVES – **pebbly** *adjective*.

pebbledash > *noun* mortar with pebbles in it, used as a coating for external walls.

pec > *noun* *informal* a pectoral muscle.

pecan /**pee**kən/ > *noun* a smooth pinkish-brown nut like a walnut, obtained from a hickory tree of the southern US.
ORIGIN – from Illinois (an American Indian language).

peccadillo*　/pekkə**dill**ō/ > *noun* (pl. **peccadilloes** or **peccadillos**) a minor sin or fault.
*SPELLING – two *c*s, two *l*s: pe*cc*adi*ll*o.
ORIGIN – Spanish, diminutive of *pecado* 'sin'.

peccant /**pekk**ənt/ > *adjective* archaic **1** at fault. **2** diseased.
ORIGIN – Latin, 'sinning'.

peccary /**pekk**əri/ > *noun* (pl. **peccaries**) a gregarious piglike mammal found from the south-western US to Paraguay.
ORIGIN – Carib.

peccavi /pe**kaa**vi/ > *exclamation* archaic used to express one's guilt.
ORIGIN – Latin, 'I have sinned'.

peck¹ > *verb* **1** (of a bird) strike or bite with its beak. **2** kiss lightly or perfunctorily. **3** (**peck at**) *informal* eat (food) listlessly or daintily. **4** type slowly and laboriously. > *noun* **1** an act of pecking. **2** a light or perfunctory kiss.
COMBINATIONS – **pecking order** a hierarchy of status among members of a group, originally as observed among hens.

peck² > *noun* a measure of capacity for dry goods, equal to a quarter of a bushel (2 imperial gallons = 9.092 litres, or 8 US quarts = 8.81 litres).
ORIGIN – Old French *pek*.

pecker > *noun* N. Amer. vulgar slang a man's penis.
IDIOMS – **keep your pecker up** Brit. informal remain cheerful. [ORIGIN – probably from *pecker* in the sense 'beak'.]

peckish > *adjective* informal hungry.

Pecksniffian /pek**sniff**ən/ > *adjective* affecting high moral principles in a hypocritical way.
ORIGIN – from Mr *Pecksniff*, the name of a character in Dickens's *Martin Chuzzlewit*.

pecorino /pekkə**ree**nō/ > *noun* an Italian cheese made from ewes' milk.
ORIGIN – Italian, 'of ewes'.

pecten /**pek**ten/ > *noun* (pl. **pectens** or **pectines** /**pek**tineez/) Zoology **1** a comb-like structure. **2** a scallop.
ORIGIN – Latin, 'a comb'.

pectin > *noun* a soluble gelatinous substance present in ripe fruits, used as a setting agent in jams and jellies.
ORIGIN – from Greek *pektos* 'congealed'.

pectoral /**pek**tərəl/ > *adjective* of, on, or relating to the breast or chest. > *noun* **1** a pectoral muscle. **2** an ornamental breastplate.
COMBINATIONS – **pectoral muscle** each of four large paired muscles which cover the front of the ribcage.
ORIGIN – Latin *pectoralis*, from *pectus* 'breast, chest'.

peculation /pekyoo**lay**sh'n/ > *noun* formal embezzlement of public funds.
ORIGIN – from Latin *peculari* 'embezzle'.

peculiar* > *adjective* **1** strange or odd. **2** (**peculiar to**) belonging exclusively to. **3** formal particular. > *noun* a parish or church exempt from the jurisdiction of the diocese in which it lies, though subject to the jurisdiction of the monarch or an archbishop.
DERIVATIVES – **peculiarly** *adverb*.
*SPELLING – -iar, not -ier: pecul*iar*. The spelling *peculier* is archaic.
SYNONYMS – *adjective* **1** bizarre, funny, odd, strange, weird.
ANTONYMS – *adjective* **1** normal, ordinary.

> **wordpower facts**
> ### Peculiar
> The word **peculiar** is related to **pecuniary** and **impecunious**. It comes from Latin *peculiaris* 'of private property', from *peculium* 'property', which is based on *pecu* 'cattle', the root of **pecuniary**, **impecunious**, and other 'money' words. Original medieval senses of **peculiar** were 'particular, special' and 'belonging to an individual, constituting private property'; the sense 'odd' dates from the early 17th century.

peculiarity > *noun* (pl. **peculiarities**) **1** an unusual or distinctive feature or habit. **2** the state of being peculiar.
SYNONYMS – **1** aberration, anomaly, foible, idiosyncrasy, oddity, quirk. **2** bizarreness, oddness, strangeness, weirdness.

pecuniary > *adjective* formal of or relating to money.
ORIGIN – Latin *pecuniarius*, from *pecunia* 'money'.

pedagogue /**pedd**əgog/ > *noun* formal or humorous a teacher, especially a strict or pedantic one.
ORIGIN – Greek *paidagōgos*, denoting a slave who accompanied a child to school (from *pais* 'boy' + *agōgos* 'guide').

pedagogy /**pedd**əgogi, **pedd**əgoji/ > *noun* the profession, science, or theory of teaching.
DERIVATIVES – **pedagogic** (also **pedagogical**) *adjective*.

pedal¹ /**pedd**'l/ > *noun* **1** each of a pair of foot-operated levers for powering a bicycle or other vehicle. **2** a foot-operated throttle, brake, or clutch control. **3** a foot-operated lever on a piano, organ, etc. for sustaining or softening the tone. **4** Music a pedal note. > *verb* (**pedalled, pedalling**; US **pedaled, pedaling**) **1** move (a bicycle or similar vehicle) by working the pedals. **2** use the pedals of a piano, organ, etc.
DERIVATIVES – **pedaller** (US **pedaler**) *noun*.
USAGE – do not confuse **pedal** and **peddle**. **Pedal** is a noun denoting a foot-operated lever; as a verb it means 'move by means of pedals'. **Peddle** is a verb meaning 'sell (goods)'. The associated noun from **pedal** is **pedaller** (US **pedaler**), and the noun from **peddle** is **pedlar** or **peddler**.
COMBINATIONS – **pedal note** Music **1** the lowest or fundamental note of a harmonic series in some brass and wind instruments. **2** (also **pedal point**) a note sustained in one part (usually the bass) through successive harmonies. **pedal pushers** women's calf-length trousers. **pedal steel guitar** a musical instrument resembling a Hawaiian

guitar but set on a stand with pedals to adjust the tension of the strings.
ORIGIN – Latin *pedalis*, from *pes* 'foot'.

pedal² /pedd'l, peed'l/ > *adjective* chiefly Medicine & Zoology of or relating to the foot or feet.
ORIGIN – Latin *pedalis*, from *pes* 'foot'.

pedalo /peddəlō/ > *noun* (pl. **pedalos** or **pedaloes**) Brit. a small pedal-operated pleasure boat.

pedant /pedd'nt/ > *noun* a person excessively concerned with minor detail or with displaying technical knowledge.
DERIVATIVES – **pedantry** *noun*.
SYNONYMS – hair-splitter, perfectionist.
ORIGIN – French *pédant*, probably related to **PEDAGOGUE**.

pedantic > *adjective* of or like a pedant.
DERIVATIVES – **pedantically** *adverb*.
SYNONYMS – donnish, fussy, hair-splitting, nit-picking, perfectionist.

peddle > *verb* 1 sell (goods) by going from place to place. 2 sell (an illegal drug or stolen item). 3 derogatory promote (an idea) persistently or widely.
SYNONYMS – 1 deal in, hawk, tout, trade in.

peddler > *noun* variant spelling of **PEDLAR**.

pederasty /peddərasti/ > *noun* sexual intercourse between a man and a boy.
DERIVATIVES – **pederast** *noun* **pederastic** *adjective*.
ORIGIN – Greek *paiderastia*, from *pais* 'boy' + *erastēs* 'lover'.

pedestal /peddəst'l/ > *noun* 1 the base or support on which a statue, obelisk, or column is mounted. 2 each of the two supports of a kneehole desk or table. 3 the supporting column of a washbasin or toilet pan.
ORIGIN – Italian *piedestallo*, from *piè* 'foot' + *di* 'of' + *stallo* 'stall'.

pedestrian > *noun* a person walking rather than travelling in a vehicle. > *adjective* dull; uninspired.
DERIVATIVES – **pedestrianly** *adverb*.
SYNONYMS – *adjective* dull, plodding, predictable, unimaginative, uninspired.
ANTONYMS – exciting, inspired.
ORIGIN – from Latin *pedester* 'going on foot'.

pedestrianise (also **pedestrianize**) > *verb* make (a street or area) accessible only to pedestrians.
DERIVATIVES – **pedestrianisation** *noun*.

pediatrics > *plural noun* US spelling of **PAEDIATRICS**.

pedicure > *noun* a cosmetic treatment of the feet and toenails. > *verb* give a pedicure to.
ORIGIN – French *pédicure*, from Latin *pes* 'foot' + *curare* 'attend to'.

pedigree > *noun* 1 the record of descent of an animal, showing it to be pure-bred. 2 a

person's lineage or ancestry. 3 the history or origins of a person or thing.

wordpower facts

Pedigree

The word **pedigree** comes from Old French *pé de grue*, which literally meant 'crane's foot'. The transfer of meaning arose from a mark used to denote succession in pedigrees or family trees, which had three branching lines and was likened to a bird's foot. The first, medieval sense of **pedigree** in English was 'family tree, genealogical table'; the modern sense 1 was not recorded until the 17th century.

pediment /peddimənt/ > *noun* Architecture the triangular upper part of the front of a classical building, typically surmounting a portico.
ORIGIN – perhaps originally an alteration of **PYRAMID**.

pedlar (also **peddler**) > *noun* 1 an itinerant trader in small goods. 2 a person who sells illegal drugs or stolen goods. 3 a person who peddles an idea or view.

pedometer /pidommitər/ > *noun* an instrument for estimating the distance travelled on foot by recording the number of steps taken.

peduncle /pidungk'l/ > *noun* 1 Botany the stalk carrying a flower or fruit. 2 Zoology a stalk-like connecting structure.
DERIVATIVES – **pedunculate** *adjective*.
ORIGIN – Latin *pedunculus*, from *pes* 'foot'.

pee informal > *verb* (**pees, peed, peeing**) urinate. > *noun* 1 an act of urinating. 2 urine.
ORIGIN – euphemistic use of the initial letter of **PISS**.

peek > *verb* 1 look quickly or furtively. 2 protrude slightly so as to be just visible. > *noun* a quick or furtive look.
SYNONYMS – *verb* 1 glance, peep.

peekaboo > *noun* a game played with a young child, which involves hiding and suddenly reappearing, saying 'peekaboo'. > *adjective* 1 (of a garment) made of transparent fabric or having a pattern of small holes. 2 (of a hairstyle) concealing one eye with a fringe or wave.

peel¹ > *verb* 1 remove the outer covering or skin from (a fruit, vegetable, etc.). 2 lose parts of its outer layer or covering in small strips or pieces. 3 (**peel away** or **off**) remove (a thin outer covering). 4 (**peel something off** or Brit. **peel off**) remove an article of clothing. 5 (**peel off**) leave a formation or group by veering away.

> *noun* the outer covering or rind of a fruit or vegetable.
DERIVATIVES – **peelings** *plural noun*.
ORIGIN – Latin *pilare* 'to strip hair from', from *pilus* 'hair'.

peel² (also **pele**) > *noun* a late medieval square defensive tower typical of the border counties of England and Scotland.
ORIGIN – Old French *pel* 'stake, palisade'.

peeler¹ > *noun* a utensil for peeling fruit and vegetables.

peeler² > *noun* Brit. informal, archaic a police officer.
ORIGIN – from the name of the British Prime Minister Sir Robert *Peel*, who established the Metropolitan Police.

peen (also **pein**) > *noun* the rounded or wedge-shaped end of a hammer head opposite the face. > *verb* 1 strike with a peen. 2 another term for *shot-peen*.

peep¹ > *verb* 1 look quickly and furtively. 2 (**peep out**) come slowly or partially into view. > *noun* 1 a quick or furtive look. 2 a momentary or partial view of something.
SYNONYMS – *verb* 1 peek, glance.
COMBINATIONS – **peeping Tom** a furtive voyeur. [ORIGIN – from the name of the person said to have watched Lady Godiva ride naked through Coventry.] **peep show** an entertainment in which pictures are viewed through a lens or hole set into a box.

peep² > *noun* a weak or brief high-pitched sound. > *verb* make a peep.
IDIOMS – **not a peep** not the slightest utterance or complaint.

peeper > *noun* 1 a person who peeps. 2 (**peepers**) informal a person's eyes.

peephole > *noun* a small hole in a door through which callers may be identified.

peepul /peep'l/ (also **pipal**) > *noun* another term for **BO TREE**.
ORIGIN – Sanskrit.

peer¹ > *verb* 1 look with difficulty or concentration. 2 be just visible.
SYNONYMS – 1 gape, gaze, squint, stare.

peer² > *noun* 1 a member of the nobility in Britain or Ireland, comprising the ranks of duke, marquess, earl, viscount, and baron. 2 a person of the same age, status, or ability as another specified person.
IDIOMS – **without peer** unrivalled.
COMBINATIONS – **peer group** a group of people of approximately the same age, status, and interests. **peer of the realm** a hereditary peer who has the right to sit in the House of Lords.
ORIGIN – Old French, from Latin *par* 'equal'.

peerage > *noun* 1 the title and rank of peer or peeress. 2 (**the peerage**) peers collectively.

peeress > *noun* **1** a woman holding the rank of a peer in her own right. **2** the wife or widow of a peer.

peerless > *adjective* unequalled or unrivalled.

peeve informal > *verb* annoy; irritate. > *noun* a cause of annoyance.

peevish > *adjective* irritable.
DERIVATIVES – **peevishly** *adverb* **peevishness** *noun*.

peewit > *noun* Brit. the lapwing.

peg > *noun* **1** a short projecting pin or bolt used for hanging things on, securing something in place, or marking a position. **2** a clip for holding things together or hanging up clothes. **3** a point or limit on a scale. **4** informal a person's leg. **5** chiefly Indian a measure of spirits. > *verb* (**pegged**, **pegging**) **1** fix, attach, or mark with a peg or pegs. **2** fix (a price, rate, etc.) at a particular level. **3** (**peg out**) informal die. **4** (**peg away**) informal work hard over a long period.
IDIOMS – **off the peg** chiefly Brit. (of clothes) ready-made. **a square peg in a round hole** a person in a situation unsuited to their abilities or character. **take someone down a peg or two** make someone less arrogant.
COMBINATIONS – **pegboard** a board with a regular pattern of small holes for pegs. **peg leg** informal a wooden leg.

Peigan /**pee**gən/ (also **Piegan**) > *noun* (pl. same or **Peigans**) a member of a North American Indian people of the Blackfoot confederacy.
ORIGIN – Blackfoot.

peignoir /**pay**nwaar/ > *noun* a woman's light dressing gown or negligee.
ORIGIN – French, from *peigner* 'to comb' (because originally worn while combing the hair).

pein > *noun* & *verb* variant spelling of **PEEN**.

pejorative* /pi**jorr**ətiv/ > *adjective* expressing contempt or disapproval.
DERIVATIVES – **pejoratively** *adverb*.
*SPELLING – the first syllable is *pej-*, not *perj-*: *pejorative*.
ORIGIN – French *péjoratif*, from Latin *pejorare* 'make worse'.

Pekinese (also **Pekingese**) > *noun* (pl. same) a small, short-legged breed of dog with long hair and a snub nose. > *adjective* relating to Beijing (Peking) in China.

pekoe /**pee**kō/ > *noun* a high-quality black tea made from young leaves.
ORIGIN – Chinese dialect.

pelage /**pell**ij/ > *noun* the fur, hair, or wool of a mammal.
ORIGIN – French, from Old French *pel* 'hair'.

pelagic /pi**la**jik/ > *adjective* **1** of or relating to the open sea. **2** (chiefly of fishes) inhabiting the upper layers of the open sea.
ORIGIN – Greek *pelagikos*, from *pelagios* 'of the sea'.

pelargonium /pellər**gō**niəm/ > *noun* a plant cultivated for its red, pink, or white flowers.
ORIGIN – Latin, from Greek *pelargos* 'stork', apparently on the pattern of *geranium*.

pele > *noun* variant spelling of **PEEL²**.

pelf > *noun* archaic money, especially when gained dishonestly.
ORIGIN – related to **PILFER**.

pelican > *noun* a large waterbird with a long bill and an extensible throat pouch for scooping up fish.
COMBINATIONS – **pelican crossing** (in the UK) a pedestrian crossing with traffic lights operated by pedestrians. [ORIGIN – from *pe(destrian)* *li(ght)* *con(trolled)* altered to conform to the bird's name.]
ORIGIN – Greek *pelekan*, probably from *pelekus* 'axe' (with reference to its bill).

pelisse /pə**leess**/ > *noun* historical **1** a woman's ankle-length cloak with armholes or sleeves. **2** a fur-lined cloak, especially as part of a hussar's uniform.
ORIGIN – French, from Latin *pellicia vestis* 'garment of fur'.

pellagra /pi**lag**rə/ > *noun* a disease characterised by dermatitis, diarrhoea, and mental disturbance, caused by a dietary deficiency.
ORIGIN – Italian, from *pelle* 'skin'.

pellet > *noun* **1** a small, rounded, compressed mass of a substance. **2** a piece of small shot or other lightweight bullet. **3** a small mass of bones and feathers regurgitated by a bird of prey. > *verb* (**pelleted**, **pelleting**) **1** form into pellets. **2** hit with pellets.
DERIVATIVES – **pelletise** (also **pelletize**) *verb*.
ORIGIN – Old French *pelote* 'metal ball'.

pellicle /**pell**ik'l/ > *noun* technical a thin skin, cuticle, or membrane.
ORIGIN – Latin *pellicula*, diminutive of *pellis* 'skin'.

pell-mell > *adjective* & *adverb* in a confused, rushed, or disorderly way.
ORIGIN – French *pêle-mêle*.

pellucid /pi**loo**sid/ > *adjective* **1** translucently clear. **2** easily understood.
ORIGIN – Latin *pellucidus*, from *perlucere* 'shine through'.

Pelmanism /**pel**məniz'm/ > *noun* **1** a system of memory training originally devised by the Pelman Institute for the Scientific Development of Mind, Memory, and Personality. **2** a card game involving finding matching pairs.

pelmet > *noun* a strip of fabric or fabric-faced wood fitted across the top of a window to conceal the curtain fittings.
ORIGIN – French *palmette* 'small palm leaf'.

pelota /pi**lō**tə/ > *noun* a Basque or Spanish ball game played in a walled court with basket-like rackets.
ORIGIN – Spanish, 'ball'.

peloton /**pell**əton/ > *noun* the main group of cyclists in a race.
ORIGIN – French, 'small ball'.

pelt¹ > *verb* **1** hurl missiles at. **2** (**pelt down**) (chiefly of rain) fall very heavily. **3** run very quickly.
IDIOMS – (at) **full pelt** as fast as possible.

pelt² > *noun* **1** the skin of an animal with the fur, wool, or hair still on it. **2** the raw skin of a sheep or goat, stripped and ready for tanning.
ORIGIN – Latin *pellis* 'skin'.

peltate /**pel**tayt/ > *adjective* shield-shaped.
ORIGIN – from Greek *peltē* 'shield'.

peltry > *noun* animal pelts collectively.

pelvis /**pel**viss/ > *noun* (pl. **pelvises** or **pelves** /**pel**veez/) **1** the large bony frame at the base of the spine to which the lower limbs are attached. **2** (**renal pelvis**) the broadened top part of the ureter into which the kidney tubules drain.
DERIVATIVES – **pelvic** *adjective*.
ORIGIN – Latin, 'basin'.

pelycosaur /**pell**ikəsawr/ > *noun* a fossil reptile with a spiny sail-like crest on the back.
ORIGIN – from Greek *pelux* 'bowl' + *sauros* 'lizard'.

Pembs. > *abbreviation* Pembrokeshire.

pemmican /**pemm**ikən/ > *noun* a cake made from a paste of pounded dried meat, melted fat, and other ingredients.
ORIGIN – Cree: pemmican was originally made by North American Indians and later adapted by Arctic explorers.

pemphigus /**pem**figəss/ > *noun* Medicine a skin disease in which watery blisters form on the skin.
ORIGIN – Latin, from Greek *pemphix* 'bubble'.

pen¹ > *noun* **1** an instrument for writing or drawing with ink. **2** an electronic device used with a writing surface to enter commands into a computer. **3** the tapering internal shell of a squid. > *verb* (**penned**, **penning**) write or compose.
IDIOMS – **the pen is mightier than the sword** proverb written words are more effective than military power or violence.
COMBINATIONS – **penlight** a small electric torch shaped like a pen. **pen name** a literary pseudonym. **pen pal** informal a penfriend. **pen-pusher** informal a clerical worker.
ORIGIN – French *penne*, from Latin *penna*

'feather': originally denoting a feather with a sharpened quill, used for writing.

pen² > *noun* **1** a small enclosure for farm animals. **2** a covered dock for a submarine or other warship. > *verb* (**penned**, **penning**) **1** put or keep in a pen. **2** (**pen someone up** or **in**) confine someone in a restricted space.

pen³ > *noun* a female swan.

penal > *adjective* **1** relating to the punishment of offenders under the legal system. **2** extremely severe: *penal rates of interest*.
SYNONYMS – **1** correctional, corrective, disciplinary, punitive, retributive.
COMBINATIONS – **penal servitude** imprisonment with hard labour.

penalise (also **penalize**) > *verb* **1** subject to a penalty or punishment. **2** Law make (an action) legally punishable. **3** put (someone) in an unfavourable position.
DERIVATIVES – **penalisation** *noun*.
SYNONYMS – **1** correct, discipline, punish.

penalty > *noun* (pl. **penalties**) **1** a punishment or disadvantage imposed for breaking a law, rule, or contract. **2** something undesirable suffered as a consequence of an event or action. **3** a penalty kick.
IDIOMS – **under** (or **on**) **penalty of** under the threat of.
SYNONYMS – **1** forfeit, punishment, sanction.
COMBINATIONS – **penalty area** (also **penalty box**) Soccer the rectangular area marked out in front of each goal, within which a foul by a defender involves the award of a penalty kick. **penalty kick 1** Soccer a free shot at the goal awarded to the attacking team after a foul within the penalty area. **2** Rugby a place kick awarded to a team after an offence by an opponent.
ORIGIN – Latin *poenalitas*, based on *poena* 'pain'.

penance > *noun* **1** voluntary self-punishment expressing repentance for wrongdoing. **2** a sacrament in which a member of the Church confesses sins to a priest and is given absolution. **3** a religious duty imposed as part of this sacrament.
ORIGIN – Old French, from Latin *paenitentia* 'repentance'.

pence plural of PENNY (used for sums of money).
USAGE – avoid using **pence** in the singular to mean 'penny', as in *the chancellor will put one pence on income tax*.

penchant /**poN**shoN/ > *noun* a strong liking or inclination: *a penchant for champagne*.
ORIGIN – French, 'leaning, inclining'.

pencil > *noun* an instrument for writing or drawing, typically consisting of a thin stick of graphite enclosed in wood or a cylindrical case. > *verb* (**pencilled**,

pencilling; US **penciled**, **penciling**) **1** write, draw, or colour with a pencil. **2** (**pencil something in**) arrange or note down something provisionally.
COMBINATIONS – **pencil skirt** a very narrow straight skirt.
ORIGIN – Old French *pincel*, from Latin *peniculus* 'small brush'.

pendant > *noun* **1** a piece of jewellery that hangs from a necklace chain. **2** a light designed to hang from the ceiling. > *adjective* pendent.

pendent > *adjective* **1** hanging down. **2** pending.
DERIVATIVES – **pendency** *noun*.

pending > *adjective* **1** awaiting a decision or settlement. **2** about to happen. > *preposition* until (something) takes place.
ORIGIN – anglicised spelling of French *pendant* 'hanging'.

pendulous > *adjective* hanging down; drooping.

pendulum > *noun* a weight hung from a fixed point so that it can swing freely, especially one regulating the mechanism of a clock.
DERIVATIVES – **pendular** *adjective*.
ORIGIN – Latin, neuter of *pendulus* 'hanging down'.

penetralia /penni**tray**lia/ > *plural noun* the innermost parts of a building.

penetrant > *noun* a substance which can penetrate cracks, pores, etc.

penetrate > *verb* **1** force a way into or through. **2** spread throughout; permeate. **3** infiltrate. **4** understand or gain insight into. **5** (of a man) insert the penis into the vagina or anus of (a sexual partner).
DERIVATIVES – **penetrable** *adjective* **penetration** *noun* **penetrative** *adjective* **penetrator** *noun*.
SYNONYMS – **1** enter, pierce, puncture. **2** impregnate, permeate, pervade, suffuse.
ORIGIN – Latin *penetrare* 'go into'.

penetrating > *adjective* **1** able to make a way through or into something. **2** (of a sound) clearly heard through or above others. **3** having or showing clear insight.
DERIVATIVES – **penetratingly** *adverb*.

penetrometer /penni**tromm**itar/ > *noun* an instrument for determining the hardness of a substance by measuring the penetration of a rod driven into it by a known force.

penfriend > *noun* a person with whom one becomes friendly by exchanging letters.

penguin > *noun* a flightless black and white seabird of the southern hemisphere, with wings used as flippers.
WORDFINDER – *kinds of penguin*: emperor, gentoo, king, macaroni, rockhopper; rookery (*penguin breeding colony*).

wordpower facts
Penguin
The origins of the oddly spelled word **penguin** are obscure. It is first recorded in the late 16th-century work *Principal Navigations, Voyages, and Discoveries of the English Nation* by the English geographer and historian Richard Hakluyt (c.1552–1616), and was then applied to the now-extinct great auk as well as to the penguin. A reference in an account of Sir Francis Drake's voyage through the southern oceans to 'fowles...which the Welsh men named penguin' has led to the suggestion that the word is from Welsh *pen gwyn* 'white head': however, most penguins have black heads. Other suggestions are that it is derived from Latin *pinguis* 'fat', or is an alteration of 'pin wing'.

penicillin > *noun* an antibiotic produced naturally by certain blue moulds, now usually prepared synthetically.
ORIGIN – from Latin *Penicillium*, name of a genus of moulds, from *penicillum* 'paintbrush'.

peninsula > *noun* a long, narrow piece of land projecting out into a sea or lake.
DERIVATIVES – **peninsular** *adjective*.
ORIGIN – Latin *paeninsula*, from *paene* 'almost' + *insula* 'island'.

penis /**pee**niss/ > *noun* (pl. **penises** or **penes** /**pee**neez/) the male organ of copulation and urination.
WORDFINDER – phallic, priapic (*of the erect penis*).
DERIVATIVES – **penile** *adjective*.
ORIGIN – Latin, 'tail'.

penitent > *adjective* feeling sorrow and regret for having done wrong. > *noun* a person who repents or submits to penance.
DERIVATIVES – **penitence** *noun* **penitential** *adjective* **penitently** *adverb*.
SYNONYMS – *adjective* contrite, remorseful, repentant, sorry.
ORIGIN – from Latin *paenitere* 'repent'.

penitentiary /penni**ten**shari/ > *noun* (pl. **penitentiaries**) **1** (in North America) a prison for people convicted of serious crimes. **2** (in the Roman Catholic Church) a priest appointed to administer penance.

penknife > *noun* a small knife with a blade which folds into the handle.

penman > *noun* **1** historical a clerk. **2** dated a person with a specified ability in handwriting. **3** an author.

pennant > *noun* **1** a tapering flag flown at the masthead of a ship in commission. **2** a long triangular or swallow-tailed flag. **3** N. Amer. a flag identifying a team or club.

ORIGIN – blend of **PENDANT** and **PENNON**.

penne /**penn**ay/ > *plural noun* pasta in the form of short wide tubes.

ORIGIN – Italian, 'quills'.

penni /**penn**i/ > *noun* (pl. **penniä** /**penn**-yaa/) a monetary unit of Finland, equal to one hundredth of a markka.

ORIGIN – Finnish.

penniless > *adjective* without money; destitute.

pennon > *noun* less common term for **PENNANT**.

ORIGIN – Old French, from Latin *penna* 'feather'.

penny > *noun* (pl. **pennies** (for separate coins); **pence** (for a sum of money)) **1** a British bronze coin worth one hundredth of a pound. **2** a former British coin worth one twelfth of a shilling and 240th of a pound. **3** N. Amer. informal a one-cent coin.

IDIOMS – **a bad penny always turns up** proverb someone or something unwelcome will always reappear. **in for a penny, in for a pound** willing to see an undertaking through, however much this entails. **look after the pennies and the pounds will look after themselves** proverb if you concentrate on saving small amounts of money, you'll soon amass a large amount. **not a penny** no money at all. **pennies from heaven** unexpected benefits. **the penny drops** informal one finally realises something. **penny wise and pound foolish** economical in small matters but extravagant in large ones. **two** (or **ten**) **a penny** plentiful and thus of little value.

COMBINATIONS – **penny dreadful** historical or humorous a cheap, sensational comic or storybook. **penny-farthing** Brit. an early type of bicycle with a very large front wheel and a small rear wheel. **penny plain** plain and simple. [ORIGIN – with reference to prints of characters sold for toy theatres, costing one penny for black-and-white ones, and two pennies for coloured ones.] **penny whistle** a tin whistle. **pennywort** a plant with small rounded leaves, growing in crevices or marshy places.

penny-pinching > *adjective* unwilling to spend money; miserly. > *noun* miserliness.

DERIVATIVES – **penny-pincher** *noun*.

pennyroyal > *noun* a small-leaved plant of the mint family, used in herbal medicine.

ORIGIN – Old French *puliol real* 'royal thyme'.

pennyweight > *noun* a unit of weight, 24 grains or one twentieth of an ounce troy.

pennyworth > *noun* **1** an amount of something worth a penny. **2** (**one's**

pennyworth) Brit. one's contribution to a discussion.

penology /pee**noll**əji/ > *noun* the study of the punishment of crime and of prison management.

DERIVATIVES – **penological** *adjective* **penologist** *noun*.

pension[1] /**pen**sh'n/ > *noun* **1** a regular payment made to retired people and to some widows and disabled people, either by the state or from an investment fund. **2** chiefly historical a regular payment made to a royal favourite or to an artist or scholar. > *verb* (**pension off**) dismiss (someone) from employment and pay them a pension.

DERIVATIVES – **pensionable** *adjective*.

ORIGIN – Latin, 'payment', from *pendere* 'to pay'.

pension[2] /**poN**syoN/ > *noun* a small hotel or boarding house in France and other European countries.

ORIGIN – French.

pensione /pensi**ō**nay/ > *noun* (pl. **pensioni** /pensi**ō**ni/) a small hotel or boarding house in Italy.

pensioner > *noun* a person receiving a pension.

pensive > *adjective* engaged in deep thought.

DERIVATIVES – **pensively** *adverb* **pensiveness** *noun*.

SYNONYMS – contemplative, introspective, reflective, thoughtful.

ORIGIN – Old French *pensif*, from *penser* 'think'.

penstemon /**pen**stimən, pen**stee**mən/ (also **pentstemon**) > *noun* a North American plant with snapdragon-like flowers.

ORIGIN – Latin, from **PENTA-** + Greek *stēmōn* 'warp', used to mean 'stamen'.

penstock > *noun* **1** a sluice for controlling the flow of water. **2** a channel for conveying water to a hydroelectric station.

ORIGIN – from **PEN**[2] (meaning 'mill dam') + **STOCK**.

penta- > *combining form* five; having five.

ORIGIN – Greek *pente* 'five'.

pentacle /**pen**tək'l/ > *noun* a pentagram.

ORIGIN – Latin *pentaculum*.

pentad > *noun* a group or set of five.

pentagon > *noun* **1** a plane figure with five straight sides and five angles. **2** (**the Pentagon**) the headquarters of the US Department of Defense, near Washington DC.

DERIVATIVES – **pentagonal** *adjective*.

pentagram > *noun* a five-pointed star drawn using a continuous line, often used as a mystic and magical symbol.

pentahedron /pentə**hee**drən/ > *noun* (pl. **pentahedra** /pentə**hee**drə/ or

pentahedrons) a solid figure with five plane faces.

DERIVATIVES – **pentahedral** *adjective*.

pentameter /pen**tamm**itər/ > *noun* a line of verse consisting of five metrical feet, or (in Greek and Latin verse) of two halves each of two feet and a long syllable.

pentane /**pen**tayn/ > *noun* Chemistry a volatile liquid hydrocarbon present in petroleum spirit.

ORIGIN – from Greek *pente* 'five' (denoting five carbon atoms).

Pentateuch /**pen**tətyook/ > *noun* the first five books of the Old Testament and Hebrew Scriptures (Genesis, Exodus, Leviticus, Numbers, and Deuteronomy).

ORIGIN – Greek *pentateukhos*, from *penta-* 'five' + *teukhos* 'implement, book'.

pentathlon /pen**tath**lən/ > *noun* an athletic event comprising five different events for each competitor, in particular (**modern pentathlon**) a men's event involving fencing, shooting, swimming, riding, and cross-country running.

DERIVATIVES – **pentathlete** *noun*.

ORIGIN – from Greek *pente* 'five' + *athlon* 'contest'.

pentatonic /pentə**tonn**ik/ > *adjective* Music of or referring to a scale of five notes.

Pentecost > *noun* **1** the Christian festival celebrating the descent of the Holy Spirit on the disciples of Jesus after his Ascension, held on Whit Sunday. **2** the Jewish festival of Shavuoth.

ORIGIN – Greek *pentēkostē hēmera* 'fiftieth day' (because the Jewish festival is held on the fiftieth day after the second day of Passover).

Pentecostal > *adjective* **1** of or relating to Pentecost. **2** (in Christian use) emphasising baptism in the Holy Spirit, evidenced by 'speaking in tongues', prophecy, healing, and exorcism.

penthouse > *noun* **1** a flat on the top floor of a tall building. **2** archaic an outhouse built on the side of a building.

pentimento /penti**men**tō/ > *noun* (pl. **pentimenti** /penti**men**ti/) a visible trace of earlier painting beneath the paint on a canvas.

ORIGIN – Italian, 'repentance'.

Pentothal* /**pen**təthal/ > *noun* trademark an anaesthetic and sedative drug reputedly used as a truth drug.

*SPELLING – note the ending is *-othal*, not *-athol* (a common misspelling).

pentstemon > *noun* variant spelling of **PENSTEMON**.

penultimate > *adjective* last but one.

ORIGIN – Latin *paenultimus*, from *paene* 'almost' + *ultimus* 'last'.

wordpower facts
Penthouse

Despite its form, the word **penthouse** is not connected with 'five' in the way that most words beginning *pent-* are, and neither is it derived from **house**! As *pentis* it entered English in the Middle Ages from Old French *apentis*, which was based on Latin *appendicium* 'appendage', from *appendere* 'hang on' (the source of **append**, **appendage**, and **appendix**). It changed its form in the 16th century because it was associated with French *pente* 'slope' and the English word **house**. At that time **penthouse** referred to an outhouse or lean-to with a sloping roof attached to the wall of a building, or any of various shelters, structures, or canopies; it did not take on its modern sense until the end of the 19th century.

penumbra /pinumbrə/ > *noun* (pl. **penumbrae** /pinumbree/ or **penumbras**) the partially shaded outer region of the shadow cast by an object.
DERIVATIVES – **penumbral** *adjective*.

penurious /pinyooriəss/ > *adjective* formal **1** extremely poor. **2** parsimonious.
DERIVATIVES – **penuriously** *adverb*.

penury /penyoori/ > *noun* extreme poverty.
ORIGIN – Latin *penuria*.

peon /peeən/ > *noun* **1** /also payon/ an unskilled Spanish-American worker. **2** /also pyōon/ (in the Indian subcontinent and SE Asia) someone of low rank.
ORIGIN – Portuguese *peão* and Spanish *peón*, from Latin *pedo* 'walker, foot soldier'.

peony /peeəni/ (also **paeony**) > *noun* a herbaceous or shrubby plant cultivated for its showy flowers.
ORIGIN – Greek *paiōnia*, from *Paiōn*, the name of the physician of the gods.

people > *plural noun* **1** human beings in general or considered collectively. **2** (**the people**) the mass of citizens; the populace. **3** (**one's people**) one's relatives, or one's employees or supporters. **4** (pl. **peoples**) (treated as sing. or pl.) the members of a particular nation, community, or ethnic group. > *verb* **1** (usu. **be peopled**) inhabit. **2** fill with a particular group of inhabitants.
WORDFINDER – demotic, plebeian (*of ordinary people*), canaille, hoi polloi, rabble, riff-raff (*common people viewed as disreputable*), proletariat (*working-class people*), vernacular (*language spoken by ordinary people*).
SYNONYMS – *noun* **1** folk, humans, individuals, persons. **2** (**the people**) the masses, the mob, the multitude, the populace, the rank and file. **4** clan, ethnic group, nation, race, tribe.
COMBINATIONS – **people carrier** a motor vehicle with three rows of seats.
ORIGIN – Old French *poeple*, from Latin *populus* 'populace'.

PEP > *abbreviation* Brit. personal equity plan.

pep informal > *noun* liveliness. > *verb* (**pepped**, **pepping**) (**pep someone** or **something up**) make someone or something more lively.
DERIVATIVES – **peppy** *adjective*.
COMBINATIONS – **pep pill** informal a pill containing a stimulant drug. **pep talk** informal a talk intended to make someone feel more courageous or enthusiastic.

peplum /pepləm/ > *noun* a short flared, gathered, or pleated strip of fabric attached at the waist of a woman's jacket, dress, or blouse.
ORIGIN – Greek *peplos* 'outer robe or shawl'.

pepper > *noun* **1** a pungent, hot-tasting powder made from peppercorns, used to flavour food. **2** a capsicum. > *verb* **1** sprinkle or season with pepper. **2** (usu. **be peppered with**) scatter liberally over or through. **3** hit repeatedly with small missiles or gunshot.
WORDFINDER – *kinds of pepper:* cayenne, paprika, pimiento; jalapeño (*very hot green chilli pepper*).
COMBINATIONS – **pepper pot** Brit. a container with a perforated top for sprinkling pepper. **pepper spray** an aerosol spray containing irritant oils derived from cayenne pepper, used as a disabling weapon.
ORIGIN – Greek *peperi*, from Sanskrit.

peppercorn > *noun* the dried berry of a climbing vine, used whole as a spice or crushed or ground to make pepper.
COMBINATIONS – **peppercorn rent** Brit. a very low or nominal rent.

peppermint > *noun* **1** a kind of mint which produces aromatic leaves and oil, used as a flavouring in food. **2** a sweet flavoured with peppermint oil.

pepperoni /peppərōni/ > *noun* beef and pork sausage seasoned with pepper.
ORIGIN – Italian *peperone* 'chilli'.

peppery > *adjective* **1** strongly flavoured with pepper or other hot spices. **2** irritable and sharp-tongued.

pepsin > *noun* the chief digestive enzyme in the stomach, which breaks down proteins into polypeptides.
ORIGIN – from Greek *pepsis* 'digestion'.

peptic > *adjective* of or relating to digestion.
COMBINATIONS – **peptic ulcer** an ulcer in the lining of the stomach or duodenum.

peptide > *noun* Biochemistry a compound consisting of two or more linked amino acids.

per > *preposition* **1** for each. **2** by means of. **3** (**as per**) in accordance with. **4** Heraldry divided by a line in the direction of.
IDIOMS – **as per usual** as usual.
ORIGIN – Latin, 'through, by means of'; partly via Old French.

per- > *prefix* **1** through; all over: *pervade*. **2** completely; very: *perfect*. **3** Chemistry having the maximum proportion of some element in combination: *peroxide*.

peradventure archaic or humorous > *adverb* perhaps. > *noun* uncertainty or doubt.
ORIGIN – from Old French *per* (or *par*) *auenture* 'by chance'.

perambulate /pərambyoolayt/ > *verb* **1** formal walk or travel from place to place. **2** Brit. historical walk round (a parish, forest, etc.) in order to designate its boundaries.
DERIVATIVES – **perambulation** *noun* **perambulatory** *adjective*.
ORIGIN – Latin *perambulare* 'walk about'.

perambulator > *noun* formal term for **PRAM**.

per annum /pər annəm/ > *adverb* for each year.
ORIGIN – Latin.

percale /pərkayl/ > *noun* a closely woven fine cotton fabric.
ORIGIN – French.

per capita /pər kappitə/ (also **per caput** /kappoŏt/) > *adverb* & *adjective* for each person; in relation to people taken individually.
ORIGIN – Latin, literally 'by heads'.

perceive* > *verb* **1** become aware or conscious of through the senses. **2** regard as: *Guy does not perceive himself as disabled*.
DERIVATIVES – **perceivable** *adjective* **perceiver** *noun*.
*SPELLING – remember, *i* before *e* except after *c*: perceive.
SYNONYMS – **1** detect, discern, distinguish, make out, sense.
ORIGIN – Latin *percipere* 'seize, understand'.

per cent > *adverb* by a specified amount in or for every hundred. > *noun* one part in every hundred.

percentage > *noun* **1** a rate, number, or amount in each hundred. **2** a proportion of a larger sum of money granted as an allowance or commission. **3** any proportion or share in relation to a whole.

percentile /pərsentīl/ > *noun* Statistics **1** each of 100 equal groups into which a population can be divided according to the distribution of values of a particular variable. **2** each of the 99 intermediate values of a variable which divide a frequency distribution into 100 such groups.

percept /persept/ > noun Philosophy **1** something that is perceived. **2** a mental concept that results from perceiving.

perceptible > adjective able to be perceived.
DERIVATIVES – **perceptibly** adverb.
SYNONYMS – detectable, discernible, evident, noticeable, visible.
ANTONYMS – imperceptible, invisible.

perception > noun **1** the ability to see, hear, or become aware of something through the senses. **2** the process of perceiving. **3** a way of understanding or interpreting something. **4** intuitive understanding and insight.

perceptive > adjective having or showing acute insight.
DERIVATIVES – **perceptively** adverb **perceptiveness** noun.
SYNONYMS – acute, discerning, insightful, penetrating, sharp.

perceptual > adjective relating to the ability to perceive.
DERIVATIVES – **perceptually** adverb.

perch¹ > noun **1** a branch, bar, etc. on which a bird rests or roosts. **2** a high or narrow seat or resting place. > verb **1** sit, rest, or place somewhere. **2** (**be perched**) (of a building) be situated above or on the edge of something.
ORIGIN – from PERCH³.

perch² > noun (pl. same or **perches**) a freshwater fish with a high spiny dorsal fin and dark vertical bars.
ORIGIN – Old French perche, from Greek perkē.

perch³ > noun historical, chiefly Brit. **1** a unit of length equal to a quarter of a chain or 5½ yards (5.029 metres). **2** (also **square perch**) a unit of area equal to one 160th of an acre or 30¼ square yards (25.29 square metres).
ORIGIN – Old French perche, from Latin pertica 'measuring rod, pole'.

perchance > adverb archaic or literary by some chance; perhaps.
ORIGIN – Old French par cheance 'by chance'.

percipient /pərsippiənt/ > adjective having a perceptive understanding. > noun (especially in philosophy or with reference to psychic phenomena) a person who is able to perceive things.
DERIVATIVES – **percipience** noun **percipiently** adverb.

percolate > verb **1** filter through a porous surface or substance. **2** (of information or ideas) spread gradually through a group of people. **3** prepare (coffee) in a percolator.
DERIVATIVES – **percolation** noun.
ORIGIN – Latin percolare 'strain through'.

percolator > noun a machine for making coffee, consisting of a pot in which boiling water is circulated through a small chamber that holds the ground beans.

percuss /pərkuss/ > verb Medicine gently tap (a part of the body) as part of a diagnosis.
ORIGIN – Latin percutere 'strike through'.

percussion > noun **1** (before another noun) (of a musical instrument) played by being struck or shaken. **2** percussion instruments forming a band or section of an orchestra. **3** the striking of one solid object with or against another.
WORDFINDER – percussion instruments: bells, castanets, celesta, cymbals, drum, glockenspiel, gong, Jew's harp, maracas, marimba, piano, tambourine, vibraphone, washboard, woodblock, xylophone; gamelan (Javanese percussion ensemble).
DERIVATIVES – **percussionist** noun **percussive** adjective **percussively** adverb **percussiveness** noun.
COMBINATIONS – **percussion cap** a small amount of explosive powder contained in metal or paper and exploded by striking.
ORIGIN – Latin, from percutere 'strike through'.

percutaneous > adjective Medicine made or done through the skin.
DERIVATIVES – **percutaneously** adverb.
ORIGIN – from Latin per cutem 'through the skin'.

per diem /pər dee-em/ > adverb & adjective for each day.
ORIGIN – Latin.

perdition /pərdish'n/ > noun (in Christian theology) a state of eternal damnation into which a sinful person who has not repented passes after death.
ORIGIN – Latin, from perdere 'destroy'.

perdurable /pərdyoorəb'l/ > adjective formal enduring continuously; permanent.

père /pair/ > noun used after a surname to distinguish a father from a son of the same name.
ORIGIN – French, 'father'.

peregrinations /perrigrinaysh'nz/ > plural noun archaic or humorous travel or wandering from place to place.
DERIVATIVES – **peregrinate** /perri-grinayt/ verb.
ORIGIN – from Latin peregrinari 'travel abroad'.

peregrine /perrigrin/ > noun a powerful falcon with bluish-grey back and wings and pale underparts, breeding chiefly on mountains and coastal cliffs.
ORIGIN – Latin, 'pilgrim falcon', because falconers' birds were caught full-grown on migration, not taken from the nest.

peremptory /pəremptəri/ > adjective **1** insisting on immediate attention or obedience; brusque and imperious. **2** Law not open to appeal or challenge; final.
DERIVATIVES – **peremptorily** adverb **peremptoriness** noun.
SYNONYMS – **1** abrupt, brisk, brusque, commanding, high-handed, imperious.
ORIGIN – Latin peremptorius 'deadly, decisive'.

perennial > adjective **1** lasting through a year or several years. **2** (of a plant) living for several years. **3** lasting or doing something for a long time or for ever. > noun a perennial plant.
DERIVATIVES – **perennially** adverb.
ORIGIN – Latin perennis 'lasting the year through'.

perestroika /perristroykə/ > noun (in the former Soviet Union) the economic and political reforms practised in the 1980s under Mikhail Gorbachev.
ORIGIN – Russian, 'restructuring'.

perfect > adjective /perfikt/ **1** having all the required elements, qualities, or characteristics. **2** free from any flaw; faultless. **3** complete; absolute: it made perfect sense. **4** Grammar (of a tense) denoting a completed action or a state or habitual action which began in the past, formed in English with have or has and the past participle, as in they have eaten. > verb /pərfekt/ **1** make perfect. **2** bring to completion.
DERIVATIVES – **perfecter** noun **perfectibility** noun **perfectible** adjective.
SYNONYMS – adjective **1** consummate, ideal, model, quintessential. **2** flawless, faultless, pristine, spotless, undamaged. verb **1** fine-tune, hone, refine.
ANTONYMS – adjective **1,2** flawed, imperfect.
COMBINATIONS – **perfect number** a number equal to the sum of its positive divisors, e.g. the number 6, whose divisors (1, 2, 3) also add up to 6. **perfect pitch** the ability to recognise the pitch of a note or produce any given note.
ORIGIN – from Latin perfectus 'completed'.

perfection > noun **1** the process or condition of perfecting or being perfect. **2** a perfect person or thing.

perfectionism > noun **1** refusal to accept any standard short of perfection. **2** Philosophy the doctrine that religious, moral, social, or political perfection is attainable.
DERIVATIVES – **perfectionist** noun & adjective.

perfectly > adverb **1** in a perfect way. **2** absolutely; completely.

perfervid /pərfervid/ > adjective literary intense and impassioned.
ORIGIN – from Latin per- 'utterly' + fervidus 'glowing hot, fiery'.

perfidious /pəfiddiəss/ > adjective literary deceitful and untrustworthy.

DERIVATIVES – **perfidiously** *adverb* **perfidiousness** *noun*.

perfidy /**per**fidi/ > *noun* literary deceitfulness; untrustworthiness.

ORIGIN – Latin *perfidia*, from *perfidus* 'treacherous'.

perforate /**per**fərayt/ > *verb* pierce and make a hole or holes in.

DERIVATIVES – **perforation** *noun* **perforator** *noun*.

SYNONYMS – pierce, puncture.

ORIGIN – Latin *perforare* 'pierce through'.

perforce > *adverb* formal necessarily; inevitably.

ORIGIN – Old French *par force* 'by force'.

perform > *verb* 1 carry out, accomplish, or fulfil (an action, task, or function). 2 work, function, or do something to a specified standard. 3 present entertainment to an audience. 4 (of an investment) yield a profitable return.

DERIVATIVES – **performable** *adjective* **performer** *noun*.

SYNONYMS – 1 accomplish, achieve, complete, discharge, do, execute, fulfil.

COMBINATIONS – **performing arts** forms of creative activity that are performed in front of an audience.

ORIGIN – Old French *parfournir*, from *par* 'through, to completion' + *fournir* 'furnish, provide'.

performance > *noun* 1 the action or process of performing. 2 an act of performing a play, concert, song, etc. 3 informal a display of exaggerated behaviour; an elaborate fuss. 4 the capabilities of a machine or product.

COMBINATIONS – **performance art** an art form that combines visual art with dramatic performance.

perfume /**per**fyoom/ > *noun* 1 a fragrant liquid used to give a pleasant smell to one's body. 2 a pleasant smell. > *verb* /also pərfyoom/ 1 give a pleasant smell to. 2 impregnate with perfume or a sweet-smelling ingredient.

DERIVATIVES – **perfumed** *adjective*.

SYNONYMS – *noun* 2 aroma, bouquet, fragrance, scent.

ORIGIN – first denoting pleasant-smelling smoke used in fumigation: from obsolete Italian *parfumare* 'to smoke through'.

perfumery > *noun* (pl. **perfumeries**) 1 the process of producing and selling perfumes. 2 a shop that sells perfumes.

DERIVATIVES – **perfumer** *noun*.

perfunctory /pərfungktəri/ > *adjective* carried out with a minimum of effort or reflection.

DERIVATIVES – **perfunctorily** *adverb*.

SYNONYMS – brief, cursory, desultory, half-hearted.

ORIGIN – Latin *perfunctorius* 'careless'.

perfuse /pəfyooz/ > *verb* permeate or suffuse with a liquid, colour, quality, etc.

DERIVATIVES – **perfusion** *noun*.

ORIGIN – Latin *perfundere* 'pour through'.

pergola /**per**gələ/ > *noun* an arched structure forming a framework for climbing or trailing plants.

ORIGIN – Latin *pergula* 'projecting roof'.

perhaps > *adverb* 1 expressing uncertainty or possibility. 2 used when making a polite request or suggestion.

ORIGIN – from PER + HAP.

peri- > *prefix* round; about: *pericardium*.

ORIGIN – from Greek *peri* 'about, around'.

perianth /**perr**ianth/ > *noun* Botany the outer part of a flower, consisting of the calyx (sepals) and corolla (petals).

ORIGIN – from Greek *peri* 'around' + *anthos* 'flower'.

pericardium /perrikaardiəm/ > *noun* (pl. **pericardia** /perrikaardiə/) Anatomy the membrane enclosing the heart.

DERIVATIVES – **pericardial** *adjective*.

ORIGIN – Latin, from Greek *peri* 'around' + *kardia* 'heart'.

pericarp /**perr**ikaarp/ > *noun* Botany the part of a fruit formed from the wall of the ripened ovary.

ORIGIN – from Greek *peri-* 'around' + *karpos* 'fruit'.

peridot /**perr**idot/ > *noun* a green semi-precious stone.

ORIGIN – French.

perigee /**perr**ijee/ > *noun* Astronomy the point in the orbit of the moon or a satellite at which it is nearest to the earth. The opposite of APOGEE.

ORIGIN – from Greek *perigeion* 'close round the earth'.

perihelion /perriheeliən/ > *noun* (pl. **perihelia** /perriheeliə/) Astronomy the point in the orbit of a planet, asteroid, or comet at which it is closest to the sun. The opposite of APHELION.

ORIGIN – from Greek *peri-* 'around' + *hēlios* 'sun'.

peril > *noun* a situation of serious and immediate danger.

IDIOMS – **at one's peril** at one's own risk. **in** (or **at**) **peril of** 1 very likely to suffer from. 2 at risk of losing or injuring.

SYNONYMS – danger, hazard, jeopardy, risk, threat.

ORIGIN – Old French, from Latin *peric(u)lum* 'danger'.

perilous > *adjective* full of danger or risk.

DERIVATIVES – **perilously** *adverb* **perilousness** *noun*.

SYNONYMS – dangerous, hazardous, risky, threatening, unsafe.

ANTONYMS – safe.

perimeter /pərimmitər/ > *noun* 1 the

continuous line forming the boundary of a closed figure. 2 the outermost parts or boundary of an area or object. 3 an instrument for measuring a person's field of vision.

DERIVATIVES – **perimetric** *adjective*.

ORIGIN – Greek *perimetros*, from *peri-* 'around' + *metron* 'measure'.

perinatal /perrinayt'l/ > *adjective* relating to the time immediately before and after a birth.

DERIVATIVES – **perinatally** *adverb*.

perineum /perrineeəm/ > *noun* (pl. **perinea**) Anatomy the area between the anus and the scrotum or vulva.

DERIVATIVES – **perineal** *adjective*.

ORIGIN – Greek *perinaion*.

period > *noun* 1 a length or portion of time. 2 a distinct portion of time with particular characteristics. 3 a major division of geological time, forming part of an era. 4 a lesson in a school. 5 (also **menstrual period**) a monthly flow of blood and other material from the lining of the uterus, occurring in women of child-bearing age when not pregnant. 6 chiefly N. Amer. a full stop. 7 the interval of time between recurrences of a phenomenon. > *adjective* belonging to or characteristic of a past historical time: *period furniture*.

SYNONYMS – *noun* 1 interval, phase, spell, stint, stretch, term.

COMBINATIONS – **period piece** an object or work that is set in or reminiscent of an earlier historical period.

ORIGIN – Greek *periodos* 'orbit, recurrence, course'.

periodic /peerioddik/ > *adjective* appearing or occurring at intervals.

DERIVATIVES – **periodicity** *noun*.

SYNONYMS – intermittent, occasional, recurrent, spasmodic, sporadic.

COMBINATIONS – **periodic table** a table of the chemical elements arranged in order of atomic number, usually in rows, with elements having similar atomic structure appearing in vertical columns.

periodical > *adjective* 1 occurring or appearing at intervals. 2 (of a magazine or newspaper) published at regular intervals. > *noun* a periodical magazine or newspaper.

DERIVATIVES – **periodically** *adverb*.

perioperative /perrioppərətiv/ > *adjective* Medicine occurring or performed at or around the time of an operation.

peripatetic /perripətettik/ > *adjective* 1 travelling from place to place. 2 working or based in a succession of places.

DERIVATIVES – **peripatetically** *adverb*.

SYNONYMS – 1 itinerant, nomadic, roving, wandering.

wordpower facts

Peripatetic

The Greek philosopher Aristotle, who lived in the 4th century BC, was famous for walking around as he taught (his Lyceum in Athens incorporated a number of covered walkways). It was this habit that, in the late 15th century, led to the use of the name **Peripatetic** for the Aristotelian school of philosophy and its members. The word was adopted for this purpose (it was not in use in English before this) from Old French *peripatetique*, coming via Latin from Greek *peripatētikos*, meaning 'walking up and down'. The more general sense, 'travelling from place to place', did not come into use until the 17th century.

peripheral > *adjective* **1** relating to or situated on the periphery. **2** of secondary or minor importance. **3** (of a device) able to be attached to and used with a computer, though not an integral part of it. **4** Anatomy near the surface of the body. > *noun* Computing a peripheral device.
DERIVATIVES – **peripherality** *noun* **peripherally** *adverb*.
SYNONYMS – *adjective* **1** outlying. **2** borderline, incidental, marginal, tangential.
COMBINATIONS – **peripheral nervous system** Anatomy the nervous system outside the brain and spinal cord.

periphery /pəriffəri/ > *noun* (pl. **peripheries**) **1** the outer limits or edge of an area or object. **2** a marginal or secondary position, part, or aspect.
SYNONYMS – **1** border, boundary, fringe, margin, perimeter.
ORIGIN – Greek *periphereia* 'circumference'.

periphrasis /pərifrəsiss/ > *noun* (pl. **periphrases** /pərifrəseez/) the use of indirect and roundabout language; circumlocution.
DERIVATIVES – **periphrastic** *adjective* **periphrastically** *adverb*.
ORIGIN – from Greek *peri-* 'around' + *phrazein* 'declare'.

periscope > *noun* a tube attached to a set of mirrors or prisms, by which an observer in a submerged submarine or behind an obstacle can see things that are otherwise out of sight.
DERIVATIVES – **periscopic** *adjective*.

perish > *verb* **1** die. **2** suffer complete ruin or destruction. **3** rot or decay. **4** (**be perished**) Brit. be suffering from extreme cold.
IDIOMS – **perish the thought** informal may the thought or idea prove unfounded.
ORIGIN – Latin *perire* 'pass away'.

perishable > *adjective* (of food) likely to rot quickly. > *noun* (**perishables**) perishable foodstuffs.

perisher > *noun* Brit. informal a mischievous or awkward person, especially a child.

perishing > *adjective* Brit. informal **1** extremely cold. **2** dated used for emphasis or to express annoyance.
DERIVATIVES – **perishingly** *adverb*.

peristalsis /perristalsiss/ > *noun* the contraction and relaxation of the muscles of the intestines, creating wave-like movements which push the contents of the intestines forward.
DERIVATIVES – **peristaltic** *adjective*.
ORIGIN – from Greek *peristallein* 'wrap around'.

peristyle > *noun* a row of columns surrounding a courtyard or internal garden or edging a veranda or porch.
ORIGIN – from Greek *peri-* 'around' + *stulos* 'pillar'.

peritoneum /perritəneeəm/ > *noun* (pl. **peritoneums** or **peritonea** /perritəneeə/) the membrane lining the cavity of the abdomen and covering the abdominal organs.
DERIVATIVES – **peritoneal** *adjective*.
ORIGIN – Greek *peritonaion*, from *peritonos* 'stretched round'.

peritonitis /perritənītiss/ > *noun* inflammation of the peritoneum.

periwig > *noun* a wig of a kind worn in the 17th and 18th centuries, retained by judges and barristers as part of their professional dress.
ORIGIN – alteration of PERUKE.

periwinkle¹ > *noun* a plant with flat five-petalled flowers and glossy leaves.
ORIGIN – Latin *pervinca*.

periwinkle² > *noun* a winkle.

perjure > *verb* (**perjure oneself**) Law commit perjury.
DERIVATIVES – **perjurer** *noun*.
ORIGIN – Latin *perjurare* 'swear falsely'.

perjured > *adjective* Law **1** (of evidence) involving deliberate untruth. **2** guilty of perjury.

perjury /perjəri/ > *noun* (pl. **perjuries**) Law the offence of wilfully telling an untruth in court when under oath.

perk¹ > *verb* (**perk up**) make or become more cheerful or lively.
ORIGIN – perhaps from Old French *percher* 'to perch': originally meaning 'perch' and 'be lively'.

perk² > *noun* informal a benefit or privilege to which an employee is entitled.
ORIGIN – abbreviation of PERQUISITE.

perk³ > *verb* informal (with reference to coffee) percolate.

perky > *adjective* (**perkier**, **perkiest**) **1** cheerful and lively. **2** cheeky.
DERIVATIVES – **perkily** *adverb* **perkiness** *noun*.

perlite /perlīt/ > *noun* a form of obsidian consisting of glassy globules.
ORIGIN – French, from *perle* 'pearl'.

perm¹ > *noun* a method of setting the hair in waves or curls and treating it with chemicals so that the style lasts for several months. > *verb* treat (the hair) in such a way.
ORIGIN – short for *permanent wave*.

perm² Brit. informal > *noun* a permutation, especially a selection of a specified number of matches in a football pool. > *verb* make a selection of (so many) from a larger number.

permaculture > *noun* the development of agricultural ecosystems intended to be sustainable and self-sufficient.

permafrost > *noun* a thick subsurface layer of soil that remains below freezing point throughout the year.

permanent > *adjective* lasting or intended to last indefinitely; not temporary.
DERIVATIVES – **permanence** *noun* **permanency** *noun* **permanently** *adverb*.
SYNONYMS – enduring, fixed, immutable, irreversible, lasting, unalterable.
ANTONYMS – ephemeral, temporary.
COMBINATIONS – **permanent magnet** a magnet that retains its magnetic properties in the absence of an inducing field or current. **Permanent Undersecretary** (also **Permanent Secretary**) (in the UK) a senior civil servant who is a permanent adviser to a Secretary of State. **permanent wave** a perm. **permanent way** Brit. the finished foundation of a railway together with the track.
ORIGIN – Latin, from *per-* 'through' + *manere* 'remain'.

permanganate /pərmanggənayt/ > *noun* Chemistry a salt containing the anion MnO_4^-, typically deep purplish-red and with strong oxidising properties.

permeable /permiəb'l/ > *adjective* allowing liquids or gases to pass through; capable of being permeated.
DERIVATIVES – **permeability** *noun*.

permeate /permiayt/ > *verb* spread throughout; pervade.
DERIVATIVES – **permeation** *noun*.
SYNONYMS – infiltrate, penetrate, pervade.
ORIGIN – Latin *permeare* 'pass through'.

Permian /permiən/ > *adjective* Geology of or relating to the last period of the Palaeozoic era (between the Carboniferous and Triassic periods), about 290 to 245 million years ago, a time when reptiles increased and many marine animals became extinct.
ORIGIN – from *Perm*, a Russian province with extensive deposits from this period.

permissible > *adjective* that is permitted.
DERIVATIVES – **permissibility** *noun*.
SYNONYMS – acceptable, allowable, allowed, legitimate, sanctioned, tolerable.
ANTONYMS – forbidden.

permission > *noun* the expression of consent or authorisation in response to a request to do something.
SYNONYMS – assent, authorisation, consent, dispensation, leave, licence, sanction.

permissive > *adjective* **1** allowing or characterised by freedom of behaviour, especially in sexual matters. **2** Law allowed but not obligatory; optional.
DERIVATIVES – **permissively** *adverb* **permissiveness** *noun*.

permit > *verb* /pərmit/ (**permitted**, **permitting**) **1** give permission to (someone) or for (something). **2** make possible. **3** (**permit of**) formal allow for; admit of. > *noun* /permit/ an official document giving permission to do something.
SYNONYMS – *verb* **1** allow, authorise, endorse, license, sanction.
ANTONYMS – *verb* **1** forbid, prohibit.
ORIGIN – Latin *permittere*, from *per-* 'through' + *mittere* 'send, let go'.

permittivity /permitivviti/ > *noun* Physics the ability of a substance to store electrical energy in an electric field.

permutation /permyootaysh'n/ > *noun* **1** each of several possible ways in which a set or number of things can be ordered or arranged. **2** Mathematics the action of changing the arrangement of a set of items. **3** Brit. a selection of a specified number of matches in a football pool.
DERIVATIVES – **permutational** *adjective*.
ORIGIN – Latin, from *permutare* 'change completely'.

permute (also **permutate**) > *verb* alter the sequence of; rearrange.

pernicious /pərnishəss/ > *adjective* having a harmful effect, especially in a gradual or subtle way.
DERIVATIVES – **perniciously** *adverb* **perniciousness** *noun*.
COMBINATIONS – **pernicious anaemia** a deficiency in the production of red blood cells through a lack of vitamin B_{12}.
ORIGIN – Latin *perniciosus* 'destructive'.

pernickety > *adjective* informal, chiefly Brit. **1** fussy; over-fastidious. **2** requiring a precise or careful approach.

Pernod /pernō/ > *noun* trademark an aniseed-flavoured aperitif.

perorate /perrərayt/ > *verb* formal **1** speak at length. **2** sum up and conclude a speech.
ORIGIN – Latin *perorare*.

peroration > *noun* the concluding part of a speech; the summing up.

peroxide > *noun* **1** Chemistry a compound containing two oxygen atoms bonded together. **2** hydrogen peroxide, especially as used as a bleach for the hair. > *verb* bleach (hair) with peroxide.

perpendicular /perpəndikyoolər/ > *adjective* **1** at an angle of 90° to a given line, plane, or surface. **2** at an angle of 90° to the ground; vertical. **3** (**Perpendicular**) denoting the latest stage of English Gothic church architecture (late 14th to mid 16th centuries), characterised by broad arches and elaborate fan vaulting. > *noun* a perpendicular line.
DERIVATIVES – **perpendicularity** *noun* **perpendicularly** *adverb*.
ORIGIN – Latin *perpendicularis*, from *perpendiculum* 'plumb line'.

perpetrate /perpitrayt/ > *verb* carry out or commit (a bad or illegal action).
DERIVATIVES – **perpetration** *noun* **perpetrator** *noun*.
ORIGIN – Latin *perpetrare* 'perform'; in English the verb was first used in the statutes referring to crime, hence the negative association.

perpetual /pərpetyooəl/ > *adjective* **1** never ending or changing. **2** occurring repeatedly; seemingly continual.
DERIVATIVES – **perpetually** *adverb*.
SYNONYMS – **1** endless, eternal, everlasting, never-ending, unchanging. **2** incessant, non-stop, relentless, unremitting.
COMBINATIONS – **perpetual motion** the motion of a hypothetical machine which, once activated, would run forever unless subject to an external force or to wear.
ORIGIN – Latin *perpetualis*, from *perpetuus* 'continuing throughout'.

perpetuate > *verb* cause to continue indefinitely.
DERIVATIVES – **perpetuation** *noun* **perpetuator** *noun*.
SYNONYMS – maintain, preserve, sustain.
ORIGIN – Latin *perpetuare* 'make permanent'.

perpetuity /perpityōoiti/ > *noun* (pl. **perpetuities**) **1** the state or quality of lasting forever. **2** a bond or other security with no fixed maturity date.
IDIOMS – **in** (or **for**) **perpetuity** for ever.

perplex > *verb* cause to feel baffled; puzzle.
DERIVATIVES – **perplexed** *adjective* **perplexing** *adjective* **perplexity** *noun*.
SYNONYMS – baffle, bewilder, confound, mystify, nonplus, puzzle.
ORIGIN – from Latin *perplexus* 'entangled'.

perquisite /perkwizit/ > *noun* **1** formal a special right or privilege enjoyed as a result of one's position. **2** historical a thing which has served its primary use and to which a subordinate has a customary right.
USAGE – do not confuse **perquisite** and **prerequisite**: a **prerequisite** is something that is required as a prior condition for something else; **prerequisite** can also be an adjective, meaning 'required as a prior condition'.
ORIGIN – Latin *perquisitum* 'acquisition'.

perry > *noun* (pl. **perries**) an alcoholic drink made from the fermented juice of pears.
ORIGIN – Old French *pere*, from Latin *pirum* 'pear'.

per se /per say/ > *adverb* by or in itself or themselves.
ORIGIN – Latin.

persecute > *verb* **1** subject to prolonged hostility and ill-treatment. **2** persistently harass or annoy.
DERIVATIVES – **persecution** *noun* **persecutor** *noun*.
SYNONYMS – **1** abuse, oppress, terrorise, tyrannise, victimise. **2** badger, harass, hound, pester, plague.
COMBINATIONS – **persecution complex** an irrational and obsessive feeling that others are scheming against one.
ORIGIN – Old French *persecuter*, from Latin *persequi* 'follow with hostility'.

persevere > *verb* continue in a course of action in spite of difficulty or lack of success.
DERIVATIVES – **perseverance** *noun*.
SYNONYMS – go the distance, persist, press on; informal soldier on.
ORIGIN – Latin *perseverare* 'abide by strictly'.

wordpower facts
Persian
Among the English words that come from Persian are several that no longer have any apparent connection with the Middle East, such as **arsenic**, **azure**, **divan**, **kiosk**, **lilac**, **orange**, **seersucker**, **shawl**, **spinach**, **taffeta**, and **talcum**. Others are perhaps more predictable, for example **bazaar**, **caravan**, **cummerbund**, **dervish**, **jackal**, **jasmine**, **kaftan**, **pashmina**, **pyjamas**, and **sitar**. **Tulip** and **turban** are actually from the same Persian word, *dulband* 'turban'. The Persian word *šāh*, meaning 'king' or **shah**, gave English **check**, **chess**, and **chequer**; **checkmate** is based on the Persian phrase *šāh māt* 'the king is dead', and the Spanish word **matador** (literally 'killer') goes back to Persian *māt* 'dead'.

Persian > *noun* **1** a person from Persia (now Iran). **2** the language of ancient Persia or modern Iran. **3** a long-haired breed of domestic cat with a broad round head and stocky body. > *adjective* relating to Persia or Iran.
COMBINATIONS – **Persian carpet** a carpet or rug with a traditional Persian design incorporating stylised symbolic imagery. **Persian lamb** the silky, tightly curled fleece of the karakul, used to make clothing.

persiflage /**per**siflaazh/ > *noun* formal light mockery or banter.

ORIGIN – from French *persifler* 'to banter'.

persimmon /pərsimmən/ > *noun* an edible fruit resembling a large tomato, with very sweet flesh.

ORIGIN – Algonquian.

persist > *verb* 1 continue doing something in spite of difficulty or opposition. 2 continue to exist.

SYNONYMS – 1 persevere, press on. 2 endure, last, linger, remain.

ORIGIN – Latin *persistere*, from *per-* 'through, steadfastly' + *sistere* 'to stand'.

persistent > *adjective* 1 persisting or having a tendency to persist. 2 continuing or recurring; prolonged. 3 Botany & Zoology (of a horn, leaf, etc.) remaining attached instead of falling off in the normal manner.

DERIVATIVES – **persistence** *noun* **persistently** *adverb*.

SYNONYMS – 1 determined, dogged, steadfast, tenacious, tireless.

COMBINATIONS – **persistent vegetative state** a condition in which a patient is kept alive by medical intervention but displays no sign of higher brain function.

persnickety > *adjective* North American term for PERNICKETY.

person > *noun* (pl. **people** (in most general contexts) or **persons** (chiefly in official and formal contexts)) 1 a human being regarded as an individual. 2 an individual's body: *concealed on his person.* 3 Grammar a category used in the classification of pronouns, verb forms, etc. according to whether they indicate the speaker (**first person**), the addressee (**second person**), or a third party (**third person**). 4 Christian Theology each of the three modes of being of God, namely the Father, the Son, and the Holy Ghost.

IDIOMS – **in person** physically present.

USAGE – the words **people** and **persons** are both used as the plural of **person**, but not in exactly the same way. **People** is by far the commoner of the two words and is used in most ordinary contexts. **Persons**, however, tends to be restricted to official or formal contexts, as in *this vehicle is authorised to carry twenty persons.*

SYNONYMS – 1 being, human, individual, personage.

ORIGIN – Latin *persona* 'actor's mask, character in a play', later 'human being'.

-person > *combining form* used as a neutral alternative to *-man* in nouns denoting status, authority, etc.: *salesperson.*

persona /persōnə/ > *noun* (pl. **personas** or **personae** /persōnee/) 1 Psychoanalysis the aspect of a person's character that is presented to or perceived by others. Compare with ANIMA. 2 a role or character adopted by an author or actor.

ORIGIN – Latin, 'mask, character played by an actor'.

personable > *adjective* having a pleasant appearance and manner.

DERIVATIVES – **personably** *adverb*.

personage > *noun* a person (used to express their importance or elevated status).

personal > *adjective* 1 of, affecting, or belonging to a particular person. 2 involving the presence or action of a particular individual. 3 concerning a person's private rather than professional life. 4 making inappropriate or offensive reference to a person's character or appearance. 5 relating to a person's body. 6 Grammar of one of the three persons. 7 existing as a self-aware entity, not as an abstraction or an impersonal force: *a personal God.* > *noun* (**personals**) chiefly N. Amer. advertisements or messages in the personal column of a newspaper.

SYNONYMS – *adjective* 1 characteristic, distinctive, individual, particular. 3 confidential, intimate, private, secret.

COMBINATIONS – **personal assistant** a secretary or administrative assistant working for one particular person. **personal column** a section of a newspaper devoted to private advertisements or messages. **personal computer** a microcomputer designed for use by one person at a time. **personal equity plan** (in the UK) a scheme whereby individuals may invest a limited sum each year in British companies without liability for tax on dividends or capital gains (discontinued in 1999). **personal identification number** a number allocated to an individual and used to validate electronic transactions. **personal organiser** a loose-leaf notebook with a diary and address book. **personal pension** a pension scheme that is independent of the contributor's employer. **personal pronoun** each of the pronouns in English (*I, you, he, she, it, we, they, me, him, her, us,* and *them*) that show contrasts of person, gender, number, and case. **personal property** Law all of someone's property except land and buildings. Compare with *real property.* **personal stereo** a small portable cassette or compact disc player, used with headphones.

personalise (also **personalize**) > *verb* 1 design or produce (something) to meet someone's individual requirements. 2 make (something) identifiable as belonging to a particular person. 3 cause (an issue or argument) to become concerned with personalities or feelings. 4 personify.

DERIVATIVES – **personalisation** *noun*.

personality > *noun* (pl. **personalities**) 1 the characteristics or qualities that form an individual's character. 2 qualities that make someone interesting or popular. 3 a celebrity.

SYNONYMS – 1 character, disposition, nature, temperament. 2 charisma, charm, magnetism.

COMBINATIONS – **personality disorder** Psychiatry a deeply ingrained pattern of inappropriate or inadequate behaviour.

personally > *adverb* 1 in person. 2 from one's own viewpoint; subjectively.

IDIOMS – **take personally** interpret (a remark or action) as directed against oneself and be upset or offended by it.

personalty /persənəlti/ > *noun* Law a person's personal property. Compare with REALTY.

persona non grata /persōnə non graatə/ > *noun* (pl. **personae non gratae** /persōnee non graatee/) an unacceptable or unwelcome person.

ORIGIN – Latin.

personate > *verb* formal play the part of or pretend to be.

DERIVATIVES – **personation** *noun*.

personify > *verb* (**personifies, personified**) 1 represent (a quality or concept) by a figure in human form. 2 attribute a personal nature or human characteristics to. 3 represent or embody (a quality or concept) in a physical form.

DERIVATIVES – **personification** *noun*

SYNONYMS – 2 anthropomorphise, humanise, personalise. 3 embody, epitomise, exemplify, typify.

personnel > *plural noun* people employed in an organisation or engaged in an undertaking.

COMBINATIONS – **personnel carrier** an armoured vehicle for transporting troops.

ORIGIN – French, 'personal'.

perspective > *noun* 1 the art of representing three-dimensional objects on a two-dimensional surface so as to convey the impression of height, width, depth, and relative distance. 2 a view or prospect. 3 a particular way of regarding something. 4 understanding of the relative importance of things.

DERIVATIVES – **perspectival** *adjective*.

SYNONYMS – 3 outlook, stance, standpoint, view, viewpoint.

ORIGIN – from Latin *perspectiva ars* 'science of optics': originally in the sense 'optics'.

perspex > *noun* trademark a tough transparent plastic used as a substitute for glass.

ORIGIN – from Latin *perspicere* 'look through'.

perspicacious /perspikayshəss/ > *adjective* having a ready insight into and understanding of things.

DERIVATIVES – **perspicaciously** *adverb* **perspicacity** *noun*.

SYNONYMS – astute, discerning, perceptive, sharp-witted, shrewd.

ORIGIN – Latin *perspicax* 'seeing clearly'.

perspicuous /pərspik'yooəss/ > *adjective* **1** clearly expressed and easily understood; lucid. **2** expressing things clearly.

DERIVATIVES – **perspicuity** *noun* **perspicuously** *adverb*.

USAGE – do not confuse **perspicuous** with **perspicacious**, which means 'having a ready understanding of things'.

ORIGIN – Latin *perspicuus* 'transparent, clear'.

perspiration > *noun* **1** sweat. **2** the process of perspiring.

perspire > *verb* give out sweat through the pores of the skin.

ORIGIN – Latin *perspirare*, from *per-* 'through' + *spirare* 'breathe'.

persuade > *verb* **1** induce (someone) to do something through reasoning or argument. **2** cause (someone) to believe something.

DERIVATIVES – **persuadable** *adjective* **persuader** *noun*.

SYNONYMS – **1** cajole, coax, induce, prevail upon. **2** convince.

ORIGIN – Latin *persuadere*, from *per-* 'through, to completion' + *suadere* 'advise'.

persuasion > *noun* **1** the process of persuading or of being persuaded. **2** a belief or set of beliefs. **3** a group or sect holding a particular belief.

persuasive > *adjective* **1** good at persuading someone to do or believe something. **2** providing sound reasoning or argument.

DERIVATIVES – **persuasively** *adverb* **persuasiveness** *noun*.

SYNONYMS – **1** eloquent, silver-tongued, smooth-tongued. **2** cogent, compelling, convincing, credible.

pert > *adjective* **1** attractively lively or cheeky. **2** (of a bodily feature or garment) neat and suggestive of jauntiness.

DERIVATIVES – **pertly** *adverb* **pertness** *noun*.

ORIGIN – first used in the sense 'manifest': from Latin *apertus* 'opened'.

pertain > *verb* **1** be appropriate, related, or applicable. **2** chiefly Law belong as a part, appendage, or accessory. **3** be in effect or existence at a particular place or time.

ORIGIN – Latin *pertinere* 'extend to, have reference to'.

pertinacious /pertinay'shəss/ > *adjective* formal stubborn; persistent.

DERIVATIVES – **pertinaciously** *adverb* **pertinacity** *noun*.

ORIGIN – Latin *pertinax* 'holding fast'.

pertinent > *adjective* relevant; appropriate.

DERIVATIVES – **pertinence** *noun* **pertinently** *adverb*.

ORIGIN – from Latin *pertinere* 'extend to, have reference to'.

perturb /pərterb'/ > *verb* **1** make anxious or unsettled. **2** alter the normal or regular state or path of.

SYNONYMS – **1** concern, disturb, trouble, unsettle, upset, worry.

ORIGIN – Latin *perturbare*, from *per-* 'completely' + *turbare* 'disturb'.

perturbation /pertərbaysh'n/ > *noun* **1** anxiety; uneasiness. **2** the action of perturbing a system, moving object, or process.

pertussis /pərtuss'iss/ > *noun* medical term for *whooping cough*.

ORIGIN – from Latin *per-* 'away, extremely' + *tussis* 'a cough'.

peruke /pərook'/ > *noun* archaic a wig or periwig.

ORIGIN – French *perruque*.

peruse /pərooz'/ > *verb* formal read or examine thoroughly or carefully.

DERIVATIVES – **perusal** *noun* **peruser** *noun*.

USAGE – **peruse** is sometimes mistakenly taken to mean 'read through quickly; glance over': when used correctly it means 'read or examine thoroughly or carefully'.

SYNONYMS – examine, inspect, scrutinise, study.

ORIGIN – first meaning 'use up, wear out': perhaps from PER- + USE.

Peruvian /pərooʹviən/ > *noun* a person from Peru. > *adjective* relating to Peru.

perv (also **perve**) informal > *noun* **1** a sexual pervert. **2** Austral./NZ a lecherous look. > *verb* Austral./NZ gaze lecherously.

DERIVATIVES – **pervy** *adjective*.

pervade /pərvayd'/ > *verb* spread or be present throughout; suffuse.

DERIVATIVES – **pervasion** *noun*.

SYNONYMS – penetrate, permeate, saturate, suffuse.

ORIGIN – Latin *pervadere*, from *per-* 'throughout' + *vadere* 'go'.

pervasive > *adjective* spreading widely through something; widespread.

DERIVATIVES – **pervasively** *adverb* **pervasiveness** *noun*.

SYNONYMS – omnipresent, prevalent, rife, ubiquitous, widespread.

perverse > *adjective* **1** showing a deliberate and obstinate desire to behave unacceptably or unhelpfully. **2** contrary to what is accepted or expected. **3** sexually perverted.

DERIVATIVES – **perversely** *adverb* **perverseness** *noun* **perversity** (pl. **perversities**) *noun*.

SYNONYMS – **1** awkward, contrary, difficult, stubborn, wayward. **3** degenerate, depraved, deviant, perverted, unnatural.

perversion > *noun* **1** the action of perverting. **2** abnormal or unacceptable sexual behaviour.

pervert > *verb* /pərvert'/ **1** alter from its original meaning or state to a corruption of what was first intended. **2** lead away from what is right, natural, or acceptable. > *noun* /perʹvert/ a person whose sexual behaviour is abnormal or unacceptable.

SYNONYMS – *verb* **1** bend, distort, misrepresent, subvert, twist. **2** corrupt, lead astray. *noun* degenerate, deviant.

ORIGIN – Latin *pervertere*, from *per-* 'thoroughly, to ill effect' + *vertere* 'to turn'.

perverted > *adjective* sexually abnormal and unacceptable.

DERIVATIVES – **pervertedly** *adverb*.

pervious /perʹviəss/ > *adjective* permeable.

ORIGIN – Latin *pervius* 'having a passage through' (based on *via* 'way').

peseta /pəsaytə/ > *noun* the basic monetary unit of Spain, equal to 100 centimos.

ORIGIN – Spanish, 'little weight'.

pesewa /peseewə/ > *noun* a monetary unit of Ghana, equal to one hundredth of a cedi.

ORIGIN – Akan, 'penny'.

pesky > *adjective* (**peskier**, **peskiest**) informal annoying.

ORIGIN – perhaps related to PEST.

peso /paysō/ > *noun* (pl. **pesos**) the basic monetary unit of several Latin American countries and of the Philippines.

ORIGIN – Spanish, 'weight'.

pessary /pessʹari/ > *noun* (pl. **pessaries**) **1** a small soluble medicinal or contraceptive block inserted into the vagina. **2** a device inserted into the vagina to support the uterus.

ORIGIN – Latin *pessarium*, from Greek *pessos* 'oval stone'.

pessimism > *noun* **1** lack of hope or confidence in the future. **2** Philosophy a belief that this world is as bad as it could be or that evil will ultimately prevail over good.

DERIVATIVES – **pessimist** *noun* **pessimistic** *adjective* **pessimistically** *adverb*.

SYNONYMS – **1** defeatism, fatalism, gloominess.

ANTONYMS – optimism.

ORIGIN – from Latin *pessimus* 'worst'.

pest > *noun* **1** a destructive animal that attacks crops, food, or livestock. **2** informal an annoying person or thing.

ORIGIN – French *peste* or Latin *pestis* 'plague'.

pester > *verb* trouble or annoy with persistent requests or interruptions.

SYNONYMS – badger, bother, harass, hound, plague.

ORIGIN – French *empestrer* 'encumber': originally meaning 'overcrowd or impede', later 'infest'.

pesticide > *noun* a substance for destroying insects or other pests.

pestiferous /pestiffʹərəss/ > *adjective* **1** literary harbouring infection and disease. **2** humorous annoying.

pestilence /**pes**tilənss/ > *noun* archaic a fatal epidemic disease, especially bubonic plague.

pestilent > *adjective* **1** deadly. **2** informal, dated annoying. **3** archaic harmful to morals or public order.

pestilential > *adjective* **1** relating to or tending to cause infectious diseases. **2** of the nature of a pest. **3** informal annoying.

pestle /**pess**'l/ > *noun* a heavy tool with a rounded end, used for crushing and grinding substances in a mortar.
ORIGIN – Latin *pistillum*, from *pinsere* 'to pound'.

pesto /**pes**tō/ > *noun* a sauce of crushed basil leaves, pine nuts, garlic, Parmesan cheese, and olive oil, served with pasta.
ORIGIN – Italian, from *pestare* 'pound, crush'.

pet¹ > *noun* **1** a domestic or tamed animal or bird kept for companionship or pleasure. **2** a person treated with special favour. **3** used as an affectionate form of address. > *adjective* **1** relating to or kept as a pet. **2** favourite or particular: *my pet hate*. > *verb* (**petted**, **petting**) **1** stroke or pat (an animal). **2** caress sexually.
COMBINATIONS – **pet name** a name used to express fondness or familiarity.

pet² > *noun* a fit of sulking or bad temper.

peta- /**pet**ə/ > *combining form* denoting a factor of one thousand million million (10^{15}).
ORIGIN – alteration of PENTA-.

petal > *noun* each of the segments of the corolla of a flower.
ORIGIN – Greek *petalon* 'leaf'.

pétanque /pə**tangk**/ > *noun* a game similar to boule, played chiefly in Provence.
ORIGIN – French, from Provençal *pèd tanco* 'foot fixed (to the ground)', describing the start position.

petard /pi**taard**/ > *noun* historical a small bomb consisting of a metal or wooden box filled with powder.
IDIOMS – **be hoist with** (or **by**) **one's own petard** have one's schemes against others backfiring on one.
ORIGIN – French, from *péter* 'break wind'.

peter > *verb* (usu. **peter out**) diminish or come to an end gradually.

Peter Pan > *noun* a person who retains youthful features, or who is immature.
ORIGIN – the hero of J. M. Barrie's play of the same name (1904).

Peter Principle > *noun* the principle that members of a hierarchy are promoted until they reach the level at which they are no longer competent.
ORIGIN – named after the American educationalist Laurence J. *Peter*.

Peters projection > *noun* a world map projection in which areas are shown in correct proportion (but at the cost of distorted shape).
ORIGIN – named after the German historian Arno *Peters* (born 1916).

pethidine /**peth**ideen/ > *noun* a painkiller used especially for women in labour.

pétillant /**petti**yoN/ > *adjective* (of wine) slightly sparkling.
ORIGIN – French.

petiole /**petti**ōl/ > *noun* Botany the stalk that joins a leaf to a stem.
ORIGIN – Latin *petiolus* 'little foot, stalk'.

petit bourgeois /petti **boor**zhwaa/ > *adjective* of or characteristic of the lower middle class, especially in being conventional and conservative. > *noun* (pl. **petits bourgeois** pronunc. same) a petit bourgeois person.
ORIGIN – French, 'little citizen'.

petite > *adjective* (of a woman) attractively small and dainty.
SYNONYMS – dainty, diminutive, small.
ORIGIN – French, feminine of *petit* 'small'.

petite bourgeoisie /pə**teet** boorzh-waa**zee**/ (also **petit bourgeoisie**) > *noun* the lower middle class.
ORIGIN – French, 'little townsfolk'.

petit four /petti **for**/ > *noun* (pl. **petits fours** /petti **forz**/) a very small fancy cake, biscuit, or sweet.
ORIGIN – French, 'little oven'.

petition > *noun* **1** a formal written request or appeal to an authority, typically one signed by many people. **2** Law an application to a court for a writ, judicial action, etc. > *verb* make or present a petition to.
DERIVATIVES – **petitioner** *noun*.
ORIGIN – Latin, from *petere* 'aim at, seek, lay claim to'.

petit mal /petti **mal**/ > *noun* a mild form of epilepsy with only momentary spells of unconsciousness. Compare with GRAND MAL.
ORIGIN – French, 'little sickness'.

petit point /**petti** poynt/ > *noun* embroidery on canvas, using small diagonal stitches.
ORIGIN – French, 'little stitch'.

petits pois /petti **pwaa**/ > *plural noun* small, high-quality peas.
ORIGIN – French, 'small peas'.

petrel /**pet**rəl/ > *noun* a seabird of a kind that typically flies far from land.
ORIGIN – from the name of St *Peter*, because of the bird's habit of flying low with legs dangling, and so appearing to walk on the water (as did St Peter in the Gospel of Matthew).

Petri dish /**pet**ri, **pee**tri/ > *noun* a shallow transparent dish with a flat lid, used for the culture of micro-organisms.
ORIGIN – named after the German bacteriologist Julius R. *Petri* (1852–1922).

petrify > *verb* (**petrifies**, **petrified**) **1** change (organic matter) into stone by encrusting or replacing its original substance with a mineral deposit. **2** (often as **petrified**) paralyse with fear. **3** deprive of vitality.
DERIVATIVES – **petrifaction** *noun* **petrification** *noun*.
ORIGIN – Latin *petrificare*, from *petra* 'rock'.

petrochemical > *adjective* **1** relating to the chemical properties and processing of petroleum and natural gas. **2** relating to the chemistry of rocks. > *noun* a chemical obtained from petroleum and natural gas.
ORIGIN – sense 1 from PETROLEUM; sense 2 from Greek *petros* 'stone', *petra* 'rock'.

petrodollar > *noun* a notional unit of currency earned from the export of petroleum.

petroglyph /**pet**rəglif/ > *noun* a rock carving.
ORIGIN – from Greek *petros* 'rock' + *glyphē* 'carving'.

petrography /pe**trog**rəfi/ > *noun* the study of the composition and properties of rocks.
DERIVATIVES – **petrographer** *noun* **petrographic** *adjective*.

petrol > *noun* Brit. refined petroleum used as fuel in motor vehicles.
WORDFINDER – octane number (*standard of comparison for kinds of petrol*).
COMBINATIONS – **petrol blue** a shade of intense greenish or greyish blue. **petrol bomb** Brit. a crude bomb made from a bottle containing petrol and a cloth wick.

petrolatum /petrə**layt**əm/ > *noun* another term for *petroleum jelly*.

petroleum > *noun* a hydrocarbon oil found in rock strata and extracted and refined to produce fuels including petrol, paraffin, and diesel oil; oil.
COMBINATIONS – **petroleum jelly** a translucent solid mixture of hydrocarbons, used as a lubricant or ointment.
ORIGIN – from Latin *petra* 'rock' + *oleum* 'oil'.

petrology /pi**troll**əji/ > *noun* the study of the origin, structure, and composition of rocks.
DERIVATIVES – **petrological** *adjective* **petrologist** *noun*.

petticoat > *noun* **1** a woman's light, loose undergarment in the form of a skirt or dress. **2** (before another noun) informal, often derogatory associated with women: *petticoat government*.
ORIGIN – from *petty coat* 'small coat'.

pettifog > *verb* (**pettifogged**, **pettifogging**) archaic **1** quibble about petty points. **2** practise legal deception or trickery.
DERIVATIVES – **pettifoggery** *noun*.

pettifogger > *noun* archaic an inferior legal practitioner.
ORIGIN – from PETTY + obsolete *fogger* 'underhand dealer', probably from *Fugger*,

the name of a family of merchants in Augsburg in the 15th and 16th centuries.

pettifogging > *adjective* petty; trivial.

pettish > *adjective* petulant.

DERIVATIVES – **pettishly** *adverb* **pettishness** *noun*.

petty > *adjective* (**pettier**, **pettiest**) **1** trivial. **2** mean; small-minded. **3** minor. **4** Law (of a crime) of lesser importance. Compare with **GRAND**.

DERIVATIVES – **pettily** *adverb* **pettiness** *noun*.

COMBINATIONS – **petty bourgeois** petit bourgeois. **petty bourgeoisie** the petite bourgeoisie. **petty cash** an accessible store of money for expenditure on small items. **petty officer** a rank of non-commissioned officer in the navy, above leading seaman or seaman and below chief petty officer.

ORIGIN – from the pronunciation of French *petit* 'small'.

petulant /**pet**yoolənt/ > *adjective* childishly sulky or bad-tempered.

DERIVATIVES – **petulance** *noun* **petulantly** *adverb*.

SYNONYMS – crabby, fractious, peevish, pettish, whiny.

ORIGIN – Latin *petulans* 'impudent'.

petunia /pityoonia/ > *noun* a South American plant with white, purple, or red funnel-shaped flowers.

ORIGIN – Guarani, 'tobacco' (to which it is related).

pew > *noun* **1** (in a church) a long bench with a back. **2 Brit. informal** a seat.

ORIGIN – first denoting a raised, enclosed place for particular worshippers: from Old French *puye* 'balcony', based on Latin *podium* 'elevated place'.

pewter > *noun* a grey alloy of tin with copper and antimony (formerly, tin and lead).

ORIGIN – Old French *peutre*.

peyote /payōti/ > *noun* **1** a small spineless cactus native to Mexico and the southern US. **2** a hallucinogenic drug prepared from this, containing mescaline.

ORIGIN – Nahuatl.

Pf. > *abbreviation* pfennig.

pfennig /**fenn**ig/ > *noun* a monetary unit of Germany, equal to one hundredth of a mark.

ORIGIN – German, related to **PENNY**.

PFI > *abbreviation* (in the UK) Private Finance Initiative, a scheme whereby public services such as the National Health Service raise funds for capital projects from commercial organisations.

PG > *abbreviation* (in film classification) parental guidance, indicating that some scenes may be considered unsuitable for children.

pH > *noun* Chemistry a figure expressing acidity or alkalinity (7 is neutral, lower values are more acid and higher values more alkaline).

ORIGIN – from *p* representing German *Potenz* 'power' + *H*, the symbol for hydrogen.

phaeton /**fay**t'n/ > *noun* **1 historical** a light, open four-wheeled horse-drawn carriage. **2 US** a vintage touring car.

ORIGIN – from *Phaethōn*, son of the sun god Helios in Greek mythology, who was allowed to drive the solar chariot for a day with fatal results.

phage /fayj/ > *noun* Biology a kind of virus which acts as a parasite of bacteria, infecting them and reproducing inside them.

ORIGIN – short for *bacteriophage*, from **BACTERIUM** + Greek *phagein* 'eat'.

phagocyte /**fagg**əsīt/ > *noun* a type of body cell which engulfs and absorbs bacteria and other small particles.

DERIVATIVES – **phagocytic** *adjective*.

ORIGIN – from Greek *phagein* 'eat' + *kutos* 'vessel'.

phalange /**fal**anj/ > *noun* **1** Anatomy another term for **PHALANX** (in sense 3). **2** (**Phalange**) a right-wing Maronite party in Lebanon. [ORIGIN – abbreviation of French *Phalanges Libanaises* 'Lebanese phalanxes'.]

DERIVATIVES – **Phalangist** *noun* & *adjective*.

phalangeal /fəlanjiəl/ > *adjective* Anatomy relating to a phalanx or the phalanges.

phalanger /fəlanjər/ > *noun* a tree-dwelling marsupial native to Australia and New Guinea.

ORIGIN – Greek *phalangion* 'spider's web' (because of their webbed toes).

phalanx /**fal**angks/ > *noun* (pl. **phalanxes**) **1** a group of similar people or things. **2** a body of troops or police officers in close formation. **3** (pl. **phalanges** /fəlanjeez/) Anatomy a bone of the finger or toe.

ORIGIN – Greek.

phalarope /**fal**ərōp/ > *noun* a small wading or swimming bird with lobed feet.

ORIGIN – from Greek *phalaris* 'coot' + *pous* 'foot'.

phallic > *adjective* relating to or resembling a phallus or erect penis.

DERIVATIVES – **phallically** *adverb*.

phallocentric /falōsentrik/ > *adjective* focused on the phallus as a symbol of male dominance.

DERIVATIVES – **phallocentrism** *noun*.

phallus /**fal**əss/ > *noun* (pl. **phalli** /falī/ or **phalluses**) **1** a penis, especially when erect. **2** a representation of an erect penis symbolising fertility or potency.

DERIVATIVES – **phallicism** *noun*.

ORIGIN – Greek *phallos*.

phantasm /**fan**taz'm/ > *noun* literary an illusion or apparition.

DERIVATIVES – **phantasmal** *adjective*.

ORIGIN – Greek *phantasma*, from *phantazein* 'make visible'.

phantasmagoria /fantazməgoriə/ > *noun* a sequence of real or imaginary images like that seen in a dream.

DERIVATIVES – **phantasmagoric** *adjective* **phantasmagorical** *adjective*.

phantasy > *noun* variant spelling of **FANTASY**.

phantom > *noun* **1** a ghost. **2** a figment of the imagination. **3** (before another noun) not really existing; illusory.

SYNONYMS – **1** apparition, ghost, spectre, spirit, wraith. **2** delusion, hallucination, illusion.

COMBINATIONS – **phantom limb** a sensation experienced by a person who has had a limb amputated that the limb is still there. **phantom pregnancy** a condition in which signs of pregnancy are present in a woman who is not pregnant.

ORIGIN – Greek *phantasma* (see **PHANTASM**).

pharaoh* /**fair**ō/ > *noun* a ruler in ancient Egypt.

DERIVATIVES – **pharaonic** /fairayonnik/ *adjective*.

*SPELLING – remember, arse over head: -*aoh*, not -*oah*: phar*aoh*.

ORIGIN – Greek *Pharaō*, from an Egyptian word meaning 'great house'.

Pharisee /**farr**isee/ > *noun* **1** a member of an ancient Jewish sect noted for their strict observance of the traditional and written law. **2** a self-righteous person.

DERIVATIVES – **Pharisaic** /farrisayik/ *adjective* **Pharisaical** *adjective*.

ORIGIN – Greek *Pharisaios*, from an Aramaic word meaning 'separated ones'.

pharmaceutical /faarməsyootik'l/ > *adjective* relating to medicinal drugs. > *noun* a compound manufactured for use as a medicinal drug.

DERIVATIVES – **pharmaceutically** *adverb*.

ORIGIN – Greek *pharmakeutikos*, from *pharmakon* 'drug'.

pharmacist > *noun* a person qualified to prepare and dispense medicinal drugs.

pharmacology > *noun* the branch of medicine concerned with the uses, effects, and action of drugs.

DERIVATIVES – **pharmacological** (also **pharmacologic**) *adjective* **pharmacologically** *adverb* **pharmacologist** *noun*.

pharmacopoeia /faarməkəpeeə/ (US also **pharmacopeia**) > *noun* **1** a book containing a list of medicinal drugs with their effects and directions for use. **2** a stock of medicinal drugs.

ORIGIN – Greek *pharmakopoiia* 'art of preparing drugs'.

pharmacy > *noun* (pl. **pharmacies**) **1** a place where medicinal drugs are prepared or sold. **2** the science or practice of preparing and dispensing medicinal drugs.

pharyngeal /farrin**jee**əl/ > *adjective* relating to the pharynx.

pharyngitis /farrin**jī**tiss/ > *noun* inflammation of the pharynx.

pharynx /**farr**ingks/ > *noun* (pl. **pharynges** /fa**rin**jeez/) the membrane-lined cavity behind the nose and mouth, connecting them to the oesophagus.
ORIGIN – Greek *pharunx*.

phase > *noun* **1** a distinct period or stage in a process of change or development. **2** each of the aspects of the moon or a planet, according to the amount of its illumination. **3** Physics the relationship between the cycles of an oscillating system and a fixed reference point or another system. **4** Chemistry a distinct and homogeneous form of matter separated by its surface from other forms. > *verb* **1** carry out in gradual stages. **2** (**phase in** or **out**) gradually introduce or withdraw (something).
IDIOMS – **in** (or **out of**) **phase** in (or out of) synchrony.
SYNONYMS – *noun* **1** chapter, period, season, spell, stage, time.
ORIGIN – French, from Greek *phasis* 'appearance'.

phasic /**fay**zik/ > *adjective* relating to a phase or phases.

phatic /**fatt**ik/ > *adjective* (of language) used for general social interaction rather than to convey specific meaning, e.g. *nice morning, isn't it?*
ORIGIN – from Greek *phatos* 'spoken' or *phatikos* 'affirming'.

PhD > *abbreviation* Doctor of Philosophy.
ORIGIN – from Latin *philosophiae doctor*.

pheasant > *noun* a large long-tailed game bird, the male of which typically has showy plumage.
ORIGIN – Greek *phasianos* 'bird of Phasis', the name of a river in the Caucasus.

phencyclidine /fen**sī**klideen/ > *noun* a drug used as a veterinary anaesthetic and in hallucinogenic drugs.

phenobarbitone /feenō**baar**bitōn/ (US **phenobarbital** /feenō**baar**bit'l/) > *noun* a narcotic and sedative barbiturate drug used to treat epilepsy.

phenol /**fee**nol/ > *noun* Chemistry **1** a toxic white crystalline solid obtained from coal tar. Compare with **CARBOLIC**. **2** any compound with a hydroxyl group linked directly to a benzene ring.
DERIVATIVES – **phenolic** *adjective*.
ORIGIN – from French *phène* 'benzene'.

phenology /fi**noll**əji/ > *noun* the study of cyclic and seasonal natural phenomena, especially in relation to climate and plant and animal life.
DERIVATIVES – **phenological** *adjective*.
ORIGIN – from **PHENOMENON** + **-LOGY**.

phenolphthalein /feenol**thay**leen/ > *noun* Chemistry a crystalline solid used as an acid–base indicator and medicinally as a laxative.

phenom > *noun* N. Amer. informal an unusually gifted person.
ORIGIN – abbreviation of **PHENOMENON**.

phenomena plural of **PHENOMENON**.

phenomenal > *adjective* **1** extraordinary. **2** perceptible by the senses or through immediate experience.
DERIVATIVES – **phenomenally** *adverb*.
SYNONYMS – **1** amazing, exceptional, extraordinary, marvellous, outstanding, remarkable, staggering.

phenomenology /finommi**noll**əji/ > *noun* Philosophy **1** the science of phenomena as distinct from that of the nature of being. **2** an approach that concentrates on the study of consciousness and the objects of direct experience.
DERIVATIVES – **phenomenological** *adjective* **phenomenologically** *adverb* **phenomenologist** *noun*.

phenomenon > *noun* (pl. **phenomena**) **1** a fact or situation that is observed to exist or happen, especially one whose cause is in question. **2** Philosophy the object of a person's perception. **3** a remarkable person or thing.
USAGE – the word **phenomenon** comes from Greek, and its plural form is **phenomena**: do not treat **phenomena** as if it were a singular form.
ORIGIN – Greek *phainomenon* 'thing appearing to view', from *phainein* 'to show'.

phenotype /**fee**nōtīp/ > *noun* Biology the observable characteristics of an individual resulting from the interaction of its genotype with the environment.
ORIGIN – from Greek *phainein* 'to show'.

phenyl /**fee**nīl, **fenn**il/ > *noun* Chemistry the radical −C_6H_5, derived from benzene.

phenylalanine /feenīl**al**əneen, fenil-/ > *noun* Biochemistry an amino acid which is widely distributed in plant proteins and is an essential nutrient in the diet.

pheromone /**ferr**əmōn/ > *noun* a chemical substance released by an animal and causing a response in others of its species.
ORIGIN – from Greek *pherein* 'convey' + **HORMONE**.

phi /fī/ > *noun* the twenty-first letter of the Greek alphabet (Φ, φ), transliterated as 'ph' or (in modern Greek) 'f'.
ORIGIN – Greek.

phial /**fī**əl/ > *noun* a small cylindrical glass bottle, typically for medicines.
ORIGIN – Greek *phialē*; compare with **VIAL**.

phil- > *combining form* variant spelling of **PHILO-** before a vowel or *h*.

philadelphus /fillə**del**fəss/ > *noun* the shrub mock orange.
ORIGIN – from Greek *philadelphos* 'loving one's brother'.

philander /fi**lan**dər/ > *verb* (of a man) enter into casual sexual relationships with women.
DERIVATIVES – **philanderer** *noun*.
ORIGIN – earlier as noun in sense 'man, husband', often used in literature as the given name of a lover: from Greek *philandros* 'fond of men'.

philanthrope /**fill**ənthrōp/ > *noun* archaic a philanthropist.

philanthropist > *noun* a person who seeks to help others, especially by donating money to good causes.
SYNONYMS – altruist, benefactor.
ANTONYMS – misanthrope.

philanthropy /fi**lan**thrəpi/ > *noun* the desire to help others, especially through donation of money to good causes.
DERIVATIVES – **philanthropic** *adjective* **philanthropically** *adverb*.
ORIGIN – Greek *philanthrōpia*, from *philanthrōpos* 'man-loving'.

philately /fi**latt**əli/ > *noun* the collection and study of postage stamps.
DERIVATIVES – **philatelic** *adjective* **philatelically** *adverb* **philatelist** *noun*.
ORIGIN – from Greek *philo-* 'loving' + *ateleia* 'exemption from payment', used in reference to a franking mark or postage stamp exempting the recipient from payment.

-phile > *combining form* denoting a person or thing having a fondness for or tendency towards a specified thing.
ORIGIN – from Greek *philos* 'loving'.

philharmonic > *adjective* (in the names of orchestras) devoted to music.

philhellene /**fil**heleen/ > *noun* **1** a lover of Greece and Greek culture. **2** historical a supporter of Greek independence.
DERIVATIVES – **philhellenic** *adjective* **philhellenism** *noun*.

-philia > *combining form* denoting fondness, especially an abnormal love for or inclination towards something: *paedophilia*.
DERIVATIVES – **-philiac** *combining form* **-philic** *combining form* **-philous** *combining form*.
ORIGIN – from Greek *philia* 'fondness'.

philippic /fi**lipp**ik/ > *noun* a bitter verbal attack or denunciation.
ORIGIN – Greek *philippikos*, the name given to Demosthenes' speeches against Philip II of Macedon, and Cicero's against Mark Antony.

Philippine /**fill**ipeen/ > *adjective* relating to the Philippines.

Philistine /**fill**istīn/ > *noun* **1** a member of a people of ancient Palestine who came into conflict with the Israelites. **2** (**philistine**) a person who is hostile or indifferent to culture and the arts.

DERIVATIVES – **philistinism** /ˈfillistiniz'm/ *noun*.

---

wordpower facts

Philistine

What is the connection between uncultured philistines and the Philistines of biblical times (who came into conflict with the Israelites during the 12th and 11th centuries BC and from whom the country of Palestine took its name)? The sense 'person hostile or indifferent to culture' arose in the 19th century (coming from the German word for Philistine, *Philister*) as a result of a confrontation between townspeople and members of the university of Jena, Germany, in the late 17th century. A sermon on the conflict quoted the phrase 'the Philistines are upon you' (Book of Judges, chapter 16), which led to an association between the townspeople and those hostile to culture.

Phillips > *adjective* trademark referring to a screw with a cross-shaped slot for turning, or a corresponding screwdriver.

ORIGIN – from the name of the American manufacturer Henry F. *Phillips*.

phillumenist /fiˈlooʊmənist/ > *noun* a collector of matchbox or matchbook labels.

DERIVATIVES – **phillumeny** *noun*.

ORIGIN – from PHIL- + Latin *lumen* 'light'.

philo- (also **phil-** before a vowel or *h*) > *combining form* denoting a liking for a specified thing: *philopatric*.

ORIGIN – from Greek *philein* 'to love' or *philos* 'loving'.

philodendron /filləˈdendrən/ > *noun* (pl. **philodendrons** or **philodendra**) a tropical American climbing plant grown as a greenhouse or indoor plant.

ORIGIN – from PHILO- + Greek *dendron* 'tree'.

philology /fiˈlolləji/ > *noun* **1** the study of the structure, historical development, and relationships of a language or languages. **2** chiefly N. Amer. literary or classical scholarship.

DERIVATIVES – **philological** *adjective* **philologically** *adverb* **philologist** *noun*.

ORIGIN – first meaning 'love of learning', from Greek *philologia*.

philoprogenitive /fillōprəˈjennitiv/ > *adjective* formal **1** having many offspring. **2** loving one's offspring.

DERIVATIVES – **philoprogenitiveness** *noun*.

philosopher > *noun* a person engaged or learned in philosophy.

COMBINATIONS – **philosopher's stone** a mythical substance supposed to change any metal into gold or silver.

philosophical > *adjective* **1** relating to the study of philosophy. **2** calm in difficult circumstances.

DERIVATIVES – **philosophic** *adjective*.

philosophise (also **philosophize**) > *verb* theorise about fundamental or serious issues.

philosophy > *noun* (pl. **philosophies**) **1** the study of the fundamental nature of knowledge, reality, and existence. **2** the theories of a particular philosopher. **3** a theory or attitude that guides one's behaviour. **4** the study of the theoretical basis of a branch of knowledge or experience.

WORDFINDER – determinism (*belief that events are determined by external forces acting on the will*), dialectic (*philosophical debate*), epistemology (*the philosophy of knowledge*), ethics (*philosophy of morals*), existentialism (*philosophical system centred on human freedom and experience*), fatalism (*belief that events are predestined*), materialism (*doctrine that nothing exists except matter and its manifestations*), metaphysics (*philosophical study of abstract concepts*), nihilism (*doctrine that nothing is real*), positivism (*system recognising only proven or logical facts*), pragmatism (*doctrine that things are justified by practical utility*), stoicism (*doctrine of remaining indifferent to changes of fortune and of suppressing emotions*), Weltanschauung (*world view, personal philosophy of life*).

ORIGIN – Greek *philosophia* 'love of wisdom'.

philtre /ˈfiltər/ (US **philter**) > *noun* a love potion.

ORIGIN – Greek *philtron*, from *philein* 'to love'.

phiz /fiz/ (also **phizog**, **fizzog** /ˈfizog/) > *noun* Brit. informal one's face or expression.

ORIGIN – abbreviation of PHYSIOGNOMY.

phlebitis /fliˈbītiss/ > *noun* Medicine inflammation of the walls of a vein.

ORIGIN – Greek *phleps* 'vein'.

phlegm /flem/ > *noun* **1** the thick viscous substance secreted by the mucous membranes of the respiratory passages. **2** (in medieval science and medicine) one of the four bodily humours, believed to be associated with a calm or apathetic temperament. **3** calmness of temperament.

DERIVATIVES – **phlegmy** *adjective*.

ORIGIN – Greek *phlegma* 'inflammation', from *phlegein* 'to burn'.

phlegmatic /flegˈmattik/ > *adjective* unemotional and stolidly calm.

phloem /ˈflōəm/ > *noun* Botany the tissue in plants which conducts food materials downwards from the leaves.

ORIGIN – from Greek *phloos* 'bark'.

phlox /floks/ > *noun* a plant with dense clusters of colourful scented flowers.

ORIGIN – Greek, 'flame'.

-phobe > *combining form* denoting a person having a fear or dislike of a specified thing: *homophobe*.

ORIGIN – from Greek *phobos* 'fear'.

phobia > *noun* an extreme or irrational fear or dislike of something.

WORDFINDER – *examples of phobias:* acrophobia (*fear of heights*), agoraphobia (*open or public places*), arachnophobia (*spiders*), claustrophobia (*confined places*), cyberphobia (*computers*), gynophobia (*women*), homophobia (*homosexuals*), hydrophobia (*water*), necrophobia (*the dead*), neophobia (*the new*), nyctophobia (*night or darkness*), technophobia (*new technology*), xenophobia (*foreigners or strangers*).

DERIVATIVES – **phobic** *adjective & noun*.

-phobia > *combining form* extreme or irrational fear or dislike of a specified thing: *arachnophobia*.

DERIVATIVES – **-phobic** *combining form*.

Phoenician /fəˈneesh'n/ > *noun* a member of an ancient people inhabiting Phoenicia in the eastern Mediterranean. > *adjective* relating to Phoenicia.

phoenix* /ˈfeeniks/ > *noun* (in classical mythology) a unique bird that periodically burned itself on a funeral pyre and was born again from the ashes.

*SPELLING – -oe-, not -eo-: ph**oe**nix.

ORIGIN – Greek *phoinix* 'Phoenician, reddish purple, or phoenix'.

phone > *noun* **1** a telephone. **2** (**phones**) informal headphones or earphones. > *verb* telephone.

COMBINATIONS – **phone book** a telephone directory. **phonecard** a prepaid card allowing the user to make calls on a public telephone.

-phone > *combining form* **1** denoting an instrument using or connected with sound: *megaphone*. **2** denoting a person who uses a specified language: *francophone*.

ORIGIN – from Greek *phōnē* 'sound, voice'.

phone-in > *noun* a radio or television programme during which listeners or viewers telephone the studio and participate.

phoneme /ˈfōneem/ > *noun* Phonetics any of the distinct units of sound that distinguish one word from another, e.g. *p*, *b*, *d*, and *t* in *pad*, *pat*, *bad*, and *bat*.

ORIGIN – Greek *phōnēma* 'sound, speech', from *phōnein* 'speak'.

phonetic > *adjective* Phonetics **1** of or relating to speech sounds. **2** (of a system of writing) having a direct correspondence between symbols and sounds.

ORIGIN – Greek *phōnētikos*, from *phōnein* 'speak'.

phonetics > *plural noun* (treated as sing.) the study and classification of speech sounds.

phoney (also **phony**) informal > *adjective* (**phonier**, **phoniest**) not genuine. > *noun* (pl. **phoneys** or **phonies**) a fraudulent person or thing.

DERIVATIVES – **phonily** adverb.

phonic /**fonn**ik/ > *adjective* relating to speech sounds.

phonics > *plural noun* (treated as sing.) a method of teaching people to read by correlating sounds with alphabetic symbols.

phono /**fonn**ō/ > *adjective* denoting a type of plug used with audio and video equipment, in which one conductor is cylindrical and the other is a central prong that extends beyond it.

phono- > *combining form* relating to sound: *phonograph*.

ORIGIN – from Greek *phōnē* 'sound, voice'.

phonograph > *noun* 1 Brit. an early form of gramophone. 2 N. Amer. a record player.

phonology /fə**noll**əji/ > *noun* the system of contrastive relationships among the fundamental speech sounds of a language.

DERIVATIVES – **phonological** adjective.

phony > *adjective & noun* variant spelling of **PHONEY**.

phooey informal > *exclamation* used to express disdain or disbelief. > *noun* nonsense.

phormium /**for**miəm/ > *noun* the flax-lily of New Zealand.

ORIGIN – Latin, from Greek *phormion* 'small basket' (the fibres were used to make baskets).

phosgene /**foz**jeen/ > *noun* Chemistry a poisonous gas formerly used in warfare.

ORIGIN – from Greek *phōs* 'light' + **-GEN** (it was originally made by the action of sunlight on chlorine and carbon monoxide).

phosphate /**fos**fayt/ > *noun* Chemistry a salt or ester of phosphoric acid.

phosphor /**fos**fər/ > *noun* 1 a synthetic fluorescent or phosphorescent substance. 2 old-fashioned term for **PHOSPHORUS**.

phosphorescence > *noun* 1 light emitted by a substance without combustion or perceptible heat. 2 Physics the emission of light by a process resembling fluorescence but continuing after excitation ceases.

DERIVATIVES – **phosphoresce** verb **phosphorescent** adjective.

phosphoric /fos**forr**ik/ > *adjective* relating to or containing phosphorus.

phosphoric acid > *noun* Chemistry a crystalline acid obtained by treating phosphates with sulphuric acid.

phosphorus* /**fos**fərəss/ > *noun* a poisonous non-metallic chemical element existing as a yellowish waxy solid which ignites spontaneously in air and glows in the dark, and as a less reactive form used in making matches.

DERIVATIVES – **phosphorous** adjective.

***SPELLING** – the noun denoting the chemical element is spelled **phosphorus**, while the related adjective is spelled **phosphorous**.

ORIGIN – Greek *phōsphoros*, from *phōs* 'light' + *-phoros* '-bringing'.

photo > *noun* (pl. **photos**) a photograph.

COMBINATIONS – **photo finish** a close finish of a race in which the winner is identifiable only from a photograph of competitors crossing the line. **photo opportunity** a photocall.

photo- > *combining form* 1 relating to light. 2 relating to photography.

ORIGIN – from Greek *phōs* 'light'.

photocall > *noun* Brit. an occasion on which famous people pose for photographers by arrangement.

photocell > *noun* a photoelectric cell.

photochemistry > *noun* the branch of chemistry concerned with the chemical effects of light.

DERIVATIVES – **photochemical** adjective.

photochromic > *adjective* (of glass, lenses, etc.) undergoing a reversible change in colour when exposed to bright light.

photocopier > *noun* a machine for making photocopies.

photocopy > *noun* (pl. **photocopies**) a photographic copy of something produced by a process involving the action of light on a specially prepared surface. > *verb* (**photocopies**, **photocopied**) make a photocopy of.

DERIVATIVES – **photocopiable** adjective.

photoelectric > *adjective* characterised by or involving the emission of electrons from a surface by the action of light.

COMBINATIONS – **photoelectric cell** a device using a photoelectric effect to generate current.

photofit > *noun* Brit. a picture of a person made from composite photographs of facial features.

photogenic /fōtə**jenn**ik/ > *adjective* 1 looking attractive in photographs. 2 Biology producing or emitting light.

photograph > *noun* a picture made with a camera, in which an image is focused on to film and then made visible and permanent by chemical treatment. > *verb* take a photograph of.

WORDFINDER – cinematography (*the art of photography in film-making*), daguerreotype (*early photograph using a silvered plate*), microfiche (*film containing greatly reduced photographs of printed matter*), paparazzi (*freelance photographers who try to photograph celebrities*), sepia (*brown colour of many early photographs*), vignette (*portrait photograph with blurred border*).

DERIVATIVES – **photographer** noun **photographic** adjective.

photographic memory > *noun* an ability to remember information or visual images in great detail.

photography > *noun* the taking and processing of photographs.

photogravure /fōtōgrə**vyoor**/ > *noun* an image produced from a photographic negative transferred to a metal plate and etched in.

ORIGIN – from French *photo-* 'relating to light' + *gravure* 'engraving'.

photojournalism > *noun* the communicating of news by photographs.

DERIVATIVES – **photojournalist** noun.

photometer /fō**tomm**itər/ > *noun* an instrument for measuring the intensity of light.

DERIVATIVES – **photometric** adjective **photometry** noun.

photomicrograph > *noun* another term for **MICROGRAPH**.

photon /**fō**ton/ > *noun* Physics a particle representing a quantum of light or other electromagnetic radiation.

DERIVATIVES – **photonic** adjective.

photophobia > *noun* extreme sensitivity to light.

DERIVATIVES – **photophobic** adjective.

photoreceptor > *noun* a structure in an organism that responds to light.

photosensitive > *adjective* responding to light.

DERIVATIVES – **photosensitivity** noun.

photostat > *noun* trademark 1 a type of machine for making photocopies on special paper. 2 a copy made by a photostat. > *verb* (**photostatted**, **photostatting**) copy with a photostat.

photosynthesis > *noun* the process by which green plants use sunlight to synthesise nutrients from carbon dioxide and water.

DERIVATIVES – **photosynthesise** (also **photosynthesize**) verb **photosynthetic** adjective.

phototropism /fōtō**trō**piz'm/ > *noun* Biology the orientation of a plant or other organism in response to light.

DERIVATIVES – **phototropic** adjective.

phrasal verb > *noun* Grammar an idiomatic phrase consisting of a verb and an adverb or preposition, as in *break down* or *see to*.

phrase > *noun* 1 a small group of words standing together as a conceptual unit. 2 Music a group of notes forming a distinct unit within a longer passage. 3 an idiomatic or pithy expression. > *verb* put into a particular form of words.

DERIVATIVES – **phrasal** adjective.

COMBINATIONS – **phrase book** a book listing useful expressions in a foreign language and their translations.

ORIGIN – Greek *phrasis*, from *phrazein* 'declare, tell'.

phraseology /frayzi**oll**əji/ > *noun* (pl. **phraseologies**) a particular or characteristic mode of expression.

phrasing > *noun* division of music into phrases.

phreaking > *noun* informal, chiefly N. Amer. the action of hacking into telecommunications systems, especially to obtain free calls.

DERIVATIVES – **phreak** *noun* **phreaker** *noun*.

ORIGIN – alteration of *freaking* by association with *phone*.

phrenology /fri**noll**əji/ > *noun* chiefly historical the study of the shape and size of the cranium as a supposed indication of character.

DERIVATIVES – **phrenologist** *noun*.

ORIGIN – from Greek *phrēn* 'mind' + -LOGY.

Phrygian /**fri**jiən/ > *noun* a person from Phrygia, an ancient region of west central Asia Minor. > *adjective* relating to Phrygia.

phthisis /**fthī**siss/ > *noun* archaic pulmonary tuberculosis or a similar progressive wasting disease.

ORIGIN – Greek, from *phthinein* 'to decay'.

phut > *exclamation* used to represent a dull abrupt sound as of a slight impact or explosion.

phyla plural of PHYLUM.

phylactery /fi**lak**təri/ > *noun* (pl. **phylacteries**) a small leather box containing Hebrew texts, worn by Jewish men at morning prayer.

ORIGIN – Greek *phulaktērion* 'amulet', from *phulassein* 'to guard'.

phyllo > *noun* variant spelling of FILO.

phylloquinone /fillō**kwinn**ōn/ > *noun* vitamin K₁, a compound found in cabbage, spinach, and other green vegetables, and essential for the blood-clotting process.

ORIGIN – from Greek *phullon* 'leaf' + QUINONE.

phylloxera /fi**lok**sərə, fillok**seer**ə/ > *noun* a plant louse that is a pest of vines.

ORIGIN – from Greek *phullon* 'leaf' + *xēros* 'dry'.

phylogeny /fī**loj**əni/ > *noun* Biology the evolutionary development and diversification of species. Compare with ONTOGENY.

phylum /**fī**ləm/ > *noun* (pl. **phyla** /**fī**lə/) Zoology a principal taxonomic category that ranks above class and below kingdom.

ORIGIN – Greek *phulon* 'race'.

physalis /fi**say**liss/ > *noun* a plant of a genus that includes the Cape gooseberry and Chinese lantern.

ORIGIN – Greek *phusallis* 'bladder'.

physic archaic > *noun* medicinal drugs or medical treatment.

ORIGIN – Latin *physica*, from Greek *phusikē*

epistēmē 'knowledge of nature', from *phusis* 'nature'.

physical > *adjective* 1 relating to the body as opposed to the mind. 2 relating to things perceived through the senses as opposed to the mind. 3 relating to physics or the operation of natural forces. 4 involving bodily contact or activity. > *noun* a medical examination to determine a person's bodily fitness.

DERIVATIVES – **physicality** *noun* **physically** *adverb*.

SYNONYMS – *adjective* 1 bodily, corporal, corporeal, fleshly, somatic. 2 material, substantial, tangible.

COMBINATIONS – **physical chemistry** the branch of chemistry concerned with the application of the techniques and theories of physics to the study of chemical systems. **physical education** instruction in physical exercise and games, especially in schools. **physical geography** the branch of geography concerned with natural features. **physical sciences** the sciences concerned with the study of inanimate natural objects, including physics, chemistry, and astronomy.

physical sciences > *plural noun* the sciences concerned with the study of inanimate natural objects, including physics, chemistry, and astronomy.

physical therapy > *noun* US term for PHYSIOTHERAPY.

DERIVATIVES – **physical therapist** *noun*.

physician > *noun* a person qualified to practise medicine.

IDIOMS – **physician, heal thyself** proverb before attempting to correct others, make sure that you aren't guilty of the same faults yourself. [ORIGIN – with biblical allusion to the Gospel of Luke, chapter 4.]

physics > *plural noun* (treated as sing.) 1 the branch of science concerned with the nature and properties of matter and energy. 2 the physical properties and phenomena of something.

DERIVATIVES – **physicist** *noun*.

physio > *noun* (pl. **physios**) informal physiotherapy or a physiotherapist.

physiognomy /fizzi**onn**əmi/ > *noun* (pl. **physiognomies**) a person's facial features or expression.

ORIGIN – Greek *phusiognōmonia* 'judging of a man's nature (by his features)', based on *phusis* 'nature' + *gnōmōn* 'judge or interpreter'.

physiology > *noun* 1 the branch of biology concerned with the normal functions of living organisms and their parts. 2 the way in which a living organism or bodily part functions.

DERIVATIVES – **physiological** *adjective* **physiologist** *noun*.

physiotherapy > *noun* the treatment of

disease, injury, or deformity by physical methods such as massage and exercise.

DERIVATIVES – **physiotherapist** *noun*.

physique > *noun* the form, size, and development of a person's body.

phytoplankton /**f**ītōplangktən/ > *noun* Biology plankton consisting of microscopic plants.

ORIGIN – from Greek *phuton* 'plant'.

pi /pī/ > *noun* 1 the sixteenth letter of the Greek alphabet (Π, π), transliterated as 'p'. 2 the numerical value of the ratio of the circumference of a circle to its diameter (approximately 3.14159).

ORIGIN – Greek; sense 2 is from the initial letter of *periphereia* 'circumference'.

pia /**pī**ə/ (in full **pia mater**) > *noun* Anatomy the delicate innermost membrane enveloping the brain and spinal cord.

ORIGIN – Latin, (in full) 'tender mother', translating an Arabic phrase.

pianism > *noun* skill or artistry in playing the piano or composing piano music.

DERIVATIVES – **pianistic** *adjective*.

pianissimo /peeə**niss**imō/ > *adverb* & *adjective* Music very soft or softly.

ORIGIN – Italian, 'softest'.

piano[1] /pi**ann**ō/ > *noun* (pl. **pianos**) a large keyboard musical instrument with metal strings, which are struck by hammers when the keys are depressed.

DERIVATIVES – **pianist** *noun*.

COMBINATIONS – **piano accordion** an accordion with the melody played on a small vertical keyboard like that of a piano.

ORIGIN – Italian, abbreviation of PIANOFORTE.

piano[2] /**pyaa**nō/ > *adverb* & *adjective* Music soft or softly.

ORIGIN – Italian, 'soft'.

pianoforte /piannō**for**tay/ > *noun* formal term for PIANO[1].

ORIGIN – from Italian *piano e forte* 'soft and loud', expressing the gradation in tone.

pianola /peeə**nō**lə/ > *noun* trademark a piano equipped to be played automatically.

piastre /pi**ast**ər/ (US also **piaster**) > *noun* a monetary unit of several Middle Eastern countries, equal to one hundredth of a pound.

ORIGIN – Italian *piastra d'argento* 'plate of silver'.

piazza /pi**at**sə/ > *noun* a public square or marketplace.

ORIGIN – Italian.

pibroch /**pee**brok, **pee**brokh/ > *noun* a form of music for the Scottish bagpipes involving elaborate variations on a theme.

ORIGIN – Scottish Gaelic *piobaireachd* 'art of piping'.

pic > *noun* informal a picture, photograph, or film.

pica /**pī**kə/ > *noun* Printing 1 a unit of type size and line length equal to 12 points (about

⅙ inch or 4.2 mm). **2** a size of letter in typewriting, with 10 characters to the inch (about 3.9 to the centimetre).

ORIGIN – Latin, literally 'magpie', commonly identified with a 15th-century book of rules about Church feasts, although there is no known copy of this book printed in 'pica' type.

picador /pikkədor/ > *noun* (in bullfighting) a person on horseback who goads the bull with a lance.

ORIGIN – Spanish, from *picar* 'to prick'.

picaresque /pikkəresk/ > *adjective* relating to fiction dealing with the adventures of a dishonest but appealing hero.

ORIGIN – Spanish *picaresco*, from *pícaro* 'rogue'.

picayune /pikkəyoon/ N. Amer. > *adjective* informal petty; worthless. > *noun* **1** informal an insignificant person or thing. **2** dated a coin of little value.

ORIGIN – French *picaillon*, denoting a Piedmontese copper coin, also used to mean 'cash'.

piccalilli /pikkəlilli/ > *noun* (pl. **piccalillies** or **piccalillis**) a pickle of chopped vegetables, mustard, and hot spices.

ORIGIN – probably from a blend of PICKLE and CHILLI.

piccaninny /pikkəninni/ (US **pickaninny**) > *noun* (pl. **picaninnies**) offensive a small black child.

ORIGIN – from a Spanish or Portuguese word meaning 'little'.

piccolo > *noun* (pl. **piccolos**) a small flute sounding an octave higher than the ordinary one.

ORIGIN – Italian, 'small flute'.

pick¹ > *verb* **1** (often **pick up**) take hold of and move. **2** remove (a flower or fruit) from where it is growing. **3** choose from a number of alternatives. **4** remove unwanted matter from (one's nose or teeth) with a finger or a pointed instrument. > *noun* **1** an act of selecting something. **2** (**the pick of**) informal the best person or thing in a particular group.

IDIOMS – **pick and choose** select only the best from among a number of alternatives. **pick at 1** repeatedly pull at (something) with one's fingers. **2** eat in small amounts. **pick someone's brains** informal obtain information by questioning someone with expertise. **pick a fight** provoke an argument or fight. **pick holes in** find fault with. **pick a lock** open a lock with an instrument other than the proper key. **pick off** shoot (one of a group) from a distance. **pick on** single out for unfair treatment. **pick out** distinguish from among a group. **pick over** (or **pick through**) sort through (a number of items) carefully. **pick someone's pockets** steal something from a person's pocket. **pick up 1** go to collect.

2 improve or increase. **3** informal casually strike up a relationship with (someone) as a sexual overture. **4** return to (an earlier point or topic). **5** obtain, acquire, or learn. **6** become aware of or sensitive to. **7** detect or receive (a signal or sound). **pick one's way** walk slowly and carefully.

SYNONYMS – *verb* **3** choose, elect, opt for, select, single out.

pick² (also **pickaxe**) > *noun* **1** a tool consisting of a curved iron bar with one or both ends pointed, mounted at right angles to its handle, used for breaking up hard ground or rock. **2** a plectrum.

ORIGIN – variant of PIKE².

picket > *noun* **1** a person or group of people standing outside a workplace trying to persuade others not to enter during a strike. **2** (also **piquet**) a soldier or small body of troops sent out to watch for the enemy. **3** a pointed wooden stake driven into the ground. > *verb* (**picketed, picketing**) act as a picket outside (a workplace).

ORIGIN – French *piquet* 'pointed stake': originally denoting a pointed stake on which a soldier was required to stand on one foot, as a military punishment.

pickings > *plural noun* **1** profits or gains, especially those made effortlessly or dishonestly. **2** scraps or leftovers.

pickle > *noun* **1** a relish consisting of vegetables or fruit preserved in vinegar, brine, or mustard. **2** liquid used to preserve food or other perishable items. **3** (**a pickle**) informal a difficult situation. > *verb* **1** preserve (food) in pickle. **2** (**pickled**) informal drunk.

pick-me-up > *noun* informal a thing that makes one feel more energetic or cheerful.

pickpocket > *noun* a person who steals from people's pockets.

pickup > *noun* **1** (also **pickup truck**) a small van or truck with low sides. **2** an act of picking up or collecting a person or goods. **3** an improvement. **4** a device on an electric guitar which converts sound vibrations into electrical signals for amplification.

picky > *adjective* (**pickier, pickiest**) informal fastidious, especially excessively so.

picnic > *noun* a packed meal eaten outdoors, or an occasion when such a meal is eaten. > *verb* (**picnicked, picnicking**) have or take part in a picnic.

IDIOMS – **be no picnic** informal be difficult or unpleasant.

DERIVATIVES – **picnicker** noun.

ORIGIN – French.

pico- > *combining form* denoting a factor of one million millionth (10^{-12}): picosecond.

ORIGIN – from Spanish *pico* 'beak, peak, little bit'.

picot /peekō/ > *noun* a small decorative loop or series of loops in lace or embroidery.

ORIGIN – French, 'small peak or point'.

picric acid /pikrik/ > *noun* Chemistry a bitter

yellow compound obtained by nitrating phenol, used in making explosives.

ORIGIN – from Greek *pikros* 'bitter'.

Pict > *noun* a member of an ancient people inhabiting northern Scotland in Roman times.

ORIGIN – Latin *Picti*, perhaps from *pingere* 'to paint or tattoo'.

pictograph (also **pictogram**) > *noun* **1** a pictorial symbol for a word or phrase. **2** a pictorial representation of statistics on a chart, graph, or computer screen.

DERIVATIVES – **pictographic** adjective.

ORIGIN – from Latin *pingere* 'to paint'.

pictorial > *adjective* of or expressed in pictures; illustrated. > *noun* a newspaper or periodical with pictures as a main feature.

DERIVATIVES – **pictorially** adverb.

ORIGIN – Latin *pictorius* from *pictor* 'painter'.

picture > *noun* **1** a painting, drawing, or photograph. **2** an image on a television screen. **3** a cinema film. **4** (**the pictures**) the cinema. **5** an impression formed from an account or description. **6** informal a state of being fully informed about something: *in the picture*. > *verb* **1** represent in a picture. **2** form a mental image of.

IDIOMS – **be** (or **look**) **a picture 1** be beautiful. **2** look amusingly startled. (**as**) **pretty as a picture** very pretty.

SYNONYMS – *noun* **5** idea, image, impression. *verb* **2** envisage, imagine, visualise.

COMBINATIONS – **picture postcard 1** a postcard with a picture on one side. **2** (**picture-postcard**) prettily picturesque. **picture window** a large window consisting of one pane of glass.

ORIGIN – Latin *pictura*, from *pingere* 'to paint'.

picturesque > *adjective* visually attractive in a quaint or charming manner.

ORIGIN – Italian *pittoresco*, from *pittore* 'painter'.

piddle > *verb* informal **1** urinate. **2** (**piddle about** or **around**) spend time in trifling activities. **3** (**piddling**) pathetically trivial.

pidgin > *noun* a grammatically simplified form of a language, used for communication between people not sharing a common language.

ORIGIN – Chinese alteration of English *business*.

pi-dog > *noun* variant spelling of PYE-DOG.

pie¹ > *noun* a baked dish of savoury or sweet ingredients encased in or topped with pastry.

IDIOMS – **pie in the sky** informal a pleasant prospect that is very unlikely to be realised.

COMBINATIONS – **pie chart** a diagram in which a circle is divided into sectors that each represent a proportion of the whole.

pie² > *noun* a former monetary unit of the Indian subcontinent, equal to one twelfth of an anna.

ORIGIN – Hindi, from Sanskrit, 'quarter'.

piebald /**pī**bawld/ > *adjective* (of a horse) having irregular patches of two colours, typically black and white. > *noun* a piebald horse.

ORIGIN – from *pie* in *magpie* + *bald* (in the obsolete sense 'streaked with white').

piece > *noun* **1** a portion separated from or regarded distinctly from the whole. **2** an item used in constructing something or forming part of a set. **3** a musical or written work. **4** a figure or token used to make moves in a board game. **5** a coin of specified value. **6** informal, chiefly N. Amer. a firearm. > *verb* (**piece together**) assemble from individual parts.

IDIOMS – **go to pieces** become so nervous or upset that one is unable to function normally. **in one piece** unharmed or undamaged. (**all**) **of a piece** entirely consistent. **piece by piece** in slow and small stages. **piece of work** informal a person of a specified kind, especially an unpleasant one. **say one's piece** give one's opinion or make a prepared statement. **tear** (or **pull**) **to pieces** criticise harshly.

SYNONYMS – *noun* **1** bit, chunk, fragment, part, portion, section, segment, slice.

ORIGIN – Old French.

pièce de résistance /pyess de ray**zist**ONss/ > *noun* the most important or remarkable feature of a creative work.

ORIGIN – French, 'piece (i.e. means) of resistance'.

piecemeal > *adjective & adverb* done piece by piece over a period of time.

piecework > *noun* work paid for according to the amount produced.

pied /pīd/ > *adjective* patterned or variegated with two or more different colours, in particular black and white.

ORIGIN – from obsolete *pie* 'magpie', from Latin *pica*.

pied-à-terre /pyaydaa**tair**/ > *noun* (pl. **pieds-à-terre** pronunc. same) a small flat, house, or room kept for occasional use, one's permanent residence being elsewhere.

ORIGIN – French, 'foot to earth'.

Pied Piper > *noun* a person who entices others to follow them, especially to their doom.

ORIGIN – from the legendary German figure who rid the town of Hamelin of rats by enticing them away with his music, and when refused the promised payment lured away the town's children.

pie-eyed > *adjective* informal very drunk.

Piegan > *noun* variant spelling of **PEIGAN**.

pier > *noun* **1** a structure leading out to sea and used as a landing stage for boats or as a place of entertainment. **2** Brit. a long, narrow structure projecting from an airport terminal and giving access to an aircraft. **3** the pillar of an arch or supporting a bridge. **4** a wall between windows or other adjacent openings.

pierce > *verb* **1** make a hole in or through with a sharp object. **2** force or cut a way through. **3** (**piercing**) very sharp, cold, or high-pitched.

SYNONYMS – **1** penetrate, perforate, puncture, skewer, spear.

ORIGIN – Latin *pertundere* 'bore through'.

Pierrot /**pi**eerō/ > *noun* a male character in French pantomime, with a sad white-painted face, a loose white costume, and a pointed hat.

ORIGIN – French, familiar form of the male given name *Pierre* 'Peter'.

pietà /pyay**taa**/ > *noun* a picture or sculpture of the Virgin Mary holding the dead body of Christ.

ORIGIN – Italian, from Latin *pietas* 'piety, compassion'.

piety /**pī**əti/ > *noun* (pl. **pieties**) **1** the quality of being pious or reverent. **2** a conventional belief accepted unthinkingly.

SYNONYMS – **1** devotion, devoutness, godliness, holiness, piousness.

ORIGIN – Old French *piete* 'compassion', from Latin *pietas* 'dutifulness', from *pius* (see **PIOUS**).

piezo /**pī**eezō/ > *adjective* piezoelectric.

piezoelectricity /pī-eezōillek**triss**iti/ > *noun* electric polarisation produced in certain crystals by the application of mechanical stress.

DERIVATIVES – **piezoelectric** *adjective*.

ORIGIN – from Greek *piezein* 'press, squeeze' + **ELECTRICITY**.

piffle > *noun* informal nonsense.

piffling > *adjective* informal trivial; unimportant.

pig > *noun* **1** a domesticated mammal with sparse bristly hair and a flat snout, kept for its meat. **2** informal a greedy, dirty, or unpleasant person. **3** a wild animal related to the domestic pig. **4** informal, derogatory a police officer. **5** an oblong mass of iron or lead from a smelting furnace. > *verb* (**pigged**, **pigging**) informal gorge oneself with food.

WORDFINDER – boar (*male pig*), farrow (*litter of pigs; give birth to this*), hog (*castrated male pig*), porcine (*of or like a pig*), sow (*female pig*), swineherd (*person who tends pigs*).

IDIOMS – **make a pig of oneself** informal overeat. **make a pig's ear of** Brit. informal handle ineptly. **a pig in a poke** something that is bought or accepted without first being seen or assessed.

DERIVATIVES – **piglet** *noun*.

COMBINATIONS – **pig-headed** stupidly obstinate. **pig iron** crude iron obtained from a smelting furnace. **pigskin** leather made from the hide of a domestic pig.

pigeon* > *noun* a medium-sized seed-eating bird with a small head, short legs, and a cooing voice, very similar to but generally larger than a dove.

WORDFINDER – columbine (*of or like a pigeon or dove*), dovecote, loft (*shelter for pigeons*), squab (*young unfledged pigeon*).

***SPELLING** – note that there is no *d*: *pigeon*.

COMBINATIONS – **pigeon-chested** (also **pigeon-breasted**) having a narrow, projecting chest. **pigeon-toed** having the toes or feet turned inwards.

ORIGIN – Old French *pijon* 'young bird', from Latin *pipio* 'young cheeping bird'.

pigeonhole > *noun* **1** a small recess for a domestic pigeon to nest in. **2** each of a set of small compartments where letters or messages may be left for individuals. **3** a rigid category to which someone or something is assigned. > *verb* assign to a particular category, especially a restrictive one.

piggery > *noun* (pl. **piggeries**) **1** a farm or enclosure where pigs are kept. **2** behaviour regarded as characteristic of pigs, especially greed or unpleasantness.

piggish > *adjective* resembling a pig, especially in being unpleasant.

piggy > *noun* (pl. **piggies**) a child's word for a pig or piglet. > *adjective* resembling a pig, especially in features or appetite.

IDIOMS – **piggy in the middle** chiefly Brit. **1** a game in which two people attempt to throw a ball to each other without a third person in the middle catching it. **2** a person who is placed in an awkward situation between two others.

COMBINATIONS – **piggy bank** a money box, especially one shaped like a pig.

piggyback > *noun* a ride on someone's back and shoulders. > *adverb* on the back and shoulders of another person. > *verb* carry by or as if by means of a piggyback.

pigment > *noun* **1** the natural colouring matter of animal or plant tissue. **2** a substance used for colouring or painting. > *verb* colour with or as if with pigment.

DERIVATIVES – **pigmentary** *adjective* **pigmentation** *noun*.

ORIGIN – Latin *pigmentum*, from *pingere* 'to paint'.

pigmy > *noun* variant spelling of **PYGMY**.

pigsty > *noun* (pl. **pigsties**) **1** a pen or enclosure for a pig or pigs. **2** a very dirty or untidy house or room.

pigswill > *noun* kitchen refuse and scraps fed to pigs.

pigtail > *noun* a plaited lock of hair worn singly at the back or on each side of the head.

DERIVATIVES – **pigtailed** *adjective*.

pike¹ > *noun* (pl. same) a long-bodied predatory freshwater fish with long teeth.
ORIGIN – from **PIKE²** (because of the fish's pointed jaw).

pike² > *noun* historical a weapon with a pointed metal head on a long wooden shaft.
ORIGIN – French *pique*, from *piquer* 'pierce', from *pic* 'pick, pike'.

pikelet > *noun* a thin kind of crumpet.
ORIGIN – Welsh *bara pyglyd* 'pitchy bread'.

piker > *noun* N. Amer. & Austral./NZ informal **1** a gambler who makes only small bets. **2** a mean or cautious person.

pikestaff > *noun* historical the wooden shaft of a pike.
IDIOMS – (as) **plain as a pikestaff** very obvious. [ORIGIN – the phrase is an altered version of *as plain as a packstaff*, the staff being that of a pedlar, on which he rested his pack of wares.]

pilaf /pilaf/ (also **pilaff**, **pilau** /pilow/, **pulao** /pəlow/) > *noun* a Middle Eastern or Indian dish of spiced rice or wheat and often meat and vegetables.
ORIGIN – Turkish *pilâv*.

pilaster /pilastər/ > *noun* a rectangular column, especially one projecting from a wall.
ORIGIN – Latin *pilastrum*, from *pila* 'pillar'.

pilchard > *noun* a small marine food fish of the herring family.

pile¹ > *noun* **1** a heap of things laid or lying one on top of another. **2** informal a large amount. **3** a large imposing building. > *verb* **1** place (things) one on top of the other. **2** (**pile up**) form a pile or very large quantity. **3** (**pile into** or **out of**) get into or out of (a vehicle) in a disorganised manner.
IDIOMS – **make a pile** informal make a lot of money. **pile on** informal intensify or exaggerate for effect.
SYNONYMS – *noun & verb* **1** heap, mound, stack.
ORIGIN – Latin *pila* 'pillar, pier'.

pile² > *noun* a heavy stake or post driven into the ground to support foundations.
COMBINATIONS – **piledriver 1** a machine for driving piles into the ground. **2** Brit. informal a forceful act, blow, or shot.

pile³ > *noun* the soft projecting surface of a carpet or a fabric, consisting of many small threads.
ORIGIN – Latin *pilus* 'hair'.

piles > *plural noun* haemorrhoids.

pile-up > *noun* informal **1** a crash involving several vehicles. **2** an accumulation of a specified thing.

pilfer > *verb* steal (things of little value).
DERIVATIVES – **pilferage** noun.
ORIGIN – Old French *pelfrer* 'to pillage'.

pilgrim > *noun* a person who journeys to a sacred place for religious reasons.
ORIGIN – Provençal *pelegrin*, from Latin *peregrinus* 'foreign'.

pilgrimage > *noun* a pilgrim's journey.

pill > *noun* **1** a small round mass of solid medicine for swallowing whole. **2** (**the Pill**) a contraceptive pill. > *verb* (of knitted fabric) form small balls of fluff on its surface.
IDIOMS – **a bitter pill** an unpleasant or painful necessity. **sugar** (or **sweeten**) **the pill** make an unpleasant or painful necessity more palatable.
COMBINATIONS – **pillbox 1** a small box for holding pills. **2** a hat of a similar shape. **3** a small, partly underground, concrete fort used as an outpost.
ORIGIN – Latin *pilula* 'little ball'.

pillage > *verb* rob or steal with violence, especially in wartime. > *noun* the action of pillaging.
SYNONYMS – *verb* despoil, loot, plunder, raid, ransack, sack.
ORIGIN – from Old French, from *piller* 'to plunder'.

pillar > *noun* **1** a tall vertical structure used as a support for a building or as an ornament. **2** a person or thing providing reliable support.
WORDFINDER – caryatid (*classical pillar in the form of a draped female*), obelisk (*pillar set up as monument*), peristyle (*row of pillars round a courtyard or other space*), pilaster (*rectangular pillar projecting from a wall*), telamon (*pillar in the form of a male figure*).
IDIOMS – **from pillar to post** from one place to another in an unsatisfactory manner.
DERIVATIVES – **pillared** adjective.
COMBINATIONS – **pillar box** (in the UK) a large red cylindrical public postbox.
ORIGIN – Latin *pila* 'pillar'.

pillbox > *noun* **1** a small box for holding pills. **2** a hat of a similar shape. **3** a small, partly underground concrete fort used as an outpost.

pillion > *noun* a seat for a passenger behind a motorcyclist.
ORIGIN – Irish *pillín* 'small cushion'.

pillock > *noun* Brit. informal a stupid person.
ORIGIN – from obsolete *pillicock* 'penis'.

pillory > *noun* (pl. **pillories**) a wooden framework with holes for the head and hands, in which offenders were formerly imprisoned and exposed to public abuse. > *verb* (**pillories**, **pilloried**) **1** put in a pillory. **2** attack or ridicule publicly.

pillow > *noun* a rectangular cloth bag stuffed with feathers or other soft materials, used to support the head when lying or sleeping. > *verb* support (one's head) as if on a pillow.
DERIVATIVES – **pillowy** adjective.
COMBINATIONS – **pillowcase** a removable cloth cover for a pillow. **pillow fight** a mock fight using pillows. **pillow talk** intimate conversation in bed.
ORIGIN – Latin *pulvinus* 'cushion'.

pilot > *noun* **1** a person who operates the flying controls of an aircraft. **2** a person with local knowledge qualified to take charge of a ship entering or leaving a harbour. **3** something done or produced as an experiment or test before wider introduction. > *verb* (**piloted**, **piloting**) **1** act as a pilot of (an aircraft or ship). **2** test (a scheme, project, etc.) before introducing it more widely.
DERIVATIVES – **pilotage** noun.
SYNONYMS – *verb* **1** direct, drive, guide, shepherd, steer.
COMBINATIONS – **pilot chute** a small parachute used to bring the main one into operation. **pilot light 1** a small gas burner kept alight permanently to light a larger burner when needed. **2** an electric indicator light or control light. **pilot officer** the lowest rank of officer in the RAF. **pilot whale** a black toothed whale with a square bulbous head.
ORIGIN – Latin *pilotus*, based on Greek *pēdon* 'oar'.

pilotfish > *noun* a fish of warm seas that often swims close to large fish such as sharks.

Pilsner /pilznər/ (also **Pilsener**) > *noun* a lager beer with a strong hop flavour, originally brewed at Pilsen (Plzeň) in the Czech Republic.

PIM > *abbreviation* personal information manager.

pimento /pimentō/ > *noun* (pl. **pimentos**) **1** variant spelling of PIMIENTO. **2** chiefly W. Indian another term for ALLSPICE.

pimiento /pimmientō/ (also **pimento**) > *noun* (pl. **pimientos**) a red sweet pepper.
ORIGIN – Latin *pigmentum* 'spice'.

pimp > *noun* **1** a man who controls prostitutes and arranges clients for them. **2** Austral. informal a telltale or informer. > *verb* **1** act as a pimp. **2** (**pimp on**) Austral. informal inform on.

pimpernel > *noun* a low-growing plant with bright five-petalled flowers.
ORIGIN – Old French *pimpernelle*, from Latin *piper* 'pepper'.

pimple > *noun* a small, hard inflamed spot on the skin.
DERIVATIVES – **pimpled** adjective **pimply** adjective.

PIN (also **PIN number**) > *abbreviation* personal identification number.

pin > *noun* **1** a thin piece of metal with a sharp point at one end and a round head at the other. **2** a metal projection from a plug or an integrated circuit. **3** a small brooch or badge. **4** Medicine a steel rod used to join the ends of fractured bones while they heal. **5** Golf a stick with a flag placed in a hole to mark its position. **6** a metal peg in a hand grenade that prevents its explosion. **7** a skittle in bowling. **8** (**pins**) informal legs. > *verb* (**pinned, pinning**) **1** attach or fasten with a pin or pins. **2** hold someone firmly so they are unable to move. **3** (**pin someone down**) force someone to be specific about their intentions. **4** (**pin something on**) fix blame or responsibility on.

IDIOMS – **pin one's hopes** (or **faith**) **on** rely heavily on.

SYNONYMS – *verb* **1** affix, attach, clip, fasten, fix, secure, tack. **2** pinion, restrain.

COMBINATIONS – **pin money** a small sum of money for spending on inessentials. [ORIGIN – first denoting an allowance to a woman from her husband for dress and other personal expenses.] **pins and needles** a tingling sensation in a limb recovering from numbness. **pin-tuck** a very narrow ornamental tuck in a garment. **pinwheel 1** a small cogwheel in which the teeth are formed by pins set into the rim. **2** a small Catherine wheel.

ORIGIN – Latin *pinna* 'point, tip, edge'.

pina colada /peenə kəlaadə/ > *noun* a cocktail made with rum, pineapple juice, and coconut.

ORIGIN – Spanish *piña colada* 'strained pineapple'.

pinafore > *noun* **1** (also **pinafore dress**) a collarless, sleeveless dress worn over a blouse or jumper. **2** Brit. a woman's loose sleeveless garment worn over clothes to keep them clean.

pinball > *noun* a game in which small metal balls are shot across a sloping board and score points by striking targets.

pince-nez /paNsnay/ > *noun* (treated as sing. or pl.) a pair of eyeglasses with a nose clip instead of earpieces.

ORIGIN – French, 'that pinches the nose'.

pincer > *noun* **1** (**pincers**) a tool made of two pieces of metal bearing blunt concave jaws arranged like the blades of scissors, used for gripping and pulling things. **2** a front claw of a lobster or similar crustacean.

COMBINATIONS – **pincer movement** a movement by two separate bodies of troops converging on the enemy.

ORIGIN – Old French *pincier* 'to pinch'.

pinch > *verb* **1** grip (the flesh) tightly between finger and thumb. **2** live in a frugal way. **3** informal, chiefly Brit. steal. **4** (of a shoe) hurt (a foot) by being too tight. **5** tighten (the lips or a part of the face). **6** informal arrest. > *noun* **1** an act of pinching. **2** an amount of an ingredient that can be held between fingers and thumb.

IDIOMS – **at** (or N. Amer. **in**) **a pinch** if absolutely necessary. **feel the pinch** experience hardship, especially financial.

SYNONYMS – *verb* **1** nip, squeeze, tweak.
ORIGIN – Old French *pincier* 'to pinch'.

pinchbeck > *noun* an alloy of copper and zinc resembling gold, used in cheap jewellery. > *adjective* appearing valuable, but actually cheap or tawdry.

ORIGIN – named after the English watchmaker Christopher *Pinchbeck* (died 1732).

pinch-hitter > *noun* Baseball a specialist batter who takes the place of another player, typically at a critical point in the game.

DERIVATIVES – **pinch-hit** *verb.*

pincushion > *noun* **1** a small pad for holding pins. **2** optical distortion in which straight lines along the edge of a screen or lens bulge towards the centre.

pine¹ > *noun* (also **pine tree**) an evergreen coniferous tree having clusters of long needle-shaped leaves.

COMBINATIONS – **pine cone** the conical or rounded woody fruit of a pine tree. **pine nut** the edible seed of various pine trees.

ORIGIN – Latin *pinus.*

pine² > *verb* **1** suffer a mental and physical decline, especially because of a broken heart. **2** (**pine for**) miss and long for the return of.

SYNONYMS – **1** decline, languish, weaken, wither. **2** (**pine for**) ache for, long for, yearn for.

ORIGIN – from Latin *poena* 'punishment'.

pineal gland /pīniəl/ (also **pineal body**) > *noun* a small gland situated at the back of the skull within the brain.

ORIGIN – from Latin *pinea* 'pine cone' (with reference to its shape).

pineapple > *noun* a large juicy tropical fruit consisting of edible yellow flesh surrounded by a tough segmented skin and topped with a tuft of leaves.

pine marten > *noun* a tree-dwelling weasel-like mammal with a dark brown coat.

ping > *noun* an abrupt high-pitched ringing sound. > *verb* make or cause to make such a sound.

ping-pong > *noun* informal term for *table tennis.*

pinhead > *noun* **1** the flattened head of a pin. **2** informal a stupid person.

pinhole > *noun* a very small hole.

COMBINATIONS – **pinhole camera** a camera with a pinhole aperture and no lens.

pinion¹ /pinyən/ > *noun* the outer part of a bird's wing including the flight feathers. > *verb* **1** tie or hold the arms or legs of. **2** cut off the pinion of (a bird) to prevent flight.

ORIGIN – Latin *pinna, penna* 'feather'.

pinion² /pinyən/ > *noun* a small cogwheel or spindle engaging with a large cogwheel.

ORIGIN – Latin *pinea* 'pine cone'.

pink¹ > *adjective* **1** of a colour intermediate between red and white, as of coral or salmon. **2** informal, often derogatory left-wing. **3** relating to or associated with homosexuals: *the pink economy.* > *noun* **1** pink colour, pigment, or material. **2** (**the pink**) informal the best condition or degree. **3** informal, often derogatory a left-wing person.

WORDFINDER – *shades of pink:* damask, rose, salmon, shocking pink.

DERIVATIVES – **pinkish** *adjective* **pinky** *adjective.*

COMBINATIONS – **pink gin** Brit. gin flavoured with angostura bitters.

wordpower facts

Pink

The colour word **pink** is probably derived from the name of the plant the **pink**, although the reverse may seem more likely. **Pink** as a plant name is first recorded in the late 16th century. It is perhaps short for *pink eye*, literally 'small or half-shut eye': *pink* in this sense is now restricted to regional use and probably derived from Dutch *pinck* 'small' (from which the informal word **pinkie** 'little finger' comes). In French the plant is called *oeillet*, which literally means 'little eye'. Many pinks have pink flowers, and thus the colour came to be known as **pink**, in the mid 17th century. **Pink** meaning 'give a zigzag edge to', as in *pinking shears*, is a completely different word, probably of Low German origin.

pink² > *noun* a plant with sweet-smelling pink or white flowers and slender grey-green leaves.

pink³ > *verb* cut a scalloped or zigzag edge on.

COMBINATIONS – **pinking shears** shears with a serrated blade, used to cut a zigzag edge in fabric.

pink⁴ > *verb* Brit. (of a vehicle engine) make rattling sounds as a result of over-rapid combustion in the cylinders.

pinkie > *noun* informal the little finger.

ORIGIN – Dutch *pink* 'the little finger'.

pinking shears > *plural noun* shears with a serrated blade, used to cut a zigzag edge in fabric.

pinko > *noun* (pl. **pinkos** or **pinkoes**) informal, derogatory, chiefly N. Amer. a person with left-wing or liberal views.

pinna /pinnə/ > *noun* (pl. **pinnae** /pinnee/) Anatomy the external part of the ear.

ORIGIN – Latin, from *penna* 'feather, wing, fin'.

pinnace /**pinn**iss/ > *noun* chiefly historical a small boat forming part of the equipment of a larger vessel.

pinnacle > *noun* **1** a high pointed piece of rock. **2** a small pointed turret built as an ornament on a roof. **3** the most successful point.

SYNONYMS – **1** apex, crest, peak, summit. **3** acme, apex, climax, culmination, zenith.

ORIGIN – Latin *pinnaculum*, from *pinna* 'wing, point'.

pinnate /**pinn**ayt/ > *adjective* Botany & Zoology having leaflets or other parts arranged on either side of a stem like the vanes of a feather.

ORIGIN – Latin *pinnatus* 'feathered'.

PIN number > *noun* see **PIN**.

pinny > *noun* (pl. **pinnies**) informal a pinafore.

Pinot /**pee**nō/ > *noun* any of several varieties of black or white wine grape.

ORIGIN – French, from *pin* 'pine' (because of the shape of the grape cluster).

pinpoint > *noun* a tiny dot or point. > *adjective* absolutely precise. > *verb* find or locate exactly.

pinstripe > *noun* a very narrow stripe in cloth, used especially for formal suits.

DERIVATIVES – **pinstriped** *adjective*.

pint > *noun* **1** a unit of liquid or dry capacity equal to one eighth of a gallon, in Britain equal to 0.568 litre and in the US equal to 0.473 litre (for liquid measure) or 0.551 litre (for dry measure). **2** Brit. informal a pint of beer.

COMBINATIONS – **pint-sized** informal very small.

pintail > *noun* a duck with a long, pointed tail.

pintle > *noun* a pin or bolt on which a rudder turns.

pinto bean /**pin**tō/ > *noun* a medium-sized speckled variety of kidney bean.

ORIGIN – Spanish *pinto* 'mottled'.

pin-up > *noun* a poster featuring a sexually attractive person.

Pinyin /**pin**yin/ > *noun* the standard system of romanised spelling for transliterating Chinese.

ORIGIN – Chinese, 'spell-sound'.

pion /**pī**on/ > *noun* Physics a meson with a mass around 270 times that of the electron.

ORIGIN – contraction of the earlier name *pi-meson*.

pioneer > *noun* **1** a person who explores or settles in a new region. **2** a developer of new ideas or techniques. > *verb* be a pioneer of.

DERIVATIVES – **pioneering** *adjective*.

ORIGIN – French *pionnier* 'foot soldier'.

pious > *adjective* **1** devoutly religious. **2** making a hypocritical display of virtue. **3** (of a hope) sincere but unlikely to be fulfilled.

DERIVATIVES – **piously** *adverb* **piousness** *noun*.

SYNONYMS – **1** devout, God-fearing, religious, reverent.

ANTONYMS – **1** impious.

ORIGIN – Latin *pius* 'dutiful'.

pip[1] > *noun* a small hard seed in a fruit.

ORIGIN – abbreviation of **PIPPIN**.

pip[2] > *noun* (**the pips**) Brit. a series of short high-pitched sounds used as a signal on the radio or within the telephone system.

pip[3] > *noun* **1** Brit. a star indicating rank on the shoulder of an army officer's uniform. **2** any of the spots on a playing card, dice, or domino. **3** an image of an object on a radar screen.

pip[4] > *noun* a disease of poultry or other birds causing thick mucus in the throat and white scale on the tongue.

ORIGIN – probably from an alteration of Latin *pituita* 'slime'.

pip[5] > *verb* (**pipped**, **pipping**) Brit. informal **1** (**be pipped**) be defeated by a small margin or at the last moment. **2** dated hit or wound with a gun.

IDIOMS – **pip someone at the post** defeat someone at the last moment.

pip[6] > *verb* (**pipped**, **pipping**) (of a young bird) crack (the shell of the egg) when hatching.

pipal > *noun* variant spelling of **PEEPUL**.

pipe > *noun* **1** a tube used to convey water, gas, oil, etc. **2** a device for smoking tobacco, consisting of a narrow tube that opens into a small bowl in which the tobacco is burned, the smoke being drawn through the tube to the mouth. **3** a wind instrument consisting of a single tube with holes along its length that are covered by the fingers to produce different notes. **4** one of the cylindrical tubes by which notes are produced in an organ. **5** (**pipes**) bagpipes. **6** a high-pitched cry or song, especially that of a bird. > *verb* **1** convey through a pipe. **2** transmit (music, a programme, a signal, etc.) by wire or cable. **3** play (a tune) on a pipe. **4** sing or say in a high, shrill voice. **5** decorate with piping.

WORDFINDER – bong, chillum (*pipes for smoking cannabis*), calumet (*North American Indian peace pipe*), dottle (*remnant of tobacco left in a pipe*), hookah (*tobacco pipe which draws the smoke through water*), meerschaum (*white clay used to make pipes*).

IDIOMS – **pipe down** informal stop talking; be less noisy. **pipe up** say something suddenly. **put that in one's pipe and smoke it** informal one will have to accept a particular fact, even if it is unwelcome.

COMBINATIONS – **pipe cleaner** a piece of wire covered with fibre, used to clean a tobacco pipe. **piped music** pre-recorded background music played through loudspeakers. **pipe dream** an unattainable or fanciful hope or scheme. [ORIGIN – referring to a dream experienced when smoking an opium pipe.] **pipe organ** an organ using pipes instead of or as well as reeds.

ORIGIN – Latin *pipare* 'to peep, chirp'.

pipeclay > *noun* a fine white clay, used especially for making tobacco pipes or for whitening leather.

pipeline > *noun* **1** a long pipe for conveying oil, gas, etc. over a distance. **2** (in surfing) the hollow formed by the breaking of a large wave. **3** Computing a linear sequence of specialised modules used for pipelining. > *verb* **1** convey by a pipeline. **2** Computing execute using the technique of pipelining.

IDIOMS – **in the pipeline** in the process of being developed.

pipelining > *noun* **1** the laying or use of pipelines. **2** Computing a form of computer organisation in which successive steps of an instruction sequence are executed in turn, so that another instruction can be begun before the previous one is finished.

piper > *noun* a person who plays a pipe or bagpipes.

pipette /pi**pet**/ > *noun* a slender tube used in a laboratory for handling small quantities of liquid, the liquid being drawn into the tube by suction. > *verb* pour or draw off using a pipette.

ORIGIN – French, 'little pipe'.

piping > *noun* **1** lengths of pipe. **2** lines of icing or cream, used to decorate cakes and desserts. **3** thin cord covered in fabric and inserted along the length of a seam or hem for decoration.

IDIOMS – **piping hot** (of food or water) very hot. [ORIGIN – with reference to the whistling sound made by very hot liquid or food.]

pipistrelle /pippi**strel**/ > *noun* a common small bat with a jerky erratic flight.

ORIGIN – French, from Latin *vespertilio* 'bat', from *vesper* 'evening'.

pipit /**pip**it/ > *noun* a ground-dwelling songbird of open country, typically having brown streaky plumage.

pipkin > *noun* a small earthenware pot.

pippin > *noun* a red and yellow dessert apple.

pipsqueak > *noun* informal an insignificant or contemptible person.

piquant /**pee**kONt/ > *adjective* **1** having a pleasantly sharp taste or appetising flavour. **2** pleasantly stimulating or exciting.

DERIVATIVES – **piquancy** *noun* **piquantly** *adverb*.

SYNONYMS – **1** flavoursome, tangy.

ANTONYMS – bland.

ORIGIN – French, 'stinging, pricking'.

pique /peek/ > *noun* irritation or resentment arising from hurt pride. > *verb* (**piques**, **piqued**, **piquing**) **1** stimulate (interest or curiosity). **2** (**be piqued**) feel hurt and irritated or resentful.

ORIGIN – French *piquer* 'prick, irritate'.

piqué /**pee**kay/ > *noun* firm fabric woven in a ribbed or raised pattern.

ORIGIN – French, 'backstitched'.

piquet[1] /pi**ket**/ > *noun* a trick-taking card game for two players.

ORIGIN – French.

piquet[2] > *noun* variant spelling of PICKET (in sense 2).

piracy > *noun* **1** the practice of attacking and robbing ships at sea. **2** the unauthorised use or reproduction of another's work.

piranha* /pi**raa**nə/ > *noun* a freshwater fish having very sharp teeth that it uses to tear flesh from prey.

*SPELLING – remember the *h*, which comes before the final *a*: piran*h*a.

ORIGIN – Portuguese, from two Tupi words meaning 'fish' and 'tooth'.

pirate > *noun* **1** a person who attacks and robs ships at sea. **2** (before another noun) denoting a text, film, recording, etc. that has been reproduced and used for profit without permission: *pirate videos*. **3** (before another noun) denoting an organisation that is broadcasting without official authorisation. > *verb* **1** dated rob or plunder (a ship). **2** reproduce (a film, recording, etc.) for profit without permission.

DERIVATIVES – **piratic** *adjective*.

ORIGIN – Greek *peiratēs*, from *peirein* 'to attempt, attack'.

piripiri /**pirr**ipirri/ > *noun* (pl. **piripiris**) a New Zealand plant of the rose family, with prickly burrs.

ORIGIN – Maori.

pirogue /pi**rōg**/ > *noun* (in Central America and the Caribbean) a long. narrow canoe made from a single tree trunk.

ORIGIN – French, from a Carib word.

pirouette /pirroo**et**/ > *noun* (in ballet) an act of spinning on one foot. > *verb* perform a pirouette.

ORIGIN – French, 'spinning top'.

piscatorial /piskə**tor**iəl/ (also **piscatory**) > *adjective* relating to fishing.

ORIGIN – Latin, from *piscator* 'fisherman', from *piscis* 'fish'.

Pisces /**pī**seez/ > *noun* **1** Astronomy a large constellation (the Fish or Fishes), said to represent a pair of fish tied together by their tails. **2** Astrology the twelfth sign of the zodiac, which the sun enters about 20 February.

DERIVATIVES – **Piscean** /**pī**seeən/ *noun & adjective*.

ORIGIN – Latin, plural of *piscis* 'fish'.

pisciculture /**piss**ikulchər/ > *noun* the controlled breeding and rearing of fish.

ORIGIN – from Latin *piscis* 'fish'.

piscina /pi**seen**ə/ > *noun* (pl. **piscinas** or **piscinae** /pi**seen**ee/) **1** a stone basin near the altar in some churches, for draining water used in the Mass. **2** (in ancient Roman architecture) a bathing pool.

ORIGIN – Latin, 'fish pond'.

piscine /**piss**īn/ > *adjective* relating to fish.

ORIGIN – from Latin *piscis* 'fish'.

piscivorous /pi**sivv**ərəss/ > *adjective* Zoology feeding on fish.

DERIVATIVES – **piscivore** *noun*.

piss vulgar slang > *verb* urinate. > *noun* **1** urine. **2** an act of urinating.

IDIOMS – **piss about** (or **around**) Brit. mess around. **piss off 1** go away. **2** annoy (someone). **take the piss** Brit. tease or mock.

DERIVATIVES – **pisser** *noun*.

COMBINATIONS – **piss artist** Brit. vulgar slang **1** a drunkard. **2** an incompetent person.

ORIGIN – Old French *pisser*.

pissed > *adjective* vulgar slang **1** Brit. drunk. **2** (**pissed off** or N. Amer. **pissed**) very annoyed.

pissoir /pi**swaar**/ > *noun* a public urinal.

ORIGIN – French.

piss-up > *noun* Brit. vulgar slang a heavy drinking session.

pissy > *adjective* vulgar slang **1** relating to urine. **2** contemptible or inferior.

pistachio /pi**staa**shiō/ > *noun* (pl. **pistachios**) a small nut with an edible pale green kernel, the seed of an Asian tree.

ORIGIN – Greek *pistakion*, from Old Persian.

piste /peest/ > *noun* a course or run for skiing.

ORIGIN – French, 'racetrack'.

pistil /**pist**il/ > *noun* Botany the female organs of a flower, comprising the stigma, style, and ovary.

ORIGIN – Latin *pistillum* 'pestle'.

pistol > *noun* a small firearm designed to be held in one hand.

COMBINATIONS – **pistol–whip** hit or beat with the butt of a pistol.

ORIGIN – French *pistole*, from Czech *pišt'ala*: originally in the sense 'whistle', hence 'a firearm' by the resemblance in shape.

piston > *noun* **1** a disc or short cylinder fitting closely within a tube in which it moves up and down against a liquid or gas, used to derive or impart motion in an internal-combustion engine or pump. **2** a valve in a brass instrument, depressed to alter the pitch of a note.

ORIGIN – Italian *pistone*, variant of *pestone* 'large pestle'.

pistou /**pee**stoo/ > *noun* a paste made from crushed basil, garlic, and cheese, used in Provençal dishes.

ORIGIN – Provençal, related to PESTO.

pit[1] > *noun* **1** a large hole in the ground. **2** a mine or excavation for coal, chalk, etc. **3** a hollow or indentation in a surface. **4** a sunken area in a workshop floor allowing access to a car's underside. **5** an area at the side of a track where racing cars are serviced and refuelled. **6** an orchestra pit. **7** a part of the floor of an exchange in which a particular stock or commodity is traded. **8** chiefly historical an enclosure in which animals are made to fight. **9** (**the pit**) literary hell. **10** (**the pits**) informal a very bad place or situation. **11** Brit. informal a person's bed. > *verb* (**pitted**, **pitting**) **1** (**pit against**) set in conflict or competition with. **2** make a hollow or indentation in the surface of.

IDIOMS – **the pit of the stomach** the region of the lower abdomen.

DERIVATIVES – **pitted** *adjective*.

COMBINATIONS – **pit bull terrier** an American variety of bull terrier, noted for its ferocity. **pithead** the top of a mineshaft and the area around it. **pit pony** Brit. historical a pony used to haul loads in a coal mine. **pit stop** Motor Racing a brief stop at a pit for servicing and refuelling.

ORIGIN – Latin *puteus* 'well, shaft'; sense 1 of the verb derives from the former practice of setting animals to fight in a pit.

pit[2] chiefly N. Amer. > *noun* the stone of a fruit. > *verb* (**pitted**, **pitting**) remove the pit from (fruit).

pita > *noun* chiefly N. Amer. variant spelling of PITTA.

pit-a-pat (also **pitapat**) > *adverb* with a sound like quick light taps. > *noun* a sound of this kind.

pitch[1] > *noun* **1** the degree of highness or lowness in a sound or tone, as governed by the rate of vibrations producing it. **2** the steepness of a roof. **3** a particular level of intensity. **4** Brit. an area of ground marked out or used for play in an outdoor team game. **5** a form of words used to persuade or influence: *a sales pitch*. **6** Brit. a place where a street vendor or performer stations themselves. **7** a swaying or oscillation of a ship, aircraft, or vehicle around a horizontal axis perpendicular to the direction of motion. > *verb* **1** set at a particular musical pitch. **2** throw or fall heavily or roughly. **3** set or aim at a particular level, target, or audience. **4** set up and fix in position. **5** (**pitch in**) informal join in enthusiastically with a task or activity. **6** (**pitch up**) informal arrive. **7** (of a moving ship, aircraft, or vehicle) rock or oscillate around a lateral axis, so that the front moves up and down. **8** (with reference to a roof) slope or cause to slope downwards.

SYNONYMS – *noun* **2** angle, gradient, slope. *verb* **2** fling, hurl, toss.

COMBINATIONS – **pitched battle** a battle in which the time and place are determined beforehand, rather than a casual or chance skirmish.

pitch[2] > *noun* a sticky resinous black or dark brown substance which hardens on cooling, obtained by distilling tar or turpentine and used for waterproofing.

COMBINATIONS – **pitch pine** a pine tree with hard, heavy, resinous wood.

pitch-black (also **pitch-dark**) > *adjective* completely dark.

pitchblende /**pich**blend/ > *noun* a mineral consisting mainly of uranium dioxide, occurring in brown or black pitch-like masses and also containing radium.

ORIGIN – *blende* from German *blenden* 'deceive' (because it resembles galena but yields no lead).

pitcher[1] > *noun* a large jug.

COMBINATIONS – **pitcher plant** a plant with a deep pitcher-shaped fluid-filled pouch in which insects are trapped and absorbed.

ORIGIN – Old French *pichier* 'pot', from Latin *picarium*.

pitcher[2] > *noun* Baseball the player who pitches the ball.

pitchfork > *noun* a farm tool with a long handle and two sharp metal prongs, used for lifting hay. > *verb* **1** lift with a pitchfork. **2** thrust suddenly into an unexpected and difficult situation.

ORIGIN – from earlier *pickfork*, influenced by **PITCH**[1] in the sense 'throw'.

pitchy > *adjective* (**pitchier**, **pitchiest**) as dark as pitch.

piteous > *adjective* deserving or arousing pity.

DERIVATIVES – **piteously** *adverb* **piteousness** *noun*.

SYNONYMS – pathetic, pitiful, sad.

ORIGIN – Old French *piteus*, from Latin *pietas* 'dutifulness'.

pitfall > *noun* **1** a hidden or unsuspected danger or difficulty. **2** a covered pit for use as a trap.

pith > *noun* **1** spongy white tissue lining the rind of citrus fruits. **2** spongy tissue in the stems and branches of many plants. **3** the true nature or essence of something. **4** vigorous and concise expression.

COMBINATIONS – **pith helmet** a head covering made from the dried pith of the sola or a similar plant, used for protection from the sun.

pithos /**pi**thoss/ > *noun* (pl. **pithoi** /**pi**thoy/) Archaeology a large earthenware storage jar.

ORIGIN – Greek.

pithy > *adjective* (**pithier**, **pithiest**) **1** (of a fruit or plant) containing much pith. **2** (of language or style) terse and vigorously expressive.

DERIVATIVES – **pithily** *adverb* **pithiness** *noun*.

SYNONYMS – **2** concise, crisp, succinct.

pitiable > *adjective* **1** deserving or arousing pity. **2** contemptibly poor or small.

DERIVATIVES – **pitiably** *adverb*.

pitiful > *adjective* **1** deserving or arousing pity. **2** very small or poor; inadequate.

DERIVATIVES – **pitifully** *adverb* **pitifulness** *noun*.

SYNONYMS – **1** pathetic, piteous, sad.

pitiless > *adjective* showing no pity; harsh or cruel.

DERIVATIVES – **pitilessly** *adverb* **pitilessness** *noun*.

SYNONYMS – merciless, remorseless, ruthless.

piton /**pee**ton/ > *noun* a peg or spike driven into a crack to support a climber or a rope.

ORIGIN – French, 'eye bolt'.

pitot /**pee**tō/ (also **pitot tube**) > *noun* a device for measuring the speed of flow of a fluid, consisting of an open-ended right-angled tube pointing against the flow.

ORIGIN – named after the French physicist Henri *Pitot* (1695–1771).

pitta /**pitt**ə/ (also chiefly N. Amer. **pita**) > *noun* flat hollow unleavened bread which can be split open to hold a filling.

ORIGIN – Modern Greek, 'cake or pie'.

pittance > *noun* a very small or inadequate amount of money.

ORIGIN – Old French *pitance*, from Latin *pietas* 'pity': originally denoting a small bequest to a religious establishment to provide extra food and wine for a festival.

pitter-patter > *noun* a sound as of quick light steps or taps. > *adverb* with this sound.

pituitary gland /pit**yoo**itəri/ (also **pituitary body**) > *noun* a pea-sized gland attached to the base of the brain, important in controlling growth and development.

ORIGIN – Latin *pituitarius* 'secreting phlegm'.

pity > *noun* (pl. **pities**) **1** a feeling of sorrow and compassion caused by the sufferings of others. **2** a cause for regret or disappointment. > *verb* (**pities**, **pitied**) feel pity for.

WORDFINDER – pathos (*quality arousing pity*).

IDIOMS – **for pity's sake** informal used to express impatience or make an urgent appeal. **more's the pity** informal used to express regret.

SYNONYMS – *noun* **1** commiseration, compassion, regret, sympathy.

ORIGIN – Old French *pite* 'compassion', from Latin *pietas* 'piety'.

pivot > *noun* **1** the central point, pin, or shaft on which a mechanism turns or oscillates. **2** a person or thing playing a central part in an activity or organisation. > *verb* (**pivoted**, **pivoting**) **1** turn on or as if on a pivot. **2** (**pivot on**) depend on.

DERIVATIVES – **pivotable** *adjective*.

ORIGIN – French.

pivotal > *adjective* **1** fixed on or as if on a pivot. **2** of crucial or central importance.

SYNONYMS – **2** critical, essential, vital.

pix > *noun* variant spelling of **PYX**.

pixel > *noun* Electronics a minute area of illumination on a display screen, one of many from which an image is composed.

ORIGIN – abbreviation of *picture element*.

pixelate /**pik**səlayt/ (also **pixellate** or **pixilate**) > *verb* **1** divide (an image) into pixels, for display or for storage in a digital format. **2** display (a person's image) as a small number of large pixels in order to disguise their identity.

DERIVATIVES – **pixelation** *noun*.

pixie (also **pixy**) > *noun* (pl. **pixies**) a supernatural being in folklore, typically portrayed as a tiny man with pointed ears and a pointed hat.

DERIVATIVES – **pixieish** *adjective*.

pixilate > *verb* variant spelling of **PIXELATE**.

pixilated (also **pixillated**) > *adjective* **1** crazy; confused. **2** informal drunk.

DERIVATIVES – **pixilation** *noun*.

ORIGIN – from *pixie-led*, 'led astray by pixies'.

pizza > *noun* a dish of Italian origin, consisting of a flat, round base of dough baked with a topping of tomatoes, cheese, and other ingredients.

ORIGIN – Italian, 'pie'.

pizzazz (also **pizazz**) > *noun* informal a combination of vitality and style.

ORIGIN – said to have been invented by Diana Vreeland, fashion editor of *Harper's Bazaar* in the 1930s.

pizzeria /peetsə**ree**ə/ > *noun* a place where pizzas are sold.

ORIGIN – Italian.

pizzicato /pitsi**kaat**ō/ Music > *adverb* & *adjective* plucking the strings of a violin or other stringed instrument with one's finger. > *noun* (pl. **pizzicatos** or **pizzicati** /pitsi**kaat**i/) this technique of playing.

ORIGIN – Italian, 'pinched'.

pizzle > *noun* dialect or archaic the penis of an animal, especially a bull.

pl. > *abbreviation* **1** (also **Pl.**) place. **2** plural.

placable /**plakk**ə'l/ > *adjective* easily calmed or placated.

placard /**plakk**aard/ > *noun* a sign for public display, either posted on a wall or carried during a demonstration. > *verb* /also pla**kaard**/ cover with placards.

ORIGIN – Old French *placquart*, from *plaquier* 'to plaster, lay flat'.

placate /plə**kayt**/ > *verb* calm, pacify, or appease.

DERIVATIVES – **placating** *adjective* **placatory** *adjective*.

SYNONYMS – appease, calm, mollify, pacify, soothe.

ORIGIN – Latin *placare* 'appease'.

place > *noun* **1** a particular position or location. **2** a portion of space available or designated for someone or something. **3** a vacancy or available position. **4** a position in a sequence or hierarchy. **5** the position of a figure in a series indicated in decimal notation. **6** informal a person's home. **7** (in place names) a square or short street. > *verb* **1** put in a particular position. **2** find an appropriate place or role for. **3** allocate or award a specified position in a sequence or hierarchy. **4** (**be placed**) Brit. achieve a specified position in a race. **5** remember the relevant background or circumstances of. **6** arrange for the implementation of (an order, bet, etc.). **7** Rugby & American Football score (a goal) by a place kick.
IDIOMS – **go places** informal **1** travel. **2** be increasingly successful. **in one's place** in one's appropriate (but inferior) position or status. **in place 1** working or ready to work. **2** N. Amer. on the spot; not travelling any distance. **in place of** instead of. **out of place 1** not in the proper position. **2** in a setting where one is or feels incongruous. **take place** occur. **take one's place** take up one's usual or recognised position. **take the place of** replace.
SYNONYMS – *noun* **1** site, situation, spot.
COMBINATIONS – **place name** the name of a geographical location, such as a town, lake, or mountain.
ORIGIN – Old French, from Latin *platea* 'open space'.

placebo /pləseebō/ > *noun* (pl. **placebos**) **1** a medicine prescribed for the psychological benefit to the patient rather than for any physiological effect. **2** a substance that has no therapeutic effect, used as a control in testing new drugs.
ORIGIN – Latin, from *placere* 'to please'.

place kick American Football, Rugby, & Soccer > *noun* a kick made after the ball is first placed on the ground. > *verb* (**place-kick**) take a place kick.
DERIVATIVES – **place-kicker** *noun*.

placement > *noun* **1** the action or fact of placing or being placed. **2** a temporary posting of someone in a workplace, especially to gain work experience.

placenta /pləsentə/ > *noun* (pl. **placentae** /pləsentee/ or **placentas**) a flattened circular organ in the uterus of a pregnant mammal, nourishing and maintaining the fetus through the umbilical cord.
DERIVATIVES – **placental** *adjective*.
COMBINATIONS – **placenta praevia** (US **placenta previa**) Medicine a condition in which the placenta partially or wholly blocks the neck of the uterus, so interfering with normal delivery of a baby. [ORIGIN – Latin *praevia* 'going before'.]
ORIGIN – Greek *plakous* 'flat cake'.

placer > *noun* a deposit of sand or gravel in the bed of a river or lake, containing particles of valuable minerals.
ORIGIN – Latin American Spanish, 'deposit, shoal'.

placid > *adjective* not easily upset or excited; calm.
DERIVATIVES – **placidity** *noun* **placidly** *adverb*.
SYNONYMS – calm, equable, even-tempered, serene.
ANTONYMS – excitable, temperamental.
ORIGIN – Latin *placidus*, from *placere* 'to please'.

placing > *noun* **1** the action or fact of placing or being placed. **2** a ranking given to a competitor.

placket > *noun* **1** an opening in a garment. **2** a flap of material used to strengthen such an opening.
ORIGIN – from **PLACARD** in an obsolete sense 'garment worn under an open coat'.

plagiarise /playjəriz/ (also **plagiarize**) > *verb* take (the work or idea of someone else) and pass it off as one's own.
DERIVATIVES – **plagiariser** *noun* **plagiarism** *noun* **plagiarist** *noun*.
ORIGIN – Latin *plagiarius* 'kidnapper'.

plague > *noun* **1** a contagious disease spread by bacteria and characterised by fever and delirium. **2** an unusually and unpleasantly large quantity: *a plague of locusts.* > *verb* (**plagues**, **plagued**, **plaguing**) **1** cause continual trouble or distress to. **2** pester or harass continually.
WORDFINDER – bubonic plague (*form of plague spread by rat fleas, black death*).
SYNONYMS – *noun* **1** contagion; archaic pestilence. **2** host, infestation, multitude, swarm. *verb* **1** afflict, bedevil, dog, torment. **2** badger, persecute, torment.
ORIGIN – Latin *plaga* 'stroke, wound'.

plaice > *noun* (pl. same) a brown flatfish with orange spots, commercially important as a food fish.
ORIGIN – Old French *plaiz*, from Greek *platus* 'broad'.

plaid /plad/ > *noun* fabric woven in a chequered or tartan design.
ORIGIN – Scottish Gaelic *plaide* 'blanket'.

plain > *adjective* **1** not decorated or elaborate; simple or ordinary. **2** without a pattern; in only one colour. **3** unmarked; without identification. **4** easy to perceive or understand; clear. **5** (of language) clearly expressed; direct. **6** (of a woman or girl) not marked by beauty; ordinary looking. **7** sheer; simple (used for emphasis): *plain stupidity.* **8** (of a knitting stitch) made by putting the needle through the front of the stitch from left to right. Compare with **PURL**[1]. > *adverb* informal **1** simply (used for emphasis): *that's just plain stupid.* **2** clearly; unequivocally. > *noun* a large area of flat land with few trees.

DERIVATIVES – **plainly** *adverb* **plainness** *noun*.
SYNONYMS – *adjective* **1** modest, ordinary, simple, unadorned. **4** apparent, clear, evident, obvious. **5** candid, direct, forthright, frank.
COMBINATIONS – **plain chocolate** Brit. dark, slightly bitter, chocolate without added milk. **plain clothes** ordinary clothes rather than uniform, especially when worn by police officers. **plain flour** Brit. flour that does not contain a raising agent. **plain sailing** smooth and easy progress. [ORIGIN – probably a popular use of *plane sailing*, denoting the practice of determining a ship's position on the theory that it is moving on a flat plane (without reference to the curvature of the earth; therefore 'straightfoward'.] **plain weave** a style of weave in which the weft alternates over and under the warp.
ORIGIN – Latin *planus*, from a base meaning 'flat'.

plainsong (also **plainchant**) > *noun* unaccompanied medieval church music sung in free rhythm corresponding to the accentuation of the words.

plaint > *noun* **1** Law, Brit. an accusation; a charge. **2** chiefly literary a complaint or lamentation.
ORIGIN – Old French *plainte*, from *plaindre* 'complain'.

plaintiff > *noun* Law a person who brings a case against another in a court of law. Compare with **DEFENDANT**.
ORIGIN – Old French *plaintif* 'plaintive'.

plaintive > *adjective* sounding sad and mournful.
DERIVATIVES – **plaintively** *adverb* **plaintiveness** *noun*.
ORIGIN – Old French, from *plaindre* 'complain'.

plait > *noun* Brit. a single length of hair, rope, or other material made up of three or more interlaced strands. > *verb* form into a plait or plaits.
ORIGIN – Old French *pleit* 'a fold', from Latin *plicare* 'to fold'.

plan > *noun* **1** a detailed proposal for doing or achieving something. **2** an intention or decision about what one is going to do. **3** a scheme for the regular payment of contributions towards a pension, insurance policy, etc. **4** a map or diagram. **5** a scale drawing of a horizontal section of a building. > *verb* (**planned**, **planning**) **1** decide on and arrange in advance. **2** (**plan for**) make preparations for. **3** make a plan of (something to be made or built).
DERIVATIVES – **planner** *noun*.
SYNONYMS – *noun* **1** scheme, strategy. **2** aim, goal, idea, intent.
COMBINATIONS – **planned economy** an economy in which production, investment,

prices, and incomes are determined centrally by the government.

ORIGIN – French, from earlier *plant* 'ground plan, plane surface'.

planar /**play**nər/ > *adjective* Mathematics relating to or in the form of a plane.

plane[1] > *noun* **1** a flat surface on which a straight line joining any two points would wholly lie. **2** a level of existence or thought. > *adjective* **1** completely level or flat. **2** relating to two-dimensional surfaces or magnitudes. > *verb* **1** soar without moving the wings; glide. **2** (of a boat, surfboard, etc.) skim over the surface of water.

ORIGIN – Latin *planum* 'flat surface', from *planus* 'plain'.

plane[2] > *noun* an aeroplane.

plane[3] (also **planer**) > *noun* a tool consisting of a block with a projecting steel blade, used to smooth a wooden surface by paring shavings from it. > *verb* smooth with a plane.

ORIGIN – from Latin *planare* 'make level'.

plane[4] (also **plane tree**) > *noun* a tall spreading tree with maple-like leaves and a peeling bark.

ORIGIN – Old French, from Greek *platanos*, from *platus* 'broad'.

planet > *noun* **1** a celestial body moving in an elliptical orbit round a star. **2** (**the planet**) the earth. **3** chiefly Astrology & historical a celestial body distinguished from the fixed stars by having an apparent motion of its own (including the moon and sun).

WORDFINDER – aphelion (*point of a planet's orbit furthest from the sun*), conjunction (*alignment of planets near the same place in the sky*), opposition (*position of planets in opposite parts of the sky*), perihelion (*point of a planet's orbit nearest to the sun*).

DERIVATIVES – **planetary** *adjective* **planetology** *noun*.

ORIGIN – Greek *planētēs* 'wanderer, planet', from *planan* 'wander'.

planetarium /planni**tair**iəm/ > *noun* (pl. **planetariums** or **planetaria** /planni**tair**iə/) a building in which images of stars, planets, and constellations are projected on to a domed ceiling.

ORIGIN – from Latin *planetarius* 'relating to the planets'.

planetesimal /planni**tess**im'l/ Astronomy > *noun* a minute planet; a body which could come together with many others under gravitation to form a planet. > *adjective* relating to such bodies.

planetoid > *noun* another term for ASTEROID.

plangent /**plan**jənt/ > *adjective* chiefly literary (of a sound) loud and resonant, with a mournful tone.

DERIVATIVES – **plangency** *noun* **plangently** *adverb*.

ORIGIN – from Latin *plangere* 'to lament'.

planimeter /plə**nimm**itər/ > *noun* an instrument for measuring the area of a plane figure.

DERIVATIVES – **planimetric** *adjective* **planimetry** *noun*.

planisphere /**plann**isfeer/ > *noun* a map formed by the projection of a sphere, especially a star map that can be adjusted to show the constellations at a specific time and place.

DERIVATIVES – **planispheric** *adjective*.

ORIGIN – from Latin *planus* 'level' + *sphaera* 'sphere'.

plank > *noun* **1** a long, flat piece of timber, used in flooring. **2** a fundamental part of a political or other programme.

IDIOMS – **walk the plank** (formerly) be forced by pirates to walk blindfold along a plank over the side of a ship to one's death in the sea.

DERIVATIVES – **planked** *adjective* **planking** *noun*.

ORIGIN – Latin *planca* 'board', from *plancus* 'flat-footed'.

plankton > *noun* small and microscopic organisms living in the sea or fresh water, consisting chiefly of diatoms, protozoans, and small crustaceans.

DERIVATIVES – **planktic** *adjective* **planktonic** *adjective*.

ORIGIN – from Greek *planktos* 'wandering', from *plazein* 'wander'.

planning > *noun* **1** the process of making plans for something. **2** the control of urban development by a local government authority.

SYNONYMS – **1** arrangement, organisation, preparation.

COMBINATIONS – **planning permission** Brit. formal permission from a local authority to construct or alter buildings.

plant > *noun* **1** a living organism (such as a tree, grass, or fern) that absorbs water and inorganic substances through its roots and makes nutrients in its leaves by photosynthesis. **2** a place where an industrial or manufacturing process takes place. **3** machinery used in an industrial or manufacturing process. **4** a person placed in a group as a spy or informer. **5** a thing put among someone's belongings to incriminate or discredit them. > *verb* **1** place (a seed, bulb, or plant) in the ground so that it can grow. **2** (**plant out**) transfer (a seedling or young plant) from a protected container to the open ground. **3** place or fix in a specified position. **4** secretly place (a bomb). **5** put or hide (something) among someone's belongings in order to incriminate or discredit them. **6** send (someone) to join a group to act as a spy or informer. **7** establish (an idea) in someone's mind.

WORDFINDER – botany (*study of plants*), chlorophyll (*green pigment of plants*), flora (*the plants of a region*), germination (*a plant's beginning to sprout and grow*), herbivorous, phytophagous (*feeding on plants*), phytopathology (*the study of plant diseases*), transpiration (*loss of water vapour from the leaves of a plant*), tropism (*growth or turning of plant in particular direction*); annual (*a plant living one year*), biennial (*two years*), perennial (*three or more years*).

DERIVATIVES – **plantlet** *noun*.

ORIGIN – Latin *planta* 'sprout, cutting' and *plantare* 'plant, fix in place'.

Plantagenet /plan**taj**init/ > *noun* a member of the English royal dynasty which held the throne from 1154 until 1485.

ORIGIN – Latin *planta genista* 'sprig of broom', said to be worn as a crest by and given as a nickname to Geoffrey, count of Anjou, the father of Henry II.

plantain[1] /**plan**tin/ > *noun* a low-growing plant, typically with a rosette of leaves and a slender green flower spike.

ORIGIN – Old French, from Latin *planta* 'sole of the foot' (because of its broad prostrate leaves).

plantain[2] /**plan**tin/ > *noun* a type of banana containing high levels of starch and little sugar, which is harvested green and widely used as a cooked vegetable in the tropics.

ORIGIN – probably by assimilation of a South American word to the Spanish *plá(n)tano* 'plane tree'.

plantar /**plan**tər/ > *adjective* Anatomy relating to the sole of the foot.

ORIGIN – from Latin *planta* 'sole'.

plantation > *noun* **1** a large estate on which crops such as coffee, sugar, and tobacco are grown. **2** an area in which trees have been planted.

planter > *noun* **1** a manager or owner of a plantation. **2** a decorative container in which plants are grown.

plantigrade /**plan**tigrayd/ > *adjective* walking on the soles of the feet, like a human or a bear. Compare with DIGITIGRADE.

ORIGIN – Latin *plantigradus*, from *planta* 'sole' + *-gradus* '-walking'.

plaque /plak, plaak/ > *noun* **1** an ornamental tablet fixed to a wall in commemoration of a person or event. **2** a sticky deposit on teeth in which bacteria proliferate. **3** Medicine a small raised patch on or within the body, caused by local damage or deposition of material. **4** a flat counter used in gambling.

ORIGIN – French, from Dutch *plak* 'tablet'.

plash > *noun* **1** a splashing sound. **2** a pool or puddle. > *verb* make or hit with a splash.

DERIVATIVES – **plashy** *adjective*.

plasma /**plaz**mə/ > *noun* **1** the colourless fluid part of blood, lymph, or milk, in which corpuscles or fat globules are suspended. **2** Physics a gas of positive ions and free electrons with little or no overall electric charge. **3** a bright green translucent ornamental variety of quartz. **4** (also **plasm** /plazz'm/) cytoplasm or protoplasm.

DERIVATIVES – **plasmatic** adjective **plasmic** adjective.

ORIGIN – Greek, from *plassein* 'to shape'.

plaster > noun **1** a soft mixture of lime with sand or cement and water for spreading on walls and ceilings to form a smooth hard surface when dried. **2** (also **plaster of Paris**) a hard white substance made by the addition of water to powdered gypsum, used for setting broken bones and making sculptures and casts. [ORIGIN – so called because the gypsum originally came from Paris.] **3** (also **sticking plaster**) an adhesive strip of material for covering cuts and wounds. > verb **1** cover with plaster; apply plaster to. **2** apply a plaster cast to. **3** coat thickly; daub. **4** (**plaster down**) make (hair) lie flat by applying a liquid or gel to it.

WORDFINDER – fresco (*painting done on wet plaster*), pargeting (*decorative plasterwork*), roughcast (*plaster of lime, cement, and gravel used outside*), stucco (*fine plaster*).

DERIVATIVES – **plasterer** noun.

COMBINATIONS – **plasterboard** board made of plaster set between two sheets of paper, used to line interior walls and ceilings. **plasterwork** plaster as part of the interior of a building, especially when formed into decorative shapes.

ORIGIN – from Greek *emplastron* 'daub, salve'.

plastered > adjective informal very drunk.

plastic > noun **1** a synthetic material made from organic polymers, that can be moulded into shape while soft and then set into a rigid or slightly elastic form. **2** informal credit cards or other plastic cards that can be used as money. > adjective **1** made of plastic. **2** easily shaped or moulded. **3** relating to moulding or modelling in three dimensions. **4** artificial; unnatural.

WORDFINDER – *kinds of plastic:* Bakelite, celluloid, epoxy, Formica, melamine, perspex, polycarbonate, polystyrene, polythene, silicone, vinyl; laminate (*coat with plastic*), Semtex (*plastic explosive*), thermoplastic (*denoting plastic becoming soft when heated*), thermosetting (*becoming harder when heated*).

DERIVATIVES – **plastically** adverb **plasticity** noun.

COMBINATIONS – **plastic bullet** a bullet made of PVC or another plastic, used for riot control. **plastic explosive** a putty-like explosive capable of being moulded by hand. **plastic surgery** the reconstruction or repair of parts of the body by the transfer of tissue, either in the treatment of injury or for cosmetic reasons.

ORIGIN – Greek *plastikos*, from *plassein* 'to mould'.

plasticine (also **Plasticine**) > noun trademark a soft modelling material.

plasticise (also **plasticize**) > verb **1** make plastic or mouldable. **2** treat or coat with plastic.

DERIVATIVES – **plasticisation** noun.

plasticiser (also **plasticizer**) > noun a substance (typically a solvent) added to a synthetic resin to promote plasticity and to reduce brittleness.

plasticky > adjective **1** resembling plastic. **2** artificial or of inferior quality.

plastique /plasteek/ > noun plastic explosive.

ORIGIN – French, 'plastic'.

plastron /plastrən/ > noun **1** a large pad worn by a fencer to protect the chest. **2** an ornamental front part of a woman's bodice, fashionable in the late 19th century. **3** a man's starched shirt front. **4** Zoology the part of a tortoise's or turtle's shell forming the underside.

DERIVATIVES – **plastral** adjective.

ORIGIN – Italian *piastra* 'breastplate'.

plat du jour /pla doo **zhoor**/ > noun (pl. **plats du jour** pronunc. same) a dish specially prepared by a restaurant on a particular day, in addition to the usual menu.

ORIGIN – French, 'dish of the day'.

plate > noun **1** a flat dish from which food is eaten or served. **2** bowls, cups, and other utensils made of gold or silver. **3** Austral./NZ a plate of food contributed by a guest to a social gathering. **4** a thin, flat piece of metal used to join or strengthen or forming part of a machine. **5** a small, flat piece of metal bearing a name or inscription and fixed to a wall or door. **6** a horizontal timber laid along the top of a wall to support the ends of joists or rafters. **7** Botany & Zoology a thin, flat organic structure or formation. **8** Geology each of the several rigid pieces of the earth's lithosphere which together make up the earth's surface. **9** a sheet of metal or other material bearing an image of type or illustrations, from which multiple copies are printed. **10** a printed photograph or illustration in a book. > verb cover (a metal object) with a thin coating of a different metal, especially silver.

IDIOMS – **be handed something on a plate** informal acquire something with little or no effort.

DERIVATIVES – **plater** noun.

COMBINATIONS – **plate armour** protective armour of metal plates, as worn by knights in the Middle Ages. **plate glass** thick fine-quality glass used for shop windows and doors, originally cast in flat plates. **plate tectonics** a theory explaining the structure of the earth's crust as resulting from the movement of lithospheric plates.

ORIGIN – Greek *platus* 'flat'; sense 1 represents Old French *plat* 'platter'.

plateau /plattō/ > noun (pl. **plateaux** /plattōz/ or **plateaus**) **1** an area of fairly level high ground. **2** a state or period of little or no change following a period of activity or progress. > verb (**plateaus, plateaued, plateauing**) reach a plateau.

ORIGIN – French, from *plat* 'level'.

platelet > noun Physiology a small colourless disc-shaped cell fragment without a nucleus, found in large numbers in blood and involved in clotting.

platen /platt'n/ > noun **1** a plate in a small letterpress printing press which presses the paper against the type. **2** a cylindrical roller in a typewriter against which the paper is held.

ORIGIN – French *platine* 'flat piece', from *plat* 'flat'.

platform > noun **1** a raised level surface on which people or things can stand. **2** a raised structure along the side of a railway track where passengers get on and off trains. **3** a raised structure standing in the sea from which oil or gas wells can be drilled. **4** Computing a standard for the hardware of a computer system, which determines the kinds of software it can run. **5** the declared policy of a political party or group. **6** an opportunity for the expression or exchange of views. **7** a very thick sole on a shoe.

ORIGIN – French *plateforme* 'ground plan', literally 'flat shape'.

platinise (also **platinize**) > verb coat with platinum.

DERIVATIVES – **platinisation** noun.

platinoid > noun an alloy of copper with zinc, nickel, and sometimes tungsten, used for its high electrical resistance.

platinum /plattinəm/ > noun **1** a precious silvery-white metallic chemical element used in jewellery and in some electrical and laboratory apparatus. **2** (before another noun) greyish-white or silvery like platinum.

COMBINATIONS – **platinum blonde** (of a woman's hair) silvery-blonde. **platinum disc** a framed platinum disc awarded to a recording artist for sales of a record exceeding a specified high figure.

ORIGIN – Spanish *platina*, from *plata* 'silver'.

platitude > noun a trite, obvious, or insincere remark or statement.

DERIVATIVES – **platitudinise** (also **platitudinize**) verb **platitudinous** adjective.

SYNONYMS – cliché, commonplace, truism.

ORIGIN – French, from *plat* 'flat'.

Platonic /plətonnik/ > adjective **1** of or associated with the Greek philosopher Plato or his ideas. **2** (**platonic**) (of love or

739

friendship) intimate and affectionate but not sexual.

DERIVATIVES – **platonically** adverb.

Platonism /playtəniz'm/ > noun the philosophy of Plato, especially his theories on the relationship between abstract ideas or entities and their corresponding objects or forms in the material world.

DERIVATIVES – **Platonist** noun & adjective.

platoon > noun a subdivision of a company of soldiers, usually commanded by a subaltern or lieutenant and divided into three sections.

ORIGIN – French peloton 'platoon', literally 'small ball'.

platter > noun 1 a large flat serving dish. 2 the rotating metal disc forming the turntable of a record player. 3 Computing a rigid rotating disk on which data is stored in a disk drive; a hard disk.

IDIOMS – **be handed something on a (silver) platter** informal acquire something with little or no effort.

ORIGIN – Old French plater, from plat; related to PLATE.

platypus /plattipəss/ (also **duck-billed platypus**) > noun (pl. **platypuses**) a semiaquatic egg-laying Australian mammal with a sensitive pliable bill like that of a duck and webbed feet with poisonous spurs.

ORIGIN – from Greek platupous 'flat-footed'.

plaudits > plural noun praise; enthusiastic approval.

SYNONYMS – acclaim, accolades, commendation, praise.

ORIGIN – from Latin plaudere 'applaud'.

plausible > adjective 1 seeming reasonable or probable. 2 skilled in producing persuasive or deceptive arguments.

DERIVATIVES – **plausibility** noun **plausibly** adverb.

SYNONYMS – convincing, credible, persuasive.

ANTONYMS – implausible.

ORIGIN – from Latin plaudere 'applaud': originally in the sense 'deserving applause'.

play > verb 1 engage in games or other activities for enjoyment rather than for a serious or practical purpose. 2 (**play with**) treat inconsiderately for one's own amusement. 3 (**play with**) tamper with. 4 take part in (a sport or contest). 5 compete against. 6 take a specified position in a sports team. 7 handle skilfully. 8 move (a piece) or display (a playing card) in one's turn in a game. 9 represent (a character) in a play or film. 10 perform on or have the skill to perform on (a musical instrument). 11 produce (notes) from a musical instrument; perform (a piece of music). 12 make (a record player, radio, etc.) produce sounds. 13 move lightly and quickly; flicker. > noun

1 games and other activities engaged in for enjoyment. 2 the progress of a sporting match. 3 a move or manoeuvre in a sport or game. 4 the state of being active, operative, or effective. 5 a dramatic work for the stage or to be broadcast. 6 light and constantly changing movement.

WORDFINDER – denouement (final part of a play in which all is resolved), dramatize (turn into a play), dramaturgy (art of writing plays), entr'acte (interval between acts of a play), epilogue (address to audience at end of play), mise en scène (scenery and properties used in a play), prologue (address to audience at start of play).

IDIOMS – **make a play for** informal attempt to attract or attain. **make great play of** ostentatiously draw attention to. **play about** (or **around**) 1 behave in a casual or irresponsible way. 2 informal (of a married person) have an affair. **play-act** engage in pretence in an attention-seeking manner. **play along** 1 perform a piece of music at the same time as it is playing on a tape or record. 2 pretend to cooperate. **play by ear** 1 perform (music) without having to read from a score. 2 (**play it by ear**) informal proceed instinctively according to circumstances rather than according to rules or a plan. **play down** disguise the importance or significance of. **play fast and loose** behave irresponsibly or immorally. **play for time** use specious excuses or unnecessary manoeuvres to gain time. **play into someone's hands** act in such a way as unintentionally to give someone an advantage. **play it cool** informal make an effort to seem unconcerned. **play off** bring (two or more people or parties) into conflict for one's own advantage. **play on** exploit (someone's weak or vulnerable point). **a play on words** a pun. **play** (or **play it**) **safe** avoid taking risks. **play up** 1 emphasise the extent or importance of. 2 (**play up to**) humour or flatter. 3 Brit. informal fail to function properly; cause problems.

DERIVATIVES – **playability** noun **playable** adjective.

COMBINATIONS – **playgroup** (also **playschool**) Brit. a regular play session for pre-school children, organised by parents. **playhouse** 1 a theatre. 2 a toy house for children to play in. **playing card** each of a set of rectangular pieces of card with numbers and symbols on one side (usually 52 cards divided into four suits), used to play various games. **playing field** a field used for outdoor team games. **playpen** a small portable enclosure in which a baby or small child can play safely. **playroom** a room in a house that is set aside for children to play in. **playscheme** a local project providing recreational facilities and activities for children. **playsuit** an all-

in-one stretchy garment for a baby or toddler, covering the body, arms, and legs.

playback > noun the replaying of previously recorded sound or moving images.

playboy > noun a wealthy man who spends his time seeking pleasure.

player > noun 1 a person taking part in a sport or game. 2 a person who is involved and influential in an activity. 3 a person who plays a musical instrument. 4 a device for playing compact discs, cassettes, etc. 5 an actor.

COMBINATIONS – **player-manager** a person who both plays in a sports team and manages it.

playful > adjective 1 fond of games and amusement. 2 intended for amusement; light-hearted.

DERIVATIVES – **playfully** adverb **playfulness** noun.

SYNONYMS – 2 facetious, humorous, jocular, light-hearted.

playground > noun an outdoor area provided for children to play on.

playlist > noun a list of recorded songs or pieces of music chosen to be broadcast on a radio station.

playmaker > noun a player in a team game who leads attacks or brings teammates into attacking positions.

playmate > noun a friend with whom a child plays.

play-off > noun an additional match played to decide the outcome of a contest.

plaything > noun 1 a toy. 2 a person who is treated as amusing but unimportant.

playwright > noun a person who writes plays.

plaza /plaazə/ > noun 1 a public square or similar open space in a built-up area. 2 N. Amer. a shopping centre.

ORIGIN – Spanish, 'place'.

plc (also **PLC**) > abbreviation Brit. public limited company.

plea > noun 1 a request made in an urgent and emotional manner. 2 Law a formal statement by or on behalf of a defendant, stating guilt or innocence in response to a charge, offering an allegation of fact, or claiming that a point of law should apply. 3 Law an excuse or claim of mitigating circumstances.

SYNONYMS – 1 appeal, entreaty.

COMBINATIONS – **plea-bargaining** Law an arrangement between prosecutor and defendant whereby the defendant pleads guilty to a lesser charge in the expectation of leniency.

ORIGIN – Old French plait 'agreement, discussion', from Latin placitum 'a decree', from placere 'to please'.

pleach /pleech/ > verb entwine (tree branches) to form a hedge or provide cover for an outdoor walkway.

ORIGIN – Old French *plaissier*, from Latin *plectere* 'plait'.

plead > *verb* (past and past participle **pleaded** or N. Amer., Scottish, or dialect **pled**) **1** make an emotional appeal. **2** present and argue for (a position), especially in court or in another public context. **3** Law state formally in court whether one is guilty or not guilty of the offence with which one is charged. **4** Law invoke (a reason or a point of law) as an accusation or defence. **5** offer or present as an excuse for doing or not doing something.
DERIVATIVES – **pleader** *noun*.
NOTE – in a law court a person can **plead guilty** or **plead not guilty**; the phrase **plead innocent** is not a recognised legal term, although often found in general use.
SYNONYMS – **1** (**plead with**) beg, beseech, entreat, implore.
ORIGIN – Old French *plaidier* 'go to law', from *plaid* 'agreement, discussion'; related to PLEA.

pleading > *noun* **1** the action of making an emotional or earnest appeal. **2** Law a formal statement of the cause of an action or defence. > *adjective* earnestly appealing.
DERIVATIVES – **pleadingly** *adverb*.

pleasance > *noun* a secluded enclosure or part of a garden.
ORIGIN – Old French *plaisance*, from *plaisir* 'please'.

pleasant > *adjective* **1** creating a response of happy satisfaction or enjoyment. **2** (of a person) friendly and likeable.
DERIVATIVES – **pleasantly** *adverb* **pleasantness** *noun*.
SYNONYMS – **1** agreeable, pleasurable, satisfying. **2** amiable, likeable, personable.
ANTONYMS – nasty, unpleasant.
ORIGIN – Old French *plaisant*, from *plaisir* 'please'.

pleasantry > *noun* (pl. **pleasantries**) an inconsequential remark made as part of a polite conversation.

please > *verb* **1** cause to feel happy and satisfied. **2** wish or desire: *do as you please.* **3** (**please oneself**) take only one's own wishes into consideration. **4** (**if you please**) used in polite requests or to express indignation. > *adverb* used in polite requests or questions, or to accept an offer.
DERIVATIVES – **pleasing** *adjective*
ORIGIN – Old French *plaisir*, from Latin *placere*.

pleased > *adjective* **1** feeling or showing pleasure and satisfaction. **2** (**pleased to do**) willing or glad to do.

pleasurable > *adjective* pleasing; enjoyable.
DERIVATIVES – **pleasurableness** *noun* **pleasurably** *adverb*.
SYNONYMS – agreeable, delightful, enjoyable, pleasing.

pleasure > *noun* **1** a feeling of happy

satisfaction and enjoyment. **2** an event or activity from which one derives enjoyment. **3** (before another noun) intended for entertainment rather than business: *pleasure boats.* **4** sensual gratification. > *verb* give pleasure (especially of a sexual nature) to.
WORDFINDER – epicurean, libertine, sybarite, voluptuary (*persons devoted to pleasure*), hedonism (*the pursuit of pleasure*), Schadenfreude (*pleasure derived from another's misfortune*).
IDIOMS – **at one's pleasure** formal as and when one wishes.
SYNONYMS – *noun* **1** contentment, enjoyment, happiness, satisfaction.
ORIGIN – from Old French *plaisir* 'to please'.

pleat > *noun* **1** a fold in a garment or other item made of cloth, held by stitching the top or side. **2** a plait. > *verb* fold or form into pleats.
ORIGIN – variant of PLAIT.

pleb > *noun* informal, derogatory a member of the lower social classes.
DERIVATIVES – **plebby** *adjective*.
ORIGIN – abbreviation of PLEBEIAN.

plebeian /pli·bee·ən/ > *noun* **1** (in ancient Rome) a commoner. **2** a member of the lower social classes. > *adjective* **1** relating to the plebeians of ancient Rome. **2** lower-class or lacking in refinement.
ORIGIN – from Latin *plebs* 'the common people'.

plebiscite /**plebb**·i·sīt/ > *noun* **1** the direct vote of all the members of an electorate on an important public question. **2** (in ancient Rome) a law enacted by the plebeians' assembly.
DERIVATIVES – **plebiscitary** /ple·**biss**·i·tər·i/ *adjective*.
ORIGIN – Latin, from *plebs* 'the common people' + *scitum* 'decree'.

plectrum > *noun* (pl. **plectrums** or **plectra**) a thin flat piece of plastic or tortoiseshell used to pluck the strings of a guitar or similar musical instrument.
ORIGIN – Greek *plēktron* 'something with which to strike', from *plēssein* 'to strike'.

pled North American, Scottish, or dialect past participle of PLEAD.

pledge > *noun* **1** a solemn promise or undertaking. **2** Law a thing that is given as security for the fulfilment of a contract or the payment of a debt and is liable to forfeiture in the event of failure. **3** (**the pledge**) a solemn undertaking to abstain from alcohol. **4** a thing given as a token of love, favour, or loyalty. **5** archaic the drinking of a person's health; a toast. > *verb* **1** solemnly undertake to do or give something. **2** Law give as security on a loan. **3** archaic drink to the health of.

SYNONYMS – *noun* **1** assurance, oath, promise, vow. *verb* **1** promise, swear, vow.
ORIGIN – Old French *plege*, from Latin *plebium*: originally denoting a person acting as surety for another.

Pleistocene /**plīs**·tə·seen/ > *adjective* Geology of or relating to the first epoch of the Quaternary period (between the Pliocene and Holocene epochs, from 1.64 million to about 10,000 years ago), a time which included the ice ages and the appearance of humans.
ORIGIN – Greek, from *pleistos* 'most' + *kainos* 'new'.

plenary /**plee**·nə·ri/ > *adjective* **1** unqualified; absolute. **2** (of a meeting at a conference or assembly) to be attended by all participants. > *noun* a plenary meeting.
ORIGIN – Latin *plenus* 'full'.

plenipotentiary /plen·ni·pə·**ten**·shə·ri/ > *noun* (pl. **plenipotentiaries**) a person appointed by a government to act on its behalf with full and independent power. > *adjective* **1** having full power to take independent action. **2** (of power) absolute.
ORIGIN – from Latin *plenus* 'full' + *potentia* 'power'.

plenitude > *noun* formal **1** an abundance. **2** the condition of being full or complete.
ORIGIN – Old French, from Latin *plenus* 'full'.

plenteous > *adjective* literary plentiful.
DERIVATIVES – **plenteously** *adverb* **plenteousness** *noun*.

plentiful > *adjective* existing in or yielding great quantities; abundant.
DERIVATIVES – **plentifully** *adverb* **plentifulness** *noun*.
SYNONYMS – abundant, copious, profuse.
ANTONYMS – scarce.

plentitude > *noun* another term for PLENITUDE.

plenty > *pronoun* a large or sufficient amount or quantity. > *noun* a situation in which food and other necessities are available in sufficiently large quantities. > *adverb* informal fully; sufficiently.
SYNONYMS – *pronoun* a great deal, lots, many. *noun* abundance, affluence, prosperity.
ORIGIN – Old French *plente*, from Latin *plenus* 'full'.

plenum /**plee**·nəm/ > *noun* **1** an assembly of all the members of a group or committee. **2** Physics a space completely filled with matter, or the whole of space so regarded.
ORIGIN – Latin, 'full space'.

pleonasm /**plee**·ō·naz·'m/ > *noun* the use of more words than are necessary to convey meaning (e.g. *see with one's eyes*).
DERIVATIVES – **pleonastic** *adjective*.

ORIGIN – Greek *pleonasmos*, from *pleonazein* 'be superfluous'.

plesiosaur /**plee**siəsawr/ > *noun* a large fossil marine reptile of the Mesozoic era, with large paddle-like limbs and a long flexible neck.
ORIGIN – from Greek *plēsios* 'near' (because closely related to the lizards) + *sauros* 'lizard'.

plessor > *noun* variant spelling of **PLEXOR**.

plethora /**pleth**ərə/ > *noun* an excess.
ORIGIN – from Greek *plēthein* 'be full'.

pleura /**ploo**rə/ > *noun* (pl. **pleurae** /**ploo**ree/) Anatomy each of a pair of membranes lining the thorax and enveloping the lungs.
DERIVATIVES – **pleural** *adjective*.
ORIGIN – Greek, 'side of the body, rib'.

pleurisy /**ploo**risi/ > *noun* inflammation of the pleurae, causing pain during breathing.
DERIVATIVES – **pleuritic** *adjective*.

plexiglas /**plek**siglaass/ > *noun* trademark a tough transparent plastic made of an acrylic resin, used as a substitute for glass.

plexor /**plek**sər/ (also **plessor**) > *noun* a small hammer with a rubber head, used to test reflexes.
ORIGIN – from Greek *plēxis* 'percussion'.

plexus /**plek**səss/ > *noun* (pl. same or **plexuses**) 1 Anatomy a network of nerves or vessels in the body. 2 an intricate network or web-like formation.
DERIVATIVES – **plexiform** *adjective*.
ORIGIN – Latin, 'plaited formation', from *plectere* 'to plait'.

pliable /**plī**əb'l/ > *adjective* 1 easily bent; flexible. 2 easily influenced or swayed.
DERIVATIVES – **pliability** *noun* **pliably** *adverb*.
SYNONYMS – 2 malleable, pliant, tractable.
ORIGIN – French, from *plier* 'to bend or fold', from Latin *plicare*.

pliant > *adjective* pliable.
DERIVATIVES – **pliancy** *noun* **pliantly** *adverb*.

plié /**plee**ay/ Ballet > *noun* a movement in which a dancer bends the knees and straightens them again, having the feet turned right out and heels firmly on the ground.
ORIGIN – French, 'bent'.

pliers > *plural noun* pincers with parallel flat jaws, used for gripping small objects or bending wire.
ORIGIN – from French *plier* 'to bend'.

plight[1] > *noun* a dangerous or difficult situation.
SYNONYMS – difficulty, predicament, trouble.
ORIGIN – Old French *plit* 'fold'.

plight[2] > *verb* archaic 1 solemnly pledge or promise (faith or loyalty). 2 (**be plighted to**) be engaged to be married to.

plimsoll (also **plimsole**) > *noun* Brit. a light rubber-soled canvas sports shoe.
ORIGIN – probably from the resemblance of the side of the sole to a *Plimsoll* line.

Plimsoll line > *noun* a marking on a ship's side showing the limit of legal submersion when loaded with cargo.
ORIGIN – named after the English politician Samuel *Plimsoll*, responsible for the Merchant Shipping Act of 1876.

plink > *verb* 1 emit a short, sharp, metallic ringing sound. 2 chiefly N. Amer. shoot at (a target) casually. > *noun* a plinking sound.
DERIVATIVES – **plinky** *adjective*.

plinth > *noun* 1 a heavy base supporting a statue or vase. 2 Architecture the lower square slab at the base of a column.
ORIGIN – Greek *plinthos* 'tile, brick, squared stone'.

Pliocene /**plī**əseen/ > *adjective* Geology of or relating to the last epoch of the Tertiary period (between the Miocene and Pleistocene epochs, 5.2 to 1.64 million years ago), a time when the first hominids appeared.
ORIGIN – from Greek *pleiōn* 'more' + *kainos* 'new'.

pliosaur /**plī**əsawr/ > *noun* a plesiosaur with a short neck, large head, and massive toothed jaws.
ORIGIN – from Greek *pleiōn* 'more' + *sauros* 'lizard' (because of its greater similarity to a lizard than the ichthyosaur).

PLO > *abbreviation* Palestine Liberation Organisation.

plod > *verb* (**plodded**, **plodding**) 1 walk doggedly and slowly with heavy steps. 2 work slowly and perseveringly at a dull task. > *noun* 1 a slow, heavy walk. 2 (also **PC Plod**) Brit. informal a police officer.
DERIVATIVES – **plodder** *noun*.
SYNONYMS – *verb* clomp, lumber, trudge.

plonk[1] informal > *verb* 1 set down heavily or carelessly. 2 play unskilfully on a musical instrument. > *noun* a sound as of something being set down heavily.

plonk[2] > *noun* Brit. informal cheap wine.
ORIGIN – Australian: probably an alteration of *blanc* in French *vin blanc* 'white wine'.

plonker > *noun* Brit. informal a foolish or inept person.

plop > *noun* a sound as of a small, solid object dropping into water without a splash. > *verb* (**plopped**, **plopping**) fall or drop with such a sound.

plosive > *adjective* Phonetics referring to a consonant that is produced by stopping the airflow using the lips, teeth, or palate, followed by a sudden release of air.

plot > *noun* 1 a secret plan to do something illegal or harmful. 2 the main sequence of events in a play, novel, or film. 3 a small piece of ground marked out for building, gardening, etc. 4 a graph showing the relation between two variables. 5 chiefly US a diagram, chart, or map. > *verb* (**plotted**, **plotting**) 1 secretly make plans to carry out (something illegal or harmful). 2 devise the plot of (a play, novel, or film). 3 mark (a route or position) on a chart or graph.
DERIVATIVES – **plotless** *adjective* **plotter** *noun*.
SYNONYMS – *noun* 1 conspiracy, intrigue, machinations. *verb* 1 collude, conspire, intrigue.

plough (US **plow**) > *noun* 1 a large farming implement with one or more blades fixed in a frame, drawn through soil to turn it over and cut furrows. 2 (**the Plough**) a prominent formation of seven stars in the constellation Ursa Major (the Great Bear). > *verb* 1 turn up (earth) with a plough. 2 (**plough through** or **into**) (of a vehicle) move in a fast or uncontrolled manner through or into. 3 (of a ship or boat) travel through (an area of water). 4 (**plough on**) advance or progress laboriously or forcibly. 5 (**plough something in**) invest or reinvest money in a business.
WORDFINDER – *parts of a plough:* coulter, mouldboard, share, yoke; arable (*denoting land able to be ploughed*), furrow (*groove made by ploughing*), lynchet (*ridge formed by ancient ploughing*).
DERIVATIVES – **ploughable** *adjective*.

ploughman's lunch > *noun* Brit. a meal of bread and cheese with pickle and salad.

ploughshare > *noun* the main cutting blade of a plough.

plover /**pluvv**ər/ > *noun* a short-billed wading bird, typically found by water but sometimes frequenting grassland.
ORIGIN – Old French, from Latin *pluvia* 'rain'.

plow > *noun & verb* US spelling of **PLOUGH**.

ploy > *noun* a cunning manoeuvre to gain an advantage.
SYNONYMS – gambit, ruse, stratagem.

pluck > *verb* 1 take hold of (something) and quickly remove it from its place. 2 pull out (a hair, feather, etc.) 3 pull the feathers from (a bird's carcass) to prepare it for cooking. 4 pull at or twitch. 5 sound (a stringed musical instrument) with one's finger or a plectrum. 6 (**pluck up**) summon up (courage) in order to do something frightening. > *noun* 1 spirited and determined courage. 2 the heart, liver, and lungs of an animal as food.

plucky > *adjective* (**pluckier**, **pluckiest**) determined and courageous in the face of difficulties.

DERIVATIVES – **pluckily** *adverb* **pluckiness** *noun*.

SYNONYMS – brave, resolute, spirited.

ANTONYMS – cowardly, feeble.

plug > *noun* **1** a piece of solid material fitting tightly into a hole and blocking it up. **2** a device consisting of an insulated casing with metal pins that fit into holes in a socket to make an electrical connection. **3** informal an electrical socket. **4** informal a piece of publicity promoting a product or event. **5** a piece of tobacco for chewing. **6** Fishing a lure with one or more hooks attached. > *verb* (**plugged**, **plugging**) **1** block or fill in (a hole or cavity). **2** (**plug in**) connect (an electrical appliance) to the mains by means of a socket. **3** (**plug into**) have or gain access to (an information system or area of activity). **4** informal promote (a product or event) by mentioning it publicly. **5** informal shoot or hit. **6** (**plug away**) informal proceed steadily and laboriously with a task.

DERIVATIVES – **plugger** *noun*.

COMBINATIONS – **plughole** Brit. a hole at the lowest point of a bath or sink, through which the water drains away. **plug-in** Computing a module or piece of software which can be added to an existing system to give extra features.

plum > *noun* **1** an oval fleshy fruit which is purple, reddish, or yellow when ripe, containing a flattish pointed stone. **2** the tree bearing this fruit. **3** a reddish-purple colour. **4** (before another noun) informal highly desirable: *a plum job*.

IDIOMS – **have a plum in one's mouth** Brit. have an upper-class accent.

COMBINATIONS – **plum duff** dated a plum pudding. **plum pudding** a rich suet pudding containing raisins, currants, and spices. **plum tomato** a plum-shaped variety of tomato.

ORIGIN – Latin *prunum*; compare with **PRUNE¹**.

plumage /ˈplo͞omij/ > *noun* a bird's feathers.

ORIGIN – Old French, from *plume* 'feather'.

plumb¹ > *verb* **1** measure (the depth of a body of water). **2** explore or experience fully or to extremes. **3** test (an upright surface) to determine the vertical. > *noun* a lead ball or other heavy object attached to a line for finding the depth of water or determining the vertical on an upright surface. > *adverb* informal **1** exactly: *plumb in the centre*. **2** N. Amer. extremely or completely. > *adjective* vertical.

COMBINATIONS – **plumb bob** a piece of lead or other heavy material forming the

weight of a plumb line. **plumb line** a line with a plumb attached to it.

---

wordpower facts

Plumb

What connects **plumb**, **plumber**, **plummet**, **plunge**, and **aplomb**? The common factor is the metal lead. The Latin word *plumbum* 'lead' is the root of all these words. A **plumber** was originally a tradesman who worked with lead, which was formerly used for water pipes. The original use of **plummet**, in medieval times, was to denote a plumb or plumb line; use as a verb to mean 'fall rapidly' is a 20th-century development. The word **aplomb** entered English from the French phrase *à plomb* 'according to a plummet': it originally meant 'perpendicularity, steadiness'.

---

plumb² > *verb* (**plumb in**) install (a bath, washing machine, etc.) and connect it to water and drainage pipes.

plumbago /plumˈbāgō/ > *noun* (pl. **plumbagos**) **1** an evergreen shrub or climber with grey or blue flowers. **2** old-fashioned term for **GRAPHITE**.

ORIGIN – Latin, from *plumbum* 'lead'.

plumber > *noun* a person who fits and repairs the pipes and fittings of water supply, sanitation, or heating systems.

ORIGIN – Old French *plommier*, from Latin *plumbum* 'lead': see **PLUMB¹**.

plumbing > *noun* **1** the system of pipes, tanks, and fittings required for the water supply, heating, and sanitation in a building. **2** the work of installing and maintaining such a system.

plumbism /ˈplumbiz'm/ > *noun* technical poisoning due to the absorption of lead into the body.

plume > *noun* **1** a long, soft feather or arrangement of feathers. **2** a long spreading cloud of smoke or vapour. **3** Geology a column of magma rising by convection in the earth's mantle. > *verb* **1** (**plumed**) decorated with feathers. **2** spread out in a shape resembling a feather.

ORIGIN – Latin *pluma* 'down'.

plummet > *verb* (**plummeted**, **plummeting**) **1** fall or drop straight down at high speed. **2** decrease rapidly in value or amount. > *noun* **1** a steep and rapid fall or drop. **2** a plumb bob or plumb line.

SYNONYMS – *verb* **1** crash, hurtle, plunge.

ORIGIN – from Old French *plommet* 'small sounding lead', from *plomb* 'lead'.

plummy > *adjective* (**plummier**, **plummiest**) **1** resembling a plum. **2** Brit.

informal (of a person's voice) typical of the English upper classes. **3** Brit. informal choice; highly desirable.

plump¹ > *adjective* **1** full and rounded in shape. **2** rather fat. > *verb* (**plump up**) make or become full and round.

DERIVATIVES – **plumpish** *adjective* **plumpness** *noun*.

SYNONYMS – *adjective* **2** ample, chubby, fat, fleshy, round.

plump² > *verb* **1** (**plump down**) set or sit down heavily or unceremoniously. **2** (**plump for**) decide in favour of (one of two or more possibilities). > *adverb* informal with a sudden or heavy fall.

plumule /ˈplo͞omyo͞ol/ > *noun* **1** Botany the rudimentary shoot or stem of an embryo plant. **2** Ornithology a bird's down feather.

ORIGIN – Latin *plumula* 'small feather'.

plumy > *adjective* resembling or decorated with feathers.

plunder > *verb* enter forcibly and steal goods from. > *noun* **1** the action of plundering. **2** goods obtained by plundering.

DERIVATIVES – **plunderer** *noun*.

SYNONYMS – *verb* despoil, loot, pillage, ransack. *noun* looting, marauding, pillaging.

ORIGIN – German *plündern* 'rob of household goods'.

plunge > *verb* **1** fall or move suddenly and uncontrollably. **2** jump or dive quickly and energetically. **3** (**plunge in**) embark impetuously on (a course of action). **4** (**plunge into**) suddenly bring into a specified condition or state. **5** push or thrust quickly. > *noun* an act of plunging.

IDIOMS – **take the plunge** informal commit oneself to a bold course of action after consideration.

COMBINATIONS – **plunge pool 1** a deep basin at the foot of a waterfall formed by the action of the falling water. **2** a small, deep swimming pool.

ORIGIN – Old French *plungier* 'thrust down', from Latin *plumbum* 'lead, plummet'.

plunger > *noun* **1** a part of a device or mechanism that works with a plunging or thrusting movement. **2** a device consisting of a rubber cup on a long handle, used to clear blocked pipes by means of suction.

plunk informal > *verb* **1** play a keyboard or pluck a stringed instrument in an unexpressive way. **2** US hit (someone) abruptly. **3** chiefly N. Amer. set down heavily or abruptly. > *noun* **1** a plunking sound. **2** US a heavy blow. **3** N. Amer. an act of setting something down heavily.

pluperfect Grammar > *adjective* (of a tense) denoting an action completed prior to some past point of time, formed in English by *had* and the past participle (as in *he had gone by then*). > *noun* a verb in the pluperfect tense.

ORIGIN – from Latin *plus quam perfectum* 'more than perfect' (referring to the perfect tense).

plural > *adjective* **1** more than one in number. **2** Grammar (of a word or form) denoting more than one. > *noun* Grammar a plural word or form.

DERIVATIVES – **plurally** *adverb*.

COMBINATIONS – **plural society** a society composed of different ethnic groups or cultural traditions.

ORIGIN – Latin *pluralis*, from *plus* 'more'.

pluralise (also **pluralize**) > *verb* **1** cause to become more numerous. **2** give a plural form to (a word).

DERIVATIVES – **pluralisation** *noun*.

pluralism > *noun* **1** the existence or toleration of a diversity of ethnic groups or differing cultures and views within a society. **2** a political system of power-sharing among a number of political parties. **3** Philosophy a theory or system that recognises more than one ultimate principle. **4** the holding of more than one ecclesiastical office or position at the same time by one person.

DERIVATIVES – **pluralist** *noun* & *adjective* **pluralistic** *adjective*.

plurality > *noun* (pl. **pluralities**) **1** the fact or state of being plural. **2** a large number of people or things. **3** US the number of votes cast for a candidate who receives more than any other but does not receive an absolute majority.

plus > *preposition* **1** with the addition of. **2** informal together with. > *adjective* **1** (after a number or amount) at least: *$500,000 plus*. **2** (after a grade) rather better than: *B plus*. **3** (before a number) above zero; positive: *plus 60 degrees centigrade*. **4** having a positive electric charge. > *noun* **1** (also **plus sign**) the symbol +, indicating addition or a positive value. **2** informal an advantage. > *conjunction* informal furthermore; also.

COMBINATIONS – **plus fours** men's baggy knickerbockers reaching below the knee, formerly worn for hunting and golf. [ORIGIN – so named because the overhang at the knee required an extra four inches of material.]

ORIGIN – Latin, 'more'.

plus ça change /plōō sa **shoɴj**/ > *exclamation* used to express the observation that certain things remain fundamentally unchanged.

ORIGIN – French, from *plus ça change, plus c'est la même chose* 'the more it changes, the more it stays the same'.

plush > *noun* a rich fabric of silk, cotton, or wool, with a long, soft nap. > *adjective* informal expensively luxurious.

DERIVATIVES – **plushy** (**plushier**, **plushiest**) *adjective*.

ORIGIN – French *peluche*, from Latin *pilus* 'hair'.

plutocracy /plōō**tok**rəsi/ > *noun* (pl. **plutocracies**) **1** government by the wealthy. **2** a society governed by the wealthy. **3** an elite or ruling class whose power derives from their wealth.

DERIVATIVES – **plutocratic** *adjective*.

ORIGIN – from Greek *ploutos* 'wealth' + *kratos* 'strength, authority'.

plutocrat > *noun* often derogatory a person whose power derives from their wealth.

Plutonian > *adjective* relating to the planet Pluto.

plutonic /plōō**tonn**ik/ > *adjective* **1** Geology (of igneous rock) formed by solidification at considerable depth beneath the earth's surface. **2** (**Plutonic**) relating to the underworld or the Greek god Pluto.

plutonium /plōō**tō**niəm/ > *noun* a radioactive metallic chemical element formed by the radioactive decay of uranium and used as a fuel in nuclear reactors and as an explosive in atomic weapons.

ORIGIN – from the planet *Pluto*, on the pattern of *neptunium* (Pluto being the next planet beyond Neptune).

pluvial /**plōō**viəl/ > *adjective* relating to or characterised by rainfall.

ORIGIN – Latin *pluvialis*, from *pluvia* 'rain'.

ply[1] > *noun* (pl. **plies**) **1** a thickness or layer of a folded or laminated material. **2** each of a number of multiple layers or strands of which something is made.

ORIGIN – French *pli* 'fold', from Latin *plicare* 'to fold'.

ply[2] > *verb* (**plies**, **plied**) **1** work steadily with (a tool) or at (one's job). **2** (of a vessel or vehicle) travel regularly over a route, typically for commercial purposes. **3** (**ply with**) provide (someone) with (food or drink) in a continuous or insistent way. **4** (**ply with**) direct (numerous questions) at someone.

SYNONYMS – **4** lavish, regale, shower. **5** assail, besiege, bombard.

ORIGIN – shortening of **APPLY**.

plywood > *noun* thin, strong board consisting of two or more layers of wood glued together.

PM > *abbreviation* **1** post-mortem. **2** Prime Minister.

Pm > *symbol* the chemical element promethium.

p.m. > *abbreviation* after noon.

ORIGIN – from Latin *post meridiem*.

PMS > *abbreviation* premenstrual syndrome.

PMT > *abbreviation* chiefly Brit. premenstrual tension.

pneumatic /nyōō**matt**ik/ > *adjective* **1** containing or operated by air or gas under pressure. **2** informal (of a woman) having large breasts.

DERIVATIVES – **pneumatically** *adverb*.

COMBINATIONS – **pneumatic drill** a large, heavy drill driven by compressed air, used for breaking up a hard surface.

ORIGIN – Greek *pneumatikos*, from *pneuma* 'wind'.

pneumatics > *plural noun* (treated as sing.) the science of the mechanical properties of gases.

pneumococcus /nyōōmə**kokk**əss/ > *noun* (pl. **pneumococci** /nyōōmə**kokk**(s)ī/) a bacterium associated with pneumonia and some forms of meningitis.

DERIVATIVES – **pneumococcal** *adjective*.

pneumonia /nyōō**mō**niə/ > *noun* a lung infection in which the air sacs fill with pus.

DERIVATIVES – **pneumonic** *adjective*.

ORIGIN – Greek, from *pneumōn* 'lung'.

PNG > *abbreviation* Papua New Guinea.

PO > *abbreviation* **1** postal order. **2** Post Office.

Po > *symbol* the chemical element polonium.

poach[1] > *verb* cook by simmering in a small amount of liquid.

ORIGIN – Old French *pochier* (earlier in the sense 'enclose in a bag'), from *poche* 'bag, pocket'.

poach[2] > *verb* **1** illegally take (game or fish) from private or protected areas. **2** take or acquire in an unfair or clandestine way.

ORIGIN – apparently related to **POKE**[1]; perhaps also partly from Old French *pochier* (see **POACH**[1]).

poacher[1] > *noun* a pan for poaching eggs or other food.

poacher[2] > *noun* a person who poaches game or fish.

pochard /**pō**chərd/ > *noun* a diving duck, the male of which typically has a reddish-brown head.

pock > *noun* a pockmark.

DERIVATIVES – **pocked** *adjective*.

ORIGIN – Old English; compare with **POX**.

pocket > *noun* **1** a small bag sewn into or on clothing, used for carrying small articles. **2** a small, isolated patch, group, or area. **3** (**one's pocket**) informal one's financial resources. **4** a pouch-like compartment providing storage space in a suitcase, car door, etc. **5** an opening at the corner or on the side of a billiard table into which balls are struck. > *adjective* of a suitable size for carrying in a pocket. > *verb* (**pocketed**,

pocketing) 1 put into one's pocket. **2** take for oneself, especially dishonestly. **3** Billiards & Snooker drive (a ball) into a pocket.

IDIOMS – **in** (or **out of**) **pocket** having gained (or lost) money in a transaction. **in someone's pocket** financially dependent on someone and therefore under their influence. **line one's pockets** make money, especially dishonestly. **put one's hand in one's pocket** spend or provide one's own money.

DERIVATIVES – **pocketable** *adjective*.

COMBINATIONS – **pocketbook 1** Brit. a notebook. **2** US a wallet, purse, or handbag. **pocket borough** (in the UK before the 1832 Reform Act) a borough in which the election of political representatives was controlled by one person or family. **pocket knife** a penknife. **pocket money** Brit. **1** a small regular allowance given to a child by their parents. **2** a small amount of money for minor expenses. **pocket watch** a watch on a chain, intended to be carried in a jacket or waistcoat pocket.

ORIGIN – Old French *pokete* 'little bag', from *poke* 'pouch'.

pockmark > *noun* **1** a pitted scar or mark on the skin left by a pustule or spot. **2** a mark or pitted area disfiguring a surface. > *verb* cover or disfigure with pockmarks.

pod¹ > *noun* **1** a long seed-case of a leguminous plant such as the pea. **2** a self-contained or detachable unit on an aircraft or spacecraft. > *verb* (**podded, podding**) **1** remove (peas or beans) from their pods prior to cooking. **2** (of a plant) bear or form pods.

ORIGIN – from dialect *podware, podder* 'field crops'.

pod² > *noun* a small herd or school of marine animals, especially whales.

podge > *noun* Brit. informal **1** a short, fat person. **2** excess weight; fat.

podgy > *adjective* (**podgier, podgiest**) Brit. informal rather fat; chubby.

podiatry /pədīətri/ > *noun* another term for CHIROPODY.

DERIVATIVES – **podiatrist** *noun*.

ORIGIN – from Greek *pous* 'foot' + *iatros* 'physician'.

podium /pōdiəm/ > *noun* (pl. **podiums** or **podia** /pōdiə/) **1** a small platform on which a person may stand to be seen by an audience. **2** N. Amer. a lectern.

ORIGIN – Latin, from Greek *podion* 'little foot'.

podzol /podzol/ (also **podsol** /podsol/) > *noun* an infertile acidic soil with a grey layer under the surface, typical of coniferous woodland.

ORIGIN – from Russian *pod* 'under' + *zola* 'ashes'.

poem > *noun* a literary composition in verse, typically concerned with the expression of feelings or imaginative description.

WORDFINDER – *forms of poem:* ballad, eclogue, elegy, epic, haiku, idyll, limerick, lyric, ode, sonnet; anthology (*a collection of poems*), blank verse (*unrhymed poetry*), metre (*rhythmic pattern of a poem*), prosody (*study of forms and rhythms of poetry*), scansion (*action of finding the metre of a poem*), stanza (*group of lines forming basic unit of a poem*).

ORIGIN – Greek *poēma*, variant of *poiēma* 'fiction, poem', from *poiein* 'create'.

poesy /pōizi/ > *noun* archaic or literary poetry.

ORIGIN – Greek *poēsis* 'making, poetry'.

poet > *noun* **1** a person who writes poems. **2** a person possessing special powers of imagination or expression.

DERIVATIVES – **poetess** *noun*.

COMBINATIONS – **Poet Laureate** (pl. **Poets Laureate** or **Poet Laureates**) a poet appointed by the British sovereign to write poems for royal and official occasions.

poetaster /pōitastər/ > *noun* a person who writes bad poetry.

poetic (also **poetical**) > *adjective* relating to or of the nature of poetry.

DERIVATIVES – **poetically** *adverb* **poeticise** (also **poeticize**) *verb*.

COMBINATIONS – **poetic justice** fitting or deserved punishment or reward. **poetic licence** departure from convention or factual accuracy for artistic effect.

poetics > *plural noun* (treated as sing.) the study of linguistic techniques in poetry and literature.

poetise (also **poetize**) > *verb* represent in poetic form.

poetry > *noun* **1** poems collectively or as a literary genre. **2** a quality of beauty and intensity of emotion regarded as characteristic of poetry.

po-faced > *adjective* Brit. humourless and disapproving.

ORIGIN – perhaps from *po* 'chamber pot', influenced by *poker-faced*.

pogo > *verb* (**pogoes, pogoed**) informal jump up and down as if on a pogo stick as a form of dancing to rock music.

pogo stick > *noun* a toy for bouncing around on, consisting of a spring-loaded pole with a handle at the top and rests for the feet near the bottom.

pogrom /pogrəm/ > *noun* an organised massacre of an ethnic group, originally that of Jews in Russia or eastern Europe.

ORIGIN – Russian, 'devastation'.

poignant /poynyənt/ > *adjective* evoking a keen sense of sadness or regret.

DERIVATIVES – **poignancy** *noun* **poignantly** *adverb*.

SYNONYMS – affecting, moving, touching.

wordpower facts

Poignant

Poignant is closely related to **pungent**, both in origin and meaning. Both words come from the Latin verb *pungere* 'to prick', the difference in form being due to the fact that **poignant** entered English from Old French. **Poignant** is the older word: in the Middle Ages it meant 'sharp in taste or smell' (i.e. the modern sense of **pungent**), 'keenly felt or suffered', 'pleasing to the senses', 'sharp-pointed', and (with reference to words) 'stinging, pointed'. **Pungent** entered English in the late 16th century and originally meant 'sharp-pointed' and 'keenly felt or suffered' (i.e. **poignant**); later it took on the meanings 'stinging, pointed', 'interesting, stimulating', and 'sharp in taste or smell'. Other words derived from Latin *pungere* are **compunction**, **counterpane**, **counterpoint**, **expunge**, and **puncture**.

poikilotherm /poykillətherm/ > *noun* Zoology an organism that cannot regulate its body temperature except by behavioural means such as basking or burrowing; a cold-blooded organism. Contrasted with HOMEOTHERM.

DERIVATIVES – **poikilothermic** *adjective*.

ORIGIN – from Greek *poikilos* 'varied'.

poinciana /poynsiaanə/ > *noun* a tropical tree with showy red or red and yellow flowers.

ORIGIN – named after M. de *Poinci*, a 17th-century governor of the French Antilles.

poinsettia /poynsettiə/ > *noun* a small shrub with large showy scarlet bracts surrounding the small yellow flowers.

ORIGIN – named after the American diplomat and botanist Joel R. *Poinsett* (1779–1851).

point > *noun* **1** the tapered, sharp end of a tool, weapon, or other object. **2** a particular spot, place, or moment. **3** an item, detail, or idea in a discussion, text, etc. **4** (**the point**) the most significant or relevant factor or element. **5** advantage or purpose: *what's the point of it all?* **6** a positive feature or characteristic. **7** a unit of scoring or of measuring value, achievement, or extent. **8** a full stop or a decimal point. **9** a very small dot or mark on a surface. **10** (in geometry) something having position but not spatial extent, magnitude, dimension, or direction. **11** each of thirty-two directions marked at equal distances round a compass. **12** a narrow piece of land jutting out into the sea. **13 (points)** Brit. a junction of two railway lines, with a pair of linked tapering rails that can be moved laterally to allow a train to pass from one line to the other. **14** Printing a unit of measurement for type sizes and spacing (in the UK and US 0.351 mm, in Europe 0.376 mm). **15** Brit. a socket in a wall for connecting a device to an electrical supply or communications network. **16** each of a set of electrical contacts in the distributor of a motor vehicle. **17** Cricket a fielding position on the off side near the batsman. **18** Ballet another term for POINTE. > *verb* **1** direct someone's attention in a particular direction by extending one's finger. **2** direct or aim (something). **3** face in or indicate a particular direction. **4** (**point out**) make someone aware of (a fact or circumstance). **5** (often **point to**) cite or function as evidence. **6** (**point up**) reveal the true nature or importance of. **7** give a sharp, tapered point to. **8** fill in or repair the joints of (brickwork or tiling) with smoothly finished mortar or cement.

WORDFINDER – acme, apex, summit, zenith (*highest point*), nadir (*lowest point*), nexus, node (*point of intersection*).

IDIOMS – **a case in point** a example that illustrates what is being discussed. **make a point of** make a special effort to do something. **on the point of** on the verge or brink of. **score points** deliberately make oneself appear superior by making clever remarks. **take someone's point** chiefly Brit. accept the validity of someone's idea or argument. **up to a point** to some extent.

SYNONYMS – *verb* **2** aim, direct, level, train. **4** (**point out**) draw attention to, identify, indicate, show.

COMBINATIONS – **point duty** Brit. the duties of a police officer stationed at a junction to control traffic. **point of order** a query in a formal debate or meeting as to whether correct procedure is being followed. **point of view 1** a particular attitude or way of considering a matter. **2** the position from which someone or something is observed. **point-to-point** (pl. **point-to-points**) an amateur cross-country steeplechase for horses used in hunting.

ORIGIN – Latin *punctum* 'something that is pricked', from *pungere* 'to prick'.

point-blank > *adjective & adverb* **1** (of a shot or missile) fired from very close to its target. **2** without explanation or qualification.

SYNONYMS – **2** bluntly, flatly, outright.

pointe /pwant/ > *noun* (pl. pronunc. same) Ballet the tips of the toes.

ORIGIN – French, 'tip'.

pointed > *adjective* **1** having a sharpened or tapered tip or end. **2** (of a remark or look) clearly directed and unambiguous in intent.

DERIVATIVES – **pointedly** *adverb*.

pointer > *noun* **1** a long, thin piece of metal on a scale or dial which moves to give a reading. **2** a rod used for pointing to features on a map or chart. **3** a hint or tip. **4** a dog of a breed that on scenting game stands rigid looking towards it. **5** Computing a cursor or a link.

pointillism /ˈpwantiliz'm/ > *noun* a technique of neo-Impressionist painting using tiny dots of pure colours, which become blended in the viewer's eye.

DERIVATIVES – **pointillist** *noun & adjective*.

ORIGIN – from French *pointiller* 'mark with dots'.

pointing > *noun* mortar or cement used to fill the joints of brickwork or tiling.

pointless > *adjective* having little or no sense or purpose.

DERIVATIVES – **pointlessly** *adverb* **pointlessness** *noun*.

SYNONYMS – futile, useless, vain.

pointy > *adjective* (**pointier**, **pointiest**) informal having a pointed tip or end.

poise[1] > *noun* **1** graceful and elegant bearing. **2** composure and dignity of manner. > *verb* **1** be or cause to be balanced or suspended. **2** (**be poised to do**) be ready and prepared to do.

SYNONYMS – *noun* **2** aplomb, assurance, composure, cool, self-possession.

ORIGIN – Old French *pois*, from Latin *pensum* 'weight'.

wordpower facts

Poise

The word **poise** originally meant 'weight' and 'measure of weight', from which arose the notion of 'equal weight, balance' and the extended senses 'composure' and 'elegant bearing'. The ultimate root of **poise** is the very productive Latin verb *pendere* 'weigh, pay out, consider'. **Poise** is thus related to such words as **compendium**, **compensate**, **dispense**, **expend**, **pension**, **ponder**, **ponderous**, and **stipend**. *Pendere* is the source of the Latin verb *pensare* 'consider' and French *penser* 'think', the sources of **pensive** and **pansy**. The monetary terms **peseta**, **peso**, and **pound** are also connected to *pendere*: they come ultimately from the idea of 'something weighed'.

poise[2] > *noun* Physics a unit used to express the viscosity of a liquid, equal to 0.1 newton seconds per square metre.

ORIGIN – named after the French physician Jean L. M. *Poiseuille* (1799–1869).

poised > *adjective* composed and elegant or self-assured.

SYNONYMS – assured, composed, cool, self-assured, unruffled.

poisha > *noun* (pl. same) a monetary unit of Bangladesh, equal to one hundredth of a taka.

ORIGIN – Bengali, alteration of PAISA.

poison > *noun* **1** a substance that causes death or injury when introduced into or absorbed by a living organism. **2** a destructive or corrupting influence. > *verb* **1** administer poison to. **2** contaminate with poison. **3** corrupt or prove harmful to.

WORDFINDER – antidote (*medicine which counteracts a poison*), toxicology (*science of poisons*), toxin (*poison produced by a micro-organism*), venom (*snake poison*).

DERIVATIVES – **poisoner** *noun*.

COMBINATIONS – **poisoned chalice** something offered which is apparently appealing or beneficial but which is likely to prove a source of problems to the recipient. **poison ivy** a North American climbing plant which secretes an irritant oil from its leaves. **poison pen letter** an anonymous letter containing malicious accusations or abuse.

ORIGIN – Old French, 'magic potion', from Latin *potio* 'potion'.

poisonous > *adjective* **1** containing or of the nature of poison. **2** extremely unpleasant or malicious.

SYNONYMS – **1** noxious, toxic, venomous. **2** malevolent, venomous, vicious.

poke[1] > *verb* **1** jab or prod with a finger or a sharp object. **2** make (a hole) by jabbing or prodding. **3** (**poke about** or **around**) look or search around a place. **4** (often **poke out**) thrust out or protrude in a particular direction. > *noun* an act of poking.

IDIOMS – **poke fun at** tease or make fun of. **poke one's nose into** informal take an intrusive interest in. **take a poke at** informal hit, punch, or criticise (someone).

COMBINATIONS – **poke bonnet** a woman's bonnet with a projecting brim, popular in the early 19th century.

poke[2] > *noun* chiefly Scottish a bag or small sack.

ORIGIN – Old French *poche* 'pocket'.

poker[1] > *noun* a metal rod with a handle, used for prodding and stirring an open fire.

poker[2] > *noun* a card game in which the players bet on the value of the hands dealt to them, sometimes using bluff.

WORDFINDER – *card combinations*: flush, full house, royal flush, straight, straight flush; ante (*player's initial stake*), stud poker (*in which first card only is dealt face down*).

COMBINATIONS – **poker face** an impassive expression that hides one's true feelings.
ORIGIN – perhaps related to German *pochen* 'to brag', *Pochspiel* 'bragging game'.

pokerwork > *noun* British term for **PYROGRAPHY**.

pokey > *noun* informal, chiefly N. Amer. prison.
ORIGIN – variant of *pogey*, a Canadian informal term meaning 'hostel for the needy', later 'unemployment benefit'; perhaps influenced by **POKY**.

poky (also **pokey**) > *adjective* (**pokier**, **pokiest**) **1** (of a room or building) uncomfortably small and cramped. **2** informal (of a car) having considerable power or acceleration. **3** N. Amer. annoyingly slow.
ORIGIN – from **POKE¹** (in the sense 'confine').

Polack /pōlak/ > *noun* derogatory, chiefly N. Amer. a person from Poland or of Polish descent.
ORIGIN – from Polish *Polak*.

polar > *adjective* **1** relating to the North or South Poles of the earth or their adjacent area. **2** having an electrical or magnetic field. **3** directly opposite in character or tendency.
COMBINATIONS – **polar bear** a large white arctic bear.

polarise (also **polarize**) > *verb* **1** divide into two sharply contrasting groups or sets of beliefs. **2** Physics restrict the vibrations of (a transverse wave, especially light) to one direction. **3** give magnetic or electric polarity to.
DERIVATIVES – **polarisation** noun.

polarity > *noun* (pl. **polarities**) **1** the state of having poles or opposites. **2** the direction of a magnetic or electric field.

Polaroid > *noun* trademark **1** a composite material with the property of polarising light, produced in thin plastic sheets. **2** (**Polaroids**) sunglasses with lenses of polaroid. **3** a type of camera that produces a finished print rapidly after each exposure. **4** a photograph taken with such a camera.

polder /pōldər/ > *noun* a piece of land reclaimed from the sea or a river, especially in the Netherlands.
ORIGIN – Dutch.

Pole > *noun* a person from Poland.

pole¹ > *noun* **1** a long, slender rounded piece of wood or metal, typically used as a support. **2** a wooden shaft fitted to the front of a cart or carriage drawn by animals and attached to their yokes or collars. **3** Brit. historical another term for **PERCH³** (in sense 1). **4** (also **square pole**) Brit. historical another term for **PERCH³** (in sense 2). > *verb* propel (a boat) with a pole.
IDIOMS – **up the pole** Brit. informal mad.
COMBINATIONS – **pole position** the most favourable position at the start of a motor race. [ORIGIN – from the use of *pole* in horse racing to mean the starting position next to the inside boundary fence.] **pole vault** an athletic event in which competitors attempt to vault over a high bar with the aid of an extremely long flexible pole.
ORIGIN – Latin *palus* 'stake'.

pole² > *noun* **1** either of the two locations (**North Pole** or **South Pole**) on the earth which are the ends of the axis of rotation. **2** Geometry each of the two points at which the axis of a circle cuts the surface of a sphere. **3** each of the two opposite points of a magnet at which magnetic forces are strongest. **4** the positive or negative terminal of an electric cell or battery. **5** each of two opposed principles or ideas.
IDIOMS – **be poles apart** have nothing in common.
COMBINATIONS – **Pole Star** a fairly bright star located within one degree of the celestial north pole, in the constellation Ursa Minor.
ORIGIN – Greek *polos* 'pivot, axis, sky'.

poleaxe (US also **poleax**) > *noun* **1** a battleaxe. **2** a butcher's axe used to slaughter animals. > *verb* **1** kill or knock down with or as if with a poleaxe. **2** shock greatly.
ORIGIN – from **POLL** + **AXE**.

polecat > *noun* **1** a weasel-like mammal with dark brown fur and an unpleasant smell. **2** N. Amer. a skunk.
ORIGIN – perhaps from Old French *pole* 'chicken' + **CAT**.

polemic /pəlemmik/ > *noun* **1** a strong verbal or written attack. **2** (also **polemics**) the practice of engaging in controversial debate. > *adjective* (also **polemical**) of or involving heated or controversial debate.
DERIVATIVES – **polemicist** noun.
SYNONYMS – *noun* **1** broadside, diatribe, sally.
ORIGIN – Greek *polemikos*, from *polemos* 'war'.

polenta /pəlentə/ > *noun* (in Italian cookery) maize flour or a dough made from this, which is boiled and then fried or baked.
ORIGIN – Latin, 'pearl barley'.

police > *noun* (treated as pl.) **1** a civil force responsible for the prevention and detection of crime and the maintenance of public order. **2** members of such a force. > *verb* **1** maintain law and order in (an area), with police or a similar force. **2** regulate, administer, or control.
COMBINATIONS – **police officer** a policeman or policewoman. **police state** a totalitarian state in which political police secretly monitor and control citizens' activities. **police station** the office of a local police force.

wordpower facts
Police

The word **police** has the same origin as **policy**, Greek *politeia* 'citizenship'; ultimately it goes back to *polis* 'city', the source of **acropolis**, **cosmopolitan**, **metropolitan**, and **politics**. 'Policy' was in fact one of the early senses of **police**, in the early 16th century; others were 'social organisation, civilisation', 'regulation of society, public order', and 'the government institutions concerned with the maintenance of public order'. Current senses date from the early 19th century.

policeman (or **policewoman**) > *noun* a member of a police force.

policy¹ > *noun* (pl. **policies**) **1** a course or principle of action adopted or proposed by an organisation or individual. **2** archaic prudent or expedient conduct or action.
SYNONYMS – **1** course, line, method, programme, strategy.
ORIGIN – Old French *policie* 'civil administration', from Greek *politeia* 'citizenship'.

policy² > *noun* (pl. **policies**) a contract of insurance.
ORIGIN – from French *police* 'bill of lading, contract of insurance'.

polio > *noun* short for **POLIOMYELITIS**.

poliomyelitis /pōliōmīəlītiss/ > *noun* an infectious disease, caused by a virus, that affects the central nervous system and can cause temporary or permanent paralysis.
ORIGIN – from Greek *polios* 'grey' + *muelos* 'marrow'.

Polish /pōlish/ > *noun* the language of Poland. > *adjective* relating to Poland.

polish /pollish/ > *verb* **1** make smooth and shiny by rubbing. **2** improve or refine. **3** (**polish off**) finish or consume quickly. > *noun* **1** a substance used to make something smooth and shiny when rubbed in. **2** an act of polishing. **3** smoothness or glossiness produced by polishing. **4** refinement or elegance.
DERIVATIVES – **polisher** noun.
SYNONYMS – *verb* **1** buff, burnish, shine. **2** enhance, hone, improve, refine. *noun* **4** elegance, grace, refinement, sophistication, urbanity.
ORIGIN – from Latin *polire* 'polish, make smooth.'

politburo /pollitbyoorō/ > *noun* (pl. **politburos**) the principal policy-making committee of a communist party, especially that of the former USSR.
ORIGIN – from Russian *politicheskoe byuro* 'political bureau'.

polite > *adjective* (**politer**, **politest**) **1** courteous and well mannered. **2** cultured and refined: *polite society*.
DERIVATIVES – **politely** *adverb* **politeness** *noun*.
SYNONYMS – **1** civil, courteous, polished, well bred, well mannered. **2** civilised, cultured, elegant, refined, sophisticated.
ANTONYMS – **1** impolite, rude. **2** savage.
ORIGIN – Latin *politus*, from *polire* 'polish, make smooth'.

politesse /polli**tess**/ > *noun* formal politeness or etiquette.
ORIGIN – French.

politic > *adjective* **1** (of an action) sensible and judicious. **2** (also **politick**) archaic prudent and shrewd. > *verb* (**politicked**, **politicking**) often derogatory engage in political activity.
SYNONYMS – *adjective* **1** astute, judicious, prudent, sensible, wise.

political > *adjective* **1** relating to the government or public affairs of a country. **2** interested in or active in politics. **3** chiefly derogatory acting in the interests of status within an organisation rather than on principle.
DERIVATIVES – **politically** *adverb*.
COMBINATIONS – **political correctness** the avoidance of terms or behaviour considered to be discriminatory or offensive to certain groups of people. **politically correct** (or **incorrect**) exhibiting (or failing to exhibit) political correctness. **political prisoner** a person imprisoned for their political beliefs or actions. **political science** the study of political activity and behaviour.
ORIGIN – Greek *politikos*, from *politēs* 'citizen', from *polis* 'city'.

politician > *noun* **1** a person who is professionally involved in politics, especially as a holder of an elected office. **2** chiefly US a person who acts in a manipulative and devious way, typically to gain advancement.

politicise (also **politicize**) > *verb* **1** make politically aware or politically active. **2** engage in or talk about politics.
DERIVATIVES – **politicisation** *noun*.

politick > *adjective* archaic spelling of **POLITIC**.

politico > *noun* (pl. **politicos**) informal, chiefly derogatory a politician, or a person with strong political views.

politics > *plural noun* (usu. treated as sing.) **1** the activities associated with governing a country or area, and with the relations between states. **2** a particular set of political beliefs or principles. **3** activities aimed at gaining power within an organisation: *office politics*. **4** the principles relating to or inherent in a sphere or activity, especially when concerned with power and status: *the politics of gender*.

polity > *noun* (pl. **polities**) **1** a form or process of civil government or constitution. **2** a state as a political entity.

polka /**polk**ə/ > *noun* a lively dance of Bohemian origin in duple time.
COMBINATIONS – **polka dot** each of a number of round dots repeated to form a regular pattern.
ORIGIN – Czech *půlka* 'half-step'.

poll /pōl/ > *noun* **1** the process of voting in an election. **2** a record of the number of votes cast. **3** dialect a person's head. > *verb* **1** record the opinion or vote of. **2** (of an electoral candidate) receive a specified number of votes. **3** cut the horns off (an animal, especially a young cow).
WORDFINDER – plebiscite, referendum (*public poll on a particular question*), straw poll (*an unofficial ballot to test opinion*).
COMBINATIONS – **poll tax 1** a tax levied on every adult, without reference to their income or resources. **2** informal (in the UK) the community charge.
ORIGIN – perhaps from Low German: originally in sense 'head', hence 'number of people ascertained by counting of heads' and then 'counting of heads or of votes'.

pollack /**poll**ək/ (also **pollock**) > *noun* an edible greenish-brown fish of the cod family.
ORIGIN – perhaps Celtic.

pollard /**poll**ərd/ > *verb* cut off the top and branches of (a tree) to encourage new growth. > *noun* a tree that has been pollarded.

pollen > *noun* a powdery substance discharged from the male part of a flower, containing the fertilising agent.
WORDFINDER – palynology (*study of ancient pollen grains*).
COMBINATIONS – **pollen count** a measure of the amount of pollen in the air.
ORIGIN – Latin, 'fine powder'.

pollinate > *verb* deposit pollen in and fertilise (a flower or plant).
DERIVATIVES – **pollination** *noun* **pollinator** *noun*.

pollock > *noun* variant spelling of **POLLACK**.

pollster /**pōl**stər/ > *noun* a person who conducts or analyses opinion polls.

pollute > *verb* **1** contaminate with harmful or poisonous substances. **2** corrupt or defile.
DERIVATIVES – **pollutant** *adjective* & *noun* **polluter** *noun* **pollution** *noun*.
SYNONYMS – **1** adulterate, poison, taint.
ORIGIN – Latin *polluere* 'pollute, defile'.

polly (also **pollie**) > *noun* (pl. **pollies**) Austral./NZ informal a politician.

Pollyanna > *noun* an excessively cheerful or optimistic person.

ORIGIN – the name of the optimistic heroine created by the American author Eleanor H. Porter (1868–1920).

polo > *noun* a game similar to hockey, played on horseback with a long-handled mallet.
COMBINATIONS – **polo neck** Brit. a high, close-fitting, turned-over collar on a sweater. **polo shirt** a casual short-sleeved shirt with a collar and two or three buttons at the neck.
ORIGIN – Balti (the language of Baltistan in the Himalayas), 'ball'.

polonaise /pollə**nayz**/ > *noun* a slow stately dance of Polish origin in triple time. > *adjective* (of a dish, especially a vegetable dish) garnished with chopped hard-boiled egg yolk, breadcrumbs, and parsley.
ORIGIN – French, literally 'Polish'.

polonium /pə**lō**niəm/ > *noun* a rare radioactive metallic chemical element.
ORIGIN – from Latin *Polonia* 'Poland' (the native country of Marie Curie, the element's co-discoverer).

polony /pə**lō**ni/ > *noun* (pl. **polonies**) Brit. another term for **BOLOGNA**.
ORIGIN – apparently an alteration of *Bologna*.

poltergeist /**polt**ərgīst/ > *noun* a supernatural being supposedly responsible for physical disturbances such as throwing objects about.
ORIGIN – German, from *poltern* 'create a disturbance' + *Geist* 'ghost'.

poltroon /pol**troōn**/ > *noun* archaic or literary an utter coward.
ORIGIN – Italian *poltrone*, perhaps from *poltro* 'lazy'.

poly > *noun* (pl. **polys**) informal **1** polythene. **2** Brit. a polytechnic.

poly- > *combining form* **1** many; much: *polychrome*. **2** Chemistry forming names of polymers: *polyester*.
ORIGIN – from Greek *polus* 'much', *polloi* 'many'.

polyandry /**poll**iandri/ > *noun* polygamy in which a woman has more than one husband.
DERIVATIVES – **polyandrous** *adjective*.
ORIGIN – from **POLY-** + Greek *anēr* 'man'.

polyanthus /polli**anth**əss/ > *noun* (pl. same) a cultivated hybrid of the wild primrose and primulas.
ORIGIN – from **POLY-** + Greek *anthos* 'flower'.

polycarbonate > *noun* a synthetic resin in which the polymer units are linked through carbonate groups.

polychlorinated biphenyl > *noun* any of a class of toxic chlorinated organic compounds, formed as waste in some industrial processes.

polychromatic > *adjective* multicoloured.

polychrome > *adjective* painted, printed, or

decorated in several colours. > *noun* varied colouring.

ORIGIN – from **POLY-** + Greek *khrōma* 'colour'.

polyester > *noun* a synthetic resin in which the polymer units are linked by ester groups, used chiefly to make textile fibres.

polyethylene /polliethileen/ > *noun* another term for **POLYTHENE**.

polygamy /pəliggəmi/ > *noun* the practice or custom of having more than one wife or husband at the same time.

DERIVATIVES – **polygamist** *noun* **polygamous** *adjective*.

ORIGIN – from Greek *polugamos* 'often marrying'.

polyglot /polliglot/ > *adjective* knowing, using, or written in several languages. > *noun* a person who knows or uses several languages.

ORIGIN – Greek *poluglōttos*, from *polu-* 'many' + *glōtta* 'tongue'.

polygon /polligən/ > *noun* Geometry a plane figure with at least three straight sides and angles, and typically five or more.

DERIVATIVES – **polygonal** *adjective*.

polygraph > *noun* a machine for recording changes in a person's physiological characteristics, such as pulse and breathing rates, used especially as a lie detector.

polygyny /pəlijini/ > *noun* polygamy in which a man has more than one wife.

DERIVATIVES – **polygynous** *adjective*.

ORIGIN – from **POLY-** + Greek *gunē* 'woman'.

polyhedron /polliheedrən/ > *noun* (pl. **polyhedra** /polliheedrə/ or **polyhedrons**) Geometry a solid figure with many plane faces, typically more than six.

DERIVATIVES – **polyhedral** *adjective*.

ORIGIN – Greek *poluedron* 'many-sided thing'.

polymath /pollimath/ > *noun* a person of wide-ranging knowledge or learning.

DERIVATIVES – **polymathic** *adjective*.

ORIGIN – from Greek *polumathēs* 'having learned much'.

polymer /pollimər/ > *noun* Chemistry a substance with a molecular structure formed from many identical small molecules bonded together.

DERIVATIVES – **polymeric** *adjective* **polymerise** (also **polymerize**) *verb*.

ORIGIN – from Greek *polumeros* 'having many parts'.

polymorphism /pollimorfiz'm/ > *noun* the occurrence of something in several different forms.

DERIVATIVES – **polymorphic** *adjective* **polymorphous** *adjective*.

Polynesian > *noun* 1 a person from Polynesia, a large group of Pacific islands including New Zealand, Hawaii, and Samoa. 2 a group of languages spoken in Polynesia. > *adjective* relating to Polynesia.

polynomial /pollinōmiəl/ > *noun* Mathematics an expression consisting of several terms, especially terms containing different powers of the same variable.

polyp /pollip/ > *noun* 1 Zoology the sedentary form of an organism such as a sea anemone or coral, in some cases forming a distinct stage in the animal's life cycle. 2 Medicine a small growth protruding from a mucous membrane.

DERIVATIVES – **polypoid** *adjective & noun*.

ORIGIN – Greek *polupous* 'cuttlefish, polyp', from *polu-* 'many' + *pous* 'foot'.

polypeptide > *noun* Biochemistry a peptide consisting of many amino-acids bonded together in a chain, e.g. in a protein.

polyphonic /pollifonnik/ > *adjective* 1 having many sounds or voices. 2 Music (especially of vocal music) in two or more parts each having a melody of its own; contrapuntal.

DERIVATIVES – **polyphony** *noun*.

ORIGIN – from Greek *polu-* 'many' + *phōnē* 'voice, sound'.

polypropylene /polliprōpileen/ > *noun* a synthetic resin which is a polymer of propylene.

polyptych /polliptik/ > *noun* a painting, especially an altarpiece, consisting of four or more panels joined by hinges or folds.

ORIGIN – from Greek *poluptukhos* 'having many folds'.

polyrhythm > *noun* Music the use of two or more different rhythms simultaneously.

DERIVATIVES – **polyrhythmic** *adjective*.

polysaccharide /pollisakkərīd/ > *noun* a carbohydrate (e.g. starch or cellulose) whose molecules consist of chains of sugar molecules.

polysemy /polliseemi, pəlisimi/ > *noun* the coexistence of many possible meanings for a word or phrase.

DERIVATIVES – **polysemous** *adjective*.

ORIGIN – from **POLY-** + Greek *sēma* 'sign'.

polystyrene /pollistīreen/ > *noun* a synthetic resin which is a polymer of styrene.

polysyllabic > *adjective* having more than one syllable.

DERIVATIVES – **polysyllable** *noun*.

polytechnic > *noun* an institution of higher education offering courses at degree level or below.

NOTE – In Britain the term **polytechnic** has largely dropped out of use: in 1989 polytechnics gained autonomy from local education authorities and in 1992 became able to call themselves **universities**.

polytheism /pollithee-iz'm/ > *noun* the belief in or worship of more than one god.

DERIVATIVES – **polytheist** *noun* **polytheistic** *adjective*.

ORIGIN – from Greek *polutheos* 'of many gods'.

polythene > *noun* chiefly Brit. a tough, light, flexible plastic made by polymerising ethylene, chiefly used for packaging.

ORIGIN – contraction of *polyethylene*.

polytunnel > *noun* an elongated polythene-covered frame under which plants are grown outdoors.

polyunsaturated > *adjective* referring to fats whose molecules contain several double or triple bonds, believed to be healthier in the diet than monounsaturated fats.

polyurethane /polliyoorəthayn/ > *noun* a synthetic resin in which the polymer units are linked by urethane groups.

polyvalent /pollivaylənt/ > *adjective* having many different functions, forms, or facets.

polyvinyl acetate > *noun* a synthetic resin made by polymerising vinyl acetate, used chiefly in paints and adhesives.

polyvinyl chloride > *noun* a tough chemically resistant synthetic resin made by polymerising vinyl chloride.

Pom > *noun* short for **POMMY**.

pomade /pəmayd/ > *noun* a scented preparation for dressing the hair.

DERIVATIVES – **pomaded** *adjective*.

ORIGIN – French *pommade*, from Latin *pomum* 'apple' (from which it was formerly made).

pomander /pəmandər/ > *noun* a ball or perforated container of mixed aromatic substances used to perfume a room or cupboard or (formerly) carried as protection against infection.

ORIGIN – Old French *pome d'embre*, Latin *pomum de ambra* 'apple of ambergris'.

pomegranate /pommigrannit/ > *noun* a round tropical fruit with a tough golden-orange outer skin and sweet red flesh containing many seeds.

ORIGIN – Old French *pome grenate*, from Latin *pomum granatum* 'apple having many seeds'.

pomelo /pomməlō, pumməlō/ (also **pummelo**) > *noun* (pl. **pomelos**) a large citrus fruit similar to a grapefruit, with a thick yellow skin and bitter pulp.

Pomeranian /pommərayniən/ > *noun* a small breed of dog with long, silky hair, a pointed muzzle, and pricked ears.

ORIGIN – from *Pomerania*, a region of central Europe.

pomfret /pomfrit/ > *noun* an edible deep-bodied sea fish.

ORIGIN – apparently from Portuguese *pampo*.

pomiculture /pōmikulchər/ > *noun* fruit-growing.

ORIGIN – from Latin *pomum* 'fruit'.

pommel /**pumm**'l/ > *noun* **1** the upwardly curving or projecting front part of a saddle. **2** a rounded knob on the end of the handle of a sword, dagger, or old-fashioned gun. > *verb* (**pommelled, pommelling**; US **pommeled, pommeling**) another term for PUMMEL.

COMBINATIONS – **pommel horse** a vaulting horse fitted with a pair of curved handgrips.

ORIGIN – Old French *pomel*, from Latin *pomum* 'fruit, apple'.

Pommy (also **Pommie**) > *noun* (pl. **Pommies**) Austral./NZ informal, derogatory a British person.

ORIGIN – said by some to be short for *pomegranate*, as a near rhyme to *immigrant*.

pomp > *noun* **1** ceremony and splendid display. **2** (**pomps**) archaic vain and boastful display.

ORIGIN – Greek *pompē* 'procession, pomp', from *pempein* 'send'.

pompadour /**pomp**ədoor/ > *noun* **1** a woman's hairstyle in which the hair is turned back off the forehead in a roll. **2** N. Amer. a men's hairstyle in which the hair is combed back from the forehead without a parting.

ORIGIN – named after Madame de *Pompadour* (1721–64), the mistress of Louis XV of France.

pompom (also **pompon**) > *noun* **1** a small woollen ball attached to a garment for decoration. **2** a dahlia, chrysanthemum, or aster with small tightly clustered petals.

ORIGIN – French *pompon* 'tuft, topknot'.

pom-pom > *noun* Brit. a ship's automatic quick-firing two-pounder anti-aircraft gun of the Second World War period.

pompous > *adjective* affectedly grand, solemn, or self-important.

DERIVATIVES – **pomposity** *noun* **pompously** *adverb*.

SYNONYMS – affected, conceited, grand, pretentious, self-important.

ANTONYMS – humble, modest, self-effacing.

ponce Brit. informal > *noun* **1** a man who lives off a prostitute's earnings. **2** derogatory an effeminate man. > *verb* **1** (**ponce about** or **around**) behave in an affected or ineffectual way. **2** (**ponce off**) ask for or obtain (something to which one is not entitled) from (someone).

DERIVATIVES – **poncey** (also **poncy**) *adjective*.

ORIGIN – perhaps from POUNCE¹.

poncho > *noun* (pl. **ponchos**) a garment made of a thick piece of woollen cloth with a slit in the middle for the head.

ORIGIN – Latin American Spanish.

pond > *noun* **1** a fairly small body of still water. **2** (**the pond**) humorous the Atlantic ocean.

COMBINATIONS – **pondweed** a submerged aquatic plant of still or running water.

ORIGIN – alteration of POUND³.

ponder > *verb* consider carefully.

SYNONYMS – contemplate, meditate on, mull over, muse on.

ORIGIN – Latin *ponderare* 'weigh', from *pondus* 'weight'.

ponderable > *adjective* literary worthy of consideration; thought-provoking.

ponderosa /pondərōzə/ (also **ponderosa pine**) > *noun* a tall North American pine tree, planted for wood and as an ornamental.

ORIGIN – feminine of Latin *ponderosus* 'massive'.

ponderous > *adjective* **1** slow and clumsy because of great weight. **2** dull or laborious.

DERIVATIVES – **ponderously** *adverb*.

SYNONYMS – **1** awkward, bulky, hulking, lumpish, unwieldy. **2** laboured, stolid, turgid.

ANTONYMS – **1** graceful. **2** lively.

ORIGIN – Latin *ponderosus*, from *pondus* 'weight'.

pong Brit. informal > *noun* a strong, unpleasant smell. > *verb* have a strongly unpleasant smell.

DERIVATIVES – **pongy** *adjective*.

ponga /pungə/ > *noun* a tree fern found in forests throughout New Zealand.

ORIGIN – Maori.

pongee /ponjee/ > *noun* a soft, unbleached type of Chinese fabric, originally made from uneven threads of raw silk and now also other fibres such as cotton.

ORIGIN – Chinese, originally meaning either 'own loom' or 'home-woven'.

poniard /**pon**yərd/ > *noun* historical a small, slim dagger.

ORIGIN – French *poignard*, from Latin *pugnus* 'fist'.

pons /ponz/ > *noun* (pl. **pontes** /**pon**teez/) Anatomy the part of the brainstem that links the medulla oblongata and the thalamus.

ORIGIN – Latin, 'bridge'.

Pontefract cake /**pon**tifrakt/ > *noun* Brit. a flat, round liquorice sweet.

ORIGIN – named after *Pontefract*, a town in Yorkshire where the sweets were first made.

pontiff /**pon**tiff/ > *noun* the Pope.

ORIGIN – Latin *pontifex* 'high priest', from *pons* 'bridge' + *-fex* (from *facere* 'to make').

pontifical /pon**tiff**ik'l/ > *adjective* **1** papal. **2** characterised by a pompous air of infallibility.

DERIVATIVES – **pontifically** *adverb*.

pontificate > *verb* /pon**tiff**ikayt/ **1** express one's opinions in a pompous and dogmatic way. **2** (in the Roman Catholic Church) officiate as bishop, especially at Mass. > *noun* /pon**tiff**ikət/ (in the Roman Catholic Church) the office or term of office of pope or bishop.

DERIVATIVES – **pontificator** *noun*.

SYNONYMS – *verb* **1** hold forth, sound off.

pontoon¹ /pon**toon**/ > *noun* Brit. a card game in which players try to acquire cards with a value totalling twenty-one.

ORIGIN – probably an alteration of French *vingt-et-un* 'twenty-one'.

pontoon² /pon**toon**/ > *noun* **1** a flat-bottomed boat or hollow metal cylinder used with others to support a temporary bridge or floating landing stage. **2** a bridge or landing stage supported by pontoons. **3** a large flat-bottomed barge or lighter equipped for careening ships and performing salvage work.

ORIGIN – French *ponton*, from Latin *ponto*, from *pons* 'bridge'.

pony > *noun* (pl. **ponies**) **1** a horse of a small breed, especially one below 15 hands. **2** Brit. informal a sum of twenty-five pounds sterling.

COMBINATIONS – **ponytail** a hairstyle in which the hair is drawn back and tied at the back of the head. **pony-trekking** Brit. the leisure activity of riding across country on a pony or horse.

ORIGIN – probably from French *poulenet* 'small foal'.

poo > *exclamation, noun, & verb* variant spelling of POOH.

pooch > *noun* informal a dog.

poodle > *noun* **1** a breed of dog with a curly coat that is usually clipped. **2** Brit. a servile or obsequious person. > *verb* Brit. informal move or travel in a leisurely manner.

ORIGIN – German *Pudelhund*, from *puddeln* 'splash in water'.

poof¹ /poof, pŏof/ (also **pouf, poofter**) > *noun* Brit. informal, derogatory an effeminate or homosexual man.

DERIVATIVES – **poofy** *adjective*.

ORIGIN – perhaps an alteration of *puff* in the obsolete sense 'braggart'.

poof² /pŏof/ (also **pouf**) > *exclamation* describing a sudden disappearance or expressing contemptuous dismissal.

pooh (also **poo**) informal > *exclamation* **1** expressing disgust at an unpleasant smell. **2** expressing impatience or contempt. > *noun* **1** excrement. **2** an act of defecating. > *verb* defecate.

pooh-bah /**pŏo**baa/ > *noun* a pompous person having much influence or holding many offices simultaneously.

ORIGIN – named after a character in Gilbert and Sullivan's *The Mikado* (1885).

pooh-pooh > *verb* informal dismiss as being foolish or impractical.

pool¹ > *noun* **1** a small area of still water. **2** (also **swimming pool**) an artificial pool for swimming in. **3** a small, shallow patch of liquid lying on a surface. **4** a deep place in a river.

pool² > *noun* **1** a shared supply of vehicles, people, commodities, or funds to be drawn on when needed. **2** the total amount of players' stakes in gambling or sweepstakes. **3** (**the pools** or **football pools**) a form of gambling on the results of football matches, in which the winners receive large sums accumulated from entry money. **4** a game played on a billiard table using sixteen balls. **5** an arrangement between competing commercial ventures to fix prices and share business so as to eliminate competition. > *verb* **1** put (money or other assets) into a common fund. **2** share for the benefit of all.

SYNONYMS – *noun* **1** fund, reservoir, stock. *verb* **1** amalgamate, combine, join.

ORIGIN – French *poule* in the sense 'stake, kitty', associated with POOL¹.

poop¹ (also **poop deck**) > *noun* a raised deck at the stern of a ship, especially a sailing ship.

ORIGIN – Latin *puppis* 'stern'.

poop² N. Amer. informal > *noun* excrement. > *verb* defecate.

pooped > *adjective* N. Amer. informal exhausted.

pooper scooper > *noun* an implement for clearing up dog excrement.

poor > *adjective* **1** lacking sufficient money to live at a comfortable or normal standard. **2** of a low or inferior standard or quality. **3** (**poor in**) lacking in. **4** deserving pity or sympathy.

WORDFINDER – impoverish (*make poor*), pauper (*poor person*).

IDIOMS – **the poor man's** —— an inferior or cheaper substitute for the thing specified. **take a poor view of** regard with disapproval.

SYNONYMS – **1** impecunious, impoverished, indigent, penurious, poverty-stricken. **2** inadequate, second-rate, substandard, unsatisfactory. **4** hapless, pitiable, unfortunate.

COMBINATIONS – **poorhouse** Brit. a workhouse. **poor relation** a person or thing that is considered inferior to others of the same type or group. **poor white** derogatory a member of an impoverished white underclass, especially one living in the southern US.

ORIGIN – Old French *poure*, from Latin *pauper*.

poorly > *adverb* in a poor manner. > *adjective* chiefly Brit. unwell.

pootle > *verb* Brit. informal move or travel in a leisurely manner.

ORIGIN – blend of TOOTLE and POODLE.

pop¹ > *verb* (**popped**, **popping**) **1** make or cause to make a sudden sharp, explosive sound. **2** go or come quickly or unexpectedly. **3** put or place quickly. **4** (of a

person's eyes) open wide and appear to bulge. **5** informal take or inject (a drug). > *noun* **1** a sudden sharp, explosive sound. **2** informal, dated or N. Amer. fizzy soft drink.

IDIOMS – **have** (or **take**) **a pop at** informal attack. **pop off** (or Brit. **pop one's clogs**) informal die. **pop the question** informal propose marriage.

pop² > *noun* (also **pop music**) popular modern commercial music, typically with a strong melody and beat. > *adjective* **1** relating to pop music. **2** often derogatory made understandable or simple for the general public: *pop psychology*.

COMBINATIONS – **pop art** art based on modern popular culture and the mass media. **pop culture** commercial culture based on popular taste.

pop³ > *noun* informal, chiefly US one's father.

ORIGIN – abbreviation of POPPA.

popadom > *noun* variant spelling of POPPADOM.

popcorn > *noun* maize kernels which swell up and burst open when heated and are then eaten as a snack.

pope > *noun* (**the Pope**) the Bishop of Rome as head of the Roman Catholic Church.

WORDFINDER – papal, pontifical (*of or relating to popes*); brief (*papal letter on a point of discipline*), bull (*papal edict*), Curia (*papal court at the Vatican*), decretal (*papal decree on a point of law*), encyclical (*letter from the pope to all Catholic bishops*), His/Your Holiness (*title given to pope*), papacy, pontificate (*tenure of office by a pope*).

IDIOMS – **is the Pope a Catholic?** informal used to indicate that something is blatantly obvious.

ORIGIN – Greek *papas* 'bishop, patriarch', variant of *pappas* 'father'.

popery > *noun* derogatory, chiefly archaic Roman Catholicism.

pop-eyed > *adjective* informal having bulging or staring eyes.

popgun > *noun* a child's toy gun which shoots a harmless pellet or cork.

popinjay /**popp**injay/ > *noun* dated a vain or foppish person.

ORIGIN – Old French *papingay* 'parrot', from Arabic.

popish > *adjective* derogatory Roman Catholic.

poplar > *noun* a tall, slender tree, often grown in shelter belts or for wood and pulp.

ORIGIN – Old French *poplier*, from Latin *populus*.

poplin > *noun* a plain-woven fabric, typically a lightweight cotton, with a corded surface.

ORIGIN – obsolete French *papeline*, perhaps from Italian *papalina* 'papal', because first made in the town of Avignon (residence of popes in exile during the 14th century).

popliteal /po**plitt**iəl/ > *adjective* Anatomy relating to or situated in the hollow at the back of the knee.

ORIGIN – Latin *popliteus*, from *poples* 'ham, hock'.

poppa > *noun* N. Amer. informal one's father.

ORIGIN – alteration of PAPA.

poppadom /**popp**ədəm/ (also **poppadum** or **popadom**) > *noun* (in Indian cookery) a large disc of unleavened spiced bread made from ground lentils and fried in oil.

ORIGIN – Tamil.

popper > *noun* **1** Brit. informal a press stud. **2** informal a small vial of amyl nitrite used for inhalation, which makes a popping sound when opened.

poppet > *noun* Brit. informal an endearingly sweet or pretty child.

ORIGIN – Latin *puppa* 'girl, doll'; related to PUPPET.

popping crease > *noun* Cricket a line across the pitch in front of the stumps, behind which the batsman must keep the bat or one foot grounded to avoid the risk of being stumped or run out.

ORIGIN – from POP¹, perhaps in the obsolete sense 'strike'.

poppy¹ > *noun* a plant with showy flowers (typically red, pink, or yellow) and large seed capsules, including species which produce drugs such as opium and codeine.

WORDFINDER – papaveraceous (*of the poppy family*).

COMBINATIONS – **Poppy Day** Brit. Remembrance Sunday.

ORIGIN – from Latin *papaver*.

poppy² > *adjective* (of popular music) tuneful and immediately appealing.

poppycock > *noun* informal nonsense.

ORIGIN – Dutch dialect *pappekak*, from *pap* 'soft' + *kak* 'dung'.

popster > *noun* informal a pop musician.

popsy (also **popsie**) > *noun* (pl. **popsies**) informal, chiefly Brit. an attractive young woman.

ORIGIN – alteration of POPPET.

populace /**pop**yooləss/ > *noun* (treated as sing. or pl.) the general public.

ORIGIN – French, from Italian *popolaccio* 'common people'.

popular > *adjective* **1** liked or admired by many or by a particular group. **2** intended for or suited to the taste or means of the general public. **3** (of a belief or attitude) widely held among the general public. **4** (of political activity) of or carried on by the people as a whole.

DERIVATIVES – **popularity** *noun* **popularly** *adverb*.

SYNONYMS – **1** approved, fashionable, favoured, well liked. **2** accessible, approachable, mass-market, non-technical. **3** common, general, widespread.

COMBINATIONS – **popular front** a political party or coalition representing left-wing elements.

ORIGIN – Latin *popularis*, from *populus* 'people'.

popularise (also **popularize**) > *verb* **1** make popular. **2** make (something scientific or academic) accessible or interesting to the general public.

DERIVATIVES – **popularisation** *noun* **populariser** *noun*.

populate > *verb* **1** form the population of. **2** cause people to settle in.

SYNONYMS – **1** inhabit, live in, occupy, people.

population > *noun* **1** all the inhabitants of a place. **2** a particular group within this: *the immigrant population*. **3** the action of populating an area. **4** Biology a community of interbreeding organisms.

WORDFINDER – demography (*the study of human populations*).

SYNONYMS – **1** citizens, people, residents.

populist > *noun* **1** a politician who tries to appeal to the views of the majority of ordinary people. **2** a person who holds or is concerned with the views of ordinary people. > *adjective* relating to or characteristic of populists.

DERIVATIVES – **populism** *noun*.

populous > *adjective* having a large population.

pop-up > *adjective* **1** (of a book or greetings card) containing folded pictures that rise up to form a three-dimensional scene or figure when opened. **2** (of an electric toaster) that pushes up pieces of toast when ready. **3** Computing (of a menu or other utility) able to be superimposed on the screen being worked on and suppressed rapidly.

porbeagle /**por**beeg'l/ > *noun* a large shark found chiefly in the North Atlantic and Mediterranean.

ORIGIN – Cornish dialect, perhaps from Cornish *porth* 'harbour' + *bugel* 'shepherd'.

porcelain /**por**səlin/ > *noun* **1** a translucent white vitrified ceramic. **2** articles made of this.

ORIGIN – Italian *porcellana* 'cowrie shell', hence 'chinaware' (from its resemblance to the polished surface of cowrie shells).

porch > *noun* **1** a covered shelter projecting over the entrance of a building. **2** N. Amer. a veranda.

ORIGIN – Old French *porche*, from Latin *porticus* 'colonnade'.

porcine /**por**sīn/ > *adjective* of or resembling a pig or pigs.

ORIGIN – Latin *porcinus*, from *porcus* 'pig'.

porcini /**por**cheeni/ > *plural noun* chiefly N. Amer. ceps (wild mushrooms).

ORIGIN – Italian, 'little pigs'.

porcupine /**por**kyoopīn/ > *noun* a large rodent with defensive spines or quills on the body and tail.

ORIGIN – Old French *porc espin*, from Latin *porcus* 'pig' + *spina* 'thorn'.

pore[1] > *noun* a minute opening in the skin or other surface through which gases, liquids, or microscopic particles may pass.

ORIGIN – Greek *poros* 'passage, pore'.

pore[2] > *verb* **1** (**pore over** or **through**) be absorbed in the reading or study of. **2** (**pore on** or **over**) archaic ponder.

SYNONYMS – **1** (**pore over** or **through**) peruse, scrutinise, study.

ORIGIN – perhaps related to PEER[1].

pork > *noun* the flesh of a pig used as food, especially when uncured.

COMBINATIONS – **pork barrel** N. Amer. informal used in reference to the use of government funds for projects designed to win votes. [ORIGIN – from the farmers' practice of keeping a reserve supply of meat in a barrel, later meaning 'a supply of money'.] **pork pie** a raised pie made with minced, cooked pork, eaten cold.

ORIGIN – Latin *porcus* 'pig'.

porker > *noun* **1** a young pig raised and fattened for food. **2** informal, derogatory a fat person.

porky > *adjective* (**porkier, porkiest**) **1** informal fleshy or fat. **2** of or resembling pork. > *noun* (pl. **porkies**) (also **porky-pie**) Brit. rhyming slang a lie.

porn (also **porno**) informal > *noun* pornography. > *adjective* pornographic.

pornography > *noun* commercially produced printed or visual material intended to stimulate sexual excitement.

DERIVATIVES – **pornographer** *noun* **pornographic** *adjective*.

ORIGIN – Greek *pornographos* 'writing about prostitutes', from *pornē* 'prostitute'.

porous /**por**ass/ > *adjective* (of a rock or other material) having minute openings through which liquid or air may pass.

DERIVATIVES – **porosity** *noun*.

ORIGIN – Old French *poreux*, from Latin *porus* 'pore'.

porphyria /porfirria/ > *noun* Medicine a rare hereditary disease in which the body fails to break down haemoglobin properly, causing mental disturbance, sensitivity to light, and excretion of dark pigments in the urine.

ORIGIN – from *porphyrin* (a pigment made by breakdown of haemoglobin), from Greek *porphura* 'purple'.

porphyry /**por**firi/ > *noun* (pl. **porphyries**) a hard, typically reddish igneous rock containing crystals of feldspar.

ORIGIN – Greek *porphuritēs*, from *porphura* 'purple'.

porpoise /**por**pass, **por**poyz/ > *noun* a small toothed whale with a blunt rounded snout.

ORIGIN – Old French *porpois*, from Latin *porcus* 'pig' + *piscis* 'fish'.

porridge > *noun* **1** a dish consisting of oatmeal or another cereal boiled with water or milk. **2** Brit. informal time spent in prison.

ORIGIN – alteration of POTTAGE.

porringer /**porr**injər/ > *noun* historical a small bowl, often with a handle, used for soup or similar dishes.

ORIGIN – Old French *potager*, from *potage* 'contents of a pot'.

port[1] > *noun* **1** a town or city with a harbour. **2** a harbour.

IDIOMS – **any port in a storm** proverb in difficult circumstances one welcomes any source of relief or escape. **port of call** a place where a ship or person stops on a journey.

ORIGIN – Latin *portus* 'harbour'.

port[2] (also **port wine**) > *noun* a sweet, dark fortified wine from Portugal.

ORIGIN – shortened form of *Oporto*, a port in Portugal from which the wine is shipped.

port[3] > *noun* the side of a ship or aircraft that is on the left when one is facing forward. The opposite of STARBOARD. > *verb* turn (a ship or its helm) to port.

wordpower facts

Port

The term **port** replaced the older *larboard* so as to avoid confusion with *starboard*. It probably derives from either **port**[1] or **port**[4]. As the steering apparatus of many early ships was on the right side (the *steereboord* or starboard—*board* was a nautical term for the side of a ship), it would have been convenient to have the entrance or loading hatch on the opposite side (the *lade board* or larboard). The ship would thus be aligned with her larboard side alongside or facing the shore or port: whichever word the term **port** came from, the larboard side would have been identified with *port*.

port[4] > *noun* **1** an opening in the side of a ship for boarding or loading. **2** a porthole. **3** an opening for the passage of steam, liquid, or gas. **4** an opening in the body of an aircraft or in a wall or armoured vehicle through which a gun may be fired. **5** Electronics a socket in a computer network into which a device can be plugged.

ORIGIN – Latin *porta* 'gate'.

port[5] > *verb* **1** Computing transfer (software) from one system or machine to another. **2** Military carry (a weapon) diagonally across and close to the body with the barrel or blade near the left shoulder. > *noun* **1** Military the position required by an order to port a weapon. **2** Computing an instance of porting software.

ORIGIN – Old French 'bearing, gait', from *porter* 'carry'.

port⁶ > *noun* Austral. informal a suitcase or travelling bag.

ORIGIN – abbreviation of **PORTMANTEAU**.

portable > *adjective* **1** able to be easily carried or moved. **2** (of a loan or pension) capable of being transferred or adapted. **3** Computing (of software) able to be ported. > *noun* a portable object.

DERIVATIVES – **portability** *noun*.

SYNONYMS – *adjective* **1** mobile, movable, transferable, transportable.

portage /**por**tij/ > *noun* **1** the carrying of a boat or its cargo between two navigable waters. **2** a place at which this is necessary. > *verb* carry (a boat or its cargo) between navigable waters.

ORIGIN – French, from *porter* 'carry'.

Portakabin > *noun* Brit. trademark a portable building used as a temporary office, classroom, etc.

portal > *noun* **1** a doorway, gate, or gateway, especially a large and imposing one. **2** Computing an Internet site providing a directory of links to other sites.

COMBINATIONS – **portal vein** a vein conveying blood to the liver from the spleen, stomach, pancreas, and intestines.

ORIGIN – from Latin *porta* 'door, gate'.

portamento /portə**men**tō/ > *noun* (pl. **portamentos** or **portamenti** /portə**men**ti/) Music a slide from one note to another, especially in singing or playing the violin.

ORIGIN – Italian, 'carrying'.

portcullis > *noun* a strong, heavy grating that can be lowered to block a gateway.

ORIGIN – from Old French *porte coleice* 'sliding door'.

portend /por**tend**/ > *verb* be a sign or warning that (something momentous or disastrous) is likely to happen.

ORIGIN – Latin *portendere*, from *pro-* 'forth' + *tendere* 'stretch'.

portent /**por**tent/ > *noun* **1** a sign or warning that something momentous or disastrous is likely to happen. **2** archaic an exceptional or wonderful person or thing.

SYNONYMS – **1** harbinger, herald, omen, presage, sign.

portentous > *adjective* **1** of or like a portent. **2** excessively or pompously solemn.

DERIVATIVES – **portentously** *adverb* **portentousness** *noun*.

porter¹ > *noun* **1** a person employed to carry luggage and other loads. **2** a hospital employee who moves equipment or patients. **3** dark brown bitter beer brewed from charred or browned malt. [ORIGIN –

so called because it was originally made for porters.] **4** N. Amer. a sleeping-car attendant.

DERIVATIVES – **porterage** *noun*.

ORIGIN – Old French *porteour*, from Latin *portare* 'carry'.

porter² > *noun* Brit. an employee in charge of the entrance of a large building.

ORIGIN – Old French *portier*, from Latin *porta* 'gate, door'.

porterhouse > *noun* historical, chiefly N. Amer. an establishment at which porter and sometimes steaks were served.

COMBINATIONS – **porterhouse steak** a thick steak cut from the thick end of a sirloin.

portfolio > *noun* (pl. **portfolios**) **1** a thin, flat case for carrying drawings, maps, etc. **2** a set of pieces of creative work intended to demonstrate a person's ability. **3** a range of investments held. **4** the position and duties of a Minister or Secretary of State.

ORIGIN – Italian *portafogli*, from *portare* 'carry' + *foglio* 'leaf'.

porthole > *noun* **1** a small window on the outside of a ship or aircraft. **2** historical an opening for firing a cannon through.

portico /**por**tikō/ > *noun* (pl. **porticoes** or **porticos**) a roof supported by columns at regular intervals, typically attached as a porch to a building.

ORIGIN – Italian, from Latin *porticus* 'porch'.

portière /porti**air**/ > *noun* a curtain hung over a door or doorway.

ORIGIN – French, from *porte* 'door'.

portion > *noun* **1** a part or share of something. **2** an amount of food suitable for or served to one person. **3** archaic a person's destiny or lot. **4** archaic a dowry. > *verb* **1** divide into portions and share out. **2** archaic give a dowry to.

SYNONYMS – *noun* **2** helping, ration, serving.

ORIGIN – Latin, from *pro portione* 'in proportion'.

Portland cement > *noun* cement which resembles Portland stone when hard.

Portland stone > *noun* limestone from the Isle of Portland in Dorset, valued as a building material.

portly > *adjective* (**portlier**, **portliest**) (especially of a man) rather fat.

DERIVATIVES – **portliness** *noun*.

SYNONYMS – corpulent, heavy, plump, rotund, stout.

ORIGIN – first meaning 'stately or dignified': from **PORT⁵** in the sense 'bearing'.

portmanteau /port**man**tō/ > *noun* (pl. **portmanteaus** or **portmanteaux** /port**man**tōz/) **1** a large travelling bag made of stiff leather and opening into two equal parts. **2** (before another noun) consisting of two or more aspects or qualities.

COMBINATIONS – **portmanteau word** a word blending the sounds and combining the meanings of two others, e.g. *brunch* from *lunch* and *breakfast*.

ORIGIN – French *portemanteau*, from *porter* 'carry' + *manteau* 'mantle'.

portrait > *noun* **1** an artistic representation of a person, especially one depicting only the face or head and shoulders. **2** a written or filmed description. **3** a format of printed matter which is higher than it is wide. Compare with **LANDSCAPE**.

DERIVATIVES – **portraitist** *noun* **portraiture** *noun*.

portray > *verb* **1** depict in a work of art or literature. **2** describe in a particular way. **3** (of an actor) play the part of.

DERIVATIVES – **portrayal** *noun* **portrayer** *noun*.

SYNONYMS – **1** depict, illustrate, render, sketch. **2** delineate, depict, describe, evoke, represent.

ORIGIN – Old French *portraire*, from *traire* 'to draw'.

Portuguese* /portyoo**geez**/ > *noun* (pl. same) **1** a person from Portugal. **2** the Romance language of Portugal and Brazil. > *adjective* relating to Portugal.

WORDFINDER – lusophone (*Portuguese-speaking*).

***SPELLING** – *-guese*, not *-gese*: Portu*guese*.

pose > *verb* **1** present or constitute (a problem, danger, question, etc.). **2** assume a particular attitude or position in order to be photographed, painted, or drawn. **3** (**pose as**) pretend to be. **4** behave affectedly in order to impress. > *noun* **1** a position assumed in order to be painted, drawn, or photographed. **2** a way of behaving adopted in order to impress or give a false impression.

SYNONYMS – *noun* **1** attitude, position, posture, stance. **2** act, affectation, pretence.

ORIGIN – Old French *poser*, from Latin *pausare* 'to pause'.

poser > *noun* **1** a person who poses; a poseur. **2** a puzzling question or problem.

poseur /pō**zör**/ > *noun* (fem. **poseuse** /pō**zöz**/) a person who behaves affectedly in order to impress.

ORIGIN – French.

posey (also **posy**) > *adjective* informal pretentious.

posh informal > *adjective* **1** elegant or stylishly luxurious. **2** chiefly Brit. upper-class. > *adverb* Brit. in an upper-class way. > *verb* (**posh up**) Brit. smarten (something) up.

DERIVATIVES – **poshly** *adverb* **poshness** *noun*.

ORIGIN – perhaps from slang *posh*, meaning either 'money' or 'a dandy'; there is no basis for the popular theory that *posh* is formed from the initials of *port out starboard home* (referring to a supposed practice of using the more comfortable accommodation, out of the heat of the sun, on ships between England and India).

posit /pozzit/ > *verb* (**posited**, **positing**) **1** put forward as fact or as a basis for argument. **2** put in position; place.

position > *noun* **1** a place where someone or something is located or has been put. **2** the correct place. **3** a way in which someone or something is placed or arranged. **4** a situation or set of circumstances. **5** high rank or social standing. **6** a job. **7** a point of view or attitude. **8** a place where part of a military force is posted. > *verb* put or arrange in a particular position.
DERIVATIVES – **positional** *adjective* **positionally** *adverb*.
SYNONYMS – *noun* **1** location, site, situation. **4** circumstances, condition, situation, state. *verb* arrange, locate, place, put, set, situate.
ORIGIN – Latin, from *ponere* 'to place'.

positive > *adjective* **1** characterised by the presence rather than the absence of distinguishing features. **2** expressing or implying affirmation, agreement, or permission. **3** constructive, optimistic, or confident. **4** with no possibility of doubt; certain. **5** (of a quantity) greater than zero. **6** of, containing, or producing the kind of electric charge opposite to that carried by electrons. **7** (of a photographic image) showing light and shade or colours true to the original. **8** Grammar (of an adjective or adverb) expressing a quality in its basic, primary degree. Contrasted with COMPARATIVE and SUPERLATIVE. > *noun* a positive quality, attribute, or image.
DERIVATIVES – **positively** *adverb* **positiveness** *noun* **positivity** *noun*.
COMBINATIONS – **positive discrimination** Brit. the deliberate favouring of individuals belonging to groups which suffer discrimination. **positive pole** the north-seeking pole of a magnet. **positive sign** the plus sign (+). **positive vetting** Brit. the investigation of the background and character of a candidate for a civil service post that involves access to secret material.

positivism > *noun* Philosophy **1** a system recognising only that which can be scientifically verified or logically proved, and therefore rejecting metaphysics and theism. **2** short for *logical positivism*.
DERIVATIVES – **positivist** *noun & adjective* **positivistic** *adjective*.

positron /pozzitron/ > *noun* Physics a subatomic particle with the same mass as an electron and a numerically equal but positive charge.

wordpower facts
Positive

The word **positive** came into the English language in the Middle Ages from Old French *positif*, which was from the Latin verb *ponere* 'to place', the source of such words as **position**, **post**, **posture**, **compose**, **dispose**, **expose**, **impose**, **oppose**, and **suppose**. The original sense of **positive** referred to laws as being formally 'laid down', which gave rise to the sense 'explicitly laid down and admitting no question', hence 'very sure, convinced'. The word was first applied to electricity in the 18th century, the static charge produced by rubbing glass with silk being designated **positive** and its opposite, produced by rubbing resin or amber, **negative**. As a result of this arbitrary choice we now regard atomic nuclei as positive and electrons as negative, but it could have been the other way round.

posse /possi/ > *noun* **1** N. Amer. historical a body of men summoned by a sheriff to enforce the law. **2** (also **posse comitatus** /possi kommitaytəss/) Brit. historical the men of a county forming a body whom the sheriff could summon. **3** informal a group of people with a common characteristic, interest, or purpose.

wordpower facts
Posse

Although it is associated principally with the American Wild West, **posse** is actually a Latin word meaning 'be able', which is the root of **possible**, **potent**, and **power**. In medieval Latin it became a noun with the meaning 'power, armed force', and in the 16th century it entered English in the phrase *posse comitatus*, literally 'force of the county'. This denoted the whole body of males over the age of 15 in a county (excluding peers, clergymen, and the infirm) who could be summoned by the sheriff for such purposes as stopping a riot. The simple form **posse** emerged at the end of the 17th century, and gradually became restricted to American use.

possess > *verb* **1** have (something) as belonging to one. **2** (also **be possessed of**) have as an ability, quality, or characteristic. **3** (of a demon or spirit) have complete power over. **4** (of an emotion, idea, etc.) dominate the mind of.
IDIOMS – **what possessed you?** used to express surprise at a very unwise action.
DERIVATIVES – **possessor** *noun* **possessory** *adjective*.
SYNONYMS – **1** have, hold, own. **2** be blessed with, boast, be endowed with, have. **4** consume, dominate, haunt, obsess, preoccupy.
ORIGIN – Old French *possesser*, from Latin *possidere* 'occupy, hold'.

possession > *noun* **1** the state of possessing something. **2** a thing owned or possessed. **3** the state of being possessed by a demon, emotion, etc. **4** (in sport) temporary control of the ball by a player or team.

possessive > *adjective* **1** demanding someone's total attention and love. **2** unwilling to share one's possessions. **3** Grammar expressing possession.
DERIVATIVES – **possessively** *adverb* **possessiveness** *noun*.
SYNONYMS – **1** controlling, dominating, jealous, overprotective, proprietorial.
COMBINATIONS – **possessive determiner** Grammar a determiner indicating possession, for example *my*. **possessive pronoun** Grammar a pronoun indicating possession, for example *mine*.

posset /possit/ > *noun* **1** a drink made of hot milk curdled with ale or wine and flavoured with spices. **2** milk regurgitated by a baby. > *verb* (**possetted**, **possetting**) (of a baby) regurgitate curdled milk.

possibility > *noun* (pl. **possibilities**) **1** a thing that is possible. **2** the state or fact of being possible. **3** (**possibilities**) unspecified qualities of a promising nature.

possible > *adjective* **1** capable of existing, happening, or being achieved. **2** that may be so, but that is not certain or probable. > *noun* **1** a possible candidate for a job or member of a team. **2** (**the possible**) that which is likely or achievable.
SYNONYMS – *adjective* **1** achievable, feasible, practicable, workable. **2** conceivable, imaginable, plausible.
ORIGIN – Latin *possibilis*, from *posse* 'be able'.

possibly > *adverb* **1** perhaps. **2** in accordance with what is possible.

possum > *noun* **1** an Australasian marsupial that lives in trees. **2** N. Amer. informal an opossum.
IDIOMS – **play possum 1** feign unconsciousness or death (as an opossum does when threatened). **2** feign ignorance.
ORIGIN – shortening of OPOSSUM.

post¹ > *noun* **1** a long, sturdy upright piece of timber or metal used as a support or a marker. **2** (**the post**) a starting post or winning post. > *verb* **1** display (a notice) in a public place. **2** announce or publish. **3** achieve or record (a score or result).

ORIGIN – Latin *postis* 'doorpost'.

post² > *noun* chiefly Brit. **1** the official service or system that delivers letters and parcels. **2** letters and parcels delivered. **3** a single collection or delivery of post. > *verb* **1** chiefly Brit. send via the postal system. **2** (in bookkeeping) enter (an item) in a ledger.

IDIOMS – **keep posted** keep (someone) informed of the latest developments or news.

COMBINATIONS – **postbag** Brit. a mailbag. **postbox** a large public box into which letters are posted for collection by the post office. **postcode** Brit. a group of letters and numbers added to a postal address to assist the sorting of mail.

ORIGIN – Italian *posta*, from Latin *ponere* 'to place'.

post³ > *noun* **1** a place where someone is on duty or where an activity is carried out. **2** a job. > *verb* **1** station in a particular place. **2** send to a place to take up an appointment.

ORIGIN – Italian *posto*, from Latin *ponere* 'to place'.

post- > *prefix* after in time or order: *post-date*.

ORIGIN – from Latin *post* 'after, behind'.

postage > *noun* **1** the sending of letters and parcels by post. **2** the amount required to send something by post.

postal > *adjective* relating to or carried out by post.

DERIVATIVES – **postally** *adverb*.

COMBINATIONS – **postal code** a postcode. **postal order** Brit. an order for payment of a specified sum to a named person, issued by the Post Office.

postbellum > *adjective* occurring or existing after a particular war.

ORIGIN – from Latin *post* 'after' and *bellum* 'war'.

postcard > *noun* a card for sending a message by post without an envelope.

WORDFINDER – deltiologist (*person who collects postcards*).

post-chaise /pōst **shayz**/ > *noun* (pl. **post-chaises** pronunc. same) historical a horse-drawn carriage for transporting passengers or mail.

post-coital > *adjective* occurring or done after sexual intercourse.

DERIVATIVES – **post-coitally** *adverb*.

post-date > *verb* **1** assign a date later than the actual one to (a document or event). **2** occur or come at a later date than.

postdoctoral > *adjective* (of research) undertaken after the completion of a doctorate.

poster > *noun* a large printed picture or notice used for decoration or advertisement.

COMBINATIONS – **poster paint** an opaque paint with a water-soluble binder.

poste restante /pōst **rest**ənt, restoNt/ > *noun* Brit. a department in a post office that keeps letters until they are collected by the person they are addressed to.

ORIGIN – French, 'mail remaining'.

posterior > *adjective* **1** chiefly Anatomy further back in position; of or nearer the rear or hind end. The opposite of ANTERIOR. **2** formal coming after in time or order; later. > *noun* humorous a person's bottom.

ORIGIN – Latin, from *posterus* 'following'.

posterity > *noun* all future generations of people.

postern /**post**ərn/ > *noun* a back or side entrance.

ORIGIN – Old French *posterne*, from Latin *posterus* 'following'.

postgraduate > *adjective* relating to study undertaken after completing a first degree. > *noun* a person engaged in postgraduate study.

post-haste > *adverb* with great speed.

ORIGIN – from the direction 'haste, post, haste', formerly given on letters.

post horn > *noun* historical a valveless horn used to signal the arrival or departure of a mounted courier or mail coach.

posthumous /**post**yooməss/ > *adjective* occurring, awarded, or appearing after the death of the originator.

DERIVATIVES – **posthumously** *adverb*.

ORIGIN – Latin *postumus* 'last', later associated with *humus* 'ground'.

postilion /pos**til**yən/ (also **postillion**) > *noun* the rider of the leading nearside horse of a team or pair drawing a coach, when there is no coachman.

ORIGIN – French *postillon*, from Italian *postiglione* 'post boy'.

post-Impressionism > *noun* a late 19th-century and early 20th-century style of art in which colour, line, and form were used to express an emotional response.

DERIVATIVES – **post-Impressionist** *noun* & *adjective*.

post-industrial > *adjective* (of an economy or society) no longer relying on heavy industry.

posting > *noun* chiefly Brit. an appointment to a job, especially one abroad or in the armed forces.

postlude > *noun* Music a concluding piece of music.

postman (or **postwoman**) > *noun* Brit. a person who is employed to deliver or collect post.

COMBINATIONS – **postman's knock** Brit. a children's game in which imaginary letters are delivered in exchange for kisses.

postmark > *noun* an official mark stamped on a letter or parcel, giving the date of

posting and cancelling the postage stamp. > *verb* stamp with a postmark.

postmaster (or **postmistress**) > *noun* a person in charge of a post office.

COMBINATIONS – **postmaster general** the head of a country's postal service.

postmillennialism > *noun* (among fundamentalist Christians) the doctrine that the Second Coming of Christ will be the culmination of the prophesied millennium of blessedness.

postmodernism > *noun* an artistic style and concept characterised by distrust of theories and ideologies and by the drawing of attention to conventions.

DERIVATIVES – **postmodern** *adjective* **postmodernist** *noun* & *adjective* **postmodernity** *noun*.

post-mortem > *noun* **1** an examination of a dead body to determine the cause of death. **2** an analysis of an event made after it has occurred. > *adjective* happening after death.

ORIGIN – Latin, 'after death'.

post-natal > *adjective* occurring in or relating to the period after childbirth.

post office > *noun* **1** the public department or corporation responsible for postal services and (in some countries) telecommunications. **2** a building where postal business is transacted.

COMBINATIONS – **post office box** a numbered box in a post office where letters are kept until called for.

post-operative > *adjective* relating to the period following a surgical operation.

postpartum /pōst**paar**təm/ > *adjective* relating to the period following childbirth or the birth of young.

ORIGIN – from Latin *post partum* 'after childbirth'.

postpone > *verb* arrange for (something) to take place at a time later than that first scheduled.

DERIVATIVES – **postponement** *noun*.

SYNONYMS – defer, delay, hold over, put back.

ORIGIN – Latin *postponere*, from *post* 'after' + *ponere* 'to place'.

postpositive > *adjective* (of a word) placed after or as a suffix on the word that it relates to.

postprandial /pōst**pran**diəl/ > *adjective* **1** formal or humorous during or relating to the period after a meal. **2** Medicine occurring after a meal.

ORIGIN – from POST- + Latin *prandium* 'a meal'.

postscript > *noun* an additional remark at the end of a letter, following the signature.

ORIGIN – Latin *postscriptum*, from *postscribere* 'write under, add'.

755

post-structuralism > *noun* an extension and critique of structuralism, especially as used in critical textual analysis.

DERIVATIVES – **post-structural** *adjective* **post-structuralist** *noun & adjective*.

post-traumatic stress disorder > *noun* a condition of persistent stress occurring as a result of injury or severe psychological shock.

postulant /**pos**tyoolənt/ > *noun* a candidate seeking admission into a religious order.

postulate > *verb* /**pos**tyoolayt/ **1** suggest or assume the existence, fact, or truth of (something) as a basis for reasoning or belief. **2** nominate or elect to an ecclesiastical office subject to the sanction of a higher authority. > *noun* /**pos**tyoolət/ a thing postulated.

DERIVATIVES – **postulation** *noun*.

SYNONYMS – *verb* **1** assume, hypothesise, posit, propose, suppose.

ORIGIN – Latin *postulare* 'ask'.

posture > *noun* **1** a particular position of the body. **2** the way in which a person holds their body. **3** an approach or attitude towards something. > *verb* behave in a way that is intended to impress or mislead others.

DERIVATIVES – **postural** *adjective*.

SYNONYMS – *noun* **1** pose, position, stance. **2** bearing, carriage, comportment, deportment.

ORIGIN – Latin *positura*, from *ponere* 'to place'.

postviral syndrome (also **postviral fatigue syndrome**) > *noun* myalgic encephalomyelitis after infection by a virus.

posy¹ > *noun* (pl. **posies**) a small bunch of flowers.

ORIGIN – contraction of **POESY**: originally meaning 'motto or line of verse inscribed inside a ring'.

posy² > *adjective* variant spelling of **POSEY**.

pot¹ > *noun* **1** a rounded or cylindrical container, especially one of ceramic, used for storage or cooking. **2** a flowerpot. **3** (**the pot**) the total sum of the bets made on a round in poker, brag, etc. **4** Billiards & Snooker a shot in which a player strikes a ball into a pocket. **5** (in rugby) an attempt to score a goal with a kick. > *verb* (**potted, potting**) **1** plant in a pot. **2** preserve (food) in a sealed pot or jar. **3** make pottery. **4** Billiards & Snooker strike (a ball) into a pocket. **5** score (a goal). **6** informal hit or kill by shooting.

IDIOMS – **go to pot** informal deteriorate through neglect. **a watched pot never boils** proverb time seems to drag endlessly when you're waiting anxiously for something to happen.

COMBINATIONS – **pot belly** a protruding stomach. **pot-bound** (of a plant) having roots which fill the pot, leaving no room for them to expand. **pot luck** the chance that whatever is available will prove to be good or acceptable. **pot roast** a piece of meat cooked slowly in a covered pot. **potting shed** a shed used for potting plants and storing garden tools and supplies.

pot² > *noun* informal cannabis.

ORIGIN – probably from Mexican Spanish *potiguaya* 'cannabis leaves'.

potable /**pō**təb'l/ > *adjective* formal drinkable.

DERIVATIVES – **potability** *noun*.

ORIGIN – French, from Latin *potare* 'to drink'.

potage /po**taazh**/ > *noun* thick soup.

ORIGIN – French; compare with **POTTAGE**.

potash > *noun* an alkaline potassium compound, especially potassium carbonate or hydroxide.

ORIGIN – from *pot-ashes*, because originally obtained by leaching vegetable ashes and evaporating the solution in iron pots.

potassium /pə**tass**iəm/ > *noun* a soft silvery-white reactive metallic chemical element of the alkali-metal group.

COMBINATIONS – **potassium hydroxide** a strongly alkaline white compound used in many industrial processes, e.g. soap manufacture.

ORIGIN – from **POTASH**.

potation /pō**tay**sh'n/ > *noun* archaic or humorous **1** the action of drinking alcohol. **2** an alcoholic drink.

ORIGIN – Latin, from *potare* 'to drink'.

potato* > *noun* (pl. **potatoes**) a starchy plant tuber which is cooked and eaten as a vegetable.

WORDFINDER – *varieties of potato:* Cara, Desiree, Estima, King Edward, Maris Piper; aquavit (*alcoholic spirit made from potatoes*), duchesse (*potatoes mashed with egg yolk and baked*), latke (*a Jewish potato pancake*), lyonnaise (*sliced potatoes cooked with onions*), rösti (*Swiss-style fried potatoes*), solanine (*a toxic substance in green potatoes*).

*****SPELLING – no *e* on the end: potat*o*.

ORIGIN – Spanish *patata* 'sweet potato', from Taino (an extinct Caribbean language).

pot-au-feu /potō**fö**/ > *noun* a French soup of meat and vegetables cooked in a large pot.

ORIGIN – French, 'pot on the fire'.

potboiler > *noun* informal a book, film, etc. produced purely to make the writer or artist a living.

poteen /po**teen**/ > *noun* chiefly Irish illicitly made whiskey.

ORIGIN – from Irish *fuisce poitín* 'little pot of whiskey'.

potent > *adjective* **1** having great power, influence, or effect. **2** (of a male) able to achieve an erection or to reach an orgasm.

DERIVATIVES – **potency** *noun* **potently** *adverb*.

SYNONYMS – **1** mighty, powerful, strong, vigorous.

ANTONYMS – **1** impotent, weak.

ORIGIN – from Latin *posse* 'be powerful, be able'.

potentate > *noun* a monarch or ruler.

potential > *adjective* having the capacity to develop into something in the future. > *noun* **1** qualities or abilities that may be developed and lead to future success or usefulness. **2** (often **potential for** or **to do**) the possibility of something happening or of someone doing something in the future. **3** Physics the quantity determining the energy of mass in a gravitational field or of charge in an electric field.

DERIVATIVES – **potentiality** *noun* **potentially** *adverb*.

SYNONYMS – *adjective* latent, possible, probable, prospective. *noun* **1** capability, promise, prospects.

COMBINATIONS – **potential difference** Physics the difference of electrical potential between two points. **potential energy** Physics energy possessed by a body by virtue of its position or state.

ORIGIN – Latin *potentialis*, from *potentia* 'power'.

potentiate /pə**ten**shiayt/ > *verb* increase the power or effect of (a drug, physiological reaction, etc.).

potentilla /pōtən**till**ə/ > *noun* a small shrub with yellow or red flowers.

ORIGIN – from Latin *posse* 'be powerful or able' (with reference to its herbal qualities).

potentiometer /pətenshi**omm**itər/ > *noun* an instrument for measuring or adjusting an electromotive force.

pother /**poth**ər/ > *noun* a commotion or fuss.

pothole > *noun* **1** a deep natural underground cave formed by the eroding action of water. **2** a hole in a road surface. > *verb* Brit. explore underground potholes as a pastime.

DERIVATIVES – **potholed** *adjective* **potholer** *noun* **potholing** *noun*.

ORIGIN – from dialect *pot* 'pit'.

potion > *noun* a liquid with healing, magical, or poisonous properties.

SYNONYMS – brew, concoction, draught, elixir, philtre.

ORIGIN – Latin, 'drink, poisonous draught'; related to *potare* 'to drink'.

potlatch > *noun* (among some North American Indian peoples) a ceremonial feast at which possessions are given away or destroyed to display wealth.

ORIGIN – Nootka (an American Indian language of Vancouver Island).

potoroo /pottə**rōō**/ > *noun* a small long-nosed marsupial with long hindlimbs, native to mainland Australia and Tasmania.

ORIGIN – probably from Dharuk (an Aboriginal language).

pot-pourri /pō pooree/ > *noun* (pl. **pot-pourris**) **1** a mixture of dried petals and spices placed in a bowl to perfume a room. **2** a mixture of things; a medley.

ORIGIN – French, 'rotten pot': originally meaning 'stew made of different kinds of meat'.

potsherd /**pot**sherd/ > *noun* a piece of broken pottery.

potshot > *noun* a shot aimed unexpectedly or at random.

ORIGIN – from the idea of a *shot* at an animal intended for the *pot*, i.e. for food, rather than for display (which would require skilled shooting).

pottage > *noun* archaic soup or stew.

ORIGIN – Old French *potage* 'that which is put into a pot'; compare with **POTAGE** and **PORRIDGE**.

potted > *adjective* **1** grown or preserved in a pot. **2** (of an account) put into a short, accessible form.

potter¹ > *verb* **1** occupy oneself in a desultory but pleasant manner. **2** move or go in a casual, unhurried way. > *noun* a spell of pottering.

ORIGIN – first meaning 'poke repeatedly': from *pote* 'to push, kick, or poke'.

potter² > *noun* a person who makes ceramic ware.

COMBINATIONS – **potter's field** historical a burial place for paupers and strangers. [ORIGIN – with biblical allusion to the Gospel of Matthew, chapter 27.] **potter's wheel** a horizontal revolving disc on which wet clay is shaped into pots, bowls, etc.

pottery > *noun* (pl. **potteries**) **1** articles made of clay hardened by heating. **2** the craft or profession of making such ware. **3** a factory or workshop where such ware is made.

WORDFINDER – *types of pottery:* china, earthenware, faience, maiolica, majolica, stoneware, terracotta; biscuit, bisque (*unglazed pottery*), ceramic (*pottery made from clay hardened by heat*), greenware (*unfired pottery*), saggar (*box to protect pottery during firing*), slip (*coloured clay used to decorate pottery*).

potty¹ > *adjective* (**pottier**, **pottiest**) informal, chiefly Brit. **1** foolish; crazy. **2** extremely enthusiastic about someone or something.

DERIVATIVES – **pottiness** *noun*.

potty² > *noun* (pl. **potties**) informal a receptacle for a child to urinate or defecate into.

pouch > *noun* **1** a small, flexible bag. **2** a pocket-like receptacle in an animal's body, especially that in which marsupials carry their young. > *verb* put, make, or form into a pouch.

DERIVATIVES – **pouched** *adjective* **pouchy** *adjective*.

ORIGIN – from Old French *poche* 'bag'.

pouf¹ > *noun* variant spelling of **POOF¹** or **POUFFE**. > *exclamation* variant spelling of **POOF²**.

pouf² /poof/ > *noun* **1** a part of a dress in which a large mass of material has been gathered so that it stands away from the body. **2** a bouffant hairstyle.

ORIGIN – French.

pouffe /poof/ (also **pouf**) > *noun* a cushioned footstool or low seat with no back.

ORIGIN – French.

poult /pōlt/ > *noun* Farming a young domestic fowl being raised for food.

ORIGIN – contraction of **PULLET**.

poulterer > *noun* Brit. a dealer in poultry.

poultice /**pōl**tiss/ > *noun* a soft, moist mass applied to a part of the body to relieve inflammation. > *verb* apply a poultice to.

ORIGIN – from Latin *puls* 'pottage, pap'.

poultry /**pōl**tri/ > *noun* chickens, turkeys, ducks, and geese; domestic fowl.

ORIGIN – Old French *pouletrie*, from *poulet* 'pullet'.

pounce¹ > *verb* **1** spring or swoop suddenly to catch prey. **2** take swift advantage of a mistake or sign of weakness. > *noun* an act of pouncing.

pounce² > *noun* **1** a fine powder formerly used to prevent ink from spreading on paper or to prepare parchment to receive writing. **2** a fine powder dusted over a perforated pattern to transfer the design to the surface beneath.

ORIGIN – French *poncer*, from Latin *pumex* 'pumice'.

pound¹ > *noun* **1** a unit of weight equal to 16 oz avoirdupois (0.4536 kg), or 12 oz troy (0.3732 kg). **2** (also **pound sterling**, pl. **pounds sterling**) the basic monetary unit of the UK, equal to 100 pence. **3** another term for **PUNT⁴**. **4** the basic monetary unit of several Middle Eastern countries, equal to 100 piastres. **5** the basic monetary unit of Cyprus, equal to 100 cents. **6** a monetary unit of the Sudan, equal to one tenth of a dinar.

IDIOMS – **one's pound of flesh** something to which one is strictly entitled, but which it is ruthless to demand. [ORIGIN – with allusion to Shakespeare's *Merchant of Venice*.]

DERIVATIVES – **pounder** *noun*.

COMBINATIONS – **pound cake** a rich cake originally made with a pound of each chief ingredient.

ORIGIN – from Latin *libra pondo*, denoting a Roman 'pound weight' of 12 ounces.

pound² > *verb* **1** strike or hit heavily and repeatedly. **2** crush or grind into a powder or paste. **3** walk or run with heavy steps. **4** beat or throb with a strong, regular rhythm. **5** (**pound out**) produce (a document or piece of music) with heavy strokes on a keyboard or instrument. **6** informal defeat resoundingly.

SYNONYMS – **1** batter, beat, hammer, pummel. **2** crush, grind, mill, pulp, pulverise.

pound³ > *noun* **1** a place where stray dogs or illegally parked vehicles may officially be taken and kept until claimed. **2** archaic a trap or prison.

poundage > *noun* Brit. **1** a commission of a particular amount of the sum involved in a transaction. **2** a percentage of the total earnings of a business, paid as wages. **3** weight.

pour > *verb* **1** flow or cause to flow in a steady stream. **2** (of rain) fall heavily. **3** prepare and serve (a drink). **4** come or go in a steady stream. **5** (**pour out**) express (one's feelings) in an unrestrained way.

IDIOMS – **pour oil on troubled waters** try to calm a dispute with placatory words. **it never rains but it pours** proverb misfortunes or difficult situations tend to arrive all at the same time.

DERIVATIVES – **pourer** *noun*.

poussin /poosaN/ > *noun* a chicken killed young for eating.

ORIGIN – French.

pout > *verb* push one's lips forward as an expression of petulant annoyance or in order to make oneself look sexually attractive. > *noun* a pouting expression.

DERIVATIVES – **pouty** *adjective*.

ORIGIN – perhaps from Swedish dialect *puta* 'be inflated'.

pouter > *noun* a kind of pigeon that is able to inflate its crop to a considerable extent.

poverty > *noun* **1** the state of being very poor. **2** the state of being inferior in quality or insufficient in amount.

SYNONYMS – **1** beggary, destitution, impoverishment, indigence, pennilessness, penury. **2** inferiority, insufficiency, paucity, scarcity.

ANTONYMS – wealth.

COMBINATIONS – **poverty trap** Brit. a situation in which an increase in someone's income is offset by a consequent loss of state benefits.

ORIGIN – Old French *poverte*, from Latin *paupertas*, from *pauper* 'poor'.

POW > *abbreviation* prisoner of war.

powder > *noun* **1** fine, dry particles produced by the grinding, crushing, or disintegration of a solid substance. **2** a facial cosmetic in the form of powder. **3** dated a medicine in the form of powder. **4** loose, dry, newly fallen snow. **5** gunpowder. > *verb* **1** sprinkle or cover with powder. **2** reduce to a powder.

WORDFINDER – pulverise (*reduce to a powder*).

IDIOMS – **keep one's powder dry** remain cautious and alert. **take a powder** N. Amer. informal depart quickly.

DERIVATIVES – **powdery** *adjective*.

COMBINATIONS – **powder blue** a soft, pale blue. **powder keg 1** a barrel of gunpowder. **2** a potentially explosive situation. **powder monkey 1** historical a boy employed on a sailing warship to carry powder to the guns. **2** N. Amer. a person who works with explosives. **powder puff 1** a soft pad for applying powder to the face. **2** informal an ineffectual person or thing. **powder room** euphemistic a women's toilet in a public building.

ORIGIN – Old French *poudre*, from Latin *pulvis* 'dust'.

power > *noun* **1** the ability to do something or act in a particular way. **2** the capacity to influence other people or the course of events. **3** a right or authority given or delegated to a person or body. **4** political authority or control. **5** physical strength or force. **6** a country viewed in terms of its international influence and its military strength: *a world power*. **7** the capacity or performance of an engine or other device. **8** energy that is produced by mechanical, electrical, or other means. **9** Physics the rate of doing work, measured in watts or horse power. **10** Mathematics the product obtained when a number is multiplied by itself a certain number of times. > *verb* **1** supply with power. **2** (**power up** or **down**) switch (a device) on or off. **3** move with speed or force.

WORDFINDER – éminence grise (*a person exercising hidden power*), megalomaniac (*a person obsessed with exercising power*), omnipotence (*unlimited power*), usurp (*seize power unlawfully*).

IDIOMS – **do someone a power of good** informal be very beneficial to someone. **the powers that be** the authorities. [ORIGIN – with biblical allusion to the Epistle to the Romans, chapter 13.]

DERIVATIVES – **powered** *adjective*.

SYNONYMS – *noun* **1** ability, capability, capacity, faculty. **2** authority, influence; informal clout. **3** authorisation, authority, licence, right, warrant. **5** force, might, potency, powerfulness, strength.

ANTONYMS – *noun* **5** impotence, weakness.

COMBINATIONS – **power broker** a person who exerts influence to affect the distribution of political or economic power. **power cut** a temporary withdrawal or failure of an electrical power supply. **power pack 1** a unit which stores and supplies electrical power. **2** a transformer for converting an alternating current (from the mains) to a direct current. **power plant 1** a power station. **2** an apparatus which provides power for a machine, building, etc. **power play 1** tactics exhibiting or intended to increase a person's power. **2** attacking tactics in a team sport involving the concentration of players in a particular area. **power station** an installation where electrical power is generated. **power steering** steering aided by power from the vehicle's engine. **power train** the mechanism that transmits the drive from the engine of a vehicle to its axle.

ORIGIN – Old French *poeir*, from Latin *posse* 'be able'.

powerboat > *noun* a fast motor boat.

powerful > *adjective* having power. > *adverb* chiefly dialect very.

DERIVATIVES – **powerfully** *adverb*.

SYNONYMS – *adjective* dominant, forceful, influential, mighty, potent, strong.

ANTONYMS – *adjective* powerless, weak.

powerhouse > *noun* a person or thing having great energy or power.

powerless > *adjective* without ability, influence, or power.

DERIVATIVES – **powerlessly** *adverb* **powerlessness** *noun*.

SYNONYMS – helpless, impotent, ineffectual, weak.

ANTONYMS – powerful, strong.

Powhatan /ˈpowətan/ > *noun* (pl. same or **Powhatans**) a member of an American Indian people of eastern Virginia.

ORIGIN – Virginia Algonquian.

powwow > *noun* **1** a North American Indian ceremony involving feasting and dancing. **2** informal a meeting for discussion among friends or colleagues. > *verb* informal hold a powwow.

ORIGIN – from a word in Narragansett meaning 'magician'.

pox > *noun* **1** any disease caused by a virus and producing a rash of pimples that become pus-filled and leave pockmarks on healing. **2** (**the pox**) historical smallpox. **3** (**the pox**) informal syphilis.

IDIOMS – **a pox on** —— archaic expressing anger with someone.

ORIGIN – alteration of *pocks*, plural of POCK.

poxy > *adjective* (**poxier, poxiest**) informal, chiefly Brit. of poor quality; worthless.

pp > *abbreviation* **1** (**pp.**) pages. **2** (also **p.p.**) per procurationem (used when signing a letter on someone else's behalf). [ORIGIN – Latin, 'through the agency of'.] **3** Music pianissimo.

NOTE – the correct way to use **pp** when signing a letter on someone else's behalf is to place **pp** before one's own name, rather than before the name of the other person. However, **pp** is now often taken to mean 'on behalf of' and placed before the name of the person who has not signed.

PPE > *abbreviation* philosophy, politics, and economics.

ppm > *abbreviation* **1** part(s) per million. **2** Computing page(s) per minute.

PPS > *abbreviation* **1** post (additional) postscript. **2** Brit. Parliamentary Private Secretary.

PPV > *abbreviation* pay-per-view.

PR > *abbreviation* **1** proportional representation. **2** public relations.

Pr > *symbol* the chemical element praseodymium.

practicable > *adjective* able to be done or put into practice successfully.

DERIVATIVES – **practicability** *noun* **practicably** *adverb*.

USAGE – although they are related, **practicable** and **practical** do not mean exactly the same thing: **practicable** means 'able to be done successfully', whereas the closest senses of **practical** are 'likely to be effective, feasible' and 'suitable for a particular purpose'.

practical > *adjective* **1** of or concerned with practice. **2** likely to be effective in real circumstances; feasible. **3** suitable for a particular purpose. **4** realistic in approach. **5** skilled at manual tasks. **6** so nearly the case that it can be regarded as so; virtual. > *noun* Brit. an examination or lesson involving the practical application of theories and procedures.

SYNONYMS – *adjective* **1** applied, empirical, experimental. **2** feasible, realistic, viable, workable. **3** functional, handy, useful, utilitarian. **4** commonsensical, pragmatic, realistic.

ANTONYMS – *adjective* **1** theoretical. **3,4** impractical.

COMBINATIONS – **practical joke** a trick played on someone in order to make them look foolish and to amuse others.

ORIGIN – from archaic *practic*, from Greek *praktikos* 'concerned with action'.

practicality > *noun* (pl. **practicalities**) **1** the quality or state of being practical. **2** (**practicalities**) the aspects of a situation that involve action or experience rather than theories or ideas.

practically > *adverb* **1** in a practical way. **2** virtually; almost.

practice > *noun* **1** the actual application of a plan or method, as opposed to the theories relating to it. **2** the customary way of doing something. **3** the practising of an activity or skill. **4** the practising of a profession. **5** the business or premises of a doctor or lawyer. > *verb* US spelling of **PRACTISE**.

USAGE – do you mean **practice** or **practise**? **Practice** is the spelling for the noun, and in America for the verb as well; **practise** is the British spelling of the verb.

SYNONYMS – *noun* **1** application, exercise, implementation. **2** convention, custom, policy, procedure.

practise (US **practice**) > *verb* **1** perform (an activity) or exercise (a skill) repeatedly in order to improve or maintain proficiency in it. **2** carry out or perform (an activity or custom) habitually or regularly. **3** be engaged in (a particular profession). **4** observe the teaching and rules of (a religion). **5** archaic scheme or plot for an evil purpose.

ORIGIN – Old French *practiser*, from Latin *practicare* 'perform, carry out'.

practised (US **practiced**) > *adjective* expert as the result of much experience.

practitioner > *noun* a person engaged in an art, discipline, or profession, especially medicine.

praenomen /preenṓmen/ > *noun* the first or personal name given to a citizen of ancient Rome.

ORIGIN – Latin, from *prae* 'before' + *nomen* 'name'.

praepostor /pripóstər/ > *noun* Brit. (at some public schools) a prefect or monitor.

ORIGIN – from Latin *praepositus* 'head, chief'; compare with **PROVOST**.

praetor /préetər, préetor/ (US also **pretor**) > *noun* each of two ancient Roman magistrates ranking below consul.

DERIVATIVES – **praetorian** *adjective* & *noun*.

COMBINATIONS – **praetorian guard** (in ancient Rome) the bodyguard of the emperor.

ORIGIN – Latin, perhaps from *prae* 'before' + *ire* 'go'.

pragmatic /pragmáttik/ > *adjective* **1** dealing with things in a practical rather than theoretical way. **2** relating to philosophical or political pragmatism.

DERIVATIVES – **pragmatically** *adverb*.

SYNONYMS – **1** businesslike, common-sensical, practical, realistic.

ORIGIN – Greek *pragmatikos* 'relating to fact', from *pragma* 'deed'.

pragmatism /prágmətiz'm/ > *noun* **1** a pragmatic attitude or policy. **2** Philosophy an approach that evaluates theories or beliefs in terms of the success of their practical application.

DERIVATIVES – **pragmatist** *noun*.

prairie > *noun* (in North America) a large open area of grassland.

COMBINATIONS – **prairie chicken** a large North American grouse found on the prairies. **prairie dog** a gregarious ground squirrel that lives in burrows in the grasslands of North America. **prairie oyster 1** a drink made with a raw egg and seasoning, drunk as a cure for a hangover. **2** (**prairie oysters**) chiefly N. Amer. the testicles of a calf as food.

ORIGIN – French, from Latin *pratum* 'meadow'.

praise > *verb* **1** express warm approval of or admiration for. **2** express respect and gratitude towards (a deity). > *noun* **1** the expression of approval or admiration. **2** the expression of respect and gratitude as an act of worship.

WORDFINDER – encomium, eulogy, panegyric (*speech or text praising someone*), laudatory (*expressing praise*).

IDIOMS – **praise be** expressing relief, joy, or gratitude.

SYNONYMS – *verb* **1** acclaim, commend, compliment, eulogise, extol; formal laud. **2** exalt, glorify, honour; archaic magnify. *noun* **1** acclaim, approbation, commendation, kudos, plaudits; formal laudation. **2** exaltation, glorification, glory, honour.

ANTONYMS – *verb* **1** censure, criticise. *noun* **1** censure, criticism.

ORIGIN – Old French *preisier* 'to prize, praise', from Latin *pretium* 'price'.

praiseworthy > *adjective* deserving of praise.

DERIVATIVES – **praiseworthily** *adverb* **praiseworthiness** *noun*.

SYNONYMS – admirable, commendable, laudable, meritorious, worthy.

praline /práaleen/ > *noun* a smooth sweet substance made from nuts boiled in sugar, used as a filling for chocolates.

ORIGIN – named after Marshal de Plessis-Praslin, the 17th-century French soldier whose cook invented it.

pram > *noun* Brit. a four-wheeled carriage for a baby, pushed by a person on foot.

ORIGIN – contraction of **PERAMBULATOR**.

prance > *verb* **1** (of a horse) move with high springy steps. **2** walk with ostentatious, exaggerated movements. > *noun* an act of prancing.

prandial /prándiəl/ > *adjective* during or relating to a meal.

ORIGIN – from Latin *prandium* 'meal'.

prang Brit. informal > *verb* crash (a motor vehicle or aircraft). > *noun* a collision or crash.

prank > *noun* a practical joke or mischievous act.

DERIVATIVES – **prankish** *adjective*.

prankster > *noun* a person fond of playing pranks.

prase /prayz/ > *noun* a translucent greenish variety of quartz.

ORIGIN – Greek *prasios* 'leek green', from *prason* 'leek'.

praseodymium /prayziədímmiəm/ > *noun* a silvery-white metallic chemical element of the lanthanide series.

ORIGIN – from Greek *prasios* 'leek green' (because of its green salts) + *didymium* (see **NEODYMIUM**).

prat > *noun* informal **1** Brit. an incompetent or stupid person. **2** a person's buttocks.

prate > *verb* talk foolishly or at tedious length.

ORIGIN – from Dutch, Low German *praten*.

pratfall > *noun* informal a fall on to one's buttocks.

prattle > *verb* talk at length in a foolish or inconsequential way. > *noun* foolish or inconsequential talk.

SYNONYMS – *verb* babble, blather, chatter, gabble, maunder.

prawn > *noun* a marine crustacean which resembles a large shrimp.

COMBINATIONS – **prawn cracker** (in Chinese cooking) a light prawn-flavoured crisp which puffs up when deep-fried.

praxis /práksiss/ > *noun* **1** practice, as distinguished from theory. **2** custom.

ORIGIN – Greek, 'doing'.

pray > *verb* **1** address a prayer to God or another deity. **2** wish or hope earnestly for a particular outcome. > *adverb* formal or archaic used in polite requests or questions: *pray continue*.

ORIGIN – Latin *precari* 'entreat'.

prayer > *noun* **1** a request for help or expression of thanks addressed to God or another deity. **2** (**prayers**) a religious service at which people gather to pray together. **3** an earnest hope or wish.

WORDFINDER – amen (*said at the conclusion of a prayer*), Ave Maria, Hail Mary (*a Roman Catholic prayer to the Virgin Mary*), collect (*a short prayer*), intercession (*a prayer said for others*), paternoster (*the Lord's Prayer, said in Latin*), rosary (*Roman Catholic prayer of repeated Hail Marys, or beads used in this*).

IDIOMS – **not have a prayer** informal have no chance.

SYNONYMS – **1** invocation; literary orison.

COMBINATIONS – **prayer wheel** a small revolving cylinder inscribed with or containing prayers, used by Tibetan Buddhists.

prayerful > *adjective* **1** characterised by the use of prayer. **2** given to praying; devout.

DERIVATIVES – **prayerfully** *adverb*.

pre- > *prefix* before (in time, place, order, degree, or importance): *pre-adolescent*.

ORIGIN – from Latin *prae-*.

preach > *verb* **1** deliver a religious address to an assembled group of people. **2** earnestly advocate (a principle). **3** (**preach at**) give moral advice to (someone) in a self-righteous way.

WORDFINDER – evangelism (*preaching the Christian gospel*), homiletics (*art of preaching*), pulpit (*platform for preaching*).

DERIVATIVES – **preacher** *noun*.

SYNONYMS – **1** evangelise, sermonise. **2** advocate, counsel, recommend, urge.

ORIGIN – Old French *prechier*, from Latin *praedicare* 'proclaim'.

preachify > *verb* (**preachifies**, **preachified**) informal preach or moralise tediously.

preachy > *adjective* giving moral advice in a self-righteous way.

preamble /**pree**amb'l/ > *noun* a preliminary statement; an introduction.
ORIGIN – Old French *preambule*, from Latin *praeambulus* 'going before'.

preamp > *noun* short for **PREAMPLIFIER**.

preamplifier > *noun* an electronic device that amplifies a very weak signal and transmits it to a main amplifier.

pre-arrange > *verb* arrange or agree in advance.

prebend /**prebb**'nd/ > *noun* historical **1** the allowance granted to a canon or member of a chapter. **2** the property from which such an allowance was derived. **3** another term for **PREBENDARY**.
DERIVATIVES – **prebendal** adjective.
ORIGIN – from Latin *praebenda* 'things to be supplied, pension'.

prebendary /**prebb**əndəri/ > *noun* (pl. **prebendaries**) **1** an honorary canon. **2** historical a canon whose income came from a prebend.

prebuttal > *noun* (in politics) a response formulated in anticipation of a criticism; a pre-emptive rebuttal.

Precambrian /pree**kam**briən/ > *adjective* Geology of or relating to the earliest aeon of the earth's history, preceding the Cambrian period and ending about 570 million years ago, and including the time when living organisms first appeared.

precancerous > *adjective* Medicine (of a cell or medical condition) likely to develop into cancer if untreated.

precarious /pri**kair**iəss/ > *adjective* **1** not securely held or in position; likely to fall. **2** dependent on chance; uncertain.
DERIVATIVES – **precariously** adverb **precariousness** noun.
SYNONYMS – insecure, risky, uncertain, unreliable, unsafe, perilous.
ORIGIN – Latin *precarius* 'obtained by entreaty', from *prex* 'prayer'.

precast > *adjective* (especially of concrete) cast in its final shape before positioning.

precaution > *noun* **1** a measure taken in advance to prevent something undesirable from happening. **2** (**precautions**) informal contraception.
DERIVATIVES – **precautionary** adjective.
ORIGIN – Latin, from *praecavere* 'beware of in advance'.

precede > *verb* **1** come or go before in time, order, or position. **2** (**precede with**) preface with.
DERIVATIVES – **preceding** adjective.
ORIGIN – Latin *praecedere* 'go before'.

precedence /**press**id'nss/ > *noun* **1** the condition of preceding others in importance, order, or rank. **2** an acknowledged or legally determined right to such precedence.

precedent > *noun* /**press**id'nt/ **1** an earlier event or action serving as an example or guide. **2** Law a previous case or legal decision that may or must be followed in subsequent similar cases. > *adjective* /pri**seed**'nt, **press**id'nt/ preceding in time, order, or importance.

precentor /pri**sen**tər/ > *noun* **1** a person who leads a congregation in its singing or (in a synagogue) prayers. **2** a minor canon who administers the musical life of a cathedral.
ORIGIN – Latin *praecentor*, from *praecinere* 'sing before'.

precept /**pree**sept/ > *noun* **1** a general rule regulating behaviour or thought. **2** a writ or warrant. **3** Brit. an order issued by one local authority to another specifying the rate of tax to be charged on its behalf.
ORIGIN – Latin *praeceptum* 'something advised'.

preceptor /pri**sep**tər/ > *noun* a teacher or instructor.

precession /pri**sesh**'n/ > *noun* **1** the slow movement of the axis of a spinning body around another axis. **2** Astronomy the slow retrograde motion of the equinoctial points along the ecliptic, resulting in the earlier occurrence of equinoxes each year.
DERIVATIVES – **precess** verb **precessional** adjective.

precinct /**pree**singkt/ > *noun* **1** the area within the walls or boundaries of a place. **2** an area of ground around a cathedral, church, or college. **3** Brit. a specially designated area in a town, especially one closed to traffic. **4** N. Amer. a district of a city or town as defined for policing or electoral purposes.
ORIGIN – Latin *praecinctum*, from *praecingere* 'encircle'.

preciosity /preshi**oss**iti/ > *noun* over-refinement in language or art.

precious > *adjective* **1** having great value. **2** greatly loved or treasured. **3** ironic great; considerable: *a precious lot you know!* **4** derogatory affectedly concerned with elegant or refined language or manners.
IDIOMS – **precious little** (or **few**) informal extremely little (or few).
DERIVATIVES – **preciously** adverb **preciousness** noun.
SYNONYMS – **1** costly, expensive, priceless, valuable. **2** adored, dear, loved, prized, treasured.
COMBINATIONS – **precious metals** gold, silver, and platinum. **precious stone** a highly attractive and valuable piece of mineral, used in jewellery.
ORIGIN – Latin *pretiosus*, from *pretium* 'price'.

precipice > *noun* a tall and very steep rock face or cliff.
ORIGIN – Latin *praecipitium*, from *praeceps* 'steep, headlong'.

precipitancy > *noun* rashness or suddenness of action.

precipitant > *noun* **1** a cause of an action or event. **2** Chemistry a substance that causes precipitation.

precipitate > *verb* /pri**sipp**itayt/ **1** cause (something bad) to happen unexpectedly or prematurely. **2** cause to move suddenly and with force. **3** Chemistry cause (a substance) to be deposited in solid form from a solution. **4** cause (moisture or dust) to be deposited from the atmosphere or from a vapour or suspension. > *adjective* /pri**sipp**itət/ done, acting, or occurring suddenly or without careful consideration. > *noun* /pri**sipp**itayt, pri**sipp**itət/ Chemistry a substance precipitated from a solution.
DERIVATIVES – **precipitately** adverb **precipitator** noun.
SYNONYMS – *verb* **1** accelerate, incite, provoke, spark, trigger. **2** catapult, hurl, project, propel.
ORIGIN – Latin *praecipitare* 'throw headlong'.

precipitation > *noun* **1** rain, snow, sleet, or hail that falls to or condenses on the ground. **2** Chemistry the action or process of precipitating. **3** archaic sudden and unthinking action.

precipitous /pri**sipp**itəss/ > *adjective* **1** dangerously high or steep. **2** (of a change in a condition or situation) sudden and dramatic. **3** hasty; precipitate.
DERIVATIVES – **precipitously** adverb.

precis /**pray**si/ > *noun* (pl. same /**pray**seez/) a summary of a text or speech. > *verb* (**precises** /**pray**seez/, **precised** /**pray**seed/, **precising** /**pray**seeing/) make a precis of.
ORIGIN – from French *précis* 'precise'.

precise > *adjective* **1** marked by exactness of expression or detail. **2** very attentive to detail. **3** exact; particular: *at that precise moment.*
DERIVATIVES – **precisely** adverb.
USAGE – strictly speaking, **precise** does not mean the same as **accurate**. Accurate means 'correct in all details', while **precise** contains a notion of trying to specify details exactly: if you say 'It's 4.04 and 12 seconds' you are being *precise*, but not necessarily *accurate* (your watch might be slow).
ORIGIN – Old French *prescis*, from Latin *praecidere* 'cut short'.

precision > *noun* **1** the quality or condition of being precise. **2** (before another noun) very accurate: *a precision instrument.*

preclude > *verb* prevent (something) from happening or (someone) from doing something.

DERIVATIVES – **preclusion** noun.

ORIGIN – Latin *praecludere*, from *prae* 'before' + *claudere* 'to shut'.

precocious /prikōshəss/ > *adjective* having developed certain abilities or inclinations at an earlier age than usual.

DERIVATIVES – **precociously** *adverb* **precociousness** *noun* **precocity** *noun*.

SYNONYMS – advanced, forward, mature, quick.

ORIGIN – Latin *praecox*, from *praecoquere* 'ripen fully'; compare with **APRICOT**.

precognition /preekognish'n/ > *noun* foreknowledge of an event, especially through supposed paranormal means.

DERIVATIVES – **precognitive** *adjective*.

precoital > *adjective* occurring before sexual intercourse.

DERIVATIVES – **precoitally** *adverb*.

pre-Columbian > *adjective* relating to the Americas before the arrival of Christopher Columbus in 1492.

preconceived > *adjective* (of an idea or opinion) formed before evidence for its truth or usefulness has been acquired.

preconception > *noun* a preconceived idea or prejudice.

precondition > *noun* a condition that must be fulfilled before other things can happen or be done. > *verb* bring into a desired or necessary state beforehand.

precursor > *noun* a person or thing that comes before another of the same kind.

DERIVATIVES – **precursory** *adjective*.

SYNONYMS – antecedent, forerunner, predecessor.

ORIGIN – Latin *praecursor*, from *praecurrere* 'run beforehand'.

predacious /pridayshəss/ (also **predaceous**) > *adjective* (of an animal) predatory.

pre-date > *verb* exist or occur at a date earlier than.

predation /pridaysh'n/ > *noun* the preying of one animal on others.

predator /preddətər/ > *noun* 1 an animal that preys on others. 2 a person who exploits others.

DERIVATIVES – **predatorily** *adverb* **predatoriness** *noun*.

ORIGIN – Latin, from *praedari* 'seize as plunder', from *praeda* 'plunder'; compare with **PREY**.

predatory > *adjective* 1 (of an animal) naturally preying on others. 2 seeking to exploit others.

predecease formal > *verb* die before (another person). > *noun* a death preceding that of another person.

predecessor > *noun* 1 a person who held a job or office before the current holder. 2 a thing that has been followed or replaced by another.

ORIGIN – Latin *praedecessor*, from *prae* 'beforehand' + *decessor* 'retiring officer'.

predestinarian /preedestinairiən/ > *noun* a person who believes in the doctrine of predestination. > *adjective* upholding or relating to the doctrine of predestination.

predestination > *noun* (in Christian theology) the divine ordaining of all that will happen, a doctrine associated particularly with Calvinism.

predestine > *verb* 1 (of God) destine (someone) for a particular fate or purpose. 2 determine (an outcome) in advance by divine will or fate.

DERIVATIVES – **predestined** *adjective*.

predetermine > *verb* 1 establish or decide in advance. 2 predestine.

DERIVATIVES – **predetermination** *noun*.

predeterminer > *noun* Grammar a word or phrase that occurs before a determiner, for example *both* in *he raised both his arms* or *a lot of* in *a lot of the time*.

predicable /preddikəb'l/ > *adjective* that may be predicated or affirmed.

predicament /pridikkəmənt/ > *noun* 1 a difficult situation. 2 Philosophy each of the ten categories in Aristotelian logic.

SYNONYMS – 1 dilemma, emergency, fix, quandary.

ORIGIN – first used to mean 'category', later 'state of being', hence 'difficult situation': from Latin *praedicamentum* 'something predicated'.

predicate > *noun* /preddikət/ 1 Grammar the part of a sentence or clause containing a verb and stating something about the subject (e.g. *went home* in *John went home*). 2 Logic something which is affirmed or denied concerning an argument of a proposition. > *verb* /preddikayt/ 1 Grammar & Logic assert (something) about the subject of a sentence or an argument of a proposition. 2 (**predicate on**) found or base (something) on (an idea, quality, circumstance, etc.).

DERIVATIVES – **predication** *noun*.

ORIGIN – Latin *praedicatum*, from *praedicare* 'make known beforehand, declare'.

predicative /pridikkətiv/ > *adjective* 1 Grammar (of an adjective or noun) forming or contained in the predicate, as *old* in *the dog is old* (but not in *the old dog*). Contrasted with **ATTRIBUTIVE**. 2 Logic acting as a predicate.

DERIVATIVES – **predicatively** *adverb*.

predict > *verb* state that (a specified event) will happen in the future.

DERIVATIVES – **predictive** *adjective* **predictor** *noun*.

SYNONYMS – forecast, foretell, presage, prophesy.

ORIGIN – Latin *praedicere* 'make known beforehand, declare'.

predictable > *adjective* 1 able to be predicted. 2 derogatory always behaving or occurring in the way expected.

DERIVATIVES – **predictability** *noun* **predictably** *adverb*.

prediction > *noun* 1 a thing predicted; a forecast. 2 the action of predicting.

SYNONYMS – 1 forecast, prognosis, projection, prophecy.

predigest > *verb* 1 treat (food) to make it easier to digest. 2 simplify (information) so that it is easier to absorb.

predilection /preedileksh'n/ > *noun* a preference or special liking for something.

SYNONYMS – fondness, liking, partiality, penchant, preference.

ORIGIN – French, from Latin *praediligere* 'prefer'.

predispose > *verb* (**predispose to** or **to do**) make (someone) liable or inclined to a specified attitude, action, or condition.

DERIVATIVES – **predisposition** *noun*.

predominant > *adjective* 1 present as the strongest or main element. 2 having the greatest control or power.

DERIVATIVES – **predominance** *noun* **predominantly** *adverb*.

predominate > *verb* 1 be the strongest or main element. 2 have or exert control or power.

predominately > *adverb* mainly; for the most part.

pre-echo > *noun* 1 a faint copy heard just before an actual sound in a recording, caused by the accidental transfer of signals. 2 a foreshadowing of something.

pre-eclampsia > *noun* a condition in pregnancy characterised especially by high blood pressure.

DERIVATIVES – **pre-eclamptic** *adjective*.

pre-embryo > *noun* a fertilised ovum in the first fourteen days after fertilisation, before implantation in the womb.

pre-eminent > *adjective* surpassing all others.

DERIVATIVES – **pre-eminence** *noun* **pre-eminently** *adverb*.

pre-empt > *verb* 1 take action in order to prevent (something) happening; forestall. 2 acquire or appropriate in advance.

DERIVATIVES – **pre-emptive** *adjective* **pre-emptor** *noun*.

pre-emption > *noun* 1 the action of pre-empting or forestalling. 2 the purchase of goods or shares before the opportunity is offered to others.

ORIGIN – Latin, from *praeemere* 'buy in advance'.

preen > *verb* 1 (of a bird) tidy and clean its feathers with its beak. 2 devote effort to making oneself look attractive. 3 (**preen oneself**) congratulate or pride oneself.

ORIGIN – probably related to obsolete *prune*, from Latin *ungere* 'anoint'.

pre-exist > *verb* exist at or from an earlier time.

DERIVATIVES – **pre-existence** *noun* **pre-existent** *adjective* **pre-existing** *adjective*.

prefab > *noun* informal a prefabricated building.

prefabricate > *verb* manufacture sections of (a building) to enable easy assembly on site.

DERIVATIVES – **prefabricated** *adjective* **prefabrication** *noun*.

preface /preffəss/ > *noun* **1** an introduction to a book, stating its subject, scope, or aims. **2** the preliminary part of a speech. > *verb* **1** provide with a preface. **2** (**preface with** or **by**) begin (a speech or event) with or by doing something.

DERIVATIVES – **prefatory** /preffətəri/ *adjective*.

SYNONYMS – *noun* foreword, introduction, preamble, prolegomenon, prologue.

ORIGIN – Old French, from Latin *praefari* 'speak before'.

prefect > *noun* **1** chiefly Brit. a senior pupil authorised to enforce discipline in a school. **2** a chief officer, magistrate, or regional governor in certain countries.

DERIVATIVES – **prefectoral** *adjective* **prefectorial** *adjective*.

ORIGIN – Latin *praefectus*, from *praeficere* 'set in authority over'.

prefecture /preefektyoor/ > *noun* **1** a district under the government of a prefect. **2** a prefect's office, tenure, or residence.

DERIVATIVES – **prefectural** *adjective*.

prefer* > *verb* (**preferred**, **preferring**) **1** like (someone or something) better than another or others; tend to choose (a particular alternative). **2** formal submit (a charge or information) for consideration. **3** archaic promote to a prestigious position.

* SPELLING – double the *r* when forming the past tense: prefe*rr*ed.

SYNONYMS – **1** favour, incline towards, be partial to.

ORIGIN – Latin *praeferre* 'to bear or carry before'.

preferable /preffərəb'l/ > *adjective* more desirable or suitable.

DERIVATIVES – **preferability** *noun*.

preferably > *adverb* ideally; if possible.

preference > *noun* **1** a greater liking for one alternative than for another or others. **2** a thing preferred. **3** favour shown to one person over another or others.

SYNONYMS – **1** bias, partiality, predilection. **3** advantage, favour, precedence, priority.

COMBINATIONS – **preference share** a share which entitles the holder to a fixed dividend whose payment takes priority over that of ordinary share dividends.

preferential > *adjective* **1** of or involving preference or partiality. **2** (of a creditor) having a claim for repayment which will be met before those of other creditors.

DERIVATIVES – **preferentially** *adverb*.

preferment > *noun* promotion or appointment to a position or office.

prefigure > *verb* **1** be an early indication or version of. **2** archaic imagine beforehand.

DERIVATIVES – **prefiguration** *noun* **prefigurative** *adjective* **prefigurement** *noun*.

prefix > *noun* **1** a word, letter, or number placed before another. **2** an element placed at the beginning of a word to alter its meaning (e.g. *non-*, *re-*) or (in some languages) as an inflection. **3** a title placed before a name (e.g. *Mr*). > *verb* **1** add as a prefix. **2** add a prefix to.

preggers > *adjective* informal pregnant.

pregnancy > *noun* (pl. **pregnancies**) the condition or period of being pregnant.

WORDFINDER – amniocentesis (*testing of fluid in the womb during pregnancy*), conceive (*become pregnant*), ectopic (*involving growth of the fetus outside the womb*), in utero (*in the womb*), in vitro (*denoting conception achieved outside the body*), multigravida (*a woman pregnant more than once*), primigravida (*a woman pregnant for the first time*), progesterone (*hormone stimulating the uterus to prepare for pregnancy*).

pregnant > *adjective* **1** (of a woman or female animal) having a child or young developing in the uterus. **2** full of meaning or significance.

ORIGIN – Latin *praegnant-*, probably from *prae* 'before' + the base of *gnasci* 'be born'.

preheat > *verb* heat beforehand.

prehensile /prihensīl/ > *adjective* (chiefly of an animal's limb or tail) capable of grasping.

ORIGIN – from Latin *prehendere* 'grasp'.

prehistoric > *adjective* relating to prehistory.

prehistory > *noun* **1** the period of time before written records. **2** the events or conditions leading up to a particular phenomenon.

DERIVATIVES – **prehistorian** *noun*.

pre-ignition > *noun* premature combustion of the fuel–air mixture in an internal-combustion engine.

pre-industrial > *adjective* before industrialisation.

prejudge > *verb* form a judgement on (an issue or person) prematurely and without having adequate information.

prejudice > *noun* **1** preconceived opinion that is not based on reason or experience. **2** unjust behaviour formed on such a basis. **3** chiefly Law harm that may result from some action or judgement. > *verb* **1** give rise to prejudice in (someone); make biased. **2** chiefly Law cause harm to (a state of affairs).

IDIOMS – **without prejudice** Law without detriment to any existing right or claim.

SYNONYMS – *noun* **2** bias, bigotry, chauvinism, discrimination, intolerance. *verb* **1** bias, influence, predispose, sway.

ORIGIN – Latin *praejudicium*, from *prae* 'in advance' + *judicium* 'judgement'.

prejudicial > *adjective* harmful or damaging to someone or something.

prelapsarian /preelapsairiən/ > *adjective* Theology or literary before the Fall of Man; innocent and unspoilt.

ORIGIN – from **PRE-** + Latin *lapsus*, from *labi* 'to slip or fall'.

prelate /prellət/ > *noun* formal or historical a bishop or other high ecclesiastical dignitary.

ORIGIN – Latin *praelatus* 'civil dignitary'.

preliminary > *adjective* preceding or done in preparation for something fuller or more important. > *noun* (pl. **preliminaries**) **1** a preliminary action or event. **2** a preliminary round in a sporting competition.

SYNONYMS – *adjective* initial, introductory, preparatory.

ORIGIN – Latin *praeliminaris*, from *prae* 'before' + *limen* 'threshold'.

preliterate > *adjective* (of a society or culture) that has not developed the use of writing.

prelude > *noun* **1** an action or event serving as an introduction to something more important. **2** a piece of music serving as an introduction to a longer piece. **3** the introductory part of a poem or other literary work. > *verb* serve as a prelude or introduction to.

SYNONYMS – *noun* **1** curtain-raiser, introduction, opener, preface, preliminary.

ORIGIN – Latin *praeludium*, from *praeludere* 'play beforehand'.

premarital > *adjective* occurring or existing before marriage.

premature > *adjective* **1** occurring or done before the proper time. **2** (of a baby) born before the end of the full term of gestation.

DERIVATIVES – **prematurely** *adverb* **prematurity** *noun*.

ORIGIN – Latin *praematurus* 'very early', from *prae* 'before' + *maturus* 'ripe'.

pre-med > *noun* **1** chiefly N. Amer. a premedical student or course of study. **2** short for PREMEDICATION.

premedication > *noun* medication given in preparation for an operation or other treatment.

premeditated > *adjective* (of an action, especially a crime) planned beforehand.

DERIVATIVES – **premeditation** *noun*.

premenopausal > *adjective* of or in the part of a woman's life just before the menopause.

premenstrual > *adjective* of, occurring, or experienced before menstruation.

COMBINATIONS – **premenstrual syndrome** a complex of symptoms (including emotional tension and fluid retention) experienced by some women prior to menstruation.

premier > *adjective* first in importance, order, or position. > *noun* a Prime Minister or other head of government.

DERIVATIVES – **premiership** *noun*.

SYNONYMS – *adjective* chief, foremost, head, leading, principal.

ORIGIN – Old French, 'first', from Latin *primarius* 'principal'.

premiere > *noun* the first performance of a musical or theatrical work or the first showing of a film. > *verb* give the premiere of.

ORIGIN – French 'first', feminine of *premier*.

premise > *noun* /**premm**iss/ (Brit. also **premiss**) Logic 1 a previous statement from which another is inferred. 2 an underlying assumption. > *verb* /pri**mīz**/ (**premise on**) base (an argument, theory, etc.) on.

ORIGIN – Old French *premisse*, from Latin *praemissa propositio* 'proposition set in front'.

premises > *plural noun* a house or building, together with its land and outbuildings, occupied by a business or considered in an official context.

premium > *noun* (pl. **premiums**) 1 an amount paid for a contract of insurance. 2 a sum added to an ordinary price or other payment. 3 (before another noun) (of a commodity) superior and more expensive.

IDIOMS – **at a premium 1** scarce and in demand. 2 above the usual price. **put** (or **place**) **a premium on** regard as particularly valuable.

ORIGIN – Latin *praemium* 'booty, reward', from *prae* 'before' + *emere* 'buy, take'.

Premium Bond (also **Premium Savings Bond**) > *noun* (in the UK) a government security offering no interest or capital gain but entered in regular draws for cash prizes.

premolar > *noun* a tooth situated between the canines and molars.

premonition /premm**ə**nish'n/ > *noun* a strong feeling that something is about to happen.

DERIVATIVES – **premonitory** *adjective*.

ORIGIN – Latin, from *praemonere* 'forewarn'.

prenatal > *adjective* before birth.

prenuptial > *adjective* before marriage.

COMBINATIONS – **prenuptial agreement** an agreement made by a couple before they marry concerning ownership of assets in the event of a divorce.

prenuptial agreement > *noun* an agreement made by a couple before they marry concerning ownership of assets in the event of a divorce.

preoccupation > *noun* 1 the state of being preoccupied. 2 a matter that preoccupies someone.

preoccupy > *verb* (**preoccupies**, **preoccupied**) dominate the mind of (someone) to the exclusion of other thoughts.

SYNONYMS – absorb, consume, engross, enthral, obsess, occupy.

preordain > *verb* decide or determine beforehand.

prep[1] > *noun* Brit. informal 1 (especially in a private school) school work done outside lessons. 2 a period set aside for this.

prep[2] informal, chiefly N. Amer. > *verb* (**prepped**, **prepping**) prepare; make ready. > *noun* preparation.

pre-packed > *adjective* (of goods) packed or wrapped on the site of production or before sale.

prepaid past and past participle of PREPAY.

preparation > *noun* 1 the action or process of preparing or being prepared. 2 a specially made-up substance, especially a medicine or food.

preparative > *adjective* preparatory.

preparatory > *adjective* 1 serving as or carrying out preparation. 2 Brit. relating to education in a preparatory school.

COMBINATIONS – **preparatory school 1** Brit. a private school for pupils between the ages of seven and thirteen. **2** N. Amer. a private school that prepares pupils for college or university.

prepare > *verb* 1 make ready for use or consideration. 2 make or get ready to do or deal with something. 3 (**be prepared to do**) be willing to do something. 4 make (a substance) by chemical reaction.

DERIVATIVES – **preparer** *noun*.

wordpower facts
Prepare
The word **prepare** comes from Latin *praeparare*, which was formed from *prae* 'before' + *parare* 'make ready'. Its derivation from *parare* means that **prepare** is related to a range of apparently unconnected English words including **apparatus**, **disparate**, **emperor**, **imperative**, **parade**, **pare**, **rampart**, **repair**, and **separate**.

preparedness > *noun* a state of readiness, especially for war.

prepay > *verb* (past and past participle **prepaid**) pay for in advance.

DERIVATIVES – **prepayment** *noun*.

pre-planned > *adjective* planned in advance.

preponderant > *adjective* predominant in influence, number, or importance.

DERIVATIVES – **preponderance** *noun*.

preponderate > *verb* be preponderant; predominate.

ORIGIN – Latin *praeponderare*, from *prae* 'before' + *ponderare* 'weigh, consider'.

preposition /prepp**ə**zish'n/ > *noun* Grammar a word governing a noun or pronoun and expressing a relation to another word or element, as in 'she arrived *after* dinner' and 'what did you do it *for*?'

DERIVATIVES – **prepositional** *adjective*.

ORIGIN – Latin *praepositio*, from *praeponere* 'to place before'.

prepossessing > *adjective* attractive or appealing in appearance.

preposterous > *adjective* utterly absurd or ridiculous.

SYNONYMS – absurd, farcical, laughable, ludicrous, ridiculous, risible.

ORIGIN – Latin *praeposterus* 'reversed, absurd', from *prae* 'before' + *posterus* 'coming after'.

preppy (also **preppie**) N. Amer. informal > *noun* (pl. **preppies**) a pupil of an expensive preparatory school. > *adjective* (**preppier**, **preppiest**) of or typical of such a person, especially with reference to their neat style of dress.

pre-production > *noun* work done on a film, broadcast programme, etc. before full-scale production begins.

pre-programmed > *adjective* programmed in advance.

prep school > *noun* a preparatory school.

pre-pubescent > *adjective* relating to or in the period preceding puberty.

prepuce /**pree**pyo͞oss/ > *noun* Anatomy 1 technical term for FORESKIN. 2 the fold of skin surrounding the clitoris.

ORIGIN – Latin *praeputium*.

prequel > *noun* a story or film containing events which precede those of an existing work.

Pre-Raphaelite /pree-**raff**əlīt/ > *noun* a member of a group of English 19th-century artists who sought to emulate the style of Italian artists from before the time of Raphael. > *adjective* 1 relating to the Pre-Raphaelites. 2 (of women) suggesting Pre-Raphaelite painting in appearance, typically with long auburn hair and pale skin.

DERIVATIVES – **Pre-Raphaelitism** *noun*.

pre-recorded > *adjective* (of sound or film) recorded in advance.

prerequisite /pree**rek**wizit/ > *noun* a thing that is required as a prior condition for something else to happen or exist. > *adjective* required as a prior condition.

SYNONYMS – *noun* condition, precondition. *adjective* essential, mandatory, necessary, obligatory, required.

prerogative /pri**rogg**ətiv/ > *noun* 1 a right or privilege exclusive to a particular individual or class. 2 (in UK law) the right of the sovereign, theoretically unrestricted but usually delegated to government or the judiciary.

ORIGIN – Latin *praerogativa* '(the verdict of) the political division which was chosen to vote first in the assembly'.

presage /**press**ij/ > *verb* /also pri**sayj**/ be a sign or warning of (an imminent event). > *noun* an omen or portent.

ORIGIN – Latin *praesagium*, from *praesagire* 'forebode'.

presbyter /**prez**bitər/ > *noun* 1 historical an elder or minister of the Christian Church. 2 formal (in presbyterian Churches) an elder.

ORIGIN – Greek *presbuteros* 'elder'.

Presbyterian /prezbi**teer**iən/ > *adjective* relating to a Protestant Church or denomination governed by elders all of equal rank. > *noun* a member of a Presbyterian Church.

DERIVATIVES – **Presbyterianism** *noun*.

presbytery /**prez**bitəri/ > *noun* (pl. **presbyteries**) 1 (treated as sing. or pl.) a body of Church elders. 2 the house of a Roman Catholic parish priest. 3 chiefly Architecture the eastern part of a church chancel.

pre-school > *adjective* relating to the time before a child is old enough to go to school.

prescient /**press**iənt/ > *adjective* having knowledge of events before they take place.

DERIVATIVES – **prescience** *noun* **presciently** *adverb*.

ORIGIN – from Latin *praescire* 'know beforehand'.

prescribe /pri**skrīb**/ > *verb* 1 advise and authorise the use of (a medicine or treatment), especially in writing. 2 state authoritatively that (an action or procedure) should be carried out.

ORIGIN – Latin *praescribere* 'direct in writing'.

prescription > *noun* 1 an instruction written by a medical practitioner authorising a patient to be issued with a medicine or treatment. 2 the action of prescribing something. 3 an authoritative recommendation or ruling. 4 (also **positive prescription**) Law the establishment of a claim founded on the basis of long usage or custom.

prescriptive > *adjective* 1 serving or seeking to impose a rule or method. 2 (of a right, title, etc.) legally established by long usage.

DERIVATIVES – **prescriptivism** *noun* **prescriptivist** *noun & adjective*.

preseason > *adjective* before the start of the season for a particular sport. > *noun* the preseason period.

presence > *noun* 1 the state or fact of being present. 2 the impressive manner or appearance of a person. 3 a person or thing that is present but not seen. 4 a group of

soldiers or police stationed in a particular place.

IDIOMS – **make one's presence felt** have a strong influence on a situation. **presence of mind** the ability to remain calm and take quick, sensible action in the face of sudden difficulty.

present[1] /**prezz**'nt/ > *adjective* 1 being or occurring in a particular place. 2 existing or occurring now. 3 Grammar (of a tense) expressing an action now going on or habitually performed, or a condition now existing. > *noun* 1 (**the present**) the period of time now occurring. 2 Grammar a present tense or form of a verb.

IDIOMS – **at present** now. **for the present** for now; temporarily. **these presents** Law this document.

SYNONYMS – *adjective* 1 at hand, in attendance. 2 contemporary, current, present-day.

ANTONYMS – *adjective* 1 absent. 2 future, past.

COMBINATIONS – **present participle** Grammar the form of a verb, ending in *-ing* in English, which is used in forming continuous tenses (e.g. *I'm thinking*), as a noun (e.g. *good thinking*), and as an adjective (e.g. *running water*).

ORIGIN – from Latin *praeesse* 'be at hand'.

present[2] /pri**zent**/ > *verb* 1 give formally or ceremonially. 2 formally introduce to someone. 3 put (a show or exhibition) before the public. 4 introduce and appear in (a television or radio show). 5 offer for acceptance or consideration. 6 be the cause of (a problem). 7 (**present oneself**) appear formally before others. 8 (**present with**) Medicine come forward for medical examination for a particular condition or symptom. 9 exhibit (a particular appearance) to others.

IDIOMS – **present arms** hold a rifle vertically in front of the body as a salute.

SYNONYMS – 1 award, bestow, confer, dispense. 3 display, exhibit, show, stage. 4 anchor, host. 5 offer, proffer, submit.

ORIGIN – Latin *praesentare* 'place before'.

present[3] /**prezz**'nt/ > *noun* a thing given to someone as a gift.

ORIGIN – Old French, originally in the phrase *mettre une chose en present à quelqu'un* 'put a thing into the presence of a person'.

presentable > *adjective* clean, smart, or decent enough to be seen in public.

presentation > *noun* 1 the action or an instance of presenting or being presented. 2 the manner or style in which something is presented. 3 a demonstration or display of a product or idea.

DERIVATIVES – **presentational** *adjective* **presentationally** *adverb*.

presenteeism > *noun* the practice of regularly being present at work for longer

than required by one's terms of employment.

presenter > *noun* a person who introduces and appears in a television or radio programme.

presentiment /pri**zen**timənt/ > *noun* an intuitive feeling or foreboding about the future.

presentism > *noun* the tendency to interpret past events in terms of modern values and concepts.

DERIVATIVES – **presentist** *adjective*.

presently > *adverb* 1 after a short time; soon. 2 at the present time; now.

preservation > *noun* the action or state of preserving or being preserved.

preservationist > *noun* a supporter of the preservation of something, especially of historic buildings or artefacts.

preservative > *noun* a substance used to preserve foodstuffs or other materials against decay. > *adjective* acting to preserve something.

preserve > *verb* 1 maintain (something) in its original or existing state. 2 keep safe from harm or injury. 3 keep alive (a memory or quality). 4 treat (food) to prevent its decomposition. 5 prepare (fruit) for long-term storage by boiling it with sugar. > *noun* 1 a foodstuff made with fruit preserved in sugar, such as jam. 2 something regarded as being reserved for a particular person or group. 3 a place where game is protected and kept for private hunting.

DERIVATIVES – **preserver** *noun*.

SYNONYMS – *verb* 1 conserve, maintain, save. 2 defend, guard, protect, safeguard. 3 continue, maintain, perpetuate, sustain. *noun* 2 area, domain, field, territory.

ORIGIN – Latin *praeservare*, from *prae-* 'before, in advance' + *servare* 'to keep'.

preset > *verb* /pree**set**/ (**presetting**; past and past participle **preset**) set (a value that controls the operation of a device) in advance of its use. > *noun* /**pree**set/ a preset value or control.

pre-shrunk > *adjective* (of a fabric or garment) shrunk during manufacture to prevent further shrinking in use.

preside > *verb* 1 be in a position of authority in a meeting, court, etc. 2 (**preside over**) be in charge of (a situation).

ORIGIN – Latin *praesidere*, from *prae* 'before' + *sedere* 'sit'.

presidency > *noun* (pl. **presidencies**) the office or tenure of a president.

president > *noun* 1 the elected head of a republican state. 2 the head of a society, council, or other organisation. 3 Christian Church the celebrant at a Eucharist.

DERIVATIVES – **presidential** *adjective*.

press[1] > *verb* 1 move into a position of contact with something by exerting continuous physical force. 2 exert continuous physical force on, especially in order to operate a device. **3** apply pressure to (something) to flatten or shape it. **4** move in a specified direction by pushing. **5** (**press on** or **ahead**) continue in one's action. **6** forcefully put forward (an opinion or claim). **7** make strong efforts to persuade or force to do something. **8** extract (juice or oil) by crushing or squeezing fruit, vegetables, etc. **9** (of time) be short. **10** (**be pressed to do**) have difficulty doing. **11** Weightlifting raise (a weight) by gradually pushing it upwards from the shoulders. > *noun* **1** a device for applying pressure in order to flatten or shape something or to extract juice or oil. **2** a printing press. **3** (**the press**) newspapers or journalists viewed collectively. **4** coverage in newspapers and magazines. **5** a printing or publishing business. **6** a closely packed mass of people or things.

IDIOMS – **go to press** go to be printed. **press** (**the**) **flesh** informal, chiefly N. Amer. greet people by shaking hands.

COMBINATIONS – **press conference** a meeting held with journalists in order to make an announcement or answer questions. **press release** an official statement issued to journalists. **press stud** Brit. a small fastener engaged by pressing its two halves together.

ORIGIN – Old French *presser*, from Latin *pressare* 'keep pressing'.

press² > *verb* **1** (**press into**) put to a specified use, especially as a makeshift measure. **2** historical force to enlist in the army or navy.

ORIGIN – alteration of obsolete *prest* 'pay given on enlistment' (by association with **PRESS¹**), from Latin *praestare* 'provide'.

press gang > *noun* historical a body of men employed to enlist men forcibly into service in the army or navy. > *verb* (**press-gang**) force into service.

pressie > *noun* variant spelling of **PREZZIE**.

pressing > *adjective* **1** requiring quick or immediate action or attention. **2** expressing something strongly or persistently. > *noun* an object, especially a record, made by moulding under pressure.

SYNONYMS – **1** acute, burning, desperate, urgent. **2** insistent, persistent.

pressman > *noun* chiefly Brit. a journalist.

press-up > *noun* Brit. an exercise in which a person lies facing the floor and raises their body by pressing down on their hands.

pressure > *noun* **1** continuous physical force exerted on or against an object by something in contact with it. **2** the use of persuasion or intimidation to make someone do something. **3** a feeling of stressful urgency. **4** the force per unit area exerted by a fluid against a surface. > *verb* attempt to persuade or coerce (someone) into doing something.

WORDFINDER – anticyclone (*a high-pressure weather system*), barometer, manometer (*devices to measure pressure*), cyclone, depression (*a low-pressure weather system*), hyperbaric (*at greater than normal pressure*), hypertension (*high blood pressure*), isobar (*a line of equal pressure on a weather map*), pneumatic (*operated by air or gas under pressure*), rarefied (*of lower than normal pressure*), sphygmomanometer (*an instrument for measuring blood pressure*).

SYNONYMS – *noun* **3** strain, stress, tension. *verb* bully, coerce, dragoon, intimidate, pressurise.

COMBINATIONS – **pressure cooker** an airtight pot in which food can be cooked quickly under steam pressure. **pressure group** a group that tries to influence public policy in the interest of a particular cause. **pressure point 1** a point on the surface of the body sensitive to pressure. **2** a point where an artery can be pressed against a bone to inhibit bleeding.

pressurise (also **pressurize**) > *verb* **1** artificially produce or maintain raised pressure in (something). **2** attempt to persuade or coerce (someone) into doing something.

prestidigitation /prestidijitaysh'n/ > *noun* formal sleight of hand performed as entertainment.

ORIGIN – from French *preste* 'nimble' + Latin *digitus* 'finger'.

prestige /pressteezh/ > *noun* respect and admiration attracted through a perception of high achievements or quality.

SYNONYMS – cachet, distinction, glory, honour, kudos.

---

wordpower facts

Prestige

The word **prestige** originally meant 'illusion, conjuring trick', and did not take on its modern sense until the 19th century. It entered English in the mid 17th century from French, and ultimately derives from the Latin plural noun *praestigiae* 'conjuring tricks'. The change of meaning in English occurred by way of the sense 'dazzling influence, glamour', which at first had a derogatory implication.

---

prestigious > *adjective* inspiring respect and admiration; having prestige.

DERIVATIVES – **prestigiously** *adverb*.

SYNONYMS – acclaimed, distinguished, esteemed, honoured, respected.

presto > *adverb* & *adjective* Music in a quick tempo. > *exclamation* (Brit. also **hey presto**) announcing the successful completion of a conjuring trick or other surprising achievement.

ORIGIN – Italian, 'quick, quickly'.

prestressed > *adjective* strengthened by the application of stress during manufacture.

presumably > *adverb* as may reasonably be presumed.

presume > *verb* **1** suppose that something is probably the case. **2** take for granted. **3** (**presume to do**) be arrogant enough to do something. **4** (**presume on**) unjustifiably regard (something) as entitling one to privileges.

USAGE – **presume** and **assume** are not interchangeable. Both mean 'suppose something to be true', but while **assume** implies something is taken for granted without proof, **presume** is used especially when the supposition is based on evidence.

SYNONYMS – **1** assume, believe, imagine, surmise, suppose. **3** be so bold as, dare, have the audacity, venture.

ORIGIN – Latin *praesumere* 'anticipate', from *prae* 'before' + *sumere* 'take'.

presumption > *noun* **1** an act or instance of presuming something to be the case. **2** an idea that is presumed to be true. **3** presumptuous behaviour. **4** chiefly Law an attitude adopted towards something in the absence of contrary factors.

presumptive > *adjective* **1** presumed in the absence of further information. **2** another term for **PRESUMPTUOUS**.

presumptuous* > *adjective* failing to observe the limits of what is permitted or appropriate.

*SPELLING – the ending is *-uous*, not *-ious*: presumpt*uous*.

SYNONYMS – brazen, familiar; informal fresh; archaic malapert.

presuppose > *verb* **1** (of a situation or argument) require (something) to be the case in order to be possible or coherent. **2** tacitly assume to be the case.

DERIVATIVES – **presupposition** *noun*.

prêt-à-porter /prett ə portay/ > *noun* designer clothing sold ready-to-wear.

ORIGIN – French, 'ready to wear'.

pretence (US **pretense**) > **1** an act or the action of pretending. **2** affected and ostentatious behaviour. **3** (**pretence to**) a claim to something, especially a false or ambitious one.

pretend > *verb* **1** make it appear that something is the case when in fact it is not. **2** engage in an imaginative game. **3** simulate (an emotion or quality). **4** (**pretend to**) lay claim to (a quality or title). > *adjective* informal imaginary; make-believe.

SYNONYMS – *verb* **1** affect, bluff, sham. **3** counterfeit, fake, feign, simulate.

ORIGIN – Latin *praetendere* 'stretch forth, claim'.

pretender > *noun* a person who claims or aspires to a title or position.

pretension > *noun* 1 (usu. **pretension to**) a claim or aspiration to a particular status or quality. 2 pretentiousness.

pretentious > *adjective* attempting to impress by affecting greater importance or merit than is actually possessed.
SYNONYMS – affected, grandiose, pompous; informal highfalutin, posey.
ANTONYMS – unaffected, unassuming.

preterite /**prett**ərit/ (US also **preterit**) Grammar > *adjective* expressing a past action or state. > *noun* a simple past tense or form.
ORIGIN – Latin *praeteritus*, past participle of *praeterire* 'pass, go by'.

preterm > *adjective & adverb* Medicine born or occurring after a pregnancy significantly shorter than normal.

preternatural /preetə**na**chərəl/ > *adjective* beyond what is normal or natural.
DERIVATIVES – **preternaturally** adverb.
ORIGIN – from Latin *praeter* 'past, beyond'.

pretext > *noun* an ostensible or false reason used to justify an action.
ORIGIN – Latin *praetextus* 'outward display', from *praetexere* 'to disguise'.

pretreat > *verb* treat with a chemical before use.
DERIVATIVES – **pretreatment** noun.

prettify > *verb* (**prettifies**, **prettified**) make superficially pretty.
DERIVATIVES – **prettification** noun.

pretty > *adjective* (**prettier**, **prettiest**) 1 attractive in a delicate way without being truly beautiful. 2 informal used ironically to express displeasure: *he led me a pretty dance.* > *adverb* informal to a moderately high degree; fairly. > *noun* (pl. **pretties**) informal a pretty thing; a trinket.
IDIOMS – **a pretty penny** informal a large sum of money. **be sitting pretty** informal be in an advantageous position.
DERIVATIVES – **prettily** adverb **prettiness** noun.
SYNONYMS – *adjective* 1 appealing, attractive, cute, fetching, good-looking.
ANTONYMS – *adjective* 1 ugly.
COMBINATIONS – **pretty boy** derogatory a foppish or effeminate man.

pretzel /**pretz**'l/ > *noun* a crisp biscuit baked as a knot or stick and flavoured with salt.
ORIGIN – German.

prevail > *verb* 1 prove more powerful; be victorious. 2 (**prevail on**) persuade (someone) to do something. 3 be widespread or current.
DERIVATIVES – **prevailing** adjective.
SYNONYMS – 1 succeed, triumph, win. 2 (**prevail on**) convince, induce, persuade.

COMBINATIONS – **prevailing wind** a wind from the predominant or most usual direction.
ORIGIN – Latin *praevalere*, from *prae* 'before' + *valere* 'have power'.

wordpower facts
Pretty
In Old English **pretty** (then spelled *prættig*) meant 'clever' in a bad way: 'cunning or crafty'. The word comes from a West Germanic base meaning 'trick'. In the Middle Ages **pretty** meant 'clever, skilful, or ingenious': one might find references to 'a praty [pretty] man of pure wit', 'a pretie philosopher', or 'a very pretty way to escape'. The sense development 'deceitful, cunning, clever, skilful, admirable, pleasing, nice' has parallels in adjectives such as **nice**.

prevalent > *adjective* widespread in a particular area at a particular time.
DERIVATIVES – **prevalence** noun.
SYNONYMS – common, current, pervasive, prevailing, widespread.

prevaricate /pri**varr**ikayt/ > *verb* speak or act evasively.
DERIVATIVES – **prevarication** noun.
USAGE – the verbs **prevaricate** and **procrastinate** have similar but not identical meanings: **prevaricate** means 'act or speak in an evasive way', whereas **procrastinate** means 'put off doing something'.
SYNONYMS – beat about the bush, equivocate, stall; archaic palter.
ORIGIN – Latin *praevaricari* 'walk crookedly, deviate'.

prevent > *verb* 1 keep (something) from happening or arising. 2 make (someone) unable to do something.
WORDFINDER – prophylactic (*intended to prevent disease*).
DERIVATIVES – **preventable** adjective **prevention** noun.
SYNONYMS – 1 avert, avoid, stop, ward off. 2 block, obstruct, stop.
ORIGIN – Latin *praevenire* 'precede, hinder', from *prae* 'before' + *venire* 'come'.

preventer > *noun* 1 a person or thing that prevents something. 2 Sailing an extra line rigged to support a piece of rigging or to prevent the boom from gybing.

preventive (also **preventative**) > *adjective* designed to prevent something from occurring. > *noun* a preventive medicine or other treatment.

preview > *noun* 1 a viewing or display of

something before it is acquired or becomes generally available. 2 a publicity article or trailer of a forthcoming film, book, etc. > *verb* provide or have a preview of (a product, film, etc.).

previous > *adjective* 1 existing or occurring before in time or order. 2 informal over-hasty.
ORIGIN – Latin *praevius* 'going before'.

prey > *noun* 1 an animal hunted and killed by another for food. 2 a victim or quarry. > *verb* (**prey on** or **upon**) 1 hunt and kill for food. 2 exploit or injure; cause trouble to.
ORIGIN – Latin *praedari* 'seize as plunder', from *praeda* 'prey'; compare with **PREDATOR**.

prezzie (also **pressie**) > *noun* Brit. informal a present.

priapic /prī**app**ik/ > *adjective* 1 phallic. 2 Medicine having a persistently erect penis.
DERIVATIVES – **priapism** noun.
ORIGIN – from *Priapos*, name of a Greek god of fertility.

price > *noun* 1 the amount of money expected, required, or given in payment for something. 2 something endured in order to achieve an objective. 3 the odds in betting. > *verb* decide the price of.
IDIOMS – **at any price** no matter what is involved. **at a price** requiring great expense or involving unwelcome consequences. **a price on someone's head** a reward offered for someone's capture or death. **what price** ——? 1 what has or would become of ——? 2 what is the chance of ——?
ORIGIN – Old French *pris*, from Latin *pretium* 'value, reward'.

priceless > *adjective* 1 so precious that its value cannot be determined. 2 informal very amusing or absurd.

pricey > *adjective* (**pricier**, **priciest**) informal expensive.

prick > *verb* 1 press briefly or puncture with a sharp point. 2 feel a sensation as though a sharp point were sticking into one. 3 (often **prick up**) (chiefly of a horse or dog) make (the ears) stand erect when alert. 4 (**prick out**) plant (seedlings) in small holes made in the earth. > *noun* 1 an act of pricking something. 2 a sharp pain caused by being pierced with a fine point. 3 a small hole or mark made by pricking. 4 vulgar slang a man's penis. 5 vulgar slang a man regarded as stupid, unpleasant, or contemptible.
IDIOMS – **kick against the pricks** hurt oneself by persisting in useless resistance. [ORIGIN – with biblical allusion to Acts of the Apostles, chapter 9.]

prickle > *noun* 1 a short spine or pointed

outgrowth on the surface of a plant or on the skin of an animal. **2** a tingling or mildly painful sensation on the skin. > *verb* experience or produce a prickle.

prickly > *adjective* (**pricklier, prickliest**) **1** covered in or resembling prickles. **2** having or causing a prickling sensation. **3** ready to take offence.

COMBINATIONS – **prickly heat** an itchy skin rash experienced in hot moist weather. **prickly pear** a cactus with flattened, jointed stems which produces prickly, pear-shaped fruits.

pride > *noun* **1** a feeling of deep pleasure or satisfaction derived from achievements, qualities, or possessions. **2** something which causes this. **3** consciousness of one's own dignity. **4** the quality of having an excessively high opinion of oneself. **5** a group of lions forming a social unit. > *verb* (**pride oneself on**) be especially proud of (a quality or skill).

WORDFINDER – hubris (*pride leading to downfall*).

IDIOMS – **one's pride and joy** a person or thing of which one is very proud. **pride goes** (or **comes**) **before a fall** *proverb* if you are too self-important, something will happen to make you look foolish. **pride of place** the most prominent or important position.

DERIVATIVES – **prideful** *adjective*.

SYNONYMS – **1** fulfilment, gratification, pleasure, satisfaction. **3** dignity, honour, self-esteem, self-respect, self-worth. **4** arrogance, conceit, self-congratulation, vanity.

ANTONYMS – **4** humility, modesty.

prie-dieu /pree djö/ > *noun* (pl. **prie-dieux** pronunc. same) a narrow desk on which to kneel for prayer.

ORIGIN – French, 'pray God'.

priest > *noun* **1** an ordained minister of the Catholic, Orthodox, or Anglican Church, authorised to perform certain ceremonies. **2** a person who performs ceremonies in a non-Christian religion.

WORDFINDER – clerical, hieratic, sacerdotal (*of priests*), neophyte (*newly ordained priest*), ordinand (*person training to be ordained as a priest*), presbytery (*house of a Roman Catholic parish priest*), seminary (*college for priests*), theocracy (*rule by priests*).

DERIVATIVES – **priesthood** *noun* **priestly** *adjective*.

ORIGIN – Old English, from Latin *presbyter* 'elder'.

priestess > *noun* a female priest of a non-Christian religion.

prig > *noun* a self-righteously moralistic person.

DERIVATIVES – **priggish** *adjective*.

wordpower facts
Prig

The word **prig** has undergone a startling change in meaning since it was first recorded in the 16th century. It was originally a slang word for 'tinker' or 'petty thief': Shakespeare used it in the latter sense in *The Winter's Tale*. It then came to mean 'a dandy or fop' or simply 'a disliked person', then 'a person of strict religious observance, a puritan or nonconformist', from which sense the modern meaning arose in the mid 18th century. **Prig** is also a verb, now restricted to dialect use, which means 'steal, haggle, or beg'.

prim > *adjective* (**primmer, primmest**) feeling or showing disapproval of anything improper; stiffly correct.

SYNONYMS – prissy, proper, prudish, strait-laced; informal starchy.

prima ballerina /**pree**mə/ > *noun* the chief female dancer in a ballet or ballet company.

primacy /**prī**məsi/ > *noun* pre-eminence.

prima donna /**pree**mə/ > *noun* **1** the chief female singer in an opera or opera company. **2** a very temperamental and self-important person.

ORIGIN – Italian, 'first lady'.

primaeval > *adjective* variant spelling of PRIMEVAL.

prima facie /**prī**mə **fay**shee/ > *adjective & adverb* Law at first sight; accepted as so until proved otherwise.

ORIGIN – Latin, from *primus* 'first' + *facies* 'face'.

primal > *adjective* **1** basic; primitive; primeval. **2** Psychology relating to feelings or behaviour that are thought to form the origins of emotional life: *primal fears.*

primarily > *adverb* for the most part; mainly.

primary > *adjective* **1** of chief importance; principal. **2** earliest in time or order. **3** relating to education for children between the ages of about five and eleven. > *noun* (pl. **primaries**) (in the US) a preliminary election to appoint delegates to a party conference or to select candidates for an election.

SYNONYMS – *adjective* **1** chief, foremost, key, main, prime, principal. **2** earliest, initial, original.

COMBINATIONS – **primary care** health care provided in the community by medical practitioners and specialist clinics. **primary colour** any of a group of colours from which all others can be obtained by mixing.

ORIGIN – Latin *primarius*, from *primus* 'first'.

primate > *noun* **1** a mammal of an order including monkeys, apes, and humans. **2** Christian Church the chief bishop or archbishop of a province.

WORDFINDER – *other primates:* bushbaby, lemur, loris, potto, tarsier.

primatology /prīmətolləji/ > *noun* the branch of zoology concerned with primates.

DERIVATIVES – **primatologist** *noun*.

primavera /preemə**verr**ə/ > *adjective* (of a pasta dish) made with lightly sautéed spring vegetables.

ORIGIN – Spanish or Italian, denoting the season of spring.

prime¹ > *adjective* **1** of first importance; main. **2** of the best possible quality; excellent. **3** (of a number) divisible only by itself and one (e.g. 2, 3, 5, 7). > *noun* **1** a time of greatest vigour or success in a person's life. **2** a prime number. **3** Printing a symbol (′) written as a distinguishing mark or to denote minutes or feet. **4** Christian Church a service traditionally said at the first hour of the day (i.e. 6 a.m.), but now little used.

SYNONYMS – *adjective* **1** chief, key, main, primary, principal. **2** choice, excellent, first-class, first-rate, select, top-quality. *noun* **1** heyday, salad days.

COMBINATIONS – **prime minister** the head of an elected government; the principal minister of a sovereign or state. **prime mover 1** the originator of a plan or project. **2** an initial source of motive power. **prime time** the time at which a radio or television audience is expected to be greatest.

ORIGIN – from Latin *prima hora* 'first hour', from *primus* 'first'.

prime² > *verb* **1** make (something, especially a firearm or bomb) ready for use or action. **2** introduce liquid into (a pump) to make it work more easily. **3** prepare (someone) for a situation. **4** cover (a surface) with primer.

primer¹ > *noun* a substance painted on a surface as a preparatory coat.

primer² > *noun* a book providing a basic introduction to a subject or used for teaching reading.

ORIGIN – from Latin *primarius liber* 'primary book' and *primarium manuale* 'primary manual'.

primeval* /prī**meev**'l/ (also **primaeval**) > *adjective* **1** of the earliest time in history. **2** (of behaviour or emotion) instinctive and unreasoning.

***SPELLING** – as with other words of similar form, such as **medieval**, the simpler -*e*-spelling is now more usual than that with -*ae*-: prim*e*val.

ORIGIN – Latin *primaevus*, from *primus* 'first' + *aevum* 'age'.

primitive > *adjective* **1** relating to the earliest times in history or stages in development. **2** denoting a preliterate society organised in a simple way. **3** offering an extremely basic level of comfort or convenience. **4** (of behaviour or emotion) instinctive and unreasoning. **5** (of art) simple, direct, and deliberately unsophisticated. > *noun* **1** a person belonging to a primitive society. **2** a painter employing a primitive style.
SYNONYMS – *adjective* **1** ancient, primeval, primordial. **3** basic, crude, elementary, rudimentary.
ORIGIN – Latin *primitivus* 'first of its kind', from *primus* 'first'.

primogeniture /preemōjennichər/ > *noun* **1** the state of being the firstborn child. **2** a rule of inheritance by the firstborn child.
ORIGIN – Latin *primogenitura*, from *primo* 'first' + *genitura* 'birth, begetting'.

primordial /prīmordiəl/ > *adjective* existing at or from the beginning of time; primitive.
ORIGIN – Latin *primordialis* 'first of all', from *primus* 'first' + *ordiri* 'begin'.

primp > *verb* make minor adjustments to (one's hair, make-up, or clothes).

primrose > *noun* **1** a woodland and hedgerow plant which produces pale yellow flowers. **2** a pale yellow colour.
IDIOMS – **primrose path** the pursuit of pleasure, especially when it brings disastrous consequences. [ORIGIN – with allusion to Shakespeare's *Hamlet* (I. iii. 50).]
ORIGIN – probably related to Latin *prima rosa* 'first rose'.

primula /primyoolə/ > *noun* a plant of a genus that includes primroses, cowslips, and polyanthuses.
ORIGIN – Latin *primulus* 'little first flower'.

Primus /prīməss/ > *noun* trademark a portable cooking stove that burns vaporised oil.

primus inter pares /preeməss intər paareez/ > *noun* the senior or representative member of a group.
ORIGIN – Latin, 'first among equals'.

prince > *noun* **1** a son or other close male relative of a monarch. **2** a male monarch of a small state. **3** (in some European countries) a nobleman.
DERIVATIVES – **princedom** *noun*.
COMBINATIONS – **Prince Charming** a handsome and honourable young male lover. [ORIGIN – from French *Roi Charmant* 'King Charming', the title of an 18th-century fairy-tale romance.] **prince consort** the husband of a reigning female sovereign who is himself a prince. **Prince of Darkness** the Devil.
ORIGIN – Old French, from Latin *princeps* 'first, chief, sovereign'.

princeling > *noun* chiefly derogatory **1** the ruler of a small principality or domain. **2** a young prince.

princely > *adjective* **1** relating to or suitable for a prince. **2** often ironic (of a sum of money) very large.

princess > *noun* **1** a daughter or other close female relative of a monarch. **2** the wife or widow of a prince. **3** a female monarch of a small state.

principal > *adjective* **1** first in order of importance; main. **2** denoting an original sum of money invested or lent. > *noun* **1** the most important person in an organisation or group. **2** the head of a school or college. **3** a sum of money lent or invested, on which interest is paid. **4** a person for whom another acts as a representative. **5** Law a person directly responsible for a crime.
USAGE – do not confuse **principal** with **principle**, which is a noun meaning chiefly 'a basis of a system of thought or belief'.
COMBINATIONS – **principal boy** Brit. a woman who takes the leading male role in a pantomime.
ORIGIN – Latin *principalis* 'first, original', from *princeps* 'first, chief'.

principality > *noun* (pl. **principalities**) **1** a state ruled by a prince. **2** (**the Principality**) Brit. Wales.

principally > *adverb* for the most part; chiefly.

principle > *noun* **1** a fundamental truth or proposition serving as the foundation for belief or action. **2** a rule or belief governing one's personal behaviour. **3** a general scientific theorem or natural law. **4** morally correct behaviour and attitudes. **5** a fundamental source or basis of something. **6** Chemistry an active or characteristic constituent of a substance.
IDIOMS – **in principle** in theory. **on principle** because of one's adherence to a particular belief.
USAGE – do not confuse **principle** with **principal**, which is an adjective meaning 'main or most important'.
SYNONYMS – **1** precept, proposition, standard, tenet, truth. **2** conviction. **4** conscience, honour, integrity, morality.
ORIGIN – Latin *principium* 'source', from *princeps* 'first, chief'.

principled > *adjective* acting in accordance with morality.
SYNONYMS – ethical, honourable, moral, noble, righteous, virtuous.

print > *verb* **1** produce (books, newspapers, etc.) by a process involving the transfer of text or designs to paper. **2** produce (text or a picture) in such a way. **3** produce a paper copy of (information stored on a computer). **4** produce (a photographic print) from a negative. **5** write clearly without joining the letters. **6** mark with a coloured design. > *noun* **1** the text appearing in a book, newspaper, etc. **2** an indentation or mark left on a surface by pressure. **3** a printed picture or design. **4** a photograph printed on paper from a negative or transparency. **5** (before another noun) relating to the printing industry or the printed media. **6** a copy of a motion picture on film. **7** a piece of fabric or clothing with a coloured pattern or design.
IDIOMS – **in print 1** (of a book) available from the publisher. **2** in published form. **out of print** (of a book) no longer available from the publisher.
DERIVATIVES – **printable** *adjective*.
COMBINATIONS – **print run** the number of copies of a book, magazine, etc. printed at one time.
ORIGIN – from Old French *preinte* 'pressed', from Latin *premere* 'to press'.

printed circuit > *noun* an electronic circuit based on thin strips of a conductor on an insulating board.

printer > *noun* **1** a person whose job is commercial printing. **2** a machine for printing text or pictures.

printing > *noun* **1** the production of books, newspapers, etc. **2** a single impression of a book. **3** handwriting in which the letters are written separately.
WORDFINDER – compositor, typesetter (*person who arranges type for printing*), font (*set of printed characters of particular design*), impression (*copies of a book printed at one time*), justification (*spacing of words to fill width of page or column*), typography (*art of printing from types*).
COMBINATIONS – **printing press** a machine for printing from type or plates.

printmaker > *noun* a person who prints pictures or designs from plates or blocks.
DERIVATIVES – **printmaking** *noun*.

printout > *noun* a page of printed material from a computer's printer.

prion /preeon/ > *noun* a submicroscopic protein particle believed to be the cause of certain brain diseases such as BSE.
ORIGIN – by rearrangement of elements from *pro*(*teinaceous*) *in*(*fectious particle*).

prior[1] > *adjective* existing or coming before in time, order, or importance.
IDIOMS – **prior to** before.
ORIGIN – Latin, 'former, elder'.

prior[2] > *noun* (fem. **prioress**) **1** (in an abbey) the person next in rank below an abbot (or abbess). **2** the head of a house of friars (or nuns).
ORIGIN – Latin (see **PRIOR**[1]).

prioritise (also **prioritize**) > *verb* **1** designate or treat as most important. **2** determine the relative importance of (items or tasks).
DERIVATIVES – **prioritisation** *noun*.

priority > *noun* (pl. **priorities**) **1** the

condition of being regarded as more important. **2** a thing regarded as more important than others. **3** the right to proceed before other traffic.

SYNONYMS – **1** precedence, pre-eminence, preference. **3** right of way.

priory > *noun* (pl. **priories**) a monastery or nunnery governed by a prior or prioress.

prise (US **prize**) > *verb* **1** use force in order to open or move apart (something). **2** (**prise out of** or **from**) obtain (something) from (someone) with effort or difficulty.

ORIGIN – from Old French *prise* 'a grasp, taking hold'.

prism > *noun* **1** a piece of glass or other transparent material of regular shape, used to separate white light into a spectrum of colours. **2** Geometry a solid geometric figure whose two ends are similar, equal, and parallel rectilinear figures, and whose sides are parallelograms.

ORIGIN – Greek *prisma* 'thing sawn', from *prizein* 'to saw'.

prismatic > *adjective* **1** relating to or having the form of a prism. **2** (of colours) formed, separated, or distributed by or as by a prism.

prison > *noun* a building for the confinement of criminals or those awaiting trial.

WORDFINDER – custodial (*of prisons and imprisonment*), dungeon, oubliette (*an underground prison cell*), hulk (*a ship used as a prison*), incarcerate (*lock up in prison*), panopticon (*a prison with cells arranged in a circle*), parole (*release from prison on promise of good behaviour*), penology (*the study of prison management*), remission (*reduction of a prison sentence*).

COMBINATIONS – **prison camp** a camp where prisoners of war or political prisoners are kept.

ORIGIN – Old French *prisun*, from Latin *prehendere* 'lay hold of'.

prisoner > *noun* **1** a person legally committed to prison. **2** a person captured and kept confined. **3** a person trapped by circumstances.

IDIOMS – **take no prisoners** be ruthlessly aggressive in the pursuit of one's objectives.

COMBINATIONS – **prisoner of conscience** a person imprisoned for their political or religious views. **prisoner of war** a person captured and imprisoned by the enemy in war.

prissy > *adjective* (**prissier**, **prissiest**) fussily respectable; prim.

DERIVATIVES – **prissily** adverb **prissiness** noun.

ORIGIN – perhaps a blend of PRIM and SISSY.

pristine /pristeen/ > *adjective* **1** in its original condition. **2** spotlessly clean.

SYNONYMS – **1** flawless, in mint condition, perfect, unused. **2** immaculate, spotless, unblemished, unsullied.

ORIGIN – first used in the senses 'original, former, undeveloped': from Latin *pristinus* 'former'.

prithee /prithee/ > *exclamation* archaic please.

ORIGIN – abbreviation of *I pray thee*.

privacy /privvəsi, prīvəsi/ > *noun* a state in which one is not observed or disturbed by others.

NOTE – in British English both pronunciations occur, although the first, beginning like *privilege*, is more widely used. The second, beginning like *private*, is standard in American English.

SYNONYMS – isolation, seclusion, solitude.

private > *adjective* **1** for or belonging to one particular person or group only. **2** (of thoughts, feelings, etc.) not to be shared or revealed. **3** (of a place) secluded or unobserved. **4** (of a service or industry) provided by an individual or commercial company rather than the state. **5** (of a person) not readily sharing their thoughts and feelings. **6** (of a person) having no official or public position. **7** not connected with one's work or official position. > *noun* **1** the lowest rank in the army, below lance corporal. **2** (**privates**) informal short for **private parts**.

IDIOMS – **in private** not done publicly; in secret.

SYNONYMS – *adjective* **1** exclusive, particular, personal. **2** confidential, intimate, personal, secret. **5** introverted, reserved, retiring, uncommunicative, unforthcoming.

ANTONYMS – public.

COMBINATIONS – **private company** Brit. a company whose shares may not be offered to the public for sale. **private detective** (also **private investigator**) a freelance detective carrying out investigations for private clients. **private enterprise** business or industry managed by independent companies rather than the state. **private eye** informal a private detective. **private life** one's personal relationships, interests, etc., as distinct from one's professional or public life. **private means** Brit. a source of income derived from investments, property, etc., rather than from employment. **private member** (in the UK, Canada, Australia, and New Zealand) a member of a parliament who is not a minister or does not hold government office. **private parts** euphemistic a person's genitals. **private practice 1** the work of a doctor, lawyer, etc. who is self-employed. **2** Brit. medical practice that is not part of the National Health Service. **private school 1** Brit. an independent school supported wholly by the payment of fees. **2** N. Amer. a school supported mainly by private individuals. **private secretary 1** a secretary who deals with the personal concerns of their employer. **2** a civil servant acting as an aide to a senior government official. **private sector** the part of the national economy not under direct state control. **private soldier** a soldier of the lowest rank (in the US, one who is also not a recruit). **private view** a chance for invited guests to see an art exhibition before it opens to the public.

ORIGIN – Latin *privatus* 'withdrawn from public life', from *privus* 'single, individual'.

privateer /prīvəteer/ > *noun* chiefly historical a privately owned armed ship holding a government commission and authorised for use in war.

privation /prīvaysh'n/ > *noun* a state in which essentials such as food and warmth are lacking.

SYNONYMS – adversity, deprivation, hardship, poverty.

ORIGIN – Latin, from *privare* 'bereave, deprive'.

privatise (also **privatize**) > *verb* transfer (a business or industry) from public to private ownership.

DERIVATIVES – **privatisation** noun.

privet /privvit/ > *noun* a shrub with small white flowers and poisonous black berries.

privilege* > *noun* **1** a special right, advantage, or immunity for a particular person. **2** a special honour. **3** the right to say or write something without the risk of punishment, especially in parliament.

*SPELLING – il not el, and no d: privilege.

SYNONYMS – **1** advantage, dispensation, entitlement, prerogative, right.

ORIGIN – Latin *privilegium* 'bill or law affecting an individual', from *privus* 'private' + *lex* 'law'.

privileged > *adjective* **1** having special rights, advantages, or immunities. **2** (of information) legally protected from being made public.

privy > *adjective* (**privy to**) sharing in the knowledge of (something secret). > *noun* (pl. **privies**) a toilet in a small shed outside a house.

COMBINATIONS – **privy purse** (in the UK) an allowance from the public revenue for the monarch's private expenses. **privy seal** (in the UK) a seal affixed to state documents.

ORIGIN – Old French *prive* 'private', from Latin *privatus*.

Privy Council > *noun* a body of advisers appointed by a sovereign or a Governor General.

DERIVATIVES – **privy counsellor** (also **privy councillor**) noun.

prix fixe /pree **fiks**/ > *noun* a meal of several courses costing a fixed price.
ORIGIN – French, 'fixed price'.

prize¹ > *noun* **1** a thing given as a reward to a winner or in recognition of an outstanding achievement. **2** something of great value that is worth struggling to achieve. > *adjective* **1** having been or likely to be awarded a prize. **2** outstanding of its kind. > *verb* value highly.
ORIGIN – the noun is a variant of **PRICE**; the verb is from Old French *preisier* 'praise, appraise'.

prize² > *verb* US spelling of **PRISE**.

prizefight > *noun* a boxing match for prize money.
DERIVATIVES – **prizefighter** *noun*.

PRO > *abbreviation* Public Record Office.

pro¹ > *noun* (pl. **pros**) informal a professional. > *adjective* professional.

pro² > *noun* (pl. **pros**) (usu. in phrase **pros and cons**) an advantage or argument in favour of something. > *preposition & adverb* in favour of.
ORIGIN – Latin, 'for, on behalf of'.

pro-¹ > *prefix* **1** favouring; supporting: *pro-choice*. **2** acting as a substitute for: *proconsul*. **3** denoting motion forwards, out, or away: *propel*.
ORIGIN – from Latin *pro* (see **PRO²**).

pro-² > *prefix* before in time, place, or order.
ORIGIN – from Greek *pro* 'before'.

proactive > *adjective* creating or controlling a situation rather than simply responding to it.

pro-am > *adjective* involving professionals and amateurs. > *noun* a pro-am event.

prob > *noun* informal a problem.

probabilistic > *adjective* based on or adapted to a theory of probability; involving chance variation.

probability > *noun* (pl. **probabilities**) **1** the extent to which something is probable. **2** a probable or the most probable event.
IDIOMS – **in all probability** most probably.

probable > *adjective* likely to happen or be the case. > *noun* a person likely to become or do something.
SYNONYMS – *adjective* anticipated, expected, likely, odds-on.
ANTONYMS – *adjective* improbable, unlikely.
COMBINATIONS – **probable cause** Law, chiefly N. Amer. reasonable grounds.
ORIGIN – Latin *probabilis*, from *probare* 'to test, demonstrate'.

probably > *adverb* almost certainly; as far as one knows or can tell.

probate /**prō**bayt/ > *noun* **1** the official proving of a will. **2** a verified copy of a will with a certificate as handed to the executors.
ORIGIN – Latin *probatum* 'something proved', from *probare* 'to test, prove'.

probation > *noun* **1** Law the release of an offender from detention, subject to a period of supervision. **2** the process of testing the character or abilities of a person in a certain role.
DERIVATIVES – **probationary** *adjective*.
COMBINATIONS – **probation officer** a person who supervises offenders on probation.
ORIGIN – Latin, from *probare* 'to test, prove'.

probationer > *noun* **1** a person serving a probationary period in a job or position. **2** an offender on probation.

probe > *noun* **1** a blunt-ended instrument for exploring a wound or part of the body. **2** an investigation. **3** a small measuring or testing device, especially an electrode. **4** (also **space probe**) an unmanned exploratory spacecraft. > *verb* **1** physically explore or examine. **2** enquire into closely.
DERIVATIVES – **probing** *adjective*.
ORIGIN – Latin *probare* 'to test'.

probity /**prō**biti/ > *noun* honesty and decency.
SYNONYMS – decency, honesty, honour, integrity, uprightness, virtue.
ORIGIN – Latin *probitas*, from *probus* 'good'.

problem > *noun* **1** an unwelcome or harmful matter needing to be dealt with. **2** a thing that is difficult to achieve. **3** Physics & Mathematics an inquiry starting from given conditions to investigate or demonstrate something.
SYNONYMS – **1** complication, difficulty, setback, snag, worry.
ORIGIN – Greek *problēma*, from *proballein* 'put forth'.

problematic > *adjective* presenting a problem.
DERIVATIVES – **problematical** *adjective* **problematically** *adverb*.
SYNONYMS – awkward, complicated, difficult, thorny, tricky, vexed.
ANTONYMS – simple, straightforward.

problematise (also **problematize**) > *verb* make into or regard as a problem.

pro bono publico /prō bonnō **poo**blikō/ > *adverb & adjective* **1** for the public good. **2** (usu. **pro bono**) chiefly N. Amer. (of legal work) undertaken without charge.
ORIGIN – Latin.

proboscis /prə**boss**is/ > *noun* (pl. **probosces** /prə**boss**eez/, **proboscides** /prə**boss**ideez/, or **proboscises**) **1** the nose of a mammal, especially when long and mobile like an elephant's trunk. **2** Zoology an elongated sucking organ or mouthpart.
ORIGIN – Greek *proboskis* 'means of obtaining food', from *pro* 'before' + *boskein* '(cause to) feed'.

procedure > *noun* **1** an established or official way of doing something. **2** a series of actions conducted in a certain manner.

DERIVATIVES – **procedural** *adjective* **procedurally** *adverb*.
SYNONYMS – **1** method, policy, practice, process, routine, strategy; informal drill.
ORIGIN – French, from Latin *procedere* (see **PROCEED**).

proceed > *verb* **1** begin a course of action. **2** go on to do something. **3** (of an action) carry on or continue. **4** move forward. **5** Law start a lawsuit against someone.
ORIGIN – Latin *procedere*, from *pro-* 'forward' + *cedere* 'go'.

proceedings > *plural noun* **1** an event or a series of activities with a set procedure. **2** Law action taken in a court to settle a dispute. **3** a report of a set of meetings or a conference.

proceeds > *plural noun* money obtained from an event or activity.

process¹ /**prō**sess/ > *noun* **1** a series of actions or steps towards achieving a particular end. **2** a natural series of changes. **3** (before another noun) Printing relating to printing using ink in three colours (cyan, magenta, and yellow) and black. **4** Law a summons to appear in court. **5** Biology & Anatomy a natural appendage or outgrowth on or in an organism. > *verb* **1** perform a series of operations to change or preserve (something). **2** Computing operate on (data) by means of a program. **3** deal with (something) using an established procedure.
SYNONYMS – *noun* **1** method, operation, procedure, technique. **2** course, development, progression.
ORIGIN – Latin *processus* 'progression, course', from *procedere* (see **PROCEED**).

process² /prə**sess**/ > *verb* walk in procession.

procession > *noun* **1** a number of people or vehicles moving forward in an orderly fashion. **2** the action of moving in such a way. **3** a relentless succession of people or things.
WORDFINDER – cortège (*funeral procession*), motorcade (*procession of cars*).
SYNONYMS – **1** cavalcade, pageant, parade. **3** series, stream, succession.
ORIGIN – Latin, from *procedere* (see **PROCEED**).

processional > *adjective* of or used in a religious or ceremonial procession. > *noun* a book of litanies and hymns used in religious processions.

processor > *noun* **1** a machine that processes something. **2** Computing a central processing unit.

pro-choice > *adjective* advocating the right of a woman to choose to have an abortion.

proclaim > *verb* **1** announce officially. **2** declare (someone) to be a particular thing. **3** indicate (something) clearly.

DERIVATIVES – **proclamation** *noun*.

SYNONYMS – **1** announce, broadcast, declare, herald, pronounce. **2** announce, declare, pronounce. **3** demonstrate, indicate, show, signify.

ORIGIN – Latin *proclamare* 'cry out', from *pro-* 'forth' + *clamare* 'to shout'.

proclivity /prəklivviti/ > *noun* (pl. **proclivities**) an inclination or predisposition towards a particular thing.

SYNONYMS – inclination, leaning, liking, predisposition, preference, tendency.

ORIGIN – Latin *proclivitas*, from *proclivis* 'inclined'.

procrastinate /prəkrastinayt/ > *verb* delay or postpone action.

DERIVATIVES – **procrastination** *noun* **procrastinator** *noun*.

USAGE – the verbs **prevaricate** and **procrastinate** have similar but not identical meanings: **prevaricate** means 'act or speak in an evasive way', whereas **procrastinate** means 'put off doing something'.

SYNONYMS – be dilatory, delay, play for time, stall, temporise.

ORIGIN – Latin *procrastinare* 'defer till the morning', from *pro-* 'forward' + *crastinus* 'belonging to tomorrow'.

procreate > *verb* produce young.

DERIVATIVES – **procreation** *noun* **procreative** *adjective*.

ORIGIN – Latin *procreare* 'generate, bring forth'.

Procrustean /prōkrustiən/ > *adjective* enforcing conformity without regard to natural variation or individuality.

ORIGIN – from the name of *Procrustes*, a robber in Greek mythology who fitted victims to a bed by stretching or cutting off parts of them.

proctology /proktolləji/ > *noun* the branch of medicine concerned with the anus and rectum.

DERIVATIVES – **proctological** *adjective* **proctologist** *noun*.

ORIGIN – from Greek *prōktos* 'anus'.

proctor > *noun* Brit. a disciplinary officer at certain universities.

ORIGIN – contraction of **PROCURATOR**.

procurator /prokyooraytər/ > *noun* Law **1** an agent representing others in a court in countries retaining Roman civil law. **2** (in Scotland) a lawyer practising before the lower courts.

COMBINATIONS – **procurator fiscal** (in Scotland) a local coroner and public prosecutor.

ORIGIN – Latin, 'administrator, finance agent', from *procurare* (see **PROCURE**).

procure > *verb* **1** obtain (something), especially with care or effort. **2** obtain (someone) as a prostitute for another person. **3** Law persuade or cause (someone) to do something.

DERIVATIVES – **procurement** *noun* **procurer** *noun*.

SYNONYMS – **1** acquire, obtain, secure.

ORIGIN – Latin *procurare* 'take care of, manage'.

Prod (also **Proddie**, **Proddy**) > *noun* informal, offensive (especially in Ireland) a Protestant.

prod > *verb* (**prodded**, **prodding**) **1** poke with a finger or pointed object. **2** stimulate or persuade to do something. > *noun* **1** a poke. **2** a stimulus or reminder. **3** a pointed implement, typically used as a goad.

prodigal > *adjective* **1** wastefully extravagant. **2** lavish. > *noun* **1** a prodigal person. **2** (also **prodigal son**) a person who leaves home to lead a prodigal life but returns repentant. [ORIGIN – with allusion to the parable in the Gospel of Luke, chapter 15.]

DERIVATIVES – **prodigality** *noun* **prodigally** *adverb*.

ORIGIN – Latin *prodigalis*, from *prodigus* 'lavish'.

prodigious /prədijəss/ > *adjective* impressively large.

SYNONYMS – enormous, fantastic, great, immense, tremendous.

ORIGIN – Latin *prodigiosus*, from *prodigium* 'portent'.

prodigy > *noun* (pl. **prodigies**) **1** a person, especially a young one, with exceptional abilities. **2** an outstanding example of a quality. **3** an amazing or very unusual thing.

SYNONYMS – **1** genius, marvel, virtuoso, wunderkind; informal whizz-kid.

ORIGIN – Latin *prodigium* 'portent'.

produce > *verb* /prədyōoss/ **1** make, manufacture, or create. **2** cause to happen or exist. **3** show or provide for inspection or use. **4** administer the financial and managerial aspects of (a film or broadcast) or the staging of (a play). **5** supervise the making of (a musical recording). > *noun* /prodyōoss/ things that have been produced or grown.

DERIVATIVES – **producer** *noun*.

ORIGIN – Latin *producere*, from *pro-* 'forward' + *ducere* 'to lead'.

product > *noun* **1** an article or substance manufactured for sale. **2** a substance produced during a natural, chemical, or manufacturing process. **3** a result of an action or process. **4** Mathematics a quantity obtained by multiplying quantities together.

SYNONYMS – **1** artefact, commodity. **3** consequence, effect, fruit, outcome, result.

COMBINATIONS – **product placement** a practice in which companies pay for their products to be featured in films and television programmes.

ORIGIN – Latin *productum* 'something produced', from *producere* (see **PRODUCE**).

production > *noun* **1** the action or process of producing or being produced. **2** the amount of something produced. **3** a film, record, or play viewed in terms of its making or staging.

COMBINATIONS – **production line** an assembly line.

productive > *adjective* **1** producing or able to produce large amounts of goods or crops. **2** achieving or producing a significant amount or result. **3** relating to or engaged in the production of goods or crops.

DERIVATIVES – **productively** *adverb*.

SYNONYMS – **1** fertile, fruitful, rich. **2** beneficial, constructive, effective, efficient, profitable, rewarding.

productivity > *noun* **1** the state or quality of producing something. **2** the effectiveness of productive effort.

profane > *adjective* **1** secular rather than religious. **2** not respectful of religious practice. **3** (of language) blasphemous or obscene. > *verb* treat with irreverence.

DERIVATIVES – **profanation** *noun* **profanely** *adverb*.

SYNONYMS – **1** lay, secular, temporal, worldly. **2** disrespectful, impious, irreligious, irreverent.

ANTONYMS – **1,2** religious, sacred.

ORIGIN – Latin *profanus* 'outside the temple, not sacred', from *fanum* 'temple'.

profanity > *noun* (pl. **profanities**) profane language or behaviour.

profess > *verb* **1** claim that one has (a quality or feeling). **2** affirm one's faith in or allegiance to (a religion).

SYNONYMS – **1** allege, assert, claim, contend, maintain.

ORIGIN – Latin *profiteri* 'declare publicly', from *pro-* 'before' + *fateri* 'confess'.

professed > *adjective* **1** (of a quality or feeling) claimed openly but typically falsely. **2** (of a person) self-acknowledged or openly declared to be.

DERIVATIVES – **professedly** *adverb*.

profession > *noun* **1** a paid occupation, especially one involving training and a formal qualification. **2** a body of people engaged in a profession. **3** an open but typically false claim. **4** a declaration of belief in a religion.

SYNONYMS – **1** business, career, métier, occupation, trade.

ORIGIN – Latin, from *profiteri* 'declare publicly'.

professional > *adjective* **1** relating to or belonging to a profession. **2** engaged in an activity as a paid occupation rather than as an amateur. **3** impressively competent. > *noun* **1** a professional person. **2** a person having impressive competence in a particular activity.

DERIVATIVES – **professionalise** (also **professionalize**) *verb* **professionally** *adverb*.

SYNONYMS – *noun* **2** expert, master, specialist.

ANTONYMS – amateur.

COMBINATIONS – **professional foul** (especially in soccer) a deliberate foul to deprive an opponent of an advantage.

professionalism > *noun* the competence or skill expected of a professional.

professor > *noun* **1** a university academic of the highest rank. **2** N. Amer. a university teacher. **3** a person who affirms a faith in or allegiance to something.

DERIVATIVES – **professorial** *adjective* **professorship** *noun*.

ORIGIN – Latin, from *profiteri* (see **PROFESS**).

proffer > *verb* hold out (something) for acceptance; offer.

ORIGIN – Old French *proffrir*, from Latin *pro-* 'before' + *offerre* 'to offer'.

proficient > *adjective* competent or skilled in doing or using something.

DERIVATIVES – **proficiency** *noun*.

SYNONYMS – able, accomplished, adept, capable, competent, efficient, skilled.

ORIGIN – from Latin *proficere* 'to advance'.

profile > *noun* **1** an outline of something, especially a face, as seen from one side. **2** a short descriptive article about someone. **3** the extent to which a person or organisation attracts public notice. > *verb* **1** describe in a short article. **2** (**be profiled**) appear in outline.

IDIOMS – **in profile** as seen from one side. **keep a low profile** remain inconspicuous.

ORIGIN – obsolete Italian *profilo*, from *profilare*, from Latin *filare*, from *filum* 'thread'.

profiling > *noun* the analysis of a person's psychological and behavioural characteristics.

profit* > *noun* **1** a financial gain, especially the difference between an initial outlay and the amount subsequently earned. **2** advantage; benefit. > *verb* (**profited**, **profiting**) benefit, especially financially.

DERIVATIVES – **profitless** *adjective*.

*SPELLING – note that the forms **profited** and **profiting** have a single rather than a double *t*.

COMBINATIONS – **profit and loss account** an account to which incomes and gains are credited and expenses and losses debited, so as to show the net profit or loss. **profit margin** the amount by which revenue from sales exceeds costs in a business. **profit-sharing** a system in which the people who work for a company receive a direct share of its profits.

ORIGIN – Latin *profectus* 'progress, profit', from *proficere* 'to advance'.

profitable > *adjective* **1** (of a business or activity) yielding profit or financial gain. **2** beneficial; useful.

DERIVATIVES – **profitability** *noun* **profitably** *adverb*.

SYNONYMS – **1** commercial, cost-effective, gainful, lucrative, money-making, remunerative.

profiteer > *verb* make an excessive or unfair profit. > *noun* a person who profiteers.

DERIVATIVES – **profiteering** *noun*.

profiterole /prəfittərōl/ > *noun* a small ball of choux pastry filled with cream and covered with chocolate sauce.

ORIGIN – French, literally 'small gain', from *profit* 'profit'.

profligate /profligət/ > *adjective* **1** recklessly extravagant or wasteful. **2** licentious; dissolute. > *noun* a profligate person.

DERIVATIVES – **profligacy** *noun*.

SYNONYMS – *adjective* **1** extravagant, prodigal, reckless, spendthrift, wasteful.

ORIGIN – Latin *profligatus* 'dissolute', from *profligare* 'overthrow, ruin'.

pro forma /prō formə/ > *adverb* as a matter of form or politeness. > *adjective* done or produced as a matter of form. > *noun* a standard document or form.

ORIGIN – Latin.

profound > *adjective* (**profounder**, **profoundest**) **1** (of a state, quality, or emotion) very great or intense. **2** showing great knowledge or insight. **3** demanding deep study or thought. **4** archaic very deep.

DERIVATIVES – **profoundly** *adverb* **profoundness** *noun* **profundity** *noun*.

SYNONYMS – **1** deep, earnest, far-reaching, fervent, great, heartfelt, intense. **2** learned, knowledgeable, penetrating, scholarly, wise. **3** complex, deep, weighty.

ANTONYMS – superficial.

ORIGIN – Latin *profundus* 'deep'.

profuse > *adjective* **1** (of something offered or discharged) plentiful; abundant. **2** archaic extravagant.

DERIVATIVES – **profusely** *adverb* **profuseness** *noun* **profusion** *noun*.

SYNONYMS – **1** abundant, copious, fulsome, lavish, plentiful, prolific.

ANTONYMS – meagre, sparse.

ORIGIN – Latin *profusus* 'lavish, spread out'.

progenitive > *adjective* formal having reproductive power.

progenitor /prōjennitər/ > *noun* **1** an ancestor or parent. **2** the originator of an artistic, political, or intellectual movement.

DERIVATIVES – **progenitorial** *adjective*.

ORIGIN – Latin, from *progignere* 'beget'.

progeniture /prōjennichər/ > *noun* formal **1** procreation. **2** offspring.

progeny /projini/ > *noun* (treated as sing. or pl.) children, descendents, or young; offspring.

progeria /prōjeeriə/ > *noun* Medicine a rare condition affecting children, who show physical symptoms suggestive of premature old age.

ORIGIN – from Greek *progērōs* 'prematurely old'.

progesterone /prəjestərōn/ > *noun* Biochemistry a steroid hormone released by the corpus luteum that stimulates the uterus to prepare for pregnancy.

progestogen /prəjestəjən/ > *noun* Biochemistry a steroid hormone that maintains pregnancy and prevents further ovulation.

prognathous /prognaythəss/ > *adjective* (of a jaw or chin) projecting.

ORIGIN – from **PRO-²** + Greek *gnathos* 'jaw'.

prognosis /prognōsiss/ > *noun* (pl. **prognoses** /prognōseez/) a forecast, especially of the likely course of a disease or ailment.

ORIGIN – Greek, from *pro-* 'before' + *gignōskein* 'know'.

prognostic /prognostik/ > *adjective* serving to predict the likely course of a disease or ailment.

DERIVATIVES – **prognostically** *adverb*.

prognosticate > *verb* foretell; prophesy.

DERIVATIVES – **prognostication** *noun* **prognosticator** *noun*.

prograde /prōgrayd/ > *adjective* chiefly Astronomy proceeding in the normal direction; not retrograde.

programmatic > *adjective* of the nature of or according to a programme, schedule, or method.

DERIVATIVES – **programmatically** *adverb*.

programme (US **program**) > *noun* **1** a planned series of events. **2** a set of related measures or activities with a long-term aim. **3** a sheet or booklet detailing items or performers at an event. **4** a radio or television broadcast. **5** (**program**) a series of coded software instructions used to control the operation of a computer or other machine. > *verb* (**programmed**, **programming**; US **programed**, **programing**) **1** (**program**) provide (a computer) with a program. **2** cause to behave in a predetermined way. **3** arrange according to a plan or schedule.

DERIVATIVES – **programmable** *adjective* **programmer** *noun*.

SYNONYMS – *noun* **1** agenda, calendar, schedule, timetable. **2** plan, project, scheme, strategy. *verb* **3** arrange, organise, plan, schedule.

COMBINATIONS – **programme music** music intended to evoke images or tell a story.

ORIGIN – Greek *programma*, from *prographein* 'write publicly'.

progress > *noun* **1** forward movement towards a destination. **2** development towards a better, more complete, or more modern condition. **3** Brit. archaic a state journey or official tour. > *verb* move or develop towards a destination or a more advanced condition.

WORDFINDER – Luddite, reactionary (*person opposed to progress*).

SYNONYMS – *noun* 1 advance, headway, progression. 2 advance, development, improvement. *verb* advance, continue, develop, mature, improve, proceed.

ANTONYMS – *noun* regression, reversal. *verb* regress.

ORIGIN – Latin *progressus*, from *progredi* 'move forward'.

progression > *noun* 1 a gradual movement or development towards a destination or a more advanced state. 2 a succession. 3 a sequence of numbers following a mathematical rule.

DERIVATIVES – **progressional** *adjective*.

progressive > *adjective* 1 proceeding gradually or in stages. 2 favouring innovation or social reform. 3 (of tax) taking a proportionally greater amount from those on higher incomes. 4 (of a card game or dance) involving successive changes of partner. 5 archaic engaging in or constituting forward motion. > *noun* a person advocating social reform.

DERIVATIVES – **progressively** *adverb* **progressiveness** *noun*.

SYNONYMS – *adjective* 1 continuing, cumulative, developing, increasing, ongoing. 2 advanced, enlightened, forward-thinking, innovative, modern. *noun* innovator, reformer.

ANTONYMS – *adjective* 2 conservative, reactionary.

prohibit > *verb* (**prohibited**, **prohibiting**) 1 formally forbid by law, rule, etc. 2 prevent.

DERIVATIVES – **prohibitory** *adjective*.

SYNONYMS – 1 ban, bar, disallow, forbid, outlaw, proscribe.

ANTONYMS – allow, permit.

ORIGIN – Latin *prohibere* 'keep in check'.

prohibition /prōhiˈbishˈn, prō-iˈbishˈn/ > *noun* 1 the action of prohibiting something. 2 an order that forbids something. 3 (**Prohibition**) the prevention by law of the manufacture and sale of alcohol in the US from 1920 to 1933.

DERIVATIVES – **Prohibitionist** *noun*.

SYNONYMS – 2 ban, bar, embargo, injunction, proscription.

prohibitive > *adjective* 1 serving to forbid, restrict, or prevent. 2 (of a price or charge) so high that it deters buyers.

DERIVATIVES – **prohibitively** *adverb*.

SYNONYMS – 1 proscriptive, repressive, restrictive. 2 excessive, exorbitant, extortionate.

project > *noun* /ˈprojekt/ 1 an enterprise carefully planned to achieve a particular aim. 2 a piece of research work by a school

or college student. 3 N. Amer. a government-subsidised estate or block of homes. > *verb* /prəˈjekt/ 1 estimate or forecast on the basis of present trends. 2 plan. 3 protrude. 4 throw or cause to move forward or outward. 5 cause (light, shadow, or an image) to fall on a surface. 6 present, promote, or display (a view or image). 7 (**project on to**) attribute (an emotion) to (another person), especially unconsciously. 8 Geometry draw straight lines through (a figure) to produce a corresponding figure on a surface or line. 9 represent (the earth's surface, the heavens, etc.) on a plane surface.

SYNONYMS – *noun* 1 enterprise, plan, programme, scheme, undertaking. *verb* 1 calculate, estimate, forecast, predict, reckon. 3 extend, jut out, protrude, stick out. 4,5 cast, propel, send, throw.

ORIGIN – Latin *projectum* 'something prominent', from *proicere* 'throw forth'.

projectile > *noun* a missile fired or thrown at a target. > *adjective* 1 relating to a projectile. 2 propelled with great force.

projection > *noun* 1 an estimate or forecast based on present trends. 2 the projecting of an image, sound, etc. 3 a mental image viewed as reality. 4 the unconscious transfer of one's own desires or emotions to another person. 5 a protruding thing. 6 a map or diagram made by projecting a given figure, area, etc.

WORDFINDER – orthographic (*denoting projection by parallel lines on to a plane*); kinds of map projection: azimuthal, conical, Mercator, Mollweide, Peters, zenithal.

DERIVATIVES – **projective** *adjective* **projectionist** *noun*.

SYNONYMS – 1 calculation, estimate, forecast, prediction, reckoning. 5 bulge, protrusion, protuberance, ridge.

projector > *noun* an apparatus for projecting slides or film on to a screen.

WORDFINDER – epidiascope (*projector giving an image of objects*).

prokaryote /prōˈkarrɪət/ > *noun* Biology a single-celled organism with neither a distinct nucleus with a membrane nor other specialised structures (i.e. a bacterium or archaean). Compare with EUKARYOTE.

DERIVATIVES – **prokaryotic** *adjective*.

ORIGIN – from PRO-2 + Greek *karuon* 'nut, kernel'.

prolactin /prōˈlaktin/ > *noun* Biochemistry a pituitary hormone which stimulates milk production after childbirth.

prolapse > *noun* /ˈprōlaps/ 1 a slipping forward or down of a part or organ of the body. 2 a prolapsed part or organ. > *verb* /also prōˈlaps/ undergo prolapse.

ORIGIN – from Latin *prolabi* 'slip forward'.

prolate /ˈprōlayt/ > *adjective* Geometry (of a

spheroid) lengthened in the direction of a polar diameter. Contrasted with OBLATE1.

ORIGIN – Latin *prolatus*, from *pro-* 'forward' + *-latus* 'carried'.

prole informal, derogatory > *noun* a member of the proletariat. > *adjective* working class.

prolegomenon /prōliˈgommɪnən/ > *noun* (pl. **prolegomena**) a critical or discursive introduction to a book.

ORIGIN – Greek, from *prolegein* 'say beforehand'.

prolepsis /prōˈlepsiss/ > *noun* (pl. **prolepses** /prōˈlepseez/) 1 Rhetoric the anticipation and answering of possible objections. 2 the representation of something as happening before it actually does, as in *he was a dead man when he entered*.

ORIGIN – Greek, from *prolambanein* 'anticipate'.

proletarian /prōliˈtairɪən/ > *adjective* relating to the proletariat. > *noun* a member of the proletariat.

ORIGIN – Latin *proletarius* (from *proles* 'offspring'), denoting a person without wealth, who served the state only by producing offspring.

proletariat > *noun* (treated as sing. or pl.) 1 workers or working-class people. 2 the lowest class of citizens in ancient Rome.

pro-life > *adjective* seeking to ban abortion and euthanasia.

DERIVATIVES – **pro-lifer** *noun*.

proliferate /prəˈliffərayt/ > *verb* reproduce rapidly; increase rapidly in number.

DERIVATIVES – **proliferation** *noun* **proliferative** *adjective*.

SYNONYMS – burgeon, escalate, multiply, mushroom, snowball.

ORIGIN – based on Latin *proles* 'offspring'.

prolific > *adjective* 1 producing much fruit or foliage or many offspring. 2 (of an artist, author, etc.) producing many works. 3 plentiful.

DERIVATIVES – **prolifically** *adverb*.

SYNONYMS – abundant, bountiful, fertile, fruitful, luxuriant, plentiful, productive.

ORIGIN – Latin *prolificus*, from *proles* 'offspring'.

proline /ˈprōleen/ > *noun* Biochemistry an amino acid which is a constituent of most proteins, especially collagen.

ORIGIN – contraction of the chemical name *pyrrolidine-2-carboxylic acid*.

prolix /ˈprōliks/ > *adjective* (of speech or writing) tediously lengthy.

DERIVATIVES – **prolixity** *noun* **prolixly** *adverb*.

SYNONYMS – long-winded, verbose, wordy.

ANTONYMS – concise.

ORIGIN – Latin *prolixus* 'poured forth, extended'.

prologue (US **prolog**) > *noun* 1 an introductory section or scene in a literary,

prolong-prong

dramatic, or musical work. **2** an event or action leading to another.

ORIGIN – Greek *prologos*, from *pro-* 'before' + *logos* 'saying'.

prolong > *verb* **1** extend the duration of. **2** technical extend in spatial length.

DERIVATIVES – **prolongation** *noun.*

SYNONYMS – **1** draw out, elongate, extend, lengthen, protract, spin out.

ANTONYMS – curtail.

ORIGIN – Latin *prolongare*, from *pro-* 'forward, onward' + *longus* 'long'.

prolonged > *adjective* continuing for a long time; lengthy.

prom > *noun* informal **1** Brit. short for **PROMENADE** (in sense 1). **2** Brit. a promenade concert. **3** N. Amer. a formal dance, especially at a high school or college.

promenade /prommənaad/ > *noun* **1** a paved public walk, especially one along a seafront. **2** a leisurely walk, ride, or drive in a public place. **3** N. Amer. old-fashioned term for **PROM** (in sense 3). > *verb* make a promenade.

COMBINATIONS – **promenade concert** Brit. a concert of classical music at which part of the audience stands in an area without seating. **promenade deck** an upper, open-air deck on a passenger ship.

ORIGIN – French, from *se promener* 'to walk'.

promenader > *noun* **1** a person who takes a promenade. **2** Brit. a person standing at a promenade concert.

Promethean /prəmeethiən/ > *adjective* daring or skilful like Prometheus, a demigod in Greek mythology who stole fire from the gods and gave it to humans.

promethium /prəmeethiəm/ > *noun* an unstable radioactive metallic chemical element of the lanthanide series, made by high-energy collisions.

prominence > *noun* **1** the state of being prominent. **2** a thing that projects.

prominent > *adjective* **1** important; famous. **2** protuberant. **3** particularly noticeable.

DERIVATIVES – **prominently** *adverb.*

SYNONYMS – **1** distinguished, eminent, famous, important, leading, notable, well known. **3** conspicuous, evident, noticeable, obvious, striking.

ANTONYMS – **1** obscure. **3** inconspicuous.

ORIGIN – from Latin *prominere* 'jut out'.

promiscuous /prəmiskyooəss/ > *adjective* **1** having or characterised by many transient sexual relationships. **2** indiscriminate or casual.

DERIVATIVES – **promiscuity** *noun* **promiscuously** *adverb.*

SYNONYMS – **1** libidinous, licentious, loose, wanton. **2** casual, indiscriminate, unconsidered, unselective.

ORIGIN – Latin *promiscuus* 'indiscriminate'.

promise > *noun* **1** an assurance that one will do something or that something will happen. **2** potential excellence. > *verb* **1** make a promise. **2** give good grounds for expecting. **3** (**promise oneself**) firmly intend.

WORDFINDER – renege (*go back on a promise*).

SYNONYMS – *noun* **1** assurance, oath, pledge, undertaking, vow, word. *verb* **1** give one's word, pledge, swear, vow.

COMBINATIONS – **promised land 1** (**the Promised Land**) (in the Bible) the land of Canaan, promised to Abraham and his descendants (Book of Genesis, chapter 12). **2** a place or situation where great happiness is expected.

ORIGIN – Latin *promissum*, from *promittere* 'put forth, promise'.

promisee > *noun* Law a person to whom a promise is made.

promising > *adjective* showing great potential.

DERIVATIVES – **promisingly** *adverb.*

SYNONYMS – auspicious, encouraging, favourable, hopeful, positive.

promisor > *noun* Law a person who makes a promise.

promissory /prommisəri/ > *adjective* chiefly Law conveying or implying a promise.

COMBINATIONS – **promissory note** a signed document containing a written promise to pay a stated sum.

promo /prōmō/ > *noun* (pl. **promos**) informal a promotional film, video, etc.

promontory /promməntəri/ > *noun* (pl. **promontories**) **1** a point of high land jutting out into the sea or a lake. **2** Anatomy a protruding part of a bodily structure.

ORIGIN – Latin *promontorium*, influenced by *mons* 'mountain'.

promote > *verb* **1** further the progress of; support or encourage. **2** publicise (a product or celebrity). **3** raise to a higher position or rank. **4** transfer (a sports team) to a higher division.

SYNONYMS – **1** advance, encourage, foster, further, support. **2** advertise, market, publicise, sell. **3** advance, elevate, upgrade.

ANTONYMS – **1** discourage, obstruct. **3,4** demote, relegate.

ORIGIN – Latin *promovere* 'move forward'.

promoter > *noun* **1** the organiser of a sporting event or theatrical production. **2** a supporter of a cause or aim.

promotion > *noun* **1** activity that supports or encourages. **2** the publicising of a product or celebrity. **3** (**promotions**) the activity or business of organising such publicity. **4** elevation to a higher position or rank. **5** the transfer of a sports team to a higher division.

DERIVATIVES – **promotional** *adjective.*

SYNONYMS – **1** advancement,

encouragement, furtherance, support. **2** advertising, marketing, publicity, selling.

prompt > *verb* **1** cause or bring about. **2** (**prompt to** or **to do**) cause (someone) to take a course of action. **3** assist or encourage (a hesitating speaker). **4** supply a forgotten word or line to (an actor). > *noun* **1** an act of prompting. **2** a word or phrase used in prompting an actor. **3** a prompter. **4** Computing a word or symbol on a VDU screen to show that input is required. > *adjective* **1** done or acting without delay. **2** punctual. > *adverb* Brit. exactly or punctually: *12 o'clock prompt.*

DERIVATIVES – **promptly** *adverb* **promptness** *noun.*

SYNONYMS – *verb* **1** bring about, cause, elicit, engender, occasion, precipitate, provoke, stimulate. **2** encourage, incline, induce, motivate, lead. *noun* cue, reminder. *adjective* **1** direct, immediate, rapid, speedy, swift, unhesitating. **2** on time, punctual.

ANTONYMS – *adjective* slow, tardy.

COMBINATIONS – **prompt book** a copy of a play used by a prompter. **prompt note** a note sent as a reminder of payment due.

ORIGIN – Latin *promptus* 'brought to light, prepared, ready', from *promere* 'to produce'.

prompter > *noun* a person who prompts the actors during the performance of a play.

promulgate /prommǝlgayt/ > *verb* **1** promote or make widely known; disseminate. **2** put (a law or decree) into effect by official proclamation.

DERIVATIVES – **promulgation** *noun* **promulgator** *noun.*

ORIGIN – Latin *promulgare*, from *pro-* 'out, publicly' + *mulgere* 'cause to come forth' (literally 'to milk').

pronate /prōnayt/ > *verb* technical put or hold (a hand, foot, or limb) with the palm or sole turned downwards. Compare with **SUPINATE**.

DERIVATIVES – **pronation** *noun.*

ORIGIN – from Latin *pronus* 'leaning forward'.

pronator > *noun* Anatomy a muscle involved in pronation.

prone > *adjective* **1** (**prone to** or **to do**) likely or liable to suffer from, do, or experience (something unfortunate). **2** lying flat, especially face downwards. **3** archaic with a downward slope or direction.

DERIVATIVES – **proneness** *noun.*

SYNONYMS – **1** (**prone to**) apt to, disposed to, inclined to, liable to, susceptible to. **2** face down, flat, horizontal, prostrate.

ORIGIN – Latin *pronus* 'leaning forward'.

prong > *noun* **1** each of two or more projecting pointed parts on a fork or other article. **2** each of the separate parts of an attack or operation. > *verb* pierce or stab with a fork.

774

DERIVATIVES – **pronged** adjective.
SYNONYMS – noun **1** point, spike, tine, tip, tooth.

pronghorn > noun a deer-like North American mammal with black horns.

pronominal /prōnomm in'l/ > adjective relating to or serving as a pronoun.
DERIVATIVES – **pronominally** adverb.

pronoun /prōnown/ > noun a word used instead of a noun to indicate someone or something already mentioned or known, e.g. I, she, this.

pronounce /prənownss/ > verb **1** make the sound of (a word or part of a word). **2** declare or announce. **3** (**pronounce on**) pass judgement or make a decision on.
DERIVATIVES – **pronounceable** adjective **pronouncement** noun **pronouncer** noun.
SYNONYMS – **1** articulate, enunciate, sound, utter. **2** announce, declare, proclaim, state.
ORIGIN – Latin pronuntiare, from pro- 'out, forth' + nuntiare 'announce'.

pronounced > adjective very noticeable.
DERIVATIVES – **pronouncedly** adverb.
SYNONYMS – conspicuous, distinct, marked, prominent, striking.
ANTONYMS – inconspicuous, indefinite.

pronto > adverb informal promptly.
ORIGIN – Spanish.

pronunciation* /prənunsiaysh'n/ > noun the way in which a word is pronounced.
WORDFINDER – homophone (word with the same pronunciation but different meaning or spelling), orthoepy (the study of correct pronunciation), received pronunciation (British English pronunciation considered standard).
NOTE – **pronunciation** is pronounced with the second syllable rhyming with **dunce**: avoid making the second syllable rhyme with **bounce**.
*SPELLING – unlike **pronounce**, **pronunciation** has no o in the middle.

pro-nuncio /prōnunsiō/ > noun (pl. **pro-nuncios**) a papal ambassador to a country that does not give the Pope's ambassador automatic precedence.

proof > noun **1** evidence establishing a fact or the truth of a statement. **2** the proving of the truth of a statement. **3** a series of stages in the resolution of a mathematical or philosophical problem. **3** archaic a test or trial. **4** Printing a trial impression of a page used for making corrections before final printing. **5** a trial photographic print. **6** a specially struck specimen coin. **7** the strength of distilled alcoholic liquor, relative to proof spirit taken as a standard of 100. > adjective resistant to the specified thing: the armour was proof against most weapons. > verb **1** make waterproof. **2** make a proof of (a printed work). **3** proof-read (a text).
IDIOMS – **the proof of the pudding is in the eating** proverb the real value of something can be judged only from practical experience or results.
SYNONYMS – noun **1** confirmation, corroboration, validation, verification.
COMBINATIONS – **proof positive** final or absolute proof of something. **proof spirit** a mixture of alcohol and water used as a standard of strength of distilled alcoholic liquor.

proof-read > verb read (printer's proofs or other material) and mark any errors.
DERIVATIVES – **proof-reader** noun.

prop¹ > noun **1** a pole or beam used as a temporary support. **2** a source of support or assistance. **3** (also **prop forward**) Rugby a forward at either end of the front row of a scrum. > verb (**propped**, **propping**) **1** support with a prop. **2** lean (something) against something else. **3** (**prop up**) support or assist (someone) to stop them failing or declining.
SYNONYMS – noun **2** backbone, buttress, cornerstone, mainstay, support. verb **3** (**prop up**) bolster, buttress, shore up, support.

prop² > noun a portable object used on the set of a play or film.
ORIGIN – abbreviation of **PROPERTY**.

prop³ > noun informal an aircraft propeller.
COMBINATIONS – **prop jet** a turboprop aircraft or engine.

propaganda* /proppəgandə/ > noun information, especially of a biased or misleading nature, used to promote a political cause or point of view.
*SPELLING – propa-, not propo-: propaganda.

wordpower facts
Propaganda
The word **propaganda** has negative connotations today, with implications of bias and deception, but such associations date only from the mid 19th century. The term derives from the phrase Congregation of the Propaganda, an English form of the Latin title congregatio de propaganda fide, literally 'congregation for propagation of the faith'. The Congregation of the Propaganda was a committee of cardinals responsible for spreading the word of Christianity through foreign missions, founded in 1622 by Pope Gregory XV. From the late 18th century **propaganda** was used to refer to a scheme or organisation for promoting a particular doctrine; it seems to have acquired its modern meaning in the 1830s.

propagandist chiefly derogatory > noun a person who disseminates propaganda.

> adjective consisting of or spreading propaganda.
DERIVATIVES – **propagandise** (also **propagandize**) verb.

propagate /proppəgayt/ > verb **1** breed by natural processes from the parent stock. **2** promote (an idea, knowledge, etc.) widely. **3** transmit in a particular direction.
DERIVATIVES – **propagation** noun.
SYNONYMS – **2** disseminate, promote, promulgate, publicise, spread.
ORIGIN – Latin propagare 'multiply from layers or shoots'.

propagator > noun **1** a covered, heated container of earth or compost, used for germinating seedlings. **2** a person who propagates an idea, knowledge, etc.

propane /prōpayn/ > noun a flammable hydrocarbon gas present in natural gas and used as bottled fuel.

propel > verb (**propelled**, **propelling**) drive or push forwards.
SYNONYMS – drive, launch, project, push, throw, thrust.
COMBINATIONS – **propelling pencil** a pencil with a thin lead that can be extended as the point is worn away.

propellant > noun **1** a compressed fluid in which the active contents of an aerosol are dispersed. **2** an explosive that fires bullets from a firearm. **3** a substance used to provide thrust in a rocket engine. > adjective (also **propellent**) capable of propelling.

propeller* > noun a revolving shaft with two or more angled blades, for propelling a ship or aircraft.
*SPELLING – -er not -or: propeller.
COMBINATIONS – **propeller shaft** a shaft transmitting power from an engine to a propeller or to the wheels of a vehicle.

propensity > noun (pl. **propensities**) an inclination or tendency.
ORIGIN – from Latin propensus 'inclined'.

proper > adjective **1** truly what something is said or regarded to be; genuine. **2** (after a noun) strictly so called: the World Cup proper. **3** suitable or appropriate; correct. **4** respectable, especially excessively so. **5** (**proper to**) belonging or relating exclusively to. **6** (usu. after a noun) Heraldry in the natural colours. > adverb Brit. informal or dialect thoroughly.
SYNONYMS – adjective **1** actual, bona fide, genuine, real, true. **3** appropriate, correct, fitting, right, suitable. **4** decorous, prim, respectable, strait-laced.
ANTONYMS – **3** improper, inappropriate.
COMBINATIONS – **proper fraction** a fraction that is less than one, with the numerator less than the denominator. **proper noun** (also **proper name**) a name for an individual person, place, or organisation, having an initial capital letter.

ORIGIN – Old French *propre*, from Latin *proprius* 'one's own, special'.

properly > *adverb* **1** in a proper manner. **2** in the strict sense. **3** informal, chiefly Brit. thoroughly.

propertied > *adjective* owning property and land.

property > *noun* (pl. **properties**) **1** a thing or things belonging to someone. **2** a building and the land belonging to it. **3** Law ownership. **4** a characteristic of something. **5** old-fashioned term for **PROP²**.

SYNONYMS – **1** belongings, effects, possessions. **2** premises. **4** attribute, characteristic, feature, hallmark, trait.

ORIGIN – Latin *proprietas*, from *proprius* 'one's own, special'.

prophecy /**proff**isi/ > *noun* (pl. **prophecies**) **1** a prediction. **2** the faculty or practice of prophesying.

SYNONYMS – **1** forecast, prediction, prognostication.

ORIGIN – Old French *profecie*, from Greek *prophēteia*, from *prophētēs* 'spokesman'.

prophesy /**proff**isī/ > *verb* (**prophesies**, **prophesied**) **1** predict. **2** speak or write by divine inspiration.

SYNONYMS – **1** foretell, predict.

ORIGIN – Old French *profecier*: the different spellings of *prophesy* and *prophecy* were established after 1700.

prophet > *noun* (fem. **prophetess**) **1** an inspired teacher or proclaimer of the will of God. **2** a person who predicts the future. **3** a person who advocates a new belief or theory.

WORDFINDER – *prophets of disaster:* Cassandra (*doomed not to be believed*), Jeremiah.

IDIOMS – **a prophet is not without honour save in his own country** proverb a person's gifts and talents are rarely appreciated by those close to him. [ORIGIN – with biblical allusion to the Gospel of Matthew, chapter 13.]

SYNONYMS – **1,2** oracle, seer, soothsayer.

ORIGIN – Greek *prophētēs* 'spokesman'.

prophetic /prə**fett**ik/ > *adjective* **1** accurately predicting the future. **2** relating to or characteristic of a prophet or prophecy.

DERIVATIVES – **prophetical** *adjective* **prophetically** *adverb*.

SYNONYMS – **1** far-seeing, oracular, prescient, revelatory.

prophylactic /proffi**lak**tik/ > *adjective* intended to prevent disease. > *noun* **1** a preventative medicine or course of action. **2** chiefly N. Amer. a condom.

prophylaxis /proffi**lak**siss/ > *noun* action taken to prevent disease.

ORIGIN – from Greek *phulaxis* 'act of guarding'.

propinquity /prə**ping**kwiti/ > *noun* **1** proximity. **2** technical close kinship.

ORIGIN – Latin *propinquitas*, from *propinquus* 'near'.

propitiate /prə**pish**iayt/ > *verb* win or regain favour with (someone) by doing something that pleases them.

DERIVATIVES – **propitiation** *noun* **propitiatory** *adjective*.

SYNONYMS – appease, conciliate, mollify, pacify, placate.

ORIGIN – Latin *propitiare* 'make favourable', from *propitius* 'favourable, gracious'.

propitious /prə**pish**əss/ > *adjective* **1** favourable. **2** archaic favourably disposed towards someone.

DERIVATIVES – **propitiously** *adverb* **propitiousness** *noun*.

SYNONYMS – **1** advantageous, auspicious, favourable, fortunate, promising.

propolis /**propp**əliss/ > *noun* a resinous substance collected by honeybees from tree buds for constructing and varnishing honeycombs.

ORIGIN – Greek, from *polis* 'city'.

proponent /prə**pō**nənt/ > *noun* a person who advocates a theory, proposal, or project.

SYNONYMS – advocate, champion, exponent, supporter, upholder.

ORIGIN – from Latin *proponere* 'put forward'.

proportion > *noun* **1** a part, share, or number considered in relation to a whole. **2** the ratio of one thing to another. **3** the correct or pleasing relation of things or between the parts of a whole. **4** (**proportions**) dimensions; size. > *verb* formal adjust so as to have a particular or suitable relationship to something else.

IDIOMS – **in** (or **out of**) **proportion 1** according (or not according) to a particular relationship in size, amount, or degree. **2** regarded without (or with) exaggeration. **sense of proportion** an ability to judge the relative importance of things.

DERIVATIVES – **proportioned** *adjective*.

SYNONYMS – *noun* **1** part, portion, section, segment, share. **3** balance, correspondence, harmony, symmetry.

ORIGIN – Latin, from *pro portione* 'in respect of a share'.

proportional > *adjective* corresponding in size or amount to something else.

DERIVATIVES – **proportionality** *noun* **proportionally** *adverb*.

SYNONYMS – commensurate, comparable, corresponding, equivalent.

COMBINATIONS – **proportional representation** an electoral system in which parties gain seats in proportion to the number of votes cast for them.

proportionate > *adjective* in proportion; proportional.

DERIVATIVES – **proportionately** *adverb*.

proposal > *noun* **1** a plan or suggestion. **2** the action of proposing something. **3** an offer of marriage.

SYNONYMS – **1** plan, proposition, recommendation, submission, suggestion.

propose > *verb* **1** put forward (an idea or plan) for consideration by others. **2** nominate for an office or position. **3** put forward (a motion) to a legislature or committee. **4** plan or intend. **5** make an offer of marriage to someone.

DERIVATIVES – **proposer** *noun*.

SYNONYMS – **1** introduce, postulate, present, recommend, submit, suggest. **4** intend, mean, plan.

ORIGIN – Latin *proponere* 'put forward'.

proposition > *noun* **1** a statement expressing a judgement or opinion. **2** a proposed scheme or plan. **3** informal an offer of sexual intercourse. **4** a matter or person to be dealt with: *it's a tough proposition*. **5** Mathematics a formal statement of a theorem or problem. > *verb* informal make an offer to (someone), especially of sexual intercourse.

DERIVATIVES – **propositional** *adjective*.

SYNONYMS – **1** argument, hypothesis, postulation, premise, theory, thesis. **2** plan, project, proposal, scheme.

propound /prə**pownd**/ > *verb* put forward (an idea, theory, etc.) for consideration.

DERIVATIVES – **propounder** *noun*.

ORIGIN – Latin *proponere* 'put forward'.

proprietary > *adjective* **1** relating to or characteristic of an owner or ownership. **2** (of a product) marketed under a registered trade name.

COMBINATIONS – **proprietary name** (also **proprietary term**) a name of a product or service registered as a trademark.

ORIGIN – from Latin *proprietarius* 'proprietor', from *proprietas* 'property'.

proprietor /prə**prī**ətər/ > *noun* (fem. **proprietress**) **1** the owner of a business. **2** a holder of property.

proprietorial /prəprīə**tor**iəl/ > *adjective* **1** relating to an owner. **2** possessive.

DERIVATIVES – **proprietorially** *adverb*.

propriety > *noun* (pl. **proprieties**) **1** correctness of behaviour or morals. **2** (**proprieties**) the details or rules of conventionally accepted behaviour. **3** appropriateness; rightness.

SYNONYMS – **1** correctness, decency, decorum, respectability. **2** (**proprieties**) etiquette, convention, formalities, niceties. **3** appropriateness, correctness, fitness, rightness, suitability.

ANTONYMS – **1,3** impropriety.

propulsion > *noun* the action of propelling or driving forward.

DERIVATIVES – **propulsive** *adjective*.

propyl /**prō**pīl/ > *noun* Chemistry the radical $-C_3H_7$, derived from propane.

propylene /**prō**pileen/ > *noun* Chemistry a gaseous hydrocarbon of the alkene series.

pro rata /prō **raa**tə/ > *adjective* proportional. > *adverb* proportionally.
ORIGIN – Latin, 'according to the rate'.

prorogue /prə**rōg**/ > *verb* (**prorogues**, **prorogued**, **proroguing**) discontinue a session of (a parliament or assembly) without dissolving it.
DERIVATIVES – **prorogation** *noun*.
ORIGIN – Latin *prorogare* 'prolong, extend'.

prosaic /prō**zay**ik/ > *adjective* **1** having the style of prose rather than poetry. **2** commonplace; unromantic.
DERIVATIVES – **prosaically** *adverb*.
SYNONYMS – **2** commonplace, humdrum, mundane, ordinary, unromantic.
ANTONYMS – **1** poetic. **2** exotic, unusual.

proscenium /prə**see**niəm/ > *noun* (pl. **prosceniums** or **proscenia**) **1** the part of a stage in front of the curtain. **2** (also **proscenium arch**) an arch framing the opening between the stage and the auditorium.
ORIGIN – Greek *proskēnion*, from *pro* 'before' + *skēnē* 'stage'.

prosciutto /prə**shoo**tō/ > *noun* raw cured Italian ham.
ORIGIN – Italian.

proscribe /prō**skrīb**/ > *verb* **1** forbid, especially by law. **2** denounce or condemn. **3** historical outlaw (someone).
DERIVATIVES – **proscription** *noun* **proscriptive** *adjective*.
USAGE – do not confuse **proscribe** with **prescribe**. **Proscribe** is a rather formal word meaning 'condemn or forbid', whereas **prescribe** means either 'issue a medical prescription' or 'recommend with authority'.
ORIGIN – Latin *proscribere* 'publish'.

prose > *noun* ordinary written or spoken language, without metrical structure. > *verb* (usu. **prose away** or **on**) talk tediously.
ORIGIN – from Latin *prosa oratio* 'straightforward discourse'.

prosecute > *verb* **1** institute legal proceedings against (someone) or with reference to (a crime). **2** formal continue (a course of action) with a view to completion. **3** archaic carry on (a trade or pursuit).
DERIVATIVES – **prosecutable** *adjective*.
SYNONYMS – **1** arraign, charge, sue, summons, take to court.
ORIGIN – Latin *prosequi* 'pursue, accompany'.

prosecution > *noun* **1** the prosecuting of someone in respect of a criminal charge. **2** (**the prosecution**) the party prosecuting someone in a lawsuit. **3** formal the continuation of a course of action.

prosecutor > *noun* **1** a person, especially a public official, who prosecutes someone. **2** a lawyer who conducts the case against a defendant.
DERIVATIVES – **prosecutorial** *adjective*.

proselyte /**pross**ilīt/ > *noun* **1** a convert from one opinion, religion, or party to another. **2** a Gentile who has converted to Judaism.
DERIVATIVES – **proselytism** *noun*.
ORIGIN – Greek *prosēluthos* 'stranger, convert'.

proselytise /**pross**ilitīz/ (also **proselytize**) > *verb* try to convert (someone) from one religion, belief, or opinion to another.
DERIVATIVES – **proselytiser** *noun*.

prosody /**pross**ədi/ > *noun* **1** the patterns of rhythm and sound used in poetry. **2** the theory or study of these patterns, or the rules governing them. **3** the patterns of stress and intonation in a language.
DERIVATIVES – **prosodic** *adjective* **prosodist** *noun*.
ORIGIN – Greek *prosōidia* 'song sung to music, tone of a syllable', from *ōidē* 'song'.

prospect > *noun* /**pros**pekt/ **1** the possibility or likelihood of some future event occurring. **2** a mental picture of a future or anticipated event. **3** (**prospects**) chances or opportunities for success. **4** a potential customer or person likely to be successful. **5** an extensive view of landscape. > *verb* /prə**spekt**/ search for mineral deposits, especially by means of drilling and excavation.
DERIVATIVES – **prospector** *noun*.
SYNONYMS – *noun* **1** chance, expectation, likelihood, possibility. **3** (**prospects**) chances, expectations, opportunities, potential, scope. **5** outlook, view, vista.
ORIGIN – Latin *prospectus* 'view', from *prospicere* 'look forward'.

prospective > *adjective* expected or likely to happen or be in the future.
DERIVATIVES – **prospectively** *adverb*.

prospectus > *noun* (pl. **prospectuses**) a printed booklet advertising a school or university or giving details of a share offer.
ORIGIN – Latin, 'view, prospect'.

prosper > *verb* succeed or flourish, especially financially.
SYNONYMS – flourish, prosper, succeed, thrive.
ANTONYMS – fail.
ORIGIN – Latin *prosperare*, from *prosperus* 'doing well'.

prosperous > *adjective* successful or flourishing, especially financially.
DERIVATIVES – **prosperity** *noun* **prosperously** *adverb*.
SYNONYMS – affluent, booming, flourishing, successful, thriving, wealthy.
ANTONYMS – failing, poor.

prostaglandin /prostə**glan**din/ > *noun* Biochemistry any of a group of compounds which have hormone-like effects such as causing uterine contractions.

prostate /**pros**tayt/ > *noun* a gland surrounding the neck of the bladder in males and releasing a component of semen.
DERIVATIVES – **prostatic** *adjective*.
ORIGIN – from Greek *prostatēs* 'one that stands before'.

prosthesis /pross**thee**siss/ > *noun* (pl. **prostheses** /pross**thee**seez/) an artificial body part.
DERIVATIVES – **prosthetic** /pross**thett**ik/ *adjective*.
ORIGIN – Greek *prosthesis*, from *prostithenai* 'add'.

prosthetics /pross**thett**iks/ > *plural noun* **1** artificial body parts; prostheses. **2** pieces of flexible material applied to actors' faces to transform their appearance. **3** (treated as sing.) the branch of surgery concerned with the making and fitting of artificial body parts.
DERIVATIVES – **prosthetist** /**pros**thitist/ *noun*.

prostitute > *noun* a person, typically a woman, who engages in sexual activity for payment. > *verb* (often **prostitute oneself**) **1** offer (someone) as a prostitute. **2** put to an unworthy or corrupt use for the sake of gain.
DERIVATIVES – **prostitution** *noun*.
ORIGIN – Latin *prostituere* 'expose publicly, offer for sale'.

prostrate > *adjective* /**pros**trayt/ **1** lying stretched out on the ground with one's face downwards. **2** completely overcome with distress or exhaustion. **3** Botany growing along the ground. > *verb* /pro**strayt**/ **1** (**prostrate oneself**) throw oneself flat on the ground in reverence or submission. **2** (of distress, exhaustion, or illness) completely overcome (someone).
DERIVATIVES – **prostration** *noun*.
SYNONYMS – *adjective* **1** prone, spreadeagled. **2** dazed, drained, exhausted, overwhelmed, stunned.
ORIGIN – Latin *prosternere* 'throw down'.

prosy /**prō**zi/ > *adjective* (**prosier**, **prosiest**) (of speech or writing) dull and unimaginative.

protactinium /prōtak**tinn**iəm/ > *noun* a rare radioactive metallic chemical element formed as a product of the natural decay of uranium.

protagonist /prə**tagg**ənist/ > *noun* **1** the leading character in a drama, film, or novel. **2** a prominent figure in a real situation. **3** an advocate or champion of a cause or idea.
ORIGIN – Greek *prōtagōnistēs*, from *prōtos* 'first in importance' + *agōnistēs* 'actor'.

protean /**prō**teeən/ > *adjective* tending or able to change or adapt; variable or versatile.

ORIGIN – from the Greek sea god *Proteus*, who was able to change shape at will.

protect > *verb* **1** keep safe from harm or injury. **2** Economics shield (a domestic industry) from competition by imposing import duties on foreign goods. **3** (**protected**) (of a threatened plant or animal species) safeguarded through legislation against collecting or hunting.

SYNONYMS – **1** guard, harbour, safeguard, shelter, shield.

ANTONYMS – **1** expose.

ORIGIN – Latin *protegere* 'cover in front'.

protection > *noun* **1** the action or state of protecting or being protected. **2** a person or thing that protects. **3** the payment of money to criminals to prevent them from attacking oneself or one's property.

SYNONYMS – **1** safekeeping, safety, security. **2** refuge, sanctuary, shelter, shield.

protectionism > *noun* Economics the theory or practice of shielding a country's domestic industries from foreign competition by taxing imports.

DERIVATIVES – **protectionist** *noun* & *adjective*.

protective > *adjective* serving, intended, or wishing to protect. > *noun* Brit. **1** a thing that protects. **2** dated a condom.

DERIVATIVES – **protectively** *adverb* **protectiveness** *noun*.

COMBINATIONS – **protective custody** the detention of a person for their own protection.

protector > *noun* **1** a person or thing that protects. **2** (**Protector**) historical a regent in charge of a kingdom during the minority, absence, or incapacity of the sovereign.

DERIVATIVES – **protectress** *noun*.

SYNONYMS – **1** custodian, defender, guard, guardian, minder.

protectorate > *noun* **1** a state that is controlled and protected by another. **2** (**Protectorate**) historical the position or period of office of a Protector, in particular that of Oliver Cromwell and his son Richard as heads of state in England 1653–9.

protégé /**prott**izhay, **prō**-/ > *noun* (fem. **protégée**) a person who is guided and supported by an older and more experienced person.

ORIGIN – French, 'protected'.

protein > *noun* any of a class of organic compounds forming structural components of body tissues and constituting an important part of the diet.

WORDFINDER – albumin (*blood protein*), amino acids (*compounds which are building blocks of proteins*), casein (*milk protein*), gluten (*cereal protein*), kwashiorkor (*protein deficiency disease*), polypeptide (*a protein or other molecule built up from amino acids*).

ORIGIN – from Greek *prōteios* 'primary'.

pro tem /prō **tem**/ > *adverb & adjective* for the time being.

ORIGIN – abbreviation of Latin *pro tempore*.

Proterozoic /prōtərəzōik/ > *adjective* Geology of or relating to the later part of the Precambrian aeon (between the Archaean aeon and the Cambrian period, about 2,500 to 570 million years ago), in which the earliest forms of life evolved.

ORIGIN – from Greek *proteros* 'former' + *zōē* 'life'.

protest > *noun* /**prō**test/ **1** a statement or action expressing disapproval or objection. **2** an organised public demonstration objecting to an official policy or course of action. > *verb* /prətest/ **1** express an objection to what someone has said or done. **2** take part in a public protest. **3** emphatically deny or state something in response to an accusation or criticism.

DERIVATIVES – **protester** (also **protestor**) *noun*.

SYNONYMS – *noun* **1** complaint, dissent, objection, opposition. *verb* **1** complain, demur, disagree, dissent, object, remonstrate. **3** assert, claim, proclaim, profess.

ANTONYMS – *noun* **1** acquiescence, agreement. *verb* **1** acquiesce, agree.

ORIGIN – Latin *protestari* 'assert formally', based on *testis* 'a witness'.

Protestant /**prott**istənt/ > *noun* a member or follower of any of the Western Christian Churches that are separate from the Roman Catholic Church in accordance with the principles of the Reformation. > *adjective* relating to or belonging to any of the Protestant Churches.

DERIVATIVES – **Protestantism** *noun*.

COMBINATIONS – **Protestant ethic** (also **Protestant work ethic**) the view that a person's duty and responsibility is to achieve success through hard work and thrift.

ORIGIN – Latin, from *protestare* 'protest'.

protestation /prottistaysh'n/ > *noun* **1** an emphatic declaration that something is or is not the case. **2** an objection or protest.

prothalamium /prōthəlaymiəm/ > *noun* (pl. **prothalamia**) literary a song or poem celebrating a forthcoming wedding.

ORIGIN – from *Prothalamion*, the title of a poem by Edmund Spenser, on the pattern of *epithalamium*.

protist /**prō**tist/ > *noun* Biology a primitive organism of a kind including the protozoans, slime moulds, and simple algae and fungi.

ORIGIN – Greek *prōtista*, from *prōtistos* 'very first'.

proto- > *combining form* **1** original; primitive: *prototype*. **2** first; relating to a precursor: *protozoon*.

ORIGIN – from Greek *prōtos* 'first'.

protocol /**prō**təkol/ > *noun* **1** the official procedure or system of rules governing affairs of state or diplomatic occasions. **2** the accepted code of behaviour in a particular situation. **3** the original draft of a diplomatic document, especially of the terms of a treaty. **4** a formal record of scientific observations. **5** Computing a set of rules governing the exchange or transmission of data between devices.

ORIGIN – first meaning 'original note of an agreement': from Greek *prōtokollon* 'first page, flyleaf'.

proton /**prō**ton/ > *noun* Physics a stable subatomic particle occurring in all atomic nuclei, with a positive electric charge equal in magnitude to that of an electron.

ORIGIN – Greek, 'first thing'.

protoplasm /**prō**təplaz'm/ > *noun* Biology the material comprising the living part of a cell, including the cytoplasm, nucleus, and other organelles.

DERIVATIVES – **protoplasmic** *adjective*.

ORIGIN – Greek *prōtoplasma*, from *protos* 'first' + *plasma* (see **PLASMA**).

prototype > *noun* **1** a first or preliminary form from which other forms are developed or copied. **2** a typical example of something.

DERIVATIVES – **prototypical** *adjective* **prototypically** *adverb*.

SYNONYMS – archetype, exemplar, model, paradigm.

protozoan /prōtəzōən/ > *noun* a single-celled microscopic animal such as an amoeba. > *adjective* relating to protozoans.

ORIGIN – from Greek *protos* 'first' + *zōion* 'animal'.

protract > *verb* prolong; draw out.

DERIVATIVES – **protracted** *adjective*.

SYNONYMS – draw out, extend, lengthen, prolong.

ANTONYMS – contract, shorten.

ORIGIN – Latin *protrahere* 'prolong'.

protraction > *noun* **1** the action or state of prolonging or being prolonged. **2** technical the action of extending a part of the body.

protractor > *noun* an instrument for measuring angles, typically in the form of a flat semicircle marked with degrees along the curved edge.

protrude > *verb* extend beyond or above a surface.

DERIVATIVES – **protrusion** *noun*.

SYNONYMS – bulge, extend, project, stick out.

ORIGIN – Latin *protrudere* 'thrust forward'.

protuberance* /prətyōōbərənss/ > *noun* **1** a thing that protrudes. **2** the state of protruding.

***SPELLING** – there is no r immediately after the t: pro**t**uberance.

SYNONYMS – **1** bulge, bump, excrescence, lump, projection.

protuberant > *adjective* protruding; bulging.

SYNONYMS – bulging, distended, prominent, protruding, swollen.

ORIGIN – from Latin *protuberare* 'swell out'.

proud > *adjective* 1 (often **proud of**) feeling pride or satisfaction in one's own or another's achievements. 2 having or showing a high opinion of oneself. 3 conscious of one's own dignity. 4 slightly projecting from a surface. 5 literary imposing; splendid.

IDIOMS – **do proud** informal 1 cause (someone) to feel pleased or satisfied. 2 treat or entertain (someone) very well.

DERIVATIVES – **proudly** *adverb*.

SYNONYMS – 2 arrogant, conceited, haughty, immodest, vain. 3 dignified, self-respecting.

ANTONYMS – 1 ashamed, disappointed. 2 humble, modest.

ORIGIN – Old French *prud* 'valiant', based on Latin *prodesse* 'be of value'.

prove /prōōv/ > *verb* (past participle **proved** or **proven** /prōōv'n, prōv'n/) 1 demonstrate by evidence or argument the truth or existence of. 2 show or be seen to be: *the scheme has proved a great success.* 3 (**prove oneself**) demonstrate one's abilities or courage. 4 Law establish the genuineness and validity of (a will). 5 subject (a gun) to a testing process. 6 (of bread dough) rise through the action of yeast.

WORDFINDER – refute (*prove to be wrong*).

IDIOMS – **not proven** Scots Law a verdict that there is insufficient evidence to establish guilt or innocence.

DERIVATIVES – **provable** *adjective*.

USAGE – the verb **prove** has two past participles, **proved** and **proven**, which can be used more or less interchangeably. However, **proven** is always used when the word is an adjective coming before the noun: *a proven talent,* not *a proved talent.*

SYNONYMS – 1 confirm, demonstrate, substantiate, validate, verify.

ANTONYMS – 1 disprove.

COMBINATIONS – **proving ground** an area or situation in which a person or thing is tested or proved.

ORIGIN – Latin *probare* 'test, approve, demonstrate'.

provenance /provvənənss/ > *noun* 1 the origin or earliest known history of something. 2 a record of ownership of a work of art or an antique.

SYNONYMS – 1 derivation, origin, root, source.

ORIGIN – French, from *provenir* 'come from'.

Provençal /provvoNsaal/ > *noun* 1 a person from Provence in southern France. 2 the language of Provence. > *adjective* relating to Provence.

provençale /provvoNsaal/ > *adjective* (after a noun) cooked in a sauce made with tomatoes, garlic, and olive oil, as characteristic of Provençal cuisine.

provender /provvindər/ > *noun* 1 animal fodder. 2 archaic or humorous food.

ORIGIN – Old French *provendre*, from Latin *praebenda* 'things to be supplied, pension'.

proverb > *noun* a short saying stating a general truth or piece of advice.

SYNONYMS – adage, maxim, motto, saying, saw.

ORIGIN – Latin *proverbium*, from *verbum* 'word'.

proverbial > *adjective* 1 referred to in a proverb or idiom. 2 well known, especially so as to be stereotypical: *their proverbial hospitality.*

DERIVATIVES – **proverbially** *adverb*.

provide > *verb* 1 make available for use; supply. 2 (**provide with**) equip or supply (someone) with. 3 (**provide for**) make adequate preparation or arrangements for. 4 stipulate in a will or other legal document.

DERIVATIVES – **provider** *noun*.

SYNONYMS – 1 dispense, furnish, give, issue, supply.

ORIGIN – Latin *providere* 'foresee, attend to'.

provided > *conjunction* on the condition or understanding that.

providence > *noun* 1 the protective care of God or of nature as a spiritual power. 2 timely preparation for future eventualities.

provident > *adjective* making or indicating timely preparation for the future.

DERIVATIVES – **providently** *adverb*.

SYNONYMS – far-sighted, judicious, prudent, shrewd.

providential > *adjective* 1 occurring at a favourable time; opportune. 2 involving divine foresight or interference.

DERIVATIVES – **providentially** *adverb*.

SYNONYMS – 1 advantageous, auspicious, fortunate, opportune, propitious.

providing > *conjunction* on the condition or understanding that.

province > *noun* 1 a principal administrative division of a country or empire. 2 (**the provinces**) the whole of a country outside the capital, especially when regarded as lacking in sophistication or culture. 3 (**one's province**) an area in which one has expertise, interest, or responsibility.

ORIGIN – Latin *provincia* 'charge, province'.

provincial > *adjective* 1 relating to a province or the provinces. 2 unsophisticated or narrow-minded. > *noun* 1 an inhabitant of a province. 2 an inhabitant of the regions outside the capital city of a country.

DERIVATIVES – **provincialism** *noun* **provinciality** *noun* **provincially** *adverb*.

SYNONYMS – *adjective* 1 outlying, rural. 2 narrow-minded, parochial, unsophisticated.

provision > *noun* 1 the action of providing or supplying. 2 something supplied or provided. 3 (**provision for** or **against**) arrangements for future eventualities or requirements. 4 (**provisions**) supplies of food, drink, or equipment, especially for a journey. 5 a condition or requirement in a legal document. > *verb* supply with provisions.

SYNONYMS – *noun* 3 arrangement, plan, precaution. 4 (**provisions**) supplies, stocks, stores. 5 condition, requirement, specification, stipulation.

provisional > *adjective* 1 arranged or existing for the present, possibly to be changed later. 2 (**Provisional**) relating to or denoting sections of the IRA and Sinn Fein which broke away from the 'official' bodies in 1969. > *noun* (**Provisional**) a member of the Provisional IRA or Sinn Fein.

DERIVATIVES – **provisionality** *noun* **provisionally** *adverb*.

SYNONYMS – *adjective* 1 conditional, interim, temporary, transitional.

ANTONYMS – *adjective* 1 permanent.

proviso /prəvīzō/ > *noun* (pl. **provisos**) a condition attached to an agreement.

SYNONYMS – caveat, condition, provision, qualification, rider, stipulation.

ORIGIN – from Latin *proviso quod* 'it being provided that'.

provisory > *adjective* 1 subject to a proviso; conditional. 2 provisional.

Provo /prōvō/ > *noun* (pl. **Provos**) informal a member of the Provisional IRA or Sinn Fein.

provocation > *noun* 1 the action of provoking. 2 action or speech that provokes.

SYNONYMS – 1 goading, incitement, taunting.

provocative > *adjective* 1 causing annoyance or anger, especially deliberately. 2 arousing sexual desire or interest, especially deliberately.

DERIVATIVES – **provocatively** *adverb*.

SYNONYMS – 1 annoying, galling, goading, inflammatory, irritating. 2 arousing, suggestive, titillating.

ANTONYMS – 1 placatory.

provoke > *verb* 1 stimulate or cause (a strong or unwelcome reaction or emotion) in someone. 2 deliberately annoy or anger. 3 incite to do or feel something, especially by arousing anger.

SYNONYMS – 1 arouse, elicit, evoke, kindle, precipitate. 2 anger, annoy, inflame, infuriate, irk, irritate, nettle. 3 goad, incite, induce, spur.

ORIGIN – Latin *provocare* 'challenge', from *vocare* 'to call'.

provost /provvəst/ > *noun* 1 Brit. the position of head in certain university colleges and public schools. 2 N. Amer. a senior administrative officer in certain universities. **3** Scottish a mayor. **4** the head of a chapter in a cathedral. **5** short for *provost marshal*. **6** historical the chief magistrate of a European town.

COMBINATIONS – **provost marshal 1** the head of military police in camp or on active service. **2** the master-at-arms of a ship in which a court martial is held.

ORIGIN – from Latin *propositus*, *praepositus* 'head, chief'.

prow /prow/ > *noun* the pointed front part of a ship; the bow.

ORIGIN – Greek *prōira*, related to Latin *pro* 'in front'.

prowess > *noun* **1** skill or expertise in a particular activity or field. **2** bravery or heroism in battle.

SYNONYMS – **1** expertise, proficiency, skill, talent.

ORIGIN – Old French *proesce*, from *prou* 'valiant'.

prowl > *verb* move about stealthily or restlessly as if in search of prey. > *noun* an act of prowling.

DERIVATIVES – **prowler** noun.

SYNONYMS – *verb* creep, lurk, slink, steal.

proximal /proksim'l/ > *adjective* chiefly Anatomy situated nearer to the centre of the body or an area or the point of attachment. The opposite of DISTAL.

DERIVATIVES – **proximally** adverb.

proximate /proksimat/ > *adjective* **1** closest in space, time, or relationship. **2** nearly accurate; approximate.

DERIVATIVES – **proximately** adverb.

ORIGIN – from Latin *proximare* 'draw near'.

proximity > *noun* nearness in space, time, or relationship.

proxy > *noun* (pl. **proxies**) **1** the authority to represent someone else, especially in voting. **2** a person authorised to act on behalf of another. **3** a figure used to represent the value of something in a calculation.

ORIGIN – contraction of *procuracy* 'management or action on behalf of another', related to PROCURE.

Prozac /prōzak/ > *noun* trademark a drug which reduces the uptake of serotonin in the brain and is taken to treat depression.

prude > *noun* a person who is easily offended or shocked by matters of sex or nudity.

DERIVATIVES – **prudery** noun.

ORIGIN – from French *prudefemme* 'good woman and true'.

prudent > *adjective* acting with or showing care and thought for the future.

DERIVATIVES – **prudence** noun **prudently** adverb.

SYNONYMS – sensible, shrewd, thoughtful, wise.

ORIGIN – Latin *prudens*, from *providens* 'foreseeing'.

prudential > *adjective* involving or showing care and forethought.

DERIVATIVES – **prudentially** adverb.

prudish > *adjective* easily offended or shocked by matters of sex or nudity.

DERIVATIVES – **prudishly** adverb **prudishness** noun.

SYNONYMS – prim, prissy, puritanical, strait-laced, stuffy.

prune[1] > *noun* **1** a plum preserved by drying and having a black, wrinkled appearance. **2** informal a disagreeable person.

ORIGIN – Latin *prunum* 'plum', from Greek *prounon*.

prune[2] > *verb* **1** trim (a tree, shrub, or bush) by cutting away dead or overgrown branches or stems. **2** remove superfluous or unwanted parts from. > *noun* an instance of pruning.

DERIVATIVES – **pruner** noun.

SYNONYMS – **1** crop, cut back, thin, trim. **2** curtail, cut, decrease, pare, reduce, trim.

ORIGIN – Old French *proignier*, possibly based on Latin *rotundus* 'round'.

prurient /prooriant/ > *adjective* having or encouraging an unwholesome curiosity regarding sexual matters.

DERIVATIVES – **prurience** noun **pruriency** noun **pruriently** adverb.

SYNONYMS – salacious, voyeuristic.

ORIGIN – from Latin *prurire* 'itch, long, be wanton': originally in the sense 'having a craving'.

pruritus /proorītəss/ > *noun* Medicine severe itching of the skin.

DERIVATIVES – **pruritic** /proorittik/ *adjective*.

ORIGIN – Latin, 'itching'.

Prussian > *noun* a person from the former German kingdom of Prussia. > *adjective* relating to Prussia.

COMBINATIONS – **Prussian blue** a deep blue pigment.

prussic acid > *noun* old-fashioned term for HYDROCYANIC ACID.

ORIGIN – from French *prussique* 'relating to Prussian blue'.

pry[1] > *verb* (**pries**, **pried**) enquire too intrusively into a person's private affairs.

DERIVATIVES – **prying** adjective.

SYNONYMS – be inquisitive, be nosy, delve, ferret, intrude, snoop.

pry[2] > *verb* (**pries**, **pried**) chiefly N. Amer. another term for PRISE.

PS > *abbreviation* **1** Police Sergeant. **2** postscript. **3** private secretary.

psalm /saam/ > *noun* a religious song or hymn, in particular any of those contained in the biblical Book of Psalms.

WORDFINDER – psalter (*book of psalms*).

DERIVATIVES – **psalmist** noun.

ORIGIN – Greek *psalmos* 'song sung to harp music'.

psalmody /saaமədi/ > *noun* the singing of psalms or similar religious verses.

DERIVATIVES – **psalmodic** adjective **psalmodist** noun.

psalter /sawltər/ > *noun* a copy of the biblical Psalms.

ORIGIN – Latin *psalterium* from Greek *psaltērion* 'stringed instrument'.

psaltery /sawltəri/ > *noun* (pl. **psalteries**) an ancient and medieval musical instrument resembling a dulcimer but played by plucking the strings.

PSBR > *abbreviation* Brit. public-sector borrowing requirement.

psephology /sefollaji/ > *noun* the statistical study of elections and trends in voting.

DERIVATIVES – **psephologist** noun.

ORIGIN – from Greek *psēphos* 'pebble, vote'.

pseud /syōod/ > *noun* informal a pretentious person; a poseur.

pseudo > *adjective* informal not genuine; fake, pretentious, or insincere.

pseudo- (also **pseud-** before a vowel) > *combining form* **1** false; not genuine: *pseudonym*. **2** resembling or imitating: *pseudo-hallucination*.

ORIGIN – from Greek *pseudēs* 'false', *pseudos* 'falsehood'.

pseudonym /syōodanim/ > *noun* a fictitious name, especially one used by an author.

SYNONYMS – alias, assumed name, nom de plume, sobriquet.

pseudonymous /syōodonnimass/ > *adjective* writing or written under a pseudonym or false name.

DERIVATIVES – **pseudonymity** noun **pseudonymously** adverb.

pseudoscience > *noun* beliefs or practices mistakenly regarded as being based on scientific method.

DERIVATIVES – **pseudoscientific** adjective.

psi /psī, sī/ > *noun* **1** the twenty-third letter of the Greek alphabet (Ψ, ψ), transliterated as 'ps'. **2** supposed psychic faculties or phenomena.

ORIGIN – Greek.

p.s.i. > *abbreviation* pounds per square inch.

psilocybin /sīlōsībin/ > *noun* a substance found in some toadstools which is able to cause hallucinations.

ORIGIN – from Latin *Psilocybe* (a genus of toadstools), from Greek *psilos* 'bald' + *kubē* 'head'.

psittacine /sittəsīn/ Ornithology > *adjective* relating to parrots. > *noun* a bird of the parrot family.

ORIGIN – from Greek *psittakos* 'parrot'.

psittacosis /sittəkōsiss/ > *noun* a contagious disease of birds which can be passed to human beings (especially from parrots) as a form of pneumonia.

psoriasis /sərīəsiss/ > *noun* a skin disease marked by red, itchy, scaly patches.
DERIVATIVES – **psoriatic** /soriattik/ *adjective*.
ORIGIN – Greek, from *psōrian* 'to itch'.

PST > *abbreviation* Pacific Standard Time.

PSV > *abbreviation* Brit. public service vehicle.

psych /sīk/ (also **psyche**) > *verb* **1** (**psych up**) informal mentally prepare (someone) for a testing task or occasion. **2** (**psych out**) intimidate an opponent or rival by appearing very confident or aggressive. **3** informal subject (someone) to psychological investigation or psychotherapy.

psyche /sīki/ > *noun* the human soul, mind, or spirit.
ORIGIN – Greek *psukhē* 'breath, life, soul'.

psychedelia /sīkədeeliə/ > *noun* music, culture, or art based on the experiences produced by psychedelic drugs.

psychedelic* /sīkədellik/ > *adjective* **1** (of drugs) producing hallucinations and apparent expansion of consciousness. **2** (of rock music) characterised by musical experimentation and drug-related lyrics. **3** having an intense, vivid colour or a swirling abstract pattern.
DERIVATIVES – **psychedelically** *adverb*.
*SPELLING – psyche- not psycho-: psychedelic.
ORIGIN – from Greek *psyche* 'soul' + *dēlos* 'clear, manifest'.

psychiatrist > *noun* a medical practitioner specialising in the diagnosis and treatment of mental illness.

psychiatry /sīkīətri/ > *noun* the branch of medicine concerned with the study and treatment of mental illness and emotional disturbance.
DERIVATIVES – **psychiatric** /sīkiatrik/ *adjective* **psychiatrically** *adverb*.
ORIGIN – from Greek *psukhē* 'soul, mind' + *iatreia* 'healing'.

psychic /sīkik/ > *adjective* **1** (of faculties or phenomena) apparently inexplicable by natural laws, especially involving telepathy or clairvoyance. **2** (of a person) appearing or considered to be telepathic or clairvoyant. **3** relating to the soul or mind. > *noun* **1** a person considered or claiming to have psychic powers; a medium. **2** (**psychics**) (treated as sing. or pl.) the study of psychic phenomena.
DERIVATIVES – **psychical** *adjective* **psychically** *adverb*.
SYNONYMS – *adjective* **1** paranormal, preternatural. **2** clairvoyant, prophetic, telepathic. **3** spiritual. *noun* **1** clairvoyant, medium, spiritualist.

psycho > *noun* (pl. **psychos**) informal a psychopath.

psycho- > *combining form* relating to the mind or psychology: *psychometrics*.
ORIGIN – from Greek *psukhē* 'breath, soul, mind'.

psychoactive > *adjective* affecting the mind.

psychoanalyse (US **psychoanalyze**) > *verb* subject (someone) to psychoanalysis in order to treat or investigate mental disorder.

psychoanalysis > *noun* a method of treating mental disorders by investigating the conscious and unconscious elements in the mind and bringing repressed fears and conflicts into the conscious mind.
DERIVATIVES – **psychoanalyst** *noun* **psychoanalytical** (also **psychoanalytic**) *adjective* **psychoanalytically** *adverb*.

psychobabble > *noun* informal, derogatory jargon used in popular psychology.

psychodrama > *noun* **1** a form of psychotherapy in which patients act out events from their past. **2** a play, film, or novel in which psychological elements are the main interest.

psychokinesis /sīkōkineesiss, -kīneesiss/ > *noun* the supposed ability to move objects by mental effort alone.
DERIVATIVES – **psychokinetic** *adjective*.

psycholinguistics > *plural noun* (treated as sing.) the study of the relationships between language and psychological processes, including the process of language acquisition.
DERIVATIVES – **psycholinguist** *noun* **psycholinguistic** *adjective*.

psychological > *adjective* **1** of, affecting, or arising in the mind. **2** relating to psychology.
DERIVATIVES – **psychologically** *adverb*.
SYNONYMS – **1** conceptual, emotional, inner, mental.
COMBINATIONS – **psychological warfare** actions intended to reduce an opponent's morale.

psychology* > *noun* **1** the scientific study of the human mind and its functions. **2** the mental characteristics or attitude of a person. **3** the mental factors governing a situation or activity.
DERIVATIVES – **psychologist** *noun*.
*SPELLING – this and all other **psycho-** words begin with psy-, not py-: psychology.

psychometrics > *plural noun* (treated as sing.) the science of measuring mental capacities and processes.

psychometry /sīkommitri/ > *noun* **1** the supposed ability to discover facts about an event or person from inanimate objects associated with them. **2** another term for **PSYCHOMETRICS**.
DERIVATIVES – **psychometric** *adjective*

psychometrically *adverb* **psychometrist** *noun*.

psychopath /sīkəpath/ > *noun* a person suffering from chronic mental disorder with abnormal or violent social behaviour.
DERIVATIVES – **psychopathic** *adjective* **psychopathically** *adverb*.

psychopathology > *noun* **1** the scientific study of mental disorders. **2** mental or behavioural disorder.
DERIVATIVES – **psychopathological** *adjective* **psychopathologist** *noun*.

psychopathy /sīkoppəthi/ > *noun* mental illness or disorder.

psychosexual > *adjective* of or involving the psychological aspects of sex.
DERIVATIVES – **psychosexually** *adverb*.

psychosis /sīkōsiss/ > *noun* (pl. **psychoses** /sīkōseez/) a severe mental disorder in which thought and emotions are so impaired that contact is lost with external reality.

psychosocial > *adjective* of or relating to the interrelation of social factors and individual thought and behaviour.
DERIVATIVES – **psychosocially** *adverb*.

psychosomatic /sīkōsəmattik/ > *adjective* **1** (of a physical illness) caused or aggravated by a mental factor such as internal conflict or stress. **2** relating to the interaction of mind and body.
DERIVATIVES – **psychosomatically** *adverb*.

psychosurgery > *noun* brain surgery used to treat mental disorder.
DERIVATIVES – **psychosurgical** *adjective*.

psychotherapy > *noun* the treatment of mental disorder by psychological rather than medical means.
DERIVATIVES – **psychotherapeutic** *adjective* **psychotherapist** *noun*.

psychotic /sīkottik/ > *adjective* suffering from a psychosis. > *noun* a psychotic person.
DERIVATIVES – **psychotically** *adverb*.

psychotropic /sīkətrōpik, -troppik/ > *adjective* (of drugs) affecting a person's mental state.

PT > *abbreviation* physical training.

Pt > *abbreviation* **1** Part. **2** (**pt**) pint. **3** (in scoring) point. **4** Printing point (as a unit of measurement). **5** (**Pt.**) Point (on maps). **6** (**pt**) port (a side of a ship or aircraft). > *symbol* the chemical element platinum.

PTA > *abbreviation* **1** parent–teacher association. **2** Passenger Transport Authority.

ptarmigan /taarmigən/ > *noun* a grouse of northern mountains and the Arctic, having grey and black plumage which changes to white in winter.
ORIGIN – Scottish Gaelic *tàrmachan*.

Pte > *abbreviation* Private (in the army).

pteranodon /terannədon/ > *noun* a large tailless pterosaur of the Cretaceous period, with a long toothless beak.

ORIGIN – from Greek *pteron* 'wing' + *an-* 'without' + *odous* 'tooth'.

pterodactyl /terrədaktil/ > *noun* a pterosaur of the late Jurassic period, with a long slender head and neck.

ORIGIN – from Greek *pteron* 'wing' + *daktulos* 'finger'.

pterosaur /terrəsawr/ > *noun* a fossil warm-blooded flying reptile of the Jurassic and Cretaceous periods, with membranous wings supported by a greatly lengthened fourth finger.

ORIGIN – from Greek *pteron* 'wing' + *sauros* 'lizard'.

PTO > *abbreviation* please turn over.

Ptolemaic /tolləmayik/ > *adjective* **1** relating to the 2nd-century Greek astronomer Ptolemy, and in particular to the formerly held theory that the earth is the stationary centre of the universe. **2** relating to the Ptolemies, rulers of Egypt 304–30 BC.

ptomaine /tōmayn/ > *noun* any of a group of amine compounds of unpleasant taste and odour formed in putrefying animal and vegetable matter and formerly thought to cause food poisoning.

ORIGIN – from Greek *ptōma* 'corpse'.

PTSD > *abbreviation* post-traumatic stress disorder.

Pu > *symbol* the chemical element plutonium.

pub > *noun* **1** Brit. an establishment for the sale and consumption of beer and other drinks. **2** Austral. a hotel.

COMBINATIONS – **pub crawl** Brit. informal a tour taking in several pubs, with one or more drinks at each.

ORIGIN – abbreviation of *public house*.

pube /pyoob/ > *noun* informal a pubic hair.

puberty > *noun* the period during which adolescents reach sexual maturity and become capable of reproduction.

DERIVATIVES – **pubertal** *adjective*.

ORIGIN – Latin *pubertas*, from *puber* 'adult'; related to PUBES.

pubes > *noun* **1** /pyoobeez/ (pl. same) the lower part of the abdomen at the front of the pelvis, covered with hair from puberty. **2** /pyoobeez/ plural of PUBIS. **3** /pyoobz/ informal plural of PUBE.

ORIGIN – Latin, 'pubic hair, groin, genitals'.

pubescence /pyoobess'nss/ > *noun* **1** the time when puberty begins. **2** Botany & Zoology soft down on the leaves and stems of plants or on animals, especially insects.

DERIVATIVES – **pubescent** *adjective* & *noun*.

ORIGIN – from Latin *pubescere* 'reach puberty'.

pubic > *adjective* relating to the pubes or pubis.

pubis /pyoobiss/ > *noun* (pl. **pubes** /pyoobeez/) either of a pair of bones forming the two sides of the pelvis.

ORIGIN – from Latin *os pubis* 'bone of the pubes'.

public > *adjective* **1** of, concerning, or open to the people as a whole. **2** involved in the affairs of the community, especially in government or entertainment. **3** done, perceived, or existing in open view. **4** of or provided by the state rather than an independent, commercial company. > *noun* **1** (**the public**) (treated as sing. or pl.) ordinary people in general; the community. **2** (**one's public**) the people who watch or are interested in an artist, writer, or performer.

IDIOMS – **go public 1** become a public company. **2** reveal details about a previously private concern. **in public** in view of other people; when others are present.

DERIVATIVES – **publicly** *adverb*.

SYNONYMS – **1** civic, communal, municipal, popular.

ANTONYMS – private.

COMBINATIONS – **public address system** a system of microphones, amplifiers, and loudspeakers used to amplify speech or music. **public analyst** Brit. a health official who analyses food. **public bar** Brit. the more plainly furnished bar in a pub. **public company** a company whose shares are traded freely on a stock exchange. **public enemy** a notorious wanted criminal. **public house** formal a pub. **public lending right** (in the UK) the right of authors to receive payment when their books are lent out by public libraries. **public limited company** (in the UK) a company with shares offered to the public subject to conditions of limited liability. **public nuisance** Brit. **1** an act that is illegal because it interferes with the rights of the public generally. **2** informal an obnoxious or dangerous person or group. **public prosecutor** a law officer who conducts criminal proceedings on behalf of the state or in the public interest. **public relations** the professional maintenance of a favourable public image by an organisation or famous person. **public sector** the part of an economy that is controlled by the state. **public servant** a person who works for the state or for local government. **public spirited** showing a willingness to promote the public good. **public transport** buses, trains, and other forms of transport that are available to the public, charge set fares, and run on fixed routes. **public utility** an organisation supplying the community with electricity, gas, water, or sewerage.

ORIGIN – Latin *publicus*, blend of *poplicus* 'of the people' and *puber* 'adult'.

publican > *noun* **1** Brit. a person who owns or manages a pub. **2** Austral. a person who owns or manages a hotel. **3** (in ancient Roman and biblical times) a tax collector.

publication > *noun* **1** the action or process of publishing something. **2** a book or journal that is published.

publicise (also **publicize**) > *verb* **1** make widely known. **2** give out publicity about; advertise or promote.

SYNONYMS – **1** announce, publish, report, reveal. **2** advertise, promote, push; informal hype.

publicist > *noun* a person responsible for publicising a product or celebrity.

publicity > *noun* **1** notice or attention given to someone or something by the media. **2** material or information used for advertising or promotional purposes.

SYNONYMS – **1** attention, exposure, notice. **2** advertising, marketing, promotion.

public school > *noun* **1** (in the UK) a private fee-paying secondary school. **2** (chiefly in North America) a school supported by public funds.

wordpower facts

Public school

The British expression **public school** causes great confusion among non-British speakers of English, since its meaning is the opposite of the American one, and since public schools are not subject to government or local authority control and are able to select their own pupils. In England *public school* (a term recorded from 1580) originally denoted a grammar school under public management, founded for the benefit of the public; such schools were contrasted with *private schools*, which were run for the profit of their proprietor. In the 19th century many of the old English grammar schools with wealthy endowments turned themselves into fee-paying boarding schools, and it is these schools, together with other foundations modelled on them, which are known as **public schools**.

publish > *verb* **1** prepare and issue (a book, newspaper, piece of music, etc.) for public sale. **2** print in a book, newspaper, or journal so as to make generally known. **3**

announce formally. **4** Law communicate (a libel) to a third party.

DERIVATIVES – **publishing** *noun*.

ORIGIN – Latin *publicare* 'make public'.

publisher > *noun* **1** a company or person that prepares and issues books, newspapers, journals, or music for sale. **2** chiefly N. Amer. a newspaper proprietor.

puce /pyooss/ > *noun* a dark red or purple-brown colour.

ORIGIN – French, literally 'flea'.

puck¹ > *noun* a black disc made of hard rubber, used in ice hockey.

puck² > *noun* a mischievous or evil spirit.

pucker > *verb* tightly gather or contract into wrinkles or small folds. > *noun* a wrinkle or small fold.

SYNONYMS – *verb* crease, crinkle, crumple, purse, rumple, shrivel, wrinkle.

ORIGIN – probably from **POKE²** and **POCKET** (suggesting the formation of small purse-like gatherings).

puckish > *adjective* playful and mischievous.

pud > *noun* Brit. informal short for **PUDDING**.

pudding > *noun* **1** a dessert, especially a cooked one. **2** chiefly Brit. the dessert course of a meal. **3** a baked or steamed savoury dish made with suet and flour or batter. **4** the intestines of a pig or sheep stuffed with oatmeal, spices, and meat and boiled. **5** informal a fat person.

IDIOMS – **in the pudding club** Brit. informal pregnant.

DERIVATIVES – **puddingy** *adjective*.

COMBINATIONS – **pudding basin 1** a deep round bowl used for cooking steamed puddings. **2** (**pudding-basin**) (of a hairstyle) produced or seemingly produced by cutting round the edge of a pudding basin inverted on a person's head.

ORIGIN – probably from Old French *boudin* 'black pudding', from Latin *botellus* 'sausage, small intestine'.

puddle > *noun* **1** a small pool of liquid, especially of rainwater on the ground. **2** clay and sand mixed with water and used as a watertight covering or lining for embankments or canals. > *verb* **1** cover with or form puddles. **2** (**puddle about** or **around**) informal occupy oneself in a disorganised or unproductive way. **3** line or cover with puddle. **4** knead (clay and sand) into puddle. **5** historical stir (molten iron) with iron oxide in a furnace, to produce wrought iron.

DERIVATIVES – **puddler** *noun*.

pudendum /pyoodendəm/ > *noun* (pl. **pudenda** /pyoodendə/) a person's external genitals, especially a woman's.

ORIGIN – from Latin *pudenda membra* 'parts to be ashamed of'.

pudgy > *adjective* (**pudgier**, **pudgiest**) informal fat or flabby.

pueblo /pweblō/ > *noun* (pl. **pueblos**) **1** a town or village in Spain, Latin America, or the south-western US, especially an American Indian settlement. **2** (**Pueblo**) (pl. same or **Pueblos**) a member of any of various American Indian peoples living in pueblos chiefly in New Mexico and Arizona.

ORIGIN – Spanish, 'people'.

puerile /pyoorīl/ > *adjective* childishly silly and trivial.

DERIVATIVES – **puerility** /pyoorilliti/ (pl. **puerilities**) *noun*.

SYNONYMS – childish, immature, infantile, juvenile.

ORIGIN – Latin *puerilis*, from *puer* 'boy'.

puerperal fever /pyooerpərəl/ > *noun* fever caused by an infection of the uterus following childbirth.

ORIGIN – from Latin *puer* 'child, boy' + *parus* 'bearing'.

Puerto Rican /pwertō reekən/ > *noun* a person from Puerto Rico. > *adjective* relating to Puerto Rico.

puff > *noun* **1** a short burst of breath or wind, or a small quantity of vapour or smoke sent out by such a burst. **2** an act of drawing quickly on a pipe, cigarette, or cigar. **3** a light pastry case, typically filled with cream or jam. **4** informal breath. **5** informal an overly enthusiastic review or promotional feature. > *verb* **1** breathe in repeated short gasps. **2** move with short, noisy puffs of air or steam. **3** smoke a pipe, cigarette, or cigar. **4** (**be puffed** or **puffed out**) be out of breath. **5** (**puff out** or **up**) swell or cause to swell. **6** informal advertise with exaggerated or false praise.

DERIVATIVES – **puffer** *noun*.

SYNONYMS – *noun* **1** blast, blow, burst, gust, whiff. *verb* **1** blow, gasp, heave, pant.

COMBINATIONS – **puff adder** a large, sluggish African viper which inflates the upper part of its body and hisses loudly when under threat. **puff pastry** light flaky pastry. **puff sleeve** a short sleeve gathered at the top and cuff and full in the middle.

puffa jacket > *noun* Brit. a type of thick padded jacket.

puffball > *noun* a fungus that produces a large round fruiting body which ruptures when ripe to release a cloud of spores.

pufferfish > *noun* a fish with a spiny body which can inflate itself like a balloon when threatened.

puffery > *noun* exaggerated praise.

puffin > *noun* a northern auk with a large head and a massive brightly coloured triangular bill.

wordpower facts
Puffin
What is the origin of the name **puffin**, and why do bird books give *Puffinus puffinus* as the Latin name for the Manx shearwater while the unrelated puffin, a kind of auk, is *Fratercula arctica*? In medieval England the **puffin** was the shearwater, in particular a fat shearwater nestling, suitable to be removed from its nest burrow and cooked. **Puffin** was derived from **puff**, and referred to the puffed-up or swollen condition of the young bird. Sometime around the 16th century the name **puffin** began to be used for the auk as well, the confusion probably arising because it also nests in burrows. Following Thomas Pennant (1768), British ornithologists have used **puffin** only for the auk, replacing colourful local alternatives like **coulterneb** ('ploughshare-bill') and **tomnoddy**. As regards the Latin name, *Puffinus* for the shearwater is a Latinised version of **puffin**, while *Fratercula* 'little brother, friar' for the puffin is a reference to the somewhat monklike impression of their upright stance, prominent head, and black and white plumage.

puffy > *adjective* (**puffier**, **puffiest**) **1** softly rounded: *puffy clouds.* **2** (of a part of the body) swollen and soft.

DERIVATIVES – **puffiness** *noun*.

SYNONYMS – **2** bloated, distended, swollen.

pug > *noun* a dog of a dwarf breed with a broad flat nose and deeply wrinkled face.

COMBINATIONS – **pug nose** a short nose with an upturned tip.

pugilist /pyoojilist/ > *noun* dated or humorous a boxer.

DERIVATIVES – **pugilism** *noun* **pugilistic** *adjective*.

ORIGIN – from Latin *pugil* 'boxer'.

pugnacious /pugnayshəss/ > *adjective* eager or quick to argue, quarrel, or fight.

DERIVATIVES – **pugnacity** *noun*.

SYNONYMS – argumentative, belligerent, combative, disputatious.

ANTONYMS – peaceable.

ORIGIN – from Latin *pugnare* 'to fight'.

puissance /pweesənss/ > *noun* **1** /also **pweesonss**/ a competitive test of a horse's ability to jump large obstacles in showjumping. **2** archaic or literary great power, influence, or prowess.

DERIVATIVES – **puissant** (archaic or literary).

ORIGIN – Old French, from Latin *posse* 'be able'.

puja /pōōjaa/ > *noun* a Hindu ceremonial offering.
ORIGIN – Sanskrit, 'worship'.

puke > *verb & noun* informal vomit.
DERIVATIVES – **pukey** *adjective*.

pukka /**pukk**ə/ > *adjective* 1 authentic. 2 socially acceptable. 3 informal excellent.
ORIGIN – Hindi, 'cooked, ripe, substantial'.

pul /pōōl/ > *noun* (pl. **puls** or **puli**) a monetary unit of Afghanistan, equal to one hundredth of an afghani.
ORIGIN – Pashto, from Persian, 'copper coin'.

pula /pōōlə/ > *noun* (pl. same) the basic monetary unit of Botswana, equal to 100 thebe.
ORIGIN – Setswana (a Bantu language), 'rain'.

pulao > *noun* variant spelling of PILAF.

pulchritude /**pul**krityōōd/ > *noun* literary beauty.
DERIVATIVES – **pulchritudinous** *adjective*.
ORIGIN – from Latin *pulcher* 'beautiful'.

pule /pyōōl/ > *verb* (often as **puling**) literary cry in a complaining or feeble manner.

pull > *verb* 1 exert force on (something) so as to move it towards oneself or the origin of the force. 2 remove by pulling. 3 informal bring out (a weapon) for use. 4 move steadily: *the bus pulled away*. 5 attract as a customer. 6 strain (a muscle, ligament, etc.). 7 (**pull at** or **on**) inhale deeply while drawing on (a cigarette). 8 informal cancel or withdraw (an entertainment or advertisement). 9 check the speed of (a horse) to make it lose a race. 10 informal succeed in attracting sexually. > *noun* 1 an act of pulling. 2 a deep draught of a drink or an inhalation on a cigarette, pipe, etc. 3 a force, influence, or compulsion.
IDIOMS – **on the pull** informal attempting to attract someone sexually. **pull back 1** retreat or withdraw. 2 improve or restore a team's position in a sporting contest. **pull down** demolish (a building). **pull in 1** succeed in securing or obtaining. 2 informal arrest. **pull someone's leg** deceive someone playfully. **pull off** informal succeed in achieving or winning (something difficult). **pull out** withdraw or retreat. **pull the plug on** informal prevent from happening or continuing. **pull (one's) punches** limit the severity of one's criticism or aggression. **pull round** chiefly Brit. recover from an illness. **pull strings** make use of one's influence to gain an advantage. **pull the strings** be in control of events or of other people's actions. **pull through** get through an illness or other difficult situation. **pull together** cooperate in an undertaking. **pull oneself together** regain one's self-control. **pull up 1** (of a vehicle) come to a halt. 2 cause to stop or

pause. 3 reprimand. **pull one's weight** do one's fair share of work.
DERIVATIVES – **puller** *noun*.
SYNONYMS – *verb* 1 drag, draw, haul, heave, lug, tug. 2 draw, jerk, wrench. *noun* 1 haul, heave, jerk, tug. 3 attraction, compulsion, enticement, force, influence, lure.

pullet > *noun* a young hen, especially one less than one year old.
ORIGIN – Old French *poulet*, from Latin *pullus* 'chicken, young animal'.

pulley > *noun* (pl. **pulleys**) a wheel with a grooved rim around which a rope, chain, or belt passes, used to raise heavy weights.
ORIGIN – Old French *polie*, probably ultimately from Greek *polos* 'pivot, axis'.

Pullman > *noun* (pl. **Pullmans**) a luxurious railway carriage.
ORIGIN – named after its American designer George M. *Pullman* (1831–97).

pull-out > *noun* a section of a magazine or newspaper that is designed to be detached and kept for rereading.

pullover > *noun* a knitted garment put on over the head and covering the top half of the body.

pullulate /**pul**yoolayt/ > *verb* 1 reproduce or spread so as to become very widespread. 2 teem with life and activity.
ORIGIN – Latin *pullulare* 'to sprout'.

pulmonary /**pul**mənəri/ > *adjective* relating to the lungs.
ORIGIN – from Latin *pulmo* 'lung'.

pulp > *noun* 1 a soft, wet mass of crushed or pounded material. 2 the soft fleshy part of a fruit. 3 a soft, wet mass of fibres derived from rags or wood, used in papermaking. 4 (before another noun) denoting popular or sensational writing, often regarded as being of poor quality. > *verb* 1 crush into a pulp. 2 withdraw (a publication) from the market and recycle the paper.
DERIVATIVES – **pulper** *noun* **pulpy** *adjective*.
SYNONYMS – *noun* 1 mash, mess, pap, purée. *verb* 1 crush, liquidise, mash, pound, squash.
ORIGIN – Latin *pulpa*; sense 4 is from the printing of such material on cheap paper.

pulpit /**pool**pit/ > *noun* a raised enclosed platform in a church or chapel from which the preacher delivers a sermon.
ORIGIN – Latin *pulpitum* 'scaffold, platform'.

pulque /**pool**kay, **pool**ki/ > *noun* an alcoholic Mexican drink made by fermenting sap from the maguey.
ORIGIN – from a Nahuatl word meaning 'decomposed'.

pulsar /**pul**saar/ > *noun* a celestial object, thought to be a rapidly rotating neutron star, that emits regular rapid pulses of radio waves.

pulsate /pul**sayt**/ > *verb* 1 expand and

contract with strong regular movements. 2 produce a regular throbbing sensation or sound. 3 (**pulsating**) very exciting.
DERIVATIVES – **pulsation** *noun* **pulsator** *noun*.
SYNONYMS – beat, pulse, pump, throb.
ORIGIN – Latin *pulsare* 'throb, pulse'.

pulse[1] > *noun* 1 the rhythmical throbbing of the arteries as blood is propelled through them. 2 each successive throb of the arteries. 3 a single vibration or short burst of sound, electric current, light, etc. 4 a musical beat or other regular rhythm. 5 the centre of activity in an area or field: *those close to the economic pulse*. > *verb* 1 pulsate. 2 convert (a wave or beam) into a series of pulses.
WORDFINDER – sphygmograph (*instrument for recording the strength and rate of the pulse*).
IDIOMS – **feel** (or **take**) **the pulse of** ascertain the mood or opinion of.
SYNONYMS – *noun* 1 beating, palpitation, throbbing. 3 blast, burst, surge, vibration. 4 beat, rhythm, tempo. *verb* 1 beat, pound, pulsate, pump, throb, vibrate.
ORIGIN – Latin *pulsus* 'beating', from *pellere* 'to drive, beat'.

pulse[2] > *noun* the edible seed of various leguminous plants, e.g. lentils or beans.
ORIGIN – Latin *puls* 'porridge of meal or pulse'.

pulverise /**pul**vərīz/ (also **pulverize**) > *verb* 1 reduce to fine particles. 2 informal defeat utterly.
DERIVATIVES – **pulveriser** *noun*.
SYNONYMS – 1 crush, grind, pound.
ORIGIN – Latin *pulverizare*, from *pulvis* 'dust'.

puma > *noun* a large American wild cat with a plain tawny to greyish coat.
ORIGIN – Quechua.

pumice /**pumm**iss/ > *noun* a light and porous form of solidified lava, used as a skin abrasive.
ORIGIN – Old French *pomis*, from Latin *pumex*; related to POUNCE[2].

pummel > *verb* (**pummelled, pummelling**; US **pummeled, pummeling**) strike repeatedly, especially with the fists.
SYNONYMS – beat, hammer, pound.
ORIGIN – variant of POMMEL.

pummelo > *noun* variant spelling of POMELO.

pump[1] > *noun* a mechanical device using suction or pressure to raise or move liquids, compress gases, or force air into inflatable objects. > *verb* 1 move or force to move as if driven by a pump. 2 (often **pump up**) fill (something) with liquid, gas, etc. 3 move or cause to move vigorously up and down. 4 informal try to obtain information from (someone) by persistent questioning.
IDIOMS – **pump iron** informal exercise with weights.

SYNONYMS – *verb* **1** jet, siphon, spout, spurt. **2** aerate, dilate, distend, inflate.

COMBINATIONS – **pump-action** denoting a repeating firearm in which a new round is brought into the breech by a slide action in line with the barrel. **pump-priming 1** the introduction of fluid into a pump to prepare it for working. **2** the stimulation of economic activity by investment.

ORIGIN – related to Dutch *pomp* 'ship's pump'.

pump² > *noun* **1** chiefly N. English a plimsoll. **2** a light shoe for dancing. **3** N. Amer. a court shoe.

pumpernickel /**pum**pərnikk'l/ > *noun* dark, dense German bread made from wholemeal rye.

ORIGIN – German, first meaning 'lout, bumpkin'.

pumpkin > *noun* **1** a large rounded orange-yellow fruit with a thick rind and edible flesh. **2** Brit. another term for SQUASH².

ORIGIN – from Greek *pepōn* 'large melon'.

pun > *noun* a joke exploiting the different meanings of a word or the fact that there are words of the same sound and different meanings. > *verb* (**punned, punning**) make a pun.

DERIVATIVES – **punster** *noun*.

ORIGIN – perhaps an abbreviation of obsolete *pundigrion*, a fanciful alteration of PUNCTILIO.

punch¹ > *verb* **1** strike with the fist. **2** press (a button or key on a machine). **3** N. Amer. drive (cattle) by prodding them with a stick. > *noun* **1** a blow with the fist. **2** informal effectiveness; impact.

IDIOMS – **punch above one's weight** informal engage in an activity perceived as beyond one's abilities.

DERIVATIVES – **puncher** *noun*.

SYNONYMS – *verb* **1** box, hammer, strike, thump, thwack, whack.

COMBINATIONS – **punchbag** Brit. a stuffed suspended bag used for punching as exercise or training, especially by boxers. **punchball** Brit. a suspended or mounted ball, used for punching as exercise or training, especially by boxers. **punch-drunk** stupefied by or as if by a series of punches.

ORIGIN – variant of POUNCE¹.

punch² > *noun* **1** a device or machine for making holes in paper, metal, leather, etc. **2** a tool or machine for impressing a design or stamping a die on a material. > *verb* **1** pierce a hole in (a material) with or as if with a punch. **2** pierce (a hole) with or as if with a punch.

COMBINATIONS – **punched card** (also **punchcard**) a card perforated according to a code, for controlling the operation of a machine, formerly used to program computers.

ORIGIN – perhaps an abbreviation of PUNCHEON, or from PUNCH¹.

punch³ > *noun* a drink made from wine or spirits mixed with water, fruit juices, spices, etc.

ORIGIN – apparently from a Sanskrit word meaning 'five, five kinds of' (because the drink had five ingredients).

punch⁴ > *noun* **1** (**Punch**) a grotesque, hook-nosed humpbacked buffoon, the chief male character of the Punch and Judy puppet show. **2** (also **Suffolk punch**) a short-legged thickset breed of draught horse.

ORIGIN – abbreviation of *Punchinello*, a similar character in an Italian puppet show and commedia dell'arte; sense 2 derives from a dialect word for a short, fat person.

punchbowl > *noun* **1** a deep bowl for mixing and serving punch. **2** chiefly Brit. a deep round hollow in a hilly area.

puncheon /**pun**chən/ > *noun* **1** a short post, especially one used for supporting the roof in a mine. **2** another term for PUNCH².

ORIGIN – Old French *poinchon*, probably from Latin *pungere* 'puncture'.

punchline > *noun* the culmination of a joke or story, providing the humour or climax.

punch-up > *noun* informal, chiefly Brit. a brawl.

punchy > *adjective* (**punchier, punchiest**) effective; forceful.

punctilio /pungk**till**iō/ > *noun* (pl. **punctilios**) **1** a minor or petty point of conduct or procedure. **2** punctilious behaviour.

ORIGIN – Italian *puntiglio* and Spanish *puntillo* 'small point'.

punctilious /pungk**till**iəss/ > *adjective* showing great attention to detail or correct behaviour.

SYNONYMS – conscientious, meticulous, painstaking, scrupulous.

ANTONYMS – casual.

punctual > *adjective* happening or keeping to the appointed time.

DERIVATIVES – **punctuality** *noun* **punctually** *adverb*.

SYNONYMS – on the dot, on time, prompt.

ORIGIN – Latin *punctualis*, from *punctum* 'a point'.

punctuate /**pungk**tyooayt/ > *verb* **1** interrupt at intervals throughout. **2** insert punctuation marks in.

SYNONYMS – **1** break up, interrupt.

ORIGIN – Latin *punctuare* 'bring to a point'.

punctuation > *noun* **1** the marks, such as full stop, comma, and brackets, used in writing to separate sentences and their elements and to clarify meaning. **2** the use of such marks.

DERIVATIVES – **punctuational** *adjective*.

puncture > *noun* a small hole caused by a sharp object, especially one in a tyre. > *verb* **1** make a puncture in. **2** cause a sudden collapse of (a mood, feeling, etc.).

ORIGIN – Latin *punctura*, from *pungere* 'to prick'.

pundit /**pun**dit/ > *noun* **1** a person who often speaks authoritatively on a subject in public. **2** variant spelling of PANDIT.

DERIVATIVES – **punditry** *noun*.

ORIGIN – from a Sanskrit word meaning 'learned'.

pungent /**pun**jənt/ > *adjective* **1** having a sharply strong taste or smell. **2** (of remarks or humour) sharp and caustic.

DERIVATIVES – **pungency** *noun* **pungently** *adverb*.

SYNONYMS – astringent, biting, caustic, penetrating, sharp, strong.

ORIGIN – from Latin *pungere* 'to prick'.

Punic /**pyoo**nik/ > *adjective* relating to ancient Carthage. > *noun* the language of ancient Carthage.

ORIGIN – Latin *Punicus*, from *Poenus*, from Greek *Phoinix* 'Phoenician'.

punish > *verb* **1** impose a penalty on (someone) for an offence. **2** impose a penalty on someone for (an offence). **3** treat harshly or unfairly.

DERIVATIVES – **punishable** *adjective*.

SYNONYMS – **1** castigate, chastise, discipline, penalise.

ORIGIN – Latin *punire*, from *poena* 'penalty'.

punishment > *noun* **1** the action of punishing or the state of being punished. **2** the penalty imposed for an offence. **3** informal harsh or rough treatment.

WORDFINDER – penal (*of punishment*), punitive (*intended as punishment*); condign (*denoting appropriate punishment*), impunity (*exemption from punishment*), nemesis (*unavoidable punishment*).

SYNONYMS – **1,2** correction, discipline, penalty, penance, retribution.

punitive /**pyoo**nitiv/ > *adjective* inflicting or intended as punishment.

Punjabi /pun**jaa**bi, poon**jaa**bi/ (also **Panjabi**) > *noun* (pl. **Punjabis**) **1** a person from Punjab, a region of NW India and Pakistan. **2** the language of Punjab. > *adjective* relating to Punjab.

punk > *noun* **1** (also **punk rock**) a loud, fast form of rock music characterised by aggressive and anarchic lyrics and behaviour. **2** (also **punk rocker**) an admirer or player of punk music, typically favouring spiky or coloured hair and ripped clothing. **3** N. Amer. informal a worthless person; a thug or criminal. **4** chiefly N. Amer. tinder. > *adjective* **1** N. Amer. informal bad; worthless. **2** relating to punk rock and its associated subculture.

DERIVATIVES – **punkish** *adjective* **punky** *adjective*.

┌ **wordpower facts** ─

Punk

To most people today **punk** refers to an aggressive form of rock music originating in the late 1970s, but the word was in fact first recorded in 1678! Originally an American word, it first denoted dry crumbly wood used for tinder, and is possibly of American Indian origin. It later developed the senses 'rubbish, nonsense' and (perhaps influenced by the obsolete word *punk* 'prostitute') 'passive male homosexual' and 'young male companion to a vagrant'. The musical use arose from the still-current American sense 'criminal or worthless person'.

punkah /pungkə/ > *noun* chiefly historical (in India) a large cloth fan on a frame suspended from the ceiling, worked by a cord or electrically.
ORIGIN – Hindi, from a Sanskrit word meaning 'wing'.

punnet > *noun* Brit. a small light basket or other container for fruit or vegetables.
ORIGIN – perhaps from dialect *pun* 'a pound'.

punt¹ /punt/ > *noun* a long, narrow flat-bottomed boat, square at both ends and propelled with a long pole. > *verb* travel or convey in a punt.
ORIGIN – Latin *ponto*, denoting a flat-bottomed ferry boat.

punt² /punt/ > *verb* **1** chiefly American Football & Rugby kick (the ball) after it has dropped from the hands and before it reaches the ground. > *noun* a kick of this kind.
ORIGIN – probably from dialect *punt* 'push forcibly'.

punt³ /punt/ > *verb* **1** Brit. informal bet or speculate. **2** (in some gambling card games) lay a stake against the bank. > *noun* informal, chiefly Brit. a bet.
ORIGIN – French *ponte* 'player against the bank'.

punt⁴ /poont/ > *noun* the basic monetary unit of the Republic of Ireland.
ORIGIN – Irish, 'a pound'.

punter > *noun* **1** informal a person who gambles or places a bet. **2** Brit. informal a customer or client.

puny /pyooni/ > *adjective* (**punier**, **puniest**) **1** small and weak. **2** meagre.
SYNONYMS – **1** feeble, frail, slight, small, weak. **2** inadequate, meagre, scanty.
ANTONYMS – **1** strong, sturdy.
ORIGIN – phonetic spelling of Old French *puisne* 'younger or junior person', 'judge of a superior court inferior in rank to chief

justices', from Latin *postea* 'afterwards' + *natus* 'born'.

pup > *noun* **1** a young dog. **2** a young wolf, seal, rat, or other mammal. **3** dated, chiefly Brit. a cheeky or arrogant boy or young man. > *verb* (**pupped**, **pupping**) give birth to a pup or pups.
IDIOMS – **sell** (or **buy**) **a pup** Brit. informal swindle (or be swindled) by selling (or buying) something worthless.
ORIGIN – back-formation from PUPPY.

pupa /pyoopə/ > *noun* (pl. **pupae** /pyoopee/) an insect in its inactive immature form between larva and adult, e.g. a chrysalis.
DERIVATIVES – **pupal** adjective.
ORIGIN – Latin, 'girl, doll'.

pupate /pyoopayt/ > *verb* become a pupa.
DERIVATIVES – **pupation** noun.

pupil¹ > *noun* **1** a person who is taught by another, especially a schoolchild in relation to a teacher. **2** Brit. a trainee barrister.
WORDFINDER – alumnus (*former pupil*).
SYNONYMS – **1** apprentice, disciple, follower, schoolchild, student.

┌ **wordpower facts** ─

Pupil

The two English words **pupil** are related to each other, and to **poppet**, **puppet**, and **pupa**, through their root, Latin *pupa* 'girl, doll'. **Pupil** in the sense 'person taught by another' entered English via Old French from the Latin forms *pupillus* (diminutive of *pupus* 'boy') and *pupilla* (diminutive of *pupa* 'girl'); it originally meant 'orphan or ward', and did not take on its modern meaning until the 16th century. **Pupil** meaning 'centre of the eye' is from the feminine form *pupilla* (literally 'little doll' or 'young girl'): it acquired its English meaning from the phenomenon whereby one can see a tiny reflected image of oneself, like a little doll, if one stares into someone's pupils.

pupil² > *noun* the dark circular opening in the centre of the iris of the eye, which regulates the amount of light reaching the retina.

pupillage /pyoopilij/ > *noun* **1** the state of being a pupil. **2** Law (in the UK) apprenticeship to a member of the Bar, which qualifies a barrister to practise independently.

puppet > *noun* **1** a movable model of a person or animal, moved either by strings or by a hand inside it, used to entertain. **2** a person under the control of another.
DERIVATIVES – **puppeteer** noun **puppetry** noun.

SYNONYMS – **1** marionette. **2** instrument, lackey, pawn, servant, tool.
ORIGIN – later form of POPPET.

puppy > *noun* (pl. **puppies**) **1** a young dog. **2** informal, dated a conceited or arrogant young man.
DERIVATIVES – **puppyish** adjective.
COMBINATIONS – **puppy fat** fat on the body of a child which disappears around adolescence. **puppy love** intense but relatively short-lived love, typically associated with adolescents.
ORIGIN – perhaps from Old French *poupee* 'doll, toy'.

purblind /purblīnd/ > *adjective* **1** partially sighted. **2** lacking in discernment or understanding.
ORIGIN – first meaning 'completely blind': from PURE 'utterly' + BLIND.

purchase > *verb* obtain by payment; buy. > *noun* **1** the action of buying. **2** a thing bought. **3** firm contact or grip. **4** a pulley or similar device for moving heavy objects.
DERIVATIVES – **purchasable** adjective **purchaser** noun.
SYNONYMS – *verb* acquire, buy, invest in. *noun* **2** acquisition, investment.
ORIGIN – Old French *pourchacier* 'seek to obtain or bring about'.

purdah /purdə/ > *noun* the practice in certain Muslim and Hindu societies of screening women from men or strangers by means of a curtain or all-enveloping clothes.
ORIGIN – Urdu and Persian, 'veil, curtain'.

pure > *adjective* **1** not mixed or adulterated with any other substance or material. **2** free of impurities. **3** innocent or morally good. **4** complete; nothing but: *a shout of pure anger*. **5** theoretical rather than practical: *pure mathematics*. **6** (of a sound) perfectly in tune and with a clear tone.
DERIVATIVES – **purely** adverb.
SYNONYMS – **1,2** clean, clear, unadulterated, uncontaminated. **3** chaste, innocent, undefiled, virtuous.
ANTONYMS – **1,2** contaminated, defiled, impure. **5** applied.
COMBINATIONS – **pure-bred** (of an animal) bred from parents of the same breed or variety.
ORIGIN – Latin *purus*.

purée /pyooray/ > *noun* a smooth pulp of liquidised, crushed, or sieved fruit or vegetables. > *verb* (**purées**, **puréed**, **puréeing**) make a purée of.
ORIGIN – French, 'purified'.

purgation /purgaysh'n/ > *noun* **1** purification. **2** evacuation of the bowels brought about by laxatives.
ORIGIN – Latin, from *purgare* 'purge'.

purgative /purgətiv/ > *adjective* strongly laxative in effect. > *noun* a laxative.
SYNONYMS – aperient, laxative.

purgatory /**pur**gətri/ > *noun* (pl. **purgatories**) 1 (in Catholic doctrine) a place or state of suffering inhabited by the souls of sinners who are atoning for their sins before going to heaven. 2 mental anguish.

DERIVATIVES – **purgatorial** *adjective*.

ORIGIN – Latin *purgatorium*, from *purgare* 'purge'.

purge > *verb* 1 rid of people or things considered undesirable or harmful. 2 evacuate one's bowels, especially as a result of taking a laxative. 3 Law atone for or wipe out (contempt of court). > *noun* 1 an act of purging. 2 dated a laxative.

SYNONYMS – **1** cleanse, clear, purify, rid.

ORIGIN – Latin *purgare* 'purify', from *purus* 'pure'.

puri /**poo**ri/ > *noun* (pl. **puris**) (in Indian cookery) a small, round piece of unleavened bread which puffs up when deep-fried.

ORIGIN – Sanskrit.

purify* > *verb* (**purifies**, **purified**) remove contaminants from; make pure.

DERIVATIVES – **purification** *noun* **purifier** *noun*.

*SPELLING – *i* not *e*: pur*i*fy.

SYNONYMS – clarify, clean, cleanse, decontaminate, sterilise.

ANTONYMS – contaminate, defile.

purism > *noun* scrupulous observance of traditional rules or structures, especially in language or style.

DERIVATIVES – **purist** *noun & adjective*.

puritan > *noun* 1 (**Puritan**) a member of a group of English Protestants in the 16th and 17th centuries who sought to simplify and regulate forms of worship. 2 a person with censorious moral beliefs, especially about self-indulgence and sex. > *adjective* 1 (**Puritan**) relating to the Puritans. 2 characteristic of a puritan.

DERIVATIVES – **puritanical** *adjective* **puritanism** (also **Puritanism**) *noun*.

purity > *noun* the state of being pure.

purl¹ > *adjective* (of a knitting stitch) made by putting the needle through the front of the stitch from right to left. Compare with **PLAIN** (in sense 8). > *verb* knit with a purl stitch.

purl² *literary* > *verb* (of a stream or river) flow with a swirling motion and babbling sound.

ORIGIN – probably imitative.

purler > *noun* Brit. informal a headlong fall.

ORIGIN – from dialect *purl* 'upset, overturn'.

purlieu /**pur**lyoo/ > *noun* (pl. **purlieus** or **purlieux**) 1 (**purlieus**) the area near or surrounding a place. 2 Brit. historical a tract on the border of a forest.

ORIGIN – probably from Old French *puralee* 'a walk round to settle boundaries'.

purlin > *noun* a horizontal beam along the length of a roof, supporting the rafters.

ORIGIN – perhaps of French origin.

purloin /pər**loyn**/ > *verb* formal or humorous steal.

ORIGIN – Old French *purloigner* 'put away'.

purple > *noun* 1 a colour intermediate between red and blue. 2 the scarlet official dress of a cardinal. 3 the dye Tyrian purple. > *adjective* of a colour intermediate between red and blue.

WORDFINDER – *shades of purple:* lavender, lilac, magenta, mauve, mulberry, plum, violet.

IDIOMS – **born in** (or **to**) **the purple** born into a reigning family or privileged class.

DERIVATIVES – **purplish** *adjective* **purply** *adjective*.

COMBINATIONS – **purple heart 1** (**Purple Heart**) (in the US) a decoration for those wounded or killed in action. 2 Brit. informal a heart-shaped mauve stimulant tablet, especially of amphetamine. **purple passage** an excessively ornate passage in a literary work. **purple patch 1** informal a run of success or good luck. 2 a purple passage. **purple prose** prose that is too ornate.

ORIGIN – from Greek *porphura*, denoting molluscs that yielded Tyrian purple, also cloth dyed with this.

purport > *verb* /pər**port**/ appear to be or do, especially falsely. > *noun* /**pur**port/ the meaning or purpose of something.

DERIVATIVES – **purported** *adjective* **purportedly** *adverb*.

ORIGIN – Latin *proportare*, from *pro-* 'forth' + *portare* 'carry, bear'.

purpose > *noun* 1 the reason for which something is done or for which something exists. 2 an intention or objective; intend. 3 resolve or determination. > *verb* formal have as one's objective; intend.

IDIOMS – **on purpose** intentionally.

SYNONYMS – *noun* **1** basis, cause, justification, raison d'être. **2** aim, goal, intention, motive, objective. **3** determination, drive, resolve, steadfastness.

ORIGIN – from Old French *porposer*, variant of *proposer* 'propose'.

purposeful > *adjective* 1 having or showing determination. 2 having a purpose.

DERIVATIVES – **purposefully** *adverb* **purposefulness** *noun*.

SYNONYMS – **1** determined, resolute. **2** directed, meaningful.

purposeless > *adjective* done with or having no purpose.

DERIVATIVES – **purposelessly** *adverb* **purposelessness** *noun*.

SYNONYMS – aimless, meaningless, pointless.

purposely > *adverb* deliberately; on purpose.

purposive > *adjective* having or done with a purpose.

DERIVATIVES – **purposively** *adverb* **purposiveness** *noun*.

purr > *verb* 1 (of a cat) make a low continuous vibratory sound expressing contentment. 2 (of a vehicle or engine) move or run smoothly while making a similar sound. > *noun* a purring sound.

purse > *noun* 1 a small pouch for carrying money. 2 N. Amer. a handbag. 3 money for spending; funds. 4 a sum of money given as a prize in a sporting contest. > *verb* (with reference to the lips) pucker or contract.

IDIOMS – **hold the purse strings** have control of expenditure.

COMBINATIONS – **purse seine** a seine net which may be drawn into the shape of a bag, used for catching shoal fish.

ORIGIN – Latin *bursa*, from Greek *bursa* 'hide, leather'.

purser > *noun* a ship's officer who keeps the accounts, especially on a passenger vessel.

purslane /**pur**slin/ > *noun* a small fleshy-leaved plant of damp or marshy habitats, some kinds of which are edible.

ORIGIN – Old French *porcelaine*, probably from Latin *porcillaca*, variant of *portulaca*.

pursuance > *noun* formal the performance or doing of something.

pursuant /pər**syoo**ənt/ > *adverb* (**pursuant to**) formal in accordance with.

ORIGIN – Old French, 'pursuing'.

pursue* > *verb* (**pursues, pursued, pursuing**) 1 follow in order to catch or attack. 2 seek to attain (a goal). 3 engage in or continue with (an activity or procedure). 4 continue to investigate or discuss.

DERIVATIVES – **pursuer** *noun*.

*SPELLING – *pur-*, not *per-*: *pur*sue.

SYNONYMS – **1** chase, follow, stalk, track, trail. **2** aspire to, seek, strive for. **3** engage in, follow, participate in, practise.

ORIGIN – Old French *pursuer*, from Latin *prosequi* 'prosecute'.

pursuit > *noun* 1 the action of pursuing. 2 a recreational or sporting activity.

SYNONYMS – **2** activity, hobby, pastime.

pursuivant /**per**sivənt/ > *noun* Brit. an officer of the College of Arms ranking below a herald.

ORIGIN – Old French *pursivant* 'follower or attendant'.

purulent /**pyoo**roŏlənt/ > *adjective* consisting of, containing, or discharging pus.

ORIGIN – Latin *purulentus*, from *pus* 'pus'.

purvey /pər**vay**/ > *verb* provide or supply (food or drink) as one's business.

DERIVATIVES – **purveyor** *noun*.

wordpower facts

Purvey

The word **purvey** is from the same root as **provide**, the Latin verb *providere* 'foresee, attend to', which was itself based on *pro-* 'before' and *videre* 'to see'. The difference in form is due to the fact that **purvey** entered English from Old French *purvieer* whereas **provide** came directly from the Latin word. Other English words from *providere* include **improvise**, **provident**, and **provision**. Both **purvey** and **provide** originally had the meanings 'foresee', 'attend to in advance', and 'prepare' before the current sense of 'supply' developed.

purview > *noun* **1** the scope of the influence or concerns of something. **2** a range of experience or thought.
ORIGIN – Old French *purveu*, from *purveier* 'purvey'.

pus > *noun* a thick yellowish or greenish opaque liquid produced in infected tissue.
ORIGIN – Latin.

push > *verb* **1** exert force on (someone or something) so as to move them away from oneself or from the source of the force. **2** move (one's body or a part of it) forcefully into a specified position. **3** move forward by using force. **4** drive oneself or urge (someone) to greater effort. **5** (**push for**) demand persistently. **6** informal promote the use, sale, or acceptance of. **7** informal sell (a narcotic drug) illegally. **8** (**be pushed for**) informal have very little of (something, especially time). **9** (**be pushing**) informal be nearly (a particular age). > *noun* **1** an act of pushing. **2** a vigorous effort. **3** forcefulness and enterprise.
IDIOMS – **at a push** Brit. informal only if necessary or with difficulty. **get** (or **give someone**) **the push** Brit. informal **1** be dismissed (or dismiss someone) from a job. **2** be rejected in (or end) a relationship. **push ahead** proceed with or continue a course of action. **push along** (or **off**) Brit. informal go away. **push in** go in front of people who are already queuing. **push one's luck** informal take a risk on the assumption that success will continue. **when push comes to shove** informal when one must commit oneself to action.
DERIVATIVES – **pusher** *noun*.
SYNONYMS – *verb* **1** propel, shove, thrust. **2** elbow, jostle, ram, shove, thrust. **4** drive, compel, impel, press, urge. *noun* **1** nudge, shove, thrust.
COMBINATIONS – **pushbike** Brit. informal a bicycle. **pushcart** a small handcart or barrow. **pushchair** Brit. a folding chair on wheels, in which a young child can be pushed along.
ORIGIN – Old French *pousser*, from Latin *pulsare* 'pulse'.

pushover > *noun* informal **1** a person who is easy to influence or defeat. **2** a thing that is easily done.

pushy > *adjective* (**pushier**, **pushiest**) excessively self-assertive or ambitious.
DERIVATIVES – **pushiness** *noun*.
SYNONYMS – bossy, brash, bumptious, forceful, overbearing, thrusting.

pusillanimous /pyōossi**lann**iməss/ > *adjective* lacking courage; timid.
DERIVATIVES – **pusillanimity** *noun*.
ORIGIN – from Latin *pusillus* 'very small' + *animus* 'mind'.

puss > *noun* informal **1** a cat. **2** a coquettish girl or young woman: *a glamour puss.*
ORIGIN – probably from Low German *pūs* or Dutch *poes*.

pussy > *noun* (pl. **pussies**) **1** (also **pussy cat**) informal a cat. **2** vulgar slang a woman's genitals. **3** vulgar slang women considered sexually.
COMBINATIONS – **pussy willow** a willow with soft fluffy catkins.

pussyfoot > *verb* **1** act very cautiously. **2** move stealthily.

pustule /**pust**yōol/ > *noun* a small blister or pimple containing pus.
ORIGIN – Latin *pustula*.

put > *verb* (**putting**; past and past participle **put**) **1** move to or place in a particular position. **2** bring into a particular state or condition: *she tried to put me at ease.* **3** (**put on** or **on to**) cause to carry or be subject to. **4** assign a value, figure, or limit to. **5** express in a particular way. **6** (of a ship) proceed in a particular direction: *the boat put out to sea.* **7** throw (a shot or weight) as an athletic sport. > *noun* a throw of the shot or weight.
IDIOMS – **put about 1** spread (information or rumours). **2** (of a ship) turn on the opposite tack. **put away** informal **1** consume (food or drink) in large quantities. **2** confine in a prison or psychiatric hospital. **put down 1** suppress (a rebellion, coup, or riot) by force. **2** kill (a sick, old, or injured animal). **3** pay (a sum) as a deposit. **4** informal humiliate by public criticism. **put down to** attribute (something) to. **put off 1** cancel or postpone an appointment with. **2** postpone. **3** cause to feel dislike or lose enthusiasm. **4** distract. **put on 1** present or provide (a play, service, etc.). **2** become heavier by (a specified amount). **3** assume (an expression, accent, etc.). **put on to** make aware of. **put one over on** informal deceive into accepting something false. **put out 1** inconvenience, upset, or annoy. **2** dislocate (a joint). **put through 1** subject to a gruelling or unpleasant experience. **2** connect (someone) by telephone to another person or place. **put to** submit (something) to (someone) for consideration. **put up 1** present, provide, or offer. **2** accommodate temporarily. **3** propose for election or adoption. **put upon** informal exploit the good nature of. **put up or shut up** informal justify oneself or remain silent. **put up to** informal encourage to do (something wrong or unwise). **put up with** tolerate or endure.

putative /**pyōo**tətiv/ > *adjective* generally considered or reputed to be; supposed.
DERIVATIVES – **putatively** *adverb*.
ORIGIN – Latin *putativus*, from *putare* 'think'.

put-down > *noun* informal a humiliating or critical remark.

put-put > *noun* & *verb* another term for **PUTTER²**.

putrefy* /**pyōo**trifī/ > *verb* (**putrefies**, **putrefied**) decay or rot and produce a fetid smell.
DERIVATIVES – **putrefaction** *noun*.
*SPELLING – *e* not *i*: putr*e*fy.
SYNONYMS – decay, decompose, fester, moulder, perish, rot.
ORIGIN – Latin *putrefacere*, from *puter* 'rotten'.

putrescent /pyōo**tress**'nt/ > *adjective* becoming putrid; rotting.

putrid /**pyōo**trid/ > *adjective* **1** decaying or rotting and emitting a fetid smell. **2** informal very unpleasant.
SYNONYMS – **1** decaying, decomposed, festering, foul, rank, rotting.
ORIGIN – Latin *putridus*, from *putrere* 'to rot'.

putsch /pŏoch/ > *noun* a violent attempt to overthrow a government.
ORIGIN – Swiss German, 'thrust, blow'.

putt /put/ > *verb* (**putted**, **putting**) strike a golf ball gently so that it rolls into or near a hole. > *noun* a stroke of this kind.
COMBINATIONS – **putting green** a smooth area of short grass surrounding a hole on a golf course.
ORIGIN – Scots form of **PUT**.

puttanesca /pŏotə**ness**kə/ > *adjective* denoting a pasta sauce of tomatoes, garlic, olives, anchovies, etc.
ORIGIN – Italian, from *puttana* 'a prostitute' (the sauce is said to have been devised by prostitutes as one which could be cooked quickly between clients' visits).

puttee /**putt**i/ > *noun* a long strip of cloth wound spirally round the leg from ankle to knee for protection and support.
ORIGIN – Hindi, 'band, bandage'.

putter¹ > *noun* a golf club designed for putting.

putter² > *noun* the rapid intermittent sound of a small petrol engine. > *verb* move with or make such a sound.

putto /**putt**ō/ > *noun* (pl. **putti** /**putt**i/) a

788

representation of a naked child, especially a cherub or a cupid in Renaissance art.

ORIGIN – Italian, 'boy'.

putty > *noun* a malleable paste that hardens as it sets, used for sealing glass in window frames, filling holes in wood, etc.

IDIOMS – **be (like) putty in someone's hands** be easily manipulated by someone.

ORIGIN – French *potée* 'potful'.

put-up job > *noun* informal something devised so as to deceive.

putz N. Amer. informal > *noun* **1** a stupid or worthless person. **2** vulgar slang a man's penis. > *verb* (often **putz around**) engage in trivial or unproductive activity.

ORIGIN – Yiddish, 'penis'.

puzzle > *verb* **1** confuse (someone) through being difficult to understand. **2** think hard about something difficult to understand. > *noun* **1** a game, toy, or problem designed to test ingenuity or knowledge. **2** a person or thing that is difficult to understand.

DERIVATIVES – **puzzlement** *noun* **puzzler** *noun*.

SYNONYMS – *verb* **1** baffle, bemuse, confound, confuse, mystify, nonplus, perplex. *noun* **2** conundrum, enigma, mystery.

PVA > *abbreviation* polyvinyl acetate.

PVC > *abbreviation* polyvinyl chloride.

PVS > *abbreviation* Medicine persistent vegetative state.

PW > *abbreviation* policewoman.

p.w. > *abbreviation* per week.

PWR > *abbreviation* pressurised-water reactor.

pya > *noun* a monetary unit of Burma (Myanmar), equal to one hundredth of a kyat.

pyaemia /pīeemiə/ (US **pyemia**) > *noun* blood poisoning caused by the release of pus-forming bacteria from an abscess.

ORIGIN – from Greek *puon* 'pus' + *haima* 'blood'.

pye-dog (also **pi-dog**) > *noun* (in Asia) a half-wild stray mongrel.

ORIGIN – from Hindi *pāhī* 'outsider' + DOG.

pygmy (also **pigmy**) > *noun* (pl. **pygmies**) **1** a member of certain peoples of very short stature in equatorial Africa. **2** chiefly derogatory a very small person or thing. **3** a person who is deficient in a particular respect: *an intellectual pygmy.* > *adjective* very small; dwarf.

ORIGIN – Greek *pugmaios* 'dwarfish', from *pugmē* 'fist, length measured from elbow to knuckles'.

pyjamas (US **pajamas**) > *plural noun* **1** a suit of loose trousers and jacket for sleeping in. **2** loose trousers with a drawstring waist, worn by both sexes in some Asian countries.

ORIGIN – from the Persian words for 'leg' + 'clothing'.

pylon > *noun* **1** (also **electricity pylon**) a tall tower-like structure for carrying electricity cables. **2** a monumental gateway to an ancient Egyptian temple, formed by two truncated pyramidal towers.

ORIGIN – Greek *pulōn* 'gateway'.

pyracantha /pīrəkanthə/ > *noun* a thorny evergreen shrub with white flowers and bright red or yellow berries.

ORIGIN – from Greek *pur* 'fire' + *akantha* 'thorn'.

pyramid > *noun* **1** a monumental stone structure with a square or triangular base and sloping sides that meet in a point at the top, especially one built as a royal tomb in ancient Egypt. **2** Geometry a polyhedron of which one face is a polygon and the other faces are triangles with a common vertex. **3** a pyramid-shaped thing or pile of things.

COMBINATIONS – **pyramid selling** a system of selling goods in which agency rights are sold to an increasing number of distributors at successively lower levels.

ORIGIN – Greek *puramis*.

pyramidal /pirammid'l/ > *adjective* resembling a pyramid in shape.

pyre > *noun* a heap of combustible material, especially one for the ritual cremation of a corpse.

ORIGIN – Greek *pur* 'fire'.

pyrethrum /pīreethrəm/ > *noun* **1** a plant of the daisy family with brightly coloured flowers. **2** an insecticide made from the dried flowers of these plants.

ORIGIN – Greek *purethron* 'feverfew'.

pyretic /pīrettik/ > *adjective* feverish or inducing fever.

ORIGIN – from Greek *puretos* 'fever'.

Pyrex > *noun* trademark a hard heat-resistant type of glass.

pyrexia /pīreksiə/ > *noun* Medicine fever.

ORIGIN – Greek *purexis*, from *puressein* 'be feverish'.

pyridoxine /pirridoksin/ > *noun* vitamin B₆, a compound present chiefly in cereals, liver oils, and yeast, and important in the metabolism of fats.

ORIGIN – from *pyridine* (a liquid chemical), from Greek *pur* 'fire' + *oxy(gen)*.

pyrites /pīrīteez/ (also **iron pyrites** or

pyrite) > *noun* a shiny yellow mineral consisting of iron sulphide.

ORIGIN – from Greek *puritēs* 'of fire'.

pyro- > *combining form* **1** relating to fire: *pyromania.* **2** Chemistry & Mineralogy formed or affected by heat: *pyroxene.*

ORIGIN – from Greek *pur* 'fire'.

pyroclastic /pīrōklastik/ > *adjective* Geology of or relating to rock fragments or ash erupted by a volcano, especially as a hot, dense, destructive flow.

ORIGIN – from Greek *klastos* 'broken in pieces'.

pyrogenic /pīrōjennik/ > *adjective* **1** Medicine inducing fever. **2** resulting from combustion or heating.

pyrography /pīrogrəfi/ > *noun* the art or technique of decorating wood or leather by burning a design on the surface with a heated metallic point.

pyromania > *noun* an obsessive desire to set fire to things.

DERIVATIVES – **pyromaniac** *noun.*

pyrophoric /pīrəforrik/ > *adjective* **1** liable to ignite spontaneously in air. **2** (of an alloy) emitting sparks when scratched or struck.

ORIGIN – Greek *purophoros* 'fire-bearing'.

pyrotechnic /pīrōteknik/ > *adjective* **1** relating to fireworks. **2** brilliant or spectacular.

DERIVATIVES – **pyrotechnical** *adjective.*

pyrotechnics > *plural noun* **1** a firework display. **2** (treated as sing.) the art of making fireworks or staging firework displays. **3** a spectacular performance or display.

pyrrhic /pirrik/ > *adjective* (of a victory) won at too great a cost to have been worthwhile for the victor.

ORIGIN – named after *Pyrrhus*, a king of Epirus whose victory over the Romans in 279 BC incurred heavy losses.

Pythagoras' theorem /pīthaggərəssiz/ > *noun* the theorem that the square on the hypotenuse of a right-angled triangle is equal in area to the sum of the squares on the other two sides.

Pythagorean /pīthaggəreeən/ > *adjective* relating to the Greek philosopher and mathematician Pythagoras (*c.*580–500 BC). > *noun* a follower of Pythagoras.

python > *noun* a large non-poisonous snake which kills prey by constriction.

ORIGIN – Greek *Puthōn*, a huge serpent killed by Apollo.

pyx /piks/ (also **pix**) > *noun* Christian Church the container in which the consecrated bread of the Eucharist is kept.

ORIGIN – Greek *puxis* 'box'.

q

Q¹ (also **q**) > *noun* (pl. **Qs** or **Q's**) the seventeenth letter of the alphabet.

Q² > *abbreviation* **1** queen (used especially in card games and chess). **2** question.

QA > *abbreviation* quality assurance.

Qabalah > *noun* variant spelling of KABBALAH.

Qatari /kataari/ > *noun* a person from Qatar, a country in the Persian Gulf. > *adjective* relating to Qatar.

QB > *abbreviation* Law Queen's Bench.

QC > *abbreviation* **1** quality control. **2** Quebec. **3** Law Queen's Counsel.

QED > *abbreviation* quod erat demonstrandum.

qi > *noun* variant spelling of CHI².

qigong /cheegong/ > *noun* a Chinese system of physical exercises and breathing control related to tai chi.
ORIGIN – Chinese.

qintar /kintaar/ > *noun* (pl. same, **qintars**, or **qindarka** /kindaarkə/) a monetary unit of Albania, equal to one hundredth of a lek.
ORIGIN – Albanian *qindar*, from *qind* 'hundred'.

QPM > *abbreviation* (in the UK) Queen's Police Medal.

qt > *abbreviation* quart(s).

q.t. > *noun* (**on the q.t.**) informal secretly.
ORIGIN – abbreviation of *quiet*.

qua /kwaa/ > *conjunction* formal in the capacity of; as being: *academics qua teachers*.
ORIGIN – Latin.

quack¹ > *noun* the characteristic harsh sound made by a duck. > *verb* make this sound.

quack² > *noun* **1** an unqualified person who dishonestly claims to have medical knowledge. **2** Brit. informal a doctor.
DERIVATIVES – **quackery** *noun*.
ORIGIN – abbreviation of earlier *quacksalver*, from Dutch, probably from obsolete *quacken* 'prattle' + *salf* 'salve'.

quad > *noun* **1** a quadrangle. **2** a quadruplet. > *adjective* quadraphonic.
COMBINATIONS – **quad bike** a motorcycle with four large tyres, for off-road use.

quadragenarian /kwodrəjinairiən/ > *noun* a person who is between 40 and 49 years old.

ORIGIN – Latin *quadragenarius* from *quadraginta* 'forty'.

Quadragesima /kwodrəjessimə/ > *noun* the first Sunday in Lent.
ORIGIN – from Latin *quadragesimus* 'fortieth' (Lent lasting forty days).

quadrangle > *noun* **1** a four-sided geometrical figure, especially a square or rectangle. **2** a square or rectangular courtyard enclosed by buildings.
DERIVATIVES – **quadrangular** *adjective*.

quadrant > *noun* **1** each of four parts of a circle, plane, body, etc. divided by two lines or planes at right angles. **2** historical an instrument for taking angular measurements of altitude in astronomy and navigation.
ORIGIN – Latin *quadrans* 'quarter', from *quattuor* 'four'.

quadraphonic /kwodrəfonnik/ (also **quadrophonic**) > *adjective* (of sound reproduction) transmitted through four channels.
DERIVATIVES – **quadraphony** *noun*.

quadrate /kwodrət/ > *adjective* roughly square or rectangular.
ORIGIN – from Latin *quadrare* 'make square'.

quadratic /kwodrattik/ > *adjective* Mathematics involving the second and no higher power of an unknown quantity or variable.

quadrennial /kwodrenniəl/ > *adjective* lasting for or recurring every four years.
ORIGIN – from Latin *quadri-* 'four' + *annus* 'year'.

quadri- > *combining form* four; having four: *quadriplegia*.
ORIGIN – from Latin *quattuor* 'four'.

quadriceps /kwodriseps/ > *noun* (pl. same) a large muscle at the front of the thigh.
ORIGIN – Latin, 'four-headed'.

quadrilateral > *noun* a four-sided figure. > *adjective* having four straight sides.

quadrille¹ /kwodril/ > *noun* a square dance performed typically by four couples and containing five figures.
ORIGIN – Spanish *cuadrilla* or Italian *quadriglia* 'troop, company', from *quadra* 'square'.

quadrille² /kwodril/ > *noun* a trick-taking card game for four players, fashionable in the 18th century.
ORIGIN – perhaps from Spanish *cuartillo*, from *cuarto* 'fourth'.

quadrillion /kwodrilyən/ > *cardinal number* a thousand raised to the power of five (10^{15}); a thousand million million.
DERIVATIVES – **quadrillionth** *ordinal number*.

quadripartite /kwodripaartīt/ > *adjective* **1** consisting of four parts. **2** shared by or involving four parties.

quadriplegia /kwodripleejə/ > *noun* Medicine paralysis of all four limbs.

DERIVATIVES – **quadriplegic** *adjective* & *noun*.
ORIGIN – from Greek *plēgē* 'blow, stroke'.

quadroon > *noun* archaic a person who is one-quarter black by descent.
ORIGIN – Spanish *cuarterón*, from *cuarto* 'quarter'.

quadrophonic > *adjective* variant spelling of QUADRAPHONIC.

quadruped /kwodrooped/ > *noun* an animal which has four feet, especially a mammal.
DERIVATIVES – **quadrupedal** *adjective*.
ORIGIN – from Latin *quadru-* 'four' + *pes* 'foot'.

quadruple > *adjective* **1** consisting of four parts or elements. **2** four times as much or as many. **3** (of time in music) having four beats in a bar. > *verb* increase or be increased fourfold. > *noun* a quadruple number or amount.
ORIGIN – Latin *quadruplus*.

quadruplet > *noun* each of four children born at one birth.

quadruplicate > *adjective* /kwodrooplikət/ consisting of four parts or elements. > *verb* /kwodrooplikayt/ **1** multiply by four. **2** make four copies of.
IDIOMS – **in quadruplicate** in four copies.

quaff /kwof/ > *verb* drink (something) heartily.
DERIVATIVES – **quaffable** *adjective* **quaffer** *noun*.

quag /kwag, kwog/ > *noun* archaic a marshy or boggy place.
ORIGIN – related to dialect *quag* 'to shake'.

quagga /kwaggə/ > *noun* an extinct South African zebra with a yellowish-brown coat with darker stripes.
ORIGIN – probably from Khoikhoi.

quagmire /kwagmīr, kwog-/ > *noun* **1** a soft boggy area of land that gives way underfoot. **2** a complex or difficult situation.

quail¹ > *noun* (pl. same or **quails**) a small short-tailed game bird.
ORIGIN – Old French *quaille*, from Latin *coacula*.

quail² > *verb* feel or show fear or apprehension.

quaint > *adjective* attractively unusual or old-fashioned.
DERIVATIVES – **quaintly** *adverb* **quaintness** *noun*.
SYNONYMS – charming, old-fashioned, picturesque.
ORIGIN – Old French *cointe*, from Latin *cognoscere* 'ascertain': originally in the sense 'wise', 'ingenious'.

quake > *verb* **1** (especially of the earth) shake or tremble. **2** shudder with fear. > *noun* informal an earthquake.

SYNONYMS – *verb* shake, shiver, shudder, tremble.

Quaker > *noun* a member of the Religious Society of Friends, a Christian movement devoted to peaceful principles and rejecting both formal ministry and all set forms of worship.

DERIVATIVES – **Quakerism** *noun*.

---

wordpower facts
Quaker

George Fox (1624–91), who founded the Society of Friends in 1650, stated in his journal that the name **Quaker** was first given to himself and his followers in 1650 by a Justice Bennet 'because I bid them tremble at the Word of the Lord'. However, there are earlier references (in a letter written in London in 1647) to 'a sect of women…come from beyond the Sea, called Quakers, and these swell, shiver, and shake', for 'Mahomett's holy-ghost hath bin conversing with them'. It is therefore probable that Bennet was using a term that was already familiar, and was appropriately descriptive of Fox's early followers. Compare this with **Shaker**: it is known that the **Shakers** were so named from the wild, ecstatic movements in which they engaged during worship.

---

qualification > *noun* **1** the action of qualifying or the fact of becoming qualified. **2** a pass of an examination or an official completion of a course. **3** a quality that makes someone suitable for a job or activity. **4** a condition that must be fulfilled before a right can be acquired. **5** a statement that qualifies another.

qualify > *verb* (**qualifies, qualified**) **1** (often **qualify for**) meet the necessary standard or conditions to be entitled to or eligible for something. **2** become officially recognised as a practitioner of a profession or activity, typically after study and passing examinations. **3** make competent or knowledgeable enough to do something. **4** modify (a statement) by adding restrictions or reservations. **5** describe or class as being. **6** Grammar (of a word or phrase) attribute a quality to (another word, especially a preceding noun).

DERIVATIVES – **qualifier** *noun*.

SYNONYMS – **1,2** be eligible, make the grade, pass. **3** authorise, empower, equip, license, permit.

ORIGIN – Latin *qualificare*, from *qualis* (see **QUALITY**).

qualitative /kwollitətiv/ > *adjective* **1** of, concerned with, or measured by quality. **2** Grammar (of an adjective) describing the quality of something in size, appearance, etc.

DERIVATIVES – **qualitatively** *adverb*.

quality > *noun* (pl. **qualities**) **1** the degree of excellence of something as measured against other similar things. **2** general excellence. **3** a distinctive attribute or characteristic. **4** archaic high social standing.

SYNONYMS – **1** calibre, class, grade, standard. **2** distinction, excellence, superiority, value, worth. **3** attribute, characteristic, feature, property, trait.

COMBINATIONS – **quality control** a system of maintaining standards in manufactured products by testing a sample against the specification. **quality time** time devoted exclusively to another person in order to strengthen a relationship.

ORIGIN – Latin *qualitas*, from *qualis* 'of what kind, of such a kind'.

qualm /kwaam/ > *noun* **1** a feeling of doubt or unease, especially about one's conduct. **2** archaic a momentary faint or sick feeling.

SYNONYMS – **1** concern, doubt, misgiving, reservation, worry.

quandary /kwondri/ > *noun* (pl. **quandaries**) a state of perplexity or uncertainty.

SYNONYMS – dilemma, plight, predicament.

ORIGIN – perhaps partly from Latin *quando* 'when'.

quango /kwanggō/ > *noun* (pl. **quangos**) Brit., chiefly derogatory an administrative body outside the civil service that is at least partly funded and appointed by the government.

ORIGIN – acronym from *quasi* (or *quasi-autonomous*) *non-governmental organisation*.

quanta plural of **QUANTUM**.

quantifier > *noun* Grammar a determiner or pronoun which indicates quantity (e.g. *all*).

quantify > *verb* (**quantifies, quantified**) express or measure the quantity of.

DERIVATIVES – **quantifiable** *adjective* **quantification** *noun*.

SYNONYMS – assess, calculate, measure, reckon.

quantise (also **quantize**) > *verb* **1** Physics divide into quanta. **2** Electronics approximate (a freely varying signal) by one whose amplitude is restricted to prescribed values.

DERIVATIVES – **quantisation** *noun* **quantiser** *noun*.

quantitative* /kwontitətiv, -taytiv/ > *adjective* of, concerned with, or measured by quantity.

DERIVATIVES – **quantitatively** *adverb*.

*SPELLING – remember the *-at-*: quanti*tat*ive.

quantity > *noun* (pl. **quantities**) **1** a certain amount or number. **2** the property of something that is measurable in number, amount, size, or weight. **3** a considerable number or amount.

SYNONYMS – **1** amount, extent, magnitude, mass, number, sum, volume.

COMBINATIONS – **quantity surveyor** Brit. a person who calculates the amount and cost of materials needed for building work.

ORIGIN – Latin *quantitas*, from *quantus* 'how great, how much'.

quantum /kwontəm/ > *noun* (pl. **quanta** /kwontə/) **1** Physics an individual quantity of energy corresponding to that involved in the absorption or emission of energy or light by an atom or other particle. **2** a total amount, especially an amount of money legally payable in damages. **3** a share.

COMBINATIONS – **quantum computer** a computer which makes use of the energy states of subatomic particles to store information. **quantum leap** (also **quantum jump**) a sudden large increase or advance. **quantum mechanics** the branch of physics concerned with describing the behaviour of subatomic particles in terms of quanta, incorporating the idea that particles can also be regarded as waves. **quantum theory** a theory of matter and energy based on the idea of quanta.

ORIGIN – from Latin *quantus* 'how great'.

quarantine > *noun* a state or period of isolation for people or animals that have arrived from elsewhere or been exposed to contagious disease. > *verb* put in quarantine.

---

wordpower facts
Quarantine

The word **quarantine** entered English in the 16th century, coming from Italian *quarantina*, meaning 'forty days', from *quaranta* 'forty'. Originally it denoted a period of forty days during which a widow who was entitled to a share of her deceased husband's estate had the right to remain in his house. It also denoted the right itself; a legal nicety quoted in a work of 1628 states: 'If she marry within the forty days she loseth her quarentine'. The current sense is first recorded in 1663, in Samuel Pepys's *Diary*, which referred to a period of quarantine of thirty days. From now on the emphasis of the word was on the state of isolation rather than the specific length of time, which varied according to the incubation period of the disease in question.

---

quark¹ /kwaark, kwawk/ > *noun* Physics any of a group of subatomic particles which carry a fractional electric charge and are believed to be building blocks of protons, neutrons, and other particles.

wordpower facts

Quark

The word **quark** was coined in 1963 by the American physicist Murray Gell-Mann. He originally used the spelling **quork**, but changed it to **quark** on coming across the line in James Joyce's *Finnegans Wake* (1939), 'Three quarks for Muster Mark'; he felt this to be particularly appropriate, given that three kinds of quark were originally proposed. In a letter written in 1978, Gell-Mann says 'I needed an excuse for retaining the pronunciation quork despite the occurrence of "Mark", "bark", "mark", and so forth in Finnegans Wake. I found that excuse by supposing that one ingredient of the line "Three quarks for Muster Mark" was a cry of "Three quarts for Mister..." heard in H. C. Earwicker's pub.' Gell-Mann's three **flavours** of quark (*up, down,* and *strange*) have now become six (including *charmed, top,* and *bottom*), each divided into three **colours** (*blue, green,* and *red*).

quark² /kwaark/ > *noun* a type of low-fat curd cheese.
ORIGIN – German, 'curd, curds'.

quarrel¹ > *noun* **1** an angry argument or disagreement. **2** a reason for disagreement. > *verb* (**quarrelled**, **quarrelling**; US **quarreled**, **quarreling**) **1** have a quarrel. **2** (**quarrel with**) disagree with.
SYNONYMS – *noun* **1** altercation, argument, dispute, squabble. *verb* **1** argue, dispute, squabble.
ORIGIN – Latin *querella* 'complaint', from *queri* 'complain'.

quarrel² > *noun* historical a short, heavy square-headed arrow or bolt for a crossbow or arbalest.
ORIGIN – Old French, from Latin *quadrus* 'square'; compare with QUARRY³.

quarrelsome > *adjective* given to or characterised by quarrelling.
SYNONYMS – argumentative, contentious, disputatious, fractious.
ANTONYMS – peaceable.

quarry¹ > *noun* (pl. **quarries**) an open excavation in the earth's surface from which stone or other materials are extracted. > *verb* (**quarries**, **quarried**) **1** extract from a quarry. **2** cut into (rock or ground) to obtain stone or other materials.
DERIVATIVES – **quarrier** *noun*.
ORIGIN – Old French *quarriere*, from Latin

quadrare 'to square (stones)', from *quadrum* 'a square'.

quarry² > *noun* (pl. **quarries**) **1** an animal being hunted. **2** a person or thing being chased or sought.
ORIGIN – first used to denote the parts of a deer placed on a hide for the hounds: from Old French *couree*, from Latin *cor* 'heart'.

quarry³ > *noun* (pl. **quarries**) **1** a diamond-shaped pane in a lattice window. **2** (also **quarry tile**) an unglazed floor tile.
ORIGIN – alteration of QUARREL², which originally denoted a lattice windowpane.

quart > *noun* **1** a unit of liquid capacity equal to a quarter of a gallon or two pints, equivalent in Britain to approximately 1.13 litres and in the US to approximately 0.94 litre. **2** N. Amer. a unit of dry capacity equivalent to approximately 1.10 litres.
IDIOMS – **you can't get a quart into a pint pot** Brit. proverb you cannot achieve the impossible.
ORIGIN – from Latin *quarta pars* 'fourth part', from *quartus* 'fourth'.

quarter > *noun* **1** each of four equal or corresponding parts into which something is or can be divided. **2** a period of three months, used especially in reference to financial transactions. **3** a quarter-hour. **4** a US or Canadian coin worth 25 cents. **5** one fourth of a pound weight (avoirdupois, equal to 4 ounces). **6** one fourth of a hundredweight (Brit. 28 lb or US 25 lb). **7** a part of a town or city with a specific character or use: *the business quarter.* **8** (**quarters**) rooms or lodgings. **9** a person, area, etc. regarded as the source of something: *help came from an unexpected quarter.* **10** (in combat) pity or mercy: *they gave the enemy no quarter.* **11** (**quarters**) the haunches or hindquarters of a horse. **12** the direction of one of the points of the compass. > *verb* **1** divide into quarters. **2** historical cut the body of (an executed person) into four parts. **3** (**be quartered**) be stationed or lodged. **4** range over (an area) in all directions. **5** Heraldry display (different coats of arms) in the four divisions of a shield.
COMBINATIONS – **quarter day** Brit. each of four days on which some tenancies begin and end and quarterly payments fall due. **quarter-final** a match of a knockout competition preceding the semi-final. **quarter-hour 1** (also **quarter of an hour**) a period of fifteen minutes. **2** a point of time fifteen minutes before or after a full hour of the clock. **quarter-light** Brit. a window in the side of a motor vehicle other than a main door window. **quarter sessions** historical (in England, Wales, and Northern Ireland) a court of limited criminal and civil jurisdiction and of appeal,

usually held quarterly. **quarter tone** Music half a semitone.
ORIGIN – Latin *quartarius* 'fourth part of a measure', from *quartus* 'fourth'.

quarterback > *noun* American Football a player stationed behind the centre who directs a team's offensive play.

quarterdeck > *noun* the part of a ship's upper deck near the stern, traditionally reserved for officers or for ceremonial use.

quarterly > *adjective & adverb* produced or occurring once every quarter of a year. > *noun* (pl. **quarterlies**) a publication produced four times a year.

quartermaster > *noun* **1** a regimental officer in charge of looking after the barracks and supplies. **2** a naval petty officer responsible for steering and signals.

quarterstaff > *noun* a stout pole 6–8 feet long, formerly used as a weapon.

quartet > *noun* **1** a group of four people playing music or singing together. **2** a composition for a quartet. **3** a set of four people or things.
ORIGIN – Italian *quartetto*, from *quarto* 'fourth'.

quartile /kwawrtīl/ > *noun* Statistics each of four equal groups into which a population can be divided according to the distribution of values of a particular variable.
ORIGIN – Latin *quartilis*, from *quartus* 'fourth'.

quarto /kwawrtō/ > *noun* (pl. **quartos**) **1** a page or paper size resulting from folding a sheet into four leaves (eight pages), typically 10 inches × 8 inches (254 × 203 mm). **2** a book of this size.
ORIGIN – from Latin *in quarto* 'in the fourth (of a sheet)'.

quartz > *noun* a hard mineral consisting of silica, typically occurring as colourless or white hexagonal prisms.
COMBINATIONS – **quartz clock** (or **watch**) a clock (or watch) regulated by vibrations of an electrically driven quartz crystal.
ORIGIN – German *Quarz*, from Polish dialect *kwardy*, corresponding to Czech *tvrdý* 'hard'.

quartzite > *noun* a compact, hard, granular rock consisting mainly of quartz.

quasar /kwayzaar/ > *noun* a massive and extremely remote celestial object which emits large amounts of energy.
ORIGIN – contraction of *quasi-stellar radio source*: telescope images of quasars are typically star-like.

quash > *verb* **1** reject as invalid, especially by legal procedure. **2** put an end to; suppress.
ORIGIN – Old French *quasser* 'annul', from Latin *cassus* 'null, void'.

quasi- /kwayzī/ > *combining form* **1**

seemingly: *quasi-scientific*. **2** being partly or almost: *quasicrystalline*.

ORIGIN – Latin, 'as if, almost'.

quassia /kwoshə/ > *noun* a South American shrub or small tree whose wood, bark, or root yields a bitter medicinal tonic and insecticide.

ORIGIN – named after Graman *Quassi*, the eighteenth-century Surinamese slave who discovered its medicinal properties.

quatercentenary /kwattərsenteenəri, -sentennəri/ > *noun* (pl. **quatercentenaries**) a four-hundredth anniversary.

ORIGIN – from Latin *quater* 'four times'.

quaternary /kwəternəri/ > *adjective* **1** fourth in order or rank. **2** (**Quaternary**) Geology relating to the most recent period in the Cenozoic era, from about 1.64 million years ago to the present.

ORIGIN – Latin *quaternarius*, from *quater* 'four times'.

quatrain /kwotrayn/ > *noun* a stanza of four lines, typically with alternate rhymes.

ORIGIN – French, from *quatre* 'four'.

quatrefoil /katrəfoyl/ > *noun* an ornamental design of four lobes or leaves, resembling a flower or clover leaf.

ORIGIN – from Old French *quatre* 'four' + *foil* 'leaf'.

quattrocento /kwatrōchentō/ > *noun* the 15th century as a period of Italian art or architecture.

ORIGIN – Italian, '400' (shortened from *milquattrocento* '1400').

quaver > *verb* (of a voice) tremble. > *noun* **1** a tremble in a voice. **2** Music, chiefly Brit. a note having the value of an eighth of a semibreve or half a crotchet, represented by a large dot with a hooked stem.

DERIVATIVES – **quavery** *adjective*.

ORIGIN – dialect *quave* 'quake, tremble', probably from an Old English word related to QUAKE.

quay /kee/ > *noun* a platform lying alongside or projecting into water for loading and unloading ships.

COMBINATIONS – **quayside** a quay and the area around it.

ORIGIN – Old French *kay*; the change of spelling in the 17th century was influenced by the modern French spelling *quai*.

queasy > *adjective* (**queasier, queasiest**) **1** feeling nauseous or inducing a feeling of nausea. **2** slightly nervous or uneasy.

DERIVATIVES – **queasily** *adverb* **queasiness** *noun*.

ORIGIN – perhaps related to Old French *coisier* 'to hurt'.

Quechua /kechwə/ > *noun* (pl. same or **Quechuas**) a member of an American Indian people of Peru and neighbouring countries.

DERIVATIVES – **Quechuan** *adjective & noun*.

ORIGIN – Quechua, 'temperate valleys'.

queen > *noun* **1** the female ruler of an independent state, especially one who inherits the position by right of birth. **2** (also **queen consort**) a king's wife. **3** the best or most important woman or thing in a sphere or group. **4** a playing card bearing a representation of a queen, ranking next below a king. **5** the most powerful chess piece, able to move in any direction. **6** a reproductive female in a colony of ants, bees, wasps, or termites. **7** informal a flamboyantly effeminate male homosexual. > *verb* **1** (**queen it**) (of a woman) act in an unpleasantly superior way. **2** Chess convert (a pawn) into a queen when it reaches the opponent's end of the board.

DERIVATIVES – **queendom** *noun* **queenly** *adjective* **queenship** *noun*.

COMBINATIONS – **Queen Anne** denoting a style of English furniture or architecture characteristic of the early 18th century. **queen bee 1** the single reproductive female in a colony of honeybees. **2** informal a dominant woman in a group. **queen dowager** the widow of a king. **queen mother** the widow of a king and mother of the sovereign. **queen post** either of two upright timbers between the tie beam and principal rafters of a roof truss. **Queen's Bench** (in the UK) a division of the High Court of Justice. **Queen's Counsel** (in the UK) a senior barrister appointed on the recommendation of the Lord Chancellor. **Queen's English** the English language as correctly written and spoken in Britain. **Queen's evidence** English Law evidence for the prosecution given by a participant in the crime being tried. **Queen's Guide** (or **Queen's Scout**) (in the UK) a Guide (or Scout) who has reached the highest rank of proficiency. **Queen's highway** Brit. the public road network. **queen-sized** (also **queen-size**) of a larger size than the standard but smaller than king-sized. **Queen's Messenger** (in the UK) a courier in the diplomatic service. **Queen's Speech** (in the UK) a statement read by the sovereign at the opening of Parliament, detailing the government's proposed legislative programme.

Queensberry Rules > *plural noun* the standard rules of boxing.

ORIGIN – named after the 8th Marquess of *Queensberry*, who supervised the preparation of the rules in 1867.

queer > *adjective* **1** strange; odd. **2** informal, derogatory (of a man) homosexual. **3** Brit. informal, dated slightly ill. > *noun* informal, derogatory a homosexual man. > *verb* informal spoil or ruin.

IDIOMS – **in Queer Street** Brit. informal, dated in difficulty or debt. **queer someone's pitch** Brit. informal spoil someone's plans or chances of doing something.

DERIVATIVES – **queerish** *adjective* **queerly** *adverb* **queerness** *noun*.

USAGE – the word **queer** was first used to mean 'homosexual' in the early 20th century. It was originally, and usually still is, a deliberately derogatory term when used by heterosexual people; in recent years, however, gay people have used it in place of **gay** or **homosexual**, in an attempt, by using the word positively, to deprive it of its negative power.

ORIGIN – perhaps from German *quer* 'oblique, perverse'.

quell > *verb* **1** put an end to (a rebellion or other disorder), typically by force. **2** subdue or suppress.

SYNONYMS – *verb* **1** check, put down, stamp out.

ORIGIN – Old English, 'kill'.

quench > *verb* **1** satisfy (thirst) by drinking. **2** satisfy (a desire). **3** extinguish (a fire). **4** stifle (a feeling). **5** rapidly cool (hot metal). **6** Physics & Electronics suppress or damp (luminescence, an oscillation, etc.).

DERIVATIVES – **quencher** *noun*.

quenelle /kənel/ > *noun* a small seasoned ball of fish or meat.

ORIGIN – French, probably from German dialect *knödel*.

quern /kwern/ > *noun* a simple hand mill for grinding grain, typically consisting of two circular stones.

querulous /kwerro'oləss/ > *adjective* complaining in a petulant or whining manner.

DERIVATIVES – **querulously** *adverb* **querulousness** *noun*.

SYNONYMS – crotchety, peevish, pettish, petulant, tetchy.

ORIGIN – Latin *querulus*, from *queri* 'complain'.

query > *noun* (pl. **queries**) **1** a question, especially one expressing doubt. **2** chiefly Printing a question mark. > *verb* (**queries, queried**) **1** ask a query. **2** N. Amer. put a query or queries to.

ORIGIN – from Latin *quaerere* 'ask, seek'.

quesadilla /kayssədeeyə/ > *noun* a hot tortilla with a spicy cheese filling.

ORIGIN – Spanish.

quest > *noun* **1** a long or arduous search. **2** (in medieval romance) an expedition by a knight to accomplish a specific task. > *verb* search for something.

DERIVATIVES – **quester** (also **questor**) *noun*.

ORIGIN – Old French *queste*, from Latin *quaerere* 'ask, seek'.

question > *noun* **1** a sentence worded or expressed so as to obtain information. **2** a doubt. **3** the raising of a doubt or objection: *he obeyed the order without question.* **4** a problem requiring resolution. **5** a matter or issue depending on conditions: *it's only a question of time before something changes.* > *verb* **1** ask questions of. **2** express doubt about; object to.

IDIOMS – **come** (or **bring**) **into question** become (or raise) an issue for further consideration or discussion. **in question 1** being considered or discussed. **2** in doubt. **no question of** no possibility of. **out of the question** not possible. **put the question** require supporters and opponents of a debated proposal to record their votes.

DERIVATIVES – **questioner** *noun*.

COMBINATIONS – **question mark** a punctuation mark (?) indicating a question. **question master** Brit. the questioner in a quiz or panel game. **question time** (in the UK) a period during proceedings in the House of Commons when MPs may question ministers.

ORIGIN – Old French, from Latin *quaerere* 'ask, seek'.

questionable > *adjective* **1** open to doubt. **2** of suspect morality, honesty, etc.

DERIVATIVES – **questionably** *adverb*.

SYNONYMS – **1** contentious, controversial, doubtful, uncertain. **2** dubious, irregular, suspicious.

questionnaire* /kwess-chə**nair**, kess-chə**nair**/ > *noun* a set of printed questions, usually with a choice of answers, devised for a survey or statistical study.

*SPELLING – note there are two *n*s: questio*nn*aire.

ORIGIN – French.

quetzal /**kwets**'l/ > *noun* a long-tailed tropical American bird with iridescent green plumage and typically red underparts.

ORIGIN – from an Aztec word meaning 'brightly coloured tail feather'.

queue > *noun* **1** a line of people or vehicles awaiting their turn to be attended to or to proceed. **2** Computing a list of data items, commands, etc., stored so as to be retrievable in a definite order. > *verb* (**queues, queued, queuing** or **queueing**) wait in a queue.

COMBINATIONS – **queue-jump** Brit. move forward out of turn in a queue.

ORIGIN – first used as a heraldic term for the tail of an animal, later meaning 'long plait or pigtail': from French, based on Latin *cauda* 'tail'. Compare with **CUE**[2].

quibble > *noun* **1** a slight objection or criticism. **2** archaic a pun. > *verb* argue about a trivial matter.

SYNONYMS – *noun* **1** cavil, grouse, grumble, moan.

---

wordpower facts

Quibble

The word **quibble** was first recorded in the sense 'a play on words; a pun'. It probably comes from the obsolete word *quib*, which was used in the same senses as **quibble** and came from the Latin word *quibus* (the dative and ablative plural of *qui, quae, quod* 'who, what, which'). The word *quibus*, being used frequently in legal documents, became associated with the subtle distinctions and verbal niceties of legal terminology.

---

quiche /keesh/ > *noun* a baked flan with a savoury filling thickened with eggs.

ORIGIN – French, from German dialect *Küchen*.

quick > *adjective* **1** moving fast. **2** lasting or taking a short time: *a quick worker.* **3** with little or no delay; prompt. **4** (of a person) understanding, thinking, or learning fast. **5** (of one's eye or ear) keenly perceptive. **6** (of temper) easily roused. > *noun* **1** (**the quick**) the tender flesh below the growing part of a fingernail or toenail. **2** the central or most sensitive part: *his laughter cut us to the quick.* **3** (**the quick**) archaic those who are living.

IDIOMS – **a quick one** informal a rapidly consumed alcoholic drink. **quick with child** archaic at a stage of pregnancy when the fetus can be felt to move.

DERIVATIVES – **quickly** *adverb* **quickness** *noun*.

SYNONYMS – *adjective* **1,2** fast, rapid, swift. **3** immediate, instantaneous, prompt. **4** clever, bright, intelligent, sharp.

COMBINATIONS – **quick fix** a speedy but inadequate solution. **quick march** a brisk military march. **quick-tempered** easily angered. **quick-witted** able to think or respond quickly.

ORIGIN – Old English, 'alive, animated, alert'.

quicken > *verb* **1** make or become quicker. **2** stimulate or be stimulated. **3** archaic reach a stage in pregnancy when the fetus can be felt to move. **4** archaic (of a fetus) begin to show signs of life.

SYNONYMS – **1** accelerate, hasten, speed up.

quick-fire > *adjective* **1** unhesitating and rapid. **2** (of a gun) firing shots in rapid succession.

quickie informal > *noun* **1** a rapidly consumed alcoholic drink. **2** a quickly performed act of sexual intercourse. > *adjective* done or made quickly.

quicklime > *noun* a white caustic alkaline substance consisting of calcium oxide, obtained by heating limestone.

quicksand (also **quicksands**) > *noun* loose wet sand that sucks in anything resting on it.

quickset > *noun* Brit. hedging, especially of hawthorn, grown from slips or cuttings.

quicksilver > *noun* liquid mercury. > *adjective* moving or changing rapidly.

quickstep > *noun* a fast foxtrot in 4/4 time.

quickthorn > *noun* hawthorn.

quid[1] > *noun* (pl. same) Brit. informal one pound sterling.

IDIOMS – **not the full quid** Austral./NZ informal not intelligent. **quids in** Brit. informal profiting or likely to profit from something.

quid[2] > *noun* a lump of chewing tobacco.

ORIGIN – variant of **CUD**.

quiddity /**kwidd**iti/ > *noun* (pl. **quiddities**) the inherent nature or essence of a person or thing.

ORIGIN – Latin *quidditas*, from *quid* 'what'.

quidnunc /**kwid**nungk/ > *noun* archaic or literary an inquisitive, gossipy person.

ORIGIN – from Latin *quid nunc?* 'what now?'

quid pro quo /kwid prō **kwō**/ > *noun* (pl. **quid pro quos**) a favour or advantage given in return for something.

ORIGIN – Latin, 'something for something'.

quiescent /kwi**ess**'nt/ > *adjective* in a state or period of inactivity.

DERIVATIVES – **quiescence** *noun* **quiescently** *adverb*.

ORIGIN – from Latin *quiescere* 'be still', from *quies* 'quiet'.

quiet > *adjective* (**quieter, quietest**) **1** making little or no noise. **2** free from activity, disturbance, or excitement. **3** without being disturbed or interrupted: *a quiet drink.* **4** discreet, moderate, or restrained. **5** (of a person) tranquil and reserved. > *noun* absence of noise or disturbance. > *verb* chiefly N. Amer. make or become quiet.

IDIOMS – **on the quiet** informal secretly or unobtrusively.

DERIVATIVES – **quietly** *adverb* **quietness** *noun*.

SYNONYMS – *adjective* **1** hushed, muted, silent. **2,3** peaceful, tranquil, undisturbed. **5** calm, equable, placid. *noun* calm, serenity, tranquillity.

ORIGIN – first used as a noun denoting peace as opposed to war: from Latin *quies* 'repose, quiet'.

quieten > *verb* chiefly Brit. make or become quiet and calm.

quietism > *noun* **1** devotional contemplation

and abandonment of the will as a form of Christian mysticism. **2** calm acceptance of things as they are.

DERIVATIVES – **quietist** noun & adjective.

quietude > noun a state of calmness and quiet.

quietus /kwīeetəss/ > noun (pl. **quietuses**) **1** literary death or a cause of death, regarded as a release from life. **2** archaic something calming or soothing.

ORIGIN – abbreviation of Latin quietus est 'he is quit or set free', originally used as a receipt on payment of a debt.

quiff > noun chiefly Brit. a man's tuft of hair brushed upwards and backwards from the forehead.

quill > noun **1** a main wing or tail feather of a bird. **2** the hollow shaft of a feather, especially the lower part that lacks barbs. **3** a pen made from a quill. **4** a hollow sharp spine of a porcupine, hedgehog, etc.

ORIGIN – probably from Low German quiele.

quilling > noun a type of ornamental craftwork involving the shaping of paper or fabric into delicate pleats or folds.

quilt > noun **1** a warm bed covering made of padding enclosed between layers of fabric and kept in place by lines of decorative stitching. **2** a bedspread of similar design. > verb join (layers of fabric or padding) with stitching to form a bed covering or garment or for decorative effect.

DERIVATIVES – **quilter** noun **quilting** noun.

ORIGIN – Old French cuilte, from Latin culcita 'mattress, cushion'.

quim > noun Brit. vulgar slang a woman's genitals.

quin > noun informal, chiefly Brit. a quintuplet.

quince > noun the hard, acid, pear-shaped fruit of an Asian shrub or small tree, used in preserves or as flavouring.

ORIGIN – Old French cooin, from Latin malum cydonium 'apple of Cydonia' (a former name for Chania, in Crete).

quincentenary /kwinsenteenəri, kwin-sentennəri/ > noun (pl. **quincentenaries**) a five-hundredth anniversary.

DERIVATIVES – **quincentennial** noun & adjective.

ORIGIN – from Latin quinque 'five'.

quincunx /**kwin**kungks/ > noun (pl. **quincunxes**) an arrangement of five objects with four at the corners of a square or rectangle and the fifth at its centre.

DERIVATIVES – **quincuncial** adjective.

ORIGIN – Latin, 'five twelfths'.

quinine /**kwin**een, kwineen/ > noun a bitter crystalline compound present in cinchona bark, used as a tonic and formerly to treat malaria.

ORIGIN – Quechua.

quinone /**kwin**ōn/ > noun Chemistry any of a class of organic compounds related to benzene but having two hydrogen atoms replaced by oxygen.

ORIGIN – from Spanish quina 'cinchona bark'.

quinquagenarian /kwingkwəji**nair**iən/ > noun a person between 50 and 59 years old.

ORIGIN – Latin quinquagenarius, from quinquaginti 'fifty'.

Quinquagesima /kwingkwə**jess**imə/ > noun the Sunday before the beginning of Lent.

ORIGIN – from Latin quinquagesimus 'fiftieth', on the pattern of Quadragesima (because it is ten days before the forty days of Lent).

quinque- > combining form five; having five.

ORIGIN – Latin.

quinquennial /kwing**kwenn**iəl/ > adjective lasting for or recurring every five years.

DERIVATIVES – **quinquennially** adverb.

ORIGIN – from Latin quinque 'five' + annus 'year'.

quinquennium /kwing**kwenn**iəm/ > noun (pl. **quinquennia** /kwing**kwenn**iə/ or **quinquenniums**) a period of five years.

quinquereme /**kwing**kwireem/ > noun an ancient Roman or Greek galley of a kind believed to have had three banks of oars, the oars in the top two banks being rowed by pairs of oarsmen and the oars in the bottom bank being rowed by single oarsmen.

ORIGIN – from Latin quinque 'five' + remus 'oar'.

quinsy /**kwin**zi/ > noun inflammation of the throat, especially an abscess near the tonsils.

ORIGIN – Greek kunankhē 'canine quinsy', from kun- 'dog' + ankhein 'to strangle'.

quinta /**kin**tə, **kwin**tə/ > noun **1** (in Spain, Portugal, and Latin America) a large country house. **2** a wine-growing estate, especially in Portugal.

ORIGIN – Spanish and Portuguese, from quinta parte 'fifth part' (with reference to the amount of a farm's produce paid in rent).

quintal /**kwin**t'l/ > noun **1** a unit of weight equal to a hundredweight (112 lb) or, formerly, 100 lb. **2** a unit of weight equal to 100 kg.

ORIGIN – Latin quintale, from centenarius 'containing a hundred'.

quintessence /kwin**tess**'nss/ > noun **1** the most perfect or typical example or embodiment of a quality or type: crystals are the quintessence of symmetry. **2** a refined essence or extract of a substance.

---

wordpower facts

Quintessence

The word **quintessence** was first used in medieval philosophy. It came from the medieval Latin term quinta essentia, meaning 'fifth essence', and denoted a fifth substance believed to exist in addition to the four elements air, earth, fire, and water. Medieval philosophers believed that this 'fifth essence' was the substance of which the celestial bodies were composed, and that it lay within all things; optimistic alchemists attempted to extract it by distillation and other experimental methods.

---

quintessential /kwinti**sen**sh'l/ > adjective representing the most perfect or typical example.

DERIVATIVES – **quintessentially** adverb.

SYNONYMS – archetypal, classic, exemplary, prototypical, typical.

quintet > noun **1** a group of five people playing music or singing together. **2** a composition for a quintet. **3** a set of five people or things.

ORIGIN – Italian quintetto, from quinto 'fifth'.

quintillion /kwin**til**yən/ > cardinal number a thousand raised to the power of six (10^{18}); a million million million.

DERIVATIVES – **quintillionth** ordinal number.

quintuple /**kwin**tyoop'l/ > adjective **1** consisting of five parts or elements. **2** five times as much or as many. **3** (of time in music) having five beats in a bar. > verb increase or be increased fivefold. > noun a quintuple number or amount.

ORIGIN – Latin quintuplus, from quintus 'fifth'.

quintuplet /**kwin**tyooplit/ > noun each of five children born at one birth.

quintuplicate /kwin**tyoo**plikət/ > adjective **1** fivefold. **2** of which five copies are made.

quip > noun a witty remark. > verb (**quipped**, **quipping**) make a quip.

DERIVATIVES – **quipster** noun.

SYNONYMS – noun jest, joke, witticism.

ORIGIN – perhaps from Latin quippe 'indeed, forsooth'.

quire /kwīr/ > noun **1** four sheets of paper or parchment folded to form eight leaves, as in medieval manuscripts. **2** 25 (formerly 24) sheets of paper; one twentieth of a ream. **3** any collection of leaves one within another in a manuscript or book.

ORIGIN – Old French quaier, from Latin quaterni 'set of four'.

quirk > *noun* **1** a peculiar behavioural habit. **2** a strange chance occurrence. **3** a sudden twist, turn, or curve.

SYNONYMS – **1** eccentricity, foible, idiosyncrasy. **2** fluke, freak.

quirky > *adjective* (**quirkier, quirkiest**) characterised by peculiar or unexpected traits.

DERIVATIVES – **quirkily** *adverb* **quirkiness** *noun*.

quirt /kwurt/ > *noun* a short-handled riding whip with a braided leather lash.

ORIGIN – Spanish *cuerda* 'cord' or Mexican Spanish *cuarta* 'whip'.

quisling /**kwiz**ling/ > *noun* a traitor collaborating with an occupying enemy force.

ORIGIN – from the Norwegian army officer Major Vidkun *Quisling* (1887–1945), who ruled Norway on behalf of the German occupying forces.

quit > *verb* (**quitting**; past and past participle **quitted** or **quit**) **1** leave (a place), especially permanently. **2** resign from (a job). **3** informal, chiefly N. Amer. stop or discontinue (an action or activity). **4** (**quit oneself**) archaic behave in a specified way. > *adjective* (**quit of**) rid of.

ORIGIN – Old French *quiter*, from Latin *quietus*, from *quiescere* 'be still'.

quitch > *noun* another term for COUCH².

quite > *adverb* **1** to the utmost or most absolute extent or degree; completely. **2** to a certain extent; moderately. **3** US very; really. > *exclamation* (also **quite so**) expressing agreement.

IDIOMS – **quite a —— ** a remarkable or impressive (person or thing). **quite a lot** (or **a bit**) a considerable number or amount. **quite some** a considerable amount of.

ORIGIN – from the obsolete adjective *quite*, variant of QUIT.

quits > *adjective* (of two people) on equal terms, especially because a debt or score has been settled.

IDIOMS – **call it quits 1** agree that terms are now equal. **2** decide to abandon an activity.

ORIGIN – first used in the sense 'freed from a liability or debt': perhaps an informal abbreviation of Latin *quittus*, from *quietus* (see QUIETUS).

quittance > *noun* archaic or literary a release from a debt or obligation.

quitter > *noun* informal a person who gives up easily.

quiver¹ > *verb* shake or vibrate with a slight rapid motion. > *noun* a quivering movement or sound.

DERIVATIVES – **quivery** *adjective*.

SYNONYMS – *verb* shiver, shudder, tremble. *noun* frisson, shiver, shudder, tremor.

ORIGIN – from an Old English word meaning 'nimble, quick'.

quiver² > *noun* an archer's portable case for arrows.

ORIGIN – Old French *quiveir*.

quiverful > *noun* **1** as much as a quiver can hold. **2** Brit. humorous a large number of offspring. [ORIGIN – with biblical allusion to Psalm 127.]

qui vive /kee **veev**/ > *noun* (in phrase **on the qui vive**) on the alert or lookout.

ORIGIN – French, '(long) live who?', i.e. 'on whose side are you?', used as a sentry's challenge.

quixotic /kwik**sott**ik/ > *adjective* impractically idealistic or fanciful.

DERIVATIVES – **quixotically** *adverb* **quixotism** /**kwik**sətiz'm/ *noun*.

SYNONYMS – romantic, unwordly.

ORIGIN – from the name of Don *Quixote*, hero of Cervantes' romance (1605–15).

quiz¹ > *noun* (pl. **quizzes**) **1** a test of knowledge, especially as a competition for entertainment. **2** informal, chiefly Brit. a period of questioning. > *verb* (**quizzes, quizzed, quizzing**) question (someone).

COMBINATIONS – **quizmaster** Brit. a question master.

quiz² archaic > *verb* (**quizzes, quizzed, quizzing**) **1** peer at. **2** make fun of. > *noun* (pl. **quizzes**) **1** a hoax. **2** an odd or eccentric person.

wordpower facts

Quiz

The origin of the archaic word **quiz** is uncertain. There is a story that a Dublin theatre proprietor called Richard Daly made a bet that a nonsense word could be made known throughout the city within forty-eight hours, and that the public would give it a meaning: he is said to have had the word written up on walls all over the city, with the result that Dubliners soon took it up. However, this stunt is supposed to have taken place in 1791, and the word is first recorded in 1782, in the sense 'an odd or eccentric person'. The more familiar modern word **quiz** or 'test of knowledge' arose in the mid 19th century. It may have developed from the older **quiz**, influenced by the word *inquisitive*.

quizzical > *adjective* indicating mild or amused puzzlement.

DERIVATIVES – **quizzically** *adverb*.

quod erat demonstrandum /kwod errat demmən**stran**dəm/ > used, especially at the conclusion of a formal proof, to convey that something demonstrates the truth of one's claim.

ORIGIN – Latin, 'which was to be demonstrated'.

quoin /koyn/ > *noun* **1** an external angle of a wall or building. **2** a cornerstone.

ORIGIN – variant of COIN, in the former senses 'cornerstone' and 'wedge'.

quoit /koyt/ > *noun* **1** a ring of iron, rope, or rubber thrown in a game to encircle or land as near as possible to an upright peg. **2** (**quoits**) (treated as sing.) a game of aiming and throwing quoits.

ORIGIN – probably French.

quokka /**kwokk**ə/ > *noun* a small short-tailed wallaby native to Western Australia.

ORIGIN – from Nyungar (an extinct Aboriginal language).

quoll /kwol/ > *noun* a catlike carnivorous marsupial with a white-spotted coat, native to Australia and New Guinea.

ORIGIN – from Guugu Yimidhirr (an Aboriginal language).

quondam /**kwon**dam/ > *adjective* formal former.

ORIGIN – Latin, 'formerly'.

Quonset hut /**kwon**sit/ > *noun* N. Amer. trademark a prefabricated building with a semicylindrical corrugated roof.

ORIGIN – named after *Quonset* Point, Rhode Island, where such huts were first made.

quorate /**kwor**ət/ > *adjective* Brit. (of a meeting) attended by a quorum.

quorum /**kwor**əm/ > *noun* (pl. **quorums**) the minimum number of members of an assembly or society that must be present at a meeting to make the proceedings valid.

ORIGIN – used in commissions in which particular people were designated as members of a body (originally of justices of the peace) by the Latin words *quorum vos … unum* (*duos*, etc.) *esse volumus* 'of whom we wish that you … be one (two, etc.)'.

quota > *noun* **1** a limited quantity of a product which may be produced, exported, or imported. **2** a share that one is entitled to receive or bound to contribute. **3** a fixed number of a group allowed to do something, e.g. of immigrants entering a country.

ORIGIN – from Latin *quota pars* 'how great a part', from *quot* 'how many'.

quotable > *adjective* suitable for or worth quoting.

DERIVATIVES – **quotability** *noun*.

quotation > *noun* **1** a passage or remark repeated by someone other than the originator. **2** the action of quoting. **3** a short musical passage or visual image taken from one piece of music or work of art and used in another. **4** a formal statement of the estimated cost of a job or service. **5** Stock Exchange a registration granted to a company enabling their shares to be officially listed and traded.

COMBINATIONS – **quotation mark** each of a set of punctuation marks, single (' ') or double (" "), used either to mark the beginning and end of a title or quotation, or to indicate slang or jargon words.

quote > *verb* **1** repeat or copy out (a passage or remark by another). **2** repeat a passage or remark from. **3** (**quote as**) put forward or describe as being. **4** give someone (an estimated price). **5** (**quote at** or **as**) name (someone or something) at specified odds. **6** give (a company) a listing on a stock exchange. > *noun* **1** a quotation. **2** (**quotes**) quotation marks.

wordpower facts

Quote

The word **quote** comes from the Latin verb *quotare*, and ultimately from *quot*, meaning 'how many'. The original sense was 'mark a book with numbers or marginal references', then 'give a reference by page or chapter', hence 'cite a text or person'. *Quot* is the root also of **quota** and **quotient**.

quoth /kwōth/ > *verb* archaic or humorous said (used only in first and third person singular before the subject).
ORIGIN – past tense of obsolete *quethe* 'say, declare'.

quotidian /kwotiddiən/ > *adjective* **1** daily. **2** ordinary or everyday.
ORIGIN – Latin *quotidianus*, from *cotidie* 'daily'.

quotient /kwōsh'nt/ > *noun* **1** Mathematics a result obtained by dividing one quantity by another. **2** a degree or amount of a specified quality.
ORIGIN – from Latin *quotiens* 'how many times', from *quot* 'how many'.

Qur'an /kəraan/ (also **Quran**) > *noun* Arabic spelling of **KORAN**.

qursh /koorsh/ > *noun* (pl. same) a monetary unit of Saudi Arabia, equal to one twentieth of a rial.
ORIGIN – Arabic, from Slavic *grossus*.

q.v. > *abbreviation* used to direct a reader to another part of a text for further information.
ORIGIN – from Latin *quod vide* 'which see'.

qwerty /kwerti/ > *adjective* denoting the standard layout on English-language typewriters and keyboards, having *q*, *u*, *e*, *r*, *t*, and *y* as the first keys on the top row of letters.

R¹ (also **r**) > *noun* (pl. **Rs** or **R's**) the eighteenth letter of the alphabet.

IDIOMS – **the three Rs** reading, writing, and arithmetic, regarded as the fundamentals of learning.

R² > *abbreviation* **1** rand. **2** Regina or Rex. **3** (®) registered as a trademark. **4** (**R.**) River. **5** roentgen(s). **6** rook (in chess). **7** Cricket (on scorecards) run(s).

r > *abbreviation* **1** radius. **2** right.

RA > *abbreviation* **1** (in the UK) Royal Academician or Royal Academy. **2** (in the UK) Royal Artillery.

Ra > *symbol* the chemical element radium.

RAAF > *abbreviation* Royal Australian Air Force.

rabbet /rabbit/ > *noun & verb* chiefly N. Amer. another term for REBATE².

ORIGIN – Old French *rabbat* 'abatement, recess'.

rabbi /rabbī/ > *noun* (pl. **rabbis**) **1** a Jewish scholar or teacher, especially of Jewish law. **2** a Jewish religious leader.

DERIVATIVES – **rabbinate** /rabbinət/ *noun*.

ORIGIN – Hebrew, 'my master'.

rabbinic /rəbinnik/ > *adjective* relating to rabbis or to Jewish law or teachings.

DERIVATIVES – **rabbinical** *adjective*.

rabbit > *noun* **1** a burrowing plant-eating mammal, with long ears and a short tail. **2** N. Amer. a hare. **3** the fur of the rabbit. **4** informal a poor performer in a sport or game. > *verb* (**rabbited**, **rabbiting**) **1** hunt rabbits. **2** Brit. informal chatter. [ORIGIN – from *rabbit and pork*, rhyming slang for 'talk'.]

WORDFINDER – buck (*male rabbit*), doe (*female rabbit*), kitten (*young rabbit*), myxomatosis (*disease of rabbits*), scut (*a rabbit's short tail*), warren (*network of rabbit burrows*).

DERIVATIVES – **rabbity** *adjective*.

COMBINATIONS – **rabbit punch** a sharp chop with the edge of the hand to the back of the neck.

ORIGIN – apparently from Old French, perhaps of Dutch origin.

rabble > *noun* **1** a disorderly crowd. **2** (**the**

rabble) ordinary people regarded as socially inferior or uncouth.

SYNONYMS – **1** horde, mass, mob.

COMBINATIONS – **rabble-rouser** a person who stirs up popular opinion, especially for political reasons.

ORIGIN – perhaps related to dialect *rabble* 'to gabble'.

Rabelaisian /rabbəlayziən/ > *adjective* of or like the French satirist François Rabelais (*c.*1494–1553) or his writings, especially in being characterised by exuberant imagination and earthy humour.

rabid /rabbid, raybid/ > *adjective* **1** extreme; fanatical. **2** relating to or affected with rabies.

DERIVATIVES – **rabidly** *adverb*.

rabies /raybeez/ > *noun* a dangerous disease of dogs and other mammals, caused by a virus transmissible through the saliva to humans and causing madness and convulsions.

ORIGIN – Latin, from *rabere* 'to rave'.

RAC > *abbreviation* **1** (in the UK) Royal Armoured Corps. **2** (in the UK) Royal Automobile Club.

raccoon /rəkōon/ (also **racoon**) > *noun* a greyish-brown omnivorous American mammal with a black facial mask and a ringed tail.

ORIGIN – Algonquian dialect.

race¹ > *noun* **1** a competition between runners, horses, vehicles, etc. to see which is fastest over a set course. **2** (**the races**) a series of races for horses or dogs, held at a fixed time on a set course. **3** a situation in which people compete to be first to achieve something. **4** a strong or rapid current flowing through a narrow channel. **5** a water channel, especially one in a mill or mine. **6** a smooth ring-shaped groove or guide for a ball bearing or roller bearing. > *verb* **1** compete in a race. **2** have a race with. **3** prepare and enter (an animal or vehicle) for races. **4** move or progress swiftly. **5** operate at excessive speed.

SYNONYMS – *verb* **4** dash, hasten, hurry, rush, speed.

COMBINATIONS – **racecard** a programme giving information about the races at a race meeting. **racecourse** a ground or track for horse or dog racing. **racehorse** a horse bred and trained for racing. **race meeting** Brit. a sporting event consisting of a series of horse races held at one course. **racetrack 1** a racecourse. **2** a track for motor racing.

ORIGIN – Old Norse *rás* 'current': the first sense in English was 'rapid forward movement'.

race² > *noun* **1** each of the major divisions of humankind, having distinct physical characteristics. **2** racial origin or distinction: *rights based on race.* **3** a group of people sharing the same culture, language, etc.; an

ethnic group. **4** a group of people or things with a common feature. **5** Biology a distinct population within a species; a subspecies.

USAGE – some people now feel that the word **race** should be avoided, because of its associations with the now discredited theories of 19th-century anthropologists and physiologists about supposed racial superiority. Terms such as **people**, **community**, or **ethnic group** are less emotionally charged.

COMBINATIONS – **race relations** relations between members of different races within a country.

ORIGIN – French, from Italian *razza*.

raceme /rəseem/ > *noun* a flower cluster with the separate flowers attached by short stalks along a central stem, the lower flowers developing first. Compare with CYME.

ORIGIN – Latin *racemus* 'bunch of grapes'.

racer > *noun* **1** an animal or vehicle used for racing. **2** a person who competes in races.

rachitic /rəkittik/ > *adjective* Medicine relating to or suffering from rickets.

ORIGIN – from Greek *rhakhitis* 'rickets', from *rhakhis* 'spine'.

Rachmanism /rakməniz'm/ > *noun* Brit. the exploitation and intimidation of tenants by unscrupulous landlords.

ORIGIN – named after the London landlord Peter *Rachman* (1919–62), whose practices became notorious in the early 1960s.

racial > *adjective* **1** of or relating to a race. **2** relating to relations or differences between races.

DERIVATIVES – **racially** *adverb*.

racialism > *noun* racism.

DERIVATIVES – **racialist** *noun & adjective*.

racing > *noun* a sport involving races. > *adjective* **1** moving swiftly. **2** (of a person) following horse racing.

COMBINATIONS – **racing car** a car built for racing. **racing driver** a driver of racing cars.

racism* > *noun* **1** the belief that there are characteristics, abilities, or qualities specific to each race. **2** discrimination against or antagonism towards other races.

DERIVATIVES – **racist** *noun & adjective*.

*****SPELLING – rac-, not rasc-: ra*c*ism.

rack¹ > *noun* **1** a framework for holding or storing things. **2** a cogged or toothed bar or rail engaging with a wheel or pinion, or using pegs to adjust the position of something. **3** (**the rack**) historical an instrument of torture consisting of a frame on which the victim was tied by the wrists and ankles and stretched. **4** a vertically barred holder for animal fodder. **5** a triangular frame for positioning pool balls. **6** a single game of pool. > *verb* **1** (also **wrack**) cause extreme physical or mental pain to. **2** place in or on a rack. **3** (**rack up**) accumulate or achieve (a score or amount).

IDIOMS – **rack (or wrack) one's brains** make a great mental effort.

SYNONYMS – *verb* **1** agonise, torment, torture.

COMBINATIONS – **rack and pinion** a mechanism using a fixed cogged or toothed bar or rail engaging with a smaller cog. **rack railway** a railway for steep slopes, having a toothed rail between the bearing rails which engages with a cogwheel under the locomotive. **rack rent** a very high rent.

ORIGIN – Dutch *rec*, Low German *rek* 'horizontal bar or shelf', probably from *recken* 'to stretch, reach'.

wordpower facts
Rack
The relationship between **rack** and its variant **wrack** is complicated. The most common noun sense of **rack**¹, 'a framework for holding or storing things', is always spelled **rack**, never **wrack**. However, the figurative senses of the verb, deriving from the type of torture in which someone is stretched on a **rack**, can be spelled either **rack** or **wrack**: thus *racked with guilt* or *wracked with guilt; rack your brains* or *wrack your brains*. In such cases **rack** is always the commoner spelling.

rack² > *noun* a joint of meat, especially lamb, including the front ribs.

rack³ (also **wrack**) > *noun* (in phrase **go to rack and ruin**) gradually deteriorate due to neglect.

ORIGIN – Old English, related to **WREAK**.

rack⁴ > *verb* draw off (wine, beer, etc.) from the sediment in the barrel.

ORIGIN – Provençal *arracar*, from *raca* 'stems and husks of grapes, dregs'.

rack⁵ > *noun* variant spelling of **WRACK³**.

racket¹ (also **racquet**) > *noun* a bat with a round or oval frame strung with catgut or nylon, used especially in tennis, badminton, and squash.

ORIGIN – French *raquette*, from an Arabic word meaning 'palm of the hand'.

racket² > *noun* **1** a loud, unpleasant noise. **2** informal a fraudulent scheme for obtaining money. **3** informal a person's line of business. > *verb* (**racketed**, **racketing**) make a loud, unpleasant noise.

DERIVATIVES – **rackety** *adjective*.

SYNONYMS – *noun* **1** din, hubbub.

ORIGIN – perhaps imitative of clattering.

racketeer /rakki**teer**/ > *noun* a person engaging in fraudulent business dealings.

DERIVATIVES – **racketeering** *noun*.

rackets > *plural noun* (treated as sing.) a ball game for two or four people played with rackets and a hard ball in a four-walled court.

raclette /ra**klet**/ > *noun* a Swiss dish of melted cheese, typically with potatoes.

ORIGIN – French, 'small scraper', from the practice of scraping the cheese on to a plate as it melts.

raconteur /rakkon**tör**/ > *noun* (fem. **raconteuse** /rakkon**töz**/) a skilful teller of anecdotes.

ORIGIN – French, from *raconter* 'relate, recount'.

racoon > *noun* variant spelling of **RACCOON**.

racquet > *noun* variant spelling of **RACKET¹**.

racy > *adjective* (**racier**, **raciest**) **1** lively and rather suggestive or risqué. **2** lively, vigorous, or spirited.

DERIVATIVES – **racily** *adverb* **raciness** *noun*.

SYNONYMS – **1** ribald, indecent, risqué, salacious, suggestive.

rad¹ > *abbreviation* radian(s).

rad² > *noun* Physics a unit of absorbed dose of ionising radiation.

ORIGIN – acronym from *radiation absorbed dose*.

rad³ > *noun* a radiator.

RADA /**raa**də/ > *abbreviation* (in the UK) Royal Academy of Dramatic Art.

radar > *noun* a system for detecting the presence, direction, and speed of aircraft, ships, etc., by sending out pulses of radio waves which are reflected back off the object.

COMBINATIONS – **radar gun** a hand-held radar device used by traffic police to estimate a vehicle's speed. **radar trap** an area of road in which radar is used by the police to detect speeding vehicles.

ORIGIN – from *radio detection and ranging*.

raddled > *adjective* (of a person) showing signs of age or fatigue.

SYNONYMS – gaunt, haggard.

ORIGIN – earlier in the sense 'coloured with rouge in an attempt to conceal signs of ageing'; variant of **RUDDLE**.

radial /**ray**diəl/ > *adjective* **1** of or arranged like rays or the radii of a circle; diverging in lines from a common centre. **2** (also **radial-ply**) (of a tyre) in which the layers of fabric have their cords running at right angles to the circumference of the tyre. **3** (of an internal-combustion engine) having its cylinders fixed like the spokes of a wheel around a rotating crankshaft. > *noun* a radial tyre.

DERIVATIVES – **radially** *adverb*.

COMBINATIONS – **radial symmetry** chiefly Biology symmetry about a central axis, as in a starfish.

ORIGIN – Latin *radialis*, from *radius* 'spoke, ray'.

radian /**ray**diən/ > *noun* a unit of measurement of angles equal to about 57.3°, equivalent to the angle subtended at the centre of a circle by an arc equal in length to the radius.

radiant > *adjective* **1** shining or glowing brightly. **2** emanating great joy, love, or health. **3** (of electromagnetic energy, especially heat) transmitted by radiation, rather than conduction or convection. **4** (of an appliance) emitting radiant energy for cooking or heating. > *noun* a point or object from which light or heat radiates.

DERIVATIVES – **radiance** *noun* **radiantly** *adverb*.

SYNONYMS – *adjective* **1** brilliant, gleaming, luminous.

radiate > *verb* **1** (with reference to light, heat, or other energy) emit or be emitted in the form of rays or waves. **2** emanate (a strong feeling or quality). **3** diverge from or as if from a central point.

DERIVATIVES – **radiative** *adjective*.

ORIGIN – Latin *radiare* 'emit in rays', from *radius* 'ray, spoke'.

radiation > *noun* **1** the action or process of radiating. **2** energy emitted in the form of electromagnetic waves or subatomic particles.

WORDFINDER – *kinds of radiation:* alpha particles, beta particles, cosmic rays, electromagnetic radiation, gamma rays, infrared, microwaves, ultraviolet, X-rays; dosimeter (*device to measure an absorbed dose of radiation*), irradiate (*expose to radiation*).

COMBINATIONS – **radiation sickness** illness caused by exposure to X-rays, gamma rays, or other radiation. **radiation therapy** radiotherapy.

radiator > *noun* **1** a thing that radiates light, heat, or sound. **2** a device that radiates heat, consisting of a metal case through which hot water circulates, or a similar one heated by electricity or oil. **3** a cooling device in a vehicle or aircraft engine consisting of a bank of thin tubes in which circulating water is cooled by the surrounding air.

radical > *adjective* **1** relating to or affecting the fundamental nature of something. **2** advocating thorough political or social reform; politically extreme. **3** departing from tradition; innovative or progressive. **4** (of surgery) thorough and intended to be completely curative. **5** Mathematics of the root of a number or quantity. **6** of or coming from the root or stem base of a plant. **7** informal, chiefly N. Amer. excellent. > *noun* **1** an advocate of radical political or social reform. **2** Chemistry a group of atoms behaving as a unit in a number of compounds.

DERIVATIVES – **radicalise** (also **radicalize**) *verb* **radicalism** *noun* **radically** *adverb* **radicalness** *noun*.

COMBINATIONS – **radical chic** the fashionable affectation of radical left-wing views. **radical sign** Mathematics the sign √ indicating the square root of the number following (or a higher root indicated by a preceding superscript numeral).

ORIGIN – Latin *radicalis*, from *radix* 'root' (see box at **ROOT**).

radicchio /radeekiō/ > *noun* (pl. **radicchios**) chicory of a variety with dark red leaves.

ORIGIN – Italian.

radices plural of **RADIX**.

radicle /raddik'l/ > *noun* the part of a plant embryo that develops into the primary root.

ORIGIN – Latin *radicula* 'little root'.

radii plural of **RADIUS**.

radio > *noun* (pl. **radios**) **1** the transmission and reception of electromagnetic waves having a frequency in the range between about ten kilohertz and a hundred thousand or a million megahertz, especially those carrying sound messages. **2** broadcasting in sound. **3** a broadcasting station or channel. **4** an apparatus for receiving radio programmes. **5** an apparatus for receiving and transmitting radio messages. > *verb* (**radioes**, **radioed**) **1** send a message by radio. **2** communicate with by radio.

COMBINATIONS – **radio astronomy** the branch of astronomy concerned with radio emissions from celestial objects. **radio-controlled** controllable from a distance by radio. **radio telescope** an instrument used to detect radio emissions from space. **radio wave** an electromagnetic wave of radio frequency.

ORIGIN – abbreviation of *radiotelephone*, ultimately from **RADIATION**.

radio- > *combining form* **1** denoting radio waves or broadcasting: *radiogram*. **2** connected with rays, radiation, or radioactivity: *radiograph*. **3** denoting artificially prepared radioisotopes: *radiocobalt*.

radioactive > *adjective* emitting or relating to the emission of ionising radiation or particles.

DERIVATIVES – **radioactively** *adverb*.

radioactivity > *noun* **1** the emission of ionising radiation or particles caused by the spontaneous disintegration of atomic nuclei. **2** radioactive particles.

radiocarbon > *noun* a radioactive isotope of carbon, especially carbon-14 used in carbon dating.

radio-element > *noun* a radioactive element or isotope.

radiogram > *noun* **1** Brit. a combined radio and record player. **2** a radiograph.

radiograph > *noun* an image produced on a sensitive plate or film by X-rays or other radiation.

DERIVATIVES – **radiographer** *noun* **radiographic** *adjective* **radiography** *noun*.

radioisotope > *noun* a radioactive isotope.

DERIVATIVES – **radioisotopic** *adjective*.

radiology > *noun* the science of X-rays and other high-energy radiation, especially as used in medicine.

DERIVATIVES – **radiologic** *adjective* **radiological** *adjective* **radiologist** *noun*.

radiometer /raydiommitər/ > *noun* an instrument for detecting or measuring radiation.

DERIVATIVES – **radiometry** *noun*.

radiometric /raydiōmetrik/ > *adjective* of or relating to the measurement of radioactivity.

DERIVATIVES – **radiometrically** *adverb*.

radionics /raydionniks/ > *plural noun* (treated as sing.) a system of alternative medicine based on the study of radiation supposedly emitted by living matter.

radionuclide /raydiōnyōoklīd/ > *noun* a radioactive nuclide.

radiophonic /raydiəfonnik/ > *adjective* relating to or denoting sound produced electronically.

radioscopy /raydioskəpi/ > *noun* the examination by X-rays of objects opaque to light.

radiotelephone > *noun* a telephone using radio transmission.

DERIVATIVES – **radiotelephony** *noun*.

radiotherapy > *noun* the treatment of cancer or other disease using X-rays or similar radiation.

DERIVATIVES – **radiotherapeutic** *adjective* **radiotherapist** *noun*.

radish > *noun* the small, pungent red root of a plant of the cabbage family, eaten raw.

ORIGIN – Latin *radix* 'root'.

radium /raydiəm/ > *noun* a reactive, radioactive metallic chemical element, formerly used as a source of radiation for medical treatment.

ORIGIN – from Latin *radius* 'ray'.

radius /raydiəss/ > *noun* (pl. **radii** /raydi-ī/ or **radiuses**) **1** a straight line from the centre to the circumference of a circle or sphere. **2** a radial line from the focus to any point of a curve. **3** a specified distance from a centre in all directions: *within a two-mile radius of the house*. **4** Anatomy & Zoology a bone of the forearm or forelimb, in humans the thicker and shorter of two. > *verb* (**radiused**, **radiusing**) make (a corner or edge) rounded.

ORIGIN – Latin, 'spoke, ray'.

radix /raydiks/ > *noun* (pl. **radices** /raydiseez/) **1** Mathematics the base of a system of numeration. **2** formal a source or origin.

ORIGIN – Latin, 'root'.

radome /raydōm/ > *noun* a dome or other structure protecting radar equipment and made from material transparent to radio waves.

radon /raydon/ > *noun* a rare radioactive gaseous chemical element produced by the radioactive decay of radium and used as a source of alpha particles in radiotherapy.

RAF > *abbreviation* (in the UK) Royal Air Force.

raffia > *noun* fibre from the leaves of a tropical palm tree of Africa and Madagascar, used for making hats, baskets, etc.

ORIGIN – Malagasy.

raffish > *adjective* slightly disreputable, especially in an attractive manner.

DERIVATIVES – **raffishly** *adverb* **raffishness** *noun*.

SYNONYMS – louche, rakish.

ORIGIN – from **RIFF-RAFF**.

raffle > *noun* a lottery with goods as prizes. > *verb* offer as a prize in a raffle.

ORIGIN – Old French: originally denoting a dice game.

raft[1] > *noun* **1** a buoyant flat structure of timber or other materials fastened together, used as a boat or floating platform. **2** a small inflatable boat. **3** a floating mass of fallen trees, ice, etc. > *verb* travel or transport on or as if on a raft.

DERIVATIVES – **rafting** *noun*.

ORIGIN – first used in the sense 'beam, rafter': from Old Norse *raptr*.

raft[2] > *noun* a large amount of something.

ORIGIN – alteration of dialect *raff* 'abundance', by association with **RAFT**[1] in the sense 'floating mess'.

rafter[1] > *noun* a beam forming part of the internal framework of a roof.

DERIVATIVES – **raftered** *adjective*.

ORIGIN – Old English, related to **RAFT**[1].

rafter[2] > *noun* a person who travels by raft.

rag[1] > *noun* **1** a piece of old cloth, especially one torn from a larger piece. **2** (**rags**) old or tattered clothes. **3** informal a low-quality newspaper. > *verb* give a decorative effect to (a painted surface) by applying paint with a rag.

IDIOMS – **lose one's rag** informal lose one's temper.

COMBINATIONS – **rag-and-bone man** Brit. a person who goes from door to door, collecting old clothes and other second-hand items for resale. **rag paper** paper made from cotton. **ragpicker** historical a person who collected and sold rags. **rag-roll** create a striped or marbled effect on (a surface) by painting it with a rag crumpled up into a roll. **rag rug** a rug made from small strips of fabric hooked into or pushed through a material such as hessian. **rag**

trade informal the clothing or fashion industry.

ORIGIN – probably from **RAGGED** or **RAGGY**.

rag² > *noun* Brit. **1** a programme of entertainments organised by students to raise money for charity. **2** informal, dated a prank. > *verb* (**ragged**, **ragging**) **1** make fun of loudly and boisterously. **2** rebuke severely.

rag³ > *noun* a ragtime composition or tune.

rag⁴ > *noun* **1** a large, coarse roofing slate. **2** (also **ragstone**) Brit. a hard, coarse sedimentary rock that can be broken into thick slabs.

raga /raagə/ > *noun* (in Indian music) a characteristic pattern of notes used as a basis for improvisation.

ORIGIN – Sanskrit, 'colour, musical tone'.

ragamuffin (also **raggamuffin**) > *noun* **1** a person in ragged, dirty clothes. **2** an exponent or follower of ragga, typically wearing scruffy clothes.

ORIGIN – probably based on **RAG¹**.

ragbag > *noun* **1** a bag for storing rags and old clothes. **2** a miscellaneous collection of things.

SYNONYMS – **2** hotchpotch, jumble, miscellany, mishmash.

rage > *noun* **1** violent, uncontrollable anger. **2** violent anger associated with conflict arising from a particular context: *air rage*. **3** a vehement desire or passion. **4** Austral./NZ informal a lively party. > *verb* **1** feel or express rage. **2** continue violently or with great force: *the argument raged for days*. **3** Austral./NZ informal enjoy oneself socially.

IDIOMS – **all the rage** temporarily very popular or fashionable.

DERIVATIVES – **raging** adjective.

SYNONYMS – *noun* **1** frenzy, fury, wrath. *verb* **1** be furious, fulminate, fume, seethe.

ORIGIN – Old French, from a variant of Latin *rabies* 'rabies'.

ragga /ragə/ > *noun* chiefly Brit. a style of dance music in which a DJ improvises lyrics over a backing track.

ORIGIN – from **RAGAMUFFIN**, because of the clothing worn by its followers.

raggamuffin > *noun* variant spelling of **RAGAMUFFIN**.

ragged /raggid/ > *adjective* **1** (of cloth or clothes) old and torn. **2** wearing ragged clothes. **3** rough or irregular. **4** lacking finish, smoothness, or uniformity. **5** suffering from exhaustion or stress.

IDIOMS – **run ragged** exhaust (someone).

DERIVATIVES – **raggedly** adverb **raggedness** noun.

SYNONYMS – **1** frayed, tattered, threadbare, torn, worn.

COMBINATIONS – **ragged robin** a pink-flowered campion with divided petals that give it a tattered appearance.

ORIGIN – Scandinavian.

raggedy > *adjective* informal, chiefly N. Amer. scruffy; shabby.

raggle-taggle > *adjective* untidy and scruffy.

ORIGIN – apparently a fanciful variant of **RAGTAG**.

raggy > *adjective* (**raggier**, **raggiest**) informal ragged.

raglan > *adjective* having or denoting sleeves continuing in one piece up to the neck of a garment.

ORIGIN – named after Lord *Raglan* (1788–1855), a British commander in the Crimean War.

ragout /ragōō/ > *noun* a highly seasoned stew of chopped meat and vegetables.

ORIGIN – French, from *ragoûter* 'revive the taste of'.

ragtag > *adjective* untidy, disorganised, or incongruously varied: *a ragtag group of idealists*.

ORIGIN – from earlier *tag-rag* and *tag and rag*.

ragtime > *noun* music characterised by a syncopated melodic line and regularly accented accompaniment, played especially on the piano.

ORIGIN – probably from the idea of 'ragged' syncopation.

ragworm > *noun* a predatory marine bristle worm, often used as bait by fishermen.

ragwort > *noun* a yellow-flowered ragged-leaved plant of the daisy family, toxic to livestock.

rai /rī/ > *noun* a style of music fusing Arabic and Algerian folk elements with Western rock.

ORIGIN – perhaps from an Arabic phrase meaning 'that's the thinking, here is the view', frequently found in the songs.

raid > *noun* **1** a rapid surprise attack on people or premises. **2** a surprise visit by police to arrest suspects or seize illicit goods. > *verb* **1** make a raid on. **2** quickly and illicitly take something from (a place).

DERIVATIVES – **raider** noun.

ORIGIN – Scots variant of **ROAD** in the early senses 'journey on horseback, foray'.

rail¹ > *noun* **1** a bar or series of bars fixed on upright supports or attached to a wall or ceiling, serving as part of a fence or barrier or used to hang things on. **2** a steel bar or continuous line of bars laid on the ground as one of a pair forming a railway track. **3** railways as a means of transport. > *verb* **1** provide or enclose with a rail or rails. **2** convey (goods) by rail.

IDIOMS – **go off the rails** informal begin behaving in an uncontrolled way. **on the rails 1** informal functioning normally. **2** (of a racehorse or jockey) in a position on the racetrack nearest the inside fence.

COMBINATIONS – **railcar** Brit. a powered railway passenger vehicle designed to operate singly or as part of a multiple unit. **railcard** Brit. a pass entitling the holder to reduced rail fares.

ORIGIN – Old French *reille* 'iron rod', from Latin *regula* 'straight stick, rule'.

rail² > *verb* (**rail against** or **at**) complain or protest strongly about or to.

ORIGIN – Old French *railler* 'to jest', from an alteration of Latin *rugire* 'to bellow'.

rail³ > *noun* a secretive marsh bird with typically drab grey and brown plumage.

ORIGIN – Old French *raille*.

railhead > *noun* **1** a point on a railway from which roads and other transport routes begin. **2** the furthest point reached in constructing a railway.

railing > *noun* a fence or barrier made of rails.

raillery /rayləri/ > *noun* good-humoured teasing.

SYNONYMS – banter, chaffing, kidding, ribbing, teasing.

ORIGIN – French *raillerie*, from *railler* 'to jest' (see **RAIL²**).

railroad > *noun* N. Amer. a railway. > *verb* informal **1** rush or coerce (someone) into doing something. **2** cause (a measure) to be approved quickly by applying pressure.

railway > *noun* chiefly Brit. **1** a track made of rails along which trains run. **2** a system of such tracks with the trains, organisation, and personnel required for its working.

raiment /raymənt/ > *noun* archaic or literary clothing.

ORIGIN – shortening of obsolete *arrayment* 'dress, outfit'.

rain > *noun* **1** the condensed moisture of the atmosphere falling visibly in separate drops. **2** (**rains**) falls of rain. **3** a large quantity of things falling or descending: *a rain of blows*. > *verb* **1** (**it rains**, **it is raining**, etc.) rain falls. **2** (**be rained off**) (of an event) be terminated or cancelled because of rain. **3** fall or cause to fall in large quantities.

WORDFINDER – ombro- (*combining form*); pluvial (*relating to or characterised by rain*); isohyet (*line on a map connecting places with equal rainfall*), precipitation (*rain, snow, sleet, or hail*), St Swithin's day (*saint's day associated with rain*).

IDIOMS – **be as right as rain** be perfectly fit and well. **rain cats and dogs** rain heavily.

DERIVATIVES – **rainless** adjective.

COMBINATIONS – **raincoat** a coat made from waterproofed or water-resistant fabric. **raindrop** a single drop of rain. **rainfall 1** the fall of rain. **2** the quantity of rain falling within a given area in a given time. **rainmaker 1** a person who attempts to

801

cause rain to fall. **2** N. Amer. informal a person who is highly successful, especially in business. **rain shadow** a relatively dry region sheltered from prevailing rain-bearing winds by a range of hills. **rainswept** frequently or recently exposed to rain and wind.

rainbow > *noun* **1** an arch of colours visible in the sky, caused by the refraction and dispersion of the sun's light by water droplets in the atmosphere. **2** a wide range of things of different colours or kinds.
WORDFINDER – *colours of the rainbow:* red, orange, yellow, green, blue, indigo, violet.
COMBINATIONS – **rainbow coalition** a political alliance of differing groups, especially one comprising minorities and other disadvantaged groups. **rainbow trout** a large trout with reddish sides, native to western North America and introduced widely elsewhere.

rain check > *noun* N. Amer. a ticket given for later use when an outdoor event is interrupted or postponed by rain.
IDIOMS – **take a rain check** politely refuse an offer, with the implication that one may take it up later.

rainforest > *noun* a luxuriant, dense forest found in tropical areas with consistently heavy rainfall.

rainy > *adjective* (**rainier, rainiest**) having or characterised by considerable rainfall.
IDIOMS – **a rainy day** a time in the future when money may be needed.

raise > *verb* **1** lift or move to a higher position or level. **2** set upright. **3** increase the amount, level, or strength of. **4** promote to a higher rank. **5** cause to be heard, felt, or considered: *doubts have been raised.* **6** build (a structure). **7** collect or levy (money or resources). **8** generate (an invoice or other document). **9** bring up (a child). **10** breed or grow (animals or plants). **11** wake from sleep or bring back from death. **12** abandon or force to abandon (a blockade, embargo, etc.). **13** drive (an animal) from its lair. **14** Brit. informal establish contact with (someone), especially by telephone or radio. **15** (**raise to**) Mathematics multiply (a quantity) to a specified power. > *noun* chiefly N. Amer. an increase in salary.
IDIOMS – **raise hell** informal make a noisy disturbance. **raise the roof** make a great deal of noise, especially cheering.
DERIVATIVES – **raisable** *adjective* **raiser** *noun.*
SYNONYMS – *verb* **1** elevate, hoist, lift up. **3** augment, boost, escalate, increase.
ORIGIN – Old Norse *reisa,* related to REAR².

raisin > *noun* a partially dried grape.
DERIVATIVES – **raisiny** *adjective.*
ORIGIN – Old French, 'grape', from an alteration of Latin *racemus* 'bunch of grapes'.

raison d'être /rayzoN detrə/ > *noun* (pl. **raisons d'être** pronunc. same) the most important reason or purpose for someone or something's existence.
ORIGIN – French, 'reason for being'.

raita /rītə/ > *noun* an Indian side dish of spiced yogurt containing chopped cucumber or other vegetables.
ORIGIN – Hindi.

Raj /raaj/ > *noun* (**the Raj**) historical British sovereignty in India.
ORIGIN – Hindi, 'reign'.

raja /raajaa/ (also **rajah**) > *noun* historical an Indian king or prince.
ORIGIN – Hindi.

Rajput /raajpoot/ > *noun* a member of a Hindu military caste.
ORIGIN – Hindi, from the Sanskrit words for 'king' + 'son'.

rake¹ > *noun* an implement consisting of a pole with a toothed crossbar or fine tines at the end, used for drawing together leaves, cut grass, etc. or smoothing loose soil or gravel. > *verb* **1** draw together with a rake. **2** make smooth with a rake. **3** scratch or scrape with a long, sweeping movement. **4** draw or drag (something) through something with a long, sweeping movement. **5** sweep with gunfire, a look, or a beam of light. **6** (**rake through**) search or rummage through.
IDIOMS – **rake it in** informal make a lot of money. **rake over old coals** (or **rake over the ashes**) chiefly Brit. revive the memory of a past event. **rake up/over** revive the memory of (an incident or period best forgotten).
DERIVATIVES – **raker** *noun.*
COMBINATIONS – **rake-off** informal a share of the profits from a deal, especially one that is disreputable.

rake² > *noun* a fashionable or wealthy man of dissolute habits.
ORIGIN – abbreviation of archaic *rakehell* in the same sense.

rake³ > *verb* **1** set at a sloping angle. **2** (of a ship's mast or funnel) incline from the perpendicular towards the stern. > *noun* **1** the angle at which a thing slopes. **2** the angle of the edge or face of a cutting tool.
ORIGIN – probably related to German *ragen* 'to project'.

rake⁴ > *noun* Brit. a number of railway carriages or wagons coupled together.
ORIGIN – from Old Norse *rák* 'stripe, streak': originally a Scots and northern English use.

raki /rəkee, rakki/ > *noun* a strong alcoholic spirit made in eastern Europe or the Middle East.
ORIGIN – Turkish.

rakish /raykish/ > *adjective* **1** having a dashing, jaunty, or slightly disreputable quality or appearance. **2** (of a boat or car) smart and streamlined.
DERIVATIVES – **rakishly** *adverb.*
SYNONYMS – **1** louche, raffish.

rallentando /raləntandō/ > *adverb & adjective* Music with a gradual decrease of speed.
ORIGIN – Italian, 'slowing down'.

rally¹ > *verb* (**rallies, rallied**) **1** (with reference to troops) bring or come together again so as to continue fighting. **2** bring or come together as support or for united action: *his family rallied round.* **3** recover or cause to recover in health, spirits, or poise. **4** (of share, currency, or commodity prices) increase after a fall. **5** drive in a motor rally. > *noun* (pl. **rallies**) **1** a mass meeting held as a protest or in support of a cause. **2** a long-distance competition for motor vehicles over public roads or rough terrain. **3** an open-air event for people who own a particular kind of vehicle. **4** a quick or marked recovery. **5** (in tennis and other racket sports) an extended exchange of strokes between players.
DERIVATIVES – **rallier** *noun* **rallyist** *noun.*
SYNONYMS – *verb* **1** reassemble, re-form, regroup. **3** improve, pick up, recover, revive.
ORIGIN – French *rallier,* from *re-* 'again' + *allier* 'to ally'.

rally² > *verb* (**rallies, rallied**) archaic tease.
ORIGIN – French *railler* (see RAIL²).

rallycross > *noun* Brit. a form of motor racing in which cars are driven in heats over rough terrain and private roads.

rallying > *noun* **1** (before another noun) having the effect of calling people to action: *a rallying cry.* **2** the action or sport of participating in a motor rally.

RAM > *abbreviation* Computing random-access memory.

ram > *noun* **1** an uncastrated male sheep. **2** a battering ram. **3** a striking or plunging device in various machines. **4** historical a projecting part of the bow of a warship, for piercing the sides of other ships. > *verb* (**rammed, ramming**) **1** roughly force into place. **2** strike or be struck with force.
WORDFINDER – Aries (*constellation and zodiac sign, the Ram*).
DERIVATIVES – **rammer** *noun.*
SYNONYMS – *verb* **1** pack, stuff, thrust. **2** collide with, crash into, run into.
COMBINATIONS – **ramjet** a type of jet engine in which the air drawn in for combustion is compressed solely by the forward motion of the aircraft. **ram raid** a robbery in which a shop window is rammed with a vehicle and looted.

Ramadan /ramməḍan/ (also **Ramadhan** /ramməzan/) > *noun* the ninth month of the Muslim year, during which strict fasting is observed from sunrise to sunset.

wordpower facts
Ramadan
The name **Ramadan** comes from the Arabic word *ramaḍa*, meaning 'be hot'. It was originally intended that the period of fasting should take place in one of the hottest months of the year, but the lunar reckoning of the Muslim calendar brings it forward annually by eleven days, with the result that, over a cycle of about thirty-three years, the month of Ramadan passes through all the seasons.

ramble > *verb* **1** walk for pleasure in the countryside. **2** (of a plant) grow over walls, fences, etc. **3** (often **ramble on**) talk or write at length in a confused or inconsequential way. > *noun* a walk taken for pleasure in the countryside.
DERIVATIVES – **rambler** *noun* **rambling** *adjective & noun*.
SYNONYMS – *verb* **3** babble, blather, prattle.
ORIGIN – probably related to Dutch *rammelen* (used of animals in the sense 'wander about on heat'), also to RAM.

Rambo /rambō/ > *noun* (pl. **Rambos**) an extremely tough and aggressive man.
ORIGIN – the name of the hero of the novel *First Blood* (1972) by David Morrell, popularised in the films *First Blood* (1982) and *Rambo: First Blood Part II* (1985).

rambunctious > *adjective* informal, chiefly N. Amer. uncontrollably exuberant.
DERIVATIVES – **rambunctiously** *adverb* **rambunctiousness** *noun*.

rambutan /rambōōt'n/ > *noun* the red, plum-sized fruit of a tropical Malaysian tree, with soft spines and a slightly acidic taste.
ORIGIN – from a Malay word meaning 'hair' (referring to the fruit's spines).

ramekin /rammikin/ > *noun* a small dish for baking and serving an individual portion of food.
ORIGIN – French *ramequin*.

ramie /rammi/ > *noun* a vegetable fibre from a tropical Asian plant, used in the manufacture of textiles.
ORIGIN – Malay.

ramification > *noun* **1** the action or state of ramifying or being ramified. **2** (usu. **ramifications**) a complex consequence of an action or event. **3** a subdivision of a complex structure or process.

ramify /rammifī/ > *verb* (**ramifies**, **ramified**) form branches or cause to branch out.
DERIVATIVES – **ramified** *adjective*.

ORIGIN – Latin *ramificare*, from *ramus* 'branch'.

ramp > *noun* **1** a sloping surface joining two different levels. **2** a movable set of steps for entering or leaving an aircraft. **3** Brit. a transverse ridge in a road to control the speed of vehicles. **4** N. Amer. an inclined slip road leading to or from a main road or motorway. > *verb* **1** provide with a ramp. **2** (**ramp up**) increase (the production of goods). **3** archaic (of an animal) rear up threateningly.
ORIGIN – Old French *ramper* 'creep, crawl'.

rampage /rampayj/ > *verb* rush around in a violent and uncontrollable manner. > *noun* an instance of rampaging.

rampant > *adjective* **1** flourishing or spreading unchecked. **2** unrestrained in action or performance. **3** (usu. after a noun) Heraldry (of an animal) represented standing on its left hind foot with its forefeet in the air.
DERIVATIVES – **rampantly** *adverb*.

wordpower facts
Rampant
The word **rampant** entered Middle English from Old French, in which it meant 'crawling' (from *ramper* 'crawl'). Following the typical construction in French, early use in English had the adjective following the noun, especially in heraldry, in which the 'lion rampant' is represented in profile, standing on its left hind foot, with forefeet and tail raised. From this early use in heraldry, and by extension its application to other wild animals rearing up in a threatening manner, **rampant** acquired the sense 'fierce', from which developed the current notion 'unrestrained'.

rampart > *noun* a defensive wall of a castle or walled city, having a broad top with a walkway.
ORIGIN – French *rempart*, from *remparer* 'fortify, take possession of again'.

ramrod > *noun* a rod for ramming down the charge of a muzzle-loading firearm.

ramshackle > *adjective* in a state of severe disrepair.
SYNONYMS – decrepit, derelict, dilapidated, rundown, tumbledown.
ORIGIN – from obsolete *ransackled* 'ransacked'.

RAN > *abbreviation* Royal Australian Navy.

ran past of RUN.

ranch > *noun* **1** a large farm, especially in the western US and Canada, where cattle or other animals are bred. **2** (also **ranch house**) N. Amer. a single-storey house. > *verb* run a ranch.

DERIVATIVES – **rancher** *noun* **ranching** *noun*.
ORIGIN – from Spanish *rancho* 'group of persons eating together'.

rancid > *adjective* (of foods containing fat or oil) smelling or tasting unpleasant as a result of being stale.
DERIVATIVES – **rancidity** *noun*.
ORIGIN – Latin *rancidus* 'stinking'.

rancour /rangkər/ (US **rancor**) > *noun* bitter or resentful feelings.
DERIVATIVES – **rancorous** *adjective*.
SYNONYMS – bitterness, rancour, resentment, spite.
ORIGIN – Latin *rancor* 'rankness', later 'bitter grudge'.

rand /rand/ > *noun* the basic monetary unit of South Africa, equal to 100 cents.
ORIGIN – from *the Rand*, the name of a goldfield district near Johannesburg.

R & B > *abbreviation* rhythm and blues.

R & D > *abbreviation* research and development.

random > *adjective* **1** made, done, or happening without method or conscious decision. **2** Statistics governed by or involving equal chances for each item.
DERIVATIVES – **randomise** (also **randomize**) *verb* **randomly** *adverb* **randomness** *noun*.
COMBINATIONS – **random access** Computing the process of transferring information to or from memory in which every memory location can be accessed directly rather than being accessed in a fixed sequence.
ORIGIN – first used in the sense 'impetuous headlong rush': from Old French *randon* 'great speed', from *randir* 'gallop'.

R & R > *abbreviation* **1** (also **R'n'R**) rock and roll. **2** informal rest and recreation.

randy > *adjective* (**randier**, **randiest**) informal, chiefly Brit. sexually aroused or excited.
ORIGIN – perhaps from obsolete Dutch *randen* 'to rant'.

rang past of RING².

rangatira /ranggəteerə/ > *noun* NZ a Maori chief or noble.
ORIGIN – Maori.

range > *noun* **1** the area of variation between limits on a particular scale. **2** a set of different things of the same general type. **3** the scope or extent of a person's or thing's abilities or capacity. **4** the distance within which something is able to operate or be effective. **5** a line or series of mountains or hills. **6** a large area of open land for grazing or hunting. **7** the area over which a plant or animal is distributed. **8** an area used as a testing ground for military equipment. **9** an area with targets for shooting practice. **10** a large cooking stove with several burners or hotplates. > *verb* **1** vary or extend between specified limits. **2** place or arrange in a row or rows or in a specified manner. **3** (**range**

against) place in opposition to. **4** travel or wander over a wide area. **5** embrace a wide number of different topics.

COMBINATIONS – **rangefinder** an instrument for estimating the distance of an object.

ORIGIN – Old French, 'row, rank', from *rangier* 'put in order'.

ranger > *noun* **1** a keeper of a park, forest, or area of countryside. **2** a member of a body of armed men. **3** (**Ranger** or **Ranger Guide**) Brit. a senior Guide.

rangy /**rayn**ji/ > *adjective* (of a person) tall, slim, and long-limbed.

rank¹ > *noun* **1** a position within a fixed hierarchy, especially that of the armed forces. **2** high social standing. **3** a single line of soldiers or police officers drawn up abreast. **4** (**the ranks**) (in the armed forces) those who are not commissioned officers. **5** (**ranks**) the people belonging to or constituting a group or class: *the ranks of the unemployed*. **6** Chess each of the eight rows of eight squares running from side to side across a chessboard. Compare with FILE¹. > *verb* **1** give (someone or something) a rank within a grading system. **2** hold a specified rank. **3** US take precedence over (someone) in respect to rank. **4** arrange in a row or rows.

IDIOMS – **break rank** (or **ranks**) **1** (of soldiers or police officers) fail to remain in line. **2** fail to maintain solidarity. **close ranks 1** (of soldiers or police officers) come closer together in a line. **2** unite in order to defend common interests. **pull rank** take unfair advantage of one's seniority. **rank and file** the ordinary members of an organisation as opposed to its leaders. [ORIGIN – referring to the 'ranks' and 'files' into which privates and non-commissioned officers form on parade.]

ORIGIN – Old French *ranc*.

rank² > *adjective* **1** (of vegetation) growing too thickly. **2** having a foul smell. **3** conspicuously undesirable; flagrant.

SYNONYMS – **2** fetid, foul, malodorous, noxious.

ORIGIN – Old English, 'proud, rebellious, sturdy', also 'fully grown'.

ranker > *noun* **1** chiefly Brit. a soldier in the ranks; a private. **2** a commissioned officer who has been in the ranks.

ranking > *noun* **1** a position in a hierarchy or scale. **2** the action of giving a rank or status to someone or something. > *adjective* having a specified rank: *high-ranking officers*.

rankle > *verb* (of a comment or fact) cause annoyance or resentment.

ORIGIN – Old French *rancler*, from *rancle* 'festering sore'.

ransack > *verb* **1** go hurriedly through (a place) stealing things and causing damage. **2** thoroughly search (a place).

SYNONYMS – **1** loot, pillage, plunder, sack. **2** comb, scour, turn inside out.

ORIGIN – Old Norse *rannsaka*, from *rann* 'house' + a second element meaning 'seek'.

ransom* > *noun* a sum of money demanded or paid for the release of a captive. > *verb* **1** obtain the release of (someone) by paying a ransom. **2** detain (someone) and demand a ransom for their release.

IDIOMS – **hold to ransom 1** hold (someone) captive and demand payment for release. **2** demand concessions from (a person or organisation) by threatening damaging action. **a king's ransom** a huge amount of money.

*SPELLING – note that **ransom** is spelled without an *e* at the end, although names often have an *e*, as in that of the English novelist Arthur Ransome (1884–1967).

ORIGIN – Old French *ransoun*, from Latin *redemptio* 'redemption'.

rant > *verb* speak or shout at length in a wild, impassioned way. > *noun* a spell of ranting.

DERIVATIVES – **ranter** *noun*.

SYNONYMS – *verb* bluster, rave, storm. *noun* diatribe, harangue, tirade.

ORIGIN – Dutch *ranten* 'talk nonsense, rave'.

ranunculus /rə**nung**kyooləss/ > *noun* (pl. **ranunculuses** or **ranunculi** /-kyoolī/) a plant of the genus that includes the buttercups and water crowfoots.

ORIGIN – Latin, 'little frog'.

rap > *verb* (**rapped**, **rapping**) **1** strike (a hard surface) with a series of rapid audible blows. **2** strike (someone or something) sharply. **3** (usu. **rap out**) say something sharply or suddenly. **4** informal rebuke or criticise sharply. **5** informal, chiefly N. Amer. talk or chat. **6** perform rap music. > *noun* **1** a quick, sharp knock or blow. **2** informal a rebuke or criticism. **3** a type of popular music of US black origin in which words are recited rapidly and rhythmically over an instrumental backing. **4** informal, chiefly N. Amer. a criminal charge.

IDIOMS – **beat the rap** informal, chiefly N. Amer. escape punishment for or be acquitted of a crime. **take the rap** informal, chiefly N. Amer. be punished or blamed for something.

DERIVATIVES – **rapper** *noun*.

SYNONYMS – *verb* **1** bang, knock, tap. **2** hit, slap, thump.

rapacious /rə**pay**shəss/ > *adjective* aggressively greedy.

DERIVATIVES – **rapaciously** *adverb* **rapaciousness** *noun* **rapacity** *noun*.

SYNONYMS – acquisitive, avaricious, grasping, predatory, voracious.

ORIGIN – Latin *rapax*, from *rapere* 'to snatch'.

rape¹ > *verb* **1** (of a man) force (another person) to have sexual intercourse with him against their will. **2** spoil or destroy (a place). > *noun* an act or the crime of raping someone.

ORIGIN – Latin *rapere* 'seize': originally denoting violent seizure of property.

rape² > *noun* a plant of the cabbage family with bright yellow flowers, especially a variety (**oilseed rape**) grown for its oil-rich seed.

COMBINATIONS – **rapeseed** seeds of the rape plant, used for oil.

ORIGIN – Latin *rapum*, *rapa* 'turnip'.

rapid > *adjective* happening in a short time or at great speed. > *noun* (usu. **rapids**) a fast-flowing and turbulent part of the course of a river.

DERIVATIVES – **rapidity** *noun* **rapidly** *adverb*.

SYNONYMS – *adjective* **1** fast, quick, speedy, swift.

COMBINATIONS – **rapid eye movement** the jerky movement of a person's eyes that occurs in REM sleep.

ORIGIN – Latin *rapidus*, from *rapere* 'take by force'.

rapier /**ray**piər/ > *noun* a thin, light sharp-pointed sword used for thrusting.

ORIGIN – French *rapière*, from *râpe* 'rasp, grater' (because the perforated hilt resembles a rasp or grater).

rapine /**rapp**īn/ > *noun* literary the violent seizure of property.

ORIGIN – Old French.

rapist > *noun* a man who commits rape.

rappel /ra**pel**/ > *noun* & *verb* (**rappelled**, **rappelling**) another term for ABSEIL.

ORIGIN – French, literally 'a recalling', from *rappeler* in the sense 'bring back to oneself' (with reference to the rope manoeuvre).

rappen /**rapp**'n/ > *noun* (pl. same) a monetary unit of the German-speaking cantons of Switzerland and of Liechtenstein, equal to one hundredth of the Swiss franc.

ORIGIN – German *Rappe* 'raven', with reference to the depiction of a raven's head on a medieval coin.

rapport /ra**por**/ > *noun* a close and harmonious relationship in which there is common understanding.

SYNONYMS – affinity, bond, link, understanding.

ORIGIN – French, from *rapporter* 'bring back'.

rapporteur /rapport**ör**/ > *noun* a person appointed by an organisation to report on its meetings.

rapprochement /ra**prosh**mon/ > *noun* the establishment or resumption of harmonious relations.

ORIGIN – French.

rapscallion /rap**skal**yən/ > *noun* archaic or humorous a mischievous person.

ORIGIN – alteration of earlier *rascallion*, perhaps from **RASCAL**.

rapt > *adjective* **1** fully absorbed and intent; fascinated. **2** filled with intense and pleasurable emotion; enraptured. **3** Austral. informal another term for **WRAPPED**.

DERIVATIVES – **raptly** *adverb* **raptness** *noun*.

SYNONYMS – **1** absorbed, engrossed, fascinated, intent. **2** enchanted, enraptured, enthralled, mesmerised.

ORIGIN – Latin *raptus* 'seized'.

raptor > *noun* a bird of prey.

DERIVATIVES – **raptorial** *adjective*.

ORIGIN – Latin, 'plunderer'.

rapture > *noun* **1** a feeling of intense pleasure or joy. **2** (**raptures**) the expression of intense pleasure or enthusiasm.

SYNONYMS – **1** bliss, ecstasy, elation.

rapturous > *adjective* characterised by, feeling, or expressing great pleasure or enthusiasm.

DERIVATIVES – **rapturously** *adverb*.

SYNONYMS – ecstatic, elated, enraptured, joyous.

rara avis /raira **ay**viss/ > *noun* (pl. **rarae aves** /rairee **ay**veez/) an exceptional person or thing.

ORIGIN – Latin, 'rare bird'.

rare¹ > *adjective* (**rarer**, **rarest**) **1** occurring very infrequently. **2** remarkable: *a player of rare skill*.

SYNONYMS – **1** infrequent, scarce, uncommon, unusual.

ANTONYMS – **1** common.

COMBINATIONS – **rare bird** an exceptional person or thing. **rare earth** Chemistry any of a group of chemically similar metallic elements including cerium, lanthanum, and the other lanthanide elements together with (usually) scandium and yttrium. **rare gas** a noble gas.

ORIGIN – Latin *rarus*.

rare² > *adjective* (**rarer**, **rarest**) (of red meat) lightly cooked, so that the inside is still red.

ORIGIN – variant of obsolete *rear* 'half-cooked'.

rarebit (also **Welsh rarebit** or **Welsh rabbit**) > *noun* a dish of melted and seasoned cheese on toast.

raree show /rairee/ > *noun* archaic a form of street entertainment, especially one carried in a box, such as a peep show.

ORIGIN – apparently representing *rare show*, as pronounced by showmen from Savoy in France.

rarefaction /rairifaksh'n/ > *noun* reduction of the density of something, especially air or a gas.

ORIGIN – Latin, from *rarefacere* 'grow thin, become rare'.

rarefied* /**rair**ifīd/ > *adjective* **1** (of air) of

lower pressure than usual; thin. **2** very esoteric or refined.

*SPELLING – note that the middle syllable is *-ref-*, not *-rif-*: ra*ref*ied.

rarely > *adverb* not often; seldom.

SYNONYMS – hardly ever, infrequently, not often, scarcely ever, seldom.

raring > *adjective* (**raring to do**) informal very eager to do something.

ORIGIN – from *rare*, dialect variant of **ROAR** or **REAR²**.

rarity > *noun* (pl. **rarities**) **1** the state or quality of being rare. **2** a rare thing.

SYNONYMS – **1** infrequency, rareness, scarcity, unusualness.

rascal > *noun* a mischievous or cheeky person.

DERIVATIVES – **rascality** *noun* **rascally** *adjective*.

ORIGIN – first used in the senses 'a mob' and 'member of the rabble': from Old French *rascaille* 'rabble'.

rase > *verb* variant spelling of **RAZE**.

rash¹ > *adjective* acting or done impetuously, without careful consideration.

DERIVATIVES – **rashly** *adverb* **rashness** *noun*.

SYNONYMS – foolhardy, impetuous, reckless, thoughtless.

rash² > *noun* **1** a reddened area on a person's skin, sometimes with raised spots. **2** an unwelcome series of things happening within a short space of time: *a rash of strikes*.

ORIGIN – probably related to Old French *rasche* 'eruptive sores, scurf'.

rasher > *noun* a thin slice of bacon.

rasp /raasp/ > *noun* **1** a coarse file for use on metal, wood, or other hard material. **2** a harsh, grating noise. > *verb* **1** file with a rasp. **2** (of a rough surface or object) scrape in a painful or unpleasant way. **3** make a harsh, grating noise.

DERIVATIVES – **rasping** *adjective* **raspy** *adjective*.

ORIGIN – Old French *rasper*.

raspberry* > *noun* **1** an edible soft fruit related to the blackberry, consisting of a cluster of reddish-pink drupels. **2** informal a sound made with the tongue and lips, expressing derision or contempt. [ORIGIN – from *raspberry tart*, rhyming slang for 'fart'.]

*SPELLING – remember the *p* in the middle: ra*sp*berry.

Rasta /**ras**tə/ > *noun & adjective* informal short for **RASTAFARIAN**.

Rastafarian /rastəfairiən/ > *adjective* of or relating to a religious movement of Jamaican origin holding that Emperor Haile Selassie of Ethiopia was the Messiah and that blacks are the chosen people. > *noun* a member of this movement.

DERIVATIVES – **Rastafarianism** *noun*.

ORIGIN – from *Ras Tafari*, the name by which Haile Selassie was known 1916–30.

raster /**ras**tə/ > *noun* a rectangular pattern of parallel scanning lines followed by the electron beam on a television screen or computer monitor.

ORIGIN – German, 'screen'.

rasterise (also **rasterize**) > *verb* Computing convert (an image stored as an outline) into pixels that can be displayed on a screen or printed.

DERIVATIVES – **rasterisation** *noun*.

rat > *noun* **1** a large, long-tailed rodent, typically considered a serious pest. **2** informal a despicable person. **3** informal an informer. **4** N. Amer. informal a person associated with or frequenting a specified place: *mall rats*. > *exclamation* (**rats**) informal expressing mild annoyance. > *verb* (**ratted**, **ratting**) **1** hunt or kill rats. **2** informal desert one's party, side, or cause. **3** (**rat on**) informal inform on (someone). **4** (**rat on**) informal break (an agreement or promise).

WORDFINDER – murine (*relating to rats or other rodents*).

COMBINATIONS – **rat-arsed** Brit. vulgar slang very drunk. **ratbag** Brit. informal an unpleasant or disliked person. **rat pack** informal a group of journalists and photographers perceived as aggressive or relentless in their pursuit of stories. **rat race** informal a way of life in which people are caught up in a fiercely competitive struggle for wealth or power. **rat run** Brit. informal a minor street used by drivers to avoid congestion on main roads. **rat's tails** Brit. informal hair hanging in lank, damp, or greasy strands.

rata /**raa**tə/ > *noun* a large New Zealand tree with crimson flowers and hard red wood.

ORIGIN – Maori.

ratable > *adjective* variant spelling of **RATEABLE**.

ratafia /rattəfeeə/ > *noun* **1** a liqueur flavoured with almonds or the kernels of peaches, apricots, or cherries. **2** an almond-flavoured biscuit like a small macaroon.

ORIGIN – French.

ratatouille /rattətwee/ > *noun* a vegetable dish consisting of onions, courgettes, tomatoes, aubergines, and peppers, stewed in oil.

ORIGIN – French.

ratchet > *noun* a device consisting of a bar or wheel with a set of angled teeth in which a pawl, cog, or tooth engages, allowing motion in one direction only. > *verb* (**ratcheted**, **ratcheting**) **1** operate by means of a ratchet. **2** (**ratchet up** or **down**) cause (something) to rise (or fall) as a step in an irreversible process.

ORIGIN – French *rochet*, originally denoting a blunt lance head, later a bobbin or ratchet.

rate¹ > *noun* **1** a measure, quantity, or frequency. **2** the speed with which something moves, happens, or changes. **3** a fixed price paid or charged for something. **4** the amount of a charge or payment expressed as a percentage of some other amount, or as a basis of calculation. **5** (**rates**) (in the UK) a tax on commercial land and buildings paid to a local authority. > *verb* **1** assign a standard or value to (something) according to a particular scale. **2** *informal* have a high opinion of. **3** be worthy of; merit.

IDIOMS – **at any rate** whatever happens or may have happened. **at this rate** if things continue in this way, or should a certain assumption be true.

SYNONYMS – *verb* **1** appraise, assess, evaluate. **3** deserve, merit, warrant.

COMBINATIONS – **ratepayer 1** (in the UK) a person liable to pay rates. **2** N. Amer. a customer of a public utility.

ORIGIN – Old French, from Latin *rata* (from *pro rata parte* 'according to the proportional share').

rate² > *verb* archaic scold angrily.

rateable (also **ratable**) > *adjective* able to be rated or estimated.

COMBINATIONS – **rateable value** (in the UK) a value ascribed to a commercial property based on its size, location, etc., used to determine the rates payable by its owner.

rather > *adverb* **1** (**would rather**) indicating one's preference in a particular matter. **2** to a certain or significant extent or degree. **3** on the contrary. **4** more precisely. **5** instead of; as opposed to. > *exclamation* Brit. dated used to express emphatic affirmation, agreement, or acceptance.

IDIOMS – **had rather** literary or archaic would rather.

ORIGIN – Old English, 'earlier, sooner'.

rathskeller /raatskellər/ > *noun* US a beer hall or restaurant in a basement.

ORIGIN – obsolete German, from *Rathaus* 'town hall' + *Keller* 'cellar'.

ratify > *verb* (**ratifies, ratified**) give formal consent to; make officially valid.

DERIVATIVES – **ratification** *noun*.

SYNONYMS – affirm, approve, endorse, sanction.

ORIGIN – Latin *ratificare*, from *ratus* 'reckoned'.

rating > *noun* **1** a classification or ranking based on quality, standard, or performance. **2** (**ratings**) the estimated audience size of a particular television or radio programme. **3** Brit. a non-commissioned sailor in the navy.

SYNONYMS – **1** categorisation, class, grade, rank.

ratio > *noun* (pl. **ratios**) the quantitative relation between two amounts showing the number of times one value contains or is contained within the other.

ORIGIN – Latin, 'reckoning'.

ratiocinate /rattiossinayt, rashiossinayt/ > *verb* formal form judgements by a process of logic; reason.

DERIVATIVES – **ratiocination** *noun* **ratiocinative** *adjective*.

ration > *noun* **1** a fixed amount of a commodity officially allowed to each person during a time of shortage. **2** (**rations**) an amount of food supplied on a regular basis to members of the armed forces during a war. **3** (**rations**) food; provisions. > *verb* **1** limit the supply of (a commodity) to fixed rations. **2** limit the amount of a commodity available to (someone).

SYNONYMS – *noun* **1** allocation, allowance, quota.

rational > *adjective* **1** based on or in accordance with reason or logic. **2** able to think sensibly or logically. **3** having the capacity to reason. **4** Mathematics (of a number or quantity) expressible as a ratio of whole numbers.

DERIVATIVES – **rationality** *noun* **rationally** *adverb*.

SYNONYMS – **1** cogent, logical. **2** coherent, lucid.

ANTONYMS – irrational.

rationale /rashənaal/ > *noun* a set of reasons or a logical basis for a course of action or a belief.

rationalise (also **rationalize**) > *verb* **1** attempt to justify (an action or attitude) with logical reasoning. **2** reorganise (a process or system) in such a way as to make it more logical and consistent. **3** make (a company or industry) more efficient by dispensing with superfluous personnel or equipment.

DERIVATIVES – **rationalisation** *noun*.

rationalism > *noun* the practice or principle of basing opinions and actions on reason and knowledge rather than on religious belief or emotional response.

DERIVATIVES – **rationalist** *noun*.

COMBINATIONS – **economic rationalism** Austral. a policy of promoting efficiency and productivity in a free-market system by privatisation, deregulation, and reduced government spending.

rat-kangaroo > *noun* a small rat-like Australian marsupial with long hindlimbs used for hopping.

rattan /rətan/ > *noun* a tropical climbing palm which yields thin, jointed stems used to make furniture.

ORIGIN – Malay.

rat-tat (also **rat-tat-tat**) > *noun* a rapping sound.

ratted > *adjective* Brit. informal very drunk.

rattle > *verb* **1** make or cause to make a rapid succession of short, sharp knocking or clinking sounds. **2** move or travel somewhere while making such sounds. **3** (**rattle about** or **around in**) be in or occupy (too large a space). **4** informal cause to feel nervous, worried, or irritated. **5** (**rattle off**) say, perform, or produce (something) quickly and effortlessly. **6** (**rattle on** or **away**) talk rapidly and at length. > *noun* **1** a rattling sound. **2** a device or plaything designed to make a rattling sound. **3** a gurgling sound in the throat.

DERIVATIVES – **rattler** *noun* **rattly** *adjective*.

SYNONYMS – *verb* **1** clank, clatter, clink. *noun* **1** clanking, clattering, clinking.

COMBINATIONS – **rattletrap** informal an old or rickety vehicle.

rattlesnake > *noun* a heavy-bodied American viper with a series of horny rings on the tail that produce a characteristic rattling sound when vibrated as a warning.

rattling > *adjective* **1** making a rattle. **2** informal, dated very good of its kind.

ratty > *adjective* **1** resembling or characteristic of a rat. **2** infested with rats. **3** informal shabby, untidy, or in bad condition. **4** Brit. informal bad-tempered and irritable.

raucous /rawkəss/ > *adjective* making or constituting a harsh, loud noise.

DERIVATIVES – **raucously** *adverb* **raucousness** *noun*.

SYNONYMS – discordant, grating, harsh, noisy, strident.

ORIGIN – Latin *raucus* 'hoarse'.

raunch > *noun* informal energetic earthiness or vulgarity.

raunchy > *adjective* (**raunchier, raunchiest**) informal energetically earthy and sexually explicit.

DERIVATIVES – **raunchily** *adverb* **raunchiness** *noun*.

ravage > *verb* cause extensive damage to; devastate. > *noun* (**ravages**) the destructive effects of something.

SYNONYMS – *verb* devastate, lay waste, ruin.

ORIGIN – French *ravager*, from earlier *ravage*, alteration of *ravine* 'rush of water'.

rave > *verb* **1** talk wildly or incoherently. **2** speak or write about someone or something with great enthusiasm or admiration. **3** informal, chiefly Brit. attend or take part in a rave party. > *noun* informal **1** chiefly N. Amer. an extremely enthusiastic appraisal of someone or something. **2** a person or thing that inspires intense and widely shared enthusiasm. **3** chiefly Brit. a very large party or event with dancing to loud, fast electronic music.

SYNONYMS – *verb* **1** babble, jabber. **2** enthuse, gush, rhapsodise, wax lyrical.

COMBINATIONS – **rave-up** Brit. informal a lively, noisy party.

ravel > *verb* (**ravelled, ravelling;** US **raveled, raveling**) 1 (**ravel out**) untangle. 2 confuse or complicate (a question or situation). > *noun* a tangle or cluster.

ORIGIN – probably from Dutch *ravelen* 'fray out, tangle'.

raven[1] /**ray**v'n/ > *noun* a large heavily built black crow. > *adjective* (especially of hair) of a glossy black colour.

raven[2] /**ravv**'n/ > *verb* archaic 1 (of a wild animal) hunt voraciously for prey. 2 devour voraciously.

ORIGIN – Old French *raviner*, from Latin *rapina* 'pillage'.

ravening /**ravv**əning/ > *adjective* voracious; rapacious.

ravenous > *adjective* voraciously hungry.

DERIVATIVES – **ravenously** *adverb*.

SYNONYMS – famished, starving.

ORIGIN – Old French *ravineus*, from *raviner* 'to ravage'.

raver > *noun* 1 informal a person who has an exciting and uninhibited social life. 2 informal, chiefly Brit. a person who regularly goes to raves. 3 a person who talks wildly or incoherently.

ravine /rə**veen**/ > *noun* a deep, narrow gorge with steep sides.

ORIGIN – French, 'violent rush'.

raving > *noun* (usu. **ravings**) wild or incoherent talk. > *adjective & adverb* informal extremely or conspicuously the thing mentioned: *raving mad*.

SYNONYMS – *noun* babbling, gibberish, rambling.

ravioli /ravvi**ō**li/ > *plural noun* small pasta envelopes containing minced meat, cheese, or vegetables.

ORIGIN – Italian.

ravish > *verb* archaic or literary 1 fill with intense delight; enrapture. 2 seize and carry off by force. 3 rape (a woman).

ORIGIN – Old French *ravir*, from Latin *rapere* 'seize'.

ravishing > *adjective* causing intense delight; entrancing.

DERIVATIVES – **ravishingly** *adverb*.

raw > *adjective* 1 (of food) uncooked. 2 (of a material or substance) in its natural state; not processed. 3 new and lacking in experience in an activity or job. 4 (of the skin) red and painful, especially as the result of abrasion. 5 (of the nerves) very sensitive. 6 (of an emotion or quality) strong and undisguised. 7 (of the weather) bleak, cold, and damp. 8 (of data) not organised, analysed, or evaluated. 9 (of the edge of a piece of cloth) not having a hem or selvedge.

IDIOMS – **in the raw** 1 in its true state. 2 informal naked.

COMBINATIONS – **raw-boned** having a bony or gaunt physique. **rawhide** 1 stiff untanned leather. 2 N. Amer. a whip or rope

made of rawhide. **raw material** a basic material from which a product is made.

Rawlplug /**rawl**plug/ > *noun* Brit. trademark a thin plastic or fibre sheath inserted into a hole in masonry in order to hold a screw.

ORIGIN – from *Rawlings* (the name of the engineers who introduced it).

ray[1] > *noun* 1 each of the lines in which light seems to stream from the sun or any luminous body. 2 the straight line in which radiation travels to a given point. 3 (**rays**) a specified form of non-luminous radiation. 4 an initial or slight indication of a positive or welcome quality: *a ray of hope*. 5 Botany any of the individual strap-shaped florets around the edge of the flower of a daisy or related plant. 6 Zoology each of the long, slender bony supports in a fish's fins.

IDIOMS – **ray of sunshine** informal a person who brings happiness into the lives of others.

COMBINATIONS – **ray gun** (in science fiction) a gun causing injury or damage by the emission of rays.

ORIGIN – Old French *rai*, from Latin *radius* 'spoke, ray'.

ray[2] > *noun* a broad flat fish with wing-like pectoral fins and a long, slender tail.

ORIGIN – Latin *raia*.

ray[3] (also **re**) > *noun* Music the second note of a major scale, coming between 'doh' and 'me'.

rayon > *noun* a textile fibre or fabric made from viscose.

raze (also **rase**) > *verb* tear down and destroy (a building, town, etc.).

SYNONYMS – demolish, flatten, level.

ORIGIN – Old French *raser* 'shave closely'.

razor > *noun* an instrument with a sharp blade, used to shave unwanted hair from the face or body. > *verb* cut with a razor.

COMBINATIONS – **razor shell** a burrowing bivalve mollusc with a long, straight shell. **razor wire** metal wire with sharp edges or studded with small, sharp blades, used as a defensive barrier.

razorback > *noun* a pig of a half-wild breed common in the southern US, with the back formed into a high, narrow ridge.

razorbill > *noun* a black-and-white auk with a deep bill.

razz > *verb* informal, chiefly N. Amer. tease playfully.

ORIGIN – from an alteration of **RASPBERRY**.

razzle > *noun* (in phrase **on the razzle**) informal out celebrating or enjoying oneself.

razzle-dazzle > *noun* another term for **RAZZMATAZZ**.

razzmatazz (also **razzamatazz**) > *noun* informal noisy, showy, and exciting activity and display.

Rb > *symbol* the chemical element rubidium.

RC > *abbreviation* 1 Red Cross. 2 Roman

Catholic. 3 Electronics resistance/capacitance (or resistor/capacitor).

RD > *abbreviation* (in the UK) Royal Naval Reserve Decoration.

Rd > *abbreviation* Road (used in street names).

RDA > *abbreviation* recommended daily (or dietary) allowance.

RDS > *abbreviation* radio data system.

RE > *abbreviation* religious education (as a school subject).

Re > *symbol* the chemical element rhenium.

re[1] /ree, ray/ > *preposition* 1 in the matter of (used in headings or to introduce a reference). 2 about; concerning.

ORIGIN – Latin, ablative of *res* 'thing'.

re[2] > *noun* variant spelling of **RAY**[3].

re- > *prefix* 1 once more; afresh; anew: *reactivate*. 2 with return to a previous state: *restore*. 3 (also **red-**) in return; mutually: *resemble*. 4 in opposition: *repel*. 5 behind or after: *relic*. 6 in a withdrawn state: *reticent*. 7 back and away; down: *recede*. 8 with frequentative or intensive force: *resound*. 9 with negative force: *recant*.

USAGE – in modern English, words formed with the prefix **re-** are unhyphenated, except when the word to which **re-** attaches begins with e; in this case a hyphen is inserted for clarity, as in **re-examine** and **re-enact**. A hyphen is also used where the word formed with **re-** would be identical to an already existing word: thus **re-cover** (meaning 'cover again') and **recover** (meaning 'get better in health').

ORIGIN – Latin *re-* 'again, back'.

're > *abbreviation* informal are (usually after the pronouns you, we, and they).

reach > *verb* 1 stretch out an arm in a specified direction in order to touch or grasp something. 2 be able to touch (something) with an outstretched arm or leg. 3 arrive at, attain, or extend to. 4 make contact with. 5 succeed in influencing or having an effect on. > *noun* 1 an act of reaching. 2 the distance to which someone can stretch out their hand. 3 the extent or range of something's application, effect, or influence. 4 (often **reaches**) a continuous extent of land or water, especially a stretch of river between two bends.

COMBINATIONS – **reach-me-down** Brit. informal, dated a second-hand or ready-made garment.

react > *verb* 1 respond to something in a particular way. 2 (**react against**) respond with hostility or a contrary course of action to. 3 suffer from adverse physiological effects after ingesting, breathing, or touching a substance. 4 Chemistry & Physics interact and undergo a chemical or physical change.

reactant > *noun* Chemistry a substance that takes part in and undergoes change during a reaction.

reaction > *noun* 1 an instance of reacting to or against something. 2 (**reactions**) a person's ability to respond physically and mentally to external stimuli. 3 opposition to political or social progress or reform. 4 a process in which substances interact causing chemical or physical change. 5 Physics a force exerted in opposition to an applied force.

reactionary > *adjective* opposing political or social progress or reform. > *noun* (pl. **reactionaries**) a person holding reactionary views.

reactivate > *verb* restore to a state of activity.
DERIVATIVES – **reactivation** *noun*.

reactive > *adjective* 1 showing a response to a stimulus. 2 acting in response to a situation rather than creating or controlling it. 3 having a tendency to react chemically.
DERIVATIVES – **reactivity** *noun*.

reactor > *noun* 1 an apparatus or structure in which fissile material can be made to undergo a controlled, self-sustaining nuclear reaction releasing energy. 2 a container or apparatus in which substances are made to react chemically.

read /reed/ > *verb* (past and past participle **read** /red/) 1 look at and comprehend the meaning of (written or printed matter) by interpreting its characters or symbols. 2 speak (written or printed words) aloud. 3 (of a passage, text, or sign) contain or consist of specified words; have a certain wording. 4 habitually read (a particular newspaper or journal). 5 discover (information) by reading. 6 understand or interpret the nature or significance of. 7 (**read into**) attribute a meaning or significance to (something) that it may not possess. 8 (**read up on**) acquire information about (a particular subject) by reading. 9 present (a bill or other measure) before a legislative assembly. 10 inspect and record the figure indicated on (a measuring instrument). 11 chiefly Brit. study (an academic subject) at a university. 12 (of a computer) copy or transfer (data). 13 hear and understand the words of (someone speaking on a radio transmitter). > *noun* 1 chiefly Brit. a period or act of reading. 2 informal a book considered in terms of its readability: *a good read*.
WORDFINDER – dyslexia (*reading disorder*), illegible (*not clear enough to be read*), illiterate (*unable to read or write*), lectern (*tall bookstand used by a reader standing upright*).
IDIOMS – **read between the lines** look for or discover a meaning that not explicitly stated. **read someone's mind** discern what someone is thinking. **read my lips** N. Amer. informal listen carefully. **take as read**

assume (something) without needing further discussion. **well read** having a high level of knowledge as a result of reading widely.
DERIVATIVES – **readable** *adjective*.
COMBINATIONS – **read-only memory** Computing memory read at high speed but not capable of being changed by program instructions.
ORIGIN – Old English; early senses included 'advise' and 'interpret (a riddle or dream)'.

reader > *noun* 1 a person who reads. 2 a person who assesses the merits of manuscripts submitted for publication. 3 (**Reader**) Brit. a university lecturer of the highest grade below professor. 4 a book containing extracts of a text or texts for teaching purposes. 5 a device that produces on a screen a readable image from a microfiche or microfilm.

readership > *noun* 1 the readers of a publication regarded collectively. 2 (**Readership**) Brit. the position of Reader at a university.

readily > *adverb* 1 without hesitation; willingly. 2 without difficulty; easily.

reading > *noun* 1 the action or skill of reading. 2 an instance of something being read to an audience. 3 an interpretation of a text. 4 a figure recorded on a measuring instrument. 5 a stage of debate in parliament through which a bill must pass before it can become law.
COMBINATIONS – **reading age** a child's reading ability expressed with reference to an average age at which a comparable ability is found.

readjust > *verb* 1 set or adjust again. 2 adjust or adapt to a changed situation or environment.
DERIVATIVES – **readjustment** *noun*.

ready > *adjective* (**readier**, **readiest**) 1 prepared for an activity or situation. 2 made suitable and available for immediate use. 3 easily available or obtained; within reach. 4 (**ready to do**) willing or eager to do something. 5 immediate, quick, or prompt. > *noun* (**readies** or **the ready**) Brit. informal available money; cash. > *verb* (**readies**, **readied**) make (something) ready.
DERIVATIVES – **readiness** *noun*.
SYNONYMS – *adjective* 2 completed, finished, prepared. 3 at hand, accessible, handy.
COMBINATIONS – **ready-made 1** made to a standard size or specification rather than to order. 2 readily available: *ready-made answers*. 3 (of food) sold ready or almost ready to be served. **ready-mixed** (of concrete, paint, food, etc.) having some or all of the constituents already mixed together. **ready money** money in the form of cash that is immediately available. **ready reckoner** a book, table, etc. listing standard

numerical calculations or other kinds of information. **ready-to-wear** (of clothes) sold through shops rather than made to order for an individual customer.

reagent /riayjənt/ > *noun* a substance or mixture for use in chemical analysis or other reactions.

real[1] /reel/ > *adjective* 1 actually existing or occurring in fact; not imagined or supposed. 2 significant; serious. 3 not artificial; genuine. 4 rightly so called; proper: *a real man*. 5 adjusted for changes in the value of money: *an increase in real terms*. 6 Mathematics (of a number or quantity) having no imaginary part. > *adverb* informal, chiefly N. Amer. really; very.
IDIOMS – **for real** informal as a serious or actual concern.
SYNONYMS – *adjective* 1 actual, existent, factual. 3 authentic, bona fide, genuine, sincere.
COMBINATIONS – **real ale** chiefly Brit. cask-conditioned beer that is served traditionally, without additional gas pressure. **real estate** chiefly N. Amer. real property; land. **real property** Law property consisting of land or buildings. Compare with *personal property*. **real tennis** the original form of tennis, played with a solid ball on an enclosed court. **real time** the actual time during which something occurs.
ORIGIN – Latin *realis*, from *res* 'thing'.

real[2] /rayaal/ > *noun* 1 the basic monetary unit of Brazil since 1994, equal to 100 centavos. 2 a former coin and monetary unit of various Spanish-speaking countries.
ORIGIN – Spanish and Portuguese, 'royal'.

realign > *verb* 1 change or restore to a different or former position or state. 2 (**realign oneself with**) change one's position or attitude with regard to.
DERIVATIVES – **realignment** *noun*.

realise (also **realize**) > *verb* 1 become fully aware of as a fact. 2 cause (something desired or anticipated) to happen; fulfil. 3 give actual or physical form to (a concept or work). 4 sell for or make a profit of.
DERIVATIVES – **realisation** *noun*.
SYNONYMS – 1 discern, grasp, notice, perceive, register, understand. 2 accomplish, achieve, fulfil.

realism > *noun* 1 the practice of accepting a situation as it is and dealing with it accordingly. 2 (in art or literature) the representation of things in a way that is accurate and true to life. 3 Philosophy the doctrine that universals or abstract concepts have an objective or absolute existence. Contrasted with NOMINALISM.
DERIVATIVES – **realist** *noun*.

realistic > *adjective* 1 having a sensible and practical idea of what can be achieved or expected. 2 representing things in a way that is accurate and true to life.

DERIVATIVES – **realistically** adverb.

SYNONYMS – **1** commonsensical, down-to-earth, matter-of-fact, pragmatic.

reality > noun (pl. **realities**) **1** the state of things as they actually exist, as opposed to an idealistic or notional idea of them. **2** a thing that is actually experienced or seen. **3** the quality of being lifelike. **4** the state or quality of having existence or substance.

really > adverb **1** in reality; in actual fact. **2** very; thoroughly. > exclamation **1** expressing interest, surprise, doubt, or protest. **2** chiefly US expressing agreement.

realm > noun **1** archaic, literary, or Law a kingdom. **2** a field or domain of activity or interest.

SYNONYMS – **2** area, domain, field, sphere, world.

ORIGIN – Old French reaume, from Latin regimen, from regere 'to rule'.

realpolitik /rayaalpolliteek/ > noun politics based on practical rather than moral or ideological considerations.

ORIGIN – German, 'practical politics'.

realtor /reeəltər/ > noun N. Amer. an estate agent.

realty /reeəlti/ > noun Law a person's real property. Compare with PERSONALTY.

ream¹ > noun **1** 500 (formerly 480) sheets of paper. **2** a large quantity of something, especially paper.

ORIGIN – Old French raime, from an Arabic word meaning 'bundle'.

ream² > verb widen (a bore or hole) with a special tool.

DERIVATIVES – **reamer** noun.

reanimate > verb restore to life or vigour; revive.

DERIVATIVES – **reanimation** noun.

reap > verb **1** cut or gather (a crop or harvest). **2** receive or suffer as a consequence of one's own or others' actions.

IDIOMS – **you reap what you sow** proverb you eventually have to face up to the consequences of your actions.

SYNONYMS – **1** garner, harvest. **2** acquire, get, obtain, receive, suffer.

reaper > noun **1** a person or machine that harvests a crop. **2** (**the Reaper** or **the Grim Reaper**) a personification of death as a cloaked skeleton wielding a large scythe.

reappear > verb appear again.

DERIVATIVES – **reappearance** noun.

reappoint > verb appoint again to a position previously held.

DERIVATIVES – **reappointment** noun.

reappraise > verb appraise again or differently.

DERIVATIVES – **reappraisal** noun.

rear¹ > noun **1** the back or hindmost part of something. **2** (also **rear end**) informal a person's bottom. > adjective at the back.

IDIOMS – **bring up the rear 1** be at the very end of a queue. **2** come last in a race.

COMBINATIONS – **rear admiral** a rank of naval officer, above commodore and below vice admiral. **rear-view mirror** a mirror fixed inside the windscreen of a motor vehicle enabling the driver to see the vehicle or road behind. **rear-wheel drive** a transmission system that provides power to the rear wheels of a motor vehicle.

ORIGIN – Old French rere, from Latin retro 'back'.

rear² > verb **1** bring up and care for (offspring). **2** breed or cultivate animals or plants. **3** (of an animal) raise itself upright on its hind legs. **4** (of a building, mountain, etc.) extend or appear to extend to a great height.

ORIGIN – Old English, 'set upright, construct, elevate'.

rearguard > noun **1** the soldiers at the rear of a body of troops, especially those protecting a retreating army. **2** a reactionary or conservative faction.

COMBINATIONS – **rearguard action** a defensive action carried out by a retreating army.

rearm > verb provide with or acquire a new supply of weapons.

DERIVATIVES – **rearmament** noun.

rearmost > adjective furthest back.

rearrange > verb arrange again in a different way.

DERIVATIVES – **rearrangement** noun.

rearrest > verb arrest again. > noun an act of rearresting someone.

rearward > adjective directed towards the back. > adverb (also **rearwards**) towards the back.

reason > noun **1** a cause, explanation, or justification. **2** good or obvious cause to do something. **3** the power of the mind to think, understand, and form judgements logically. **4** (**one's reason**) one's sanity. **5** what is right, practical, or possible. > verb **1** think, understand, and form judgements logically. **2** (**reason out**) find a solution (to a problem) by considering possible options. **3** (**reason with**) conduct a rational argument with (someone).

WORDFINDER – a posteriori (denoting reasoning based on known facts), a priori (reasoning based on theory rather than observation), deduction (the inference of particular instances by reference to a general law), fallacy (a failure in reasoning), induction (the inference of a general law from particular instances).

IDIOMS – **by reason of** formal because of. **listen to reason** be persuaded to act sensibly. **it stands to reason** it is obvious or logical.

DERIVATIVES – **reasoned** adjective.

SYNONYMS – noun **1** basis, grounds, motive, rationale.

ORIGIN – Old French reisun, from Latin reri 'consider'.

reasonable > adjective **1** having or based on sound judgement; fair and sensible. **2** as much as is appropriate or fair; moderate. **3** fairly good; average.

DERIVATIVES – **reasonably** adverb.

SYNONYMS – **1** judicious, logical, rational, sensible.

reassemble > verb assemble again; put back together.

DERIVATIVES – **reassembly** noun.

reassert > verb assert again.

DERIVATIVES – **reassertion** noun.

reassess > verb assess again, especially differently.

DERIVATIVES – **reassessment** noun.

reassign > verb assign again or differently.

DERIVATIVES – **reassignment** noun.

reassure > verb allay the doubts and fears of (someone).

DERIVATIVES – **reassurance** noun **reassuring** adjective **reassuringly** adverb.

reattach > verb attach again.

DERIVATIVES – **reattachment** noun.

reattempt > verb attempt again.

reawaken > verb awaken again.

rebar /reebaar/ > noun reinforcing steel, especially as rods in concrete.

rebarbative /ribaarbətiv/ > adjective formal unattractive and objectionable.

wordpower facts

Rebarbative

Although the word **rebarbative** may be applied to women as well as men, and to concepts or inanimate objects, it is rooted in the notion of the male beard. It comes from French rébarbatif, from Old French se rebarber, which means 'face each other beard to beard', or 'confront each other aggressively', from barbe 'beard'.

rebate¹ /reebayt/ > noun **1** a partial refund to someone who has paid too much for tax, rent, etc. **2** a deduction or discount on a sum due. > verb pay back as a rebate.

ORIGIN – Old French rebatre 'beat back', also 'deduct'.

rebate² /reebayt/ > noun a step-shaped recess cut in a piece of wood, typically forming a match to the edge or tongue of another piece. > verb (**rebated, rebating**) **1** make a rebate in. **2** join or fix with a rebate.

ORIGIN – alteration of RABBET.

rebec /reebek/ (also **rebeck**) > *noun* a medieval three-stringed instrument played with a bow.
ORIGIN – French, from Arabic.

rebel > *noun* /rebb'l/ a person who rebels. > *verb* /ribel/ (**rebelled**, **rebelling**) 1 rise in opposition or armed resistance to an established government or ruler. 2 resist authority, control, or convention.
SYNONYMS – *verb* 1 mutiny, revolt, riot, rise up.
ORIGIN – first used in reference to a fresh declaration of war by the defeated: from Latin *rebellis*, from *bellum* 'war'.

rebellion > *noun* 1 armed resistance to an established government or ruler. 2 defiance of authority or control.
SYNONYMS – 1 insurrection, mutiny, revolt, uprising. 2 disobedience, insubordination, subversion.

rebellious > *adjective* 1 engaged in rebellion or showing a desire to rebel. 2 (of a thing) unmanageable.
DERIVATIVES – **rebelliously** *adverb* **rebelliousness** *noun*.

rebid > *verb* (**rebidding**; past and past participle **rebid**) bid again. > *noun* a further bid.

rebind > *verb* (past and past participle **rebound**) give a new binding to (a book).

rebirth > *noun* 1 reincarnation. 2 a revival.

reboot > *verb* boot (a computer system) again. > *noun* an act of rebooting.

rebore > *verb* make a new or wider boring in (the cylinders of an internal-combustion engine). > *noun* 1 an act of reboring. 2 an engine with rebored cylinders.

reborn > *adjective* 1 brought back to life or activity. 2 born again as a Christian.

rebound¹ > *verb* /ribownd/ 1 bounce back after hitting a hard surface. 2 recover in value, amount, or strength. 3 (**rebound on**) have an unexpected adverse consequence for. > *noun* /reebownd/ 1 a ball or shot that rebounds. 2 an instance of recovering in value, amount, or strength.
IDIOMS – **on the rebound** while still distressed after the ending of a romantic relationship.
ORIGIN – Old French *rebondir*, from *bondir* 'bounce up'.

rebound² past and past participle of **REBIND**.

rebrand > *verb* change the corporate image of (a company or organisation).

rebroadcast > *verb* (past **rebroadcast** or **rebroadcasted**; past participle **rebroadcast**) broadcast again. > *noun* a repeated broadcast.

rebuff > *verb* reject in an abrupt or ungracious manner. > *noun* an abrupt rejection.
SYNONYMS – *verb* refuse, reject, repulse, snub, spurn. *noun* rejection, repulse, snub.

ORIGIN – obsolete French *rebuffer*, from Italian *buffo* 'a gust, puff'.

rebuild > *verb* (past and past participle **rebuilt**) build again.

rebuke > *verb* criticise or reprimand sharply. > *noun* a sharp criticism.
SYNONYMS – *verb* admonish, berate, chastise, upbraid. *noun* admonition, censure, reproof.

> ## wordpower facts
> ### Rebuke
> The source of the word **rebuke** is the Old French word for 'log', *busche*. Entering Middle English in the sense 'force back, repress', **rebuke** comes from Old Northern French *rebuker*, from re- 'back, down' and *bukier* 'to beat'; *bukier* is based on *busche* and originally meant, specifically, 'cut down wood'.

rebus /reebəss/ > *noun* (pl. **rebuses**) a puzzle in which words are represented by combinations of pictures and letters.
ORIGIN – Latin, 'by things', from *de rebus quae geruntur*, literally 'concerning the things that are taking place', a title formerly given to satirical pieces containing riddles in picture form.

rebut /ribut/ > *verb* (**rebutted**, **rebutting**) claim or prove to be false.
ORIGIN – Old French *rebuter*, from *boter* 'to butt'.

rebuttal > *noun* a refutation or contradiction.

recalcitrant /rikalsitrənt/ > *adjective* obstinately uncooperative. > *noun* a recalcitrant person.
DERIVATIVES – **recalcitrance** *noun* **recalcitrantly** *adverb*.
ORIGIN – from Latin *recalcitrare* 'kick out with the heels'.

recalculate > *verb* calculate again.
DERIVATIVES – **recalculation** *noun*.

recall /rikawl/ > *verb* 1 remember. 2 cause one to remember or think of. 3 officially order to return. 4 call up (stored computer data). 5 (of a manufacturer) request the return of (faulty products). 6 reselect (a sports player) as a member of a team. > *noun* /also reekawl/ 1 the action or faculty of remembering. 2 an act of officially recalling someone or something.
IDIOMS – **beyond recall** in such a way that restoration is impossible.
SYNONYMS – *verb* 2 bring to mind, conjure up, evoke. *noun* 1 memory, recollection, remembrance.

recant /rikant/ > *verb* renounce a former opinion or belief.
DERIVATIVES – **recantation** *noun*.

SYNONYMS – disavow, repudiate.
ORIGIN – Latin *recantare* 'revoke', from *cantare* 'sing, chant'.

recap informal > *verb* (**recapped**, **recapping**) recapitulate. > *noun* a recapitulation.

recapitulate /reekəpityoolayt/ > *verb* 1 summarise and state again the main points of. 2 Biology repeat (an evolutionary or other process) during development and growth.
SYNONYMS – 1 reiterate, review, sum up.
ORIGIN – Latin *recapitulare* 'go through heading by heading', from *capitulum* 'chapter'.

recapitulation > *noun* 1 an act or instance of recapitulating something. 2 Music a part of a movement in which themes from the exposition are restated.

recapture > *verb* 1 capture (an escapee). 2 recover (something taken or lost). 3 recreate (a past time, event, or feeling). > *noun* an act of recapturing.

recast > *verb* (past and past participle **recast**) 1 cast (metal) again or differently. 2 present in a different form or style. 3 allocate roles in (a play or film) to different actors.

recce /rekki/ informal, chiefly Brit. > *noun* reconnaissance. > *verb* (**recced**, **recceing**) reconnoitre.

recede /riseed/ > *verb* 1 move back or further away. 2 gradually diminish. 3 (of a man's hair) cease to grow at the temples and above the forehead. 4 (of a facial feature) slope backwards.
SYNONYMS – 1 move back, retreat, withdraw. 2 dwindle, fade, lessen.
ORIGIN – Latin *recedere* 'go back'.

receipt > *noun* 1 the action of receiving something or the fact of its being received. 2 a written acknowledgement of receiving something. 3 (**receipts**) an amount of money received over a period by an organisation.
ORIGIN – Old French *receite*, from Latin *recepta* 'received'.

receivable > *adjective* able to be received. > *noun* (**receivables**) amounts owed to a business, regarded as assets.

receive* > *verb* 1 be given, presented with, or paid. 2 accept or take delivery of. 3 chiefly Brit. buy or accept (goods known to be stolen). 4 detect or pick up (broadcast signals). 5 (in tennis and similar games) be the player to whom the server serves (the ball). 6 serve as a receptacle for. 7 suffer, experience, or be subject to. 8 meet with (a specified reaction). 9 (**received**) widely accepted as authoritative or true. 10 entertain as a guest. 11 admit as a member.
IDIOMS – **be at** (or **on**) **the receiving end** informal be subjected to something unpleasant.
*SPELLING – remember, the rule is *i* before *e* except after *c*: receive.

COMBINATIONS – **received pronunciation** (also **received standard**) the standard form of British English pronunciation, based on educated speech in southern England.
ORIGIN – Latin *recipere*, from *capere* 'take'.

receiver > *noun* **1** a person or thing that receives something. **2** a piece of radio or television apparatus converting broadcast signals into sound or images. **3** a telephone handset, in particular the part that converts electrical signals into sounds. **4** (Brit. also **official receiver**) a person appointed to manage the financial affairs of a bankrupt business.

receivership > *noun* the state of being managed by an official receiver.

recension /risensh'n/ > *noun* **1** a revised edition of a text. **2** the revision of a text.
ORIGIN – Latin, from *recensere* 'revise'.

recent > *adjective* **1** having happened or been done lately; belonging to a period of time not long ago. **2** (**Recent**) Geology another term for HOLOCENE.
DERIVATIVES – **recently** adverb.
SYNONYMS – **1** contemporary, current, late, modern, present-day.
ANTONYMS – **1** former, old.
ORIGIN – Latin *recens*.

receptacle /riseptak'l/ > *noun* **1** an object or space used to contain something. **2** Botany the base of a flower or flower head.
SYNONYMS – **1** container, holder, vessel.

reception > *noun* **1** the action or process of receiving someone or something. **2** the way in which something is received. **3** a formal social occasion held to welcome someone or celebrate an event. **4** the area in a hotel, office, etc. where visitors are greeted. **5** the quality with which broadcast signals are received.
COMBINATIONS – **reception room 1** a function room in a hotel or other building. **2 Brit.** a room in a private house suitable for entertaining visitors.

receptionist > *noun* a person who greets and deals with clients and visitors to a surgery, office, hotel, etc.

receptive > *adjective* **1** able or willing to receive something. **2** willing to consider new suggestions and ideas.
DERIVATIVES – **receptivity** noun.
SYNONYMS – **2** amenable, open-minded, responsive.

receptor /riseptər/ > *noun* Physiology an organ or cell that responds to external stimuli and transmits signals to a sensory nerve.

recess /risess, reesess/ > *noun* **1** a small space set back in a wall. **2** a hollow in something. **3** (**recesses**) remote, secluded, or secret places. **4** a break between sessions of a parliament, law court, etc. **5 chiefly N. Amer.** a break between school classes.
> *verb* **1** set (a fitment) back into a wall or other surface. **2** temporarily suspend (proceedings).
ORIGIN – Latin *recessus*, from *recedere* 'go back'.

recession /risesh'n/ > *noun* a temporary economic decline during which trade and industrial activity are reduced.
DERIVATIVES – **recessionary** adjective.

recessional > *adjective* relating to recession. > *noun* a hymn sung while the clergy and choir withdraw after a service.

recessive Genetics > *adjective* (of a heritable characteristic) controlled by a gene that is expressed in offspring only when inherited from both parents. Compare with DOMINANT. > *noun* a recessive trait or gene.

recharge > *verb* **1** charge (a battery or device) again. **2** (also **recharge one's batteries**) return to a normal state of mind or strength after exertion.

recheck > *verb* check again. > *noun* an act of rechecking.

recherché /rəshairshay/ > *adjective* rare, exotic, or obscure.
ORIGIN – French, literally 'carefully sought out'.

rechristen > *verb* give a new name to.

recidivist /risiddivist/ > *noun* a convicted criminal who reoffends.
DERIVATIVES – **recidivism** noun.
ORIGIN – French *récidiviste*, from Latin *recidivus* 'falling back'.

recipe /ressipi/ > *noun* **1** a set of instructions for preparing a dish. **2** something likely to lead to a particular outcome: *a recipe for disaster*.
ORIGIN – Latin, literally 'receive!'

recipient /risippiənt/ > *noun* a receiver of something.

reciprocal /risiprək'l/ > *adjective* **1** given, felt, or done in return. **2** (of an agreement or arrangement) bearing on or binding two parties equally. **3** Grammar (of a pronoun or verb) expressing mutual action or relationship (e.g. *each other, they kissed*). > *noun* Mathematics the quantity obtained by dividing the number one by a given quantity.
DERIVATIVES – **reciprocally** adverb.
SYNONYMS – *adjective* **1** common, mutual, shared.

reciprocate /risiprəkayt/ > *verb* respond to (a gesture, action, or emotion) with a corresponding one.
COMBINATIONS – **reciprocating engine** a piston engine.
ORIGIN – Latin *reciprocare* 'move backwards and forwards'.

reciprocity /ressiprossiti/ > *noun* the practice of exchanging things with others for mutual benefit.

recirculate > *verb* circulate again.
DERIVATIVES – **recirculation** noun.

recital > *noun* **1** the performance of a programme of music by a soloist or small group. **2** the enumeration of connected names, facts, or elements.
SYNONYMS – **2** catalogue, enumeration, list.

recitative /ressitəteev/ > *noun* musical declamation of the kind usual in the narrative and dialogue parts of opera and oratorio.

recite > *verb* **1** repeat aloud or declaim from memory before an audience. **2** state (names, facts, etc.) in order.
ORIGIN – Latin *recitare* 'read out'.

reck > *verb* archaic **1** pay heed to something: *ye reck not of lands or goods*. **2** (**it recks**) it is important.

reckless > *adjective* without thought or care for the consequences of an action.
DERIVATIVES – **recklessly** adverb **recklessness** noun.
SYNONYMS – careless, heedless, rash, thoughtless.
ORIGIN – Old English, from the base (meaning 'care') of RECK.

reckon > *verb* **1** establish by counting or calculation; calculate. **2** informal be of the opinion. **3** regard in a specified way. **4** (**reckon on** or **to**) informal have a specified view or opinion of. **5** (**reckon on**) rely on or be sure of. **6** (**reckon with** or **without**) take (or fail to take) into account.
IDIOMS – **to be reckoned with** not to be ignored or underestimated.
SYNONYMS – **1** calculate, compute, count up, work out.
ORIGIN – Old English, 'recount, relate', later 'give an account of items received', hence the notion of 'calculation'.

reckoning > *noun* **1** the action of calculating or estimating something. **2** an opinion or judgement. **3** the working out of consequences or retribution for one's actions.
IDIOMS – **into** (or **out of**) **the reckoning** into or out of contention for selection, victory, etc.

reclaim > *verb* **1** retrieve or recover. **2** reform (a wicked or corrupt person). **3** bring (waste land or land formerly under water) under cultivation. > *noun* the action of reclaiming or being reclaimed.
DERIVATIVES – **reclamation** noun.

reclassify > *verb* (**reclassifies, reclassified**) classify differently.
DERIVATIVES – **reclassification** noun.

recline > *verb* **1** lean or lie back in a relaxed position. **2** (of a seat) have a back able to move into a sloping position.
DERIVATIVES – **reclinable** adjective **recliner** noun.
SYNONYMS – **1** be recumbent, loll, repose.

ORIGIN – Latin *reclinare*, from *clinare* 'to bend'.

recluse /rik**loo**ss/ > *noun* a person who avoids others and lives a solitary life.

DERIVATIVES – **reclusive** *adjective*.

ORIGIN – from Latin *recludere* 'enclose'.

recognisance /rik**og**niz'nss/ (also **recognizance**) > *noun* Law a bond undertaken before a court or magistrate that requires the observation of a condition, e.g. to appear when summoned.

recognise (also **recognize**) > *verb* **1** identify as already known; know again. **2** acknowledge the existence, validity, or legality of. **3** reward formally.

DERIVATIVES – **recognisable** *adjective*.

SYNONYMS – **1** know, place, remember. **2** accept, acknowledge, concede, realise.

ORIGIN – Latin *recognoscere*, from *cognoscere* 'to learn'.

recognition > *noun* **1** the action of recognising or the process of being recognised. **2** appreciation or acknowledgement. **3** (also **diplomatic recognition**) formal acknowledgement by a country that a particular place qualifies to be recognised as a state.

recoil > *verb* **1** suddenly spring back or flinch in fear, horror, or disgust. **2** feel such emotions at the thought of something. **3** spring back through force of impact or elasticity. **4** (**recoil on**) (of an action) have an adverse consequence for (the originator). > *noun* the action of recoiling.

SYNONYMS – *verb* **1,2** draw back, shrink back, shy away.

wordpower facts

Recoil

The **-coil** part of **recoil** has nothing to do with the word **coil**. In fact it comes from Latin *culus*, which means 'buttocks, bottom'! **Recoil** came into English from Old French *reculer* 'move back', and first meant 'drive or force back' or 'retreat'. *Culus* gave rise to the French word *cul*, the source of **cul-de-sac** (literally 'bottom of a sack'), **culottes**, and (via the children's word *cucu* 'botty, bum') **tutu**.

recollect /rekk**ə**lekt/ > *verb* **1** remember. **2** (**recollect oneself**) compose oneself.

recollection > *noun* **1** the action or faculty of remembering. **2** a memory.

recombinant /rik**om**binənt/ > *adjective* Genetics of or relating to genetic material formed by recombination.

recombination > *noun* **1** the process of recombining things. **2** Genetics the rearrangement of genetic material, especially by exchange between chromosomes or by the artificial joining of DNA segments.

recombine > *verb* combine again or differently.

recommence > *verb* begin again.

recommend* > *verb* **1** put forward with approval as being suitable for a purpose or role. **2** advise as a course of action. **3** make appealing or desirable.

DERIVATIVES – **recommendation** *noun*.

*SPELLING – one *c* and two *m*s: re*c*o*mm*end.

SYNONYMS – **1** advocate, commend, endorse. **2** advise, advocate, propose.

recommission > *verb* commission again.

recompense /**rekk**əmpenss/ > *verb* **1** compensate (someone) for loss or harm suffered. **2** pay or reward for effort or work. > *noun* compensation or reward.

SYNONYMS – *verb* **1** compensate, indemnify, reimburse, repay.

ORIGIN – Latin *recompensare*, from *compensare* 'weigh one thing against another'.

recon /**ri**kon/ informal, chiefly N. Amer. > *noun* short for **RECONNAISSANCE**. > *verb* (**reconned**, **reconning**) short for **RECONNOITRE**.

reconcile /**rekk**ənsīl/ > *verb* **1** restore friendly relations between. **2** make or show to be compatible. **3** (**reconcile to**) make (someone) accept (a disagreeable thing).

DERIVATIVES – **reconciliation** *noun*.

ORIGIN – Latin *reconciliare*, from *conciliare* 'bring together'.

recondite /**rekk**əndīt, ri**kon**dīt/ > *adjective* (of a subject or knowledge) obscure.

SYNONYMS – abstruse, arcane, esoteric, obscure, recherché.

ORIGIN – Latin *reconditus* 'hidden, put away'.

recondition > *verb* **1** condition again. **2** Brit. overhaul or renovate.

reconfigure > *verb* configure differently.

DERIVATIVES – **reconfiguration** *noun*.

reconnaissance /ri**konn**is'nss/ > *noun* **1** military observation of a region to locate an enemy or ascertain strategic features. **2** preliminary surveying or research.

ORIGIN – French, from *reconnoître* 'recognise'.

reconnect > *verb* connect again.

DERIVATIVES – **reconnection** *noun*.

reconnoitre /rekk**ə**noytər/ (US **reconnoiter**) > *verb* make a military observation of (a region). > *noun* informal an act of reconnoitring.

ORIGIN – obsolete French *reconnoître*, from Latin *recognoscere* 'to recognise'.

reconsider > *verb* consider again.

DERIVATIVES – **reconsideration** *noun*.

reconstitute > *verb* **1** reconstruct. **2** change the form and organisation of (an institution). **3** restore (something dried) to its original state by adding water.

DERIVATIVES – **reconstitution** *noun*.

reconstruct > *verb* **1** construct again. **2** form an impression, model, or re-enactment of (something) from evidence.

DERIVATIVES – **reconstruction** *noun* **reconstructive** *adjective*.

reconvene > *verb* convene again.

reconvert > *verb* convert back to a former state.

DERIVATIVES – **reconversion** *noun*.

record > *noun* /**rekk**ord/ **1** a piece of evidence or information constituting an account of something that has occurred or been said. **2** a person or thing's previous conduct or performance. **3** (also **gramophone record**) a thin plastic disc carrying recorded sound in grooves on each surface, for reproduction by a record player. **4** a criminal record. **5** the best performance or most remarkable event of its kind officially recognised. > *verb* /ri**kord**/ **1** make a record of. **2** convert (sound, a broadcast, etc.) into permanent form for later reproduction.

IDIOMS – **for the record** so that the true facts are recorded or known. **on record** officially measured and noted. **on** (or **off**) **the record** made (or not made) as an official or attributable statement. **put** (or **set**) **the record straight** correct a misapprehension.

DERIVATIVES – **recording** *noun* **recordist** *noun*.

SYNONYMS – *noun* **1** account, document, documentation, mention, note.

COMBINATIONS – **recorded delivery** Brit. a service in which the Post Office obtains a signature from the recipient as a record that an item of post has been delivered. **record player** an apparatus for reproducing sound from gramophone records, with a turntable and a stylus that picks up sound from the groove.

ORIGIN – Old French, 'remembrance', from Latin *recordari* 'remember'.

recorder > *noun* **1** an apparatus for recording sound, pictures, or data. **2** a person who keeps records. **3** (**Recorder**) (in England and Wales) a barrister appointed to serve as a part-time judge. **4** a simple woodwind instrument without keys, played by blowing air through a shaped mouthpiece.

recount[1] /ri**kownt**/ > *verb* give an account of (something).

SYNONYMS – describe, narrate, relate, tell.

ORIGIN – Old French *reconter* 'tell again'.

recount[2] > *verb* /ree**kownt**/ count again. > *noun* /**ree**kownt/ an act of counting something again.

recoup /rikōōp/ > verb regain (something lost).

SYNONYMS – get back, recover, retrieve.

ORIGIN – French recouper 'retrench, cut back'.

recourse > noun 1 a source of help in a difficult situation. 2 (**recourse to**) use of (something) as a recourse.

ORIGIN – Latin recursus, from cursus 'course, running'.

recover > verb 1 return to a normal state of health, mind, or strength. 2 find or regain possession of. 3 regain or secure (compensation). 4 remove or extract (an energy source, chemical, etc.) for use, reuse, or waste treatment.

DERIVATIVES – **recoverable** adjective.

SYNONYMS – 1 get better, mend, rally, recuperate. 2 get back, recoup, retrieve.

ORIGIN – Latin recuperare 'get again'.

re-cover > verb put a new cover or covering on.

recovery > noun (pl. **recoveries**) 1 an act or the process of recovering. 2 the action of taking a vehicle that has broken down or crashed for repair.

SYNONYMS – 1 convalescence, recuperation, rehabilitation.

COMBINATIONS – **recovery position** Brit. a position used to prevent an unconscious person from choking, the body being placed face downwards and slightly to the side, supported by bent limbs.

recreate > verb 1 create again. 2 reproduce or re-enact (a situation or event).

recreation¹ /rekriaysh'n/ > noun enjoyable leisure activity.

DERIVATIVES – **recreational** adjective **recreationally** adverb.

COMBINATIONS – **recreation ground** Brit. a piece of public land used for sports and games.

ORIGIN – Latin, from recreare 'create again, renew'.

recreation² /reekriaysh'n/ > noun the action of recreating something.

recriminate /rikrimminayt/ > verb make recriminations.

ORIGIN – Latin recriminari 'accuse in return', from re- (expressing opposition) + criminare 'accuse'.

recrimination > noun (usu. **recriminations**) an accusation in response to one from someone else.

recrudesce /reekrōōdess/ > verb formal break out again; recur.

DERIVATIVES – **recrudescence** noun.

ORIGIN – Latin recrudescere 'become raw again'.

recruit > verb 1 enlist (someone) in the armed forces. 2 enrol (someone) as a member or worker in an organisation. 3 informal persuade (someone) to do or help

with something. > noun a newly recruited person.

DERIVATIVES – **recruiter** noun **recruitment** noun.

SYNONYMS – verb 1 conscript, enrol, sign up.

ORIGIN – obsolete French recrute, from Latin recrescere 'grow again'.

recta plural of RECTUM.

rectal > adjective relating to or affecting the rectum.

rectangle > noun a plane figure with four straight sides and four right angles, and with unequal adjacent sides.

DERIVATIVES – **rectangular** adjective.

ORIGIN – Latin rectangulum, from rectus 'straight' + angulus 'an angle'.

rectifier > noun an electrical device converting an alternating current into a direct one by allowing it to flow in one direction only.

rectify > verb (**rectifies**, **rectified**) 1 put right; correct. 2 convert (alternating current) to direct current.

DERIVATIVES – **rectifiable** adjective.

ORIGIN – Latin rectificare, from rectus 'right'.

rectilinear /rektilinniər/ (also **rectilineal** /rektilinniəl/) > adjective contained by, consisting of, or moving in a straight line or lines.

rectitude > noun formal morally correct behaviour.

recto /rektō/ > noun (pl. **rectos**) a right-hand page of an open book, or the front of a loose document. Contrasted with VERSO.

ORIGIN – Latin, 'on the right'.

rector > noun 1 (in the Church of England) the incumbent of a parish where all tithes formerly passed to the incumbent. 2 (in other Anglican Churches) a member of the clergy in charge of a parish. 3 (in the Roman Catholic Church) a priest in charge of a church or a religious institution. 4 the head of certain universities, colleges, and schools. 5 (in Scotland) a person elected to represent students on a university's governing body.

ORIGIN – Latin, 'ruler'.

rectory > noun (pl. **rectories**) 1 a rector's house. 2 a Church of England benefice held by a rector.

rectum /rektəm/ > noun (pl. **rectums** or **recta** /rektə/) the final section of the large intestine, terminating at the anus.

WORDFINDER – enema (procedure in which fluid is injected into the rectum), proctology (branch of medicine concerned with the rectum), rectal (relating to the rectum).

ORIGIN – Latin, 'straight'.

recumbent /rikumbənt/ > adjective 1 lying down. 2 (of a plant) growing close to the ground.

ORIGIN – from Latin recumbere 'recline'.

recuperate /rikōōpərayt/ > verb 1 recover from illness or exertion. 2 regain (something lost).

DERIVATIVES – **recuperation** noun **recuperative** adjective.

SYNONYMS – 1 convalesce, get better, rally. 2 get back, recover, retrieve.

ORIGIN – Latin recuperare 'regain'.

recur > verb (**recurred, recurring**) 1 occur again. 2 (of a thought, image, etc.) come back to one's mind.

DERIVATIVES – **recurrence** noun **recurring** adjective.

SYNONYMS – 1 happen again, reoccur, repeat itself.

COMBINATIONS – **recurring decimal** a decimal fraction in which a figure or group of figures is repeated indefinitely, as in 0.666 …

ORIGIN – Latin recurrere, from currere 'run'.

recurrent /rikurrənt/ > adjective occurring often or repeatedly.

DERIVATIVES – **recurrently** adverb.

recursion /rikursh'n/ > noun chiefly Mathematics & Linguistics 1 the repeated application of a procedure or rule to successive results of the process. 2 a recursive procedure or rule.

DERIVATIVES – **recursive** adjective.

recusant /rekyooz'nt/ > noun 1 a person who refuses to submit to authority or comply with a regulation. 2 historical a person who refused to attend services of the Church of England.

DERIVATIVES – **recusancy** noun.

ORIGIN – from Latin recusare 'refuse'.

recuse /rikyōōz/ > verb (**recuse oneself**) chiefly N. Amer. & S. African (of a judge) excuse oneself from a case because of a possible lack of impartiality.

DERIVATIVES – **recusal** noun.

recycle > verb 1 convert (waste) into reusable material. 2 use again.

DERIVATIVES – **recyclable** adjective **recycler** noun.

red > adjective (**redder, reddest**) 1 of a colour at the end of the spectrum next to orange and opposite violet, as of blood, fire, or rubies. 2 (of a person's face) red due to embarrassment, anger, or heat. 3 (of hair or fur) of a reddish-brown colour. 4 (of wine) made from dark grapes and coloured by their skins. 5 informal, chiefly derogatory communist or socialist. 6 archaic or literary involving bloodshed or violence. > noun 1 red colour, pigment, or material. 2 informal, chiefly derogatory a communist or socialist. 3 (**the red**) the situation of having spent more than is in one's bank account.

WORDFINDER – shades of red: auburn, burgundy, cerise, cherry, claret, coral, coralline, crimson, damask, fuchsia, maroon, mulberry, puce, ruby, scarlet, strawberry, terracotta, vermilion.

IDIOMS – **see red** informal become very angry suddenly.

DERIVATIVES – **reddish** adjective **reddy** adjective **redly** adverb **redness** noun.

COMBINATIONS – **red admiral** a butterfly having dark wings with red bands and white spots. **redback** a highly poisonous Australasian spider with a bright red stripe down the back. **red-blooded** (of a man) vigorous or virile. **redbreast** informal, chiefly Brit. a robin. **red-brick 1** built with red bricks. **2** (of a British university) founded in the late 19th or early 20th century. **redcap 1** Brit. informal a member of the military police. **2** N. Amer. a railway porter. **red card** (especially in soccer) a red card shown by the referee to a player being sent off the field. **red carpet** a long, narrow red carpet for a distinguished visitor to walk along. **red cell** an erythrocyte. **red cent** N. Amer. **1** a one-cent coin, formerly made of copper. **2** the smallest amount of money: *some of the people don't deserve a single red cent*. **redcoat 1** historical a British soldier. **2** (in the UK) an organiser and entertainer at a Butlin's holiday camp. **Red Crescent** a national branch in Muslim countries of the Red Cross. **Red Cross** the International Movement of the Red Cross and the Red Crescent, an organisation bringing relief to victims of war or natural disaster. **redcurrant** the small edible red berry of a shrub related to the blackcurrant. **red deer** a deer with a rich red-brown summer coat that turns brownish-grey in winter, the male having large antlers. **red dwarf** Astronomy a small, old, relatively cool star. **red ensign** a red flag with the Union Jack in the top corner next to the flagstaff, flown by British-registered ships. **red-eye 1** the effect in photography of people appearing to have red eyes, caused by a reflection from the retina when the flashgun is too near the camera lens. **2** (also **red-eye flight**) informal, chiefly N. Amer. a flight on which one cannot expect much sleep. **3** US informal cheap whisky. **red-faced** embarrassed or ashamed. **red-figure** a type of ancient Greek pottery in which the background is painted black, leaving figures in the red colour of the clay. Compare with *black-figure*. **red flag 1** a warning of danger. **2** the symbol of socialist revolution. **red giant** Astronomy a very large luminous star of low surface temperature. **red grouse** a British moorland grouse with reddish-brown plumage. **red-handed** in or just after the act of doing something wrong. **red heat** the temperature or state of something so hot that it emits red light. **red herring 1** a dried smoked herring. **2** a misleading clue or distraction. [ORIGIN – so named from the practice of using the scent of red herring in training hounds.] **red lead** red lead oxide used as a pigment. **red-letter day** a noteworthy or memorable day. [ORIGIN – from the practice of highlighting a festival in red on a calendar.] **red light** a red light instructing moving vehicles to stop. **red-light district** an area with many brothels, strip clubs, etc. [ORIGIN – from the use of a red light as the sign of a brothel.] **redline** N. Amer. informal **1** drive with (the car engine) at its maximum rpm. **2** refuse (a loan or insurance) to someone due to their area of residence. **red meat** meat that is red when raw, e.g. beef or lamb. **red mullet** an elongated food fish with long barbels on the chin, living in warmer seas. **red pepper** the ripe red fruit of a sweet pepper. **the red planet** Mars. **red rose** the emblem of Lancashire or the Lancastrians. **red salmon** the sockeye salmon. **red setter** an Irish setter. **red shift** Astronomy a displacement of the spectrum to longer wavelengths in the light from a distant galaxy or other object moving away from the observer. **redskin** dated or offensive an American Indian. **red snapper** an reddish edible marine fish. **red squirrel** a small squirrel with a reddish coat. **red tape** excessive bureaucracy or adherence to rules, especially in public business. [ORIGIN – so named because of the red or pink tape used to bind official documents.] **red top** Brit. a tabloid newspaper. [ORIGIN – from the red background on which the titles of certain British newspapers are printed.]

redact /rɪdakt/ > verb rare edit for publication.

DERIVATIVES – **redaction** noun **redactor** noun.

ORIGIN – from Latin *redigere* 'bring back'.

redden > verb **1** make or become red. **2** blush.

reddle > noun red ochre, used to mark sheep.

ORIGIN – variant of *ruddle*, from obsolete *rud* 'red colour'.

redecorate > verb decorate again or differently.

DERIVATIVES – **redecoration** noun.

rededicate > verb dedicate again.

DERIVATIVES – **rededication** noun.

redeem > verb **1** compensate for the faults or bad aspects of. **2** (**redeem oneself**) make up for one's poor past performance or behaviour. **3** save from sin, error, or evil. **4** fulfil (a pledge or promise). **5** gain or regain possession of (something) in exchange for payment. **6** exchange (a coupon) for goods or money. **7** repay (a stock, bond, etc.) or clear (a debt). **8** archaic buy the freedom of.

DERIVATIVES – **redeemable** adjective.

ORIGIN – Latin *redimere*, from *re-* 'back' + *emere* 'buy'.

redeemer > noun **1** a person who redeems someone or something. **2** (**the Redeemer**) Christ.

redefine > verb define again or differently.

DERIVATIVES – **redefinition** noun.

redemption > noun **1** the action of redeeming or of being redeemed. **2** a thing that saves someone from error or evil.

DERIVATIVES – **redemptive** adjective.

redeploy > verb deploy again or differently.

DERIVATIVES – **redeployment** noun.

redesign > verb design again or differently. > noun the action or process of redesigning something.

redetermine > verb determine again or differently.

DERIVATIVES – **redetermination** noun.

redevelop > verb develop again or differently.

DERIVATIVES – **redeveloper** noun **redevelopment** noun.

redhead > noun a person, especially a woman, with red hair.

red-hot > adjective **1** so hot as to glow red. **2** extremely exciting or popular. **3** very passionate.

COMBINATIONS – **red-hot poker** a plant with tall, erect spikes of tubular flowers, the upper ones of which are red and the lower ones yellow.

redial > verb (**redialled**, **redialling**; US **redialed**, **redialing**) dial (a telephone number) again.

redid past of REDO.

rediffusion > noun Brit. the relaying of broadcast programmes, especially by cable from a central receiver.

Red Indian > noun old-fashioned term for **AMERICAN INDIAN**.

USAGE – avoid using the term **Red Indian**: it is now associated with the stereotypes of cowboys and Indians and the Wild West, and may cause offence. The normal terms in current use are **American Indian** and **Native American** or, if appropriate, the name of the specific people (**Cherokee**, **Iroquois**, and so on).

redingote /reddɪnggōt/ > noun a woman's long coat with a cutaway or contrasting front.

ORIGIN – from *riding coat*.

redirect > verb direct differently.

DERIVATIVES – **redirection** noun.

rediscover > verb discover again.

DERIVATIVES – **rediscovery** noun.

redistribute > verb distribute again or differently.

DERIVATIVES – **redistribution** noun **redistributive** adjective.

redivide > verb divide again or differently.

DERIVATIVES – **redivision** noun.

redivivus /reddɪveevəss/ > adjective (after a noun) literary come back to life; reborn.

ORIGIN – Latin, from *re-* 'again' + *vivus* 'living'.

redneck > *noun* N. Amer. informal, derogatory a working-class white person from the southern US, especially a politically conservative one.

redo > *verb* (**redoes**; past **redid**; past participle **redone**) **1** do again or differently. **2** informal redecorate.

redolent /**redd**ələnt/ > *adjective* **1** (**redolent of** or **with**) strongly reminiscent or suggestive of. **2** (**redolent of** or **with**) literary strongly smelling of. **3** archaic or literary fragrant.
DERIVATIVES – **redolence** *noun* **redolently** *adverb*.
ORIGIN – from Latin *redolere* 'give out a strong smell', from *olere* 'to smell'.

redouble > *verb* make or become much greater, more intense, or more numerous.

redoubt > *noun* a temporary or supplementary fortification, typically square or polygonal and without flanking defences.
ORIGIN – Latin *reductus* 'refuge', from *reducere* 'withdraw'.

redoubtable > *adjective* often humorous (of a person) formidable, especially as an opponent.
DERIVATIVES – **redoubtably** *adverb*.
ORIGIN – Old French *redoutable*, from *redouter* 'to fear'.

redound /ri**downd**/ > *verb* **1** (**redound to**) formal contribute greatly to (a person's credit or honour). **2** (**redound upon**) archaic rebound on.
ORIGIN – Latin *redundare* 'surge', from *unda* 'a wave'.

redox /**ree**doks, **redd**oks/ > *adjective* Chemistry involving both oxidation and reduction.

redpoll /**red**pōl/ > *noun* **1** a small, mainly brown finch with a red forehead. **2** (**red poll**) an animal of a breed of red-haired polled cattle.

redraft > *verb* draft differently.

redraw > *verb* (past **redrew**; past participle **redrawn**) draw or draw up again or differently.

redress > *verb* **1** remedy or set right (an undesirable or unfair situation). **2** archaic set upright again. > *noun* remedy or compensation for a wrong or grievance.
IDIOMS – **redress the balance** restore equality in a situation.
ORIGIN – Old French *redresser*.

re-dress > *verb* dress again or differently.

redshank > *noun* a large sandpiper with long red legs.

redstart > *noun* a small songbird of the thrush family with a reddish tail.
ORIGIN – from **RED** + **START** in the obsolete sense 'tail'.

reduce > *verb* **1** make or become smaller or less in amount, degree, or size. **2** (**reduce to**) change (something) to (a simpler or more basic form). **3** (**reduce to**) bring to (an undesirable state or action). **4** boil (a sauce or other liquid) so that it becomes thicker and more concentrated. **5** archaic conquer (a place). **6** Chemistry cause to combine chemically with hydrogen. **7** Chemistry cause to undergo a reaction in which electrons are gained from another substance or molecule. The opposite of **OXIDISE**. **8** restore (a dislocated body part) to its proper position.
IDIOMS – **reduced circumstances** poverty after relative prosperity. **reduce to the ranks** demote (a non-commissioned officer) to an ordinary soldier.
DERIVATIVES – **reducer** *noun* **reducible** *adjective*.
SYNONYMS – **1** decrease, diminish, lessen, lower, shrink.
ORIGIN – Latin *reducere* 'bring or lead back'.

reductio ad absurdum /ri**duk**tiō ad ab**sur**dəm/ > *noun* Philosophy a method of proving that a premise is false by showing that its logical consequence is absurd or contradictory.
ORIGIN – Latin, 'reduction to the absurd'.

reduction > *noun* **1** the action of reducing something. **2** the amount by which something is reduced. **3** a smaller copy of a picture or photograph. **4** a thick and concentrated liquid or sauce.

reductionism > *noun* often derogatory the analysis and description of a complex phenomenon in terms of its simple or fundamental constituents.
DERIVATIVES – **reductionist** *noun* & *adjective*.

reductive > *adjective* **1** tending to present a subject or problem in a simplified form, especially one viewed as crude. **2** relating to chemical reduction.
DERIVATIVES – **reductively** *adverb* **reductiveness** *noun*.

reductivism > *noun* **1** minimalism. **2** reductionism.

redundant > *adjective* **1** not or no longer needed or useful; superfluous. **2** chiefly Brit. unemployed.
DERIVATIVES – **redundancy** (pl. **redundancies**) *noun* **redundantly** *adverb*.
SYNONYMS – **1** expendable, inessential, superfluous, unnecessary.
ANTONYMS – **1** essential, necessary.
ORIGIN – first used in the sense 'abundant': from Latin *redundare* 'surge'.

reduplicate > *verb* **1** repeat or copy so as to form another of the same kind. **2** repeat (a linguistic element) exactly or with a slight change (e.g. *hurly-burly*).
DERIVATIVES – **reduplication** *noun*.

redux /**ree**duks/ > *adjective* (after a noun) revived; restored.
ORIGIN – Latin, from *reducere* 'bring back'.

redwing > *noun* a small migratory thrush of northern Europe, with red underwings.

redwood > *noun* a giant coniferous tree with reddish wood, native to California and Oregon.

reebok > *noun* variant spelling of **RHEBOK**.

re-echo > *verb* (**re-echoes**, **re-echoed**) echo again or repeatedly.

reed > *noun* **1** a tall, slender-leaved plant growing in water or on marshy ground. **2** reeds or straw used for thatching. **3** literary a rustic musical pipe made from reeds or straw. **4** a piece of thin cane or metal which vibrates in a current of air to produce the sound of various musical instruments, as in the mouthpiece of a clarinet or at the base of some organ pipes. **5** a wind instrument played with a reed.
DERIVATIVES – **reeded** *adjective*.
COMBINATIONS – **broken reed** a weak or impressionable person. **reed mace** a tall reed-like water plant with a dark brown velvety cylindrical flower head. **reed organ** a keyboard instrument similar to a harmonium, in which air is drawn upwards past metal reeds.

re-edit > *verb* (**re-edited**, **re-editing**) edit again.

re-educate > *verb* educate or train to behave or think differently.
DERIVATIVES – **re-education** *noun*.

reedy > *adjective* (**reedier**, **reediest**) **1** (of a sound or voice) high and thin in tone. **2** full of or edged with reeds. **3** (of a person) tall and thin.

reef[1] > *noun* **1** a ridge of jagged rock or coral just above or below the surface of the sea. **2** a vein of gold or other ore.
ORIGIN – Old Norse *rif* 'rib'; compare with **REEF**[2].

reef[2] Sailing > *noun* each of several strips across a sail which can be taken in or rolled up to reduce the area exposed to the wind. > *verb* take in one or more reefs of (a sail).
COMBINATIONS – **reef knot** a double knot made symmetrically to hold securely and cast off easily.
ORIGIN – Old Norse *rif* 'rib'; compare with **REEF**[1].

reefer[1] > *noun* informal a cannabis cigarette.
ORIGIN – perhaps related to Mexican Spanish *grifo* 'smoker of cannabis'.

reefer[2] > *noun* a person who reefs a sail.
COMBINATIONS – **reefer jacket** a thick close-fitting double-breasted jacket.

reefer[3] > *noun* informal a refrigerated truck, railway wagon, or ship.

reek > *verb* **1** have a foul smell. **2** (**reek of**) be suggestive of (something unpleasant). **3** archaic give off smoke, steam, or fumes. > *noun* **1** a foul smell. **2** chiefly Scottish smoke.
DERIVATIVES – **reeky** *adjective*.

ORIGIN – Old English, 'give out smoke or vapour'.

reel > *noun* **1** a cylinder on which film, wire, thread, etc. can be wound. **2** a part of a film. **3** a lively Scottish or Irish folk dance with music in simple or duple time. > *verb* **1** (**reel in**) wind on or bring towards one by turning a reel. **2** (**reel off**) say or recite rapidly and effortlessly. **3** dance a reel. **4** stagger or lurch violently. **5** feel giddy or bewildered.

DERIVATIVES – **reeler** *noun*.

COMBINATIONS – **reel-to-reel** (of a tape recorder) having tape that passes between two reels mounted separately rather than within a cassette.

re-elect > *verb* elect again.

DERIVATIVES – **re-election** *noun*.

re-emerge > *verb* emerge again.

DERIVATIVES – **re-emergence** *noun* **re-emergent** *adjective*.

re-emphasise (also **re-emphasize**) > *verb* emphasise again.

DERIVATIVES – **re-emphasis** *noun*.

re-enact > *verb* **1** act out (a past event). **2** enact (a repealed law) once more.

DERIVATIVES – **re-enactment** *noun*.

re-engineer > *verb* **1** redesign (a machine). **2** restructure (a company).

re-enter > *verb* enter again.

DERIVATIVES – **re-entrance** *noun*.

re-entrant > *adjective* (of an angle) pointing inwards. The opposite of SALIENT.

re-entry > *noun* (pl. **re-entries**) **1** the action or process of re-entering. **2** the return of a spacecraft or missile into the earth's atmosphere.

reeve[1] > *noun* historical a local official, in particular the chief magistrate of a town or district in Anglo-Saxon England.

reeve[2] > *verb* (past and past participle **rove** or **reeved**) Nautical thread (a rope or rod) through a ring or other aperture.

ORIGIN – probably from Dutch *reven*, related to REEF[2].

reeve[3] > *noun* a female ruff (bird).

re-examine > *verb* **1** examine again or further. **2** Law examine (a witness) again, after cross-examination by the opposing counsel.

DERIVATIVES – **re-examination** *noun*.

re-export > *verb* /ree-ik**sport**/ export (imported goods), typically after further processing or manufacture. > *noun* /ree-ek**sport**/ **1** the action of re-exporting. **2** a thing that has or will be re-exported.

DERIVATIVES – **re-exportation** *noun* **re-exporter** *noun*.

ref > *noun* informal (in sports) a referee.

ref. > *abbreviation* **1** reference. **2** refer to.

reface > *verb* put a new facing on (a building).

refection > *noun* literary or archaic **1** refreshment by food or drink. **2** a meal or snack.

ORIGIN – Latin, from *reficere* 'refresh, renew'.

refectory > *noun* (pl. **refectories**) a room used for communal meals, especially in an educational or religious institution.

COMBINATIONS – **refectory table** a long, narrow table.

refer > *verb* (**referred**, **referring**) **1** (**refer to**) mention or allude to. **2** (**refer to**) direct the attention of (someone) to. **3** (**refer to**) (of a word or phrase) describe or denote. **4** (**refer to**) pass (a person or matter) to (a higher body) for a decision. **5** (**refer to**) archaic trace or attribute something to (a cause or source). **6** fail (a candidate in an examination).

IDIOMS – **refer to drawer** Brit. a phrase used by banks when suspending payment of a cheque.

DERIVATIVES – **referable** *adjective* **referrer** *noun*.

COMBINATIONS – **referred pain** Medicine pain felt in a part of the body other than its actual source.

ORIGIN – Latin *referre* 'carry back'.

referee > *noun* **1** an official who supervises a game or match to ensure that the rules are adhered to. **2** a person willing to testify about the character or ability of a person applying for a job. **3** a person appointed to examine and assess an academic work for publication. > *verb* (**referees**, **refereed**, **refereeing**) be a referee of.

reference > *noun* **1** the action of referring to something. **2** a mention or citation of a source of information in a book or article. **3** a letter from a previous employer testifying to someone's ability or reliability. > *verb* provide (a book or article) with references.

WORDFINDER – *textual references:* ff. (*following pages*), ibid. (*in the same source*), loc. cit. (*in the passage already cited*), op. cit. (*in the work already cited*), passim (*at various places*), vide (*see*).

IDIOMS – **terms of reference** the scope and limitations of an activity or area of knowledge. **with** (or **in**) **reference to** in relation to; as regards.

COMBINATIONS – **reference library** a library in which the books are to be consulted rather than borrowed. **reference point** a basis or standard for evaluation or comparison.

referendum /reffə**ren**dəm/ > *noun* (pl. **referendums** or **referenda** /reffə**ren**də/) a general vote by the electorate on a single political question which has been referred to them for a direct decision.

ORIGIN – Latin, 'something to be referred'.

referent /**reff**ərənt/ > *noun* Linguistics the thing in the world that a word or phrase denotes or stands for.

referential > *adjective* **1** containing or of the nature of a reference or references. **2** Linguistics relating to a referent, in particular having the external world rather than a text or language as a referent.

DERIVATIVES – **referentiality** *noun* **referentially** *adverb*.

referral > *noun* the action of referring someone or something for consultation or review, especially the directing of a patient by a GP to a specialist.

refill > *verb* /ree**fill**/ fill or become full again. > *noun* /**ree**fill/ an act of refilling or a glass that is refilled.

DERIVATIVES – **refillable** *adjective*.

refinance > *verb* finance again, typically with new loans at a lower rate of interest.

refine > *verb* **1** remove impurities or unwanted elements from. **2** make minor changes so as to improve (a theory or method).

DERIVATIVES – **refiner** *noun*.

SYNONYMS – **1** cleanse, distil, purify. **2** fine-tune, hone, polish.

ORIGIN – from RE- + FINE[1].

refined > *adjective* **1** with impurities or unwanted elements having been removed by processing. **2** elegant and cultured.

SYNONYMS – **1** distilled, purified. **2** civilised, cultivated, cultured, genteel, polished.

ANTONYMS – **1** crude. **2** coarse, common.

refinement > *noun* **1** the process of refining. **2** an improvement or clarification brought about by the making of small changes. **3** cultured elegance or superior taste.

refinery > *noun* (pl. **refineries**) an industrial installation where a substance is refined.

refinish > *verb* apply a new finish to (a surface or object). > *noun* an act of refinishing a surface or object.

refit > *verb* (**refitted**, **refitting**) replace or repair machinery, equipment, and fittings in (a ship, building, etc.). > *noun* an act of refitting.

reflate > *verb* (of a government) expand the level of output of (an economy).

DERIVATIVES – **reflation** *noun* **reflationary** *noun*.

reflect > *verb* **1** throw back (heat, light, or sound) without absorbing it. **2** (of a mirror or shiny surface) show an image of. **3** represent in a faithful or appropriate way. **4** (**reflect well** or **badly on**) bring about a good or bad impression of. **5** (often **reflect on**) think deeply or carefully about (something).

SYNONYMS – **3** demonstrate, evidence, exhibit, illustrate, reveal, show. **5** (**reflect on**) chew over, contemplate, mull over, ponder, ruminate on.

COMBINATIONS – **reflecting telescope** a

telescope in which a mirror is used to collect and focus light.

ORIGIN – Latin *reflectere* 'to bend back'.

reflectance > *noun* Physics a property of a surface equal to the proportion of light shining on it which it reflects or scatters.

reflection > *noun* 1 the phenomenon of light, heat, sound, etc. being reflected. 2 something reflected or an image so formed. 3 (usu. **reflection on**) a thing bringing discredit. 4 serious thought or consideration.

reflective > *adjective* 1 providing or produced by reflection. 2 thoughtful.

DERIVATIVES – **reflectively** *adverb* **reflectiveness** *noun* **reflectivity** *noun*.

reflector > *noun* 1 a piece of reflective material, e.g. a red one on the back of a motor vehicle or bicycle. 2 an object or device which reflects radio waves, sound, or other waves. 3 a reflecting telescope.

reflex > *noun* 1 an action performed without conscious thought as a response to a stimulus. 2 a thing that reproduces the essential features or qualities of something else. 3 archaic a reflected source of light. > *adjective* 1 performed as a reflex. 2 (of an angle) exceeding 180°. 3 archaic (of light) reflected. 4 archaic bent or turned backwards.

DERIVATIVES – **reflexly** *adverb*.

SYNONYMS – *adjective* 1 automatic, instinctive, involuntary, mechanical, unconscious.

COMBINATIONS – **reflex camera** a camera with a ground-glass focusing screen on which the image is formed by a combination of lens and mirror, enabling a scene to be correctly composed and focused.

reflexible > *adjective* chiefly technical capable of being reflected.

reflexion > *noun* archaic spelling of REFLECTION.

reflexive > *adjective* 1 Grammar (of a pronoun) referring back to the subject of the clause in which it is used, e.g. *myself*. 2 Grammar (of a verb or clause) having a reflexive pronoun as its object, e.g. *wash oneself*. 3 performed without conscious thought; reflex.

DERIVATIVES – **reflexively** *adverb* **reflexivity** *noun*.

reflexology /reefleks**oll**əji/ > *noun* a system of massage used to relieve tension and treat illness, based on the theory that there are points on the feet, hands, and head linked to every part of the body.

DERIVATIVES – **reflexologist** *noun*.

refloat > *verb* set afloat again.

refluent /**ref**looənt/ > *adjective* literary flowing back; ebbing.

DERIVATIVES – **refluence** *noun*.

reflux /**ree**fluks/ > *noun* 1 Chemistry the process of boiling a liquid so that any vapour is liquefied and returned to the stock. 2 technical the flowing back of a bodily fluid.

refocus > *verb* (**refocused, refocusing** or **refocussed, refocussing**) 1 adjust the focus of (a lens or one's eyes). 2 focus (attention or resources) on something new or different.

reforest > *verb* replant with trees; cover again with forest.

DERIVATIVES – **reforestation** *noun*.

reform > *verb* 1 make changes in (something) in order to improve it. 2 cause (someone) to abandon an immoral or criminal lifestyle. > *noun* the action or process of reforming.

DERIVATIVES – **reformable** *adjective* **reformative** *adjective* **reformed** *adjective* **reformer** *noun*.

SYNONYMS – *verb* 1 improve, reconstitute, remodel, reorganise, revolutionise.

COMBINATIONS – **Reformed Church** a Church that has accepted the principles of the Reformation, especially a Calvinist Church (as distinct from Lutheran). **Reform Judaism** a form of Judaism which has reformed or abandoned aspects of Orthodox Jewish worship and ritual. **reform school** historical an institution to which young offenders were sent as an alternative to prison.

ORIGIN – Latin *reformare* 'form or shape again'.

re-form > *verb* form or cause to form again.

DERIVATIVES – **re-formation** *noun*.

reformat > *verb* (**reformatted, reformatting**) chiefly Computing give a new format to.

reformation /refferr**may**sh'n/ > *noun* 1 the action or process of reforming. 2 (**the Reformation**) a 16th-century movement to reform abuses in the Roman Catholic Church, ending in the establishment of the Reformed and Protestant Churches.

reformatory > *noun* (pl. **reformatories**) N. Amer. dated an institution to which young offenders are sent as an alternative to prison. > *adjective* tending or intended to produce reform.

reformist > *adjective* supporting or advocating gradual reform rather than abolition or revolution. > *noun* a supporter or advocate of such a policy.

DERIVATIVES – **reformism** *noun*.

reformulate > *verb* formulate again or differently.

DERIVATIVES – **reformulation** *noun*.

refract > *verb* (of water, air, or glass) make (a ray of light) change direction when it enters at an angle.

COMBINATIONS – **refracting telescope** a telescope which uses a lens to collect and focus the light.

ORIGIN – Latin *refringere* 'break up'.

refraction > *noun* the fact or phenomenon of being refracted.

refractive > *adjective* of or involving refraction.

DERIVATIVES – **refractively** *adverb*.

COMBINATIONS – **refractive index** the ratio of the velocity of light in a vacuum to its velocity in a specified medium.

refractor > *noun* 1 a lens or other object which causes refraction. 2 a refracting telescope.

refractory > *adjective* 1 formal stubborn or unmanageable. 2 Medicine not yielding to treatment. 3 technical heat-resistant; hard to melt or fuse.

DERIVATIVES – **refractoriness** *noun*.

ORIGIN – Latin *refractarius* 'stubborn'.

refrain[1] > *verb* (usu. **refrain from**) stop oneself from doing something.

SYNONYMS – (**refrain from**) abstain from, avoid, desist from, eschew, forbear from.

ORIGIN – Latin *refrenare*, from *frenum* 'bridle'.

refrain[2] > *noun* a repeated line or section in a poem or song, typically at the end of each verse.

ORIGIN – from Latin *refringere* 'break up' (because the refrain 'broke' the sequence).

refrangible > *adjective* able to be refracted.

DERIVATIVES – **refrangibility** *noun*.

refresh > *verb* 1 give new strength or energy to. 2 stimulate (someone's memory) by going over previous information. 3 revise or update (skills, knowledge, etc.).

SYNONYMS – 1 energise, enliven, reinvigorate, rejuvenate, revitalise, revive. 2 jog, prompt.

refresher > *noun* 1 an activity that refreshes one's skills or knowledge. 2 Law, Brit. an extra fee payable to counsel in a prolonged case.

refreshing > *adjective* 1 serving to refresh. 2 welcome or stimulating because new or different.

DERIVATIVES – **refreshingly** *adverb*.

SYNONYMS – 1 energising, invigorating, restorative, revitalising, reviving, stimulating. 2 different, fresh, novel.

refreshment > *noun* 1 a light snack or drink. 2 the giving of fresh strength or energy.

refried beans > *plural noun* (in Mexican cooking) pinto beans boiled and fried in advance and reheated when required.

refrigerant > *noun* a substance used for refrigeration. > *adjective* causing cooling or refrigeration.

refrigerate > *verb* subject (food or drink) to cold in order to chill or preserve it.

DERIVATIVES – **refrigeration** *noun*.

ORIGIN – Latin *refrigerare* 'make cool', from *frigus* 'cold'.

817

refrigerator > *noun* an appliance or compartment which is artificially kept cool and used to store food and drink.

refuel > *verb* (**refuelled, refuelling; US refueled, refueling**) supply or be supplied with more fuel.

refuge > *noun* **1** a place or state of safety from danger or trouble. **2** Brit. a traffic island.
SYNONYMS – **1** asylum, sanctuary, shelter.
ORIGIN – Latin *refugium*, from *fugere* 'flee'.

refugee > *noun* a person who has been forced to leave their country in order to escape war, persecution, or natural disaster.
SYNONYMS – asylum seeker, displaced person, exile, outcast.

refulgent /rifulʒənt/ > *adjective* literary shining very brightly.
DERIVATIVES – **refulgence** *noun* **refulgently** *adverb*.
ORIGIN – from Latin *refulgere* 'shine out'.

refund > *verb* /rifund/ pay back (money) to (someone). > *noun* /reefund/ a refunded sum of money.
DERIVATIVES – **refundable** *adjective*.
SYNONYMS – *verb* reimburse, repay. *noun* rebate, reimbursement, repayment.
ORIGIN – Latin *refundere* 'pour back'.

refurbish > *verb* renovate and redecorate (a building).
DERIVATIVES – **refurbishment** *noun*.

refuse[1] /rifyōoz/ > *verb* **1** indicate that one is unwilling to do, accept, or grant (something). **2** informal (of a thing) fail to perform a required action: *the car refused to start*. **3** (of a horse) decline to jump (a fence or other obstacle).
DERIVATIVES – **refusal** *noun* **refuser** *noun*.
SYNONYMS – **1** decline, rebuff, reject, spurn.
ORIGIN – Old French *refuser*, probably an alteration of Latin *recusare* 'to refuse'.

refuse[2] /refyōoss/ > *noun* matter thrown away as worthless.
SYNONYMS – detritus, garbage, litter, rubbish, waste; chiefly N. Amer. trash.
ORIGIN – perhaps from Old French *refusé* 'refused'.

refusenik /rifyōoznik/ > *noun* **1** a Jew in the former Soviet Union who was refused permission to emigrate to Israel. **2** a person who refuses to comply with orders or the law as a protest.

refute /rifyōot/ > *verb* prove (a statement or the person advancing it) to be wrong.
DERIVATIVES – **refutable** *adjective* **refutation** *noun*.
USAGE – strictly speaking, **refute** means 'prove (a statement) to be wrong'; it does not mean simply 'deny', although many people use it in this sense.
SYNONYMS – discredit, disprove, invalidate, negate, rebut.
ANTONYMS – confirm.
ORIGIN – Latin *refutare* 'repel, rebut'.

regain > *verb* **1** obtain possession or use of (something) again after losing it. **2** get back to (a place or position).
SYNONYMS – **1** recapture, reclaim, recoup, recover, repossess, retrieve.

regal > *adjective* of, resembling, or fit for a king or queen, especially in being magnificent or dignified.
DERIVATIVES – **regally** *adverb*.
SYNONYMS – kingly, majestic, princely, queenly, royal.
ORIGIN – Latin *regalis*, from *rex* 'king'.

regale /rigayl/ > *verb* **1** entertain with conversation. **2** lavishly supply with food or drink.
ORIGIN – French *régaler*, from Old French *gale* 'pleasure'.

regalia /rigaylia/ > *plural noun* (treated as sing. or pl.) **1** the insignia of royalty, especially the crown and other ornaments used at a coronation. **2** the distinctive clothing and trappings of high office, worn at formal occasions.
USAGE – the word **regalia** comes from Latin and is, technically speaking, the plural of the adjective *regalis* 'royal'. However, in modern English use it behaves as a collective noun, similarly to words like **staff** or **government**, which means that it can be used with either a singular or plural verb.
ORIGIN – Latin, 'royal privileges'.

regality > *noun* (pl. **regalities**) **1** the state of being a monarch. **2** regal manner or bearing. **3** historical (in Scotland) territorial jurisdiction granted by the king to a powerful subject.

regard > *verb* **1** consider in a particular way. **2** gaze at in a specified fashion. **3** archaic pay attention to. > *noun* **1** heed or concern. **2** high opinion; esteem. **3** (**regards**) best wishes (used especially at the end of letters). **4** a steady look.
IDIOMS – **as regards** concerning. **in this** (or **that**) **regard** in connection with the point previously mentioned. **with** (or **in** or **having**) **regard to** as concerns.
SYNONYMS – *verb* **1** account, consider, deem, perceive, view. **2** contemplate, gaze at, look at, study, view.
ORIGIN – Old French *regarder* 'to watch', from *garder* 'to guard'.

regardful > *adjective* (**regardful of**) formal mindful of.

regarding > *preposition* about; concerning.

regardless > *adverb* despite the prevailing circumstances.
IDIOMS – **regardless of** without regard for.

regatta > *noun* a sporting event consisting of a series of boat or yacht races.
ORIGIN – Italian, 'a fight or contest'.

regency /reejənsi/ > *noun* (pl. **regencies**) **1** the office or period of government by a regent. **2** a commission acting as regent. **3** (**the Regency**) the period of the regency in Britain (1811–20) or France (1715–23). > *adjective* (**Regency**) in the neoclassical style of British architecture, clothing, and furniture popular during the late 18th and early 19th centuries.

regenerate > *verb* /rijennərayt/ **1** regrow (new tissue). **2** bring new and more vigorous life to (an area or institution). **3** (especially in Christian use) give a new and higher spiritual nature to. > *adjective* /rijennərət/ reborn, especially in a spiritual or moral sense.
DERIVATIVES – **regeneration** *noun* **regenerative** *adjective* **regenerator** *noun*.

regent > *noun* a person appointed to administer a state because the monarch is a minor or is absent or unfit to rule. > *adjective* (**after a noun**) acting as regent: *Prince Regent*.
ORIGIN – from Latin *regere* 'to rule'.

reggae /reggay/ > *noun* a style of popular music with a strongly accented subsidiary beat, originating in Jamaica.
ORIGIN – perhaps related to Jamaican English *rege-rege* 'quarrel, row'.

regicide /rejisīd/ > *noun* **1** the killing of a king. **2** a person who kills a king.
DERIVATIVES – **regicidal** *adjective*.
ORIGIN – from Latin *rex* 'king'.

regime /rayzheem/ > *noun* **1** a government, especially an authoritarian one. **2** a systematic or ordered way of doing something. **3** the conditions under which a scientific or industrial process occurs.
ORIGIN – French, from Latin *regimen* 'rule'; 'regimen' was the original sense in English.

regimen /rejimən/ > *noun* **1** a therapeutic course of medical treatment, often including recommendations as to diet and exercise. **2** archaic a system of government.
ORIGIN – Latin, from *regere* 'to rule'.

regiment > *noun* /rejimənt/ **1** a permanent unit of an army, typically divided into several smaller units and often into two battalions. **2** a large number of people or things. **3** archaic rule or government. > *verb* /rejiment/ organise according to a strict system.
DERIVATIVES – **regimentation** *noun*.
ORIGIN – Latin *regimentum* 'rule', from *regere* 'to rule'.

regimental > *adjective* relating to a regiment. > *noun* (**regimentals**) military uniform, especially that of a particular regiment.
DERIVATIVES – **regimentally** *adverb*.

Regina /rijīnə/ > *noun* the reigning queen (used following a name or in the titles of lawsuits, e.g. *Regina v. Jones*, the Crown versus Jones).
ORIGIN – Latin, 'queen'.

region > *noun* **1** an area of a country or the world having definable characteristics but not always fixed boundaries. **2** an administrative district of a city or country. **3** (**the regions**) the parts of a country outside the capital or chief seat of government. **4** a part of the body, especially around or near an organ.
IDIOMS – **in the region of** approximately.
ORIGIN – Latin, 'direction, district', from *regere* 'to rule, direct'.

regional > *adjective* **1** relating to or characteristic of a region. **2** relating to the regions of a country rather than the capital: *a regional accent*.
DERIVATIVES – **regionalise** (also **regionalize**) *verb* **regionally** *adverb*.

regionalism > *noun* **1** regional rather than central administration or economic, cultural, or political affiliation. **2** a linguistic feature peculiar to a particular region.
DERIVATIVES – **regionalist** *noun* & *adjective*.

register > *noun* **1** an official list or record. **2** a record of attendance, for example of pupils in a class. **3** a particular part of the range of a voice or instrument. **4** a variety of a language in terms of its degree of formality. **5** (in printing and photography) exact correspondence of the position of colour components or of printed matter. **6** a sliding device controlling a set of organ pipes, or a set of organ pipes so controlled. **7** a plate for widening or narrowing an opening and regulating a draught, especially in a fire grate. **8** (in electronic devices) a location in a store of data. > *verb* **1** enter in or place on a register. **2** put one's name on a register, especially as an eligible voter or as a guest in a hotel. **3** express (an opinion or emotion). **4** (of an emotion) show in a person's face or gestures. **5** become aware of: *he had not even registered her presence.* **6** (of an instrument) detect and show (a reading) automatically.
DERIVATIVES – **registrable** *adjective*.
COMBINATIONS – **registered post** Brit. a postal procedure with special precautions for safety and for compensation in case of loss.
ORIGIN – Latin *registrum*, from *regesta* 'things recorded', from *regerere* 'enter, record'.

register office > *noun* (in the UK) a local government building where civil marriages are conducted and births, marriages, and deaths are recorded.
NOTE – the official term is **register office**, although the form **registry office** is commonly used in unofficial and informal contexts.

registrant > *noun* a person who registers.

registrar /**rej**istraar, reji**straar**/ > *noun* **1** an official responsible for keeping a register or official records. **2** the chief administrative officer in a university. **3** (in the UK) the judicial and administrative officer of the High Court. **4** Brit. a middle-ranking hospital doctor undergoing training as a specialist.
COMBINATIONS – **Registrar General** a government official responsible for holding a population census.

registration > *noun* **1** the action or process of registering or of being registered. **2** (also **registration mark** or **registration number**) Brit. the series of letters and figures used to indentify a motor vehicle, displayed on a number plate.

registry > *noun* (pl. **registries**) **1** a place where registers are kept. **2** registration.

registry office > *noun* see **REGISTER OFFICE**.

Regius professor /**ree**jəss/ > *noun* (in the UK) the holder of a university chair founded by a sovereign or filled by Crown appointment.
ORIGIN – from Latin *regius* 'royal'.

regnal /**reg**n'l/ > *adjective* of a reign or monarch.

regnant /**reg**nənt/ > *adjective* **1** reigning. **2** formal dominant.

regrade > *verb* grade again or differently.

regress > *verb* /ri**gress**/ **1** return to a former state. **2** return mentally to a former stage of life or a supposed previous life. > *noun* /**ree**gress/ the action of regressing.
SYNONYMS – *verb* **1** relapse, retrogress, revert.
ORIGIN – Latin *regredi* 'go back, return'.

regression > *noun* **1** a return to a former state. **2** a return to an earlier stage of life or a supposed previous life.

regressive > *adjective* **1** tending to regress or characterised by regression. **2** (of a tax) taking a proportionally greater amount from those on lower incomes.
DERIVATIVES – **regressively** *adverb* **regressiveness** *noun*.

regret > *verb* (**regretted, regretting**) feel or express sorrow, repentance, or disappointment over. > *noun* **1** a feeling of sorrow, repentance, or disappointment. **2** (often **one's regrets**) used in polite formulas to express apology or sadness.
SYNONYMS – *noun* **1** contrition, remorse, repentance, sadness, sorrow.
ORIGIN – Old French *regreter* 'lament the dead'.

regretful > *adjective* feeling or showing regret.
DERIVATIVES – **regretfulness** *noun*.
USAGE – do not confuse **regretful** with **regrettable**, which means 'giving rise to regret; undesirable'.

regretfully > *adverb* **1** in a regretful manner. **2** it is regrettable that.
USAGE – the established sense of **regretfully** is 'in a regretful manner', as in *he sighed regretfully.* However, it is now sometimes used with the meaning 'it is regrettable that, regrettably', as in *regretfully, the trustees must turn down your request,* although traditionalists object to this use. For more information on disputed use of adverbs of this type, see the note at **HOPEFULLY**.

regrettable > *adjective* giving rise to regret; undesirable.
DERIVATIVES – **regrettably** *adverb*.
USAGE – do not confuse **regrettable** with **regretful**, which means 'feeling or showing regret'.
SYNONYMS – lamentable, reprehensible, undesirable, unfortunate, unwelcome.

regroup > *verb* reassemble into organised groups, typically after being attacked or defeated.
DERIVATIVES – **regroupment** *noun*.

regrow > *verb* (past **regrew**; past participle **regrown**) grow again.
DERIVATIVES – **regrowth** *noun*.

regular > *adjective* **1** arranged or recurring in a constant or definite pattern, especially with the same space between individual instances. **2** doing the same thing often or at uniform intervals. **3** done or happening frequently. **4** conforming to or governed by an accepted standard of procedure or convention. **5** usual or customary. **6** Grammar (of a word) following the normal pattern of inflection. **7** (of merchandise) of average size. **8** of or belonging to the permanent professional armed forces of a country. **9** chiefly N. Amer. of an ordinary kind. **10** Geometry (of a figure) having all sides and all angles equal. **11** Christian Church subject to or bound by religious rule. **12** informal, dated rightly so called; complete; absolute: *this place is a regular fisherman's paradise.* > *noun* **1** a regular customer, member of a team, etc. **2** a regular member of the armed forces.
DERIVATIVES – **regularity** *noun* (pl. **regularities**) **regularly** *adverb*.
COMBINATIONS – **regular canon** see **CANON²**. **regular guy** N. Amer. informal an ordinary, uncomplicated, sociable man.
ORIGIN – Latin *regularis*, from *regula* 'rule'.

regularise (also **regularize**) > *verb* **1** make (something) regular. **2** establish (a hitherto temporary or provisional arrangement) on an official or correct basis.
DERIVATIVES – **regularisation** *noun*.

regulate > *verb* **1** control or maintain the rate or speed of (a machine or process). **2** control or supervise by means of rules and regulations.
DERIVATIVES – **regulative** *adjective* **regulator** *noun* **regulatory** *adjective*.
SYNONYMS – **2** administer, control, govern, monitor, oversee, supervise.

regulation > *noun* **1** a rule or directive made and maintained by an authority. **2** (before another noun) informal of a familiar or predictable type. **3** the action or process of regulating or being regulated.

regulo /**reg**yoolō/ > *noun* Brit. trademark used before a numeral to denote a setting on a temperature scale in a gas oven.

regurgitate /ri**gur**jitayt/ > *verb* **1** bring (swallowed food) up again to the mouth. **2** repeat (information) without analysing or comprehending it.
DERIVATIVES – **regurgitation** *noun*.
ORIGIN – Latin *regurgitare*, from *gurges* 'whirlpool'.

rehab /**ree**hab/ > *noun* informal rehabilitation.

rehabilitate /reehə**bill**itayt/ > *verb* **1** restore to health or normal life by training and therapy after imprisonment, addiction, or illness. **2** restore the standing or reputation of. **3** restore to a former condition.
DERIVATIVES – **rehabilitation** *noun* **rehabilitative** *adjective*.
ORIGIN – Latin *rehabilitare*, from *habilitare* 'make able'.

rehash > *verb* reuse (old ideas or material) without significant change or improvement. > *noun* an instance of rehashing.

rehearsal > *noun* **1** a trial performance of a play or other work for later public performance. **2** the action or process of rehearsing.

rehearse > *verb* **1** practise (a play, piece of music, or other work) for later public performance. **2** state (a list of points that have been made many times before).
SYNONYMS – **1** go over, practise, run through. **2** recapitulate, reiterate, repeat, restate.
ORIGIN – first used in the sense 'repeat aloud': from Old French *rehercier*, perhaps from *hercer* 'to harrow'; see also **HEARSE**.

reheat > *verb* heat again. > *noun* the use of the hot exhaust to burn extra fuel in a jet engine and produce extra power.

rehoboam /reehə**bō**əm/ > *noun* a wine bottle of about six times the standard size.
ORIGIN – from the name of *Rehoboam*, a king of ancient Israel.

rehouse > *verb* provide with new housing.

rehydrate > *verb* absorb or cause to absorb moisture after dehydration.
DERIVATIVES – **rehydration** *noun*.

Reich /rīk, rīkh/ > *noun* the former German state, in particular the **Third Reich** (the Nazi regime, 1933–45).
ORIGIN – German, 'empire'.

reify /**ree**ifī/ > *verb* (**reifies**, **reified**) formal make (something abstract) more concrete or real.
DERIVATIVES – **reification** *noun*.
ORIGIN – from Latin *res* 'thing'.

reign > *verb* **1** rule as monarch. **2** prevail: *confusion reigned*. **3** (**reigning**) (of a sports player or team) currently holding a particular title. > *noun* **1** the period of rule of a monarch. **2** the period during which someone or something is predominant or pre-eminent.
WORDFINDER – interregnum (*period between two successive reigns*), regnal (*relating to a reign*).
ORIGIN – Old French *reignier* 'to reign', from Latin *regnum* 'kingdom, reign'.

reimburse /ree-im**burss**/ > *verb* repay (money) to (a person who has spent or lost it).
DERIVATIVES – **reimbursement** *noun*.
ORIGIN – from obsolete *imburse* 'put in a purse', from Latin *bursa* 'purse'.

reimport > *verb* /ree-im**port**/ import (goods processed or made from exported materials). > *noun* /ree**im**port/ **1** the action of reimporting. **2** a reimported item.
DERIVATIVES – **reimportation** *noun*.

rein > *noun* **1** a long, narrow strap attached at one end to a horse's bit, used in pairs to guide or check a horse. **2** (**reins**) the power to direct and control. > *verb* **1** check or guide (a horse) by pulling on its reins. **2** (often **rein in** or **back**) restrain.
IDIOMS – (**a**) **free rein** freedom of action or expression. **keep a tight rein on** exercise strict control over.
USAGE – note that the correct idiomatic phrase is **free rein** or **a free rein**, deriving from the literal meaning of using reins to control a horse, not **free reign**.
ORIGIN – Old French *rene*, from Latin *retinere* 'retain'.

reincarnate > *verb* /ree-in**kaar**nayt/ (usu. **be reincarnated**) cause (someone) to undergo rebirth in another body. > *adjective* /ree-in**kaar**nət/ (after a noun) reborn in another body.

reincarnation > *noun* **1** the rebirth of a soul in a new body. **2** a person in whom a soul is believed to have been reborn. **3** a new version of something from the past.

reindeer > *noun* (pl. same or **reindeers**) a deer with large branching antlers, native to the northern tundra and subarctic.
ORIGIN – from Old Norse *hreinn* 'reindeer' + *dýr* 'deer'.

reinforce > *verb* **1** strengthen (a military force) with additional personnel or material. **2** give added strength to.
DERIVATIVES – **reinforcer** *noun*.
SYNONYMS – **2** bolster, buttress, fortify, strengthen, toughen.
COMBINATIONS – **reinforced concrete** concrete in which metal bars or wire are embedded to strengthen it.
ORIGIN – French *renforcer*, influenced by *inforce*, an obsolete spelling of **ENFORCE**.

reinforcement > *noun* **1** the action or process of reinforcing. **2** (**reinforcements**) extra personnel sent to strengthen a military force.

reinstate > *verb* restore to a former position or state.
DERIVATIVES – **reinstatement** *noun*.

reinsure > *verb* (of an insurer) transfer (all or part of a risk) to another insurer to provide protection against the risk of the first insurance.
DERIVATIVES – **reinsurance** *noun* **reinsurer** *noun*.

reinterpret > *verb* (**reinterpreted**, **reinterpreting**) interpret in a new or different light.
DERIVATIVES – **reinterpretation** *noun*.

reintroduce > *verb* **1** bring (something) into effect again. **2** put (a species of animal or plant) back into a former habitat.
DERIVATIVES – **reintroduction** *noun*.

reinvent > *verb* change (something) so much that appears entirely new.
IDIOMS – **reinvent the wheel** waste a great deal of time or effort in creating something that already exists.
DERIVATIVES – **reinvention** *noun*.

reinvest > *verb* put (the profit on a previous investment) back into the same scheme.
DERIVATIVES – **reinvestment** *noun*.

reinvigorate > *verb* give new energy or strength to.
DERIVATIVES – **reinvigoration** *noun*.

reissue > *verb* (**reissues**, **reissued**, **reissuing**) make a new supply or different form of (a book, record, or other product) available for sale. > *noun* a new issue of such a product.

reiterate > *verb* say something again or repeatedly.
DERIVATIVES – **reiteration** *noun*.
ORIGIN – Latin *reiterare* 'go over again'.

reive /reev/ > *verb* historical (in the Scottish Borders) carry out raids to plunder and steal cattle.
DERIVATIVES – **reiver** *noun*.
ORIGIN – variant of archaic *reave* 'to plunder'.

reject > *verb* /ri**jekt**/ **1** dismiss as inadequate or faulty. **2** refuse to consider or agree to. **3** fail to show due affection or concern for. **4** Medicine show a damaging immune response to (a transplanted organ or tissue). > *noun* /**ree**jekt/ a rejected person or thing.
DERIVATIVES – **rejection** *noun*.
ORIGIN – Latin *reicere* 'throw back'.

rejig > *verb* (**rejigged**, **rejigging**) chiefly Brit. **1** organise differently; rearrange. **2** dated re-equip or refit.

rejoice > *verb* feel or show great joy.
DERIVATIVES – **rejoicing** *noun* & *adjective*.
SYNONYMS – celebrate, delight, exult, glory, triumph.
ORIGIN – Old French *rejoir*, from *joir* 'experience joy'.

rejoin[1] /ree**joyn**/ > *verb* **1** join together again. **2** return to (a companion or route that one has left).

rejoin² /riˈjoyn/ > *verb* say in reply; retort.

ORIGIN – Old French *rejoindre*, from *joindre* 'to join'.

rejoinder > *noun* **1** a sharp or witty reply. **2** Law, dated a defendant's answer to the plaintiff's reply.

rejuvenate /riˈjoovənayt/ > *verb* make or cause to appear younger, fresher, or more lively.

DERIVATIVES – **rejuvenation** *noun* **rejuvenator** *noun*.

SYNONYMS – invigorate, refresh, revitalise, revive.

ORIGIN – from Latin *juvenis* 'young'.

rekindle > *verb* **1** relight (a fire). **2** revive (something lapsed or lost).

relaid past and past participle of **RELAY²**.

relapse /riˈlaps/ > *verb* **1** (of a sick or injured person) deteriorate after a period of improvement. **2** (**relapse into**) return to (a worse or less active state). > *noun* /also **ree**laps/ a deterioration in health after a temporary improvement.

ORIGIN – Latin *relabi* 'slip back'.

relate > *verb* **1** give an account of. **2** (**be related**) be connected by blood or marriage. **3** establish a causal connection between. **4** (**relate to**) have reference to; concern. **5** (**relate to**) feel sympathy with.

DERIVATIVES – **relater** (also **relator**) *noun*.

SYNONYMS – **1** communicate, impart, narrate, recount, report, tell. **3** associate, connect, link. **5** (**relate to**) empathise with, identify with, respond to, sympathise with.

ORIGIN – Latin *referre* 'bring back'.

related > *adjective* belonging to the same family, group, or type; connected.

DERIVATIVES – **relatedness** *noun*.

relation > *noun* **1** the way in which two or more people or things are connected or related. **2** (**relations**) the way in which two or more people or groups feel about and behave towards each other. **3** a relative. **4** (**relations**) formal sexual intercourse. **5** the action of telling a story.

IDIOMS – **in relation to** in connection with.

DERIVATIVES – **relational** *adjective*.

relationship > *noun* **1** the way in which two or more people or things are connected, or the state of being connected. **2** the way in which two or more people or groups regard and behave towards each other. **3** an emotional and sexual association between two people.

relative /ˈrellətiv/ > *adjective* **1** considered in relation or in proportion to something else. **2** existing or possessing a characteristic only in comparison to something else; not absolute. **3** Grammar (of a pronoun, determiner, or adverb) referring to an expressed or implied antecedent and attaching a subordinate clause to it, e.g. *which*. **4** Grammar (of a clause) attached to an antecedent by a relative word. > *noun* **1** a person connected to another by blood or marriage. **2** a species related to another by common origin.

IDIOMS – **relative to 1** compared with or in relation to. **2** concerning.

COMBINATIONS – **relative atomic mass** the ratio of the average mass of one atom of an element to one twelfth of the mass of an atom of carbon-12. **relative density** the ratio of the density of a substance to a standard density, usually that of water or air. **relative humidity** the amount of water vapour present in air, expressed as a percentage of the amount needed for saturation at the same temperature. **relative molecular mass** the ratio of the average mass of one molecule of an element or compound to one twelfth of the mass of an atom of carbon-12.

relatively > *adverb* **1** in relation, comparison, or proportion to something else. **2** quite; fairly.

relativise (also **relativize**) > *verb* **1** make or treat as relative. **2** Physics treat according to the principles of relativity.

DERIVATIVES – **relativisation** *noun*.

relativism > *noun* the doctrine that knowledge, truth, and morality exist in relation to culture, society, or historical context, and are not absolute.

DERIVATIVES – **relativist** *noun*.

relativistic > *adjective* Physics accurately described only by the theory of relativity.

DERIVATIVES – **relativistically** *adverb*.

relativity > *noun* **1** the absence of standards of absolute and universal application. **2** Physics a description of matter, energy, space, and time according to Einstein's theories based on the importance of relative motion and the principle that the speed of light is constant for all observers.

relaunch > *verb* /riˈlawnch/ launch again or in a different form. > *noun* /ˈreelawnch/ an instance of relaunching.

relax > *verb* **1** make or become less tense, anxious, or rigid. **2** rest from work or engage in a recreational activity. **3** make (a rule or restriction) less strict.

DERIVATIVES – **relaxed** *adjective*.

ORIGIN – Latin *relaxare*, from *laxus* 'lax, loose'.

relaxant > *noun* a drug or other thing that promotes relaxation or reduces tension. > *adjective* causing relaxation.

relaxation > *noun* the action of relaxing or the state of being relaxed.

relay¹ /ˈreelay/ > *noun* **1** a group of people or animals engaged in a task for a period of time and then replaced by a similar group. **2** a race between teams of runners, each team member in turn covering part of the total distance. **3** an electrical device which opens or closes a circuit in response to a current in another circuit. **4** a device which receives, reinforces, and retransmits a signal. > *verb* /also riˈlay/ **1** receive and pass on (information or a message). **2** broadcast by means of a relay.

ORIGIN – Old French *relayer*, from Latin *laxare* 'slacken'.

relay² /ˈreelay/ > *verb* (past and past participle **relaid**) lay again or differently.

release > *verb* **1** allow to escape from confinement; set free. **2** allow to move or flow freely. **3** allow (information) to be generally available. **4** make (a film or recording) available to the public. **5** make over (property, money, or a right) to another. > *noun* **1** the action or process of releasing or being released. **2** a film or other product released to the public. **3** a handle or catch that releases part of a mechanism. **4** a document making over property, money, or a right to another.

DERIVATIVES – **releasable** *adjective* **releaser** *noun*.

SYNONYMS – *verb* **1** deliver, emancipate, free, liberate; historical manumit.

ORIGIN – Old French *relesser*, from Latin *relaxare* 'slacken, relax'.

relegate > *verb* **1** assign an inferior rank or position to. **2** (usu. **be relegated**) Brit. transfer (a sports team) to a lower division of a league.

DERIVATIVES – **relegation** *noun*.

SYNONYMS – demote, downgrade.

ANTONYMS – promote, upgrade.

ORIGIN – Latin *relegare* 'send away'.

relent > *verb* **1** abandon or mitigate a harsh intention or cruel treatment. **2** become less intense.

ORIGIN – from Latin *re-* 'back' + *lentare* 'to bend'.

relentless > *adjective* **1** oppressively constant. **2** harsh or inflexible.

DERIVATIVES – **relentlessly** *adverb* **relentlessness** *noun*.

SYNONYMS – **1** incessant, perpetual, persistent, unremitting.

relevant > *adjective* closely connected or appropriate to the matter in hand.

DERIVATIVES – **relevance** *noun* **relevancy** *noun* **relevantly** *adverb*.

SYNONYMS – applicable, apposite, germane, material, pertinent, to the point.

ANTONYMS – irrelevant.

ORIGIN – first used as a Scots legal term meaning 'legally pertinent': from Latin *relevare* 'raise up'.

reliable > *adjective* able to be relied on.

DERIVATIVES – **reliability** *noun* **reliably** *adverb*.

821

SYNONYMS – consistent, dependable, infallible, sound, stable.

reliance > *noun* dependence on or trust in someone or something.
DERIVATIVES – **reliant** *adjective*.

relic > *noun* **1** an object of interest surviving from an earlier time. **2** a surviving but outdated object, custom, or belief. **3** a part of a holy person's body or belongings kept and revered after their death.
ORIGIN – Old French *relique*, from Latin *reliquiae* 'remains'.

relict /**rell**ikt/ > *noun* **1** an organism or other thing which has survived from an earlier period. **2** archaic a widow.
ORIGIN – from Latin *relictus* 'left behind'.

relief > *noun* **1** a feeling of reassurance and relaxation following release from anxiety or distress. **2** a cause of relief. **3** the action of relieving. **4** (usu. **light relief**) a temporary break in a generally tense or tedious situation. **5** financial or practical assistance given to those in special need or difficulty. **6** a person or group of people replacing others who have been on duty. **7** distinct appearance due to being accentuated in some way. **8** a method of moulding, carving, or stamping in which the design stands out from the surface, to a greater (**high relief**) or lesser (**low relief**) extent.
IDIOMS – **on relief** chiefly N. Amer. receiving state assistance because of need.
COMBINATIONS – **relief map 1** a map indicating hills and valleys by shading rather than by contour lines alone. **2** a map model with elevations and depressions representing hills and valleys. **relief road** Brit. a road taking traffic around, rather than through, a congested urban area.
ORIGIN – Old French, from Latin *relevare* 'raise again, alleviate'.

relieve > *verb* **1** alleviate or remove (pain, distress, or difficulty). **2** release (someone) from duty by taking their place. **3** (usu. **be relieved**) cause (someone) to stop feeling distressed or anxious. **4** (**relieve of**) take (a burden or responsibility) from (someone). **5** bring military support for (a besieged place). **6** make less tedious or monotonous. **7** (**relieve oneself**) formal or euphemistic urinate or defecate.
DERIVATIVES – **relieved** *adjective* **relievedly** *adverb* **reliever** *noun*.
SYNONYMS – **1** allay, alleviate, assuage, ease, mitigate, palliate, soothe.

relight > *verb* (past and past participle **relighted** or **relit**) light again.

religion > *noun* **1** the belief in and worship of a superhuman controlling power, especially a personal God or gods. **2** a particular system of faith and worship. **3** a pursuit or interest followed with devotion.
WORDFINDER – *major religions:* Baha'i, Buddhism, Christianity, Islam, Jainism, Judaism, Shinto, Sikhism, Zoroastrianism.
ORIGIN – Latin *religio* 'obligation, reverence': originally in the sense 'life under monastic vows'.

religiose /rilijiōss/ > *adjective* excessively religious.
DERIVATIVES – **religiosity** *noun*.

religious > *adjective* **1** of, concerned with, or believing in a religion. **2** treated or regarded with care and devotion appropriate to worship. > *noun* (pl. same) a person bound by monastic vows.
DERIVATIVES – **religiously** *adverb* **religiousness** *noun*.

relinquish > *verb* voluntarily cease to keep or claim; give up.
DERIVATIVES – **relinquishment** *noun*.
SYNONYMS – forsake, give up, renounce, yield.
ORIGIN – Latin *relinquere*, from *linquere* 'to leave'.

reliquary /**rell**ikwəri/ > *noun* (pl. **reliquaries**) a container for holy relics.

reliquiae /ri**lik**wi-ee/ > *plural noun* formal remains.
ORIGIN – Latin, from *reliquus* 'remaining'.

relish > *noun* **1** great enjoyment. **2** pleasurable anticipation. **3** a piquant sauce or pickle eaten with plain food to add flavour. **4** archaic an appetising flavour. > *verb* **1** enjoy greatly. **2** anticipate with pleasure. **3** archaic make pleasant to the taste.
SYNONYMS – *noun* **1** delight, enthusiasm, gusto, pleasure, zest. *verb* **1** appreciate, delight in, savour.
ORIGIN – Old French *reles* 'remainder': originally in the sense 'odour, taste'.

relive > *verb* live through (an experience or feeling) again in one's imagination.

reload > *verb* load (something, especially a gun) again.

relocate > *verb* move to a new place and establish one's home or business there.
DERIVATIVES – **relocation** *noun*.

reluctance > *noun* unwillingness or disinclination to do something.

reluctant > *adjective* unwilling and hesitant.
DERIVATIVES – **reluctantly** *adverb*.
SYNONYMS – chary, disinclined, hesitant, loath, unenthusiastic, unwilling.
ANTONYMS – eager, keen.
ORIGIN – first used in the sense 'offering opposition': from Latin *reluctari* 'struggle against'.

rely > *verb* (**relies, relied**) (**rely on** or **upon**) **1** depend on with full trust. **2** be dependent on.
SYNONYMS – (**rely on** or **upon**) **1** bank on, believe in, count on, depend on. **2** count on, depend on.

wordpower facts
Rely
The word **rely** comes from Old French *relier*, meaning 'bind together', from Latin *religare* (from *ligare* 'to bind'). In English the original sense was 'gather together, assemble (soldiers, followers, etc.)', later 'turn to, associate with', from which developed the current sense, 'depend on with full trust'. The Latin root *ligare* is the source of a number of words that are now distant in meaning, including **ally**, **furl**, **league**, **liable**, **ligament**, and **oblige**.

rem > *noun* (pl. same) a unit of effective absorbed dose of radiation in human tissue, approximately equivalent to one roentgen of X-rays.
ORIGIN – acronym from *roentgen equivalent man*.

remain > *verb* **1** continue to exist. **2** be in the same place during further time. **3** continue in the same state or condition: *he remained alert.* **4** be left over after others or other parts have been completed, used, or dealt with.
SYNONYMS – **1** abide, continue, endure, linger, persist, survive. **2,3** stay.

wordpower facts
Remain
Remain comes from Latin *remanere*, from *manere* 'to stay', a root shared by **permanent**. *Manere* is the source also of words relating to imposing dwelling places, such as **manor**, **manse**, and **mansion**, and the French word for 'household', **ménage**, which has been adopted into English in the phrase **ménage à trois**.

remainder > *noun* **1** a part, number, or quantity that is left over. **2** a part that is still to come. **3** the number which is left over in a division in which one quantity does not exactly divide another. **4** a copy of a book left unsold when demand has fallen. > *verb* (often **be remaindered**) dispose of (an unsold book) at a reduced price.

remains > *plural noun* **1** things remaining. **2** historical or archaeological relics. **3** a person's body after death.

remake > *verb* /reemayk/ (past and past participle **remade**) make again or differently. > *noun* /**ree**mayk/ a film or piece of music that has been filmed or recorded again and re-released.

remand Law > *verb* place (a defendant) on bail

or in custody, especially when a trial is adjourned. > *noun* a committal to custody.
ORIGIN – Latin *remandare* 'commit again'.

remark > *verb* **1** say as a comment; mention. **2** regard with attention; notice. > *noun* **1** a comment. **2** the action of noticing or commenting.
SYNONYMS – *verb* **1** comment, declare, mention, observe, say. **2** mark, note, notice, observe. *noun* **1** comment, declaration, observation, statement, utterance.
ORIGIN – French *remarquer* 'note again'.

remarkable > *adjective* extraordinary or striking.
DERIVATIVES – **remarkably** *adverb*.
SYNONYMS – astonishing, exceptional, extraordinary, outstanding, striking.

remarry > *verb* (**remarries, remarried**) marry again.
DERIVATIVES – **remarriage** *noun*.

remaster > *verb* make a new or improved master of (a sound recording).

rematch > *noun* a second match or game between two sports teams or players.

remedial /rimeediəl/ > *adjective* **1** giving or intended as a remedy. **2** provided or intended for children with learning difficulties.

remediation /rimeediaysh'n/ > *noun* **1** the action of remedying something, in particular environmental damage. **2** the giving of remedial teaching or therapy.
DERIVATIVES – **remediate** *verb*.

remedy > *noun* (pl. **remedies**) **1** a medicine or treatment for a disease or injury. **2** a means of counteracting or eliminating something undesirable. **3** a means of legal reparation. > *verb* (**remedies, remedied**) make good (an undesirable situation); rectify.
DERIVATIVES – **remediable** *adjective*.
SYNONYMS – *noun* **1** cure, medication, medicine, restorative, treatment. **2** antidote, corrective, cure, solution. *verb* correct, fix, rectify, repair.
ORIGIN – Latin *remedium*, from *mederi* 'heal'.

remember > *verb* **1** have in or be able to bring to one's mind (someone or something from the past). **2** keep (something necessary or advisable) in mind. **3** bear (someone) in mind by making them a gift, mentioning them in prayer, or otherwise acknowledging them. **4** (**remember oneself**) recover one's manners after a lapse. **5** (**remember to**) convey greetings from (one person) to (another).
SYNONYMS – **1** recall, recollect. **2** memorise, retain.
ANTONYMS – **1,2** forget.
ORIGIN – Latin *rememorari* 'call to mind'.

remembrance > *noun* **1** the action of remembering. **2** a memory. **3** a thing kept or given as a reminder or in commemoration of someone.
COMBINATIONS – **Remembrance Sunday** (also **Remembrance Day**) (in the UK) the Sunday nearest 11 November (the anniversary of the armistice in the First World War), when those who were killed in the two world wars and later conflicts are commemorated.

remind > *verb* **1** cause (someone) to remember something or to do something. **2** (**remind of**) cause (someone) to think of (something) because of a resemblance.

reminder > *noun* **1** a thing that causes someone to remember something. **2** a letter sent to remind someone to pay a bill.

reminisce /remminiss/ > *verb* indulge in recollection of the past.

reminiscence > *noun* **1** a story told about a past event remembered by the narrator. **2** enjoyable recollection of the past. **3** a characteristic of one thing suggestive of another.
ORIGIN – Latin, from *reminisci* 'remember'.

reminiscent > *adjective* **1** (usu. **reminiscent of**) tending to remind one of something. **2** absorbed in memories.
DERIVATIVES – **reminiscently** *adverb*.

remiss /rimiss/ > *adjective* lacking care or attention to duty.
SYNONYMS – careless, lax, neglectful, negligent, slack.
ORIGIN – first used in the senses 'weakened in colour or consistency' and (in describing sound) 'faint': from Latin *remittere* 'slacken'.

remission > *noun* **1** the cancellation of a debt, charge, or penalty. **2** Brit. the reduction of a prison sentence, especially as a reward for good behaviour. **3** a temporary lessening of the severity of disease or pain. **4** formal forgiveness of sins.

remit > *verb* /rimit/ (**remitted, remitting**) **1** refrain from exacting or inflicting (a debt or punishment). **2** send (money) in payment for something. **3** refer (a matter for decision) to an authority. **4** Theology pardon (a sin). **5** archaic diminish. > *noun* /reemit/ **1** the task or area of activity officially assigned to an individual or organisation. **2** an item referred for consideration.
ORIGIN – Latin *remittere* 'send back, restore'.

remittance > *noun* **1** a sum of money sent in payment. **2** the sending of a payment.
COMBINATIONS – **remittance man** chiefly historical an emigrant supported or assisted by money sent from home.

remix > *verb* **1** mix again. **2** produce a different version of (a musical recording) by altering the balance of the separate tracks. > *noun* a remixed musical recording.
DERIVATIVES – **remixer** *noun*.

remnant > *noun* **1** a small remaining quantity. **2** a piece of cloth left when the greater part has been used or sold. **3** a surviving trace. > *adjective* remaining.

remodel > *verb* (**remodelled, remodelling**; US **remodeled, remodeling**) **1** change the structure or form of. **2** shape (a figure or object) again or differently.

remold > *verb* US spelling of REMOULD.

remonstrance /rimonstrənss/ > *noun* a forcefully reproachful protest.

remonstrate /remmənstrayt/ > *verb* make a forcefully reproachful protest.
DERIVATIVES – **remonstration** *noun*.
ORIGIN – Latin *remonstrare* 'demonstrate': originally in the sense 'make plain'.

remora /remmərə/ > *noun* a slender sea fish which attaches itself to large fish by means of a sucker on top of the head.
ORIGIN – Latin, literally 'hindrance' (because of the former belief that the fish slowed down ships).

remorse > *noun* deep regret or guilt for a wrong committed.
SYNONYMS – compunction, contrition, guilt, regret, repentance.
ORIGIN – Latin *remorsus*, from *mordere* 'to bite'.

remorseful > *adjective* filled with remorse or repentance.
DERIVATIVES – **remorsefully** *adverb*.
SYNONYMS – contrite, guilt-ridden, regretful, repentant, sorry.
ANTONYMS – remorseless, unrepentant.

remorseless > *adjective* **1** without remorse. **2** (of something unpleasant) relentless.
DERIVATIVES – **remorselessly** *adverb* **remorselessness** *noun*.
SYNONYMS – **1** cruel, heartless, merciless, pitiless, ruthless.
ANTONYMS – **1** compassionate, remorseful.

remortgage > *verb* take out another or a different mortgage on. > *noun* a different or additional mortgage.

remote > *adjective* (**remoter, remotest**) **1** far away in space or time. **2** situated far from the main centres of population. **3** distantly related. **4** (often **remote from**) having very little connection. **5** (of a chance or possibility) unlikely to occur. **6** aloof or distant in manner. **7** (of an electronic device) operating or operated by means of radio or infrared signals. **8** Computing (of a device) that can only be accessed by means of a network.
DERIVATIVES – **remotely** *adverb* **remoteness** *noun*.
SYNONYMS – **1** distant. **2** isolated, off the beaten track, secluded, unfrequented. **5** faint, improbable, slight, unlikely.
COMBINATIONS – **remote sensing** the scanning of the earth by satellite or high-flying aircraft.
ORIGIN – Latin *remotus* 'removed'.

remote control > *noun* **1** control of a machine or apparatus from a distance by means of signals transmitted from a radio or electronic device. **2** (also **remote controller**) a device that controls an apparatus in this way.

DERIVATIVES – **remote-controlled** *adjective*.

remoulade /remmŏŏlaad/ > *noun* salad or seafood dressing made with hard-boiled egg yolks, oil, vinegar, and seasoning.

ORIGIN – French.

remould (US **remold**) > *verb* /reemōld/ **1** mould again or differently. **2** Brit. put a new tread on (a worn tyre). > *noun* /reemōld/ a remoulded tyre.

remount > *verb* /reemownt/ **1** get on (a horse or vehicle) again. **2** attach (a picture, photograph, etc.) to a new frame or setting. **3** initiate (a course of action) again. > *noun* /reemownt/ a fresh horse for a rider.

removal > *noun* **1** the action of removing. **2** chiefly Brit. the transfer of furniture and other contents when moving house.

removalist > *noun* Austral. a person or firm engaged in household or business removals.

remove > *verb* **1** take off or away from the position occupied. **2** abolish or get rid of. **3** dismiss from a post. **4** (**be removed**) be very different from. **5** (**remove to**) dated relocate to (another place). **6** (**removed**) separated by a particular number of steps of descent: *his second cousin once removed.* > *noun* **1** a degree of remoteness or separation: *at this remove, the whole incident seems insane.* **2** a form or division in some British schools.

DERIVATIVES – **removable** *adjective* **remover** *noun*.

SYNONYMS – **1** detach, extract, separate. **2** abolish, eliminate, erase, obliterate. **3** discharge, dismiss, expel, oust.

ORIGIN – Latin *removere*, from *movere* 'to move'.

REM sleep > *noun* a kind of sleep that occurs at intervals during the night and is characterised by rapid eye movement (thus 'REM'), more dreaming and bodily movement, and faster pulse and breathing.

remunerate /rimyŏŏnərayt/ > *verb* pay (someone) for services rendered or work done.

DERIVATIVES – **remunerative** *adjective*.

ORIGIN – Latin *remunerari* 'reward, recompense'.

remuneration > *noun* money paid for work or a service.

Renaissance /rinaysoNss, rinaysənss/ > *noun* **1** the revival of art and literature under the influence of classical models in the 14th–16th centuries. **2** (**renaissance**) a revival of or renewed interest in something.

COMBINATIONS – **Renaissance man** a person with a wide range of talents or interests.

ORIGIN – French, 'rebirth'.

renal /reen'l/ > *adjective* technical relating to the kidneys.

ORIGIN – Latin *renalis*, from *renes* 'kidneys'.

rename > *verb* give a new name to.

renascence /rinass'nss, rinays'nss/ > *noun* **1** the revival of something that has been dormant. **2** another term for **RENAISSANCE**.

renascent > *adjective* becoming active again.

ORIGIN – Latin, from *renasci* 'be born again'.

rend > *verb* (past and past participle **rent**) literary **1** tear to pieces. **2** cause great emotional pain to.

IDIOMS – **rend the air** sound piercingly.

render > *verb* **1** provide or give (a service, help, etc.). **2** submit for inspection, consideration, or payment. **3** literary hand over; surrender. **4** cause to be or become. **5** represent, interpret, or perform artistically. **6** translate. **7** melt down (fat), typically in order to clarify it. **8** process (the carcass of an animal) in order to extract proteins, fats, and other usable parts. **9** cover (stone or brick) with a coat of plaster. > *noun* a first coat of plaster applied to a brick or stone surface.

DERIVATIVES – **renderer** *noun*.

ORIGIN – Old French *rendre*, from Latin *reddere* 'give back'.

rendering > *noun* **1** a performance of a piece of music or drama. **2** a translation. **3** the action of applying render to a wall. **4** a first coat of plaster. **5** the action of giving or surrendering something.

rendezvous /rondayvŏŏ/ > *noun* (pl. same /rondayvŏŏz/) **1** a meeting at an agreed time and place. **2** a meeting place. > *verb* (**rendezvouses** /rondayvŏŏz/, **rendezvoused** /rondayvŏŏd/, **rendezvousing** /rondayvŏŏing/) meet at an agreed time and place.

ORIGIN – French *rendez-vous!* 'present yourselves!'.

rendition > *noun* **1** a rendering of a dramatic, musical, or artistic work. **2** a translation.

renegade /rennigayd/ > *noun* a person who deserts and betrays an organisation, country, or set of principles. > *adjective* having treacherously changed allegiance.

ORIGIN – Spanish *renegado*, from Latin *renegare* 'renounce'.

renege /rinayg, rineeg/ (also **renegue**) > *verb* go back on a promise, undertaking, or contract.

DERIVATIVES – **reneger** *noun*.

ORIGIN – Latin *renegare*, from *re-* (expressing intensive force) + *negare* 'deny'.

renegotiate > *verb* negotiate again in order to change the original agreed terms.

DERIVATIVES – **renegotiable** *adjective* **renegotiation** *noun*.

renew > *verb* **1** resume or re-establish after an interruption. **2** give fresh life or strength to. **3** extend the period of validity of (a licence, subscription, or contract). **4** replace or restore (something broken or worn out).

DERIVATIVES – **renewal** *noun* **renewer** *noun*.

renewable > *adjective* **1** capable of being renewed. **2** (of energy or its source) not depleted when used.

DERIVATIVES – **renewability** *noun*.

renminbi /renminbi/ > *noun* (pl. same) the national currency of the People's Republic of China.

ORIGIN – from the Chinese words for 'people' and 'currency'.

rennet /rennit/ > *noun* **1** curdled milk from the stomach of an unweaned calf, containing rennin and used in curdling milk for cheese. **2** a preparation containing rennin.

ORIGIN – probably related to **RUN**.

rennin /rennin/ > *noun* an enzyme secreted into the stomach of unweaned mammals, causing the curdling of milk.

ORIGIN – from **RENNET**.

renounce > *verb* **1** formally declare one's abandonment of (a claim, right, or possession). **2** refuse to recognise any longer. **3** abandon (a cause, bad habit, or way of life).

DERIVATIVES – **renounceable** *adjective* **renouncement** *noun* **renouncer** *noun*.

ORIGIN – Old French *renoncer*, from Latin *renuntiare* 'protest against'.

renovate /rennəvayt/ > *verb* restore (something old) to a good state of repair.

DERIVATIVES – **renovation** *noun* **renovator** *noun*.

ORIGIN – Latin *renovare* 'make new again'.

renown /rinown/ > *noun* the state of being famous.

DERIVATIVES – **renowned** *adjective*.

ORIGIN – from Old French *renomer* 'make famous', from *nom* 'name'.

rent[1] > *noun* **1** a tenant's regular payment to a landlord for the use of property or land. **2** a sum paid for the hire of equipment. > *verb* **1** pay someone for the use of. **2** let someone use (something) in return for payment.

DERIVATIVES – **rentable** *adjective*.

COMBINATIONS – **rent boy** Brit. informal a young male prostitute.

ORIGIN – Old French *rente*, from a root shared by **RENDER**.

rent[2] > *noun* a large tear in a piece of fabric.

ORIGIN – from **REND**.

rent[3] past and past participle of **REND**.

rental > *noun* **1** an amount paid or received

as rent. **2** the action of renting. **3** N. Amer. a rented house or car. > *adjective* relating to or available for rent.

renter > *noun* **1** a person who rents a flat, car, etc. **2** (in the UK) a person who distributes cinema films. **3** US a rented car or video cassette. **4** Brit. informal a male prostitute.

rentier /**ron**tiay/ > *noun* a person living on income from property or investments.

ORIGIN – French, from *rente* 'dividend'.

renumber > *verb* change the number or numbers assigned to.

renunciation > *noun* the action of renouncing.

reoccupy > *verb* (**reoccupies**, **reoccupied**) occupy again.

DERIVATIVES – **reoccupation** *noun*.

reoccur > *verb* (**reoccurred**, **reoccurring**) occur again or repeatedly.

DERIVATIVES – **reoccurrence** *noun*.

reoffend > *verb* commit a further offence.

DERIVATIVES – **reoffender** *noun*.

reopen > *verb* open again.

reorder > *verb* **1** order again. **2** arrange again. > *noun* a renewed or repeated order for goods.

reorganise (also **reorganize**) > *verb* change the organisation of.

DERIVATIVES – **reorganisation** *noun* **reorganiser** *noun*.

reorient /ree**or**ient/ > *verb* **1** change the focus or direction of. **2** (**reorient oneself**) find one's bearings again.

DERIVATIVES – **reorientate** *verb* **reorientation** *noun*.

Rep. > *abbreviation* **1** (in the US Congress) Representative. **2** Republic. **3** US a Republican.

rep¹ informal > *noun* a representative. > *verb* (**repped**, **repping**) act as a sales representative.

rep² > *noun* informal **1** repertory. **2** a repertory theatre or company.

rep³ (also **repp**) > *noun* a fabric with a ribbed surface, used in curtains and upholstery.

ORIGIN – French *reps*.

rep⁴ > *noun* N. Amer. informal short for **REPUTATION**.

rep⁵ > *noun* (in bodybuilding) a repetition of a set of exercises. > *verb* (as an instruction in knitting patterns) repeat.

repackage > *verb* package again or differently.

repaid past and past participle of **REPAY**.

repaint > *verb* cover with a new coat of paint. > *noun* an act of repainting.

repair¹ > *verb* **1** restore (something damaged, worn, or faulty) to a good condition. **2** set right (a rift in relations). > *noun* **1** the action of repairing. **2** a result of this. **3** the relative physical condition of an object: *the cottages were in good repair.*

DERIVATIVES – **repairable** *adjective* **repairer** *noun*.

SYNONYMS – *verb* **1,2** fix, mend, patch up, restore.

ORIGIN – Old French *reparer*, from Latin *reparare*, from *re-* 'back' + *parare* 'make ready'.

repair² > *verb* (**repair to**) formal or humorous go to (a place).

ORIGIN – Old French *repairer*, from Latin *repatriare* 'return to one's country'.

reparable /**repp**ərəb'l/ > *adjective* able to be repaired or rectified.

reparation /reppə**ray**sh'n/ > *noun* **1** the making of amends for a wrong. **2** (**reparations**) compensation for war damage paid by a defeated state. **3** the action of repairing something.

DERIVATIVES – **reparative** /**repp**ərətiv, ri**parr**ətiv/ *adjective*.

repartee /reppaar**tee**/ > *noun* conversation or speech characterised by quick, witty comments or replies.

ORIGIN – French *repartie* 'replied promptly', from *repartir*, from *re-* 'again' + *partir* 'set off'.

repast /ri**paast**/ > *noun* formal a meal.

ORIGIN – Old French, from Latin *repascere*, from *pascere* 'to feed'.

repatriate /ree**pat**riayt/ > *verb* send (someone) back to their own country. > *noun* a person who has been repatriated.

DERIVATIVES – **repatriation** *noun*.

ORIGIN – Latin *repatriare* 'return to one's country'.

repay > *verb* (past and past participle **repaid**) **1** pay back (a loan). **2** pay back money owed to (someone). **3** do or give something as recompense for (a favour or kindness received). **4** be worth subjecting to (a specified action): *these sites would repay more detailed investigation.*

DERIVATIVES – **repayable** *adjective* **repayment** *noun*.

COMBINATIONS – **repayment mortgage** a mortgage in which the borrower repays the capital and interest together in fixed instalments over a fixed period.

repeal > *verb* revoke or annul (a law or act of parliament). > *noun* the action of repealing.

DERIVATIVES – **repealable** *adjective*.

ORIGIN – Old French *repeler*, from *re-* (expressing reversal) + *apeler* 'to call, appeal'.

repeat > *verb* **1** say or do again. **2** (**repeat oneself**) say the same thing again. **3** (**repeat itself**) occur again in the same way or form. **4** (of food) be tasted again after being swallowed, as a result of indigestion. > *noun* **1** an instance of repeating or being repeated. **2** a repeated broadcast of a television or radio programme. **3** (before

another noun) occurring, done, or used more than once: *a repeat prescription.* **4** a decorative pattern which is repeated uniformly over a surface. **5** Music a passage intended to be repeated.

DERIVATIVES – **repeatable** *adjective* **repeated** *adjective* **repeatedly** *adverb* **repeater** *noun*.

ORIGIN – Latin *repetere*, from *re-* 'back' + *petere* 'seek'.

repel > *verb* (**repelled**, **repelling**) **1** drive or force back or away. **2** be repulsive or distasteful to. **3** formal refuse to accept; reject. **4** (of a magnetic pole or electric field) force (something similarly magnetised or charged) away. **5** (of a substance) resist mixing with or be impervious to.

DERIVATIVES – **repeller** *noun*.

ORIGIN – Latin *repellere*, from *re-* 'back' + *pellere* 'to drive'.

repellent (also **repellant**) > *adjective* **1** able to repel or impervious to a particular thing: *water-repellent nylon.* **2** causing disgust or distaste. > *noun* **1** a substance that deters insects or other pests. **2** a substance used to treat something to make it impervious to water.

DERIVATIVES – **repellence** *noun* **repellency** *noun* **repellently** *adverb*.

repent > *verb* feel or express sincere regret or remorse.

DERIVATIVES – **repentance** *noun* **repentant** *adjective* **repenter** *noun*.

ORIGIN – Old French *repentir*, from Latin *paenitere* 'cause to repent'.

repercussion > *noun* a consequence of an event or action.

DERIVATIVES – **repercussive** *adjective*.

---

wordpower facts

Repercussion

The verb **repercuss** entered late Middle English as a medical term, meaning 'drive back' or 'repress'; such conditions as swellings and unhealthy bodily 'humours', or infections, were treated by **repercussion**, a term used also for the medicines or medical applications themselves. These words came via Old French from Latin *repercutere* 'cause to rebound, push back', from *percutere* 'to strike'. The early use of **repercussion** to mean 'driving back, rebounding' led to the sense 'a blow given in return', from which the modern sense developed. The current medical term **percuss**, meaning 'tap (a part of the body)', which was first used in the early 19th century, comes from the same Latin root.

repertoire /**repp**ərtwaar/ > *noun* the body of pieces known or regularly performed by a performer or company.
ORIGIN – Latin *repertorium*, from *reperire* 'find, discover'.

repertory /**repp**ərtri/ > *noun* (pl. **repertories**) **1** the performance by a company of the plays, operas, or ballets in its repertoire at regular short intervals. **2** another term for **REPERTOIRE**. **3** a repository or collection.
COMBINATIONS – **repertory company** a theatrical company that performs plays from its repertoire for regular, short periods of time, moving on from one play to another.
ORIGIN – first denoting an index or catalogue: from Latin *repertorium*, from *reperire* 'find, discover'.

repetition* > *noun* **1** the act or an instance of repeating or being repeated. **2** a thing that repeats another.
DERIVATIVES – **repetitional** *adjective* **repetitious** *adjective*.
*SPELLING – note the second syllable is *pet*, not *pit*: repe*ti*tion.

repetitive > *adjective* containing or characterised by repetition.
DERIVATIVES – **repetitively** *adverb* **repetitiveness** *noun*.
COMBINATIONS – **repetitive strain injury** a condition in which the prolonged performance of repetitive actions, typically with the hands, causes pain or impairment of function in the tendons and muscles involved.

rephrase > *verb* express in an alternative way.

repine > *verb* literary be discontented; fret.

replace > *verb* **1** take the place of. **2** provide a substitute for. **3** put back in a previous place or position.
DERIVATIVES – **replaceable** *adjective* **replacement** *noun* **replacer** *noun*.
SYNONYMS – **1** oust, succeed, supersede, supplant. **3** reinstate, restore, return.

replant > *verb* **1** plant in a new pot or site. **2** provide (an area) with new plants or trees.

replay > *verb* **1** play back (a recording). **2** play (a match) again. > *noun* **1** the act or an instance of replaying. **2** a replayed match. **3** an occurrence which closely follows the pattern of a previous event.

replenish > *verb* **1** fill up again. **2** restore to a former level or condition.
DERIVATIVES – **replenisher** *noun* **replenishment** *noun*.
SYNONYMS – **1** recharge, refill, restock, top up.
ORIGIN – Old French *replenir*, from *re-* 'again' + *plenir* 'fill'.

replete > /ri**pleet**/ > *adjective* **1** filled or well-supplied with something. **2** very full with food; sated.

DERIVATIVES – **repletion** *noun*.
ORIGIN – Latin *repletus* 'filled up', from *re-* 'back, again' + *plere* 'fill'.

replica > *noun* an exact copy or model of something, especially one on a smaller scale.
ORIGIN – Italian, from *replicare* 'to reply': originally as a musical term in the sense 'a repeat'.

replicate > *verb* /**rep**likayt/ **1** make an exact copy of; reproduce. **2** (**replicate itself**) (of genetic material or a living organism) reproduce or give rise to a copy of itself. **3** repeat (a scientific experiment or trial) to obtain a consistent result. > *adjective* /**rep**likət/ **1** of the nature of a copy. **2** relating to a replicated experiment or trial. > *noun* /**rep**likət/ **1** a close or exact copy; a replica. **2** a replicated experiment or trial. **3** Music a tone one or more octaves above or below the given tone.
DERIVATIVES – **replicable** /**rep**likəb'l/ *adjective* **replication** *noun* **replicative** *adjective* **replicator** *noun*.
ORIGIN – Latin *replicare*, from *re-* 'back, again' + *plicare* 'to fold'.

reply > *verb* (**replies**, **replied**) **1** say or write something in response to something said or written. **2** respond with a similar action. > *noun* (pl. **replies**) **1** the action of replying. **2** a spoken or written response.
DERIVATIVES – **replier** *noun*.
SYNONYMS – *verb* **1** answer, respond.
ORIGIN – Old French *replier*, from Latin *replicare* 'repeat', later 'make a reply'.

repo /**ree**pō/ N. Amer. informal > *noun* (pl. **repos**) a car or other item which has been repossessed. > *verb* (**repo's**, **repo'd**) repossess.

repopulate > *verb* introduce a population into (an area previously deserted or taken by occupying forces).
DERIVATIVES – **repopulation** *noun*.

report > *verb* **1** give a spoken or written account of something. **2** convey information about an event or situation. **3** make a formal complaint about. **4** present oneself as having arrived somewhere or as ready to do something. **5** (**report to**) be responsible to (a supervisor or manager). **6** Brit. formally announce that a parliamentary committee has dealt with (a bill). > *noun* **1** an account given of a matter after investigation or consideration. **2** a piece of information about an event or situation. **3** Brit. a teacher's written assessment of a pupil's work and progress. **4** a sudden loud noise of or like an explosion or gunfire.
DERIVATIVES – **reportable** *adjective* **reported** *adjective* **reportedly** *adverb*.
COMBINATIONS – **reported speech** a speaker's words reported in a subordinate clause, with the required changes of person and tense (e.g. *he said that he would go*, based

on *I will go*). Contrasted with *direct speech*.
report stage (in the UK and Canada) the stage in the process of a bill becoming law at which it is debated after being reported.
ORIGIN – Latin *reportare* 'bring back'.

reportage /**repport**aa**zh**/ > *noun* **1** the reporting of news by the press and the broadcasting media. **2** factual, journalistic presentation in a book or other text.

reporter > *noun* a person who reports news for a newspaper or broadcasting company.

repose¹ /ri**pōz**/ > *noun* **1** a state of restfulness or tranquillity. **2** composure. > *verb* **1** rest. **2** be situated or kept in a particular place.
ORIGIN – Old French *reposer*, from Latin *repausare*, from *pausare* 'to pause'.

repose² /ri**pōz**/ > *verb* (**repose in**) place (something, especially one's confidence or trust) in.
ORIGIN – first meaning 'put back in the same position': from **POSE**, suggested by Latin *reponere* 'replace'.

reposition > *verb* place in a different position; adjust or alter the position of.

repository /ri**pozz**itəri/ > *noun* (pl. **repositories**) **1** a place in which things are stored. **2** a place where something is found in significant quantities.
ORIGIN – Latin *repositorium*, from *reponere* 'replace'.

repossess > *verb* retake possession of (something) when a buyer defaults on payments.
DERIVATIVES – **repossession** *noun* **repossessor** *noun*.

repot > *verb* (**repotted**, **repotting**) put (a plant) in another pot.

repoussé /rə**poo**ssay/ > *adjective* (of metalwork) hammered into relief from the reverse side. > *noun* ornamental metalwork fashioned in this way.
ORIGIN – French, 'pushed back'.

repp > *noun* variant spelling of **REP³**.

reprehend /repri**hend**/ > *verb* reprimand.
DERIVATIVES – **reprehension** *noun*.
ORIGIN – Latin *reprehendere* 'seize, check, rebuke'.

reprehensible > *adjective* deserving condemnation.
DERIVATIVES – **reprehensibility** *noun* **reprehensibly** *adverb*.
SYNONYMS – blameworthy, deplorable, disgraceful, objectionable, shameful.
ANTONYMS – commendable, praiseworthy.

represent /repri**z**ent/ > *verb* **1** be entitled or appointed to act and speak for. **2** be an elected Member of Parliament or member of a legislature for. **3** constitute; amount to. **4** be a specimen or example of; typify. **5** (**be represented**) be present to a particular degree. **6** portray in a particular way. **7** depict in a work of art. **8** signify, symbolise, or embody.

ORIGIN – Latin *repraesentare*, from *praesentare* 'to present'.

re-present /reepri**zent**/ > *verb* present again.

DERIVATIVES – **re-presentation** *noun*.

representation > *noun* **1** the action or an instance of representing or being represented. **2** an image, model, or other depiction of something. **3** (**representations**) statements made to an authority to communicate an opinion or register a protest.

representational > *adjective* **1** relating to or characterised by representation. **2** relating to art which depicts the physical appearance of things.

representationalism > *noun* the practice or advocacy of representational art.

DERIVATIVES – **representationalist** *adjective & noun*.

representative > *adjective* **1** typical of a class or group. **2** containing typical examples of many or all types. **3** (of a legislative or deliberative assembly) consisting of people chosen to act and speak on behalf of a wider group. **4** serving as a portrayal or symbol of something. > *noun* **1** a person chosen to act and speak for another or others. **2** an agent of a firm who travels to potential clients to sell its products. **3** an example of a class or group.

DERIVATIVES – **representativeness** *noun*.

SYNONYMS – *adjective* **1** characteristic, prototypical, typical. **4** emblematic, symbolic.

ANTONYMS – *adjective* **1** atypical, unrepresentative.

repress > *verb* **1** subdue by force. **2** restrain, prevent, or inhibit. **3** suppress (a thought or feeling) in oneself so that it becomes or remains unconscious.

DERIVATIVES – **represser** *noun* **repressible** *adjective* **repression** *noun*.

ORIGIN – Latin *reprimere* 'press back, check'.

repressed > *adjective* **1** oppressed. **2** (of a thought or feeling) kept suppressed and unconscious in one's mind. **3** tending to suppress one's feelings and desires.

repressive > *adjective* inhibiting or restraining personal freedom; oppressive.

DERIVATIVES – **repressively** *adverb* **repressiveness** *noun*.

reprieve > *verb* **1** cancel the punishment of. **2** stop or postpone the cancellation or closure of. > *noun* **1** the cancellation of a punishment. **2** a respite from difficulty or danger.

---

wordpower facts

Reprieve

The sense development of **reprieve** underwent a complete reversal, from the original 15th-century meaning 'send back to prison', via 'postpone (a legal process)', to the sense 'rescue from impending punishment', which developed a century later. The word itself comes from Old French *reprendre*, from Latin *re-* 'back' and *prehendere* 'seize'. It is related to **reprise**, which comes from the same root.

reprimand /**rep**rimaand/ > *noun* a formal expression of disapproval; a rebuke. > *verb* address a reprimand to.

ORIGIN – from Latin *reprimenda* 'things to be held in check', from *reprimere* 'press back, check'.

reprint > *verb* /ree**print**/ print again or in a revised form. > *noun* /**ree**print/ **1** an act of reprinting. **2** a copy of a book or other material that has been reprinted.

reprisal /ri**prīz**'l/ > *noun* **1** an act of retaliation. **2** historical the forcible seizure of a citizen of a foreign country or their goods as an act of retaliation.

ORIGIN – Old French *reprisaille*, from Latin *reprehendere* 'seize, check, rebuke'.

reprise * /ri**preez**/ > *noun* **1** a repeated passage in music. **2** a further performance of something. > *verb* repeat (a piece of music or a performance).

*SPELLING – **reprise** cannot be spelled with an *-ize* ending.

ORIGIN – French, 'taken up again'.

reproach > *verb* **1** express to (someone) one's disapproval of or disappointment in their actions. **2** (**reproach with**) accuse of. > *noun* an expression of disapproval or disappointment.

IDIOMS – **above** (or **beyond**) **reproach** such that no criticism can be made; perfect.

DERIVATIVES – **reproachable** *adjective* **reproachful** *adjective*.

SYNONYMS – *verb* **1** censure, chide, rebuke, scold, upbraid.

ORIGIN – Old French *reprochier*, from a base meaning 'bring back close'.

reprobate /**rep**rəbayt/ > *noun* an unprincipled person; a scoundrel. > *adjective* unprincipled or roguish.

ORIGIN – from Latin *reprobare* 'disapprove'.

reprocess > *verb* process (something, especially spent nuclear fuel) again or differently, in order to reuse it.

reproduce > *verb* **1** produce a copy or representation of. **2** recreate in a different medium or context. **3** (of an organism) produce offspring.

DERIVATIVES – **reproducer** *noun* **reproducible** *adjective*.

reproduction > *noun* **1** the action or process of reproducing. **2** a copy of a work of art, especially a print made of a painting. **3** (before another noun) made to imitate the style of an earlier period or particular craftsman: *reproduction furniture*.

DERIVATIVES – **reproductive** *adjective*.

reprogram (also **reprogramme**) > *verb* (**reprogrammed**, **reprogramming**; US also **reprogramed**, **reprograming**) program (a computer) again.

DERIVATIVES – **reprogrammable** *adjective*.

reprography /ree**prog**rəfi/ > *noun* the science and practice of reproducing documents and graphic material.

DERIVATIVES – **reprographic** *adjective*.

ORIGIN – from REPRODUCE + -GRAPHY.

reproof[1] /ri**proof**/ > *noun* a rebuke or reprimand.

reproof[2] /ree**proof**/ > *verb* **1** Brit. render waterproof again. **2** make a fresh proof of (printed matter).

reprove /ri**proov**/ > *verb* rebuke or reprimand.

DERIVATIVES – **reproving** *adjective* **reprovingly** *adverb*.

ORIGIN – Old French *reprover*.

reptile > *noun* **1** a cold-blooded vertebrate animal of a class that includes snakes, lizards, crocodiles, turtles, and tortoises, typically having a dry scaly skin and laying soft-shelled eggs on land. **2** informal a person regarded with loathing and contempt.

WORDFINDER – herpetology (*the branch of zoology concerned with reptiles and amphibians*).

DERIVATIVES – **reptilian** *adjective & noun*.

ORIGIN – from Latin *repere* 'crawl'.

republic > *noun* a state in which supreme power is held by the people and their elected representatives, and which has an elected or nominated president rather than a monarch.

ORIGIN – Latin *respublica*, from *res* 'concern' + *publicus* 'of the people, public'.

republican > *adjective* **1** belonging to or characteristic of a republic. **2** advocating republican government. **3** (**Republican**) (in the US) supporting the Republican Party. > *noun* **1** a person advocating republican government. **2** (**Republican**) (in the US) a member or supporter of the Republican Party. **3** (**Republican**) an advocate of a united Ireland.

DERIVATIVES – **republicanism** *noun*.

repudiate /ri**pyoo**diayt/ > *verb* **1** refuse to accept or be associated with. **2** deny the truth or validity of. **3** archaic disown or divorce (one's wife).

DERIVATIVES – **repudiation** *noun* **repudiator** *noun*.

ORIGIN – from Latin *repudiatus* 'divorced, cast off', from *repudium* 'divorce'.

repugnance /ri**pug**nənss/ > *noun* intense disgust.

DERIVATIVES – **repugnancy** *noun*.

ORIGIN – first meaning 'opposition': from Latin *repugnare* 'oppose'.

repugnant > *adjective* extremely distasteful; unacceptable.

SYNONYMS – abhorrent, disgusting, repellent, repulsive, revolting.

repulse > *verb* **1** drive back (an attacking enemy) by force. **2** rebuff or refuse to accept. **3** cause to feel intense distaste or disgust. > *noun* the action or an instant of repulsing or being repulsed.

ORIGIN – from Latin *repellere*, from *re-* 'back' + *pellere* 'to drive'.

repulsion > *noun* **1** a feeling of intense distaste or disgust. **2** Physics a force under the influence of which objects tend to move away from each other, e.g. through having the same magnetic polarity or electric charge.

repulsive > *adjective* **1** arousing intense distaste or disgust. **2** Physics of or relating to repulsion between physical objects.

DERIVATIVES – **repulsively** *adverb* **repulsiveness** *noun*.

SYNONYMS – **1** abhorrent, disgusting, odious, repellent, repugnant, revolting, vile.

repurchase > *verb* buy (something) back. > *noun* the action of buying something back.

reputable /**rep**yootəb'l/ > *adjective* having a good reputation.

DERIVATIVES – **reputably** *adverb*.

reputation > *noun* **1** the beliefs or opinions that are generally held about someone or something. **2** a widespread belief that someone or something has a particular characteristic: *it earned him a reputation as an expert.*

repute /ri**pyoot**/ > *noun* **1** the opinion generally held of someone or something. **2** the state of being highly regarded. > *verb* **1** (**be reputed**) be generally regarded as having done something or as having particular characteristics. **2** (**reputed**) generally believed to exist: *the reputed flatness of the country.*

DERIVATIVES – **reputedly** *adverb*.

ORIGIN – from Latin *reputare* 'think over'.

request > *noun* **1** an act of asking politely or formally for something. **2** a thing that is asked for in such a way. > *verb* **1** politely or formally ask for. **2** politely or formally ask (someone) to do something.

DERIVATIVES – **requester** *noun*.

SYNONYMS – *noun* **1,2** appeal, entreaty, petition, plea. *verb* **1** appeal for, ask for, call for, solicit. **2** beg, beseech, entreat, implore, importune.

COMBINATIONS – **request stop** Brit. a bus stop at which the bus halts only if requested by a passenger or if hailed.

ORIGIN – from Latin *requirere* 'require'.

requiem /**rek**wiəm/ > *noun* **1** (especially in the Roman Catholic Church) a Mass for the repose of the souls of the dead. **2** a musical composition setting parts of such a Mass.

ORIGIN – Latin, from *requies* 'rest'.

require > *verb* **1** need or depend on. **2** wish to have. **3** instruct or expect (someone) to do something. **4** (**require of**) regard (an action or quality) as due from. **5** specify as compulsory.

DERIVATIVES – **requirement** *noun*.

SYNONYMS – **1** call for, demand, necessitate, need. **2** desire, want, wish for.

ORIGIN – Latin *requirere*, from *re-* (expressing intensive force) + *quaerere* 'seek'.

requisite /**rek**wizit/ > *adjective* made necessary by particular circumstances or regulations. > *noun* a thing that is necessary for the achievement of a specified end.

requisition /rekwi**zish**'n/ > *noun* **1** an official order laying claim to the use of property or materials. **2** the appropriation of goods for military or public use. **3** a formal written demand that something should be performed or put into operation. > *verb* demand the use, supply, or performance of through the issue of a requisition.

requite /ri**kwit**/ > *verb* formal **1** make appropriate return for (a favour or demonstration of affection, or a wrongdoing). **2** return a favour to (someone).

DERIVATIVES – **requital** *noun*.

ORIGIN – from **RE-** + obsolete *quite* 'quit oneself'.

reran past of **RERUN**.

reread > *verb* (past and past participle **reread**) read (a text) again. > *noun* an act of rereading.

reredos /**reer**doss/ > *noun* (pl. same) an ornamental screen at the back of an altar in a church.

ORIGIN – Old French *areredos*, from *arere* 'behind' + *dos* 'back'.

re-release > *verb* release (a recording or film) again. > *noun* a re-released recording or film.

re-route > *verb* send by or along a different route.

rerun > *verb* /ree**run**/ (**rerunning**; past **reran**; past participle **rerun**) show, stage, or perform again. > *noun* /**ree**run/ a rerun event, competition, or programme.

resale > *noun* the sale of a thing previously bought.

DERIVATIVES – **resaleable** (also **resalable**) *adjective*.

resat past and past participle of **RESIT**.

reschedule > *verb* **1** change the time of (a planned event). **2** arrange a new scheme of repayments of (a debt).

rescind /ri**sind**/ > *verb* revoke, cancel, or repeal (a law, order, or agreement).

DERIVATIVES – **rescindable** *adjective*.

ORIGIN – Latin *rescindere*, from *re-* (expressing intensive force) + *scindere* 'to divide, split'.

rescission /ri**sizh**'n/ > *noun* formal the rescinding of a law, order, or agreement.

rescue > *verb* (**rescues, rescued, rescuing**) save from a dangerous or distressing situation. > *noun* an act of rescuing or being rescued.

DERIVATIVES – **rescuer** *noun*.

ORIGIN – Old French *rescoure*, from Latin *re-* (expressing intensive force) + *excutere* 'shake out, discard'.

reseal > *verb* seal again.

DERIVATIVES – **resealable** *adjective*.

research /ri**serch**/ > *noun* the systematic study of materials and sources in order to establish facts and reach new conclusions. > *verb* **1** carry out research into. **2** use research to discover or verify information to be presented in (a book, programme, etc.).

DERIVATIVES – **researcher** *noun*.

NOTE – the traditional pronunciation in British English puts the stress on the second syllable, **-search**, while in US English the stress comes on the **re-**. The US pronunciation is becoming more common in British English and, though still a matter of some controversy, is now generally accepted as a standard variant.

COMBINATIONS – **research and development** (in industry) work directed towards innovation in and improvement of products and processes.

ORIGIN – obsolete French *recercher*, from *re-* (expressing intensive force) + *cerchier* 'to search'.

reselect > *verb* select again or differently.

DERIVATIVES – **reselection** *noun*.

resell > *verb* (past and past participle **resold**) sell (something one has bought) to someone else.

DERIVATIVES – **reseller** *noun*.

resemblance > *noun* **1** the state of resembling. **2** a way in which things resemble each other.

SYNONYMS – **1** affinity, likeness, similarity.

resemble > *verb* have a similar appearance to or features in common with.

ORIGIN – Old French *resembler*, from Latin *similare*, from *similis* 'like'.

resent > *verb* feel bitterness or indignation towards.

ORIGIN – obsolete French *resentir*, from *re-* (expressing intensive force) + *sentir* 'feel', from Latin *sentire*.

resentful > *adjective* feeling or expressing bitterness or indignation.

DERIVATIVES – **resentfully** *adverb* **resentfulness** *noun*.

SYNONYMS – aggrieved, bitter, embittered, indignant, rancorous, sour.

resentment > *noun* bitterness; indignation.

reservation > *noun* **1** the action of reserving. **2** an arrangement whereby something has been reserved. **3** an area of land set aside for occupation by North American Indians or Australian Aboriginals. **4** a qualification or expression of doubt attached to a statement or claim.

reserve > *verb* **1** retain for future use. **2** arrange for (a seat, ticket, etc.) to be kept for the use of a particular person. **3** retain or hold (a right or entitlement). **4** refrain from delivering (a judgement or decision) without due consideration or evidence. > *noun* **1** a reserved supply of a commodity. **2** funds kept available by a bank, company, or government. **3** a force or body of troops withheld from action to reinforce or protect others, or additional to the regular forces and available in an emergency. **4** an extra player in a team, serving as a possible substitute. **5** (**the reserves**) the second-choice team. **6** an area of land set aside for occupation by an indigenous people. **7** a protected area for wildlife. **8** a lack of warmth or openness. **9** qualification or doubt attached to a statement or claim.

DERIVATIVES – **reservable** *adjective*.

SYNONYMS – *verb* **1** earmark, keep, preserve, put aside, retain, save. **2** book. *noun* **1** stock, store, supply. **8** aloofness, detachment, remoteness, reticence.

COMBINATIONS – **reserve bank 1** (in the US) a regional bank operating under and implementing the policies of the Federal Reserve. **2** Austral./NZ a central bank. **reserve currency** a strong currency widely used in international trade that a central bank is prepared to hold as part of its foreign exchange reserves. **reserve price** the price stipulated as the lowest acceptable by the seller for an item sold at auction.

ORIGIN – Latin *reservare* 'keep back'.

re-serve > *verb* serve again.

reserved > *adjective* slow to reveal emotion or opinions.

DERIVATIVES – **reservedly** *adverb* **reservedness** *noun*.

reservist > *noun* a member of a military reserve force.

reservoir* /**rezz**ərvwaar/ > *noun* **1** a large natural or artificial lake used as a source of water supply. **2** a place where fluid collects, especially in rock strata or in the body. **3** a receptacle or part of a machine designed to hold fluid. **4** a supply or source of something.

*SPELLING – remember to include an *r* before the *v*: reservoir.

ORIGIN – French *réservoir*, from *réserver* 'to reserve, keep'.

reset > *verb* (**resetting**; past and past participle **reset**) **1** set again or differently. **2** set (a counter, clock, etc.) to zero.

DERIVATIVES – **resettable** *adjective*.

resettle > *verb* settle or cause to settle in a different place.

DERIVATIVES – **resettlement** *noun*.

reshape > *verb* shape or form differently or again.

reshuffle > *verb* **1** interchange the positions of (members of a team, especially government ministers). **2** rearrange. > *noun* an act of reshuffling.

reside > *verb* **1** have one's permanent home in a particular place. **2** (of a right or legal power) belong to a person or body. **3** (of a quality) be present or inherent in something.

residence > *noun* **1** the fact of residing somewhere. **2** the place where a person resides; a person's home. **3** the official house of a government minister or other official figure.

IDIOMS – **artist** (or **writer**) **in residence** an artist or writer who is based for a set period within an institution and is available for teaching purposes.

residency > *noun* (pl. **residencies**) **1** the fact of living in a place. **2** a residential post held by an artist or writer. **3** Brit. a musician's regular engagement at a club or other venue. **4** N. Amer. a period of specialised medical training in a hospital; the position of a resident. **5** a group or organisation of intelligence agents in a foreign country. **6** historical the official residence of a British government agent in a semi-independent state.

resident > *noun* **1** a person who lives somewhere on a long-term basis. **2** Brit. a guest in a hotel who stays for one or more nights. **3** US a pupil who boards at a boarding school. **4** N. Amer. a medical graduate engaged in specialised practice under supervision in a hospital. **5** an intelligence agent in a foreign country. **6** historical a British government agent in any semi-independent state, especially the Governor General's representative at the court of an Indian state. **7** a bird, butterfly, or other animal of a species that does not migrate. > *adjective* **1** living somewhere on a long-term basis. **2** having living quarters on the premises of one's work. **3** attached to and working regularly for a particular institution. **4** (of a bird, butterfly or other animal) non-migratory.

ORIGIN – from Latin *residere* 'remain'.

residential > *adjective* **1** designed for people to live in. **2** providing accommodation in addition to other services. **3** occupied by private houses. **4** concerning or relating to residence: *land for residential use.*

DERIVATIVES – **residentially** *adverb*.

residua plural of RESIDUUM.

residual /ri**zid**yooəl/ > *adjective* remaining after the greater part or quantity has gone or been subtracted. > *noun* **1** a residual quantity. **2** a royalty paid to a performer or writer for a repeat of a play, television show, or advertisement. **3** the resale value of a new car or other item at a specified time after purchase.

DERIVATIVES – **residually** *adverb*.

residue /**rezz**idyoō/ > *noun* **1** a small amount of something that remains after the main part has gone or been taken or used. **2** a substance that remains after a process such as combustion or evaporation. **3** Law the part of an estate that is left after the payment of charges, debts, and bequests.

ORIGIN – Latin *residuum*, from *residere* 'remain'.

residuum /ri**zid**yooəm/ > *noun* (pl. **residua** /ri**zid**yooə/) technical a chemical residue.

ORIGIN – Latin, from *residere* 'remain'.

resign > *verb* **1** voluntarily leave a job or position of office. **2** (**be resigned**) accept that something undesirable cannot be avoided.

DERIVATIVES – **resigned** *adjective*.

ORIGIN – Latin *resignare* 'unseal, cancel'.

re-sign > *verb* sign (a document or contract) again.

resignation > *noun* **1** an act of resigning. **2** a document conveying an intention to resign. **3** acceptance of something undesirable but inevitable.

resilient /ri**zill**iənt/ > *adjective* **1** able to recoil or spring back into shape after bending, stretching, or being compressed. **2** (of a person) able to withstand or recover quickly from difficult conditions.

DERIVATIVES – **resilience** *noun* **resiliently** *adverb*.

SYNONYMS – **1** elastic, pliant. **2** buoyant, irrepressible, strong, tough.

ORIGIN – Latin, 'leaping back'.

resin /**rezz**in/ > *noun* **1** a sticky substance exuded by some trees. **2** a synthetic polymer used as the basis of plastics, adhesives, varnishes, etc. > *verb* (**resined**, **resining**) rub or treat with resin.

DERIVATIVES – **resinous** *adjective*.

ORIGIN – Latin *resina*; related to Greek *rhētinē* 'pine resin'.

resinate > *verb* impregnate or flavour with resin.

DERIVATIVES – **resinated** *adjective*.

resist > *verb* **1** withstand the action or effect of. **2** try to prevent by action or argument. **3** refrain from (something tempting). **4** struggle against someone or something. > *noun* a resistant substance used to protect parts of a surface during the application of dye, glaze, etc.

DERIVATIVES – **resistible** *adjective*.

SYNONYMS – *verb* **1** endure, weather, withstand. **2** block, hinder, obstruct, oppose. **3** abstain from, forgo, refuse.

ORIGIN – Latin *resistere*, from *re-* (expressing opposition) + *sistere* 'stop'.

resistance > *noun* **1** the action of resisting. **2** armed or violent opposition. **3** (also **resistance movement**) a secret organisation resisting political authority. **4** the impeding effect exerted by one material thing on another. **5** the ability not to be affected by something. **6** Medicine & Biology lack of sensitivity to a drug, insecticide, etc., especially as a result of continued exposure or genetic change. **7** the degree to which a material or device opposes the passage of an electric current.

IDIOMS – **the line** (or **path**) **of least resistance** the easiest course of action.

DERIVATIVES – **resistant** *adjective*.

resistive > *adjective* **1** technical able to resist something. **2** Physics of or concerning electrical resistance.

DERIVATIVES – **resistivity** *noun*.

resistor > *noun* Physics a device having resistance to the passage of an electric current.

resit Brit. > *verb* /reesit/ (**resitting**; past and past participle **resat**) take (an examination) again after failing. > *noun* /reesit/ an examination held for this purpose.

resize > *verb* alter the size of (something, especially a computer window or image).

reskill > *verb* teach or equip with new skills.

resold past and past participle of RESELL.

re-soluble > *adjective* able to dissolve or be dissolved again.

resolute /rezzaloot/ > *adjective* determined; unwavering.

DERIVATIVES – **resolutely** *adverb* **resoluteness** *noun*.

ORIGIN – Latin *resolutus* 'loosened, released, paid': originally in the sense 'paid', describing a rent.

resolution > *noun* **1** the quality of being resolute. **2** a firm decision. **3** an expression of opinion or intention agreed on by a legislative body. **4** the action of solving a problem or dispute. **5** the process of reducing or separating something into components. **6** the smallest interval measurable by a telescope or other scientific instrument. **7** the degree of detail visible in a photographic or television image.

resolve > *verb* **1** settle or find a solution to. **2** decide firmly on a course of action. **3** (of a legislative body) take a decision by a formal vote. **4** (**resolve into**) reduce into (separate elements or a more elementary form). **5** (of something seen at a distance) turn into a different form when seen more clearly. **6** (of

optical or photographic equipment) separate or distinguish between (closely adjacent objects). > *noun* **1** firm determination. **2** US a formal resolution by a legislative body or public meeting.

DERIVATIVES – **resolvable** *adjective* **resolved** *adjective* **resolver** *noun*.

SYNONYMS – *verb* **1** clear up, settle, solve, sort out. **2** decide, determine. *noun* **1** dedication, determination, purpose, resoluteness, tenacity.

COMBINATIONS – **resolving power** the ability of an optical instrument or type of film to separate or distinguish small or closely adjacent images.

ORIGIN – first in the senses 'dissolve, disintegrate' and 'solve (a problem)': from Latin *resolvere*, from *re-* (expressing intensive force) + *solvere* 'loosen'.

resonance > *noun* **1** the quality of being resonant. **2** Physics the reinforcement or prolongation of sound by reflection or synchronous vibration.

resonant > *adjective* **1** (of sound) deep, clear, and continuing to sound or ring. **2** (of a room, musical instrument, or hollow body) tending to reinforce or prolong sounds. **3** (**resonant with**) filled or resounding with. **4** evoking or suggesting enduring images, memories, or emotions.

DERIVATIVES – **resonantly** *adverb*.

ORIGIN – from Latin *resonare* 'sound again, resound'.

resonate /rezzanayt/ > *verb* **1** be resonant. **2** chiefly US (of an idea or action) meet with someone's agreement.

DERIVATIVES – **resonator** *noun*.

resorb /risorb/ > *verb* **1** absorb again. **2** Physiology remove (cells, tissue, etc.) by gradual breakdown and dispersal in the circulation.

ORIGIN – Latin *resorbere*.

resorption /rizorpsh'n/ > *noun* the process or action of resorbing or being resorbed.

DERIVATIVES – **resorptive** *adjective*.

resort > *verb* (**resort to**) turn to and adopt (a strategy or course of action) so as to resolve a difficult situation. > *noun* **1** a place frequented for holidays or recreation. **2** the action of resorting to something. **3** a strategy or course of action.

IDIOMS – **as a first** (or **last** or **final**) **resort** before anything else is attempted (or when all else has failed).

ORIGIN – Old French *resortir* 'come or go out again'.

resound /rizownd/ > *verb* **1** fill or be filled with a ringing, booming, or echoing sound. **2** (of fame, success, etc.) be much talked of. **3** (**resounding**) emphatic; unmistakable.

DERIVATIVES – **resoundingly** *adverb*.

resource /risorss, rizorss/ > *noun* **1** a stock or supply of materials or assets. **2** an action

or strategy adopted in adverse circumstances. **3** (**resources**) personal attributes and capabilities that sustain one in adverse circumstances. **4** a teaching aid. > *verb* provide with resources.

ORIGIN – from Old French *resourdre* 'rise again, recover'.

resourceful > *adjective* able to find quick and clever ways to overcome difficulties.

DERIVATIVES – **resourcefully** *adverb* **resourcefulness** *noun*.

SYNONYMS – enterprising, imaginative, inventive, quick-witted.

respect > *noun* **1** a feeling of admiration for someone elicited by their qualities or achievements. **2** due regard for the feelings or rights of others. **3** (**respects**) polite greetings. **4** a particular aspect, point, or detail. > *verb* **1** feel or have respect for. **2** avoid harming or interfering with. **3** agree to recognise and abide by.

IDIOMS – **in respect of** (or **with respect to**) as regards; with reference to.

DERIVATIVES – **respecter** *noun* **respectful** *adjective* **respectfully** *adverb* **respectfulness** *noun*.

SYNONYMS – *noun* **1** admiration, esteem, regard, reverence. **2** consideration, politeness, thoughtfulness. *verb* **1** admire, esteem, hold in high regard, revere, think highly of.

ORIGIN – Latin *respectus*, from *respicere* 'look back at, regard'.

respectable > *adjective* **1** regarded by society as being proper, correct, and good. **2** of some merit or importance. **3** adequate or acceptable in number, size, or amount.

DERIVATIVES – **respectability** *noun* **respectably** *adverb*.

SYNONYMS – **1** decent, honourable, proper, upright, upstanding. **2** considerable, noteworthy. **3** decent, passable, reasonable.

ANTONYMS – **1** disreputable.

respecting > *preposition* with reference or regard to.

respective > *adjective* belonging or relating separately to each of two or more people or things.

respectively > *adverb* separately or individually and in the order already mentioned.

respell > *verb* (past and past participle **respelled** or chiefly Brit. **respelt**) spell (a word) differently, especially in order to indicate its pronunciation.

respirate /respirayt/ > *verb* Medicine & Biology assist to breathe by means of artificial respiration.

respiration > *noun* **1** the action of breathing. **2** a single breath. **3** Biology a process in living organisms involving the production of energy and the release of carbon dioxide from the oxidation of complex organic substances.

respirator > *noun* **1** an apparatus worn over the face to prevent the inhalation of dust, smoke, or other harmful substances. **2** an apparatus used to induce artificial respiration.

respiratory /riˈspirrətri/ > *adjective* relating to respiration or the organs of respiration.

respire /riˈspīr/ > *verb* **1** breathe. **2** (of a plant) carry out respiration.

DERIVATIVES – **respirable** *adjective*.

ORIGIN – Latin *respirare* 'breathe out'.

respite /ˈrespīt, riˈspīt/ > *noun* a short period of rest or relief from something difficult or unpleasant.

SYNONYMS – break, breathing space, lull, pause, reprieve, rest.

COMBINATIONS – **respite care** temporary care of a sick, elderly, or disabled person, providing relief for their usual carer.

ORIGIN – Old French *respit*, from Latin *respectus* 'refuge, consideration'.

resplendent /riˈsplendənt/ > *adjective* attractive and impressive through being richly colourful or sumptuous.

DERIVATIVES – **resplendence** *noun* **resplendency** *noun* **resplendently** *adverb*.

ORIGIN – Latin, from *resplendere* 'shine out'.

respond > *verb* say or do something in reply or as a reaction.

DERIVATIVES – **responder** *noun*.

ORIGIN – Latin *respondere* 'pledge again'.

respondent > *noun* **1** a defendant in a lawsuit, especially one in an appeal or divorce case. **2** a person who responds to a questionnaire or an advertisement. > *adjective* **1** in the position of defendant in a lawsuit. **2** responding to something.

response > *noun* **1** an instance of responding; an answer or reaction. **2** an excitation of a nerve impulse.

responsibility > *noun* (pl. **responsibilities**) **1** the state or fact of being responsible. **2** the opportunity or ability to act independently and take decisions without authorisation. **3** a thing which one is required to do as part of a job, role, or legal obligation.

responsible > *adjective* **1** having an obligation to do something, or having control over or care for someone. **2** being the primary cause of something and so able to be blamed or credited for it. **3** morally accountable for one's behaviour. **4** capable of being trusted. **5** (of a job or position) involving important duties or decisions or control over others. **6** (**responsible to**) reporting to; answerable to.

DERIVATIVES – **responsibleness** *noun* **responsibly** *adverb*.

ORIGIN – from Latin *respondere* 'respond, pledge again'.

responsive > *adjective* **1** responding readily and positively. **2** in response; answering.

DERIVATIVES – **responsively** *adverb* **responsiveness** *noun*.

respray > *verb* /reeˈspray/ spray with a new coat of paint. > *noun* /ˈreespray/ an instance of respraying.

res publica /rayz ˈpoobblikə/ > *noun* the state, republic, or commonwealth.

ORIGIN – Latin, 'public matter'.

rest[1] > *verb* **1** cease work or movement in order to relax or recover strength. **2** allow to be inactive in order to regain or save strength or energy. **3** place or be placed so as to stay in a specified position. **4** (**rest on**) be based on or grounded in; depend on. **5** (**rest with**) (of power, responsibility, etc.) belong to. **6** (of a problem or subject) be left without further investigation or discussion. **7** N. Amer. conclude the case for the prosecution or defence in a court of law. > *noun* **1** the action or a period of resting. **2** a motionless state. **3** Music an interval of silence of a specified duration. **4** an object that is used to hold or support something.

IDIOMS – **rest one's case** conclude one's presentation of evidence and arguments in a lawsuit.

DERIVATIVES – **restful** *adjective* **restfully** *adverb* **restfulness** *noun* **restless** *adjective* **restlessly** *adverb* **restlessness** *noun*.

COMBINATIONS – **rest home** a residential institution where old or frail people are cared for. **restroom** chiefly N. Amer. a toilet in a public building.

ORIGIN – Old English, from a root meaning 'league' or 'mile' (referring to a distance after which one rests).

rest[2] > *noun* **1** the remaining part of something. **2** (treated as pl.) the remaining people or things; the others. > *verb* remain or be left in a specified condition.

ORIGIN – Latin *restare* 'remain'.

restart > *verb* start again.

restaurant /ˈrestəroN, ˈrestəront/ > *noun* a place where people pay to sit and eat meals that are cooked on the premises.

ORIGIN – French, from *restaurer* 'provide food for' (literally 'restore to a former state').

restaurateur* /restərəˈtör/ > *noun* a person who owns and manages a restaurant.

***SPELLING** – note that there is no *n*: restau*rat*eur. This is because the word is taken directly from the French verb *restaurer*. (The word **restaurant** reflects the spelling in French of the present participle of the same verb.)

restitution > *noun* **1** the restoration of something lost or stolen to its proper owner. **2** recompense for injury or loss. **3** the restoration of something to its original state.

DERIVATIVES – **restitutive** *adjective*.

ORIGIN – Latin, from *restituere* 'restore'.

restive > *adjective* **1** unable to keep still or silent; restless. **2** (of a horse) refusing to advance; stubbornly standing still or moving backwards or sideways.

DERIVATIVES – **restively** *adverb* **restiveness** *noun*.

wordpower facts

Restive

The adjective **restive** comes via Old French *restif* from Latin *restare*, meaning 'remain'. The original sense was 'inclined to rest or remain still'; when this was applied to a horse it took on the additional notion of stubbornness, leading to the sense 'obstinately moving backwards or to the side' and later 'restless, unable to settle'. This sense was then extended into general use, bringing about a complete reversal of the original, 17th-century, meaning of the word.

restock > *verb* replenish with fresh stock or supplies.

restoration > *noun* **1** the action of returning something to a former condition, place, or owner. **2** the process of repairing or renovating a building, work of art, etc. **3** the reinstatement of a previous practice, right, or situation. **4** the return of a monarch to a throne, a head of state to government, or a regime to power. **5** (**the Restoration**) the re-establishment of Charles II as King of England in 1660, or the period following this. **6** a structure provided to replace or repair dental tissue.

restorative /riˈstorrətiv/ > *adjective* **1** having the ability to restore health, strength, or a feeling of well-being. **2** relating to the restoration of a damaged tooth or other part of the body. > *noun* a medicine or drink that restores health, strength, or well-being.

DERIVATIVES – **restoratively** *adverb*.

restore > *verb* **1** return to a former condition, place, or owner. **2** repair or renovate (a building, work of art, etc.). **3** bring back (a previous practice, right, or situation); reinstate.

DERIVATIVES – **restorable** *adjective* **restorer** *noun*.

ORIGIN – Latin *restaurare* 'rebuild, restore'.

restrain > *verb* **1** keep under control or within limits. **2** deprive of freedom of movement or personal liberty. **3** repress (a strong emotion).

DERIVATIVES – **restrainable** *adjective* **restrainer** *noun*.

SYNONYMS – **1** check, contain, control, curb, limit, restrict. **2** bind, confine, pinion. **3** contain, curb, repress, stifle, suppress.

ORIGIN – Latin *restringere* 'tie back'.

restrained > *adjective* **1** reserved, unemotional, or dispassionate. **2** understated and subtle; not ornate or brightly coloured.

DERIVATIVES – **restrainedly** *adverb*.

restraint > *noun* **1** the action of restraining. **2** a measure or condition that restrains. **3** a device which limits or prevents freedom of movement. **4** dispassionate or moderate behaviour; self-control.

restrict > *verb* **1** put a limit on; keep under control. **2** deprive of freedom of movement or action.

SYNONYMS – **1** circumscribe, confine, constrain, control, limit. **2** constrict, cramp, hinder, impede, obstruct, restrain.

ORIGIN – Latin *restringere* 'tie back'.

restricted > *adjective* **1** limited in extent, number, or scope. **2** not revealed or made open to the public for reasons of national security.

restriction > *noun* **1** a limiting condition or measure. **2** the action or state of restricting or being restricted.

restrictive > *adjective* imposing restrictions.

DERIVATIVES – **restrictively** *adverb* **restrictiveness** *noun*.

COMBINATIONS – **restrictive practice** Brit. **1** an arrangement by a group of workers to limit output or restrict the entry of new workers in order to protect their own interests. **2** an arrangement in industry or trade that restricts or controls competition between firms.

restring > *verb* (past and past participle **restrung**) **1** fit new strings to. **2** string (beads) again.

restructure > *verb* **1** organise differently. **2** Finance convert (a debt) into debt that is repayable at a later time.

restyle > *verb* /reestīl/ **1** rearrange or remake in a new shape or layout. **2** give a new name or description to. > *noun* /reestīl/ an instance of restyling.

result > *noun* **1** something that is produced by an activity or operation. **2** an item of information or a quantity or formula obtained by experiment or calculation. **3** a final score, mark, or placing in a sporting event or examination. **4** a satisfactory or favourable outcome. **5** the outcome of a business's trading over a given period, expressed as a statement of profit or loss. > *verb* **1** occur or follow as a result. **2** (**result in**) have (a specified outcome).

SYNONYMS – *noun* **1** consequence, effect, product, outcome.

ORIGIN – Latin *resultare* 'to result', earlier in the sense 'spring back', from *salire* 'to jump'.

resultant > *adjective* occurring or produced as a result.

resume > *verb* **1** begin again or continue after a pause or interruption. **2** take or put on again; return to the use of.

DERIVATIVES – **resumption** *noun*.

SYNONYMS – **1** continue, recommence, reconvene, renew, reopen, restart.

ORIGIN – Latin *resumere* 'take back'.

résumé /rezyoomay/ > *noun* **1** a summary. **2** N. Amer. a curriculum vitae.

ORIGIN – French, 'resumed'.

resurface > *verb* **1** put a new coating on (a surface). **2** come back up to the surface of deep water. **3** arise or become evident again.

resurgent /risurjənt/ > *adjective* increasing or reviving after a period of little activity, popularity, or occurrence.

DERIVATIVES – **resurgence** *noun*.

ORIGIN – Latin, from *resurgere* 'rise again'.

resurrect > *verb* **1** restore to life. **2** revive the practice, use, or memory of.

resurrection > *noun* **1** the action or fact of resurrecting or being resurrected. **2** (**the Resurrection**) (in Christian belief) Christ's rising from the dead.

ORIGIN – Latin, from *resurgere* 'rise again'.

resuscitate* /risussitayt/ > *verb* **1** revive from unconsciousness. **2** make active or vigorous again.

DERIVATIVES – **resuscitation** *noun* **resuscitative** *adjective* **resuscitator** *noun*.
***SPELLING** – note that it is *-susc-*, not *-suss-*: re*susc*itate.

ORIGIN – Latin *resuscitare* 'raise again'.

ret /ret/ (also **rate**) > *verb* (**retted, retting**) soak (flax or hemp) in water to soften it.

ORIGIN – related to ROT.

retail > *noun* the sale of goods to the general public (rather than to a wholesaler). > *adverb* being sold in such a way. > *verb* **1** sell (goods) in such a way. **2** (**retail at** or **for**) be sold in this way for (a specified price). **3** recount or relate details of.

DERIVATIVES – **retailer** *noun*.

COMBINATIONS – **retail price index** (in the UK) an index of the variation in the prices of retail goods and other items.

ORIGIN – Old French *retaillier*, from *tailler* 'to cut'.

retain > *verb* **1** continue to have; keep possession of. **2** absorb and continue to hold (a substance). **3** keep in place; hold fixed. **4** keep engaged in one's service. **5** secure the services of (a barrister) with a preliminary payment.

DERIVATIVES – **retainable** *adjective*.

COMBINATIONS – **retaining wall** a wall that holds back earth or water on one side of it.

ORIGIN – Latin *retinere* 'hold back'.

retainer > *noun* **1** a thing that holds something in place. **2** a fee paid in advance to a barrister, in order to secure their services. **3** Brit. a reduced rent paid to retain accommodation during a period of non-occupancy. **4** a servant who has worked for a person or family for a long time.

retake > *verb* /reetayk/ (past **retook**; past participle **retaken**) **1** take (a test or examination) again. **2** regain possession of. > *noun* /reetayk/ **1** a test or examination that is retaken. **2** an instance of filming a scene or recording a piece of music again.

retaliate /ritaliayt/ > *verb* make an attack or assault in return for a similar attack.

DERIVATIVES – **retaliation** *noun* **retaliative** *adjective* **retaliator** *noun* **retaliatory** *adjective*.

ORIGIN – Latin *retaliare* 'return in kind'.

retard > *verb* /ritaard/ hold back the development or progress of. > *noun* /reetaard/ derogatory a mentally handicapped person.

DERIVATIVES – **retardation** *noun* **retarder** *noun*.

ORIGIN – Latin *retardare*, from *tardus* 'slow'.

retardant > *adjective* preventing or inhibiting. > *noun* a fabric or substance that prevents or inhibits the outbreak of fire.

DERIVATIVES – **retardancy** *noun*.

retardataire /ritaardətair/ > *adjective* (of a work of art or architecture) executed in an earlier style.

ORIGIN – French.

retarded > *adjective* less advanced in mental, physical, or social development than is usual for one's age.

retch > *verb* make the sound and movement of vomiting. > *noun* an instance of retching.

ORIGIN – from a Germanic word meaning 'spittle'.

retell > *verb* (past and past participle **retold**) tell (a story) again or differently.

retention > *noun* **1** the act of retaining or state of being retained. **2** failure to eliminate a substance from the body.

retentive > *adjective* **1** (of a person's memory) effective in retaining facts and impressions. **2** able to retain or hold in place.

DERIVATIVES – **retentively** *adverb* **retentiveness** *noun* **retentivity** *noun*.

rethink > *verb* (past and past participle **rethought**) assess or consider (a policy or course of action) again. > *noun* an instance of rethinking.

reticent /rettis'nt/ > *adjective* not revealing one's thoughts or feelings readily.

DERIVATIVES – **reticence** *noun* **reticently** *adverb*.

SYNONYMS – inhibited, reserved, unforthcoming, withdrawn.

ORIGIN – Latin, from *reticere* 'remain silent'.

reticulated /ritikyoolaytid/ > *adjective*

constructed, arranged, or marked like a net or network.

ORIGIN – Latin *reticulatus*, from *rete* 'net'.

reticule /**rett**ikyool/ > *noun* chiefly historical a woman's small drawstring handbag.

ORIGIN – French *réticule*.

retina /**rett**inə/ > *noun* (pl. **retinas** or **retinae** /**rett**inee/) a layer at the back of the eyeball containing cells that are sensitive to light and from which impulses are sent to the brain, where they are interpreted as visual images.

DERIVATIVES – **retinal** *adjective*.

ORIGIN – Latin, from *rete* 'net'.

retinitis /**rett**inītiss/ > *noun* inflammation of the retina.

COMBINATIONS – **retinitis pigmentosa** Medicine a hereditary eye disease characterised by black pigmentation and gradual degeneration of the retina. [ORIGIN – *pigmentosa* from Latin *pigmentum* 'pigment'.]

retinol /**rett**inol/ > *noun* vitamin A, a yellow compound which is essential for vision in dim light and bodily growth and is found in vegetables, egg yolk, and fish-liver oil.

retinopathy /rettinoppəthi/ > *noun* Medicine disease of the retina which results in impairment or loss of vision.

retinue /**rett**inyoo/ > *noun* a group of advisers or assistants accompanying an important person.

ORIGIN – from Old French *retenir* 'keep back, retain'.

retire > *verb* 1 leave one's job and cease to work, especially because one has reached a particular age. 2 (of a sports player) cease to play competitively. 3 withdraw from a race or match because of accident or injury. 4 withdraw to or from a particular place. 5 (of a jury) leave the courtroom to decide the verdict of a trial. 6 go to bed.

DERIVATIVES – **retired** *adjective*.

ORIGIN – French *retirer*, from *re-* 'back' + *tirer* 'draw'.

retirement > *noun* 1 the action or fact of retiring. 2 the period of one's life after retiring from work. 3 seclusion.

retiring > *adjective* tending to avoid company; shy.

DERIVATIVES – **retiringly** *adverb*.

retold past and past participle of RETELL.

retook past of RETAKE.

retool > *verb* 1 equip (a factory) with new or adapted tools. 2 chiefly N. Amer. adapt, alter, or prepare for a new purpose or challenge.

retort[1] > *verb* say something sharp or witty in answer to a remark or accusation. > *noun* a sharp or witty reply.

ORIGIN – Latin *retorquere* 'twist back'.

retort[2] > *noun* 1 a container or furnace for carrying out a chemical process on a large or industrial scale. 2 historical a glass container

with a long neck, used in distilling liquids and other chemical operations. > *verb* heat in a retort.

ORIGIN – from Latin *retorquere* 'twist back' (with reference to the long recurved neck of the glass container).

retouch > *verb* improve or repair (a painting, photograph, etc.) by making slight additions or alterations.

DERIVATIVES – **retoucher** *noun*.

retrace > *verb* 1 go back over (the same route that one has just taken). 2 discover and follow (a route or course taken by someone else). 3 trace (something) back to its source or beginning.

retract > *verb* 1 draw or be drawn back. 2 withdraw (a statement or accusation) as untrue or unjustified. 3 withdraw or go back on (an undertaking or promise).

DERIVATIVES – **retractable** *adjective* **retraction** *noun* **retractive** *adjective*.

ORIGIN – Latin *retrahere* 'draw back'.

retractile /ritraktīl/ > *adjective* Zoology capable of being retracted.

DERIVATIVES – **retractility** *noun*.

retractor > *noun* 1 a device for retracting something. 2 (also **retractor muscle**) chiefly Zoology a muscle serving to retract a part of the body.

retrain > *verb* teach or learn new skills.

retread > *verb* /reetred/ 1 (past **retrod**; past participle **retrodden**) go back over (a path or one's steps). 2 (past and past participle **retreaded**) put a new tread on (a worn tyre). > *noun* /reetred/ a tyre that has been given a new tread; a remould.

retreat > *verb* 1 (of an army) withdraw from confrontation with enemy forces. 2 move back from a difficult situation. 3 withdraw to a quiet or secluded place. > *noun* 1 an act of retreating. 2 a quiet or secluded place. 3 a period or place of seclusion for the purposes of prayer and meditation. 4 a military musical ceremony carried out at sunset.

SYNONYMS – *verb* **1,2** draw back, flee, give ground, pull back, retire, withdraw. *noun* **2** haven, hideaway, refuge, sanctuary.

ORIGIN – Latin *retrahere* 'draw back'.

retrench > *verb* 1 reduce costs or spending in response to economic difficulty. 2 chiefly Austral. make (an employee) redundant in order to reduce costs. 3 formal reduce or diminish.

DERIVATIVES – **retrenchment** *noun*.

ORIGIN – French *retrancher* 'cut out'.

retrial > *noun* Law a second or further trial.

retribution /retribyoosh'n/ > *noun* punishment inflicted in the spirit of moral outrage or personal vengeance.

DERIVATIVES – **retributive** /ritribyootiv/ *adjective* **retributory** /ritribyootəri/ *adjective*.

ORIGIN – Latin, from *retribuere* 'assign again'.

retrieve > *verb* 1 get or bring back. 2 (of a dog) find and bring back (game that has been shot). 3 find or extract (information stored in a computer). 4 rescue from a state of difficulty or collapse. > *noun* an act of retrieving.

DERIVATIVES – **retrievable** *adjective* **retrieval** *noun*.

ORIGIN – Old French *retrover* 'find again'.

retriever > *noun* a dog of a breed used for retrieving game.

retro /retrō/ > *adjective* imitative of a style from the recent past. > *noun* retro clothes, music, or style.

ORIGIN – French, from *rétrograde* 'retrograde'.

retro- > *combining form* 1 denoting action that is directed backwards or is reciprocal: *retrogress*. 2 denoting location behind: *retrorocket*.

ORIGIN – Latin *retro* 'backwards'.

retroactive > *adjective* (especially of legislation) taking effect from a date in the past.

DERIVATIVES – **retroaction** *noun* **retroactively** *adverb*.

retrod past of RETREAD (in sense 1).

retrodden past participle of RETREAD (in sense 1).

retrofit > *verb* (**retrofitted**, **retrofitting**) fit with a component or accessory not fitted during manufacture. > *noun* an act of retrofitting.

ORIGIN – blend of RETROACTIVE and REFIT.

retroflex (also **retroflexed**) > *adjective* Anatomy & Medicine turned backwards.

DERIVATIVES – **retroflexion** *noun*.

ORIGIN – Latin *retroflectere* 'bend backwards'.

retrograde > *adjective* 1 directed or moving backwards. 2 (of the order of something) reversed; inverse. 3 reverting to an earlier and inferior condition. 4 chiefly Astronomy proceeding in a reverse direction from normal, especially (of planetary motion) from east to west. > *verb* 1 go back in position or time. 2 revert to an earlier and inferior condition. 3 Astronomy show retrograde motion.

DERIVATIVES – **retrogradation** *noun* **retrogradely** *adverb*.

ORIGIN – Latin *retrogradus*, from *retro* 'backwards' + *gradus* 'step'.

retrogress /retrəgress/ > *verb* go back to an earlier and typically inferior state; engage in retrogression.

retrogression > *noun* 1 the process of retrogressing. 2 Astronomy retrogradation.

DERIVATIVES – **retrogressive** *adjective*.

retrorocket > *noun* a small auxiliary rocket on a spacecraft or missile, fired in the direction of travel to slow it down.

retrospect > *noun* a survey or review of a past course of events or period of time.

IDIOMS – **in retrospect** when looking back on a past event or situation; with hindsight.

DERIVATIVES – **retrospection** *noun*.

retrospective > *adjective* **1** looking back on or dealing with past events or situations. **2** (of an exhibition or compilation) showing the development of an artist's work over a period of time. **3** (of a statute or legal decision) taking effect from a date in the past. > *noun* a retrospective exhibition or compilation.

DERIVATIVES – **retrospectively** *adverb*.

retroussé /rətroōsay/ > *adjective* (of a person's nose) turned up at the tip.

ORIGIN – French, 'tucked up'.

retroverted /retrəvertid/ > *adjective* Anatomy (of the uterus) tilted backwards.

DERIVATIVES – **retroversion** *noun*.

ORIGIN – from Latin *retrovertere* 'turn backwards'.

retrovirus /retrōvīrəss/ > *noun* Biology any of a group of RNA viruses which insert a DNA copy of their genome into the host cell in order to replicate, e.g. HIV.

ORIGIN – from the initial letters of *reverse transcriptase* + VIRUS.

retsina /retseenə/ > *noun* a Greek white wine flavoured with resin.

ORIGIN – modern Greek.

retune > *verb* tune again or differently.

return > *verb* **1** come or go back to a place. **2** (**return to**) go back to (a particular state or activity). **3** give or send back or put back in place. **4** feel, say, or do (the same feeling, action, etc.) in response. **5** (in tennis) hit or send (the ball) back to an opponent. **6** (of a judge or jury) state or present (a verdict). **7** yield or make (a profit). **8** (of an electorate) elect to office. > *noun* **1** an act of returning. **2** chiefly Brit. a ticket allowing travel to a place and back again. **3** (in sport) a second contest between the same opponents. **4** a ticket (for an event) that has been returned because no longer wanted. **5** a profit from an investment. **6** a key on a computer keyboard used to move a cursor to the start of a new line. **7** a mechanism or key on a typewriter that returns the carriage to the start of a new line. **8** Architecture a part receding from the line of the front, for example the side of a house or of a window opening.

IDIOMS – **by return of post** Brit. in the next available mail delivery to the sender. **many happy returns of the day** a greeting to someone on their birthday.

DERIVATIVES – **returnable** *adjective* **returner** *noun*.

COMBINATIONS – **returning officer** Brit. the official in each constituency or electorate who conducts an election and announces the result.

ORIGIN – Old French *returner*, from Latin *re-* 'back' + *tornare* 'to turn'.

returnee > *noun* **1** a refugee returning from abroad. **2** a person returning to work after an extended absence.

retype > *verb* type (text) again.

reunify > *verb* (**reunifies**, **reunified**) restore political unity to.

DERIVATIVES – **reunification** *noun*.

reunion > *noun* **1** the process or an instance of reuniting. **2** a social gathering attended by members of a group of people who have not seen each other for some time.

reunite > *verb* bring or come together again after a period of separation or disunity.

reuse > *verb* /reeyōoz/ use again or more than once. > *noun* /reeyōoss/ the action of using something again.

DERIVATIVES – **reusable** *adjective*.

Rev. > *abbreviation* Reverend.

rev informal > *noun* (**revs**) the number of revolutions of an engine per minute. > *verb* (**revved**, **revving**) increase the running speed of (an engine) by pressing the accelerator.

COMBINATIONS – **rev counter** an instrument that measures the rate of revolutions of an engine.

revalue > *verb* (**revalues**, **revalued**, **revaluing**) **1** value again. **2** Economics adjust the value of (a currency) in relation to other currencies.

DERIVATIVES – **revaluation** *noun*.

revamp > *verb* give new and improved form, structure, or appearance to. > *noun* a new and improved version.

revanchism /rivanchiz'm/ > *noun* a policy of retaliation, especially to recover lost territory.

DERIVATIVES – **revanchist** *adjective* & *noun*.

ORIGIN – from French *revanche* 'revenge'.

Revd > *abbreviation* Reverend.

reveal[1] > *verb* **1** disclose (information). **2** cause or allow to be seen.

DERIVATIVES – **revealer** *noun*.

SYNONYMS – **1** disclose, divulge, impart, leak, tell. **2** expose, uncover, unveil.

ORIGIN – Latin *revelare*, from *velum* 'veil'.

reveal[2] > *noun* either side surface of an aperture in a wall for a door or window.

ORIGIN – from Old French *revaler* 'lower'.

revealing > *adjective* **1** divulging interesting or significant information. **2** (of a garment) allowing more of the wearer's body to be seen than is usual or acceptable.

DERIVATIVES – **revealingly** *adverb*.

revegetate > *verb* produce new vegetation on (disturbed or barren ground).

DERIVATIVES – **revegetation** *noun*.

reveille /rivali/ > *noun* a military waking signal sounded on a bugle, drum, etc.

ORIGIN – from French *réveillez!* 'wake up!'.

revel > *verb* (**revelled**, **revelling**; US **reveled**, **reveling**) **1** engage in lively and noisy festivities. **2** (**revel in**) gain great pleasure from. > *noun* (**revels**) lively and noisy festivities.

DERIVATIVES – **reveller** *noun* **revelry** (pl. **revelries**) *noun*.

SYNONYMS – *verb* **1** carouse, celebrate, make merry, roister. **2** (**revel in**) bask in, delight in, enjoy, lap up, relish.

ORIGIN – Old French *reveler* 'rise up in rebellion', from Latin *rebellare* 'to rebel'.

revelation > *noun* **1** the revealing of something that was previously unknown, secret, or hidden. **2** a surprising or remarkable thing.

DERIVATIVES – **revelational** *adjective*.

revelatory /revvəlaytəri/ > *adjective* revealing.

revenge > *noun* **1** retaliation for an injury or wrong. **2** the desire to inflict this. > *verb* **1** (**revenge oneself** or **be revenged**) inflict revenge for an injury or wrong done to oneself. **2** inflict revenge on behalf of (someone else). **3** inflict revenge for (a wrong or injury).

IDIOMS – **revenge is a dish best served** (or **eaten**) **cold** proverb vengeance is often more satisfying if it is not exacted immediately.

SYNONYMS – *noun* **1** reprisal, retaliation, retribution, vengeance. **2** vengefulness.

ORIGIN – Old French *revencher*, from Latin *revindicare*, from *vindicare* 'claim, avenge'.

revengeful > *adjective* eager for revenge.

DERIVATIVES – **revengefully** *adverb* **revengefulness** *noun*.

revenue > *noun* **1** the income received by an organisation. **2** a state's annual income from which public expenses are met.

ORIGIN – from Latin *revenire* 'return'.

reverberate > *verb* **1** (of a loud noise) be repeated as an echo. **2** have continuing serious effects.

DERIVATIVES – **reverberant** *adjective* **reverberation** *noun* **reverberative** *adjective* **reverberator** *noun* **reverberatory** *adjective*.

ORIGIN – Latin *reverberare* 'strike again'.

revere /riveer/ > *verb* respect or admire deeply.

SYNONYMS – admire, esteem, idolise, venerate, worship.

ANTONYMS – despise.

ORIGIN – Latin *revereri*, from *vereri* 'to fear'.

reverence > *noun* **1** deep respect. **2** archaic a bow or curtsy. **3** (**His** or **Your Reverence**) a title given to a member of the clergy, especially a priest in Ireland. > *verb* regard or treat with reverence.

SYNONYMS – **1** admiration, esteem, idolisation, veneration, worship.

reverend > *adjective* a title or form of address to members of the clergy. > *noun* informal a clergyman.

COMBINATIONS – **Reverend Mother** the title of the Mother Superior of a convent.

reverent > *adjective* showing reverence.

DERIVATIVES – **reverential** *adjective* **reverently** *adverb*.

reverie /**revv**əri/ > *noun* **1** a daydream. **2** Music an instrumental piece suggesting a dreamy or musing state.

ORIGIN – Old French, 'rejoicing, revelry', from *rever* 'be delirious'.

revers /ri**veer**/ > *noun* (pl. same /ri**veerz**/) the turned-back edge of a garment revealing the underside, especially at the lapel.

ORIGIN – French, 'reverse'.

reversal > *noun* **1** a change to an opposite direction, position, or course of action. **2** an adverse change of fortune.

reverse > *verb* **1** move backwards. **2** (of an engine) work in a contrary direction. **3** turn the other way round or up or inside out. **4** undo, revoke, or counteract. > *adjective* going in or turned towards the opposite direction. > *noun* **1** a complete change of direction or action. **2** reverse gear. **3** (**the reverse**) the opposite or contrary. **4** a setback or defeat. **5** the opposite side or face to the observer. **6** the side of a coin or medal bearing the value or secondary design.

IDIOMS – **reverse the charges** chiefly Brit. make the recipient of a telephone call responsible for payment.

DERIVATIVES – **reversible** *adjective*.

COMBINATIONS – **reverse engineering** the reproduction of another manufacturer's product after detailed examination of its construction or composition. **reverse gear** a gear making a vehicle or piece of machinery move or work backwards. **reverse takeover** a takeover of a public company by a smaller company. **reversing light** Brit. a white light at the rear of a vehicle that shines when the vehicle is reversing.

ORIGIN – Latin *revertere* 'turn back'.

reversion /ri**ver**sh'n/ > *noun* **1** a return to a previous state, practice, or belief. **2** Biology the action of reverting to a former or ancestral type. **3** Law the right to possess or succeed to property on the death of the present possessor or at the end of a lease. **4** a sum payable on a person's death by way of life insurance.

DERIVATIVES – **reversionary** *adjective*.

revert > *verb* (**revert to**) **1** return to (a previous state, condition, etc.). **2** Biology return to (a former or ancestral type). **3** Law

(of property) return or pass to by reversion.

ORIGIN – Latin *revertere* 'turn back'.

revetment /ri**vet**mənt/ > *noun* **1** a retaining wall or facing of masonry, supporting or protecting a rampart, wall, etc. **2** a barricade of earth or sandbags providing protection from blast or to prevent aircraft from overrunning when landing.

ORIGIN – French *revêtement*, from Latin *revestire* 'reclothe'.

review > *noun* **1** a formal assessment of something with the intention of instituting change if necessary. **2** a critical appraisal of a book, play, or other work. **3** a retrospective survey or report. **4** a ceremonial display and formal inspection of military or naval forces. > *verb* **1** carry out or write a review of. **2** view or inspect again.

DERIVATIVES – **reviewable** *adjective* **reviewer** *noun*.

SYNONYMS – *noun* **1** analysis, appraisal, assessment, examination, inspection. **2** critique, notice, write-up. *verb* **2** reassess, reconsider, re-evaluate, re-examine.

ORIGIN – obsolete French *reveue*, from *revoir* 'see again'.

revile > *verb* (usu. **be reviled**) criticise with angry insults.

DERIVATIVES – **revilement** *noun* **reviler** *noun*.

ORIGIN – Old French *reviler*, based on *vil* 'vile'.

revise* > *verb* **1** examine and improve or amend (text). **2** reconsider and alter (an opinion or judgement). **3** Brit. reread work done previously in order to prepare for an examination. > *noun* Printing a proof including corrections made in an earlier proof.

DERIVATIVES – **reviser** *noun*.

*****SPELLING – **revise** cannot be spelled with an *-ize* ending.

SYNONYMS – *verb* **1** edit, recast, redraft, rework, rewrite. **2** alter, change, modify.

ORIGIN – Latin *revisere* 'look at again'.

revision > *noun* **1** the action of revising. **2** a revised edition or form.

DERIVATIVES – **revisionary** *adjective*.

revisionism > *noun* often derogatory the revision or modification of accepted theories or principles.

DERIVATIVES – **revisionist** *noun* & *adjective*.

revisit > *verb* (**revisited**, **revisiting**) come back to or visit again.

revitalise (also **revitalize**) > *verb* imbue with new life and vitality.

DERIVATIVES – **revitalisation** *noun*.

revival > *noun* **1** an improvement in the condition, strength, or popularity of something. **2** a reawakening of religious fervour brought about by evangelistic

meetings. **3** a new production of an old play.

revivalism > *noun* **1** a movement to reawaken religious faith and fervour. **2** a tendency or desire to revive a former custom or practice.

DERIVATIVES – **revivalist** *noun* & *adjective*.

revive > *verb* **1** restore to or regain life, consciousness, or strength. **2** restore interest in or the popularity of.

DERIVATIVES – **revivable** *adjective* **reviver** *noun*.

ORIGIN – Latin *revivere*, from *vivere* 'live'.

revivify /ri**vivv**ifī/ > *verb* (**revivifies**, **revivified**) give new life or vigour to.

DERIVATIVES – **revivification** *noun*.

revoke > *verb* end the validity or operation of (a decree, decision, or promise).

DERIVATIVES – **revocable** *adjective* **revocation** *noun* **revoker** *noun*.

ORIGIN – Latin *revocare* 'call back'.

revolt > *verb* **1** rebel against or defy an authority. **2** cause to feel disgust. > *noun* an act of rebellion or defiance.

DERIVATIVES – **revolting** *adjective*.

SYNONYMS – *verb* **1** dissent, mutiny, rebel, riot, rise up. **2** disgust, nauseate, repel, sicken. *noun* insurrection, mutiny, rebellion, rising, uprising.

ORIGIN – Latin *revolvere* 'roll back'.

revolution > *noun* **1** a forcible overthrow of a government or social order, in favour of a new system. **2** a dramatic and wide-reaching change. **3** the action of revolving or rotating. **4** a single completion of an orbit or rotation.

DERIVATIVES – **revolutionism** *noun* **revolutionist** *noun*.

ORIGIN – Latin, from *revolvere* 'roll back'.

revolutionary > *adjective* **1** involving or causing dramatic change or innovation. **2** engaged in, promoting, or relating to political revolution. > *noun* (pl. **revolutionaries**) a person who introduces a major change or who starts or supports a political revolution.

revolutionise (also **revolutionize**) > *verb* change radically or fundamentally.

revolve > *verb* **1** move in a circle on a central axis. **2** (**revolve about** or **around**) move in a circular orbit around. **3** (**revolve around**) treat as the most important point or element.

ORIGIN – Latin *revolvere* 'roll back'.

revolver > *noun* a pistol with revolving chambers enabling several shots to be fired without reloading.

revue > *noun* a light theatrical entertainment of short sketches, songs, and dances, typically dealing satirically with topical issues.

ORIGIN – French, 'review'.

revulsion > *noun* a sense of disgust and loathing.

ORIGIN – Latin, from *revellere* 'tear out'.

reward > *noun* **1** a thing given in recognition of service, effort, or achievement. **2** a fair return for good or bad behaviour. **3** a sum offered for the detection of a criminal, the restoration of lost property, etc. > *verb* **1** give a reward to. **2** show one's appreciation of (an action or quality) with a reward. **3** (**be rewarded**) receive what one deserves.

SYNONYMS – *noun* **1** award, bonus, prize. *verb* **1** honour.

ORIGIN – from Old French *reguard* 'regard, heed'.

rewarding > *adjective* providing satisfaction.

DERIVATIVES – **rewardingly** *adverb*.

SYNONYMS – fulfilling, gratifying, pleasing, satisfying, worthwhile.

rewind > *verb* /ree**wīnd**/ (past and past participle **rewound**) wind (a film or tape) back to the beginning. > *noun* /**ree**wīnd/ a mechanism for rewinding a film or tape.

DERIVATIVES – **rewinder** *noun*.

rewire > *verb* provide with new electric wiring.

DERIVATIVES – **rewirable** *adjective*.

reword > *verb* put into different words.

rework > *verb* alter, revise, or reshape.

rewound past and past participle of REWIND.

rewrite > *verb* (past **rewrote**; past participle **rewritten**) write again in an altered or improved form. > *noun* **1** an instance of rewriting something. **2** a text that has been rewritten.

Rex > *noun* the reigning king (following a name or in the titles of lawsuits, e.g. *Rex v. Jones*: the Crown versus Jones).

ORIGIN – Latin, 'king'.

Rf > *symbol* the chemical element rutherfordium.

r.f. > *abbreviation* radio frequency.

RFC > *abbreviation* Rugby Football Club.

Rh > *abbreviation* rhesus (factor). > *symbol* the chemical element rhodium.

RHA > *abbreviation* (in the UK) regional health authority.

rhapsodise (also **rhapsodize**) > *verb* enthuse about someone or something.

rhapsody /**rap**sədi/ > *noun* (pl. **rhapsodies**) **1** an enthusiastic or ecstatic expression of feeling. **2** a piece of music in one extended movement, typically emotional in character. **3** (in ancient Greece) an epic poem of a suitable length for recitation at one time.

DERIVATIVES – **rhapsodic** *adjective*.

ORIGIN – Greek *rhapsōidia*, from *rhaptein* 'to stitch' + *ōidē* 'song, ode'.

rhea /**ree**ə/ > *noun* a large flightless bird of South American grasslands, resembling a small ostrich with greyish-brown plumage.

ORIGIN – from *Rhea*, the mother of Zeus in Greek mythology.

rhebok /**ree**bok/ (also **reebok**) > *noun* a small South African antelope with a brownish-grey coat, a long slender neck, and short straight horns.

ORIGIN – Dutch *reebok* 'roebuck'.

Rhenish /**renn**ish/ > *adjective* of the river Rhine and adjacent regions.

ORIGIN – Latin *Rhenanus*, from *Rhenus* 'Rhine'.

rhenium /**ree**niəm/ > *noun* a rare silvery-white metallic chemical element.

ORIGIN – from Latin *Rhenus* 'Rhine'.

rheology /ree**oll**əji/ > *noun* the branch of physics concerned with the deformation and flow of matter.

DERIVATIVES – **rheological** *adjective* **rheologist** *noun*.

ORIGIN – from Greek *rheos* 'stream'.

rheostat /**ree**əstat/ > *noun* an electrical instrument used to control a current by varying the resistance.

DERIVATIVES – **rheostatic** *adjective*.

ORIGIN – from Greek *rheos* 'stream'.

rhesus factor /**ree**ssəss/ > *noun* a substance occurring on red blood cells which can cause disease in a newborn baby whose blood contains the factor (i.e. is **rhesus-positive**) while the mother's blood does not (i.e. is **rhesus-negative**).

ORIGIN – from *rhesus monkey*, in which the antigen was first observed.

rhesus monkey > *noun* a small brown macaque with red skin on the face and rump, native to southern Asia.

ORIGIN – Latin *Rhesus*, from Greek *Rhēsos*, a mythical king of Thrace.

rhetoric /**rett**ərik/ > *noun* **1** the art of effective or persuasive speaking or writing. **2** language with a persuasive or impressive effect, but often lacking sincerity or meaningful content.

ORIGIN – Greek *rhētorikē tekhnē* 'art of rhetoric'.

rhetorical /ri**torr**ik'l/ > *adjective* **1** relating to or concerned with rhetoric. **2** expressed in terms intended to persuade or impress. **3** (of a question) asked for effect or to make a statement rather than to obtain an answer.

DERIVATIVES – **rhetorically** *adverb*.

rhetorician > *noun* **1** an expert in formal rhetoric. **2** a speaker whose words are intended to impress or persuade.

rheum /**roo**m/ > *noun* chiefly literary a watery fluid that collects in or drips from the nose or eyes.

DERIVATIVES – **rheumy** *adjective*.

ORIGIN – Greek *rheuma* 'stream'.

rheumatic /roo**matt**ik/ > *adjective* relating to, caused by, or suffering from rheumatism. > *noun* a person with rheumatism.

DERIVATIVES – **rheumaticky** *adjective* (informal).

COMBINATIONS – **rheumatic fever** an acute fever marked by inflammation and pain in the joints, caused by a streptococcal infection.

ORIGIN – first used in reference to an infection characterised by rheum.

rheumatics > *plural noun* (usu. treated as sing.) informal rheumatism.

rheumatism > *noun* any disease marked by inflammation and pain in the joints, muscles, or fibrous tissue, especially rheumatoid arthritis.

ORIGIN – Greek *rheumatismos*, from *rheuma* 'stream' (because it was believed to be caused by the internal flow of 'watery' humours).

rheumatoid /**roo**mətoyd/ > *adjective* relating to, affected by, or resembling rheumatism.

COMBINATIONS – **rheumatoid arthritis** a chronic progressive disease causing inflammation in the joints and resulting in painful deformity and immobility.

rheumatology /roomə**toll**əji/ > *noun* the study of rheumatism, arthritis, and other disorders of the joints, muscles, and ligaments.

DERIVATIVES – **rheumatological** *adjective* **rheumatologist** *noun*.

rhinestone > *noun* an imitation diamond.

ORIGIN – translating French *caillou du Rhin* 'pebble of the Rhine'.

rhinitis /rī**nī**tiss/ > *noun* inflammation of the mucous membrane of the nose, caused by infection with a virus or an allergic reaction.

ORIGIN – from Greek *rhis* 'nose'.

rhino > *noun* (pl. same or **rhinos**) informal a rhinoceros.

rhinoceros /rī**noss**ərəss/ > *noun* (pl. same or **rhinoceroses**) a large, heavily built plant-eating mammal with one or two horns on the nose and thick folded skin, native to Africa and South Asia.

ORIGIN – from Greek *rhis* 'nose' + *keras* 'horn'.

rhinoplasty /**rī**nōplasti/ > *noun* (pl. **rhinoplasties**) Medicine plastic surgery performed on the nose.

rhizome /**rī**zōm/ > *noun* a horizontal underground plant stem with lateral shoots and adventitious roots at intervals.

ORIGIN – Greek *rhizōma*, from *rhiza* 'root'.

rho /rō/ > *noun* the seventeenth letter of the Greek alphabet (P, ρ), transliterated as 'r' or 'rh'.

ORIGIN – Greek.

Rhodesian /rō**dee**zhən/ historical > *noun* a person from Rhodesia (now Zimbabwe). > *adjective* relating to Rhodesia.

Rhodes Scholarship > *noun* any of several scholarships awarded annually and tenable at Oxford University by students from certain Commonwealth countries, the US, and Germany.

DERIVATIVES – **Rhodes Scholar** *noun*.

ORIGIN – named after the South African statesman Cecil *Rhodes* (1853–1902), who founded the scholarships.

rhodium /rōdiəm/ > *noun* a hard, dense silvery-white metallic chemical element.

ORIGIN – from Greek *rhodon* 'rose' (from the colour of its salts).

rhododendron /rōdədendrən/ > *noun* a shrub with large clusters of showy trumpet-shaped flowers and typically with large evergreen leaves.

ORIGIN – from Greek *rhodon* 'rose' + *dendron* 'tree'.

rhombi plural of RHOMBUS.

rhombohedron /rombōheedrən/ > *noun* (pl. **rhombohedra** /rombōheedrə/ or **rhombohedrons**) a solid figure whose faces are six equal rhombuses.

DERIVATIVES – **rhombohedral** *adjective*.

ORIGIN – from RHOMBUS + –HEDRON.

rhomboid /romboyd/ > *adjective* having or resembling the shape of a rhombus. > *noun* a quadrilateral of which only the opposite sides and angles are equal.

DERIVATIVES – **rhomboidal** *adjective*.

rhombus /rombəss/ > *noun* (pl. **rhombuses** or **rhombi** /rombī/) Geometry a parallelogram with oblique angles and equal sides.

ORIGIN – Latin, from Greek *rhombos* 'thing that can be spun round, a rhombus'.

rhubarb > *noun* 1 the thick leaf stalks of a plant of the dock family, which are reddish or green and eaten as a fruit after cooking. 2 Brit. informal noise made by a group of actors to give the impression of indistinct background conversation. 3 nonsense.

ORIGIN – Latin *rheubarbarum*, alteration of *rhabarbarum* 'foreign rhubarb', from Greek *rha* (also meaning 'rhubarb') + *barbaros* 'foreign'.

rhumb /rum/ > *noun* Nautical 1 (also **rhumb line**) an imaginary line on the earth's surface cutting all meridians at the same angle, used to plot a ship's course on a chart. 2 any of the thirty-two points of the compass.

ORIGIN – French *rumb* (earlier *ryn de vent* 'point of the compass').

rhumba > *noun* variant spelling of RUMBA.

rhyme > *noun* 1 correspondence of sound between words or the endings of words, especially when used in poetry. 2 a short poem with rhyming lines. 3 rhyming poetry or verse. 4 a word with the same sound as another. > *verb* 1 (of a word, syllable, or line) have or end with a sound that corresponds to another. 2 literary compose verse or poetry.

IDIOMS – **rhyme or reason** logical explanation: *there's no rhyme or reason to it.*

DERIVATIVES – **rhymer** *noun*.

COMBINATIONS – **rhyming slang** a type of slang originating in Cockney speech that

replaces words with rhyming words or phrases, typically with the rhyming element omitted (e.g. *butcher's*, short for *butcher's hook*, meaning 'look').

---

wordpower facts

Rhyme

The word **rhyme** entered Middle English in the form **rime**, coming via Old French from Latin *rhythmus*, ultimately from Greek *rhuthmos*, meaning 'measured motion or time; rhythm' (the source of the word **rhythm** itself). From around 1560 awareness of the Latin form led to new spellings incorporating the *h* and the *y*, including **rhythm**, which for a period was used to denote both rhyme and rhythm (and was pronounced in the same way as 'rhyme'). From about 1600 the forms **rhime** and **rhyme** were favoured, probably from a desire to distinguish the usage from that of **rhythm**; the spelling **rhyme** became established as the standard form from the late 18th century.

---

rhymester > *noun* a composer of rhymes.

rhyolite /rīəlīt/ > *noun* a pale fine-grained volcanic rock of granitic composition.

ORIGIN – German *Rhyolit*, from Greek *rhuax* 'lava stream' + *lithos* 'stone'.

rhythm* /rithəm/ > *noun* 1 a strong, regular repeated pattern of movement or sound. 2 the systematic arrangement of musical sounds, according to duration and periodical stress. 3 a particular pattern formed by such arrangement: *a slow waltz rhythm.* 4 the measured flow of words and phrases in verse or prose as determined by the length of and stress on syllables. 5 a regularly recurring sequence of events or actions.

DERIVATIVES – **rhythmless** *adjective*.

*SPELLING – remember the first *h*, following the *r*: r*h*ythm.

COMBINATIONS – **rhythm and blues** popular music of US black origin, arising from a combination of blues with jazz rhythms. **rhythm method** a method of birth control involving the avoidance of sexual intercourse when ovulation is likely to occur. **rhythm section** the part of a pop or jazz group supplying the rhythm, in particular the bass and drums.

ORIGIN – French *rhythme* or Latin *rhythmus*, ultimately from Greek *rhuthmos*: originally also meaning 'rhyme'.

rhythmic > *adjective* 1 having or relating to rhythm. 2 occurring regularly.

DERIVATIVES – **rhythmical** *adjective* **rhythmically** *adverb* **rhythmicity** *noun*.

RI > *abbreviation* Rhode Island.

rial /reeaal/ (also **riyal**) > *noun* 1 the basic monetary unit of Iran and Oman. 2 (usu. **riyal**) the basic monetary unit of Saudi Arabia, Qatar, and Yemen.

ORIGIN – Arabic, from Spanish *real* 'royal'.

rib > *noun* 1 each of a series of slender curved bones articulated in pairs to the spine, protecting the thoracic cavity and its organs. 2 Architecture a curved member supporting a vault or defining its form. 3 a curved transverse strut of metal or timber in a ship, forming part of the framework of the hull. 4 each of the hinged rods supporting the fabric of an umbrella. 5 a vein of a leaf or an insect's wing. 6 Knitting alternate plain and purl stitches producing a ridged, slightly elastic fabric. > *verb* (**ribbed**, **ribbing**) 1 (usu. **be ribbed**) mark with or form into raised bands or ridges. 2 informal tease good-naturedly.

WORDFINDER – costal (*relating to the ribs*), intercostal (*situated between the ribs*).

COMBINATIONS – **ribcage** the bony frame formed by the ribs. **rib-tickler** informal a very amusing joke or story.

ribald /ribb'ld/ > *adjective* coarsely or irreverently humorous.

SYNONYMS – bawdy, earthy, racy, risqué; informal naughty.

ORIGIN – Old French *ribauld*, from *riber* 'indulge in licentious pleasures': originally as a noun denoting a licentious or irreverent person.

ribaldry > *noun* ribald talk or behaviour.

riband /ribb'nd/ > *noun* archaic a ribbon.

ORIGIN – Old French *riban*, probably related to BAND¹.

ribbed > *adjective* 1 having a pattern of raised bands. 2 Architecture strengthened with ribs.

ribbing > *noun* 1 a rib-like structure or pattern. 2 informal good-natured teasing.

ribbon > *noun* 1 a long, narrow strip of fabric, used for tying something or for decoration. 2 a ribbon of a special colour or design awarded as a prize or worn to indicate the holding of an honour. 3 a long, narrow strip. 4 a narrow band of inked material wound on a spool and used to produce the characters in some typewriters and computer printers.

IDIOMS – **cut** (or **tear**) **to ribbons** cut (or tear) into ragged strips.

DERIVATIVES – **ribboned** *adjective*.

COMBINATIONS – **ribbon development** Brit. the building of houses along a main road.

ORIGIN – variant of RIBAND.

ribby > *adjective* having prominent ribs.

riboflavin /rībōflayvin/ > *noun* vitamin B₂, a yellow compound essential for energy production and present especially in milk, liver, and green vegetables.

ORIGIN – from **RIBOSE** + Latin *flavus* 'yellow'.

ribonucleic acid /rībōnyōōkleeik, -klay̆ik/ > *noun* see **RNA**.

ORIGIN – from **RIBOSE** + **NUCLEIC ACID**.

ribose /rībōz/ > *noun* a sugar which is a constituent of DNA and several vitamins and enzymes.

ORIGIN – arbitrary alteration of *arabinose*, a related sugar.

ribosome /rībəsōm/ > *noun* Biochemistry a minute particle of RNA and protein found in cells, involved in the synthesis of polypeptides and proteins.

DERIVATIVES – **ribosomal** *adjective*.

ORIGIN – from **RIBONUCLEIC ACID** + Greek *soma* 'body'.

rice > *noun* 1 a swamp grass which is cultivated as a source of food in warm countries. 2 the grains of this cereal used as food. > *verb* N. Amer. force (cooked potatoes or other vegetables) through a sieve or similar utensil.

WORDFINDER – basmati (*long-grain Indian rice*), paddy (*field where rice is grown; rice in its husk*), paella (*Spanish rice dish*), pilaf (*Middle Eastern or Indian rice dish*), risotto (*Italian rice dish*), sake (*Japanese alcoholic drink made from rice*).

DERIVATIVES – **ricer** *noun* (N. Amer.).

COMBINATIONS – **rice paper** thin edible paper made from the flattened and dried pith of a shrub, used in oriental painting and in baking biscuits and cakes.

ORIGIN – Old French *ris*, from Greek *oruza*.

rich > *adjective* 1 having a great deal of money or assets. 2 (of a country or region) having valuable natural resources or a successful economy. 3 of expensive materials or workmanship. 4 plentiful; abundant. 5 having or producing something in large amounts: *fruits rich in vitamins*. 6 (of food) containing much fat, sugar, etc. 7 (of a colour, sound, or smell) pleasantly deep and strong. 8 full of interesting diversity or complexity: *a rich, full life*. 9 (of soil or land) fertile. 10 (of the mixture in an internal-combustion engine) containing a high proportion of fuel. 11 informal (of a remark) causing ironic amusement or indignation.

DERIVATIVES – **richen** *verb* **richness** *noun*.

SYNONYMS – 1 affluent, moneyed, wealthy, well-off; informal well-heeled. 3 luxurious, opulent, plush, sumptuous. 4 abundant, bountiful, copious, plentiful, profuse. 7 deep, full, intense, strong, warm. 9 fecund, fertile, fruitful, productive.

ANTONYMS – 1,2,4,5 poor. 10 lean.

ORIGIN – Old English, 'powerful, wealthy'.

riches > *plural noun* 1 material wealth. 2 valuable natural resources.

richly > *adverb* 1 in a rich way. 2 fully.

Richter scale /rik̆tər/ > *noun* a logarithmic scale for expressing the magnitude of an earthquake on the basis of seismograph oscillations.

ORIGIN – named after the American geologist Charles F. *Richter* (1900–85).

ricin /rīsin, rissin/ > *noun* Chemistry a highly toxic protein obtained from the pressed seeds of the castor oil plant.

ORIGIN – from Latin *Ricinus communis* (denoting the castor oil plant).

rick[1] > *noun* a stack of hay, corn, or straw, especially one built into a regular shape and thatched.

rick[2] > *noun* a slight sprain or strain, especially in the neck or back. > *verb* strain (one's neck or back) slightly.

ORIGIN – dialect.

rickets /rikk̆its/ > *noun* (treated as sing. or pl.) a disease of children caused by vitamin D deficiency, characterised by softening and distortion of the bones.

WORDFINDER – rachitic (*relating to or suffering from rickets*).

ORIGIN – perhaps an alteration of Greek *rhakhitis* 'rickets'.

rickety > *adjective* 1 poorly made and likely to collapse. 2 suffering from rickets.

DERIVATIVES – **ricketiness** *noun*.

SYNONYMS – 1 flimsy, frail, insecure, shaky, unsteady, wobbly.

rickrack > *noun* braided trimming in a zigzag pattern, used on clothes.

rickshaw > *noun* a light two-wheeled hooded vehicle drawn by one or more people, chiefly used in Asian countries.

ORIGIN – Japanese, 'person-strength-vehicle'.

ricochet /rikk̆əshay, rikk̆əshet/ > *verb* (**ricocheted** /rikk̆əshayd/, **ricocheting** /rikk̆əshaying/ or **ricochetted** /rikk̆əshetid/, **ricochetting** /rikk̆əsheting/) 1 (of a bullet or other projectile) rebound off a surface. 2 move or appear to move in such a way. > *noun* 1 a shot or hit that ricochets. 2 the ricocheting action of a bullet or other projectile.

ORIGIN – French.

ricotta /rikott̆ə/ > *noun* a soft white unsalted Italian cheese.

ORIGIN – Italian, 'recooked, cooked twice'.

rictus /rikt̆əss/ > *noun* a fixed grimace or grin.

DERIVATIVES – **rictal** *adjective*.

ORIGIN – Latin, 'open mouth', from *ringi* 'to gape'.

rid > *verb* (**ridding**; past and past participle **rid**) 1 (**rid of**) make (someone or something) free of (an unwanted person or thing). 2 (**be** or **get rid of**) be freed or relieved of.

ORIGIN – Old Norse.

riddance > *noun* the action of getting rid of someone or something.

IDIOMS – **good riddance** expressing relief at being rid of someone or something.

ridden past participle of **RIDE**. > *adjective* full of or dominated by a particular thing: *guilt-ridden*.

riddle[1] > *noun* 1 a question or statement phrased so as to require ingenuity in ascertaining its answer or meaning. 2 a puzzling person or thing. > *verb* archaic speak in or pose riddles.

DERIVATIVES – **riddler** *noun*.

ORIGIN – Old English, related to **READ**.

riddle[2] > *verb* (usu. **be riddled**) 1 make many holes in, especially with gunshot. 2 fill or permeate with something undesirable: *a policy riddled with inadequacies*. 3 pass through a riddle. > *noun* a large coarse sieve, especially one for separating ashes from cinders or sand from gravel.

riddling > *adjective* expressed in riddles; enigmatic.

ride > *verb* (past **rode**; past participle **ridden**) 1 sit on and control the movement of (a horse, bicycle, or motorcycle). 2 (usu. **ride in** or **on**) travel in or on a vehicle or horse. 3 travel over on horseback or on a bicycle or motorcycle: *ride the six-mile scenic trail*. 4 be carried or supported by: *surfers rode the waves*. 5 sail or float: *a ship rode at anchor in the dock*. 6 (**ride up**) (of a garment) gradually move upwards out of its proper position. 7 (**ride on**) depend on. 8 (**ride out**) come safely through. 9 yield to (a blow) so as to reduce its impact. 10 (**be ridden**) be full of or dominated by: *people ridden by ill health*. > *noun* 1 an act of riding. 2 a roller coaster, roundabout, etc. ridden at a fair or amusement park. 3 a path for horse riding. 4 N. Amer. a person giving a lift in a vehicle.

IDIOMS – **be riding for a fall** informal be acting in a reckless way that invites failure. **let something ride** take no immediate action over something. **ride high** be successful. **ride to hounds** chiefly Brit. go fox-hunting on horseback. **a rough** (or **easy**) **ride** a difficult (or easy) time. **take someone for a ride** informal deceive someone.

DERIVATIVES – **rideable** (also **ridable**) *adjective*.

rider > *noun* 1 a person who rides a horse, bicycle, motorcycle, etc. 2 an added condition or proviso.

DERIVATIVES – **riderless** *adjective*.

ridge > *noun* 1 a long, narrow hilltop, mountain range, or watershed. 2 a narrow raised band on a surface. 3 Meteorology an elongated region of high atmospheric pressure. 4 the edge formed where the two sloping sides of a roof meet at the top. > *verb* mark with or form into ridges.

DERIVATIVES – **ridged** *adjective* **ridgy** *adjective*.

COMBINATIONS – **ridge tent** a tent with a central ridge supported by a pole or frame at each end. **ridgeway** a road or track along the ridge of a hill.

ORIGIN – Old English, 'spine, crest'.

ridicule > *noun* mockery or derision. > *verb* make fun of; mock.

SYNONYMS – *noun* contempt, derision, disdain, scorn. *verb* deride, guy, lampoon, mock, pillory, scorn.

ridiculous > *adjective* inviting mockery or derision; absurd.

DERIVATIVES – **ridiculously** *adverb* **ridiculousness** *noun*.

SYNONYMS – absurd, farcical, laughable, ludicrous, preposterous.

ORIGIN – Latin *ridiculus* 'laughable', from *ridere* 'to laugh'.

riding[1] > *noun* **1** the sport or activity of riding horses. **2** a path for horse riding.

COMBINATIONS – **riding crop** a short flexible whip with a loop for the hand, used when riding horses. **riding habit** a woman's riding dress, consisting of a skirt and a double-breasted jacket.

riding[2] > *noun* **1** (usu. **the East** or **North** or **West Riding**) one of three former administrative divisions of Yorkshire. **2** an electoral district of Canada.

ORIGIN – Old Norse, 'third part'.

riel /reeəl/ > *noun* the basic monetary unit of Cambodia, equal to 100 sen.

ORIGIN – Khmer.

Riesling* /reesling/ > *noun* **1** a variety of wine grape grown especially in Germany and Austria. **2** a dry white wine made from this grape.

*SPELLING – the spelling with *Rei-*, and the corresponding pronunciation of the first syllable as **rye**, is incorrect: R*ie*sling.

ORIGIN – German.

rife > *adjective* **1** (especially of something undesirable) widespread. **2** (**rife with**) full of.

DERIVATIVES – **rifeness** *noun*.

riff > *noun* a short repeated phrase in popular music or jazz. > *verb* play riffs.

ORIGIN – abbreviation of RIFFLE.

riffle > *verb* **1** turn over something, especially pages, quickly and casually. **2** (**riffle through**) search quickly through. **3** shuffle (playing cards) by flicking up and releasing the corners of two piles of cards so that they intermingle. > *noun* an act of riffling.

ORIGIN – perhaps from a variant of RUFFLE, influenced by RIPPLE.

riff-raff > *noun* disreputable or undesirable people.

ORIGIN – from Old French *rif et raf* 'one and all, every bit'.

rifle[1] > *noun* **1** a gun, especially one fired from shoulder level, having a long spirally grooved barrel to make a bullet spin and thereby increase accuracy over a long distance. **2** (**rifles**) troops armed with rifles. > *verb* **1** make spiral grooves in (a gun or its barrel or bore). **2** hit or kick (a ball) hard and straight.

WORDFINDER – bayonet (*a blade fixed to the muzzle of a rifle*), bolt (*sliding piece of a breech mechanism of a rifle*), breech (*back part of a rifle barrel*), carbine (*a light automatic rifle*).

COMBINATIONS – **rifleman** a soldier armed with a rifle. **rifle range** a place for practising rifle shooting.

ORIGIN – from French *rifler* 'graze, scratch'.

rifle[2] > *verb* **1** search through something hurriedly to find or steal something. **2** steal.

ORIGIN – Old French *rifler* 'graze, plunder'.

rifling > *noun* spiral grooves on the inside of a rifle barrel.

rift > *noun* **1** a crack, split, or break. **2** a serious break in friendly relations.

COMBINATIONS – **rift valley** a steep-sided valley formed by subsidence of the earth's surface between nearly parallel faults.

ORIGIN – Scandinavian.

rig[1] > *verb* (**rigged**, **rigging**) **1** provide (a boat) with sails and rigging. **2** assemble and adjust (the equipment of a sailing boat, aircraft, etc.) in readiness for operation. **3** (often **rig up**) set up (a device or structure), typically in a makeshift way. **4** (often **rig out**) provide with clothes of a particular type. > *noun* **1** the arrangement of a boat's sails and rigging. **2** an apparatus or device for a particular purpose: *a lighting rig*. **3** an oil rig. **4** a person's costume or outfit. **5** chiefly N. Amer. & Austral./NZ a truck.

IDIOMS – **full rig** informal smart or ceremonial clothes.

DERIVATIVES – **rigged** *adjective*.

rig[2] > *verb* (**rigged**, **rigging**) manage or conduct fraudulently so as to gain an advantage.

rigatoni /riggətōni/ > *plural noun* pasta in the form of short hollow fluted tubes.

ORIGIN – Italian.

rigger[1] > *noun* **1** a ship rigged in a particular way: *a square-rigger*. **2** a person who attends to the rigging of a sailing ship, aircraft, or parachute. **3** a person who erects and maintains scaffolding, cranes, etc. **4** a person who works on an oil rig.

rigger[2] > *noun* a person who rigs something to their advantage.

rigging > *noun* **1** the system of ropes or chains supporting a ship's masts and controlling or setting the yards and sails. **2** the ropes and wires supporting the structure of an airship, biplane, hang-glider, or parachute. **3** the cables and fittings controlling the flight surfaces and engines of an aircraft.

right > *adjective* **1** on, towards, or relating to the side of a human body or of a thing which is to the east when the person or thing is facing north. **2** morally good, justified, or acceptable. **3** factually correct. **4** most appropriate: *the right man for the job*. **5** in a satisfactory, sound, or normal state or condition. **6** socially fashionable or important: *he was seen in all the right places*. **7** relating to a right-wing person or group. **8** informal, chiefly Brit. complete; absolute. > *adverb* **1** on or to the right side. **2** to the furthest or most complete extent or degree. **3** exactly; directly. **4** correctly or satisfactorily. **5** informal immediately. > *noun* **1** that which is morally right. **2** a moral or legal entitlement to have or do something. **3** (**rights**) the authority to perform, publish, or film a particular work or event. **4** (**the right**) the right-hand part, side, or direction. **5** a right turn. **6** a person's right fist, or a blow given with it. **7** (often **the Right**) (treated as sing. or pl.) a group or political party favouring conservative views. > *verb* **1** restore to a normal or upright position. **2** restore to a normal or correct condition. **3** make reparation for (a wrong).

WORDFINDER – dextral (*relating to the right hand or right side*).

IDIOMS – **bang to rights** informal (of a criminal) with positive proof of guilt. **by rights** if things were fair or correct. **in one's own right** as a result of one's own claims, qualifications, or efforts. **put** (or **set**) **right** tell the true facts to. **put** (or **set**) **to rights** restore to the correct or normal state. **right** (or **straight**) **away** immediately. **right on** informal **1** expressing support, approval, or encouragement. **2** (**right-on**) informal, often derogatory in keeping with fashionable liberal or left-wing opinions and values. **a right one** Brit. informal a silly or foolish person. **she's** (or **she'll be**) **right** Austral./NZ informal don't worry.

DERIVATIVES – **righter** *noun* **rightish** *adjective* **rightmost** *adjective* **rightness** *noun* **rightward** *adjective* & *adverb* **rightwards** *adverb*.

SYNONYMS – *adjective* **2** ethical, fair, honest, just. **3** accurate, correct, true. **4** ideal. *noun* **1** fairness, goodness, righteousness, virtue. **2** entitlement, prerogative, warrant. *verb* **2** fix, mend, rectify, remedy.

ANTONYMS – *adjective* **2** unjust, wrong. **3** incorrect, wrong. *noun* **1** wrong.

COMBINATIONS – **right ascension** Astronomy position measured along the celestial equator, expressed in hours, minutes, and seconds. **right back** a defender in soccer or field hockey who plays primarily on the right of the field. **right bank** the bank of a river on the right as one faces downstream. **Right Honourable** Brit. a title given to certain high officials such as government ministers. **right-minded** having sound views and principles. **right of way 1** the legal right to pass along a specific route through another's property. **2** a path subject to such a right. **3** the right of a pedestrian, vehicle, or ship to proceed with precedence over others in a situation or place. **Right Reverend** a title given to a bishop. **rights issue** an issue of shares offered at a special price by a company to its existing shareholders. **right-thinking** right-minded. **right-to-life** opposing abortion; pro-life. **right whale** a whale with a large head and a deeply curved jaw, of Arctic and temperate waters. [ORIGIN – so named because it was regarded as the 'right' whale to hunt.]

right angle > *noun* an angle of 90°, as in a corner of a square.

IDIOMS – **at right angles to** forming an angle of 90° with.

DERIVATIVES – **right-angled** *adjective*.

righteous /**rī**chəss/ > *adjective* morally right or justifiable.

DERIVATIVES – **righteously** *adverb* **righteousness** *noun*.

SYNONYMS – ethical, good, moral, principled, upright, virtuous.

rightful > *adjective* **1** having a legitimate right to something. **2** legitimately claimed; fitting.

DERIVATIVES – **rightfully** *adverb* **rightfulness** *noun*.

right hand > *noun* **1** the hand of a person's right side. **2** the region or direction on the right side. **3** the most important position next to someone. > *adjective* **1** on or towards the right side. **2** done with or using the right hand.

COMBINATIONS – **right-hand drive** a motor-vehicle steering system with the steering wheel and other controls fitted on the right side, for use in countries where vehicles drive on the left. **right-handed 1** using or done with the right hand. **2** turning to the right; towards the right. **3** (of a screw) advanced by turning clockwise. **right-hander 1** a right-handed person. **2** a blow struck with the right hand. **right-hand man** an indispensable helper or chief assistant.

rightism > *noun* the political views or policies of the right.

DERIVATIVES – **rightist** *noun & adjective*.

rightly > *adverb* **1** in accordance with what is true or just. **2** with good reason.

right side > *noun* the side of something intended to be uppermost or foremost.

IDIOMS – **on the right side of 1** in favour with. **2** somewhat less than (a specified age).

rightsize > *verb* chiefly US convert to an appropriate or optimum size, in particular shed staff from (an organisation).

right wing > *noun* **1** the conservative or reactionary section of a political party or system. [ORIGIN – see LEFT WING.] **2** the right side of a sports team on the field or of an army.

DERIVATIVES – **right-winger** *noun*.

rigid > *adjective* **1** unable to bend or be forced out of shape. **2** (of a person) stiff and unmoving. **3** not able to be changed or adapted.

DERIVATIVES – **rigidify** *verb* **rigidity** *noun* **rigidly** *adverb* **rigidness** *noun*.

SYNONYMS – **1** hard, firm, inflexible, stiff. **2** inflexible, intransigent, uncompromising, unrelenting. **3** cast-iron, fixed, set, unalterable.

ANTONYMS – flexible.

ORIGIN – Latin *rigidus*, from *rigere* 'be stiff'.

rigmarole /**rig**mərōl/ > *noun* **1** a lengthy and complicated procedure. **2** a long, rambling story.

ORIGIN – apparently an alteration of *ragman roll*, originally denoting a legal document recording a list of offences.

rigor mortis /**rigg**ər **mor**tiss/ > *noun* stiffening of the joints and muscles a few hours after death, lasting from one to four days.

ORIGIN – Latin, 'stiffness of death'.

rigorous > *adjective* **1** extremely thorough, exhaustive, or accurate. **2** (of a rule, system, etc.) strictly applied or adhered to. **3** adhering strictly to a belief, opinion, or system. **4** harsh or severe: *rigorous military training.*

DERIVATIVES – **rigorously** *adverb* **rigorousness** *noun*.

SYNONYMS – **1** meticulous, painstaking, punctilious, scrupulous. **2** rigid, strict, stringent. **4** demanding, exacting, harsh, severe, tough.

rigour /**rigg**ər/ (US **rigor**) > *noun* **1** the quality of being rigorous. **2** (**rigours**) demanding, difficult, or extreme conditions.

ORIGIN – Latin *rigor* 'stiffness'.

rig-out > *noun* informal, chiefly Brit. an outfit of clothes.

rile > *verb* informal annoy or irritate.

ORIGIN – variant of ROIL.

Riley > *noun* (in phrase **the life of Riley**) informal a luxurious or carefree existence.

rill > *noun* a small stream.

ORIGIN – probably Low German.

rillettes /**ree**yet/ > *plural noun* (treated as sing. or pl.) pâté of minced pork or other light meat combined with fat.

ORIGIN – French, from Old French *rille* 'strip of pork'.

rim > *noun* **1** the upper or outer edge of something, typically something circular. **2** (also **wheel rim**) the outer edge of a wheel, on which the tyre is fitted. **3** a limit

or boundary. **4** an encircling stain or deposit. > *verb* (**rimmed**, **rimming**) (usu. **be rimmed**) provide or mark with a rim.

DERIVATIVES – **rimless** *adjective* **rimmed** *adjective*.

ORIGIN – Old English, 'a border, coast'.

rime[1] /rīm/ > *noun* technical & literary hoar frost. > *verb* literary cover with hoar frost.

DERIVATIVES – **rimy** *adjective* (literary).

rime[2] > *noun & verb* archaic spelling of **RHYME**.

rimu /**ree**moo/ > *noun* a tall conifer which is the chief native softwood tree of New Zealand.

ORIGIN – Maori.

rind > *noun* **1** a tough outer layer or covering, especially of fruit, cheese, or bacon. **2** the bark of a tree.

DERIVATIVES – **rinded** *adjective* **rindless** *adjective*.

rinderpest /**rin**dərpest/ > *noun* an infectious disease of ruminants, especially cattle, transmitted by a virus and characterised by fever and dysentery.

ORIGIN – German, from *Rinder* 'cattle' + *Pest* 'plague'.

ring[1] > *noun* **1** a small circular band, typically of precious metal, worn on a finger. **2** a circular band, object, or mark. **3** an enclosed space in which a sport, performance, or show takes place. **4** a group of people or things arranged in a circle. **5** a group of people with a shared interest or goal, especially one involving illegal activity: *a drug ring.* **6** a flat circular heating device forming part of a gas or electric hob. **7** Chemistry a number of atoms bonded together to form a closed loop in a molecule. > *verb* **1** surround. **2** draw a circle round. **3** put an aluminium strip around the leg of (a bird) so as to identify it.

WORDFINDER – annular (*in the shape of a ring*).

IDIOMS – **hold the ring** monitor a dispute or conflict without becoming involved. **run** (or **make**) **rings round** (or **around**) informal outclass or outwit easily.

DERIVATIVES – **ringed** *adjective* **ringless** *adjective*.

COMBINATIONS – **ring binder** a loose-leaf binder with ring-shaped clasps that can be opened to pass through holes in the paper. **ringdove** Brit. a wood pigeon. **ring finger** the finger next to the little finger, especially of the left hand, on which the wedding ring is worn. **ring main** Brit. **1** an electrical supply serving a series of consumers and returning to the original source. **2** an electric circuit serving a number of power points, with one fuse in the supply. **ringmaster** the person directing a circus performance. **ring ouzel** an upland bird resembling a blackbird, with a white crescent across the breast. **ring pull** a ring on a can that is pulled to open it. **ring road** a bypass encircling a town.

ORIGIN – Old English, related to RANK[1].

ring² > *verb* (past **rang**; past participle **rung**) **1** make or cause to make a clear resonant or vibrating sound. **2** (**ring with**) reverberate with (a sound). **3** chiefly Brit. call by telephone. **4** (**ring off**) Brit. end a telephone call by replacing the receiver. **5** call for attention by sounding a bell. **6** (of the ears) be filled with a buzzing or humming sound due to a blow or loud noise. **7** sound (the hour, a peal, etc.) on a bell or bells. **8** (**ring in** or **out**) usher (someone or something) in (or out) by or as if by ringing a bell. **9** (**ring up**) record (an amount) on a cash register. **10** convey a specified impression or quality: *her honesty rings true.* > *noun* **1** an act or instance of ringing. **2** a loud clear sound or tone. **3** Brit. informal a telephone call. **4** a quality conveyed by something heard: *the tale had a ring of truth.* **5** a set of bells, especially church bells.

IDIOMS – **ring down** (or **up**) **the curtain** **1** lower (or raise) a theatre curtain. **2** mark the end (or beginning) of something.

ringer > *noun* **1** a person or device that rings. **2** informal a person's or thing's double. **3** informal an athlete or horse fraudulently substituted for another in a competition. **4** Austral./NZ a shearer with the highest tally of sheep shorn. **5** Austral./NZ a person who looks after livestock.

ring fence > *noun* **1** a fence completely enclosing a piece of land. **2** an effective barrier. > *verb* (**ring-fence**) **1** enclose with a ring fence. **2** guard securely. **3** guarantee that (funds for a particular purpose) will not be spent on anything else.

ringgit > *noun* (pl. same or **ringgits**) the basic monetary unit of Malaysia, equal to 100 sen.

ORIGIN – Malay.

ringing > *adjective* **1** having a clear resonant sound. **2** (of a statement) forceful and unequivocal.

WORDFINDER – tinnitus (*ringing in the ears*).

DERIVATIVES – **ringingly** *adverb*.

ringleader > *noun* a person who leads a rebellious or illicit activity.

ringlet > *noun* a corkscrew-shaped curl of hair.

DERIVATIVES – **ringletted** (also **ringleted**) *adjective*.

ringside > *noun* the area beside a boxing ring or circus ring.

DERIVATIVES – **ringsider** noun.

COMBINATIONS – **ringside seat** an advantageous position from which to observe something.

ringtail > *noun* **1** a mammal or bird having a tail marked with a ring or rings. **2** an

Australian possum that habitually curls its tail into a ring. – **ring-tailed** *adjective*.

ringworm > *noun* a contagious itching skin disease occurring in small circular patches, caused by various fungi and affecting chiefly the scalp or feet.

rink > *noun* **1** (also **ice rink**) an enclosed area of ice for skating, ice hockey, or curling. **2** (also **roller rink**) a smooth enclosed floor for roller skating. **3** (also **bowling rink**) the strip of a bowling green used for a match. **4** a team in curling or bowls.

ORIGIN – Scots, in the sense 'jousting ground': perhaps from Old French *renc* 'rank'.

rinse > *verb* **1** wash with clean water to remove soap or dirt. **2** (often **rinse off** or **out**) remove (soap or dirt) by rinsing. > *noun* **1** an act of rinsing. **2** an antiseptic solution for cleansing the mouth. **3** a preparation for conditioning or tinting the hair.

DERIVATIVES – **rinser** noun.

ORIGIN – Old French *rincer*.

Rioja /riˈokhə/ > *noun* a wine produced in La Rioja, Spain.

riot > *noun* **1** a violent disturbance of the peace by a crowd. **2** a confused or lavish combination or display: *a riot of colour.* **3** (**a riot**) informal a highly amusing or entertaining person or thing. > *verb* **1** take part in a riot. **2** behave in an unrestrained way.

IDIOMS – **read** (or **read someone**) **the Riot Act** give someone a severe warning or reprimand. [ORIGIN – with reference to a former act of the British Parliament, parts of which were officially read out as a legal preliminary to taking action to disperse rioters.] **run riot 1** behave in a violent and unrestrained way. **2** proliferate or spread uncontrollably.

DERIVATIVES – **rioter** noun.

SYNONYMS – *noun* **1** disturbance, fracas, furore, rumpus, uproar. *verb* **1** rampage, rise up, run riot.

ORIGIN – Old French *riote* 'debate', from *rioter* 'to quarrel'.

riotous > *adjective* **1** marked by or involving public disorder. **2** involving wild and uncontrolled behaviour. **3** having a vivid, varied appearance.

DERIVATIVES – **riotously** *adverb* **riotousness** noun.

SYNONYMS – **1** anarchic, disorderly, disruptive, lawless. **2** boisterous, lively, rowdy, unruly, wild.

RIP > *abbreviation* rest in peace (used on graves).

ORIGIN – from Latin *requiescat* (or (plural) *requiescant*) *in pace*.

rip¹ > *verb* (**ripped**, **ripping**) **1** tear or pull forcibly away from something or someone.

2 tear. **3** move forcefully and rapidly. **4** (**rip off**) informal cheat (someone), especially financially. **5** (**rip off**) informal steal or plagiarise. **6** (**rip into**) informal make a vehement verbal attack on. > *noun* a long tear or cut.

IDIOMS – **let rip** informal **1** proceed vigorously or without restraint. **2** express oneself vehemently.

COMBINATIONS – **ripcord** a cord that is pulled to open a parachute. **rip-off** informal **1** an article that is greatly overpriced. **2** an inferior imitation. **ripsaw** a coarse saw for cutting wood along the grain. **ripstop** nylon fabric that is woven so that a tear will not spread.

rip² (also **rip tide**) > *noun* a stretch of fast-flowing and rough water caused by the meeting of currents.

ORIGIN – perhaps related to RIP[1].

rip³ > *noun* informal, dated **1** a dissolute immoral man. **2** a worthless horse.

ORIGIN – perhaps from *rep*, an abbreviation of REPROBATE.

riparian /rɪˈpɛːrɪən/ > *adjective* of, relating to, or situated on the banks of a river.

ORIGIN – from Latin *riparius*, from *ripa* 'bank'.

ripe > *adjective* **1** (of fruit or grain) ready for harvesting and eating. **2** (of a cheese or wine) fully matured. **3** (**ripe for**) arrived at a fitting time for. **4** (of a person's age) advanced. **5** (**ripe with**) full of.

DERIVATIVES – **ripely** *adverb* **ripeness** *noun*.

ripen > *verb* become or make ripe.

riposte /rɪˈpɒst/ > *noun* **1** a quick clever reply. **2** a quick return thrust in fencing. > *verb* make a riposte.

ORIGIN – French, from Italian *risposta* 'response'.

ripper > *noun* **1** a person or thing that rips. **2** informal a thing that is particularly admirable or excellent.

ripping > *adjective* Brit. informal, dated excellent.

ripple > *noun* **1** a small wave or series of waves. **2** a gentle rising and falling sound of conversation, laughter, etc. that spreads through a group of people. **3** a feeling that spreads through someone or something. **4** a type of ice cream with wavy lines of coloured flavoured syrup running through it. **5** a small periodic variation in voltage. > *verb* **1** form or cause to form ripples. **2** (of a sound or feeling) spread through a person or place.

DERIVATIVES – **ripply** *adjective*.

rip-roaring > *adjective* full of vigour.

DERIVATIVES – **rip-roaringly** *adverb*.

ripsnorting > *adjective* informal showing great vigour or intensity.

DERIVATIVES – **ripsnorter** *noun*.

RISC > *abbreviation* reduced instruction set computer (or computing).

rise > *verb* (past **rose**; past participle **risen**) **1** come or go up. **2** get up from lying, sitting, or kneeling. **3** increase in number, size, intensity, or quality. **4** (of land) slope upwards. **5** (of the sun, moon, or stars) appear above the horizon. **6** reach a higher social or professional position. **7** (**rise above**) succeed in not being constrained by. **8** (**rise to**) respond adequately to (a challenging situation). **9** (often **rise up**) rebel. **10** (of a river) have its source. **11** be restored to life. **12** chiefly Brit. (of a meeting or a session of a court) adjourn. > *noun* **1** an act or instance of rising. **2** an upward slope or hill. **3** Brit. an increase in salary or wages. **4** the vertical height of a step, arch, or incline.

IDIOMS – **get** (or **take**) **a rise out of** informal provoke an angry or irritated response from. **on the rise 1** increasing. **2** becoming more successful. **rise and shine** informal wake up and get out of bed promptly.

SYNONYMS – *verb* **1** arise, ascend, mount, soar. **3** grow, increase. **6** advance, climb.

ANTONYMS – *verb* **1** descend, fall.

ORIGIN – Old English, 'make an attack', 'get out of bed'.

riser > *noun* **1** a person who habitually gets out of bed at a particular time of the morning: *an early riser.* **2** a vertical section between the treads of a staircase. **3** a vertical pipe for the upward flow of liquid or gas. **4** a low platform on a stage or in an auditorium.

risible /**rizz**ib'l/ > *adjective* provoking laughter or mockery.

DERIVATIVES – **risibility** *noun* **risibly** *adverb.*

SYNONYMS – absurd, farcical, laughable, ludicrous, ridiculous.

ORIGIN – Latin *risibilis*, from *ridere* 'to laugh'.

rising > *adjective* approaching a specified age. > *noun* a revolt.

COMBINATIONS – **rising damp** Brit. moisture absorbed from the ground into a wall.

risk > *noun* **1** a situation involving exposure to danger. **2** the possibility that something unpleasant will happen. **3** a person or thing causing a risk or regarded in relation to risk: *a fire risk.* > *verb* **1** expose to danger or loss. **2** act in such a way as to incur the risk of. **3** incur risk by engaging in (an action).

IDIOMS – **at one's** (**own**) **risk** taking responsibility for one's own safety or possessions. **run** (or **take**) **a risk** (or **risks**) act in such a way as to expose oneself to danger.

SYNONYMS – *noun* **2** chance, danger, peril, threat. *verb* **1** endanger, hazard, imperil, jeopardise.

COMBINATIONS – **risk capital** venture capital.

ORIGIN – Italian *risco* 'danger'.

risky > *adjective* (**riskier**, **riskiest**) involving risk.

DERIVATIVES – **riskily** *adverb* **riskiness** *noun.*

SYNONYMS – dangerous, hazardous, perilous; informal chancy, dicey.

ANTONYMS – safe.

risotto* /ri**zott**ō/ > *noun* (pl. **risottos**) an Italian dish of rice cooked in stock with ingredients such as meat or seafood.

*SPELLING – note that there is only one *s*: risotto.

ORIGIN – Italian, from *riso* 'rice'.

risqué /**ris**kay/ > *adjective* slightly indecent and liable to shock.

ORIGIN – French, from *risquer* 'to risk'.

rissole > *noun* a compressed mixture of meat and spices, coated in breadcrumbs and fried.

ORIGIN – French, ultimately from Latin *russeolus* 'reddish'.

ritardando /rittaar**dan**dō/ > *adverb* & *adjective* Music another term for **RALLENTANDO**.

ORIGIN – Italian.

rite > *noun* **1** a religious or other solemn ceremony or act. **2** a body of customary observances characteristic of a Church or a part of it.

IDIOMS – **rite of passage** a ceremony or event, e.g. marriage, marking an important stage in someone's life.

ORIGIN – Latin *ritus* '(religious) usage'.

ritual > *noun* **1** a religious or solemn ceremony involving a series of actions performed according to a set order. **2** a set order of performing such a ceremony. **3** a series of actions habitually and invariably followed by someone. > *adjective* relating to or done as a ritual.

DERIVATIVES – **ritually** *adverb.*

ritualise (also **ritualize**) > *verb* make into a ritual by following a pattern of actions or behaviour.

DERIVATIVES – **ritualisation** *noun.*

ritualism > *noun* the regular observance or practice of ritual, especially when excessive or without regard to its function.

DERIVATIVES – **ritualist** *noun* **ritualistic** *adjective.*

ritz > *noun* informal ostentatious luxury and glamour.

ORIGIN – from *Ritz*, a name associated with luxury hotels, from the Swiss hotel owner César *Ritz* (1850–1918).

ritzy > *adjective* (**ritzier**, **ritziest**) informal expensively stylish.

rival > *noun* **1** a person or thing competing with another for superiority or the same objective. **2** a person or thing equal to another in quality: *she has no rivals as a*

female rock singer. > *verb* (**rivalled**, **rivalling**; US **rivaled**, **rivaling**) be comparable to.

DERIVATIVES – **rivalrous** *adjective* **rivalry** (pl. **rivalries**) *noun.*

SYNONYMS – *noun* **1** adversary, challenger, competitor, opponent. **2** counterpart, equal, match, peer. *verb* compete with, equal, match, measure up to, vie with.

ORIGIN – Latin *rivalis*: see box at **RIVER**.

rive /rīv/ > *verb* (past **rived**; past participle **riven** /**rivv**'n/) (usu. **be riven**) tear apart.

ORIGIN – Old Norse.

river > *noun* **1** a large natural flow of water travelling along a channel to the sea, a lake, or another river. **2** a large quantity of a flowing substance.

WORDFINDER – confluence (*conjunction of two rivers*), delta (*triangular area where a river branches at its mouth*), Eridanus (*constellation, the River*), estuary (*tidal mouth of a large river*), fluvial (*of or found in a river*), riparian (*relating to or situated on the banks of a river*), tributary (*river or stream flowing into a larger river*).

IDIOMS – **sell someone down the river** informal betray someone. [ORIGIN – first used in reference to the sale of a troublesome slave to a plantation owner on the lower Mississippi, where conditions were relatively more harsh.]

wordpower facts

River

There is a connection between the words **river** and **rival**, although they do not come from exactly the same root. **River** comes via Old French *rivere* from Latin *riparius*, from *ripa* 'bank of a river'. It is related to **arrive**, which originally meant 'bring a ship to shore', and to **riparian**, used in law and ecology to refer to regions adjacent to a river. **Rival** derives from Latin *rivalis*, originally meaning 'person using the same stream as another', from *rivus* 'stream'. *Rivus* is the root also of **derive** and **rivulet**.

riverine /**rivv**ərīn/ > *adjective* technical or literary relating to or situated on a river or riverbank.

rivet /**rivv**it/ > *noun* a short metal pin or bolt for holding together two metal plates, its headless end being beaten out or pressed down when in place. > *verb* (**riveted**, **riveting**) **1** join or fasten with a rivet or rivets. **2** (usu. **be riveted**) completely engross. **3** direct (one's eyes or attention) intently.

DERIVATIVES – **riveter** *noun.*

ORIGIN – Old French, from *river* 'fix, clinch'.

riviera /rivvi**air**ə/ > *noun* a coastal region

with a subtropical climate and vegetation, especially that of southern France and northern Italy.

ORIGIN – Italian, 'seashore'.

rivulet /**riv**yoolit/ > *noun* a very small stream.

ORIGIN – alteration of obsolete French *riveret* 'small river', from Latin *rivus* 'stream'.

riyal > *noun* variant spelling of **RIAL**.

RL > *abbreviation* rugby league.

RM > *abbreviation* (in the UK) Royal Marines.

RN > *abbreviation* (in the UK) Royal Navy.

Rn > *symbol* the chemical element radon.

RNA > *noun* ribonucleic acid, a substance in living cells which carries instructions from DNA for controlling the synthesis of proteins and in some viruses carries genetic information instead of DNA.

RNLI > *abbreviation* (in the UK) Royal National Lifeboat Institution.

RNZAF > *abbreviation* Royal New Zealand Air Force.

RNZN > *abbreviation* Royal New Zealand Navy.

roach¹ > *noun* (pl. same) a common freshwater fish of the carp family.

ORIGIN – Old French *roche*.

roach² > *noun* informal 1 chiefly N. Amer. a cockroach. 2 a roll of card or paper that forms the butt of a cannabis cigarette. [ORIGIN – of unknown origin.]

road > *noun* 1 a way by which one can travel from one place to another, especially one surfaced for use by vehicles. 2 a way to achieving a particular outcome. 3 a partly sheltered stretch of water near the shore in which ships can ride at anchor.

IDIOMS – **down the road** informal, chiefly N. Amer. in the future. **in** (or **out of**) **the** (or **one's**) **road** informal in (or out of) someone's way. **one for the road** informal a final alcoholic drink before leaving. **on the road 1** on a long journey or series of journeys. **2** (of a car) able to be driven.

DERIVATIVES – **roadless** *adjective*.

COMBINATIONS – **road fund licence** Brit. a disc displayed on a vehicle certifying payment of road tax. **road hog** informal an inconsiderate motorist. **roadholding** the ability of a moving vehicle to remain stable, especially when cornering at high speeds. **roadhouse** a pub, club, or restaurant on a country road. **road hump** a hump in the road intended to cause traffic to reduce speed. **road kill** chiefly N. Amer. the killing of an animal on the road by a vehicle; animals killed in this way. **road pricing** the practice of charging motorists to use busy roads at certain times, especially to relieve congestion. **road rage** violent anger arising from conflict with the driver of another vehicle. **roadshow 1** each of a series of

radio or television programmes broadcast on location from different venues. **2** a touring political or promotional campaign. **3** a touring show of pop musicians. **road tax** Brit. a periodic tax payable on motor vehicles using public roads. **road test 1** a test of the performance of a vehicle or engine on the road. **2** a test of equipment carried out in working conditions. **roadway 1** a road. **2** the part of a road intended for vehicles, in contrast to the pavement or verge.

ORIGIN – Old English, 'journey on horseback', 'foray'; related to **RIDE**.

roadblock > *noun* a barrier put across a road by the police or army to stop and investigate traffic.

roadie > *noun* informal a person employed by a touring band of musicians to set up and maintain equipment.

roadrunner > *noun* a fast-running long-tailed bird found chiefly in arid country from the southern US to Central America.

roadstead > *noun* another term for **ROAD** (in sense 3).

ORIGIN – from **ROAD** + **STEAD** in the sense 'a place'.

roadster > *noun* 1 an open-top car with two seats. 2 a bicycle designed for use on the road.

roadworks > *plural noun* Brit. repairs to roads or to utilities under roads.

roadworthy > *adjective* (of a vehicle) fit to be used on the road.

DERIVATIVES – **roadworthiness** *noun*.

roam > *verb* 1 travel aimlessly over a wide area. 2 wander over, through, or about (a place). > *noun* an aimless walk.

DERIVATIVES – **roamer** *noun*.

SYNONYMS – *verb* drift, meander, ramble, range, wander.

roan > *adjective* (of a horse or cow) having a bay, chestnut, or black coat thickly interspersed with hairs of another colour, typically white. > *noun* a roan animal.

COMBINATIONS – **red roan** (of an animal's coat) bay or chestnut mixed with white or grey.

ORIGIN – Old French.

roar > *noun* 1 a full, deep, prolonged sound as made by a lion, natural force, or engine. 2 a loud, deep sound uttered by a person, especially as an expression of pain, anger, or great amusement. > *verb* 1 make or utter a roar. 2 laugh loudly. 3 move, act, or happen very fast.

DERIVATIVES – **roarer** *noun*.

roaring > *adjective* informal complete; unqualified: *a roaring success.*

IDIOMS – **do a roaring trade** (or **business**) informal do very good business. **the roaring forties** stormy ocean tracts between latitudes 40° and 50° south. **the**

roaring twenties the prosperous years of the 1920s.

DERIVATIVES – **roaringly** *adverb*.

roast > *verb* 1 (with reference to food, especially meat) cook or be cooked by prolonged exposure to heat in an oven or over a fire. 2 process (a foodstuff) by subjecting it to intense heat. 3 make or become very warm. 4 criticise or reprimand severely. > *adjective* (of food) having been roasted. > *noun* 1 a joint of meat that has been roasted or that is intended for roasting. 2 the process of roasting something, especially coffee. 3 an outdoor party at which meat is roasted: *a pig roast.*

DERIVATIVES – **roaster** *noun*.

ORIGIN – Old French *rostir*.

roasting informal > *adjective* very hot and dry. > *noun* a severe criticism or reprimand.

rob > *verb* (**robbed**, **robbing**) 1 take property unlawfully from (a person or place) by force or threat of force. 2 deprive of something needed, deserved, or significant. 3 informal overcharge.

IDIOMS – **rob Peter to pay Paul** deprive one person of something in order to pay another. [ORIGIN – probably with reference to the saints and apostles *Peter* and *Paul*; the allusion is uncertain.]

DERIVATIVES – **robber** *noun*.

SYNONYMS – 1 burgle, loot, mug, plunder, steal from. 2 deprive, divest, strip.

ORIGIN – Old French *rober*.

robbery > *noun* (pl. **robberies**) 1 the action of robbing a person or place. 2 informal unashamed swindling or overcharging.

robe > *noun* 1 a loose outer garment reaching to the ankles, worn on formal or ceremonial occasions as an indication of the wearer's rank, office, or profession. 2 a bathrobe or dressing gown. > *verb* clothe in or put on a robe or robes.

wordpower facts

Robe

The word **robe** is actually related to **rob**: both are from Old French words that go back to the same Germanic base. In Old French *robe* meant 'spoils, booty' as well as 'garment', because clothing was a typical example of the sort of thing that might be looted by victorious troops. The base of **rob** and **robe** is also the source of **bereave**, **reave**, and possibly **rubbish** and **rubble**.

robin > *noun* 1 a small European songbird of the thrush family, with a red breast and brown back and wings. 2 (also **American**

robin) a large North American thrush with an orange-red breast.

ORIGIN – Old French, familiar form of the given name *Robert*.

robot /rōbot/ > *noun* a machine capable of carrying out a complex series of actions automatically, especially one programmable by a computer.

DERIVATIVES – **robotise** (also **robotize**) *verb*.

ORIGIN – from Czech *robota* 'forced labour'; the term was coined in Karel Čapek's play *R.U.R.* 'Rossum's Universal Robots' (1920).

robotic /rōbottik/ > *adjective* **1** relating to robots. **2** mechanical, stiff, or unemotional.

DERIVATIVES – **robotically** *adverb*.

robotics > *plural noun* (treated as sing.) the branch of technology concerned with the design, construction, and application of robots.

robust > *adjective* **1** sturdy or resilient. **2** strong and healthy. **3** uncompromising and forceful; not subtle: *a robust defence.* **4** (of wine or food) strong and rich in flavour or smell.

DERIVATIVES – **robustly** *adverb* **robustness** *noun*.

SYNONYMS – **1** durable, hard-wearing, resilient, sturdy, tough. **2** hardy, hearty, rugged, vigorous.

ANTONYMS – **1** fragile. **2** frail, weak.

ORIGIN – Latin *robustus* 'firm and hard'.

robusta /rōbustə/ > *noun* coffee beans from a West African species of coffee plant (*Coffea canephora*, formerly *robusta*).

ORIGIN – Latin, feminine of *robustus* 'robust'.

roc > *noun* a gigantic mythological bird described in the *Arabian Nights*.

ORIGIN – ultimately from Persian.

rock¹ > *noun* **1** the hard mineral material of the earth's crust, exposed on the surface or underlying the soil. **2** a mass of rock projecting out of the ground or water. **3** a boulder. **4** Geology any natural material with a distinct composition of minerals. **5** Brit. a kind of hard confectionery in the form of cylindrical peppermint-flavoured sticks. **6** informal a diamond or other precious stone.

WORDFINDER – petrography (*study of composition and properties of rocks*), petrology (*study of origin, structure, and composition of rocks*); types of rock: igneous (*solidified from lava or magma*), metamorphic (*having been transformed by heat or pressure*), sedimentary (*formed from sediment*).

IDIOMS – **on the rocks** informal **1** experiencing difficulties and likely to fail. **2** (of a drink) served undiluted and with ice cubes.

COMBINATIONS – **rock-bottom** at the lowest possible level. **rock cake** chiefly Brit. a small currant cake with a hard rough surface. **rock climbing** the sport or pastime of climbing rock faces, especially with the aid of ropes and special equipment. **rock crystal** transparent quartz, typically in the form of colourless hexagonal crystals. **rock garden** a rockery. **rock plant** a plant that grows on or among rocks. **rock pool** a pool of water among rocks, typically along a shoreline. **rock rose** a herbaceous or shrubby plant with rose-like flowers, native to temperate and warm regions. **rock salmon** Brit. dogfish or wolf fish as food. **rock salt** common salt occurring naturally as a mineral. **rock solid** completely firm or stable. **rock wool** inorganic material made into matted fibre, used especially for insulation or soundproofing.

ORIGIN – Latin *rocca*.

rock² > *verb* **1** move gently to and fro or from side to side. **2** shake violently, especially because of an earthquake or explosion. **3** shock or distress greatly. **4** informal dance to or play rock music. **5** informal have an atmosphere of excitement or busy social activity. > *noun* **1** (also **rock music**) a form of popular music derived from rock and roll and pop music but characterised by a more serious approach. **2** rock and roll. **3** a rocking movement.

COMBINATIONS – **rock and roll** (also **rock 'n' roll**) a type of popular dance music originating in the 1950s and characterised by a heavy beat and simple melodies. **rocking chair** a chair mounted on rockers or springs. **rocking horse** a model of a horse mounted on rockers or springs for a child to ride on.

rockabilly > *noun* a type of popular music, originating in the south-eastern US, combining elements of rock and roll and country music.

ORIGIN – blend of *rock and roll* and *hillbilly*.

rocker > *noun* **1** a person who performs, dances to, or enjoys rock music. **2** Brit. a young person, especially in the 1960s, belonging to a subculture characterised by leather clothing, riding motorcycles, and a liking for rock music. **3** a rocking chair. **4** a curved bar or similar support on which something such as a chair can rock. **5** a rocking device forming part of a mechanism.

IDIOMS – **off one's rocker** informal mad.

rockery > *noun* (pl. **rockeries**) a heaped arrangement of rocks with soil between them, planted with rock plants.

rocket¹ > *noun* **1** a cylindrical projectile that can be propelled to a great height or distance by the combustion of its contents. **2** a missile or spacecraft propelled by an engine providing thrust on the same principle. **3** Brit. informal a severe reprimand. > *verb* (**rocketed**, **rocketing**) **1** increase very rapidly and suddenly. **2** move or progress very rapidly. **3** attack with rocket-propelled missiles.

COMBINATIONS – **rocket scientist** informal, chiefly N. Amer. a very intelligent person.

ORIGIN – Italian *rocchetto* 'small distaff (for spinning)', with reference to its cylindrical shape.

rocket² > *noun* an edible Mediterranean plant of the cabbage family, eaten in salads.

ORIGIN – French *roquette*, ultimately from Latin *eruca* 'downy-stemmed plant'.

rocketeer > *noun* a person who designs or operates rockets.

rocketry > *noun* the branch of science and technology concerned with rockets.

rocky¹ > *adjective* (**rockier**, **rockiest**) **1** consisting or formed of rock. **2** full of rocks.

rocky² > *adjective* (**rockier**, **rockiest**) unsteady or unstable.

rococo /rəkōkō/ > *adjective* **1** in or relating to an elaborately ornate late baroque style of European furniture or architecture of the 18th century. **2** (of music or literature) highly ornamented and florid. > *noun* the rococo style.

ORIGIN – French, humorous alteration of *rocaille*, an 18th-century style of decoration based on shells and pebbles.

rod > *noun* **1** a thin straight bar, especially of wood or metal. **2** a fishing rod. **3** a slender straight stick or shoot growing on or cut from a tree or bush. **4** (**the rod**) the use of a stick for caning or flogging. **5** historical, chiefly Brit. a perch or square perch (see PERCH³). **6** Anatomy one of two types of light-sensitive cell in the retina of the eye, responsible mainly for monochrome vision in poor light. Compare with CONE.

IDIOMS – **make a rod for one's own back** do something likely to cause difficulties for oneself later. **spare the rod and spoil the child** proverb if children are not punished when they do wrong their personal development will suffer.

DERIVATIVES – **rodlet** *noun*.

rode past of RIDE.

rodent /rōdənt/ > *noun* a mammal of a large group (the order Rodentia) including rats, mice, and squirrels and distinguished by strong constantly growing incisors and no canine teeth.

WORDFINDER – rodents: beaver, capybara, chinchilla, coypu, dormouse, gerbil, gopher, hamster, jerboa, lemming, marmot, mouse, muskrat, porcupine, rat, squirrel, vole, water rat.

ORIGIN – from Latin *rodere* 'gnaw'.

rodenticide /rōdentisīd/ > *noun* a poison used to kill rodents.

rodeo /rōdiō, rədayō/ > *noun* (pl. **rodeos**) **1**

a contest or entertainment in which cowboys show their skill at riding broncos, roping calves, etc. **2** a competitive display of other skills, such as motorcycle riding. **3** a round-up of cattle on a ranch for branding and counting.

ORIGIN – Spanish, from *rodear* 'go round', from Latin *rotare* 'rotate'.

rodomontade /roddəmon**tayd**/ > *noun* boastful or inflated talk or behaviour.

ORIGIN – from Italian *rodomonte* 'boaster', from the name of a boastful character in the medieval *Orlando* epics.

roe[1] > *noun* **1** (also **hard roe**) the mass of eggs contained in the ovaries of a female fish or shellfish, especially when ripe and used as food. **2** (**soft roe**) the ripe testes of a male fish, especially when used as food.

ORIGIN – related to Low German, Dutch *roge*.

roe[2] (also **roe deer**) > *noun* (pl. same or **roes**) a small deer with a reddish summer coat that turns greyish in winter.

roebuck > *noun* a male roe deer.

roentgen /**runt**yən/ > *noun* a unit of quantity of ionising radiation.

ORIGIN – named after the German physicist and discoverer of X-rays Wilhelm Conrad *Röntgen* (1845–1923).

rogan josh /**rō**gən **jōsh**/ > *noun* an Indian dish of curried meat, typically lamb, in a rich tomato-based sauce.

ORIGIN – Urdu.

rogations /rō**gay**sh'nz/ > *plural noun* (in the Christian Church) a special litany chanted on the three days before Ascension Day.

ORIGIN – from Latin *rogare* 'ask'.

roger > *exclamation* your message has been received and understood (used in radio communication). > *verb* Brit. vulgar slang (of a man) have sexual intercourse with.

ORIGIN – from the given name *Roger*; the verb is from an obsolete sense ('penis') of the noun.

rogue > *noun* **1** a dishonest or unprincipled man. **2** a mischievous but likeable person. **3** an elephant or other large wild animal with destructive tendencies driven away or living apart from the herd. **4** a person or thing that is defective or unpredictable.

SYNONYMS – **1** charlatan, reprobate, scoundrel, villain; archaic varlet. **2** imp, rascal, scamp; informal scallywag.

COMBINATIONS – **rogues' gallery** informal a collection of photographs of known criminals, used by police to identify suspects.

ORIGIN – first denoting an idle vagrant: probably from Latin *rogare* 'beg, ask'.

roguery > *noun* (pl. **rogueries**) behaviour characteristic of a rogue.

roguish > *adjective* characteristic of a rogue, especially in being playfully mischievous: *a roguish smile.*

DERIVATIVES – **roguishly** *adverb* **roguishness** *noun*.

SYNONYMS – cheeky, devilish, impish, mischievous, wicked.

roil /royl/ > *verb* **1** make (a liquid) muddy by disturbing the sediment. **2** (of a liquid) move in a turbulent manner.

ORIGIN – perhaps from Old French *ruiler* 'mix mortar', from Latin *regulare* 'regulate'.

roister /**roy**stər/ > *verb* enjoy oneself or celebrate in a noisy or boisterous way.

DERIVATIVES – **roisterer** *noun* **roisterous** *adjective*.

ORIGIN – from obsolete *roister* 'roisterer', from French *rustre* 'ruffian'.

role > *noun* **1** an actor's part in a play, film, etc. **2** a person's or thing's function in a particular situation.

COMBINATIONS – **role model** a person looked to by others as an example to be imitated. **role playing** (also **role play**) the acting out of a particular role, either consciously (as a technique in psychotherapy or training) or unconsciously (in accordance with the perceived expectations of society).

ORIGIN – from obsolete French *roule* 'roll', referring originally to the roll of paper on which an actor's part was written.

roll > *verb* **1** move by turning over and over on an axis. **2** move forward on wheels or with a smooth, undulating motion. **3** (of a moving ship, aircraft, or vehicle) sway on an axis parallel to the direction of motion. **4** (of a machine or device) begin operating. **5** (often **roll up**) turn (something flexible) over and over on itself to form a cylindrical or spherical shape. **6** (**roll up**) curl up tightly. **7** flatten (something) by passing a roller over it or by passing it between rollers. **8** (of a loud, deep sound such as that of thunder) reverberate. **9** pronounce (a consonant, typically an *r*) with a trill. **10** (**rolling**) (of land) extending in gentle undulations. **11** (**rolling**) steady and continuous: *a rolling programme of reforms.* **12** informal rob (a drunk or sleeping person). > *noun* **1** a cylinder formed by rolling flexible material. **2** a rolling movement. **3** a gymnastic exercise in which the body is rolled into a tucked position and turned in a forward or backward circle. **4** a prolonged, deep, reverberating sound. **5** (in drumming) a sustained, rapid alternation of single or double strokes of each stick. **6** a round item of bread baked as an individual portion. **7** a roller used to shape metal in a rolling mill. **8** an official list or register of names. **9** a document in scroll form. **10** N. Amer. & Austral. a quantity of banknotes rolled together.

IDIOMS – **a roll in the hay** (or **the sack**) informal an act of sexual intercourse. **be rolling in it** (or **money**) informal be very rich. **on a roll** informal experiencing a prolonged spell of success or good luck. **roll in** informal **1** be received in large amounts. **2** arrive in a casual way in spite of being late. **a rolling stone gathers no moss** proverb a person who does not settle in one place will not accumulate responsibilities or commitments. **roll of honour** a list of people whose deeds are honoured, especially a list of those who have died in battle. **roll out** officially launch (a new product). **roll up** informal arrive. **roll up one's sleeves** prepare to fight or work. **roll with the punches 1** (of a boxer) move one's body away from an opponent's blows so as to lessen the impact. **2** adapt oneself to adverse circumstances.

COMBINATIONS – **roll bar** a metal bar running up the sides and across the top of a sports car, protecting the occupants if the vehicle overturns. **roll-call** the process of calling out a list of names to establish who is present. **rolled gold** gold in the form of a thin coating applied to a baser metal by rolling. **rolled oats** oats that have been husked and crushed. **rolling hitch** a kind of hitch knot used to attach a rope to a spar or larger rope. **rolling mill** a factory or machine for rolling steel or other metal into sheets. **rolling pin** a cylinder for rolling out dough. **rolling stock 1** locomotives, carriages, or other vehicles used on a railway. **2** US the road vehicles of a trucking company. **roll neck** a high loosely turned-over collar. **roll-on** (of a deodorant or cosmetic) applied by means of a rotating ball in the neck of the container. **roll-on roll-off** referring to a ferry in which vehicles are driven directly on at the start of the voyage and off at the end of it. **roll-out 1** the unveiling or launch of a new aircraft, spacecraft, or product. **2** Aeronautics the stage of an aircraft's landing during which it travels along the runway while losing speed. **rollover** (in a lottery) the accumulative carry-over of prize money to the following draw. **roll-top desk** a writing desk with a semicircular flexible cover sliding in curved grooves. **roll-up** informal **1** Brit. a hand-rolled cigarette. **2** Austral. an assembly.

ORIGIN – from Latin *rotulus* 'a roll, little wheel'.

roller > *noun* **1** a cylinder that rotates about a central axis and is used to move, flatten, or spread something. **2** a small cylinder on which hair is rolled to produce curls. **3** a long swelling wave that appears to roll steadily towards the shore. **4** a brightly coloured crow-sized bird with a characteristic tumbling display flight.

COMBINATIONS – **rollerball 1** a ballpoint pen using relatively thin ink. **2** Computing an input device containing a ball which is moved with the fingers to control the cursor. **roller bearing** a bearing similar to a ball bearing but using small cylindrical rollers instead of balls. **roller blind** a window blind fitted on a roller. **roller coaster** a fairground attraction consisting of a light railway track with many tight turns and steep slopes, on which people ride in small open carriages. **roller towel** a long towel with the ends joined and hung on a roller.

Rollerblade > *noun* trademark a roller skate in which the wheels are fixed in a single line. > *verb* skate using Rollerblades.

DERIVATIVES – **rollerblader** *noun*.

roller skate > *noun* each of a pair of boots or metal frames fitted to shoes, having four or more small wheels and used for gliding across a hard surface.

DERIVATIVES – **roller skater** *noun* **roller skating** *noun*.

rollicking¹ > *adjective* exuberantly lively and amusing.

ORIGIN – perhaps a blend of **ROMP** and **FROLIC**.

rollicking² (also **rollocking**) > *noun* Brit. informal a severe reprimand.

ORIGIN – euphemistic alteration of **BOLLOCKING**.

rollmop > *noun* a rolled uncooked pickled herring fillet.

ORIGIN – German *Rollmops*.

roly-poly > *noun* (also **roly-poly pudding**) Brit. a pudding made of a sheet of suet pastry covered with jam or fruit, formed into a roll, and steamed or baked. > *adjective* informal round and plump.

ROM > *abbreviation* Computing read-only memory.

romaine /rəmayn/ > *noun* a cos lettuce.

ORIGIN – French, feminine of *romain* 'Roman'.

Roman > *adjective* **1** relating to ancient Rome or its empire or people. **2** relating to medieval or modern Rome. **3** referring to the alphabet used for writing Latin, English, and most European languages, developed in ancient Rome. **4** (**roman**) (of type) of a plain upright kind used in ordinary print. > *noun* **1** an inhabitant of ancient or modern Rome. **2** (**roman**) roman type.

WORDFINDER – *principal Roman gods:* Jupiter (*supreme god*), Cupid (*love*), Mars (*war*), Mercury (*messenger of the gods*), Morpheus (*dreams or sleep*), Neptune (*the sea*), Saturn (*agriculture*), Vulcan (*fire*); *goddesses:* Juno (*wife of Jupiter*), Aurora (*dawn*), Ceres (*crops*), Diana (*hunting*), Minerva (*crafts*), Pax (*peace*), Vesta (*hearth and household*), Venus (*love*).

COMBINATIONS – **Roman candle** a firework giving off flaming coloured balls and sparks. **Roman Empire** the empire under Roman rule established in 27 BC and divided in AD 395 into the Western or Latin and Eastern or Greek Empire. **Roman holiday** an occasion on which enjoyment or profit is derived from the suffering of others. [ORIGIN – from Byron's *Childe Harold*, originally with reference to a holiday given for a gladiatorial combat.] **Roman law** the law code of the ancient Romans forming the basis of civil law in many countries today. **Roman nose** a nose with a high bridge. **Roman numeral** any of the letters representing numbers in the Roman numerical system: I = 1, V = 5, X = 10, L = 50, C = 100, D = 500, M = 1,000.

roman-à-clef /rōmoNaaklay/ > *noun* (pl. **romans-à-clef** pronunc. same) a novel in which real people or events appear with invented names.

ORIGIN – French, 'novel with a key'.

Roman Catholic > *adjective* relating to the Roman Catholic Church. > *noun* a member of this Church.

DERIVATIVES – **Roman Catholicism** *noun*.

COMBINATIONS – **Roman Catholic Church** the part of the Christian Church which acknowledges the Pope as its head, especially as it has developed since the Reformation.

ORIGIN – translation of Latin *Ecclesia Romana Catholica et Apostolica* 'Roman Catholic and Apostolic Church', apparently first used in place of the earlier *Roman*, *Romanist*, or *Romish*, which were considered derogatory.

Romance /rəmanss/ > *noun* the group of languages descended from Latin, principally French, Spanish, Portuguese, Italian, and Romanian.

ORIGIN – from Latin *Romanicus* 'Roman': originally denoting the ordinary language of France as opposed to Latin.

romance /rəmanss, rōmans/ > *noun* **1** a pleasurable feeling of excitement and wonder associated with love. **2** a love affair. **3** a book or film dealing with love in a sentimental or idealised way. **4** a quality or feeling of mystery, excitement, and remoteness from everyday life. **5** a medieval tale dealing with a hero of chivalry, of the kind common in the Romance languages. > *verb* **1** court or pursue amorously. **2** dated be involved in an amorous relationship with. **3** informal court the favour of. **4** romanticise.

romancer /rōmansər/ > *noun* **1** a person prone to wild exaggeration or falsehood. **2** a writer of medieval romances.

Romanesque /rōmənesk/ > *adjective* relating to a style of architecture which prevailed in Europe *c*.900–1200, with massive vaulting and round arches.

roman-fleuve /rōmoNflöv/ > *noun* (pl. **romans-fleuves** pronunc. same) a novel or sequence of novels dealing with the lives of a family or other group over a prolonged period of time.

ORIGIN – French, 'river novel'.

Romanian /rōōmayniən/ (also **Rumanian**) > *noun* **1** a person from Romania. **2** the language of Romania. > *adjective* relating to Romania or its language.

Romanic /rōmannik/ > *noun* less common term for **ROMANCE** (the language group).

romanise /rōmənīz/ (also **romanize**) > *verb* **1** historical bring under Roman influence or authority. **2** make Roman Catholic in character. **3** put (text) into the Roman alphabet or into roman type.

DERIVATIVES – **romanisation** *noun*.

Romansh /rōmansh/ > *noun* the language spoken in the Swiss canton of Grisons, an official language of Switzerland.

ORIGIN – from Latin *romanice* 'in the Romanic manner'.

romantic > *adjective* **1** inclined towards or suggestive of love or romance. **2** of, characterised by, or suggestive of an idealised view of reality. **3** (**Romantic**) relating to the artistic and literary movement of Romanticism. > *noun* **1** a person with romantic beliefs or attitudes. **2** (**Romantic**) a writer or artist of the Romantic movement.

DERIVATIVES – **romantically** *adverb*.

romanticise (also **romanticize**) > *verb* deal with or describe in an idealised or unrealistic fashion.

DERIVATIVES – **romanticisation** *noun*.

Romanticism > *noun* a literary and artistic movement which began in the late 18th century and emphasised inspiration and subjectivity.

DERIVATIVES – **Romanticist** *noun*.

Romany /romməni, rōməni/ > *noun* (pl. **Romanies**) **1** the language of the gypsies. **2** a gypsy.

---

wordpower facts

Romany

Romany, the language of the gypsies, is an Indo-European language related to Hindi: gypsies are now found mostly in Europe, North Africa, and North America, but they are believed to have originated in the Indian subcontinent. Romany is spoken by a widely scattered group of about one million people, and has many dialects. The word **Romany** has nothing to do with Romans: it comes from the Romany word *Rom*, meaning 'man, husband'. Several slang words have entered English from Romany, among them **cove** (as in *he is an odd cove*), **nark**, **pal**, and **stir** (meaning 'prison').

Romeo /rōmiō/ > *noun* (pl. **Romeos**) an attractive, passionate male seducer or lover.
ORIGIN – from the name of the hero of Shakespeare's romantic tragedy *Romeo and Juliet*.

Romish /rōmish/ > *adjective* chiefly derogatory Roman Catholic.

romp > *verb* **1** play about roughly and energetically. **2** informal achieve something easily. **3** (**romp home** or **in**) informal finish as the easy winner of a race or other contest. **4** informal engage in sexual activity. > *noun* **1** a spell of romping. **2** a light-hearted film or other work. **3** informal an easy victory.
SYNONYMS – *verb* **1** caper, cavort, frisk, frolic, sport.
ORIGIN – perhaps an alteration of RAMP.

rompers (also **romper suit**) > *plural noun* a young child's one-piece outer garment.

rondeau /rondō/ > *noun* (pl. **rondeaux** pronunc. same or /rondōz/) a poem of ten or thirteen lines with only two rhymes throughout and with the opening words used twice as a refrain.
ORIGIN – French.

rondel /rond'l/ > *noun* a rondeau, especially one of three stanzas of thirteen or fourteen lines with a two-line refrain.
ORIGIN – Old French, from *rond* 'round'.

rondo /rondō/ > *noun* (pl. **rondos**) a musical form with a recurring leading theme, often found in the final movement of a sonata or concerto.
ORIGIN – Italian, from French *rondeau*.

röntgen > *noun* variant spelling of ROENTGEN.

roo > *noun* Austral. informal a kangaroo.

rood /rōōd/ > *noun* **1** a crucifix, especially one positioned above the rood screen of a church or on a beam over the entrance to the chancel. **2** chiefly Brit. a former measure of land area equal to a quarter of an acre.
COMBINATIONS – **rood screen** a screen of wood or stone separating the nave from the chancel of a church.

roof > *noun* (pl. **roofs** or **rooves**) **1** the structure forming the upper covering of a building or vehicle. **2** the top inner surface of a covered area or space. **3** the upper limit or level of prices or wages. > *verb* (usu. **be roofed**) cover with or as a roof.
WORDFINDER – bargeboard (*an ornamental board fixed to the gable end of a roof*), eaves (*part of a roof that meets or overhangs the walls of a building*), finial (*a distinctive section or ornament at the highest point of a roof*), gable (*triangular part of a wall at the end of a ridged roof*), gambrel, mansard (*roofs in which the lower part of the slope is steeper than the upper part*), hip (*edge where two sloping sides of a roof meet*), purlin (*horizontal beam along the length of a roof*).
IDIOMS – **go through the roof** informal (of prices or figures) reach extreme levels. **hit** (or **go through**) **the roof** informal suddenly become very angry.
DERIVATIVES – **roofless** *adjective*.
USAGE – although the plural **rooves** is sometimes used and is not incorrect, the form **roofs** is now much more common.
COMBINATIONS – **roof of the mouth** the palate. **roof rack** a framework for carrying luggage on the roof of a vehicle. **roof tree** the ridge piece of a roof.

roofer > *noun* a person who constructs or repairs roofs.

roofing > *noun* **1** material for constructing a building's roof. **2** the process of constructing a roof or roofs.

rook¹ > *noun* a gregarious crow with black plumage and a bare face, nesting in colonies in treetops. > *verb* informal defraud, swindle, or overcharge.

rook² > *noun* a chess piece, typically with its top in the shape of a battlement, that can move in any direction along a rank or file on which it stands.
ORIGIN – Arabic.

rookery > *noun* (pl. **rookeries**) **1** a breeding colony of rooks, typically a collection of nests high in a clump of trees. **2** a breeding colony of seabirds (especially penguins), seals, or turtles.

rookie > *noun* informal a new recruit or member, especially in the army or police or a sports team; a novice.
ORIGIN – perhaps an alteration of RECRUIT.

room /rōōm, rŏŏm/ > *noun* **1** space viewed in terms of its capacity to accommodate contents or allow action. **2** opportunity or scope: *room for improvement*. **3** a part of a building enclosed by walls, floor, and ceiling. **4** (**rooms**) a set of rooms rented out to a lodger or lodgers. > *verb* chiefly N. Amer. share lodgings, especially at a college or similar institution.
IDIOMS – **no room to swing a cat** humorous a very confined space. [ORIGIN – *cat* in the sense 'cat-o'-nine-tails'.]
DERIVATIVES – **roomed** *adjective*.
COMBINATIONS – **rooming house** chiefly N. Amer. a lodging house. **room-mate 1** a person occupying the same room as another. **2** N. Amer. a person occupying the same room, flat, or house as another. **room service** provision of food and drink to hotel guests in their rooms. **room temperature** a comfortable ambient temperature, generally taken as about 20°C.

roomy > *adjective* (**roomier**, **roomiest**) having plenty of room; spacious.
DERIVATIVES – **roominess** *noun*.
SYNONYMS – big, capacious, commodious, sizeable, spacious.
ANTONYMS – cramped, poky.

roost > *noun* a place where birds or bats regularly settle to rest. > *verb* (of a bird or bat) settle or congregate for rest.
IDIOMS – **curses, like chickens, come home to roost** proverb one's past mistakes or wrongdoings will eventually be the cause of present troubles.

rooster > *noun* chiefly N. Amer. a male domestic fowl.

wordpower facts
Root
The word **root** entered Old English in the form *rōt*. It comes from Old Norse *rót*, and is from the same Germanic base as the Old English word *wyrt* 'plant', which occurs as the element **-wort** in many plant names (**ragwort**, **woundwort**, etc.) and is the source of the term **wort** 'infusion of grain used in brewing'. Ultimately **root** is from an Indo-European source shared by Latin *radix* 'root', and is therefore also related to words such as **radical** ('forming the root', hence 'basic, fundamental'), **radish**, and **eradicate** (literally 'tear up by the roots').

root¹ > *noun* **1** a part of a plant normally below ground, which acts as a support and collects water and nourishment. **2** the embedded part of a bodily organ or structure such as a hair. **3** (also **root vegetable**) a turnip, carrot, or other vegetable which grows as the root of a plant. **4** the basic cause, source, or origin: *money is the root of all evil*. **5** (**roots**) family, ethnic, or cultural origins. **6** (also **root note**) Music the fundamental note of a chord. **7** Linguistics a form from which words have been made by the addition of prefixes or suffixes or by other modification. **8** Mathematics a number or quantity that when multiplied by itself one or more times gives a specified number or quantity. **9** Austral./NZ & Irish vulgar slang an act of sexual intercourse. > *verb* **1** cause (a plant or cutting) to establish roots. **2** (usu. **be rooted**) establish deeply and firmly. **3** (**be rooted in**) have as a source or origin. **4** (**be rooted**) stand immobile through fear or amazement. **5** (**root out** or **up**) find and get rid of. **6** Austral./NZ & Irish vulgar slang have sexual intercourse with.
IDIOMS – **at root** fundamentally. **put down roots** begin to have a settled life in a place. **root and branch** (of a process or operation) thorough or radical. **take root** become fixed or established.
DERIVATIVES – **rootless** *adjective*.
COMBINATIONS – **root beer** N. Amer. a fizzy drink made from an extract of the roots and bark of certain plants. **root canal 1** the

pulp-filled cavity in the root of a tooth. **2** N. Amer. a procedure to replace infected pulp in a root canal with an inert material. **root mean square** Mathematics the square root of the arithmetic mean of the squares of a set of values. **root sign** Mathematics the radical sign √.

root² > *verb* **1** (of an animal) turn up the ground with its snout in search of food. **2** rummage. **3** (**root for**) informal support enthusiastically.

ORIGIN – Old English, related to *wrōt* 'snout'.

rootin'-tootin' > *adjective* N. Amer. informal boisterous, noisy, or lively.

rootle > *verb* Brit. informal root or rummage.

rootstock > *noun* **1** a rhizome. **2** a plant on to which another variety is grafted. **3** a primary form or source from which offshoots have arisen.

rootsy > *adjective* informal (of music) unpolished and emphasising its traditional or ethnic origins.

rope > *noun* **1** a length of stout cord made by twisting together strands of hemp, sisal, nylon, etc. **2** a quantity of roughly spherical objects strung together. **3** (**the ropes**) the ropes enclosing a boxing or wrestling ring. **4** (**the ropes**) informal the established procedures in an organisation or area of activity: *I showed her the ropes.* > *verb* **1** catch, fasten, or secure with rope. **2** (**rope in** or **into**) persuade (someone) to take part in something.

IDIOMS – **give a man enough rope** (or **plenty of rope**) **and he will hang himself** proverb given enough freedom of action a person will bring about their own downfall. **on the ropes 1** Boxing forced against the ropes by the opponent's attack. **2** in a state of near collapse. **a rope of sand** literary illusory security.

COMBINATIONS – **rope ladder** two long ropes connected by short crosspieces, used as a ladder.

ropeable /rōpəb'l/ (also **ropable**) > *adjective* Austral./NZ informal very angry; furious.

ORIGIN – from the notion that the person requires to be restrained.

ropy (also **ropey**) > *adjective* (**ropier**, **ropiest**) **1** resembling a rope. **2** Brit. informal poor in quality or health.

DERIVATIVES – **ropily** adverb **ropiness** noun.

Roquefort /rokfor/ > *noun* trademark a soft blue cheese made from ewes' milk.

ORIGIN – from the name of a village in southern France.

ro-ro > *abbreviation* Brit. roll-on roll-off.

rorqual /rorkwəl/ > *noun* a baleen whale of a small group with pleated skin on the underside, e.g. the blue, fin, and humpback whales.

ORIGIN – Norwegian *røyrkval* 'fin whale'.

Rorschach test /rorshaak/ > *noun* a test used in psychoanalysis, in which a standard set of symmetrical ink blots is presented to the subject, who is asked to describe what they suggest or resemble.

ORIGIN – named after the Swiss psychiatrist Hermann *Rorschach* (1884–1922).

rort /rort/ > *noun* Austral. informal **1** a fraudulent or dishonest act or practice. **2** a wild party.

rorty > *adjective* (**rortier**, **rortiest**) Brit. informal boisterous and high-spirited.

rosacea /rōzayshiə/ > *noun* a condition in which some facial blood vessels enlarge, giving the cheeks and nose a flushed appearance.

ORIGIN – Latin, 'rose-coloured'.

rosaceous /rōzayshəss/ > *adjective* Botany relating to plants of the rose family (Rosaceae).

rosary /rōzəri/ > *noun* (pl. **rosaries**) **1** (in the Roman Catholic Church) a form of devotion in which five (or fifteen) sets of ten Hail Marys are repeated. **2** a string of beads for keeping count in such a devotion or in the devotions of some other religions.

ORIGIN – Latin *rosarium*: originally in the sense 'rose garden'.

rose¹ > *noun* **1** a fragrant flower (typically red, pink, yellow, or white) borne on a prickly bush or shrub. **2** a bush or shrub producing such flowers. **3** a perforated cap attached to a shower, the spout of a watering can, or the end of a hose to produce a spray. **4** a warm pink or light crimson colour. **5** (**roses**) favourable circumstances or ease of success: *everything was coming up roses.*

IDIOMS – **under the rose** archaic another way of saying SUB ROSA. **Wars of the Roses** the 15th-century English civil wars between the Houses of York and Lancaster, represented by white and red roses respectively.

COMBINATIONS – **rose-coloured** (also **rose-tinted**) **1** of a warm pink colour. **2** referring to a naively optimistic or unfoundedly favourable viewpoint: *you are still seeing the profession through rose-coloured spectacles.* **rose hip** the fruit of a rose. **rose madder** a pale shade of pink. **rose of Jericho** a desert plant whose dead branches fold inwards to form a ball. **rose of Sharon 1** a low shrub with dense foliage and large golden-yellow flowers. **2** (in biblical use) a flowering plant of unknown identity. [ORIGIN – from *Sharon*, a region of fertile coastal plain in present-day Israel.] **rose water** scented water made with rose petals. **rose window** a circular window with mullions or tracery radiating in a form suggestive of a rose. **rosewood** a close-grained tropical timber used for making furniture and musical instruments.

ORIGIN – Latin *rosa*.

rose² past of RISE.

rosé /rōzay/ > *noun* light pink wine made from red grapes, coloured by only brief contact with the skins.

ORIGIN – French, 'pink'.

roseate /rōziət/ > *adjective* rose-coloured.

rosebay > *noun* **1** (also **rosebay willowherb**) a tall willowherb with pink flowers. **2** N. Amer. an azalea.

rosebud > *noun* **1** the bud of a rose. **2** Brit. dated a pretty young woman.

rosella /rəzellə/ > *noun* an Australian parakeet with brightly coloured plumage.

ORIGIN – alteration of *Rosehill*, New South Wales, where the bird was first found.

rosemary > *noun* an evergreen aromatic shrub of southern Europe, the leaves of which are used as a herb in cooking.

ORIGIN – from Latin *ros marinus*, from *ros* 'dew' + *marinus* 'of the sea'.

roseroot > *noun* a yellow-flowered stonecrop whose roots smell of roses when dried or bruised.

rosette > *noun* **1** a rose-shaped decoration made of ribbon, worn by supporters of a team or political party or awarded as a prize. **2** a design or growth resembling a rose. **3** a radiating arrangement of spreading leaves at the base of a low-growing plant.

Rosh Hashana /rosh həshaanə/ (also **Rosh Hashanah**) > *noun* the Jewish New Year festival.

ORIGIN – Hebrew, 'head of the year'.

Rosicrucian /rōzikrōōsh'n/ > *noun* a member of a secretive 17th- and 18th-century society devoted to the study of metaphysical, mystical, and alchemical lore. > *adjective* relating to the Rosicrucians.

DERIVATIVES – **Rosicrucianism** noun.

ORIGIN – from the Latin form of the name of Christian *Rosenkreuz*, legendary 15th-century founder of the movement.

rosin /rozzin/ > *noun* resin, especially the solid amber residue obtained after distilling oil of turpentine and used for treating the bows of stringed instruments. > *verb* (**rosined**, **rosining**) rub or treat with rosin.

ORIGIN – Latin *rosina*, from *resina* 'resin'.

RoSPA /rospə/ > *abbreviation* (in the UK) Royal Society for the Prevention of Accidents.

roster /rostər/ > *noun* **1** a list or plan showing turns of duty or leave in an organisation. **2** a list of names, in particular of sports players available for team selection. > *verb* (usu. **be rostered**) assign according to a duty roster.

ORIGIN – Dutch *rooster* 'list', earlier 'gridiron', with reference to its parallel lines.

rösti /rōsti/ > *noun* a Swiss dish of grated

potatoes formed into a small flat cake and fried.

ORIGIN – Swiss German.

rostrum /rostrəm/ > *noun* (pl. **rostra** /rostrə/ or **rostrums**) **1** a raised platform on which a person stands to make a public speech, play music, or conduct an orchestra. **2** a platform for supporting a film or television camera. **3** chiefly Zoology a beak-like projection.

DERIVATIVES – **rostral** *adjective* (chiefly Zoology).

ORIGIN – Latin, 'beak'; the word was originally used to denote an orator's platform in the Forum in Rome, which was decorated with the beaks of captured galleys.

rosy > *adjective* (**rosier**, **rosiest**) **1** (especially of a person's skin) rose-red or pink, typically as an indication of health or youthfulness. **2** promising or suggesting good fortune; hopeful.

DERIVATIVES – **rosily** *adverb* **rosiness** *noun*.

rot > *verb* (**rotted**, **rotting**) **1** decompose by the action of bacteria and fungi; decay. **2** gradually deteriorate or decline. > *noun* **1** the process of decaying. **2** rotten or decayed matter. **3** (**the rot**) Brit. a process of deterioration or decline in standards. **4** a fungal or bacterial disease that causes tissue deterioration, especially in plants. **5** informal nonsense; rubbish: *don't talk rot.*

SYNONYMS – *verb* **1** decay, decompose, fester, moulder, putrefy. **2** decay, decline, degenerate, deteriorate, go to seed.

rota > *noun* chiefly Brit. a list showing times and names for people to take their turn to undertake duties.

⌐ wordpower facts ¬
Rota

In Latin *rota* means 'wheel'. It acquired its English meaning from the idea of people performing duties in 'rotation': the **Rota** was a political club, founded in 1659 by James Harrington, which advocated rotation in the offices of government. Latin *rota* and its associated verb *rotare* have given rise to many English words, including **control**, **roll**, **rotary**, **rotate**, **rotund**, **round**, and **roulette**. Another word derived from *rota* is **rodeo**. This entered English from a Spanish word meaning 'riding round' or 'ring': the notion is of 'rounding up' cattle.

Rotarian /rōtairiən/ > *noun* a member of a Rotary club. > *adjective* relating to Rotary.

rotary > *adjective* **1** revolving around a centre or axis; rotational. **2** acting by means of

rotation; having a rotating part or parts: *a rotary mower.* > *noun* (pl. **rotaries**) **1** a rotary machine or device. **2** N. Amer. a traffic roundabout. **3** (**Rotary**) a worldwide charitable society of business and professional people organised into local Rotary clubs.

COMBINATIONS – **rotary wing** an aerofoil that rotates in an approximately horizontal plane, providing all or most of the lift in a helicopter or autogiro.

rotate /rōtayt/ > *verb* **1** move in a circle round an axis. **2** move or pass on in a regularly recurring order or succession. **3** grow (different crops) in succession on a particular piece of land.

DERIVATIVES – **rotatable** *adjective* **rotating** *adjective* **rotatory** /rōtətəri, rōtaytəri/ *adjective*.

SYNONYMS – **1** circle, gyrate, pivot, revolve, spin.

ORIGIN – Latin *rotare* 'turn in a circle', from *rota* 'wheel'.

rotation > *noun* the action or process of rotating.

DERIVATIVES – **rotational** *adjective* **rotationally** *adverb*.

rotator > *noun* **1** a thing which rotates or which causes something to rotate. **2** Anatomy a muscle whose contraction causes or assists in the rotation of a part of the body.

rotavator /rōtəvaytər/ > *noun* trademark a machine with rotating blades for breaking up or tilling the soil.

DERIVATIVES – **rotavate** *verb*.

ORIGIN – blend of **ROTARY** + **CULTIVATOR**.

rote > *noun* mechanical or habitual repetition: *a poem learnt by rote.*

rotgut > *noun* informal poor-quality and potentially harmful alcoholic liquor.

rotisserie /rōtissəri/ > *noun* **1** a restaurant specialising in roasted or barbecued meat. **2** a rotating spit for roasting and barbecuing meat.

ORIGIN – French, from *rôtir* 'to roast'.

rotogravure /rōtəgrəvyoor/ > *noun* a printing system using a rotary press with engraved cylinders.

ORIGIN – German *Rotogravur*, part of the name of a printing company.

rotor > *noun* **1** the rotating part of a turbine, electric motor, or other device. **2** a hub with a number of radiating blades that is rotated to provide the lift for a helicopter.

rotten > *adjective* **1** suffering from decay. **2** corrupt. **3** informal very bad or unpleasant. > *adverb* informal very much: *your mother spoiled you rotten.*

DERIVATIVES – **rottenness** *noun*.

SYNONYMS – **1** bad, decaying, mouldy, putrid. **2** bad, base, corrupt, immoral, wicked.

COMBINATIONS – **rotten borough** Brit.

historical (before the Reform Act of 1832) a borough that was able to elect an MP though having very few voters.

ORIGIN – Old Norse.

rotter > *noun* informal, dated a cruel, mean, or unkind person.

Rottweiler /rotvīlər/ > *noun* a large powerful dog of a tall black-and-tan breed.

ORIGIN – from *Rottweil*, the name of a town in SW Germany.

rotund /rōtund/ > *adjective* **1** large and plump. **2** round; spherical.

DERIVATIVES – **rotundity** *noun* **rotundly** *adverb*.

SYNONYMS – **1** chubby, fat, heavy, plump, portly, stout.

ORIGIN – Latin *rotundus*, from *rotare* 'rotate'.

rotunda /rōtundə/ > *noun* a round building or room, especially one with a dome.

ORIGIN – from Italian *rotonda camera* 'round chamber'.

rouble /roob'l/ (also **ruble**) > *noun* the basic monetary unit of Russia and some other former republics of the USSR, equal to 100 kopeks.

ORIGIN – Russian.

roué /rooay/ > *noun* a debauched man, especially an elderly one.

ORIGIN – French, literally 'broken on a wheel', referring to the instrument of torture thought to be deserved by such a person.

rouge /roozh/ > *noun* a red powder or cream used as a cosmetic for colouring the cheeks or lips. > *verb* colour with rouge.

ORIGIN – French, 'red'.

rough > *adjective* **1** having an uneven or irregular surface; not smooth or level. **2** not gentle; violent or boisterous: *rough treatment.* **3** (of weather or the sea) wild and stormy. **4** lacking sophistication or refinement. **5** not finished tidily; plain and basic. **6** harsh and rasping in sound or taste. **7** not worked out or correct in every detail; approximate: *a rough guess.* **8** informal difficult and unpleasant. > *noun* **1** a rough, preliminary state: *jot things down in rough first.* **2** a preliminary sketch for a design. **3** chiefly Brit. a disreputable and violent person. **4** (on a golf course) the area of longer grass around the fairway and the green. > *verb* **1** work or shape in a rough, preliminary fashion. **2** make uneven. **3** (**rough it**) informal live in discomfort with only basic necessities. **4** (**rough up**) informal beat (someone) up.

IDIOMS – **in the rough 1** in a natural state; without decoration or other treatment. **2** in difficulties. **rough and ready 1** crude but effective. **2** unsophisticated or unrefined. **the rough edge** (or **side**) **of one's tongue** a scolding. **rough edges** small imperfections in something that is otherwise satisfactory. **rough justice** treatment that is not scrupulously fair or in accordance with the law. **sleep rough** Brit. sleep in uncomfortable conditions, typically out of doors. **take the rough with the smooth** accept the difficult or unpleasant aspects of life as well as the good.

DERIVATIVES – **roughness** *noun*.

SYNONYMS – *adjective* **1** bumpy, irregular, uneven. **2** boisterous, brutal, rowdy, unruly, violent. **3** tempestuous, turbulent. **4** boorish, coarse, uncouth, unrefined.

ANTONYMS – *adjective* **1** smooth. **2** gentle.

COMBINATIONS – **rough and tumble** a situation without rules or organisation. **rough diamond 1** an uncut diamond. **2** a person who is of good character but lacks manners or education. **rough-hewn** (of a person) uncultivated or uncouth. **rough-rider** N. Amer. a person who breaks in or can ride unbroken horses. **rough trade** informal male homosexual prostitution, especially when involving brutality or sadism.

roughage > *noun* fibrous indigestible material in vegetable foodstuffs which aids the passage of food and waste products through the gut.

roughcast > *noun* plaster of lime, cement, and gravel, used on outside walls. > *adjective* **1** coated with roughcast. **2** (of a person) lacking refinement. > *verb* coat with roughcast.

roughen > *verb* make or become rough.

rough house informal > *noun* a violent disturbance. > *verb* (**rough-house**) chiefly N. Amer. act or treat in a rough, violent manner.

roughly > *adverb* **1** in a rough or harsh manner. **2** approximately.

roughneck > *noun* **1** informal a rough, uncouth person. **2** an oil-rig worker.

roughshod > *adjective* archaic (of a horse) having shoes with nail heads projecting to prevent slipping.

IDIOMS – **ride roughshod over** arrogantly or inconsiderately disregard.

roughy /**ruffi**/ > *noun* (pl. **roughies**) Austral./NZ a marine fish with large rough-edged scales which become spiny on the belly.

roulade /rōōlaad/ > *noun* a piece of meat, sponge, or other food, spread with a filling and rolled up.

ORIGIN – French, from *rouler* 'to roll'.

roulette > *noun* a gambling game in which a ball is dropped on to a revolving wheel with numbered compartments, the players betting on the number at which the ball comes to rest.

ORIGIN – French, 'small wheel'.

round > *adjective* **1** shaped like a circle or cylinder. **2** shaped like a sphere. **3** having a curved surface with no sharp projections. **4** (of a person's shoulders) bent forward. **5** (of a voice or musical tone) rich and mellow. **6** (of a number) expressed in convenient units rather than exactly, for example to the nearest whole number. **7** (of a figure) completely and exactly reached: *a round 100*. **8** frank and truthful: *she berated him in round terms*. > *noun* **1** a circular piece or section. **2** a route or sequence by which a number of people or places are visited or inspected in turn: *a newspaper round*. **3** a regularly recurring sequence of activities: *the daily round*. **4** each of a sequence of sessions in a process, especially in a sports contest. **5** a single division of a boxing or wrestling match. **6** a song for three or more unaccompanied voices or parts, each singing the same theme but starting one after another. **7** the amount of ammunition needed to fire one shot. **8** a set of drinks bought for all the members of a group. **9** Brit. a slice of bread. **10** Brit. the quantity of sandwiches made from two slices of bread. > *adverb* chiefly Brit. **1** so as to rotate or cause rotation. **2** so as to cover the whole area surrounding a particular centre. **3** so as to rotate and face in the opposite direction. **4** used in describing the relative position of something: *it's the wrong way round*. **5** so as to surround or give support. **6** so as to reach a new place or position. > *preposition* chiefly Brit. **1** on every side of (a focal point). **2** so as to encircle. **3** from or on the other side of. **4** so as to cover the whole of. > *verb* **1** pass and go round. **2** make (a figure) less exact but more convenient for calculations: *we'll round the weight up to the nearest kilo*. **3** make or become round in shape.

IDIOMS – **in the round 1** (of sculpture) standing free, rather than carved in relief. **2** (of theatre) with the audience placed on at least three sides of the stage. **3** fully and thoroughly; with all aspects shown. **round off 1** smooth the edges of. **2** complete in a satisfying or suitable way. **round on** make a sudden attack on. **round up** drive or collect (a number of people or animals) together.

DERIVATIVES – **roundness** *noun*.

USAGE – when are **round** and **around** interchangeable and when are they not? They are interchangeable in sentences such as *she put her arm round him* and *she put her arm around him*. However, **round** tends to be used for definite, specific movement, as in *she turned round*, whereas **around** is used in contexts which are less definite (*she wandered around for ages*; *costing around £3,000*). In US English **around** is the normal form in most contexts.

SYNONYMS – *adjective* **1** annular, circular, cylindrical. **2** globular, spherical.

COMBINATIONS – **round dance 1** a folk dance in which the dancers form one large circle. **2** a ballroom dance such as a waltz or polka in which couples move in circles round the ballroom. **roundhouse 1** a railway locomotive maintenance shed built around a turntable. **2** informal a blow given with a wide sweep of the arm. **3** a cabin or set of cabins on the quarterdeck of a sailing ship. **round robin 1** a tournament in which each competitor plays in turn against every other. **2** a petition, especially one with signatures written in a circle to conceal the order of writing. **round table** an assembly where parties meet on equal terms for discussion. **round trip** a journey to a place and back again. **round-up 1** a systematic gathering together of people or things. **2** a summary of facts or events.

ORIGIN – Old French, from Latin *rotundus* 'rotund'.

roundabout > *noun* Brit. **1** a road junction at which traffic moves in one direction round a central island to reach one of the roads converging on it. **2** a large revolving device in a playground, for children to ride on. **3** a merry-go-round. > *adjective* not following a short direct route; circuitous.

rounded > *adjective* **1** round or curved. **2** well developed in all aspects; complete and balanced: *a rounded human being*.

roundel /**rown**d'l/ > *noun* **1** a small disc, especially a decorative medallion. **2** a circular identifying mark painted on military aircraft.

roundelay /**rown**dəlay/ > *noun* literary **1** a short simple song with a refrain. **2** a circle dance.

ORIGIN – Old French *rondelet*, from *rondel* 'roundel, circle'.

rounders > *plural noun* (treated as sing.) a ball game similar to baseball, in which players run round a circuit of bases after hitting the ball with a cylindrical wooden bat, scoring a **rounder** if all four bases are reached before the ball is fielded.

Roundhead > *noun* historical a member or supporter of the parliamentary party in the English Civil War (1642–9).

ORIGIN – with reference to their short-cropped hair.

roundly > *adverb* **1** in a vehement, emphatic, or thorough manner. **2** in a circular or roughly circular shape.

roundsman > *noun* **1** Brit. a trader's employee who goes round delivering and taking orders. **2** US a police officer in charge of a patrol. **3** Austral. a journalist covering a specified subject.

roundworm > *noun* a nematode worm, especially a parasitic one found in the intestines of mammals.

rouse /rowz/ > *verb* **1** bring or come out of sleep; awaken or wake up. **2** bring out of inactivity. **3** excite; provoke: *his evasiveness roused my curiosity*.

ORIGIN – first used as a hawking and hunting term: probably from Old French.

rouseabout > *noun* Austral./NZ an unskilled labourer on a farm.

rousing > *adjective* **1** stirring: *a rousing speech*. **2** archaic (of a fire) blazing strongly.
DERIVATIVES – **rousingly** adverb.

roust /rowst/ > *verb* **1** cause to get up or start moving; rouse. **2** N. Amer. informal treat roughly; harass.

roustabout /rowstəbowt/ > *noun* an unskilled or casual labourer, especially a labourer on an oil rig.

rout[1] /rowt/ > *noun* **1** a disorderly retreat of defeated troops. **2** a decisive defeat. **3** archaic a disorderly or tumultuous crowd of people. > *verb* defeat utterly and force to retreat.
ORIGIN – obsolete French *route*, from Latin *rumpere* 'break'.

rout[2] /rowt/ > *verb* **1** cut a groove in (a surface). **2** rummage; root. **3** (**rout out**) root out.

route /rōōt/ > *noun* **1** a way or course taken in getting from a starting point to a destination. **2** N. Amer. a round travelled in delivering, selling, or collecting goods. > *verb* (**routed**; **routeing** or **routing**) send or direct along a specified course.
SYNONYMS – *noun* **1** course, direction, itinerary, path, road, way.
ORIGIN – Old French *rute* 'road', from Latin *rupta via* 'broken way'.

router /rowtər/ > *noun* a power tool with a shaped cutter, used in carpentry.

routine > *noun* **1** a sequence of actions regularly followed; a fixed unvarying programme. **2** a set sequence in a theatrical or comic performance. > *adjective* **1** performed as part of a regular procedure: *a routine inspection*. **2** characteristic of routine; without variety.
DERIVATIVES – **routinely** adverb.
SYNONYMS – *noun* **1** pattern, practice, procedure, regime, system; informal drill. *adjective* **2** humdrum, pedestrian, run-of-the-mill, tedious.
ORIGIN – French, from *route* 'route'.

roux /rōō/ > *noun* (pl. same) Cookery a mixture of fat (especially butter) and flour used in making sauces.
ORIGIN – from French *beurre roux* 'browned butter'.

ROV > *abbreviation* remotely operated vehicle.

rove[1] > *verb* **1** travel constantly without a fixed destination; wander. **2** (of eyes) look around in all directions.
COMBINATIONS – **roving commission** Brit. an authorisation given to someone conducting an inquiry to travel as necessary. **roving eye** a tendency to look out for potential sexual partners.
ORIGIN – first used as a term in archery in the sense 'shoot at a casual mark of undetermined range': perhaps from dialect *rave* 'to stray'.

rove[2] past of REEVE[2].

rover[1] > *noun* **1** a person who spends their time wandering. **2** a vehicle for driving over rough terrain.

rover[2] > *noun* archaic a pirate.
ORIGIN – Low German and Dutch, from *rōven* 'rob'.

row[1] /rō/ > *noun* a number of people or things in a more or less straight line.
IDIOMS – **in a row 1** forming a line. **2** informal in succession.
SYNONYMS – chain, column, file, line, series.
COMBINATIONS – **row house** N. Amer. a terrace house.

row[2] /rō/ > *verb* **1** propel (a boat) with oars. **2** engage in the sport of rowing. > *noun* a spell of rowing.
DERIVATIVES – **rower** noun **rowing** noun.
COMBINATIONS – **rowing machine** an exercise machine which causes one to use the movements involved in rowing.
ORIGIN – Old English, related to RUDDER.

row[3] /row/ informal, chiefly Brit. > *noun* **1** an acrimonious quarrel. **2** a loud noise or uproar. **3** Brit. a severe reprimand. > *verb* **1** have a row. **2** Brit. rebuke severely.

rowan /rōən, rowən/ > *noun* a small tree with white flowers and red berries.
ORIGIN – Scandinavian.

rowdy > *adjective* (**rowdier**, **rowdiest**) noisy and disorderly. > *noun* (pl. **rowdies**) a rowdy person.
DERIVATIVES – **rowdily** adverb **rowdiness** noun **rowdyism** noun.
SYNONYMS – *adjective* disorderly, noisy, obstreperous, undisciplined, unruly, wild.
ANTONYMS – *adjective* peaceful.
ORIGIN – first used in the US, in the sense 'lawless backwoodsman'.

rowel /rowəl/ > *noun* a spiked revolving disc at the end of a spur.
ORIGIN – Latin *rotella* 'little wheel'.

rowlock /rollək/ > *noun* a fitting on the gunwale of a boat which serves as a fulcrum for an oar and keeps it in place.
ORIGIN – alteration of earlier *oarlock*, influenced by ROW[2].

royal > *adjective* **1** relating to or having the status of a king or queen or a member of their family. **2** of a quality or size suitable for a king or queen; splendid. > *noun* informal a member of the royal family.
DERIVATIVES – **royally** adverb.
COMBINATIONS – **royal assent** assent of the sovereign to a bill which has been passed by Parliament, and which thus becomes an Act of Parliament. **royal blue** a deep, vivid blue. **Royal Commission** (in the UK) a commission of inquiry appointed by the Crown on the recommendation of the government. **royal flush** Poker the highest straight flush, including ace, king, queen, jack, and ten all in the same suit. **royal icing** chiefly Brit. hard white icing, typically used to decorate fruit cakes. **royal jelly** a substance secreted by honeybee workers and fed by them to larvae which are being raised as potential queen bees. **royal mast** a section of a sailing ship's mast above the topgallant. **royal tennis** real tennis. **royal warrant** a warrant issued by the sovereign, in particular one authorising a company to display the royal arms, indicating that goods or services are supplied to the royal family. **royal 'we'** the use of 'we' instead of 'I' by a single person, as traditionally used by a sovereign.
ORIGIN – Latin *regalis* 'regal'.

royalist > *noun* **1** a person who supports the principle of monarchy. **2** a supporter of the King against Parliament in the English Civil War (1642–9).
DERIVATIVES – **royalism** noun.

royalty > *noun* (pl. **royalties**) **1** people of royal blood or status. **2** the status or power of a king or queen. **3** a sum paid for the use of a patent or to an author or composer for each copy of a work sold or for each public performance. **4** a royal right (now especially over minerals) granted by the sovereign. **5** a payment made by a producer of minerals, oil, or natural gas to the owner of the site.

rozzer > *noun* Brit. informal a police officer.

RP > *abbreviation* received pronunciation.

RPG > *abbreviation* rocket-propelled grenade.

RPI > *abbreviation* retail price index.

rpm > *abbreviation* revolutions per minute.

RPV > *abbreviation* remotely piloted vehicle.

RRP > *abbreviation* Brit. recommended retail price.

Rs > *abbreviation* rupee(s).

RSA > *abbreviation* **1** Republic of South Africa. **2** Royal Scottish Academy; Royal Scottish Academician. **3** Royal Society of Arts.

RSC > *abbreviation* Royal Shakespeare Company.

RSI > *abbreviation* repetitive strain injury.

RSJ > *abbreviation* rolled steel joist.

RSM > *abbreviation* (in the British army) Regimental Sergeant Major.

RSPB > *abbreviation* (in the UK) Royal Society for the Protection of Birds.

RSPCA > *abbreviation* (in the UK) Royal Society for the Prevention of Cruelty to Animals.

RSV > *abbreviation* Revised Standard Version (of the Bible).

RSVP > *abbreviation* répondez s'il vous plaît; please reply (used at the end of invitations).
ORIGIN – French.

RTE > *abbreviation* Radio Telefís Éireann (the broadcasting authority of the Republic of Ireland).

RTF > *abbreviation* Computing rich text format.

Rt Hon. > *abbreviation* Brit. Right Honourable.

Rt Revd (also **Rt Rev.**) > *abbreviation* Right Reverend.

RU > *abbreviation* rugby union.

Ru > *symbol* the chemical element ruthenium.

rub > *verb* (**rubbed**, **rubbing**) 1 apply firm pressure to (a surface) with a repeated back and forth motion. 2 move to and fro against a surface. 3 apply with a rubbing action. 4 (**rub down**) dry, smooth, or clean by rubbing. 5 (**rub in** or **into**) work (fat) into (a mixture) by breaking and blending it with the fingertips. 6 reproduce the design of (a sepulchral brass or a stone) by rubbing paper laid on it with pencil or chalk. > *noun* 1 an act of rubbing. 2 an ointment designed to be rubbed on the skin. 3 (usu. **the rub**) the central or most important difficulty. [ORIGIN – from Shakespeare's *Hamlet* (III. i. 65).]

IDIOMS – **rub along** Brit. informal cope or get along without undue difficulty. **the rub of the green 1** Golf an accidental or unpredictable influence on the course or position of the ball. **2** good fortune. **rub one's hands** rub one's hands together to show keen satisfaction. **rub it in** (or **rub someone's nose in something**) informal emphatically draw someone's attention to an embarrassing or painful fact. **rub noses** rub one's nose against someone else's in greeting (as is traditional among Maoris and some other peoples). **rub off** be transferred by contact or association. **rub out 1** erase (pencil marks) with a rubber. **2** N. Amer. informal kill (someone). **rub shoulders** (or N. Amer. **elbows**) associate or come into contact. **rub (up) the wrong way** anger or irritate (someone).

COMBINATIONS – **rubbing alcohol** denatured alcohol used as an antiseptic or in massage.

rubato /roobaatō/ (also **tempo rubato**) > *noun* (pl. **rubatos** or **rubati** /roobaati/) Music temporary disregard for strict tempo to allow an expressive quickening or slackening.

ORIGIN – Italian, 'robbed'.

rubber¹ > *noun* 1 a tough, elastic substance made from the latex of a tropical plant or synthetically. 2 Brit. a piece of such material used for erasing pencil marks. 3 N. Amer. informal a condom. 4 (**rubbers**) N. Amer. rubber boots; galoshes.

DERIVATIVES – **rubberise** (also **rubberize**) *verb* **rubbery** *adjective*.

COMBINATIONS – **rubber band** a loop of rubber for holding things together. **rubber bullet** a bullet made of rubber, used especially in riot control. **rubber plant** an evergreen tree with large dark green shiny leaves, formerly grown as a source of rubber. **rubber tree** a tree that produces latex from which rubber is made, native to the Amazonian rainforest.

ORIGIN – from **RUB**; an early use of rubber was to rub out pencil marks.

rubber² > *noun* 1 a contest consisting of a series of matches between the same sides in cricket, tennis, and other games. 2 Bridge a unit of play in which one side scores bonus points for winning two out of a possible three games.

ORIGIN – first used as a term in bowls.

rubberneck informal > *noun* a person who turns their head to stare at something in a foolish manner. > *verb* stare in such a way.

DERIVATIVES – **rubbernecker** *noun*.

rubber stamp > *noun* 1 a hand-held device for imprinting dates, addresses, etc. 2 a person who automatically authorises another's actions. > *verb* (**rubber-stamp**) 1 apply a rubber stamp to. 2 approve (something) automatically without proper consideration.

rubbing > *noun* 1 the action of rubbing. 2 an impression of a design on brass or stone, made by rubbing.

rubbish > *noun* chiefly Brit. 1 waste material; refuse or litter. 2 unimportant or valueless material. 3 nonsense; worthless talk or ideas. > *verb* Brit. informal criticise and reject as worthless. > *adjective* Brit. informal very bad.

DERIVATIVES – **rubbishy** *adjective*.

SYNONYMS – *noun* 1 detritus, garbage, junk, litter, refuse, waste; chiefly N. Amer. trash.

ORIGIN – Old French *rubbous*, perhaps related to *robe* 'spoils'; compare with **RUBBLE**.

rubble > *noun* rough fragments of stone, brick, concrete, etc., especially as the debris from the demolition of buildings.

DERIVATIVES – **rubbly** *adjective*.

ORIGIN – perhaps from Old French *robe* 'spoils'; compare with **RUBBISH**.

rube /roob/ > *noun* N. Amer. informal a country bumpkin.

ORIGIN – abbreviation of the given name *Reuben*.

rubella /roobellə/ > *noun* a contagious disease spread by a virus, with symptoms like mild measles; German measles.

ORIGIN – Latin, literally 'reddish things'.

rubescent /roobess'nt/ > *adjective* literary reddening; blushing.

ORIGIN – from Latin *rubescere* 'redden'.

Rubicon /roobikon/ > *noun* a point of no return.

wordpower facts

Rubicon

Why do we speak of *crossing the Rubicon* when we are referring to passing a point of no return? The **Rubicon** is a stream in north-east Italy which marked the ancient boundary between Italy and Cisalpine Gaul. Julius Caesar led his army across it into Italy in 49 BC, breaking the law that forbade a general to lead an army out of his province, and so committing himself to war against the Senate and his rival Pompey. The ensuing civil war resulted in victory for Caesar after three years.

rubicund /roobikənd/ > *adjective* having a ruddy complexion.

ORIGIN – Latin *rubicundus*, from *rubere* 'be red'.

rubidium /roobiddiəm/ > *noun* a soft, silvery, reactive metallic chemical element.

ORIGIN – from Latin *rubidus* 'red' (because it has characteristic lines in the red part of the spectrum).

Rubik's cube /roobiks/ > *noun* trademark a puzzle in the form of a plastic cube covered with coloured squares, which the player attempts to turn so that all the squares on each face are of the same colour.

ORIGIN – named after its Hungarian inventor Erno *Rubik* (born 1944).

ruble > *noun* variant spelling of **ROUBLE**.

rubric /roobrik/ > *noun* 1 a heading on a document. 2 a set of instructions or rules. 3 a direction in a liturgical book as to how a church service should be conducted.

ORIGIN – from Latin *rubrica terra* 'red earth or ochre as writing material': originally referring to text written in red for emphasis.

ruby > *noun* (pl. **rubies**) 1 a precious stone consisting of corundum in colour varieties varying from deep crimson or purple to pale rose. 2 an intense deep red colour.

COMBINATIONS – **ruby wedding** the fortieth anniversary of a wedding.

ORIGIN – Latin *rubinus*, from *rubeus* 'red'.

RUC > *abbreviation* Royal Ulster Constabulary.

ruche /roosh/ > *noun* a frill or pleat of fabric.

DERIVATIVES – **ruched** *adjective* **ruching** *noun*.

ORIGIN – French, from Latin *rusca* 'tree bark'.

ruck¹ > *noun* 1 Rugby a loose scrum formed around a player with the ball on the ground. 2 Australian Rules a group of three players who follow the play without fixed positions. 3 a tightly packed crowd of people. > verb **Rugby & Australian Rules** take part in a ruck.

ORIGIN – first in the sense 'stack of fuel, heap': probably of Scandinavian origin.

ruck² > verb make or form wrinkles, creases, or folds. > noun a crease or wrinkle.

ORIGIN – Old Norse.

ruck³ > noun Brit. informal a brawl.

ORIGIN – perhaps a shortened form of **RUCTION** or **RUCKUS**.

ruckle > verb & noun Brit. another term for **RUCK²**.

rucksack /ruksak/ > noun a bag with two shoulder straps which allow it to be carried on the back, used by hikers.

ORIGIN – German, from dialect *rucken* 'back' + *Sack* 'bag, sack'.

ruckus /rukkəss/ > noun a row or commotion.

ORIGIN – perhaps related to **RUCTION** and **RUMPUS**.

ruction > noun informal **1** a disturbance or quarrel. **2** (**ructions**) trouble.

ORIGIN – perhaps from **INSURRECTION**.

rudd > noun (pl. same) a freshwater fish of the carp family with a silvery body and red fins.

ORIGIN – probably from archaic *rud* 'red colour'.

rudder > noun **1** a flat piece hinged vertically near the stern of a boat for steering. **2** a vertical aerofoil pivoted from the tailplane of an aircraft, for controlling movement about the vertical axis.

ORIGIN – Old English, 'paddle, oar'.

rudderless > adjective **1** lacking a rudder. **2** lacking direction.

ruddle > noun another term for **REDDLE**.

ruddy > adjective (**ruddier, ruddiest**) **1** reddish. **2** (of a person's face) having a healthy red colour. **3** Brit. informal, dated used as a euphemism for 'bloody'.

DERIVATIVES – **ruddiness** noun.

COMBINATIONS – **ruddy duck** an American duck of which the male has mainly deep red-brown plumage and white cheeks.

ORIGIN – Old English, from the same base as archaic *rud* 'red colour'; related to **RED**.

rude > adjective **1** offensively impolite or ill-mannered. **2** referring to sex in a way considered improper and offensive. **3** very abrupt: *a rude awakening*. **4** chiefly Brit. vigorous or hearty: *rude health*. **5** dated roughly made or done; lacking sophistication. **6** archaic ignorant and uneducated.

DERIVATIVES – **rudely** adverb **rudeness** noun **rudery** noun.

SYNONYMS – **1** bad-mannered, discourteous, disrespectful, ill-mannered, impolite, uncivil. **2** coarse, crude, lewd, smutty, vulgar.

ANTONYMS – **1** civil, courteous, polite.

COMBINATIONS – **rude boy** (in Jamaica) a lawless urban youth who likes ska or reggae.

ORIGIN – Latin *rudis* 'unwrought, uncultivated'; related to *rudus* 'broken stone'.

rudiment /roodimənt/ > noun **1** (**rudiments**) the first principles of a subject. **2** (**rudiments**) an elementary or primitive form of something. **3** Biology an undeveloped or immature part or organ.

ORIGIN – Latin *rudimentum*, from *rudis* 'unwrought'.

rudimentary /roodimentri/ > adjective **1** involving or limited to basic principles. **2** immature, undeveloped, or basic.

DERIVATIVES – **rudimentarily** adverb.

SYNONYMS – **1** basic, elementary, essential. **2** basic, crude, immature, primitive, simple, undeveloped.

rue¹ > verb (**rues, rued, rueing** or **ruing**) bitterly regret (a past event or action). > noun archaic **1** repentance; regret. **2** compassion; pity.

rue² > noun a perennial evergreen shrub with bitter, strong-scented leaves which are used in herbal medicine.

ORIGIN – Greek *rhutē*.

rueful > adjective expressing regret, especially in a wry or humorous way.

DERIVATIVES – **ruefully** adverb **ruefulness** noun.

ruff¹ > noun **1** a projecting starched frill worn round the neck, characteristic of Elizabethan and Jacobean costume. **2** a ring of feathers or hair round the neck of a bird or mammal. **3** (pl. same or **ruffs**) a wading bird, the male of which has a large ruff and ear tufts in the breeding season.

ORIGIN – probably from a variant of **ROUGH**.

ruff² > verb (in bridge and whist) play a trump in a trick which was led in a different suit. > noun an act of ruffing or opportunity to ruff.

ORIGIN – Old French *rouffle*, perhaps an alteration of Italian *trionfo* 'a trump': originally the name of a card game.

ruffian > noun a violent or lawless person.

DERIVATIVES – **ruffianism** noun **ruffianly** adjective.

SYNONYMS – delinquent, hoodlum, hooligan, lout, thug.

ORIGIN – Old French, from Italian *ruffiano*, perhaps from dialect *rofia* 'scab, scurf'.

ruffle > verb **1** make or become disarranged; disrupt the smooth surface of. **2** disconcert or upset the composure of. **3** (**ruffled**) ornamented with or gathered into a frill. > noun an ornamental gathered frill on a garment.

SYNONYMS – **1** disarrange, disturb, ripple, rumple. **2** disconcert, fluster, unnerve.

rufiyaa /roofeeyaa/ > noun (pl. same) the basic monetary unit of the Maldives, equal to 100 laris.

ORIGIN – Maldivian.

rufous /roofəss/ > adjective reddish brown in colour. > noun a reddish-brown colour.

ORIGIN – Latin *rufus* 'red, reddish'.

rug > noun **1** a small carpet. **2** chiefly Brit. a thick woollen blanket. **3** informal, chiefly N. Amer. a toupee or wig.

IDIOMS – **pull the rug out from under** abruptly expose or withdraw support from.

ORIGIN – probably Scandinavian; related to **RAG¹**.

rugby (also **rugby football**) > noun a team game played with an oval ball that may be kicked, carried, and passed by hand, in which points are won by scoring a try or by kicking the ball over the crossbar of the opponents' goal.

COMBINATIONS – **rugby league** a form of rugby played in teams of thirteen, in which professionalism has always been allowed. **rugby union** a form of rugby played in teams of fifteen, traditionally strictly amateur but now open to professionalism.

ORIGIN – named after *Rugby* School, where the game was first played.

rugged /ruggid/ > adjective **1** having a rocky and uneven surface. **2** having or requiring toughness and determination. **3** (of a man) having attractively masculine, rough-hewn features.

DERIVATIVES – **ruggedly** adverb **ruggedness** noun.

ORIGIN – first meaning 'shaggy': probably of Scandinavian origin.

ruggedised (also **ruggedized**) > adjective chiefly N. Amer. designed or improved to be hard-wearing.

rugger > noun Brit. informal rugby.

rugose /roogōss/ > adjective chiefly Biology wrinkled; corrugated.

ORIGIN – Latin *rugosus*, from *ruga* 'wrinkle'.

ruin > noun **1** physical destruction or collapse. **2** a building (or the remains of a building) that has suffered much damage. **3** a dramatic decline; a downfall. > verb **1** damage irreparably; reduce to a state of ruin. **2** reduce to poverty or bankruptcy.

SYNONYMS – noun **1** decay, decrepitude, disintegration. **2** downfall, fall, undoing. verb **1** destroy, devastate, shatter, wreck. **2** bankrupt, cripple, impoverish.

ORIGIN – Latin *ruina*, from *ruere* 'to fall'.

ruination > noun the action or fact of ruining or the state of being ruined.

ruinous > adjective **1** disastrous or destructive. **2** in ruins; dilapidated.

DERIVATIVES – **ruinously** adverb.

rule > noun **1** a regulation or principle governing conduct or procedure within a particular sphere. **2** control or government:

British rule. **3** a code of practice and discipline for a religious community. **4** (**the rule**) the normal or customary state of things. **5** a straight strip of rigid material used for measuring; a ruler. **6** a thin printed line or dash. > *verb* **1** exercise ultimate power over (a people or nation). **2** exert a powerful and restricting influence on. **3** pronounce authoritatively and legally to be the case. **4** make parallel lines on (paper).

IDIOMS – **as a rule** usually, but not always. **rule of thumb** a broadly accurate guide or principle, based on practice rather than theory. **rule out** (or **in**) exclude (or include) as a possibility. **rule the roost** be in complete control. **run the rule over** Brit. examine cursorily.

SYNONYMS – *noun* **1** decree, guideline, law, precept, principle, regulation. *verb* **1** administer, command, control, direct, govern.

ORIGIN – Latin *regula* 'straight stick'.

ruler > *noun* **1** a person who rules a people or nation. **2** a straight-edged strip of rigid material, marked at regular intervals and used to draw lines or measure distances.

ruling > *noun* an authoritative decision or pronouncement. > *adjective* exercising government or control.

rum[1] > *noun* **1** an alcoholic spirit distilled from sugar-cane residues or molasses. **2** N. Amer. any intoxicating liquor.

COMBINATIONS – **rum baba** see BABA. **rum butter** a rich, sweet, rum-flavoured sauce made with butter and sugar.

ORIGIN – perhaps an abbreviation of obsolete *rumbullion*.

rum[2] > *adjective* (**rummer**, **rummest**) Brit. informal, dated odd; peculiar.

Rumanian > *adjective* & *noun* variant spelling of ROMANIAN.

rumba /rumbə/ (also **rhumba**) > *noun* **1** a rhythmic dance with Spanish and African elements, originating in Cuba. **2** a ballroom dance based on this. > *verb* (**rumbas**, **rumbaed** /rumbəd/ or **rumba'd**, **rumbaing** /rumbəing/) dance the rumba.

ORIGIN – Latin American Spanish.

rumble > *verb* **1** make a continuous deep, resonant sound. **2** move with such a sound. **3** (**rumble on**) (of a dispute) continue in a persistent but low-key way. **4** Brit. informal discover (an illicit activity or its perpetrator). > *noun* **1** a continuous deep, resonant sound like distant thunder. **2** US informal a street fight between rival gangs.

DERIVATIVES – **rumbler** *noun* **rumbling** *adjective*.

COMBINATIONS – **rumble seat** N. Amer. an uncovered folding seat in the rear of a motor car. **rumble strip** a series of raised strips set in a road to warn drivers of speed restrictions or an approaching hazard.

rumbustious /rumbusschəss/ > *adjective* informal, chiefly Brit. boisterous or unruly.

ORIGIN – probably an alteration of archaic *robustious* 'boisterous, robust'.

ruminant > *noun* a mammal of a type that chews the cud, comprising cattle, sheep, antelopes, deer, giraffes, and their relatives. > *adjective* relating to ruminants.

ORIGIN – from Latin *ruminari* 'chew over again', from *rumen* 'throat, first stomach of a ruminant'.

ruminate /roominayt/ > *verb* **1** think deeply about something. **2** (of a ruminant) chew the cud.

DERIVATIVES – **rumination** *noun* **ruminative** *adjective*.

SYNONYMS – **1** contemplate, consider, meditate, mull over, ponder.

rummage > *verb* search unsystematically and untidily for something. > *noun* an act of rummaging.

COMBINATIONS – **rummage sale** chiefly N. Amer. a jumble sale.

wordpower facts
Rummage
The word **rummage** is connected to **room**, through the shared Middle Dutch root *ruim* 'room'. **Rummage** came into English in the late 15th century, from the Old French word *arrumage*, which was based on *arrumer* 'stow in a hold'. In early use it meant 'arrange items such as casks in the hold of a ship', which gave rise to the sense 'make a search of a vessel' (which is still used in the context of customs officers going about their duties) and then to the main modern meaning, 'search unsystematically and untidily for something'.

rummy > *noun* a card game in which the players try to form sets and sequences of cards.

rumour (US **rumor**) > *noun* a currently circulating story or report of unverified or doubtful truth. > *verb* (**be rumoured**) be circulated as a rumour.

ORIGIN – Latin *rumor* 'noise'.

rump > *noun* **1** the rear part of the body of a mammal or the lower back of a bird. **2** a small or unimportant remnant.

ORIGIN – probably Scandinavian.

rumple > *verb* give a ruffled or dishevelled appearance to. > *noun* an untidy state.

DERIVATIVES – **rumpled** *adjective*.

ORIGIN – Dutch *rompel*: originally in the sense 'wrinkle'.

rumpus > *noun* (pl. **rumpuses**) a noisy disturbance.

SYNONYMS – brouhaha, commotion, disturbance, furore, ruckus, uproar.

COMBINATIONS – **rumpus room** N. Amer. & Austral./NZ a room for playing games or other noisy activities.

rumpy pumpy > *noun* informal, humorous sexual relations.

run > *verb* (**running**; past **ran** ; past participle **run**) **1** move at a speed faster than a walk, never having both or all feet on the ground at the same time. **2** move about in a hurried and hectic way. **3** pass or cause to pass. **4** move forcefully: *the tanker ran aground.* **5** (of a bus, train, etc.) make a regular journey on a particular route. **6** be in charge of; manage or organise. **7** continue, operate, or proceed. **8** be in or cause to be in operation; function or cause to function. **9** pass into or reach a specified state or level. **10** (**run in**) (of a quality or trait) be common or inherent in. **11** emit or exude a liquid. **12** (of dye or colour) dissolve and spread when wet. **13** enter or be entered in a race. **14** stand as a candidate. **15** publish or be published in a newspaper or magazine. **16** smuggle (goods). **17** transport in a car. **18** chiefly N. Amer. (of a stocking or pair of tights) develop a ladder. > *noun* **1** an act or spell of running. **2** a running pace. **3** a journey or route. **4** a short excursion made in a car. **5** a course or track made or regularly used: *a ski run.* **6** a length, spell, or stretch of something: *a run of bad luck.* **7** an enclosed area in which animals or birds may run freely in the open. **8** Austral./NZ a large open stretch of land used for pasture or livestock. **9** a rapid series of musical notes. **10** a sequence of cards of the same suit. **11** (**the run**) the average or usual type. **12** (**the run of**) free and unrestricted use of or access to somewhere. **13** Cricket a unit of scoring achieved by hitting the ball so that both batsmen are able to run between the wickets. **14** Baseball a point scored by the batter returning to the home plate after touching the bases. **15** a ladder in stockings or tights. **16** (**the runs**) informal diarrhoea.

IDIOMS – **be run off one's feet** be extremely busy. **a (good) run for one's money** **1** challenging competition or opposition. **2** reward or enjoyment in return for one's efforts. **on the run** **1** escaping from arrest. **2** while running or moving. **run across** meet or find (someone or something) by chance. **run after** informal pursue persistently. **run along** informal go away. **run away** **1** take flight; escape. **2** try to avoid facing up to danger or difficulty. **run away with** **1** escape the control of. **2** win (a competition or prize) easily. **run before one can walk** attempt something difficult before one has grasped the basic skills. **run by** (or **past**) tell (someone) about (something) to find out their opinion. **run**

down 1 knock over (a person or animal) with a vehicle. **2** criticise unfairly or unkindly. **3** reduce or become reduced in size or resources. **4** lose or cause to lose power; stop functioning. **5** gradually deteriorate. **run in 1** Brit. use (something new) in such a way as not to make maximum demands upon it. **2** informal arrest (someone). **run into 1** collide with. **2** meet by chance. **3** experience (a problem or difficult situation). **run off 1** produce (a copy) on a machine. **2** write or recite (something) quickly and with little effort. **run on** continue without stopping; go on longer than is expected. **run out 1** use up or be used up. **2** become no longer valid. **3** extend; project. **4** Cricket dismiss (a batsman) by dislodging the bails with the ball while the batsman is still running. **run over 1** knock down (a person or animal) with a vehicle. **2** overflow. **3** exceed (a limit). **run through 1** stab (someone) so as to kill them. **2** (also **run over**) go over quickly or briefly as a rehearsal or reminder. **run to 1** extend to or reach. **2** show a tendency towards. **run up 1** allow (a bill, score, etc.) to accumulate. **2** make (something) quickly or hurriedly. **3** raise (a flag). **run up against** experience or meet (a difficulty or problem). **you can't run with the hares and hunt with the hounds** proverb you can't be loyal to both sides in a conflict or dispute.

COMBINATIONS – **run-in 1** the approach to an action or event. **2** informal a disagreement or fight. **run-off 1** a further contest after a tie or inconclusive result. **2** rainfall or other liquid that drains away from the surface of an area. **run-out 1** Cricket the dismissal of a batsman by being run out. **2** informal a short session of play or practice in a sport. **run-through 1** a rehearsal. **2** a brief outline or summary. **run-up 1** the preparatory period before a notable event. **2** an act of running briefly to gain momentum before bowling, performing a jump, etc.

runabout > noun a small car or light aircraft, especially one used for short journeys.

runaround > noun informal **1** (**the runaround**) deceitful or evasive treatment. **2** a runabout.

runaway > noun a person who has run away from their home or an institution. > adjective **1** (of an animal or vehicle) running out of control. **2** happening or done quickly or uncontrollably: a runaway success.

runcible spoon /runsib'l/ > noun a fork curved like a spoon, with three broad prongs, one of which has a sharpened outer edge for cutting.

ORIGIN – used by the English humorist Edward Lear (1812–88), perhaps suggested by obsolete rouncival, denoting a large variety of pea.

rundown > noun a brief analysis or summary. > adjective (**run-down**) **1** in a poor or neglected state. **2** tired and rather unwell, especially through overwork.

rune /roon/ > noun **1** a letter of an ancient Germanic alphabet used especially in Scandinavia. **2** a mysterious symbol, especially in a spell or incantation. **3** an ancient Scandinavian poem or part of one.
DERIVATIVES – **runic** adjective.
ORIGIN – Old English, 'secret, mystery'.

rung[1] > noun **1** a horizontal support on a ladder for a person's foot. **2** a strengthening crosspiece in the structure of a chair. **3** a level in a hierarchical structure.

rung[2] past participle of RING[2].

runnel > noun **1** a gutter. **2** a brook or stream.

runner > noun **1** a person or animal that runs. **2** a messenger, collector, or agent for a bank, bookmaker, etc. **3** an orderly in the army. **4** a rod, groove, blade, or roller on which something slides. **5** a ring capable of sliding or being drawn along a strap or rod. **6** a shoot which grows along the ground and can take root at points along its length. **7** a climbing plant, or one that spreads by means of runners. **8** a long, narrow rug or strip of carpet.
IDIOMS – **do a runner** Brit. informal leave hastily to escape or avoid something.
COMBINATIONS – **runner bean** chiefly Brit. a climbing bean plant with scarlet flowers and long green edible pods.

runner-up > noun (pl. **runners-up**) a competitor or team taking second place in a contest.

running > noun **1** the activity or movement of a runner. **2** the action or business of managing or operating. > adjective **1** (of water) flowing naturally or supplied through pipes and taps. **2** exuding liquid or pus. **3** continuous or recurring: a running joke. **4** done while running. **5** (after a noun) consecutive; in succession: the third week running.
IDIOMS – **in** (or **out of**) **the running** in (or no longer in) contention. **make** (or **take up**) **the running** set the pace.
COMBINATIONS – **running back** American Football an offensive player who specialises in carrying the ball. **running battle** a military engagement which does not occur at a fixed location. **running board** a footboard extending along the side of a vehicle. **running commentary** a verbal description of events, given as they occur. **running dog** informal a servile follower, especially of a political system. **running head** a heading printed at the top of each page of a book or chapter. **running knot** a knot that slips along the rope and changes the size of a noose. **running lights 1** navigation lights. **2** small lights on a motor vehicle that remain illuminated while the vehicle is running. **running mate 1** chiefly US an election candidate for the lesser of two closely associated political offices. **2** chiefly N. Amer. a horse entered in a race in order to set the pace for another horse which is intended to win. **running repairs** minor or temporary repairs carried out on machinery while it is in use. **running stitch** a simple needlework stitch consisting of a line of small even stitches which run back and forth through the cloth.

runny > adjective (**runnier**, **runniest**) **1** more liquid in consistency than is usual or expected. **2** (of a person's nose) producing or discharging mucus.

run-of-the-mill > adjective lacking unusual or special aspects; ordinary.

runt > noun a small pig or other animal, especially the smallest in a litter.
DERIVATIVES – **runtish** adjective **runty** adjective.
ORIGIN – first meaning 'old or decayed tree stump', later 'small ox or cow'.

runway > noun **1** a strip of hard ground along which aircraft take off and land. **2** a raised gangway extending into an auditorium, especially as used for fashion shows. **3** an animal run. **4** a chute down which logs are slid.

rupee /roopee/ > noun the basic monetary unit of India, Pakistan, Sri Lanka, Nepal, Mauritius, and the Seychelles.
ORIGIN – Hindi, from a Sanskrit word meaning 'wrought silver'.

rupiah /roopeeə/ > noun the basic monetary unit of Indonesia, equal to 100 sen.
ORIGIN – Indonesian, from Hindi rupyah 'rupee'.

rupture > verb **1** break or burst suddenly. **2** (**be ruptured** or **rupture oneself**) suffer an abdominal hernia. **3** breach or disturb (a harmonious situation). > noun **1** an instance of rupturing. **2** an abdominal hernia.
SYNONYMS – verb **1** break, crack, fracture. noun **1** break, burst, fissure.
ORIGIN – Latin ruptura, from rumpere 'to break'.

rural > adjective relating to or characteristic of the countryside rather than the town.
DERIVATIVES – **ruralise** (also **ruralize**) verb **ruralism** noun **ruralist** noun **rurality** noun **rurally** adverb.
SYNONYMS – bucolic, pastoral, rustic.
ANTONYMS – urban.
ORIGIN – Latin ruralis, from rus 'country'.

Ruritanian /rooritaynian/ > adjective relating to or characteristic of romantic adventure or its setting.
ORIGIN – from Ruritania, the imaginary setting for the novels of courtly intrigue

and romance written by the English novelist Anthony Hope (1863–1933).

ruse /rooz/ > *noun* a stratagem or trick.
SYNONYMS – device, ploy, stratagem, trick.

wordpower facts
Ruse
The word **ruse** was originally a hunting term referring to the dodging or doubling back of an animal to elude hounds. It comes from Old French, from the verb *ruser*, which meant 'use trickery' or 'drive back'. *Ruser* is also the source of **rush**, which used to mean 'drive back'.

rush¹ > *verb* **1** move or act with urgent haste. **2** transport or produce with urgent haste. **3** deal with hurriedly. **4** (of air or a liquid) flow strongly. **5** dash towards in an attempt to attack or capture. > *noun* **1** the action or an instance of rushing. **2** a flurry of hasty activity. **3** a sudden strong demand for a commodity. **4** a sudden intensity of feeling. **5** a sudden thrill experienced after taking certain drugs. **6** (**rushes**) the first prints made of a film after a period of shooting.
IDIOMS – **rush one's fences** Brit. act with undue haste. **a rush of blood to the head** a sudden attack of wild irrationality.
SYNONYMS – *verb* **1** dash, hurry, scramble.
COMBINATIONS – **rush hour** a time at the start and end of the working day when traffic is at its heaviest.
ORIGIN – Old French *ruser* 'drive back'; related to RUSE.

rush² > *noun* a marsh or waterside plant with slender pith-filled leaves, some kinds of which are used for matting, baskets, etc.
DERIVATIVES – **rushy** *adjective*.

rushlight > *noun* historical a candle made by dipping the pith of a rush in tallow.

rusk > *noun* a dry biscuit or piece of rebaked bread.
ORIGIN – Spanish or Portuguese *rosca* 'twist, coil, roll of bread'.

russet > *adjective* reddish brown. > *noun* **1** a reddish-brown colour. **2** a variety of dessert apple with a slightly rough greenish-brown skin. **3** historical a coarse homespun reddish-brown or grey cloth.
DERIVATIVES – **russety** *adjective*.
ORIGIN – Old French *rousset*, from Latin *russus* 'red'.

Russian > *noun* **1** a person from Russia. **2** the Slavic language of Russia, written in the Cyrillic alphabet. > *adjective* relating to Russia.

COMBINATIONS – **Russian doll** each of a set of brightly painted hollow wooden dolls that fit inside each other. **Russian Orthodox Church** the national Church of Russia. **Russian roulette** a dangerous game of chance in which a single bullet is loaded into the chamber of a revolver, the cylinder is spun, and people take it in turns to hold the gun to their own head and fire it. **Russian vine** a fast-growing Asian climbing plant with long clusters of white or pink flowers.

Russki /ruski/ (also **Russky**) > *noun* (pl. **Russkis** or **Russkies**) informal, chiefly derogatory a Russian.

rust > *noun* **1** a reddish- or yellowish-brown flaky coating of iron oxide that is formed on iron or steel by oxidation, especially in the presence of moisture. **2** a fungal disease of plants which results in reddish or brownish patches. **3** a reddish-brown colour. > *verb* be affected with rust.
WORDFINDER – ferruginous (*containing rust or rust-coloured*).
DERIVATIVES – **rustless** *adjective*.
COMBINATIONS – **rust belt** informal (especially in the American Midwest and NE states) a region characterised by declining industry and a falling population. **rust bucket** informal a vehicle or ship which is old and badly rusted.
ORIGIN – Old English, related to RED.

rustic > *adjective* **1** of or characteristic of life in the country. **2** having a simplicity and charm that is considered typical of the countryside. **3** (of furniture) made of rough branches or timber. > *noun* often derogatory an unsophisticated country person.
DERIVATIVES – **rustically** *adverb* **rusticity** *noun*.
SYNONYMS – *adjective* **1** bucolic, pastoral, rural.
ORIGIN – Latin *rusticus*, from *rus* 'the country'.

rusticate /rustikayt/ > *verb* **1** Brit. suspend from a university as a punishment (used chiefly at Oxford and Cambridge). **2** fashion (masonry) in large blocks with sunken joints and a roughened surface. **3** archaic go to or live in the country.
DERIVATIVES – **rustication** *noun*.

rustle > *verb* **1** make a soft crackling sound like that caused by the movement of dry leaves or paper. **2** move in a particular direction with such a sound. **3** round up and steal (cattle, horses, or sheep). **4** (**rustle up**) informal produce (food or a drink) quickly. **5** N. Amer. informal move or act quickly or energetically. > *noun* a rustling sound.
DERIVATIVES – **rustler** *noun*.

rustproof > *adjective* not susceptible to corrosion by rust. > *verb* make rustproof.

rusty > *adjective* (**rustier, rustiest**) **1** affected by rust. **2** rust-coloured. **3** (of knowledge or a skill) impaired by lack of recent practice.
DERIVATIVES – **rustily** *adverb* **rustiness** *noun*.

rut¹ > *noun* **1** a long deep track made by the repeated passage of the wheels of vehicles. **2** a routine or pattern of activity that has become dull but is hard to change.
DERIVATIVES – **rutted** *adjective* **rutty** *adjective*.
ORIGIN – probably from Old French *rute*, from Latin *rupta via* 'broken way', from *rumpere* 'break'.

rut² > *noun* an annual period of sexual activity in deer and some other mammals, during which the males fight each other for access to the females. > *verb* (**rutted, rutting**) engage in such activity.
DERIVATIVES – **ruttish** *adjective*.
ORIGIN – Old French, from Latin *rugire* 'to roar'.

rutabaga /rootəbaygə/ > *noun* chiefly N. Amer. a swede (vegetable).
ORIGIN – Swedish dialect *rotabagge*.

ruth > *noun* archaic a feeling of pity, distress, or grief.
ORIGIN – from RUE¹.

ruthenium /rootheeniəm/ > *noun* a hard, silvery-white metallic chemical element.
ORIGIN – from *Ruthenia*, the name of a region of eastern Europe, because it was discovered in ores from the Urals.

rutherfordium /ruthərfordiəm/ > *noun* a very unstable chemical element made by high-energy atomic collisions.
ORIGIN – named after the New Zealand physicist Ernest *Rutherford* (1871–1937).

ruthless > *adjective* having or showing no compassion.
DERIVATIVES – **ruthlessly** *adverb* **ruthlessness** *noun*.
SYNONYMS – cruel, merciless, pitiless, unrelenting.

RV > *abbreviation* N. Amer. recreational vehicle (especially a motorised caravan).

Rwandan /rooandən/ (also **Rwandese** /rooandeez/) > *noun* a person from Rwanda, a country in central Africa. > *adjective* relating to Rwanda.

rye > *noun* **1** a wheat-like cereal plant which tolerates poor soils and low temperatures. **2** whisky in which a significant amount of the grain used in distillation is fermented rye.
COMBINATIONS – **rye bread** a dense, chewy bread made with rye flour. **ryegrass** a grass used for fodder and lawns.
ORIGIN – Old English *ryge*; *ryegrass* is an alteration of obsolete *ray-grass*.

S¹ (also **s**) > *noun* (pl. **Ss** or **S's**) the nineteenth letter of the alphabet.

S² > *abbreviation* **1** (chiefly in Catholic use) Saint. **2** siemens. **3** small (as a clothes size). **4** South or Southern. > *symbol* the chemical element sulphur.

s > *abbreviation* **1** second or seconds. **2** shilling or shillings. **3** Grammar singular. **4** (in genealogies) son or sons.

's > *contraction informal* **1** is. **2** has. **3** us. **4** does.

-s¹ > *suffix* denoting the plurals of nouns: *wagons.*

-s² > *suffix* forming the third person singular of the present of verbs: *sews.*

-'s¹ > *suffix* denoting possession in singular nouns, also in plural nouns not having a final *-s*: *John's book.*

-'s² > *suffix* denoting the plural of a letter or symbol: *9's.*

SA > *abbreviation* **1** Salvation Army. **2** South Africa. **3** South America. **4** South Australia.

sabbatarian /sabbətairiən/ > *noun* a strict observer of the sabbath. > *adjective* relating to or upholding the observance of the sabbath.
DERIVATIVES – **sabbatarianism** *noun.*

sabbath > *noun* **1** (often **the Sabbath**) a day of religious observance and abstinence from work, kept by Jews from Friday evening to Saturday evening, and by most Christians on Sunday. **2** (also **witches' sabbath**) a midnight pagan ritual held by witches.
ORIGIN – from a Hebrew word meaning 'to rest'.

sabbatical /səbattik'l/ > *noun* a period of paid leave granted to a university teacher for study or travel (traditionally one year for every seven years worked). > *adjective* **1** relating to a sabbatical. **2** archaic of or appropriate to the sabbath.
ORIGIN – from Greek *sabbatikos.*

saber > *noun & verb* US spelling of SABRE.

Sabine /sabbīn/ > *noun* a member of an ancient people of the central Apennines in Italy.
ORIGIN – Latin *Sabinus.*

sable¹ /sayb'l/ > *noun* **1** a marten with a short tail and dark brown fur, native to Siberia and Japan. **2** the fur of the sable.
ORIGIN – Old French, from Latin *sabelum.*

sable² /sayb'l/ > *adjective* literary or Heraldry black. > *noun* **1** literary or Heraldry black. **2** (**sables**) archaic mourning garments.
ORIGIN – Old French, generally taken to be identical with SABLE¹, although sable fur is dark brown.

sabot /sabbō/ > *noun* a kind of simple shoe, shaped and hollowed out from a single block of wood.
ORIGIN – French, blend of *savate* 'shoe' and *botte* 'boot'.

sabotage /sabbətaazh/ > *verb* deliberately destroy or wreck (something), especially for military or political advantage. > *noun* the action of sabotaging something.

wordpower facts
Sabotage
The word **sabotage** is directly linked with a word for a heavy wooden clog, **sabot**. Both words are French in origin: **sabot**, a much older word, entered English in the 17th century; **sabotage** was not adopted until the early 20th century. **Sabotage** comes from the verb *saboter*, meaning 'wilfully destroy', originally 'kick or strike with sabots'. It was first used in English in the context of industrial action, in reference to the wilful destruction of their employer's property by workmen during a strike.

saboteur /sabbətör/ > *noun* a person who engages in sabotage.
ORIGIN – French.

sabra /sabrə/ > *noun* a Jew born in Israel (or before 1948 in Palestine).
ORIGIN – from a Hebrew word meaning 'opuntia fruit' (opuntias being common in coastal regions of Israel).

sabre /saybər/ (US **saber**) > *noun* **1** a heavy cavalry sword with a curved blade and a single cutting edge. **2** a light fencing sword with a tapering, typically curved blade.
COMBINATIONS – **sabre-rattling** the display or threat of military force.
ORIGIN – French, from German *Sabel*, from Hungarian *szablya.*

sabretooth > *noun* a large extinct carnivore of the cat family with massive curved upper canine teeth.
DERIVATIVES – **sabre-toothed** *adjective.*

sac /sak/ > *noun* **1** a hollow, flexible structure resembling a bag or pouch. **2** a cavity enclosed by a membrane within a living organism.
ORIGIN – Latin *saccus* 'sack, bag'.

saccharide /sakkərīd/ > *noun* Biochemistry another term for SUGAR (in sense 2).

saccharin /sakkərin/ > *noun* a sweet-tasting synthetic compound used as a low-calorie substitute for sugar.
ORIGIN – from Greek *sakkharon* 'sugar'.

saccharine /sakkərīn, -rin/ > *adjective* **1** excessively sweet or sentimental. **2** relating to or containing sugar. > *noun* another term for SACCHARIN.
SYNONYMS – *adjective* **1** cloying, mawkish, syrupy.

sacerdotal /sakkərdōt'l/ > *adjective* relating to priests or the priesthood.
DERIVATIVES – **sacerdotalism** *noun.*
ORIGIN – Latin *sacerdotalis*, from *sacerdos* 'priest'.

sachem /saychem/ > *noun* **1** (among some American Indian peoples) a chief. **2** N. Amer. informal a boss or leader.
ORIGIN – Narragansett, 'chief'.

Sachertorte /zakhərtortə/ > *noun* (pl. **Sachertorten** /zakhərtortən/) a chocolate gateau with apricot jam filling.
ORIGIN – German, from the name of the chef Franz *Sacher* + *Torte* 'tart, pastry'.

sachet /sashay/ > *noun* chiefly Brit. a small sealed bag or packet containing a small quantity of something.
ORIGIN – French, 'little bag', from Latin *saccus* 'sack, bag'.

wordpower facts
Sack
The word **sack** comes from Latin *saccus*, meaning 'bag or sack' and also 'sackcloth', from Greek *sakkos*. It is related to **sac** and **sachet**, which come from the same source. The sense 'dismissal from one's job' is first recorded in the early 19th century: it probably arose from the idea of a dismissed worker taking away his belongings in a sack. **Sack** meaning 'plunder' comes from the French phrase *mettre à sac* 'put to sack', on the model of Italian *mettere a sacco*, which perhaps originally referred to filling a sack with plunder.

sack¹ > *noun* **1** a large bag made of a material such as hessian or thick paper, used for storing and carrying goods. **2** (**the sack**) informal dismissal from employment. **3** (**the sack**) informal bed. > *verb* **1** informal dismiss from employment. **2** (**sack out**) informal, chiefly N. Amer. go to sleep or bed. **3** put into a sack or sacks.
IDIOMS – **hit the sack** informal go to bed.
DERIVATIVES – **sackable** *adjective.*
COMBINATIONS – **sack dress** a woman's loose unwaisted dress, originally fashionable in the 1950s. **sack race** a children's race in

which each competitor stands in a sack and moves forward by jumping.

sack² > *verb* plunder and destroy (used chiefly in historical contexts). > *noun* the sacking of a town or city.

sack³ > *noun* historical a dry white wine formerly imported into Britain from Spain and the Canaries.

ORIGIN – from French *vin sec* 'dry wine'.

sackbut /sakbut/ > *noun* an early form of trombone used in Renaissance music.

ORIGIN – obsolete French *saquebute*, first meaning 'hook for pulling a man off a horse'.

sackcloth > *noun* a coarse fabric woven from flax or hemp.

IDIOMS – **sackcloth and ashes** an expression of extreme sorrow or remorse. [ORIGIN – with allusion to the wearing of sackcloth and having ashes sprinkled on the head as a sign of penitence or mourning (Gospel of Matthew, chapter 11).]

sacking > *noun* **1** an act of dismissing someone from employment. **2** coarse material for making sacks; sackcloth.

sacra plural of SACRUM.

sacral /saykrəl/ > *adjective* **1** Anatomy relating to the sacrum. **2** relating to sacred rites or symbols.

sacrament /sakrəmənt/ > *noun* **1** (in the Christian Church) a religious ceremony or ritual regarded as imparting divine grace, such as baptism and the Eucharist. **2** (also **the Blessed Sacrament** or **the Holy Sacrament**) (in Catholic use) the consecrated elements of the Eucharist, especially the bread. **3** a thing of mysterious or sacred significance; a religious symbol.

ORIGIN – Latin *sacramentum* 'solemn oath'.

sacramental > *adjective* relating to or constituting a sacrament. > *noun* (in the Christian Church) an observance that is comparable to but not itself considered to be a sacrament, such as the use of holy water or the sign of the cross.

DERIVATIVES – **sacramentalise** (also **sacramentalize**) *verb* **sacramentalism** *noun* **sacramentally** *adverb*.

sacré bleu /sakray blö/ > *exclamation* a French expression of surprise, exasperation, or dismay.

ORIGIN – alteration of *sacré Dieu* 'holy God'.

sacred /saykrid/ > *adjective* **1** connected with a deity and so deserving veneration; holy. **2** (of a text) embodying the doctrines of a religion. **3** religious rather than secular.

WORDFINDER – blaspheme (*speak irreverently of sacred things*), consecrate (*make or declare sacred*), hierophant (*a person who interprets sacred mysteries*), ineffable (*too sacred to be uttered*).

DERIVATIVES – **sacredly** *adverb* **sacredness** *noun*.

SYNONYMS – **1** consecrated, hallowed, holy.

COMBINATIONS – **sacred cow** an idea, custom, or institution held to be above criticism (with reference to the respect of Hindus for the cow as a sacred animal).

ORIGIN – from Latin *sacrare* 'consecrate', from *sacer* 'holy'.

sacrifice > *noun* **1** the practice or an act of killing an animal or person or surrendering a possession as an offering to a deity. **2** an animal, person, or object offered in this way. **3** an act of giving up something of value for the sake of something considered more worthy or important. > *verb* offer or give up as a sacrifice.

DERIVATIVES – **sacrificial** *adjective*.

ORIGIN – Latin *sacrificium*, from *sacer* 'holy'.

sacrilege* /sakrilij/ > *noun* violation or misuse of something regarded as sacred.

DERIVATIVES – **sacrilegious** *adjective*.

*SPELLING – the last part of the word is commonly misspelled as *-relige* or *-rilige*; it should be sac*rilege* (and sac*rilegious*).

ORIGIN – Latin *sacrilegium*, from *sacer* 'sacred' + *legere* 'take possession of'.

sacristan /sakristən/ > *noun* a person in charge of a sacristy.

sacristy /sakristi/ > *noun* (pl. **sacristies**) a room in a church where a priest prepares for a service, and where vestments and other things used in worship are kept.

ORIGIN – Latin *sacristia*, from *sacer* 'sacred'.

sacroiliac /saykrōilliak/ > *adjective* Anatomy **1** relating to the sacrum and the ilium. **2** denoting the rigid joint at the back of the pelvis between the sacrum and the ilium.

sacrosanct /sakrōsankt/ > *adjective* regarded as too important or valuable to be interfered with.

DERIVATIVES – **sacrosanctity** *noun*.

SYNONYMS – inviolable, untouchable.

ORIGIN – Latin *sacrosanctus*, from *sacro* 'by a sacred rite' + *sanctus* 'holy'.

sacrum /saykrəm/ > *noun* (pl. **sacra** /saykrə/ or **sacrums**) Anatomy a triangular bone in the lower back formed from fused vertebrae and situated between the two hip bones of the pelvis.

ORIGIN – Latin *os sacrum*, translation of Greek *hieron osteon* 'sacred bone' (from the belief that the soul resided in it).

SAD > *abbreviation* seasonal affective disorder.

sad > *adjective* (**sadder**, **saddest**) **1** feeling sorrow; unhappy. **2** causing or characterised by sorrow or regret. **3** informal pathetically inadequate or unfashionable.

DERIVATIVES – **sadness** *noun*.

SYNONYMS – **1** downcast, miserable, sorrowful, unhappy. **2** pitiful, tragic, unfortunate.

ORIGIN – Old English, from an Indo-European root shared by Latin *satis* 'enough', and related to SATISFY: first meaning 'sated, weary', 'weighty, dense', later 'steadfast, firm', 'serious, sober', 'sorrowful'.

sadden > *verb* cause to feel sad.

SYNONYMS – depress, dispirit, grieve.

saddle > *noun* **1** a seat with a raised ridge at the front and back, fastened on the back of a horse for riding. **2** a seat on a bicycle or motorcycle. **3** a low part of a hill or mountain ridge between two higher points or peaks. **4** a shaped support for a cable, pipe, or other object. **5** the lower part of the back in a mammal or fowl. **6** a joint of meat consisting of the two loins. > *verb* **1** put a saddle on (a horse). **2** (**saddle with**) burden with (a responsibility or task).

WORDFINDER – cantle (*the raised curved part at the back of a saddle*), crupper (*strap on the back of a saddle*), girth (*band attached to a saddle and fastened round the horse's belly*), pommel (*projecting front part of a saddle*), stirrup (*device attacked to the side of a saddle, to support the rider's foot*).

IDIOMS – **in the saddle 1** on horseback. **2** in a position of control or responsibility.

COMBINATIONS – **saddlebag** a bag attached to a saddle. **saddle horse 1** a wooden stand on which saddles are cleaned or stored. **2** chiefly N. Amer. a horse kept for riding only. **saddle soap** soft soap containing neat's-foot oil, used for cleaning leather. **saddle-sore** chafed by a saddle. **saddle stitch 1** a stitch of thread or a wire staple passed through the fold of a magazine or booklet. **2** (in needlework) a decorative stitch made with long stitches on the upper side of the cloth alternated with short stitches on the underside.

saddleback > *noun* **1** a hill with a ridge along the top that dips in the middle. **2** a pig of a black breed with a white stripe across the back.

DERIVATIVES – **saddlebacked** *adjective*.

saddler > *noun* someone who makes, repairs, or deals in saddlery.

saddlery > *noun* (pl. **saddleries**) **1** saddles, bridles, and other equipment for horses. **2** the making or repairing of such equipment. **3** a saddler's business or premises.

saddo > *noun* (pl. **saddos**) Brit. informal a person perceived as pathetically inadequate.

Sadducee /sadyosee/ > *noun* a member of an ancient Jewish sect that denied the resurrection of the dead and the existence of spirits, and that emphasised acceptance of the written Law rather than oral tradition.

DERIVATIVES – **Sadducean** *adjective*.

ORIGIN – from a Hebrew word meaning 'descendant of Zadok' (high priest in the time of kings David and Solomon).

sadhu /**saa**doo/ > *noun* Indian a holy man, sage, or ascetic.

ORIGIN – Sanskrit.

sadism /**say**diz'm/ > *noun* the tendency to derive pleasure or sexual gratification from inflicting pain, suffering, or humiliation on others.

DERIVATIVES – **sadist** *noun* **sadistic** *adjective* **sadistically** *adverb*.

ORIGIN – named after the French writer the Marquis de *Sade* (1740–1814).

sadly > *adverb* **1** in a sad manner. **2** it is sad or regrettable that; regrettably.

sadomasochism /saydō**mass**əkiz'm/ > *noun* the psychological tendency or sexual practice characterised by a combination of sadism and masochism.

DERIVATIVES – **sadomasochist** *noun* **sadomasochistic** *adjective*.

sae > *abbreviation* Brit. stamped addressed envelope.

safari > *noun* (pl. **safaris**) (especially in East Africa) an expedition to observe or hunt animals in their natural habitat.

COMBINATIONS – **safari park** an area of parkland where wild animals are kept in the open and may be observed by visitors driving through. **safari suit** a lightweight suit consisting of a belted jacket with patch pockets and matching trousers, shorts, or skirt.

ORIGIN – from an Arabic word meaning 'to travel'.

safe > *adjective* **1** protected from danger or risk. **2** not causing or leading to harm or injury. **3** (of a place) affording security or protection. **4** often derogatory cautious and unenterprising. **5** (of an assertion, verdict, bet, etc.) based on good reasons or evidence and not likely to be proved wrong. **6** informal excellent. > *noun* **1** a strong fireproof cabinet with a complex lock, used for the storage of valuables. **2** N. Amer. informal a condom.

IDIOMS – **safe and sound** uninjured; with no harm done. **to be on the safe side** in order to have a margin of security against risks.

DERIVATIVES – **safely** *adverb* **safeness** *noun*.

SYNONYMS – *adjective* **1** guarded, secure, shielded. **3** impregnable, secure, sound.

COMBINATIONS – **safe conduct** immunity from arrest or harm when passing through an area. **safe deposit** a strongroom or safe in a bank or hotel. **safe house** a house in a secret location, used by spies or criminals in hiding. **safekeeping** preservation in a safe place. **safe period** the time during and near a woman's menstrual period when conception is least likely. **safe seat** a parliamentary seat that is likely to be retained with a large majority in an election. **safe sex** sexual activity engaged in by people who have taken precautions to protect themselves against sexually transmitted diseases such as Aids.

ORIGIN – Old French *sauf*, from Latin *salvus* 'uninjured'.

safeguard > *noun* a measure taken to protect or prevent something. > *verb* protect with a safeguard.

SYNONYMS – *noun* defence, precaution, protection. *verb* defend, guard, preserve, shelter.

ORIGIN – Old French *sauve garde*, from *sauve* 'safe' + *garde* 'guard'.

safety > *noun* (pl. **safeties**) **1** the condition of being safe. **2** (before another noun) designed to prevent injury or damage: *a safety barrier*. **3** US informal a condom.

IDIOMS – **there's safety in numbers** proverb being in a group of people makes you feel more confident or secure.

SYNONYMS – **1** protection, security, soundness.

COMBINATIONS – **safety belt** a belt or strap securing a person to their seat in a vehicle or aircraft. **safety catch** a device that prevents a gun being fired or a machine being operated accidentally. **safety curtain** a fireproof curtain that can be lowered between the stage and the main part of a theatre to prevent the spread of fire. **safety deposit** a safe deposit. **safety glass** glass that has been toughened or laminated so that it is less likely to splinter when broken. **safety match** a match that ignites only when struck on a specially prepared surface, such as that on the side of a matchbox. **safety net 1** a net placed to catch an acrobat in case of a fall. **2** a safeguard against adversity. **safety pin** a pin with a point that is bent back to the head and is held in a guard when closed. **safety razor** a razor with a guard to reduce the risk of cutting the skin. **safety valve 1** a valve that opens automatically to relieve excessive pressure. **2** a means of giving harmless vent to feelings of tension or stress.

safflower > *noun* an orange-flowered thistle-like plant with seeds that yield an edible oil and petals that were formerly used to produce a red or yellow dye.

ORIGIN – Dutch *saffloer* or German *Saflor*, from an Arabic word meaning 'yellow'.

saffron > *noun* an orange-yellow spice used for flavouring and colouring food, made from the dried stigmas of a crocus.

ORIGIN – Arabic.

sag¹ > *verb* (**sagged**, **sagging**) **1** sink, subside, or bulge downwards gradually under weight or pressure or through lack of strength. **2** hang down loosely or unevenly. > *noun* **1** an instance of sagging.

DERIVATIVES – **saggy** *adjective*.

ORIGIN – Low German *sacken*, Dutch *zakken* 'subside'.

sag² > *noun* variant spelling of SAAG.

saga > *noun* **1** a long story of heroic achievement, especially a medieval prose narrative in Old Norse or Old Icelandic. **2** a long, involved account or series of incidents.

ORIGIN – Old Norse, 'narrative'.

sagacious /sə**gay**shəss/ > *adjective* having or showing good judgement.

DERIVATIVES – **sagaciously** *adverb* **sagacity** *noun*.

ORIGIN – from Latin *sagax* 'wise'.

sage¹ > *noun* an aromatic plant with greyish-green leaves used as a culinary herb, native to southern Europe and the Mediterranean.

COMBINATIONS – **sage green** a greyish-green colour like that of sage leaves.

ORIGIN – Old French *sauge*, from Latin *salvia* 'healing plant', from *salvus* 'safe'.

sage² > *noun* (especially in ancient history or legend) a man recognised for his wisdom. > *adjective* wise; judicious.

DERIVATIVES – **sagely** *adverb* **sageness** *noun*.

SYNONYMS – *adjective* intelligent, judicious, sagacious, shrewd, wise.

ORIGIN – Old French, from Latin *sapere* 'be wise'.

sagebrush > *noun* **1** a shrubby, aromatic North American plant of the daisy family. **2** semi-arid country dominated by this plant.

saggar /**sagg**ər/ (also **sagger**) > *noun* a protective fireclay box for pottery while it is being fired.

ORIGIN – probably a contraction of SAFEGUARD.

Sagittarius /saji**tair**iəss/ > *noun* **1** Astronomy a large constellation (the Archer), said to represent a centaur carrying a bow and arrow. **2** Astrology the ninth sign of the zodiac, which the sun enters about 22 November.

DERIVATIVES – **Sagittarian** *noun* & *adjective*.

ORIGIN – Latin, 'archer'.

sago /**say**gō/ > *noun* **1** edible starch obtained from a palm, dried and processed to produce a flour or granules. **2** a sweet dish made from sago and milk.

ORIGIN – Malay.

Saharan /sə**haar**ən/ > *adjective* relating to the Sahara Desert in North Africa.

Sahelian /sə**heel**iən/ > *adjective* relating to the Sahel, a semi-arid region bordering the southern Sahara Desert in North Africa.

sahib /saab, saa**hib**/ > *noun* Indian a polite title or form of address for a man.

ORIGIN – Urdu, from an Arabic word meaning 'friend, lord'.

said past and past participle of SAY. > *adjective* denoting someone or something already mentioned: *the said agreement*.

sail > *noun* **1** a piece of material extended on a mast to catch the wind and propel a boat or ship. **2** a wind-catching apparatus attached to the arm of a windmill. **3** a voyage or excursion in a sailing boat or ship. > *verb* **1** travel in a sailing boat as a sport or for recreation. **2** travel in a ship or boat using sails or engine power. **3** begin a voyage; leave a harbour. **4** travel by ship on or across (a sea) or on (a route). **5** navigate or control (a boat or ship). **6** move in a stately and confident manner. **7** move smoothly and rapidly. **8** (**sail through**) *informal* succeed easily at.

IDIOMS – **sail close to the wind 1** sail as nearly against the wind as possible. **2** behave or operate in a risky way. **under sail** with the sails hoisted.

COMBINATIONS – **sailcloth 1** a canvas or other strong fabric used for making sails. **2** a similar fabric used for making durable clothes. **sailfish** an edible marine fish with a high sail-like dorsal fin. **sailing boat** (**N. Amer. sailboat**) a boat propelled by sails. **sailing ship** a ship propelled by sails. **sailplane** a glider designed for sustained flight.

sailboard > *noun* a board with a mast and a sail, used in windsurfing.

DERIVATIVES – **sailboarder** *noun* **sailboarding** *noun*.

sailor > *noun* **1** a person who works as a member of the crew of a commercial or naval ship or boat. **2** a person who sails as a sport or for recreation. **3** (**a good** or **bad sailor**) a person who rarely (or often) becomes sick at sea in rough weather.

COMBINATIONS – **sailor collar** a collar cut deep and square at the back, tapering to a V-neck at the front, resembling the collar in the uniform traditionally worn by sailors. **sailor suit** a suit of blue and white material resembling the traditional uniform of a sailor.

sainfoin /**sayn**foyn/ > *noun* a pink-flowered Asian plant, grown for fodder.

ORIGIN – obsolete French *saintfoin*, from Latin *sanum foenum* 'wholesome hay'.

saint /saynt, before a name usually sənt/ > *noun* **1** a very virtuous or holy person who is regarded as being in heaven after death. **2** (in the Catholic and Orthodox Churches) such a person who is formally recognised and may be the object of veneration and prayers for intercession. **3** *informal* a very virtuous person. > *verb* **1** formally recognise as a saint; canonise. **2** (**sainted**) worthy of being a saint; very virtuous.

WORDFINDER – beatification (*the first step towards making someone a saint*), canonise (*officially declare someone a saint*), hagiography (*writing of the lives of saints*), hagiolatry (*worship of saints*), nimbus (*a luminous cloud or halo surrounding a saint*).

DERIVATIVES – **sainthood** *noun* **saintliness** *noun* **saintly** *adjective*.

COMBINATIONS – **saint's day** (in the Christian Church) a day on which a saint is particularly commemorated.

ORIGIN – from Latin *sanctus* 'holy'.

St Anthony's fire > *noun* **1** erysipelas. **2** ergotism.

St Bernard > *noun* a very large dog of a breed originally kept to rescue travellers by the monks of the hospice on the Great St Bernard, a pass across the Alps.

St Elmo's fire /**el**mōz/ > *noun* a phenomenon in which a luminous electrical discharge appears on a ship or aircraft during a storm.

ORIGIN – regarded as a sign of protection given by *St Elmo*, the patron saint of sailors.

St George's cross > *noun* a +-shaped cross, red on a white background (especially as a national emblem of England).

St John's wort > *noun* a herbaceous plant or shrub with yellow flowers and paired oval leaves.

ORIGIN – so named because some species come into flower near the feast day of St John the Baptist (24 June).

St Lucian /**loo**sh'n/ > *noun* a person from the Caribbean island of St Lucia. > *adjective* relating to St Lucia.

saintpaulia /sənt**paw**liə/ > *noun* an African violet.

ORIGIN – from the name of the German explorer Baron W. von *Saint Paul* (1860–1910), who discovered it.

St Swithin's day > *noun* 15 July, a Church festival commemorating St Swithin and popularly said to be a day on which, if it rains, it will continue raining for forty days.

St Vitus's dance /**vī**təsiz/ > *noun* old-fashioned term for SYDENHAM'S CHOREA.

ORIGIN – so named because a visit to the shrine of the Christian martyr *St Vitus* (died c.300) was believed to alleviate the disease.

saith /seth/ *archaic* third person singular present of SAY.

saithe /sayth/ > *noun* a North Atlantic food fish of the cod family.

ORIGIN – Old Norse.

sake¹ /sayk/ > *noun* **1** (**for the sake of**) for the purpose of or in the interest of; in order to achieve or preserve. **2** (**for the sake of**) out of consideration for or in order to help. **3** (**for old times' sake**) in memory of former times. **4** (**for God's** or **goodness sake**) expressing impatience or despair.

ORIGIN – Old English, 'contention, crime', from a base meaning 'affair, legal action, thing'.

sake² /**saa**ki, **sakk**ay/ > *noun* a Japanese alcoholic drink made from fermented rice.

ORIGIN – Japanese.

salaam /sə**laam**/ > *noun* a gesture of greeting or respect in Arabic-speaking and Muslim countries, consisting of a low bow of the head and body with the hand or fingers touching the forehead. > *verb* make a salaam.

ORIGIN – from an Arabic phrase meaning 'peace be upon you'.

salable > *adjective* variant spelling of SALEABLE.

salacious /sə**lay**shəss/ > *adjective* having or conveying undue or indecent interest in sexual matters.

DERIVATIVES – **salaciously** *adverb* **salaciousness** *noun*.

SYNONYMS – indecent, lewd, prurient.

ORIGIN – from Latin *salax*, from *salire* 'to leap'.

salad > *noun* a dish containing cold, typically uncooked vegetables, often with a dressing.

COMBINATIONS – **salad cream** Brit. a creamy dressing resembling mayonnaise. **salad days 1** (**one's salad days**) the period when one is young and inexperienced. **2** the peak or heyday of something. [ORIGIN – from Shakespeare's *Antony and Cleopatra* (I. v. 72).]

ORIGIN – Old French *salade*, from Latin *sal* 'salt'.

salamander /**sal**əmandər/ > *noun* **1** a long-tailed amphibian resembling a newt, typically with bright markings. **2** a mythical lizard-like creature said to live in or be able to withstand fire. **3** a metal plate heated and placed over food to brown it.

DERIVATIVES – **salamandrine** /salə**man**drin/ *adjective*.

ORIGIN – Greek *salamandra*.

salami /sə**laa**mi/ > *noun* (pl. same or **salamis**) a type of highly seasoned preserved sausage, originally from Italy.

ORIGIN – Italian, from Latin *salare* 'to salt'.

sal ammoniac /sal ə**mō**niak/ > *noun* dated ammonium chloride, a white crystalline salt.

ORIGIN – Latin *sal ammoniacus* 'salt of Ammon', from Greek *ammōniakos* (because the salt was obtained near the temple of Jupiter *Ammon* at Siwa in Egypt).

salaried > *adjective* earning or offering a salary: *a salaried job*.

salary > *noun* (pl. **salaries**) a fixed regular payment made by an employer to an employee, especially a professional or white-collar worker.

ORIGIN – Latin *salarium*, originally denoting a Roman soldier's allowance to buy salt, from *sal* 'salt'.

salchow /**sal**kō/ > *noun* a jump in figure skating from the backward inside edge of one skate to the backward outside edge of the other, with one or more full turns in the air.

ORIGIN – named after the Swedish skater Ulrich *Salchow* (1877–1949).

sale > *noun* **1** the exchange of a commodity for money; the process of selling something. **2** (**sales**) the activity or profession of selling. **3** a period in which goods are sold at reduced prices. **4** a public event at which goods are sold or auctioned.

IDIOMS – **for** (or **on**) **sale** offered for purchase. **sale or return** Brit. an arrangement by which a retailer takes a quantity of goods with the right to return unsold items without payment.

COMBINATIONS – **saleroom** (also **salesroom**) chiefly Brit. a room in which auctions are held. **sales clerk** N. Amer. a shop assistant.

saleable (also **salable**) > *adjective* fit or able to be sold.

DERIVATIVES – **saleability** noun.

salesman (or **saleswoman**) > *noun* a person whose job involves selling or promoting commercial products.

DERIVATIVES – **salesmanship** noun.

salesperson > *noun* a salesman or saleswoman.

salicylic acid /salisillik/ > *noun* Chemistry a bitter compound present in certain plants, used as a fungicide and in the manufacture of aspirin and dyestuffs.

DERIVATIVES – **salicylate** /səlissilayt/ noun.

ORIGIN – from Latin *salix* 'willow' (salicylic acid was originally derived from willow bark).

salient /sayliənt/ > *adjective* **1** most noticeable or important. **2** (of an angle) pointing outwards. The opposite of **RE-ENTRANT**. > *noun* **1** a piece of land or section of fortification that juts out to form an angle. **2** an outward bulge in a military line.

DERIVATIVES – **salience** noun **saliency** noun **saliently** adverb.

SYNONYMS – *adjective* **1** main, notable, principal, prominent.

ORIGIN – Latin, from *salire* 'to leap'.

saline /saylīn/ > *adjective* **1** containing or impregnated with salt. **2** chiefly Medicine (of a solution) containing sodium chloride and/or other salts, especially in the same concentration as in the body. > *noun* a saline solution.

DERIVATIVES – **salinity** noun.

ORIGIN – from Latin *sal* 'salt'.

Salish /saylish/ > *noun* (pl. same) a member of a group of American Indian peoples of the north-western US and the west coast of Canada.

DERIVATIVES – **Salishan** adjective.

ORIGIN – a local name, literally 'Flatheads'.

saliva /səlīvə/ > *noun* a watery liquid secreted into the mouth by glands, providing lubrication for chewing and swallowing, and aiding digestion.

DERIVATIVES – **salivary** /səlīvəri, salivəri/ adjective.

ORIGIN – Latin.

salivate /salivayt/ > *verb* **1** secrete saliva, especially in anticipation of food. **2** display great relish at the sight or prospect of something.

DERIVATIVES – **salivation** noun.

sallow¹ > *adjective* (of a person's face or complexion) of a yellowish or pale brown colour. > *verb* make sallow.

DERIVATIVES – **sallowness** noun.

ORIGIN – Old English, 'dusky'.

sallow² > *noun* chiefly Brit. a willow tree of a low-growing or shrubby kind.

ORIGIN – Old English, related to Latin *salix* 'willow'.

sally > *noun* (pl. **sallies**) **1** a sortie. **2** a witty or lively retort. > *verb* (**sallies**, **sallied**) make a sortie; set forth.

SYNONYMS – *noun* **1** assault, charge, foray, sortie.

ORIGIN – from Old French *salir* 'to leap', from Latin *salire*.

Sally Lunn > *noun* a sweet, light teacake.

ORIGIN – said to be from the name of a woman selling such cakes in Bath *c*.1800.

salmagundi /salmagundi/ > *noun* (pl. **salmagundis**) **1** a dish of chopped meat, anchovies, eggs, onions, and seasoning. **2** a miscellaneous collection or mixture of things.

ORIGIN – French *salmigondis*.

salmon /sammən/ > *noun* (pl. same) a large fish with edible pink flesh, that matures in the sea and migrates to freshwater streams to spawn.

WORDFINDER – gravlax (*a Swedish dish of dry-cured salmon marinated in herbs*), grilse (*a salmon that has returned to fresh water after a single winter at sea*), kelt (*a salmon after spawning and before returning to the sea*), parr (*a young salmon*), smolt (*a young salmon after the parr stage*).

DERIVATIVES – **salmony** adjective.

COMBINATIONS – **salmon pink** a pale orange-pink colour like that of the flesh of salmon. **salmon trout** a sea trout or other fish resembling a small salmon.

ORIGIN – Latin *salmo*.

salmonella /salmənellə/ > *noun* (pl. **salmonellae** /salmənellee/) **1** a bacterium that occurs mainly in the gut and can cause food poisoning. **2** food poisoning caused by this.

DERIVATIVES – **salmonellosis** noun.

ORIGIN – named after the American veterinary surgeon Daniel E. *Salmon* (1850–1914).

salon > *noun* **1** an establishment where a hairdresser, beautician, or couturier conducts their trade. **2** a reception room in a large house. **3** chiefly historical a regular gathering of writers, artists, etc., held in a fashionable household. **4** (**Salon**) an annual exhibition of the work of living artists held by the Royal Academy of Painting and Sculpture in Paris (originally in the Salon d'Apollon in the Louvre).

ORIGIN – French, from Italian *salone* 'large hall'.

saloon > *noun* **1** a public room or building used for a specified purpose. **2** Brit. another term for *lounge bar*. **3** a large public room for use as a lounge on a ship. **4** N. Amer. historical or humorous a place where alcoholic drinks may be bought and drunk. **5** Brit. a car having a closed body and separate boot. **6** (also **saloon car**) Brit. a luxurious railway carriage used as a lounge or restaurant.

ORIGIN – first meaning 'drawing room': from French *salon*, from Italian *salone* 'large hall'.

salopettes /saləpets/ > *plural noun* padded or fleecy trousers with a high waist and shoulder straps, worn for skiing.

ORIGIN – French *salopette*.

salsa /salsə/ > *noun* **1** a type of Latin American dance music with elements of jazz and rock. **2** a dance performed to this music. **3** (especially in Latin American cookery) a spicy tomato sauce.

ORIGIN – Spanish, 'sauce'.

salsa verde /salsə verdi/ > *noun* **1** an Italian sauce of olive oil, garlic, capers, anchovies, vinegar or lemon juice, and parsley. **2** a Mexican sauce of chopped onion, garlic, coriander, parsley, and hot peppers.

ORIGIN – Spanish, 'green sauce'.

salsify /salsifi/ > *noun* a plant of the daisy family, with a long edible root like that of a parsnip.

ORIGIN – French *salsifis*.

SALT /sawlt/ > *abbreviation* Strategic Arms Limitation Talks.

salt > *noun* **1** (also **common salt**) sodium chloride, a white crystalline substance which gives seawater its characteristic taste and is used for seasoning or preserving food. **2** Chemistry any compound formed by the reaction of an acid with a base, with the hydrogen of the acid replaced by a metal or equivalent group. **3** (usu. **old salt**) informal an experienced sailor. **4** something which adds freshness or piquancy. > *adjective* **1** impregnated with salt. **2** (of a plant) growing on the coast or in salt marshes. > *verb* **1** season or preserve with salt. **2** sprinkle (a road or path) with salt in order to melt snow or ice. **3** (**salt away**) informal put by (money) secretly. **4** make piquant or more interesting.

WORDFINDER – brackish (*denoting slightly salty water*), brine (*very salty water*), halite (*rock salt*), saline (*containing or impregnated with salt*).

IDIOMS – **rub salt into the wound** make a painful experience even more painful. **the salt of the earth** a person of great goodness and strength of character. [ORIGIN – with reference to the Gospel of Matthew, chapter 5.] **sit below the salt** be of lower social standing. [ORIGIN – from the former custom of placing a salt cellar in the middle of a dining table with the host at one end.] **take something with a pinch** (or **grain**) **of salt** regard something as exaggerated. **worth one's salt** good or competent at one's job or allotted task.

DERIVATIVES – **saltless** adjective **saltness** noun.

COMBINATIONS – **saltbush** a salt-tolerant plant, sometimes planted on saline soils. **salt cellar** a dish or container for storing salt. [ORIGIN – cellar is from Old French salier 'salt-box', changed by association with CELLAR.] **salt flats** areas of flat land covered with a layer of salt. **salt glaze** a hard glaze with a pitted surface, produced on stoneware by adding salt to the kiln during firing. **salt lick 1** a place where animals go to lick salt from the ground. **2** a block of salt provided for animals to lick. **salt marsh** an area of coastal grassland regularly flooded by seawater. **salt pan** a shallow container or depression in the ground in which salt water evaporates to leave a deposit of salt. **saltwater** of or found in salt water; living in the sea.

wordpower facts

Salt

The word **salt** comes from the Old English noun sealt, ultimately from an Indo-European root shared by the Latin and Greek words for 'salt', sal and hals. Latin sal is the source of a number of words: **salad** and **sauce**, both of which come from the verb salare 'to salt'; **salsa**, which is the Spanish word for **sauce** and comes from the same root; **saline**; and **salary**, from Latin salarium, denoting a Roman soldier's allowance to buy salt. Greek hals is the source of the name of the mineral **halite**, 'rock salt', and of the chemical term **halogen**, denoting a group of similar elements including fluorine, chlorine, bromine, and iodine, which form simple crystalline salts.

saltimbocca /saltimbokkə/ > noun a dish consisting of rolled pieces of veal or poultry cooked with herbs, bacon, and other flavourings.

ORIGIN – Italian, 'leap into the mouth'.

salting /sawlting/ > noun (usu. **saltings**) Brit.

an area of coastal land that is regularly covered by the tide.

saltire /sawltīr/ > noun a diagonal cross as a simple design in heraldry.

ORIGIN – Old French saultoir 'stirrup cord, stile, saltire', from Latin saltare 'to dance'.

saltpetre /sawltpeetər/ (US **saltpeter**) > noun potassium nitrate or (**Chile saltpetre**) sodium nitrate.

ORIGIN – Latin salpetra, probably representing sal petrae 'salt of rock'.

salty > adjective (**saltier**, **saltiest**) **1** tasting of, containing, or preserved with salt. **2** down-to-earth; coarse: salty language.

DERIVATIVES – **saltily** adverb **saltiness** noun.

salubrious /səloobriəss/ > adjective **1** health-giving; healthy. **2** (of a place) pleasant; not run-down.

DERIVATIVES – **salubriously** adverb **salubriousness** noun **salubrity** noun.

SYNONYMS – adjective **1** beneficial, health-giving, healthy, wholesome.

ORIGIN – Latin salubris, from salus 'health'.

saluki /səlooki/ > noun (pl. **salukis**) a tall, swift, slender breed of dog with a silky coat and large drooping ears.

ORIGIN – Arabic.

salutary /salyootəri/ > adjective **1** (of something disadvantageous) beneficial in providing an opportunity for learning from experience. **2** archaic health-giving.

ORIGIN – Latin salutaris, from salus 'health'.

salutation > noun a greeting.

DERIVATIVES – **salutational** adjective **salutatory** adjective.

ORIGIN – Latin, from salutare 'greet'.

salute > noun **1** a gesture of respect and recognition. **2** a raising of a hand to the head, made as a formal gesture of respect by a member of a military or similar force. **3** the discharge of a gun or guns as a ceremonial sign of respect or celebration. > verb **1** make a formal salute to. **2** greet. **3** show or express admiration and respect for.

DERIVATIVES – **saluter** noun.

ORIGIN – Latin salutare 'greet, pay one's respects to', from salus 'health, welfare, greeting'.

Salvadorean /salvədoriən/ > noun a person from El Salvador, a country in Central America. > adjective relating to El Salvador.

salvage > verb **1** rescue (a ship or its cargo) from loss at sea. **2** retrieve or preserve from loss or destruction. > noun **1** the rescue of a ship or its cargo. **2** the cargo saved from a wrecked or sunken ship. **3** Law payment made or due to a person who has salvaged a ship or its cargo. **4** the rescue of property or a plan from potential loss, destruction, or failure.

DERIVATIVES – **salvageable** adjective **salvager** noun.

SYNONYMS – verb **2** preserve, recoup, recapture, retain.

COMBINATIONS – **salvage yard** a place where disused machinery, vehicles, etc. are broken up and parts salvaged.

ORIGIN – Latin salvagium, from salvare 'to save': originally denoting payment for saving a ship or its cargo.

salvation > noun **1** Theology deliverance from sin and its consequences, believed by Christians to be brought about by faith in Christ. **2** preservation or deliverance from harm, ruin, or loss. **3** (**one's salvation**) a source or means of being saved in this way.

ORIGIN – Latin, from salvare 'to save'.

salvationist > noun (**Salvationist**) a member of the Salvation Army, a Christian evangelical organisation. > adjective **1** relating to salvation. **2** (**Salvationist**) relating to the Salvation Army.

DERIVATIVES – **salvationism** noun.

salve > noun **1** an ointment used to soothe or promote healing of the skin. **2** something that soothes wounded feelings or an uneasy conscience. > verb apply a salve to; soothe.

salver > noun a tray, typically one made of silver and used in formal circumstances.

ORIGIN – French salve 'tray for presenting food to the king', from Spanish salvar 'make safe'.

salvia /salviə/ > noun a plant of a large group that includes sage, especially one cultivated for its spikes of bright flowers.

ORIGIN – Latin, 'sage'.

salvo > noun (pl. **salvos** or **salvoes**) **1** a simultaneous discharge of artillery or other guns in a battle. **2** a sudden vigorous series of aggressive statements or acts.

ORIGIN – Italian salva 'salutation'.

sal volatile /sal vəlattili/ > noun a scented solution of ammonium carbonate in alcohol, used as smelling salts.

ORIGIN – Latin, 'volatile salt'.

salwar /sulwaar/ (also **shalwar** /shulwaar/) > noun a pair of light, loose, trousers tapering to a tight fit around the ankles, worn by women from the Indian subcontinent, typically with a kameez.

ORIGIN – Persian and Urdu.

SAM > abbreviation surface-to-air missile.

Samaritan > noun **1** a member of a people inhabiting Samaria, an ancient city of Palestine, in biblical times. **2** (usu. **good Samaritan**) a charitable or helpful person. [ORIGIN – with biblical reference to the story of the Samaritan who helped a man in need whom others had passed by, in the Gospel of Luke.] **3** (**the Samaritans**) (in the UK) an organisation which counsels those in distress, mainly through a telephone service.

DERIVATIVES – **Samaritanism** noun.

samarium /səmairiəm/ > noun a hard, silvery-white, metallic chemical element of the lanthanide series.

ORIGIN – from *samarskite*, a mineral in which its spectrum was first observed (named after a 19th-century Russian official called *Samarsky*).

samba /sambə/ > noun a Brazilian dance of African origin. > verb (**sambas, sambaed** /sambəd/ or **samba'd, sambaing** /sambə(r)ing/) dance the samba.

ORIGIN – Portuguese, of African origin.

Sam Browne > noun a leather belt with a supporting strap that passes over the right shoulder, worn by army and police officers.

ORIGIN – named after the British general Sir *Samuel Browne* (1824–1901).

sambuca /sambōōkə/ > noun an Italian aniseed-flavoured liqueur.

ORIGIN – Italian, from Latin *sambucus* 'elder tree'.

same > adjective **1** (**the same**) identical; unchanged. **2** (**this** or **that same**) referring to a person or thing just mentioned. > pronoun **1** (**the same**) the same thing as previously mentioned. **2** (**the same**) identical people or things. **3** the person or thing just mentioned. > adverb in the same way.

WORDFINDER – coeval (*having the same age or date of origin*), concurrent (*existing or happening at the same time*), consanguineous (*descended from the same ancestor*), coterminous (*having the same boundaries or extent*), isobar (*line on a map connecting points with the same atmospheric pressure*), isochronous (*occurring at the same time*), isotherm (*lines on a map connecting points with the same temperature*), synchronous (*existing or occurring at the same time*), synonym (*word that means that same as another word*).

IDIOMS – **all** (or **just**) **the same 1** nevertheless. **2** anyway. **at the same time 1** simultaneously. **2** on the other hand.

DERIVATIVES – **sameness** noun.

ORIGIN – Old Norse.

samey > adjective (**samier, samiest**) Brit. informal monotonous.

DERIVATIVES – **sameyness** noun.

Samhain /sown, sowin/ > noun a festival held by the ancient Celts on 1 November, marking the beginning of winter and the Celtic new year.

ORIGIN – Old Irish *samain*.

Sami /saami/ > plural noun the Lapps of northern Scandinavia.

USAGE – **Sami** is the term by which the Lapps themselves prefer to be known.

ORIGIN – Lappish.

samizdat /sammizdat/ > noun (especially in the former Soviet Union) the clandestine copying and distribution of literature banned by the state.

ORIGIN – Russian, 'self-publishing house'.

Samoan /səmōən/ > noun **1** a person from Samoa. **2** the Polynesian language of Samoa. > adjective relating to Samoa.

samosa /səmōsə/ > noun a triangular fried pastry containing spiced vegetables or meat.

ORIGIN – Persian and Urdu.

samovar /samməvaar/ > noun a highly decorated Russian tea urn.

ORIGIN – Russian, 'self-boiler'.

Samoyed /samməyed/ > noun **1** a member of a group of mainly nomadic peoples of northern Siberia. **2** a dog of a white Arctic breed.

ORIGIN – Russian *samoed*.

sampan /sampan/ > noun a small boat propelled with an oar at the stern, used in the Far East.

ORIGIN – Chinese.

samphire /samfīr/ > noun a fleshy-leaved plant which grows near the sea.

ORIGIN – from French *herbe de Saint Pierre* 'St Peter's herb'.

sample > noun **1** a small part or quantity intended to show what the whole is like. **2** Statistics a portion of a population, serving as a basis for estimates of the attributes of the whole population. **3** a specimen taken for scientific testing or analysis. **4** a sound created by sampling. > verb **1** take a sample or samples of. **2** get a representative experience of. **3** Electronics ascertain the momentary value of (an analogue signal) many times a second so as to convert the signal to digital form.

DERIVATIVES – **sampling** noun.

SYNONYMS – noun **1** example, selection, snippet, specimen.

ORIGIN – Old French *essample* 'example'.

sampler > noun **1** a piece of embroidery worked in various stitches as a specimen of skill. **2** a representative collection or example of something. **3** a device for sampling music and sound.

samurai /samyoorī/ > noun (pl. same) historical a member of a powerful military caste in feudal Japan.

ORIGIN – Japanese.

San /saan/ > noun (pl. same) **1** a member of the Bushmen (a number of aboriginal peoples) of southern Africa. **2** the languages spoken by these peoples.

ORIGIN – Nama, 'aboriginals, settlers'.

sanatorium /sannətoriəm/ > noun (pl. **sanatoriums** or **sanatoria**) **1** an establishment for the care of convalescent or chronically ill people. **2** Brit. a place in a boarding school for children who are unwell.

ORIGIN – Latin, from *sanare* 'heal'.

Sancerre /soNsair/ > noun a light white wine produced in Sancerre, in the upper Loire region of France.

sanctify /sangktifī/ > verb (**sanctifies, sanctified**) **1** consecrate. **2** make legitimate or binding by religious sanction. **3** free from sin. **4** give (something) the appearance of being right or good.

DERIVATIVES – **sanctification** noun **sanctifier** noun.

SYNONYMS – **1** bless, consecrate, hallow, make holy.

ORIGIN – Latin *sanctificare*, from *sanctus* 'holy'.

sanctimonious /sangktimōniəss/ > adjective derogatory making a show of being morally superior.

DERIVATIVES – **sanctimoniously** adverb **sanctimoniousness** noun **sanctimony** /sangktiməni/ noun.

SYNONYMS – holier-than-thou, pious, self-righteous.

ORIGIN – from Latin *sanctimonia* 'sanctity'.

sanction > noun **1** a threatened penalty for disobeying a law or rule. **2** (**sanctions**) measures taken by a state to coerce another to conform to an international agreement or norms of conduct. **3** official permission or approval. > verb **1** give official sanction for. **2** impose a sanction or penalty on.

DERIVATIVES – **sanctionable** adjective.

SYNONYMS – noun **1** deterrent, punishment, sentence. **3** authorisation, dispensation, ratification, validation. verb **1** allow, authorise, permit. **2** discipline, penalise.

ORIGIN – Latin, from *sancire* 'ratify'.

sanctity > noun **1** holiness; saintliness. **2** ultimate importance and inviolability.

SYNONYMS – **1** godliness, holiness, sacredness, saintliness.

ORIGIN – Old French *sainctite*, from Latin *sanctus* 'holy'.

sanctuary > noun (pl. **sanctuaries**) **1** a place of refuge or safety. **2** a nature reserve. **3** a place where injured or unwanted animals are cared for. **4** a holy place. **5** the part of the chancel of a church containing the high altar.

SYNONYMS – **1** asylum, haven, refuge, shelter.

ORIGIN – Latin *sanctuarium*, from *sanctus* 'holy': originally denoting a holy place in which, by law, a fugitive was immune from arrest.

sanctum /sangktəm/ > noun (pl. **sanctums**) **1** a sacred place, especially a shrine in a temple or church. **2** a private place.

ORIGIN – from Latin *sanctus* 'holy'.

Sanctus /sangktəss/ > noun Christian Church a hymn beginning Sanctus, sanctus, sanctus (Holy, holy, holy) forming part of the Mass.

sand > noun **1** a substance consisting of fine particles of eroded rocks, forming a major constituent of beaches, river beds, the seabed, and deserts. **2** (**sands**) an expanse of sand. > *verb* **1** smooth with sandpaper or a sander. **2** sprinkle or overlay with sand.

IDIOMS – **the sands (of time) are running out** the allotted time is nearly at an end. [ORIGIN – with reference to the sand of an hourglass.]

COMBINATIONS – **sandbank** a deposit of sand forming a shallow area in the sea or a river. **sandbar** a long, narrow sandbank. **sandcastle** a model of a castle built out of sand. **sandfly 1** a small hairy biting fly of tropical and subtropical regions, which transmits a number of diseases. **2** Austral./NZ another term for *blackfly* (in sense 2). **sandglass** an hourglass. **sand martin** a small gregarious swallow with dark brown and white plumage, excavating nest holes in sandy banks. **sandpit 1** Brit. a shallow box or hollow, containing sand for children to play in. **2** a quarry from which sand is excavated. **sandshoe** a plimsoll.

sandal > *noun* a shoe with an openwork upper or straps attaching the sole to the foot.

DERIVATIVES – **sandalled** (US **sandaled**) *adjective.*

ORIGIN – Greek *sandalon* 'wooden shoe'.

sandalwood > *noun* the fragrant wood of an Indian or SE Asian tree.

ORIGIN – Latin *sandalum*, from Sanskrit.

sandbag > *noun* a bag of sand, used for defensive purposes or as ballast in a boat. > *verb* (**sandbagged**, **sandbagging**) **1** barricade with sandbags. **2** hit or fell with or as if with a blow from a sandbag. **3** N. Amer. bully.

DERIVATIVES – **sandbagger** *noun.*

sandblast > *verb* roughen or clean with a jet of sand driven by compressed air or steam.

DERIVATIVES – **sandblaster** *noun.*

sandboy > *noun* (in phrase **as happy as a sandboy**) extremely happy or carefree.

ORIGIN – probably first denoting a boy hawking sand.

sander > *noun* a power tool used for smoothing a surface with sandpaper or other abrasive material.

sanderling /**sand**ərling/ > *noun* a small migratory sandpiper, typically seen running after receding waves on the beach.

Sandinista /sandə**nee**stə/ > *noun* a member of a Nicaraguan left-wing political organisation, in power 1979–90.

ORIGIN – named after a similar organisation founded by the nationalist leader Augusto César *Sandino* (1893–1934).

sandlot > *noun* N. Amer. **1** a piece of unoccupied land used by children for games. **2** (before another noun) denoting sport played by amateurs.

sandman > *noun* (**the sandman**) a fictional man supposed to make children sleep by sprinkling sand in their eyes.

sandpaper > *noun* paper with sand or another abrasive stuck to it, used for smoothing wooden or other surfaces. > *verb* smooth with sandpaper.

DERIVATIVES – **sandpapery** *adjective.*

sandpiper > *noun* a wading bird with a long bill and long legs, frequenting coastal areas.

sandstone > *noun* sedimentary rock consisting of sand or quartz grains cemented together, typically red, yellow, or brown in colour.

sandstorm > *noun* a strong wind in a desert carrying clouds of sand.

sandwich > *noun* **1** an item of food consisting of two pieces of bread with a filling between them. **2** Brit. a sponge cake of two or more layers with jam or cream between them. > *verb* **1** (**sandwich between**) insert between (two people or things). **2** (**sandwich together**) squeeze (two things) together.

COMBINATIONS – **sandwich board** a pair of advertisement boards connected by straps by which they are hung over a person's shoulders. **sandwich course** Brit. a training course with alternate periods of formal instruction and practical experience.

ORIGIN – named after the 4th Earl of *Sandwich* (1718–92), an English nobleman said to have eaten food in this form.

sandy > *adjective* (**sandier**, **sandiest**) **1** covered in or consisting of sand. **2** light yellowish brown.

DERIVATIVES – **sandiness** *noun.*

sane > *adjective* **1** of sound mind; not mad. **2** reasonable; sensible.

DERIVATIVES – **sanely** *adverb* **saneness** *noun.*

SYNONYMS – **1** balanced, lucid, rational. **2** advisable, prudent, reasonable, sensible.

ORIGIN – Latin *sanus* 'healthy'.

sang past of SING.

sangfroid /soN **frwaa**/ > *noun* composure or coolness under trying circumstances.

ORIGIN – French, 'cold blood'.

Sangiovese /sanjiə**vayzi**/ > *noun* a variety of black wine grape used to make Chianti and other Italian red wines.

ORIGIN – Italian.

sangria /sang**gree**ə/ > *noun* a Spanish drink of red wine, lemonade, fruit, and spices.

ORIGIN – Spanish, literally 'bleeding'.

sanguinary /**sang**gwinəri/ > *adjective* chiefly archaic involving or causing much bloodshed.

sanguine /**sang**gwin/ > *adjective* **1** cheerfully optimistic. **2** (in medieval medicine) having a predominance of blood among the bodily humours, supposedly marked by a ruddy complexion and an optimistic disposition.

SYNONYMS – **1** buoyant, positive.

ANTONYMS – **1** gloomy.

ORIGIN – Old French, 'blood red', from Latin *sanguis* 'blood'.

Sanhedrin /**sann**idrin/ (also **Sanhedrim** /**sann**idrim/) > *noun* the highest court of justice and the supreme council in ancient Jerusalem.

ORIGIN – Hebrew, from Greek *sunedrion* 'council'.

sanitarium /sanni**tair**iəm/ > *noun* (pl. **sanitariums** or **sanitaria**) North American term for SANATORIUM.

sanitary > *adjective* **1** relating to conditions affecting hygiene and health. **2** hygienic.

COMBINATIONS – **sanitary protection** sanitary towels and tampons collectively. **sanitary towel** (N. Amer. **sanitary napkin**) an pad worn by women to absorb menstrual blood. **sanitaryware** toilet bowls, cisterns, and other fittings.

ORIGIN – from Latin *sanitas* 'health'.

sanitation > *noun* conditions relating to public health.

sanitise (also **sanitize**) > *verb* **1** make hygienic. **2** derogatory make more acceptable.

DERIVATIVES – **sanitisation** *noun.*

SYNONYMS – **1** clean, disinfect, sterilise.

sanity > *noun* **1** the condition of being sane. **2** reasonable and rational behaviour.

SYNONYMS – **1** balance, lucidity, rationality, soundness of mind.

ORIGIN – Latin *sanitas* 'health'.

sank past of SINK[1].

USAGE – on the use of **sank**, **sunk**, and **sunken**, see the note at SINK[1].

sans /sanz/ > *preposition* literary or humorous without: *a picture of Maughan sans specs.*

ORIGIN – French, from Latin *sine*.

sans-culotte /sanzkyoo**lot**, soN-/ > *noun* **1** a lower-class Parisian republican in the French Revolution. **2** an extreme republican or revolutionary.

ORIGIN – French, 'without knee breeches'.

Sanskrit /**san**skrit/ > *noun* an ancient language of India, still used as a language of religion and scholarship, and the source of many Indian languages.

ORIGIN – Sanskrit, 'composed, elaborated'.

sans serif /san **serr**if/ (also **sanserif**) Printing > *noun* a style of type without serifs. > *adjective* without serifs.

Santa Claus (also informal **Santa**) > *noun* Father Christmas.

ORIGIN – alteration of Dutch *Sante Klaas* 'St Nicholas': originally a US usage.

santim /**san**teem/ > *noun* a monetary unit of Latvia, equal to one hundredth of a lat.

ORIGIN – Latvian, from French *centime*.

sap[1] > *noun* **1** the fluid circulating in the vascular system of a plant. **2** vigour or energy. > *verb* (**sapped**, **sapping**) **1** gradually weaken (a person's strength or power). **2** (**sap someone of**) drain someone of (strength or power).

SYNONYMS – *verb* **1** deplete, erode, exhaust, wear down. **2** drain, empty, exhaust.

sap² historical > *noun* a tunnel or trench to conceal an assailant's approach to a fortified place. > *verb* (**sapped**, **sapping**) dig a sap.

ORIGIN – French *saper*, from Italian *zappa* 'spade, spadework'.

sap³ > *noun* informal, chiefly N. Amer. a foolish and gullible person.

ORIGIN – abbreviation of *sapskull* 'person with a head like sapwood'.

sapid /**sapp**id/ > *adjective* chiefly N. Amer. **1** flavoursome. **2** pleasant or interesting.

ORIGIN – Latin *sapidus*, from *sapere* 'to taste'.

sapient /**say**piənt/ > *adjective* formal wise, or attempting to appear wise.

ORIGIN – from Latin *sapere* 'to be wise'.

sapling > *noun* **1** a young, slender tree. **2** literary a young and slender or inexperienced person.

sapodilla /sappə**dilla**/ > *noun* **1** a large, evergreen, tropical American tree which has hard, durable wood and yields chicle. **2** (also **sapodilla plum**) the sweet, brownish, bristly fruit of this tree.

ORIGIN – Spanish *zapotillo*.

saponify /sə**ponn**ifī/ > *verb* (**saponifies**, **saponified**) Chemistry turn (fat or oil) into soap by reaction with an alkali.

DERIVATIVES – **saponification** *noun*.

ORIGIN – from Latin *sapo* 'soap'.

sapper > *noun* **1** a military engineer who lays or detects and disarms mines. **2** Brit. a soldier in the Corps of Royal Engineers.

sapphic /**saff**ik/ > *adjective* **1** (**Sapphic**) relating to the Greek lyric poet Sappho (early 7th century BC), or her poetry expressing love and affection for women. **2** relating to lesbians or lesbianism.

DERIVATIVES – **sapphism** *noun*.

sapphire /**saff**īr/ > *noun* **1** a transparent precious stone, typically blue, which is a form of corundum. **2** a bright blue colour.

ORIGIN – Greek *sappheiros*, probably denoting lapis lazuli.

sappy > *adjective* (**sappier**, **sappiest**) **1** informal, chiefly N. Amer. over-sentimental. **2** (of a plant) containing a lot of sap.

saprophyte /**sa**prəfīt/ > *noun* Biology a plant, fungus, or micro-organism that lives on decaying matter.

DERIVATIVES – **saprophytic** *adjective*.

ORIGIN – from Greek *sapros* 'putrid' + *phuton* 'plant'.

sapwood > *noun* the soft outer layers of new wood between the heartwood and the bark of a tree.

saraband /**sarr**əband/ (also **sarabande**) > *noun* a slow, stately Spanish dance in triple time.

ORIGIN – French, from Spanish and Italian *zarabanda*.

Saracen /**sarr**ə's'n/ > *noun* **1** an Arab or Muslim, especially at the time of the Crusades. **2** (in ancient times) a nomad of the Syrian and Arabian desert.

ORIGIN – Greek *Sarakēnos*, perhaps from an Arabic word meaning 'eastern'.

sarape > *noun* variant of **SERAPE**.

sarcasm > *noun* the use of irony to mock someone or convey contempt.

ORIGIN – Greek *sarkasmos*, from *sarkazein* 'tear flesh', later 'gnash the teeth, speak bitterly'.

sarcastic > *adjective* marked by or given to sarcasm.

DERIVATIVES – **sarcastically** *adverb*.

sarcenet > *noun* variant spelling of **SARSENET**.

sarcoma /saar**kō**mə/ > *noun* (pl. **sarcomas** or **sarcomata** /saar**kō**mətə/) Medicine a malignant tumour of a kind found chiefly in connective tissue.

ORIGIN – Greek *sarkōma*, from *sarkoun* 'become fleshy'.

sarcophagus /saar**koff**əgəss/ > *noun* (pl. **sarcophagi** /saar**koff**əgī/) a stone coffin.

ORIGIN – Latin, from Greek *sarkophagos* 'flesh-consuming'.

sard /saard/ > *noun* a yellow or brownish-red variety of chalcedony.

ORIGIN – Greek *sardios*, probably from *Sardō* 'Sardinia'.

sardar /**ser**daar/ (also **sirdar**) > *noun* chiefly Indian **1** a leader. **2** a Sikh.

ORIGIN – Persian and Urdu.

sardine > *noun* a young pilchard or other young or small herring-like fish. > *verb* informal pack closely together.

IDIOMS – **packed like sardines** crowded close together, as sardines in tins.

ORIGIN – Latin *sardina*, probably from Greek *Sardō* 'Sardinia'.

Sardinian /saar**dinn**iən/ > *adjective* relating to Sardinia, its people, or their language. > *noun* **1** a person from Sardinia. **2** the language of Sardinia.

sardonic /saar**donn**ik/ > *adjective* grimly mocking or cynical.

DERIVATIVES – **sardonically** *adverb* **sardonicism** *noun*.

ORIGIN – French *sardonique*, from Greek *sardonios* 'of Sardinia', alteration of *sardanios*, used by Homer to describe bitter or scornful laughter.

sardonyx /saar**dənnik**s/ > *noun* onyx in which white layers alternate with sard.

ORIGIN – Greek *sardonux*.

sargassum /saar**gass**əm/ (also **sargasso**) > *noun* a brown seaweed with berry-like air bladders, typically floating in large masses.

ORIGIN – Portuguese *sargaço*.

sarge > *noun* informal sergeant.

sari /**saar**i/ (also **saree**) > *noun* (pl. **saris** or **sarees**) a garment consisting of a length of cotton or silk elaborately draped around the body, traditionally worn by women from the Indian subcontinent.

ORIGIN – Hindi.

sarin /**saar**in/ > *noun* a nerve gas, developed during the Second World War.

ORIGIN – German.

sarky > *adjective* (**sarkier**, **sarkiest**) Brit. informal sarcastic.

DERIVATIVES – **sarkily** *adverb* **sarkiness** *noun*.

sarnie > *noun* Brit. informal a sandwich.

sarong /sə**rong**/ > *noun* a garment consisting of a long piece of cloth wrapped round the body and tucked at the waist or under the armpits.

ORIGIN – Malay, 'sheath'.

sarsaparilla /saasəpə**rilla**/ > *noun* **1** a preparation of the dried roots of various plants, used to flavour drinks and medicines and formerly as a tonic. **2** a sweet drink flavoured with this.

ORIGIN – Spanish *zarzaparilla*, from *zarza* 'bramble' + *parra* 'vine'.

sarsen /**saar**s'n/ > *noun* a sandstone boulder of a kind used at Stonehenge and other prehistoric monuments in southern England.

ORIGIN – probably a variant of **SARACEN**.

sarsenet /**saar**sənit/ (also **sarcenet**) > *noun* a fine soft silk fabric.

ORIGIN – Old French *sarzinett*, perhaps from *sarzin* 'Saracen', suggested by *drap sarrasinois* 'Saracen cloth'.

sartorial /saar**tor**iəl/ > *adjective* relating to tailoring, clothes, or style of dress.

DERIVATIVES – **sartorially** *adverb*.

ORIGIN – from Latin *sartor* 'tailor'.

SAS > *abbreviation* Special Air Service.

sash¹ > *noun* a long strip or loop of cloth worn over one shoulder or round the waist.

ORIGIN – earlier as *shash*, denoting fabric worn as a turban, from Arabic.

sash² > *noun* a frame holding the glass in a window.

COMBINATIONS – **sash window** a window with one or two sashes which can be slid vertically to open it.

ORIGIN – alteration of **CHASSIS**.

sashay /**sa**shay/ > *verb* informal, chiefly N. Amer. walk ostentatiously, with exaggerated hip and shoulder movements.

ORIGIN – alteration of **CHASSÉ**.

sashimi /**sa**shimi/ > *noun* a Japanese dish of bite-sized pieces of raw fish eaten with soy sauce and horseradish paste.

ORIGIN – Japanese.

Sasquatch /**sas**kwach/ > *noun* another name for **BIGFOOT**.

ORIGIN – Salish.

sass N. Amer. informal > *noun* cheek. > *verb* be cheeky to.

ORIGIN – variant of SAUCE.

sassafras /**sass**əfrass/ > *noun* 1 a deciduous North American tree with aromatic leaves and bark. 2 an extract of the leaves or bark of this tree, used medicinally or in perfumery.

ORIGIN – Spanish *sasafrás*, based on Latin *saxifraga* 'saxifrage'.

Sassenach /**sass**ənak/ Scottish & Irish derogatory > *noun* an English person. > *adjective* English.

ORIGIN – Scottish Gaelic *Sasunnoch*, Irish *Sasanach*, from Latin *Saxones* 'Saxons'.

sassy > *adjective* (**sassier**, **sassiest**) informal, chiefly N. Amer. bold and spirited; cheeky.

SAT > *abbreviation* standard assessment task.

sat past and past participle of SIT.

USAGE – on the use of the participles **sitting** and **sat**, see the note at SIT.

Satan > *noun* the Devil; Lucifer.

ORIGIN – Hebrew, 'adversary'.

satang /**satt**ang/ > *noun* (pl. same or **satangs**) a monetary unit of Thailand, equal to one hundredth of a baht.

ORIGIN – Thai, from Pali (an ancient language related to Sanskrit), 'hundred'.

satanic /sə**tann**ik/ > *adjective* 1 characteristic of Satan. 2 connected with satanism.

SYNONYMS – 1 devilish, diabolical, evil, fiendish.

satanism > *noun* the worship of Satan, typically involving a travesty of Christian symbols and practices.

DERIVATIVES – **satanist** noun & adjective.

satay /**satt**ay/ (also **saté**) > *noun* an Indonesian and Malaysian dish consisting of small pieces of meat grilled on a skewer and served with spiced sauce.

ORIGIN – Malay and Indonesian.

satchel > *noun* a shoulder bag with a long strap, used especially for school books.

ORIGIN – Latin *saccellus* 'small bag'.

sate /sayt/ > *verb* 1 satisfy fully. 2 supply with as much as or more than is desired or can be managed.

ORIGIN – probably an alteration of dialect *sade*, from Old English *sadian* 'become sated or weary' (related to SAD).

saté > *noun* variant spelling of SATAY.

sateen /sa**teen**/ > *noun* a cotton fabric woven like satin with a glossy surface.

ORIGIN – alteration of SATIN.

satellite > *noun* 1 an artificial body placed in orbit round the earth or another planet to collect information or for communication. 2 Astronomy a celestial body orbiting a planet. 3 a thing separate from something else but dependent on or controlled by it.

COMBINATIONS – **satellite dish** a bowl-shaped aerial with which signals are transmitted to or received from a communications satellite. **satellite tele-**

vision television in which the signals are broadcast via satellite.

ORIGIN – from Latin *satelles* 'attendant'.

sati > *noun* variant spelling of SUTTEE.

satiate /**say**shiayt/ > *verb* another term for SATE.

ORIGIN – Latin *satiare*, from *satis* 'enough'.

satiety /sə**tī**əti/ > *noun* the feeling or state of being sated.

satin > *noun* 1 a smooth, glossy fabric, usually of silk. 2 (before a noun) denoting or having a smooth, glossy surface or finish.

DERIVATIVES – **satiny** adjective.

COMBINATIONS – **satin stitch** a long straight embroidery stitch, giving the appearance of satin.

ORIGIN – from the Arabic word for *Tsinkiang*, a town in China.

satinwood > *noun* glossy yellowish wood valued for high-quality woodwork.

satire /**satt**īr/ > *noun* 1 the use of humour, irony, exaggeration, or ridicule to expose and criticise people's stupidity or vices. 2 a play, novel, etc. using satire. 3 (in Latin literature) a literary miscellany, especially a poem ridiculing prevalent vices or follies.

DERIVATIVES – **satirist** noun.

ORIGIN – Latin *satira* 'poetic medley'.

satirical /sə**tirr**ik'l/ (also **satiric**) > *adjective* 1 containing or using satire. 2 sarcastic; humorously critical.

DERIVATIVES – **satirically** adverb.

satirise /**satt**irīz/ (also **satirize**) > *verb* mock and criticise by means of satire.

SYNONYMS – lampoon, pillory.

satisfaction > *noun* 1 the state of being satisfied. 2 Law the payment of a debt or fulfilment of an obligation or claim. 3 what is felt to be owed or due to one.

SYNONYMS – 1 contentment, fulfilment, gratification.

satisfactory > *adjective* fulfilling expectations or needs; acceptable.

DERIVATIVES – **satisfactorily** adverb.

SYNONYMS – acceptable, adequate, good enough, sufficient.

satisfy > *verb* (**satisfies**, **satisfied**) 1 meet the expectations, needs, or desires of. 2 fulfil (a desire or need). 3 provide with adequate information about or proof of something. 4 comply with (a condition, obligation, or demand).

DERIVATIVES – **satisfied** adjective **satisfying** adjective.

SYNONYMS – 1 appease, assuage, fulfil, gratify. 2 assure, convince, persuade. 3 comply with, conform to, fulfil.

ORIGIN – Latin *satisfacere*, from *satis* 'enough' + *facere* 'make'.

satori /sə**tor**i/ > *noun* Buddhism sudden enlightenment.

ORIGIN – Japanese, 'awakening'.

satrap /**sa**trap/ > *noun* 1 a provincial

governor in the ancient Persian empire. 2 a subordinate or local ruler.

ORIGIN – Latin *satrapa*, from a Persian word meaning 'country-protector'.

satsuma /sat**soo**mə/ > *noun* a tangerine of a loose-skinned variety, originally grown in Japan.

ORIGIN – named after the former Japanese province of *Satsuma*.

saturate > *verb* /**sa**chərayt/ 1 soak thoroughly with water or other liquid. 2 cause to combine with, dissolve, or hold the greatest possible quantity of another substance. 3 magnetise or charge (a substance or device) fully. 4 supply (a market) beyond the point at which the demand for a product is satisfied. 5 overwhelm (an area) by concentrated bombing. > *noun* /**sa**chərət/ a saturated fat.

SYNONYMS – verb 1 drench, souse, waterlog.

ORIGIN – Latin *saturare* 'fill, glut', from *satur* 'full'.

saturated > *adjective* 1 Chemistry (of a solution) containing the largest possible amount of dissolved substance. 2 Chemistry (of an organic molecule) containing the greatest possible number of hydrogen atoms, without double or triple bonds. 3 (of colour) bright and rich.

saturation > *noun* 1 the action of saturating or state of being saturated. 2 (before another noun) to the fullest extent: *saturation bombing*.

COMBINATIONS – **saturation point** the stage beyond which no more can be absorbed or accepted.

Saturday > *noun* the day of the week before Sunday and following Friday.

ORIGIN – Old English, translation of Latin *Saturni dies* 'day of Saturn'.

Saturnalia /sattər**nay**liə/ > *noun* (treated as sing. or pl.) 1 the ancient Roman festival of Saturn in December, a period of unrestrained merrymaking. 2 (**saturnalia**) an occasion of wild revelry.

DERIVATIVES – **saturnalian** adjective.

Saturnian > *adjective* relating to the planet Saturn.

saturnine /**satt**ərnīn/ > *adjective* 1 gloomy. 2 (of looks, temperament, etc.) dark and brooding.

SYNONYMS – 1 dour, gloomy, melancholy, sombre.

ORIGIN – Latin *Saturninus* 'of Saturn' (associated with slowness and gloom by astrologers).

satyr /**satt**ər/ > *noun* 1 Greek Mythology one of a class of lustful, drunken woodland gods, represented as a man with a horse's ears and tail or (in Roman representations) with a goat's ears, tail, legs, and horns. 2 a man with strong sexual desires.

DERIVATIVES – **satyric** /sətirrik/ *adjective*.
ORIGIN – Greek *saturos*.

satyriasis /sattirīəsiss/ > *noun* excessive sexual desire in a man.

sauce > *noun* **1** thick liquid served with food to add moistness and flavour. **2 N. Amer.** stewed fruit, especially apples. **3** informal, chiefly **Brit.** impertinence. > *verb* **1** (usu. **be sauced**) season with a sauce. **2** make more interesting and exciting. **3** informal be impudent to.
WORDFINDER – *sauces:* barbecue sauce, Béarnaise, béchamel, carbonara, coulis, Cumberland sauce, harissa, hoisin sauce, hollandaise, ketchup, Marie Rose, marinara, Melba sauce, mole, mousseline, puttanesca, salsa, salsa verde, soy, supreme, Tabasco, tamari, tartare sauce, velouté, Worcester sauce.
IDIOMS – **what's sauce for the goose is sauce for the gander** proverb what is appropriate in one case is also appropriate in the other case in question.
COMBINATIONS – **sauce boat** a long, narrow jug for serving sauce.
ORIGIN – Old French, from Latin *salsus* 'salted'.

saucepan > *noun* a deep cooking pan, with one long handle and a lid.

saucer > *noun* a shallow dish with a central circular indentation, on which a cup is placed.
ORIGIN – Old French *saussier* 'sauce boat'.

saucy > *adjective* (**saucier**, **sauciest**) informal **1** chiefly **Brit.** sexually suggestive in a light-hearted way. **2** chiefly **N. Amer.** bold, lively, and spirited.
DERIVATIVES – **saucily** adverb **sauciness** noun.

Saudi /sowdi/ > *noun* (pl. **Saudis**) a person from Saudi Arabia, or a member of its ruling dynasty. > *adjective* relating to Saudi Arabia or its ruling dynasty.
ORIGIN – from the name of Abdul-Aziz ibn *Saud*, first king of Saudi Arabia.

Saudi Arabian > *noun* a person from Saudi Arabia. > *adjective* relating to Saudi Arabia.

sauerkraut /sowərkrowt/ > *noun* a dish of chopped pickled cabbage.
ORIGIN – German, from *sauer* 'sour' + *Kraut* 'vegetable'.

sauna /sawnə/ > *noun* **1** a small room used as a hot-air or steam bath for cleaning and refreshing the body. **2** a session in a sauna.
ORIGIN – Finnish.

saunter > *verb* walk in a slow, relaxed manner. > *noun* a leisurely stroll.
SYNONYMS – *verb* amble, stroll, wander. *noun* amble, ramble, wander.

-saur > *combining form* forming names of reptiles, especially extinct ones: *ichthyosaur*.
ORIGIN – Latin, from Greek *sauros* 'lizard'.

saurian /sawriən/ > *adjective* of or like a lizard.

saurischian /sawriskiən/ > *noun* Palaeontology a dinosaur of a group with pelvic bones resembling those of lizards. Compare with **ORNITHISCHIAN**.
ORIGIN – from Greek *sauros* 'lizard' + *iskhion* 'hip joint'.

sauropod /sawrəpod/ > *noun* an apatosaurus, brachiosaurus, or similar huge dinosaur with a long neck and tail.
ORIGIN – from Greek *sauros* 'lizard' + *pous* 'foot'.

-saurus > *combining form* forming genus names of reptiles, especially extinct ones: *stegosaurus*.

sausage > *noun* **1** a short cylindrical tube of minced meat encased in a skin, sold raw and grilled or fried before eating. **2** a cylindrical tube of minced meat seasoned and cooked or preserved, eaten cold in slices. **3** a sausage-shaped object.
WORDFINDER – *types of sausage:* andouille, black pudding, bologna, bratwurst, chipolata, chorizo, Cumberland sausage, frankfurter, knackwurst, mortadella, pepperoni, salami, saveloy, wurst.
IDIOMS – **not a sausage** Brit. informal nothing at all.
COMBINATIONS – **sausage dog** Brit. informal a dachshund. **sausage meat** minced meat with spices and a binder such as cereal, used in sausages or as a stuffing. **sausage roll** a piece of sausage meat baked in a roll of pastry.
ORIGIN – Old French *saussiche*, from Latin *salsus* 'salted'.

sauté /sōtay/ > *adjective* fried quickly in a little hot fat. > *noun* a dish cooked in such a way. > *verb* (**sautés**, **sautéed** or **sautéd**, **sautéing**) cook in such a way.
ORIGIN – French, 'jumped'.

Sauternes /sōtern/ > *noun* a sweet white wine from Sauternes in the Bordeaux region of France.

Sauvignon /sōvinyoN/ (also **Sauvignon Blanc**) > *noun* a variety of white wine grape grown originally in France.

savage > *adjective* **1** fierce, violent, and uncontrolled. **2** aggressively hostile. **3** primitive or uncivilised. **4** (of a place) wild; uncultivated. > *noun* **1** a member of a people regarded as primitive and uncivilised. **2** a brutal or vicious person. > *verb* **1** (especially of a dog) attack ferociously. **2** criticise brutally.
DERIVATIVES – **savagely** adverb **savagery** noun.
SYNONYMS – *adjective* **1** ferocious. **2** brutal, cruel, vicious, violent. **3** barbarian, barbaric, primitive, uncivilised, unenlightened. **4** rugged, inhospitable, uncultivated, wild. *noun* **2** animal, beast, monster. *verb* **2** flay, lambaste, revile.
ORIGIN – Old French *sauvage* 'wild', from Latin *silvaticus* 'of the woods'.

savannah (also **savanna**) > *noun* a grassy plain in tropical and subtropical regions, with few trees.
ORIGIN – Spanish *sabana*, from Taino (an extinct Caribbean language).

savant /savv'nt/ > *noun* (fem. **savante**) a learned person.
ORIGIN – French, 'knowing'.

save¹ > *verb* **1** keep safe or rescue from harm or danger. **2** prevent from dying. **3** (in Christian use) preserve (a soul) from damnation. **4** store up for future use. **5** Computing keep (data) by moving a copy to a storage location. **6** avoid the need to use up or spend. **7** avoid, lessen, or guard against. **8** prevent an opponent from scoring (a goal or point). > *noun* chiefly Soccer an act of preventing an opponent scoring.
IDIOMS – **save one's breath** not bother to say something pointless. **save the day** (or **situation**) provide a solution to a problem. **save someone's skin** (or **neck** or **bacon**) rescue someone from difficulty.
SYNONYMS – *verb* **1** conserve, deliver, free, preserve. **4** conserve, put aside, put by, set aside. **6** forestall, obviate, prevent.
ORIGIN – Latin *salvare*, from *salvus* 'safe'.

save² > *preposition & conjunction* formal or literary except; other than.
ORIGIN – from Latin *salvus* 'safe', used in phrases such as *salvo jure, salva innocentia* 'with no violation of right or innocence'.

saveloy /savvəloy/ > *noun* Brit. a seasoned red pork sausage, dried and smoked and sold ready to eat.
ORIGIN – Italian *cervellata*.

saver > *noun* **1** a person who regularly saves money through a bank or recognised scheme. **2** something that prevents a particular resource from being used up: *sliding doors are a space-saver.*

saving > *noun* **1** an economy of or reduction in money, time, etc. **2** (**savings**) money saved, especially over a long period. > *adjective* (in combination) preventing waste of a particular resource: *energy-saving.* > *preposition* **1** except. **2** archaic with due respect to.
COMBINATIONS – **saving grace 1** the redeeming grace of God. **2** a redeeming quality or characteristic. **savings account** a deposit account. **savings and loan (association)** (in the US) an institution which accepts savings at interest and lends money to savers. **savings bank** a non-profit-making bank receiving small deposits at interest. **Savings Bond** a Premium Bond.

saviour (US **savior**) > *noun* **1** a person who saves someone or something from danger or harm. **2** (**the/our Saviour**) (in Christianity) God or Jesus Christ.
SYNONYMS – **1** deliverer, liberator, rescuer.

savoir faire /savwaar **fair**/ > *noun* the ability to act appropriately in social situations.

ORIGIN – French, literally 'know how to do'.

savory¹ > *noun* an aromatic plant of the mint family, used as a culinary herb.

ORIGIN – Latin *satureia*.

savory² > *adjective & noun* US spelling of **SAVOURY**.

savour (US **savor**) > *verb* **1** appreciate and enjoy the taste of (food or drink). **2** enjoy or appreciate to the full. **3** (**savour of**) have a suggestion or trace of. > *noun* **1** a characteristic taste, flavour, or smell. **2** a suggestion or trace.

ORIGIN – Old French, from Latin *sapere* 'to taste'.

savoury (US **savory**) > *adjective* **1** (of food) salty or spicy rather than sweet. **2** morally wholesome or acceptable. > *noun* (pl. **savouries**) chiefly Brit. a savoury snack.

savoy > *noun* a cabbage of a hardy variety with densely wrinkled leaves.

ORIGIN – from *Savoy*, a region of SE France.

savvy informal > *noun* shrewdness. > *verb* (**savvies, savvied**) know or understand. > *adjective* (**savvier, savviest**) shrewd and knowledgeable.

ORIGIN – black and pidgin English, imitating Spanish *sabe usted* 'you know'.

saw¹ > *noun* **1** a hand tool for cutting wood or other hard materials, having a long, thin serrated blade and operated using a backwards and forwards movement. **2** a mechanical power-driven cutting tool with a toothed rotating disc or moving band. > *verb* (past participle chiefly Brit. **sawn** or chiefly N. Amer. **sawed**) **1** cut or form with a saw. **2** cut roughly. **3** make rapid sawlike motions.

WORDFINDER – *types of saw:* bandsaw, chainsaw, circular saw, cross-cut saw, frame saw, fretsaw, hacksaw, jigsaw, padsaw, panel saw, ripsaw, tenon saw, trephine, whipsaw.

COMBINATIONS – **sawbuck** N. Amer. a sawhorse. [ORIGIN – Dutch *zaagbok*, from *zaag* 'saw' + *bok* 'vaulting horse'.] **sawhorse** N. Amer. a rack supporting wood for sawing. **sawmill** a factory in which logs are sawn by machine.

saw² past of **SEE¹**.

saw³ > *noun* a proverb or maxim.

ORIGIN – Old English, related to **SAY** and **SAGA**.

sawbones > *noun* (pl. same) informal, dated a doctor or surgeon.

sawdust > *noun* powdery particles of wood produced by sawing.

sawfish > *noun* a large fish of tropical seas, with a long flattened snout bearing large blunt teeth along each side.

sawfly > *noun* an insect related to the wasps,

with a saw-like tube used in laying eggs in plant tissues.

sawn past participle of **SAW¹**.

sawn-off (N. Amer. **sawed-off**) > *adjective* **1** (of a gun) having a shortened barrel for ease of handling and a wider field of fire. **2** informal (of a garment) having been cut short.

sawtooth (also **sawtoothed**) > *adjective* shaped like the teeth of a saw.

sawyer > *noun* a person who saws wood.

sax > *noun* informal **1** a saxophone. **2** a saxophone player.

DERIVATIVES – **saxist** noun.

saxe > *noun* a light blue colour with a greyish tinge.

ORIGIN – French, 'Saxony', the source of a dye of this colour.

saxhorn > *noun* a brass instrument with valves and a funnel-shaped mouthpiece, used mainly in military and brass bands.

ORIGIN – named after the Belgian instrument-makers Charles *Sax* (1791–1865) and his son Adolphe *Sax* (1814–94).

saxifrage /**sak**sifrayj/ > *noun* a low-growing plant of rocky or stony ground, bearing small white, yellow, or red flowers.

ORIGIN – Latin *saxifraga*, from *saxum* 'rock' + *frangere* 'break'.

Saxon > *noun* **1** a member of a Germanic people that conquered and settled in much of southern England in the 5th–6th centuries. **2** a native of modern Saxony in Germany. **3** (**Old Saxon**) the language of the ancient Saxons. **4** another term for **OLD ENGLISH**. > *adjective* **1** relating to the Anglo-Saxons, their language, or their period of dominance in England (5th–11th centuries). **2** relating to Saxony.

ORIGIN – Greek *Saxones*, perhaps from the base of Old English *seax* 'knife'.

saxophone /**sak**səfōn/ > *noun* a member of a family of metal wind instruments with a reed like a clarinet, used especially in jazz and dance music.

DERIVATIVES – **saxophonic** /saksə**fonn**ik/ *adjective* **saxophonist** /sak**soff**ənist/ *noun*.

ORIGIN – named after Adolphe *Sax* (see **SAXHORN**).

say > *verb* (**says**; past and past participle **said**) **1** utter (words) so as to convey information, an opinion, an instruction, etc. **2** (of a text or symbol) convey specified information or instructions. **3** (of a clock or watch) indicate (a time). **4** (**be said**) be asserted or reported. **5** (**say for**) present (a consideration) in favour of or excusing: *he had nothing to say for himself.* **6** assume as a hypothesis. > *noun* **1** an opportunity to state one's opinion or feelings. **2** an opportunity to influence events.

IDIOMS – **go without saying** be obvious. **how say you?** Law how do you find? (used to request a jury's verdict). **say the word** give permission or instructions. **there is no**

saying it is impossible to know. **they say** it is rumoured. **when all is said and done** when everything is taken into account.

SYNONYMS – *verb* **1** pronounce, speak, utter. **6** assume, imagine, presume, suppose. *noun* **2** influence, sway, voice.

saying > *noun* a short, commonly known expression containing advice or wisdom.

say-so > *noun* informal **1** the power or action of deciding or allowing something. **2** mere assertion.

Sb > *symbol* the chemical element antimony.

ORIGIN – from Latin *stibium*.

SBS > *abbreviation* Special Boat Service.

SC > *abbreviation* South Carolina.

Sc > *symbol* the chemical element scandium.

sc. > *abbreviation* scilicet.

scab > *noun* **1** a dry, rough protective crust that forms over a cut or wound during healing. **2** mange or a similar skin disease in animals. **3** a fungal disease of plants in which rough patches develop. **4** informal a person or thing regarded with contempt. **5** a person who refuses to strike or who takes the place of a striker. > *verb* (**scabbed, scabbing**) **1** become encrusted with a scab or scabs. **2** act or work as a scab.

DERIVATIVES – **scabby** *adjective*.

ORIGIN – Old Norse.

scabbard /**skabb**ərd/ > *noun* **1** a sheath for the blade of a sword or dagger. **2** a sheath for a gun or other weapon or tool.

ORIGIN – Old French *escalberc*.

scabies /**skay**beez/ > *noun* a contagious skin disease marked by itching and small raised red spots, caused by the itch mite.

ORIGIN – Latin, from *scabere* 'to scratch'.

scabious /**skay**biəss/ > *noun* a plant of the daisy family with blue, pink, or white flowers.

ORIGIN – from Latin *scabiosa* 'rough, scabby'; it was formerly regarded as a cure for skin disease.

scabrous /**skay**brəss/ > *adjective* **1** rough and covered with scabs. **2** salacious or sordid.

ORIGIN – Latin *scabrosus*, from *scaber* 'rough'.

scads > *plural noun* informal, chiefly N. Amer. a large number or quantity.

scaffold > *noun* **1** a raised wooden platform used formerly for public executions. **2** a structure made using scaffolding. > *verb* attach scaffolding to.

DERIVATIVES – **scaffolder** noun.

ORIGIN – Old French *eschaffaut*.

scaffolding > *noun* **1** a temporary structure on the outside of a building, made of wooden planks and metal poles, used while building, repairing, or cleaning. **2** the materials used in such a structure.

scag > *noun* variant spelling of **SKAG**.

scalable > *adjective* **1** able to be scaled or climbed. **2** able to be changed in size or scale. **3** technical able to be graded according to a scale.

DERIVATIVES – **scalability** noun.

scalar /**skay**lər/ Mathematics & Physics > adjective having only magnitude, not direction. > noun a scalar quantity (especially as opposed to a vector).

ORIGIN – Latin scalaris, from scala 'ladder'.

scalawag > noun variant spelling of SCALLYWAG.

scald > verb **1** injure with very hot liquid or steam. **2** heat (a liquid) to near boiling point. **3** immerse briefly in boiling water. > noun a burn or other injury caused by hot liquid or steam.

IDIOMS – **like a scalded cat** very fast.

DERIVATIVES – **scalding** adjective.

ORIGIN – Latin excaldare, from calidus 'hot'.

scale[1] > noun **1** each of the small overlapping plates protecting the skin of fish and reptiles. **2** a thick dry flake of skin. **3** a white deposit formed in a kettle, boiler, etc. by the evaporation of water containing lime. **4** tartar formed on teeth. > verb **1** remove scale or scales from. **2** (especially of the skin) form or flake off in scales.

IDIOMS – **the scales fall from one's eyes** one is no longer deceived. [ORIGIN – with biblical reference to Acts of the Apostles, chapter 9.]

COMBINATIONS – **scale insect** a small bug which secretes a protective shield-like scale and spends its life attached to a plant.

ORIGIN – Old French escale.

scale[2] > noun **1** (usu. **scales**) an instrument or device for weighing. **2** either of the dishes on a simple balance. > verb have a weight of (a specified amount).

IDIOMS – **throw on** (or **into**) **the scale** contribute (something) to one side of an argument or debate. **tip** (or **turn**) **the scales** be the deciding factor; make the critical difference.

ORIGIN – Old Norse, 'bowl'.

scale[3] > noun **1** a graduated range of values forming a standard system for measuring or grading something. **2** a measuring device based on such a system. **3** the relative size or extent of something. **4** a ratio of size in a map, model, drawing, or plan. **5** Music an arrangement of the notes in any system of music in ascending or descending order of pitch. > verb **1** climb up or over (something high and steep). **2** represent or draw according to a common scale. **3** (of a quantity or property) be variable according to a particular scale. **4** (**scale back** or **down**) reduce (something) in size, number, or extent. **5** (**scale up**) increase (something) in size, number, or extent.

IDIOMS – **to scale** with a uniform reduction or enlargement. **in scale** in proportion to the surroundings.

ORIGIN – Latin scala 'ladder'.

scalene /**skay**leen/ > adjective (of a triangle) having all sides unequal in length.

ORIGIN – Greek skalēnos 'unequal'.

scallion /**skal**yən/ > noun a long-necked onion with a small bulb, in particular a shallot or spring onion.

ORIGIN – Old French scaloun, from Latin Ascalonia 'of Ascalon', a port in ancient Palestine.

scallop /**skoll**əp, **skal**əp/ > noun **1** an edible bivalve mollusc with a ribbed fan-shaped shell. **2** each of a series of projections shaped like a scallop shell, forming an ornamental edging in material, knitting, etc. > verb (**scalloped**, **scalloping**) **1** ornament with scallops. **2** N. Amer. gather or dredge for scallops.

ORIGIN – Old French escalope.

scally > noun (pl. **scallies**) informal (in NW English dialect) a rascal; a rogue.

ORIGIN – abbreviation of SCALLYWAG.

scallywag (US also **scalawag**) > noun informal a mischievous person; a rascal.

scalp > noun **1** the skin covering the top and back of the head. **2** historical the scalp with the hair cut away from an enemy's head as a battle trophy, a former practice among American Indians. > verb **1** take the scalp of (an enemy). **2** informal punish severely. **3** informal, chiefly N. Amer. resell (shares or tickets) at a large or quick profit.

DERIVATIVES – **scalper** noun.

scalpel > noun a knife with a small sharp blade, as used by a surgeon.

ORIGIN – Latin scalpellum 'small chisel', from scalpere 'to scratch'.

scaly > adjective (**scalier**, **scaliest**) **1** covered in scales. **2** (of skin) dry and flaking.

scam informal > noun a dishonest scheme; a fraud. > verb (**scammed**, **scamming**) swindle.

DERIVATIVES – **scammer** noun.

scamp[1] > noun informal a mischievous person, especially a child.

DERIVATIVES – **scampish** adjective.

wordpower facts

Scamp

The word **scamp** originally denoted a highwayman. The noun developed from the now obsolete verb scamp, meaning 'rob on the highway', which probably comes from Middle Dutch schampen 'slip away, decamp', from Old French eschamper. While **scamp** now tends to be used affectionately, in its early use it was always derogatory.

scamp[2] > verb dated perform in a perfunctory or inadequate way.

ORIGIN – perhaps from SCAMP[1], but associated in sense with SKIMP.

scamper > verb run with quick light steps, especially through fear or excitement. > noun an act of scampering.

scampi > noun (treated as sing. or pl.) a kind of small lobster prepared for eating, especially fried in breadcrumbs.

ORIGIN – Italian.

scan > verb (**scanned**, **scanning**) **1** look at quickly in order to identify relevant features or information. **2** traverse with a detector or an electromagnetic beam, especially to obtain an image. **3** convert (a document or picture) into digital form for storage or processing on a computer. **4** analyse the metre of (a line of verse). **5** (of verse) conform to metrical principles. > noun **1** an act of scanning. **2** a medical examination using a scanner. **3** an image obtained by scanning or with a scanner.

DERIVATIVES – **scannable** adjective.

wordpower facts

Scan

The word **scan** entered English at the beginning of the 15th century in the sense relating to poetry, 'analyse the metre of (a line of verse)'. From this arose the senses 'estimate the correctness of' and 'examine minutely', which led to 'look at searchingly' and then recently, in contrast, 'look at quickly for information'. The word itself comes from Latin scandere, meaning 'to climb', which in late Latin had developed the sense 'scan (verse)', by analogy with the raising and lowering of one's foot when marking rhythm.

scandal > noun **1** an action or event regarded as morally or legally wrong and causing general public outrage. **2** outrage, rumour, or gossip arising from this.

SYNONYMS – **1** impropriety, misconduct, wrongdoing. **2** disgrace, ignominy, shame.

ORIGIN – Latin scandalum 'cause of offence', from Greek skandalon 'snare, stumbling block'.

scandalise (also **scandalize**) > verb shock or horrify by a violation of propriety or morality.

SYNONYMS – appal, offend, outrage.

scandalous > adjective **1** causing general public outrage by a perceived offence against morality or law. **2** (of a state of affairs) disgracefully bad.

DERIVATIVES – **scandalously** adverb.

SYNONYMS – **1,2** disgraceful, outrageous, shameful, shocking.

Scandinavian > adjective relating to Scandinavia, its people, or their languages. > noun **1** a person from Scandinavia or of Scandinavian descent. **2** the northern branch of the Germanic languages, comprising Danish, Norwegian, Swedish, Icelandic, and Faroese, all descended from Old Norse.

scandium /**skan**diəm/ > *noun* a soft, silvery-white, metallic chemical element resembling the rare-earth elements.

ORIGIN – Latin, from *Scandinavia* (where minerals are found containing this element).

scanner > *noun* 1 Medicine a machine that examines the body by means of radiation, ultrasound etc., used to aid diagnosis. 2 a device that scans documents or images and converts them into digital data.

scansion /**skan**sh'n/ > *noun* 1 the action of scanning a line of verse to determine its rhythm. 2 the rhythm of a line of verse.

scant > *adjective* 1 barely sufficient or adequate. 2 barely amounting to the amount specified. > *verb* chiefly N. Amer. provide for or deal with insufficiently.

DERIVATIVES – **scantly** *adverb* **scantness** *noun*.

SYNONYMS – *adjective* 1 meagre, minimal, negligible.

ANTONYMS – *adjective* 1 abundant, ample.

ORIGIN – Old Norse, 'short'.

scantling > *noun* 1 a timber beam of small cross section. 2 (often **scantlings**) a set of standard dimensions for parts of a structure, especially in shipbuilding.

ORIGIN – alteration of obsolete *scantillon*, from Old French *escantillon* 'sample'.

scanty > *adjective* (**scantier**, **scantiest**) small or insufficient in quantity or amount.

DERIVATIVES – **scantily** *adverb*.

scapegoat > *noun* 1 a person who is blamed for the wrongdoings or mistakes of others. 2 (in the Bible) a goat sent into the wilderness after the Jewish chief priest had symbolically laid the sins of the people upon it (Leviticus, chapter 16). > *verb* make a scapegoat of.

ORIGIN – from archaic *scape* 'escape'.

scapegrace > *noun* archaic a person who lacks the grace of God; a rascal.

scapula /**skap**yoolə/ > *noun* (pl. **scapulae** /**skap**yoolee/ or **scapulas**) Anatomy technical term for **shoulder blade**.

ORIGIN – Latin.

scapular /**skap**yoolər/ > *adjective* Anatomy & Zoology relating to the shoulder or shoulder blade. > *noun* a short monastic cloak covering the shoulders.

scar¹ > *noun* 1 a mark left on the skin or within body tissue after the healing of a wound or burn. 2 a mark left at the point of separation of a leaf, frond, or other part from a plant. 3 a lasting effect left following an unpleasant experience. > *verb* (**scarred**, **scarring**) mark or be marked with a scar or scars.

ORIGIN – Greek *eskhara* 'scab'.

scar² > *noun* a steep high cliff or rock outcrop.

ORIGIN – Old Norse, 'low reef'.

scarab /**skarr**əb/ > *noun* 1 a large dung beetle, regarded as sacred in ancient Egypt. 2 an ancient Egyptian gem in the form of a scarab beetle, engraved with hieroglyphs on the flat underside.

ORIGIN – Greek *skarabeios*.

scarce > *adjective* 1 (of a resource) insufficient for the demand. 2 rare.

IDIOMS – **make oneself scarce** informal leave a place, especially so as to avoid a difficult situation.

DERIVATIVES – **scarcely** *adverb* **scarcity** *noun*.

SYNONYMS – 1 deficient, inadequate, in short supply. 2 infrequent, rare, uncommon.

ORIGIN – Old French *escars*, from a word meaning 'selected'.

scare > *verb* 1 cause great fear or nervousness in; frighten. 2 (**scare away** or **off**) drive or keep (someone) away by fear. 3 become scared. > *noun* 1 a sudden attack of fright. 2 a period of general anxiety or alarm about something.

SYNONYMS – *verb* 1 frighten, panic, petrify, terrify. *noun* 1 fright, shock, start.

ORIGIN – Old Norse, 'frighten'.

scarecrow > *noun* an object made to resemble a human figure, set up to scare birds away from a field where crops are growing.

scared > *adjective* feeling or showing fear or nervousness.

scaredy-cat > *noun* informal a timid person.

scarf¹ > *noun* (pl. **scarves** or **scarfs**) a length or square of fabric worn around the neck or head.

DERIVATIVES – **scarfed** (also **scarved**) *adjective*.

ORIGIN – probably from Old French *escharpe* 'pilgrim's pouch'.

scarf² > *verb* join the ends of (two pieces of timber or metal) by bevelling or notching them so that they fit together. > *noun* an instance of scarfing; a joint made by scarfing.

ORIGIN – Old Norse.

scarf³ > *verb* N. Amer. informal eat or drink hungrily or enthusiastically.

scarify¹ /**skarr**ifī, **skair**-/ > *verb* (**scarifies**, **scarified**) 1 cut and remove debris from (a lawn). 2 break up the surface of (soil or a road or pavement). 3 make shallow incisions in (the skin). 4 criticise severely and hurtfully.

DERIVATIVES – **scarification** *noun*.

ORIGIN – Greek *skariphasthai* 'scratch an outline', from *skariphos* 'stylus'.

scarify² /**skair**ifī/ > *verb* (**scarifies**, **scarified**) informal frighten.

ORIGIN – formed irregularly from **SCARE**.

scarlatina /skaarlə**teen**ə/ (also **scarletina**) > *noun* another term for *scarlet fever*.

ORIGIN – Latin.

scarlet > *noun* a brilliant red colour.

COMBINATIONS – **scarlet fever** an infectious bacterial disease affecting especially children, and causing fever and a scarlet rash. **scarlet woman** a notoriously promiscuous or immoral woman.

ORIGIN – Latin *scarlata*, from *sigillatus* 'decorated with small images': originally denoting any brightly coloured cloth.

scarp > *noun* a very steep bank or slope; an escarpment. > *verb* cut or erode so as to form a scarp.

ORIGIN – Italian *scarpa*.

scarper > *verb* Brit. informal run away.

ORIGIN – probably from Italian *scappare* 'to escape', influenced by rhyming slang *Scapa Flow* 'go'.

Scart (also **SCART**) > *noun* a 21-pin socket used to connect video equipment.

ORIGIN – acronym from French *Syndicat des Constructeurs des Appareils Radiorécepteurs et Téléviseurs*, the committee which designed the connector.

scarves plural of SCARF¹.

scary > *adjective* (**scarier**, **scariest**) informal frightening; causing fear.

DERIVATIVES – **scarily** *adverb*.

scat¹ > *verb* (**scatted**, **scatting**) informal go away; leave.

scat² > *noun* improvised jazz singing in which the voice is used in imitation of an instrument. > *verb* (**scatted**, **scatting**) sing in such a way.

scathing > *adjective* witheringly scornful; severely critical.

DERIVATIVES – **scathingly** *adverb*.

SYNONYMS – blistering, devastating, trenchant, withering.

ORIGIN – from obsolete *scathe* 'harm, injure'.

scatology /ska**toll**əji/ > *noun* a preoccupation with excrement and excretion.

DERIVATIVES – **scatological** *adjective*.

ORIGIN – from Greek *skōr* 'dung'.

scatter > *verb* 1 throw in various random directions. 2 separate and move off in different directions. 3 (**be scattered**) occur or be found at various places rather than all together. 4 Physics deflect or diffuse (electromagnetic radiation or particles). > *noun* a small, dispersed amount of something.

DERIVATIVES – **scattering** *noun*.

SYNONYMS – *verb* 1 shower, sprinkle, strew.

COMBINATIONS – **scatter cushion** a small cushion placed randomly so as to create a casual effect.

ORIGIN – probably a variant of **SHATTER**.

scatterbrained > *adjective* tending to be disorganised and lacking in concentration.

scattergun > *noun* **1** chiefly N. Amer. a shotgun. **2** (also **scattershot**) (before another noun) covering a broad range in a random and unsystematic way.

scatty > *adjective* (**scattier**, **scattiest**) informal absent-minded and disorganised.

ORIGIN – abbreviation of *scatterbrained*.

scaup /skawp/ > *noun* a diving duck, the male of which has a black head with a green or purple gloss.

ORIGIN – short for *scaup duck*, from Scots and northern English *scalp* 'mussel bed'.

scavenge /**skavv**inj/ > *verb* **1** search for and collect (anything usable) from discarded waste. **2** search for (carrion) as food. **3** technical combine with and remove (a particular substance) from a medium.

scavenger > *noun* **1** a person or animal that scavenges. **2** Chemistry a substance that combines with and removes particular molecules, ions, etc.

wordpower facts

Scavenger

One might expect the noun **scavenger** to have developed from the verb **scavenge**, but in fact it was the other way round. **Scavenge** dates from the 17th century, when it had the sense 'clean out (dirt)', while **scavenger** is a century older. A **scavenger** (originally spelled **scavager**) was an official employed to collect *scavage*, that is, a toll on foreign goods being sold in a town: the word comes from Anglo-Norman French *scawager*, from Old Northern French *escauwer*, meaning 'to inspect'. In time, a **scavenger** was also charged with keeping the streets swept and clean, and it is from this action that the verb derives.

SCE > *abbreviation* Scottish Certificate of Education.

scenario /sɪnaariō/ > *noun* (pl. **scenarios**) **1** a written outline of a film, novel, or stage work giving details of the plot and individual scenes. **2** a postulated sequence or development of events.

ORIGIN – Italian, from Latin *scena* 'scene'.

scene > *noun* **1** the place where an incident in real life or fiction occurs or occurred. **2** a landscape. **3** an incident or representation of an incident of a specified nature. **4** a sequence of continuous action in a play, film, opera, etc. **5** the pieces of scenery used in a play or opera. **6** a public display of emotion or anger. **7** a specified area of activity or interest: *the literary scene*.

IDIOMS – **behind the scenes** out of public view. **change of scene** a move to different surroundings. **come** (or **appear** or **arrive**) **on the scene** arrive; appear. **not one's scene** informal not something one enjoys or is interested in.

SYNONYMS – **1** location, site, spot. **3** episode, event, situation. **6** commotion, outburst, performance.

ORIGIN – Latin *scena*, from Greek *skēnē* 'tent, stage'.

scenery > *noun* **1** the natural features of a landscape considered in terms of their appearance. **2** the painted background used to represent the fictional surroundings on a stage or film set.

scenic > *adjective* **1** relating to impressive or beautiful natural scenery. **2** relating to theatrical scenery. **3** (of a picture) representing an incident.

DERIVATIVES – **scenically** *adverb*.

SYNONYMS – **1** attractive, picturesque, pleasing, pretty.

COMBINATIONS – **scenic railway** an attraction at a fair consisting of a miniature railway that goes past natural features and artificial scenery.

scent > *noun* **1** a distinctive smell, especially one that is pleasant. **2** pleasant-smelling liquid worn on the skin; perfume. **3** a trail indicated by the characteristic smell of an animal. > *verb* **1** give a pleasant scent to. **2** discern by the sense of smell. **3** sense the presence or approach of.

DERIVATIVES – **scented** *adjective*.

SYNONYMS – *noun* **1** aroma, fragrance, odour, perfume. *verb* **3** detect, discern, perceive.

COMBINATIONS – **scent gland** an animal gland that secretes an odorous pheromone or defensive substance.

wordpower facts

Scent

The word **scent** entered English in the 15th century, spelled as **sent**. It comes via Old French *sentir*, meaning 'perceive, smell', from Latin *sentire* 'to feel'. A number of words share this same Latin root, including **assent**, **consent**, **resent**, **sense**, **sensitive**, and **sentiment**. It is not clear why the letter c was inserted in the spelling of **scent**, around the 17th century.

sceptic /**skep**tik/ (US **skeptic**) > *noun* **1** a person inclined to question or doubt accepted opinions. **2** a person who doubts the truth of Christianity and other religions.

DERIVATIVES – **scepticism** *noun*.

ORIGIN – Greek *skeptikos*, from *skepsis* 'inquiry, doubt'.

sceptical > *adjective* not easily convinced; having doubts or reservations.

SYNONYMS – disbelieving, dubious, suspicious.

sceptre /**sep**tər/ (US **scepter**) > *noun* a staff carried by rulers on ceremonial occasions as a symbol of sovereignty.

DERIVATIVES – **sceptred** *adjective*.

ORIGIN – Greek *skēptron*, from *skēptein* 'lean on'.

Schadenfreude /**shaa**dənfroydə/ > *noun* pleasure derived from another's misfortune.

ORIGIN – German, from *Schaden* 'harm' + *Freude* 'joy'.

schedule /**shed**yool, chiefly US **sked**yool/ > *noun* **1** a plan for carrying out a process or procedure, giving lists of intended events and times. **2** a timetable. **3** chiefly Law an appendix to a formal document or statute, especially as a list, table, or inventory. **4** (in Britain) any of the forms (named 'A', 'B', etc.) issued relating to various classes of taxable income. > *verb* **1** arrange or plan to take place at a particular time. **2** include in a schedule. **3** Brit. include (a building) in a list for legal preservation or protection.

IDIOMS – **to** (or **on** or **according to**) **schedule** on time; as planned.

ORIGIN – Latin *schedula* 'slip of paper', from Greek *skhedē* 'papyrus leaf'.

scheduled > *adjective* **1** forming part of a schedule. **2** (of an airline or flight) forming part of a regular service rather than specially chartered. **3** Brit. (of a building) included in a list for legal preservation and protection.

COMBINATIONS – **scheduled caste** the official name given in India to the lowest caste, who are given special concessions in recognition of their disadvantaged status.

schema /**skee**mə/ > *noun* (pl. **schemata** /**skee**mətə/ or **schemas**) technical a representation of a plan or theory in the form of an outline or model.

ORIGIN – Greek *skhēma* 'form, figure'.

schematic > *adjective* **1** (of a diagram or representation) symbolic and simplified. **2** (of thought, ideas, etc.) simplistic or formulaic in character.

DERIVATIVES – **schematically** *adverb*.

schematise (also **schematize**) > *verb* arrange or represent in a schematic form.

scheme > *noun* **1** a systematic plan or arrangement for achieving a particular object or effect. **2** a secret or underhand plan; a plot. > *verb* **1** form a scheme, especially a devious one or with intent to do something wrong. **2** arrange according to a colour scheme.

DERIVATIVES – **schemer** *noun* **scheming** *adjective* & *noun*.

SYNONYMS – *noun* **1** programme, project, strategy. **2** conspiracy, plot, ruse, subterfuge. *verb* **1** conspire, intrigue, plot.

ORIGIN – Greek *skhēma* 'form, figure'.

schemozzle > *noun* variant spelling of SHEMOZZLE.

scherzo /skairtsō/ > *noun* (pl. **scherzos** or **scherzi** /skairtsi/) Music a vigorous, light, or playful composition, typically comprising a movement in a symphony or sonata.

ORIGIN – Italian, 'jest'.

schilling /**shil**ling/ > *noun* the basic monetary unit of Austria, equal to 100 groschen.

ORIGIN – German, related to SHILLING.

schism /**sizz**'m, **skizz**'m/ > *noun* **1** a division between strongly opposed parties, caused by differences in opinion or belief. **2** the formal separation of a Church into two Churches or the secession of a group owing to doctrinal and other differences.

SYNONYMS – **1** breach, rift, split.

ORIGIN – Greek *skhisma* 'cleft', from *skhizein* 'to split'.

schismatic > *adjective* characterised by or favouring schism. > *noun* chiefly historical an adherent of a schismatic group.

schist /shist/ > *noun* Geology a coarse-grained metamorphic rock which consists of layers of different minerals and can be split into thin irregular plates.

ORIGIN – from Greek *skhistos* 'split'.

schistosome /**shis**təsōm/ > *noun* a parasitic flatworm which causes bilharzia, infesting freshwater snails when immature and the blood vessels of birds and mammals when adult.

ORIGIN – from Greek *skhistos* 'divided' + *sōma* 'body'.

schistosomiasis /shistəsəmīəsiss/ > *noun* another term for BILHARZIA.

schizo > *adjective & noun* (pl. **schizos**) informal schizophrenic.

schizoid /**skit**zoyd/ > *adjective* Psychiatry **1** denoting a personality type characterised by emotional aloofness and solitary habits. **2** informal resembling schizophrenia in having contradictory elements; mad or crazy. > *noun* a schizoid person.

schizophrenia /skitsəfreeniə/ > *noun* a long-term mental disorder involving faulty perception, inappropriate actions and feelings, and withdrawal from reality into fantasy and delusion.

ORIGIN – Latin, from Greek *skhizein* 'to split' + *phrēn* 'mind'.

schizophrenic /skitsəfrennik/ > *adjective* **1** suffering from schizophrenia. **2** (in general use) characterised by inconsistent or contradictory elements. > *noun* a schizophrenic person.

schlep /shlep/ (also **schlepp**) informal, chiefly N. Amer. > *verb* (**schlepped, schlepping**) **1** haul or carry with difficulty. **2** go or move

reluctantly or with effort. > *noun* **1** a tedious or difficult journey. **2** (also **schlepper**) an inept or stupid person.

ORIGIN – Yiddish, 'drag'.

schlock /shlok/ > *noun* informal, chiefly N. Amer. cheap or inferior goods; trash.

ORIGIN – apparently from Yiddish words for 'an apoplectic stroke' and 'wretch, untidy person'.

schloss /shloss/ > *noun* (chiefly in Germany or Austria) a castle.

ORIGIN – German.

schmaltz /shmolts/ > *noun* informal excessive sentimentality.

DERIVATIVES – **schmaltzy** *adjective*.

ORIGIN – Yiddish, from German *Schmalz* 'dripping, lard'.

schmooze /shmōōz/ chiefly N. Amer. > *verb* **1** chat; gossip. **2** chat to (someone) in order to gain an advantage. > *noun* an intimate conversation.

DERIVATIVES – **schmoozer** *noun* **schmoozy** *adjective*.

ORIGIN – Yiddish.

schmuck /shmuk/ > *noun* N. Amer. informal a foolish or contemptible person.

ORIGIN – Yiddish *shmok* 'penis'.

schnapps /shnaps/ > *noun* a strong alcoholic drink resembling gin.

ORIGIN – German *Schnaps* 'dram of liquor'.

schnauzer /**shnow**zər/ > *noun* a German breed of dog with a close wiry coat and heavy whiskers round the muzzle.

ORIGIN – German, from *Schnauze* 'muzzle, snout'.

schnitzel /**shnit**z'l/ > *noun* a thin slice of veal or other pale meat, coated in breadcrumbs and fried.

ORIGIN – German, 'slice'.

schnozz /shnoz/ (also **schnozzle** or **schnozzola**) > *noun* N. Amer. informal a person's nose.

ORIGIN – Yiddish, from German *Schnauze* 'snout'.

scholar > *noun* **1** a specialist in a particular branch of study, especially the humanities; a distinguished academic. **2** chiefly archaic a person who is highly educated or has an aptitude for study. **3** a university student holding a scholarship.

ORIGIN – Old English *scolere* 'student', from Greek *skholē*.

scholarly > *adjective* **1** relating to serious academic study. **2** having or showing knowledge, learning, or devotion to academic pursuits.

SYNONYMS – **2** bookish, erudite, intellectual, learned.

scholarship > *noun* **1** academic achievement; learning of a high level. **2** a grant made to support a student's education, awarded on the basis of achievement.

scholastic /skəlastik/ > *adjective* **1** concerning schools and education. **2** Philosophy & Theology relating to medieval scholasticism. > *noun* Philosophy & Theology, historical an adherent of scholasticism.

scholasticism > *noun* the system of theology and philosophy taught in medieval European universities, based on Aristotelian logic and early Christian writings.

school¹ > *noun* **1** an institution for educating children. **2** a day's work at school; lessons. **3** any institution at which instruction is given in a particular discipline. **4** N. Amer. informal a university. **5** a department or faculty of a university. **6** a group of people sharing similar ideas, methods, or style. **7** Brit. a group of people gambling together. > *verb* chiefly formal or N. Amer. send to school; educate. **2** train in a particular skill or activity. **3** Riding train (a horse) on the flat or over fences.

IDIOMS – **school of thought** a particular way of thinking.

SYNONYMS – *verb* **2** coach, instruct, teach, train, tutor.

COMBINATIONS – **schoolhouse 1** a building used as a school, especially in a rural community. **2** Brit., chiefly historical a house adjoining a school, lived in by the schoolteacher. **schoolmate** informal a fellow pupil.

ORIGIN – Greek *skholē* 'leisure, philosophy, lecture-place'.

school² > *noun* a large group of fish or sea mammals. > *verb* (of fish or sea mammals) form a school.

ORIGIN – Low German, Dutch *schōle*; compare with SHOAL¹.

schooling > *noun* **1** education received at school. **2** Riding the training of a horse on the flat or over fences.

schoolmarm > *noun* chiefly N. Amer. a schoolmistress, especially one regarded as prim and strict.

DERIVATIVES – **schoolmarmish** *adjective*.

schoolmaster (or **schoolmistress**) > *noun* a male (or female) teacher in a school.

schoolteacher > *noun* a person who teaches in a school.

DERIVATIVES – **schoolteaching** *noun*.

schooner /**skōō**nər/ > *noun* **1** a sailing ship with two or more masts, typically with the foremast smaller than the mainmast. **2** Brit. a large glass for sherry. **3** N. Amer. & Austral./NZ a tall beer glass.

ORIGIN – perhaps from dialect *scun* 'skim along'.

schottische /shoteesh/ > *noun* a dance resembling a slow polka.

ORIGIN – from German *der schottische Tanz* 'the Scottish dance'.

schtuck > *noun* variant spelling of SHTOOK.

schtum > *adjective* variant spelling of SHTUM.

schuss /shooss/ > *noun* a straight downhill run on skis. > *verb* perform a schuss.
ORIGIN – German, literally 'shot'.

sciatic /sīattik/ > *adjective* 1 relating to the hip. 2 affecting the sciatic nerve. 3 suffering from or liable to sciatica.
COMBINATIONS – **sciatic nerve** Anatomy a major nerve running from the lower spinal cord down the back of the thigh.
ORIGIN – Greek *iskhiadikos* 'relating to the hips'.

sciatica /sīattikə/ > *noun* pain affecting the back, hip, and outer side of the leg, caused by compression of the sciatic nerve root in the lower back.

science > *noun* 1 the intellectual and practical activity encompassing the systematic study of the structure and behaviour of the physical and natural world through observation and experiment. 2 a systematically organised body of knowledge on any subject.
COMBINATIONS – **science fiction** fiction based on imagined future or alien worlds portraying scientific or technological changes. **science park** an area devoted to scientific research or the development of science-based industries.

wordpower facts
Science
The word **science** entered English in the 14th century, in the sense 'the state of knowing; knowledge'. It comes via French from Latin *scientia*, from the verb *scire* 'to know'. *Scire* is the source of a number of words relating to knowledge and awareness, including **conscience**, **omniscient**, and **prescient**.

scientific > *adjective* 1 relating to or based on science. 2 systematic; methodical.
DERIVATIVES – **scientifically** *adverb*.

scientism > *noun* 1 thought or expression regarded as characteristic of scientists. 2 excessive belief in the power of scientific knowledge and techniques.

scientist > *noun* a person who has expert knowledge of one or more of the natural or physical sciences.

Scientology > *noun* trademark a religious system founded by the American science-fiction writer L. Ron Hubbard (1911–86) in 1955, based on the seeking of self-knowledge and spiritual fulfilment through study and training.
DERIVATIVES – **Scientologist** *noun*.

sci-fi > *noun* informal short for *science fiction*.

scilicet /sīliset, skeeliket/ > *adverb* that is to say; namely.

ORIGIN – from Latin *scire licet* 'one is permitted to know'.

scimitar /simmitər/ > *noun* a short sword with a curved blade that broadens towards the point, used originally in Eastern countries.
ORIGIN – from French *cimeterre* or Italian *scimitarra*.

scintilla /sintillə/ > *noun* a tiny trace or amount: *not a scintilla of doubt.*
ORIGIN – Latin, 'spark'.

scintillate /sintilayt/ > *verb* emit flashes of light; sparkle.
DERIVATIVES – **scintillant** *adjective & noun* **scintillation** *noun*.
ORIGIN – Latin *scintillare* 'to sparkle', from *scintilla* 'spark'.

scintillating > *adjective* 1 sparkling or shining brightly. 2 brilliant and exciting.

scion /sīən/ > *noun* 1 a young shoot or twig of a plant, especially one cut for grafting or rooting. 2 a descendant of a notable family.
ORIGIN – Old French *ciun* 'shoot, twig'.

scissor > *verb* 1 cut with scissors. 2 move in a way resembling the action of scissors.

scissors > *plural noun* 1 (also **a pair of scissors**) an instrument used for cutting cloth and paper, consisting of two crossing blades pivoted in the middle. 2 (also **scissor**) (before another noun) referring to an action in which two things cross each other or open and close like a pair of scissors: *a scissor kick.*
ORIGIN – Old French *cisoires*, from Latin *cisorium* 'cutting instrument'.

sclera /skleerə/ > *noun* Anatomy the white outer layer of the eyeball.
ORIGIN – Latin, from Greek *sklēros* 'hard'.

scleritis /skleerītiss/ > *noun* Medicine inflammation of the sclera of the eye.

scleroderma /skleerədermə/ > *noun* Medicine a chronic hardening and contraction of the skin and connective tissue.

sclerose /skleerōss/ > *verb* Medicine affect with sclerosis.

sclerosis /sklərōsiss/ > *noun* Medicine 1 abnormal hardening of body tissue. 2 (in full **multiple sclerosis**) a chronic progressive disease involving damage to the sheaths of nerve cells in the brain and spinal cord.
ORIGIN – Greek *sklērōsis*, from *sklēroun* 'harden'.

sclerotic /sklərottik/ > *adjective* 1 Medicine of or having sclerosis. 2 rigid; unable to adapt.

scoff[1] > *verb* speak about something in a scornfully derisive way. > *noun* an expression of scornful derision.
DERIVATIVES – **scoffer** *noun* **scoffing** *adjective*.
SYNONYMS – *verb* (**scoff at**) deride, jeer at, mock, ridicule, sneer at.

scoff[2] > *verb* informal, chiefly Brit. eat quickly and greedily.
ORIGIN – from Dutch *schoft* 'quarter of a day, meal'.

scold > *verb* angrily remonstrate with or rebuke. > *noun* archaic a woman who nags or grumbles constantly.
SYNONYMS – admonish, berate, castigate, rebuke, reprove, upbraid.
ORIGIN – probably from Old Norse *skáld* 'a composer and reciter of heroic poems'.

scollop > *noun & verb* archaic spelling of SCALLOP.

sconce > *noun* a candle holder attached to a wall with an ornamental bracket.
ORIGIN – Old French *esconse* 'lantern', from Latin *absconsa laterna* 'dark lantern', from *abscondere* 'to hide'.

scone /skon, skōn/ > *noun* a small unsweetened or lightly sweetened cake made from flour, fat, and milk.
NOTE – there are two standard pronunciations of **scone**, the first rhyming with *gone* and the second with *tone*. Traditionally the first is associated with Scotland and the north of England, although at times the middle classes in those areas may have favoured the second, while the second is associated with the south. In recent years, however, the first pronunciation, as *gone*, has become widespread in middle-class speech in both north and south.
ORIGIN – perhaps from Dutch *schoonbroot* 'fine bread'.

scoop > *noun* 1 a utensil resembling a spoon, having a short handle and a deep bowl. 2 the bowl-shaped part of a digging machine or dredger. 3 informal a piece of news published or broadcast in advance of being released by other newspapers or broadcast stations. > *verb* 1 pick up with a scoop. 2 create (a hollow) with or as if with a scoop. 3 pick or gather up in a swift, fluid movement. 4 informal publish a news story before (a rival). 5 win.
COMBINATIONS – **scoop neck** a deeply curved wide neckline on a woman's garment.
ORIGIN – Low German *schōpe* 'waterwheel bucket'.

scoot > *verb* informal 1 go or leave somewhere quickly. 2 move with a rapid, darting motion.

scooter > *noun* 1 (also **motor scooter**) a light two-wheeled motorcycle. 2 any small light vehicle able to travel quickly across water or snow. 3 a child's toy consisting of a footboard mounted on two wheels and a long steering handle, propelled by pushing one foot against the ground. > *verb* travel or ride on a scooter.

scope[1] > *noun* 1 the extent of the area or subject matter that something deals with or to which it is relevant. **2** the opportunity or possibility for doing something.

SYNONYMS – **1** ambit, extent, range, reach, span. **2** capacity, freedom, latitude, leeway, opportunity, possibility.

ORIGIN – Italian *scopo* 'aim', from Greek *skopos* 'target'.

scope² > *noun informal* a telescope or other device having a name ending in *-scope*.

-scope > *combining form* denoting an instrument for observing or examining: *telescope*.

DERIVATIVES – **-scopic** *combining form*.

ORIGIN – from Greek *skopein* 'look at'.

scopolamine /skəpolləmeen/ > *noun* another term for HYOSCINE.

ORIGIN – from *Scopolia* (genus name) + AMINE.

-scopy > *combining form* indicating observation or examination: *microscopy*.

ORIGIN – from Greek *skopia* 'observation', from *skopein* 'examine, look at'.

scorbutic /skorbyootik/ > *adjective* relating to or affected with scurvy.

ORIGIN – from Latin *scorbutus* 'scurvy'.

scorch > *verb* **1** become burnt or cause to become burnt on the surface or edges. **2** (**scorched**) dried out and withered as a result of extreme heat. **3** *informal* move very fast. > *noun* the burning or charring of the surface of something.

COMBINATIONS – **scorched earth policy** a military strategy of burning or destroying all crops and resources that might be of use to an invading enemy force.

scorcher > *noun informal* **1** a day or period of very hot weather. **2** Brit. a remarkable or powerful example of something.

scorching > *adjective* **1** very hot. **2** (of criticism) very harsh. **3** *informal* very fast.

DERIVATIVES – **scorchingly** *adverb*.

score > *noun* **1** the number of points, goals, runs, etc. achieved in a game or by an individual. **2** (pl. same) a group or set of twenty. **3** a large amount or number. **4** a written representation of a musical composition showing all the vocal and instrumental parts. **5** a notch or line cut or scratched into a surface. **6** (**the score**) *informal* the state of affairs; the real facts. > *verb* **1** gain (a point, goal, run, etc.) in a competitive game. **2** be worth (a number of points). **3** record the score during a game. **4** cut or scratch a mark on (a surface). **5** (**score out** or **through**) delete (text) by drawing a line through it. **6** orchestrate or arrange (a piece of music). **7** *informal* secure (a success or an advantage). **8** *informal* succeed in obtaining (illegal drugs). **9** *informal* succeed in attracting a sexual partner.

IDIOMS – **on that** (or **this**) **score** so far as that (or this) is concerned. **settle a score** take revenge on someone.

DERIVATIVES – **scoreless** *adjective* **scorer** *noun*.

ORIGIN – Old Norse, 'notch, tally, twenty'; related to SHEAR.

scorecard > *noun* **1** (also **scoresheet** or **scorebook**) a card, sheet, or book in which scores are entered. **2** a card listing the names and positions of players in a team.

scoreline > *noun* the number of points or goals scored in a match.

scoria /skoriə/ > *noun* (pl. **scoriae** /skoriee/) **1** basaltic lava ejected as fragments from a volcano. **2** slag separated from molten metal during smelting.

DERIVATIVES – **scoriaceous** *adjective*.

ORIGIN – Greek *skōria* 'refuse', from *skōr* 'dung'.

scorn > *noun* contempt or disdain expressed openly. > *verb* **1** express scorn for. **2** reject in a contemptuous way.

DERIVATIVES – **scorner** *noun* **scornful** *adjective* **scornfully** *adverb*.

SYNONYMS – *noun* contempt, derision, disdain, disparagement, mockery, ridicule. *verb* **1** deride, disdain, disparage, mock, ridicule, sneer at. **2** rebuff, shun, spurn.

ORIGIN – Old French *escarn* (noun), *escharnir* (verb).

Scorpio > *noun* Astrology the eighth sign of the zodiac (the Scorpion), which the sun enters about 23 October.

DERIVATIVES – **Scorpian** *noun* & *adjective*.

NOTE – in astronomy, the corresponding constellation is called *Scorpius*.

ORIGIN – Latin.

scorpion > *noun* an arachnid with lobster-like pincers and a poisonous sting at the end of its tail.

ORIGIN – Greek *skorpios* 'scorpion'.

Scot > *noun* **1** a person from Scotland. **2** a member of a Gaelic people that migrated from Ireland to Scotland around the late 5th century.

ORIGIN – Latin *Scottus*.

Scotch > *adjective* old-fashioned term for SCOTTISH. > *noun* **1** short for *Scotch whisky*. **2** (**the Scotch**) dated the people of Scotland. **3** dated the form of English spoken in Scotland.

COMBINATIONS – **Scotch bonnet** W. Indian & N. Amer. a small chilli pepper which is the hottest variety available. **Scotch broth** a traditional Scottish soup made from meat stock with pearl barley and vegetables. **Scotch egg** a hard-boiled egg enclosed in sausage meat, rolled in breadcrumbs, and fried. **Scotch mist** a thick drizzly mist of a kind common in the Scottish Highlands. **Scotch pancake** a drop scone. **Scotch tape** trademark, chiefly N. Amer. transparent adhesive tape. **Scotch whisky** whisky distilled in Scotland.

ORIGIN – contraction of SCOTTISH.

scotch > *verb* **1** decisively put an end to. **2** archaic injure and render harmless.

ORIGIN – perhaps related to SKATE¹.

Scotchgard > *noun* trademark a preparation for giving a waterproof stain-resistant finish to textiles and other materials.

scoter /skōtər/ > *noun* a northern diving duck, the male of which has mainly black plumage.

ORIGIN – probably an error for *sooter*, relating to its black plumage.

scot-free > *adverb* without suffering any punishment or injury.

ORIGIN – from obsolete *scot* 'tax'.

scotoma /skotōmə/ > *noun* (pl. **scotomas** or **scotomata** /skotōmətə/) Medicine a partial loss of vision or blind spot in an otherwise normal visual field.

ORIGIN – Greek *skotōma*, from *skotos* 'darkness'.

Scots > *adjective* another term for SCOTTISH. > *noun* the form of English used in Scotland.

COMBINATIONS – **Scots pine** a pine tree, now widely planted for commercial use, dominant in the old Caledonian pine forest of the Scottish Highlands.

Scotsman (or **Scotswoman**) > *noun* a person from Scotland.

Scotticism /skottisiz'm/ (also **Scoticism**) > *noun* a characteristically Scottish phrase, word, or idiom.

Scottie (also **Scottie dog**) > *noun informal* a Scottish terrier.

Scottish > *adjective* relating to Scotland or its people. > *noun* (**the Scottish**) the people of Scotland.

DERIVATIVES – **Scottishness** *noun*.

COMBINATIONS – **Scottish Nationalist** a member or supporter of Scottish nationalism or of the Scottish National Party. **Scottish terrier** a small rough-haired breed of terrier.

scoundrel > *noun* a dishonest or unscrupulous person.

DERIVATIVES – **scoundrelism** *noun* **scoundrelly** *adjective*.

SYNONYMS – blackguard, cad, good-for-nothing, rascal, rogue; archaic knave.

scour¹ > *verb* **1** clean or brighten by vigorous rubbing with an abrasive or detergent. **2** (of running water) erode (a channel or pool). > *noun* **1** the action of scouring or the state of being scoured. **2** (also **scours**) diarrhoea in livestock.

DERIVATIVES – **scourer** *noun*.

ORIGIN – Old French *escurer*, from Latin *excurare* 'clean (off)'.

scour² > *verb* **1** subject to a thorough search. **2** move rapidly.

ORIGIN – related to obsolete *scour* 'moving hastily'.

wordpower facts

Scottish

The terms **Scottish**, **Scot**, **Scots**, and **Scotch** are all variants of the same word, but in modern English they have developed different uses and connotations. The everyday adjective meaning 'of or relating to Scotland or its people' is **Scottish**, as in *Scottish hills* or *she's English, not Scottish*. The normal, neutral word for a person from Scotland is **Scot**, along with **Scotsman**, **Scotswoman**, and the plural form **the Scots** (or, less commonly, **the Scottish**). The word **Scotch**, used as an adjective meaning 'of or relating to Scotland' or as a noun meaning 'a person (or people) from Scotland', though widely used in the past by Scottish writers such as Robert Burns and Sir Walter Scott, is now disliked by many Scottish people and is regarded as old-fashioned in most contexts (though it survives in certain fixed phrases, such as *Scotch mist* and *Scotch whisky*). The adjective **Scots** tends to be used specifically in reference to the form of English spoken in Scotland, as in *a Scots accent*.

scourge > *noun* **1** historical a whip used as an instrument of punishment. **2** a person or thing causing great trouble or suffering. > *verb* **1** historical whip with a scourge. **2** cause great suffering to.
SYNONYMS – *noun* **2** affliction, bane, plague. *verb* **2** afflict, plague, torment.
ORIGIN – from Latin *ex-* 'thoroughly' + *corrigia* 'thong, whip'.

Scouse Brit. informal > *noun* **1** the dialect or accent of people from Liverpool. **2** (also **Scouser**) a person from Liverpool. > *adjective* relating to Liverpool.
ORIGIN – abbreviation of *lobscouse*, a stew formerly eaten by sailors.

scout > *noun* **1** a soldier or other person sent ahead of a main force to gather information about the enemy. **2** an instance of scouting. **3** (also **Scout**) a member of the Scout Association, a boys' organisation founded with the aim of developing character through outdoor activities. **4** a talent scout. > *verb* **1** make a detailed search of a place. **2** explore or examine so as to gather information. **3** act as a scout.
DERIVATIVES – **scouter** *noun* **scouting** *noun*.
ORIGIN – Old French *escouter* 'listen', from Latin *auscultare*.

scow /skow/ > *noun* a wide-beamed sailing dinghy.
ORIGIN – Dutch *schouw* 'ferry boat'.

scowl > *noun* an angry or bad-tempered expression. > *verb* frown in an angry or bad-tempered way.
SYNONYMS – frown, glare, glower, lour.

SCR > *abbreviation* Brit. Senior Common (or Combination) Room.

scrabble > *verb* **1** scratch or grope around with one's fingers to find or hold on to something. **2** move quickly and in a disorderly manner; scramble. > *noun* **1** an act of scrabbling. **2** (**Scrabble**) trademark a board game in which players build up words from small lettered squares or tiles.
ORIGIN – Dutch *schrabbelen*, from *schrabben* 'to scrape'.

scrag > *verb* (**scragged**, **scragging**) informal chiefly Brit. handle roughly; beat up. > *noun* **1** an unattractively thin person or animal. **2** archaic, informal the neck.
ORIGIN – perhaps an alteration of Scots and northern English *crag* 'neck'.

scrag-end > *noun* Brit. the inferior end of a neck of mutton.

scraggy > *adjective* (**scraggier**, **scraggiest**) **1** scrawny. **2** (also chiefly N. Amer. **scraggly**) ragged or untidy in form or appearance.

scram > *verb* (**scrammed**, **scramming**) informal go away or leave quickly.
ORIGIN – probably from **SCRAMBLE**.

scramble > *verb* **1** move or make one's way quickly and awkwardly, typically by using one's hands as well as one's feet. **2** make or become jumbled or muddled. **3** informal act in a hurried, disorderly, or undignified manner: *editors scrambled to finish the new dictionary*. **4** cook (beaten eggs with a little liquid) in a pan. **5** make (a broadcast transmission or telephone conversation) unintelligible unless received by an appropriate decoding device. **6** (with reference to fighter aircraft) take off or cause to take off immediately in an emergency or for action. > *noun* **1** an act of scrambling. **2** Brit. a motorcycle race over rough and hilly ground. **3** a disordered mixture.
SYNONYMS – *verb* **1** clamber, crawl, scrabble. **2** confuse, disorganise, jumble, mix up, muddle.
COMBINATIONS – **scrambled egg** (also **scrambled eggs**) a dish of eggs prepared by beating with a little liquid and then cooking and stirring gently.

scrambler > *noun* **1** a device for scrambling a transmission or conversation. **2** Brit. a motorcycle for racing over rough ground.

scrap¹ > *noun* **1** a small piece or amount of something, especially one that is left over after the greater part has been used. **2** (**scraps**) bits of uneaten food left after a meal. **3** material discarded for reprocessing. > *verb* (**scrapped**, **scrapping**) **1** remove from use or service, especially for conversion to scrap metal. **2** abolish or cancel (a plan, policy, or law).
SYNONYMS – *noun* **1** bit, fragment, piece, remnant, shred, snippet. *verb* **1** discard, dispose of, dump; informal junk. **2** abandon, abolish, axe, cancel, withdraw.
COMBINATIONS – **scrap heap** a pile of discarded materials or articles. **scrapyard** Brit. a place where scrap is collected before being discarded, reused, or recycled.

scrap² informal > *noun* a fight or quarrel, especially a minor or spontaneous one. > *verb* (**scrapped**, **scrapping**) **1** engage in such a fight or quarrel. **2** compete fiercely.
DERIVATIVES – **scrapper** *noun*.
ORIGIN – perhaps from **SCRAPE**.

scrapbook > *noun* a book of blank pages for sticking cuttings, drawings, or pictures in.

scrape > *verb* **1** drag or pull a hard or sharp implement across (a surface or object) **2** use a sharp or hard implement to remove (dirt or unwanted matter). **3** rub against a rough or hard surface. **4** just manage to achieve, succeed, or pass. **5** (**scrape by** or **along**) manage to live with difficulty. **6** (**scrape together** or **up**) collect or accumulate with difficulty. > *noun* **1** an act or sound of scraping. **2** an injury or mark caused by scraping. **3** informal an embarrassing or difficult predicament. **4** archaic an obsequious bow in which one foot is drawn backwards along the ground.
IDIOMS – **scrape the barrel** (or **the bottom of the barrel**) informal be reduced to using the last and poorest resources.
DERIVATIVES – **scraper** *noun* **scraping** *adjective & noun*.
ORIGIN – Old English 'scratch with the fingernails'.

scrapie /skraypi/ > *noun* a disease of sheep involving the central nervous system, characterised by a lack of coordination causing affected animals to rub against objects for support.
ORIGIN – from **SCRAPE**.

scrappy > *adjective* (**scrappier**, **scrappiest**) consisting of disorganised, untidy, or incomplete parts.
DERIVATIVES – **scrappily** *adverb* **scrappiness** *noun*.

scratch > *verb* **1** make a long superficial mark or wound on (a surface) with something sharp or pointed. **2** rub (a part of one's body) with one's fingernails to relieve itching. **3** (of a bird or mammal) rake the ground with the beak or claws in search of food. **4** (**scratch out**) cancel or strike out (writing). **5** withdraw from a competition. **6** cancel or abandon (an undertaking or project). **7** (**scratch around** or **along**) make a living or find resources with difficulty. > *noun* **1** a mark or wound made by scratching. **2** an act or spell of scratching. **3** informal a slight or insignificant wound or injury. > *adjective* assembled or made from whatever is available.

IDIOMS – **from scratch** from the very beginning. **scratch the surface** deal with a matter only in the most superficial way. **up to scratch** up to the required standard; satisfactory.

DERIVATIVES – **scratcher** *noun*.

SYNONYMS – *verb* **1** abrade, cut, score, scrape. *noun* **1** abrasion, cut, scratch.

COMBINATIONS – **scratch card** a card with a section or sections coated in an opaque waxy substance which may be scraped away to reveal whether a prize has been won.

ORIGIN – probably a blend of the synonymous dialect words *scrat* and *cratch*.

scratching > *noun* a technique used in rap music which involves stopping a record by hand and moving it back and forwards to give a rhythmic scratching effect.

scratchy > *adjective* (**scratchier**, **scratchiest**) **1** causing or characterised by scratching. **2** (of a voice or sound) rough; grating. **3** (of a record) making a crackling sound because of scratches on the surface.

scrawl > *verb* write in a hurried, careless way. > *noun* hurried, careless handwriting.

ORIGIN – apparently an alteration of CRAWL.

scrawny > *adjective* (**scrawnier**, **scrawniest**) unattractively thin and bony.

SYNONYMS – bony, emaciated, gaunt, scraggy, skeletal, skinny.

scream > *verb* **1** make a long, loud, piercing cry, especially expressing fear, pain, or excitement. **2** (of the wind, a machine, etc.) make a loud, high-pitched sound. **3** move very rapidly with or as if with such a sound. > *noun* **1** a screaming cry or sound. **2** (**a scream**) informal an irresistibly funny person or thing.

SYNONYMS – *verb* & *noun* **1** cry, howl, screech, shriek, squeal.

screamer > *noun* **1** a person or thing that makes a screaming sound. **2** informal a thing remarkable for speed or impact.

screamingly > *adverb* to a very great extent; extremely: *screamingly obvious*.

scree > *noun* a mass of small loose stones that form or cover a slope on a mountain.

ORIGIN – first as *screes*, probably from Old Norse *skritha* 'landslip'.

screech > *noun* a loud, harsh, piercing cry or sound. > *verb* **1** make a screech. **2** move rapidly with a screech.

DERIVATIVES – **screecher** *noun* **screechy** (**screechier**, **screechiest**) *adjective*.

COMBINATIONS – **screech owl** Brit. the barn owl.

screed > *noun* **1** a long speech or piece of writing. **2** a levelled layer of material applied to a floor or other surface.

DERIVATIVES – **screeding** *noun*.

ORIGIN – probably a variant of SHRED.

screen > *noun* **1** an upright partition used to divide a room, give shelter, or provide concealment. **2** something that provides shelter or concealment: *his car was parked behind a screen of trees.* **3** the surface of a cathode ray tube or similar electronic device, especially that of a television, VDU, or monitor, on which images and data are displayed. **4** a blank surface on which a photographic image is projected. **5** (**the screen**) films or television. **6** a windscreen of a motor vehicle. **7** a frame with fine wire netting used to keep out flying insects. > *verb* **1** conceal, protect, or shelter with a screen. **2** show (a film or video) or broadcast (a television programme). **3** protect from something dangerous or unpleasant. **4** test for the presence or absence of a disease. **5** investigate (someone), typically to ascertain suitability for a job.

DERIVATIVES – **screener** *noun* **screenful** *noun*.

SYNONYMS – *verb* **2** air, broadcast, show, televise, transmit. **3** guard, protect, safeguard, shelter, shield. **4** check, examine, scan, test. **5** check out, vet.

COMBINATIONS – **screen saver** Computing a program which replaces an unchanging screen display with a moving image to prevent damage to the phosphor.

ORIGIN – Old French *escren*.

screenplay > *noun* the script of a film, including acting instructions and scene directions.

screen-print > *verb* force ink on to (a surface) through a prepared screen of fine material so as to create a picture or pattern. > *noun* (**screen print**) a picture or design produced by screen-printing.

screen test > *noun* a filmed test to ascertain whether an actor is suitable for a film role. > *verb* (**screen-test**) give such a test to.

screenwriter > *noun* a person who writes a screenplay.

DERIVATIVES – **screenwriting** *noun*.

screw > *noun* **1** a thin, sharp-pointed metal pin with a spiral thread running around it and a slotted head, used to join things together by being rotated in under pressure. **2** a cylinder with a spiral ridge or thread running round the outside that can be turned to seal an opening, apply pressure, adjust position, etc. **3** an act of turning a screw. **4** (also **screw propeller**) a ship's or aircraft's propeller. **5** informal, derogatory a prison warder. **6** vulgar slang an act of sexual intercourse. > *verb* **1** fasten or tighten with a screw or screws. **2** rotate (something) so as to attach or remove it by means of a spiral thread. **3** informal cheat or swindle. **4** vulgar slang have sexual intercourse with.

WORDFINDER – countersink (*enlarge a hole so a screw can be inserted flush with the surface*),

grub screw (*small headless screw*), tap (*cut a thread to accept a screw*).

IDIOMS – **have one's head screwed on (the right way)** informal have common sense. **have a screw loose** informal be slightly eccentric or mentally disturbed. **screw up 1** crush into a tight mass. **2** informal cause to fail or go wrong. **3** informal make emotionally or mentally disturbed. **4** summon up (one's courage).

DERIVATIVES – **screwer** *noun*.

ORIGIN – Old French *escroue* 'female screw, nut', from Latin *scrofa* 'sow'.

screwball informal, chiefly N. Amer. > *noun* a crazy or eccentric person. > *adjective* **1** crazy; absurd. **2** referring to a style of fast-moving comedy film involving eccentric characters or ridiculous situations.

screwdriver > *noun* **1** a tool with a shaped tip that fits into the head of a screw to turn it. **2** a cocktail made from vodka and orange juice.

screwy > *adjective* (**screwier**, **screwiest**) informal, chiefly N. Amer. rather odd or eccentric.

scribble > *verb* **1** write or draw carelessly or hurriedly. **2** informal write for a living or as a hobby. > *noun* a piece of writing or a picture produced carelessly or hurriedly.

DERIVATIVES – **scribbler** *noun*.

ORIGIN – Latin *scribillare*, from *scribere* 'write'.

scribe > *noun* **1** historical a person who copied out documents. **2** informal, often humorous a writer, especially a journalist. **3** Jewish History an ancient Jewish record-keeper or, later, a professional theologian and jurist. **4** (also **scriber**) an awl used for making marks to guide a saw or in signwriting. > *verb* **1** chiefly literary write. **2** mark with a pointed instrument.

DERIVATIVES – **scribal** *adjective*.

ORIGIN – Latin *scriba*, from *scribere* 'write'.

scrim > *noun* **1** strong, coarse fabric used for heavy-duty lining or upholstery. **2** Theatre a piece of gauze cloth that appears opaque until lit from behind, used as a screen or backcloth. **3** chiefly N. Amer. something that conceals or obscures.

scrimmage > *noun* **1** a confused struggle or fight. **2** American Football a sequence of play beginning with the placing of the ball on the ground with its longest axis at right angles to the goal line. > *verb* American Football engage in a scrimmage.

ORIGIN – variant of SKIRMISH.

scrimp > *verb* be thrifty or parsimonious; economise.

ORIGIN – Scots, 'meagre'.

scrimshaw > *verb* adorn (shells, ivory, or other materials) with carved designs. > *noun* work done in such a way.

scrip > *noun* **1** a provisional certificate of money subscribed to a bank or company, entitling the holder to a formal certificate and dividends. **2** certificates of this type collectively. **3 Finance** an issue of additional shares to shareholders in proportion to the shares already held.

ORIGIN – abbreviation of *subscription receipt*.

script > *noun* **1** handwriting as distinct from print. **2** the written text of a play, film, or broadcast. **3** writing using a particular alphabet. **4 Brit.** a candidate's written answers in an examination. > *verb* write a script for.

ORIGIN – Latin *scriptum*, from *scribere* 'write'.

scriptural > *adjective* relating to the Bible.

scripture (also **scriptures**) > *noun* **1** the sacred writings of Christianity contained in the Bible. **2** the sacred writings of another religion.

WORDFINDER – *scriptures of major world religions:* Adi Granth (*Sikhism*), Avesta (*Zoroastrianism*), Bible (*Christianity*), Koran (*Islam*), Torah (*Judaism*), Tripitaka (*Theravada Buddhism*), Veda (*Hinduism*).

ORIGIN – Latin *scriptura* 'writings', from *scribere* 'write'.

scriptwriter > *noun* a person who writes a script for a play, film, or broadcast.

DERIVATIVES – **scriptwriting** *noun*.

scrivener /skrivvənər/ > *noun* historical a clerk, scribe, or notary.

ORIGIN – Old French *escrivein*, from Latin *scriba* (see SCRIBE).

scrofula /skrofyoolə/ > *noun* chiefly historical a disease with glandular swellings, probably a form of tuberculosis.

DERIVATIVES – **scrofulous** *adjective*.

ORIGIN – from Latin *scrofa* 'breeding sow' (said to be subject to the disease).

scroll > *noun* **1** a roll of parchment or paper for writing or painting on. **2** an ornamental design or carving resembling a partly unrolled scroll of parchment. > *verb* **1** move displayed text or graphics on a computer screen in order to view different parts of them. **2** cause to move like paper rolling or unrolling.

DERIVATIVES – **scrollable** *adjective* **scroller** *noun* **scrolling** *noun*.

COMBINATIONS – **scroll bar** a long, thin section at the edge of a computer display by which material can be scrolled using a mouse. **scrollwork** decoration consisting of spiral lines or patterns.

ORIGIN – alteration of obsolete *scrow* 'roll', shortening of ESCROW.

scrolled > *adjective* having an ornamental design or carving resembling a scroll.

Scrooge > *noun* a person who is mean with money.

ORIGIN – from the name of Ebenezer *Scrooge*, a miserly curmudgeon in Charles Dickens's story *A Christmas Carol* (1843).

scrotum /skrōtəm/ > *noun* (pl. **scrota**

/skrōtə/ or **scrotums**) a pouch of skin containing the testicles.

DERIVATIVES – **scrotal** *adjective*.

ORIGIN – Latin.

scrounge informal > *verb* seek to obtain (something) at the expense of others or by stealth. > *noun* an act or the action of scrounging.

DERIVATIVES – **scrounger** *noun*.

ORIGIN – variant of dialect *scrunge* 'steal'.

scrub¹ > *verb* (**scrubbed**, **scrubbing**) **1** rub hard so as to clean. **2** informal cancel or abandon. **3** (**scrub up**) thoroughly clean one's hands and arms before performing surgery. > *noun* **1** an act of scrubbing. **2** a semi-abrasive cosmetic lotion used to cleanse the skin. **3** (**scrubs**) hygienic clothing worn by surgeons during operations.

ORIGIN – probably from Low German or Dutch.

scrub² > *noun* **1** vegetation consisting mainly of brushwood or stunted forest growth. **2** (also **scrubs**) land covered with such vegetation. **3** (before another noun) denoting a shrubby or small form of a plant.

DERIVATIVES – **scrubby** *adjective*.

ORIGIN – from SHRUB¹.

scrubber > *noun* **1** a person or thing that scrubs. **2** an apparatus using water or a solution for purifying gases or vapours. **3** Brit. informal, derogatory a sexually promiscuous woman.

scruff¹ > *noun* the back of a person's or animal's neck.

scruff² > *noun* Brit. informal a scruffy person.

ORIGIN – variant of SCURF.

scruffy > *adjective* (**scruffier**, **scruffiest**) shabby and untidy or dirty.

DERIVATIVES – **scruffily** *adverb* **scruffiness** *noun*.

SYNONYMS – bedraggled, dishevelled, frowzy, messy, raggle-taggle, unkempt.

ANTONYMS – smart, tidy.

scrum > *noun* **1** Rugby an ordered formation of players in which the forwards of each team push against each other with heads down and the ball is thrown in. **2** Brit. informal a disorderly crowd.

scrummage > *noun* fuller form of SCRUM.

ORIGIN – variant of SCRIMMAGE.

scrummy > *adjective* (**scrummier**, **scrummiest**) informal delicious.

ORIGIN – from SCRUMPTIOUS.

scrump > *verb* Brit. informal steal (fruit) from an orchard or garden.

ORIGIN – from dialect *scrump* 'withered apple'.

scrumptious > *adjective* informal extremely delicious or attractive.

scrumpy > *noun* Brit. rough strong cider, especially as made in the West Country of England.

scrunch > *verb* **1** make a loud crunching

noise. **2** crush or squeeze into a compact mass. > *noun* a loud crunching noise.

scrunchy > *adjective* making a loud crunching noise when crushed or compressed. > *noun* (also **scrunchie**) (pl. **scrunchies**) chiefly Brit. a circular band of fabric-covered elastic for fastening the hair.

scruple > *noun* **1** a feeling of doubt as to the morality or propriety of an action. **2** historical a unit of weight equal to 20 grains used by apothecaries. > *verb* hesitate to do something that one thinks may be wrong.

SYNONYMS – *noun* **1** doubt, misgiving, qualm, reservation.

ORIGIN – Latin *scrupus* 'rough pebble', (figuratively) 'anxiety'.

scrupulous /skrōōpyooləss/ > *adjective* **1** diligent and thorough. **2** very concerned to avoid doing wrong.

DERIVATIVES – **scrupulosity** *noun* **scrupulously** *adverb* **scrupulousness** *noun*.

SYNONYMS – **1** conscientious, diligent, fastidious, meticulous, punctilious, thorough. **2** honest, honourable, principled, upright, upstanding.

ANTONYMS – **1** careless. **2** dishonest, unscrupulous.

scrutineer > *noun* **1** a person who examines something closely and thoroughly. **2** chiefly Brit. a person who supervises the conduct of an election or competition.

scrutinise (also **scrutinize**) > *verb* examine closely and thoroughly.

SYNONYMS – analyse, examine, inspect, study; formal peruse.

scrutiny > *noun* (pl. **scrutinies**) critical observation or examination.

SYNONYMS – analysis, appraisal, examination, inspection, study; formal perusal.

ORIGIN – Latin *scrutinium*, from *scrutari* 'to search' (originally 'sort rubbish', from *scruta* 'rubbish').

scry /skrī/ > *verb* (**scries**, **scried**) foretell the future, especially using a crystal ball.

ORIGIN – shortening of DESCRY.

SCSI /skuzzi/ > *abbreviation* Computing small computer system interface.

scuba /skōōbə/ > *noun* an aqualung.

ORIGIN – acronym from *self-contained underwater breathing apparatus*.

scuba-diving > *noun* the sport or pastime of swimming underwater using a scuba.

DERIVATIVES – **scuba-dive** *verb* **scuba-diver** *noun*.

scud > *verb* (**scudded**, **scudding**) move fast in a straight line because or as if driven by the wind. > *noun* **1** chiefly literary vaporous clouds or spray driven fast by the wind. **2** the action of scudding.

ORIGIN – perhaps from SCUT, reflecting the sense 'race like a hare'.

scuff > *verb* **1** scrape (a shoe or other object) against something. **2** mark by scuffing. **3** drag (one's feet) when walking. > *noun* a mark made by scuffing.

scuffle > *noun* a short, confused fight or struggle. > *verb* **1** engage in a scuffle. **2** move in a hurried, confused, or shuffling manner.
ORIGIN – probably of Scandinavian origin.

scull > *noun* **1** each of a pair of small oars used by a single rower. **2** an oar placed over the stern of a boat to propel it with a side to side motion. **3** a light, narrow boat propelled with a scull or a pair of sculls. > *verb* propel a boat with sculls.
DERIVATIVES – **sculler** *noun*.

scullery > *noun* (pl. **sculleries**) a small kitchen or room at the back of a house used for washing dishes and other dirty household work.
ORIGIN – from Old French *escuele* 'dish', from Latin *scutella* 'salver'.

scullion /**skul**yən/ > *noun* archaic a servant assigned the most menial kitchen tasks.
ORIGIN – perhaps related to **SCULLERY**.

sculpt > *verb* create or represent by sculpture.

sculptor > *noun* (fem. **sculptress**) an artist who makes sculptures.

sculpture > *noun* **1** the art of making three-dimensional representative or abstract forms, especially by carving or casting. **2** a work of such a kind. > *verb* **1** make or represent by sculpture. **2** (**sculptured**) formed or shaped as if by sculpture, especially with strong, smooth curves.
DERIVATIVES – **sculptural** *adjective* **sculpturing** *noun*.
ORIGIN – from Latin *sculpere* 'carve'.

scum > *noun* **1** a layer of dirt or froth on the surface of a liquid. **2** informal a worthless or contemptible person or group of people. > *verb* (**scummed**, **scumming**) cover or become covered with a layer of scum.
DERIVATIVES – **scummy** (**scummier**, **scummiest**) *adjective*.
COMBINATIONS – **scumbag** informal a contemptible person.
ORIGIN – Low German or Dutch.

scumble Art > *verb* give a softer or duller effect to (a picture or colour) by applying a very thin coat of opaque paint. > *noun* paint applied in this way.
ORIGIN – perhaps from the verb **SCUM**.

scunge /skunj/ > *noun* Austral./NZ informal a disagreeable person.
DERIVATIVES – **scungy** (**scungier**, **scungiest**) *adjective*.

scupper[1] > *noun* a hole in a ship's side to allow water to run away from the deck.
ORIGIN – perhaps from Old French *escopir* 'to spit'.

scupper[2] > *verb* chiefly Brit. **1** scuttle (a ship). **2**

informal prevent from working or succeeding; thwart.
ORIGIN – first used as military slang in the sense 'kill, especially in an ambush'.

scurf > *noun* flakes on the surface of the skin that form as fresh skin develops below, occurring especially as dandruff.
DERIVATIVES – **scurfy** *adjective*.
ORIGIN – Old English, from the base of words meaning 'gnaw' and 'cut to shreds'.

scurrilous /**skurr**iləss/ > *adjective* making scandalous claims about someone in order to damage their reputation.
DERIVATIVES – **scurrility** (pl. **scurrilities**) *noun*.
SYNONYMS – calumnious, defamatory, denigratory, deprecatory, disparaging.
ORIGIN – Latin *scurrilus*, from *scurra* 'buffoon'.

scurry > *verb* (**scurries**, **scurried**) move hurriedly with short quick steps. > *noun* a situation of hurried and confused movement.
SYNONYMS – *verb* bustle, scamper, scuttle; informal beetle.
ORIGIN – abbreviation of *hurry-scurry*, from **HURRY**.

scurvy > *noun* a disease caused by a deficiency of vitamin C, characterised by bleeding gums and the opening of previously healed wounds. > *adjective* (**scurvier**, **scurviest**) archaic worthless or contemptible.
ORIGIN – from **SCURF**.

scut > *noun* the short tail of a hare, rabbit, or deer.

scutter chiefly Brit. > *verb* move hurriedly with short steps. > *noun* an act or sound of scuttering.
ORIGIN – perhaps from **SCUTTLE**[2].

scuttle[1] > *noun* **1** a metal container used to store coal for a domestic fire. **2** Brit. the part of a car's bodywork between the windscreen and the bonnet.
ORIGIN – Latin *scutella* 'dish'.

scuttle[2] > *verb* run hurriedly or furtively with short quick steps. > *noun* an act or sound of scuttling.
ORIGIN – from **SCUD**.

scuttle[3] > *verb* **1** sink (one's own ship) deliberately. **2** deliberately cause (a scheme) to fail. > *noun* an opening with a lid in a ship's deck or side.
ORIGIN – perhaps from Spanish *escotilla* 'hatchway'.

scuttlebutt > *noun* informal, chiefly N. Amer. rumour; gossip.
ORIGIN – from *scuttled butt*: originally referring to a water butt on the deck of a ship, providing drinking water.

scuzz > *noun* informal, chiefly N. Amer. a disgusting person or thing.
DERIVATIVES – **scuzzy** *adjective*.

ORIGIN – probably an abbreviation of *disgusting*.

scythe > *noun* a tool used for cutting crops such as grass or corn, with a long curved blade at the end of a long pole. > *verb* **1** cut with a scythe. **2** move through or penetrate rapidly and forcefully.

Scythian /**si**thiən/ > *noun* a person from Scythia, an ancient region of SE Europe and Asia. > *adjective* relating to Scythia.

SD > *abbreviation* South Dakota.

SDI > *abbreviation* Strategic Defense Initiative.

SDLP > *abbreviation* (in Northern Ireland) Social Democratic and Labour Party.

SE > *abbreviation* **1** south-east. **2** south-eastern.

Se > *symbol* the chemical element selenium.

sea > *noun* **1** the expanse of salt water that covers most of the earth's surface and surrounds its land masses. **2** a roughly definable area of this. **3** a vast expanse or quantity.
WORDFINDER – marine, thalassic (*relating to the sea*), maritime (*relating to shipping or the sea*); oceanography (*scientific study of the sea*), pelagic (*of or inhabiting the open sea*), plankton (*tiny organisms floating in the sea*), thalassotherapy (*therapeutic or cosmetic use of seawater*).
IDIOMS – **at sea 1** sailing on the sea. **2** (also **all at sea**) confused; uncertain. **one's sea legs** one's ability to keep one's balance and not feel seasick on board a ship.
DERIVATIVES – **seaward** *adjective* & *adverb* **seawards** *adverb*.
COMBINATIONS – **sea anchor** an object dragged in the water behind a boat in order to keep its bows pointing into the waves or to lessen leeway. **sea anemone** a marine coelenterate with a tube-shaped body which bears a ring of stinging tentacles around the mouth. **sea bass** a marine fish with a spiny dorsal fin, resembling the freshwater perch. **seabird** a bird that frequents the sea or coast. **sea bream** a deep-bodied marine fish that resembles the freshwater bream. **sea breeze** a breeze blowing towards the land from the sea. **sea change** a profound or notable transformation. [ORIGIN – from Shakespeare's *Tempest* (I. ii. 403).] **sea cow** a sirenian, especially a manatee. **sea cucumber** an echinoderm having a thick worm-like body with tentacles around the mouth. **sea dog** informal an old or experienced sailor. **seagrass** eelgrass or a similar grass-like plant that grows near the sea. **sea green** a pale bluish green colour. **seagull** a gull. **sea horse** a small marine fish with an upright posture and a head and neck suggestive of a horse. **seakale** a maritime plant of the cabbage family cultivated for its edible young shoots. **sea**

level the level of the sea's surface, used in reckoning the height of geographical features and as a barometric standard. **sea lion** an eared seal, the large male of which has a mane on the neck and shoulders. **Sea Lord** either of two senior officers in the Royal Navy (**First Sea Lord, Second Sea Lord**) serving originally as members of the Admiralty Board (now of the Ministry of Defence). **sea mile** a unit of distance equal to a minute of arc of a great circle, varying between approximately 2,014 yards (1,842 metres) at the equator and 2,035 yards (1,861 metres) at the pole. **sea room** clear space at sea for a ship to turn or manoeuvre in. **sea salt** salt produced by the evaporation of seawater. **sea slug** a shell-less marine mollusc with external gills and a number of appendages on the upper surface. **sea squirt** a marine animal (a tunicate) which has a bag-like body with orifices through which water flows in and out. **sea trout** Brit. a brown trout of a salmon-like migratory race. **sea urchin** a marine echinoderm which has a shell covered in mobile spines. **sea wall** a wall or embankment erected to prevent the sea encroaching on an area of land.

seabed > *noun* the ground under the sea; the ocean floor.

seaboard > *noun* a region bordering the sea; the coastline.

seaborgium /see**bor**giəm/ > *noun* a very unstable chemical element made by high-energy atomic collisions.

ORIGIN – named after the American nuclear chemist Glenn *Seaborg* (1912–99).

SeaCat > *noun* trademark a large, high-speed catamaran used as a passenger and car ferry on short sea crossings.

seafaring > *adjective* travelling by sea. > *noun* travel by sea.

DERIVATIVES – **seafarer** *noun.*

seafood > *noun* shellfish and sea fish served as food.

seafront > *noun* the part of a coastal town next to and directly facing the sea.

seagoing > *adjective* **1** (of a ship) suitable for voyages on the sea. **2** relating to sea travel.

seal¹ > *noun* **1** a device or substance used to join two things together or render something impervious. **2** the state of being joined or rendered impervious with a seal. **3** a piece of wax with an individual design stamped into it, attached to a document as a guarantee of authenticity. **4** a confirmation or guarantee: *a seal of approval.* **5** an engraved device used for stamping a seal. > *verb* **1** fasten or close securely. **2** (**seal off**) isolate (an area) by preventing entrance to and exit from it. **3** apply a non-porous coating to (a surface) to make it impervious. **4** conclude, establish, or secure

definitively. **5** authenticate (a document) with a seal.

DERIVATIVES – **sealable** *adjective.*

SYNONYMS – *verb* **1** close, fasten, lock, plug, secure, shut. **2** (**seal off**) close off, cordon off, fence off, isolate, shut off. **4** clinch, close, settle.

COMBINATIONS – **sealing wax** a mixture of shellac and rosin with turpentine and pigment, softened by heating and used to make seals.

ORIGIN – Latin *sigillum* 'small picture', from *signum* 'a sign'.

seal² > *noun* a fish-eating aquatic mammal with a streamlined body and feet developed as flippers. > *verb* hunt for seals.

sealant > *noun* material used for rendering something airtight or watertight.

sealer¹ > *noun* a device or substance used to seal something.

sealer² > *noun* a ship or person engaged in hunting seals.

seam > *noun* **1** a line where two pieces of fabric are sewn together in a garment or other article. **2** an underground layer of a mineral such as coal or gold. **3** a line where the edges of two pieces of wood or other material touch each other. > *verb* join with a seam.

seaman > *noun* **1** a sailor, especially one below the rank of officer. **2** the lowest rank in the US navy, below petty officer.

DERIVATIVES – **seamanlike** *adjective* **seamanship** *noun.*

seam bowler > *noun* Cricket a bowler who makes the ball deviate by causing it to bounce on its seam.

DERIVATIVES – **seam bowling** *noun.*

seamless > *adjective* smooth and without seams or obvious joins.

DERIVATIVES – **seamlessly** *adverb.*

seamstress /**seem**strəss/ > *noun* a woman who sews, especially as a job.

ORIGIN – from archaic *seamster* 'tailor, seamstress'.

seamy > *adjective* (**seamier, seamiest**) sordid and disreputable.

seance /**say**ONss/ > *noun* a meeting at which people attempt to make contact with the dead.

ORIGIN – French, from Latin *sedere* 'sit'.

seaplane > *noun* an aircraft with floats or skis instead of wheels, designed to land on and take off from water.

seaport > *noun* a town or city with a harbour for seagoing ships.

sear > *verb* **1** burn or scorch with a sudden intense heat. **2** (of pain) be experienced as a sudden burning sensation. **3** brown (food) quickly at a high temperature. > *adjective* (also **sere**) literary withered.

DERIVATIVES – **searingly** *adverb.*

search > *verb* **1** (often **search for**) try to find something by looking or otherwise seeking

carefully and thoroughly. **2** examine (a place or person) thoroughly in order to find something. **3** (**searching**) scrutinising thoroughly, especially in a disconcerting way. > *noun* an act of searching.

IDIOMS – **search me!** informal I do not know.

DERIVATIVES – **searchable** *adjective* **searcher** *noun* **searchingly** *adverb.*

SYNONYMS – *verb* **1** forage, hunt, look, seek. **2** comb, examine, ransack, scour.

COMBINATIONS – **search engine** Computing a program for the retrieval of data, files, or documents from a database or network, especially the Internet. **search party** a group of people organised to look for someone or something. **search warrant** a legal document authorising a police officer or other official to enter and search premises.

wordpower facts
Search

The change in spelling undergone by the word **search**, following its adoption into English from French, obscures its origins. It is actually linked etymologically, as well as notionally, with the concept of 'going round in circles'. It comes via Old French *cerchier* from Latin *circare*, meaning 'go round', from *circus* 'circle, ring' (ultimately from Greek *kuklos*). The words **circle** and **cycle**, and **circus** itself, are from the same source.

searchlight > *noun* a powerful outdoor electric light with a concentrated beam that can be turned in the required direction.

seascape > *noun* a view or picture of an expanse of sea.

seashell > *noun* the shell of a marine mollusc.

seashore > *noun* **1** an area of sandy, stony, or rocky land bordering and level with the sea. **2** Law the land between high- and low-water marks.

seasick > *adjective* suffering from nausea caused by the motion of a ship at sea.

DERIVATIVES – **seasickness** *noun.*

seaside > *noun* a place by the sea, especially a beach area or holiday resort.

season > *noun* **1** each of the four divisions of the year (spring, summer, autumn, and winter) marked by particular weather patterns and daylight hours. **2** a period of the year characterised by an activity or event, especially a particular sport. **3** the time of year when a particular fruit, vegetable, etc., is plentiful and in good condition. **4** (usu. in phrase **in season**) a period when a female mammal is ready to mate. **5** (**the season**) the time of year traditionally marked by fashionable upper-class social events. **6** archaic a proper or suitable time. > *verb* **1** add salt, herbs, or spices to (food). **2** add an enlivening quality or feature to. **3** keep (wood) so as to dry it for use as timber. **4** (**seasoned**) accustomed to particular conditions; experienced.

COMBINATIONS – **season ticket** a ticket allowing travel within a particular period or admission to a series of events.

ORIGIN – Old French *seson*, from Latin *satio* 'sowing', later 'time of sowing'.

seasonable > *adjective* **1** appropriate to a particular season of the year. **2** archaic coming at the right time; opportune.

USAGE – **seasonable** and **seasonal** do not mean exactly the same thing: **seasonable** means 'appropriate to a particular season of the year', as in *a seasonable Christmas Carol*, whereas **seasonal**, a much commoner word, means 'determined by or characteristic of the time of year', as in *a seasonal climate* or *seasonal employment*.

seasonal > *adjective* **1** relating to or characteristic of a particular season of the year. **2** fluctuating according to the season.

DERIVATIVES – **seasonality** *noun* **seasonally** *adverb*.

COMBINATIONS – **seasonal affective disorder** depression associated with late autumn and winter and thought to be caused by a lack of light.

seasoning > *noun* salt, herbs, or spices added to food to enhance the flavour.

seat > *noun* **1** a thing made or used for sitting on. **2** the horizontal part of a chair. **3** a sitting place for a passenger in a vehicle or for a member of an audience. **4** a person's buttocks. **5** chiefly Brit. a place in an elected parliament or council. **6** Brit. a parliamentary constituency. **7** a site or location. **8** a large country house and estate belonging to an aristocratic family. **9** a part of a machine that supports or guides another part. **10** a manner of sitting on a horse. > *verb* **1** arrange for (someone) to sit somewhere. **2** (**seat oneself** or **be seated**) sit down. **3** (of a place) have sufficient seats for.

DERIVATIVES – **seating** *noun* **seatless** *adjective*.

COMBINATIONS – **seat belt** a belt used to secure someone in the seat of a motor vehicle or aircraft.

ORIGIN – Old Norse, related to SIT.

seaway > *noun* a waterway or channel used by or capable of accommodating ships.

seaweed > *noun* large algae growing in the sea or on rocks below the high-water mark.

WORDFINDER – bladderwrack, carragean, fucus, kelp, laver, sargassum, wrack (*types of seaweed*).

seaworthy > *adjective* (of a boat) in a good enough condition to sail on the sea.

DERIVATIVES – **seaworthiness** *noun*.

sebaceous /si**bay**shəss/ > *adjective* technical relating to oil, fat, or sebum.

COMBINATIONS – **sebaceous gland** a gland in the skin which secretes oily matter into the hair follicles to lubricate the skin and hair.

ORIGIN – Latin *sebaceus*, from *sebum* 'tallow'.

sebum /**see**bəm/ > *noun* the oily secretion of the sebaceous glands.

ORIGIN – Latin *sebum* 'grease'.

sec[1] > *abbreviation* secant.

sec[2] > *noun* informal a second or a very short space of time.

sec[3] > *adjective* (of wine) dry.

ORIGIN – from Latin *siccus*.

secant /**see**kənt/ > *noun* **1** Mathematics the ratio of the hypotenuse (in a right-angled triangle) to the shorter side adjacent to an acute angle. **2** Geometry a straight line that cuts a curve in two or more parts.

ORIGIN – from Latin *secare* 'to cut'.

secateurs /sekkə**turz**/ > *plural noun* chiefly Brit. a pair of pruning clippers for use with one hand.

ORIGIN – from French *sécateur* 'cutter', from Latin *secare* 'to cut'.

secede /si**seed**/ > *verb* withdraw formally from membership of a federal union or a political or religious organisation.

ORIGIN – Latin *secedere*, from *se-* 'apart' + *cedere* 'go'.

secession /si**sesh**'n/ > *noun* the action of seceding from a federation or organisation.

DERIVATIVES – **secessionism** *noun*.

seclude > *verb* keep (someone) away from other people.

ORIGIN – Latin *secludere*, from *se-* 'apart' + *claudere* 'to shut'.

secluded > *adjective* (of a place) not seen or visited by many people; sheltered and private.

SYNONYMS – concealed, hidden, isolated, private, sheltered, unfrequented.

seclusion > *noun* the state of being private and away from other people.

second[1] /**sekk**ənd/ > *ordinal number* **1** constituting number two in a sequence; 2nd. **2** subordinate or inferior in position, rank, or importance. **3** secondly. **4** (**seconds**) goods of an inferior quality. **5** (**seconds**) informal a second course or second helping of food at a meal. **6** Brit. denoting the second highest division in the results of the examinations for a university degree. **7** an attendant assisting a combatant in a duel or boxing match. > *verb* **1** formally support or endorse (a nomination or resolution) before adoption or further discussion. **2** express agreement with.

DERIVATIVES – **seconder** *noun* **secondly** *adverb*.

COMBINATIONS – **second chamber** the upper house of a parliament with two chambers. **Second Coming** Christian Theology the prophesied return of Christ to Earth at the Last Judgement. **second-degree 1** Medicine denoting burns that cause blistering but not permanent scars. **2** Law, chiefly N. Amer. denoting a category of a crime that is less serious than a first-degree crime. **second-generation 1** referring to the offspring of parents who have immigrated to a particular country. **2** of a more advanced stage of technology than previous models or systems. **second in command** the officer next in authority to the commanding or chief officer. **second lieutenant** a rank of officer in the army and the US air force, above warrant officer or chief warrant officer and below lieutenant or first lieutenant. **second name** Brit. a surname. **second nature** a tendency or habit that has become instinctive. **second officer** (also **second mate**) an assistant mate on a merchant ship. **second person** see PERSON (sense 3). **second sight** the supposed ability to perceive future or distant events; clairvoyance. **second string** an alternative resource or course of action in case another one fails. **second thoughts** a change of opinion or resolve reached after reconsideration. **second wind** regained ability to breathe freely during exercise, after having been out of breath.

ORIGIN – Latin *secundus* 'following, second', from *sequi* 'follow'.

second[2] /**sekk**ənd/ > *noun* **1** the unit of time in the SI system, equal to one-sixtieth of a minute. **2** informal a very short time. **3** (also **arc second** or **second of arc**) a sixtieth of a minute of angular distance.

COMBINATIONS – **second hand** an extra hand in some watches and clocks which moves round to indicate the seconds.

ORIGIN – Latin *secunda minuta* 'second minute', from *secundus*, referring to the 'second' operation of dividing an hour by sixty.

second[3] /si**kond**/ > *verb* Brit. temporarily transfer (a worker) to another position.

DERIVATIVES – **secondee** *noun* **secondment** *noun*.

ORIGIN – from French *en second* 'in the second rank (of officers)'.

secondary > *adjective* **1** coming after, less important than, or resulting from something primary. **2** relating to education for children from the age of eleven to sixteen or eighteen.

DERIVATIVES – **secondarily** *adverb*.

COMBINATIONS – **secondary industry** industry that converts raw materials into commodities and products; manufacturing industry. **secondary modern school** chiefly historical (in the UK) a secondary school for children not selected for grammar or technical schools. **secondary picketing** Brit. picketing of a firm not directly involved in a particular dispute. **secondary sexual characteristics** physical characteristics developed at puberty which distinguish between the sexes but are not involved in reproduction.

second best > *adjective* next after the best. > *noun* a less adequate or less desirable alternative.

second class > *noun* 1 a set of people or things grouped together as the second best. 2 the second-best accommodation in an aircraft, train, or ship. 3 Brit. the second-highest division in the results of the examinations for a university degree. > *adjective & adverb* of the second-best quality or in the second class.

second-guess > *verb* 1 anticipate or predict (someone's actions or thoughts) by guesswork. 2 judge (someone) with hindsight.

second-hand > *adjective & adverb* 1 (of goods) having had a previous owner; not new. 2 accepted on another's authority and not from original investigation.

IDIOMS – **at second hand** by hearsay rather than direct observation or experience.

second hand > *noun* an extra hand in some watches and clocks which moves round to indicate the seconds.

second-rate > *adjective* of mediocre or inferior quality.

DERIVATIVES – **second-rater** *noun*.

secret > *adjective* 1 not known or seen or not meant to be known or seen by others. 2 fond of having or keeping secrets; secretive. > *noun* 1 something kept or meant to be kept secret. 2 a valid but not commonly known method of achieving something: *the secret of a happy marriage.* 3 something not properly understood; a mystery: *the secrets of the universe.*

DERIVATIVES – **secrecy** *noun* **secretly** *adverb*.

SYNONYMS – *adjective* 1 clandestine, classified, concealed, covert, hidden, private. 2 enigmatic, furtive, mysterious, secretive, tight-lipped.

ANTONYMS – *adjective* 1 public. 2 open.

COMBINATIONS – **secret agent** a spy acting for a country. **secret police** a police force working in secret against a government's political opponents. **secret service** 1 a government department concerned with espionage. 2 (**Secret Service**) (in the US) a branch of the Treasury Department dealing with counterfeiting and providing protection for the President. **secret society**

an organisation whose members are sworn to secrecy about its activities.

ORIGIN – Latin *secretus* 'separate, set apart', from *secernere*, from *se-* 'apart' + *cernere* 'sift'.

secretaire /sekri**tair**/ > *noun* a small writing desk.

ORIGIN – French, 'secretary'.

secretariat /sekri**tair**iət/ > *noun* a governmental administrative office or department.

secretary /**sekk**rəteri/ > *noun* (pl. **secretaries**) 1 a person employed to assist with correspondence, keep records, etc. 2 an official of a society or other organisation who conducts its correspondence and keeps its records. 3 the principal assistant of a UK government minister or ambassador.

DERIVATIVES – **secretarial** *adjective*.

COMBINATIONS – **secretary bird** a slender long-legged African bird of prey that feeds on snakes, having a crest likened to a quill pen stuck behind the ear. **Secretary General** (pl. **Secretaries General**) the title of the principal administrator of some organisations. **Secretary of State** 1 (in the UK) the head of a major government department. 2 (in the US) the head of the State Department, responsible for foreign affairs.

ORIGIN – Latin *secretarius* 'confidential officer', from *secretum* 'a secret': originally in the sense 'person entrusted with a secret'.

secrete¹ /si**kreet**/ > *verb* (of a cell, gland, or organ) produce by secretion: *insulin is secreted by the pancreas.*

DERIVATIVES – **secretor** *noun* **secretory** *adjective*.

secrete² /si**kreet**/ > *verb* conceal; hide.

ORIGIN – from the obsolete verb *secret* 'keep secret'.

secretion > *noun* 1 a process by which substances are produced and discharged from a cell, gland, or organ for a particular function in the organism or for excretion. 2 a substance discharged in such a way.

ORIGIN – Latin 'separation', from *secernere* 'move apart'.

secretive /**see**kritiv/ > *adjective* inclined to conceal feelings and intentions or not to disclose information.

DERIVATIVES – **secretively** *adverb* **secretiveness** *noun*.

SYNONYMS – enigmatic, mysterious, reserved, tight-lipped, uncommunicative.

ANTONYMS – communicative, open.

sect > *noun* 1 a religious group or faction regarded as heretical or as deviating from orthodox tradition. 2 a group with extreme or dangerous philosophical or political ideas.

ORIGIN – Latin *secta* 'following', from *sequi* 'follow'.

sectarian > *adjective* 1 concerning or deriving from a sect or sects. 2 carried out on the grounds of membership of a sect or other group: *sectarian killings.* > *noun* a member or follower of a sect.

DERIVATIVES – **sectarianism** *noun*.

section > *noun* 1 any of the more or less distinct parts into which something is divided or from which it is made up. 2 a distinct group within a larger body of people or things. 3 the shape resulting from cutting a solid by or along a plane. 4 a representation of the internal structure of something as if it has been cut through. 5 Biology a thin slice of plant or animal tissue prepared for microscopic examination. 6 Surgery a separation by cutting. 7 NZ a building plot. > *verb* 1 divide into sections. 2 Surgery divide by cutting. 3 Brit. (often **be sectioned**) commit compulsorily to a psychiatric hospital (in accordance with a section of the Mental Health Act).

DERIVATIVES – **sectional** *adjective*.

SYNONYMS – *noun* 1,2 component, division, part, piece, portion, segment.

ORIGIN – Latin, from *secare* 'to cut'.

sectionalism > *noun* 1 restriction of interest to parochial rather than general concerns. 2 undue concern with petty distinctions.

DERIVATIVES – **sectionalist** *noun* & *adjective*.

sector > *noun* 1 an area or portion that is distinct from others. 2 a distinct part of an economy, society, or sphere of activity. 3 a subdivision of an area for military operations. 4 the plane figure enclosed by two radii of a circle or ellipse and the arc between them. 5 a mathematical instrument consisting of two arms hinged at one end and marked with sines, tangents, etc. for making diagrams.

DERIVATIVES – **sectoral** *adjective*.

ORIGIN – Latin, 'cutter'.

secular /**sek**yoolər/ > *adjective* 1 having no religious, sacred, or spiritual aspect. 2 (of clergy) not subject to or bound by religious rule. 3 occurring once every century or similarly long period. 4 Economics (of a fluctuation or trend) occurring or persisting over an indefinitely long period. > *noun* a secular priest.

DERIVATIVES – **secularise** (also **secularize**) *verb* **secularism** *noun* **secularist** *noun* **secularity** *noun* **secularly** *adverb*.

SYNONYMS – 1 earthly, lay, non-religious, profane, temporal, worldly.

ANTONYMS – 1 religious, sacred.

ORIGIN – Latin *saecularis* 'relating to an age or period', from *saeculum* 'generation', used in Christian Latin to mean 'the world'.

secure > *adjective* 1 certain to remain safe and unthreatened. 2 fixed or fastened so as not to give way, become loose, or be lost. 3

feeling free from fear or anxiety. **4** protected against attack, burglary, etc. **5** (of a place of detention) having provisions against the escape of inmates. > *verb* **1** protect against danger or threat. **2** make secure; fix or fasten securely. **3** succeed in obtaining. **4** seek to guarantee repayment of (a loan) by having a right to take possession of an asset in the event of non-payment.

DERIVATIVES – **securable** *adjective* **securely** *adverb* **securement** *noun* **secureness** *noun*.

SYNONYMS – *adjective* **1** certain, safe, sound, steady. **2** fast, fastened, firm, fixed, solid, tight. **3** at ease, safe, unworried. **4** defended, guarded, protected, safe. *verb* **1** defend, guard, preserve, protect, shelter, shield. **3** acquire, gain, get, obtain.

ANTONYMS – *adjective* **1** insecure, uncertain.

ORIGIN – Latin *securus*, from *se-* 'without' + *cura* 'care'.

securitise (also **securitize**) > *verb* convert (an asset, especially a loan) into marketable securities, typically for the purpose of raising cash.

DERIVATIVES – **securitisation** *noun*.

security > *noun* (pl. **securities**) **1** the state of being or feeling secure. **2** the safety of a state or organisation against criminal activity such as terrorism or espionage. **3** a thing deposited or pledged as a guarantee of the fulfilment of an undertaking or the repayment of a loan, to be forfeited in case of default. **4** a certificate attesting credit, the ownership of stocks or bonds, etc.

COMBINATIONS – **security blanket 1** a blanket or other familiar object which is a comfort to a child. **2** Brit. an official sanction imposed on information in order to maintain complete secrecy.

sedan /si**dan**/ > *noun* **1** an enclosed chair carried between two horizontal poles, common in the 17th and 18th centuries. **2** chiefly N. Amer. a car for four or more people.

ORIGIN – Latin *sella* 'saddle'.

sedate[1] > *adjective* **1** calm and unhurried. **2** staid and rather dull.

DERIVATIVES – **sedately** *adverb* **sedateness** *noun*.

SYNONYMS – **1** calm, comfortable, gentle, leisurely, relaxed, unhurried. **2** conventional, sober, staid, stuffy.

ORIGIN – from Latin *sedare* 'settle', from *sedere* 'sit': originally used also as a medical term in the sense 'not sore or painful'.

sedate[2] > *verb* put under sedation.

sedation > *noun* the administering of a sedative drug to produce a state of calm or sleep.

ORIGIN – Latin, from *sedare* 'settle'.

sedative /**sedd**ətiv/ > *adjective* promoting calm or inducing sleep. > *noun* a sedative drug.

sedentary /**sedd**əntri/ > *adjective* **1** sitting; seated. **2** tending to sit down a lot; taking little physical exercise. **3** tending to stay in the same place for much of the time.

DERIVATIVES – **sedentarily** *adverb* **sedentariness** *noun*.

ORIGIN – Latin *sedentarius*, from *sedere* 'sit': originally in the sense 'not migratory'.

sedge > *noun* a grass-like plant with triangular stems and inconspicuous flowers, growing typically in wet ground.

COMBINATIONS – **sedge warbler** a common migratory songbird with streaky brown plumage, frequenting marshes and reed beds.

sediment > *noun* **1** matter that settles to the bottom of a liquid. **2** Geology material carried in particles by water or wind and deposited on the land surface or seabed. > *verb* settle or deposit as sediment.

WORDFINDER – alluvium (*fertile sedimentary deposit*), delta (*triangular area of sediment at the mouth of a river*), lees (*sediment of wine*), moraine (*a mass of rock and sediment carried down and deposited by a glacier*), silt (*fine material carried by running water and deposited as sediment*).

DERIVATIVES – **sedimentation** *noun*.

ORIGIN – Latin *sedimentum* 'settling'.

sedimentary > *adjective* **1** relating to sediment. **2** Geology (of rock) formed from sediment deposited by water or wind.

sedition > *noun* conduct or speech inciting rebellion against the authority of a state or monarch.

DERIVATIVES – **seditious** *adjective* **seditiously** *adverb*.

ORIGIN – Latin, from *sed-* 'apart' + *itio* 'going'.

seduce > *verb* **1** persuade to do something inadvisable. **2** entice into sexual activity.

DERIVATIVES – **seducer** *noun* **seducible** *adjective* **seduction** *noun* **seductress** *noun*.

ORIGIN – Latin *seducere*, from *se-* 'away' + *ducere* 'to lead'.

seductive > *adjective* having a quality that attracts or tempts people.

DERIVATIVES – **seductively** *adverb* **seductiveness** *noun*.

SYNONYMS – alluring, attractive, enticing, inviting, tantalising, tempting.

sedulous /**sed**yooləss/ > *adjective* showing dedication and diligence.

DERIVATIVES – **sedulity** /si**dyōo**liti/ *noun* **sedulously** *adverb* **sedulousness** *noun*.

ORIGIN – Latin *sedulus* 'zealous'.

sedum /**see**dəm/ > *noun* a plant of a large group having fleshy leaves and small star-shaped flowers.

ORIGIN – Latin.

see[1] > *verb* (**sees**, **seeing**; past **saw**; past participle **seen**) **1** perceive with the eyes. **2** experience or witness. **3** deduce after reflection or from information. **4** regard in a specified way. **5** regard as a possibility; envisage. **6** meet (someone one knows) socially or by chance. **7** meet regularly as a boyfriend or girlfriend. **8** consult (a specialist or professional). **9** give an interview or consultation to. **10** escort to a specified place. **11** (**see to**) attend to. **12** (**see that**) ensure that.

IDIOMS – **see about** attend to; deal with. **see off 1** accompany (a person who is leaving) to their point of departure. **2** Brit. repel or deter (an intruder, aggressor, etc.). **see out** Brit. **1** last longer than the life of. **2** come to the end of (a period of time or undertaking). **see over** tour and examine. **see right** Brit. informal reward or look after appropriately. **see something of** spend some time with (someone) socially. **see through 1** support (a person) for the duration of a difficult time. **2** persist with (an undertaking) until it is completed. **3** detect the true nature of.

DERIVATIVES – **seeable** *adjective*.

SYNONYMS – **1** discern, glimpse, perceive; literary behold, espy. **3** appreciate, apprehend, comprehend, grasp, understand. **5** anticipate, envisage, foresee, visualise.

see[2] > *noun* the seat of authority of a bishop or archbishop, centred on a cathedral church.

ORIGIN – Latin *sedes* 'seat'.

seed > *noun* **1** a flowering plant's unit of reproduction, capable of developing into another such plant. **2** the beginning of a feeling, process, or condition. **3** archaic a man's semen. **4** archaic (chiefly in biblical use) offspring or descendants. **5** any of a number of stronger competitors in a sports tournament who have been assigned a position in an ordered list to ensure they do not play each other in the early rounds. > *verb* **1** sow (land) with seeds. **2** produce or drop seeds. **3** remove the seeds from. **4** initiate the development or growth of. **5** give (a competitor) the status of seed in a tournament. **6** drop crystals into (a cloud) to cause rain.

WORDFINDER – seminal (*relating to or derived from a seed*).

IDIOMS – **go** (or **run**) **to seed 1** cease flowering as the seeds develop. **2** deteriorate; weaken. **3** fail to maintain one's appearance or standards.

DERIVATIVES – **seeded** *adjective* **seedless** *adjective*.

COMBINATIONS – **seed cake** cake containing caraway seeds. **seed corn 1** good-quality corn kept for seed. **2** Brit. assets set aside for the generation of future profit. **seed head** a flower head in seed. **seed leaf** Botany a cotyledon. **seed money** (also **seed capital**) money allocated to initiate a project. **seed pearl** a very small pearl. **seed**

potato a potato intended for replanting to produce a new plant.

ORIGIN – Old English, related to SOW[1].

seedbed > *noun* a bed of fine soil in which seedlings are germinated.

seeder > *noun* **1** a machine for sowing seed. **2** a plant that produces seeds in a particular way or under particular conditions.

seedling > *noun* a young plant raised from seed.

seedsman > *noun* a person who deals in seeds as a profession.

seedy > *adjective* (**seedier**, **seediest**) **1** unkempt or dirty, and generally not respectable in appearance. **2** dated unwell.

DERIVATIVES – **seedily** *adverb* **seediness** *noun*.

SYNONYMS – **1** disreputable, seamy, sleazy, sordid, squalid, unsavoury.

seeing > *conjunction* (usu. **seeing as** or **that**) because; since. > *noun* **1** the action of perceiving or observing. **2** Astronomy the quality of observed images as determined by atmospheric conditions.

IDIOMS – **seeing is believing** proverb you need to see something before you can accept that it really exists or occurs.

seek > *verb* (past and past participle **sought**) **1** try to find or obtain. **2** (**seek out**) search for and find. **3** (**seek to**) make an effort to (do something). **4** ask for.

DERIVATIVES – **seeker** *noun*.

SYNONYMS – **1** hunt for, inquire after, look for, search for. **3** (**seek to**) aim to, aspire to, endeavour to, strive to. **4** request, solicit.

seem > *verb* **1** give the impression of being. **2** (**cannot seem to**) appear to be unable to (do something), despite having tried.

ORIGIN – from an Old Norse word meaning 'fitting': originally also in the sense 'be appropriate'.

seeming > *adjective* **1** apparent. **2** giving the impression of having a specified quality: *an angry-seeming man*.

DERIVATIVES – **seemingly** *adverb*.

seemly > *adjective* conforming to propriety or good taste.

DERIVATIVES – **seemliness** *noun*.

SYNONYMS – appropriate, becoming, correct, decent, decorous, proper.

ANTONYMS – improper, unseemly.

seen past participle of SEE[1].

seep > *verb* (of a liquid) flow or leak slowly through porous material or small holes.

DERIVATIVES – **seepage** *noun*.

seer /seer/ > *noun* a person of supposed supernatural insight who sees visions of the future.

seersucker > *noun* a fabric with a puckered surface.

ORIGIN – from a Persian phrase meaning 'milk and sugar' (with reference to the alternating stripes in which the fabric was originally woven).

see-saw > *noun* **1** a long plank balanced on a fixed support, on each end of which children sit and move up and down by pushing the ground with their feet. **2** a situation characterised by repeated alternation between two states or positions. > *verb* repeatedly change from one state or position to another and back again.

ORIGIN – from SAW[1].

seethe > *verb* **1** (of a liquid) boil or be turbulent as if boiling. **2** be filled with intense but unexpressed anger. **3** be crowded with people or things.

SYNONYMS – **1** boil, bubble, foam, simmer. **2** fume, rage, simmer. **3** swarm, teem.

ORIGIN – Old English, 'make or keep boiling'.

see-through > *adjective* transparent or translucent.

segment /**seg**mənt/ > *noun* **1** each of the parts into which something is divided. **2** Geometry a part of a circle cut off by a chord, or a part of a sphere cut off by a plane not passing through the centre. **3** Zoology each of a series of similar anatomical units of which the body and appendages of some animals are composed. > *verb* /usu. seg**ment**/ divide into segments.

DERIVATIVES – **segmental** *adjective* **segmentary** *adjective* **segmentation** *noun*.

SYNONYMS – *noun* **1** bit, division, part, piece, portion, section.

ORIGIN – Latin *segmentum*, from *secare* 'to cut'.

segregate /**seg**rigayt/ > *verb* **1** set apart from the rest or from each other. **2** separate along racial, sexual, or religious lines.

DERIVATIVES – **segregation** *noun* **segregational** *adjective* **segregationist** *adjective* & *noun*.

ORIGIN – Latin *segregare* 'separate from the flock'.

segue /**seg**way/ > *verb* (**segues**, **segued**, **segueing**) (in music and film) move without interruption from one song, melody, or scene to another. > *noun* an instance of this.

ORIGIN – Italian, 'follows'.

seicento /say**chen**tō/ > *noun* the style of Italian art and literature of the 17th century.

DERIVATIVES – **seicentist** *noun*.

ORIGIN – Italian, '600', shortened from *mille seicento* '1600'.

seigneur /say**nyör**/ (also **seignior** /**say**nyər/) > *noun* a feudal lord; the lord of a manor.

DERIVATIVES – **seigneurial** *adjective*.

ORIGIN – Old French, from Latin *senior* 'older, elder'.

seine /sayn/ > *noun* a fishing net which hangs vertically in the water with floats at the top and weights at the bottom edge, the ends being drawn together to encircle the fish. > *verb* fish or catch with a seine.

DERIVATIVES – **seiner** *noun*.

ORIGIN – Greek *sagēnē*.

seismic /**sīz**mik/ > *adjective* **1** relating to earthquakes or other vibrations of the earth and its crust. **2** of enormous proportions or effect.

DERIVATIVES – **seismical** *adjective* **seismically** *adverb*.

ORIGIN – from Greek *seismos* 'earthquake'.

seismicity /sīz**miss**iti/ > *noun* Geology the occurrence or frequency of earthquakes in a region.

seismogram /**sīz**məgram/ > *noun* a record produced by a seismograph.

seismograph /**sīz**məgraaf/ > *noun* an instrument that measures and records the force and duration of earthquakes.

DERIVATIVES – **seismographic** *adjective*.

seismology /sīz**moll**əji/ > *noun* the branch of science concerned with earthquakes and related phenomena.

DERIVATIVES – **seismological** *adjective* **seismologist** *noun*.

seismometer /sīz**momm**itər/ > *noun* another term for SEISMOGRAPH.

seismosaurus /sīzməsə**saw**rəss/ > *noun* a huge late Jurassic plant-eating dinosaur with a long neck and tail.

ORIGIN – from Greek *seismos* 'earthquake' + *sauros* 'lizard'.

seize* > *verb* **1** take hold of suddenly and forcibly. **2** take forcible possession of. **3** (of the police or another authority) take possession of by warrant or legal right. **4** take (an opportunity) eagerly and decisively. **5** (**seize on** or **upon**) take eager advantage of. **6** (of a machine or part in a machine) become jammed.

DERIVATIVES – **seizable** *adjective* **seizer** *noun*.

*SPELLING – contrary to the usual rule, the *e* comes before the *i*: seize.

SYNONYMS – **1** grab, grasp, snatch. **2** appropriate, capture, commandeer, take. **3** confiscate, impound, requisition, sequester, sequestrate.

ORIGIN – Latin *sacire*, in the phrase *ad proprium sacire* 'claim as one's own'.

seizure > *noun* **1** the action of seizing. **2** a sudden attack of illness, especially a stroke or an epileptic fit.

seldom > *adverb* not often; rarely. > *adjective* dated infrequent.

ORIGIN – Old English, from a base meaning 'strange, wonderful'.

select > *verb* carefully choose as being the best or most suitable. > *adjective* **1** carefully chosen as being among the best. **2** used by or consisting of a wealthy or sophisticated elite.

DERIVATIVES – **selectable** *adjective* **selectness** *noun*.

SYNONYMS – *verb* choose, decide on, pick, settle on, single out. *adjective* **1** choice, chosen, favoured, hand-picked. **2** elite, exclusive, privileged.

COMBINATIONS – **select committee** a small parliamentary committee appointed for a special purpose.

ORIGIN – Latin *seligere* 'choose'.

selection > *noun* **1** the action or fact of selecting. **2** a number of selected things. **3** a range of things from which a choice may be made. **4** a horse or horses tipped as worth bets in a race or meeting. **5** Biology the evolutionary process which determines which types of organism thrive; natural selection.

selective > *adjective* **1** relating to or involving selection. **2** tending to choose carefully. **3** (of a process or agent) affecting some things and not others.

DERIVATIVES – **selectively** *adverb* **selectiveness** *noun* **selectivity** *noun*.

selector > *noun* **1** a person appointed to select a team in a sport. **2** a device for selecting a particular gear or other setting of a machine or device.

selenite /ˈselɪnʌɪt/ > *noun* a form of gypsum occurring as transparent crystals or thin plates.

ORIGIN – Greek *selēnitēs lithos* 'moonstone'.

selenium /sɪˈliːnɪəm/ > *noun* a grey, crystalline, non-metallic chemical element with semiconducting properties.

DERIVATIVES – **selenide** *noun*.

ORIGIN – from Greek *selēnē* 'moon'.

self > *noun* (pl. **selves**) **1** a person's essential being that distinguishes them from others. **2** a person's particular nature or personality: *he was back to his old self.* > *pronoun* (pl. **selves**) **1** oneself. **2** used on counterfoils, cheques, and other papers to refer to the holder or person who has signed. > *adjective* (of a trimming, woven design, etc.) of the same material or colour as the rest. > *verb* chiefly Botany self-pollinate; self-fertilise.

self- > *combining form* **1** of or directed towards oneself or itself: *self-hatred.* **2** by one's own efforts; by its own action: *self-adjusting.* **3** on, in, for, or relating to oneself or itself: *self-adhesive.*

self-abandonment (also **self-abandon**) > *noun* the action of completely surrendering oneself to a desire or impulse.

DERIVATIVES – **self-abandoned** *adjective*.

self-absorption > *noun* preoccupation with one's own emotions, interests, or situation.

DERIVATIVES – **self-absorbed** *adjective*.

self-abuse > *noun* **1** behaviour which causes damage or harm to oneself. **2** euphemistic masturbation.

self-addressed > *adjective* (of an envelope) bearing one's own address.

self-adhesive > *adjective* adhering without requiring moistening.

self-adjusting > *adjective* (chiefly of machinery) adjusting itself to meet varying requirements.

DERIVATIVES – **self-adjustment** *noun*.

self-advertisement > *noun* the active publicising of oneself.

DERIVATIVES – **self-advertiser** *noun* **self-advertising** *adjective*.

self-affirmation > *noun* the recognition and assertion of the existence and value of one's individual self.

self-appointed > *adjective* having assumed a position or role without the endorsement of others.

self-assembly > *noun* the construction of a piece of furniture from materials sold as a set of parts.

DERIVATIVES – **self-assemble** *verb*.

self-assertion > *noun* the confident and forceful expression or promotion of oneself or one's views.

DERIVATIVES – **self-assertive** *adjective* **self-assertiveness** *noun*.

self-assessment > *noun* **1** assessment of oneself or one's performance in relation to an objective standard. **2** calculation of one's own taxable liability.

self-assurance > *noun* confidence in one's own abilities or character.

DERIVATIVES – **self-assured** *adjective*.

self-awareness > *noun* conscious knowledge of one's own character, feelings, motives, and desires.

DERIVATIVES – **self-aware** *adjective*.

self-cancelling > *adjective* **1** having elements which contradict or negate one another. **2** (of a mechanical device) designed to stop working automatically when no longer required.

self-catering Brit. > *adjective* (of a holiday or accommodation) offering facilities for people to cook their own meals. > *noun* the action of catering for oneself.

self-censorship > *noun* the exercising of control over what one says and does.

self-centred > *adjective* preoccupied with oneself and one's affairs.

DERIVATIVES – **self-centredly** *adverb* **self-centredness** *noun*.

self-certification > *noun* **1** the practice of attesting something about oneself in a formal statement, rather than asking a disinterested party to do so. **2** the practice, for the purpose of claiming sick pay, by which an employee rather than a doctor declares in writing that an absence was due to illness.

DERIVATIVES – **self-certificate** *noun*.

self-certify > *verb* Brit. **1** attest (one's financial standing) in a formal statement. **2**

(**self-certified**) (of a loan or mortgage) obtained as a result of such self-certification.

self-colour > *noun* **1** a single uniform colour. **2** the natural colour of something.

DERIVATIVES – **self-coloured** *adjective*.

self-conceit > *noun* another term for SELF-CONGRATULATION.

self-confessed > *adjective* openly admitting to having certain characteristics.

DERIVATIVES – **self-confessedly** *adverb*.

self-confidence > *noun* a feeling of trust in one's abilities, qualities, and judgement.

DERIVATIVES – **self-confident** *adjective* **self-confidently** *adverb*.

SYNONYMS – aplomb, assurance, composure, poise, self-assurance.

ANTONYMS – diffidence.

self-congratulation > *noun* undue pride regarding one's achievements or qualities.

DERIVATIVES – **self-congratulatory** *adjective*.

self-conscious > *adjective* **1** nervous or awkward because unduly aware of oneself or one's actions. **2** (especially of an action) deliberate and with full awareness.

DERIVATIVES – **self-consciously** *adverb* **self-consciousness** *noun*.

SYNONYMS – **1** awkward, embarrassed, uncomfortable.

self-consistent > *adjective* not having conflicting parts or aspects; consistent.

DERIVATIVES – **self-consistency** *noun*.

self-contained > *adjective* **1** complete, or having all that is needed, in itself. **2** chiefly Brit. (of accommodation) having its own kitchen and bathroom, and typically its own private entrance. **3** not depending on or influenced by others.

DERIVATIVES – **self-containment** *noun*.

self-contradiction > *noun* inconsistency between aspects or parts of a whole.

DERIVATIVES – **self-contradicting** *adjective* **self-contradictory** *adjective*.

self-control > *noun* the ability to control one's emotions or behaviour in difficult situations.

DERIVATIVES – **self-controlled** *adjective*.

SYNONYMS – composure, coolness, restraint, self-discipline.

self-deception > *noun* the action or practice of deceiving oneself into believing that a false or unvalidated feeling, idea, or situation is true.

DERIVATIVES – **self-deceit** *noun* **self-deceiver** *noun* **self-deceiving** *adjective* **self-deceptive** *adjective*.

self-defeating > *adjective* (of an action or policy) unable to achieve the end it is designed to bring about.

self-defence > *noun* the defence of oneself or one's interests, especially the defence of one's person through physical force, permitted in certain cases as an answer to a charge of violent crime.

DERIVATIVES – **self-defensive** *adjective*.

self-denial > *noun* the denial of one's own interests and needs.

DERIVATIVES – **self-denying** *adjective*.

self-deprecating > *adjective* modest about or critical of oneself.

DERIVATIVES – **self-deprecatingly** *adverb* **self-deprecation** *noun* **self-deprecatory** *adjective*.

self-depreciatory > *adjective* another term for **SELF-DEPRECATING**.

DERIVATIVES – **self-depreciation** *noun*.

self-destruct > *verb* explode or disintegrate automatically, having been preset to do so.

self-destructive > *adjective* destroying or causing harm to oneself.

DERIVATIVES – **self-destruction** *noun* **self-destructively** *adverb*.

self-determination > *noun* **1** the process by which a country determines its own statehood and forms its own allegiances and government. **2** the process by which a person controls their own life.

self-directed > *adjective* **1** (of an emotion, statement, or activity) directed at one's self. **2** (of an activity) under one's own control.

DERIVATIVES – **self-direction** *noun*.

self-discipline > *noun* the ability to control one's feelings and overcome one's weaknesses.

DERIVATIVES – **self-disciplined** *adjective*.

self-doubt > *noun* lack of confidence in oneself and one's abilities.

self-drive > *adjective* **1** Brit. (of a hired vehicle) driven by the hirer. **2** (of a holiday) involving use of one's own car rather than transport arranged by the operator.

self-educated > *adjective* educated largely through one's own efforts, rather than by formal instruction.

DERIVATIVES – **self-education** *noun*.

self-effacing > *adjective* not claiming attention for oneself.

DERIVATIVES – **self-effacement** *noun* **self-effacingly** *adverb*.

self-employed > *adjective* working for oneself as a freelance or the owner of a business rather than for an employer.

DERIVATIVES – **self-employment** *noun*.

self-enclosed > *adjective* (of a person, community, or system) not choosing or able to communicate with others or with external systems.

self-esteem > *noun* confidence in one's own worth or abilities.

SYNONYMS – confidence, pride, self-confidence, self-respect, self-worth.

self-evaluation > *noun* another term for **SELF-ASSESSMENT**.

self-evident > *adjective* not needing to be demonstrated or explained; clearly perceived or understood.

DERIVATIVES – **self-evidence** *noun* **self-evidently** *adverb*.

self-examination > *noun* **1** the study of one's behaviour and motivations. **2** the examination of one's body for signs of illness.

self-explanatory > *adjective* not needing explanation; clearly understood.

self-expression > *noun* the expression of one's feelings or thoughts, especially in writing, art, music, or dance.

DERIVATIVES – **self-expressive** *adjective*.

self-fertile > *adjective* Botany (of a plant) capable of self-fertilisation.

DERIVATIVES – **self-fertility** *noun*.

self-fertilisation (also **self-fertilization**) > *noun* Biology the fertilisation of plants and some invertebrate animals by their own pollen or sperm.

DERIVATIVES – **self-fertilise** *verb*.

self-financing > *adjective* (of an organisation or enterprise) having or generating enough income to finance itself.

DERIVATIVES – **self-financed** *adjective*.

self-fulfilling > *adjective* (of an opinion or prediction) bound to be proved correct or to come true as a result of behaviour caused by its being expressed.

self-governing > *adjective* responsible for administering its own affairs; independent or autonomous.

DERIVATIVES – **self-governed** *adjective* **self-government** *noun*.

self-heal > *noun* a purple-flowered plant of the mint family, formerly used for healing wounds.

self-help > *noun* the use of one's own efforts and resources to achieve things without relying on others.

selfhood > *noun* the quality that constitutes one's individuality.

self-identification > *noun* the action of regarding certain characteristics or qualities as belonging to oneself.

self-image > *noun* the idea one has of one's abilities, appearance, and personality.

self-immolation > *noun* the offering of oneself as a sacrifice, especially by burning.

self-importance > *noun* an exaggerated sense of one's own value or importance.

DERIVATIVES – **self-important** *adjective* **self-importantly** *adverb*.

SYNONYMS – arrogance, bumptiousness, conceit, pomposity, sententiousness.

ANTONYMS – humility.

self-improvement > *noun* the improvement of one's knowledge, status, or character by one's own efforts.

self-induced > *adjective* brought about by oneself.

self-indulgent > *adjective* indulging or tending to indulge one's desires.

DERIVATIVES – **self-indulgence** *noun* **self-indulgently** *adverb*.

SYNONYMS – decadent, extravagant, hedonistic, indulgent, sybaritic.

self-inflicted > *adjective* (of a wound or other harm) inflicted on oneself by one's own actions.

self-interest > *noun* one's personal interest or advantage, especially when pursued without regard for others.

DERIVATIVES – **self-interested** *adjective*.

self-involved > *adjective* wrapped up in oneself or one's own thoughts.

DERIVATIVES – **self-involvement** *noun*.

selfish > *adjective* concerned chiefly with one's own personal profit or pleasure at the expense of consideration for others.

DERIVATIVES – **selfishly** *adverb* **selfishness** *noun*.

SYNONYMS – egocentric, inconsiderate, self-centred, self-serving.

ANTONYMS – selfless, unselfish.

selfless > *adjective* concerned more with the needs and wishes of others than with one's own.

DERIVATIVES – **selflessly** *adverb* **selflessness** *noun*.

SYNONYMS – altruistic, considerate, self-denying, self-sacrificing, unselfish.

ANTONYMS – inconsiderate, selfish.

self-limiting > *adjective* Medicine (of a condition) ultimately resolving itself without treatment.

self-love > *noun* regard for one's own well-being and happiness.

self-made > *adjective* **1** having become successful or rich by one's own efforts. **2** made by oneself.

self-management > *noun* **1** management of or by oneself. **2** the distribution of political control to individual regions of a state, especially as a form of socialism.

DERIVATIVES – **self-managing** *adjective*.

self-motivated > *adjective* motivated to do something because of one's own enthusiasm or interest, without needing pressure from others.

DERIVATIVES – **self-motivating** *adjective* **self-motivation** *noun*.

self-mutilation > *noun* deliberate injury to one's own body.

self-opinionated > *adjective* having an arrogantly high regard for oneself or one's own opinions.

self-parody > *noun* the intentional or inadvertent parodying of one's own behaviour, style, etc.

DERIVATIVES – **self-parodic** *adjective* **self-parodying** *adjective*.

self-perpetuating > *adjective* perpetuating itself without external intervention.

DERIVATIVES – **self-perpetuation** *noun*.

self-pity > *noun* excessive concern with and unhappiness over one's own troubles.

DERIVATIVES – **self-pitying** *adjective* **self-pityingly** *adverb*.

self-policing > *noun* the process of keeping order or maintaining control within a community without accountability or reference to an external authority.

self-pollination > *noun* Botany the pollination of a flower by pollen from the same plant.

DERIVATIVES – **self-pollinate** *verb* **self-pollinator** *noun*.

self-portrait > *noun* a portrait by an artist of himself or herself.

DERIVATIVES – **self-portraiture** *noun*.

self-possessed > *adjective* calm, confident, and in control of one's feelings.

DERIVATIVES – **self-possession** *noun*.

self-preservation > *noun* the protection of oneself from harm or death, especially regarded as a basic instinct in human beings and animals.

self-proclaimed > *adjective* proclaimed to be such by oneself, without endorsement by others.

self-propelled > *adjective* moving or able to move without external propulsion or intervention.

DERIVATIVES – **self-propelling** *adjective*.

self-raising flour > *noun* Brit. flour that has a raising agent already added.

self-realisation (also **self-realization**) > *noun* fulfilment of one's own potential.

self-referential > *adjective* (especially of a literary or other creative work) making reference to itself, its creator, or their other work.

DERIVATIVES – **self-referentiality** *noun* **self-referentially** *adverb*.

self-regard > *noun* **1** consideration for oneself. **2** vanity.

DERIVATIVES – **self-regarding** *adjective*.

self-regulating > *adjective* regulating itself without intervention from external bodies.

DERIVATIVES – **self-regulation** *noun* **self-regulatory** *adjective*.

self-reliance > *noun* reliance on one's own powers and resources rather than those of others.

DERIVATIVES – **self-reliant** *adjective*.

self-respect > *noun* pride and confidence in oneself.

DERIVATIVES – **self-respecting** *adjective*.

SYNONYMS – confidence, dignity, pride, self-esteem.

self-restraint > *noun* self-control.

DERIVATIVES – **self-restrained** *adjective*.

self-revealing > *adjective* revealing one's character or motives, especially inadvertently.

DERIVATIVES – **self-revelation** *noun* **self-revelatory** *adjective*.

self-righteous > *adjective* certain that one is totally correct or morally superior.

DERIVATIVES – **self-righteously** *adverb* **self-righteousness** *noun*.

SYNONYMS – holier-than-thou, priggish, sanctimonious, superior.

self-righting > *adjective* (of a boat) designed to right itself when capsized.

self-rule > *noun* self-government.

self-sacrifice > *noun* the giving up of one's own interests or wishes in order to help others or advance a cause.

DERIVATIVES – **self-sacrificial** *adjective* **self-sacrificing** *adjective*.

selfsame > *adjective* (**the selfsame**) the very same.

self-satisfied > *adjective* smugly complacent.

DERIVATIVES – **self-satisfaction** *noun*.

self-seal (also **self-sealing**) > *adjective* (of an envelope) having a self-adhesive flap.

self-seed > *verb* (of a plant) propagate itself by seed.

DERIVATIVES – **self-seeder** *noun*.

self-seeking > *adjective* pursuing one's own welfare and interests before those of others.

DERIVATIVES – **self-seeker** *noun*.

self-selection > *noun* **1** the action of putting oneself forward for something. **2** the action of selecting something for oneself.

DERIVATIVES – **self-selecting** *adjective*.

self-service > *adjective* (of a shop, restaurant, etc.) at which customers select goods for themselves and pay at a checkout. > *noun* a self-service system or outlet.

self-serving > *adjective* self-seeking.

self-sow > *verb* (of a plant) self-seed.

self-starter > *noun* a self-motivated and ambitious person who acts on their own initiative.

self-styled > *adjective* using a description or title that one has given oneself: *self-styled experts.*

self-sufficient > *adjective* **1** able to satisfy one's basic needs without outside help, especially with regard to the production of food. **2** emotionally and intellectually independent.

DERIVATIVES – **self-sufficiency** *noun* **self-sufficiently** *adverb*.

self-supporting > *adjective* **1** having the resources to be able to survive without outside assistance. **2** staying up or upright without support.

DERIVATIVES – **self-support** *noun*.

self-surrender > *noun* the surrender of oneself or one's will to an emotion or to some external influence.

self-sustaining > *adjective* able to continue in a healthy state without outside assistance.

DERIVATIVES – **self-sustained** *adjective*.

self-tapping > *adjective* (of a screw) able to

cut a thread in the material into which it is inserted.

self-taught > *adjective* having acquired knowledge or skill on one's own initiative rather than through formal instruction or training.

self-timer > *noun* a mechanism in a camera that introduces a delay between the operation of the shutter release and the opening of the shutter, enabling the photographer to be included in the photograph.

self-willed > *adjective* determinedly pursuing one's own wishes.

DERIVATIVES – **self-will** *noun*.

self-worth > *noun* self-esteem.

sell > *verb* (past and past participle **sold**) **1** hand over in exchange for money. **2** deal in. **3** (of goods) attain sales. **4** (**sell out**) sell all of one's stock of something. **5** (**sell up**) sell all of one's property or assets. **6** persuade someone of the merits of. **7** (**sell out**) betray (someone) for one's own financial or material benefit. **8** (**sell short**) fail to recognise or state the true value of. **9** (**sell out**) abandon one's principles for reasons of expedience.

IDIOMS – **sell one's soul (to the devil)** be willing to do anything, no matter how wrong it is, in order to achieve one's objective.

DERIVATIVES – **sellable** *adjective*.

SYNONYMS – **1,2** barter, exchange, peddle, trade.

COMBINATIONS – **selling point** a feature of a product for sale that makes it attractive to customers.

sell-by date > *noun* **1** chiefly Brit. a date marked on a perishable product indicating the recommended time by which it should be sold. **2** informal a time after which something or someone is no longer considered desirable or effective.

seller > *noun* **1** a person who sells. **2** a product that sells in a specified way.

IDIOMS – **seller's market** an economic situation in which goods or shares are scarce and sellers can ask high prices.

sell-off > *noun* a sale of assets, typically at a low price, carried out in order to dispose of them rather than as normal trade.

Sellotape Brit. > *noun* trademark transparent adhesive tape. > *verb* fasten or stick with Sellotape.

ORIGIN – from CELLULOSE + TAPE.

sell-out > *noun* **1** the selling of an entire stock of something. **2** an event for which all tickets are sold. **3** a sale of a business or company. **4** a betrayal.

seltzer /seltsər/ > *noun* dated carbonated mineral water.

ORIGIN – from German *Selterser*, from *Niederselters* in Germany, where a medicinal mineral water was produced.

selvedge /**sel**vij/ (chiefly N. Amer. also **selvage**) > *noun* an edge produced on woven fabric during manufacture that prevents it from unravelling.
ORIGIN – from **SELF** + **EDGE**, on the pattern of Dutch *selfegghe*.

selves plural of **SELF**.

semantic /si**man**tik/ > *adjective* relating to meaning in language or logic.
DERIVATIVES – **semantically** *adverb* **semanticity** *noun*.
ORIGIN – Greek *sēmantikos* 'significant'.

semantics > *plural noun* (usu. treated as sing.) **1** the branch of linguistics and logic concerned with meaning. **2** the meaning of a word, phrase, sentence, or text.
DERIVATIVES – **semanticist** *noun*.

semaphore > *noun* **1** a system of sending messages by holding the arms or two flags or poles in certain positions according to an alphabetic code. **2** an apparatus for signalling in this way, consisting of an upright with movable parts. > *verb* send by semaphore.
DERIVATIVES – **semaphoric** *adjective* **semaphorically** *adverb*.
ORIGIN – French *sémaphore*, from Greek *sēma* 'sign' + *-phoros* 'bearing'.

semblance > *noun* the outward appearance or apparent form of something.
ORIGIN – from Old French *sembler* 'seem', from Latin *similare* 'simulate'.

semen /**see**mən/ > *noun* the male reproductive fluid, containing spermatozoa in suspension.
ORIGIN – Latin, 'seed'.

semester /si**mes**tər/ > *noun* a half-year term in a school or university, especially in North America, typically lasting for fifteen to eighteen weeks.
ORIGIN – from Latin *semestris* 'six-monthly'.

semi > *noun* (pl. **semis**) informal **1** Brit. a semi-detached house. **2** a semi-final.

semi- > *prefix* **1** half: *semicircular*. **2** partly; in some degree: *semi-conscious*.
ORIGIN – Latin.

semiaquatic > *adjective* **1** (of an animal) living partly on land and partly in water. **2** (of a plant) growing in very wet or waterlogged ground.

semi-automatic > *adjective* **1** partially automatic. **2** (of a firearm) having a mechanism for automatic loading but not for continuous firing.

semi-basement > *noun* a storey of a building partly below ground level.

semibreve /**semm**ibreev/ > *noun* Music, chiefly Brit. a note having the time value of two minims or four crotchets, represented by a ring with no stem.

semicircle > *noun* a half of a circle or of its circumference.

semicircular > *adjective* having the form of a semicircle.
COMBINATIONS – **semicircular canals** a system of three fluid-filled bony channels in the inner ear, involved in sensing and maintaining balance.

semicolon /**semm**i**kō**lən/ > *noun* a punctuation mark (;) indicating a more pronounced pause than that indicated by a comma.

semiconductor > *noun* a solid, e.g. silicon, whose conductivity is between that of an insulator and a conductive metal and increases with temperature.
DERIVATIVES – **semi-conducting** *adjective*.

semi-conscious > *adjective* partially conscious.

semi-detached > *adjective* (of a house) joined to another house on one side by a common wall.

semi-double > *adjective* (of a flower) intermediate between single and double in having only the outer stamens converted to petals.

semi-final > *noun* (in sport) a match or round immediately preceding the final.
DERIVATIVES – **semi-finalist** *noun*.

semi-fluid > *adjective* having a thick consistency between solid and liquid. > *noun* a semi-fluid substance.

semi-invalid > *noun* a partially disabled or somewhat infirm person.

semi-liquid > *adjective & noun* another term for **SEMI-FLUID**.

Semillon /**semm**iyoN/ > *noun* a variety of white wine grape grown in France, Australia, and South America.
ORIGIN – French, from Latin *semen* 'seed'.

semilunar > *adjective* chiefly Anatomy shaped like a half-moon or crescent.

seminal > *adjective* **1** (of a work, event, or idea) strongly influencing later developments. **2** relating to or denoting semen. **3** Botany relating to or derived from the seed of a plant.
DERIVATIVES – **seminally** *adverb*.
ORIGIN – Latin *seminalis*, from *semen* 'seed'.

seminar /**semm**inaar/ > *noun* **1** a conference or other meeting for discussion or training. **2** a small group of students at university, meeting to discuss topics with a teacher.
ORIGIN – German *Seminar*, from Latin *seminarium* 'seed plot, seminary'.

seminary /**semm**inəri/ > *noun* (pl. **seminaries**) a training college for priests or rabbis.
DERIVATIVES – **seminarian** /semmi**nair**iən/ *noun* **seminarist** *noun*.
ORIGIN – Latin *seminarium* 'seed plot', from *semen* 'seed': originally denoting a piece of ground in which seeds are sown.

Seminole /**sem**inōl/ > *noun* (pl. same or **Seminoles**) a member of an American Indian people of the Creek confederacy.
ORIGIN – from American Spanish *cimarrón* 'wild'.

semiology /seemi**oll**əji, semmi**oll**əji/ > *noun* another term for **SEMIOTICS**.
DERIVATIVES – **semiological** *adjective* **semiologist** *noun*.
ORIGIN – Greek *sēmeion* 'sign'.

semiotics /seemi**ott**iks, semi**ott**iks/ > *plural noun* (treated as sing.) the study of signs and symbols and their use or interpretation.
DERIVATIVES – **semiotic** *adjective* **semiotician** *noun*.
ORIGIN – Greek *sēmeiotikos* 'of signs'.

semipermeable /semmi**per**miəb'l/ > *adjective* permeable only to certain substances, especially allowing the passage of a solvent but not of the solute.

semi-precious > *adjective* denoting minerals which can be used as gems but are considered to be less valuable than precious stones.

semiquaver /**semm**ikwayvər/ > *noun* Music, chiefly Brit. a note having the time value of a sixteenth of a semibreve or half a quaver, represented by a large dot with a two-hooked stem.

semi-retired > *adjective* having retired from employment or an occupation but continuing to work part-time or occasionally.
DERIVATIVES – **semi-retirement** *noun*.

semi-skimmed > *adjective* Brit. (of milk) having had some of the cream removed.

semi-solid > *adjective* highly viscous; slightly thicker than semi-fluid.

semi-submersible > *adjective* denoting an oil or gas drilling platform or barge with submerged hollow pontoons able to be flooded when the vessel is anchored on site in order to provide stability.

Semite /**see**mīt/ > *noun* a member of a people speaking a Semitic language, in particular the Jews and Arabs.
ORIGIN – from the name of *Shem*, son of Noah in the Bible, from whom these people are traditionally descended.

Semitic /si**mitt**ik/ > *noun* a family of languages that includes Hebrew, Arabic, and Aramaic and certain ancient languages such as Phoenician. > *adjective* relating to these languages or their speakers.

semitone > *noun* Music the smallest interval used in classical Western music, equal to a twelfth of an octave or half a tone.

semolina /semmə**lee**nə/ > *noun* the hard grains left after the milling of flour, used in puddings and in pasta.
ORIGIN – Italian *semolino*, from *semola* 'bran'.

sempiternal /sempi**ter**n'l/ > *adjective* eternal and unchanging; everlasting.

DERIVATIVES – **sempiternally** *adverb* **sempiternity** *noun*.

ORIGIN – Latin *sempiternus*, from *semper* 'always' + *aeternus* 'eternal'.

sempre /**sem**pray/ > *adverb* Music throughout; always.

ORIGIN – Italian.

sempstress > *noun* another term for **SEAMSTRESS**.

Semtex > *noun* a pliable, odourless plastic explosive.

ORIGIN – probably a blend of *Semtin* (the name of a village in the Czech Republic near the place of production) and **EXPLOSIVE**.

SEN > *abbreviation* (in the UK) State Enrolled Nurse.

sen > *noun* (pl. same) **1** a monetary unit of Brunei, Cambodia, Indonesia, and Malaysia, equal to one hundredth of the basic unit. **2** a former monetary unit of Japan, equal to one hundredth of a yen.

ORIGIN – sense 1 represents **CENT**; sense 2 from Japanese.

senate > *noun* **1** a legislative or governing body, especially the smaller upper assembly in the US, US states, France, and other countries. **2** the governing body of a university or college. **3** the state council of the ancient Roman republic and empire.

ORIGIN – Latin *senatus*, from *senex* 'old man'.

senator > *noun* a member of a senate.

DERIVATIVES – **senatorial** *adjective* **senatorship** *noun*.

send > *verb* (past and past participle **sent**) **1** cause to go or be taken to a particular destination. **2** cause to move sharply or quickly; propel. **3** cause to be in a specified state: *it nearly sent me crazy*.

IDIOMS – **send down** Brit. **1** expel (a student) from a university. **2** informal sentence to imprisonment. **send for 1** order (someone) to come. **2** order by post. **send off** (of a soccer or rugby referee) order (a player) to leave the field and take no further part in the game. **send to Coventry** see **COVENTRY**. **send up 1** ridicule (someone) by imitating them in an exaggerated manner. **2** US sentence to imprisonment. **send word** send a message.

DERIVATIVES – **sender** *noun*.

SYNONYMS – **1** convey, direct, dispatch, transmit. **2** catapult, project, propel, shoot. **3** drive, make.

send-off > *noun* a celebratory demonstration of goodwill at a person's departure.

send-up > *noun* a parody or exaggerated imitation of someone or something.

sene /**sen**i/ > *noun* (pl. same or **senes**) a monetary unit of Samoa, equal to one hundredth of a tala.

ORIGIN – Samoan.

Seneca /**sen**ikə/ > *noun* (pl. same or

Senecas) a member of an American Indian people forming part of the Iroquois confederacy.

ORIGIN – Algonquian.

Senegalese /sennigəleez/ > *noun* a person from Senegal. > *adjective* relating to Senegal.

senesce /si**ness**/ > *verb* (of a living organism) deteriorate with age.

DERIVATIVES – **senescence** *noun* **senescent** *adjective*.

ORIGIN – Latin *senescere*, from *senex* 'old'.

seneschal /**senn**ish'l/ > *noun* **1** historical the steward or major-domo of a medieval great house. **2** chiefly historical a governor or other administrative or judicial officer.

ORIGIN – Latin *seniscalus*, from words meaning 'old' and 'servant'.

senile /**see**nīl/ > *adjective* having the weaknesses or diseases of old age, especially a loss of mental faculties. > *noun* a senile person.

DERIVATIVES – **senility** *noun*.

COMBINATIONS – **senile dementia** severe mental deterioration in old age, characterised by loss of memory and lack of control of bodily functions.

ORIGIN – Latin *senilis*, from *senex* 'old man'.

senior > *adjective* **1** of or relating to a more advanced age. **2** Brit. of, for, or denoting schoolchildren above a certain age, typically eleven. **3** US of the final year at a university or high school. **4** (after a name) denoting the elder of two with the same name in a family. **5** high or higher in rank or status. > *noun* **1** a person who is a specified number of years older than someone else: *she was two years his senior.* **2** a student in one of the higher forms of a senior school. **3** (in sport) a competitor of above a certain age or of the highest status. **4** an elderly person, especially an old-age pensioner.

WORDFINDER – doyen (*most senior or respected person in a group*).

DERIVATIVES – **seniority** *noun*.

COMBINATIONS – **senior aircraftman** (or **senior aircraftwoman**) a rank in the RAF, above leading aircraftman (or leading aircraftwoman) and below junior technician. **senior citizen** an elderly person, especially an old-age pensioner. **senior common room** Brit. a room used for social purposes by fellows, lecturers, and other senior members of a college. **senior nursing officer** Brit. the person in charge of nursing services in a hospital. **senior registrar** Brit. a hospital doctor receiving specialist training, one grade below that of consultant. **Senior Service** Brit. the Royal Navy. [ORIGIN – *Senior* with reference to the fact that it pre-dated the East India Company, a trading company formed in 1600.]

ORIGIN – Latin, 'older, older man', from *senex* 'old man, old'.

seniti /**senn**iti/ > *noun* (pl. same) a monetary unit of Tonga, equal to one hundredth of a pa'anga.

ORIGIN – Tongan.

senna > *noun* a laxative prepared from the dried pods of the cassia tree.

ORIGIN – Arabic.

señor /se**nyor**/ > *noun* (pl. **señores** /se**nyor**ayz/) (in Spanish-speaking countries) a form of address for a man, corresponding to *Mr* or *sir*.

ORIGIN – Spanish, from Latin *senior* 'older, older man'.

señora /se**nyor**ə/ > *noun* (in Spanish-speaking countries) a form of address for a woman, corresponding to *Mrs* or *madam*.

señorita /senyə**ree**tə/ > *noun* (in Spanish-speaking countries) a form of address for an unmarried woman, corresponding to *Miss*.

sensate /**sen**sayt/ > *adjective* perceiving or perceived with the senses.

sensation > *noun* **1** a physical feeling or perception resulting from something that happens to or comes into contact with the body. **2** the capacity to have such feelings or perceptions. **3** an inexplicable awareness or impression. **4** a widespread reaction of interest and excitement, or a person or thing causing it.

sensational > *adjective* **1** causing or seeking to cause great public interest and excitement. **2** informal very impressive or attractive.

DERIVATIVES – **sensationalise** (also **sensationalize**) *verb* **sensationally** *adverb*.

sensationalism > *noun* the deliberate use of sensational stories or language.

DERIVATIVES – **sensationalist** *noun* & *adjective* **sensationalistic** *adjective*.

sense > *noun* **1** a faculty by which the body perceives an external stimulus; one of the faculties of sight, smell, hearing, taste, and touch. **2** an awareness of something; a feeling that something is the case. **3** (**a sense of**) an awareness or appreciation of: *a sense of direction.* **4** a sane and realistic attitude to situations and problems. **5** a reasonable or comprehensible rationale. **6** a way in which an expression or situation can be interpreted; a meaning. > *verb* **1** perceive by a sense or senses. **2** be vaguely or indefinably aware of. **3** (of a machine or similar device) detect.

WORDFINDER – insensate (*deprived of all senses*), synaesthesia (*production of a sense impression by stimulation of another sense or part of the body*).

IDIOMS – **come to one's senses 1** be restored to consciousness. **2** regain one's good sense or sound judgement. **make sense** be intelligible, justifiable, or practicable. **make sense of** find meaning or coherence in.

SYNONYMS – *noun* **2** awareness, consciousness, feeling, perception, sensation. **4** common sense, discernment, level-headedness, practicality, wisdom. **5** point, purpose, reason, use. *verb* **1,2** detect, discern, feel, perceive.

COMBINATIONS – **sense organ** an organ of the body which responds to external stimuli by conveying impulses to the sensory nervous system.

ORIGIN – Latin *sensus* 'faculty of feeling, thought, meaning', from *sentire* 'feel'.

sensei /sensay/ > *noun* (pl. same) (in martial arts) a teacher.

ORIGIN – Japanese, from *sen* 'previous' + *sei* 'birth'.

senseless > *adjective* **1** unconscious or incapable of sensation. **2** without discernible meaning or purpose. **3** lacking common sense; wildly foolish.

DERIVATIVES – **senselessly** *adverb* **senselessness** *noun*.

sensibility > *noun* (pl. **sensibilities**) (also **sensibilities**) the ability to appreciate and respond to complex emotional or aesthetic influences; sensitivity.

sensible > *adjective* **1** wise and prudent; having or showing common sense. **2** practical and functional rather than decorative. **3** (**sensible of** or **to**) formal or dated aware of.

DERIVATIVES – **sensibleness** *noun* **sensibly** *adverb*.

SYNONYMS – **1** balanced, level-headed, prudent, responsible.

ORIGIN – Latin *sensibilis*, from *sensus* 'faculty of feeling, thought'.

sensitise (also **sensitize**) > *verb* cause to respond to certain stimuli; make sensitive.

DERIVATIVES – **sensitisation** *noun* **sensitiser** *noun*.

sensitive > *adjective* **1** quick to detect, respond to, or be affected by slight changes, signals, or influences. **2** delicately appreciating the feelings of others. **3** easily offended or upset. **4** kept secret or with restrictions on disclosure.

DERIVATIVES – **sensitively** *adverb* **sensitiveness** *noun*.

SYNONYMS – **1** perceptive, receptive, responsive. **2** considerate, sympathetic, tactful, thoughtful. **3** delicate, fragile, thin-skinned, touchy.

ANTONYMS – **1** insensitive, unresponsive. **2** insensitive, tactless. **3** thick-skinned.

COMBINATIONS – **sensitive plant** a tropical American plant of the pea family, whose leaflets fold together and leaves bend down when touched.

ORIGIN – Latin *sensitivus*, from *sentire* 'feel'.

sensitivity > *noun* (pl. **sensitivities**) **1** the quality or condition of being sensitive. **2** (**sensitivities**) a person's feelings when readily offended or hurt.

sensor > *noun* a device which detects or measures a physical property.

sensory > *adjective* relating to sensation or the senses.

DERIVATIVES – **sensorily** *adverb*.

sensual /senshooəl, sensyooəl/ > *adjective* relating to the physical senses as a source of pleasure, especially sexual pleasure.

DERIVATIVES – **sensualise** (also **sensualize**) *verb* **sensualism** *noun* **sensualist** *noun* **sensuality** *noun* **sensually** *adverb*.

USAGE – strictly speaking there is a difference between **sensual** and **sensuous**. **Sensual** is used in relation to gratification of the senses, especially sexual gratification, while **sensuous** is a more neutral term, meaning 'relating to the senses rather than the intellect'.

sensuous > *adjective* relating to or affecting the senses rather than the intellect.

DERIVATIVES – **sensuously** *adverb* **sensuousness** *noun*.

sent[1] past and past participle of SEND.

sent[2] > *noun* a monetary unit of Estonia, equal to one hundredth of a kroon.

ORIGIN – respelling of CENT.

sente /senti/ > *noun* (pl. **lisente** /lisenti/) a monetary unit of Lesotho, equal to one hundredth of a loti.

ORIGIN – Sesotho, a Bantu language.

sentence > *noun* **1** a set of words that is complete in itself, conveying a statement, question, exclamation, or command, and typically containing a subject and predicate. **2** the punishment assigned to someone found guilty by a court. > *verb* declare the punishment decided for (an offender).

WORDFINDER – *parts of a sentence:* adverbial, clause, complement, object, predicate, subject, verb; pangram (*sentence containing all letters of the alphabet*), parse (*analyse structure of a sentence*), syntax (*arrangement of words to make well-formed sentence*).

COMBINATIONS – **sentence adverb** Grammar an adverb that expresses an attitude to the content of the sentence in which it occurs or places the sentence in a particular context.

ORIGIN – Latin *sententia* 'opinion': originally used also in the sense 'way of thinking, opinion'.

sententious /sentenshəss/ > *adjective* given to moralising in a pompous or affected manner.

DERIVATIVES – **sententiously** *adverb* **sententiousness** *noun*.

ORIGIN – from Latin *sententia* 'opinion': originally in the sense 'full of meaning or wisdom'.

sentient /sensh'nt/ > *adjective* able to perceive or feel things.

DERIVATIVES – **sentience** *noun* **sentiently** *adverb*.

ORIGIN – Latin, from *sentire* 'to feel'.

sentiment > *noun* **1** a view, opinion, or feeling. **2** exaggerated and self-indulgent feelings of tenderness, sadness, or nostalgia.

ORIGIN – Latin *sentimentum*, from *sentire* 'feel': originally in the senses 'personal experience' and 'physical feeling, sensation'.

sentimental > *adjective* **1** deriving from feelings of tenderness, sadness, or nostalgia. **2** (of a person) prone to feelings of tenderness or nostalgia; emotional. **3** having or arousing such feelings in an exaggerated and self-indulgent way.

IDIOMS – **sentimental value** the value of an object that comes from personal or emotional associations rather than material worth.

DERIVATIVES – **sentimentalism** *noun* **sentimentalist** *noun* **sentimentality** *noun* **sentimentally** *adverb*.

SYNONYMS – **3** cloying, mawkish, saccharine, sickly; informal corny.

ANTONYMS – **3** gritty, unsentimental.

sentimentalise (also **sentimentalize**) > *verb* treat or regard (something) in a sentimental way.

DERIVATIVES – **sentimentalisation** *noun*.

sentinel /sentin'l/ > *noun* a soldier or guard whose job is to stand and keep watch. > *verb* (**sentinelled**, **sentinelling**; US **sentineled**, **sentineling**) station a sentinel to keep watch over.

ORIGIN – Italian *sentinella*.

sentry > *noun* (pl. **sentries**) a soldier stationed to keep guard or to control access to a place.

COMBINATIONS – **sentry box** a structure providing shelter for a standing sentry.

ORIGIN – perhaps from obsolete *centrinel*, from SENTINEL.

sepal /sepp'l/ > *noun* Botany each of the leaf-like parts of a flower that surround the petals, enclosing them when the flower is in bud.

ORIGIN – from Greek *skepē* 'covering', influenced by French *pétale* 'petal'.

separable > *adjective* able to be separated or treated separately.

DERIVATIVES – **separability** *noun* **separableness** *noun* **separably** *adverb*.

separate* > *adjective* /seppərət/ **1** forming or viewed as a unit apart or by itself; not joined or united with others. **2** different; distinct. > *verb* /seppərayt/ **1** move or come apart; make or become detached or disconnected. **2** stop living together as a couple. **3** divide into constituent or distinct elements. **4** extract or remove for use or rejection. **5** distinguish between or from another; consider individually. **6** form a distinction or boundary between. > *noun* /**sep**pərət/ (**separates**) individual items of clothing that may be worn in different combinations.

DERIVATIVES – **separately** *adverb* **separateness** *noun* **separative** *adjective* **separator** *noun*.

***SPELLING** – the middle syllable is *-par-*, not *-per-*: separate.

SYNONYMS – *adjective* **1** discrete, independent, individual, unconnected, unrelated. *verb* **1** detach, disconnect, divide, part, sever, split. **6** divide, partition, stand between.

ORIGIN – from Latin *separare* 'disjoin, divide'.

separation > *noun* **1** the action or state of separating or being separated. **2** the state in which a husband and wife remain married but live apart.

separatism > *noun* the advocacy or practice of separation of a group of people from a larger body on the basis of ethnicity, religion, or gender.

DERIVATIVES – **separatist** *noun & adjective*.

Sephardi /si**faar**di/ > *noun* (pl. **Sephardim** /si**faar**dim/) a Jew of Spanish or Portuguese descent. Compare with **ASHKENAZI**.

DERIVATIVES – **Sephardic** *adjective*.

ORIGIN – Hebrew, from the name of a country mentioned in the Bible (Obadiah 20) and taken to be Spain.

sepia /**see**piə/ > *noun* **1** a reddish-brown colour, associated particularly with early monochrome photographs. **2** a brown pigment prepared from cuttlefish ink, used in drawing and in watercolours. **3** cuttlefish ink.

ORIGIN – Greek, 'cuttlefish' (the original meaning of the word in English).

sepoy /**see**poy/ > *noun* historical an Indian soldier serving under British or other European orders.

ORIGIN – Urdu and Persian, 'soldier'.

seppuku /se**poo**koo/ > *noun* another term for **HARA-KIRI**.

ORIGIN – Japanese, from 'to cut' + 'abdomen'.

sepsis /**sep**siss/ > *noun* Medicine the presence in tissues of harmful bacteria, typically through infection of a wound.

ORIGIN – Greek *sēpsis*, from *sēpein* 'make rotten'.

Sept. > *abbreviation* September.

sept- > *combining form* variant spelling of **SEPTI-**.

septa plural of **SEPTUM**.

septal > *adjective* **1** Anatomy & Biology relating to a septum or septa. **2** Archaeology (of a large stone or stone slab) separating compartments in a burial chamber.

September > *noun* the ninth month of the year.

ORIGIN – from Latin *septem* 'seven' (being originally the seventh month of the Roman year).

septennial > *adjective* lasting for or recurring every seven years.

ORIGIN – Latin *septennis*, from *septem* 'seven' + *annus* 'year'.

septet /sep**tet**/ > *noun* a group of seven people playing music or singing together.

ORIGIN – from Latin *septem* 'seven'.

septi- (also **sept-**) > *combining form* seven; having seven: *septivalent*.

ORIGIN – from Latin *septem* 'seven'.

septic /**sep**tik/ > *adjective* **1** (of a wound or a part of the body) infected with bacteria. **2** denoting a drainage system incorporating a septic tank.

DERIVATIVES – **septically** *adverb* **septicity** /sep**tiss**iti/ *noun*.

COMBINATIONS – **septic tank** an underground tank in which sewage is allowed to decompose through bacterial activity before draining by means of a soakaway.

ORIGIN – Greek *sēptikos*, from *sēpein* 'make rotten'.

septicaemia /septi**see**miə/ (US **septicemia**) > *noun* blood poisoning caused by bacteria.

DERIVATIVES – **septicaemic** *adjective*.

septillion /sep**til**yən/ > *cardinal number* a thousand raised to the eighth power (10^{24}); a million million million million.

DERIVATIVES – **septillionth** *ordinal number*.

septimal /**sep**tim'l/ > *adjective* relating to the number seven.

ORIGIN – Latin *septimus* 'seventh'.

septuagenarian /septyooəji**nair**iən/ > *noun* a person who is between 70 and 79 years old.

ORIGIN – Latin *septuagenarius*, from *septuaginta* 'seventy'.

Septuagesima /septyooə**jess**imə/ > *noun* the Sunday before Sexagesima.

ORIGIN – from Latin *septuagesimus* 'seventieth'.

Septuagint /**sep**tyooəjint/ > *noun* a Greek version of the Hebrew Bible (or Old Testament), including the Apocrypha, produced in the 3rd and 2nd centuries BC.

ORIGIN – Latin *septuaginta* 'seventy', because of the tradition that it was produced by seventy-two independent translators.

septum /**sep**təm/ > *noun* (pl. **septa** /**sep**tə/) chiefly Anatomy & Biology a partition separating two chambers, such as that between the nostrils or the chambers of the heart.

ORIGIN – Latin, from *sepire* 'enclose'.

septuple /sep**toop**'l/ > *adjective* **1** consisting of seven parts or elements. **2** (of time in music) having seven beats in a bar. **3** consisting of seven times as much or as

many as usual. > *verb* multiply by seven; increase sevenfold.

ORIGIN – from Latin *septem* 'seven'.

septuplet /**sep**tyooplit/ > *noun* **1** each of seven children born at one birth. **2** Music a group of seven notes to be performed in the time of four or six.

sepulchral /si**pul**krəl/ > *adjective* **1** relating to a tomb or burial. **2** gloomy; dismal.

DERIVATIVES – **sepulchrally** *adverb*.

sepulchre /**sep**əlkər/ (US **sepulcher**) > *noun* a stone tomb or monument in which a dead person is laid or buried. > *verb* chiefly literary lay or bury in a sepulchre.

ORIGIN – Latin *sepulcrum* 'burial place', from *sepelire* 'bury'.

seq. (also **seqq.**) > *adverb* short for ET SEQ.

sequel > *noun* **1** a published, broadcast, or recorded work that continues the story or develops the theme of an earlier one. **2** something that takes place after or as a result of an earlier event.

> ## wordpower facts
> ### Sequel
> The word **sequel** originally meant 'a body of followers' and 'descendants', then 'a consequence'. It comes via Old French *sequelle* from Latin *sequi*, meaning 'to follow', an important source of English words. **Consequence, ensue, execute, persecute, prosecute, second, sect, sequence, sue, suit,** and **suitor** are among the large number of words deriving from *sequi*.

sequela /si**kway**lə/ > *noun* (pl. **sequelae** /si**kway**lee/) Medicine a condition which is the consequence of a previous disease or injury.

ORIGIN – Latin, from *sequi* 'follow'.

sequence > *noun* **1** a particular order in which related events, movements, etc., follow each other. **2** a set of related events, movements, etc., that follow each other in a particular order. **3** a part of a film dealing with one particular event or topic. **4** Music a repetition of a phrase or melody at a higher or lower pitch. > *verb* **1** arrange in a sequence. **2** play or record (music) with a sequencer. **3** Biochemistry ascertain the sequence of molecular residues in (DNA, a protein, etc.).

SYNONYMS – *noun* **2** chain, course, series, string, succession, train.

ORIGIN – from Latin *sequi* 'to follow'.

sequencer > *noun* a programmable electronic device for storing sequences of musical notes, chords, or rhythms and transmitting them to an electronic musical instrument.

sequential /sikwensh'l/ > *adjective* forming or following in a logical order or sequence.

DERIVATIVES – **sequentiality** *noun* **sequentially** *adverb*.

sequester /sikwestər/ > *verb* 1 isolate or hide away. 2 another term for **SEQUESTRATE**.

ORIGIN – Latin *sequestrare* 'commit for safekeeping', from *sequester* 'trustee'.

sequestrate /sikwestrayt, seekwistrayt/ > *verb* 1 take legal possession of (assets) until a debt has been paid or other claims have been met. 2 take forcible possession of; confiscate.

DERIVATIVES – **sequestration** *noun* **sequestrator** /seekwistraytər/ *noun*.

sequin /seekwin/ > *noun* a small, shiny disc sewn on to clothing for decoration.

DERIVATIVES – **sequinned** (also **sequined**) *adjective*.

ORIGIN – first denoting a former Venetian gold coin: from Italian *zecchino*, from an Arabic word meaning 'a die for coining'.

sequoia /sikwoyə/ > *noun* a redwood tree.

ORIGIN – named after *Sequoya*, a Cherokee Indian scholar.

sera plural of **SERUM**.

seraglio /səraaliō/ > *noun* (pl. **seraglios**) 1 the women's apartments in a Muslim house or palace. 2 a harem.

ORIGIN – Italian *serraglio*, from a Persian word meaning 'palace'.

serai /sərī/ > *noun* a caravanserai.

serape /seraapay/ (also **sarape**) > *noun* a shawl or blanket worn as a cloak by people from Latin America.

ORIGIN – Mexican Spanish.

seraph /serrəf/ > *noun* (pl. **seraphim** /serrəfim/ or **seraphs**) an angelic being associated with light, ardour, and purity.

DERIVATIVES – **seraphic** *adjective* **seraphically** *adverb*.

ORIGIN – Hebrew.

Serb > *noun* a person from Serbia.

Serbian > *noun* 1 the language of the Serbs. 2 a Serb. > *adjective* relating to Serbia.

Serbo-Croat /serbō krōat/ (also **Serbo-Croatian** /serbō krōaysh'n/) > *noun* the language spoken in Serbia, Croatia, and elsewhere in the former Yugoslavia.

sere > *adjective* variant spelling of **SEAR**.

serenade > *noun* a piece of music sung or played in the open air at night, especially by a man under the window of his beloved. > *verb* entertain with a serenade.

DERIVATIVES – **serenader** *noun*.

ORIGIN – Italian *serenata*, from *sereno* 'serene'.

serendipity /serrəndippiti/ > *noun* the occurrence and development of events by chance in a happy or beneficial way.

DERIVATIVES – **serendipitous** *adjective* **serendipitously** *adverb*.

ORIGIN – from *Serendip* (a former name for Sri Lanka): coined by the English politician and writer Horace Walpole (1717–97), after *The Three Princes of Serendip*, a fairy tale in which the heroes were always making fortunate discoveries.

serene > *adjective* not troubled or disturbed; tranquil.

DERIVATIVES – **serenely** *adverb* **serenity** *noun*.

SYNONYMS – calm, peaceful, tranquil, undisturbed, untroubled.

ANTONYMS – disturbed, troubled.

ORIGIN – Latin *serenus*.

serf > *noun* (in the feudal system) an agricultural labourer who was tied to working on a particular estate.

DERIVATIVES – **serfdom** *noun*.

ORIGIN – Latin *servus* 'slave'.

serge /serj/ > *noun* a durable twilled woollen or worsted fabric.

ORIGIN – Old French *sarge*, from a variant of Latin *serica lana* 'silken wool'.

sergeant /saarjənt/ > *noun* 1 a rank of non-commissioned officer in the army or air force, above corporal and below staff sergeant. 2 Brit. a police officer ranking below an inspector.

COMBINATIONS – **sergeant major** a warrant officer in the British army whose job is to assist the adjutant of a regiment or battalion or a subunit commander.

ORIGIN – Old French *sergent*, from Latin *servire* 'serve': originally in the senses 'servant' and 'common soldier'.

sergeant-at-arms > *noun* variant spelling of **SERJEANT-AT-ARMS**.

serial > *adjective* 1 consisting of, forming part of, or taking place in a series. 2 repeatedly committing the same offence or following a characteristic behaviour pattern: *a serial killer*. 3 Computing (of a device) involving the transfer of data as a single sequence of bits. > *noun* 1 a story or play published or broadcast in regular instalments. 2 (in a library) a periodical.

DERIVATIVES – **seriality** *noun* **serially** *adverb*.

COMBINATIONS – **serial number** an identification number showing the position of a manufactured or printed item in a series.

serialise (also **serialize**) > *verb* 1 publish or broadcast (a story or play) in regular instalments. 2 arrange in a series.

DERIVATIVES – **serialisation** *noun*.

serialism > *noun* a technique of musical composition using the twelve notes of the chromatic scale in a fixed order which is subject to change only in specific ways.

DERIVATIVES – **serialist** *adjective & noun*.

sericulture /serrikulchər/ > *noun* the production of silk and the rearing of silkworms for this purpose.

ORIGIN – from Latin *sericum* 'silk' + French *culture* 'cultivation'.

series > *noun* (pl. same) 1 a number of similar or related things coming one after another. 2 a sequence of related television or radio programmes. 3 Geology a range of strata corresponding to an epoch in time.

IDIOMS – **in series** (of electrical components or circuits) arranged so that the current passes through each successively.

SYNONYMS – 1 chain, course, sequence, string, succession, train.

ORIGIN – Latin, 'row, chain', from *serere* 'join, connect'.

serif /serrif/ > *noun* a slight projection finishing off a stroke of a letter, as in T contrasted with T.

ORIGIN – perhaps from Dutch *schreef* 'dash, line'.

serine /serreen/ > *noun* Biochemistry an amino acid which is a constituent of most proteins.

ORIGIN – from Latin *sericum* 'silk'.

serio-comic /seeriō/ > *adjective* combining the serious and the comic.

serious > *adjective* 1 demanding or characterised by careful consideration or application. 2 solemn or thoughtful. 3 sincere and in earnest, rather than joking or half-hearted. 4 significant or worrying in terms of danger or risk: *serious injury*. 5 informal substantial in terms of size, number, or quality: *serious money*.

DERIVATIVES – **seriousness** *noun*.

SYNONYMS – 1 important, significant, weighty. 2 grave, humourless, sober, solemn, sombre, thoughtful.

ANTONYMS – 1 trivial, unimportant. 2 jovial, light-hearted.

ORIGIN – Latin *seriosus*, from *serius* 'earnest, serious'.

seriously > *adverb* in a serious manner or to a serious extent.

serjeant > *noun* (in official lists) a sergeant in the Foot Guards.

ORIGIN – variant of **SERGEANT**.

serjeant-at-arms (also **sergeant-at-arms**) > *noun* (pl. **serjeants-at-arms**) an official of a legislative assembly whose duties include maintaining order and security.

serjeant-at-law > *noun* (pl. **serjeants-at-law**) historical a barrister of the highest rank.

sermon > *noun* 1 a talk on a religious or moral subject, especially one given during a church service. 2 informal a long talk about how one should perform or behave.

WORDFINDER – homiletic (*of or like a sermon*).

DERIVATIVES – **sermonic** *adjective* **sermonise** (also **sermonize**) *verb* **sermoniser** (also **sermonizer**) *noun*.
ORIGIN – Latin, 'discourse, talk'.

serology /seerollǝji/ > *noun* the scientific study or diagnostic examination of blood serum.
DERIVATIVES – **serologic** *adjective* **serological** *adjective* **serologist** *noun*.

seropositive (or **seronegative**) > *adjective* giving a positive (or negative) result in a test of blood serum, especially for the presence of a virus.

serotonin /serrǝtōnin/ > *noun* a compound present in blood which constricts the blood vessels and acts as a neurotransmitter.
ORIGIN – from **SERUM** + **TONIC**.

serous /seerǝss/ > *adjective* of, resembling, or producing serum.

serpent > *noun* **1** literary a large snake. **2** a sly or treacherous person. **3** historical a bass wind instrument made of leather-covered wood in three U-shaped turns.
WORDFINDER – Ophiuchus (*constellation, the Serpent Bearer*).
ORIGIN – from Latin *serpere* 'to creep'.

serpentine /serpǝntīn/ > *adjective* **1** of or like a serpent or snake, especially in being winding or twisting. **2** complex, cunning, or treacherous. > *noun* a dark green mineral consisting of a silicate of magnesium, sometimes mottled like a snake's skin.

SERPS /serps/ > *abbreviation* (in the UK) state earnings-related pension scheme.

serrated /sǝraytid/ > *adjective* having or denoting a jagged edge like the teeth of a saw.
ORIGIN – Latin *serratus*, from *serra* 'saw'.

serration > *noun* a tooth or point of a serrated edge or surface.

serried > *adjective* (of rows of people or things) standing close together.
ORIGIN – from archaic *serry* 'press close', probably from French *serré* 'close together'.

serum /seerǝm/ > *noun* (pl. **sera** /seerǝ/ or **serums**) the amber-coloured, protein-rich liquid which separates out when blood coagulates.
ORIGIN – Latin, 'whey'.

servant > *noun* **1** a person employed to perform domestic duties in a household or as a personal attendant. **2** a person regarded as providing support or service for an organisation or person: *a government servant*.
ORIGIN – Old French, 'person serving', from *servir* 'to serve'.

serve > *verb* **1** perform duties or services for. **2** be employed as a member of the armed forces. **3** spend (a period) in office, in an apprenticeship, or in prison. **4** present food or drink to. **5** attend to (a customer in a shop). **6** be of use in fulfilling (a purpose). **7** treat in a specified way. **8** (of food or drink)

be enough for. **9** Law formally deliver (a summons or writ) to the person to whom it is addressed. **10** (in tennis and other racket sports) hit the ball or shuttlecock to begin play for each point of a game. **11** (of a male breeding animal) copulate with (a female). > *noun* **1** an act of serving in tennis, badminton, etc. **2** Austral. informal a reprimand.
IDIOMS – **serve someone right** be someone's deserved punishment or misfortune. **serve one's** (or **its**) **turn** be useful.
ORIGIN – Latin *servire*, from *servus* 'slave'.

server > *noun* **1** a person or thing that serves. **2** a computer or computer program which manages access to a centralised resource or service in a network.

servery > *noun* (pl. **serveries**) Brit. a counter, hatch, or room from which meals are served.

service > *noun* **1** the action or process of serving. **2** a period of employment with an organisation. **3** an act of assistance. **4** a ceremony of religious worship according to a prescribed form. **5** a system supplying a public need such as transport, or a utility such as water. **6** a public department or organisation run by the state: *the probation service*. **7** (**the services**) the armed forces. **8** (often in phrase **in service**) employment as a servant. **9** a set of matching crockery used for serving a particular meal. **10** (in tennis, badminton, etc.) a serve. **11** a periodic routine inspection and maintenance of a vehicle or other machine. > *verb* **1** perform routine maintenance or repair work on. **2** provide a service or services for. **3** pay interest on (a debt). **4** (of a male animal) mate with (a female animal).
IDIOMS – **be at someone's service** be ready to assist someone whenever required. **be of service** be available to assist someone. **in** (or **out of**) **service** available (or not available) for use.
COMBINATIONS – **service area** chiefly Brit. a roadside area where services are available to motorists. **service charge 1** a charge added to a bill for service in a restaurant. **2** a charge made for banking or other services. **service flat** Brit. a rented flat in which domestic service and sometimes meals are provided by the management. **service industry** a business that provides a service for a customer, but is not involved in manufacturing. **service provider** Computing a company which gives its subscribers access to the Internet. **service road** a subsidiary road running parallel to a main road and giving access to houses, shops, or businesses. **service station** a roadside establishment selling petrol and oil and sometimes offering vehicle maintenance.
ORIGIN – Latin *servitium* 'slavery'.

serviceable > *adjective* **1** fulfilling its function adequately; usable or in working order. **2** functional and durable rather than attractive.
DERIVATIVES – **serviceability** *noun*.

serviceman (or **servicewoman**) > *noun* **1** a person serving in the armed forces. **2** a person providing maintenance for machinery.

service tree > *noun* a tree resembling a rowan, with brown berries.
ORIGIN – from obsolete *serves* (plural), from Latin *sorbus*.

serviette > *noun* Brit. a table napkin.
ORIGIN – Old French, from *servir* 'to serve'.

servile /servīl/ > *adjective* **1** excessively willing to serve or please others. **2** of or characteristic of a slave or slaves.
DERIVATIVES – **servilely** *adverb* **servility** *noun*.
SYNONYMS – **1** fawning, obsequious, slavish, subservient, sycophantic, toadying.
ORIGIN – Latin *servilis*, from *servus* 'slave'.

serving > *noun* a quantity of food suitable for or served to one person.

servitor /servitǝr/ > *noun* archaic a servant or attendant.

servitude /servityōōd/ > *noun* **1** the state of being a slave. **2** the state of being completely subject to someone more powerful than oneself.
ORIGIN – Latin *servitudo*, from *servus* 'slave'.

servo > *noun* (pl. **servos**) short for **SERVOMECHANISM** or **SERVOMOTOR**.
ORIGIN – Latin *servus* 'slave'.

servomechanism > *noun* a powered mechanism producing motion or forces at a higher level of energy than the input level, e.g. in the brakes and steering of large motor vehicles.

servomotor > *noun* the motive element in a servomechanism.

sesame /sessǝmi/ > *noun* a tall herbaceous plant of tropical and subtropical areas, cultivated for its oil-rich seeds.
WORDFINDER – halva (*a sweet made from sesame seeds*), tahini (*paste made from sesame seeds*).
IDIOMS – **open sesame** a free or unrestricted means of admission or access. [ORIGIN – from the magic formula in the tale of Ali Baba and the Forty Thieves.]
ORIGIN – Greek *sēsamon*, *sēsamē*.

sesqui- > *combining form* denoting one and a half: *sesquicentenary*.
ORIGIN – from Latin *semi-* 'half' + *que* 'and'.

sesquicentenary /seskwisenteenǝri, -sentennǝri/ > *noun* (pl. **sesquicentenaries**) the one-hundred-and-fiftieth anniversary of a significant event.
DERIVATIVES – **sesquicentennial** *adjective* & *noun*.

sesquipedalian /seskwipi**day**liən/ > *adjective* formal 1 (of a word) having many syllables; long. 2 characterised by long words; long-winded.

ORIGIN – from Latin *sesquipedalis* 'a foot and a half long'.

sessile /**sess**īl/ > *adjective* 1 (of an organism) fixed in one place; immobile. 2 (of a structure) attached directly by its base without a stalk or peduncle.

ORIGIN – Latin *sessilis*, from *sedere* 'sit'.

session > *noun* 1 a period devoted to a particular activity: *a training session*. 2 a meeting of a council, court, or legislative body to conduct its business. 3 a period during which such meetings are regularly held. 4 an academic year. 5 informal a period of heavy or sustained drinking.

DERIVATIVES – **sessional** *adjective*.

COMBINATIONS – **session musician** a freelance musician hired to play at recording sessions.

ORIGIN – Latin, from *sedere* 'sit'.

sestet /ses**tet**/ > *noun* the last six lines of a sonnet.

ORIGIN – Italian *sestetto*, from Latin *sextus* 'a sixth'.

set¹ > *verb* (**setting**; past and past participle **set**) 1 put, lay, or stand in a specified place or position. 2 put, bring, or place into a specified state. 3 cause or instruct (someone) to do something. 4 give someone (a task). 5 decide on or fix (a time, value, or limit). 6 establish as (an example or record). 7 adjust (a device) as required. 8 prepare (a table) for a meal by placing cutlery, crockery, etc., on it. 9 harden into a solid, semi-solid, or fixed state. 10 arrange (damp hair) into the required style. 11 put (a broken or dislocated bone or limb) into the correct position for healing. 12 (of the sun, moon, etc.) appear to move towards and below the earth's horizon as the earth rotates. 13 Printing arrange (type or text) as required. 14 (**set something to**) provide (music) so that a written work can be produced in a musical form. 15 (of a tide or current) take or have a specified direction or course. 16 (of blossom or a tree) form into or produce (fruit).

IDIOMS – **set about** 1 start doing something with vigour or determination. 2 Brit. informal attack. **set apart** give (someone) an air of unusual superiority. **set aside** 1 save or keep for a particular purpose. 2 annul (a legal decision or process). **set back** informal cost (someone) a particular amount of money. **set down** record in writing or as an authoritative rule or principle. **set forth** 1 begin a journey or trip. 2 state or describe in writing or speech. **set in** (of something unwelcome) begin and seem likely to continue. **set off** 1 begin a journey. 2 cause (a bomb or alarm) to go off. 3 serve as

decorative embellishment to. **set on** attack or urge to attack violently. **set out** 1 begin a journey. 2 aim or intend to do something. 3 arrange or display in a particular order or position. **set out one's stall** display one's abilities or attributes. **set sail** 1 hoist the sails of a boat. 2 begin a voyage. **set one's teeth** become resolute. **set to** begin doing something vigorously. **set up** 1 place or erect in position. 2 establish (a business, institution, etc.). 3 establish (someone) in a particular capacity or role. 4 begin making (a loud sound). 5 informal make (an innocent person) appear guilty. **set the wheels in motion** begin a process or put a plan into action.

ORIGIN – Old English, related to SIT.

set² > *noun* 1 a number of things or people grouped together as similar or forming a unit. 2 a group of people with common interests or occupations: *the literary set*. 3 the way in which something is arranged or positioned: *that cold set of his jaw*. 4 a radio or television receiver. 5 (in tennis, darts, and other games) a group of games counting as a unit towards a match. 6 a collection of scenery, stage furniture, etc., used for a scene in a play or film. 7 (in jazz or popular music) a sequence of songs or pieces constituting or forming part of a live show or recording. 8 Mathematics a collection of distinct entities satisfying specified conditions and regarded as a unit. 9 a cutting, young plant, or bulb used in the propagation of new plants: *an onion set*. 10 (also **dead set**) (in reference to a setter) the action of suddenly standing still when scenting game. 11 variant spelling of SETT.

IDIOMS – **make a dead set at** Brit. make a determined attempt to win the affections of. [ORIGIN – by association with hunting (see sense 10 above).]

COMBINATIONS – **set point** (in tennis) a point which if won by the player in the lead will also win them the set.

ORIGIN – partly from Old French *sette*, from Latin *secta* 'sect', partly from SET¹.

set³ > *adjective* 1 fixed or arranged in advance. 2 firmly fixed and unchanging. 3 having a conventional or predetermined wording. 4 ready, prepared, or likely to do something. 5 (of a book) prescribed for study.

COMBINATIONS – **set phrase** an unvarying phrase having a specific meaning or being the only context in which a word appears.

set-aside > *noun* 1 the policy of taking land out of production to reduce crop surpluses. 2 land taken out of production in this way.

setback > *noun* a difficulty or problem that prevents the progress of something.

SYNONYMS – blow, complication, difficulty, hitch, problem.

SETI /**set**i/ > *abbreviation* search for extraterrestrial intelligence.

set piece > *noun* 1 a formal or elaborate arrangement, especially part of a novel, film, etc., arranged for maximum effect. 2 a carefully organised and practised move in a team game.

set square > *noun* a right-angled triangular plate for drawing lines, especially at 90°, 45°, 60°, or 30°.

sett (also **set**) > *noun* 1 the earth or burrow of a badger. 2 a granite paving block.

ORIGIN – variant of SET².

settee > *noun* a long upholstered seat for more than one person, typically with a back and arms.

ORIGIN – perhaps a variant of SETTLE².

setter > *noun* 1 a large long-haired breed of dog that is trained to stand rigid when scenting game. 2 a person or thing that sets something.

set theory > *noun* the branch of mathematics concerned with the formal properties and applications of sets.

setting > *noun* 1 the way or place in which something is set. 2 a piece of metal in which a precious stone or gem is fixed to form a piece of jewellery. 3 a piece of vocal or choral music composed for particular words. 4 (also **place setting**) a complete set of crockery and cutlery for one person at a meal.

settle¹ > *verb* 1 reach an agreement or decision about (an argument or problem). 2 (often **settle down**) adopt a more steady or secure life, especially through establishing a permanent home. 3 sit, come to rest, or arrange comfortably or securely. 4 become or make calmer or quieter. 5 (often **settle in**) begin to feel comfortable or established in a new situation. 6 (**settle down to**) apply oneself to. 7 pay (a debt or account). 8 (**settle for**) accept or agree to (something less than one had wanted). 9 (**settle something on**) give money or property to (someone) through a deed of settlement or a will. 10 fall or sink down. 11 (of suspended particles) sink slowly in a liquid to form sediment.

DERIVATIVES – **settleable** *adjective*.

ORIGIN – Old English, 'to seat, place', from SETTLE².

settle² > *noun* a wooden bench with a high back and arms, typically incorporating a box under the seat.

ORIGIN – Old English, related to SIT.

settlement > *noun* 1 the action or process of settling. 2 an official agreement intended to settle a dispute or conflict. 3 a place where people establish a community. 4 Law an arrangement whereby property passes to a person or succession of people as dictated by the settlor.

settler > *noun* a person who settles in an area, especially an area with no or few previous inhabitants.

settlor /setlər/ > *noun* Law a person who makes a settlement, especially of a property.

set-to > *noun* (pl. **set-tos**) informal a fight or argument.

set-up > *noun* informal **1** the way in which something is organised or arranged. **2** an organisation or arrangement. **3** a scheme or trick intended to incriminate or deceive someone.

seven > *cardinal number* one more than six; 7. (Roman numeral: **vii** or **VII**.)

WORDFINDER – heptad (*group or set of seven*), heptagon (*plane figure with seven straight sides and angles*), heptahedron (*three-dimensional shape with seven faces*), septennial (*lasting for or recurring every seven years*), septet (*group of seven musicians*).

IDIOMS – **the seven deadly sins** (in Christian tradition) the sins of pride, covetousness, lust, anger, gluttony, envy, and sloth. **the seven seas** all the oceans of the world (conventionally the Arctic, Antarctic, North Pacific, South Pacific, North Atlantic, South Atlantic, and Indian Oceans). **the Seven Wonders of the World** the seven most spectacular man-made structures of the ancient world. **the seven-year itch** a supposed tendency to infidelity after seven years of marriage.

DERIVATIVES – **sevenfold** adjective & adverb.

seventeen > *cardinal number* one more than sixteen; 17. (Roman numeral: **xvii** or **XVII**.)

DERIVATIVES – **seventeenth** *ordinal number*.

seventh > *ordinal number* **1** constituting number seven in a sequence; 7th. **2** (**a seventh** or **one seventh**) each of seven equal parts into which something is or may be divided. **3** Music an interval spanning seven consecutive notes in a diatonic scale. **4** Music the note which is higher by this interval than the tonic of a diatonic scale or root of a chord.

DERIVATIVES – **seventhly** adverb.

COMBINATIONS – **Seventh-Day Adventist** a member of a strict Protestant sect which preaches the imminent return of Christ to Earth and observes Saturday as the sabbath.

seventy > *cardinal number* (pl. **seventies**) ten less than eighty; 70. (Roman numeral: **lxx** or **LXX**.)

WORDFINDER – septuagenarian (*person aged 70–79*).

DERIVATIVES – **seventieth** *ordinal number*.

COMBINATIONS – **seventy-eight** an old gramophone record designed to be played at 78 rpm.

sever > *verb* **1** divide by cutting or slicing. **2** put an end to (a connection or relationship).

DERIVATIVES – **severable** adjective.

ORIGIN – Old French *severer*, from Latin *separare* 'disjoin, divide'.

several > *determiner & pronoun* more than two but not many. > *adjective* separate or respective.

DERIVATIVES – **severally** adverb.

ORIGIN – Old French, from Latin *separ* 'separate, different'.

severance /sevvərənss/ > *noun* **1** the action of ending a connection or relationship. **2** the state of being separated or cut off.

COMBINATIONS – **severance pay** money paid to an employee on the early termination of a contract.

severe > *adjective* **1** (of something bad, undesirable, or difficult) very great; intense. **2** strict or harsh. **3** very plain in style or appearance.

DERIVATIVES – **severely** adverb **severity** noun.

SYNONYMS – **1** acute, critical, extreme, grave, intense, serious. **2** brutal, hard, harsh, rigorous, stern, strict. **3** austere, bare, plain, stark.

ANTONYMS – **1** minor. **2** gentle, mild.

ORIGIN – Latin *severus*.

Seville orange /sevvil/ > *noun* a bitter orange used for marmalade.

ORIGIN – from *Seville* in Spain.

sew > *verb* (past participle **sewn** or **sewed**) **1** join, fasten, or repair by making stitches with a needle and thread or a sewing machine. **2** (**sew up**) informal bring to a favourable state or conclusion.

WORDFINDER – embroidery (*art of decorative sewing*), haberdasher (*seller of sewing materials*), needlewoman, seamstress, sempstress (*woman skilled at sewing*); backstitch (*sew with overlapping stitches*), baste, tack (*sew loosely with long stitches*).

COMBINATIONS – **sewing machine** a machine with a mechanically driven needle for sewing or stitching cloth.

sewage /sooij/ > *noun* waste water and excrement conveyed in sewers.

COMBINATIONS – **sewage farm** (also **sewage works**) a place where sewage is treated, especially for use as fertiliser.

ORIGIN – from **SEWER**[1].

sewer[1] /sooər/ > *noun* an underground conduit for carrying off drainage water and waste matter.

ORIGIN – Old French *seuwiere* 'channel to drain the overflow from a fish pond', from Latin *ex-* 'out of' + *aqua* 'water'.

sewer[2] /sōər/ > *noun* a person who sews.

sewerage > *noun* **1** the provision of drainage by sewers. **2** US term for **SEWAGE**.

sewn past participle of **SEW**.

sex > *noun* **1** either of the two main categories (male and female) into which humans and most other living things are divided on the basis of their reproductive functions. **2** the fact of belonging to one of these categories. **3** sexual activity, or, more specifically, sexual intercourse. **4** the group of all members of either sex. > *verb* determine the sex of.

WORDFINDER – androgynous, epicene (*appearing partly male and partly female*), aphrodisiac (*arousing sexual desire*), celibate, chaste (*abstaining from sexual relations*), concupiscence, erotomania, nymphomania, satyriasis (*excessive sexual desire*), hermaphrodite (*biologically both male and female*), libido (*sexual desire*), Platonic (*denoting non-sexual love*), post-coital (*after sexual intercourse*), prurient (*unhealthily interested in sexual matters*), venereal disease (*transmitted by sexual intercourse*).

DERIVATIVES – **sexer** noun.

USAGE – the words **sex** and **gender** both mean 'the state of being male or female'; however, when used in this sense, **sex** tends to refer to biological differences, while **gender** refers to cultural or social ones.

COMBINATIONS – **sex appeal** the quality of being attractive in a sexual way. **sex bomb** informal a woman who is very sexually attractive. **sex chromosome** a chromosome concerned in determining the sex of an organism (in mammals the X and Y chromosomes). **sex hormone** a hormone affecting sexual development or reproduction, such as oestrogen or testosterone. **sex kitten** informal a young woman who asserts or exploits her sexual attractiveness. **sex life** a person's sexual activity and relationships considered as a whole. **sex object** a person regarded purely in terms of their sexual attractiveness or availability. **sexpot** informal a sexy person. **sex symbol** a person widely noted for their sexual attractiveness. **sex tourism** travel to certain countries with the aim of taking advantage of the lack of restrictions on sexual activity and prostitution. **sex worker** euphemistic a prostitute.

ORIGIN – Latin *sexus*.

sex- > *combining form* variant spelling of **SEXI-**, shortened before a vowel.

sexagenarian /seksəjinairiən/ > *noun* a person between 60 and 69 years old.

ORIGIN – Latin *sexagenarius*, from *sexaginta* 'sixty'.

Sexagesima /seksəjessimə/ > *noun* the Sunday before Quinquagesima.

ORIGIN – from Latin *sexagesima* 'sixtieth'.

sexagesimal /seksəjessim'l/ > *adjective* relating to or based on sixtieths.

sexed > *adjective* having specified sexual appetites: *highly sexed*.

sexennial /seksenniəl/ > *adjective* lasting for or recurring every six years.

ORIGIN – from Latin *sex* 'six' + *annus* 'year'.

sexi- (also **sex-**) > *combining form* six; having six: *sextuplet*.

ORIGIN – from Latin *sex* 'six'.

sexism > *noun* prejudice, stereotyping, or discrimination, typically against women, on the basis of sex and gender.

DERIVATIVES – **sexist** *adjective* & *noun*.

sexless > *adjective* **1** not sexually desirable, attractive, or active. **2** neither male nor female.

DERIVATIVES – **sexlessly** *adverb* **sexlessness** *noun*.

sexology > *noun* the study of human sexual behaviour.

DERIVATIVES – **sexological** *adjective* **sexologist** *noun*.

sext > *noun* a service forming part of the Divine Office of the Western Christian Church, traditionally said at the sixth hour of the day (i.e. noon).

ORIGIN – from Latin *sexta hora* 'sixth hour'.

sextant /**seks**tənt/ > *noun* an instrument with a graduated arc of 60° and a sighting mechanism, used for measuring the angular distances between objects and especially for taking altitudes in navigation and surveying.

ORIGIN – first denoting the sixth part of a circle: from Latin *sextans* 'sixth part'.

sextet (also **sextette**) > *noun* **1** a group of six people playing music or singing together. **2** a composition for a sextet. **3** a set of six.

ORIGIN – alteration of **SESTET**, suggested by Latin *sex* 'six'.

sextillion /seks**til**yən/ > *cardinal number* a thousand raised to the seventh power (10^{21}); a thousand million million million.

DERIVATIVES – **sextillionth** *ordinal number*.

sexton > *noun* a person who looks after a church and churchyard, typically acting as bell-ringer and gravedigger.

ORIGIN – Old French *segrestein*, from Latin *sacristanus* 'sacristan'.

sextuple /**seks**tyoop'l/ > *adjective* **1** consisting of six parts or elements. **2** six times as much or as many.

ORIGIN – Latin *sextuplus*, from *sex* 'six'.

sextuplet /**seks**tyooplit/ > *noun* **1** each of six children born at one birth. **2** Music a group of six notes to be performed in the time of four.

sexual > *adjective* **1** relating to the instincts and activities connected with physical attraction or intimate physical contact between individuals. **2** relating to the sexes or to gender. **3** (of reproduction) involving the fusion of gametes. **4** Biology being of one sex or the other; capable of sexual reproduction.

DERIVATIVES – **sexualise** (also **sexualize**) *verb* **sexually** *adverb*.

COMBINATIONS – **sexual harassment** the repeated making of unwanted sexual advances or obscene remarks to a person, especially in a workplace. **sexual politics** relations between the sexes regarded in terms of power.

sexuality > *noun* (pl. **sexualities**) **1** capacity for sexual feelings. **2** a person's sexual orientation or preference.

sexy > *adjective* (**sexier**, **sexiest**) **1** sexually attractive or exciting. **2** sexually aroused. **3** informal very exciting or appealing.

DERIVATIVES – **sexily** *adverb* **sexiness** *noun*.

Seychellois /sayshel**waa**/ > *noun* a person from the Seychelles. > *adjective* relating to the Seychelles.

SF > *abbreviation* science fiction.

sforzando /sfor**tsan**dō/ (also **sforzato** /sfor**tsaa**tō/) > *adverb* & *adjective* Music with sudden emphasis.

ORIGIN – Italian, 'using force'.

SFX > *abbreviation* special effects.

ORIGIN – *FX* representing a pronunciation of *effects*.

SG > *abbreviation* Physics specific gravity.

Sg > *symbol* the chemical element seaborgium.

SGML > *abbreviation* Computing Standard Generalised Mark-up Language, a system for encoding electronic texts so that they can be displayed in any desired format.

shabby > *adjective* (**shabbier**, **shabbiest**) **1** worn out or dilapidated. **2** dressed in old or worn clothes. **3** mean and unfair: *a shabby trick*.

DERIVATIVES – **shabbily** *adverb* **shabbiness** *noun*.

ORIGIN – from dialect *shab* 'scab'.

shack > *noun* a roughly built hut or cabin. > *verb* (**shack up**) informal live with someone as a lover.

ORIGIN – perhaps from the Mexican or Nahuatl words for 'wooden hut'.

shackle > *noun* **1** (**shackles**) a pair of fetters connected by a chain, used to fasten a prisoner's wrists or ankles together. **2** (**shackles**) restraints or impediments. **3** a metal link or loop, closed by a bolt and used to secure a chain or rope to something. > *verb* **1** chain with shackles. **2** restrain; limit.

shad > *noun* (pl. same or **shads**) an edible herring-like marine fish that enters rivers to spawn.

shaddock /**shadd**ək/ > *noun* another term for **POMELO**.

ORIGIN – named after Captain *Shaddock*, who introduced it to the West Indies in the 17th century.

shade > *noun* **1** comparative darkness and coolness caused by shelter from direct sunlight. **2** a colour, especially with regard to how light or dark it is. **3** a position of relative inferiority or obscurity: *your bravery puts me in the shade*. **4** a slightly differing variety. **5** a slight amount: *a shade anxious*. **6** a lampshade. **7** (**shades**) informal sunglasses. **8** literary a ghost. > *verb* **1** screen from direct light. **2** cover or moderate the light of. **3** darken or intensify using a pencil, charcoal, etc., or a darker colour. **4** pass or change by degrees: *outrage began to shade into dismay*.

IDIOMS – **shades of** —— suggestive or reminiscent of.

DERIVATIVES – **shadeless** *adjective* **shader** *noun*.

shading > *noun* **1** the representation of light and shade on a drawing or map. **2** a very slight variation. **3** something providing shade.

shadow > *noun* **1** a dark area or shape produced by an object coming between light rays and a surface. **2** partial or complete darkness. **3** a position of relative inferiority or obscurity. **4** sadness or gloom. **5** the slightest trace: *without a shadow of a doubt*. **6** a weak or inferior remnant or version: *a shadow of her former self*. **7** an inseparable attendant or companion. **8** a person secretly following and observing another. **9** (before another noun) Brit. denoting the opposition counterpart of a government minister. > *verb* **1** cast a shadow over. **2** follow and observe secretly. **3** accompany (a worker) in their daily activities for experience of or insight into a job.

WORDFINDER – tenebrous (*shadowy*); Brocken spectre (*shadow projected on to mist or cloud*), penumbra (*area of partial shadow*), umbra (*area of full shadow*).

DERIVATIVES – **shadower** *noun* **shadowless** *adjective*.

COMBINATIONS – **shadowland 1** a place in shadow. **2** an indeterminate borderland between places or states.

shadow-box > *verb* spar with an imaginary opponent as a form of training.

shadowy > *adjective* (**shadowier**, **shadowiest**) **1** full of shadows. **2** of uncertain identity or nature.

DERIVATIVES – **shadowiness** *noun*.

shady > *adjective* (**shadier**, **shadiest**) **1** situated in or full of shade. **2** giving shade. **3** informal of doubtful honesty or legality.

DERIVATIVES – **shadiness** *noun*.

shaft > *noun* **1** a long, narrow part forming the handle of a tool or club, the body of a spear or arrow, or similar. **2** a ray of light or bolt of lightning. **3** a long, narrow, typically vertical hole giving access to a mine, accommodating a lift, etc. **4** each of the pair of poles between which a horse is harnessed to a vehicle. **5** a long cylindrical rotating rod for the transmission of motive power in a machine. **6** a column, especially the part between the base and capital. **7** a sudden flash of a quality or feeling. **8** a witty, wounding, or provoking remark. > *verb* **1** (of light) shine in beams. **2** informal treat harshly or unfairly. **3** vulgar slang (of a man) have sexual intercourse with.

DERIVATIVES – **shafted** adjective.

shag[1] > noun **1** a carpet or rug with a long, rough pile. **2** (before another noun) (of pile) long and rough. **3** a thick, tangled hairstyle. **4** coarse cut tobacco.

shag[2] > noun a cormorant with greenish-black plumage and a long curly crest in the breeding season.

ORIGIN – perhaps from **SHAG**[1], with reference to the bird's 'shaggy' crest.

shag[3] Brit. vulgar slang > verb (**shagged**, **shagging**) have sexual intercourse with. > noun an act of sexual intercourse.

DERIVATIVES – **shagger** noun.

shag[4] > noun a dance originating in the US, characterised by vigorous hopping from one foot to the other.

ORIGIN – perhaps from obsolete *shag* 'waggle'.

shagged > adjective Brit. vulgar slang **1** exhausted. **2** damaged or ruined.

shaggy > adjective (**shaggier**, **shaggiest**) **1** (of hair or fur) long, thick, and unkempt. **2** having shaggy hair or fur.

IDIOMS – **shaggy-dog story** a long, rambling story or joke, amusing only because it is absurdly inconsequential.

DERIVATIVES – **shaggily** adverb **shagginess** noun.

shagreen /sha**green**/ > noun **1** sharkskin used for decoration or as an abrasive. **2** untanned leather with a rough granulated surface.

ORIGIN – variant of **CHAGRIN** in the literal sense 'rough skin'.

shah /shaa/ > noun historical a title of the former monarch of Iran.

ORIGIN – Persian, 'king'.

shake > verb (past **shook**; past participle **shaken**) **1** move quickly and jerkily up and down or to and fro. **2** tremble uncontrollably with strong emotion. **3** make a threatening gesture with: *he shook his fist.* **4** remove or dislodge by shaking. **5** shock or astonish. **6** weaken (confidence, a belief, etc.). **7** get rid of or put an end to: *old habits he couldn't shake off.* > noun **1** an act of shaking. **2** an amount sprinkled from a container. **3** informal a milkshake. **4** (**the shakes**) informal a fit of trembling or shivering.

IDIOMS – **in two shakes (of a lamb's tail)** informal very quickly. **no great shakes** informal not very good. **shake down 1** settle down. **2** N. Amer. informal extort money from. **shake someone's hand** clasp someone's right hand in one's own and shake it a little, in greeting or as a sign of agreement or reconciliation. **shake hands** (of two people) shake each other's hand. **shake the dust off one's feet** leave indignantly or disdainfully. **shake a leg** informal make a start; rouse oneself. **shake on** informal confirm (an

agreement) by shaking hands. **shake up 1** rouse from lethargy or apathy. **2** make radical changes to (an institution or system).

SYNONYMS – *verb* **1,2** agitate, jiggle, quiver, shiver, shudder, tremble. **3** brandish. **5** astonish, disconcert, disturb, perturb, shock, unnerve. **6** damage, harm, undermine, weaken.

COMBINATIONS – **shakedown** informal, chiefly N. Amer. **1** a radical change or restructuring. **2** a thorough search. **3** a swindle. **4** a makeshift bed.

shaker > noun **1** a container used for mixing ingredients by shaking. **2** a container with a pierced top from which a powder or granules are poured by shaking. **3** (**Shaker**) a member of an American Christian sect living simply in celibate mixed communities. [ORIGIN – so named from the wild, ecstatic movements engaged in during worship.] **4** (**Shaker**) (before another noun) denoting a style of elegantly functional furniture traditionally produced by Shakers.

DERIVATIVES – **Shakerism** noun.

Shakespearean /shayk**speer**iən/ (also **Shakespearian**) > adjective relating to or in the style of William Shakespeare or his works. > noun an expert in or student of Shakespeare's works.

wordpower facts
Shakespeare's English
The dramatist William Shakespeare (1564–1616) introduced a great many new words and phrases into the English language, and also gave new life to existing words by using them in a new way. For example, he was the first to borrow the word **anchovy** from Spanish (*Henry IV, Part I*), the first to use the verb **bellow** in reference to a human being rather than an animal (*Hamlet*), the first to refer to the start of something as a **birth** (*Love's Labours Lost*), and the first to use **scream** as a noun (*Macbeth*). The *Oxford English Dictionary* attributes over 7,000 new words and senses to Shakespeare. He also enriched the store of idioms, coining such phrases as **this mortal coil** (*Hamlet*), **the dogs of war** (*Julius Caesar*), **in one fell swoop** (*Macbeth*), **the green-eyed monster** (*Othello*), **the milk of human kindness** (*Macbeth*), **the world is your oyster** (*The Merry Wives of Windsor*), and many more.

shake-up (also **shake-out**) > noun informal a radical reorganisation.

shako /**shay**kō/ > noun (pl. **shakos**) a peaked cylindrical military hat with a plume or pompom.

ORIGIN – Hungarian *csákó* (*süveg*) 'peaked (cap)'.

shaky > adjective (**shakier**, **shakiest**) **1** shaking or trembling. **2** unstable. **3** not safe or reliable.

DERIVATIVES – **shakily** adverb **shakiness** noun.

shale > noun soft stratified sedimentary rock formed from consolidated mud or clay.

DERIVATIVES – **shaly** (also **shaley**) adjective.

ORIGIN – probably from German *Schale*.

shall > modal verb (3rd sing. present **shall**) **1** (in the first person) expressing the future tense. **2** expressing a strong assertion or intention. **3** expressing an instruction or command. **4** used in questions indicating offers or suggestions.

USAGE – what is the difference between **shall** and **will**? Strictly speaking **shall** should be used with **I** and **we** to form the future tense, as in *I shall be late*, while **will** should be used with **you**, **he**, **she**, **it**, and **they**, as in *she will not be there*. This, however, is reversed when strong determination is being expressed, as in *I will not tolerate this*, and *you shall go to school*. In speech the distinction tends to be obscured, through the use of the contracted forms **I'll**, **she'll**, etc.

ORIGIN – Old English, from a base meaning 'owe'.

shallot /shə**lot**/ > noun the small bulb of a plant of the onion family, used in cookery and pickling.

ORIGIN – French *eschalotte*, alteration of Old French *eschaloigne*, *scaloun* 'scallion'.

shallow > adjective **1** of little depth. **2** not showing, requiring, or capable of serious thought. > noun (**shallows**) a shallow area of water.

DERIVATIVES – **shallowly** adverb **shallowness** noun.

SYNONYMS – **2** facile, slight, superficial, trivial.

ANTONYMS – **1** deep. **2** profound, serious.

ORIGIN – obscurely related to **SHOAL**[2].

shalom /shə**lom**/ > exclamation used as a greeting by Jews at meeting or parting.

ORIGIN – Hebrew, 'peace'.

shalt archaic second person singular of **SHALL**.

shalwar > noun variant spelling of **SALWAR**.

sham > noun **1** a person or thing that is not what they appear or are claimed to be. **2** the action of pretending; deception. > adjective bogus; false. > verb (**shammed**, **shamming**) pretend or pretend to be.

DERIVATIVES – **shammer** noun.

SYNONYMS – **1** charlatan, fake, fraud,

impostor; informal phoney. **2** act, counterfeit, deception, fiction, pretence.

ORIGIN – perhaps a northern English dialect variant of SHAME.

shaman /**shay**mən, **shamm**ən/ > *noun* (pl. **shamans**) (especially among some peoples of northern Asia and North America) a person regarded as having access to, and influence in, the world of good and evil spirits.

DERIVATIVES – **shamanic** /shə**mann**ik/ *adjective* **shamanism** *noun* **shamanistic** *adjective*.

ORIGIN – Tungus (a language of Siberia).

shamateur > *noun* derogatory a sports player who makes money from sporting activities though classified as amateur.

DERIVATIVES – **shamateurism** *noun*.

ORIGIN – blend of SHAM and AMATEUR.

shamble > *verb* move with a slow, shuffling, awkward gait. > *noun* a shambling gait.

ORIGIN – probably from dialect *shamble* 'ungainly', perhaps from *shamble legs*, with reference to the legs of trestle tables typical of meat markets (see SHAMBLES).

shambles > *noun* **1** informal a chaotic state. **2** archaic a butcher's slaughterhouse. **3** a scene of carnage.

ORIGIN – first used in the sense 'meat market': plural of earlier *shamble* 'stool, stall', from Latin *scamellum* 'little bench'.

shambolic > *adjective* informal, chiefly Brit. chaotic or disorganised.

ORIGIN – from SHAMBLES, probably on the pattern of *symbolic*.

shame > *noun* **1** a feeling of humiliation or distress caused by awareness of one's wrong or foolish behaviour. **2** loss of respect or esteem. **3** a cause of shame. **4** a regrettable or unfortunate thing. > *verb* cause to feel ashamed.

IDIOMS – **put to shame** shame (someone) by outdoing or surpassing them. **shame on you!** you should be ashamed.

SYNONYMS – *noun* **1** chagrin, distress, embarrassment, guilt, humiliation, mortification. **2** disgrace, dishonour, disrepute, ignominy, opprobrium. **4** pity. *verb* disgrace, embarrass, humiliate.

ANTONYMS – *noun* **1** pride. **2** glory, honour.

shamefaced > *adjective* feeling and showing shame.

DERIVATIVES – **shamefacedly** *adverb* **shamefacedness** *noun*.

SYNONYMS – abashed, ashamed, mortified, penitent, red-faced, sheepish.

shameful > *adjective* worthy of or causing shame.

DERIVATIVES – **shamefully** *adverb* **shamefulness** *noun*.

SYNONYMS – contemptible, disgraceful, dishonourable, ignoble, ignominious, scandalous.

ANTONYMS – admirable, honourable.

shameless > *adjective* showing a lack of shame or constraint.

DERIVATIVES – **shamelessly** *adverb* **shamelessness** *noun*.

SYNONYMS – barefaced, blatant, brazen, flagrant, forward, unabashed.

shammy (also **shammy leather**) > *noun* (pl. **shammies**) informal chamois leather.

ORIGIN – a phonetic spelling.

shampoo > *noun* **1** a liquid preparation for washing the hair. **2** a similar substance for cleaning a carpet, car, etc. **3** an act of washing with shampoo. > *verb* (**shampoos**, **shampooed**) wash or clean with shampoo.

ORIGIN – from a Hindi word meaning 'to press': originally used in the sense 'massage'.

shamrock > *noun* a clover-like plant with three-lobed leaves, the national emblem of Ireland.

ORIGIN – Irish *seamróg* 'trefoil'.

shamus /**shay**məss/ > *noun* N. Amer. informal a private detective.

shandy > *noun* (pl. **shandies**) beer mixed with lemonade or ginger beer.

ORIGIN – abbreviation of *shandygaff*, in the same sense, of unknown origin.

shanghai[1] /shang**hī**/ > *verb* (**shanghais**, **shanghaied**, **shanghaiing**) **1** historical force to join a ship's crew by underhand means. **2** informal coerce or trick into a place or action.

ORIGIN – from *Shanghai*, a major Chinese seaport.

shanghai[2] /shang**hī**/ Austral./NZ > *noun* (pl. **shanghais**) a catapult. > *verb* (**shanghais**, **shanghaied**, **shanghaiing**) shoot with or as with a catapult.

ORIGIN – probably an alteration of Scots dialect *shangan* 'a stick cleft at one end'.

Shangri-La /shanggri**laa**/ > *noun* an earthly paradise.

ORIGIN – named after a Tibetan utopia in James Hilton's *Lost Horizon* (1933), from *Shangri* (an invented name) + Tibetan *la* 'mountain pass'.

shank > *noun* **1** a person's leg, especially the lower part. **2** the lower part of an animal's foreleg, especially as a cut of meat. **3** the shaft or stem of a tool or implement. **4** the band of a ring.

DERIVATIVES – **shanked** *adjective*.

Shanks's pony (also **Shanks's mare**) > *noun* one's own legs as a means of transport.

shan't > *contraction* shall not.

shantung /shan**tung**/ > *noun* a type of soft silk with a coarse surface.

ORIGIN – from *Shantung* in China, where it was originally made.

shanty[1] > *noun* (pl. **shanties**) a makeshift shack or dwelling, improvised from available materials.

COMBINATIONS – **shanty town** an impoverished area consisting of large numbers of shanty dwellings.

ORIGIN – perhaps from Canadian French *chantier* 'lumberjack's cabin, logging camp'.

shanty[2] (also **chanty** or **sea shanty**) > *noun* (pl. **shanties**) a song with alternating solo and chorus, of a kind originally sung by sailors working together.

ORIGIN – probably from French *chantez!* 'sing!'.

shape > *noun* **1** the external form or appearance of someone or something as produced by their outline. **2** a piece of material, paper, etc., made or cut in a particular form. **3** a particular condition or state: *the house was in poor shape*. **4** a specific form or guise assumed by someone or something: *a fiend in human shape*. **5** definite or orderly arrangement. > *verb* **1** give a shape or form to. **2** determine the nature of. **3** (often **shape up**) develop in a particular way. **4** (**shape up**) become physically fit. **5** (**shape up**) informal improve (something).

WORDFINDER – amorphous (*having no definite shape*), malformation (*abnormality of shape*), morphology (*the study of shape*).

IDIOMS – **in (good) shape** in good physical condition. **in the shape of** by way of. **lick (or knock) into shape** act forcefully to bring into a better state. **out of shape 1** not having its usual or original shape. **2** in poor physical condition. **take shape** assume a distinct form.

DERIVATIVES – **shaped** *adjective* **shaper** *noun*.

SYNONYMS – *verb* **1** fashion, form, model, mould. **2** determine, direct, form, influence, mould.

COMBINATIONS – **shape-shifter** an imaginary being who is able to change their physical form at will.

shapeless > *adjective* lacking definite or attractive shape.

DERIVATIVES – **shapelessly** *adverb* **shapelessness** *noun*.

shapely > *adjective* (**shapelier**, **shapeliest**) having an attractive or well-proportioned shape.

DERIVATIVES – **shapeliness** *noun*.

shard > *noun* a sharp piece of broken ceramic, metal, glass, etc.

ORIGIN – Old English 'gap, notch, potsherd'; related to SHEAR.

share[1] > *noun* **1** a part of a larger amount which is divided among or contributed by a number of people. **2** any of the equal parts into which a company's capital is divided, entitling the holder to a proportion of the profits. **3** the allotted or due amount

S share–sheath

expected to be had or done: *more than their fair share of problems.* **4** a person's contribution to an enterprise. > *verb* **1** have or give a share of. **2** possess or use in common with others. **3** (**share in**) participate in. **4** tell someone about.

WORDFINDER – ordinary share (*share yielding variable dividend*), preference share (*yielding fixed dividend*); blue-chip, gilt-edged (*denoting shares regarded as very reliable investments*), equity (*value of the shares issued by a company*), flotation (*offering a company's shares for sale on the stock market for the first time*), scrip (*provisional certificate of shares held*); index of figures showing share prices: FTSE (*UK*), Dow Jones (*US*), Hang Seng (*Hong Kong*), Nikkei (*Japan*).

DERIVATIVES – **shareable** (also **sharable**) *adjective* **sharer** *noun*.

SYNONYMS – *noun* **1** allocation, allowance, bit, division, part, portion, quota.

COMBINATIONS – **share option** an option for an employee to buy shares in their company at a discount or at a stated fixed price. **shareware** computer software that is available free of charge and often distributed informally for evaluation.

ORIGIN – Old English, related to SHEAR.

share² > *noun* a ploughshare.

sharecropper > *noun* chiefly N. Amer. a tenant farmer who gives a part of each crop as rent.

shareholder > *noun* an owner of shares in a company.

DERIVATIVES – **shareholding** *noun*.

sharia /shəreeə/ > *noun* Islamic canonical law based on the teachings of the Koran and the traditions of Muhammad.

ORIGIN – Arabic.

shark¹ > *noun* a long-bodied cartilaginous marine fish, typically predatory and voracious, with a prominent dorsal fin.

COMBINATIONS – **sharkskin** a stiff, slightly lustrous synthetic fabric.

shark² > *noun* informal a person who exploits or swindles others.

ORIGIN – perhaps from German *Schurke* 'worthless rogue', influenced by SHARK¹.

sharon fruit /sharrən/ > *noun* a persimmon, especially one of an orange variety grown in Israel.

ORIGIN – from *Sharon*, a fertile coastal plain in Israel.

sharp > *adjective* **1** having a cutting or piercing edge or point. **2** tapering to a point or edge. **3** sudden and marked: *a sharp increase.* **4** making a sudden change of direction. **5** clearly defined. **6** producing a sudden, piercing sensation or effect: *a sharp pain.* **7** quick to understand, notice, or respond. **8** quick to take advantage, especially in a dishonest way. **9** (of a food, taste, or smell) acidic and intense. **10** (of a sound) sudden and penetrating. **11** critical

or hurtful. **12** informal smart and stylish. **13** (of musical sound) above true or normal pitch. **14** (after a noun) (of a note or key) higher by a semitone than a specified note or key. > *adverb* **1** precisely: *at 7.30 sharp.* **2** suddenly or abruptly. **3** above the true or normal pitch of musical sound. > *noun* **1** a musical note raised a semitone above natural pitch. **2** the sign (♯) indicating this. **3** a thing with a sharp edge or point.

WORDFINDER – acuity (*sharpness of vision*).

DERIVATIVES – **sharply** *adverb* **sharpness** *noun*.

SYNONYMS – **1** cutting, keen, piercing. **6** intense, piercing, searing, stabbing, stinging. **7** alert, astute, keen, perceptive, quick. **8** artful, crafty, cunning. **9** piquant, tart.

ANTONYMS – **1** blunt. **3** gradual. **6** mild. **9** mellow, mild.

COMBINATIONS – **sharp practice** dishonest or barely honest dealings. **sharp-tongued** given to using harsh or critical language. **sharp-witted** perceptive or intelligent.

sharpen > *verb* make or become sharp.

DERIVATIVES – **sharpener** *noun*.

sharper > *noun* informal a swindler, especially at cards.

sharpish informal > *adjective* fairly sharp. > *adverb* chiefly Brit. quickly; soon.

sharpshooter > *noun* a person skilled in shooting.

shat past and past participle of SHIT.

shatter > *verb* **1** break suddenly and violently into pieces. **2** damage or destroy: *their hopes were shattered.* **3** upset greatly. **4** informal exhaust completely.

DERIVATIVES – **shatterer** *noun* **shattered** *adjective* **shattering** *adjective*.

SYNONYMS – **1** disintegrate, smash, splinter. **2** crush, damage, dash, destroy, wreck. **3** devastate, shock, stun.

ORIGIN – perhaps imitative; compare with SCATTER.

shave > *verb* **1** cut the hair off one's face with a razor. **2** cut the hair off (part of the body) with a razor. **3** cut (a thin slice or slices) off something. **4** reduce by a small amount. **5** pass or send something very close to. > *noun* **1** an act of shaving. **2** a tool for shaving very thin slices or layers from wood.

shaven > *adjective* shaved.

shaver > *noun* **1** an electric razor. **2** informal, dated a young lad.

Shavian /shayviən/ > *adjective* relating to the Irish dramatist George Bernard Shaw (1856–1950) or his works or ideas. > *noun* an admirer of Shaw or his work.

ORIGIN – from *Shavius*, the Latinised form of *Shaw*.

shaving > *noun* **1** a thin strip cut off a

surface. **2** (before another noun) used when shaving: *shaving foam.*

shawl > *noun* a large piece of fabric worn by women over the shoulders or head or wrapped round a baby.

DERIVATIVES – **shawled** *adjective*.

COMBINATIONS – **shawl collar** a rounded collar without lapel notches that extends down the front of a garment.

ORIGIN – from Urdu and Persian, probably from *Shāliāt*, a town in India.

shawm /shawm/ > *noun* a medieval and Renaissance wind instrument, forerunner of the oboe, with a double reed in a wooden mouthpiece.

ORIGIN – Old French *chalemel*, from Greek *kalamos* 'reed'.

Shawnee /shawnee/ > *noun* (pl. same or **Shawnees**) a member of an American Indian people formerly living in the eastern US.

ORIGIN – the name in Delaware.

shaykh > *noun* variant spelling of SHEIKH.

she > *pronoun* (third person sing.) **1** used to refer to a woman, girl, or female animal previously mentioned or easily identified. **2** used to refer to a ship, country, or other inanimate thing regarded as female. **3** any female person (in modern use, now largely replaced by 'anyone' or 'the person'). **4** Austral./NZ informal it; the state of affairs. > *noun* a female; a woman.

COMBINATIONS – **she-devil** a malicious or spiteful woman.

sheaf > *noun* (pl. **sheaves**) **1** a bundle of grain stalks laid lengthways and tied together after reaping. **2** a bundle of objects, especially papers. > *verb* bundle into sheaves.

ORIGIN – Old English, related to SHOVE.

shear > *verb* (past participle **shorn** or **sheared**) **1** cut the wool off (a sheep or other animal). **2** cut off with scissors or shears. **3** (**be shorn of**) be deprived or stripped of. **4** break off or cause to break off, owing to a structural strain. > *noun* a strain produced by pressure in the structure of a substance, when its layers are laterally shifted in relation to each other.

DERIVATIVES – **shearer** *noun*.

USAGE – do not confuse **shear** with **sheer**, which means 'swerve or change course quickly', as in *the boat sheers off the bank*, and 'avoid an unpleasant topic', as in *her mind sheered away from these unwelcome images.*

shears (also **a pair of shears**) > *plural noun* a cutting instrument in which two blades move past each other, like very large scissors.

shearwater > *noun* a long-winged seabird related to the petrels, often flying low over the water.

sheath /sheeth/ > *noun* (pl. **sheaths** /sheethz, sheeths/) **1** a cover for the blade of a knife or sword. **2** a condom. **3** a structure in living tissue which closely envelops another. **4** a protective covering around an electric cable. **5** (also **sheath dress**) a close-fitting dress.

COMBINATIONS – **sheath knife** a short knife similar to a dagger, carried in a sheath.

ORIGIN – Old English, related to **SHED²**.

sheathe /sheeth/ > *verb* **1** put (a knife or sword) into a sheath. **2** (often **be sheathed in**) encase in a close-fitting or protective covering.

sheathing /sheething/ > *noun* protective casing or covering.

sheave > *verb* make into sheaves.

sheaves plural of **SHEAF**.

shebang /shibang/ > *noun informal* a matter, operation, or situation: *the whole shebang.*

ORIGIN – first used in the US, in the sense 'a rough hut or shelter'.

shebeen /shibeen/ > *noun* (especially in Ireland, Scotland, and South Africa) an unlicensed establishment or private house selling alcoholic liquor.

ORIGIN – Anglo-Irish *síbín*, from *séibe* 'mugful'.

shed¹ > *noun* **1** a simple roofed structure, typically of wood and used for storage or to shelter animals. **2** a larger structure, typically with one or more sides open, for storing vehicles or machinery.

COMBINATIONS – **shedload** Brit. informal a large amount or number.

ORIGIN – apparently a variant of **SHADE**.

shed² > *verb* (**shedding**; past and past participle **shed**) **1** lose (leaves, hair, skin, etc.) as a result of their falling off naturally. **2** discard; get rid of. **3** take off (clothes). **4** cast or give off (light). **5** accidentally drop or spill. **6** resist the absorption of.

IDIOMS – **shed tears** cry.

DERIVATIVES – **shedder** *noun.*

ORIGIN – Old English, 'separate out, divide', also 'scatter'; related to **SHEATH**.

she'd > *contraction* she had; she would.

sheen > *noun* a soft lustre on a surface.

DERIVATIVES – **sheeny** *adjective.*

SYNONYMS – gleam, gloss, lustre, polish, shine.

ORIGIN – from obsolete *sheen* 'beautiful, resplendent'; apparently related to **SHINE**.

sheep > *noun* (pl. same) **1** a domesticated ruminant mammal with a thick woolly coat, kept in flocks for its wool or meat. **2** a person who is too easily influenced or led. **3** a member of a minister's congregation. [ORIGIN – with allusion to the Gospel of Luke, chapter 15.]

WORDFINDER – ovine (*of or like a sheep*); ewe (*female sheep*), ram, tup (*male sheep*), shearling (*sheep that has been shorn once*), wether (*castrated male sheep*).

IDIOMS – **make sheep's eyes at** look at in a foolishly amorous way.

DERIVATIVES – **sheeplike** *adjective.*

COMBINATIONS – **sheep dip 1** a liquid preparation for cleansing sheep of parasites or preserving their wool. **2** a place where sheep are dipped in this liquid. **sheepdog 1** a dog trained to guard and herd sheep. **2** a dog of a breed suitable for this. **sheepskin** a sheep's skin with the wool on, especially when made into a garment or rug.

sheepish > *adjective* embarrassed as an effect of shame or shyness.

DERIVATIVES – **sheepishly** *adverb* **sheepishness** *noun.*

SYNONYMS – abashed, ashamed, embarrassed, shamefaced.

sheepshank > *noun* a knot used to shorten a rope temporarily.

sheer¹ > *adjective* **1** nothing but; absolute: *sheer hard work.* **2** (of a cliff, wall, etc.) perpendicular or nearly so. **3** (of a fabric) very thin. > *adverb* perpendicularly.

DERIVATIVES – **sheerly** *adverb* **sheerness** *noun.*

SYNONYMS – *adjective* **1** absolute, complete, plain, pure, simple, utter. **2** perpendicular, precipitous, vertical. **3** diaphanous, fine, flimsy, gauzy, gossamer.

ORIGIN – probably an alteration of dialect *shire* 'pure, clear', from the base of **SHINE**.

sheer² > *verb* **1** (especially of a boat) swerve or change course quickly. **2** avoid or move away from an unpleasant topic.

USAGE – although they are related historically **sheer** and **shear** have different meanings. **Shear** means 'cut the wool off (a sheep)', or 'cut or break off' as in *the pins broke and the wing sheared off.*

ORIGIN – perhaps from Low German *scheren* 'to shear'.

sheet¹ > *noun* **1** a large rectangular piece of cotton or other fabric, used on a bed to cover the mattress or as a layer beneath blankets. **2** a broad flat piece of metal or glass. **3** a rectangular piece of paper. **4** an extensive layer or moving mass of water, ice, flame, etc. > *verb* **1** cover with or wrap in a sheet or sheeting. **2** (of rain) fall heavily.

COMBINATIONS – **sheet lightning** lightning with its brightness diffused by reflection within clouds. **sheet metal** metal formed into thin sheets. **sheet music 1** printed music, as opposed to performed or recorded music. **2** music published on separate sheets, that are not fastened together.

ORIGIN – Old English, related to **SHOOT**.

sheet² > *noun* **1** a rope attached to the lower corner of a sail. **2** (**sheets**) the space at the bow or stern of an open boat.

IDIOMS – **two** (or **three**) **sheets to the wind** informal drunk. [ORIGIN – nautical: if the *sheets* or ropes used for controlling the

sails are flapping in the wind the vessel is likely to be sailing erratically.]

ORIGIN – Old English, related to **SHEET¹**.

sheet anchor > *noun* **1** an additional anchor for use in emergencies. **2** a person or thing that can be relied on if all else fails.

ORIGIN – perhaps related to obsolete *shot*, denoting two cables spliced together, later influenced by **SHEET²**.

sheeting > *noun* material of extra width, used for making sheets.

sheikh /shayk/ (also **shaykh** or **sheik**) > *noun* **1** an Arab leader, especially the chief or head of a tribe, family, or village. **2** a leader in a Muslim community or organisation.

DERIVATIVES – **sheikhdom** *noun.*

ORIGIN – Arabic, 'old man, sheikh'.

sheila > *noun* Austral./NZ informal a girl or woman.

ORIGIN – first spelt as *shaler*: of unknown origin, later assimilated to the given name *Sheila.*

shekel /shekk'l/ > *noun* **1** the basic monetary unit of modern Israel. **2** (**shekels**) informal money; wealth.

ORIGIN – Hebrew.

shelduck /shelduk/ > *noun* (pl. same or **shelducks**) a large goose-like duck with boldly marked plumage.

ORIGIN – probably from dialect *sheld* 'pied' (related to Dutch *schillede* 'variegated') + **DUCK¹**.

shelf > *noun* (pl. **shelves**) **1** a flat length of wood or other rigid material attached to a wall or forming part of a piece of furniture, providing a surface for storage or display. **2** a ledge of rock or protruding strip of land.

IDIOMS – **off the shelf** taken from existing stock, not designed or made to order. **on the shelf 1** no longer useful or desirable. **2** past an age when one might expect to be married.

COMBINATIONS – **shelf life** the length of time for which an item remains usable, edible, or saleable.

ORIGIN – Low German *schelf.*

shell > *noun* **1** the hard protective outer case of an animal such as a snail, shellfish, or turtle. **2** the outer covering of an egg, nut kernel, or seed. **3** an explosive artillery projectile or bomb. **4** a hollow metal or paper case used as a container for fireworks, explosives, or cartridges. **5** N. Amer. a cartridge. **6** something resembling or likened to a shell, especially a hollow case. **7** the walls of an unfinished or gutted building. **8** a light racing boat. **9** (also **shell program**) Computing a program providing an interface between the user and the operating system. > *verb* **1** bombard with explosive shells. **2** remove the shell or pod from. **3** (**shell out**) informal pay (an amount of money).

WORDFINDER – conchology (*study of mollusc shells*).

IDIOMS – **come out of one's shell** cease to be shy.

DERIVATIVES – **shelled** adjective **shell-less** adjective **shell-like** adjective **shelly** adjective.

COMBINATIONS – **shell company** a non-trading company used as a vehicle for various financial manoeuvres. **shellfire** bombardment by shells. **shell game** N. Amer. **1** the game of thimblerig. **2** a deceptive and evasive action or ploy. **shell pink** a delicate pale pink. **shell suit** a casual outfit consisting of a loose jacket and trousers with a soft lining and a shiny polyester outer shell.

ORIGIN – Old English, related to SCALE¹.

she'll > *contraction* she shall; she will.

shellac /shə**lak**/ > *noun* lac resin melted into thin flakes, used for making varnish. > *verb* (**shellacked**, **shellacking**) varnish with shellac.

ORIGIN – from SHELL + LAC¹, translating French *laque en écailles* 'lac in thin plates'.

shellfish > *noun* an aquatic shelled mollusc or crustacean, especially an edible one.

shell shock > *noun* psychological disturbance caused by prolonged exposure to active warfare.

DERIVATIVES – **shell-shocked** adjective.

Shelta /**shel**tə/ > *noun* an ancient secret language used by Irish and Welsh tinkers and gypsies, based on altered Irish or Gaelic words.

shelter > *noun* **1** a place giving protection from bad weather or danger. **2** a place providing food and accommodation for the homeless. **3** a shielded condition; protection. > *verb* **1** provide with shelter. **2** find refuge or take cover. **3** (**sheltered**) protected from having to do or face something difficult.

DERIVATIVES – **shelterer** noun **shelterless** adjective.

SYNONYMS – noun **1** refuge, sanctuary. **3** protection, refuge, safety, sanctuary, security. verb **1** cover, protect, screen, shield.

COMBINATIONS – **sheltered housing** (also **sheltered accommodation**) Brit. accommodation for elderly or handicapped people, consisting of private independent units with some shared facilities and a warden.

ORIGIN – perhaps an alteration of obsolete *sheltron* 'phalanx', from an Old English word meaning 'shield troop'.

shelve¹ > *verb* **1** place on a shelf. **2** defer (a plan or project). **3** fit with shelves.

DERIVATIVES – **shelver** noun.

SYNONYMS – **2** defer, delay, hold over, postpone, put off, suspend.

ORIGIN – from *shelves*, plural of SHELF.

shelve² > *verb* (of ground) slope downwards.

ORIGIN – perhaps from SHELF.

shelves plural of SHELF.

shelving > *noun* lengths of wood to be made into shelves, or shelves collectively.

shemozzle /shi**mozz**'l/ (also **schemozzle**) > *noun* informal a muddle.

ORIGIN – Yiddish, suggested by a Hebrew word meaning 'of no luck'.

shenanigans /shi**nann**igənz/ > *plural noun* informal **1** secret or dishonest activity. **2** mischief.

Sheol /**shee**ōl/ > *noun* the Hebrew underworld, abode of the dead.

ORIGIN – Hebrew.

shepherd > *noun* **1** a person who tends sheep. **2** a member of the clergy providing spiritual care and guidance for a congregation. > *verb* **1** tend (sheep). **2** guide or direct somewhere. **3** give spiritual or other guidance to.

DERIVATIVES – **shepherdess** noun.

COMBINATIONS – **shepherd's pie** a dish of minced meat under a layer of mashed potato. **shepherd's purse** a white-flowered weed with triangular or heart-shaped seed pods.

ORIGIN – Old English, from SHEEP + obsolete *herd* 'herdsman'.

Sheraton /**sherr**ət'n/ > *adjective* (of furniture) designed by or in the simple, graceful style of the English furniture-maker Thomas Sheraton (1751–1806).

sherbet* > *noun* **1** Brit. a flavoured sweet fizzing powder eaten alone or made into a drink. **2** (especially in Arab countries) a drink of sweet diluted fruit juices. **3** N. Amer. water ice; sorbet. **4** Austral. humorous beer.

*SPELLING – -*bet*, not -*bert*: sher*bet.

ORIGIN – Arabic, 'drink'; related to SORBET and SYRUP.

sherd /sherd/ > *noun* another term for POTSHERD.

ORIGIN – variant of SHARD.

sheriff > *noun* **1** (also **high sheriff**) (in England and Wales) the chief executive officer of the Crown in a county. **2** an honorary officer elected annually in some English towns. **3** (in Scotland) a judge. **4** US an elected officer in a county, responsible for keeping the peace.

WORDFINDER – shrieval (*relating to a sheriff*), shrievalty (*sheriff's tenure of office*).

COMBINATIONS – **sheriff court** (in Scotland) a court for civil cases, equivalent to a county court.

ORIGIN – Old English, 'shire reeve'.

Sherpa /**sher**pə/ > *noun* (pl. same or **Sherpas**) a member of a Himalayan people living on the borders of Nepal and Tibet.

ORIGIN – Tibetan, 'inhabitant of an Eastern country'.

sherry > *noun* (pl. **sherries**) a fortified wine originally and mainly from southern Spain.

WORDFINDER – *kinds of sherry*: amontillado, amoroso, fino, manzanilla, oloroso; *glasses for sherry*: copita, schooner.

ORIGIN – from Spanish *vino de Xeres* 'Xeres wine' (Xeres being the former name of the city of *Jerez de la Frontera*).

she's > *contraction* she is; she has.

Shetlander /**shet**ləndər/ > *noun* a person from the Shetland Islands.

Shetland pony > *noun* a small, hardy, rough-coated breed of pony.

shew > *verb* old-fashioned variant of SHOW.

Shia /**shee**ə/ (also **Shi'a**) > *noun* (pl. same or **Shias**) **1** one of the two main branches of Islam, regarding Ali, the fourth caliph, as Muhammad's first true successor. Compare with SUNNI. **2** a Muslim who adheres to this branch of Islam.

ORIGIN – Arabic, 'party (of Ali)'.

shiatsu /shi**at**sōō/ > *noun* a Japanese therapy in which pressure is applied with the hands to points on the body.

ORIGIN – Japanese, 'finger pressure'.

shibboleth /**shibb**əleth/ > *noun* a custom, principle, or belief distinguishing a particular class or group of people.

---

wordpower facts

Shibboleth

The word **shibboleth** comes from Hebrew, in which it means 'ear of corn'. According to the Bible, it was used in ancient Israel as a test of nationality because of its difficult pronunciation. In the Book of Judges (chapter 12), the ruler Jephthah describes how he was able to distinguish (and subsequently massacre) the fleeing Ephraimites because they could not pronounce the *sh*, unlike his own men, the Gileadites. The word was adopted in English in the 17th century in the sense 'a word or sound which a foreigner is unable to pronounce'. From this developed the sense 'a peculiarity of pronunciation or accent', leading, by the early 19th century, to the sense 'a custom, habit, or mode of dress which distinguishes a particular class or set of people'. In its current use a **shibboleth** is likely to denote a custom, taboo, or piece of received wisdom identifiable with a particular group of people.

---

shied past and past participle of SHY².

shield > *noun* **1** a broad piece of armour held for protection against blows or missiles. **2** a sporting trophy consisting of an engraved metal plate mounted on a piece of wood. **3** Heraldry a stylised representation of a shield used for displaying a coat of arms. **4** a US police officer's badge. **5** a protective plate, screen, etc. **6** a source of protection. > *verb* **1** protect from a danger, risk, etc. **2** prevent from being seen. **3** enclose or screen (machinery or a source of sound, light, radiation, etc.) to protect the user.

WORDFINDER – peltate (*shield-shaped*); escutcheon (*shield bearing coat of arms*).

SYNONYMS – *verb* **1** cover, defend, guard, protect, safeguard, shelter. **2** screen.

shift > *verb* **1** move or change from one position to another. **2** Brit. informal move quickly. **3** (**shift oneself**) Brit. informal move or rouse oneself. **4** Brit. remove (a stain). **5** informal sell (merchandise) quickly or in large quantities. **6** Brit. informal eat or drink hastily or in large amounts. **7** chiefly N. Amer. change gear. > *noun* **1** a slight change in position, direction, or tendency. **2** a key used to switch between two sets of characters or functions on a keyboard. **3** each of two or more periods in which different groups of workers do the same jobs in relay. **4** N. Amer. a gear lever or gear-changing mechanism. **5** a straight unwaisted dress. **6** historical a long, loose undergarment. **7** archaic an ingenious or devious device or stratagem.

IDIOMS – **make shift** dated manage or contrive to do something. **shift for oneself** manage alone as best one can. **shift one's ground** change one's position in an argument.

DERIVATIVES – **shifter** noun.

ORIGIN – Old English, 'arrange, apportion' and 'change, replace'.

shiftless > *adjective* lazy, indolent, and lacking ambition.

DERIVATIVES – **shiftlessness** noun.

shifty > *adjective* (**shiftier**, **shiftiest**) informal deceitful or evasive.

DERIVATIVES – **shiftily** adverb **shiftiness** noun.

shigella /shiˈgellə/ > *noun* (pl. same or **shigellae** /shiˈgellee/) a bacterium of a genus including some kinds responsible for dysentery.

ORIGIN – from the name of the Japanese bacteriologist Kiyoshi *Shiga* (1870–1957).

shih-tzu /sheetsoo/ > *noun* a breed of dog with long, silky, erect hair and short legs.

ORIGIN – Chinese, 'lion'.

shiitake /shiˈtaakay/ > *noun* an edible mushroom cultivated in Japan and China.

ORIGIN – Japanese, from *shii*, denoting a kind of oak, + *take* 'mushroom'.

Shiite /sheeīt/ (also **Shi'ite**) > *noun* an adherent of the Shia branch of Islam. > *adjective* relating to Shia.

DERIVATIVES – **Shiism** /sheeiz'm/ (also **Shi'ism**) noun.

shiksa /shiksə/ > *noun* derogatory (in Jewish use) a gentile girl or woman.

ORIGIN – Hebrew, 'detested thing'.

shill > *noun* N. Amer. informal an accomplice of a hawker, gambler, or swindler who acts as an enthusiastic customer to entice others.

shillelagh /shiˈlaylə/ > *noun* (in Ireland) a cudgel of blackthorn or oak.

ORIGIN – from the name of the town *Shillelagh*, in County Wicklow, Ireland.

shilling > *noun* **1** a former British coin and monetary unit equal to one twentieth of a pound or twelve pence. **2** the basic monetary unit of Kenya, Tanzania, and Uganda.

IDIOMS – **not the full shilling** Brit. informal not very clever. **take the King's** (or **Queen's**) **shilling** Brit. enlist as a soldier. [ORIGIN – with reference to the former practice of paying a shilling to a new recruit.]

shilly-shally > *verb* (**shilly-shallies**, **shilly-shallied**) be indecisive. > *noun* indecisive behaviour.

DERIVATIVES – **shilly-shallyer** (also **shilly-shallier**) noun.

ORIGIN – from *shill I, shall I*, reduplication of *shall I?*

shim > *noun* a washer or thin strip of material used to align parts, make them fit together, or reduce wear. > *verb* (**shimmed**, **shimming**) wedge or fill up with a shim.

shimmer > *verb* shine with a soft tremulous light. > *noun* a light with such qualities.

DERIVATIVES – **shimmery** adjective.

SYNONYMS – *verb* glimmer, glint, glisten, glitter, sparkle, twinkle.

ORIGIN – Old English, related to SHINE.

shimmy > *noun* (pl. **shimmies**) **1** a kind of ragtime dance in which the whole body shakes or sways. **2** abnormal vibration of the wheels of a motor vehicle. > *verb* (**shimmies**, **shimmied**) **1** dance the shimmy. **2** shake or vibrate abnormally. **3** move swiftly and effortlessly.

shin > *noun* **1** the front of the leg below the knee. **2** a cut of beef from the lower part of a cow's leg. > *verb* (**shinned**, **shinning**) (**shin up** or **down**) climb quickly up or down by gripping with one's arms and legs.

COMBINATIONS – **shin bone** the tibia. **shin pad** a protective pad worn on the shins when playing soccer and other sports. **shin splints** acute pain in the shin and lower leg caused by prolonged running on hard surfaces.

shindig > *noun* informal **1** a large, lively party. **2** a noisy disturbance or quarrel.

shindy > *noun* (pl. **shindies**) informal **1** a noisy disturbance or quarrel. **2** a large, lively party.

ORIGIN – perhaps an alteration of SHINTY.

shine > *verb* (past and past participle **shone** or

shined) **1** give out a bright light, or glow with reflected light. **2** direct (a torch or other light) somewhere. **3** (of a person's eyes) be bright with the expression of emotion. **4** excel at something. **5** (**shine through**) (of a quality or skill) be clearly evident. **6** (past and past participle **shined**) polish. > *noun* **1** a quality of brightness, especially through reflecting light. **2** an act of polishing.

IDIOMS – **take the shine off** spoil the brilliance or excitement of. **take a shine to** informal develop a liking for.

SYNONYMS – *verb* **1** blaze, flare, gleam, glow.

shiner > *noun* informal a black eye.

shingle[1] > *noun* a mass of small rounded pebbles, especially on a seashore.

DERIVATIVES – **shingly** adjective.

shingle[2] > *noun* **1** a rectangular wooden tile used on walls or roofs. **2** dated a woman's short haircut, tapering from the back of the head to the nape of the neck. **3** N. Amer. a small signboard, especially one outside an office. > *verb* **1** roof or clad with shingles. **2** dated cut (hair) in a shingle.

ORIGIN – probably from Latin *scindula* 'a split piece of wood'.

shingles > *plural noun* (treated as sing.) an acute painful inflammation of nerve endings, with a skin eruption often forming a girdle around the body.

ORIGIN – from Latin *cingulum* 'girdle'.

shinny[1] > *verb* (**shinnies**, **shinnied**) (**shinny up** or **down**) N. Amer. shin up or down.

shinny[2] > *noun* N. Amer. an informal form of ice hockey played on the street or on ice.

ORIGIN – variant of SHINTY.

Shinola /shīnōlə/ > *noun* US trademark a brand of boot polish.

IDIOMS – **not know shit from Shinola** vulgar slang be ignorant or innocent.

Shinto /shintō/ > *noun* a Japanese religion incorporating the worship of ancestors and nature spirits.

DERIVATIVES – **Shintoism** noun.

ORIGIN – Japanese, from a Chinese word meaning 'way of the gods'.

shinty > *noun* a Scottish game resembling hockey, played with curved sticks and taller goalposts and derived from hurling.

ORIGIN – first spelled *shinny*: apparently from the cry *shin ye, shin you, shin t' ye*, used in the game.

shiny > *adjective* (**shinier**, **shiniest**) reflecting light through being very smooth, clean, or polished.

DERIVATIVES – **shinily** adverb **shininess** noun.

SYNONYMS – bright, glossy, lustrous, reflective.

ANTONYMS – matt.

ship > *noun* **1** a large seagoing boat. **2** a sailing vessel with a bowsprit and three or more square-rigged masts. **3** a spaceship. **4** N. Amer. an aircraft. > *verb* (**shipped, shipping**) **1** transport on a ship or by other means. **2** make (a product) available for purchase. **3** (of a sailor) take service on a ship. **4** (of a boat) take in (water) over the side. **5** take (oars) from the rowlocks and lay them inside a boat. **6** fix (a rudder, mast, etc.) in place on a ship.

WORDFINDER – *kinds of ship:* bulk carrier, coaster, collier, container ship, ferry, freighter, liner, reefer, tanker, warship; naval architect (*designer of ships*); load line, Plimsoll line (*line on ship's side showing legal limit of submersion*).

IDIOMS – **when one's ship comes in** when one's fortune is made.

DERIVATIVES – **shipload** *noun* **shipper** *noun.*

COMBINATIONS – **ship canal** a canal large enough for use by ships. **ship money** historical a tax raised in medieval England to provide ships for the navy. **ship of the desert** literary a camel. **ship of the line** historical a sailing warship of the largest size, used in the line of battle. **ship's biscuit** a hard, coarse kind of biscuit formerly used as food on long sea voyages. **ship's company** the crew of a ship. **shipworm** a teredo. **shipyard** a place where ships are built and repaired.

-ship > *suffix* forming nouns: **1** denoting a quality or condition: *companionship.* **2** denoting status, office, or honour: *citizenship.* **3** denoting a skill in a certain capacity: *workmanship.* **4** denoting the collective individuals of a group: *membership.*

shipboard > *noun* (before another noun) used or occurring on board a ship.

IDIOMS – **on shipboard** on board a ship.

shipbroker > *noun* a broker who arranges charters, cargo space, and passenger bookings on ships.

shipbuilder > *noun* a person or company that designs and builds ships.

DERIVATIVES – **shipbuilding** *noun.*

shiplap > *verb* fit (boards) together by halving so that each overlaps the one below. > *noun* shiplapped boards, used for cladding.

shipmate > *noun* a fellow member of a ship's crew.

shipment > *noun* **1** the action of shipping goods. **2** a consignment of goods shipped.

shipping > *noun* **1** ships collectively. **2** the transport of goods by sea or other means.

shippon /shippən/ (also **shippen**) > *noun* dialect a cattle shed.

shipshape (also **shipshape and Bristol fashion**) > *adjective* orderly and neat.

ORIGIN – *Bristol fashion* refers to the commercial prosperity of Bristol when its shipping trade was thriving.

shipway > *noun* a slope on which a ship is built and down which it slides to be launched.

shipwreck > *noun* **1** the destruction of a ship at sea by sinking or breaking up. **2** a ship so destroyed. > *verb* (**be shipwrecked**) suffer a shipwreck.

shipwright > *noun* a shipbuilder.

shiralee /shirrəlee/ > *noun* Austral. informal a bundle of belongings carried by a tramp.

Shiraz /shiraz/ > *noun* a variety of black wine grape.

ORIGIN – from *Shiraz* in Iran, apparently an alteration of French *syrah*, from the belief that the vine was brought from Iran by the Crusades.

shire /shīr/ > *noun* **1** Brit. a county, especially in England. **2** (**the Shires**) the parts of England regarded as strongholds of traditional rural culture, especially the rural Midlands. **3** a medieval administrative district ruled jointly by an alderman and a sheriff. **4** Austral. a rural area with its own elected council.

COMBINATIONS – **shire county** (in the UK since 1974) a non-metropolitan county. **shire horse** a heavy, powerful horse of a draught breed, originally from the English Midlands.

ORIGIN – Old English, 'care, official charge, county'.

shirk > *verb* avoid or neglect (a duty or responsibility).

DERIVATIVES – **shirker** *noun.*

SYNONYMS – avoid, dodge, evade, neglect, shun, sidestep.

ORIGIN – from obsolete *shirk* 'sponger', perhaps from German *Schurke* 'scoundrel'.

shirr /shur/ > *verb* **1** gather (fabric) by means of drawn or elasticised threads in parallel rows. **2** US bake (an egg without its shell).

shirt > *noun* **1** a garment for the upper body, with a collar and sleeves and buttons down the front. **2** a similar garment of stretchable material without full fastenings, worn for sports.

IDIOMS – **keep your shirt on** informal stay calm. **lose one's shirt** informal lose all one's possessions. **put one's shirt on** Brit. informal bet all one has on.

DERIVATIVES – **shirted** *adjective.*

COMBINATIONS – **shirt dress** a dress with a collar and button fastening in the style of a shirt, without a seam at the waist. **shirtwaist** N. Amer. **1** a woman's blouse resembling a shirt. **2** (also **shirtwaister**) a shirt dress with a seam at the waist.

ORIGIN – Old English, related to **SKIRT** and **SHORT**; probably from a base meaning 'short garment'.

shirtsleeve > *noun* the sleeve of a shirt.

IDIOMS – **in (one's) shirtsleeves** wearing a shirt with nothing over it.

DERIVATIVES – **shirtsleeved** *adjective.*

shirty > *adjective* (**shirtier, shirtiest**) Brit. informal bad-tempered or annoyed.

DERIVATIVES – **shirtily** *adverb* **shirtiness** *noun.*

shish kebab /shish kibab/ > *noun* a dish of pieces of marinated meat and vegetables cooked and served on skewers.

ORIGIN – Turkish.

shit vulgar slang > *verb* (**shitting; past and past participle shitted** or **shit** or **shat**) **1** defecate. **2** (**shit oneself**) be very frightened. > *noun* **1** faeces. **2** something worthless; rubbish. **3** a contemptible person. > *exclamation* expressing disgust or annoyance.

IDIOMS – **be scared shitless** be extremely frightened. **be up shit creek (without a paddle)** be in an awkward predicament. **when the shit hits the fan** when the disastrous consequences of something become known.

COMBINATIONS – **shit-eating** US smug; self-satisfied. **shit-faced** under the influence of alcohol or drugs. **shit-hot** excellent. **shitkicker** N. Amer. an unsophisticated or oafish person.

ORIGIN – Old English, 'diarrhoea'.

shite > *noun & exclamation* vulgar slang another term for **SHIT**.

shitty > *adjective* (**shittier, shittiest**) vulgar slang **1** contemptible or awful. **2** covered with excrement.

shive /shīv/ > *noun* a broad bung hammered into a hole in the top of a cask when the cask has been filled.

ORIGIN – first used in sense 'slice of bread', later 'piece of split wood'.

shiver[1] > *verb* shake slightly and uncontrollably as a result of being cold, frightened, or excited. > *noun* **1** a momentary trembling movement. **2** (**the shivers**) a spell or attack of shivering.

DERIVATIVES – **shivery** *adjective.*

SYNONYMS – *verb* quake, quiver, shake, shudder, tremble.

ORIGIN – perhaps an alteration of dialect *chavele* 'to chatter', from Old English *ceafl* 'jaw'.

shiver[2] > *noun* a splinter. > *verb* break into shivers.

IDIOMS – **shiver my timbers** an oath attributed to sailors.

Shoah /shōə/ > *noun* (in Jewish use) the Holocaust.

ORIGIN – modern Hebrew, 'catastrophe'.

shoal[1] > *noun* **1** a large number of fish swimming together. **2** informal, chiefly Brit. a large number of people. > *verb* (of fish) form shoals.

ORIGIN – probably from Dutch *schōle* 'troop'; compare with **SCHOOL**[2].

shoal[2] > *noun* **1** an area of shallow water. **2** a submerged sandbank visible at low water. > *verb* (of water) become shallower.

ORIGIN – Old English, related to **SHALLOW**.

shock¹ > *noun* **1** a sudden upsetting or surprising event or experience, or the resulting feeling. **2** an acute medical condition associated with a fall in blood pressure, caused by loss of blood, severe burns, sudden emotional stress, etc. **3** a violent shaking movement caused by an impact, explosion, or tremor. **4** an electric shock. > *verb* **1** cause (someone) to feel surprised and upset. **2** offend the moral feelings of; outrage. **3** affect with physiological shock, or with an electric shock.

WORDFINDER – electroconvulsive therapy (*treatment of mental illness by applying electric shocks to the brain*), electrocute (*kill by electric shock*); trauma (*shock causing psychological harm*).

DERIVATIVES – **shockable** adjective.

SYNONYMS – *noun* **1** blow, bombshell, fright, scare, surprise. *verb* **1** distress, disturb, traumatise, upset. **2** appal, horrify, outrage, scandalise.

COMBINATIONS – **shock absorber** a device for absorbing jolts and vibrations, especially on a vehicle. **shock tactics** the use of sudden violent or extreme action to shock someone into doing something. **shock therapy** (also **shock treatment**) treatment of chronic mental conditions by electroconvulsive therapy or by inducing physiological shock. **shock troops** troops trained for carrying out sudden assaults. **shock wave** an intense travelling pressure wave caused by explosion or by a body moving faster than sound.

ORIGIN – French *choc*; the original senses were 'throw (troops) into confusion by charging at them' and 'an encounter between charging forces', giving rise to the notion of 'sudden violent blow or impact'.

shock² > *noun* a group of twelve sheaves of grain placed upright and supporting each other to allow the grain to dry and ripen.

shock³ > *noun* an unkempt or thick mass of hair.

COMBINATIONS – **shock-headed** having thick, shaggy, and unkempt hair.

shocker > *noun informal* **1** a person or thing that shocks, especially through being unacceptable or sensational. **2** Brit. a shock absorber.

shocking > *adjective* **1** causing shock or disgust. **2** Brit. informal very bad.

DERIVATIVES – **shockingly** adverb.

SYNONYMS – **1** appalling, disgraceful, outrageous, scandalous, terrible.

COMBINATIONS – **shocking pink** a vibrant shade of pink.

shod past and past participle of **SHOE**.

shoddy > *adjective* (**shoddier**, **shoddiest**) **1** badly made or done. **2** lacking moral principle; sordid. > *noun* an inferior yarn or fabric made from shredded woollen waste.

DERIVATIVES – **shoddily** adverb **shoddiness** noun.

SYNONYMS – **1** inferior, low-grade, second-rate, sloppy.

shoe > *noun* **1** a covering for the foot having a sturdy sole and not reaching above the ankle. **2** a horseshoe. **3** a brake shoe or a drag for a wheel. **4** a socket on a camera for fitting a flash unit. **5** a metal rim or ferrule, especially on the runner of a sledge. **6** a step for a mast. > *verb* (**shoes**, **shoeing**; past and past participle **shod**) **1** fit (a horse) with a shoe or shoes. **2** (**be shod**) be wearing shoes of a specified kind. **3** protect with a metal shoe.

IDIOMS – **be** (or **put oneself**) **in another person's shoes** imagine oneself in another's situation or predicament. **dead men's shoes** property or a position coveted by a prospective successor but available only on a person's death or departure.

COMBINATIONS – **shoebox 1** a box in which a pair of shoes is delivered or sold. **2** informal a very cramped room or space. **shoelace** a cord or leather strip passed through eyelets or hooks on opposite sides of a shoe and pulled tight and fastened. **shoemaker** a person who makes shoes and other footwear as a profession. **shoe tree** a shaped block inserted into a shoe when it is not being worn to keep it in shape.

shoeblack > *noun* dated a person who cleans the shoes of passers-by for payment.

shoehorn > *noun* a curved instrument used for easing one's heel into a shoe. > *verb* force into an inadequate space.

shoeshine > *noun* chiefly N. Amer. an act of polishing someone's shoes.

shoestring > *noun* **1** N. Amer. a shoelace. **2** (before another noun) informal made or working with a small or inadequate budget: *a shoestring edition*.

IDIOMS – **on a shoestring** informal using very little money.

shogun /shōgŏon/ > *noun* (in feudal Japan) a hereditary commander-in-chief.

DERIVATIVES – **shogunate** noun.

ORIGIN – Japanese, from a Chinese word meaning 'general'.

Shona /shōnə/ > *noun* (pl. same or **Shonas**) a member of a group of peoples inhabiting parts of southern Africa, particularly Zimbabwe.

shone past and past participle of **SHINE**.

shonky Austral./NZ informal > *adjective* (**shonkier**, **shonkiest**) dishonest, unreliable, or illegal. > *noun* (also **shonk**) a person engaged in suspect business activities.

shoo-in > *noun* chiefly N. Amer. a person or thing that is certain to succeed or win.

shook past of **SHAKE**.

shoot > *verb* (past and past participle **shot**) **1** kill or wound (a person or animal) with a bullet or arrow. **2** cause (a gun) to fire. **3** move suddenly and rapidly. **4** direct (a glance, question, or remark) at someone. **5** film or photograph (a scene, film, etc.). **6** (**shooting**) (of a pain) sudden and piercing. **7** (of a boat) sweep swiftly down or under (rapids, a waterfall, or a bridge). **8** move (a door bolt) to fasten or unfasten a door. **9** informal drive past (a traffic light at red). **10** (in sport) kick, hit, or throw the ball or puck in an attempt to score a goal. **11** informal make (a specified score) for a round of golf. **12** send out buds or shoots; germinate. > *noun* **1** a young branch or sucker springing from the main stock of a tree or other plant. **2** an occasion when a group of people hunt and shoot game for sport. **3** Brit. land used for shooting game. **4** an occasion of taking photographs professionally or making a film or video: *a fashion shoot*. **5** variant spelling of **CHUTE¹**. > *exclamation* N. Amer. used as a euphemism for 'shit'.

IDIOMS – **shoot the breeze** (or **the bull**) N. Amer. informal have a casual conversation. **shoot one's cuffs** pull one's shirt cuffs out to project beyond the cuffs of one's jacket or coat. **shoot down** bring down (an aircraft or person) by shooting. **shoot oneself in the foot** informal inadvertently make a situation worse for oneself. **shoot a line** Brit. informal describe something in an exaggerated, untruthful, or boastful way. **shoot one's mouth off** informal talk boastfully or indiscreetly. **the whole shooting match** informal everything. **shoot through** Austral./NZ informal depart, especially hurriedly. **shoot up** informal inject oneself with a narcotic drug.

COMBINATIONS – **shooting box** Brit. a lodge used by hunters in the shooting season. **shooting brake** Brit. dated an estate car. **shooting gallery** a room or fairground booth for recreational shooting at targets. **shooting iron** informal, chiefly US a firearm. **shooting star** a small, rapidly moving meteor burning up on entering the earth's atmosphere. **shooting stick** a walking stick with a handle that unfolds to form a seat and a sharpened end which can be stuck firmly in the ground.

shooter > *noun* **1** a person who uses a gun. **2** informal a gun. **3** (in netball, basketball, etc.) a player whose role is to attempt to score goals.

shoot-out > *noun* **1** informal a decisive gun battle. **2** (usu. **penalty shoot-out**) Soccer a tiebreaker decided by each side taking a specified number of penalty kicks.

shop > *noun* **1** a building or part of a building where goods or services are sold. **2** a place where things are manufactured or repaired;

shopaholic-shortcake

a workshop. **3** (often in phrase **talk shop**) matters concerning one's work, especially when discussed at an inappropriate time. > *verb* (**shopped**, **shopping**) **1** go to a shop or shops to buy goods. **2** (**shop around**) look for the best available price or rate for something. **3** informal, chiefly Brit. inform on (someone).

WORDFINDER – *shops and their products:* boutique (*fashionable clothes*), chandler (*supplies and equipment for ships*), clothier (*clothes or cloth*), confectioner (*confectionery*), delicatessen (*cooked and prepared foods*), draper (*fabrics*), furrier (*furs*), greengrocer (*fruit and vegetables*), grocer (*food and household goods*), haberdasher (*dressmaking and sewing goods*), hatter (*hats*), herbalist (*medicinal herbs*), ironmonger (*hardware*), mercer (*textile fabrics*), milliner (*women's hats*), patisserie (*cakes and pastries*), poulterer (*poultry*), stationer (*writing and office materials*).

COMBINATIONS – **shop assistant** Brit. a person who serves customers in a shop. **shopfitter** a person whose job it is to fit the counters, shelves, etc. with which a shop is equipped. **shop floor** the part of a workshop or factory where production as distinct from administrative work is carried out. **shopfront** the facade of a shop. **shop-soiled** (N. Amer. **shopworn**) Brit. (of an article) made dirty or imperfect by being displayed or handled in a shop. **shop steward** a person elected by workers in a factory to represent them in dealings with management. **shopwalker** Brit. dated a senior employee in a large shop who supervises assistants and directs customers. **shop window 1** a display window of a shop. **2** a position that allows a person or organisation to demonstrate their strengths.

ORIGIN – shortening of Old French *eschoppe* 'lean-to booth'.

shopaholic > *noun* informal a compulsive shopper.

shopkeeper > *noun* the owner and manager of a shop.

shoplifting > *noun* the theft of goods from a shop by someone pretending to be a customer.

DERIVATIVES – **shoplift** *verb* **shoplifter** *noun*.

shopper > *noun* **1** a person who is shopping. **2** Brit. a bag for holding shopping, attached to wheels and pushed or pulled along. **3** a small-wheeled bicycle with a basket.

shopping > *noun* **1** the purchasing of goods from shops. **2** goods bought from shops, especially food and household goods.

COMBINATIONS – **shopping centre** an area or complex of shops. **shopping list 1** a list of purchases to be made. **2** a list of items to be considered or acted on.

shore[1] > *noun* **1** the land along the edge of a

sea, lake, etc. **2** (also **shores**) literary a country or other geographic area bounded by a coast: *distant shores.*

DERIVATIVES – **shoreward** *adjective & adverb* **shorewards** *adverb.*

COMBINATIONS – **shore leave** leisure time spent ashore by a sailor. **shoreline** the line along which a large body of water meets the land.

ORIGIN – Dutch, Low German *schōre.*

shore[2] > *noun* a prop or beam set up against something weak or unstable as a support. > *verb* (often **shore up**) support or hold up with shores.

DERIVATIVES – **shoring** *noun.*

ORIGIN – Dutch, Low German *schore* 'prop'.

shorn past participle of SHEAR.

short > *adjective* **1** of a small length or duration. **2** relatively small in extent. **3** (of a person) small in height. **4** (**short of** or **on**) not having enough of (something); lacking or deficient in. **5** in insufficient supply. **6** (of a person) rudely terse. **7** (of a ball in sport) travelling only a small distance, or not far enough. **8** (of odds or a chance) reflecting or representing a high level of probability. **9** Phonetics (of a vowel) categorised as short with regard to quality and length (e.g. in standard British English the vowel sound in *good*). **10** (of pastry) containing a high proportion of fat to flour and therefore crumbly. > *adverb* (in sport) at, to, or over a short distance, or not as far as the point aimed at. > *noun* **1** Brit. informal a strong alcoholic drink, especially spirits, served in small measures. **2** a short film as opposed to a feature film. **3** a short circuit. > *verb* short-circuit.

IDIOMS – **be caught short 1** be put at a disadvantage. **2** Brit. informal urgently need to urinate or defecate. **bring** (or **pull**) **up short** cause (someone) to stop or pause abruptly. **for short** as an abbreviation or nickname. **get** (or **have**) **by the short and curlies** informal have complete control of (a person). **go short** not have enough of something. **in short** to sum up; briefly. **in the short run** (or **term**) in the near future. **in short supply** (of a commodity) scarce. **make short work of** accomplish, consume, or destroy quickly. **short for** an abbreviation or nickname for. **short of 1** less than. **2** not reaching as far as. **3** without going so far as (some extreme action). **stop short** stop suddenly or abruptly.

DERIVATIVES – **shortish** *adjective* **shortness** *noun.*

SYNONYMS – *adjective* **2** abbreviated, brief, compact, concise. **3** diminutive, little, petite, small; informal pint-sized. **6** abrupt, blunt, brusque, curt, sharp, terse, uncivil. ANTONYMS – *adjective* **1,2** long. **3** tall.

COMBINATIONS – **short back and sides**

Brit. a man's haircut in which the hair is cut short at the back and the sides. **shortcrust pastry** Brit. crumbly pastry made with flour, fat, and a little water. **short cut 1** an alternative route that is shorter than the one usually taken. **2** an accelerated but somewhat irregular way of doing something. **short-dated** (of a stock or bond) due for early payment or redemption. **short division** division in which the quotient is written directly without a succession of intermediate workings. **short fuse** informal a quick temper. **short-handed** without enough or the usual number of staff or crew. **short haul** a relatively short distance in terms of travel or the transport of goods. **short head** Brit. Horse Racing a distance less than the length of a horse's head. **short measure** an amount less than that which is declared or paid for. **short-order** N. Amer. relating to food dishes which can be quickly prepared and served: *a short-order cook.* **short-range 1** able to be used or be effective only over short distances. **2** of or over a short period of future time. **short shrift** rapid and unsympathetic dismissal; curt treatment. [ORIGIN – first meaning 'little time allowed for making confession between being condemned and executed or punished'.] **short sight** the inability to see things clearly unless they are relatively close to the eyes; myopia. **short-sighted 1** having short sight. **2** lacking imagination or foresight. **short-staffed** not having enough or the usual number of staff. **short story** a story with a fully developed theme but significantly shorter and less elaborate than a novel. **short-tempered** having a tendency to lose one's temper quickly. **short time** the condition of working fewer than the regular hours per day or days per week. **short-waisted** (of a dress or a person's body) having a high waist. **short wave 1** a radio wave of a wavelength between about 10 and 100 metres (and a frequency of about 3 to 30 megahertz). **2** broadcasting using radio waves of this wavelength. **short weight** weight that is less than that declared. **short-winded** out of breath, or tending to run out of breath quickly.

ORIGIN – Old English, related to SHIRT, SKIRT.

shortage > *noun* a situation in which something needed cannot be obtained in sufficient amounts.

SYNONYMS – dearth, deficiency, lack, paucity, scarcity.

shortbread > *noun* a crisp, rich, crumbly type of biscuit made with butter, flour, and sugar.

shortcake > *noun* **1** another term for SHORTBREAD. **2** N. Amer. a rich dessert made

904

from short pastry and topped with fruit and whipped cream.

short change > *noun* insufficient money given as change. > *verb* (**short-change**) **1** cheat (someone) by giving short change. **2** treat unfairly by withholding something of value.

short circuit > *noun* an electrical circuit of lower than usual resistance, especially one formed unintentionally. > *verb* (**short-circuit**) **1** cause or suffer a short circuit. **2** shorten (a process or activity) by using a more direct but irregular method.

shortcoming > *noun* a failure to meet a certain standard; a fault or defect.
SYNONYMS – defect, drawback, failing, fault, flaw, imperfection, weakness.

shorten > *verb* **1** make or become shorter. **2** Sailing reduce the amount of (sail spread).
SYNONYMS – **1** compress, contract, shrink.

shortening > *noun* fat used for making pastry.

shortfall > *noun* a deficit of something required or expected.

shorthand > *noun* **1** a method of rapid writing by means of abbreviations and symbols, used for taking dictation. **2** a short and simple way of expressing or referring to something.
WORDFINDER – stenographer (*North American term for shorthand typist*).

shorthold > *adjective* English Law denoting a tenancy whereby the tenant agrees to rent a property for a stated term, at the end of which the landlord may recover it.

shorthorn > *noun* a breed of cattle with short horns.

shortlist > *noun* a list of selected candidates from which a final choice is made. > *verb* put on a shortlist.

short-lived > *adjective* lasting only a short time.

shortly > *adverb* **1** in a short time; soon. **2** in a few words; briefly. **3** abruptly, sharply, or curtly.

shorts > *plural noun* **1** short trousers that reach only to the knees or thighs. **2 N. Amer.** men's underpants.

shortstop > *noun* Baseball a fielder positioned between second and third base.

short-term > *adjective* occurring in or relating to a relatively short period of future time: *a short-term investment.*

short-termism > *noun* concentration on immediate profit or advantage at the expense of long-term security.

shorty (also **shortie**) > *noun* (pl. **shorties**) informal **1** a short person. **2** a short dress, nightdress, or raincoat.

Shoshone /shəˈshōni/ > *noun* (pl. same or **Shoshones**) a member of an American Indian people living chiefly in Wyoming, Idaho, and Nevada.

shot¹ > *noun* **1** the firing of a gun or cannon.

2 a person with a specified level of ability in shooting: *he was an excellent shot.* **3** a hit, stroke, or kick of the ball in sports, in particular an attempt to score. **4** informal an attempt to do something. **5** (pl. same) a ball of stone or metal fired from a large gun or cannon. **6** (also **lead shot**) tiny lead pellets used in a single charge or cartridge in a shotgun. **7** a heavy ball thrown by a shot-putter. **8** a photograph. **9** a film sequence photographed continuously by one camera. **10** informal a small drink of spirits. **11** the launch of a rocket: *a moon shot.* **12** an injection of a drug or vaccine. **13 Brit. informal**, dated a bill or one's share of it, especially in a pub.
IDIOMS – **give it one's best shot** informal do the best that one can. **like a shot** informal without hesitation; very willingly. **a shot in the arm** informal an encouraging stimulus.
COMBINATIONS – **shot-blast** clean or strip (a surface) by directing a high-speed stream of steel particles at it. **shot glass N. Amer.** a small glass used for serving spirits. **shot-peen** shape (sheet metal) by bombarding it with a stream of metal shot.

shot² past and past participle of **SHOOT**. > *adjective* **1** (of coloured cloth) woven with different colours, giving a contrasting effect when looked at from different angles. **2** informal ruined or worn out. **3 US & Austral./NZ** informal drunk.
IDIOMS – **get** (or **be**) **shot of** Brit. informal get (or be) rid of. **shot through with** suffused with.

shotgun > *noun* a smooth-bore gun for firing small shot at short range.
COMBINATIONS – **shotgun marriage** (also **shotgun wedding**) informal an enforced or hurried wedding, especially because the bride is pregnant.

shot put > *noun* an athletic contest in which a very heavy round ball is thrown as far as possible.
DERIVATIVES – **shot-putter** *noun* **shot-putting** *noun.*

should > *modal verb* (3rd sing. **should**) **1** used to indicate obligation, duty, or correctness. **2** used to indicate what is probable. **3** formal expressing the conditional mood. **4** used in a clause with 'that' after a main clause describing feelings. **5** used in a clause with 'that' expressing purpose. **6** (in the first person) expressing a polite request or acceptance. **7** (in the first person) expressing a conjecture or hope.
USAGE – what is the difference between **should** and **would**? Strictly speaking **should** is used with **I** and **we**, as in *I should be grateful if you would let me know*, while **would** is used with **you**, **he**, **she**, **it**, and **they**, as in *you didn't say you would be late.* In practice, however, **would** is normally used instead of **should** in reported speech and

conditional clauses, such as *I said I would be late.* In speech the distinction tends to be obscured anyway, through the use of the contracted forms **I'd**, **we'd**, etc.
ORIGIN – past of **SHALL**.

shoulder > *noun* **1** the joint between the upper arm or forelimb and the main part of the body. **2** a part of something resembling a shoulder, in particular a point at which a steep slope descends from a plateau or highland area. **3** short for **hard shoulder**. > *verb* **1** put (something heavy) over one's shoulder or shoulders to carry. **2** take on (a burden or responsibility). **3** push out of one's way with one's shoulder.
WORDFINDER – scapular (*of the shoulder*); deltoid, trapezius (*muscles of the shoulder*), epaulette (*ornamental shoulder piece*).
IDIOMS – **put one's shoulder to the wheel** set to work vigorously. **shoulder arms** hold a rifle against the right side of the body, barrel upwards. **shoulder to shoulder** side by side or acting together.
DERIVATIVES – **shouldered** *adjective.*
COMBINATIONS – **shoulder bag** a bag with a long strap that is hung over the shoulder. **shoulder blade** either of the large, flat, triangular bones which lie against the ribs in the upper back; the scapula. **shoulder pad** a pad sewn into the shoulder of a garment to provide shape or give protection. **shoulder strap 1** a narrow strip of material going over the shoulder from front to back of a garment. **2** a long strap attached to a bag for carrying it over the shoulder. **3** a strip of cloth from shoulder to collar on a military uniform or coat.

shouldn't > *contraction* should not.

shout > *verb* **1** speak or call out very loudly. **2** (**shout at**) reprimand loudly. **3** (**shout down**) prevent (someone) from speaking or being heard by shouting. **4 Austral./NZ** informal treat (someone) to (something, especially a drink). > *noun* **1** a loud cry or call. **2** (**one's shout**) Brit. informal one's turn to buy a round of drinks.
IDIOMS – **all over bar the shouting** informal (of a contest) almost finished and therefore virtually decided. **give someone a shout** informal call on or get in touch with someone. **in with a shout** informal having a good chance. **shout the odds** talk loudly and in an opinionated way.
SYNONYMS – *verb* **1** bawl, bellow, cry, howl, roar, yell; informal holler.

shove > *verb* **1** push roughly. **2** informal put (something) somewhere carelessly or roughly. > *noun* a strong push.
IDIOMS – **shove off 1** informal go away. **2** push away from the shore in a boat. **shove up** informal move oneself to make room for someone.
SYNONYMS – *verb* **1** barge, elbow, push, shunt, thrust.

COMBINATIONS – **shove-halfpenny** a game in which coins are struck so that they slide across a marked board on a table.

shovel > *noun* a tool resembling a spade with a broad blade and upturned sides, used for moving coal, earth, snow, etc. > *verb* (**shovelled, shovelling;** US **shoveled, shoveling**) 1 move with a shovel. 2 (**shovel down** or **in**) informal eat (food) quickly and in large quantities.

COMBINATIONS – **shovel hat** a black felt hat with a low round crown and a broad brim turned up at the sides, formerly worn by clergymen.

shovelboard > *noun* Brit. a game played by pushing discs with the hand or with a long-handled shovel over a marked surface.

ORIGIN – alteration of obsolete *shoveboard*.

shoveler (also **shoveller**) > *noun* a kind of duck with a long, broad bill.

show > *verb* (past participle **shown** or **showed**) 1 be, allow, or cause to be visible. 2 exhibit or produce for inspection or viewing. 3 represent or depict in art. 4 display or allow (a quality, emotion, or characteristic) to be perceived. 5 demonstrate or prove. 6 treat (someone) with (a specified quality). 7 explain or demonstrate (something) to. 8 conduct or lead: *show them in, please.* 9 (also **show up**) informal arrive for an appointment or at a gathering. 10 N. Amer. finish third or in the first three in a race. > *noun* 1 a spectacle or display. 2 a play or other stage performance, especially a musical. 3 a light entertainment programme on television or radio. 4 an event or competition involving the public display of animals, plants, or products. 5 informal an undertaking, project, or organisation: *I run the show.* 6 an outward appearance or display of a quality or feeling. 7 (often in phrase **for show**) an outward display intended to give a false impression.

IDIOMS – **all over the show** another way of saying *all over the place* (see ALL). **get the show on the road** informal begin an undertaking or enterprise. **good** (or **bad** or **poor**) **show!** informal, dated used to express approval (or disapproval or dissatisfaction). **on show** being exhibited. **show someone a clean pair of heels** informal run away from someone extremely fast. **show someone the door** dismiss or eject someone. **show one's hand** (or **cards**) disclose one's plans. **show off** 1 boastfully display one's abilities or accomplishments. 2 display (something) that is a source of pride. **show of force** a demonstration of the forces at one's command and of one's readiness to use them. **show of hands** a vote by the raising of hands. **show oneself** (or **one's face**) allow oneself to be seen; appear in public. **show someone round** point out interesting features in a place or building to someone. **show one's teeth** Brit. use one's

power or authority in an aggressive or intimidating way. **show up** 1 expose as being bad or faulty. 2 informal embarrass or humiliate (someone). **show willing** display a willingness to help.

COMBINATIONS – **showband** 1 a band which plays cover versions of popular songs. 2 a jazz band which performs with theatrical extravagance. **show business** the theatre, films, television, and pop music as a profession or industry. **showgirl** an actress who sings and dances in musicals, variety acts, etc. **show house** (also **show home**) Brit. a house on a newly built estate which is furnished and decorated to be shown to prospective buyers. **showplace** a place of beauty or interest attracting many visitors. **show trial** a judicial trial held in public with the intention of influencing or satisfying public opinion, rather than of ensuring justice.

showbiz > *noun* informal term for *show business*.

DERIVATIVES – **showbizzy** *adjective*.

showboat > *noun* 1 (in the US) a river steamer on which theatrical performances are given. 2 N. Amer. informal a show-off. > *verb* informal, chiefly N. Amer. show off.

showcase > *noun* 1 a glass case used for displaying articles in a shop or museum. 2 a place or occasion for presenting something to general attention. > *verb* exhibit or display prominently.

showdown > *noun* 1 a final test or confrontation intended to settle a dispute. 2 (in poker or brag) the requirement at the end of a round that the players should show their cards to determine which is the strongest hand.

shower /showr/ > *noun* 1 a brief and usually light fall of rain or snow. 2 a mass of small things falling or moving at once. 3 a large number of things happening or given at the same time: *a shower of awards.* 4 a cubicle or bath in which a person stands under a spray of water to wash. 5 an act of washing oneself in a shower. 6 Brit. informal an incompetent or worthless group of people. 7 N. Amer. a party at which presents are given to a woman who is about to get married or have a baby. > *verb* 1 fall, throw, or be thrown in a shower. 2 (**shower on** or **with**) give (a great number of things) to (someone). 3 wash oneself in a shower.

showerproof > *adjective* (of a garment) resistant to light rain. > *verb* make showerproof.

showery > *adjective* characterised by frequent showers of rain.

showground > *noun* an area of land on which a show takes place.

showing > *noun* 1 a presentation of a cinema film or television programme. 2 a

performance of a specified quality: *a poor showing in the opinion polls.*

showjumping > *noun* the competitive sport of riding horses over a course of fences and other obstacles in an arena.

DERIVATIVES – **showjump** *verb* **showjumper** *noun*.

showman > *noun* 1 the manager or presenter of a circus, fair, etc. 2 a person who is skilled at entertaining, theatrical presentation, or performance.

DERIVATIVES – **showmanship** *noun*.

shown past participle of SHOW.

show-off > *noun* informal a person who boastfully displays their abilities or accomplishments.

showpiece > *noun* 1 an outstanding example of its type. 2 an item of work presented for exhibition or display.

showroom > *noun* a room used to display cars, furniture, or other goods for sale.

show-stopper > *noun* informal a performance or item receiving prolonged applause.

DERIVATIVES – **show-stopping** *adjective*.

showy > *adjective* (**showier, showiest**) strikingly bright, colourful, or ostentatious.

DERIVATIVES – **showily** *adverb* **showiness** *noun*.

SYNONYMS – conspicuous, flamboyant, ostentatious.

ANTONYMS – discreet, restrained.

shrank past of SHRINK.

shrapnel /shrapnəl/ > *noun* 1 small metal fragments thrown out by the explosion of a shell, bomb, etc. 2 shells designed to burst short of the target and shower it with shrapnel. 3 informal coins of low denomination; small change.

ORIGIN – named after the British soldier General Henry *Shrapnel* (1761–1842), inventor of shrapnel shells.

shred > *noun* 1 a strip of material that has been torn, cut, or scraped from something larger. 2 a very small amount. > *verb* (**shredded, shredding**) tear or cut into shreds.

ORIGIN – Old English, 'piece cut off'; related to SHROUD.

shredder > *noun* a device for shredding something, especially documents.

shrew > *noun* 1 a small mouse-like insectivorous mammal with a long pointed snout and tiny eyes. 2 a bad-tempered or aggressively assertive woman.

shrewd > *adjective* having or showing sharp powers of judgement; astute.

DERIVATIVES – **shrewdly** *adverb* **shrewdness** *noun*.

SYNONYMS – acute, astute, canny, discriminating, sharp.

shrewish > *adjective* (of a woman) bad-tempered or nagging.

DERIVATIVES – **shrewishly** *adverb* **shrewishness** *noun*.

---

wordpower facts

Shrew

The name of the animal the **shrew**, which comes ultimately from a Germanic source, is recorded in Old English as early as the 8th century. People felt superstitious about the shrew in the Middle Ages, regarding it as a dangerous, malignant creature (the general sense 'malignant being' is found in the Germanic sources); in the 13th century the word started to be used in the new sense 'an evil person or thing'. The adjective **shrewd**, first recorded in the 14th century, was originally used in the sense 'evil in nature or character', and it is likely that it derives from **shrew**; it may, however, have started as a past participle of the obsolete verb to *shrew*, meaning 'to curse'. Over the next two to three hundred years **shrewd** developed a range of unfavourable senses, such as 'malevolent', 'mischievous', 'dangerous', and 'irksome'. Its current favourable sense 'astute', which eventually replaced these, first arose in the early 16th century.

---

shriek > *verb* utter a piercing high-pitched sound, cry, or words. > *noun* a piercing high-pitched cry or sound.

DERIVATIVES – **shrieker** *noun*.

shrift > *noun* archaic **1** confession, especially to a priest. **2** absolution by a priest.

ORIGIN – Old English, 'penance imposed after confession', from **SHRIVE**.

shrike > *noun* a predatory songbird with a hooked bill, often impaling its prey on thorns.

shrill > *adjective* **1** (of a voice or sound) high-pitched and piercing. **2** derogatory (of a complaint or demand) loud and forceful. > *verb* make a shrill noise.

DERIVATIVES – **shrillness** *noun* **shrilly** *adverb*.

shrimp > *noun* **1** (pl. same or **shrimps**) a small, mainly marine edible crustacean with ten legs. **2** informal, derogatory a small, physically weak person. > *verb* fish for shrimps.

DERIVATIVES – **shrimper** *noun*.

ORIGIN – probably related to Low German *schrempen* 'to wrinkle'.

shrine > *noun* **1** a place regarded as holy because of its associations with a god, goddess, or sacred person. **2** a casket containing sacred relics; a reliquary. **3** a niche or enclosure containing a religious statue or other object. > *verb* literary enshrine.

ORIGIN – Old English, 'cabinet, chest, reliquary'.

shrink > *verb* (past **shrank**; past participle **shrunk** or (especially as adjective) **shrunken**) **1** become or make smaller in size or amount; contract. **2** (of clothes or material) become smaller as a result of being immersed in water. **3** move back or away in fear or disgust. **4** (**shrink from**) be averse to or unwilling to do (something). > *noun* informal a psychiatrist. [ORIGIN – from *headshrinker*.]

DERIVATIVES – **shrinkable** *adjective*.

COMBINATIONS – **shrinking violet** informal an exaggeratedly shy person. **shrink wrap** clinging transparent plastic film used to enclose an article as packaging. **shrink-wrap** enclose in shrink wrap.

shrinkage > *noun* **1** the process or amount of shrinking. **2** an allowance made for reduction in the takings of a business due to wastage or theft.

shrive /shrīv/ > *verb* (past **shrove**; past participle **shriven**) archaic **1** (of a priest) hear the confession of, assign penance to, and absolve (someone). **2** (**shrive oneself**) present oneself to a priest for confession, penance, and absolution.

ORIGIN – Old English, from Latin *scribere* 'write'.

shrivel > *verb* (**shrivelled**, **shrivelling**; US **shriveled**, **shriveling**) wrinkle and contract through loss of moisture.

shroud > *noun* **1** a length of cloth or an enveloping garment in which a dead person is wrapped for burial. **2** a thing that envelops or obscures. **3** technical a protective casing or cover. **4** (**shrouds**) a set of ropes forming part of the rigging of a sailing boat and supporting the mast or topmast. **5** each of the lines joining the canopy of a parachute to the harness. > *verb* **1** wrap or dress in a shroud. **2** cover or envelop so as to conceal from view.

WORDFINDER – sindonology (*investigation of the Turin Shroud, supposed shroud of Christ*).

ORIGIN – Old English, 'garment, clothing'; related to **SHRED**.

shrove past of **SHRIVE**.

Shrove Tuesday > *noun* the day before Ash Wednesday, traditionally marked by feasting before the Lenten fast.

shrub¹ > *noun* a woody plant which is smaller than a tree and has several main stems arising at or near the ground.

DERIVATIVES – **shrubby** *adjective*.

shrub² > *noun* **1** a drink made of sweetened fruit juice and rum or brandy. **2** N. Amer. a slightly acid cordial made from fruit juice and water.

ORIGIN – Arabic, related to **SHERBET** and **SYRUP**.

shrubbery > *noun* (pl. **shrubberies**) an area in a garden planted with shrubs.

shrug > *verb* (**shrugged**, **shrugging**) **1** raise (one's shoulders) slightly and momentarily as an expression of doubt, ignorance, or indifference. **2** (**shrug off**) dismiss as unimportant. > *noun* **1** an act of shrugging one's shoulders. **2** a woman's close-fitting cardigan or jacket cut short at the front and back so that only the arms and shoulders are covered.

shrunk (also **shrunken**) past participle of **SHRINK**.

shtick /shtik/ > *noun* informal an attention-getting or theatrical routine, gimmick, or talent.

ORIGIN – Yiddish, from German *Stück* 'piece'.

shtook /shtook/ (also **schtuck**) > *noun* informal trouble.

shtum /shtoom/ (also **schtum**) > *adjective* informal silent; non-communicative.

ORIGIN – Yiddish, from German *stumm*.

shubunkin /shoobungkin/ > *noun* an ornamental variety of goldfish with black spots, red patches, and long fins and tail.

ORIGIN – Japanese.

shuck /shuk/ chiefly N. Amer. > *noun* **1** a husk or pod, especially the husk of an ear of maize. **2** the shell of an oyster or clam. > *verb* **1** remove the shucks from. **2** informal abandon; get rid of. **3** informal take off (a garment).

shucks > *exclamation* informal, chiefly N. Amer. used to express surprise, regret, etc.

shudder > *verb* tremble or shake convulsively, especially as a result of fear or repugnance. > *noun* an act of shuddering.

DERIVATIVES – **shuddery** *adjective*.

SYNONYMS – *verb* convulse, jerk, quake, quiver, shake, tremble.

ORIGIN – Dutch *schüderen*.

shuffle > *verb* **1** walk by dragging one's feet along or without lifting them fully from the ground. **2** restlessly shift one's position. **3** rearrange (a pack of cards) by sliding them over each other quickly. **4** (**shuffle through**) sort or look through (a number of things) hurriedly. **5** move (people or things) around into different positions or a different order. **6** (**shuffle off** or **out of**) get out of or avoid (a responsibility or obligation). > *noun* **1** a shuffling movement, walk, or sound. **2** a quick dragging or scraping movement of the feet in dancing. **3** an act of shuffling a pack of cards. **4** a change of order or relative positions; a reshuffle. **5** a facility on a CD player for playing tracks in an arbitrary order.

DERIVATIVES – **shuffler** *noun*.

COMBINATIONS – **shuffleboard** North American term for **SHOVELBOARD**.

shufti /shoofti/ > *noun* (pl. **shuftis**) Brit. informal a quick look or reconnoitre.

ORIGIN – Second World War military slang: from an Arabic word meaning 'try to see'.

shun > *verb* (**shunned**, **shunning**) persistently avoid, ignore, or reject.

shunt > *verb* **1** slowly push or pull (a railway vehicle or vehicles) so as to make up or remove from a train. **2** push or shove. **3** direct or divert to a less important place or position. > *noun* **1** an act of shunting. **2** Brit. informal a motor accident, especially a collision of vehicles travelling one close behind the other. **3** an electrical conductor joining two points of a circuit.

shunter > *noun* **1** a small locomotive used for shunting. **2** a railway worker engaged in such work.

shut > *verb* (**shutting**; past and past participle **shut**) **1** move into position to block an opening. **2** (**shut in** or **out**) confine or exclude by closing something such as a door. **3** fold or bring together the sides or parts of. **4** chiefly Brit. make or become unavailable for business or service.
IDIOMS – **be** (or **get**) **shut of** informal be (or get) rid of. **shut down** cease business or operation. **shut off** stop flowing or working. **shut out** prevent (an opponent) from scoring in a game. **shut up** informal stop talking.
ORIGIN – Old English, 'put (a bolt) in position to hold fast'.

shutdown > *noun* a closure of a factory or instance of turning off a machine or computer.

shut-eye > *noun* informal sleep.

shutout > *noun* a match or period in which the opposition is prevented from scoring.

shutter > *noun* **1** each of a pair of hinged panels fixed inside or outside a window that can be closed for security or privacy or to keep out the light. **2** a device that opens and closes to expose the film in a camera. **3** the blind enclosing the swell box in an organ, used for controlling the volume of sound. > *verb* close the shutters of (a window or building).

shuttle > *noun* **1** a form of transport that travels regularly between two places. **2** a bobbin with two pointed ends used for carrying the weft thread across between the warp threads in weaving. **3** a bobbin carrying the lower thread in a sewing machine. **4** a shuttlecock. > *verb* **1** travel regularly between two or more places. **2** transport in a shuttle.
COMBINATIONS – **shuttle diplomacy** negotiations conducted by a mediator who travels between two or more parties that are reluctant to hold direct discussions.
ORIGIN – Old English, 'dart, missile'; related to **SHOOT**.

shuttlecock > *noun* a light cone-shaped object struck with rackets in the games of badminton and battledore, traditionally of cork with feathers attached.

shy[1] > *adjective* (**shyer**, **shyest**) **1** nervous or timid in the company of other people. **2** (**shy of** or **about**) slow or reluctant to do. **3** having a specified dislike or aversion: *camera-shy.* **4** (**shy of**) informal less than; short of or before. > *verb* (**shies**, **shied**) **1** (especially of a horse) start suddenly aside in fright. **2** (**shy from**) avoid (something) through nervousness or lack of confidence. > *noun* a sudden startled movement, especially of a frightened horse.
DERIVATIVES – **shyly** *adverb* **shyness** *noun*.
SYNONYMS – *adjective* **1** bashful, inhibited, nervous, retiring, self-conscious, timid.
ANTONYMS – *adjective* **1** brash, confident.

shy[2] > *verb* (**shies**, **shied**) fling or throw at a target. > *noun* (pl. **shies**) an act of shying.

shyster /**shī**stər/ > *noun* informal a person, especially a lawyer, who uses unscrupulous methods.
ORIGIN – said to be from *Scheuster*, the name of a lawyer.

SI > *abbreviation* **1** Système International, the international system of units of measurement based on the metre, kilogram, second, ampere, kelvin, candela, and mole. **2** Law statutory instrument.

Si > *symbol* the chemical element silicon.

si > *noun* Music another term for **TE**.

Siamese > *noun* (pl. same) **1** dated a native of Siam (now Thailand) in SE Asia. **2** (also **Siamese cat**) a lightly built short-haired breed of cat characterised by slanting blue eyes and pale fur with darker points. > *adjective* dated relating to Siam.
COMBINATIONS – **Siamese twins** twins that are physically joined at birth, in some cases sharing organs. [ORIGIN – with reference to the *Siamese* men Chang and Eng (1811–74), who were joined at the waist.]

sib > *noun* chiefly Zoology a brother or sister; a sibling.

Siberian /sī**beer**iən/ > *noun* a person from Siberia. > *adjective* relating to Siberia.

sibilant > *adjective* **1** making or characterised by a hissing sound. **2** Phonetics (of a speech sound) sounded with a hissing effect, for example *s, sh*. > *noun* Phonetics a sibilant speech sound.
DERIVATIVES – **sibilance** *noun*.
ORIGIN – from Latin *sibilare* 'hiss'.

siblicide /**sib**lisīd/ > *noun* Zoology the killing of a sibling or siblings.

sibling > *noun* each of two or more children or offspring having one or both parents in common; a brother or sister.
ORIGIN – Old English, 'relative'.

sibyl > *noun* **1** (in ancient times) a woman supposedly able to utter the messages and prophecies of a god. **2** literary a woman able to foretell the future.
DERIVATIVES – **sibylline** *adjective*.
ORIGIN – Greek *Sibulla*.

sic /sik/ > *adverb* (after a copied or quoted word) written exactly as it stands in the original.
ORIGIN – Latin, 'so, thus'.

Sicilian > *noun* a person from Sicily. > *adjective* relating to Sicily.

sick[1] > *adjective* **1** affected by physical or mental illness. **2** feeling nauseous and wanting to vomit. **3** informal disappointed, mortified, or miserable. **4** (**sick of**) bored by or annoyed with through excessive exposure; weary of. **5** informal having abnormal or unnatural tendencies; perverted. **6** informal (of humour) dealing offensively with unpleasant or upsetting subjects. **7** archaic pining or longing. > *noun* Brit. informal vomit. > *verb* (**sick up**) Brit. informal bring up by vomiting.
IDIOMS – **be sick 1** be ill. **2** Brit. vomit. **get sick 1** be ill. **2** N. Amer. vomit.
USAGE – what is the difference between **sick** and **ill**? In British English there is a distinction according to the position of the adjective: if **sick** is used before the noun, as in *a sick child*, it means the same as *a child who is ill*, i.e. unwell in some way; if it stands alone after the verb, as in *a child who is feeling sick*, it means 'nauseous'. In American English, **sick** in *my daughter was sick yesterday* means 'ill, unwell', while in British English it may mean either 'ill, unwell' or 'nauseous', according to the context. Finally, it is not good English to use **ill** before a noun, as in *ill children*; it is better to say *sick children*.
SYNONYMS – *adjective* **1** ailing, ill, indisposed, unwell; chiefly Brit. poorly. **2** bilious, nauseous, queasy.
ANTONYMS – *adjective* **1** healthy, well.
COMBINATIONS – **sick building syndrome** a condition marked by headaches, respiratory problems, etc. that affects office workers, attributed to factors such as poor ventilation in the working environment. **sick headache** a headache accompanied by nausea, particularly a migraine. **sick leave** leave of absence granted because of illness. **sickroom** a room occupied by or set apart for people who are unwell.

sick[2] > *verb* (**sick on**) **1** set (a dog) on. **2** set (someone) to pursue, keep watch on, or accompany.
ORIGIN – dialect variant of **SEEK**.

sickbay > *noun* a room or building set aside for sick people, especially on a ship.

sickbed > *noun* an invalid's bed.

sicken > *verb* **1** make or become disgusted or appalled. **2** become ill. **3** (**sicken for**) begin to show symptoms of (a particular illness). **4**

(**sickening**) informal very irritating or annoying. **5** archaic feel disgust or horror.

DERIVATIVES – **sickeningly** adverb.

sickener > *noun* informal something which causes disgust or severe disappointment.

sickie > *noun* informal **1** chiefly Brit. a period of sick leave taken when one is not actually ill. **2** another word for SICKO.

sickle > *noun* a short-handled farming tool with a semicircular blade, used for cutting corn, lopping, or trimming.

WORDFINDER – falcate, falciform (*curved like a sickle*).

COMBINATIONS – **sickle-cell anaemia** (also **sickle-cell disease**) a severe hereditary form of anaemia in which a mutated form of haemoglobin distorts the red blood cells into a crescent shape at low oxygen levels.

ORIGIN – Old English, from Latin *secula*, from *secare* 'to cut'.

sickly > *adjective* (**sicklier, sickliest**) **1** often ill; in poor health. **2** causing, characterised by, or indicative of poor health. **3** (of flavour, colour, etc.) so garish or sweet as to induce nausea. **4** excessively sentimental or mawkish.

DERIVATIVES – **sickliness** noun.

SYNONYMS – **1** delicate, frail, unhealthy, weak. **4** cloying, mawkish, sugary, syrupy; informal mushy, schmaltzy.

sickness > *noun* **1** the state of being ill. **2** a particular type of illness or disease. **3** nausea or vomiting.

COMBINATIONS – **sickness benefit** (in the UK) benefit paid weekly by the state to an individual for sickness which interrupts paid employment.

sicko > *noun* (pl. **sickos**) informal a mentally ill or perverted person, especially a dangerous one.

side > *noun* **1** a position to the left or right of an object, place, or central point. **2** either of the two halves of something regarded as divided by an imaginary central line. **3** an upright or sloping surface of a structure or object that is not the top or bottom and generally not the front or back. **4** each of the flat surfaces of a solid object. **5** each of the lines forming the boundary of a plane rectilinear figure. **6** each of the two surfaces of something flat and thin, e.g. paper. **7** each of the two faces of a record or of the two separate tracks on a cassette tape. **8** a part or region near the edge and away from the middle of something. **9** (before another noun) subsidiary or less important: *a side dish*. **10** a person or group opposing another or others in a dispute or contest. **11** a particular aspect: *he had a disagreeable side*. **12** a person's kinship or line of descent as traced through either their father or mother. **13** a sports team. **14** Brit. informal a television channel. **15** Brit. informal boastful or

pretentious manner or attitude. > *verb* (**side with** or **against**) support or oppose in a conflict or dispute.

WORDFINDER – lateral (*of or at the side*); collateral (*situated side by side*), equilateral (*having equal sides*), juxtapose (*place side by side*), polygon (*figure with many sides*).

IDIOMS – **from side to side 1** alternately left and right from a central point. **2** across the entire width; right across. **no side** Rugby the end of a game. **on the side 1** informal in addition to one's regular job. **2** informal secretly, especially as an illicit sexual relationship. **3** N. Amer. served separately from the main dish. **side by side** close together and facing the same way. **take sides** support one person or cause against another or others.

DERIVATIVES – **sided** adjective **sideward** adjective & adverb **sidewards** adverb.

COMBINATIONS – **side arms** weapons worn at a person's side, such as pistols. **side drum** a small drum with a membrane at each end, the upper one being struck with sticks and the lower one often fitted with rattling cords or wires (snares). **side effect** a secondary, typically undesirable effect of a drug or medical treatment. **side-foot** kick (a ball) with the inside of the foot. **side issue** a subsidiary point or topic connected to some other issue. **sidelight 1** Brit. a small supplementary light on either side of a motor vehicle's headlights. **2** (**sidelights**) a ship's navigation lights. **3** a narrow pane of glass alongside a door or larger window. **side road** a minor or subsidiary road joining or diverging from a main road. **side-saddle** (of a woman rider) sitting with both feet on the same side of the horse. **side-splitting** informal extremely amusing. **side street** a minor or subsidiary street. **sidestroke** a swimming stroke similar to the breaststroke, in which the swimmer lies on their side. **sidewall** the side of a tyre. **side whiskers** whiskers or sideburns on a man's cheeks. **side wind** a wind blowing predominantly from one side.

sidebar > *noun* a short note or supplement placed alongside a main article of text.

sideboard > *noun* **1** a flat-topped piece of furniture with cupboards and drawers, used for storing crockery, glasses, etc. **2** Brit. a sideburn.

sideburn > *noun* a strip of hair grown by a man down each side of the face in front of his ears.

ORIGIN – first as *burnside*, from the name of the American general Ambrose *Burnside* (1824–81), who affected this style.

sidecar > *noun* a small, low vehicle attached to the side of a motorcycle for carrying passengers.

sidekick > *noun* informal a person's assistant or junior associate.

sideline > *noun* **1** an activity done in addition to one's main job. **2** either of the two lines bounding the longer sides of a football field, basketball court, etc. **3** (**the sidelines**) a position of observing a situation rather than being directly involved in it. > *verb* remove or bar from a team, game, or active position.

sidelong > *adjective & adverb* directed to or from one side; sideways.

sideman > *noun* a supporting musician in a jazz band or rock group.

side-on > *adjective & adverb* on, from, or towards a side.

sidereal /sīˈdeerɪəl/ > *adjective* relating to the distant stars or their apparent positions in the sky.

COMBINATIONS – **sidereal time** time reckoned from the motion of the earth (or a planet) relative to the distant stars (rather than with respect to the sun).

ORIGIN – Latin *sidereus*, from *sidus* 'star'.

sideshow > *noun* **1** a small show or stall at an exhibition, fair, or circus. **2** a minor but diverting incident or issue.

sidesman > *noun* Brit. a churchwarden's assistant.

sidestep > *verb* (**sidestepped, sidestepping**) **1** avoid by stepping sideways. **2** avoid dealing with or discussing (a problem). > *noun* an instance of sidestepping.

sideswipe > *noun* **1** a passing critical remark. **2** chiefly N. Amer. a glancing blow from or on the side, especially of a vehicle. > *verb* chiefly N. Amer. strike with a glancing blow.

sidetrack > *verb* **1** distract from an immediate or important issue. **2** chiefly N. Amer. direct (a train) into a branch line or siding. > *noun* chiefly N. Amer. a railway branch line or siding.

sidewalk > *noun* N. Amer. a pavement.

sideways > *adverb & adjective* **1** to, towards, or from the side. **2** unconventional or unorthodox: *a sideways look at daily life*.

DERIVATIVES – **sidewise** US adverb & adjective.

sidewinder /ˈsīdwīndər/ > *noun* a nocturnal burrowing rattlesnake that moves sideways over sand by throwing its body into S-shaped curves.

siding > *noun* **1** a short track at the side of and opening on to a railway line, where trains are shunted or left. **2** N. Amer. a loop line. **3** N. Amer. cladding material for the outside of a building.

sidle /ˈsīd'l/ > *verb* walk in a furtive or stealthy manner, especially sideways or obliquely. > *noun* an instance of sidling.

ORIGIN – from obsolete *sideling* 'sidelong'.

SIDS > *abbreviation* sudden infant death syndrome.

siege* > *noun* **1** a military operation in which enemy forces surround a town or building, cutting off essential supplies, with the aim of compelling those inside to surrender. **2** a similar operation by a police team to compel an armed person to surrender.

IDIOMS – **lay siege to** conduct a siege of. **siege mentality** a defensive or paranoid attitude based on the belief that others are hostile towards one. **under siege** undergoing a siege.

*SPELLING – remember, *i* before e: *siege*.

ORIGIN – Old French *sege*, from *asegier* 'besiege'.

siemens /seemənz/ > *noun* Physics the unit of conductance in the SI system, equivalent to the reciprocal of one ohm of resistance.

ORIGIN – named after the German-born British engineer Sir Charles William *Siemens* (1823–83).

sienna /sienna/ > *noun* a kind of earth used as a pigment in painting, normally yellowish-brown in colour (**raw sienna**) or deep reddish-brown when roasted (**burnt sienna**).

ORIGIN – from Italian *terra di Sienna* 'earth of Siena'.

sierra /sierrə/ > *noun* (especially in Spanish-speaking countries or the western US) a long jagged mountain chain.

ORIGIN – Spanish.

Sierra Leonean /sierrə liōniən/ > *noun* a person from Sierra Leone, a country in West Africa. > *adjective* relating to Sierra Leone.

siesta /siestə/ > *noun* an afternoon rest or nap, especially one habitually taken in a hot climate.

ORIGIN – Spanish, from Latin *sexta hora* 'sixth hour'.

sieve* /siv/ > *noun* a utensil consisting of a wire or plastic mesh held in a frame, used for straining solids from liquids or separating coarser from finer particles. > *verb* **1** put through a sieve. **2** (**sieve through**) examine in detail.

*SPELLING – remember, *i* before e: *sieve*.

sievert /seevərt/ > *noun* Physics the unit of dose equivalent in the SI system, defined as a dose of radiation which delivers a joule of energy per kilogram of the mass of the recipient body.

ORIGIN – named after the Swedish physicist Rolf M. *Sievert* (1896–1966).

sift > *verb* **1** put (a dry substance) through a sieve so as to remove lumps or large particles. **2** examine thoroughly to isolate what is important or useful. **3** (**sift down**) (of snow, ash, etc.) descend lightly or sparsely. > *noun* an act of sifting.

DERIVATIVES – **sifter** *noun*.

sigh > *noun* **1** a long, deep audible exhalation expressing sadness, tiredness, relief, etc. **2** a sound resembling this. > *verb* **1** emit a sigh. **2** (**sigh for**) literary yearn for.

sight > *noun* **1** the faculty or power of seeing.

2 the action or fact of seeing someone or something. **3** the area or distance within which someone can see or something can be seen. **4** a thing that one sees or that can be seen. **5** (**sights**) places of interest to tourists and other visitors. **6** (**a sight**) informal a person or thing having a ridiculous or unattractive appearance. **7** (also **sights**) a device on a gun or optical instrument used for assisting in precise aim or observation. > *verb* **1** manage to see or briefly observe. **2** take aim by looking through the sights of a gun. **3** take a detailed visual measurement with a sight. **4** adjust the sight of (a gun or optical instrument).

IDIOMS – **at first sight** at the first glimpse; on the first impression. **catch sight of** glimpse for a moment. **in sight 1** visible. **2** near at hand; close to being achieved or realised. **in** (or **within**) **sight of 1** so as to see or be seen from. **2** within reach of; close to attaining. **in** (or **within**) **one's sights 1** visible through the sights of one's gun. **2** within the scope of one's ambitions or expectations. **lose sight of 1** be no longer able to see. **2** fail to consider, be aware of, or remember. **on** (or **at**) **sight** as soon as someone or something has been seen. **out of sight 1** not visible. **2** informal extremely good; excellent. **out of sight, out of mind** proverb you soon forget people or things that are no longer visible or present. **raise** (or **lower**) **one's sights** become more (or less) ambitious; increase (or lower) one's expectations. **set one's sights on** hope strongly to achieve or reach. **a sight** informal considerably: *she is a sight cleverer than Sarah.* **a sight for sore eyes** informal a person or thing that one is extremely pleased or relieved to see.

DERIVATIVES – **sighter** *noun* **sighting** *noun*.

COMBINATIONS – **sight line** a hypothetical line from someone's eye to what is seen. **sight-read** read and perform (music) at sight, without preparation. **sight unseen** without the opportunity to look at the object in question beforehand.

sighted > *adjective* **1** having the ability to see; not blind. **2** having a specified kind of sight: *keen-sighted*.

sightless > *adjective* unable to see; blind.

sightseeing > *noun* the activity of visiting places of interest in a particular location.

DERIVATIVES – **sightseer** *noun*.

sigil /sijil/ > *noun* a sign or symbol.

ORIGIN – Latin *sigillum* 'sign'.

sigma /sigmə/ > *noun* the eighteenth letter of the Greek alphabet (Σ, σ, or at the end of a word ς), transliterated as 's'.

ORIGIN – Greek.

sign > *noun* **1** a thing whose presence or occurrence indicates the probable presence, occurrence, or arrival of something else. **2** a

signal, gesture, or notice conveying information or an instruction. **3** a symbol or word used to represent something in algebra, music, or other subjects. **4** Astrology each of the twelve equal sections into which the zodiac is divided. > *verb* **1** write one's name on (something) for the purposes of identification or authorisation. **2** engage for or commit oneself to work by signing a contract. **3** use gestures to convey information or instructions.

IDIOMS – **sign off 1** conclude a letter, broadcast, or other message. **2** authorise (someone) to miss work. **sign on 1** commit oneself to something. **2** Brit. register as unemployed. **3** employ (someone). **sign out** sign to indicate that one has borrowed or hired (something). **sign up** commit oneself to a course, job, etc.

DERIVATIVES – **signer** *noun*.

SYNONYMS – *noun* **1** indication, signal, symptom. *verb* **1** autograph, endorse, witness. **3** gesticulate, gesture, indicate, signal.

COMBINATIONS – **signboard** a board displaying the name or logo of a business or product. **sign language** a system of communication used among and with deaf people, consisting of gestures and signs made by the hands and face.

ORIGIN – Latin *signum* 'mark, token'.

signage > *noun* chiefly N. Amer. signs collectively, especially commercial or public display signs.

signal¹ > *noun* **1** a gesture, action, or sound conveying information or an instruction. **2** an indication of a state of affairs. **3** an event or statement that provides the impulse or occasion for something to happen. **4** a light or semaphore on a railway, giving indications to train drivers of whether or not to proceed. **5** an electrical impulse or radio wave sent or received. > *verb* (**signalled**, **signalling**; US **signaled**, **signaling**) **1** transmit a signal. **2** instruct or indicate by means of a signal.

DERIVATIVES – **signaller** *noun*.

SYNONYMS – *noun* **1** gesticulation, gesture, sign, wave. **2** indication, pointer, symptom. **3** cue, prompt, stimulus.

COMBINATIONS – **signal box** Brit. a building beside a railway track from which signals and points are controlled. **signalman 1** a railway worker responsible for operating signals and points. **2** a person responsible for sending and receiving naval or military signals. **signal-to-noise ratio** the ratio of the strength of an electrical or other signal carrying information to that of unwanted interference, expressed in decibels.

ORIGIN – Latin *signalis*, from *signum* 'mark, token'.

signal² > *adjective* striking; outstanding.

DERIVATIVES – **signally** *adverb*.

ORIGIN – French *signalé*, from Italian *segnalato* 'distinguished', from *segnale* 'a signal'.

signalise (also **signalize**) > *verb* **1** mark or indicate. **2** archaic make noteworthy or remarkable.

signatory /**sig**nətri/ > *noun* (pl. **signatories**) a party that has signed an agreement.

signature > *noun* **1** a person's name written in a distinctive way as a form of identification or authorisation. **2** the action of signing something. **3** a distinctive product or characteristic by which someone or something can be identified. **4** Music a key signature or time signature.

COMBINATIONS – **signature tune** chiefly Brit. a distinctive piece of music associated with a particular programme or performer on television or radio.

signet /**sig**nit/ > *noun* historical a small seal, especially one set in a ring, used to give authentication to an official document.

COMBINATIONS – **signet ring** a ring with a seal set into it.

ORIGIN – Latin *signetum*, from *signum* 'token, seal'.

significance > *noun* **1** the quality of being significant; importance. **2** the unstated meaning to be found in words or events.

SYNONYMS – **1** gravity, import, importance, seriousness. **2** implication, import, thrust.

ORIGIN – Latin *significantia*, from *significare* 'indicate, portend'.

significant > *adjective* **1** having an unstated meaning; indicative of something. **2** extensive or important enough to merit attention.

DERIVATIVES – **significantly** adverb.

SYNONYMS – **1** knowing, meaningful, suggestive. **2** important, notable, serious, weighty.

ANTONYMS – **1** meaningless. **2** insignificant.

COMBINATIONS – **significant figure** Mathematics each of the digits of a number that are used to express it to the required degree of accuracy.

signify > *verb* (**signifies**, **signfied**) **1** be an indication of. **2** be a symbol of; have as meaning. **3** indicate or declare (a feeling or intention). **4** be of importance: *the locked door doesn't necessarily signify.*

DERIVATIVES – **signification** noun.

SYNONYMS – **1** be evidence of, mark, mean, signal. **2** denote, designate, represent, symbolise. **3** express, indicate, show.

ORIGIN – Latin *significare* 'indicate, portend', from *signum* 'token'.

signing > *noun* **1** Brit. a person who has recently been signed to join a sports team, record company, etc. **2** an event at which an author signs copies of their book to gain publicity and sales. **3** sign language.

signor /see**nyor**/ > *noun* (pl. **signori** /see**nyor**ee/) a title or form of address used of or to an Italian-speaking man, corresponding to *Mr* or *sir*.

ORIGIN – Italian, from Latin *senior* 'older man'.

signora /see**nyor**ə/ > *noun* a title or form of address used of or to an Italian-speaking married woman, corresponding to *Mrs* or *madam*.

ORIGIN – Italian, feminine of SIGNOR.

signorina /seenyə**ree**nə/ > *noun* a title or form of address used of or to an Italian-speaking unmarried woman, corresponding to *Miss*.

ORIGIN – Italian, from SIGNORA.

signpost > *noun* a sign on a post, giving information such as the direction and distance to a nearby town. > *verb* **1** provide (an area) with a signpost or signposts. **2** chiefly Brit. indicate (a place or feature) with a signpost.

signwriter > *noun* a person who paints commercial signs and advertisements.

DERIVATIVES – **signwriting** noun.

sika /**see**kə/ > *noun* a deer with a greyish coat that turns yellowish-brown with white spots in summer, native to Japan and SE Asia.

ORIGIN – Japanese.

Sikh /seek/ > *noun* an adherent of Sikhism. > *adjective* relating to Sikhs or Sikhism.

ORIGIN – Punjabi, 'disciple'.

Sikhism /**seek**iz'm/ > *noun* a religion founded in Punjab in the 15th century by Guru Nanak.

Siksika /**sik**sikə/ > *plural noun* the northernmost of the three peoples forming the Blackfoot confederacy.

ORIGIN – Blackfoot, 'black foot'.

silage /**sī**lij/ > *noun* green fodder that is compacted and stored in airtight conditions, without first being dried, and used as animal feed in the winter.

ORIGIN – from Spanish *ensilar* 'put into a silo'.

silence > *noun* **1** complete absence of sound. **2** the fact or state of abstaining from speech. > *verb* **1** make silent. **2** fit with a silencer.

IDIOMS – **silence is golden** proverb it is often wise to say nothing.

DERIVATIVES – **silenced** adjective.

SYNONYMS – *noun* **1** hush, quietness, soundlessness. **2** muteness, speechlessness, taciturnity.

ORIGIN – Latin *silentium*, from *silere* 'be silent'.

silencer > *noun* a device for reducing the noise emitted by a mechanism, especially a gun or exhaust system.

silent > *adjective* **1** not making or accompanied by any sound. **2** not speaking or not spoken aloud. **3** (of a film) without an accompanying soundtrack. **4** (of a letter)

written but not pronounced, e.g. *b* in *doubt*. **5** tending not to speak much.

DERIVATIVES – **silently** adverb.

SYNONYMS – **1** hushed, inaudible, noiseless, quiet, soundless.

COMBINATIONS – **silent partner** North American term for *sleeping partner*.

silhouette /silloo**et**/ > *noun* **1** the dark shape and outline of someone or something visible in restricted light against a brighter background. **2** a representation of someone or something that shows the shape and outline only. > *verb* cast or show as a silhouette.

ORIGIN – named after the French author and politician Étienne de *Silhouette* (1709–67).

silica /**sill**ikə/ > *noun* silicon dioxide, a hard, unreactive, colourless compound which occurs as quartz and in sandstone and many other rocks.

DERIVATIVES – **siliceous** /si**lish**əss/ adjective.

COMBINATIONS – **silica gel** hydrated silica in a hard granular hygroscopic form used as a drying agent.

ORIGIN – from Latin *silex* 'flint', on the pattern of words such as *alumina*.

silicate > *noun* a salt or mineral containing silica combined with a base.

silicic /si**liss**ik/ > *adjective* Geology (of rocks) rich in silica.

silicon > *noun* a grey non-metallic chemical element with semiconducting properties, used in making electronic circuits.

COMBINATIONS – **silicon carbide** a hard refractory compound of silicon and carbon; carborundum. **silicon chip** a microchip.

ORIGIN – from Latin *silex* 'flint', on the pattern of *carbon* and *boron*.

silicone* > *noun* a durable synthetic resin with a structure based on chains of silicon and oxygen atoms with organic side chains.

*****SPELLING** – remember the final *-e* to distinguish **silicone** from **silicon**. Silicon is a chemical element used in electronic circuits and microchips, while **silicone** is the material used in cosmetic implants and in polishes and lubricants.

silicosis /silli**kō**siss/ > *noun* Medicine lung fibrosis caused by the inhalation of dust containing silica.

silk > *noun* **1** a fine, soft lustrous fibre produced by silkworms. **2** thread or fabric made from silk. **3** (**silks**) garments made from silk, especially as worn by a jockey. **4** Brit. informal a Queen's (or King's) Counsel. [ORIGIN – so named because of having the right to wear a gown made of silk.]

WORDFINDER – sericulture (*silk production by rearing of silkworms*).

DERIVATIVES – **silken** adjective.

ORIGIN – from Latin *sericus*, from Greek *Sēres*, the name given to the inhabitants of the Far Eastern countries from which silk first came overland to Europe.

silk screen > *noun* a screen of fine mesh used in screen printing. > *verb* (**silk-screen**) print, decorate, or reproduce using a silk screen.

silkworm > *noun* a caterpillar of a domesticated silk moth, which spins a silk cocoon that is processed to yield silk fibre.

silky > *adjective* (**silkier**, **silkiest**) **1** of or resembling silk. **2** suave and smooth.
DERIVATIVES – **silkily** *adverb* **silkiness** *noun*.

sill (also chiefly Building **cill**) > *noun* **1** a shelf or slab of stone, wood, or metal at the foot of a window or doorway. **2** a strong horizontal member at the base of any structure. **3** Geology a sheet of igneous rock intruded between and parallel with existing strata. Compare with **DYKE**[1].
ORIGIN – Old English, 'horizontal beam forming a foundation'.

silly > *adjective* (**sillier**, **silliest**) **1** lacking in common sense or judgement; foolish. **2** trivial or frivolous. **3** Cricket denoting fielding positions very close to the batsman. > *noun* (pl. **sillies**) informal a silly person.
IDIOMS – **the silly season** chiefly Brit. high summer, when newspapers often publish trivial material because of a lack of important news.
DERIVATIVES – **silliness** *noun*.
SYNONYMS – *adjective* **1** foolish, idiotic, stupid, witless.
ANTONYMS – *adjective* **1** sensible. **2** serious.

wordpower facts

Silly

The current senses of **silly** have moved a long way from the original meaning of the word. Spelled as **seely**, it entered English in the 13th century from a Germanic source, in the senses 'happy, blissful' and 'lucky, auspicious'. From this the senses 'spiritually blessed' and 'pious and holy' arose. A subtle development in meaning from 'innocent, harmless' (often referring to animals, for example 'The Woolfe shall fawne upon the silly Sheepe') to 'deserving of pity; pitiable' led to 'feeble' and then, from the early 16th century, 'foolish, simple'. By this time shortening of the sound of the vowel had led to the spelling changing to **silly**, which is recorded from the 15th century.

silo /sīlō/ > *noun* (pl. **silos**) **1** a tall tower or pit on a farm, used to store grain. **2** a pit or other airtight structure in which green

crops are stored as silage. **3** an underground chamber in which a guided missile is kept ready for firing.
ORIGIN – Spanish, from Greek *siros* 'corn pit'.

silt > *noun* fine sand, clay, or other material carried by running water and deposited as a sediment. > *verb* fill or block with silt.
DERIVATIVES – **siltation** *noun* **silting** *noun* **silty** *adjective*.
ORIGIN – related to **SALT**: probably originally denoting a salty deposit.

siltstone > *noun* fine-grained sedimentary rock consisting of consolidated silt.

Silurian /sīlyooriən/ > *adjective* Geology relating to the third period in the Palaeozoic era (between the Ordovician and Devonian periods, about 439 to 409 million years ago), a time when the first fish and land plants appeared.
ORIGIN – from *Silures*, the Latin name of a people of ancient Wales.

silver > *noun* **1** a precious greyish-white metallic chemical element. **2** a shiny grey-white colour or appearance like that of silver. **3** silver dishes, containers, or cutlery. **4** coins made from silver or from a metal that resembles silver. **5** household cutlery of any material. > *verb* **1** coat or plate with silver. **2** provide (mirror glass) with a backing of a silver-coloured material in order to make it reflective.
WORDFINDER – argentiferous (*containing silver*), argentine (*like silver*).
IDIOMS – **be born with a silver spoon in one's mouth** be born into a wealthy family of high social standing. **every cloud has a silver lining** proverb every difficult or sad situation has a comforting or more hopeful aspect, even though this may not be immediately apparent. **the silver screen** the cinema industry.
DERIVATIVES – **silvered** *adjective* **silverware** *noun* **silvery** *adjective*.
COMBINATIONS – **silver birch** a birch with silver-grey bark. **silver fern 1** another term for **PONGA**. **2** a stylised fern leaf in silver, as an emblem of New Zealand. **silver jubilee** the twenty-fifth anniversary of a significant event. **silver medal** a medal made of or coloured silver, customarily awarded for second place in a race or competition. **silver plate 1** a thin layer of silver applied as a coating to another metal. **2** plates, dishes, etc. made of or plated with silver. **silver sand** Brit. a fine, white sand used in gardening. **silver service** a style of serving food at formal meals in which the server uses a silver spoon and fork in one hand to place food on the diner's plate. **silver wedding** the twenty-fifth anniversary of a wedding.

silverfish > *noun* a small silvery wingless insect that lives in buildings.

silverside > *noun* Brit. the upper side of a round of beef from the outside of the leg.

silversmith > *noun* a person who makes silver articles.

silver tongue > *noun* an ability to be eloquent and persuasive in speaking.
DERIVATIVES – **silver-tongued** *adjective*.

silviculture /silvikulchər/ > *noun* the growing and cultivation of trees.
DERIVATIVES – **silvicultural** *adjective*.
ORIGIN – from Latin *silva* 'wood'.

sim > *noun* informal a video game that simulates an activity such as flying an aircraft or playing a sport.

simian /simmiən/ > *adjective* relating to or resembling apes or monkeys. > *noun* an ape or monkey.
ORIGIN – from Latin *simia* 'ape', perhaps from Greek *simos* 'flat-nosed'.

similar > *adjective* **1** of the same kind in appearance, character, or quantity, without being identical. **2** Geometry (of geometrical figures) having the same angles and proportions, though of different sizes.
DERIVATIVES – **similarity** *noun* **similarly** *adverb*.
USAGE – use the construction **similar to**, as in *I've had problems similar to yours*; it is not good English to say **similar as**, as in *I've had similar problems as yourself*.
SYNONYMS – **1** akin, alike, related.
ANTONYMS – **1** dissimilar.
ORIGIN – Latin *similaris*, from *similis* 'like'.

simile /simmili/ > *noun* a figure of speech involving the comparison of one thing with another thing of a different kind (e.g. *as solid as a rock*).
ORIGIN – Latin, from *similis* 'like'.

similitude /similityōod/ > *noun* the quality or state of being similar.

SIMM > *abbreviation* Computing single in-line memory module.

simmer > *verb* **1** stay or cause to stay just below boiling point while bubbling gently. **2** be in a state of suppressed anger or excitement. **3** (**simmer down**) become calmer and quieter. > *noun* a state or temperature just below boiling point.
ORIGIN – from dialect *simper* (in the same sense).

simnel cake > *noun* chiefly Brit. a rich fruit cake with a layer of marzipan on top, eaten especially at Easter or during Lent.
ORIGIN – Old French *simenel*, from Latin *simila* or Greek *semidalis* 'fine flour'.

simony /sīməni, simməni/ > *noun* chiefly historical the buying or selling of pardons, benefices, and other ecclesiastical privileges.
ORIGIN – Latin *simonia*, from *Simon* Magus in the Bible (Acts of the Apostles), in allusion to his offer of money to the Apostles.

simoom /simōōm/ (also **simoon**

/si**moon**/) > *noun* a hot, dry dust-laden wind blowing in the desert.

ORIGIN – Arabic, from a word meaning 'to poison'.

simpatico /sim**patt**ikō/ > *adjective* likeable; congenial.

ORIGIN – Italian and Spanish.

simper > *verb* smile in an ingratiating manner. > *noun* an ingratiating smile.

DERIVATIVES – **simpering** *adjective* **simperingly** *adverb*.

simple > *adjective* (**simpler**, **simplest**) **1** easily understood or done; not difficult. **2** plain and uncomplicated in form, nature, or design. **3** composed of a single element; not compound. **4** humble and unpretentious. **5** of very low intelligence. **6** (in English grammar) denoting a tense formed without an auxiliary. **7** (of interest) payable on the sum loaned only. Compare with **COMPOUND**[1]. **8** Botany (of a leaf or stem) not divided or branched. **9** (of a lens, microscope, etc.) consisting of a single lens or component. > *noun* chiefly historical a medicinal herb, or a medicine made from one.

DERIVATIVES – **simpleness** *noun*.

SYNONYMS – *adjective* **1** easy, effortless, straightforward, undemanding. **2** accessible, clear, comprehensible. **4** no-nonsense, plain, unostentatious, unpretentious.

ANTONYMS – *adjective* **1** difficult. **2** complex. **4** affected, pretentious.

COMBINATIONS – **simple eye** a small eye of an insect or other arthropod which has only one lens. **simple fracture** a fracture of the bone only, without damage to the surrounding tissues or breaking of the skin. **simple-minded** having or showing very little intelligence or judgement. **simple time** musical rhythm or metre in which each beat in a bar may be subdivided simply into halves or quarters. Compare with *compound time*.

ORIGIN – Old French, from Latin *simplus*.

simpleton > *noun* a foolish or gullible person.

SYNONYMS – dimwit, dunce, fool.

ORIGIN – from **SIMPLE**, on the pattern of surnames derived from place names ending in *-ton*.

simplex > *adjective* technical composed of or characterised by a single part or structure.

ORIGIN – Latin, 'single', from *simplus* 'simple'.

simplicity > *noun* the quality or condition of being simple.

simplify > *verb* (**simplifies**, **simplified**) make more simple.

DERIVATIVES – **simplification** *noun*.

simplistic > *adjective* treating complex issues and problems as simpler they really are.

DERIVATIVES – **simplistically** *adverb*.

simply > *adverb* **1** in a simple manner. **2** merely; just. **3** absolutely; completely.

simulacrum /simyoo**layk**rəm/ > *noun* (pl. **simulacra** /simyoo**layk**rə/ or **simulacrums**) **1** an image or representation of someone or something. **2** an unsatisfactory imitation or substitute.

ORIGIN – Latin, from *simulare* 'copy, represent'.

simulate > *verb* imitate or reproduce the appearance, character, or conditions of.

DERIVATIVES – **simulant** *noun* **simulation** *noun*.

SYNONYMS – counterfeit, duplicate, mimic, replicate.

ORIGIN – Latin *simulare* 'copy, represent'.

simulator > *noun* a machine that simulates the controls and conditions of a real vehicle, process, etc., for training or testing.

simulcast /**simm**əlkaast/ > *noun* **1** a simultaneous broadcast of the same programme on radio and television, or on two or more channels. **2** N. Amer. a live transmission of a public celebration or sports event. > *verb* broadcast (such a transmission).

simultaneous* /simməl**tay**niəss/ > *adjective* occurring, operating, or done at the same time.

DERIVATIVES – **simultaneity** /simməl-tə**nay**iti/ *noun* **simultaneously** *adverb* **simultaneousness** *noun*.

*****SPELLING** – the ending is *-eous*, not *-ious*: simultan*eous*.

SYNONYMS – concurrent, contemporaneous, synchronous.

COMBINATIONS – **simultaneous equations** equations involving two or more unknowns that are to have the same values in each equation.

ORIGIN – from Latin *simul* 'at the same time'.

sin[1] /sin/ > *noun* **1** an immoral act considered to violate divine law. **2** an act regarded as a serious offence. > *verb* (**sinned**, **sinning**) commit a sin.

WORDFINDER – mortal (*denoting serious sin believed to deprive the soul of divine grace*), venial (*less serious, not depriving the soul of divine grace*).

IDIOMS – **live in sin** informal, dated (of an unmarried couple) live together.

DERIVATIVES – **sinless** *adjective*.

COMBINATIONS – **sin bin** informal **1** (in sport) a box or bench to which offending players can be sent as a penalty during a game. **2** Brit. a detention centre for offenders.

ORIGIN – Old English; probably related to Latin *sons* 'guilty'.

sin[2] /sīn/ > *abbreviation* sine.

since > *preposition* in the period between (the time mentioned) and the time under consideration. > *conjunction* **1** during or in

the time after. **2** for the reason that; because. > *adverb* **1** from the time mentioned until the present or the time under consideration. **2** ago.

ORIGIN – from dialect *sithen* 'thereupon, afterwards, ever since'.

sincere > *adjective* (**sincerer**, **sincerest**) proceeding from or characterised by genuine feelings; free from deceit.

DERIVATIVES – **sincerity** *noun*.

SYNONYMS – frank, genuine, heartfelt, honest, straightforward.

ANTONYMS – disingenuous, insincere.

ORIGIN – Latin *sincerus* 'clean, pure'.

sincerely > *adverb* in a sincere or genuine way.

IDIOMS – **yours sincerely** (US also **sincerely yours**) a formula used to end a formal letter in which the recipient is addressed by name.

sine /sīn/ > *noun* Mathematics (in a right-angled triangle) the ratio of the side opposite a particular acute angle to the hypotenuse.

COMBINATIONS – **sine curve** (also **sine wave**) a curve representing periodic oscillations of constant amplitude, as given by a graph of the value of the sine plotted as a function of angle.

ORIGIN – Latin *sinus* 'curve'.

sinecure /**sī**nikyoor, **sin**ikyoor/ > *noun* a position requiring little or no work but giving the holder status or financial benefit.

ORIGIN – from Latin *sine cura* 'without care'.

sine die /seenay **dee**ay, sīni **dī**ee/ > *adverb* Law (with reference to an adjournment) with no appointed date for resumption.

ORIGIN – Latin, 'without a day'.

sine qua non /seenay kwaa **nōn**/ > *noun* a thing that is absolutely essential.

ORIGIN – Latin, 'without which not'.

sinew /**sin**yoo/ > *noun* **1** a piece of tough fibrous tissue uniting muscle to bone; a tendon or ligament. **2** (**sinews**) the parts of a structure or system that give it strength or bind it together.

DERIVATIVES – **sinewy** *adjective*.

ORIGIN – Old English, 'tendon'.

sinfonia /sin**fō**niə, sinfə**nee**ə/ > *noun* Music **1** a symphony. **2** (in baroque music) an orchestral piece used as an introduction to an opera, cantata, or suite. **3** a small symphony orchestra.

ORIGIN – Italian.

sinful > *adjective* **1** wicked and immoral. **2** highly reprehensible: *a sinful waste*.

DERIVATIVES – **sinfully** *adverb* **sinfulness** *noun*.

sing > *verb* (past **sang**; past participle **sung**) **1** make musical sounds with the voice, especially words with a set tune. **2** perform (a song) in this way. **3** (of a bird) make characteristic melodious whistling and twittering sounds. **4** (**sing along**) sing in accompaniment to a song or piece of music. **5** make a high-pitched sound. **6** recount or celebrate, especially in poetry: *sing someone's praises.*

DERIVATIVES – **singable** *adjective* **singer** *noun* **singing** *noun & adjective.*

singalong > *noun* an informal occasion when people sing together in a group.

Singaporean /singəpōriən/ > *noun* a person from Singapore. > *adjective* relating to Singapore.

singe > *verb* (**singed**, **singeing**) **1** burn or be burnt lightly or superficially. **2** burn the bristles or down off (the carcass of a pig or fowl) to prepare it for cooking. > *noun* a light or superficial burn.

Singhalese > *noun & adjective* variant spelling of **SINHALESE**.

single > *adjective* **1** only one; not one of several. **2** designed or suitable for one person. **3** consisting of one part. **4** regarded as distinct from others in a group. **5** even one (used for emphasis): *not a single mention.* **6** not involved in an established romantic or sexual relationship. **7** Brit. (of a ticket) valid for an outward journey only. > *noun* **1** a single person or thing. **2** a short record or CD with one song on each side. **3** (**singles**) a game or competition for individual players. **4** Cricket one run. > *verb* (**single out**) choose (someone or something) from a group for special treatment.

DERIVATIVES – **singleness** *noun* **singly** *adverb.*

SYNONYMS – *adjective* **1** lone, sole, solitary, unique. **4** individual, particular, separate.

COMBINATIONS – **single bond** a chemical bond in which one pair of electrons is shared between two atoms. **single-breasted** (of a jacket or coat) fastened by one row of buttons at the centre of the front. **single combat** fighting between two people. **single cream** Brit. thin cream with a relatively low fat content. **single-lens reflex** denoting a reflex camera in which the lens that forms the image on the film also provides the image in the viewfinder. **single malt** whisky that has not been blended with any other malt. **single market** an association of countries trading with each other without restrictions or tariffs. **single parent** a person bringing up a child or children without a partner. **single transferable vote** an electoral system of proportional representation in which a person's vote can be transferred to a further choice of candidate.

ORIGIN – Old French, from Latin *singulus.*

single file > *noun* a line of people or things arranged one behind another. > *adverb* one behind another.

single-handed > *adverb & adjective* **1** done

without help from others. **2** done or designed to be used with one hand.

DERIVATIVES – **single-handedly** *adverb.*

SYNONYMS – **1** alone, by oneself, solo, unaided.

single-minded > *adjective* concentrating purposefully on one particular thing.

DERIVATIVES – **single-mindedly** *adverb* **single-mindedness** *noun.*

SYNONYMS – committed, determined, unswerving.

ANTONYMS – half-hearted.

singlet > *noun* chiefly Brit. a vest or similar sleeveless garment.

ORIGIN – first used to denote a man's short jacket: from **SINGLE** (because the garment was unlined).

singleton > *noun* **1** a single person or thing of the kind under consideration. **2** informal a person who is not in a long-term relationship. **3** (in card games) a card that is the only one of its suit in a hand.

ORIGIN – from **SINGLE**, on the pattern of *simpleton.*

sing-song > *adjective* (of a person's voice) having a repeated rising and falling rhythm. > *noun* Brit. informal an informal gathering for singing.

singular > *adjective* **1** exceptionally good or great; remarkable. **2** single; unique. **3** Grammar (of a word or form) denoting or referring to just one person or thing. **4** strange or eccentric in some respect. > *noun* Grammar the singular form of a word.

DERIVATIVES – **singularly** *adverb.*

SYNONYMS – *adjective* **1** exceptional, extraordinary, outstanding, remarkable.

ORIGIN – Latin *singularis*, from *singulus* 'single'.

singularity > *noun* (pl. **singularities**) **1** the state or quality of being singular. **2** Physics a point of infinite density within a black hole.

Sinhalese /sinhəleez, sinnəleez/ (also **Singhalese** /singgəleez/, **Sinhala** /sinhaalə/) > *noun* (pl. same) **1** a member of an Indian people now forming the majority of the population of Sri Lanka. **2** the language spoken by this people. > *adjective* relating to the Sinhalese or Sinhalese.

ORIGIN – from Sanskrit *Siṅhala* 'Sri Lanka'.

sinister > *adjective* **1** suggestive of evil or harm. **2** archaic & Heraldry on or towards the left-hand side and the observer's right of a coat of arms. The opposite of **DEXTER**.

DERIVATIVES – **sinisterly** *adverb.*

SYNONYMS – **1** menacing, ominous, threatening.

ORIGIN – Latin, 'left'.

sink[1] > *verb* (past **sank**; past participle **sunk**) **1** become submerged in liquid. **2** (with reference to a ship) go or cause to go to the bottom of the sea. **3** disappear and not be

seen or heard of again. **4** drop downwards. **5** lower oneself or drop down gently. **6** (**sink in**) become fully understood. **7** insert beneath a surface. **8** (**sink into**) cause (something sharp) to penetrate (a surface). **9** gradually decrease or decline in amount or intensity. **10** pass or fall into a particular state or condition: *she sank into sleep.* **11** (**sink in** or **into**) put (money or energy) into.

IDIOMS – **a sinking feeling** an unpleasant bodily sensation caused by apprehension or dismay. **sink or swim** fail or succeed by one's own efforts.

USAGE – in modern English the past tense of **sink** is **sank**, as in *the boat sank*, and the past participle is **sunk**, as in *the boat had already sunk.* The form **sunken**, formerly also used as a past participle, now only survives as an adjective, as in *sunken garden.*

COMBINATIONS – **sinking fund** a fund formed by periodically setting aside money for the gradual repayment of a debt.

sink[2] > *noun* **1** a fixed basin with a water supply and outflow pipe. **2** short for **SINKHOLE**. **3** (before another noun) denoting a school or estate situated in a socially deprived area: *a sink school.* **4** a body or process by which something is removed from a system: *a heat sink.* The opposite of **SOURCE**.

ORIGIN – from **SINK**[1].

sinker > *noun* a weight used to sink a fishing line or sounding line.

sinkhole > *noun* a cavity in the ground caused by water erosion and enabling surface water to disappear underground.

sinner > *noun* a person who sins.

Sino- /sīnō/ > *combining form* Chinese; Chinese and …: *Sino-American.*

ORIGIN – from Latin *Sinae*, from an Arabic word denoting the Chinese empire.

sinology /sīnolləji, sinolləji/ > *noun* the study of Chinese language, history, and culture.

DERIVATIVES – **sinologist** *noun.*

sinter > *noun* Geology a hard siliceous or calcareous deposit precipitated from mineral springs. > *verb* cause (a powdered material) to coalesce by heating (and usually also by compression), without melting.

ORIGIN – German, 'cinder'.

sinuous /sinyooəss/ > *adjective* **1** having many curves and turns. **2** lithe and supple.

DERIVATIVES – **sinuosity** *noun.*

SYNONYMS – **1** serpentine, snaking, winding.

ORIGIN – Latin *sinuosus*, from *sinus* 'a bend'.

sinus /sīnəss/ > *noun* Anatomy & Zoology a cavity within a bone or other tissue, especially one in the bones of the face or skull connecting with the nasal cavities.

DERIVATIVES – **sinusitis** /sīnəsītiss/ *noun*.

ORIGIN – Latin, 'a recess, bend'.

sinusitis /sīnəsītiss/> *noun* inflammation of a nasal sinus.

Sioux /sōō/ > *noun* (pl. same) another term for the Dakota people of North America.

ORIGIN – Ojibwa.

sip > *verb* (**sipped, sipping**) drink (something) by taking small mouthfuls. > *noun* a small mouthful of liquid.

DERIVATIVES – **sipper** *noun*.

ORIGIN – perhaps from SUP¹.

siphon (also **syphon**) > *noun* **1** a tube used to convey liquid upwards from a container and then down to a lower level, the flow being maintained by atmospheric pressure. **2** Zoology a tubular organ in an aquatic animal, especially a mollusc, through which water is drawn in or expelled. > *verb* **1** draw off or convey (liquid) by means of a siphon. **2** draw off (small amounts of money) over a period of time, especially illicitly.

DERIVATIVES – **siphonage** *noun* **siphonal** *adjective* (Zoology) **siphonic** *adjective*.

ORIGIN – Greek, 'pipe'.

sir > *noun* **1** a polite or respectful form of address to a man. **2** used to address a man at the beginning of a formal letter. **3** used as a title before the forename of a knight or baronet.

ORIGIN – reduced form of SIRE.

sire /sīr/ > *noun* **1** the male parent of an animal. **2** archaic or literary a father or other male forebear. **3** archaic a respectful form of address to someone of high social status, especially a king. > *verb* be the sire of.

ORIGIN – Old French, from Latin *senior* 'older'.

siren > *noun* **1** a device that makes a loud prolonged signal or warning sound. **2** Greek Mythology each of a number of women or winged creatures whose singing lured unwary sailors on to rocks. **3** a woman who is considered to be alluring but also dangerous.

ORIGIN – Greek *Seirēn*.

sirenian /sīreeniən/ > *noun* Zoology a large aquatic plant-eating mammal of a group (the order Sirenia) that includes the dugong and manatee.

sirloin > *noun* the choicer part of a loin of beef.

ORIGIN – Old French (see SUR-¹, LOIN).

sirocco /sirokkō/ > *noun* (pl. **siroccos**) a hot wind blowing from North Africa across the Mediterranean to southern Europe.

ORIGIN – Arabic, 'east wind'.

sirrah /sirrə/ > *noun* archaic a term of address to a man or boy, especially one of lower status than the speaker.

sirup > *noun* US spelling of SYRUP.

SIS > *abbreviation* (in the UK) Secret Intelligence Service.

sis > *noun* informal sister.

sisal /sīs'l/ > *noun* **1** a Mexican agave with large fleshy leaves, cultivated for the fibre it yields. **2** the fibre made from the sisal plant, used especially for ropes or matting.

ORIGIN – from *Sisal*, the name of a port in Yucatán, Mexico.

siskin > *noun* a small yellowish-green finch.

ORIGIN – Dutch *siseken*.

sissy (also **cissy**) informal > *noun* (pl. **sissies**) a person regarded as feeble or effeminate. > *adjective* (**sissier, sissiest**) feeble or effeminate.

DERIVATIVES – **sissified** *adjective*.

ORIGIN – from SIS.

sister > *noun* **1** a woman or girl in relation to other children of her parents. **2** a female friend or associate. **3** (before another noun) denoting an organisation or a place which bears a relationship to another of common origin or allegiance. **4** a member of a religious order of women. **5** Brit. a senior female nurse.

WORDFINDER – sororal (*of or like a sister*), sorority (*sisterhood*). See also BROTHER.

DERIVATIVES – **sisterly** *adjective*.

COMBINATIONS – **sister-in-law** (pl. **sisters-in-law**) **1** the sister of one's wife or husband. **2** the wife of one's brother or brother-in-law.

sisterhood > *noun* **1** the relationship between sisters. **2** a feeling of kinship with and closeness to a group of women or all women. **3** an association or community of women linked by a common interest, religion, or trade.

Sisyphean /sissifeeən/ > *adjective* (of a task) unending.

ORIGIN – from the name of *Sisyphus*, a character in Greek mythology who was condemned to the eternal task of rolling a large stone to the top of a hill, from which it always rolled down again.

sit > *verb* (**sitting**; past and past participle **sat**) **1** be or cause to be in a position in which one's weight is supported by one's buttocks and one's back is upright. **2** be or remain in a particular position or state: *the fridge was sitting in a pool of water.* **3** (of an animal) rest with the hind legs bent and the body close to the ground. **4** (of a parliament, committee, court of law, etc.) be engaged in its business. **5** Brit. take (an examination). **6** serve as a member of a council, jury, or other official body. **7** (of a table or room) have enough seats for. **8** (**sit for**) pose for (an artist or photographer). > *noun* a period of sitting.

WORDFINDER – sedentary (*involving much sitting*).

IDIOMS – **sit in** occupy a place as a form of protest. **sit in for** temporarily carry out the duties of. **sit on** informal **1** fail to deal with. **2** subdue or suppress. **sit out** not take part in (an event or activity). **sit tight** informal **1** remain firmly in one's place. **2** refrain from taking action or changing one's mind. **sit up** refrain from going to bed until later than usual.

USAGE – use the participle **sitting** rather than **sat** with the verb 'to be': *we were sitting there for hours* rather than *we were sat there for hours*.

wordpower facts

Sit

The word **sit** comes from Old English *sittan*, from a Germanic source. Ultimately it derives from an Indo-European root shared by Latin *sedere*, also meaning 'to sit', which gave rise to words such as **preside**, **reside**, **seance**, **sedate**, **sedentary**, and **session**. **Saddle** and **settle** almost certainly come from the same root; like **sit**, they entered English from a Germanic rather than Latin source.

sitar /sittaar, sitaar/ > *noun* a large, long-necked Indian lute played with a wire pick.

DERIVATIVES – **sitarist** *noun*.

ORIGIN – from Persian words meaning 'three' and 'string'.

sitcom > *noun* informal a situation comedy.

sit-down > *adjective* **1** (of a meal) eaten sitting at a table. **2** denoting a protest in which demonstrators occupy their workplace or sit down on the ground in a public place. > *noun* **1** a period of sitting down. **2** a sit-down protest.

site > *noun* **1** an area of ground on which something is located. **2** a place where a particular event or activity is occurring or has occurred. > *verb* fix or build in a particular place.

SYNONYMS – *noun* **2** location, position, setting. *verb* locate, place, put, situate.

ORIGIN – Latin *situs* 'local position'.

Sitka /sitkə/ > *noun* a fast-growing North American spruce tree, cultivated for its strong, lightweight wood.

ORIGIN – named after the town of *Sitka* in Alaska.

sitter > *noun* **1** a person who sits, especially for a portrait or examination. **2** a person who looks after children, pets, or a house while the parents or owners are away. **3** informal (in sport) an easy catch or shot.

sitting > *noun* **1** a period or spell of sitting. **2** a period of time when a group of people are served a meal. **3** a period of time during which a committee, court, etc. is engaged in its business. > *adjective* **1** in a seated position. **2** currently present or in office.

COMBINATIONS – **sitting duck** informal a person or thing with no protection against attack. **sitting room** chiefly Brit. a room that is furnished for sitting and relaxing in. **sitting tenant** Brit. a tenant already in occupation of premises.

situate > verb **1** place in a particular location or context. **2** (**be situated**) be in a specified financial or marital position.
SYNONYMS – **1** locate, position, set, site.
ORIGIN – Latin situare 'place', from situs 'site'.

situation > noun **1** a set of circumstances in which one finds oneself. **2** the location and surroundings of a place. **3** a job. **4** N. Amer. informal a very difficult set of circumstances; a crisis.
IDIOMS – **situations vacant** (or **wanted**) chiefly Brit. jobs currently available (or sought).
DERIVATIVES – **situational** adjective **situationally** adverb.
SYNONYMS – **1** condition, state, state of affairs. **2** environment, place, site, spot.
COMBINATIONS – **situation comedy** a television or radio series in which the same set of characters are involved in various amusing situations.

situationism > noun **1** the theory that human behaviour is determined by surrounding circumstances rather than by personal qualities. **2** a revolutionary political theory which regards modern industrial society as being inevitably oppressive and exploitative.
DERIVATIVES – **situationist** noun & adjective.

sit-up > noun a physical exercise designed to strengthen the abdominal muscles, in which a person sits up from a lying position without using the arms for leverage.

sitz bath > noun a bath in which only the buttocks and hips are immersed in water.
ORIGIN – partial translation of German Sitzbad, from sitzen 'sit' + Bad 'bath'.

six > cardinal number **1** one more than five; 6. (Roman numeral: **vi** or **VI**.) **2** Cricket a hit that reaches the boundary without first striking the ground, scoring six runs. **3** a group of six Brownies or Cubs.
WORDFINDER – hexad (group or set of six), hexagon (plane figure with six straight sides and angles), hexagram (six-pointed star), hexahedron (three-dimensional shape with six faces), sexennial (lasting for or recurring every six years), sextet (group of six musicians).
IDIOMS – **at sixes and sevens** in a state of confusion or disarray. **knock for six** Brit. informal utterly surprise or overcome (someone). **six feet under** informal dead and buried. **six of one and half a dozen of the other** a situation in which there is little difference between two alternatives.
DERIVATIVES – **sixfold** adjective & adverb.
COMBINATIONS – **six-shooter** a revolver with six chambers.

sixer > noun the leader of a group of six Brownies or Cubs.

six-pack > noun **1** a pack of six cans of beer. **2** informal a set of well-developed abdominal muscles.

sixpence > noun Brit. **1** a small coin worth six old pence (2½ p), withdrawn in 1980. **2** the sum of six pence, especially before decimalisation (1971).

sixpenny > adjective Brit. costing or worth six pence, especially before decimalisation (1971).

sixteen > cardinal number one more than fifteen; 16. (Roman numeral: **xvi** or **XVI**.)
DERIVATIVES – **sixteenth** ordinal number.

sixth > ordinal number **1** constituting number six in a sequence; 6th. **2** (**a sixth** or **one sixth**) each of six equal parts into which something is or may be divided. **3** Music an interval spanning six consecutive notes in a diatonic scale.
COMBINATIONS – **sixth-form college** Brit. a college for pupils in their final years of secondary education, starting at the age of 16. **sixth sense** a supposed intuitive faculty giving awareness not explicable in terms of normal perception.

sixty > cardinal number (pl. **sixties**) ten more than fifty; 60. (Roman numeral: **lx** or **LX**.)
WORDFINDER – sexagenarian (person aged 60–69).
DERIVATIVES – **sixtieth** ordinal number.

size¹ > noun **1** a thing's overall dimensions or magnitude. **2** each of the classes into which articles are divided according to how large they are. > verb alter or sort in terms of size or according to size.
IDIOMS – **size up 1** estimate or measure the dimensions of. **2** informal form an estimate or rough judgement of. **to size** to the dimensions wanted.
SYNONYMS – noun **1** dimensions, magnitude, measurements, proportions.
ORIGIN – from Old French assise 'ordinance', or a shortening of ASSIZE.

size² > noun a gelatinous solution used in glazing paper, stiffening textiles, and preparing plastered walls for decoration. > verb treat with size.
ORIGIN – perhaps the same word as SIZE¹.

sizeable (also **sizable**) > adjective fairly large.

sizzle > verb **1** (of food) make a hissing sound when frying or roasting. **2** informal be very hot. > noun an instance or the sound of sizzling.
DERIVATIVES – **sizzler** noun **sizzling** adjective.

sjambok /sham bok/ > noun (in South Africa) a long, stiff whip, originally made of rhinoceros hide.

ORIGIN – South African Dutch tjambok, from Urdu.

SK > abbreviation Saskatchewan.

ska /skaa/ > noun a style of fast popular music having a strong offbeat and originating in Jamaica in the 1960s.

skag (also **scag**) > noun informal, chiefly N. Amer. heroin.

skank /skangk/ > noun **1** a dance performed to reggae music, characterised by rhythmically bending forward, raising the knees, and extending the hands palms-downwards. **2** informal, chiefly N. Amer. a sleazy or unpleasant person. > verb **1** play or dance to reggae music. **2** informal walk or move in a sexually suggestive way.
DERIVATIVES – **skanking** adjective.

skanky > adjective informal, chiefly N. Amer. very unpleasant.

skate¹ > noun **1** an ice skate or roller skate. **2** a wheeled device used to move a heavy or unwieldy object. > verb **1** move on ice skates or roller skates in a gliding fashion. **2** ride on a skateboard. **3** (**skate over** or **round** or **around**) pass over or refer only fleetingly to (a subject or problem). **4** (**skate through**) make quick and easy progress through.
WORDFINDER – axel, lutz, salchow, toe loop (jumps in ice skating).
IDIOMS – **get one's skates on** Brit. informal hurry up.
DERIVATIVES – **skater** noun **skating** noun.
COMBINATIONS – **skatepark** an area equipped for skateboarding.
ORIGIN – Dutch schaats, from Old French eschasse 'stilt'.

skate² > noun (pl. same or **skates**) an edible marine fish with a diamond-shaped body.
ORIGIN – Old Norse skata.

skateboard > noun a short, narrow board with two small wheels fixed to the bottom of either end, on which a person can ride in a standing position. > verb ride on a skateboard.
DERIVATIVES – **skateboarder** noun **skateboarding** noun.

skedaddle > verb informal depart hurriedly.

skeet (also **skeet shooting**) > noun a shooting sport in which a clay target is thrown from a trap.
ORIGIN – apparently a pseudo-archaic alteration of the verb **SHOOT**.

skein /skayn/ > noun **1** a length of thread or yarn, loosely coiled and knotted. **2** a flock of wild geese or swans in flight.
ORIGIN – from Old French escaigne.

skeletal /skell it'l/ > adjective **1** relating to or functioning as a skeleton. **2** existing only in outline or as a framework. **3** very thin; emaciated.
DERIVATIVES – **skeletally** adverb.

skeleton > noun **1** an internal or external framework of bone, cartilage, or other rigid material supporting or containing the body of an animal or plant. **2** a very thin or emaciated person or animal. **3** a supporting framework, basic structure, or essential part. **4** (before another noun) denoting an essential or minimum number of people or things: *a skeleton staff.*

WORDFINDER – osteology (*study of the skeleton*).

IDIOMS – **skeleton in the cupboard** a discreditable fact that someone wishes to keep secret.

COMBINATIONS – **skeleton key** a key designed to fit many locks by having the interior of the bit hollowed.

ORIGIN – Greek, from *skeletos* 'dried up'.

skep (also **skip**) > *noun* **1** a straw or wicker beehive. **2** archaic a wooden or wicker basket.

ORIGIN – Old English, 'basket'.

skeptic > *noun* US spelling of SCEPTIC.

skerrick > *noun* Austral./NZ informal the smallest bit: *there's not a skerrick of food in the house.*

skerry > *noun* (pl. **skerries**) Scottish a reef or rocky island.

ORIGIN – Orkney dialect.

sketch > *noun* **1** a rough or unfinished drawing or painting. **2** a short humorous play or performance. **3** a brief written or spoken account or description. > *verb* **1** make a sketch of. **2** give a brief account or general outline of.

DERIVATIVES – **sketcher** *noun.*

ORIGIN – Italian *schizzo*, from Greek *skhedios* 'done extempore'.

sketchbook (also **sketch pad**) > *noun* a pad of drawing paper for sketching on.

sketchy > *adjective* (**sketchier, sketchiest**) not thorough or detailed.

SYNONYMS – cursory, imprecise, perfunctory, superficial, vague.

skew > *adjective* neither parallel nor at right angles to a specified or implied line; askew. > *noun* **1** an oblique angle; a slant. **2** a bias towards one particular group or subject. > *verb* **1** suddenly change direction or move at an angle. **2** make biased or distorted.

DERIVATIVES – **skewness** *noun.*

ORIGIN – from Old French *eschiver* 'eschew'.

skewbald > *adjective* (of a horse) with irregular patches of white and another colour (properly not black). > *noun* a skewbald horse.

ORIGIN – from obsolete *skewed* 'skewbald', on the pattern of *piebald*.

skewer > *noun* a long piece of wood or metal used for holding pieces of food together during cooking. > *verb* fasten together or pierce with a pin or skewer.

skew-whiff > *adverb & adjective* informal, chiefly Brit. not straight; askew.

ski* > *noun* (pl. **skis**) **1** each of a pair of long, narrow pieces of hard flexible material

fastened under the feet for travelling over snow. **2** a similar device attached beneath a vehicle or aircraft. > *verb* (**skis, skied, skiing**) travel over snow on skis.

WORDFINDER – Alpine skiing (*fast downhill skiing*), langlauf (*cross-country skiing*), Nordic skiing (*cross-country skiing and ski jumping*), piste (*ski slope with compacted snow*), schuss (*straight downhill run on skis*), slalom (*ski race down a winding course*).

DERIVATIVES – **skiable** *adjective* **skiing** *noun.*

*SPELLING – note that the plural of the noun is **skis**, without an *e*.

COMBINATIONS – **ski jump 1** a steep slope levelling off before a sharp drop to allow a skier to leap through the air. **2** a leap made from such a slope. **ski lift** a system used to transport skiers up a slope to the top of a run, typically consisting of moving seats attached to an overhead cable. **ski mask** a protective covering for the head and face, with holes for the eyes, nose, and mouth. **ski pants** women's trousers made of stretchy fabric with tapering legs and an elastic stirrup under each foot.

skid > *verb* (**skidded, skidding**) **1** (of a vehicle) slide, typically sideways, on slippery ground or as a result of stopping or turning too quickly. **2** slip or slide. > *noun* **1** an act of skidding. **2** a runner attached to the underside of an aircraft for use when landing on snow or grass. **3** a braking device consisting of a wooden or metal shoe that prevents a wheel from revolving. **4** (**skids**) N. Amer. a set of wooden rollers used for moving logs or other heavy objects.

IDIOMS – **put the skids under** informal hasten the decline or failure of.

COMBINATIONS – **skidpan** a slippery road surface prepared for drivers to practise control of skidding. **skid road** N. Amer. a line of skids along which logs are hauled.

skidoo /skiˈdoo/ trademark, chiefly N. Amer. > *noun* a motorised toboggan. > *verb* (**skidoos, skidooed**) ride on a skidoo.

ORIGIN – an arbitrary formation from SKI.

skid row > *noun* informal, chiefly N. Amer. a run-down part of a town frequented by vagrants and alcoholics.

ORIGIN – alteration of *skid road*.

skier > *noun* a person who skis.

skiff > *noun* a light rowing boat, typically for one person.

ORIGIN – Italian *schifo*; related to SHIP.

skiffle > *noun* Brit. a kind of folk music popular in the 1950s, incorporating improvised instruments such as washboards.

skilful* (also N. Amer. **skillful**) > *adjective* having or showing skill.

DERIVATIVES – **skilfully** *adverb.*

*SPELLING – the British spelling has only one *l* in the middle: *skilful.*

SYNONYMS – accomplished, adept, deft, dexterous, proficient, skilled.

ANTONYMS – inept.

skill > *noun* **1** the ability to do something well; expertise or dexterity. **2** a particular ability. > *verb* train (a worker) to do a particular task.

SYNONYMS – *noun* **1** adeptness, dexterity, expertise, expertness, proficiency, prowess.

ORIGIN – Old Norse *skil* 'discernment, knowledge'.

skilled > *adjective* **1** having or showing skill; skilful. **2** (of work) requiring special abilities or training.

skillet > *noun* **1** a frying pan. **2** Brit. historical a small metal cooking pot with a long handle.

ORIGIN – perhaps from Latin *scutella* 'dish, platter'.

skim > *verb* (**skimmed, skimming**) **1** remove (a substance) from the surface of a liquid. **2** move quickly and lightly over or on a surface or through the air. **3** read (something) quickly, noting only the important points. **4** (**skim over** or **through**) deal with or treat briefly or superficially. **5** throw (a flat stone) so that it bounces several times on the surface of water. > *noun* **1** a thin layer of a substance on the surface of a liquid. **2** an act of reading something quickly or superficially.

DERIVATIVES – **skimmer** *noun.*

COMBINATIONS – **skimmed milk** (N. Amer. also **skim milk**) milk from which the cream has been removed.

ORIGIN – Old French *escumer*, from *escume* 'scum, foam'.

skimmia /ˈskimmiə/ > *noun* an evergreen East Asian shrub with creamy-white flowers and red berries.

ORIGIN – modern Latin, from Japanese.

skimp > *verb* expend fewer resources on something than are necessary in an attempt to economise.

SYNONYMS – be frugal with, scrimp on, stint on.

skimpy > *adjective* (**skimpier, skimpiest**) **1** providing or consisting of less than is necessary; meagre. **2** (of clothes) flimsy and revealing.

SYNONYMS – **1** insufficient, meagre, paltry, scanty.

skin > *noun* **1** the thin layer of tissue forming the natural outer covering of the body of a person or animal. **2** the skin of a dead animal used as material for clothing or other items. **3** the peel or outer layer of a fruit or vegetable. **4** an outer layer of something. **5** (before another noun) informal referring to pornography: *the skin trade.* **6** Brit. informal a skinhead. > *verb* (**skinned,**

skinning) 1 remove the skin from. **2** graze (a part of one's body).

WORDFINDER – cutaneous (*of the skin*), dermatology (*branch of medicine concerned with the skin*), dermis, epidermis (*layers of the skin*), dermatitis, eczema (*inflammation of the skin*).

IDIOMS – **by the skin of one's teeth** by only a very narrow margin. **get under someone's skin** informal **1** annoy someone intensely. **2** reach or display a deep understanding of someone. **have a thick** (or **thin**) **skin** be insensitive (or oversensitive) to criticism or insults. **it's no skin off my nose** informal I am not offended or adversely affected. **there's more than one way to skin a cat** proverb there's more than one way of achieving one's aim.

DERIVATIVES – **skinless** adjective **skinned** adjective **skinner** noun.

COMBINATIONS – **skin-deep** not deep or lasting; superficial. **skin test** a test to determine whether an immune reaction is elicited when a substance is applied to or injected into the skin. **skintight** (of a garment) very close-fitting.

skinflint > *noun* informal a person who spends as little money as possible; a miser.

skinful > *noun* Brit. informal enough alcoholic drink to make one drunk.

skinhead > *noun* a young person of a subculture characterised by close-cropped hair and heavy boots, often perceived as aggressive and racist.

skink > *noun* a smooth-bodied lizard with short or absent limbs.

ORIGIN – Greek *skinkos*.

skinny > *adjective* (**skinnier**, **skinniest**) **1** (of a person) unattractively thin. **2** (of an article of clothing) tight-fitting.

DERIVATIVES – **skinniness** noun.

SYNONYMS – **1** emaciated, gaunt, scrawny, skeletal.

skinny-dip informal > *verb* swim naked. > *noun* a naked swim.

skint > *adjective* Brit. informal having little or no money available.

ORIGIN – variant of colloquial *skinned*, in the same sense.

skip¹ > *verb* (**skipped**, **skipping**) **1** move along lightly, stepping from one foot to the other with a hop or bounce. **2** jump repeatedly over a rope which is held at both ends and turned over the head and under the feet. **3** jump lightly over. **4** omit or move quickly over (a stage or point). **5** fail to attend or deal with; miss. > *noun* a skipping movement.

SYNONYMS – *verb* **1** caper, gambol, prance. **4** bypass, leave out, pass over, skim over. **5** absent oneself from, miss, play truant from.

skip² > *noun* **1** Brit. a large transportable open-topped container for bulky refuse. **2** a cage

or bucket in which workers or materials are lowered and raised in mines and quarries.

ORIGIN – variant of **SKEP**.

skipjack > *noun* (also **skipjack tuna**) a small tuna with dark horizontal stripes.

ORIGIN – from **SKIP¹** + **JACK** (with reference to the fish's habit of jumping out of the water).

skipper informal > *noun* **1** the captain of a ship, boat, or aircraft. **2** the captain of a side in a game or sport. > *verb* act as captain of.

ORIGIN – Dutch, Low German *schipper*, from *schip* 'ship'.

skirl > *noun* a shrill sound, especially that of bagpipes. > *verb* (of bagpipes) make such a sound.

skirmish > *noun* an episode of irregular or unpremeditated fighting. > *verb* engage in a skirmish.

DERIVATIVES – **skirmisher** noun.

ORIGIN – from Old French *eskirmir*, from a root meaning 'defend'.

skirt > *noun* **1** a woman's outer garment fastened around the waist and hanging down around the legs. **2** the part of a coat or dress that hangs below the waist. **3** a surface that conceals or protects the wheels or underside of a vehicle or aircraft. **4** an animal's diaphragm and other membranes as food. **5** Brit. a cut of meat from the lower flank of an animal. **6** informal women regarded as objects of sexual desire. > *verb* (also **skirt along** or **around**) **1** go round or past the edge of. **2** avoid dealing with.

ORIGIN – Old Norse *skyrta* 'shirt'; related to **SHORT**.

skirting (also **skirting board**) > *noun* Brit. a wooden board running along the base of an interior wall.

skit > *noun* a short comedy sketch or piece of humorous writing, especially a parody.

ORIGIN – related to the rare verb *skit* 'move lightly and rapidly'.

skite /skīt/ informal > *verb* **1** Austral./NZ boast. **2** Scottish & dialect move or glance off quickly and forcefully. > *noun* Austral./NZ **1** a boaster. **2** boasting or boastfulness.

skitter > *verb* move lightly and quickly or hurriedly.

skittery > *adjective* restless; skittish.

skittish > *adjective* **1** (of a horse) nervous; inclined to shy. **2** lively and unpredictable; playful.

DERIVATIVES – **skittishly** adverb **skittishness** noun.

SYNONYMS – **2** frisky, high-spirited, lively, playful.

ORIGIN – perhaps from the rare verb *skit* (see **SKIT**).

skittle > *noun* **1** (**skittles**) (treated as sing.) a game played with wooden pins set up at the end of an alley to be bowled down. **2** a pin used in the game of skittles. **3** (also **table skittles**) a game played with similar pins set

up on a board to be knocked down by swinging a suspended ball. > *verb* knock over as if in a game of skittles.

skive /skīv/ Brit. informal > *verb* avoid work or a duty; shirk. > *noun* an instance of shirking.

DERIVATIVES – **skiver** noun.

ORIGIN – perhaps from French *esquiver* 'slink away'.

skivvy > *noun* (pl. **skivvies**) **1** Brit. informal a low-ranking female domestic servant. **2** a person doing menial work. > *verb* (**skivvies**, **skivvied**) informal do menial household tasks.

skua /skyōōə/ > *noun* a large predatory seabird which pursues other birds to make them disgorge fish.

ORIGIN – Faroese.

skulduggery (also **skullduggery**) > *noun* underhand or unscrupulous behaviour.

ORIGIN – alteration of Scots *sculduddery*.

skulk > *verb* hide or move around secretly, typically with a sinister or cowardly motive.

DERIVATIVES – **skulker** noun.

SYNONYMS – loiter, lurk, sneak.

skull > *noun* **1** a bone framework enclosing the brain of a vertebrate. **2** informal a person's head or brain.

WORDFINDER – cranial (*of the skull*); cephalic index (*ratio of breadth to length of skull*), cranium (*part of skull containing brain*), fontanelle (*soft area in a baby's skull*), phrenology (*study of skull shape as supposed indicator of character*), suture (*joint between skull bones*), trepan or trephine (*surgeon's saw for cutting hole in skull*).

IDIOMS – **out of one's skull** informal **1** mad; insane. **2** very drunk. **skull and crossbones** a representation of a skull with two thigh bones crossed below it as an emblem of piracy or death.

COMBINATIONS – **skullcap** a small close-fitting peakless cap or protective helmet.

skunk > *noun* a black-and-white striped American mammal able to spray foul-smelling irritant liquid at attackers.

ORIGIN – Abnaki (an American Indian language).

sky > *noun* (pl. **skies**) **1** the region of the atmosphere and outer space seen from the earth. **2** literary heaven or heavenly power. > *verb* (**skies**, **skied**) informal hit (a ball) high into the air.

IDIOMS – **the sky is the limit** there is practically no limit.

DERIVATIVES – **skyward** adjective & adverb **skywards** adverb.

COMBINATIONS – **sky blue** a bright clear blue. **skybox** N. Amer. a luxurious enclosed seating area high up in a sports arena. **sky-high 1** as if reaching the sky; very high. **2** at or to a very high level. **skyscape** a view or picture of an expanse of sky. **skyway** chiefly

N. Amer. **1** a recognised route followed by aircraft. **2** (also **skywalk**) a covered overhead walkway between buildings. **skywriting** words in the form of smoke trails made by an aircraft.

ORIGIN – Old Norse *ský* 'cloud'.

skydiving > *noun* the sport of jumping from an aircraft and performing acrobatic manoeuvres in the air before landing by parachute.

DERIVATIVES – **skydive** *verb* **skydiver** *noun*.

skyjack > *verb* hijack (an aircraft). > *noun* an act of skyjacking.

skylark > *noun* a common lark of open country, noted for its prolonged song given in hovering flight. > *verb* play practical jokes or indulge in horseplay.

skylight > *noun* a window set in a roof or ceiling at the same angle.

skyline > *noun* the outline of land and buildings defined against the sky.

skyrocket > *noun* a rocket designed to explode high in the air as a signal or firework. > *verb* (**skyrocketed**, **skyrocketing**) informal (of a price or amount) increase very rapidly.

skyscraper > *noun* a very tall building with many storeys.

slab > *noun* **1** a large, thick, flat piece of solid material, in particular stone, concrete, or heavy food. **2** a table used for laying a body on in a mortuary. **3** an outer piece of timber sawn from a log. > *verb* (**slabbed**, **slabbing**) remove slabs from (a log or tree) to prepare it for sawing into planks.

slabber chiefly Scottish & Irish > *verb* dribble at the mouth; slaver. > *noun* a dribble of saliva.

slack¹ > *adjective* **1** not taut or held tightly in position; loose. **2** (of business or trade) not busy; quiet. **3** lacking care or effort; negligent. **4** (of a tide) neither ebbing nor flowing. > *noun* **1** the part of a rope or line which is not held taut. **2** (**slacks**) casual trousers. **3** informal a spell of inactivity or laziness. > *verb* **1** loosen or reduce the intensity or speed of; slacken. **2** (**slack off** or **up**) decrease in intensity or speed. **3** Brit. informal work slowly or lazily.

IDIOMS – **cut some slack** N. Amer. informal allow (someone) some leeway in conduct. **slack water** the state of the tide when it is turning. **take** (or **pick**) **up the slack 1** improve the use of resources to avoid an undesirable lull in business. **2** pull on the loose part of a rope to make it taut.

DERIVATIVES – **slacken** *verb* **slackly** *adverb* **slackness** *noun*.

SYNONYMS – *adjective* **1** limp, loose, relaxed, sagging. **2** flat, quiet, slow, sluggish. **3** lax, neglectful, negligent, remiss, slapdash.

slack² > *noun* coal dust or small pieces of coal.

slacker > *noun* informal **1** a person who avoids work or effort. **2** chiefly N. Amer. a young person of a subculture characterised by apathy and aimlessness.

slag > *noun* **1** stony waste matter separated from metals during the smelting or refining of ore. **2** Brit. informal, derogatory a promiscuous woman. > *verb* (**slagged**, **slagging**) **1** produce deposits of slag. **2** (often **slag off**) Brit. informal criticise abusively.

COMBINATIONS – **slag heap** a hill or area of refuse from a mine or industrial site.

ORIGIN – Low German *slagge*, perhaps from *slagen* 'strike', with reference to fragments formed by hammering.

slain past participle of **SLAY**.

slainte /**slaan**chə/ > *exclamation* used as a toast before drinking.

ORIGIN – Scottish Gaelic, 'health'.

slake > *verb* **1** satisfy (a desire, thirst, etc.). **2** combine (quicklime) with water to produce calcium hydroxide.

SYNONYMS – **1** assuage, gratify, quench.

COMBINATIONS – **slaked lime** calcium hydroxide.

ORIGIN – Old English, 'become less eager'.

slalom /**slaa**ləm/ > *noun* a skiing, canoeing, or sailing race following a winding course marked out by poles. > *verb* move or race in a winding path, avoiding obstacles.

ORIGIN – Norwegian, 'sloping track'.

slam¹ > *verb* (**slammed**, **slamming**) **1** shut forcefully and loudly. **2** push or put somewhere with great force. **3** (often **slam into**) crash or strike heavily into. **4** put into action suddenly or forcefully. **5** informal criticise severely. **6** N. Amer. informal easily score points against or defeat. > *noun* a loud bang caused by the forceful shutting of something.

COMBINATIONS – **slam-bang** informal, chiefly N. Amer. **1** exciting and energetic. **2** direct and forceful. **slam-dancing** chiefly N. Amer. a form of dancing to rock music in which the dancers deliberately collide with one another.

ORIGIN – probably Scandinavian.

slam² > *noun* Bridge the feat of bidding and winning all thirteen tricks in a hand (a **grand slam**), or all but one (a **small slam**), for which bonus points are scored.

ORIGIN – perhaps from obsolete *slampant* 'trickery'.

slam dunk > *noun* **1** Basketball a shot thrust down through the basket. **2** N. Amer. informal a foregone conclusion or certainty. > *verb* (**slam-dunk**) **1** Basketball thrust (the ball) down through the basket. **2** N. Amer. informal defeat or dismiss decisively.

slammer > *noun* **1** (**the slammer**) informal prison. **2** (also **tequila slammer**) a cocktail of tequila and champagne or another fizzy drink, which is covered, slammed on the table, and then drunk in one.

slander Law > *noun* **1** the action or crime of making a false spoken statement damaging to a person's reputation. Compare with **LIBEL**. **2** a false and malicious spoken statement. > *verb* make such statements about.

DERIVATIVES – **slanderer** *noun* **slanderous** *adjective*.

ORIGIN – Old French *esclandre*, from Latin *scandalum* 'cause of offence'.

slang > *noun* informal language that is more common in speech than in writing and is typically restricted to a particular context or group. > *verb* informal attack (someone) using abusive language.

DERIVATIVES – **slangy** *adjective*.

COMBINATIONS – **slanging match** chiefly Brit. a prolonged exchange of insults.

slant > *verb* **1** diverge from the vertical or horizontal; slope or lean. **2** present or view (information) from a particular angle, especially in a biased or unfair way. > *noun* **1** a sloping position. **2** a point of view. > *adjective* sloping.

DERIVATIVES – **slantwise** *adjective* & *adverb*.

slap > *verb* (**slapped**, **slapping**) **1** hit or strike with the palm of one's hand or a flat object. **2** hit against with a slapping sound. **3** (**slap down**) informal reprimand forcefully. **4** (**slap on**) apply (something) quickly, carelessly, or forcefully. **5** (**slap on**) informal impose (a fine or penalty) on. > *noun* **1** an act or sound of slapping. **2** informal make-up. > *adverb* (also **slap bang**) informal suddenly and directly, especially with great force.

IDIOMS – **slap and tickle** Brit. informal physical amorous play. **slap in the face** an unexpected rejection or affront. **slap on the back** an expression of congratulation or commendation. **slap on the wrist** a mild reprimand or punishment.

SYNONYMS – *verb* **1** hit, smack, strike.

COMBINATIONS – **slap-happy** informal **1** cheerfully casual or flippant. **2** dazed or stupefied from happiness or relief.

slapdash > *adjective* & *adverb* done too hurriedly and carelessly.

SYNONYMS – careless, casual, lackadaisical, perfunctory, slipshod.

ANTONYMS – meticulous.

slaphead > *noun* Brit. informal, humorous a bald or balding man.

slapper > *noun* Brit. informal, derogatory a promiscuous or vulgar woman.

slapstick > *noun* **1** comedy based on deliberately clumsy actions and humorously embarrassing events. **2** a device consisting of two flexible pieces of wood joined at one end, used by clowns and in pantomime to produce a loud slapping sound.

slap-up > *adjective* informal, chiefly Brit. (of a meal) large and sumptuous.

slash > *verb* **1** cut with a violent sweeping movement. **2** informal reduce (a price, quantity, etc.) greatly. **3** archaic lash, whip, or thrash severely. > *noun* **1** a cut made with a wide, sweeping stroke. **2** a bright patch or flash of colour or light. **3** an oblique stroke (/) used between alternatives, in fractions and ratios, or between separate elements of a text. **4** Brit. informal an act of urinating.
DERIVATIVES – **slasher** *noun*.
COMBINATIONS – **slash-and-burn** denoting agriculture in which vegetation is cut down and burned off before new seeds are sown.
ORIGIN – Old French *esclachier* 'break in pieces'.

slashed > *adjective* (of a garment) having slits to show the lining material or skin beneath.

slat > *noun* a thin, narrow piece of wood or other material, especially one of a series which overlap or fit into each other.
DERIVATIVES – **slatted** *adjective*.
ORIGIN – shortening of Old French *esclat* 'splinter'.

slate > *noun* **1** a fine-grained grey, green, or bluish-purple rock easily split into smooth, flat plates, used as roofing material. **2** a plate of slate formerly used in schools for writing on. **3** a bluish-grey colour. **4** a list of candidates for election to a post or office. **5** Brit. a record of a person's debt or credit. **6** a board showing the identifying details of a take of a film, held in front of the camera at the beginning and end of the take. > *verb* **1** cover (a roof) with slates. **2** Brit. informal criticise severely. **3** chiefly N. Amer. schedule; plan.
ORIGIN – shortening of Old French *esclate* 'splinter'.

slather /slaᴛʜər/ > *verb* informal spread or smear thickly or liberally.
IDIOMS – **open slather** Austral./NZ informal freedom to act without restriction; free rein.

slattern /slattərn/ > *noun* dated a dirty, untidy woman.
DERIVATIVES – **slatternly** *adjective*.
ORIGIN – related to *slattering* 'slovenly', from dialect *slatter* 'to spill or slop'.

slaughter /slawtər/ > *noun* **1** the killing of farm animals for food. **2** the killing of a large number of people in a cruel or violent way. **3** informal a thorough defeat. > *verb* **1** kill (animals) for food. **2** kill (people) in a cruel or violent way. **3** informal defeat (an opponent) thoroughly.
DERIVATIVES – **slaughterer** *noun*.
SYNONYMS – *noun* **2** bloodbath, butchery, carnage, massacre. *verb* **2** butcher, exterminate, massacre.
COMBINATIONS – **slaughterhouse** a place where animals are slaughtered for food.
ORIGIN – Old Norse *slátr* 'butcher's meat'.

Slav /slaav/ > *noun* a member of a group of peoples in central and eastern Europe speaking Slavic languages.

slave > *noun* **1** historical a person who is the legal property of another and is forced to obey them. **2** a person who is excessively dependent on or controlled by something: *a slave to fashion*. > *verb* work excessively hard.
WORDFINDER – servile (*of or like a slave*); emancipate, enfranchise, manumit (*release from slavery*).
COMBINATIONS – **slave-driver** a person who works others very hard. **slave labour** labour which is coerced and inadequately rewarded. **slave state** historical any of the Southern states of the US in which slavery was legal before the Civil War. **slave trade** historical the procuring, transporting, and selling of human beings, especially black Africans, as slaves.

> ## wordpower facts
> ### Slave
> The word **slave** comes via Old French *esclave* from medieval Latin *Sclavus*, 'a Slav'. The Slavonic people were subjected in the Dark Ages to repeated attacks and conquests: as a result their name was adopted as a general term for a captive, or **slave**.

slaver¹ /slayvər/ > *noun* historical **1** a person dealing in or owning slaves. **2** a ship used for transporting slaves.

slaver² /slavvər/ > *noun* **1** saliva running from the mouth. **2** archaic excessive or obsequious flattery. > *verb* **1** let saliva run from the mouth. **2** (usu. **slaver over**) show excessive desire.

slavery > *noun* **1** the state of being a slave. **2** the practice or system of owning slaves.
SYNONYMS – bondage, enslavement, servitude.

Slavic /slaavik/ > *noun* the branch of the Indo-European language family that includes Russian, Polish, Czech, Bulgarian, and Serbo-Croat. > *adjective* relating to this branch of languages or their speakers.

slavish > *adjective* **1** showing no attempt at originality. **2** servile or submissive.
DERIVATIVES – **slavishly** *adverb*.

Slavonic /sləvonnik/ > *noun* & *adjective* another term for **Slavic**.

slaw > *noun* N. Amer. coleslaw.
ORIGIN – Dutch *sla*, from *salade* 'salad'.

slay > *verb* (past **slew**; past participle **slain**) **1** archaic or literary kill (someone) in a violent way. **2** N. Amer. murder (someone).
DERIVATIVES – **slayer** *noun*.

sleaze informal > *noun* **1** immoral, sordid, and corrupt behaviour or material. **2** (also

sleazebag or **sleazeball**) informal, chiefly N. Amer. a sordid, corrupt, or immoral person.

sleazy > *adjective* (**sleazier, sleaziest**) **1** sordid, corrupt, or immoral. **2** (of a place) squalid and seedy. **3** dated (of textiles or clothing) flimsy.
DERIVATIVES – **sleazily** *adverb* **sleaziness** *noun*.

sled > *noun* & *verb* (**sledded, sledding**) North American term for **sledge¹**.
ORIGIN – Low German *sledde*.

sledge¹ > *noun* **1** a vehicle on runners for travelling over snow or ice. **2** Brit. a toboggan. > *verb* ride or carry on a sledge.
ORIGIN – Dutch *sleedse*.

sledge² > *noun* a sledgehammer.

sledgehammer > *noun* **1** a large, heavy hammer used for breaking rocks, driving in posts, etc. **2** (before another noun) very powerful, forceful, or unsubtle: *sledgehammer blows*.
ORIGIN – from a base meaning 'to strike', related to **slay**.

sledging > *noun* Cricket the practice by fielders of making offensive remarks to opposing batsmen in order to break their concentration.

sleek > *adjective* **1** (of hair or fur) smooth, glossy, and healthy-looking. **2** wealthy and well-groomed in appearance. **3** elegant and streamlined. > *verb* make (the hair) sleek by applying pressure or moisture.
DERIVATIVES – **sleekly** *adverb* **sleekness** *noun*.
ORIGIN – a later variant of **slick**.

sleep > *noun* **1** a regularly recurring condition of body and mind in which the nervous system is inactive, the eyes closed, the muscles relaxed, and consciousness practically suspended. **2** a gummy secretion found in the corners of the eyes after sleep. > *verb* (past and past participle **slept**) **1** rest in such a condition. **2** (**sleep off**) recover from (something) by going to sleep. **3** (**sleep in**) remain asleep or in bed later than usual in the morning. **4** provide (a specified number of people) with beds or bedrooms. **5** (**sleep together** or **with**) have sexual intercourse or be involved in a sexual relationship (with). **6** (**sleep around**) have many casual sexual partners.
WORDFINDER – hypnotic, sedative (*inducing sleep*), insomnia (*inability to sleep*), narcolepsy (*abnormal tendency to fall asleep suddenly*), noctambulist (*a sleepwalker*), REM sleep (*periods of lighter sleep with rapid eye movements and dreaming*), somnambulism (*sleepwalking*), somnolent, soporific (*tending to cause sleep*).
IDIOMS – **let sleeping dogs lie** proverb avoid interfering in a situation that is currently causing no problems but may well do so as a result of such interference. **put to sleep** kill (an animal) painlessly. **sleep like a log** sleep very soundly.

DERIVATIVES – **sleepless** adjective.

COMBINATIONS – **sleeping bag** a warm lined padded bag to sleep in, especially when camping. **sleeping car** (Brit. also **sleeping carriage**) a railway carriage provided with beds or berths. **sleeping draught** Brit. dated a drink or drug intended to induce sleep. **sleeping partner** Brit. a partner not sharing in the actual work of a firm. **sleeping pill** a tablet of a sleep-inducing drug. **sleeping policeman** Brit. a hump in the road intended to cause vehicles to reduce speed. **sleeping sickness** a tropical disease transmitted by the bite of the tsetse fly, marked by extreme lethargy.

sleeper > noun **1** a sleeping car or a train carrying sleeping cars. **2** a film, book, play, etc. that suddenly achieves success after initially attracting little attention. **3** Brit. a ring or bar worn in a pierced ear to keep the hole from closing. **4** chiefly Brit. a wooden or concrete beam laid transversely under railway track to support it.

sleepover > noun chiefly N. Amer. an occasion of spending the night away from home.

sleepwalk > verb walk around and sometimes perform other actions while asleep.

DERIVATIVES – **sleepwalker** noun.

sleepy > adjective (**sleepier**, **sleepiest**) **1** needing or ready for sleep. **2** (of a place) without much activity. **3** not dynamic or able to respond to change.

DERIVATIVES – **sleepily** adverb **sleepiness** noun.

SYNONYMS – **1** drowsy, somnolent, tired.

COMBINATIONS – **sleepyhead** informal a sleepy or inattentive person.

sleet > noun **1** rain containing some ice, or snow melting as it falls. **2** US a thin coating of ice formed by sleet or rain freezing on coming into contact with a cold surface. > verb (**it sleets**, **it is sleeting**, etc.) sleet falls.

DERIVATIVES – **sleety** adjective.

sleeve > noun **1** the part of a garment that wholly or partly covers a person's arm. **2** a protective paper or cardboard cover for a record. **3** a protective or connecting tube fitting over a rod, spindle, or smaller tube. **4** a windsock.

IDIOMS – **up one's sleeve** kept secret and in reserve for use when needed.

DERIVATIVES – **sleeved** adjective **sleeveless** adjective.

sleigh > noun a sledge drawn by horses or reindeer. > verb ride on a sleigh.

COMBINATIONS – **sleigh bell** a tinkling bell attached to the harness of a sleigh horse.

ORIGIN – Dutch slee; related to SLED.

sleight /slīt/ > noun literary the use of dexterity or cunning, especially so as to deceive.

IDIOMS – **sleight of hand 1** manual

dexterity, especially in performing conjuring tricks. **2** skilful deception.

ORIGIN – Old Norse, sloegth, from sloegr 'sly, cunning'.

slender > adjective (**slenderer**, **slenderest**) **1** gracefully thin. **2** barely sufficient.

DERIVATIVES – **slenderly** adverb **slenderness** noun.

SYNONYMS – **1** lissom, slim, svelte, willowy. **2** limited, meagre, narrow, scant, sparse.

slept past and past participle of SLEEP.

sleuth /slooth/ informal > noun a detective. > verb carry out a search or investigation in the manner of a detective.

COMBINATIONS – **sleuth-hound 1** dated a bloodhound. **2** informal an investigator or detective.

ORIGIN – first used in sleuth-hound, in the sense 'track'; from Old Norse slóth 'trail'.

S level > noun (in the UK except Scotland) an examination taken together with an A level in the same subject but having a more advanced syllabus.

ORIGIN – abbreviation of Special level or (formerly) Scholarship level.

slew[1] (also **slue**) > verb turn or slide violently or uncontrollably. > noun a slewing movement.

slew[2] past of SLAY.

slew[3] > noun informal, chiefly N. Amer. a large number or quantity of something.

ORIGIN – Irish sluagh.

slice > noun **1** a thin, broad piece of food cut from a larger portion. **2** a portion or share of something. **3** a utensil with a broad, flat blade for lifting foods such as cake and fish. **4** (in sports) a sliced stroke or shot. > verb **1** cut into slices. **2** (often **slice off** or **from**) cut with or as if with a sharp implement. **3** (often **slice through**) move easily and quickly. **4** Golf strike (the ball) so that it curves away to the right (for a left-handed player, the left). **5** (in other sports) propel (the ball) with a glancing contact so that it travels forward spinning.

ORIGIN – shortening of Old French esclice 'splinter'.

slick > adjective **1** done or operating in an impressively smooth and efficient way. **2** glibly assured. **3** (of skin or hair) smooth and glossy. **4** (of a surface) smooth, wet, and slippery. > noun a smooth patch of oil, especially on the sea. > verb **1** make (hair) flat and slick with water, oil, or cream. **2** (**slick up**) N. Amer. make smart, tidy, or stylish.

DERIVATIVES – **slickly** adverb **slickness** noun.

SYNONYMS – adjective **1** efficient, polished, smooth, streamlined. **2** fluent, glib, pat.

slicker > noun chiefly N. Amer. **1** informal a convincing rogue. **2** a raincoat made of smooth material.

slide > verb (past and past participle **slid**) **1** move

along a smooth surface while maintaining continuous contact with it. **2** move smoothly, quickly, or unobtrusively. **3** change gradually to a worse condition or lower level. > noun **1** a structure with a smooth sloping surface for children to slide down. **2** a smooth stretch of ice or packed snow for sliding or tobogganing on. **3** an act of sliding. **4** a rectangular piece of glass on which an object is mounted or placed for examination under a microscope. **5** a mounted transparency, especially one placed in a projector for viewing on a screen. **6** Brit. a hairslide.

SYNONYMS – verb **1** glide, skim, slither. **3** decline, degenerate, deteriorate.

COMBINATIONS – **slide guitar** a style of guitar playing in which a glissando effect is produced by moving a bottleneck or similar device over the strings. **slide rule** a ruler with a sliding central strip, marked with logarithmic scales and used for making rapid calculations. **sliding scale** a scale of fees, wages, etc., that varies in accordance with the variation of some standard.

slight > adjective **1** small in degree; inconsiderable. **2** not profound or substantial. **3** not sturdy and strongly built. > verb insult (someone) by treating them without proper respect or attention. > noun an insult caused by a failure to show someone proper respect or attention.

DERIVATIVES – **slighting** adjective.

SYNONYMS – adjective **1** imperceptible, inconsiderable, minute, small, tiny. **2** inconsequential, minor, trivial.

wordpower facts
Slight
Some subtle changes of meaning have taken place in the history of the word **slight**. It entered English from Old Norse in the early 14th century, the adjective in the sense 'smooth, glossy, sleek' and the verb meaning 'make smooth'. From there developed the meanings 'slender, thin', then 'of light, thin, or poor texture or material' and 'of little worth', and then, by the early 16th century, 'small in amount, quantity, or degree'. The verb sense 'treat with disrespect' dates from the late 16th century.

slightly > adverb **1** to a small degree. **2** (with reference to a person's build) in a slender way.

slily > adverb variant spelling of slyly.

slim > adjective (**slimmer**, **slimmest**) **1** gracefully thin; slenderly built. **2** small in width and long and narrow in shape. **3** very small: a slim chance. > verb (**slimmed**,

slimming) make or become thinner, especially by dieting.

DERIVATIVES – **slimmer** noun.

SYNONYMS – *adjective* **1** lissom, slender, svelte, willowy. **3** faint, slender, slight.

ORIGIN – Low German or Dutch.

slime > *noun* an unpleasantly moist, soft, and slippery substance. > *verb* cover with slime.

COMBINATIONS – **slimeball** informal a repulsive or despicable person.

slimline > *adjective* **1** slender in design or build. **2** (of food or drink) low in calories.

slimy > *adjective* (**slimier, slimiest**) **1** covered by or having the feel or consistency of slime. **2** informal repulsively obsequious.

sling¹ > *noun* **1** a flexible strap, bandage, or pouch used in the form of a loop to support or raise a hanging weight. **2** a simple weapon in the form of a strap or loop, used to hurl stones or other small missiles. **3** Austral./NZ informal a bribe or gratuity. > *verb* (past and past participle **slung**) **1** suspend or carry loosely with or a sling or strap. **2** informal throw; fling. **3** hurl from a sling or similar weapon. **4** Austral./NZ informal pay a bribe or gratuity. **5** (**sling off**) Austral./NZ informal mock; make fun.

COMBINATIONS – **slingback** a shoe held in place by a strap around the ankle above the heel. **slingshot** a hand-held catapult.

sling² > *noun* a sweetened drink of spirits, especially gin, and water.

slink > *verb* (past and past participle **slunk**) **1** move quietly with gliding steps, in a stealthy or sensuous manner. **2** come or go unobtrusively or furtively. > *noun* an act of slinking.

SYNONYMS – *verb* creep, sneak, steal.

ORIGIN – Old English, 'crawl, creep'.

slinky > *adjective* (**slinkier, slinkiest**) informal graceful and sinuous in movement or form.

slip¹ > *verb* (**slipped, slipping**) **1** lose one's balance or footing and slide unintentionally for a short distance. **2** accidentally slide or move out of position or from someone's grasp. **3** fail to grip or make proper contact with a surface. **4** pass gradually to a worse condition. **5** (usu. **slip up**) make a careless error. **6** move or place quietly, quickly, or stealthily. **7** escape or get loose from (a means of restraint). **8** fail to be remembered by (one's mind or memory). **9** release (the clutch of a motor vehicle) slightly or for a moment. **10** Knitting move (a stitch) to the other needle without knitting it. > *noun* **1** an act or instance of slipping. **2** (also **slip-up**) a minor or careless mistake. **3** a loose-fitting garment, especially a short petticoat. **4** Cricket a fielding position close behind the batsman on the off side.

IDIOMS – **give someone the slip** informal evade or escape from someone. **let slip** reveal (something) inadvertently in the course of a conversation. **slip of the pen** (or **the tongue**) a minor mistake in writing (or speech). **there's many a slip 'twixt cup and lip** proverb many things can go wrong between the start of a project and its completion; nothing is certain until it has happened.

DERIVATIVES – **slippage** noun.

SYNONYMS – *verb* **1** fall over, stumble, tumble. **4** decline, degenerate, deteriorate, slide, worsen.

COMBINATIONS – **slip case** a close-fitting case open at one side or end for an object such as a book. **slip cover 1** a detachable cover for a chair or sofa. **2** a jacket or slip case for a book. **slip knot 1** a knot that can be undone by a pull. **2** a running knot. **slipped disc** a cartilaginous disc between vertebrae in the spine that is displaced or partly protruding, pressing on nearby nerves and causing back pain or sciatica. **slip road** Brit. a road entering or leaving a motorway or dual carriageway. **slip stitch 1** (in sewing) a loose stitch joining layers of fabric and not visible externally. **2** Knitting a type of stitch in which the stitches are moved from one needle to the other without being knitted.

ORIGIN – probably from Low German *slippen*.

slip² > *noun* **1** a small piece of paper for writing on or that gives printed information. **2** a cutting taken from a plant for grafting or planting; a scion.

IDIOMS – **a slip of a girl** (or **thing**) a small, slim young girl.

slip³ > *noun* a creamy mixture of clay, water, and typically a pigment of some kind, used for decorating earthenware.

COMBINATIONS – **slipware** pottery decorated with slip.

slip-on > *adjective* (of shoes or clothes) having no fastenings and therefore able to be put on and taken off quickly.

slipover > *noun* a pullover, typically one without sleeves.

slipper > *noun* **1** a comfortable slip-on shoe that is worn indoors. **2** a light slip-on shoe, especially one used for dancing.

DERIVATIVES – **slippered** adjective.

COMBINATIONS – **slipper orchid** a lady's slipper (orchid).

slippery > *adjective* **1** difficult to hold firmly or stand on through being smooth, wet, or slimy. **2** (of a person) evasive and unpredictable. **3** (of a word or concept) changing in meaning according to context or point of view.

DERIVATIVES – **slipperiness** noun.

COMBINATIONS – **slippery elm** a North American elm with slimy inner bark, used medicinally. **slippery slope** a course of action likely to lead to something bad.

slippy > *adjective* (**slippier, slippiest**) informal slippery.

slipshod > *adjective* **1** lacking in care, thought, or organisation. **2** archaic (of shoes) worn down at the heel.

SYNONYMS – **1** careless, lackadaisical, slapdash.

ANTONYMS – **1** meticulous.

slipstream > *noun* **1** a current of air or water driven back by a revolving propeller or jet engine. **2** the partial vacuum created in the wake of a moving vehicle. **3** an assisting force regarded as drawing something along in its wake. > *verb* follow in the slipstream of a vehicle, especially in motor racing.

slipway > *noun* a slope leading into water, used for launching and landing boats and ships or for building and repairing them.

slit > *noun* a long, narrow cut or opening. > *verb* (**slitting**; past and past participle **slit**) **1** make a slit in. **2** (past and past participle **slitted**) form (one's eyes) into slits.

slither > *verb* **1** move smoothly over a surface with a twisting or oscillating motion. **2** slide or slip unsteadily on a loose or slippery surface. > *noun* **1** a slithering movement. **2** a sliver.

DERIVATIVES – **slithery** adjective.

slitty > *adjective* (**slittier, slittiest**) chiefly derogatory (of the eyes) long and narrow.

sliver /slivər, slīvər/ > *noun* a small, narrow, sharp piece cut or split off a larger piece. > *verb* cut or break into slivers.

SYNONYMS – *noun* chip, shard, splinter.

slivovitz /slivvəvits/ > *noun* a type of plum brandy made chiefly in the former Yugoslavia and in Romania.

ORIGIN – Serbo-Croat *šljivovica*, from *šljiva* 'plum'.

Sloane (also **Sloane Ranger**) > *noun* Brit. informal a fashionable upper-class young woman.

DERIVATIVES – **Sloaney** adjective.

ORIGIN – from *Sloane* Square, London + Lone *Ranger*, the name of a fictitious cowboy hero.

slob > *noun* **1** informal a lazy and slovenly person. **2** Irish muddy land. > *verb* informal behave in a lazy and slovenly manner.

DERIVATIVES – **slobbish** adjective **slobby** adjective.

ORIGIN – from Irish *slab* 'mud'.

slobber > *verb* **1** have saliva dripping copiously from the mouth. **2** (**slobber over**) show excessive enthusiasm for. > *noun* saliva dripping copiously from the mouth.

DERIVATIVES – **slobbery** adjective.

ORIGIN – probably from Dutch *slobberen* 'walk through mud', also 'feed noisily'.

sloe > *noun* **1** another term for **BLACKTHORN**. **2** the small bluish-black fruit of the blackthorn, with a sharp sour taste.

COMBINATIONS – **sloe-eyed** having attractive dark almond-shaped eyes. **sloe gin** a liqueur made by steeping sloes in gin.

slog > *verb* (**slogged, slogging**) 1 work hard over a period of time. 2 walk or move with difficulty or effort. 3 hit or strike forcefully. 4 (**slog it out**) fight or compete fiercely. > *noun* 1 a spell of difficult, tiring work or travelling. 2 a forceful hit or strike.

SYNONYMS – *verb* 1 labour, slave, toil. 2 plod, traipse, trudge, tramp. *noun* 1 exertion, labour, toil.

slogan > *noun* 1 a short, memorable phrase used in advertising or associated with a political party or group. 2 historical a Scottish Highland war cry.

ORIGIN – Scottish Gaelic *sluagh-ghairm*, from *sluagh* 'army' + *gairm* 'shout'.

sloganeer chiefly N. Amer. > *verb* use or invent slogans, especially in a political context. > *noun* a person who does this.

slo-mo > *noun* short for *slow motion*.

sloop > *noun* 1 a one-masted sailing boat with a mainsail and jib rigged fore and aft. 2 a small anti-submarine warship used for convoy escort in the Second World War.

ORIGIN – Dutch *sloep*.

sloosh Brit. informal > *noun* a rushing of water or energetic rinsing. > *verb* flow, pour, or rinse with a rush.

slop > *verb* (**slopped, slopping**) 1 (of a liquid) spill or flow over the edge of a container. 2 apply casually or carelessly. 3 (**slop out**) (especially in prison) empty the contents of a chamber pot. 4 (**slop through**) wade through (a wet or muddy area). 5 (**slop about** or **around**) chiefly Brit. dress in an untidy or casual manner. 6 chiefly N. Amer. speak or write in a sentimentally effusive manner; gush. > *noun* 1 (**slops**) waste water or liquid that has to be emptied by hand. 2 (**slops**) semi-liquid kitchen refuse used as animal food. 3 (**slops**) unappetising weak, semi-liquid food. 4 chiefly N. Amer. sentimental language or material.

slope > *noun* 1 a surface of which one end or side is at a higher level than another. 2 a part of the side of a hill or mountain, especially as a place for skiing. > *verb* 1 be inclined from a horizontal or vertical line; slant up or down. 2 informal move in an idle or aimless manner. 3 (**slope off**) leave unobtrusively, typically in order to evade work or duty.

WORDFINDER – acclivity (*upward slope*), clinometer, gradiometer (*instruments for measuring slopes*), declivity (*downward slope*).

sloppy > *adjective* (**sloppier, sloppiest**) 1 (of semi-fluid matter) containing too much liquid; watery. 2 careless and unsystematic; excessively casual. 3 (of a garment) casual and loose-fitting. 4 weakly or foolishly sentimental.

DERIVATIVES – **sloppily** *adverb* **sloppiness** *noun*.

SYNONYMS – 1 runny, watery, thin. 2 careless, negligent, slapdash, slipshod. 4 cloying, mawkish, saccharine.

slosh > *verb* 1 (of liquid in a container) move irregularly with a splashing sound. 2 move through liquid with a splashing sound. 3 pour (liquid) clumsily. 4 Brit. informal hit hard. > *noun* 1 an act or sound of splashing. 2 Brit. informal a heavy blow.

ORIGIN – variant of SLUSH.

sloshed > *adjective* informal drunk.

sloshy > *adjective* (**sloshier, sloshiest**) 1 wet and sticky; slushy. 2 excessively sentimental; sloppy.

slot > *noun* 1 a long, narrow aperture or slit into which something may be fitted or inserted. 2 an allotted place in an arrangement or scheme. > *verb* (**slotted, slotting**) 1 place or be placed into a slot. 2 (**slot in** or **into**) fit easily into (a new role or situation).

DERIVATIVES – **slotted** *adjective*.

COMBINATIONS – **slot machine** a fruit machine or (Brit.) vending machine.

ORIGIN – Old French *esclot*.

sloth /slōth/ > *noun* 1 reluctance to work or make an effort; laziness. 2 a slow-moving tropical American mammal that hangs upside down from branches using its long limbs and hooked claws.

DERIVATIVES – **slothful** *adjective*.

SYNONYMS – 1 idleness, indolence, laziness.

ANTONYMS – 1 industriousness.

ORIGIN – Old English: from SLOW.

slouch > *verb* stand, move, or sit in a lazy, drooping way. > *noun* 1 a lazy, drooping posture or movement. 2 informal an incompetent person: *he was no slouch at making a buck.*

DERIVATIVES – **slouchy** *adjective*.

SYNONYMS – *verb* 1 hunch, loll, slump.

COMBINATIONS – **slouch hat** a hat with a wide flexible brim.

slough[1] /slow/ > *noun* 1 a swamp. 2 a situation characterised by lack of progress or activity.

DERIVATIVES – **sloughy** *adjective*.

slough[2] /sluf/ > *verb* (of an animal, especially a snake) cast off or shed (an old skin). > *noun* the dropping off of dead tissue from living flesh.

Slovak /slōvak/ > *noun* 1 a person from Slovakia, a country in central Europe that was formerly part of Czechoslovakia. 2 the language of Slovakia.

Slovakian /sləvakkiən/ > *noun* a person from Slovakia. > *adjective* relating to Slovakia.

sloven /sluvv'n/ > *noun* dated a person who is habitually untidy or careless.

ORIGIN – perhaps from Flemish *sloef* 'dirty' or Dutch *slof* 'careless, negligent'.

Slovene /slōveen/ > *noun* 1 a person from Slovenia, a country in SE Europe that was formerly part of Yugoslavia. 2 the language of Slovenia.

DERIVATIVES – **Slovenian** *noun & adjective*.

slovenly > *adjective* 1 untidy and dirty. 2 careless; excessively casual.

DERIVATIVES – **slovenliness** *noun*.

SYNONYMS – 1 dishevelled, messy, scruffy, unkempt. 2 careless, slapdash, slipshod.

slow > *adjective* 1 moving or capable of moving only at a low speed. 2 lasting or taking a long time. 3 (of a clock or watch) showing a time earlier than the correct time. 4 not prompt to understand, think, or learn. 5 uneventful; showing little activity. 6 Photography (of a film) needing long exposure. 7 (of a fire or oven) burning or giving off heat gently. > *verb* (often **slow down** or **up**) 1 reduce one's speed or the speed of a vehicle or process. 2 live or work less actively or intensely.

IDIOMS – **slow but sure** not quick but achieving the required result eventually.

DERIVATIVES – **slowly** *noun* **slowness** *noun*.

USAGE – **slow** is normally used as an adjective, as in *a slow learner* and *the journey was slow*. It should only be used as an adverb in certain specific contexts, which include the compound **slow-moving** and the expression **go slow**. Instead, use the adverb **slowly**, as in *he drives too slowly*. Note that in this respect **slow** does not behave in the same way as **fast**.

SYNONYMS – *adjective* 1 dawdling, plodding, ponderous, sluggish, unhurried. 2 interminable, prolonged, protracted. 4 dull-witted, obtuse, stupid.

ANTONYMS – *adjective* 1 fast, quick, rapid. 2 brief. 4 astute, bright, quick.

COMBINATIONS – **slow cooker** a large electric pot used for cooking food very slowly. **slow handclap** a slow, rhythmic clapping by an audience as a sign of displeasure or impatience. **slow march** a military marching pace approximately half the speed of the quick march. **slow motion** the showing of film or video more slowly than it was made or recorded, so that the action appears much slower than in real life. **slow puncture** chiefly Brit. a puncture causing only gradual deflation of a tyre.

slowcoach (N. Amer. **slowpoke**) > *noun* Brit. informal a person who acts or moves slowly.

slow-worm > *noun* a small snake-like legless lizard that gives birth to live young.

ORIGIN – Old English, from *wyrm* 'snake'; the origin of the first element is uncertain.

923

SLR > *abbreviation* **1** self-loading rifle. **2** single-lens reflex.

slub > *noun* **1** a lump or thick place in yarn or thread. **2** fabric woven from yarn that has such lumps. > *adjective* (of fabric) having an irregular appearance caused by uneven thickness of the warp.
DERIVATIVES – **slubbed** *adjective*.

sludge > *noun* **1** thick, soft, wet mud or a similar viscous mixture. **2** dirty oil or industrial waste. **3** an unattractive muddy shade of brown or green.
DERIVATIVES – **sludgy** *adjective*.

slue > *verb & noun* variant spelling of SLEW[1].

slug[1] > *noun* **1** a tough-skinned terrestrial mollusc which lacks a shell and secretes a film of mucus for protection. **2** an amount of an alcoholic drink that is gulped or poured. **3** a bullet. > *verb* (**slugged**, **slugging**) gulp (something, typically alcohol).
COMBINATIONS – **slug pellet** a pellet containing a substance poisonous to slugs, placed among growing plants to prevent them being damaged.

slug[2] informal, chiefly N. Amer. > *verb* (**slugged**, **slugging**) **1** strike with a hard blow. **3** (**slug it out**) settle a dispute or contest by fighting or competing fiercely. > *noun* a hard blow.
DERIVATIVES – **slugger** *noun*.

sluggard > *noun* a lazy, sluggish person.
ORIGIN – from the rare verb *slug* 'be lazy or slow'.

sluggish > *adjective* **1** slow-moving or inactive. **2** lacking energy or alertness.
DERIVATIVES – **sluggishly** *adverb* **sluggishness** *noun*.
SYNONYMS – **2** apathetic, lethargic, torpid.

sluice /slooss/ > *noun* **1** (also **sluice gate**) a sliding gate or other device for controlling the flow of water. **2** (also **sluiceway**) an artificial channel for carrying off overflow or surplus water. **3** an act of rinsing or showering with water. > *verb* wash or rinse freely with a stream or shower of water.
ORIGIN – Old French *escluse*, from Latin *excludere* 'exclude'.

slum > *noun* **1** a squalid and overcrowded urban area inhabited by very poor people. **2** a house or building unfit for human habitation. > *verb* (**slummed**, **slumming**) (often **slum it**) informal voluntarily spend time in uncomfortable conditions or at a lower social level than one's own.

slumber literary > *verb* sleep. > *noun* a sleep.
DERIVATIVES – **slumberous** (also **slumbrous**) *adjective*.
ORIGIN – from Scots and northern English *sloom*.

slump > *verb* **1** sit, lean, or fall heavily and limply. **2** fail or decline substantially or over a prolonged period. > *noun* **1** an instance of slumping. **2** a prolonged period of abnormally low economic activity.
DERIVATIVES – **slumped** *adjective*.
SYNONYMS – *verb* **1** flop, sag, slouch.

slung past and past participle of SLING[1].

slunk past and past participle of SLINK.

slur > *verb* (**slurred**, **slurring**) **1** utter (words) indistinctly so that the sounds run into one another. **2** pass over (a fact or aspect) so as to conceal or minimise it. **3** Music perform (a group of two or more notes) legato. **4** chiefly US make insinuations or allegations about. > *noun* **1** an insinuation or allegation. **2** an indistinct utterance. **3** Music a curved line indicating that notes are to be slurred.
DERIVATIVES – **slurred** *adjective*.
SYNONYMS – *verb* **1** garble, mumble, stumble over.
ORIGIN – first used as a noun in the sense 'thin mud', later a verb meaning 'smear'.

slurp > *verb* eat or drink with a loud sucking sound. > *noun* an act or sound of slurping.
ORIGIN – Dutch *slurpen*.

slurry > *noun* (pl. **slurries**) a semi-liquid mixture, especially of fine particles of manure, cement, or coal and water.

slush > *noun* **1** partially melted snow or ice. **2** watery mud. **3** informal excessive sentiment. > *verb* make a soft splashing sound.
DERIVATIVES – **slushy** *adjective*.

slush fund > *noun* a reserve of money used for illicit purposes, especially political bribery.
ORIGIN – nautical slang denoting money collected to buy luxuries, from the sale of watery food known as *slush*.

slut > *noun* a slovenly or promiscuous woman.
DERIVATIVES – **sluttish** *adjective*.

sly > *adjective* (**slyer**, **slyest**) **1** having a cunning and deceitful nature. **2** (of a remark, glance, or expression) insinuating. **3** (of an action) surreptitious.
IDIOMS – **on the sly** in a surreptitious fashion.
DERIVATIVES – **slyly** (also **slily**) *adverb* **slyness** *noun*.
SYNONYMS – **1** crafty, guileful, wily.
ORIGIN – Old Norse *sloegr* 'cunning'; compare with SLEIGHT.

SM > *abbreviation* **1** sadomasochism. **2** Sergeant Major.

Sm > *symbol* the chemical element samarium.

smack[1] > *noun* **1** a sharp blow or slap, typically one given with the palm of the hand. **2** a loud, sharp sound made by such a blow. **3** a loud kiss. > *verb* **1** hit with a smack. **2** smash, drive, or put forcefully into or on to something. **3** part (one's lips) noisily. > *adverb* (Brit. also **smack bang**) informal **1** in a sudden and violent way. **2** (N. Amer. also **smack dab**) exactly; precisely.
SYNONYMS – *noun* **1** blow, slap, swat. *verb* **1** cuff, slap, spank, strike. **2** bang, crash, thump.
ORIGIN – Dutch *smacken*.

smack[2] > *verb* (**smack of**) **1** have a flavour or smell of. **2** suggest the presence or effects of. > *noun* (**a smack of**) a flavour, smell, or suggestion of.
SYNONYMS – *verb* (**smack of**) **2** give the impression of, hint at, suggest.
ORIGIN – Old English, 'flavour, smell'.

smack[3] > *noun* a single-masted sailing boat used for coasting or fishing.
ORIGIN – Dutch *smak*.

smack[4] > *noun* informal heroin.
ORIGIN – probably an alteration of Yiddish *shmek* 'a sniff'.

smacker (also **smackeroo**) > *noun* informal **1** a loud kiss. **2** Brit. one pound sterling. **3** N. Amer. one dollar.

small > *adjective* **1** of a size that is less than normal or usual. **2** not great in amount, number, strength, or power. **3** not fully grown or developed; young. **4** insignificant; unimportant. **5** (of a business) operating on a modest scale. > *noun* (**smalls**) Brit. informal underwear. > *adverb* **1** into small pieces. **2** in a small manner or size.
IDIOMS – **feel** (or **look**) **small** feel (or look) contemptibly weak or insignificant. **small beer** chiefly Brit. something unimportant. **the small of the back** the part of a person's back where the spine curves in at the level of the waist. **the small screen** television as a medium.
DERIVATIVES – **smallness** *noun*.
SYNONYMS – *adjective* **1** little, miniature, tiny.
ANTONYMS – *adjective* **1** big, large.
COMBINATIONS – **small arms** portable firearms. **small-bore** (of a firearm) having a narrow bore. **small change 1** money in the form of coins of low value. **2** something trivial. **small claims court** a local court in which claims for small sums of money can be heard and decided quickly and cheaply, without legal representation. **small fry 1** young or small fish. **2** young or insignificant people or things. **the small hours** the early hours of the morning after midnight. **small intestine** the part of the intestine that runs between the stomach and the large intestine. **small-minded** having a narrow outlook; petty. **small print 1** printed matter in small type. **2** inconspicuous but binding details or conditions printed in an agreement or contract. **small-scale** of limited size or extent. **small talk** polite conversation about uncontroversial matters. **small-time** informal unimportant; minor.

smallholding > *noun* Brit. an agricultural holding that is smaller than a farm.

smallpox > *noun* an acute contagious disease spread by a virus, with fever and pustules usually leaving permanent scars.

smarm informal > *verb* **1** chiefly Brit. behave in an ingratiating way. **2** smooth down (one's hair), especially with oil or gel. > *noun* ingratiating behaviour.

smarmy > *adjective* ingratiating and wheedling in an insincere way.
DERIVATIVES – **smarmily** *adverb* **smarminess** *noun*.
SYNONYMS – obsequious, oily, sycophantic, unctuous.

smart > *adjective* **1** clean, tidy, and stylish. **2** bright and fresh in appearance. **3** (of a place) fashionable and upmarket. **4** informal having a quick intelligence. **5** chiefly N. Amer. impertinently clever or sarcastic. **6** quick; brisk. > *verb* **1** give a sharp, stinging pain. **2** feel upset and annoyed. > *noun* **1** (**smarts**) N. Amer. informal intelligence; acumen. **2** a smarting pain. > *adverb* archaic in a quick or brisk manner.
IDIOMS – **look smart** chiefly Brit. be quick.
DERIVATIVES – **smarting** *adjective* **smartly** *adverb*.
SYNONYMS – *adjective* **1** dapper, debonair, spruce, trim. **3** chic, high-class, stylish, trendy.
COMBINATIONS – **smart alec** (also **smart aleck**, **smart-arse**, US **smart-ass**) informal a person considered irritating in always having a clever answer to a question. **smart card** a plastic card with a built-in microprocessor, used for financial transactions and personal identification.

wordpower facts
Smart
The word **smart** comes from the Old English verb *smeortan*, which was used of wounds and injuries in the sense 'be a source of sharp pain; be acutely painful'. The adjective dates from the early 11th century, when it meant 'inflicting pain; sharp, biting, stinging'. From this developed the senses 'cutting, acrimonious' and 'brisk and vigorous', then, in the 17th century, 'clever, capable, and adept' and 'neat in a brisk, sharp style'. The sense 'neatly dressed' dates from the late 18th century.

smarten > *verb* (often **smarten up**) make or become smarter.

smartish > *adverb* informal, chiefly Brit. quickly; briskly.

smash > *verb* **1** break violently into pieces. **2** crash and severely damage (a vehicle). **3** (often **smash into**) hit or collide with something forcefully. **4** (in sport) strike (the ball) with great force. **5** completely defeat, destroy, or foil. **6** informal, dated (of a business) fail financially. > *noun* **1** an act, instance, or sound of smashing. **2** (also **smash hit**) informal a very successful song, film, or show. > *adverb* with a sudden smash.
SYNONYMS – *verb* **1** disintegrate, shatter, splinter. **3** (**smash into**) crash into, hit, plough into, ram. **5** crush, demolish, ruin, wreck.
COMBINATIONS – **smash-and-grab** (of a robbery) in which the thief smashes a shop window and seizes goods.

smashed > *adjective* informal very drunk.

smasher > *noun* **1** a person or device that smashes something. **2** Brit. informal a very attractive or impressive person or thing.

smashing > *adjective* informal, chiefly Brit. excellent; wonderful.

smattering (also **smatter**) > *noun* **1** a small amount. **2** a slight knowledge of a language or subject.
ORIGIN – from *smatter* 'talk ignorantly, prate'.

smear > *verb* **1** coat or mark with a greasy or sticky substance. **2** blur or smudge. **3** damage the reputation of (someone) by false or unwarranted accusations. > *noun* **1** a greasy or sticky mark. **2** a false or unwarranted accusation. **3** a sample thinly spread on a microscopic slide.
DERIVATIVES – **smeary** *adjective*.
SYNONYMS – *verb* **1** mark, stain, streak. *noun* **1** blotch, daub, smudge, streak.
COMBINATIONS – **smear test** a test to detect signs of cervical cancer, conducted by taking a cervical smear.

smegma /smegmə/ > *noun* an oily secretion in the folds of the skin, especially under a man's foreskin.
ORIGIN – Greek, 'soap'.

smell > *noun* **1** the faculty of perceiving odours by means of the organs in the nose. **2** a quality in something that is perceived by this faculty; an odour. **3** an act of inhaling in order to perceive an odour. > *verb* (past and past participle **smelt** or **smelled**) **1** perceive or detect the odour of. **2** sniff at (something) in order to ascertain its odour. **3** emit an odour of a specified kind. **4** have a strong or unpleasant odour. **5** detect or suspect by means of instinct or intuition. **6** be suggestive of something: *it smells like a hoax to me*.
WORDFINDER – anosmia (*loss of the sense of smell*), fragrant (*having a sweet smell*), malodorous (*smelling very unpleasant*), olfaction (*the sense of smell*), olfactory (*relating to the sense of smell*).
IDIOMS – **smell a rat** informal suspect trickery.
SYNONYMS – *noun* **2** aroma, fragrance, odour, scent. *verb* **4** reek, stink.
COMBINATIONS – **smelling salts** chiefly historical ammonium carbonate mixed with perfume, sniffed by someone who feels faint.

smelly > *adjective* (**smellier**, **smelliest**) having a strong or unpleasant smell.
SYNONYMS – fetid, malodorous, rank.

smelt¹ > *verb* extract (metal) from its ore by a process involving heating and melting.
DERIVATIVES – **smelter** *noun* **smelting** *noun*.
ORIGIN – Dutch, Low German *smelten*.

smelt² past and past participle of SMELL.

smelt³ > *noun* (pl. same or **smelts**) a small silvery fish of both marine and fresh water.

smew /smyoo/ > *noun* a small northern diving duck, the male of which is white with black markings.

smidgen (also **smidgeon** or **smidgin**) > *noun* informal a tiny amount.
ORIGIN – perhaps from Scots *smitch* in the same sense.

smile > *verb* **1** form one's features into a pleased, friendly, or amused expression, with the corners of the mouth turned up. **2** (**smile at** or **on** or **upon**) regard favourably or indulgently. > *noun* an act of smiling; a smiling expression.
DERIVATIVES – **smiling** *adjective*.

smiley > *adjective* informal smiling; cheerful.

smirch /smurch/ > *verb* **1** make dirty. **2** discredit; taint. > *noun* **1** a dirty mark or stain. **2** a flaw.

smirk > *verb* smile in an irritatingly smug or silly way. > *noun* a smug or silly smile.
DERIVATIVES – **smirking** *adjective* **smirky** *adjective*.

smite > *verb* (past **smote**; past participle **smitten**) **1** archaic or literary strike with a firm blow. **2** archaic or literary defeat or conquer. **3** (usu. **be smitten**) (especially of a disease) attack or affect (someone) severely. **4** (**be smitten**) be strongly attracted to someone or something.
ORIGIN – Old English, 'to smear or blemish'.

smith > *noun* **1** a worker in metal. **2** a blacksmith. > *verb* treat (metal) by heating, hammering, and forging it.

-smith > *combining form* denoting a person skilled in creating something with a specified material: *goldsmith*.

smithereens /smithəreenz/ > *plural noun* informal small pieces.
ORIGIN – probably from Irish *smidirín*.

smithy /smithi/ > *noun* (pl. **smithies**) a blacksmith's workshop; a forge.

smitten past participle of SMITE.

smock > *noun* **1** a loose dress or blouse having the upper part closely gathered in smocking. **2** a loose overall worn to protect one's clothes. > *verb* decorate with smocking.
DERIVATIVES – **smocked** *adjective*.

smocking > *noun* decoration on a garment created by gathering a section of the material into tight pleats and holding them together with parallel stitches in an ornamental pattern.

smog > *noun* fog or haze intensified by smoke or other atmospheric pollutants.

DERIVATIVES – **smoggy** *adjective*.

ORIGIN – blend of SMOKE and FOG.

smoke > *noun* 1 a visible suspension of carbon or other particles in the air, emitted from a burning substance. 2 an act of smoking tobacco. 3 informal a cigarette or cigar. 4 (**the Smoke** or **the Big Smoke**) Brit. informal a big city, especially London. > *verb* 1 emit smoke. 2 inhale and exhale the smoke of tobacco or a drug. 3 cure or preserve (meat or fish) by exposure to smoke. 4 treat (glass) so as to darken it. 5 (**smoke out**) drive out of a place by using smoke.

IDIOMS – **go up in smoke** informal 1 be destroyed by fire. 2 (of a plan) come to nothing. **smoke and mirrors** N. Amer. the use of misleading or irrelevant information to obscure or embellish the truth. **there is no smoke without fire** proverb rumours usually have some basis in fact.

DERIVATIVES – **smoked** *adjective* **smoking** *adjective & noun*.

COMBINATIONS – **smoke alarm** a device that detects and gives a warning of the presence of smoke. **smokehouse** a shed or room for smoking fish or meat. **smoke signal** a column of smoke used to convey a message to a distant person. **smokestack** a chimney or funnel for discharging smoke from a locomotive, ship, factory, etc. **smoking gun** a piece of undeniable incriminating evidence. **smoking jacket** a man's comfortable jacket, formerly worn while smoking after dinner.

smoker > *noun* 1 a person who smokes tobacco regularly. 2 a person or device that smokes fish or meat. 3 chiefly N. Amer. an informal social gathering for men.

smokescreen > *noun* 1 a cloud of smoke created to conceal military operations. 2 an irrelevant activity designed to disguise someone's real intentions or activities.

smoky > *adjective* (**smokier**, **smokiest**) 1 producing, filled with, or smelling of smoke. 2 resembling smoke in colour or appearance. 3 having the taste or aroma of smoked food.

DERIVATIVES – **smokily** *adverb* **smokiness** *noun*.

smolder > *verb* US spelling of SMOULDER.

smolt /smōlt/ > *noun* a young salmon or trout after the parr stage, when it becomes silvery and migrates to the sea.

smooch informal > *verb* 1 kiss and cuddle amorously. 2 Brit. dance slowly in a close embrace. > *noun* a spell of smooching.

DERIVATIVES – **smoocher** *noun* **smoochy** (**smoochier**, **smoochiest**) *adjective*.

ORIGIN – an alteration of dialect *smouch* 'kiss, sidle up to'.

smoodge (also **smooge**) Austral./NZ informal > *verb* 1 behave amorously. 2 behave in an ingratiating manner. > *noun* 1 a display of amorous affection. 2 an act or instance of being ingratiating.

DERIVATIVES – **smoodger** *noun*.

smooth > *adjective* 1 having an even and regular surface; free from projections or indentations. 2 (of a liquid) having an even consistency; without lumps. 3 (of movement) without jerks. 4 without problems or difficulties. 5 (of a flavour) without harshness or bitterness. 6 charming in a suave or excessively ingratiating way. > *verb* (also **smoothe**) 1 make smooth. 2 (often **smooth over**) deal successfully with (a problem).

DERIVATIVES – **smoothly** *adverb* **smoothness** *noun*.

COMBINATIONS – **smooth-bore** (of a gun) having an unrifled barrel. **smoothing iron** historical a flat iron. **smooth-tongued** insincerely flattering.

smoothie > *noun* 1 informal a man with a smooth, suave manner. 2 N. Amer. & Austral./NZ a thick, smooth drink of fresh fruit puréed with milk, yogurt, or ice cream.

smooth talk > *noun* persuasively charming or flattering language. > *verb* (**smooth-talk**) informal address or persuade with smooth talk.

DERIVATIVES – **smooth-talker** *noun* **smooth-talking** *adjective*.

smorgasbord /ˈsmɔːgəsbɔːd/ > *noun* a range of open sandwiches and savoury delicacies served as hors d'oeuvres or a buffet.

ORIGIN – Swedish, from *smörgås* 'slice of bread and butter' + *bord* 'table'.

smorzando /smɔːrˈtsandō/ > *adverb & adjective* Music dying away.

ORIGIN – Italian, 'extinguishing'.

smote past of SMITE.

smother > *verb* 1 suffocate by covering the nose and mouth. 2 extinguish (a fire) by covering it. 3 (**smother in** or **with**) cover entirely with. 4 cause to feel trapped and oppressed. 5 suppress (a feeling or action). 6 (in sport) stop the motion of (the ball or a shot). > *noun* a mass of something that stifles or obscures.

SYNONYMS – *verb* 2 dampen, douse, snuff out. 5 muffle, repress, restrain, stifle.

smoulder (US also **smolder**) > *verb* 1 burn slowly with smoke but no flame. 2 feel intense and barely suppressed anger, hatred, lust, etc. > *noun* an instance of smouldering.

DERIVATIVES – **smouldering** *adjective* **smoulderingly** *adverb*.

smudge > *verb* make or become blurred or smeared. > *noun* a smudged mark or image.

DERIVATIVES – **smudgy** (**smudgier**, **smudgiest**) *adjective*.

smudging > *noun* N. Amer. a ceremony or ritual, allegedly of North American Indian origin, involving the burning of twigs to purify a person or place.

ORIGIN – related to obsolete *smudge* 'cure (herring) by smoking'.

smug > *adjective* (**smugger**, **smuggest**) irritatingly pleased with oneself; self-satisfied.

DERIVATIVES – **smugly** *adverb* **smugness** *noun*.

SYNONYMS – complacent, self-congratulatory, self-satisfied, superior.

ORIGIN – first used in the sense 'neat, spruce'; from Low German *smuk* 'pretty'.

smuggle > *verb* 1 move (goods) secretly into or out of a country, avoiding customs and excise duties or legal restrictions. 2 convey secretly and illicitly.

DERIVATIVES – **smuggler** *noun* **smuggling** *noun*.

ORIGIN – Low German *smuggelen*.

smut > *noun* 1 a small flake of soot or dirt. 2 indecent or obscene talk, writing, or pictures. 3 a disease of cereals caused by a fungus, in which parts of the ear change to black powder. > *verb* (**smutted**, **smutting**) 1 mark with smuts. 2 infect with smut.

smutty > *adjective* 1 indecent or obscene. 2 soiled with or characterised by smut or soot.

Sn > *symbol* the chemical element tin.

ORIGIN – from Latin *stannum* 'tin'.

snack > *noun* 1 a small quantity of food eaten between meals or in place of a meal. 2 Austral. informal a thing that is easy to accomplish. > *verb* eat a snack.

ORIGIN – Dutch, from *snacken* 'to bite'.

snaffle > *noun* a simple bit on a bridle, used with a single set of reins. > *verb* informal illicitly take for oneself.

snafu /snaˈfuː/ informal, chiefly N. Amer. > *noun* a confused or chaotic state; a mess. > *verb* throw into confusion or chaos.

ORIGIN – acronym from *situation normal: all fouled* (or *fucked*) *up*.

snag[1] > *noun* 1 an unexpected or hidden obstacle or drawback. 2 a sharp, angular, or jagged projection. 3 a small rent or tear. 4 N. Amer. a dead tree. > *verb* (**snagged**, **snagging**) 1 catch or tear on a snag. 2 N. Amer. informal catch; obtain.

DERIVATIVES – **snaggy** *adjective*.

SYNONYMS – *noun* 1 catch, complication, drawback, hitch, problem, stumbling block.

ORIGIN – probably Scandinavian (in sense 2): the early sense 'stump sticking out from a tree trunk' gave rise to a US sense 'submerged piece of timber obstructing navigation', of which sense 1 was originally a figurative use.

snag² > *noun* Austral./NZ informal a sausage.

snaggle > *noun* a tangled or knotted mass. > *verb* become knotted or tangled.

COMBINATIONS – **snaggle-toothed** having irregular or projecting teeth.

snail > *noun* a slow-moving mollusc with a spiral shell into which the whole body can be withdrawn.

COMBINATIONS – **snail mail** informal the ordinary post as opposed to email.

snake > *noun* 1 a predatory reptile with a long, slender limbless body, many kinds of which have a poisonous bite. 2 (also **snake in the grass**) a treacherous or deceitful person. > *verb* move or extend with the twisting motion of a snake.

WORDFINDER – colubrine, serpentine (*of or like a snake*); constrictor (*snake that kills by squeezing*); *types of snake:* adder, anaconda, boa, cobra, grass snake, mamba, python, rattlesnake, sidewinder, viper; Hydra (*constellation, the Water Snake or Sea Monster*).

COMBINATIONS – **snakebite** Brit. a drink consisting of draught cider and lager in equal proportions. **snake charmer** an entertainer who appears to make snakes move by playing music. **snake oil** informal, chiefly N. Amer. a substance with no real medicinal value sold as a cure-all. **snakes and ladders** a board game in which players proceed up ladders or fall back down snakes depicted on the board.

snaky > *adjective* (**snakier, snakiest**) 1 long and sinuous like a snake. 2 cold and cunning. 3 Austral./NZ informal angry; irritable.

snap > *verb* (**snapped, snapping**) 1 break with a sharp cracking sound. 2 (of an animal) make a sudden audible bite. 3 (**snap up**) quickly secure (something that is in short supply). 4 open or close with a brisk movement or sharp sound. 5 suddenly lose one's self-control. 6 say something quickly and irritably. 7 (**snap out of**) informal get out of (a bad mood) by a sudden effort. 8 take a snapshot of. > *noun* 1 an act of snapping; a sudden snapping sound or movement. 2 a brief spell of cold or otherwise distinctive weather. 3 vigour; liveliness. 4 a snapshot. 5 Brit. a card game in which players compete to call 'snap' as soon as two cards of the same type are exposed. 6 a crisp, brittle biscuit. > *adjective* done or taken on the spur of the moment: *a snap decision.*

SYNONYMS – *verb* 1 break, crack, fracture, splinter. 6 bark, growl, snarl.

COMBINATIONS – **snap-brim** (of a hat) having a brim that can be turned up and down at opposite sides. **snap fastener** a press stud. **snap-lock** (of a device or component) fastened automatically when pushed into position.

ORIGIN – probably from Dutch or Low German *snappen* 'seize'.

snapdragon > *noun* a plant bearing spikes of brightly coloured two-lobed flowers which gape like a mouth when a bee lands on the curved lip.

snapper > *noun* a marine fish noted for snapping its toothed jaws.

snappish > *adjective* 1 (of a dog) irritable and inclined to bite. 2 (of a person) irritable and curt.

DERIVATIVES – **snappishly** *adverb* **snappishness** *noun.*

snappy > *adjective* (**snappier, snappiest**) informal 1 irritable and curt; snappish. 2 cleverly concise. 3 neat and stylish.

IDIOMS – **make it snappy** do it quickly.

DERIVATIVES – **snappily** *adverb.*

SYNONYMS – 1 crotchety, ill-tempered, snappish, tetchy, waspish. 2 catchy, concise, pithy, succinct.

snapshot > *noun* an informal photograph, taken quickly.

snare > *noun* 1 a trap for catching small animals, consisting of a loop of wire or cord that pulls tight. 2 a thing likely to lure someone into harm or error. 3 a length of wire, gut, or hide stretched across a drumhead to produce a rattling sound. 4 (also **snare drum**) another term for *side drum.* > *verb* catch in a snare or trap.

snarf > *verb* informal, chiefly N. Amer. consume quickly or greedily.

snarky > *adjective* (**snarkier, snarkiest**) N. Amer. informal sharply critical.

ORIGIN – from dialect *snark* 'snore, snort, find fault'.

snarl¹ > *verb* 1 growl with bared teeth. 2 say something aggressively. > *noun* an act or sound of snarling.

DERIVATIVES – **snarling** *adjective* **snarly** *adjective.*

snarl² > *verb* (**snarl up**) entangle or become entangled. > *noun* a knot or tangle.

ORIGIN – from SNARE.

snarl-up > *noun* informal 1 a traffic jam. 2 a muddle.

snatch > *verb* 1 seize quickly and deftly. 2 informal steal or kidnap by seizing suddenly. 3 (**snatch at**) hastily or ineffectually attempt to seize (something). > *noun* 1 an act of snatching. 2 a fragment of music or talk. 3 Weightlifting the rapid raising of a weight from the floor to above the head in one movement.

snazzy > *adjective* (**snazzier, snazziest**) informal smart; stylish.

DERIVATIVES – **snazzily** *adverb* **snazziness** *noun.*

sneak > *verb* (past and past participle **sneaked**; US also **snuck**) 1 move, go, or convey in a furtive or stealthy manner. 2 stealthily acquire or obtain: *she sneaked a glance at her watch.* 3 Brit. informal inform someone in

authority of a person's misdeeds. > *noun* informal 1 a furtive person. 2 Brit. a telltale. > *adjective* acting or done surreptitiously: *a sneak preview.*

USAGE – the usual past tense of **sneak** is **sneaked**: **snuck** is American.

SYNONYMS – *verb* 1 creep, slink, steal.

sneaker > *noun* chiefly N. Amer. a soft shoe worn for sports or casual occasions.

sneaking > *adjective* (of a feeling) persistent in one's mind but reluctantly held; nagging.

sneaky > *adjective* furtive or sly.

DERIVATIVES – **sneakily** *adverb* **sneakiness** *noun.*

sneck Scottish & N. English > *noun* a latch on a door or window. > *verb* close or fasten with a latch.

ORIGIN – related to SNATCH.

sneer > *noun* a contemptuous or mocking smile, remark, or tone. > *verb* smile or speak in a contemptuous or mocking manner.

DERIVATIVES – **sneering** *adjective.*

sneeze > *verb* make a sudden involuntary expulsion of air from the nose and mouth due to irritation of one's nostrils. > *noun* an act or the sound of sneezing.

IDIOMS – **not to be sneezed at** informal not to be rejected without careful consideration.

ORIGIN – Old English: apparently an alteration of *fnese* due to misreading or misprinting (after initial *fn-* had become unfamiliar), later adopted because it sounded appropriate.

snib chiefly Scottish & Irish > *noun* 1 a lock, latch, or fastening for a door or window. 2 a small catch on a lock which holds the bolt in or out. > *verb* (**snibbed, snibbing**) fasten or lock.

ORIGIN – perhaps from Low German *snibbe* 'beak-like point'.

snick > *verb* 1 cut a small notch or incision in. 2 Cricket deflect (the ball) slightly with the edge of the bat. > *noun* 1 a small notch or cut. 2 Cricket a slight deflection of the ball by the bat.

ORIGIN – probably from obsolete *snick* or *snee* 'fight with knives'.

snicker > *verb* 1 snigger. 2 (of a horse) whinny. > *noun* a snigger or whinny.

snicket > *noun* chiefly N. English a narrow alley between houses.

snide > *adjective* 1 derogatory or mocking in an indirect way. 2 chiefly N. Amer. devious and underhand. 3 counterfeit or inferior. > *noun* a snide person or remark.

DERIVATIVES – **snidely** *adverb* **snidey** *adjective.*

sniff > *verb* 1 draw air audibly through the nose. 2 (**sniff at**) show contempt or dislike for. 3 (**sniff around** or **round**) informal investigate something secretly. 4 (**sniff out**) informal discover (something) by secret or

S

hidden investigation. > *noun* **1** an act or sound of sniffing. **2** *informal* a hint or sign. **3** *informal* a slight chance.

DERIVATIVES – **sniffer** *noun*.

COMBINATIONS – **sniffer dog** *informal* a dog trained to find drugs or explosives by smell.

sniffle > *verb* sniff slightly or repeatedly, typically because of a cold or fit of crying. > *noun* **1** an act of sniffling. **2** a slight head cold.

DERIVATIVES – **sniffly** *adjective*.

sniffy > *adjective* (**sniffier**, **sniffiest**) *informal* scornful; contemptuous.

DERIVATIVES – **sniffily** *adverb*.

snifter > *noun informal* **1** a small quantity of an alcoholic drink. **2** *chiefly N. Amer.* a balloon glass for brandy.

snigger > *noun* a smothered or half-suppressed laugh. > *verb* give such a laugh.

snip > *verb* (**snipped**, **snipping**) cut with scissors or shears, with small, quick strokes. > *noun* **1** an act of snipping. **2** a small piece that has been cut off. **3** *Brit. informal* a bargain. **4** *informal* a thing that is easily achieved. **5** (**snips**) hand shears for cutting metal.

ORIGIN – Low German, 'small piece'.

snipe /snīp/ > *noun* (pl. same or **snipes**) a wading bird with brown camouflaged plumage and a long straight bill. > *verb* **1** shoot at someone from a hiding place at long range. **2** make a sly or petty verbal attack.

DERIVATIVES – **sniper** *noun*.

snippet > *noun* a small piece or brief extract.

SYNONYMS – excerpt, extract, scrap.

snippy > *adjective* (**snippier**, **snippiest**) *informal* curt or sharp.

snit > *noun N. Amer. informal* a fit of irritation or pique.

snitch *informal* > *verb* **1** steal. **2** inform on someone. > *noun* an informer.

snivel > *verb* (**snivelled**, **snivelling**; US **sniveled**, **sniveling**) **1** cry and sniffle. **2** complain in a whining or tearful way. > *noun* a spell of snivelling.

ORIGIN – Old English, 'mucus'.

snob > *noun* **1** a person who has an exaggerated respect for high social position or wealth and who looks down on those regarded as socially inferior. **2** a person with a similar respect for tastes considered superior in a particular area: *a wine snob.*

DERIVATIVES – **snobbery** *noun* **snobbism** *noun* **snobby** *adjective*.

snobbish > *adjective* characteristic of or like a snob.

DERIVATIVES – **snobbishly** *adverb*.

SYNONYMS – condescending, elitist, patronising, superior.

snog *Brit. informal* > *verb* (**snogged**, **snogging**) kiss and caress amorously. > *noun* an act or spell of snogging.

Snob

When it first appeared, as a dialect word in the late 18th century, **snob** meant 'cobbler' or 'cobbler's apprentice'. It next surfaced as a Cambridge University slang term for a townsman or non-member of the university, and then came to refer to any ordinary person lacking high rank or status. The main modern sense, of a person who looks down on those regarded as socially inferior, is first recorded in 1848, in *The Book of Snobs* by William Makepeace Thackeray. Folk etymology connects **snob** with the Latin phrase *sine nobilitate* 'without nobility', but the first recorded sense has no connection with this.

snood /snood/ > *noun* **1** an ornamental hairnet or pouch worn over the hair at the back of a woman's head. **2** a wide ring of knitted material worn as a hood or scarf.

snook /snook/ > *noun* (in phrase **cock a snook**) *informal, chiefly Brit.* **1** place one's hand so that the thumb touches one's nose and the fingers are spread out, as a gesture of contempt. **2** openly show contempt or a lack of respect for someone or something.

snooker > *noun* **1** a game played with cues on a billiard table, in which the players use a white cue ball to pocket the other balls in a set order. **2** a position in a game of snooker or pool in which a player cannot make a direct shot at any permitted ball. > *verb* **1** subject to a snooker. **2** (**be snookered**) *informal* be ruined or placed in an impossible position.

wordpower facts
Snooker

The origin of the word **snooker** is uncertain. It may, however, be related to the army slang term *snooker*, meaning 'new recruit', which was current at the Royal Military Academy, Woolwich, in the late 19th century. The game was invented by British army officers in India, and is said to have acquired its name from a remark made by Colonel Sir Neville Chamberlain, who was a subaltern in the Devonshire Regiment at Jabalpur in 1875. Chamberlain is supposed to have referred to one of his fellow officers as a *snooker*, meaning a 'beginner' at the game.

snoop *informal* > *verb* investigate or look

around furtively in an attempt to find out something. > *noun* **1** an act of snooping. **2** a person who snoops.

DERIVATIVES – **snooper** *noun*.

ORIGIN – Dutch *snœpen* 'eat on the sly'.

snoot > *noun informal* **1** a person's nose. **2** a snob.

ORIGIN – variant of SNOUT.

snooty > *adjective* (**snootier**, **snootiest**) *informal* showing disapproval of or contempt towards others, especially those considered to be socially inferior.

DERIVATIVES – **snootily** *adverb* **snootiness** *noun*.

snooze *informal* > *noun* a short, light sleep. > *verb* have a snooze.

DERIVATIVES – **snoozer** *noun* **snoozy** *adjective*.

COMBINATIONS – **snooze button** a control on a clock which sets an alarm to repeat after a short interval.

snore > *noun* a snorting or grunting sound in a person's breathing while they are asleep. > *verb* make such a sound while asleep.

DERIVATIVES – **snorer** *noun*.

snorkel /snork'l/ > *noun* a tube for a swimmer to breathe through while under water. > *verb* (**snorkelled**, **snorkelling**; US **snorkeled**, **snorkeling**) swim using a snorkel.

DERIVATIVES – **snorkeller** *noun*.

ORIGIN – German *Schnorchel*.

snort > *noun* **1** an explosive sound made by the sudden forcing of breath through the nose. **2** *informal* an inhaled dose of cocaine. **3** *informal* a measure of an alcoholic drink. > *verb* **1** make a snort. **2** express indignation or derision by making a snort. **3** *informal* inhale (cocaine).

DERIVATIVES – **snorter** *noun*.

snot > *noun informal* **1** nasal mucus. **2** a contemptible person.

COMBINATIONS – **snot-nosed** *informal* **1** childish and inexperienced. **2** considering oneself superior; snobbish.

ORIGIN – probably from Dutch and Low German; related to SNOUT.

snotty > *adjective* (**snottier**, **snottiest**) *informal* **1** full of or covered with nasal mucus. **2** having a superior or conceited attitude.

DERIVATIVES – **snottily** *adverb* **snottiness** *noun*.

snout > *noun* **1** the projecting nose and mouth of an animal. **2** the projecting front or end of something such as a pistol. **3** *Brit. informal* tobacco or a cigarette. **4** *Brit. informal* a police informer.

DERIVATIVES – **snouted** *adjective*.

ORIGIN – Dutch, Low German *snūt*; related to SNOT.

snow > *noun* **1** atmospheric water vapour frozen into ice crystals and falling in light white flakes or lying on the ground as a white layer. **2** (**snows**) falls of snow. **3** a mass of flickering white spots on a television or radar screen, caused by interference or a poor signal. > *verb* **1** (**it snows**, **it is snowing**, etc.) snow falls. **2** (**be snowed in** or **up**) be confined or blocked by a large quantity of snow. **3** (**be snowed under**) be overwhelmed with a large quantity of something, especially work.

WORDFINDER – niveous (*snowy or resembling snow*).

DERIVATIVES – **snowless** *adjective*.

COMBINATIONS – **snow blindness** temporary blindness caused by the glare of light reflected by a large expanse of snow. **snowdrift** a bank of deep snow heaped up by the wind. **snowfall 1** a fall of snow. **2** the quantity of snow falling within a given area in a given time. **snowfield** a permanent wide expanse of snow in mountainous or polar regions. **snow goose** a gregarious goose that breeds in Arctic Canada and Greenland, typically having white plumage with black wing tips. **snow leopard** a rare large cat which has pale grey fur patterned with dark blotches and rings, living in mountainous parts of central Asia. **snowline** the altitude above which some snow remains on the ground throughout the year. **snowmobile** a motor vehicle, especially one with runners or caterpillar tracks, for travelling over snow. **snowplough** (US **snowplow**) **1** an implement or vehicle for clearing roads of snow. **2** Skiing an act of turning the points of one's skis inwards in order to slow down or turn. **snowshoe** a flat device resembling a racket, which is attached to the sole of a boot and used for walking on snow. **snowstorm** a heavy fall of snow accompanied by a high wind.

snowball > *noun* **1** a ball of packed snow. **2** a cocktail containing advocaat and lemonade. > *verb* **1** throw snowballs at. **2** increase rapidly in size, intensity, or importance.

snowboard > *noun* a board resembling a short, broad ski, used for sliding downhill on snow.

DERIVATIVES – **snowboarder** *noun* **snowboarding** *noun*.

snowbound > *adjective* **1** prevented from travelling or going out by snow. **2** cut off or inaccessible because of snow.

snowcat (also US trademark **Sno-Cat**) > *noun* a tracked vehicle for travelling over snow.

snowdrop > *noun* a plant which bears drooping white flowers during the late winter.

snowflake > *noun* each of the many feathery ice crystals that fall as snow.

WORDFINDER – fractal (*denoting a repeating pattern such as the outline of a snowflake*).

snowman > *noun* a representation of a human figure created with compressed snow.

snowy > *adjective* (**snowier**, **snowiest**) **1** covered with snow. **2** (of weather or a period of time) characterised by snowfall. **3** of or like snow, especially in being pure white.

DERIVATIVES – **snowily** *adverb*.

COMBINATIONS – **snowy owl** a large owl that breeds mainly in the Arctic tundra, the male being entirely white.

snub > *verb* (**snubbed**, **snubbing**) ignore or spurn disdainfully. > *noun* an act of snubbing. > *adjective* (of a person's nose) short and turned up at the end.

SYNONYMS – *verb* brush off, ignore, rebuff, spurn.

ORIGIN – Old Norse *snubba* 'chide, check the growth of'.

snuck US past and past participle of SNEAK.

snuff¹ > *verb* **1** extinguish (a candle). **2** (**snuff out**) abruptly put an end to. **3** (**snuff it**) Brit. informal die. > *noun* the charred part of a candle wick.

COMBINATIONS – **snuff movie** informal a pornographic film or video recording of an actual murder.

snuff² > *noun* powdered tobacco that is sniffed up the nostril rather than smoked. > *verb* inhale or sniff at.

IDIOMS – **up to snuff** informal **1** up to the required standard. **2** in good health.

ORIGIN – from Dutch *snuffen* 'to snuffle'.

snuffer > *noun* a small hollow metal cone on the end of a handle, used to extinguish a candle by smothering the flame.

snuffle > *verb* **1** breathe noisily through a partially blocked nose. **2** (of an animal) make repeated sniffing sounds. > *noun* **1** a snuffling sound. **2** (**the snuffles**) informal a cold.

DERIVATIVES – **snuffly** *adjective*.

snug > *adjective* (**snugger**, **snuggest**) **1** warm and cosy. **2** close-fitting. > *noun* Brit. a small, cosy public room in a pub or small hotel.

DERIVATIVES – **snugly** *adverb* **snugness** *noun*.

SYNONYMS – *adjective* **1** comfortable, cosy, sheltered, warm.

ORIGIN – first in nautical use in the sense 'shipshape, compact, prepared for bad weather': probably of Low German or Dutch origin.

snuggery > *noun* (pl. **snuggeries**) a cosy place, especially someone's private room.

snuggle > *verb* settle into a warm, comfortable position.

so¹ > *adverb* **1** to such a great extent. **2** extremely; very much. **3** to the same extent: *he isn't so bad as you'd think*. **4** referring back to something previously mentioned. **5** similarly. **6** in the way described or demonstrated; thus.

> *conjunction* **1** and for this reason; therefore. **2** (**so that**) with the result or aim that. **3** and then. **4** introducing a question or concluding statement. **5** in the same way; correspondingly.

IDIOMS – **and so on** (or **forth**) and similar things; et cetera. **or so** approximately. **so be it** an expression of acceptance or resignation. **so long!** informal goodbye. **so much as** even: *without so much as a word*. **so to speak** (or **say**) indicating that one is talking in an exaggerated or metaphorical way.

so² > *noun* variant spelling of SOH.

soak > *verb* **1** make or become thoroughly wet by immersion in liquid. **2** (of a liquid) penetrate or permeate completely. **3** (**soak up**) absorb (a liquid). **4** (**soak up**) expose oneself to (something beneficial or enjoyable). **5** (**soak oneself in**) immerse oneself in (a particular experience). **6** informal impose heavy charges or taxation on. > *noun* **1** an act or spell of soaking. **2** informal a heavy drinker. **3** Austral. a hollow where rainwater collects.

DERIVATIVES – **soaked** *adjective* **soaking** *adjective*.

SYNONYMS – *verb* **1** immerse, marinate, souse, steep. **2** drench, saturate, waterlog.

ORIGIN – Old English, related to *sūcan* 'to suck'.

so-and-so > *noun* (pl. **so-and-sos**) informal **1** a person or thing whose name the speaker does not know, remember, or need to specify. **2** euphemistic a person who is disliked or considered to have an objectionable characteristic (used instead of a vulgar word): *a nosy so-and-so*.

soap > *noun* **1** a substance used with water for washing and cleaning, made of natural oils or fats combined with an alkali, and typically perfumed. **2** informal a soap opera. > *verb* wash with soap.

WORDFINDER – saponaceous (*referring to soap; soapy*).

COMBINATIONS – **soapbox 1** a box or crate used as a makeshift stand for public speaking. **2** an opportunity for someone to air their views publicly.

soap opera > *noun* a television or radio drama serial dealing with daily events in the lives of the same group of characters.

ORIGIN – so named because such serials were originally sponsored in the US by soap manufacturers.

soapstone > *noun* a soft rock consisting largely of talc.

soapy > *adjective* (**soapier**, **soapiest**) **1** containing or covered with soap. **2** of or like soap. **3** unpleasantly flattering and ingratiating. **4** informal characteristic of a soap opera.

soar > *verb* **1** fly or rise high into the air. **2** maintain height in the air by gliding. **3** increase rapidly above the usual level.
DERIVATIVES – **soarer** *noun*.
SYNONYMS – **1** ascend, climb, fly, rise. **2** drift, glide. **3** escalate, shoot up, skyrocket.
ORIGIN – Old French *essorer*, from Latin *ex-* 'out of' + *aura* 'breeze'.

Soave /sōaavay/ > *noun* a dry white wine produced in the region of northern Italy around Soave.

sob > *verb* (**sobbed**, **sobbing**) **1** cry making loud, convulsive gasps. **2** say while sobbing. > *noun* an act or sound of sobbing.
SYNONYMS – *verb* cry, howl, weep.
COMBINATIONS – **sob story** informal a story intended to arouse sympathy.

sober > *adjective* (**soberer**, **soberest**) **1** not affected by alcohol; not drunk. **2** serious and restrained. **3** (of a colour) not bright or conspicuous. > *verb* (usu. **sober up**) **1** make or become sober after drinking alcohol. **2** make or become serious.
DERIVATIVES – **soberly** *adverb*.
SYNONYMS – *adjective* **1** abstemious, clear-headed, teetotal, temperate. **2** grave, moderate, restrained, serious, steady. **3** drab, dull, plain, sombre.
ORIGIN – Latin *sobrius*.

sobriety /səbrīəti/ > *noun* the state of being sober.

sobriquet /sōbrikay/ (also **soubriquet** /sōōbrikay/) > *noun* a person's nickname.
ORIGIN – French, originally in the sense 'a tap under the chin'.

soca /sōkə/ > *noun* calypso music with elements of soul, originally from Trinidad.
ORIGIN – blend of SOUL and CALYPSO.

so-called > *adjective* called by the name or term specified (often, in the speaker's view, inappropriately).

soccer > *noun* a form of football played with a round ball which may not be handled during play except by the goalkeepers, the object being to score goals by kicking or heading the ball into the opponents' goal.
ORIGIN – shortening of *Assoc* from *Association Football* + -ER³.

sociable > *adjective* **1** willing to talk and engage in activities with others. **2** (of a place, occasion, or activity) marked by friendliness.
DERIVATIVES – **sociability** *noun* **sociably** *adverb*.
USAGE – **sociable** and **social** do not mean quite the same thing. **Sociable** tends to mean 'willing to engage with others, friendly', while **social** means, more neutrally, 'relating to society' or 'done or living with others, communal'.
SYNONYMS – **1** convivial, extrovert, friendly, gregarious, outgoing.
ANTONYMS – **1** solitary, unsociable.

ORIGIN – Latin *sociabilis*, from *sociare* 'unite', from *socius* 'companion'.

social > *adjective* **1** relating to society or its organisation or hierarchy. **2** relating to or designed for activities in which people meet each other for pleasure. **3** needing companionship; suited to living in communities. **4** (of animals) breeding or living in colonies or organised communities. > *noun* an informal social gathering organised by the members of a club or group.
DERIVATIVES – **sociality** *noun* **socially** *adverb*.
SYNONYMS – *adjective* **1** collective, communal, popular, public.
ANTONYMS – *adjective* **1** individual, solitary.
COMBINATIONS – **social climber** derogatory a person who is anxious to gain a higher social status. **social contract** (also **social compact**) an implicit agreement among the members of a society to cooperate for mutual benefit, for example by sacrificing some individual freedom for state protection. **social democracy** a socialist system of government achieved by democratic means. **social fund** (in the UK) a social security fund from which loans or grants are made to people in need. **social market** an economic system based on a free market operated in conjunction with state provision for those unable to sell their labour, such as the elderly or unemployed. **social realism** the realistic depiction in art of contemporary life, as a means of social or political comment. **social science 1** the scientific study of human society and social relationships. **2** a subject within this field, such as economics. **social security** (in the UK) state financial assistance for people with an inadequate or no income. **social service 1** (**social services**) services provided by the state for the community, such as education and medical care. **2** activity aiming to promote the welfare of others. **social studies** the study of human society.
ORIGIN – Latin *socialis* 'allied', from *socius* 'companion'.

socialise (also **socialize**) > *verb* **1** mix socially with others. **2** make (someone) behave in a way that is acceptable to society. **3** organise according to the principles of socialism.
DERIVATIVES – **socialisation** *noun*.
SYNONYMS – **1** consort, fraternise, interact, mingle, mix.

socialism > *noun* a political and economic theory of social organisation which advocates that the means of production, distribution, and exchange should be owned or regulated by the community as a whole.

DERIVATIVES – **socialist** *noun* & *adjective* **socialistic** *adjective*.

socialite > *noun* a person who mixes in fashionable society.

social work > *noun* work carried out by trained staff with the aim of improving the conditions of people suffering from social deprivation.
DERIVATIVES – **social worker** *noun*.

society > *noun* (pl. **societies**) **1** the aggregate of people living together in a more or less ordered community. **2** a particular community of people living in a country or region, and having shared customs, laws, and organisations. **3** (also **high society**) people who are fashionable, wealthy, and influential, regarded as a distinct social group. **4** an organisation or club formed for a particular purpose or activity. **5** the situation of being in the company of other people.
DERIVATIVES – **societal** *adjective*.
SYNONYMS – **1** the community, the people, the public. **3** the beau monde, the crème de la crème, the elite, the smart set. **4** association, club, group, guild, union. **5** companionship, company, fellowship.
ORIGIN – Latin *societas*, from *socius* 'companion'.

sociobiology > *noun* the scientific study of the biological (especially ecological and evolutionary) aspects of social behaviour in animals and humans.
DERIVATIVES – **sociobiological** *adjective* **sociobiologist** *noun*.

socio-economic > *adjective* relating to or concerned with the interaction of social and economic factors.

sociolinguistics > *plural noun* (treated as sing.) the study of language in relation to social factors.
DERIVATIVES – **sociolinguist** *noun* **sociolinguistic** *adjective*.

sociology > *noun* the study of the development, structure, and functioning of human society.
DERIVATIVES – **sociological** *adjective* **sociologist** *noun*.

sociopath /sōsiōpath, sōshiōpath/ > *noun* a person with a personality disorder manifesting itself in extreme antisocial attitudes and behaviour.
DERIVATIVES – **sociopathic** *adjective* **sociopathy** *noun*.

sock > *noun* **1** a knitted garment for the foot and lower part of the leg. **2** an insole. **3** informal a hard blow. > *verb* informal hit forcefully.
IDIOMS – **knock** (or **blow**) **someone's socks off** informal amaze or impress someone. **knock the socks off** informal surpass or beat easily. **pull one's socks up** informal make an effort to improve. **put a**

sock in it Brit. informal stop talking. **sock it to** informal make a forceful impression on (someone).

ORIGIN – Latin *soccus* 'comic actor's shoe, light low-heeled slipper', from Greek *sukkhos*.

socket > *noun* 1 a hollow in which something fits or revolves. 2 an electrical device receiving a plug or light bulb to make a connection. > *verb* (**socketed**, **socketing**) place in or fit with a socket.

ORIGIN – Old French *soket* 'small ploughshare'.

sockeye > *noun* a commercially valuable salmon of the North Pacific region.

ORIGIN – Salish, 'fish of fishes'.

Socratic /səkrattik/ > *adjective* relating to the Athenian philosopher Socrates (469–399 BC) or his philosophy or methods.

sod[1] > *noun* 1 grass-covered ground; turf. 2 a piece of turf.

IDIOMS – **under the sod** dead and buried.

ORIGIN – Dutch or Low German *sode*.

sod[2] vulgar slang, chiefly Brit. > *noun* 1 an unpleasant person. 2 a person of a specified kind: *poor sod*. 3 a difficult or problematic thing. > *verb* (**sodded**, **sodding**) 1 used to express anger or annoyance. 2 (**sod off**) go away. 3 (**sodding**) used as a general term of contempt.

IDIOMS – **sod all** absolutely nothing.

ORIGIN – abbreviation of **SODOMITE**.

soda > *noun* 1 (also **soda water**) carbonated water (originally made with sodium bicarbonate). 2 N. Amer. a sweet carbonated drink. 3 sodium carbonate. 4 sodium in chemical combination.

COMBINATIONS – **soda bread** bread leavened with baking soda. **soda fountain** N. Amer. 1 a device dispensing soda water or soft drinks. 2 a shop or counter selling drinks from such a device. **soda siphon** a bottle from which carbonated water is dispensed by allowing the gas pressure to force it out.

ORIGIN – Latin, from an Arabic word meaning 'saltwort'.

sodality /sōdaliti/ > *noun* (pl. **sodalities**) a fraternity or association, especially a Roman Catholic religious guild or brotherhood.

ORIGIN – Latin *sodalitas*, from *sodalis* 'comrade'.

sodden > *adjective* 1 soaked through. 2 having drunk an excessive amount of an alcoholic drink: *whisky-sodden*.

SYNONYMS – 1 drenched, saturated, soaked, sopping, wringing.

ORIGIN – archaic past participle of **SEETHE**: originally used in the sense 'boiled'.

sodium > *noun* a soft silver-white reactive metallic chemical element of which common salt and soda are compounds.

COMBINATIONS – **sodium bicarbonate** a soluble white powder used chiefly in effervescent drinks and as a raising agent in baking. **sodium carbonate** a white alkaline compound used in making soap and glass. **sodium chloride** the chemical name for salt. **sodium hydroxide** a strongly alkaline white deliquescent compound used in many industrial processes; caustic soda. **sodium lamp** a lamp in which an electrical discharge in sodium vapour gives a yellow light.

ORIGIN – from **SODA**.

sodomite /soddəmīt/ > *noun* a person who engages in sodomy.

DERIVATIVES – **sodomitic** *adjective* **sodomitical** *adjective*.

sodomy > *noun* anal intercourse.

DERIVATIVES – **sodomise** (also **sodomize**) *verb*.

ORIGIN – from Latin *peccatum Sodomiticum* 'sin of Sodom' (after the Book of Genesis, chapter 19, which implies that the men of the town of Sodom in ancient Palestine practised homosexual rape).

Sod's Law > *noun* another name for **MURPHY'S LAW**.

sofa > *noun* a long upholstered seat with a back and arms, for two or more people.

WORDFINDER – *types of sofa*: canapé, chaise longue, chesterfield, davenport, divan, love seat.

COMBINATIONS – **sofa bed** a sofa that can be converted into a bed.

ORIGIN – French, from Arabic.

soffit /soffit/ > *noun* the underside of an arch, a balcony, overhanging eaves, etc.

ORIGIN – Italian *soffitto*, from Latin *suffixus* 'fastened below'.

soft > *adjective* 1 easy to mould, cut, compress, or fold. 2 not rough or coarse in texture. 3 quiet and gentle. 4 (of light or colour) pleasingly subtle; not harsh. 5 sympathetic, lenient, or compassionate, especially excessively so. 6 informal (of a job or way of life) requiring little effort. 7 informal foolish. 8 (**soft on**) informal infatuated with. 9 (of a drink) not alcoholic. 10 (of a drug) not likely to cause addiction. 11 (of water) free from mineral salts. 12 denoting a faction within a political party that is willing to compromise. 13 (also **soft-core**) (of pornography) suggestive but not explicit.

IDIOMS – **have a soft spot for** be fond of.

DERIVATIVES – **softish** *adjective* **softly** *adverb* **softness** *noun*.

SYNONYMS – 1 compressible, elastic, malleable, pliable, yielding. 2 satiny, silky, smooth, velvety. 4 delicate, muted, subdued, warm.

ANTONYMS – 1 firm, hard. 2 coarse, harsh, rough. 4 bright, harsh.

COMBINATIONS – **softback** a paperback. **softball** a modified form of baseball played on a smaller field with a larger, softer ball. **soft-boiled** (of an egg) lightly boiled, leaving the yolk soft or liquid. **soft copy** a legible version of a piece of information, stored or displayed on a computer. **soft focus** deliberate slight blurring or lack of definition in a photograph or film. **soft fruit** Brit. a small stoneless fruit, e.g. a strawberry. **soft furnishings** Brit. curtains, chair coverings, and other cloth items used to decorate a room. **soft-headed** not intelligent. **soft-hearted** kind and compassionate. **soft palate** the fleshy, flexible part towards the back of the roof of the mouth. **the soft sell** subtly persuasive selling. **soft target** a relatively vulnerable person or thing. **soft-top** a motor vehicle with a roof that can be folded back. **softwood** the wood from a conifer as distinguished from that of broadleaved trees.

soften > *verb* 1 make or become soft or softer. 2 (often **soften up**) undermine the resistance of.

DERIVATIVES – **softener** *noun*.

softie (also **softy**) > *noun* (pl. **softies**) informal a weak or soft-hearted person.

softly-softly > *adjective* cautious and patient.

soft pedal > *noun* a pedal on a piano that can be pressed to soften the tone. > *verb* (**soft-pedal**) play down the unpleasant aspects of (something).

soft soap > *noun* 1 a semi-fluid soap. 2 informal persuasive flattery. > *verb* (**soft-soap**) informal use flattery to persuade.

software > *noun* programs and other operating information used by a computer. Compare with **HARDWARE**.

softy > *noun* variant spelling of **SOFTIE**.

soggy > *adjective* (**soggier**, **soggiest**) very wet and soft.

DERIVATIVES – **soggily** *adverb* **sogginess** *noun*.

SYNONYMS – boggy, marshy, mushy, sloppy, squelchy.

ORIGIN – from dialect *sog* 'a swamp'.

soh /sō/ (also **so** or **sol**) > *noun* Music the fifth note of a major scale, coming between 'fah' and 'lah'.

soi-disant /swaadeezoN/ > *adjective* self-styled: *a soi-disant novelist*.

ORIGIN – French, from *soi* 'oneself' + *disant* 'saying'.

soigné /**swaan**yay/ > *adjective* (fem. **soignée** pronunc. same) elegant and well groomed.
ORIGIN – French, from *soigner* 'take care of'.

soil¹ > *noun* **1** the upper layer of earth in which plants grow, typically consisting of organic remains, clay, and rock particles. **2** the territory of a particular nation.
WORDFINDER – agronomy (*science of soil management and crop production*), humus (*organic component of soil*), hydroponics (*growing of plants without soil*), loam (*soil of clay and sand containing humus*), marl (*soil consisting of clay and lime*), pedologist or soil scientist (*scientist who studies the soil*), sward (*upper layer of soil*), telluric (*of the soil*).

wordpower facts
Soil

The two English words **soil**, identical in form and related in meaning, are of totally different origin. **Soil** in the sense 'layer of earth in which plants grow' is an Old French word meaning 'land', which probably came from Latin *solium* 'seat' but acquired the meaning 'earth' by association with *solum* 'ground'. **Soil** meaning 'make dirty', on the other hand, is based on Latin *sucula* 'little pig' (a diminutive of *sus* 'pig', connected to **sow²**). This word entered English via the Old French verb *soiller*, which may be related to **sully**; the earliest use of the noun was 'muddy place for wild boar to wallow in'.

soil² > *verb* **1** make dirty. **2** bring discredit to. > *noun* waste matter, especially sewage.
SYNONYMS – *verb* **1** begrime, dirty, foul, stain, sully.

soirée /**swaa**ray/ > *noun* an evening social gathering, typically in a private house, for conversation or music.
ORIGIN – French, from *soir* 'evening'.

sojourn /**so**jurn/ *literary* > *noun* a temporary stay. > *verb* stay temporarily.
DERIVATIVES – **sojourner** *noun*.
ORIGIN – from Old French *sojourner*, from Latin *sub-* 'under' + *diurnum* 'day'.

sol¹ > *noun* variant of **SOH**.

sol² > *noun* Chemistry a fluid suspension of a colloidal solid in a liquid.
ORIGIN – abbreviation of **SOLUTION**.

sol³ /sol/ > *noun* (pl. **soles**) the basic monetary unit of Peru, equal to 100 cents.
ORIGIN – Spanish, 'sun'.

sola /**sō**lə/ > *noun* an Indian swamp plant with pithy stems.
ORIGIN – Hindi.

solace /**soll**əss/ > *noun* comfort or consolation in time of distress. > *verb* give solace to.
SYNONYMS – *noun* cheer, comfort, consolation, relief, support.
ORIGIN – Old French *solas*, from Latin *solari* 'to console'.

solar /**sō**lər/ > *adjective* relating to or determined by the sun or its rays.
COMBINATIONS – **solar battery** (also **solar cell**) a device converting solar radiation into electricity. **solar eclipse** an eclipse in which the sun is obscured by the moon. **solar energy** (also **solar power**) radiant energy emitted by the sun. **solar panel** a panel designed to absorb the sun's rays as a source of energy for generating electricity or heating. **solar plexus** a complex of ganglia and radiating nerves at the pit of the stomach. **solar wind** a continuous flow of charged particles from the sun, permeating the solar system. **solar year** the time between successive spring or autumn equinoxes, or winter or summer solstices (365 days, 5 hours, 48 minutes, and 46 seconds).
ORIGIN – Latin *solaris*, from *sol* 'sun'.

solarium /sə**lair**iəm/ > *noun* (pl. **solariums** or **solaria** /sə**lair**iə/) **1** a room equipped with sunlamps or sunbeds. **2** a room with extensive areas of glass to admit sunlight.
ORIGIN – Latin, 'sundial, place for sunning oneself'.

solar system > *noun* the sun together with the planets, asteroids, comets, etc. in orbit around it.
WORDFINDER – cosmogony (*science of the origin of the universe, especially the solar system*), orrery (*clockwork model of the solar system*).

sola topi /**sō**lə **tō**pi/ > *noun* an Indian sun hat made from the pith of the sola plant.
ORIGIN – Hindi, 'sola hat'.

sold past and past participle of **SELL**.

solder /**sō**ldər, **sold**ər/ > *noun* an alloy that melts at a low temperature, especially one based on lead and tin, used for joining less fusible metals. > *verb* join with solder.
COMBINATIONS – **soldering iron** an electrical tool for melting and applying solder.
ORIGIN – Old French *soudure*, from Latin *solidare* 'fasten together'.

soldi plural of **SOLDO**.

soldier > *noun* **1** a person who serves in an army. **2** (also **common soldier** or **private soldier**) a private in an army. **3** Brit. informal a strip of bread or toast, dipped into a soft-boiled egg. > *verb* **1** serve as a soldier. **2** (**soldier on**) informal persevere.
IDIOMS – **soldier of fortune** a mercenary.
DERIVATIVES – **soldierly** *adjective*.
SYNONYMS – *noun* **1** fighter, serviceman/woman, trooper, warrior.

wordpower facts
Soldier

Soldier is an Old French word derived from *soulde* 'soldier's pay', a *soldier* being someone who is paid to fight. *Soulde* came from Latin *solidus*, which is the ancestor of the English word **solid** but was also the name of a gold coin of the later Roman Empire: it was short for *solidus nummus*, which meant literally 'solid coin'. *Solidus* is also the root of **solder** and of **sou**, a former French coin of low value.

soldiery > *noun* **1** soldiers collectively. **2** military training or knowledge.

soldo /**sold**ō/ > *noun* (pl. **soldi** /**sold**i/) a former Italian coin and monetary unit worth the twentieth part of a lira.
ORIGIN – Italian, from Latin *solidus* 'solid'.

sole¹ > *noun* **1** the underside of a person's foot. **2** the section forming the underside of a piece of footwear. **3** the underside of a tool or implement, e.g. a plane. > *verb* (usu. **be soled**) put a new sole on (a shoe).
WORDFINDER – bastinado (*punishment of caning the soles of the feet*), plantar (*relating to the soles*), plantigrade (*walking on the soles*).
ORIGIN – Latin *solea* 'sandal, sill'.

sole² > *noun* an edible marine flatfish.
ORIGIN – Latin *solea* (see **SOLE¹**); named from its shape.

sole³ > *adjective* **1** one and only. **2** belonging or restricted to one person or group.
DERIVATIVES – **solely** *adverb*.
SYNONYMS – **1** lone, only, single, solitary, unique.
ORIGIN – Latin *sola*, feminine of *solus* 'alone'.

solecism /**soll**isiz'm/ > *noun* **1** a grammatical mistake. **2** an instance of bad manners or incorrect behaviour.
DERIVATIVES – **solecistic** /solli**sist**ik/ *adjective*.
ORIGIN – Greek *soloikismos*, from *soloikos* 'speaking incorrectly'.

solemn > *adjective* **1** formal and dignified. **2** not cheerful; serious. **3** deeply sincere.
DERIVATIVES – **solemnly** *adverb*.
SYNONYMS – **1** ceremonious, dignified, formal, grand, stately. **2** earnest, grave, grim, serious, stern. **3** earnest, genuine, heartfelt, sincere, wholehearted.
ANTONYMS – **1** frivolous, informal. **2** jolly, light-hearted.
ORIGIN – first used in the sense 'associated with religious rites': from Latin *sollemnis* 'customary, celebrated at a fixed date'.

solemnise /**soll**əmnīz/ (also **solemnize**) > *verb* **1** duly perform (a ceremony, especially that of marriage). **2** mark with a formal ceremony.

DERIVATIVES – **solemnisation** noun.

solemnity /səlemniti/ > noun (pl. **solemnities**) **1** the state or quality of being solemn. **2** a solemn rite or ceremony.

solenoid /sōlənoyd, solənoyd/ > noun a cylindrical coil of wire acting as a magnet when carrying electric current.

DERIVATIVES – **solenoidal** adjective.

ORIGIN – from Greek sōlēn 'channel, pipe'.

soleplate > noun **1** a metal plate forming the base of an electric iron, machine saw, or other machine. **2** a horizontal timber at the base of a wall frame.

sol-fa /solfaa/ (also **tonic sol-fa**) > noun Music a system of naming the notes of the scale used to teach singing, with doh as the keynote of all major keys and lah as the keynote of all minor keys.

ORIGIN – from French sol 'soh' + fa 'fah'.

soli plural of SOLO.

solicit > verb (**solicited**, **soliciting**) **1** ask for or try to obtain (something) from someone. **2** ask for something from (someone). **3** accost someone and offer one's or someone else's services as a prostitute.

DERIVATIVES – **solicitation** noun.

SYNONYMS – **1** ask for, request, seek. **2** beg, call on, entreat, petition.

ORIGIN – Latin sollicitare 'agitate'.

solicitor > noun **1** Brit. a lawyer qualified to deal with conveyancing, draw up wills, advise clients and instruct barristers, and represent clients in lower courts. Compare with BARRISTER. **2** N. Amer. the chief law officer of a city, town, or government department.

COMBINATIONS – **Solicitor General** (pl. **Solicitors General**) (in the UK) the Crown law officer below the Attorney-General or (in Scotland) below the Lord Advocate.

solicitous > adjective showing interest or concern about a person's well-being.

DERIVATIVES – **solicitously** adverb **solicitousness** noun.

SYNONYMS – attentive, caring, concerned, considerate, sympathetic.

solicitude > noun care or concern.

solid > adjective (**solider**, **solidest**) **1** firm and stable in shape; not liquid or fluid. **2** strongly built or made. **3** not hollow or having spaces or gaps. **4** consisting of the same substance throughout. **5** (of time) continuous. **6** able to be relied on; dependable or sound. **7** Geometry three-dimensional. > noun **1** a solid substance or object. **2** (**solids**) food that is not liquid. **3** a three-dimensional body or geometric figure.

DERIVATIVES – **solidity** noun **solidly** adverb **solidness** noun.

SYNONYMS – adjective **1** concrete, firm, hard, rigid, set. **2** durable, sound, stout, strong, sturdy.

ANTONYMS – adjective **1** fluid, liquid. **2** flimsy.

COMBINATIONS – **solid-state** (of an electronic device) employing solid semiconductors, e.g. transistors, as opposed to valves.

ORIGIN – Latin solidus.

solidarity > noun unity resulting from common interests, feelings, or sympathies.

solidify > verb (**solidifies**, **solidified**) make or become hard or solid.

DERIVATIVES – **solidification** noun **solidifier** noun.

SYNONYMS – congeal, clot, coagulate, gel, harden, set.

ANTONYMS – liquefy, melt.

solidus /sollidəss/ > noun (pl. **solidi** /sollidī/) a slash or oblique stroke (/).

ORIGIN – from Latin solidus nummus 'solid coin'; solidus was formerly a name for a shilling, and a slash or solidus was used to separate shillings and pence in writing.

soliloquy /səliləkwi/ > noun (pl. **soliloquies**) an act of speaking one's thoughts aloud when alone or regardless of hearers, especially in a play.

DERIVATIVES – **soliloquise** (also **soliloquize**) verb **soliloquist** noun.

ORIGIN – Latin soliloqium, from solus 'alone' + loqui 'speak'.

solipsism /sollipsiz'm/ > noun the view that the self is all that can be known to exist.

DERIVATIVES – **solipsist** noun **solipsistic** adjective.

ORIGIN – from Latin solus 'alone' + ipse 'self'.

solitaire /sollitair, sollitair/ > noun **1** a game for one player played by removing pegs from a board one at a time by jumping others over them from adjacent holes, the object being to be left with only one peg. **2** the card game patience. **3** a single diamond or other gem in a piece of jewellery.

ORIGIN – French, from Latin solitarius 'solitary'.

solitary > adjective **1** done or existing alone. **2** secluded or isolated. **3** single; only. **4** (of a bee, wasp, etc.) not social or colonial. > noun (pl. **solitaries**) **1** a recluse or hermit. **2** informal solitary confinement.

DERIVATIVES – **solitarily** adverb **solitariness** noun.

SYNONYMS – adjective **1** alone, lonely, single.

COMBINATIONS – **solitary confinement** the isolation of a prisoner in a separate cell as a punishment.

ORIGIN – Latin solitarius, from solus 'alone'.

solitude > noun **1** the state of being alone. **2** a lonely or uninhabited place.

SYNONYMS – **1** isolation, loneliness, retirement, seclusion.

solmisation /solmizaysh'n/ (also **solmization**) > noun Music a system of associating each note of a scale with a particular syllable (typically the sequence doh, ray, me, fah, so, la, te), especially to teach singing.

ORIGIN – French, from sol 'soh' + mi 'me': the names for these and other notes were taken from the words of a Latin hymn.

solo > noun (pl. **solos**) **1** (pl. **solos** or **soli**) a piece of music, song, or dance for one performer. **2** an unaccompanied flight by a pilot. **3** (also **solo whist**) a card game resembling whist in which the players make bids and the highest bidder plays against the others. > adjective & adverb for or done by one person. > verb (**soloes**, **soloed**) **1** perform a solo. **2** fly an aircraft unaccompanied.

ORIGIN – Italian, from Latin solus 'alone'.

soloist > noun a performer of a solo.

Solomon /solləmən/ > noun a very wise person.

DERIVATIVES – **Solomonic** /solləmonnik/ adjective.

COMBINATIONS – **Solomon's seal** a plant with arching stems bearing broad leaves and drooping green and white flowers.

ORIGIN – the name of a king of ancient Israel c.970–c.930 BC, famed for his wisdom.

solstice /solstiss/ > noun each of the two times in the year (at midsummer and midwinter) when the sun reaches its highest or lowest point in the sky at noon, marked by the longest and shortest days.

DERIVATIVES – **solstitial** adjective.

ORIGIN – Latin solstitium, from sol 'sun' + sistere 'stop, be stationary'.

soluble > adjective **1** (of a substance) able to be dissolved, especially in water. **2** able to be solved.

DERIVATIVES – **solubility** noun.

SYNONYMS – **2** explicable, manageable, solvable, understandable.

ANTONYMS – **2** insoluble.

ORIGIN – Latin solubilis, from solvere 'loosen'.

solute /solyoot/ > noun the minor component in a solution, dissolved in the solvent.

solution > noun **1** a means of solving a problem. **2** the correct answer to a puzzle. **3** a liquid mixture in which a quantity of a substance (the solute, often normally a solid) is incorporated within a liquid (the solvent). **4** the process of dissolving or the state of being dissolved.

SYNONYMS – **1** answer, explanation, remedy, resolution.

solve > verb find an answer to, explanation for, or way of dealing with (a problem or mystery).

DERIVATIVES – **solvable** *adjective* **solver** *noun*.

SYNONYMS – answer, explain, remedy, resolve, work out.

ORIGIN – Latin *solvere* 'loosen, unfasten'.

solvent > *adjective* **1** having assets in excess of liabilities. **2** able to dissolve other substances. > *noun* a liquid in which another substance is dissolved to form a solution.

DERIVATIVES – **solvency** *noun*.

COMBINATIONS – **solvent abuse** the use of certain volatile solvents as intoxicants by inhalation, e.g. glue-sniffing.

Som. > *abbreviation* Somerset.

som /sōm/ > *noun* (pl. same) the basic monetary unit of Kyrgyzstan, equal to 100 tiyin.

Somali /səmaali/ > *noun* (pl. same or **Somalis**) **1** a member of a mainly Muslim people of Somalia. **2** the language of this people. **3** a person from Somalia. > *adjective* relating to Somalia.

DERIVATIVES – **Somalian** *adjective & noun*.

somatic /səmattik/ > *adjective* relating to the body, especially as distinct from the mind.

DERIVATIVES – **somatically** *adverb*.

ORIGIN – Greek *sōmatikos*, from *sōma* 'body'.

somatotrophin /sōmətətrōfin/ > *noun* a growth hormone secreted by the pituitary gland.

sombre (US also **somber**) > *adjective* **1** dark or dull in colour or tone. **2** oppressively solemn or sober.

DERIVATIVES – **sombrely** *adverb* **sombreness** *noun*.

SYNONYMS – **1** dark, drab, dull, sober, subdued. **2** grave, serious, sober, solemn, unsmiling.

ANTONYMS – **1** bright. **2** cheerful.

wordpower facts
Sombre

Unlikely as it may seem, the words **sombre** and **sombrero** come from the same source, Latin *umbra* 'shade'. **Sombre** entered English from French and is based on Latin *sub* 'under' + *umbra*, whereas **sombrero**, a hat that provides shade from the sun, is a Spanish word that comes from *sombra* 'shade', which is descended from *umbra*. The same root is shared by the English words **adumbrate**, **penumbra**, **umbrage** (originally 'shadowy outline', then 'ground for suspicion' and thus 'offence'), and **umbrella** (originally a word for a parasol or similar article giving protection from the sun).

sombrero /sombrairō/ > *noun* (pl. **sombreros**) a broad-brimmed felt or straw hat, typically worn in Mexico and the south-western US.

some > *determiner* **1** an unspecified amount or number of. **2** referring to an unknown or unspecified person or thing. **3** (used with a number) approximately. **4** a considerable amount or number of. **5** at least a small amount or number of. **6** expressing admiration. > *pronoun* **1** an unspecified number or amount of people or things. **2** at least a small number or amount of people or things.

IDIOMS – **and then some** informal and plenty more than that.

-some[1] > *suffix* forming adjectives meaning: **1** productive of: *loathsome*. **2** characterised by being: *wholesome*. **3** apt to: *tiresome*.

-some[2] > *suffix* (forming nouns) denoting a group of a specified number: *foursome*.

somebody > *pronoun* someone.

some day (also **someday**) > *adverb* at some time in the future.

somehow > *adverb* **1** by one means or another. **2** for an unknown or unspecified reason.

someone > *pronoun* **1** an unknown or unspecified person. **2** a person of importance or authority.

someplace > *adverb & pronoun* informal, chiefly N. Amer. somewhere.

somersault > *noun* **1** an acrobatic movement in which a person turns head over heels in the air or on the ground and finishes on their feet. **2** a dramatic upset or reversal of policy or opinion. > *verb* perform a somersault.

ORIGIN – Old French *sombresault*, from Latin *supra* 'above' + *saltus* 'a leap'.

something > *pronoun* **1** an unspecified or unknown thing. **2** an unspecified or unknown amount or degree. > *adverb* informal used for emphasis with a following adjective.

IDIOMS – **quite** (or **really**) **something** informal something impressive or notable. **something else** informal an exceptional person or thing. **something of** to some degree. **thirty-something** (or **forty-something**, etc.) informal an unspecified age between thirty and forty (or forty and fifty, etc.).

sometime > *adverb* at some unspecified or unknown time. > *adjective* former.

sometimes > *adverb* occasionally, rather than all the time.

somewhat > *adverb* to some extent.

IDIOMS – **somewhat of** something of.

somewhere > *adverb* **1** in or to an unspecified or unknown place. **2** used to indicate an approximate amount. > *pronoun* some unspecified place.

IDIOMS – **get somewhere** informal make progress.

sommelier /somməlyay, səmelyay/ > *noun* a waiter who serves wine.

ORIGIN – French, 'butler'.

somnambulism /somnambyooliz'm/ > *noun* sleepwalking.

DERIVATIVES – **somnambulant** *adjective* **somnambulist** *noun* **somnambulistic** *adjective*.

ORIGIN – from Latin *somnus* 'sleep' + *ambulare* 'to walk'.

somnolent /somnələnt/ > *adjective* **1** sleepy; drowsy. **2** inducing drowsiness.

DERIVATIVES – **somnolence** *noun* **somnolently** *adverb*.

ORIGIN – Latin *somnolentus*, from *somnus* 'sleep'.

son > *noun* **1** a boy or man in relation to his parents. **2** a male descendant. **3** (**the Son**) (in Christian belief) the second person of the Trinity; Christ. **4** (also **my son**) used as a form of address for a boy or younger man.

WORDFINDER – filial (*relating to a son*), filicide (*murder of one's own son*).

IDIOMS – **son-in-law** (pl. **sons-in-law**) the husband of one's daughter. **son of a bitch** (pl. **sons of bitches**) informal used as a general term of abuse. **son of a gun** (pl. **sons of guns**) informal a humorous way of addressing or referring to someone. [ORIGIN – with reference to the guns carried on ships: said to have been applied originally to babies born at sea to women allowed to accompany their husbands.] **Son of Man** Jesus Christ.

sonar /sōnaar/ > *noun* **1** a system for the detection of objects under water based on the emission and measured reflection of sound pulses. **2** an apparatus used for this.

ORIGIN – from *so(und) na(vigation and) r(anging)*, on the pattern of *radar*.

sonata /sənaatə/ > *noun* a classical composition for an instrumental soloist, often with a piano accompaniment.

ORIGIN – Italian, 'sounded'.

son et lumière /son ay loomyair/ > *noun* an entertainment held by night at a historic monument or building, telling its history by the use of lighting effects and recorded sound.

ORIGIN – French, 'sound and light'.

song > *noun* **1** a poem or other set of words set to music. **2** singing or vocal music. **3** the musical phrases uttered by some birds, whales, and insects. **4** a poem, especially one in rhymed stanzas.

WORDFINDER – *kinds of song:* anthem, aria, ballad, calypso, ditty, fado, glee, hymn, lament, lied, lullaby, madrigal, psalm, round, roundelay, shanty, spiritual.

IDIOMS – **for a song** informal very cheaply.

on song Brit. informal performing well. **a song and dance** informal a fuss.

SYNONYMS – **1** air, ditty, melody, number, tune.

COMBINATIONS – **songbird** a bird with a musical song. **song cycle** a set of related songs forming a single musical entity. **songsmith** informal a writer of popular songs. **song thrush** a thrush with a buff spotted breast and a song in which phrases are repeated three or four times. **songwriter** a writer of songs or the music for them.

ORIGIN – Old English, related to SING.

songster > *noun* (fem. **songstress**) **1** a person who sings. **2** a songbird.

sonic > *adjective* relating to or using sound waves.

DERIVATIVES – **sonically** *adverb*.

COMBINATIONS – **sonic boom** an explosive noise caused by the shock wave from an aircraft or other object travelling faster than the speed of sound.

ORIGIN – from Latin *sonus* 'sound'.

sonics > *plural noun* musical sounds artificially produced or reproduced.

sonnet > *noun* a poem of fourteen lines using any of a number of formal rhyme schemes, in English typically having ten syllables per line.

ORIGIN – French, or Italian *sonetto* 'little sound'.

sonneteer /sonni**teer**/ > *noun* a writer of sonnets.

sonny > *noun* informal **1** a familiar form of address to a young boy. **2** (also **Sonny Jim**) a humorous or patronising way of addressing a man.

sonogram > *noun* **1** a graph showing the distribution of energy at different frequencies in a sound. **2** a visual image produced from an ultrasound examination.

DERIVATIVES – **sonograph** *noun* **sonographic** *adjective* **sonography** *noun*.

ORIGIN – from Latin *sonus* 'sound'.

sonorous /**sonn**ərəss, sə**nōr**əss/ > *adjective* **1** (of a sound) deep and full. **2** (of speech) using imposing or grandiose language.

DERIVATIVES – **sonority** *noun* **sonorously** *adverb* **sonorousness** *noun*.

SYNONYMS – **1** booming, resonant, resounding, rich.

ORIGIN – Latin *sonorus*, from *sonor* 'sound'.

sool /sool/ > *verb* chiefly Austral./NZ **1** (of a dog) attack or worry. **2** urge or goad into doing something.

ORIGIN – variant of dialect *sowl* 'seize by the ears'.

soon > *adverb* **1** in or after a short time. **2** relatively early: *it's a pity you have to leave so soon.* **3** used to indicate a preference: *I'd just as soon Tim did it.*

IDIOMS – **no sooner than** at the very moment that. **sooner or later** eventually.

DERIVATIVES – **soonish** *adverb*.

ORIGIN – Old English, 'immediately'.

soot > *noun* a black powdery or flaky substance produced by the incomplete burning of organic matter.

WORDFINDER – fuliginous (*relating to soot*).

sooth /sooth/ > *noun* archaic truth.

IDIOMS – **in sooth** truly.

ORIGIN – Old English, 'genuine, true'.

soothe > *verb* **1** gently calm (a person or their feelings); appease. **2** relieve (pain or discomfort).

DERIVATIVES – **soother** *noun* **soothing** *adjective* **soothingly** *adverb*.

SYNONYMS – **1** appease, calm, pacify, quieten, subdue. **2** alleviate, assuage, ease, relieve.

ANTONYMS – **1** agitate. **2** aggravate.

ORIGIN – Old English, 'verify, show to be true', from SOOTH; early senses included 'corroborate (a statement)' and 'humour (a person) by agreeing with them'.

soothsayer > *noun* a person supposed to be able to foresee the future.

DERIVATIVES – **soothsaying** *noun*.

ORIGIN – from SOOTH: originally in the sense 'person who speaks the truth'.

sooty > *adjective* (**sootier**, **sootiest**) covered with or coloured like soot.

sop > *noun* **1** a thing given or done to appease or bribe someone. **2** a piece of bread dipped in gravy, soup, or sauce. > *verb* (**sopped**, **sopping**) (**sop up**) soak up (liquid).

> ### wordpower facts
> #### Sop
> In Old English a **sop** (then spelled *sopp*) was a piece of bread dipped in water, wine, or other liquid before being eaten or cooked. The word is probably from the base of Old English *sūpan* 'sup', the base of **sip**, **soup**, **sup**, and **supper**. The main modern sense, of something given or done to appease or bribe someone, alludes to a story in the *Aeneid* by the Roman poet Virgil: when Aeneas visited the Underworld he managed to pass Cerberus, the monstrous three-headed watchdog, by throwing the creature a piece of bread soaked in honey.

sophism /**soff**iz'm/ > *noun* a false argument, especially one used to deceive.

ORIGIN – Greek *sophisma* 'clever device', from *sophizesthai* 'devise, become wise'.

sophist /**soff**ist/ > *noun* a person who uses clever but false arguments.

DERIVATIVES – **sophistic** /sə**fist**ik/ *adjective* **sophistical** /sə**fist**ik'l/ *adjective*.

sophisticate > *verb* **1** make more discerning and aware of complex issues through education or experience. **2** make more complex or refined. > *noun* a sophisticated person.

DERIVATIVES – **sophistication** *noun*.

> ### wordpower facts
> #### Sophisticate
> The words **sophisticate** and **sophisticated** entered English in the Middle Ages, the verb meaning 'mix with a foreign substance' and the adjective 'adulterated'. The root is the medieval Latin verb *sophisticare* 'tamper with', which goes back to Greek *sophistēs* 'deviser, sophist' and ultimately to *sophos* 'wise': the **sophists** were paid teachers of philosophy and rhetoric who became associated with moral scepticism and clever but dishonest reasoning, or **sophistry**. Until the late 19th century, when it acquired the sense 'worldly and experienced', **sophisticated** meant 'adulterated' or 'deprived of natural simplicity', and did not take on the positive modern meaning 'highly developed and complex' until 1945. The shift of sense probably occurred first in the adjective *unsophisticated*, which moved from 'uncorrupted' via 'innocent' to 'inexperienced, uncultured'.

sophisticated > *adjective* **1** (of a machine, system, or technique) highly developed and complex. **2** having or showing worldly experience and taste in matters of culture or fashion. **3** appealing to sophisticated people.

DERIVATIVES – **sophisticatedly** *adverb*.

SYNONYMS – **1** advanced, complex, elaborate, innovative, intricate. **2** cosmopolitan, cultivated, stylish, urbane, worldly.

sophistry /**soff**istri/ > *noun* (pl. **sophistries**) **1** the use of false arguments, especially to deceive. **2** a false argument.

sophomore /**soff**əmor/ > *noun* N. Amer. a second-year university or high-school student.

DERIVATIVES – **sophomoric** *adjective*.

ORIGIN – probably from *sophum*, *sophom* (obsolete variants of SOPHISM).

soporific /soppə**riff**ik/ > *adjective* inducing drowsiness or sleep. > *noun* a soporific drug or other agent.

DERIVATIVES – **soporifically** *adverb*.

SYNONYMS – *adjective* deadening, hypnotic, sedative, somnolent.

ORIGIN – from Latin *sopor* 'sleep'.

sopping > *adjective* wet through.

soppy > *adjective* (**soppier, soppiest**) Brit. informal **1** self-indulgently sentimental. **2** lacking spirit; feeble.

DERIVATIVES – **soppily** *adverb* **soppiness** *noun*.

ORIGIN – from **SOP**: originally in the sense 'soaked with water'.

soprano /səˈpraanō/ > *noun* (pl. **sopranos**) **1** the highest singing voice. **2** (before another noun) denoting an instrument of a high or the highest pitch in its family: *a soprano saxophone*.

ORIGIN – Italian, from *sopra* 'above'.

sorbet /ˈsorbay, ˈsorbit/ > *noun* a water ice.

ORIGIN – French, from an Arabic word meaning 'to drink'; related to **SHERBET**.

sorcerer > *noun* (fem. **sorceress**) a person believed to practise magic; a wizard.

DERIVATIVES – **sorcerous** *adjective* **sorcery** *noun*.

SYNONYMS – magician, magus, warlock, witch, wizard.

ORIGIN – Old French *sorcier*, from Latin *sors* 'lot', also (in plural) 'responses made by an oracle'.

sordid > *adjective* **1** involving dishonourable actions and motives. **2** dirty or squalid.

DERIVATIVES – **sordidly** *adverb* **sordidness** *noun*.

SYNONYMS – **1** dishonourable, ignoble, seedy, shabby, sleazy, squalid.

ANTONYMS – **1** respectable, wholesome.

ORIGIN – Latin *sordidus*, from *sordere* 'be dirty'.

sore > *adjective* **1** (of part of one's body) giving pain. **2** suffering pain. **3** severe; urgent: *in sore need*. **4** informal, chiefly N. Amer. upset and angry. > *noun* **1** a raw or painful place on the body. **2** a source of distress or annoyance. > *adverb* archaic extremely; severely: *sore afraid*.

IDIOMS – **sore point** an issue about which someone feels distressed or annoyed. **stand (or stick) out like a sore thumb** be quite obviously different.

DERIVATIVES – **soreness** *noun*.

SYNONYMS – *adjective* **1** aching, hurting, painful, sensitive.

sorely > *adverb* extremely; badly.

sorghum /ˈsorgəm/ > *noun* a cereal native to warm regions, grown for grain and animal feed.

ORIGIN – Italian *sorgo*, perhaps from a variant of Latin *syricum* 'Syrian'.

sororal /səˈrorəl/ > *adjective* formal of or like a sister or sisters.

ORIGIN – from Latin *soror* 'sister'.

sorority /səˈrorriti/ > *noun* (pl. **sororities**) N. Amer. a society for female students in a university or college.

sorrel¹ > *noun* an edible plant of the dock family with arrow-shaped leaves and a bitter flavour.

COMBINATIONS – **wood sorrel** a woodland plant with clover-like leaves and pink or white flowers.

ORIGIN – Old French *sorele*; related to **SOUR**.

sorrel² > *noun* **1** a light reddish-brown colour. **2** a horse with a sorrel coat.

ORIGIN – Old French *sorel*, from *sor* 'yellowish'.

sorrow > *noun* **1** deep distress caused by loss or disappointment. **2** a cause of sorrow. > *verb* feel sorrow.

SYNONYMS – *noun* grief, heartache, misery, sadness, unhappiness.

ANTONYMS – happiness, joy.

sorrowful > *adjective* **1** feeling or showing sorrow. **2** causing sorrow.

DERIVATIVES – **sorrowfully** *adverb* **sorrowfulness** *noun*.

SYNONYMS – **1** grief-stricken, melancholy, miserable, sad, unhappy.

ANTONYMS – cheerful, happy.

sorry > *adjective* (**sorrier, sorriest**) **1** feeling distress or pity through sympathy with someone else's misfortune. **2** feeling or expressing regret or penitence. **3** in a poor or pitiful state. **4** unpleasant and regrettable: *a sorry business*.

DERIVATIVES – **sorriness** *noun*.

SYNONYMS – **1** compassionate, concerned, sympathetic, understanding. **2** apologetic, contrite, penitent, regretful, remorseful.

ANTONYMS – **1** uncaring, unsympathetic. **2** unconcerned, unrepentant.

ORIGIN – Old English, 'pained, distressed'; related to **SORE**.

sort > *noun* **1** a category of people or things with common features. **2** informal a person with a specified nature: *a friendly sort*. **3** Computing the arrangement of data in a prescribed sequence. > *verb* **1** arrange systematically in groups. **2** (often **sort out**) separate from a mixed group. **3** (**sort out**) resolve (a problem or difficulty). **4** (**sort out**) informal deal with (a troublesome person).

IDIOMS – **in some sort** to some extent. **it takes all sorts to make a world** proverb people vary greatly in character, tastes, and abilities, and one should be tolerant of what may appear to be strange behaviour. **of a sort** (or **of sorts**) of a somewhat unusual or inferior kind. **out of sorts** slightly unwell or unhappy. **sort of** informal to some extent.

DERIVATIVES – **sortable** *adjective* **sorter** *noun*.

USAGE – when using **sort** to refer to a plural noun, avoid the ungrammatical construction *these sort*: say *these sorts of questions are not relevant* rather than *these sort of questions are not relevant*.

SYNONYMS – *noun* **1** category, class, division, kind, order, variety. *verb* **1** arrange, classify, grade, order, rank. **3** (**sort out**) deal with, manage, resolve, solve, straighten out.

ORIGIN – Old French *sorte*, from Latin *sors* 'lot, condition'.

sorted > *adjective* Brit. informal **1** organised; arranged. **2** emotionally well balanced.

sortie > *noun* **1** an attack by troops coming out from a position of defence. **2** an operational flight by a single military aircraft. **3** a short trip. > *verb* (**sorties, sortied, sortieing**) make a sortie.

ORIGIN – French, from *sortir* 'go out'.

SOS > *noun* **1** an international coded signal of extreme distress, used especially by ships at sea. **2** an urgent appeal for help.

ORIGIN – letters chosen as easy to transmit and recognise in Morse code; by folk etymology an abbreviation of *save our souls*.

so-so > *adjective* neither very good nor very bad; mediocre.

sot > *noun* a habitual drunkard.

DERIVATIVES – **sottish** *adjective*.

ORIGIN – Latin *sottus* 'foolish person'.

sotto voce /ˌsottō ˈvōchay/ > *adverb & adjective* in a quiet voice.

ORIGIN – from Italian *sotto* 'under' + *voce* 'voice'.

sou /soo/ > *noun* **1** a former French coin of low value. **2** informal a very small amount of money.

ORIGIN – French, from Latin *solidus* 'solid': see **SOLDIER**.

soubrette /sooˈbret/ > *noun* a pert maidservant or similar minor female role in a comedy.

ORIGIN – Provençal *soubreto*, feminine of *soubret* 'coy'.

soubriquet > *noun* variant spelling of **SOBRIQUET**.

soufflé > *noun* a light, spongy baked dish made by mixing egg yolks and another ingredient such as cheese or fruit with stiffly beaten egg whites.

ORIGIN – French, 'blown'.

sough /sow, suf/ > *verb* literary (of the wind, sea, etc.) make a moaning, whistling, or rushing sound.

sought past and past participle of **SEEK**.

COMBINATIONS – **sought after** much in demand.

souk /sook/ (also **suq**) > *noun* an Arab market.

ORIGIN – Arabic.

soukous /ˈsookooss/ > *noun* a style of African popular music with syncopated rhythms and intricate contrasting guitar melodies.

ORIGIN – perhaps from French *secouer* 'to shake'.

soul > *noun* **1** the spiritual element of a person, regarded as an immortal entity. **2** a person's moral or emotional nature. **3** emotional or intellectual energy or integrity. **4** a person regarded as the embodiment of a particular quality. **5** an individual, often of a specified type: *poor soul.* **6** (also **soul music**) a kind of music incorporating elements of gospel music and rhythm and blues, popularised by American blacks.

WORDFINDER – animism (*belief that inanimate objects have souls*), metempsychosis (*supposed movement of the soul into a different body at death*), psychic (*relating to the soul or mind*), reincarnation (*supposed rebirth of a soul in a new body*).

IDIOMS – **lost soul** a soul that is damned. **upon my soul** *dated* an exclamation of surprise.

SYNONYMS – **1** inner self, psyche, spirit.

COMBINATIONS – **soul-destroying** (of an activity) unbearably monotonous. **soul food** food traditionally associated with black people of the southern US. **soulmate** a person ideally suited to another. **soul-searching** close examination of one's emotions and motives.

soulful > *adjective* expressing deep and typically sorrowful feeling.

DERIVATIVES – **soulfully** *adverb* **soulfulness** *noun.*

soulless > *adjective* **1** lacking character and individuality. **2** (of an activity) tedious and uninspiring. **3** lacking human feelings.

DERIVATIVES – **soullessly** *adverb* **soullessness** *noun.*

sound¹ > *noun* **1** vibrations which travel through the air or another medium and are sensed by the ear. **2** a thing that can be heard. **3** music, speech, and sound effects accompanying a film or broadcast. **4** an idea or impression conveyed by words. > *verb* **1** emit or cause to emit sound. **2** say (something); utter: *he sounded a warning.* **3** convey a specified impression: *the job sounds great.* **4** (**sound off**) express one's opinions loudly or forcefully.

DERIVATIVES – **soundless** *adjective* **soundlessly** *adverb.*

SYNONYMS – *noun* **2** noise, report, tone.

COMBINATIONS – **sound barrier** the speed of sound, regarded as presenting problems of drag, controllability, etc. for aircraft. **soundboard** (also **sounding board**) a thin board under the strings of a piano or similar instrument to increase the sound produced. **soundbox** the hollow chamber forming the body of a stringed instrument and providing resonance. **sound effect** a sound other than speech or music made artificially for use in a play, film, etc. **sound system** a set of equipment for the reproduction and amplification of sound. **sound wave** a wave of alternate compression and rarefaction by which sound travels through a medium.

ORIGIN – Latin *sonus.*

sound² > *adjective* **1** in good condition. **2** based on reason or judgement. **3** financially secure. **4** competent or reliable. **5** (of sleep) deep and unbroken. **6** severe or thorough: *a sound thrashing.* > *adverb* soundly.

DERIVATIVES – **soundly** *adverb* **soundness** *noun.*

SYNONYMS – **1** solid, strong, sturdy, undamaged, unimpaired. **2** cogent, convincing, logical, plausible, sensible.

ANTONYMS – **1** flimsy, unsound, weak. **2** unsound.

sound³ > *verb* **1** ascertain the depth of water in (the sea, a lake, etc.) by means of a line or pole or using sound echoes. **2** (**sound out**) question (someone) discreetly or cautiously as to their opinions or feelings. **3** Medicine examine (the bladder or other internal cavity) with a long surgical probe.

DERIVATIVES – **sounder** *noun.*

ORIGIN – Old French *sonder*, from Latin *sub-* 'below' + *unda* 'wave'.

sound⁴ > *noun* a narrow stretch of water forming an inlet or connecting two larger bodies of water.

ORIGIN – Old Norse *sund* 'swimming, strait'; related to SWIM.

sound bite > *noun* a short extract from a recorded interview, chosen for its aptness or expressive impact.

sounding¹ > *noun* **1** the action of sounding the depth of water. **2** a measurement taken by sounding. **3** (**soundings**) information or evidence ascertained before taking action.

COMBINATIONS – **sounding line** a weighted line used to measure the depth of water under a boat.

sounding² > *adjective* archaic producing sound, especially of a loud or resonant nature.

COMBINATIONS – **sounding board 1** a board over or behind a pulpit or stage to reflect a speaker's voice forward. **2** a soundboard. **3** a person or group whose reactions to ideas or opinions are used as a test of their validity or likely success.

soundproof > *adjective* preventing the passage of sound. > *verb* make soundproof.

soundscape > *noun* a piece of music considered in terms of its component sounds.

soundtrack > *noun* the sound accompaniment to a film.

soup > *noun* a savoury liquid dish made by boiling meat, fish, or vegetables in stock or water. > *verb* (**soup up**) *informal* **1** increase the power and efficiency of (an engine). **2** make more elaborate or impressive.

WORDFINDER – *types of soup:* bird's nest soup, bisque, borscht, bouillabaisse, bouillon, chowder, cock-a-leekie, consommé, gazpacho, gumbo, minestrone, mock turtle soup, mulligatawny, oxtail, pot-au-feu, Scotch broth, vichyssoise.

IDIOMS – **in the soup** *informal* in trouble.

COMBINATIONS – **soup kitchen** a place where free food is served to the homeless or destitute.

ORIGIN – Old French *soupe* 'sop, broth (poured on slices of bread)', from Latin *suppa.*

soupçon /ˈsoopson/ > *noun* a very small quantity.

ORIGIN – French, from Latin *suspectio* 'suspicion'.

soupy > *adjective* (**soupier**, **soupiest**) **1** having the appearance or consistency of soup. **2** *informal* mawkishly sentimental.

DERIVATIVES – **soupily** *adverb* **soupiness** *noun.*

sour > *adjective* **1** having a sharp taste like lemon or vinegar. **2** tasting or smelling rancid from fermentation or staleness. **3** resentful, bitter, or angry. > *noun* a cocktail made by mixing a spirit with lemon or lime juice. > *verb* make or become sour.

IDIOMS – **go** (or **turn**) **sour** become less pleasant; turn out badly. **sour grapes** an attitude in which someone pretends to despise something because they cannot have it themselves. [ORIGIN – with allusion to Aesop's fable *The Fox and the Grapes.*]

DERIVATIVES – **sourish** *adjective* **sourly** *adverb* **sourness** *noun.*

SYNONYMS – *adjective* **1** acid, acidic, sharp, tart.

COMBINATIONS – **sour cream** cream deliberately fermented by adding certain bacteria. **sourdough 1** leaven for making bread, consisting of fermenting dough, originally that left over from a previous baking. **2** bread made using such leaven.

source > *noun* **1** a place, person, or thing from which something originates. **2** a spring or other place from which a river or stream issues. **3** a person, book, or document that provides information or evidence. **4** *technical* a body or process by which something enters a system. The opposite of SINK². > *verb* obtain from a particular source.

SYNONYMS – *noun* **1** derivation, origin, root, starting point.

ORIGIN – Old French *sourse*, from Latin *surgere* 'to rise'.

sourpuss > *noun* *informal* a bad-tempered or sullen person.

soursop > *noun* a large acidic custard apple with white fibrous flesh.

sousaphone /ˈsoozəfōn/ > *noun* an American form of tuba with a wide bell pointing forward above the player's head.

ORIGIN – named after the American composer J. P. *Sousa* (1854–1932), on the pattern of *saxophone.*

souse /sowss/ > *verb* **1** soak in or drench with liquid. **2** (**soused**) (of gherkins, fish, etc.) pickled or marinaded: *soused herring.* **3** (**soused**) *informal* drunk. > *noun* **1** liquid used for pickling. **2** *informal* a drunkard.

ORIGIN – Old French *sous* 'pickle'; related to **SALT**.

soutane /sootaan/ > *noun* a type of cassock worn by Roman Catholic priests.

ORIGIN – Italian *sottana*, from *sotto* 'under'.

south > *noun* 1 the direction towards the horizon on the right-hand side of a person facing east, opposite the north. 2 the southern part of a country, region, or town. > *adjective* 1 lying towards, near, or facing the south. 2 (of a wind) blowing from the south. > *adverb* to or towards the south.

WORDFINDER – meridional (*relating to the south*).

IDIOMS – **south by east** (or **west**) between south and south-south-east (or south-south-west).

DERIVATIVES – **southbound** *adjective & adverb*.

COMBINATIONS – **south-south-east** (or **south-south-west**) the compass point or direction midway between south and south-east (or south-west).

South African > *noun* a person from South Africa. > *adjective* relating to South Africa.

South American > *noun* a person from South America. > *adjective* relating to South America.

south-east > *noun* 1 the point of the horizon midway between south and east. 2 the south-eastern part of a country, region, or town. > *adjective* 1 lying towards, near, or facing the south-east. 2 (of a wind) from the south-east. > *adverb* to or towards the south-east.

DERIVATIVES – **south-eastern** *adjective*.

south-easterly > *adjective & adverb* in a south-eastward position or direction. > *noun* a wind blowing from the south-east.

south-eastward > *adverb* (also **south-eastwards**) towards the south-east. > *adjective* situated in, directed toward, or facing the south-east.

southerly > *adjective & adverb* 1 in a southward position or direction. 2 (of a wind) blowing from the south. > *noun* a wind blowing from the south.

southern > *adjective* 1 situated in, directed towards, or facing the south. 2 (usu. **Southern**) living in, coming from, or characteristic of the south.

DERIVATIVES – **southernmost** *adjective*.

COMBINATIONS – **Southern Lights** the aurora australis.

southerner > *noun* a person from the south of a particular region or country.

southing > *noun* 1 distance travelled or measured southward. 2 a figure or line representing southward distance on a map.

southpaw > *noun* 1 a left-handed boxer who leads with the right hand. 2 informal, chiefly N. Amer. a left-hander in any sphere.

southward > *adjective* in a southerly direction. > *adverb* (also **southwards**) towards the south.

south-west > *noun* 1 the point of the horizon midway between south and west. 2 the south-western part of a country, region, or town. > *adjective* 1 lying towards, near, or facing the south-west. 2 (of a wind) from the south-west. > *adverb* to or towards the south-west.

DERIVATIVES – **south-western** *adjective*.

south-westerly > *adjective & adverb* in a south-westward position or direction. > *noun* a wind blowing from the south-west.

south-westward > *adverb* (also **south-westwards**) towards the south-west. > *adjective* situated in, directed towards, or facing the south-west.

souvenir /soovəneer/ > *noun* a thing that is kept as a reminder of a person, place, or event.

SYNONYMS – keepsake, memento, reminder, token.

ORIGIN – French, from *souvenir* 'remember'.

sou'wester /sow-westər/ > *noun* a waterproof hat with a broad brim or flap covering the back of the neck.

sovereign > *noun* 1 a king or queen who is the supreme ruler of a country. 2 a former British gold coin worth one pound sterling. > *adjective* 1 possessing supreme or ultimate power. 2 (of a nation or its affairs) acting or done independently and without outside interference.

SYNONYMS – emperor, king, monarch, queen, ruler.

ORIGIN – Old French *soverain*, from Latin *super* 'above'.

sovereignty > *noun* (pl. **sovereignties**) 1 supreme power or authority. 2 a self-governing state.

soviet /sōviet, soviet/ > *noun* 1 (**Soviet**) a citizen of the former Soviet Union. 2 an elected council in the former Soviet Union. 3 a revolutionary council of workers or peasants in Russia before 1917. > *adjective* (**Soviet**) of or concerning the former Soviet Union.

DERIVATIVES – **Sovietise** (also **Sovietize**) *verb* **Sovietism** *noun*.

ORIGIN – Russian *sovet* 'council'.

Sovietologist /sōviətolləjist, sov-/ > *noun* an expert on the former Soviet Union.

sow[1] /sō/ > *verb* (past **sowed** /sōd/; past participle **sown** /sōn/ or **sowed**) 1 plant (seed) by scattering it on or in the earth. 2 plant (an area) with seed. 3 disseminate or introduce (something unwelcome).

DERIVATIVES – **sower** *noun*.

sow[2] /sow/ > *noun* an adult female pig.

IDIOMS – **you can't make a silk purse out of a sow's ear** proverb you can't create a fine product from inferior materials.

soy > *noun* 1 (also **soy sauce**) a sauce made with fermented soya beans, used in Chinese and Japanese cooking. 2 another term for **SOYA**.

ORIGIN – Japanese, from Chinese words meaning 'salted beans' and 'oil'.

soya > *noun* an Asian plant of the pea family which produces an edible bean that is high in protein.

WORDFINDER – tofu (*soya bean curd*).

COMBINATIONS – **soya milk** a suspension of soya bean flour in water, used as a fat-free substitute for milk.

sozzled > *adjective* informal very drunk.

SP > *abbreviation* starting price.

spa > *noun* 1 a mineral spring considered to have health-giving properties. 2 a place or resort with a mineral spring.

ORIGIN – from *Spa*, a small town in eastern Belgium noted for its mineral springs.

space > *noun* 1 unoccupied ground or area. 2 a free or unoccupied area or expanse. 3 the dimensions of height, depth, and width within which all things exist and move. 4 a blank between typed or written words or characters. 5 (also **outer space**) the physical universe beyond the earth's atmosphere. 6 an interval of time: *both cars were stolen in the space of a few hours*. 7 the freedom and scope to live and develop as one wishes. > *verb* 1 position (two or more items) at a distance from one another. 2 (**be spaced out** or chiefly N. Amer. **space out**) informal be or become euphoric or disorientated, especially from taking drugs.

DERIVATIVES – **spacer** *noun* **spacing** *noun*.

SYNONYMS – 1 capacity, latitude, room, scope. 2 area, expanse, gap, interval, stretch.

COMBINATIONS – **space bar** a long key on a typewriter or computer keyboard for making a space between words. **space cadet** informal a person perceived as being out of touch with reality. **space capsule** a small spacecraft or the part of a larger one that contains the instruments or crew, designed to be returned to earth. **spacecraft** a vehicle used for travelling in space. **spaceman** a male astronaut. **space probe** an unmanned exploratory spacecraft. **spaceship** a manned spacecraft. **space shuttle** a rocket-launched spacecraft able to land like an unpowered aircraft, used for journeys between earth and craft orbiting the earth. **space station** a large artificial satellite used as a long-term base for manned operations in space. **spacesuit** a sealed and pressurised suit designed to allow an astronaut to survive in space. **space–time** Physics time and three-dimensional space regarded as fused in a four-dimensional continuum. **space walk** an excursion by an astronaut outside a spacecraft.

ORIGIN – Old French *espace*, from Latin *spatium*.

space age > *noun* (**the space age**) the era starting when the exploration of space became possible. > *adjective* (**space-age**) very modern; technologically advanced.

spacey (also **spacy**) > *adjective* (**spacier**, **spaciest**) informal 1 out of touch with reality. 2 (of popular music) drifting and ethereal.

spacial > *adjective* variant spelling of SPATIAL.

spacious > *adjective* (of a room or building) having plenty of space.
DERIVATIVES – **spaciously** *adverb* **spaciousness** *noun*.
SYNONYMS – capacious, commodious, generous, roomy, sizeable.
ANTONYMS – cramped, poky.

spade¹ > *noun* a tool with a rectangular metal blade and a long handle, used for digging. > *verb* 1 dig over with a spade. 2 move or lift with a spade.
IDIOMS – **call a spade a spade** speak plainly and frankly.
COMBINATIONS – **spadework** hard or routine preparatory work.

spade² > *noun* 1 (**spades**) one of the four suits in a pack of playing cards, denoted by a black inverted heart-shaped figure with a small stalk. 2 informal, offensive a black person.
IDIOMS – **in spades** informal in large amounts or to a high degree.
ORIGIN – Italian, plural of *spada* 'sword', from Greek *spathē*.

spadix /**spay**diks/ > *noun* (pl. **spadices** /**spay**diseez/) Botany a spike of minute flowers closely arranged round a fleshy axis and typically enclosed in a spathe, characteristic of the arums.
ORIGIN – Greek, 'palm branch'.

spaghetti /spə**getti**/ > *plural noun* pasta made in solid strings, between macaroni and vermicelli in thickness.
COMBINATIONS – **spaghetti western** informal a western film made in Europe by an Italian director.
ORIGIN – Italian, 'little strings'.

spaghetti Bolognese /bollə**nayz**/ > *noun* a dish of spaghetti with a sauce of minced beef, tomato, onion, and herbs.
ORIGIN – Italian, 'spaghetti of Bologna'.

spake archaic or literary past of SPEAK.

spall /spawl/ > *noun* a splinter or chip of rock. > *verb* break into spalls.

spam > *noun* 1 trademark a canned meat product made mainly from ham. 2 informal irrelevant or inappropriate messages sent on the Internet to a large number of users. > *verb* (**spammed**, **spamming**) informal send the same email message indiscriminately to (large numbers of users).
DERIVATIVES – **spammer** *noun*.
ORIGIN – apparently from the first two and last two letters of *spiced ham*; the Internet sense is thought to derive from a sketch by the British 'Monty Python' comedy group, set in a cafe in which every item on the menu includes spam.

span > *noun* 1 the full extent of something from end to end. 2 the length of time for which something lasts. 3 a wingspan. 4 a part of a bridge between piers or supports. 5 the maximum distance between the tips of the thumb and little finger, taken as the basis of a measurement equal to 9 inches. > *verb* (**spanned**, **spanning**) extend across or over.
SYNONYMS – *noun* 1 extent, length, reach, spread, width. 2 duration, length, period, space, stretch.
ORIGIN – Old English, 'distance between thumb and little finger'.

spandrel /**span**dril/ > *noun* Architecture the almost triangular space between the curve of an arch, a wall or an adjoining arch, and the ceiling or framework above.
ORIGIN – perhaps from Old French *espaundre* 'expand'.

spangle > *noun* 1 a small, thin piece of glittering material used to ornament a garment; a sequin. 2 a spot of bright colour or light. > *verb* cover with spangles.
DERIVATIVES – **spangly** *adjective*.
ORIGIN – from obsolete *spang* 'glittering ornament', from Dutch *spange* 'buckle'.

Spaniard /**span**yərd/ > *noun* a person from Spain.
ORIGIN – Old French *Espaignart*, from *Espaigne* 'Spain'.

spaniel > *noun* a breed of dog with a long silky coat and drooping ears.
ORIGIN – Old French *espaigneul* 'Spanish dog', from Latin *Hispaniolus* 'Spanish'.

Spanish > *noun* the main language of Spain and of much of Central and South America. > *adjective* relating to Spain or the Spanish language.
WORDFINDER – Hispanic (*a Spanish-speaking person, especially in America*).
DERIVATIVES – **Spanishness** *noun*.
COMBINATIONS – **Spanish guitar** the standard six-stringed acoustic guitar, used especially for classical and folk music. **Spanish omelette** an omelette containing potatoes and onions. **Spanish onion** a large onion with a mild flavour.

Spanish-American > *noun* a person from the Spanish-speaking countries of Central and South America. > *adjective* relating to the Spanish-speaking countries or peoples of Central and South America.

spank > *verb* slap with one's open hand or a flat object, especially on the buttocks as a punishment. > *noun* a slap or series of slaps of this type.

spanking > *noun* a series of spanks. > *adjective* informal 1 lively; brisk. 2 very good; impressive or pleasing.

spanner > *noun* chiefly Brit. a tool with a shaped opening or jaws for gripping and turning a nut or bolt.
IDIOMS – **spanner in the works** a person or thing that prevents the successful implementation of a plan.
ORIGIN – from German *spannen* 'draw tight'.

spar¹ > *noun* 1 a thick, strong pole such as is used for a mast or yard on a ship. 2 the main longitudinal beam of an aeroplane wing.
ORIGIN – shortening of Old French *esparre*, or from Old Norse *sperra*.

spar² > *verb* (**sparred**, **sparring**) 1 make the motions of boxing without landing heavy blows, as a form of training. 2 engage in argument without marked hostility. > *noun* a period or bout of sparring.
ORIGIN – Old English, 'strike out'.

spar³ > *noun* a crystalline translucent or transparent mineral that is easily broken apart.
ORIGIN – Low German.

spare > *adjective* 1 additional to what is required for ordinary use. 2 not currently in use or occupied. 3 with no excess fat; thin. 4 elegantly simple in style or presentation. > *noun* an item kept in case another item of the same type is lost, broken, or worn out. > *verb* 1 give (something of which one has enough) to someone. 2 make (something) free or available for (someone). 3 refrain from killing or harming. 4 refrain from inflicting (harm) on.
IDIOMS – **go spare** Brit. informal become extremely angry or distraught. **spare no expense** be prepared to pay any amount. **to spare** left over.
DERIVATIVES – **sparely** *adverb* **spareness** *noun*.
SYNONYMS – *adjective* 1 additional, auxiliary, extra, supplementary, surplus. 2 redundant, superfluous, surplus, unused. *verb* 3 have mercy on, pardon, preserve, reprieve, save.
COMBINATIONS – **spare ribs** trimmed ribs of pork. **spare tyre** 1 an extra tyre carried in a motor vehicle for use in case of puncture. 2 informal a roll of fat round a person's waist.
ORIGIN – Old English *spær* 'not plentiful, meagre' and *sparian* 'refrain from injuring or using'.

sparing > *adjective* moderate; economical.
DERIVATIVES – **sparingly** *adverb*.

spark > *noun* 1 a small fiery particle thrown off from a fire, alight in ashes, or caused by friction. 2 a light produced by a sudden disrupted electrical discharge through the air. 3 a discharge such as this serving to ignite the explosive mixture in an internal-combustion engine. 4 a small bright object or point. **5** a small but concentrated amount or trace: *a tiny spark of anger.* **6** a sense of liveliness and excitement. > *verb* **1** emit sparks. **2** produce sparks at the point where an electric circuit is interrupted. **3** ignite. **4** (usu. **spark off**) provide the stimulus for; trigger.

IDIOMS – **bright spark** often ironic a clever person. **spark out** Brit. informal unconscious.

DERIVATIVES – **sparky** adjective.

COMBINATIONS – **spark plug** (also **sparking plug**) a device for firing the explosive mixture in an internal-combustion engine.

sparkle > *verb* **1** shine brightly with flashes of light. **2** be vivacious and witty. **3** (**sparkling**) (of a drink) effervescent. > *noun* **1** a glittering flash of light. **2** vivacity and wit.

DERIVATIVES – **sparkly** adjective.

SYNONYMS – *verb* **1** flash, gleam, glint, glisten, shimmer.

sparkler > *noun* a hand-held firework that emits sparks.

sparrow > *noun* a small bird with brown and grey plumage.

COMBINATIONS – **sparrow grass** dialect asparagus. [ORIGIN – corruption of obsolete *sparagus* 'asparagus'.]

sparrowhawk > *noun* **1** a small hawk that preys on small birds. **2** N. Amer. the American kestrel.

sparse > *adjective* **1** thinly dispersed or scattered. **2** austere or meagre.

DERIVATIVES – **sparsely** adverb **sparseness** noun **sparsity** noun.

SYNONYMS – **1** scanty, scarce, scattered.

ANTONYMS – **1** abundant, plentiful, thick.

ORIGIN – Latin *sparsus*, from *spargere* 'scatter'.

Spartan > *adjective* **1** relating to Sparta, a city state in ancient Greece whose inhabitants were traditionally indifferent to comfort or luxury. **2** (**spartan**) lacking in comfort or luxury; austere. > *noun* a citizen of Sparta.

SYNONYMS – *adjective* **2** (**spartan**) ascetic, austere, frugal, harsh, simple.

ANTONYMS – *adjective* **2** (**spartan**) luxurious, opulent.

spasm > *noun* **1** a sudden involuntary muscular contraction or convulsive movement. **2** a sudden brief spell of an activity or sensation.

SYNONYMS – **1** attack, convulsion, fit, paroxysm, seizure.

ORIGIN – Greek *spasmos*, from *span* 'pull'.

spasmodic > *adjective* **1** occurring or done in brief, irregular bursts. **2** of or caused by a spasm or spasms.

DERIVATIVES – **spasmodically** adverb.

SYNONYMS – **1** fitful, intermittent, irregular, patchy, sporadic.

spastic > *adjective* **1** relating to or affected by muscle spasm. **2** of or having a form of

muscular weakness typical of cerebral palsy, involving reflex resistance to passive movement of the limbs and difficulty in initiating and controlling muscular movement. **3** informal, offensive incompetent or uncoordinated. > *noun* **1** a person with cerebral palsy. **2** informal, offensive an incompetent or uncoordinated person.

DERIVATIVES – **spastically** adverb **spasticity** noun.

USAGE – avoid using the term **spastic**, as it is likely to cause offence. Use phrasing such as *people with cerebral palsy* instead.

ORIGIN – Greek *spastikos* 'pulling'.

spat¹ past and past participle of SPIT¹.

spat² > *noun* a short cloth gaiter covering the instep and ankle.

ORIGIN – from *spatterdash*, a long gaiter or legging formerly worn when riding.

spat³ informal > *noun* a petty quarrel. > *verb* (**spatted**, **spatting**) quarrel pettily.

spatchcock > *noun* a chicken or game bird split open and grilled or roasted. > *verb* **1** prepare (a bird) in this way.

ORIGIN – perhaps related to DISPATCH + COCK¹; compare with SPITCHCOCK.

spate > *noun* **1** a large number of similar things or events coming in quick succession. **2** chiefly Brit. a sudden flood in a river.

IDIOMS – **in** (**full**) **spate** (of a river) full of rushing water.

SYNONYMS – **1** deluge, flood, flurry, rush, torrent.

spathe /spayth/ > *noun* Botany a large sheathing bract enclosing the flower cluster of certain plants, especially the spadix of arums and palms.

ORIGIN – Greek, 'broad blade'.

spatial /spaysh'l/ (also **spacial**) > *adjective* relating to space.

DERIVATIVES – **spatialise** (also **spatialize**) verb **spatiality** noun **spatially** adverb.

ORIGIN – from Latin *spatium* 'space'.

spatter > *verb* **1** cover with drops or spots. **2** splash or be splashed over a surface. > *noun* **1** a spray or splash. **2** a short outburst of sound.

spatula /spatyoolə/ > *noun* an implement with a broad, flat, blunt blade, used especially for mixing or spreading.

ORIGIN – Latin, variant of *spathula* 'small spathe'.

spatulate /spatyoolət/ > *adjective* having a broad, rounded end.

spavin /spavvin/ > *noun* a disorder of a horse's hock.

DERIVATIVES – **spavined** adjective.

ORIGIN – Old French *espavin*.

spawn > *verb* **1** (of a fish, frog, etc.) release or deposit eggs. **2** produce or generate; give rise to. > *noun* **1** the eggs of fish, frogs, etc. **2** the mycelium of a fungus, especially a cultivated mushroom.

DERIVATIVES – **spawner** noun.

ORIGIN – Old French *espaundre* 'to shed roe', from *espandre* 'pour out'.

spay > *verb* sterilise (a female animal) by removing the ovaries.

ORIGIN – Old French *espeer* 'cut with a sword', from *espee* 'sword', from Latin *spatha* 'broad blade'.

speak > *verb* (past **spoke**; past participle **spoken**) **1** say something. **2** (**speak to**) talk to (someone) in order to advise, pass on information, etc. **3** communicate in or be able to communicate in (a specified language). **4** make a speech. **5** (**speak for**) express the views or position of. **6** (**speak out** or **up**) express one's opinions frankly and publicly. **7** (**speak up**) speak more loudly. **8** (of behaviour, an event, etc.) serve as evidence for something. **9** (**speak to**) appeal or relate to.

IDIOMS – **speak in tongues** speak in an unknown language during religious worship, regarded as a gift of the Holy Spirit (Acts of the Apostles, chapter 2). **speak one's mind** express one's opinions frankly. **speak volumes** convey a great deal without using words.

SYNONYMS – **1** articulate, enunciate, talk, verbalise, vocalise.

speakeasy > *noun* (pl. **speakeasies**) informal (in the US during Prohibition) an illicit liquor shop or drinking club.

speaker > *noun* **1** a person who speaks. **2** a person who speaks a specified language. **3** a person who makes a speech at a formal occasion. **4** (**Speaker**) the presiding officer in a legislative assembly, especially the House of Commons. **5** a loudspeaker.

speaking > *noun* the action of expressing oneself in speech or giving speeches. > *adjective* **1** used for or engaged in speech. **2** able to communicate in a specified language: *an English-speaking guide.*

IDIOMS – **on speaking terms 1** slightly acquainted. **2** sufficiently friendly to talk to each other.

COMBINATIONS – **speaking clock** Brit. a telephone service giving the correct time in recorded speech.

spear > *noun* **1** a weapon with a pointed tip and a long wooden shaft, used for thrusting or throwing. **2** a plant shoot, especially a pointed stem of asparagus or broccoli. **3** (before another noun) denoting the male side or members of a family. Compare with DISTAFF. > *verb* pierce or strike with a spear or other pointed object.

WORDFINDER – *types of spear:* assegai, gaff, halberd, javelin, trident.

COMBINATIONS – **speargun** a gun used to propel a spear in underwater fishing.

spearhead > *noun* **1** the point of a spear. **2** an individual or group leading an attack or movement. > *verb* lead (an attack or movement).

spearmint > *noun* the common garden mint, which is used as a herb and in flavouring.

spec¹ > *noun* (in phrase **on spec**) informal in the hope of success but without any specific preparation or plan.
ORIGIN – abbreviation of *speculation*.

spec² > *noun* informal a detailed working description; a specification.

special > *adjective* **1** better, greater, or otherwise different from what is usual. **2** designed for or belonging to a particular person, place, or event. **3** exceptionally good, precious, or memorable. > *noun* **1** something designed or organised for a particular occasion or purpose. **2** a dish not on the regular menu in a cafe or restaurant but served on a particular day. **3** a person assigned to a special duty.
DERIVATIVES – **specialness** *noun*.
SYNONYMS – *adjective* **1** exceptional, extra, particular, unusual. **2** distinct, distinctive, individual, particular, peculiar. **3** important, memorable, momentous, significant.
ANTONYMS – *adjective* **1** ordinary. **2** general. **3** average, ordinary.
COMBINATIONS – **special constable** (in the UK) a person who is trained to act as a police officer on particular occasions, especially in times of emergency. **special effects** illusions created for films and television by props, camerawork, computer graphics, etc. **special needs** particular educational requirements resulting from learning difficulties, physical disability, or emotional and behavioural difficulties. **special pleading** argument in which the speaker deliberately ignores aspects that are unfavourable to their point of view. **special school** (in the UK) a school catering for children with special needs.
ORIGIN – Latin *specialis*, from *species* 'appearance'.

specialise (also **specialize**) > *verb* **1** (often **specialise in**) concentrate on and become expert in a particular skill or area. **2** make a habit of engaging in.
DERIVATIVES – **specialisation** *noun*.

specialised (also **specialized**) > *adjective* **1** requiring or involving detailed and specific knowledge or training. **2** concentrating on a small area of a subject; specialist. **3** Biology (of an organ or part) adapted or set apart to serve a special function.

specialist > *noun* a person who is highly skilled or knowledgeable in a particular field. > *adjective* relating to or involving detailed knowledge or a specific focus within a field.
DERIVATIVES – **specialism** *noun*.

SYNONYMS – *noun* authority, connoisseur, expert, master.
ANTONYMS – *noun* generalist, layman.

speciality* /speshialiti/ (chiefly US & Medicine also **specialty** /spesh'lti/) > *noun* (pl. **specialities**) **1** a pursuit, area of study, or skill to which someone has devoted themselves and in which they are expert. **2** a product for which a person or region is famous. **3** (usu. **specialty**) a branch of medicine or surgery.
***SPELLING** – the standard spelling is special*ity*; special*ty* is American, and is also used in technical medical contexts.
SYNONYMS – **1** field, forte, strength, strong point, talent.

specially > *adverb* **1** for a special purpose. **2** particularly.
USAGE – **specially** and **especially** are not interchangeable, although both can mean 'particularly'. Only **especially** means 'in particular', as in *he despised them all, especially Thomas*, and only **specially** means 'for a special purpose', as in *the car was specially made for the occasion*.

speciation /speeshiaysh'n, speessiaysh'n/ > *noun* Biology the formation of new and distinct species in the course of evolution.
DERIVATIVES – **speciate** *verb*.

specie /speeshi, speesee/ > *noun* money in the form of coins rather than notes.
ORIGIN – from the Latin phrase *in specie* 'in kind', later 'in the coin specified'.

species /speesheez, speeseez/ > *noun* (pl. same) **1** Biology a group of living organisms consisting of similar individuals capable of exchanging genes or interbreeding. **2** a kind or sort. **3** (before another noun) denoting a plant of a distinct species rather than a hybrid variety: *species roses*.

wordpower facts
Species
Species was originally a Latin word meaning 'appearance, form, beauty' and derived from *specere* 'to look'; among its early senses in English were 'appearance, form', 'reflection', and 'vision, illusion', as well as 'class of things having common features'. The Latin word *species* is the source of **special, specific, specious** (via *speciosus* 'fair, plausible'), and **spice** (via a late Latin meaning, 'wares'). The root verb *specere* is the source of a great many English words, such as **aspect, auspice, circumspect, expect, inspect, perspective, prospect, respect, specimen, spectacle, spectrum**, and **suspect**.

speciesism > *noun* the assumption of

human superiority over other creatures, leading to the exploitation of animals.
DERIVATIVES – **speciesist** *adjective* & *noun*.

specific /spəsiffik/ > *adjective* **1** clearly defined or identified. **2** precise and clear. **3** (**specific to**) belonging or relating uniquely to. **4** Biology relating to species or a species. > *noun* (**specifics**) precise details.
DERIVATIVES – **specifically** *adverb* **specificity** /spessifissiti/ *noun*.
SYNONYMS – *adjective* **1** definite, fixed, particular, precise, set. **2** clear, exact, explicit, precise, unequivocal.
ANTONYMS – *adjective* **1** general. **2** vague.
COMBINATIONS – **specific gravity** Physics relative density.
ORIGIN – Latin *specificus*, from *species* 'appearance, form'.

specification > *noun* **1** the action of specifying. **2** (usu. **specifications**) a detailed description of the design and materials used to make something. **3** a standard of workmanship, materials, etc. required to be met in a piece of work.

specify > *verb* (**specifies, specified**) **1** make specific; state or identify clearly and definitely. **2** include in an architect's or engineer's specifications.
DERIVATIVES – **specifiable** *adjective* **specifier** *noun*.
SYNONYMS – **1** define, detail, enumerate, lay down, stipulate.

specimen > *noun* **1** an individual animal, plant, object, etc. used as an example of its species or type for scientific study or display. **2** a sample for medical testing, especially of urine. **3** an example of something regarded as typical of its class or group. **4** humorous a person or animal of a specified kind: *he was confronted by a sorry specimen*.
SYNONYMS – **1** example, model, representative, sample, selection.
ORIGIN – Latin, from *specere* 'to look': originally in the sense 'pattern, model'.

specious /speeshəss/ > *adjective* **1** superficially plausible, but actually wrong. **2** misleading in appearance.
DERIVATIVES – **speciously** *adverb* **speciousness** *noun*.
ORIGIN – first used in the sense 'beautiful': from Latin *speciosus* 'fair, plausible'.

speck > *noun* a tiny spot or particle. > *verb* mark with small spots.
SYNONYMS – *noun* dot, fleck, mark, spot.

speckle > *noun* a small spot or patch of colour. > *verb* mark with speckles.
DERIVATIVES – **speckled** *adjective*.

specs > *plural noun* informal a pair of spectacles.

spectacle > *noun* a visually striking performance or display.
IDIOMS – **make a spectacle of oneself** draw attention to oneself by behaving in a ridiculous way in public.

941

SYNONYMS – display, exhibition, show, sight, vision.

ORIGIN – Latin *spectaculum* 'public show', from *spectare* 'gaze at, observe'.

spectacled > *adjective* wearing spectacles.

spectacles > *plural noun* Brit. a pair of glasses.

spectacular > *adjective* very impressive, striking, or dramatic. > *noun* a performance or event produced on a large scale and with striking effects.

DERIVATIVES – **spectacularly** *adverb*.

SYNONYMS – *adjective* impressive, magnificent, sensational, striking, stunning.

spectate > *verb* be a spectator.

spectator > *noun* a person who watches at a show, game, or other event.

SYNONYMS – bystander, observer, onlooker, viewer, watcher.

ORIGIN – Latin, from *spectare* 'gaze at, observe'.

spectra plural of SPECTRUM.

spectral > *adjective* **1** of or like a spectre. **2** of or concerning spectra or the spectrum.

DERIVATIVES – **spectrally** *adverb*.

SYNONYMS – **1** eerie, ghostly, phantasmal, wraithlike.

spectre (US **specter**) > *noun* **1** a ghost. **2** something unpleasant or dangerous that is imagined or expected.

ORIGIN – French, from Latin *spectrum* 'image, apparition'.

spectrogram > *noun* a visual or electronic record of a spectrum.

spectrograph > *noun* an apparatus for photographing or otherwise recording spectra.

DERIVATIVES – **spectrographic** *adjective*.

spectrometer > *noun* an apparatus used for recording and measuring spectra, especially as a method of analysis.

DERIVATIVES – **spectrometric** *adjective* **spectrometry** *noun*.

spectroscope > *noun* an apparatus for producing and recording spectra for examination.

spectroscopy > *noun* the branch of science concerned with the investigation and measurement of spectra produced when matter interacts with or emits electromagnetic radiation.

DERIVATIVES – **spectroscopic** *adjective* **spectroscopist** *noun*.

spectrum /**spek**trəm/ > *noun* (pl. **spectra** /**spek**trə/) **1** a band of colours produced by separation of the components of light by their different degrees of refraction, e.g. in a rainbow. **2** the entire range of wavelengths of electromagnetic radiation. **3** a characteristic series of frequencies of electromagnetic radiation emitted or absorbed by a substance. **4** the components of a sound or other phenomenon arranged according to frequency, energy, etc. **5** a

scale extending between two points; a range: *the political spectrum*.

ORIGIN – Latin, 'image, apparition', from *specere* 'to look'.

speculate /**spek**yoolayt/ > *verb* **1** form a theory or conjecture without firm evidence. **2** invest in stocks, property, or other ventures in the hope of financial gain but with the risk of loss.

DERIVATIVES – **speculation** *noun* **speculator** *noun*.

SYNONYMS – **1** conjecture, hypothesise, postulate, surmise, theorise.

ORIGIN – Latin *speculari* 'observe', from *specula* 'watchtower', from *specere* 'to look'.

speculative > *adjective* **1** engaged in or based on conjecture rather than knowledge. **2** (of an investment) involving a high risk of loss.

DERIVATIVES – **speculatively** *adverb*.

SYNONYMS – **1** conjectural, hypothetical, notional, suppositional, theoretical.

speculum /**spek**yoolam/ > *noun* (pl. **specula** /**spek**yoola/) Medicine a metal instrument that is used to dilate an orifice or canal in the body to allow inspection.

ORIGIN – Latin, 'mirror', from *specere* 'to look'.

sped past and past participle of SPEED.

speech > *noun* **1** the expression of thoughts and feelings by articulate sounds. **2** a formal address delivered to an audience. **3** a sequence of lines written for one character in a play.

WORDFINDER – aphasia (*inability to understand or produce speech, as a result of brain damage*), lingual (*relating to speech or language*), locution (*person's style of speech*), oral (*spoken rather than written*), oratory (*public speaking*), phonetic, phonic (*relating to speech sounds*), phonetics (*study and classification of speech sounds*).

SYNONYMS – **1** articulation, speaking, talking, utterance, verbal communication. **2** address, discourse, lecture, oration, talk.

COMBINATIONS – **speech recognition** the process of enabling a computer to identify and respond to the sounds produced in human speech.

speechify > *verb* (**speechifies**, **speechified**) deliver a speech, especially in a tedious or pompous way.

DERIVATIVES – **speechifier** *noun*.

speechless > *adjective* unable to speak, especially as the temporary result of shock or strong emotion.

DERIVATIVES – **speechlessly** *adverb* **speechlessness** *noun*.

SYNONYMS – dumbfounded, dumbstruck, mute, thunderstruck, voiceless.

speech therapy > *noun* treatment to help people with speech and language problems.

DERIVATIVES – **speech therapist** *noun*.

speed > *noun* **1** the rate at which someone or something moves or operates. **2** rapidity of movement or action. **3** each of the possible gear ratios of a bicycle or car. **4** the light-gathering power or f-number of a camera lens. **5** the sensitivity of photographic film to light. **6** informal an amphetamine drug, especially methamphetamine. **7** archaic success; prosperity. > *verb* (past and past participle **speeded** or **sped**) **1** move quickly. **2** (**speed up**) move or work more quickly. **3** (of a motorist) travel at a speed greater than the legal limit. **4** informal take or be under the influence of an amphetamine drug. **5** archaic make prosperous or successful: *may God speed you*.

WORDFINDER – anemometer (*instrument for measuring wind speed*), Beaufort scale (*scale of wind speed*), Mach number (*indicating ratio of speed to the speed of sound*), pitot (*device for measuring speed of flow of a fluid*), subsonic (*slower than the speed of sound*), supersonic (*faster than the speed of sound*), tachometer (*instrument measuring the working speed of an engine*), tempo (*speed at which a piece of music is played*).

IDIOMS – **at speed** quickly. **up to speed 1** operating at full speed or capacity. **2** fully informed or up to date.

DERIVATIVES – **speeder** *noun*.

SYNONYMS – *noun* **1** pace, rate, tempo, velocity. **2** dispatch, haste, quickness, rapidity, swiftness, velocity. *verb* **1** dash, hasten, hurry, race, rush.

COMBINATIONS – **speedball** informal a mixture of cocaine with heroin. **speedboat** a motor boat designed for high speed. **speed bump** (Brit. also **speed hump**) a ridge set in a road to control the speed of vehicles. **speed camera** a roadside camera designed to catch speeding vehicles by taking video footage or a photograph. **speed limit** the maximum speed at which a vehicle may legally travel on a particular stretch of road.

ORIGIN – Old English, from a base meaning 'prosper, succeed'.

speedo > *noun* (pl. **speedos**) informal short for SPEEDOMETER.

speedometer /speedommitər/ > *noun* an instrument on a vehicle's dashboard indicating its speed.

speedster > *noun* informal a person or thing that operates well at high speed.

speedway > *noun* **1** a form of motorcycle racing in which the riders race laps around an oval dirt track. **2** N. Amer. a highway for fast motor traffic.

speedwell > *noun* a small creeping plant with blue or pink flowers.

speedy > *adjective* (**speedier**, **speediest**) **1** done or occurring quickly. **2** moving quickly.

speleology–spiccato

DERIVATIVES – **speedily** *adverb* **speediness** *noun*.

SYNONYMS – fast, quick, rapid, swift.

ANTONYMS – slow, sluggish.

speleology /speeli**oll**əji/ > *noun* the study or exploration of caves.

DERIVATIVES – **speleological** *adjective* **speleologist** *noun*.

ORIGIN – from Greek *spēlaion* 'cave'.

spell[1] > *verb* (past and past participle **spelled** or chiefly Brit. **spelt**) **1** write or name the letters that form (a word) in correct sequence. **2** (of letters) make up or form (a word). **3** be a sign of; lead to. **4** (**spell out**) explain clearly and in detail.

ORIGIN – Old French *espeller*; related to **SPELL**[2].

spell[2] > *noun* **1** a form of words used as a magical charm or incantation. **2** a state of enchantment induced by a spell.

ORIGIN – Old English, 'narration'.

spell[3] > *noun* **1** a short period of time. **2** Austral./NZ a period of rest from work. > *verb* Austral./NZ take a brief rest.

SYNONYMS – *noun* **1** interval, period, phase, season, time.

ORIGIN – from dialect *spele* 'take the place of'.

spellbind > *verb* (past and past participle **spellbound**) hold the complete attention of (someone), as if by a spell; entrance.

DERIVATIVES – **spellbinder** *noun* **spellbinding** *adjective* **spellbindingly** *adverb*.

spellchecker (also **spelling checker**) > *noun* a computer program which checks the spelling of words in files of text by comparing them with a stored list of words.

DERIVATIVES – **spellcheck** *verb & noun*.

speller > *noun* **1** a person of a specified spelling ability. **2** a spellchecker.

spelling > *noun* **1** the process or activity of writing or naming the letters of a word. **2** the way in which a word is spelled. **3** a person's ability to spell.

WORDFINDER – homographs (*words with the same spelling but different meanings and origins*), homonyms (*words with the same spelling and pronunciation but different meanings and origins*), orthography (*spelling system of a language*).

spelt past and past participle of **SPELL**[1].

spencer > *noun* **1** a short, close-fitting jacket worn by women and children in the early 19th century. **2** a thin woollen vest.

ORIGIN – probably named after the second Earl *Spencer* (1758–1834).

spend > *verb* (past and past participle **spent**) **1** pay out (money) in buying or hiring goods or services. **2** use or use up (energy or resources); exhaust. **3** pass (time) in a specified way. > *noun* informal an amount of money paid out.

IDIOMS – **spend a penny** Brit. informal, euphemistic urinate. [ORIGIN – with reference to the coin-operated locks of public toilets.]

DERIVATIVES – **spendable** *adjective* **spender** *noun*.

SYNONYMS – *verb* **1** disburse, expend, lay out, pay out.

ORIGIN – Latin *expendere* 'pay out'.

spendthrift > *noun* a person who spends money in an extravagant, irresponsible way.

SYNONYMS – prodigal, profligate, squanderer, waster, wastrel.

spent past and past participle of **SPEND**. > *adjective* used up; exhausted.

sperm > *noun* (pl. same or **sperms**) **1** semen. **2** a spermatozoon.

COMBINATIONS – **sperm bank** a place where semen is kept in cold storage for use in artificial insemination. **sperm count** the number of spermatozoa in a measured amount of semen, used as an indication of a man's fertility.

ORIGIN – Greek *sperma* 'seed'.

spermaceti /spermə**see**ti, spermə**setti**/ > *noun* a white waxy substance obtained from an organ in the head of the sperm whale, which focuses acoustic signals and aids in the control of buoyancy, and was formerly used in candles and ointments.

ORIGIN – from Latin *sperma* 'sperm' + *ceti* 'of a whale' (from Greek *kētos* 'whale'), from the belief that it was whale spawn.

spermatozoon /spermətə**zō**on/ > *noun* (pl. **spermatozoa** /spermətə**zō**ə/) Biology the motile male sex cell of an animal by which the ovum is fertilised, typically having a compact head and one or more long flagella for swimming.

DERIVATIVES – **spermatozoal** *adjective* **spermatozoan** *adjective*.

ORIGIN – from Greek *sperma* 'seed' + *zōion* 'animal'.

spermicide > *noun* a substance that kills spermatozoa, used as a contraceptive.

DERIVATIVES – **spermicidal** *adjective*.

sperm oil > *noun* an oil found with spermaceti in the head of the sperm whale, used formerly as a lubricant.

sperm whale > *noun* a toothed whale with a massive head, feeding at great depths largely on squid.

ORIGIN – abbreviation of **SPERMACETI**.

spew > *verb* **1** expel or be expelled in large quantities rapidly and forcibly. **2** informal vomit. > *noun* informal vomit.

DERIVATIVES – **spewer** *noun*.

SPF > *abbreviation* sun protection factor.

sphagnum /**sfag**nəm/ > *noun* a plant of a genus that comprises the peat mosses.

ORIGIN – Greek *sphagnos*.

sphere > *noun* **1** a round solid figure, in which every point on the surface is equidistant from the centre. **2** an area of activity, interest, or expertise. **3** each of a series of revolving concentrically arranged spherical shells in which the planets and other celestial bodies were formerly thought to be fixed.

IDIOMS – **music** (or **harmony**) **of the spheres** the natural harmonic tones supposedly produced by the regular movement of the celestial bodies.

SYNONYMS – **1** ball, globe, orb.

ORIGIN – Greek *sphaira* 'ball'.

spherical > *adjective* **1** shaped like a sphere. **2** relating to the properties of spheres.

DERIVATIVES – **spheric** *adjective* **spherically** *adverb* **sphericity** *noun*.

SYNONYMS – **1** globular, round, spheroidal.

spheroid /**sfeer**oyd/ > *noun* a sphere-like but not perfectly spherical body.

DERIVATIVES – **spheroidal** *adjective*.

spherule /**sferr**ool/ > *noun* a small sphere.

DERIVATIVES – **spherular** *adjective*.

sphincter /**sfingk**tər/ > *noun* Anatomy a ring of muscle surrounding and serving to guard or close an opening, such as the anus.

ORIGIN – Greek *sphinktēr*, from *sphingein* 'bind tight'.

sphinx > *noun* **1** an ancient Egyptian stone figure having a lion's body and a human or animal head. **2** an enigmatic or inscrutable person.

ORIGIN – the name of a winged monster in Greek mythology, having a woman's head and a lion's body, who asked travellers a riddle and killed those who failed to solve it.

sphygmomanometer /sfigmōmə**nomm**itər/ > *noun* an instrument for measuring blood pressure, consisting of an inflatable rubber cuff which is applied to the arm and connected to a column of mercury next to a graduated scale.

DERIVATIVES – **sphygmomanometry** *noun*.

ORIGIN – from Greek *sphugmos* 'pulse'.

spic > *noun* US informal, offensive a Spanish-speaking person from Central or South America or the Caribbean, especially a Mexican.

ORIGIN – abbreviation of US slang *spiggoty*, in the same sense: perhaps from *speak the* in 'no speak the English'.

spiccato /spi**kaa**tō/ > *noun* Music a style of staccato playing on stringed instruments

943

involving bouncing the bow on the strings.

ORIGIN – Italian, 'detailed, distinct'.

spice > *noun* **1** an aromatic or pungent vegetable substance used to flavour food. **2** an element providing interest and excitement. > *verb* **1** flavour with spice. **2** (**spice up**) make more exciting or interesting.

WORDFINDER – *types of spice:* allspice, cardamom, cinnamon, clove, cumin, fenugreek, ginger, mace, nutmeg, paprika, peppercorn, saffron, star anise.

ORIGIN – Old French *espice*, from Latin *species* 'sort, kind', in late Latin 'wares'.

spick and span (also **spic and span**) > *adjective* neat, clean, and well looked after.

ORIGIN – first used in the sense 'brand new': from *spick and span new*, emphatic extension of dialect *span new*, from Old Norse *spánn* 'chip'.

spicule /**spik**yo͞ol/ > *noun* **1** chiefly Zoology a small needle-like structure, in particular any of those making up the skeleton of a sponge. **2** Astronomy a short-lived jet of gas in the sun's corona.

DERIVATIVES – **spicular** *adjective* **spiculate** /**spik**yo͞olət/ *adjective* **spiculation** *noun*.

ORIGIN – Latin *spicula* 'little ear of grain'.

spicy (also **spicey**) > *adjective* (**spicier**, **spiciest**) **1** strongly flavoured with spice. **2** titillating or mildly indecent.

DERIVATIVES – **spicily** *adverb* **spiciness** *noun*.

SYNONYMS – **1** hot, peppery, piquant, pungent.

spider > *noun* **1** an eight-legged predatory arachnid with an unsegmented body consisting of a fused head and thorax and a rounded abdomen, most kinds of which spin webs in which to capture insects. **2** Billiards & Snooker a long-legged rest for a cue that can be placed over a ball without touching it. > *verb* **1** move in a scuttling manner suggestive of a spider. **2** form a pattern suggestive of a spider or its web.

WORDFINDER – arachnophobia (*extreme fear of spiders*).

COMBINATIONS – **spider crab** a crab with long, thin legs and a compact pear-shaped body. **spider mite** a plant-feeding mite resembling a minute spider. **spider monkey** a South American monkey with very long limbs and a long prehensile tail. **spider plant** a plant of the lily family having long, narrow leaves with a central yellow stripe, popular as a house plant.

ORIGIN – Old English, from *spinnan* 'spin'.

spidery > *adjective* resembling a spider, especially in having long, thin, angular lines like a spider's legs.

spiel /shpeel, speel/ informal > *noun* an elaborate and glib speech or story, such as that used by a salesperson. > *verb* speak or reel off at length or glibly.

ORIGIN – German, 'a game'.

spieler > *noun* informal **1** a glib or voluble speaker. **2** Austral./NZ a gambler or swindler. **3** a gambling club.

spiff > *verb* (**spiff up**) informal make smart or stylish.

ORIGIN – perhaps from dialect *spiff* 'well dressed, a well-dressed man'.

spiffing > *adjective* Brit. informal, dated excellent; splendid.

spiffy > *adjective* (**spiffier**, **spiffiest**) N. Amer. informal smart or stylish.

DERIVATIVES – **spiffily** *adverb*.

spigot /**spigg**ət/ > *noun* **1** a small peg or plug, especially for insertion into the vent of a cask. **2** US a tap. **3** the plain end of a section of a pipe fitting into the socket of the next one.

ORIGIN – perhaps from Provençal *espigou*, from Latin *spiculum* 'little ear of corn'.

spike[1] > *noun* **1** a thin, pointed piece of metal. **2** each of several metal points set into the sole of a sports shoe to prevent slipping. **3** chiefly Brit. a pointed metal rod fixed to a base, used for impaling and storing notes or papers. **4** a sharp increase in the magnitude or intensity of something. > *verb* **1** impale on or pierce with a spike. **2** form into or cover with sharp points. **3** reject (a submitted paper or report) by or as if by impaling it on a spike. **4** informal surreptitiously lace (drink or food) with alcohol or a drug. **5** increase and then decrease sharply.

IDIOMS – **spike someone's guns** thwart someone's plans.

ORIGIN – perhaps from Low German, Dutch *spiker*; related to **spoke**[1].

spike[2] > *noun* Botany a flower cluster formed of many flower heads attached directly to a long stem.

ORIGIN – Latin *spica* 'ear of corn' (its original sense in English).

spikelet > *noun* Botany the basic unit of a grass flower, consisting of two outer bracts at the base and one or more florets above.

spikenard /**spīk**naard/ > *noun* a Himalayan plant of which the root was used in ancient times to make a highly valued perfumed ointment.

ORIGIN – from Latin *spica nardi*, from Greek *nardostakhus*.

spiky > *adjective* (**spikier**, **spikiest**) **1** like a spike or spikes or having many spikes. **2** informal easily annoyed; irritable.

DERIVATIVES – **spikily** *adverb* **spikiness** *noun*.

spile /spīl/ > *noun* **1** a small wooden peg or spigot. **2** a large, heavy timber driven into the ground to support a superstructure.

ORIGIN – Dutch, Low German; sense 2 is apparently from **pile**[2].

spill[1] > *verb* (past and past participle **spilt** or **spilled**) **1** flow or cause to flow over the edge of a container. **2** be discharged or emptied from a place or container. **3** informal reveal (confidential information). > *noun* **1** an instance of a liquid spilling or being spilt. **2** the quantity of liquid spilt. **3** a fall from a horse or bicycle. **4** Austral. a reorganisation of posts in a cabinet or parliamentary party after one important change of office.

IDIOMS – **spill the beans** informal reveal secret information unintentionally or indiscreetly. **spill blood** kill or wound people.

DERIVATIVES – **spillage** *noun* **spiller** *noun*.

ORIGIN – Old English, 'kill, waste, shed (blood)'.

spill[2] > *noun* a thin strip of wood or paper used for lighting a fire.

ORIGIN – first used in the sense 'sharp fragment of wood': related to **spile**.

spillikin /**spill**ikin/ > *noun* **1** (**spillikins**) (treated as sing.) a game played with a heap of small rods of wood, bone, or plastic, in which players try to remove one at a time without disturbing the others. **2** a splinter or fragment.

ORIGIN – from **spill**[2].

spin > *verb* (**spinning**; past and past participle **spun**) **1** turn round quickly. **2** (of a person's head) give a sensation of dizziness. **3** (of a ball) move through the air with a revolving motion. **4** draw out and twist (the fibres of wool, cotton, etc.) to convert them into yarn. **5** (of a spider or a silkworm or other insect) produce (gossamer or silk) or construct (a web or cocoon) by extruding a fine viscous thread from a special gland. **6** (**spin out**) make (something) last as long as possible. **7** give (a news story) a favourable emphasis or slant. > *noun* **1** a spinning motion. **2** informal a brief trip in a vehicle for pleasure. **3** a favourable emphasis or slant given to a news story. **4** Austral./NZ informal a piece of good or bad luck.

IDIOMS – **flat spin 1** a spin in which an aircraft descends in tight circles while remaining horizontal. **2** Brit. informal a state of agitation. **spin a yarn** tell a far-fetched story.

SYNONYMS – *verb* **1** go round, gyrate, revolve, rotate, whirl. **2** reel, swim, whirl.

COMBINATIONS – **spin dryer** a machine for extracting water from wet clothes by spinning them in a revolving perforated drum. **spinning jenny** historical a machine for spinning with more than one spindle at a time. **spinning mule** see **mule**[1] (sense 4). **spinning top** see **top**[2]. **spinning**

wheel an apparatus for spinning yarn or thread with a spindle driven by a wheel attached to a crank or treadle.
ORIGIN – Old English, 'draw out and twist (fibre)'.

spina bifida /spīnə **biff**idə/ > *noun* a congenital defect in which part of the spinal cord is exposed through a gap in the backbone, and which can cause paralysis and other problems.
ORIGIN – modern Latin, from **SPINE** and Latin *bifidus* 'doubly split'.

spinach > *noun* a plant with large dark green leaves which are eaten as a vegetable.
WORDFINDER – Florentine (*dish served on a bed of spinach*).
COMBINATIONS – **spinach beet** beet of a variety with spinach-like leaves.
ORIGIN – probably from Old French *espinache*, from Persian.

spinal > *adjective* relating to the spine.
DERIVATIVES – **spinally** *adverb*.
COMBINATIONS – **spinal column** the spine. **spinal cord** the cylindrical bundle of nerve fibres which is enclosed in the spine and connected to the brain, with which it forms the central nervous system. **spinal tap** North American term for *lumbar puncture*.

spindle > *noun* **1** a slender rounded rod with tapered ends, used in hand spinning to twist and wind fibres from a mass of wool, flax, etc. held on a distaff. **2** a rod or pin serving as an axis that revolves or on which something revolves. **3** a turned piece of wood used as a banister or chair leg. **4** N. Amer. a spike for filing papers.
ORIGIN – Old English, from **SPIN**.

spindle-shanks > *plural noun* informal, dated **1** long, thin legs. **2** (treated as sing.) a person with such legs.

spindly > *adjective* long or tall and thin.

spin doctor > *noun* informal a spokesperson for a political party or politician employed to give a favourable interpretation of events to the media.

spindrift > *noun* **1** spray blown from the crests of waves by the wind. **2** driving snow.
ORIGIN – from archaic *spoondrift*, from *spoon* 'run before wind or sea' + **DRIFT**.

spine > *noun* **1** a series of vertebrae extending from the skull to the small of the back, enclosing the spinal cord and providing support for the thorax and abdomen; the backbone. **2** a central feature or main source of strength. **3** the part of a book that encloses the inner edges of the pages. **4** chiefly Zoology & Botany a prickle or other hard pointed projection or structure.
DERIVATIVES – **spined** *adjective*.

COMBINATIONS – **spine-chilling** (of a story or film) inspiring terror and excitement. **spine-tingling** thrilling or pleasurably frightening.
ORIGIN – Latin *spina* 'thorn, backbone'.

spinel /spi**nel**/ > *noun* a hard glassy mineral consisting chiefly of magnesium and aluminium oxides.
ORIGIN – Italian *spinella* 'little thorn'.

spineless > *adjective* **1** having no spine; invertebrate. **2** (of an animal or plant) lacking spines. **3** weak and purposeless.
DERIVATIVES – **spinelessly** *adverb* **spinelessness** *noun*.
SYNONYMS – **3** feeble, lily-livered, pathetic, pusillanimous, weak.

spinet /spi**net**, **spinn**it/ > *noun* **1** a small harpsichord with the strings set obliquely to the keyboard, popular in the 18th century. **2** US a type of small upright piano.
ORIGIN – Italian *spinetta* 'virginal, spinet', from Latin *spina* 'thorn, spine, quill', the strings being plucked by quills.

spinifex /**spinn**ifeks/ > *noun* a grass with spiny flower heads which break off and are blown about, occurring from east Asia to Australia.
ORIGIN – Latin, from *spina* 'thorn'.

spinnaker /**spinn**ikər/ > *noun* a large three-cornered sail set forward of the mainsail of a racing yacht when running before the wind.
ORIGIN – apparently a fanciful formation from *Sphinx*, the name of the yacht first using it, perhaps influenced by *spanker*, a fore-and-aft sail.

spinner > *noun* **1** a person occupied in spinning thread. **2** Cricket a bowler who is expert in spinning the ball. **3** (also **spinnerbait**) Fishing a lure designed to revolve when pulled through the water.

spinneret /**spinn**əret/ > *noun* **1** Zoology any of a number of different organs through which the silk, gossamer, or thread of spiders, silkworms, and certain other insects is produced. **2** (in the production of man-made fibres) a cap or plate with a number of small holes through which a fibre-forming solution is forced.

spinney > *noun* (pl. **spinneys**) Brit. a small area of trees and bushes.
ORIGIN – Old French *espinei*, from Latin *spinetum* 'thicket'.

spin-off > *noun* **1** a product or incidental benefit produced during or after a primary activity. **2** a subsidiary of a parent company that has been sold off, creating a new company.

spinster > *noun* chiefly derogatory an unmarried woman, typically an older woman beyond the usual age for marriage.

DERIVATIVES – **spinsterhood** *noun* **spinsterish** *adjective*.

wordpower facts

Spinster

The development of the word **spinster** is a good example of the way in which a word acquires such strong connotations that it can no longer be used in a neutral sense. In the Middle Ages a **spinster** was 'a woman who spins'. From the 17th century the word was added to names as the official legal description of an unmarried woman: *Elizabeth Harris of London, Spinster*; this type of use survives today in some legal and religious contexts. In modern everyday English, however, **spinster** does not signify simply 'unmarried woman'; it is now always a derogatory term referring to a stereotype of an older woman who is unmarried, childless, prissy, and repressed.

spiny > *adjective* (**spinier**, **spiniest**) **1** full of or covered with prickles. **2** informal difficult to understand or handle.
DERIVATIVES – **spininess** *noun*.
COMBINATIONS – **spiny anteater** the echidna.

spiracle /**spī**rək'l/ > *noun* Zoology an external respiratory opening in insects, cartilaginous fish, and other animals.
DERIVATIVES – **spiracular** *adjective*.
ORIGIN – Latin *spiraculum*, from *spirare* 'breathe'.

spiraea /spī**ree**ə/ (chiefly US also **spirea**) > *noun* a shrub with clusters of small white or pink flowers.
ORIGIN – Greek *speiraia*, from *speira* 'a coil'.

spiral > *adjective* winding in a continuous curve around a central point or axis. > *noun* **1** a spiral curve, shape, or pattern. **2** a progressive rise or fall of prices, wages, etc., each responding to an upward or downward stimulus provided by a previous one. **3** a progressive, rise, fall, or deterioration. > *verb* (**spiralled**, **spiralling**; US **spiraled**, **spiraling**) **1** take or cause to follow a spiral course. **2** show a continuous and dramatic increase or decrease.
DERIVATIVES – **spirally** *adverb*.
COMBINATIONS – **spiral-bound** (of a book or notepad) bound with a spiral wire threaded through a row of holes along one edge.
ORIGIN – Latin *spiralis*, from Greek *speira* 'a coil'.

spire > *noun* a tapering conical or pyramidal structure on the top of a building, especially a church tower.

DERIVATIVES – **spired** adjective.
ORIGIN – Old English, 'stem of a plant'.

spirea > noun chiefly US variant spelling of SPIRAEA.

spirit > noun 1 a person's non-physical being as opposed to their body. 2 this regarded as surviving after the death of the body, often manifested as a ghost. 3 a supernatural being. 4 prevailing or typical quality or mood. 5 (**spirits**) a person's mood. 6 courage, energy, and determination. 7 the real meaning or intention of something as opposed to its strict verbal interpretation. 8 chiefly Brit. strong distilled liquor such as rum. 9 a volatile liquid, especially a fuel, prepared by distillation. > verb (**spirited**, **spiriting**) (**spirit away**) convey rapidly and secretly.
WORDFINDER – types of spirit: aquavit, brandy, gin, ouzo, raki, rum, tequila, vodka, whisky.
IDIOMS – **in spirit** in thought or intention though not physically. **when the spirit moves one** when one feels inclined to do something. [ORIGIN – a phrase originally in Quaker use, with reference to the Holy Spirit.]
SYNONYMS – noun 1 inner self, psyche, soul. 2 apparition, ghost, phantom, spectre, wraith.
COMBINATIONS – **spirit gum** a quick-drying solution of gum, chiefly used by actors to attach false hair to their faces. **spirit lamp** a lamp burning methylated or other volatile spirits instead of oil. **spirit level** a device consisting of a sealed glass tube partially filled with alcohol or other liquid, containing an air bubble whose position reveals whether a surface is perfectly level.

wordpower facts
Spirit
The word **spirit** comes via Old French esperit from Latin spiritus, literally 'breath' but used in Christian Latin to denote the spirit, soul, or 'breath of life'. Its ultimate root is the verb spirare 'to breathe', the source of English verbs such as **aspire**, **conspire**, **expire**, **inspire**, and **perspire**. Sprite and **spirit** are the same word, **sprite** being formed by a change of spelling in the Middle Ages; spright, the source of **sprightly**, is itself a variant of **sprite**, which was formed in the 16th century.

spirited > adjective 1 full of energy, enthusiasm, and determination. 2 having a specified character or mood: a generous-spirited man.
DERIVATIVES – **spiritedly** adverb.

spiritless > adjective lacking courage, energy, or determination.
DERIVATIVES – **spiritlessly** adverb.

spiritual /spirrityooəl/ > adjective 1 relating to or affecting the human spirit as opposed to material or physical things. 2 relating to religion or religious belief. > noun (also **negro spiritual**) a religious song of a kind associated with black Christians of the southern US.
DERIVATIVES – **spiritualise** (also **spiritualize**) verb **spirituality** noun **spiritually** adverb.
SYNONYMS – adjective 1 immaterial, incorporeal, inner, mystical, psychic.

spiritualism > noun a system of belief and practice based on supposed communication with the spirits of the dead, especially through mediums.
DERIVATIVES – **spiritualist** noun **spiritualistic** adjective.

spirituous /spirrityooəss/ > adjective formal or archaic containing much alcohol.

spirogyra /spīrəjīrə/ > noun Botany algae of a genus found in blanket weed, consisting of long green filaments.
ORIGIN – from Greek speira 'coil' + guros 'round'.

spirometer /spīrommitər/ > noun an instrument for measuring the air capacity of the lungs.
DERIVATIVES – **spirometry** noun.

spit¹ > verb (**spitting**; past and past participle **spat** or **spit**) 1 eject saliva forcibly from one's mouth. 2 forcibly eject (food or liquid) from one's mouth. 3 utter in a hostile way. 4 (of a fire or something being cooked) emit small bursts of sparks or hot fat with a series of explosive noises. 5 (**it spits, it is spitting**, etc.) Brit. light rain falls. 6 (**spit up**) N. Amer. (especially of a baby) vomit. > noun 1 saliva that has been ejected from someone's mouth. 2 an act of spitting.
IDIOMS – **be the spitting image of** (or **be the spit of**) informal look exactly like. [ORIGIN – first as the spit of or the spit and image of: perhaps from the idea of a person apparently being formed from the spit of another, so great is the similarity between them.] **spit and polish** thorough cleaning and polishing. **spit-and-sawdust** Brit. informal (of a pub) dirty or run-down. **spit blood** (or Austral. **chips**) feel or express vehement anger. **spit in the eye** (or **face**) **of** show contempt or scorn for.
DERIVATIVES – **spitter** noun.
SYNONYMS – verb 1 expectorate, hawk. noun 1 dribble, saliva, spittle, sputum.

spit² > noun 1 a long, thin metal rod pushed through meat in order to hold and turn it while it is being roasted. 2 a narrow point of land projecting into the sea. > verb (**spitted**, **spitting**) put a spit through (meat).

COMBINATIONS – **spit-roasted** cooked on a spit.

spit³ > noun (pl. same or **spits**) a layer of earth whose depth is equal to the length of the blade of a spade.
ORIGIN – from Dutch and Low German; probably related to SPIT².

spitball > noun N. Amer. a ball of chewed paper used as a missile.

spitchcock > noun an eel that has been split and grilled or fried. > verb prepare (an eel or other fish) in this way.

spite > noun a desire to hurt, annoy, or offend. > verb deliberately hurt, annoy, or offend (someone).
IDIOMS – **in spite of** without being affected by. **in spite of oneself** although one did not want or expect to do so.
SYNONYMS – noun animosity, ill will, malevolence, malice, nastiness.
ORIGIN – Old French despit 'contempt'.

spiteful > adjective showing or caused by malice.
DERIVATIVES – **spitefully** adverb **spitefulness** noun.
SYNONYMS – malevolent, malicious, nasty, unkind, vindictive.

spitfire > noun a person with a fierce temper.

spittle > noun saliva, especially as ejected from the mouth.
ORIGIN – from dialect spattle, altered by association with SPIT¹.

spittoon /spitoon/ > noun a container for spitting into.

spiv > noun Brit. informal a flashily dressed man who makes a living by disreputable dealings.
DERIVATIVES – **spivvish** adjective **spivvy** adjective.
ORIGIN – perhaps related to SPIFFY.

splash > verb 1 (of a liquid) fall or fly about in scattered drops. 2 make wet or cover with scattered drops of liquid. 3 move around in or strike water, causing it to fly about. 4 (**splash down**) (of a spacecraft) land on water. 5 informal prominently feature (a story or photograph) in a newspaper or magazine. 6 (**splash out**) Brit. informal spend money freely. > noun 1 an instance of splashing or the sound made by this. 2 a small quantity of liquid that has splashed on to a surface. 3 a small quantity of liquid added to a drink. 4 a bright patch of colour. 5 informal a prominent news feature or story.
IDIOMS – **make a splash** informal attract a great deal of attention.
SYNONYMS – verb 1,2 dash, spatter, spray, sprinkle, wet.

splashback > noun Brit. a panel behind a sink

or cooker that protects the wall from splashes.

splat¹ > *noun* a piece of thin wood in the centre of a chair back.

ORIGIN – from obsolete *splat* 'split up'.

splat² informal > *noun* a sound of something soft and wet or heavy striking a surface. > *adverb* with a splat. > *verb* (**splatted**, **splatting**) hit or land with a splat.

splatter > *verb* 1 splash with a sticky or viscous liquid. 2 (of such a liquid) splash. > *noun* 1 a splash of a sticky or viscous liquid. 2 (before another noun) informal (of a film) featuring many violent and gruesome deaths: *a splatter movie*.

COMBINATIONS – **splatterpunk** informal a literary genre characterised by the explicit description of horrific, violent, or pornographic scenes.

splay > *verb* 1 spread or be spread out or further apart. 2 construct (a window, doorway, or other aperture) so that it is wider at one side of the wall than the other. > *noun* 1 a tapered widening. 2 a surface making an oblique angle with another. > *adjective* turned outward or widened.

COMBINATIONS – **splay-footed** having a broad, flat foot turned outward.

ORIGIN – shortening of **DISPLAY**.

spleen > *noun* 1 Anatomy an abdominal organ involved in the production and removal of blood cells and forming part of the immune system. 2 bad temper; spite.

ORIGIN – Greek *splēn*; sense 2 derives from the former belief that the spleen was the seat of bad temper.

splendid > *adjective* 1 magnificent; very impressive. 2 informal excellent.

DERIVATIVES – **splendidly** adverb.

SYNONYMS – 1 dazzling, glorious, grand, magnificent, spectacular, superb.

ORIGIN – Latin *splendidus*, from *splendere* 'shine'.

splendiferous > *adjective* informal, humorous splendid.

splendour (US **splendor**) > *noun* splendid appearance.

SYNONYMS – grandeur, impressiveness, magnificence, sumptuousness.

splenetic /splɪˈnettɪk/ > *adjective* bad-tempered or spiteful.

ORIGIN – Latin *spleneticus*, from Greek *splēn* 'spleen'.

splenic /ˈsplennɪk, ˈspleenɪk/ > *adjective* relating to the spleen.

splice > *verb* 1 join (a rope or ropes) by interweaving the strands at the ends. 2 join (pieces of timber, film, or tape) at the ends. 3 Genetics join or insert (a gene or gene fragment). > *noun* a spliced join.

IDIOMS – **get spliced** informal get married.

splice the main brace Brit. historical (in the navy) serve out an extra tot of rum.

DERIVATIVES – **splicer** noun.

ORIGIN – probably from Dutch *splissen*.

spliff > *noun* informal a cannabis cigarette.

spline > *noun* 1 a rectangular key fitting into grooves in the hub and shaft of a wheel. > *verb* secure by means of a spline.

splint > *noun* 1 a strip of rigid material for supporting a broken bone when it has been set. 2 a long, thin strip of wood used in basketwork or to light a fire. > *verb* secure with a splint or splints.

ORIGIN – Dutch, Low German *splinte* 'metal plate or pin'.

splinter > *noun* a small, thin, sharp piece of wood, glass, etc. broken off from a larger piece. > *verb* break or cause to break into splinters.

DERIVATIVES – **splintery** adjective.

COMBINATIONS – **splinter group** a small organisation that has broken away from a larger one.

ORIGIN – Dutch.

split > *verb* (**splitting**; past and past participle **split**) 1 break forcibly into parts. 2 divide into parts or groups. 3 (often **split up**) end a marriage or other relationship. 4 informal (of one's head) suffer great pain from a headache. 5 (**split on**) Brit. informal betray the secrets of or inform on someone. > *noun* 1 a tear, crack, or fissure. 2 an instance of splitting or being split. 3 (**the splits**) (in gymnastics and dance) an act of leaping in the air or sitting down with the legs straight and at right angles to the body.

IDIOMS – **split one's sides** informal be convulsed with laughter.

DERIVATIVES – **splitter** noun.

SYNONYMS – *verb* 1 break, chop, cleave. 2 break up, divide, separate.

COMBINATIONS – **split end** a tip of a person's hair which has split from dryness or ill-treatment. **split-level** 1 (of a room or building) having the floor level of one part about half a storey above or below the floor level of an adjacent part. 2 (of a cooker) having the oven and hob in separately installed units. **split pea** a pea dried and split in half for cooking. **split pin** a metal cotter pin with two arms passed through a hole, held in place by the springing apart of the arms. **split screen** a cinema, television, or computer screen on which two or more separate images are displayed.

ORIGIN – Dutch *splitten* '(of a storm or rock) break up (a ship)'.

split infinitive > *noun* a construction (regarded as an error by traditionalists) consisting of an infinitive with an adverb or other word inserted between *to* and the verb, as in *she seems to really like it*.

wordpower facts
Split infinitive
The long-standing dislike of split infinitives results from a comparison with Latin. In Latin, infinitives consist of only one word (e.g. *amare* 'to love') and so are impossible to split: therefore, so the argument goes, they should not be split in English either. However, English is not the same as Latin. Today the prohibition on the split infinitive is less strong than it used to be, and it is recognised that its use can be effective, for example in *Star Trek*'s mission *to boldly go where no one has gone before*. However, in careful writing or speech it is better to avoid the problem, e.g. by writing *to go boldly* ....

split second > *noun* a very brief moment of time. > *adjective* (**split-second**) very rapid or accurate.

splodge > *noun* & *verb* Brit. informal another term for **SPLOTCH**.

splosh informal > *verb* move with a soft splashing sound. > *noun* a splash or splashing sound.

splotch informal > *noun* a spot, splash, or smear. > *verb* make a splotch on.

DERIVATIVES – **splotchy** adjective.

splurge informal > *noun* 1 a sudden burst of extravagance. 2 a large or excessive amount. > *verb* spend extravagantly.

splutter > *verb* 1 make a series of short, explosive spitting or choking sounds. 2 say in a rapid, indistinct way. > *noun* a spluttering sound.

DERIVATIVES – **splutterer** noun.

spoil > *verb* (past and past participle **spoilt** (chiefly Brit.) or **spoiled**) 1 diminish or destroy the value or quality of. 2 (of food) become unfit for eating. 3 harm the character of (a child) by being too indulgent. 4 treat with great or excessive kindness. 5 (**be spoiling for**) be extremely or aggressively eager for. 6 mark (a ballot paper) incorrectly so as to invalidate one's vote. > *noun* 1 (**spoils**) stolen goods. 2 waste material brought up during the course of an excavation or a dredging or mining operation.

IDIOMS – **be spoilt for choice** Brit. have so many options that it is difficult to make a choice.

DERIVATIVES – **spoilage** noun.

SYNONYMS – *verb* 1 blight, damage, mar, mess up, ruin, wreck. 2 go bad, go off, perish. 3 coddle, cosset, indulge, mollycoddle, overindulge, pamper.

ANTONYMS – *verb* 1 enhance, improve.

ORIGIN – Latin *spoliare*, from *spolium* 'plunder, skin stripped from an animal', or a shortening of **DESPOIL**.

spoiler > *noun* **1** a person or thing that spoils. **2** a flap on an aircraft wing which can be projected to create drag and so reduce speed. **3** a similar device on a motor vehicle intended to improve road-holding at high speeds. **4** a news story published with the intention of reducing the impact of a related item published in a rival paper.

spoilsport > *noun* a person who spoils the pleasure of others.

spoke¹ > *noun* **1** each of the bars or wire rods connecting the centre of a wheel to its rim. **2** each of a set of radial handles projecting from a ship's wheel. **3** each of the metal rods in an umbrella to which the material is attached.
ORIGIN — Old English, related to SPIKE¹.

spoke² past of SPEAK.

spoken past participle of SPEAK. > *adjective* speaking in a specified way: *a soft-spoken man.*
IDIOMS — **be spoken for 1** be already claimed or reserved. **2** already have a romantic commitment.

spokeshave > *noun* a small plane with a handle on each side of its blade, used for shaping curved surfaces.

spokesman (or **spokeswoman**) > *noun* a person who makes statements on behalf of a group.
ORIGIN — formed irregularly from SPOKE², on the pattern of words such as *craftsman*.

spokesperson > *noun* (pl. **spokespersons** or **spokespeople**) a spokesman or spokeswoman (used as a neutral alternative).

spoliation /spōliaysh'n/ > *noun* **1** the action of spoiling. **2** the action of plundering.

spondee /**spon**dee/ > *noun* Poetry a foot consisting of two long (or stressed) syllables.
ORIGIN — from Greek *spondeios pous* 'foot of a libation', from *spondē* 'libation' (being characteristic of music accompanying libations).

spondulicks /spondōōliks/ > *plural noun* Brit. informal money.

spondylitis /spondilītiss/ > *noun* Medicine arthritis in the backbone, especially (**ankylosing spondylitis**) a form in which vertebrae become fused.
ORIGIN — from Latin *spondylus* 'vertebra'.

sponge > *noun* **1** an aquatic invertebrate animal with a soft porous body. **2** a piece of a light, absorbent substance originally consisting of the fibrous skeleton of a sponge but now usually made of synthetic material, used for washing, as padding, etc. **3** a very light cake made with eggs, sugar, and flour but little or no fat. **4** a piece of sponge impregnated with spermicide and inserted into a woman's vagina as a form of barrier contraceptive. **5** informal a person who lives at someone else's expense. > *verb*

(**sponged**, **sponging** or **spongeing**) **1** wipe or clean with a wet sponge or cloth. **2** informal obtain money or food from others without giving anything in return.
COMBINATIONS — **sponge bag** Brit. a toilet bag. **sponge pudding** Brit. a steamed or baked pudding of fat, flour, and eggs.
ORIGIN — Greek *spongos.*

sponger > *noun* informal a person who lives at others' expense.

spongiform /**spun**jiform/ > *adjective* technical having a porous structure or consistency like that of a sponge.

spongy > *adjective* (**spongier**, **spongiest**) like a sponge, especially in being porous, compressible, or absorbent.
DERIVATIVES — **sponginess** *noun.*

sponsor > *noun* **1** a person or organisation that pays for or contributes to the costs of a sporting or artistic event or a radio or television programme in return for advertising. **2** a person who pledges a certain amount of money to a charity after another person has participated in a fund-raising event. **3** a person who introduces and supports a proposal for legislation. **4** a person taking official responsibility for the actions of another. **5** a godparent at a child's baptism. > *verb* be a sponsor for.
DERIVATIVES — **sponsorship** *noun.*

wordpower facts

Sponsor
Sponsor was originally a Latin word derived from *spondere* 'promise solemnly'. In English the first sense was 'godparent', a person who promises to look after and guide a child. From there it came to mean 'a person who takes responsibility for the actions of another'; the main modern meaning (sense 1) is not recorded until 1931. Its root, *spondere*, is the source of the English words **despondent**, **respond**, and **spouse.**

spontaneous > *adjective* **1** performed or occurring as a result of an unpremeditated inner impulse and without external stimulus. **2** open, natural, and uninhibited. **3** (of a process or event) occurring without apparent external cause. **4** Biology (of movement or activity) instinctive or involuntary.
DERIVATIVES — **spontaneity** *noun* **spontaneously** *adverb.*
SYNONYMS — **1** impromptu, impulsive, off the cuff, unplanned, unpremeditated, unsolicited.
ANTONYMS — **1** calculated, planned.
COMBINATIONS — **spontaneous**

combustion the ignition of organic matter without apparent cause.
ORIGIN — Latin *spontaneus*, from *sua sponte* 'of one's own accord'.

spoof informal > *noun* **1** a parody. **2** a hoax. > *verb* **1** parody. **2** hoax.
DERIVATIVES — **spoofer** *noun* **spoofery** *noun.*
ORIGIN — coined by the English comedian Arthur Roberts (1852–1933).

spook informal > *noun* **1** a ghost. **2** chiefly N. Amer. a spy. > *verb* frighten or become frightened.
ORIGIN — Dutch.

spooky > *adjective* (**spookier**, **spookiest**) informal sinister or ghostly.
DERIVATIVES — **spookily** *adverb* **spookiness** *noun.*

spool > *noun* a cylindrical device on which thread, film, fishing line, etc. can be wound. > *verb* **1** wind on to a spool. **2** Computing send (data for printing or peripheral processing) to an intermediate store.
ORIGIN — from Old French *espole* or Low German *spōle.*

spoon > *noun* **1** an implement consisting of a small, shallow bowl on a long handle, used for eating, stirring, and serving food. **2** (also **spoon bait**) a fishing lure designed to wobble when pulled through the water. > *verb* **1** transfer with a spoon. **2** hit (a ball) up into the air with a soft or weak stroke. **3** informal, dated (of a couple) behave in an amorous way.
COMBINATIONS — **spoon-feed 1** feed (a baby or infirm adult) using a spoon. **2** provide (someone) with so much help or information that they do not need to think for themselves.
ORIGIN — Old English, 'chip of wood'.

spoonbill > *noun* a tall wading bird having a long bill with a very broad flat tip.

spoonerism > *noun* an error in speech in which the initial sounds or letters of two or more words are accidentally transposed, often to humorous effect, as in *you have hissed the mystery lectures.*
ORIGIN — named after the English scholar Revd W. A. *Spooner* (1844–1930), who reputedly made such errors in speaking.

spoor > *noun* the track or scent of an animal.
ORIGIN — Dutch *spor.*

sporadic /spe**radd**ik/ > *adjective* occurring at irregular intervals or only in a few places.
DERIVATIVES — **sporadically** *adverb.*
SYNONYMS — infrequent, irregular, occasional, patchy, periodic, scattered.
ANTONYMS — frequent, regular.
ORIGIN — Greek *sporadikos*, from *sporas* 'scattered'.

spore > *noun* Biology a minute structure, typically a single cell, produced by lower plants, fungi, or protozoans and capable of giving rise to a new individual asexually.

ORIGIN – Greek *spora* 'sowing, seed'.

sporran /*sporr*ən/ > *noun* a small pouch worn around the waist so as to hang in front of the kilt as part of men's Scottish Highland dress.

ORIGIN – Scottish Gaelic.

sport > *noun* 1 an activity involving physical exertion and skill in which an individual or team competes against another or others. 2 *informal* a person who behaves well in response to teasing, defeat, etc. 3 success or pleasure derived from an activity such as hunting. 4 *dated* entertainment; fun. 5 *chiefly Austral./NZ* a friendly form of address, especially between unacquainted men. 6 Biology a spontaneously mutated animal or plant showing abnormal or striking variation from the parent type. > *verb* 1 wear or display (a distinctive item). 2 amuse oneself or play in a lively way.

IDIOMS – **the sport of kings** horse racing.

DERIVATIVES – **sporter** *noun*.

COMBINATIONS – **sports bar** a bar where televised sport is shown continuously. **sports car** a low-built car designed for performance at high speeds. **sports jacket** a man's jacket resembling a suit jacket, for informal wear. **sportswear** clothes worn for sport or for casual outdoor use.

wordpower facts

Sport

Sport is a shortening of the archaic word **disport**, which as a verb meant 'enjoy oneself, frolic' and as a noun 'diversion, amusement' and 'a pastime, game, or sport'. In the Middle Ages **sport** meant 'entertainment, amusement', and did not take on the notion of athletic competition until the 16th century. Until the mid 20th century, a **sportsman** was primarily someone devoted to hunting, shooting, and fishing rather than athletics or 'games'. As a verb **sport** meant 'amuse oneself, be at leisure' and 'take part in sports'; the main modern sense, 'wear or display ostentatiously', arose in the 18th century, originally as a colloquial use. Through **disport** and its Latin source, *portare* 'to carry', **sport** is connected to such English words as **deport**, **export**, **import**, **portable**, **report**, **support**, and **transport**.

sporting > *adjective* 1 connected with or interested in sport. 2 fair and generous in one's behaviour.

DERIVATIVES – **sportingly** *adverb*.

sportive > *adjective* playful; light-hearted.

sportsman (or **sportswoman**) > *noun* 1 a person who takes part in a sport, especially as a professional. 2 a person who behaves sportingly.

DERIVATIVES – **sportsmanlike** *adjective* **sportsmanship** *noun*.

sportster > *noun* a sports car.

sporty > *adjective* (**sportier**, **sportiest**) *informal* 1 fond of or good at sport. 2 (of clothing) suitable for wearing for sport or for casual use. 3 (of a car) compact and with fast acceleration.

spot > *noun* 1 a small round mark differing in colour or texture from the surface around it. 2 a pimple. 3 a particular place, point, or position. 4 a place for an individual item in a show. 5 *informal, chiefly Brit.* a small amount: *a spot of lunch*. > *verb* (**spotted**, **spotting**) 1 notice or recognise (someone or something) that is difficult to detect. 2 mark with spots. 3 (**it spots, it is spotting**, etc.) it is raining slightly.

IDIOMS – **in a spot** *informal* in a difficult situation. **on the spot 1** immediately. **2** at the scene of an action or event. **put on the spot** *informal* force (someone) into a situation in which they must respond or act. **spot on** *Brit. informal* completely accurate.

DERIVATIVES – **spotted** *adjective*.

COMBINATIONS – **spotted dog 1** a Dalmatian dog. **2** (also **spotted dick**) *Brit.* a suet pudding containing currants. **spotted fever** a disease characterised by fever and skin spots, especially (in full **Rocky Mountain spotted fever**) a bacterial disease transmitted by ticks. **spot-weld** join by welding at a number of separate points.

ORIGIN – perhaps from Dutch *spotte*.

spot check > *noun* a test made without warning on a randomly selected subject. > *verb* (**spot-check**) subject to a spot check.

spotless > *adjective* absolutely clean or pure.

DERIVATIVES – **spotlessly** *adverb*.

SYNONYMS – flawless, immaculate, pristine, unblemished, unsullied.

ANTONYMS – dirty, impure.

spotlight > *noun* 1 a lamp projecting a narrow, intense beam of light directly on to a place or person. 2 (**the spotlight**) intense public attention. > *verb* (past and past participle **spotlighted** or **spotlit**) 1 illuminate with a spotlight. 2 direct attention on.

spotter > *noun* 1 a person who observes or looks for a particular thing as a hobby or job: *a bus-spotter*. 2 an aviator or aircraft employed in spotting enemy positions.

spotty > *adjective* (**spottier**, **spottiest**) 1 marked with or having spots. 2 *chiefly N. Amer.* of uneven quality.

spousal /*spowz*'l/ > *adjective* Law, chiefly N. Amer. relating to marriage or to a husband or wife.

spouse /*spowz*, *spows*/ > *noun* a husband or wife.

ORIGIN – Latin *sponsus*, from *spondere* 'promise solemnly, betroth'.

spout > *noun* 1 a projecting tube or lip through or over which liquid can be poured from a container. 2 a stream of liquid issuing from somewhere with great force. 3 a pipe, trough, or chute for conveying liquid, grain, etc. > *verb* 1 send out or issue forcibly in a stream. 2 express (one's views) in a lengthy or declamatory way.

IDIOMS – **up the spout** *Brit. informal* 1 useless or ruined. 2 (of a woman) pregnant.

DERIVATIVES – **spouted** *adjective* **spouter** *noun*.

ORIGIN – from Old Norse *spýta* 'to spit'.

sprain > *verb* wrench the ligaments of (a joint) violently so as to cause pain and swelling but not dislocation. > *noun* the result of such a wrench.

sprang past of SPRING.

sprat > *noun* 1 a small marine fish of the herring family, caught for food and fish products. 2 *informal* any small sea fish.

sprawl > *verb* 1 sit, lie, or fall with one's limbs spread out in an ungainly way. 2 spread out irregularly over a large area. > *noun* 1 a sprawling position or movement. 2 a sprawling group or mass. 3 the disorganised expansion of an urban or industrial area into the adjoining countryside.

DERIVATIVES – **sprawling** *adjective*.

ORIGIN – Old English, 'move the limbs convulsively'.

spray[1] > *noun* 1 liquid sent through the air in tiny drops. 2 a liquid preparation which can be forced out of an aerosol or other container in a spray. > *verb* 1 apply (liquid) in a spray. 2 cover or treat with a spray. 3 (of liquid) be sent through the air in a spray. 4 scatter over an area with force.

DERIVATIVES – **sprayer** *noun*.

COMBINATIONS – **spray gun** a device resembling a gun which is used to spray a liquid such as paint under pressure.

ORIGIN – related to Dutch *spraeyen* 'sprinkle'.

spray[2] > *noun* 1 a stem or small branch of a tree or plant, bearing flowers and foliage. 2 a bunch of cut flowers arranged in an attractive way.

spread > *verb* (past and past participle **spread**) 1 open out so as to increase in surface area, width, or length. 2 stretch out (limbs, hands, fingers, or wings) so that they are far apart. 3 extend or distribute over a wide area or a specified period of time. 4 make or become more widely known: *panic spread*. 5 apply (a substance) in an even

949

layer. > *noun* **1** the fact or action of spreading. **2** the extent, width, or area covered by something. **3** the range of something. **4** a soft paste that can be spread on bread. **5** an article or advertisement covering several columns or pages of a newspaper or magazine. **6** informal a large and elaborate meal. **7** N. Amer. a large farm or ranch.

IDIOMS – **spread oneself too thin** be involved in so many different activities that one's time and energy are not used to good effect.

DERIVATIVES – **spreadable** *adjective* **spreader** *noun*.

SYNONYMS – *verb* **1** lay out, open out, unfurl, unroll. **2** extend, fan out, stretch out, unfurl. **3** disperse, scatter, strew.

COMBINATIONS – **spread betting** a form of betting in which money is won or lost according to the degree by which the score or result of a sporting fixture varies from the spread of expected values quoted by the bookmaker.

spreadeagle > *verb* (usu. **be spreadeagled**) stretch (someone) out with their arms and legs extended.

spreadsheet > *noun* a computer program used chiefly for accounting, in which figures arranged in a grid can be manipulated and used in calculations.

spree > *noun* a spell of unrestrained activity of a particular kind.

sprig¹ > *noun* **1** a small stem bearing leaves or flowers, taken from a bush or plant. **2** a descendant or younger member of a family or social class. **3** a small moulded decoration applied to a piece of pottery before firing. > *verb* decorate with sprigs.

ORIGIN – Low German *sprick*.

sprig² > *noun* a small tapering tack with no head, used chiefly to hold glass in a window frame until the putty dries.

sprightly (also **spritely**) > *adjective* (**sprightlier**, **sprightliest**) (especially of an old person) lively; energetic.

DERIVATIVES – **sprightliness** *noun*.

SYNONYMS – active, energetic, lively, perky, spry.

ORIGIN – from *spright*, a rare variant of **SPRITE**.

spring > *verb* (past **sprang** or chiefly N. Amer. **sprung**; past participle **sprung**) **1** move suddenly or rapidly upwards or forwards. **2** move suddenly by or as if by the action of a spring. **3** operate by means of a spring mechanism: *spring a trap*. **4** (**spring from**) originate or appear from. **5** (**spring up**) suddenly develop or appear. **6** (**sprung**) (of a vehicle or item of furniture) having springs. **7** (**spring on**) present (something) suddenly or unexpectedly to. **8** informal bring about the escape or release of (a prisoner). **9** cause (a game bird) to rise from cover.

> *noun* **1** the season after winter and before summer. **2** an elastic device, typically a spiral metal coil, that can be pressed or pulled but returns to its former shape when released. **3** a sudden jump upwards or forwards. **4** a place where water wells up from an underground source. **5** the quality of being elastic.

IDIOMS – **spring a leak** (of a boat or container) develop a leak. [ORIGIN – a nautical use, referring to timbers springing out of position.]

DERIVATIVES – **springlike** *adjective*.

USAGE – the standard past tense of **spring** is **sprang** (*the water tank sprang a leak*): **sprung** is American. However, the past participle is always **sprung** (*the tank has sprung a leak*).

COMBINATIONS – **spring chicken 1** a young chicken for eating (originally available only in spring). **2** informal a young person: *I'm no spring chicken*. **spring fever** a feeling of restlessness and excitement felt at the beginning of spring. **spring greens** the leaves of young cabbage plants of a variety that does not develop a heart. **spring-loaded** containing a compressed or stretched spring pressing one part against another. **spring lock** a type of lock with a spring-loaded bolt which requires a key only to open it, as distinct from a deadlock. **spring onion** chiefly Brit. an onion taken from the ground before the bulb has formed. **spring roll** a Chinese pancake filled with vegetables and sometimes meat, rolled into a cylinder and fried. **spring tide** a tide just after a new or full moon, when there is the greatest difference between high and low water.

springboard > *noun* **1** a strong, flexible board from which a diver or gymnast may jump in order to gain impetus. **2** a thing providing impetus to an action or enterprise.

springbok > *noun* **1** a southern African gazelle with a characteristic habit of leaping when disturbed. **2** (**Springbok**) a member of a sports team selected to represent South Africa.

ORIGIN – from Dutch *springen* 'to spring' + *bok* 'antelope'.

spring clean > *noun* Brit. a thorough cleaning of a house or room, typically undertaken in spring. > *verb* (**spring-clean**) clean thoroughly.

springer spaniel > *noun* a small breed of spaniel originally used to spring game.

springy > *adjective* (**springier**, **springiest**) **1** springing back quickly when squeezed or stretched. **2** (of movements) light and confident.

DERIVATIVES – **springily** *adverb* **springiness** *noun*.

sprinkle > *verb* **1** scatter or pour small drops or particles over. **2** scatter or pour (small drops or particles) over an object or surface. **3** distribute something randomly throughout. > *noun* a small amount that is sprinkled.

sprinkler > *noun* **1** a device for watering lawns. **2** an automatic fire extinguisher installed in a ceiling.

sprinkling > *noun* a small, thinly distributed amount.

sprint > *verb* run at full speed over a short distance. > *noun* **1** an act or spell of sprinting. **2** a short, fast race.

DERIVATIVES – **sprinter** *noun* **sprinting** *noun*.

sprit > *noun* Sailing a small spar reaching diagonally from a mast to the upper outer corner of a sail.

COMBINATIONS – **spritsail 1** a sail extended by a sprit. **2** a sail extended by a yard set under a ship's bowsprit.

ORIGIN – Old English, 'punting pole'.

sprite > *noun* **1** an elf or fairy. **2** Computing a graphical figure which can be moved and manipulated as a single entity.

ORIGIN – a contraction of **SPIRIT**.

spritely > *adjective* variant spelling of **SPRIGHTLY**.

spritz chiefly N. Amer. > *verb* squirt or spray in quick, short bursts. > *noun* an act or instance of spritzing.

ORIGIN – German *spritzen* 'to squirt'.

spritzer > *noun* a mixture of wine and soda water.

ORIGIN – German, 'a splash'.

sprocket > *noun* **1** each of several projections on the rim of a wheel that engage with the links of a chain or with holes in film, tape, or paper. **2** (also **sprocket wheel**) a wheel with projections of this kind.

sprog > *noun* Brit. informal a child.

ORIGIN – perhaps from obsolete *sprag* 'lively young man'.

sprout > *verb* **1** produce shoots. **2** grow (plant shoots or hair). **3** start to grow or develop. > *noun* **1** a shoot of a plant. **2** short for **BRUSSELS SPROUT**.

spruce¹ > *adjective* neat and smart. > *verb* (**spruce up**) make (a person or place) smarter.

spruce² > *noun* a widespread coniferous tree which has a distinctive conical shape and hanging cones.

sprue¹ > *noun* **1** a channel through which metal or plastic is poured into a mould. **2** a piece of metal or plastic which has solidified in a sprue.

sprue² > *noun* a disease characterised by ulceration of the mouth and chronic enteritis, suffered by visitors to tropical regions.

ORIGIN – Dutch *spruw* 'thrush'.

wordpower facts
Spruce

The two English words **spruce** are completely different in meaning, but may have a shared origin. **Spruce**, the name of a coniferous tree, is an alteration of obsolete *Pruce* 'Prussia'. The word entered English in the medieval period with the meaning 'Prussia' or 'Prussian'; its application to the tree dates from the early 17th century. **Spruce** meaning 'neat and smart' may have come from the phrase *spruce leather jerkin*, a leather jacket made of fine Prussian leather.

spruik /sprook/ > *verb* Austral. informal speak in public, especially to advertise a show.
DERIVATIVES – **spruiker** *noun*.

sprung past participle and (especially in North America) past of **SPRING**.

spry > *adjective* (**spryer**, **spryest**) (especially of an old person) lively.
SYNONYMS – active, energetic, lively, perky, sprightly.

spud > *noun* **1** informal a potato. **2** a small, narrow spade for cutting the roots of weeds. > *verb* (**spudded**, **spudding**) **1** dig up or cut (weeds) with a spud. **2** make the initial drilling for (an oil well).

spumante /spoomanti/ > *noun* an Italian sparkling white wine.
ORIGIN – Italian, 'sparkling'.

spume /spyoom/ literary > *noun* froth or foam, especially that found on waves. > *verb* froth or foam.
ORIGIN – Latin *spuma*.

spun past and past participle of **SPIN**.

spunk > *noun* **1** informal courage and determination. **2** Brit. vulgar slang semen. **3** Austral. informal a sexually attractive person.
ORIGIN – perhaps a blend of **SPARK**[1] and obsolete *funk* 'spark'.

spunky > *adjective* (**spunkier**, **spunkiest**) informal **1** courageous and determined. **2** Austral. sexually attractive.
DERIVATIVES – **spunkily** *adverb*.

spur > *noun* **1** a device with a small spike or a spiked wheel, worn on a rider's heel for urging a horse forward. **2** something that prompts or encourages; an incentive. **3** a projection from a mountain or mountain range. **4** Botany a slender tubular projection from the base of a flower. **5** a short branch road or railway line. > *verb* (**spurred**, **spurring**) (often **spur on**) **1** urge (a horse) forward with spurs. **2** encourage; give an incentive to.
IDIOMS – **on the spur of the moment** on a momentary impulse.
SYNONYMS – *noun* **2** encouragement, goad, impetus, incentive, motivation, stimulus.

verb **2** encourage, inspire, motivate, prompt, stimulate.
COMBINATIONS – **spur wheel** (also **spur gear**) a gearwheel with teeth projecting parallel to the wheel's axis.

spurge > *noun* a plant or shrub with milky latex and small flowers.
ORIGIN – Old French *espurge*, from Latin *expurgare* 'cleanse' (because of the purgative properties of the milky latex).

spurious /spyooriass/ > *adjective* **1** false or fake. **2** (of a line of reasoning) apparently but not actually valid.
DERIVATIVES – **spuriously** *adverb*.
ORIGIN – Latin *spurius* 'false'.

spurn > *verb* reject with contempt.
SYNONYMS – brush off, rebuff, reject, scorn, shun, snub.
ORIGIN – Old English; related to Latin *spernere* 'to scorn'.

spurt* > *verb* **1** gush out in a sudden stream. **2** move with a sudden burst of speed. > *noun* **1** a sudden gushing stream. **2** a sudden burst of activity or speed.
*SPELLING – -u-, not -i-: spurt. Spirt is an old-fashioned spelling.

sputnik /sputnik, spootnik/ > *noun* each of a series of Soviet satellites, the first of which was the first artificial satellite to be placed in orbit.
ORIGIN – Russian, 'fellow-traveller'.

sputter > *verb* **1** make a series of soft explosive sounds. **2** speak in a series of incoherent bursts. > *noun* a sputtering sound.
ORIGIN – Dutch *sputteren*.

sputum > *noun* a mixture of saliva and mucus coughed up from the respiratory tract.
ORIGIN – Latin, from *spuere* 'to spit'.

spy > *noun* (pl. **spies**) **1** a person employed to collect and report secret information on an enemy or competitor. **2** a person who observes others secretly. > *verb* (**spies**, **spied**) **1** be a spy. **2** (**spy on**) observe furtively. **3** observe or notice.
WORDFINDER – espionage (*the practice of spying or using spies*).
ORIGIN – shortening of Old French *espie* 'espying', *espier* 'espy'.

spyglass > *noun* a small telescope.

spyhole > *noun* Brit. a peephole.

sq > *abbreviation* square.

SQL > *abbreviation* Computing Structured Query Language, an international standard for database manipulation.

squab /skwob/ > *noun* **1** a young unfledged pigeon. **2** Brit. the padded back or side of a vehicle seat. **3** a thick cushion, especially one covering the seat of a chair or sofa.

squabble > *noun* a trivial noisy quarrel. > *verb* engage in a squabble.
SYNONYMS – *noun* argument, quarrel, row. *verb* argue, bicker, quarrel, row.

squad > *noun* **1** a small number of soldiers assembled for drill or assigned to a particular task. **2** a group of sports players from which a team is chosen. **3** a division of a police force dealing with a particular type of crime.
COMBINATIONS – **squad car** a police patrol car.
ORIGIN – from Italian *squadra* 'square'.

squaddie > *noun* (pl. **squaddies**) Brit. informal a private soldier.

squadron > *noun* **1** an operational unit in an air force consisting of two or more flights of aircraft. **2** a principal division of an armoured or cavalry regiment, consisting of two or more troops. **3** a group of warships detached on a particular duty or under the command of a flag officer.
COMBINATIONS – **squadron leader** a rank of officer in the RAF, above flight lieutenant and below wing commander.
ORIGIN – Italian *squadrone*, from *squadra* 'square': originally referring to a group of soldiers in square formation.

squalid > *adjective* **1** extremely dirty and unpleasant. **2** showing a contemptible lack of moral standards: *a squalid attempt to buy votes*.
SYNONYMS – **1** dingy, filthy, foul, seedy, sordid. **2** base, cheap, low, seedy, sleazy, sordid.
ORIGIN – Latin *squalidus*, from *squalere* 'be rough or dirty'.

squall > *noun* **1** a sudden violent gust of wind or localised storm. **2** a loud cry. > *verb* (of a baby or small child) cry noisily and continuously.
DERIVATIVES – **squally** *adjective*.
ORIGIN – probably an alteration of **SQUEAL**.

squalor > *noun* the state of being squalid.
SYNONYMS – dirt, filth, muck.

squamous /skwaymass/ > *adjective* **1** technical covered with or resembling scales. **2** Anatomy relating to a layer of epithelium consisting of very thin flattened cells.
ORIGIN – Latin *squamosus*, from *squama* 'scale'.

squander > *verb* waste in a reckless or foolish manner.
SYNONYMS – dissipate, fritter, waste.

square > *noun* **1** a plane figure with four equal straight sides and four right angles. **2** an open area, typically with four sides, surrounded by buildings. **3** an area within a military barracks or camp used for drill. **4** the product of a number multiplied by itself. **5** an L-shaped or T-shaped instrument used for obtaining or testing right angles. **6** informal an old-fashioned or boringly conventional person. > *adjective* **1** having the shape of a square. **2** having or forming a right angle. **3** denoting a unit of measurement equal to the area of a square whose side is of the unit specified. **4** (after a noun) denoting the length of each side of a square shape or object. **5** at right angles. **6** broad and solid in shape. **7** level or parallel. **8** fair and honest. **9** informal old-fashioned or boringly conventional. > *adverb* directly; straight. > *verb* **1** make square or rectangular. **2** (**squared**) marked out in squares. **3** multiply (a number) by itself. **4** make or be compatible. **5** balance (an account) or settle (a bill or debt). **6** make the score of (a match or game) even. **7** informal secure the co-operation of (someone) by offering an inducement. **8** bring (one's shoulders) into a position in which they appear square and broad.

IDIOMS – **back to square one** informal back to where one started. **square the circle 1** construct a square equal in area to a given circle (a problem incapable of geometrical solution). **2** do something considered to be impossible. **a square deal** see DEAL¹. **a square peg in a round hole** see PEG. **square up 1** assume the attitude of a person about to fight. **2** (**square up to**) face and tackle (a difficulty) resolutely.

DERIVATIVES – **squareness** *noun* **squarer** *noun* **squarish** *adjective*.

COMBINATIONS – **square-bashing** Brit. informal military drill performed repeatedly on a barrack square. **square dance** a country dance that starts with four couples facing one another in a square. **square eyes** Brit. humorous eyes supposedly affected by excessive television viewing. **square leg** Cricket a fielding position level with the batsman approximately halfway towards the boundary on the leg side. **square meal** a substantial and balanced meal. [ORIGIN – said to derive from nautical use, with reference to the square platters on which meals were served.] **square measure** a unit of measurement relating to area. **square number** a number which is equal to another number squared, e.g. 1, 4, 9, 16. **square-rigged** (of a sailing ship) having the principal sails at right angles to the length of the ship. **square root** a number which produces a specified quantity when multiplied by itself.

squarely > *adverb* without deviation or equivocation; directly.

squarial > *noun* Brit. trademark a type of diamond-shaped dish aerial for receiving satellite television broadcasts.

squash¹ > *verb* **1** crush or squeeze (something) so that it becomes flat, soft, or out of shape. **2** squeeze or force into a restricted space. **3** suppress or subdue. > *noun* **1** a state of being squashed. **2** Brit. a concentrated liquid made from fruit juice and sugar, diluted to make a drink. **3** (also **squash rackets**) a game in which two players use rackets to hit a small rubber ball

against the walls of a closed court. **4** dated a social gathering or informal meeting.

ORIGIN – from QUASH.

wordpower facts

Square

The word **square** entered English from Old French *esquare*, which came from Latin *quadra*, *quadrus* 'square' and ultimately from *quattuor* 'four', the root of the word **four** in many European languages. A number of English words are formed from *quadrus*, including **cadre**, **quadrille**, and **quarry**; the related Latin element *quadri-*, meaning 'four', is the root of words such as **quadrangle** and **quadrilateral**. **Squad** and **squadron** are also connected to **square**, via Italian: a **squadron** was originally a group of soldiers in square formation.

squash² > *noun* (pl. same or **squashes**) a gourd with flesh that can be cooked and eaten as a vegetable.

ORIGIN – Narragansett.

squashy > *adjective* (**squashier**, **squashiest**) easily crushed or squeezed into a different shape.

squat > *verb* (**squatted**, **squatting**) **1** crouch or sit with the knees bent and the heels close to the bottom or thighs. **2** unlawfully occupy an uninhabited building or area of land. > *adjective* (**squatter**, **squattest**) short or low, and disproportionately broad or wide. > *noun* **1** a squatting position or movement. **2** a building occupied by squatters. **3** an act of squatting in an uninhabited building. **4** N. Amer. informal short for DIDDLY-SQUAT.

COMBINATIONS – **squat thrust** an exercise in which the legs are thrust backwards to their full extent from a squatting position with the hands on the floor.

ORIGIN – Old French *esquatir* 'flatten', from Latin *cogere* 'compel'.

squatter > *noun* **1** a person who squats in a building or on unused land. **2** Austral./NZ a large-scale sheep or cattle farmer.

squaw /skwaw/ > *noun* offensive an American Indian woman or wife.

USAGE – avoid using the word **squaw**: the derogatory attitudes of the past towards American Indian women have meant that it cannot now be used without being regarded as offensive and old-fashioned.

ORIGIN – Narragansett, 'woman'.

squawk > *verb* **1** (of a bird) make a loud, harsh noise. **2** say something in a loud, discordant tone. > *noun* an act of squawking.

COMBINATIONS – **squawk box** informal, chiefly N. Amer. a loudspeaker.

squeak > *noun* **1** a short, high-pitched sound or cry. **2** a single remark or communication: *I didn't hear a squeak from him for months.* > *verb* **1** make a squeak. **2** say something in a high-pitched tone. **3** (often **squeak through**) informal narrowly succeed in achieving something.

IDIOMS – **a narrow squeak** Brit. informal something that is only narrowly achieved.

DERIVATIVES – **squeaker** *noun*.

squeaky > *adjective* (**squeakier**, **squeakiest**) making a high-pitched sound or cry.

DERIVATIVES – **squeakily** *adverb*.

COMBINATIONS – **squeaky clean** informal **1** completely clean. **2** beyond reproach.

squeal > *noun* a long, high-pitched cry or noise. > *verb* **1** make a squeal. **2** say something in a high-pitched, excited tone. **3** complain. **4** informal inform on someone.

DERIVATIVES – **squealer** *noun*.

squeamish > *adjective* **1** easily nauseated or disgusted. **2** having fastidious moral views.

DERIVATIVES – **squeamishness** *noun*.

SYNONYMS – **2** high-minded, particular, principled, scrupulous, upright.

ORIGIN – Old French *escoymos*.

squeegee /skweejee/ > *noun* a scraping implement with a rubber-edged blade, typically used for cleaning windows. > *verb* (**squeegees**, **squeegeed**, **squeegeeing**) clean or scrape with a squeegee.

ORIGIN – from archaic *squeege* 'to press', from SQUEEZE.

squeeze > *verb* **1** firmly press from opposite or all sides. **2** extract (liquid or a soft substance) from something by squeezing. **3** (usu. **squeeze out of**) obtain from someone with difficulty. **4** (**squeeze in** or **into** or **through**) manage to get into or through (a restricted space). **5** (**squeeze in**) manage to find time for. **6** (**squeeze off**) informal shoot (a round or shot) from a gun. > *noun* **1** an act of squeezing or state of being squeezed. **2** a hug. **3** a small amount of liquid extracted by squeezing. **4** a strong financial demand or pressure. **5** (often **main squeeze**) N. Amer. informal a person's girlfriend or boyfriend.

IDIOMS – **put the squeeze on** informal coerce or pressurise.

DERIVATIVES – **squeezable** *adjective* **squeezer** *noun*.

COMBINATIONS – **squeeze box** informal an accordion or concertina.

ORIGIN – from obsolete *queise*.

squeezy > *adjective* (especially of a container) flexible and able to be squeezed to force out the contents.

squelch > *verb* **1** make a soft sucking sound like that made by treading in thick mud. **2**

informal forcefully silence or suppress. > *noun* a squelching sound.

DERIVATIVES – **squelchy** *adjective*.

squib > *noun* **1** a small firework that hisses before exploding. **2** a short piece of satirical writing.

squid > *noun* (pl. same or **squids**) **1** an elongated cephalopod mollusc with eight arms and two long tentacles. **2** the flesh of this animal as food.

WORDFINDER – calamari (*squid served as food*).

squidge > *verb* informal **1** squash or crush. **2** squelch.

squidgy > *adjective* (**squidgier, squidgiest**) informal, chiefly Brit. soft and moist.

squiffy > *adjective* (**squiffier, squiffiest**) informal **1** chiefly Brit. slightly drunk. **2** askew; awry.

squiggle > *noun* a short line that curls and loops irregularly.

DERIVATIVES – **squiggly** *adjective*.

ORIGIN – perhaps a blend of **SQUIRM** and **WIGGLE** or **WRIGGLE**.

squill > *noun* **1** (also **sea squill**) a bulbous Mediterranean plant with broad leaves and white flowers. **2** a small plant resembling a hyacinth, with clusters of violet-blue or blue-striped flowers.

ORIGIN – Greek *skilla*.

squillion > *cardinal number* informal an indefinite very large number.

DERIVATIVES – **squillionth** *ordinal number*.

ORIGIN – fanciful formation on the pattern of *billion* and *trillion*.

squinch > *verb* chiefly N. Amer. tense up the muscles of (one's eyes or face).

ORIGIN – perhaps a blend of **SQUEEZE** and **PINCH**.

squint > *verb* **1** look at someone or something with partly closed eyes. **2** partly close (one's eyes). **3** have a squint affecting one eye. > *noun* **1** a permanent deviation in the direction of the gaze of one eye. **2** informal a quick or casual look.

DERIVATIVES – **squinty** *adjective*.

ORIGIN – perhaps related to Dutch *schuinte* 'slant'.

squire > *noun* **1** a country gentleman, especially the chief landowner in an area. **2** Brit. informal used as a friendly form of address by one man to another. **3** historical a young nobleman acting as an attendant to a knight before becoming a knight himself. > *verb* **1** (of a man) accompany or escort (a woman). **2** dated (of a man) have a romantic relationship with (a woman).

ORIGIN – Old French *esquier* 'esquire'.

squirearchy > *noun* landowners collectively.

ORIGIN – from **SQUIRE**, on the pattern of words such as *hierarchy*.

squirm > *verb* **1** wriggle or twist the body from side to side, especially because of

nervousness or discomfort. **2** be embarrassed or ashamed. > *noun* a wriggling movement.

DERIVATIVES – **squirmy** *adjective*.

ORIGIN – probably associated with **WORM**.

squirrel > *noun* an agile tree-dwelling rodent with a bushy tail, typically feeding on nuts and seeds. > *verb* (**squirrelled, squirrelling**; US also **squirreled, squirreling**) **1** (**squirrel away**) hide (money or valuables) in a safe place. **2** move about inquisitively or busily.

WORDFINDER – sciurine (*squirrel-like*); drey (*squirrel's nest*).

COMBINATIONS – **squirrel monkey** a small South American monkey with a non-prehensile tail.

ORIGIN – Old French *esquireul*, from Greek *skiouros*, from *skia* 'shade' + *oura* 'tail'.

squirrelly > *adjective* **1** relating to or resembling a squirrel. **2** informal, chiefly N. Amer. restless or nervous.

squirt > *verb* **1** (with reference to a liquid) be or cause to be ejected in a thin jet from a small opening. **2** wet with a jet of liquid. > *noun* **1** a thin jet of liquid. **2** informal a puny or insignificant person. **3** a device from which liquid may be squirted.

squish > *verb* **1** make a soft squelching sound. **2** informal squash. > *noun* a soft squelching sound.

DERIVATIVES – **squishy** (**squishier, squishiest**) *adjective*.

squiz > *noun* Austral./NZ informal a look or glance.

ORIGIN – probably a blend of **QUIZ²** and **SQUINT**.

SR > *abbreviation* historical (in the UK) Southern Railway.

Sr > *symbol* the chemical element strontium.

sr > *abbreviation* steradian(s).

SRAM > *abbreviation* Electronics static random-access memory.

Sri Lankan /sri **lang**kən, shri/ > *noun* a person from Sri Lanka (formerly Ceylon). > *adjective* relating to Sri Lanka.

SRN > *abbreviation* State Registered Nurse.

SS¹ > *abbreviation* **1** Saints. **2** steamship.

SS² > *noun* the Nazi special police force.

ORIGIN – abbreviation of German *Schutzstaffel* 'defence squadron'.

SSE > *abbreviation* south-south-east.

SSP > *abbreviation* (in the UK) statutory sick pay.

SSSI > *abbreviation* (in the UK) Site of Special Scientific Interest.

SSW > *abbreviation* south-south-west.

St > *abbreviation* **1** Saint. **2** Street.

st > *abbreviation* stone (in weight).

stab > *verb* (**stabbed, stabbing**) **1** thrust a knife or other pointed weapon into. **2** thrust a pointed object at. **3** (of a pain or painful thing) cause a sudden sharp sensation. > *noun* **1** an act of stabbing. **2** a

sudden sharp feeling or pain. **3** (**a stab at**) informal an attempt to do.

IDIOMS – **stab in the back** betray.

DERIVATIVES – **stabber** *noun* **stabbing** *noun & adjective*.

SYNONYMS – *verb* **1** perforate, pierce, puncture, skewer, spike.

stabilise (also **stabilize**) > *verb* make or become stable.

DERIVATIVES – **stabilisation** *noun*.

stabiliser (also **stabilizer**) > *noun* **1** the horizontal tailplane of an aircraft. **2** a gyroscopic device used to reduce the rolling of a ship. **3** (**stabilisers**) Brit. a pair of small supporting wheels fitted on a child's bicycle. **4** a substance preventing the breakdown of emulsions, especially in food or paint.

stability > *noun* the state of being stable.

SYNONYMS – balance, constancy, equilibrium, firmness, solidity, steadiness.

stable¹ > *adjective* (**stabler, stablest**) **1** not likely to give way or overturn; firmly fixed. **2** not deteriorating in health after an injury or operation. **3** emotionally well balanced. **4** not likely to change or fail. **5** not liable to undergo chemical decomposition or radioactive decay.

DERIVATIVES – **stably** *adverb*.

SYNONYMS – **1,4** firm, secure, solid, steady. **3** balanced, reasonable, sensible, sound.

ANTONYMS – **1,4** unstable. **3** unbalanced, unstable.

ORIGIN – Latin *stabilis*, from *stare* 'to stand'.

stable² > *noun* **1** a building for housing horses. **2** an establishment where racehorses are kept and trained. **3** an establishment producing particular types of people or things. > *verb* put or keep (a horse) in a stable.

COMBINATIONS – **stable boy** (or **stable girl**, also Brit. **stable lad**) a boy or man (or girl or woman) employed in a stable. **stable door** a door of a kind found in a stable, divided into two parts horizontally. **stablemate 1** a horse from the same stable as another. **2** a person or product from the same organisation or background as another.

ORIGIN – Old French *estable* 'stable, pigsty', from Latin *stabulum*.

stabling > *noun* accommodation for horses.

staccato /stə**kaa**tō/ > *adverb & adjective* Music with each sound or note sharply separated from the others. > *noun* (pl. **staccatos**) **1** Music a staccato passage or performance. **2** a series of short, detached sounds or words.

ORIGIN – Italian, 'detached'.

stack > *noun* **1** a neat pile. **2** a rectangular or cylindrical pile of hay, straw, etc. **3** informal a large quantity. **4** a chimney or vertical exhaust pipe. **5** a number of aircraft flying in circles at different altitudes around the

same point while waiting to land at an airport. **6** (also **sea stack**) Brit. a column of rock standing in the sea. > *verb* **1** arrange in a stack. **2** fill or cover with stacks of things. **3** cause (aircraft) to fly in stacks. **4** shuffle or arrange (a pack of cards) dishonestly. **5** (**be stacked against** or **in favour of**) (of a situation) be overwhelmingly likely to produce an unfavourable or favourable outcome for.
DERIVATIVES – **stackable** *adjective* **stacker** *noun*.
ORIGIN – Old Norse *stakkr* 'haystack'.

stacked > *adjective* **1** arranged in a stack or stacks. **2** filled or covered with goods. **3** (of a pack of cards) shuffled or arranged dishonestly.

stadium /staydiəm/ > *noun* (pl. **stadiums** or **stadia** /staydiə/) **1** an athletic or sports ground with tiers of seats for spectators. **2** (in ancient Rome or Greece) a racing track.
ORIGIN – first used to denote an ancient Greek and Roman measure of length, about 185 metres (equivalent to the length of a stadium): Latin, from Greek *stadion*.

staff > *noun* **1** the employees of an organisation. **2** a long stick used as a support or weapon. **3** a rod or sceptre held as a sign of office or authority. **4** a group of officers assisting an officer in command of an army formation or administration headquarters. **5** Music another term for STAVE (in sense 3). > *verb* provide with staff.
WORDFINDER – *types of staff:* crook, crozier, mace, sceptre.
IDIOMS – **the staff of life** a staple food, especially bread.
COMBINATIONS – **staff college** a college at which military officers are trained for staff duties. **staff nurse** Brit. an experienced nurse less senior than a sister or charge nurse. **staff officer** a military officer serving on the staff of a headquarters or government department. **staffroom** chiefly Brit. a common room for teachers in a school or college. **staff sergeant 1** a rank of non-commissioned officer in the army, above sergeant and below warrant officer. **2** a rank of non-commissioned officer in the US air force.

staffer > *noun* chiefly N. Amer. a member of a staff, especially of a newspaper.

Staffordshire bull terrier > *noun* a small, stocky breed of terrier with a short, broad head and dropped ears.

Staffs. > *abbreviation* Staffordshire.

stag > *noun* **1** a fully adult male deer. **2** an adult male turkey. **3** (before another noun) denoting a social gathering attended by men only. **4** Brit. Stock Exchange a person who applies for shares in a new issue with a view to selling at once for a profit. > *verb* (**stagged**, **stagging**) Brit. Stock Exchange buy

(shares in a new issue) and sell them at once for a profit.
COMBINATIONS – **stag beetle** a very large dark beetle, the male of which has large branched jaws resembling antlers. **staghound** a large breed of dog used for hunting deer. **stag night** (also **stag party**) an all-male celebration, especially one held for a man about to be married.
ORIGIN – related to Old Norse *steggr* 'male bird'.

stage > *noun* **1** a point, period, or step in a process or development. **2** a raised floor or platform on which actors, entertainers, or speakers perform. **3** (**the stage**) the acting or theatrical profession. **4** a scene of action or forum of debate. **5** a floor of a building. **6** each of two or more sections of a rocket or spacecraft that are jettisoned in turn when their propellant is exhausted. **7** Electronics a part of a circuit containing a single amplifying transistor or valve. **8** Geology a range of strata corresponding to an age in time, forming a subdivision of a series. **9** archaic a stagecoach. > *verb* **1** present a performance of (a play or other show). **2** organise and participate in (a public event). **3** cause (something dramatic or unexpected) to happen.
IDIOMS – **hold the stage** dominate a scene of action or forum of debate. **set the stage for** prepare the conditions for.
SYNONYMS – *noun* **1** juncture, period, phase, point, step, time. *verb* **1** mount, perform, present, produce, put on. **2** arrange, coordinate, mount, orchestrate, organise.
COMBINATIONS – **stagecraft** skill in writing or staging plays. **stage direction** an instruction in a play script indicating the position or tone of an actor, or specifying sound effects, lighting, etc. **stage door** an actors' and workmen's entrance from the street to the backstage area of a theatre. **stage fright** nervousness before or during a performance. **stagehand** a person dealing with scenery or props during a play. **stage manager** the person responsible for lighting and other technical arrangements for a stage play. **stage name** a name assumed for professional purposes by an actor. **stage-struck** having a passionate love of the theatre and wishing to become an actor. **stage whisper** a loud whisper by an actor on stage, intended to be heard by the audience. **staging area** a stopping place or assembly point en route to a destination. **staging post** a place at which people or vehicles regularly stop during a journey.
ORIGIN – Old French *estage* 'dwelling', from Latin *stare* 'to stand'.

stagecoach > *noun* a large horse-drawn vehicle formerly used to carry passengers and often mail along a regular route.

stage-manage > *verb* **1** be the stage manager of. **2** arrange carefully to create a certain effect.
DERIVATIVES – **stage management** *noun*.

stagey > *adjective* variant spelling of STAGY.

stagflation > *noun* Economics persistent high inflation combined with high unemployment and stagnant demand in a country's economy.

stagger > *verb* **1** walk or move unsteadily, as if about to fall. **2** astonish or deeply shock (someone). **3** spread over a period of time. **4** arrange (objects or parts) so that they are not in line. > *noun* an act of staggering.
DERIVATIVES – **staggering** *noun & adjective* **staggeringly** *adverb*.
SYNONYMS – *verb* **1** lurch, reel, stumble, totter, wobble. **2** amaze, astonish, astound, flabbergast, stun, surprise.
ORIGIN – Old Norse *staka* 'push, stagger'.

staggers > *plural noun* (usu. treated as sing.) **1** a diseased condition of farm animals manifested by staggering or loss of balance. **2** (**the staggers**) the inability to stand or walk steadily.

staghorn (also **stag's horn**) > *noun* the material of a stag's antler, used to make handles for cutlery.

staging > *noun* **1** an instance or method of staging something. **2** a stage or set of stages or platforms for performers or between levels of scaffolding. **3** Brit. shelving for plants in a greenhouse.

stagnant > *adjective* **1** (of water or air) motionless and often having an unpleasant smell as a consequence. **2** showing little activity.
DERIVATIVES – **stagnancy** *noun*.
SYNONYMS – **1** motionless, stale, standing, still. **2** inactive, slow, sluggish, static.
ANTONYMS – **1** flowing, fresh. **2** active, vibrant.
ORIGIN – from Latin *stagnare* 'form a pool of standing water', from *stagnum* 'pool'.

stagnate > *verb* **1** (of water or air) become stagnant. **2** cease developing; become inactive or dull.
DERIVATIVES – **stagnation** *noun*.

stagy (also **stagey**) > *adjective* (**stagier**, **stagiest**) excessively theatrical or exaggerated.
DERIVATIVES – **stagily** *adverb* **staginess** *noun*.

staid > *adjective* respectable and unadventurous.
DERIVATIVES – **staidness** *noun*.
SYNONYMS – conventional, respectable, sedate, sober, steady, unadventurous.
ANTONYMS – adventurous, daring, wild.
ORIGIN – archaic past participle of STAY[1].

stain > *verb* **1** mark or discolour with something that is not easily removed. **2** damage (the reputation of someone or something). **3** colour with a penetrative dye or chemical. > *noun* **1** a stubborn discoloured patch or dirty mark. **2** a thing that damages the reputation of someone or something. **3** a dye or chemical used to colour materials. **4** Biology a dye used to colour organic tissue so as to make the structure visible for microscopic examination.

DERIVATIVES – **stainable** *adjective* **stainer** *noun*.

SYNONYMS – *verb* **1** blemish, blot, dirty, discolour, mark, soil. **2** besmirch, damage, sully, taint, tarnish. *noun* **1** blemish, blot, blotch, discoloration, mark, spot. **2** blemish, blot, smear, stigma.

COMBINATIONS – **stained glass** coloured glass used to form decorative or pictorial designs, especially in church windows.

ORIGIN – shortening of archaic *distain*, from Old French *desteindre* 'tinge with a different colour'.

stainless > *adjective* **1** unmarked by or resistant to stains. **2** (of a person or their reputation) free from wrongdoing or disgrace.

COMBINATIONS – **stainless steel** a form of steel containing chromium, resistant to tarnishing and rust.

stair > *noun* **1** each of a set of fixed steps. **2** (**stairs**) a set of such steps leading from one floor of a building to another.

COMBINATIONS – **stairlift** a lift in the form of a chair that can be raised or lowered at the edge of a domestic staircase. **stairwell** a shaft in which a staircase is built.

ORIGIN – Old English, from a Germanic word meaning 'climb'.

staircase > *noun* a set of stairs and its surrounding structure.

stairway > *noun* a staircase.

staithe /stayth/ > *noun* (in the north and east of England) a landing stage for loading or unloading cargo boats.

ORIGIN – Old Norse, 'landing stage'.

stake[1] > *noun* **1** a strong post with a point at one end, driven into the ground to support a tree, form part of a fence, etc. **2** historical a wooden post to which a person was tied before being burned alive. > *verb* **1** support (a plant) with a stake. **2** (**stake out**) mark (an area) with stakes so as to claim ownership. **3** (**stake out**) informal keep (a place or person) under surveillance.

IDIOMS – **stake a claim** assert one's right to something.

ORIGIN – Old English, related to STICK[2].

stake[2] > *noun* **1** a sum of money gambled on a risky game or venture. **2** a share or interest in a business or situation. **3** (**stakes**) prize money. **4** (**stakes**) a competitive situation: *one step ahead in the fashion stakes.* > *verb* gamble (money or something of value).

IDIOMS – **at stake 1** at risk. **2** at issue or in question.

ORIGIN – perhaps from STAKE[1], from the notion of an object being placed as a wager on a post or stake.

stakeholder > *noun* **1** an independent party with whom money or counters wagered are deposited. **2** a person with an interest or concern in something.

stake-out > *noun* informal a period of secret surveillance.

Stakhanovite /stəkaanəvīt/ > *noun* a worker, especially in the former USSR, who is exceptionally productive or zealous.

ORIGIN – from the name of the Russian coal miner Aleksei Grigorevich *Stakhanov* (1906–77).

stalactite /stalәktīt/ > *noun* a tapering structure hanging from the roof of a cave, formed of calcium salts deposited by dripping water.

---

wordpower facts

Stalactite, stalagmite

How do you remember the difference between a **stalagmite** and a **stalactite**? Perhaps the easiest is the idea that a stalactite has to hang on *tight*; alternatively, stalagmite contains *g* for ground, while stalactite contains *c* for ceiling. Both words are formed from Greek roots, **stalactite** from *stalaktos* 'dripping' and **stalagmite** from *stalagma* 'a drop' (and both ultimately from *stalassein* 'to drip'). The technical term which covers all cave formations deposited from water, including stalactites and stalagmites, is **speleothem**, from Greek *spēlaion* 'cave' + *thema* 'deposit', while the material of which they are made is called **dripstone**.

Stalag > *noun* (in the Second World War) a German prison camp, especially for non-commissioned officers and privates.

ORIGIN – German, contraction of *Stammlager*, from *Stamm* 'base, main stock' + *Lager* 'camp'.

stalagmite /stalәgmīt/ > *noun* a mound or tapering column rising from the floor of a cave, formed of calcium salts deposited by dripping water.

stale > *adjective* (**staler, stalest**) **1** (of food) no longer fresh or pleasant to eat. **2** no longer new and interesting. **3** (of a person) no longer performing well because of having done something for too long. > *verb* make or become stale.

DERIVATIVES – **stalely** *adverb* **staleness** *noun*.

SYNONYMS – *adjective* **1** mouldy, musty, off,

rancid. **2** banal, hackneyed, tired, trite, overworked.

ANTONYMS – *adjective* fresh.

ORIGIN – first used to describe beer in the sense 'clear from long standing': probably from Old French, from *estaler* 'to halt'.

stalemate > *noun* **1** Chess a position counting as a draw, in which a player is not in check but can only move into check. **2** a situation in which further progress by opposing parties seems impossible. > *verb* bring to stalemate.

SYNONYMS – *noun* **2** deadlock, impasse, stand-off, standstill.

ORIGIN – from obsolete *stale* (from Old French *estale* 'position') + MATE[2].

Stalinism > *noun* the ideology and policies adopted by the Soviet Communist Party leader and head of state Joseph Stalin (1879–1953), based on centralisation, totalitarianism, and the pursuit of communism.

DERIVATIVES – **Stalinist** *noun* & *adjective*.

stalk[1] > *noun* **1** the main stem of a herbaceous plant. **2** the attachment or support of a leaf, flower, or fruit. **3** a slender support or stem. **4** (in a vehicle) a lever on the steering column.

DERIVATIVES – **stalk-like** *adjective* **stalky** *adjective*.

ORIGIN – probably from *stale* 'rung of a ladder, long handle'.

stalk[2] > *verb* **1** pursue or approach stealthily. **2** harass or persecute with unwanted and obsessive attention. **3** stride in a proud, stiff, or angry manner. **4** chiefly literary move silently or threateningly through. > *noun* **1** a stealthy pursuit. **2** a stiff, striding gait.

DERIVATIVES – **stalker** *noun*.

COMBINATIONS – **stalking horse 1** a screen in the shape of a horse behind which a hunter hides when stalking prey. **2** a false pretext that conceals someone's real intentions. **3** a candidate for the leadership of a political party who stands only in order to provoke the election and thus allow a stronger candidate to come forward.

ORIGIN – Old English, 'walk cautiously or stealthily'.

stall > *noun* **1** a stand, booth, or compartment for the sale of goods in a market. **2** an individual compartment for an animal in a stable or cowshed, enclosed on three sides. **3** a stable or cowshed. **4** (also **starting stall**) a cage-like compartment in which a horse is held prior to the start of a race. **5** a compartment for one person in a set of toilets, shower cubicles, etc. **6** (**stalls**) Brit. the ground-floor seats in a theatre. **7** a seat in the choir or chancel of a church, enclosed at the back and sides. > *verb* **1** (with reference to a motor vehicle or its engine) stop running. **2** (of an aircraft) slow down to a speed too low to allow effective operation of the controls. **3** stop making progress. **4** speak or act evasively in order to gain time; prevaricate.

COMBINATIONS – **stallholder** Brit. a person in charge of a market stall.

ORIGIN – Old English, related to **STAND**.

stallion > *noun* an uncastrated adult male horse.

ORIGIN – Old French *estalon*; related to **STALL**.

stalwart /**stawl**wərt/ > *adjective* **1** loyal, reliable, and hard-working. **2** dated sturdy. > *noun* a stalwart supporter or participant in an organisation.

SYNONYMS – *adjective* **1** dedicated, dependable, faithful, loyal, reliable, staunch, steadfast.

ORIGIN – Scots variant of obsolete *stalworth*, from Old English *stæl* 'place' + *weorth* 'worth'.

stamen /**stay**mən/ > *noun* Botany a male fertilising organ of a flower, typically consisting of a pollen-containing anther and a filament.

ORIGIN – Latin, 'warp in an upright loom, thread'.

stamina > *noun* the ability to sustain prolonged physical or mental effort.

SYNONYMS – endurance, resilience, staying power.

ORIGIN – Latin, plural of **STAMEN** in the sense 'threads spun by the Fates'.

stammer > *verb* **1** speak with sudden involuntary pauses and a tendency to repeat the initial letters of words. **2** utter (words) in such a way. > *noun* a tendency to stammer.

DERIVATIVES – **stammerer** *noun* **stammering** *noun & adjective.*

stamp > *verb* **1** bring down (one's foot) heavily on the ground or an object. **2** crush, flatten, or remove with a heavy blow from one's foot. **3** walk with heavy, forceful steps. **4** (**stamp out**) suppress or put an end to. **5** impress with a device that leaves a mark or pattern. **6** impress (a pattern or mark). **7** cut out using a die or mould. **8** fix a postage stamp to. > *noun* **1** (also **postage stamp**) a small adhesive piece of paper attached to a letter or parcel to record payment of postage. **2** an instrument for stamping a pattern or mark. **3** a mark or pattern made by a stamp. **4** a characteristic or distinctive impression or quality. **5** a particular type of person or thing. **6** an act or sound of stamping the foot.

WORDFINDER – philatelist (*person who collects postage stamps*), philately (*the collection and study of postage stamps*).

DERIVATIVES – **stamper** *noun.*

COMBINATIONS – **stamp duty** a duty levied on the legal recognition of certain documents. **stamping ground** a place one regularly frequents.

stampede > *noun* **1** a sudden panicked rush of a number of horses, cattle, etc. **2** a sudden rapid movement or reaction of a mass of people due to interest or panic. > *verb* take part or cause to take part in a stampede.

DERIVATIVES – **stampeder** *noun.*

ORIGIN – Spanish *estampida* 'crash, uproar'.

stance /staanss, stanss/ > *noun* **1** the way in which someone stands. **2** an attitude or standpoint towards something. **3** Scottish a street site for a market, stall, or taxi rank.

SYNONYMS – **1** attitude, bearing, pose, posture. **2** attitude, opinion, outlook, point of view, standpoint, viewpoint.

stanch > *verb* chiefly US variant spelling of **STAUNCH²**.

stanchion /**stan**sh'n/ > *noun* an upright bar, post, or frame forming a support or barrier.

ORIGIN – Old French *stanchon*, from *estance* 'a support'.

stand > *verb* (past and past participle **stood**) **1** be in or rise to an upright position, supported by one's feet. **2** place or be situated in a particular position. **3** remain stationary or without disturbance. **4** be in a specified state or condition. **5** move in a standing position to a specified place: *stand aside.* **6** remain valid or unaltered. **7** adopt a particular attitude towards an issue. **8** be likely to do something: *investors stood to lose heavily.* **9** act in a specified capacity: *he stood security for the government's borrowings.* **10** tolerate, withstand, or like: *I can't stand it.* **11** Brit. be a candidate in an election. **12** provide (food or drink) for (someone) at one's expense. **13** (of a ship) remain on a specified course. > *noun* **1** an attitude towards a particular issue. **2** a determined effort to hold one's ground or resist something. **3** a stopping of motion or progress. **4** a large raised tiered structure for spectators. **5** a raised platform for a band, orchestra, or speaker. **6** a rack, base, or item of furniture for holding or displaying something. **7** a small temporary stall or booth from which promotional goods are sold or displayed. **8** (**the stand**) a witness box. **9** a place where vehicles wait for passengers. **10** a group of trees or other plants. **11** Cricket a partnership.

IDIOMS – **stand alone** be unequalled. **stand and deliver!** a highwayman's order to hand over money and valuables. **stand by 1** look on without intervening. **2** support, remain loyal to, or abide by. **3** be ready to take action if required. **stand down 1** (also **stand aside**) resign from or leave a position or office. **2** relax after a state of readiness. **stand for 1** be an abbreviation of or symbol for. **2** endure or tolerate: *I won't stand for any nonsense.* **stand in** deputise. **stand off** move or keep away.

stand on be scrupulous in the observance of. **stand on one's own (two) feet** be or become self-reliant or independent. **stand out 1** project or be easily noticeable. **2** be clearly better. **stand to** Military stand ready for an attack. **stand trial** be tried in a court of law. **stand up** informal fail to keep a date with (someone). **stand up and be counted** state publicly one's support for someone or something. **stand up for** speak or act in support of. **stand up to 1** make a spirited defence against. **2** be resistant to the harmful effects of.

USAGE – it is not good English to use the past participle **stood** with the verb 'to be', as in *we were stood in a line for hours*; the correct form is *we were standing....*

ORIGIN – Old English, from a root shared by Latin *stare* and Greek *histanai*, also by **STEAD**.

stand-alone > *adjective* (of computer hardware or software) able to operate independently of other hardware or software.

standard > *noun* **1** a level of quality or attainment. **2** a required or agreed level of quality or attainment. **3** something used as a measure, norm, or model in comparative evaluations. **4** (**standards**) principles of honourable, decent behaviour. **5** a military or ceremonial flag. **6** an upright water or gas pipe. **7** a tree growing on an erect stem of full height, or a shrub grafted on such a stem. > *adjective* **1** used or accepted as normal or average. **2** (of a size, measure, etc.) regularly used or produced. **3** (of a work, writer, etc.) viewed as authoritative and so widely read.

DERIVATIVES – **standardly** *adverb.*

SYNONYMS – *noun* **1** level, quality. **2** benchmark, criterion, guideline, measure, norm, requirement, specification. **3** archetype, ideal, model, paradigm. **5** banner, flag, pennant. *adjective* **1** accepted, average, conventional, normal, routine, usual.

COMBINATIONS – **standard assessment task** (in the UK) a standard test given to schoolchildren to assess their progress in a core subject of the national curriculum. **standard-bearer 1** a soldier carrying the standard of a unit, regiment, or army. **2** a leading figure in a cause or movement. **standard deviation** Statistics a quantity calculated to indicate the extent of deviation for a group as a whole. **Standard Grade** (in Scotland) an examination equivalent to the GCSE. **standard lamp** chiefly Brit. a lamp with a tall stem whose base stands on the floor. **standard of living** the degree of material comfort available to a person or community. **standard time** a uniform time for places in approximately the same longitude.

ORIGIN – Old French *estendart*, from *estendre* 'extend'.

standardise (also **standardize**) > *verb* **1** cause to conform to a standard. **2** determine the properties of by comparison with a standard.

DERIVATIVES – **standardisation** *noun*.

standby > *noun* (pl. **standbys**) **1** readiness for duty or immediate action. **2** a person or thing ready to be deployed in an emergency. > *adjective* (of tickets for a journey or performance) unreserved and sold only at the last minute if still available.

standee /stan**dee**/ > *noun* chiefly N. Amer. a person who is standing.

stand-in > *noun* a substitute.

standing > *noun* **1** position, status, or reputation. **2** duration: *a problem of long standing*. > *adjective* **1** (of a jump or start of a race) performed from rest or an upright position. **2** long-term or regularly repeated: *a standing invitation*. **3** (of water) stagnant or still. **4** (of corn) not yet reaped.

IDIOMS – **leave standing** informal be much better or faster than.

COMBINATIONS – **standing committee** a permanent committee meeting regularly. **standing joke** something that regularly causes amusement or provokes ridicule. **standing order 1** Brit. an instruction to a bank to make regular fixed payments to someone. **2** Brit. an order placed on a regular basis with a retailer. **3** (**standing orders**) rulings governing the procedures of a parliament, council, etc. **standing ovation** a period of prolonged applause during which the audience rise to their feet. **standing stone** a menhir. **standing wave** Physics a vibration of a system in which some particular points remain fixed while others between them vibrate with the maximum amplitude.

stand-off > *noun* **1** a deadlock between two equally matched opponents. **2** (also **stand-off half**) Rugby a halfback who forms a link between the scrum half and the three-quarters.

stand-offish > *adjective* informal distant and cold in manner.

standout > *noun* informal, chiefly N. Amer. an outstanding person or thing.

standpipe > *noun* a vertical pipe extending from a water supply, especially one connecting a temporary tap to the mains.

standpoint > *noun* **1** an attitude towards a particular issue. **2** the position from which a scene or an object is viewed.

SYNONYMS – **1** attitude, opinion, point of view, stance, view, viewpoint.

standstill > *noun* a situation or condition without movement or activity.

stand-to > *noun* Military **1** the action or state

of standing to. **2** the beginning of a spell of duty.

stand-up > *adjective* **1** involving or used by people standing up. **2** (of comedy or a comedian) performed or performing by standing in front of an audience and telling jokes. **3** (of a fight or argument) involving direct confrontation; loud or violent. **4** designed to stay upright or erect.

stank past of STINK.

Stanley knife > *noun* Brit. trademark a utility knife with a short, strong replaceable blade.

stannary /**stann**əri/ > *noun* (pl. **stannaries**) Brit., chiefly historical a tin-mining district in Cornwall or Devon.

ORIGIN – Latin *stannaria* (plural), from *stannum* 'tin'.

stanza /**stan**zə/ > *noun* a group of lines forming the basic recurring metrical unit in a poem.

ORIGIN – Italian, 'standing place, stanza'.

staphylococcus /staffilə**kokk**əss/ > *noun* (pl. **staphylococci** /staffilə**kokk**ī/) a bacterium of a genus including many kinds that cause pus to be formed.

DERIVATIVES – **staphylococcal** *adjective*.

ORIGIN – from Greek *staphulē* 'bunch of grapes' + *kokkos* 'berry'.

┌─────────────────────────────┐
wordpower facts

Staple

The two English words **staple** are totally different in meaning, but come from the same root, a Germanic word meaning 'pillar'. **Staple**[1] was an Old English word (meaning 'pillar'), while **staple**[2] entered English in the Middle Ages from Old French *estaple*, 'market'. In English **staple**[2] first referred to a town or area appointed by royal authority as an official market for certain important classes of goods, such as wool. From about 1390 to 1558 the chief staple was at Calais, then an English possession. It is uncertain why a word meaning 'pillar' should have come to denote a market (which it also did in Old French and in Middle Low German and Middle Dutch): perhaps it referred to the pillared market halls in which trading would often have taken place. From 'official market for important goods' it was a short step to the modern sense of 'a main item of trade or production'. Why **staple**[1] came to mean 'piece of wire for fastening papers together' is unclear, however.
└─────────────────────────────┘

staple[1] > *noun* **1** a small flattened U-shaped piece of wire used to fasten papers together. **2** a small U-shaped metal bar with pointed

ends for driving into wood. > *verb* secure with a staple or staples.

staple[2] > *noun* **1** a main item of trade or production. **2** a main or important element of something. **3** the fibre of cotton or wool considered with regard to its length and fineness. > *adjective* main or most important: *a staple diet*.

SYNONYMS – *adjective* basic, chief, main, primary, principal.

stapler > *noun* a device for fastening papers together with staples.

star > *noun* **1** a fixed luminous point in the night sky which is a large, remote incandescent body like the sun. **2** a stylised representation of a star, typically with five or more points. **3** a famous or exceptionally talented entertainer or sports player. **4** Astrology a planet, constellation, or configuration regarded as influencing one's fortunes or personality. > *verb* (**starred**, **starring**) **1** (of a film, play, etc.) have (someone) as a principal performer. **2** (of a performer) have a principal role in a film, play, etc. **3** mark, decorate, or cover with star-shaped marks or objects.

WORDFINDER – astral, stellar (*of a star or stars*), binary (*a system of two stars*), constellation (*group of stars forming a pattern*), interstellar (*occurring or situated between stars*), magnitude (*brightness of a star*), nova (*star undergoing an increase in brightness*), sidereal (*relating to the stars or their positions in the sky*), stellate (*arranged in a star-like pattern*), supernova (*exploding star*).

IDIOMS – **see stars** seem to see flashes of light as a result of a blow on the head.

COMBINATIONS – **star anise** a small star-shaped fruit with an aniseed flavour, used in Asian cookery. **starburst 1** a pattern of lines or rays radiating from a central point. **2** an explosion producing such an effect. **3** Astronomy an intense episode of star formation. **star-crossed** literary ill-fated. **stardust** magical or charismatic quality or feeling. **starfruit 1** a golden-yellow fruit with a star-shaped cross section; a carambola. **2** a small aquatic plant with tiny white flowers and six-pointed star-shaped fruit. **starlight** light coming from the stars. **starlit** lit by stars. **Star of David** a six-pointed figure consisting of two interlaced equilateral triangles, used as a Jewish and Israeli symbol. **Stars and Bars** historical the flag of the Confederate States of America. **Stars and Stripes** the national flag of the US. **star shell** an explosive projectile which bursts in the air to light up an enemy's position. **starship** (in science fiction) a large manned spaceship for interstellar travel. **star sign** a sign of the zodiac. **star-spangled 1** literary covered or decorated with stars. **2** informal very successful or celebrated. **star-struck** fascinated and greatly impressed by famous people. **star-studded 1** (of the sky) filled with stars. **2** informal featuring a number of famous people. **star turn** the principal act or performer in a programme.

starboard /staarbərd/ > *noun* the side of a ship or aircraft on the right when one is facing forward. The opposite of **PORT**³. > *verb* turn (a ship or its helm) to starboard.

ORIGIN – Old English, 'rudder side', because early Teutonic sailing vessels were steered with a paddle on the right side; related to **STEER**¹.

starch > *noun* **1** an odourless, tasteless carbohydrate which is obtained chiefly from cereals and potatoes and is an important constituent of the human diet. **2** powder or spray made from this substance, used to stiffen fabric. **3** stiffness of manner. > *verb* stiffen with starch.

starchy > *adjective* (**starchier, starchiest**) **1** (of food) containing a lot of starch. **2** (of clothing) stiff with starch. **3** informal very stiff, formal, or prim in manner or character.

DERIVATIVES – **starchily** *adverb* **starchiness** *noun*.

stardom > *noun* the state or status of being a star in entertainment, sport, or other sphere.

stare > *verb* **1** look fixedly at someone or something with the eyes wide open. **2** (**stare out** or **down**) look fixedly at (someone) until they feel forced to look away. > *noun* an act of staring.

IDIOMS – **be staring one in the face** be glaringly obvious.

SYNONYMS – *verb* **1** gape, gaze, goggle; Brit. informal gawp.

starfish > *noun* a marine animal (an echinoderm) having a flattened body with five or more radiating arms bearing tube feet.

stargazer > *noun* informal an astronomer or astrologer.

DERIVATIVES – **stargaze** *verb*.

stark > *adjective* **1** severe or bare in appearance. **2** unpleasantly or sharply clear. **3** complete; sheer: *stark terror*.

IDIOMS – **stark naked** completely naked. **stark raving** (or **staring**) **mad** informal completely mad.

DERIVATIVES – **starkly** *adverb* **starkness** *noun*.

SYNONYMS – **1** austere, bare, bleak, desolate, grim, severe. **2** clear, evident, obvious, plain, sharp.

ORIGIN – Old English, 'unyielding, severe'.

starkers > *adjective* informal, chiefly Brit. completely naked.

starlet > *noun* informal a promising young actress or performer.

starling > *noun* a gregarious songbird with dark lustrous or iridescent plumage.

starry > *adjective* (**starrier, starriest**) **1** full of or lit by stars. **2** informal relating to stars in entertainment.

COMBINATIONS – **starry-eyed** naively enthusiastic or idealistic.

START > *abbreviation* Strategic Arms Reduction Talks.

start > *verb* **1** begin to do, happen, or engage in. **2** begin to operate or work. **3** cause to operate or happen. **4** begin to move or travel. **5** give a small jump or jerking movement from surprise. **6** literary move or appear suddenly. **7** rouse (game) from its lair. **8** (of eyes) bulge. **9** displace or be displaced by pressure or shrinkage. > *noun* **1** the beginning of something, or an act of beginning. **2** an advantage given to a competitor at the beginning of a race. **3** a sudden movement of surprise.

IDIOMS – **for a start** in the first place. **start at** cost at least (a specified amount). **start on 1** begin to work on or deal with. **2** informal begin to talk to in a critical or hostile way. **start over** N. Amer. make a new beginning. **start out** (or **up**) embark on a venture or undertaking. **start something** informal cause trouble. **to start with** as the first thing to be taken into account.

SYNONYMS – *verb* **1** begin, commence. **2** activate, set in motion. **4** depart, embark, get under way, proceed, set out. **5** flinch, jump, twitch. *noun* **1** beginning, commencement, dawn, inception, launch, outset.

ANTONYMS – *verb* **1** finish. **4** stop. *noun* end, finish.

COMBINATIONS – **starting block** a shaped rigid block for bracing the feet of a runner at the start of a race. **starting gate** a barrier raised at the start of a horse race to ensure a simultaneous start. **starting pistol** a pistol used to signal the start of a race. **starting price** the final odds at the start of a horse race.

starter > *noun* **1** a person or thing that starts. **2** chiefly Brit. the first course of a meal. **3** an automatic device for starting a machine. **4** a competitor taking part in a race or game at the start.

IDIOMS – **for starters** informal first of all. **under starter's orders** waiting for the signal to start a race.

startle > *verb* cause to feel sudden shock or alarm.

DERIVATIVES – **startled** *adjective*.

SYNONYMS – agitate, alarm, frighten, scare, shock, surprise.

startling > *adjective* **1** alarming. **2** very surprising or remarkable.

DERIVATIVES – **startlingly** *adverb*.

starve > *verb* **1** suffer or die from hunger. **2** cause to starve. **3** (**be starving** or **starved**) informal feel very hungry. **4** (usu. **be starved of** or US **for**) deprive of.

DERIVATIVES – **starvation** *noun*.

ORIGIN – Old English, 'to die', later 'die of hunger' and 'be freezing cold'.

starveling /staarvling/ archaic > *adjective* starving or emaciated. > *noun* a starveling person or animal.

stash informal > *verb* store safely in a secret place. > *noun* **1** a secret store of something. **2** dated a hiding place.

stasis /staysiss, stasiss/ > *noun* **1** formal or technical a period or state of inactivity or equilibrium. **2** Medicine a stoppage of flow of a body fluid.

ORIGIN – Greek, 'standing, stoppage'.

state > *noun* **1** the condition of someone or something. **2** a nation or territory considered as an organised political community under one government. **3** a community or area forming part of a federal republic. **4** (**the States**) the United States. **5** the civil government of a country. **6** pomp and ceremony associated with monarchy or government. **7** (**a state**) informal an agitated, disorderly, or dirty condition. > *verb* express definitely or clearly in speech or writing.

IDIOMS – **state of affairs** (or **things**) a situation. **state of emergency** a situation of national danger or disaster in which a government suspends normal constitutional procedures. **state of grace** a state of being free from sin. **the state of play** Brit. **1** the score at a particular time in a cricket or football match. **2** the current situation. **state-of-the-art** incorporating the newest ideas and most up-to-date features.

DERIVATIVES – **statehood** *noun*.

SYNONYMS – *noun* **1** condition, shape, situation. **2** country, land, nation. *verb* announce, assert, declare, proclaim, report, say.

COMBINATIONS – **state capitalism** a political system in which the state has control of production and the use of capital. **State Department** (in the US) the department of foreign affairs. **state house 1** (in the US) the building where the legislature of a state meets. **2** NZ a private house owned and let by the government. **state school** Brit. a school funded and controlled by the state. **state's evidence** US Law evidence for the prosecution given by a participant in or accomplice to the crime being tried. **state socialism** a political system in which the state has control of industries and services.

ORIGIN – partly a shortening of **ESTATE**, partly from Latin *status* 'standing'.

statecraft > *noun* the skilful management of state affairs.

stateless > *adjective* not recognised as a citizen of any country.

DERIVATIVES – **statelessness** *noun*.

stately > *adjective* (**statelier, stateliest**) dignified, imposing, and rather grand.

DERIVATIVES – **stateliness** noun.

SYNONYMS – dignified, grand, imposing, majestic, noble, splendid.

COMBINATIONS – **stately home** Brit. a large and fine house occupied or formerly occupied by an aristocratic family.

statement > noun **1** a definite or clear expression of something in speech or writing. **2** a formal account of facts or events, especially one given to the police or in court. **3** a document setting out items of debit and credit between a bank or other organisation and a customer.

stateroom > noun **1** a large room in a palace or public building, for use on formal occasions. **2** a private compartment on a ship.

stateside > adjective & adverb informal, chiefly US of, in, or towards the United States.

statesman (or **stateswoman**) > noun a skilled, experienced, and respected political leader or figure.

DERIVATIVES – **statesmanlike** adjective **statesmanship** noun.

static /stattik/ > adjective **1** lacking movement, action, or change. **2** Physics concerned with bodies at rest or forces in equilibrium. Contrasted with DYNAMIC. **3** (of an electric charge) acquired by objects that cannot conduct a current. > noun **1** static electricity. **2** crackling or hissing on a telephone, radio, etc.

DERIVATIVES – **statically** adverb.

SYNONYMS – adjective **1** fixed, immobile, inert, motionless, stable, still, unmoving.

ANTONYMS – adjective **1** active, mobile.

statics > plural noun **1** (usu. treated as sing.) the branch of mechanics concerned with bodies at rest and forces in equilibrium. **2** another term for STATIC (in sense 2).

station > noun **1** a place where passenger trains stop on a railway line, typically with platforms and buildings. **2** a place where a specified activity or service is based: a radar station. **3** a broadcasting company of a specified kind. **4** the place where someone or something stands or is placed for a particular purpose or duty. **5** Austral./NZ a large sheep or cattle farm. **6** dated one's social rank or position. > verb assign to a station.

COMBINATIONS – **station hand** Austral./NZ a worker on a large sheep or cattle farm. **station house** N. Amer. a police or fire station. **stationmaster** an official in charge of a railway station. **Station of the Cross** each of a series of fourteen pictures representing incidents during Jesus' progress from Pilate's house to his crucifixion at Calvary. **station wagon** N. Amer. & Austral./NZ an estate car.

ORIGIN – Latin, from stare 'to stand'.

stationary > adjective **1** not moving. **2** not changing in quantity or condition.

USAGE – take care to distinguish between

stationary and stationery: **stationary** is an adjective meaning 'not moving or changing', whereas **stationery** is a noun meaning 'paper and other writing materials'.

SYNONYMS – **1** inert, motionless, static, still, unmoving. **2** constant, invariable, stable, unchanging, unvarying.

stationer > noun a seller of stationery.

---

wordpower facts

Stationer

The word **stationer**, like **station** and **stationary**, comes from the very productive Latin verb stare 'to stand'. What do **stationer** and its derivative **stationery** have to do with **station** and other words related to 'stand'? In medieval times a **stationer** was a bookseller. The word entered English from medieval Latin stationarius, 'tradesman at a fixed location', i.e. as opposed to an itinerant vendor. In the Middle Ages the most common type of permanent shop was a bookseller's, especially an officially licensed one in a university town, and thus the Latin term came to have the sense 'bookseller' in English. Some of the other words from Latin stare are **circumstance**, **constant**, **distant**, **estate**, **instance**, **obstacle**, **resist**, **rest**, **stable**, **stage**, **stay**, and **stand** itself.

---

stationery > noun paper and other materials needed for writing.

statism /staytiz'm/ > noun a political system in which the state has substantial central control over social and economic affairs.

DERIVATIVES – **statist** noun & adjective.

statistic > noun a fact or piece of data obtained from a study of a large quantity of numerical data.

statistical > adjective relating to statistics.

DERIVATIVES – **statistically** adverb.

statistics > plural noun (treated as sing.) the collection and analysis of numerical data in large quantities.

DERIVATIVES – **statistician** noun.

statoscope > noun an aneroid barometer measuring minute variations of pressure, used especially to indicate aircraft altitude.

ORIGIN – from Greek statos 'standing'.

stats > plural noun informal statistics.

statuary /statyooəri/ > noun statues collectively.

statue > noun a carved or cast figure of a person or animal, especially one that is life-size or larger.

ORIGIN – Latin statua, from stare 'to stand'.

statuesque /statyooesk/ > adjective

(especially of a woman) attractively tall, graceful, and dignified.

DERIVATIVES – **statuesquely** adverb.

statuette > noun a small statue.

stature > noun **1** a person's natural height when standing. **2** importance or reputation gained by ability or achievement.

status > noun **1** relative social or professional standing. **2** high rank or social standing. **3** the position of affairs at a particular time. **4** official classification.

SYNONYMS – **1** position, rank, standing, stature. **2** cachet, kudos, prestige, stature.

COMBINATIONS – **status symbol** a possession taken to indicate a person's wealth or high status.

ORIGIN – Latin, 'standing'.

status quo /staytəss kwō/ > noun the existing state of affairs.

ORIGIN – Latin, 'the state in which'.

statute /statyoot/ > noun **1** a written law passed by a legislative body. **2** a rule of an organisation or institution.

COMBINATIONS – **statute book 1** a book in which laws are written. **2** (**the statute book**) a nation's laws collectively. **statute law** the body of principles and rules of law laid down in statutes. **statute of limitations** Law a statute limiting the period for the bringing of certain kinds of actions.

ORIGIN – Latin statutum 'thing set up'.

statutory > adjective **1** required, permitted, or enacted by statute. **2** having come to be required or expected due to being done regularly.

DERIVATIVES – **statutorily** adverb.

COMBINATIONS – **statutory instrument** Law a government or executive order of subordinate legislation. **statutory rape** US Law the offence of having sexual intercourse with a minor.

staunch[1] /stawnch/ > adjective **1** very loyal and committed. **2** archaic strong or watertight.

DERIVATIVES – **staunchly** adverb **staunchness** noun.

SYNONYMS – **1** committed, dedicated, loyal, stalwart, steadfast, trusty.

ORIGIN – Old French estanche 'watertight', from a base meaning 'dried up, weary'.

staunch[2] /stawnch, staanch/ (US also **stanch**) > verb stop or restrict (a flow of blood from a wound); stop from bleeding.

ORIGIN – Old French estanchier, from the base of STAUNCH[1].

stave > noun **1** any of the lengths of wood fixed side by side to make a barrel, bucket, etc. **2** a strong stick, post, or pole. **3** (also **staff**) Music a set of five parallel lines on or between any of which a note is written to indicate its pitch. **4** a verse or stanza of a poem. > verb **1** (past and past participle **staved** or **stove**) (**stave in**) break (something) by forcing it inwards or piercing it roughly with a hole. **2** (past and past participle **staved**) (**stave off**) avert or delay (something bad or dangerous).

ORIGIN – from *staves*, variant plural of **STAFF**[1].

stay[1] > *verb* **1** remain in the same place. **2** remain in a specified state or position. **3** live somewhere temporarily as a visitor or guest. **4** *Scottish & S. African* live permanently. **5** stop, delay, or prevent. **6** *literary* support or prop up. > *noun* **1** a period of staying somewhere. **2** a curb or check, especially a suspension or postponement of judicial proceedings: *a stay of execution.* **3** a device used as a brace or support. **4** (**stays**) *historical* a corset made of two pieces laced together and stiffened by strips of whalebone.

IDIOMS – **stay the course** (or **distance**) **1** keep going to the end of a race or contest. **2** pursue a difficult task or activity to the end. **stay on** continue to study, work, or be somewhere after others have left. **stay over** stay for the night at someone's home or a hotel. **stay put** remain somewhere without moving. **stay up** not go to bed. **stay with** continue, persevere, or keep up with (an activity or person).

DERIVATIVES – **stayer** *noun.*

COMBINATIONS – **staying power** endurance or stamina.

ORIGIN – Old French *ester*, from Latin *stare* 'to stand'.

stay[2] > *noun* **1** a large rope, wire, or rod used to support a ship's mast or other upright pole. **2** a supporting wire or cable on an aircraft. > *verb* secure or steady with a stay.

COMBINATIONS – **staysail** a triangular fore-and-aft sail extended on a stay.

ORIGIN – Old English, from a base meaning 'be firm'.

STD > *abbreviation* **1** sexually transmitted disease. **2** *Brit.* subscriber trunk dialling.

stead > *noun* the place or role that someone or something should have or fill: *she was appointed in his stead.*

IDIOMS – **stand someone in good stead** be advantageous to someone over time or in the future.

ORIGIN – Old English, 'place'.

steadfast > *adjective* resolutely or dutifully firm and unwavering.

DERIVATIVES – **steadfastly** *adverb* **steadfastness** *noun.*

SYNONYMS – determined, firm, resolute, stalwart, staunch, steady, unwavering.

ORIGIN – Old English, 'standing firm' (see **STEAD, FAST**[1]).

steading > *noun Scottish & N. English* a farmstead.

steady > *adjective* (**steadier, steadiest**) **1** firmly fixed, supported, or balanced. **2** not faltering or wavering; controlled. **3** sensible

and reliable. **4** regular, even, and continuous in development, frequency, or intensity. > *verb* (**steadies, steadied**) make or become steady. > *exclamation* (also **steady on!**) a warning to keep calm or take care.

IDIOMS – **go steady** *informal* have a regular romantic or sexual relationship with someone.

DERIVATIVES – **steadier** *noun* **steadily** *adverb* **steadiness** *noun.*

SYNONYMS – *adjective* **1** firm, secure, solid, stable. **3** balanced, dependable, level-headed, reliable, sensible, sound.

ANTONYMS – *adjective* **1** unstable, unsteady. **3** fickle, flighty. **4** fluctuating.

COMBINATIONS – **steady state** an unchanging condition in a physical process; an equilibrium.

steak > *noun* **1** high-quality beef from the hindquarters of the animal, cut into thick slices for grilling or frying. **2** a thick slice of other meat or fish. **3** poorer-quality beef for braising or stewing.

COMBINATIONS – **steak tartare** a dish consisting of raw minced steak mixed with raw egg.

ORIGIN – Old Norse *steik.*

steal > *verb* (past **stole**; past participle **stolen**) **1** take (something) without permission or legal right and without intending to return it. **2** give or take surreptitiously or without permission: *I stole a look at my watch.* **3** move somewhere quietly or surreptitiously. **4** (in various sports) gain (a point, advantage, etc.) unexpectedly or by exploiting the temporary distraction of an opponent. > *noun* **1** *informal* a bargain. **2** *chiefly N. Amer.* an act of stealing.

IDIOMS – **steal a march on** gain an advantage over by taking early action. **steal the show** attract the most attention and praise. **steal someone's thunder** win praise or attention for oneself by pre-empting someone else's attempt to impress.

DERIVATIVES – **stealer** *noun.*

SYNONYMS – *verb* **1** embezzle, misappropriate, pilfer, poach, thieve; *informal* filch, nick, pinch. **2** snatch, sneak. **3** creep, slip, sneak, tiptoe.

stealth /stelth/ > *noun* **1** cautious and surreptitious action or movement. **2** (before another noun) (of aircraft) designed to make detection by radar or sonar difficult: *a stealth bomber.*

ORIGIN – first used in the sense 'theft': probably from an Old English word related to **STEAL**.

stealthy > *adjective* (**stealthier, stealthiest**) characterised by stealth.

DERIVATIVES – **stealthily** *adverb.*

SYNONYMS – clandestine, covert, furtive, secretive, surreptitious.

wordpower facts

Steal someone's thunder

The phrase **steal someone's thunder** is thought to derive from an exclamation by the English dramatist John Dennis (1657–1734). Dennis invented a new method of simulating the sound of thunder as a theatrical sound effect, which he used in his unsuccessful play *Appius and Virginia.* Shortly after his play came to the end of its short run he attended a performance of *Macbeth*, at which he heard his new thunder effects used. He is said to have exclaimed: 'Damn them! They will not let my play run, but they steal my thunder!'

steam > *noun* **1** the hot vapour into which water is converted when heated, which condenses in the air into a mist of minute water droplets. **2** the expansive force of this vapour used as a source of power for machines. **3** momentum; impetus: *the dispute gathered steam.* > *verb* **1** give off or produce steam. **2** (**steam up**) mist over with steam. **3** cook (food) by heating it in steam from boiling water. **4** clean or otherwise treat with steam. **5** (of a ship or train) travel somewhere under steam power. **6** (**be** or **get steamed up**) be or become extremely agitated or angry. **7** *informal* move somewhere rapidly or forcefully.

IDIOMS – **get up steam 1** generate enough pressure to drive a steam engine. **2** gradually gain impetus. **have steam coming out of one's ears** *informal* be extremely angry. **let off steam** *informal* get rid of pent-up energy or strong emotion. **run out of steam** *informal* lose impetus or enthusiasm. **under one's own steam** without assistance from others.

COMBINATIONS – **steam bath** a room filled with hot steam for cleaning and refreshing the body. **steamboat** a boat propelled by a steam engine, especially (in the US) a paddle-wheel craft of a type used on rivers in the 19th century. **steam engine 1** an engine that uses the expansion or rapid condensation of steam to generate power. **2** a steam locomotive. **steam hammer** a large steam-powered hammer used in forging. **steam iron** an electric iron that emits steam from holes in its flat surface. **steam turbine** a turbine in which a rapid jet of steam rotates a bladed disc or drum.

steamed > *adjective* **1** *Brit. informal* very drunk. **2** *informal, chiefly N. Amer.* angry; upset.

steamer > *noun* **1** a ship or boat powered by steam. **2** a type of saucepan in which food can be steamed.

steaming > *adjective* **1** giving off steam. **2** Brit. informal extremely drunk. **3** Brit. informal very angry.

steamroller > *noun* a heavy, slow-moving vehicle with a roller, used to flatten the surfaces of roads during construction. > *verb* (also **steamroll**) **1** forcibly pass (a measure) by restricting debate or otherwise overriding opposition. **2** force (someone) into doing or accepting something.

steamy > *adjective* (**steamier, steamiest**) **1** producing, filled with, or clouded with steam. **2** hot and humid. **3** informal of or involving passionate sexual activity.

DERIVATIVES – **steamily** *adverb* **steaminess** *noun*.

stearic acid /steerik/ > *noun* Chemistry a solid saturated fatty acid obtained from animal or vegetable fats.

ORIGIN – from Greek *stear* 'tallow'.

stearin /steerin/ > *noun* a white crystalline substance which is the main constituent of tallow and suet.

steatite /steeətīt/ > *noun* the mineral talc in bulk form, especially soapstone.

steatopygia /steeətəpijiə/ > *noun* accumulation of large amounts of fat on the buttocks, especially as a normal condition in the Khoikhoi and other peoples of arid parts of southern Africa.

DERIVATIVES – **steatopygous** /steeətəpīgəss, steeətoppigəss/ *adjective*.

ORIGIN – from Greek *stear* 'tallow' + *pugē* 'rump'.

steed > *noun* archaic or literary a horse.

steel > *noun* **1** a hard, strong grey or bluish-grey alloy of iron with carbon and usually other elements, used as a structural material and in manufacturing. **2** a rod of roughened steel on which knives are sharpened. **3** strength and determination: *nerves of steel*. > *verb* (**steel oneself**) mentally prepare oneself to do or face something difficult.

COMBINATIONS – **steel band** a band that plays music on steel drums. **steel drum** (also **steel pan**) a percussion instrument originating in Trinidad, made out of an oil drum with one end beaten down and divided into sections to give different notes. **steel wool** fine strands of steel matted together into a mass, used as an abrasive.

steelworks > *plural noun* (usu. treated as sing.) a factory where steel is manufactured.

steely > *adjective* (**steelier, steeliest**) **1** resembling steel in colour, brightness, or strength. **2** coldly determined; severe.

DERIVATIVES – **steeliness** *noun*.

steelyard > *noun* an apparatus for weighing that has a short arm taking the item to be weighed and a long graduated arm along which a weight is moved until it balances.

ORIGIN – from **STEEL** + **YARD**[1] in obsolete sense 'rod, measuring stick'.

steep[1] > *adjective* **1** rising or falling sharply; almost perpendicular. **2** (of a rise or fall in an amount) very large or rapid. **3** informal (of a price or demand) not reasonable; excessive. **4** informal (of a claim or account) exaggerated. > *noun* chiefly literary a steep mountain slope.

DERIVATIVES – **steeply** *adverb* **steepness** *noun*.

SYNONYMS – **1** abrupt, precipitous, sheer. **2** precipitate, sharp, sudden.

ORIGIN – Old English, 'extending to a great height'; related to **STEEPLE** and **STOOP**[1].

steep[2] > *verb* **1** soak or be soaked in water or other liquid. **2** (usu. **be steeped in**) fill or imbue with a particular quality.

steepen > *verb* become or cause to become steeper.

steeple > *noun* **1** a church tower and spire. **2** a spire on the top of a church tower or roof.

DERIVATIVES – **steepled** *adjective*.

steeplechase > *noun* **1** a horse race run on a racecourse having ditches and hedges as jumps. **2** a running race in which runners must clear hurdles and water jumps.

DERIVATIVES – **steeplechaser** *noun* **steeplechasing** *noun*.

ORIGIN – so named because originally the race was run across country, with a steeple marking the finishing point.

steeplejack > *noun* a person who climbs tall structures such as chimneys and steeples in order to carry out repairs.

steer[1] > *verb* **1** guide or control the movement of (a vehicle, ship, etc.). **2** direct or guide in a particular direction. > *noun* **1** the type of steering of a vehicle. **2** informal a piece of advice or information.

IDIOMS – **steer clear of** take care to avoid.

DERIVATIVES – **steerable** *adjective* **steerer** *noun*.

SYNONYMS – *verb* **1** control, direct, drive, guide, navigate, pilot. **2** direct, escort, guide, lead, shepherd, usher.

COMBINATIONS – **steering column** a shaft that connects the steering wheel of a vehicle to the rest of the steering mechanism. **steering committee** (also **steering group**) a committee that decides on the priorities or order of business of an organisation. **steering wheel** a wheel that a driver rotates in order to steer a vehicle.

steer[2] > *noun* a bullock.

steerage > *noun* **1** historical the part of a ship providing accommodation for passengers with the cheapest tickets. **2** archaic or literary the action of steering a boat.

COMBINATIONS – **steerage way** the rate of headway required if a ship is to be controlled by the helm.

steering > *noun* **1** the action of steering. **2** the mechanism in a vehicle, vessel, or aircraft which allows it to be steered.

steersman > *noun* a person who steers a boat or ship.

stegosaur /steggəsawr/ (also **stegosaurus** /steggəsawrəss/) > *noun* a plant-eating dinosaur with a double row of large bony plates along the back.

ORIGIN – from Greek *stegē* 'covering' + *sauros* 'lizard'.

stein /stīn/ > *noun* a large earthenware beer mug.

ORIGIN – German, 'stone'.

stela /steelə/ (also **stele** /steel, steeli/) > *noun* (pl. **stelae** /steelee/) Archaeology an upright stone slab or column bearing an inscription or design.

ORIGIN – Greek.

stellar /stellə/ > *adjective* **1** relating to a star or stars. **2** informal of or having the quality of a star performer.

ORIGIN – Latin *stellaris*, from *stella* 'star'.

stellate /stellayt/ > *adjective* arranged in a radiating pattern like that of a star.

DERIVATIVES – **stellated** *adjective*.

stem[1] > *noun* **1** the main body or stalk of a plant or shrub. **2** the stalk supporting a fruit, flower, or leaf. **3** a long, thin supportive or main section of something, such as that of a wine glass or tobacco pipe. **4** a rod or cylinder in a mechanism. **5** a vertical stroke in a letter or musical note. **6** Grammar the root or main part of a word, to which inflections or formative elements are added. **7** the main upright timber or metal piece at the bow of a ship. > *verb* (**stemmed, stemming**) **1** (**stem from**) originate in or be caused by. **2** remove the stems from (fruit or tobacco leaves). **3** (of a boat) make headway against (the tide or current).

IDIOMS – **from stem to stern** from one end to the other, especially of a ship.

DERIVATIVES – **stemmed** *adjective*.

COMBINATIONS – **stem ginger** pieces of crystallised or preserved ginger. **stem stitch** an embroidery stitch forming a continuous line of long, overlapped stitches. **stemware** N. Amer. goblets and stemmed glasses regarded collectively.

stem[2] > *verb* (**stemmed, stemming**) **1** stop or restrict (the flow of something). **2** Skiing slide the tail of one ski or both skis outwards in order to turn or slow down.

ORIGIN – Old Norse.

stench > *noun* a strong and very unpleasant smell.

stencil > *noun* a thin sheet of card, plastic, or metal with a pattern or letters cut out of it, used to produce the cut design on the surface below by the application of ink or paint through the holes. > *verb* (**stencilled, stencilling**; US **stenciled, stenciling**) decorate or form with a stencil.

ORIGIN – from earlier *stansel* 'ornament with various colours', from Latin *scintilla* 'spark'.

Sten gun > *noun* a type of lightweight British sub-machine gun.

ORIGIN – from the initials of the inventors' surnames, Shepherd and *T*urpin, suggested by **Bren gun**.

stenography /ste**nog**rəfi/ > *noun* N. Amer. the action or process of writing in shorthand and transcribing the shorthand on a typewriter.

DERIVATIVES – **stenographer** *noun* **stenographic** *adjective*.

ORIGIN – from Greek *stenos* 'narrow'.

stentorian /sten**tor**iən/ > *adjective* (of a person's voice) loud and powerful.

ORIGIN – from *Stentor*, the name of a Greek herald in the Trojan War.

step > *noun* **1** an act or movement of putting one leg in front of the other in walking or running. **2** the distance covered by a step. **3** informal a short and easily walked distance. **4** a flat surface on which to place one's foot when moving from one level to another. **5** a position or grade in a scale or hierarchy. **6** a measure or action taken to deal with or achieve a particular thing. **7** (**steps** or **a pair of steps**) Brit. a stepladder. **8** a block fixed to a boat's keel to take the base of a mast or other fitting. **9** Music, chiefly US an interval in a scale; a tone (whole step) or semitone (half step). > *verb* (**stepped**, **stepping**) **1** lift and set down one's foot or one foot after the other to walk somewhere or move to a new position. **2** set up (a mast) in its step.

IDIOMS – **in** (or **out of**) **step 1** walking, marching, or dancing in the same (or a different) rhythm and pace as others. **2** conforming (or not conforming) to what others are doing or thinking. **3** in (or out of) synchrony. **follow in someone's steps** do as someone else did before. **mind** (or **watch**) **one's step** walk or act carefully. **step on it** informal go faster. **step out 1** leave a room or building briefly. **2** N. Amer. informal have a romantic or sexual relationship. **3** walk with long or vigorous steps. **step out of line** behave inappropriately or disobediently. **step up** increase the amount, speed, or intensity of.

DERIVATIVES – **stepped** *adjective* **stepper** *noun* **stepwise** *adjective*.

SYNONYMS – *noun* **1** footstep, pace, stride. **5** grade, level, notch, rung, stage. **6** act, action, measure, motion, move, procedure. *verb* **1** stride, tread, walk.

COMBINATIONS – **step aerobics** a type of aerobics that involves stepping up on to and down from a portable block. **stepladder** a short folding ladder with flat steps and a small platform. **stepping stone 1** a raised stone on which to step when crossing a

stream or muddy area. **2** an action that helps one to make progress towards a goal.

step- > *combining form* denoting a relationship resulting from a remarriage: *stepmother*.

ORIGIN – Old English, from a base meaning 'bereaved, orphaned'.

stepbrother > *noun* a son of one's step-parent, by a marriage other than that with one's own father or mother.

stepchild > *noun* a child of one's husband or wife by a previous marriage.

stepdaughter > *noun* a daughter of one's husband or wife by a previous marriage.

stepfather > *noun* a man who is married to one's mother after the divorce of one's parents or the death of one's father.

stephanotis /steffə**nō**tiss/ > *noun* a climbing plant with fragrant waxy white flowers.

ORIGIN – Greek, 'fit for a wreath', from *stephanos* 'wreath'.

stepmother > *noun* a woman who is married to one's father after the divorce of one's parents or the death of one's mother.

steppe /step/ > *noun* a large area of flat unforested grassland, especially in SE Europe or Siberia.

ORIGIN – Russian.

stepsister > *noun* a daughter of one's step-parent, by a marriage other than that with one's own father or mother.

stepson > *noun* a son of one's husband or wife by a previous marriage.

-ster > *suffix* **1** denoting a person engaged in or associated with a particular activity or thing: *songster*. **2** denoting a person having a particular quality: *youngster*.

steradian /stə**ray**diən/ > *noun* the unit of solid angle in the SI system, equal to the angle at the centre of a sphere subtended by a part of the surface equal in area to the square of the radius.

ORIGIN – from Greek *stereos* 'solid' + **RADIAN**.

stereo /**ster**riō/ > *noun* (pl. **stereos**) **1** stereophonic sound. **2** a stereophonic CD player, record player, etc. > *adjective* **1** stereophonic. **2** stereoscopic.

stereographic > *adjective* representing three-dimensional things on a two-dimensional surface, as in cartography.

stereophonic > *adjective* (of sound reproduction) using two or more channels so that the reproduced sound seems to surround the listener and to come from more than one source. Compare with **MONOPHONIC**.

DERIVATIVES – **stereophonically** *adverb* **stereophony** *noun*.

ORIGIN – from Greek *stereos* 'solid'.

stereoscope > *noun* a device by which two photographs of the same object taken at slightly different angles are viewed

together, creating an impression of depth and solidity.

DERIVATIVES – **stereoscopic** *adjective*.

stereotype > *noun* **1** an image or idea of a particular type of person or thing that has become fixed through being widely held. **2** a relief printing plate cast in a mould made from composed type or an original plate. > *verb* view or represent as a stereotype.

DERIVATIVES – **stereotypy** *noun*.

stereotypical > *adjective* relating to or resembling a stereotype.

DERIVATIVES – **stereotypic** *adjective* **stereotypically** *adverb*.

sterile > *adjective* **1** not able to produce children, young, crops, or fruit. **2** lacking in imagination, creativity, or excitement. **3** free from bacteria or other living micro-organisms.

DERIVATIVES – **sterilely** *adverb* **sterility** *noun*.

SYNONYMS – **1** barren, infertile, unproductive. **2** dry, lifeless, stale.

ANTONYMS – **1** fertile. **2** creative, imaginative.

ORIGIN – Latin *sterilis*, related to Greek *steira* 'barren cow'.

sterilise (also **sterilize**) > *verb* **1** make sterile. **2** deprive of the ability to produce offspring by removing or blocking the sex organs.

WORDFINDER – tubal ligation (*female sterilisation by tying the Fallopian tubes*), vasectomy (*male sterilisation by cutting the vas deferens*).

DERIVATIVES – **sterilisation** *noun*.

sterling > *noun* British money. > *adjective* chiefly Brit. excellent; of great value.

COMBINATIONS – **sterling silver** silver of at least 92¼ per cent purity.

ORIGIN – probably from Old English *steorra* 'star' (because some early Norman pennies bore a small star).

stern[1] > *adjective* **1** grimly serious or strict, especially in the exercise of discipline. **2** severe; demanding.

DERIVATIVES – **sternly** *adverb* **sternness** *noun*.

SYNONYMS – **1** forbidding, grim, hard, serious, sombre, strict. **2** demanding, harsh, rigorous, severe, stringent.

stern[2] > *noun* the rearmost part of a ship or boat.

DERIVATIVES – **sternmost** *adjective* **sternwards** *adverb*.

COMBINATIONS – **sternpost** the central upright support at the stern of a boat, traditionally bearing the rudder.

ORIGIN – probably from Old Norse *stjórn* 'steering'.

sternal > *adjective* relating to the sternum.

sternum /**ster**nəm/ > *noun* (pl. **sternums** or **sterna** /**ster**nə/) the breastbone.

ORIGIN – Greek *sternon* 'chest'.

sternutation /sternyootaysh'n/ > *noun* formal the action of sneezing.

ORIGIN – Latin, from *sternutare* 'to sneeze'.

steroid /**steer**oyd, **sterr**oyd/ > *noun* 1 any of a large class of organic compounds that includes certain hormones and vitamins, with a molecule containing four rings of carbon atoms. 2 short for ANABOLIC STEROID.

DERIVATIVES – **steroidal** adjective.

sterol /**steer**ol, **sterr**ol/ > *noun* Biochemistry any of a group of naturally occurring steroid alcohols, typically waxy solids.

stertorous /**stert**ərəss/ > *adjective* (of breathing) noisy and laboured.

DERIVATIVES – **stertorously** adverb.

ORIGIN – from Latin *stertere* 'to snore'.

stet > *verb* let it stand (used as an instruction on a printed proof to ignore a correction).

ORIGIN – Latin.

stethoscope /**steth**əskōp/ > *noun* a medical instrument for listening to the action of someone's heart or breathing, having a small disc that is placed against the chest and two tubes connected to earpieces.

WORDFINDER – auscultation (*the action of listening to bodily sounds with a stethoscope*).

ORIGIN – from Greek *stēthos* 'breast' + *skopein* 'look at'.

Stetson /**stets**ən/ > *noun* (trademark in the US) a hat with a high crown and a very wide brim, traditionally worn by cowboys and ranchers in the US.

ORIGIN – named after the American hat manufacturer John B. *Stetson*.

stevedore /**steev**ədor/ > *noun* a person employed at a dock to load and unload ships.

ORIGIN – Spanish *estivador*, from *estivar* 'stow a cargo'.

stew¹ > *noun* 1 a dish of meat and vegetables cooked slowly in liquid in a closed dish or pan. 2 informal a state of anxiety or agitation. 3 archaic a public steam bath. 4 archaic a brothel. > *verb* 1 cook slowly in liquid in a closed dish or pan. 2 Brit. (of tea) become strong and bitter with prolonged brewing. 3 informal be in a heated or stifling atmosphere. 4 informal be in an anxious or agitated state.

IDIOMS – **stew in one's own juice** informal be left to suffer the consequences of one's own actions.

ORIGIN – Old French *estuve*, related to *estuver* 'heat in steam'.

stew² > *noun* Brit. 1 a pond or large tank for keeping fish for eating. 2 an artificial oyster bed.

ORIGIN – Old French *estui*, from *estoier* 'confine'.

steward > *noun* 1 a person who looks after the passengers on a ship or aircraft. 2 a person responsible for supplies of food to a college, club, etc. 3 an official who supervises arrangements at a large public event. 4 a person employed to manage a large house or estate. 5 chiefly historical an officer of the British royal household, especially an administrator of Crown estates. > *verb* act as a steward of.

DERIVATIVES – **stewardship** noun.

stewardess > *noun* a woman who looks after the passengers on a ship or aircraft.

stewed > *adjective* informal drunk.

stick¹ > *noun* 1 a thin piece of wood that has fallen or been cut off a tree. 2 a stick used for support in walking or as a weapon. 3 (in hockey, polo, etc.) a long, thin implement used to hit or direct the ball or puck. 4 a long, thin object or piece of something: *a stick of dynamite.* 5 a group of bombs or paratroopers dropped from an aircraft. 6 the threat of punishment as a means of persuasion (as contrasted with the 'carrot' or enticement). 7 Brit. informal severe criticism or treatment. 8 (**the sticks**) informal, derogatory rural areas. 9 informal, dated a person of a specified kind: *Janet's not a bad old stick.*

IDIOMS – **up sticks** Brit. informal go to live elsewhere. [ORIGIN – from nautical slang *to up sticks* 'set up a boat's mast' (ready for departure).]

COMBINATIONS – **stick insect** a long, slender, slow-moving insect that resembles a twig. **stick shift** N. Amer. a gear lever or manual transmission.

stick² > *verb* (past and past participle **stuck**) 1 insert, thrust, or push (something pointed) into or through something. 2 (**stick in** or **into** or **through**) be or remain fixed with its point embedded in. 3 stab or pierce with a sharp object. 4 protrude or extend in a certain direction. 5 adhere or cause to adhere. 6 informal put somewhere in a quick or careless way. 7 (**be stuck**) be fixed in a particular position or unable to move or be moved. 8 (**be stuck**) be unable to progress with a task or find the answer or solution. 9 Brit. informal accept; tolerate; endure.

IDIOMS – **be stuck for** be at a loss for or in need of. **be stuck on** informal be infatuated with. **be stuck with** informal be unable to get rid of or escape from. **get stuck in** (or **into**) Brit. informal start doing something with determination. **stick around** informal remain in or near a place. **stick at** informal persevere with. **stick by** continue to support or be loyal to. **stick in one's throat** (or **craw**) be difficult or impossible to accept. **stick it out** informal put up with or persevere with something difficult or disagreeable. **stick one's neck out** informal risk criticism or anger by acting or speaking boldly. **stick out** be extremely noticeable. **stick out for** refuse to accept less than. **stick to** continue or confine oneself to doing, using, or practising. **stick together** informal remain united or mutually loyal. **stick up** informal,

chiefly N. Amer. rob at gunpoint. **stick up for** support or defend. **stick with** informal persevere or continue with.

COMBINATIONS – **stick-in-the-mud** informal a person who resists change. **stickpin** N. Amer. a straight pin with an ornamental head, worn to keep a tie in place or as a brooch.

sticker > *noun* 1 an adhesive label or notice. 2 informal a determined or persistent person.

stickleback > *noun* a small freshwater or coastal fish with sharp spines along its back.

ORIGIN – from Old English *sticel* 'thorn, sting' + *bæc* 'back'.

stickler > *noun* a person who insists on a certain quality or type of behaviour.

ORIGIN – first used in the sense 'umpire': from obsolete *stickle* 'be umpire'.

stick-up > *noun* informal, chiefly US an armed robbery in which a gun is used to threaten people.

sticky > *adjective* (**stickier**, **stickiest**) 1 tending or designed to stick; adhesive. 2 glutinous; viscous. 3 (of the weather) hot and humid; muggy. 4 informal difficult; awkward. 5 informal (of a website) attracting a long visit or repeat visits from users.

IDIOMS – **come to a sticky end** informal be led by one's own actions to ruin or an unpleasant death. **sticky fingers** informal a tendency to steal.

DERIVATIVES – **stickily** adverb **stickiness** noun.

SYNONYMS – 1 adhesive, tacky. 2 gluey, glutinous, gummy, viscous; informal gooey. 3 clammy, close, humid, muggy, steamy, sultry.

stickybeak Austral./NZ informal > *noun* an inquisitive person. > *verb* pry.

stiff > *adjective* 1 not easily bent; rigid. 2 not moving freely; difficult to turn or operate. 3 unable to move easily and without pain. 4 not relaxed or friendly; constrained. 5 severe or strong: *stiff fines* | *a stiff drink.* 6 (**stiff with**) informal full of. 7 (—— **stiff**) informal having a specified unpleasant feeling to an extreme extent: *scared stiff.* > *noun* informal 1 a dead body. 2 chiefly N. Amer. a boring, conventional person. > *verb* N. Amer. informal kill.

DERIVATIVES – **stiffly** adverb **stiffness** noun.

SYNONYMS – *adjective* 1 inflexible, rigid. 4 constrained, formal, reserved, stand-offish, wooden.

COMBINATIONS – **stiff upper lip** a quality of uncomplaining endurance. **stiff-necked** haughty and stubborn.

stiffen > *verb* 1 make or become stiff. 2 make or become stronger or more steadfast.

DERIVATIVES – **stiffener** noun.

stifle¹ > *verb* **1** prevent from breathing freely; suffocate. **2** smother or suppress. **3** prevent or constrain (an activity or idea).
DERIVATIVES – **stifling** *adjective* **stiflingly** *adverb*.
SYNONYMS – **1** asphyxiate, smother, suffocate. **2** contain, muffle, quench, smother, suppress. **3** constrain, curb, hamper, hinder, inhibit, prevent.

stifle² > *noun* a joint in the legs of horses and other animals, equivalent to the knee in humans.

stigma /stigmə/ > *noun* (pl. **stigmas** or especially in sense 2 **stigmata** /stigmaatə, stigmətə/) **1** a mark or sign of disgrace or discredit. **2** (**stigmata**) (in Christian tradition) marks corresponding to those left on Christ's body by the Crucifixion, said to have been impressed by divine favour on the bodies of St Francis of Assisi and others. **3** Medicine a visible sign or characteristic of a disease. **4** Botany the part of a pistil that receives the pollen during pollination.
ORIGIN – Greek, 'a mark made by a pointed instrument, a dot'.

stigmatic > *adjective* relating to a stigma or stigmas. > *noun* a person bearing stigmata.

stigmatise (also **stigmatize**) > *verb* **1** regard as worthy of disgrace. **2** mark with stigmata.
DERIVATIVES – **stigmatisation** *noun*.

stile > *noun* an arrangement of steps set into a fence or wall that allows people to climb over.
ORIGIN – Old English, from a root meaning 'to climb'.

stiletto > *noun* (pl. **stilettos**) **1** chiefly Brit. a thin, high tapering heel on a woman's shoe. **2** a short dagger with a tapering blade. **3** a sharp-pointed tool for making eyelet holes.
ORIGIN – Italian, 'little dagger'.

still¹ > *adjective* **1** not moving. **2** (of air or water) undisturbed by wind, sound, or current. **3** (of a drink) not fizzy. > *noun* **1** a state of deep and quiet calm. **2** a photograph or a single shot from a cinema film. > *adverb* **1** even now or at a particular time. **2** nevertheless. **3** even: *better still*. > *verb* make or become still.
DERIVATIVES – **stillness** *noun*.
SYNONYMS – *adjective* **1** immobile, inert, motionless, static, stationary, unmoving. **2** calm, peaceful, tranquil.
COMBINATIONS – **still life** a painting or drawing of an arrangement of objects such as flowers or fruit.

still² > *noun* an apparatus for distilling alcoholic drinks such as whisky.

stillbirth > *noun* the birth of a baby that has died in the womb.
NOTE – strictly, a stillbirth is distinguished from a miscarriage: **miscarriage** refers to the expulsion of a fetus within the first 28 weeks of pregnancy, and **stillbirth** to the birth of a baby that has died in the womb after surviving at least the first 28 weeks.

stillborn > *adjective* **1** (of an infant) born dead. **2** (of a proposal or plan) having failed to develop or succeed; unrealised.

stilly literary > *adverb* /still-li/ quietly and with little movement. > *adjective* /stilli/ still and quiet.

stilt > *noun* **1** either of a pair of upright poles with supports for the feet enabling the user to walk raised above the ground. **2** each of a set of posts or piles supporting a building. **3** a long-billed wading bird with very long slender legs.

stilted > *adjective* **1** (of speech or writing) stiff and self-conscious or unnatural. **2** standing on stilts.
DERIVATIVES – **stiltedly** *adverb* **stiltedness** *noun*.

Stilton > *noun* trademark a kind of strong, rich blue cheese originally made in Leicestershire.
ORIGIN – so named because it was formerly sold at a coaching inn in *Stilton*, Cambridgeshire.

stimulant > *noun* **1** a substance that acts to increase physiological or nervous activity in the body. **2** something that promotes activity, interest, or enthusiasm. > *adjective* acting as a stimulant.

stimulate > *verb* **1** apply or act as a stimulus to. **2** animate or excite.
DERIVATIVES – **stimulation** *noun* **stimulator** *noun* **stimulatory** *adjective*.
SYNONYMS – **1** activate, motivate. **2** animate, encourage, excite, fire, inspire, rouse.
ORIGIN – Latin *stimulare* 'urge, goad'.

stimulus /stimyooləss/ > *noun* (pl. **stimuli** /stimyoolī/) **1** something that evokes a specific reaction in an organ or tissue. **2** something that promotes activity, interest, or enthusiasm.
SYNONYMS – **2** impetus, incentive, motivation, prompt, spur.
ORIGIN – Latin, 'goad, spur, incentive'.

sting > *noun* **1** a small sharp-pointed organ of an insect, capable of inflicting a painful wound by injecting poison. **2** any of a number of minute hairs on certain plants, causing inflammation if touched. **3** a wound from a sting. **4** a sharp tingling sensation or hurtful effect. **5** informal a carefully planned undercover operation. > *verb* (past and past participle **stung**) **1** wound with a sting. **2** produce a stinging sensation. **3** hurt; upset. **4** (**sting into**) provoke (someone) to do (something) by causing annoyance or offence. **5** informal swindle or exorbitantly overcharge.
IDIOMS – **sting in the tail** an unexpected and unpleasant end to something.
DERIVATIVES – **stinger** *noun*

COMBINATIONS – **stinging nettle** a nettle covered in stinging hairs. **stingray** a marine ray with a long poisonous serrated spine at the base of the tail.

stingy /stinji/ > *adjective* (**stingier**, **stingiest**) informal mean; ungenerous.
DERIVATIVES – **stingily** *adverb* **stinginess** *noun*.

stink > *verb* (past **stank** or **stunk**; past participle **stunk**) **1** have a strong unpleasant smell. **2** informal be contemptible or scandalous. > *noun* **1** a strong, unpleasant smell. **2** informal a row or fuss.
IDIOMS – **like stink** informal extremely hard or intensely.
COMBINATIONS – **stink bomb** a small container holding a sulphurous compound that is released when the container is broken, giving off a very unpleasant smell. **stinkhorn** a fungus with a rounded head that turns into a foul-smelling slime containing the spores.

stinker > *noun* informal **1** a person or thing that stinks. **2** a contemptible or very unpleasant person or thing.

stinking > *adjective* **1** foul-smelling. **2** informal contemptible or very unpleasant. > *adverb* informal extremely: *stinking rich*.

stinky > *adjective* (**stinkier**, **stinkiest**) informal having a strong unpleasant smell.

stint¹ > *verb* **1** (often **stint on**) supply an inadequate or ungenerous amount of something. **2** deprive (someone) of an adequate or generous amount of something. > *noun* **1** an allotted period of work. **2** limited supply or effort.
ORIGIN – Old English, 'make blunt'.

stint² > *noun* a very small short-legged northern sandpiper.

stipend /stīpend/ > *noun* a fixed regular sum paid as a salary or as expenses to a clergyman, teacher, or public official.
ORIGIN – Latin *stipendium*, from *stips* 'wages' + *pendere* 'to pay'.

stipendiary /stīpendiəri/ > *adjective* **1** receiving a stipend; working for pay rather than voluntarily. **2** relating to or of the nature of a stipend.

stipple > *verb* **1** mark (a surface) with numerous small dots or specks. **2** produce a decorative effect on (paint or other material) by roughening its surface when wet. > *noun* the process, technique, or effect of stippling.
ORIGIN – Dutch *stippelen* 'to prick'.

stipulate /stipyoolayt/ > *verb* demand or specify as part of a bargain or agreement.
DERIVATIVES – **stipulation** *noun*.
SYNONYMS – demand, dictate, insist on, require, specify.
ORIGIN – Latin *stipulari* 'demand as a formal promise'.

stir¹ > *verb* (**stirred**, **stirring**) **1** move an implement round and round in (a liquid or other substance) to mix it thoroughly. **2** move slightly or begin to be active. **3** wake or rise from sleep. **4** (often **stir up**) arouse (a strong feeling) in someone. **5** Brit. informal deliberately cause trouble by spreading rumours or gossip. > *noun* **1** an act of stirring or being stirred. **2** a disturbance or commotion.

DERIVATIVES – **stirrer** *noun*.

COMBINATIONS – **stir-crazy** informal psychologically disturbed as a result of being confined or imprisoned. **stir-fry** fry rapidly over a high heat while stirring briskly.

stir² > *noun* informal prison.

ORIGIN – perhaps from Romany *sturbin* 'jail'.

stirring > *adjective* causing great excitement or strong emotion; rousing. > *noun* an initial sign of activity, movement, or emotion.

DERIVATIVES – **stirringly** *adverb*.

SYNONYMS – *adjective* affecting, dramatic, exciting, moving, rousing, thrilling.

stirrup > *noun* **1** each of a pair of devices attached at either side of a horse's saddle, in the form of a loop with a flat base to support the rider's foot. **2** (also **lithotomy stirrups**) a pair of metal supports for the ankles used during gynaecological examinations and childbirth.

COMBINATIONS – **stirrup cup** an alcoholic drink offered to a person on horseback who is about to depart. **stirrup pump** a hand-operated water pump with a foot rest resembling a stirrup, used to extinguish small fires.

stitch > *noun* **1** a loop of thread or yarn resulting from a single pass of the needle in sewing, knitting, or crocheting. **2** a method of sewing, knitting, or crocheting producing a particular pattern. **3** informal the smallest item of clothing: *swimming around with not a stitch on.* **4** a sudden sharp pain in the side of the body, caused by strenuous exercise. > *verb* **1** make or mend with stitches; apply a stitch or stitches to.

IDIOMS – **in stitches** informal laughing uncontrollably. **a stitch in time saves nine** proverb if you sort out a problem immediately it may save a lot of extra work later. **stitch up** Brit. informal **1** manipulate (a situation) to someone's disadvantage. **2** cheat or falsely incriminate (someone).

DERIVATIVES – **stitcher** *noun* **stitchery** *noun* **stitching** *noun*.

stitchwort > *noun* a plant with white starry flowers, formerly thought to cure a stitch in the side.

stoa /stōə/ > *noun* (in ancient Greek architecture) a portico or roofed colonnade.

ORIGIN – Greek.

stoat > *noun* a small carnivorous mammal of the weasel family, with chestnut fur (white in northern animals in winter) with white underparts and a black-tipped tail.

WORDFINDER – ermine (*white stoat's fur*).

stochastic /stəkastik/ > *adjective* having a random pattern that can be analysed statistically but not predicted precisely.

DERIVATIVES – **stochastically** *adverb*.

ORIGIN – Greek *stokhastikos*, from *stokhazesthai* 'aim at, guess'.

stock > *noun* **1** a supply of goods or materials available for sale or use. **2** farm animals bred and kept for their meat or milk; livestock. **3** the capital of a company raised through the issue and subscription of shares. **4** (usu. **stocks**) a portion of a company's capital held by an individual or group as an investment. **5** securities issued by the government in fixed units with a fixed rate of interest. **6** water in which bones, meat, fish, or vegetables have been slowly simmered. **7** the raw material from which a specified commodity can be manufactured. **8** a person's ancestry. **9** a breed, variety, or population of an animal or plant. **10** the trunk or woody stem of a tree or shrub. **11** a plant cultivated for its fragrant flowers, which are typically lilac, pink, or white. **12** (**the stocks**) (treated as sing. or pl.) historical a wooden structure with holes for securing a person's feet and hands, in which criminals were locked as a method of public punishment. **13** the part of a firearm to which the barrel and firing mechanism are attached. **14** a band of material worn round the neck. **15** (**stocks**) a frame used to support a ship or boat when out of water. > *adjective* **1** usually kept in stock and thus regularly available for sale. **2** commonly used or occurring; conventional. > *verb* **1** have or keep a stock of. **2** provide or fill with a stock of something. **3** (**stock up**) amass stocks of something.

IDIOMS – **in** (or **out of**) **stock** available (or unavailable) for immediate sale or use. **put stock in** have a specified amount of belief or faith in. **take stock** make an overall assessment of a particular situation.

SYNONYMS – *noun* **1** reserve, reservoir, store. *verb* **1** carry, offer, sell. **3** (**stock up**) accumulate, collect, stockpile.

COMBINATIONS – **stock car** an ordinary car that has been strengthened for use in a race in which competing cars collide with each other. **stock cube** a cube of concentrated dehydrated meat, vegetable, or fish stock for use in cooking. **stock exchange** a market in which securities are bought and sold. **stockholder** chiefly N. Amer. a shareholder. **stock-in-trade** the typical subject or commodity a person, company, or profession uses or deals in. **stockman 1** a person who looks after livestock. **2** US an owner of livestock. **stock market** a stock

exchange. **stockpot** a pot in which stock is prepared by long, slow cooking. **stockyard** N. Amer. a large yard containing pens and sheds in which livestock is kept and sorted.

ORIGIN – Old English, 'trunk, block of wood, post'.

stockade > *noun* **1** a barrier or enclosure formed from upright wooden posts. **2** chiefly N. Amer. a military prison. > *verb* enclose with a stockade.

ORIGIN – obsolete French *estocade*, from the base of STAKE¹.

stockbreeder > *noun* a farmer who breeds livestock.

DERIVATIVES – **stockbreeding** *noun*.

stockbroker > *noun* a broker who buys and sells securities on a stock exchange on behalf of clients.

DERIVATIVES – **stockbroking** *noun*.

COMBINATIONS – **stockbroker belt** Brit. an affluent residential area outside a large city.

stockinet (also **stockinette**) > *noun* a soft, loosely knitted stretch fabric.

ORIGIN – probably an alteration of *stocking-net*.

stocking > *noun* **1** either of a pair of separate close-fitting nylon garments covering the foot and leg, worn especially by women. **2** US or archaic a long sock worn by men. **3** a real or ornamental stocking hung up for children on Christmas Eve for Father Christmas to fill with presents. **4** a white marking of the lower part of a horse's leg.

DERIVATIVES – **stockinged** *adjective*.

COMBINATIONS – **stocking cap** a knitted hat with a long tapered end that hangs down. **stocking filler** (N. Amer. **stocking stuffer**) Brit. a small present suitable for putting in a Christmas stocking. **stocking stitch** a knitting stitch consisting of alternate rows of plain and purl stitch.

stockist > *noun* Brit. a retailer that stocks goods of a particular type for sale.

stockpile > *noun* a large accumulated stock of goods or materials. > *verb* accumulate a large stock of.

SYNONYMS – *noun* hoard, pool, reserve. *verb* amass, collect, gather, hoard.

stock-still > *adverb* without any movement; completely still.

stocktaking > *noun* the action or process of recording the amount of stock held by a business.

stocky > *adjective* (**stockier**, **stockiest**) (especially of a person) short and sturdy.

DERIVATIVES – **stockily** *adverb* **stockiness** *noun*.

stodge > *noun* informal, chiefly Brit. **1** food that is heavy, filling, and high in carbohydrates. **2** dull and uninspired material or work.

DERIVATIVES – **stodginess** *noun* **stodgy** *adjective*.

stogy /stōgi/ (also **stogie**) > *noun* (pl. **stogies**) N. Amer. a long, thin, cheap cigar.
ORIGIN – first in the form *stoga*: short for *Conestoga* in Pennsylvania.

stoic /stōik/ > *noun* **1** a stoical person. **2** (**Stoic**) a member of the ancient philosophical school of Stoicism. > *adjective* **1** stoical. **2** (**Stoic**) relating to the Stoics or Stoicism.
ORIGIN – Latin, from Greek *stōïkos*, from **STOA** (with reference to the teaching of the ancient Greek philosopher Zeno, in the *Stoa Poikilē* or Painted Porch, at Athens).

stoical /stōik'l/ > *adjective* enduring pain and hardship without showing one's feelings or complaining.
DERIVATIVES – **stoically** adverb.
SYNONYMS – forbearing, phlegmatic, self-controlled, stoic.

stoicism /stōisiz'm/ > *noun* **1** stoical behaviour. **2** (**Stoicism**) an ancient Greek school of philosophy which taught that it is wise to remain indifferent to changes of fortune and to pleasure and pain.

stoke > *verb* **1** add coal to (a fire, furnace, etc.). **2** encourage or incite (a strong emotion). **3** (**stoke up**) informal consume a large quantity of food to give one energy.
DERIVATIVES – **stoker** noun.
ORIGIN – Dutch *stoken* 'stoke', earlier 'push, poke'; related to **STICK**[1].

STOL > *abbreviation* Aeronautics short take-off and landing.

stole[1] > *noun* **1** a woman's long scarf or shawl, worn loosely over the shoulders. **2** a priest's vestment worn over the shoulders.
ORIGIN – Greek *stolē* 'clothing'.

stole[2] past of **STEAL**.

stolen past participle of **STEAL**.

stolid > *adjective* calm, dependable, and showing little emotion or animation.
DERIVATIVES – **stolidity** noun **stolidly** adverb.
SYNONYMS – impassive, phlegmatic, placid.
ANTONYMS – emotional.
ORIGIN – Latin *stolidus*, perhaps related to *stultus* 'foolish'.

stollen /shtollən, stollən/ > *noun* a rich German fruit and nut loaf.
ORIGIN – German.

stolon /stōlon/ > *noun* Botany a creeping horizontal stem or runner that takes root at several points to form new plants.
ORIGIN – Latin *stolo* 'shoot, scion'.

stoma /stōmə/ > *noun* (pl. **stomas** or **stomata** /stōmətə/) **1** Botany a minute pore in the epidermis of the leaf or stem of a plant, allowing movement of gases in and out. **2** Zoology a small mouth-like opening in some lower animals. **3** Medicine an artificial opening made into a hollow organ, especially the gut or trachea.
ORIGIN – Greek, 'mouth'.

stomach > *noun* **1** an internal organ in which the first part of the process of digestion occurs. **2** the abdominal area of the body; the belly. **3** an appetite or desire for something. > *verb* **1** consume (food or drink) without feeling or being sick. **2** endure or accept: *what I won't stomach is thieving.*
WORDFINDER – gastric (*of the stomach*); four stomachs of a ruminant: rumen, reticulum, omasum, abomasum.
ORIGIN – Greek *stomakhos* 'gullet'.

stomp > *verb* **1** tread heavily and noisily. **2** dance with heavy stamping steps.
DERIVATIVES – **stomping** adjective.
COMBINATIONS – **stomping ground** N. Amer. another term for *stamping ground*.

stone > *noun* **1** hard, solid non-metallic mineral matter of which rock is made. **2** a small piece of stone found on the ground. **3** a piece of stone shaped for a purpose, especially to commemorate something or for demarcation. **4** a gem. **5** a hard seed in certain fruits. **6** (pl. same) Brit. a unit of weight equal to 14 lb (6.35 kg). **7** a whitish or brownish-grey colour. > *verb* **1** throw stones at in order to injure or kill. **2** remove the stone from (a fruit). > *adverb* extremely or totally: *stone cold.*
WORDFINDER – lapidary (*relating to the cutting and polishing of stones*), lithic (*of or relating to stone*), megalith (*large standing stone in a monument*), monolith (*single large standing stone*), petrify (*turn into stone*), scree (*loose stones on a hillside*); calculus (*a stone in the kidney or gall bladder*), lithiasis (*formation of stones in the body*).
IDIOMS – **leave no stone unturned** try every possible course of action in order to achieve something. **a stone's throw** a short distance. **stone me!** (or **stone the crows!**) Brit. informal an exclamation of surprise or shock.
COMBINATIONS – **Stone Age** a prehistoric period when weapons and tools were made of stone, preceding the Bronze Age. **stone circle** a megalithic monument consisting of stones arranged in a circle. **stone-faced** informal revealing no emotions through the expressions of the face. **stonemason** a person who cuts, prepares, and builds with stone. **stoneware** a type of pottery which is impermeable and partly vitrified but opaque. **stonewashed** (also **stonewash**) (of a garment or fabric) washed with abrasives to produce a worn or faded appearance. **stonework 1** the parts of a building that are made of stone. **2** the work of a mason.

stonechat > *noun* a small heathland bird with a call like two stones being knocked together.

stonecrop > *noun* a plant with star-shaped yellow or white flowers which grows among rocks or on walls.

stoned > *adjective* informal under the influence of drugs or alcohol.

stonewall > *verb* **1** delay or block by refusing to answer questions or by giving evasive replies, especially in politics. **2** Cricket bat extremely defensively.

stonker > *noun* Brit. informal something very large or impressive of its kind.
DERIVATIVES – **stonking** adjective.

stonkered > *adjective* Austral./NZ informal **1** utterly exhausted or defeated. **2** drunk.
ORIGIN – from Scots and northern English *stonk* 'game of marbles'.

stony > *adjective* (**stonier, stoniest**) **1** full of stones. **2** of or resembling stone. **3** cold and unfeeling.
IDIOMS – **fall on stony ground** (of words or a suggestion) be ignored or badly received. [ORIGIN – with biblical reference to the parable of the sower in the Gospel of Matthew.]
DERIVATIVES – **stonily** adverb.
COMBINATIONS – **stony broke** Brit. informal entirely without money.

stood past and past participle of **STAND**.

stooge > *noun* **1** derogatory a subordinate used by another to do routine or unpleasant work. **2** a performer whose act involves being the butt of a comedian's jokes. > *verb* **1** informal move about aimlessly. **2** be a comedian's stooge.
SYNONYMS – *noun* **1** lackey, minion, underling.

stook /stook, stook/ Brit. > *noun* a group of sheaves of grain stood on end in a field. > *verb* arrange in stooks.
ORIGIN – Low German *stūke*.

stool > *noun* **1** a seat without a back or arms. **2** chiefly Medicine a piece of faeces. **3** a root or stump of a tree or plant from which shoots spring. **4** US a decoy bird in hunting.
IDIOMS – **fall between two stools** Brit. fail to be or take either of two satisfactory alternatives.
COMBINATIONS – **stool pigeon 1** a police informer. **2** a person acting as a decoy. [ORIGIN – so named from the original use of a pigeon fixed to a stool as a decoy.]

stoop[1] > *verb* **1** bend one's head or body forwards and downwards. **2** have the head and shoulders habitually bent forwards. **3** lower one's standards so far as to do something morally wrong. **4** (of a bird of prey) swoop down on a quarry. > *noun* **1** a stooping posture. **2** the downward swoop of a bird of prey.

stoop[2] > *noun* N. Amer. a porch with steps in front of a building.
ORIGIN – Dutch *stoep*.

stoor > *noun* variant of **STOUR**.

stop > *verb* (**stopped, stopping**) **1** come or cause to come to an end. **2** prevent from happening or from doing something. **3** cease or cause to cease moving or operating. **4** (in full **stop payment of** or **on**) instruct a bank to withhold payment on (a cheque). **5** withhold or deduct. **6** (of a bus or train) call at a designated place to pick up or set down passengers. **7** Brit. informal stay somewhere for a short time. **8** block or close up (a hole or leak). **9** obtain the required pitch from (the string of a musical instrument) by pressing at the appropriate point with the finger. > *noun* **1** an act of stopping. **2** a place designated for a bus or train to stop. **3** an object or part of a mechanism which prevents movement. **4** a set of organ pipes of a particular tone and range of pitch. **5** a knob or lever in an organ or harpsichord which activates a set of pipes or strings of a particular tone and range of pitch. **6** Photography the effective diameter of a lens.

IDIOMS – **pull out all the stops** make a very great effort to achieve something. [ORIGIN – with reference to the stops of an organ.] **put a stop to** cause (an activity) to end. **stop dead** (or **short**) suddenly cease moving, speaking, or acting. **stop off** (or **over**) pay a short visit en route to one's ultimate destination.

SYNONYMS – *verb* **1,2** finish, halt, terminate. *noun* **1** cessation, halt, stoppage.

COMBINATIONS – **stop light** a red traffic signal. **stop-motion** a technique of film animation whereby the camera is repeatedly stopped and started to give the impression of movement. **stop press** Brit. late news inserted in a newspaper or periodical either just before printing or after printing has begun.

ORIGIN – Latin *stuppare* 'to stuff'.

stopcock > *noun* an externally operated valve regulating the flow of a liquid or gas through a pipe.

stopgap > *noun* a temporary solution or substitute.

stoppage > *noun* **1** an instance of stopping. **2** an instance of industrial action. **3** a blockage. **4** (**stoppages**) Brit. deductions from wages by an employer for the payment of tax, National Insurance, etc.

SYNONYMS – **1** cessation, halt, interruption, suspension.

COMBINATIONS – **stoppage time** another term for *injury time*.

stopper > *noun* **1** a plug for sealing a hole. **2** a person or thing that stops. > *verb* seal with a stopper.

stopwatch > *noun* a special watch with buttons that start and stop the display, used to time races.

storage > *noun* **1** the action of storing. **2** space available for storing. **3** a charge for storing things in a warehouse.

COMBINATIONS – **storage battery** (also

storage cell) a battery (or cell) used for storing electrical energy. **storage heater** Brit. an electric heater in which special bricks are heated up at night, releasing heat during the day.

store > *noun* **1** a quantity or supply kept for use as needed. **2** (**stores**) supplies of equipment and food kept for use by members of an army, navy, or other institution. **3** a place where things are kept for future use or sale. **4** chiefly N. Amer. a shop. **5** Brit. a large shop selling different types of goods. **6** Brit. a computer memory. > *verb* **1** keep or accumulate for future use. **2** retain or enter (information) in the memory of a computer. **3** (**be stored with**) have a useful supply of.

IDIOMS – **in store** about to happen. **set** (or **lay** or **put**) **store by** (or **on**) consider to be of a particular degree of importance.

SYNONYMS – *noun* **1** fund, pool, reserve, stock. *verb* **1** hoard, keep, save, stockpile.

COMBINATIONS – **storefront** chiefly N. Amer. **1** a shopfront. **2** a room or rooms facing the street on the ground floor of a commercial building, typically used as a shop. **storehouse 1** a building used for storing goods. **2** a repository: *an enormous storehouse of facts*.

ORIGIN – Old French *estore*, from Latin *instaurare* 'renew'.

storey (N. Amer. also **story**) > *noun* (pl. **storeys** or **stories**) a part of a building comprising all the rooms that are on the same level.

DERIVATIVES – **storeyed** (N. Amer. also **storied**) *adjective*.

wordpower facts
Storey

The words **storey** 'floor of a building' and **story** 'tale or account' are often confused, and in America the spelling **story** is sometimes used for **storey**. Although similar in form, the two words are totally different in meaning, so it may come as a surprise that they are from the same root, Latin *historia* 'history', from Greek. In Greek *historia* meant 'finding out, narrative, history'; it came from *histōr* 'learned, wise man', and was based on a root shared by **wit**[2]. It is not certain why **storey** acquired its English sense: the word perhaps originally denoted a tier of windows with painted mullions or sculptures on the front of a building, representing a historical subject.

storied > *adjective* literary celebrated in or associated with stories or legends.

stork > *noun* a tall long-legged bird with a

long heavy bill and white and black plumage.

storm > *noun* **1** a violent disturbance of the atmosphere with strong winds and usually rain, thunder, lightning, or snow. **2** an uproar or controversy. **3** a sudden violent display of strong feeling. > *verb* **1** move angrily or forcefully in a specified direction. **2** (of troops) suddenly attack and capture (a place). **3** shout angrily.

IDIOMS – **go down a storm** be enthusiastically received. **a storm in a teacup** Brit. great anger or excitement about a trivial matter. **take by storm 1** capture (a place) by a sudden and violent attack. **2** have great and rapid success in (a place).

SYNONYMS – *noun* **2** commotion, furore, uproar. *verb* **1** charge, march, stalk. **3** rant, rave, thunder.

COMBINATIONS – **storm cloud 1** a heavy, dark rain cloud. **2** (**storm clouds**) an ominous state of affairs. **storm door** (or **window**) chiefly N. Amer. an additional outer door (or window) for protection in bad weather or winter. **storm drain** (US **storm sewer**) a drain built to carry away excess water in times of heavy rain. **storm lantern** chiefly Brit. a hurricane lamp. **storm petrel** a small petrel with blackish plumage, formerly believed to be a sign of bad weather to come.

stormbound > *adjective* prevented by storms from starting or continuing a journey.

stormer > *noun* Brit. informal a thing which is particularly impressive of its kind.

DERIVATIVES – **storming** *adjective*.

storm troops > *plural noun* another term for *shock troops*.

DERIVATIVES – **storm trooper** *noun*.

stormy > *adjective* (**stormier**, **stormiest**) **1** affected or disturbed by a storm. **2** full of angry or violent outbursts of feeling.

DERIVATIVES – **stormily** *adverb* **storminess** *noun*.

SYNONYMS – **2** tempestuous, turbulent, volatile.

story[1] > *noun* (pl. **stories**) **1** an account of imaginary or real people and events told for entertainment. **2** an account of past events, experiences, etc. **3** an item of news. **4** a storyline. **5** informal a lie.

WORDFINDER – allegory (*story with symbolic meaning*), fable, parable (*story illustrating moral lesson*), folklore, legend, mythology (*traditional stories in a culture*), narrator (*storyteller*), raconteur (*skilled storyteller*).

SYNONYMS – **1** anecdote, narrative, tale. **4** plot, scenario, storyline.

COMBINATIONS – **storyboard** a sequence of drawings representing the shots planned for a film or television production. **storybook 1** a book containing a story or stories for children. **2** idyllically perfect: *a storybook romance.*

ORIGIN – Old French *estorie*, from Latin *historia* 'history'.

story² > *noun* N. Amer. variant spelling of **STOREY**.

storyline > *noun* the plot of a novel, play, film, etc.

stotin /stoteen/ > *noun* a monetary unit of Slovenia, equal to one hundredth of a tolar.

ORIGIN – Slovene.

stotinka /stotingkə/ > *noun* (pl. **stotinki** /stotingki/) a monetary unit of Bulgaria, equal to one hundredth of a lev.

ORIGIN – Bulgarian, 'one hundredth'.

stoup /stoop/ > *noun* a basin for holy water in a church.

ORIGIN – Old Norse.

stour /stoor/ (also **stoor**) > *noun* Scottish & N. English dust forming a cloud or deposited in a mass.

DERIVATIVES – **stoury** *adjective.*

stout > *adjective* **1** rather fat or heavily built. **2** (of an object) sturdy and thick. **3** brave and determined. > *noun* a kind of strong, dark beer brewed with charred malt or barley.

DERIVATIVES – **stoutly** *adverb.*

SYNONYMS – *adjective* **1** fattish, plump, portly, rotund. **3** forceful, staunch, vigorous.

ORIGIN – Old French.

stove¹ > *noun* an apparatus for cooking or heating that operates by burning fuel or using electricity.

ORIGIN – Dutch or Low German.

stove² past and past participle of **STAVE**.

stovepipe > *noun* a pipe taking the smoke and gases from a stove up through a roof or to a chimney.

COMBINATIONS – **stovepipe hat** a type of tall top hat.

stovies /stoviz/ > *plural noun* Scottish a dish of stewed potatoes.

stow > *verb* **1** pack or store (an object) tidily in an appropriate place. **2** (**stow away**) conceal oneself on a ship, aircraft, etc. so as to travel secretly or without paying.

DERIVATIVES – **stowage** *noun.*

SYNONYMS – **1** deposit, load, stash.

ORIGIN – shortening of **BESTOW**.

stowaway > *noun* a person who stows away.

strabismus /strəbizməss/ > *noun* the condition of having a squint.

ORIGIN – Latin, from Greek *strabismos*, from *strabizein* 'to squint'.

straddle > *verb* **1** sit or stand with one leg on either side of. **2** extend across both sides of. > *noun* an act of straddling.

Stradivarius /straddivairiəss/ > *noun* a violin or other stringed instrument made by the Italian violin-maker Antonio Stradivari (*c.*1644–1737) or his followers.

strafe /strayf, straaf/ > *verb* attack with machine-gun fire or bombs from low-flying aircraft. > *noun* an act of strafing.

ORIGIN – humorous adaptation of the German First World War catchphrase *Gott strafe England* 'may God punish England'.

straggle > *verb* **1** trail slowly behind the person or people in front. **2** grow or spread out in an irregular, untidy way. > *noun* an irregular and untidy group.

DERIVATIVES – **straggler** *noun* **straggly** *adjective.*

straight > *adjective* **1** extending uniformly in one direction only; without a curve or bend. **2** properly positioned so as to be level, upright, or symmetrical. **3** in proper order or condition. **4** honest or not evasive. **5** (of a choice) simple. **6** (of thinking) clear and logical. **7** in continuous succession: *his fourth straight win.* **8** (of an alcoholic drink) undiluted. **9** (of drama) serious as opposed to comic or musical. **10** informal conventional or respectable. **11** informal heterosexual. > *adverb* **1** in a straight line or in a straight manner. **2** without delay or diversion. > *noun* **1** the straight part of something. **2** Poker a continuous sequence of five cards. **3** informal a conventional person. **4** informal a heterosexual.

IDIOMS – **go straight** live an honest life after being a criminal. **keep a straight face** keep a blank or serious facial expression when trying not to laugh. **the straight and narrow** the honest and morally acceptable way of living. **straight away** immediately. **a straight fight** Brit. a contest between just two opponents. **straight from the shoulder 1** dated (of a blow) swift and well delivered. **2** (of words) frank or direct. **straight off** (or **out**) informal without hesitation or deliberation. **straight up** informal **1** Brit. honestly. **2** chiefly N. Amer. undiluted or unadulterated.

DERIVATIVES – **straightness** *noun.*

SYNONYMS – *adjective* **1** linear, undeviating, unswerving. **2** aligned, even, true. **3** neat, organised, shipshape, tidy. **4** candid, direct, forthright, frank. **6** cogent, lucid, rational. **7** consecutive, successive, unbroken. *adverb* **2** at once, immediately, right away.

ANTONYMS – *adjective* **1** curved, winding. **2** askew. **3** untidy. **4** evasive. **6** irrational.

COMBINATIONS – **straight angle** Mathematics an angle of 180°. **straight edge** a bar with one edge accurately straight, used for testing straightness. **straight flush** (in poker or brag) a hand of cards all of one suit and in a continuous sequence. **straight-laced** variant spelling of **STRAIT-LACED**. **straight man** a comedian's stooge. **straight shooter** informal, chiefly N. Amer. an honest and forthright person.

ORIGIN – archaic past participle of **STRETCH**.

straighten > *verb* **1** make or become straight. **2** stand or sit erect after bending.

straightforward > *adjective* **1** easy to do or understand. **2** honest and open.

DERIVATIVES – **straightforwardly** *adverb.*

SYNONYMS – **1** logical, uncomplicated. **2** frank, honest, open, sincere, truthful.

ANTONYMS – **1** complicated. **2** disingenuous.

straightjacket > *noun* variant spelling of **STRAITJACKET**.

strain¹ > *verb* **1** force (a part of one's body or oneself) to make an unusually great effort. **2** injure (a limb, muscle, or organ) by overexertion. **3** make severe or excessive demands on. **4** pull or push forcibly at something. **5** pour (a mainly liquid substance) through a sieve or similar device to separate out any solid matter. > *noun* **1** a force tending to strain something to an extreme degree. **2** an injury caused by straining a muscle, limb, etc. **3** a severe demand on strength or resources. **4** a state of tension or exhaustion caused by severe demands or pressures. **5** the sound of a piece of music as it is played or performed.

SYNONYMS – *verb* **3** overburden, overextend, overtax. **5** filter, sieve. *noun* **3** burdens, demands, pressure.

ORIGIN – Old French *estreindre*, from Latin *stringere* 'draw tight'.

strain² > *noun* **1** a distinct breed or variety of an animal, plant, or other organism. **2** a tendency in a person's character.

ORIGIN – Old English, 'acquisition, gain'.

strained > *adjective* **1** not relaxed or comfortable; showing signs of strain. **2** produced by deliberate effort; artificial or laboured.

SYNONYMS – **1** awkward, fraught, tense. **2** constrained, forced, laboured.

strainer > *noun* a device for straining liquids, having holes punched in it or made of wire net.

strait > *noun* **1** (also **straits**) a narrow passage of water connecting two seas or other large areas of water. **2** (**straits**) a situation characterised by a specified degree of trouble or difficulty. > *adjective* archaic **1** narrow or cramped. **2** strict or rigorous.

ORIGIN – Old French *estreit* 'tight, narrow', from Latin *strictus* 'tighten'.

straiten > *verb* **1** (**straitened**) restricted in range. **2** (**straitened**) restricted because of poverty: *they lived in straitened circumstances.* **3** archaic make or become narrow.

straitjacket (also **straightjacket**) > *noun* **1** a strong garment with long sleeves which can be tied together at the back to confine the arms of a violent prisoner or mental patient. **2** a severe restriction.

strait-laced (also **straight-laced**)

> *adjective* having or showing very strict moral attitudes.

SYNONYMS – moralistic, prim, prissy.

strake > *noun* **1** a continuous line of planking or plates from the stem to the stern of a ship or boat. **2** a protruding ridge fitted to an aircraft or other structure to improve aerodynamic stability.

ORIGIN – Latin *stracus*.

stramash /strəmash/ > *noun* Scottish & N. English an uproar; a row.

strand¹ > *verb* **1** drive or leave aground on a shore. **2** leave (someone) without the means to move from a place. > *noun* literary the shore of a sea, lake, or large river.

DERIVATIVES – **stranded** *adjective*.

strand² > *noun* **1** a single thin length of thread, wire, etc. **2** an element that forms part of a complex whole.

DERIVATIVES – **stranded** *adjective*.

strange > *adjective* **1** unusual or surprising. **2** not previously visited, seen, or encountered. **3** (**strange to** or **at** or **in**) archaic unaccustomed to or unfamiliar with. **4** Physics denoting one of the six flavours of quark.

DERIVATIVES – **strangely** *adverb* **strangeness** *noun*.

SYNONYMS – *adjective* **1** bizarre, curious, peculiar, surprising, unusual. **2** alien, unfamiliar, unknown.

ANTONYMS – *adjective* **1** ordinary.

ORIGIN – Old French *estrange*, from Latin *extraneus* 'external, strange'.

stranger > *noun* **1** a person whom one does not know. **2** a person who does not know, or is not known in, a particular place. **3** (**a stranger to**) a person entirely unaccustomed to (a feeling, experience, or situation).

WORDFINDER – xenophobia (*dislike or fear of strangers*).

strangle > *verb* **1** squeeze or constrict the throat of, especially so as to cause death. **2** suppress or hinder (an impulse, action, or sound).

WORDFINDER – garrotte (*execute by strangling*).

DERIVATIVES – **strangler** *noun*.

ORIGIN – Old French *estrangler*, from Greek *strangalē* 'halter'.

stranglehold > *noun* **1** a grip around the neck of a person that can kill by asphyxiation if held for long enough. **2** complete or overwhelming control.

strangulation > *noun* **1** the action of strangling or the state of being strangled. **2** Medicine a condition in which circulation of blood to a part of the body is cut off by constriction.

DERIVATIVES – **strangulated** *adjective*.

ORIGIN – from Latin *strangulare* 'choke'.

strap > *noun* **1** a strip of flexible material used for fastening, securing, carrying, or

holding on to. **2** (**the strap**) punishment by beating with a leather strap. > *verb* (**strapped, strapping**) **1** fasten or secure with a strap. **2** Brit. bind (an injured part of the body) with adhesive plaster. **3** beat with a leather strap. **4** (**strapped**) informal short of money.

DERIVATIVES – **strapless** *adjective* **strappy** *adjective*.

COMBINATIONS – **strapline** a subheading or caption in a newspaper or magazine.

ORIGIN – dialect form of **STROP¹**.

strapping¹ > *adjective* (of a person) big and strong.

strapping² > *noun* **1** adhesive plaster for strapping injuries. **2** a length of narrow material to be used for straps, or straps collectively.

strata plural of **STRATUM**.

stratagem /strattəjəm/ > *noun* **1** a plan or scheme intended to outwit an opponent. **2** archaic cunning.

SYNONYMS – **1** gambit, manoeuvre, ruse, wile.

ORIGIN – Greek *stratēgēma*, from *stratēgein* 'be a general': originally denoting a military ploy.

strategic /strəteejik/ > *adjective* **1** forming part of a long-term plan or aim to achieve a specific purpose. **2** relating to the gaining of overall or long-term military advantage. **3** used against an enemy's territory or infrastructure: *strategic bombing*. Contrasted with **TACTICAL**.

DERIVATIVES – **strategically** *adverb*.

strategy /strattiji/ > *noun* (pl. **strategies**) **1** a plan designed to achieve a particular long-term aim. **2** the art of planning and directing military activity in a war or battle. Contrasted with *tactics*.

DERIVATIVES – **strategist** *noun*.

SYNONYMS – **1** master plan, programme, scheme.

ORIGIN – Greek *stratēgia* 'generalship'.

strath /strath/ > *noun* Scottish a broad river valley.

ORIGIN – Scottish Gaelic *srath*.

strathspey /strathspay/ > *noun* a slow Scottish dance.

ORIGIN – named after *Strathspey* in Scotland.

stratify /strattifī/ > *verb* (**stratifies, stratified**) **1** form or arrange into strata. **2** arrange or classify.

DERIVATIVES – **stratification** *noun*.

stratigraphy /strətigrəfi/ > *noun* **1** the branch of geology concerned with the order and relative dating of strata. **2** the analysis of the order and position of layers of archaeological remains.

DERIVATIVES – **stratigrapher** *noun* **stratigraphic** *adjective*.

stratocumulus /strattōkyōomyooləss/

> *noun* cloud forming a low layer of clumped or broken grey masses.

stratosphere /strattəsfeer/ > *noun* **1** the layer of the earth's atmosphere above the troposphere and below the mesosphere. **2** informal the very highest levels of something.

DERIVATIVES – **stratospheric** /strattəsferrik/ *adjective*.

stratum /straatəm, straytəm/. > *noun* (pl. **strata**) **1** a layer or a series of layers of rock. **2** a thin layer within any structure. **3** a level or class of society.

DERIVATIVES – **stratal** *adjective*.

USAGE – it is incorrect to use **strata** as a singular or to create the form **stratas** as the plural. In this case English follows Latin, in which one layer is a **stratum** and more than one are **strata**.

ORIGIN – Latin, 'something spread or laid down'.

stratus /straatəss, straytəss/ > *noun* cloud forming a continuous horizontal grey sheet, often with rain or snow.

ORIGIN – Latin, 'strewn'.

straw > *noun* **1** dried stalks of grain, used as fodder or for thatching, packing, or weaving. **2** a single dried stalk of grain. **3** a thin hollow tube of paper or plastic for sucking drink from a container. **4** a pale yellow colour.

IDIOMS – **clutch at straws** resort in desperation to unlikely or inadequate means of salvation. [ORIGIN – from the proverb *a drowning man will clutch at a straw.*] **draw the short straw** be chosen to perform an unpleasant task. **the last** (or **final**) **straw** a further minor difficulty that comes after a series of difficulties and makes a situation unbearable. [ORIGIN – from the proverb *the last straw breaks the (laden) camel's back.*] **a straw in the wind** a slight hint of future developments.

COMBINATIONS – **straw man** another term for *man of straw*. **straw poll** (N. Amer. also **straw vote**) an unofficial ballot conducted as a test of opinion.

strawberry > *noun* **1** a sweet soft red fruit with a seed-studded surface. **2** a deep pinkish-red colour.

COMBINATIONS – **strawberry blonde** (of hair) having a light reddish-blonde colour. **strawberry mark** a soft red birthmark.

stray > *verb* **1** move away aimlessly from a group or from the right course or place. **2** (of the eyes or a hand) move idly in a specified direction. **3** informal be unfaithful to a spouse or partner. > *adjective* **1** not in the right place; separated from a group. **2** (of a domestic animal) having no home or having wandered away from home. > *noun* a stray person or thing, especially a domestic animal.

ORIGIN – Old French *estrayer*, from Latin *extra* 'out of bounds' + *vagari* 'wander'.

streak > *noun* **1** a long, thin mark of a different substance or colour from its surroundings. **2** an element of a specified kind in someone's character: *a ruthless streak*. **3** a spell of specified success or luck: *a winning streak*. > *verb* **1** mark with streaks. **2** move very fast in a specified direction. **3** informal run naked in a public place so as to shock or amuse.

DERIVATIVES – **streaker** *noun* **streaking** *noun*.

SYNONYMS – *noun* **1** band, strip, stripe. *verb* **1** band, fleck, stripe.

streaky > *adjective* (**streakier**, **streakiest**) **1** having streaks. **2** Brit. (of bacon) having alternate strips of fat and lean.

DERIVATIVES – **streakily** *adverb* **streakiness** *noun*.

stream > *noun* **1** a small, narrow river. **2** a continuous flow of liquid, air, gas, people, etc. **3** Brit. a group in which schoolchildren of the same age and ability are taught. > *verb* **1** run or move in a continuous flow. **2** (usu. **be streaming**) run with tears, sweat, or other liquid. **3** float at full extent in the wind. **4** Brit. put (schoolchildren) in streams.

IDIOMS – **against** (or **with**) **the stream** against (or with) the prevailing view or tendency. **on stream** in or into operation or existence.

COMBINATIONS – **stream of consciousness 1** Psychology a person's thoughts and reactions to events, perceived as a continuous flow. **2** a literary style which records as a continuous flow the thoughts and reactions in the mind of a character.

streamer > *noun* **1** a long, narrow strip of material used as a decoration or flag. **2** a banner headline in a newspaper. **3** Fishing a fly with feathers attached.

streaming > *adjective* (of a cold) accompanied by copious running of the nose and eyes. > *noun* a method of relaying data (especially video and audio material) over a computer network as a steady continuous stream.

streamline > *verb* **1** (usu. as **streamlined**) design or form in a way that presents very little resistance to a flow of air or water. **2** make (an organisation or system) more efficient by employing faster or simpler working methods.

street > *noun* **1** a public road in a city, town, or village. **2** (before another noun) relating to the subculture of fashionable urban youth: *street style*. **3** (before another noun) homeless: *street children*.

IDIOMS – **not in the same street** Brit. informal far inferior in terms of ability. **on the streets 1** homeless. **2** working as a prostitute. **streets ahead** Brit. informal greatly superior. **up** (or **right up**) **one's street** (or N. Amer. **alley**) informal well suited to one's tastes, interests, or abilities.

COMBINATIONS – **street Arab** archaic a raggedly dressed homeless child wandering the streets. **streetcar** N. Amer. a tram. **streetsmart** chiefly N. Amer. streetwise. **street value** the price a commodity would fetch if sold illicitly. **streetwalker** a prostitute who seeks clients in the street.

ORIGIN – Latin *strāta* 'paved'.

streetwise > *adjective* informal having the skills and knowledge necessary for dealing with modern urban life.

Strega /straygə/ > *noun* trademark an orange-flavoured Italian liqueur.

ORIGIN – Italian, literally 'witch'.

strelitzia /strəlitsiə/ > *noun* a southern African plant of a genus including the bird of paradise flower.

ORIGIN – named after Charlotte of Mecklenburg-*Strelitz* (1744–1818), queen of George III.

strength /strength, strengkth/ > *noun* **1** the quality or state of being strong. **2** a good or beneficial quality or attribute. **3** literary a source of mental or emotional support. **4** the number of people comprising a group. **5** a full complement of people: *below strength*.

IDIOMS – **go from strength to strength** progress with increasing success. **on the strength of** on the basis or with the justification of. **tower** (or **pillar**) **of strength** a person who can be relied upon to support and comfort others.

SYNONYMS – **1** brawn, power, sturdiness. **2** advantage, asset, strong point, virtue.

ANTONYMS – **1,2** weakness.

strengthen > *verb* make or become stronger.

DERIVATIVES – **strengthener** *noun*.

SYNONYMS – buttress, fortify, reinforce, toughen.

strenuous /strenyooəss/ > *adjective* requiring or using great exertion.

DERIVATIVES – **strenuously** *adverb* **strenuousness** *noun*.

SYNONYMS – arduous, demanding, exacting, taxing.

ORIGIN – Latin *strenuus* 'brisk'.

strep > *noun* Medicine, informal short for STREPTOCOCCUS.

streptococcus /streptəkokkəss/ > *noun* (pl. **streptococci** /streptəkokkī/) a bacterium of a large genus including those causing scarlet fever, pneumonia, souring of milk, and dental decay.

DERIVATIVES – **streptococcal** *adjective*.

ORIGIN – from Greek *streptos* 'twisted'.

streptomycin /streptəmīsin/ > *noun* Medicine an antibiotic used against tuberculosis.

ORIGIN – from Latin *Streptomyces* (name of the bacterium which produces streptomycin), from Greek *streptos* 'twisted' + *mukēs* 'fungus'.

stress > *noun* **1** pressure or tension exerted on a material object. **2** a state of mental, emotional, or other strain. **3** particular emphasis. **4** emphasis given to a syllable or word in speech. > *verb* **1** emphasise. **2** give emphasis to (a syllable or word) when pronouncing it. **3** subject to stress.

SYNONYMS – *noun* **2** anxiety, strain, trauma, worry. *verb* **1** emphasise, highlight, underline, underscore.

ORIGIN – shortening of DISTRESS, or partly from Old French *estresse* 'narrowness, oppression'.

stressful > *adjective* causing mental or emotional stress.

SYNONYMS – fraught, taxing, traumatic.

ANTONYMS – relaxing.

stretch > *verb* **1** (of something soft or elastic) be made or be able to be made longer or wider without tearing or breaking. **2** pull (something) tightly from one point to another. **3** extend one's body or a part of one's body to its full length. **4** last longer than expected. **5** (of finances or resources) be sufficient for a particular purpose. **6** extend over an area or period of time. **7** make demands on. > *noun* **1** an act of stretching. **2** the fact or condition of being stretched. **3** the capacity to stretch or be stretched; elasticity. **4** a continuous expanse or period. **5** informal a period of time spent in prison. **6** (before another noun) informal a motor vehicle or aircraft modified with extended seating or storage capacity: *a stretch limo*. **7** a difficult or demanding task.

IDIOMS – **at full stretch** using the maximum amount of one's resources or energy. **at a stretch 1** in one continuous period. **2** just possible but with difficulty. **stretch one's legs** go for a short walk. **stretch a point** allow or do something not usually acceptable.

DERIVATIVES – **stretchy** (**stretchier**, **stretchiest**) *adjective*.

COMBINATIONS – **stretch marks** marks on the skin, especially on the abdomen, caused by stretching of the skin during pregnancy or as a result of a rapid gain in weight.

stretcher > *noun* **1** a framework of two poles with a long piece of canvas slung between them, used for carrying sick, injured, or dead people. **2** a wooden frame over which a canvas is stretched ready for painting. **3** a brick or stone laid with its long side along the face of a wall. Compare with HEADER (in sense 3). > *verb* carry on a stretcher.

strew > *verb* (past participle **strewn** or **strewed**) **1** (usu. **be strewn**) scatter untidily over a surface or area. **2** (usu. **be strewn with**) cover (a surface or area) with untidily scattered things.

strewth (also **struth**) > *exclamation* informal used to express surprise or dismay.
ORIGIN – contraction of *God's truth*.

stria /strīə/ > *noun* (pl. **striae** /strīee/) **1** technical a linear mark, ridge, or groove, especially one of a number of similar parallel features. **2** Anatomy a longitudinal collection of nerve fibres in the brain.
ORIGIN – Latin, 'furrow'.

striate /strīət/ (also **striated**) > *adjective* marked with striae.
DERIVATIVES – **striation** noun.

stricken North American or archaic past participle of **STRIKE**. > *adjective* **1** seriously affected by an undesirable condition or unpleasant feeling. **2** (of a face or look) showing great distress.
SYNONYMS – afflicted, distressed, troubled.

strict > *adjective* **1** demanding that rules concerning behaviour are obeyed. **2** (of a rule or discipline) demanding total compliance; rigidly enforced. **3** following rules or beliefs exactly. **4** clearly and exactly defined: *a strict interpretation of the law.*
DERIVATIVES – **strictly** adverb **strictness** noun.
SYNONYMS – **1** severe, stern, unbending, uncompromising. **2** exacting, harsh, rigid, rigorous, stringent. **3** meticulous, punctilious, scrupulous. **4** accurate, exact, precise, literal.

wordpower facts

Strict

Derived as it is from Latin *stringere* 'tighten, draw tight', **strict** is related to such words as **astringent**, **restrain**, **strait**, **stress**, **stricture**, and **stringent**. Its original senses were 'restricted in space or extent', 'pressed closely together, tight', and 'restricted or limited'.

stricture /strikchər/ > *noun* **1** a rule restricting behaviour or action. **2** a sternly critical remark.

stride > *verb* (past **strode**; past participle **stridden**) **1** walk with long, decisive steps. **2** (**stride across** or **over**) cross (an obstacle) with one long step. > *noun* **1** a long, decisive step. **2** the length of a step or manner of taking steps. **3** a step in progress towards an aim. **4** (**one's stride**) a good or regular rate of progress, especially after a slow start. **5** (**strides**) Brit. informal trousers.
IDIOMS – **take something in one's stride** deal with something difficult in a calm way.
SYNONYMS – verb **1** march, pace, stalk.

strident > *adjective* **1** loud and harsh. **2** presenting a point of view in an excessively forceful way.
DERIVATIVES – **stridency** noun **stridently** adverb.
SYNONYMS – **1** discordant, grating, raucous.
ORIGIN – from Latin *stridere* 'creak'.

stridulate /stridyoolayt/ > *verb* (of a grasshopper or other insect) make a shrill sound by rubbing the legs, wings, or other parts of the body together.
DERIVATIVES – **stridulation** noun.
ORIGIN – from Latin *stridulus* 'creaking'.

strife > *noun* **1** angry or bitter disagreement; conflict. **2** Austral./NZ trouble or difficulty of any kind.
SYNONYMS – **1** conflict, discord, dissension, friction.
ORIGIN – Old French *estrif*.

strike > *verb* (past and past participle **struck**) **1** deliver a blow to. **2** come into forcible contact with. **3** (in sport) hit or kick (a ball) so as to score a run, point, or goal. **4** ignite (a match) by rubbing it briskly against an abrasive surface. **5** (of a disaster, disease, etc.) occur suddenly and have harmful effects on. **6** attack suddenly. **7** (**strike into**) cause (a strong emotion) in. **8** cause to become suddenly: *he was struck dumb.* **9** suddenly come into the mind of. **10** (**strike on** or **upon**) discover or think of, especially unexpectedly. **11** (**be struck by** or **with**) find particularly interesting or impressive. **12** (of employees) refuse to work, as a form of organised protest. **13** cancel or remove by crossing out with a pen. **14** (**strike off**) officially remove (someone) from membership of a professional group. **15** move or proceed vigorously or purposefully. **16** (**strike out**) start out on a new or independent course. **17** reach (an agreement, balance, or compromise). **18** (of a clock) indicate the time by sounding a chime or stroke. **19** make (a coin or medal) by stamping metal. **20** discover (gold, minerals, or oil) by drilling or mining. **21** take down or dismantle (a tent, camp, or theatrical scenery). > *noun* **1** an act of striking by employees. **2** a refusal to do something, as part of an organised protest: *a rent strike.* **3** a sudden attack. **4** (in sport) an act of striking a ball. **5** (in tenpin bowling) an act of knocking down all the pins with one's first ball. **6** an act of striking gold, minerals, or oil.
IDIOMS – **strike an attitude** (or **pose**) hold one's body in a particular position to create an impression. **strike a blow for** (or **against**) do something to help (or hinder) a cause, belief, or principle. **strike up 1** begin to play a piece of music. **2** begin (a friendship or conversation) with (someone). **strike while the iron is hot** make use of an opportunity immediately. [ORIGIN – with reference to smithing.]

SYNONYMS – *verb* **1** hit, knock, smack, thump. **2** collide with, hit, smash into.
COMBINATIONS – **strike-breaker** a person who works or is employed in place of others who are on strike. **strike pay** money paid to strikers by their trade union. **strike rate** the success rate of a sports team in scoring goals or runs.

striker > *noun* **1** an employee on strike. **2** the player who is to strike the ball in a game. **3** (chiefly in soccer) a forward or attacker.

striking > *adjective* **1** readily perceived; noticeable. **2** dramatically good-looking or beautiful.
DERIVATIVES – **strikingly** adverb.
SYNONYMS – **1** conspicuous, distinct, noticeable, obvious.

strimmer > *noun* trademark an electrically powered grass trimmer with a cutting cord which rotates rapidly on a spindle.

Strine /strīn/ > *noun* informal Australian English or the Australian accent.
ORIGIN – representing the pronunciation of *Australian* in Strine.

string > *noun* **1** material consisting of threads twisted together to form a thin length. **2** a piece of such material. **3** a length of catgut or wire on a musical instrument, producing a note by vibration. **4** (**strings**) the stringed instruments in an orchestra. **5** a piece of catgut, nylon, etc., interwoven with others to form the head of a sports racket. **6** a set of things tied or threaded together on a thin cord. **7** a sequence of similar items or events. **8** a tough piece of fibre in vegetables, meat, or other food. > *verb* (past and past participle **strung**) **1** arrange on a string. **2** (**be strung** or **be strung out**) be arranged in a long line. **3** fit a string or strings to (a musical instrument, a racket, or a bow).
WORDFINDER – *stringed instruments:* balalaika, banjo, cello, double bass, guitar, harp, lute, lyre, mandolin, sitar, ukulele, viola, violin, zither.
IDIOMS – **no strings attached** informal there are no special conditions or restrictions. **second string 1** an alternative resource or course of action. **2** a reserve team. **string along** informal **1** stay with a person or group as long as it is convenient. **2** mislead (someone) deliberately over a length of time. **string out** prolong (something). **string up 1** kill (someone) by hanging. **2** (**be strung up**) Brit. be tense or nervous.
DERIVATIVES – **stringed** adjective.
COMBINATIONS – **string bass** (especially among jazz musicians) a double bass. **string bean** any of various beans eaten in their pods. **string quartet** a chamber music ensemble consisting of first and second violins, viola, and cello. **string vest** a man's undergarment made of a meshed fabric.

stringent /ˈstrinjənt/ > *adjective* (of regulations or requirements) strict, precise, and exacting.
DERIVATIVES – **stringency** *noun* **stringently** *adverb*.
SYNONYMS – rigid, rigorous, severe, strict.
ANTONYMS – flexible, lenient.
ORIGIN – from Latin *stringere* 'draw tight'.

stringer > *noun* **1** a structural piece running lengthwise in a framework, especially that of a ship or aircraft. **2** *informal* a journalist who is not on the regular staff of a newspaper, but who reports part-time on a particular place.

stringy > *adjective* (**stringier, stringiest**) **1** resembling string. **2** tall, wiry, and thin. **3** (of food) tough and fibrous.

stringybark > *noun* Austral. a eucalyptus with tough fibrous bark.

strip¹ > *verb* (**stripped, stripping**) **1** remove all coverings or clothes from. **2** take off one's clothes. **3** leave bare of accessories or fittings. **4** remove (paint) from a surface with solvent. **5** (**strip of**) deprive (someone) of (rank, power, or property). **6** sell off (the assets of a company) for profit. **7** tear the thread or teeth from (a screw, gearwheel, etc.). > *noun* **1** an act of undressing, especially in a striptease. **2** *Brit.* the identifying outfit worn by the members of a sports team while playing.
SYNONYMS – *verb* **1** denude. **2** disrobe, undress.
COMBINATIONS – **strip poker** a form of poker in which a player with a losing hand takes off an item of clothing as a forfeit. **strip-search** search (someone) for concealed drugs, weapons, or other items, by stripping off their clothes.

strip² > *noun* **1** a long, narrow piece of cloth, paper, etc. **2** a long, narrow area of land. **3** chiefly *N. Amer.* a main road lined with shops and other facilities.
COMBINATIONS – **strip light** *Brit.* a tubular fluorescent lamp. **strip mine** chiefly *N. Amer.* an opencast mine.
ORIGIN – Low German *strippe* 'strap, thong'.

stripe > *noun* **1** a long, narrow band or strip of a different colour or texture from the surface on either side of it. **2** a chevron sewn on to a uniform to denote military rank. **3** chiefly *N. Amer.* a type or category. > *verb* (usu. **be striped**) mark with stripes.
DERIVATIVES – **striped** *adjective* **stripy** (also **stripey**) *adjective*.

stripling > *noun* archaic or humorous a young man.

stripper > *noun* **1** a device or substance for stripping. **2** a striptease performer.

strippergram > *noun* a novelty greetings message delivered by a man or woman who accompanies it with a striptease act.

striptease > *noun* a form of entertainment in which a performer gradually undresses to music in a sexually provocative way.

strive > *verb* (past **strove** or **strived**; past participle **striven** or **strived**) **1** make great efforts. **2** (**strive against**) fight vigorously against.
DERIVATIVES – **striver** *noun*.
SYNONYMS – **1** endeavour, exert oneself, make every effort, try hard. **2** battle, combat, struggle.
ORIGIN – Old French *estriver*.

strobe /strōb/ *informal* > *noun* **1** a stroboscope. **2** a stroboscopic lamp. **2** *N. Amer.* an electronic flash for a camera. > *verb* **1** flash intermittently. **2** show or cause strobing.

strobing > *noun* **1** irregular movement and loss of continuity of lines and stripes in a television picture. **2** jerkiness in what should be a smooth movement of a cinematographic image.

stroboscope /ˈstrōbəskōp/ > *noun* Physics an instrument which shines a bright light at rapid intervals so that a moving or rotating object appears stationary.
DERIVATIVES – **stroboscopic** *adjective*.
ORIGIN – from Greek *strobos* 'whirling'.

strode past of STRIDE.

stroganoff /ˈstrogənof/ > *noun* a dish in which the central ingredient, typically strips of beef, is cooked in a sauce containing sour cream.
ORIGIN – named after the Russian diplomat Count Pavel *Stroganov* (1772–1817).

stroke > *noun* **1** an act of hitting. **2** *Golf* an act of hitting the ball with a club, as a unit of scoring. **3** a sound made by a striking clock. **4** a mark made by drawing a pen, pencil, or paintbrush once across paper or canvas. **5** a line forming part of a written or printed character. **6** a short diagonal line separating characters or figures. **7** an act of stroking. **8** one of a series of repeated movements. **9** a style of moving the arms and legs in swimming. **10** the mode or action of moving the oar in rowing. **11** a sudden disabling attack or loss of consciousness caused by an interruption in the flow of blood to the brain. > *verb* move one's hand with gentle pressure over (a surface).
IDIOMS – **at a stroke** by a single action having immediate effect. **not do a stroke of work** do no work at all. **put someone off their stroke** disconcert someone so that they make a mistake or hesitate. **stroke of genius** an outstandingly original idea. **a stroke of luck** something that happens unexpectedly and is of great benefit.
SYNONYMS – *noun* **1** blow, hit, knock, thump. *verb* caress, fondle.
COMBINATIONS – **stroke play** play in golf in which the score is reckoned by counting the number of strokes taken overall. Compare with *match play*.

stroll > *verb* **1** walk in a leisurely way. **2** achieve a sporting victory easily. > *noun* **1** a short leisurely walk. **2** a victory easily achieved.
SYNONYMS – *verb* **1** amble, saunter, wander. *noun* **1** amble, promenade, wander.
ORIGIN – first used in the sense 'roam as a vagrant': probably from German *strollen*, from *Strolch* 'vagabond'.

stroller > *noun* N. Amer. a pushchair.

stromatolite /strəˈmatəlīt/ > *noun* Biology a mound built up of layers of blue-green algae and lime-rich sediment, especially as fossilised in Precambrian rocks.
ORIGIN – from Latin *stroma* 'layer, covering' + -LITE.

strong > *adjective* (**stronger, strongest**) **1** physically powerful. **2** done with or exerting great force. **3** able to withstand great force or pressure. **4** secure, stable, or firmly established. **5** great in power, influence, or ability. **6** great in intensity or degree. **7** (of language or actions) forceful and extreme. **8** (of something seen or heard) not soft or muted. **9** pungent and full-flavoured. **10** (of a solution or drink) containing a large proportion of a substance. **11** used after a number to indicate the size of a group: *a crowd several thousands strong*. **12** Grammar (of verbs) forming the past tense and past participle by a change of vowel within the stem rather than by addition of a suffix (e.g. *swim, swam, swum*).
IDIOMS – **come on strong** informal behave aggressively or assertively. **going strong** informal continuing to be healthy, vigorous, or successful. **strong on 1** good at. **2** possessing large quantities of. **strong meat** Brit. ideas or language likely to be found unacceptably forceful or extreme.
DERIVATIVES – **strongly** *adverb*.
SYNONYMS – **1** brawny, muscular, powerful. **3** durable, resilient, sturdy. **4** firmly established, impregnable, secure, solid, stable. **6** fervent, forceful, vehement.
ANTONYMS – **1** puny. **3,4** weak. **6** half-hearted.
COMBINATIONS – **strong-arm** using or characterised by force or violence. **strongbox** a small lockable metal box in which valuables may be kept. **strongman 1** a man of great physical strength, especially one who performs feats of strength for entertainment. **2** a leader who rules by the exercise of threats, force, or violence. **strong point 1** a specially fortified defensive position. **2** a thing at which one excels. **strong suit 1** (in bridge or whist) a holding of a number of high cards of one suit in a hand. **2** a thing at which a person excels.

stronghold > *noun* **1** a place that has been

fortified against attack. **2** a place of strong support for a cause or political party.

strontium /**stron**tiəm/ > *noun* a soft silver-white metallic chemical element .

ORIGIN – named after *Strontian*, a village in Scotland, where a mineral containing strontium was discovered.

strop¹ > *noun* **1** a device, typically a strip of leather, for sharpening razors. **2** Nautical a collar of leather, spliced rope, or iron, used for handling cargo. > *verb* (**stropped, stropping**) sharpen on or with a strop.

ORIGIN – probably from Latin *stroppus* 'thong'.

strop² > *noun* Brit. informal a temper.

stroppy > *adjective* (**stroppier, stroppiest**) Brit. informal bad-tempered; argumentative.

ORIGIN – perhaps an abbreviation of **OBSTREPEROUS**.

strove past of **STRIVE**.

struck past and past participle of **STRIKE**.

structural > *adjective* relating to or forming part of a structure.

DERIVATIVES – **structurally** *adverb*.

structuralism > *noun* a method of interpretation and analysis of human cognition, behaviour, culture, and experience, which focuses on relationships of contrast between elements in a conceptual system.

DERIVATIVES – **structuralist** *noun & adjective*.

structure > *noun* **1** the arrangement of and relations between the parts of something complex. **2** a building or other object constructed from several parts. **3** the quality of being well organised. > *verb* give structure to.

ORIGIN – Latin *structura*, from *struere* 'to build'.

strudel /**strōō**d'l/ > *noun* a confection of thin pastry rolled up round a fruit filling and baked.

ORIGIN – German, literally 'whirlpool'.

struggle > *verb* **1** make forceful efforts to get free. **2** strive under difficult circumstances to do something. **3** have difficulty in gaining recognition or a living. **4** contend or compete. **5** make one's way with difficulty. > *noun* **1** an act of struggling. **2** a very difficult task.

DERIVATIVES – **struggler** *noun*.

SYNONYMS – *verb* **2** battle, endeavour, labour, strive. **5** flounder, scramble, stumble. *noun* **1** effort, exertion, labour.

strum > *verb* (**strummed, strumming**) play (a guitar or similar instrument) by sweeping the thumb or a plectrum up or down the strings. > *noun* an instance or the sound of strumming.

strumpet > *noun* archaic or humorous a female prostitute or a promiscuous woman.

strung past and past participle of **STRING**.

strut > *noun* **1** a bar forming part of a framework and designed to resist compression. **2** a strutting gait. > *verb* (**strutted, strutting**) **1** walk with a stiff, erect, and conceited gait. **2** brace with a strut or struts.

IDIOMS – **strut one's stuff** informal dance or behave in a confident and expressive way.

DERIVATIVES – **strutting** *adjective*.

struth > *exclamation* variant spelling of **STREWTH**.

strychnine /**strik**neen/ > *noun* a bitter and highly poisonous substance obtained from nux vomica and related plants.

ORIGIN – from Greek *strukhnos*, denoting a kind of nightshade.

Stuart (also **Stewart**) > *adjective* belonging or relating to the royal family ruling Scotland 1371–1714 and Britain 1603–1714 (interrupted by the Commonwealth 1649–60). > *noun* a member of this family.

stub > *noun* **1** the remnant of a pencil, cigarette, or similar-shaped object after use. **2** a shortened or unusually short thing. **3** the counterfoil of a cheque, ticket, or other document. > *verb* (**stubbed, stubbing**) **1** accidentally strike (one's toe) against something. **2** extinguish (a cigarette) by pressing the lighted end against something.

ORIGIN – Old English, 'stump of a tree'.

stubble > *noun* **1** the cut stalks of cereal plants left in the ground after harvesting. **2** short, stiff hairs growing on a man's face when he has not shaved for a while.

DERIVATIVES – **stubbly** *adjective*.

ORIGIN – Old French *stuble*, from Latin *stipula* 'straw'.

stubborn > *adjective* **1** determined not to change one's attitude or position. **2** difficult to move, remove, or cure.

DERIVATIVES – **stubbornly** *adverb* **stubbornness** *noun*.

SYNONYMS – **1** intransigent, mulish, obdurate, obstinate.

stubby > *adjective* (**stubbier, stubbiest**) short and thick. > *noun* (pl. **stubbies**) Austral./ NZ informal a small squat bottle of beer.

stucco /**stukk**ō/ > *noun* fine plaster used for coating wall surfaces or moulding into architectural decorations. > *verb* (**stuccoes, stuccoed**) coat or decorate with stucco.

ORIGIN – Italian.

stuck past participle of **STICK²**.

stuck-up > *adjective* informal snobbishly aloof.

stud¹ > *noun* **1** a large-headed piece of metal that pierces and projects from a surface, especially for decoration. **2** a small projection fixed to the base of a shoe or boot to provide better grip. **3** a small piece of jewellery which is pushed through a pierced ear, nostril, etc. **4** a fastener consisting of two buttons joined with a bar, used to fasten a shirt front or to fasten a collar to a shirt. > *verb* (**studded,**

studding) (usu. **be studded**) **1** decorate with studs or similar small objects. **2** strew or scatter: *the sky was studded with stars*.

DERIVATIVES – **studding** *noun*.

ORIGIN – Old English, 'post, upright prop'.

stud² > *noun* **1** an establishment where horses or other domesticated animals are kept for breeding. **2** (also **stud horse**) a stallion. **3** informal a sexually active or virile young man. **4** (also **stud poker**) a form of poker in which the first card of a player's hand is dealt face down and the others face up, with betting after each round of the deal.

student > *noun* **1** a person studying at a university or other place of higher education. **2** chiefly N. Amer. a school pupil. **3** (before another noun) denoting someone who is studying to enter a particular profession: *a student nurse*. **4** a person who takes a particular interest in a subject.

studio > *noun* (pl. **studios**) **1** a room where an artist works or where dancers practise. **2** a room from which television or radio programmes are broadcast, or in which they are recorded. **3** a place where film or sound recordings are made. **4** a film production company.

COMBINATIONS – **studio flat** Brit. a flat containing one main room.

ORIGIN – Italian, from Latin *studium* 'zeal, painstaking application'.

studious > *adjective* **1** spending a lot of time studying or reading. **2** done deliberately or with great care.

DERIVATIVES – **studiously** *adverb* **studiousness** *noun*.

SYNONYMS – **1** bookish, scholarly. **2** assiduous, diligent, painstaking, thorough.

study > *noun* (pl. **studies**) **1** the devotion of time and attention to acquiring knowledge. **2** a detailed investigation and analysis of a subject or situation. **3** a room for reading, writing, or academic work. **4** a piece of work done for practice or as an experiment. > *verb* (**studies, studied**) **1** acquire knowledge on. **2** make a study of. **3** apply oneself to study. **4** look at closely in order to observe or read. **5** (**studied**) done with deliberate and careful effort.

IDIOMS – **a study in** a good example of (a quality or emotion). **in a brown study** absorbed in one's thoughts. [ORIGIN – apparently from *brown* in an early sense 'gloomy'.]

DERIVATIVES – **studiedly** *adverb*.

SYNONYMS – *noun* **2** analysis, enquiry, examination, investigation, research. *verb* **4** examine, inspect, scrutinise.

ORIGIN – Latin *studium* 'zeal, painstaking application'.

stuff > *noun* **1** matter, material, articles, or activities of a specified or indeterminate kind. **2** (**one's stuff**) informal one's area of expertise. **3** basic characteristics; substance. **4** Brit. dated woollen fabric, especially as distinct from silk, cotton, and linen. **5** Brit. informal, dated nonsense; rubbish. > *verb* **1** fill tightly with something. **2** force tightly or hastily into a receptacle or space. **3** fill out the skin of (a dead animal or bird) with material to restore the original shape and appearance. **4** (**be stuffed up**) have one's nose blocked up with catarrh. **5** (**stuff oneself**) informal eat greedily. **6** Brit. informal defeat heavily in sport.

WORDFINDER – taxidermist (*a person who stuffs dead animals for display*).

IDIOMS – **get stuffed** Brit. informal said to express dismissal or contempt. **stuffed shirt** informal a conservative, pompous person.

SYNONYMS – *verb* **1** fill, pack, pad. **2** cram, shove, squeeze, thrust.

ORIGIN – Old French *estoffe* 'material, furniture', from Greek *stuphein* 'draw together'.

stuffing > *noun* **1** a mixture used to stuff poultry or meat before cooking. **2** padding used to stuff cushions, furniture, or soft toys.

IDIOMS – **knock** (or **take**) **the stuffing out of** informal severely damage the confidence or strength of.

stuffy > *adjective* (**stuffier, stuffiest**) **1** lacking fresh air or ventilation. **2** conventional and narrow-minded. **3** (of a person's nose) blocked up.

DERIVATIVES – **stuffily** *adverb* **stuffiness** *noun*.

SYNONYMS – **1** airless, musty, stale. **2** conservative, prim, staid.

stultify /stultifī/ > *verb* (**stultifies, stultified**) **1** cause to feel bored or drained of energy. **2** cause to appear foolish or absurd.

ORIGIN – Latin *stultificare*, from *stultus* 'foolish'.

stumble > *verb* **1** trip or momentarily lose one's balance. **2** walk unsteadily. **3** make a mistake or repeated mistakes in speaking. **4** (**stumble across** or **on**) find by chance. > *noun* an act of stumbling.

DERIVATIVES – **stumbling** *adjective*.

SYNONYMS – *verb* **1** founder, lose one's footing, slip. **2** lurch, stagger, teeter, totter. **4** (**stumble across or on**) chance on, come across, happen on.

COMBINATIONS – **stumbling block** an obstacle to progress.

ORIGIN – Old Norse.

stump > *noun* **1** the part of a tree trunk left projecting from the ground after the rest has fallen or been felled. **2** a projecting remnant of something worn away or cut or broken off. **3** Cricket each of the three upright pieces of wood which form a wicket. > *verb* **1** baffle. **2** Cricket dismiss (a batsman) by

dislodging the bails with the ball while the batsman is out of the crease but not running. **3** walk stiffly and noisily. **4** (**stump up**) Brit. informal pay (a sum of money).

IDIOMS – **on the stump** informal engaged in political campaigning. [ORIGIN – from the use of a tree stump as a platform for a speaker.]

ORIGIN – Low German *stumpe* or Dutch *stomp*.

stumper > *noun* informal a puzzling question.

stumpy > *adjective* (**stumpier, stumpiest**) short and thick; squat.

stun > *verb* (**stunned, stunning**) **1** knock unconscious or into a dazed or semi-conscious state. **2** astonish or shock (someone) so that they are temporarily unable to react.

SYNONYMS – *verb* **1** daze, knock out. **2** amaze, astound, dumbfound, stupefy.

COMBINATIONS – **stun gun** a device that delivers an electric shock, used to immobilise an attacker without causing serious injury.

ORIGIN – from Old French *estoner* 'astonish'.

stung past and past participle of STING.

stunk past and past participle of STINK.

stunner > *noun* informal **1** a strikingly beautiful or impressive person or thing. **2** an amazing turn of events.

stunning > *adjective* extremely impressive or attractive.

DERIVATIVES – **stunningly** *adverb*.

stunt[1] > *verb* **1** retard the growth or development of. **2** frustrate and spoil.

ORIGIN – first used in the sense 'bring to an abrupt halt': from dialect *stunt* 'foolish, stubborn'.

stunt[2] > *noun* **1** an action displaying spectacular skill and daring. **2** something unusual done to attract attention.

COMBINATIONS – **stuntman** (or **stuntwoman**) a person taking an actor's place in performing dangerous stunts.

ORIGIN – US college slang.

stupa /stōopə/ > *noun* a dome-shaped building erected as a Buddhist shrine.

ORIGIN – Sanskrit.

stupefy /styōopifī/ > *verb* (**stupefies, stupefied**) **1** make (someone) unable to think or feel properly. **2** astonish and shock.

DERIVATIVES – **stupefaction** *noun* **stupefying** *adjective* **stupefyingly** *adverb*.

ORIGIN – from Latin *stupefacere*, from *stupere* 'be struck senseless'.

stupendous /styoopendəss/ > *adjective* extremely impressive.

DERIVATIVES – **stupendously** *adverb*.

SYNONYMS – amazing, extraordinary.

ORIGIN – from Latin *stupendus* 'to be wondered at'.

stupid > *adjective* (**stupider, stupidest**) **1** lacking intelligence or common sense. **2** informal used to express exasperation or boredom: *your stupid paintings!* **3** dazed and unable to think clearly.

DERIVATIVES – **stupidity** *noun* **stupidly** *adverb*.

SYNONYMS – **1** foolish, unintelligent, witless.

ORIGIN – Latin *stupidus*, from *stupere* 'be amazed or stunned'.

stupor /styōopər/ > *noun* a state of near-unconsciousness or insensibility.

DERIVATIVES – **stuporous** *adjective*.

SYNONYMS – daze, torpor.

ORIGIN – from Latin *stupere* 'be amazed or stunned'.

sturdy > *adjective* (**sturdier, sturdiest**) **1** strongly and solidly built or made. **2** confident and determined: *a sturdy independence*.

DERIVATIVES – **sturdily** *adverb* **sturdiness** *noun*.

SYNONYMS – **1** durable, robust, strong, substantial. **2** resolute, staunch, steadfast.

ANTONYMS – frail.

wordpower facts

Sturdy

In medieval times **sturdy** meant 'reckless, violent' and 'intractable, obstinate'. The word is a shortening of Old French *esturdi* 'stunned, dazed', and is thought to be based on Latin *turdus* 'a thrush': thrushes were formerly associated with drunkenness, possibly because of eating wine grapes. Interestingly, there is an old French phrase *soûl comme une grive*, which means 'drunk as a thrush'.

sturgeon /sturjən/ > *noun* a very large fish with bony plates on the body, found in seas and rivers and commercially important for its caviar and flesh.

ORIGIN – Old French.

Sturm und Drang /shtoorm oont **drang**/ > *noun* an 18th-century German literary and artistic movement characterised by the expression of emotional unrest.

ORIGIN – German, 'storm and stress'.

stutter > *verb* **1** talk with continued involuntary repetition of sounds, especially initial consonants. **2** (of a machine or gun) produce a series of short, sharp sounds. > *noun* a tendency to stutter while speaking.

DERIVATIVES – **stutterer** *noun* **stuttering** *adjective*.

ORIGIN – from dialect *stut*.

sty[1] > *noun* (pl. **sties**) a pigsty.

ORIGIN – Old English, 'sty pig'.

sty[2] (also **stye**) > *noun* (pl. **sties** or **styes**) an inflamed swelling on the edge of an eyelid.

ORIGIN – dialect *styany*, from *styan* (from Old English *stīgend* 'riser') + EYE.

Stygian /stijiən/ > *adjective* literary very dark or gloomy.

ORIGIN – from the name of the River *Styx*, an underworld river in Greek mythology.

style > *noun* 1 a manner of doing something. 2 a distinctive appearance, design, or arrangement. 3 a way of painting, writing, etc., characteristic of a particular period, person, etc. 4 elegance and sophistication. 5 an official or legal title. 6 Botany a narrow extension of the ovary, bearing the stigma. > *verb* 1 design, make, or arrange in a particular form. 2 designate with a particular name, description, or title.

DERIVATIVES – **styleless** *adjective* **styler** *noun*.

SYNONYMS – *noun* 1 method, technique, way. 3 genre, school, type. 4 elegance, finesse, grace, poise. *verb* 1 design, fashion, tailor.

ORIGIN – Latin *stilus*.

styli plural of STYLUS.

stylised (also **stylized**) > *adjective* depicted or treated in a mannered and non-realistic style.

DERIVATIVES – **stylisation** *noun*.

stylish > *adjective* 1 having or displaying a good sense of style. 2 fashionably elegant.

DERIVATIVES – **stylishly** *adverb* **stylishness** *noun*.

stylist > *noun* 1 a person who designs fashionable clothes or cuts hair. 2 a writer noted for their literary style.

stylistic > *adjective* of or concerning style, especially literary style.

DERIVATIVES – **stylistically** *adverb*.

stylistics > *plural noun* (treated as sing.) the study of the literary styles of particular genres or writers.

stylus /stīləss/ > *noun* (pl. **styli** /stīlī/) 1 a pointed implement used for scratching or tracing letters or engraving. 2 a pen-like device used to input handwriting or drawings directly into a computer. 3 a hard point following a groove in a gramophone record and transmitting the recorded sound for reproduction.

ORIGIN – an erroneous spelling of Latin *stilus*.

stymie /stīmi/ > *verb* (**stymies, stymied, stymying** or **stymieing**) informal prevent or hinder the progress of.

ORIGIN – first used as a golfing term, denoting a situation on the green where a ball obstructs the shot of another player.

styptic /stiptik/ Medicine > *adjective* causing bleeding to stop. > *noun* a styptic substance.

ORIGIN – Greek *stuptikos*, from *stuphein* 'to contract'.

styrene /stīreen/ > *noun* Chemistry an unsaturated liquid hydrocarbon obtained as a petroleum by-product and used to make plastics and resins.

ORIGIN – from *styrax*, a gum resin.

styrofoam /stīrəfōm/ > *noun* (trademark in the US) a kind of expanded polystyrene, used especially for making food containers.

ORIGIN – from POLYSTYRENE + FOAM.

suasion /swayzh'n/ > *noun* formal persuasion as opposed to force or compulsion.

ORIGIN – from Latin *suadere* 'to urge'.

suave /swaav/ > *adjective* (**suaver, suavest**) (of a man) charming, confident, and elegant.

DERIVATIVES – **suavely** *adverb* **suaveness** *noun* **suavity** *noun*.

SYNONYMS – poised, polished, refined, urbane.

ORIGIN – Latin *suavis* 'agreeable'.

sub informal > *noun* 1 a submarine. 2 a subscription. 3 a substitute, especially in a sporting team. 4 a subeditor. 5 Brit. an advance or loan against expected income. > *verb* (**subbed, subbing**) 1 act as a substitute. 2 Brit. lend or advance a sum to. 3 subedit.

sub- (also **suc-** before *c*; **suf-** before *f*; **sug-** before *g*; **sup-** before *p*; **sur-** before *r*; **sus-** before *c, p, t*) > *prefix* 1 at, to, or from a lower level or position: *subalpine*. 2 lower in rank or importance: *subdeacon*. 3 somewhat; nearly: *subantarctic*. 4 denoting subsequent or secondary action of the same kind: *subdivision*. 5 denoting support: *subsidy*.

ORIGIN – from Latin *sub* 'under, close to'.

subacute > *adjective* Medicine between acute and chronic.

subadult > *noun* Zoology an animal that is not fully adult.

subalpine > *adjective* of or situated on the higher slopes of mountains just below the treeline.

subaltern /subbəltərn/ > *noun* an officer in the British army below the rank of captain, especially a second lieutenant. > *adjective* of lower status.

ORIGIN – from Latin *sub-* 'next below' + *alternus* 'every other'.

subantarctic > *adjective* relating to the region immediately north of the Antarctic Circle.

sub-aqua > *adjective* relating to swimming or exploring under water, especially with an aqualung.

subaqueous > *adjective* existing, formed, or taking place under water.

subarctic > *adjective* relating to the region immediately south of the Arctic Circle.

subatomic > *adjective* smaller than or occurring within an atom.

subcategory > *noun* (pl. **subcategories**) a secondary or subordinate category.

sub-clause > *noun* chiefly Law a subsidiary section of a clause of a bill, contract, or treaty.

subconscious > *adjective* of or concerning the part of the mind of which one is not fully aware but which influences one's actions and feelings. > *noun* (**one's** or **the subconscious**) this part of the mind.

DERIVATIVES – **subconsciously** *adverb* **subconsciousness** *noun*.

subcontinent > *noun* a large distinguishable part of a continent, especially the part of Asia south of the Himalayas (consisting of India, Pakistan, and Bangladesh).

DERIVATIVES – **subcontinental** *adjective*.

subcontract > *verb* /subkəntrakt/ 1 employ a firm or person outside one's company to do (work). 2 carry out work for a company as part of a larger project. > *noun* /subkontrakt/ a contract to do work for another company as part of a larger project.

subcontractor > *noun* a firm or person that carries out work for a company as part of a larger project.

subcostal > *adjective* Anatomy beneath a rib; below the ribs.

subculture > *noun* a cultural group within a larger culture, often having beliefs or interests at variance with those of the larger culture.

DERIVATIVES – **subcultural** *adjective*.

subcutaneous > *adjective* Anatomy & Medicine situated or applied under the skin.

DERIVATIVES – **subcutaneously** *adverb*.

subdeacon > *noun* (in some Christian Churches) a minister of an order ranking below deacon.

subdivide > *verb* divide (something that has already been divided or that is a separate unit).

subdivision > *noun* 1 the action of subdividing or being subdivided. 2 a secondary or subordinate division. 3 N. Amer. & Austral./NZ an area of land divided into plots for sale.

subduction > *noun* Geology the sideways and downward movement of the edge of a plate of the earth's crust into the mantle beneath another plate.

DERIVATIVES – **subduct** verb.

ORIGIN – from Latin subducere 'draw from below'.

subdue > verb (**subdues, subdued, subduing**) 1 overcome, quieten, or bring under control. 2 bring (a country) under control by force.

SYNONYMS – 1 contain, curb, quell, suppress.

ORIGIN – Old French suduire, from Latin subducere 'draw from below'.

subdued > adjective 1 (of a person) quiet and rather reflective or depressed. 2 (of colour or lighting) soft; muted.

SYNONYMS – 1 pensive, sombre, thoughtful.

subedit > verb (**subedited, subediting**) chiefly Brit. check and correct (newspaper or magazine text) before printing.

DERIVATIVES – **subeditor** noun.

subfloor > noun the foundation for a floor in a building.

subframe > noun a supporting frame.

subfusc /subfusk/ > adjective literary dull or gloomy. > noun Brit. the formal clothing worn for examinations and formal occasions at some universities.

ORIGIN – Latin subfuscus, from sub- 'somewhat' + fuscus 'dark brown'.

subgroup > noun a subdivision of a group.

sub-heading (also **sub-head**) > noun a heading given to a subsection of a piece of writing.

subhuman > adjective 1 of a lower order of being than the human. 2 Zoology (of a primate) closely related to humans. 3 derogatory not worthy of a human being; debased or depraved. > noun a subhuman creature or person.

subject > noun /subjikt/ 1 a person or thing that is being discussed, studied, or dealt with. 2 a branch of knowledge studied or taught. 3 Grammar the word or words in a sentence that name who or what performs the action of the verb. 4 a member of a state owing allegiance to its monarch or supreme ruler. 5 Music a theme, leading phrase, or motif. > adjective /subjikt/ (**subject to**) 1 likely or prone to be affected by (something bad). 2 dependent or conditional upon. 3 under the control or authority of. > adverb /subjikt/ (**subject to**) conditionally upon. > verb /səbjekt/ (usu. **subject to**) 1 cause to undergo. 2 bring under one's control or jurisdiction.

DERIVATIVES – **subjection** noun.

SYNONYMS – noun 1 issue, question, theme, topic. 2 area, discipline, field. adjective (**subject to**) 1 liable to, prone to,

susceptible to. 2 conditional on, contingent on, dependent on, depending on. 3 accountable to, bound by, constrained by.

COMBINATIONS – **subject matter** the topic dealt with or the subject represented in a debate, exposition, or work of art.

ORIGIN – from Latin subicere 'bring under'.

subjective > adjective 1 based on or influenced by personal feelings, tastes, or opinions. 2 dependent on the mind for existence. 3 Grammar relating to or denoting a case of nouns and pronouns used for the subject of a sentence.

DERIVATIVES – **subjectively** adverb **subjectivity** noun.

sub judice /sub jōodisi/ > adjective Law under judicial consideration and therefore prohibited from public discussion elsewhere.

ORIGIN – Latin, 'under a judge'.

subjugate /subjoogayt/ > verb bring under domination or control, especially by conquest.

DERIVATIVES – **subjugation** noun.

ORIGIN – Latin subjugare 'bring under a yoke', from jugum 'yoke'.

subjunctive Grammar > adjective (of a form of a verb) expressing what is imagined or wished or possible (as in if I were you). > noun a verb in the subjunctive mood.

ORIGIN – Latin subjunctivus, from subjungere, from sub- 'in addition' + jungere 'to join'.

sublet > verb /sublet/ (**subletting**; past and past participle **sublet**) lease (a property) to a subtenant. > noun /sublet/ a lease of a property by a tenant to a subtenant.

sub lieutenant > noun a rank of officer in the Royal Navy, above midshipman and below lieutenant.

sublimate /sublimayt/ > verb 1 (in psychoanalytic theory) divert or modify (an instinctual impulse) into a culturally higher or socially more acceptable activity. 2 transform into a purer or idealised form. 3 Chemistry another term for SUBLIME. > noun /also sublimət/ Chemistry a solid deposit of a substance which has sublimed.

DERIVATIVES – **sublimation** noun.

ORIGIN – Latin sublimare 'raise up'.

sublime > adjective (**sublimer, sublimest**) 1 of such excellence, grandeur, or beauty as to inspire great admiration or awe. 2 extreme or unparalleled: sublime confidence. > verb Chemistry (with reference to a solid substance) change directly into vapour when heated, typically forming a solid deposit again on cooling.

DERIVATIVES – **sublimely** adverb **sublimity** noun.

SYNONYMS – adjective 1 awe-inspiring, exalted, lofty, noble. 2 complete, supreme, utter.

wordpower facts

Sublime

The source of the word **sublime**, Latin sublimis 'high, elevated, eminent', was formed from sub- and probably limen 'threshold'. Sub- normally means 'under, below', but in this case seems to mean up to, so that the word literally means 'as high as the top of the door'. In medieval English **sublime** was a verb meaning 'heat (a solid substance) so that it changes into vapour'. Early uses as an adjective (16th century) were in the senses 'dignified, aloof', 'elevated, grand', and '(of a building or similar) high, towering'. The related word **subliminal** was formed in the 19th century from sub- and limen, but in this case sub- has its usual meaning of 'under, below', so that the idea is 'below the threshold of sensation or consciousness'.

subliminal /səblimmin'l/ > adjective Psychology (of a stimulus or mental process) perceived by or affecting someone's mind without their being aware of it.

DERIVATIVES – **subliminally** adverb.

COMBINATIONS – **subliminal advertising** advertising that uses images and sounds to influence consumers subliminally.

sublunary > adjective literary belonging to this world rather than a better or more spiritual one.

ORIGIN – Latin sublunaris, from luna 'moon'.

sub-machine gun > noun a hand-held lightweight machine gun.

submarine > noun a streamlined warship designed to operate completely submerged in the sea for long periods. > adjective existing, occurring, done, or used under the surface of the sea.

DERIVATIVES – **submariner** noun.

submerge > verb 1 cause to be under water. 2 descend below the surface of water. 3 completely cover or obscure.

DERIVATIVES – **submergence** noun.

ORIGIN – Latin submergere, from sub- 'under' + mergere 'to dip'.

submerse > verb technical submerge.

submersible > adjective designed to operate while submerged. > noun a small boat or craft that is submersible.

submersion > noun the action or state of submerging or being submerged.

submicroscopic > adjective too small to be seen by an ordinary light microscope.

submission > noun 1 the action or fact of

submitting. **2** a proposal or application submitted for consideration.

submissive > *adjective* meekly obedient or passive.

DERIVATIVES – **submissively** *adverb* **submissiveness** *noun*.

SYNONYMS – docile, meek, slavish, timid.

submit > *verb* (**submitted, submitting**) **1** accept or yield to a superior force or stronger person. **2** subject to a particular process, treatment, or condition. **3** present (a proposal or application) for consideration or judgement. **4** (especially in judicial contexts) suggest; argue.

SYNONYMS – **1** accede, capitulate, give in, surrender.

ORIGIN – Latin *submittere*, from *sub-* 'under' + *mittere* 'send, put'.

subnormal > *adjective* not reaching a level regarded as usual, especially with respect to intelligence or development.

DERIVATIVES – **subnormality** *noun*.

suboptimal > *adjective* technical of less than the highest standard or quality.

subordinate > *adjective* /səˈbordinət/ **1** lower in rank or position. **2** of less or secondary importance. > *noun* /səˈbordinət/ a person under the authority or control of another. > *verb* /səˈbordinayt/ **1** treat or regard as subordinate. **2** make subservient or dependent.

DERIVATIVES – **subordinately** *adverb* **subordination** *noun*.

COMBINATIONS – **subordinate clause** a clause that forms part of and is dependent on a main clause (e.g. 'when it rang' in 'she answered the phone when it rang').

ORIGIN – Latin *subordinatus* 'placed in an inferior rank', from *sub-* 'below' + *ordinare* 'ordain'.

suborn /səˈborn/ > *verb* bribe or otherwise induce (someone) to commit an unlawful act such as perjury.

ORIGIN – Latin *subornare* 'incite secretly', from *sub-* 'secretly' + *ornare* 'equip'.

sub-plot > *noun* a subordinate plot in a play, novel, etc.

subpoena /səˈpeenə/ Law > *noun* a writ ordering a person to attend a court. > *verb* (**subpoenas, subpoenaed** or **subpoena'd, subpoenaing**) summon with a subpoena.

ORIGIN – from Latin *sub poena* 'under penalty' (the first words of the writ).

sub-post office > *noun* (in the UK) a small local post office offering fewer services than a main post office.

sub rosa /sub ˈrōzə/ > *adjective & adverb* formal happening or done in secret.

ORIGIN – Latin, 'under the rose', as an emblem of secrecy.

subroutine > *noun* Computing a set of instructions designed to perform a frequently used operation within a program.

sub-Saharan > *adjective* from or forming part of the African regions south of the Sahara desert.

subscribe > *verb* **1** (usu. **subscribe to**) arrange to receive something, especially a periodical, regularly by paying in advance. **2** (**subscribe to**) contribute (a sum of money) to a project or cause. **3** apply to participate in. **4** (**subscribe to**) express agreement with (an idea or proposal).

DERIVATIVES – **subscriber** *noun*.

COMBINATIONS – **subscriber trunk dialling** Brit. the automatic connection of long-distance telephone calls by dialling without the assistance of an operator.

ORIGIN – Latin *subscribere* 'write below'.

subscript > *adjective* (of a letter, figure, or symbol) written or printed below the line. > *noun* a subscript letter, figure, or symbol.

subscription > *noun* **1** the action or fact of subscribing. **2** a payment to subscribe to something. **3** formal a signature or short piece of writing at the end of a document.

subsection > *noun* a division of a section.

subsequent > *adjective* coming after something in time.

DERIVATIVES – **subsequently** *adverb*.

SYNONYMS – ensuing, following, succeeding.

ORIGIN – from Latin *subsequi* 'follow after'.

subserve > *verb* formal help to further or promote.

ORIGIN – Latin *subservire* (see **SUB-, SERVE**).

subservient > *adjective* **1** prepared to obey others unquestioningly; obsequious. **2** less important; subordinate.

DERIVATIVES – **subservience** *noun*.

SYNONYMS – **1** deferential, obedient, obsequious, servile.

subset > *noun* **1** a part of a larger group of related things. **2** Mathematics a set of which all the elements are contained in another set.

subside > *verb* **1** become less intense, violent, or severe. **2** (of water) go down to a lower or the normal level. **3** (of a building) sink lower into the ground. **4** (of the ground) cave in; sink. **5** (**subside into**) give way to (an overwhelming feeling).

SYNONYMS – **1** abate, calm, moderate, slacken.

ORIGIN – Latin *subsidere*, from *sub-* 'below' + *sidere* 'settle'.

subsidence /ˈsubsidˈnss, səbˈsīdˈnss/ > *noun* the gradual caving in or sinking of an area of land.

NOTE – both of the pronunciations given above are found in British and American English: the second is older, but the first is probably now more widely used.

subsidiarity /səbsiddiˈarriti/ > *noun* (in politics) the principle that a central authority should perform only those tasks which cannot be performed at a more local level.

subsidiary > *adjective* **1** less important than but related or supplementary to. **2** (of a company) controlled by a holding or parent company. > *noun* (pl. **subsidiaries**) a subsidiary company.

ORIGIN – Latin *subsidiarius*, from *subsidium* 'assistance'.

subsidise (also **subsidize**) > *verb* **1** support (an organisation or activity) financially. **2** pay part of the cost of producing (something) to reduce its price.

DERIVATIVES – **subsidisation** *noun*.

subsidy > *noun* (pl. **subsidies**) **1** a sum of money granted from public funds to help an industry or business keep the price of a commodity or service low. **2** a sum of money granted to support an undertaking held to be in the public interest. **3** a grant or contribution of money. **4** historical a parliamentary grant to the sovereign for state needs.

ORIGIN – Old French *subsidie*, from Latin *subsidium* 'assistance'.

subsist > *verb* **1** maintain or support oneself, especially at a minimal level. **2** chiefly Law remain in being, force, or effect. **3** (**subsist in**) be attributable to.

ORIGIN – Latin *subsistere* 'stand firm'.

subsistence > *noun* **1** the action or fact of subsisting. **2** the means of doing this. **3** (before another noun) referring to production at a level sufficient only for one's own use, without any surplus for trade: *subsistence agriculture*.

COMBINATIONS – **subsistence level** (or **wage**) a standard of living (or wage) that provides only the bare necessities of life.

subsoil > *noun* the soil lying immediately under the surface soil.

subsonic > *adjective* relating to or flying at a speed or speeds less than that of sound.

subspace > *noun* **1** Mathematics a space that is wholly contained in another space. **2** (in science fiction) a hypothetical space–time continuum used for communication at a speed faster than that of light.

subspecies > *noun* (pl. same) Biology a subdivision of a species, usually a geographically isolated variety.

DERIVATIVES – **subspecific** *adjective*.

substance > *noun* **1** a particular kind of matter with uniform properties. **2** the real physical matter of which a person or thing consists. **3** solid basis in reality or fact: *the claim has no substance.* **4** the quality of being important, valid, or significant. **5** the most important or essential part or meaning. **6** the subject matter of a text or work of art. **7** an intoxicating or narcotic drug.

IDIOMS – **in substance** essentially.

ORIGIN – Latin *substantia* 'being, essence', from *substare* 'stand firm'.

substandard > *adjective* below the usual or required standard.

substantial > *adjective* **1** of considerable importance, size, or worth. **2** strongly built or made. **3** concerning the essentials of something. **4** real and tangible rather than imaginary.

DERIVATIVES – **substantiality** *noun*.

SYNONYMS – **1** material, significant, sizeable. **2** durable, stout, sturdy. **4** actual, existing, physical.

substantially > *adverb* **1** to a great or significant extent. **2** for the most part; essentially.

substantiate /səbˈstanshiayt/ > *verb* provide evidence to support or prove the truth of.

DERIVATIVES – **substantiation** *noun*.

ORIGIN – Latin *substantiare* 'give substance'.

substantive /ˈsubstəntiv/ > *adjective* /also səbˈstantiv/ **1** having a firm basis in reality and so important or meaningful. **2** having a separate and independent existence. > *noun* **Grammar, dated** a noun.

DERIVATIVES – **substantively** *adverb*.

substation > *noun* **1** a set of equipment reducing the high voltage of electrical power transmission to that suitable for supply to consumers. **2** a subordinate police station or fire station.

substituent /səbˈstityooənt/ > *noun* **Chemistry** an atom or group of atoms taking the place of another or occupying a specified position in a molecule.

substitute > *noun* **1** a person or thing acting or serving in place of another. **2** a sports player eligible to replace another after a match has begun. > *verb* **1** use, add, or serve in place of. **2** replace with another. **3** replace (a sports player) with a substitute during a match.

DERIVATIVES – **substitutable** *adjective* **substitution** *noun* **substitutive** *adjective*.

USAGE – **substitute** is traditionally followed by **for** and means 'put (someone or something) in place of another', as in *she substituted the fake vase for the real one.* It may also be used with **with** or **by** to mean 'replace (something) with something else', as in *she substituted the real vase with the fake one.* This can be confusing, since the two sentences shown above mean the same thing, yet the object of the verb and the object of the preposition have swapped positions. Despite the potential confusion, the second, newer use is acceptable, although still disapproved of by some people.

SYNONYMS – *noun* **1** proxy, replacement, surrogate. *verb* **2** exchange, replace, switch.

ORIGIN – Latin *substituere* 'put in place of'.

substrate /ˈsubstrayt/ > *noun* **1** the surface or material on which an organism lives, grows, or feeds. **2** the substance on which an enzyme acts.

ORIGIN – anglicised form of **SUBSTRATUM**.

substratum > *noun* (pl. **substrata**) **1** an underlying layer or substance, in particular a layer of rock or soil beneath the surface of the ground. **2** a foundation or basis.

substructure > *noun* an underlying or supporting structure.

subsume > *verb* include or absorb in something else.

DERIVATIVES – **subsumable** *adjective*.

ORIGIN – Latin *subsumere*, from *sub-* 'from below' + *sumere* 'take'.

subtenant > *noun* a person who leases property from a tenant.

subtend > *verb* (of a line, arc, etc.) form (an angle) at a particular point when straight lines from its extremities meet.

ORIGIN – Latin *subtendere*, from *sub-* 'under' + *tendere* 'stretch'.

subterfuge /ˈsubtərfyooj/ > *noun* a trick or deception used in order to achieve one's goal.

ORIGIN – from Latin *subterfugere* 'escape secretly', from *subter-* 'beneath' + *fugere* 'flee'.

subterranean /subtəˈrayniən/ > *adjective* existing or occurring under the earth's surface.

ORIGIN – Latin *subterraneus*, from *sub-* 'below' + *terra* 'earth'.

subtext > *noun* an underlying theme in a piece of writing or speech.

subtitle > *noun* **1** (**subtitles**) captions displayed at the bottom of a cinema or television screen that translate or transcribe the dialogue or narrative. **2** a subordinate title of a published work. > *verb* provide with a subtitle or subtitles.

subtle > *adjective* (**subtler**, **subtlest**) **1** so delicate or precise as to be difficult to analyse or describe. **2** capable of making fine distinctions. **3** delicately complex and understated. **4** making use of clever and indirect methods to achieve something.

DERIVATIVES – **subtleness** *noun* **subtlety** *noun* **subtly** *adverb*.

SYNONYMS – **1** delicate, fine, minute. **3** low-key, muted, subdued. **4** crafty, ingenious, wily.

---

wordpower facts

Subtle

The word **subtle** entered English via Old French *sotil* from Latin *subtilis*. Although it had many of the meanings of **subtle**, *subtilis* was probably originally a weaving term with the sense 'fine in texture'. It seems to go back to *sub-* 'under, below' and *tela* 'woven material, web', which means that **subtle** is related to such words as **text**, **textile**, **texture**, and **tissue**. Medieval senses of **subtle** that are now obsolete include 'of fine texture', '(of a smell, colour, etc.) faint or delicate', 'not easily understood', and 'crafty, cunning'.

---

subtotal > *noun* the total of one set of a larger group of figures to be added.

subtract > *verb* take away (a number or amount) from another to calculate the difference.

DERIVATIVES – **subtraction** *noun* **subtractive** *adjective*.

ORIGIN – Latin *subtrahere* 'draw away'.

subtropics > *plural noun* the regions adjacent to or bordering on the tropics.

DERIVATIVES – **subtropical** *adjective*.

subunit > *noun* a distinct component of something.

suburb > *noun* an outlying district of a city, especially a residential one.

DERIVATIVES – **suburban** *adjective* **suburbanisation** (also **suburbanization**) *noun* **suburbanise** (also **suburbanize**) *verb* **suburbanite** *noun*.

ORIGIN – Latin *suburbium*, from *sub-* 'near to' + *urbs* 'city'.

suburbia > *noun* the suburbs viewed collectively.

subvention > *noun* a grant of money, especially from a government.

ORIGIN – from Latin *subvenire* 'assist'.

subversive > *adjective* seeking or intended to subvert an established system or institution. > *noun* a subversive person.

DERIVATIVES – **subversively** *adverb* **subversiveness** *noun*.

SYNONYMS – *adjective* disruptive, dissident, seditious. *noun* agitator, dissident, troublemaker.

subvert > *verb* undermine the power and authority of (an established system or institution).

DERIVATIVES – **subversion** *noun*.

SYNONYMS – destabilise, disrupt, weaken.

ORIGIN – Latin *subvertere*, from *sub-* 'from below' + *vertere* 'to turn'.

subway > *noun* **1 Brit.** a tunnel under a road for use by pedestrians. **2 chiefly N. Amer.** an underground railway.

subwoofer > *noun* a loudspeaker

component designed to reproduce very low bass frequencies.

sub-zero > *adjective* (of temperature) lower than zero; below freezing.

succeed > *verb* **1** achieve an aim or purpose. **2** attain fame, wealth, or social status. **3** take over an office, title, etc., from (someone). **4** (usu. **succeed to**) become the new rightful holder of an office, title, etc. **5** come after and take the place of.
ORIGIN – Latin *succedere* 'come close after'.

succès d'estime /sooksay desteem/ > *noun* (pl. same) a success in terms of critical appreciation, as opposed to popularity or commercial gain.
ORIGIN – French, 'success of opinion'.

success > *noun* **1** the accomplishment of an aim or purpose. **2** the attainment of fame, wealth, or social status. **3** a person or thing that achieves success.
COMBINATIONS – **success story** informal a successful person or thing.
ORIGIN – Latin *successus*, from *succedere* 'come close after'.

successful* > *adjective* **1** accomplishing an aim or purpose. **2** having achieved fame, wealth, or social status.
DERIVATIVES – **successfully** *adverb*.
*SPELLING – double *c*, double *s*, one *l*: su*ccessful*.

succession* > *noun* **1** a number of people or things following one after the other. **2** the action, process, or right of inheriting an office, title, etc. **3** Ecology the process by which a plant community successively gives way to another until stability is reached.
IDIOMS – **in quick succession** following one another at short intervals. **in succession** following one after the other without interruption.
DERIVATIVES – **successional** *adjective*.
*SPELLING – double *c*, double *s*: su*ccession*.

successive* > *adjective* following one another or following others.
DERIVATIVES – **successively** *adverb*.
*SPELLING – double *c*, double *s*: su*ccessive*.
SYNONYMS – consecutive, sequential, succeeding.

successor > *noun* a person or thing that succeeds another.

succinct /səksingkt/ > *adjective* briefly and clearly expressed.
DERIVATIVES – **succinctly** *adverb* **succinctness** *noun*.
SYNONYMS – clear, concise, pithy.
ANTONYMS – verbose.
ORIGIN – from Latin *succingere* 'tuck up', from *sub-* 'from below' + *cingere* 'gird'.

succour /sukkər/ (US **succor**) > *noun* assistance and support in times of hardship and distress. > *verb* give assistance to.
ORIGIN – Latin *succursus*, from *succurrere* 'run to the help of'.

succubus /sukyoobəss/ > *noun* (pl. **succubi** /sukyoobī/) a female demon believed to have sexual intercourse with sleeping men.
ORIGIN – Latin 'prostitute', from *succubare*, from *sub-* 'under' + *cubare* 'to lie'.

succulent > *adjective* **1** (of food) tender, juicy, and tasty. **2** Botany (of a plant) having thick fleshy leaves or stems adapted to storing water. > *noun* Botany a succulent plant.
DERIVATIVES – **succulence** *noun* **succulently** *adverb*.
ORIGIN – Latin *succulentus*, from *succus* 'juice'.

succumb > *verb* **1** fail to resist (pressure, temptation, etc.). **2** die from the effect of a disease or injury.
SYNONYMS – **1** cave in, give in, submit, yield.
ORIGIN – Latin *succumbere*, from *sub-* 'under' + a verb related to *cubare* 'to lie'.

such > *determiner, predeterminer, & pronoun* **1** of the type previously mentioned. **2** (**such —— as** or **that**) of the type about to be mentioned. **3** to so high a degree; so great.
IDIOMS – **as such** in the exact sense of the word. **such-and-such** an unspecified person or thing. **such as 1** for example. **2** of a kind that; like. **such as it is** what little there is; for what it's worth. **such that** to the extent that.
ORIGIN – Old English, related to **so¹** and **ALIKE**.

suchlike > *pronoun* things of the type mentioned: *old chairs, tables, and suchlike.* > *determiner* of the type mentioned: *food, clothing, and suchlike provisions.*

suck > *verb* **1** draw into the mouth by contracting the muscles of the lip and mouth to make a partial vacuum. **2** hold (something) in the mouth and draw at it by contracting the lip and cheek muscles. **3** draw in a specified direction by creating a vacuum. **4** (**suck in** or **into**) involve (someone) in something without their choosing. **5** (**suck up to**) informal attempt to gain advantage by behaving obsequiously towards. **6** N. Amer. informal be very bad or disagreeable. > *noun* an act or sound of sucking. > *exclamation* (**sucks**) Brit. informal used to express derision and defiance.
IDIOMS – **give suck** archaic suckle. **suck someone dry** exhaust someone's physical, material, or emotional resources.
ORIGIN – Old English, related to **SOAK**.

sucker > *noun* **1** a rubber cup that adheres to a surface by suction. **2** a flat or concave organ enabling an animal to cling to a surface by suction. **3** informal a gullible person. **4** (**a sucker for**) informal a person especially susceptible to or fond of (a

specified thing). **5** a shoot springing from the base of a tree or other plant, especially one arising from the root at some distance from the trunk. > *verb* **1** (of a plant) produce suckers. **2** N. Amer. informal, fool or trick.

sucker punch > *noun* an unexpected punch or blow. > *verb* (**sucker-punch**) hit with a sucker punch.

suckle > *verb* (with reference to a baby or young animal) feed from the breast or teat.
DERIVATIVES – **suckler** *noun*.
ORIGIN – probably from **SUCKLING**.

suckling > *noun* an unweaned child or animal.
ORIGIN – from **SUCK** + **-LING**.

sucre /sookray/ > *noun* the basic monetary unit of Ecuador, equal to 100 centavos.
ORIGIN – named after the Venezuelan revolutionary Antonio José de *Sucre* (1795–1830).

sucrose /sookrōz, syookrōz/ > *noun* Chemistry a compound which is the chief component of cane or beet sugar.
ORIGIN – from French *sucre* 'sugar' + **-OSE²**.

suction > *noun* the production of a partial vacuum by the removal of air in order to force fluid into a vacant space or produce adhesion. > *verb* remove using suction.
COMBINATIONS – **suction pump** a pump for drawing liquid through a pipe into a chamber emptied by a piston.
ORIGIN – from Latin *sugere* 'suck'.

Sudanese /soodəneez/ > *noun* a person from the Sudan. > *adjective* relating to the Sudan.

sudarium /soodairiəm, syoodairiəm/ > *noun* (pl. **sudaria** /soodairiə, syoodairiə/) (in the Roman Catholic Church) another term for **VERONICA** (in sense 2).
ORIGIN – Latin, 'napkin', from *sudor* 'sweat'.

sudden > *adjective* occurring or done quickly and unexpectedly.
IDIOMS – (**all**) **of a sudden** suddenly.
DERIVATIVES – **suddenness** *noun*.
COMBINATIONS – **sudden death** a means of deciding the winner in a tied match, in which play continues and the winner is the first side or player to score. **sudden infant death syndrome** technical term for *cot death*.
ORIGIN – Old French *sudein*, from Latin *subitaneus*, from *subitus* 'sudden'.

suddenly > *adverb* quickly and unexpectedly.

sudorific /syoodəriffik, soodəriffik/ Medicine > *adjective* relating to or causing sweating. > *noun* a sudorific drug.
ORIGIN – from Latin *sudor* 'sweat'.

Sudra /sōōdrə/ > *noun* a member of the worker caste, lowest of the four Hindu castes.

ORIGIN – Sanskrit.

suds > *plural noun* **1** froth made from soap and water. **2** N. Amer. informal beer. > *verb* chiefly N. Amer. cover or wash in soapy water.

DERIVATIVES – **sudsy** *adjective*.

sue > *verb* (**sues, sued, suing**) **1** institute legal proceedings against (a person or institution), typically for redress. **2** formal appeal formally to a person for something.

ORIGIN – Old French *suer*, from Latin *sequi* 'follow'.

suede > *noun* leather, especially the skin of a young goat, with the flesh side rubbed to make a velvety nap.

ORIGIN – from French *gants de Suède* 'gloves of Sweden'.

suet > *noun* the hard white fat on the kidneys and loins of cattle, sheep, and other animals, used in making foods.

COMBINATIONS – **suet pudding** a boiled or steamed pudding of suet and flour.

ORIGIN – from Latin *sebum* 'tallow'.

suffer > *verb* **1** experience or be subjected to (something bad or unpleasant). **2** (**suffer from**) be affected by or subject to (an illness or ailment). **3** become or appear worse in quality. **4** archaic tolerate. **5** archaic allow (someone) to do something.

DERIVATIVES – **sufferer** *noun*.

SYNONYMS – **1** bear, endure, undergo.

ORIGIN – Latin *sufferre*, from *sub-* 'from below' + *ferre* 'to bear'.

sufferance > *noun* absence of objection rather than genuine approval; toleration.

suffice /səfïss/ > *verb* **1** be enough or adequate. **2** meet the needs of.

IDIOMS – **suffice** (**it**) **to say** used to indicate that one is withholding something for reasons of discretion or brevity.

ORIGIN – Latin *sufficere* 'put under, meet the need of'.

sufficiency > *noun* (pl. **sufficiencies**) **1** the condition or quality of being sufficient. **2** an adequate amount, especially of something essential.

sufficient > *adjective & determiner* enough; adequate.

DERIVATIVES – **sufficiently** *adverb*.

SYNONYMS – abundant, adequate, enough, satisfactory.

suffix /suffiks/ > *noun* an element added at the end of a word to form a derivative (e.g. *-ation*). > *verb* /also səfiks/ append, especially as a suffix.

ORIGIN – Latin *suffixum*, from *suffigere*, from *sub-* 'subordinately' + *figere* 'fasten'.

suffocate > *verb* **1** die or cause to die from lack of air or inability to breathe. **2** have or cause to have difficulty in breathing.

DERIVATIVES – **suffocating** *adjective* **suffocatingly** *adverb* **suffocation** *noun*.

ORIGIN – Latin *suffocare* 'stifle', from *sub-* 'below' + *fauces* 'throat'.

suffragan /sufrəgən/ (also **suffragan bishop**) > *noun* a bishop appointed to help a diocesan bishop.

ORIGIN – Latin *suffraganeus* 'assistant', from *suffragium* 'suffrage'.

suffrage /sufrij/ > *noun* the right to vote in political elections.

ORIGIN – Latin *suffragium*: originally in the sense 'intercessory prayers', also 'assistance'.

suffragette /sufrəjet/ > *noun* historical a woman seeking the right to vote through organised protest.

suffragist > *noun* chiefly historical a person advocating the extension of suffrage, especially to women.

suffuse /səfyōōz/ > *verb* gradually spread through or over.

DERIVATIVES – **suffusion** *noun*.

SYNONYMS – imbue, permeate, pervade.

ORIGIN – Latin *suffundere* 'pour into'.

Sufi /sōōfi/ > *noun* (pl. **Sufis**) a Muslim ascetic and mystic.

DERIVATIVES – **Sufic** *adjective* **Sufism** *noun*.

ORIGIN – perhaps from an Arabic word meaning 'wool', referring to the woollen garment worn.

sugar > *noun* **1** a sweet crystalline substance obtained especially from sugar cane and sugar beet. **2** Biochemistry any of a class of soluble crystalline sweet-tasting carbohydrates, including glucose and sucrose. **3** informal, chiefly N. Amer. used as a term of endearment. > *verb* **1** sweeten, sprinkle, or coat with sugar. **2** make more agreeable or palatable.

WORDFINDER – saccharine (*relating to sugar*); bagasse (*sugar cane residue from which juice has been extracted*), molasses (*thick brown liquid containing sugar*), muscovado (*unrefined sugar made from sugar cane*); diabetes (*disease with excess sugar in the blood and urine*), hyperglycaemia (*excess of sugar in the blood*).

DERIVATIVES – **sugarless** *adjective*.

COMBINATIONS – **sugar beet** beet of a variety from which sugar is extracted. **sugar cane** a tropical grass with tall stout stems from which sugar is extracted. **sugar daddy** informal a rich older man who lavishes gifts on a young woman. **sugar maple** a North American maple, the sap of which is used to make maple sugar and maple syrup. **sugar snap** mangetout, especially of a variety with thicker and more rounded pods. **sugar soap** Brit. an alkaline preparation containing washing soda and soap, used for cleaning or removing paint.

ORIGIN – Italian *zucchero*, probably from Arabic.

sugar-coated > *adjective* superficially attractive or excessively sentimental.

DERIVATIVES – **sugar-coat** *verb*.

sugarloaf > *noun* a conical moulded mass of sugar.

sugary > *adjective* **1** resembling or containing much sugar. **2** excessively sentimental.

suggest > *verb* **1** put forward for consideration. **2** cause one to think that (something) exists or is the case. **3** state or express indirectly. **4** (**suggest itself**) (of an idea) come into one's mind.

SYNONYMS – **1** advocate, propose, recommend. **3** hint, imply, insinuate.

ORIGIN – Latin *suggerere* 'suggest, prompt', from *sub-* 'from below' + *gerere* 'bring'.

suggestible > *adjective* open to suggestion; easily swayed.

DERIVATIVES – **suggestibility** *noun*.

suggestion > *noun* **1** an idea or plan put forward for consideration. **2** the action of suggesting. **3** something that implies or indicates a certain fact or situation. **4** a slight trace or indication: *a suggestion of a smile*. **5** Psychology the influencing of a person to accept a belief or impulse uncritically.

SYNONYMS – **1** proposal, proposition, recommendation. **4** hint, suspicion, trace.

suggestive > *adjective* **1** tending to suggest or evoke something. **2** hinting at or bringing to mind sexual matters.

DERIVATIVES – **suggestively** *adverb* **suggestiveness** *noun*.

suicide > *noun* **1** the action of killing oneself intentionally. **2** a person who does this. **3** (before another noun) referring to a military operation carried out by people who do not expect to survive it: *a suicide bombing*. **4** a course of action which is disastrously damaging to one's own interests. > *verb* intentionally kill oneself.

WORDFINDER – parasuicide (*apparent suicide attempt to gain attention*).

DERIVATIVES – **suicidal** *adjective* **suicidally** *adverb*.

COMBINATIONS – **suicide pact** an agreement between two or more people to commit suicide together.

ORIGIN – Latin *suicidium* 'person who commits suicide', from *sui* 'of oneself' + *caedere* 'kill'.

sui generis /sōō-i jennəriss/ > *adjective* unique.

ORIGIN – Latin, 'of its own kind'.

suit > *noun* **1** a set of outer clothes made of the same fabric and designed to be worn together, typically consisting of a jacket and trousers or a jacket and skirt. **2** a set of clothes for a particular activity. **3** any of the sets into which a pack of playing cards is divided (spades, hearts, diamonds, and clubs). **4** short for *lawsuit*. **5** informal a high-ranking business executive. **6** the process of trying to win a woman's affection with a view to marriage. **7** literary a petition or entreaty made to a person in authority. > *verb* **1** be convenient for or acceptable to. **2** go well with or enhance the features, figure, or character of (someone). **3** (**suit oneself**) act entirely according to one's own wishes. **4** (**suited**) appropriate or fitting.

IDIOMS – **suit down to the ground** Brit. be extremely convenient or appropriate for (someone).

DERIVATIVES – **suited** *adjective* **suiting** *noun*.

ORIGIN – Old French *siwte*, from Latin *sequi* 'follow'.

suitable > *adjective* right or appropriate for a particular person, purpose, or situation.

DERIVATIVES – **suitability** *noun* **suitableness** *noun* **suitably** *adverb*.

SYNONYMS – acceptable, apt, fitting, seemly.

suitcase > *noun* a case with a handle and a hinged lid, used for carrying clothes and other personal possessions.

suite /sweet/ > *noun* **1** a set of rooms for one person's or family's use or for a particular purpose. **2** a set of furniture of the same design. **3** Music a set of instrumental compositions to be played in succession. **4** a set of pieces from an opera or musical arranged as one instrumental work.

ORIGIN – Old French *siwte*, from Latin *sequi* 'follow'.

suitor /soōtər, syoōtər/ > *noun* **1** a man who pursues a relationship with a woman with a view to marriage. **2** a prospective buyer of a business or corporation.

ORIGIN – Latin *secutor*, from *sequi* 'follow'.

sukiyaki /soōkiyaaki/ > *noun* a Japanese dish of sliced meat fried rapidly with vegetables and sauce.

ORIGIN – Japanese.

sulfur etc. US spelling of SULPHUR etc.

sulk > *verb* be silent, morose, and bad-tempered through annoyance or disappointment. > *noun* a period of sulking.

DERIVATIVES – **sulker** *noun*.

ORIGIN – perhaps from SULKY.

sulky > *adjective* (**sulkier, sulkiest**) morose, bad-tempered, and resentful.

DERIVATIVES – **sulkily** *adverb* **sulkiness** *noun*.

ORIGIN – perhaps from obsolete *sulke* 'hard to dispose of'.

sullen > *adjective* bad-tempered and sulky.

DERIVATIVES – **sullenly** *adverb* **sullenness** *noun*.

SYNONYMS – churlish, glowering, sulky, surly.

wordpower facts
Sullen

The word **sullen** comes from Old French *sol, soule* 'sole, alone', the root of English **sole**; the ultimate root is Latin *solus*, the base of **desolate, soliloquy, solitary, solitude,** and **solo.** As well as its modern meaning, **sullen** had the senses 'single, sole', 'solitary', and 'averse to company' when it entered English in the Middle Ages.

sully > *verb* (**sullies, sullied**) literary or ironic damage the purity or integrity of; defile.

ORIGIN – perhaps from French *souiller* 'to soil'.

sulpha /sulfə/ (US **sulfa**) > *noun* short for SULPHONAMIDE.

sulphate (US **sulfate**) > *noun* Chemistry a salt or ester of sulphuric acid.

sulphide /sulfīd/ (US **sulfide**) > *noun* Chemistry a compound of sulphur with another element or group.

sulphite /sulfīt/ (US **sulfite**) > *noun* Chemistry a salt of sulphurous acid.

sulphonamide /sulfonnəmīd/ (US **sulfonamide**) > *noun* Medicine any of a class of sulphur-containing drugs which are able to prevent the multiplication of some disease-causing bacteria.

sulphonic acid (US **sulfonic**) > *noun* Chemistry an organic acid containing the group $-SO_2OH$.

sulphur* (US & Chemistry **sulfur**) > *noun* **1** a combustible non-metallic chemical element which typically occurs as yellow crystals. **2** the material of which hellfire and lightning were formerly believed to consist. **3** a pale greenish-yellow colour.

*SPELLING – the usual British spelling is **sulphur: sulfur** is used in America and is standard in technical contexts.

COMBINATIONS – **sulphur dioxide** Chemistry a colourless pungent toxic gas formed by burning sulphur.

ORIGIN – Latin *sulfur, sulphur*.

sulphuric /sulfyoorik/ (US **sulfuric**) > *adjective* containing sulphur or sulphuric acid.

COMBINATIONS – **sulphuric acid** a strong acid made by oxidising solutions of sulphur dioxide.

sulphurous (US **sulfurous**) > *adjective* **1** containing or derived from sulphur. **2** pale yellow.

COMBINATIONS – **sulphurous acid** Chemistry an unstable weak acid formed when sulphur dioxide dissolves in water.

sultan > *noun* a Muslim sovereign.

DERIVATIVES – **sultanate** *noun*.

ORIGIN – Arabic, 'power, ruler'.

sultana > *noun* **1** a small light brown seedless raisin. **2** a wife or concubine of a sultan.

ORIGIN – Italian, feminine of *sultano* 'sultan'.

sultry > *adjective* (**sultrier, sultriest**) **1** (of the weather) hot and humid. **2** displaying or suggesting passion; provocative.

ORIGIN – from obsolete *sulter* 'swelter'.

sum > *noun* **1** a particular amount of money. **2** (also **sum total**) the total amount resulting from the addition of two or more numbers or amounts. **3** an arithmetical problem, especially at an elementary level. > *verb* (**summed, summing**) (**sum up**) **1** concisely describe the nature or character of. **2** summarise briefly. **3** Law (of a judge) review the evidence at the end of a case, and direct the jury regarding points of law.

IDIOMS – **in sum** to sum up.

COMBINATIONS – **summing-up 1** a summary. **2** Law a judge's review of evidence at the end of a case, with a direction to the jury regarding points of law.

ORIGIN – Latin *summa* 'main part, sum total', from *summus* 'highest'.

sumac /soōmak, shoōmak/ (also **sumach**) > *noun* a shrub or small tree with conical clusters of fruits and bright autumn colours.

ORIGIN – Arabic.

Sumatran /soōmaatrən/ > *noun* a person from the Indonesian island of Sumatra. > *adjective* relating to Sumatra.

Sumerian /soōmeeriən/ > *noun* a member of a people of ancient Sumer in Babylonia. > *adjective* relating to Sumer or the Sumerians.

summa cum laude /soōmmə koōm lowday/ > *adverb & adjective* chiefly N. Amer. (of a degree, diploma, etc.) with the highest distinction.

ORIGIN – Latin, 'with highest praise'.

summarise (also **summarize**) > *verb* give a summary of (something).

DERIVATIVES – **summariser** *noun*.

summary > *noun* (pl. **summaries**) a brief statement of the main points of something. > *adjective* **1** dispensing with needless details or formalities. **2** Law (of a judicial process) conducted without the customary legal formalities.

DERIVATIVES – **summarily** *adverb*.

SYNONYMS – *noun* abstract, digest, precis, synopsis.

ORIGIN – Latin *summarius*, from *summa* (see SUM).

summation /səmaysh'n/ > *noun* **1** the process of adding things together. **2** the action of summing up. **3** a summary.

DERIVATIVES – **summative** *adjective*.

summer > *noun* the season after spring and before autumn, when the weather is warmest. > *verb* spend the summer in a particular place.

WORDFINDER – aestival (*of or relating to summer*).

DERIVATIVES – **summery** adjective.

COMBINATIONS – **summer house** a small building in a garden, used for relaxation during fine weather. **summer pudding Brit.** a pudding of soft summer fruit encased in bread. **summer school** a course of lectures held during school and university summer vacations. **summer season** the summer period when most people take holidays.

summertime > *noun* **1** the season or period of summer. **2** (**summer time**) Brit. time as advanced one hour ahead of standard time to achieve longer evening daylight in summer.

summit > *noun* **1** the highest point of a hill or mountain. **2** the highest attainable level of achievement. **3** a meeting between heads of government.

ORIGIN – Old French *somete*, from *som* 'top', from Latin *summus* 'highest'.

summiteer > *noun* a participant in a government summit.

summon > *verb* **1** authoritatively call on (someone) to be present, especially to appear in a law court. **2** call people to attend (a meeting). **3** cause (a quality or reaction) to emerge from within oneself: *she managed to summon up a smile.*

ORIGIN – Latin *summonere* 'give a hint', from *sub-* 'secretly' + *monere* 'warn'.

summons > *noun* (pl. **summonses**) **1** an order to appear in a law court. **2** an act of summoning. > *verb* chiefly Law serve with a summons.

sumo /sōōmō/ > *noun* (pl. **sumos**) Japanese wrestling in which a wrestler must not go outside a circle or touch the ground with any part of his body except the soles of his feet.

ORIGIN – Japanese.

sump > *noun* **1** the base of an internal-combustion engine, which serves as a reservoir of oil for the lubrication system. **2** a depression in the floor of a mine or cave in which water collects. **3** a cesspool.

ORIGIN – from Dutch or Low German *sump*, or (in the mining sense) from German *Sumpf*; originally in the sense 'marsh'.

sumptuary /**sump**tyoori/ > *adjective* chiefly historical referring to laws that limit private expenditure on food and personal items.

ORIGIN – Latin *sumptuarius*, from *sumptus* 'cost'.

sumptuous > *adjective* splendid and expensive-looking.

DERIVATIVES – **sumptuously** adverb **sumptuousness** noun.

SYNONYMS – lavish, luxurious, opulent, rich.

ORIGIN – Latin *sumptuosus*, from *sumptus* 'cost'.

sun > *noun* **1** (also **Sun**) the star round which the earth orbits. **2** any similar star, with or without planets. **3** the light or warmth received from the sun. > *verb* (**sunned, sunning**) (**sun oneself**) sit or lie in the light and warmth received from the sun.

WORDFINDER – solar (*of or relating to the sun*); heliocentric (*having the sun at the centre*), heliograph (*device for signalling by reflecting flashes of sunlight; telescope for photographing the sun*), heliotropism (*growth or movement towards sunlight*), insolation (*exposure to sunlight*), parhelion (*bright spot close to the sun*), zenith (*sun's highest point in the sky*).

IDIOMS – **under the sun** in existence.

DERIVATIVES – **sunless** adjective **sunlike** adjective **sunward** adjective & adverb.

COMBINATIONS – **sun-baked** exposed to the heat of the sun. **sunbed** Brit. **1** a lounger used for sunbathing. **2** an apparatus for acquiring a tan, consisting of two banks of sunlamps between which one lies or stands. **sunbelt** a strip of territory receiving high levels of sunshine, especially the southern US from California to Florida. **suncream** a creamy preparation for protecting the skin from sunburn. **sun dance** a dance performed by North American Indians in honour of the sun. **sun deck** the deck of a yacht or cruise ship that is open to the sky. **sundress** a light sleeveless dress, typically having a wide neckline and thin shoulder straps. **sunglasses** glasses tinted to protect the eyes from sunlight or glare. **sun-kissed** made warm or brown by the sun. **sunlamp** a lamp emitting ultraviolet rays, used chiefly to produce an artificial suntan or in therapy. **sunray** a radiating line or broadening stripe resembling a ray of the sun. **sunroof** a panel in the roof of a car that can be opened for extra ventilation. **sunshade** a parasol, awning, or other device giving protection from the sun. **suntrap** Brit. a place sheltered from the wind and positioned to receive much sunshine. **sun visor** a small hinged screen above a vehicle's windscreen that can be lowered to shield the occupants' eyes from bright sunlight.

sunbathe > *verb* sit or lie in the sun to get a suntan.

DERIVATIVES – **sunbather** noun.

sunbeam > *noun* a ray of sunlight.

sunblock > *noun* a cream or lotion for protecting the skin from sunburn.

sunburn > *noun* inflammation of the skin caused by overexposure to the ultraviolet rays of the sun. > *verb* (past and past participle **sunburned** or **sunburnt**) (**be sunburned**) suffer from sunburn.

sunburst > *noun* **1** a sudden brief appearance of the full sun from behind clouds. **2** a design or ornament representing the sun and its rays.

sundae* > *noun* a dish of ice cream with added ingredients such as fruit, nuts, and syrup.

*SPELLING – *-ae*, not *-ay*: sund*ae*.

ORIGIN – perhaps from **SUNDAY**, either because the dish was made with ice cream left over from Sunday, or because it was sold only on Sundays.

Sunday > *noun* the day of the week before Monday and following Saturday, observed by Christians as a day of rest and religious worship.

WORDFINDER – dominical (*of Sundays*).

COMBINATIONS – **Sunday best** a person's best clothes. **Sunday school** a class held on Sundays to teach children about Christianity and the Bible.

ORIGIN – Old English, 'day of the sun', translation of Latin *dies solis*.

sunder > *verb* literary split apart.

sundew > *noun* a small carnivorous plant of boggy places, with leaves bearing sticky hairs for trapping insects.

sundial > *noun* an instrument showing the time by the shadow cast by a pointer.

sundown > *noun* chiefly N. Amer. sunset.

sundowner > *noun* Brit. informal an alcoholic drink taken at sunset.

sun-dried > *adjective* dried in the sun, rather than by artificial heat.

sundry > *adjective* of various kinds. > *noun* (pl. **sundries**) (**sundries**) various items not important enough be mentioned individually.

ORIGIN – Old English, 'distinct, separate'.

sunfish > *noun* a large, short-tailed sea fish with tall dorsal and anal fins.

sunflower > *noun* a tall plant with very large golden-rayed flowers, grown for its edible seeds which yield oil.

sung past participle of SING.

sunk past and past participle of SINK[1].

USAGE – on the use of **sunk**, **sunken**, and **sank**, see the note at SINK[1].

sunken past participle of SINK[1]. > *adjective* **1** having sunk. **2** at a lower level than the surrounding area. **3** (of a person's eyes or cheeks) deeply recessed.

sunlight > *noun* light from the sun.

DERIVATIVES – **sunlit** adjective.

Sunna /sōōnnə, sunnə/ > *noun* the traditional portion of Muslim law based on Muhammad's words or acts, accepted as authoritative by Muslims.

ORIGIN – Arabic, 'form, way, rule'.

Sunni /sōōnni, sunni/ > *noun* (pl. same or **Sunnis**) **1** one of the two main branches of Islam, differing from Shia in its understanding of the Sunna and in its acceptance of the first three caliphs.

Compare with SHIA. **2** a Muslim who adheres to this branch of Islam.

ORIGIN – Arabic, 'custom, normative rule'.

sunny > *adjective* (**sunnier, sunniest**) **1** bright with or receiving much sunlight. **2** cheerful.

IDIOMS – **sunny side up** N. Amer. (of an egg) fried on one side only.

DERIVATIVES – **sunniness** *noun*.

sunrise > *noun* **1** the time in the morning when the sun rises. **2** the colours and light visible in the sky at sunrise.

COMBINATIONS – **sunrise industry** a new and growing industry.

sunscreen > *noun* a cream or lotion rubbed on to the skin to protect it from the sun.

sunset > *noun* **1** the time in the evening when the sun sets. **2** the colours and light visible in the sky at sunset. **3** the final declining phase of something.

sunshine > *noun* **1** sunlight unbroken by cloud. **2** cheerfulness or happiness. **3** Brit. informal used as a familiar form of address.

DERIVATIVES – **sunshiny** *adjective*.

sunspot > *noun* Astronomy a temporary darker and cooler patch on the sun's surface, associated with the sun's magnetic field.

sunstroke > *noun* heatstroke brought about by excessive exposure to the sun.

suntan > *noun* a golden-brown colouring of the skin caused by exposure to the sun.

DERIVATIVES – **suntanned** *adjective*.

sunup > *noun* chiefly N. Amer. sunrise.

sup[1] > *verb* (**supped, supping**) dated or N. English take (drink or liquid food) by sips or spoonfuls. > *noun* a sip.

sup[2] > *verb* (**supped, supping**) dated eat supper.

IDIOMS – **he who sups with the devil should have a long spoon** proverb a person who has dealings with a dangerous or wily person should be cautious.

ORIGIN – Old French *super*; related to SUP[1].

super > *adjective* informal excellent. > *noun* informal a superintendent.

super- > *combining form* **1** above; over; beyond: *superstructure*. **2** to a great or extreme degree: *superabundant*. **3** extra large of its kind: *supercontinent*. **4** of a higher kind (especially in names of classificatory divisions): *superordinate*.

ORIGIN – from Latin *super* 'above, beyond'.

superabundant > *adjective* formal excessive in quantity.

DERIVATIVES – **superabundance** *noun*.

superadd > *verb* add to what has already been added.

superannuate > *verb* **1** retire with a pension. **2** (**superannuated**) belonging to a superannuation scheme. **3** (**superannuated**) too old to be effective or useful.

ORIGIN – from Latin *super-* 'over' + *annus* 'year'.

superannuation > *noun* regular payment made into a fund by an employee towards a future pension.

superb > *adjective* of impressive quality or effect; excellent.

DERIVATIVES – **superbly** *adverb*.

SYNONYMS – excellent, outstanding, remarkable, superlative.

ORIGIN – Latin *superbus* 'proud, magnificent'.

superbike > *noun* a high-performance motorcycle.

superbug > *noun* informal a bacterium, insect, etc. regarded as having enhanced qualities, especially of resistance to antibiotics or pesticides.

supercar > *noun* a high-performance sports car.

supercargo > *noun* (pl. **supercargoes** or **supercargos**) a representative of the ship's owner on board a merchant ship, responsible for the cargo.

ORIGIN – Spanish *sobrecargo*, from *sobre* 'over' + *cargo* 'cargo'.

supercharge > *verb* **1** provide with a supercharger. **2** (**supercharged**) having powerful emotional associations.

supercharger > *noun* a device that increases the pressure of the fuel-air mixture in an internal-combustion engine, thereby giving greater efficiency.

supercilious > *adjective* having an air of contemptuous superiority.

DERIVATIVES – **superciliously** *adverb* **superciliousness** *noun*.

SYNONYMS – arrogant, condescending, haughty, patronising, superior.

ORIGIN – Latin *superciliosus* 'haughty', from *supercilium* 'eyebrow'.

supercomputer > *noun* a particularly powerful mainframe computer.

DERIVATIVES – **supercomputing** *noun*.

superconductivity > *noun* Physics the property of zero electrical resistance in some substances at very low temperatures.

DERIVATIVES – **superconducting** *adjective* **superconductive** *adjective* **superconductor** *noun*.

supercontinent > *noun* a large land mass believed to have divided in the geological past to form some of the present continents.

supercool > *verb* Chemistry cool (a liquid) below its freezing point without solidification or crystallisation.

supercritical > *adjective* Physics greater than or above a critical threshold such as critical mass or temperature.

super-duper > *adjective* informal, humorous excellent; super.

superego > *noun* (pl. **superegos**) Psychoanalysis the part of the mind that acts as a self-critical conscience, reflecting social standards that have been learned. Compare with EGO and ID.

supererogation /sōōpərerrəgaysh'n/ > *noun* the performance of more work than duty requires.

DERIVATIVES – **supererogatory** /sōōpəriroggətəri/ *adjective*.

ORIGIN – Latin, from *supererogare* 'pay in addition'.

superficial > *adjective* **1** existing or occurring at or on the surface. **2** apparent rather than actual. **3** not thorough or deep; cursory. **4** lacking depth of character or understanding.

DERIVATIVES – **superficiality** (pl. **superficialities**) *noun* **superficially** *adverb*.

SYNONYMS – **1** cosmetic, external, surface. **2** apparent, ostensible, specious. **3** casual, cursory, desultory, perfunctory. **4** frivolous, shallow, trivial.

ANTONYMS – **1** deep. **2** genuine. **3** thorough. **4** profound, serious.

ORIGIN – Latin *superficialis*, from *superficies* 'top, surface'.

superfluidity > *noun* Physics the property of flowing without friction or viscosity, as shown by liquid helium close to absolute zero.

DERIVATIVES – **superfluid** *noun* & *adjective*.

superfluous > *adjective* unnecessary, especially through being more than is needed or wanted.

DERIVATIVES – **superfluity** (pl. **superfluities**) *noun* **superfluously** *adverb*.

SYNONYMS – dispensable, expendable, needless, redundant, surplus, unnecessary.

ORIGIN – Latin *superfluus*, from *super-* 'over' + *fluere* 'to flow'.

supergiant > *noun* Astronomy a star that is greater and more luminous than a giant.

superglue > *noun* a very strong quick-setting adhesive.

supergrass > *noun* Brit. informal a police informer who implicates a large number of people.

superheat > *verb* Physics **1** heat (a liquid) under pressure above its boiling point without vaporisation. **2** heat (steam or other vapour) above the temperature of the liquid from which it was formed.

superhighway > *noun* N. Amer. a dual carriageway with controlled access.

superhuman > *adjective* having or showing ability or powers above those of a normal human being.

DERIVATIVES – **superhumanly** *adverb*.

superimpose > *verb* place or lay (one thing) over another.

DERIVATIVES – **superimposition** *noun*.

superintend > *verb* be responsible for the management or arrangement of.

DERIVATIVES – **superintendence** *noun* **superintendency** *noun*.

ORIGIN – Latin *superintendere*.

superintendent > *noun* **1** a person who supervises or is in charge of an organisation, department, etc. **2** (in the UK) a police officer ranking above chief inspector. **3** (in the US) the chief of a police department. **4** N. Amer. the caretaker of a building.

superior > *adjective* **1** higher in status, quality, or power. **2** of high standard or quality. **3** (**superior to**) above yielding to or being influenced by. **4** having or showing an overly high opinion of oneself; supercilious. **5** (of a letter, figure, or symbol) written or printed above the line. **6** chiefly Anatomy further above or out; higher in position. > *noun* **1** a person of superior rank. **2** the head of a monastery or other religious institution. **3** Printing a superior letter, figure, or symbol.

SYNONYMS – *adjective* **1** better, greater, higher, senior. **2** choice, fine, first-class, first-rate, select. **3** (**superior to**) above, better than. **4** arrogant, condescending, haughty, patronising, supercilious.

ANTONYMS – *adjective* **1,2** inferior. **4** humble, modest.

ORIGIN – Latin, 'higher', from *super* 'above'.

superiority > *noun* the state of being superior.

COMBINATIONS – **superiority complex** an attitude of superiority which conceals actual feelings of inferiority and failure.

superlative /sooˈperlətiv, syooˈperlətiv/ > *adjective* **1** of the highest quality or degree. **2** Grammar (of an adjective or adverb) expressing the highest or a very high degree of a quality (e.g. *bravest*, *most fiercely*). Contrasted with **POSITIVE** and **COMPARATIVE**. > *noun* an exaggerated expression of praise.

DERIVATIVES – **superlatively** *adverb* **superlativeness** *noun*.

ORIGIN – Latin *superlativus*, from *superferre* 'carry beyond'.

superlunary /sooˈperloonəri, syooˈper-/ > *adjective* literary belonging to a higher world; celestial.

ORIGIN – Latin *superlunaris*, from *luna* 'moon'.

superman > *noun* **1** another term for **ÜBERMENSCH**. **2** informal a man with exceptional physical or mental ability.

supermarket > *noun* a large self-service shop selling foods and household goods.

supermodel > *noun* a very successful and famous fashion model.

supernal /sooˈpern'l/ > *adjective* chiefly literary **1** relating to the sky or the heavens. **2** supremely excellent.

ORIGIN – Latin *supernalis*, from *super* 'above'.

supernatural > *adjective* **1** attributed to some force beyond scientific understanding or the laws of nature. **2** exceptionally or extraordinarily great. > *noun* (**the supernatural**) supernatural manifestations or events.

DERIVATIVES – **supernaturally** *adverb*.

SYNONYMS – **1** magical, miraculous, occult, paranormal, preternatural, psychic.

ANTONYMS – **1** natural.

supernormal > *adjective* beyond what is normal.

supernova /sooˈpernōva, syooˈpər-/ > *noun* (pl. **supernovae** /sooˈpernōvee, syooˈpər-/ or **supernovas**) Astronomy a star that undergoes a catastrophic explosion, becoming suddenly very much brighter.

supernumerary /sooˈpernyoomərəri, syooˈpər-/ > *adjective* **1** present in excess of the normal or required number. **2** not belonging to a regular staff but engaged for extra work. > *noun* (pl. **supernumeraries**) a supernumerary person or thing.

ORIGIN – Latin *supernumerarius* 'soldier added to a legion after it is complete'.

superordinate /sooˈperordinət, syooˈpər-/ > *noun* **1** a thing that represents a higher order or category within a system of classification. **2** a person of higher rank or status. > *adjective* higher in status.

superpose > *verb* place (something) on or above something else, especially so that they coincide.

DERIVATIVES – **superposed** *adjective* **superposition** *noun*.

ORIGIN – French *superposer*.

superpower > *noun* any of the few most powerful and influential nations of the world.

supersaturate > *verb* Chemistry increase the concentration of (a solution) beyond saturation point.

DERIVATIVES – **supersaturation** *noun*.

superscribe > *verb* **1** write or print (an inscription) at the top of or on the outside of a document. **2** write or print (a character or word) above an existing one.

DERIVATIVES – **superscription** *noun*.

superscript > *adjective* (of a letter, figure, or symbol) written or printed above the line.

supersede* /sooˈpərseed/ > *verb* take the place of; supplant.

*SPELLING – *-sede* not *-cede*: super*sede*.

SYNONYMS – replace, succeed, supplant.

ORIGIN – Latin *supersedere* 'be superior to'.

supersonic > *adjective* involving or referring to a speed greater than that of sound.

DERIVATIVES – **supersonically** *adverb*.

supersonics > *plural noun* (treated as sing.) another term for **ULTRASONICS**.

superstar > *noun* an extremely famous and successful performer or sports player.

DERIVATIVES – **superstardom** *noun*.

superstition > *noun* **1** excessively credulous belief in the supernatural. **2** a widely held but irrational belief in supernatural influences, especially as bringing good or bad luck.

wordpower facts

Superstition

The words **superstition** and **superstitious** are derived from Latin *superstitio*, which comes ultimately from *super-* 'over' + *stare* 'to stand' (the source of **circumstance, constant, estate, rest, stable, stay**, etc.). How did a word that referred to 'standing over' something come to refer to superstition? The notion is perhaps one of 'standing over' something in awe; alternatively, the connection could be the idea of an excess of religious ceremony or devotion, or the survival of old ideas into more modern times.

superstitious > *adjective* characterised or influenced by superstition.

DERIVATIVES – **superstitiously** *adverb*.

superstore > *noun* a very large out-of-town supermarket.

superstructure > *noun* **1** a structure built on top of something else. **2** the part of a building above its foundations. **3** the parts of a ship, other than masts and rigging, above its hull and main deck. **4** a concept or idea based on others.

supertanker > *noun* a very large oil tanker.

supertax > *noun* an additional tax on something already taxed.

supervene > *verb* occur as an interruption or change to an existing situation.

DERIVATIVES – **supervenient** *adjective* **supervention** *noun*.

ORIGIN – Latin *supervenire venire* 'come in addition'.

supervise* > *verb* observe and direct the performance of (a task or activity) or the work of (a person).

DERIVATIVES – **supervision** *noun* **supervisor** *noun* **supervisory** *adjective*.

*SPELLING – unlike most verbs ending in *-ise*, **supervise** cannot be spelled with an *-ize* ending.

SYNONYMS – manage, oversee, preside over, superintend.

ORIGIN – Latin *supervidere* 'survey, supervise'.

superwoman > *noun* informal a woman with exceptional physical or mental ability.

supinate /sooˈpinayt, syooˈpinayt/ > *verb* technical put or hold (a hand, foot, or limb) with the palm or sole turned upwards. Compare with **PRONATE**.

DERIVATIVES – **supination** *noun*.

ORIGIN – from Latin *supinare* 'lay backwards'.

supinator > *noun* Anatomy a muscle involved in supination.

supine /sōōpīn, syōōpīn/ > *adjective* 1 lying face upwards. 2 failing to act as a result of laziness or lack of courage; passive.

DERIVATIVES – **supinely** *adverb* **supineness** *noun*.

ORIGIN – from Latin *supinus* 'bent backwards'.

supper > *noun* 1 a light or informal evening meal. 2 Scottish & N. English a meal consisting of the specified food with chips: *a fish supper*.

IDIOMS – **sing for one's supper** provide a service in return for a benefit.

ORIGIN – from Old French *super* 'to sup'.

supplant > *verb* supersede and replace.

DERIVATIVES – **supplanter** *noun*.

SYNONYMS – displace, oust, replace, succeed, supersede, usurp.

ORIGIN – Latin *supplantare* 'trip up'.

supple > *adjective* (**suppler**, **supplest**) flexible or pliant.

DERIVATIVES – **supplely** *adverb* **suppleness** *noun*.

SYNONYMS – flexible, limber, lithe, pliable, pliant, resilient.

ORIGIN – Latin *supplex* 'submissive'.

supplement > *noun* 1 a thing added to something else to enhance or complete it. 2 a separate section added to a newspaper or periodical. 3 an additional charge payable for an extra service or facility. > *verb* provide a supplement for.

DERIVATIVES – **supplemental** *adjective* **supplementation** *noun*.

SYNONYMS – *noun* 1 addition, adjunct, extra. *verb* augment, boost, complement, increase.

ORIGIN – Latin *supplementum*, from *supplere* 'fill up'.

supplementary > *adjective* completing or enhancing something.

SYNONYMS – added, additional, ancillary, auxiliary, complementary, extra.

COMBINATIONS – **supplementary benefit** (in the UK) payment made by the state to those on a low income, now replaced by income support.

suppliant /*sup*liənt/ > *noun* a person who supplicates. > *adjective* making or expressing a humble or earnest plea.

supplicate /*sup*likayt/ > *verb* ask or beg for something earnestly or humbly.

DERIVATIVES – **supplicant** *adjective* & *noun* **supplication** *noun* **supplicatory** *adjective*.

ORIGIN – Latin *supplicare* 'implore', from *sub-* 'from below' + *placere* 'propitiate'.

supply > *verb* (**supplies**, **supplied**) 1 make (something needed) available to someone. 2 provide (someone) with something needed. 3 be adequate to satisfy (a requirement or demand). > *noun* (pl. **supplies**) 1 a stock or amount of something supplied or available. 2 the action of supplying. 3 (**supplies**) provisions and equipment necessary for an army or expedition. 4 (before another noun) acting as a temporary substitute for another: *a supply teacher*.

IDIOMS – **supply and demand** the amount of goods or services available and the desire of buyers for them, considered as factors regulating its price. **supply-side** Economics designed to increase output and employment by reducing taxation and other forms of restriction.

DERIVATIVES – **supplier** *noun*.

SYNONYMS – *verb* 1 bestow, dispense, give, issue, provide. 2 equip, furnish, issue, provide. 3 fill, fulfil, meet, satisfy. *noun* 1 reserve, stock, store. 2 distribution, provision.

ORIGIN – Latin *supplere* 'fill up'.

support > *verb* 1 bear all or part of the weight of. 2 give assistance, encouragement, or approval to. 3 be actively interested in (a sports team). 4 provide with a home and the necessities of life. 5 be capable of sustaining. 6 suggest or confirm the truth of. 7 manage to endure or tolerate. 8 (**supporting**) of secondary importance to the leading roles in a play or film. 9 (of a pop or rock group or performer) function as a secondary act to (another) at a concert. > *noun* 1 a person or thing that supports. 2 the action or state of supporting or being supported. 3 assistance, encouragement, or approval.

DERIVATIVES – **supportable** *adjective*.

SYNONYMS – *verb* 1 bear, buttress, carry, hold up, prop up. 2 comfort, encourage, fortify, hearten, sustain. 6 attest to, back up, bear out, corroborate, substantiate. 7 bear, endure, stand, stomach, suffer, tolerate.

ORIGIN – Latin *supportare*, from *sub-* 'from below' + *portare* 'carry'.

supporter > *noun* a person who supports a sports team, policy, etc.

supportive > *adjective* providing encouragement or emotional help.

DERIVATIVES – **supportively** *adverb* **supportiveness** *noun*.

SYNONYMS – caring, concerned, encouraging, helpful, sympathetic, understanding.

suppose > *verb* 1 think or assume that something is true or probable, but without proof. 2 (of a theory or argument) assume or require that something is the case as a precondition. 3 (**be supposed to do**) be required or expected to do.

SYNONYMS – 1 assume, believe, guess, judge, presume, surmise, think.

ORIGIN – Latin *supponere*, from *sub-* 'from below' + *ponere* 'to place'.

supposedly > *adverb* according to what is generally believed or supposed.

supposition > *noun* an assumption or hypothesis.

suppositious > *adjective* based on assumption rather than fact.

supposititious /səpozzi**tish**əss/ > *adjective* substituted for the real thing; counterfeit.

ORIGIN – Latin *supposititius*, from *supponere* 'to substitute'.

suppository /sə**pozz**itri/ > *noun* (pl. **suppositories**) a solid medical preparation in a roughly conical or cylindrical shape, designed to dissolve after insertion into the rectum or vagina.

ORIGIN – Latin *suppositorium* 'thing placed underneath'.

suppress* > *verb* 1 forcibly put an end to. 2 prevent from being expressed or published. 3 Psychoanalysis consciously avoid thinking of (an unpleasant idea or memory). 4 partly or wholly eliminate (electrical interference).

DERIVATIVES – **suppressible** *adjective* **suppression** *noun* **suppressive** *adjective* **suppressor** *noun*.

*SPELLING – two *ps*: su*ppress*.

SYNONYMS – 1 crush, quash, quell, squash, stamp out, subdue. 2 muffle, smother, stifle.

ORIGIN – Latin *supprimere* 'press down'.

suppressant > *adjective* acting to suppress or restrain someone or something. > *noun* a substance which acts to suppress something, especially a drug which suppresses the appetite.

suppurate /*sup*yərayt/ > *verb* form or discharge pus.

DERIVATIVES – **suppuration** *noun* **suppurative** /*sup*yərətiv/ *adjective*.

ORIGIN – from Latin *sub-* 'below' + *pus* 'pus'.

supra- /sōōprə/ > *prefix* 1 above: *suprarenal*. 2 beyond; transcending: *supranational*.

ORIGIN – from Latin *supra* 'above, beyond, before in time'.

supranational > *adjective* having power or influence that transcends national boundaries or governments.

supremacist > *noun* an advocate of the supremacy of a particular group, especially one determined by race or sex. > *adjective* relating to or advocating such supremacy.

DERIVATIVES – **supremacism** *noun*.

supremacy /sōō**premm**əsi, syōō**premm**əsi/ > *noun* the state or condition of being superior to all others in authority, power, or status.

supreme > *adjective* 1 highest in authority or rank. 2 very great or greatest; most important. > *noun* (also **suprême**) a rich cream sauce or a dish served in this.

DERIVATIVES – **supremely** *adverb*.

COMBINATIONS – **Supreme Being** an all-powerful creator and ruler of the universe; God. **supreme court** the highest judicial court in a country or state. **Supreme**

Soviet the governing council of the former USSR or one of its constituent republics.

ORIGIN – Latin *supremus* 'highest'.

supremo /sōōˈpreemō, syōōˈpreemō/ > *noun* (pl. **supremos**) Brit. informal **1** a person in overall charge. **2** a person with great authority or skill in a certain area.

ORIGIN – Spanish, 'supreme'.

suq > *noun* variant spelling of **SOUK**.

sur-¹ > *prefix* equivalent to **SUPER-**.

ORIGIN – French.

sur-² > *prefix* variant spelling of **SUB-** before *r*: *surrogate*.

surcease > *noun* archaic or N. Amer. **1** cessation. **2** relief. > *verb* archaic cease.

ORIGIN – Old French *surseoir* 'refrain, delay', from Latin *supersedere* 'be superior to, refrain from, omit'.

surcharge > *noun* **1** an additional charge or payment. **2** a mark printed on a postage stamp changing its value. > *verb* **1** exact a surcharge from. **2** mark (a postage stamp) with a surcharge.

surcoat /ˈsurkōt/ > *noun* historical an outer coat or garment worn over armour, in particular a short sleeveless garment worn as part of the insignia of an order of knighthood.

ORIGIN – Old French *surcot*, from *sur* 'over' + *cot* 'coat'.

surd /surd/ > *noun* **1** Mathematics an irrational number. **2** Phonetics a speech sound uttered with the breath and not the voice (e.g. *f*, *k*, and *p*).

ORIGIN – from Latin *surdus* 'deaf, mute'.

sure /shoor, shor/ > *adjective* **1** completely confident that one is right. **2** (**sure of** or **to do**) certain to receive, get, or do. **3** undoubtedly true; completely reliable. > *adverb* informal certainly.

IDIOMS – **for sure** informal without doubt. **make sure** confirm or ensure. **sure thing** informal **1** a certainty. **2** chiefly N. Amer. certainly. **to be sure** certainly; it must be admitted.

DERIVATIVES – **sureness** *noun*.

SYNONYMS – *adjective* **1** certain, convinced, definite, positive. **3** guaranteed, infallible, proven, true, undeniable, undoubted.

ANTONYMS – *adjective* **1** uncertain, unsure.

COMBINATIONS – **sure-footed 1** unlikely to stumble or slip. **2** confident and competent.

ORIGIN – Old French *sur*, from Latin *securus* 'free from care'.

sure-fire > *adjective* informal certain to succeed: *a sure-fire way of getting attention*.

surely > *adverb* **1** it must be true that. **2** certainly. **3** with assurance. **4** N. Amer. informal of course.

surety /ˈshooriti, ˈshoriti/ > *noun* (pl. **sureties**) **1** a person who takes responsibility for another's undertaking, such as the payment of a debt. **2** money

given as a guarantee that someone will do something. **3** the state of being sure.

surf > *noun* the mass or line of foam formed by waves breaking on a seashore or reef. > *verb* **1** stand or lie on a surfboard and ride on the crest of a wave towards the shore. **2** occupy oneself by moving from site to site on (the Internet).

DERIVATIVES – **surfer** *noun* **surfing** *noun*.

ORIGIN – apparently from obsolete *suff*.

surface > *noun* **1** the outside part or uppermost layer of something. **2** the upper limit of a body of liquid. **3** outward appearance as distinct from less obvious aspects. > *adjective* **1** relating to or occurring on the surface. **2** outward or superficial: *surface politeness*. **3** (of transportation) by sea or overland rather than by air. > *verb* **1** rise or come up to the surface. **2** become apparent. **3** provide (something, especially a road) with a particular surface. **4** informal appear after having been asleep.

WORDFINDER – superficial (*on the surface*); patina, veneer (*a surface film or layer*); adsorb (*hold molecules on a surface*).

COMBINATIONS – **surface tension** the tension of the surface film of a liquid, which tends to minimise surface area. **surface-to-air** (of a missile) designed to be fired from the ground or a vessel at an aircraft.

ORIGIN – French, from *sur-* 'above' + *face* 'form, appearance, face'.

surfactant /surˈfaktənt/ > *noun* a substance which tends to reduce surface tension.

ORIGIN – from *surface-active*.

surfboard > *noun* a long, narrow board used in surfing.

surfeit /ˈsurfit/ > *noun* **1** an excess. **2** archaic an illness caused by excessive eating or drinking. > *verb* (**surfeited**, **surfeiting**) **1** cause to be wearied of something through excess. **2** archaic overeat.

SYNONYMS – *noun* **1** excess, glut, superabundance, superfluity, surplus.

ORIGIN – Old French, from Latin *super-* 'above, in excess' + *facere* 'do'.

surge > *noun* **1** a sudden powerful forward or upward movement. **2** a sudden large temporary increase. **3** a powerful rush of an emotion or feeling. > *verb* **1** move in a surge. **2** increase suddenly and powerfully.

ORIGIN – from Latin *surgere* 'to rise'.

surgeon > *noun* **1** a medical practitioner qualified to practise surgery. **2** a doctor in the navy.

COMBINATIONS – **surgeon general** (pl. **surgeons general**) (in the US) the head of a public health service or of the medical service of the armed forces.

ORIGIN – Old French *serurgien*, ultimately from Greek *kheirourgia* 'handiwork, surgery'.

surgery > *noun* (pl. **surgeries**) **1** the branch

of medicine concerned with treatment of bodily injuries or disorders by incision or manipulation. **2** Brit. a place where a medical practitioner treats or advises patients. **3** Brit. an occasion on which an MP, lawyer, or other professional person gives advice.

WORDFINDER – ablation, amputation (*surgical removal of a part*), ligature (*cord used in surgery to tie an artery*), microsurgery (*very intricate surgery using a microscope*), prosthetics (*surgical fitting of artificial body parts*).

surgical > *adjective* **1** relating to or used in surgery. **2** worn to correct or relieve an injury, illness, or deformity. **3** (especially of a military attack from the air) done with great precision.

DERIVATIVES – **surgically** *adverb*.

COMBINATIONS – **surgical spirit** Brit. methylated spirit used for cleansing the skin before injections or surgery.

surly > *adjective* (**surlier**, **surliest**) bad-tempered and unfriendly.

DERIVATIVES – **surlily** *adverb* **surliness** *noun*.

SYNONYMS – bad-tempered, churlish, grumpy, sulky, sullen, unfriendly.

ORIGIN – alteration of obsolete *sirly*, from **SIR**: originally in the sense 'lordly, haughty'.

surmise* /sərˈmīz/ > *verb* suppose without having evidence. > *noun* a supposition or guess.

*SPELLING – **surmise** cannot be spelled with an *-ize* ending.

SYNONYMS – *verb* conjecture, guess, infer, presume, suspect.

ORIGIN – from Old French *surmise* 'accused': originally in the senses 'formal allegation' and 'allege formally'.

surmount > *verb* **1** overcome (a difficulty or obstacle). **2** stand or be placed on top of.

DERIVATIVES – **surmountable** *adjective*.

surname > *noun* a hereditary name common to all members of a family, as distinct from a forename. > *verb* give a surname to.

surpass > *verb* **1** be greater or better than. **2** (**surpassing**) archaic or literary incomparable or outstanding.

DERIVATIVES – **surpassable** *adjective* **surpassingly** *adverb*.

surplice /ˈsurpliss/ > *noun* a loose white linen robe worn over a cassock by clergy and choristers at Christian church services.

ORIGIN – Latin *superpellicium*, from *super-* 'above' + *pellicia* 'fur garment'.

surplus > *noun* **1** an amount left over when requirements have been met. **2** an excess of income or assets over expenditure or liabilities in a given period. > *adjective* excess; extra.

SYNONYMS – *noun* **1** excess, oversupply, surfeit. *adjective* additional, excess, extra, leftover, remaining, spare.

ORIGIN – Latin *superplus*, from *super-* 'in addition' + *plus* 'more'.

surprise* > *noun* **1** a feeling of mild astonishment or shock caused by something unexpected. **2** an unexpected or astonishing thing. > *verb* **1** cause to feel surprise. **2** capture, attack, or discover suddenly and unexpectedly.

IDIOMS – **take by surprise 1** attack or capture unexpectedly. **2** happen unexpectedly to (someone).

DERIVATIVES – **surprised** *adjective* **surprising** *adjective* **surprisingly** *adverb*.

*SPELLING – do not forget the first *r*, and note also that **surprise** cannot be spelled with an *-ize* ending: su*r*prise.

SYNONYMS – *noun* **1** amazement, astonishment, shock. **2** bolt from the blue, bombshell, eye-opener, thunderbolt. *verb* **1** amaze, astonish, flabbergast, shock, stagger, startle, stun.

ORIGIN – Old French, from Latin *superprehendere* 'seize'.

surreal > *adjective* having the qualities of surrealism; bizarre.

DERIVATIVES – **surreally** *adverb*.

surrealism > *noun* an avant-garde 20th-century movement in art and literature which sought to release the creative potential of the unconscious mind, for example by the distortion or irrational juxtaposition of images.

DERIVATIVES – **surrealist** *noun* & *adjective* **surrealistic** *adjective* **surrealistically** *adverb*.

surrender > *verb* **1** stop resisting an opponent and submit to their authority. **2** give up (a person, right, or possession) on compulsion or demand. **3** (**surrender to**) abandon oneself entirely to (a powerful emotion or influence). **4** cancel (a life insurance policy) and receive back a proportion of the premiums paid. > *noun* the action of surrendering.

SYNONYMS – *verb* **1** capitulate, give in, give up, submit, yield. **2** cede, forgo, relinquish, renounce.

surreptitious /surrəptishəss/ > *adjective* done secretly or furtively; clandestine.

DERIVATIVES – **surreptitiously** *adverb*.

SYNONYMS – clandestine, covert, furtive, secret, secretive.

ORIGIN – Latin *surreptitius*, from *sub-* 'secretly' + *rapere* 'seize'.

surrey > *noun* (pl. **surreys**) historical (in the US) a light four-wheeled carriage with two seats facing forwards.

ORIGIN – from *Surrey cart*, a carriage first made in *Surrey*, England.

surrogate /surrəgət/ > *noun* **1** a substitute, especially a person deputising for another in a role or office. **2** (in the Christian Church) a bishop's deputy who grants marriage licences.

DERIVATIVES – **surrogacy** *noun*.

COMBINATIONS – **surrogate mother** a woman who bears a child on behalf of another woman, either from her own egg or from having a fertilised egg from the other woman implanted in her womb.

ORIGIN – from Latin *surrogare* 'elect as a substitute'.

surround > *verb* **1** be all round; encircle. **2** be associated with. > *noun* **1** a border or edging. **2** (**surrounds**) surroundings.

ORIGIN – first used in the sense 'overflow': from Latin *superundare*, from *undare* 'to flow'.

surroundings > *plural noun* the conditions or area around a person or thing.

surtax > *noun* an additional tax on something already taxed, especially a higher rate of tax on incomes above a certain level.

surtitle > *noun* a caption projected on a screen above the stage in an opera, translating the text being sung. > *verb* provide with surtitles.

surveillance /survaylənss/ > *noun* close observation, especially of a suspected spy or criminal.

ORIGIN – French, from *sur-* 'over' + *veiller* 'watch'.

survey > *verb* /sərvay/ **1** look carefully and thoroughly at. **2** examine (an area of land) to produce a map, plan, or description. **3** Brit. examine and report on the condition of (a building), especially for a prospective buyer. **4** conduct a survey among (a group of people). > *noun* /survay/ **1** a general view, examination, or description. **2** an investigation of the opinions or experience of a group of people, based on a series of questions. **3** an act of surveying. **4** a map, plan, or report obtained by surveying.

WORDFINDER – benchmark (*surveyor's mark used as reference point*), sextant, theodolite (*surveying instruments*), triangulation (*surveying system based on measuring triangles*).

SYNONYMS – *verb* **1** contemplate, examine, inspect, observe, regard, scrutinise, study.

ORIGIN – Old French *surveier*, from Latin *super-* 'over' + *videre* 'to see'.

surveyor > *noun* **1** a person who surveys land, buildings, etc. as a profession. **2** Brit. an official inspector of something for purposes of measurement and valuation.

survival > *noun* **1** the state or fact of surviving. **2** an object or practice that has survived from an earlier time.

IDIOMS – **survival of the fittest** Biology the continued existence of the organisms best adapted to their environment; natural selection.

survivalism > *noun* **1** the policy of trying to ensure one's own survival or that of one's social or national group. **2** the practising of outdoor survival skills as a sport or hobby.

DERIVATIVES – **survivalist** *noun* & *adjective*.

survive > *verb* **1** continue to live or exist. **2** continue to live or exist in spite of (an accident or ordeal). **3** remain alive after the death of.

DERIVATIVES – **survivable** *adjective*.

SYNONYMS – **1** continue, endure, last, persist, remain. **2** live through. **3** outlast, outlive.

ORIGIN – Old French *sourvivre*, from Latin *super-* 'in addition' + *vivere* 'live'.

survivor > *noun* a person who has survived.

sus- > *prefix* variant spelling of **SUB-** before *c*, *p*, *t*.

susceptibility > *noun* (pl. **susceptibilities**) **1** the state or fact of being susceptible. **2** (**susceptibilities**) a person's feelings, regarded as being easily hurt.

susceptible /səseptib'l/ > *adjective* **1** (often **susceptible to**) likely to be influenced or harmed by a particular thing. **2** (often **susceptible to**) easily influenced by feelings or emotions. **3** (**susceptible of**) capable or admitting of.

DERIVATIVES – **susceptibly** *adverb*.

ORIGIN – Latin *susceptibilis*, from *suscipere* 'take up, sustain'.

sushi /sooshi/ > *noun* a Japanese dish consisting of small balls or rolls of cold rice with vegetables, egg, or raw seafood.

ORIGIN – Japanese.

suspect > *verb* /səspekt/ **1** believe (something) to be probable or possible. **2** believe (someone) to be guilty of a crime or offence, without certain proof. **3** doubt the genuineness or truth of. > *noun* /suspekt/ a person suspected of a crime or offence. > *adjective* /suspekt/ possibly dangerous or false.

SYNONYMS – *verb* **1** fancy, suppose, surmise, think. **3** distrust, doubt, mistrust, be wary of.

ORIGIN – Latin *suspicere* 'mistrust'.

suspend > *verb* **1** halt temporarily. **2** temporarily remove (someone) from a post as a punishment or during investigation. **3** hang from somewhere. **4** defer or delay (an action, event, or judgement). **5** (**be suspended**) be dispersed in a suspension. **6** (**suspended**) Law (of a sentence) not enforced as long as no further offence is committed within a specified period.

SYNONYMS – **1** adjourn, break off, freeze, hold up, interrupt. **3** dangle, hang, swing. **4** defer, delay, postpone, put off.

COMBINATIONS – **suspended animation** temporary stopping of most vital functions, without death. **suspended ceiling** a ceiling with a space between it and the floor above from which it hangs.

ORIGIN – Latin *suspendere*, from *sub-* 'from below' + *pendere* 'hang'.

suspender > *noun* **1** Brit. an elastic strap attached to a belt or garter, fastened to the top of a stocking to hold it up. **2** (**suspenders**) N. Amer. braces for holding up trousers.

COMBINATIONS – **suspender belt** Brit. a woman's undergarment consisting of a decorative belt and suspenders.

suspense > *noun* a state or feeling of excited or anxious uncertainty about what may happen.

DERIVATIVES – **suspenseful** *adjective*.

suspension > *noun* **1** the action of suspending or the condition of being suspended. **2** the system of springs and shock absorbers by which a vehicle is supported on its wheels. **3** a mixture in which particles are dispersed throughout a fluid.

COMBINATIONS – **suspension bridge** a bridge in which the deck is suspended from cables running between towers.

suspicion > *noun* **1** a feeling that something wrong or undesirable is taking or has taken place. **2** a feeling that someone is guilty of a crime or offence. **3** a very slight trace: *a suspicion of a smile*.

IDIOMS – **above suspicion** too good or honest to be thought capable of wrongdoing. **under suspicion** suspected of wrongdoing.

SYNONYMS – **1** feeling, hunch, impression, intuition. **2** distrust, doubt, misgiving, mistrust, wariness. **3** hint, suggestion, touch, trace.

suspicious > *adjective* **1** having or showing suspicion or distrust. **2** having the impression that someone is involved in an illegal or dishonest activity. **3** giving an impression of being dishonest or dangerous in character.

DERIVATIVES – **suspiciously** *adverb* **suspiciousness** *noun*.

SYNONYMS – **1,2** chary, distrustful, doubtful, mistrustful, uncertain, wary. **3** dubious, suspect; informal fishy, shady.

suss Brit. informal > *verb* (**sussed, sussing**) **1** (often **suss out**) realise or understand the true character or nature of. **2** (**sussed**) clever and well informed. > *noun* knowledge or awareness of a specified kind: *business suss.*

ORIGIN – abbreviation of **SUSPECT**.

sustain > *verb* **1** strengthen or support physically or mentally. **2** bear (the weight of an object). **3** keep (something) going over time or continuously. **4** suffer (something unpleasant). **5** confirm that (something) is just or valid.

DERIVATIVES – **sustainer** *noun* **sustainment** *noun*.

ORIGIN – Latin *sustinere*, from *sub-* 'from below' + *tenere* 'hold'.

sustainable > *adjective* **1** able to be sustained. **2** (of industry, development, or agriculture) avoiding depletion of natural resources.

DERIVATIVES – **sustainability** *noun* **sustainably** *adverb*.

sustenance > *noun* **1** food and drink regarded as sustaining life. **2** the process of sustaining or keeping alive.

susurration /sōōssə**ray**sh'n, syōōss-/ (also **susurrus** /soo**surr**əss, syoo-/) > *noun* literary whispering or rustling.

ORIGIN – Latin, from *susurrare* 'to murmur, hum'.

sutler /**sut**lər/ > *noun* historical a person who followed an army and sold provisions to the soldiers.

ORIGIN – obsolete Dutch *soeteler*, from *soetelen* 'perform mean duties'.

sutra /**soo**trə/ > *noun* **1** a rule or aphorism in Sanskrit literature, or a set of these on grammar or Hindu law or philosophy. **2** a Buddhist or Jainist scripture.

ORIGIN – Sanskrit, 'thread, rule'.

suttee /**su**tee, **sutt**i/ (also **sati**) > *noun* the former Hindu practice of a widow burning herself to death on her husband's funeral pyre.

ORIGIN – Sanskrit, 'faithful wife'.

suture /**soo**chər/ > *noun* **1** a stitch or row of stitches holding together the edges of a wound or surgical incision. **2** a thread or wire used for this. **3** a seam-like junction between two parts, especially between bones of the skull. > *verb* stitch up with a suture.

DERIVATIVES – **sutural** *adjective*.

ORIGIN – Latin *sutura*, from *suere* 'sew'.

suzerain /**soo**zərayn/ > *noun* **1** a sovereign or state having some control over another state that is internally autonomous. **2** a feudal overlord.

DERIVATIVES – **suzerainty** *noun*.

ORIGIN – French, from *sus* 'above', suggested by *souverain* 'sovereign'.

Sv > *abbreviation* sievert(s).

s.v. > *abbreviation* (in textual references) under the word or heading given.

ORIGIN – from Latin *sub voce* or *sub verbo* 'under the word or voice'.

svelte /svelt/ > *adjective* slender and elegant.

ORIGIN – Italian *svelto*.

Svengali /sven**gaa**li/ > *noun* a person who exercises a controlling influence on another, especially for a sinister purpose.

ORIGIN – from the name of *Svengali*, a musician in George du Maurier's novel *Trilby* (1894) who controls Trilby's stage singing hypnotically.

S-VHS > *abbreviation* super video home system, an improved version of VHS.

SW > *abbreviation* **1** south-west. **2** south-western.

swab > *noun* **1** an absorbent pad used for cleaning wounds or applying medication. **2** a specimen of a secretion taken with a swab. **3** a mop or other absorbent device for cleaning or mopping up. **4** archaic a contemptible person. > *verb* (**swabbed, swabbing**) clean or absorb with a swab.

ORIGIN – from *swabber* 'sailor detailed to swab decks', from Dutch *zwabber*.

swaddle > *verb* wrap in garments or cloth.

COMBINATIONS – **swaddling clothes** cloth bands formerly wrapped round a newborn child to calm it.

ORIGIN – from **SWATHE²**.

swag > *noun* **1** an ornamental festoon of flowers, fruit, and greenery. **2** a curtain or drape fastened to hang in a drooping curve. **3** informal money or goods taken by a thief or burglar. **4** Austral./NZ a traveller's or miner's bundle of personal belongings. > *verb* (**swagged, swagging**) **1** arrange in or decorate with swags. **2** chiefly literary hang or sway heavily.

swagger > *verb* walk or behave in a very confident and stylish or arrogant manner. > *noun* a very confident and stylish or arrogant gait or manner.

COMBINATIONS – **swagger stick** a short cane carried by a military officer.

swagman > *noun* Austral./NZ a tramp or itinerant worker carrying a bundle of belongings.

Swahili /swə**hee**li/ > *noun* (pl. same) **1** a Bantu language widely used as a lingua franca in East Africa. **2** a member of a people of Zanzibar and nearby coastal regions.

ORIGIN – from an Arabic word meaning 'coasts'.

swain > *noun* **1** archaic a country youth. **2** literary a young lover or suitor.

ORIGIN – Old English, denoting a young man attending a knight, from Old Norse *sveinn* 'lad'.

swallow¹ > *verb* **1** cause or allow (food, drink, or saliva) to pass down the throat. **2** make a similar movement of the throat, especially through fear or nervousness. **3** (often **swallow up**) take in and cause to disappear; engulf. **4** put up with or meekly accept. **5** resist expressing: *he swallowed his pride.* **6** believe (an untrue or unlikely statement) unquestioningly. > *noun* an act of swallowing.

DERIVATIVES – **swallower** *noun*.

COMBINATIONS – **swallow hole** a sinkhole.

swallow² > *noun* a swift-flying migratory insect-eating songbird with a forked tail.

IDIOMS – **one swallow does not make a summer** proverb a single fortunate event doesn't mean that what follows will also be good (from the popular notion that the swallow is a herald of summer).

COMBINATIONS – **swallow dive** Brit. a dive performed with one's arms outspread until close to the water.

swallowtail > *noun* **1** a deeply forked tail. **2** a large brightly coloured butterfly with tail-like projections on the hindwings.

swam past of SWIM.

swami /swaami/ > *noun* (pl. **swamis**) a male Hindu religious teacher.

ORIGIN – Hindi, 'master, prince'.

swamp > *noun* an area of waterlogged ground; a bog or marsh. > *verb* **1** overwhelm or flood with water. **2** overwhelm with too much of something; inundate.

DERIVATIVES – **swampy** adjective.

swan > *noun* a large waterbird, typically white, with a long flexible neck, short legs, and webbed feet. > *verb* (**swanned**, **swanning**) Brit. informal move or go in a casual, irresponsible, or ostentatious way.

WORDFINDER – cob (*male swan*), cygnet (*young swan*), pen (*female swan*); Cygnus (*constellation, the Swan*).

COMBINATIONS – **swan dive** N. Amer. a swallow dive. **swansdown 1** the fine down of a swan. **2** a thick cotton fabric with a soft nap on one side. **swan-upping** Brit. the annual practice of catching swans on the River Thames and marking them to indicate ownership by the Crown or a corporation.

swank informal > *verb* display one's wealth, knowledge, or achievements in an attempt to impress others. > *noun* behaviour, talk, or display intended to impress others. > *adjective* North American term for SWANKY.

swanky > *adjective* (**swankier**, **swankiest**) informal **1** stylishly luxurious and expensive. **2** inclined to show off.

swannery > *noun* (pl. **swanneries**) Brit. a place where swans are kept or bred.

swansong > *noun* the final performance or activity of a person's career.

ORIGIN – suggested by German *Schwanengesang*, denoting a song fabled to be sung by a dying swan.

swap (also **swop**) > *verb* (**swapped**, **swapping**) exchange or substitute. > *noun* an act of exchanging one thing for another.

ORIGIN – first used in the sense 'throw forcibly': the current sense arose from an early use meaning 'strike hands as a token of agreement'.

SWAPO /swaapō/ > *abbreviation* South West Africa People's Organisation.

sward /swawrd/ > *noun* **1** an expanse of short grass. **2** the upper layer of soil, especially when covered with grass.

swarf /swaarf/ > *noun* fine chips or filings produced by machining.

swarm > *noun* **1** a large or dense group of flying insects. **2** a large number of honeybees that leave a hive with a queen in order to establish a new colony. **3** a large group of people or things. > *verb* **1** move in or form a swarm. **2** (**swarm with**) be crowded or overrun with. **3** (**swarm up**) climb rapidly by gripping with one's hands and feet.

swart /swawrt/ > *adjective* archaic or literary swarthy.

swarthy > *adjective* (**swarthier**, **swarthiest**) dark-complexioned.

DERIVATIVES – **swarthiness** noun.

swash > *verb* **1** (of water) move with a splashing sound. **2** archaic flamboyantly swagger about or wield a sword. > *noun* the rush of seawater up the beach after the breaking of a wave.

swashbuckling > *adjective* engaging in daring and romantic adventures with ostentatious bravado or flamboyance.

DERIVATIVES – **swashbuckler** noun.

swastika /swostikə/ > *noun* an ancient symbol in the form of an equal-armed cross with each arm continued at a right angle, used (in clockwise form) as the emblem of the German Nazi party.

ORIGIN – from a Sanskrit word meaning 'well-being'.

swat > *verb* (**swatted**, **swatting**) hit or crush with a sharp blow from a flat object.

ORIGIN – northern English dialect and US variant of SQUAT: originally in the sense 'sit down'.

swatch > *noun* **1** a piece of fabric used as a sample. **2** a number of fabric samples bound together.

wordpower facts
Swathe
The two English words **swathe** both date back to Old English, but are unrelated. **Swathe** in the sense 'line of cut grass or corn' originally meant 'track, trace'; the term later denoted a measure of the width of grassland, probably reckoned by a sweep of the mower's scythe. **Swathe** meaning 'wrap in layers of fabric' is related to **swaddle**.

swathe¹ /swayth/ (chiefly N. Amer. also **swath** /swawth/) > *noun* (pl. **swathes** /swaythz/ or **swaths** /swawths/) **1** a row or line of grass, corn, etc. as it falls when mown or reaped. **2** a broad strip or area: *vast swathes of countryside.*

swathe² /swayth/ > *verb* wrap in several layers of fabric. > *noun* a strip of material in which something is wrapped.

sway > *verb* **1** move slowly and rhythmically backwards and forwards or from side to side. **2** cause (someone) to change their opinion; influence. **3** literary rule; govern. > *noun* **1** a rhythmical movement from side to side. **2** influence; rule.

IDIOMS – **hold sway** have great power or influence.

SYNONYMS – *verb* **1** oscillate, swing. **2** affect, bias, influence, persuade, swing.

Swazi /swaazi/ > *noun* (pl. same or **Swazis**) a person from Swaziland.

ORIGIN – from the name of *Mswati*, a 19th-century king of the Swazis.

swear > *verb* (past **swore**; past participle **sworn**) **1** state or promise solemnly or on oath. **2** compel (someone) to observe a certain course of action: *I am sworn to secrecy.* **3** use offensive or obscene language, especially to express anger.

IDIOMS – **swear blind** Brit. informal affirm something emphatically. **swear by** informal have or express great confidence in. **swear in** admit (someone) to a position or office by directing them to take a formal oath. **swear off** informal promise to abstain from. **swear to** give an assurance that something is the case.

DERIVATIVES – **swearer** noun.

SYNONYMS – **1** give one's word, pledge, promise, vow. **3** curse; informal cuss; archaic execrate.

COMBINATIONS – **swear word** an offensive or obscene word.

ORIGIN – Old English, related to ANSWER.

sweat > *noun* **1** moisture exuded through the pores of the skin, especially as a reaction to heat, physical exertion, or anxiety. **2** informal a state of anxiety or distress. **3** informal hard work or a laborious undertaking. > *verb* (past and past participle **sweated** or N. Amer. **sweat**) **1** exude sweat. **2** exert a great deal of strenuous effort. **3** be in a state of extreme anxiety. **4** (of a substance) exude moisture. **5** cook (chopped vegetables) slowly in a pan with a small amount of fat.

WORDFINDER – antiperspirant (*substance reducing sweating*), diaphoretic, sudorific (*inducing sweating*), perspiration (*process of sweating*).

IDIOMS – **break sweat** informal exert oneself physically. **by the sweat of one's brow** by one's own hard labour. **no sweat** informal all right; no problem. **old sweat** informal a veteran soldier. **sweat blood** informal make an extraordinarily strenuous effort.

COMBINATIONS – **sweatband** a band of absorbent material worn to soak up sweat. **sweatpants** loose trousers with an elasticated or drawstring waist, worn for exercise or leisure. **sweatshirt** a loose cotton sweater worn for exercise or leisure.

sweated > *adjective* (of goods or workers) produced by or subjected to long hours of work under poor conditions.

sweater > *noun* a pullover with long sleeves.

sweatshop > *noun* a factory or workshop employing workers for long hours in poor conditions.

sweaty > *adjective* (**sweatier, sweatiest**) exuding, soaked in, or inducing sweat.
DERIVATIVES – **sweatily** *adverb* **sweatiness** *noun*.

Swede > *noun* a person from Sweden.

swede > *noun* Brit. a large, round yellow-fleshed root vegetable originally introduced into Scotland from Sweden; rutabaga.

Swedish > *noun* the Scandinavian language of Sweden. > *adjective* relating to Sweden or its language.

sweep > *verb* (past and past participle **swept**) **1** clean (an area) by brushing away dirt or litter. **2** move or push with great force. **3** (**sweep away** or **aside**) remove or abolish swiftly and suddenly. **4** search or survey (an area). **5** pass or traverse swiftly and smoothly. **6** affect swiftly and widely: *violence swept the country.* **7** extend continuously in an arc or curve. **8** (**swept** or **swept back**) (of an aircraft's wings) directed backwards from the fuselage. **9** N. Amer. be victorious in (a series of games). > *noun* **1** an act of sweeping. **2** a long, swift, curving movement. **3** a long curved stretch of road, river, etc. **4** the range or scope of something. **5** (also **chimney sweep**) a person whose job is cleaning out the soot from chimneys. **6** informal a sweepstake. **7** N. Amer. a victory in every event, award, or place in a contest.
IDIOMS – **sweep the board** win every event or prize in a contest.

sweeper > *noun* **1** a person or device that cleans by sweeping. **2** Soccer a player stationed behind the other defenders, free to defend at any point across the field.

sweeping > *adjective* **1** extending or performed in a long, continuous curve. **2** wide in range or effect. **3** (of a statement) too general. > *noun* (**sweepings**) dirt or refuse collected by sweeping.
DERIVATIVES – **sweepingly** *adverb*.

sweepstake > *noun* (also **sweepstakes**) a form of gambling, especially on sporting events, in which all the stakes are divided among the winners.

sweet > *adjective* **1** having the pleasant taste characteristic of sugar or honey; not salt, sour, or bitter. **2** fragrant. **3** (of air, water, etc.) fresh, pure, and untainted. **4** melodious or harmonious. **5** pleasing in general; delightful. **6** working, moving, or done smoothly or easily. **7** pleasant and kind

or thoughtful. **8** charming and endearing. **9** dear; beloved. **10** (**sweet on**) informal, dated infatuated or in love with. > *noun* **1** Brit. a small shaped piece of confectionery made with sugar. **2** Brit. a sweet dish forming a course of a meal; a pudding or dessert. **3** (**sweets**) literary the pleasures or delights found in something.
WORDFINDER – saccharine (*excessively sweet*).
IDIOMS – **she's sweet** Austral./NZ informal all is well.
DERIVATIVES – **sweetish** *adjective* **sweetly** *adverb*.
SYNONYMS – *adjective* **2** aromatic, fragrant, perfumed, sweet-smelling. **4** dulcet, harmonious, honeyed, mellifluous, melodious. **5** delightful, fine, good, pleasant, pleasing. **7** considerate, good-natured, kind, nice, pleasant, thoughtful. **8** adorable, charming, cute, endearing, lovable.
ANTONYMS – *adjective* **1** bitter, savoury, sour. **4,5** harsh. **7** nasty.
COMBINATIONS – **sweet-and-sour** cooked with both sugar and a sour substance, such as vinegar or lemon. **sweetmeal** Brit. sweetened wholemeal. **sweet pea** a climbing plant of the pea family with colourful fragrant flowers. **sweet pepper** a large green, yellow, orange, or red variety of capsicum with a mild or sweet flavour. **sweet potato** the edible tuber of a tropical climbing plant, with pinkish-orange, slightly sweet flesh. **sweet-talk** informal persuade to do something by insincere flattery or kind words. **sweet tooth** (pl. **sweet tooths**) a liking for sweet-tasting foods. **sweet william** a fragrant plant with flattened clusters of vivid red, pink, or white flowers.

sweetbread > *noun* the thymus gland or pancreas of an animal, used for food.

sweetbriar > *noun* a wild rose with fragrant leaves and flowers.

sweetcorn > *noun* maize of a variety with kernels that have a high sugar content, eaten as a vegetable.

sweeten > *verb* **1** make or become sweet or sweeter. **2** make more agreeable or acceptable.

sweetener > *noun* **1** a substance used to sweeten food or drink. **2** informal, chiefly Brit. an inducement or bribe.

sweetheart > *noun* **1** a person that one is in a romantic relationship with. **2** (before another noun) informal agreed privately by two sides in their own interests: *a sweetheart deal.*
COMBINATIONS – **sweetheart neckline** a low neckline shaped like the top of a heart.

sweetie > *noun* informal **1** Brit. a sweet. **2** (also **sweetie-pie**) used as a term of endearment.

sweetmeat > *noun* archaic an item of confectionery or sweet food.

sweetness > *noun* the quality of being sweet.
IDIOMS – **sweetness and light** good-natured benevolence or harmony. [ORIGIN – taken from Jonathan Swift's *The Battle of the Books*, originally by Matthew Arnold in *Culture and Anarchy* (1869).]

swell > *verb* (past participle **swollen** or **swelled**) **1** become larger or rounder in size. **2** increase in intensity, amount, or volume. > *noun* **1** a full or gently rounded form. **2** a gradual increase in sound, amount, or intensity. **3** a slow, regular movement of the sea in rolling waves that do not break. **4** a mechanism for producing a crescendo or diminuendo in an organ or harmonium. **5** informal, dated a fashionable person of high social position. > *adjective* **1** N. Amer. informal, dated excellent; very good. **2** archaic smart; fashionable. > *adverb* N. Amer. informal, dated excellently; very well.
WORDFINDER – aneurysm (*localised swelling of an artery*), detumescence (*subsidence from a swollen state*), dropsy, oedema (*swelling due to liquid in the tissues*), goitre (*swelling of the neck due to thyroid disorder*).

swelling > *noun* an abnormal enlargement of a part of the body as a result of an accumulation of fluid.

swelter > *verb* be uncomfortably hot: *Barney sweltered in his uniform.* > *noun* an uncomfortably hot atmosphere.
DERIVATIVES – **sweltering** *adjective* **swelteringly** *adverb*.
ORIGIN – from dialect *swelt* 'perish'.

swept past and past participle of **SWEEP**.

swerve > *verb* abruptly diverge from a straight course. > *noun* such a change of course.
ORIGIN – Old English, 'depart, leave, turn aside'.

swift > *adjective* **1** happening quickly or promptly. **2** moving or capable of moving at high speed. > *noun* a fast-flying insect-eating bird with long, slender wings, spending most of its life on the wing.
DERIVATIVES – **swiftly** *adverb* **swiftness** *noun*.
SYNONYMS – *adjective* **1** prompt, quick, rapid. **2** fast, fleet, quick, speedy.
ORIGIN – Old English, from a base meaning 'move in a course, sweep'.

swig informal > *verb* (**swigged, swigging**) drink in large draughts. > *noun* a large draught of drink.

swill > *verb* **1** Brit. rinse out with large amounts of water. **2** Brit. (of liquid) swirl round in a container or cavity. **3** informal drink greedily or in large quantities. > *noun* **1** kitchen refuse and waste food mixed with water for feeding to pigs. **2** informal alcohol of inferior quality.

swim > *verb* (**swimming;** past **swam;** past

participle **swum**) **1** propel oneself through water by bodily movement. **2** be immersed in or covered with liquid. **3** experience a dizzily confusing sensation. > *noun* **1** an act or period of swimming. **2** a pool in a river which is a particularly good spot for fishing.

WORDFINDER – aqualung, scuba (*swimmer's underwater breathing apparatus*), lido (*public open-air swimming pool*), natation (*technical word for swimming*), nekton (*aquatic animals able to swim, as opposed to plankton*).

IDIOMS – **in the swim** involved in or aware of current affairs or events.

DERIVATIVES – **swimmer** noun **swimming** *noun*.

USAGE – note that the past tense of **swim** is **swam** (*she swam to the shore*) and the past participle is **swum** (*she had never swum there before*).

COMBINATIONS – **swim bladder** a gas-filled sac in a fish's body, used to maintain buoyancy. **swimming costume** Brit. a garment worn for swimming, especially a woman's one-piece swimsuit. **swimming trunks** shorts worn by men for swimming. **swimsuit** a woman's one-piece garment worn for swimming. **swimwear** clothing worn for swimming.

swimmingly > *adverb* informal smoothly and satisfactorily.

swindle > *verb* use deception to obtain or deprive of money or possessions. > *noun* a fraudulent scheme or action.

DERIVATIVES – **swindler** noun.

SYNONYMS – *verb* cheat, defraud, dupe; informal diddle, fleece, sting. *noun* fraud, racket, ruse; informal con, sting.

ORIGIN – German *schwindeln* 'be giddy', also 'tell lies'.

swine > *noun* **1** (pl. same) formal or N. Amer. a pig. **2** (pl. same or **swines**) informal a contemptible or disgusting person.

DERIVATIVES – **swinish** *adjective*.

COMBINATIONS – **swine fever** an intestinal disease of pigs. **swine vesicular disease** an infectious disease of pigs causing blisters around the mouth and feet.

swineherd > *noun* chiefly historical a person who tends pigs.

swing > *verb* (past and past participle **swung**) **1** move back and forth or from side to side while or as if suspended. **2** move by grasping a support and leaping. **3** move in a smooth, curving line. **4** (**swing at**) attempt to hit or punch. **5** shift from one opinion, mood, or state of affairs to another. **6** have a decisive influence on (a vote, judgement, etc.). **7** informal succeed in bringing about. **8** play music with an easy flowing but vigorous rhythm. **9** informal be lively, exciting, or fashionable. **10** informal be promiscuous, especially by swapping sexual partners. **11** informal be executed by hanging.

> *noun* **1** a seat suspended by ropes or chains, on which someone can sit and swing back and forth. **2** an act of swinging. **3** a discernible change in public opinion, especially in an election. **4** a style of jazz or dance music with an easy flowing but vigorous rhythm. **5** the manner in which a golf club or a bat is swung.

IDIOMS – **get into the swing of things** informal become accustomed to an activity or routine. **go with a swing** informal be lively and enjoyable. **in full swing** at the height of activity. **swing the lead** Brit. informal shirk one's duty. [ORIGIN – with nautical allusion to using a lump of lead on a line to ascertain the depth of water.] **swings and roundabouts** Brit. a situation in which different options result in no eventual gain or loss. [ORIGIN – from the phrase *to gain on the swings and lose on the roundabouts*.]

DERIVATIVES – **swinger** noun **swingy** *adjective*.

COMBINATIONS – **swing bridge** a bridge that can be swung to one side to allow ships to pass. **swing door** a door that can be opened in either direction and swings back when released. **swing-wing** denoting an aircraft wing that can move from a right-angled to a swept-back position.

ORIGIN – Old English, 'to beat, whip', also 'rush'.

swingeing > *adjective* chiefly Brit. severe or otherwise extreme.

ORIGIN – from archaic *swinge* 'strike hard, beat'.

swinging > *adjective* informal **1** lively, exciting, and fashionable. **2** sexually liberated or promiscuous.

swingle > *noun* **1** a wooden tool for beating flax and removing the woody parts. **2** the swinging part of a flail.

swingletree /**swing**g'ltree/ > *noun* a pivoted crossbar to which the traces are attached in a horse-drawn cart or plough.

swipe informal > *verb* **1** hit or try to hit with a swinging blow. **2** steal. **3** pass (a swipe card) through an electronic reader. > *noun* **1** a sweeping blow. **2** an attack or criticism.

COMBINATIONS – **swipe card** a plastic card bearing magnetically encoded information which is read when the card is slid through an electronic device.

swirl > *verb* move in a twisting or spiralling pattern. > *noun* a swirling movement or pattern.

DERIVATIVES – **swirly** *adjective*.

swish > *verb* move with a hissing or rushing sound. > *noun* a swishing sound or movement. > *adjective* Brit. informal impressively smart and fashionable.

Swiss > *adjective* relating to Switzerland or its people. > *noun* (pl. same) a person from Switzerland.

COMBINATIONS – **Swiss cheese plant** a house plant with perforated leaves (supposedly resembling the holes in a Swiss cheese). **Swiss roll** Brit. a cake made from a sponge cake spread with a filling such as jam and rolled up.

switch > *noun* **1** a device for making and breaking an electrical connection. **2** a change or exchange. **3** a slender, flexible shoot cut from a tree. **4** N. Amer. a set of points on a railway track. **5** a tress of hair used in hairdressing to supplement natural hair. > *verb* **1** change in position, direction, or focus. **2** adopt instead of something else; exchange. **3** (**switch off** or **on**) turn an electrical device off (or on). **4** (**switch off**) informal cease to pay attention. **5** archaic beat with a stick.

DERIVATIVES – **switchable** *adjective*.

COMBINATIONS – **switched-on** Brit. informal aware of what is going on or up to date.

switchback > *noun* **1** Brit. a road, railway, etc. with alternate sharp ascents and descents. **2** a roller coaster. **3** N. Amer. a hairpin bend.

switchblade > *noun* chiefly N. Amer. a flick knife.

switchboard > *noun* **1** an installation for manually controlling telephone connections in a large building. **2** an apparatus for varying connections between electric circuits.

switcher > *noun* **1** US a shunting engine. **2** a device used to select or combine different video and audio signals.

switchgear > *noun* electrical switching equipment.

swive /swīv/ > *verb* archaic or humorous have sexual intercourse with.

swivel > *noun* a coupling between two parts enabling one to revolve without turning the other. > *verb* (**swivelled, swivelling**; US **swiveled, swiveling**) turn on or as if on a swivel.

swizz > *noun* Brit. informal an instance of being mildly cheated or disappointed.

swizzle[1] > *noun* a mixed alcoholic drink, especially a frothy one of rum or gin and bitters. > *verb* stir with a swizzle stick.

COMBINATIONS – **swizzle stick** a stick used for frothing up or taking the fizz out of drinks.

swizzle[2] > *noun* Brit. informal another term for SWIZZ.

swollen past participle of SWELL.

swoon literary > *verb* faint, especially from extreme emotion. > *noun* an occurrence of swooning.

swoop > *verb* **1** move rapidly downwards through the air. **2** carry out a sudden raid. **3** (often **swoop up**) informal seize with a sweeping motion. > *noun* an act of swooping.

IDIOMS – **at** (or **in**) **one fell swoop** see FELL[4].

swoosh > *noun* the sound produced by a sudden rush of air or liquid.

swop > *verb & noun* variant spelling of **SWAP**.

sword > *noun* **1** a weapon with a long metal blade and a hilt with a handguard, used for thrusting or striking. **2** (**the sword**) literary military power; violence.
WORDFINDER – kinds of sword: broadsword, claymore, cutlass, épée, foil, rapier, sabre, scimitar; baldric (*sword belt worn over the shoulder*), hilt (*sword handle*), pommel (*knob on sword handle*), scabbard (*sheath for sword*).
IDIOMS – **beat** (or **turn**) **swords into ploughshares** devote resources to peaceful rather than warlike ends. [ORIGIN – with biblical allusion to the books of Isaiah (chapter 2) and Micah (chapter 4).] **he who lives by the sword dies by the sword** *proverb* those who commit violent acts must expect to suffer violence themselves. **put to the sword** kill, especially in war. **sword of Damocles** an impending danger. [ORIGIN – with reference to *Damocles*, who flattered the Greek ruler Dionysius I so much that the king made him feast sitting under a sword suspended by a single hair, to show him how precarious the king's good fortune was.]
COMBINATIONS – **swordplay** fencing with swords or foils.

swordfish > *noun* a large marine fish with a streamlined body and a long sword-like snout.

swordsman > *noun* a man who fights with a sword.
DERIVATIVES – **swordsmanship** *noun*.

swore past of **SWEAR**.

sworn past participle of **SWEAR**. > *adjective* **1** given under oath. **2** determined to remain the specified thing: *sworn enemies*.

swot Brit. informal, derogatory > *verb* (**swotted**, **swotting**) (also **swot up**) study intensively. > *noun* a person who spends a lot of time studying.
ORIGIN – dialect variant of **SWEAT**.

swum past participle of **SWIM**.

swung past and past participle of **SWING**.

sybarite /**sibb**ərīt/ > *noun* a person who is self-indulgently fond of sensuous luxury.
DERIVATIVES – **sybaritic** *adjective*.
ORIGIN – first denoting an inhabitant of Sybaris, an ancient Greek city in southern Italy which was noted for its luxury.

sycamore > *noun* **1** a large maple native to central and southern Europe. **2** N. Amer. a plane tree.
ORIGIN – Greek *sukomoros*, from *sukon* 'fig' + *moron* 'mulberry'.

sycophant /**sikk**əfant/ > *noun* a person who flatters someone important in a servile way.
DERIVATIVES – **sycophancy** *noun*

sycophantic *adjective* **sycophantically** *adverb*.
SYNONYMS – crawler, creep, flatterer, lickspittle, toady, yes-man.

---

wordpower facts

Sycophant

A **sycophant** was originally an informer, the sense the word had in its original Greek. The Greek word *sukophantēs* is formed, oddly, from *sukon* 'fig' and *phainein* 'to show'. Why did it develop in this way? There are two main theories. One connects the word to people who informed against those exporting figs from ancient Athens, which at one time was illegal. The other theory derives it from the insulting gesture known as the *fig*, made by thrusting the thumb between two closed fingers. It could be that the Greek word referred to an informer 'giving the fig' (rather like *showing two fingers*) to the criminals he informed against.

Sydenham's chorea > *noun* a form of chorea chiefly affecting children, associated with rheumatic fever.
ORIGIN – named after the English physician Thomas *Sydenham* (*c*.1624–89).

syllabary /**sill**əbəri/ > *noun* (pl. **syllabaries**) a set of written characters representing syllables, serving the purpose of an alphabet.

syllabic /si**labb**ik/ > *adjective* **1** relating to or based on syllables. **2** (of a consonant) constituting a whole syllable.
DERIVATIVES – **syllabically** *adverb*.

syllabify > *verb* (**syllabifies**, **syllabified**) divide words into syllables.
DERIVATIVES – **syllabification** *noun*.

syllable /**sill**əb'l/ > *noun* a unit of pronunciation having one vowel sound, with or without surrounding consonants, and forming all or part of a word.
ORIGIN – Greek *sullabē*, from *sun-* 'together' + *lambanein* 'take'.

syllabub /**sill**əbub/ > *noun* a whipped cream dessert, typically flavoured with white wine or sherry.

syllabus /**sill**əbəss/ > *noun* (pl. **syllabuses** or **syllabi** /**sill**əbī/) the topics in a course of study or teaching.
ORIGIN – first used in sense 'table of headings': Latin, from Greek *sittuba* 'title slip, label'.

syllepsis /si**lep**siss/ > *noun* (pl. **syllepses** /si**lep**seez/) a figure of speech in which a word is applied to two others of which it grammatically suits only one (e.g. *neither they nor it is working*).
ORIGIN – Greek *sullēpsis* 'taking together'.

syllogism /**sill**əjiz'm/ > *noun* a form of reasoning in which a conclusion is drawn from two given or assumed propositions (premises).
DERIVATIVES – **syllogistic** *adjective*.
ORIGIN – Greek *sullogismos*, from *sullogizesthai* 'to reason with'.

sylph /silf/ > *noun* **1** an imaginary spirit of the air. **2** a slender woman or girl.
ORIGIN – Latin *sylphes* (plural), perhaps from *sylvestris* 'of the woods' + *nympha* 'nymph'.

sylphlike > *adjective* (of a woman or girl) slender and graceful.

sylvan /**silv**ən/ > *adjective* chiefly literary **1** consisting of or associated with woods; wooded. **2** pleasantly rural or pastoral.
ORIGIN – from Latin *Silvanus* the name of a woodland deity, from *silva* 'a wood'.

symbiont /**sim**biənt/ > *noun* Biology an organism living in symbiosis with another.

symbiosis /simbi**ō**siss, simbī**ō**siss/ > *noun* (pl. **symbioses** /simbi**ō**seez, -bī**ō**seez/) Biology an interaction between two different organisms living in close association, especially to the advantage of both.
DERIVATIVES – **symbiotic** /simbi**ottik**, -bī**ottik**/ *adjective* **symbiotically** *adverb*.
ORIGIN – Greek *sumbiōsis*, from *sumbioun* 'live together'.

symbol > *noun* **1** a thing that represents or stands for something else, especially a material object representing something abstract. **2** a mark or character used as a conventional representation of something.
SYNONYMS – **1** emblem, figure, sign, token.
ORIGIN – Greek *sumbolon* 'mark, token'.

symbolic > *adjective* **1** serving as a symbol. **2** involving the use of symbols or symbolism.
DERIVATIVES – **symbolically** *adverb*.
SYNONYMS – **1** emblematic, representative. **2** allegorical, figurative, metaphorical.
COMBINATIONS – **symbolic logic** the use of symbols to denote propositions, terms, and relations in order to assist reasoning.

symbolise (also **symbolize**) > *verb* **1** be a symbol of. **2** represent by means of symbols.
DERIVATIVES – **symbolisation** *noun*.

symbolism > *noun* **1** the use of symbols to represent ideas or qualities. **2** symbolic meaning. **3** (**Symbolism**) an artistic and poetic movement or style using symbolic images and indirect suggestion to express ideas, emotions, and states of mind.
DERIVATIVES – **symbolist** *noun & adjective*.

symbology > *noun* **1** the study or use of symbols. **2** symbols collectively.

symmetrical > *adjective* made up of exactly similar parts facing each other or around an axis; showing symmetry.

DERIVATIVES – **symmetric** *adjective* **symmetrically** *adverb.*

symmetry /**simm**ətri/ > *noun* (pl. **symmetries**) **1** the quality of being made up of exactly similar parts facing each other or around an axis. **2** correct or pleasing proportion of parts. **3** similarity or exact correspondence.

ORIGIN – Latin *symmetria*, from Greek *sun-* 'with' + *metron* 'measure'.

sympathetic > *adjective* **1** feeling, showing, or expressing sympathy. **2** showing approval of an idea or action. **3** pleasing, likeable, or sensitively designed. **4** Physiology referring to the part of the autonomic nervous system supplying the internal organs, blood vessels, and glands, and balancing the action of the parasympathetic nerves. **5** arising in response to a similar action elsewhere.

DERIVATIVES – **sympathetically** *adverb.*

SYNONYMS – **1** caring, compassionate, solicitous, supportive, understanding.

sympathise (also **sympathize**) > *verb* (often **sympathise with**) **1** feel or express sympathy. **2** agree with a sentiment or opinion.

DERIVATIVES – **sympathiser** *noun.*

SYNONYMS – **1** (**sympathise with**) commiserate with, console, feel for, feel sorry for, pity.

sympathy > *noun* (pl. **sympathies**) **1** feelings of pity and sorrow for someone else's misfortune. **2** (**one's sympathies**) expressions of sympathy for a loss; condolences. **3** understanding between people; common feeling. **4** (also **one's sympathies**) support or favourable attitude.

IDIOMS – **in sympathy 1** relating harmoniously to something else; in keeping. **2** responding in a way corresponding to an action elsewhere.

USAGE – on the difference between **sympathy** and **empathy**, see the note at **EMPATHY**.

SYNONYMS – **1** compassion, concern, pity. **3** affinity, fellow feeling, rapport. **4** agreement, approval, favour, support.

ORIGIN – Greek *sumpatheia*, from *sun-* 'with' + *pathos* 'feeling'.

symphonist > *noun* a composer of symphonies.

symphony > *noun* (pl. **symphonies**) an elaborate musical composition for full orchestra, typically in four movements.

DERIVATIVES – **symphonic** *adjective.*

COMBINATIONS – **symphony orchestra** a large classical orchestra.

ORIGIN – Greek *sumphōnia*, from *sumphōnos* 'harmonious'.

symposium /simpō̄ziəm/ > *noun* (pl. **symposia** /simpō̄ziə/ or **symposiums**) **1** a conference or meeting to discuss a particular academic or specialist subject. **2** a

collection of related papers by a number of contributors. **3** (in ancient Greece) a party with drinking and discussion.

ORIGIN – Latin, from Greek *sumposion*, from *sumpotēs* 'fellow drinker'.

symptom > *noun* **1** a feature which indicates a condition of disease, in particular one apparent to the patient. **2** an indication of an undesirable situation.

USAGE – in medical use, a **symptom** (which is apparent to the patient) is distinguished from a **sign** (which is not).

ORIGIN – Greek *sumptōma* 'chance, symptom', from *sumpiptein* 'happen'.

symptomatic > *adjective* serving as a symptom or sign of something.

syn- > *prefix* united; acting together: *synchrony.*

ORIGIN – from Greek *sun* 'with'.

synaesthesia /sinniss**thee**ziə/ (US **synesthesia**) > *noun* Physiology & Psychology the production of a sense impression relating to one sense or part of the body by stimulation of another sense or part of the body.

DERIVATIVES – **synaesthetic** *adjective.*

ORIGIN – Latin, from **SYN-**, on the pattern of *anaesthesia.*

synagogue /**sinn**əgog/ > *noun* a building where a Jewish assembly or congregation meets for religious observance and instruction.

ORIGIN – Greek *sunagōgē* 'meeting', from *sun-* 'together' + *agein* 'bring'.

synapse /**sī**naps, **sin**aps/ > *noun* a gap between two nerve cells, across which nerve impulses are conducted.

DERIVATIVES – **synaptic** *adjective.*

ORIGIN – Greek *sunapsis*, from *sun-* 'together' + *hapsis* 'joining'.

sync (also **synch**) informal > *noun* synchronisation. > *verb* synchronise.

IDIOMS – **in** (or **out of**) **sync** working well (or badly) together.

synchro /**sing**krō/ > *noun* synchronised or synchronisation.

synchromesh > *noun* a system of gear changing in which the driving and driven gearwheels are made to revolve at the same speed during engagement.

synchronic /sing**kronn**ik/ > *adjective* concerned with something (especially a language) as it exists at one point in time. Contrasted with **DIACHRONIC**.

DERIVATIVES – **synchronically** *adverb.*

synchronicity > *noun* the simultaneous occurrence of events.

synchronise (also **synchronize**) > *verb* cause to occur or operate at the same time or rate.

DERIVATIVES – **synchronisation** *noun.*

COMBINATIONS – **synchronised swimming** a sport in which teams of swimmers perform coordinated movements in time to music.

synchronous /**sing**krənəss/ > *adjective* **1** existing or occurring at the same time. **2** (of a satellite) revolving in its orbit in exactly the same time as the primary body rotates on its axis.

DERIVATIVES – **synchronously** *adverb.*

ORIGIN – Greek *sunkhronos*, from *sun-* 'together' + *khronos* 'time'.

synchrony /**sing**krəni/ (also **synchronism**) > *noun* simultaneous action, development, or occurrence.

syncline > *noun* Geology a trough or fold of stratified rock in which the strata slope upwards from the axis. Compare with **ANTICLINE**.

ORIGIN – from **SYN-** + Greek *klinein* 'to lean', on the pattern of *incline.*

syncopated /**sing**kəpaytid/ > *adjective* (of music or a rhythm) having the beats or accents displaced so that strong beats become weak and vice versa.

DERIVATIVES – **syncopation** *noun.*

ORIGIN – from Latin *syncopare* 'faint, affect with syncope'.

syncope /**sing**kəpi/ > *noun* **1** Medicine temporary loss of consciousness caused by low blood pressure. **2** Grammar the omission of sounds or letters from within a word, e.g. when *library* is pronounced /**lī**bri/.

ORIGIN – Greek *sunkopē*, from *sun-* 'together' + *koptein* 'strike, cut off'.

syncretise /**sing**krītīz/ (also **syncretize**) > *verb* attempt to amalgamate (differing religious beliefs, schools of thought, etc.).

DERIVATIVES – **syncretisation** *noun.*

syncretism /**sing**krītiz'm/ > *noun* the amalgamation of different religions, cultures, or schools of thought.

DERIVATIVES – **syncretic** *adjective* **syncretist** *noun.*

ORIGIN – Greek *sunkrētismos*, from *sunkrētizein* 'unite against a third party'.

syndicalism > *noun* historical a movement for transferring the ownership and control of the means of production and distribution to workers' unions.

DERIVATIVES – **syndicalist** *noun & adjective.*

syndicate > *noun* /**sin**dikət/ **1** a group of individuals or organisations combined to promote some common interest. **2** an agency supplying material simultaneously to a number of news media. > *verb* /**sin**dikayt/ **1** control or manage by a syndicate. **2** publish or broadcast (material) simultaneously in a number of media.

DERIVATIVES – **syndication** *noun.*

ORIGIN – Latin *syndicatus*, from Greek *sundikos*, from *sun-* 'together' + *dikē* 'justice'.

syndrome > *noun* **1** a group of symptoms which consistently occur together. **2** a characteristic combination of opinions, emotions, or behaviour.

ORIGIN – Greek *sundromē*, from *sun-* 'together' + *dramein* 'to run'.

syne /sīn/ > *adverb* Scottish ago.

ORIGIN – dialect *sithen* 'ever since'.

synecdoche /sinekdəki/ > *noun* a figure of speech in which a part is made to represent the whole or vice versa, as in *England lost by six wickets* (meaning 'the English cricket team').

ORIGIN – Greek *sunekdokhē*, from *sun-* 'together' + *ekdekhesthai* 'take up'.

synergist > *noun* an agent that participates in synergy.

DERIVATIVES – **synergistic** *adjective* **synergistically** *adverb*.

synergy /sinnərji/ (also **synergism**) > *noun* interaction or cooperation of two or more agents to produce a combined effect greater than the sum of their separate effects.

DERIVATIVES – **synergetic** *adjective*.

ORIGIN – from Greek *sunergos* 'working together'.

synesthesia > *noun* US spelling of SYNAESTHESIA.

synod /sinnəd/ > *noun* an assembly of the clergy (and sometimes also the laity) in a division of a Christian Church.

ORIGIN – Greek *sunodos* 'meeting', from *sun-* 'together' + *hodos* 'way'.

synodic /sinoddik/ > *adjective* Astronomy relating to or involving a conjunction.

synodical > *adjective* Christian Church relating to or constituted as a synod.

synonym /sinnənim/ > *noun* a word or phrase that means the same as another word or phrase in the same language.

DERIVATIVES – **synonymy** *noun*.

ORIGIN – Greek *sunōnumon*, from *sun-* 'with' + *onoma* 'name'.

synonymous /sinonniməss/ > *adjective* **1** (of a word or phrase) having the same meaning as another word or phrase in the same language. **2** closely associated with something: *his name was synonymous with victory*.

DERIVATIVES – **synonymously** *adverb*.

synopsis /sinopsiss/ > *noun* (pl. **synopses** /sinopseez/) a brief summary of something.

ORIGIN – Greek, from *sun-* 'together' + *opsis* 'seeing'.

synoptic > *adjective* **1** of, forming, or involving a synopsis or general view. **2** (**Synoptic**) referring to the Gospels of Matthew, Mark, and Luke, which describe events from a similar point of view.

synovial /sīnōviəl, sinōviəl/ > *adjective* relating to joints of the body enclosed in a thick flexible membrane containing a lubricating fluid (**synovial fluid**).

ORIGIN – from Latin *synovia*, a word

probably invented by the Swiss physician Paracelsus (c.1493–1541).

syntax > *noun* **1** the arrangement of words and phrases to create well-formed sentences. **2** the structure of statements in a computer language.

DERIVATIVES – **syntactic** *adjective* **syntactical** *adjective* **syntactically** *adverb*.

ORIGIN – Greek *suntaxis*, from *sun-* 'together' + *tassein* 'arrange'.

synth > *noun* short for SYNTHESISER.

synthesis /sinthəsiss/ > *noun* (pl. **syntheses** /sinthəseez/) **1** the combination of components to form a connected whole. **2** the production of chemical compounds by reaction from simpler materials.

ORIGIN – Greek *sunthesis*, from *suntithenai* 'place together'.

synthesise /sinthəsīz/ (also **synthesize**, **synthetise**, **synthetize**) > *verb* **1** make by synthesis. **2** combine into a coherent whole. **3** produce (sound) electronically.

synthesiser (also **synthesizer**) > *noun* an electronic musical instrument producing sounds by generating and combining signals of different frequencies.

synthetic /sinthettik/ > *adjective* **1** made by chemical synthesis, especially to imitate a natural product. **2** not genuine; unnatural. > *noun* a synthetic textile fibre.

DERIVATIVES – **synthetically** *adverb*.

syphilis > *noun* a sexually transmitted disease, spread by bacteria and progressing if untreated from infection of the genitals to the bones, muscles, and brain.

DERIVATIVES – **syphilitic** *adjective & noun*.

ORIGIN – Latin, from *Syphilus*, the subject of a 16th-century poem who was the supposed first sufferer of the disease.

syphon > *noun & verb* variant spelling of SIPHON.

Syrah /seerə/ > *noun* another term for SHIRAZ.

Syrian > *noun* a person from Syria. > *adjective* relating to Syria.

syringe /sirinj/ > *noun* a tube with a nozzle and piston for sucking in and ejecting liquid in a thin stream, often fitted with a hollow needle. > *verb* (**syringed**, **syringing**) spray liquid into or over with a syringe.

ORIGIN – Latin *syringa*, from *syrinx* (see SYRINX).

syrinx /sirringks/ > *noun* (pl. **syrinxes**) **1** a set of pan pipes. **2** Ornithology the lower larynx or voice organ, especially in songbirds.

ORIGIN – Greek *surinx* 'pipe, channel'.

syrup (US also **sirup**) > *noun* **1** a thick, sweet liquid made by dissolving sugar in boiling water, used for preserving fruit. **2** a thick, sweet liquid containing medicine or used as a drink.

DERIVATIVES – **syrupy** *adjective*.

ORIGIN – Arabic, 'beverage'; related to SHERBET and SHRUB[2].

sysop /sissop/ > *noun* Computing a system operator.

system > *noun* **1** a set of things working together as a mechanism or interconnecting network; a complex whole. **2** an organised scheme or method. **3** orderliness; method. **4** (**the system**) the prevailing political or social order, especially when regarded as oppressive. **5** Geology a major range of strata corresponding to a period in time.

IDIOMS – **get something out of one's system** informal get rid of a preoccupation or anxiety.

SYNONYMS – **1** network, organisation, structure. **2** arrangement, method, practice, procedure, process, scheme.

COMBINATIONS – **system operator** (also **systems operator**) a person who manages the operation of a computer system.

ORIGIN – Greek *sustēma*, from *sun-* 'with' + *histanai* 'set up'.

systematic > *adjective* done or acting according to a fixed plan or system; methodical.

DERIVATIVES – **systematically** *adverb* **systematist** *noun*.

SYNONYMS – methodical, orderly, organised, structured, systematised.

ANTONYMS – chaotic, disorganised.

systematics > *plural noun* (treated as sing.) the branch of biology concerned with classification and nomenclature; taxonomy.

systematise (also **systematize**) > *verb* arrange according to an organised system; make systematic.

DERIVATIVES – **systematisation** *noun*.

systemic /sistemmik, sisteemik/ > *adjective* **1** relating to a system as a whole. **2** Physiology referring to the part of the circulatory system not involving the lungs. **3** (of an insecticide, fungicide, etc.) entering the plant via the roots or shoots and passing through the tissues.

DERIVATIVES – **systemically** *adverb*.

systems analyst > *noun* a person who analyses a complex process or operation in order to improve its efficiency.

systole /sistəli/ > *noun* Physiology the phase of the heartbeat when the heart muscle contracts and pumps blood into the arteries. Contrasted with DIASTOLE.

DERIVATIVES – **systolic** *adjective*.

ORIGIN – Greek *sustolē*, from *sustellein* 'to contract'.

syzygy /sizziji/ > *noun* (pl. **syzygies**) Astronomy a conjunction or opposition, especially of the moon with the sun.

ORIGIN – Greek *suzugia*, from *suzugos* 'yoked, paired'.

T¹ (also **t**) > *noun* (pl. **Ts** or **T's**) the twentieth letter of the alphabet.

IDIOMS – **to a T** informal exactly; to perfection.

COMBINATIONS – **T-bar** a type of ski lift in the form of a series of inverted T-shaped bars for towing two skiers at a time uphill. **T-bone** a large choice piece of loin steak containing a T-shaped bone. **T-junction** a road junction at which one road joins another at right angles without crossing it. **T-square** a T-shaped instrument for drawing or testing right angles.

T² > *abbreviation* 1 tera- (10¹²). 2 tesla.

t > *abbreviation* ton(s).

TA > *abbreviation* (in the UK) Territorial Army.

Ta > *symbol* the chemical element tantalum.

ta > *exclamation* Brit. informal thank you.

tab¹ > *noun* 1 a small flap or strip of material attached to something, for holding, manipulation, identification, etc. 2 informal, chiefly N. Amer. a restaurant bill. 3 Brit. Military a collar marking distinguishing an officer of high rank. 4 N. Amer. a ring pull on a can. 5 N. English & informal a cigarette. > *verb* (**tabbed**, **tabbing**) mark with a tab.

IDIOMS – **keep tabs on** informal monitor the activities of. **pick up the tab** informal, chiefly N. Amer. pay for something.

DERIVATIVES – **tabbed** adjective.

ORIGIN – perhaps related to TAG¹.

tab² > *noun* short for TABULATOR. > *verb* (**tabbed**, **tabbing**) short for TABULATE.

tab³ > *noun* informal a tablet, especially one containing an illicit drug.

tabard /tabbərd/ > *noun* 1 a sleeveless jerkin consisting only of front and back pieces with a hole for the head. 2 a herald's official coat emblazoned with the arms of the sovereign.

ORIGIN – Old French *tabart*.

Tabasco /təbaskō/ > *noun* trademark a pungent sauce made from capsicums.

ORIGIN – named after the state of *Tabasco* in Mexico.

tabbouleh /tabboolay, təboōlay/ > *noun* a salad of cracked wheat mixed with finely chopped tomatoes, onions, parsley, etc.

ORIGIN – Arabic.

tabby > *noun* (pl. **tabbies**) 1 a grey or brownish cat with dark stripes. 2 silk or other fabric with a watered pattern. 3 a plain weave.

wordpower facts

Tabby

What connects a striped cat, a kind of cloth, and an area of Baghdad? **Tabby** originally referred to a kind of silk taffeta, at first specifically striped cloth but later also material of a uniform colour with a watered pattern. The **tabby cat** is thought to have got its name because its striped or streaked coat was reminiscent of the fabric. The word **tabby** comes from French *tabis*, which was based on *al-'Attābiyya*, the name of the quarter of Baghdad where tabby was manufactured. **Tabby** used also to be a rather derogatory term for an old unmarried woman: in this sense it may have been a shortening of the name *Tabitha*.

tabernacle /tabbərnakk'l/ > *noun* 1 (in biblical use) a fixed or movable habitation, typically of light construction. 2 a tent used as a sanctuary for the Ark of the Covenant by the Israelites during the Exodus. 3 a meeting place for Nonconformist or Mormon worship. 4 (in Catholic churches) an ornamented receptacle or cabinet in which the container holding the consecrated bread of the Eucharist may be placed.

ORIGIN – Latin *tabernaculum* 'tent'.

tabla /tablə/ > *noun* a pair of small hand drums fixed together, used in Indian music.

ORIGIN – Arabic, 'drum'.

tablature /tabləchər/ > *noun* a form of musical notation indicating fingering rather than the pitch of notes.

ORIGIN – French, probably from Italian *tavolare* 'set to music'.

table > *noun* 1 a piece of furniture with a flat top and one or more legs, for eating, writing, or working at. 2 a set of facts or figures systematically displayed. 3 (**tables**) multiplication tables. 4 food provided in a restaurant or household. > *verb* Brit. present formally for discussion or consideration at a meeting.

IDIOMS – **on the table** available for discussion. **turn the tables** reverse a situation disadvantageous to oneself so that it becomes advantageous.

COMBINATIONS – **tablecloth** a cloth spread over a table, especially during meals. **table manners** behaviour that is conventionally required while eating at table. **table tennis** an indoor game played with small bats and a small, hollow ball bounced on a table divided by a net. **tableware** crockery, cutlery, and glassware used for serving and eating meals at a table. **table wine** wine of moderate quality considered suitable for drinking with a meal.

ORIGIN – Latin *tabula* 'plank, tablet, list'.

tableau /tablō/ > *noun* (pl. **tableaux** /tablōz/) a group of models or motionless figures representing a scene.

ORIGIN – French, 'picture', from *table* 'table'.

table d'hôte /taablə dōt/ > *noun* a restaurant meal offered at a fixed price and with few if any choices.

ORIGIN – French, 'host's table'.

tableland > *noun* a broad, high, level region; a plateau.

tablespoon > *noun* a large spoon for serving food.

DERIVATIVES – **tablespoonful** noun.

tablet > *noun* 1 a slab of stone, clay, or wood, used especially for an inscription. 2 a small disc or cylinder of a compressed solid substance, typically a medicine or drug; a pill. 3 Brit. a small flat piece of soap.

ORIGIN – Old French *tablete*, from Latin *tabula* 'plank, tablet, list'.

tabloid > *noun* a newspaper having pages half the size of those of the average broadsheet, typically popular in style.

ORIGIN – from TABLET, originally a proprietary term for a medicinal tablet: the current sense reflects the notion of 'concentrated, easily assimilable'.

taboo (also **tabu**) > *noun* (pl. **taboos** or **tabus**) a social or religious custom prohibiting or restricting a particular practice or forbidding association with a particular thing or person. > *adjective* 1 prohibited or restricted by social custom. 2 designated as sacred and prohibited. > *verb* (**taboos**, **tabooed** or **tabus**, **tabued**) place under such prohibition.

ORIGIN – Tongan, 'set apart, forbidden'.

tabor /taybər/ > *noun* historical a small drum, especially one used simultaneously by the player of a simple pipe.

ORIGIN – Old French *tabour* 'drum'.

tabular /tabyoolər/ > *adjective* 1 (of data) consisting of or presented in columns or tables. 2 broad and flat like the top of a table.

tabula rasa /tabyoolə raazə/ > *noun* (pl. **tabulae rasae** /tabyoolee raazee/) 1 an absence of preconceived ideas or predetermined goals; a clean slate. 2 the human mind, especially at birth, viewed as having no innate ideas.

ORIGIN – Latin, 'scraped tablet', i.e. a tablet with the writing erased, ready to be used again.

tabulate /**tab**yoolayt/ > *verb* arrange (data) in tabular form.

DERIVATIVES – **tabulation** *noun*.

tabulator > *noun* a facility in a word-processing program, or a device on a typewriter, for advancing to set positions in tabular work.

tach /tak/ > *noun* N. Amer. informal short for TACHOMETER.

tache > *noun* variant spelling of TASH.

tacho /**tak**kō/ > *noun* (pl. **tachos**) Brit. short for TACHOGRAPH or TACHOMETER.

tachograph > *noun* a tachometer used in commercial road vehicles to provide a record of engine speed over a period.

tachometer /ta**komm**itər/ > *noun* an instrument which measures the working speed of an engine, typically in revolutions per minute.

tachycardia /takki**kaar**diə/ > *noun* an abnormally rapid heart rate.

ORIGIN – from Greek *takhus* 'swift' + *kardia* 'heart'.

tachyon /**takki**on/ > *noun* Physics a hypothetical particle that travels faster than light.

tacit /**tass**it/ > *adjective* understood or implied without being stated.

DERIVATIVES – **tacitly** *adverb*.

SYNONYMS – implicit, implied, undeclared, understood, unsaid, unspoken.

ORIGIN – Latin *tacitus* 'silent'.

taciturn /**tass**iturn/ > *adjective* reserved or uncommunicative in speech; saying little.

DERIVATIVES – **taciturnity** *noun* **taciturnly** *adverb*.

SYNONYMS – quiet, reserved, silent, uncommunicative, unforthcoming.

ANTONYMS – loquacious, talkative.

ORIGIN – Latin *taciturnus*, from *tacitus* 'silent'.

tack¹ > *noun* **1** a small, sharp broad-headed nail. **2** N. Amer. a drawing pin. **3** a long stitch used to fasten fabrics together temporarily. **4** a method of dealing with a situation; a course of action. **5** Sailing an act of tacking. **6** a boat's course relative to the direction of the wind: *the ketch swung to the opposite tack.* > *verb* **1** fasten or fix with tacks. **2** (**tack on**) add (something) to something already existing. **3** change course by turning a boat's head into and through the wind. **4** make a series of such changes of course while sailing.

ORIGIN – probably related to Old French *tache* 'clasp, large nail'.

tack² > *noun* equipment used in horse riding, including the saddle and bridle.

ORIGIN – contraction of TACKLE.

tack³ > *noun* informal cheap, shoddy, or tasteless material.

ORIGIN – from TACKY².

tackle > *noun* **1** the equipment required for a task or sport. **2** a mechanism consisting of ropes, pulley blocks, and hooks for lifting heavy objects. **3** the running rigging and pulleys used to work a boat's sails. **4** (in sport) an act of tackling an opponent. **5** Brit. vulgar slang a man's genitals. > *verb* **1** make determined efforts to deal with (a difficult task). **2** initiate discussion with (someone) about a sensitive issue. **3** (in soccer, hockey, rugby, etc.) intercept (an opponent in possession of the ball).

DERIVATIVES – **tackler** *noun*.

SYNONYMS – *noun* **1** apparatus, equipment, gear, kit. **4** block, challenge, interception. *verb* **1** combat, face up to, get to grips with, grapple with, handle, take on. **3** block, challenge, intercept.

ORIGIN – probably from Low German *takel*, from *taken* 'lay hold of'.

tacky¹ > *adjective* (**tackier, tackiest**) (of glue, paint, etc.) slightly sticky because not fully dry.

DERIVATIVES – **tackiness** *noun*.

tacky² > *adjective* (**tackier, tackiest**) informal showing poor taste and quality.

DERIVATIVES – **tackiness** *noun*.

ORIGIN – first used in reference to a horse of little value, later to a poor white person in the southern US.

taco /**takk**ō/ > *noun* (pl. **tacos**) a Mexican dish consisting of a folded tortilla filled with seasoned meat or beans.

ORIGIN – Spanish, 'plug, wad'.

tact > *noun* adroitness and sensitivity in dealing with others or with difficult issues.

SYNONYMS – delicacy, diplomacy, discretion, sensitivity, understanding.

ORIGIN – Latin *tactus* 'touch, sense of touch', from *tangere* 'to touch'.

Tactel /**tak**tel/ > *noun* trademark a synthetic fabric or fibre with a soft, silky feel.

tactful > *adjective* having or showing tact.

DERIVATIVES – **tactfully** *adverb* **tactfulness** *noun*.

SYNONYMS – considerate, diplomatic, discreet, sensitive, thoughtful.

ANTONYMS – insensitive, tactless.

tactic > *noun* **1** an action or strategy planned to achieve a specific end. **2** (**tactics**) the art of disposing armed forces in order of battle and of organising operations. Contrasted with STRATEGY.

DERIVATIVES – **tactician** *noun*.

SYNONYMS – **1** action, manoeuvre, measure, move, ploy, stratagem, strategy.

ORIGIN – from Greek *taktikē tekhnē* 'art of tactics', from *taktos* 'ordered, arranged'.

tactical > *adjective* **1** done or planned to gain a specific military end. **2** (of bombing or weapons) done or for use in immediate support of military or naval operations. Contrasted with STRATEGIC. **3** planned in order to achieve an end beyond the immediate action. **4** (of voting) aimed at preventing a particular candidate from winning by supporting another, without regard to one's true political allegiance.

DERIVATIVES – **tactically** *adverb*.

tactile > *adjective* **1** of or connected with the sense of touch. **2** perceptible or designed to be perceived by touch. **3** (of a person) given to touching others in a friendly or sympathetic way.

DERIVATIVES – **tactility** *noun*.

ORIGIN – Latin *tactilis*, from *tangere* 'to touch'.

tactless > *adjective* having or showing a lack of tact.

DERIVATIVES – **tactlessly** *adverb* **tactlessness** *noun*.

SYNONYMS – clumsy, inconsiderate, indiscreet, insensitive, thoughtless, undiplomatic.

ANTONYMS – diplomatic, tactful.

tad informal > *adverb* (**a tad**) to a minor extent; somewhat. > *noun* a small amount.

ORIGIN – first referring to a small child; perhaps from TADPOLE.

Tadjik (also **Tadzhik**) > *noun & adjective* variant spelling of TAJIK.

tadpole > *noun* the tailed aquatic larva of an amphibian, breathing through gills and lacking legs until the later stages of its development.

ORIGIN – from Old English *tāda* 'toad' + POLL (probably because the tadpole seems to consist of a large head and a tail in its early development stage).

tae kwon do /tī kwon **dō**/ > *noun* a modern Korean martial art similar to karate.

ORIGIN – Korean, 'art of hand and foot fighting'.

taffeta > *noun* a fine lustrous silk or similar synthetic fabric.

ORIGIN – Latin, from a Persian word meaning 'to shine'.

taffrail > *noun* a rail round a ship's stern.

ORIGIN – from obsolete *tafferel* 'panel', used to denote the flat part of a ship's stern above the transom, from Dutch *tafereel*.

Taffy (also **Taff**) > *noun* (pl. **Taffies**) Brit. informal, often offensive a Welshman.

ORIGIN – representing a supposed Welsh pronunciation of the given name *Davy* or *David* (Welsh *Dafydd*).

taffy > *noun* (pl. **taffies**) N. Amer. a sweet similar to toffee.

ORIGIN – earlier form of TOFFEE.

tag¹ > *noun* **1** a label providing identification or giving other information. **2** an electronic device attached to someone or something for monitoring purposes. **3** a small piece or part that is attached to a main body. **4** a metal or plastic point at the end of a shoelace. **5** a frequently repeated quotation or stock phrase. **6** a nickname or popular description. **7** Computing a character or set of characters appended to an item of data in order to identify it. > *verb* (**tagged**, **tagging**) **1** attach a tag to. **2** (**tag on** or **to**) add to something as an afterthought. **3** (**tag along**) accompany someone without invitation.

COMBINATIONS – **tag end** chiefly N. Amer. the last remaining part of something. **tag line** informal, chiefly N. Amer. a catchphrase, slogan, or punchline.

tag² > *noun* a children's game in which one chases the rest, and anyone who is caught then becomes the pursuer. > *verb* (**tagged**, **tagging**) touch (someone being chased) in a game of tag.

COMBINATIONS – **tag team** a pair of wrestlers who fight as a team, taking the ring alternately.

Tagalog /təgaalog/ > *noun* **1** a member of a people from the Philippine Islands. **2** the Austronesian language of this people, the basis of the national language of the Philippines (Filipino).

ORIGIN – the name in Tagalog, from words meaning 'native' and 'river'.

tagine /tazheen/ > *noun* a North African stew of spiced meat and vegetables prepared by slow cooking in a shallow earthenware dish.

ORIGIN – Arabic, 'frying pan'.

tagliatelle /talyətelli/ > *plural noun* pasta in narrow ribbons.

ORIGIN – Italian, from *tagliare* 'to cut'.

tahini /taaheeni/ > *noun* a Middle Eastern paste or spread made from ground sesame seeds.

ORIGIN – modern Greek *takhini*, from an Arabic word meaning 'to crush'.

Tahitian /təheesh'n/ > *noun* **1** a person from Tahiti. **2** the Polynesian language of Tahiti. > *adjective* relating to Tahiti, its people, or their language.

t'ai chi ch'uan /tī chee chwaan/ (also **t'ai chi**) > *noun* a Chinese martial art and system of callisthenics, consisting of sequences of very slow controlled movements.

ORIGIN – Chinese, 'great ultimate boxing'.

Taig /tayg/ > *noun* informal, offensive (in Northern Ireland) a Protestant name for a Catholic.

ORIGIN – variant of *Teague*, anglicised spelling of the Irish name *Tadhg*, used as a nickname for an Irishman.

taiga /tīgə/ > *noun* swampy coniferous forest of high northern latitudes, especially that between the tundra and steppes of Siberia.

ORIGIN – Mongolian.

tail¹ > *noun* **1** the hindmost part of an animal, especially when extended beyond the rest of the body. **2** something extending downwards, outwards, or back like an animal's tail. **3** the rear part of an aircraft, with the tailplane and rudder. **4** the final, more distant, or weaker part. **5** (**tails**) the side of a coin without the image of a head on it. **6** (**tails**) informal a tailcoat, or a man's formal evening suit with such a coat. **7** informal a person secretly following another to observe their movements. > *verb* **1** informal secretly follow and observe. **2** (**tail off** or **away**) gradually diminish in amount, strength, or intensity. **3** (**tail back**) Brit. (of traffic) become congested and form a tailback.

WORDFINDER – caudal (*of or like a tail*).

IDIOMS – **on someone's tail** informal following someone closely. **with one's tail between one's legs** informal in a state of dejection or humiliation. **with one's tail up** informal in a confident or cheerful mood.

DERIVATIVES – **tailed** *adjective* **tailless** *adjective*.

COMBINATIONS – **tailboard** Brit. a tailgate. **tailcoat** Brit. a man's formal morning or evening coat, with a long skirt divided at the back into tails and cut away in front. **tail end** the last or hindmost part of something, in particular the batting order in cricket. **tail fin 1** Zoology a fin at the posterior end of a fish's body. **2** a projecting vertical surface on the tail of an aircraft, housing the rudder. **3** an upswept projection on each rear corner of a motor car, popular in the 1950s. **tail light** a red light at the rear of a vehicle. **tailpiece 1** the final or end part of something. **2** a small decorative design at the foot of a page or the end of a chapter or book. **3** a part added to the end of a piece of writing. **tailpipe** the rear section of the exhaust pipe of a motor vehicle. **tailplane** Brit. a horizontal aerofoil at the tail of an aircraft. **tailspin** a spin by an aircraft. **tailwind** a wind blowing in the direction of travel of a vehicle or aircraft.

ORIGIN – Old English, from a base meaning 'hair, hairy tail'.

tail² > *noun* Law, chiefly historical limitation of ownership, especially of an estate or title limited to a person and their heirs.

ORIGIN – Old French *taille* 'notch, tax', from *taillier* 'to cut'.

tailback > *noun* Brit. a long queue of traffic extending back from a junction or obstruction.

tailgate > *noun* **1** a hinged flap giving access to the back of a truck. **2** the door at the back of an estate or hatchback car. > *verb* informal, chiefly N. Amer. drive too closely behind (another vehicle).

DERIVATIVES – **tailgater** noun.

tailor > *noun* a person whose occupation is making clothes, especially men's outer garments for individual customers. > *verb* **1** (of a tailor) make (clothes) to fit individual customers. **2** make or adapt (something) for a particular purpose or person.

WORDFINDER – sartorial (*relating to tailoring or clothes*).

DERIVATIVES – **tailoring** noun.

COMBINATIONS – **tailor-made 1** (of clothes) made by a tailor for a particular customer. **2** made or adapted for a particular purpose or person.

ORIGIN – Old French *taillour* 'cutter', from Latin *taliare* 'to cut'.

tailored > *adjective* (of clothes) smart, fitted, and well cut.

taimen /tīmən/ > *noun* (pl. same) a large food fish found in Siberia and east Asia.

ORIGIN – Russian.

taint > *noun* **1** a trace of a bad or undesirable quality or substance. **2** a contaminating influence or effect. > *verb* **1** contaminate or pollute (something). **2** affect with a bad or undesirable quality.

SYNONYMS – *verb* **1** contaminate, corrupt, infect, poison, pollute. **2** besmirch, blacken, smirch, sully, tarnish.

ORIGIN – from Old French *teint* 'tinged', from Latin *tingere* 'to dye, tinge'.

taipan /tīpan/ > *noun* a foreigner who is head of a business in China.

ORIGIN – Chinese.

Taiwanese /tīwəneez/ > *noun* (pl. same) a person from Taiwan. > *adjective* relating to Taiwan.

Tajik /tajeek/ (also **Tadjik** or **Tadzhik**) > *noun* **1** a member of a mainly Muslim people inhabiting Tajikistan and parts of neighbouring countries. **2** a person from the republic of Tajikistan.

ORIGIN – Persian, 'a Persian, someone who is neither an Arab nor a Turk'.

taka /taakaa/ > *noun* (pl. same) the basic monetary unit of Bangladesh, equal to 100 poisha.

ORIGIN – Bengali.

takahe /taakəhi/ > *noun* a large, rare flightless rail found in New Zealand.

ORIGIN – Maori.

take > *verb* (past **took**; past participle **taken**) **1** lay hold of with one's hands; reach for and hold. **2** occupy (a place or position). **3** capture or gain possession of by force. **4** carry or bring with one; convey. **5** remove from a place. **6** subtract. **7** consume as food, drink, medicine, or drugs. **8** bring into a specified state. **9** experience or be affected by. **10** use as a route or a means of transport. **11** accept or receive. **12** acquire or assume (a position, state, or form). **13** require or use up. **14** hold or accommodate. **15** act on (an opportunity). **16** regard, view, or deal with in a specified way. **17** submit to, tolerate, or endure. **18** make, undertake, or perform (an action or task). **19** be taught or examined in (a subject). > *noun* **1** a sequence of sound or vision photographed or recorded continuously. **2** a particular version of or approach to something: *his whimsical take on life.* **3** an amount gained or acquired from one source or in one session.

IDIOMS – **take after** resemble (a parent or ancestor). **take as read** Brit. assume that (something) is the case without considering or discussing it. **take back** retract (a statement). **take five** informal, chiefly N. Amer. have a short break. **take in 1** cheat or deceive. **2** make (a garment) tighter by altering its seams. **3** encompass, understand, or absorb. **take in hand 1** undertake to control or reform (someone). **2** start doing or dealing with (a task). **take it on one** (or **oneself**) **to do** decide to do (something) without asking for permission or advice. **take it out of** exhaust the strength of. **take off 1** become airborne. **2** remove (clothing). **3** mimic (someone). **4** depart hastily. **take on 1** engage (an employee). **2** undertake (a task). **3** acquire (a particular meaning or quality). **take out on** relieve (frustration or anger) by mistreating (someone). **take over 1** assume control of or responsibility for. **2** (of a company) buy out (another). **take one's time** not hurry. **take to 1** fall into the habit of. **2** form a liking or develop an ability for. **3** go to (a place) to escape danger. **take up 1** become interested or engaged in (a pursuit). **2** occupy (time, space, or attention). **3** pursue (a matter) further. **take up on** accept an offer or challenge from (someone). **take up with** begin to associate with (someone).

DERIVATIVES – **taker** *noun.*

COMBINATIONS – **take-home pay** the pay received by an employee after the deduction of tax and insurance.

takeaway > *noun* **1** Brit. a restaurant or shop selling cooked food to be eaten elsewhere. **2** a meal or dish of such food.

take-off > *noun* the action of becoming airborne.

takeout > *noun* chiefly N. Amer. a takeaway.

takeover > *noun* an act of assuming control of something, especially the buying-out of one company by another.

taking > *noun* **1** the action or process of taking. **2** (**takings**) the amount of money earned by a business from the sale of goods or services. > *adjective* dated captivating in manner; charming.

IDIOMS – **for the taking** ready or available to take advantage of.

tala /ˈtaːlə/ > *noun* (pl. same or **talas**) the basic monetary unit of Samoa, equal to 100 sene.

ORIGIN – Samoan.

talc > *noun* **1** talcum powder. **2** a soft mineral consisting of a hydrated silicate of magnesium.

talcum powder > *noun* a preparation for the body and face consisting of the mineral talc in powdered form. > *verb* (**talcumed, talcuming**) powder with this substance.

ORIGIN – Arabic, from Persian.

tale > *noun* **1** a narrative or story, especially one that is imaginatively recounted. **2** an untrue account; a lie.

SYNONYMS – **1** account, anecdote, chronicle, narrative, story, yarn.

ORIGIN – Old English, 'telling, something told'.

taleggio /taˈlejiō/ > *noun* a soft Italian cheese made from cows' milk.

ORIGIN – named after the *Taleggio* valley in Lombardy.

talent > *noun* **1** natural aptitude or skill. **2** people possessing such aptitude or skill. **3** informal sexually attractive people. **4** an ancient weight and unit of currency.

DERIVATIVES – **talentless** *adjective.*

SYNONYMS – **1** ability, aptitude, flair, gift, prowess, skill.

COMBINATIONS – **talent scout** a person whose job is to search for talented performers in sport and entertainment.

ORIGIN – Latin *talentum* 'weight, sum of money', from Greek *talanton.*

wordpower facts

Talent

A **talent** was a unit of weight used by the Greeks, Romans, and other ancient peoples, and also a unit of currency equivalent to the value of a talent's weight of gold or silver. The weight of a talent varied, but two established Greek talents were 37.8 kg (83 lb 3 oz) and 25.8 kg (56 lb 14 oz): thus a talent was a considerable amount of money. In medieval times the word **talent** referred to this ancient use and also meant 'mental inclination'. The main modern sense arose as an allusion to the biblical story of the parable of the talents (Gospel of Matthew, chapter 25). A man about to undertake a long journey divided his money between his servants, one servant receiving five talents, one two, and the other man one talent. The first two servants used their money to make a profit and were rewarded on their master's return, but the man who had received the single talent cautiously buried it and displeased his master. From this story of 'using one's talents' the word took on the meaning 'natural aptitude or skill'.

talented > *adjective* having a natural aptitude or skill for something.

SYNONYMS – able, accomplished, gifted, skilful, skilled.

ANTONYMS – inept, talentless.

talisman /ˈtalɪzmən/ > *noun* (pl. **talismans**) an object thought to have magic powers and to bring good luck.

DERIVATIVES – **talismanic** /talɪzˈmannɪk/ *adjective.*

ORIGIN – apparently from an alteration of Greek *telesma* 'completion, religious rite'.

talk > *verb* **1** speak in order to give information or express ideas or feelings. **2** have the power of speech. **3** (**talk over** or **through**) discuss (something) thoroughly. **4** (**talk back**) reply defiantly or insolently. **5** (**talk down to**) speak patronisingly or condescendingly to. **6** (**talk round**) convince (someone) that they should adopt a particular point of view. **7** (**talk into** or **out of**) persuade or dissuade (someone) to or from. **8** reveal secret or private information. > *noun* **1** conversation; discussion. **2** an address or lecture. **3** (**talks**) formal discussions or negotiations over a period. **4** rumour, gossip, or speculation.

IDIOMS – **you can't** (or **can**) **talk** (also **look who's talking**) informal used to convey that a criticism made applies equally well to the person making it.

DERIVATIVES – **talker** *noun.*

COMBINATIONS – **talking book** a recorded reading of a book. **talking drum** each of a set of West African drums which are beaten to transmit a tonal language. **talking head** informal a presenter or reporter on television who addresses the camera and is viewed in close-up. **talking point** a topic that invites discussion or argument. **talking shop** Brit. a place or group regarded as a centre for unproductive talk rather than action. **talking-to** informal a sharp reprimand. **talk radio** chiefly N. Amer. a type of radio broadcast in which topical issues are discussed by the presenter and by listeners who phone in. **talk show** a chat show.

ORIGIN – related to TALE or TELL.

talkative > *adjective* fond of or given to talking.

DERIVATIVES – **talkatively** *adverb* **talkativeness** *noun.*

SYNONYMS – chatty, communicative, garrulous, loquacious, voluble.

ANTONYMS – taciturn.

talkback > *noun* **1** a system of two-way communication by loudspeaker. **2** another term for PHONE-IN.

talkfest > *noun* informal, chiefly N. Amer. a lengthy discussion or debate, especially as part of a television chat show.

talkie > *noun* informal a film with a soundtrack, as distinct from a silent film.

tall > *adjective* **1** of great or more than average

height. **2** measuring a specified distance from top to bottom. **3** fanciful and difficult to believe; unlikely: *a tall story.*

DERIVATIVES – **tallish** *adjective* **tallness** *noun.*

SYNONYMS – **1** big, high, towering.

ANTONYMS – **1** short, small.

COMBINATIONS – **a tall order** an unreasonable or difficult demand. **tall ship** a sailing ship with a high mast or masts.

ORIGIN – probably from Old English *getæl* 'swift, prompt'.

tallboy > *noun* Brit. a tall chest of drawers in two sections, one standing on the other.

tallow /tal**ō**/ > *noun* **1** a hard fatty substance made from rendered animal fat, used in making candles and soap. **2** (**vegetable tallow**) vegetable fat used for similar purposes.

COMBINATIONS – **tallow tree** a tree with fatty seeds from which vegetable tallow or other oils are extracted.

tally > *noun* (pl. **tallies**) **1** a current score or amount. **2** a record of a score or amount. **3** a particular number taken as a group or unit to facilitate counting. **4** a mark registering such a number. **5** (also **tally stick**) historical a piece of wood scored across with notches for the items of an account. > *verb* (**tallies**, **tallied**) **1** agree or correspond. **2** calculate the total number of.

COMBINATIONS – **tallyman** Brit. a person who sells goods on credit, especially from door to door.

ORIGIN – Old French *tallie*, from Latin *talea* 'twig, cutting'.

tally-ho > *exclamation* a huntsman's cry to the hounds on sighting a fox.

ORIGIN – apparently from French *taïaut.*

Talmud /tal**mŏod**/ > *noun* the body of Jewish civil and ceremonial law and legend.

DERIVATIVES – **Talmudic** *adjective* **Talmudist** *noun.*

ORIGIN – Hebrew, 'instruction'.

talon > *noun* a claw, especially one belonging to a bird of prey.

DERIVATIVES – **taloned** *adjective.*

ORIGIN – Old French, 'heel', from Latin *talus* 'ankle bone, heel'.

talus /**tay**ləss/ > *noun* (pl. **taluses**) **1** a sloping mass of rock fragments at the foot of a cliff. **2** the sloping side of an earthwork or tapering wall.

ORIGIN – French.

tam > *noun* a tam-o'-shanter.

tamagotchi /tamməgochi/ > *noun* trademark an electronic toy displaying a digital image of a creature, which has to be looked after by the 'owner' as if it were a pet.

ORIGIN – Japanese.

tamale /təmaali/ > *noun* a Mexican dish of seasoned meat and maize flour steamed or baked in maize husks.

ORIGIN – Mexican Spanish *tamal*, from Nahuatl.

tamari /təmaari/ > *noun* a variety of rich, naturally fermented soy sauce.

ORIGIN – Japanese.

tamarin /tammərin/ > *noun* a small forest-dwelling South American monkey.

ORIGIN – Carib.

tamarind /tammərind/ > *noun* sticky brown acidic pulp from the pod of a tropical African tree, used as a flavouring in Asian cookery.

ORIGIN – Latin *tamarindus*, from an Arabic word meaning 'Indian date'.

tamarisk /tammərisk/ > *noun* a shrub or small tree with tiny scale-like leaves borne on slender branches.

ORIGIN – Latin *tamariscus.*

tambala /tambaalə/ > *noun* (pl. same or **tambalas**) a monetary unit of Malawi, equal to one hundredth of a kwacha.

ORIGIN – Nyanja (a Bantu language), 'cockerel'.

tambour /tamboor/ > *noun* **1** historical a small drum. **2** a circular frame for holding fabric taut while it is being embroidered.

ORIGIN – French, 'drum'.

tambourine /tambəreen/ > *noun* a percussion instrument resembling a shallow drum with metal discs around the edge, played by being shaken or hit with the hand.

ORIGIN – French *tambourin*, from *tambour* 'drum'.

tame > *adjective* **1** (of an animal) not dangerous or frightened of people; domesticated. **2** not exciting or adventurous. **3** informal (of a person) willing to cooperate. > *verb* **1** domesticate (an animal). **2** make less powerful and easier to control.

DERIVATIVES – **tamely** *adverb* **tameness** *noun* **tamer** *noun.*

SYNONYMS – *adjective* **1** docile, domestic, domesticated. **2** bland, boring, insipid, safe, vapid. *verb* **1** break in, domesticate, train. **2** curb, discipline, humble, master, subdue.

ANTONYMS – *adjective* **1** fierce, wild.

Tamil /tammil/ > *noun* **1** a member of a people inhabiting parts of South India and Sri Lanka. **2** the Dravidian language of the Tamils.

ORIGIN – the name in Tamil.

Tammany /tamməni/ (also **Tammany Hall**) > *noun* N. Amer. a corrupt political organisation or group.

ORIGIN – from the name of a powerful organisation within the US Democratic Party that was widely associated with corruption and had headquarters at *Tammany* Hall, New York.

tam-o'-shanter /tamməshantər/ > *noun* a round Scottish cap with a bobble in the centre.

ORIGIN – named after the hero of Robert Burns's poem *Tam o' Shanter* (1790).

tamoxifen /təmoksifen/ > *noun* a synthetic drug used to treat breast cancer and infertility in women.

tamp > *verb* **1** pack (a blast hole) full of clay or sand to concentrate the force of the explosion. **2** firmly ram or pack (a substance) down or into something.

ORIGIN – probably from French *tampon.*

Tampax > *noun* (pl. same) trademark a sanitary tampon.

tamper > *verb* (**tamper with**) interfere with (something) without authority or so as to cause damage.

DERIVATIVES – **tamperer** *noun.*

SYNONYMS – (**tamper with**) doctor, fiddle with, interfere with, meddle with, tinker with.

ORIGIN – alteration of the verb TEMPER.

tampon > *noun* a plug of soft material inserted into the vagina to absorb menstrual blood.

ORIGIN – French, from *tapon* 'plug, stopper'.

tam-tam > *noun* a large metal gong.

ORIGIN – perhaps from the same Hindi word as TOM-TOM.

tan¹ > *noun* **1** a yellowish-brown colour. **2** a golden-brown shade of skin developed by pale-skinned people after exposure to the sun. **3** (also **tanbark**) bark of oak or other trees, used as a source of tannin for converting hides into leather. > *verb* (**tanned**, **tanning**) **1** give or acquire a tan after exposure to the sun. **2** convert (animal skin) into leather, especially by soaking in a liquid containing tannic acid. **3** informal, dated beat (someone) as a punishment.

ORIGIN – Old English, 'convert into leather'.

tan² > *abbreviation* tangent.

tanager /tannəjər/ > *noun* a brightly coloured American songbird of the bunting family.

ORIGIN – Tupi.

tandem > *noun* **1** a bicycle with seats and pedals for two riders, one behind the other. **2** a carriage drawn by two animals harnessed one in front of the other. > *adverb* one behind another.

IDIOMS – **in tandem 1** alongside each other; together. **2** one behind another.

ORIGIN – humorously from Latin *tandem* 'at length'.

tandoor /tandoor/ > *noun* a clay oven of a type used originally in northern India and Pakistan.

ORIGIN – Arabic, 'oven'.

tandoori /tandoori/ > *noun* a style of Indian cooking based on the use of a tandoor.

tang > *noun* **1** a strong taste, flavour, or smell. **2** the projection on the blade of a knife or other tool by which the blade is held firmly in the handle.

ORIGIN – Old Norse *tangi* 'point, tang of a knife'.

tanga /tanggə/ > *noun* Brit. a pair of briefs consisting of small panels connected by strings at the sides.

ORIGIN – first denoting a loincloth worn by indigenous peoples in tropical America: Portuguese, of Bantu origin.

tangelo /tanjəlō/ > *noun* (pl. **tangelos**) a hybrid of the tangerine and grapefruit.

ORIGIN – blend of **TANGERINE** and **POMELO**.

tangent /tanjənt/ > *noun* **1** a straight line or plane that touches a curve or curved surface at a point, but if extended does not cross it at that point. **2** Mathematics the trigonometric function that is equal to the ratio of the sides (other than the hypotenuse) opposite and adjacent to an angle in a right-angled triangle. **3** a completely different line of thought or action. > *adjective* (of a line or plane) touching, but not intersecting, a curve or curved surface.

DERIVATIVES – **tangency** *noun*.

ORIGIN – from Latin *tangere* 'to touch'.

tangential /tanjensh'l/ > *adjective* **1** relating to or along a tangent. **2** having only a slight connection or relevance; peripheral. **3** diverging from a previous course; erratic.

DERIVATIVES – **tangentially** *adverb*.

tangerine > *noun* **1** a small citrus fruit with a loose skin, especially one of a variety with deep orange-red skin. **2** a deep orange-red colour.

ORIGIN – from *Tanger* (former name of *Tangier*, from where the fruit was exported).

tangible /tanjib'l/ > *adjective* **1** perceptible by touch. **2** clear and definite; real.

DERIVATIVES – **tangibility** *noun* **tangibly** *adverb*.

SYNONYMS – **1** palpable, tactile, touchable. **2** actual, concrete, real, solid, substantial.

ORIGIN – Latin *tangibilis*, from *tangere* 'to touch'.

tangle > *verb* **1** twist (strands) together into a confused mass. **2** (**tangle with**) informal become involved in a conflict with. > *noun* **1** a confused mass of something twisted together. **2** a confused or complicated state; a muddle.

DERIVATIVES – **tangly** *adjective*.

ORIGIN – probably Scandinavian.

tango > *noun* (pl. **tangos**) **1** a ballroom dance originating in Buenos Aires, characterised by marked rhythms and postures and abrupt pauses. **2** a piece of music in the style of this dance. > *verb* (**tangoes**, **tangoed**) dance the tango.

ORIGIN – Latin American Spanish.

tangy > *adjective* (**tangier**, **tangiest**) having a strong, piquant flavour or smell.

tank > *noun* **1** a large receptacle or storage chamber, especially for liquid or gas. **2** the container holding the fuel supply in a motor vehicle. **3** a receptacle with transparent sides in which to keep fish; an aquarium. **4** a heavy armoured fighting vehicle carrying guns and moving on a continuous metal track. > *verb* **1** (**be** or **get tanked up**) informal drink heavily or become drunk. **2** US informal fail completely or disastrously.

DERIVATIVES – **tankful** *noun*.

COMBINATIONS – **tank engine** a steam locomotive with fuel and water tanks in its own frame, not in a tender.

ORIGIN – perhaps from a Gujarati or Marathi (a central Indian language) word meaning 'underground cistern'.

tankard > *noun* a tall beer mug, typically made of silver or pewter, with a handle and sometimes a hinged lid.

tanker > *noun* a ship, road vehicle, or aircraft for carrying liquids, especially mineral oils, in bulk.

tank top > *noun* a close-fitting sleeveless top worn over a shirt or blouse.

tanner¹ > *noun* a person employed to tan animal hides.

tanner² > *noun* Brit. informal, historical a sixpence.

tannery > *noun* (pl. **tanneries**) a place where animal hides are tanned.

tannic acid > *noun* another term for **TANNIN**.

tannin > *noun* a yellowish or brownish bitter-tasting organic substance present in tea and some grapes, galls, barks, etc.

DERIVATIVES – **tannic** *adjective*.

ORIGIN – French *tanin*, from *tan* 'tanbark'.

tannoy Brit. > *noun* trademark a type of public address system.

ORIGIN – contraction of *tantalum alloy*, which is used as a rectifier in the system.

tansy > *noun* a plant with yellow flat-topped button-like flower heads.

ORIGIN – Old French *tanesie*, probably from Latin *athanasia* 'immortality'.

tantalise (also **tantalize**) > *verb* torment or tease (someone) with the sight or promise of something that is unobtainable or withheld.

DERIVATIVES – **tantalising** *adjective* **tantalisingly** *adverb*.

ORIGIN – from *Tantalus* in Greek mythology, who was punished for his crimes by being provided with fruit and water which receded when he reached for them.

tantalum /tantələm/ > *noun* a hard, silver-grey metallic chemical element.

ORIGIN – from *Tantalus* (see **TANTALISE**), with reference to its frustrating insolubility in acids.

tantalus /tantələss/ > *noun* Brit. a stand in which spirit decanters may be locked up though still visible.

ORIGIN – from *Tantalus* (see **TANTALISE**).

tantamount > *adjective* (**tantamount to**) equivalent in seriousness to; virtually the same as.

ORIGIN – from the earlier verb *tantamount* 'amount to as much', from Italian *tanto montare*.

tantra /tantrə/ > *noun* **1** a Hindu or Buddhist mystical or magical text. **2** adherence to the doctrines or principles of the tantras, involving mantras, meditation, yoga, and ritual.

DERIVATIVES – **tantric** *adjective* **tantrism** *noun*.

ORIGIN – Sanskrit, 'loom, groundwork, doctrine'.

tantrum > *noun* an uncontrolled outburst of anger and frustration, typically in a young child.

Tanzanian /tanzəneeən/ > *noun* a person from Tanzania, a country in East Africa. > *adjective* relating to Tanzania.

Taoiseach /teeshəkh/ > *noun* the Prime Minister of the Irish Republic.

ORIGIN – Irish, 'chief, leader'.

Taoism /towiz'm/ > *noun* a Chinese philosophy based on the interpretation of the writer Lao-Tzu (6th century BC) of the Tao, or fundamental principle underlying the universe, incorporating the principles of yin and yang and advocating humility and religious piety.

DERIVATIVES – **Taoist** *noun* & *adjective*.

ORIGIN – from Chinese *tao* 'the right way'.

tap¹ > *noun* **1** a device by which a flow of liquid or gas from a pipe or container can be controlled. **2** an instrument for cutting a threaded hole in a material. **3** a device connected to a telephone for listening secretly to conversations. **4** Brit. a taproom. > *verb* (**tapped**, **tapping**) **1** draw liquid through the tap or spout of (a cask, barrel, etc.). **2** draw sap from (a tree) by cutting into it. **3** exploit or draw a supply from (a resource). **4** informal obtain money or information from. **5** connect a device to (a telephone) so that conversations can be listened to secretly. **6** cut a thread in (something) to accept a screw.

IDIOMS – **on tap 1** ready to be poured from a tap. **2** informal freely available whenever needed. **3** N. Amer. informal on schedule to occur.

COMBINATIONS – **taproom** a room in a pub or hotel where beer is available on tap.

ORIGIN – Old English, 'stopper for a cask'.

tap² > *verb* (**tapped**, **tapping**) **1** strike or knock with a quick, light blow or blows. **2** strike lightly and repeatedly against something else. **3** US informal designate or select for a task or honour. > *noun* **1** a quick, light blow or the sound of such a blow. **2** tap dancing. **3** a piece of metal attached to the toe and heel of a tap dancer's shoe to make a tapping sound.

DERIVATIVES – **tapper** *noun*.

SYNONYMS – *verb* **1,2** knock, pat, rap. *noun* **1** knock, pat, rap.

tapas /**tapp**əss/ > *plural noun* small Spanish savoury dishes, typically served with drinks at a bar.

ORIGIN – Spanish, 'cover, lid' (because the dishes were formerly given free with the drink, served on a dish balanced on the glass).

tap dance > *noun* a dance performed wearing shoes fitted with metal taps, characterised by rhythmical tapping of the toes and heels. > *verb* (**tap-dance**) perform such a dance.

DERIVATIVES – **tap dancer** *noun* **tap-dancing** *noun*.

tape > *noun* **1** light, flexible material in a narrow strip, used to hold, fasten, or mark off something. **2** (also **adhesive tape**) a strip of paper or plastic coated with adhesive, used to stick things together. **3** long, narrow material with magnetic properties, used for recording sound, pictures, or computer data. **4** a cassette or reel containing such material. > *verb* **1** record (sound or pictures) on audio or video tape. **2** fasten, attach, or mark off with tape.

COMBINATIONS – **tape deck** a piece of equipment for playing audio tapes, as part of a stereo system. **tape measure** a length of tape marked at graded intervals for measuring.

ORIGIN – Old English; perhaps related to Low German *teppen* 'pluck, tear'.

tapenade /**tapp**ənaad/ > *noun* a Provençal savoury paste or dip made from black olives, capers, and anchovies.

ORIGIN – French, from Provençal.

taper > *verb* **1** diminish or reduce in thickness towards one end. **2** (**taper off**) gradually lessen. > *noun* a slender tapered candle, used for conveying a flame.

ORIGIN – Old English, formed, by alteration of *p-* to *t-*, from Latin *papyrus* 'papyrus plant', the pith of which was used for candle wicks.

tape recorder > *noun* an apparatus for recording sounds on magnetic tape and afterwards reproducing them.

DERIVATIVES – **tape-record** *verb* **tape recording** *noun*.

tapestry > *noun* (pl. **tapestries**) a piece of thick textile fabric with pictures or designs formed by weaving coloured weft threads or by embroidering on canvas.

DERIVATIVES – **tapestried** *adjective*.

ORIGIN – Old French *tapisserie*, from *tapis* 'carpet'.

tapeworm > *noun* a parasitic flatworm with a long ribbon-like body, the adult of which lives in the intestines.

tapioca /tappiŌkə/ > *noun* a starchy substance in the form of hard white grains, obtained from cassava and used for puddings and other dishes.

ORIGIN – from a Tupi-Guarani word meaning 'squeezed-out dregs'.

tapir /**tay**pər, **tay**peer/ > *noun* a hoofed mammal with a short, flexible proboscis, native to tropical America and Malaysia.

ORIGIN – Tupi.

tappet > *noun* a lever or projecting part on a machine which intermittently makes contact with a cam or other part so as to give or receive motion.

ORIGIN – from **TAP²**.

taproot > *noun* a straight, tapering root growing vertically downwards, from which subsidiary rootlets spring.

tapu /**taa**poo/ > *adjective* **NZ** forbidden; taboo.

ORIGIN – Maori.

tar¹ > *noun* **1** a dark, thick flammable liquid distilled from wood or coal, used in road-making and for coating and preserving timber. **2** a similar substance formed by burning tobacco or other material. > *verb* (**tarred**, **tarring**) cover with tar.

IDIOMS – **tar and feather** smear with tar and then cover with feathers as a punishment. **tar with the same brush** consider to have the same faults.

COMBINATIONS – **tar baby** informal a difficult problem which is made worse by attempts to solve it. [ORIGIN – with allusion to the doll smeared with tar as a trap for Brer Rabbit, in J. C. Harris's *Uncle Remus: His Songs and His Sayings* (1880).]

tar² > *noun* informal, dated a sailor.

ORIGIN – perhaps an abbreviation of **TARPAULIN**, used as a nickname for a sailor.

tarakihi /tarrəkeehi/ > *noun* a silver marine fish with a black band behind the head, caught off New Zealand coasts.

ORIGIN – Maori.

taramasalata /tarrəməsəlaatə/ (also **tarama** /tarrəmə/) > *noun* a paste or dip made from fish roe, mixed with olive oil and seasoning.

ORIGIN – from modern Greek *taramas* 'roe' + *salata* 'salad'.

tarantella /tarrəntellə/ (also **tarantelle** /tarrəntel/) > *noun* a rapid whirling dance originating in southern Italy.

tarantula /tərantyoolə/ > *noun* **1** a very large hairy spider found chiefly in tropical and subtropical America. **2** a large black wolf spider of southern Europe.

wordpower facts

Tarantula

The word **tarantula** comes from the name of the seaport *Taranto* in southern Italy. It was first applied to the smaller European tarantula spider rather than to the huge, hairy tropical creature that most people think of as a tarantula. The bite of the tarantula (which is in fact fairly harmless) was formerly regarded as very dangerous. From time to time between the 15th and 17th centuries a psychological illness characterised by an extreme impulse to dance swept through southern Italy: this became known as *tarantism*, either because it was ascribed to the spider's bite or because dancing until exhausted was thought to alleviate the bite's effects. The rapid whirling dance the *tarantella* gained its name for similar reasons.

tardy > *adjective* (**tardier**, **tardiest**) **1** delaying or delayed beyond the right or expected time; late. **2** slow in action or response.

DERIVATIVES – **tardily** *adverb* **tardiness** *noun*.

ORIGIN – Latin *tardus* 'slow'.

tare¹ /tair/ > *noun* **1** the common vetch. **2** (**tares**) (in biblical use) a weed that resembles corn when young.

tare² /tair/ > *noun* **1** an allowance made for the weight of the packaging in determining the net weight of goods. **2** the weight of a vehicle without its fuel or load.

ORIGIN – French, 'deficiency, tare', from an Arabic word meaning 'reject, deduct'.

target* > *noun* **1** a person, object, or place selected as the aim of an attack. **2** a board marked with concentric circles, aimed at in archery or shooting. **3** an objective or result towards which efforts are directed. > *verb* (**targeted**, **targeting**) **1** select as an object of attention or attack. **2** aim or direct.

IDIOMS – **on** (or **off**) **target** succeeding (or not succeeding) in hitting or achieving the thing aimed at.

DERIVATIVES – **targetable** *adjective*.

*****SPELLING – note that **targeted** and **targeting** have only a single *t* in the middle.

SYNONYMS – *noun* **3** aim, goal, objective. *verb* **2** aim, direct, focus, level, position.

tariff > *noun* **1** a tax or duty to be paid on a particular class of imports or exports. **2** a table of the fixed charges made by a business, especially in a hotel or restaurant. **3** Law a scale of sentences and damages for crimes and injuries of different severities.

> *verb* fix the price of (something) according to a tariff.

ORIGIN – Italian *tariffa*, from an Arabic word meaning 'notify'.

tarmac > *noun* (trademark in the UK) **1** material used for surfacing roads or other outdoor areas, consisting of broken stone mixed with tar. **2** a runway or other area surfaced with such material. > *verb* (**tarmacked**, **tarmacking**) surface with tarmac.

ORIGIN – abbreviation of earlier *tarmacadam*, from TAR¹ + MACADAM.

tarn > *noun* a small mountain lake.

ORIGIN – northern English dialect: from Old Norse *tjǫrn*.

tarnation > *noun & exclamation* chiefly N. Amer. used as a euphemism for 'damnation'.

tarnish > *verb* **1** lose or cause to lose lustre, especially as a result of exposure to air or moisture. **2** make or become less valuable or respected. > *noun* **1** a film or stain formed on an exposed surface of a mineral or metal. **2** dullness of colour; loss of brightness.

DERIVATIVES – **tarnishable** *adjective*.

SYNONYMS – *verb* **2** besmirch, sully, taint.

ORIGIN – French *ternir*, from *terne* 'dark, dull'.

taro /taarō/ > *noun* a tropical Asian plant with edible starchy corms and fleshy leaves, grown as a staple in the Pacific.

ORIGIN – Polynesian.

tarot /tarrō/ > *noun* a set of playing cards with a special suit of trumps, used for fortune telling and games.

ORIGIN – French, from Italian *tarocchi*.

tarpaulin /taarpawlin/ > *noun* **1** heavy-duty waterproof cloth, originally of tarred canvas. **2** a sheet or covering of this.

ORIGIN – probably from TAR¹ + PALL¹ + -ING¹.

tarpon /taarpon/ > *noun* a large tropical marine fish of herring-like appearance.

ORIGIN – probably from Dutch *tarpoen*.

tarragon /tarrəgən/ > *noun* a plant with narrow aromatic leaves, used as a herb in cooking.

ORIGIN – Latin *tragonia* and *tarchon*, perhaps via Arabic from Greek *drakōn* 'dragon'.

tarry¹ /taari/ > *adjective* of, like, or covered with tar.

DERIVATIVES – **tarriness** *noun*.

tarry² /tarri/ > *verb* (**tarries**, **tarried**) archaic stay longer than intended; delay leaving a place.

tarsal /taars'l/ Anatomy & Zoology > *adjective* relating to the tarsus. > *noun* a bone of the tarsus.

tarsier /taarsiər/ > *noun* a small tree-dwelling insectivorous primate with very large eyes, a long tufted tail, and very long hindlimbs, native to the islands of SE Asia.

ORIGIN – French, from *tarse* 'tarsus', with reference to the animal's long tarsal bones.

tarsus /taarsəss/ > *noun* (pl. **tarsi** /taarsī/) **1** the group of small bones in the ankle and upper foot. **2** Zoology the shank of the leg of a bird or reptile.

ORIGIN – Greek *tarsos* 'flat of the foot, the eyelid'.

tart¹ > *noun* an open pastry case containing a sweet or savoury filling.

DERIVATIVES – **tartlet** *noun*.

ORIGIN – Old French *tarte*.

tart² informal > *noun* derogatory a prostitute or promiscuous woman. > *verb* **1** (**tart oneself up**) chiefly Brit. dress or make oneself up in order to look attractive. **2** (**tart up**) decorate or improve the appearance of.

ORIGIN – probably from SWEETHEART.

tart³ > *adjective* **1** sharp or acid in taste. **2** (of a remark or tone of voice) cutting, bitter, or sarcastic.

DERIVATIVES – **tartly** *adverb* **tartness** *noun*.

ORIGIN – Old English, 'harsh, severe'.

tartan > *noun* a woollen cloth woven in one of several patterns of coloured checks and intersecting lines, especially of a design associated with a particular Scottish clan.

ORIGIN – perhaps from Old French *tertaine*, denoting a kind of cloth; there may be a connection with *tartarin*, a rich fabric formerly imported from the east through the ancient region of Tartary, in Asia and eastern Europe.

Tartar /taartər/ > *noun* **1** historical a member of the combined forces of central Asian peoples, including Mongols and Turks, who conquered much of Asia and eastern Europe in the 13th century. **2** (**tartar**) a harsh, fierce, or intractable person.

ORIGIN – from *Tatar*, the local name of a tribe formerly living in parts of Russia and Ukraine.

tartar /taartər/ > *noun* **1** a hard calcified deposit that forms on the teeth and contributes to their decay. **2** a deposit of impure potassium hydrogen tartrate formed during the fermentation of wine.

IDIOMS – **cream of tartar** potassium hydrogen tartrate, an acidic crystalline compound used in baking powder.

ORIGIN – Greek *tartaron*.

tartare /taartaar/ > *adjective* (of fish or meat) served raw, typically seasoned and shaped into small cakes: *steak tartare*.

COMBINATIONS – **tartare sauce** (also **tartar sauce**) a cold sauce, typically eaten with fish, consisting of mayonnaise mixed with chopped onions, gherkins, and capers.

ORIGIN – French, 'Tartar'.

tartaric acid > *noun* Chemistry a crystalline organic acid present especially in unripe grapes and used in baking powder and as a food additive.

tartrate /taartrayt/ > *noun* Chemistry a salt or ester of tartaric acid.

tartrazine /taartrəzeen/ > *noun* Chemistry a brilliant yellow synthetic dye derived from tartaric acid and used to colour food, drugs, and cosmetics.

tarty > *adjective* (**tartier**, **tartiest**) informal (of a woman or her clothing) sexually provocative in a way considered to be in bad taste.

DERIVATIVES – **tartily** *adverb* **tartiness** *noun*.

Tarzan > *noun* a very strong and agile man.

ORIGIN – from the name of a fictitious character, created by the American writer Edgar Rice Burroughs (1875–1950), who is reared by apes in the African jungle.

tash (also **tache**) > *noun* informal a moustache.

task > *noun* a piece of work. > *verb* **1** (**task with**) assign (a particular task) to. **2** make great demands on.

IDIOMS – **take to task** reprimand or criticise (someone).

SYNONYMS – *noun* chore, duty, job.

COMBINATIONS – **task force 1** an armed force organised for a special operation. **2** a unit specially organised for a task.

ORIGIN – Old French *tasche*, from Latin *taxare* 'censure, charge'.

taskmaster > *noun* a person who imposes a demanding workload on someone.

Tasmanian /tazmayniən/ > *noun* a person from the Australian state of Tasmania. > *adjective* relating to Tasmania.

COMBINATIONS – **Tasmanian devil** a mainly black marsupial with a large head and powerful jaws, found only in Tasmania and eating mainly carrion.

tassel > *noun* **1** a tuft of hanging threads, knotted together at one end and used for decoration in soft furnishing and clothing. **2** the tufted head of some plants.

DERIVATIVES – **tasselled** *adjective*.

ORIGIN – Old French, 'clasp'.

taste > *noun* **1** the sensation of flavour perceived in the mouth on contact with a substance. **2** the faculty of perceiving this. **3** a small portion of food or drink taken as a sample. **4** a brief experience of something. **5** a person's liking for something. **6** the ability to discern what is of good quality or of a high aesthetic standard. **7** conformity to a specified degree with generally held views on what is appropriate or offensive: *a joke in bad taste*. > *verb* **1** perceive or experience the flavour of. **2** have a specified flavour. **3** sample or test the flavour of. **4** eat or drink a small portion of. **5** have a brief experience of.

WORDFINDER – gustatory (*relating to tasting or the sense of taste*).

IDIOMS – **to taste** according to personal liking.

DERIVATIVES – **tasting** *noun*.

COMBINATIONS – **taste bud** any of the clusters of nerve endings on the tongue and in the lining of the mouth which provide the sense of taste.

ORIGIN – Old French *taster* 'touch, try, taste', perhaps based on a blend of Latin *tangere* 'to touch' and *gustare* 'to taste'.

tasteful > *adjective* showing good aesthetic judgement or appropriate behaviour.

DERIVATIVES – **tastefully** *adverb* **tastefulness** *noun*.

SYNONYMS – cultivated, discriminating, refined.

tasteless > *adjective* 1 lacking flavour. 2 lacking in aesthetic judgement or constituting inappropriate behaviour.

DERIVATIVES – **tastelessly** *adverb* **tastelessness** *noun*.

SYNONYMS – 1 bland, flavourless, insipid. 2 garish, tawdry, uncouth, vulgar.

taster > *noun* 1 a person who tests food or drink by tasting it. 2 a sample or brief experience of something.

tasty > *adjective* (**tastier, tastiest**) 1 (of food) having a pleasant, distinct flavour. 2 informal, chiefly Brit. attractive; appealing.

DERIVATIVES – **tastily** *adverb* **tastiness** *noun*.

tat > *noun* Brit. informal tasteless or shoddy articles.

ORIGIN – probably from **TATTY**.

tater /**tay**tər/ (Brit. also **tatie** /**tay**ti/) > *noun* informal a potato.

tatterdemalion /tatərdim**ayl**iən/ > *noun* a person in tattered clothing. > *adjective* tattered or dilapidated.

ORIGIN – from **TATTERS** or **TATTERED**: the ending remains unexplained.

tattered > *adjective* old and torn; in poor condition.

tatters > *plural noun* irregularly torn pieces of cloth, paper, etc.

IDIOMS – **in tatters** informal 1 torn; in shreds. 2 destroyed; ruined.

SYNONYMS – rags, scraps, shreds.

ORIGIN – Old Norse *tǫtrar* 'rags'.

tattersall /**tatt**ərsawl/ > *noun* a woollen fabric with a pattern of coloured checks and intersecting lines, resembling a tartan.

ORIGIN – named after *Tattersalls*, a firm of horse auctioneers, by association with the traditional design of horse blankets.

tatting > *noun* 1 a kind of knotted lace made by hand with a small shuttle. 2 the process of making such lace.

tattle > *noun* gossip; idle talk. > *verb* engage in tattle.

DERIVATIVES – **tattler** *noun*.

ORIGIN – Middle Flemish *tatelen, tateren*.

tattletale US > *noun* a telltale. > *verb* tell tales.

tattoo¹ > *noun* (pl. **tattoos**) 1 an evening drum or bugle signal recalling soldiers to their quarters. 2 a military display consisting of music, marching, and exercises. 3 a rhythmic tapping or drumming.

ORIGIN – from Dutch *taptoe!* 'close the tap of the cask!'.

tattoo² > *verb* (**tattoos, tattooed**) mark with an indelible design by inserting pigment into punctures in the skin. > *noun* (pl. **tattoos**) a design made in such a way.

DERIVATIVES – **tattooer** *noun* **tattooist** *noun*.

ORIGIN – Polynesian.

tatty > *adjective* (**tattier, tattiest**) informal worn and shabby; in poor condition.

DERIVATIVES – **tattily** *adverb* **tattiness** *noun*.

ORIGIN – from Old English *tættec* 'rag'.

tau > /tow, taw/ > *noun* the nineteenth letter of the Greek alphabet (Τ, τ), transliterated as 't'.

ORIGIN – Greek.

taught past and past participle of TEACH.

taunt > *noun* a jeering or mocking remark made in order to wound or provoke. > *verb* provoke or wound with taunts.

DERIVATIVES – **taunter** *noun* **taunting** *adjective* **tauntingly** *adverb*.

SYNONYMS – *noun* insult, jeer, jibe, sneer. *verb* insult, jeer at, sneer at.

ORIGIN – from French *tant pour tant* 'like for like, tit for tat', from *tant* 'so much', from Latin *tantus*.

taupe /tōp/ > *noun* a grey colour tinged with brown.

ORIGIN – French, 'mole, moleskin'.

taurine¹ /**taw**reen/ > *noun* Biochemistry a sulphur-containing amino acid important in the metabolism of fats.

ORIGIN – from Greek *tauros* 'bull' (because it was originally obtained from ox bile).

taurine² /**taw**rīn/ > *adjective* 1 of or like a bull. 2 relating to bullfighting.

ORIGIN – Latin *taurinus*, from *taurus* 'bull'.

Taurus /**taw**rəss/ > *noun* 1 Astronomy a constellation (the Bull), said to represent a bull tamed by Jason (a hero of Greek mythology). 2 Astrology the second sign of the zodiac, which the sun enters about 21 April.

DERIVATIVES – **Taurean** /taw**ree**ən/ *noun* & *adjective*.

ORIGIN – Latin, 'bull'.

taut > *adjective* 1 stretched or pulled tight. 2 (of muscles or nerves) tense. 3 (of writing, music, etc.) concise and controlled. 4 (of a ship) having a disciplined crew.

DERIVATIVES – **tauten** *verb* **tautly** *adverb* **tautness** *noun*.

ORIGIN – from *tought* 'distended', perhaps originally a variant of TOUGH.

tautology /taw**toll**əji/ > *noun* (pl. **tautologies**) the unnecessary repetition within a statement of the same thing in different words.

DERIVATIVES – **tautological** *adjective* **tautologist** *noun* **tautologous** *adjective*.

ORIGIN – Greek *tautologos*, from *tauto-* 'same' + *logos* 'word, telling'.

tavern > *noun* chiefly archaic or N. Amer. an inn or public house.

ORIGIN – Old French *taverne*, from Latin *taberna* 'hut, tavern'.

taverna /tə**ver**nə/ > *noun* a small Greek restaurant.

ORIGIN – modern Greek.

tawa /**taa**wə/ > *noun* a tall New Zealand forest tree, which bears damson-like fruit.

ORIGIN – Maori.

tawdry > *adjective* (**tawdrier, tawdriest**) 1 showy but cheap and of poor quality. 2 sordid; sleazy.

DERIVATIVES – **tawdriness** *noun*.

---

wordpower facts
Tawdry

Tawdry is short for *tawdry lace*, a kind of fine silk lace or ribbon worn as a necklace in the 16th and 17th centuries. The word is a contraction of *Saint Audrey's lace*, named after St Audrey (died 679), the patron saint of Ely: *Audrey* was a later form of the Old English name *Etheldrida*. St Audrey, the daughter of a king of East Anglia, built a monastery on the site of the present Ely Cathedral. She is said to have died of a tumour of the neck, which she considered to be retribution for her liking for necklaces in her youth. 'Tawdry laces' were sold at the fairs held every year in her memory, along with other items of clothing and decoration: much of the merchandise would have been of low quality, a fact which gave rise to the negative associations of the word **tawdry**.

---

tawny > *adjective* (**tawnier, tawniest**) of an orange-brown or yellowish-brown colour. > *noun* this colour.

DERIVATIVES – **tawniness** *noun*.

COMBINATIONS – **tawny owl** a common owl with reddish-brown or grey plumage, and a quavering hoot.

ORIGIN – Old French *tane*, from *tan* 'tanbark'; related to TAN¹.

tax > *noun* 1 a compulsory contribution to state revenue, levied by the government on personal income and business profits or added to the cost of some goods, services, and transactions. 2 a strain or heavy demand. > *verb* 1 impose a tax on. 2 pay tax on (a vehicle). 3 make heavy demands on. 4 charge with a fault or wrongdoing.

WORDFINDER – fiscal (*relating to taxes*).

DERIVATIVES – **taxable** *adjective*.

SYNONYMS – *noun* **2** burden, demand, strain. *verb* **3** encumber, overload, strain, weigh down. **4** accuse, call to account.

COMBINATIONS – **tax avoidance** Brit. the arrangement of one's financial affairs to minimise tax liability within the law. **tax break** informal a tax concession or advantage allowed by government. **tax-deductible** permitted to be deducted from taxable income. **tax disc** Brit. a circular label displayed on the windscreen of a vehicle, certifying payment of road tax. **tax evasion** the illegal non-payment or underpayment of tax. **tax exile** a person with a high taxable income who chooses to live in a country or area with low rates of taxation. **tax haven** a country or autonomous area where taxes are levied at a low rate. **tax return** a form on which a taxpayer makes a statement of income and personal circumstances, used to assess liability for tax. **tax year** a year as reckoned for taxation (in Britain from 6 April).

ORIGIN – from Latin *taxare* 'to censure, charge, compute'.

taxa plural of TAXON.

taxation > *noun* **1** the levying of tax. **2** money paid as tax.

taxi > *noun* (pl. **taxis**) a motor vehicle licensed to transport passengers in return for payment of a fare. > *verb* (**taxies, taxied, taxiing** or **taxying**) **1** (of an aircraft) move slowly along the ground before take-off or after landing. **2** travel in a taxi.

COMBINATIONS – **taxi rank** (N. Amer. **taxi stand**) a place where taxis park while waiting to be hired.

ORIGIN – abbreviation of *taxicab* or *taximeter cab* (see TAXIMETER).

taxicab > *noun* a taxi.

taxidermy /taksidermi/ > *noun* the art of preparing, stuffing, and mounting the skins of animals so that they appear lifelike.

DERIVATIVES – **taxidermist** noun.

ORIGIN – from Greek *taxis* 'arrangement' + *derma* 'skin'.

taximeter > *noun* a device used in taxis that automatically records the distance travelled and the fare payable.

ORIGIN – French *taximètre*, from *taxe* 'tariff' + *mètre* 'meter'.

taxing > *adjective* physically or mentally demanding.

SYNONYMS – arduous, exacting, onerous, strenuous.

taxiway > *noun* a route along which an aircraft taxies when moving to or from a runway.

taxman > *noun* informal an inspector or collector of taxes.

taxon /taksən/ > *noun* (pl. **taxa** /taksə/) Biology a taxonomic group of any rank, such as a family, genus, or species.

taxonomy /taksonnəmi/ > *noun* chiefly Biology **1** the branch of science concerned with classification. **2** a scheme of classification.

DERIVATIVES – **taxonomic** adjective **taxonomical** adjective **taxonomist** noun.

ORIGIN – from Greek *taxis* 'arrangement' + *-nomia* 'distribution'.

tayberry > *noun* (pl. **tayberries**) a dark red soft fruit produced by crossing a blackberry and a raspberry.

ORIGIN – named after the River *Tay* in Scotland, near where it was introduced.

TB > *abbreviation* tubercle bacillus or tuberculosis.

Tb > *symbol* the chemical element terbium.

t.b.a. > *abbreviation* to be announced.

tbsp (also **tbs**) (pl. same or **tbsps**) > *abbreviation* tablespoonful.

Tc > *symbol* the chemical element technetium.

TCP/IP > *abbreviation* Computing, trademark transmission control protocol/Internet protocol, used to govern the connection of computer systems to the Internet.

TD > *abbreviation* **1** (in the Republic of Ireland) Teachta Dála, Member of the Dáil. **2** technical drawing. **3** (in the UK) Territorial (Officer's) Decoration.

Te > *symbol* the chemical element tellurium.

te (N. Amer. **ti**) > *noun* Music the seventh note of a major scale, coming after 'lah'.

ORIGIN – alteration of SI, adopted to avoid having two notes (*soh* and *si*) beginning with the same letter.

tea > *noun* **1** a hot drink made by infusing the dried, crushed leaves of the tea plant in boiling water. **2** the dried leaves used to make tea. **3** the evergreen shrub or small tree which produces these leaves, native to south and east Asia. **4** a drink made from the leaves, fruits, or flowers of other plants. **5** chiefly Brit. a light afternoon meal consisting of sandwiches, cakes, etc., with tea to drink. **6** Brit. a cooked evening meal.

COMBINATIONS – **tea bag** a small porous sachet containing tea leaves, on to which boiling water is poured in order to make tea. **tea bread** a type of cake containing dried fruit that has been soaked in tea before baking. **tea break** Brit. a short rest period during the working day. **tea ceremony** an elaborate Japanese ritual of serving and drinking tea, as an expression of Zen Buddhist philosophy. **tea chest** a light metal-lined wooden box in which tea is transported. **tea cloth** a tea towel. **tea cosy** a thick or padded cover placed over a teapot to keep the tea hot. **tea dance** an afternoon tea with dancing. **tea lady** Brit. a woman employed to make and serve tea in a workplace. **tea leaf 1** (**tea leaves**) dried leaves of tea. **2** Brit. rhyming slang a thief. **tea room** a small restaurant or cafe where tea and other light refreshments are served. **tea rose** a garden rose having flowers that are pale yellow tinged with pink, and a delicate scent resembling that of tea. **tea set** a set of crockery for serving tea. **tea towel** chiefly Brit. a cloth for drying washed crockery, cutlery, and glasses.

ORIGIN – probably Malay, from Chinese *te*; related to CHAR³.

teacake > *noun* Brit. a light yeast-based sweet bun containing dried fruit, typically served toasted and buttered.

teach > *verb* (past and past participle **taught**) **1** impart knowledge to or instruct in how to do something, especially in a school or as part of a recognised programme. **2** give instruction in (a subject or skill). **3** cause to learn by example or experience. **4** advocate as a practice or principle.

WORDFINDER – pedagogy (*the profession, science, or theory of teaching*).

DERIVATIVES – **teachable** adjective **teaching** noun.

SYNONYMS – **1** educate, instruct, train, tutor. **3** demonstrate, guide, show.

COMBINATIONS – **teaching hospital** a hospital affiliated to a medical school, in which medical students receive training.

ORIGIN – Old English, 'show, present, point out'.

teacher > *noun* a person who teaches in a school.

DERIVATIVES – **teacherly** adjective.

Teachta Dála /tyokhtə dawlə/ > *noun* (pl. **Teachti** /tyokhti/) (in the Republic of Ireland) a member of the Dáil or lower House of Parliament.

ORIGIN – Irish.

teacup > *noun* a cup from which tea is drunk.

teak > *noun* hard, durable wood used in shipbuilding and for making furniture, obtained from a large deciduous tree native to India and SE Asia.

ORIGIN – Portuguese *teca*, from Tamil.

teal > *noun* **1** a small freshwater duck, typically with a bright blue-green patch on the wing plumage. **2** (also **teal blue**) a dark greenish-blue colour.

team > *noun* **1** a group of players forming one side in a competitive game or sport. **2** two or more people working together. **3** two or more horses harnessed together to pull a vehicle. > *verb* **1** (**team up**) come together as a team to achieve a common goal. **2** (**team with**) match or coordinate with.

COMBINATIONS – **teammate** a fellow member of a team. **team player** a person who plays or works well as a member of a team. **team spirit** feelings of camaraderie among the members of a team. **teamwork** the combined effective action of a group.

ORIGIN – Old English, 'team of draught animals'; related to TEEM¹ and TOW¹.

teamster > *noun* **1** N. Amer. a truck driver. **2** a driver of a team of animals.

teapot > *noun* a pot with a handle, spout, and lid, in which tea is prepared.

tear¹ /tair/ > *verb* (past **tore**; past participle **torn**) **1** rip a hole or split in. **2** (usu. **tear up**) pull or rip apart or to pieces. **3** damage (a muscle or ligament) by overstretching it. **4** (usu. **tear down**) energetically demolish or destroy. **5** (**tear apart**) disrupt and force apart. **6** (**be torn**) be in a state of conflict and uncertainty between two opposing options or parties. **7** (**tear oneself away**) leave despite a strong desire to stay. **8** move very quickly and in a reckless or excited manner. **9** (**tear into**) attack verbally. > *noun* a hole or split caused by tearing.
IDIOMS – **tear one's hair out** informal feel extreme desperation. **tear someone off a strip** (or **tear a strip off someone**) Brit. informal rebuke someone angrily. **that's torn it** Brit. informal said to express dismay when something has happened to disrupt someone's plans.
DERIVATIVES – **tearable** *adjective*.
SYNONYMS – *verb* **1** gash, lacerate, slash, shred. **4** (**tear down**) bulldoze, flatten, level, raze. **5** (**tear apart**) divide, rupture, sever. *noun* cut, rip, slash.

tear² /teer/ > *noun* a drop of clear salty liquid secreted from glands in a person's eye when they are crying or the eye is irritated.
WORDFINDER – lachrymal (*related to weeping or tears*).
IDIOMS – **in tears** crying.
DERIVATIVES – **teary** *adjective*.
COMBINATIONS – **tear duct** a passage through which tears pass from the lachrymal glands to the eye or from the eye to the nose. **tear gas** gas that causes severe irritation to the eyes, used in warfare and riot control. **tear-jerker** informal a story, film, or song that is calculated to evoke sadness or sympathy.

tearaway > *noun* Brit. a person who behaves in a wild or reckless manner.

teardrop > *noun* **1** a single tear. **2** (before another noun) shaped like a tear.

tearful > *adjective* **1** crying or inclined to cry. **2** causing tears; sad.
DERIVATIVES – **tearfully** *adverb* **tearfulness** *noun*.
SYNONYMS – **1** close to tears, sobbing, weeping, weepy; formal or literary lachrymose.

tearing /tairing/ > *adjective* violent; extreme: *a tearing hurry*.

tearless > *adjective* not crying.
DERIVATIVES – **tearlessly** *adverb*.

tease > *verb* **1** playfully make fun of or attempt to provoke. **2** tempt (someone) sexually. **3** gently pull or comb (tangled wool, hair, etc.) into separate strands. **4** archaic comb (the surface of woven cloth) to raise a nap. **5** (**tease out**) find out by searching through a mass of information. > *noun* informal **1** an act of teasing. **2** a person who teases.
DERIVATIVES – **teasing** *adjective* & *noun* **teasingly** *adverb*.
SYNONYMS – *verb* **1** chaff, deride, make fun of, mock, ridicule.
ORIGIN – Old English, related to TEASEL. Compare with HECKLE.

teasel (also **teazle** or **teazel**) > *noun* **1** a tall prickly plant with spiny purple flower heads. **2** a dried head from a teasel, or a similar man-made device, used to raise a nap on woven cloth. > *verb* chiefly archaic raise a nap on (cloth) with a teasel.
ORIGIN – Old English, related to TEASE.

teaser > *noun* **1** a person who teases others. **2** informal a tricky question or task.

teaspoon > *noun* a small spoon used for adding sugar to and stirring hot drinks or for eating some foods.

teat > *noun* **1** a nipple of the mammary gland of a female mammal. **2** Brit. a perforated plastic nipple-shaped device by which an infant or young animal can suck milk from a bottle.
ORIGIN – Old French *tete*.

tea tree > *noun* **1** an Australasian flowering shrub or small tree with leaves that are sometimes used for tea.
COMBINATIONS – **tea-tree oil** an oil obtained from a species of tea tree, used in soaps and other products for its refreshing fragrance and antiseptic properties.

teazle (also **teazel**) > *noun* variant spelling of TEASEL.

TEC > *abbreviation* (in the UK) Training and Enterprise Council.

tech (also **tec**) > *noun* informal **1** Brit. a technical college. **2** technology. **3** a technician.

techie /tekki/ (also **techy**) > *noun* (pl. **techies**) informal a person who is an expert in technology, especially computing.

technetium /tekneeshiəm/ > *noun* an unstable radioactive metallic chemical element made by high-energy collisions.
ORIGIN – from Greek *tekhnētos* 'artificial'.

technic /teknik/ > *noun* **1** /also tekneek/ chiefly US technique. **2** (**technics**) (treated as sing. or pl.) technical terms, details, and methods; technology.

technical > *adjective* **1** relating to a particular subject, art, or craft, or its techniques. **2** requiring specialised knowledge in order to be understood. **3** of or concerned with applied and industrial sciences. **4** according to a strict application or interpretation of the law or rules.
DERIVATIVES – **technically** *adverb*.
COMBINATIONS – **technical college** a college of further education providing courses in applied sciences and other practical subjects.
ORIGIN – Latin *technicus*, from Greek *tekhnē* 'art, craft'.

technicality > *noun* (pl. **technicalities**) **1** a small formal detail specified within a set of rules. **2** (**technicalities**) details of theory or practice within a particular field. **3** the use of technical terms or methods.

technician > *noun* **1** a person employed to look after technical equipment or do practical work in a laboratory. **2** an expert in the practical application of a science. **3** a person skilled in the technique of an art or craft.

Technicolor > *noun* trademark **1** a process of colour cinematography using synchronised monochrome films, each of a different colour, to produce a colour print. **2** (**technicolor** or Brit. also **technicolour**) informal vivid colour.
DERIVATIVES – **technicolored** (Brit. also **technicoloured**) *adjective*.

technique > *noun* **1** a way of carrying out a particular task, especially the execution of an artistic work or a scientific procedure. **2** a procedure that is effective in achieving an aim.
SYNONYMS – **1** approach, method, procedure, process.
ORIGIN – French, from Latin *technicus*, from Greek *tekhnē* 'art, craft'.

techno > *noun* a style of fast, heavy electronic dance music, with few or no vocals.
ORIGIN – abbreviation of *technological*.

technobabble > *noun* informal incomprehensible technical jargon.

technocracy /teknokrəsi/ > *noun* (pl. **technocracies**) the control of society or industry by an elite of technical experts.
DERIVATIVES – **technocrat** *noun* **technocratic** *adjective*.

technology > *noun* (pl. **technologies**) **1** the application of scientific knowledge for practical purposes. **2** the branch of knowledge concerned with applied sciences.
DERIVATIVES – **technological** *adjective* **technologically** *adverb* **technologist** *noun*.
COMBINATIONS – **technology transfer** the transfer of new technology from the originator to a secondary user, especially from developed to underdeveloped countries.
ORIGIN – Greek *tekhnologia* 'systematic treatment', from *tekhnē* 'art, craft'.

technophile > *noun* a person who is enthusiastic about new technology.
DERIVATIVES – **technophilia** *noun* **technophilic** *adjective*.

technophobe > *noun* a person who dislikes or fears new technology.
DERIVATIVES – **technophobia** *noun* **technophobic** *adjective*.

technospeak > *noun* informal incomprehensible technical jargon.

techy > *noun* variant spelling of TECHIE.

tectonic /tektonnik/ > *adjective* **1** Geology relating to the structure of the earth's crust and the large-scale processes which take place within it. **2** relating to building or construction.
DERIVATIVES – **tectonically** *adverb*.
ORIGIN – Greek *tektonikos*, from *tektōn* 'carpenter, builder'.

tectonics > *plural noun* (treated as sing. or pl.) Geology large-scale processes affecting the structure of the earth's crust.

teddy > *noun* (pl. **teddies**) **1** (also **teddy bear**) a soft toy bear. **2** a woman's all-in-one undergarment.
ORIGIN – from *Teddy*, familiar form of the given name *Theodore*: in sense 1 alluding to the US President *Theodore* Roosevelt (1858–1919), an enthusiastic bear-hunter.

Teddy boy > *noun* Brit. (in the 1950s) a young man of a subculture characterised by a style of dress based on Edwardian fashion, by hair slicked up in a quiff, and by a liking for rock-and-roll music.
ORIGIN – from *Teddy*, familiar form of the given name *Edward* (with reference to the Edwardian style of dress).

tedious > *adjective* too long, slow, or dull.
DERIVATIVES – **tediously** *adverb* **tediousness** *noun*.
SYNONYMS – boring, dull, monotonous, uninteresting.
ORIGIN – from Latin *taedium* 'tedium', from *taedere* 'be weary of'.

tedium > *noun* the state of being tedious.
SYNONYMS – dullness, monotony.

tee¹ > *noun* **1** a cleared space on a golf course, from which the ball is struck at the beginning of play for each hole. **2** a small peg with a concave head which is placed in the ground to support a golf ball before it is struck from a tee. **3** a mark aimed at in bowls, quoits, curling, and other similar games. > *verb* (**tees, teed, teeing**) Golf **1** (**tee up**) place the ball on a tee ready to make the first stroke of the round or hole. **2** (**tee off**) begin a round or hole by playing the ball from a tee.

tee² > *noun* informal, chiefly N. Amer. a T-shirt.

tee-hee > *noun* a titter or giggle. > *verb* (**tee-hees, tee-heed, tee-heeing**) titter or giggle.

teem¹ > *verb* (**teem with**) be full of or swarming with.
DERIVATIVES – **teeming** *adjective*.
ORIGIN – Old English, 'give birth to' or 'be or become pregnant'.

teem² > *verb* (especially of rain) pour down; fall heavily.
ORIGIN – Old Norse *toema* 'to empty' (the original sense in English).

teen informal > *adjective* relating to teenagers. > *noun* a teenager.

-teen > *suffix* forming the names of numerals from 13 to 19.
ORIGIN – Old English, inflected form of TEN.

teenage > *adjective* denoting, relating to, or characteristic of a teenager or teenagers.
DERIVATIVES – **teenaged** *adjective*.

teenager > *noun* a person aged between 13 and 19 years.

teens > *plural noun* the years of a person's age from 13 to 19.

teensy > *adjective* (**teensier, teensiest**) informal very tiny.

teeny > *adjective* (**teenier, teeniest**) informal tiny.

teeny-bopper > *noun* informal a young teenager who follows the latest fashions in clothes and pop music.

teeny-weeny (also **teensy-weensy**) > *adjective* informal very tiny.

teepee > *noun* variant spelling of TEPEE.

tee shirt > *noun* variant spelling of T-SHIRT.

teeter > *verb* **1** move or balance unsteadily. **2** waver between different courses.
ORIGIN – Old Norse *titra* 'shake, shiver'.

teeth plural of TOOTH.

teethe > *verb* cut one's milk teeth.
DERIVATIVES – **teething** *noun*.
COMBINATIONS – **teething ring** a small ring for an infant to bite on while teething. **teething troubles** (also **teething problems**) short-term problems that occur in the early stages of a new project.

teetotal > *adjective* choosing or characterised by abstinence from alcohol.
DERIVATIVES – **teetotalism** *noun* **teetotaller** *noun*.
ORIGIN – emphatic extension of TOTAL, apparently first used by Richard Turner, a worker from Preston, in a speech (1833) urging total abstinence from all alcohol.

TEFL /teff'l/ > *abbreviation* teaching of English as a foreign language.

Teflon /teflon/ > *noun* **1** trademark a tough synthetic resin used to make seals and bearings and to coat non-stick cooking utensils. **2** (before another noun) informal (of a politician) retaining an undamaged reputation, despite having been associated with scandal or misjudgement.

tein /tayin/ > *noun* (pl. same or **teins**) a monetary unit of Kazakhstan, equal to one hundredth of a tenge.

tektite /tektīt/ > *noun* Geology a small black glassy object believed to have been formed in numbers as molten debris in a meteorite impact and scattered through the air.
ORIGIN – from Greek *tēktos* 'molten'.

tele- /telli/ > *combining form* **1** to or at a distance: *telecommunication*. **2** relating to television: *telegenic*. **3** done by means of the telephone: *telemarketing*.
ORIGIN – Greek *tēle-* 'far off'.

telecast > *noun* a television broadcast. > *verb* transmit by television.
DERIVATIVES – **telecaster** *noun*.

telecentre > *noun* another term for TELECOTTAGE.

telecommunication > *noun* **1** communication over a distance by cable, telegraph, telephone, or broadcasting. **2** (**telecommunications**) (treated as sing.) the branch of technology concerned with this.

telecommute > *verb* work from home, communicating with a central workplace by telephone, email, and fax.
DERIVATIVES – **telecommuter** *noun*.

telecomputer > *noun* a device which combines the capabilities of a computer with those of a television and a telephone.
DERIVATIVES – **telecomputing** *noun*.

telecoms (also **telecomms**) > *plural noun* (treated as sing.) telecommunications.

teleconference > *noun* a conference with participants in different locations linked by telecommunication devices.
DERIVATIVES – **teleconferencing** *noun*.

telecottage > *noun* a place, especially in a rural area, where computer equipment is available for communal use.

tele-evangelist > *noun* variant spelling of TELEVANGELIST.

telegenic /tellijennik/ > *adjective* having an appearance or manner that is attractive on television.

telegram > *noun* a message sent by telegraph and delivered in written or printed form, used in the UK only for international messages since 1981.

telegraph > *noun* a system or device for transmitting messages from a distance along a wire, especially one creating signals by making and breaking an electrical connection. > *verb* **1** send (someone) a message by telegraph. **2** send (a message) by telegraph. **3** convey (an intentional or unconscious message) with facial expression or body language.
DERIVATIVES – **telegrapher** *noun* **telegraphist** *noun* **telegraphy** *noun*.
COMBINATIONS – **telegraph pole** a tall pole used to carry telegraph or telephone wires above the ground.

telegraphese > *noun* informal the terse, abbreviated style of language used in telegrams.

telegraphic > *adjective* **1** of or by telegraphs or telegrams. **2** (of language) omitting inessential words; concise.
DERIVATIVES – **telegraphically** *adverb*.

telekinesis /tellikīneesiss, tellikineesiss/ > *noun* the supposed ability to move objects at a distance by mental power or other non-physical means.

DERIVATIVES – **telekinetic** adjective.

telemarketing > noun the marketing of goods or services by telephone calls to potential customers.

DERIVATIVES – **telemarketer** noun.

telematics > plural noun (treated as sing.) the branch of information technology which deals with the long-distance transmission of computerised information.

DERIVATIVES – **telematic** adjective.

telemedicine > noun the remote diagnosis and treatment of patients by means of telecommunications technology.

telemessage > noun a message sent by telephone or telex and delivered in written form, which replaced the telegram for inland messages in the UK in 1981.

telemeter > noun an apparatus for recording the readings of an instrument and transmitting them by radio. > verb transmit (readings) to a distant receiving set or station.

DERIVATIVES – **telemetric** adjective **telemetry** noun.

teleology /telliˈolləji, teeliˈolləji/ > noun 1 Philosophy the doctrine that the existence of phenomena may be explained with reference to the purpose they serve. 2 Theology the doctrine that there is evidence of design and purpose in the natural world.

DERIVATIVES – **teleological** adjective **teleologist** noun.

ORIGIN – from Greek telos 'end'.

telepathy > noun the supposed communication of thoughts or ideas by means other than the known senses.

DERIVATIVES – **telepath** noun **telepathic** adjective **telepathically** adverb **telepathist** noun.

telephone > noun 1 a system for transmitting voices over a distance using wire or radio, by converting acoustic vibrations to electrical signals. 2 an instrument used as part of such a system, typically including a handset with a transmitting microphone and a dial or set of numbered buttons by which a connection can be made to another such instrument. > verb 1 ring or speak to (someone) using the telephone. 2 make a telephone call.

DERIVATIVES – **telephonic** adjective **telephonically** adverb.

COMBINATIONS – **telephone box** chiefly Brit. a public booth or enclosure housing a payphone. **telephone directory** a book listing the names, addresses, and telephone numbers of the people in a particular area. **telephone exchange** a set of equipment that connects telephone lines during a call. **telephone number** a number assigned to a

particular telephone and used in making connections to it.

ORIGIN – from Greek tēle- 'far off'.

telephonist > noun Brit. an operator of a telephone switchboard.

telephony /tiˈleffəni/ > noun the working or use of telephones.

telephoto lens > noun a lens with a longer focal length than standard, giving a narrow field of view and a magnified image.

teleport > noun a centre providing interconnections between different forms of telecommunications, especially one linking satellites to ground-based communications. > verb (especially in science fiction) transport or be transported across space and distance instantly.

DERIVATIVES – **teleportation** noun.

telepresence > noun the use of virtual reality technology, especially for remote control of machinery or for apparent participation in distant events.

teleprinter > noun Brit. a device for transmitting telegraph messages as they are keyed, and for printing messages received.

teleprompter > noun North American term for AUTOCUE.

telescope > noun an optical instrument designed to make distant objects appear nearer, containing an arrangement of lenses, or of curved mirrors and lenses, by which rays of light are collected and focused and the resulting image magnified. > verb 1 (with reference to an object made of concentric tubular parts) slide or cause to slide into itself, so that it becomes smaller. 2 condense or conflate so as to occupy less space or time.

DERIVATIVES – **telescopic** adjective **telescopically** adverb.

teletext > noun a news and information service transmitted to televisions with appropriate receivers.

telethon > noun a long television programme broadcast to raise money for a charity.

teletype > noun trademark 1 a kind of teleprinter. 2 a message received and printed by a teleprinter. > verb send (a message) by means of a teleprinter.

televangelist (also **tele-evangelist**) > noun chiefly N. Amer. an evangelical preacher who appears regularly on television.

DERIVATIVES – **televangelical** adjective **televangelism** noun.

televise* > verb record for or transmit by television.

***SPELLING** – **televise** cannot be spelled with an -ize ending.

ORIGIN – back-formation from TELEVISION.

television > noun 1 a system for converting visual images (with sound) into electrical signals, transmitting them by radio or other

means, and displaying them electronically on a screen. 2 the activity, profession, or medium of broadcasting on television. 3 (also **television set**) a device with a screen for receiving television signals.

ORIGIN – from Greek tēle- 'far off'.

televisual > adjective relating to or suitable for television.

DERIVATIVES – **televisually** adverb.

telework > verb another term for TELECOMMUTE.

DERIVATIVES – **teleworker** noun.

telex > noun 1 an international system of telegraphy with printed messages transmitted and received by teleprinters using the public telecommunications network. 2 a device used for this. 3 a message sent by this system. > verb 1 communicate with by telex. 2 send (a message) by telex.

tell > verb (past and past participle told) 1 communicate information to. 2 instruct to do something. 3 relate (a story). 4 (tell on) informal inform on. 5 (tell off) informal reprimand. 6 determine correctly or with certainty. 7 perceive (a distinction). 8 (of an experience or period of time) have a noticeable effect on someone.

IDIOMS – **tell tales** gossip about another person's secrets or faults. **tell the time** (or N. Amer. **tell time**) be able to ascertain the time from reading the face of a clock or watch. **tell someone where to get off** informal angrily dismiss or rebuke someone. **there is no telling** it is not possible to know what has happened or will happen. **you're telling me** informal I am in complete agreement.

SYNONYMS – 1 apprise, inform, notify. 2 command, direct, order. 3 chronicle, describe, narrate, recount, relate. 6 ascertain, discern, identify.

COMBINATIONS – **telling-off** (pl. **tellings-off**) informal a reprimand.

ORIGIN – Old English, 'relate, count, estimate'; related to TALE.

teller > noun 1 a person who deals with customers' transactions in a bank. 2 a person appointed to count votes. 3 a person who tells something.

telling > adjective having a striking or revealing effect; significant.

DERIVATIVES – **tellingly** adverb.

telltale > adjective revealing or betraying something. > noun a person who tells tales.

telluric /telˈyoorik/ > adjective 1 of the earth as a planet. 2 of the soil.

ORIGIN – from Latin tellus 'earth'.

tellurium /telˈyooriəm/ > noun a silvery-white crystalline non-metallic chemical element with semiconducting properties, resembling selenium.

DERIVATIVES – **telluride** /tel-yoor-īd/ *noun.*

ORIGIN – from Latin *tellus* 'earth'.

telly > *noun* (pl. **tellies**) Brit. informal term for **TELEVISION**.

telnet Computing > *noun* a network protocol or program that allows a user on one computer to log in to another computer that is part of the same network. > *verb* (**telnetted**, **telnetting**) informal log into a remote computer using a telnet program.

temazepam /tə-mazz-i-pam/ > *noun* Medicine a tranquillising drug of the benzodiazepine group.

temblor /tem-blor/ > *noun* US an earthquake.

ORIGIN – American Spanish.

temerity /ti-merr-i-ti/ > *noun* excessive confidence or boldness.

SYNONYMS – audacity, effrontery, gall.

ORIGIN – Latin *temeritas*, from *temere* 'rashly'.

temp informal > *noun* an employee, especially an office worker, who is employed on a temporary basis. > *verb* work as a temp.

temper > *noun* **1** a person's state of mind in terms of their being angry or calm. **2** a tendency to become angry easily. **3** an angry state of mind. **4** the degree of hardness and elasticity in steel or other metal. > *verb* **1** improve the temper of (a metal) by reheating and then cooling it. **2** (often **be tempered with**) serve as a neutralising or counterbalancing force to.

IDIOMS – **keep** (or **lose**) **one's temper** retain (or fail to retain) composure or restraint when angry.

DERIVATIVES – **temperer** *noun.*

SYNONYMS – *noun* **3** fury, mood, passion, paroxysm, rage. *verb* **2** lessen, moderate, modify.

ORIGIN – from Latin *temperare* 'mingle, restrain'; the noun originally denoted a proportionate mixture of elements, also the combination of the four bodily humours, formerly believed to be the basis of temperament.

tempera /tem-pə-rə/ > *noun* **1** a method of painting with pigments dispersed in an emulsion that mixes with water, typically egg yolk. **2** emulsion used in tempera.

ORIGIN – from the Italian phrase *pingere a tempera* 'paint in distemper'.

temperament > *noun* a person's nature with regard to the effect it has on their behaviour.

SYNONYMS – character, disposition, nature, personality.

ORIGIN – Latin *temperamentum* 'correct mixture', from *temperare* 'mingle'; related to **TEMPER**.

temperamental > *adjective* **1** relating to or caused by temperament. **2** liable to unreasonable changes of mood.

DERIVATIVES – **temperamentally** *adverb.*

SYNONYMS – **2** capricious, mercurial, moody, unpredictable, volatile.

ANTONYMS – calm, even-tempered, placid.

temperance > *noun* abstinence from alcoholic drink.

ORIGIN – Old French *temperaunce*, from Latin *temperantia* 'moderation', from *temperare* 'restrain'.

temperate > *adjective* **1** (of a region or climate) characterised by mild temperatures. **2** showing moderation or self-restraint.

DERIVATIVES – **temperately** *adverb* **temperateness** *noun.*

SYNONYMS – **2** disciplined, moderate, restrained, self-controlled.

ANTONYMS – **2** intemperate.

COMBINATIONS – **temperate zone** each of the two belts of latitude between the torrid zone and the northern and southern frigid zones.

ORIGIN – Latin *temperatus*, from *temperare* 'mingle, restrain'.

temperature > *noun* **1** the degree or intensity of heat present in a substance or object. **2** informal a body temperature above the normal. **3** the degree of excitement or tension present in a situation or discussion. WORDFINDER – absolute temperature (*temperature measured from absolute zero in kelvins*), absolute zero (*lowest temperature theoretically possible: −273.15°C*), Celsius, centigrade (*denoting temperature scale on which water freezes at 0° and boils at 100°*), Fahrenheit (*denoting temperature scale on which water freezes at 32° and boils at 212°*), isotherm (*line of equal temperature on a map*), thermostat (*device that automatically regulates temperature*); thermometer, thermocouple, pyrometer (*instruments for measuring temperature*); homeotherm (*organism that maintains a constant body temperature*), poikilotherm (*organism that cannot regulate its body temperature*).

ORIGIN – first used in the sense 'the state of being tempered or mixed', later synonymous with **TEMPERAMENT**: from Latin *temperatura*, from *temperare* 'restrain'.

tempest > *noun* a violent windy storm.

ORIGIN – Old French *tempeste*, from Latin *tempestas* 'season, weather, storm'.

tempestuous /tem-pes-tyoo-əss/ > *adjective* **1** very stormy. **2** characterised by strong and turbulent emotion.

DERIVATIVES – **tempestuously** *adverb* **tempestuousness** *noun.*

SYNONYMS – **2** emotional, explosive, passionate, stormy, tumultuous, turbulent.

tempi plural of **TEMPO**.

Templar /tem-plər/ > *noun* historical a member of the Knights Templars, a powerful medieval religious and military order.

ORIGIN – Latin *templarius*, from *templum* 'temple'.

template /tem-playt, tem-plit/ (also **templet**) > *noun* **1** a shaped piece of rigid material used as a pattern for processes such as cutting out, shaping, or drilling. **2** something that serves as a model or example.

ORIGIN – probably from *temple* 'a device in a loom for keeping the cloth stretched', influenced by **PLATE**.

temple[1] > *noun* a building devoted to the worship of a god or gods.

ORIGIN – Latin *templum* 'open or consecrated space'.

temple[2] > *noun* the flat part either side of the head between the forehead and the ear.

ORIGIN – Old French, from Latin *tempus*.

tempo /tem-pō/ > *noun* (pl. **tempos** or **tempi** /tem-pi/) **1** Music the speed at which a passage of music is played. **2** the pace of an activity or process.

ORIGIN – Italian, from Latin *tempus* 'time'.

temporal[1] /tem-pə-rəl/ > *adjective* **1** relating to time. **2** relating to worldly affairs; secular.

DERIVATIVES – **temporally** *adverb.*

COMBINATIONS – **temporal power** the power of a bishop or cleric, especially the Pope, in secular matters.

ORIGIN – Latin *temporalis*, from *tempus* 'time'.

temporal[2] /tem-pə-rəl/ > *adjective* Anatomy of or situated in the temples of the head.

COMBINATIONS – **temporal bone** either of a pair of bones which form part of the side of the skull on each side and enclose the middle and inner ear. **temporal lobe** each of the paired lobes of the brain lying beneath the temples, including areas concerned with the understanding of speech.

temporality > *noun* (pl. **temporalities**) the state of existing within or having some relationship with time.

temporary > *adjective* lasting for only a limited period. > *noun* (pl. **temporaries**) a person employed on a temporary basis.

DERIVATIVES – **temporarily** *adverb* **temporariness** *noun.*

SYNONYMS – *adjective* ephemeral, impermanent, makeshift, provisional, short-term.

ORIGIN – Latin *temporarius*, from *tempus* 'time'.

temporise (also **temporize**) > *verb* avoid making a decision or committing oneself in order to gain time.

DERIVATIVES – **temporisation** *noun* **temporiser** *noun.*

SYNONYMS – equivocate, procrastinate, prevaricate.

ORIGIN – French *temporiser* 'bide one's time'.

tempo rubato > *noun* see **RUBATO**.

Tempranillo /tempra**nee**yō/ > *noun* a variety of black wine grape grown in Spain, used to make Rioja wine.

ORIGIN – named after a village in northern Spain.

tempt > *verb* **1** entice (someone) to do something against their better judgement. **2** (**be tempted to do**) have an urge or inclination to do. **3** attract or charm someone.

IDIOMS – **tempt fate** (or **providence**) do something that is risky or dangerous.

DERIVATIVES – **tempting** *adjective* **temptingly** *adverb*.

ORIGIN – Latin *temptare* 'handle, test, try'.

temptation > *noun* **1** a desire to do something, especially something wrong or unwise. **2** a tempting thing.

SYNONYMS – **1** impulse, inclination, urge. **2** attraction, enticement, lure.

tempter > *noun* a person or thing that tempts.

temptress > *noun* a sexually alluring woman.

tempura /tem**poo**ra/ > *noun* a Japanese dish of fish, shellfish, or vegetables, fried in batter.

ORIGIN – Japanese, probably from Portuguese *têmpero* 'seasoning'.

ten > *cardinal number* one more than nine; 10. (Roman numeral: **x** or **X**.)

WORDFINDER – decade (*period of ten years*), decagon (*plane figure with ten straight sides and angles*), decahedron (*solid figure with ten plane faces*), Decalogue (*the Ten Commandments*), decathlon (*athletic event in which each competitor takes part in the same ten events*), decennial (*lasting for or recurring every ten years*), decimal (*relating to a number system based on the number ten*), denary (*relating to or based on the number ten*), tithe (*one tenth of annual produce or earnings*).

IDIOMS – **ten out of ten** denoting an excellent performance. **ten to one** very probably.

DERIVATIVES – **tenfold** *adjective & adverb*.

COMBINATIONS – **Ten Commandments** (in the Bible) the divine rules of conduct given by God to Moses on Mount Sinai. **ten-gallon hat** a large, broad-brimmed hat, traditionally worn by cowboys.

tenable > *adjective* **1** able to be maintained or defended against attack or objection. **2** (of a post, grant, etc.) able to be held or used for a specified period: *a scholarship tenable for three years*.

DERIVATIVES – **tenability** *noun*.

ORIGIN – French, from *tenir* 'to hold'.

tenacious /ti**nay**shass/ > *adjective* **1** not readily relinquishing something; keeping a firm hold. **2** persisting in existence or in a course of action.

DERIVATIVES – **tenaciously** *adverb* **tenacity** /ti**nass**iti/ *noun*.

ORIGIN – Latin *tenax*, from *tenere* 'to hold'.

tenancy > *noun* (pl. **tenancies**) possession of land or property as a tenant.

tenant > *noun* **1** a person occupying rented land or property. **2** Law a person holding real property by private ownership. > *verb* (usu. **be tenanted**) occupy (property) as a tenant.

COMBINATIONS – **tenant farmer** a person who farms rented land.

ORIGIN – Old French, 'holding', from Latin *tenere* 'to hold'.

tench > *noun* (pl. same) a freshwater fish of the carp family, popular with anglers.

ORIGIN – Old French *tenche*, from Latin *tinca*.

tend¹ > *verb* **1** (**tend to do**) regularly or frequently behave in a particular way or have a certain characteristic. **2** (**tend to** or **towards**) be liable to possess or display. **3** go or move in a particular direction.

SYNONYMS – **1** be apt, be disposed, be inclined. **3** gravitate, incline, lean.

wordpower facts

Tend

Tend in the sense 'frequently behave in a particular way' is one of many English words derived from the Latin verb *tendere* 'stretch, strive, hold out'. Other words from the same root include **attend**, **extend**, **intend**, **ostensible**, **tender**, **tense**, and **tension**. Also from *tendere* is **tent**: the link between the words is the idea of fabric being stretched over a frame. **Tend** in the sense 'look after' is a shortening of **attend**, so is ultimately from the same root as **tend¹**.

tend² > *verb* **1** care for or look after. **2** US direct or manage.

tendency > *noun* (pl. **tendencies**) **1** (often **tendency to** or **towards**) an inclination towards a particular characteristic or type of behaviour. **2** a group within a larger political party or movement.

SYNONYMS – **1** inclination, leaning, proclivity, propensity.

tendentious /ten**den**shass/ > *adjective* calculated to promote a particular cause or point of view.

DERIVATIVES – **tendentiously** *adverb* **tendentiousness** *noun*.

tender¹ > *adjective* (**tenderer**, **tenderest**) **1** gentle and caring or sympathetic. **2** (of food) easy to cut or chew. **3** (of a part of the body) sensitive. **4** young and vulnerable. **5** requiring tact or careful handling.

DERIVATIVES – **tenderly** *adverb* **tenderness** *noun*.

SYNONYMS – **1** caring, compassionate, warm.

COMBINATIONS – **tender-hearted** having a kind, gentle, or sentimental nature.

ORIGIN – Old French *tendre*, from Latin *tener* 'tender, delicate'.

tender² > *verb* **1** offer or present formally. **2** make a formal written offer to carry out work, supply goods, etc. for a stated fixed price. **3** offer as payment. > *noun* a tendered offer.

IDIOMS – **put something out to tender** seek tenders to carry out work, supply goods, etc.

DERIVATIVES – **tenderer** *noun*.

ORIGIN – Old French *tendre*, from Latin *tendere* 'stretch, strive'.

tender³ > *noun* **1** a vehicle used by a fire service or the armed forces for carrying supplies or fulfilling a specified role. **2** a boat used to ferry people and supplies to and from a ship. **3** a truck closely coupled to a steam locomotive to carry fuel and water. **4** a person who looks after a machine, place, or other people.

ORIGIN – first used in the sense 'attendant, nurse': from **TEND²** or **ATTEND**.

tenderfoot > *noun* (pl. **tenderfoots** or **tenderfeet**) informal **1** chiefly N. Amer. a newcomer or novice. **2** dated a newly enrolled member of the Scout or Guide movement.

tenderise (also **tenderize**) > *verb* make (meat) more tender by beating or slow cooking.

DERIVATIVES – **tenderiser** *noun*.

tenderloin > *noun* **1** the tenderest part of a loin of beef, pork, etc., taken from under the short ribs in the hindquarters. **2** US the undercut of a sirloin. **3** N. Amer. informal a district of a city where vice and corruption are prominent. [ORIGIN – first applied to a district of New York, seen as a 'choice' assignment by police because of the bribes offered to them to turn a blind eye.]

tendinitis /tendi**nī**tiss/ (also **tendonitis**) > *noun* inflammation of a tendon.

tendon /**ten**dan/ > *noun* **1** a flexible but inelastic cord of strong fibrous tissue attaching a muscle to a bone. **2** the hamstring of a four-legged mammal.

WORDFINDER – Achilles tendon (*connecting the calf muscle to the heel*), hamstring (*tendon at the back of the knee*), tendinitis (*inflammation of a tendon*), tennis elbow (*inflammation of the tendons of the elbow*), tenosynovitis (*inflammation and swelling of a tendon*).

ORIGIN – Greek *tenōn* 'sinew', from *teinein* 'to stretch'.

tendril > *noun* **1** a slender thread-like appendage of a climbing plant, which stretches out and twines round any suitable support. **2** a slender ringlet of hair.
ORIGIN – probably from Old French *tendron* 'young shoot', from Latin *tener* 'tender'.

tenebrous /tennibrəss/ > *adjective* literary dark; shadowy.
ORIGIN – Latin *tenebrosus*, from *tenebrae* 'darkness'.

tenement /tennəmənt/ > *noun* **1** (especially in Scotland or the US) a separate residence within a house or block of flats. **2** (also **tenement house**) a house divided into several separate residences. **3** a piece of land held by an owner.
ORIGIN – Latin *tenementum*, from *tenere* 'to hold'.

tenet /tennit/ > *noun* a principle or belief.
SYNONYMS – belief, credo, doctrine, precept, principle.
ORIGIN – Latin, literally 'he holds'.

tenge /tenggay/ > *noun* (pl. same or **tenges**) **1** the basic monetary unit of Kazakhstan, equal to 100 teins. **2** a monetary unit of Turkmenistan, equal to one hundredth of a manat.

tenner > *noun* Brit. informal a ten-pound note.

tennis > *noun* a game in which two or four players strike a hollow rubber ball with rackets over a net stretched across a court.
COMBINATIONS – **tennis elbow** inflammation of the tendons of the elbow caused by overuse of the forearm muscles. **tennis shoe** a light canvas or leather soft-soled shoe suitable for tennis or casual wear.
ORIGIN – first as *tenetz, tenes*, denoting the game of real tennis, apparently from Old French *tenez* 'take, receive' (called by the server to an opponent).

tenon /tennən/ > *noun* a projecting piece of wood made for insertion into a mortise in another piece of wood.
COMBINATIONS – **tenon saw** a small saw with a strong brass or steel back for precise work.
ORIGIN – French, from *tenir* 'to hold'.

tenor¹ > *noun* **1** a singing voice between baritone and alto or countertenor, the highest of the ordinary adult male range. **2** (before another noun) referring to an instrument of the second or third lowest pitch in its family. **3** the largest and deepest bell of a ring or set.
COMBINATIONS – **tenor clef** Music a clef placing middle C on the second-highest line of the stave, used chiefly for cello and bassoon music.
ORIGIN – Latin, from *tenere* 'to hold'; so named because the tenor part 'held' the melody.

tenor² > *noun* **1** the general meaning, sense, or content of something. **2** a prevailing character or direction.
ORIGIN – Latin, 'course, substance', from *tenere* 'to hold'.

tenosynovitis /tennōsīnəvītiss/ > *noun* Medicine inflammation and swelling of a tendon, especially in the wrist and typically caused by repetitive movement.
ORIGIN – from Greek *tenōn* 'tendon' + *synovitis*, 'inflammation of a synovial membrane'.

tenpin > *noun* **1** a skittle used in tenpin bowling. **2** (**tenpins**) (treated as sing.) N. Amer. tenpin bowling.
COMBINATIONS – **tenpin bowling** a game in which ten skittles are set up at the end of a track and bowled down with hard balls.

tenrec /tenrek/ > *noun* a small insectivorous mammal of Madagascar and the Comoro Islands.
ORIGIN – Malagasy.

TENS > *abbreviation* transcutaneous electrical nerve stimulation, a technique designed to provide pain relief by applying electrodes to the skin.

tense¹ > *adjective* **1** stretched tight or rigid. **2** feeling, causing, or showing anxiety and nervousness. > *verb* make or become tense.
DERIVATIVES – **tensely** *adverb* **tenseness** *noun*.
ORIGIN – Latin *tensus*, from *tendere* 'stretch'.

tense² > *noun* Grammar a set of forms taken by a verb to indicate the time, continuance, or completeness of the action.
ORIGIN – Old French *tens*, from Latin *tempus* 'time'.

tensile /tensīl/ > *adjective* **1** relating to tension. **2** capable of being drawn out or stretched.
COMBINATIONS – **tensile strength** the resistance of a material to breaking under tension.

tension > *noun* **1** the state of being tense. **2** mental or emotional strain. **3** a strained political or social state. **4** the degree of stitch tightness in knitting and machine sewing. **5** voltage of specified magnitude: *high tension*. > *verb* subject (something) to tension.
DERIVATIVES – **tensional** *adjective*.

tent > *noun* a portable shelter made of cloth, supported by one or more poles and stretched tight by cords attached to pegs driven into the ground. > *verb* **1** cover with or arrange like a tent. **2** (**tented**) composed of or provided with tents.
COMBINATIONS – **tent stitch** a series of parallel diagonal stitches.
ORIGIN – Old French *tente*, from Latin *tendere* 'stretch'.

tentacle > *noun* a long, slender, flexible appendage of an animal, used for grasping or moving about, or bearing sense organs.
DERIVATIVES – **tentacled** *adjective* **tentacular** *adjective*.
ORIGIN – Latin *tentaculum*, from *temptare* 'to feel, try'.

tentage > *noun* tents collectively.

tentative > *adjective* **1** done without confidence; hesitant. **2** not certain or fixed; provisional.
DERIVATIVES – **tentatively** *adverb* **tentativeness** *noun*.
SYNONYMS – **1** faltering, hesitant, uncertain, unsure, wavering. **2** indefinite, provisional, unconfirmed.
ANTONYMS – **1** confident. **2** definite.
ORIGIN – Latin *tentativus*, from *temptare* 'handle, try'.

tenterhook > *noun* (in phrase **on tenterhooks**) in a state of agitated suspense.
ORIGIN – first denoting a hook used to fasten cloth on a *tenter*, a framework on which fabric could be held taut during manufacture.

tenth > *ordinal number* **1** constituting number ten in a sequence; 10th. **2** (**a tenth** or **one tenth**) each of ten equal parts into which something is divided. **3** Music an interval spanning an octave and a third in the diatonic scale.
DERIVATIVES – **tenthly** *adverb*.

tenuous > *adjective* **1** very slight or insubstantial: *a tenuous distinction*. **2** very slender or fine.
DERIVATIVES – **tenuously** *adverb* **tenuousness** *noun*.
SYNONYMS – **1** flimsy, negligible, sketchy.
ORIGIN – Latin *tenuis* 'thin'.

tenure /tenyər/ > *noun* **1** the conditions under which land or buildings are held or occupied. **2** the holding of an office.
ORIGIN – Old French, from Latin *tenere*.

tenured > *adjective* (especially of a teacher or lecturer) having a permanent post.

tenurial > *adjective* relating to the tenure of land.

tepee /teepee/ (also **teepee** or **tipi**) > *noun* a conical tent made of skins or cloth on a frame of poles, used by American Indians.
ORIGIN – Sioux, 'dwelling'.

tephra /tefrə/ > *noun* rock fragments and particles ejected by a volcanic eruption.
ORIGIN – Greek, 'ash, ashes'.

tepid > *adjective* **1** (especially of a liquid) lukewarm. **2** unenthusiastic.
DERIVATIVES – **tepidity** *noun* **tepidly** *adverb*.
ORIGIN – Latin *tepidus*, from *tepere* 'be warm'.

tequila /təkeelə/ > *noun* a Mexican liquor made from an agave.
COMBINATIONS – **tequila sunrise** a cocktail of tequila, orange juice, and grenadine.

ORIGIN – named after the town of *Tequila* in Mexico.

ter- > *combining form* three; having three: *tercentenary*.

ORIGIN – from Latin *ter* 'thrice'.

tera- /terrə/ > *combining form* **1** denoting a factor of one million million (10^{12}): *terawatt*. **2** Computing denoting a factor of 2^{40}: *terabyte*.

ORIGIN – from Greek *teras* 'monster'.

terabyte > *noun* Computing a unit of information equal to one million million (10^{12}) or (strictly) 2^{40} bytes.

teraflop > *noun* Computing a unit of computing speed equal to one million million floating-point operations per second.

terai /tərī/ > *noun* a wide-brimmed felt hat, typically with a double crown, worn chiefly by travellers in subtropical regions.

ORIGIN – from *Terai*, the name of a belt of marshy jungle near the Himalayan foothills.

teratogen /tərattəjən/ > *noun* an agent or factor causing malformation of an embryo.

DERIVATIVES – **teratogenic** *adjective* **teratogenicity** *noun*.

ORIGIN – from Greek *teras* 'monster'.

teratology /terrətolləji/ > *noun* **1** the branch of medicine concerned with congenital abnormalities. **2** mythology relating to fantastic creatures and monsters.

DERIVATIVES – **teratological** *adjective* **teratologist** *noun*.

terbium /terbiəm/ > *noun* a silvery-white metallic chemical element.

ORIGIN – named after *Ytterby* in Sweden (see **YTTERBIUM**).

terce /terss/ > *noun* a service forming part of the Divine Office of the Western Christian Church, traditionally said at the third hour of the day (9 a.m.).

ORIGIN – Latin *tertia*, from *tertius* 'third'.

tercel /ters'l/ (also **tiercel** /teers'l/) > *noun* Falconry a male hawk, especially a peregrine. Compare with **FALCON**.

ORIGIN – Old French, from Latin *tertius* 'third', perhaps from the belief that the third egg of a clutch produced a male.

tercentenary > *noun* (pl. **tercentenaries**) a three-hundredth anniversary.

DERIVATIVES – **tercentennial** *adjective* & *noun*.

terebinth /terrəbinth/ > *noun* a small tree which was formerly a source of turpentine.

ORIGIN – Greek *terebinthos*.

teredo /təreedō/ > *noun* (pl. **teredos**) a worm-like marine bivalve mollusc which bores into wood.

ORIGIN – Greek *teredōn*, related to *teirein* 'rub hard, wear away'.

tergiversate /terjiversayt/ > *verb* **1** use ambiguous or evasive language. **2** change one's loyalties.

DERIVATIVES – **tergiversation** *noun*.

ORIGIN – Latin *tergiversari* 'turn one's back'.

teriyaki /terriyaaki/ > *noun* a Japanese dish of fish or meat marinated in soy sauce and grilled.

ORIGIN – Japanese.

term > *noun* **1** a word or phrase used to describe a thing or to express a concept. **2** (**terms**) language used on a particular occasion: *a protest in the strongest possible terms*. **3** a period for which something lasts or is intended to last. **4** each of the periods in the year during which instruction is given in a school or college or during which a law court holds sessions. **5** (**terms**) stipulated or agreed requirements or conditions. **6** (**terms**) relationship or footing: *we're on good terms*. **7** (also **full term**) the completion of a normal length of pregnancy. **8** Logic a word or words that may be the subject or predicate of a proposition. **9** Mathematics each of the quantities in a ratio, series, or mathematical expression. > *verb* call by a specified term.

WORDFINDER – binomial (*consisting of two terms*), hapax legomenon (*term of which only one instance of use is recorded*), nomenclature (*the term or terms applied to someone or something*), polynomial (*in mathematics, an expression consisting of several terms*), trinomial (*consisting or three terms or names*).

IDIOMS – **come to terms with** reconcile oneself to. **in terms of** (or **in —— terms**) with regard to the aspect or subject specified. **the —— term** a period that is a specified way into the future: *in the long term*. **on terms 1** in a state of friendship or equality. **2** (in sport) level in score. **terms of reference** Brit. the scope of an inquiry or discussion.

DERIVATIVES – **termly** *adjective* & *adverb*.

SYNONYMS – *noun* **2** (**terms**) language, phraseology, words. **5** (**terms**) particulars, provisions, stipulations. *verb* call, entitle, name, title.

COMBINATIONS – **terms of trade** Economics the ratio of an index of a country's export prices to an index of its import prices.

ORIGIN – Old French *terme*, from Latin *terminus* 'end, boundary, limit'.

termagant /terməgənt/ > *noun* a bad-tempered or overbearing woman.

ORIGIN – from the name of *Termagant*, a violent imaginary deity often appearing in medieval morality plays, from Italian *Trivagante* 'thrice-wandering'.

terminable > *adjective* **1** able to be terminated. **2** coming to an end after a certain time.

terminal > *adjective* **1** of, forming, or situated at the end of something. **2** (of a disease) predicted to lead to death. **3** informal extreme and irreversible. **4** done or occurring each school or college term.

> *noun* **1** the station at the end of a railway or other transport route. **2** a departure and arrival building for passengers at an airport. **3** a point of connection for closing an electric circuit. **4** a device at which data or commands for a computer may be entered, and which displays the received output. **5** an installation where oil or gas is stored.

DERIVATIVES – **terminally** *adverb*.

COMBINATIONS – **terminal velocity** Physics the constant speed that a freely falling object reaches when the resistance of the medium through which it is falling prevents further acceleration.

terminate > *verb* **1** bring to an end. **2** (of a train or bus service) end its journey. **3** (**terminate in**) have an end at or resolution in. **4** end (a pregnancy) before term by artificial means. **5** chiefly N. Amer. end the employment of. **6** euphemistic, chiefly N. Amer. assassinate.

DERIVATIVES – **termination** *noun* **terminator** *noun*.

SYNONYMS – **1** close, conclude, end, finish.

terminology > *noun* (pl. **terminologies**) the body of terms used in a subject of study, profession, etc.

DERIVATIVES – **terminological** *adjective* **terminologically** *adverb*.

COMBINATIONS – **terminological inexactitude** humorous a lie. [ORIGIN – first used by Winston Churchill in 1906.]

terminus > *noun* (pl. **termini** or **terminuses**) **1** chiefly Brit. a railway or bus terminal. **2** an end or extremity. **3** an oil or gas terminal.

ORIGIN – Latin, 'end, limit, boundary'.

terminus ante quem /terminəss anti kwem/ > *noun* the latest possible date.

ORIGIN – Latin, literally 'end before which'.

termite /termīt/ > *noun* a small, soft-bodied insect which feeds on wood and lives in complex colonies in large nests of earth.

ORIGIN – Latin *termes* 'woodworm'.

tern /tern/ > *noun* a seabird resembling a gull but smaller and more slender, with long pointed wings and a forked tail.

ORIGIN – Scandinavian.

ternary /ternəri/ > *adjective* **1** composed of three parts. **2** Mathematics using three as a base.

ORIGIN – Latin *ternarius*, from *terni* 'three at once'.

terpene /terpeen/ > *noun* Chemistry any of a large group of volatile unsaturated hydrocarbons with cyclic molecules, found in the essential oils of conifers and other plants.

DERIVATIVES – **terpenoid** *noun* & *adjective*.

ORIGIN – from German *Terpentin* 'turpentine'.

terpsichorean /terpsikəreeən/ formal or humorous > *adjective* relating to dancing. > *noun* a dancer.

ORIGIN – from *Terpsichore*, the ancient Greek and Roman Muse of dance.

terrace > *noun* 1 each of a series of flat areas on a slope, used for cultivation. 2 a patio. 3 chiefly Brit. a row of houses built in one block in a uniform style. 4 Brit. a flight of wide, shallow steps providing standing room for spectators in a stadium. > *verb* make or form (sloping land) into terraces.

DERIVATIVES – **terracing** noun.

---

wordpower facts

Terrace

Terrace is one of several English words that derive ultimately from Latin *terra* 'earth'. These include **inter** or 'bury', **Mediterranean**, **subterranean**, **terrestrial**, and **territory**. The related pair **terrine** and **tureen** are also from this source: the underlying notion is of an earthenware pot.

Terrace entered English from Old French, in which it meant 'rubble' or 'platform'; in English it first referred to an open gallery, and later to a platform or balcony in a theatre.

---

terraced > *adjective* 1 (of a house) forming part of a terrace. 2 (of land) having been formed into terraces.

terracotta /terrəkottə/ > *noun* 1 unglazed, typically brownish-red earthenware, used as an ornamental building material and in modelling. 2 a strong brownish-red colour.

ORIGIN – from Italian *terra cotta* 'baked earth'.

terra firma /terrə furmə/ > *noun* dry land; the ground.

ORIGIN – Latin, 'firm land'.

terraform > *verb* (in science fiction) transform (a planet) so it resembles the earth.

ORIGIN – from Latin *terra* 'earth' + FORM.

terrain /terayn/ > *noun* a stretch of land, especially with regard to its physical features.

ORIGIN – French, from Latin *terrenus* 'of or like earth'.

terra incognita /terrə inkognitə, inkogneetə/ > *noun* unknown territory.

ORIGIN – Latin, 'unknown land'.

terrapin > *noun* a small freshwater turtle.

ORIGIN – Algonquian.

terrarium /terairiəm/ > *noun* (pl. **terrariums** or **terraria** /terairiə/) 1 a glass-fronted case for keeping smaller land animals, e.g. reptiles or amphibians. 2 a sealed transparent globe or similar container in which plants are grown.

ORIGIN – from Latin *terra* 'earth', on the pattern of *aquarium*.

terrazzo /teratsō/ > *noun* flooring material consisting of chips of marble or granite set in concrete and polished smooth.

ORIGIN – Italian, 'terrace'.

terrene /tereen/ > *adjective* archaic 1 of or like earth. 2 occurring on or inhabiting dry land. 3 worldly.

terrestrial /tərestriəl/ > *adjective* 1 of, on, or relating to the earth or dry land. 2 (of an animal or plant) living on or in the ground. 3 (of television broadcasting) not using a satellite. > *noun* an inhabitant of the earth.

DERIVATIVES – **terrestrially** adverb.

terrible > *adjective* 1 extremely bad, serious, or unpleasant. 2 causing terror. 3 troubled or guilty. 4 extremely unwell.

DERIVATIVES – **terribleness** noun.

SYNONYMS – 1 appalling, awful, dreadful, horrible.

ORIGIN – Latin *terribilis*, from *terrere* 'frighten'.

terribly > *adverb* 1 extremely. 2 very badly.

terrier > *noun* 1 a small breed of dog originally used for turning out foxes and other animals from their earths. 2 a tenacious or eager person.

ORIGIN – from Old French *chien terrier* 'earth dog'.

terrific > *adjective* 1 of great size, amount, or intensity. 2 informal excellent. 3 archaic causing terror.

DERIVATIVES – **terrifically** adverb.

SYNONYMS – 1 enormous, gigantic, huge, tremendous.

ORIGIN – Latin *terrificus*, from *terrere* 'frighten'.

terrify > *verb* (**terrifies**, **terrified**) cause (someone) to feel terror.

DERIVATIVES – **terrifying** adjective **terrifyingly** adverb.

SYNONYMS – frighten, petrify, scare.

terrine /təreen/ > *noun* 1 a meat, fish, or vegetable mixture prepared in advance and allowed to cool or set in a container. 2 an earthenware container for such a dish.

ORIGIN – French, 'large earthenware pot'; related to TUREEN.

territorial > *adjective* 1 relating to the ownership of land or sea. 2 relating to a territory or area. 3 (of an animal) tending to defend a territory. > *noun* (**Territorial**) (in the UK) a member of the Territorial Army.

DERIVATIVES – **territoriality** noun **territorially** adverb.

COMBINATIONS – **Territorial Army** (in the UK) a volunteer force locally organised to provide a trained military reserve for use in an emergency. **territorial waters** the waters under the jurisdiction of a state, especially those within a stated distance from its coast.

territory > *noun* (pl. **territories**) 1 an area under the jurisdiction of a ruler or state. 2 (**Territory**) an organised division of a country not having the full rights of a state. 3 an area defended by an animal against others of the same sex or species. 4 an area defended by a team or player in a game or sport. 5 an area in which one has certain rights or responsibilities. 6 an area of knowledge or experience.

ORIGIN – Latin *territorium*, from *terra* 'land'.

terror > *noun* 1 extreme fear. 2 a cause of terror. 3 the use of terror to intimidate people. 4 (also **holy terror**) informal a person causing trouble or annoyance.

ORIGIN – Latin, from *terrere* 'frighten'.

terrorise (also **terrorize**) > *verb* create and maintain a feeling of terror in (a person or area).

terrorist > *noun* a person who uses violence and intimidation in the pursuit of political aims.

DERIVATIVES – **terrorism** noun.

terry > *noun* (pl. **terries**) fabric with raised uncut loops of thread on both sides, used especially for towels.

terse > *adjective* (**terser**, **tersest**) sparing in the use of words; abrupt.

DERIVATIVES – **tersely** adverb **terseness** noun.

SYNONYMS – abrupt, blunt, curt.

ORIGIN – first used in the sense 'polished, trim', hence 'concise and to the point': from Latin *tersus* 'wiped, polished'.

tertiary /tershəri/ > *adjective* 1 third in order or level. 2 chiefly Brit. (of education) at a level beyond that provided by schools. 3 (of medical treatment) provided at a specialist institution. 4 (**Tertiary**) Geology relating to the first period of the Cenozoic era, about 65 to 1.64 million years ago.

COMBINATIONS – **tertiary industry** the service industry of a country.

ORIGIN – Latin *tertiarius* 'of the third part or rank'.

terylene /terileen/ > *noun* Brit. trademark a polyester fibre used to make clothing, bed linen, etc.

TESL > *abbreviation* teaching of English as a second language.

tesla /teslə/ > *noun* Physics the unit of magnetic flux density in the SI system.

ORIGIN – named after the US electrical engineer Nikola *Tesla* (1856–1943).

TESOL /tessol/ > *abbreviation* teaching of English to speakers of other languages.

TESSA > *noun* (in the UK) a tax-exempt special savings account allowing savers to invest a certain amount without paying tax on the interest (replaced in 1999 by the ISA).

tessellate /tessəlayt/ > *verb* 1 decorate (a floor) with mosaics. 2 Mathematics cover (a plane surface) by repeated use of a single shape.

DERIVATIVES – **tessellated** *adjective* **tessellation** *noun*.

ORIGIN – Latin *tessellare*, from *tessera*.

tessera /tessərə/ > *noun* (pl. **tesserae** /tessəree/) **1** a small block of stone, tile, etc. used in a mosaic. **2** (in ancient Greece and Rome) a small tablet of wood or bone used as a token.

ORIGIN – via Latin from Greek, from *tessares* 'four'.

tessitura /tessityoorə/ > *noun* Music the range within which most notes of a vocal part fall.

ORIGIN – Italian, 'texture'.

test[1] > *noun* **1** a procedure intended to establish the quality, performance, or reliability of something. **2** a short examination of proficiency or knowledge. **3** a means of testing something. **4** a difficult situation that reveals the strength or quality of someone or something. **5** an examination of part of the body or a body fluid for medical purposes. **6** Chemistry a procedure for identifying a substance or revealing whether it is present. **7** a test match. > *verb* **1** subject to a test. **2** touch or taste before proceeding further. **3** try severely; tax (a person's endurance or patience).

IDIOMS – **test the water** ascertain feelings or opinions before proceeding further.

DERIVATIVES – **testable** *adjective*.

SYNONYMS – *noun* **1** experiment, pilot study, trial. **3** criterion, touchstone, yardstick. *verb* **1** check, examine, trial, try out.

COMBINATIONS – **test card** Brit. a still television picture transmitted outside normal programme hours to aid in judging the quality of the image. **test case** Law a case setting a precedent for other cases. **test match** an international cricket or rugby match played between teams representing two different countries. **test pilot** a pilot who flies new or modified aircraft to test their performance.

ORIGIN – first denoting a container used for treating gold or silver alloys or ore: from Latin *testum* 'earthen pot'.

test[2] > *noun* Zoology the shell of some invertebrates and protozoans.

ORIGIN – Latin *testa* 'tile, shell'.

testa /testə/ > *noun* (pl. **testae** /testee/) Botany the protective outer covering of a seed.

ORIGIN – Latin, 'tile, shell'.

testament > *noun* **1** a person's will. **2** evidence or proof of a fact, event, or quality. **3** (in biblical use) a covenant or dispensation. **4** (**Testament**) a division of the Bible (see *Old Testament*, *New Testament*).

SYNONYMS – **2** demonstration, monument, testimony.

ORIGIN – Latin *testamentum* 'a will', from *testari* 'testify', from *testis* 'a witness'.

testamentary > *adjective* of, in, or through a will.

testate /testayt/ > *adjective* having made a valid will before one dies. > *noun* a person who dies testate.

ORIGIN – from Latin *testari* 'testify, witness'.

testator /testaytər/ > *noun* (fem. **testatrix** /testaytriks/, pl. **testatrices** /testaytriseez/ or **testatrixes**) Law a person who has made a will or given a legacy.

test bed > *noun* a piece of equipment for testing new machinery, especially aircraft engines.

test-drive > *verb* drive (a motor vehicle) to determine its qualities.

tester[1] > *noun* **1** a person or device that tests. **2** a sample of a product allowing customers to try it before purchase.

tester[2] > *noun* a canopy over a four-poster bed.

ORIGIN – Latin *testerium*, from a base meaning 'head'.

testicle > *noun* either of the two oval organs that produce sperm in male mammals, enclosed in the scrotum behind the penis.

WORDFINDER – castrate (*remove the testicles of*), monorchid (*having only one testicle*), orchidectomy (*surgical removal of one or both testicles*), orchitis (*inflammation of one or both testicles*).

DERIVATIVES – **testicular** *adjective*.

wordpower facts

Testicle

The English word **testicle** is connected to a number of apparently unrelated words, for example **attest**, **contest**, **intestate**, **testament**, and **testify**. The link is the Latin word *testis*, which means 'a witness': the idea seems to have been that a testicle was a witness to a man's virility. *Testis* could also mean 'testicle' in Latin, and is used today in medical contexts with the same meaning. The Greek word for testicle is *orkhis*; this gave rise to medical terms such as **orchidectomy**, as well as **orchid** the name of the plant: the tubers of orchids were said to resemble testicles.

testify > *verb* (**testifies**, **testified**) **1** give evidence as a witness in a law court. **2** serve as evidence or proof of something.

testimonial /testimōniəl/ > *noun* **1** a formal statement testifying to someone's

character and qualifications. **2** a public tribute to a person and their achievements.

testimony > *noun* (pl. **testimonies**) **1** a formal statement, especially one given in a court of law. **2** evidence or proof of something.

ORIGIN – Latin *testimonium*, from *testis* 'a witness'.

testis /testiss/ > *noun* (pl. **testes** /testeez/) Anatomy & Zoology an organ which produces sperm.

ORIGIN – Latin (see TESTICLE).

testosterone /testostərōn/ > *noun* a steroid hormone stimulating development of male secondary sexual characteristics.

ORIGIN – from TESTIS + *sterone* (blend of STEROL and KETONE).

test tube > *noun* a thin glass tube closed at one end, used to hold material for laboratory testing or experiments.

COMBINATIONS – **test-tube baby** informal a baby conceived by in vitro fertilisation.

testy > *adjective* easily irritated; irritable.

DERIVATIVES – **testily** *adverb* **testiness** *noun*.

SYNONYMS – crotchety, dyspeptic, irascible, irritable, peevish, tetchy.

ORIGIN – first used in the sense 'headstrong, impetuous': from Old French *teste* 'head'.

tetanic /titannik/ > *adjective* relating to or characteristic of tetanus.

tetanus /tettənəss/ > *noun* a disease causing muscle rigidity and spasms, spread by bacteria.

ORIGIN – Latin, from Greek *tetanos* 'muscular spasm'.

tetany /tettəni/ > *noun* a condition of intermittent muscular spasms, caused by parathyroid malfunction and consequent calcium deficiency.

tetchy > *adjective* bad-tempered and irritable.

DERIVATIVES – **tetchily** *adverb* **tetchiness** *noun*.

SYNONYMS – crotchety, dyspeptic, irascible, irritable, peevish, testy.

ORIGIN – probably from Scots *tache* 'blotch, fault'.

tête-à-tête /tetaatet/ > *noun* (pl. same or **tête-à-têtes** pronunc. same) a private conversation between two people. > *adjective & adverb* involving or happening privately between two people.

ORIGIN – French, 'head-to-head'.

tether > *noun* a rope or chain with which an animal is tied to restrict its movement. > *verb* tie with a tether.

ORIGIN – Old Norse *tjóthr*, from a base meaning 'fasten'.

tetra- (also **tetr-** before a vowel) > *combining form* four; having four: *tetragram*.

ORIGIN – from Greek *tettares* 'four'.

tetrad /tetrad/ > *noun* technical a group or set of four.
ORIGIN – Greek *tetras*.

tetraethyl lead /tetrəeethīl/ > *noun* Chemistry an oily organic compound of lead, used as an anti-knock agent in leaded petrol.

Tetragrammaton /tetrəgrammətton/ > *noun* the Hebrew name of God transliterated in four letters as *YHWH* or *JHVH* and articulated as *Yahweh* or *Jehovah*.
ORIGIN – Greek, 'thing having four letters'.

tetrahedron /tetrəheedrən/ > *noun* (pl. **tetrahedra** or **tetrahedrons**) a solid having four plane triangular faces.
DERIVATIVES – **tetrahedral** *adjective*.

tetralogy /titraləji/ > *noun* (pl. **tetralogies**) a group of four related literary or operatic works.

tetrameter /titrammitər/ > *noun* Poetry a verse of four measures.

tetraplegia /tetrəpleejə/ > *noun* another term for QUADRIPLEGIA.
DERIVATIVES – **tetraplegic** *adjective* & *noun*.

tetrapod > *noun* 1 Zoology an animal of a group which includes all vertebrates apart from fishes. 2 an object or structure with four feet, legs, or supports.
ORIGIN – from Greek *tetrapous* 'four-footed'.

tetrarch /tetraark/ > *noun* (in the Roman Empire) the governor of one of four divisions of a country or province.
DERIVATIVES – **tetrarchy** (pl. **tetrarchies**) *noun*.
ORIGIN – Greek *tetrarkhēs*, from *tetra-* 'four' + *arkhein* 'to rule'.

tetrathlon /tetrathlən/ > *noun* a sporting contest in which participants compete in four events, typically riding, shooting, swimming, and running.

tetrode /tetrōd/ > *noun* a thermionic valve with four electrodes.

Teuton /tyoot'n/ > *noun* 1 a member of an ancient Germanic people who lived in Jutland. 2 often derogatory a German.
ORIGIN – from Latin *Teutones* (plural), from a root meaning 'people' or 'country'.

Teutonic /tyootonnik/ > *adjective* 1 relating to the Teutons. 2 informal, often derogatory displaying characteristics that are popularly attributed to Germans.

Texan > *noun* a person from the US state of Texas. > *adjective* relating to Texas.

Tex-Mex > *adjective* associated with both Mexico and the southern US. > *noun* Tex-Mex music or food.

text > *noun* 1 a written or printed work regarded in terms of content rather than form. 2 the main body of a book or other work as distinct from appendices, illustrations, etc. 3 written or printed words or computer data. 4 a written work chosen as a subject of study. 5 a passage from the Bible, especially as the subject of a sermon.

wordpower facts
Text
A **text** is literally 'something woven'. The word comes from Latin *textus* 'tissue, literary style', which is from *texere* 'to weave'. The change of meaning came about from the idea of a literary work being 'woven' together. The root word *texere* is the source of many English words, among them **context, pretext, texture, textile, texture,** and **tissue.**

textbook > *noun* a book used as a standard work for the study of a subject. > *adjective* conforming to an established standard; exemplary.

textile > *noun* 1 a type of cloth or woven fabric. 2 informal (among nudists) a person who wears clothes. > *adjective* relating to fabric or weaving.
ORIGIN – Latin *textilis*, from *texere* 'weave'.

textual > *adjective* relating to a text or texts.
DERIVATIVES – **textually** *adverb*.
COMBINATIONS – **textual criticism** the process of attempting to ascertain the original wording of a text.

textualist > *noun* a person adhering strictly to a text, especially that of the scriptures.
DERIVATIVES – **textualism** *noun*.

textuality > *noun* 1 the quality or use of language characteristic of written works as opposed to spoken usage. 2 textualism.

texture > *noun* 1 the feel, appearance, or consistency of a surface, substance, or fabric. 2 the quality created by the combination of elements in a work of music or literature. > *verb* give a rough or raised texture to.
DERIVATIVES – **textural** *adjective*.
COMBINATIONS – **textured vegetable protein** a protein obtained from soya beans and made to resemble minced meat.
ORIGIN – Latin *textura* 'weaving', from *texere* 'weave'.

texturise (also **texturize**) > *verb* give (something) a particular texture.

T-group > *noun* Psychology a group of people observing and seeking to improve their own interpersonal behaviour.
ORIGIN – *T* for *training*.

TGV > *noun* a French high-speed passenger train.
ORIGIN – abbreviation of French *train à grande vitesse*.

Th > *symbol* the chemical element thorium.

-th¹ (also **-eth**) > *suffix* forming ordinal and fractional numbers from *fourth* onwards.

-th² > *suffix* forming nouns: 1 (from verbs) denoting an action or process: *growth*. 2 (from adjectives) denoting a state: *filth*.

Thai /tī/ > *noun* (pl. same or **Thais**) 1 a person from Thailand. 2 the official language of Thailand.
ORIGIN – Thai, 'free'.

thalamus /thaləməss/ > *noun* (pl. **thalami** /thaləmī/) Anatomy each of two masses of grey matter in the forebrain, relaying sensory information.
ORIGIN – Greek *thalamos*.

thalassaemia /thaləseemiə/ (US **thalassemia**) > *noun* a hereditary disease in which the blood contains an abnormal form of the pigment haemoglobin, widespread in Mediterranean, African, and Asian countries.
ORIGIN – from Greek *thalassa* 'sea' (because the disease was first known around the Mediterranean).

thalassic /thəlassik/ > *adjective* literary or technical relating to the sea.

thalassotherapy > *noun* the use of seawater in cosmetic and health treatment.

thalidomide /thəliddəmīd/ > *noun* a drug formerly used as a sedative, but found to cause malformation of the fetus when taken in early pregnancy.

thallium /thaliəm/ > *noun* a soft silvery-white metallic chemical element whose compounds are very poisonous.
ORIGIN – from Greek *thallos* 'green shoot', because of a green line in its spectrum.

thallus /thaləss/ > *noun* (pl. **thalli** /thalī/) Botany a simple plant body not differentiated into stem, leaves, and roots and without a vascular system, typical of algae, fungi, lichens, and some liverworts.
ORIGIN – Greek *thallos* 'green shoot'.

than > *conjunction* & *preposition* 1 introducing the second element in a comparison. 2 used to introduce an exception or contrast. 3 used in expressions indicating one thing happening immediately after another.
USAGE – some people insist that it is wrong to use *me* and *us* rather than *I* and *we* after **than**: *she's younger than I* rather than *she's younger than me*. In modern English, however, the use with *me* and *us* is quite acceptable, while *I* and *we* are generally used only in formal situations.
ORIGIN – Old English, originally the same word as THEN.

thanatology /thannətolləji/ > *noun* the scientific study of death and practices associated with it.
ORIGIN – from Greek *thanatos* 'death'.

thane /thayn/ > *noun* 1 (in Anglo-Saxon England) a man granted land by the king or a nobleman, ranking between a freeman and a hereditary noble. 2 (in Scotland) a man who held land from a Scottish king and ranked with an earl's son.

ORIGIN – Old English, 'servant, soldier'.

thank > *verb* **1** express gratitude to. **2** *ironic* blame or hold responsible: *you have only yourself to thank.*

IDIOMS – **thank goodness** (or **God** or **heavens**) an expression of relief. **thank one's lucky stars** feel grateful for one's good fortune.

COMBINATIONS – **thank-offering** an offering made as an act of thanksgiving. **thank you** a polite expression of gratitude.

thankful > *adjective* **1** pleased and relieved. **2** expressing gratitude; grateful.

DERIVATIVES – **thankfulness** *noun*.

thankfully > *adverb* **1** in a thankful manner. **2** fortunately.

thankless > *adjective* **1** (of a job or task) unpleasant and unlikely to gain the appreciation of others. **2** not showing or feeling gratitude.

thanks > *plural noun* **1** an expression of gratitude. **2** another way of saying *thank you.*

IDIOMS – **no thanks to** despite the unhelpfulness of. **thanks to** due to.

thanksgiving > *noun* **1** the expression of gratitude, especially to God. **2** (**Thanksgiving**) (in North America) an annual holiday commemorating a harvest festival celebrated by the Pilgrim Fathers in 1621, held in the US on the fourth Thursday in November and in Canada usually on the second Monday in October.

that > *pronoun & determiner* (pl. **those**) **1** used to identify a specific person or thing observed or heard by the speaker. **2** referring to the more distant of two things near to the speaker. **3** referring to a specific thing previously mentioned or known. **4** used in singling out someone or something with a particular feature. **5** (**as pronoun**) (pl. **that**) used instead of which, who, when, etc. to introduce a defining clause. > *adverb* **1** to such a degree. **2** *informal* very: *he wasn't that far away.* > *conjunction* **1** introducing a subordinate clause. **2** *literary* expressing a wish or regret.

IDIOMS – **and all that** (or **and that**) *informal* and so on. **like that** *informal* instantly or effortlessly. **that is** (or **that is to say**) a formula introducing or following an explanation or further clarification. **that said** even so. **that's that** there is nothing more to do or say about the matter.

USAGE – is there any difference between the use of **that** and **which** in sentences such as *any book that/which gets children reading is worth having*? The general rule is that, in relative clauses serving to define or restrict the reference to the particular one

described, **which** or **that** can be used, but in clauses serving only to give additional information, **that** cannot be: *this book, which is set in the last century, is very popular with teenagers* but not *this book, that is set in the last century, is very popular with teenagers.* Some people hold that **that** should be used for non-human references, while **who** should be used for human references: *a house that overlooks the park* but *the woman who lives next door.* In practice, while it is true to say that **who** is restricted to human references, **that** is interchangeable with **who** in this context.

thatch > *noun* **1** a roof covering of straw, reeds, or similar material. **2** *informal* the hair on a person's head. > *verb* cover with thatch.

DERIVATIVES – **thatcher** *noun*.

ORIGIN – Old English, 'cover'.

Thatcherism > *noun* the political and economic policies advocated by the British Conservative politician Margaret Thatcher, Prime Minister 1979–90.

DERIVATIVES – **Thatcherite** *noun & adjective*.

thaumaturge /**thaw**məturj/ > *noun* a person who works wonders or miracles.

DERIVATIVES – **thaumaturgical** *adjective* **thaumaturgy** *noun*.

ORIGIN – Greek *thaumatourgos*, from *thauma* 'marvel' + *-ergos* '-working'.

thaw > *verb* **1** (of ice, snow, or a frozen thing) become liquid or soft as a result of warming up. **2** (**it thaws, it is thawing**, etc.) the weather becomes warmer and causes snow and ice to melt. **3** (of a part of the body) become warm enough to stop feeling numb. **4** make or become friendlier or more cordial. > *noun* **1** a period of warmer weather that thaws ice and snow. **2** an increase in friendliness or cordiality.

the > *determiner* **1** denoting one or more people or things already mentioned or assumed to be common knowledge; the definite article. **2** used to refer to a person, place, or thing that is unique. **3** used to point forward to a following qualifying or defining clause or phrase. **4** used to make a generalised reference rather than identifying a particular instance. **5** enough of. **6** (pronounced stressing 'the') used to indicate that someone or something is the best known or most important of that name or type. **7** used with comparatives to indicate how one amount or degree of something varies in relation to another.

theatre (US **theater**) > *noun* **1** a building in which plays and other performances are given. **2** the writing and production of plays. **3** a play or other activity considered in terms of its dramatic quality. **4** (also **lecture theatre**) a room for lectures with seats in tiers. **5** *Brit.* an operating theatre. **6**

the area in which something happens: *a theatre of war.* **7** (before another noun) (of weapons) intermediate between tactical and strategic.

WORDFINDER – thespian (*of the theatre*); impresario (*a person who finances theatrical productions*), repertory (*performance of a repertoire of plays by a theatre company*); *seats in a theatre, lowest to highest:* stalls, dress circle, circle, gallery (or balcony or gods).

ORIGIN – Greek *theatron*, from *theasthai* 'behold'.

theatric /thiatrik/ > *adjective* theatrical. > *noun* (**theatrics**) theatricals.

theatrical > *adjective* **1** of, for, or relating to acting, actors, or the theatre. **2** excessively dramatic. > *noun* **1** a professional actor or actress. **2** (**theatricals**) theatrical performances or behaviour.

DERIVATIVES – **theatricality** *noun* **theatrically** *adverb*.

SYNONYMS – *adjective* **2** histrionic, melodramatic, stagy.

thebe /**thay**bay/ > *noun* (pl. same) a monetary unit of Botswana, equal to one hundredth of a pula.

ORIGIN – Setswana (a Bantu language), 'shield'.

thecodont /**thee**kədont/ > *noun* Palaeontology a Triassic fossil reptile thought to be an evolutionary ancestor of the dinosaurs.

ORIGIN – from Greek *thēkē* 'case' + *odous* 'tooth' (because the teeth were fixed in sockets in the jaw).

thee > *pronoun* (**second person sing.**) archaic or dialect form of **YOU**, as the singular object of a verb or preposition.

theft > *noun* the action or crime of stealing.

thegn /thayn/ > *noun* an English thane.

their > *possessive determiner* **1** belonging to or associated with the people or things previously mentioned or easily identified. **2** belonging to or associated with a person of unspecified sex (used in place of either 'his' or 'his or her'). **3** (**Their**) used in titles: *Their Majesties.*

USAGE – on the use of **their** in the singular to mean 'his or her', see the note at **THEY**.

theirs* > *possessive pronoun* used to refer to something belonging to or associated with two or more people or things previously mentioned.

***SPELLING – no apostrophe: theirs.

theism /**thee**iz'm/ > *noun* belief in the existence of a god or gods, specifically of a creator who intervenes in the universe. Compare with **DEISM**.

DERIVATIVES – **theist** *noun* **theistic** /theeistik/ *adjective*.

ORIGIN – from Greek *theos* 'god'.

them > *pronoun* (**third person pl.**) **1** used as the object of a verb or preposition to refer to two or more people or things previously mentioned or easily identified. **2** referring to a person of unspecified sex (used in place of either 'him' or 'him or her'). **3** archaic themselves.

USAGE – on the use of **them** in the singular to mean 'his or her', see the note at **THEY**.

thematic > *adjective* having or relating to subjects or a particular subject. > *noun* (**thematics**) (treated as sing. or pl.) a body of topics for study or discussion.

DERIVATIVES – **thematically** *adverb*.

theme > *noun* **1** a subject or topic on which a person speaks, writes, or thinks. **2** Music a prominent or frequently recurring melody or group of notes in a composition. **3** an idea that recurs in or pervades a work of art or literature. **4** (before another noun) (of music) accompanying the beginning and end of a film or programme. **5** (before another noun) (of a restaurant or pub) designed to be suggestive of a particular country, historical period, etc. **6** US an essay on a set subject. > *verb* give a particular setting or ambience to.

SYNONYMS – *noun* **1** issue, motif, subject matter.

COMBINATIONS – **theme park** an amusement park with a unifying setting or idea.

ORIGIN – Greek, 'proposition'.

themself > *pronoun* (third person sing.) informal used instead of 'himself' or 'herself' to refer to a person of unspecified sex.

USAGE – the standard reflexive form corresponding to **they** and **them** is **themselves**, as in *they can do it themselves*. The singular form **themself**, first recorded in the 14th century, has re-emerged in recent years to correspond to the singular gender-neutral use of **they**, as in *this is the first step in helping someone to help themself*. It is not generally accepted as good English, however: use **themselves**.

themselves > *pronoun* (third person pl.) **1** used as the object of a verb or preposition to refer to a group of people or things previously mentioned as the subject of the clause. **2** used to emphasise a particular group of people or things mentioned. **3** used instead of 'himself' or 'herself' to refer to a person of unspecified sex.

then > *adverb* **1** at that time. **2** after that; next. **3** also. **4** therefore.

IDIOMS – **but then (again)** on the other hand. **then and there** immediately.

thence (also **from thence**) > *adverb* formal **1** from a place or source previously mentioned. **2** as a consequence.

USAGE – **thence** means 'from that place', as in *he travelled across France to Spain and thence to England*. Strictly speaking, the preposition **from**, as in *they proceeded from thence to Scotland*, is redundant, but nevertheless **from thence** is usually accepted as good English.

thenceforth (also **from thenceforth**)

> *adverb* archaic or literary from that time, place, or point onward.

thenceforward > *adverb* thenceforth.

theocentric /thee-ōsentrik/ > *adjective* having God as a central focus.

theocracy /thiokrəsi/ > *noun* (pl. **theocracies**) a system of government in which priests rule in the name of God or a god.

DERIVATIVES – **theocratic** *adjective*.

ORIGIN – from Greek *theos* 'god'.

theodicy /thioddisi/ > *noun* the justification of God and divine providence in view of the existence of evil.

ORIGIN – from Greek *theos* 'god' + *dikē* 'justice'.

theodolite /thioddəlīt/ > *noun* a surveying instrument with a rotating telescope for measuring horizontal and vertical angles.

ORIGIN – modern Latin *theodelitus*.

theogony /thioggəni/ > *noun* (pl. **theogonies**) the genealogy of a group or system of gods.

ORIGIN – from Greek *theos* 'god' + *-gonia* '-begetting'.

theologian /thiəlōjən/ > *noun* a person expert in or studying theology.

theology > *noun* (pl. **theologies**) **1** the study of God and religious belief. **2** religious beliefs and theory when systematically developed.

WORDFINDER – divinity (*study of religion*), ecclesiology (*theology applied to the nature and structure of the Christian Church*), eschatology (*the part of theology concerned with death, judgement, and destiny*), liberation theology (*movement in Christian theology which attempts to address problems of poverty and social injustice*), original sin (*tendency to evil of all human beings*), predestination (*divine ordaining of all that will happen*).

DERIVATIVES – **theological** *adjective* **theologically** *adverb* **theologist** *noun*.

theophany /thioffəni/ > *noun* (pl. **theophanies**) a visible manifestation to humankind of God or a god.

ORIGIN – from Greek *theos* 'god' + *phainein* 'to show'.

theorem /theeərəm/ > *noun* **1** Physics & Mathematics a general proposition not self-evident but proved by a chain of reasoning. **2** Mathematics a rule expressed by symbols or formulae.

ORIGIN – Greek *theōrēma* 'speculation, proposition'.

theoretical (also **theoretic**) > *adjective* **1** concerned with or involving theory rather than its practical application. **2** based on or calculated through theory.

DERIVATIVES – **theoretically** *adverb*.

SYNONYMS – **2** abstract, academic, hypothetical, speculative.

theoretician /theeərətish'n/ > *noun* a

person who develops or studies the theoretical framework of a subject.

theorise (also **theorize**) > *verb* form a theory or theories about something.

DERIVATIVES – **theorisation** *noun*.

theorist > *noun* a theoretician.

theory > *noun* (pl. **theories**) **1** a system of ideas intended to explain something, especially one based on general principles independent of the thing to be explained. **2** an idea accounting for or justifying something. **3** a set of principles on which an activity is based.

IDIOMS – **in theory** in an ideal or hypothetical situation.

ORIGIN – Greek *theōria* 'contemplation, speculation'.

theosophy /thiossəfi/ > *noun* a philosophy maintaining that a knowledge of God may be achieved through spiritual ecstasy, direct intuition, or special individual relations.

DERIVATIVES – **theosophical** *adjective* **theosophist** *noun*.

ORIGIN – from Greek *theosophos* 'wise concerning God'.

therapeutic /therrəpyōōtik/ > *adjective* **1** relating to the healing of disease. **2** having a good effect on the body or mind.

DERIVATIVES – **therapeutically** *adverb*.

therapsid /therapsid/ > *noun* Palaeontology a fossil reptile of a large group including the cynodonts, related to the evolutionary ancestors of mammals.

ORIGIN – from Greek *thēr* 'beast' + *hapsis* 'arch' (referring to the structure of the skull).

therapy > *noun* (pl. **therapies**) **1** treatment intended to relieve or heal a disorder. **2** the treatment of mental or psychological disorders by psychological means.

DERIVATIVES – **therapist** *noun*.

ORIGIN – Greek *therapeia* 'healing', from *therapeuein* 'minister to, treat medically'.

Theravada /therrəvaadə/ > *noun* the more conservative of the two major traditions of Buddhism (the other being Mahayana), practised mainly in Sri Lanka, Burma (Myanmar), Thailand, Cambodia, and Laos.

ORIGIN – Pali (an ancient language related to Sanskrit), 'doctrine of the elders'.

there > *adverb* **1** in, at, or to that place or position. **2** in that respect; on that issue. **3** used in attracting attention to someone or something. **4** (usu. **there is** or **are**) used to indicate the fact or existence of something. > *exclamation* **1** used to focus attention. **2** used to comfort someone.

IDIOMS – **here and there** in various places. **so there** informal used to express defiance. **there and then** immediately.

thereabouts (also **thereabout**) > *adverb* **1** near that place. **2** used to indicate that a date or figure is approximate.

thereafter > *adverb* formal after that time.

thereat > *adverb* archaic or formal **1** at that place. **2** on account of or after that.

thereby > *adverb* by that means; as a result of that.

therefore > *adverb* for that reason; consequently.

therefrom > *adverb* archaic or formal from that or that place.

therein > *adverb* archaic or formal in that place, document, or respect.

thereinafter (or **thereinbefore**) > *adverb* archaic or formal in a later (or an earlier) part of that document.

thereof > *adverb* formal of the thing just mentioned; of that.

thereon > *adverb* formal on or following from the thing just mentioned.

there's > *contraction* **1** there is. **2** there has.

thereto (also **thereunto**) > *adverb* archaic or formal to that or that place.

thereupon > *adverb* formal immediately or shortly after that.

therewith > *adverb* archaic or formal **1** with or in the thing mentioned. **2** soon or immediately after that; forthwith.

therm > *noun* a unit of heat, especially as the former statutory unit of gas supplied in the UK equivalent to 100,000 British thermal units or 105.5 million joules.
ORIGIN – from Greek *thermē* 'heat'.

thermal > *adjective* **1** relating to heat. **2** (of a garment) made of a fabric that provides good insulation to keep the body warm. > *noun* **1** an upward current of warm air, used by birds, gliders, and balloonists to gain height. **2** (**thermals**) thermal garments, especially underwear.
DERIVATIVES – **thermally** *adverb*.
COMBINATIONS – **thermal capacity** the quantity of heat needed to raise the temperature of a body by one degree. **thermal imaging** the technique of using the heat given off by an object to produce an image of it or locate it. **thermal spring** a spring of naturally hot water.

thermic > *adjective* relating to heat.

thermionic /thermionnik/ > *adjective* of or relating to the emission of electrons from substances heated to very high temperatures.
COMBINATIONS – **thermionic valve** a vacuum tube giving a flow of thermionic electrons in one direction, used in rectifying a current and in radio reception.

thermistor /thermistər/ > *noun* an electrical resistor whose resistance is greatly reduced by heating, used for measurement and control.

thermochromic > *adjective* undergoing a reversible change of colour when heated or cooled.

thermocline /thermōklīn/ > *noun* a temperature gradient in a lake or other body of water, separating layers at different temperatures.

thermocouple > *noun* a device for measuring or sensing a temperature difference, consisting of two wires of different metals connected at two points, between which a voltage is developed in proportion to any temperature difference.

thermodynamics > *plural noun* (treated as sing.) the branch of science concerned with the relations between heat and other forms of energy involved in physical and chemical processes.
DERIVATIVES – **thermodynamic** *adjective* **thermodynamically** *adverb*.

thermoelectric > *adjective* producing electricity by a difference of temperatures.

thermogram > *noun* a record made by a thermograph.

thermograph > *noun* an instrument that produces a record of the varying temperature or infrared radiation over an area or during a period of time.
DERIVATIVES – **thermographic** *adjective* **thermography** *noun*.

thermoluminescence > *noun* the property of some materials of becoming luminescent when treated and heated, used as a means of dating ancient artefacts.
DERIVATIVES – **thermoluminescent** *adjective*.

thermometer > *noun* an instrument for measuring and indicating temperature, typically consisting of a graduated glass tube containing mercury or alcohol which expands when heated.

thermonuclear > *adjective* relating to or using nuclear fusion reactions that occur at very high temperatures.

thermopile /thermōpīl/ > *noun* a set of thermocouples arranged for measuring small quantities of radiant heat.

thermoplastic > *adjective* (of a substance) becoming plastic when heated.

thermoregulation > *noun* Physiology the regulation of bodily temperature.

Thermos > *noun* trademark a vacuum flask.
ORIGIN – Greek, literally 'hot'.

thermosetting > *adjective* (of a substance) setting permanently when heated.

thermosphere > *noun* the upper region of the atmosphere above the mesosphere.

thermostat /therməstat/ > *noun* a device that automatically regulates temperature or activates a device at a set temperature.
DERIVATIVES – **thermostatic** *adjective* **thermostatically** *adverb*.

theropod /theerəpod/ > *noun* a dinosaur of a group including bipedal carnivores such as the carnosaurs and dromaeosaurs.
ORIGIN – from Greek *thēr* 'beast' + *pous* 'foot'.

thesaurus /thəsawrəss/ > *noun* (pl. **thesauri** /thisawrī/ or **thesauruses**) a book that lists words in groups of synonyms and related concepts.
ORIGIN – Latin, from Greek *thēsauros* 'storehouse, treasure'.

these plural of **THIS**.

thesis /theesiss/ > *noun* (pl. **theses** /theeseez/) **1** a statement or theory put forward to be maintained or proved. **2** a long essay or dissertation involving personal research, written as part of a university degree.
SYNONYMS – **1** argument, hypothesis, proposal, proposition, theory.
ORIGIN – Greek, 'placing, a proposition'.

thespian /thespiən/ > *adjective* relating to drama and the theatre. > *noun* an actor or actress.
ORIGIN – from the name of the Greek dramatic poet *Thespis* (6th century BC).

theta /theetə/ > *noun* the eighth letter of the Greek alphabet (Θ, θ), transliterated as 'th'.
COMBINATIONS – **theta rhythm** Physiology low-frequency electrical activity observed in the brain under certain conditions.
ORIGIN – Greek.

thew /thyoo/ (also **thews**) > *noun* literary muscle or muscular strength.
ORIGIN – Old English, 'usage, custom', later 'a virtue or good quality', (in plural) 'physical endowments, strength'.

they > *pronoun* (third person pl.) **1** used to refer to two or more people or things previously mentioned or easily identified. **2** people in general. **3** informal people in authority regarded collectively. **4** used to refer to a person of unspecified sex (in place of either 'he' or 'he or she').
USAGE – in recent years many people have come to dislike the traditional use of **he** to refer to a person of either sex, and **they** has increasingly been used to refer to a single person of unspecified sex. **They** is now generally accepted in contexts where it follows an indefinite pronoun such as **anyone, no one, someone,** or **a person,** as in *anyone can join if they are a resident* and *each to their own.* It is less widely accepted when it comes after a singular noun: sentences such as *ask a friend if they could help* are still criticised for being ungrammatical, although **they** (with its counterparts **them, their,** and **themselves**) has actually been used in such a way since at least the 16th century. **They** is used in this dictionary in many cases where **he** would have been used formerly.

they'd > *contraction* **1** they had. **2** they would.

they'll > *contraction* **1** they shall. **2** they will.

they're > *contraction* they are.

they've > *contraction* they have.

thiamine /thīəmeen/ (also **thiamin** /thīəmin/) > *noun* vitamin B_1, a compound found in unrefined cereals, beans, and liver, a deficiency of which causes beriberi.

ORIGIN – from Greek *theion* 'sulphur' + **AMINE**.

thick > *adjective* **1** with opposite sides or surfaces relatively far apart. **2** (of a garment or fabric) made of heavy material. **3** made up of a large number of things or people close together. **4** (**thick with**) densely filled or covered with. **5** (of the air or atmosphere) opaque, heavy, or stuffy. **6** (of a liquid or a semi-liquid substance) relatively firm in consistency; not flowing freely. **7** informal of low intelligence; stupid. **8** (of a voice) not clear or distinct; hoarse or husky. **9** (of an accent) very marked and difficult to understand. **10** informal having a very close, friendly relationship. > *noun* (**the thick of**) the middle or the busiest part of (something).

IDIOMS – **a bit thick** Brit. informal unfair or unreasonable. **thick and fast** rapidly and in great numbers. (**as**) **thick as thieves** informal very close or friendly. (**as**) **thick as two short planks** (or **as a plank**) Brit. informal very stupid. **the thick end of** Brit. the greater part of (something). **through thick and thin** under all circumstances, no matter how difficult.

DERIVATIVES – **thickly** adverb.

SYNONYMS – *adjective* **1** broad, bulky, large, wide.

COMBINATIONS – **thickheaded** (also **thick-skulled** or **thick-witted**) informal dull and stupid.

thicken > *verb* make or become thick or thicker.

IDIOMS – **the plot thickens** the situation is becoming more complicated and puzzling.

DERIVATIVES – **thickener** noun.

thickening > *noun* **1** the process or result of becoming thicker. **2** a thicker area or part. **3** a substance added to a liquid to make it thicker.

thicket > *noun* a dense group of bushes or trees.

thickness > *noun* **1** the distance through an object, as distinct from width or height. **2** the state or quality of being thick. **3** a layer of material. **4** a thicker part of something.

thickset > *adjective* heavily or solidly built; stocky.

thief* > *noun* (pl. **thieves**) a person who steals another person's property.

***SPELLING** – remember, the usual rule is *i* before *e* except after *c*: thief.

thieve > *verb* be a thief; steal things.

DERIVATIVES – **thievery** noun **thieving** noun & adjective **thievish** adjective.

thigh > *noun* the part of the leg between the hip and the knee.

COMBINATIONS – **thigh bone** the femur. **thigh-slapper** informal a very funny joke or anecdote.

thimble > *noun* a metal or plastic cap with a closed end, worn to protect the finger and push the needle in sewing.

thimblerig > *noun* a game in which three inverted thimbles or cups are moved about, contestants having to spot which one has a pea or other object underneath.

ORIGIN – from **THIMBLE** + **RIG²** in the sense 'trick, dodge'.

thin > *adjective* (**thinner**, **thinnest**) **1** having opposite surfaces or sides close together. **2** (of a garment or fabric) made of light material. **3** having little flesh or fat on the body. **4** having few parts or members relative to the area covered or filled; sparse. **5** not dense or heavy. **6** containing much liquid and not much solid substance. **7** (of a sound) faint and high-pitched. **8** (of a smile) weak and forced. **9** lacking substance; weak and inadequate. > *verb* (**thinned**, **thinning**) **1** make or become less thick. **2** remove some plants from (a row or area) to allow the others more room to grow.

IDIOMS – **have a thin time** Brit. informal have a miserable or uncomfortable time.

DERIVATIVES – **thinly** adverb **thinness** noun.

SYNONYMS – *adjective* **1** fine, narrow, slender. **3** lean, slender, slim, svelte. **6** dilute, watery, weak. **9** flimsy, insubstantial, weak.

ANTONYMS – *adjective* **1,6** thick. **2** heavy, thick. **3** fat, plump.

thine > *possessive pronoun* archaic form of **YOURS**. > *possessive determiner* form of **THY** used before a vowel.

thing > *noun* **1** an inanimate material object, especially as distinct from a living sentient being. **2** an unspecified object. **3** (**things**) personal belongings or clothing. **4** an action, activity, concept, or thought. **5** (**things**) unspecified circumstances or matters. **6** (**the thing**) informal what is needed, required, acceptable, or fashionable. **7** (**one's thing**) informal one's special interest or concern.

thingamabob (also **thingamajig** or **thingumajig**) > *noun* another term for **THINGUMMY**.

thingummy /ˈθɪŋəmi/ (also **thingamy**) > *noun* (pl. **thingummies**) informal a person or thing whose name one has forgotten, does not know, or does not wish to mention.

thingy > *noun* (pl. **thingies**) another term for **THINGUMMY**.

think > *verb* (past and past participle **thought**) **1** have a particular opinion, belief, or idea about someone or something. **2** direct one's mind towards someone or something; use one's mind actively to form connected ideas. **3** (**think of** or **about**) take into account or consideration. **4** (**think of** or **about**) consider the possibility or

advantages of. **5** (**think of**) have a particular opinion of. **6** (usu. **think of** or **to do**) call something to mind; remember. > *noun* informal an act of thinking.

IDIOMS – **think better of** decide not to do (something) after reconsideration. **think big** see **BIG**. **think nothing** (or **little**) **of** consider (an activity others regard as odd, wrong, or difficult) as straightforward or normal. **think over** consider (something) carefully. **think through** consider (something) in all its aspects before taking action. **think twice** consider a course of action carefully before embarking on it. **think up** informal invent or devise.

DERIVATIVES – **thinker** noun.

SYNONYMS – *verb* **1** believe, suppose, surmise; informal reckon. **2** cogitate, contemplate, deliberate, meditate, reflect. **6** recall, recollect, remember.

COMBINATIONS – **think tank** a body of experts providing advice and ideas on specific political or economic problems.

thinking > *adjective* using thought or rational judgement; intelligent. > *noun* a person's ideas or opinions.

IDIOMS – **put on one's thinking cap** informal meditate on a problem.

thinner > *noun* a volatile solvent used to make paint or other solutions less viscous.

thinnings > *plural noun* seedlings, trees, or fruit which have been thinned out to improve the growth of those remaining.

thiosulphate (US **thiosulfate**) > *noun* Chemistry a salt containing the anion $S_2O_3^{2-}$, i.e. a sulphate with one oxygen atom replaced by sulphur.

third > *ordinal number* **1** constituting number three in a sequence; 3rd. **2** (**a third** or **one third**) each of three equal parts into which something is or may be divided. **3** Music an interval spanning three consecutive notes in a diatonic scale, e.g. C to E. **4** Brit. a place in the third grade in the examinations for a university degree.

WORDFINDER – tertiary (*third in order or level*).

IDIOMS – **third time lucky** (or US **third time is the charm**) used to express the hope that one may succeed on the third attempt.

DERIVATIVES – **thirdly** adverb.

COMBINATIONS – **third age** Brit. the period in life of active retirement, following middle age. **third estate** the third order or class in a country or society, made up of the common people. **third eye** Hinduism & Buddhism the 'eye of insight' in the forehead of an image of a deity. **third man** Cricket a fielding position near the boundary behind the slips. **third person 1** a third party. **2** see **PERSON** (sense 3). **third rail** an additional rail supplying electric current, used in some electric railway systems. **third way** any option regarded as an alternative to two extremes, especially a political agenda which is moderate and based on general agreement rather than left- or right-wing.

third class > *noun* **1** a group of people or things considered together as the third best. **2** Brit. the third-highest division in the results of the examinations for a university degree. **3** US a cheap class of mail for unsealed printed material. **4** chiefly historical the cheapest and least comfortable accommodation in a train or ship. > *adjective & adverb* of the third-best quality or in the third class.

third-degree > *adjective* **1** (of burns) being of the most severe kind, affecting tissue below the skin. **2** Law, chiefly N. Amer. (of a crime) in the least serious category: *third-degree murder.* > *noun* (**the third degree**) long and harsh questioning to obtain information or a confession.

third party > *noun* a person or group besides the two primarily involved in a situation or dispute. > *adjective* Brit. (of insurance) covering damage or injury suffered by a person other than the insured.

third-rate > *adjective* of inferior or very poor quality.

Third World > *noun* the developing countries of Asia, Africa, and Latin America.

ORIGIN – first used to distinguish the developing countries from the capitalist and Communist blocs.

thirst > *noun* **1** a feeling of needing or wanting to drink. **2** lack of the liquid needed to sustain life. **3** (**thirst for**) a strong desire for. > *verb* **1** archaic feel a need to drink. **2** (**thirst for** or **after**) have a strong desire for.

thirsty > *adjective* (**thirstier, thirstiest**) **1** feeling thirst. **2** (of land, plants, etc.) in need of water; dry or parched. **3** (of an engine, plant, or crop) consuming a lot of fuel or water. **4** informal causing thirst: *modelling is thirsty work.* **5** (**thirsty for**) having or showing a strong desire for.

DERIVATIVES – **thirstily** *adverb* **thirstiness** *noun.*

thirteen > *cardinal number* one more than twelve; 13. (Roman numeral: **xiii** or **XIII.**)

DERIVATIVES – **thirteenth** *ordinal number.*

thirty > *cardinal number* (pl. **thirties**) ten less than forty; 30. (Roman numeral: **xxx** or **XXX.**)

DERIVATIVES – **thirtieth** *ordinal number.*

this > *pronoun & determiner* (pl. **these**) **1** used to identify a specific person or thing close at hand or being indicated or experienced. **2** referring to the nearer of two things close to the speaker. **3** referring to a specific thing or situation just mentioned. **4** used

with periods of time related to the present: *how are you this morning?* > *adverb* to the degree or extent indicated.

thistle > *noun* a plant with a prickly stem and leaves and rounded heads of purple flowers.

COMBINATIONS – **thistledown** the light fluffy down of thistle seeds, which enable them to be blown about in the wind.

thither > *adverb* archaic or literary to or towards that place.

thixotropic /thiksətroppik/ > *adjective* Chemistry becoming more fluid when subjected to an applied stress, such as being shaken or stirred.

ORIGIN – from Greek *thixis* 'touching' + *tropē* 'turning'.

tho' (also **tho**) > *conjunction & adverb* informal spelling of THOUGH.

thole¹ /thōl/ (also **thole pin**) > *noun* a pin fitted to the gunwale of a rowing boat to act as the fulcrum for an oar.

thole² /thōl/ > *verb* Scottish or archaic endure without complaint; tolerate.

thong > *noun* **1** a narrow strip of leather or other material, used as a fastening or as the lash of a whip. **2** a skimpy bathing garment or pair of knickers like a G-string. **3** chiefly N. Amer. a flip-flop (shoe).

thoracic /thorassik/ > *adjective* Anatomy & Zoology relating to the thorax.

thorax /thoraks/ > *noun* (pl. **thoraces** /thorəseez/ or **thoraxes**) **1** Anatomy & Zoology the part of the body between the neck and the abdomen. **2** the middle section of an insect's body, bearing the legs and wings.

ORIGIN – Greek.

thorium /thoriəm/ > *noun* a white radioactive metallic chemical element of the actinide series.

ORIGIN – named after *Thor,* the Scandinavian god of thunder.

thorn > *noun* **1** a stiff, sharp-pointed woody projection on the stem or other part of a plant. **2** a thorny bush, shrub, or tree. **3** an Old English and Icelandic runic letter, þ or Þ, eventually superseded by *th.*

IDIOMS – **there is no rose without a thorn** proverb every apparently desirable situation has its share of trouble or difficulty. **a thorn in someone's side** (or **flesh**) a source of continual annoyance or trouble.

thorny > *adjective* (**thornier, thorniest**) **1** having many thorns or thorn bushes. **2** causing distress, difficulty, or trouble.

thorough > *adjective* **1** complete with regard to every detail. **2** performed with or showing great care and completeness. **3** absolute; utter: *he is a thorough nuisance.*

DERIVATIVES – **thoroughly** *adverb* **thoroughness** *noun.*

SYNONYMS – **1** comprehensive, exhaustive, full, thoroughgoing. **2** conscientious, diligent, meticulous, painstaking.

thoroughbred > *adjective* **1** of pure breed. **2** informal of outstanding quality. > *noun* **1** a thoroughbred animal. **2** informal an outstanding or first-class person or thing.

thoroughfare > *noun* a road or path forming a route between two places.

thoroughgoing > *adjective* **1** involving or attending to every detail or aspect. **2** complete; absolute.

thorp (also **thorpe**) > *noun* (in place names) a village or hamlet.

those plural of THAT.

thou¹ > *pronoun* (second person sing.) archaic or dialect form of YOU, as the singular subject of a verb.

thou² > *noun* (pl. same or **thous**) **1** informal a thousand. **2** one thousandth of an inch.

though > *conjunction* **1** despite the fact that; although. **2** however; but. > *adverb* however: *I was hunting for work. Jobs were scarce though.*

thought¹ > *noun* **1** an idea or opinion produced by thinking or occurring suddenly in the mind. **2** the action or process of thinking. **3** (**one's thoughts**) one's mind or attention. **4** an act of considering or remembering: *she hadn't given a thought to Max for some time.* **5** careful consideration or attention. **6** (**thought of**) an intention, hope, or idea of. **7** the formation of opinions, especially as a philosophy or system of ideas, or the opinions so formed.

WORDFINDER – noetic (*relating to thought or the intellect*).

SYNONYMS – **1** concept, idea, notion, opinion, view. **2** cogitation, contemplation, consideration, deliberation, reflection.

IDIOMS – **not give something a second thought** fail to give something more than the slightest consideration. **the thought police** informal people who aim to suppress ideas that deviate from the way of thinking that they believe to be correct.

thought² past and past participle of THINK.

thoughtful > *adjective* **1** absorbed in or involving thought. **2** showing careful consideration or attention. **3** showing regard for other people.

DERIVATIVES – **thoughtfully** *adverb* **thoughtfulness** *noun.*

SYNONYMS – **1** contemplative, meditative, pensive, reflective. **2** intelligent, serious, studious, weighty. **3** attentive, caring, considerate, helpful, kind.

ANTONYMS – **1** vacant. **3** inconsiderate, thoughtless.

thoughtless > *adjective* **1** not showing consideration for other people. **2** without consideration of the consequences.

DERIVATIVES – **thoughtlessly** *adverb* **thoughtlessness** *noun.*

SYNONYMS – **1** inconsiderate, insensitive, selfish, uncaring. **2** careless, heedless, mindless, reckless, unthinking.

ANTONYMS – **1** considerate, thoughtful.

thousand ▸ *cardinal number* (pl. **thousands** or (with numeral or quantifying word) same) **1** (**a** or **one thousand**) the number equivalent to the product of a hundred and ten; 1,000. (Roman numeral: **m** or **M**.) **2** (**thousands**) informal an unspecified large number.

DERIVATIVES – **thousandth** ordinal number.

Thousand Island dressing ▸ *noun* a dressing for salad or seafood consisting of mayonnaise with ketchup and chopped pickles.

ORIGIN – named after a large group of islands in the St Lawrence River between the US and Canada.

Thracian /ˈthraysh'n/ ▸ *noun* a person from Thrace, an ancient country lying west of the Black Sea and north of the Aegean. ▸ *adjective* relating to Thrace.

thrall /thrawl/ ▸ *noun* the state of being in another's power: *she was in thrall to her abusive husband.*

DERIVATIVES – **thraldom** (also **thralldom**) *noun*.

ORIGIN – Old English, 'slave', from Old Norse.

thrash ▸ *verb* **1** beat repeatedly and violently with a stick or whip. **2** move in a violent or uncontrolled way. **3** informal defeat heavily. **4** (**thrash out**) discuss (something) frankly and thoroughly. ▸ *noun* **1** a violent or noisy movement of beating or thrashing. **2** Brit. informal a loud or lavish party. **3** (also **thrash metal**) a style of fast, loud, harsh-sounding rock music.

DERIVATIVES – **thrasher** *noun*.

thread ▸ *noun* **1** a long, thin strand of cotton, nylon, or other fibres used in sewing or weaving. **2** a long, thin line or piece of something. **3** (also **screw thread**) a spiral ridge on the outside of a screw, bolt, etc. or on the inside of a cylindrical hole, to allow two parts to be screwed together. **4** a theme or characteristic running throughout a situation or piece of writing. **5** (**threads**) informal, chiefly N. Amer. clothes. ▸ *verb* **1** pass a thread through (something, especially a needle). **2** move or weave in and out of obstacles. **3** cut a screw thread in or on (a hole, screw, or other object).

DERIVATIVES – **threader** *noun*.

threadbare ▸ *adjective* thin and tattered with age; worn out.

threadworm ▸ *noun* a very slender parasitic nematode worm.

thready ▸ *adjective* (**threadier**, **threadiest**) **1** relating to or resembling a thread. **2** Medicine (of a person's pulse) scarcely perceptible.

threat ▸ *noun* **1** a statement of an intention to inflict injury, damage, or other hostile action. **2** a person or thing likely to cause damage or danger. **3** the possibility of trouble or danger.

ORIGIN – Old English, 'oppression'.

threaten ▸ *verb* **1** make or express a threat to (someone) or to do (something). **2** put at risk; endanger. **3** seem likely to produce an unwelcome result: *the sky threatened rain.*

DERIVATIVES – **threatening** *adjective*.

SYNONYMS – **1** browbeat, bully, intimidate, terrorise. **2** endanger, imperil, jeopardise.

three ▸ *cardinal number* one more than two; 3. (Roman numeral: **iii** or **III**.)

WORDFINDER – hat-trick (*three successes of the same kind*), ternary (*composed of three parts*), trefoil (*thing having three parts*), triad (*group or set of three people or things*), triathlon (*athletic contest consisting of three different events*), triennial (*lasting for or recurring every three years*), triennium (*period of three years*), trifurcate (*divide into three branches or forks*), trio (*group or set of three*), triumvirate (*group of three powerful or notable people or things*).

IDIOMS – **three parts** three out of four equal parts; three quarters.

DERIVATIVES – **threefold** *adjective & adverb*.

COMBINATIONS – **three-dimensional** having or appearing to have length, breadth, and depth. **three-legged race** a race run by pairs of people, one member of each pair having their left leg tied to the right leg of the other. **three-line whip** (in the UK) a written notice, underlined three times to stress its urgency, to members of a political party to attend a parliamentary vote. **three-piece 1** consisting of three matching items. **2** (of a set of furniture) consisting of a sofa and two armchairs. **3** (of a suit) consisting of trousers or a skirt, a waistcoat, and jacket. **three-point turn** a method of turning a vehicle round in a narrow space by moving forwards, backwards, and forwards again in a sequence of arcs. **three-quarter** consisting of three quarters of something in terms of length, angle, time, etc. **three-ring circus** chiefly US **1** a circus with three rings for simultaneous performances. **2** a confused situation; a shambles.

threepence /ˈthreppənss, ˈthrooppənss/ ▸ *noun* Brit. the sum of three pence, especially before decimalisation (1971).

threepenny bit ▸ *noun* Brit. historical a coin worth three old pence (1¼ p).

threescore ▸ *cardinal number* literary sixty.

threesome ▸ *noun* a group of three people or things.

threnody /ˈthrennədi/ ▸ *noun* (pl. **threnodies**) a song or piece of music expressing grief.

ORIGIN – Greek *thrēnōidia*, from *thrēnos* 'wailing' + *ōidē* 'song'.

threonine /ˈthreeəneen/ ▸ *noun* Biochemistry an amino acid which is an essential nutrient in the diet.

ORIGIN – from *threose* (the name of a sugar).

thresh ▸ *verb* separate grain from (wheat or other crops).

thresher /ˈthreshər/ ▸ *noun* **1** a person or machine that threshes. **2** a shark with a long upper lobe to the tail, used to lash the water to herd its prey.

threshold* /ˈthreshōld, ˈthresh-hōld/ ▸ *noun* **1** a strip of wood or stone forming the bottom of a doorway and crossed in entering a house or room. **2** a level or point at which something would start or cease to happen or come into effect.

*****SPELLING – note there is only one *h* in the middle: thre*s*hold.

threw past of **THROW**.

thrice /thrīss/ ▸ *adverb* archaic or literary **1** three times. **2** extremely; very: *I was thrice blessed.*

thrift ▸ *noun* **1** the quality of being careful and not wasteful with money and other resources. **2** a plant which forms low-growing tufts of slender leaves with rounded pink flower heads, growing chiefly on sea cliffs and mountains.

SYNONYMS – **1** economy, frugality, thriftiness.

ANTONYMS – **1** extravagance.

COMBINATIONS – **thrift shop** (also **thrift store**) N. Amer. a shop selling second-hand clothes and other household goods.

ORIGIN – Old Norse, from a word meaning 'grasp, get hold of'.

thriftless ▸ *adjective* spending money in an extravagant and wasteful way.

thrifty ▸ *adjective* (**thriftier**, **thriftiest**) careful and prudent with money.

DERIVATIVES – **thriftily** *adverb* **thriftiness** *noun*.

SYNONYMS – careful, economical, frugal, prudent, sparing.

ANTONYMS – extravagant.

thrill ▸ *noun* **1** a sudden feeling of excitement and pleasure. **2** an exciting or pleasurable experience. **3** a wave or nervous tremor of emotion or sensation. ▸ *verb* **1** have or cause to have a thrill. **2** (of an emotion or sensation) pass with a nervous tremor.

IDIOMS – **thrills and spills** excitement and exhilaration.

DERIVATIVES – **thrilling** *adjective* **thrillingly** *adverb*.

SYNONYMS – noun **1** frisson; informal buzz, kick. verb **1** delight, excite, exhilarate, stimulate.

ORIGIN – alteration of dialect *thirl* 'pierce, bore'.

thriller ▸ *noun* a novel, play, or film with an exciting plot, typically involving crime or espionage.

thrips /thrips/ (also **thrip**) ▸ *noun* (pl.

thrips) a tiny black insect which sucks plant sap, noted for swarming on warm still summer days.

ORIGIN – Greek, 'woodworm'.

thrive > *verb* (past **thrived** or **throve**; past participle **thrived** or **thriven**) 1 grow or develop well or vigorously. 2 prosper; flourish.

SYNONYMS – bloom, blossom, burgeon, flourish, prosper.

ORIGIN – Old Norse, from a word meaning 'grasp, get hold of'.

thro' > *preposition, adverb, & adjective* literary or informal spelling of THROUGH.

throat > *noun* 1 the passage which leads from the back of the mouth of a person or animal. 2 the front part of the neck. 3 literary the voice of a person or a songbird.

IDIOMS – **be at each other's throats** quarrel or fight. **force something down someone's throat** force something on a person's attention. **stick in one's throat** be unwelcome or unacceptable.

throaty > *adjective* (**throatier, throatiest**) (of a voice or other sound) deep and husky.

DERIVATIVES – **throatily** *adverb* **throatiness** *noun*.

throb > *verb* (**throbbed, throbbing**) 1 beat or sound with a strong, regular rhythm; pulsate steadily. 2 feel pain in a series of pulsations. > *noun* a strong, regular beat or sound.

SYNONYMS – *verb* 1 beat, palpitate, pound, pulsate, pulse, thump.

throes /thrōz/ > *plural noun* intense or violent pain and struggle.

IDIOMS – **in the throes of** struggling in the midst of.

thrombocyte > *noun* a blood platelet.

thrombocytopenia /thrombəsītəpeeniə/ > *noun* Medicine deficiency of platelets in the blood, leading to bleeding into the tissues, bruising, and slow blood clotting after injury.

ORIGIN – from Greek *thrombos* 'blood clot' + *penia* 'poverty'.

thrombosis /thrombōsiss/ > *noun* (pl. **thromboses** /thrombōseez/) a local coagulation or clotting of the blood in an artery or vein.

DERIVATIVES – **thrombotic** *adjective*.

ORIGIN – Greek, 'curdling', from *thrombos* 'blood clot'.

thrombus /thrombəss/ > *noun* (pl. **thrombi** /thrombī/) a blood clot in an artery or vein, impeding blood flow.

ORIGIN – Greek *thrombos*.

throne > *noun* 1 a ceremonial chair for a sovereign, bishop, or similar figure. 2 (**the throne**) the power or rank of a sovereign. > *verb* literary place on a throne.

ORIGIN – Greek *thronos* 'elevated seat'.

throng > *noun* a large, densely packed crowd.

> *verb* gather in large numbers in (a place).

throstle /thross'l/ > *noun* Brit. old-fashioned term for THRUSH.

throttle > *noun* 1 a device controlling the flow of fuel or power to an engine. 2 archaic a person's throat, gullet, or windpipe. > *verb* 1 attack or kill by choking or strangling. 2 control (an engine or vehicle) with a throttle.

through > *preposition & adverb* 1 moving in one side and out of the other side of (an opening or location). 2 so as to make a hole or passage in. 3 (preposition) expressing the position or location of something beyond (an opening or an obstacle). 4 expressing the extent of changing orientation. 5 continuing in time to or towards completion of. 6 so as to inspect all or part of. 7 (preposition) N. Amer. up to and including (a particular point in a sequence). 8 by means of. 9 (adverb) so as to be connected by telephone. > *adjective* 1 (of public transport or a ticket) continuing or valid to the final destination. 2 (of traffic, roads, etc.) passing continuously from one side and out of the other side. 3 having successfully passed to the next stage of a competition. 4 informal, chiefly N. Amer. having finished an activity, relationship, etc.

IDIOMS – **through and through** thoroughly or completely.

throughout > *preposition & adverb* all the way through.

throughput > *noun* the amount of material or items passing through a system or process.

throve past of THRIVE.

throw > *verb* (past **threw**; past participle **thrown**) 1 propel with force through the air by a rapid movement of the arm and hand. 2 move or put into place quickly, hurriedly, or roughly. 3 send suddenly into a particular position or condition. 4 disconcert or confuse. 5 project, direct, or cast (light, an expression, etc.) in a particular direction. 6 form (ceramic ware) on a potter's wheel. 7 have (a fit or tantrum). 8 informal give or hold (a party). 9 informal lose (a race or contest) intentionally. 10 send (one's opponent) to the ground in wrestling, judo, etc. 11 (of a horse) unseat (its rider). 12 project (one's voice) so that it appears to come from somewhere else. > *noun* 1 an act of throwing. 2 a small rug or light cover for furniture. 3 (**a throw**) informal a single turn, round, or item.

IDIOMS – **throw away** 1 discard as useless or unwanted. 2 waste or fail to make use of (an opportunity or advantage). **be thrown back on** be forced to rely on (something) because there is no alternative. **throw good money after bad** incur further loss in a hopeless attempt to recoup a previous loss.

throw one's hand in 1 withdraw from a card game because one has a poor hand. 2 withdraw; give up. **throw in** 1 include (something extra) with something that is being sold or offered. 2 make (a remark) casually as an interjection in a conversation. **throw in the towel** (or **sponge**) 1 (in boxing) throw a towel (or sponge) into the ring as a token of defeat. 2 admit defeat. **throw oneself into** start to do (something) with enthusiasm and vigour. **throw open** make generally accessible. **throw out** 1 discard as unwanted. 2 expel unceremoniously. 3 (of a court, legislature, or other body) dismiss or reject. 4 cause numbers or calculations to become inaccurate. **throw over** abandon or reject (someone) as a lover. **throw together** 1 bring people into contact, especially by chance. 2 make or produce hastily or without careful planning. **throw up** vomit. **throw up one's hands** raise both hands in the air as an indication of one's exasperation.

SYNONYMS – *verb* 1 cast, fling, hurl, launch, lob, pitch, toss. 4 bewilder, confuse, disconcert, fluster, unsettle.

ORIGIN – Old English, 'to twist, turn'.

throwaway > *adjective* 1 intended to be discarded after being used once or a few times. 2 (of a remark) expressed in a casual or understated way.

throwback > *noun* a reversion to an earlier ancestral type or characteristic.

throw-in > *noun* Soccer & Rugby the act of throwing the ball from the sideline to restart the game after the ball has gone out of play.

throw-over > *adjective* (of a bedspread or cloth) used as a loose-fitting decorative cover.

thru > *preposition, adverb, & adjective* chiefly US informal spelling of THROUGH.

thrum¹ > *verb* (**thrummed, thrumming**) 1 make a continuous rhythmic humming sound. 2 strum (the strings of a musical instrument) in a rhythmic way. > *noun* a continuous rhythmic humming sound.

thrum² > *noun* (in weaving) an unwoven end of a warp thread, or a fringe of such ends, left in the loom when the finished cloth is cut away. > *verb* (**thrummed, thrumming**) adorn with thrums.

thrush¹ > *noun* a songbird with a brown back and spotted breast.

thrush² > *noun* infection of the mouth and throat or the female genitals by a yeast-like fungus of the genus *Candida*.

thrust > *verb* (past and past participle **thrust**) 1 push suddenly or violently. 2 make one's way forcibly. 3 project conspicuously: *the jetty thrust out into the water.* 4 (**thrust on** or **upon**) impose (something) unwelcome on. > *noun* 1 a sudden or violent lunge or attack. **2** the principal purpose or theme of a course of action or line of reasoning. **3** the force which propels a jet or rocket engine.

DERIVATIVES – **thruster** noun.

SYNONYMS – verb **1** force, impel, propel, push, ram, shove.

ORIGIN – Old Norse.

thrusting > adjective **1** aggressively ambitious. **2** projecting conspicuously.

thud > noun a dull, leaden sound, such as that made by a heavy object falling to the ground. > verb (**thudded**, **thudding**) move, fall, or strike something with a thud.

DERIVATIVES – **thudding** noun.

thug > noun a violent and uncouth man.

DERIVATIVES – **thuggery** noun **thuggish** adjective.

SYNONYMS – hoodlum, hooligan, lout, ruffian.

wordpower facts

Thug

The word **thug** has a fairly modern feel to it, but in fact comes from the Hindi word *thag* 'swindler, thief', and beyond that goes back to ancient Sanskrit. The original Thugs were an organisation of robbers and assassins in India who were followers of the goddess Kali. The Thugs waylaid and strangled their victims, usually travellers, in a ritually prescribed manner, until they were suppressed by the British in the 1830s. The modern sense, denoting any violent and uncouth man, arose surprisingly early, being first recorded in 1839.

thuggee /thugee/ > noun historical the robbery and murder practised by the Thugs in accordance with their ritual.

DERIVATIVES – **thuggism** noun.

thulium /thyōoliəm/ > noun a soft silvery-white metallic chemical element of the lanthanide series.

ORIGIN – Latin, from *Thule*, the name of a country identified by the ancients as the northernmost part of the world.

thumb > noun the short, thick first digit of the hand, set lower and apart from the other four and opposable to them. > verb **1** press, touch, or indicate with one's thumb. **2** turn over (pages) with one's thumb. **3** (**thumbed**) (of a book's pages) worn or soiled by repeated handling. **4** request or obtain (a free ride in a passing vehicle) by signalling with one's thumb.

IDIOMS – **thumb one's nose at** informal show disdain or contempt for. [ORIGIN – with reference to the gesture of putting one's thumb on one's nose and spreading the fingers.] **thumbs up** (or **down**) informal

an indication of satisfaction or approval (or of rejection or failure). [ORIGIN – with reference to the signal of approval or disapproval used by spectators at a Roman amphitheatre (although the Romans used the symbols in reverse).] **under someone's thumb** completely under someone's influence or control.

COMBINATIONS – **thumb index** a set of lettered indentations cut down the side of a book for easy reference. **thumbscrew** an instrument of torture that crushes the thumbs. **thumbtack** N. Amer. a drawing pin.

thumbnail > noun **1** the nail of the thumb. **2** (before another noun) brief or concise: *a thumbnail sketch.*

thump > verb **1** hit heavily with the fist or a blunt implement. **2** put down forcefully, noisily, or decisively. **3** (of a person's heart or pulse) beat or pulsate strongly. **4** (**thump out**) play (a tune) enthusiastically but heavy-handedly. **5** informal defeat heavily. > noun a heavy dull blow or noise.

DERIVATIVES – **thumper** noun.

thumping > adjective **1** pounding; throbbing. **2** informal impressively large: *a thumping 64 per cent majority.*

thunder > noun **1** a loud rumbling or crashing noise heard after a lightning flash due to the expansion of rapidly heated air. **2** a resounding loud deep noise. > verb **1** (**it thunders, it is thundering**, etc.) thunder sounds. **2** move heavily and forcefully. **3** speak loudly, angrily, and forcefully.

DERIVATIVES – **thundery** adjective.

COMBINATIONS – **thunderbug** (also **thunderfly**) a thrips. **thunderclap** a crash of thunder. **thundercloud** a cumulus cloud with a towering or spreading top, charged with electricity and producing thunder and lightning. **thunderhead** a rounded, projecting head of a cumulus cloud.

thunderbolt > noun a flash of lightning with a simultaneous crash of thunder.

thunderflash > noun a noisy but harmless pyrotechnic device used especially in military exercises.

thundering > adjective **1** making a resounding, loud, deep noise. **2** informal extremely great, severe, or impressive: *a thundering bore.*

DERIVATIVES – **thunderingly** adverb.

thunderous > adjective **1** relating to or resembling thunder. **2** (of a person's expression or behaviour) very angry or menacing.

DERIVATIVES – **thunderously** adverb.

thunderstorm > noun a storm with thunder and lightning.

thunderstruck > adjective extremely surprised or shocked.

thurible /thyoorib'l/ > noun a container in which incense is burnt; a censer.

ORIGIN – Latin *thuribulum*, from *thus* 'incense'.

Thursday > noun the day of the week before Friday and following Wednesday.

ORIGIN – Old English, 'day of thunder' (named after the Germanic thunder god *Thor*), translation of Latin *Jovis dies* 'day of Jupiter'.

thus > adverb literary or formal **1** as a result or consequence of this; therefore. **2** in the manner now being indicated or exemplified; in this way. **3** to this point; so.

thwack > verb strike forcefully with a sharp blow. > noun a sharp blow.

thwaite /thwayt/ > noun (in place names) a piece of wild land cleared or reclaimed for cultivation.

ORIGIN – Old Norse, 'paddock'.

thwart /thwawrt/ > verb prevent from succeeding in or accomplishing something. > noun a crosspiece forming a seat for a rower in a boat.

SYNONYMS – verb block, foil, frustrate, hinder, impede, obstruct.

ORIGIN – Old Norse, 'transverse'.

thy (also **thine** before a vowel) > possessive determiner archaic or dialect form of YOUR.

thyme /tīm/ > noun a low-growing aromatic plant of the mint family, used in cooking.

ORIGIN – Greek *thumon*, from *thuein* 'burn, sacrifice'.

thymine /thīmeen/ > noun Biochemistry a compound which is one of the four constituent bases of DNA.

thymol /thīmol/ > noun Chemistry a white crystalline compound present in oil of thyme and used as a flavouring and preservative.

thymus /thīməss/ > noun (pl. **thymi** /thīmī/) a gland situated in the neck, which produces white blood cells for the immune system.

DERIVATIVES – **thymic** adjective.

ORIGIN – Greek *thumos* 'excrescence, thymus gland'.

thyristor /thīristər/ > noun Electronics a kind of solid-state rectifier containing four layers of semiconductor material.

ORIGIN – blend of *thyratron*, denoting a kind of thermionic valve (from Greek *thura* 'gate'), and TRANSISTOR.

thyroid /thīroyd/ > noun (also **thyroid gland**) a large gland in the neck which secretes hormones regulating growth and development through the rate of metabolism.

COMBINATIONS – **thyroid-stimulating hormone** thyrotropin.

ORIGIN – Greek *thureoeidēs* 'shield-shaped', from *thureos* 'oblong shield'.

thyrotoxicosis /thīrōtoksikōsiss/ > noun another term for HYPERTHYROIDISM.

thyrotropin /thīrətrōpin/ > noun Biochemistry

a hormone secreted by the pituitary gland which regulates the production of hormones by the thyroid.

thyroxine /thīrokseen/ > *noun* Biochemistry the main growth hormone produced by the thyroid gland.

thyself > *pronoun* (second person sing.) archaic or dialect form of YOURSELF, corresponding to the subject THOU[1].

Ti > *symbol* the chemical element titanium.

ti > *noun* North American form of TE.

Tia Maria /teeə məreeə/ > *noun* trademark a coffee-flavoured liqueur based on rum.
ORIGIN – Spanish, literally 'Aunt Mary'.

tiara > *noun* 1 a jewelled ornamental band worn on the front of a woman's hair. 2 a three-crowned diadem worn by a pope.
ORIGIN – Greek.

Tibetan > *noun* 1 a person from Tibet. 2 the language of Tibet. > *adjective* relating to Tibet.

tibia /tibbiə/ > *noun* (pl. **tibiae** /tibbi-ee/) Anatomy the inner and typically larger of the two bones between the knee and the ankle, parallel with the fibula.
DERIVATIVES – **tibial** *adjective*.
ORIGIN – Latin, 'shin bone'.

tic > *noun* a habitual contraction of the muscles caused by spasm, most often in the face.
ORIGIN – Italian *ticchio*.

tich /tich/ > *noun* variant spelling of TITCH.

tick[1] > *noun* 1 a mark (✓) used to indicate that an item in a text is correct or has been chosen or checked. 2 a regular short, sharp sound. 3 Brit. informal a moment. > *verb* 1 mark with a tick. 2 make regular ticking sounds. 3 (**tick away** or **by** or **past**) (of time) pass inexorably. 4 (**tick over**) (of an engine) run slowly in neutral. 5 (**tick off**) Brit. informal reprimand or rebuke (someone).
IDIOMS – **make someone tick** informal motivate someone.

tick[2] > *noun* 1 a parasitic spider-like creature (an arachnid) which attaches itself to the skin, from which it sucks blood. 2 informal a parasitic blood-sucking fly, especially the sheep ked.

tick[3] > *noun* (in phrase **on tick**) on credit.
ORIGIN – apparently a shortening of *on the ticket*, referring to a promise to pay.

tick[4] > *noun* 1 a fabric case stuffed to form a mattress or pillow. 2 short for TICKING.
ORIGIN – probably from Greek *thēkē* 'case'.

ticker > *noun* 1 informal a watch. 2 informal a person's heart. 3 N. Amer. a telegraphic or electronic machine that prints out data on a strip of paper.
COMBINATIONS – **ticker tape** a paper strip on which messages are recorded in a telegraphic tape machine.

ticket > *noun* 1 a piece of paper or card giving the holder a right to admission to a place or event or to travel on public transport. 2 a certificate or warrant. 3 an official notice of a traffic offence. 4 a label attached to a retail product, giving its price, size, etc. 5 chiefly N. Amer. a set of principles supported by a party in an election. 6 (**the ticket**) informal the desirable thing. > *verb* (**ticketed, ticketing**) issue with a ticket.
ORIGIN – Old French *estiquet*, from *estiquier* 'to fix'.

tickety-boo > *adjective* Brit. informal, dated in good order.

ticking > *noun* a strong, durable material used to cover mattresses.

tickle > *verb* 1 lightly touch in a way that causes itching or twitching and often laughter. 2 be appealing or amusing to. 3 catch (a trout) by lightly rubbing it so that it moves backwards into the hand. > *noun* an act of tickling or sensation of being tickled.
IDIOMS – **be tickled pink** informal be extremely amused or pleased. **tickle the ivories** informal play the piano.
DERIVATIVES – **tickler** *noun* **tickly** *adjective*.

ticklish > *adjective* 1 sensitive to being tickled. 2 (of a cough) characterised by persistent irritation in the throat. 2 (of a situation or problem) sensitive or difficult to deal with.

tic-tac (also **tick-tack**) > *noun* (in the UK) a kind of manual semaphore used by racecourse bookmakers to exchange information.

tic-tac-toe (also **tick-tack-toe**) > *noun* North American term for *noughts and crosses*.
ORIGIN – from *tick-tack*, used earlier to denote games in which the pieces made clicking sounds.

tidal > *adjective* relating to or affected by tides.
DERIVATIVES – **tidally** *adverb*.
COMBINATIONS – **tidal basin** a basin accessible or navigable only at high tide. **tidal bore** a large wave caused by the constriction of the spring tide as it enters a long, narrow, shallow inlet. **tidal wave** 1 a very large ocean wave; a tsunami. 2 a widespread manifestation of an emotion or phenomenon.

tidbit > *noun* US spelling of TITBIT.

tiddler > *noun* Brit. informal 1 a small fish. 2 a young or unusually small person or thing.

tiddly[1] > *adjective* (**tiddlier, tiddliest**) informal, chiefly Brit. slightly drunk.
ORIGIN – perhaps from slang *tiddlywink*, meaning an unlicensed public house.

tiddly[2] > *adjective* (**tiddlier, tiddliest**) Brit. informal little; tiny.

tiddlywinks (US also **tiddledywinks**) > *plural noun* a game in which small plastic counters are flicked into a central receptacle, using a larger counter.

tide > *noun* 1 the alternate rising and falling of the sea due to the attraction of the moon and sun. 2 a powerful surge of feeling or trend of events. > *verb* (**tide over**) help (someone) through a difficult period.
WORDFINDER – ebb (*outflow of the tide as it falls*), flood (*inflow of the rising tide*), neap tide (*tide when there is least difference between high and low water*), spring tide (*when there is the greatest difference between high and low water*).
COMBINATIONS – **tideline** a line left or reached by the sea on a shore at the highest point of a tide. **tidemark** 1 a tideline. 2 Brit. a grimy mark left around the inside of a bath or washbasin at the level reached by the water. **tidewater** water brought or affected by tides. **tideway** a channel in which a tide runs.
ORIGIN – Old English, 'time, period, era'.

-tide > *combining form* 1 literary denoting a specified time or season: *springtide*. 2 denoting a festival of the Christian Church: *Shrovetide*.

tidings > *plural noun* literary news; information.

tidy > *adjective* (**tidier, tidiest**) 1 arranged neatly and in order. 2 not messy; neat and controlled. 3 informal (of an amount) considerable. > *noun* (pl. **tidies**) 1 (also **tidy-up**) an act or spell of tidying. 2 a receptacle for holding small objects. > *verb* (**tidies, tidied**) 1 (often **tidy up**) make tidy. 2 (**tidy away**) put (something) away for the sake of tidiness.
DERIVATIVES – **tidily** *adverb* **tidiness** *noun*.
SYNONYMS – *adjective* 1 neat, orderly, presentable, shipshape, spick and span.
ANTONYMS – *adjective* 1 messy, untidy.
ORIGIN – first used in the sense 'timely, opportune': from TIDE.

tie > *verb* (**tying**) 1 attach or fasten with string, cord, etc. 2 form into a knot or bow. 3 restrict; limit. 4 connect; link. 5 achieve the same score or ranking as another competitor. 6 hold together by a crosspiece or tie. 7 Music unite (written notes) by a tie. > *noun* (pl. **ties**) 1 a thing that ties. 2 a strip of material worn beneath a collar, tied in a knot at the front. 3 a result in a game or match in which two or more competitors have tied. 4 Brit. a sports match in which the winners proceed to the next round of the competition. 5 a rod or beam holding parts of a structure together. 6 Music a curved line above or below two notes of the same pitch indicating that they are to be played for the combined duration of their time values. 7 Cricket a game in which the scores are level and both sides have completed their innings. Compare with DRAW.
IDIOMS – **tie down** restrict (someone) to a particular situation or place. **tie in** be or cause to be in harmony with something. **tie**

up 1 restrict (someone's) movement by binding their limbs or binding them to something. 2 bring (something) to a satisfactory conclusion. 3 informal occupy (someone) to the exclusion of other activity. 4 invest or reserve (capital) so that it is not immediately available for use.

COMBINATIONS – **tie-dye** a method of producing textile patterns by tying parts of the fabric to shield it from the dye.

tie-back > *noun* a decorative strip of fabric or cord used for holding an open curtain back from the window.

tie-break (also **tie-breaker**) > *noun* a means of deciding a winner from competitors who have tied.

tied > *adjective* 1 Brit. (of a house) occupied subject to the tenant's working for its owner. 2 (of a public house) owned and controlled by a brewery.

tie-in > *noun* 1 a connection or association. 2 a product produced to take commercial advantage of a related work in another medium.

tier > *noun* 1 one of a series of rows or levels placed one above and behind the other. 2 a level or grade within a hierarchy.

DERIVATIVES – **tiered** *adjective*.

ORIGIN – French *tire* 'sequence, order'.

tierce /teerss/ > *noun* another term for TERCE.

tiercel > *noun* variant spelling of TERCEL.

tie-up > *noun* a link or connection.

TIFF > *abbreviation* Computing tagged image file format.

tiff > *noun* informal a quarrel.

tiffin > *noun* (in India) a light midday meal.

ORIGIN – apparently from dialect *tiffing* 'sipping'.

tig > *noun & verb* chiefly Brit. another term for TAG².

tiger > *noun* a large solitary cat with a yellow-brown coat striped with black, native to the forests of Asia.

COMBINATIONS – **tiger economy** a dynamic economy of one of the smaller East Asian countries, especially Singapore, Taiwan, or South Korea. **tiger lily** a tall Asian lily which has orange flowers spotted with black or purple. **tiger moth** a moth which has boldly spotted and streaked wings and a hairy caterpillar. **tiger prawn** (also **tiger shrimp**) a large edible prawn marked with dark bands.

ORIGIN – Greek *tigris*.

tight > *adjective* 1 fixed or fastened firmly; hard to move, undo, or open. 2 (of clothes) close-fitting. 3 well sealed against something such as water or air. 4 (of a rope, fabric, or surface) stretched so as to leave no slack. 5 (of an area or space) allowing little room for manoeuvre. 6 (of a bend, turn, or angle) changing direction sharply. 7 tense: *a tight smile.* 8 (of a form of control) strictly

imposed. 9 (of a written work or form) concise. 10 (of an organisation or group) disciplined and well coordinated. 11 (of a group of people) having close relations. 12 (of money or time) limited; restricted. 13 informal miserly. 14 informal drunk. > *adverb* very firmly, closely, or tensely.

DERIVATIVES – **tighten** *verb* **tightly** *adverb* **tightness** *noun*.

SYNONYMS – *adjective* 1 fast, firm, fixed, secure. 4 rigid, taut, tense.

ANTONYMS – *adjective* 1 loose. 4 slack.

COMBINATIONS – **a tight corner** (or **spot**) a difficult situation. **tight-fisted** informal not willing to spend or give much money; miserly. **tight-knit** (also **tightly knit**) (of a group of people) bound together by strong relationships and common interests. **tight-lipped** with the lips firmly closed, as a sign of suppressed emotion or unwillingness to divulge information. **a tight ship** a strictly controlled and disciplined organisation or operation.

tightrope > *noun* a rope or wire stretched high above the ground, on which acrobats balance.

tights > *plural noun* a close-fitting garment made of a knitted yarn, covering the legs, hips, and bottom.

tightwad > *noun* informal, chiefly N. Amer. a miserly person.

tigress > *noun* a female tiger.

tike > *noun* variant spelling of TYKE.

tiki /tikki/ > *noun* (pl. **tikis**) NZ a large wooden or small greenstone image of a human figure.

ORIGIN – Maori, 'image'.

tikka /tikkə, teekə/ > *noun* an Indian dish of small pieces of meat or vegetables marinated in a spice mixture.

ORIGIN – Punjabi.

tilapia /tilaypiə/ > *noun* an African freshwater fish, introduced in other parts of the world for food.

ORIGIN – Latin, of unknown origin.

tilde /tildə/ > *noun* an accent (˜) placed over Spanish *n* when pronounced *ny* (as in *señor*) or Portuguese *a* or *o* when nasalised (as in *São Paulo*).

ORIGIN – Spanish, from Latin *titulus* 'inscription, title'.

tile > *noun* 1 a thin square or rectangular slab of baked clay, concrete, etc., used for covering roofs, floors, or walls. 2 a thin, flat piece used in Scrabble, mah-jong, and other games. > *verb* cover with tiles.

IDIOMS – **on the tiles** informal, chiefly Brit. having a lively night out.

DERIVATIVES – **tiler** *noun*.

ORIGIN – Latin *tegula*, from a root meaning 'cover'.

tiling > *noun* 1 the action of laying tiles. 2 a surface covered by tiles.

till¹ > *preposition & conjunction* less formal way of saying UNTIL.

ORIGIN – Old English (not, as is commonly assumed, a shortened form of *until*).

till² > *noun* a cash register or drawer for money in a shop, bank, or restaurant.

till³ > *verb* prepare and cultivate (land) for crops.

DERIVATIVES – **tillable** *adjective* **tillage** *noun*.

ORIGIN – Old English, 'strive for, obtain by effort'; ultimately related to TILL¹.

till⁴ > *noun* Geology boulder clay or other unstratified sediment deposited by melting glaciers or ice sheets.

tiller¹ > *noun* a horizontal bar fitted to the head of a boat's rudder post and used for steering.

ORIGIN – Latin *telarium* 'weaver's beam, stock of a crossbow', from *tela* 'web'.

tiller² > *noun* an implement or machine for breaking up soil.

tilt > *verb* 1 move into a sloping position. 2 incline towards a particular opinion. 3 (**tilt at**) historical (in jousting) thrust at with a lance or other weapon. > *noun* 1 a tilting position or movement. 2 an inclination or bias. 3 historical a joust.

IDIOMS – (**at**) **full tilt** with maximum speed or force. **tilt at windmills** attack imaginary enemies. [ORIGIN – with allusion to the story of Don Quixote thrusting at windmills with his sword, believing they were giants.]

DERIVATIVES – **tilter** *noun*.

tilth > *noun* 1 cultivation of land; tillage. 2 the condition of tilled soil.

timbale /tambaal/ > *noun* a dish of finely minced meat or fish cooked with other ingredients in a pastry shell or in a mould.

ORIGIN – French, 'drum'.

timber > *noun* 1 wood prepared for use in building and carpentry. 2 trees grown for such wood. 3 informal, chiefly US suitable quality or character: *she is hailed as presidential timber.* > *exclamation* used to warn that a tree is about to fall after being cut.

DERIVATIVES – **timbered** *adjective* **timbering** *noun*.

COMBINATIONS – **timberline** chiefly N. Amer. the treeline. **timber wolf** a wolf of a large variety found mainly in northern North America, with grey brindled fur.

timbre /tambər/ > *noun* the character or quality of a musical sound or voice as distinct from its pitch and intensity.

ORIGIN – Greek *timbanon*, from *tumpanon* 'drum'.

timbrel /timbrəl/ > *noun* archaic a tambourine or similar instrument.

time > *noun* 1 the indefinite continued progress of existence and events in the past, present, and future, regarded as a whole. 2 a point of time as measured in hours and minutes past midnight or noon. **3** the favourable or appropriate moment to do something. **4** (**a time**) an indefinite period. **5** (also **times**) a portion of time characterised by particular events or circumstances. **6** (**one's time**) a period regarded as characteristic of a particular stage of one's life. **7** the length of time taken to complete an activity. **8** time as allotted, available, or used. **9** an instance of something happening or being done. **10** Brit. the moment at which the opening hours of a public house end. **11** informal a prison sentence. **12** an apprenticeship. **13** the normal rate of pay for time spent working. **14** (**times**) (following a number) expressing multiplication. **15** the rhythmic pattern or tempo of a piece of music. > *verb* **1** arrange a time for. **2** perform at a particular time. **3** measure the time taken by. **4** (**time out**) Computing (of a computer or a program) cancel (an operation) automatically because a predefined interval of time has passed. **5** (**times**) informal multiply (a number).

WORDFINDER – anachronism (*something placed in the wrong time period*), chronological (*relating to dates and time sequences*), chronometry (*science of time measurement*), diachronic (*concerned with things changing through time*), horology (*the study and measurement of time*), synchronic (*concerned with things as they are now, or at one particular time*), synchronicity (*occurrence of things at the same time*), temporal (*relating to time*).

IDIOMS – **about time** conveying that something should have happened earlier. **all the time 1** at all times. **2** very frequently or regularly. **at the same time 1** simultaneously. **2** nevertheless. **at a time** proceeding separately in the specified groups or numbers. **behind the times** not aware of or using the latest ideas or techniques. **for the time being** until some other arrangement is made. **from time to time** occasionally. **have no time for 1** be unable or unwilling to spend time on. **2** dislike or disapprove of. **in time 1** not late. **2** eventually. **3** in accordance with the appropriate musical rhythm or tempo. **keep good** (or **bad**) **time 1** (of a clock or watch) record time accurately (or inaccurately). **2** (of a person) be habitually punctual (or not punctual). **keep time** play or accompany music in time. **on time** punctual; punctually. **pass the time of day** exchange greetings or casual remarks. **time and tide wait for no man** proverb if you don't make use of a favourable opportunity, you may never get the same chance again. **time immemorial** a point of time in the distant past beyond recall or knowledge. **time is money** proverb time is a valuable resource, therefore it's better to do things as quickly as possible. **the time of one's life** a period

or occasion of exceptional enjoyment. **time out of mind** another way of saying *time immemorial*. **time will tell** the truth about something will be established in the future.

COMBINATIONS – **time-and-motion study** an evaluation of the efficiency of an industrial or other operation. **time bomb** a bomb designed to explode at a preset time. **time capsule** a container storing a selection of objects chosen as being typical of the present time, buried for discovery in the future. **time frame** a specified period of time. **timekeeper 1** a person who records the amount of time taken by a process or activity. **2** a person regarded in terms of their punctuality. **3** a watch or clock regarded in terms of its accuracy. **time-lapse** (of a photographic technique) taking a sequence of frames at set intervals to record changes that take place slowly over time. **time lock** a lock fitted with a device that prevents it from being unlocked until a set time. **time machine** (in science fiction) a machine capable of time travel. **time-release** (of a drug preparation) releasing an active substance gradually. **time-server 1** a person who changes their views to suit the prevailing circumstances or fashion. **2** a person who makes very little effort at work because they are waiting to leave or retire. **time sheet** a piece of paper for recording the number of hours worked. **time signature** Music an indication of rhythm following a clef. **times table** informal a multiplication table. **time switch** a switch automatically activated at a preset time. **time travel** (in science fiction) travel through time into the past or the future. **time trial** (in various sports) a test of a competitor's individual speed over a set distance. **time warp** an imaginary distortion of space in relation to time whereby people or objects of one period can be moved to another.

ORIGIN – Old English; related to TIDE.

time-honoured > *adjective* (of a custom or tradition) respected or valued because it has existed for a long time.

timeless > *adjective* not affected by the passage of time or changes in fashion.
DERIVATIVES – **timelessly** *adverb* **timelessness** *noun*.
SYNONYMS – ageless, classic, enduring, lasting, unfading.

timely > *adjective* done or occurring at a favourable or appropriate time.
DERIVATIVES – **timeliness** *noun*.

time off > *noun* time for rest or recreation away from one's usual work or studies.

timeous /tīməss/ > *adjective* chiefly Scottish in good time; sufficiently early.

time out > *noun* chiefly N. Amer. **1** time for rest

or recreation. **2** (**timeout**) a brief break from play in a game or sport.

timepiece > *noun* an instrument for measuring time; a clock or watch.

timer > *noun* **1** an automatic mechanism for activating a device at a preset time. **2** a person or device that records the amount of time taken by a process or activity. **3** indicating how many times someone has done something: *a first-timer*.

timescale > *noun* the time allowed for or taken by a process or sequence of events.

timeshare > *noun* an arrangement whereby joint owners use a property as a holiday home at different specified times.

timetable > *noun* a list or plan of times at which events are scheduled to take place. > *verb* schedule to take place at a particular time.

time-worn > *adjective* impaired or made less striking as a result of age or long use.

timid > *adjective* (**timider**, **timidest**) lacking in courage or confidence.
DERIVATIVES – **timidity** *noun* **timidly** *adverb* **timidness** *noun*.
SYNONYMS – fearful, meek, nervous, pusillanimous, reticent, shy, timorous.
ANTONYMS – bold, confident.
ORIGIN – Latin *timidus*, from *timere* 'to fear'.

timing > *noun* **1** the choice, judgement, or control of when something should be done. **2** a particular time when something happens.

Timorese /teemoreez/ > *noun* (pl. same) a person from Timor, an island in the southern Malay Archipelago. > *adjective* relating to Timor.

timorous > *adjective* lacking in courage or confidence; nervous.
DERIVATIVES – **timorously** *adverb* **timorousness** *noun*.
SYNONYMS – apprehensive, faint-hearted, fearful, nervous, timid.
ORIGIN – Latin *timorosus*, from *timor* 'fear'.

timothy > *noun* a grass which is widely grown for grazing and hay.
ORIGIN – named after the 18th-century American farmer *Timothy* Hanson.

timpani /timpəni/ (also **tympani**) > *plural noun* kettledrums.
DERIVATIVES – **timpanist** *noun*.
ORIGIN – Italian, from Latin *tympanum* 'drum'.

tin > *noun* **1** a silvery-white metallic chemical element. **2** a lidded airtight container made of tinplate or aluminium. **3** chiefly Brit. a sealed tinplate or aluminium container for preserving food; a can. **4** an open metal container for baking food. > *verb* (**tinned**, **tinning**) **1** cover with a thin layer of tin. **2** (**tinned**) chiefly Brit. preserved in a tin; canned.

IDIOMS – **have a tin ear** informal be tone-deaf.

COMBINATIONS – **tin god 1** a person who is pompous and self-important. **2** an object of unjustified veneration or respect. **tin hat** informal, chiefly Brit. a soldier's steel helmet. **tin-opener** chiefly Brit. a tool for opening tins of food. **tinsnips** a pair of clippers for cutting sheet metal. **tin whistle** a small flute-like instrument made from a thin metal tube, with six finger holes of varying size.

tincture /ˈtɪŋkchər/ > *noun* **1** a medicine made by dissolving a drug in alcohol. **2** a slight trace. **3** Heraldry any of the conventional colours used in coats of arms. > *verb* (**be tinctured**) be tinged or flavoured with a slight trace.
ORIGIN – Latin *tinctura* 'dyeing'.

tinder > *noun* dry, flammable material used for lighting a fire.

tinderbox > *noun* historical a box containing tinder, flint, a steel, and other items for kindling fires.

tine /tīn/ > *noun* a prong or sharp point.
DERIVATIVES – **tined** *adjective*.

tinea /ˈtinniə/ > *noun* technical term for RINGWORM.
ORIGIN – Latin, 'worm'.

tinfoil > *noun* metal foil used for covering or wrapping food.

ting > *noun* a sharp, clear ringing sound. > *verb* emit a ting.

tinge > *verb* (**tinged**; **tinging** or **tingeing**) (often **be tinged**) **1** colour slightly. **2** have a slight influence on: *a visit tinged with sadness*. > *noun* a slight trace.
ORIGIN – Latin *tingere* 'to dip or colour'.

tingle > *noun* a slight prickling or stinging sensation. > *verb* experience or cause to experience a tingle.
DERIVATIVES – **tingly** *adjective*.

tinker > *noun* **1** a travelling mender of pots, kettles, etc. **2** Brit., chiefly derogatory a gypsy or other person living in a travelling community. **3** Brit. informal a mischievous child. **4** an act of tinkering with something. > *verb* (**tinker with**) attempt in a casual manner to repair or improve.
IDIOMS – **not give a tinker's curse** informal not care at all.
DERIVATIVES – **tinkerer** *noun*.

tinkle > *verb* **1** make or cause to make a light, clear ringing sound. **2** informal urinate. > *noun* **1** a tinkling sound. **2** informal an act of urinating.
DERIVATIVES – **tinkly** *adjective*.

tinnitus /tiˈnītəss, ˈtinnitəss/ > *noun* Medicine ringing or buzzing in the ears.
ORIGIN – Latin, from *tinnire* 'to ring, tinkle'.

tinny > *adjective* **1** having a thin, metallic sound. **2** made of thin or poor-quality metal. **3** having an unpleasantly metallic taste. **4** Austral./NZ informal lucky. [ORIGIN –

from *tin* 'luck' (literally 'money, cash').] > *noun* (pl. **tinnies**) Austral./NZ informal a can of beer.
DERIVATIVES – **tinnily** *adverb* **tinniness** *noun*.

tinplate > *noun* sheet steel or iron coated with tin. > *verb* coat with tin.
DERIVATIVES – **tin-plated** *adjective*.

tinpot > *adjective* informal (of a country or its leader) having or showing poor leadership or organisation.

tinsel > *noun* **1** a form of decoration consisting of thin strips of shiny metal foil attached to a length of thread. **2** superficial attractiveness or glamour.
DERIVATIVES – **tinselled** *adjective* **tinselly** *adjective*.
COMBINATIONS – **Tinseltown** derogatory the superficially glamorous world of Hollywood and its film industry.
ORIGIN – Old French *estincele* 'spark', from Latin *scintilla*.

tinsmith > *noun* a person who makes or repairs articles of tin or tinplate.

tint > *noun* **1** a shade or variety of colour. **2** a trace of something. **3** the process or dye used in artificial colouring of the hair. **4** Printing an area of faint colour printed as a half-tone. > *verb* **1** colour slightly; tinge. **2** dye (hair) with a tint.
ORIGIN – Latin *tinctus* 'dyeing', from *tingere* 'to dye or colour'.

tintinnabulation /ˌtintinabyooˈlaysh'n/ > *noun* a ringing or tinkling sound.
ORIGIN – Latin *tintinnabulum* 'tinkling bell'.

tiny > *adjective* (**tinier, tiniest**) very small. > *noun* (pl. **tinies**) informal a very young child.
DERIVATIVES – **tinily** *adverb* **tininess** *noun*.
SYNONYMS – *adjective* infinitesimal, microscopic, minuscule, minute.
ANTONYMS – *adjective* enormous, huge.

-tion > *suffix* forming nouns of action, condition, etc. such as *completion*.

tip¹ > *noun* **1** the pointed or rounded extremity of something slender or tapering. **2** a small part fitted to the end of an object. > *verb* (**tipped, tipping**) attach to or cover the tip of.
IDIOMS – **on the tip of one's tongue** almost but not quite spoken or coming to mind.
DERIVATIVES – **tipped** *adjective*.
ORIGIN – Old Norse.

tip² > *verb* (**tipped, tipping**) **1** overbalance so as to fall or turn over. **2** be or put in a sloping position. **3** empty out (the contents of a container) by holding it at an angle. **4** (**it tips down, it is tipping down**, etc.) Brit. informal rain heavily. **5** strike or touch lightly. > *noun* **1** Brit. a place where rubbish is left. **2** informal a dirty or untidy place.
IDIOMS – **tip one's hand** N. Amer. informal reveal one's intentions inadvertently. **tip**

one's hat raise or touch one's hat as a greeting or mark of respect.

tip³ > *noun* **1** a small sum of money given as a reward for services rendered. **2** a piece of practical advice. **3** a prediction or piece of expert information about the likely winner of a race or contest. > *verb* (**tipped, tipping**) **1** give a tip to. **2** Brit. predict as likely to win or achieve something. **3** (**tip off**) informal give (someone) confidential information.
IDIOMS – **tip the wink** Brit. informal secretly give (someone) confidential information.

tipi > *noun* variant spelling of TEPEE.

tip-off > *noun* informal a piece of confidential information.

tipper > *noun* **1** a truck having a rear platform which can be raised at its front end, thus enabling a load to be tipped off. **2** a person who leaves a tip as a reward: *a good tipper*.

tippet > *noun* **1** a woman's fur cape or woollen shawl. **2** a ceremonial garment worn by the clergy.

Tipp-Ex (also **Tippex**) > *noun* Brit. trademark an opaque liquid painted over a typed or written error, allowing for correction. > *verb* delete with such a liquid.
ORIGIN – German, from *tippen* 'to type' and Latin *ex* 'out'.

tipple > *verb* drink alcohol regularly. > *noun* informal an alcoholic drink.

tippler > *noun* a habitual drinker of alcohol.

tippy > *adjective* N. Amer. inclined to tilt or overturn; unsteady.

tippy-toe > *verb* informal, chiefly N. Amer. tiptoe.

tipstaff > *noun* a sheriff's officer; a bailiff.
ORIGIN – contraction of *tipped staff* (carried by a bailiff).

tipster > *noun* a person who gives tips, especially about the likely winner of a race or contest.

tipsy > *adjective* (**tipsier, tipsiest**) slightly drunk.
DERIVATIVES – **tipsily** *adverb* **tipsiness** *noun*.
ORIGIN – from the verb TIP².

tiptoe > *verb* (**tiptoes, tiptoed, tiptoeing**) walk quietly and carefully with one's heels raised and one's weight on the balls of the feet.

tip-top > *adjective* of the very best; excellent. > *noun* the highest part or point of excellence.

tirade /ˈtīrayd, tiˈrayd/ > *noun* a long speech of angry criticism or accusation.
SYNONYMS – diatribe, harangue, rant.
ORIGIN – French, from Italian *tirato* 'volley'.

tiramisu /ˌtirrəmiˈsoo/ > *noun* an Italian dessert consisting of layers of sponge cake soaked in coffee and brandy or liqueur, with powdered chocolate and mascarpone cheese.

ORIGIN – Italian, from the phrase *tira mi sù* 'pick me up'.

tire[1] > *verb* **1** become or cause to become in need of rest or sleep. **2** exhaust the patience or interest of. **3** (**tire of**) become impatient or bored with.

tire[2] > *noun* US spelling of **TYRE**.

tired > *adjective* **1** in need of sleep or rest; weary. **2** (**tired of**) bored with. **3** (of a statement or idea) boring or uninteresting because overfamiliar: *tired clichés.*

IDIOMS – **tired and emotional** humorous drunk; intoxicated.

DERIVATIVES – **tiredly** *adverb* **tiredness** *noun.*

SYNONYMS – **1** exhausted, fatigued, sleepy, weary, worn out. **3** hackneyed, stale, trite.

tireless > *adjective* having or showing great effort or energy.

DERIVATIVES – **tirelessly** *adverb* **tirelessness** *noun.*

SYNONYMS – dynamic, indefatigable, inexhaustible, unflagging, vigorous.

tiresome > *adjective* causing one to feel bored or impatient.

DERIVATIVES – **tiresomely** *adverb* **tiresomeness** *noun.*

SYNONYMS – boring, dull, monotonous, tedious, wearisome.

tiro > *noun* variant spelling of **TYRO**.

'tis > *contraction* chiefly literary it is.

tisane /tizan/ > *noun* a herb tea.

ORIGIN – French.

tissue /tishoo, tisyoo/ > *noun* **1** any of the distinct types of material of which animals or plants are made. **2** tissue paper. **3** a piece of absorbent paper, used as a disposable handkerchief. **4** fabric of a delicate gauzy texture. **5** a web-like structure or network: *a tissue of lies.*

WORDFINDER – histology (*branch of biology concerned with living tissues*).

DERIVATIVES – **tissuey** *adjective.*

COMBINATIONS – **tissue paper** very thin, soft paper.

ORIGIN – from Old French *tissu* 'woven', from Latin *texere* 'to weave'.

tit[1] > *noun* a titmouse.

tit[2] > *noun* **1** vulgar slang a woman's breast. **2** Brit. informal a foolish or ineffectual person. **3** military slang a push-button used to fire a gun or release a bomb.

ORIGIN – Old English, 'teat, nipple'.

tit[3] > *noun* (in phrase **tit for tat**) the infliction of an injury or insult in retaliation for one received.

Titan /tītən/ > *noun* **1** any of a family of giant gods in Greek mythology. **2** (**titan**) a person or thing of very great strength, intellect, or importance.

titanic > *adjective* of exceptional strength, size, or power.

DERIVATIVES – **titanically** *adverb.*

titanium /tītayniəm, tītayniəm/ > *noun* a hard silver-grey metal used in strong, light, corrosion-resistant alloys.

titbit (N. Amer. **tidbit**) > *noun* **1** a small piece of tasty food. **2** a small and particularly interesting item of gossip or information.

titch (also **tich**) > *noun* Brit. informal a small person.

wordpower facts
Titch

The word **titch** has been used since the 1930s as a name for a small person. It comes from *Little Tich*, the stage name of Harry Relph (1868–1928), an English music-hall comedian of small stature. Relph was given the nickname because he resembled Arthur Orton, the *Tichborne claimant*. The case of the Tichborne claimant was a celebrated one in Victorian England. Arthur Orton, an English butcher, emigrated to Australia in 1852, but returned in 1866 claiming to be the heir to the Tichborne estate; he asserted that he was the eldest son of the 10th baronet, who was presumed lost at sea, and convinced the lost heir's mother that he was her son. After a long trial he lost his claim and was tried and imprisoned for perjury.

titchy > *adjective* (**titchier, titchiest**) Brit. informal very small.

titer > *noun* US spelling of **TITRE**.

titfer > *noun* Brit. informal a hat.

ORIGIN – abbreviation of rhyming slang *tit for tat.*

tithe /tīth/ > *noun* **1** one tenth of annual produce or earnings, formerly taken as a tax for the support of the Church and clergy. **2** archaic a tenth of a specified thing. > *verb* subject to or pay as a tithe.

COMBINATIONS – **tithe barn** a barn built to hold produce made over as tithes.

ORIGIN – Old English, 'tenth'.

Titian /tish'n/ > *adjective* (of hair) bright golden auburn.

ORIGIN – from the name of the 16th-century Italian painter *Titian*, by association with the bright auburn hair portrayed in many of his works.

titillate* /tittillayt/ > *verb* **1** arouse (someone) to mild excitement or interest. **2** archaic lightly touch; tickle.

DERIVATIVES – **titillating** *adjective* **titillation** *noun.*

USAGE – do not confuse **titillate** and **titivate**: **titillate** means 'excite', whereas **titivate** means 'adorn or smarten up'.

*SPELLING – one *t*, two *l*s: tit*ill*ate.

ORIGIN – Latin *titillare* 'tickle'.

titivate* /tittivayt/ > *verb* adorn or smarten up.

DERIVATIVES – **titivation** *noun.*

*SPELLING – *tit*-, not *titt*-: ti*t*ivate.

ORIGIN – in early use also spelled *tidivate*: perhaps from **TIDY**.

title > *noun* **1** the name of a book, musical composition, or other artistic work. **2** a name that describes someone's position or job. **3** a word used before or instead of someone's name to indicate rank, profession, or status. **4** a name or description that is earned or chosen. **5** the position of being the champion of a major sports competition. **6** a caption or credit in a film or broadcast. **7** Law a right or claim to the ownership of property or to a rank or throne. > *verb* give a title to.

COMBINATIONS – **title deed** a legal document constituting evidence of a right, especially to ownership of property. **title music** music accompanying the credits at the beginning or end of a television programme or film. **title role** the part in a play or film from which the work's title is taken.

ORIGIN – Latin *titulus* 'inscription, title'.

titled > *adjective* having a title indicating nobility or rank.

titmouse > *noun* (pl. **titmice**) a small songbird, typically foraging acrobatically among foliage and branches.

ORIGIN – from **TIT**[1] + obsolete *mose* 'titmouse'.

titrate /tītrayt/ > *verb* Chemistry ascertain the amount of a substance in (a solution) by measuring the volume of a standard reagent required to react with it.

DERIVATIVES – **titration** *noun.*

ORIGIN – from French *titre* 'fineness of alloyed gold or silver'.

titre /tītər/ (US **titer**) > *noun* Chemistry the concentration of a solution as determined by titration.

titter > *noun* a short, half-suppressed laugh. > *verb* give a titter.

tittle > *noun* a tiny amount or part of something.

ORIGIN – from Latin *titulus* 'title' in the sense 'small stroke, accent'.

tittle-tattle > *noun* gossip. > *verb* engage in gossip.

tittup /tittəp/ > *verb* (**tittuped, tittuping** or **tittupped, tittupping**) (in horse riding) proceed with jerky or exaggerated movements.

titular /tityoolər/ > *adjective* **1** relating to a title. **2** holding or constituting a formal position or title without any real authority.

tiyin /teeyin/ > *noun* (pl. same or **tiyins**) a monetary unit of Kyrgyzstan, equal to one hundredth of a som.

tizzy (also **tizz**) > *noun* (pl. **tizzies**) informal a state of nervous excitement or agitation.

TKO > *abbreviation* Boxing technical knockout.

Tl > *symbol* the chemical element thallium.

TLC > *abbreviation* informal tender loving care.

TM > *abbreviation* (**trademark in the US**) Transcendental Meditation.

Tm > *symbol* the chemical element thulium.

TN > *abbreviation* Tennessee.

TNT > *abbreviation* trinitrotoluene, a high explosive made by nitrating toluene.

to > *preposition* **1** expressing direction or position in relation to a particular location, point, or condition. **2** chiefly Brit. (in telling the time) before (the hour specified). **3** identifying the person or thing affected. **4** identifying a particular relationship between one person or thing and another. **5** indicating a rate of return on something. **6** indicating that two things are attached. **7** governing a phrase expressing someone's reaction to something. **8** used to introduce the second element in a comparison. > *infinitive marker* used with the base form of a verb to indicate that the verb is in the infinitive. > *adverb* so as to be closed or nearly closed.
IDIOMS – **to and fro** in a constant movement backwards and forwards or from side to side.

toad > *noun* **1** a tailless amphibian with a short stout body and short legs, typically having dry warty skin that can exude poison. **2** a detestable person.
WORDFINDER – batrachian (*relating to frogs and toads*).
COMBINATIONS – **toad-in-the-hole** Brit. a dish consisting of sausages baked in batter.

toadflax > *noun* a plant with yellow or purplish snapdragon-like flowers and slender leaves.

toadstool > *noun* the spore-bearing fruiting body of a fungus, typically in the form of a rounded cap on a stalk.

toady > *noun* (pl. **toadies**) a person who behaves obsequiously towards others. > *verb* (**toadies**, **toadied**) act obsequiously.
ORIGIN – said to be a contraction of *toad-eater*, a charlatan's assistant who appeared to eat a toad (regarded as poisonous) in order to demonstrate the charlatan's remedy.

toast > *noun* **1** sliced bread browned on both sides by exposure to radiant heat. **2** an act of raising glasses at a gathering and drinking together in honour of a person or thing. **3** a person who is toasted or held in high regard. > *verb* **1** cook or brown by exposure to radiant heat. **2** drink a toast to. **3** (of a DJ) accompany reggae music with improvised rhythmic speech.
DERIVATIVES – **toasted** *adjective* **toasty** *adjective*.
COMBINATIONS – **toasting fork** a long-handled fork for making toast in front of a

fire. **toastmaster** (or **toastmistress**) an official responsible for proposing toasts and making other formal announcements at a large social event.

wordpower facts

Toast

The verb **toast** first meant 'burn as the sun does, parch'; it came from Old French *toster* 'roast', from Latin *torrere* 'parch' (past participle *tostus*). The notion of drinking a *toast* goes back to the late 17th century. It originated in the practice of naming a lady whose health the company was requested to drink, the idea being that the lady's name flavoured the drink like the pieces of spiced toast, rather like croutons, that were formerly put in wine and other drinks.

toaster > *noun* an electrical device for making toast.

toastie > *noun* Brit. informal a toasted sandwich or snack.

tobacco > *noun* (pl. **tobaccos**) a preparation of the dried and fermented nicotine-rich leaves of an American plant, used for smoking or chewing.
ORIGIN – Spanish *tabaco*.

tobacconist > *noun* chiefly Brit. a shopkeeper who sells cigarettes and tobacco.

toboggan > *noun* a light, narrow vehicle on runners, used for sliding downhill over snow or ice. > *verb* ride on a toboggan.
DERIVATIVES – **tobogganist** *noun*.
ORIGIN – Micmac.

toby jug > *noun* a beer jug or mug in the form of a stout old man wearing a three-cornered hat.
ORIGIN – said to come from an 18th-century poem about *Toby Philpot* (with a pun on *fill pot*), a soldier who liked to drink.

toccata /təˈkaːtə/ > *noun* a musical composition for a keyboard instrument designed to exhibit the performer's touch and technique.
ORIGIN – Italian, literally 'touched'.

tocopherol /tɒˈkɒfərɒl/ > *noun* vitamin E, a compound found in wheatgerm oil, egg yolk, and leafy vegetables and important in stabilising cell membranes.
ORIGIN – from Greek *tokos* 'offspring' + *pherein* 'to bear'.

tocsin /ˈtɒksɪn/ > *noun* archaic an alarm bell or signal.
ORIGIN – Provençal *tocasenh*, from *tocar* 'to touch' + *senh* 'signal bell'.

tod > *noun* (in phrase **on one's tod**) Brit. informal on one's own.

ORIGIN – from rhyming slang *Tod Sloan*, the name of an American jockey (1873–1933).

today > *adverb* **1** on or in the course of this present day. **2** at the present period of time; nowadays. > *noun* **1** this present day. **2** the present period of time.
ORIGIN – Old English, 'on this day'.

toddle > *verb* **1** (of a young child) move with short unsteady steps while learning to walk. **2** informal walk or go in a casual or leisurely way. > *noun* an act of toddling.

toddler > *noun* a young child who is just beginning to walk.

toddy > *noun* (pl. **toddies**) **1** a drink made of spirits with hot water and sugar. **2** the sap of some kinds of palm, fermented to produce the alcoholic spirit arrack.
ORIGIN – Sanskrit.

todger > *noun* Brit. vulgar slang a man's penis.

to-do > *noun* informal a commotion or fuss.
ORIGIN – from *to do* as in *much to do*, originally meaning 'much needing to be done' but later interpreted as the adjective *much* and a noun; compare with **ADO**.

toe > *noun* **1** any of the five digits at the end of the foot. **2** the lower end, tip, or point of something. > *verb* (**toes**, **toed**, **toeing**) push, touch, or kick with one's toes.
WORDFINDER – bourré (*series of ballet steps performed on the tips of the toes*), digitigrade (*walking on the toes*), hammer toe (*toe that is bent downwards*), pedicure (*cosmetic treatment of the feet and toenails*), pointe (*in ballet, the tips of the toes*), polydactyly (*condition of having more than five toes on a foot*).
IDIOMS – **make someone's toes curl** informal cause an extreme reaction of delight or disgust in someone. **on one's toes** ready and alert. **toe the line** comply with authority. **turn up one's toes** informal die.
DERIVATIVES – **toed** *adjective*.
COMBINATIONS – **toecap** a piece of steel or leather on the front part of a boot or shoe. **toe loop** Skating a jump in which the skater makes a full turn in the air, taking off from and landing on the outside edge of the same foot. **toenail** a nail on the upper surface of the tip of each toe.

toea /ˈtoʊə/ > *noun* (pl. same) a monetary unit of Papua New Guinea, equal to one hundredth of a kina.
ORIGIN – Motu (a Melanesian language), 'cone-shaped shell'.

toehold > *noun* a small foothold.

toerag > *noun* Brit. informal a contemptible person.
ORIGIN – first denoting a rag wrapped round the foot as a sock or the wearer of such a rag, such as a vagrant.

toff > *noun* Brit. informal, derogatory a rich or upper-class person.
ORIGIN – perhaps an alteration of **TUFT**, used to denote a gold tassel worn on the

cap by titled undergraduates at Oxford and Cambridge.

toffee > *noun* a kind of firm or hard sweet which softens when sucked or chewed, made by boiling together sugar and butter.
COMBINATIONS – **toffee apple** Brit. an apple coated with a thin layer of toffee and fixed on a stick. **toffee-nosed** informal, chiefly Brit. pretentiously superior; snobbish.

tofu /ˈtōfoō/ > *noun* curd made from mashed soya beans, used in Asian and vegetarian cookery.
ORIGIN – Chinese, 'rotten beans'.

tog¹ informal > *noun* (**togs**) clothes. > *verb* (**togged, togging**) (**be togged up** or **out**) be fully dressed for a particular occasion or activity.

wordpower facts
Tog
The informal expressions **togs**, meaning 'clothes', and **be togged up**, 'be dressed up', date back to the late 18th century, although **tog** or the fuller form *togman* or *togeman* was used earlier as thieves' slang for a coat or cloak. It is thought to come ultimately from the same Latin source as **toga**. **Tog** as a unit expressing the insulating properties of clothes and quilts is basically the same word; it was adopted in this sense in the 1940s, on the pattern of an earlier unit called the *clo* (which was from the first part of *clothes*).

tog² > *noun* Brit. a unit of thermal resistance used to express the insulating properties of clothes and quilts.

toga /ˈtōgə/ > *noun* a loose flowing outer garment worn by the citizens of ancient Rome, made of a single piece of cloth and covering the whole body apart from the right arm.
ORIGIN – Latin; related to *tegere* 'to cover'.

together > *adverb* 1 with or in proximity to another person or people. 2 so as to touch, combine, or be united. 3 in combination; collectively. 4 (of two people) married or in a sexual relationship. 5 at the same time. 6 without interruption. > *adjective* informal level-headed and well organised.
IDIOMS – **together with** as well as.
DERIVATIVES – **togetherness** *noun*.

toggle > *noun* 1 a narrow piece of wood or plastic attached to a garment, pushed through a loop to act as a fastener. 2 Computing a key or command that is operated the same way but with opposite effect on successive occasions. > *verb* Computing switch from one effect, feature, or state to another by using a toggle.
COMBINATIONS – **toggle switch** an

electric switch operated by means of a projecting lever that is moved up and down.

Togolese /ˌtōgəˈleez/ > *noun* (pl. same) a person from Togo, a country in West Africa. > *adjective* relating to Togo.

toil > *verb* 1 work extremely hard or incessantly. 2 move somewhere slowly and with difficulty. > *noun* exhausting work.
DERIVATIVES – **toiler** *noun*.
SYNONYMS – *verb* 1 grind, labour, slave, slog. 2 labour, plod, struggle. *noun* drudgery, labour.
ORIGIN – Old French *toiler* 'strive, dispute', from Latin *tudiculare* 'stir about', from *tudicula* 'machine for crushing olives'.

toile /twaal/ > *noun* 1 an early version of a garment made up in cheap material so that the design can be tested. 2 a translucent fabric.
ORIGIN – French, 'cloth, web'.

toilet > *noun* 1 a large bowl for urinating or defecating into, typically plumbed into a sewage system. 2 the process of washing oneself, dressing, and attending to one's appearance.
COMBINATIONS – **toilet bag** Brit. a waterproof bag for holding toothpaste, soap, etc. when travelling. **toilet-train** teach (a young child) to use the toilet. **toilet water** a dilute form of perfume.

wordpower facts
Toilet
The word **toilet** has shifted a long way in sense since it entered English in the mid 16th century. It came from French *toilette* 'cloth, wrapper' and ultimately from Latin *tela* 'woven material, web' (and so is related to such words as **text, textile, texture,** and **tissue**). In English a **toilet** was originally a cloth or cloth bag used for wrapping clothes; the word then began to refer to a cloth cover for a dressing table, the articles used in dressing, and the process of dressing and later also of washing oneself. In the 19th century it came to denote a dressing room, and, in the US, one with washing facilities; from this the modern meaning of 'lavatory' arose in the early 20th century.

toiletries > *plural noun* articles used in washing and taking care of one's body, such as soap and shampoo.

toilette /twaaˈlet/ > *noun* old-fashioned term for **TOILET** (in sense 2).

toils > *plural noun* literary a situation regarded as a trap.
ORIGIN – first denoting a net into which a

hunted animal is driven: from Old French *toile* 'cloth, web'.

toilsome > *adjective* archaic or literary involving hard work.

Tokay /ˈtōkī/ > *noun* a sweet aromatic wine, originally made near Tokaj in Hungary.

toke informal > *noun* a pull on a cigarette or pipe, especially one containing cannabis. > *verb* smoke cannabis or tobacco.

token > *noun* 1 a thing serving to represent a fact, quality, feeling, etc. 2 a voucher that can be exchanged for goods or services. 3 a disc used to operate a machine or in exchange for particular goods or services. 4 a device given to a train driver on a single-track railway as authority to proceed. > *adjective* 1 done for the sake of appearances or as a symbolic gesture. 2 chosen by way of tokenism to represent a particular group.
IDIOMS – **by the same** (or **that** or **this**) **token** in the same way or for the same reason. **in token of** as a sign or symbol of.
SYNONYMS – *noun* 1 emblem, mark, sign, symbol. *adjective* 1 nominal, symbolic.

tokenism > *noun* the making of a perfunctory or symbolic effort to do a particular thing, especially by recruiting a small number of people from under-represented groups to give the appearance of sexual or racial equality within a workforce.
DERIVATIVES – **tokenistic** *adjective*.

tolar /ˈtollaar/ > *noun* the basic monetary unit of Slovenia, equal to 100 stotins.
ORIGIN – Slovene; related to German *Thaler* (see **DOLLAR**).

told past and past participle of **TELL**.

tolerable > *adjective* 1 able to be tolerated. 2 fairly good.
DERIVATIVES – **tolerability** *noun* **tolerably** *adverb*.
SYNONYMS – 1 bearable, endurable, sufferable, supportable. 2 acceptable, adequate, passable, satisfactory.
ANTONYMS – 1 intolerable, unbearable.

tolerance > *noun* 1 the ability, willingness, or capacity to tolerate something. 2 an allowable amount of variation of a specified quantity, especially in the dimensions of a machine or part.
SYNONYMS – 1 forbearance, patience, sufferance, toleration, understanding.
ANTONYMS – 1 intolerance.

tolerant > *adjective* 1 showing tolerance. 2 able to endure specified conditions or treatment.
DERIVATIVES – **tolerantly** *adverb*.
SYNONYMS – 1 broad-minded, forbearing, liberal, patient, understanding.
ANTONYMS – 1 intolerant, unsympathetic.

tolerate > *verb* 1 allow (something that one dislikes or disagrees with) to exist or occur without interference. **2** patiently endure (something unpleasant). **3** be capable of continued exposure to (a drug, toxin, etc.) without adverse reaction.

DERIVATIVES – **toleration** noun.

SYNONYMS – **1** accept, allow, brook, countenance, put up with. **2** bear, endure, stand, suffer; informal abide.

ORIGIN – Latin tolerare 'endure'.

toll¹ /tōl/ > noun **1** a charge payable to use a bridge or road or (N. Amer.) for a long-distance telephone call. **2** the number of deaths or casualties arising from an accident, disaster, etc. **3** the cost or damage resulting from something.

IDIOMS – **take its toll** (or **take a heavy toll**) have an adverse effect.

COMBINATIONS – **tollbooth 1** a roadside kiosk where tolls are paid. **2** Scottish archaic a town hall or town jail. **toll gate** a barrier across a road where one must pay a toll in order to proceed further.

ORIGIN – Greek telōnion 'toll house', from telos 'tax'.

toll² /tōl/ > verb **1** (of a bell) sound with a slow, uniform succession of strokes. **2** announce (the time, a service, or a person's death) in this way. > noun a single ring of a bell.

ORIGIN – probably a special use of dialect toll 'drag, pull'.

Toltec /toltek/ > noun a member of an American Indian people that flourished in Mexico before the Aztecs.

DERIVATIVES – **Toltecan** adjective.

ORIGIN – Nahuatl, 'person from Tula (a town and former Toltec site in central Mexico)'.

toluene /tolyoo-een/ > noun Chemistry a colourless liquid hydrocarbon resembling benzene, present in coal tar and petroleum.

ORIGIN – from tolu, a fragrant balsam obtained from a South American tree, named after Santiago de Tolú in Colombia.

tom > noun the male of various animals, especially a domestic cat.

ORIGIN – first denoting an ordinary man: abbreviation of the given name Thomas.

tomahawk /tomməhawk/ > noun **1** a light axe formerly used as a tool or weapon by American Indians. **2** Austral./NZ a hatchet. > verb strike or cut with a tomahawk.

ORIGIN – from an Algonquian language.

tomato* > noun (pl. **tomatoes**) a glossy red or yellow edible fruit, eaten as a vegetable or in salads.

*SPELLING – no e on the end: tomato.

ORIGIN – Nahuatl.

tomb > noun **1** a burial place, especially a large underground vault. **2** a monument to a dead person, erected over their burial place. **3** (**the tomb**) literary death.

WORDFINDER – catacomb (underground cemetery), cromlech, dolmen (megalithic tomb), epitaph (inscription on a tomb), inter (place someone in a tomb), mausoleum (building housing a tomb or tombs), monumental mason (person who makes tombstones), sepulchral (relating to tombs or burial), sepulchre (stone tomb or monument).

COMBINATIONS – **tombstone** a large, flat inscribed stone standing or laid over a grave.

ORIGIN – Greek tumbos.

tombola /tombōlə/ > noun Brit. a game in which tickets are drawn from a revolving drum to win prizes.

ORIGIN – Italian, from tombolare 'turn a somersault'.

tomboy > noun a girl who enjoys rough, noisy activities traditionally associated with boys.

DERIVATIVES – **tomboyish** adjective.

tomcat > noun a male domestic cat.

Tom Collins > noun a cocktail made from gin mixed with soda, sugar, and lemon or lime juice.

ORIGIN – said to have been named after a 19th-century London bartender.

Tom, Dick, and Harry > noun ordinary people in general.

tome > noun chiefly humorous a book, especially a large, scholarly one.

ORIGIN – Greek tomos 'section, roll of papyrus, volume'.

tomfoolery > noun foolish or silly behaviour.

Tommy > noun (pl. **Tommies**) informal a British private soldier.

ORIGIN – familiar form of the given name Thomas; from a use of the name Thomas Atkins in specimens of completed official forms in the British army.

tommy gun > noun informal a type of sub-machine gun.

ORIGIN – contraction of Thompson gun, named after John T. Thompson (1860–1940), the American army officer who conceived the idea for it.

tommyrot > noun informal, dated nonsense.

tomography /təmogrəfi/ > noun a technique for displaying a cross section through a human body or other solid object using X-rays or ultrasound.

DERIVATIVES – **tomogram** noun **tomographic** adjective.

ORIGIN – from Greek tomos 'slice, section'.

tomorrow* > adverb **1** on the day after today. **2** in the near future. > noun **1** the day after today. **2** the near future.

IDIOMS – **like there was no tomorrow** informal completely without restraint.

*SPELLING – one m, two rs: tomorrow.

tomtit > noun a small, active titmouse or similar bird, especially (Brit.) the blue tit.

tom-tom > noun **1** a medium-sized cylindrical drum, of which one to three may be used in a drum kit. **2** a drum beaten with the hands, associated with North American Indian, African, or Eastern cultures.

ORIGIN – Hindi.

-tomy > combining form cutting, especially as part of a surgical process: hysterectomy.

ORIGIN – from Greek -tomia 'cutting'.

ton /tun/ > noun **1** (also **long ton**) a unit of weight equal to 2,240 lb avoirdupois (1016.05 kg). **2** (also **short ton**) chiefly N. Amer. a unit of weight equal to 2,000 lb avoirdupois (907.19 kg). **3** short for **metric ton**. **4** (also **displacement ton**) a unit of measurement of a ship's weight equal to 2,240 lb or 35 cu. ft (0.99 cubic metres). **5** informal a large number or amount. **6** informal, chiefly Brit. a hundred, in particular a speed of 100 mph, a score of 100 or more, or a sum of £100. > adverb (**tons**) Brit. informal much; a lot.

ORIGIN – variant of TUN.

tonal /tōn'l/ > adjective **1** relating to tone. **2** (of music) written using conventional keys and harmony.

DERIVATIVES – **tonally** adverb.

tonality > noun (pl. **tonalities**) **1** the character of a piece of music as determined by the key in which it is played or the relations between the notes of a scale or key. **2** the use of conventional keys and harmony as the basis of musical composition. **3** the range of tones used in a picture.

tone > noun **1** a musical or vocal sound with reference to its pitch, quality, and strength. **2** the sound of a person's voice, expressing a feeling or mood. **3** general character: trust her to lower the tone of the conversation. **4** (also **whole tone**) a basic interval in classical Western music, equal to two semitones; a major second. **5** the particular quality of brightness, deepness, or hue of a colour. **6** the general effect of colour or of light and shade in a picture. **7** the normal level of firmness or slight contraction in a resting muscle. > verb **1** (often **tone up**) give greater strength or firmness to (the body or a muscle). **2** (**tone down**) make (something) less harsh, extreme, or intense. **3** (**tone with**) harmonise with in terms of colour.

DERIVATIVES – **toned** adjective **toneless** adjective.

SYNONYMS – noun **3** character, feel, flavour, mood, quality, spirit. verb **2** (**tone down**) moderate, modify, soften, subdue, temper.

COMBINATIONS – **tone arm** the movable arm supporting the pickup of a record player. **tone-deaf** unable to perceive differences of musical pitch accurately. **tonepad** a device generating specific tones to control another device at the other end of a telephone line. **tone poem** a piece of orchestral music, typically in one movement, on a descriptive or rhapsodic theme.

ORIGIN – Greek *tonos* 'tension, tone', from *teinein* 'to stretch'.

toner > *noun* **1** a liquid applied to the skin to reduce oiliness and improve its condition. **2** a powder used in xerographic copying processes. **3** a chemical bath for changing the tone of a photographic print.

tong > *noun* a Chinese association or secret society associated with organised crime.

ORIGIN – Chinese, 'meeting place'.

Tongan /**tong**gən, **tong**ən/ > *noun* **1** a person from Tonga, an island group in the South Pacific. **2** the Polynesian language spoken in Tonga. > *adjective* relating to Tonga.

tongs > *plural noun* **1** a tool with two movable arms that are joined at one end, used for picking up and holding things. **2** short for *curling tongs*.

tongue > *noun* **1** the fleshy muscular organ in the mouth, used for tasting, licking, swallowing, and (in humans) articulating speech. **2** the tongue of an ox or lamb, as food. **3** a person's style or manner of speaking. **4** a particular language. **5** a strip of leather or fabric under the laces in a shoe. **6** the free-swinging metal piece inside a bell which strikes the bell to produce the sound. **7** a long, low promontory of land. **8** a projecting strip on a wooden board fitting into a groove on another. **9** the vibrating reed of a musical instrument or organ pipe. > *verb* (**tongues, tongued, tonguing**) **1** Music sound (a note) distinctly on a wind instrument by interrupting the air flow with the tongue. **2** lick or caress with the tongue.

WORDFINDER – lingual (*relating to the tongue*).

IDIOMS – **the gift of tongues** the power of speaking in unknown languages, regarded as one of the gifts of the Holy Spirit. **give tongue 1** (of hounds) bark, especially on finding a scent. **2** express one's feelings or opinions freely. (**with**) **tongue in cheek** insincerely or ironically. **one's tongue is hanging out** one is very eager for something.

COMBINATIONS – **tongue and groove** wooden planking in which adjacent boards are joined by means of interlocking ridges and grooves down their sides. **tongue-lashing** a loud or severe scolding. **tongue-tied** too shy or embarrassed to speak. **tongue-twister** a sequence of words that are difficult to pronounce quickly and correctly.

tonic > *noun* **1** a medicinal substance taken to give a feeling of vigour or well-being. **2** something with an invigorating effect. **3** short for *tonic water*. **4** Music the first note in a scale which, in conventional harmony,

provides the keynote of a piece of music. > *adjective* Music referring to the first note of a scale.

COMBINATIONS – **tonic sol-fa** see **SOL-FA**. **tonic water** a carbonated soft drink with a bitter flavour, used as a mixer with gin or other spirits.

ORIGIN – Greek *tonikos* 'of or for stretching', from *tonos* 'tension, tone'.

tonicity /tə**niss**iti/ > *noun* muscle tone.

tonight > *adverb* on the present or approaching evening or night. > *noun* the evening or night of the present day.

tonnage > *noun* **1** weight in tons. **2** the size or carrying capacity of a ship measured in tons.

tonne /tun/ > *noun* another term for **metric ton**.

ORIGIN – French.

tonneau /**tonn**ō/ > *noun* **1** the part of an open car occupied by the back seats. **2** a protective cover for the seats in an open car or cabin cruiser when they are not in use.

ORIGIN – French, 'cask': originally denoting a unit of capacity for wine.

tonsil > *noun* either of two small masses of tissue in the throat, one on each side of the root of the tongue.

ORIGIN – from Latin *tonsillae* (plural).

tonsillectomy /tonsi**lekt**əmi/ > *noun* (pl. **tonsillectomies**) a surgical operation to remove the tonsils.

tonsillitis /tonsi**lī**tiss/ > *noun* inflammation of the tonsils.

tonsorial /ton**sor**iəl/ > *adjective* formal or humorous relating to hairdressing.

ORIGIN – from Latin *tonsorius*, from *tonsor* 'barber', from *tondere* 'clip'.

tonsure /**ton**syər/ > *noun* a part of a monk's or priest's head left bare on top by shaving off the hair. > *verb* give a tonsure to.

ORIGIN – Latin *tonsura*, from *tondere* 'shear, clip'.

ton-up > *adjective* Brit. informal achieving a speed of 100 mph or a score of 100 or more.

Tony > *noun* (pl. **Tonys**) (in the US) any of a number of awards given annually for outstanding achievement in the theatre.

ORIGIN – from the nickname of the American actress and director Antoinette Perry.

tony > *adjective* (**tonier, toniest**) N. Amer. informal fashionable, stylish, or high-class.

too > *adverb* **1** to a higher degree than is desirable, permissible, or possible. **2** in addition. **3** informal very.

IDIOMS – **none too ——** not very.

toodle-oo > *exclamation* informal, dated goodbye.

ORIGIN – perhaps an alteration of French *à tout à l'heure* 'see you soon'.

took past of **TAKE**.

tool > *noun* **1** a device or implement used to carry out a particular function. **2** a thing used to help perform a job. **3** a person used by another. > *verb* **1** (usu. **be tooled**) impress a design on (a leather book cover) with a heated tool. **2** equip with tools for industrial production. **3** (**tool up** or **be tooled up**) Brit. informal be or become armed. **4** informal drive or ride in a casual or leisurely manner.

COMBINATIONS – **toolbar** Computing a strip of icons used to perform certain functions. **toolmaker** a person who makes and maintains tools for use in a manufacturing process.

toot > *noun* **1** a short, sharp sound made by a horn, trumpet, or similar instrument. **2** informal, chiefly N. Amer. a snort of a drug, especially cocaine. > *verb* **1** make or cause to make a toot. **2** informal, chiefly N. Amer. snort (cocaine).

tooth > *noun* (pl. **teeth**) **1** each of a set of hard, bony enamel-coated structures in the jaws, used for biting and chewing. **2** a similar projecting part, especially a cog on a gearwheel or a point on a saw or comb. **3** (**teeth**) genuine force or effectiveness.

WORDFINDER – *adult human teeth:* eight incisors, four canines, eight premolars, twelve molars (including four wisdom teeth); bruxism (*involuntary habitual grinding of the teeth*), dental (*relating to teeth*), edentulous (*lacking teeth*), odontology (*scientific study of teeth*), orthodontics (*treatment of irregularities of the teeth*).

IDIOMS – **armed to the teeth** formidably armed. **fight tooth and nail** fight very fiercely. **get** (or **sink**) **one's teeth into** work energetically and productively on. **in the teeth of 1** directly against (the wind). **2** in spite of (opposition or difficulty).

DERIVATIVES – **toothed** *adjective*.

COMBINATIONS – **toothache** pain in a tooth or teeth. **toothbrush** a small brush with a long handle, used for cleaning the teeth. **toothed whale** any of the large group of predatory whales with teeth, including sperm whales, killer whales, dolphins, porpoises, etc. **tooth fairy** a fairy said to collect from under a child's pillow a milk tooth placed there after falling out, and to leave a coin in its place. **toothpaste** a paste used on a brush for cleaning the teeth.

toothcomb > *noun* Brit. used with reference to a very thorough search: *the police went over the area with a fine toothcomb.*

USAGE – the forms **toothcomb** and **fine toothcomb** arose from a misreading of the compound noun *fine-tooth comb*, i.e. a comb with narrow, closely spaced teeth. Despite the absurdity of the idea of combing one's teeth, **toothcomb** is accepted as standard English.

toothless > *adjective* **1** having no teeth. **2** lacking genuine force or effectiveness.

toothpick > *noun* a short pointed piece of wood or plastic used for removing bits of food lodged between the teeth.

toothsome > *adjective* **1** (of food) temptingly tasty. **2** *informal* attractive; alluring.

toothy > *adjective* (**toothier**, **toothiest**) having or showing numerous or prominent teeth.
DERIVATIVES – **toothily** *adverb*.

tootle > *verb* **1** casually make a series of sounds on a horn, trumpet, etc. **2** *informal* go or travel in a leisurely way. > *noun* **1** an act or sound of tootling. **2** *informal* a leisurely journey.

tootsie (also **tootsy**) > *noun* (pl. **tootsies**) *informal* **1** a person's foot. **2** a young woman.

top¹ > *noun* **1** the highest or uppermost point, part, or surface. **2** something placed on, fitted to, or covering the upper part of something. **3** (**the top**) the highest or most important rank, level, or position. **4** the utmost degree: *the top of her voice.* **5** *chiefly Brit.* the end that is furthest from the speaker or a point of reference. **6** a garment covering the upper part of the body. **7** (**tops**) *informal* a particularly good person or thing. **8** the high-frequency component of reproduced sound. **9** a platform at the head of a ship's mast. > *adjective* **1** highest in position, rank, or degree. **2** *chiefly Brit.* furthest away from the speaker or a point of reference. > *verb* (**topped**, **topping**) **1** be more, better, or taller than. **2** be at the highest place or rank in. **3** reach the top of (a hill, rise, etc.). **4** (usu. **be topped**) provide with a top or topping. **5** *informal* kill. **6** *Golf* mishit (the ball) by hitting above its centre. > *adverb* (**tops**) *informal* at the most.
IDIOMS – **get on top of** be more than (someone) can bear or cope with. **on top 1** on the highest point or surface. **2** in a leading or the dominant position. **3** in addition. **on top of 1** so as to cover. **2** in close proximity to. **3** in command or control of. **4** in addition to. **on top of the world** *informal* happy and elated. **over the top 1** *informal, chiefly Brit.* to an excessive or exaggerated degree. **2** *chiefly historical* over the parapet of a trench and into battle. **top and tail** *Brit.* remove the top and bottom of (a fruit or vegetable) while preparing it as food. **top off** finish (something) in a memorable way. **top out 1** put the highest structural feature on (a building). **2** reach an upper limit. **top up 1** add to (a number or

amount) to bring it up to a certain level. **2** fill up (a partly full container).
DERIVATIVES – **topmost** *adjective*.
SYNONYMS – *noun* **1** apex, crest, head, peak, pinnacle, summit, surface, tip.
ANTONYMS – *noun* **1** base, bottom.
COMBINATIONS – **top boot** *chiefly historical* a high boot with a broad band of a different material or colour at the top. **top brass** see **BRASS** (sense 5). **topcoat 1** an overcoat. **2** an outer coat of paint. **top dog** *informal* a person who is successful or dominant in their field. **top drawer** *informal* high social position or class. **top dressing** an application of manure or fertiliser to the surface layer of soil or a lawn. **top flight** the highest rank or level. **top hat** a man's formal hat with a high cylindrical crown. **top-heavy 1** disproportionately heavy at the top so as to be unstable. **2** (of an organisation) having a disproportionately large number of senior executives. **top-hole** *Brit. informal, dated* excellent. **top-level** (also **top-line**) of the highest quality or ranking. **topmast** the second section of a square-rigged sailing ship's mast, immediately above the lower mast. **topsail 1** a sail set on a ship's topmast. **2** a fore-and-aft sail set above the gaff. **top secret** of the highest secrecy. **topsoil** the top layer of soil. **topspin** a fast forward spin given to a moving ball, often resulting in a curved path or a strong forward motion on rebounding.

top² (also **spinning top**) > *noun* a conical, spherical, or pear-shaped toy that may be set to spin.

topaz /tōpaz/ > *noun* **1** a colourless, yellow, or pale blue precious stone. **2** a dark yellow colour.
ORIGIN – Greek *topazos*.

tope¹ > *verb archaic or literary* habitually drink alcohol to excess.
DERIVATIVES – **toper** *noun*.

tope² > *noun* a small shark of inshore waters.
ORIGIN – perhaps Cornish.

tope³ > *noun* another term for **STUPA**.
ORIGIN – Punjabi, 'barrow, mound'.

topgallant /topgalənt, təgalənt/ > *noun* **1** the section of a square-rigged sailing ship's mast immediately above the topmast. **2** a sail set on such a mast.

Tophet /tōfit/ > *noun literary* hell.
ORIGIN – from the name of a place near Jerusalem used in biblical times for the worship of idols, including the sacrifice of children.

topiary /tōpiəri/ > *noun* (pl. **topiaries**) **1** the art of clipping shrubs or trees into ornamental shapes. **2** shrubs or trees clipped in such a way.

ORIGIN – Latin *topiarius* 'ornamental gardener'.

topic > *noun* a subject of a text, speech, conversation, etc.
SYNONYMS – issue, matter, question, subject, theme.
ORIGIN – from Greek *ta topika*, literally 'matters concerning commonplaces' (the title of a treatise by Aristotle).

topical > *adjective* **1** relating to or dealing with current affairs. **2** relating to a particular subject.
DERIVATIVES – **topicality** *noun* **topically** *adverb*.
SYNONYMS – **1** current, timely.

topknot > *noun* **1** a knot of hair arranged on the top of the head. **2** a decorative knot or bow of ribbon worn on the top of the head, popular in the 18th century. **3** a tuft or crest of hair or feathers on the head of an animal or bird.

topless > *adjective* having or leaving the breasts uncovered.

top-notch > *adjective informal* of the highest quality.

topography /təpogrəfi/ > *noun* **1** the arrangement of the natural and artificial physical features of an area. **2** a detailed description or representation on a map of such features.
DERIVATIVES – **topographer** *noun* **topographic** *adjective* **topographical** *adjective* **topographically** *adverb*.
ORIGIN – from Greek *topos* 'place'.

topology /təpolləji/ > *noun* **1** *Mathematics* the study of geometrical properties and spatial relations which remain unaffected by smooth changes in shape or size of figures. **2** the way in which constituent parts are interrelated or arranged.
DERIVATIVES – **topological** *adjective* **topologically** *adverb* **topologist** *noun*.

toponym /toppənim/ > *noun* a place name, especially one derived from a topographical feature.
DERIVATIVES – **toponymic** *adjective* **toponymy** *noun*.

topos /topposs/ > *noun* (pl. **topoi** /toppoy/) a traditional theme or formula in literature.
ORIGIN – Greek, 'place'.

topper > *noun informal* **1** a top hat. **2** *Brit. dated* an exceptionally good person or thing.

topping > *noun* a layer of food poured or spread over another food. > *adjective* *Brit. informal, dated* excellent.

topple > *verb* overbalance and fall, or cause to fall in this way.

topside > *noun* **1** *Brit.* the outer side of a round of beef. **2** the upper part of a ship's side, above the waterline.

topsy-turvy > *adjective & adverb* **1** upside down. **2** in a state of confusion.

toque /tōk/ > *noun* **1** a woman's small hat, typically having a narrow, closely turned-up brim. **2** a tall white hat with a full pouched crown, worn by chefs.
ORIGIN – French.

tor > *noun* a hill or rocky peak.
ORIGIN – perhaps Celtic.

Torah /torə/ > *noun* (in Judaism) the law of God as revealed to Moses and recorded in the Pentateuch.
ORIGIN – Hebrew, 'instruction, doctrine, law'.

torc /tork/ (also **torque**) > *noun* a neck ornament consisting of a band of twisted metal, worn by the ancient Gauls and Britons.
ORIGIN – Latin *torques* (see **TORCH**).

torch > *noun* **1** Brit. a portable battery-powered electric lamp. **2** chiefly historical a piece of wood or cloth soaked in tallow and ignited. **3** something valuable which needs to be protected and maintained: *the torch of freedom.* **4** chiefly N. Amer. a blowlamp. > *verb* informal set fire to.
IDIOMS – **carry a torch for** suffer from unrequited love for. **put to the torch** (or **put a torch to**) destroy by burning.
COMBINATIONS – **torch song** a sad or sentimental song of unrequited love.
ORIGIN – Latin *torqua*, *torques* 'necklace, wreath', from *torquere* 'to twist' (torches having been made originally from twisted flax fibres dipped in pitch).

tore past of **TEAR**[1].

toreador /torriədor/ > *noun* a bullfighter, especially one on horseback.
COMBINATIONS – **toreador pants** chiefly N. Amer. women's tight-fitting calf-length trousers.
ORIGIN – Spanish, from *toro* 'bull'.

torero /torairō/ > *noun* (pl. **toreros**) a bullfighter, especially one on foot.
ORIGIN – Spanish.

tori plural of **TORUS**.

toric /torrik/ > *adjective* Geometry having the form of a torus or part of a torus.

torment > *noun* /torment/ **1** severe physical or mental suffering. **2** a cause of torment. > *verb* /torment/ **1** subject to torment. **2** annoy or tease unkindly.
DERIVATIVES – **tormented** *adjective* **tormentor** *noun*.
SYNONYMS – *noun* **1** agony, anguish, distress, pain, suffering, torture. **2** affliction, nightmare, ordeal, worry. *verb* **1** afflict, distress, plague, torture. **2** annoy, bother, bully, harass, taunt, tease.
ORIGIN – Latin *tormentum* 'instrument of torture', from *torquere* 'to twist'.

torn past participle of **TEAR**[1].

tornado /tornaydō/ > *noun* (pl. **tornadoes** or **tornados**) a violently rotating wind storm having the appearance of a funnel-shaped cloud.
ORIGIN – perhaps from Spanish *tronada* 'thunderstorm'.

toroid /toroyd/ > *noun* Geometry a figure having the shape of a torus.
DERIVATIVES – **toroidal** *adjective*.

torpedo > *noun* (pl. **torpedoes**) a tubular, round-nosed, self-propelled underwater missile designed to be fired from a ship, submarine, or an aircraft. > *verb* (**torpedoes**, **torpedoed**) **1** attack with a torpedo or torpedoes. **2** ruin (a plan or project).
COMBINATIONS – **torpedo boat** a small, fast, light warship armed with torpedoes. **torpedo net** a net made of steel wire, formerly hung round an anchored ship to intercept torpedoes. **torpedo ray** an electric ray (fish).

wordpower facts

Torpedo

In Latin **torpedo** meant 'stiffness, numbness', and also denoted the electric ray, with reference to the effects of the shock this fish could inflict. The ultimate root was the verb *torpere* 'be numb or sluggish', the source of **torpor** and **torpid**. The word entered English in the early 16th century as a name for the fish; the modern noun sense dates from the late 18th century, and first described a timed explosive device or mine detonated under water, likening its effect to that of the torpedo ray. It was such mines that the American admiral David Farragut was referring to when he commanded 'Damn the torpedoes! Full speed ahead' at the battle of Mobile Bay in 1864.

torpid > *adjective* **1** mentally or physically inactive. **2** (of an animal) dormant, especially during hibernation.
DERIVATIVES – **torpidity** *noun* **torpidly** *adverb*.
SYNONYMS – **1** idle, inactive, inert, lethargic, listless, sluggish.
ORIGIN – Latin *torpidus*, from *torpere* 'be numb or sluggish'.

torpor /torpər/ > *noun* physical or mental inactivity; lethargy.
SYNONYMS – inactivity, inertia, lethargy, listlessness, sluggishness, torpidity.
ORIGIN – Latin.

torque /tork/ > *noun* **1** Mechanics a force that tends to cause rotation. **2** variant spelling of **TORC**. > *verb* apply torque to.
DERIVATIVES – **torquey** *adjective*.
COMBINATIONS – **torque converter** a device that transmits or multiplies torque generated by an engine.
ORIGIN – from Latin *torquere* 'to twist'.

torr /tor/ > *noun* (pl. same) a unit of pressure equivalent to 1 mm of mercury in a barometer and equal to 133.32 pascals.
ORIGIN – named after the Italian mathematician and physicist Evangelista *Torricelli* (1608–47).

torrent > *noun* **1** a strong and fast-moving stream of water or other liquid. **2** a copious outpouring: *a torrent of abuse.*
ORIGIN – from Latin *torrere* 'scorch, boil, roar'.

torrential > *adjective* (of rain) falling rapidly and heavily.
DERIVATIVES – **torrentially** *adverb*.

torrid > *adjective* **1** very hot and dry. **2** full of intense emotions arising from sexual love. **3** full of difficulty.
DERIVATIVES – **torridly** *adverb*.
COMBINATIONS – **torrid zone** the hot central belt of the earth bounded by the tropics of Cancer and Capricorn.
ORIGIN – Latin *torridus*, from *torrere* 'parch, scorch'.

torsion /torsh'n/ > *noun* the action of twisting or the state of being twisted, especially of one end of an object relative to the other.
DERIVATIVES – **torsional** *adjective*.
COMBINATIONS – **torsion bar** a bar in a vehicle suspension, which twists in response to the motion of the wheels and absorbs their vertical movement.
ORIGIN – Latin, from *torquere* 'to twist'.

torso > *noun* (pl. **torsos** or US also **torsi**) **1** the trunk of the human body. **2** an unfinished or mutilated thing, especially a work of art or literature.
ORIGIN – Italian, 'stalk, stump'.

tort > *noun* Law a wrongful act or an infringement of a right (other than under contract) leading to legal liability.
ORIGIN – Latin *tortum* 'wrong, injustice'.

torte /torte/ > *noun* (pl. **torten** /tortən/ or **tortes**) a sweet cake or tart.
ORIGIN – German.

tortellini /tortəleeni/ > *noun* small stuffed pasta parcels rolled and formed into small rings.
ORIGIN – Italian, from *tortello* 'small cake, fritter'.

tortilla /torteeyə/ > *noun* **1** (in Mexican cookery) a thin, flat maize pancake. **2** (in Spanish cookery) a thick omelette containing potato.
ORIGIN – Spanish, 'little cake'.

tortious /**tor**shəss/ > *adjective* Law constituting a tort; wrongful.

tortoise /**tor**təss, **tor**toyz/ > *noun* a slow-moving land reptile with a scaly or leathery domed shell into which it can retract its head and legs.
ORIGIN – Latin *tortuca*.

tortoiseshell > *noun* **1** the semi-transparent mottled yellow and brown shell of certain turtles, used to make jewellery or ornaments. **2** a cat with markings resembling tortoiseshell. **3** a butterfly with mottled orange, yellow, and black markings.

tortuous /**tor**tyooəss, **tor**chooəss/ > *adjective* **1** full of twists and turns. **2** excessively lengthy and complex.
DERIVATIVES – **tortuosity** *noun* **tortuously** *adverb* **tortuousness** *noun*.
USAGE – do not confuse **tortuous** with **torturous**, which means 'characterised by pain or suffering'.
SYNONYMS – **1** labyrinthine, meandering, sinuous, winding. **2** complicated, convoluted, involved, roundabout.
ORIGIN – Latin *tortuosus*, from *torquere* 'to twist'.

torture > *noun* **1** the infliction of severe pain as a punishment or a forcible means of persuasion. **2** great suffering or anxiety. > *verb* subject to torture.
DERIVATIVES – **torturer** *noun*.
SYNONYMS – **1** abuse, torment. **2** agony, anguish, distress, pain, suffering. *verb* abuse, torment.
ORIGIN – Latin *tortura* 'twisting, torment', from *torquere* 'to twist'.

torturous > *adjective* characterised by pain or suffering.
DERIVATIVES – **torturously** *adverb*.
USAGE – do not confuse **torturous** with **tortuous**, which means 'full of twists and turns'.

torus /**tor**əss/ > *noun* (pl. **tori** /**tor**ī/ or **toruses**) **1** Geometry a surface or solid resembling a ring doughnut, formed by rotating a closed curve about a line which lies in the same plane but does not intersect it. **2** a ring-shaped object or chamber. **3** Architecture a large convex moulding with a semicircular cross section.
ORIGIN – Latin, 'swelling, round moulding'.

Tory > *noun* (pl. **Tories**) **1** a member or supporter of the British Conservative Party. **2** a member of the English political party that opposed the exclusion of James II from the succession and later gave rise to the Conservative Party. **3** US a colonist who supported the British side during the American Revolution.
DERIVATIVES – **Toryism** *noun*.

wordpower facts
Tory
The word **Tory** has a long history, and has certainly changed a lot in meaning! It is probably derived from the Irish word *toraidhe* 'outlaw, highwayman', and was originally used of Irish peasants dispossessed by English settlers and living as robbers. It was extended to other marauders, especially in the Scottish Highlands, and was then adopted in about 1679 as an abusive nickname for supporters of the future James II (a Catholic). After James's deposition it lost its negative connotations and started to be applied to members of the English, later British, parliamentary party which supported the established religious and political order and opposed the Whigs. This party became the Conservative Party in the 1830s, but the term **Tory** is still used as a more informal term for a Conservative.

tosh > *noun* Brit. informal rubbish; nonsense.

Tosk /tosk/ > *noun* (pl. same or **Tosks**) **1** a member of one of the main ethnic groups of Albania, living chiefly in the south of the country. Compare with **GHEG**. **2** the dialect of Albanian spoken by this people.
ORIGIN – Albanian *Toskë*.

toss > *verb* **1** throw lightly or casually. **2** move from side to side or back and forth. **3** jerk (one's head or hair) sharply backwards. **4** throw (a coin) into the air so as to make a choice, based on which side of the coin faces uppermost when it lands. **5** shake or turn (food) in a liquid to coat it lightly. > *noun* an act of tossing.
IDIOMS – **give** (or **care**) **a toss** Brit. informal care at all. **toss off 1** produce rapidly or without thought or effort. **2** drink (something) rapidly or all at once. **3** Brit. vulgar slang masturbate.
DERIVATIVES – **tosser** *noun*.

toss-up > *noun* informal **1** the tossing of a coin to make a choice. **2** a situation in which any of two or more outcomes or options is equally possible.

tot¹ > *noun* **1** a very young child. **2** chiefly Brit. a small drink of spirits.

tot² > *verb* (**totted**, **totting**) (**tot up**) chiefly Brit. **1** add up (numbers or amounts). **2** accumulate over time.
ORIGIN – from archaic *tot* 'set of figures to be added up', abbreviation of **TOTAL** or of Latin *totum* 'the whole'.

total > *adjective* **1** comprising the whole number or amount. **2** complete; absolute. > *noun* a total number or amount. > *verb* (**totalled**, **totalling**; US **totaled**, **totaling**) **1** amount to (a total number). **2** find the total of. **3** informal, chiefly N. Amer. destroy or kill.
DERIVATIVES – **totally** *adverb*.
SYNONYMS – *adjective* **1** complete, comprehensive, entire, full, gross, whole. **2** absolute, complete, outright, thorough, utter. *verb* **1** amount to, come to, equal, number. **2** add up, calculate, count, tot up.
ANTONYMS – *adjective* partial.
COMBINATIONS – **total eclipse** an eclipse in which the whole of the disc of the sun or moon is obscured. **total war** a war which is unrestricted in terms of the weapons used, the territory or combatants involved, or the objectives pursued.
ORIGIN – Latin *totalis*, from *totum* 'the whole'.

totalisator /**tō**təlīzaytər/ (also **totalizator**) > *noun* **1** a device showing the number and amount of bets staked on a race. **2** another term for **TOTE¹**.

totalise (also **totalize**) > *verb* **1** combine into a total. **2** calculate the total of.
DERIVATIVES – **totalisation** *noun* **totaliser** *noun*.

totalitarian /**tō**talitairiən/ > *adjective* (of government) centralised, dictatorial, and requiring complete subservience to the state. > *noun* a person advocating such a system.
DERIVATIVES – **totalitarianism** *noun*.

totality > *noun* **1** the whole of something. **2** Astronomy the time during which the sun or moon is totally obscured during an eclipse.

tote¹ > *noun* (**the tote**) informal a system of betting based on the totalisator, in which dividends are calculated according to the amount staked rather than odds offered.

tote² > *verb* informal, chiefly N. Amer. carry.
DERIVATIVES – **toter** *noun*.
COMBINATIONS – **tote bag** a large bag for carrying a number of items.

totem /**tō**təm/ > *noun* a natural object or animal believed by a particular society to have spiritual significance and adopted by it as an emblem.
DERIVATIVES – **totemic** /tō**temm**ik/ *adjective*.
COMBINATIONS – **totem pole** a pole on which totems are hung or on which the images of totems are carved.
ORIGIN – Ojibwa.

totter¹ > *noun* Brit. informal a person who salvages saleable items from dustbins or rubbish heaps.
DERIVATIVES – **totting** *noun*.
ORIGIN – from slang *tot* 'bone'.

totter² > *verb* **1** move in an unsteady way. **2** shake or rock as if about to collapse. **3** be insecure or about to collapse. > *noun* a tottering gait.
DERIVATIVES – **tottery** *adjective*.

ORIGIN – Dutch *touteren* 'to swing' (the original sense in English).

totty > *noun* Brit. informal girls or women collectively regarded as sexually desirable.

toucan /tōōkən/ > *noun* a tropical American fruit-eating bird with a massive bill and brightly coloured plumage.

ORIGIN – Tupi.

touch > *verb* 1 come into or be in contact with or in mutual contact. 2 bring one's hand or another part of one's body into contact with. 3 harm, interfere with, or use. 4 have an effect on. 5 (often **be touched**) produce feelings of affection, gratitude, or sympathy in. 6 have any dealings with. 7 informal approach in excellence: *no one can touch him at judo.* 8 (**touched**) informal slightly mad. > *noun* 1 an act or manner of touching. 2 the faculty of perception through physical contact, especially with the fingers. 3 a small amount. 4 a distinctive detail or feature. 5 a distinctive or skilful manner or method of dealing with something. 6 Rugby & Soccer the area beyond the sidelines, out of play.

WORDFINDER – palpable (*able to be touched or felt*), tactile (*relating to the sense of touch*), tangible (*perceptible by touch*).

IDIOMS – **in touch** 1 in or into communication. 2 possessing up-to-date knowledge. **lose touch** 1 cease to be in communication. 2 cease to be informed. **out of touch** lacking up-to-date knowledge or awareness. **soft** (or **easy**) **touch** informal a person who is easily persuaded or imposed upon. **touch-and-go** (of an outcome) possible but very uncertain. **touch at** (of a ship) call briefly at (a port). **touch down** 1 (of an aircraft or spacecraft) land. 2 Rugby touch the ground with the ball behind the opponents' goal line, scoring a try. 3 American Football score six points by being in possession of the ball behind the opponents' goal line. **touch for** informal ask (someone) for (money) as a loan or gift. **touch in** lightly mark in (details) with a brush or pencil. **touch off** 1 cause (something) to ignite or explode by touching it with a match. 2 cause to happen suddenly. **touch on** 1 deal briefly with (a subject). 2 come near to being. **touch up** 1 make small improvements to. 2 Brit. informal caress (someone) without their consent for sexual pleasure.

SYNONYMS – *verb* 1 abut, adjoin, connect, converge, join, meet. 2 brush, caress, feel, graze, pat, stroke, tap. 4 affect, move, stir. *noun* 3 hint, spot, trace, whisper.

COMBINATIONS – **touch football** a form of American football in which a ball-carrier is downed by touching instead of tackling. **touch judge** Rugby a linesman. **touch screen** a display device which allows the user to interact with a computer by touching areas on the screen. **touch-tone** (of a telephone) generating tones to dial rather than pulses.

ORIGIN – Old French *tochier*.

touchdown > *noun* 1 the moment at which an aircraft touches down. 2 Rugby & American Football an act of touching down.

touché /tōōshay/ > *exclamation* 1 (in fencing) used to acknowledge a hit by one's opponent. 2 used to acknowledge a good or clever point made at one's expense.

ORIGIN – French, 'touched'.

touching > *adjective* arousing emotion; moving. > *preposition* concerning.

DERIVATIVES – **touchingly** adverb.

touchline > *noun* Rugby & Soccer the boundary line on each side of the field.

touchpaper > *noun* a strip of paper impregnated with nitre, for setting light to fireworks or gunpowder.

touchstone > *noun* 1 a piece of fine-grained dark schist or jasper formerly used for testing alloys of gold by observing the colour of the mark which they made on it. 2 a standard or criterion.

touch-type > *verb* type using all of one's fingers and without looking at the keys.

touchy > *adjective* (**touchier, touchiest**) 1 quick to take offence; oversensitive. 2 (of a situation or issue) requiring careful handling.

DERIVATIVES – **touchily** adverb **touchiness** noun.

touchy-feely > *adjective* informal, often derogatory openly expressing affection or other emotions, especially through physical contact.

tough > *adjective* 1 strong enough to withstand wear and tear. 2 able to endure hardship, adversity, or pain. 3 strict and uncompromising. 4 involving considerable difficulty or hardship. 5 rough or violent. 6 used to express a lack of sympathy. > *noun* informal a rough and violent man.

IDIOMS – **tough it out** informal endure a period of hardship or difficulty.

DERIVATIVES – **toughly** adverb **toughness** noun.

SYNONYMS – *adjective* 1 durable, hard-wearing, resilient, strong, sturdy. 2 gritty, hardy, resilient, strong. 3 firm, hard, harsh, severe, strict, uncompromising. 4 arduous, demanding, difficult, hard, taxing.

ANTONYMS – *adjective* 1,2 weak. 3 light, soft. 4 easy.

COMBINATIONS – **tough love** promotion of a person's welfare by enforcing certain constraints on them or requiring them to take responsibility for their actions. **tough-minded** strong, realistic, and unsentimental.

toughen > *verb* make or become tough.

toupee /tōōpay/ > *noun* a small wig or artificial hairpiece worn to cover a bald spot.

ORIGIN – French, from *toupet* 'hair-tuft'.

tour > *noun* 1 a journey for pleasure in which several different places are visited. 2 a short trip to view or inspect something. 3 a series of performances or matches in several different places by performers or sports players. 4 (also **tour of duty**) a spell of duty on military or diplomatic service. > *verb* make a tour of.

COMBINATIONS – **tour operator** a travel agent specialising in package holidays.

ORIGIN – Old French, 'turn', from Greek *tornos* 'lathe'.

tour de force /toor də forss/ > *noun* (pl. **tours de force** pronunc. same) a performance or achievement accomplished with great skill.

ORIGIN – French, 'feat of strength'.

tourer > *noun* a car, caravan, or bicycle designed for touring.

Tourette's syndrome /tōōrets/ > *noun* Medicine a neurological disorder characterised by involuntary tics and often the compulsive utterance of obscenities.

ORIGIN – named after the French neurologist Gilles de la *Tourette* (1857–1904).

tourism > *noun* the commercial organisation and operation of holidays and visits to places of interest.

tourist > *noun* 1 a person who travels for pleasure. 2 a member of a touring sports team.

DERIVATIVES – **touristic** adjective.

SYNONYMS – 1 day tripper, sightseer, visitor; Brit holidaymaker, tripper.

COMBINATIONS – **tourist class** the cheapest accommodation or seating in a ship, aircraft, or hotel.

touristy > *adjective* informal, often derogatory relating to, appealing to, or visited by tourists.

tourmaline /toorməleen/ > *noun* a brittle grey or black mineral with piezoelectric and polarising properties.

ORIGIN – Sinhalese, 'carnelian'.

tournament > *noun* 1 a series of contests between a number of competitors, competing for an overall prize. 2 a medieval sporting event in which knights jousted with blunted weapons for a prize.

ORIGIN – Old French *torneiement*, from *torneier* (see **TOURNEY**).

tournedos /toornədō/ > *noun* (pl. same /toornədōz/) a small round thick cut from a fillet of beef.

ORIGIN – French, from *tourner* 'to turn' + *dos* 'back'.

tourney /toorni/ > *noun* (pl. **tourneys**) a medieval joust. > *verb* (**tourneys, tourneyed**) take part in a tourney.

ORIGIN – Old French *tornei* (noun), *torneier* (verb), from Latin *tornus* 'a turn'.

tourniquet /**toor**nikay/ > *noun* a device for stopping the flow of blood through an artery, typically by compressing a limb with a cord or tight bandage.

ORIGIN – French, probably from Old French *tournicle* 'coat of mail'.

tousle /**towz**'l/ > *verb* make (something, especially a person's hair) untidy.

ORIGIN – from dialect *touse* 'handle roughly'.

tout /towt/ > *verb* **1** attempt to sell (something), typically by a direct or persistent approach. **2** attempt to persuade people of the merits of. **3** Brit. sell (a ticket) for a popular event at a price higher than the official one. > *noun* (also **ticket tout**) Brit. a person who buys up tickets for an event to resell them at a profit.

ORIGIN – Middle English *tute* 'look out', of Germanic origin; in the 18th century it acquired the sense 'solicit custom'.

tout court /tōō **koor**/ > *adverb* briefly; simply.

ORIGIN – French, 'very short'.

tout de suite /tōō də **sweet**/ > *adverb* at once.

ORIGIN – French, 'quite in sequence'.

tow¹ > *verb* use a vehicle or boat to pull (another vehicle or boat) along. > *noun* an act of towing.

IDIOMS – **in tow 1** (also **on tow**) being towed. **2** accompanying or following someone.

DERIVATIVES – **towable** *adjective* **towage** *noun*.

COMBINATIONS – **tow bar** a bar fitted to the back of a vehicle, used in towing a trailer or caravan. **towline** a tow rope. **towpath** a path beside a river or canal, originally used as a pathway for horses towing barges. **tow rope** a rope, cable, etc. used in towing.

ORIGIN – Old English, 'draw, drag'.

tow² > *noun* **1** the coarse and broken part of flax or hemp prepared for spinning. **2** a bundle of untwisted natural or man-made fibres.

toward > *preposition* variant of **TOWARDS**.

towards (chiefly N. Amer. also **toward**) > *preposition* **1** in the direction of. **2** getting nearer to (a time or goal). **3** in relation to. **4** contributing to the cost of.

ORIGIN – Old English (see **TO**, **-WARD**).

towel > *noun* a piece of thick absorbent cloth or paper used for drying. > *verb* (**towelled**, **towelling**; US **toweled**, **toweling**) dry with a towel.

ORIGIN – Old French *toaille*.

towelling (US **toweling**) > *noun* thick absorbent cloth, typically cotton with uncut loops, used for towels and bathrobes.

tower > *noun* **1** a tall, narrow building, either free-standing or forming part of a building such as a church or castle. **2** a tall structure that houses machinery, operators, etc. **3** a tall structure used as a receptacle or for storage. > *verb* **1** rise to or reach a great height. **2** (of a bird) soar up to a great height. **3** (**towering**) very important or influential. **4** (**towering**) very intense: *a towering rage*.

WORDFINDER – *types of tower:* belfry, campanile, donjon, keep, minaret, peel, steeple, turret, watchtower, ziggurat.

COMBINATIONS – **tower block** Brit. a tall modern building containing numerous floors of offices or flats.

town > *noun* **1** a built-up area with a name, defined boundaries, and local government, that is larger than a village and generally smaller than a city. **2** the central part of a neighbourhood, with its business or shopping area. **3** densely populated areas, especially as contrasted with the country or suburbs. **4** the permanent residents of a university town. Contrasted with **GOWN**.

IDIOMS – **go to town** informal do something thoroughly or enthusiastically. **on the town** informal enjoying the nightlife of a city or town.

DERIVATIVES – **townlet** *noun*.

COMBINATIONS – **town car** US a limousine. **town clerk 1** N. Amer. a public official in charge of the records of a town. **2** (in the UK, until 1974) the secretary and legal adviser of a town corporation. **town crier** historical a person employed to make public announcements in the streets. **town hall** a building used for the administration of local government. **town house 1** a tall, narrow traditional terrace house, generally having three or more floors. **2** an urban residence of a person owning another property in the country. **townland** (especially in Ireland) a territorial division of land; a township. **town meeting** US a meeting of the voters of a town for the transaction of public business.

ORIGIN – Old English, 'enclosed piece of land, homestead, village'.

town council > *noun* (especially in the UK) the elected governing body in a municipality.

DERIVATIVES – **town councillor** *noun*.

townie (also **townee**) > *noun* informal a person who lives in a town (used especially with reference to their supposed ignorance of rural affairs).

town planning > *noun* the planning and control of the construction, growth, and development of a town or other urban area.

DERIVATIVES – **town planner** *noun*.

townscape > *noun* an urban landscape.

township > *noun* **1** (in South Africa) a suburb or city of predominantly black occupation, formerly officially designated for black occupation by apartheid legislation. **2** S. African a new area being developed for residential or industrial use by speculators. **3** N. Amer. a division of a county with some corporate powers. **4** Brit. historical a manor or parish as a territorial division. **5** Austral./NZ a small town.

ORIGIN – Old English, 'the inhabitants of a village'.

townsman (or **townswoman**) > *noun* a person living in a particular town or city.

townspeople (also **townsfolk**) > *plural noun* the people living in a particular town or city.

toxaemia /tok**see**miə/ (US **toxemia**) > *noun* Medicine **1** blood poisoning by toxins from a local bacterial infection. **2** pre-eclampsia.

ORIGIN – from Latin *toxicum* 'poison' + **-AEMIA**.

toxic > *adjective* **1** poisonous. **2** relating to or caused by poison. > *noun* (**toxics**) poisonous substances.

DERIVATIVES – **toxicity** *noun*.

COMBINATIONS – **toxic shock syndrome** acute septicaemia in women, typically caused by bacterial infection from a retained tampon or IUD.

ORIGIN – Latin *toxicus* 'poisoned', from *toxicum* 'poison'.

toxicant > *noun* a toxic substance introduced into the environment, e.g. a pesticide.

toxicology /toksi**koll**əji/ > *noun* the branch of science concerned with the nature, effects, and detection of poisons.

DERIVATIVES – **toxicological** *adjective* **toxicologist** *noun*.

toxin > *noun* a poison produced by a micro-organism or other organism and acting as an antigen in the body.

ORIGIN – from **TOXIC**.

toxocara /toksə**kaar**ə/ > *noun* a nematode worm which is a parasite of dogs, cats, and other animals and can be transmitted to humans.

DERIVATIVES – **toxocariasis** *noun*.

ORIGIN – from Latin *toxicum* 'poison' + Greek *kara* 'head'.

toxophilite /tok**soff**ilīt/ rare > *noun* a student or lover of archery. > *adjective* relating to archers and archery.

ORIGIN – from *Toxophilus*, a name invented by the English scholar and writer Roger Ascham, used as the title of his treatise on archery (1545), from Greek *toxon* 'bow' + *-philos* 'loving'.

toxoplasmosis /toksōplaz**mō**siss/ > *noun* Medicine a disease caused by a parasitic protozoan, transmitted chiefly through undercooked meat, soil, or in cat faeces.

ORIGIN – from *Toxoplasma* (genus name).

toy > *noun* **1** an object for a child to play with. **2** (before another noun) denoting a model or miniature replica of something, used for playing with: *a toy car.* **3** a gadget or machine regarded as providing amusement for an adult. **4** (before another noun) denoting a diminutive breed or variety of dog. > *verb* (**toy with**) **1** consider (an idea or proposal) casually or indecisively. **2** move or handle absent-mindedly or nervously. **3** eat or drink in an unenthusiastic or restrained way.
DERIVATIVES – **toylike** *adjective.*
COMBINATIONS – **toy boy** Brit. informal a male lover who is much younger than his partner. **toytown 1** resembling a quaint or simplified model of a town. **2** having no real value or substance.
ORIGIN – first referring to a funny story or remark.

TQM > *abbreviation* Total Quality Management.

trace¹ > *verb* **1** find by investigation. **2** find or describe the origin or development of. **3** follow the course or position of with one's eye, mind, or finger. **4** copy (a drawing, map, or design) by drawing over its lines on a superimposed piece of transparent paper. **5** draw (a pattern or line). **6** give an outline of. > *noun* **1** a mark or other indication of the existence or passing of something. **2** a very small quantity. **3** a barely discernible indication: *a trace of a smile.* **4** a line or pattern corresponding to something which is being recorded or measured. **5** a procedure to find, or investigate the source of, something.
DERIVATIVES – **traceable** *adjective* **traceless** *adjective.*
SYNONYMS – *verb* **1** discover, find, track down. *noun* **1** evidence, mark, sign, vestige. **3** ghost, hint, suggestion, suspicion.
COMBINATIONS – **trace element** a chemical element present or required only in minute amounts.
ORIGIN – Old French *trace* (noun), *tracier* (verb), from Latin *tractus* (see **TRACT¹**).

trace² > *noun* each of the two side straps, chains, or ropes by which a horse is attached to a vehicle that it is pulling.
IDIOMS – **kick over the traces** become rebellious or reckless.
ORIGIN – Old French *trais*, from *trait* (see **TRAIT**).

tracer > *noun* **1** a bullet or shell whose course is made visible by a trail of flames or smoke, used to assist in aiming. **2** a substance introduced into a system so that its subsequent distribution can be followed from its colour, radioactivity, or other distinctive property.

tracery > *noun* (pl. **traceries**) **1** Architecture ornamental stone openwork. **2** a delicate branching pattern.
DERIVATIVES – **traceried** *adjective.*

trachea /trəkeeə, traykiə/ > *noun* (pl. **tracheae** /trəkee-ee, trayki-ee/ or **tracheas**) Anatomy the tube conveying air between the larynx and the bronchial tubes; the windpipe.
DERIVATIVES – **tracheal** *adjective.*
ORIGIN – from Greek *trakheia artēria* 'rough artery'.

tracheotomy /trakkiottəmi/ (also **tracheostomy** /trakkiostəmi/) > *noun* (pl. **tracheotomies**) Medicine an incision in the windpipe made to relieve an obstruction to breathing.

trachoma /trəkōmə/ > *noun* a contagious bacterial infection causing inflammation of the inner surface of the eyelids.
ORIGIN – Greek *trakhōma* 'roughness'.

tracing > *noun* **1** a copy of a drawing, map, etc. made by tracing. **2** a faint or delicate mark or pattern.

track > *noun* **1** a rough path or minor road. **2** a prepared course or circuit for racing. **3** a mark or line of marks left by a person, animal, or vehicle in passing. **4** a continuous line of rails on a railway. **5** a section of a record, compact disc, or cassette tape containing one song or piece of music. [ORIGIN – first used in reference to a groove on a gramophone record.] **6** a strip or rail along which something (e.g. a curtain) may be moved. **7** a continuous articulated metal band around the wheels of a heavy vehicle. > *verb* **1** follow the course or movements of. **2** (**track down**) find after a thorough or difficult search. **3** follow a particular course. **4** (of a film or television camera) move in relation to the subject being filmed. [ORIGIN – with reference to early filming when a camera was moved along a track.]
IDIOMS – **keep** (or **lose**) **track of** keep (or fail to keep) fully aware of or informed about. **stop** (or **be stopped**) **in one's tracks** informal be brought to a sudden and complete halt. **track and field** chiefly N. Amer. athletics. **the wrong side of the tracks** informal a poor or less prestigious part of town. [ORIGIN – with reference to the railway tracks of American towns, once serving as a line of demarcation between rich and poor quarters.]
DERIVATIVES – **trackless** *adjective.*
COMBINATIONS – **trackball** a small ball, set in a holder, that can be rotated by hand to move a cursor on a computer screen. **trackbed** the foundation structure on which railway tracks are laid. **track events** athletic events that take place on a running track. **track record** the past achievements or performance of a person, organisation,

or product. **trackway** a path formed by the repeated treading of people or animals.
ORIGIN – Old French *trac*, perhaps from Low German or Dutch *trek* 'draught, drawing'.

tracker > *noun* a person who tracks.

tracking > *noun* **1** Electronics the maintenance of a constant difference in frequency between connected devices. **2** the formation of an electrically conducting path over the surface of an insulator.

tracksuit > *noun* a loose, warm outfit consisting of a sweatshirt and trousers.

tract¹ > *noun* **1** a large area of land. **2** a major passage in the body or other continuous elongated anatomical structure.
ORIGIN – Latin *tractus* 'drawing, draught', from *trahere* 'draw, pull'.

tract² > *noun* a written work produced in pamphlet form, typically on a religious subject.
ORIGIN – apparently an abbreviation of Latin *tractatus* (see **TRACTATE**).

tractable > *adjective* **1** easy to control or influence. **2** (of a situation or problem) easy to deal with.
DERIVATIVES – **tractability** *noun.*
SYNONYMS – **1** amenable, biddable, impressionable, malleable, pliable. **2** manageable.
ANTONYMS – **1** obstinate.
ORIGIN – Latin *tractabilis*, from *tractare* 'to handle'.

tractate /traktayt/ > *noun* formal a piece of writing in which a subject is formally discussed.
ORIGIN – Latin *tractatus*, from *tractare* 'to handle'.

traction > *noun* **1** the action of pulling a thing along a surface. **2** the motive power used for pulling. **3** Medicine the application of a sustained pull on a limb or muscle, especially in order to maintain the position of a fractured bone or to correct a deformity. **4** the grip of a tyre on a road or a wheel on a rail.
COMBINATIONS – **traction engine** a steam or diesel-powered road vehicle used (especially formerly) for pulling very heavy loads.
ORIGIN – from Latin *trahere* 'draw, pull'.

tractor > *noun* a powerful motor vehicle with large rear wheels, used chiefly on farms for hauling equipment and trailers.
ORIGIN – from Latin *trahere* 'to pull'.

trad informal > *adjective* (especially of music) traditional. > *noun* traditional jazz or folk music.

trade > *noun* **1** the buying and selling of goods and services. **2** a business of a particular kind: *the tourist trade.* **3** a job

requiring manual skills and special training. **4** (**the trade**) (treated as sing. or pl.) the people engaged in a particular area of business. **5** dated, chiefly derogatory the practice of making one's living in business. > verb **1** buy and sell goods and services. **2** buy or sell (a particular item or product). **3** exchange, typically as a commercial transaction. **4** (**trade in**) exchange (a used article) in part payment for another. **5** (**trade on**) take advantage of. **6** (**trade off**) exchange (something of value).
DERIVATIVES – **tradable** (or **tradeable**) adjective.
SYNONYMS – noun **1** business, commerce, traffic. **3** craft. verb **1** deal, do business, traffic. **3** barter, exchange, swap, switch. **5** (**trade on**) abuse, exploit, use.
COMBINATIONS – **trade deficit** (also **trade gap**) the amount by which the cost of a country's imports exceeds the value of its exports. **trade name 1** a name that has the status of a trademark. **2** a name by which something is known in a particular trade or profession. **trade price** the price paid for goods by a retailer to a manufacturer or wholesaler. **trade surplus** the amount by which the value of a country's exports exceeds the cost of its imports. **trading estate** Brit. a specially designed industrial and commercial area. **trading post** a store or small settlement established for trading, typically in a remote place.
ORIGIN – Low German, 'track'; related to **TREAD**.

trademark > noun **1** a symbol, word, or words legally registered or established by use as representing a company or product. **2** a distinctive characteristic or object. > verb provide with a trademark.

trader > noun **1** a person who trades goods, currency, or shares. **2** a merchant ship.

tradescantia /traddiˈskantiə/ > noun an American plant with triangular three-petalled flowers.
ORIGIN – modern Latin, named in honour of the English botanist John Tradescant (1570–1638).

tradesman > noun a person engaged in trading or a trade, typically on a small scale.

trade union (Brit. also **trades union**) > noun an organised association of workers, formed to protect and further their rights and interests.
DERIVATIVES – **trade unionism** noun **trade unionist** noun.

trade wind > noun a wind blowing steadily towards the equator from the north-east in the northern hemisphere or the south-east in the southern hemisphere, especially at sea.

wordpower facts
Trade wind
The expression **trade wind** is first recorded in use from the mid 17th century. It comes from the obsolete phrase blow trade 'blow steadily in the same direction': **trade** formerly meant 'course, direction' and 'track, trail' before it acquired its modern meanings of 'an occupation' and 'buying and selling'. Because of the importance of the trade winds to navigation and therefore to the transport of goods by sea, 18th-century etymologists incorrectly connected the word trade with 'commerce'.

tradition > noun **1** the transmission of customs or beliefs from generation to generation. **2** a long-established custom or belief passed on in this way. **3** an artistic or literary method or style established by an artist, writer, or movement, and subsequently followed by others.
SYNONYMS – **2** belief, convention, custom, observance, practice, ritual.
ORIGIN – from Latin tradere 'deliver, betray', from trans- 'across' + dare 'give'.

traditional > adjective **1** of, relating to, or following tradition. **2** (of jazz) in the style of the early 20th century.
DERIVATIVES – **traditionally** adverb.
SYNONYMS – **1** conventional, customary, established, orthodox.

traditionalism > noun the upholding of tradition, especially so as to resist change.
DERIVATIVES – **traditionalist** noun & adjective.

traduce /trəˈdyooss/ > verb speak badly of or tell lies about.
ORIGIN – Latin traducere 'lead in front of others, expose to ridicule'.

traffic > noun **1** vehicles moving on a public highway. **2** the movement of ships or aircraft. **3** the commercial transportation of goods or passengers. **4** the messages or signals transmitted through a communications system. **5** the action of trafficking. > verb (**trafficked**, **trafficking**) deal or trade in something illegal.
DERIVATIVES – **trafficker** noun.
COMBINATIONS – **traffic calming** the deliberate slowing of traffic in residential areas, by building road humps or other obstructions. **traffic island** a small raised area in the middle of a road which provides a safe place for pedestrians to stand. **traffic jam** a line or lines of traffic at or virtually at a standstill. **traffic lights** (also **traffic light** or **traffic signal**) a set of automatically operated coloured lights for controlling traffic. **traffic warden** Brit. a uniformed

official who locates and reports on infringements of parking regulations.
ORIGIN – from French traffique, Spanish tráfico, or Italian traffico.

tragedian /trəˈjeediən/ > noun **1** (fem. **tragedienne** /trəˈjeedien/) a tragic actor or actress. **2** a writer of tragedies.

tragedy > noun (pl. **tragedies**) **1** an event causing great sadness or suffering. **2** a serious play with an unhappy ending.
SYNONYMS – **1** calamity, cataclysm, catastrophe, disaster, misfortune.
ORIGIN – Greek tragōidia, apparently from tragos 'goat' (the reason remains unexplained) + ōidē 'song, ode'.

tragic > adjective **1** causing great sadness or suffering. **2** suffering extreme distress or sadness. **3** relating to tragedy in a literary work.
DERIVATIVES – **tragical** adjective **tragically** adverb.
SYNONYMS – **1** devastating, disastrous, dreadful, sad, terrible. **2** sad, sorrowful, woeful, wretched.

tragicomedy > noun (pl. **tragicomedies**) a play or novel containing elements of both comedy and tragedy.
DERIVATIVES – **tragicomic** adjective **tragicomically** adverb.

trail > noun **1** a mark or a series of signs left behind by the passage of someone or something. **2** a track or scent used in following someone or hunting an animal. **3** a long, thin part stretching behind or hanging down from something. **4** a beaten path through rough country. **5** a route planned or followed for a particular purpose: the tourist trail. > verb **1** draw or be drawn along behind. **2** walk or move slowly or wearily. **3** follow the trail of. **4** (of a plant) grow along the ground or so as to hang down. **5** (**trail away** or **off**) (of the voice or a speaker) fade gradually before stopping. **6** be losing to an opponent in a contest. **7** advertise with a trailer.
COMBINATIONS – **trailing edge** the rear edge of a moving body, especially an aircraft wing or propeller blade. **trail mix** a mixture of dried fruit and nuts eaten as a snack food.
ORIGIN – from Old French trailler 'to tow' or Low German treilen 'haul (a boat)', from Latin trahere 'to pull'.

trailblazer > noun **1** a person who makes a new track through wild country. **2** an innovator.
DERIVATIVES – **trailblazing** noun & adjective.

trailer > noun **1** an unpowered vehicle towed by another. **2** the rear section of an articulated truck. **3** N. Amer. a caravan. **4** an extract from a film or programme used to advertise it. > *verb* **1** advertise with a trailer. **2** transport by trailer.

COMBINATIONS – **trailer park 1** N. Amer. a caravan site. **2** (**trailer-park**) US lacking refinement, taste, or quality: *a trailer-park floozy*. **trailer truck** US an articulated truck.

train > *verb* **1** teach (a person or animal) a particular skill or type of behaviour through regular practice and instruction. **2** be taught in such a way. **3** make or become physically fit through a course of exercise and diet. **4** (**train on**) point (something) at. **5** make (a plant) grow in a particular direction or into a required shape. > *noun* **1** a series of railway carriages or wagons moved as a unit by a locomotive or by integral motors. **2** a number of vehicles or pack animals moving in a line. **3** a series of connected events, thoughts, etc. **4** a long piece of trailing material attached to the back of a formal dress or robe. **5** a retinue of attendants accompanying an important person.

IDIOMS – **in train** in progress.

DERIVATIVES – **trainable** *adjective* **training** *noun* **trainload** *noun*.

SYNONYMS – *verb* **1** coach, drill, instruct, teach, tutor. *noun* **3** chain, sequence, series, string.

COMBINATIONS – **training college** (in the UK) a college where people, especially prospective teachers, are trained. **training shoes** trainers.

wordpower facts

Train

The word **train** has many senses, and the connection between the core meanings 'teach' and 'series of linked vehicles' is not readily apparent. The word entered English as a noun in the sense 'delay', coming via Old French from the Latin verb *trahere* 'pull, draw' (the root of words such as **abstract**, **attract**, **contract**, **distract**, **portray**, **traction**, **trail**, and **treat**). Early noun senses were 'trailing part of a robe' and 'retinue'; the latter gave rise to 'line of travelling people or vehicles', later 'a connected series of things'. The early verb sense 'cause (a plant) to grow in a desired shape' was the basis of the sense 'educate, instruct, teach'.

trainee > *noun* a person undergoing training for a particular job or profession.

DERIVATIVES – **traineeship** *noun*.

trainer > *noun* **1** a person who trains people or animals. **2** Brit. a soft shoe, suitable for sports or casual wear.

trainspotter > *noun* Brit. **1** a person who collects locomotive numbers as a hobby. **2**

derogatory a person who obsessively studies the minutiae of a hobby or subject.

DERIVATIVES – **trainspotting** *noun*.

traipse > *verb* walk or move wearily, reluctantly, or aimlessly. > *noun* a tedious or tiring walk.

trait /tray, trayt/ > *noun* **1** a distinguishing quality or characteristic. **2** a genetically determined characteristic.

NOTE – **trait** has two pronunciations. The first, sounding like *tray*, is the traditional one (corresponding to the sound of *trait* in French), but the newer one, rhyming with *rate*, is increasingly used and is standard in the US.

SYNONYMS – **1** attribute, characteristic, feature, property, quality.

ORIGIN – French, from Latin *tractus* (see **TRACT**[1]).

traitor > *noun* a person who betrays their country, a cause, etc.

DERIVATIVES – **traitorous** *adjective* **traitorously** *adverb*.

ORIGIN – Latin *traditor*, from *tradere* 'hand over'.

trajectory /trəˈjektəri/ > *noun* (pl. **trajectories**) the path described by a projectile flying or an object moving under the action of given forces.

ORIGIN – Latin *trajectoria*, from *traicere* 'throw across'.

tram (also **tramcar**) > *noun* Brit. a passenger vehicle powered by electricity conveyed by overhead cables, and running on rails laid in a public road.

ORIGIN – Low German and Dutch *trame* 'beam, barrow shaft', the original sense in English; it also denoted a barrow or cart used in coal mines, later the tracks on which such carts ran.

tramlines > *plural noun* Brit. **1** rails for a tramcar. **2** informal a pair of parallel lines at the sides of a tennis court or at the side or back of a badminton court.

trammel > *noun* **1** (**trammels**) literary restrictions or impediments to freedom of action. **2** (also **trammel net**) a three-layered net, designed so that a pocket forms when fish attempt to swim through, thus trapping them. > *verb* (**trammelled**, **trammelling**; US **trammeled**, **trammeling**) constrain or impede.

ORIGIN – from Latin *trimaculum*, perhaps from *tri-* 'three' + *macula* 'mesh'.

tramontana /traamonˈtaanə/ > *noun* a cold north wind blowing in Italy or the adjoining regions of the Adriatic and Mediterranean.

ORIGIN – Italian, 'north wind, Pole Star', from Latin *transmontanus* 'beyond the mountains'.

tramp > *verb* **1** walk heavily or noisily. **2** walk wearily or reluctantly over a long distance. > *noun* **1** an itinerant homeless

person who lives by begging or doing casual work. **2** the sound of heavy steps. **3** a long walk. **4** a cargo vessel running between many different ports rather than sailing a fixed route. **5** N. Amer. informal a promiscuous woman.

DERIVATIVES – **tramper** *noun*.

ORIGIN – probably of Low German origin.

trample > *verb* **1** tread on and crush. **2** (**trample on** or **over**) treat with contempt.

trampoline > *noun* a strong fabric sheet connected by springs to a frame, used as a springboard and landing area in doing acrobatic or gymnastic exercises. > *verb* (**trampolining**) use a trampoline.

ORIGIN – Italian *trampolino*, from *trampoli* 'stilts'.

tramway > *noun* **1** Brit. a set of rails for a tram. **2** a tram system.

trance /traanss/ > *noun* **1** a half-conscious state characterised by an absence of response to external stimuli, typically as induced by hypnosis. **2** a state of abstraction. **3** (also **trance music**) a type of electronic dance music characterised by hypnotic rhythms. > *verb* literary put into a trance.

ORIGIN – from Old French *transir* 'depart, fall into a trance', from Latin *transire* 'go across'.

tranche /traansh/ > *noun* a portion, especially of money.

ORIGIN – Old French, 'slice'.

trank > *noun* informal a tranquillising drug.

tranny (also **trannie**) > *noun* (pl. **trannies**) informal **1** chiefly Brit. a transistor radio. **2** a transvestite.

tranquil > *adjective* free from disturbance; calm.

DERIVATIVES – **tranquillity** (also **tranquility**) *noun* **tranquilly** *adverb*.

SYNONYMS – calm, peaceful, quiet, serene, still, undisturbed.

ORIGIN – Latin *tranquillus*.

tranquillise (also **tranquillize**; US **tranquilise**) > *verb* **1** (of a drug) have a calming or sedative effect on. **2** administer such a drug to.

DERIVATIVES – **tranquilliser** *noun*.

trans- > *prefix* **1** across; beyond: *transcontinental*. **2** on or to the other side of: *transatlantic*. **3** into another state or place: *translate*.

ORIGIN – from Latin *trans* 'across'.

transaction > *noun* **1** an instance of buying or selling. **2** the action of conducting business. **3** an exchange or interaction between people.

DERIVATIVES – **transact** *verb* **transactional** *adjective*.

ORIGIN – from Latin *transigere* 'drive through'.

1039

transatlantic > *adjective* **1** crossing the Atlantic. **2** concerning countries on both sides of the Atlantic, typically Britain and the US. **3** relating to or situated on the other side of the Atlantic; **Brit.** American; **N. Amer.** British or European.

transaxle > *noun* an integral driving axle and differential gear in a motor vehicle.

transceiver > *noun* a combined radio transmitter and receiver.

transcend > *verb* **1** be or go beyond the range or limits of. **2** surpass.
ORIGIN – Latin *transcendere*, from *trans-* 'across' + *scandere* 'climb'.

transcendent > *adjective* **1** transcending normal or physical human experience. **2** (of God) existing apart from and not subject to the limitations of the material universe.
DERIVATIVES – **transcendence** *noun* **transcendently** *adverb*.

transcendental > *adjective* **1** relating to a spiritual realm. **2** relating to or denoting Transcendentalism.
DERIVATIVES – **transcendentally** *adverb*.
COMBINATIONS – **Transcendental Meditation** (trademark in the US) a technique for detaching oneself from anxiety and promoting harmony and self-realisation by meditation and repetition of a mantra.

Transcendentalism > *noun* a 19th-century idealistic philosophical and social movement which taught that divinity pervades all nature and humanity.
DERIVATIVES – **transcendentalist** *noun* & *adjective*.

transcontinental > *adjective* crossing or extending across a continent or continents.

transcribe > *verb* **1** put (thoughts, speech, or data) into written or printed form. **2** make a copy of, especially in another alphabet or language. **3** arrange (music) for a different instrument, voice, etc.
DERIVATIVES – **transcriber** *noun*.
ORIGIN – Latin *transcribere*, from *trans-* 'across' + *scribere* 'write'.

transcript > *noun* a written or printed version of material originally presented in another medium.
ORIGIN – Latin *transcriptum*, from *transcribere* (see TRANSCRIBE).

transcriptase /tran**skrip**tayz/ > *noun* **Biochemistry** an enzyme which promotes the formation of RNA from a DNA template, or (**reverse transcriptase**), the formation of DNA from an RNA template.

transcription > *noun* **1** a transcript. **2** the action or process of transcribing. **3** a piece of music transcribed for a different instrument, voice, etc.

transducer /tranz**dyoo**sər/ > *noun* a device that converts variations in a physical quantity (such as pressure or brightness) into an electrical signal, or vice versa.
DERIVATIVES – **transduction** *noun*.

ORIGIN – from Latin *transducere* 'lead across'.

transect technical > *verb* cut across or make a transverse section in. > *noun* a straight line or narrow cross section along which observations or measurements are made.
DERIVATIVES – **transection** *noun*.
ORIGIN – from TRANS- + Latin *secare* 'divide by cutting'.

transept /**tran**sept/ > *noun* (in a cross-shaped church) either of the two parts forming the arms of the cross shape, projecting at right angles from the nave.
ORIGIN – Latin *transeptum* (see TRANS-, SEPTUM).

transfer > *verb* (**transferred**, **transferring**) **1** move from one place to another. **2** move to another department, occupation, etc. **3** change to another place, route, or means of transport during a journey. **4** make over the possession of (property, a right, or a responsibility) to another. > *noun* **1** an act of transferring. **2** **Brit.** a small coloured picture or design on paper, which can be transferred to another surface by being pressed or heated.
DERIVATIVES – **transferability** *noun* **transferable** *adjective* **transferee** *noun*.
SYNONYMS – *verb* **1** convey, move, relocate, shift, transport. **3** change, switch. **4** consign, devolve, hand over, make over, pass on.
COMBINATIONS – **transfer fee** **Brit.** a fee paid by one soccer or rugby club to another for the transfer of a player.
ORIGIN – Latin *transferre*, from *trans-* 'across' + *ferre* 'to bear'.

transference > *noun* **1** the action of transferring or the process of being transferred. **2** **Psychoanalysis** the redirection of emotions originally felt in childhood.

transfiguration > *noun* **1** a complete transformation into a more beautiful or spiritual state. **2** (**the Transfiguration**) Christ's appearance in radiant glory to three of his disciples (in the gospels of Matthew and Mark).

transfigure > *verb* (**be transfigured**) be transformed into something more beautiful or spiritual.
ORIGIN – Latin *transfigurare*, from *trans-* 'across' + *figura* 'figure'.

transfix > *verb* **1** make motionless with horror, wonder, or astonishment. **2** pierce with a sharp implement.
ORIGIN – Latin *transfigere* 'pierce through'.

transform > *verb* **1** subject to or undergo transformation. **2** change the voltage of (an electric current) by electromagnetic induction.
DERIVATIVES – **transformative** *adjective*.
ORIGIN – Latin *transformare* (see TRANS-, FORM).

transformation > *noun* a marked change in nature, form, or appearance.
DERIVATIVES – **transformational** *adjective*.

transformer > *noun* a device for changing the voltage of an alternating current by electromagnetic induction.

transfuse > *verb* **1** Medicine transfer (blood) from one person or animal to another. **2** permeate or infuse. **3** inject (liquid) into a blood vessel to replace lost fluid.
DERIVATIVES – **transfusion** *noun*.
ORIGIN – Latin *transfundere* 'pour from one container to another'.

transgender (also **transgendered**) > *adjective* transsexual.

transgenic /tranz**jenn**ik/ > *adjective* Biology containing genetic material into which DNA from a different organism has been artificially introduced.

transgress > *verb* go beyond the limits set by (a moral principle, standard, law, etc.).
DERIVATIVES – **transgression** *noun* **transgressive** *adjective* **transgressor** *noun*.
ORIGIN – Latin *transgredi* 'step across'.

tranship > *verb* variant spelling of TRANS-SHIP.

transhumance /tranz**hyoo**mənss/ > *noun* the action or practice of moving livestock seasonally from one grazing ground to another.
DERIVATIVES – **transhumant** *adjective*.
ORIGIN – French, from *transhumer*, from Latin *trans-* 'across' + *humus* 'ground'.

transient /**tran**ziənt/ > *adjective* **1** lasting only for a short time. **2** staying or working in a place for a short time only. > *noun* a transient person.
DERIVATIVES – **transience** *noun* **transiency** *noun* **transiently** *adverb*.
SYNONYMS – *adjective* **1** ephemeral, short-lived, temporary, transitory.
ANTONYMS – *adjective* **1** lasting, permanent.
ORIGIN – from Latin *transire* 'go across'.

transistor > *noun* **1** a semiconductor device with three connections, capable of amplification and rectification. **2** (also **transistor radio**) a portable radio using circuits containing transistors.
DERIVATIVES – **transistorise** (also **transistorize**) *verb*.
ORIGIN – from TRANSFER + RESISTOR.

transit > *noun* **1** the carrying of people or things from one place to another. **2** an act of passing through or across a place. > *verb* (**transited**, **transiting**) pass across or through.
ORIGIN – Latin *transitus*, from *transire* 'go across'.

transition > *noun* **1** the process of changing from one state or condition to another. **2** a period of such change.
DERIVATIVES – **transitional** *adjective*.
COMBINATIONS – **transition metals**

Chemistry the set of metallic elements occupying the central block in the periodic table, including for example iron, manganese, chromium, and copper.
ORIGIN – from Latin *transire* 'go across'.

transitive /**tran**zitiv/ > *adjective* Grammar (of a verb) able to take a direct object, e.g. *saw* in *he saw the donkey*. The opposite of **INTRANSITIVE**.
DERIVATIVES – **transitively** *adverb* **transitiveness** *noun* **transitivity** *noun*.
ORIGIN – Latin *transitivus*: originally in the sense 'transitory'.

transitory /**tran**zitəri/ > *adjective* not permanent; short-lived.
DERIVATIVES – **transitorily** *adverb* **transitoriness** *noun*.
SYNONYMS – ephemeral, passing, short-lived, temporary, transient.
ANTONYMS – lasting, permanent.
ORIGIN – Latin *transitorius*, from *transire* 'go across'.

translate > *verb* **1** express the sense of (words or text) in another language. **2** be expressed or be capable of being expressed in another language. **3** (**translate into**) convert or be converted into another form or medium.
DERIVATIVES – **translatable** *adjective*.
SYNONYMS – **1** convert, interpret, render.
ORIGIN – Latin *transferre* (see **TRANSFER**).

translation > *noun* **1** the action or process of translating. **2** a text or word that is translated.

translator > *noun* **1** a person who translates from one language into another. **2** Computing a program that translates from one programming language into another.

transliterate /**tran**z**litt**ərayt/ > *verb* write or print (a letter or word) using the closest corresponding letters of a different alphabet or language.
DERIVATIVES – **transliteration** *noun*.

translocate > *verb* chiefly technical move from one place to another.
DERIVATIVES – **translocation** *noun*.

translucent /tranz**loo**sənt/ > *adjective* allowing a diffuse light to pass through.
DERIVATIVES – **translucence** *noun* **translucency** *noun*.
ORIGIN – from Latin *translucere* 'shine through'.

transmigrate > *verb* (of the soul) pass into a different body after death.
DERIVATIVES – **transmigration** *noun*.

transmission > *noun* **1** the action or process of transmitting or the state of being transmitted. **2** a programme or signal that is transmitted. **3** the mechanism by which power is transmitted from an engine to the axle in a motor vehicle.
COMBINATIONS – **transmission line** a conductor or conductors carrying

electricity over large distances with minimum losses.

transmit > *verb* (**transmitted, transmitting**) **1** cause to pass on from one place or person to another. **2** communicate (an idea or emotion). **3** broadcast or send out (an electrical signal or a radio or television programme). **4** allow (heat, light, etc.) to pass through a medium.
DERIVATIVES – **transmissible** *adjective* (chiefly Medicine) **transmittal** *noun*.
SYNONYMS – **1** pass on, send, transfer. **2** communicate, convey, impart, relay.
ORIGIN – Latin *transmittere*, from *trans-* 'across' + *mittere* 'send'.

transmitter > *noun* a device used to generate and transmit electromagnetic waves carrying messages or signals, especially those of radio or television.

transmogrify /tranz**mog**rifī/ > *verb* (**transmogrifies, transmogrified**) chiefly humorous transform in a surprising or magical manner.
DERIVATIVES – **transmogrification** *noun*.

transmutation /tranzmyoo**taysh**'n/ > *noun* **1** the action of transmuting or the state of being transmuted. **2** the changing of one chemical element into another, either by a nuclear process or as a supposed operation in alchemy.

transmute /tranz**myoot**/ > *verb* **1** change in form, nature, or substance. **2** change (a chemical element) into another, either by a nuclear process or as a supposed operation in alchemy.
DERIVATIVES – **transmutation** *noun*.
ORIGIN – Latin *transmutare*, from *trans-* 'across' + *mutare* 'to change'.

transnational > *adjective* extending or operating across national boundaries. > *noun* a multinational company.
DERIVATIVES – **transnationalism** *noun*.

transoceanic > *adjective* crossing an ocean.

transom /**tran**səm/ > *noun* **1** the flat surface forming the stern of a boat. **2** a strengthening crossbar, in particular one set above a window or door.
ORIGIN – Old French *traversin*, from *traverser* (see **TRAVERSE**).

transonic > *adjective* referring to speeds close to that of sound.

trans-Pacific > *adjective* **1** crossing the Pacific. **2** relating to an area beyond the Pacific.

transparency > *noun* (pl. **transparencies**) **1** the condition of being transparent. **2** a positive transparent photograph printed on plastic or glass, and viewed using a slide projector.

transparent /tran**sparr**ənt, tran**spair**ənt/ > *adjective* **1** allowing light to pass through so that objects behind can be distinctly seen. **2** obvious or evident.
DERIVATIVES – **transparently** *adverb*.

SYNONYMS – **1** clear, pellucid, see-through, translucent. **2** clear, evident, manifest, obvious, plain.
ANTONYMS – **1** opaque.
ORIGIN – from Latin *transparere* 'shine through'.

transpersonal > *adjective* relating to or dealing with states of consciousness beyond the limits of personal identity.

transpire /tran**spīr**/ > *verb* **1** come to be known; prove to be so. **2** happen. **3** Botany (of a plant or leaf) give off water vapour through the stomata.
DERIVATIVES – **transpiration** *noun*.
SYNONYMS – **1** come to light, emerge. **2** arise, come to pass, happen, occur, take place.
ORIGIN – Latin *transpirare*, from *trans-* 'through' + *spirare* 'breathe'.

transplant > *verb* /traans**plaant**, trans**plaant**/ **1** transfer to another place or situation. **2** take (living tissue or an organ) and implant it in another part of the body or in another body. > *noun* /**traans**plaant, **trans**plaant/ **1** an operation in which an organ or tissue is transplanted. **2** a thing that has been transplanted.
DERIVATIVES – **transplantable** *adjective* **transplantation** *noun*.
SYNONYMS – *verb* **1** move, relocate, resettle, shift, transfer, transport.
ORIGIN – Latin *transplantare*, from *trans-* 'across' + *plantare* 'to plant'.

transponder /tran**spon**dər/ > *noun* a device for receiving a radio signal and automatically transmitting a different signal.
ORIGIN – blend of **TRANSMIT** and **RESPOND**.

transport > *verb* /trans**port**, traans**port**/ **1** take or carry from one place to another by means of a vehicle, aircraft, or ship. **2** (**be transported**) be overwhelmed with a strong emotion, especially joy. **3** historical send (a convict) to a penal colony. > *noun* /**tran**sport, **traan**sport/ **1** a system or means of transporting. **2** the action of transporting or the state of being transported. **3** a large vehicle, ship, or aircraft for carrying troops or stores. **4** (**transports**) overwhelmingly strong emotions.
DERIVATIVES – **transportation** *noun*.
SYNONYMS – *verb* **1** bear, carry, convey, haul, move, shift, take. *noun* **1,2** carriage, conveyance, transportation.
COMBINATIONS – **transport cafe** Brit. a roadside cafe for drivers of lorries.
ORIGIN – Latin *transportare* 'carry across'.

transportable > *adjective* able to be carried or moved.
DERIVATIVES – **transportability** *noun*.

transporter > *noun* a large vehicle used to carry heavy objects.

transpose > *verb* **1** cause to exchange places. **2** transfer to a different place or context. **3** write or play (music) in a different key from the original.

DERIVATIVES – **transposable** *adjective* **transposition** *noun*.

ORIGIN – Old French *transposer*, from *trans-* 'across' + *poser* 'to place'.

transputer > *noun* a microprocessor with integral memory designed for parallel processing.

transsexual (also **transexual**) > *noun* a person born with the physical characteristics of one sex who emotionally and psychologically feels that they belong to the opposite sex. > *adjective* relating to such a person.

DERIVATIVES – **transsexualism** *noun* **transsexuality** *noun*.

trans-ship > *verb* (**trans-shipped, trans-shipping**) transfer (cargo) from one ship or other form of transport to another.

DERIVATIVES – **trans-shipment** *noun*.

transubstantiation > *noun* Christian Theology the doctrine that the bread and wine of the Eucharist are converted into the body and blood of Christ at consecration.

transuranic /tranzyooʳannik/ > *adjective* Chemistry (of an element) having a higher atomic number than uranium (92).

transverse > *adjective* situated or extending across something.

DERIVATIVES – **transversely** *adverb*.

ORIGIN – from Latin *transvertere* 'turn across'.

transvestite > *noun* a person, typically a man, who derives pleasure from dressing in clothes considered appropriate to the opposite sex.

DERIVATIVES – **transvestism** *noun*

ORIGIN – German *Transvestit*, from Latin *trans-* 'across' + *vestire* 'clothe'.

Transylvanian /transilvayniən/ > *adjective* relating to Transylvania, a large region of Romania.

trap¹ > *noun* **1** a device or enclosure designed to catch and retain animals. **2** an unpleasant situation from which it is hard to escape. **3** a trick leading someone into acting contrary to their interests or intentions. **4** a container or device used to collect a specified thing. **5** a curve in the waste pipe from a bath, basin, or toilet that is always full of liquid to prevent the upward passage of gases and smells. **6** a bunker or other hollow on a golf course. **7** the compartment from which a greyhound is released at the start of a race. **8** a device for hurling an object such as a clay pigeon into the air. **9** chiefly historical a light, two-wheeled carriage pulled by a horse or pony. **10** informal a person's mouth. > *verb* (**trapped, trapping**) **1** catch or hold in or as in a trap. **2** trick into doing something.

ORIGIN – Old English *træppe* (in *coltetræppe* 'Christ's thorn').

trap² > *verb* (**trapped, trapping**) archaic put trappings on (a horse).

ORIGIN – from the obsolete noun *trap* 'trappings', from Old French *drap* 'drape'.

trap³ (also **traprock**) > *noun* N. Amer. basalt or a similar dark, fine-grained igneous rock.

ORIGIN – Swedish *trapp*, from *trappa* 'stair' (because of the often stair-like appearance of its outcroppings).

trapdoor > *noun* a hinged or removable panel in a floor, ceiling, or roof.

trapeze > *noun* (also **flying trapeze**) a horizontal bar hanging by two ropes and free to swing, used by acrobats in a circus.

wordpower facts

Trapeze

The word **trapeze** comes via French and Latin from Greek *trapeza*, which means 'table' (literally 'four-footed thing', from *tetra-* 'four' and *peza* 'foot'). The word was applied to the acrobatic equipment because of the rectangular shape formed by the trapeze's crossbar and ropes and the roof. **Trapezium** is from the same root but is a Latin form, as is the anatomical term **trapezius**: this was adopted because of the shape formed by the trapezius muscles.

trapezium /trəpeeziəm/ > *noun* (pl. **trapezia** /trəpeeziə/ or **trapeziums**) Geometry **1** Brit. a quadrilateral with one pair of sides parallel. **2** N. Amer. a quadrilateral with no sides parallel.

trapezius /trəpeeziəss/ > *noun* (pl. **trapezii** /trəpeeziī/) Anatomy either of a pair of large triangular muscles extending over the back of the neck and shoulders and moving the head and shoulder blade.

trapezoid /trappizoyd/ > *noun* Geometry **1** Brit. a quadrilateral with no sides parallel. **2** N. Amer. a quadrilateral with one pair of sides parallel.

DERIVATIVES – **trapezoidal** *adjective*.

trapper > *noun* a person who traps wild animals, especially for their fur.

trappings > *plural noun* **1** the visible signs or objects associated with a particular situation or role: *the trappings of success.* **2** a horse's ornamental harness.

ORIGIN – from **TRAP²**.

Trappist > *adjective* referring to a branch of the Cistercian order of monks noted for an austere rule including a vow of silence. > *noun* a member of this order.

ORIGIN – French *trappiste*, from *La Trappe* in Normandy, where the order was founded.

trash > *noun* chiefly N. Amer. **1** waste material; refuse. **2** worthless writing, art, etc. **3** a person or people regarded as being of very low social standing. > *verb* informal, chiefly N. Amer. wreck or destroy.

DERIVATIVES – **trashiness** *noun* **trashy** (**trashier, trashiest**) *adjective*.

COMBINATIONS – **trash can** N. Amer. a dustbin.

trash talk US informal > *noun* insulting or boastful speech intended to demoralise, intimidate, or humiliate. > *verb* (**trash-talk**) use such speech.

DERIVATIVES – **trash talker** *noun*.

trattoria /trattəreeə/ > *noun* an Italian restaurant.

ORIGIN – Italian.

trauma /trawmə/ > *noun* (pl. **traumas**) **1** a deeply distressing experience. **2** Medicine physical injury. **3** emotional shock following a stressful event.

DERIVATIVES – **traumatic** *adjective* **traumatically** *adverb* **traumatise** (also **traumatize**) *verb*.

ORIGIN – Greek, 'wound'.

travail /travvayl/ literary > *noun* (also **travails**) **1** painful or laborious effort. **2** labour pains. > *verb* undergo such effort.

ORIGIN – Latin *trepalium* 'instrument of torture', from *tres* 'three' + *palus* 'stake'.

travel > *verb* (**travelled, travelling**; US also **traveled, traveling**) **1** make a journey. **2** journey along (a road) or through (a region). **3** move or go. **4** withstand a journey without impairment. > *noun* **1** the action of travelling. **2** (**travels**) journeys, especially abroad. **3** (before another noun) (of a device) sufficiently compact for use when travelling: *a travel iron.* **4** the range, rate, or mode of motion of a part of a machine.

SYNONYMS – *verb* **1** journey, tour, voyage. **2** cover, cross, traverse. **3** advance, go, move, proceed, progress. *noun* **2** (**travels**) excursions, expeditions, journeys, odysseys, trips, voyages.

COMBINATIONS – **travelling salesman** a representative of a firm who visits businesses to show samples and gain orders.

ORIGIN – variant of **TRAVAIL** and originally in the same sense.

travel agency > *noun* an agency that makes the necessary arrangements for travellers.

DERIVATIVES – **travel agent** *noun*.

travelator (also **travolator**) > *noun* a moving walkway, typically at an airport.

ORIGIN – from **TRAVEL**, suggested by **ESCALATOR**.

travelled > *adjective* **1** having travelled to many places. **2** used by people travelling: *a well-travelled route.*

traveller (US also **traveler**) > *noun* **1** a person who is travelling or who often travels. **2** a gypsy. **3** (also **New Age traveller**) a person who holds New Age values and leads an itinerant and unconventional lifestyle.

COMBINATIONS – **traveller's cheque** a cheque for a fixed amount that may be cashed or used in payment abroad after endorsement by the holder's signature. **traveller's joy** a wild clematis with small flowers and tufts of grey hairs around the seeds.

travelogue > *noun* a film, book, or illustrated lecture about a person's travels.

ORIGIN – from TRAVEL, on the pattern of *monologue*.

travel-sick > *adjective* suffering from nausea caused by the motion of a moving vehicle, boat, or aircraft.

DERIVATIVES – **travel-sickness** *noun*.

traverse /travvərss, trəverss/ > *verb* 1 travel or extend across or through. 2 move back and forth or sideways. > *noun* 1 an act of traversing. 2 a part of a structure that extends or is fixed across something.

DERIVATIVES – **traversable** *adjective* **traversal** *noun*.

ORIGIN – Latin *traversare*.

travertine /travvərteen/ > *noun* white or light-coloured calcareous rock deposited from mineral springs, used in building.

ORIGIN – Italian *travertino*, from Latin *tiburtinus* 'of Tibur' (now Tivoli, near Rome).

travesty /travvisti/ > *noun* (pl. **travesties**) an absurd or grotesque misrepresentation. > *verb* (**travesties**, **travestied**) represent in such a way.

ORIGIN – from French *travestir* 'to disguise'.

travolator > *noun* variant spelling of **TRAVELATOR**.

trawl > *verb* 1 fish or catch with a trawl net or seine. 2 search thoroughly. > *noun* 1 an act of trawling. 2 (also **trawl net**) a large wide-mouthed fishing net dragged by a boat along the bottom of the sea or a lake.

ORIGIN – probably from Dutch *traghelen* 'to drag'.

trawler > *noun* a fishing boat used for trawling.

tray > *noun* a flat, shallow container with a raised rim, typically used for carrying or holding things.

ORIGIN – Old English, related to TREE and TROUGH.

treacherous > *adjective* 1 guilty of or involving betrayal. 2 having hidden or unpredictable dangers: *treacherous currents*.

DERIVATIVES – **treacherously** *adverb* **treacherousness** *noun* **treachery** *noun*.

SYNONYMS – 1 disloyal, duplicitous, false, perfidious, traitorous.

ANTONYMS – 1 faithful, loyal.

ORIGIN – Old French *trecherous*, from *trechier* 'to cheat'.

treacle > *noun* chiefly Brit. 1 molasses. 2 golden syrup.

DERIVATIVES – **treacly** *adjective*.

> ### wordpower facts
> #### Treacle
> The origins of the word **treacle** are extraordinary: it means literally 'antidote against wild beasts'! When the word entered English in the Middle Ages it meant 'antidote against poison, venomous bites, and disease': it came via Old French and Latin from Greek *thēriakē* 'antidote against venom', from *thērion* 'wild beast'. **Treacle** seems to have had this sense until the beginning of the 19th century; in the meantime it broadened its meaning somewhat to 'medicine or remedy' in general: the use of syrup to make medicine taste better led to the current senses in the late 17th century.

tread > *verb* (past **trod**; past participle **trodden** or **trod**) 1 walk in a specified way. 2 press down or crush with the feet. 3 walk on or along. > *noun* 1 a manner or the sound of walking. 2 (also **tread board**) the top surface of a step or stair. 3 the thick moulded part of a vehicle tyre that grips the road. 4 the part of the sole of a shoe that rests on the ground.

IDIOMS – **tread on someone's toes** offend someone by encroaching on their area of responsibility. **tread water** 1 maintain an upright position in deep water by moving the feet with a walking movement and the hands with a downward circular motion. 2 fail to make progress.

treadle > *noun* a lever worked by the foot and imparting motion to a machine. > *verb* operate by a treadle.

ORIGIN – Old English, 'stair, step'.

treadmill > *noun* 1 a large wheel turned by the weight of people or animals treading on steps fitted into its inner surface, formerly used to drive machinery. 2 a device used for exercise consisting of a continuous moving belt on which to walk or run. 3 a job or situation that is tiring, boring, or unpleasant.

treason (also **high treason**) > *noun* the crime of betraying one's country, especially by attempting to kill or overthrow the sovereign or government.

DERIVATIVES – **treasonable** *adjective* **treasonably** *adverb* **treasonous** *adjective*.

NOTE – formerly, there were two types of crime to which the term **treason** was applied: **petty treason**, the crime of murdering one's master, and **high treason**, the crime of betraying one's country. The designation **petty treason** was abolished in 1828 and **high treason** is now often simply called **treason**.

ORIGIN – Old French *treisoun*, from Latin *tradere* 'hand over'.

treasure > *noun* 1 a quantity of precious metals, gems, or other valuable objects. 2 a very valuable object. 3 informal a much loved or highly valued person. > *verb* 1 keep carefully (a valuable or valued item). 2 value highly.

COMBINATIONS – **treasure hunt** a game in which players search for hidden objects by following a trail of clues. **treasure trove** 1 English Law (abolished in 1996) valuables of unknown ownership that are found hidden and declared the property of the Crown. 2 a hidden store of valuable or delightful things. [ORIGIN – from Old French *tresor trové* 'found treasure'.]

ORIGIN – Old French *tresor*, from Greek *thēsauros* (see THESAURUS).

treasurer > *noun* a person appointed to administer or manage the financial assets and liabilities of a society, company, etc.

treasury > *noun* (pl. **treasuries**) 1 the funds or revenue of a state, institution, or society. 2 (**Treasury**) (in some countries) the government department responsible for the overall management of the economy. 3 a place where treasure is stored. 4 a collection of valuable or delightful things.

COMBINATIONS – **Treasury bill** a short-dated UK or US government security, yielding no interest but issued at a discount on its redemption price.

ORIGIN – Old French *tresorie* (see TREASURE).

treat > *verb* 1 behave towards or deal with in a certain way. 2 give medical care or attention to. 3 apply a process or a substance to. 4 present or discuss (a subject). 5 (**treat someone to**) provide someone with (food, drink, or entertainment) at one's expense. 6 (**treat oneself**) do or have something very pleasurable. 7 (**treat with**) negotiate terms with. > *noun* 1 a surprise gift, event, etc. that gives great pleasure. 2 (**one's treat**) an act of treating someone to something.

IDIOMS – —— **a treat** Brit. informal doing something specified very well: *their tactics worked a treat*.

DERIVATIVES – **treatable** *adjective* **treater** *noun*.

ORIGIN – Old French *traitier*, from Latin *trahere* 'draw, pull'.

treatise /treetiss/ > *noun* a written work dealing formally and systematically with a subject.

ORIGIN – from Old French *traitier* (see TREAT).

treatment > *noun* 1 the process or manner of treating someone or something. 2

medical care for an illness or injury. **3** the use of a substance or process to preserve or give particular properties to something. **4** the presentation or discussion of a subject.

treaty > *noun* (pl. **treaties**) a formally concluded and ratified agreement between states.
ORIGIN – Old French *traite*, from Latin *tractatus* (see TRACTATE).

treble[1] > *adjective* **1** consisting of three parts. **2** multiplied or occurring three times. > *predeterminer* three times as much or as many. > *noun* **1** Brit. three sporting victories or championships in the same season, event, etc. **2** Darts a hit on the narrow ring enclosed by the two large inner circles of a dartboard, scoring treble. > *pronoun* an amount which is three times as large as usual. > *verb* make or become treble.
ORIGIN – from Latin *triplus* (see TRIPLE).

treble[2] > *noun* **1** a high-pitched voice, especially a boy's singing voice. **2** the high-frequency output of a radio or audio system.
COMBINATIONS – **treble clef** Music a clef placing G above middle C on the second-lowest line of the stave.
ORIGIN – from TREBLE[1], because it was the highest part in a three-part contrapuntal composition.

trebly > *adjective* (of sound, especially recorded music) having too much treble. > *adverb* three times as much.

tree > *noun* **1** a woody perennial plant typically with a single stem or trunk growing to a considerable height and bearing lateral branches. **2** a wooden structure or part of a structure. **3** (also **tree diagram**) a diagram with a structure of branching connecting lines. **4** archaic or literary the cross on which Christ was crucified.
WORDFINDER – arboreal (*relating to trees; living in trees*), broadleaved (*denoting trees with relatively wide flat leaves*), conifer (*tree bearing its seeds in cones*), deciduous (*tree shedding its leaves annually*), dendrochronology (*dating the past by means of tree rings*), dendrology (*scientific study of trees*), evergreen (*tree retaining green leaves throughout the year*), silviculture (*growing and cultivation of trees*).
DERIVATIVES – **treeless** adjective **tree-like** adjective.
COMBINATIONS – **tree fern** a large palm-like fern with a trunk-like stem. **tree house** a structure built in the branches of a tree for children to play in. **Tree of Knowledge** (in the Bible) the tree in the Garden of Eden bearing the forbidden fruit which Adam and Eve disobediently ate. **Tree of Life** (in the Bible) a tree in the Garden of Eden whose fruit imparts eternal life. **tree ring** each of a number of concentric rings

in the cross section of a tree trunk, representing a single year's growth.

treecreeper > *noun* a small brown bird which creeps about on the trunks of trees to search for insects.

tree-hugger > *noun* informal, chiefly derogatory an environmental campaigner (used in reference to the practice of embracing a tree to prevent it from being felled).
DERIVATIVES – **tree-hugging** noun.

treeline > *noun* the altitude above which no trees grow on a mountain.

treen > *noun* (treated as pl.) small domestic wooden objects, especially antiques.
ORIGIN – Old English, 'wooden'.

tree surgeon > *noun* a person who prunes and treats old or damaged trees in order to preserve them.
DERIVATIVES – **tree surgery** noun.

trefoil /**tref**foyl, **tree**foyl/ > *noun* **1** a small plant with yellow flowers and three-lobed cloverlike leaves. **2** architectural tracery in the form of three rounded lobes like a clover leaf. **3** a thing having three parts.
ORIGIN – Latin *trifolium*, from *tri-* 'three' + *folium* 'leaf'.

trek > *noun* a long arduous journey, especially one made on foot. > *verb* (**trekked, trekking**) go on a trek.
DERIVATIVES – **trekker** noun.
ORIGIN – from South African Dutch *trekken* 'to pull, travel'.

Trekkie > *noun* (pl. **Trekkies**) informal a fan of the US science-fiction television programme *Star Trek*.

trellis > *noun* a framework of light wooden or metal bars used as a support for trees or creepers. > *verb* (**trellised, trellising**) provide or support with a trellis.
ORIGIN – from Latin *trilix* 'three-ply', from *tri-* 'three' + *licium* 'warp thread'.

trematode /**tremm**ətōd/ > *noun* Zoology a kind of parasitic flatworm.
ORIGIN – from Greek *trēmatōdēs* 'perforated', from *trēma* 'hole'.

tremble > *verb* **1** shake involuntarily, typically as a result of fear, excitement, or frailty. **2** be in a state of extreme apprehension. **3** (of a thing) shake slightly. > *noun* a trembling feeling, movement, or sound.
DERIVATIVES – **trembling** adjective **tremblingly** adverb **trembly** adjective (informal).
SYNONYMS – *verb* **1** quake, quiver, shake, shiver, shudder.
ORIGIN – Latin *tremere* 'tremble'.

trembler > *noun* Brit. an automatic vibrator for making and breaking an electric circuit.

tremendous > *adjective* **1** very great in

amount, scale, or intensity. **2** informal extremely good or impressive.
DERIVATIVES – **tremendously** adverb.
SYNONYMS – **1** fantastic, great, immense, monumental, prodigious.
ORIGIN – Latin *tremendus*, from *tremere* 'tremble'.

tremolo > *noun* (pl. **tremolos**) Music **1** a wavering effect in singing or playing some musical instruments. **2** (also **tremolo arm**) a lever on an electric guitar used to produce such an effect.
ORIGIN – Italian.

tremor > *noun* **1** an involuntary quivering movement. **2** (also **earth tremor**) a slight earthquake. **3** a sudden feeling of fear or excitement.
ORIGIN – Latin, from *tremere* 'to tremble'.

tremulous > *adjective* **1** shaking or quivering slightly. **2** timid; nervous.
DERIVATIVES – **tremulously** adverb **tremulousness** noun.
ORIGIN – Latin *tremulus*, from *tremere* 'tremble'.

trench > *noun* **1** a long, narrow ditch. **2** a ditch dug by troops to provide shelter from enemy fire. **3** (also **ocean trench**) a long, narrow, deep depression in the ocean bed. > *verb* **1** dig a trench or trenches in. **2** turn over the earth of (a field or garden) by digging a succession of adjoining ditches.
COMBINATIONS – **trench coat 1** a belted double-breasted raincoat. **2** a lined or padded waterproof coat worn by soldiers. **trench fever** a highly contagious bacterial disease transmitted by lice, that infested soldiers in the trenches in the First World War. **trench foot** a painful condition of the feet caused by long immersion in cold water or mud and marked by blackening and death of surface tissue. **trench warfare** a type of combat in which opposing troops fight from trenches facing each other.
ORIGIN – Old French *trenche*, from Latin *truncare* 'truncate, cut, maim'.

trenchant /**tren**chənt/ > *adjective* **1** vigorous or incisive in expression or style. **2** archaic or literary (of a weapon or tool) having a sharp edge.
DERIVATIVES – **trenchancy** noun **trenchantly** adverb.
SYNONYMS – **1** cutting, incisive, keen, penetrating, pointed, sharp, vigorous.
ORIGIN – Old French, 'cutting', from Latin *truncare* 'truncate, cut, maim'.

trencher[1] > *noun* **1** historical a wooden plate or platter. **2** old-fashioned term for *mortar board* (in sense 1).
ORIGIN – Old French *trenchour*, from *trenchier* 'to cut' (because meat was cut and served on a trencher).

trencher[2] > *noun* a machine or attachment used in digging trenches.

trencherman > *noun* humorous a person who eats heartily.

trend > *noun* **1** a general direction in which something is developing or changing. **2** a fashion. > *verb* turn in a specified direction.

SYNONYMS – *noun* **1** drift, shift, tendency. **2** craze, fashion, vogue; informal fad.

ORIGIN – Old English, 'revolve, rotate'; related to TRUNDLE.

trendsetter > *noun* a person who leads the way in fashion or ideas.

DERIVATIVES – **trendsetting** *adjective*.

trendy informal > *adjective* (**trendier,** **trendiest**) very fashionable or up to date. > *noun* (pl. **trendies**) a person of this type.

DERIVATIVES – **trendily** *adverb* **trendiness** *noun*.

trepan /tripan/ > *noun* chiefly historical a trephine used by surgeons for perforating the skull. > *verb* (**trepanned, trepanning**) perforate (a person's skull) with a trepan.

DERIVATIVES – **trepanation** *noun*.

ORIGIN – from Greek *trupan* 'to bore', from *trupē* 'hole'.

trephine /trifīn, trifeen/ > *noun* a cylindrical saw used in surgery to remove a circle of tissue or bone. > *verb* operate on with a trephine.

DERIVATIVES – **trephination** *noun*.

ORIGIN – from Latin *tres fines* 'three ends', apparently influenced by TREPAN.

trepidation > *noun* a feeling of fear or agitation about something that may happen.

SYNONYMS – agitation, anxiety, apprehension, dread, fear, unease.

ORIGIN – Latin, from *trepidare* 'be agitated, tremble'.

trespass > *verb* **1** enter someone's land or property without their permission. **2** (**trespass on**) make unfair claims on or take advantage of. **3** (**trespass against**) archaic or literary commit an offence against. > *noun* **1** Law entry to a person's land or property without their permission. **2** archaic or literary a sin; an offence.

DERIVATIVES – **trespasser** *noun*.

ORIGIN – Old French *trespasser* 'pass over, trespass', from Latin *transpassare*.

tress > *noun* a long lock of a woman's hair.

ORIGIN – Old French *tresse*, perhaps based on Greek *trikha* 'threefold': originally also in the sense 'a plait or braid'.

trestle > *noun* **1** a framework consisting of a horizontal beam supported by two pairs of sloping legs, used in pairs to support a flat surface such as a table top. **2** (also **trestlework**) an open braced framework used to support an elevated structure such as a bridge.

COMBINATIONS – **trestle table** a table consisting of a board or boards laid on trestles.

ORIGIN – Old French *trestel*, from Latin *transtrum* 'beam'.

trews /trooz/ > *plural noun* chiefly Brit. trousers.

ORIGIN – Irish *triús*, Scottish Gaelic *triubhas*; related to TROUSERS.

tri- /trī/ > *combining form* three; having three: *triathlon*.

ORIGIN – from Latin *tres*, Greek *treis* 'three'.

triable /trīəb'l/ > *adjective* Law (of an offence or case) liable to a judicial trial.

triacetate /trīassitayt/ (also **cellulose triacetate**) > *noun* a form of the polymer cellulose acetate, used as a basis for man-made fibres.

triad /trīad/ > *noun* **1** a group or set of three connected people or things. **2** a Chinese secret society involved in organised crime.

DERIVATIVES – **triadic** *adjective*.

ORIGIN – Greek *trias*, from *treis* 'three'.

triage /treeaaj/ > *noun* **1** the action of sorting according to quality. **2** Medicine the assignment of degrees of urgency to wounds or illnesses to decide the order of treatment of a large number of patients.

ORIGIN – French, from *trier* 'separate out'.

trial > *noun* **1** a formal examination of evidence in order to decide guilt in a case of criminal or civil proceedings. **2** a test of performance, qualities, or suitability. **3** (**trials**) an event in which horses or dogs compete or perform. **4** something that tests a person's endurance or tolerance. > *verb* (**trialled, trialling;** US **trialed, trialing**) **1** test (something) to assess its suitability or performance. **2** (of a horse or dog) compete in trials.

IDIOMS – **on trial 1** being tried in a court of law. **2** undergoing tests or scrutiny. **trial and error** the process of experimenting with various methods until one finds the most successful.

COMBINATIONS – **trial run** a first use of a new system or product.

ORIGIN – Latin *triallum*.

trialist (Brit. also **triallist**) > *noun* a person who participates in a sports trial or a trial of a new product.

triangle > *noun* **1** a plane figure with three straight sides and three angles. **2** something having this shape. **3** a musical instrument consisting of a steel rod bent into a triangle, sounded with a rod. **4** an emotional relationship involving a couple and a third person with whom one of them is involved.

WORDFINDER – *types of triangle:* equilateral (*having sides of equal length*), isosceles (*having two sides equal*), scalene (*having all sides unequal*).

ORIGIN – Latin *triangulum*, from *tri-* 'three' + *angulus* 'corner'.

triangular > *adjective* **1** shaped like a triangle. **2** involving three people or parties. **3** (of a pyramid) having a three-sided base.

DERIVATIVES – **triangularity** *noun* **triangularly** *adverb*.

triangulate > *verb* /trīanggyoolayt/ **1** divide (an area) into triangles for surveying purposes. **2** measure and map (an area) by the use of triangles with a known base length and base angles. **3** determine (a height, distance, or location) in this way. **4** form into a triangle or triangles.

triangulation > *noun* **1** (in surveying) the tracing and measurement of a series or network of triangles in order to determine the distances and relative positions of points spread over a territory or region. **2** formation of or division into triangles.

COMBINATIONS – **triangulation point** a trig point.

Triassic /trīassik/ > *adjective* Geology relating to or denoting the earliest period of the Mesozoic era (between the Permian and Jurassic periods, about 245 to 208 million years ago), a time when the first dinosaurs, ammonites, and primitive mammals appeared.

ORIGIN – from Latin *trias* 'set of three', because the strata fell into three groups.

triathlon /trīathlən/ > *noun* an athletic contest consisting of three different events, typically swimming, cycling, and long-distance running.

DERIVATIVES – **triathlete** *noun*.

triatomic /trīətommik/ > *adjective* Chemistry consisting of three atoms.

tribal > *adjective* of or characteristic of a tribe or tribes. > *noun* (**tribals**) members of tribal communities.

DERIVATIVES – **tribalism** *noun* **tribalist** *noun* **tribalistic** *adjective* **tribally** *adverb*.

tribe > *noun* **1** a social division in a traditional society consisting of linked families or communities with a common culture and dialect. **2** (in ancient Rome) each of several (originally three) political divisions. **3** derogatory a distinctive close-knit social or political group. **4** (**tribes**) informal large numbers of people.

USAGE – it is best to avoid using the word **tribe** to refer to traditional societies in contemporary contexts, as it is associated with past attitudes of white colonialists towards so-called primitive or uncivilised peoples; alternative terms such as **community** or **people** are better. In historical contexts, as in *the area was inhabited by Slavic tribes*, it is acceptable.

wordpower facts

Tribe

The word **tribe** comes from Latin *tribus*, which is perhaps related to *tri-* 'three' (as in **triple**, **tricycle**, **trident**, etc.). The link is to be found in the early history of Rome, when the people were supposedly divided into three tribes called Ramnes, Tities, and Luceres. Little is known about these tribes, although the Roman cavalry was divided into companies or 'centuries' corresponding to these names. **Tribunal**, **tribune**, and **tribute** are all connected to **tribe**, while the related verb *tribuere* 'assign, divide between tribes' is the root of such words as **attribute**, **contribute**, **distribute**, and **retribution**.

tribesman (or **tribeswoman**) > *noun* a member of a tribe in a traditional society.

tribology /trɪbollǝji/ > *noun* the branch of science and technology concerned with surfaces in relative motion, as in bearings.

DERIVATIVES – **tribological** *adjective* **tribologist** *noun*.

ORIGIN – from Greek *tribos* 'rubbing'.

tribulation /tribyoolaysh'n/ > *noun* **1** a state of great trouble or suffering. **2** a cause of this.

ORIGIN – Latin, from *tribulare* 'press, oppress', based on *terere* 'rub'.

tribunal /trɪbyōōn'l/ > *noun* **1** Brit. a body established to settle certain types of dispute. **2** a court of justice.

ORIGIN – Latin, 'raised platform provided for a magistrate's seat', from *tribunus* 'head of a tribe'.

tribune[1] > *noun* **1** (in ancient Rome) an official chosen by the plebeians to protect their interests. **2** a popular leader; a champion of the people.

DERIVATIVES – **tribunate** *noun* **tribuneship** *noun*.

ORIGIN – Latin *tribunus* 'head of a tribe', from *tribus* 'tribe'.

tribune[2] > *noun* **1** an apse in a basilica. **2** a dais or rostrum, especially in a church.

ORIGIN – Latin *tribunal* (see **TRIBUNAL**): first denoting the principal room in an Italian mansion.

tributary /tribyootri/ > *noun* (pl. **tributaries**) **1** a river or stream flowing into a larger river or lake. **2** historical a person or state that pays tribute to another state or ruler.

tribute > *noun* **1** an act, statement, or gift that is intended to show gratitude, respect, or admiration. **2** something resulting from and indicating the worth of something else: *his victory was a tribute to his persistence.* **3**

historical payment made periodically by a state to another on which it is dependent.

ORIGIN – Latin *tributum*, from *tribuere* 'assign, divide between tribes', from *tribus* 'tribe'.

trice /trīss/ > *noun* (in phrase **in a trice**) in a moment; very quickly.

ORIGIN – from Dutch *trīsen* 'pull sharply': originally as *a trice* in the sense 'a tug', figuratively 'an instant'.

tricentenary /trīsenteenǝri, trīsentennǝri/ > *noun* (pl. **tricentenaries**) another term for TERCENTENARY.

DERIVATIVES – **tricentennial** *adjective* & *noun*.

triceps /trīseps/ > *noun* (pl. same) Anatomy the large muscle at the back of the upper arm.

ORIGIN – Latin, 'three-headed', because the muscle has three points of attachment at one end.

triceratops /trīserrǝtops/ > *noun* a large herbivorous dinosaur living at the end of the Cretaceous period, having a massive head with three horns and a bony frill above the neck.

ORIGIN – Latin, from Greek *trikeratos* 'three-horned' + *ōps* 'face'.

trichina /trikeenǝ/ > *noun* (pl. **trichinae** /trikeenee/) a parasitic nematode worm of humans and other mammals, the adults of which live in the small intestine.

ORIGIN – from Greek *trikhinos* 'of hair'.

trichinosis /trikkinōsiss/ > *noun* a disease caused by trichinae, typically from infected meat, characterised by digestive disturbance, fever, and muscular rigidity.

trichology /trikollǝji/ > *noun* the branch of medical and cosmetic study and practice concerned with the hair and scalp.

DERIVATIVES – **trichological** *adjective* **trichologist** *noun*.

ORIGIN – from Greek *thrix* 'hair'.

trichromatic /trīkrǝmattik/ > *adjective* **1** having or using three colours. **2** having normal colour vision, which is sensitive to all three primary colours.

DERIVATIVES – **trichromatism** *noun*.

trick > *noun* **1** a cunning or skilful act or scheme intended to deceive or outwit someone. **2** a skilful act performed for entertainment. **3** an illusion: *a trick of the light.* **4** (before another noun) intended to mystify or create an illusion: *a trick question.* **5** a peculiar or characteristic habit or mannerism. **6** (in bridge, whist, etc.) a sequence of cards forming a single round of play. > *verb* **1** deceive or outwit with cunning or skill. **2** (**trick into** or **out of**) deceive into doing or parting with.

IDIOMS – **do the trick** informal achieve the required result. **trick or treat** chiefly N. Amer. a children's custom of calling at houses at Halloween with the threat of pranks if they are not given a small gift. **tricks of the**

trade special ingenious techniques used in a profession or craft. **up to one's** (**old**) **tricks** informal misbehaving in a characteristic way.

DERIVATIVES – **tricker** *noun* **trickery** *noun*.

SYNONYMS – *noun* **1** deceit, hoax, ploy, ruse, scheme, swindle. **2** feat, stunt. *verb* **1** deceive, dupe, fool, hoax, hoodwink, outwit, swindle.

ORIGIN – Old French *triche*, from *trichier* 'deceive'.

trickle > *verb* **1** (of a liquid) flow in a small stream. **2** (**trickle down**) (of wealth) gradually benefit the poorest as a result of the increasing wealth of the richest. **3** come or go slowly or gradually. > *noun* **1** a small flow of liquid. **2** a small group or number of people or things moving slowly.

trickster > *noun* a person who cheats or deceives people.

tricksy > *adjective* (**tricksier**, **tricksiest**) **1** clever in an ingenious or deceptive way. **2** (of a person) playful or mischievous.

DERIVATIVES – **tricksily** *adverb* **tricksiness** *noun*.

tricky > *adjective* (**trickier**, **trickiest**) **1** requiring care and skill because difficult or awkward. **2** cleverly deceitful; crafty.

DERIVATIVES – **trickily** *adverb* **trickiness** *noun*.

SYNONYMS – **1** awkward, complex, difficult, knotty, problematic, thorny, vexed.

ANTONYMS – **1** straightforward, uncomplicated.

tricolour /trikkǝlǝr, trīkuller/ (US **tricolor**) > *noun* a flag with three bands or blocks of different colours, especially the French national flag with equal upright bands of blue, white, and red. > *adjective* (also **tricoloured**) having three colours.

tricorne /trīkorn/ (also **tricorn**) > *adjective* (of a hat) having a brim turned up on three sides. > *noun* a tricorne hat.

ORIGIN – Latin *tricornis*, from *tri-* 'three' + *cornu* 'horn'.

tricot /treekō/ > *noun* a fine knitted fabric.

ORIGIN – French, 'knitting', from *tricoter* 'to knit'.

tricuspid /trīkuspid/ > *adjective* **1** denoting a tooth with three cusps or points. **2** denoting a valve formed of three triangular segments situated between the right atrium and ventricle of the heart.

ORIGIN – from Latin *tri-* 'three' + *cuspis* 'sharp point'.

tricycle > *noun* a vehicle similar to a bicycle, but having three wheels, two at the back and one at the front.

tricyclic /trīsīklik/ > *adjective* Chemistry having three rings of atoms in its molecule. > *noun* Medicine any of a class of antidepressant drugs having tricyclic molecules.

trident > *noun* a three-pronged spear.
ORIGIN – Latin, from *tri-* 'three' + *dens* 'tooth'.

tried past and past participle of TRY.

triennial /trīenniəl/ > *adjective* lasting for or recurring every three years.
DERIVATIVES – **triennially** *adverb*.

triennium /trīenniəm/ > *noun* (pl. **triennia** or **trienniums**) a period of three years.
ORIGIN – Latin, from *tri-* 'three' + *annum* 'year'.

trier > *noun* **1** a person who always makes an effort, however unsuccessful they may be. **2** a person or body responsible for trying a judicial case.

trifecta /trīfektə/ > *noun* N. Amer. & Austral./NZ a bet in which the person betting correctly forecasts the first three finishers in the correct order.

trifid /trīfid/ > *adjective* chiefly Biology partly or wholly split into three divisions or lobes.
ORIGIN – Latin *trifidus*, from *tri-* 'three' + *findere* 'split, divide'.

trifle > *noun* **1** a thing of little value or importance. **2** a small amount. **3** Brit. a cold dessert of sponge cake and fruit covered with layers of custard, jelly, and cream. > *verb* **1** (**trifle with**) treat without seriousness or respect. **2** archaic talk or act frivolously.
DERIVATIVES – **trifler** *noun*.
ORIGIN – Old French *truffler* 'mock, deceive'.

trifling > *adjective* unimportant or trivial.
DERIVATIVES – **triflingly** *adverb*.
SYNONYMS – footling, inconsequential, insignificant, minor, trivial, unimportant.

trifocal > *adjective* (of a pair of glasses) having lenses with three parts with different focal lengths. > *noun* (**trifocals**) a pair of trifocal glasses.

trifoliate /trīfōliət/ > *adjective* (of a compound leaf) having three leaflets.

triforium /trīforiəm/ > *noun* (pl. **triforia**) a gallery or arcade above the arches of the nave, choir, and transepts of a church.
ORIGIN – Latin.

triform > *adjective* technical composed of three parts.

trifurcate > *verb* /trīfərkayt/ divide into three branches or forks. > *adjective* /trīfurkət/ divided in this way.
DERIVATIVES – **trifurcation** *noun*.
ORIGIN – Latin *trifurcus* 'three-forked', from *tri-* 'three' + *furca* 'fork'.

trigger > *noun* **1** a device that releases a spring or catch and so sets off a mechanism, especially in order to fire a gun. **2** an event that causes something to happen. > *verb* **1** cause (a device) to function. **2** cause to happen or exist.
COMBINATIONS – **trigger-happy** apt to fire a gun or take other drastic action on the slightest provocation.

ORIGIN – Dutch *trekker*, from *trekken* 'to pull'.

triglyceride /trīglissərīd/ > *noun* Chemistry a compound formed from glycerol and three fatty acid groups, e.g. the main constituents of natural fats and oils.

triglyph /trīglif/ > *noun* Architecture a tablet in a Doric frieze with three vertical grooves alternating with metopes.
ORIGIN – Greek *trigluphos*, from *tri-* 'three' + *gluphē* 'carving'.

trigonometry /triggənommitri/ > *noun* the branch of mathematics concerned with the relations of the sides and angles of triangles and with the relevant functions of any angles.
DERIVATIVES – **trigonometric** (also **trigonometrical**) *adjective*.
ORIGIN – from Greek *trigōnos* 'three-cornered' + *-metrēs* 'measurer'.

trig point > *noun* Brit. a reference point on high ground used in surveying, typically marked by a small pillar.

trigram /trīgram/ > *noun* **1** a trigraph. **2** each of the eight figures formed of three parallel lines that combine to form the sixty-four hexagrams of the I Ching.

trigraph /trīgraaf/ > *noun* a group of three letters representing one sound, for example German *sch-*.

trihedron /trīheedrən/ > *noun* (pl. **trihedra** /trīheedrə/ or **trihedrons**) a solid figure having three sides or faces (in addition to the base or ends).
DERIVATIVES – **trihedral** *adjective & noun*.

trike > *noun* informal **1** a tricycle. **2** a kind of ultralight aircraft.

trilateral > *adjective* **1** shared by or involving three parties. **2** Geometry of, on, or with three sides. > *noun* a triangle.

trilby > *noun* (pl. **trilbies**) chiefly Brit. a soft felt hat with a narrow brim and indented crown.
ORIGIN – from the name of George du Maurier's novel *Trilby* (1894), in the stage version of which such a hat was worn.

trilingual > *adjective* **1** speaking three languages fluently. **2** written or conducted in three languages.
DERIVATIVES – **trilingualism** *noun*.

trill > *noun* a quavering or vibratory sound, especially a rapid alternation of notes in music. > *verb* produce a quavering or warbling sound; sing or pronounce with a trill.
DERIVATIVES – **triller** *noun*.
ORIGIN – Italian *trillo* (noun), *trillare* (verb).

trillion > *cardinal number* **1** a million million (1,000,000,000,000 or 10^{12}). **2** dated, chiefly Brit. a million million million (1,000,000,000,000,000,000 or 10^{18}).
DERIVATIVES – **trillionth** *ordinal number*.

trilobite /trīləbīt/ > *noun* a fossil marine arthropod of the Palaeozoic era, with a

segmented hindpart divided longitudinally into three lobes.
ORIGIN – from Greek *tri-* 'three' + *lobos* 'lobe'.

trilogy /trilləji/ > *noun* (pl. **trilogies**) a group of three related novels, plays, or films.

trim > *verb* (**trimmed, trimming**) **1** make neat by cutting away irregular or unwanted parts. **2** cut off (irregular or unwanted parts). **3** reduce the size, amount, or number of. **4** decorate (something), especially along its edges. **5** adjust (a sail) to take advantage of the wind. > *noun* **1** additional decoration, especially along something's edges. **2** the upholstery or interior lining of a car. **3** an act of trimming. **4** the state of being in good order. > *adjective* (**trimmer, trimmest**) neat and smart; in good order.
IDIOMS – **in trim 1** slim and fit. **2** Nautical in good order. **trim one's sails** (**to the wind**) make changes to suit one's new circumstances.
DERIVATIVES – **trimly** *adverb* **trimmer** *noun* **trimness** *noun*.
SYNONYMS – *verb* **1** clip, crop, cut, prune, shape, shear. **2** cut off, lop off, remove, take off. **4** decorate, edge. *noun* **1** border, edging.
ORIGIN – Old English, 'make firm, arrange'.

trimaran /trīməran/ > *noun* a yacht with three hulls in parallel.
ORIGIN – from TRI- + CATAMARAN.

trimer /trīmər/ > *noun* Chemistry a polymer comprising three monomer units.
DERIVATIVES – **trimeric** *adjective*.

trimester /trīmestər/ > *noun* **1** a period of three months, especially as a division of the duration of pregnancy. **2** N. Amer. each of the three terms in an academic year.
DERIVATIVES – **trimestral** *adjective* **trimestrial** *adjective*.
ORIGIN – Latin *trimestris*, from *tri-* 'three' + *mensis* 'month'.

trimming > *noun* **1** (**trimmings**) small pieces trimmed off. **2** ornamentation or decoration, especially for clothing or furniture. **3** (**the trimmings**) informal the traditional accompaniments to something.

Trinidadian /trinnidaydiən, trinnidaddiən/ > *noun* a person from the Caribbean island of Trinidad. > *adjective* relating to Trinidad.

Trinitarian /trinnitairiən/ > *adjective* referring to belief in the doctrine of the Trinity. > *noun* a person who believes in the doctrine of the Trinity.
DERIVATIVES – **Trinitarianism** *noun*.

trinitrotoluene /trīnītrōtolyoo-een/ > *noun* fuller form of TNT.

trinity > *noun* (pl. **trinities**) **1** (**the Trinity** or **the Holy Trinity**) the three persons of the

Christian Godhead; Father, Son, and Holy Spirit. **2** a group of three people or things.
ORIGIN – Latin *trinitas* 'triad', from *trinus* 'threefold'.

trinket > *noun* a small ornament or item of jewellery that is of little value.
DERIVATIVES – **trinketry** *noun*.
SYNONYMS – bauble, bibelot, knick-knack, novelty; *archaic* bijou.

trinomial /trīnōmiəl/ > *adjective* technical consisting of three terms or names. > *noun* a trinomial expression or name.

trio > *noun* (pl. **trios**) **1** a set or group of three. **2** a group of three musicians.
ORIGIN – Italian, from Latin *tres* 'three'.

triode /trīōd/ > *noun* **1** a thermionic valve having three electrodes. **2** a semiconductor rectifier having three connections.

trioxide /trīoksīd/ > *noun* Chemistry an oxide containing three atoms of oxygen.

trip > *verb* (**tripped**, **tripping**) **1** catch one's foot on something and stumble or fall. **2** (**trip up**) make a mistake. **3** walk, run, or dance with quick light steps. **4** activate (a mechanism), especially by contact with a switch. **5** (of part of an electric circuit) disconnect automatically as a safety measure. **6** informal experience hallucinations induced by taking a psychedelic drug, especially LSD. > *noun* **1** a journey or excursion. **2** an instance of tripping or falling. **3** informal a hallucinatory experience caused by taking a psychedelic drug. **4** a self-indulgent attitude or activity: *a power trip.* **5** a device that trips a mechanism, circuit, etc.
IDIOMS – **trip the light fantastic** humorous dance. [ORIGIN – from 'Trip it as you go On the light fantastic toe' (Milton's *L'Allegro*).]
SYNONYMS – *verb* **1** fall, lose one's footing, stumble, topple, tumble. *noun* **1** excursion, expedition, jaunt, journey, outing, voyage.
COMBINATIONS – **trip hammer** a large, heavy pivoted hammer used in forging. **tripmeter** a vehicle instrument that can be set to record the distance of individual journeys. **tripwire** a wire that is stretched close to the ground and activates a trap, explosion, or alarm when disturbed.
ORIGIN – Old French *triper*, from Dutch *trippen* 'to skip, hop'.

tripartite /trīpaartīt/ > *adjective* **1** consisting of three parts. **2** shared by or involving three parties.

tripe > *noun* **1** the first or second stomach of a cow or other ruminant used as food. **2** informal nonsense; rubbish.
ORIGIN – Old French, 'entrails of an animal'.

triphthong /trifthong/ > *noun* **1** a union of three vowels (letters or sounds) pronounced in one syllable (as in *fire*). **2** three written vowel characters representing the sound of a single vowel (as in b*eau*).
ORIGIN – French *triphtongue*, after *diphtongue*, from Greek *diphthongos* (see **DIPHTHONG**).

triplane > *noun* an early type of aircraft with three pairs of wings, one above the other.

triple > *adjective* **1** consisting of or involving three parts, things, or people. **2** having three times the usual size, quality, or strength. > *predeterminer* three times as much or as many. > *noun* a thing that is three times as large as usual or is made up of three parts. > *verb* make or become three times as much or as many.
DERIVATIVES – **triply** *adverb*.
COMBINATIONS – **triple bond** Chemistry a chemical bond in which three pairs of electrons are shared between two atoms. **triple crown 1** (**Triple Crown**) an award or honour for winning a group of three important events in a sport. **2** the papal tiara. **triple jump 1** an athletic event in which competitors attempt to jump as far as possible by performing a hop, a step, and a jump from a running start. **2** Skating a jump in which the skater makes three full turns while in the air. **triple time** musical time with three beats to the bar.
ORIGIN – Old French, from Latin *triplus*, from Greek *triplous*.

triplet > *noun* **1** one of three children or animals born at the same birth. **2** Music a group of three equal notes to be performed in the time of two or four. **3** a set of three rhyming lines of verse.
ORIGIN – from **TRIPLE**, on the pattern of *doublet*.

triplex /tripleks/ > *noun* N. Amer. a residential building divided into three apartments. > *adjective* having three parts.
ORIGIN – Latin, from *tri-* 'three' + *plicare* 'to fold'.

triplicate > *adjective* /triplikət/ existing in three copies or examples. > *verb* /triplikayt/ **1** make three copies of. **2** multiply by three.
DERIVATIVES – **triplication** /triplikaysh'n/ *noun* **triplicity** /triplissiti/ *noun*.
ORIGIN – from Latin *triplicare* 'make three'.

triploid /triployd/ > *adjective* Genetics (of a cell or nucleus) containing three complete sets of chromosomes.

tripod /trīpod/ > *noun* **1** a three-legged stand for supporting a camera or other apparatus. **2** archaic a stool, table, or cauldron set on three legs.
ORIGIN – Greek, from *tri-* 'three' + *pous* 'foot'.

tripos /trīposs/ > *noun* the final honours examination for a BA degree at Cambridge University.
ORIGIN – from Latin *tripus* 'tripod', with reference to the stool on which a designated graduate sat to deliver a satirical speech at the degree ceremony.

tripper > *noun* Brit. informal a person who goes on a pleasure trip or excursion.

triptych /triptik/ > *noun* **1** a picture or carving on three panels, typically hinged together vertically and used as an altarpiece. **2** a set of three associated artistic, literary, or musical works.
ORIGIN – first denoting a set of three writing tablets hinged or tied together: from **TRI-**, on the pattern of *diptych*.

trireme /trīreem/ > *noun* an ancient Greek or Roman war galley with three banks of oars.
ORIGIN – Latin *triremis*, from *tri-* 'three' + *remus* 'oar'.

trisect /trīsekt/ > *verb* divide into three parts.
DERIVATIVES – **trisection** *noun* **trisector** *noun*.
ORIGIN – from **TRI-** + Latin *secare* 'divide, cut'.

trishaw /trīshaw/ > *noun* a light three-wheeled vehicle with pedals, used in the Far East.
ORIGIN – from **TRI-** + **RICKSHAW**.

trisyllable /trīsilləb'l/ > *noun* a word or metrical foot of three syllables.
DERIVATIVES – **trisyllabic** *adjective*.

trite > *adjective* (of a remark or idea) lacking originality or freshness; dull on account of overuse.
DERIVATIVES – **tritely** *adverb* **triteness** *noun*.
SYNONYMS – banal, clichéd, commonplace, hackneyed, platitudinous, stale.
ANTONYMS – fresh, original.
ORIGIN – Latin *tritus* 'rubbed', from the verb *terere*.

triticale /trittikayli/ > *noun* a hybrid cereal produced by crossing wheat and rye, grown as a fodder crop.
ORIGIN – Latin, from a blend of the genus names *Triticum* 'wheat' and *Secale* 'rye'.

tritium /trittiəm/ > *noun* Chemistry a radioactive isotope of hydrogen with a mass three times that of the usual isotope.
ORIGIN – from Greek *tritos* 'third'.

triturate /trityoorayt/ > *verb* technical **1** grind to a fine powder. **2** chew or grind (food) thoroughly.
DERIVATIVES – **trituration** *noun* **triturator** *noun*.
ORIGIN – Latin '(of corn) threshed', from *tritura* 'rubbing', from the verb *terere*.

triumph > *noun* **1** a great victory or achievement. **2** the state of being victorious or successful. **3** joy or satisfaction resulting from a success or victory. **4** a highly successful example: *the arrest was a triumph of international co-operation.* **5** the processional entry of a victorious general into ancient Rome. > *verb* **1** achieve a triumph. **2** rejoice or exult at a triumph.

DERIVATIVES – **triumphal** *adjective*.

SYNONYMS – *noun* **1** achievement, feat, success, victory. **3** delight, elation, exultation, joy, jubilation, satisfaction. *verb* **1** carry the day, prevail, succeed. **2** celebrate, exult, glory, rejoice.

ANTONYMS – *noun* **1** defeat. **3** disappointment.

ORIGIN – Latin *triumphus*, probably from Greek *thriambos* 'hymn to Bacchus'.

triumphalism > *noun* excessive exultation over one's success or achievements.

DERIVATIVES – **triumphalist** *adjective* & *noun*.

triumphant > *adjective* **1** having won a battle or contest; victorious. **2** jubilant after a victory or achievement.

DERIVATIVES – **triumphantly** *adverb*.

USAGE – **triumphant** and **triumphal** do not mean exactly the same thing: **triumphant** means 'victorious' or 'jubilant after a victory or achievement', whereas **triumphal** means 'done or made to celebrate a victory', as in *a triumphal procession.*

SYNONYMS – **1** successful, victorious. **2** elated, exultant, joyful, jubilant, rejoicing.

ANTONYMS – **1** defeated, unsuccessful. **2** disappointed.

triumvir /trīumvər, trīəmvər/ > *noun* (pl. **triumvirs** or **triumviri** /trīumvərī/) (in ancient Rome) each of three public officers jointly responsible for overseeing any of the administrative departments.

DERIVATIVES – **triumviral** *adjective*.

ORIGIN – Latin, from *trium virorum* 'of three men'.

triumvirate /trīumvirət/ > *noun* **1** a group of three powerful or notable people or things. **2** (in ancient Rome) a group of three men holding power.

trivet > *noun* **1** an iron tripod placed over a fire for a cooking pot or kettle to stand on. **2** a metal stand on which hot dishes are placed.

ORIGIN – apparently from Latin *tripes* 'three-legged'.

trivia > *plural noun* unimportant details or pieces of information.

trivial > *adjective* of little value or importance.

DERIVATIVES – **triviality** (pl. **trivialities**) *noun* **trivially** *adverb*.

SYNONYMS – inconsequential, insignificant, minor, paltry, pettifogging, petty, trifling.

ANTONYMS – important, serious.

---

wordpower facts

Trivial

The adjective **trivial** comes from Latin *trivium* 'place where three roads meet', from *tri-* 'three' and *via* 'road, way'; it is therefore related to such words as **deviate** and **viaduct**. Trivial was originally used to describe things belonging to the **trivium**, an introductory course at a medieval university involving the study of grammar, rhetoric, and logic. In the Middle Ages seven 'liberal arts' were recognised, of which the *trivium* contained the lower three and the *quadrivium* the upper four, the 'mathematical arts' of arithmetic, geometry, astronomy, and music. This association of the trivium with elementary subjects led to **trivial** being used to mean 'of little value or importance' from the 16th century. The plural of **trivium, trivia**, has been used since the early 20th century to mean 'trivial items'.

---

trivialise (also **trivialize**) > *verb* make (something) seem less important or complex than it really is.

DERIVATIVES – **trivialisation** *noun*.

trochaic /trōkayik/ Poetry > *adjective* consisting of or featuring trochees. > *noun* (**trochaics**) trochaic verse.

trochee /trōkee/ > *noun* Poetry a foot consisting of one long or stressed syllable followed by one short or unstressed syllable.

ORIGIN – from Greek *trokhaios pous* 'running foot', from *trekhein* 'to run'.

trod past and past participle of **TREAD**.

trodden past participle of **TREAD**.

trog > *verb* (**trogged, trogging**) Brit. informal walk heavily or laboriously; trudge.

troglodyte /troglədīt/ > *noun* **1** a cave-dweller. **2** a person who is deliberately ignorant or old-fashioned.

DERIVATIVES – **troglodytic** *adjective* **troglodytism** *noun*.

ORIGIN – Greek *trōglodutēs*, from the name of an Ethiopian people, influenced by *trōglē* 'hole'.

troika /troykə/ > *noun* **1** a Russian vehicle pulled by a team of three horses abreast. **2** a team of three horses. **3** a group of three people working together, especially as administrators or managers.

ORIGIN – Russian, from *troe* 'set of three'.

troilism /troyliz'm/ > *noun* sexual activity involving three participants.

ORIGIN – perhaps based on French *trois* 'three'.

Trojan /trōjən/ > *noun* an inhabitant of ancient Troy in Asia Minor. > *adjective* relating to Troy.

IDIOMS – **work like a Trojan** work extremely hard.

COMBINATIONS – **Trojan Horse** something intended to undermine or secretly overthrow an enemy or opponent. [ORIGIN – from the hollow wooden statue of a horse in which the ancient Greeks are said to have concealed themselves in order to enter Troy.]

troll¹ /trōl, trol/ > *noun* (in folklore) an ugly cave-dwelling being depicted as either a giant or a dwarf.

ORIGIN – first meaning 'witch': from Old Norse and Swedish *troll*, Danish *trold*.

troll² /trōl, trol/ > *verb* **1** fish by trailing a baited line along behind a boat. **2** chiefly Brit. walk; stroll. > *noun* **1** an act or instance of trolling. **2** a line or bait used in such fishing.

DERIVATIVES – **troller** *noun*.

trolley > *noun* (pl. **trolleys**) **1** Brit. a large wheeled metal basket or frame used for transporting heavy or unwieldy items such as luggage or supermarket purchases. **2** a small table on wheels or castors, used especially to convey food and drink. **3** (also **trolley wheel**) a wheel attached to a pole, used for collecting current from an overhead electric wire to drive a tram. **4** short for **trolleybus** or **trolley car**.

IDIOMS – **off one's trolley** Brit. informal mad; insane.

COMBINATIONS – **trolleybus** a bus powered by electricity obtained from overhead wires by means of a trolley wheel. **trolley car** US a tram powered by electricity obtained from overhead wires by means of a trolley wheel.

ORIGIN – perhaps from **TROLL²**.

trollop > *noun* dated or humorous a sexually disreputable or promiscuous woman.

trombone > *noun* a large brass wind instrument having an extendable slide with which different notes are made.

DERIVATIVES – **trombonist** *noun*.

ORIGIN – French or Italian, from Italian *tromba* 'trumpet'.

trompe l'œil /tromp loy/ > *noun* (pl. **trompe l'œils** pronunc. same) a painting or method of painting that creates the illusion of a three-dimensional object or space.

ORIGIN – French, 'deceives the eye'.

troop > *noun* **1** (**troops**) soldiers or armed forces. **2** a unit of an armoured or cavalry division. **3** a group of three or more Scout patrols. **4** a group of people or animals of a particular kind. > *verb* (of a group of people) come or go together or in large numbers.

IDIOMS – **troop the colour** Brit. perform the ceremony of parading a regiment's flag along ranks of soldiers.

COMBINATIONS – **troop carrier** a large aircraft or armoured vehicle designed for transporting troops. **troopship** a ship for transporting troops.

ORIGIN – French *troupe*, from Latin *troppus* 'flock'.

trooper > *noun* **1** a private soldier in a cavalry or armoured unit. **2** chiefly Brit. a troopship. **3** Austral./NZ & US a mounted police officer. **4** US a state police officer.

IDIOMS – **swear like a trooper** swear a great deal.

trope /trōp/ > *noun* a figurative or metaphorical use of a word or expression.

ORIGIN – Greek *tropos* 'turn, way', from *trepein* 'to turn'.

trophic /trōfik, troffik/ > *adjective* **1** Ecology relating to feeding and nutrition. **2** (also **tropic**) Physiology (of a hormone or its effect) stimulating the secretion of another hormone or product.

ORIGIN – Greek *trophikos*, from *trophē* 'nourishment', from *trephein* 'nourish'.

trophy > *noun* (pl. **trophies**) **1** a cup or other decorative object awarded as a prize for a victory or success. **2** a souvenir of an achievement, especially a head of an animal taken when hunting.

wordpower facts

Trophy

Trophy and **tropic** are related to each other: both words are based on the Greek *tropē* 'turning, rout', from *trepein* 'to turn'. A **trophy** (from Greek *tropaion* via Latin *trophaeum* and French *trophée*) was originally something awarded to celebrate the enemy having turned tail and run away. The word **tropic** (from Latin *tropicus*) is connected to 'turning' because the tropic of Cancer and the tropic of Capricorn are the lines of latitude at which the sun appears to 'turn', moving back towards the equator after reaching its most northerly or southerly point at the solstice.

tropic¹ /troppik/ > *noun* **1** the parallel of latitude 23° 26′ north (**tropic of Cancer**) or south (**tropic of Capricorn**) of the equator. **2** (**the tropics**) the region between the tropics of Cancer and Capricorn. **3** Astronomy each of two corresponding circles on the celestial sphere, marking the northern and southern limits of the ecliptic. > *adjective* tropical.

tropic² /trōpik/ > *adjective* **1** Biology relating to, consisting of, or exhibiting tropism. **2** Physiology variant spelling of **TROPHIC**.

tropical > *adjective* **1** relating to the tropics. **2** very hot and humid.

DERIVATIVES – **tropically** *adverb*.

COMBINATIONS – **tropical storm** (also **tropical cyclone**) a localised, very intense low-pressure wind system with winds of hurricane force, forming over tropical oceans.

tropism /trōpiz'm/ > *noun* Biology the turning of all or part of an organism in response to an external stimulus.

ORIGIN – from Greek *tropos* 'turning'.

troposphere /troppəsfeer, trōp-/ > *noun* the lowest region of the atmosphere, extending from the earth's surface to a height of about 6–10 km (the lower boundary of the stratosphere).

DERIVATIVES – **tropospheric** *adjective*.

ORIGIN – from Greek *tropos* 'turning'.

troppo¹ /troppō/ > *adverb* Music too much; excessively.

ORIGIN – Italian.

troppo² /troppō/ > *adjective* Austral./NZ informal mentally disturbed, supposedly as a result of spending too long in a tropical climate.

ORIGIN – from **TROPIC**¹.

trot > *verb* (**trotted**, **trotting**) **1** (of a horse) proceed at a pace faster than a walk, lifting each diagonal pair of legs alternately. **2** (of a person) run at a moderate pace with short steps. **3** informal go or walk briskly. **4** (**trot out**) informal produce (a story, explanation, etc.) that has been produced many times before. > *noun* **1** a trotting pace. **2** an act or period of trotting. **3** (**the trots**) informal diarrhoea. **4** informal, chiefly Austral./NZ a run of good or bad luck.

IDIOMS – **on the trot** informal **1** Brit. in succession. **2** continually busy.

ORIGIN – Latin *trottare*.

troth /trōth, troth/ > *noun* **1** archaic or formal faith or loyalty when pledged in a solemn agreement or undertaking. **2** archaic truth.

IDIOMS – **pledge** (or **plight**) **one's troth** make a solemn pledge of commitment or loyalty, especially in marriage.

ORIGIN – variant of **TRUTH**.

Trotskyism > *noun* the political or economic principles of the Russian revolutionary Leon Trotsky (1879–1940), especially the theory that socialism should be established throughout the world by continuing revolution.

DERIVATIVES – **Trotskyist** *noun & adjective* **Trotskyite** *noun & adjective* (derogatory).

trotter > *noun* **1** a horse bred or trained for the sport of trotting. **2** a pig's foot.

trotting > *noun* a form of racing for horses pulling a two-wheeled vehicle and driver.

troubadour /trōobədor/ > *noun* (in medieval France) a performing poet who composed and sang in Provençal, especially on the theme of courtly love.

ORIGIN – French, from Provençal *trobador*, from *trobar* 'find, invent, compose in verse'.

trouble > *noun* **1** difficulty or problems. **2** effort or exertion. **3** a cause of worry or inconvenience. **4** public unrest or disorder. > *verb* **1** cause distress, pain, or inconvenience to. **2** (**troubled**) showing or experiencing problems or anxiety. **3** (**trouble about** or **over** or **with**) be distressed or anxious about. **4** (**trouble to**) make the effort required to (do something).

IDIOMS – **ask for trouble** informal act in a way that is likely to incur problems or difficulties. **in trouble** in a situation in which one is liable to incur punishment or blame. **look for trouble** informal behave in a way that is likely to provoke an argument or fight. **trouble and strife** Brit. rhyming slang wife. **a trouble shared is a trouble halved** proverb talking to someone else about one's problems helps to alleviate them.

SYNONYMS – *noun* **1** bother, difficulty, inconvenience, problems. **2** care, effort, exertion, labour, pains. *verb* **1** agitate, bother, concern, distress, disturb, upset, worry.

COMBINATIONS – **trouble spot** a place where difficulties or conflict regularly occur.

ORIGIN – Old French *truble*, from Latin *turbidus* 'turbulent', from *turba* 'a crowd, a disturbance'.

troublemaker > *noun* a person who habitually causes trouble, especially by inciting others to defy those in authority.

troubleshoot > *verb* **1** analyse and solve problems for an organisation. **2** trace and correct faults in a mechanical or electronic system.

DERIVATIVES – **troubleshooter** *noun*.

troublesome > *adjective* causing difficulty or annoyance.

DERIVATIVES – **troublesomeness** *noun*.

SYNONYMS – annoying, bothersome, irksome, irritating, trying, vexing.

troublous > *adjective* archaic or literary full of troubles.

trough /troff/ > *noun* **1** a long, narrow open container for animals to eat or drink out of. **2** a channel used to convey a liquid. **3** Meteorology an elongated region of low atmospheric pressure. **4** a hollow between two wave crests in the sea. **5** a point of low activity or achievement.

ORIGIN – Old English, related to **TREE**.

trounce > *verb* **1** defeat heavily in a contest. **2** rebuke or punish severely.

DERIVATIVES – **trouncer** *noun*.

SYNONYMS – **1** crush, demolish, overwhelm, rout; informal thrash.

troupe /trōop/ > *noun* a group of dancers, actors, or other entertainers who tour to different venues.

ORIGIN – French, from Latin *troppus* 'flock'; related to **TROOP**.

trouper > *noun* **1** an actor or other entertainer with long experience. **2** informal a reliable and uncomplaining person.

trouser > *noun* (before another noun) relating to trousers: *his trouser pocket.* > *verb* Brit. informal receive or take for oneself; pocket.

COMBINATIONS – **trouser suit** Brit. a pair of trousers and a matching jacket, worn by women.

trousers > *plural noun* an outer garment covering the body from the waist to the ankles, with a separate part for each leg.

IDIOMS – **wear the trousers** informal be the dominant partner in a relationship.

DERIVATIVES – **trousered** *adjective*.

ORIGIN – Irish *triús*, Scottish Gaelic *triubhas*; related to **TREWS**.

trousseau /trōosō/ > *noun* (pl. **trousseaux** or **trousseaus** /trōosōz/) the clothes, linen, and other belongings collected by a bride for her marriage.

ORIGIN – French, 'small bundle'.

trout > *noun* (pl. same) an edible fish of the salmon family, chiefly inhabiting fresh water.

IDIOMS – **old trout** informal an annoying or bad-tempered old woman.

ORIGIN – Old English, from Greek *trōgein* 'gnaw'.

trove > *noun* a store of valuable or delightful things.

ORIGIN – from *treasure trove*.

trow /trō/ > *verb* archaic think or believe.

ORIGIN – Old English, 'to trust'; related to **TRUCE**.

trowel > *noun* **1** a small hand-held tool with a curved scoop for lifting plants or earth. **2** a small hand-held tool with a flat, pointed blade, used to apply and spread mortar or plaster. > *verb* (**trowelled**, **trowelling**; US **troweled**, **troweling**) apply or spread with or as if with a trowel.

ORIGIN – Latin *truella*, from *trulla* 'scoop'.

troy (also **troy weight**) > *noun* a system of weights used mainly for precious metals and gems, with a pound of 12 ounces or 5,760 grains. Compare with **AVOIRDUPOIS**.

ORIGIN – from a weight used at the fair of *Troyes* in France.

truant > *noun* a pupil who stays away from school without permission or explanation. > *adjective* wandering; straying. > *verb* (also **play truant**) (of a pupil) stay away from school without permission or explanation.

DERIVATIVES – **truancy** *noun*.

ORIGIN – from Old French: first meaning a person begging through choice rather than necessity.

truce > *noun* an agreement between enemies to stop fighting for a certain time.

ORIGIN – Old English, 'belief, trust'; related to **TRUE**.

truck¹ > *noun* **1** chiefly N. Amer. a large road vehicle, used for carrying goods, materials, or troops. **2** Brit. an open railway vehicle for carrying freight. > *verb* chiefly N. Amer. **1** convey by truck. **2** informal go or proceed in a casual or leisurely way.

WORDFINDER – *types of truck:* bogie, dray, dumper, juggernaut, low-loader, pickup, tipper.

COMBINATIONS – **truck stop** N. Amer. a transport cafe.

ORIGIN – perhaps from **TRUCKLE** in the sense 'wheel, pulley': originally denoting a solid wooden wheel.

truck² > *noun* **1** archaic barter. **2** chiefly archaic small wares. **3** N. Amer. market-garden produce, especially vegetables. > *verb* archaic barter or exchange.

IDIOMS – **have no truck with** choose to avoid dealings or association with.

trucker > *noun* a long-distance truck driver.

truckle > *noun* a small barrel-shaped cheese, especially cheddar.

COMBINATIONS – **truckle bed** chiefly Brit. a low bed on wheels that can be stored under a larger bed.

ORIGIN – Old French *trocle*, from Latin *trochlea* 'sheaf of a pulley': originally denoting a wheel or pulley.

truculent /trukyoolənt/ > *adjective* quick to argue or fight; defiant.

DERIVATIVES – **truculence** *noun* **truculently** *adverb*.

SYNONYMS – argumentative, antagonistic, belligerent, combative, confrontational, defiant.

ORIGIN – Latin *truculentus*, from *trux* 'fierce'.

trudge > *verb* walk slowly and with heavy steps. > *noun* a difficult or laborious walk.

true > *adjective* (**truer**, **truest**) **1** in accordance with fact or reality. **2** rightly or strictly so called; genuine: *true love.* **3** real or actual. **4** accurate and exact. **5** (of a note) exactly in tune. **6** correctly positioned or aligned; upright or level. **7** loyal or faithful. **8** (**true to**) accurately conforming to (a standard or expectation). > *verb* (**trues**, **trued**, **truing** or **trueing**) bring into the exact shape or position required.

IDIOMS – **come true** actually happen or become the case. **many a true word is spoken in jest** proverb a humorous remark not intended to be taken seriously may turn out to be accurate after all. **out of true** not in the correct or exact shape or alignment. **true to form** (or **type**) being or behaving as expected. **true to life** accurately representing real events or objects.

DERIVATIVES – **trueness** *noun*.

SYNONYMS – *adjective* **1** factual, real; formal veracious. **2** authentic, genuine, veritable. **4** accurate, exact, faithful, realistic. **7** constant, dedicated, devoted, faithful, firm, loyal, trusty.

ANTONYMS – *adjective* **1** false, untrue. **4** inaccurate. **7** disloyal.

COMBINATIONS – **true north** north according to the earth's axis, as opposed to magnetic north.

ORIGIN – Old English, 'steadfast, loyal'; related to **TRUCE**.

true-blue > *adjective* **1** N. Amer. extremely loyal or orthodox. **2** Brit. staunchly loyal to the Conservative Party.

true-born > *adjective* of a specified kind by birth; genuine.

truffle > *noun* **1** an underground fungus that resembles a rough-skinned potato and is considered a culinary delicacy. **2** a soft chocolate sweet. > *verb* (**truffling**) hunting for truffles.

ORIGIN – obsolete French, perhaps from Latin *tuber* 'hump, swelling'.

trug > *noun* Brit. a shallow oblong wooden basket, traditionally used for carrying garden flowers and produce.

ORIGIN – perhaps a dialect form of **TROUGH**.

truism > *noun* a statement that is obviously true and says nothing new or interesting.

truly > *adverb* **1** in a truthful way. **2** to the fullest degree; absolutely or completely. **3** genuinely or properly. **4** in actual fact; really.

IDIOMS – **yours truly 1** used as a formula for ending a letter. **2** humorous used to refer to oneself.

trump¹ > *noun* **1** (in bridge, whist, etc.) a playing card of the suit chosen to rank above the others, which can win a trick where a card of a different suit has been led. **2** (usu. **trump card**) a valuable resource that may be used, especially as a surprise, to gain an advantage. **3** informal, dated a helpful or admirable person. **4** Austral./NZ informal a person in authority. > *verb* **1** play a trump on (a card of another suit). **2** outdo by saying or doing something better. **3** (**trump up**) invent (a false accusation or excuse).

IDIOMS – **come** (or **turn**) **up trumps** informal, chiefly Brit. **1** have a better performance or outcome than expected. **2** be especially generous or helpful.

ORIGIN – from **TRIUMPH**, once used in card games in the same sense.

trump² > *noun* archaic a trumpet or a trumpet blast.

ORIGIN – Old French *trompe*.

trumpery archaic > *noun* (pl. **trumperies**) articles, practices, or beliefs of superficial appeal but little real value or worth. > *adjective* showy but worthless; illusory.

ORIGIN – Old French *tromperie*, from *tromper* 'deceive': originally in the sense 'trickery'.

trumpet > *noun* **1** a brass musical instrument with a flared bell and a bright, penetrating tone. **2** something shaped like a trumpet, especially the tubular central part of a daffodil flower. **3** the loud, strident cry of an elephant. > *verb* (**trumpeted**, **trumpeting**) **1** play a trumpet. **2** (of an elephant) make its characteristic loud cry. **3** proclaim widely or loudly.

IDIOMS – **blow one's own trumpet** talk openly and boastfully about one's achievements.

COMBINATIONS – **trumpet major** the chief trumpeter of a cavalry regiment.

ORIGIN – Old French *trompette*.

trumpeter > *noun* a person who plays a trumpet.

truncate > *verb* /trung**kayt**/ shorten by cutting off the top or the end.

DERIVATIVES – **truncation** *noun*.

ORIGIN – Latin *truncare* 'maim'.

truncheon /**trun**chən/ > *noun* chiefly Brit. a short, thick stick carried as a weapon by a police officer.

ORIGIN – Old French *tronchon* 'stump', from Latin *truncus* 'trunk'.

trundle > *verb* move slowly and unevenly on or as if on wheels. > *noun* an act of trundling.

COMBINATIONS – **trundle bed** chiefly N. Amer. a truckle bed.

ORIGIN – first meaning a small wheel or roller: related to obsolete or dialect *trendle* 'revolve', and to **TREND**.

trunk > *noun* **1** the main woody stem of a tree as distinct from its branches and roots. **2** a person's or animal's body apart from the limbs and head. **3** the elongated, prehensile nose of an elephant. **4** a large box with a hinged lid for storing or transporting clothes and other articles. **5** N. Amer. the boot of a car. **6** (before another noun) relating to the main routes of a transport or communication network: *a trunk road.*

COMBINATIONS – **trunk call** dated, chiefly Brit. a long-distance telephone call made within the same country.

ORIGIN – Latin *truncus*.

trunking > *noun* a system of shafts or conduits for cables or ventilation.

trunks > *plural noun* men's shorts, worn especially for swimming or boxing.

trunnion /**trun**yən/ > *noun* a pin or pivot forming one of a pair on which something is supported.

ORIGIN – French *trognon* 'core, tree trunk'.

truss > *noun* **1** a framework of rafters, posts, and struts which supports a roof, bridge, or other structure. **2** a padded belt worn against the skin to support a hernia. **3** a large projection of stone or wood, typically one supporting a cornice. **4** Brit., chiefly historical a bundle of old hay (56 lb), new hay (60 lb), or straw (36 lb). **5** a compact cluster of flowers or fruit growing on one stalk. > *verb* **1** support with a truss or trusses. **2** bind or tie up tightly. **3** tie up the wings and legs of (a chicken or other bird) before cooking.

ORIGIN – Old French *trusser* 'pack up, bind in', from Latin *torquere* 'to twist'.

trust > *noun* **1** firm belief in someone or something. **2** acceptance of the truth of a statement without evidence or investigation. **3** the state of being responsible for someone or something. **4** Law an arrangement whereby a person (a trustee) is made the nominal owner of property to be held or used for the benefit of one or more others. **5** a body of trustees. **6** an organisation or company managed by trustees. > *verb* **1** believe in the reliability, truth, ability, or strength of. **2** (**trust someone with**) have the confidence to allow someone to have, use, or look after. **3** (**trust to**) commit (someone or something) to the safekeeping of (someone). **4** (**trust to**) place reliance on (luck, fate, etc.). **5** have confidence; hope: *I trust that you have enjoyed this book.*

IDIOMS – **trust someone to ——!** it is characteristic or predictable for someone to act in the specified way.

DERIVATIVES – **trusted** *adjective* **trustful** *adjective*.

SYNONYMS – *noun* **1** belief, confidence, faith. *verb* **1** believe in, have confidence in, have faith in, rely on, be sure of. **5** assume, expect, hope, imagine.

ANTONYMS – *noun & verb* **1** distrust, mistrust.

COMBINATIONS – **trust company** a company formed to act as a trustee or to deal with trusts. **trust fund** a fund consisting of assets belonging to a trust, held by the trustees for the beneficiaries. **trust territory** a territory under the trusteeship of the United Nations or of a state designated by them.

ORIGIN – from Old Norse *traust*, an adjective meaning 'strong'.

trustee > *noun* **1** Law an individual or member of a board given powers of administration of property in trust with a legal obligation to administer it solely for the purposes specified. **2** a state made responsible for the government of an area by the United Nations.

DERIVATIVES – **trusteeship** *noun*.

trusting > *adjective* tending to trust others; not suspicious.

DERIVATIVES – **trustingly** *adverb* **trustingness** *noun*.

trustworthy > *adjective* able to be relied on as honest, truthful, or reliable.

DERIVATIVES – **trustworthiness** *noun*.

SYNONYMS – dependable, honest, reliable, responsible, steadfast, true, upright.

trusty > *adjective* (**trustier**, **trustiest**) archaic or humorous reliable or faithful.

DERIVATIVES – **trustiness** *noun*.

truth > *noun* (pl. **truths** /trōoths, trōothz/) **1** the quality or state of being true. **2** (also **the truth**) that which is true as opposed to false. **3** a fact or belief that is accepted as true.

IDIOMS – **in truth** really; in fact. **to tell the truth** (or **truth to tell** or **if truth be told**) to be frank.

SYNONYMS – **1** accuracy, factuality, veracity, verity. **3** certainty, fact, verity.

ANTONYMS – **1** falsity. **3** falsehood, lie.

COMBINATIONS – **truth drug** a drug supposedly able to induce a state in which a person answers questions truthfully.

ORIGIN – Old English, 'faithfulness, constancy'.

truthful > *adjective* **1** telling or expressing the truth; honest. **2** (of a representation) true to life.

DERIVATIVES – **truthfully** *adverb* **truthfulness** *noun*.

SYNONYMS – **1** candid, frank, genuine, honest, sincere. **2** accurate, faithful, true.

try > *verb* (**tries**, **tried**) **1** make an attempt or effort to do something. **2** (also **try out**) test (something new or different) in order to see if it is suitable, effective, or pleasant. **3** attempt to operate (a device), open (a door), contact (someone), etc. **4** (**try on**) put on (an item of clothing) to see if it fits or suits one. **5** make severe demands on. **6** subject (someone) to trial. **7** investigate and decide (a case or issue) in a formal trial. > *noun* (pl. **tries**) **1** an effort to accomplish something; an attempt. **2** an act of testing something new or different. **3** Rugby an act of touching the ball down behind the opposing goal line, scoring points and entitling the scoring side to a kick at goal.

IDIOMS – **tried and tested** (or **true**) having proved effective or reliable before. **try one's hand at** attempt to do for the first time. **try it on** Brit. informal deliberately test or attempt to deceive or seduce someone.

USAGE – the constructions **try to** and **try and** (as in *we should try to* (or *try and*) *help them*) mean the same thing, but **try and** is less formal: use **try to** in careful writing or speech.

COMBINATIONS – **try square** an implement used to check and mark right angles in constructional work.

ORIGIN – Old French *trier* 'sift'.

trying > *adjective* difficult or annoying; hard to endure.

DERIVATIVES – **tryingly** *adverb*.

trypanosome /**tripp**ənəsōm, tri**pann**ə-/ > *noun* Medicine & Zoology a single-celled parasitic organism with a whip-like appendage, infesting the blood.

ORIGIN – from Greek *trupanon* 'borer' + *sōma* 'body'.

trypanosomiasis /trippənōsə**mī**əsiss/

> *noun* Medicine any tropical disease caused by trypanosomes, especially sleeping sickness or Chagas' disease.

trypsin /**tripp**sin/ > *noun* a digestive enzyme which breaks down proteins in the small intestine.

ORIGIN – from Greek *tripsis* 'friction' (because it was first obtained by rubbing down the pancreas with glycerine).

tryptophan /**trip**təfan/ > *noun* Biochemistry an amino acid which is an essential nutrient in the diet.

ORIGIN – from *tryptic* 'relating to trypsin' + Greek *phainein* 'appear'.

tryst /trist/ literary > *noun* a private, romantic rendezvous between lovers. > *verb* keep or arrange a tryst.

ORIGIN – from obsolete *trist* 'an appointed place in hunting', from French *triste* or Latin *trista*.

tsar /zaar/ (also **czar** or **tzar**) > *noun* an emperor of Russia before 1917.

DERIVATIVES – **tsardom** *noun* **tsarism** *noun* **tsarist** *noun* & *adjective*.

ORIGIN – Russian, representing Latin *Caesar*.

tsarevich /**zaa**rivich/ (also **czarevich** or **tzarevich**) > *noun* historical the eldest son of a Russian tsar.

ORIGIN – Russian, 'son of a tsar'.

tsarina /zaa**ree**nə/ (also **czarina** or **tzarina**) > *noun* an empress of Russia before 1917.

tsetse /**tet**si, **tset**si/ (also **tsetse fly**) > *noun* an African bloodsucking fly which transmits sleeping sickness.

ORIGIN – from a southern African language.

T-shirt (also **tee shirt**) > *noun* a short-sleeved casual top, having the shape of a T when spread out flat.

tsp > *abbreviation* (pl. same or **tsps**) teaspoonful.

TSR > *abbreviation* Computing terminate and stay resident, denoting a type of program that remains in the memory of a microcomputer after it has finished running.

TSS > *abbreviation* toxic shock syndrome.

tsubo /**tsoo**bō/ > *noun* (pl. same or **tsubos**) (in complementary medicine) a point on the face or body to which pressure or other stimulation is applied during treatment.

ORIGIN – Japanese.

tsunami /tsoo**naa**mi/ > *noun* (pl. same or **tsunamis**) an exceptionally large ocean wave caused by an underwater earthquake or other disturbance.

ORIGIN – Japanese, 'harbour wave'.

TT > *abbreviation* 1 teetotal or teetotaller. 2 Tourist Trophy.

TTL > *abbreviation* 1 Electronics transistor transistor logic, a technology for making integrated circuits. 2 Photography (of a camera focusing system) through-the-lens.

Tuareg /**twaa**reg/ > *noun* (pl. same or

Tuaregs) a member of a Berber people of the western and central Sahara.

ORIGIN – the name in Berber.

tuatara /tōō**ə**taarə/ > *noun* a lizard-like reptile with a crest of soft spines, now confined to some small islands off New Zealand.

ORIGIN – Maori.

tub > *noun* 1 a low, wide, open container with a flat bottom. 2 a small lidded plastic or cardboard container for food. 3 informal, chiefly N. Amer. a bath. 4 informal, derogatory a short, broad boat that handles awkwardly. > *verb* (**tubbed**, **tubbing**) plant, put, or wash in a tub.

tuba > *noun* a large, low-pitched, brass wind instrument with a broad bell.

ORIGIN – Latin, 'trumpet'.

tubal > *adjective* relating to or occurring in a tube, especially the Fallopian tubes.

tubby > *adjective* (**tubbier**, **tubbiest**) informal (of a person) short and rather fat.

DERIVATIVES – **tubbiness** *noun*.

tube > *noun* 1 a long, hollow cylinder for conveying or holding liquids or gases. 2 a flexible metal or plastic container sealed at one end and having a cap at the other. 3 a hollow cylindrical organ or structure in an animal or plant. 4 Brit. informal (**the tube**) the underground railway system in London. 5 a sealed container containing two electrodes between which an electric current can be made to flow. 6 a cathode ray tube, especially in a television set. 7 (**the tube**) N. Amer. informal television. 8 N. Amer. a thermionic valve. 9 Austral. informal a can of beer. > *verb* 1 provide with a tube or tubes. 2 convey in a tube.

IDIOMS – **go down the tube** (or **tubes**) informal be completely lost or wasted; fail utterly.

ORIGIN – Latin *tubus*.

tubectomy > *noun* (pl. **tubectomies**) surgical removal of the Fallopian tubes.

tuber > *noun* 1 a thickened underground part of a stem or rhizome, e.g. that of the potato, bearing buds from which new plants grow. 2 a thickened fleshy root, e.g. of the dahlia.

ORIGIN – Latin, 'hump, swelling'.

tubercle /**tyōō**bərk'l/ > *noun* 1 a small rounded projection on a bone or on the surface of an animal or plant. 2 a small rounded swelling in the lungs or other tissues, characteristic of tuberculosis.

COMBINATIONS – **tubercle bacillus** the bacterium that causes tuberculosis.

ORIGIN – Latin *tuberculum* 'small lump or swelling'.

tubercular /tyoo**ber**kyoolər/ > *adjective* 1 relating to or affected with tuberculosis. 2 having or covered with tubercles.

tuberculin > *noun* a sterile protein extract

from cultures of tubercle bacillus, used to test for tuberculosis.

tuberculosis /tyooberkyoo**lō**siss/ > *noun* an infectious bacterial disease characterised by the growth of tubercles in the tissues, especially the lungs.

tuberculous > *adjective* another term for **TUBERCULAR**.

tuberose > *noun* /**tyōō**bərōz/ a Mexican plant with heavily scented white waxy flowers and a bulb-like base, formerly cultivated as a flavouring for chocolate. > *adjective* /**tyōō**bərōss/ another term for **TUBEROUS**.

tuberous /**tyōō**bərass/ > *adjective* 1 resembling, forming, or having a tuber or tubers. 2 characterised by or affected by rounded swellings.

tubifex worm /**tyōō**bifeks/ > *noun* a small red worm that lives in fresh water, partly buried in the mud.

ORIGIN – from Latin *tubus* 'tube' + *-fex* '-making'.

tubing > *noun* a length or lengths of material in tubular form.

tub-thumping informal, derogatory > *adjective* expressing opinions in a loud and violent or dramatic manner. > *noun* the expression of opinions in such a way.

DERIVATIVES – **tub-thumper** *noun*.

tubular > *adjective* 1 long, round, and hollow like a tube. 2 made from a tube or tubes.

COMBINATIONS – **tubular bells** an orchestral instrument consisting of a row of vertically suspended metal tubes struck with a mallet.

tubule /**tyōō**byōōl/ > *noun* a minute tube, especially in an animal or plant.

TUC > *abbreviation* (in the UK) Trades Union Congress.

tuck > *verb* 1 push, fold, or turn under or between two surfaces or into a confined space. 2 make a flattened, stitched fold in (a garment or material). 3 (**tuck away**) store in a secure place. 4 (**tuck in** or **up**) settle (someone) in bed by pulling the edges of the bedclothes firmly under the mattress. 5 (**tuck in** or **into**) informal eat food heartily. > *noun* 1 a flattened, stitched fold in a garment or material. 2 Brit. informal food eaten by children at school as a snack.

ORIGIN – Old English, 'to punish, ill-treat'.

tucker > *noun* 1 Austral./NZ informal food. 2 historical a piece of lace or linen worn on a bodice or as an insert at the front of a low-cut dress. > *verb* (**be tuckered out**) N. Amer. informal be exhausted or worn out.

-tude > *suffix* forming abstract nouns such as *beatitude*, *solitude*.

ORIGIN – from Latin *-tudo*.

Tudor > *adjective* 1 relating or belonging to the English royal dynasty which held the throne from the accession of Henry VII in

1485 until the death of Elizabeth I in 1603. **2** referring to the prevalent architectural style of the Tudor period, characterised by half-timbering. > *noun* a member of the Tudor dynasty.

COMBINATIONS – **Tudor rose** a stylised figure of a rose used in architectural decoration in the Tudor period, especially one combining the red and white roses of Lancaster and York.

Tuesday > *noun* the day of the week before Wednesday and following Monday.

ORIGIN – Old English, named after the Germanic god *Tiw* (associated with the Roman god Mars); translation of Latin *dies Marti* 'day of Mars'.

tufa /tyōōfə/ > *noun* **1** a porous rock composed of calcium carbonate and formed by precipitation from water, e.g. around mineral springs. **2** another term for TUFF.

ORIGIN – Italian.

tuff > *noun* a light, porous rock formed by consolidation of volcanic ash.

ORIGIN – Latin *tofus*.

tuffet > *noun* **1** a tuft or clump. **2** a footstool or low seat.

ORIGIN – alteration of TUFT.

tuft > *noun* a bunch of threads, grass, or hair, held or growing together at the base.

DERIVATIVES – **tufted** *adjective* **tufty** *adjective*.

COMBINATIONS – **tufted duck** a freshwater diving duck with a drooping crest and black and white (or brown) plumage.

ORIGIN – probably from Old French *tofe*.

tug > *verb* (**tugged**, **tugging**) pull (something) hard or suddenly. > *noun* **1** a hard or sudden pull. **2** (also **tugboat**) a small, powerful boat for towing larger boats and ships, especially in harbour.

SYNONYMS – *verb* jerk, pluck, wrench. *noun* **1** jerk, pluck, wrench.

COMBINATIONS – **tug of war** a contest in which two teams pull at opposite ends of a rope until one drags the other over a central line.

tugrik /tōōgrik/ > *noun* (pl. same or **tugriks**) the basic monetary unit of Mongolia, equal to 100 mongos.

ORIGIN – Mongolian.

tui /tōōi/ > *noun* a large New Zealand bird with glossy blackish plumage and two white tufts at the throat.

ORIGIN – Maori.

tuition > *noun* teaching or instruction, especially of individuals or small groups.

SYNONYMS – coaching, instruction, teaching, tutoring.

ORIGIN – Latin, from *tueri* 'to watch, guard'.

tulip > *noun* a spring-flowering plant with boldly coloured cup-shaped flowers.

COMBINATIONS – **tulip tree 1** a North American tree with large distinctively lobed leaves and insignificant tulip-like flowers. **2** a magnolia tree.

ORIGIN – Persian, 'turban' (from the shape of the flower).

tulle /tyōōl/ > *noun* a soft, fine net material, used for making veils and dresses.

ORIGIN – from *Tulle*, a town in SW France.

tumble > *verb* **1** fall suddenly, clumsily, or headlong. **2** move or rush in a headlong manner. **3** decrease rapidly in amount or value. **4** rumple; disarrange. **5** (**tumble to**) *informal* come to understand; realise. > *noun* **1** an instance of tumbling. **2** an untidy or confused arrangement or state. **3** a handspring or other acrobatic feat.

SYNONYMS – *verb* **1** collapse, topple over, trip. **2** rush, scramble, scuttle. *noun* **1** fall, spill, tumble.

COMBINATIONS – **tumble-dryer** a machine that dries washed clothes by spinning them in hot air inside a rotating drum. **tumbling barrel** a revolving device containing an abrasive substance, in which castings, gemstones, or other hard objects can be cleaned.

ORIGIN – Low German *tummelen*, related to Old English *tumbian* 'to dance'.

tumbledown > *adjective* falling or fallen into ruin; dilapidated.

SYNONYMS – decrepit, dilapidated, ramshackle.

tumblehome > *noun* the inward slope of the upper part of a boat's sides.

tumbler > *noun* **1** a drinking glass with straight sides and no handle or stem. [ORIGIN – formerly having a rounded bottom so as not to stand upright.] **2** an acrobat. **3** a pivoted piece in a lock that holds the bolt until lifted by a key. **4** an electrical switch worked by pushing a small sprung lever. **5** a tumbling barrel.

tumbleweed > *noun* N. Amer. & Austral./NZ a plant of dry regions which breaks off near the ground in late summer, forming light masses blown about by the wind.

tumbril /tumbril/ (also **tumbrel**) > *noun* historical an open cart that tilted backwards to empty out its load, in particular one used to convey prisoners to the guillotine during the French Revolution.

ORIGIN – Old French *tomberel*, from *tomber* 'to fall'.

tumefy /tyōōmifī/ > *verb* (**tumefies**, **tumefied**) become swollen.

DERIVATIVES – **tumefaction** *noun*.

ORIGIN – Latin *tumefacere*, from *tumere* 'to swell'.

tumescent /tyōōmess'nt/ > *adjective* swollen or becoming swollen.

DERIVATIVES – **tumescence** *noun*.

tumid /tyōōmid/ > *adjective* **1** (of a part of the body) swollen or bulging. **2** pompous or bombastic.

ORIGIN – Latin *tumidus*, from *tumere* 'to swell'.

tummy > *noun* (pl. **tummies**) *informal* a person's stomach or abdomen.

COMBINATIONS – **tummy button** *informal* a person's navel.

ORIGIN – a child's pronunciation of STOMACH.

tumour (US **tumor**) > *noun* a swelling of a part of the body caused by an abnormal growth of tissue, whether benign or malignant.

WORDFINDER – metastasis (*development of secondary tumours away from primary site of cancer*), neoplasm (*tumour or other abnormal growth of tissue*), oncogenic (*causing development of a tumour*).

DERIVATIVES – **tumorous** *adjective*.

ORIGIN – Latin *tumor*, from *tumere* 'to swell'.

tump > *noun* chiefly dialect a small rounded hill or clump.

tumult > *noun* **1** a loud, confused noise, as caused by a large mass of people. **2** confusion or disorder.

SYNONYMS – **1** din, racket, uproar. **2** confusion, disorder, turmoil.

ORIGIN – Latin *tumultus*.

tumultuous /tyōōmultyōōəss/ > *adjective* **1** very loud or uproarious. **2** excited, confused, or disorderly.

DERIVATIVES – **tumultuously** *adverb*.

SYNONYMS – **1** clamorous, ear-shattering, thunderous. **2** confused, disorderly, excited, rowdy, turbulent, unruly.

tumulus /tyōōmyōōləss/ > *noun* (pl. **tumuli** /tyōōmyōōlī/) an ancient burial mound; a barrow.

ORIGIN – Latin.

tun > *noun* **1** a large beer or wine cask. **2** a brewer's fermenting-vat.

ORIGIN – Latin *tunna*.

tuna > *noun* (pl. same or **tunas**) a large predatory fish of warm seas, fished commercially.

ORIGIN – Spanish *atún*.

tundish > *noun* Brit. a broad open container or large funnel with one or more holes at the bottom, used especially in plumbing or metal-founding.

tundra /tundrə/ > *noun* a vast, flat, treeless Arctic region of Europe, Asia, and North America in which the subsoil is permanently frozen.

ORIGIN – Lappish.

tune > *noun* a melody or melodious piece of music. > *verb* **1** adjust (a musical instrument) to the correct or a uniform pitch. **2** adjust (a radio or television) to the frequency of the required signal. **3** adjust (an engine) or balance (mechanical parts) so that they run smoothly and efficiently. **4** (often **be tuned to**) adjust or adapt to a purpose or situation.

IDIOMS – **in** (or **out of**) **tune 1** with correct (or incorrect) pitch or intonation. **2** (of a motor engine) properly (or poorly) adjusted. **there's many a good tune played on an old fiddle** proverb someone's abilities do not depend on their being young. **to the tune of** informal amounting to or involving.

DERIVATIVES – **tunable** (also **tuneable**) *adjective* **tuning** *noun*.

COMBINATIONS – **tunesmith** informal a composer of popular music or songs. **tuning fork** a two-pronged steel device used for tuning instruments, which vibrates when struck to give a note of specific pitch.

ORIGIN – alteration of **TONE**.

tuneful > *adjective* having a pleasing tune; melodious.

DERIVATIVES – **tunefully** *adverb* **tunefulness** *noun*.

SYNONYMS – mellifluous, melodious, musical.

ANTONYMS – discordant.

tuneless > *adjective* not having a pleasing tune; unmelodious.

DERIVATIVES – **tunelessly** *adverb* **tunelessness** *noun*.

SYNONYMS – discordant, dissonant, unmelodious, unmusical.

tuner > *noun* **1** a person who tunes musical instruments, especially pianos. **2** an electronic device used for tuning. **3** a unit for detecting and preamplifying a broadcast radio signal and supplying it to an audio amplifier.

tungsten /**tung**stən/ > *noun* a hard, steel-grey metallic chemical element with a very high melting point, used to make electric light filaments.

COMBINATIONS – **tungsten carbide** a very hard grey compound used in making engineering dies, cutting and drilling tools, etc.

ORIGIN – Swedish, from *tung* 'heavy' + *sten* 'stone'.

tunic > *noun* **1** a loose sleeveless garment reaching to the thigh or knees. **2** a close-fitting short coat worn as part of a uniform. **3** a gymslip.

ORIGIN – Latin *tunica*.

tunicate /**tyoo**nikət, -kayt/ > *noun* a marine animal of a group which includes the sea squirts, with a rubbery or hard outer coat.

Tunisian /tyoo**nizz**iən/ > *noun* a person from Tunisia. > *adjective* relating to Tunisia.

tunnel > *noun* an artificial underground passage, built through a hill or under a building or by a burrowing animal. > *verb* (**tunnelled**, **tunnelling**; US **tunneled**, **tunneling**) dig or force a passage underground or through something.

DERIVATIVES – **tunneller** *noun*.

COMBINATIONS – **tunnel vision 1** defective sight in which things cannot be seen properly if they are not close to the centre of the field of view. **2** informal the tendency to focus exclusively on a single or limited objective or view.

ORIGIN – Old French *tonel* 'small cask': first meaning 'flue of a chimney' and 'tunnel-shaped net'.

tunny > *noun* (pl. same or **tunnies**) a tuna.

ORIGIN – Greek *thunnos*.

tup /tup/ chiefly Brit. > *noun* a ram. > *verb* (**tupped**, **tupping**) (of a ram) copulate with (a ewe).

Tupi /**too**pi/ > *noun* (pl. same or **Tupis**) **1** a member of a group of American Indian peoples of the Amazon valley. **2** any of the languages of these peoples.

DERIVATIVES – **Tupian** *adjective*.

ORIGIN – a local name.

Tupi-Guarani > *noun* a South American Indian language family whose principal members are Guarani and the Tupian languages.

tuppence > *noun* Brit. variant spelling of **TWOPENCE**.

tuppenny > *adjective* Brit. variant spelling of **TWOPENNY**.

turban > *noun* a man's headdress consisting of a long length of material wound round a cap or the head, worn especially by Muslims and Sikhs.

DERIVATIVES – **turbaned** (also **turbanned**) *adjective*.

ORIGIN – Persian.

turbid /**tur**bid/ > *adjective* **1** (of a liquid) cloudy, opaque, or thick with suspended matter. **2** turbulent; confused.

DERIVATIVES – **turbidity** *noun*.

USAGE – do not confuse **turbid** and **turgid**: **turbid** is generally used in reference to a liquid and means 'cloudy or opaque'; **turgid** tends to mean 'tediously pompous' or, in reference to a river, 'swollen, overflowing'.

ORIGIN – Latin *turbidus*, from *turba* 'a crowd, a disturbance'.

turbine /**tur**bīn/ > *noun* a machine for producing power in which a wheel or rotor is made to revolve by a fast-moving flow of water, steam, gas, or air.

ORIGIN – from Latin *turbo* 'spinning top, whirl'.

turbo /**tur**bō/ > *noun* (pl. **turbos**) short for **TURBOCHARGER**.

turbocharge > *verb* equip with a turbocharger.

DERIVATIVES – **turbocharged** *adjective*.

turbocharger > *noun* a supercharger driven by a turbine powered by the engine's exhaust gases.

turbofan > *noun* a jet engine in which a turbine-driven fan provides additional thrust.

turbojet > *noun* a jet engine in which the jet gases also operate a turbine-driven compressor for compressing the air drawn into the engine.

turboprop > *noun* a jet engine in which a turbine is used to drive a propeller.

turboshaft > *noun* a gas turbine engine in which the turbine drives a shaft other than a propeller shaft.

turbot /**tur**bət/ > *noun* (pl. same) an edible flatfish of inshore waters, which has large bony tubercles on the body.

ORIGIN – Scandinavian.

turbulence > *noun* **1** violent or unsteady movement of air, water, or other fluid. **2** conflict or confusion.

SYNONYMS – **2** conflict, confusion, tumult, turmoil, upheaval.

ANTONYMS – calmness.

turbulent /**tur**byoolənt/ > *adjective* **1** disorderly or confused; not calm or controlled. **2** technical (of the flow of fluids) irregularly fluctuating.

DERIVATIVES – **turbulently** *adverb*.

ORIGIN – Latin *turbulentus* 'full of commotion', from *turba* 'crowd'.

Turcoman > *noun* variant spelling of **TURKOMAN**.

turd > *noun* vulgar slang **1** a lump of excrement. **2** an obnoxious or contemptible person.

tureen /tyoo**reen**/ > *noun* a deep covered dish from which soup is served.

ORIGIN – French *terrine* (see **TERRINE**).

turf > *noun* (pl. **turfs** or **turves**) **1** grass and the surface layer of earth held together by its roots. **2** a piece of such grass and earth cut from the ground. **3** (**the turf**) horse racing or racecourses generally. **4** (**one's turf**) informal one's territory; one's sphere of influence or activity. > *verb* **1** (**turf off** or **out**) informal, chiefly Brit. force to leave somewhere. **2** cover with turf.

COMBINATIONS – **turf accountant** Brit. formal a bookmaker.

turgescent /tur**jess**'nt/ > *adjective* chiefly technical becoming or seeming swollen or distended.

DERIVATIVES – **turgescence** *noun*.

turgid /**tur**jid/ > *adjective* **1** swollen and distended or congested. **2** (of language or style) tediously pompous or bombastic.

DERIVATIVES – **turgidity** *noun* **turgidly** *adverb*.

USAGE – do not confuse **turgid** and **turbid**: **turgid** tends to mean 'tediously pompous' or, in reference to a river, 'swollen, overflowing'; **turbid** is generally used in reference to a liquid and means 'cloudy or opaque'.

SYNONYMS – **2** inflated, orotund, overblown.

ANTONYMS – **2** plain.

ORIGIN – Latin *turgidus*, from *turgere* 'to swell'.

Turk > *noun* **1** a person from Turkey or of Turkish descent. **2** a member of any of the ancient peoples who spoke languages related to Turkish, such as the Ottomans.

turkey > *noun* (pl. **turkeys**) **1** a large mainly domesticated game bird native to North America, having a bald head and (in the male) red wattles. **2** informal, chiefly N. Amer. something extremely unsuccessful, especially a play or film. **3** informal, chiefly N. Amer. a stupid or inept person.

IDIOMS – **talk turkey** N. Amer. informal talk frankly and openly.

COMBINATIONS – **turkeycock** a male turkey. **turkey trot** a kind of ballroom dance to ragtime music, popular in the early 20th century.

---

wordpower facts

Turkey

Why is the **turkey** so called, when it is originally an American bird? The name **turkey**, originally in the longer form *turkeycock* or *turkeyhen*, was at first applied to the guineafowl, an African bird which was imported by the Portuguese through Turkey. When the American turkey was encountered by Europeans it was identified with the guineafowl or considered to be a related species: the two birds were eventually distinguished and given their own names, but the American bird was wrongly called the **turkey**.

Turkic > *noun* a large group of languages of western and central Asia, including Turkish. > *adjective* relating to these languages.

Turkish > *noun* the language of Turkey. > *adjective* relating to Turkey or its language.

COMBINATIONS – **Turkish bath 1** a cleansing treatment that involves sitting in a room filled with very hot air or steam, followed by washing and massage. **2** a building or room where such a treatment is available. **Turkish coffee** very strong black coffee served with the fine grounds in it. **Turkish delight** a sweet consisting of flavoured gelatin coated in icing sugar.

Turkmen /**turk**mən/ > *noun* (pl. same or **Turkmens**) a member of a group of peoples inhabiting the region east of the Caspian Sea and south of the Aral Sea.

ORIGIN – Turkish.

Turkoman /**turk**ōmən/ (also **Turcoman**) > *noun* (pl. **Turkomans**) **1** another term for **TURKMEN**. **2** a kind of large, soft, richly coloured rug made by the Turkmens.

turmeric /**tur**mərik/ > *noun* a bright yellow powder obtained from a plant of the ginger family, used for flavouring and colouring in Asian cookery.

ORIGIN – perhaps from French *terre mérite* 'deserving earth'.

turmoil > *noun* a state of great disturbance, confusion, or uncertainty.

SYNONYMS – disruption, tumult, upheaval, unrest.

turn > *verb* **1** move in a circular direction wholly or partly around an axis. **2** move into a different position, especially so as to face or move in the opposite direction. **3** change in nature, state, form, or colour; make or become. **4** shape on a lathe. **5** give a graceful or elegant form to. **6** make (a profit). **7** (of the tide) change from flood to ebb or vice versa. **8** twist or sprain (an ankle). **9** (of leaves) change colour in the autumn. **10** (of milk) become sour. > *noun* **1** an act of turning. **2** a bend or curve in a road, path, river, etc. **3** a place where a road meets or branches off another; a turning. **4** a time when one period of time ends and another begins. **5** a development or change in circumstances. **6** a short walk or ride. **7** a brief feeling or experience of illness: *a funny turn*. **8** an opportunity or obligation to do something that comes successively to each of a number of people. **9** a short performance, especially one of a number given by different performers. **10** one round in a coil of rope or other material.

IDIOMS – **at every turn** on every occasion; continually. **by turns** alternately. **do someone a good** (or **bad**) **turn** do something that is helpful (or unhelpful) for someone. **in turn** in succession; one after the other. **one good turn deserves another** proverb if someone does you a favour, you should take the chance to repay it. **out of turn** at a time when it is inappropriate or not one's turn. **take turns** (or **take it in turns**) (of two or more people) do something alternately or in succession. **to a turn** to exactly the right degree. **turn against** become or make hostile towards. **turn and turn about** chiefly Brit. one after another; in succession. **turn away** refuse admittance to. **turn down 1** reject an offer or application of or from. **2** adjust a control on (a device) to reduce the volume, heat, etc. **turn in 1** hand over to the authorities. **2** informal go to bed in the evening. **turn off 1** stop (something) operating by means of a tap, switch, or button. **2** leave one road in order to join another. **3** informal cause to feel bored or repelled. **turn of mind** a particular way of thinking. **turn of speed** the ability to go fast when necessary. **turn on 1** start (something) operating by means of a tap, switch, or button. **2** suddenly attack. **3** have as the main focus. **4** informal excite or stimulate, especially sexually. **turn out 1**

extinguish (an electric light). **2** produce (something). **3** empty (one's pockets). **4** prove to be the case. **5** eject or expel from a place. **6** go somewhere to attend a meeting, vote, play in a game, etc. **7** (**be turned out**) be dressed in the manner specified. **turn over 1** (of an engine) start or continue to run properly. **2** (of a business) have a turnover of. **3** change or transfer custody or control of. **turn round** (or **around**) reverse the previously poor performance of. **turn tail** informal turn round and run away. **turn to 1** start doing or becoming involved with. **2** go to for help or information. **3** have recourse to. **turn up 1** increase the volume or strength of (a device) by turning a knob or switch. **2** be found, especially by chance. **3** put in an appearance; arrive. **4** reveal or discover.

SYNONYMS – *verb* **1** circle, revolve, rotate. **3** become, change into, metamorphose, turn in to. *noun* **1** revolution, rotation, spin.

ORIGIN – Latin *tornare*, from *tornus* 'lathe'.

turnaround (also **turnround**) > *noun* **1** an abrupt or unexpected change. **2** the process of completing a task.

turnbuckle > *noun* a coupling with internal screw threads used to connect two rods, lengths of boat's rigging, etc. lengthwise or to regulate their length or tension.

turncoat > *noun* a person who deserts one party or cause in order to join an opposing one.

turnery > *noun* **1** the action or skill of turning objects on a lathe. **2** objects made on a lathe.

turning > *noun* **1** a place where a road branches off another. **2** the action or skill of using a lathe. **3** (**turnings**) shavings of wood resulting from turning wood on a lathe.

COMBINATIONS – **turning circle** the smallest circle in which a vehicle or vessel can turn without reversing.

turnip > *noun* a round root with white or cream flesh which is eaten as a vegetable.

ORIGIN – from a first element of unknown origin + NEEP.

turnkey > *noun* (pl. **turnkeys**) archaic a jailer.

turn-off > *noun* **1** a junction at which a road branches off. **2** informal a person or thing that causes one to feel bored or repelled.

turn-on > *noun* informal a person or thing that causes one to feel excited or sexually aroused.

turnout > *noun* the number of people attending or taking part in an event.

turnover > *noun* **1** the amount of money taken by a business in a particular period. **2** the rate at which employees leave a workforce and are replaced. **3** the rate at which goods are sold and replaced in a shop. **4** a small pie made by folding a piece of pastry over on itself to enclose a filling.

turnpike > *noun* **1** historical a toll gate. **2** historical a road on which a toll was collected. **3** US a motorway on which a toll is charged.

ORIGIN – from **PIKE**², originally in the sense 'spiked barrier fixed across a road as a defence against sudden attack'.

turnstile > *noun* a mechanical gate with revolving horizontal arms that allow only one person at a time to pass through.

turnstone > *noun* a small short-billed sandpiper noted for turning over stones to find small animals.

turntable > *noun* **1** a circular revolving plate supporting a gramophone record as it is played. **2** a circular revolving platform for turning a railway locomotive.

turn-up > *noun* Brit. **1** the end of a trouser leg folded upwards on the outside. **2** informal an unusual or unexpected event.

turpentine /**tur**pətīn/ > *noun* **1** (also **crude** or **gum turpentine**) a resinous oily substance secreted by certain pines and other trees and distilled to make rosin and oil of turpentine. **2** (also **oil of turpentine**) a volatile pungent oil distilled from this, used in mixing paints and varnishes and in liniment.

ORIGIN – from Latin *terebinthina resina* 'resin of the terebinth'.

turpitude /**tur**pityōōd/ > *noun* formal depravity; wickedness.

ORIGIN – Latin *turpitudo*, from *turpis* 'disgraceful, base'.

turps > *noun* informal turpentine.

turquoise /**tur**kwoyz, -kwaaz/ > *noun* **1** a semi-precious stone, typically opaque and of a greenish-blue or sky-blue colour. **2** a greenish-blue colour.

ORIGIN – Old French *turqueise* 'Turkish stone'.

turret > *noun* **1** a small tower at the corner of a building or wall, especially of a castle. **2** an armoured, usually revolving tower for a gun and gunners in a ship, aircraft, fort, or tank. **3** a rotating holder for tools, especially on a lathe.

DERIVATIVES – **turreted** *adjective*.

ORIGIN – Old French *tourete* 'small tower'.

turtle > *noun* **1** a marine or freshwater reptile with a bony or leathery shell and flippers or webbed toes. **2** Computing a directional cursor in a computer graphics system which can be instructed to move around a screen.

IDIOMS – **turn turtle** (chiefly of a boat) turn upside down.

ORIGIN – apparently an alteration of French *tortue* 'tortoise'.

turtle dove > *noun* a small dove with a soft purring call, noted for the apparent affection shown for its mate.

ORIGIN – from Latin *turtur*.

turtleneck > *noun* **1** Brit. a high, round, close-fitting neck on a knitted garment. **2** North American term for *polo neck*.

turves plural of **TURF**.

Tuscan /**tusk**ən/ > *adjective* **1** relating to Tuscany in central Italy. **2** referring to a classical order of architecture resembling the Doric but lacking all ornamentation. > *noun* a person from Tuscany.

ORIGIN – Latin *Tuscanus*, from *Tuscus* 'an Etruscan'.

Tuscarora /tuskə**ror**ə/ > *noun* (pl. same or **Tuscaroras**) an American Indian people forming part of the Iroquois confederacy.

ORIGIN – the name in Iroquois.

tush¹ /tush/ > *exclamation* archaic or humorous expressing disapproval, impatience, or dismissal.

tush² /tush/ > *noun* a long pointed tooth, in particular a canine tooth of a male horse.

tush³ /tŏŏsh/ > *noun* informal, chiefly N. Amer. a person's buttocks.

ORIGIN – Yiddish *tokhes*, from a Hebrew word meaning 'beneath'.

tusk > *noun* a long, pointed tooth, especially one which protrudes from the closed mouth, as in the elephant, walrus, or wild boar.

DERIVATIVES – **tusked** *adjective*.

tusker > *noun* an elephant or wild boar with well-developed tusks.

tussle > *noun* a vigorous struggle or scuffle. > *verb* engage in a tussle.

SYNONYMS – brawl, fight, skirmish.

ORIGIN – perhaps from dialect *touse* 'handle roughly', the root also of **TOUSLE**.

tussock /**tuss**ək/ > *noun* a dense clump or tuft of grass.

DERIVATIVES – **tussocky** *adjective*.

COMBINATIONS – **tussock grass** a coarse grass which grows in tussocks.

tussore /**tuss**or, **tuss**ər/ > *noun* a strong but coarse kind of silk.

ORIGIN – Hindi, from a Sanskrit word meaning 'shuttle'.

tutee /tyŏŏ**tee**/ > *noun* a student or pupil of a tutor.

tutelage /**tyŏŏ**tilij/ > *noun* **1** protection of or authority over someone or something; guardianship. **2** instruction; tuition.

ORIGIN – from Latin *tutela* 'keeping', from *tueri* 'watch'.

tutelary /**tyŏŏ**tiləri/ (also **tutelar** /**tyŏŏ**tilər/) > *adjective* **1** serving as a protector, guardian, or patron. **2** relating to protection or a guardian.

tutor > *noun* **1** a private teacher, typically one who teaches a single pupil or a very small group. **2** chiefly Brit. a university or college teacher responsible for assigned students. **3** Brit. a book of instruction in a particular subject. > *verb* act as a tutor to.

SYNONYMS – educate, instruct, school, teach.

ORIGIN – Latin, from *tueri* 'to watch, guard'.

tutorial > *noun* **1** a period of tuition given by a university or college tutor. **2** an account or explanation of a subject, intended for private study. > *adjective* relating to a tutor or a tutor's tuition.

Tutsi /**tŏŏt**si/ > *noun* (pl. same or **Tutsis**) a member of a people forming a minority of the population of Rwanda and Burundi.

ORIGIN – a local name.

tutti /**tŏŏt**ti/ > *adverb & adjective* Music with all voices or instruments together.

ORIGIN – Italian, from *tutto* 'all', from Latin *totus*.

tutti-frutti /tŏŏti**frŏŏt**i/ > *noun* (pl. **tutti-fruttis**) a type of ice cream or confectionery containing mixed fruits.

ORIGIN – Italian, 'all fruits'.

tutu /**tŏŏt**ŏŏ/ > *noun* a female ballet dancer's costume consisting of a bodice and a very short, stiff attached skirt incorporating numerous layers of fabric and projecting horizontally from the waist.

ORIGIN – French, child's alteration of *cucu*, informal word for *cul* 'buttocks'.

Tuvaluan /tŏŏvə**lŏŏ**ən, tŏŏvə**lŏŏ**ən/ > *noun* a person from Tuvalu, a country made up of a number of islands in the SW Pacific. > *adjective* relating to Tuvalu.

tux > *noun* informal, chiefly N. Amer. a tuxedo.

tuxedo /tuk**see**dō/ > *noun* (pl. **tuxedos** or **tuxedoes**) chiefly N. Amer. **1** a man's dinner jacket. **2** a formal evening suit including such a jacket.

DERIVATIVES – **tuxedoed** *adjective*.

ORIGIN – from *Tuxedo Park*, the site of a country club in New York.

TV > *abbreviation* television.

TVP > *abbreviation* trademark textured vegetable protein.

twaddle > *noun* informal trivial or foolish speech or writing.

twain > *cardinal number* archaic term for **TWO**.

IDIOMS – **never the twain shall meet** the two things in question are too different to exist alongside each other. [ORIGIN – from Rudyard Kipling's 'Oh, East is East, and West is West, and never the twain shall meet' (*Barrack-room Ballads*, 1892).]

twang > *noun* **1** a strong ringing sound such as that made by the plucked string of a musical instrument or a released bowstring. **2** a distinctive nasal pronunciation characteristic of the speech of an individual or region. > *verb* make or cause to make a twang.

DERIVATIVES – **twangy** *adjective*.

'twas > *contraction* archaic or literary it was.

twat /twat, twot/ > *noun* vulgar slang **1** a woman's genitals. **2** a stupid or obnoxious person. > *verb* (**twatted**, **twatting**) Brit. informal hit; punch.

tweak > *verb* **1** twist or pull with a small but sharp movement. **2** informal improve by making fine adjustments. > *noun* an act of tweaking.

SYNONYMS – *verb* **1** jerk, tug, twitch.

twee > *adjective* Brit. excessively or affectedly quaint, pretty, or sentimental.

DERIVATIVES – **tweely** *adverb* **tweeness** *noun*.

ORIGIN – representing a child's pronunciation of SWEET.

tweed > *noun* **1** a rough-surfaced woollen cloth, typically of mixed flecked colours. **2** (**tweeds**) clothes made of tweed.

ORIGIN – a misreading of *tweel*, Scots form of TWILL, influenced by association with the river *Tweed*.

tweedy > *adjective* (**tweedier**, **tweediest**) **1** made of tweed cloth. **2** informal of a robust conservative or rural character.

DERIVATIVES – **tweediness** *noun*.

'tween > *contraction* archaic or literary between.

tweet > *noun* the chirp of a small or young bird. > *verb* make a chirping noise.

tweeter > *noun* a loudspeaker designed to reproduce high frequencies.

tweezers > *plural noun* (also **pair of tweezers**) a small instrument like a pair of pincers for plucking out hairs and picking up small objects.

ORIGIN – from obsolete *tweeze* 'case of surgical instruments'.

twelfth /twelfth/ > *ordinal number* **1** constituting number twelve in a sequence; 12th. **2** (**a twelfth** or **one twelfth**) each of twelve equal parts into which something is or may be divided. **3** Music an interval spanning an octave and a fifth in the diatonic scale. **4** (**the** (**Glorious**) **Twelfth**) (in the UK) 12 August, the day on which the grouse-shooting season begins.

DERIVATIVES – **twelfthly** *adverb*.

COMBINATIONS – **twelfth man** Cricket a player acting as a reserve in a game. **Twelfth Night 1** 6 January, the feast of the Epiphany. **2** the evening of 5 January, formerly the twelfth and last day of Christmas festivities.

twelve > *cardinal number* two more than ten; 12. (Roman numeral: **xii** or **XII**.)

WORDFINDER – dodecagon (*plane figure with twelve straight sides and angles*), dodecahedron (*three-dimensional shape with twelve faces*), duodecimal (*relating to a counting system based on twelve*), gross (*twelve dozen, 144*).

COMBINATIONS – **twelvemonth** archaic a year. **twelve-note** (also **twelve-tone**) (of musical composition) using the twelve chromatic notes of the octave on an equal basis without dependence on a key system, a technique central to serialism.

---

wordpower facts

Twelve

Twelve is an Old English word that was formed from the base of **two** and a second element, probably expressing the sense 'left over', that also occurs in **eleven**. The base of **two**, *twi-*, is the source of many English words that begin with *twi*, including some that appear to have no connection with 'two'. Predictable ones include **twice** and **twin**. Among the less obvious words are **twilight**: here *twi-* is probably used in the sense 'between', a word which itself is related to **two**. Also derived from *twi-* are **twill**, **twine**, and **twist**. The link between these words and 'two' is the idea of thread being made from two or more strands twisted together.

---

twenty > *cardinal number* (pl. **twenties**) ten less than thirty; 20. (Roman numeral: **xx** or **XX**.)

WORDFINDER – icosahedron (*three-dimensional shape having twenty faces*), score (*group or set of twenty*), vigesimal (*relating to the number twenty*).

DERIVATIVES – **twentieth** *ordinal number*.

COMBINATIONS – **twenty-twenty** (also **20/20**) (of vision) of normal sharpness. [ORIGIN – with reference to the fraction for normal sharpness of vision in eyesight tests.]

'twere > *contraction* archaic or literary it were.

twerp > *noun* informal a silly or annoying person.

twice > *adverb* **1** two times. **2** double in degree or quantity.

twiddle > *verb* play or fiddle with (something) in a purposeless or nervous way. > *noun* **1** an act of twiddling. **2** a rapid or intricate series of musical notes.

IDIOMS – **twiddle one's thumbs** be idle; have nothing to do.

DERIVATIVES – **twiddler** *noun* **twiddly** *adjective*.

twig[1] > *noun* a slender woody shoot growing from a branch or stem of a tree or shrub.

DERIVATIVES – **twigged** *adjective* **twiggy** *adjective*.

twig[2] > *verb* (**twigged**, **twigging**) Brit. informal come to understand or realise something.

twilight > *noun* **1** the soft glowing light from the sky when the sun is not far below the horizon, especially after sunset. **2** a period or state of obscurity or gradual decline: *the twilight of his career*.

COMBINATIONS – **twilight zone 1** an undefined, ambiguous, or intermediate state or area. **2** a dilapidated urban area.

ORIGIN – from Old English *twi-* 'two'

(probably here meaning 'between') + LIGHT[1].

twilit > *adjective* dimly illuminated by or as if by twilight.

twill > *noun* a fabric so woven as to have a surface of diagonal parallel ridges.

DERIVATIVES – **twilled** *adjective*.

'twill > *contraction* archaic or literary it will.

twin > *noun* **1** one of two children or animals born at the same birth. **2** something containing or consisting of two matching or corresponding parts. > *adjective* forming or being one of a pair of twins or matching things. > *verb* (**twinned**, **twinning**) **1** link or combine as a pair. **2** Brit. link (a town) with another in a different country, for the purposes of cultural exchange.

WORDFINDER – dizygotic (*denoting non-identical twins, derived from two separate ova*), monozygotic (*denoting identical twins, derived from one ovum*); Gemini (*constellation and zodiac sign, the Twins*).

SYNONYMS – *noun* **2** counterpart, double, duplicate, match. *adjective* identical, matching, paired. *verb* **1** couple, match, yoke.

COMBINATIONS – **twin-tub** a type of washing machine having two top-loading drums, one for washing and the other for spin-drying.

twine > *noun* strong thread or string consisting of strands of hemp or cotton twisted together. > *verb* wind round something.

twinge > *noun* **1** a sudden, sharp localised pain. **2** a brief, sharp pang of emotion. > *verb* (**twinged**, **twingeing** or **twinging**) suffer a twinge.

twinkle > *verb* **1** (of a star or light) shine with a gleam that changes constantly from bright to faint. **2** (of a person's eyes) sparkle with amusement or vivacity. **3** move lightly and rapidly. > *noun* a twinkling sparkle or gleam.

IDIOMS – **in a twinkling** (**of an eye**) in an instant.

DERIVATIVES – **twinkly** *adjective*.

SYNONYMS – *verb* **1,2** glimmer, glitter, sparkle. *noun* glint, glitter, shimmer.

twinset > *noun* chiefly Brit. a woman's matching cardigan and jumper.

twirl > *verb* spin quickly and lightly round. > *noun* **1** an act of twirling. **2** a spiralling or swirling shape, especially a flourish made with a pen.

DERIVATIVES – **twirler** *noun* **twirly** *adjective*.

SYNONYMS – *verb* gyrate, pirouette, whirl.

twist > *verb* **1** form into a bent, curled, or distorted shape. **2** force out of the natural position by a twisting action: *he twisted his ankle*. **3** turn or bend round or into a different direction. **4** take or have a winding course. **5** distort or misrepresent the meaning of. **6** (**twisted**) unpleasantly or unhealthily abnormal. **7** Brit. informal cheat; defraud. **8** dance the twist. **9** (in pontoon) request, deal, or be dealt a card face upwards. > *noun* **1** an act or instance of twisting. **2** a thing with a spiral shape. **3** Brit. a paper packet with twisted ends. **4** force producing twisting; torque. **5** a new or unexpected development or treatment. **6** a fine strong thread consisting of twisted fibres. **7** a carpet with a tightly curled pile. **8** (**the twist**) a dance with a twisting movement of the body, popular in the 1960s.

IDIOMS – **round the twist** Brit. informal crazy. **twist someone's arm** informal forcefully persuade someone to do something that they are reluctant to do.

DERIVATIVES – **twisty** *adjective*.

SYNONYMS – *verb* **1** bend, curl, distort. **3** rotate, spin, swivel. **4** curve, meander, weave. **5** falsify, pervert, warp. *noun* **1** spin, turn, twirl.

twister informal > *noun* **1** Brit. a swindler or dishonest person. **2** N. Amer. a tornado.

twit[1] > *noun* informal, chiefly Brit. a silly or foolish person.

DERIVATIVES – **twittish** *adjective*.

ORIGIN – a dialect word, first meaning 'tale-bearer'.

twit[2] > *verb* (**twitted, twitting**) informal tease (someone) good-humouredly.

twitch > *verb* make a short, sudden jerking movement. > *noun* **1** a twitching movement. **2** a pang: *he felt a twitch of annoyance.*

SYNONYMS – *verb* convulse, jerk, spasm. *noun* **1** convulsion, jerk, spasm.

twitcher > *noun* Brit. informal a birdwatcher devoted to spotting rare birds.

twitchy > *adjective* (**twitchier, twitchiest**) **1** informal nervous. **2** given to twitching.

twite /twīt/ > *noun* a moorland finch with streaky brown plumage and a pink rump.

twitter > *verb* **1** (of a bird) make a series of high-pitched chattering sounds. **2** talk rapidly in a nervous or trivial way. > *noun* **1** a twittering sound. **2** informal an agitated or excited state.

DERIVATIVES – **twittery** *adjective*.

SYNONYMS – *verb* **2** babble, jabber, prattle.

'twixt > *contraction* betwixt.

twizzle informal or dialect > *verb* spin around. > *noun* a twisting or spinning movement.

two > *cardinal number* one less than three; 2. (Roman numeral: **ii** or **II**.)

WORDFINDER – à deux (*for or involving two people*), biennial (*taking place every two years*), bifurcate (*divide into two branches or forks*), binary (*composed of or involving two things*), bisect (*divide into two parts*), dichotomy (*separation or contrast between two things*), dual (*consisting of two parts, elements, or aspects*),

dyad (*something consisting of two elements or parts*).

IDIOMS – **put two and two together** draw an obvious conclusion from what is known or evident. **two by two** (or **two and two**) side by side in pairs. **two-horse race** a contest in which only two of the competitors are likely winners. **two's company, three's a crowd** proverb the presence of a third person is not welcomed by two lovers. **two heads are better than one** proverb it's helpful to have the advice or opinion of a second person.

DERIVATIVES – **twofold** *adjective & adverb*.

COMBINATIONS – **two-bit** N. Amer. informal insignificant, cheap, or worthless. **two-by-four** a length of wood with a rectangular cross section measuring two inches by four inches. **two-dimensional 1** having or appearing to have length and breadth but no depth. **2** lacking depth; superficial. **two-faced** insincere and deceitful. **two-piece** consisting of two matching items. **two shot** a cinema or television shot of two people together. **two-step** a round dance with a sliding step in march or polka time. **two-stroke** (of an internal-combustion engine) having its power cycle completed in one up-and-down movement of the piston. **two-up** (in Australia and New Zealand) a gambling game in which two coins are tossed in the air and bets are laid as to whether both will fall heads or tails uppermost. **two-up two-down** Brit. informal a house with two reception rooms downstairs and two bedrooms upstairs.

twoc /twok/ > *verb* (**twocced, twoccing**) Brit. informal steal (a car).

ORIGIN – police slang: acronym from *taken without owner's consent*.

twopence /tuppənss/ (also **tuppence**) > *noun* Brit. **1** the sum of two pence, especially before decimalisation (1971). **2** informal anything at all: *he didn't care twopence.*

twopenn'orth /toopennərth/ > *noun* an amount that is worth or costs twopence; a very small amount.

IDIOMS – **add** (or **put in**) **one's twopenn'orth** informal contribute one's opinion.

twopenny /tuppəni/ (also **tuppenny**) > *adjective* Brit. costing two pence, especially before decimalisation (1971).

COMBINATIONS – **twopenny-halfpenny** Brit. informal insignificant or worthless.

twosome > *noun* a pair of people or things considered together.

two-time > *verb* informal be unfaithful to (a lover or husband or wife).

'twould > *contraction* archaic it would.

two-way > *adjective* **1** involving movement or communication in opposite directions. **2**

(of a switch) permitting a current to be switched on or off from either of two points.

COMBINATIONS – **two-way mirror** a panel of glass that can be seen through from one side and is a mirror on the other. **two-way street** a situation involving mutual or reciprocal action or obligation.

TX > *abbreviation* Texas.

-ty[1] > *suffix* forming nouns denoting quality or condition such as *beauty*.

ORIGIN – from Latin *-tas*.

-ty[2] > *suffix* denoting specified groups of ten: *forty*.

tycoon > *noun* a wealthy, powerful person in business or industry.

SYNONYMS – baron, captain of industry, magnate.

ORIGIN – Japanese, 'great lord': a title applied by foreigners to the shogun of Japan.

tying present participle of TIE.

tyke (also **tike**) > *noun* **1** informal a small child, especially a mischievous one. **2** a dog, especially a mongrel. **3** Brit. informal a person from Yorkshire.

ORIGIN – Old Norse, 'bitch'.

tympani > *plural noun* variant spelling of TIMPANI.

tympanum /timpənəm/ > *noun* (pl. **tympanums** or **tympana** /timpənə/) **1** Anatomy & Zoology the eardrum. **2** Architecture a vertical recessed triangular space forming the centre of a pediment or over a door.

DERIVATIVES – **tympanic** *adjective*.

ORIGIN – Greek *tumpanon* 'drum'.

Tynwald /tinwəld/ > *noun* the parliament of the Isle of Man.

ORIGIN – Old Norse, 'place of assembly'.

type > *noun* **1** a category of people or things having common characteristics. **2** a person or thing symbolising or exemplifying the defining characteristics of something. **3** informal a person of a specified character or nature: *a sporty type*. **4** printed characters or letters. **5** pieces of metal with raised letters or characters on their upper surface, for use in letterpress printing. > *verb* **1** write using a typewriter or word processor. **2** Medicine determine the type to which (a person or their blood or tissue) belongs.

DERIVATIVES – **typing** *noun*.

SYNONYMS – *noun* **1** category, class, kind, sort, variety. **2** archetype, exemplar, model, quintessence.

ORIGIN – Greek *tupos* 'impression, figure, type'.

typecast > *verb* (past and past participle **typecast**) (usu. **be typecast**) **1** repeatedly cast (an actor) in the same type of role because their appearance is appropriate or they are known for such roles. **2** regard as fitting a stereotype.

typeface > *noun* Printing a particular design of type.

typescript > *noun* a typed copy of a text.

typeset > *verb* (**typesetting**; past and past participle **typeset**) arrange or generate the type for (text to be printed).
DERIVATIVES – **typesetter** *noun* **typesetting** *noun*.

typewriter > *noun* an electric, electronic, or manual machine with keys for producing print-like characters.
DERIVATIVES – **typewriting** *noun* **typewritten** *adjective*.

typhoid (also **typhoid fever**) > *noun* an infectious bacterial fever with an eruption of red spots on the chest and abdomen and severe intestinal irritation.
ORIGIN – from **TYPHUS**.

typhoon /tīfoon/ > *noun* a tropical storm in the region of the Indian or western Pacific oceans.
ORIGIN – partly from Arabic, partly from a Chinese dialect word meaning 'big wind'.

typhus /tīfəss/ > *noun* an infectious bacterial disease characterised by a purple rash, headaches, fever, and usually delirium.
ORIGIN – Greek *tuphos* 'smoke, stupor'.

typical > *adjective* **1** having the distinctive qualities of a particular type. **2** characteristic of a particular person or thing.
DERIVATIVES – **typicality** *noun* **typically** *adverb*.
SYNONYMS – **1** distinctive, distinguishing, particular. **2** characteristic, normal, usual.
ANTONYMS – atypical.

typify > *verb* (**typifies**, **typified**) be typical or representative of.
DERIVATIVES – **typification** *noun*.
SYNONYMS – epitomise, exemplify, represent.

typist > *noun* a person skilled in typing, especially one employed for this purpose.

typo /tīpō/ > *noun* (pl. **typos**) informal a typographical error.

typography /tīpogrəfi/ > *noun* **1** the art or process of setting and arranging types and printing from them. **2** the style and appearance of printed matter.
DERIVATIVES – **typographer** *noun*

typographic *adjective* **typographical** *adjective* **typographically** *adverb*.

typology /tīpolləji/ > *noun* (pl. **typologies**) **1** a classification according to general type. **2** the study and interpretation of types and symbols.
DERIVATIVES – **typological** *adjective* **typologist** *noun*.

tyrannical > *adjective* ruling as or behaving like a tyrant.
DERIVATIVES – **tyrannically** *adverb*.
SYNONYMS – autocratic, despotic, dictatorial, oppressive.

tyrannicide /tirannisīd, tī-/ > *noun* **1** the killing of a tyrant. **2** the killer of a tyrant.
DERIVATIVES – **tyrannicidal** *adjective*.

tyrannise /tirrənīz/ (also **tyrannize**) > *verb* rule or treat despotically or cruelly.

tyrannosaurus /tirannəsorəss/ (also **tyrannosaurus rex**, **tyrannosaur** /ti-rannəsor/) > *noun* a very large carnivorous dinosaur with powerful jaws and small claw-like front legs.
ORIGIN – Latin, from Greek *turannos* 'tyrant' + *sauros* 'lizard' (+ Latin *rex* 'king').

tyranny* /tirrəni/ > *noun* (pl. **tyrannies**) **1** the rule of a tyrant; cruel and oppressive government. **2** a state under such rule. **3** cruel and arbitrary exercise of power or control.
DERIVATIVES – **tyrannous** *adjective*.
*SPELLING – one *r*, two *ns* : ty*ra*nny.
SYNONYMS – **1** despotism, totalitarianism.

tyrant > *noun* **1** a cruel and oppressive ruler. **2** a person exercising power or control in a cruel and arbitrary way. **3** (especially in ancient Greece) a ruler who seized absolute power without legal right.
SYNONYMS – **1,2** autocrat, despot, dictator.
ORIGIN – Greek *turannos*.

tyre (US **tire**) > *noun* **1** a rubber covering, typically inflated or surrounding an inflated inner tube, placed round a wheel to form a soft contact with the road. **2** a strengthening band of metal fitted around the rim of a wheel, especially of a railway vehicle.
COMBINATIONS – **tyre gauge** a portable pressure gauge for measuring the air pressure in a tyre.

wordpower facts

Tyre

The word **tyre** first referred collectively to the curved pieces of iron plate with which cart and carriage wheels were reinforced. The word is probably derived, rather punningly, from **attire**, because the tyre was the 'clothing' of the wheel. The original spelling, from the late 15th century, was either **tyre** or **tire**: by about 1700 **tyre** had fallen out of use and been replaced by **tire**, which was the form taken to America by settlers. In Britain the spelling **tyre** was revived at the end of the 18th century and applied to new kinds of tyre, first to metal tyres fitted to the wheels of railway vehicles and then to pneumatic tyres for early bicycles and cars.

Tyrian purple /tirriən/ > *noun* a crimson dye obtained from some molluscs, used for robes worn by an emperor or senior magistrate in ancient Rome or Byzantium.
ORIGIN – from the name of *Tyre*, a former Phoenician port now in southern Lebanon.

tyro /tīrō/ (also **tiro**) > *noun* (pl. **tyros**) a beginner or novice.
ORIGIN – Latin, 'recruit'.

tyrosine /tīrəseen/ > *noun* Biochemistry an amino acid which is a constituent of most proteins and is important in the production of some hormones.
ORIGIN – from Greek *turos* 'cheese'.

tzar etc. variant spelling of **TSAR** etc.

tzatziki /tsatseeki/ > *noun* a Greek side dish of yogurt with cucumber, garlic, and often mint.
ORIGIN – Greek.

tzigane /tsigaan/ > *noun* (pl. same or **tziganes**) a Hungarian gypsy.
ORIGIN – Hungarian.

U¹ /yoō/ (also **u**) > *noun* (pl. **Us** or **U's**) the twenty-first letter of the alphabet.

COMBINATIONS – **U-bend** a section of a pipe, in particular of a waste pipe, shaped like a U. **U-lock** another term for **D-lock**.

U² /yoō/ > *abbreviation* **1** (in names of sports clubs) United. **2** Brit. universal (denoting films classified as suitable without restriction). > *symbol* the chemical element uranium.

U³ /yoō/ > *adjective* informal, chiefly Brit. characteristic of or appropriate to the upper social classes.

ORIGIN – abbreviation of **upper class**; coined in 1954 by Alan S. C. Ross, a professor of linguistics, and popularised by Nancy Mitford's *Noblesse Oblige* (1956).

U⁴ /ōō/ > *noun* a Burmese title of respect before a man's name, equivalent to Mr.

UAE > *abbreviation* United Arab Emirates.

Übermensch /ōōbərmensh/ > *noun* the ideal superior man of the future who could rise above conventional Christian morality to create and impose his own values, originally described by Nietzsche in *Thus Spake Zarathustra* (1883–5).

ORIGIN – German, 'superhuman person'.

ubiquitous /yoōbikwitəss/ > *adjective* present, appearing, or found everywhere.

DERIVATIVES – **ubiquitously** *adverb* **ubiquitousness** *noun* **ubiquity** *noun*.

SYNONYMS – ever-present, omnipresent, universal.

ORIGIN – from Latin *ubique* 'everywhere'.

U-boat > *noun* a German submarine of the First or Second World War.

ORIGIN – German *U-boot*, abbreviation of *Unterseeboot* 'undersea boat'.

UBR > *abbreviation* uniform business rate (a tax on business property in England and Wales).

UCAS /yoōkass/ > *abbreviation* (in the UK) Universities and Colleges Admissions Service.

UDA > *abbreviation* Ulster Defence Association.

udder > *noun* the mammary gland of female cattle, sheep, goats, horses, etc., hanging near the hind legs as a bag-like organ with two or more teats.

DERIVATIVES – **uddered** *adjective*.

UDI > *abbreviation* unilateral declaration of independence.

UDR > *abbreviation* Ulster Defence Regiment.

UEFA /yoōeefə, -ayfə/ > *abbreviation* Union of European Football Associations.

UFO > *noun* (pl. **UFOs**) a mysterious object seen in the sky for which it is claimed no orthodox scientific explanation can be found, popularly said to be a vehicle carrying extraterrestrials.

DERIVATIVES – **ufologist** /yoofolləjist/ *noun* **ufology** *noun*.

ORIGIN – abbreviation of *unidentified flying object*.

Ugandan /yoōgandən/ > *noun* a person from Uganda. > *adjective* relating to Uganda.

ugli fruit /ugli/ > *noun* (pl. same) trademark a mottled green and yellow citrus fruit which is a hybrid of a grapefruit and tangerine.

ORIGIN – alteration of *ugly fruit*.

ugly > *adjective* (**uglier**, **ugliest**) **1** unpleasant or repulsive in appearance. **2** hostile or threatening; likely to involve unpleasantness: *the mood in the room turned ugly.*

DERIVATIVES – **uglify** *verb* **ugliness** *noun*.

SYNONYMS – **1** hideous, ill-favoured, unsightly. **2** hostile, menacing, ominous, threatening.

ANTONYMS – **1** beautiful.

COMBINATIONS – **ugly duckling** a person who turns out to be beautiful or talented against all expectations. [ORIGIN – from the title of one of Hans Christian Andersen's fairy tales, in which the 'ugly duckling' becomes a swan.]

ORIGIN – from Old Norse *uggligr* 'to be dreaded'.

UHF > *abbreviation* ultra-high frequency.

uhlan /ōōlaan/ > *noun* historical (in various European armies) a cavalryman armed with a lance.

ORIGIN – Turkish *oğlan* 'youth, servant'.

UHT > *abbreviation* ultra heat treated (a process used to extend the shelf life of milk).

uillean pipes /illin/ > *plural noun* Irish bagpipes played using bellows worked by the elbow.

ORIGIN – from Irish *píob uilleann* 'pipe of the elbow'.

UK > *abbreviation* United Kingdom.

ukase /yoōkayz/ > *noun* **1** (in tsarist Russia) a decree with the force of law. **2** an arbitrary or peremptory command.

ORIGIN – Russian, 'ordinance, edict'.

ukiyo-e /ōōkeeyō-ay/ > *noun* a school of Japanese art depicting subjects from everyday life.

ORIGIN – Japanese, from words meaning 'fleeting world' and 'picture'.

Ukrainian /yoōkrayniən/ > *noun* **1** a person from Ukraine. **2** the language of Ukraine. > *adjective* relating to Ukraine or its language.

ukulele* /yoōkəlayli/ > *noun* a small four-stringed guitar of Hawaiian origin.

*SPELLING – the spelling is *uku-*, not *uke-*: uk*u*lele.

ORIGIN – Hawaiian, 'jumping flea'.

ulcer > *noun* an open sore on the body, caused by a break in the skin or mucous membrane which fails to heal.

DERIVATIVES – **ulcered** *adjective* **ulcerous** *adjective*.

ORIGIN – Latin *ulcus*.

ulcerate > *verb* develop into or become affected by an ulcer.

DERIVATIVES – **ulceration** *noun* **ulcerative** *adjective*.

-ule > *suffix* forming diminutive nouns such as *capsule*.

ORIGIN – from Latin *-ulus, -ula, -ulum*.

ullage /ullij/ > *noun* **1** the amount by which a container falls short of being full. **2** loss of liquid by evaporation or leakage.

ORIGIN – from Old French *euillier* 'fill up', from Latin *oculus* 'eye' (with reference to a container's bunghole).

ulna /ulnə/ > *noun* (pl. **ulnae** /ulnee/ or **ulnas**) a bone of the forearm or forelimb, in humans the thinner and longer of two.

DERIVATIVES – **ulnar** *adjective*.

ORIGIN – Latin; related to ELL.

ulster > *noun* a man's long, loose overcoat of rough cloth.

ORIGIN – from the former province of *Ulster* in Ireland, where such coats were originally sold.

Ulsterman (or **Ulsterwoman**) > *noun* a person from Ulster.

ulterior > *adjective* **1** other than what is obvious or admitted: *she had some ulterior motive in coming.* **2** beyond what is immediate or present.

SYNONYMS – **1** hidden, private, underlying.

ANTONYMS – overt.

ORIGIN – Latin, 'further, more distant'.

ultimate > *adjective* **1** being or happening at the end of a process. **2** being the best or most extreme example of its kind: *the ultimate accolade.* **3** basic or fundamental. > *noun* **1** (**the ultimate**) the best achievable or imaginable of its kind. **2** a final or fundamental fact or principle.

DERIVATIVES – **ultimacy** *noun* **ultimately** *adverb*.

SYNONYMS – *adjective* **1** final. **2** greatest, paramount, supreme. **3** basic, elementary, fundamental, primary.

ORIGIN – Latin *ultimatus*, from *ultimare* 'come to an end'.

ultima Thule /ultime tōōlee/ > *noun* a distant unknown region; the extreme limit of travel and discovery.

ORIGIN – Latin, 'furthest Thule', a country to the north of Britain (probably Norway) believed by ancient Greeks and Romans to be the northernmost part of the world.

ultimatum /ultimaytəm/ > *noun* (pl. **ultimatums** or **ultimata** /ultimaytə/) a final demand or statement of terms, the rejection of which will result in retaliation or a breakdown in relations.

ORIGIN – Latin, 'thing that has come to an end'.

ultra informal > *adverb* very. > *noun* an extremist.

ultra- > *prefix* **1** beyond; on the other side of: *ultramontane*. **2** extreme; to an extreme degree: *ultramicroscopic*.

ORIGIN – from Latin *ultra* 'beyond'.

ultra-high frequency > *noun* a radio frequency in the range 300 to 3,000 megahertz.

ultramarine /ultrəmərreen/ > *noun* **1** a brilliant deep blue pigment originally obtained from lapis lazuli. **2** a brilliant deep blue colour.

ORIGIN – from obsolete Italian *azzurro oltramarino* 'azure from overseas' (because the lapis lazuli was imported), from Latin *ultramarinus* 'beyond the sea'.

ultramicroscope > *noun* an optical microscope used to detect very small particles by observing light scattered from them.

ultramicroscopic > *adjective* **1** too small to be seen by an ordinary optical microscope. **2** relating to an ultramicroscope.

ultramontane /ultrəmontayn/ > *adjective* **1** advocating supreme papal authority in matters of faith and discipline. **2** situated on the other side of the Alps from the point of view of the speaker. > *noun* an advocate of supreme papal authority.

DERIVATIVES – **ultramontanism** noun.

ORIGIN – from Latin *ultra* 'beyond' + *mons* 'mountain': originally referring to a representative of the Roman Catholic Church north of the Alps.

ultrasonic > *adjective* involving sound waves with a frequency above the upper limit of human hearing.

DERIVATIVES – **ultrasonically** adverb.

ultrasonics > *plural noun* **1** (treated as sing.) the science and application of ultrasonic waves. **2** (treated as sing. or pl.) ultrasound.

ultrasound > *noun* sound or other vibrations having an ultrasonic frequency.

ultraviolet > *noun* electromagnetic radiation having a wavelength just shorter than that of violet light but longer than that of X-rays. > *adjective* of or relating to such radiation.

ultra vires /ultrə vīreez/ > *adjective & adverb* Law beyond one's legal power or authority.

ORIGIN – Latin, 'beyond the powers'.

ululate /yōōlyoolayt, ul-/ > *verb* howl or wail.

DERIVATIVES – **ululation** noun.

ORIGIN – Latin *ululare* 'howl, shriek'.

umbel /umb'l/ > *noun* Botany a flower cluster in which stalks spring from a common centre and form a flat or curved surface.

DERIVATIVES – **umbellate** adjective.

ORIGIN – Latin *umbella* 'sunshade'.

umbellifer /umbellifər/ > *noun* Botany a plant of the parsley family (Umbelliferae).

DERIVATIVES – **umbelliferous** adjective.

umber /umbər/ > *noun* a natural pigment, normally dark yellowish-brown in colour (**raw umber**) or dark brown when roasted (**burnt umber**).

ORIGIN – French *ombre* or Italian *ombra* 'shadow'.

umbilical /umbillik'l, umbilīk'l/ > *adjective* relating to or affecting the navel or umbilical cord.

DERIVATIVES – **umbilically** adverb.

COMBINATIONS – **umbilical cord** a flexible cord-like structure containing blood vessels, attaching a fetus to the placenta during gestation.

umbilicus /umbillikəss, umbilīkəss/ > *noun* (pl. **umbilici** /umbillisī, umbilīsī/ or **umbiliuses**) **1** Anatomy the navel. **2** Zoology a central cavity in the whorl of some gastropod molluscs and many ammonites.

ORIGIN – Latin.

umbra /umbrə/ > *noun* (pl. **umbras** or **umbrae** /umbree/) the fully shaded inner region of a shadow, especially the area on the earth or moon experiencing totality in an eclipse.

DERIVATIVES – **umbral** adjective.

ORIGIN – Latin, 'shade'.

umbrage /umbrij/ > *noun* (usu. in phrase **take umbrage**) offence or annoyance.

DERIVATIVES – **umbrageous** adjective.

ORIGIN – from Latin *umbra* 'shade': an early sense was 'shadowy outline', giving rise to 'ground for suspicion', whence the current notion of 'offence'.

umbrella > *noun* **1** a device consisting of a circular fabric canopy on a folding metal frame supported by a central rod, used as protection against rain. **2** a protecting force or influence. **3** (before another noun) including or containing many different parts: *an umbrella organisation*.

ORIGIN – Italian *ombrella*, from *ombra* 'shade'.

Umbrian /umbriən/ > *noun* a person from Umbria, a region of central Italy. > *adjective* relating to Umbria.

umlaut /ōōmlowt/ > *noun* Linguistics a mark (¨) used over a vowel, especially in German, to indicate a different vowel quality.

ORIGIN – German, from *um* 'about' + *Laut* 'sound'.

umma /ōōmə/ (also **ummah**) > *noun* the whole community of Muslims bound together by ties of religion.

ORIGIN – Arabic, 'people, community'.

umph > *noun* variant spelling of OOMPH.

umpire > *noun* **1** (in certain sports) an official who enforces the rules of a game and settles disputes arising from the play. **2** a person chosen to settle a dispute between contending parties. > *verb* act as an umpire.

ORIGIN – first as *noumpere*: from Old French *nonper* 'not equal'.

umpteen > *cardinal number* informal indefinitely many.

DERIVATIVES – **umpteenth** ordinal number.

UN > *abbreviation* United Nations.

un-¹ > *prefix* **1** (added to adjectives, participles, and their derivatives) denoting the absence of a quality or state; not: *unacademic*. **2** the reverse of: *unselfish*. **3** (added to nouns) a lack of: *untruth*.

USAGE – the prefixes **un-** and **non-** both mean 'not', but tend to be used with a difference of emphasis, **un-** being stronger and less neutral than **non-**. Compare, for example, **non-christian**, which means simply 'not Christian', and **unchristian**, which usually carries bad connotations and can mean 'ungenerous or unfair'.

un-² > *prefix* added to verbs: **1** denoting the reversal or cancellation of an action or state: *unsettle*. **2** denoting deprivation, separation, or reduction to a lesser state: *unmask*. **3** denoting release: *unhand*.

'un > *contraction* informal one.

unabashed > *adjective* not embarrassed, disconcerted, or ashamed.

DERIVATIVES – **unabashedly** adverb.

unabated > *adjective* without any reduction in intensity or strength.

DERIVATIVES – **unabatedly** adverb.

unable > *adjective* lacking the skill, means, or opportunity to do something.

SYNONYMS – inadequate, incapable, ineffectual.

unabridged > *adjective* (of a text) not cut or shortened; complete.

unaccented > *adjective* having no accent, stress, or emphasis.

unacceptable > *adjective* not satisfactory or allowable.

DERIVATIVES – **unacceptability** noun **unacceptably** adverb.

unaccompanied > *adjective* **1** having no companion or escort. **2** without instrumental accompaniment. **3** without something occurring at the same time.

unaccountable > *adjective* **1** unable to be explained. **2** not responsible for or required to justify consequences.

DERIVATIVES – **unaccountability** *noun* **unaccountably** *adverb*.

SYNONYMS – **1** inexplicable, incomprehensible, unfathomable.

unaccounted > *adjective* (**unaccounted for**) not taken into consideration or explained.

unaccustomed > *adjective* **1** not customary; unusual. **2** (**unaccustomed to**) not familiar with or used to.

DERIVATIVES – **unaccustomedly** *adverb*.

unacknowledged > *adjective* **1** existing or having taken place but not accepted or admitted to. **2** deserving but not receiving recognition.

unacquainted > *adjective* **1** (**unacquainted with**) having no experience of or familiarity with. **2** not having met before.

unadjusted > *adjective* (especially of statistics) not adjusted or refined.

unadopted > *adjective* Brit. (of a road) not taken over for maintenance by a local authority.

unadulterated > *adjective* **1** having no inferior added substances. **2** complete; utter: *pure, unadulterated jealousy.*

unadventurous > *adjective* not offering, involving, or eager for new or stimulating things.

DERIVATIVES – **unadventurously** *adverb*.

unadvisable > *adjective* another term for INADVISABLE.

unadvisedly > *adverb* in an unwise or rash manner.

unaffected > *adjective* **1** feeling or showing no effects. **2** sincere and genuine.

DERIVATIVES – **unaffectedly** *adverb* **unaffectedness** *noun*.

SYNONYMS – **1** unaltered, unchanged. **2** frank, honest, natural, unassuming, unfeigned.

unaffiliated > *adjective* not officially attached to or connected with an organisation.

unaffordable > *adjective* too expensive to be afforded by the average person.

unafraid > *adjective* feeling no fear.

unaided > *adjective* needing or having no assistance.

unalienable > *adjective* another term for INALIENABLE.

unaligned > *adjective* **1** not placed or arranged in a straight line or in correct relative positions. **2** not allied with or supporting an organisation or cause.

unalike > *adjective* differing from each other.

unalloyed > *adjective* **1** (of metal) not alloyed. **2** complete and unreserved.

unalterable > *adjective* not able to be changed.

DERIVATIVES – **unalterably** *adverb*.

unaltered > *adjective* remaining the same.

unambiguous > *adjective* without ambiguity.

DERIVATIVES – **unambiguously** *adverb*.

unambitious > *adjective* **1** not motivated by a strong desire to succeed. **2** not involving anything new, exciting, or demanding.

un-American > *adjective* **1** not in accordance with American characteristics. **2** US, chiefly historical against the interests of the US and therefore treasonable.

unanimous /yoonannimoss/ > *adjective* **1** fully in agreement. **2** (of an opinion, decision, or vote) held or carried by everyone involved.

DERIVATIVES – **unanimity** /yoononimmiti/ *noun* **unanimously** *adverb*.

ORIGIN – Latin *unanimus*, from *unus* 'one' + *animus* 'mind'.

unannounced > *adjective* **1** not publicised. **2** without warning; unexpected.

unanswerable > *adjective* **1** unable to be answered. **2** unable to be refuted.

DERIVATIVES – **unanswerably** *adverb*.

unanswered > *adjective* not answered or responded to.

unapologetic > *adjective* not acknowledging or expressing regret.

DERIVATIVES – **unapologetically** *adverb*.

unappealing > *adjective* not inviting or attractive.

DERIVATIVES – **unappealingly** *adverb*.

unappetising (also **unappetizing**) > *adjective* not inviting or attractive.

DERIVATIVES – **unappetisingly** *adverb*.

unappreciated > *adjective* not fully understood, recognised, or valued.

unappreciative > *adjective* not fully understanding or recognising something.

unapproachable > *adjective* **1** not welcoming or friendly. **2** archaic (of a place) remote and inaccessible.

unapproved > *adjective* not officially accepted or sanctioned.

unarguable > *adjective* **1** not open to disagreement; certain. **2** not able to be argued.

DERIVATIVES – **unarguably** *adverb*.

unarmed > *adjective* not equipped with or carrying weapons.

unashamed > *adjective* feeling or showing no guilt or embarrassment.

DERIVATIVES – **unashamedly** *adverb*.

unasked > *adjective* **1** (of a question) not asked. **2** (often **unasked for**) not requested or sought.

unassailable > *adjective* unable to be attacked, questioned, or defeated.

DERIVATIVES – **unassailability** *noun* **unassailably** *adverb*.

unassertive > *adjective* not having or showing a confident and forceful personality.

unassisted > *adjective* not helped by anyone or anything.

unassociated > *adjective* not connected or associated.

unassuming > *adjective* not pretentious or arrogant.

DERIVATIVES – **unassumingly** *adverb*.

SYNONYMS – diffident, modest, self-effacing.

unattached > *adjective* **1** not working for or belonging to a particular organisation. **2** without a husband or wife or established lover.

unattainable > *adjective* not able to be reached or achieved.

DERIVATIVES – **unattainably** *adverb*.

unattended > *adjective* **1** not dealt with. **2** not looked after.

unattractive > *adjective* not pleasing, appealing, or inviting.

DERIVATIVES – **unattractively** *adverb* **unattractiveness** *noun*.

SYNONYMS – plain, ugly, unsightly.

unattributed > *adjective* (of a quotation, story, or work of art) of unknown or unpublished origin.

DERIVATIVES – **unattributable** *adjective*.

unauthorised (also **unauthorized**) > *adjective* not having official permission or approval.

unavailable > *adjective* **1** not at someone's disposal. **2** not free to do something.

DERIVATIVES – **unavailability** *noun*.

unavailing > *adjective* achieving little or nothing.

DERIVATIVES – **unavailingly** *adverb*.

unavoidable > *adjective* not able to be avoided or prevented; inevitable.

DERIVATIVES – **unavoidability** *noun* **unavoidably** *adverb*.

unaware > *adjective* having no knowledge of a situation or fact.

DERIVATIVES – **unawareness** *noun*.

SYNONYMS – ignorant, oblivious, unknowing, unmindful.

unawares (also **unaware**) > *adverb* so as to surprise; unexpectedly.

unbalance > *verb* **1** upset the balance of. **2** (**unbalanced**) upset the mental balance of; derange. **3** (**unbalanced**) treating aspects of something unequally; partial.

unbearable > *adjective* not able to be endured or tolerated.

DERIVATIVES – **unbearably** *adverb*.

SYNONYMS – insufferable, intolerable, unendurable.

unbeatable > *adjective* **1** not able to be surpassed or defeated. **2** extremely good.

unbeaten > *adjective* not defeated or surpassed.

unbecoming > *adjective* **1** not appropriate; unseemly. **2** (especially of clothing) not flattering.

DERIVATIVES – **unbecomingly** *adverb*.

unbeknown (also **unbeknownst**) > *adjective* (**unbeknown to**) without the knowledge of (someone).

unbelief > *noun* lack of religious belief.
DERIVATIVES – **unbeliever** *noun* **unbelieving** *adjective* **unbelievingly** *adverb*.

unbelievable > *adjective* **1** unlikely to be true. **2** extraordinary.
DERIVATIVES – **unbelievably** *adverb*.
SYNONYMS – **1** implausible, inconceivable, incredible.

unbend > *verb* (past and past participle **unbent**) **1** straighten. **2** become less reserved, formal, or strict.

unbending > *adjective* austere and inflexible.

unbiased (also **unbiassed**) > *adjective* showing no prejudice; impartial.
SYNONYMS – dispassionate, impartial, neutral, non-partisan, objective.

unbidden > *adjective* **1** without having been invited. **2** arising without conscious effort.
SYNONYMS – **1** unasked, uninvited, unsolicited. **2** spontaneous, unprompted, voluntary.

unbleached > *adjective* (especially of paper, cloth, or flour) not bleached.

unblock > *verb* remove an obstruction from.

unblushing > *adjective* not feeling or showing embarrassment or shame.
DERIVATIVES – **unblushingly** *adverb*.

unbolt > *verb* open by drawing back a bolt.

unborn > *adjective* (of a baby) not yet born.

unbound > *adjective* **1** not bound or restricted. **2** (of printed sheets) not bound together. **3** (of a bound book) not provided with a permanent cover.

unbounded > *adjective* having no limits.

unbowed > *adjective* not having submitted to pressure, demands, or accusations.

unbreakable > *adjective* not liable to break or able to be broken.

unbreathable > *adjective* (of air) not fit or pleasant to breathe.

unbridgeable > *adjective* (of a gap or difference) not able to be bridged or made less significant.

unbridled > *adjective* uncontrolled; unconstrained.

unbroken > *adjective* **1** not broken; intact. **2** not interrupted. **3** not surpassed. **4** (of a horse) not broken in.

unbuckle > *verb* unfasten the buckle of.

unburden > *verb* **1** relieve of a burden. **2** (**unburden oneself**) be relieved of a cause of anxiety or distress through confiding in someone.

unburnt (also **unburned**) > *adjective* not damaged or destroyed by fire.

unbutton > *verb* **1** unfasten the buttons of. **2** informal relax and become less inhibited.

uncalled > *adjective* **1** not summoned or invited. **2** (**uncalled for**) undesirable and unnecessary.

uncanny > *adjective* (**uncannier**, **uncanniest**) strange or mysterious.
DERIVATIVES – **uncannily** *adverb*.
SYNONYMS – bizarre, eerie, mysterious, strange, unnatural.

uncapped > *adjective* chiefly Brit. (of a player) never having been chosen as a member of a national sports team.

uncared > *adjective* (**uncared for**) not looked after properly.

uncaring > *adjective* **1** not displaying sympathy or concern for others. **2** not interested; unconcerned.
DERIVATIVES – **uncaringly** *adverb*.

unceasing > *adjective* not ceasing; continuous.
DERIVATIVES – **unceasingly** *adverb*.

unceremonious > *adjective* discourteous or abrupt.
DERIVATIVES – **unceremoniously** *adverb*.

uncertain > *adjective* **1** not known, reliable, or definite. **2** not completely confident or sure.
IDIOMS – **in no uncertain terms** clearly and forcefully.
DERIVATIVES – **uncertainly** *adverb*.

uncertainty > *noun* (pl. **uncertainties**) **1** the state of being uncertain. **2** something that is uncertain or causes one to feel uncertain.
COMBINATIONS – **uncertainty principle** Physics the principle, stated by the German physicist Werner Heisenberg (1901–76), that the momentum and position of a particle cannot both be precisely determined at the same time.

unchallengeable > *adjective* not able to be disputed, opposed, or defeated.
DERIVATIVES – **unchallengeably** *adverb*.

unchallenged > *adjective* **1** not disputed, opposed, or defeated. **2** not called on to prove one's identity.

unchallenging > *adjective* not presenting a challenge.

unchangeable > *adjective* not liable to variation or able to be altered.

unchanged > *adjective* not changed; unaltered.

unchanging > *adjective* remaining the same.
DERIVATIVES – **unchangingly** *adverb*.

uncharacteristic > *adjective* not typical of a particular person or thing.
DERIVATIVES – **uncharacteristically** *adverb*.

uncharismatic > *adjective* lacking charisma.

uncharitable > *adjective* unkind or unsympathetic to others.
DERIVATIVES – **uncharitably** *adverb*.
SYNONYMS – inconsiderate, uncaring, unkind, unsympathetic.

uncharted > *adjective* (of an area of land or sea) not mapped or surveyed.

unchaste > *adjective* not chaste.
SYNONYMS – dissolute, immoral, licentious, promiscuous.

unchastened > *adjective* not restrained or demoralised by a reproof or misfortune.

unchecked > *adjective* (of something undesirable) not controlled or restrained.

unchivalrous > *adjective* (of a man) discourteous, especially towards women.
DERIVATIVES – **unchivalrously** *adverb*.

unchristian > *adjective* **1** not in accordance with the teachings of Christianity. **2** ungenerous or unfair.

uncial /ˈʌnsɪəl, ʌnʃ'l/ > *adjective* written in a majuscule script with rounded separated letters, from which modern capital letters are derived. > *noun* an uncial letter, script, or manuscript.
ORIGIN – Latin *uncialis*, from *uncia* 'inch'.

uncircumcised > *adjective* (of a boy or man) not circumcised.

uncivil > *adjective* discourteous; impolite.
SYNONYMS – discourteous, disrespectful, ill-mannered, impolite, rude.

uncivilised (also **uncivilized**) > *adjective* **1** not socially or culturally advanced. **2** impolite; bad-mannered.

unclaimed > *adjective* not having been claimed.

unclasp > *verb* **1** unfasten the clasp of (an object or device). **2** release the grip of.

unclassifiable > *adjective* not able to be classified.

unclassified > *adjective* not classified.

uncle > *noun* the brother of one's father or mother or the husband of one's aunt.
WORDFINDER – avuncular (*like an uncle*).
ORIGIN – Latin *aunculus*, alteration of *avunculus* 'maternal uncle'.

unclean > *adjective* **1** dirty. **2** immoral. **3** (of food) regarded in a particular religion as impure and unfit for use or consumption. **4** (in biblical use, of a spirit) evil.

uncleanliness > *noun* the state of being dirty.

unclear > *adjective* **1** not easy to see, hear, or understand. **2** not obvious, definite, or certain.

uncleared > *adjective* **1** (of a cheque) not having passed through a clearing house and been paid into the payee's account. **2** (of land) not cleared of vegetation.

unclench > *verb* release (a clenched part of the body).

Uncle Sam > *noun* a personification of the federal government or citizens of the US.
ORIGIN – said to have arisen as a flippant expansion of the letters US.

Uncle Tom > *noun* derogatory, chiefly N. Amer. a black man considered to be excessively obedient or servile.
ORIGIN – from the name of the hero of

Harriet Beecher Stowe's *Uncle Tom's Cabin* (1852).

unclimbed > *adjective* (of a mountain or rock face) not previously climbed.

DERIVATIVES – **unclimbable** *adjective*.

unclog > *verb* (**unclogged, unclogging**) remove accumulated matter from.

unclothed > *adjective* wearing no clothes; naked.

unclouded > *adjective* **1** (of the sky) not dark or overcast. **2** not troubled or spoiled by anything.

uncluttered > *adjective* not cluttered by too many objects or elements.

uncoil > *verb* straighten from a coiled or curled position.

uncoloured (US **uncolored**) > *adjective* **1** having no colour. **2** not influenced.

uncombed > *adjective* (of a person's hair) not combed.

uncomfortable > *adjective* **1** not physically comfortable. **2** uneasy or awkward.

DERIVATIVES – **uncomfortably** *adverb*.

SYNONYMS – **2** awkward, edgy, ill at ease, tense, uneasy.

uncommercial > *adjective* not making, intended to make, or allowing a profit.

uncommon > *adjective* **1** out of the ordinary; unusual. **2** remarkably great: *an uncommon amount of noise*.

DERIVATIVES – **uncommonly** *adverb*.

SYNONYMS – **1** infrequent, rare, unusual.

uncommunicative > *adjective* unwilling to talk or impart information.

uncompetitive > *adjective* not competitive or marked by fair competition.

uncomplaining > *adjective* not complaining; stoical.

DERIVATIVES – **uncomplainingly** *adverb*.

uncomplicated > *adjective* simple or straightforward.

uncomplimentary > *adjective* not complimentary; negative or insulting.

uncomprehending > *adjective* unable to comprehend something.

DERIVATIVES – **uncomprehendingly** *adverb*.

uncompromising > *adjective* **1** unwilling to make concessions; resolute. **2** harsh or relentless.

DERIVATIVES – **uncompromisingly** *adverb*.

unconcealed > *adjective* (especially of an emotion) not concealed; obvious.

unconcern > *noun* a lack of worry or interest.

DERIVATIVES – **unconcerned** *adjective* **unconcernedly** *adverb*.

unconditional > *adjective* not subject to any conditions.

DERIVATIVES – **unconditionally** *adverb*.

unconditioned > *adjective* **1** unconditional. **2** (of behaviour) instinctive, not formed or influenced by conditioning or learning. **3** not subjected to a conditioning process.

unconfident > *adjective* not confident; hesitant.

unconfined > *adjective* **1** not confined to a limited space. **2** (of joy or excitement) very great.

unconfirmed > *adjective* not confirmed as to truth or validity.

uncongenial > *adjective* **1** (of a person) not friendly or pleasant to be with. **2** unsuitable and therefore unlikely to promote success or well-being.

unconnected > *adjective* **1** not joined together or to something else. **2** not associated or linked in a sequence.

unconquerable > *adjective* not conquerable.

DERIVATIVES – **unconquered** *adjective*.

unconscionable /unˈkonshənəb'l/ > *adjective* not right or reasonable.

DERIVATIVES – **unconscionably** *adverb*.

unconscious > *adjective* **1** not awake and aware of and responding to one's environment. **2** done or existing without one realising. **3** (**unconscious of**) unaware of. > *noun* (**the unconscious**) the part of the mind which is inaccessible to the conscious mind but which affects behaviour and emotions.

WORDFINDER – catalepsy, catatonia (*sudden unconsciousness with rigid bodily posture*), coma (*a state of deep unconsciousness*), comatose (*deeply unconscious*), narcosis (*drug-induced unconsciousness*), resuscitate (*revive someone from unconsciousness*).

DERIVATIVES – **unconsciously** *adverb* **unconsciousness** *noun*.

unconsecrated > *adjective* not consecrated.

unconsidered > *adjective* **1** disregarded and unappreciated. **2** not thought about in advance; rash.

unconsolable > *adjective* inconsolable.

DERIVATIVES – **unconsolably** *adverb*.

unconstitutional > *adjective* not in accordance with the political constitution or with procedural rules.

DERIVATIVES – **unconstitutionally** *adverb*.

unconstrained > *adjective* not restricted or limited.

unconsummated > *adjective* (of a marriage) not having been consummated.

uncontainable > *adjective* (especially of an emotion) very strong.

uncontaminated > *adjective* not contaminated; pure.

uncontentious > *adjective* not contentious; uncontroversial.

uncontested > *adjective* not contested.

uncontrived > *adjective* not artificially created.

uncontrollable > *adjective* not able to be controlled.

DERIVATIVES – **uncontrollably** *adverb*.

SYNONYMS – out of control, ungovernable, unmanageable, wild.

uncontrolled > *adjective* not controlled.

uncontroversial > *adjective* not controversial; avoiding controversy.

DERIVATIVES – **uncontroversially** *adverb*.

unconventional > *adjective* not based on or conforming to what is generally done or believed.

DERIVATIVES – **unconventionality** *noun* **unconventionally** *adverb*.

SYNONYMS – eccentric, irregular, unorthodox.

unconvinced > *adjective* not certain that something is true or can be relied on.

unconvincing > *adjective* failing to convince or impress.

DERIVATIVES – **unconvincingly** *adverb*.

uncooked > *adjective* not cooked; raw.

uncool > *adjective* informal not fashionable or impressive.

uncooperative > *adjective* unwilling to help others or do what they ask.

DERIVATIVES – **uncooperatively** *adverb*.

uncoordinated > *adjective* **1** badly organised. **2** (of a person or their movements) clumsy.

uncork > *verb* pull the cork out of.

uncorroborated > *adjective* not supported or confirmed by evidence.

uncountable > *adjective* too many to be counted.

uncounted > *adjective* **1** not counted. **2** very numerous.

uncouple > *verb* disconnect or become disconnected.

uncouth > *adjective* lacking good manners, refinement, or grace.

SYNONYMS – boorish, coarse, oafish, uncivilised.

ORIGIN – Old English, 'unknown'.

uncover > *verb* **1** remove a cover or covering from. **2** discover (something previously secret or unknown).

uncritical > *adjective* not expressing criticism or using one's critical faculties.

DERIVATIVES – **uncritically** *adverb*.

uncross > *verb* **1** move (something) back from a crossed position. **2** (**uncrossed**) Brit. (of a cheque) not crossed.

uncrowded > *adjective* not crowded.

uncrowned > *adjective* not formally crowned as a monarch.

unction /ˈungksh'n/ > *noun* **1** formal the action of anointing someone with oil or ointment as a religious rite or as a symbol of investiture as a monarch. **2** a fervent manner of expression apparently arising from deep emotion.

ORIGIN – Latin, from *unguere* 'anoint'.

unctuous /ˈungktyooəss/ > *adjective* excessively flattering or ingratiating.

DERIVATIVES – **unctuously** *adverb* **unctuousness** *noun*.

SYNONYMS – fawning, obsequious, servile, sycophantic.

uncultivated > *adjective* **1** (of land) not used for growing crops. **2** (of a person) not highly educated.

uncultured > *adjective* not characterised by good taste, manners, or education.

uncured > *adjective* not preserved by salting, drying, or smoking.

uncurl > *verb* straighten from a curled position.

uncut > *adjective* not cut.

undamaged > *adjective* not harmed or damaged.

undated > *adjective* not provided or marked with a date.

undaunted > *adjective* not intimidated or discouraged by difficulty, danger, or disappointment.

SYNONYMS – unabashed, unafraid, undismayed.

undead > *adjective* (of a fictional being) technically dead but still animate.

undecagon /unˈdekkəgən/ > *noun* another term for HENDECAGON.

ORIGIN – from Latin *undecim* 'eleven'.

undeceive > *verb* tell (someone) that an idea or belief is mistaken.

undecided > *adjective* **1** not having made a decision; uncertain. **2** not settled or resolved.

DERIVATIVES – **undecidedly** *adverb*.

undecipherable > *adjective* (of speech or writing) not able to be read or understood.

undefeated > *adjective* not defeated.

undefended > *adjective* not defended.

undefined > *adjective* not clear or defined.

DERIVATIVES – **undefinable** *adjective* **undefinably** *adverb*.

undemanding > *adjective* (especially of a task) not demanding.

undemocratic > *adjective* not relating or according to democratic principles.

DERIVATIVES – **undemocratically** *adverb*.

undemonstrative > *adjective* not tending to express feelings openly.

SYNONYMS – impassive, reserved, unemotional.

undeniable > *adjective* unable to be denied or disputed.

DERIVATIVES – **undeniably** *adverb*.

under > *preposition* **1** extending or directly below. **2** below or behind (something covering or protecting). **3** at a lower level, layer, or grade than. **4** expressing submission or subordination. **5** as provided for by the rules of; in accordance with. **6** used to express grouping or classification. **7** lower than (a specified amount, rate, or norm). **8** undergoing (a process). > *adverb* **1**

extending or directly below something. **2** affected by an anaesthetic; unconscious.

IDIOMS – **under age** too young to engage legally in a particular activity. **under way 1** (of a boat) moving through the water. **2** having started and making progress.

under- > *prefix* **1** below; beneath: *undercover*. **2** lower in status; subordinate: *undersecretary*. **3** insufficiently; incompletely: *underfed*.

underachieve > *verb* do less well than is expected.

DERIVATIVES – **underachievement** *noun* **underachiever** *noun*.

underarm > *adjective* & *adverb* (of a throw, stroke with a racket, etc.) made with the arm or hand below shoulder level. > *noun* a person's armpit.

underbelly > *noun* (pl. **underbellies**) **1** the soft underside or abdomen of an animal, especially vulnerable to attack. **2** a hidden unpleasant or criminal part of society.

underbid > *verb* (**underbidding**; **past and past participle underbid**) (in an auction) make a bid lower than another.

underbite > *noun* the projection of the lower teeth beyond the upper.

underbrush > *noun* N. Amer. undergrowth in a forest.

undercarriage > *noun* **1** a wheeled structure beneath an aircraft which supports the aircraft on the ground. **2** the supporting frame under the body of a vehicle.

undercharge > *verb* charge (someone) a price or amount that is too low.

underclass > *noun* the lowest social class in a country or community, consisting of the poor and unemployed.

undercliff > *noun* a terrace or lower cliff formed by a landslip.

underclothes > *plural noun* clothes worn under others next to the skin.

DERIVATIVES – **underclothing** *noun*.

undercoat > *noun* **1** a layer of paint applied after the primer and before the topcoat. **2** an animal's under layer of fur or down.

undercook > *verb* cook (something) insufficiently.

undercover > *adjective* & *adverb* involving secret work for investigation or espionage.

undercroft > *noun* the crypt of a church.

ORIGIN – from the rare term *croft* 'crypt', from Latin *crypta*.

undercurrent > *noun* **1** a current of water below the surface and moving in a different direction from any surface current. **2** an underlying feeling or influence.

undercut > *verb* (**undercutting**; **past and past participle undercut**) **1** offer goods or services at a lower price than (a competitor). **2** cut or wear away the part under (something). **3** weaken; undermine. > *noun* **1** a space formed by the removal or absence of material from the lower part of something. **2** Brit. the underside of a sirloin of beef.

underdeveloped > *adjective* **1** not fully developed. **2** (of a country or region) not advanced economically.

DERIVATIVES – **underdevelopment** *noun*.

underdog > *noun* a competitor thought to have little chance of winning a fight or contest.

underdone > *adjective* (of food) insufficiently cooked.

underdress > *verb* (also **be underdressed**) dress too plainly or too informally for a particular occasion.

underemphasise (also **underemphasize**) > *verb* place insufficient emphasis on.

underemployed > *adjective* not having sufficient or sufficiently demanding paid work.

DERIVATIVES – **underemployment** *noun*.

underestimate > *verb* **1** estimate (something) to be smaller or less important than it really is. **2** regard (someone) as less capable than they really are. > *noun* an estimate that is too low.

DERIVATIVES – **underestimation** *noun*.

underexpose > *verb* Photography expose (film) for too short a time.

DERIVATIVES – **underexposure** *noun*.

underfed > *adjective* insufficiently fed or nourished.

underfelt > *noun* Brit. felt laid under a carpet for protection or support.

underflow > *noun* an undercurrent.

underfoot > *adverb* **1** under one's feet; on the ground. **2** constantly present and in one's way.

underfund > *verb* provide with insufficient funding.

DERIVATIVES – **underfunding** *noun*.

undergarment > *noun* an article of underclothing.

underglaze > *noun* colour or decoration applied to pottery before the glaze is applied.

undergo > *verb* (**undergoes**; **past underwent**; **past participle undergone**) experience or be subjected to (something unpleasant or arduous).

ORIGIN – Old English, 'undermine'.

undergrad > *noun* informal an undergraduate.

undergraduate > *noun* a student at a university who has not yet taken a first degree.

underground > *adjective* & *adverb* **1** beneath the surface of the ground. **2** in secrecy or hiding. **3** seeking to explore alternative forms of lifestyle or artistic expression; radical and experimental. > *noun* **1** Brit. an underground railway. **2** a group or movement organised secretly to work against an existing regime.

undergrowth > *noun* a dense growth of shrubs and other plants.

underhand (also **underhanded**) > *adjective*

1 acting or done in a secret or dishonest way. **2** underarm.

SYNONYMS – **1** deceitful, devious, fraudulent, scheming.

underlay¹ > *verb* (past and past participle **underlaid**) place something under (something else), especially to support or raise it. > *noun* material laid under a carpet for protection or support.

underlay² past tense of UNDERLIE.

underlie > *verb* (**underlying**; past **underlay**; past participle **underlain**) lie or be situated under.

DERIVATIVES – **underlying** *adjective*.

underline > *verb* **1** draw a line under (a word or phrase) to give emphasis or indicate special type. **2** emphasise. > *noun* a line drawn under a word or phrase.

underling > *noun* chiefly derogatory a subordinate.

underlip > *noun* the lower lip of a person or animal.

underlying present participle of UNDERLIE.

underman > *verb* (**undermanned**, **undermanning**) fail to provide with enough workers or crew.

undermine > *verb* **1** wear away or destroy the base or foundation of. **2** dig or excavate beneath (a building or fortification) so as to make it collapse. **3** weaken gradually or insidiously.

underneath > *preposition & adverb* **1** situated directly below. **2** so as to be partly or wholly concealed by. > *noun* the part or side facing towards the ground; the underside.

undernourished > *adjective* having insufficient food for good health and condition.

DERIVATIVES – **undernourishment** *noun*.

underpaid past and past participle of UNDERPAY.

underpants > *plural noun* an undergarment covering the lower part of the body and having two holes for the legs.

underpart > *noun* a lower part or portion.

underpass > *noun* a road or pedestrian tunnel passing under another road or a railway.

underpay > *verb* (past and past participle **underpaid**) **1** pay too little to (someone). **2** pay less than is due for.

DERIVATIVES – **underpayment** *noun*.

underperform > *verb* perform less well than expected.

DERIVATIVES – **underperformance** *noun*.

underpin > *verb* (**underpinned**, **underpinning**) **1** support (a structure) from below by laying a solid foundation or substituting stronger for weaker materials. **2** support, justify, or form the basis for.

DERIVATIVES – **underpinning** *noun*.

underplay > *verb* **1** perform (a role or part)

in a restrained way. **2** represent (something) as being less important than it really is.

underpopulated > *adjective* having an insufficient or very small population.

DERIVATIVES – **underpopulation** *noun*.

underpowered > *adjective* lacking sufficient mechanical, electrical, or other power.

underprice > *verb* sell or offer at too low a price.

underprivileged > *adjective* not enjoying the same rights or standard of living as the majority of the population.

underrate > *verb* underestimate the extent, value, or importance of.

DERIVATIVES – **underrated** *adjective*.

under-represent > *verb* provide with insufficient or inadequate representation.

under-resourced > *adjective* provided with insufficient resources.

underscore > *verb & noun* another term for UNDERLINE.

undersea > *adjective* relating to or situated below the sea or the surface of the sea.

undersecretary > *noun* (pl. **undersecretaries**) **1** (in the UK) a junior minister or senior civil servant. **2** (in the US) the principal assistant to a member of the cabinet.

undersell > *verb* (past and past participle **undersold**) **1** sell something at a lower price than (a competitor). **2** promote or rate (something) insufficiently.

undershirt > *noun* chiefly N. Amer. an undergarment worn under a shirt; a vest.

undershoot > *verb* (past and past participle **undershot**) **1** (of an aircraft) land short of (the runway). **2** fall short of (a point or target).

underside > *noun* the bottom or lower side or surface of something.

undersigned formal > *noun* (**the undersigned**) the person or people who have signed the document in question.

undersized (also **undersize**) > *adjective* of less than the usual size.

underskirt > *noun* a petticoat.

undersold past and past participle of UNDERSELL.

underspend > *verb* (past and past participle **underspent**) spend too little or less than has been planned. > *noun* an act of underspending.

understaff > *verb* provide (an organisation) with too few members of staff to operate effectively.

DERIVATIVES – **understaffing** *noun*.

understand > *verb* (past and past participle **understood**) **1** perceive the intended meaning of (words, a language, or a speaker). **2** perceive the significance, explanation, or cause of. **3** interpret or view in a particular way. **4** infer from information received. **5** assume that (something) is present or is the case.

SYNONYMS – **1** apprehend, comprehend, grasp. **2** appreciate, realise, recognise.

understandable > *adjective* **1** able to be understood. **2** to be expected; natural, reasonable, or forgivable.

DERIVATIVES – **understandably** *adverb*.

understanding > *noun* **1** the ability to understand something; comprehension. **2** the power of abstract thought; intellect. **3** an individual's perception or judgement of a situation. **4** sympathetic awareness or tolerance. **5** an informal or unspoken agreement or arrangement. > *adjective* sympathetically aware of other people's feelings; tolerant and forgiving.

DERIVATIVES – **understandingly** *adverb*.

SYNONYMS – *noun* **1** apprehension, comprehension, grasp, perception. **2** intellect, intelligence, reason. **3** belief, impression, view. **4** compassion, concern, consideration, sympathy. *adjective* compassionate, humane, kind, sympathetic.

understate > *verb* describe or represent (something) as being smaller or less significant than it really is.

DERIVATIVES – **understatement** *noun*.

understated > *adjective* presented or expressed in a subtle and effective way.

DERIVATIVES – **understatedly** *adverb*.

understeer > *verb* (of a motor vehicle) have a tendency to turn less sharply than is intended.

understood past and past participle of UNDERSTAND.

understorey (N. Amer. **understory**) > *noun* Ecology a layer of vegetation beneath the main canopy of a forest.

understudy > *noun* (pl. **understudies**) an actor who learns another's role in order to be able to act in their absence. > *verb* (**understudies**, **understudied**) study (a role or actor) as an understudy.

undersubscribed > *adjective* (of a course or event) having more places available than applications.

undertake > *verb* (past **undertook**; past participle **undertaken**) **1** commit oneself to and begin (an enterprise or responsibility); take on. **2** formally guarantee, pledge, or promise.

SYNONYMS – **1** assume, engage in, tackle, take on.

undertaker > *noun* a person whose business is preparing dead bodies for burial or cremation and making arrangements for funerals.

undertaking > *noun* **1** a formal pledge or promise to do something. **2** a task that is taken on; an enterprise. **3** the management of funerals as a profession.

undertone > *noun* **1** a subdued or muted tone of sound or colour. **2** an underlying quality or feeling.

1067

undertow > *noun* another term for **UNDERCURRENT**.

underuse > *verb* /undər**yōōz**/ use (something) below the optimum level. > *noun* /undər**yōōss**/ insufficient use.
DERIVATIVES – **underused** *adjective*.

underutilise (also **underutilize**) > *verb* underuse.

undervalue > *verb* (**undervalues**, **undervalued**, **undervaluing**) 1 rate insufficiently highly; fail to appreciate. 2 underestimate the financial value of.
DERIVATIVES – **undervaluation** *noun*.

underwater > *adjective & adverb* situated or occurring beneath the surface of the water.

underwear > *noun* clothing worn under other clothes next to the skin.

underweight > *adjective* below a weight considered normal or desirable.

underwent past of **UNDERGO**.

underwhelm > *verb* humorous fail to impress or make a positive impact on.

underwired > *adjective* (of a bra) having a semicircular wire support stitched under each cup.

underwood > *noun* small trees and shrubs growing beneath taller timber trees.

underworld > *noun* 1 the world of criminals or of organised crime. 2 the mythical abode of the dead, imagined as being under the earth.

underwrite > *verb* (past **underwrote**; past participle **underwritten**) 1 sign and accept liability under (an insurance policy). 2 undertake to finance or otherwise support or guarantee.
DERIVATIVES – **underwriter** *noun*.

undescended > *adjective* Medicine (of a testicle) remaining in the abdomen instead of descending normally into the scrotum.

undeserved > *adjective* not warranted, merited, or earned.
DERIVATIVES – **undeservedly** *adverb*.

undeserving > *adjective* not deserving or worthy of something positive.

undesirable > *adjective* not wanted or desirable because harmful, objectionable, or unpleasant. > *noun* an objectionable person.
DERIVATIVES – **undesirability** *noun* **undesirably** *adverb*.

undesired > *adjective* not wanted or desired.

undetectable > *adjective* not able to be detected.
DERIVATIVES – **undetectably** *adverb*.

undetected > *adjective* not detected or discovered.

undetermined > *adjective* not firmly decided or settled.

undeterred > *adjective* persevering despite setbacks.

undeveloped > *adjective* not having developed or been developed.

undeviating > *adjective* showing no deviation; constant and steady.

undiagnosed > *adjective* not diagnosed.

undid past of **UNDO**.

undies > *plural noun* informal articles of underwear.

undifferentiated > *adjective* not different or differentiated.

undigested > *adjective* 1 (of food) not digested. 2 not having been properly understood or absorbed.

undignified > *adjective* appearing foolish and unseemly; lacking in dignity.
SYNONYMS – degrading, demeaning, humiliating, ignominious.

undiluted > *adjective* 1 (of a liquid) not diluted. 2 not moderated or weakened.

undiminished > *adjective* not diminished, reduced, or lessened.

undiplomatic > *adjective* insensitive and tactless.
DERIVATIVES – **undiplomatically** *adverb*.

undirected > *adjective* without a coherent plan or purpose.

undiscerning > *adjective* lacking judgement, insight, or taste.

undisciplined > *adjective* lacking in discipline; uncontrolled in behaviour or manner.
SYNONYMS – disorderly, unrestrained, unruly, wayward.

undisclosed > *adjective* not revealed or made known.

undiscovered > *adjective* not discovered.

undiscriminating > *adjective* lacking good judgement or taste.

undisguised > *adjective* (of a feeling) not disguised or concealed; open.
SYNONYMS – evident, obvious, open, unconcealed.

undismayed > *adjective* not dismayed or discouraged by a setback.

undisputed > *adjective* not disputed or called in question; accepted.

undistinguished > *adjective* lacking distinction; unexceptional.

undistributed > *adjective* not distributed.

undisturbed > *adjective* not disturbed.

undivided > *adjective* 1 not divided, separated, or broken into parts. 2 devoted completely to one object: *my undivided attention*.

undo > *verb* (**undoes**; past **undid**; past participle **undone**) 1 unfasten or loosen. 2 cancel or reverse the effects of (a previous action or measure). 3 formal cause the downfall or ruin of (someone).
SYNONYMS – 2 overrule, overturn, retract, revoke.

undocumented > *adjective* not recorded in or proved by documents.

undoing > *noun* a person's ruin or downfall.

undomesticated > *adjective* 1 (of an animal) not tamed. 2 not accustomed to domestic tasks.

undone > *adjective* 1 not tied or fastened. 2 not done or finished. 3 formal or humorous ruined by a disastrous setback.

undoubted > *adjective* not questioned or doubted by anyone.
DERIVATIVES – **undoubtedly** *adverb*.

undramatic > *adjective* 1 lacking the qualities expected in drama. 2 unexciting.

undraped > *adjective* 1 not covered with cloth or drapery. 2 (of a model or subject in art) naked.

undreamed /un**dreemd**, un**dremt**/ (Brit. also **undreamt** /un**dremt**/) > *adjective* (**undreamed of**) not previously thought to be possible.

undress > *verb* 1 (also **get undressed**) take off one's clothes. 2 take the clothes off (someone else). > *noun* 1 the state of being naked or only partially clothed. 2 Military ordinary clothing or uniform, as opposed to full dress.

undressed > *adjective* 1 wearing no clothes; naked. 2 not treated, processed, or prepared for use. 3 (of food) not having a dressing.

undrinkable > *adjective* not fit to be drunk because of impurity or poor quality.

undue > *adjective* excessive or disproportionate.
DERIVATIVES – **unduly** *adverb*.
SYNONYMS – disproportionate, excessive, extreme, immoderate, inordinate.

undulant /**un**dyoolənt/ > *adjective* undulating.
COMBINATIONS – **undulant fever** brucellosis in humans. [ORIGIN – so named because of the intermittent fever associated with the disease.]

undulate > *verb* /**un**dyoolayt/ 1 move with a smooth wave-like motion. 2 have a wavy form or outline.
DERIVATIVES – **undulating** *adjective* **undulation** *noun* **undulatory** *adjective*.
ORIGIN – Latin *undulatus*, from *unda* 'a wave'.

undyed > *adjective* (of fabric) not dyed; of its natural colour.

undying > *adjective* lasting forever.

unearned > *adjective* not earned or deserved.
COMBINATIONS – **unearned income** income from investments rather than from work.

unearth > *verb* 1 find in the ground by digging. 2 discover by investigation or searching.

unearthly > *adjective* 1 unnatural or mysterious. 2 informal unreasonably early or inconvenient: *we got up at an unearthly hour*.

unease > *noun* anxiety or discontent.

uneasy > *adjective* (**uneasier**, **uneasiest**) causing or feeling anxiety; troubled or uncomfortable.
DERIVATIVES – **uneasily** *adverb* **uneasiness** *noun*.
SYNONYMS – anxious, ill at ease, nervous, worried.

uneatable > *adjective* not fit to be eaten.

uneaten > *adjective* not eaten.

uneconomic > *adjective* not profitable or making efficient use of resources.

uneconomical > *adjective* wasteful of money or other resources; not economical.
DERIVATIVES – **uneconomically** *adverb*.

unedifying > *adjective* distasteful or unpleasant.

unedited > *adjective* (of material for publication or broadcasting) not edited.

uneducated > *adjective* having had no or very little education.

unelectable > *adjective* not able or likely to win an election.

unelected > *adjective* (of an official) not elected.

unembarrassed > *adjective* not feeling or showing embarrassment.

unembellished > *adjective* not embellished or decorated.

unemotional > *adjective* not having or showing strong feelings.
DERIVATIVES – **unemotionally** *adverb*.
SYNONYMS – clinical, passionless, reserved, undemonstrative.

unemphatic > *adjective* not emphatic.

unemployable > *adjective* not able or likely to get paid employment because of a lack of skills or qualifications.

unemployed > *adjective* **1** without a paid job but available to work. **2** (of a thing) not in use.

unemployment > *noun* **1** the state of being unemployed. **2** the number or proportion of unemployed people.
COMBINATIONS – **unemployment benefit** payment made by the state or a trade union to an unemployed person.

unenclosed > *adjective* (especially of land) not enclosed.

unencumbered > *adjective* not having any burden or impediment.

unending > *adjective* **1** having or seeming to have no end. **2** countless or continual: *unending demands.*

unendowed > *adjective* not endowed.

unendurable > *adjective* not able to be tolerated or endured.
SYNONYMS – insufferable, intolerable, unbearable.

unenforceable > *adjective* impossible to enforce.

un-English > *adjective* not characteristic of English people or the English language.

unenlightened > *adjective* not enlightened in outlook.
DERIVATIVES – **unenlightening** *adjective*.

unenterprising > *adjective* lacking initiative or entrepreneurial ability.

unenthusiastic > *adjective* not having or showing enthusiasm.
DERIVATIVES – **unenthusiastically** *adverb*.

unenviable > *adjective* difficult, undesirable, or unpleasant.

unequal > *adjective* **1** not equal in quantity, size, or value. **2** not fair, evenly balanced, or having equal advantage. **3** (usu. **unequal to**) not having the ability or resources to meet a challenge.
DERIVATIVES – **unequally** *adverb*.

unequalled (US **unequaled**) > *adjective* superior to all others in performance or extent.

unequipped > *adjective* not equipped with the necessary items or skills.

unequivocal > *adjective* leaving no doubt; unambiguous.
DERIVATIVES – **unequivocally** *adverb*.
SYNONYMS – clear, explicit, unambiguous.

unerring > *adjective* always right or accurate.
DERIVATIVES – **unerringly** *adverb*.

unescapable > *adjective* unable to be avoided or denied.

UNESCO /yooneskō/ > *abbreviation* United Nations Educational, Scientific, and Cultural Organisation.

unescorted > *adjective* not escorted.

unessential > *adjective* inessential.

unethical > *adjective* not morally correct.
DERIVATIVES – **unethically** *adverb*.
SYNONYMS – immoral, unprincipled, unscrupulous.

uneven > *adjective* **1** not level or smooth. **2** not regular, consistent, or equal.
DERIVATIVES – **unevenly** *adverb* **unevenness** *noun*.
SYNONYMS – **1** bumpy, lumpy, rough. **2** inconsistent, irregular, unbalanced, unequal.

uneventful > *adjective* not marked by interesting or exciting events.
DERIVATIVES – **uneventfully** *adverb* **uneventfulness** *noun*.

unexamined > *adjective* not investigated or examined.

unexceptionable > *adjective* not open to objection, but not particularly new or exciting; inoffensive.
DERIVATIVES – **unexceptionably** *adverb*.
USAGE – do not confuse **unexceptionable** 'that cannot be taken exception to, inoffensive' with **unexceptional** 'not exceptional; ordinary'.

unexceptional > *adjective* not out of the ordinary; usual.
DERIVATIVES – **unexceptionally** *adverb*.

unexcitable > *adjective* not easily excited.

unexciting > *adjective* not exciting; dull.

unexercised > *adjective* **1** not made use of or put into practice. **2** (of a person) not taking exercise; unfit.

unexpected > *adjective* not expected or regarded as likely to happen.
DERIVATIVES – **unexpectedly** *adverb* **unexpectedness** *noun*.
SYNONYMS – sudden, surprising, unforeseen.

unexpired > *adjective* (of an agreement or period of time) not yet having come to an end.

unexplained > *adjective* not made clear or accounted for.
DERIVATIVES – **unexplainable** *adjective* **unexplainably** *adverb*.

unexploded > *adjective* (of a bomb, shell, etc.) not having exploded.

unexploited > *adjective* available to be exploited.

unexplored > *adjective* not explored, investigated, or evaluated.

unexposed > *adjective* **1** not exposed. **2** (**unexposed to**) not introduced to or acquainted with.

unexpressed > *adjective* (of a thought or feeling) not communicated or made known.

unexpurgated > *adjective* (of a text) complete and containing all the original material; not censored.

unfailing > *adjective* **1** without error. **2** reliable or constant.
DERIVATIVES – **unfailingly** *adverb*.
SYNONYMS – **2** constant, dependable, reliable, steadfast.

unfair > *adjective* not based on or showing fairness; unjust.
DERIVATIVES – **unfairly** *adverb* **unfairness** *noun*.
SYNONYMS – inequitable, unjust.

unfaithful > *adjective* **1** not faithful; disloyal. **2** engaging in sexual relations with a person other than one's lover or spouse.
DERIVATIVES – **unfaithfully** *adverb* **unfaithfulness** *noun*.

unfaltering > *adjective* not faltering; steady or resolute.
DERIVATIVES – **unfalteringly** *adverb*.

unfamiliar > *adjective* **1** not known or recognised; uncharacteristic. **2** (**unfamiliar with**) not having knowledge or experience of.
DERIVATIVES – **unfamiliarity** *noun*.

unfancied > *adjective* not considered likely to win.

unfashionable > *adjective* not fashionable or popular.
DERIVATIVES – **unfashionableness** *noun* **unfashionably** *adverb*.

unfasten > *verb* open the fastening of; undo.

unfathomable > *adjective* **1** incapable of being fully explored or understood. **2** impossible to measure the depth or extent of.
DERIVATIVES – **unfathomably** *adverb* **unfathomed** *adjective*.
SYNONYMS – **1** incomprehensible, inscrutable, mystifying.

unfavourable (US **unfavorable**) > *adjective* **1** expressing lack of approval or support. **2** adverse; inauspicious.
DERIVATIVES – **unfavourably** *adverb*.

unfazed > *adjective* informal not disconcerted or perturbed.

unfeasible > *adjective* inconvenient or impractical.
DERIVATIVES – **unfeasibility** *noun* **unfeasibly** *adverb*.

unfeeling > *adjective* **1** unsympathetic, harsh, or callous. **2** lacking physical sensation.
SYNONYMS – **1** callous, hard-hearted, harsh, uncaring, sympathetic.

unfeigned > *adjective* genuine; sincere.
SYNONYMS – authentic, genuine, honest, sincere, unaffected.

unfeminine > *adjective* lacking feminine qualities.

unfermented > *adjective* not fermented.

unfertilised (also **unfertilized**) > *adjective* not fertilised.

unfettered > *adjective* unrestrained or uninhibited.

unfilled > *adjective* not filled; vacant or empty.

unfiltered > *adjective* not filtered.

unfinished > *adjective* **1** not finished; incomplete. **2** not having been given an attractive surface appearance in manufacture.

unfit > *adjective* **1** unsuitable or inadequate for something. **2** not in good physical condition.

unfitted > *adjective* **1** unfit for something. **2** (of furniture, linen, etc.) not fitted.

unfitting > *adjective* unsuitable or unbecoming.
DERIVATIVES – **unfittingly** *adverb*.

unfixed > *adjective* **1** unfastened; loose. **2** uncertain or variable.

unflagging > *adjective* tireless or persistent.
DERIVATIVES – **unflaggingly** *adverb*.

unflappable > *adjective* informal calm in a crisis.

unflattering > *adjective* not flattering.
DERIVATIVES – **unflatteringly** *adverb*.

unflinching > *adjective* not afraid or hesitant.
DERIVATIVES – **unflinchingly** *adverb*.

unfocused (also **unfocussed**) > *adjective* **1** not focused; out of focus. **2** without a specific aim or direction.

unfold > *verb* **1** open or spread out from a folded position. **2** make or become revealed or disclosed.

unforced > *adjective* **1** produced naturally and without effort. **2** not compelled.

unforeseen > *adjective* not anticipated or predicted.
DERIVATIVES – **unforeseeable** *adjective*.

unforgettable > *adjective* unable to be forgotten; highly memorable.
DERIVATIVES – **unforgettably** *adverb*.

unforgivable > *adjective* so bad as to be unable to be forgiven or excused.
DERIVATIVES – **unforgivably** *adverb*.

unforgiven > *adjective* not forgiven.

unforgiving > *adjective* **1** not willing to forgive or excuse faults. **2** (of conditions) harsh; hostile.

unformed > *adjective* **1** without a definite form. **2** not fully developed.

unforthcoming > *adjective* **1** not willing to divulge information. **2** not available when needed.

unfortunate > *adjective* **1** having bad fortune; unlucky. **2** regrettable or inappropriate. > *noun* a person who suffers bad fortune.
DERIVATIVES – **unfortunately** *adverb*.
SYNONYMS – **1** hapless, luckless, unlucky.

unfounded > *adjective* having no foundation or basis in fact.

unfree > *adjective* deprived or devoid of liberty.

unfreeze > *verb* (past **unfroze**; past participle **unfrozen**) **1** thaw. **2** remove restrictions on the use of (an asset).

unfrequented > *adjective* visited only rarely.

unfriendly > *adjective* (**unfriendier**, **unfriendliest**) not friendly.
DERIVATIVES – **unfriendliness** *noun*.
SYNONYMS – antagonistic, disagreeable, hostile.

unfrock > *verb* another term for DEFROCK.

unfroze past of UNFREEZE.

unfrozen past participle of UNFREEZE.

unfulfilled > *adjective* not fulfilled.
DERIVATIVES – **unfulfilling** *adjective*.

unfunded > *adjective* not receiving funds; not having a fund.

unfunny > *adjective* (**unfunnier**, **unfunniest**) not amusing.

unfurl > *verb* spread out from a furled state.

unfurnished > *adjective* **1** without furniture. **2** archaic not supplied.

ungainly > *adjective* clumsy; awkward.
DERIVATIVES – **ungainliness** *noun*.
SYNONYMS – awkward, clumsy, graceless, maladroit, ungainly.
ANTONYMS – elegant, graceful.
ORIGIN – from obsolete *gainly* 'graceful', based on an Old Norse word meaning 'straight'.

ungenerous > *adjective* not generous; mean.
DERIVATIVES – **ungenerously** *adverb*.

ungentlemanly > *adjective* not appropriate to or behaving like a gentleman.

unglazed > *adjective* not glazed.

unglued > *adjective* **1** not or no longer stuck. **2** informal confused and emotionally strained.

ungodly > *adjective* **1** irreligious or immoral. **2** informal unreasonably early or inconvenient.
DERIVATIVES – **ungodliness** *noun*.

ungovernable > *adjective* impossible to control or govern.
DERIVATIVES – **ungovernability** *noun* **ungovernably** *adverb*.

ungraceful > *adjective* lacking in grace; clumsy.
DERIVATIVES – **ungracefully** *adverb*.

ungracious > *adjective* not gracious.
DERIVATIVES – **ungraciously** *adverb*.
SYNONYMS – discourteous, impolite, rude, uncivil.

ungrammatical > *adjective* not conforming to grammatical rules.
DERIVATIVES – **ungrammatically** *adverb*.

ungrateful > *adjective* not feeling or showing gratitude.
DERIVATIVES – **ungratefully** *adverb* **ungratefulness** *noun*.

ungrounded > *adjective* **1** groundless. **2** not electrically earthed. **3** (**ungrounded in**) not properly instructed or proficient in.

unguarded > *adjective* **1** without protection or a guard. **2** not well considered; careless.

unguent /**ung**gwənt/ > *noun* a soft greasy or viscous substance used as ointment or for lubrication.
ORIGIN – Latin *unguentum*, from *unguere* 'anoint'.

ungulate /**ung**gyoolət, -layt/ > *noun* Zoology a hoofed mammal.
ORIGIN – Latin *ungulatus*, from *ungula* 'hoof'.

unhand > *verb* archaic or humorous release from one's grasp.

unhappy > *adjective* (**unhappier**, **unhappiest**) **1** not happy. **2** unfortunate.
DERIVATIVES – **unhappily** *adverb* **unhappiness** *noun*.
SYNONYMS – **1** dejected, miserable, sad, sorrowful.

unharmed > *adjective* not harmed; uninjured.

unharness > *verb* remove a harness from.

unhatched > *adjective* not yet hatched.

UNHCR > *abbreviation* United Nations High Commission for Refugees.

unhealthy > *adjective* (**unhealthier**, **unhealthiest**) **1** in poor health. **2** not conducive to health.
DERIVATIVES – **unhealthily** *adverb* **unhealthiness** *noun*.

unheard > *adjective* **1** not heard or listened to. **2** (**unheard of**) previously unknown.

unheated > *adjective* not heated.

unheeded > *adjective* heard or noticed but disregarded.

unheeding > *adjective* not paying attention.

unhelpful > *adjective* not helpful.
DERIVATIVES – **unhelpfully** *adverb* **unhelpfulness** *noun*.

unheralded > *adjective* not previously announced, expected, or recognised.

unhesitating > *adjective* without doubt or hesitation.
DERIVATIVES – **unhesitatingly** *adverb*.

unhinge > *verb* (**unhinged, unhingeing** or **unhinging**) **1** make mentally unbalanced. **2** take (a door) off its hinges.
DERIVATIVES – **unhinged** *adjective*.

unhistorical > *adjective* not in accordance with history or historical analysis.
DERIVATIVES – **unhistorically** *adverb*.

unhitch > *verb* unhook or unfasten.

unholy > *adjective* (**unholier, unholiest**) **1** sinful; wicked. **2** unnatural and potentially harmful: *an unholy alliance*. **3** *informal* dreadful: *there was an unholy row about it*.
DERIVATIVES – **unholiness** *noun*.

unhook > *verb* unfasten or detach (something held by a hook).

unhoped > *adjective* (**unhoped for**) exceeding hope or expectation.

unhorse > *verb* drag or cause to fall from a horse.

unhoused > *adjective* having no accommodation or shelter.

unhurried > *adjective* moving, acting, or taking place without haste or urgency.
DERIVATIVES – **unhurriedly** *adverb*.

unhurt > *adjective* not hurt or harmed.

unhygienic > *adjective* not hygienic.
DERIVATIVES – **unhygienically** *adverb*.

unhyphenated > *adjective* not written with a hyphen.

uni > *noun* (pl. **unis**) *informal* university.

uni- > *combining form* one; having or consisting of one: *unicycle*.
ORIGIN – from Latin *unus*.

Uniate /yōoniayt/ (also **Uniat** /yōoniat/) > *adjective* denoting a Christian community in eastern Europe acknowledging papal supremacy but with its own liturgy.
ORIGIN – Russian *uniat*, from Latin *unio* 'unity'.

unicameral /yōonikammərəl/ > *adjective* (of a legislative body) having a single legislative chamber.
ORIGIN – from Latin *camera* 'chamber'.

UNICEF /yōonisef/ > *abbreviation* United Nations Children's (originally International Children's Emergency) Fund.

unicellular > *adjective* Biology consisting of a single cell.

unicorn > *noun* a mythical animal represented as a horse with a single straight horn projecting from its forehead.
ORIGIN – Latin *unicornis*, from *cornu* 'horn'.

unicycle > *noun* a cycle with a single wheel, chiefly used by acrobats.
DERIVATIVES – **unicyclist** *noun*.

unidentifiable > *adjective* unable to be identified.

unidentified > *adjective* not recognised or identified.

unidirectional > *adjective* moving or operating in a single direction.

unification > *noun* the process of being united.
DERIVATIVES – **unificatory** *adjective*.
COMBINATIONS – **Unification Church** an evangelistic religious and political organisation founded in 1954 in Korea by Sun Myung Moon.

uniform > *adjective* not varying; the same in all cases and at all times. > *noun* the distinctive clothing worn by members of the same organisation or body or by children attending certain schools.
DERIVATIVES – **uniformed** *adjective* **uniformity** *noun* **uniformly** *adverb*.
SYNONYMS – *adjective* consistent, constant, steady, unchanging, unvarying.
ANTONYMS – *adjective* changeable, variable.
ORIGIN – Latin *uniformis*.

unify /yōonifī/ > *verb* (**unifies, unified**) make or become united or uniform.
DERIVATIVES – **unifier** *noun*.
ORIGIN – Latin *unificare*.

unilateral > *adjective* **1** performed by or affecting only one person, group, etc. **2** relating to or affecting only one side of an organ, the body, etc.
DERIVATIVES – **unilateralism** *noun* **unilateralist** *noun & adjective* **unilaterally** *adverb*.

unimaginable > *adjective* impossible to imagine or comprehend.
DERIVATIVES – **unimaginably** *adverb*.

unimaginative > *adjective* not using or displaying imagination; stolid and dull.
DERIVATIVES – **unimaginatively** *adverb* **unimaginativeness** *noun*.

unimpaired > *adjective* not weakened or damaged.

unimpeachable > *adjective* beyond reproach.
DERIVATIVES – **unimpeachably** *adverb*.

unimpeded > *adjective* not obstructed or hindered.

unimportant > *adjective* lacking in importance.
DERIVATIVES – **unimportance** *noun*.
SYNONYMS – inconsequential, insignificant, trivial.

unimpressed > *adjective* not impressed.

unimpressive > *adjective* not impressive.
DERIVATIVES – **unimpressively** *adverb* **unimpressiveness** *noun*.

unimproved > *adjective* not improved.

unincorporated > *adjective* **1** not formed into a legal corporation. **2** not included as part of a whole.

uninflected > *adjective* not varied by inflection.

uninfluenced > *adjective* not influenced.

uninformative > *adjective* not providing useful or interesting information.

uninformed > *adjective* lacking awareness or understanding of the facts.

uninhabitable > *adjective* unsuitable for living in.

uninhabited > *adjective* without inhabitants.

uninhibited > *adjective* expressing oneself or acting without restraint.
DERIVATIVES – **uninhibitedly** *adverb* **uninhibitedness** *noun*.

uninitiated > *adjective* without special knowledge or experience.

uninjured > *adjective* not harmed or damaged.

uninspired > *adjective* **1** unimaginative; dull. **2** not filled with excitement.

uninspiring > *adjective* not producing excitement or interest.
DERIVATIVES – **uninspiringly** *adverb*.

uninsurable > *adjective* not eligible for insurance cover.

uninsured > *adjective* not covered by insurance.

unintelligent > *adjective* lacking intelligence.
DERIVATIVES – **unintelligence** *noun* **unintelligently** *adverb*.
SYNONYMS – asinine, foolish, stupid, witless.

unintelligible > *adjective* impossible to understand.
DERIVATIVES – **unintelligibility** *noun* **unintelligibly** *adverb*.

unintended > *adjective* not planned or meant.

unintentional > *adjective* not done on purpose.
DERIVATIVES – **unintentionally** *adverb*.

uninterested > *adjective* not interested or concerned.
USAGE – be aware of the difference between **uninterested** and **disinterested**: **disinterested** means 'impartial, unbiased' rather than 'not interested or concerned', although the earliest use of **disinterested** is actually in the sense 'not interested'.

uninteresting > *adjective* not interesting.
DERIVATIVES – **uninterestingly** *adverb*.
SYNONYMS – boring, dull, tedious, unexciting.

uninterrupted > *adjective* **1** continuous. **2** unobstructed.
DERIVATIVES – **uninterruptedly** *adverb*.

uninventive > *adjective* not inventive.
DERIVATIVES – **uninventively** *adverb*.

uninvited > *adjective* arriving or acting without invitation.

uninviting > *adjective* not attractive; unpleasant.

DERIVATIVES – **uninvitingly** *adverb*.

uninvolved > *adjective* not involved.

union > *noun* **1** the action or fact of uniting or being united. **2** a state of harmony or agreement. **3** marriage; sexual coupling. **4** a club, society, or association formed by people with a common interest or purpose. **5** (also **Union**) a political unit consisting of a number of states or provinces with the same central government. **6** (**the Union**) the northern states of the US in the American Civil War. **7** a fabric made of different yarns, typically cotton and linen or silk.

SYNONYMS – **1** combining, joining, unification. **2** accord, unison, unity.

COMBINATIONS – **Union Jack** (also **Union flag**) the national flag of the United Kingdom.

ORIGIN – Latin, 'unity'.

unionise (also **unionize**) > *verb* become or cause to become members of a trade union.

DERIVATIVES – **unionisation** *noun* **unionised** *adjective*.

unionist > *noun* **1** a member of a trade union. **2** (**Unionist**) a person in Northern Ireland in favour of union with Great Britain.

DERIVATIVES – **unionism** *noun*.

unipolar > *adjective* having or relating to a single pole or extremity.

unique > *adjective* **1** being the only one of its kind; unlike anything else. **2** (**unique to**) belonging or connected to (one particular person, group, or place). **3** remarkable or unusual.

DERIVATIVES – **uniquely** *adverb* **uniqueness** *noun*.

USAGE – adjectives such as **unique**, **complete**, **equal**, and **infinite** contain the idea of something that is absolute and which by definition cannot be more or less than it is. Strictly speaking, a thing is either unique or it isn't: it cannot be *quite unique* or *very unique*. However, in practice these adjectives have acquired secondary, less precise senses, which can be modified by adverbs. For example, one of the secondary meanings of **unique** is 'remarkable or unusual'; it is this sense that is being modified in the example *a really unique opportunity*, and this usage is accepted in informal contexts.

ORIGIN – Latin *unicus*, from *unus* 'one'.

unisex > *adjective* designed to be suitable for both sexes.

unisexual > *adjective* **1** of one sex. **2** Botany having either stamens or pistils but not both.

DERIVATIVES – **unisexuality** *noun*.

unison > *noun* **1** simultaneous action or utterance. **2** Music a coincidence in pitch of sounds or notes. > *adjective* performed in unison.

ORIGIN – Latin *unisonus*, from *uni-* 'one' + *sonus* 'sound'.

unit > *noun* **1** an individual thing or person regarded as single and complete; each of the individual components making up a larger whole. **2** a device or part with a specified function: *a sink unit*. **3** a self-contained or distinct section of a building or group of buildings. **4** a subdivision of a larger military grouping. **5** a standard quantity in terms of which other quantities may be expressed. **6** a number or quantity equal to one.

DERIVATIVES – **unitise** (also **unitize**) *verb*.

COMBINATIONS – **unit trust** Brit. a trust managing a portfolio of stock exchange securities, in which small investors can buy units.

ORIGIN – from Latin *unus*, probably suggested by DIGIT.

unitard /yoōnitaard/ > *noun* a tight-fitting one-piece garment covering the whole body.

ORIGIN – from UNI- + LEOTARD.

Unitarian /yoōnitairiən/ Christian Theology > *adjective* referring to belief in the unity of God and rejection of the doctrine of the Trinity. > *noun* a Christian holding this belief.

DERIVATIVES – **Unitarianism** *noun*.

ORIGIN – from Latin *unitarius*, from *unitas* 'unity'.

unitary > *adjective* **1** single; uniform. **2** relating to a unit or units.

COMBINATIONS – **unitary authority** (also **unitary council**) (chiefly in the UK) a division of local government established in place of a two-tier system of local councils.

unite > *verb* **1** come or bring together for a common purpose or to form a whole. **2** archaic join in marriage.

DERIVATIVES – **united** *adjective* **unitedly** *adverb* **unitive** *adjective*.

SYNONYMS – **1** amalgamate, combine, fuse, integrate, join, link, unify.

ANTONYMS – **1** divide, separate.

ORIGIN – Latin *unire* 'join together', from *unus* 'one'.

unity > *noun* (pl. **unities**) **1** the state of being united or forming a whole. **2** a thing forming a complex whole. **3** Mathematics the number one.

ORIGIN – Old French *unite*, from Latin *unus* 'one'.

universal > *adjective* of, affecting, or done by all people or things in the world or in a particular group; applicable to all cases.

DERIVATIVES – **universality** *noun* **universally** *adverb*.

COMBINATIONS – **universal joint** a joint which can transmit rotary power by a shaft at any selected angle. **universal suffrage** the right of all adults (with minor exceptions) to vote in political elections.

ORIGIN – Latin *universalis*, from *universus* (see UNIVERSE).

universalise (also **universalize**) > *verb* make universal.

universalist > *noun* **1** Christian Theology a person who believes that all humankind will eventually be saved. **2** a person advocating concern for everyone without regard to national or sectional allegiances.

DERIVATIVES – **universalism** *noun* **universalistic** *adjective*.

universe > *noun* **1** all existing matter and space considered as a whole; the cosmos. **2** a particular sphere of activity or experience.

WORDFINDER – cosmology, cosmogony (*science of the origin and development of the universe*); anthropic principle (*that theories of the universe must allow for human existence*).

ORIGIN – from Latin *universus* 'combined into one, whole', from *uni-* 'one' + *versus* 'turned'.

university > *noun* (pl. **universities**) a high-level educational institution in which students study for degrees and academic research is done.

WORDFINDER – alma mater (*university where one was educated*), alumnus (*former student of a particular university*), campus (*university site and buildings*), don (*university teacher*), extramural (*denoting teaching for non-members of a university*), fresher (*newly arrived first-year student*), graduation (*the action of receiving a degree*), matriculation (*enrolment in a university*).

ORIGIN – Latin *universitas* 'the whole', later 'guild', from *universus* (see UNIVERSE).

unjoined > *adjective* not joined together.

unjointed > *adjective* lacking a joint or joints; consisting of a single piece.

unjust > *adjective* not just; unfair.

DERIVATIVES – **unjustly** *adverb*.

unjustifiable > *adjective* impossible to justify.

DERIVATIVES – **unjustifiably** *adverb*.

unjustified > *adjective* not justified.

unkempt > *adjective* having an untidy or dishevelled appearance.

SYNONYMS – bedraggled, dishevelled, messy, scruffy, slovenly, untidy.

ORIGIN – from UN-¹ + kempt 'combed' (from archaic kemb, related to COMB).

unkept > *adjective* **1** (of an undertaking) not honoured. **2** not tidy or cared for.

unkind > *adjective* inconsiderate and harsh.

DERIVATIVES – **unkindly** *adverb* **unkindness** *noun*.

SYNONYMS – harsh, heartless, hurtful,

inconsiderate, insensitive, mean, nasty, uncharitable.

SYNONYMS – benevolent, caring, kind.

unkink > *verb* make or become straight.

unknowable > *adjective* not able to be known.

DERIVATIVES – **unknowability** noun.

unknowing > *adjective* not knowing or aware. > *noun* literary ignorance.

DERIVATIVES – **unknowingly** adverb.

unknown > *adjective* not known or familiar. > *noun* 1 an unknown person or thing. 2 Mathematics an unknown quantity or variable.

IDIOMS – **unknown to** without the knowledge of.

COMBINATIONS – **unknown quantity** a person or thing whose nature, value, or significance is not known. **Unknown Soldier** an unidentified representative member of a country's armed forces killed in war, buried with special honours in a national memorial.

unlabelled (US **unlabeled**) > *adjective* without a label.

unlace > *verb* undo the laces of.

unladen > *adjective* not carrying a load.

unladylike > *adjective* not appropriate to or behaving like a lady.

unlaid > *adjective* not laid.

unlamented > *adjective* not mourned or regretted.

unlash > *verb* unfasten (something securely tied down).

unlatch > *verb* unfasten the latch of.

unlawful > *adjective* not conforming to or permitted by law or rules.

DERIVATIVES – **unlawfully** adverb **unlawfulness** noun.

USAGE – what is the difference between **unlawful** and **illegal**? Both can mean 'contrary to or forbidden by law', but **unlawful** has a broader meaning 'not permitted by rules': thus handball in soccer is **unlawful**, but not **illegal**.

unleaded > *adjective* (especially of petrol) without added lead.

unlearn > *verb* (past and past participle **unlearned** or **unlearnt**) aim to discard (something learned) from one's memory.

unlearned[1] /unˈlernid/ > *adjective* not well educated.

unlearned[2] /unˈlernd/ (also **unlearnt** /unˈlernt/) > *adjective* not having been learned.

unleash > *verb* release from a leash or restraint.

unleavened /unˈlevv'nd/ > *adjective* made without yeast or other raising agent.

unless > *conjunction* except when; if not.

ORIGIN – from **ON** or **IN** (assimilated to **UN-**[1]) + **LESS**.

unlettered > *adjective* poorly educated or illiterate.

unlicensed > *adjective* not having an official licence, especially for the sale of alcoholic liquor.

unlike > *preposition* 1 different from; not like. 2 in contrast to. 3 uncharacteristic of. > *adjective* dissimilar or different from each other.

DERIVATIVES – **unlikeness** noun.

USAGE – it is not good English to use **unlike** as a conjunction, as in *she was behaving unlike she'd ever behaved before*; it is better to use **as** and a negative, as in *she was behaving as she'd never behaved before*.

unlikely > *adjective* (**unlikelier**, **unlikeliest**) not likely; improbable.

DERIVATIVES – **unlikelihood** noun.

SYNONYMS – doubtful, dubious, implausible, improbable, questionable.

ANTONYMS – likely, probable.

unlimited > *adjective* not limited or restricted; infinite.

unlined[1] > *adjective* not marked with lines or wrinkles.

unlined[2] > *adjective* without a lining.

unlink > *verb* make no longer connected.

unlisted > *adjective* not included on a list, especially of stock exchange prices or telephone numbers.

unlit > *adjective* 1 not provided with lighting. 2 not having been lit.

unlivable > *adjective* uninhabitable.

unlived-in > *adjective* not appearing to be inhabited.

unload > *verb* 1 remove a load from. 2 remove (goods) from a vehicle, ship, etc. 3 informal get rid of (something unwanted). 4 remove (ammunition) from a gun or (film) from a camera.

DERIVATIVES – **unloader** noun.

unlock > *verb* 1 undo the lock of (something) using a key. 2 make (something) available.

unlooked > *adjective* (**unlooked for**) unexpected; unforeseen.

unloose (also **unloosen**) > *verb* undo; let free.

unloved > *adjective* loved by no one.

unlovely > *adjective* not attractive; ugly.

unlucky > *adjective* (**unluckier**, **unluckiest**) having, bringing, or resulting from bad luck.

DERIVATIVES – **unluckily** adverb.

SYNONYMS – luckless, unfortunate.

unmade > *adjective* 1 (of a bed) not arranged tidily. 2 Brit. (of a road) without a hard, smooth surface.

unmake > *verb* (past and past participle **unmade**) reverse or undo the making of; annul or destroy.

unman > *verb* (**unmanned**, **unmanning**) literary deprive of manly qualities such as self-control or courage.

unmanageable > *adjective* difficult or impossible to manage or control.

DERIVATIVES – **unmanageably** adverb.

unmanned > *adjective* not having or needing a crew or staff.

unmannerly > *adjective* not well mannered.

unmarked > *adjective* 1 not marked. 2 not noticed.

unmarried > *adjective* not married; single.

unmask > *verb* expose the true character of.

unmatched > *adjective* not matched or equalled.

unmeasurable > *adjective* not able to be measured objectively.

unmeasured > *adjective* not having been measured.

unmelodious > *adjective* not melodious; discordant.

unmentionable > *adjective* too embarrassing or offensive to be spoken about. > *noun* chiefly humorous an unmentionable thing.

unmerciful > *adjective* showing no mercy.

DERIVATIVES – **unmercifully** adverb.

unmerited > *adjective* not deserved or merited.

unmetalled > *adjective* Brit. (of a road) not having a hard surface.

unmetrical > *adjective* not composed in or using metre.

unmindful > *adjective* (**unmindful of**) not conscious or aware of.

unmissable > *adjective* that should not or cannot be missed.

unmistakable (also **unmistakeable**) > *adjective* not able to be mistaken for anything else.

DERIVATIVES – **unmistakably** adverb.

unmitigated > *adjective* absolute; unqualified.

DERIVATIVES – **unmitigatedly** adverb.

unmixed > *adjective* not mixed.

unmodulated > *adjective* not modulated.

unmoor > *verb* release the moorings of.

unmotivated > *adjective* 1 not motivated. 2 without apparent motive.

unmoved > *adjective* 1 not affected by emotion or excitement. 2 not changed in purpose or position.

unmoving > *adjective* 1 not moving; still. 2 not stirring any emotion.

unmusical > *adjective* 1 not pleasing to the ear. 2 unskilled in or indifferent to music.

unmuzzle > *verb* 1 remove a muzzle from. 2 allow freedom of expression to.

unnameable (also **unnamable**) > *adjective* unmentionable.

unnatural > *adjective* 1 contrary to nature; abnormal. 2 affected; not spontaneous.

DERIVATIVES – **unnaturally** adverb **unnaturalness** noun.

unnavigable > *adjective* not able to be sailed on by ships or boats.

unnecessary > *adjective* 1 not necessary. 2 more than is necessary.

DERIVATIVES – **unnecessarily** *adverb*.

SYNONYMS – **1** dispensable, expendable, inessential, needless, pointless, superfluous.

ANTONYMS – **1** essential, necessary.

unnerve > *verb* deprive of courage or confidence.

DERIVATIVES – **unnerving** *adjective* **unnervingly** *adverb*.

unnoticeable > *adjective* not easily observed or noticed.

DERIVATIVES – **unnoticeably** *adverb*.

unnoticed > *adjective* not noticed.

unnumbered > *adjective* **1** not assigned a number. **2** not counted; countless.

unobliging > *adjective* not helpful or cooperative.

unobserved > *adjective* not observed; unseen.

unobstructed > *adjective* not obstructed.

unobtainable > *adjective* not able to be obtained.

unobtrusive > *adjective* not conspicuous or attracting attention.

DERIVATIVES – **unobtrusively** *adverb* **unobtrusiveness** *noun*.

unoccupied > *adjective* not occupied.

unofficial > *adjective* not officially authorised or confirmed.

DERIVATIVES – **unofficially** *adverb*.

unopened > *adjective* not opened.

unopposed > *adjective* not opposed; unchallenged.

unorganised (also **unorganized**) > *adjective* **1** not organised. **2** not unionised.

unoriginal > *adjective* lacking originality; derivative.

DERIVATIVES – **unoriginality** *noun* **unoriginally** *adverb*.

unorthodox > *adjective* contrary to what is usual, traditional, or accepted; not orthodox.

DERIVATIVES – **unorthodoxy** *noun*.

SYNONYMS – alternative, irregular, nonconformist, radical, unconventional, unusual.

ANTONYMS – conventional, orthodox.

unostentatious > *adjective* not ostentatious.

DERIVATIVES – **unostentatiously** *adverb*.

unpack > *verb* **1** open and remove the contents of (a suitcase or container). **2** remove from a packed container. **3** analyse into component elements.

unpaid > *adjective* **1** (of a debt) not yet paid. **2** (of work or leave) undertaken without payment. **3** (of a person) not receiving payment for work done.

unpaired > *adjective* **1** not arranged in pairs. **2** not forming one of a pair.

unpalatable > *adjective* **1** not pleasant to taste. **2** difficult to put up with or accept.

DERIVATIVES – **unpalatability** *noun* **unpalatably** *adverb*.

unparalleled > *adjective* having no parallel or equal; exceptional.

unpardonable > *adjective* (of a fault or offence) unforgivable.

DERIVATIVES – **unpardonably** *adverb*.

unparliamentary > *adjective* (especially of language) contrary to the rules or procedures of parliament.

unpasteurised (also **unpasteurized**) > *adjective* not pasteurised.

unpatriotic > *adjective* not patriotic.

DERIVATIVES – **unpatriotically** *adverb*.

unpaved > *adjective* lacking a metalled or paved surface.

unpeopled > *adjective* emptied of people; depopulated.

unperson > *noun* (pl. **unpersons**) a person whose name or existence is officially denied or ignored.

unperturbed > *adjective* not perturbed or concerned.

unpick > *verb* **1** undo the sewing of (stitches or a garment). **2** carefully analyse the different elements of (something).

unpin > *verb* (**unpinned**, **unpinning**) unfasten or detach by removing a pin or pins.

unpitying > *adjective* not feeling or showing pity.

DERIVATIVES – **unpityingly** *adverb*.

unplaced > *adjective* **1** not having or assigned to a specific place. **2** *chiefly Horse Racing* not one of the first three (sometimes four) to finish in a race.

unplanned > *adjective* not planned.

unplayable > *adjective* **1** not able to be played or played on. **2** (of music) too difficult or bad to perform.

unpleasant > *adjective* not pleasant; disagreeable.

DERIVATIVES – **unpleasantly** *adverb*.

SYNONYMS – disagreeable, distasteful, foul, irksome, nasty, objectionable, unsavoury.

ANTONYMS – agreeable, pleasant.

unpleasantness > *noun* **1** the state or quality of being unpleasant. **2** bad feeling or quarrelling between people.

unploughed (US **unplowed**) > *adjective* (of land) not having been ploughed.

unplug > *verb* (**unplugged**, **unplugging**) **1** disconnect (an electrical device) by removing its plug from a socket. **2** remove an obstacle or blockage from.

unplugged > *adjective* trademark (of pop or rock music) performed or recorded with acoustic rather than electrically amplified instruments.

unplumbed > *adjective* **1** not provided with plumbing. **2** not fully explored or understood.

DERIVATIVES – **unplumbable** *adjective*.

unpolished > *adjective* **1** not having a polished surface. **2** (of a work) not polished.

unpolled > *adjective* **1** (of a voter) not having voted, or registered to vote, at an election. **2** (of a vote) not cast at or registered for an election. **3** (of a person) not included in an opinion poll.

unpopular > *adjective* not liked or popular.

DERIVATIVES – **unpopularity** *noun*.

SYNONYMS – disliked, friendless, out of favour, unloved, unwanted.

unpopulated > *adjective* without inhabitants.

unpowered > *adjective* having no fuel-burning source of power for propulsion.

unpractised (US **unpracticed**) > *adjective* not trained or experienced.

unprecedented > *adjective* never done or known before.

DERIVATIVES – **unprecedentedly** *adverb*.

unpredictable > *adjective* not able to be predicted; changeable.

DERIVATIVES – **unpredictability** *noun* **unpredictably** *adverb*.

unprejudiced > *adjective* without prejudice; unbiased.

unpremeditated > *adjective* not thought out or planned beforehand.

unprepared > *adjective* **1** not ready or able to deal with something. **2** (of a thing) not made ready for use.

unprepossessing > *adjective* not attractive or appealing to the eye.

unpretending > *adjective* archaic not pretentious or false.

unpretentious > *adjective* not pretentious; modest.

DERIVATIVES – **unpretentiously** *adverb* **unpretentiousness** *noun*.

SYNONYMS – humble, modest, simple, unaffected, unassuming.

unprincipled > *adjective* not acting in accordance with moral principles.

SYNONYMS – amoral, immoral, reprobate, unethical, unscrupulous.

unprintable > *adjective* (of words, comments, or thoughts) too offensive or shocking to be published.

unproblematic > *adjective* not presenting a problem or difficulty.

DERIVATIVES – **unproblematically** *adverb*.

unprocessed > *adjective* not processed.

unproductive > *adjective* **1** not producing or able to produce large amounts of goods, crops, etc. **2** not achieving much; not very useful.

unprofessional > *adjective* below or contrary to the standards expected in a particular profession.

DERIVATIVES – **unprofessionally** *adverb*.

unprofitable > *adjective* **1** not yielding a profit. **2** not beneficial or useful.

unpromising > *adjective* not giving hope of future success or good results.

DERIVATIVES – **unpromisingly** *adverb*.

unprompted ▷ *adjective* without being prompted.

unpronounceable ▷ *adjective* too difficult to pronounce.

unprotected ▷ *adjective* 1 not protected or kept safe from harm. 2 (of sexual intercourse) performed without a condom.

unproven /un**prōō**v'n, -**prō**-/ (also **unproved**) ▷ *adjective* 1 not demonstrated by evidence or argument as true or existing. 2 not tried and tested.

unprovoked ▷ *adjective* (of an attack, crime, etc.) not directly provoked.

unpublished ▷ *adjective* 1 (of a work) not published. 2 (of an author) having no writings published.
DERIVATIVES – **unpublishable** *adjective*.

unpunished ▷ *adjective* (of an offence or offender) not receiving any punishment or penalty.

unputdownable ▷ *adjective* informal (of a book) so engrossing that one cannot stop reading it.

unqualified ▷ *adjective* 1 not having the necessary qualifications. 2 without reservation or limitation; total: *an unqualified success.*

unquantifiable ▷ *adjective* impossible to express or measure.

unquenchable ▷ *adjective* not able to be quenched.

unquestionable ▷ *adjective* not able to be disputed or doubted.
DERIVATIVES – **unquestionably** *adverb*.

unquestioned ▷ *adjective* 1 not disputed or doubted; certain. 2 accepted without question. 3 not subjected to questioning.
DERIVATIVES – **unquestioning** *adjective* **unquestioningly** *adverb*.

unquiet ▷ *adjective* 1 unable to be still; restless. 2 uneasy; anxious.
DERIVATIVES – **unquietly** *adverb*.

unquote ▷ *verb* (in phrase **quote —— unquote**) see QUOTE.

unquoted ▷ *adjective* not quoted or listed on a stock exchange.

unravel ▷ *verb* (**unravelled, unravelling; US unraveled, unraveling**) 1 undo (twisted, knitted, or woven threads); unwind. 2 become undone. 3 investigate and solve (a mystery or puzzle). 4 begin to fail or collapse.

unreachable ▷ *adjective* unable to be reached or contacted.

unreactive ▷ *adjective* having little tendency to react chemically.

unread ▷ *adjective* not having been read.

unreadable ▷ *adjective* 1 not clear enough to read; illegible. 2 too dull or difficult to be worth reading.
DERIVATIVES – **unreadability** *noun* **unreadably** *adverb*.

unready ▷ *adjective* not ready or prepared.

unreal ▷ *adjective* 1 imaginary; not seeming real. 2 unrealistic. 3 informal, chiefly N. Amer. incredible; amazing.
DERIVATIVES – **unreality** *noun* **unreally** *adverb*.

unrealised (also **unrealized**) ▷ *adjective* 1 not achieved or created. 2 not converted into money: *unrealised assets.*

unrealistic ▷ *adjective* not realistic.
DERIVATIVES – **unrealistically** *adverb*.
SYNONYMS – fanciful, impracticable, impractical, unfeasible, unworkable.

unreason ▷ *noun* irrationality; lack of reasonable thought.
DERIVATIVES – **unreasoned** *adjective*.

unreasonable ▷ *adjective* 1 not guided by or based on good sense. 2 beyond the limits of acceptability.
DERIVATIVES – **unreasonableness** *noun* **unreasonably** *adverb*.
SYNONYMS – 1 absurd, illogical, irrational, senseless. 2 excessive, immoderate, unacceptable, unjustified, unwarranted.

unreasoning ▷ *adjective* not guided by or based on reason; illogical.

unreceptive ▷ *adjective* not receptive.

unreciprocated ▷ *adjective* not reciprocated; unrequited.

unrecognisable (also **unrecognizable**) ▷ *adjective* not able to be recognised.
DERIVATIVES – **unrecognisably** *adverb*.

unrecognised (also **unrecognized**) ▷ *adjective* 1 not identified from previous encounters or knowledge. 2 not acknowledged as valid; not officially recognised.

unreconciled ▷ *adjective* not reconciled.

unreconstructed ▷ *adjective* not reconciled or converted to the current political theory or movement.

unrecorded ▷ *adjective* not recorded.

unredeemed ▷ *adjective* not redeemed.

unreel ▷ *verb* 1 unwind. 2 (of a film) wind from one reel to another during projection.

unrefined ▷ *adjective* 1 not processed to remove impurities. 2 not elegant or cultured.

unregenerate /unri**jenn**ərət/ ▷ *adjective* not reforming or showing repentance; obstinately wrong or bad.

unregistered ▷ *adjective* not officially recognised and recorded.

unregulated ▷ *adjective* not controlled or supervised by regulations or laws.

unrehearsed ▷ *adjective* not rehearsed.

unrelated ▷ *adjective* not related.

unreleased ▷ *adjective* (especially of a film or recording) not released.

unrelenting ▷ *adjective* not yielding in strength, severity, or determination.
DERIVATIVES – **unrelentingly** *adverb*.

unreliable ▷ *adjective* not able to be relied upon.
DERIVATIVES – **unreliability** *noun* **unreliably** *adverb*.
SYNONYMS – erratic, inconsistent, irresponsible, undependable, unstable, untrustworthy.

unrelieved ▷ *adjective* 1 lacking variation or change; monotonous. 2 not provided with relief; not aided or assisted.
DERIVATIVES – **unrelievedly** *adverb*.

unremarkable ▷ *adjective* not particularly interesting or surprising.

unremarked ▷ *adjective* not remarked upon; unnoticed.

unremitting ▷ *adjective* never relaxing or slackening.
DERIVATIVES – **unremittingly** *adverb*.

unremunerative ▷ *adjective* bringing little or no profit or income.

unrepeatable ▷ *adjective* 1 not able to be repeated. 2 too offensive or shocking to be said again.

unrepentant ▷ *adjective* showing no regret for one's wrongdoings.
DERIVATIVES – **unrepentantly** *adverb*.
SYNONYMS – impenitent, shameless, unapologetic, unashamed, unregenerate.

unreported ▷ *adjective* not reported.

unrepresentative ▷ *adjective* not typical of a class, group, or body of opinion.

unrequited ▷ *adjective* (of a feeling, especially love) not returned or rewarded.
DERIVATIVES – **unrequitedly** *adverb*.

unreserved ▷ *adjective* 1 without reservations; complete. 2 frank and open. 3 not set apart or booked in advance.
DERIVATIVES – **unreservedly** *adverb*.

unresolved ▷ *adjective* (of a problem, dispute, etc.) not resolved.

unresponsive ▷ *adjective* not responsive.
DERIVATIVES – **unresponsively** *adverb* **unresponsiveness** *noun*.

unrest ▷ *noun* 1 a state of rebellious dissatisfaction in a group of people. 2 a state of uneasiness or disturbance.

unrestrained ▷ *adjective* not restrained or restricted.
DERIVATIVES – **unrestrainedly** *adverb*.

unrestricted ▷ *adjective* not limited or restricted.

unrewarding ▷ *adjective* not rewarding or satisfying.

unripe ▷ *adjective* not ripe.

unrivalled (US **unrivaled**) ▷ *adjective* surpassing all others.

unroll ▷ *verb* open out from a rolled-up state.

unromantic ▷ *adjective* not romantic.

unruffled ▷ *adjective* 1 not disordered or disturbed. 2 (of a person) not agitated; calm.

unruly ▷ *adjective* (**unrulier, unruliest**) disorderly and disruptive; difficult to control.
DERIVATIVES – **unruliness** *noun*.

SYNONYMS – disorderly, disruptive, lawless, obstreperous, riotous, rowdy.

ORIGIN – from **UN-**[1] + archaic *ruly* 'disciplined; orderly' (from **RULE**).

unsaddle > *verb* remove the saddle from.

unsafe > *adjective* **1** not safe; dangerous. **2** Law (of a verdict or conviction) not based on reliable evidence and likely to constitute a miscarriage of justice.

COMBINATIONS – **unsafe sex** sexual activity engaged in by people who have not taken precautions to protect themselves against sexually transmitted diseases such as Aids.

unsaid past and past participle of **UNSAY**. > *adjective* not said or uttered.

unsaleable (also **unsalable**) > *adjective* not able to be sold.

unsalted > *adjective* not salted.

unsanitary > *adjective* not sanitary.

unsatisfactory > *adjective* **1** unacceptable because poor or not good enough. **2** Law another term for **UNSAFE**.

DERIVATIVES – **unsatisfactorily** *adverb*.

SYNONYMS – **1** disappointing, dissatisfying, inadequate, substandard, unacceptable.

unsatisfied > *adjective* not satisfied.

USAGE – the words **unsatisfied** and **dissatisfied** have different meanings: if you are **unsatisfied** you lack or do not have enough of something you want or need; if you are **dissatisfied** you are unhappy because what you have is not what you want.

unsatisfying > *adjective* not satisfying.

DERIVATIVES – **unsatisfyingly** *adverb*.

unsaturated > *adjective* Chemistry (of organic molecules) having carbon–carbon double or triple bonds and therefore not containing the greatest possible number of hydrogen atoms.

DERIVATIVES – **unsaturation** *noun*.

unsaved > *adjective* not saved, in particular (in Christian use) not saved from damnation.

unsavoury (US **unsavory**) > *adjective* **1** disagreeable to taste, smell, or look at. **2** objectionable; disreputable.

unsay > *verb* (past and past participle **unsaid**) withdraw or retract (a statement).

unsayable > *adjective* not able to be said, especially because considered too controversial or offensive.

unscarred > *adjective* not scarred or damaged.

unscathed > *adjective* without suffering any injury, damage, or harm.

unscented > *adjective* not scented.

unscheduled > *adjective* not scheduled.

unschooled > *adjective* **1** lacking schooling or training. **2** not affected; natural and spontaneous.

unscientific > *adjective* **1** not in accordance with scientific principles or methodology. **2** lacking knowledge of or interest in science.

DERIVATIVES – **unscientifically** *adverb*.

unscramble > *verb* restore or convert to an intelligible or readable state.

unscrew > *verb* unfasten by twisting.

unscripted > *adjective* said or delivered without a prepared script; impromptu.

unscrupulous > *adjective* without moral scruples.

DERIVATIVES – **unscrupulously** *adverb* **unscrupulousness** *noun*.

SYNONYMS – amoral, conscienceless, immoral, unethical, unprincipled.

unseal > *verb* remove or break the seal of.

unsealed > *adjective* not sealed.

unseasonable > *adjective* (of weather) unusual for the time of year.

DERIVATIVES – **unseasonableness** *noun*.

unseasonal > *adjective* unusual or inappropriate for the season; unseasonable.

unseasoned > *adjective* **1** (of food) not flavoured with salt, pepper, or other spices. **2** (of wood) not treated or matured. **3** (of a person) inexperienced.

unseat > *verb* **1** cause to fall from a saddle or seat. **2** remove from a position of power.

unsecured > *adjective* **1** (of a loan) made without an asset given as security. **2** not made secure or safe.

unseeded > *adjective* **1** (chiefly of a competitor in a sports tournament) not seeded. **2** without seeds; not sown with seeds.

unseeing > *adjective* with one's eyes open but without noticing or seeing anything.

DERIVATIVES – **unseeingly** *adverb*.

unseemly > *adjective* (of behaviour or actions) not proper or appropriate.

DERIVATIVES – **unseemliness** *noun*.

SYNONYMS – improper, inappropriate, indecorous, indelicate, unbecoming, undignified.

unseen > *adjective* **1** not seen or noticed. **2** chiefly Brit. (of a text in an examination) not previously read or prepared.

unselfconscious > *adjective* without self-consciousness; not shy or embarrassed.

DERIVATIVES – **unselfconsciously** *adverb* **unselfconsciousness** *noun*.

unselfish > *adjective* not selfish.

DERIVATIVES – **unselfishly** *adverb* **unselfishness** *noun*.

SYNONYMS – altruistic, charitable, considerate, disinterested, generous, selfless.

unsentimental > *adjective* not displaying or influenced by sentimental feelings.

DERIVATIVES – **unsentimentally** *adverb*.

unserious > *adjective* not serious; light-hearted.

unserviceable > *adjective* not in working order; unfit for use.

unsettle > *verb* cause to be anxious or uneasy; disturb.

DERIVATIVES – **unsettlement** *noun* **unsettling** *adjective*.

SYNONYMS – disconcert, discountenance, disquiet, disturb, perturb, unnerve.

unsettled > *adjective* **1** lacking stability; changeable or liable to change. **2** agitated; uneasy. **3** not yet resolved. **4** (of an area) having no settlers or inhabitants.

unsex > *verb* deprive of gender, sexuality, or the characteristic attributes of one or other sex.

unshackle > *verb* release from shackles or other restraints.

unshakeable (also **unshakable**) > *adjective* (of a belief, feeling, etc.) firm and unable to be changed or disputed.

unshaken > *adjective* steadfast and unwavering.

unshaven > *adjective* not having shaved or been shaved.

unsheathe > *verb* draw or pull out (a knife or similar weapon) from a sheath.

unshed > *adjective* (of tears) welling in a person's eyes but not falling.

unshelled > *adjective* not extracted from its shell.

unship > *verb* (**unshipped**, **unshipping**) chiefly Nautical **1** remove (an oar, mast, or other object) from a fixed or regular position. **2** unload (a cargo) from a ship or boat.

unshockable > *adjective* impossible to shock.

unshorn > *adjective* (of hair or wool) not cut or shorn.

unsighted > *adjective* **1** lacking the power of sight. **2** (especially in sport) prevented from having a clear view.

unsightly > *adjective* unpleasant to look at; ugly.

DERIVATIVES – **unsightliness** *noun*.

unsigned > *adjective* **1** not bearing a person's signature. **2** (of a musician or sports player) not having signed a contract of employment.

unsinkable > *adjective* unable to be sunk.

unskilful (also chiefly US **unskillful**) > *adjective* not having or showing skill.

DERIVATIVES – **unskilfully** *adverb*.

unskilled > *adjective* not having or requiring special skill or training.

unsling > *verb* (past and past participle **unslung**) remove from a position of being slung or suspended.

unsmiling > *adjective* not smiling; serious or unfriendly.

DERIVATIVES – **unsmilingly** *adverb*.

unsmoked > *adjective* **1** (of meat or fish) not cured by exposure to smoke. **2** (of tobacco or a cigarette) not having been smoked.

unsnap > *verb* (**unsnapped**, **unsnapping**) unfasten or open with a brisk movement and a sharp sound.

unsociable > *adjective* **1** not enjoying the company of or engaging in activities with others. **2** not conducive to friendly social relations.

USAGE – do not confuse **unsociable** with **unsocial** and **antisocial**: **unsocial** usually means 'socially inconvenient' and typically refers to the hours of work of a job; **antisocial** means 'contrary to accepted social customs and therefore annoying'.

unsocial > *adjective* **1** (of the hours of work of a job) falling outside the normal working day and thus socially inconvenient. **2** not seeking the company of others.
DERIVATIVES – **unsocially** *adverb*.

unsold > *adjective* (of an item) not sold.

unsolicited > *adjective* not asked for; given or done voluntarily.

unsolved > *adjective* not solved.

unsophisticated > *adjective* **1** lacking refined worldly knowledge or tastes. **2** not complicated or highly developed; basic.
SYNONYMS – **1** innocent, naive, natural, simple, unworldly. **2** basic, crude, primitive, rudimentary, simple, unrefined.

unsorted > *adjective* not sorted or arranged.

unsound > *adjective* **1** not safe or robust; in poor condition. **2** not based on sound evidence or reasoning; unreliable or unacceptable.
DERIVATIVES – **unsoundness** *noun*.

unsparing > *adjective* merciless; severe.
DERIVATIVES – **unsparingly** *adverb*.

unspeakable > *adjective* **1** not able to be expressed in words. **2** too bad or horrific to express in words.
DERIVATIVES – **unspeakably** *adverb*.

unspecialised (also **unspecialized**) > *adjective* not specialised.

unspecific > *adjective* not specific; vague.

unspecified > *adjective* not stated clearly or exactly.

unspectacular > *adjective* not spectacular; unremarkable.

unspoilt (also **unspoiled**) > *adjective* not spoilt, in particular (of a place) not marred by development.

unspoken > *adjective* not expressed in speech; tacit.

unspool > *verb* **1** unwind from or as if from a spool. **2** (of a film) be screened.

unsporting > *adjective* not fair or sportsmanlike.
DERIVATIVES – **unsportingly** *adverb*.

unsportsmanlike > *adjective* unsporting.

unsprung > *adjective* not provided with springs.

unstable > *adjective* (**unstabler, unstablest**) **1** prone to change or collapse; not stable. **2** prone to psychiatric problems or sudden changes of mood.
SYNONYMS – **1** changeable, erratic, insecure, unsettled, unsteady. **2** disturbed, unbalanced, unhinged.

unstained > *adjective* not stained.

unstated > *adjective* not stated or declared.

unsteady > *adjective* (**unsteadier, unsteadiest**) **1** liable to fall or shake; not firm. **2** not uniform or regular.
DERIVATIVES – **unsteadily** *adverb* **unsteadiness** *noun*.
SYNONYMS – **1** insecure, shaky, unsafe, unstable, wobbly. **2** inconstant, irregular, uneven, variable.

unstick > *verb* (past and past participle **unstuck**) cause to become no longer stuck together.
IDIOMS – **come unstuck** informal fail.

unstinting > *adjective* given or giving without restraint; unsparing.
DERIVATIVES – **unstinted** *adjective* **unstintingly** *adverb*.

unstoppable > *adjective* impossible to stop or prevent.
DERIVATIVES – **unstoppably** *adverb*.

unstopper > *verb* remove the stopper from (a container).

unstressed > *adjective* **1** Phonetics (of a syllable) not pronounced with stress. **2** not subjected to stress.

unstring > *verb* (past and past participle **unstrung**) **1** remove or relax the string or strings of. **2** (**unstrung**) unnerved.

unstructured > *adjective* without formal organisation or structure.

unstuck past and past participle of UNSTICK.

unstudied > *adjective* not laboured or artificial; natural.

unstuffy > *adjective* friendly, informal, and approachable.

unsubstantial > *adjective* having little or no solidity, reality, or factual basis.

unsubstantiated > *adjective* not supported or proven by evidence.

unsubtle > *adjective* not subtle; obvious; clumsy.
DERIVATIVES – **unsubtly** *adverb*.

unsuccessful > *adjective* not successful.
DERIVATIVES – **unsuccessfully** *adverb*.

unsuitable > *adjective* not fitting or appropriate.
DERIVATIVES – **unsuitability** *noun* **unsuitably** *adverb*.

unsuited > *adjective* not right or appropriate.

unsullied > *adjective* not spoiled or made impure.

unsung > *adjective* not celebrated or praised: *unsung heroes*.

unsupervised > *adjective* not done or acting under supervision.

unsupportable > *adjective* insupportable.

unsupported > *adjective* **1** not supported. **2** not borne out by evidence or facts.

unsure > *adjective* **1** lacking confidence. **2** not fixed or certain.
DERIVATIVES – **unsureness** *noun*.

unsurfaced > *adjective* (of a road or path) not provided with a durable upper layer.

unsurpassable > *adjective* not able to be surpassed.

unsurpassed > *adjective* better or greater than any other.

unsurprising > *adjective* not unexpected and so not causing surprise.
DERIVATIVES – **unsurprisingly** *adverb*.

unsuspected > *adjective* **1** not known or thought to exist; not imagined as possible. **2** not regarded with suspicion.

unsuspecting > *adjective* not aware of the presence of danger; feeling no suspicion.
DERIVATIVES – **unsuspectingly** *adverb*.

unsustainable > *adjective* **1** not able to be sustained. **2** not able to be upheld or defended. **3** Ecology upsetting the ecological balance by depleting natural resources.
DERIVATIVES – **unsustainably** *adverb*.

unswayed > *adjective* not influenced or affected.

unsweetened > *adjective* (of food or drink) without added sugar or sweetener.

unswerving > *adjective* not changing or becoming weaker.
DERIVATIVES – **unswervingly** *adverb*.

unsymmetrical > *adjective* not symmetrical; asymmetrical.

unsympathetic > *adjective* **1** not sympathetic. **2** not showing approval of an idea or action. **3** not likeable.
DERIVATIVES – **unsympathetically** *adverb*.

unsystematic > *adjective* not done or acting according to a fixed plan or system.
DERIVATIVES – **unsystematically** *adverb*.

untainted > *adjective* not contaminated or tainted.

untameable (also **untamable**) > *adjective* not capable of being tamed or controlled.

untamed > *adjective* not tamed or controlled.

untangle > *verb* **1** free from tangles. **2** free from complications or confusion.

untapped > *adjective* (of a resource) not yet exploited or used.

untarnished > *adjective* **1** not tarnished. **2** not spoiled or ruined.

untasted > *adjective* (of food or drink) not sampled.

untaught > *adjective* **1** not having been taught or educated. **2** not acquired by teaching; natural or spontaneous.

unteachable > *adjective* (of a pupil or skill) unable to be taught.

untempered > *adjective* not moderated or lessened.

untenable > *adjective* not able to be maintained or defended against attack or objection.

untended > *adjective* not cared for or looked after; neglected.

untenured > *adjective* (of a college teacher or post) without tenure.

Untermensch /ŏŏntərmensh/ > noun (pl. **Untermenschen** /ŏŏntərmenshən/) a person considered racially or socially inferior.

ORIGIN – German, 'underperson'.

untested > adjective not subjected to testing; unproven.

DERIVATIVES – **untestable** adjective.

unthinkable > adjective too unlikely or undesirable to be considered a possibility.

DERIVATIVES – **unthinkably** adverb.

unthinking > adjective without proper consideration.

DERIVATIVES – **unthinkingly** adverb **unthinkingness** noun.

unthought > adjective (**unthought of**) not imagined or dreamed of.

unthreatening > adjective not threatening.

untidy > adjective (**untidier, untidiest**) 1 not arranged tidily. 2 (of a person) not inclined to be neat.

DERIVATIVES – **untidily** adverb **untidiness** noun.

SYNONYMS – 1 chaotic, cluttered, disorderly, messy. 2 bedraggled, dishevelled, scruffy, slovenly, unkempt.

untie > verb (**untying**) undo or unfasten (something tied).

untied > adjective not fastened or knotted.

until > preposition & conjunction up to (the point in time or the event mentioned).

ORIGIN – from Old Norse und 'as far as' + **TILL**[1] (the sense thus duplicated).

untimely > adjective 1 happening or done at an unsuitable time; inappropriate. 2 (of a death or end) happening too soon or sooner than normal.

DERIVATIVES – **untimeliness** noun.

untiring > adjective continuing at the same rate without loss of vigour.

DERIVATIVES – **untiringly** adverb.

untitled > adjective 1 (of a book or other work) having no title. 2 not having a title indicating high social or official rank.

unto > preposition 1 archaic term for **TO**. 2 archaic term for **UNTIL**.

ORIGIN – from **UNTIL**, with **TO** replacing **TILL**[1] (in its northern dialect meaning 'to').

untold > adjective 1 too much or too many to be counted; indescribable. 2 not narrated or recounted.

ORIGIN – Old English, 'not counted' (see **UN-**[1], **TOLD**).

untouchable > adjective 1 not able to be touched or affected. 2 unable to be matched or rivalled. > noun historical a member of the lowest-caste Hindu group.

DERIVATIVES – **untouchability** noun.

NOTE – in senses relating to the traditional Hindu caste system, the term **untouchable** and the social restrictions accompanying it were declared illegal in the constitution of India in 1949 and of Pakistan in 1953. The official term in India today is **scheduled caste**.

untouched > adjective 1 not handled, used, or tasted. 2 (of a subject) not treated or discussed. 3 not affected, changed, or damaged in any way.

untoward > adjective unexpected and inappropriate or adverse.

untraceable > adjective unable to be found or traced.

untracked > adjective (of land) not previously traversed; without tracks.

untrained > adjective not having been trained.

untrammelled (US **untrammeled**) > adjective not restricted or hampered.

untranslatable > adjective not able to be translated.

untreatable > adjective for whom or which no medical care is available or possible.

untreated > adjective 1 not given treatment. 2 not treated by the use of a chemical, physical, or biological agent.

untried > adjective not yet tested; inexperienced.

untrodden > adjective not having been walked on.

untroubled > adjective not troubled.

SYNONYMS – carefree, serene, unconcerned, unperturbed.

untrue > adjective 1 false or incorrect. 2 not faithful or loyal.

SYNONYMS – 1 erroneous, fallacious, false, incorrect, wrong. 2 disloyal, faithless, false, unfaithful.

untrustworthy > adjective unable to be trusted.

DERIVATIVES – **untrustworthiness** noun.

SYNONYMS – deceitful, dishonest, dubious, undependable, unreliable.

untruth > noun (pl. **untruths**) 1 a lie. 2 the quality of being false.

untruthful > adjective not truthful.

DERIVATIVES – **untruthfully** adverb **untruthfulness** noun.

untuck > verb free (something) from being tucked in or up.

untuned > adjective not tuned or in tune.

unturned > adjective not turned.

untutored > adjective not formally taught.

untwist > verb open from a twisted position.

untying present participle of **UNTIE**.

untypical > adjective not typical; unusual.

DERIVATIVES – **untypically** adverb.

unusable > adjective not fit to be used.

unused > adjective 1 not used. 2 (**unused to**) not accustomed to.

unusual > adjective 1 not habitually or commonly done or occurring. 2 remarkable; exceptional.

DERIVATIVES – **unusually** adverb.

SYNONYMS – 1 abnormal, atypical, curious, extraordinary, irregular, uncommon,

unorthodox. 2 exceptional, extraordinary, notable, outstanding, remarkable.

ANTONYMS – 1 common, normal, usual.

unutterable > adjective too great or awful to describe.

DERIVATIVES – **unutterably** adverb.

unuttered > adjective not spoken or expressed.

unvalued > adjective not valued.

unvaried > adjective not varied.

unvarnished > adjective 1 not varnished. 2 plain and straightforward.

unvarying > adjective not varying.

DERIVATIVES – **unvaryingly** adverb.

unveil > verb 1 remove a veil or covering from. 2 show or announce publicly for the first time.

unventilated > adjective not ventilated.

unverifiable > adjective unable to be verified.

unverified > adjective not verified.

unversed > adjective (**unversed in**) not versed in.

unviable > adjective not viable.

unvisited > adjective not visited.

unvoiced > adjective 1 unuttered. 2 Phonetics (of a speech sound) uttered without vibration of the vocal cords.

unwaged > adjective chiefly Brit. 1 unemployed or doing unpaid work. 2 (of work) unpaid.

unwalled > adjective without walls.

unwanted > adjective not wanted.

unwarrantable > adjective unjustifiable.

DERIVATIVES – **unwarrantably** adverb.

unwarranted > adjective not warranted.

unwary > adjective not cautious.

DERIVATIVES – **unwarily** adverb.

SYNONYMS – careless, heedless, inattentive, incautious, unobservant.

unwashed > adjective not washed.

IDIOMS – **the (great) unwashed** derogatory the multitude of ordinary people.

unwatchable > adjective too bad, disturbing, or uninteresting to watch.

unwatched > adjective not watched.

unwavering > adjective not wavering.

DERIVATIVES – **unwaveringly** adverb.

unweaned > adjective not weaned.

unwearable > adjective not fit to be worn.

unwearied > adjective not wearied.

unwearying > adjective never tiring or slackening.

unwed (also **unwedded**) > adjective not married.

unweighted > adjective not weighted.

unwelcome > adjective not welcome.

unwelcoming > adjective inhospitable.

unwell > adjective ill.

SYNONYMS – ailing, indisposed, ill, sick; Brit. poorly.

unwholesome > adjective not wholesome.

unwieldy* > adjective (**unwieldier,**

unwieldiest) hard to move or manage because of its size, shape, or weight.

DERIVATIVES – **unwieldiness** noun.

*SPELLING – remember, i before e, and only one l: unwieldy.

SYNONYMS – awkward, cumbersome, unmanageable.

ORIGIN – first meaning 'weak, infirm', from obsolete wieldy 'vigorous' (from **WIELD**).

unwilling > adjective not willing.

DERIVATIVES – **unwillingly** adverb **unwillingness** noun.

unwind > verb (past and past participle **unwound**) 1 undo after winding. 2 relax after a period of work or tension.

unwinking > adjective (of a stare or light) unwavering.

unwinnable > adjective not winnable.

unwisdom > noun folly.

unwise > adjective foolish.

DERIVATIVES – **unwisely** adverb.

SYNONYMS – foolhardy, foolish, ill-advised, imprudent, injudicious, silly.

ANTONYMS – sensible, wise.

unwitting > adjective 1 not aware of the full facts. 2 unintentional.

DERIVATIVES – **unwittingly** adverb.

ORIGIN – Old English, 'not knowing or realising'.

unwomanly > adjective not womanly.

unwonted /unwōntid/ > adjective unaccustomed or unusual.

DERIVATIVES – **unwontedly** adverb.

unworkable > adjective impractical.

unworked > adjective not cultivated, mined, or carved.

unworldly > adjective 1 having little awareness of the realities of life. 2 not seeming to belong to this world.

DERIVATIVES – **unworldliness** noun.

unworn > adjective not worn.

unworried > adjective not worried.

unworthy > adjective (**unworthier**, **unworthiest**) not worthy.

DERIVATIVES – **unworthily** adverb **unworthiness** noun.

unwound¹ > adjective (of a clock or watch) not wound or wound up.

unwound² past and past participle of **UNWIND**.

unwounded > adjective not wounded.

unwrap > verb (**unwrapped**, **unwrapping**) remove the wrapping from.

unwrinkled > adjective not wrinkled.

unwritable > adjective not able to be written.

unwritten > adjective 1 not written. 2 (of a law) based originally on custom or judicial decision rather than on statute.

unyielding > adjective not yielding.

unyoke > verb release (animals) from a yoke.

unzip > verb (**unzipped**, **unzipping**) 1 unfasten the zip of. 2 Computing decompress (a compressed file).

up > adverb 1 towards a higher place or position. 2 to or at a place perceived as higher. 3 at or to a higher level or value. 4 to the place where someone is. 5 out of bed. 6 in a publicly visible place. 7 (of the sun) visible in the sky. 8 towards the north. 9 Brit. towards or in the capital or a major city. 10 into the desired or a proper condition. 11 into a happy mood. 12 winning by a specified margin. 13 Brit. at or to a university, especially Oxford or Cambridge. > preposition 1 from a lower to a higher point of. 2 from one end to another of (a street or other area). > adjective 1 directed or moving towards a higher place or position. 2 at an end. 3 (of the road) being repaired. 4 cheerful. 5 (of a computer system) working properly. > noun informal a period of good fortune. > verb (**upped**, **upping**) 1 (**up and do something**) informal do something abruptly or boldly. 2 increase (a level or amount).

IDIOMS – **it is all up with** informal it is the end or there is no hope for. **on the up and up** Brit. informal steadily improving. **something is up** informal something unusual or undesirable is happening. **up against 1** close to or touching. 2 informal confronted with. **up and down** in various places throughout. **up and running** functioning. **up before** appearing for a hearing in the presence of (a judge, magistrate, etc.). **up for 1** available for. 2 due or being considered for. 3 informal ready to take part in. **up on** well informed about. **up to 1** as far as. 2 (also **up until**) until. 3 indicating a maximum amount. 4 good enough for. 5 capable of. 6 the duty or choice of. 7 informal occupied with. **up top** Brit. informal in the way of intelligence. **up yours** vulgar slang expressing contemptuous defiance or rejection. **what's up?** informal 1 what is going on? 2 what is the matter?

up- > prefix 1 (added to verbs and their derivatives) upwards: upturned. 2 (added to verbs and their derivatives) to a more recent time: update. 3 (added to nouns) denoting motion up: uphill. 4 (added to nouns) higher: upland.

up-and-coming > adjective likely to become successful.

DERIVATIVES – **up-and-comer** noun.

up-and-over > adjective (of a door) opened by being raised and pushed back into a horizontal position.

upbeat > noun (in music) an unaccented beat preceding an accented beat. > adjective informal cheerful; optimistic.

upbraid > verb scold or reproach.

SYNONYMS – admonish, chide, reprimand, reproach, reprove, scold.

ORIGIN – Old English, 'allege as a basis for censure', based on **BRAID** in the obsolete sense 'brandish'.

upbringing > noun the treatment and instruction received throughout one's childhood.

upcast > noun a shaft through which air leaves a mine.

upchuck > verb & noun N. Amer. informal vomit.

upcoming > adjective forthcoming.

upcountry > adverb & adjective inland.

update > verb /updayt/ 1 make more modern. 2 give the latest information to. > noun /**up**dayt/ an act of updating or an updated version.

DERIVATIVES – **updatable** adjective (Computing).

updraught (US **updraft**) > noun an upward current of air.

upend > verb set or turn on its end or upside down.

upfield > adverb (in sport) in or to a position nearer to the opponents' end of a field.

upfront informal > adverb (usu. **up front**) 1 at the front; in front. 2 (of a payment) in advance. > adjective 1 bold and frank. 2 (of a payment) made in advance.

upgrade > verb raise to a higher standard or rank. > noun an act of upgrading or an upgraded version.

DERIVATIVES – **upgradeability** (also **upgradability**) noun **upgradeable** (also **upgradable**) adjective.

upheaval > noun a violent or sudden change or disruption.

upheave > verb literary heave or lift up.

uphill > adverb towards the top of a slope. > adjective 1 sloping upwards. 2 difficult: an uphill struggle. > noun an upward slope.

uphold > verb (past and past participle **upheld**) 1 confirm or support. 2 maintain (a custom or practice).

DERIVATIVES – **upholder** noun.

upholster /uphōlstər/ > verb 1 provide (furniture) with a soft, padded covering. 2 cover the walls or furniture in (a room) with textiles.

upholsterer > noun a person who upholsters furniture.

ORIGIN – from the obsolete noun upholster (from **UPHOLD** in the obsolete sense 'keep in repair').

upholstery > noun 1 soft, padded textile used to upholster furniture. 2 the art or practice of upholstering.

upkeep > noun 1 the process of keeping something in good condition. 2 the cost of this or of supporting a person.

upland > noun (also **uplands**) an area of high or hilly land.

uplift > verb 1 raise. 2 (**be uplifted**) (of an island, mountain, etc.) be created by an upward movement of the earth's surface. 3 elevate morally or spiritually. > noun 1 an act of uplifting. 2 support from a garment, especially for a woman's bust. **3** a morally or spiritually uplifting influence.

DERIVATIVES – **uplifter** noun.

uplighter > noun a lamp designed to throw light upwards.

DERIVATIVES – **uplighting** noun.

uplink > noun a communications link to a satellite. > verb provide with or send by such a link.

upload Computing > verb transfer (data) to a larger computer system. > noun the action or process of uploading.

upmarket > adjective & adverb chiefly Brit. towards or relating to the more expensive or affluent sector of the market.

upon > preposition more formal term for ON.

upper[1] > adjective **1** situated above another part. **2** higher in position or status. **3** situated on higher ground. **4** (in place names) situated to the north. > noun the part of a boot or shoe above the sole.

IDIOMS – **have the upper hand** have an advantage or control. **on one's uppers** informal extremely short of money.

COMBINATIONS – **upper case** capital letters. **upper class** the social group with the highest status, especially the aristocracy. **the upper crust** informal the upper classes. **uppercut** a punch delivered with an upwards motion and the arm bent. **upper house** (also **upper chamber**) **1** the higher house in a bicameral parliament or similar legislature. **2** (**the Upper House**) (in the UK) the House of Lords. **upper school 1** a secondary school for children aged from about fourteen upwards. **2** the section of a school comprising or catering for the older pupils.

ORIGIN – from the adjective **UP** + **-ER**[2].

upper[2] > noun informal a stimulating drug, especially amphetamine.

ORIGIN – from the verb **UP** + **-ER**[1].

uppermost > adjective highest in place, rank, or importance. > adverb at or to the uppermost position.

uppish > adjective informal arrogantly self-assertive.

uppity > adjective informal self-important.

upraise > verb raise to a higher level.

uprate > verb **1** increase the value of. **2** improve the performance of.

upright > adjective **1** vertical; erect. **2** greater in height than breadth. **3** strictly honourable or honest. **4** (of a piano) having vertical strings. > adverb in or into an upright position. > noun **1** a vertical post, structure, or line. **2** an upright piano.

DERIVATIVES – **uprightly** adverb **uprightness** noun.

uprise > verb (past **uprose**; past participle **uprisen**) archaic or literary rise up.

uprising > noun an act of resistance or rebellion.

upriver > adverb & adjective towards or

situated at a point nearer the source of a river.

uproar > noun **1** a loud and impassioned noise or disturbance. **2** a public expression of outrage.

SYNONYMS – **1** bedlam, commotion, disorder, hullabaloo, mayhem, outrage, pandemonium. **2** furore, hue and cry, outcry.

ORIGIN – Dutch *uproer*, from *op* 'up' + *roer* 'confusion'.

uproarious > adjective **1** characterised by or provoking loud noise or uproar. **2** very funny.

DERIVATIVES – **uproariously** adverb **uproariousness** noun.

uproot > verb **1** pull (a plant, tree, etc.) out of the ground. **2** move (someone) from their home or a familiar location. **3** eradicate.

uprush > noun a sudden upward surge or flow.

UPS > abbreviation Computing uninterruptible power supply.

upscale > adjective & adverb N. Amer. upmarket.

upset > verb /up*set*/ (**upsetting**; past and past participle **upset**) **1** make unhappy, disappointed, or worried. **2** knock over. **3** disrupt or disturb. > noun /*up*set/ **1** a state of being upset. **2** an unexpected result or situation. > adjective **1** /up*set*/ unhappy, disappointed, or worried. **2** /*up*set/ (of a person's stomach) having disturbed digestion.

DERIVATIVES – **upsetting** adjective.

SYNONYMS – verb **1** agitate, alarm, dismay, distress, unsettle, worry. **2** capsize, overturn, top over, topple. noun **1** agitation, alarm, dismay, distress, worry.

upshift > verb **1** change to a higher gear. **2** increase. > noun **1** a change to a higher gear. **2** an increase.

upshot > noun the eventual outcome or conclusion.

upside > noun the positive aspect of something.

WORDFINDER – invert (turn *upside* down).

COMBINATIONS – **upside down 1** with the upper part where the lower part should be. **2** in or into total disorder. [ORIGIN – from *up so down*, perhaps in the sense 'up as if down'.]

upsides > adverb (especially in horse racing) alongside.

upsilon > /up*sīl*ən/ > noun the twentieth letter of the Greek alphabet (**Y, υ**), transliterated as 'u' or (chiefly in English words derived through Latin) as 'y'.

ORIGIN – Greek, 'slender U', from *psilos* 'slender'.

upslope > noun an upward slope. > adverb &

adjective at or towards a higher point on a slope.

upstage > adverb & adjective at or towards the back of a stage. > verb **1** divert attention from (someone) towards oneself. **2** (of an actor) move towards the back of a stage to make (another actor) face away from the audience.

upstairs > adverb on or to an upper floor. > adjective (also **upstair**) situated on an upper floor. > noun an upper floor.

upstand > noun an upright structure or object.

upstanding > adjective **1** honest and respectable. **2** standing straight; erect.

SYNONYMS – **1** decent, honourable, respectable, upright. **2** erect, upright, vertical.

upstart > noun derogatory a person who has risen suddenly to prominence, especially one who behaves arrogantly.

upstate US > adjective & adverb of, in, or to a part of a state remote from its large cities, especially the northern part. > noun an upstate area.

upstream > adverb & adjective situated or moving in the direction opposite to that in which a stream or river flows.

upstroke > noun an upwards stroke.

upsurge > noun an increase.

upswept > adjective **1** curved, sloping, or directed upwards. **2** (of the hair) brushed upwards and off the face.

upswing > noun an upward trend.

upsy-daisy > exclamation expressing encouragement to a child who has fallen or is being lifted.

ORIGIN – alteration of earlier *up-a-daisy*.

uptake > noun the action of taking up or making use of something.

IDIOMS – **be quick** (or **slow**) **on the uptake** informal be quick (or slow) to understand something.

uptempo > adjective & adverb Music played with a fast or increased tempo.

upthrust > noun **1** Physics the upward force that a fluid exerts on a body floating in it. **2** Geology the upward movement of part of the earth's surface. > adjective thrust upwards.

uptick > noun N. Amer. a small increase.

uptight > adjective informal **1** nervously tense or angry. **2** conventional or repressed.

uptime > noun time during which a machine, especially a computer, is in operation.

up to date > adjective incorporating or aware of the latest developments and trends.

uptown chiefly N. Amer. > adjective & adverb of, in, or into the residential or more affluent area of a town or city. > *noun* an uptown area.

upturn > *noun* an improvement or upward trend. > *verb* (**upturned**) turned upwards or upside down.

uPVC > *abbreviation* unplasticised polyvinyl chloride.

upward > *adverb* (also **upwards**) towards a higher point or level. > *adjective* moving or leading towards a higher point or level.
IDIOMS – **upwards of** more than.
DERIVATIVES – **upwardly** *adverb*.

upwind > *adverb & adjective* into the wind.

ur- /oor/ > *combining form* primitive; original; earliest.
ORIGIN – German.

Uranian /yoo**ray**niən/ > *adjective* relating to the planet Uranus.

uranium /yoo**ray**niəm/ > *noun* a grey, dense, radioactive, metallic chemical element used as a fuel in nuclear reactors.
ORIGIN – Latin, from the name of the planet *Uranus*.

urban > *adjective* relating to a town or city.
DERIVATIVES – **urbanisation** (also **urbanization**) *noun* **urbanise** (also **urbanize**) *verb*.
COMBINATIONS – **urban myth** (also **urban legend**) an entertaining story or piece of information of uncertain origin that is circulated as if true. **urban renewal** the redevelopment of slum areas in a large city.
ORIGIN – Latin *urbanus*, from *urbs* 'city'.

urbane /ur**bayn**/ > *adjective* (especially of a man) suave, courteous, and refined.
DERIVATIVES – **urbanely** *adverb*.
ORIGIN – first meaning 'urban': from Latin *urbanus*.

urbanite > *noun* informal a town or city dweller.

urbanity > *noun* **1** an urbane quality or manner. **2** urban life.

urchin > *noun* **1** a mischievous child, especially a raggedly dressed one. **2** archaic a goblin. **3** short for **sea urchin**.
ORIGIN – Old French *herichon* 'hedgehog', from Latin *hericius*.

Urdu /oordꝏ, urdꝏ/ > *noun* a language related to Hindi but written in the Persian script.

-ure > *suffix* forming nouns: **1** denoting an action, process, or result: *closure*. **2** denoting an office or function: *judicature*. **3** denoting a collective: *legislature*.
ORIGIN – Latin *-ura*.

urea /yoo**ree**ə/ > *noun* Biochemistry a colourless crystalline compound which is the main nitrogenous breakdown product of proteins in the body and is excreted in urine.

wordpower facts
Urdu
Urdu is now the official language of Pakistan and is also widely used in India. Following the Muslim invasions of India in the 12th century, **Urdu** developed as a lingua franca between the occupying armies and the people of Delhi. The name itself, **Urdu**, is the Persian word for 'camp', coming from Turkish *ordu*, 'royal camp' (the source of **horde**). A number of Urdu words have been adopted into English: some, such as **balti** and **biriani**, denote foods and other items associated with the Indian subcontinent. A number date from the period of British rule in India: these include **cummerbund**, **gymkhana**, and **khaki**, and words adopted in military jargon, such as **Blighty**, **cushy**, and **doolally**.

ureter /yoo**ree**tə/ > *noun* Anatomy & Zoology the duct by which urine passes from the kidney to the bladder or cloaca.
ORIGIN – Greek *ourētēr*, from *ourein* 'urinate'.

urethane /**yoo**rithayn/ > *noun* **1** Chemistry a synthetic compound used to make pesticides and fungicides. **2** polyurethane.

urethra /yoo**ree**thrə/ > *noun* Anatomy & Zoology the duct by which urine is conveyed out of the body, and which in male vertebrates also conveys semen.
DERIVATIVES – **urethral** *adjective*.
ORIGIN – Greek *ourēthra*.

urethritis /yooree**thrī**tiss/ > *noun* Medicine inflammation of the urethra.

urge > *verb* **1** encourage or implore earnestly to do something. **2** strongly recommend. > *noun* a strong desire or impulse.
SYNONYMS – *verb* **1** encourage, entreat, exhort, implore, press. **2** advise, advocate, counsel, recommend. *noun* compulsion, desire, impulse, longing, wish.
ORIGIN – Latin *urgere* 'press, drive'.

urgent > *adjective* **1** requiring immediate action or attention. **2** earnest and insistent.
DERIVATIVES – **urgency** *noun* **urgently** *adverb*.
SYNONYMS – **1** acute, desperate, grave, pressing. **2** determined, earnest, importunate, insistent.
ORIGIN – from Latin *urgere* 'press, drive'.

uric acid > *noun* Biochemistry an insoluble compound which is the main excretory product of birds, reptiles, and insects.

urinal /yoo**rī**n'l/ > *noun* a receptacle into which men may urinate, typically attached to the wall in a public toilet.

urinary > *adjective* relating to urine; involved in the production and discharge of urine.

urinate > *verb* discharge urine.
DERIVATIVES – **urination** *noun*.
ORIGIN – Latin *urinare* 'urinate'.

urine /**yoo**rin/ > *noun* a pale yellowish fluid stored in the bladder and discharged through the urethra, consisting of excess water and waste substances removed from the blood by the kidneys.
WORDFINDER – diuretic (*causing increased urination*).
ORIGIN – Latin *urina*.

URL > *abbreviation* uniform (or universal) resource locator, the address of a World Wide Web page.

urn > *noun* **1** a tall, rounded vase with a stem and base, especially one for storing a cremated person's ashes. **2** a large metal container with a tap, in which tea or coffee is made and kept hot.
ORIGIN – Latin *urna*.

urogenital > *adjective* referring to both the urinary and genital organs.

urology > *noun* the branch of medicine concerned with the urinary system.
DERIVATIVES – **urological** *adjective* **urologist** *noun*.

ursine /**ur**sīn/ > *adjective* relating to bears; resembling a bear.
ORIGIN – Latin *ursinus*, from *ursus* 'bear'.

Ursuline /**ur**syoolīn/ > *noun* a nun of an order founded in northern Italy in 1535 for nursing the sick and teaching girls. > *adjective* relating to this order.
ORIGIN – named after St *Ursula*, the founder's patron saint.

urticaria /urti**kair**iə/ > *noun* Medicine a rash of round, red weals on the skin which itch intensely, caused by an allergic reaction.
ORIGIN – Latin, from *urtica* 'nettle'.

Uruguayan /yoorə**gwī**ən/ > *noun* a person from Uruguay. > *adjective* relating to Uruguay.

US > *abbreviation* United States.

us > *pronoun* (**first person pl.**) **1** used by a speaker to refer to himself or herself and one or more others as the object of a verb or preposition. **2** used after the verb 'to be' and after 'than' or 'as'. **3** informal me.

USA > *abbreviation* United States of America.

usable (also **useable**) > *adjective* able to be used.
DERIVATIVES – **usability** *noun*.

USAF > *abbreviation* United States Air Force.

usage > *noun* **1** the action of using something or the fact of being used. **2** habitual or customary practice.

USB > *abbreviation* Computing universal serial bus, a connector which enables peripheral devices to be plugged in to a computer.

use > *verb* /yꝏz/ **1** take, hold, or deploy as a means of accomplishing or achieving something. **2** (**use up**) consume or expend the whole of. **3** treat in a particular way. **4**

exploit unfairly. **5** /yōost/ (**used to**) did repeatedly or existed in the past. **6** /yōost/ (**be** or **get used to**) be or become familiar with through experience. **7** informal take (an illegal drug). > *noun* /yōoss/ **1** the action of using or state of being used. **2** the ability or power to exercise or manipulate something: *he lost the use of his legs.* **3** a purpose for or way in which something can be used. **4** value; advantage.

COMBINATIONS – **use-by date** chiefly Brit. the recommended date by which a perishable product should be used or consumed.

ORIGIN – Old French *user* 'to use', from Latin *uti.*

useable > *adjective* variant spelling of USABLE.

used > *adjective* **1** having already been used. **2** second-hand.

useful > *adjective* **1** able to be used for a practical purpose or in several ways. **2** informal very able or competent.

DERIVATIVES – **usefully** *adverb* **usefulness** *noun.*

SYNONYMS – **1** beneficial, constructive, handy, helpful, practical, productive, utilitarian.

useless > *adjective* **1** serving no purpose. **2** informal having little ability or skill.

DERIVATIVES – **uselessly** *adverb* **uselessness** *noun.*

SYNONYMS – **1** fruitless, futile, pointless, vain, worthless.

Usenet > *noun* Computing an Internet service consisting of thousands of newsgroups.

user > *noun* **1** a person who uses or operates something. **2** a person who exploits others.

user-friendly > *adjective* easy to use or understand.

DERIVATIVES – **user-friendliness** *noun.*

usher > *noun* **1** a person who shows people to their seats in a theatre or cinema or at a wedding. **2** Brit. a person employed to walk before a person of high rank on special occasions. **3** an official in a law court who swears in jurors and witnesses and keeps order. > *verb* show or guide somewhere.

ORIGIN – Old French *usser* 'doorkeeper', from Latin *ostiarius,* from *ostium* 'door'.

usherette > *noun* a woman who shows people to their seats in a cinema or theatre.

USN > *abbreviation* United States Navy.

USS > *abbreviation* United States Ship.

USSR > *abbreviation* historical Union of Soviet Socialist Republics.

usual > *adjective* habitually or typically occurring or done. > *noun* informal **1** the drink someone habitually prefers. **2** the thing which is typically done or present.

DERIVATIVES – **usually** *adverb.*

SYNONYMS – *adjective* customary, habitual, normal, regular, traditional, typical.

usufruct /yōozyoofrukt/ > *noun* Roman Law the right to enjoy the use of another's property short of the destruction or waste of its substance.

ORIGIN – from Latin *usus et fructus* 'use and enjoyment'.

usurer /yōozhərər/ > *noun* a person who lends money at unreasonably high rates of interest.

usurious /yōozhooriəss/ > *adjective* relating to usury.

usurp /yoozurp/ > *verb* **1** take (a position of power) illegally or by force. **2** supplant.

DERIVATIVES – **usurpation** *noun* **usurper** *noun.*

ORIGIN – Latin *usurpare* 'seize for use'.

usury /yōozhəri/ > *noun* the practice of lending money at unreasonably high rates of interest.

ORIGIN – Latin *usura,* from *usus* (see USE).

UT > *abbreviation* **1** Universal Time. **2** Utah.

Ute /yōot/ > *noun* (pl. same or **Utes**) a member of an American Indian people of Colorado, Utah, and New Mexico.

ute /yōot/ > *noun* N. Amer. & Austral./NZ informal a utility vehicle.

utensil > *noun* a tool or container, especially for household use.

ORIGIN – from Latin *utensilis* 'usable', from *uti* 'to use'.

uterine /yōotərīn/ > *adjective* **1** relating to the uterus. **2** having the same mother but not the same father.

uterus /yōotərəss/ > *noun* (pl. **uteri** /yōotərī/) the womb.

ORIGIN – Latin.

utilise (also **utilize**) > *verb* make practical and effective use of.

DERIVATIVES – **utilisation** *noun.*

utilitarian /yōotilitairiən/ > *adjective* **1** useful or practical rather than attractive. **2** relating to or adhering to utilitarianism. > *noun* an adherent of utilitarianism.

utilitarianism > *noun* **1** the doctrine that actions are right if they serve a purpose. **2** the doctrine that the greatest happiness of the greatest number should be the guiding principle of conduct.

utility > *noun* (pl. **utilities**) **1** the state of being useful, profitable, or beneficial. **2** a public utility. **3** Computing a program for carrying out a routine function. > *adjective* useful, especially through having several functions.

COMBINATIONS – **utility knife** a knife with a small sharp blade, designed to cut wood, cardboard, and other materials. **utility room** a room with appliances for washing and other domestic work. **utility vehicle** (also **utility truck**) a truck having low sides and used for small loads.

ORIGIN – Latin *utilitas,* from *utilis* 'useful'.

utmost > *adjective* most extreme; greatest.

> *noun* (**the utmost**) the greatest or most extreme extent or amount.

ORIGIN – Old English, 'outermost'.

Utopia /yootōpiə/ > *noun* an imagined perfect place or state of things.

ORIGIN – the title of a book (1516) by Sir Thomas More, from Greek *ou* 'not' + *topos* 'place'.

utopian > *adjective* relating to a Utopia; idealistic. > *noun* an idealistic reformer.

DERIVATIVES – **utopianism** *noun.*

utter[1] > *adjective* complete; absolute.

DERIVATIVES – **utterly** *adverb.*

SYNONYMS – absolute, complete, perfect, sheer, thorough, total.

ORIGIN – Old English, 'outer'.

utter[2] > *verb* **1** make (a sound) or say (something). **2** Law put (forged money) into circulation.

DERIVATIVES – **utterable** *adjective* **utterer** *noun.*

SYNONYMS – **1** articulate, declare, express, say, speak, voice.

ORIGIN – Dutch *ūteren* 'speak, make known, give currency to (coins)'.

utterance > *noun* **1** a word, statement, or sound uttered. **2** the action of uttering.

uttermost > *adjective* & *noun* another term for UTMOST.

U-turn > *noun* **1** the turning of a vehicle in a U-shaped course so as to face the opposite way. **2** a reversal of policy.

UV > *abbreviation* ultraviolet.

UVA > *abbreviation* ultraviolet radiation of relatively long wavelengths.

UVB > *abbreviation* ultraviolet radiation of relatively short wavelengths.

UVC > *abbreviation* ultraviolet radiation of very short wavelengths, which does not penetrate the earth's ozone layer.

uvula /yōovyoolə/ > *noun* (pl. **uvulae** /yōovyoolee/) a fleshy extension at the back of the soft palate which hangs above the throat.

ORIGIN – Latin, from *uva* 'grape'.

uxoricide /uksorrisīd/ > *noun* **1** the killing of one's wife. **2** a man who kills his wife.

ORIGIN – from Latin *uxor* 'wife'.

uxorious /uksoriəss/ > *adjective* showing great or excessive fondness for one's wife.

DERIVATIVES – **uxoriousness** *noun.*

Uzbek /oozbek/ > *noun* **1** a member of a people living mainly in Uzbekistan. **2** a person from Uzbekistan. **3** the language of Uzbekistan.

Uzi /oozi/ > *noun* a type of sub-machine gun.

ORIGIN – from *Uziel* Gal, the Israeli army officer who designed it.

V¹ (also **v**) > *noun* (pl. **Vs** or **V's**) **1** the twenty-second letter of the alphabet. **2** denoting the next after U in a set. **3** the Roman numeral for five.

V² > *abbreviation* **1** volt(s). **2** volume. > *symbol* the chemical element vanadium.

v > *abbreviation* **1** velocity. **2** Grammar verb. **3** versus. **4** very.

VA > *abbreviation* **1** (in the UK) Order of Victoria and Albert. **2** Virginia.

vac > *noun* Brit. informal **1** a vacation. **2** a vacuum cleaner.

vacancy > *noun* (pl. **vacancies**) **1** an unoccupied position or job. **2** an available room in a hotel, guest house, etc. **3** empty space. **4** lack of intelligence or understanding.

vacant > *adjective* **1** not occupied; empty. **2** (of a position) not filled. **3** showing no intelligence or interest.
DERIVATIVES – **vacantly** *adverb*.
SYNONYMS – **1** available, empty, free, uninhabited, unoccupied. **3** absent, blank, expressionless, vacuous.
COMBINATIONS – **vacant possession** Brit. ownership of a property on completion of a sale, any previous occupant having moved out.

vacate /vay**kayt**/ > *verb* **1** leave (a place). **2** give up (a position or job).
ORIGIN – Latin *vacare* 'leave empty'.

vacation > *noun* **1** a holiday period between terms in universities and law courts. **2** chiefly N. Amer. a holiday. **3** the action of vacating. > *verb* chiefly N. Amer. take a holiday.
DERIVATIVES – **vacationer** *noun* **vacationist** *noun*.

vaccinate* /**vak**sinayt/ > *verb* treat with a vaccine to produce immunity against a disease.
DERIVATIVES – **vaccination** *noun*.
*SPELLING – note the double c: va*ccinate*.

vaccine /**vak**seen/ > *noun* Medicine a substance given to stimulate the body's production of antibodies and provide immunity against a disease, prepared from the agent that causes the disease, or a synthetic substitute.
ORIGIN – Latin *vaccinus*, from *vacca* 'cow'

(because of the early use of the cowpox virus against smallpox).

vaccinia /vak**sinn**iə/ > *noun* Medicine cowpox, or the virus causing it.

vacillate /**vass**ilayt/ > *verb* waver between different opinions or actions.
DERIVATIVES – **vacillation** *noun*.
SYNONYMS – dither, hesitate, sway, waver.
ORIGIN – Latin *vacillare* 'sway'.

vacuole /**vak**yoo-ōl/ > *noun* Biology a space or vesicle inside a cell, enclosed by a membrane and typically containing fluid.
ORIGIN – from Latin *vacuus* 'empty'.

vacuous /**vak**yooəss/ > *adjective* showing a lack of thought or intelligence.
DERIVATIVES – **vacuity** /və**kyoo**iti/ *noun* **vacuously** *adverb* **vacuousness** *noun*.
ORIGIN – Latin *vacuus* 'empty'.

vacuum /**vak**yoom/ > *noun* (pl. **vacuums** or **vacua** /**vak**yooə/) **1** a space entirely devoid of matter. **2** a space from which the air has been completely or partly removed. **3** a gap left by the loss or departure of someone or something important. **4** (pl. **vacuums**) informal a vacuum cleaner. > *verb* informal clean with a vacuum cleaner.
IDIOMS – **in a vacuum** in isolation from the normal context.
COMBINATIONS – **vacuum cleaner** an electrical apparatus that collects dust from floors and other surfaces by means of suction. **vacuum flask** chiefly Brit. a container that keeps a substance hot or cold by means of a double wall enclosing a vacuum. **vacuum-pack** seal (a product) in a pack or wrapping with the air removed. **vacuum tube** a sealed glass tube containing a near-vacuum which allows the free passage of electric current.
ORIGIN – Latin *vacuus* 'empty'.

vade mecum /vaadi **may**kəm/ > *noun* a handbook or guide kept constantly at hand.
ORIGIN – Latin, 'go with me'.

vagabond > *noun* **1** a vagrant. **2** informal, dated a rogue. > *adjective* having no settled home.
ORIGIN – Latin *vagabundus*, from *vagari* 'wander'.

vagary /**vay**gəri/ > *noun* (pl. **vagaries**) an unexpected and inexplicable change.
ORIGIN – from Latin *vagari* 'wander'.

vagina /və**jī**nə/ > *noun* (pl. **vaginas** or **vaginae** /və**jī**nee/) the muscular canal leading from an outer opening to the womb in women and most female mammals, into which the penis is inserted during sexual intercourse and from which the baby emerges in childbirth.
DERIVATIVES – **vaginal** *adjective*.
ORIGIN – Latin, literally 'sheath, scabbard'.

vaginismus /vaji**niz**məss/ > *noun* painful contraction of the vagina in response to physical contact or pressure.

vaginitis /vaji**nī**tiss/ > *noun* inflammation of the vagina.

vagrant /**vay**grənt/ > *noun* **1** a person without a home or job. **2** archaic a wanderer. > *adjective* relating to or living like a vagrant; wandering.
DERIVATIVES – **vagrancy** *noun*.
SYNONYMS – *noun* **1** beggar, down-and-out, drifter, itinerant, tramp, vagabond.
ORIGIN – from Old French *vagarant* 'wandering about', from *vagrer* 'wander'.

vague > *adjective* **1** of uncertain or indefinite character or meaning. **2** imprecise in thought or expression.
DERIVATIVES – **vaguely** *adverb* **vagueness** *noun*.
SYNONYMS – **1** hazy, indefinite, indistinct, nebulous, unclear. **2** ambiguous, equivocal, imprecise, inexact, loose.
ANTONYMS – clear, precise.
ORIGIN – Latin *vagus* 'wandering, uncertain'.

vagus /**vay**gəss/ > *noun* (pl. **vagi** /**vay**gī/) Anatomy each of the pair of cranial nerves supplying the heart, lungs, and other organs of the chest and abdomen.
DERIVATIVES – **vagal** *adjective*.
ORIGIN – Latin.

vain > *adjective* **1** having or showing an excessively high opinion of one's appearance or abilities. **2** having no meaning or likelihood of fulfilment: *a vain hope*.
IDIOMS – **in vain** without success. **take someone's name in vain** use someone's name in a disrespectful way.
DERIVATIVES – **vainly** *adverb*.
SYNONYMS – **1** arrogant, conceited, egotistical, narcissistic; informal big-headed. **2** fruitless, futile, pointless, useless.
ANTONYMS – **1** modest.
ORIGIN – Latin *vanus* 'empty, without substance'.

vainglory > *noun* literary excessive vanity.
DERIVATIVES – **vainglorious** *adjective* **vaingloriously** *adverb*.

Vaisya /**vīs**yə/ (also **Vaishya**) > *noun* a member of the third of the four Hindu castes, comprising merchants and farmers.
ORIGIN – Sanskrit, 'peasant, labourer'.

valance /**val**ənss/ (also **valence**) > *noun* a length of decorative drapery attached to a bedframe or bedcover, or covering the curtain fittings above a window.
DERIVATIVES – **valanced** *adjective*.
ORIGIN – perhaps from Old French *avaler* 'lower, descend'.

vale > *noun* literary (except in place names) a valley.
IDIOMS – **vale of tears** literary the world as a scene of trouble or sorrow.
ORIGIN – Latin *vallis*.

valediction /validiksh'n/ > *noun* **1** the action of saying farewell. **2** a farewell address or statement.

ORIGIN – from Latin *vale* 'goodbye' + *dicere* 'to say'.

valedictorian /validiktoriən/ > *noun* (in North America) a student who delivers the valedictory at a graduation ceremony.

valedictory /validiktəri/ > *adjective* serving as a farewell. > *noun* (pl. **valedictories**) a farewell address.

valence¹ /vaylənss/ > *noun* Chemistry another term for VALENCY.

valence² > *noun* variant spelling of VALANCE.

valency /vaylənsi/ > *noun* Chemistry the combining power of an element, especially as measured by the number of hydrogen atoms it can displace or combine with.

ORIGIN – Latin *valentia* 'power, competence'.

valentine > *noun* **1** a card sent, often anonymously, on St Valentine's Day (14 February) to a person one loves or is attracted to. **2** a person to whom one sends such a card.

valerian /vəleeriən/ > *noun* **1** a plant bearing clusters of small pink, red, or white flowers. **2** a sedative drug obtained from a valerian root.

ORIGIN – Latin *valeriana*, apparently from *Valerianus* 'of Valerius' (a personal name).

valet /valit, valay/ > *noun* **1** a man's personal male attendant, responsible for his clothes and appearance. **2** a hotel employee performing such duties for guests. **3** a person employed to clean or park cars. > *verb* (**valeted, valeting**) **1** act as a valet to. **2** clean (a car).

ORIGIN – French; related to VASSAL.

valetudinarian /valityoodinairiən/ > *noun* a person in poor health or who is unduly anxious about their health. > *adjective* in poor health or showing undue concern about one's health.

ORIGIN – from Latin *valetudinarius* 'in ill health'.

Valhalla /valhalə/ > *noun* Scandinavian Mythology a palace in which heroes killed in battle are feasted for eternity.

ORIGIN – Latin, from Old Norse 'hall of the slain'.

valiant > *adjective* showing courage or determination.

DERIVATIVES – **valiantly** adverb.

SYNONYMS – bold, brave, courageous, heroic, plucky, valorous.

ORIGIN – Old French *vaillant*, from Latin *valere* 'be strong'.

valid > *adjective* **1** actually supporting the intended point or claim. **2** executed in compliance with the law.

DERIVATIVES – **validity** noun **validly** adverb.

SYNONYMS – **1** justifiable, legitimate, sound, well founded, well grounded. **2** bona fide, legitimate.

ANTONYMS – invalid.

ORIGIN – Latin *validus* 'strong'.

validate > *verb* **1** check or prove the validity of. **2** make or declare legally valid.

DERIVATIVES – **validation** noun.

valine /vayleen/ > *noun* Biochemistry an amino acid which is a constituent of most proteins and is an essential nutrient in the diet.

ORIGIN – from *valeric acid*, a related compound, from VALERIAN.

valise /vəleez/ > *noun* a small travelling bag or suitcase.

ORIGIN – French, from Italian *valigia*.

Valium /valiəm/ > *noun* trademark for DIAZEPAM.

Valkyrie /valkeeri, valkiri/ > *noun* Scandinavian Mythology each of Odin's twelve handmaids who conducted slain warriors of their choice to Valhalla.

ORIGIN – Old Norse, 'chooser of the slain'.

valley > *noun* (pl. **valleys**) a low area between hills or mountains, typically with a river or stream flowing through it.

WORDFINDER – *kinds of valley:* basin, canyon, cirque, combe, corrie, cwm, dale, dell, dene, dingle, glen, gorge, ravine, strath, wadi; dry valley (*having no permanent stream*), hanging valley (*cut across by a deeper valley or cliff*), rift valley (*steep-sided valley formed by subsidence*).

ORIGIN – Latin *vallis*.

valor > *noun* US spelling of VALOUR.

valorise /valəriz/ (also **valorize**) > *verb* give or ascribe value or validity to.

DERIVATIVES – **valorisation** noun.

ORIGIN – French *valorisation*, from *valeur* 'value'.

valour (US **valor**) > *noun* courage in the face of danger.

DERIVATIVES – **valorous** adjective.

SYNONYMS – bravery, courage, fearlessness, heroism, pluck.

ORIGIN – Latin *valor*, from *valere* 'be strong'.

valuable > *adjective* **1** worth a great deal of money. **2** extremely useful or important. > *noun* (**valuables**) valuable items.

DERIVATIVES – **valuably** adverb.

SYNONYMS – **1** precious. **2** helpful, invaluable, profitable, useful, worthwhile.

ANTONYMS – worthless.

valuation > *noun* an estimation of something's worth.

DERIVATIVES – **valuate** verb (chiefly N. Amer.).

value > *noun* **1** the regard that something is held to deserve; importance or worth. **2** material or monetary worth. **3** (**values**) principles or standards of behaviour. **4** the numerical amount denoted by an algebraic term; a magnitude, quantity, or number. **5** Music the relative duration of the sound signified by a note. > *verb* (**values, valued, valuing**) **1** estimate the value of. **2** consider to be important or beneficial.

DERIVATIVES – **valueless** adjective **valuer** noun.

SYNONYMS – noun **1** importance, merit, significance, usefulness, worth. **3** (**values**) ethics, morals, principles, standards. verb **1** assess, evaluate, price, rate. **2** appreciate, esteem, prize, respect.

COMBINATIONS – **value added tax** a tax on the amount by which the value of an article has been increased at each stage of its production or distribution. **value judgement** an assessment of something as good or bad in terms of one's own standards or priorities.

ORIGIN – Old French, from Latin *valere*.

valve > *noun* **1** a device for controlling the passage of fluid through a pipe or duct. **2** a cylindrical mechanism to vary the effective length of the tube in a brass musical instrument. **3** Anatomy & Zoology a membranous fold which allows blood or other fluid to flow in one direction through a vessel. **4** Zoology each of the halves of the hinged shell of a bivalve mollusc or brachiopod.

DERIVATIVES – **valved** adjective.

ORIGIN – Latin *valva*.

valvular > *adjective* relating to, having, or acting as a valve or valves.

vamoose /vəmooss/ > *verb* informal depart hurriedly.

ORIGIN – Spanish *vamos* 'let us go'.

vamp¹ > *noun* **1** the upper front part of a boot or shoe. **2** (in jazz and popular music) a short, simple introductory passage, usually repeated several times until otherwise instructed. > *verb* **1** repeat a short, simple passage of music. **2** (**vamp up**) informal repair or improve (something). **3** attach a new upper to (a boot or shoe).

ORIGIN – Old French *avantpie*, from *avant* 'before' + *pie* 'foot'.

vamp² informal > *noun* a woman who uses sexual attraction to exploit men. > *verb* blatantly set out to attract (a man).

DERIVATIVES – **vampish** adjective **vampy** adjective.

ORIGIN – abbreviation of VAMPIRE.

vampire /vampir/ > *noun* **1** (in folklore) a corpse supposed to leave its grave at night to drink the blood of the living. **2** a small bat that feeds on blood by piercing the skin with its incisor teeth, found mainly in tropical America.

DERIVATIVES – **vampiric** /vampirrik/ adjective **vampirism** noun.

ORIGIN – Hungarian *vampir*, perhaps from Turkish *uber* 'witch'.

van¹ > *noun* **1** a covered motor vehicle used for transporting goods or people. **2** Brit. a railway carriage for conveying luggage, mail, etc. **3** Brit. a caravan.

ORIGIN – shortening of **CARAVAN**.

van² > *noun* (**the van**) **1** the foremost part of an advancing group of people. **2** the forefront.

ORIGIN – abbreviation of **VANGUARD**.

vanadium /vəˈnaydiəm/ > *noun* a hard grey metallic chemical element, used to make alloy steels.

ORIGIN – modern Latin, from an Old Norse name of the Scandinavian goddess Freyja.

Van Allen belt > *noun* each of two regions of intense radiation partly surrounding the earth at heights of several thousand kilometres.

ORIGIN – named after the American physicist James A. *Van Allen* (born 1914).

vandal > *noun* **1** a person who deliberately destroys or damages public or private property. **2** (**Vandal**) a member of a Germanic people that ravaged Gaul, Spain, Rome, and North Africa in the 4th–5th centuries.

DERIVATIVES – **vandalism** *noun*

ORIGIN – Latin *Vandalus*.

vandalise (also **vandalize**) > *verb* deliberately destroy or damage (property).

Vandyke /vanˈdīk/ > *noun* **1** a broad lace or linen collar with an edge deeply cut into large points, fashionable in the 18th century. **2** (also **Vandyke beard**) a neat pointed beard.

ORIGIN – named after the 17th-century Flemish painter Sir Anthony *Van Dyck*, whose portraits often depict such styles.

vane > *noun* **1** a broad blade attached to a rotating axis or wheel which pushes or is pushed by wind or water, forming part of a device such as a windmill, propeller, or turbine. **2** a weathervane. **3** a projecting surface designed to guide the motion of a projectile, e.g. a feather on an arrow.

DERIVATIVES – **vaned** *adjective*.

ORIGIN – dialect variant of obsolete *fane* 'banner'.

vanguard > *noun* **1** the foremost part of an advancing army or naval force. **2** a group of people leading the way in new developments or ideas.

ORIGIN – Old French *avantgarde*, from *avant* 'before' + *garde* 'guard'.

vanilla > *noun* a substance obtained from the pods of a tropical climbing orchid or produced artificially, used as a flavouring and in the manufacture of cosmetics.

ORIGIN – Spanish *vainilla* 'pod', from Latin *vagina* 'sheath'.

vanillin > *noun* Chemistry a fragrant substance which is the essential constituent of vanilla.

vanish > *verb* **1** disappear suddenly and completely. **2** gradually cease to exist. **3** Mathematics become zero.

DERIVATIVES – **vanishing** *adjective* & *noun* **vanishingly** *adverb*.

SYNONYMS – **1** disappear; literary evanesce. **2** dissolve, fade away, melt away.

COMBINATIONS – **vanishing point 1** the point at which receding parallel lines viewed in perspective appear to converge. **2** the point at which something that has been growing smaller or increasingly faint disappears altogether.

ORIGIN – Old French *esvanir*, from Latin *evanescere* 'die away'.

vanity > *noun* (pl. **vanities**) **1** excessive pride in or admiration of one's own appearance or achievements. **2** the quality of being worthless or futile.

SYNONYMS – **1** conceit, egotism, narcissism, self-love; literary vainglory. **2** futility, pointlessness, uselessness, worthlessness.

ANTONYMS – **1** modesty.

COMBINATIONS – **vanity case** a small case fitted with a mirror and compartments for toiletries. **vanity table** a dressing table. **vanity unit** a unit consisting of a washbasin set into a flat top with cupboards beneath.

ORIGIN – Latin *vanitas*, from *vanus* 'empty, without substance'.

vanquish /ˈvangkwish/ > *verb* defeat thoroughly.

DERIVATIVES – **vanquisher** *noun*.

SYNONYMS – conquer, overcome, overwhelm, rout, trounce.

ORIGIN – Old French *vainquir*, from Latin *vincere* 'conquer'.

vantage /ˈvaantij/ > *noun* (usu. **vantage point**) a place or position affording a good view.

ORIGIN – Old French *avantage* 'advantage'.

Vanuatuan /vanōōˈaatōōən/ > *noun* a person from Vanuatu, a country in the SW Pacific. > *adjective* relating to Vanuatu.

vapid /ˈvappid/ > *adjective* offering nothing that is stimulating or challenging.

DERIVATIVES – **vapidity** *noun* **vapidly** *adverb*.

SYNONYMS – banal, colourless, dull, insipid, limp, uninspired.

ORIGIN – Latin *vapidus*.

vapor > *noun* US spelling of **VAPOUR**.

vaporetto /vappəˈrettō/ > *noun* (pl. **vaporetti** /vappəˈretti/ or **vaporettos**) (in Venice) a power-driven canal boat for public transport.

ORIGIN – Italian, 'little steam'.

vaporise (also **vaporize**) > *verb* convert into vapour.

DERIVATIVES – **vaporisation** *noun*.

vaporiser (also **vaporizer**) > *noun* a device that generates a vapour, especially for medicinal inhalation.

vapour (US **vapor**) > *noun* **1** moisture or another substance diffused or suspended in the air. **2** Physics a gaseous substance that can be liquefied by pressure alone. **3** (**the vapours**) dated a fit of faintness, nervousness, or depression

DERIVATIVES – **vaporous** *adjective*.

COMBINATIONS – **vapour trail** a trail of condensed water from an aircraft or rocket at high altitude, seen as a white streak against the sky.

ORIGIN – Latin *vapor* 'steam, heat'.

vaquero /vəˈkairō/ > *noun* (pl. **vaqueros**) (in Spanish-speaking parts of the USA) a cowboy; a cattle driver.

ORIGIN – Spanish, from *vaca* 'cow'.

variable > *adjective* **1** not consistent or having a fixed pattern; liable to vary. **2** Mathematics (of a quantity) able to assume different numerical values. **3** able to be changed or adapted. > *noun* **1** a variable element, feature, or quantity. **2** Astronomy a star whose brightness changes (regularly or irregularly). **3** (**variables**) the region of light, variable winds to the north of the NE trade winds or (in the southern hemisphere) between the SE trade winds and the westerlies.

DERIVATIVES – **variability** *noun* **variably** *adverb*.

SYNONYMS – *adjective* **1** changeable, fluctuating, fluid, inconstant, mutable, unstable. **3** adaptable, changeable.

ANTONYMS – *adjective* **1** constant.

variance > *noun* **1** (usu. in phrase **at variance with**) the fact or quality of being different or inconsistent. **2** the state of disagreeing or quarrelling. **3** chiefly Law a discrepancy between two statements or documents.

variant > *noun* a form or version that varies from other forms of the same thing or from a standard.

variation > *noun* **1** a change or slight difference in condition, amount, or level. **2** a different or distinct form or version. **3** Music a new but still recognisable version of a theme.

DERIVATIVES – **variational** *adjective*.

varicella /varriˈsellə/ > *noun* Medicine technical term for **CHICKENPOX**.

ORIGIN – Latin, from **VARIOLA**.

varicoloured (US **varicolored**) > *adjective* consisting of several different colours.

varicose /ˈvarrikōss, ˈvarrikəss/ > *adjective* (of a vein, especially in the leg) swollen, twisted, and lengthened as a result of poor circulation.

ORIGIN – Latin *varicosus*.

varied > *adjective* incorporating a number of different types or elements; showing variation or variety.

DERIVATIVES – **variedly** *adverb*.

variegated* /**vair**igaytid/ > *adjective* exhibiting different colours, especially as irregular patches or streaks.

DERIVATIVES – **variegation** /vairi**gay**sh'n/ *noun*.

*SPELLING – remember the *-e-* in the middle: variegated.

ORIGIN – from Latin *variegare* 'make varied'.

varietal /və**riet**'l/ > *adjective* **1** (of a wine or grape) made from or belonging to a single specified variety of grape. **2** chiefly Botany & Zoology of, forming, or characteristic of a variety.

variety > *noun* (pl. **varieties**) **1** the quality or state of being different or diverse. **2** (**a variety of**) a number of things of the same general class that are distinct in character or quality. **3** a thing which differs in some way from others of the same general class; a type. **4** Biology a subspecies or cultivar. **5** a form of entertainment consisting of a series of different types of act, such as singing, dancing, and comedy.

IDIOMS – **variety is the spice of life** proverb new and exciting experiences make life more interesting.

SYNONYMS – **1** difference, diversity, heterogeneity, variation. **3** kind, sort, type.

varifocal /vairi**fōk**'l/ > *adjective* (of a lens) allowing a number of focusing distances for near, intermediate, and far vision. > *noun* (**varifocals**) varifocal glasses.

variform /**vair**iform/ > *adjective* **1** (of a group of things) differing from one another in form. **2** (of a single thing or a mass) consisting of a variety of forms or things.

variola /və**rī**ələ/ > *noun* Medicine technical term for **SMALLPOX**.

ORIGIN – Latin, 'pustule, pock'.

variorum /vairi**or**əm/ > *adjective* **1** (of an edition of an author's works) having notes by various editors or commentators. **2** including variant readings from manuscripts or earlier editions. > *noun* a variorum edition.

ORIGIN – from Latin *editio cum notis variorum* 'edition with notes by various (commentators)'.

various > *adjective* different from one another; of different kinds or sorts. > *determiner & pronoun* more than one; individual and separate.

DERIVATIVES – **variously** *adverb*.

SYNONYMS – *adjective* assorted, diverse, miscellaneous, multifarious, sundry.

ORIGIN – Latin *varius* 'changing, diverse'.

varlet /**vaar**lit/ > *noun* **1** archaic an unprincipled rogue. **2** historical an attendant or servant.

ORIGIN – Old French, variant of *valet* (see **VALET**).

varmint /**vaar**mint/ > *noun* N. Amer. informal or dialect a troublesome or mischievous person or wild animal.

ORIGIN – alteration of **VERMIN**.

varna /**vaar**nə/ > *noun* each of the four Hindu castes, Brahman, Kshatriya, Vaisya, and Sudra.

ORIGIN – Sanskrit, 'colour, class'.

varnish > *noun* a substance consisting of resin dissolved in a liquid, applied to wood to give a hard, clear, shiny surface when dry. > *verb* apply varnish to.

ORIGIN – Old French *vernis*, from Latin *veronix* 'fragrant resin'.

varsity > *noun* (pl. **varsities**) **1** Brit. dated or S. African university. **2** chiefly N. Amer. a sports team representing a university or college.

vary > *verb* (**varies**, **varied**) **1** differ in size, degree, or nature from something else of the same general class. **2** change from one form or state to another. **3** modify or change (something) to make it less uniform.

DERIVATIVES – **varying** *adjective* **varyingly** *adverb*.

SYNONYMS – **2** alter, change, fluctuate, shift. **3** adapt, alter, change, diversify, modify.

ORIGIN – Latin *variare*, from *varius* 'diverse'.

vas /vass/ > *noun* (pl. **vasa** /**vay**sə/) Anatomy a vessel or duct.

ORIGIN – Latin, 'vessel'.

vascular /**vas**kyoolər/ > *adjective* relating to or denoting the system of vessels for carrying blood or (in plants) sap, water, and nutrients.

DERIVATIVES – **vascularise** (also **vascularize**) *verb* **vascularity** *noun*.

COMBINATIONS – **vascular plants** plants with vascular tissue, i.e. all plants apart from algae, mosses, and liverworts.

ORIGIN – Latin *vascularis*, from *vasculum* 'small vessel'.

vas deferens /vass **deff**ərenz/ > *noun* (pl. **vasa deferentia** /vaysə deffə**ren**shə/) Anatomy the duct which conveys sperm from the testicle to the urethra.

ORIGIN – from **VAS** + Latin *deferens* 'carrying away'.

vase > *noun* a decorative container without handles, used as an ornament or for displaying cut flowers.

ORIGIN – French, from Latin *vas* 'vessel'.

vasectomy /və**sek**təmi/ > *noun* (pl. **vasectomies**) the surgical cutting and sealing of part of each vas deferens, especially as a means of sterilisation.

vaseline /**vass**ileen/ > *noun* trademark a type of petroleum jelly used as an ointment and lubricant.

ORIGIN – from German *Wasser* 'water' + Greek *elaion* 'oil'.

vasoactive > *adjective* another term for **VASOMOTOR**.

vasoconstriction > *noun* the constriction of blood vessels, which increases blood pressure.

DERIVATIVES – **vasoconstrictive** *adjective*.

vasodilation /vayzōdī**lay**sh'n/ (also **vasodilatation**) > *noun* the dilatation of blood vessels, which decreases blood pressure.

DERIVATIVES – **vasodilatory** *adjective*.

vasomotor > *adjective* affecting the diameter of blood vessels (and hence blood pressure).

vassal /**vass**'l/ > *noun* **1** historical a holder of land by feudal tenure on conditions of homage and allegiance. **2** a person or country in a subordinate position to another.

DERIVATIVES – **vassalage** *noun*.

ORIGIN – Latin *vassallus* 'retainer'.

vast > *adjective* of very great extent or quantity; immense.

DERIVATIVES – **vastly** *adverb* **vastness** *noun*.

SYNONYMS – boundless, colossal, enormous, extensive, huge, immense.

ORIGIN – Latin *vastus* 'empty, immense'.

VAT > *abbreviation* value added tax.

vat > *noun* a large tank or tub used to hold liquid.

vatic /**vatt**ik/ > *adjective* literary predicting what will happen in the future.

ORIGIN – from Latin *vates* 'prophet'.

Vatican > *noun* the palace and official residence of the Pope in Rome.

vatu /**vatt**ōō/ > *noun* (pl. same) the basic monetary unit of Vanuatu, equal to 100 centimes.

ORIGIN – Bislama, the official language of Vanuatu.

vaudeville /**vaw**dəvil, **vō**deəvil/ > *noun* a type of entertainment featuring a mixture of musical and comedy acts.

DERIVATIVES – **vaudevillian** *adjective* & *noun*.

vault[1] > *noun* **1** a roof in the form of an arch or a series of arches. **2** a large room or chamber used for storage, especially an underground one. **3** a chamber beneath a church or in a graveyard used for burials. **4** Anatomy the arched roof of a cavity. > *verb* provide with or form into an arched roof.

DERIVATIVES – **vaulted** *adjective*.

ORIGIN – Old French *voute*, from Latin *volvere* 'to roll'.

vault[2] > *verb* leap or spring while supporting or propelling oneself with the hands or a pole. > *noun* an act of vaulting.

DERIVATIVES – **vaulter** *noun*.

COMBINATIONS – **vaulting horse** a padded wooden block used for vaulting over by gymnasts and athletes.

ORIGIN – Old French *volter* 'to turn (a horse), to gambol'.

vaulting > *noun* ornamental work in a vaulted roof or ceiling.

wordpower facts
Vaudeville

The word **vaudeville** appears to owe its existence to a Frenchman living in Calvados, Normandy, in the 15th century, a worker in the cloth trade, who enjoyed composing songs. His name was Olivier Basselin and he lived in the valley of Vire, in Calvados. The name by which each of his songs was known was *chanson du Vau de Vire*, or 'song of the valley of Vire'; this was shortened to *vau de vire*, which became *vau de ville*, and eventually *vaudeville*. The word **vaudeville** was adopted into English in the 18th century, when it denoted a light popular song, especially a song of a satirical nature performed on the stage.

vaunt /vawnt/ > *verb* boast about or praise (something).
DERIVATIVES – **vaunted** *adjective*.
ORIGIN – Latin *vantare*, from *vanus* 'vain, empty'.

VC > *abbreviation* Victoria Cross.

V-chip > *noun* a computer chip installed in a television receiver that can be programmed to block violent or sexually explicit material.

VCR > *abbreviation* video cassette recorder.

VD > *abbreviation* venereal disease.

VDU > *abbreviation* visual display unit.

've > *abbreviation* informal have.

veal > *noun* the flesh of a calf, used as food.
ORIGIN – Old French *veel*, from Latin *vitellus* 'small calf'.

vector /vektər/ > *noun* 1 Mathematics & Physics a quantity which possesses a direction as well as a magnitude. 2 an organism that transmits a particular disease or parasite from one animal or plant to another. 3 a course to be taken by an aircraft. > *verb* direct (an aircraft in flight) to a desired point.
DERIVATIVES – **vectorial** *adjective*.
ORIGIN – Latin, 'carrier'.

Veda /vaydə, veedə/ > *noun* (treated as sing. or pl.) the most ancient Hindu scriptures.
ORIGIN – Sanskrit, 'sacred knowledge'.

VE day > *noun* the day (8 May) marking the Allied victory in Europe in 1945.
ORIGIN – abbreviation of *Victory in Europe*.

Vedic /vaydik, veedik/ > *noun* the language of the Veda, an early form of Sanskrit. > *adjective* relating to the Veda.

veejay > *noun* informal, chiefly N. Amer. a person who introduces and plays popular music videos.
ORIGIN – representing a pronunciation of *VJ*, short for *video jockey*.

veep > *noun* N. Amer. informal a vice-president.
ORIGIN – from the initials *VP*.

veer > *verb* 1 change direction suddenly. 2 (of the wind) change direction clockwise around the points of the compass. The opposite of **BACK**. 3 suddenly change in opinion, subject, etc. > *noun* a sudden change of direction.
ORIGIN – French *virer*.

veg[1] /vej/ > *noun* (pl. same) Brit. informal a vegetable or vegetables.

veg[2] /vej/ > *verb* (**vegges, vegging, vegged**) (often **veg out**) informal relax to the point of doing nothing at all; vegetate.

vegan > *noun* a person who does not eat or use animal products.

Vegemite /vejimīt/ > *noun* Austral./NZ trademark a type of savoury spread made from concentrated yeast extract.

vegetable* /vejitəb'l, vejtəb'l/ > *noun* 1 a plant or part of a plant used as food. 2 informal, derogatory a person who is incapable of normal mental or physical activity, especially through brain damage.
*SPELLING – *vege-*, not *vega-*: vegetable.
COMBINATIONS – **vegetable oil** an oil derived from plants, e.g. olive oil or sunflower oil.
ORIGIN – first used in the sense 'growing as a plant': from Latin *vegetabilis* 'animating', from *vegetare* 'enliven'.

vegetal /vejit'l/ > *adjective* formal relating to plants.
ORIGIN – Latin *vegetalis*, from *vegetare* 'animate'.

vegetarian > *noun* a person who does not eat meat for moral, religious, or health reasons. > *adjective* eating or including no meat.
DERIVATIVES – **vegetarianism** *noun*.

vegetate > *verb* 1 live or spend a period of time in a dull, inactive, unchallenging way. 2 dated (of a plant or seed) grow or sprout.
ORIGIN – Latin *vegetare* 'enliven'.

vegetated > *adjective* covered with vegetation or plant life.

vegetation > *noun* plants collectively.
DERIVATIVES – **vegetational** *adjective*.

vegetative /vejitətiv/ > *adjective* 1 relating to vegetation or the growth of plants. 2 Biology relating to or denoting reproduction or propagation achieved by asexual means. 3 Medicine alive but comatose and without apparent brain activity or responsiveness.

veggie (also **vegie**) > *noun & adjective* informal another term for **VEGETARIAN** or **VEGETABLE**.
COMBINATIONS – **veggie burger** (also trademark **Vegeburger**) a savoury cake resembling a hamburger but made with vegetable protein or soya instead of meat.

vehement /veeəmənt/ > *adjective* showing strong feeling; forceful or intense.
DERIVATIVES – **vehemence** *noun* **vehemently** *adverb*.

SYNONYMS – ardent, fierce, forceful, heated, impassioned, intense, passionate.
ORIGIN – Latin, 'impetuous, violent'.

vehicle /veeik'l/ > *noun* 1 a thing used for transporting people or goods on land. 2 a means of expressing, embodying, or fulfilling something. 3 a substance that facilitates the use of a drug, pigment, or other material mixed with it. 4 a film, programme, song, etc., intended to display the leading performer to the best advantage.
DERIVATIVES – **vehicular** /vihikyoolər/ *adjective*.
ORIGIN – Latin *vehiculum*, from *vehere* 'carry'.

veil > *noun* 1 a piece of fine material worn to protect or conceal the face. 2 a piece of fabric forming part of a nun's headdress, resting on the head and shoulders. 3 a thing that conceals, disguises, or obscures. > *verb* 1 cover with or as though with a veil. 2 partially conceal, disguise, or obscure.
IDIOMS – **draw a veil over** avoid discussing or calling attention to (something embarrassing or unpleasant). **take the veil** become a nun.
DERIVATIVES – **veiled** *adjective* **veiling** *noun*.
ORIGIN – Latin *velum*.

vein > *noun* 1 any of the tubes forming part of the circulation system by which blood is conveyed from all parts of the body towards the heart. 2 (in general use) a blood vessel. 3 (in plants) a slender rib running through a leaf, containing vascular tissue. 4 (in insects) a hollow rib forming part of the supporting framework of a wing. 5 a streak or stripe of a different colour in wood, marble, cheese, etc. 6 a fracture in rock containing a deposit of minerals or ore. 7 a source of a specified quality or other abstract resource: *a rich vein of satire*. 8 a distinctive quality, style, or tendency: *he closes his article in a humorous vein*.
WORDFINDER – venous (*relating to a vein or the veins*).
DERIVATIVES – **veined** *adjective* **veining** *noun* **veiny** (**veinier, veiniest**) *adjective*.
ORIGIN – Old French *veine*, from Latin *vena*.

veinous > *adjective* having prominent or noticeable veins.

vela plural of **VELUM**.

velar /veelər/ > *adjective* 1 relating to a veil or velum. 2 Phonetics (of a speech sound) pronounced with the back of the tongue near the soft palate, as in *k* and *g* in English.

Velcro > *noun* trademark a fastener consisting of two strips of fabric which adhere when pressed together, by means of tiny loops and hooks.
DERIVATIVES – **Velcroed** *adjective*.

ORIGIN – from French *velours croché* 'hooked velvet'.

veld /velt/ (also **veldt**) > *noun* open, uncultivated country or grassland in southern Africa.

ORIGIN – Afrikaans, literally 'field'.

vellum /**vell**əm/ > *noun* fine parchment made originally from the skin of a calf.

ORIGIN – Old French *velin*, from *veel* 'veal', from Latin *vitellus* 'small calf'.

velocipede /vi**loss**ipeed/ > *noun* **1** historical an early form of bicycle propelled by working pedals on cranks fitted to the front axle. **2** US a child's tricycle.

ORIGIN – French *vélocipède*, from Latin *velox* 'swift' + *pes* 'foot'.

velociraptor /vi**loss**i**rapt**ər/ > *noun* a small, agile, carnivorous dinosaur with a large slashing claw on each foot.

ORIGIN – Latin, from *velox* 'swift' + *raptor* 'plunderer'.

velocity /vi**loss**iti/ > *noun* (pl. **velocities**) **1** the speed of something in a given direction. **2** (in general use) speed.

ORIGIN – Latin *velocitas*, from *velox* 'swift'.

velodrome /**vell**ədrōm/ > *noun* a cycle-racing track with steeply banked curves.

ORIGIN – French, from *vélo* 'bicycle'.

velour /və**loor**/ (also **velours**) > *noun* a plush woven fabric resembling velvet.

ORIGIN – French *velours* 'velvet'.

velouté /və**loo**tay/ > *noun* a sauce made from a roux of butter and flour with chicken, veal, or pork stock.

ORIGIN – French, literally 'velvety'.

velum /**vee**ləm/ > *noun* (pl. **vela** /**vee**lə/) **1** Zoology a membrane bordering a cavity, especially in certain molluscs and other invertebrates. **2** Anatomy the soft palate.

ORIGIN – Latin, 'sail, covering, veil'.

velvet > *noun* **1** a closely woven fabric (originally of silk, now also of cotton or man-made fibres) with a thick short pile on one side. **2** soft downy skin that covers a deer's antler while it is growing.

DERIVATIVES – **velvety** *adjective*.

ORIGIN – Old French *veluotte*, from Latin *villus* 'tuft, down'.

velveteen > *noun* a fabric with a pile resembling velvet (but originally made of cotton rather than silk).

vena cava /veenə **kay**və/ > *noun* (pl. **venae cavae** /veenee **kay**vee/) each of two large veins carrying deoxygenated blood into the heart.

ORIGIN – Latin, 'hollow vein'.

venal /**vee**n'l/ > *adjective* susceptible to bribery; corruptible.

DERIVATIVES – **venality** *noun*

USAGE – do not confuse **venal** with **venial**, which is used in Christian theology in reference to sin (a **venial** sin, unlike a **mortal** sin, is not regarded as depriving the soul of divine grace).

ORIGIN – Latin *venalis*, from *venum* 'thing for sale': originally in the sense 'available for purchase'.

vend > *verb* **1** offer (small items) for sale. **2** Law or formal sell.

COMBINATIONS – **vending machine** a machine that dispenses small articles when a coin or token is inserted.

ORIGIN – Latin *vendere* 'sell'.

vendetta /ven**dett**ə/ > *noun* **1** a blood feud in which the family of a murdered person seeks vengeance on the murderer or the murderer's family. **2** a prolonged bitter quarrel with or campaign against someone.

ORIGIN – Italian, from Latin *vindicta* 'vengeance'.

vendor (US also **vender**) > *noun* **1** a person or company offering something for sale. **2** Law the seller in a sale, especially of property.

veneer /və**neer**/ > *noun* **1** a thin decorative covering of fine wood applied to a coarser wood or other material. **2** an attractive appearance that covers or disguises true nature or feelings. > *verb* cover with a veneer.

ORIGIN – German *furnieren*, from Old French *fournir* 'furnish'.

venerable > *adjective* **1** accorded great respect because of age, wisdom, or character. **2** (in the Anglican Church) a title given to an archdeacon. **3** (in the Roman Catholic Church) a title given to a deceased person who has attained a certain degree of sanctity but has not been fully beatified or canonised.

venerate /**venn**ərayt/ > *verb* regard with great respect.

DERIVATIVES – **veneration** *noun* **venerator** *noun*.

SYNONYMS – esteem, honour, respect, revere, worship.

ORIGIN – Latin *venerari* 'adore, revere'.

venereal /vi**neer**iəl/ > *adjective* **1** relating to venereal disease. **2** formal relating to sexual desire or sexual intercourse.

COMBINATIONS – **venereal disease** a disease contracted by sexual intercourse with a person already infected.

ORIGIN – Latin *venereus*, from *venus* 'sexual love'.

venereology /vineeri**oll**əji/ > *noun* the branch of medicine concerned with venereal diseases.

Venetian /və**nee**sh'n/ > *adjective* relating to Venice or its people. > *noun* a person from Venice.

COMBINATIONS – **venetian blind** a window blind consisting of horizontal slats which can be pivoted to control the amount of light that passes through.

Venezuelan /venni**zway**lən/ > *noun* a person from Venezuela. > *adjective* relating to Venezuela.

vengeance /**ven**jənss/ > *noun* revenge taken for an injury or wrong.

IDIOMS – **with a vengeance** with great intensity.

SYNONYMS – reprisal, retaliation, retribution, revenge.

ORIGIN – Old French, from *venger* 'avenge'.

vengeful > *adjective* seeking to harm someone in return for a perceived injury.

DERIVATIVES – **vengefully** *adverb* **vengefulness** *noun*.

SYNONYMS – avenging, bitter, rancorous, revengeful, unforgiving, vindictive.

venial /**vee**niəl/ > *adjective* **1** Christian Theology (of a sin) not regarded as depriving the soul of divine grace. Contrasted with **MORTAL**. **2** (of a fault or offence) slight and pardonable.

DERIVATIVES – **venially** *adverb*.

USAGE – do not confuse **venial** with **venal**, which means 'susceptible to bribery; corruptible'.

ORIGIN – Latin *venialis*, from *venia* 'forgiveness'.

venison /**venn**is'n/ > *noun* meat from a deer.

ORIGIN – Old French *venesoun*, from Latin *venatio* 'hunting'.

Venn diagram > *noun* a diagram representing mathematical or logical sets as circles, common elements of the sets being represented by intersections of the circles.

ORIGIN – named after the English logician John *Venn* (1834–1923).

venom > *noun* **1** poisonous fluid secreted by animals such as snakes and scorpions and typically injected into prey or aggressors by biting or stinging. **2** extreme malice, bitterness, or aggression.

ORIGIN – Old French *venim*, from Latin *venenum* 'poison'.

venomous > *adjective* **1** secreting or capable of injecting venom. **2** very malicious, bitter, or aggressive.

DERIVATIVES – **venomously** *adverb*.

venous /**vee**nəss/ > *adjective* relating to a vein or the veins.

vent[1] > *noun* **1** an opening that allows air, gas, or liquid to pass out of or into a confined space. **2** (usu. in phrase **give vent to**) the release or expression of a strong emotion or burst of energy. **3** the anus or cloaca of a fish or other animal. > *verb* **1** give free expression to (a strong emotion). **2** discharge (air, gas, or liquid) through an outlet.

ORIGIN – partly from French *vent* 'wind', reinforced by *éventer* 'expose to air'.

vent[2] > *noun* a slit in a garment.

ORIGIN – Old French *fente* 'slit', from Latin *findere* 'cleave'.

ventilate > *verb* **1** cause air to enter and circulate freely in (a room or building). **2** discuss (an opinion or issue) in public. **3** Medicine subject to artificial respiration.

DERIVATIVES – **ventilation** *noun*.

ORIGIN – Latin *ventilare* 'blow, winnow', from *ventus* 'wind'.

ventilator > *noun* **1** an appliance or opening for ventilating a room or other space. **2** Medicine an appliance for artificial respiration; a respirator.

DERIVATIVES – **ventilatory** *adjective*.

ventral > *adjective* Anatomy, Zoology, & Botany on or relating to the underside of an animal or plant; abdominal. Compare with **DORSAL**.

DERIVATIVES – **ventrally** *adverb*.

ORIGIN – from Latin *venter* 'belly'.

ventricle /**ven**trik'l/ > *noun* Anatomy **1** each of the two larger and lower cavities of the heart. **2** each of four connected fluid-filled cavities in the centre of the brain.

DERIVATIVES – **ventricular** /ven**trik**-yoolər/ *adjective*.

ORIGIN – Latin *ventriculus*, from *venter* 'belly'.

ventriloquist /ven**trill**əkwist/ > *noun* an entertainer who makes their voice seem to come from a doll or puppet.

DERIVATIVES – **ventriloquial** /ventri-**lō**kwiəl/ *adjective* **ventriloquism** *noun* **ventriloquy** *noun*.

ORIGIN – Latin *ventriloquium*, from *venter* 'belly' + *loqui* 'speak'.

venture > *noun* **1** a risky or daring journey or undertaking. **2** a business enterprise involving considerable risk. > *verb* **1** undertake a risky or daring journey or course of action. **2** dare to say something that is bold or controversial.

IDIOMS – **nothing ventured, nothing gained** *proverb* you can't expect to achieve anything if you never take any risks.

COMBINATIONS – **venture capital** capital invested in a project in which there is a substantial element of risk.

ORIGIN – shortening of **ADVENTURE**.

venturesome > *adjective* willing to take risks or embark on difficult or unusual courses of action.

venturi /ven**tyoor**i/ > *noun* (pl. **venturis**) a short piece of narrow tube between wider sections, for measuring flow rate or exerting suction.

ORIGIN – named after the Italian physicist Giovanni B. *Venturi* (1746–1822).

venue /**ven**yoo/ > *noun* the place where an event or meeting is held.

ORIGIN – Old French, literally 'a coming', from *venir* 'come'.

venule /**ven**yool/ > *noun* Anatomy a very small vein.

ORIGIN – Latin *venula*.

Venus flytrap > *noun* a plant with hinged leaves that spring shut on and digest insects which land on them.

Venusian /vi**nyoo**ziən/ > *adjective* relating to the planet Venus. > *noun* a supposed inhabitant of Venus.

veracious /və**ray**shəss/ > *adjective* formal speaking or representing the truth.

ORIGIN – Latin *verax*, from *verus* 'true'.

veracity /və**rass**iti/ > *noun* **1** conformity to facts; accuracy. **2** habitual truthfulness.

veranda (also **verandah**) > *noun* a roofed platform along the outside of a house, level with the ground floor.

ORIGIN – Portuguese *varanda* 'railing, balustrade'.

verb > *noun* Grammar a word used to describe an action, state, or occurrence, such as *carry*, *hear*, *become*, or *happen*.

ORIGIN – Latin *verbum* 'word, verb'.

verbal > *adjective* **1** relating to or in the form of words. **2** spoken rather than written; oral. **3** Grammar relating to or derived from a verb. > *noun* **1** Grammar a word or words functioning as a verb. **2** (also **verbals**) Brit. informal abuse; insults.

DERIVATIVES – **verbally** *adverb*.

COMBINATIONS – **verbal noun** Grammar a noun formed as an inflection of a verb and partly sharing its constructions, such as *smoking* in *smoking is forbidden*.

verbalise (also **verbalize**) > *verb* express in words, especially by speaking aloud.

verbatim /ver**bay**tim/ > *adverb* & *adjective* in exactly the same words as were used originally.

ORIGIN – Latin, from *verbum* 'word'.

verbena /ver**bee**nə/ > *noun* an ornamental plant with heads of bright showy flowers.

ORIGIN – Latin, 'sacred bough'.

verbiage /**ver**bi-ij/ > *noun* excessively lengthy or technical speech or writing.

ORIGIN – French, from obsolete *verbeier* 'to chatter'.

verbose /ver**bōss**/ > *adjective* using or expressed in more words than are needed.

DERIVATIVES – **verbosely** *adverb* **verbosity** *noun*.

SYNONYMS – diffuse, long-winded, prolix, rambling, wordy.

ANTONYMS – laconic, succinct.

ORIGIN – Latin *verbosus*, from *verbum* 'word'.

verboten /ver**bōt**'n/ > *adjective* forbidden.

ORIGIN – German.

verdant /**ver**d'nt/ > *adjective* green with grass or other lush vegetation.

DERIVATIVES – **verdancy** *noun* **verdantly** *adverb*.

ORIGIN – perhaps from Old French *verdeant*, present participle of *verdoier* 'be green'.

verderer /**ver**dərər/ > *noun* Brit. a judicial officer of a royal forest.

ORIGIN – Old French, from Latin *viridis* 'green'.

verdict > *noun* **1** a decision on an issue of fact in a civil or criminal case or an inquest. **2** an opinion or judgement.

ORIGIN – Old French *verdit*, from *veir* 'true' + *dit* 'saying'.

verdigris /**ver**digree/ > *noun* a bright bluish-green encrustation or patina formed on copper or brass by atmospheric oxidation.

ORIGIN – Old French *vert de Grece* 'green of Greece'.

verdure /**ver**dyər/ > *noun* lush green vegetation.

ORIGIN – from Old French *verd* 'green'.

verge > *noun* **1** an edge or border. **2** Brit. a grass edging by the side of a road or path. **3** an extreme limit beyond which something specified will happen: *I was on the verge of tears.* > *verb* (**verge on**) be very close or similar to.

ORIGIN – Latin *virga* 'rod'.

verger > *noun* **1** an official in a church who acts as a caretaker and attendant. **2** an officer who carries a rod before a bishop or dean as a symbol of office.

ORIGIN – Old French, from Latin *virga* 'rod'.

Vergilian > *adjective* variant spelling of **VIRGILIAN**.

verify /**verr**ifī/ > *verb* (**verifies**, **verified**) **1** make sure or demonstrate that (something) is true, accurate, or justified. **2** Law swear to or support (a statement) by affidavit.

DERIVATIVES – **verifiable** *adjective* **verification** *noun* **verifier** *noun*.

SYNONYMS – **1** authenticate, confirm, check, corroborate, substantiate.

ORIGIN – Latin *verificare*, from *verus* 'true'.

verily > *adverb* archaic truly; certainly.

verisimilitude /verrisi**mill**ityŏod/ > *noun* the appearance of being true or real.

ORIGIN – Latin *verisimilitudo*, from *verisimilis* 'probable'.

verismo /ve**riz**mō/ > *noun* realism or authenticity, especially in the arts.

ORIGIN – Italian.

veritable > *adjective* genuine; actual; properly so called (used to qualify a metaphor): *a veritable price explosion.*

DERIVATIVES – **veritably** *adverb*.

vérité /**verr**itay/ > *noun* a genre of film and television which emphasises realism and naturalism.

ORIGIN – French, 'truth'.

verity > *noun* (pl. **verities**) **1** a true principle or belief. **2** truth.
ORIGIN – Latin *veritas*, from *verus* 'true'.

vermicelli /vermi**chell**i/ > *plural noun* **1** pasta made in long slender threads. **2** Brit. shreds of chocolate used to decorate cakes.
ORIGIN – Italian, literally 'little worms'.

vermicide /**ver**misīd/ > *noun* a substance that is poisonous to worms.

vermiculated /vər**mik**yoolaytid/ > *adjective* **1** marked with sinuous or wavy lines. **2** archaic worm-eaten.

vermiculite /vər**mik**yoolīt/ > *noun* a yellow or brown mineral found as an alteration product of mica and used for insulation or as a moisture-retentive medium for growing plants.
ORIGIN – from Latin *vermiculari* 'be full of worms' (because when heated it expands, producing small worm-like projections).

vermiform > *adjective* chiefly Zoology or Anatomy resembling or having the form of a worm.

vermifuge /**ver**mifyooj/ > *noun* Medicine an anthelmintic medicine.

vermilion /vər**mil**yən/ (also **vermillion**) > *noun* **1** a brilliant red pigment made from mercury sulphide (cinnabar). **2** a brilliant red colour.

wordpower facts
Vermilion
There is a tiny grub-like insect from the Mediterranean region called the **kermes** which, when crushed, yields a bright red dye. The word **vermilion**, from Old French *vermeillon*, derives from Latin *vermiculus*, meaning 'little worm', a reference to these little grubs. *Kermes* itself is originally an Arabic word, and the names of the colours **carmine** and **crimson** are derived from it. The food colouring **cochineal** is similarly made from the crushed bodies of insects; the name **cochineal**, which comes via French or Spanish from Latin *coccinus*, meaning 'scarlet', derives ultimately from Greek *kokkos*, 'berry', because the insect bodies were originally mistaken for grains or berries.

vermin > *noun* (treated as pl.) **1** wild mammals and birds which are harmful to crops, farm animals, or game, or which carry disease. **2** parasitic worms or insects. **3** very unpleasant and destructive people.
DERIVATIVES – **verminous** adjective.
ORIGIN – Old French, from Latin *vermis* 'worm'.

vermouth /**ver**məth, vər**mooth**/ > *noun* a red or white wine flavoured with aromatic herbs.

ORIGIN – French *vermout*, from German *Wermut* 'wormwood'.

vernacular /vər**nak**yoolər/ > *noun* **1** the language or dialect spoken by the ordinary people of a country or region. **2** informal the specialised terminology of a group or activity. > *adjective* **1** spoken as or using one's mother tongue rather than a second language. **2** (of architecture) concerned with domestic and functional buildings rather than grand or monumental ones.
ORIGIN – from Latin *vernaculus* 'domestic, native'.

vernal /**ver**n'l/ > *adjective* of, in, or appropriate to spring.
COMBINATIONS – **vernal equinox** the spring equinox.
ORIGIN – Latin *vernalis*, from *ver* 'spring'.

vernalisation (also **vernalization**) > *noun* the cooling of seed during germination in order to accelerate flowering when it is planted.

vernier /**ver**niər/ > *noun* a small movable graduated scale for obtaining fractional parts of subdivisions on a fixed main scale of a measuring instrument.
ORIGIN – named after the French mathematician Pierre *Vernier* (1580–1637).

vernix /**ver**niks/ > *noun* a greasy deposit covering the skin of a baby at birth.
ORIGIN – Latin, from *veronix* 'fragrant resin'.

veronica > *noun* **1** a herbaceous plant with upright stems bearing narrow pointed leaves and spikes of blue or purple flowers. **2** a cloth supposedly impressed with an image of Christ's face.
ORIGIN – Latin, from the given name *Veronica*; sense 2 refers to St *Veronica*, who offered her headcloth to Christ on the way to Calvary, to wipe his face.

verruca /və**roo**kə/ > *noun* (pl. **verrucae** /və**roo**see/ or **verrucas**) **1** a contagious wart on the sole of the foot. **2** (in medical use) a wart of any kind.
ORIGIN – Latin.

versatile > *adjective* able to adapt or be adapted to many different functions or activities.
DERIVATIVES – **versatility** noun.
ORIGIN – Latin *versatilis*, from *versare* 'turn about, revolve', from *vertere* 'to turn'.

verse > *noun* **1** writing arranged with a metrical rhythm. **2** a group of lines that form a unit in a poem or song. **3** each of the short numbered divisions of a chapter in the Bible or other scripture.
WORDFINDER – blank verse (*verse without rhyme*), couplet (*a pair of successive lines of verse*), doggerel (*irregular comic verse; badly written verse*), scansion (*the rhythm of a line of verse*).

wordpower facts
Verse
The word **verse** is recorded in Old English in the form *fers*. It comes from Latin *versus*, from the verb *vertere* 'to turn'. The noun *versus* means both 'a turn of the plough, a furrow' and also 'a line of writing', from the notion of 'turning' at the end of the line. *Vertere* is an important source of English words, linking many whose meanings are quite unrelated, such as **adverse**, **anniversary**, **controversy**, **universe**, and **versatile**; it is also the root of verbs such as **avert**, **convert**, **divert**, **invert**, and **pervert**.

versed > *adjective* (**versed in**) experienced or skilled in; knowledgeable about.
ORIGIN – Latin *versatus*, past participle of *versari* 'be engaged in'.

versicle /**ver**sik'l/ > *noun* a short sentence said or sung by the minister in a church service, to which the congregation gives a response.

versify > *verb* (**versifies**, **versified**) turn into or express in verse.
DERIVATIVES – **versification** noun **versifier** noun.

version > *noun* **1** a particular form of something differing in certain respects from an earlier form or from other forms of the same type of thing. **2** an account of a matter from a particular person's point of view.
ORIGIN – Latin *versio*, from *vertere* 'to turn': originally in the sense 'translation'.

verso /**ver**sō/ > *noun* (pl. **versos**) a left-hand page of an open book, or the back of a loose document. Contrasted with **RECTO**.
ORIGIN – from Latin *verso folio* 'on the turned leaf'.

versus > *preposition* **1** against. **2** as opposed to; in contrast to.
ORIGIN – Latin *versus* 'towards'.

vert /vert/ > *noun* green, as a conventional heraldic colour.
ORIGIN – Old French, from Latin *viridis* 'green'.

vertebra /**ver**tibrə/ > *noun* (pl. **vertebrae** /**ver**tibray, **ver**tibree/) each of the series of small bones forming the backbone.
DERIVATIVES – **vertebral** adjective.
ORIGIN – Latin, from *vertere* 'to turn'.

vertebrate /**ver**tibrət/ > *noun* an animal having a backbone, including mammals, birds, reptiles, amphibians, and fishes. > *adjective* relating to such animals.

vertex /**ver**teks/ > *noun* (pl. **vertices** /**ver**tiseez/ or **vertexes**) **1** the highest point; the top or apex. **2** Geometry each angular point of a polygon, polyhedron, or other figure. **3** a meeting point of two lines that form an angle. **4 Anatomy** the crown of the head.

ORIGIN – Latin, 'whirlpool, crown of a head, vertex'.

vertical > *adjective* at right angles to a horizontal plane; having the top directly above the bottom. > *noun* **1** a vertical line or plane. **2** an upright structure.

DERIVATIVES – **verticality** *noun* **vertically** *adverb*.

ORIGIN – Latin *verticalis*, from **VERTEX**.

vertiginous /vərtijinəss/ > *adjective* **1** causing vertigo, especially by being extremely high or steep. **2** relating to or affected by vertigo.

DERIVATIVES – **vertiginously** *adverb*.

vertigo /vertigō/ > *noun* a sensation of whirling and loss of balance, caused by looking down from a great height or by disease affecting the inner ear.

ORIGIN – Latin, 'whirling'.

vervain /vervayn/ > *noun* a herbaceous plant with small blue, white, or purple flowers, used in herbal medicine.

ORIGIN – Old French *verveine*, from Latin *verbena* 'sacred bough'.

verve > *noun* vigour, spirit, and style.

ORIGIN – French, 'vigour'.

vervet monkey /vervit/ > *noun* a common African monkey with greenish-brown upper parts and a black face.

ORIGIN – French.

very > *adverb* **1** in a high degree. **2** (with superlative or **own**) without qualification: *the very best quality.* > *adjective* **1** actual; precise: *those were his very words.* **2** emphasising an extreme point in time or space: *the very end.* **3** with no addition; mere. **4** archaic real; genuine.

COMBINATIONS – **Very Reverend** a title given to a dean in the Anglican Church.

ORIGIN – from Latin *verus* 'true'.

Very light /verri, veeri/ > *noun* a flare fired into the air from a pistol for signalling or for temporary illumination.

ORIGIN – named after the American naval officer Edward W. *Very* (1847–1910).

vesicle /vessik'l/ > *noun* **1 Anatomy & Zoology** a small fluid-filled sac or cyst. **2 Medicine** a blister full of clear fluid. **3 Botany** an air-filled swelling in a seaweed or other plant. **4 Geology** a small cavity in volcanic rock, produced by gas bubbles.

DERIVATIVES – **vesicular** *adjective* **vesiculated** *adjective* **vesiculation** *noun*.

ORIGIN – Latin *vesicula* 'small bladder'.

vesper > *noun* evening prayer.

ORIGIN – Latin, 'evening'.

vespers > *noun* a service of evening prayer, especially in the Western Christian Church.

ORIGIN – Latin *vesperas* 'evensong'.

vessel > *noun* **1** a ship or large boat. **2** a hollow container used to hold liquid. **3** a

tube or duct conveying a fluid within an animal body or plant structure. **4** (chiefly in biblical use) a person regarded as embodying a particular quality: *giving honour unto the wife, as unto the weaker vessel.*

ORIGIN – Old French *vessele*, from Latin *vas* 'vessel'.

vest > *noun* **1 Brit.** an undergarment worn on the upper part of the body, typically having no sleeves. **2** a similar garment worn for a particular purpose: *a bulletproof vest.* **3 N. Amer. & Austral.** a waistcoat or sleeveless jacket. > *verb* **1** (**vest something in**) confer or bestow power, property, etc. on. **2** give (someone) the legal right to power, property, etc.

COMBINATIONS – **vest-pocket N. Amer.** small enough to fit into a pocket.

ORIGIN – Latin *vestis* 'garment'.

vesta > *noun* chiefly historical a short wooden or wax match.

ORIGIN – from the name of *Vesta*, the Roman goddess of the hearth.

vestal > *adjective* **1** relating to the Roman goddess Vesta. **2 literary** chaste; pure. > *noun* a vestal virgin.

COMBINATIONS – **vestal virgin** (in ancient Rome) a virgin consecrated to the goddess Vesta and vowed to chastity.

vested interest > *noun* **1 Law** an interest (usually in land or money held in trust) recognised as belonging to a particular person. **2** a material interest in the outcome of an undertaking or the continuance of a state of affairs. **3** a person or group with such an interest.

vestibule /vestibyool/ > *noun* **1** a small hallway just inside the outer door of a building. **2 Anatomy** a chamber or channel opening into another.

DERIVATIVES – **vestibular** *adjective* (Anatomy).

ORIGIN – Latin *vestibulum* 'entrance court'.

vestige /vestij/ > *noun* **1** a trace of something. **2** the smallest amount.

ORIGIN – Latin *vestigium* 'footprint'.

vestigial /vestijiəl/ > *adjective* **1** forming a very small remnant or trace of something. **2 Biology** (of an organ or part of the body) having lost its function in the course of evolution; rudimentary or atrophied.

DERIVATIVES – **vestigially** *adverb*.

vestment > *noun* **1** a robe worn by the clergy or choristers during services. **2 archaic** a garment, especially a ceremonial or official robe.

ORIGIN – Latin *vestimentum*, from *vestire* 'to clothe'.

vestry > *noun* (pl. **vestries**) a room in or attached to a church, used as an office and for changing into ceremonial vestments.

ORIGIN – Latin *vestiarium*.

vet¹ > *noun* a veterinary surgeon. > *verb*

(**vetted**, **vetting**) make a careful and critical examination of (someone or something, especially of a person prior to employment).

ORIGIN – abbreviation of **VETERINARY** or **VETERINARIAN**.

vet² > *noun* N. Amer. informal a veteran.

vetch > *noun* a leguminous plant with purple, pink, or yellow flowers, some kinds of which are grown for silage or fodder.

ORIGIN – Old French *veche*, from Latin *vicia*.

veteran > *noun* **1** a person who has had long experience in a particular field. **2** an ex-serviceman or -servicewoman.

COMBINATIONS – **veteran car Brit.** an old style or model of car, specifically one made before 1919 or (strictly) before 1905.

ORIGIN – Latin *veteranus*, from *vetus* 'old'.

veterinarian > *noun* N. Amer. a veterinary surgeon.

veterinary* /vettərinəri/ > *adjective* relating to the diseases, injuries, and treatment of farm and domestic animals.

*****SPELLING** – note the *-er-* before the *-in-*: veterinary.

COMBINATIONS – **veterinary surgeon Brit.** a person qualified to treat diseased or injured animals.

ORIGIN – Latin *veterinarius*, from *veterinae* 'cattle'.

vetiver /vettivər/ > (also **vetivert**) > *noun* a fragrant extract or essential oil obtained from the root of an Indian grass, used in perfumery and aromatherapy.

ORIGIN – Tamil, 'root'.

veto /veetō/ > *noun* (pl. **vetoes**) **1** a constitutional right to reject a decision or proposal made by a law-making body. **2** any prohibition. > *verb* (**vetoes**, **vetoed**) exercise a veto against.

ORIGIN – Latin, 'I forbid' (used by Roman tribunes of the people when opposing measures of the Senate).

vex > *verb* cause to feel annoyed or worried.

DERIVATIVES – **vexation** *noun* **vexing** *adjective*.

SYNONYMS – annoy, bother, exasperate, irritate, trouble, worry.

ORIGIN – Latin *vexare* 'shake, disturb'.

vexatious /veksayshəss/ > *adjective* **1** causing annoyance or worry. **2 Law** (of an action, or the bringer of an action) brought without sufficient grounds for winning, in order to cause annoyance to the defendant.

vexed > *adjective* **1** difficult and much debated; problematic. **2** annoyed or worried.

VGA > *abbreviation* videographics array, a standard for defining colour display screens for computers.

vgc > *abbreviation* very good condition.

VHF > *abbreviation* very high frequency.

VHS > *abbreviation* **trademark** video home system (as used by domestic video recorders).

VI > *abbreviation* Virgin Islands.

via > *preposition* **1** travelling through (a place) en route to a destination. **2** by way of; through. **3** by means of.
ORIGIN – Latin, 'way, road'.

viable /vīab'l/ > *adjective* **1** capable of working successfully; feasible. **2** Biology (of a plant, animal, or cell) capable of surviving or living successfully.
DERIVATIVES – **viability** *noun* **viably** *adverb*.
SYNONYMS – **1** feasible, manageable, possible, practical, realistic, workable.
ORIGIN – French, from *vie* 'life', from Latin *vita*.

viaduct /vīədukt/ > *noun* a long bridge-like structure carrying a road or railway across a valley or other low ground.
ORIGIN – from Latin *via* 'way', on the pattern of *aqueduct*.

Viagra /vīagrə/ > *noun* **trademark** a synthetic compound used to enhance male potency.
ORIGIN – apparently a blend of *virility* and the name *Niagara*.

vial /vīəl/ > *noun* a small container used especially for holding liquid medicines.
ORIGIN – alteration of **PHIAL**.

via media /veeə meddiə/ > *noun* **formal** a middle way or compromise between extremes.
ORIGIN – Latin.

viand /vīənd/ > *noun* **archaic** an item of food.
ORIGIN – Old French *viande* 'food', from Latin *vivere* 'to live'.

viaticum /vīattikəm/ > *noun* (pl. **viatica** /vīattikə/) the Eucharist as given to a person near or in danger of death.
ORIGIN – Latin, from *via* 'road'.

vibe > *noun* **informal 1** the atmosphere or aura of a person or place as communicated to and felt by others. **2** (**vibes**) short for **VIBRAPHONE**.

vibrant > *adjective* **1** full of energy and enthusiasm. **2** (of colour or sound) bold and strong. **3** quivering; pulsating.
DERIVATIVES – **vibrancy** *noun* **vibrantly** *adverb*.
SYNONYMS – **1** dynamic, energetic, lively, spirited, vigorous, vivacious.
ORIGIN – Latin, from *vibrare* 'move to and fro, vibrate'.

vibraphone /vībrəfōn/ > *noun* a musical percussion instrument with a double row of tuned metal bars, each above a tubular resonator containing a motor-driven rotating vane, giving a vibrato effect.
DERIVATIVES – **vibraphonist** *noun*.
ORIGIN – from **VIBRATO** + **-PHONE**.

vibrate > *verb* **1** move with small movements rapidly to and fro. **2** (of a sound) resonate.
DERIVATIVES – **vibrating** *adjective*.
SYNONYMS – **1** judder, quake, quiver, shake, shiver, shudder, tremble.
ORIGIN – Latin *vibrare* 'move to and fro'.

vibration > *noun* **1** an instance or the state of vibrating. **2** (**vibrations**) **informal** an emotional state or atmosphere, as communicated to and felt by others.
DERIVATIVES – **vibrational** *adjective*.

vibrato /vibraatō/ > *noun* **Music** a rapid, slight variation in pitch in singing or playing some musical instruments, producing a stronger or richer tone.
ORIGIN – Italian, from *vibrare* 'vibrate'.

vibrator > *noun* **1** a device that vibrates or causes vibration. **2** a vibrating device used for massage or sexual stimulation.
DERIVATIVES – **vibratory** *adjective*.

vibrio /vibriō, vībriō/ > *noun* (pl. **vibrios**) **Medicine** a curved, rod-like bacterium of a group including that causing cholera.
ORIGIN – from Latin *vibrare* 'vibrate'.

viburnum /vīburnəm, viburnəm/ > *noun* a shrub or small tree, typically bearing clusters of small white flowers.
ORIGIN – Latin, 'wayfaring tree'.

vicar > *noun* **1** (in the Church of England) a priest in charge of a parish (formerly a parish where tithes passed to a person or group other than the priest himself). **2** (in other Anglican Churches) a member of the clergy deputising for another. **3** (in the Roman Catholic Church) a representative or deputy of a bishop.
ORIGIN – Old French *vicaire*, from Latin *vicarius* 'substitute'.

vicarage > *noun* the residence of a vicar.

vicariate /vikairiət/ > *noun* the office or authority of a vicar.

vicarious /vikairiəss/ > *adjective* **1** experienced in the imagination through the feelings or actions of another person. **2** acting or done for another.
DERIVATIVES – **vicariously** *adverb*.
ORIGIN – from Latin *vicarius* 'substitute'.

vice¹ > *noun* **1** immoral or wicked behaviour. **2** criminal activities involving prostitution, pornography, or drugs. **3** an immoral or wicked personal characteristic. **4** a weakness of character; a bad habit.
SYNONYMS – **1** badness, corruption, evil, immorality, wickedness, wrongdoing. **3,4** defect, failing, flaw, shortcoming, weakness.
ANTONYMS – **1,3,4** virtue.
ORIGIN – Latin *vitium*.

vice² (US **vise**) > *noun* a metal tool with movable jaws which are used to hold an object firmly in place while work is done on it.
DERIVATIVES – **vice-like** *adjective*.
ORIGIN – Old French *vis*, from Latin *vitis* 'vine': first meaning 'a screw or winch'.

vice- > *combining form* next in rank to (typically denoting capacity to deputise for): *vice-president*.
ORIGIN – from Latin *vice* 'in place of'.

vice admiral > *noun* a high rank of naval officer, above rear admiral and below admiral.

vice chancellor > *noun* a deputy chancellor, especially one of a British university who is in charge of its administration.

vice-president > *noun* an official or executive ranking below and deputising for a president.
DERIVATIVES – **vice-presidential** *adjective*.

viceregal > *adjective* relating to a viceroy.

viceroy > *noun* a ruler exercising authority in a colony on behalf of a sovereign.
DERIVATIVES – **viceroyal** *adjective*.
ORIGIN – archaic French, from *vice-* 'in place of' + *roi* 'king'.

vice versa /vīss versə, vīsi versə/ > *adverb* with the main items in the preceding statement the other way round.
ORIGIN – Latin, 'in-turned position'.

vichyssoise /veesheeswaaz/ > *noun* a soup made with potatoes, leeks, and cream and typically served chilled.
ORIGIN – French 'of *Vichy*', a town in central France.

vicinity > *noun* (pl. **vicinities**) the area near or surrounding a particular place.
ORIGIN – Latin *vicinitas*, from *vicinus* 'neighbour'.

vicious > *adjective* **1** cruel or violent. **2** (of an animal) wild and dangerous. **3** **dated** immoral.
DERIVATIVES – **viciously** *adverb* **viciousness** *noun*.
SYNONYMS – **1** brutal, callous, cruel, heartless, savage, violent. **2** aggressive, dangerous, ferocious, fierce, savage, wild.
COMBINATIONS – **vicious circle** a sequence of cause and effect in which one problem or need leads to another, which then makes the first one worse.
ORIGIN – Latin *vitiosus*, from *vitium* 'vice'.

vicissitude /visissityōōd/ > *noun* **1** a change of circumstances or fortune. **2** **literary** alternation between opposite or contrasting things.
ORIGIN – Latin *vicissitudo*, from *vicissim* 'by turns', from *vic-* 'turn, change'.

vicomte /veekoNt/ > *noun* (pl. pronunc. same) a French nobleman corresponding in rank to a British or Irish viscount.
ORIGIN – French.

victim > *noun* **1** a person harmed, injured, or killed as a result of a crime or accident. **2** a person who is tricked or cheated on. **3** an animal or person killed as a religious sacrifice.
IDIOMS – **fall victim to** be hurt, killed, or destroyed by.
ORIGIN – Latin *victima*.

victimise (also **victimize**) > *verb* single (someone) out for cruel or unjust treatment.

DERIVATIVES – **victimisation** *noun* **victimiser** *noun*.

SYNONYMS – bully, persecute, pick on, prey on, terrorise, torment.

victimless > *adjective* (of a crime) in which there is no injured party.

victimology > *noun* (pl. **victimologies**) the study of the victims of crime and the psychological effects on them.

victor > *noun* a person who defeats an enemy or opponent in a battle, game, or competition.

ORIGIN – Latin, from *vincere* 'conquer'.

Victorian > *adjective* **1** relating to the reign of Queen Victoria (1837–1901). **2** relating to the attitudes and values associated with the Victorian period, especially those of prudishness and high moral tone. > *noun* a person who lived during the Victorian period.

DERIVATIVES – **Victorianism** *noun*.

Victoriana > *plural noun* articles, especially collectors' items, from the Victorian period.

Victoria plum > *noun* Brit. a large red dessert plum.

Victoria sandwich (also **Victoria sponge**) > *noun* Brit. a cake consisting of two layers of sponge with a jam filling.

victorious > *adjective* having won a victory; triumphant.

DERIVATIVES – **victoriously** *adverb*.

SYNONYMS – conquering, successful, triumphant, winning.

victory > *noun* (pl. **victories**) an act of defeating an opponent in a battle or competition.

SYNONYMS – conquest, success, triumph, win.

ORIGIN – Latin *victoria*.

victual /vitt'l/ archaic > *noun* (**victuals**) food or provisions. > *verb* (**victualled**, **victualling**; US **victualed**, **victualing**) provide with food or other stores.

ORIGIN – Latin *victualis*, from *victus* 'food'; the pronunciation represents the early spelling *vittel*.

victualler /vitt'lər/ (US **victualer**) > *noun* **1** Brit. a person who is licensed to sell alcoholic liquor. **2** dated a person providing or selling food or other provisions.

vicuña /vikoōnyə/ > *noun* **1** a wild relative of the llama, valued for its fine silky wool. **2** cloth made from this wool.

ORIGIN – Quechua.

vid > *noun* informal short for **VIDEO**.

video > *noun* (pl. **videos**) **1** the system of recording, reproducing, or broadcasting moving visual images on or from videotape. **2** a film or other recording on videotape. **3** a video cassette. **4** Brit. a video recorder. > *verb* (**videoes**, **videoed**) film or make a video recording of.

COMBINATIONS – **videodisc** a CD-ROM or other disc used to store visual images. **video game** a game played by electronically manipulating images produced by a computer program. **video jockey** a person who introduces and plays music videos on television. **video-on-demand** a system in which viewers choose their own filmed entertainment, by means of a PC or interactive TV system. **videophone** a telephone device transmitting and receiving a visual image as well as sound. **VideoPlus** trademark a system for identifying broadcast television programmes by a numerical code which can be input into a video recorder in order to preset recording.

ORIGIN – from Latin *videre* 'to see', on the pattern of *audio*.

videoconference > *noun* an arrangement in which televisions linked to telephone lines are used to enable a group of people to communicate with each other in sound and vision.

DERIVATIVES – **videoconferencing** *noun*.

videography > *noun* the process or art of making video films.

DERIVATIVES – **videographer** *noun*.

videophile > *noun* an enthusiast for or devotee of video recordings or video technology.

video recorder > *noun* a device which, when linked to a television set, can be used to record programmes and play videotapes.

DERIVATIVES – **video recording** *noun*.

videotape > *noun* **1** magnetic tape for recording and reproducing visual images and sound. **2** a video cassette. > *verb* record on video.

vie > *verb* (**vied**, **vying**) compete eagerly with others in order to do or achieve something.

ORIGIN – probably a shortening of obsolete *envy*, from Latin *invitare* 'challenge'.

Viennese /veeəneez/ > *noun* a person from Vienna. > *adjective* relating to Vienna.

Vietcong /viətkong/ > *noun* the Communist guerrilla force in Vietnam which fought the South Vietnamese government forces between 1954 and 1975 and opposed the South Vietnam and US forces in the Vietnam War.

ORIGIN – Vietnamese, 'Vietnamese Communist'.

Vietnamese /viətnəmeez/ > *noun* (pl. same) **1** a person from Vietnam. **2** the language of Vietnam. > *adjective* relating to Vietnam.

view > *noun* **1** vision or sight, as from a particular position. **2** a sight or prospect from a particular position, typically an appealing one. **3** a particular way of regarding something; an attitude or opinion. **4** an inspection of things for sale by prospective purchasers. > *verb* **1** look at or inspect. **2** regard in a particular light or with a particular attitude. **3** inspect (a house or other property) with the prospect of buying or renting. **4** watch on television.

IDIOMS – **in full view** clearly visible. **in view 1** visible. **2** in one's mind or as one's aim. **in view of** because or as a result of. **with a view to** with the hope or intention of.

DERIVATIVES – **viewable** *adjective* **viewing** *noun*.

SYNONYMS – *noun* **2** outlook, panorama, prospect, vista. **3** attitude, belief, conviction, opinion, point of view, thought. *verb* **1** contemplate, examine, inspect, observe, regard, survey. **2** consider, look on, perceive, regard.

ORIGIN – Old French *vieue*, from Latin *videre* 'to see'.

viewer > *noun* **1** a person who views something. **2** a device for looking at film transparencies or similar photographic images.

viewership > *noun* (treated as sing. or pl.) the audience for a particular television programme or channel.

viewfinder > *noun* a device on a camera showing the field of view of the lens, used in framing and focusing the picture.

viewpoint > *noun* **1** a position affording a good view. **2** a point of view; an opinion.

viga /veegə/ > *noun* US a rough-hewn roof timber, especially in an adobe building.

ORIGIN – Spanish.

vigil /vijil/ > *noun* a period of staying awake during the time usually spent asleep, especially to keep watch or pray.

ORIGIN – Latin *vigilia*, from *vigil* 'awake'.

vigilant > *adjective* keeping careful watch for possible danger or difficulties.

DERIVATIVES – **vigilance** *noun* **vigilantly** *adverb*.

SYNONYMS – alert, attentive, eagle-eyed, observant, wary, watchful.

ORIGIN – Latin, from *vigilare* 'keep awake'.

vigilante /vijilanti/ > *noun* a member of a self-appointed group of people who undertake law enforcement in their community without legal authority.

DERIVATIVES – **vigilantism** *noun*.

ORIGIN – Spanish, 'vigilant'.

vigneron /veenyəroN/ > *noun* a person who cultivates grapes for winemaking.

ORIGIN – French, from *vigne* 'vine'.

vignette /vee**nyet**/ > *noun* **1** a brief evocative description, account, or episode. **2** a small illustration or portrait photograph which fades into its background without a definite border. > *verb* portray in the style of a vignette.

ORIGIN – French, from *vigne* 'vine': originally also denoting a carved representation of a vine.

vigor > *noun* US spelling of **VIGOUR**.

vigorous > *adjective* **1** strong, healthy, and full of energy. **2** characterised by or involving physical strength, effort, or energy. **3** (of language) forceful.

DERIVATIVES – **vigorously** *adverb*.

SYNONYMS – **1** dynamic, hearty, robust, sturdy, vital. **2** strenuous.

vigour (US **vigor**) > *noun* **1** physical strength and good health. **2** effort, energy, and enthusiasm.

SYNONYMS – **1** energy, robustness, vitality. **2** brio, gusto, verve, zest.

ORIGIN – Latin *vigor*, from *vigere* 'be lively'.

Viking > *noun* any of the Scandinavian seafaring pirates and traders who raided and settled in many parts of NW Europe in the 8th to 11th centuries.

ORIGIN – Old Norse *víkingr*, from *vík* 'creek' or Old English *wīc* 'camp, dwelling place'.

vile > *adjective* **1** extremely unpleasant. **2** morally bad; wicked.

DERIVATIVES – **vilely** *adverb* **vileness** *noun*.

SYNONYMS – **1** disgusting, foul, nasty, odious, repellent, sickening. **2** base, depraved, low, wicked.

ORIGIN – Latin *vilis* 'cheap, base'.

vilify /**vill**if ī/ > *verb* (**vilifies**, **vilified**) speak or write about in an abusively disparaging manner.

DERIVATIVES – **vilification** *noun*.

SYNONYMS – calumniate, defame, denigrate, disparage, traduce.

ORIGIN – Latin *vilificare*, from *vilis* 'ignoble'.

villa > *noun* **1** (especially in continental Europe) a large country residence in its own grounds. **2** Brit. a detached, semi-detached, or terraced house in a suburban area, typically having decorative architectural features. **3** a rented holiday home abroad. **4** (in Roman times) a large country house, having an estate and consisting of buildings arranged around a courtyard.

ORIGIN – Latin, 'country house'.

village > *noun* **1** a group of houses situated in a rural area, larger than a hamlet and smaller than a town. **2** a self-contained district or community within a town or city.

DERIVATIVES – **villager** *noun* **villagey** *adjective*.

ORIGIN – Old French, from Latin *villa* 'country house'.

villain > *noun* **1** a wicked person or a person guilty of a crime. **2** (in a play or novel) a character whose evil actions or motives are important to the plot.

DERIVATIVES – **villainous** *adjective* **villainously** *adverb* **villainousness** *noun* **villainy** *noun*.

SYNONYMS – **1** criminal, malefactor, miscreant, reprobate, rogue, scoundrel. **2** informal baddy.

ORIGIN – Old French *vilein*, based on Latin *villa* 'country house': originally in the sense 'a rustic'.

villein /**vill**in/ > *noun* (in medieval England) a feudal tenant entirely subject to a lord or manor to whom he paid dues and services in return for land.

ORIGIN – variant of **VILLAIN**.

villus /**vill**əss/ > *noun* (pl. **villi** /**vill**ī/) Anatomy any of numerous tiny elongated projections set closely together in the absorbent lining of the small intestine.

DERIVATIVES – **villous** *adjective*.

ORIGIN – Latin, 'shaggy hair'.

vim > *noun* informal energy; enthusiasm.

ORIGIN – perhaps from Latin *vis* 'energy'.

vinaigrette /vinni**gret**/ > *noun* salad dressing of oil, wine vinegar, and seasoning.

ORIGIN – French, from *vinaigre* 'vinegar'.

vinca /**ving**kə/ > *noun* another term for **PERIWINKLE**[1].

ORIGIN – Latin, from *pervinca* 'periwinkle'.

vindaloo /vində**loo**/ > *noun* a very hot Indian curry made with meat or fish.

ORIGIN – probably from Portuguese *vin d'alho* 'wine and garlic (sauce)', from *vinho* 'wine' + *alho* 'garlic'.

vindicate /**vin**dikayt/ > *verb* **1** clear of blame or suspicion. **2** show to be right or justified.

DERIVATIVES – **vindication** *noun*.

ORIGIN – Latin *vindicare* 'claim, avenge'.

vindictive > *adjective* having or showing a strong or unreasoning desire for revenge.

DERIVATIVES – **vindictively** *adverb* **vindictiveness** *noun*.

SYNONYMS – bitter, revengeful, spiteful, unforgiving, vengeful.

ORIGIN – from Latin *vindicta* 'vengeance'.

vine > *noun* **1** a climbing or trailing woody-stemmed plant. **2** the slender stem of a trailing or climbing plant.

ORIGIN – Latin *vinea* 'vineyard, vine', from *vinum* 'wine'.

vinegar > *noun* **1** a sour-tasting liquid containing acetic acid, obtained by fermenting dilute alcoholic liquids and used as a condiment or for pickling. **2** sourness or peevishness of behaviour.

DERIVATIVES – **vinegary** *adjective*.

ORIGIN – from Old French *vyn egre*, from Latin *vinum* 'wine' + *acer* 'sour'.

vineyard > *noun* a plantation of grapevines, typically producing grapes used in winemaking.

vingt-et-un /vaNtay**ön**/ > *noun* the card game pontoon or blackjack.

ORIGIN – French, 'twenty-one'.

vinho verde /veenō **vair**di/ > *noun* a young Portuguese wine that has not been allowed to mature.

ORIGIN – Portuguese, 'green wine'.

viniculture /**vinn**ikulchər/ > *noun* the cultivation of grapevines for winemaking.

vining /**vī**ning/ > *noun* the separation of crops such as peas or beans from their vines and pods. > *adjective* (of a plant) having climbing or trailing woody stems like a vine.

vino > *noun* (pl. **vinos**) informal, chiefly Brit. wine, especially cheap wine.

ORIGIN – Spanish and Italian, 'wine'.

vin ordinaire /vaN ordi**nair**/ > *noun* (pl. **vins ordinaires**) cheap table wine for everyday use.

ORIGIN – French, 'ordinary wine'.

vinous /**vī**nəss/ > *adjective* of, resembling, or associated with wine.

ORIGIN – from Latin *vinum* 'wine' + **-OUS**.

vintage > *noun* **1** the year or place in which wine was produced. **2** a wine of high quality made from the crop of a single identified district in a good year. **3** the grapes or wine of a particular season. **4** the time that something was produced. > *adjective* **1** referring to vintage wine. **2** referring to something of high quality from the past.

COMBINATIONS – **vintage car** Brit. an old style or model of car, specifically one made between 1919 and 1930.

ORIGIN – Old French *vendange*, from Latin *vindemia* (from *vinum* 'wine' + *demere* 'remove').

vintner /**vint**nər/ > *noun* a wine merchant.

ORIGIN – Old French *vinetier*, from Latin *vinetum* 'vineyard'.

vinyl /**vī**n'l/ > *noun* **1** synthetic resin or plastic based on polyvinyl chloride, used e.g. for wallpaper and emulsion paint and formerly for gramophone records. **2** /also **vī**nīl/ Chemistry the unsaturated hydrocarbon radical $-CH=CH_2$, derived from ethylene.

ORIGIN – from Latin *vinum* 'wine' (suggested by the relationship of ethylene to ethyl alcohol).

viol /**vī**əl/ > *noun* a musical instrument of the Renaissance and baroque periods, typically six-stringed, held vertically and played with a bow.

ORIGIN – Provençal *viola*.

viola¹ /vi-ō-lə/ > *noun* an instrument of the violin family, larger than the violin and tuned a fifth lower.

ORIGIN – Italian and Spanish; compare with **VIOL**.

viola² /vī-ə-lə/ > *noun* a plant of a genus that includes the pansies and violets.

ORIGIN – Latin, 'violet'.

violaceous /vī-ə-lay-shəss/ > *adjective* of a violet colour.

viola da gamba /vi-ō-lə da **gam**-bə/ > *noun* a bass viol, corresponding to the modern cello.

ORIGIN – Italian, 'viol for the leg'.

violate > *verb* 1 break or fail to comply with (a rule or formal agreement). 2 treat with disrespect. 3 rape or sexually assault.

DERIVATIVES – **violation** *noun* **violator** *noun*.

SYNONYMS – 1 breach, break, contravene, infringe, transgress. 2 defile, desecrate, profane.

ORIGIN – Latin *violare* 'treat violently'.

violence > *noun* 1 behaviour involving physical force intended to hurt, damage, or kill. 2 strength of emotion or an unpleasant or destructive natural force.

violent > *adjective* 1 using or involving violence. 2 very intense, forceful, or powerful.

DERIVATIVES – **violently** *adverb*.

SYNONYMS – 1 aggressive, brutal, rough, savage.

ORIGIN – Latin, 'vehement, violent'.

violet > *noun* 1 a small plant typically with purple, blue, or white five-petalled flowers. 2 a bluish-purple colour seen at the end of the spectrum opposite red.

ORIGIN – Old French *violette*, from Latin *viola* 'violet'.

violin > *noun* a stringed musical instrument of treble pitch, having four strings and a body narrowed at the middle, played with a bow.

DERIVATIVES – **violinist** *noun*.

ORIGIN – Italian *violino*, from *viola* (see **VIOLA¹**).

violist > *noun* 1 /vi-ō-list/ a viola player. 2 /vī-ə-list/ a viol player.

violoncello /vī-ə-lən-**chell**-ō, vee-ə-lən-**chell**-ō/ > *noun* formal term for **CELLO**.

ORIGIN – Italian, from *viola* (see **VIOLA**).

VIP > *abbreviation* very important person.

viper > *noun* 1 a poisonous snake with large hinged fangs, typically having a light-coloured body with dark patterns on it. 2 a spiteful or treacherous person.

DERIVATIVES – **viperish** *adjective* **viperous** *adjective*.

ORIGIN – Latin *vipera*, from *vivus* 'alive' + *parere* 'bring forth' (because of a former belief that vipers bore live young).

viraemia /vī-ree-miə/ (also **viremia**) > *noun* Medicine the presence of viruses in the blood.

virago /vi-raa-gō/ > *noun* (pl. **viragos** or **viragoes**) a domineering, violent, or bad-tempered woman.

wordpower facts
Virago

The word **virago** is first recorded in Old English, as the name given by Adam to Eve in the Vulgate version of the Bible (that is, the Latin version of the text prepared in the late 4th century). The Latin word *virago* (from *vir* 'man') means 'a man-like or heroic woman'; according to Genesis (chapter 2), Adam chose this name because Eve was made from the body of a man. The word was adopted as a general term for a heroic female warrior in the late 14th century, leading to the much less favourable sense 'bold and impudent woman', from which the current sense 'domineering, violent, or bad-tempered woman' developed.

viral > *adjective* of the nature of, caused by, or relating to a virus or viruses.

DERIVATIVES – **virally** *adverb*.

vireo /virr-iō/ > *noun* (pl. **vireos**) a small American warbler-like songbird, typically green or grey.

ORIGIN – Latin, referring to a greenfinch or similar bird.

Virgilian /vur-**jill**-iən/ (also **Vergilian**) > *adjective* relating to or in the style of the Roman poet Virgil (70–19 BC).

virgin > *noun* 1 a person who has never had sexual intercourse. 2 (**the Virgin**) the Virgin Mary. 3 a person who is naive or inexperienced in a particular context. > *adjective* 1 being, relating to, or appropriate for a virgin. 2 not yet used or exploited. 3 (of olive oil) obtained from the first pressing of olives.

WORDFINDER – Virgo (*constellation and zodiac sign, the Virgin*).

COMBINATIONS – **Virgin Birth** the doctrine of Christ's birth from a mother, Mary, who was a virgin.

ORIGIN – Latin *virgo*.

virginal > *adjective* relating to or appropriate for a virgin. > *noun* an early spinet with the strings parallel to the keyboard. [ORIGIN –

perhaps so called because it was usually played by young women.]

Virginia > *noun* a type of tobacco grown and manufactured in Virginia.

Virginia creeper > *noun* a North American vine planted for its red autumn foliage.

virginity > *noun* the state of being a virgin.

Virgo > *noun* 1 Astronomy a large constellation (the Virgin), said to represent a maiden or goddess associated with the harvest. 2 Astrology the sixth sign of the zodiac, which the sun enters about 23 August.

DERIVATIVES – **Virgoan** *noun & adjective*.

ORIGIN – Latin.

viridian > *noun* 1 a bluish-green pigment containing chromium hydroxide. 2 a bluish-green colour.

ORIGIN – from Latin *viridis* 'green'.

virile /vi-rīl/ > *adjective* 1 (of a man) having strength, energy, and a strong sex drive. 2 vigorous, strong, and manly.

DERIVATIVES – **virility** *noun*.

ORIGIN – Latin *virilis*, from *vir* 'man'.

virology /vī-**roll**-əji/ > *noun* the branch of science concerned with the study of viruses.

DERIVATIVES – **virological** *adjective* **virologist** *noun*.

virtual > *adjective* 1 almost or nearly as described, but not completely or according to strict definition. 2 Computing not physically existing as such but made by software to appear to do so. 3 Optics relating to the points at which rays would meet if extended backwards.

DERIVATIVES – **virtuality** *noun*.

COMBINATIONS – **virtual memory** (also **virtual storage**) Computing memory that appears to exist as main storage although most of it is supported by data held in secondary storage. **virtual reality** Computing the computer-generated simulation of a three-dimensional image or environment that can be interacted with by using special electronic equipment.

ORIGIN – Latin *virtualis*, from *virtus* 'virtue'.

virtually > *adverb* 1 nearly; almost. 2 Computing by means of virtual reality techniques.

virtue /vur-tyōō/ > *noun* 1 behaviour showing high moral standards. 2 a quality considered morally good or desirable. 3 a good or useful quality of a thing. 4 archaic virginity or chastity.

IDIOMS – **by virtue of** because or as a result of.

SYNONYMS – 1 decency, goodness, integrity, morality, rectitude, righteousness. 3 advantage, good point, merit, strength.

ANTONYMS – 1,2 vice. 3 failing.

wordpower facts

Virtue

It may be a surprise to some that there is a relationship between **virtue** and **virility**! Both these words come from Latin *vir*, 'a man'. *Vir* gave rise to the Latin noun *virtus*, meaning 'manliness, valour, moral perfection', and this was adopted in English in the 13th century as **vertue**, via Old French. Its early meanings in English were 'divine power' and 'moral excellence; uprightness', the latter being the usual modern meaning. *Vir* is also the source of **virago**.

virtuoso /vurtyooōsō/ > *noun* (pl. **virtuosi** /vurtyooōsi/ or **virtuosos**) a person highly skilled in music or another artistic pursuit.
DERIVATIVES – **virtuosic** *adjective* **virtuosity** *noun*.
ORIGIN – Italian, 'learned, skilful'.

virtuous > *adjective* **1** having or showing high moral standards. **2** archaic chaste.
DERIVATIVES – **virtuously** *adverb* **virtuousness** *noun*.
SYNONYMS – **1** ethical, good, moral, principled, righteous, upright.
ANTONYMS – **1** bad, sinful.
COMBINATIONS – **virtuous circle** a recurring cycle of events, the result of each one being to increase the beneficial effect of the next.

virulent /virrŏŏlənt, virryŏŏ-/ > *adjective* **1** (of a disease or poison) extremely severe or harmful in its effects. **2** (of a pathogen, especially a virus) highly infective. **3** bitterly hostile.
DERIVATIVES – **virulence** *noun* **virulently** *adverb*.
ORIGIN – Latin *virulentus*, from *virus* 'slimy liquid, poison': originally describing a poisoned wound.

virus /vīrəss/ > *noun* **1** a submicroscopic infective particle which is able to multiply within the cells of a host organism and typically consists of nucleic acid coated in protein. **2** informal an infection or disease caused by such an agent. **3** (also **computer virus**) a piece of code surreptitiously introduced into a system in order to corrupt it or destroy data.
ORIGIN – Latin, 'slimy liquid, poison'.

visa /veezə/ > *noun* an endorsement on a passport indicating that the holder is allowed to enter, leave, or stay for a specified period of time in a country.
ORIGIN – Latin, from *videre* 'to see'.

visage /vizzij/ > *noun* literary **1** a person's face, with reference to the form of the features. **2** a person's facial expression.
DERIVATIVES – **visaged** *adjective*.

ORIGIN – Old French, from Latin *visus* 'sight', from *videre* 'to see'.

vis-à-vis /veezaavee/ > *preposition* in relation to. > *adverb* archaic in a position facing a specified or implied subject.
ORIGIN – French, 'face to face'.

viscera /vissərə/ > *plural noun* (sing. **viscus**) the internal organs in the main cavities of the body, especially those in the abdomen.
ORIGIN – Latin, plural of *viscus*.

visceral > *adjective* **1** relating to the viscera. **2** (of a feeling) deep and instinctive rather than rational.
DERIVATIVES – **viscerally** *adverb*.

viscid /vissid/ > *adjective* glutinous; sticky.
ORIGIN – Latin *viscidus*, from *viscum* 'birdlime'.

viscoelastic /viskōilastik/ > *adjective* Physics exhibiting both elastic and viscous behaviour.
DERIVATIVES – **viscoelasticity** *noun*.

viscose /viskōs/ > *noun* **1** a viscous orange-brown liquid obtained by chemical treatment of cellulose and used as the basis of manufacturing rayon and transparent cellulose film. **2** rayon fabric or fibre made from this.
ORIGIN – Latin *viscosus*, from *viscum* 'birdlime'.

viscosity /viskossiti/ > *noun* (pl. **viscosities**) **1** the state of being viscous. **2** Physics a quantity expressing the magnitude of internal friction in a fluid, as measured by the force per unit area resisting uniform flow.

viscount /vīkownt/ > *noun* a British nobleman ranking above a baron and below an earl.
ORIGIN – Old French *visconte*, from Latin *vicecomes* (see VICE-, COUNT²).

viscountess /vīkowntiss/ > *noun* the wife or widow of a viscount, or a woman holding the rank of viscount in her own right.

viscous /viskəss/ > *adjective* having a thick, sticky consistency between solid and liquid; having a high viscosity.
ORIGIN – Latin *viscosus*, from *viscum* 'birdlime'.

viscus /viskəss/ singular form of VISCERA.
ORIGIN – Latin.

vise > *noun* US spelling of VICE².

visibility > *noun* **1** the state of being able to see or be seen. **2** the distance one can see as determined by light and weather conditions.

visible > *adjective* **1** able to be seen. **2** Physics (of light) within the range of wavelengths to which the eye is sensitive.
DERIVATIVES – **visibly** *adverb*.
SYNONYMS – **1** discernible, evident, noticeable, observable, perceptible.
ORIGIN – Latin *visibilis*, from *videre* 'to see'.

Visigoth /vizzigoth/ > *noun* a member of the branch of the Goths who invaded the Roman Empire between the 3rd and 5th centuries AD.
ORIGIN – Latin *Visigothus*, possibly meaning 'West Goth'. Compare with OSTROGOTH.

vision > *noun* **1** the faculty or state of being able to see. **2** the ability to think about the future with imagination or wisdom. **3** a mental image of what the future will or could be like. **4** an experience of seeing something in a dream or trance, or as a supernatural apparition. **5** a person or sight of unusual beauty. **6** the images seen on a television screen.
SYNONYMS – **1** eyesight, sight. **2** far-sightedness, foresight. **3** conception, dream, fantasy, idea.
ORIGIN – Latin, from *videre* 'to see'.

visionary > *adjective* **1** thinking about the future with imagination or wisdom. **2** relating to supernatural or dreamlike visions. > *noun* (pl. **visionaries**) a visionary person.

visit > *verb* (**visited**, **visiting**) **1** go to see and spend some time with (someone) socially or as a guest. **2** go to see and spend some time in (a place) as a tourist or guest. **3** go to see for any specific purpose. **4** (with reference to something harmful or unpleasant) inflict or be inflicted on someone. **5** N. Amer. informal chat. > *noun* **1** an act of visiting. **2** a temporary stay at a place. **3** N. Amer. an informal conversation.
DERIVATIVES – **visiting** *adjective*.
COMBINATIONS – **visiting card** Brit. a card bearing a person's name and address, sent or left in lieu of a formal visit.
ORIGIN – Latin *visitare* 'go to see'.

visitant > *noun* **1** chiefly literary a supernatural being; an apparition. **2** archaic a visitor or guest.

visitation > *noun* **1** the appearance of a divine or supernatural being. **2** US Law a divorced person's right to spend time with their children in the custody of a former spouse. **3** (in Church use) an official visit of inspection. **4** US a gathering with the family of a deceased person before the funeral. **5** a disaster or difficulty regarded as a divine punishment.

visitor > *noun* **1** a person visiting a person or place. **2** a migratory bird present in a locality for only part of the year: *a winter visitor.*

visor /vīzər/ (also **vizor**) > *noun* **1** a movable part of a helmet that can be pulled down to cover the face. **2** a screen for protecting the eyes from unwanted light. **3** N. Amer. a stiff peak at the front of a cap.
DERIVATIVES – **visored** *adjective*.
ORIGIN – from Old French *vis* 'face', from Latin *visus* 'sight'.

vista > *noun* **1** a pleasing view, especially one seen through a long, narrow opening. **2** a mental view of an imagined future event or situation.

ORIGIN – Italian, 'view'.

visual > *adjective* relating to seeing or sight. > *noun* a picture, piece of film, or display used to illustrate or accompany something.

DERIVATIVES – **visually** *adverb*.

COMBINATIONS – **visual display unit** Computing, chiefly Brit. a device for displaying input signals as characters on a screen.

ORIGIN – Latin *visualis*, from *videre* 'to see'.

visualise (also **visualize**) > *verb* form a mental image of; imagine.

DERIVATIVES – **visualisation** *noun*.

visuospatial /vizhyoo-ōspaysh'l/ > *adjective* Psychology referring to the visual perception of the spatial relationships of objects.

vital > *adjective* **1** absolutely necessary; essential. **2** indispensable to the continuance of life. **3** full of energy; lively. > *noun* (**vitals**) the body's important internal organs.

DERIVATIVES – **vitally** *adverb*.

SYNONYMS – *adjective* **1** critical, crucial, essential, imperative. **3** dynamic, energetic, lively, vigorous, zestful.

COMBINATIONS – **vital capacity** the greatest volume of air that can be expelled from the lungs after taking the deepest possible breath. **vital force** the energy or spirit which animates living creatures. **vital signs** clinical measurements, specifically pulse rate, temperature, respiration rate, and blood pressure, that indicate the state of a patient's essential body functions. **vital statistics 1** quantitative data concerning the population, such as the number of births, marriages, and deaths. **2** informal the measurements of a woman's bust, waist, and hips.

ORIGIN – Latin *vitalis*, from *vita* 'life'.

vitalise (also **vitalize**) > *verb* give strength and energy to.

vitalism > *noun* the theory that the origin and phenomena of life are dependent on a force or principle distinct from purely chemical or physical forces.

DERIVATIVES – **vitalist** *noun* & *adjective* **vitalistic** *adjective*.

vitality > *noun* **1** the state of being strong and active; energy. **2** the power giving continuance of life, present in all living things.

SYNONYMS – **1** energy, liveliness, vigour, zest.

vitamin /vittəmin, vītəmin/ > *noun* any of a group of organic compounds which are essential for normal nutrition and have to be supplied in the diet because they cannot be synthesised by the body.

WORDFINDER – *the main vitamins:* retinol (*vitamin A*), thiamine (*vitamin B₁*), riboflavin (*vitamin B₂*), pyridoxine (*vitamin B₆*), cyanocobalamin (*vitamin B₁₂*), ascorbic acid (*vitamin C*), calciferol (*vitamin D₂*), cholecalciferol (*vitamin D₃*), tocopherol (*vitamin E*), phylloquinone (*vitamin K₁*), menaquinone (*vitamin K₂*); *diseases caused by lack of a vitamin:* beriberi (*vitamin B₁*), pernicious anaemia (*vitamin B₁₂*), rickets (*vitamin D*), scurvy (*vitamin C*).

ORIGIN – from Latin *vita* 'life' + AMINE, because vitamins were originally thought to contain an amino acid.

vitelline /vitellīn, vītellīn/ > *adjective* Zoology & Embryology referring to the yolk (or yolk sac) of an egg or embryo, or to yolk-producing organs.

ORIGIN – Latin *vitellinus*, from *vitellus* 'yolk'.

vitiate /vishiayt/ > *verb* formal **1** spoil or impair the quality or efficiency of. **2** destroy or impair the legal validity of.

ORIGIN – Latin *vitiare* 'impair'.

viticulture > *noun* **1** the cultivation of grapevines. **2** the study of grape cultivation.

DERIVATIVES – **viticultural** *adjective* **viticulturist** *noun*.

ORIGIN – from Latin *vitis* 'vine'.

vitiligo /vitilīgō/ > *noun* Medicine a condition in which the pigment is lost from areas of the skin, causing whitish patches.

ORIGIN – Latin.

vitreous /vitriəss/ > *adjective* **1** like glass in appearance or physical properties. **2** derived from or containing glass.

COMBINATIONS – **vitreous humour** the transparent jelly-like tissue filling the eyeball behind the lens.

ORIGIN – Latin *vitreus*, from *vitrum* 'glass'.

vitrify /vitrifī/ > *verb* (**vitrifies, vitrified**) convert into glass or a glass-like substance, typically by exposure to heat.

DERIVATIVES – **vitrifaction** *noun* **vitrification** *noun*.

ORIGIN – from Latin *vitrum* 'glass'.

vitrine /vitreen/ > *noun* a glass display case.

ORIGIN – French, from *vitre* 'glass pane'.

vitriol /vitriəl/ > *noun* **1** archaic or literary sulphuric acid. **2** extreme bitterness or malice.

DERIVATIVES – **vitriolic** *adjective* **vitriolically** *adverb*.

ORIGIN – Latin *vitriolum*, from *vitrum* 'glass': originally denoting the sulphate of various metals.

vittle > *noun* archaic variant spelling of VICTUAL.

vituperation /vityoōpəraysh'n/ > *noun* bitter and abusive language.

ORIGIN – from Latin *vituperare* 'censure, disparage'.

vituperative /vityoōpərətiv/ > *adjective* bitter and abusive.

viva¹ /vīvə/ > *noun* Brit. an oral examination, typically for an academic qualification.

ORIGIN – abbreviation of VIVA VOCE.

viva² /veevə/ > *exclamation* long live! (used to express acclaim or support).

ORIGIN – Italian.

vivace /vivaachay/ > *adverb* & *adjective* Music in a lively and brisk manner.

ORIGIN – Italian, 'brisk, lively'.

vivacious /vivayshəss/ > *adjective* attractively lively and animated.

DERIVATIVES – **vivaciously** *adverb* **vivaciousness** *noun* **vivacity** *noun*.

SYNONYMS – animated, bubbly, ebullient, high-spirited, lively, vibrant.

ORIGIN – Latin *vivax* 'lively, vigorous'.

vivarium /vīvairiəm, vivairiəm/ > *noun* (pl. **vivaria**) an enclosure or container used for keeping small animals in semi-natural conditions for study or as pets.

ORIGIN – Latin, 'warren, fish pond'.

viva voce /vīvə vōchi/ > *adjective* (especially of an examination) oral rather than written. > *noun* Brit. full form of VIVA¹.

ORIGIN – Latin, 'with the living voice'.

vivid > *adjective* **1** producing powerful feelings or strong, clear images in the mind. **2** (of a colour) intensely deep or bright.

DERIVATIVES – **vividly** *adverb* **vividness** *noun*.

SYNONYMS – **1** arresting, colourful, evocative, graphic, striking. **2** bold, brilliant, intense, rich, strong, vibrant.

ORIGIN – Latin *vividus*, from *vivere* 'to live': originally in the sense 'lively, vigorous'.

vivify /vivvifī/ > *verb* (**vivifies, vivified**) enliven or animate.

DERIVATIVES – **vivification** *noun*.

ORIGIN – Latin *vivificare*, from *vivere* 'to live'.

viviparous /vivippərəss, vīvippərəss/ > *adjective* **1** (of an animal) bringing forth live young which have developed inside the body of the parent. Compare with OVIPAROUS and OVOVIVIPAROUS. **2** (of a plant) reproducing from buds which form plantlets while still attached to the parent plant, or from seeds which germinate within the fruit.

DERIVATIVES – **viviparity** *noun*.

ORIGIN – Latin *viviparus*, from *vivus* 'alive' + *-parus* 'bearing'.

vivisection /vivviseksh'n/ > *noun* the practice of performing operations on live animals for scientific research (a term used by those opposed to such work).

DERIVATIVES – **vivisectionist** *noun* & *adjective* **vivisector** *noun*.

ORIGIN – from Latin *vivus* 'living', on the pattern of *dissection*.

vixen > *noun* **1** a female fox. **2** a spiteful or quarrelsome woman.

DERIVATIVES – **vixenish** *adjective*.

ORIGIN – Old English *fixen* 'of a fox'.

Viyella /vīellə/ > *noun* trademark a fabric made from a twilled mixture of cotton and wool.

ORIGIN – from *Via Gellia*, a valley in Derbyshire where it was first made.

viz. > *adverb* namely; in other words (used to introduce an explanation).

ORIGIN – abbreviation of Latin *videlicet*, *z* being a Latin symbol for *-et*.

vizier /viˈzeer/ > *noun* historical a high official in some Muslim countries.

ORIGIN – Arabic, 'caliph's chief counsellor'.

vizor > *noun* variant spelling of **VISOR**.

vizsla /ˈvizlə/ > *noun* a dog of a breed of golden-brown pointer with large drooping ears.

ORIGIN – named after the town of *Vizsla* in Hungary.

VJ day > *noun* the day (15 August) in 1945 on which Japan ceased fighting in the Second World War, or the day (2 September) when Japan formally surrendered.

VLF > *abbreviation* very low frequency (denoting radio waves of frequency 3–30 kilohertz).

VLSI > *abbreviation* Electronics very large-scale integration.

V-neck > *noun* a neckline having straight sides meeting at a point to form a V-shape.

DERIVATIVES – **V-necked** *adjective*.

VO > *abbreviation* (in the UK) Royal Victorian Order.

vocabulary /vōˈkabyooləri/ > *noun* (pl. **vocabularies**) 1 the body of words used in a particular language or in a particular sphere. 2 the body of words known to an individual person. 3 a list of words with an explanation of their meanings. 4 a range of artistic or stylistic forms or techniques.

ORIGIN – Latin *vocabularius*, from *vocare* 'to call'.

vocal > *adjective* 1 relating to the human voice. 2 expressing opinions or feelings freely or loudly. 3 (of music) consisting of or incorporating singing. > *noun* 1 (also **vocals**) a musical performance involving singing. 2 a part of a piece of music that is sung.

DERIVATIVES – **vocally** *adverb*.

SYNONYMS – *adjective* 2 candid, forthright, frank, outspoken, vociferous.

COMBINATIONS – **vocal cords** (also **vocal folds**) folds of the lining of the larynx whose edges vibrate in the airstream to produce the voice.

ORIGIN – Latin *vocalis*, from *vox* 'voice'.

vocalese /vōkəˈleez/ > *noun* a style of singing in which singers put words to jazz tunes or solos.

vocalic /vōˈkalik/ > *adjective* Phonetics relating to or consisting of a vowel or vowels.

vocalise¹ /ˈvōkəlīz/ (also **vocalize**) > *verb* 1 utter (a sound or word). 2 express

(something) with words. 3 Music sing with several notes to one vowel.

DERIVATIVES – **vocalisation** *noun*.

vocalise² /vōkəˈleez/ > *noun* Music 1 a singing exercise using individual syllables or vowel sounds. 2 a vocal passage consisting of a melody without words.

vocalist > *noun* a singer, especially in jazz or popular music.

vocation > *noun* 1 a strong feeling that one would like to follow a particular career or occupation. 2 a person's employment or main occupation, especially one requiring dedication.

ORIGIN – Latin, from *vocare* 'to call'.

vocational > *adjective* 1 relating to an occupation or employment. 2 (of education or training) directed at a particular occupation and its skills.

DERIVATIVES – **vocationally** *adverb*.

vocative /ˈvokkətiv/ Grammar > *adjective* referring to a case of nouns, pronouns, and adjectives used in addressing a person or thing. > *noun* a word in the vocative case.

vociferous /vəˈsiffərəss/ > *adjective* (of a person or statement) expressing something or being expressed loudly or vehemently.

DERIVATIVES – **vociferously** *adverb* **vociferousness** *noun*.

ORIGIN – from Latin *vociferari* 'exclaim'.

vocoder /ˈvōkōdər/ > *noun* a synthesiser that produces sounds from an analysis of speech input.

ORIGIN – from **VOICE** + **CODE**.

VOD > *abbreviation* video-on-demand.

vodka > *noun* an alcoholic spirit of Russian origin made by distillation of rye, wheat, or potatoes.

ORIGIN – Russian, 'little water', from *voda* 'water'.

vodun /vōˈdoōn/ > *noun* another term for **VOODOO**.

ORIGIN – Fon (a language of Benin), 'fetish'.

voe /vō/ > *noun* a small bay or creek in Orkney or Shetland.

ORIGIN – Norwegian *våg*.

vogue > *noun* the prevailing fashion or style at a particular time.

DERIVATIVES – **voguish** *adjective*.

ORIGIN – Italian *voga* 'rowing, fashion'.

voice > *noun* 1 the sound produced in a person's larynx and uttered through the mouth, as speech or song. 2 the ability to speak or sing. 3 Music the range of pitch or type of tone with which a person sings. 4 Music a vocal part in a composition. 5 an opinion or attitude, or a means or agency by which it is expressed. 6 Grammar a form of a verb showing the relation of the subject to the action. 7 Phonetics sound uttered with resonance of the vocal cords. > *verb* 1 express in words. 2 (**voiced**) Phonetics (of a

speech sound) uttered with resonance of the vocal cords.

WORDFINDER – vocal (*relating to the human voice*); *adult male singing voices, from lowest in pitch to highest:* basso profundo, bass, baritone, tenor, alto or countertenor; *female singing voices, from lowest in pitch to highest:* contralto, mezzo, soprano.

COMBINATIONS – **voice box** the larynx. **voicemail** a centralised electronic system which can store messages from telephone callers. **voiceprint** a visual record of speech, analysed with respect to frequency, duration, and amplitude.

ORIGIN – Old French *vois*, from Latin *vox*.

voiceless > *adjective* 1 lacking a voice; speechless. 2 Phonetics (of a speech sound) uttered without resonance of the vocal cords.

voice-over > *noun* a piece of narration in a film or broadcast not accompanied by an image of the speaker.

void > *adjective* 1 not valid or legally binding. 2 completely empty. 3 (**void of**) free from; lacking. > *noun* a completely empty space. > *verb* 1 chiefly N. Amer. declare to be not valid or legally binding. 2 discharge or drain away (water, gases, etc.). 3 chiefly Medicine excrete (waste matter).

DERIVATIVES – **voidable** *adjective*.

SYNONYMS – *adjective* 1 invalid, null. 2 blank, clear, empty, vacant. *noun* space, vacancy, vacuum. *verb* 1 annul, invalidate, nullify.

ORIGIN – Old French *vuide*; related to Latin *vacare* 'vacate'.

voila /vwaaˈlaa/ > *exclamation* there it is; there you are.

ORIGIN – French.

voile /voyl, vwaal/ > *noun* a thin, semi-transparent fabric of cotton, wool, or silk.

ORIGIN – French, 'veil'.

volatile /ˈvollətīl/ > *adjective* 1 (of a substance) easily evaporated at normal temperatures. 2 liable to change rapidly and unpredictably, especially for the worse. > *noun* a volatile substance.

DERIVATIVES – **volatilise** (also **volatilize**) *verb* **volatility** *noun*.

ORIGIN – Latin *volatilis*, from *volare* 'to fly': originally in the senses 'creature that flies', 'birds'.

vol-au-vent /ˈvolləvoN/ > *noun* a small round case of puff pastry filled with a savoury mixture.

ORIGIN – French, 'flight in the wind'.

volcanic /volˈkannik/ > *adjective* 1 relating to or produced by a volcano or volcanoes. 2 (of a feeling or emotion) bursting out or liable to burst out violently.

DERIVATIVES – **volcanically** *adverb*.

COMBINATIONS – **volcanic glass** obsidian.

volcanism (also **vulcanism**) > *noun* Geology volcanic activity or phenomena.

volcano > *noun* (pl. **volcanoes** or **volcanos**) a mountain or hill having a crater or vent through which lava, rock fragments, hot vapour, and gas erupt or have erupted in the past from the earth's crust.
WORDFINDER – caldera (*large volcanic crater*), dormant (*not currently erupting*), extinct (*not active in recorded history*), fumarole (*gas vent in or near a volcano*), pyroclastic flow (*destructive and rapid flow of hot rock fragments or ash erupted by a volcano*).
ORIGIN – from Latin *Volcanus* 'Vulcan', the Roman god of fire.

volcanology (also **vulcanology**) > *noun* the scientific study of volcanoes.
DERIVATIVES – **volcanologist** *noun*.

vole > *noun* a small mouse-like rodent with a rounded muzzle.
ORIGIN – Norwegian *vollmus* 'field mouse'.

volition /vəlish'n/ > *noun* (often in phrase **of one's own volition**) the faculty or power of using one's will.
DERIVATIVES – **volitional** *adjective*.
ORIGIN – Latin, from *volo* 'I wish'.

volley > *noun* (pl. **volleys**) 1 a number of bullets, arrows, or other projectiles discharged at one time. 2 a series of utterances directed at someone in quick succession. 3 (in sport) a strike or kick of the ball made before it touches the ground. > *verb* (**volleys**, **volleyed**) 1 strike or kick (the ball) before it touches the ground. 2 utter or discharge in quick succession.
DERIVATIVES – **volleyer** *noun*.
ORIGIN – French *volée*, from Latin *volare* 'to fly'.

volleyball > *noun* a game for two teams in which a ball is hit by hand over a net and points are scored if the ball touches the ground on the opponents' side.

volt > *noun* the unit of electromotive force in the SI system, the difference of potential that would carry one ampere of current against a resistance of one ohm.
COMBINATIONS – **voltmeter** an instrument for measuring electric potential in volts.
ORIGIN – named after the Italian physicist Alessandro *Volta* (1745–1827).

voltage > *noun* an electromotive force or potential difference expressed in volts.

voltaic /voltayik/ > *adjective* referring to electricity produced by chemical action in a primary battery; galvanic.

volte-face /voltfass/ > *noun* 1 an act of turning round so as to face in the opposite direction. 2 an abrupt and complete reversal of attitude, opinion, or position.
ORIGIN – Italian *voltafaccia*, from Latin *volvere* 'to roll' + *facies* 'appearance, face'.

voluble /volyoob'l/ > *adjective* speaking or spoken incessantly and fluently.
DERIVATIVES – **volubility** *noun* **volubly** *adverb*.
ORIGIN – first meaning 'rotating about an

axis' and 'tending to change': from Latin *volvere* 'to roll'.

volume > *noun* 1 a book forming part of a work or series. 2 a single book or a bound collection of printed sheets. 3 a consecutive sequence of issues of a periodical. 4 the amount of space occupied by a substance or object or enclosed within a container. 5 the amount or quantity of something. 6 fullness or expansive thickness. 7 quantity or power of sound; degree of loudness.
ORIGIN – Latin *volumen* 'a roll', from *volvere* 'to roll'.

volumetric /volyoometrik/ > *adjective* relating to the measurement of volume.
DERIVATIVES – **volumetrically** *adverb*.

voluminous /vəlyoominəss/ > *adjective* 1 (of clothing or drapery) loose and ample. 2 (of writing) very lengthy and full.
DERIVATIVES – **voluminously** *adverb* **voluminousness** *noun*.
ORIGIN – Latin, partly from *voluminosus* 'having many coils', partly from *volumen* 'a roll' from *volvere* 'to roll'.

volumise /volyoomīz/ (also **volumize**) > *verb* give volume or body to (hair).

voluntarism /volləntəriz'm/ > *noun* the principle of relying on voluntary action.
DERIVATIVES – **voluntarist** *adjective*.

voluntary > *adjective* 1 done, given, or acting of one's own free will. 2 working or done without payment. 3 Physiology under the conscious control of the brain. > *noun* (pl. **voluntaries**) an organ solo played before, during, or after a church service.
DERIVATIVES – **voluntarily** *adverb*.
SYNONYMS – *adjective* 1 discretionary, optional, volitional.
ANTONYMS – *adjective* 1 compulsory, obligatory.
COMBINATIONS – **voluntary-aided** (in the UK) referring to a voluntary school funded mainly by the local authority. **voluntary school** (in the UK) a school which, though not established by the local education authority, is funded mainly or entirely by it, and which typically encourages a particular set of religious beliefs.
ORIGIN – Latin *voluntarius*, from *voluntas* 'will'.

volunteer > *noun* 1 a person who freely offers to do something. 2 a person who works for an organisation without being paid. 3 a person who freely enrols for military service rather than being conscripted. > *verb* 1 freely offer to do something. 2 say or suggest something without being asked. 3 work for an organisation without being paid. 4 freely enrol for military service rather than being conscripted.

volunteerism > *noun* chiefly N. Amer. the use or involvement of volunteer labour, especially in community services.

voluptuary /vəluptyoori/ > *noun* (pl. **voluptuaries**) a person devoted to luxury and sensual pleasure. > *adjective* concerned with luxury and sensual pleasure.

voluptuous /vəluptyooəss/ > *adjective* 1 relating to or characterised by luxury or sensual pleasure. 2 (of a woman) curvaceous and sexually attractive.
DERIVATIVES – **voluptuously** *adverb* **voluptuousness** *noun*.
ORIGIN – Latin *voluptuosus*, from *voluptas* 'pleasure'.

volute /vəlyoot/ > *noun* Architecture a spiral scroll characteristic of Ionic capitals and also used in Corinthian and composite capitals.
ORIGIN – Latin *voluta*, from *volvere* 'to roll'.

vomer /vōmər/ > *noun* Anatomy the thin bone between the left and right nasal cavities.
ORIGIN – Latin, 'ploughshare' (because of the shape).

vomit > *verb* (**vomited**, **vomiting**) 1 eject matter from the stomach through the mouth. 2 emit in an uncontrolled stream or flow. > *noun* matter vomited from the stomach.
WORDFINDER – emetic (*causing vomiting*).
ORIGIN – Latin *vomere* 'to vomit'.

vomitous > *adjective* nauseating.

voodoo > *noun* a black religious cult practised in the Caribbean and the southern US, combining elements of Roman Catholic ritual with traditional African rites and characterised by sorcery and spirit possession.
DERIVATIVES – **voodooism** *noun* **voodooist** *noun*.
ORIGIN – Kwa (a Niger-Congo language).

voracious /vərayshəss/ > *adjective* 1 wanting or devouring great quantities of food. 2 eagerly consuming something: *voracious reading*.
DERIVATIVES – **voraciously** *adverb* **voraciousness** *noun* **voracity** *noun*.
ORIGIN – Latin *vorax*, from *vorare* 'devour'.

-vorous /vərəss/ > *combining form* feeding on a specified food: *carnivorous*.
DERIVATIVES – **-vora** *combining form* in corresponding nouns denoting groups of animals. **-vore** *combining form* in corresponding nouns denoting animals.
ORIGIN – Latin *-vorus*, from *vorare* 'devour'.

vortex /vorteks/ > *noun* (pl. **vortexes** or **vortices** /vortiseez/) a whirling mass, especially a whirlpool or whirlwind.
DERIVATIVES – **vortical** *adjective* **vorticity** *noun*.
ORIGIN – Latin, 'eddy'.

Vorticism /vortisiz'm/ > *noun* a British artistic movement of 1914-15 formed in response to Futurism, favouring machine-like forms and the adoption of avant-garde art as a model for life in the future.
DERIVATIVES – **Vorticist** *noun & adjective*.

votary /vōtəri/ > *noun* (pl. **votaries**) **1** a person who has made vows of dedication to religious service. **2** a devoted follower, adherent, or advocate.
ORIGIN – from Latin *vovere* 'vow' + **-ARY**.

vote > *noun* **1** a formal indication of a choice between two or more candidates or courses of action. **2** an act of voting. **3** (**the vote**) the choice expressed collectively by a body of electors: *the Green vote*. **4** (**the vote**) the right to indicate a choice in an election. > *verb* **1** give or register a vote. **2** grant or confer by vote. **3** informal express a wish or suggestion.
WORDFINDER – abstain (*formally choose not to vote*), disenfranchise (*deprive of the right to vote*), enfranchise (*give someone the right to vote*), floating voter (*person who does not consistently vote for the same party*), franchise (*the right to vote*), plebiscite (*a direct vote of all members of an electorate on a question*), referendum (*a general vote by the electorate on a single question*), suffrage (*the right to vote in political elections*), suffragette (*a woman seeking through protest the right to vote*).
IDIOMS – **vote of (no) confidence** a vote showing that a majority continues to support (or no longer supports) the policy of a leader or governing body. **vote with one's feet** informal indicate an opinion implicitly by being present or absent.
DERIVATIVES – **voteless** *adjective* **voter** *noun*.
ORIGIN – Latin *votum* 'a vow, wish', from *vovere* 'to vow'.

votive > *adjective* offered or consecrated in fulfilment of a vow.
ORIGIN – Latin *votivus*, from *votum* 'vow'.

vouch /vowch/ > *verb* (**vouch for**) **1** assert or confirm the truth or accuracy of. **2** confirm the identity or good character of.
ORIGIN – Old French *voucher* 'summon', from Latin *vocare* 'to call'.

voucher > *noun* **1** a piece of paper that entitles the holder to a discount, or that may be exchanged for goods or services. **2** a receipt.

vouchsafe > *verb* give, grant, or disclose in a gracious or condescending manner.
ORIGIN – first forming the phrase *vouch something safe* on someone, i.e. 'warrant the secure conferment of'.

vow > *noun* a solemn promise. > *verb* solemnly promise to do something.
SYNONYMS – *noun* oath, pledge, promise. *verb* pledge, promise, swear.
ORIGIN – Old French *vou*, from Latin *votum*.

vowel > *noun* **1** a speech sound in which the mouth is open and the tip of the tongue is not touching the top of the mouth, the teeth, or the lips. **2** a letter representing such a sound (in English, *a, e, i, o, u,* and in some circumstances *y*).
ORIGIN – Old French *vouel*, from Latin *vocalis littera* 'vocal letter'.

vox pop > *noun* Brit. informal popular opinion as represented by informal comments from members of the public.

vox populi /voks **pop**yoolee/ > *noun* the opinions or beliefs of the majority.
ORIGIN – Latin, 'the people's voice'.

voyage > *noun* a long journey involving travel by sea or in space. > *verb* go on a voyage.
DERIVATIVES – **voyager** *noun*.
ORIGIN – Old French *voiage*, from Latin *viaticum* 'provisions for a journey'.

voyeur /vwaa**yör**, voy**yör**/ > *noun* **1** a person who gains sexual pleasure from watching others when they are naked or engaged in sexual activity. **2** a person who enjoys seeing the pain or distress of others.
DERIVATIVES – **voyeurism** *noun* **voyeuristic** *adjective*.
ORIGIN – French, from *voir* 'see'.

VP > *abbreviation* Vice-President.

VR > *abbreviation* virtual reality.

VRML > *abbreviation* Computing virtual reality modelling language.

vs > *abbreviation* versus.

V-sign > *noun* **1** Brit. a sign resembling the letter V made with the first two fingers pointing up and the back of the hand facing outwards, used as a gesture of abuse or contempt. **2** a similar sign made with the palm of the hand facing outwards, used as a symbol or gesture of victory.

VSO > *abbreviation* Voluntary Service Overseas.

VSOP > *abbreviation* Very Special Old Pale, a kind of brandy.

VT > *abbreviation* Vermont.

VTOL > *abbreviation* vertical take-off and landing.

vulcanise /**vul**kənīz/ (also **vulcanize**) > *verb* harden (rubber) by treating it with sulphur at a high temperature.
DERIVATIVES – **vulcanisation** *noun*.

vulcanism > *noun* variant spelling of **VOLCANISM**.

vulcanite /**vul**kənīt/ > *noun* hard black vulcanised rubber.
ORIGIN – from *Vulcan*, the Roman god of fire.

vulcanology > *noun* variant spelling of **VOLCANOLOGY**.

vulgar > *adjective* **1** lacking sophistication or good taste. **2** making explicit and inappropriate reference to sex or bodily functions. **3** dated characteristic of or belonging to ordinary people.
DERIVATIVES – **vulgarity** *noun* **vulgarly** *adverb*.
SYNONYMS – **1** common, crass, gross, tasteless, unrefined; informal tacky. **2** crude, indecent, obscene, offensive, rude.
COMBINATIONS – **vulgar fraction** Brit. a fraction expressed by numerator and denominator, not decimally. **vulgar Latin** informal Latin of classical times. **vulgar tongue** the national or vernacular language of a people (especially as contrasted with Latin).
ORIGIN – Latin *vulgaris*, from *vulgus* 'common people'.

vulgarian /vul**gair**iən/ > *noun* an unrefined person, especially one with newly acquired power or wealth.

vulgarise (also **vulgarize**) > *verb* **1** make less refined. **2** make commonplace or less subtle or complex.
DERIVATIVES – **vulgarisation** *noun*.

vulgarism > *noun* **1** a word or expression that is considered vulgar. **2** archaic an instance of rude or offensive behaviour.

Vulgate /**vul**gayt/ > *noun* the principal Latin version of the Bible, the official text for the Roman Catholic Church.
ORIGIN – from Latin *vulgata editio* 'edition prepared for the public'.

vulnerable > *adjective* exposed to the chance of being attacked or harmed, either physically or emotionally.
DERIVATIVES – **vulnerability** *noun* **vulnerably** *adverb*.
SYNONYMS – defenceless, helpless, unguarded, unprotected, weak.
ANTONYMS – invulnerable.
ORIGIN – Latin *vulnerabilis*, from *vulnerare* 'to wound'.

vulpine /**vul**pīn/ > *adjective* relating to or reminiscent of a fox or foxes.
ORIGIN – Latin *vulpinus*, from *vulpes* 'fox'.

vulture /**vul**chər/ > *noun* **1** a large bird of prey feeding chiefly on carrion, with the head and neck more or less bare of feathers. **2** a contemptible person who preys on or exploits others.
ORIGIN – Latin *vulturius*.

vulva /**vul**və/ > *noun* the female external genitals.
DERIVATIVES – **vulval** *adjective*.
ORIGIN – Latin, 'womb'.

vying present participle of **VIE**.

W¹ (also **w**) > *noun* (pl. **Ws** or **W's**) the twenty-third letter of the alphabet.

W² > *abbreviation* **1** watt(s). **2** West or Western. **3** Cricket (on scorecards) wicket(s). **4** (in tables of sports results) games won. > *symbol* the chemical element tungsten. [ORIGIN – from Latin *wolframium*.]

w > *abbreviation* **1** with. **2** Cricket (on scorecards) wide(s).

WA > *abbreviation* **1** Washington (State). **2** Western Australia.

Waaf /waf/ > *noun* historical (in the UK) a member of the Women's Auxiliary Air Force (1939–48).

wacko (also **whacko**) informal, chiefly N. Amer. > *adjective* mad; insane. > *noun* (pl. **wackos** or **wackoes**) a crazy person.

wacky (also **whacky**) > *adjective* (**wackier**, **wackiest**) informal funny or amusing in a slightly odd or peculiar way.
DERIVATIVES – **wackily** adverb **wackiness** noun.

wad /wod/ > *noun* **1** a lump or bundle of a soft material, as used for padding, stuffing, or wiping. **2** chiefly historical a disc of felt or another material used to keep powder or shot in place in a gun barrel. **3** a bundle of paper, banknotes, or documents. **4** informal a large amount of something, especially money. > *verb* (**wadded**, **wadding**) **1** compress (a soft material) into a wad. **2** line, stuff, or stop with soft material.
DERIVATIVES – **wadding** noun.

waddle > *verb* walk with short steps and a clumsy swaying motion. > *noun* a waddling gait.

waddy /woddi/ > *noun* (pl. **waddies**) **1** an Australian Aboriginal's war club. **2** Austral./NZ a club or stick, especially a walking stick.
ORIGIN – Dharuk (an Aboriginal language).

wade > *verb* **1** walk through a liquid or viscous substance. **2** (**wade through**) read laboriously through (a long piece of writing). **3** (**wade in** or **into**) informal attack or intervene in a vigorous or forceful way. > *noun* an act of wading.

Wade–Giles /wayd jīlz/ > *noun* a system of romanised spelling for transliterating Chinese, largely superseded by Pinyin.
ORIGIN – named after Sir T. F. *Wade* (1818–95) and H. A. *Giles* (1845–1935), professors of Chinese at Cambridge, who devised it.

wader > *noun* **1** a sandpiper, plover, or other wading bird. **2** (**waders**) high waterproof boots, used by anglers.

wadi /waadi, woddi/ > *noun* (pl. **wadis**) (in Arabic-speaking countries) a ravine or channel that is dry except in the rainy season.
ORIGIN – Arabic.

wafer > *noun* **1** a very thin light, crisp sweet biscuit. **2** a thin disc of unleavened bread used in the Eucharist. **3** a disc of red paper stuck on a legal document as a seal. **4** Electronics a very thin slice of a semiconductor crystal used in solid-state circuitry.
COMBINATIONS – **wafer-thin** very thin or thinly.
ORIGIN – Old French *gaufre* 'honeycomb'; related to **WAFFLE²**.

Waffen SS /vaff'n/ > *noun* the combat units of the Nazi special police force (SS), which served alongside but independently of the German army during the Second World War.
ORIGIN – German *Waffen* 'armed'.

waffle¹ informal > *verb* speak or write at length in a vague or trivial manner. > *noun* lengthy but vague or trivial talk or writing.
DERIVATIVES – **waffler** noun **waffly** adjective.
ORIGIN – from dialect *waff* 'yelp'.

waffle² > *noun* a small crisp cake made of batter, baked in a waffle iron and eaten hot with butter or syrup.
COMBINATIONS – **waffle iron** a utensil for baking waffles, consisting of two shallow metal pans hinged together.
ORIGIN – Dutch *wafel*; related to **WAFER** and **GOFFER**.

waft /woft, waaft/ > *verb* pass easily or gently through the air. > *noun* **1** a gentle movement of air. **2** a scent carried in the air.

wag¹ > *verb* (**wagged**, **wagging**) move rapidly to and fro. > *noun* a wagging movement.

wag² > *noun* informal **1** a person who makes facetious jokes. **2** Austral./NZ informal a truant.
ORIGIN – first denoting a young man or mischievous boy: probably from obsolete *waghalter* 'person likely to be hanged'.

wage > *noun* (also **wages**) **1** a fixed regular payment for work, typically paid on a daily or weekly basis. **2** the result or effect of doing something wrong or unwise: *the wages of sin*. > *verb* carry on (a war or campaign).
DERIVATIVES – **waged** adjective.

ORIGIN – Old French; related to **GAGE¹** and **WED**.

wordpower facts
Waft
The form **waft** is first found (in the 15th century) in the obsolete noun *wafter* 'armed convoy vessel', which came from the Low German and Dutch word *wachten* 'to guard'. The first use of **waft** as a word in English was as a verb meaning 'escort (a ship)' or 'convey by water': this latter sense was generally used with reference to the wind, as for example in 'The gale that afterwards wafted us to the shore' (1773), and thus gave rise to the current verb sense. As a noun **waft** formerly meant 'flavour or scent' and 'rush of air'; in nautical use it referred to a flag hoisted as a signal.

wager > *noun & verb* more formal term for **BET**.

waggish > *adjective* informal humorous, playful, or facetious.
DERIVATIVES – **waggishly** adverb **waggishness** noun.

waggle > *verb* move with short quick movements from side to side or up and down. > *noun* an act of waggling.
DERIVATIVES – **waggler** noun **waggly** adjective.

Wagnerian /vaagneerian/ > *adjective* relating to the German composer Richard Wagner (1813–83).

wagon (Brit. also **waggon**) > *noun* **1** a vehicle, especially a horse-drawn one, for transporting goods. **2** Brit. a railway freight vehicle; a truck. **3** chiefly N. Amer. a wheeled cart or hut used as a food stall.
IDIOMS – **on the wagon** informal teetotal.
DERIVATIVES – **wagonload** noun.
COMBINATIONS – **wagon train** historical a convoy of covered horse-drawn wagons, as used by pioneers or settlers in North America.
ORIGIN – Dutch *wagen*; related to **WAIN**.

wagoner (Brit. also **waggoner**) > *noun* the driver of a horse-drawn wagon.

wagon-lit /vaggoNlee/ > *noun* (pl. **wagons-lits** pronunc. same) a sleeping car on a train in continental Europe.
ORIGIN – French, from *wagon* 'railway coach' + *lit* 'bed'.

wagtail > *noun* a slender songbird with a long tail that is frequently wagged up and down.

Wahhabi /wəhaabi/ (also **Wahabi**) > *noun* (pl. **Wahabis**) a member of a strictly orthodox Sunni Muslim sect, the predominant religious force in Saudi Arabia.

DERIVATIVES – **Wahhabism** *noun*.

ORIGIN – named after Muhammad ibn Abd al-*Wahhab* (1703–92), the sect's founder.

wahine /waa**hee**ni/ > *noun* NZ a Maori woman or wife.

ORIGIN – Maori.

wah-wah > *noun* a musical effect achieved on brass instruments by alternately applying and removing a mute and on an electric guitar by use of a pedal.

waif > *noun* a homeless and helpless person, especially a neglected or abandoned child.

DERIVATIVES – **waifish** *adjective*.

wordpower facts

Waif

The word **waif** comes from Old Northern French *gaif*, which was probably from a Scandinavian root meaning 'something loose or wandering'. In medieval English it was a legal term used in the phrase *waif and stray* to refer to a piece of property found without an owner, for example an article washed up on the seashore or a stray animal; if unclaimed after a certain period, the property fell to the lord of the manor. From the early 17th century **waif** began to occur in reference to other things, and by the late 18th century it had assumed its modern meaning. The verb **waive** is related to **waif**: it comes from Old French *gaiver* 'allow to become a waif, abandon', and was originally a legal term relating to removal of the protection of the law.

wail > *noun* **1** a prolonged high-pitched cry of pain, grief, or anger. **2** a sound resembling this. > *verb* give or utter a wail.

DERIVATIVES – **wailer** *noun*.

ORIGIN – Old Norse; related to WOE.

wain > *noun* archaic a wagon or cart.

ORIGIN – Old English, related to WAY and WEIGH.

wainscot /**waynz**kət/ > *noun* an area of wooden panelling on the lower part of the walls of a room. > *verb* (**wainscoted**, **wainscoting** or **wainscotted**, **wainscotting**) line (a room or wall) with such wooden panelling.

DERIVATIVES – **wainscoting** (also **wainscotting**) *noun*.

ORIGIN – Low German *wagenschot*, apparently from *wagen* 'wagon' + *schot*, probably meaning 'partition'.

wainwright > *noun* historical a wagon-builder.

waist > *noun* **1** the part of the human body between the ribs and the hips. **2** a narrow part in the middle of something such as a violin or hourglass.

DERIVATIVES – **waisted** *adjective*.

COMBINATIONS – **waistband** a strip of cloth encircling the waist, attached to a skirt or a pair of trousers.

waistcoat /**wayst**kōt, **wes**kit/ > *noun* Brit. a close-fitting waist-length garment with no sleeves or collar and buttoning down the front, typically worn over a shirt.

waistline > *noun* **1** the measurement around a person's body at the waist. **2** the part of a garment that is shaped or constructed to fit at or near the waist.

wait > *verb* **1** stay where one is or delay action until a particular time or occurrence. **2** be delayed or deferred. **3** (**wait on** or **upon**) act as an attendant to. **4** act as a waiter or waitress. > *noun* **1** a period of waiting. **2** (**waits**) Brit. archaic people who sang Christmas carols in the streets.

IDIOMS – **in wait** watching for someone and preparing to attack them.

SYNONYMS – *verb* **1** bide one's time, delay, linger, mark time, remain, stay.

COMBINATIONS – **waiting list** (N. Amer. **wait list**) a list of people waiting for something not immediately available. **waiting room** a room for people waiting to see a medical practitioner or to catch a bus or train.

ORIGIN – Old French *waitier*; related to WAKE¹.

waiter > *noun* a man whose job is to serve customers at their tables in a restaurant.

WORDFINDER – maître d'hôtel (*head waiter*), sommelier (*wine waiter*).

waitress > *noun* a woman whose job is to serve customers at their tables in a restaurant.

DERIVATIVES – **waitressing** *noun*.

waive /wayv/ > *verb* refrain from insisting on or applying (a right or claim).

ORIGIN – Old French *gaiver* 'allow to become a waif, abandon'.

waiver > *noun* **1** an act or instance of waiving a right or claim. **2** a document recording this.

wake¹ > *verb* (past **woke** or US, dialect, or archaic **waked**; past participle **woken** or US, dialect, or archaic **waked**) **1** (often **wake up**) emerge or cause to emerge from a state of sleep; stop sleeping. **2** cause to stir or come to life. **3** (**wake up to**) become alert to or aware of. > *noun* **1** a watch or vigil held beside the body of someone who has died. **2** (especially in Ireland) a party held after a funeral. **3** (**wakes**) (treated as sing.) an annual festival and holiday in some parts of northern England.

WORDFINDER – hypnopompic (*of the state

immediately before waking up*); reveille (*military waking signal*).

wake² > *noun* a trail of disturbed water or air left by the passage of a ship or aircraft.

IDIOMS – **in the wake of** following as a consequence or result.

ORIGIN – probably from Old Norse *vaka* 'opening in ice' (as made by a ship).

wakeful > *adjective* **1** unable or not needing to sleep. **2** alert and vigilant.

DERIVATIVES – **wakefully** *adverb* **wakefulness** *noun*.

waken > *verb* wake from sleep.

Waldenses /wol**den**seez/ > *plural noun* a puritan religious sect originating in southern France.

DERIVATIVES – **Waldensian** *adjective* & *noun*.

ORIGIN – named after the founder, Peter *Valdes* (died 1205).

Waldorf salad /**wawl**dorf/ > *noun* a salad made from apples, walnuts, celery, and mayonnaise.

ORIGIN – named after the *Waldorf*-Astoria Hotel in New York, where it was first served.

wale > *noun* **1** a ridge on a textured woven fabric such as corduroy. **2** Nautical a horizontal wooden strip fitted as strengthening to a boat's side. **3** a horizontal band around a woven basket.

ORIGIN – Old English, 'stripe, weal'.

walk > *verb* **1** move at a regular, moderate pace by lifting and setting down each foot in turn. **2** travel over (a route or area) on foot. **3** guide, accompany, or escort (someone) on foot. **4** take (a dog) out for exercise. **5** (of a quadruped) proceed with the slowest gait, always having at least two feet on the ground at once. **6** N. Amer. informal be released from suspicion or from a charge. > *noun* **1** an excursion or act of travelling on foot. **2** an unhurried rate of movement on foot. **3** the slowest gait of an animal. **4** a route for walking.

WORDFINDER – ambulant (*denoting a patient able to walk*), ambulatory (*relating to walking; able to walk*), circumambulate (*walk all the way round*), digitigrade (*walking on the toes*), pedestrian (*a person walking on a road*), perambulate (*walk from place to place*), plantigrade (*walking on the soles*), promenade (*a place for public walking; a leisurely walk*).

IDIOMS – **walk (all) over** informal **1** treat in a thoughtless and exploitative manner. **2** defeat easily. **walk it** informal achieve a victory easily. **walk of life** the position within society that someone holds. **walk out 1** depart suddenly or angrily. **2** Brit. informal, dated go for walks in courtship.

DERIVATIVES – **walkable** *adjective* **walker** *noun*.

SYNONYMS – *verb* **1** amble, promenade,

saunter, step, stride, stroll, tread; formal perambulate.

COMBINATIONS – **walking frame** Brit. a frame used by disabled or infirm people for support while walking. **walking stick** a stick with a curved handle used for support when walking. **walking wounded** people who have been injured in a battle or major accident but who are still able to walk.

ORIGIN – Old English, 'roll, toss', also 'wander'.

walkabout > noun 1 chiefly Brit. an informal stroll among a crowd conducted by an important visitor. 2 Austral. a journey on foot undertaken by an Australian Aboriginal in order to live in the traditional manner.

walkathon > noun informal a long-distance walk organised as a fund-raising event.

walkie-talkie > noun a portable two-way radio.

walk-in > adjective (of a storage area) large enough to walk into.

Walkman > noun (pl. **Walkmans** or **Walkmen**) trademark a type of personal stereo.

walk-on > adjective (of a part in a play or film) small and not involving any speaking.

walkout > noun a sudden angry departure, especially as a protest or strike.

walkover > noun an easy victory.

walkway > noun a passageway or path for walking along.

wall > noun 1 a continuous vertical brick or stone structure that encloses or divides an area of land. 2 a side of a building or room. 3 a protective or restrictive barrier: *a wall of silence*. 4 Soccer a line of defenders forming a barrier against a free kick taken near the penalty area. 5 (in the body) the outer layer or lining of an organ or cavity. > verb 2 enclose within walls. 2 (**wall in** or **off** or **up**) block or seal by building a wall.

WORDFINDER – mural (*of or relating to a wall*), parietal (*relating to the wall of a body cavity*); espalier (*a tree trained to grow against a wall*), graffiti (*writing on a wall*), precinct (*a walled area*), rampart (*a defensive wall*).

IDIOMS – **drive up the wall** informal make (someone) very irritated. **go to the wall** informal (of a business) fail. **off the wall** informal 1 eccentric or unconventional. 2 angry. 3 (of an accusation) without basis or foundation. **walls have ears** proverb be careful what you say as people may be eavesdropping. **wall-to-wall 1** (of a carpet) fitted to cover an entire floor. 2 informal very numerous or plentiful.

COMBINATIONS – **wall bars** Brit. parallel horizontal bars attached to the wall of a gymnasium, on which exercises are performed.

ORIGIN – Latin *vallum* 'rampart'.

wallaby > noun (pl. **wallabies**) 1 an Australasian marsupial similar to but smaller than a kangaroo. 2 (**the Wallabies**) informal the Australian international rugby union team.

ORIGIN – Dharuk (an Aboriginal language).

wallah /wollə/ > noun Indian or informal a person of a specified kind or having a specified role: *a rickshaw-wallah*.

ORIGIN – from the Hindi suffix -*vālā* 'doer'.

wallet > noun 1 a pocket-sized, flat, folding holder for money and plastic cards. 2 archaic a bag for holding provisions when travelling.

ORIGIN – probably from a Germanic word related to WELL².

wall eye > noun 1 an eye squinting outwards. 2 an eye with a streaked or opaque white iris. 3 (**walleye**) a large, predatory North American perch with opaque silvery eyes.

DERIVATIVES – **wall-eyed** adjective.

ORIGIN – from Old Norse *vagleygr*; related to Icelandic *vagl* 'film over the eye'.

wallflower > noun 1 a plant with fragrant flowers that bloom in early spring. 2 informal a shy or excluded person at a dance or party, especially a girl without a partner.

Walloon /woloon/ > noun 1 a member of a people who speak a French dialect and live in southern and eastern Belgium and neighbouring parts of France. Compare with FLEMING. 2 the French dialect spoken by this people.

ORIGIN – French *Wallon*; related to WELSH.

wallop informal > verb (**walloped**, **walloping**) 1 strike or hit very hard. 2 heavily defeat (an opponent). 3 (**walloping**) strikingly large. > noun 1 a heavy blow or punch. 2 Brit. alcoholic drink, especially beer.

ORIGIN – first denoting a horse's gallop: from Old French *waloper* 'gallop'; related to WELL¹, LEAP, and GALLOP.

wallow > verb 1 roll about or lie in mud or water. 2 (of a boat or aircraft) roll from side to side. 3 (**wallow in**) indulge without restraint in (something pleasurable). > noun 1 an act of wallowing. 2 an area of mud or shallow water where mammals go to wallow.

ORIGIN – Old English, 'to roll about'.

wallpaper > noun 1 paper pasted in strips over the walls of a room to provide a decorative or textured surface. 2 something, especially music, providing a bland or unvaried background. > verb apply wallpaper to (a wall or room).

wally > noun (pl. **wallies**) Brit. informal a silly or inept person.

wordpower facts
Wally
The word **wally** is first recorded in 1969, and by the mid 1970s had become established in the language. It is presumably a shortened form of the name *Walter*, used rather like **charlie** to mean 'a silly or inept person'. There are many theories about its origin. One story tells of a *Wally* who became separated from companions at a 1960s pop festival; the name, announced many times over the public address system, was taken up as a chant by the crowd. 'Wally' was certainly heard as an exuberant call or chant at pop festivals of the 1970s.

walnut > noun 1 an edible wrinkled nut enclosed by a hard shell, produced inside a green fruit. 2 the tree which produces this nut, a source of valuable ornamental wood.

ORIGIN – Old English, from a compound meaning 'foreign nut'.

Walpurgis night /valpoorgiss/ > noun (in German folklore) the night of April 30 (May Day's eve), when witches meet on the Brocken mountain and hold pagan rituals.

ORIGIN – named after St *Walburga*, whose feast day coincided with an ancient pagan festival.

walrus > noun a large marine mammal having two large downward-pointing tusks, found in the Arctic Ocean.

COMBINATIONS – **walrus moustache** a long, thick, drooping moustache.

ORIGIN – probably Dutch, perhaps from Old Norse *hrosshvalr* 'horse-whale'.

waltz /wawlts/ > noun a dance in triple time performed by a couple, who turn rhythmically round and round as they progress around the dance floor. > verb 1 dance a waltz. 2 move or act lightly, casually, or inconsiderately.

ORIGIN – German *Walzer*, from *walzen* 'revolve'.

waltzer > noun 1 a person who dances the waltz. 2 a fairground ride in which cars spin round as they are carried round an undulating track.

wampum /wompəm/ > noun historical a quantity of small cylindrical beads made by North American Indians from shells, strung together and worn as a decorative belt or used as money.

ORIGIN – Algonquian.

WAN > abbreviation Computing wide area network.

wan /won/ > adjective 1 (of a person) pale and giving the impression of illness or exhaustion. **2** (of light) pale; weak. **3** (of a smile) weak; strained.

DERIVATIVES – **wanly** *adverb* **wanness** *noun*.

SYNONYMS – **1** ashen, pale, pallid, peaky. **2** faint, feeble, pale, watery, weak.

ORIGIN – Old English, 'dark, black', later 'of an unhealthy greyish colour, as if bruised'.

wand > *noun* **1** a stick or rod thought to have magic properties, used in casting spells or performing tricks. **2** a slender staff or rod, especially one held as a symbol of office. **3** a hand-held electronic device passed over a bar code to read the encoded data.

ORIGIN – Old Norse; related to **WEND** and **WIND²**.

wander > *verb* **1** walk or move in a leisurely, casual, or aimless way. **2** move slowly away from a fixed point or place. > *noun* an act or spell of wandering.

DERIVATIVES – **wanderer** *noun*.

SYNONYMS – *verb* **1** meander, ramble, roam, saunter, stroll. **2** drift, stray.

COMBINATIONS – **wandering Jew 1** a legendary person said to have been condemned by Christ to wander the earth until the second coming. **2** a trailing plant with striped leaves suffused with purple.

ORIGIN – Old English, related to **WEND** and **WIND²**.

wanderlust > *noun* a strong desire to travel.

ORIGIN – German.

wane > *verb* **1** (of the moon) have a progressively smaller part of its visible surface illuminated, so that it appears to decrease in size. **2** decrease in vigour or extent; become weaker.

IDIOMS – **on the wane** becoming weaker or less vigorous.

ORIGIN – Old English, 'lessen'; related to Latin *vanus* 'vain'.

wangle *informal* > *verb* obtain (something desired) by persuading others to comply or by manipulating events. > *noun* an instance of obtaining something in such a way.

DERIVATIVES – **wangler** *noun*.

ORIGIN – 19th-century printers' slang.

wank *Brit. vulgar slang* > *verb* masturbate. > *noun* an act of masturbating.

wanker > *noun Brit. vulgar slang* a stupid or contemptible person.

wanna > *contraction informal* want to; want a.

wannabe /**wonn**əbee/ > *noun informal, derogatory* a person who tries to be like someone else or to fit in with a particular group of people.

want > *verb* **1** have a desire to possess or do (something); wish for. **2** desire (someone) sexually. **3** (**be wanted**) (of a suspected criminal) be sought by the police. **4** *informal, chiefly Brit.* (of a thing) require to be attended to. **5** *informal, chiefly Brit.* ought to, should, or

need to do something. **6** (often **want for**) lack or be short of something desirable or essential. > *noun* **1** a desire for something. **2** lack or deficiency. **3** lack of essentials; poverty.

SYNONYMS – *verb* **1** crave, desire, fancy, wish for. *noun* **1** craving, desire, fancy, wish. **2** dearth, deficiency, lack, scarcity. **3** need, poverty, privation.

ORIGIN – Old Norse, 'be lacking'.

wanting > *adjective* **1** lacking in something required, necessary, or usual. **2** absent; not provided.

wanton /**won**tən/ > *adjective* **1** (of a cruel or violent action) deliberate and unprovoked. **2** sexually immodest or promiscuous. **3** *literary* growing profusely; luxuriant. > *noun archaic* a sexually immodest or promiscuous woman.

DERIVATIVES – **wantonly** *adverb* **wantonness** *noun*.

SYNONYMS – *adjective* **1** deliberate, gratuitous, groundless, motiveless, wilful. **2** dissolute, immodest, immoral, licentious, loose, promiscuous.

ORIGIN – from *wan-* 'badly' + Old English *togen* 'trained': originally in the sense 'rebellious, lacking discipline'.

WAP > *abbreviation* Wireless Application Protocol, a means of enabling a mobile phone to browse the Internet and display data.

wapentake /**wopp**əntayk/ > *noun historical* a subdivision of certain northern and midland English counties, corresponding to a hundred in other counties.

ORIGIN – Old English, from Old Norse *vápn* 'weapon' + *taka* 'take', perhaps with reference to voting in an assembly by a show of weapons.

wapiti /**wopp**iti/ > *noun* (pl. **wapitis**) a red deer of a large North American subspecies.

ORIGIN – Shawnee, 'white rump'.

War. > *abbreviation* Warwickshire.

war > *noun* **1** a state of armed conflict between nations, states, or armed groups. **2** a sustained contest between rivals. **3** a campaign against something undesirable. > *verb* (**warred, warring**) engage in a war.

WORDFINDER – martial (*of war, warlike*); antebellum (*existing before a particular war*), belligerent, combatant (*engaged in war*), casus belli (*something provoking a war*), jihad (*a holy war*), kriegspiel (*a war game*).

IDIOMS – **be on the warpath** be very angry with someone. [ORIGIN – with reference to American Indians heading towards a battle.]

COMBINATIONS – **war baby** a child born in wartime, especially one fathered

illegitimately by a serviceman. **war chest** a reserve of funds used for fighting a war. **war crime** an action carried out during the conduct of a war that violates accepted international rules of war. **war dance** a ceremonial dance performed before a battle or to celebrate victory. **war game 1** a military exercise carried out to test or improve tactical expertise. **2** a simulated military conflict carried out as a game or sport. **war loan** stock issued by the British government to raise funds at a time of war. **warpaint 1** paint traditionally used to decorate the face and body before battle, especially by North American Indians. **2** *informal* elaborate or excessive make-up. **warplane** an aircraft designed to engage in air combat or to drop bombs. **wartime** a period during which a war is taking place.

ORIGIN – from a variant of Old French *guerre* 'war'; related to **WORSE**.

waratah /**worr**ətaa/ > *noun* an Australian shrub with slender leathery leaves and clusters of crimson flowers.

ORIGIN – Dharuk (an Aboriginal language).

warble¹ > *verb* **1** (of a bird) sing softly and with a succession of constantly changing notes. **2** (of a person) sing in a trilling or quavering voice. > *noun* a warbling sound or utterance.

ORIGIN – Old French *werbler*; related to **WHIRL**.

warble² > *noun* a swelling or abscess beneath the skin of cattle, horses, and other mammals, caused by the presence of the larva of the parasitic **warble fly**.

warbler > *noun* a small songbird typically living in trees and bushes and having a warbling song.

ward > *noun* **1** a room or division in a hospital for one or more patients. **2** an administrative division of a city or borough, represented by a councillor or councillors. **3** a child or young person under the care and control of a guardian appointed by their parents or a court. **4** any of the internal ridges or bars in a lock which prevent the turning of any key without corresponding grooves. **5** *historical* an area of ground enclosed by the encircling walls of a fortress or castle. > *verb* (**ward off**) prevent from harming or affecting one.

DERIVATIVES – **wardship** *noun*.

COMBINATIONS – **ward of court** a child or young person for whom a guardian has been appointed by the Court of Chancery or who has become directly subject to the authority of that court.

ORIGIN – Old English, 'keep safe, guard'; related to **AWARD** and **GUARD**.

-ward (also **-wards**) > *suffix* **1** (usu. **-wards**) (forming adverbs) towards the specified place or direction: *homewards*. **2** (usu. **-ward**) (forming adjectives) turned or tending towards: *upward*.

warden > *noun* **1** a person responsible for the supervision of a particular place or procedure. **2** Brit. the head of certain schools, colleges, or other institutions. **3** chiefly N. Amer. a prison governor.
DERIVATIVES – **wardenship** *noun*.
ORIGIN – Old French *wardein*, *guarden* 'guardian'.

warder > *noun* (fem. **wardress**) chiefly Brit. a prison guard.

wardrobe > *noun* **1** a large, tall cupboard in which clothes may be hung or stored. **2** a person's entire collection of clothes. **3** the costume department or costumes of a theatre or film company. **4** a department of a royal or noble household in charge of clothing.
ORIGIN – first in the sense 'private chamber': from Old French *warderobe*, variant of *garderobe*, from *garder* 'to keep' and *robe* 'robe, dress'.

wardroom > *noun* a commissioned officers' mess on board a warship.

ware¹ > *noun* **1** pottery, typically that of a specified type. **2** manufactured articles of a specified type. **3** (**wares**) articles offered for sale.
ORIGIN – Old English, 'commodities'.

ware² (also **'ware**) > *verb* beware (used as a warning cry).

warehouse /**wair**howss/ > *noun* **1** a large building where raw materials or manufactured goods are stored. **2** a large wholesale or retail store. > *verb* /**wair**howz/ store (goods) in a warehouse.

warfare > *noun* engagement in or the state of war.

warfarin /**wawr**fərin/ > *noun* a substance which prevents blood from clotting, used as a rat poison and in the treatment of thrombosis.
ORIGIN – from the initial letters of *Wisconsin Alumni Research Foundation* + *-arin*.

warhead > *noun* the explosive head of a missile, torpedo, or similar weapon.

warhorse > *noun* informal a veteran soldier, politician, sports player, etc. who has fought many campaigns or contests.

warlike > *adjective* **1** disposed towards or threatening war; hostile. **2** directed towards or prepared for war.

warlock > *noun* a man who practises witchcraft.

warlord > *noun* a military commander, especially one who autonomously commands a region.

wordpower facts
Warlock
The word **warlock** is not connected to either **war** or **lock**. Spelled *wǣrloga* in Old English, it came from *wǣr* 'covenant' and an element related to *lēogan* 'belie, deny'. In Old English it seems to have meant 'traitor', 'wicked person', 'savage creature, monster', and also 'the Devil'. It came in Middle English to refer to a person in league with the Devil, and hence a sorcerer. In this sense it was chiefly Scottish until it gained wider currency through its frequent use in the novels of Sir Walter Scott.

warm > *adjective* **1** of or at a fairly or comfortably high temperature. **2** (of clothes or coverings) made of a material that helps the body to retain heat. **3** having or showing enthusiasm, affection, or kindness. **4** (of a colour) containing red, yellow, or orange tones. **5** (of a scent or trail) fresh; strong. **6** close to finding or guessing what is sought. > *verb* **1** make or become warm. **2** (**warm to** or **towards**) become more interested in or enthusiastic about. > *noun* **1** (**the warm**) a warm place or area. **2** an act of warming.
IDIOMS – **warm up 1** prepare for physical exertion by doing gentle stretches and exercises. **2** (of an engine or electrical appliance) reach a temperature high enough to allow it to operate efficiently. **3** amuse or entertain (an audience or crowd) to make them more receptive to an act that is to follow.
DERIVATIVES – **warmer** *noun* **warmly** *adverb*.
SYNONYMS – *adjective* **1** mild, temperate. **3** cordial, friendly, kind, welcoming.
ANTONYMS – *adjective* **1,3** cold, cool.
COMBINATIONS – **warm-blooded 1** (of animals, chiefly mammals and birds) maintaining a constant body temperature by their metabolism. **2** ardent; passionate. **warm-hearted** sympathetic and kind. **warming pan** historical a wide, flat brass pan on a long handle, filled with hot coals and used for warming a bed.

warmonger > *noun* a person who seeks to bring about or promote war.

warmth > *noun* **1** the quality, state, or sensation of being warm. **2** enthusiasm, affection, or kindness. **3** intensity of emotion.

warn > *verb* **1** inform of a possible danger, problem, etc. **2** give (someone) cautionary advice about actions or conduct. **3** (**warn off**) order (someone) to keep away or to refrain from doing something.

SYNONYMS – **1** alert, apprise, inform, notify. **2** advise, caution, counsel.

warning > *noun* **1** a statement or event that warns or serves as a cautionary example. **2** cautionary advice. **3** advance notice.
DERIVATIVES – **warningly** *adverb*.

warp /wawrp/ > *verb* **1** make or become bent or twisted, typically from the action of heat or damp. **2** make abnormal; distort. **3** move (a ship) along by hauling on a rope attached to a stationary object ashore. > *noun* **1** a distortion or twist in shape. **2** the lengthwise threads on a loom over and under which the weft threads are passed to make cloth. **3** a rope attached at one end to a fixed point and used for moving or mooring a ship.
SYNONYMS – **1** bend, buckle, contort, distort, twist. **2** corrupt, distort, pervert.

warrant > *noun* **1** an official authorisation enabling the police or some other body to make an arrest, search premises, etc. **2** a document entitling the holder to receive goods, money, or services. **3** justification or authority. **4** an official certificate of appointment issued to an officer of lower rank than a commissioned officer. > *verb* **1** justify or necessitate. **2** officially affirm or guarantee.
IDIOMS – **I** (or **I'll**) **warrant** dated no doubt.
DERIVATIVES – **warrantable** *adjective*.
COMBINATIONS – **warrant officer** a rank of officer in the army, RAF, or US navy, below the commissioned officers and above the NCOs.
ORIGIN – first used in the senses 'protector', 'safeguard', and 'protect from danger': from variants of Old French *guarant*, *guarantir*; related to GUARANTEE.

warranty > *noun* (pl. **warranties**) **1** a written guarantee promising to repair or replace an article if necessary within a specified period. **2** a formal statement by an insured party that certain statements are true or that certain conditions shall be fulfilled.

warren > *noun* **1** a network of interconnecting rabbit burrows. **2** a densely populated or labyrinthine building or district.
ORIGIN – Old French *garenne* 'game park'.

warrior > *noun* (especially in former times) a brave or experienced soldier or fighter.

warship > *noun* a ship equipped with weapons and designed to take part in warfare at sea.

wart /wawrt/ > *noun* **1** a small, hard, benign growth on the skin. **2** any rounded protuberance on the skin of an animal or the surface of a plant.
IDIOMS – **warts and all** informal including faults or unattractive qualities.
DERIVATIVES – **warty** *adjective*.

warthog-waste

warthog > *noun* an African wild pig with a large head, warty lumps on the face, and curved tusks.

wary > *adjective* (**warier, wariest**) (often **wary of**) cautious about possible dangers or problems.
DERIVATIVES – **warily** *adverb* **wariness** *noun*.
SYNONYMS – alert, apprehensive, cautious, circumspect, watchful.
ANTONYMS – incautious, unwary.
ORIGIN – from **WARE**².

was first and third person singular past of **BE**.

wasabi /wəsaabi/ > *noun* a Japanese plant with a thick green root which tastes like strong horseradish and is used in cookery.
ORIGIN – Japanese.

wash > *verb* 1 clean with water and, typically, soap or detergent. 2 (of flowing water) carry or move in a particular direction. 3 (**wash over**) take place around (someone) without affecting them. 4 *literary* wet or moisten. 5 brush with a thin coat of dilute paint or ink. 6 *informal* seem convincing or genuine: *excuses just don't wash with us.* > *noun* 1 an act of washing or an instance of being washed. 2 a quantity of clothes needing to be or just having been washed. 3 the water or air disturbed by a moving boat or aircraft. 4 a medicinal or cleansing solution. 5 a thin coating of paint or metal. 6 silt or gravel carried by water and deposited as sediment. 7 malt fermenting in preparation for distillation.
IDIOMS – **wash one's dirty linen** (or **laundry**) **in public** *informal* discuss or argue about one's personal affairs in public. **wash one's hands of** disclaim responsibility for. [ORIGIN – with biblical allusion to Pontius Pilate washing his hands after the condemnation of Christ (Gospel of Matthew, chapter 27).] **washed out** 1 faded by or as if by repeated washing. 2 pale and tired. 3 postponed or cancelled because of rain. **wash up** 1 *chiefly Brit.* clean crockery and cutlery after use. 2 *N. Amer.* clean one's hands and face. **washed-up** *informal* no longer effective or successful.
DERIVATIVES – **washable** *adjective*.
COMBINATIONS – **washbag** *Brit.* a toilet bag. **washbasin** a basin used for washing one's hands and face. **washboard** 1 a board made of ridged wood or a sheet of corrugated zinc, against which clothes are scrubbed during washing. 2 a similar board played as a percussion instrument by scraping. 3 (of a man's stomach) lean and with well-defined muscles. **washroom** *N. Amer.* a room with washing and toilet facilities. **washstand** *chiefly historical* a piece of furniture designed to hold a jug, bowl, or basin for washing one's hands and face.

washer > *noun* 1 a person or device that washes. 2 a small flat ring fixed between two joining surfaces or between a nut and bolt to spread the pressure or act as a spacer. 3 *Austral.* a facecloth.
COMBINATIONS – **washer-dryer** a washing machine with an inbuilt tumble-dryer.

washerwoman > *noun* a woman whose occupation is washing clothes.

washing > *noun* a quantity of clothes, bedlinen, etc. that is to be washed or has just been washed.
WORDFINDER – ablution (*action of washing*).
COMBINATIONS – **washing machine** a machine for washing clothes, bedlinen, etc. **washing powder** *chiefly Brit.* powdered detergent for washing laundry. **washing soda** sodium carbonate, used dissolved in water for washing and cleaning. **washing-up** *Brit.* crockery, cutlery, and other kitchen utensils that are to be washed.

washout > *noun* 1 *informal* a disappointing failure. 2 a breach in a road or railway track caused by flooding.

washy > *adjective* (**washier, washiest**) 1 too watery: *washy ale.* 2 insipid or pale.

wasn't > *contraction* was not.

WASP /wosp/ > *noun* *N. Amer.* an upper- or middle-class American white Protestant, regarded as a member of the most powerful social group.
ORIGIN – from *white Anglo-Saxon Protestant*.

wasp > *noun* a stinging winged insect which typically nests in complex colonies and has a black and yellow striped body.
WORDFINDER – hymenopteran (*wasp, bee, ant, or related insect*), vespine (*relating to wasps*).
COMBINATIONS – **wasp-waisted** having a very narrow waist.
ORIGIN – Old English; perhaps related to **WEAVE**¹ (from the web-like form of its nest).

waspie > *noun* (pl. **waspies**) a woman's corset or belt designed to accentuate a slender waist.

waspish > *adjective* sharply irritable.
DERIVATIVES – **waspishly** *adverb* **waspishness** *noun*.
SYNONYMS – irascible, irritable, snappish, testy, touchy.

wassail /wossayl, woss'l/ *archaic* > *noun* 1 spiced ale or mulled wine drunk during celebrations for Twelfth Night and Christmas Eve. 2 lively festivities involving drinking. > *verb* 1 make merry with much alcohol. 2 go from house to house at Christmas singing carols.
DERIVATIVES – **wassailer** *noun*.

wast /wost, wəst/ *archaic* or *dialect* second person singular past of **BE**.

wordpower facts
Wassail
Wassail means literally 'be in (good) health!'. It derives from the Old Norse phrase *ves heill*, *ves* meaning 'be' and *heill* 'healthy' (the root of **HAIL**², and related to **HALE**¹, **HEALTH**, and **WHOLE**). In Old Norse and medieval English **wassail** was a toast made when drinking: the polite reply was *drinkhail*, 'drink good health'. Both expressions were probably introduced by Danish-speaking inhabitants of England, and then spread, so that by the 12th century the usage was considered by the Normans to be characteristic of Englishmen. Indeed, around 1190 English students at the University of Paris were praised for their generosity and other virtues, but were said to be too fond of *wassail* and *drinkhail*! From around 1300 the word **wassail** was also applied to the spiced ale drunk during celebrations on Twelfth Night and Christmas Eve, but it was not until the 17th century that it came to mean 'a Christmas carol'.

wastage > *noun* 1 the action or process of wasting. 2 an amount wasted. 3 (also **natural wastage**) the reduction in the size of a workforce as a result of voluntary resignation or retirement rather than enforced redundancy.

waste > *verb* 1 use carelessly, extravagantly, or to no purpose. 2 (often **be wasted on**) give (something) to or direct (something) towards someone who does not appreciate it. 3 fail to make full or good use of. 4 (often **waste away**) become progressively weaker and more emaciated. 5 *literary* lay waste to. 6 *N. Amer. informal* kill or severely injure. 7 (**wasted**) *informal* under the influence of alcohol or illegal drugs. > *adjective* 1 eliminated or discarded as no longer useful or required. 2 (of an area of land) not used, cultivated, or built on. > *noun* 1 an act or instance of wasting. 2 unusable or unwanted material. 3 a large area of barren, uninhabited land.
WORDFINDER – atrophy, cachexia, dystrophy (*wasting away*).
IDIOMS – **go to waste** be wasted. **lay waste (to)** completely destroy. **waste not, want not** *proverb* if you use commodities or resources carefully and without extravagance you will never be in need.
SYNONYMS – *verb* 1 dissipate, fritter, squander. 4 atrophy, shrivel, weaken, wither. *adjective* 1 excess, scrap, superfluous. 2 barren, derelict, uncultivated.
COMBINATIONS – **waste-disposal unit** an

electrically operated device fitted to the waste pipe of a kitchen sink for grinding up food waste.

ORIGIN – Old French, from Latin *vastus* 'unoccupied, uncultivated'.

wasteful > *adjective* using or expending something carelessly, extravagantly, or to no purpose.

DERIVATIVES – **wastefully** *adverb* **wastefulness** *noun*.

SYNONYMS – prodigal, profligate, thriftless, uneconomical.

wasteland > *noun* a barren or empty area of land.

waster > *noun* 1 a wasteful person or thing. 2 *informal* a person who does little or nothing of value.

wastrel /**way**strəl/ > *noun* literary a wasteful or worthless person.

watch > *verb* 1 look at attentively. 2 keep under careful or protective observation. 3 exercise care, caution, or restraint about. 4 (**watch for**) look out for. 5 (**watch out**) be careful. 6 maintain an interest in. > *noun* 1 a small timepiece worn typically on a strap on one's wrist. 2 an act or instance of watching. 3 a period of vigil, typically during the night. 4 a fixed period of duty on a ship, usually lasting four hours. 5 a shift worked by firefighters or police officers. 6 (also **night watch**) historical a watchman or group of watchmen who patrolled and guarded the streets of a town at night.

WORDFINDER – analogue (*denoting a watch with hands*), digital (*denoting a watch with a numerical display*); chronometer (*a very accurate watch*), fob (*chain for a watch*), hunter (*type of watch with a hinged opaque cover over the glass*), half-hunter (*similar watch with a small opening in the cover*), synchronise (*set a watch to the same time as another*).

IDIOMS – **keep watch** stay on the lookout for danger or trouble. **watch one's back** protect oneself against danger from an unexpected quarter. **the watches of the night** literary waking hours during the night.

DERIVATIVES – **watcher** *noun*.

SYNONYMS – *verb* 1 contemplate, gaze at, look at, mark, observe, regard. 2 keep an eye on, monitor. 3 attend to, heed, pay attention to.

COMBINATIONS – **watching brief 1** Brit. Law a brief held by a barrister to follow a case on behalf of a client who is not directly involved. 2 an interest in a proceeding in which one is not directly concerned.

ORIGIN – Old English, related to WAKE¹.

watchable > *adjective* moderately enjoyable to watch.

watchdog > *noun* 1 a dog kept to guard private property. 2 a group or person that

monitors the practices of companies providing a particular service or utility.

watchful > *adjective* 1 alert and vigilant. 2 archaic wakeful.

DERIVATIVES – **watchfully** *adverb* **watchfulness** *noun*.

SYNONYMS – 1 alert, attentive, eagle-eyed, observant, vigilant.

watchman > *noun* 1 a man employed to look after an empty building, especially at night. 2 historical a member of a night watch.

watchtower > *noun* a tower built to create an elevated observation point.

watchword > *noun* 1 a word or phrase expressing a core aim or belief. 2 archaic a military password.

water > *noun* 1 the liquid which forms the seas, lakes, rivers, and rain and is the basis of the fluids of living organisms. 2 (**waters**) the water of a mineral spring as used medicinally. 3 (**waters**) an area of sea regarded as under the jurisdiction of a particular country. 4 (**waters**) amniotic fluid, especially as discharged at the onset of labour. 5 urine. 6 one of the four elements (air, earth, fire, and water) in ancient and medieval philosophy and in astrology. 7 the quality of transparency and brilliance shown by a diamond or other gem. > *verb* 1 pour water over (a plant or an area of ground). 2 (of a river) flow through (an area). 3 (of the eyes or mouth) produce tears or saliva. 4 give a drink of water to (an animal). 5 dilute (a drink) with water. 6 (**water down**) make less forceful or controversial by changing or leaving out certain details.

WORDFINDER – aquatic (*living in water*), aqueduct (*a bridge carrying water*), aqueous, hydrous (*containing water*), aquifer (*a body of water in rocks*), dehydrate (*remove water from*), hydraulic (*operated by water*), hydrocephalus (*water on the brain*), hydrography (*the science of surveying bodies of water*), hydrology (*the science of the earth's water*), hydrolysis (*chemical breakdown of substances in water*), hydropathy, hydrotherapy (*treatment of illness using water*), hydrophilic (*tending to mix with water*), hydrophobia (*extreme or irrational fear of water*), hydrophobic (*suffering from hydrophobia; tending not to mix with water*); Aquarius (*constellation and zodiac sign, the Water-Carrier*).

IDIOMS – **hold water** (of a theory) appear sound. **of the first water 1** (of a diamond or pearl) of the greatest brilliance and transparency. 2 unsurpassed of their kind: *she was a bore of the first water*. **under water** submerged; flooded. **water on the brain** informal hydrocephalus. **water under the bridge** (or N. Amer. **water over the dam**) past events that are over and done with.

DERIVATIVES – **waterless** *adjective*.

COMBINATIONS – **water bailiff** Brit. 1 an

official who enforces fishing laws. 2 historical a customs officer at a port. **waterbed** a bed with a water-filled rubber or plastic mattress. **water birth** a birth in which the mother spends the final stages of labour in a birthing pool. **water biscuit** a thin, crisp unsweetened biscuit made from flour and water. **water boatman** a predatory aquatic bug that swims on its back using its long back legs as oars. **water buffalo** a large black buffalo with heavy swept-back horns, used throughout the tropics for carrying loads. **water cannon** a device that ejects a powerful jet of water, used to disperse a crowd. **water chestnut** the crisp, white-fleshed tuber of a tropical aquatic sedge, used in oriental cookery. **water clock** historical a clock that used the flow of water to measure time. **water closet** dated a flush toilet. **water cure** chiefly historical a session of treatment by hydropathy. **watered silk** silk that has been treated in such a way as to give it a wavy lustrous finish. **waterfowl** ducks, geese, or other large aquatic birds. **water ice** a frozen dessert consisting of fruit juice or purée in a sugar syrup. **watering can** a portable water container with a long spout and a detachable perforated cap, used for watering plants. **watering hole 1** a waterhole from which animals regularly drink. 2 informal a pub or bar. **watering place 1** a watering hole. 2 a spa or seaside resort. **water level 1** the height reached by a body of water. 2 the water table. **water lily** an ornamental aquatic plant with large round floating leaves and large cup-shaped flowers. **water meadow** a meadow that is periodically flooded by a stream or river. **watermelon** a large melon-like fruit with smooth green skin, red pulp, and watery juice. **watermill** a mill worked by a waterwheel. **water nymph** (in folklore and classical mythology) a nymph inhabiting or presiding over water, especially a naiad or nereid. **water pistol** a toy pistol that shoots a jet of water. **water polo** a seven-a-side game played by swimmers in a pool, with a ball like a football that is thrown into the opponents' net. **water rail** a secretive rail (bird) inhabiting reedbeds, with a squealing call. **water rat 1** a large semiaquatic rat-like rodent. 2 Brit. a water vole. **water-resistant** able to resist the penetration of water to some degree but not entirely. **water splash** Brit. a water-filled dip in a road. **waterspout** a rotating column of water and spray formed by a whirlwind occurring over the sea or other body of water. **water table** the level below which the ground is saturated with water. **water torture** a form of torture in which the victim is exposed to the incessant dripping of water on the head or to the sound of dripping. **water tower** a tower supporting an elevated water tank, whose height creates the pressure required to distribute the water through a piped system. **water vole** a large semiaquatic vole which excavates burrows in the banks of rivers. **waterwheel** a large wheel driven by flowing water, used to work machinery or to raise water to a higher level. **water wings** inflated floats fixed to the arms of someone learning to swim to give increased buoyancy.

wordpower facts

Water

The word **water** comes from Old English *wæter*, from a Germanic source. Ultimately it stems from an important Indo-European root shared by the Greek word for 'water', *hudōr*, which is the source of such words as **hydrangea**, **hydrate**, **hydraulic**, and (shortened from *hydropsy*) **dropsy**. Sharing the same Indo-European root is Latin *unda*, meaning 'wave', which gave rise to **abound** and **abundant**, **inundate**, **redundant**, **sound** (in the sense 'ascertain the depth of'), **surround**, and **undulate**. Finally, the Russian word for 'water', *voda*, the source of **vodka**, derives from the same root.

watercolour (US **watercolor**) > *noun* **1** artists' paint made with a water-soluble binder, and thinned with water rather than oil. **2** a picture painted with watercolours. **3** the art of painting with watercolours.
DERIVATIVES – **watercolourist** *noun*.

watercourse > *noun* a river of stream, or an artificially constructed water channel.

watercress > *noun* a cress which grows in running water and whose pungent leaves are used in salad.

waterfall > *noun* a cascade of water falling from a height, formed when a river or stream flows over a precipice or steep incline.

waterfront > *noun* a part of a town or city alongside a body of water.

waterhole > *noun* a depression in which water collects, typically one at which animals drink.

waterline > *noun* **1** the level normally reached by the water on the side of a ship. **2** a line on a shore, riverbank, etc. marking the level reached by the sea or a river.

waterlogged > *adjective* saturated with or full of water.
ORIGIN – past participle of the verb *waterlog* 'make a ship unmanageable by flooding', from **WATER** + **LOG**[1].

Waterloo /wawtərloo/ > *noun* (usu. **meet**

one's **Waterloo**) a decisive defeat or failure.
ORIGIN – from the name of *Waterloo*, a village in what is now Belgium, site of a battle in 1815 in which Napoleon was finally defeated.

waterman > *noun* **1** a boatman. **2** an oarsman of a specified level of knowledge or skill.

watermark > *noun* a faint design made in some paper during manufacture that is visible when held against the light, identifying the maker. > *verb* mark with such a design.

waterproof > *adjective* impervious to water. > *noun* Brit. a waterproof garment. > *verb* make waterproof.

watershed > *noun* **1** an area or ridge of land that separates waters flowing to different rivers, basins, or seas. **2** a turning point in a state of affairs. **3** Brit. the time after which programmes that are unsuitable for children are broadcast on television.
ORIGIN – from **WATER** + *shed* in the sense 'ridge of high ground' (related to **SHED**[2]).

waterside > *noun* the area adjoining a sea, lake, or river.

waterski > *noun* (pl. **waterskis**) each of a pair of skis enabling the wearer to skim the surface of the water when towed by a motor boat. > *verb* travel on waterskis.
DERIVATIVES – **waterskier** *noun*.

watertight > *adjective* **1** closely sealed, fastened, or fitted so as to prevent the passage of water. **2** (of an argument or account) unable to be disputed or questioned.

waterway > *noun* a river, canal, or other route for travel by water.

waterweed > *noun* vegetation growing in water.

waterworks > *plural noun* **1** (treated as sing.) an establishment for managing a water supply. **2** informal the shedding of tears. **3** Brit. euphemistic, humorous the urinary system.

watery > *adjective* **1** consisting of, containing, or resembling water. **2** dilute or tasteless as a result of containing too much water. **3** weak or pale.

watt /wot/ > *noun* the unit of power in the SI system, equivalent to one joule per second and corresponding to the rate of energy consumption in an electric circuit where the potential difference is one volt and the current one ampere.
COMBINATIONS – **watt-hour** a measure of electrical energy equivalent to a power consumption of one watt for one hour.
ORIGIN – named after the Scottish engineer James *Watt* (1736–1819).

wattage > *noun* an amount of electrical power expressed in watts.

wattle[1] /wott'l/ > *noun* **1** a material for making fences, walls, etc., consisting of rods

or stakes interlaced with twigs or branches. **2** an Australian acacia with long pliant branches and cream, yellow, or golden flowers.
COMBINATIONS – **wattle and daub** wattle covered with mud or clay, formerly used to make walls.

wattle[2] /wott'l/ > *noun* a fleshy lobe hanging from the head or neck of the turkey and some other birds.
COMBINATIONS – **wattlebird** **1** an Australian songbird with a wattle hanging from each cheek. **2** a New Zealand songbird with wattles hanging from the base of the bill.

Watusi /wətoosi/ (also **Watutsi** /wətootsi/) > *noun* **1** (treated as pl.) the Tutsi people collectively (now dated in English use). **2** an energetic dance popular in the 1960s.

wave > *verb* **1** move one's hand to and fro in greeting or as a signal. **2** move (one's hand or arm, or something held in one's hand) to and fro. **3** move to and fro with a swaying motion while remaining fixed to one point. **4** style (hair) so that it curls slightly. > *noun* **1** a ridge of water curling into an arched form and breaking on the shore or between two depressions in open water. **2** a sudden occurrence of or increase in a phenomenon or emotion. **3** a gesture or signal made by waving one's hand. **4** a slightly curling lock of hair. **5** Physics a periodic disturbance of the particles of a substance which is propagated without net movement of the particles, as in the passage of undulating motion or sound. **6** Physics a similar variation of an electromagnetic field in the propagation of light or other radiation.
WORDFINDER – crest (*the summit of the ridge of a wave*), spindrift (*spray blown from waves*), spume (*froth on waves*), trough (*the hollow between waves*), tsunami (*a very large ocean wave produced by an earthquake*).
IDIOMS – **make waves** informal **1** create a significant impression. **2** cause trouble.
COMBINATIONS – **wave equation** Mathematics a differential equation expressing the properties of motion in waves. **wave mechanics** Physics a method of analysis of the behaviour of atomic phenomena with particles represented by wave equations.
ORIGIN – Old English, related to **WAVER**.

waveband > *noun* a range of wavelengths between two given limits, used in radio transmission.

waveform > *noun* Physics a curve showing the shape of a wave at a given time.

wavelength > *noun* **1** Physics the distance between successive crests of a wave, especially as a distinctive feature of sound, light, radio waves, etc. **2** a person's way of thinking when communicated to another: *we weren't on the same wavelength*.

wavelet > *noun* a small wave.

waver > *verb* **1** move quiveringly; flicker. **2** begin to weaken; falter. **3** be irresolute.

DERIVATIVES – **waverer** *noun* **wavery** *adjective*.

SYNONYMS – **1** flicker, quiver, tremble. **2** falter, wobble. **3** dither, equivocate, hesitate, vacillate.

ORIGIN – Old Norse, 'flicker'.

wavy > *adjective* (**wavier**, **waviest**) having or consisting of a series of wave-like curves.

DERIVATIVES – **waviness** *noun*.

wax¹ > *noun* **1** beeswax. **2** a soft, solid oily substance that melts easily, used for making candles or polishes. > *verb* **1** polish or treat with wax. **2** remove hair from (a part of the body) by applying wax and then peeling it off with the hairs. **3** informal make a recording of.

WORDFINDER – ceroplastic (*of modelling in wax*).

DERIVATIVES – **waxer** *noun* **waxing** *noun*.

COMBINATIONS – **waxbill** a finch-like songbird with a red bill that resembles sealing wax in colour. **waxcloth** (also **waxed cloth**) cloth treated with wax to make it waterproof. **waxed jacket** an outdoor jacket made of a waxed waterproof fabric. **waxed paper** paper treated with wax to make it waterproof or greaseproof. **waxwing** a crested songbird, mainly pinkish-brown and with bright red tips to some wing feathers.

wax² > *verb* **1** (of the moon) have a progressively larger part of its visible surface illuminated, so that it appears to increase in size. **2** literary become larger or stronger. **3** speak or write in the specified manner: *they waxed lyrical about the old days.*

wax³ > *noun* Brit. informal, dated a fit of anger.

waxen > *adjective* **1** having a smooth, pale, translucent surface like that of wax. **2** archaic or literary made of wax.

waxwork > *noun* **1** a lifelike dummy modelled in wax. **2** (**waxworks**) (treated as sing.) an exhibition of waxworks.

waxy > *adjective* (**waxier**, **waxiest**) resembling wax in consistency or appearance.

DERIVATIVES – **waxiness** *noun*.

way > *noun* **1** a method, style, or manner of doing something. **2** a road, track, path, or street. **3** a route or means taken in order to reach, enter, or leave a place. **4** the route along which someone or something is travelling or would travel if unobstructed. **5** a specified direction. **6** the distance in space or time between two points. **7** informal a particular area or locality. **8** a particular aspect or respect. **9** a specified condition or state. **10** (**ways**) parts into which something divides or is divided. **11** forward motion or momentum of a ship or boat through water. > *adverb* informal at or to a considerable distance or extent.

IDIOMS – **by the way** incidentally. **by way of 1** via. **2** as a form of. **3** by means of. **come one's way** happen or become available to one. **get** (or **have**) **one's** (**own**) **way** get or do what one wants in spite of opposition. **give way 1** yield. **2** be unable to carry a load or withstand a force and collapse or break. **3** allow another to be or go first. **4** (**give way to**) be replaced or superseded by. **go one's own way** act independently or as one wishes, especially against contrary advice. **go one's way 1** (of events, circumstances, etc.) be favourable to one. **2** leave. **have a way with** have a particular talent for dealing with or ability in. **have one's way with** humorous have sexual intercourse with. **in a way** (or **in some ways** or **in one way**) to a certain extent. **lead the way 1** go first along a route to show someone the way. **2** be a pioneer. **one way and another** (or **one way or the other**) **1** taking most aspects or considerations into account. **2** by some means. **3** whichever of two given alternatives is the case. **on the** (or **its**) **way** about to arrive or happen. **on the** (or **one's**) **way out** informal **1** going out of fashion or favour. **2** dying. **the other way round** (or **around**; Brit. also **about**) **1** in the opposite position or direction. **2** the opposite of what is expected or supposed. **out of the way 1** (of a place) remote. **2** dealt with or finished. **3** no longer an obstacle to someone's plans. **4** unusual or exceptional. **ways and means** the methods and resources for achieving something.

COMBINATIONS – **way station** N. Amer. a stopping place on a journey.

waybill > *noun* a list of passengers or goods being carried on a vehicle.

wayfarer > *noun* literary a person who travels on foot.

DERIVATIVES – **wayfaring** *noun*.

wayfaring tree > *noun* a white-flowered shrub which has berries turning from green through red to black.

waylay > *verb* (past and past participle **waylaid**) **1** intercept in order to attack. **2** intercept and detain with questions, conversation, etc.

waymark > *noun* (also **waymarker**) a sign forming one of a series used to mark out a footpath or similar route.

way-out > *adjective* informal unconventional or avant-garde.

-ways > *suffix* forming adjectives and adverbs of direction or manner: *lengthways.* Compare with **-WISE**.

wayside > *noun* the edge of a road.

IDIOMS – **fall by the wayside** fail to persist in an undertaking. [ORIGIN – with biblical allusion to the Gospel of Luke, chapter 8.]

wayward > *adjective* self-willed and not easily controlled.

DERIVATIVES – **waywardly** *adverb* **waywardness** *noun*.

SYNONYMS – headstrong, perverse, recalcitrant, unruly.

ORIGIN – shortening of obsolete *awayward* 'turned away'.

wazzock /**wazz**ək/ > *noun* Brit. informal a stupid or annoying person.

Wb > *abbreviation* weber(s).

WBA > *abbreviation* World Boxing Association.

WBC > *abbreviation* World Boxing Council.

WC > *abbreviation* Brit. water closet.

we > *pronoun* (first person pl.) **1** used by a speaker to refer to himself or herself and one or more other people considered together. **2** people in general. **3** used in formal contexts for or by a royal person, or by a writer, to refer to himself or herself. **4** you (used condescendingly): *how are we today?*

weak > *adjective* **1** lacking physical strength and energy. **2** liable to break or give way under pressure. **3** not secure, stable, or firmly established. **4** lacking power, influence, or ability. **5** lacking intensity. **6** (of a liquid or solution) heavily diluted. **7** Grammar (of verbs) forming the past tense and past participle by addition of a suffix (in English, typically *-ed*).

IDIOMS – **the weaker sex** dated women regarded collectively. **weak at the knees** helpless with emotion.

SYNONYMS – **1** feeble, frail, puny. **2** delicate, fragile, frail.

ANTONYMS – strong.

COMBINATIONS – **weak-kneed 1** weak and shaky from fear or excitement. **2** lacking in resolve or courage.

ORIGIN – Old English, 'pliant', 'of little worth', 'not steadfast'.

weaken > *verb* make or become weak.

SYNONYMS – debilitate, enfeeble, erode.

weakling > *noun* a weak person or animal.

weakly > *adverb* in a weak manner. > *adjective* (**weaklier**, **weakliest**) weak or sickly.

weakness > *noun* **1** the state or condition of being weak. **2** a disadvantage or fault. **3** a person or thing that one is unable to resist. **4** (**weakness for**) a self-indulgent liking for.

SYNONYMS – **1** enfeeblement, feebleness, frailty. **2** disadvantage, fault, flaw, imperfection, shortcoming.

weal¹ /weel/ (also chiefly Medicine **wheal**) > *noun* a red, swollen mark left on the body by a blow or pressure.

ORIGIN – variant of **WALE**, influenced by obsolete *wheal* 'suppurate'.

weal² /weel/ > *noun* formal that which is best for someone or something: *guardians of the public weal.*

ORIGIN – Old English, 'wealth, well-being'; related to **WELL¹**.

Wealden /weeldən/ > *adjective* Brit. relating to the Weald, a wooded district including parts of Kent, Surrey, and East Sussex.

wealth > *noun* **1** an abundance of valuable possessions or money. **2** the state of being rich. **3** an abundance or profusion of something desirable.

WORDFINDER – plutocracy (*rule by rich people*), plutocrat (*a wealthy and influential person*); magnate, tycoon (*a very wealthy businessman*), nouveau riche, parvenu (*a person who has recently become wealthy*); avarice (*excessive greed for wealth*), bonanza, golden goose, gold mine (*a source of wealth*), Croesus (*a legendary wealthy person*), El Dorado (*a place of great wealth*), Mammon (*wealth regarded as an evil influence*).

SYNONYMS – **2** affluence, prosperity, substance. **3** plenitude, plethora, treasury.

wealthy > *adjective* (**wealthier, wealthiest**) having a great deal of money, resources, or assets; rich.

SYNONYMS – affluent, moneyed, prosperous, rich.

wean¹ > *verb* **1** accustom (a young mammal) to food other than its mother's milk. **2** (often **wean off**) make (someone) give up a habit or addiction. **3** (**be weaned on**) be strongly influenced by (something) from an early age.

wean² > *noun* Scottish & N. English a young child.

ORIGIN – contraction of *wee ane* 'little one'.

weanling > *noun* a newly weaned animal.

weapon > *noun* **1** a thing designed or used for inflicting bodily harm or physical damage. **2** a means of gaining an advantage or defending oneself.

DERIVATIVES – **weaponry** *noun*.

wear > *verb* (past **wore**; past participle **worn**) **1** have on one's body as clothing, decoration, or protection. **2** exhibit or present (a particular facial expression or appearance). **3** undergo or cause damage or destruction by friction or use. **4** withstand continued use to a specified degree: *the fabric wears well wash after wash.* **5** (**wear off**) lose effectiveness or intensity. **6** (**wear down**) overcome through the persistent application of influence or pressure. **7** (**wear out**) exhaust. **8** (**wearing**) mentally or physically tiring. **9** (**wear on**) (of time) pass slowly or tediously. **10** (of a ship) fly (a flag). > *noun* **1** clothing suitable for a particular purpose or of a particular type. **2** damage sustained from continuous use. **3** the capacity for withstanding such damage.

WORDFINDER – attrition (*gradual wearing down*), corrosion (*wearing away by chemical action*), durable (*resistant to wear*), erosion (*wearing away by natural forces*).

IDIOMS – **wear thin** gradually dwindle or be used up.

DERIVATIVES – **wearable** *adjective* **wearer** *noun*.

wearisome > *adjective* causing one to feel tired or bored.

weary > *adjective* (**wearier, weariest**) **1** tired. **2** causing tiredness. **3** reluctant to experience any more of something. > *verb* (**wearies, wearied**) **1** make weary. **2** (**weary of**) grow tired of.

DERIVATIVES – **wearily** *adverb* **weariness** *noun* **wearying** *adjective*.

SYNONYMS – *adjective* **1** exhausted, fatigued, tired, worn out. **2** exhausting, fatiguing, tiring. *verb* **1** exhaust, fatigue, tire.

weasel > *noun* **1** a small slender carnivorous mammal related to the stoat, with reddish-brown fur. **2** informal, dated a deceitful or treacherous person. > *verb* (**weaselled, weaselling;** US **weaseled, weaseling**) achieve through cunning or deceit.

WORDFINDER – mustelid (*animal of the weasel family, e.g. marten, otter, polecat*).

DERIVATIVES – **weaselly** *adjective*.

COMBINATIONS – **weasel words** statements that are intentionally ambiguous or misleading.

weather > *noun* **1** the state of the atmosphere at a place and time as regards temperature, wind, rain, etc. **2** (before another noun) denoting the side from which the wind is blowing; windward. Contrasted with LEE. > *verb* **1** wear away or change in form or appearance by long exposure to the weather. **2** come safely through. **3** make (boards or tiles) overlap downwards to keep out rain.

WORDFINDER – meteorology (*the study of weather*); *types of meteorological instruments:* anemometer, barograph, barometer, hygrometer, hygroscope, thermometer; anticyclone (*a high-pressure weather system*), cyclone, depression (*low-pressure weather system*), front (*the boundary of a mass of air*), occluded front (*cold and warm fronts merged*).

IDIOMS – **keep a weather eye on** be watchful for developments in. **make heavy weather of** informal have unnecessary difficulty in dealing with (a task or problem). [ORIGIN – a nautical phrase referring to a ship in a storm.] **under the weather** informal slightly unwell or depressed.

COMBINATIONS – **weather-beaten** damaged, worn, or tanned by exposure to the weather. **weather house** a toy hygroscope in the form of a small house with figures of a man and woman standing in two porches, the man coming out in wet weather and the woman in dry. **weather station** an observation post where weather conditions and meteorological data are observed and recorded. **weatherstrip** a strip of material used to seal the edges of a door or window against rain and wind.

weatherboard chiefly Brit. > *noun* **1** a sloping board attached to the bottom of an outside door to keep out the rain. **2** each of a series of horizontal boards nailed to outside walls with edges overlapping to keep out the rain. > *verb* fit with weatherboards.

weathercock > *noun* a weathervane in the form of a cockerel.

weatherman (or **weatherwoman**) > *noun* a person who broadcasts a description and forecast of weather conditions.

weathervane > *noun* a revolving pointer to show the direction of the wind.

weave¹ > *verb* (past **wove**; past participle **woven** or **wove**) **1** form (fabric) by interlacing long threads passing in one direction with others at a right angle to them. **2** make fabric in this way. **3** make (basketwork or a wreath) by interlacing rods or flowers. **4** (**weave into**) make (interconnected elements) into (a story). > *noun* a particular style or manner in which fabric is woven.

WORDFINDER – warp (*the threads running lengthways in weaving*), weft or woof (*threads running crosswise*).

weave² > *verb* move from side to side to progress around obstructions.

weaver > *noun* **1** a person who weaves fabric. **2** (also **weaver bird**) a finch-like songbird of tropical Africa and Asia, which builds elaborately woven nests.

web > *noun* **1** a network of threads constructed by a spider, used to catch prey. **2** a complex system of interconnected elements. **3** a membrane between the toes of a swimming bird or other aquatic animal. **4** a roll of paper used in a continuous printing process. **5** a piece of woven fabric. **6** (**the Web**) short for WORLD WIDE WEB.

COMBINATIONS – **webmaster** a person who is responsible for a particular server on the World Wide Web. **web page** a hypertext document accessible via the World Wide Web.

ORIGIN – Old English, 'woven fabric'; related to WEAVE¹.

webbed > *adjective* **1** (of an animal's feet) having the toes connected by a web. **2** Medicine (of fingers or toes) abnormally united by a fold of skin.

webbing > *noun* strong, closely woven fabric used chiefly for making straps and belts and for supporting the seats of upholstered chairs.

webcam (also **Webcam**) > *noun* (trademark in the US) a video camera connected to a computer, so that its output may be viewed on the Internet.

webcast > *noun* a live video broadcast of an event transmitted across the Internet.

weber /vaybər/ > *noun* the unit of magnetic

flux in the SI system, sufficient to cause an electromotive force of one volt in a circuit of one turn when generated or removed in one second.

ORIGIN – named after the German physicist Wilhelm Eduard *Weber* (1804–91).

website > *noun* a location on the Internet that maintains one or more web pages.

wed > *verb* (**wedding**; past and past participle **wedded** or **wed**) **1** formal or literary marry. **2** formal or literary give or join in marriage. **3** (**wedded**) of or concerning marriage. **4** combine (two desirable factors or qualities). **5** (**be wedded to**) be entirely devoted to (an activity, belief, etc.).

ORIGIN – Old English, from the base of Scots *wed* 'a pledge'; related to **GAGE**[1].

we'd > *contraction* **1** we had. **2** we should or we would.

wedding > *noun* a marriage ceremony.

COMBINATIONS – **wedding band** chiefly N. Amer. a wedding ring. **wedding breakfast** Brit. a celebratory meal eaten just after a wedding (at any time of day) by the couple and their guests. **wedding cake** a rich iced cake served at a wedding reception. **wedding march** a piece of march music played at the entrance of the bride or the exit of the couple at a wedding. **wedding ring** a ring worn by a married person, given to them by their spouse at their wedding.

wedge > *noun* **1** a piece of wood, metal, etc. with a thick end that tapers to a thin edge, that is driven between two objects or parts of an object to secure or separate them. **2** a wedge-shaped thing or piece. **3** a golf club with a low, angled face for maximum loft. **4** a shoe with a fairly high heel forming a solid block with the sole. > *verb* **1** fix in position using a wedge. **2** force into a narrow space.

WORDFINDER – cuneate, cuneiform (*wedge-shaped*).

IDIOMS – **drive a wedge between** cause a breach between. **the thin end of the wedge** informal an action or situation of little importance in itself but likely to lead to more serious developments.

Wedgwood /**wej**woŏd/ > *noun* **1** trademark ceramic ware made by the English potter Josiah Wedgwood (1730–95) and his successors, especially a kind of powder-blue stoneware with white embossed cameos. **2** a powder-blue colour characteristic of this stoneware.

wedlock > *noun* the state of being married.

IDIOMS – **born in** (or **out of**) **wedlock** born of married (or unmarried) parents.

ORIGIN – Old English, 'marriage vow'.

Wednesday > *noun* the day of the week before Thursday and following Tuesday.

ORIGIN – Old English, named after the

Germanic god *Odin*; translation of Latin *Mercurii dies* 'day of Mercury'.

wee[1] > *adjective* (**weer**, **weest**) chiefly Scottish little.

wee[2] informal, chiefly Brit. > *noun* **1** an act of urinating. **2** urine. > *verb* (**wees**, **weed**) urinate.

weed > *noun* **1** a wild plant growing where it is not wanted and in competition with cultivated plants. **2** informal cannabis. **3** (**the weed**) informal tobacco. **4** informal a weak or skinny person. > *verb* **1** remove weeds from. **2** (**weed out**) remove (inferior or unwanted items or members) from something.

weedkiller > *noun* a substance used to destroy weeds.

weedy > *adjective* (**weedier**, **weediest**) **1** containing or covered with many weeds. **2** informal thin and puny.

week > *noun* **1** a period of seven days. **2** the period of seven days generally reckoned from and to midnight on Saturday night. **3** chiefly Brit. (preceded by a specified day) a week after (that day). **4** the five days from Monday to Friday, or the time spent working during this period.

WORDFINDER – hebdomadal (*taking place weekly*).

weekday > *noun* a day of the week other than Saturday or Sunday.

weekend > *noun* Saturday and Sunday. > *verb* informal spend a weekend somewhere.

weekender > *noun* a person who spends weekends away from their main home.

weekly > *adjective* **1** done, produced, or occurring once a week. **2** calculated in terms of a week. > *adverb* once a week. > *noun* (pl. **weeklies**) a newspaper or periodical issued every week.

weeny > *adjective* (**weenier**, **weeniest**) informal tiny.

weep > *verb* (past and past participle **wept**) **1** shed tears. **2** exude liquid. **3** (**weeping**) used in names of tree and shrub varieties with drooping branches, e.g. **weeping cherry**. > *noun* a fit or spell of shedding tears.

DERIVATIVES – **weeping** noun & adjective.

SYNONYMS – *verb* **1** cry, shed tears, sob.

COMBINATIONS – **weeping willow** a willow with trailing branches and foliage reaching down to the ground.

weepie (also **weepy**) > *noun* (pl. **weepies**) informal a sentimental or emotional film, novel, or song.

weepy > *adjective* (**weepier**, **weepiest**) informal **1** tearful; inclined to weep. **2** sentimental.

DERIVATIVES – **weepily** adverb **weepiness** noun.

weevil /**wee**vil/ > *noun* a small beetle with an elongated snout, several kinds of which are pests of crops or stored foodstuffs.

ORIGIN – Old English, 'beetle', from a base meaning 'move briskly'.

wee-wee informal, chiefly Brit. > *noun* a child's word for urine. > *verb* urinate.

w.e.f. > *abbreviation* Brit. with effect from.

weft[1] > *noun* (in weaving) the crosswise threads that are passed over and under the warp threads on a loom to make cloth.

weft[2] > *noun* variant spelling of **WAFT** (in sense 2).

Wehrmacht /**vair**maakht/ > *noun* the German armed forces from 1921 to 1945.

ORIGIN – German, 'defensive force'.

weigh > *verb* **1** find out how heavy (someone or something) is. **2** have a specified weight. **3** (**weigh out**) measure and take out (a portion of a particular weight). **4** (**weigh down**) be heavy and cumbersome or oppressive to (someone). **5** (**weigh on**) be depressing or worrying to. **6** (**weigh in**) (of a boxer or jockey) be officially weighed before or after a contest. **7** (often **weigh up**) assess the nature or importance of. **8** (often **weigh against**) influence a decision or action. **9** (**weigh in**) informal make a forceful contribution to a competition or argument. **10** (**weigh into**) join in or attack forcefully or enthusiastically.

IDIOMS – **weigh anchor** Nautical take up the anchor when ready to sail.

SYNONYMS – *verb* **5** (**weigh on**) burden, depress, oppress, trouble. **7** (**weigh up**) appraise, consider, examine, scrutinise.

weighbridge > *noun* a machine for weighing vehicles, set into the ground to be driven on to.

weigh-in > *noun* an official weighing, e.g. of boxers before a fight.

weight > *noun* **1** a body's relative mass or the quantity of matter contained by it, giving rise to a downward force; heaviness. **2** Physics the force exerted on the mass of a body by a gravitational field. **3** the quality of being heavy. **4** a unit or system of units used for expressing how much something weighs. **5** a piece of metal known to weigh a definite amount and used on scales to determine how heavy something is. **6** a heavy object. **7** (**weights**) heavy blocks or discs used in weightlifting or weight training. **8** the surface density of cloth, used as a measure of its quality. **9** ability to influence decisions or actions. **10** the importance attached to something. **11** a feeling of oppression or pressure: *a weight on one's mind.* > *verb* **1** hold (something) down by placing a heavy object on top of it. **2** attach importance or value to. **3** plan or arrange so as to give someone or something an advantage. **4** assign a handicap weight to (a horse).

WORDFINDER – gravimetric (*relating to the measurement of weight*), ponderous (*slow because of great weight*).

IDIOMS – **be worth one's weight in gold** be exceedingly useful or helpful. **throw one's weight about** (or **around**) informal be unpleasantly self-assertive.

COMBINATIONS – **weight training** physical training that involves lifting weights. **weight-watcher** a person who is on a diet in order to lose weight.

weighting > *noun* **1** allowance or adjustment made to take account of special circumstances or compensate for a distorting factor. **2** Brit. additional wages or salary paid to allow for a higher cost of living in a particular area.

weightless > *adjective* (of a body) not apparently acted on by gravity.
DERIVATIVES – **weightlessly** *adverb* **weightlessness** *noun*.

weightlifting > *noun* the sport or activity of lifting barbells or other heavy weights.

weighty > *adjective* (**weightier**, **weightiest**) **1** weighing a great deal; heavy. **2** of great importance. **3** very influential.
DERIVATIVES – **weightily** *adverb* **weightiness** *noun*.
SYNONYMS – **2** consequential, crucial, momentous, serious.
ANTONYMS – **2** trivial.

weir > *noun* **1** a low dam built across a river to raise the level of water upstream or regulate its flow. **2** an enclosure of stakes set in a stream as a trap for fish.

weird* > *adjective* **1** suggesting something supernatural; uncanny. **2** informal very strange; bizarre.
DERIVATIVES – **weirdly** *adverb* **weirdness** *noun*.
*SPELLING – contrary to the usual rule, the e comes before the i: weird.
SYNONYMS – **1** eerie, uncanny, unearthly, unnatural.

wordpower facts
Weird
In Old English **weird**, then spelled *wyrd*, was a noun meaning 'destiny, fate', or, in the plural, 'the Fates' (the three goddesses supposed to determine the course of human life); it also meant 'an event or occurrence'. The adjective, first recorded in Middle English, meant 'having the power to control destiny', and was used especially in the phrase *the Weird Sisters*, originally with reference to the Fates and later to the witches in Shakespeare's *Macbeth*. The modern sense 'strange, uncanny' did not develop until the early 19th century: it was apparently used first by the poet Shelley.

weirdo > *noun* (pl. **weirdos**) informal a strange or eccentric person.

weka /wekkə/ > *noun* a large flightless New Zealand rail.
ORIGIN – Maori, imitative of its cry.

Welch > *adjective* archaic spelling of **WELSH**.

welch > *verb* variant spelling of **WELSH**.

welcome > *noun* **1** an instance or manner of greeting someone. **2** a pleased or approving reaction. > *exclamation* used to greet someone in a glad or friendly way. > *verb* **1** greet (someone arriving) in a glad, polite, or friendly way. **2** be glad to receive or hear of. > *adjective* **1** (of a guest or new arrival) gladly received. **2** very pleasing because much needed or desired. **3** allowed or invited to do a specified thing. **4** (**welcome to**) used to indicate relief at relinquishing something to someone else: *you're welcome to it!*
DERIVATIVES – **welcomer** *noun* **welcoming** *adjective*.

weld > *verb* **1** join together (metal parts) by heating the surfaces to the point of melting and pressing or hammering them together. **2** forge (an article) by such means. **3** cause to combine and form a whole. > *noun* a welded joint.
DERIVATIVES – **welder** *noun*.

welfare > *noun* **1** the health, happiness, and fortunes of a person or group. **2** a system or procedure designed to promote the basic physical and material well-being of people in need. **3** chiefly N. Amer. financial support given for this purpose.
COMBINATIONS – **welfare state** a system whereby the state undertakes to protect the health and well-being of its citizens by means of grants, pensions, and other benefits.

well¹ > *adverb* (**better**, **best**) **1** in a good or satisfactory way. **2** in a condition of prosperity or comfort. **3** in a thorough manner. **4** to a great extent or degree; very much. **5** Brit. informal very; extremely: *he was well out of order.* **6** very probably; in all likelihood. **7** without difficulty. **8** with good reason. **9** archaic luckily; opportunely: *hail fellow, well met.* > *adjective* (**better**, **best**) **1** in good health; free or recovered from illness. **2** in a satisfactory state or position. **3** sensible; advisable. > *exclamation* used to express surprise, anger, resignation, etc., or when pausing in speech.
IDIOMS – **as well** in addition; too. **as well** (or **just as well**) **1** with equal reason or an equally good result. **2** sensible, appropriate, or desirable. **be well out of** Brit. informal be fortunate to be no longer involved in. **be well up on** know a great deal about. **leave** (or **let**) **well alone** refrain from interfering with or trying to improve something. **well and truly** completely.

USAGE – when you use **well** with a past participle, such as 'built', and the resulting compound precedes the noun, it is advisable in order to avoid ambiguity to use a hyphen, as in *a tall, well-built man*; usually a hyphen is not used when the compound stands alone, as in *her remarks were well intentioned*.
SYNONYMS – *adverb* **1** correctly, nicely, properly, satisfactorily. **3** deeply, intimately, profoundly, thoroughly. **4** considerably, substantially, very much. **7** easily, effortlessly, readily.
COMBINATIONS – **well advised** sensible; wise. **well appointed** (of a building or room) having a high standard of equipment or furnishing. **well disposed** having a positive, sympathetic, or friendly attitude. **well earned** fully merited or deserved. **well endowed 1** having plentiful supplies of a resource. **2** informal, humorous (of a man) having large genitals. **3** informal, humorous (of a woman) large-breasted. **well-heeled** informal wealthy. **well hung** informal, humorous (of a man) having large genitals. **well knit** (of a person) strongly and compactly built. **well known** known widely or thoroughly. **well meaning** (also **well meant**) having good intentions but not necessarily the desired effect. **well oiled 1** operating smoothly. **2** informal drunk. **well preserved** (of an old person) showing little sign of ageing. **well rounded 1** having a pleasing curved shape. **2** (of a person) plump. **3** having a mature personality and varied interests. **well spoken** speaking in an educated and refined manner. **well thumbed** (of a book) having been read often and bearing marks of frequent handling. **well travelled 1** (of a person) having travelled widely. **2** (of a route) much frequented by travellers. **well trodden** much frequented by travellers. **well turned 1** (of a phrase or compliment) elegantly expressed. **2** (of a woman's ankle or leg) attractively shaped. **well worn 1** showing the signs of extensive use or wear. **2** (of a phrase or idea) used or repeated so often that it no longer has interest or significance.

well² > *noun* **1** a shaft sunk into the ground to obtain water, oil, or gas. **2** a depression made to hold liquid. **3** a plentiful source or supply. **4** an enclosed space in the middle of a building, giving room for stairs or a lift or allowing light or ventilation. > *verb* (often **well up**) **1** (of a liquid) rise up to the surface and spill or be about to spill. **2** (of an emotion) arise and become more intense.
WORDFINDER – artesian well (*drilled into rock strata from which water rises by pressure.*)

we'll > *contraction* we shall; we will.

well-being > *noun* the state of being comfortable, healthy, or happy.

well done > *adjective* **1** carried out successfully or satisfactorily. **2** (of food) thoroughly cooked. > *exclamation* used to express congratulation or approval.

wellington (also **wellington boot**) > *noun* chiefly Brit. a knee-length waterproof rubber or plastic boot.

ORIGIN − named after the British soldier and Prime Minister the 1st Duke of *Wellington* (1769–1852).

well-nigh > *adverb* chiefly literary almost.

well off > *adjective* **1** wealthy. **2** in a favourable situation or circumstances.

wellspring > *noun* literary the place where a spring comes out of the ground.

well-to-do > *adjective* wealthy; prosperous.

well-wisher > *noun* a person who desires happiness or success for another, or who expresses such a desire.

welly (also **wellie**) > *noun* (pl. **wellies**) Brit. informal **1** short for WELLINGTON. **2** power or vigour.

Welsh > *noun* the language of Wales. > *adjective* relating to Wales, its people, or their language.

WORDFINDER − Cymru (*Welsh name for Wales*); Cymric, Cambrian (*of Wales*); hwyl (*stirring emotional feeling associated with the Welsh*).

DERIVATIVES − **Welshman** noun **Welshness** noun.

COMBINATIONS − **Welsh dresser** a piece of wooden furniture with cupboards and drawers in the lower part and open shelves in the upper part. **Welsh rarebit** (also **Welsh rabbit**) another term for RAREBIT.

wordpower facts

Welsh

Welsh is an Old English word from a base meaning 'foreigner' that also gave rise to **Walloon**. **Welsh** comes ultimately from Latin *Volcae*, the name of a Celtic people, and in Old English originally meant 'belonging to the native Celtic population rather than the Anglo-Saxons'. It was formerly often spelled **Welch**, which survives only in long-established names such as *The Royal Welch Fusiliers*. The Welsh language is descended from the Celtic language spoken in most of Britain in Roman times. Among the English words derived from Welsh are **bard**[1], **coracle**, **corgi**, **cwm**, **eisteddfod**, and probably **flannel**.

welsh (also **welch**) > *verb* (**welsh on**) fail to honour (a debt or obligation).

welt > *noun* **1** a leather rim round the edge of the upper of a shoe, to which the sole is attached. **2** a ribbed, reinforced, or decorative border of a garment or pocket. **3** a weal.

welter > *verb* literary **1** move in a turbulent fashion. **2** lie injured and covered in blood. > *noun* a large number of items in no order; a confused mass.

ORIGIN − Dutch, Low German *welteren*: originally in the sense 'writhe, wallow'.

welterweight > *noun* a weight in boxing and other sports intermediate between lightweight and middleweight.

wen[1] > *noun* **1** a boil or other swelling or growth on the skin. **2** (often **Great Wen**) archaic a very large or overcrowded city.

wen[2] (also **wyn**) > *noun* a runic letter used in Old and Middle English and later replaced by *u*.

ORIGIN − Old English, 'joy'; so named because it is the first letter of this word.

wench /wench/ > *noun* archaic or humorous a girl or young woman.

ORIGIN − abbreviation of obsolete *wenchel* 'child, servant, prostitute'.

wend > *verb* (**wend one's way**) go slowly or by an indirect route.

ORIGIN − Old English, 'to turn, depart'; related to WIND[2].

Wendy house > *noun* Brit. a toy house large enough for children to play in.

ORIGIN − named after the house built around *Wendy* in J. M. Barrie's play *Peter Pan* (1904).

Wensleydale /**wenz**lidayl/ > *noun* a type of white cheese with a crumbly texture.

ORIGIN − named after *Wensleydale* in Yorkshire.

went past of GO[1].

wept past and past participle of WEEP.

were second person singular past, plural past, and past subjunctive of BE.

we're > *contraction* we are.

weren't > *contraction* were not.

werewolf /**weer**woolf, **wair**woolf/ > *noun* (pl. **werewolves**) (in folklore) a person who periodically changes into a wolf, typically when there is a full moon.

ORIGIN − Old English; the first element is probably Old English *wer* 'man'.

wert /wert/ archaic second person singular past of BE.

Wesleyan /**wez**liən/ > *adjective* relating to the teachings of the English preacher John Wesley (1703–91) or the main branch of the Methodist Church which he founded. > *noun* a follower of Wesley or adherent of the main Methodist tradition.

DERIVATIVES − **Wesleyanism** noun.

west > *noun* (usu. **the west**) **1** the direction towards the point of the horizon where the sun sets at the equinoxes. **2** the western part of a country, region, or town. **3** (**the West**) Europe and North America seen in contrast to other civilisations. **4** (**the West**) historical the non-Communist states of Europe and North America. > *adjective* **1** lying towards, near, or facing the west. **2** (of a wind) blowing from the west. > *adverb* to or towards the west.

WORDFINDER − Occident (*the West, as opposed to the Orient*).

DERIVATIVES − **westbound** adjective & adverb.

COMBINATIONS − **west-north-west** (or **west-south-west**) the direction or compass point midway between west and north-west (or south-west).

westerly > *adjective* & *adverb* **1** in a westward position or direction. **2** (of a wind) blowing from the west. > *noun* **1** a wind blowing from the west. **2** (**westerlies**) the belt of prevailing westerly winds in medium latitudes in the southern hemisphere.

western > *adjective* **1** situated in, directed towards, or facing the west. **2** (usu. **Western**) living in, coming from, or characteristic of the west, in particular Europe and North America. > *noun* a film or novel about cowboys in western North America.

DERIVATIVES − **westernmost** adjective.

COMBINATIONS − **Western Church** the part of the Christian Church originating in the Western Roman Empire, including the Roman Catholic, Anglican, Lutheran, and Reformed Churches.

westerner > *noun* a person from the west of a particular region or country.

westernise (also **westernize**) > *verb* bring or come under the influence of the cultural, economic, or political systems of Europe and North America.

DERIVATIVES − **westernisation** noun **westerniser** noun.

West Indian > *noun* a person from the West Indies, or a person of West Indian descent. > *adjective* relating to the West Indies or its people.

westing > *noun* **1** distance travelled or measured westward. **2** a figure or line representing westward distance on a map.

westward > *adjective* towards the west. > *adverb* (also **westwards**) in a westerly direction.

wet > *adjective* (**wetter**, **wettest**) **1** covered or saturated with liquid. **2** (of the weather) rainy. **3** involving the use of water or liquid. **4** (of paint, ink, etc.) not yet having dried or hardened. **5** Brit. informal lacking forcefulness or strength of character; feeble. **6** informal (of an area) allowing the free sale of alcoholic drink. > *verb* (**wetting**; past and past participle **wet** or **wetted**) **1** cover or touch with liquid. **2** (especially of a young child) urinate in or on. **3** (**wet oneself**) urinate involuntarily. > *noun* **1** liquid that makes something damp. **2** (**the wet**) rainy weather. **3** Brit. informal a feeble person. **4** Brit.

a Conservative politician (especially in the 1980s) with liberal tendencies.

IDIOMS – **wet the baby's head** Brit. informal celebrate a baby's birth with a drink. **wet behind the ears** informal lacking experience; immature. **wet one's whistle** informal have a drink.

DERIVATIVES – **wetly** adverb **wetness** noun.

SYNONYMS – adjective **1** damp, drenched, moist, saturated, soaked.

COMBINATIONS – **wet blanket** informal a person who spoils other people's enjoyment through having a disapproving or unenthusiastic manner. **wet dream** an erotic dream that causes involuntary ejaculation of semen. **wet fly** an artificial fishing fly designed to sink below the surface of the water. **wet look** a shiny appearance possessed by a clothing fabric or achieved by applying gel to the hair. **wet nurse** chiefly historical a woman employed to suckle another woman's child. **wet rot** a brown fungus causing decay in moist timber.

weta /wetə/ > noun a large brown wingless insect with wood-boring larvae, found in New Zealand.

ORIGIN – Maori.

wether /wethər/ > noun a castrated ram.

wetland > noun (also **wetlands**) swampy or marshy land.

wetsuit > noun a close-fitting rubber garment covering the entire body, worn for warmth in water sports or diving.

we've > contraction we have.

whack informal > verb **1** strike forcefully with a sharp blow. **2** defeat heavily. **3** place or insert roughly or carelessly. **4** N. Amer. murder. > noun **1** a sharp or resounding blow. **2** a try or attempt. **3** Brit. a specified share of or contribution to something.

IDIOMS – **out of whack** chiefly N. Amer. & Austral./NZ not working. **top** (or **full**) **whack** chiefly Brit. the maximum price or rate.

whacked (also **whacked out**) > adjective informal **1** chiefly Brit. completely exhausted. **2** chiefly N. Amer. under the influence of drugs.

whacking > adjective Brit. informal very large.

whacko > adjective & noun (pl. **whackos**) variant spelling of **WACKO**.

whacky > adjective variant spelling of **WACKY**.

whale > noun (pl. same or **whales**) a very large marine mammal with a horizontal tail fin and a blowhole on top of the head for breathing.

WORDFINDER – baleen whales (with whalebone for feeding on plankton, as opposed to toothed whales), cetacean (a whale or related mammal, e.g. dolphin or porpoise), Cetus (constellation, the Whale), krill (shrimp-like crustaceans eaten by whales), pod (a group of whales), spermaceti (waxy substance in head of sperm whale); kinds of whale: beluga, blue, bottlenose, bowhead, fin whale, grey, humpback, killer whale or orca, minke, narwhal, pilot whale, right whale, rorqual, sei, sperm whale.

IDIOMS – **a whale of a** —— informal an exceedingly good example of something. **have a whale of a time** informal enjoy oneself very much.

COMBINATIONS – **whalebone 1** an elastic horny substance which grows as thin parallel plates in the upper jaw of some whales and is used by them to trap plankton. **2** strips of this substance, formerly used as stays in corsets and dresses.

whaler > noun **1** a whaling ship. **2** a seaman engaged in whaling.

whaling > noun the practice or industry of hunting and killing whales for their oil, meat, or whalebone.

wham informal > exclamation used to express the sound of a forcible impact or the idea of a sudden and dramatic occurrence. > verb (**whammed**, **whamming**) strike something forcefully.

whammy > noun (pl. **whammies**) informal **1** an event with a powerful and unpleasant effect. **2** chiefly US an evil or unlucky influence.

whanau /waanow/ > noun (pl. same) NZ an extended family or group of families living together in the same area.

ORIGIN – Maori.

whap > verb (**whapped**, **whapping**) & noun chiefly N. Amer. variant spelling of **WHOP**.

whare /worri/ > noun a Maori hut or house.

ORIGIN – Maori.

wharf /wawrf/ > noun (pl. **wharves** or **wharfs**) a level quayside area to which a ship may be moored to load and unload.

wharfie > noun Austral./NZ informal a dock labourer.

what > pronoun & determiner **1** asking for information specifying something. **2** (as pronoun) asking for repetition of something not heard or confirmation of something not understood. **3** (as pronoun) the thing or things that. **4** whatever. **5** used to emphasise something surprising or remarkable. > adverb **1** to what extent? **2** informal, dated used for emphasis or to invite agreement.

IDIOMS – **give someone what for** informal, chiefly Brit. punish or scold someone severely. **what for?** informal for what reason? **what with** because of.

whatever > pronoun & determiner used to emphasise a lack of restriction in referring to any thing, no matter what. > pronoun used for emphasis instead of 'what' in questions. > adverb **1** at all; of any kind: he had no help whatever. **2** informal no matter what happens.

whatnot > noun informal used to refer to an unidentified item or items that have something in common with items already named.

whatsit > noun informal a person or thing whose name one cannot recall, does not know, or does not wish to specify.

whatsoever > adverb at all: I had no doubt whatsoever. > determiner & pronoun archaic whatever.

wheal > noun variant spelling of **WEAL**[1].

wheat > noun a cereal widely grown in temperate countries, the grain of which is ground to make flour.

WORDFINDER – durum, einkorn, emmer, spelt (varieties of wheat), gluten (protein present in wheat grains).

ORIGIN – Old English, related to **WHITE**.

wheatear > noun a songbird with black and grey, buff, or white plumage and a white rump.

ORIGIN – apparently from **WHITE** + **ARSE**.

wheaten > adjective made of wheat.

wheatgerm > noun a nutritious foodstuff consisting of the extracted embryos of grains of wheat.

wheatgrass > noun another term for **COUCH**[2].

wheatmeal > noun flour made from wheat from which some of the bran and germ has been removed.

wheedle > verb employ endearments or flattery to persuade someone to do something.

DERIVATIVES – **wheedler** noun **wheedling** adjective.

ORIGIN – perhaps from German wedeln 'cringe, fawn'.

wheel > noun **1** a circular object that revolves on an axle, fixed below a vehicle to enable it to move over the ground or forming part of a machine. **2** something resembling a wheel or having a wheel as its essential part. **3** (**wheels**) informal a car. **4** an instance of wheeling; a turn or rotation. **5** a set of short lines concluding the stanza of a poem. > verb **1** push or pull (a vehicle with wheels). **2** carry in or on a vehicle with wheels. **3** fly or turn in a wide circle or curve. **4** turn round quickly to face another way. **5** (**wheel in** or **on** or **out**) informal produce (something that is unimpressive because it has been frequently seen or heard before).

WORDFINDER – felloes (outer rim of a wheel with spokes), flange (projecting rim on a railway wheel), hub, nave (centre of a wheel), sprocket (projecting tooth on a wheel).

IDIOMS – **wheel and deal** engage in commercial or political scheming. **the wheel of Fortune** the wheel which the goddess Fortune is fabled to turn as a symbol of random luck or change. **wheels**

within wheels secret or indirect influences affecting a complex situation.

COMBINATIONS – **wheelchair** a mobile wheeled chair for an invalid or disabled person. **wheel clamp** a device for immobilising an unlawfully parked car. **wheelhouse** a shelter for the person at the wheel of a boat or ship. **wheelspin** rotation of a vehicle's wheels without traction.

wheelbarrow > *noun* a small cart with a single wheel at the front and two supporting legs and two handles at the rear, used for carrying loads in building or gardening.

wheelbase > *noun* the distance between the front and rear axles of a vehicle.

wheeler > *noun* a vehicle having a specified number of wheels: *a three-wheeler*.

wheeler-dealer (also **wheeler and dealer**) > *noun* a person who engages in commercial or political scheming.

DERIVATIVES – **wheeler-dealing** noun.

wheelie > *noun* informal a manoeuvre whereby a bicycle or motorcycle is ridden for a short distance with the front wheel raised off the ground.

wheelie bin (also **wheely bin**) > *noun* Brit. informal a large refuse bin set on wheels.

wheelwright > *noun* chiefly historical a person who makes or repairs wooden wheels.

wheeze > *verb* **1** breathe with a whistling or rattling sound in the chest, as a result of obstruction in the air passages. **2** (of a device) make an irregular rattling or spluttering sound. > *noun* **1** a sound of a person wheezing. **2** Brit. informal a clever or amusing scheme or trick.

DERIVATIVES – **wheezily** adverb **wheeziness** noun **wheezy** adjective.

ORIGIN – probably from Old Norse *hvæsa* 'to hiss'.

whelk > *noun* a predatory marine mollusc with a heavy pointed spiral shell.

whelp /welp/ > *noun* chiefly archaic **1** a puppy. **2** derogatory a boy or young man. > *verb* give birth to (a puppy).

when > *adverb* **1** at what time? **2** how soon? **3** in what circumstances? **4** at which time or in which situation. > *conjunction* **1** at or during the time that. **2** at any time that; whenever. **3** after which; and just then. **4** in view of the fact that; considering that. **5** although; whereas.

whence (also **from whence**) > *adverb* formal or archaic **1** from what place or source? **2** from which; from where. **3** to the place from which. **4** as a consequence of which.

whenever > *conjunction* **1** at whatever time; on whatever occasion. **2** every time that. > *adverb* used for emphasis instead of 'when' in questions.

whensoever > *conjunction & adverb* formal word for **WHENEVER**.

where > *adverb* **1** in or to what place or position? **2** in what direction or respect? **3** at, in, or to which. **4** the place or situation in which. **5** in or to a place or situation in which.

whereabouts > *adverb* where or approximately where? > *noun* (treated as sing. or pl.) the place where someone or something is.

whereafter > *adverb* formal after which.

whereas > *conjunction* **1** in contrast or comparison with the fact that. **2** taking into consideration the fact that.

whereat > *adverb & conjunction* archaic or formal at which.

whereby > *adverb* by which.

wherefore archaic > *adverb* for what reason? > *adverb & conjunction* as a result of which.

wherefrom > *adverb* archaic from which or from where.

wherein > *adverb* formal **1** in which. **2** in what place or respect?

whereof > *adverb* formal of what or which.

whereon > *adverb* archaic on which.

wheresoever > *adverb & conjunction* formal word for **WHEREVER**.

whereto > *adverb* archaic or formal to which.

whereupon > *conjunction* immediately after which.

wherever > *adverb* **1** in or to whatever place. **2** used for emphasis instead of 'where' in questions. > *conjunction* in every case when.

wherewith > *adverb* formal or archaic with or by which.

wherewithal /**wair**withawl/ > *noun* the money or other resources needed for a particular purpose.

wherry /**werr**i/ > *noun* (pl. **wherries**) **1** a light rowing boat used chiefly for carrying passengers. **2** Brit. a large light barge.

whet /wet/ > *verb* (**whetted**, **whetting**) **1** sharpen the blade of (a tool or weapon). **2** excite or stimulate (someone's desire, interest, or appetite).

whether > *conjunction* **1** expressing a doubt or choice between alternatives. **2** expressing an enquiry or investigation. **3** indicating that a statement applies whichever of the alternatives mentioned is the case.

USAGE – **whether** and **if** are more or less interchangeable in sentences like *I'll see whether he left an address* and *I'll see if he left an address*, although **whether** is more formal and more suitable for written use.

whetstone > *noun* a fine-grained stone used for sharpening cutting tools.

whey /way/ > *noun* the watery part of milk that remains after the formation of curds.

COMBINATIONS – **whey-faced** (of a person) pale.

which > *pronoun & determiner* **1** asking for information specifying one or more people or things from a definite set. **2** used to refer to something previously mentioned when introducing a clause giving further information.

whichever > *determiner & pronoun* **1** used to emphasise a lack of restriction in selecting one of a definite set of alternatives. **2** regardless of which.

whicker > *verb* (of a horse) give a soft breathy whinny. > *noun* a sound of this type.

whiff > *noun* **1** a smell that is smelt only briefly or faintly. **2** Brit. informal an unpleasant smell. **3** a trace or hint of something bad or exciting. **4** a puff or breath of air or smoke. > *verb* **1** get a brief or faint smell of. **2** Brit. informal give off an unpleasant smell.

whiffle > *verb* **1** (of the wind) blow lightly. **2** blow or move with a puff of air. > *noun* a slight movement of air.

whiffy > *adjective* (**whiffier**, **whiffiest**) Brit. informal having an unpleasant smell.

Whig /wig/ > *noun* **1** a member of the British reforming party that sought the supremacy of Parliament, succeeded in the 19th century by the Liberal Party. **2** a supporter of the American Revolution. **3** a 17th-century Scottish Presbyterian.

DERIVATIVES – **Whiggery** noun **Whiggish** adjective **Whiggism** noun.

wordpower facts
Whig

Like the related word **Tory**, **Whig** started life with negative connotations before becoming the accepted name for a member of one of the two major English (and later British) political parties and then being replaced by another word. It is probably a shortening of the Scots term *whiggamore*, which is thought to have been formed from *whig* 'to drive' and **mare**[1]. The first **Whiggamores** or **Whigs** were the Covenanters, Scottish Presbyterians who fought for the belief that the Church should be governed by elected elders rather than bishops. From about 1679 the term was applied to those who opposed the right of the future James II (James VII of Scotland, a Catholic) to succeed to the throne; those who supported James were called *Tories*. After James II had become king and been deposed, **Whig** and **Tory** came to denote members of the two main parliamentary parties. In the mid 19th century **Whig** was replaced by **Liberal**, and unlike **Tory** is rarely used today in a political context.

while > *noun* **1** (**a while**) a period of time. **2** (**a while**) for some time. **3** (**the while**) at the same time; meanwhile. **4** (**the while**) literary during the time that. > *conjunction* **1** at the same time as. **2** whereas (indicating a contrast). **3** although. > *adverb* during which. > *verb* (**while time away**) pass time in a leisurely manner.

IDIOMS – **worth while** (or **worth one's while**) worth the time or effort spent.

whilst > *conjunction & adverb* chiefly Brit. while.

whim > *noun* a sudden desire or change of mind.

SYNONYMS – caprice, fancy, impulse, urge.

whimbrel /ˈwimbrəl/ > *noun* a small curlew with a striped crown and a trilling call.

ORIGIN – from **WHIMPER** or dialect *whimp* (referring to the bird's call).

whimper > *verb* make a series of low, feeble sounds expressive of fear, pain, or discontent. > *noun* a whimpering sound.

DERIVATIVES – **whimpering** *noun*.

SYNONYMS – cry, groan, moan, whine.

whimsical > *adjective* **1** playfully quaint or fanciful. **2** acting or behaving in a fickle or capricious manner.

DERIVATIVES – **whimsicality** *noun* **whimsically** *adverb*.

whimsy (also **whimsey**) > *noun* (pl. **whimsies** or **whimseys**) **1** playfully quaint or fanciful behaviour or humour. **2** a thing that is fanciful or odd. **3** a whim.

whin > *noun* chiefly N. English gorse.

whinchat /ˈwinchat/ > *noun* a small songbird related to the stonechat, with a brown back and orange-buff underparts.

whine > *noun* **1** a long, high-pitched complaining cry. **2** a long, high-pitched unpleasant sound. **3** a feeble or petulant complaint. > *verb* **1** give or make a whine. **2** complain in a feeble or petulant way.

DERIVATIVES – **whiner** *noun* **whining** *noun* **whiny** *adjective*.

ORIGIN – Old English, 'whistle through the air'; related to **WHINGE**.

whinge* /winj/ Brit. informal > *verb* (**whinged**, **whingeing**) complain persistently and peevishly. > *noun* an act of whingeing.

DERIVATIVES – **whinger** *noun*.

*SPELLING – remember the *h*: w*h*inge.

whinny > *noun* (pl. **whinnies**) a gentle, high-pitched neigh made by a horse. > *verb* (**whinnies**, **whinnied**) make such a sound.

whip > *noun* **1** a strip of leather or length of cord fastened to a handle, used for beating a person or urging on an animal. **2** an official of a political party appointed to enforce discipline among its members in parliament. **3** Brit. a written notice from such an official requesting attendance for voting. **4** a dessert made from cream or eggs beaten into a light fluffy mass. **5** a violent striking or beating movement. **6** a slender, unbranched shoot or plant. > *verb* (**whipped**, **whipping**) **1** beat with a whip. **2** (of a flexible object or rain or wind) strike or beat violently. **3** move or take out fast or suddenly. **4** beat (cream, eggs, etc.) into a froth. **5** Brit. informal steal.

WORDFINDER – cat-o'-nine-tails (*rope whip with knotted cords*), flagellation (*whipping for religious punishment or sexual gratification*), sjambok (*South African whip, originally of rhinoceros hide*).

IDIOMS – **the whip hand** a position of power or control. **whip up 1** make or prepare (something) very quickly. **2** deliberately excite or provoke (someone). **3** stimulate (a particular feeling).

DERIVATIVES – **whipping** *noun*.

SYNONYMS – *verb* **1** beat, flagellate, flog, lash.

COMBINATIONS – **whipping boy** a person who is blamed or punished for the faults or incompetence of others. [ORIGIN – first denoting a boy educated with a young prince and punished instead of him.]

ORIGIN – probably from Low German and Dutch *wippen* 'swing, leap, dance'.

whipcord > *noun* **1** thin, tough, tightly twisted cord used for making the flexible end part of whips. **2** a closely woven ribbed worsted fabric.

whiplash > *noun* **1** the lashing action of a whip. **2** the flexible part of a whip. **3** injury to the tissues of the neck caused by a severe jerk to the head. > *verb* jerk suddenly.

whippersnapper > *noun* informal a young and inexperienced person who is presumptuous or overconfident.

whippet > *noun* a small, slender breed of dog, bred for racing.

ORIGIN – partly from obsolete *whippet* 'move briskly'.

whippoorwill /ˈwipərwill/ > *noun* a North and Central American nightjar with a distinctive call.

whippy > *adjective* flexible; springy.

whip-round > *noun* Brit. informal a collection of contributions of money for a particular purpose.

whipsaw > *noun* a saw with a narrow blade and a handle at both ends. > *verb* (past participle **whipsawn** or **whipsawed**) N. Amer. **1** cut with a whipsaw. **2** informal subject to two difficult situations or opposing pressures at the same time.

whirl > *verb* **1** move or cause to move rapidly round and round. **2** (of the head or mind) seem to spin round. > *noun* **1** a rapid movement round and round. **2** frantic activity: *the mad social whirl*. **3** a sweet or biscuit with a spiral shape.

IDIOMS – **give something a whirl** informal give something a try. **in a whirl** in a state of confusion.

DERIVATIVES – **whirling** *adjective*.

SYNONYMS – *verb* **1** circle, rotate, revolve. **2** reel, swim. *noun* **1** flurry, swirl. **2** bustle, flurry, rush.

whirligig > *noun* **1** a toy that spins round, such as a top or windmill. **2** a roundabout for children to play on.

COMBINATIONS – **whirligig beetle** a small black water beetle which typically swims rapidly in circles on the surface.

ORIGIN – from **WHIRL** + obsolete *gig* 'toy for whipping'.

whirlpool > *noun* **1** a quickly rotating mass of water in a river or sea into which objects may be drawn. **2** (also **whirlpool bath**) a heated pool in which hot aerated water is continuously circulated.

whirlwind > *noun* **1** a column of air moving rapidly round and round in a cylindrical or funnel shape. **2** a very energetic or tumultuous person or process. **3** (before another noun) very rapid and unexpected: *a whirlwind romance*.

IDIOMS – (**sow the wind and**) **reap the whirlwind** suffer serious consequences as a result of one's actions. [ORIGIN – with biblical allusion to the Book of Hosea, chapter 8.]

whirr /wur/ (also **whir**) > *verb* (**whirred**, **whirring**) (of something rapidly rotating or moving to and fro) make a low, continuous, regular sound. > *noun* a whirring sound.

whisk > *verb* **1** beat (a substance) with a light, rapid movement. **2** move or take suddenly, quickly, and lightly. > *noun* **1** a utensil for whipping eggs or cream. **2** a bunch of grass, twigs, or bristles for flicking away dust or flies. **3** a brief, rapid action or movement.

whisker > *noun* **1** a long projecting hair or bristle growing from the face or snout of an animal. **2** (**whiskers**) the hair growing on a man's face. **3** (**a whisker**) informal a very small amount.

DERIVATIVES – **whiskered** *adjective* **whiskery** *adjective*.

wordpower facts

Whisky

Like the names for several other spirits, **whisky** means literally 'water of life'. It is a shortening of the obsolete form *whiskybae*, itself a variant of *usquebaugh*, which comes from Irish and Scottish Gaelic *uisge beatha*. Other 'waters of life' are **aqua vitae** (Latin), **aquavit** (the same word, but filtered through Scandinavian languages), and **eau de vie** (French); **usquebaugh**, the root of **whisky**, is sometimes used as a synonym for the drink. Similarly, **vodka** comes from the Russian word for 'water', *voda*.

whisky* (also Irish & US **whiskey**) > *noun* (pl.

whiskies) a spirit distilled from malted grain, especially barley or rye.

*SPELLING – Scotch whis*ky*, but Irish whis*key*. In America the spelling tends to be whis*key*.

whisper > *verb* **1** speak very softly using one's breath rather than one's throat. **2** literary rustle or murmur softly. > *noun* **1** a whispered word or phrase, or a whispering tone of voice. **2** literary a soft rustling or murmuring sound. **3** a rumour or piece of gossip. **4** a slight trace; a hint.

DERIVATIVES – **whisperer** *noun* **whispery** *adjective*.

COMBINATIONS – **whispering campaign** a systematic circulation of a rumour, especially in order to damage someone's reputation.

whist /wist/ > *noun* a card game in which points are scored according to the number of tricks won.

ORIGIN – perhaps from **WHISK** (the original form), with reference to whisking away the tricks.

whistle > *noun* **1** a clear, high-pitched sound made by forcing breath through a small hole between partly closed lips, or between one's teeth. **2** any similar sound. **3** an instrument used to produce such a sound. > *verb* **1** emit or produce a whistle. **2** produce (a tune) in such a way. **3** move rapidly through the air or a narrow opening with a whistling sound. **4** blow a whistle. **5** (**whistle for**) wish for or expect (something) in vain.

IDIOMS – **blow the whistle on** informal bring (an illicit activity) to an end by informing on the person responsible. (**as**) **clean as a whistle** extremely clean or clear. **whistle down the wind** let go or abandon (something).

DERIVATIVES – **whistler** *noun*.

COMBINATIONS – **whistle-blower** informal a person who informs on someone engaged in an illicit activity. **whistle-stop** very fast and with only brief pauses: *a whistle-stop tour.* [ORIGIN – first in American use, with reference to a small, unimportant town on a railway at which trains would stop only if a signal was given on a whistle.]

whit /wit/ > *noun* a very small part or amount.

white > *adjective* **1** of the colour of milk or fresh snow, due to the reflection of all visible rays of light. **2** (of a person) very pale. **3** Brit. (of coffee or tea) served with milk or cream. **4** (of food such as bread or rice) light in colour through having been refined. **5** relating to or denoting a human group having light-coloured skin, especially of European ancestry. **6** morally or spiritually pure. **7** (of wine) made from white grapes, or dark grapes with the skins removed, and having a yellowish colour.

> *noun* **1** white colour or pigment. **2** (also **whites**) white clothes or material. **3** the visible pale part of the eyeball around the iris. **4** the outer part which surrounds the yolk of an egg; the albumen. **5** a member of a light-skinned people. **6** a white or cream butterfly. > *verb* (**white out**) **1** turn (something) white. **2** obliterate (a mistake) with white correction fluid. **3** lose colour vision as a prelude to losing consciousness.

WORDFINDER – *shades of white:* alabaster, ivory, lily-white, milk-white, off-white, oyster white, pearl, snow-white; albino (*person or animal with white skin and hair as congenital abnormality*).

IDIOMS – **bleed white** drain of wealth or resources. **whited sepulchre** literary a hypocrite. [ORIGIN – with biblical allusion to the Gospel of Matthew, chapter 23.]

DERIVATIVES – **whitely** *adverb* **whiteness** *noun* **whitish** *adjective*.

COMBINATIONS – **white admiral** a butterfly with dark brown wings bearing a broad white band. **white ant** a termite. **white belt** a white belt worn by a beginner in judo or karate. **whiteboard** a wipeable board with a white surface used for teaching or presentations. **white cell** a leucocyte. **white Christmas** a Christmas during which there is snow on the ground. **white-collar** relating to the work done or people who work in an office or other professional environment. **white dwarf** Astronomy a small, very dense star that is typically the size of a planet. **white elephant** a possession that is useless or troublesome. [ORIGIN – from the story that the kings of Siam gave such animals to courtiers they disliked, in order to ruin the recipient by the great expense of maintaining the animal.] **white feather** a white feather given to someone as a sign that they are considered a coward. [ORIGIN – with reference to a white feather in the tail of a game bird, regarded as a mark of bad breeding.] **white flag** a white flag or cloth used as a symbol of surrender, truce, or a desire to negotiate. **white gold** a silver-coloured alloy of gold with another metal. **white goods** large domestic electrical goods such as refrigerators and washing machines. Compare with *brown goods.* **white heat** the temperature or state of something that is so hot that it emits white light. **white hope** (also **great white hope**) a person expected to bring much success to a team or organisation. **white horses** white-crested waves at sea. **white-hot** so hot as to glow white. **white knight** a person or thing that comes to someone's aid. **white-knuckle** (especially of a fairground ride) causing great nervous excitement. **white lie** a harmless lie told to avoid hurting someone's feelings. **white light** apparently colourless light containing all the wavelengths of the visible spectrum at equal intensity. **white magic** magic used only for good purposes. **white meat** pale meat such as poultry, veal, and rabbit. **white metal** a white or silvery alloy. **white noise** Physics noise containing many frequencies with equal intensities. **White Paper** (in the UK) a government report giving information or proposals on an issue. **white rose** the emblem of Yorkshire or the House of York. **white sauce** a sauce consisting of flour blended and cooked with butter and milk or stock. **white slave** a woman tricked or forced into prostitution in a foreign country. **white spirit** Brit. a volatile colourless liquid distilled from petroleum, used as a paint thinner and solvent. **white tie 1** a white bow tie worn by men as part of full evening dress. **2** full evening dress. **white trash** N. Amer. derogatory poor white people. **white-van man** Brit. informal an aggressive male driver of a delivery or workman's van (typically white in colour). **white water** a fast, shallow stretch of water in a river. **white wedding** Brit. a traditional wedding at which the bride wears a formal white dress. **white witch** a person who practises witchcraft for good purposes.

ORIGIN – Old English, related to **WHEAT**.

whitebait > *noun* the small silvery-white young of herrings, sprats, and similar marine fish as food.

whitebeam > *noun* a tree related to the rowan, with red berries and hairy oval leaves that are white underneath.

whitefish > *noun* a mainly freshwater fish of the salmon family, used as food.

whitefly > *noun* a minute winged bug covered with powdery white wax, which damages plants by feeding on sap and coating them with honeydew.

whitehead > *noun* informal a pale or white-topped pustule on the skin.

whiten > *verb* make or become white.

DERIVATIVES – **whitener** *noun*.

white-out > *noun* **1** a dense blizzard. **2** a weather condition in which the features and horizon of snow-covered country are indistinguishable due to uniform light diffusion.

White Russian > *noun* **1** a Belorussian. **2** an opponent of the Bolsheviks during the Russian Civil War. > *adjective* relating to White Russians.

whitethroat > *noun* a migratory warbler with a grey head and white throat.

whitewash > *noun* **1** a solution of lime and water or of whiting, size, and water, used for painting walls white. **2** a deliberate concealment of someone's mistakes or faults. **3** a victory by the same side in every game of a series. > *verb* **1** paint with whitewash. **2** conceal (mistakes or faults). **3** defeat with a whitewash.

SYNONYMS – *noun* **2** camouflage, cover-up, disguise. *verb* **2** camouflage, conceal, cover up, disguise, sweep under the carpet.

whitey > *noun* (pl. **whiteys**) informal, derogatory a white person.

whither archaic or literary > *adverb* **1** to what place or state? **2** what is the likely future of? **3** to which (with reference to a place). **4** to whatever place.

whiting¹ /wītíng/ > *noun* (pl. same) a slender-bodied marine fish with edible white flesh.

whiting² /wītíng/ > *noun* ground chalk used for purposes such as whitewashing and cleaning metal plate.

whitlow /witlō/ > *noun* an abscess in the soft tissue near a fingernail or toenail.
ORIGIN – possibly from **WHITE** + **FLAW**.

Whitsun /witsən/ (also **Whitsuntide**) > *noun* the weekend or week including Whit Sunday.
ORIGIN – from **WHIT SUNDAY**, reduced as if from *Whitsun Day*.

Whit Sunday > *noun* the seventh Sunday after Easter, a Christian festival commemorating the descent of the Holy Spirit at Pentecost (Acts, chapter 2).
ORIGIN – Old English, 'white Sunday', probably with reference to the white robes of those newly baptised at Pentecost.

whittle > *verb* **1** carve (wood) by repeatedly cutting small slices from it. **2** make by whittling. **3** (**whittle away** or **down**) reduce (something) by degrees.
SYNONYMS – **3** (**whittle away** or **down**) eat away, erode, wear away.
ORIGIN – from dialect *whittle* 'knife'.

whiz-bang (also **whizz-bang**) > *adjective* informal, chiefly N. Amer. impressively lively and fast-paced.

whizz (also **whiz**) > *verb* (**whizzed**, **whizzing**) **1** move quickly through the air with a whistling or rushing sound. **2** move or cause to move or go fast. **3** (**whizz through**) do or deal with quickly. > *noun* **1** a whizzing sound. **2** informal a fast movement or brief journey. **3** (also **wiz**) informal a person who is extremely clever at something. [ORIGIN – influenced by **WIZARD**.] **4** Brit. informal amphetamines.
DERIVATIVES – **whizzy** *adjective*.

whizz-kid (also **whiz-kid**) > *noun* informal a young person who is very successful or highly skilled.

WHO > *abbreviation* World Health Organization.

who > *pronoun* **1** what or which person or people? **2** introducing a clause giving further information about a person or people previously mentioned.
USAGE – strictly, **who** should be used as the subject of a verb (*who decided this?*) and

whom as the object of a verb or preposition (*to whom do you wish to speak?*); however, in spoken and informal English **who** is often used instead of **whom**, as in *who should we support?*, and most people consider this to be acceptable.

whoa /wō/ (also **wo**) > *exclamation* used as a command to a horse to stop or slow down.

who'd > *contraction* **1** who had. **2** who would.

whodunnit (US **whodunit**) > *noun* informal a story or play about a murder in which the identity of the murderer is not revealed until the end.

whoever > *pronoun* **1** the person or people who; any person who. **2** regardless of who. **3** used for emphasis instead of 'who' in questions.

whole > *adjective* **1** complete; entire. **2** emphasising a large extent or number: *a whole range of issues*. **3** in an unbroken or undamaged state. > *noun* **1** a thing that is complete in itself. **2** (**the whole**) all of something. > *adverb* informal emphasising the novelty or distinctness of something: *a whole new meaning*.
WORDFINDER – holistic (*treating the whole person, not just the part affected by disease*).
IDIOMS – **on the whole** taking everything into account; in general. **the whole nine yards** informal, chiefly N. Amer. everything possible or available.
DERIVATIVES – **wholeness** *noun*.
COMBINATIONS – **whole number** a number without fractions; an integer.

wholefood (also **wholefoods**) > *noun* Brit. food that has been minimally processed and is free from additives.

wholehearted > *adjective* completely sincere and committed.
DERIVATIVES – **wholeheartedly** *adverb*.

wholemeal > *adjective* Brit. (of flour or bread) made from wholewheat, including the husk.

wholesale > *noun* the selling of goods in large quantities to be retailed by others. > *adverb* **1** being sold in such a way. **2** on a large scale. > *adjective* done on a large scale; extensive. > *verb* sell (goods) wholesale.
DERIVATIVES – **wholesaler** *noun*.
SYNONYMS – *adjective* extensive, large-scale, wide-ranging, widespread.

wholesome > *adjective* conducive to or promoting good health and physical or moral well-being.
DERIVATIVES – **wholesomely** *adverb* **wholesomeness** *noun*.

wholewheat > *noun* whole grains of wheat including the husk.

wholly* /hōlli/ > *adverb* entirely; fully.
***SPELLING** – two *l*s, no *e*: whol*ly*, not *-ely*.

whom > *pronoun* used instead of 'who' as the object of a verb or preposition.

USAGE – on the use of **who** and **whom**, see the note at **WHO**.

whomever > *pronoun* chiefly formal used instead of 'whoever' as the object of a verb or preposition.

whomp /womp/ informal > *verb* **1** strike heavily; thump. **2** (**whomp up**) N. Amer. produce quickly. > *noun* a thump.

whomsoever > *relative pronoun* formal used instead of 'whosoever' as the object of a verb or preposition.

whoomph /woomf/ (also **whoomp** /woomp/) > *noun* a loud muffled sound.

whoop /hoop, woop/ > *noun* **1** a loud cry of joy or excitement. **2** a long, rasping indrawn breath. > *verb* give or make a whoop.
IDIOMS – **whoop it up** informal **1** enjoy oneself or celebrate unrestrainedly. **2** N. Amer. create a stir.
COMBINATIONS – **whooping cough** /hooping/ a contagious bacterial disease chiefly affecting children, characterised by convulsive coughs followed by a whoop.

whoopee informal > *exclamation* /woopee/ expressing wild excitement or joy. > *noun* /woopee/ wild revelry.
IDIOMS – **make whoopee 1** celebrate wildly. **2** have sexual intercourse.
COMBINATIONS – **whoopee cushion** a rubber cushion that makes a sound like the breaking of wind when sat on.

whooper swan /hoopər/ > *noun* a large swan with a black and yellow bill and a loud trumpeting call, breeding in northern Eurasia and Greenland.

whoops (also **whoops-a-daisy**) > *exclamation* informal used to express mild dismay.
ORIGIN – probably from **UPSY-DAISY**.

whoosh /woosh/ (also **woosh**) > *verb* move quickly or suddenly and with a rushing sound. > *noun* a whooshing movement.

whop /wop/ (chiefly N. Amer. also **whap**) informal > *verb* (**whopped**, **whopping**) hit hard. > *noun* a heavy blow or its sound.
ORIGIN – from dialect *wap* 'strike'.

whopper > *noun* informal **1** a thing that is extremely large. **2** a gross or blatant lie.

whopping > *adjective* informal extremely large.

whore /hor/ > *noun* derogatory a prostitute or promiscuous woman. > *verb* **1** work as a prostitute. **2** use the services of prostitutes.
DERIVATIVES – **whorish** *adjective*.
COMBINATIONS – **whorehouse** a brothel.

whorl /worl, wurl/ > *noun* **1** Zoology each of the convolutions in the shell of a mollusc. **2** Botany a set of leaves, flowers, or branches springing from a stem at the same level and encircling it. **3** a complete circle in a fingerprint.
DERIVATIVES – **whorled** *adjective*.
ORIGIN – apparently from **WHIRL**.

whortleberry /**wur**t'lbəri, -beri/ > *noun* a bilberry.

who's > *contraction* 1 who is. 2 who has.

USAGE – do not confuse **who's** with **whose**; **who's** is a contraction of **who is** or **who has**, while **whose** is used in questions such as *whose is this?* and *whose turn is it?*

whose > *possessive determiner & pronoun* 1 belonging to or associated with which person. 2 of whom or which.

whosesoever > *relative pronoun & determiner* formal whoever's.

whosever > *relative pronoun & determiner* belonging to or associated with whichever person; whoever's.

whosoever > *pronoun* formal term for **WHOEVER**.

whump /wump, wŏŏmp/ > *noun* a dull thud. > *verb* make a whump.

whup /wup/ > *verb* (**whupped, whupping**) informal, chiefly N. Amer. beat; thrash.

why > *adverb* 1 for what reason or purpose? 2 (with reference to a reason) on account of which; for which. 3 the reason for which. > *exclamation* 1 expressing surprise or indignation. 2 used to add emphasis to a response. > *noun* (pl. **whys**) a reason or explanation.

WI > *abbreviation* 1 West Indies. 2 Wisconsin. 3 Brit. Women's Institute.

wibble > *verb* informal 1 wobble. 2 Brit. speak or write at length.

DERIVATIVES – **wibbly** *adjective*.

ORIGIN – from the reduplication *wibble-wobble*; sense 2 is perhaps a different word and influenced by **DRIVEL**.

Wicca /**wikkə**/ > *noun* a modern religious cult claiming its origins in pre-Christian pagan religions.

DERIVATIVES – **Wiccan** *adjective & noun*.

ORIGIN – from Old English *wicca* 'witch'.

wick¹ > *noun* 1 a strip of porous material up which liquid fuel is drawn by capillary action to the flame in a candle, lamp, or lighter. 2 Medicine a gauze strip inserted in a wound to drain it. > *verb* absorb or draw off (liquid) by capillary action.

IDIOMS – **get on someone's wick** Brit. informal annoy someone.

wick² > *noun* (in place names) a town, hamlet, or district.

ORIGIN – Old English, 'dwelling place', probably from Latin *vicus* 'street, village'.

wicked > *adjective* 1 evil or morally wrong. 2 playfully mischievous. 3 informal excellent; wonderful.

DERIVATIVES – **wickedly** *adverb* **wickedness** *noun*.

SYNONYMS – 1 bad, evil, immoral, sinful, wrongful. 2 impish, rascally, roguish.

ANTONYMS – 1 good, virtuous.

ORIGIN – probably from Old English *wicca* 'witch'.

wicker > *noun* pliable twigs, typically of willow, plaited or woven to make items such as furniture and baskets.

DERIVATIVES – **wickerwork** *noun*.

ORIGIN – Scandinavian.

wicket > *noun* 1 Cricket each of the sets of three stumps with two bails across the top at either end of the pitch, defended by a batsman. 2 a small door or gate, especially one beside or in a larger one.

IDIOMS – **at the wicket** Cricket 1 batting. 2 by the wicketkeeper. **sticky wicket** 1 Cricket a pitch that has been drying after rain and is difficult to bat on. 2 informal a tricky or awkward situation.

ORIGIN – Old French *wiket*; probably related to Old Norse *víkja* 'to turn, move'.

wicketkeeper > *noun* Cricket a fielder stationed close behind a batsman's wicket.

widdershins /**widd**ərshinz/ (also **withershins**) > *adverb* chiefly Scottish in a direction contrary to the sun's course (or anticlockwise), considered as unlucky.

ORIGIN – High German *widersinnes*, from *wider* 'against' + *sin* 'direction'; the second element was associated with Scots *sin* 'sun'.

widdle informal > *verb* urinate. > *noun* an act of urinating.

wide > *adjective* (**wider, widest**) 1 of great or more than average width. 2 (after a measurement and in questions) from side to side. 3 open to the full extent. 4 including a great variety of people or things. 5 spread among a large number or over a large area. 6 extending over the whole of: *industry-wide*. 7 at a considerable or specified distance from a point or mark. 8 (especially in football) at or near the side of the field. > *adverb* 1 to the full extent. 2 far from a particular point or mark. 3 (especially in football) at or near the side of the field. > *noun* (also **wide ball**) Cricket a ball that is judged to be too wide of the stumps for the batsman to play.

IDIOMS – **wide awake** fully awake. **wide of the mark** 1 a long way from an intended target. 2 inaccurate. **wide open** 1 (of a contest) of which the outcome is not predictable. 2 vulnerable to attack.

DERIVATIVES – **widely** *adverb* **wideness** *noun* **widish** *adjective*.

SYNONYMS – *adjective* 1 broad, expansive, extensive, outspread, spacious.

COMBINATIONS – **wide-angle** (of a lens) having a short focal length and hence a field covering a wide angle. **wide boy** Brit. informal a man involved in petty criminal activities. **wide-eyed** 1 having one's eyes wide open in amazement. 2 inexperienced; innocent. **widescreen** (of a cinema or television screen) presenting a wide field of vision in relation to height.

ORIGIN – Old English *wīd* 'spacious, extensive', *wīde* 'over a large area'.

widen > *verb* make or become wider.

DERIVATIVES – **widener** *noun*.

SYNONYMS – broaden, dilate, expand, extend.

widespread > *adjective* spread among a large number or over a large area.

widgeon > *noun* variant spelling of **WIGEON**.

widget /**wi**jit/ > *noun* informal a small gadget or mechanical device.

widow > *noun* 1 a woman who has lost her husband by death and has not married again. 2 humorous a woman whose husband is often away participating in a specified sport or activity: *a golf widow*. 3 Printing a last word or short last line of a paragraph falling at the top of a page or column. > *verb* (**be widowed**) become a widow or widower.

WORDFINDER – dowager (*widow with title from her late husband*), dower (*widow's share of her husband's estate*).

COMBINATIONS – **widow's mite** a small monetary contribution from someone who is poor. [ORIGIN – with biblical allusion to the Gospel of Mark, chapter 12.] **widow's peak** a V-shaped growth of hair towards the centre of the forehead. **widow's weeds** black clothes worn by a widow in mourning. [ORIGIN – *weeds* is used in the now obsolete sense 'garments'.]

ORIGIN – Old English, from a root meaning 'be empty'.

widower > *noun* a man who has lost his wife by death and has not married again.

widowhood > *noun* the state or period of being a widow or widower.

width /witth, width/ > *noun* 1 the measurement or extent of something from side to side; the lesser of two or the least of three dimensions of a body. 2 a piece of something at its full extent from side to side. 3 wide range or extent.

widthways (also **widthwise**) > *adverb* in a direction parallel with a thing's width.

wield* /weeld/ > *verb* 1 hold and use (a weapon or tool). 2 have and be able to use (power or influence).

DERIVATIVES – **wielder** *noun*.

*****SPELLING – remember, the usual rule is *i* before *e* except after *c*: wield.

SYNONYMS – 1 brandish, flourish, use. 2 command, exercise, exert.

ORIGIN – Old English, 'govern, subdue, direct'.

Wiener schnitzel /**vee**nər shnits'l/ > *noun* a thin slice of veal coated with bread and fried.

ORIGIN – German, 'Vienna cutlet'.

wife > *noun* (pl. **wives**) 1 a married woman considered in relation to her husband. 2 archaic or dialect a woman, especially an old or uneducated one.

WORDFINDER – polygyny (*the practice of having more than one wife*), uxoricide (*murder* of one's wife), uxorious (greatly fond of one's wife).

DERIVATIVES – **wifely** adjective.

ORIGIN – Old English, 'woman'.

wig¹ > noun a covering for the head made of real or artificial hair.

DERIVATIVES – **wigged** adjective.

ORIGIN – shortening of PERIWIG.

wig² > verb (**wigged**, **wigging**) informal **1** Brit. dated rebuke severely. **2** (**wig out**) chiefly N. Amer. become deliriously excited.

DERIVATIVES – **wigging** noun.

ORIGIN – apparently from WIG¹, perhaps from *bigwig* and associated with a rebuke given by a person in authority.

wigeon /ˈwiʒən/ (also **widgeon**) > noun a duck with mainly reddish-brown and grey plumage, the male having a whistling call.

wiggle > verb move or cause to move with short movements up and down or from side to side. > noun a wiggling movement.

DERIVATIVES – **wiggler** noun **wiggly** (**wigglier**, **wiggliest**) adjective.

SYNONYMS – verb jiggle, wobble.

ORIGIN – Low German and Dutch *wiggelen*.

wigwam > noun a dome-shaped or conical dwelling made by fastening mats, skins, or bark over a framework of poles (as used formerly by some North American Indian peoples).

ORIGIN – Algonquian, from a word meaning 'their house'.

wild > adjective **1** (of animals or plants) living or growing in the natural environment; not domesticated or cultivated. **2** (of people) not civilised. **3** (of scenery or a region) desolate-looking and remote. **4** out of control; unrestrained. **5** informal very enthusiastic or excited. **6** informal very angry. **7** (of looks, appearance, etc.) indicating distraction. > noun **1** (**the wild**) a natural state or uncultivated or uninhabited region. **2** (**the wilds**) a remote area.

IDIOMS – **run wild** grow or behave without restraint or discipline.

DERIVATIVES – **wildly** adverb **wildness** noun.

SYNONYMS – adjective **1** uncultivated, undomesticated, untamed. **2** primitive, savage, uncivilised. **4** uncontrolled, undisciplined, unrestrained, wayward.

COMBINATIONS – **wild card 1** a playing card that can have any value, suit, colour, or other property in a game at the discretion of the player holding it. **2** a person or thing whose qualities are uncertain. **3** Computing a character that will match any character or sequence of characters in a search. **4** an opportunity to enter a sports competition without taking part in qualifying matches or being ranked at a particular level. **wild cherry** a tall woodland cherry tree bearing white blossom, the ancestor of cultivated sweet cherries. **wild goose chase** a foolish and hopeless search for or pursuit of something unattainable. **wild oat** a grass which is related to the cultivated oat and is found as a weed of other cereals. **wild rice** a tall aquatic American grass with edible grains, related to rice. **wild silk** coarse silk produced by wild silkworms, especially tussore.

wildcat > noun **1** (usu. **wild cat**) a small Eurasian and African cat, typically grey with black markings and a bushy tail, believed to be the ancestor of the domestic cat. **2** a hot-tempered or ferocious person. **3** an exploratory oil well. > adjective **1** (of a workers' strike) sudden and unofficial. **2** commercially unsound or risky. > verb US prospect for oil.

DERIVATIVES – **wildcatter** noun.

wildebeest /ˈwildəbeest, ˈvildəbeest/ > noun another term for GNU.

ORIGIN – Afrikaans, 'wild beast'.

wilderness > noun **1** an uncultivated, uninhabited, and inhospitable region. **2** (**the wilderness**) a position of disfavour.

IDIOMS – **a voice in the wilderness** an unheeded advocate of reform. [ORIGIN – with biblical allusion to the Gospel of Matthew, chapter 3.]

SYNONYMS – **1** wasteland, wastes, wilds.

ORIGIN – Old English, 'land inhabited only by wild animals', from *wild dēor* 'wild deer'.

wildfire > noun historical a highly flammable liquid used in warfare.

IDIOMS – **spread like wildfire** spread with great speed.

wildfowl > plural noun game birds, especially aquatic ones; waterfowl.

wildlife > noun the native fauna (and sometimes flora) of a region.

wile /wīl/ > noun a devious or cunning stratagem.

SYNONYMS – ploy, ruse, trick.

ORIGIN – perhaps from an Old Norse word related to *vél* 'craft'.

wilful* (US also **willful**) > adjective **1** intentional; deliberate. **2** stubborn and determined.

DERIVATIVES – **wilfully** adverb **wilfulness** noun.

***SPELLING** – the usual spelling is wi*l*ful: wi*ll*ful is American.

SYNONYMS – **1** deliberate, intended, intentional, planned, premeditated. **2** headstrong, obstinate, self-willed.

will¹ > modal verb (3rd sing. present **will**; past **would**) **1** expressing the future tense. **2** expressing a strong intention or assertion about the future. **3** expressing inevitable events. **4** expressing a request. **5** expressing desire, consent, or willingness. **6** expressing facts about ability or capacity. **7** expressing habitual behaviour. **8** expressing probability or expectation about something in the present.

USAGE – on the difference between **will** and **shall**, see the note at SHALL.

will² > noun **1** the faculty by which a person decides on and initiates action. **2** (also **will power**) control or restraint deliberately exerted. **3** a desire or intention. **4** a legal document containing instructions as to what should be done with one's money and property after one's death. > verb **1** chiefly formal or literary intend or desire to happen. **2** bring about by the exercise of mental powers. **3** bequeath in one's will.

WORDFINDER – abulia (loss of will power), volition (power of using one's will); codicil (a supplement to a will), executor (a person appointed to carry out the terms of a will), intestate (having left no will), legacy (something left to someone in a will), nuncupative (denoting a spoken will), probate (official validation of a will), testamentary (of a will), testate (having made a valid will), testator (a person making a will).

IDIOMS – **at will** at whatever time or in whatever way one pleases. **have a will of one's own** have a wilful character. **where there's a will there's a way** proverb determination will overcome any obstacle. **with a will** energetically and resolutely. **with the best will in the world** however good one's intentions.

SYNONYMS – noun **2** determination, resolution, resolve, single-mindedness. **3** decision, desire, inclination, intention, wish. verb **2** decree, ordain, order.

ORIGIN – Old English, related to WILL¹ and the adverb WELL¹.

willful > adjective US variant spelling of WILFUL.

willie > noun variant spelling of WILLY.

willies > plural noun (**the willies**) informal a strong feeling of nervous discomfort: *the room gave him the willies.*

willing > adjective **1** ready, eager, or prepared to do something. **2** given or done readily.

DERIVATIVES – **willingly** adverb **willingness** noun.

SYNONYMS – **1** disposed, inclined, keen, minded, prepared. **2** glad, happy, ungrudging.

ANTONYMS – **1** reluctant. **2** grudging.

will-o'-the-wisp > noun **1** a dim, flickering light seen hovering or floating at night on marshy ground, thought to result from the combustion of natural gases. **2** a person or thing that is difficult or impossible to reach or catch.

ORIGIN – from *Will with the wisp*, the sense of *wisp* being 'handful of lighted hay'.

willow > noun a tree or shrub with narrow leaves and pliant branches, typically growing near water.

COMBINATIONS – **willow pattern** a

conventional design in pottery featuring a Chinese scene depicted in blue on white, typically including figures on a bridge, a willow tree, and birds.

willowherb > *noun* a plant with long, narrow leaves and pink or pale purple flowers.

willowy > *adjective* 1 bordered, shaded, or covered by willows. 2 (of a person) tall, slim, and lithe.

willy (also **willie**) > *noun* (pl. **willies**) Brit. informal a penis.

ORIGIN – familiar form of the given name *William*.

willy-nilly > *adverb* 1 whether one likes it or not. 2 without direction or planning; haphazardly.

ORIGIN – later spelling of *will I, nill I* 'I am willing, I am unwilling'.

willy-willy > *noun* (pl. **willy-willies**) Austral. a whirlwind or dust storm.

ORIGIN – Yindjibarndi (an Aboriginal language of western Australia).

wilt[1] > *verb* 1 (of a plant) become limp through loss of water, heat, or disease; droop. 2 (of a person) lose one's energy or vigour. > *noun* any of a number of fungal or bacterial diseases of plants characterised by wilting of the foliage.

SYNONYMS – *verb* 1 droop, flop, sag. 2 fade, flag, weaken.

ORIGIN – perhaps from dialect *welk* 'lose freshness', from Low German.

wilt[2] archaic second person singular of **WILL**[1].

Wilts. > *abbreviation* Wiltshire.

wily /wīli/ > *adjective* (**wilier**, **wiliest**) skilled at gaining an advantage, especially deceitfully.

DERIVATIVES – **wilily** *adverb* **wiliness** *noun*.

SYNONYMS – canny, crafty, cunning.

wimp informal > *noun* a weak and cowardly person. > *verb* (**wimp out**) withdraw from something in a cowardly way.

DERIVATIVES – **wimpish** *adjective* **wimpishly** *adverb* **wimpishness** *noun* **wimpy** *adjective*.

wimple > *noun* a cloth headdress covering the head, neck, and sides of the face, formerly worn by women and still by some nuns.

DERIVATIVES – **wimpled** *adjective*.

win > *verb* (**winning**; past and past participle **won**) 1 be successful or victorious in (a contest or conflict). 2 acquire as a result of a contest, conflict, etc. 3 gain (someone's attention, support, or love). 4 (**win over**) gain the support or favour of. 5 (**win out** or **through**) manage to succeed or achieve something by effort. > *noun* a victory in a game or contest.

IDIOMS – **win the day** be victorious. **win** (or **earn**) **one's spurs** 1 historical gain a

knighthood by an act of bravery. 2 informal gain one's first distinction or honours.

DERIVATIVES – **winless** *adjective* **winnable** *adjective*.

SYNONYMS – *verb* 1 be the victor in, be the winner in, triumph in. 4 (**win over**) convince, persuade, talk round.

ORIGIN – Old English, 'strive, contend', also 'subdue and take possession of, acquire'.

wince > *verb* give a slight involuntary grimace or flinch due to pain or distress. > *noun* an instance of wincing.

DERIVATIVES – **wincer** *noun*.

SYNONYMS – grimace, recoil, start.

ORIGIN – Old French *guenchir* 'turn aside'.

winceyette /winsiet/ > *noun* Brit. a lightweight brushed cotton fabric, used especially for nightclothes.

ORIGIN – from *wincey*, a lightweight wool and cotton fabric, from **LINSEY-WOOLSEY**.

winch > *noun* 1 a hauling or lifting device consisting of a rope or chain winding around a horizontal rotating drum, turned by a crank or by motor. 2 the crank of a wheel or axle. > *verb* hoist or haul with a winch.

DERIVATIVES – **wincher** *noun*.

ORIGIN – Old English, 'reel, pulley'; related to **WINK**.

wind[1] /wind/ > *noun* 1 the perceptible natural movement of the air, especially in the form of a current blowing from a particular direction. 2 breath as needed in physical exertion, speech, playing an instrument, etc. 3 Brit. air swallowed while eating or gas generated in the stomach and intestines by digestion. 4 meaningless talk. 5 (also **winds**) (treated as sing. or pl.) wind or woodwind instruments forming a band or section of an orchestra. 6 a scent carried by the wind, indicating the proximity of an animal or person. > *verb* 1 cause (someone) to have difficulty breathing because of exertion or a blow to the stomach. 2 Brit. make (a baby) bring up wind after feeding by patting its back.

WORDFINDER – aeolian (*caused by the wind*), anemometer (*instrument for measuring wind speed*), anemophilous (*pollinated by the wind*), Beaufort Scale (*scale of wind speeds*), leeward (*on or towards the side sheltered from the wind*), windward (*on or towards the side facing the wind*); *local winds*: bora, chinook, föhn, haboob, harmattan, khamsin, levanter, mistral, monsoon, simoom, sirocco, tramontana.

IDIOMS – **get wind of** informal hear a rumour of. **it's an ill wind that blows nobody any good** proverb few things are so bad that no one profits from them. **put the wind up** Brit. informal alarm or frighten. **sail close to** (or **near**) **the wind** 1 sail as nearly against the wind as is consistent with using its force. 2 informal verge on indecency,

dishonesty, or disaster. **take the wind out of someone's sails** frustrate someone by anticipating an action or remark. **to the wind**(**s**) (or **the four winds**) in all directions. [ORIGIN – from 'And fear of death deliver to the winds' (Milton's *Paradise Lost*).]

DERIVATIVES – **windless** *adjective*.

COMBINATIONS – **windbreak** a row of trees, wall, or screen providing shelter from the wind. **windcheater** chiefly Brit. a wind-resistant jacket with a close-fitting neck, waistband, and cuffs. **wind chill** the cooling effect of wind on a surface. **wind chimes** pieces of glass, metal rods, or similar items, suspended from a frame and typically hung near a door or window so as to chime in the draught. **wind farm** an area containing a group of windmills or wind turbines that produce energy. **windflower** a wood anemone. **wind instrument** 1 a musical instrument in which sound is produced by the vibration of air. 2 a woodwind instrument as distinct from a brass instrument. **wind machine** 1 a machine used in the theatre or in film-making for producing a blast of air or imitating the sound of wind. 2 a wind-driven turbine. **wind shear** variation in wind velocity along a direction at right angles to the wind's direction, tending to exert a turning force. **windshield** N. Amer. a windscreen. **windsock** a light, flexible cylinder or cone mounted on a mast to show the direction and strength of the wind, especially at an airfield. **windstorm** chiefly N. Amer. a gale. **wind tunnel** a tunnel-like apparatus for producing an airstream past models of aircraft, buildings, etc., in order to investigate flow or the effect of wind on the full-size object.

wind[2] /wīnd/ > *verb* (past and past participle **wound** /wownd/) 1 move in or take a twisting or spiral course. 2 pass (something) around a thing or person so as to encircle or enfold them. 3 (with reference to a length of something) twist or be twisted around itself or a core. 4 make (a clockwork device) operate by turning a key or handle. 5 turn (a key or handle) repeatedly. 6 move (an audio or video tape or a film) back or forwards to a desired point. 7 hoist or draw with a windlass, winch, etc. > *noun* 1 a twist or turn in a course. 2 a single turn made when winding.

IDIOMS – **wind down** 1 (of a clockwork mechanism) gradually lose power. 2 draw or bring gradually to a close. 3 informal relax. **wind up** 1 gradually bring to a conclusion. 2 informal end up in a specified state, situation, or place. 3 Brit. informal tease or irritate (someone). 4 informal increase the tension or power of.

SYNONYMS – *verb* **1** loop, snake, twist, zigzag. **2** entwine, furl, wrap.

ORIGIN – Old English, 'go rapidly', 'twine'; related to **WANDER** and **WEND**.

windbag > *noun* informal a person who talks a lot but says little of any value.

windburn > *noun* reddening and soreness of the skin caused by prolonged exposure to the wind.

winder /wīndər/ > *noun* a device or mechanism for winding something, especially a watch, clock, or camera film.

windfall > *noun* **1** an apple or other fruit blown from a tree by the wind. **2** a piece of unexpected good fortune, especially a legacy.

COMBINATIONS – **windfall tax** a tax levied on an unexpectedly large profit, especially one regarded to be excessive or unfairly obtained.

winding /wīnding/ > *noun* **1** a twisting movement or course. **2** a thing that winds or is wound round something. > *adjective* having a twisting or spiral course.

COMBINATIONS – **winding sheet** a shroud.

windlass /windləss/ > *noun* a winch, especially one on a ship or in a harbour. > *verb* haul or lift with a windlass.

ORIGIN – probably from Old Norse *vindáss* 'winding pole'.

windmill > *noun* a building or structure with sails or vanes that turn in the wind, used to generate power to grind corn into flour, to generate electricity, or to draw water. > *verb* **1** move (one's arms) in a manner suggestive of the sails of a windmill. **2** (of a propeller, rotor, or aircraft) spin unpowered.

window > *noun* **1** an opening in a wall or roof, fitted with glass in a frame to admit light or air and allow people to see out. **2** an opening through which customers are served in a bank, ticket office, etc. **3** the window area of a shop, where goods are displayed. **4** a transparent panel in an envelope to show an address. **5** Computing a framed area on a display screen for viewing information. **6** (**window on** or **into** or **to**) a means of observing and learning about. **7** an interval or opportunity for action.

WORDFINDER – *types of window:* bay, casement, clerestory, dormer, fanlight, lancet, oculus, oriel, rose window, sash window, skylight; defenestration (*throwing someone out of a window*), fenestration (*the arrangement of windows in a building*).

IDIOMS – **go out of the window** informal (of a plan or behaviour) be abandoned or cease to exist. **windows of the soul** the eyes.

DERIVATIVES – **windowless** *adjective*.

COMBINATIONS – **window box** a long, narrow box in which flowers and other plants are grown on an outside window sill. **window dressing 1** the arrangement of a display in a shop window. **2** an adroit but superficial or misleading presentation of something. **window frame** a frame holding the glass of a window. **window ledge** a window sill. **windowpane** a pane of glass in a window. **window seat 1** a seat below a window, especially one in a bay or alcove. **2** a seat next to a window in an aircraft or train. **window sill** a ledge or sill forming the bottom part of a window.

ORIGIN – Old Norse *vindauga*, from *vindr* 'wind' + *auga* 'eye'.

window-shop > *verb* look at the goods displayed in shop windows, especially without intending to buy.

DERIVATIVES – **window-shopper** *noun*.

windpipe > *noun* the trachea.

windscreen > *noun* Brit. a glass screen at the front of a motor vehicle.

COMBINATIONS – **windscreen wiper** Brit. a device for keeping a windscreen clear of rain, having a rubber blade on an arm that sweeps across in an arc.

windsurfing > *noun* the sport of riding on water on a sailboard.

DERIVATIVES – **windsurf** *verb* **windsurfer** *noun*.

windswept > *adjective* **1** exposed to strong winds. **2** (of a person's hair or appearance) untidy after being exposed to the wind.

wind-up > *noun* **1** Brit. informal an attempt to tease or irritate someone. **2** an act of concluding something.

windward > *adjective* & *adverb* facing the wind or on the side facing the wind. Contrasted with **LEEWARD**. > *noun* the side from which the wind is blowing.

windy¹ /windi/ > *adjective* (**windier, windiest**) **1** marked by or exposed to strong winds. **2** Brit. suffering from, marked by, or causing wind in the alimentary canal. **3** informal using or expressed in numerous words of little substance. **4** Brit. informal nervous or anxious.

DERIVATIVES – **windily** *adverb* **windiness** *noun*.

windy² /wīndi/ > *adjective* (of a road or river) following a winding course.

wine > *noun* **1** an alcoholic drink made from fermented grape juice. **2** a fermented alcoholic drink made from other fruits or plants. > *verb* (**wine and dine**) entertain (someone) with drinks and a meal.

WORDFINDER – oenologist (*a person who studies wines*), oenophile (*a lover of wines*), viniculture (*growing of grapes for winemaking*), vinous (*of or like wine*); bouquet, nose (*the scent of a wine*), carafe (*a flask for serving wine*), cuvée (*a type or blend of wine*), lees (*sediment in wine*), sommelier (*a wine waiter*), vintage (*the year or place in which wine was produced*), vintner (*a wine merchant*); brut (*denoting very dry sparkling wine*), demi-sec (*medium dry*), pétillant (*slightly sparkling*), robust (*strong and rich*), sec (*dry*).

IDIOMS – **good wine needs no bush** proverb there's no need to advertise or boast about something of good quality as people will always discover its merits. **wine, women, and song** the life of drinking, sexual pleasure, and carefree entertainment proverbially required by men.

DERIVATIVES – **winey** (also **winy**) *adjective*.

COMBINATIONS – **wine bar** a bar or small restaurant that specialises in serving wine. **wine bottle** a glass bottle for wine, the standard size holding 75 cl or 26⅔ fl. oz. **wine cellar 1** a cellar for storing wine. **2** a stock of wine. **wine glass** a glass with a stem and foot, used for drinking wine. **winegrower** a grower of grapes for wine. **wine gum** a small coloured fruit-flavoured sweet made with gelatin. **wine list** a list of the wines available in a restaurant. **wineskin** an animal skin sewn up and used to hold wine. **wine tasting** an event at which people judge the quality of wines by tasting them. **wine vinegar** vinegar made from wine rather than malt.

wordpower facts

Wine

The Latin root of **wine**, *vinum*, is the source of the words **vine**, **vinegar**, **vintage**, and **vintner**, and also, through chemistry, **vinyl**. **Vindaloo**, a hot Indian curry, also goes back to the Latin word: it probably entered English from Portuguese *vin d'alho* 'wine and garlic sauce'. *Vinum* comes from the same ancient root as its Greek equivalent, *oinos*, the source of **oenology**, the word for the study of wine.

winemaker > *noun* a producer of wine.

DERIVATIVES – **winemaking** *noun*.

winery > *noun* (pl. **wineries**) an establishment where wine is made.

wing > *noun* **1** a modified forelimb or other appendage enabling a bird, bat, insect, or other creature to fly. **2** a rigid horizontal structure projecting from both sides of an aircraft and supporting it in the air. **3** Brit. a raised part of the body of a vehicle above the wheel. **4** a part of a large building, especially one that projects from the main part. **5** Botany a thin appendage of a fruit or seed dispersed by the wind. **6** a group within an organisation having particular views or a particular function. **7** (**the wings**) the sides of a theatre stage out of view of the audience. **8** the part of a soccer, rugby, or hockey field close to the sidelines. **9** (also **wing forward**) an attacking player positioned near the sidelines. **10** an air force unit of several squadrons or groups. > *verb* **1** fly, or move quickly as if flying. **2** shoot (a bird) in the wing, so as to prevent flight. **3** (**wing it**) informal speak or act without preparation. [ORIGIN – theatrical slang referring to the playing of a role without proper knowledge of the text (by relying on a prompter in the wings or by studying in the wings between scenes.]

WORDFINDER – alar (*of or like a wing*), aliform (*wing-shaped*), apterous (*wingless*), pinion (*the outer part of a bird's wing*), span (*the maximum extent across wings*); chord (*the width of an aircraft wing*), dihedral (*the upward slant of an aircraft wing*).

IDIOMS – **in the wings** ready for use or action at the appropriate time. **on the wing** (of a bird) in flight. **on a wing and a prayer** with only a small chance of success. [ORIGIN – with reference to an emergency landing by an aircraft.] **spread** (or **stretch**) **one's wings** extend one's activities and interests. **take wing** fly away. **under one's wing** in or into one's protective care.

DERIVATIVES – **winged** adjective **wingless** adjective.

COMBINATIONS – **wing case** each of a pair of modified toughened forewings covering the functional wings of a beetle or other insect. **wing chair** an armchair with side pieces projecting forwards from a high back. **wing collar** a high, stiff shirt collar with turned-down corners. **wing commander** a rank of RAF officer, above squadron leader and below group captain. **wing mirror** a rear-view mirror projecting from the side of a vehicle. **wing nut** a nut with a pair of projections for the fingers to turn it on a screw.

ORIGIN – Old Norse *vængr*.

wingbeat (also **wingstroke**) > *noun* one complete set of the motions of a wing in flying.

winger > *noun* **1** an attacking player on the wing in soccer, hockey, etc. **2** a member of a specified political wing: *a Tory right-winger*.

wingspan (also **wingspread**) > *noun* the maximum extent across the wings of an aircraft, bird, etc. from tip to tip.

wink > *verb* **1** close and open one eye quickly, typically as a signal of affection or greeting or to convey a message. **2** shine or flash intermittently. > *noun* an act of winking.

IDIOMS – **as easy as winking** informal very easy or easily. **in the wink of an eye** (or **in a wink**) very quickly. **not sleep** (or **get**) **a wink** (or **not get a wink of sleep**) not sleep at all.

ORIGIN – Old English, 'close the eyes'; related to WINCE.

winkle > *noun* a small shore-dwelling mollusc with a spiral shell. > *verb* (**winkle out**) chiefly Brit. extract or obtain with difficulty.

DERIVATIVES – **winkler** noun.

COMBINATIONS – **winkle-picker** Brit. informal a shoe with a long pointed toe, popular in the 1950s.

ORIGIN – shortening of PERIWINKLE².

winner > *noun* **1** a person or thing that wins. **2** informal a successful or highly promising thing.

SYNONYMS – **1** champion, conqueror, victor.

winning > *adjective* **1** gaining, resulting in, or relating to victory. **2** attractive and endearing. > *noun* (**winnings**) money won, especially by gambling.

DERIVATIVES – **winningly** adverb.

SYNONYMS – *adjective* **1** successful, triumphant, victorious. **2** attractive, charming, endearing, engaging, fetching.

COMBINATIONS – **winning post** a post marking the end of a race.

winnow /winnō/ > *verb* **1** blow air through (grain) in order to remove the chaff. **2** remove (chaff) from grain. **3** identify and remove (the least valuable members of a group).

DERIVATIVES – **winnower** noun.

ORIGIN – Old English, related to WIND¹.

wino /wīnō/ > *noun* (pl. **winos**) informal a person who drinks excessive amounts of cheap wine or other alcohol.

winsome > *adjective* attractive or appealing in an innocent or naive way.

DERIVATIVES – **winsomely** adverb **winsomeness** noun.

SYNONYMS – appealing, charming, engaging, fetching, winning.

ORIGIN – Old English, from *wyn* 'joy'.

winter > *noun* **1** the coldest season of the year, after autumn and before spring. **2** Astronomy the period from the winter solstice to the vernal equinox. > *adjective* **1** (of fruit) ripening late in the year. **2** (of crops) sown in autumn for harvesting the following year. > *verb* **1** spend the winter in a particular place. **2** keep or feed (plants or cattle) during winter.

WORDFINDER – hibernate (*spend the winter in a dormant state*).

COMBINATIONS – **Winter Olympics** an international contest of winter sports held every four years at a two-year interval from the Olympic games. **winter sports** sports performed on snow or ice. **wintertime** (also literary **wintertide**) the season or period of winter.

wintergreen > *noun* **1** a low-growing plant with spikes of white bell-shaped flowers. **2** an American shrub whose leaves produce oil. **3** (also **oil of wintergreen**) a pungent oil obtained from these plants or from birch bark, used medicinally and as a flavouring.

winterise (also **winterize**) > *verb* chiefly N. Amer. adapt or prepare for use in cold weather.

DERIVATIVES – **winterisation** noun.

wintry (also **wintery**) > *adjective* (**wintrier**, **wintriest**) characteristic of winter, especially in being very cold or bleak.

DERIVATIVES – **wintrily** adverb **wintriness** noun.

wipe > *verb* **1** clean or dry by rubbing with a cloth or one's hand. **2** remove (dirt or moisture) in this way. **3** spread (liquid) over a surface by rubbing. **4** erase (data) from a magnetic medium. **5** pass over an electronic reader, bar code, etc. > *noun* **1** an act of wiping. **2** an absorbent disposable cleaning cloth.

IDIOMS – **wipe the floor with** informal inflict a humiliating defeat on. **wipe out 1** remove or eliminate. **2** kill (a large number of people). **3** ruin financially. **4** informal exhaust or intoxicate. **wipe the slate clean** make a fresh start.

DERIVATIVES – **wipeable** adjective **wiper** noun.

ORIGIN – Old English, related to WHIP.

wire > *noun* **1** metal drawn out into a thin, flexible thread or rod. **2** a length or quantity of wire used for fencing, to carry an electric current, etc. **3** a concealed electronic listening device. **4** informal a telegram. > *verb* **1** install electric circuits or wires in. **2** provide, fasten, or reinforce with wire. **3** informal, chiefly N. Amer. send a telegram to.

IDIOMS – **by wire** by telegraph. **down to the wire** informal until the very last minute.

DERIVATIVES – **wirer** noun.

COMBINATIONS – **wire brush** a brush with tough wire bristles for cleaning hard surfaces. **wire grass** chiefly N. Amer. & Austral. grass with tough wiry stems. **wire-haired** (especially of a dog breed) having wiry hair. **wire service** N. Amer. a news agency that supplies syndicated news by teleprinter or other electronic means to newspapers, radio, and television stations. **wire wool** Brit. steel wool.

ORIGIN – Old English, probably from Latin *viere* 'plait, weave'.

wired > *adjective* informal **1** making use of computers and information technology to transfer or receive information. **2** nervous, tense, or edgy. **3** intoxicated by drugs or alcohol.

wireless > *noun* dated, chiefly Brit. **1** a radio receiving set. **2** broadcasting or telegraphy using radio signals. > *adjective* lacking or not requiring wires.

wiretapping > *noun* the practice of tapping a telephone line to monitor conversations secretly.

DERIVATIVES – **wiretapper** noun.

wireworm > *noun* the worm-like larva of a type of beetle, which feeds on roots and can cause damage to crops.

wiring > *noun* a system of wires providing electric circuits for a device or building.

wiry > *adjective* (**wirier**, **wiriest**) **1** resembling wire in form and texture. **2** lean, tough, and sinewy.
DERIVATIVES – **wiriness** *noun*.

wisdom > *noun* **1** the quality of being wise. **2** the soundness or advisability of an action or decision. **3** the body of knowledge and experience that develops within a specified society or period.
SYNONYMS – **1** cleverness, intelligence, judgement, sagacity, sageness, understanding.
ANTONYMS – **1** folly.
COMBINATIONS – **wisdom tooth** each of the four hindmost molars in humans, which usually appear at about the age of twenty.

wise[1] > *adjective* **1** having or showing experience, knowledge, and good judgement. **2** responding sensibly or shrewdly to a particular situation. **3** (**wise to**) informal aware of. > *verb* (**wise up**) informal become alert or aware.
IDIOMS – **be wise after the event** understand and assess something only after its implications have become obvious.
DERIVATIVES – **wisely** *adverb*.
SYNONYMS – *adjective* **1** clever, intelligent, judicious, sagacious, sage, sensible.
ANTONYMS – *adjective* **1** foolish.
COMBINATIONS – **wise guy** informal a person who makes sarcastic or insolent remarks so as to demonstrate their cleverness.
ORIGIN – Old English, related to WIT[2].

wise[2] > *noun* archaic manner, way, or extent.
IDIOMS – **in no wise** not at all.
ORIGIN – Old English, related to WIT[2].

-wise > *suffix* **1** forming adjectives and adverbs of manner or respect: *clockwise*. Compare with **-WAYS**. **2** informal with respect to: *price-wise*.

wiseacre /wīzaykər/ > *noun* a person who pretentiously tries to give the impression of being wise or knowledgeable.
ORIGIN – Dutch *wijsseggher* 'soothsayer'.

wisecrack informal > *noun* a witty remark or joke. > *verb* make a wisecrack.
DERIVATIVES – **wisecracker** *noun*.

wish > *verb* **1** desire something that cannot or probably will not happen. **2** want to do something. **3** ask (someone) to do something or that (something) be done. **4** express a hope that (someone) has (happiness, success, etc.). **5** (**wish on**) hope that (something unpleasant) will happen to. > *noun* **1** a desire or hope. **2** (**wishes**) an expression of a hope for someone's happiness, success, or welfare. **3** an invocation or recitation of a desire or hope. **4** a thing wished for.
IDIOMS – **if wishes were horses, beggars would ride** proverb if you could achieve your aims simply by wishing for them, life

would be very easy. **the wish is father to the thought** proverb we believe a thing because we wish it to be true.
SYNONYMS – *verb* **2** be inclined, desire, want.
COMBINATIONS – **wish-fulfilment** the satisfying of wishes or desires in dreams or fantasies. **wishing well** a well into which one drops a coin and makes a wish.

wishbone > *noun* a forked bone between the neck and breast of a bird, especially one from a cooked bird which, when broken by two people, entitles the holder of the longer portion to make a wish.

wishful > *adjective* **1** having or expressing a wish for something to happen. **2** based on impractical wishes rather than facts.
DERIVATIVES – **wishfully** *adverb* **wishfulness** *noun*.

wishy-washy > *adjective* **1** (of a drink or soup) weak or thin. **2** feeble or insipid.

wisp > *noun* **1** a small, thin bunch, strand, or amount of something. **2** a small, thin person.
DERIVATIVES – **wispily** *adverb* **wispiness** *noun* **wispy** (**wispier**, **wispiest**) *adjective*.

wist past and past participle of WIT[2].

wisteria /wisteeriə/ (also **wistaria** /wistairiə/) > *noun* a climbing shrub of East Asia and North America, with hanging clusters of pale bluish-lilac flowers.
ORIGIN – named after Caspar *Wistar* (or *Wister*) (1761–1818), American anatomist.

wistful > *adjective* having or showing a feeling of vague or regretful longing.
DERIVATIVES – **wistfully** *adverb* **wistfulness** *noun*.
SYNONYMS – longing, melancholy, plaintive, regretful, yearning.
ORIGIN – apparently from obsolete *wistly* 'intently', influenced by WISHFUL.

wit[1] > *noun* **1** (also **wits**) the capacity for inventive thought and quick understanding; keen intelligence. **2** a natural aptitude for using words and ideas in a quick and inventive way to create humour. **3** a person with this aptitude.
IDIOMS – **be at one's wits' end** be completely at a loss as to what to do. **be frightened out of one's wits** be extremely frightened. **gather one's wits** allow oneself to think calmly and clearly in a demanding situation. **have** (or **keep**) **one's wits about one** be constantly alert. **live by one's wits** earn money by clever and sometimes dishonest means.
DERIVATIVES – **witted** *adjective*.
SYNONYMS – **1** acuteness, cleverness, sharpness, sharp-wittedness.
ORIGIN – Old English, denoting the mind as the seat of consciousness; related to WIT[2].

wit[2] > *verb* (**wot**, **witting**; past and past participle

wist) **1** archaic know. **2** (**to wit**) that is to say.

witch > *noun* **1** a woman thought to have evil magic powers. **2** a follower or practitioner of modern witchcraft. **3** informal an ugly or unpleasant old woman. > *verb* archaic **1** practise witchcraft. **2** cast an evil spell on. **3** (of a girl or woman) enchant (a man).
WORDFINDER – coven (*a group of witches*), familiar (*a witch's attendant spirit*), sabbath (*a midnight ritual held by witches*), Wicca (*the pagan religion of modern witchcraft*).
DERIVATIVES – **witchy** *adjective*.
COMBINATIONS – **witch doctor** a tribal magician credited with powers of healing, divination, and protection against the magic of others. **witches' broom** dense twiggy growth in a tree caused by infection with fungus, mites, or viruses. **the witching hour** midnight, regarded as the time when witches are supposedly active. [ORIGIN – with allusion to *the witching time of night* from Shakespeare's *Hamlet* (III. ii. 377).]
ORIGIN – Old English *wicca*, *wicce*.

witchcraft > *noun* **1** the practice of magic, especially the use of spells and the invocation of evil spirits. **2** the modern religious cult of Wicca.

witch elm > *noun* variant spelling of WYCH ELM.

witchery > *noun* **1** the practice of magic. **2** bewitching quality or power.

witch hazel (also **wych hazel**) > *noun* **1** a shrub with fragrant yellow or orange flowers. **2** a lotion made from the bark and leaves of this plant.
ORIGIN – from *wych* (see WYCH ELM).

witch-hunt > *noun* a campaign directed against a person or group holding views considered unorthodox or a threat to society.

with > *preposition* **1** accompanied by. **2** in the same direction as. **3** possessing; having. **4** indicating the instrument used to perform an action or the material used for a purpose. **5** in opposition to or competition with. **6** indicating the manner or attitude in which a person does something. **7** indicating responsibility. **8** in relation to. **9** employed by. **10** using the services of. **11** affected by (a particular fact or condition). **12** indicating separation or removal from something.
IDIOMS – **be with someone** informal follow someone's meaning. **with it** informal **1** up to date or fashionable. **2** alert and comprehending.
ORIGIN – Old English, probably related to obsolete *wither* 'adverse, opposite'.

withal /withawl/ archaic > *adverb* **1** in addition. **2** nevertheless. > *preposition* with.

withdraw > *verb* (past **withdrew**; past participle **withdrawn**) **1** remove or take away (something) from a place or position. **2** take (money) out of an account. **3** retract (a statement or accusation). **4** leave or cause to leave a place, especially a war zone. **5** cease to participate in an activity or be a member of a team or organisation. **6** depart to another place in search of quiet or privacy. **7** cease to take an addictive drug.

DERIVATIVES – **withdrawal** *noun*.

SYNONYMS – **1** extract, pull back, remove, take away, take out.

ANTONYMS – **1** insert.

withdrawn past participle of **WITHDRAW**. > *adjective* unusually shy or reserved.

SYNONYMS – introverted, inward-looking, uncommunicative.

ANTONYMS – extrovert.

withe /with, wīth/ > *noun* variant spelling of **WITHY**.

wither > *verb* **1** (of a plant) become dry and shrivelled. **2** become shrunken or wrinkled from age or disease. **3** fall into decay or decline. **4** mortify (someone) with a scornful look or manner. **5** (**withering**) scornful.

DERIVATIVES – **witheringly** *adverb*.

ORIGIN – apparently originally a variant of **WEATHER**.

withers > *plural noun* the highest part of a horse's back, lying at the base of the neck above the shoulders.

ORIGIN – apparently from *widersome*, from obsolete *wither-* 'against' (as the part that resists the strain of the collar).

withershins > *adverb* variant spelling of **WIDDERSHINS**.

withhold* > *verb* (past and past participle **withheld**) **1** refuse to give (something due to or desired by another). **2** suppress or restrain (an emotion or reaction).

DERIVATIVES – **withholder** *noun*.

*SPELLING – remember to double the *h*: wit*h*hold.

SYNONYMS – **1** hold back, keep back. **2** hold back, repress, restrain, suppress.

within > *preposition* **1** inside. **2** inside the range or bounds of. **3** occurring inside (a particular period of time). > *adverb* **1** inside; indoors. **2** internally or inwardly.

without > *preposition* **1** not accompanied by or having the use of. **2** in which the action mentioned does not happen. **3** archaic or literary outside. > *adverb* archaic or literary outside. > *conjunction* archaic or dialect **1** without it being the case that. **2** unless.

withstand > *verb* (past and past participle **withstood**) **1** remain undamaged or unaffected by. **2** offer strong resistance or opposition to.

DERIVATIVES – **withstander** *noun*.

withy /wi<u>th</u>i/ (also **withe**) > *noun* (pl. **withies** or **withes**) **1** a tough, flexible branch of an osier or other willow, used for tying, binding, or basketry. **2** an osier.

witless > *adjective* foolish; stupid.

DERIVATIVES – **witlessly** *adverb* **witlessness** *noun*.

witness > *noun* **1** a person who sees an event take place. **2** a person giving sworn testimony to a court of law or the police. **3** a person who is present at the signing of a document and signs it themselves to confirm this. **4** (**witness to**) evidence or proof of. **5** open profession of one's religious faith through words or actions. > *verb* **1** be a witness to. **2** be the place, period, etc. in which (a particular event) takes place.

SYNONYMS – *noun* **1** eyewitness, observer, onlooker. *verb* **1** observe, see, view, watch.

COMBINATIONS – **witness box** (N. Amer. **witness stand**) Law the place in a court where a witness stands to give evidence.

witter > *verb* (usu. **witter on**) Brit. informal speak at length about trivial matters.

witticism > *noun* a witty remark.

ORIGIN – coined by the English writer John Dryden (1631–1700) from *witty*, on the pattern of *criticism*.

witting > *adjective* **1** deliberate. **2** aware of the full facts of the situation.

DERIVATIVES – **wittingly** *adverb*.

witty > *adjective* (**wittier**, **wittiest**) showing or characterised by quick and inventive verbal humour.

DERIVATIVES – **wittily** *adverb* **wittiness** *noun*.

SYNONYMS – amusing, clever, funny, humorous, quick-witted.

wives plural of **WIFE**.

wiz > *noun* variant of **WHIZZ** (in sense 3).

wizard > *noun* **1** (especially in legends and fairy tales) a man who has magical powers. **2** a person who is very skilled in a particular field or activity. > *adjective* Brit. informal, dated excellent.

DERIVATIVES – **wizardly** *adjective*.

ORIGIN – from **WISE**¹: originally in the sense 'philosopher, sage'.

wizardry > *noun* **1** the art or practice of magic. **2** great skill in a particular field or activity.

wizened /ˈwizz'nd/ > *adjective* shrivelled or wrinkled with age.

ORIGIN – from archaic *wizen* 'shrivel'.

WLTM > *abbreviation* would like to meet.

WNW > *abbreviation* west-north-west.

WO > *abbreviation* Warrant Officer.

wo > *exclamation* variant spelling of **WHOA**.

woad /wōd/ > *noun* a yellow-flowered plant whose leaves were formerly used to make blue dye.

wobble > *verb* **1** move unsteadily from side to side. **2** (of the voice) tremble. **3** waver between different courses of action. > *noun* a wobbling movement or sound.

SYNONYMS – *verb* **1** rock, shake, sway.

COMBINATIONS – **wobbleboard** Austral. a piece of fibreboard used as a musical instrument, producing a low booming sound when flexed.

ORIGIN – first spelled *wabble*; related to **WAVE**.

wobbler > *noun* **1** a person or thing that wobbles. **2** another term for **WOBBLY**.

wobbly > *adjective* (**wobblier**, **wobbliest**) **1** tending to wobble. **2** weak and unsteady from illness, tiredness, or anxiety. **3** uncertain or insecure. > *noun* Brit. informal a fit of temper or panic.

DERIVATIVES – **wobbliness** *noun*.

wodge > *noun* Brit. informal a large piece or amount of something.

woe > *noun* literary **1** great sorrow or distress. **2** (**woes**) troubles.

IDIOMS – **woe betide** —— humorous the person in question will be in trouble if they do a specified thing. **woe is me!** humorous an exclamation of sorrow or distress.

woebegone /ˈwōbigon/ > *adjective* sad or miserable in appearance.

SYNONYMS – crestfallen, dejected, downcast, forlorn.

ORIGIN – from **WOE** + *begone* 'surrounded'.

woeful > *adjective* **1** full of sorrow; miserable. **2** very bad; deplorable.

DERIVATIVES – **woefully** *adverb* **woefulness** *noun*.

SYNONYMS – **1** dejected, forlorn, miserable, sad, sorrowful, unhappy. **2** atrocious, deplorable, dreadful, frightful, shameful.

wog¹ > *noun* Brit. informal, offensive a person who is not white.

wog² > *noun* Austral. informal a minor illness or infection.

woggle > *noun* a loop or ring of leather or cord through which the ends of a Scout's neckerchief are threaded.

wok > *noun* a bowl-shaped frying pan used in Chinese cookery.

ORIGIN – Chinese.

woke past of **WAKE**¹.

woken past participle of **WAKE**¹.

wold /wōld/ > *noun* (especially in British place names) a piece of high, open, uncultivated land or moor.

ORIGIN – Old English, 'wooded upland'.

wolf > *noun* (pl. **wolves**) **1** a carnivorous mammal that lives and hunts in packs and is the largest member of the dog family. **2** a rapacious or ferocious person. **3** informal a man who habitually seduces women. > *verb* (usu. **wolf down**) devour (food) greedily.

WORDFINDER – lupine (*of or like a wolf*), lycanthropy (*transformation into a werewolf*).

IDIOMS – **cry wolf** raise repeated false alarms, so that a real cry for help is ignored. [ORIGIN – with allusion to the fable of the shepherd boy who deluded people with false cries of 'Wolf!'] **keep the wolf from the door** have enough money to be able to buy food. **throw someone to the wolves** sacrifice someone in order to avoid trouble for oneself. **a wolf in sheep's clothing** a person who appears friendly but is really hostile. [ORIGIN – with biblical allusion to the Gospel of Matthew, chapter 7.]

DERIVATIVES – **wolfish** *adjective* **wolfishly** *adverb*.

COMBINATIONS – **Wolf Cub** chiefly Brit. former term for *Cub Scout*. **wolfhound** a dog of a large breed originally used to hunt wolves.

wolfram /ˈwoolfrəm/ > *noun* tungsten or its ore, especially as a commercial commodity.

ORIGIN – German, perhaps from *Wolf* 'wolf' and an old word meaning 'soot': probably at first a pejorative term used by miners.

wolf whistle > *noun* a whistle with a rising and falling pitch, used to express sexual attraction or admiration. > *verb* (**wolf-whistle**) whistle in such a way at.

wolverine /ˈwoolvəreen/ > *noun* a heavily built short-legged carnivorous mammal of northern tundra and forests.

woman > *noun* (pl. **women**) 1 an adult human female. 2 a female worker or employee. 3 a wife or lover.

WORDFINDER – feminist (*a person advocating women's rights*), gynaecology (*the branch of medicine concerned with health problems specific to women*), gynarchy, gynaecocracy (*rule by women or a woman*), gynophobia (*irrational fear of women*), misogynist (*a man who hates women*).

IDIOMS – **woman of the streets** euphemistic, dated a prostitute.

DERIVATIVES – **womanliness** *noun* **womanly** *adjective*.

ORIGIN – Old English *wīfmon, wīfman* (see **WIFE, MAN**); the ancient word for 'woman' was **WIFE**.

womanhood > *noun* 1 the state or condition of being a woman. 2 women considered collectively. 3 the qualities traditionally associated with women.

womanise (also **womanize**) > *verb* (of a man) enter into numerous casual sexual relationships with women.

DERIVATIVES – **womaniser** *noun*.

womanish > *adjective* derogatory 1 suitable for or characteristic of a woman. 2 (of a man) effeminate.

DERIVATIVES – **womanishly** *adverb* **womanishness** *noun*.

womankind > *noun* women considered collectively.

womb > *noun* the organ in the lower body of a woman or female mammal where offspring are conceived and in which they gestate before birth; the uterus.

wombat /ˈwombat/ > *noun* a burrowing plant-eating Australian marsupial which resembles a small bear with short legs.

ORIGIN – Dharuk (an extinct Aboriginal language).

women plural of **WOMAN**.

COMBINATIONS – **women's liberation** the liberation of women from inequalities and subservient status in relation to men, and from attitudes causing these (now generally replaced by the term *feminism*).

womenfolk > *plural noun* the women of a family or community considered collectively.

won[1] /wun/ past and past participle of **WIN**.

won[2] /won/ > *noun* (pl. same) the basic monetary unit of North and South Korea, equal to 100 jun in North Korea and 100 jeon in South Korea.

ORIGIN – Korean.

wonder > *noun* 1 a feeling of surprise and admiration, caused by something beautiful, unexpected, or unfamiliar. 2 a person or thing that causes such a feeling. 3 (before another noun) having remarkable properties or abilities: *a wonder drug*. > *verb* 1 feel curious; desire to know. 2 feel doubt. 3 feel wonder.

IDIOMS – **I shouldn't wonder** informal I think it likely. **no** (or **little** or **small**) **wonder** it is not surprising. **nine-day** (or **seven-day**) **wonder** something that attracts great interest for a short while but is then forgotten. **wonders will never cease** often ironic an exclamation of surprise and pleasure. **work** (or **do**) **wonders** have a very beneficial effect.

DERIVATIVES – **wonderer** *noun* **wondering** *adjective* **wonderingly** *adverb*.

SYNONYMS – *noun* 1 amazement, awe, surprise, wonderment. 2 marvel, miracle, phenomenon.

wonderful > *adjective* extremely good, pleasant, or remarkable.

DERIVATIVES – **wonderfully** *adverb* **wonderfulness** *noun*.

SYNONYMS – fabulous, fantastic, glorious, magnificent, marvellous, superb.

ANTONYMS – awful, dreadful.

wonderland > *noun* a place full of wonderful things.

wonderment > *noun* a state of awed admiration or respect.

wondrous > *adjective* literary inspiring wonder. > *adverb* archaic wonderfully.

DERIVATIVES – **wondrously** *adverb* **wondrousness** *noun*.

wonk > *noun* N. Amer. informal, derogatory a studious or hard-working person.

COMBINATIONS – **policy wonk** a person having a great interest in minor details of political policy.

wonky > *adjective* (**wonkier, wonkiest**) informal 1 crooked; askew. 2 unsteady or faulty.

DERIVATIVES – **wonkily** *adverb* **wonkiness** *noun*.

wont /wōnt/ > *adjective* archaic or literary accustomed. > *noun* (**one's wont**) formal or

humorous one's customary behaviour. > *verb* (3rd sing. present **wonts** or **wont**; past and past participle **wont** or **wonted**) archaic make or become accustomed.

ORIGIN – Old English, from *wunian* 'dwell, be accustomed'.

won't > *contraction* will not.

wonted /ˈwōntid/ > *adjective* archaic or literary usual.

wonton /ˈwonton/ > *noun* (in Chinese cookery) a small round dumpling with a savoury filling, typically served in soup.

ORIGIN – Chinese.

woo > *verb* (**woos, wooed**) 1 try to gain the love of (a woman). 2 seek the support or custom of.

DERIVATIVES – **wooer** *noun*.

wood > *noun* 1 the hard fibrous material forming the main substance of the trunk or branches of a tree or shrub, used for fuel or timber. 2 a small forest. 3 (**the wood**) wooden barrels used for storing alcoholic drinks. 4 a golf club with a wooden or other head that is relatively broad from face to back.

WORDFINDER – ligneous (*of or relating to wood*), marquetry (*furniture decoration of inlaid wood*), parquet (*flooring of wooden blocks*), treen (*wooden antiques*), veneer (*a thin decorative covering of wood*), wainscot (*an area of wooden panelling in a room*); coppice (*a wood with trees periodically cut back to stimulate growth*), dryad (*a wood nymph*), sylvan (*of woods*).

IDIOMS – **be unable to see the wood** (or N. Amer. **the forest**) **for the trees** fail to grasp the main issue because of over-attention to details. **out of the woods** out of danger or difficulty. **touch** (or chiefly N. Amer. **knock on**) **wood** touch something wooden to ward off bad luck.

COMBINATIONS – **wood anemone** a spring-flowering anemone with pink-tinged white flowers, growing in woodland and shady places. **woodblock** 1 a block of wood from which woodcut prints are made. 2 a hollow wooden block used as a percussion instrument. **woodchip** chiefly Brit. wallpaper with small chips of wood embedded in it to give a grainy surface texture. **wood fibre** fibre obtained from wood and used especially in the manufacture of paper. **woodgrain** (of a surface or finish) imitating the grain pattern of wood. **wood pigeon** a common large pigeon, mainly grey with white patches forming a ring round its neck. **wood pulp** wood fibre reduced chemically or mechanically to pulp and used in the manufacture of paper. **wood stain** a commercially produced substance for colouring wood. **woodyard** a yard where wood is chopped or stored.

woodbine > *noun* **1** Brit. the common honeysuckle. **2** N. Amer. Virginia creeper.

woodchuck > *noun* a North American marmot with a heavy body and short legs.
ORIGIN – an alteration (by association with *wood*) of an American Indian name.

woodcock > *noun* (pl. same) a long-billed woodland bird of the sandpiper family, with brown plumage.

woodcut > *noun* a print of a type made from a design cut in relief in a block of wood.

woodcutter > *noun* **1** a person who cuts down wood. **2** a person who makes woodcuts.
DERIVATIVES – **woodcutting** *noun*.

wooded > *adjective* (of land) covered with woods.

wooden > *adjective* **1** made of wood. **2** like or characteristic of wood. **3** stiff and awkward in movement or manner.
DERIVATIVES – **woodenly** *adverb* **woodenness** *noun*.
COMBINATIONS – **wooden spoon** chiefly Brit. a real or notional prize awarded for coming last in a race or competition; a booby prize. [ORIGIN – from the practice of giving a spoon to the candidate coming last in the Cambridge mathematical tripos.]

wood engraving > *noun* **1** a print made from a finely detailed design cut into the end grain of a block of wood. **2** the technique of making such prints.

woodland > *noun* (also **woodlands**) land covered with trees.

woodlouse > *noun* (pl. **woodlice**) a small land crustacean with a greyish segmented body which it is able to roll into a ball.

woodpecker > *noun* a bird with a strong bill and a stiff tail, typically pecking at tree trunks to find insects and drumming on dead wood.

woodruff (also **sweet woodruff**) > *noun* a white-flowered plant with sweet-scented leaves used to flavour drinks and in perfumery.

woodshed > *noun* a shed where firewood is stored.
IDIOMS – **something nasty in the woodshed** Brit. informal a shocking or distasteful thing that has been kept secret. [ORIGIN – from the novel *Cold Comfort Farm* by Stella Gibbons (1933).]

woodsman > *noun* a forester, hunter, or woodcutter.

woodsy > *adjective* N. Amer. relating to or characteristic of wood or woodland.

woodturning > *noun* the activity of shaping wood with a lathe.
DERIVATIVES – **woodturner** *noun*.

woodwind > *noun* (treated as sing. or pl.) wind instruments other than brass instruments forming a section of an orchestra.
WORDFINDER – *woodwind instruments:* bassoon, clarinet, cor anglais, flute, oboe, piccolo, recorder.

woodwork > *noun* **1** the wooden parts of a room, building, or other structure. **2** Brit. the activity or skill of making things from wood.
IDIOMS – **come out of the woodwork** (of an unpleasant person or thing) emerge from obscurity.
DERIVATIVES – **woodworker** *noun* **woodworking** *noun*.

woodworm > *noun* **1** the wood-boring larva of the furniture beetle. **2** the damaged condition of wood resulting from infestation with this larva.

woody > *adjective* (**woodier**, **woodiest**) **1** covered with trees. **2** made of, resembling, or suggestive of wood.
DERIVATIVES – **woodiness** *noun*.
COMBINATIONS – **woody nightshade** a climbing plant with purple flowers and poisonous red berry-like fruit.

woof[1] /wo͝of/ > *noun* the barking sound made by a dog. > *verb* (of a dog) bark.

woof[2] /wo͞of/ > *noun* another term for **WEFT**[1].
ORIGIN – Old English, from the base of **WEAVE**[1].

woofer /wo͞ofər/ > *noun* a loudspeaker designed to reproduce low frequencies.

wool > *noun* **1** the fine, soft curly or wavy hair forming the coat of a sheep, goat, or similar animal, especially when shorn and made into cloth or yarn. **2** a metal or mineral made into a mass of fine fibres.
IDIOMS – **pull the wool over someone's eyes** deceive someone.
COMBINATIONS – **wool-gathering** aimless meditation or daydreaming. **wool grower** a breeder of sheep for wool. **woolshed** Austral./NZ a large shed for shearing and baling wool.

woollen (US **woolen**) > *adjective* made wholly or partly of wool. > *noun* (**woollens**) woollen garments.

woolly > *adjective* (**woollier**, **woolliest**) **1** made of wool. **2** (of an animal or plant) covered with wool or hair resembling wool. **3** resembling wool in texture or appearance. **4** vague or confused. **5** (of a sound) indistinct or distorted. > *noun* (pl. **woollies**) informal **1** chiefly Brit. a woollen garment, especially a pullover. **2** Austral./NZ a sheep.
DERIVATIVES – **woolliness** *noun*.
COMBINATIONS – **woolly bear** a large hairy caterpillar, especially that of a tiger moth.

woomera /wo͞omərə/ > *noun* Austral. a stick used by Aboriginals to throw a dart or spear more forcibly.
ORIGIN – Dharuk (an Aboriginal language).

woomph /wo͝omf, wo͞omf/ > *adverb* & *exclamation* used to imitate a sound like that of a sudden blow or impact accompanied by an expulsion of air.

Woop Woop /wo͝op wo͝op/ > *noun* Austral. informal a humorous name for a remote outback town or district.

woosh > *verb, noun, & exclamation* variant spelling of **WHOOSH**.

woozy > *adjective* (**woozier**, **wooziest**) informal unsteady, dizzy, or dazed.
DERIVATIVES – **woozily** *adverb* **wooziness** *noun*.

wop > *noun* informal, offensive an Italian or other southern European.
ORIGIN – perhaps from Italian *guappo* 'bold, showy'.

wop-wops > *noun* NZ informal a very remote district; the wilds.

Worcester sauce /wo͝ostər/ (also **Worcestershire sauce**) > *noun* a pungent sauce containing soy sauce and vinegar, first made in Worcester in England.

Worcs. > *abbreviation* Worcestershire.

word > *noun* **1** a single distinct meaningful element of speech or writing, used to form sentences with others. **2** a remark or statement. **3** (**a word**) even the smallest amount of something spoken or written: *don't believe a word.* **4** (**words**) angry talk. **5** (**the word**) a command, slogan, or signal. **6** (**one's word**) a person's account of the truth, especially when it differs from that of another person. **7** (**one's word**) a promise or assurance. **8** a message; news. > *verb* express (something) in particular words.
WORDFINDER – verbal (*of or in words*), lexical (*of vocabulary*); acronym (*a word formed from initial letters*), anagram (*a word formed from the letters of another*), coinage (*the introduction of new word*), diction, parlance (*the choice and use of words*), hapax legomenon (*a word or term used only once*), loanword (*a word taken directly from another language*), malapropism (*the use of a similar-sounding but wrong word*), neologism (*a newly invented word*), nonce word (*a word coined for a particular occasion*), onomatopoeic (*denoting a word imitating the sound of what it refers to*), palindrome (*a word or phrase spelled the same backwards*), phraseology (*words used by a particular person or group*), verbatim (*in exactly the same words*).
IDIOMS – **be as good as one's word** do what one has promised. **have a word** speak briefly to someone. **have a word in someone's ear** speak to someone privately and discreetly. **in other words** that is to say. **in so many words** precisely in the way mentioned. **in a word** briefly. **a man** (or **woman**) **of his** (or **her**) **word** a person who keeps their promises. **on** (or **upon**) **my word** an exclamation of surprise or emphasis. **put words into someone's mouth 1** inaccurately report what someone has said. **2** prompt someone to say

something inadvertently. **take someone at their word** assume that a person is speaking honestly or sincerely. **take the words out of someone's mouth** say what someone else was about to say. **take someone's word (for it)** believe what someone says or writes without checking for oneself. **too —— for words** informal extremely ——. **waste words** talk in vain. **word for word** in exactly the same or, when translated, exactly equivalent words. **one's word of honour** a solemn promise. **word of mouth** spoken communication as a means of transmitting information.

DERIVATIVES – **wordless** adjective **wordlessly** adverb.

COMBINATIONS – **word association** the spontaneous production of other words in response to a given word, used as a technique in psychiatric evaluation. **word class** a category of words of similar form or function; a part of speech. **word-perfect** (of an actor or speaker) knowing one's part or speech by heart. **word processor** a computer or program for storing, manipulating, and formatting text entered from a keyboard and providing a printout.

wording > noun the words used to express something; the way in which something is expressed.

wordplay > noun the witty exploitation of the meanings and ambiguities of words.

wordsmith > noun a skilled user of words.

wordy > adjective (**wordier, wordiest**) using or expressed in too many words.

DERIVATIVES – **wordily** adverb **wordiness** noun.

wore past of **WEAR**.

work > noun **1** activity involving mental or physical effort done in order to achieve a result. **2** such activity as a means of earning income. **3** a task or tasks to be undertaken. **4** a thing or things done or made; the result of an action. **5** (**works**) (treated as sing.) chiefly Brit. a factory or other place where industrial or manufacturing processes are carried out. **6** (**works**) chiefly Brit. operations of building or repair. **7** (also **works**) Military a defensive structure. **8** (**works**) the mechanism of a clock or other machine. **9** Physics the exertion of force overcoming resistance or producing molecular change. **10** (**the works**) informal everything needed, desired, or expected. > verb (past and past participle **worked** or archaic **wrought**) **1** do work, especially as one's job. **2** set to or keep at work. **3** (of a machine or system) function, especially properly or effectively. **4** (of a machine) be in operation. **5** have or bring about the desired result. **6** bring (a material or mixture) to a desired shape or consistency. **7** produce (an article or design) using a specified material or sewing stitch. **8** cultivate (land) or extract materials from (a

mine or quarry). **9** move gradually or with difficulty into another position. **10** (of a person's features) move violently or convulsively. **11** bring into a specified emotional state.

IDIOMS – **have one's work cut out** be faced with a hard or lengthy task. **in the works** being planned, worked on, or produced. **work in** try to include (something). **work off** reduce or eliminate (something) by activity. **work on** exert influence on. **work one's passage** pay for one's journey on a ship with work instead of money. **work out 1** solve or be capable of being solved. **2** develop in a good or specified way. **3** plan (something) in detail. **4** understand the character of (someone). **5** engage in vigorous physical exercise. **work out at** be calculated at. **work over** informal beat (someone) up. **work to rule** chiefly Brit. follow official working rules and hours exactly in order to reduce output and efficiency, as a form of industrial action. **work up** develop or improve (something) gradually. **work up to** proceed gradually towards (something more advanced). **get worked up** gradually come into a state of intense excitement, anger, or anxiety.

DERIVATIVES – **workless** adjective.

SYNONYMS – noun **1** labour, toil; informal graft, grind. **2** employment. verb **1** labour, toil. **3,4** function, go, operate, perform, run. **5** succeed.

COMBINATIONS – **workbench** a bench at which carpentry or other mechanical or practical work is done. **work ethic** the principle that hard work is intrinsically virtuous or worthy of reward. **workmate** chiefly Brit. a person with whom one works; a colleague. **work of art** a creative product with strong imaginative or aesthetic appeal. **work permit** an official document giving a foreigner permission to take a job in a country. **workpiece** an object being worked on with a tool or machine. **works council** chiefly Brit. a group of employees representing a workforce in discussions with their employers. **worksheet 1** a paper listing questions or tasks for students. **2** a paper or table recording work done or in progress. **work-shy** disinclined to work. **workspace 1** an area rented or sold for commercial purposes. **2** Computing a memory storage facility for temporary use. **workstation** a desktop computer terminal, typically networked and more powerful than a personal computer. **worktop** Brit. a flat surface for working on, especially in a kitchen.

workable > adjective **1** able to be worked. **2** capable of producing the desired result.

DERIVATIVES – **workability** noun **workably** adverb.

workaday > adjective not unusual or interesting; ordinary.

workaholic > noun informal a person who compulsively works excessively hard.

DERIVATIVES – **workaholism** noun.

worker > noun **1** a person who works. **2** a neuter or undeveloped female bee, wasp, ant, etc., large numbers of which perform the basic work of a colony. **3** a person who achieves a specified thing: a miracle-worker.

workfare > noun a welfare system which requires some work or attendance for training from those receiving benefits.

workforce > noun the people engaged in or available for work in a particular area, firm, or industry.

workhorse > noun a person or machine that works hard and reliably over a long period.

workhouse > noun **1** historical (in the UK) a public institution in which poor people received board and lodging in return for work. **2** US a prison in which petty offenders are expected to work.

working > adjective **1** having paid employment. **2** engaged in manual labour. **3** functioning or able to function. **4** good enough as the basis for work or argument and likely to be developed or improved later: a working title. > noun **1** a mine or a part of a mine from which minerals are being extracted. **2** (**workings**) the way in which a machine, organisation, or system operates. **3** (**workings**) a record of the successive calculations made in solving a mathematical problem. **4** a scheduled duty or trip performed by a locomotive, bus, or other vehicle.

COMBINATIONS – **working capital** the capital of a business which is used in its day-to-day trading operations. **working class** the social group consisting of people who are employed in manual or industrial work. **working party** (also **working group**) Brit. a group appointed to study and report on a particular question and make recommendations.

workload > noun the amount of work to be done by someone or something.

workman > noun **1** a man employed to do manual labour. **2** a person who works in a specified way.

IDIOMS – **a bad workman always blames his tools** proverb a person who has done something badly will seek to lay the blame on their equipment rather than admit their own lack of skill.

workmanlike > adjective showing efficient competence.

workmanship > noun the degree of skill with which a product is made or a job done.

workout > noun a session of vigorous physical exercise.

workshop > *noun* **1** a room or building in which goods are manufactured or repaired. **2** a meeting at which a group engages in intensive discussion and activity on a particular subject or project.

world > *noun* **1** (**the world**) the earth with all its countries and peoples. **2** all that belongs to a particular area, period, or sphere of activity: *the theatre world*. **3** (**one's world**) a person's life and activities. **4** (**the world**) secular or material matters as opposed to spiritual ones. **5** a planet. **6** (**a** or **the world**) a very large amount of: *that makes a world of difference*.
IDIOMS – **the best of both** (or **all possible**) **worlds** the benefits of widely differing situations, enjoyed at the same time. **bring into the world** give birth to or assist at the birth of. **man** (or **woman**) **of the world** a person who is experienced in the ways of sophisticated society. **out of this world** informal extremely enjoyable or impressive. **the world and his wife** Brit. informal everybody. **the world, the flesh, and the devil** all forms of temptation to sin.
COMBINATIONS – **world-beater** a person or thing that is better than all others in its field. **world-class** of or among the best in the world. **world English** the English language including all of its regional varieties, such as North American, Australian, and South African English. **world music** music from the developing world incorporating traditional and/or popular elements. **world order** a set of arrangements established internationally for preserving global political stability. **world power** a country that has significant influence in international affairs. **world-ranking** among the best in the world. **world-shaking** of very great importance; momentous. **world view** a particular philosophy of life or conception of the world. **world war** a war involving many large nations in all different parts of the world, especially the wars of 1914–18 and 1939–45. **world-weary** bored with or cynical about life.

worldly > *adjective* (**wordlier, wordliest**) **1** of or concerned with material affairs rather than spiritual ones. **2** experienced and sophisticated.
IDIOMS – **worldly goods** (or **possessions** or **wealth**) everything that someone owns.
DERIVATIVES – **worldliness** *noun*.
SYNONYMS – **1** earthly, mortal, mundane, temporal, terrestrial. **2** cosmopolitan, experienced, seasoned, sophisticated, urbane.
ANTONYMS – **2** naive, unsophisticated.
COMBINATIONS – **worldly-wise** having sufficient experience not to be easily shocked or deceived.

worldwide > *adjective* extending or applicable throughout the world. > *adverb* throughout the world.

World Wide Web > *noun* Computing an extensive information system on the Internet providing facilities for documents to be connected to other documents by hypertext links.

worm > *noun* **1** an earthworm or other creeping or burrowing invertebrate animal having a long, slender, soft body and no limbs. **2** (**worms**) intestinal or other internal parasites. **3** (**worms**) maggots regarded as eating dead bodies buried in the ground. **4** informal a weak or despicable person. > *verb* **1** move by crawling or wriggling. **2** (**worm one's way into**) insinuate one's way into. **3** (**worm out of**) obtain (information) from (someone) by cunning persistence. **4** treat (an animal) with a preparation designed to expel parasitic worms.
WORDFINDER – annelid (*an earthworm, leech, or related creature*), anthelmintic, vermifuge (*a medicine used against parasitic worms*), vermicide (*a substance poisonous to worms*), vermiform (*long and thin like a worm*).
IDIOMS – (**even**) **a worm will turn** proverb even a meek person will resist or retaliate if pushed too far. **worm's-eye view** a view from below or from a very low position.
COMBINATIONS – **worm cast** a convoluted mass of soil, mud, or sand thrown up at the surface by a burrowing worm. **worm-eaten** (of wood) full of holes made by woodworm. **worm gear** a mechanical arrangement consisting of a toothed wheel worked by a short revolving cylinder (worm) bearing a screw thread. **wormwheel** the wheel of a worm gear.

wormery > *noun* (pl. **wormeries**) a container in which worms are bred or kept for study.

wormhole > *noun* **1** a hole made by a burrowing insect larva or worm in wood, fruit, etc. **2** Physics a hypothetical connection between widely separated regions of space–time.

wormwood > *noun* **1** a woody shrub with a bitter aromatic taste, used as an ingredient of vermouth and absinthe and in medicine. **2** bitterness or grief, or a source of this.
ORIGIN – Old English; compare with **VERMOUTH**.

wormy > *adjective* (**wormier, wormiest**) worm-eaten or full of worms.

worn past participle of **WEAR**. > *adjective* **1** suffering from wear. **2** very tired.
IDIOMS – **worn out 1** exhausted. **2** worn to the point of being no longer usable.
SYNONYMS – **1** shabby, tattered, threadbare; informal tatty.

worried > *adjective* feeling, showing, or expressing anxiety.
DERIVATIVES – **worriedly** adverb.
SYNONYMS – anxious, apprehensive, concerned, nervous, tense, troubled.
ANTONYMS – calm, carefree.

worrisome > *adjective* causing anxiety or concern.

worry > *verb* (**worries, worried**) **1** cause (someone) to feel troubled over actual or potential difficulties. **2** feel troubled or anxious. **3** annoy or disturb. **4** (of a dog or other carnivorous animal) tear at or pull about with the teeth. **5** (of a dog) chase and attack (livestock, especially sheep). **6** (**worry at**) pull at or fiddle with repeatedly. **7** (**worry out**) discover or devise (a solution) by persistent thought. > *noun* (pl. **worries**) **1** the state of being worried. **2** a source of anxiety.
IDIOMS – **no worries** informal, chiefly Austral. all right; fine.
DERIVATIVES – **worrier** noun **worrying** adjective **worryingly** adverb.
SYNONYMS – verb **1** bother, concern, perturb, trouble, unsettle. **2** agonise, brood, lose sleep. **3** annoy, bother, disturb, harass, pester, trouble, vex. noun **1** anxiety, apprehension, concern, disquiet, fretfulness, nervousness, unease. **2** cause for concern, headache, problem, trouble.
COMBINATIONS – **worry beads** a string of beads that one fingers to calm oneself.

wordpower facts
Worry
The main current meanings of the verb **worry** (senses 1 and 2) actually arose surprisingly recently, and the sense 'tear at with the teeth' is much earlier. **Worry** (or *wyrgan*, as it was then) was an Old English word meaning 'strangle'. In Middle English it took on the meanings 'choke with a mouthful of food', 'seize by the throat and tear', and 'swallow greedily', and in the 16th century 'harass with repeated aggression'. This gave rise to 'annoy or disturb' in the late 17th century and 'cause anxiety to' in the early 19th century; the sense 'feel anxious or troubled', as in *he worried about his son*, is not recorded until the end of the 19th century.

worse > *adjective* **1** less good, satisfactory, or pleasing. **2** more ill or unhappy. > *adverb* **1** less well. **2** more seriously or severely. > *noun* a worse event or circumstance: *worse was to follow*.
IDIOMS – **none the worse for** not adversely affected by. **the worse for drink** rather drunk. **the worse for wear** informal **1** worn. **2** feeling rather unwell, especially as

a result of drinking too much alcohol. **worse off** less fortunate or prosperous.

worsen > *verb* make or become worse.

worship > *noun* 1 the feeling or expression of reverence and adoration for a god or goddess. 2 religious rites and ceremonies. 3 great admiration or devotion. 4 (**His or Your Worship**) chiefly Brit. a title of respect for a magistrate or mayor. > *verb* (**worshipped**, **worshipping**; US also **worshiped**, **worshiping**) 1 show reverence and adoration for (a god or goddess). 2 feel great admiration or devotion for.
DERIVATIVES – **worshipper** *noun*.
SYNONYMS – *noun* 1 adoration, devotion, homage, reverence, veneration. *verb* 1 exalt, extol, glorify, revere, reverence, venerate. 2 admire, hero-worship, idolise.
ORIGIN – Old English, 'worthiness, acknowledgement of worth'.

worshipful > *adjective* 1 feeling or showing reverence and admiration. 2 (**Worshipful**) Brit. a title given to justices of the peace and to certain old companies or their officers.

worst > *adjective* most bad, severe, or serious. > *adverb* 1 most severely or seriously. 2 least well. > *noun* the worst part, event, or circumstance. > *verb* get the better of.
IDIOMS – **at worst** in the worst possible case. **do one's worst** do as much damage as one can. **get** (or **have**) **the worst of it** suffer the most. **if the worst comes to the worst** if the most serious or difficult circumstances arise.

worsted /ˈwo͝ostid/ > *noun* 1 a fine, smooth yarn spun from combed long-staple wool. 2 fabric made from such yarn.
ORIGIN – from *Worstead*, the name of a parish in Norfolk, England.

wort /wurt/ > *noun* the sweet infusion of ground malt or other grain before fermentation, used to produce beer and distilled malt liquors.
ORIGIN – Old English, related to **ROOT**¹.

-wort > *suffix* used in names of plants and herbs, especially those used formerly as food or medicinally: *lungwort*.

worth > *adjective* 1 equivalent in value to the sum or item specified. 2 deserving to be treated or regarded in the way specified. 3 having income or property amounting to a specified sum. > *noun* 1 the value or merit of someone or something. 2 an amount of a commodity equivalent to a specified sum of money: *hundreds of pounds worth of clothes*.
IDIOMS – **for all one is worth** informal as energetically or enthusiastically as one can.
SYNONYMS – *noun* 1 importance, merit, quality, value, virtue.

worthless > *adjective* 1 having no real value or use. 2 (of a person) having no good qualities.

DERIVATIVES – **worthlessly** *adverb* **worthlessness** *noun*.
SYNONYMS – 1 futile, meaningless, pointless, trivial, useless, valueless. 2 contemptible, despicable, good-for-nothing.

worthwhile > *adjective* worth the time, money, or effort spent.
SYNONYMS – beneficial, fruitful, rewarding, satisfying, valuable.

worthy > *adjective* (**worthier**, **worthiest**) 1 (often **worthy of**) deserving or good enough. 2 deserving effort, attention, or respect. 3 showing good intent but lacking in humour or imagination. > *noun* (pl. **worthies**) often humorous a person important in a particular sphere: *local worthies*.
DERIVATIVES – **worthily** *adverb* **worthiness** *noun*.
SYNONYMS – *adjective* 2 commendable, decent, deserving, estimable, good, respectable.

-worthy > *combining form* 1 deserving of a specified thing: *newsworthy*. 2 suitable for a specified thing: *roadworthy*.

wot singular present of **WIT**².

would > *modal verb* (3rd sing. present **would**) 1 past of **WILL**¹, in various senses. 2 (expressing the conditional mood) indicating the consequence of an imagined event. 3 expressing a desire or inclination. 4 expressing a polite request. 5 expressing a conjecture or opinion. 6 literary expressing a wish or regret.
USAGE – on the difference between **would** and **should**, see the note at **SHOULD**.

would-be > *adjective* often derogatory desiring or aspiring to be a specified type of person.

wouldn't > *contraction* would not.

wouldst archaic second person singular of **WOULD**.

wound¹ /wo͞ond/ > *noun* 1 an injury to living tissue caused by a cut, blow, or other impact. 2 an injury to a person's feelings or reputation. > *verb* inflict a wound on.
SYNONYMS – *noun* 1 cut, gash, injury, laceration, lesion. 2 blow, hurt, injury, pain. *verb* damage, harm, hurt, injure.

wound² past and past participle of **WIND**².

wove past of **WEAVE**¹.

woven past participle of **WEAVE**¹.

wow¹ informal > *exclamation* (also **wowee**) expressing astonishment or admiration. > *noun* a sensational success. > *verb* impress and excite greatly.

wow² > *noun* Electronics slow pitch fluctuation in sound reproduction, perceptible in long notes. Compare with **FLUTTER**.

wowser /ˈwowzər/ > *noun* Austral./NZ informal a puritanical person; a killjoy.

WP > *abbreviation* word processing or word processor.

WPC > *abbreviation* (in the UK) woman police constable.

wpm > *abbreviation* words per minute (used after a number to indicate typing speed).

wrack¹ > *verb* variant spelling of **RACK**¹, **RACK**³.
USAGE – the complicated relationship between **wrack** and **rack** is explained at **RACK**¹.

wrack² > *noun* a coarse brown seaweed which grows on the shoreline, often with air bladders providing buoyancy.
ORIGIN – apparently from archaic and dialect *wrack* 'shipwreck'.

wrack³ (also **rack**) > *noun* a mass of high, thick, fast-moving cloud.
ORIGIN – probably Scandinavian: originally denoting a rush or collision.

wraith /rayth/ > *noun* 1 a ghost or ghostly image of someone, especially one seen shortly before or after their death. 2 literary a wisp or faint trace.
DERIVATIVES – **wraithlike** *adjective*.

wrangle > *noun* a long and complicated dispute or argument. > *verb* 1 engage in a wrangle. 2 N. Amer. round up or take charge of (livestock).
DERIVATIVES – **wrangler** *noun*.

wrap > *verb* (**wrapped**, **wrapping**) 1 cover or enclose in paper or soft material. 2 arrange (paper or soft material) round something. 3 Computing cause (a word or unit of text) to be carried over to a new line automatically. 4 informal finish filming or recording. > *noun* 1 a loose outer garment or piece of material. 2 paper or material used for wrapping. 3 informal the end of a session of filming or recording. 4 Brit. informal a small packet of a powdered illegal drug. 5 a tortilla wrapped around a cold filling, eaten as a sandwich.
IDIOMS – **under wraps** kept secret. **wrap up** 1 put on or dress in warm clothes. 2 complete or conclude (a meeting or other process). 3 Brit. informal be quiet; stop talking. 4 (**wrapped up**) engrossed or absorbed to the exclusion of other things.
DERIVATIVES – **wrapping** *noun*.

wrapped > *adjective* Austral. informal overjoyed; delighted.

wrapper > *noun* 1 a piece of paper or other material used for wrapping something. 2 chiefly N. Amer. a loose robe or gown.

wrasse /rass/ > *noun* (pl. same or **wrasses**) a brightly coloured marine fish with thick lips and strong teeth.
ORIGIN – Cornish *wrah*; related to Welsh *gwrach* 'old woman'.

wrath /roth, rawth/ > *noun* extreme anger.

wrathful > *adjective* literary full of or characterised by intense anger.
DERIVATIVES – **wrathfully** *adverb*.

wreak /reek/ > *verb* 1 cause (a large amount of damage or harm). 2 inflict (vengeance).
USAGE – the past tense of the verb **wreak** is **wreaked**, as in *torrential rainstorms wreaked*

havoc, not **wrought**. When **wrought** is used in the phrase **wrought havoc**, it is in fact an archaic past tense of **work**.

ORIGIN – Old English, 'drive (out), avenge'; related to **WRECK** and **WRETCH**.

wreath /reeth/ > *noun* (pl. **wreaths** /reeths, reethz/) **1** an arrangement of flowers, leaves, or stems fastened in a ring and used for decoration or for laying on a grave. **2** a curl or ring of smoke or cloud.

USAGE – do not confuse **wreath** and **wreathe**: **wreath** with no *e* at the end means 'arrangement of flowers', while **wreathe** with an *e* is a verb meaning 'envelop, surround, or encircle'.

ORIGIN – Old English, related to **WRITHE**.

wreathe /reeth/ > *verb* **1** (usu. **be wreathed in** or **with**) envelop, surround, or encircle. **2** (of smoke) move with a curling motion.

ORIGIN – from **WRITHE**, reinforced by **WREATH**.

wreck > *noun* **1** the destruction of a ship at sea; a shipwreck. **2** a ship destroyed at sea. **3** a building, vehicle, etc. that has been destroyed or badly damaged. **4** N. Amer. a road or rail crash. **5** a person in a very bad physical or mental state. > *verb* **1** cause the destruction of (a ship) by sinking or breaking up. **2** destroy or severely damage. **3** spoil completely. **4** (**wrecking**) historical the practice of causing a ship to run aground in order to steal the cargo.

ORIGIN – Old French *wrec*; related to **WREAK**.

wreckage > *noun* the remains of something that has been badly damaged or destroyed.

wrecked > *adjective* informal **1** exhausted. **2** drunk.

wrecker > *noun* **1** a person or thing that wrecks something. **2** chiefly N. Amer. a person who breaks up damaged vehicles or demolishes old buildings to obtain usable spares or scrap.

Wren > *noun* (in the UK) a member of the former Women's Royal Naval Service.

ORIGIN – from the abbreviation *WRNS*.

wren > *noun* a very small short-winged songbird with a cocked tail.

wrench > *verb* **1** pull or twist suddenly and violently. **2** injure (a part of the body) as a result of a sudden twisting movement. **3** turn or adjust with a wrench. > *noun* **1** a sudden violent twist or pull. **2** a feeling of abrupt pain and distress caused by one's own or another's departure. **3** an adjustable tool like a spanner, used for gripping and turning nuts or bolts.

wrest /rest/ > *verb* **1** forcibly pull from a person's grasp. **2** take (power or control) after effort or resistance.

ORIGIN – Old English, 'twist, tighten'; related to **WRIST**.

wrestle > *verb* **1** take part in a fight or contest that involves close grappling with

one's opponent. **2** struggle with a difficulty or problem. **3** extract or manipulate (an object) with difficulty and some physical effort. > *noun* **1** a wrestling bout or contest. **2** a hard struggle.

WORDFINDER – armlock, hammerlock, headlock, nelson (*wrestling holds*), Graeco-Roman (*style of wrestling with no holds below the waist*), sumo (*traditional Japanese wrestling*).

DERIVATIVES – **wrestler** noun **wrestling** noun.

wretch > *noun* **1** an unfortunate person. **2** informal a contemptible person.

wretched > *adjective* (**wretcheder**, **wretchedest**) **1** in a very unhappy or unfortunate state; miserable. **2** used to express anger or annoyance: *she disliked the wretched man intensely.*

DERIVATIVES – **wretchedly** *adverb* **wretchedness** *noun*.

SYNONYMS – **1** dejected, depressed, downhearted, miserable, sad, unhappy.

wriggle > *verb* **1** twist and turn with quick writhing movements. **2** (**wriggle out of**) avoid by devious means. > *noun* a wriggling movement.

DERIVATIVES – **wriggler** noun **wriggly** *adjective*.

ORIGIN – Low German *wriggelen*.

wright > *noun* a maker or builder of something: *playwright | shipwright.*

ORIGIN – Old English, related to **WORK**.

wring > *verb* (past and past participle **wrung**) **1** squeeze and twist to force liquid from. **2** break (an animal's neck) by twisting forcibly. **3** squeeze (someone's hand) tightly. **4** (**wring from** or **out of**) obtain with difficulty or effort. **5** cause great pain or distress to. > *noun* an act of wringing.

IDIOMS – **wring one's hands** clasp and twist one's hands together as a gesture of distress or despair.

wringer > *noun* a device for wringing water from wet clothes or other objects.

wringing > *adjective* extremely wet; soaked.

wrinkle > *noun* **1** a slight line or fold, especially in fabric or the skin of the face. **2** informal a clever innovation, or useful piece of information or advice. > *verb* make or become wrinkled.

DERIVATIVES – **wrinkled** *adjective*.

wrinkly > *adjective* (**wrinklier**, **wrinkliest**) having many wrinkles. > *noun* (pl. **wrinklies**) Brit. informal, derogatory an old person.

wrist > *noun* the joint connecting the hand with the forearm.

WORDFINDER – carpus (*the group of bones in the wrist*).

COMBINATIONS – **wristband** a band worn round the wrist, especially for identity purposes or as a sweatband. **wristwatch** a watch worn on a strap round the wrist.

writ[1] > *noun* **1** a form of written command in the name of a court or other legal authority. **2** (**one's writ**) one's power to enforce compliance or submission.

COMBINATIONS – **writ of execution** Law a judicial order that a judgement be enforced.

writ[2] > *verb* archaic past participle of **WRITE**.

IDIOMS – **writ large** in an obvious or exaggerated form.

write > *verb* (past **wrote**; past participle **written**) **1** mark (letters, words, or other symbols) on a surface, with a pen, pencil, or similar implement. **2** write in a cursive hand, as opposed to printing individual letters. **3** write and send (a letter) to someone. **4** compose (a text or work) in writing. **5** compose (a musical work). **6** Computing enter (data) into a specified storage medium or location in store. **7** underwrite (an insurance policy).

IDIOMS – **be written all over one's face** informal be obvious from one's expression. **write off 1** dismiss as insignificant. **2** cancel the record of (a bad debt); acknowledge the failure to recover (an asset). **3** Brit. damage (a vehicle) so badly that it cannot be repaired or is not worth repairing.

DERIVATIVES – **writable** *adjective* (chiefly Computing).

ORIGIN – Old English, 'score, form (letters) by carving, write'.

write-off > *noun* **1** a vehicle that is too badly damaged to be repaired. **2** a worthless or ineffectual person or thing.

writer > *noun* **1** a person who has written a particular text, or who writes books or articles as an occupation. **2** Computing a device that writes data to a storage medium.

COMBINATIONS – **writer's block** the condition of being unable to think of what to write or how to proceed with writing. **writer's cramp** pain or stiffness in the hand caused by excessive writing.

writerly > *adjective* **1** of or characteristic of a professional author. **2** consciously literary.

write-up > *noun* a newspaper article giving an opinion of a recent event, performance, etc.; a review.

writhe /rīth/ > *verb* twist or squirm in pain or as if in pain.

ORIGIN – Old English, 'make into coils, plait'.

writing > *noun* **1** the activity or skill of writing. **2** written work. **3** (**writings**) books or other written works. **4** a sequence of letters or symbols forming coherent words.

WORDFINDER – calligraphy (*decorative handwriting*), cursive (*denoting joined-up writing*), graphologist (*a person who examines handwriting for psychological indications*), palaeographer (*an expert in ancient writing systems*).

IDIOMS – **the writing is on the wall** there are clear signs that something unpleasant or unwelcome is going to happen. [ORIGIN – with biblical allusion to Belshazzar's feast (Book of Daniel, chapter 5), at which mysterious writing appeared on the wall foretelling Belshazzar's overthrow.]

wrong > *adjective* **1** not correct or true; mistaken or in error. **2** unjust, dishonest, or immoral. **3** in a bad or abnormal condition; amiss. > *adverb* **1** in an unsuitable or undesirable manner or direction. **2** with an incorrect result. > *noun* **1** an unjust, dishonest, or immoral action. **2** that which is morally wrong. > *verb* **1** act unjustly or dishonestly towards. **2** mistakenly attribute bad motives to; misrepresent.

IDIOMS – **get wrong** misunderstand (someone), especially by falsely believing them to be malicious. **get hold of the wrong end of the stick** misunderstand something. **in the wrong** responsible for a mistake or offence. **on the wrong side of 1** out of favour with. **2** somewhat more than (a specified age). **two wrongs don't make a right** proverb the fact that someone has done something unjust or dishonest is no justification for acting in a similar way.

DERIVATIVES – **wrongly** *adverb* **wrongness** *noun*.

SYNONYMS – *adjective* **1** erroneous, inaccurate, incorrect, mistaken, untrue. *noun* **1** crime, injustice, misdeed, offence, sin. **2** evil, immorality, injustice, sin, wickedness.

ANTONYMS – *adjective* **1** correct, right. **2** ethical, right.

COMBINATIONS – **wrong-headed** having or showing bad judgement; misguided.

ORIGIN – Old Norse *rangr* 'awry, unjust'.

wrongdoing > *noun* illegal or dishonest behaviour.

DERIVATIVES – **wrongdoer** *noun*.

wrong-foot > *verb* Brit. **1** (in a game) play so as to catch (an opponent) off balance. **2** place (someone) in a difficult or embarrassing situation by saying or doing something unexpected.

wrongful > *adjective* not fair, just, or legal.

DERIVATIVES – **wrongfully** *adverb*.

wrote past tense of **WRITE**.

wroth /rōth, roth/ > *adjective* archaic angry.

wrought /rawt/ > *adjective* **1** (of metals) beaten out or shaped by hammering. **2** made or fashioned in the specified way: *well-wrought*. **3** (**wrought up**) upset and anxious.

COMBINATIONS – **wrought iron** a tough, malleable form of iron suitable for forging or rolling rather than casting.

ORIGIN – archaic past and past participle of **WORK**.

wrung past and past participle of **WRING**.

wry /rī/ > *adjective* (**wryer**, **wryest** or **wrier**, **wriest**) **1** using or expressing dry, especially mocking, humour. **2** (of a person's face) twisted into an expression of disgust, disappointment, or annoyance. **3** bending or twisted to one side.

DERIVATIVES – **wryly** *adverb* **wryness** *noun*.

SYNONYMS – **1** droll, dry, ironic, mocking, sardonic.

ORIGIN – from Old English *wrīgian* 'tend, incline', later 'deviate, swerve, contort'.

wrybill > *noun* a small New Zealand plover with a bill that bends to the right.

wryneck > *noun* a bird of the woodpecker family, with brown plumage and a habit of twisting its head backwards.

WSW > *abbreviation* west-south-west.

WTO > *abbreviation* World Trade Organisation.

wunderkind /voŏndərkind/ > *noun* (pl. **wunderkinds** or **wunderkinder** /voŏn-dərkindər/) a person who achieves great success when relatively young.

ORIGIN – German, from *Wunder* 'wonder' + *Kind* 'child'.

Wurlitzer /**wur**litsər/ > *noun* trademark a large pipe organ or electric organ.

ORIGIN – named after the American instrument-maker Rudolf *Wurlitzer* (1831–1914).

wurst /voorst, wurst/ > *noun* German or Austrian sausage.

ORIGIN – German.

wuss /woŏss/ > *noun* N. Amer. informal a weak or ineffectual person.

DERIVATIVES – **wussy** *noun* (pl. **wussies**) & *adjective*.

WV > *abbreviation* West Virginia.

WWI > *abbreviation* World War I.

WWII > *abbreviation* World War II.

WWF > *abbreviation* **1** World Wide Fund for Nature. **2** World Wrestling Federation.

WWW > *abbreviation* World Wide Web.

WY > *abbreviation* Wyoming.

wych elm /wich/ (also **witch elm**) > *noun* a European elm with large, rough leaves.

ORIGIN – *wych*, used in names of trees with pliant branches, is from Old English, apparently from a root meaning 'bend'.

wych hazel > *noun* variant spelling of **WITCH HAZEL**.

wyn /win/ > *noun* variant spelling of **WEN**².

WYSIWYG /**wizz**iwig/ > *adjective* Computing denoting the representation of text on-screen in a form exactly corresponding to its appearance on a printout.

ORIGIN – acronym from *what you see is what you get*.

wyvern /**wī**vərn/ > *noun* Heraldry a winged two-legged dragon with a barbed tail.

ORIGIN – Old French *wivre*, from Latin *vipera* 'viper' (the original sense in English).

X¹ (also **x**) > *noun* (pl. **Xs** or **X's**) **1** the twenty-fourth letter of the alphabet. **2** denoting an unknown or unspecified person or thing. **3** (usu. *x*) the first unknown quantity in an algebraic expression. **4** referring to the principal or horizontal axis in a system of coordinates. **5** a cross-shaped written symbol, used to indicate an incorrect answer or to symbolise a kiss. **6** the Roman numeral for ten.
COMBINATIONS – **X chromosome** Genetics (in humans and other mammals) a sex chromosome, two of which are normally present in female cells (designated XX) and only one in male cells (designated XY). Compare with **Y chromosome**.

X² > *symbol* denoting films classified as suitable for adults only (replaced in the UK in 1983 by *18*, and in the US in 1990 by *NC–17*).

xanthine /**zan**theen/ > *noun* Biochemistry any of a class of organic compounds including caffeine and other alkaloids.
ORIGIN – from Greek *xanthos* 'yellow'.

Xe > *symbol* the chemical element xenon.

xeno- > *combining form* **1** relating to a foreigner or foreigners: *xenophobia*. **2** other; different in origin: *xenograft*.
ORIGIN – from Greek *xenos* 'stranger', 'strange'.

xenobiotic /zennōbī**ott**ik/ > *adjective* (of a substance) foreign to the body or to an ecological system.

xenograft /**zenn**əgraaft/ > *noun* a tissue graft or organ transplant from a donor of a different species from the recipient.

xenolith /**zenn**əlith/ > *noun* Geology a piece of rock within an igneous mass which is not derived from the original magma but has been introduced from elsewhere.

xenology /zenn**oll**əji/ > *noun* (chiefly in science fiction) the scientific study of alien biology, cultures, etc.
DERIVATIVES – **xenologist** *noun*.

xenon /**zenn**on/ > *noun* an inert gaseous chemical element, present in trace amounts in the air and used in some kinds of electric light.
ORIGIN – from Greek *xenos* 'strange'.

xenophobia /zennə**fōb**iə/ > *noun* intense or irrational dislike or fear of people from other countries.
DERIVATIVES – **xenophobe** *noun* **xenophobic** *adjective*.

xenotransplantation > *noun* the process of grafting or transplanting organs or tissues between members of different species.
DERIVATIVES – **xenotransplant** *noun*.

xeriscape /**zeer**iskayp, **zerr**iskayp/ > *noun* chiefly N. Amer. a style of landscape design requiring little or no irrigation or other maintenance, used in arid regions.
DERIVATIVES – **xeriscaping** *noun*.
ORIGIN – from Greek *xēros* 'dry'.

xerography > *noun* a dry copying process in which powder adheres to parts of a surface remaining electrically charged after being exposed to light from an image of the document to be copied.
DERIVATIVES – **xerographic** *adjective*.

xerophyte /**zeer**əfīt, **zerr**əfīt/ > *noun* Botany a plant which needs very little water.
DERIVATIVES – **xerophytic** *adjective*.

Xerox /**zeer**oks/ > *noun* trademark **1** a xerographic copying process. **2** a copy made using such a process. > *verb* (**xerox**) copy (a document) by such a process.

Xhosa /**kō**sə, **kaw**sə/ > *noun* (pl. same or **Xhosas**) **1** a member of a South African people traditionally living in the Eastern Cape Province. **2** the Bantu language of this people.
ORIGIN – the name in Xhosa.

xi /ksī/ > *noun* the fourteenth letter of the Greek alphabet (Ξ, ξ), transliterated as 'x'.
ORIGIN – Greek.

XL > *abbreviation* extra large (as a clothes size).

Xmas /**kris**məss, **eks**məss/ > *noun* informal term for **Christmas**.
ORIGIN – *X* representing the initial *Kh* (Greek chi) of Greek *Khristos* 'Christ'.

XML > *abbreviation* Extensible Markup Language.

XOR > *noun* Electronics exclusive OR (a Boolean operator).

X-rated > *adjective* **1** pornographic or indecent. **2** (formerly) denoting a film given an X classification.

X-ray > *noun* **1** an electromagnetic wave of very short wavelength, able to pass through many materials opaque to light. **2** a photograph or other image of the internal structure of an object produced by passing X-rays through the object. > *verb* photograph or examine with X-rays.
WORDFINDER – barium meal (*a preparation swallowed to allow X-rays to be made of the stomach or intestines*), mammography (*the use of X-rays to diagnose tumours of the breasts*), radiograph (*an image produced by X-rays*), radiology (*the science of X-rays*), radioscopy (*examination by X-rays of objects opaque to light*), radiotherapy (*the treatment of cancer or other disease using X-rays*), tomography (*a technique for displaying a cross section of a human body using X-rays or ultrasound*).
COMBINATIONS – **X-ray astronomy** the branch of astronomy concerned with the detection and measurement of high-energy electromagnetic radiation emitted by celestial objects.
ORIGIN – from *X*- (because, when discovered in 1895, the nature of the rays was unknown).

xu /soo/ > *noun* (pl. same) a monetary unit of Vietnam, equal to one hundredth of a dong.
ORIGIN – Vietnamese, from French *sou*.

xylem /**zī**ləm/ > *noun* Botany the vascular tissue in plants which conducts water and dissolved nutrients upwards from the root and also helps to form the woody element in the stem.
ORIGIN – from Greek *xulon* 'wood'.

xylene /**zī**leen/ > *noun* Chemistry a volatile liquid hydrocarbon resembling benzene, obtained by distilling wood, coal tar, or petroleum.

xylophone > *noun* a musical instrument played by striking a row of wooden bars of graduated length with small beaters.
ORIGIN – from Greek *xulon* 'wood'.

Y¹ (also **y**) > *noun* (pl. **Ys** or **Y's**) **1** the twenty-fifth letter of the alphabet. **2** referring to an unknown or unspecified person or thing (coming second after 'x'). **3** (usu. *y*) the second unknown quantity in an algebraic expression. **4** referring to the secondary or vertical axis in a system of coordinates.
COMBINATIONS – **Y chromosome** Genetics (in humans and other mammals) a sex chromosome which is normally present only in male cells, which are designated XY. Compare with **X chromosome**. **Y-fronts** Brit. trademark men's or boys' underpants with a seam at the front in the shape of an upside-down Y.

Y² > *abbreviation* yen. > *symbol* the chemical element yttrium.

y > *abbreviation* year(s).

-y¹ > *suffix* forming adjectives: **1** full of; having the quality of: *messy*. **2** inclined to; apt to: *sticky*.

-y² (also **-ey** or **-ie**) > *suffix* **1** forming diminutive nouns, pet names, etc.: *aunty*. **2** forming verbs: *shinny*.

-y³ > *suffix* forming nouns: **1** referring to a state or quality: *jealousy*. **2** referring to an action or its result: *victory*.
ORIGIN – French *-ie*, from Greek *-eia*, *-ia*.

Y2K > *abbreviation* year 2000.

yabby (also **yabbie**) > *noun* (pl. **yabbies**) Austral. **1** a small freshwater crayfish. **2** a burrowing marine prawn, used as bait.
ORIGIN – Wemba-wemba (an Aboriginal language).

yacht /yot/ > *noun* **1** a medium-sized sailing boat equipped for cruising or racing. **2** a powered boat equipped for cruising. > *verb* race or cruise in a yacht.
DERIVATIVES – **yachting** noun.
ORIGIN – Dutch *jaghte*, from *jaghtschip* 'fast pirate ship', from *jaght* 'hunting' + *schip* 'ship'.

yachtie > *noun* informal a person who sails yachts.

yack > *noun & verb* variant spelling of **YAK²**.

yacker > *noun* variant spelling of **YAKKA**.

yah¹ > *exclamation* yes (used in representations of upper-class speech).

yah² > *exclamation* expressing derision.

yahoo /yaahoo, yəhoo/ > *noun* informal a rude, coarse, or brutish person.
ORIGIN – from the name of an imaginary race in Jonathan Swift's *Gulliver's Travels* (1726).

Yahweh /yaaway/ > *noun* a form of the Hebrew name of God used in the Bible.
ORIGIN – Hebrew.

yak¹ > *noun* a large ox with shaggy hair and large horns, used in Tibet as a pack animal and for its milk, meat, and hide.
ORIGIN – Tibetan.

yak² (also **yack**) informal > *verb* (**yakked**, **yakking**) talk at length about trivial or boring subjects. > *noun* a trivial or unduly persistent conversation.

yakka (also **yacker**) > *noun* Austral./NZ informal work; hard labour.
ORIGIN – Jagara (an Aboriginal language).

yakuza /yəkoozə/ > *noun* (pl. same) **1** (**the Yakuza**) a powerful Japanese criminal organisation. **2** a member of this.
ORIGIN – Japanese, from words meaning 'eight' + 'nine' + 'three', referring to the worst hand in a gambling game.

Yale > *noun* trademark a type of lock with a latch bolt and a flat key with a serrated edge.
ORIGIN – named after the American locksmith Linus *Yale* Jr (1821–68).

yam > *noun* **1** the edible starchy tuber of a climbing plant, grown in tropical and subtropical countries. **2** N. Amer. a sweet potato.
ORIGIN – from Portuguese *inhame* or obsolete Spanish *iñame*.

yammer informal > *verb* **1** talk loudly and incessantly. **2** make a loud, incessant noise. > *noun* loud and sustained noise.
ORIGIN – from Old English *geōmrian* 'to lament'.

yang > *noun* (in Chinese philosophy) the active male principle of the universe. Contrasted with **YIN**.
ORIGIN – Chinese, literally 'male genitals', 'sun', 'positive'.

Yank > *noun* informal **1** often derogatory an American. **2** US another term for **YANKEE** (in senses 2 and 3).

yank informal > *verb* pull with a jerk. > *noun* a sudden hard pull.

Yankee > *noun* informal **1** often derogatory an American. **2** US an inhabitant of New England or one of the northern states. **3** historical a Federal soldier in the Civil War. **4** a bet on four or more horses to win (or be placed) in different races.
ORIGIN – perhaps from Dutch *Janke*, diminutive form of the common Dutch name *Jan*.

Yanqui /yangki/ > *noun* variant spelling of **YANKEE**, as used in Latin American contexts.

yap > *verb* (**yapped, yapping**) **1** give a sharp, shrill bark. **2** informal talk at length in an irritating manner. > *noun* a sharp, shrill bark.
DERIVATIVES – **yappy** *adjective* (informal).

yard¹ > *noun* **1** a unit of linear measure equal to 3 feet (0.9144 metre). **2** a square or cubic yard, especially of sand or other building materials. **3** a cylindrical spar slung across a ship's mast for a sail to hang from.
IDIOMS – **by the yard** in large numbers or quantities.

wordpower facts
Yard
The two English words **yard** are distinct, although both go back to Old English. **Yard** in the sense 'three feet' originally meant 'twig, stick, or cane' and 'spar supporting a ship's sail'. Its first use as a unit was as a measure of land equal to about five metres; it did not mean 'three feet' until the late Middle Ages. **Yard** in the sense 'ground adjoining a building' meant 'building, home, region' in Saxon times; it comes from a base related to **garden** and **orchard** and also to Russian *gorod* 'town' (as found in Russian place names such as *Novgorod* and *Leningrad*).

yard² > *noun* **1** chiefly Brit. a piece of uncultivated ground adjoining a building. **2** an area of land used for a particular purpose or business: *a builder's yard*. **3** N. Amer. the garden of a house.
COMBINATIONS – **yardman 1** a person working in a railway or timber yard. **2** US a person who does various outdoor jobs. **yard sale** N. Amer. a sale of miscellaneous second-hand items held in the grounds of a private house.

yardage > *noun* a distance or length measured in yards.

yardarm > *noun* the outer extremity of a ship's yard.

Yardie > *noun* informal **1** (among Jamaicans) a fellow Jamaican. **2** (in the UK) a member of a Jamaican or West Indian gang of criminals.
ORIGIN – from Jamaican English *yard* 'house, home', also 'Jamaica'.

yardstick > *noun* **1** a measuring rod a yard long. **2** a standard used for comparison.

yarmulke /yaarmoolkə/ (also **yarmulka**) > *noun* a skullcap worn in public by Orthodox Jewish men or during prayer by other Jewish men.
ORIGIN – Yiddish.

yarn > *noun* **1** spun thread used for knitting, weaving, or sewing. **2** informal a long or rambling story. **3** Austral./NZ a chat. > *verb* **1** informal tell a yarn. **2** Austral./NZ chat; talk.

yarrow > *noun* a plant with feathery leaves and heads of small white or pale pink flowers, used in herbal medicine.

yashmak /yashmak/ > *noun* a veil concealing all of the face except the eyes, worn by some Muslim women in public.
ORIGIN – Arabic, from Turkish.

yatter informal > *verb* talk incessantly; chatter. > *noun* incessant talk.

yaw > *verb* (of a moving ship or aircraft) twist or oscillate about a vertical axis. > *noun* twisting or oscillation of a moving ship or aircraft about a vertical axis.

yawl > *noun* a two-masted fore-and-aft-rigged sailing boat with the mizzenmast stepped far aft so that the mizzen boom overhangs the stern.
ORIGIN – Low German *jolle* or Dutch *jol*.

yawn > *verb* **1** involuntarily open one's mouth wide and inhale deeply due to tiredness or boredom. **2** be wide open: *a yawning chasm*. > *noun* **1** an act of yawning. **2** informal a boring or tedious thing or event.

yawp > *noun* a harsh or hoarse cry or yelp. > *verb* shout or exclaim hoarsely.

yaws > *plural noun* (treated as sing.) a contagious tropical disease caused by a bacterium that enters skin abrasions and causes small lesions which may develop into deep ulcers.
ORIGIN – probably from Carib.

yay /yay/ (also **yea**) > *adverb* informal, chiefly N. Amer. (with measurements) so; to this extent: *I knew him when he was yay big.*
ORIGIN – probably a variant of **YEA**.

Yb > *symbol* the chemical element ytterbium.

yd > *abbreviation* yard (measure).

ye¹ > *pronoun* (second person pl.) archaic or dialect plural of **THOU¹**.

ye² > *determiner* pseudo-archaic term for **THE**.

---

wordpower facts

Ye

The word **ye** is often used today to give a quaintly old-fashioned effect, as in phrases like *Ye Olde Cock Tavern*. It is a genuinely medieval form of *the*, but its modern use has arisen from a misunderstanding. In Old English the sound th- was represented by a letter called the *thorn*, which was written þ. In medieval times this character came to be written identically with y, so that *the* could be written ye. This spelling (usually yᵉ) was kept as a convenient abbreviation in handwriting down to the 19th century, and in printing during the 15th and 16th centuries, but it was never pronounced as 'ye'.

---

yea archaic or formal > *adverb* yes. > *noun* an affirmative answer.

yeah (also **yeh**) > *exclamation* & *noun* non-standard spelling of **YES**.

year > *noun* **1** the time taken by the earth to make one revolution around the sun. **2** (also **calendar year**) the period of 365 days (or 366 days in leap years) starting from the first of January, used for reckoning time in ordinary affairs. **3** a period of the same length as this starting at a different point. **4** a similar period used for reckoning time according to other calendars. **5** (**one's years**) one's age or time of life. **6** (**years**) informal a very long time. **7** a set of students grouped together as being of roughly similar ages.
WORDFINDER – annal (*a history of events year by year; a record of events of one year*), annual (*occurring once a year; covering a year*), annuity (*a yearly allowance*), biannual (*occurring twice a year*), biennial (*occurring every other year*), per annum (*for each year*), perennial (*lasting through a year or several years*).
IDIOMS – **in the year of grace** (or **Our Lord**) —— in the specified year AD. [ORIGIN – *year of grace* from Latin *anno gratiae*, used by chroniclers.] **year in, year out** continuously or repeatedly over a period of years. **year-on-year** (of figures, prices, etc.) as compared with the corresponding ones from a year earlier.

year-round happening or continuing throughout the year.

yearbook > *noun* **1** an annual publication giving current information about and listing events of the previous year. **2** N. Amer. an annual publication of the graduating class in a school or university, giving photographs of students and details of school activities in the previous year.

yearling > *noun* **1** an animal of a year old, or in its second year. **2** a racehorse in the calendar year after its year of foaling. > *adjective* having lived or existed for a year.

yearly > *adjective* & *adverb* happening or produced once a year or every year.

yearn /yern/ > *verb* have an intense feeling of loss and longing for something.
DERIVATIVES – **yearning** *noun* **yearningly** *adverb*.
SYNONYMS – ache, hunger, long, pine.
ORIGIN – Old English, from a Germanic base meaning 'eager'.

yeast > *noun* **1** a microscopic single-celled fungus capable of converting sugar into alcohol and carbon dioxide. **2** a preparation of this obtained chiefly from fermented beer, used as a fermenting agent, to raise bread dough, and as a food supplement. **3** Biology any unicellular fungus that reproduces vegetatively by budding or fission.

yeasty > *adjective* (**yeastier**, **yeastiest**) **1** of, resembling, or containing yeast. **2** turbulent or restless.

yell > *noun* **1** a loud, sharp cry, especially of pain, surprise, or delight. **2** N. Amer. an organised rhythmic cheer, especially one used to support a sports team. > *verb* shout in a loud or piercing way.
SYNONYMS – *noun* **1** cry, howl, shout, wail.

yellow > *adjective* **1** of the colour between green and orange in the spectrum, a primary colour complementary to blue. **2** offensive having a yellowish or olive skin (as used to describe Chinese or Japanese people). **3** informal cowardly. **4** (of a book or newspaper) unscrupulously sensational. > *noun* **1** yellow colour or pigment. **2** used in names of yellow butterflies and moths. > *verb* become a yellow colour, especially with age.
WORDFINDER – shades of yellow: amber, blonde, canary, cream, flaxen, gold, lemon, mustard, primrose, straw, sulphur, topaz.
DERIVATIVES – **yellowed** *adjective* **yellowing** *adjective* **yellowish** *adjective* **yellowness** *noun* **yellowy** *adjective*.
COMBINATIONS – **yellow card** (especially in soccer) a yellow card shown by the referee to a player being cautioned. **yellow dog** N. Amer. informal a contemptible person or thing. **yellow fever** a tropical virus disease transmitted by mosquitoes, which affects the liver and kidneys, causing fever and jaundice, and is often fatal. **yellow flag** a ship's yellow or quarantine flag, used to indicate the presence or absence of disease aboard. **yellow jersey** (in a cycling race involving stages) a yellow jersey worn each day by the rider who is ahead on time over the whole race, and presented to the rider with the shortest overall time at the finish of the race. **Yellow Pages** (trademark in the UK) a telephone directory printed on yellow paper and listing businesses and other organisations according to the goods or services they offer. **the yellow peril** offensive the political or military threat regarded as being posed by the Chinese or by the peoples of SE Asia. **yellow rattle** a partly parasitic yellow-flowered plant whose ripe seeds are shed into a pouch which rattles when shaken.
ORIGIN – Old English, related to **GOLD**.

yellow-belly > *noun* informal **1** a coward. **2** any of a number of animals with yellow underparts.
DERIVATIVES – **yellow-bellied** *adjective*.

yellowfin > *noun* a widely distributed, commercially important tuna that has yellow anal and dorsal fins.

yellowhammer > *noun* a common Eurasian bunting, the male of which has a yellow head, neck, and breast.
ORIGIN – -*hammer* is perhaps from Old English *amore* (a kind of bird), perhaps conflated with *hama* 'feathers'.

yelp > *noun* a short, sharp cry. > *verb* utter a yelp or yelps.
ORIGIN – Old English, 'to boast'.

Yemeni /yemmə ni/ > *noun* a person from Yemen. > *adjective* relating to Yemen.

Yemenite /yemmə nīt/ > *noun* & *adjective* another term for **YEMENI**.

yen¹ > *noun* (pl. same) the basic monetary unit of Japan.
ORIGIN – Japanese, 'round'; compare with **YUAN**.

yen² informal > *noun* a longing or yearning.
ORIGIN – Chinese: originally in the sense 'craving for a drug'.

yenta /yentə/ > *noun* N. Amer. informal a female gossip and busybody.
ORIGIN – Yiddish: originally a given name.

yeoman /yōmən/ > *noun* (pl. **yeomen**) historical **1** a man holding a small landed estate; a freeholder. **2** a servant in a royal or noble household. **3** a member of the yeomanry force.
IDIOMS – **yeoman service** efficient help.
DERIVATIVES – **yeomanly** *adjective*.
COMBINATIONS – **Yeoman of the Guard** a member of the British sovereign's bodyguard, now having only ceremonial duties and wearing Tudor dress as uniform.

Yeoman Warder a warder at the Tower of London.

ORIGIN – probably from YOUNG + MAN.

yeomanry > *noun* historical a body of yeomen, or yeomen collectively.

yerba buena /yerbə **bway**nə/ > *noun* a trailing aromatic herb related to savory, with whitish or lilac flowers.

ORIGIN – Spanish, 'good herb'.

yerba maté > *noun* variant of MATÉ.

yes > *exclamation* **1** used to give an affirmative response. **2** said in response to someone addressing one or attracting one's attention. **3** said when questioning a remark. **4** expressing delight. > *noun* (pl. **yeses** or **yesses**) an affirmative answer, decision, or vote.

ORIGIN – Old English, probably from an unrecorded phrase meaning 'may it be so'.

yeshiva /yə**shee**və/ > *noun* an Orthodox Jewish college or seminary.

ORIGIN – Hebrew.

yes-man > *noun* informal a person who always agrees with their superiors.

yessir /**yess**ər, **yess** sur/ > *exclamation* informal expressing assent, especially to a superior.

ORIGIN – alteration of *yes sir*.

yesterday > *adverb* on the day before today. > *noun* **1** the day before today. **2** the recent past.

yesteryear > *noun* literary last year or the recent past.

yet > *adverb* **1** up until the present or a specified or implied time; by now or then. **2** as soon as the present or a specified or implied time: *wait, don't go yet*. **3** from now into the future for a specified length of time. **4** referring to something that will or may happen in the future. **5** still; even (emphasising increase or repetition). **6** nevertheless; in spite of that. > *conjunction* but at the same time; but nevertheless.

IDIOMS – **as yet** until now or that time. **nor yet** and also not.

USAGE – avoid the unnecessarily long phrase *as of yet*: *as yet* is the proper form.

yeti /**yett**i/ > *noun* a large, hairy manlike creature said to live in the highest part of the Himalayas.

ORIGIN – Tibetan, 'little manlike animal'.

yew > *noun* a coniferous tree with poisonous red berry-like fruit and dense, springy wood.

Yid > *noun* informal, offensive a Jew.

ORIGIN – from YIDDISH.

Yiddish /**yidd**ish/ > *noun* a language used by Jews in or from central and eastern Europe, originally a German dialect with words from Hebrew and several modern languages. > *adjective* relating to this language.

DERIVATIVES – **Yiddisher** *noun*.

---

wordpower facts

Yiddish

Yiddish is the language that was used by Jews in central and eastern Europe before the Holocaust; today its speakers live mainly in the US, Israel, and Russia. The word comes from the Yiddish phrase *yidish daytsh* 'Jewish German', which reflects the fact that the language is based on a German dialect. Yiddish words that have entered English include food terms such as **bagel**, **gefilte fish**, **halva**, and **pastrami**, and slang words like **klutz**, **nebbish**, **shtick**, and **shtum**. Words from Yiddish in widespread use include **chutzpah**, **nosh**, and **gazump**: this entered English in the 1920s, when it meant 'to swindle'.

Yiddishism > *noun* a Yiddish word or idiom.

yield* > *verb* **1** produce or provide (a natural, agricultural, or industrial product). **2** produce or deliver (a result or gain). **3** generate (a specified financial return). **4** give way to demands or pressure. **5** relinquish possession of; give up. **6** (of a mass or structure) give way under force or pressure. > *noun* an amount or result yielded.

DERIVATIVES – **yielder** *noun* **yielding** *adjective*.

*SPELLING – remember, *i* before *e* except after *c*: yield.

SYNONYMS – *verb* **1** bear, generate, produce, provide. **4** capitulate, give in, submit, surrender. **5** give up, relinquish, sacrifice, surrender.

ORIGIN – Old English, 'pay, repay'.

yikes > *exclamation* informal used to express exaggerated shock and alarm, for humorous effect.

yin > *noun* (in Chinese philosophy) the passive female principle of the universe. Contrasted with YANG.

ORIGIN – Chinese, literally 'feminine', 'moon', 'shade'.

yip > *noun* a short, sharp cry or yelp, especially of excitement or delight. > *verb* (**yipped**, **yipping**) give a yip.

yippee > *exclamation* expressing wild excitement or delight.

yippie > *noun* (pl. **yippies**) a member of a group of young politically active hippies in the 1960s, originally in the US.

ORIGIN – acronym from *Youth International Party* + the suffix *-ie*, suggested by HIPPY[1].

ylang-ylang /eelangeelang/ > *noun* a sweet-scented essential oil obtained from the flowers of a tropical tree, used in perfumery and aromatherapy.

ORIGIN – Tagalog.

YMCA > *abbreviation* Young Men's Christian Association.

-yne > *suffix* Chemistry forming names of unsaturated hydrocarbons containing a triple bond.

yob > *noun* Brit. informal a rude and loutish young man.

DERIVATIVES – **yobbery** *noun* **yobbish** *adjective* **yobby** *adjective*.

ORIGIN – from BOY (spelled backwards).

yobbo > *noun* (pl. **yobbos** or **yobboes**) Brit. informal a yob.

yocto- /**yokt**ō/ > *combining form* used in units of measurement to indicate a factor of one million million million millionth (10^{-24}).

ORIGIN – alteration of OCTO-.

yodel /**yō**d'l/ > *verb* (**yodelled**, **yodelling**; US **yodeled**, **yodeling**) practise a form of singing or calling marked by rapid alternation between the normal voice and falsetto. > *noun* a song or call delivered in such a way.

DERIVATIVES – **yodeller** *noun*.

ORIGIN – German *jodeln*.

yoga > *noun* a Hindu spiritual and ascetic discipline, a part of which, including breath control, simple meditation, and the adoption of specific bodily postures, is widely practised for health and relaxation.

DERIVATIVES – **yogic** *adjective*.

ORIGIN – Sanskrit, 'union'.

yogi > *noun* (pl. **yogis**) a person who is proficient in yoga.

yogic flying > *noun* a technique of Transcendental Meditation involving thrusting oneself off the ground while in the lotus position.

yogurt /**yogg**ərt, **yō**gərt/ (also **yoghurt** or **yoghourt**) > *noun* a semi-solid slightly sour food prepared from milk fermented by added bacteria.

ORIGIN – Turkish.

yoke > *noun* **1** a wooden crosspiece that is fastened over the necks of two animals and attached to a plough or cart that they pull in unison. **2** (pl. same or **yokes**) a pair of yoked animals. **3** a frame fitting over the neck and shoulders of a person, used for carrying pails or baskets. **4** something that represents a bond between two parties: *the yoke of marriage*. **5** something regarded as oppressive or burdensome: *the yoke of imperialism*. **6** a part of a garment that fits over the shoulders and to which the main part of the garment is attached. > *verb* put a yoke on; couple or attach with or to a yoke.

ORIGIN – Old English, from a root shared by Latin *jungere* 'to join'.

yokel > *noun* an unsophisticated country person.

ORIGIN – perhaps from dialect *yokel* 'green woodpecker'.

yolk /yōk/ > *noun* the yellow internal part of a bird's egg, which is rich in protein and fat and nourishes the developing embryo.

DERIVATIVES – **yolked** *adjective* **yolky** *adjective*.

COMBINATIONS – **yolk sac** Zoology a membranous sac containing yolk attached to the embryos of reptiles and birds and the larvae of some fishes.

ORIGIN – Old English, from *geolu* 'yellow'.

Yom Kippur /yom **kipp**ər, ki**poor**/ > *noun* the most solemn religious fast of the Jewish year, the last of the ten days of penitence that begin with Rosh Hashana (the Jewish New Year).

ORIGIN – Hebrew.

yon literary or dialect > *determiner & adverb* yonder; that. > *pronoun* yonder person or thing.

yonder archaic or dialect > *adverb* at some distance in the direction indicated; over there. > *determiner* that or those (referring to something situated at a distance). > *noun* (**the yonder**) the far distance.

yoni /yōnee/ > *noun* (pl. **yonis**) Hinduism the vulva, regarded as a symbol of divine procreative energy and conventionally represented by a circular stone.

ORIGIN – Sanskrit, 'source, womb, female genitals'.

yonks > *plural noun* Brit. informal a very long time.

ORIGIN – perhaps related to *donkey's years*.

yore > *noun* (in phrase **of yore**) literary of former times or long ago: *a great empire in days of yore*.

yorker > *noun* Cricket a ball bowled so that it pitches immediately under the bat.

ORIGIN – probably from *York*, suggesting its introduction by Yorkshire players.

Yorkist > *noun* a follower of the House of York in the Wars of the Roses. > *adjective* relating to the House of York.

Yorks. > *abbreviation* Yorkshire.

Yorkshire pudding > *noun* a baked batter pudding typically eaten with roast beef.

Yorkshire terrier > *noun* a small long-haired blue-grey and tan breed of terrier.

Yoruba /**yorr**oobə/ > *noun* (pl. same or **Yorubas**) **1** a member of an African people of SW Nigeria and Benin. **2** the language of this people.

ORIGIN – the name in Yoruba.

yotta- /**yott**ə/ > *combining form* used in units of measurement to indicate a factor of one million million million million (10^{24}).

ORIGIN – from Italian *otto* 'eight'.

you > *pronoun* (second person sing. or pl.) **1** used to refer to the person or people that the speaker is addressing. **2** used to refer to the person being addressed together with other

people regarded in the same class. **3** used to refer to any person in general.

you'd > *contraction* **1** you had. **2** you would.

you'll > *contraction* you will; you shall.

young > *adjective* (**younger**, **youngest**) **1** having lived or existed for only a short time; not far advanced in life. **2** relating to or characteristic of young people. > *noun* (treated as pl.) young children or animals; offspring.

WORDFINDER – jeunesse dorée (*wealthy, fashionable young people*), juvenilia (*works produced by a writer or artist when young*), nonage (*a period of immaturity or youth*), rejuvenate (*make younger or more energetic*), wunderkind (*a very successful young person*).

DERIVATIVES – **youngish** *adjective*.

SYNONYMS – *adjective* **1** immature, juvenile, youthful.

ANTONYMS – *adjective* **1** elderly, mature, old.

COMBINATIONS – **young gun** informal an energetic and assertive young man. **young offender** Law (in the UK) a criminal between 14 and 17 years of age. **Young Turk** a young person eager for radical change to the established order. [ORIGIN – with reference to a revolutionary party active in the Ottoman Empire in the late 19th and early 20th centuries.]

youngster > *noun* a child, young person, or young animal.

your > *possessive determiner* **1** belonging to or associated with the person or people that the speaker is addressing. **2** belonging to or associated with any person in general. **3** (**Your**) used when addressing the holder of certain titles.

USAGE – do not confuse **your** with **you're**; **you're** is a contraction of **you are**, while **your** is a possessive determiner used in phrases such as *your turn*.

you're > *contraction* you are.

yours > *possessive pronoun* used to refer to something belonging to or associated with the person or people that the speaker is addressing.

yourself > *pronoun* (second person sing.) (pl. **yourselves**) **1** used as the object of a verb or preposition when this is the same as the subject of the clause and the subject is the person or people being addressed. **2** (emphatic) you personally.

youse /yōoz/ (also **yous**) > *pronoun* dialect you (usually more than one person).

youth > *noun* (pl. **youths**) **1** the period between childhood and adult age. **2** the qualities of vigour, freshness, immaturity, etc. associated with being young. **3** (treated as sing. or pl.) young people. **4** a young man.

SYNONYMS – **1** adolescence.

COMBINATIONS – **youth club** (also **youth**

centre) a place or organisation providing leisure activities for young people.

ORIGIN – Old English, related to **YOUNG**.

youthful > *adjective* **1** young or seeming young. **2** characteristic of young people.

DERIVATIVES – **youthfully** *adverb* **youthfulness** *noun*.

SYNONYMS – **1** fresh, lively, sprightly, spry, vigorous, young.

youth hostel > *noun* a place providing cheap accommodation, aimed mainly at young people on holiday. > *verb* (**youth-hostel**) take a holiday in which one stays overnight in youth hostels.

DERIVATIVES – **youth-hosteller** *noun*.

you've > *contraction* you have.

yowl /yowl/ > *noun* a loud wailing cry of pain or distress. > *verb* make such a cry.

yo-yo > *noun* (pl. **yo-yos**) **1** (trademark in the UK) a toy consisting of a pair of joined discs with a deep groove between them in which string is attached and wound, which is spun alternately downward and upward by its weight and momentum as the string unwinds and rewinds. **2** a thing that repeatedly falls and rises again. > *verb* (**yo-yoes**, **yo-yoed**) move up and down repeatedly; fluctuate.

YT > *abbreviation* Yukon Territory.

YTS > *abbreviation* Youth Training Scheme.

ytterbium /i**ter**biəm/ > *noun* a silvery-white metallic chemical element of the lanthanide series.

ORIGIN – from *Ytterby* in Sweden, where minerals containing several rare-earth elements were found; compare with **ERBIUM, TERBIUM, YTTRIUM**.

yttrium /i**tri**əm/ > *noun* a greyish-white metallic chemical element resembling the rare-earth elements.

ORIGIN – from *Ytterby* (see **YTTERBIUM**).

yuan /yoo**aan**/ > *noun* (pl. same) the basic monetary unit of China, equal to 10 jiao or 100 fen.

ORIGIN – Chinese, literally 'round'; compare with **YEN¹**.

yuca /**yōo**kə/ > *noun* chiefly US another term for **CASSAVA**.

ORIGIN – Carib.

yucca /**yukk**ə/ > *noun* a plant of the agave family with sword-like leaves and spikes of white bell-shaped flowers, native to warm regions of the US and Mexico.

ORIGIN – variant of **YUCA**.

yuck (also **yuk**) informal > *exclamation* used to express strong distaste or disgust. > *noun* something messy or disgusting.

DERIVATIVES – **yucky** (also **yukky**) *adjective*.

Yugoslav /**yōo**gəslaav/ > *noun* a person from Yugoslavia.

DERIVATIVES – **Yugoslavian** *noun & adjective*.

ORIGIN – Austrian German *Jugoslav*, from Serbo-Croat *jug* 'south' + **SLAV**.

Yule (also **Yuletide**) > *noun* archaic term for **CHRISTMAS**.

COMBINATIONS – **yule log 1** a large log traditionally burnt in the hearth on Christmas Eve. **2** a log-shaped chocolate cake eaten at Christmas.

ORIGIN – Old English, corresponding to Old Norse *jól*, originally applied to a pagan midwinter festival lasting twelve days; perhaps related to **JOLLY**.

yummy > *adjective* (**yummier**, **yummiest**) informal delicious.

Yupik /yōopik/ > *noun* (pl. same or **Yupiks**) **1** a member of an Eskimo people of Siberia, the Aleutian Islands, and Alaska. **2** any of the languages of this people.

ORIGIN – Alaskan Yupik, 'real person'.

yuppie (also **yuppy**) > *noun* (pl. **yuppies**) informal, derogatory a well-paid young middle-class professional working in a city.

DERIVATIVES – **yuppiedom** *noun* **yuppification** *noun* **yuppify** *verb*.

COMBINATIONS – **yuppie flu** informal, derogatory chronic fatigue syndrome.

ORIGIN – elaboration of the acronym from *young urban professional*.

yurt /yoort, yert/ > *noun* a circular tent of felt or skins used by nomads in Mongolia, Siberia, and Turkey.

ORIGIN – Russian *yurta*.

YWCA > *abbreviation* Young Women's Christian Association.

Z /zed, US zee/ (also **z**) > *noun* (pl. **Zs** or **Z's**) **1** the twenty-sixth letter of the alphabet. **2** (usu. *z*) the third unknown quantity in an algebraic expression. **3** used in repeated form to represent buzzing or snoring.

zabaglione /zabbalyōni/ > *noun* an Italian dessert made of whipped egg yolks, sugar, and Marsala wine.

ORIGIN – Italian.

zag > *noun* a sharp change of direction in a zigzag course. > *verb* (**zagged**, **zagging**) make a zag.

ORIGIN – shortening of **ZIGZAG**.

zaire /zīeer/ > *noun* (pl. same) the basic monetary unit of Zaire (Democratic Republic of Congo).

Zairean /zīeeriən/ (also **Zairian**) > *noun* a person from Zaire (Democratic Republic of Congo). > *adjective* relating to Zaire.

Zambian /zambiən/ > *noun* a person from Zambia. > *adjective* relating to Zambia.

zander /zandər/ > *noun* (pl. same) a large freshwater perch native to northern and central Europe.

ORIGIN – German.

zany /zayni/ > *adjective* (**zanier**, **zaniest**) amusingly unconventional and idiosyncratic. > *noun* (pl. **zanies**) **1** a zany person. **2** historical a comic performer partnering a clown, whom he imitated in an amusing way.

DERIVATIVES – **zanily** *adverb* **zaniness** *noun*.

ORIGIN – Italian *zani* or *zanni*, Venetian form of *Gianni*, *Giovanni*, the stock name of the servants acting as clowns in the commedia dell'arte.

zap informal > *verb* (**zapped**, **zapping**) **1** destroy or obliterate. **2** move or propel suddenly and rapidly. **3** use a remote control to change television channels, operate a video recorder, etc. > *noun* a sudden burst of energy or sound, or other sudden dramatic event.

DERIVATIVES – **zapper** *noun* **zappy** *adjective*.

zarzuela /thaarthwaylə, saarswaylə/ > *noun* **1** a traditional Spanish form of musical comedy. **2** a Spanish dish of seafood cooked in a rich sauce.

ORIGIN – Spanish.

zeal /zeel/ > *noun* great energy or enthusiasm for a cause or objective.

SYNONYMS – ardour, energy, enthusiasm, fervour, passion.

ORIGIN – Greek *zēlos*.

zealot /zellət/ > *noun* a fanatical and uncompromising follower of a religion or policy.

DERIVATIVES – **zealotry** *noun*.

ORIGIN – Greek *zēlōtēs*, from *zēloun* 'be jealous', from *zēlos* 'zeal'.

zealous /zelləss/ > *adjective* having or showing zeal.

DERIVATIVES – **zealously** *adverb* **zealousness** *noun*.

SYNONYMS – ardent, enthusiastic, fervent, keen, passionate.

zebra /zebrə, zeebrə/ > *noun* an African wild horse with black-and-white stripes and an erect mane.

COMBINATIONS – **zebra crossing** Brit. a pedestrian street crossing marked with broad white stripes.

ORIGIN – Italian, Spanish, or Portuguese, originally in the sense 'wild ass'; perhaps ultimately from Latin *equiferus* 'wild horse'.

zeitgeist /zītgīst/ > *noun* the defining spirit or mood of a particular period of history.

ORIGIN – German, from *Zeit* 'time' + *Geist* 'spirit'.

Zen > *noun* a Japanese school of Mahayana Buddhism emphasising the value of meditation and intuition.

ORIGIN – Sanskrit, 'meditation'.

zenith /zennith/ > *noun* **1** the point in the sky directly overhead. **2** the highest point in the sky reached by a given celestial object. **3** the time at which something is most powerful or successful.

DERIVATIVES – **zenithal** *adjective*.

SYNONYMS – **3** acme, climax, height, peak, pinnacle.

ANTONYMS – **3** nadir.

ORIGIN – from an Arabic phrase meaning 'path over the head'.

zeolite /zeeəlīt/ > *noun* any of a large group of silicate minerals used as cation exchangers and molecular sieves.

ORIGIN – from Greek *zein* 'to boil' (from their characteristic swelling when heated).

zephyr /zeffər/ > *noun* literary a soft, gentle breeze.

ORIGIN – Greek *zephuros* 'west wind'.

Zeppelin /zeppəlin/ > *noun* historical a large German dirigible airship of the early 20th century.

ORIGIN – named after Ferdinand, Count von *Zeppelin* (1838–1917), German airship pioneer.

zepto- /zeptō/ > *combining form* used in units of measurement to indicate a factor of one thousand million million millionth (10^{-21}).

ORIGIN – alteration of **SEPTI-**.

zero /zeerō/ > *cardinal number* (pl. **zeros**) **1** the figure 0; nought. **2** a temperature of 0°C (32°F), marking the freezing point of water. > *verb* (**zeroes**, **zeroed**) **1** adjust (an instrument) to zero. **2** set the sights of (a gun) for firing. **3** (**zero in on**) take aim at or focus attention on.

COMBINATIONS – **zero hour** the time at which a military or other operation is set to begin. **zero tolerance** strict enforcement of the law regarding any form of anti-social behaviour.

ORIGIN – Arabic, 'cipher'.

zest > *noun* **1** great enthusiasm and energy. **2** excitement or piquancy. **3** the outer, coloured part of the peel of citrus fruit, used as flavouring.

DERIVATIVES – **zestful** *adjective* **zesty** *adjective*.

SYNONYMS – **1** appetite, enthusiasm, gusto, relish, vigour, vitality.

ORIGIN – French *zeste* 'orange or lemon peel'.

zester > *noun* a kitchen utensil for scraping or peeling zest from citrus fruit.

zeta /zeetə/ > *noun* the sixth letter of the Greek alphabet (Z, ζ), transliterated as 'z'.
ORIGIN – Greek.

zetta- /zettə/ > *combining form* used in units of measurement to indicate a factor of one thousand million million million (10^{21}).
ORIGIN – from Italian *sette* 'seven'.

zeugma /zyoōgmə/ > *noun* a figure of speech in which a word applies to two others in different senses (e.g. *John and his driving licence expired last week*).
DERIVATIVES – **zeugmatic** *adjective*.
ORIGIN – Greek, from *zeugnunai* 'to yoke'.

zidovudine /zidovyoodeen/ > *noun* Medicine an antiviral drug used to slow the growth of HIV infection in the body.

zig > *noun* a sharp change of direction in a zigzag course. > *verb* (**zigged**, **zigging**) make a zig.
ORIGIN – shortening of ZIGZAG.

ziggurat /ziggərat/ > *noun* (in ancient Mesopotamia) a rectangular stepped tower.
ORIGIN – Akkadian (an ancient Semitic language).

zigzag > *noun* a line or course having abrupt alternate right and left turns. > *adjective & adverb* veering to right and left alternately. > *verb* (**zigzagged**, **zigzagging**) take a zigzag course.
ORIGIN – from German *Zickzack*, first applied to fortifications.

zilch /zilch/ informal, chiefly N. Amer. > *pronoun* nothing. > *determiner* not any; no.
ORIGIN – perhaps from a Mr *Zilch*, a character in the 1930s magazine *Ballyhoo*.

zillion > *cardinal number* informal an extremely large number of people or things.
DERIVATIVES – **zillionaire** *noun* **zillionth** *ordinal number*.

Zimbabwean /zimbaabwiən/ > *noun* a person from Zimbabwe. > *adjective* relating to Zimbabwe.

Zimmer /zimmər/ (also **Zimmer frame**) > *noun* trademark a kind of walking frame.
ORIGIN – from *Zimmer* Orthopaedic Limited, the name of the manufacturer.

zinc > *noun* 1 a silvery-white metallic chemical element which is a constituent of brass and is used for galvanising iron and steel. 2 galvanised iron or steel. > *verb* (**zinced** /zingkt/, **zincing** /zingking/) coat with zinc.
ORIGIN – German *Zink*.

Zinfandel /zinfandel/ > *noun* a variety of black wine grape grown in California, from which a red or blush wine is made.

zing informal > *noun* energy, enthusiasm, or liveliness. > *verb* 1 move swiftly. 2 N. Amer. criticise sharply.
DERIVATIVES – **zingy** *adjective*.

zinger > *noun* informal, chiefly N. Amer. an outstanding person or thing.

zinnia /zinniə/ > *noun* a plant of the daisy

family, cultivated for its bright showy flowers.
ORIGIN – named after the 18th-century German physician and botanist Johann G. *Zinn*.

Zion /zīən/ (also **Sion**) > *noun* 1 the hill of Jerusalem on which the city of David was built. 2 the Jewish people or religion. 3 (in Christian thought) the heavenly city or kingdom of heaven. 4 the Christian Church.
ORIGIN – Hebrew.

Zionism /zīəniz'm/ > *noun* a movement for the development and protection of a Jewish nation in Israel.
DERIVATIVES – **Zionist** *noun & adjective*.

zip > *noun* 1 chiefly Brit. a fastener consisting of two flexible strips of metal or plastic with interlocking projections closed or opened by pulling a slide along them. 2 informal energy; vigour. > *pronoun* N. Amer. informal nothing at all. > *verb* (**zipped**, **zipping**) 1 fasten with a zip. 2 informal move or propel at high speed. 3 Computing compress (a file) so that it takes up less space.

zip code (also **ZIP code**) > *noun* (in the US) a postal code consisting of five or nine digits.
ORIGIN – acronym from *zone improvement plan*.

zipper chiefly N. Amer. > *noun* a zip fastener. > *verb* fasten with a zipper.

zippo > *pronoun* N. Amer. informal nothing at all.

zippy > *adjective* (**zippier**, **zippiest**) informal 1 bright, fresh, or lively. 2 speedy.
DERIVATIVES – **zippily** *adverb* **zippiness** *noun*.

zip-up > *adjective* chiefly Brit. fastened with a zip.

zircon /zurkən/ > *noun* a mineral consisting of zirconium silicate, typically brown but sometimes in translucent forms of gem quality.
ORIGIN – German *Zirkon*.

zirconium /zərkōniəm/ > *noun* a hard silver-grey metallic chemical element.
ORIGIN – from ZIRCON.

zit > *noun* informal, chiefly N. Amer. a spot on the skin.

zither /zithər/ > *noun* a musical instrument consisting of a flat wooden soundbox with numerous strings stretched across it, placed horizontally and played with the fingers and a plectrum.
DERIVATIVES – **zitherist** *noun*.
ORIGIN – German, from Latin *cithara*, from Greek *kithara*, denoting a kind of harp; related to CITTERN.

zizz informal, chiefly Brit. > *noun* 1 a whizzing or buzzing sound. 2 a short sleep. > *verb* 1

make a whizzing or buzzing sound. 2 doze; sleep.

zloty /zlotti/ > *noun* (pl. same, **zlotys**, or **zloties**) the basic monetary unit of Poland.
ORIGIN – Polish, 'golden'.

Zn > *symbol* the chemical element zinc.

zodiac /zōdiak/ > *noun* a belt of the heavens within about 8° of the ecliptic, including all apparent positions of the sun, moon, and planets and divided by astrologers into twelve equal divisions or signs.
WORDFINDER – *signs of the zodiac:* Aries (*Ram*), Taurus (*Bull*), Gemini (*Twins*), Cancer (*Crab*), Leo (*Lion*), Virgo (*Virgin*), Libra (*Scales/Balance*), Scorpio (*Scorpion*), Sagittarius (*Archer*), Capricorn (*Goat*), Aquarius (*Water Bearer*), Pisces (*Fish/Fishes*).
DERIVATIVES – **zodiacal** /zədīək'l/ *adjective*.
ORIGIN – Greek *zōidiakos*, from *zōidion* 'sculptured animal figure', from *zōion* 'animal'.

zoetrope /zōitrōp/ > *noun* a cylinder with a series of pictures on the inner surface that, when viewed through slits with the cylinder rotating, give an impression of continuous motion.
ORIGIN – from Greek *zōē* 'life' + -*tropos* 'turning'.

zombie > *noun* 1 a corpse supposedly revived by witchcraft, especially in certain African and Caribbean religions. 2 informal a lifeless, apathetic, or completely unresponsive person.
DERIVATIVES – **zombify** *verb*.
ORIGIN – West African.

zonation /zōnaysh'n/ > *noun* distribution in or division into distinct zones.

zone > *noun* 1 an area distinguished on the basis of a particular characteristic, use, restriction, etc. 2 (also **time zone**) a range of longitudes where a common standard time is used. 3 chiefly Botany & Zoology an encircling band or stripe of distinctive colour, texture, etc. > *verb* divide into or assign to zones.
DERIVATIVES – **zonal** *adjective*.
SYNONYMS – *noun* 1 area, belt, region, section, sector, sphere, territory.
ORIGIN – Greek *zōnē* 'girdle'.

zonk > *verb* informal 1 hit or strike heavily. 2 (usu. **zonk out**) fall suddenly and heavily asleep.

zonked > *adjective* informal under the influence of drugs or alcohol.

zoo > *noun* an establishment which keeps wild animals for study, conservation, or display to the public.
COMBINATIONS – **zookeeper** an animal attendant employed in a zoo.

wordpower facts

Zoo

Zoo, like all the other words in this dictionary beginning with zoo- (apart from **zoom**), is based on Greek *zōion* 'animal', which is also the root of **zodiac** and such technical terms as **protozoan**. **Zoo** itself is an abbreviation of 'zoological garden', and originally referred specifically to the zoo at Regent's Park, London (properly the gardens of the London Zoological Society). The colloquial shortening used to be **Zoological** rather than **zoo**, as in the quotation 'I...passed three hours...at the Zoological, which is the best lounge of London' (*Correspondence of Joseph Jekyll*, 1831).

zoogeography /zōəjiogrəfi, zōōəjiogrəfi/ > *noun* the branch of zoology concerned with the geographical distribution of animals.

DERIVATIVES – **zoogeographer** *noun* **zoogeographic** *adjective* **zoogeographical** *adjective*.

zooid /zō-oyd, zōō-oyd/ > *noun* Zoology an animal arising from another by budding or division, especially each of the individuals which make up a colonial organism.

zoology /zōōolləji, zōollə ji/ > *noun* **1** the scientific study of the behaviour, structure, physiology, classification, and distribution of animals. **2** the animal life of a particular region or geological period.

DERIVATIVES – **zoological** *adjective* **zoologically** *adverb* **zoologist** *noun*.

NOTE – **zoology** and related words are usually pronounced with the first syllable **zoo**, reflecting the association with animals and zoos. However, the second pronunciation given here, with the first syllable pronounced to rhyme with **go**, is more correct etymologically.

zoom > *verb* **1** move or travel very quickly. **2** (of a camera) change smoothly from a long shot to a close-up or vice versa. > *noun* the action of a camera zooming.

SYNONYMS – *verb* **1** dart, dash, hurry, race, rush, shoot, speed.

COMBINATIONS – **zoom lens** a lens allowing a camera to zoom by varying the focal length.

zoomorphic /zōəmorfik, zōōmorfik/ > *adjective* having or representing animal forms or gods of animal form.

DERIVATIVES – **zoomorphism** *noun*.

ORIGIN – from Greek *zōion* 'animal' + *morphē* 'form'.

zoonosis /zōənōsiss, zōōənōsiss/ > *noun* (pl. **zoonoses** /zōənōseez, zōōənōseez/) Medicine any disease which can be transmitted to humans from animals.

DERIVATIVES – **zoonotic** *adjective*.

ORIGIN – from Greek *zōion* 'animal' + *nosos* 'disease'.

Zoroastrianism /zorrōastriəniz'm/ > *noun* a religion of ancient Persia based on the worship of a single god, founded by the prophet Zoroaster (also called Zarathustra) in the 6th century BC.

DERIVATIVES – **Zoroastrian** *adjective* & *noun*.

Zouave /zōōaav, zwaav/ > *noun* **1** a member of a French light-infantry corps, originally formed of Algerians and long retaining an oriental uniform. **2** (**zouaves**) women's trousers with wide tops, tapering to a narrow ankle.

ORIGIN – French, from *Zouaoua*, the name of a Berber tribe living in Algeria.

zouk /zōōk/ > *noun* an exuberant style of popular music combining Caribbean and Western elements.

ORIGIN – Guadeloupian Creole, literally 'to have a party'.

zounds /zowndz/ > *exclamation* archaic or humorous expressing surprise or indignation.

ORIGIN – a contraction from *God's wounds*.

Zr > *symbol* the chemical element zirconium.

zucchetto /tsōōkettō/ > *noun* (pl. **zucchettos**) a Roman Catholic cleric's skullcap: black for a priest, purple for a bishop, red for a cardinal, and white for the Pope.

ORIGIN – Italian *zucchetta* 'little gourd or head'.

zucchini /zōōkeeni/ > *noun* (pl. same or **zucchinis**) chiefly N. Amer. a courgette.

ORIGIN – Italian, plural of *zucchino* 'little gourd'.

Zulu /zōōlōō/ > *noun* **1** a member of a South African people living mainly in KwaZulu/Natal province. **2** the Bantu language of this people.

WORDFINDER – impi (*group of Zulu warriors*).

Zyban /zīban/ > *noun* trademark an antidepressant drug used to relieve nicotine withdrawal symptoms in those giving up smoking.

zydeco /zīdikō/ > *noun* a kind of black American dance music originally from southern Louisiana, typically featuring accordion and guitar.

ORIGIN – Louisiana Creole, possibly from a pronunciation of French *les haricots* ('the beans') in a dance-tune title.

zygoma /zīgōmə, zigōmə/ > *noun* (pl. **zygomata** /zīgōmətə, zigōmətə/) Anatomy the bony arch of the cheek, formed by connection of the zygomatic and temporal bones.

DERIVATIVES – **zygomatic** *adjective*.

COMBINATIONS – **zygomatic bone** the bone forming the prominent part of the cheek and the outer side of the eye socket.

ORIGIN – Greek *zugōma*, from *zugon* 'yoke'.

zygote /zīgōt/ > *noun* Biology a cell resulting from the fusion of two gametes.

DERIVATIVES – **zygotic** /zīgottik/ *adjective*.

ORIGIN – from Greek *zugōtos* 'yoked'.

Guide to good English

1. Parts of speech

In this section the traditional names are used for parts of speech (*noun*, *verb*, *adjective*, *adverb*, *pronoun*, *conjunction*, and *preposition*). Two other terms are sometimes used in describing grammar. One is *modifier*, which means any word that modifies the meaning of another word (usually a noun). It is broader in scope than adjective and includes, for example, *table* in *table lamp* as well as *bright* in *a bright lamp* or *the lamp was bright*. The other is *determiner*, which means any word such as *a*, *the*, *this*, *those*, and *every* which you put before a noun to show how you are using the noun (as in *a fire*, *the fire*, *this fire*, *those fires*, and *every fire*).

Nouns

A noun is a word that names something: a person (*woman*, *boy*, *Frances*), a thing (*building*, *tree*), or an idea (*birth*, *happiness*). A common noun names things generally, whereas a proper noun names a particular person, place, or thing when there is only one example. Collective nouns, such as *audience*, *family*, *generation*, *government*, *team*, are nouns which refer to groups of people or things. They can be treated as singular or plural: see the section on **AGREEMENT**.

Proper nouns

Proper nouns are normally spelled with a capital initial letter and refer to persons or things of which there is only one example (*Asia*, *Ark Royal*, *Dickens*). The term is sometimes understood more broadly to include geographical and ethnic designations such as *American* and *Ashanti*, which behave like common nouns, for example in allowing the forms *an American* and *the Ashanti*. Some genuinely proper names can also behave like common nouns in certain uses, for example *a fine Picasso* (= a painting by Picasso) and *three Picassos* (plural), *another Callas* (= a singer comparable to Callas). In these uses it is usual to retain the capital initial letter.

Verbal nouns

A verbal noun (also called a gerund) is a form of a verb ending with *-ing* that acts as a noun, for example *smoking* in the phrase no smoking and in the sentence Smoking annoys people. It should be distinguished from *smoking* used as an adjective (a smoking man) and as the present participle of the verb (The man was smoking).

Because a verbal noun is a part of a verb as well as being a noun, it keeps some of the characteristics of verbs in its grammatical behaviour; for example the forms They objected to me swearing (non-possessive) and They objected to my swearing (possessive) are both established in ordinary usage, although the second, in which swearing is treated as a full noun, is often preferred in more formal writing. In current use, certain patterns are clear:

The possessive is the more normal choice when the word preceding the *-ing* form is a personal name or a noun denoting a person:

She did not know what to think about Richard's constantly leaving her in the lurch.

I was now counting on my father's being able to make some provision somehow.

When the noun is non-personal or in the plural, the possessive is not normally used:

They turned a blind eye to toffee apples going missing.

Then we had our old conversation about the house being haunted.

With personal pronouns, usage varies between the possessive and non-possessive, the possessive being more usual at the start of a sentence:

His being so capable was the only pleasant thing about the whole dreadful day.

Fancy him minding that you went to the Summer Exhibition.

With indefinite pronouns the possessive sounds less natural, and a non-possessive form is more usual:

☑ He didn't think for a time of anyone clawing at his back.

☐ There are many sound reasons, then, for everyone's wanting to join in this new Gold Rush.

You can also use an infinitive with *to* as a verbal noun (To err is human, to forgive divine), and choice between this and an *-ing* form is largely a matter of idiom. For example, you *hope to do something* but you *think of doing something*, *have a fondness for doing something*, and *have an aversion to doing something*. You need to be careful not to confuse these patterns, especially when more than one is used in the same sentence.

Related nouns and verbs

Some words exist as both nouns and verbs, in some cases with no difference of form and pronunciation (e.g. *insult*, *master*, *score*) and in others with differences of form (e.g. *cloth* / *clothe*, *half* / *halve*, *licence* / *license*) or pronunciation (usually stress, with the noun stressed on the first syllable and the verb on the second, e.g. *conduct*, *record*, *transfer*). Some nouns have affected the pronunciation of their corresponding verbs, so that (for example) *decrease* and *export* are increasingly heard with a stress on the first rather than the second syllable as verbs as well as nouns. Conversely, and more controversially, some nouns are now heard stressed on the first syllable when the traditional pronunciation has been a second-syllable stress as both noun and verb (e.g. *dispute*).

For verbs ending with *-ise* formed from nouns, see **VERBS** below.

Verbs

A verb is a word that describes an action (*go*, *sit*, *put*) or state (*be*, *become*, *live*) and is normally an essential element in a clause or sentence. A verb is classified as transitive when the action affects a person or thing called the object (We lit a fire), and as intransitive when there is no object (She smiled).

Using the correct tense

Tense is the location in time of the state or action expressed by a verb. English verbs properly have only two tenses, the present

(*I am*) and the past (*I was*). The future is formed with *shall* or *will*, other forms of the past are formed with auxiliary verbs (*I have been* / *I was being*), and the past perfect is formed with the past tense of *have* (*I had been*).

The tense used mostly corresponds to actual time, apart from conventional uses such as the so-called 'historic present', used for dramatic effect in narratives (as in **George gets up and walks over to the window**), and the future used in polite requests (as in **Will that be all for now?**).

However, choice of tense (called 'sequence of tenses') becomes more complex in reported speech. If a simple statement such as **I'm afraid I haven't finished** is put into indirect speech by means of a reporting verb such as *said, thought*, etc., the tense of the reported action changes in accordance with the time perspective of the speaker: **He said he was afraid he hadn't finished**.

The tense of the reported verb can stay the same if the time relative to the speaker is the same as that relative to the person reported: **She likes beans** can be converted either to **She said she liked beans** or to **She said she likes beans**, and **I won't be here tomorrow** can be converted either to **I said I wouldn't be here tomorrow** or to **I said I won't be here tomorrow**.

shall *and* will

With *I* and *we*, *shall* should be used to form the simple future tense (expressing a prediction of a future action), while *will* is used to express an intention to do something:

- ☑ **I shall be late for work.**
- ☑ **We will not tolerate this rudeness.**

With *you, he, she, it*, and *they*, the situation is reversed; simple future action is expressed with *will*, while *shall* expresses an intention or command:

- ☑ **He will be late for work.**
- ☑ **You shall join us or die!**

In speech, these distinctions are often not observed. Contractions like *I'll* and *she'll* are commonly used, and strong determination is more likely to be conveyed by intonation than by strictly correct syntax.

should *and* would

The situation is similar with *should* and *would*. Strictly speaking *should* is used with *I* and *we*, while *would* is used with *you, he, she, it*, and *they*:

- ☑ **I should be grateful if you would let me know.**
- ☑ **You didn't say you would be late.**

In practice, however, it is normal to use *would* instead of *should* in reported speech and conditional clauses, such as **I said I would be late**. In speech the distinction is also often obscured through the use of the contracted forms *I'd, we'd*, etc.

Active and passive

Verbs can be either active, in which the subject is the person or thing performing the action (as in **France beat Brazil in the final**), or passive, in which the subject undergoes the action (**Brazil were beaten by France**). In the passive voice the subject is expressed as an agent introduced by the preposition *by*.

Passive verbs are usually formed with the verb *be*. Other forms of the passive include:

- impersonal constructions with *it*:

  It is believed that no action should be taken.

  It is felt that your complaint arises from a misunderstanding.

  This is a style found in official documents and reports, which usually seek to avoid the personal responsibility that is implied by the active voice (**We feel that your complaint arises from a misunderstanding**). It is not suitable for ordinary writing and speaking.

- other verbs besides *be* can be used to form so-called 'semi-passives' (as in **He got changed, They seem bothered**). Here *changed* and *bothered* are behaving almost more like adjectives.

- double passive. This awkward construction occurs with verbs such as *attempt, begin, desire, endeavour, propose, threaten*, and others involving constructions with a passive infinitive:

  - ☐ **The order was attempted to be carried out.**

  Avoid this construction when there is no corresponding active form (✗ **They attempted the order to be carried out**). Use a fully active construction instead:

  - ☑ **They attempted to carry out the order.**

  In some cases the sentence can be rephrased, for example:

  - ☑ **There was an attempt to carry out the order.**

  Other verbs, such as *expect, intend*, and *order*, which are grammatically more versatile, will allow a double passive construction. For example, we can say:

  - ☑ **They ordered the deserters to be shot.**

  and therefore a double passive form is allowed:

  - ☑ **The deserters were ordered to be shot.**

Sentences with no verb

Verbs are occasionally left out of sentences, for example in radio and television announcements (**This report from our Washington correspondent.**) or as stylistic devices, afterthoughts, ways of avoiding repetition, etc.:

Friday morning. By tube to a lecture at the London School of Economics. (written like an entry in a diary)

That way, they can work out their aggressions. Once a year.

Participles

There are two kinds of participle in English: the present participle ending with *-ing* as in **We are going**, and the past participle ending with *-d* or *-ed* for many verbs and with *-t* or *-en* or some other form for others, as in **Have you decided?**, **New houses are being built**, and **It's not broken**.

Participles are often used to introduce subordinate clauses that are attached to other words in a sentence, e.g.

Her mother, opening the door quietly, came into the room.

Hearing a noise I went out to look.

Born in Rochdale, he spent most of his life in the area.

Participles at the beginning of a sentence, as in the last two examples, are acceptable grammatically but when overdone can produce a poor style, especially when the clause they introduce bears little relation to the main one:

- ☐ **Being blind from birth, she became a teacher and travelled widely.**

A worse stylistic error occurs with so-called 'unattached', 'mis-related', or 'dangling' participles, when the participle does not refer to the noun to which it is attached, normally the subject of the sentence:

> ✗ Recently converted into apartments, I passed by the house where I grew up.

Grammatically, this sentence implies that the writer has recently been converted into apartments. Here is another example:

> ✗ Driving near home recently, a thick pall of smoke turned out to be a bungalow well alight.

Although everyone knows what these two examples mean, unattached participles can distract and sometimes mislead the reader, and are best avoided.

Certain participles, such as *considering, assuming, excepting, given, provided, seeing, speaking (of)*, etc., have virtually become prepositions or conjunctions in their own right, and their use in a grammatically free role is now standard:

> ☑ 'Speaking of money,' said Beryl, 'do you mind my asking what you did with yours?'

Verbs from nouns

By a process called 'conversion', verbs have for several centuries been formed from nouns (and occasionally adjectives), by using the same word (e.g. *to question, to knife, to quiz, to service*), by adding a suffix such as *-ise* (*prioritise, randomise*), or by a shortening of the noun in a process called 'back-formation' (*to diagnose* from *diagnosis, to televise* from *television*). Although traditionalists may object to some of these words (especially the longer ones such as *hospitalise* and *privatise*), it is an established process and generally a useful one.

Adjectives and adverbs

Position

Most adjectives can be used in two positions: either before the noun they describe, where they are called 'attributive', as in **a black cat** and **a gloomy outlook**, or after a verb such as *be, become, grow, look,* or *seem*, where they are called predicative, as in **the cat was black** and **the prospect looks gloomy**. A few adjectives used to denote status stand immediately after the noun and are called 'postpositive', as in *the body politic* and *the president elect*. You will find information about these later in this section.

Some adjectives are nearly always used in the predicative position and cannot stand before a noun (e.g. *afraid*). Others by contrast are found in attributive position, either always (e.g. *main* as in **the main reason**, *mere* as in **This is mere repetition**) or in certain meanings (e.g. *big* as in **He is a big eater**, *whole* as in **Have you told the whole truth?**).

In these last examples, the adjective can only be made predicative by repeating the noun or by using the pronoun *one*:

> The truth I have told is the whole truth.
> This reason is the main one.

Other adjectives that have been restricted in the past are now becoming more mobile; for example, *aware* and *ill* are increas-ingly heard in the attributive position, as in **a highly aware person** and **an ill woman**.

Comparatives and superlatives

An adjective has three forms, called a positive (or absolute), e.g. *hot, splendid,* a comparative, e.g. *hotter, more splendid,* and a superlative, e.g. *hottest, most splendid*.

Adjectives of one syllable and some adjectives of two syllables can form their comparative and superlative forms by adding *-er* and *-est*, sometimes with a change of spelling such as *y* to *i* (*soft, softer, softest; happy, happier, happiest*). Adjectives of more than two syllables are normally preceded by *more* or *most* instead of changing their form (*more frightening; most remarkable*).

Some adjectives (such as *dead, infinite,* and *unique*) have an all-or-nothing kind of meaning and cannot logically be qualified by *more* or *most*. These are called 'absolute' or 'non-gradable' adjectives. They are not normally used in comparative or superlative forms and cannot be qualified by adverbs that intensify or moderate such as *fairly, largely, more, rather,* or *very*.

There are exceptions to this rule, but these are normally obvious special cases:

> All animals are equal but some animals are more equal than others.
> His profile is most utterly perfect.

Absolute adjectives can be regularly qualified by adverbs that denote an extreme or completeness, such as *absolutely, completely,* and *utterly*, since these are consistent with the absolute nature of the adjectives concerned:

> ☑ The ghosts made the place utterly impossible.

In this sentence, *utterly impossible* is acceptable, and so is *completely* or *absolutely impossible*, but *fairly* or *rather impossible* is much less so, except conversationally.

Adjectives following a noun

In many fixed standard expressions, adjectives denoting status are placed immediately after the nouns they describe, e.g. in *court martial, heir apparent, poet laureate, president elect, situations vacant,* and *the village proper*. In other cases, an adjective follows a noun as a matter of sentence structure rather than peculiarity of expression:

> The waiter picked up our dirty glasses in his fingertips, his eyes impassive.

or for rhetorical effect:

> The loving hands of the Almighty cradled him in bliss eternal.

Adjectives used as adverbs

Some adjectives have corresponding adverbs that are identical, e.g. *fast, late, straight,* and the type *monthly, weekly,* etc. So you can say **He left in the late afternoon** or **He left late in the afternoon** (*lately* has a different meaning).

In other cases, adjectives are used as adverbs only informally, often in fixed expressions such as *come clean* and *hold tight*. To these we can add *real* and *sure*, which are characteristic of informal North American speech (**That was real nice** and **I sure liked seeing you**) and are also found in non-standard and dialect use in Britain.

Position of adverbs

The position of adverbs in phrases and clauses follows fairly clear rules, i.e. they normally come between the subject and its verb, or between an auxiliary verb and a main verb:

> She dutifully observes all its quaint rules.
>
> Roosevelt's financial policy was roundly criticised in 1933.
>
> He had inadvertently joined a lonely-hearts club.

But for emphasis, or when the adverb belongs closely to what follows the main verb, it comes after the verb and before a following adverbial phrase:

> There is little chance that the student will function effectively after he returns home.
>
> Gradually the Chinese communists abandoned the Soviet methods.
>
> Did he hear her correctly?
>
> They aim to set each subject briefly in context.

Sentence adverbs

Some adverbs (such as *clearly*, *happily*, *hopefully*, *thankfully*, *unhappily*) refer to a whole statement, and form a comment associated more closely with the speaker or writer than with what is said. In this role they are called 'sentence adverbs'. This use can be seen by comparing the use of *unhappily* as an ordinary adverb of manner (She went unhappily to bed) with its use as a sentence adverb (She was, unhappily, too ill to leave the house). Sentence adverbs often stand at the beginning of the sentence:

> Clearly, we will have to think again.

Sentence adverbs are well established in English, although the use of *thankfully* and (in particular) *hopefully* can arouse controversy:

> ? All that lay before a young lady of breeding were duty to parents and hopefully a good marriage.
>
> ? It was five o'clock by the time he reached the house, which was thankfully empty.

The reason for this appears to be that unlike other adverbs such as *clearly* and *happily*, *thankfully* and *hopefully* do not correspond to an equivalent phrase such as 'as is clear' (or 'it is clear that') or 'as is a happy circumstance' (or 'it is a happy circumstance that'). Although this objection is artificial, and such use is now very familiar, be aware that some people may take exception to these words, especially in written or formal contexts.

Pronouns

A pronoun is a word such as *I*, *we*, *they*, *me*, *you*, *them*, etc., and other forms such as the possessive *hers* and *theirs* and the reflexive *myself* and *themselves*. They are used to refer to (and take the place of) a noun or noun phrase that has already been mentioned or is known, especially in order to avoid repetition, as in the sentence When she saw her husband again, she wanted to hit him.

When a pronoun refers back to a person or thing previously named, it is important that the gap is not so large that the reader or hearer might have difficulty relating the two, and that ambiguity is avoided when more than one person might be referred to, as

in the following exchange in a play (where the ambiguity is deliberate):

> SEPTIMUS: Geometry, Hobbes assures us in the Leviathan, is the only science God has been pleased to bestow on mankind.
> LADY CROOM: And what does he mean by it?
> SEPTIMUS: Mr Hobbes or God?
>
> (Tom Stoppard)

Reflexive pronouns

Reflexive pronouns are the type formed with *-self*, e.g. *myself*, *herself*, and *ourselves*, used in sentences in which the subject of the verb and the object are the same person or thing, as in We enjoyed ourselves and Make yourself at home.

A problem occurs when a reflexive pronoun refers back to a singular noun or pronoun of unknown or irrelevant gender:

> ? Take the case of someone who is still too young to look after themselves.

The use of the plural form *themselves* is the solution that is often used in ordinary speaking and writing, and it is generally acceptable.

In more precise writing, and in cases where the individuality of the person referred to is significant, the more cumbersome (and traditional) alternative is:

> ☑ Take the case of a person who is still too young to look after himself or herself.

This is a particular instance of a problem discussed further in the section on **AGREEMENT**.

Conjunctions

A conjunction is a word such as *and*, *because*, *but*, *for*, *if*, *or*, and *when*, used to connect words, phrases, clauses, and sentences.

There are some conjunctions that are used in British English but not in American English:

- *now* (Now the tourist season's starting it's better to have someone there, like a caretaker)

- *and nor* (His septic tank did not work, and nor did most others in the village)

- *but nor* (I am not a trained architect but nor was Sir Edwin Lutyens).

On the use of *and* and *but* at the beginning of a sentence, see the section on **SENTENCES**.

and/or

And/or is a formula indicating that the items connected by it can be taken either together or as alternatives. Its principal uses are in legal and other formal documents, but in general use it is often clumsy:

> The Press has rather plumped for the scholar as writer, and/or as bibliophile.

A more comfortable way of expressing the same idea is to use *X or Y or both*, and in some cases *or* by itself will do.

but

But is both a preposition and a conjunction:

Everyone seems to know but me.

(preposition, equivalent to 'except for')

Everyone seems to know but I don't.

(conjunction, equivalent to 'except that')

Confusion between these overlapping roles can cause uncertainty about whether to say:

Everyone but she can see the answer.

or Everyone but her can see the answer.

Usage varies on this point, but here are some guidelines:

- when the phrase introduced by *but* is associated with the subject of the sentence, treat the pronoun as a subject form (i.e. No one saw him but I) and when the phrase is associated with the object, treat it like an object (i.e. I saw no one but him).

- when the association is not as clear-cut, the case of the pronoun is determined by the position of the *but*-phrase in the sentence: when the *but*-phrase is in the subject area, treat the pronoun as a subject form (i.e. Everyone but she can see the answer) and when the *but*-phrase is in the object area treat the pronoun as an object (Everyone can see the answer but her).

- usage is unstable when the verb is intransitive: Everyone knows but her is somewhat more natural than Everyone knows but she.

for

As a conjunction *for* overlaps with *because* and *since*. It is generally more formal in effect, but it suffers from two limitations:

- it normally comes at the beginning of a sentence, following a main clause:

He picked his way down carefully, step by step, for the steps were narrow.

- it is normally preceded by a comma, except occasionally when the sentence is short:

It was gloomy and damp, for the sun could hardly shine through the tops of the trees.

He did not cry any more for it did not help.

Prepositions

A preposition is a word such as *after*, *in*, *to*, and *with*, which usually stands before a noun or pronoun and establishes the way it relates to what has gone before (The man on the platform, They came after dinner, and What did you do it for?).

The superstition that a preposition should always precede the word it governs and should not end a sentence (as in the last example given) seems to have developed from an observation of the 17th-century poet John Dryden, although Dryden himself did not always follow the rule in his own prose. It is not based on a real appreciation of the structure of English, which regularly separates words that are grammatically related.

There are cases when it is either impossible or not natural to organise the sentence in a way that avoids a final preposition:

- in relative clauses and questions featuring verbs with linked adverbs or prepositions:

What did Marion think she was up to?

They must be convinced of the commitment they are taking on.

Budget cuts themselves are not damaging: the damage depends on where the cuts are coming from.

- in passive constructions:

The dress had not even been paid for.

- in short sentences including an infinitive with *to* or a verbal noun:

There are a couple of things I want to talk to you about.

In spring the gardens are a joy to look at.

2. Inflection

Basic rules

Inflection is the process by which words (principally nouns, verbs, adjectives, and adverbs) change their form, especially their ending, in accordance with their grammatical role in a sentence. The typical patterns of inflection in English are as follows:

- nouns add -*s* or -*es* to form plurals (*book, books; church, churches*)

- verbs add -*s* or -*es*, and -*ed*, and -*ing* to form third-person present-tense forms (*change, changes; want, wants*), past tenses (*changed; wanted*), past participles (*changed; wanted*), and present participles (*changing; wanting*)

- adjectives and adverbs add -*er* and -*est* to form their comparative and superlative forms, sometimes also changing the stem (the main part of the word) as in *funnier, funniest*.

Some words that end in a vowel or a single consonant, or that have certain other features of spelling in the stem, can cause uncertainty in their inflections (e.g. *shellac, shellacked; samba, sambaed* or *samba'ed*).

Some verbs, called strong verbs, form tenses by changing their stem (*throw, threw, thrown*); and others are completely irregular (*have, had, had; go, went, gone*).

A verb ending in a double consonant usually has the following inflections:

- the past and past participle form -*ed* (as in *filled*)

- the present participle form -*ing* (as in *filling*)

- the adjective form -*able* (as in *fillable*) and its derived forms -*ably* and -*ability*

- the agent form -*er* (denoting a person or thing that does the action, as in *filler*).

Verbs of one syllable ending in a single consonant double the consonant when adding any of the suffixes given above: *beg*, *begged, begging; clap, clapped, clapping; rub, rubbed, rubbing.* (An exception is the verb *bus*, which has forms *bused, busing*.)

When the final consonant is *w*, *x*, or *y* this is not doubled: *tow, towed, towing; vex, vexed, vexing; toy, toyed, toying.*

When the final consonant is preceded by more than one vowel (other than *u* in *qu*), the consonant is not normally doubled: *boil, boiled, boiling; clean, cleaned, cleaning.*

Verbs of more than one syllable ending in a single consonant double the consonant when the stress (i.e. the natural emphasis used in pronouncing it) is placed on the final syllable: *allot, allotted, allotting; begin, beginning; occur, occurred, occurring.*

When the final consonant is *w*, *x*, or *y* this is again not doubled: *guffaw, guffawed, guffawing; relax, relaxed, relaxing; array, arrayed, arraying.*

Verbs that do not have their stress on the final syllable do not double the consonant unless it is an *l*: *audit, audited, auditing; gallop, galloped, galloping; offer, offered, offering.*

Exceptions in British English are: *input, inputting; output, outputting; kidnap, kidnapped, kidnapping; worship, worshipped, worshipping.* (In American English the forms are usually *kidnaped, kidnaping* and *worshiped, worshiping*.)

Verbs ending in *-l* normally double the *l* in British English regardless of where the stress occurs in the word: *annul, annulled, annulling; enrol, enrolled, enrolling; grovel, grovelled, grovelling, groveller; travel, travelled, travelling, traveller.* In American English the final *l* only doubles when the stress is on the final syllable (as in *annul* and *enrol* but not *grovel* and *travel*), and the basic form of the verb is sometimes spelled with *-ll* as well (as in *enroll, fulfill,* and *instill*).

Exceptions in British English are: *appeal, appealed, appealing; conceal, concealed, concealing; reveal, revealed, revealing; parallel, paralleled, paralleling.*

The verb *focus* also sometimes has the forms *focussed, focussing*; but the forms recommended here are *focused, focusing*.

Verbs: dropping final silent e

Verbs drop a final silent *e* when the suffix begins with a vowel (as in *blue, bluish; brave, bravest; continue, continuous; queue, queued*). But a final *e* is usually retained in *ageing*, to preserve the soft sound of the *g* in *changeable* (but not in *changing*), *twingeing*, and *whingeing*, and in *dyeing* (from *dye*), *singeing* (from *singe*), and *swingeing*, to distinguish these from the corresponding forms *dying* (from *die*), *singing* (from *sing*), and *swinging* (from *swing*).

More about plurals of nouns

English nouns normally form their plurals by adding *-s*, or *-es* if the singular form ends in *-s*, *-x*, *-z*, *-sh*, or soft *-ch* (as in *church* but not *loch*).

Words ending in *-y* form plurals with *-ies* (*policy, policies*) unless the ending is *-ey* in which case the plural form is normally *-eys* (*valley, valleys*); an exception is *money*, which has two plural forms *moneys* and *monies* in the meaning 'sums of money'.

Difficulties occur mainly when the singular form is unusual and does not allow you to use the normal rules or when the word is of foreign origin (or both).

Nouns ending in *-f* and *-fe* form plurals sometimes with *-fes*, sometimes *-ves*, and occasionally both *-fes* and *-ves* (in some cases with a difference in meaning). Many of these words also have corresponding verbs:

noun	-fs plural	-ves plural	verb form
calf		calves	calve, calved
dwarf	dwarfs	dwarves	dwarf, dwarfed
elf		elves	
half		halves	halve, halved
handkerchief	handkerchiefs		
hoof	hoofs	hooves	hoof, hoofed
knife		knives	knife, knifed
leaf		leaves	leaf, leafed
life		lives	live, lived
loaf		loaves	loaf, loafed
oaf	oafs		
proof	proofs		prove, proved
roof	roofs	rooves	roof, roofed
scarf	scarfs	scarves	
self		selves	
sheaf		sheaves	sheave, sheaved
shelf		shelves	shelve, shelved
thief		thieves	thieve, thieved
turf	turfs	turves	turf, turfed
wharf	wharfs	wharves	
wife		wives	
wolf		wolves	wolf, wolfed

The following tables list other plural forms that cause difficulties of various kinds.

Irregular plurals

singular	plural	singular	plural
child	children	man	men
foot	feet	mouse	mice
goose	geese	tooth	teeth
louse	lice	woman	women

Animal names the same in the plural

singular	plural	singular	plural
bison	bison	salmon	salmon
cod	cod	sheep	sheep
deer	deer	squid	squid
grouse	grouse	swine	swine

Nouns only having a plural form: tools

bellows	gallows	pliers	tongs
binoculars	glasses	scissors	tweezers
clippers	goggles	shears	
forceps	pincers	spectacles (= glasses)	

Nouns only having a plural form: articles of clothing

braces	jeans	pyjamas (US pajamas)	tights
breeches	knickers	shorts	trousers
briefs	leggings	slacks	
flannels	pants	suspenders	

Compound nouns

singular	plural
Attorney-General	Attorneys-General
brother-in-law	brothers-in-law
commander-in-chief	commanders-in-chief
court martial	courts martial*
daughter-in-law	daughters-in-law
father-in-law	fathers-in-law
Governor-General	Governors-General
lay-by	lay-bys
man-of war	men-of-war
mother-in-law	mothers-in-law
passer-by	passers-by
Poet Laureate	Poets Laureate*
sister-in-law	sisters-in-law
son-in-law	sons-in-law

*The forms court martials and Poet Laureates are also used.

For plurals of abbreviated forms (such as *MP*) see the section on **ABBREVIATIONS**.

Nouns ending in *-ful*

-ful is a suffix forming nouns that denote amounts, as in *handful*, *mouthful*, etc. Often these nouns develop meanings that are remote from the word that forms the first element; for example, a *handful* means 'a small number' as well as 'an amount that can be held in the hand'. The plurals of these words are *handfuls*, *mouthfuls*, etc.

Nouns ending in -o

Plurals of nouns ending in *-o* cause difficulty in English because there are few convenient rules for choosing between *-os* (as in *ratios*) and *-oes* (as in *heroes*). But here are some guidelines:

- when a vowel (usually *i* or *e*) precedes the final *-o*, the plural is normally *-os* (*trios*, *videos*), probably because of the bizarre look of *-ioes* etc.

- names of animals and plants normally form plurals with *–oes* (*buffaloes*, *tomatoes*).

- words that are shortenings of other words invariably form plurals with *-os* (*demos*, *hippos*).

- words introduced from foreign languages, especially recently, form plurals with *-os* (*boleros*, *placebos*).

- words of many syllables tend to have *-os* plurals (*aficionados*, *manifestos*).

- proper names used allusively, i.e. to refer to people of a certain type or character, form plurals with *-os* (*Neros*, *Romeos*).

In other cases practice varies quite unpredictably: we refer to *kilos* and *pianos*, *dominoes* and *vetoes*. With some words things are not settled, e.g. both *mementoes* and *mementos* are widely used.

Nouns: Latin plurals

Plurals of Latin words used in English are formed according to the rules either of Latin (*apex*, *apices*; *stratum*, *strata*) or of English (*gymnasium*, *gymnasiums*; *arena*, *arenas*). Often more than one form is in use, sometimes with a usage distinction (*appendix*, *appendices* or *appendixes*; *formula*, *formulae* or *formulas*) and sometimes with no clear distinction (*cactus*, *cacti* or *cactuses*).

Words ending in *-is* usually follow the original Latin form (*basis*, *bases*; *crisis*, *crises*) because they sound best that way, and the same rule operates in other cases (*nucleus*, *nuclei*). A more alien form is the plural *-mata* of words ending in *-ma* in the singular (*carcinoma*, *carcinomata*; *stigma*, *stigmata*).

Some Latinate nouns ending in *-us* cannot form plurals in *-i* for technical reasons: *hiatus* (a fourth-declension noun in Latin whose plural is the same, *hiatus*), *ignoramus* (a first-person plural verb in Latin, not a noun), *octopus* (a Romanised form of a Greek word *octopous*), *vademecum* (*cum* being a preposition meaning 'with'): their English plurals are *hiatuses*, *ignoramuses*, *octopuses*, and *vademecums*.

Adjectives and adverbs: comparatives and superlatives

Adjectives

Adjectives that form comparatives and superlatives using *-er* and *-est* in preference to (or as well as) *more* and *most* are:

- words of one syllable (e.g. *fast*, *hard*, *rich*, *wise*). Words of one syllable ending in a single consonant double the consonant when it is preceded by a single vowel (*glad*, *gladder*, *gladdest*; *hot*, *hotter*, *hottest*) but not when it is preceded by more than one vowel (*clean*, *cleaner*, *cleanest*; *loud*, *louder*, *loudest*).

- words of two syllables ending in *-y* and *-ly* (e.g. *angry*, *early*, *happy*, *holy*, *likely*, *lively*) and corresponding *un-* forms when these exist (e.g. *unhappy*, *unlikely*). Words ending in *-y* change the *y* to *i* (e.g. *angrier*, *earliest*). In some cases only the *-est* form is used (e.g. *unholiest* but *more unholy*).

- words of two syllables ending in *-le* (e.g. *able*, *humble*, *noble*, *simple*).

- words of two syllables ending in *-ow* (e.g. *mellow*, *narrow*, *shallow*).

- some words of two syllables ending in *-er* (e.g. *bitter*, *clever*, *slender*, *tender*, but not *eager*). In some cases only the *-est* form is used (e.g. *bitterest* but *more bitter*).

- some words of two syllables pronounced with the stress on the second syllable (e.g. *polite*, *profound*, but not *antique*, *bizarre*, *secure*, and others).

- other words of two syllables that do not belong to any classifiable group (e.g. *common*, *cruel*, *pleasant*, *quiet*); some words can take -er and -est although the forms sound some-what less natural (e.g. *awkward*, *crooked*).

Words of two syllables ending in -l double the l (e.g. *cruel, crueller, cruellest*); words ending in other consonants do not double them.

Adjectives of three or more syllables need to use forms with *more* and *most* (*more beautiful*, *most interesting*, etc.).

Adverbs

Adverbs that take -er and -est in preference to (or as well as) *more* and *most* are:

- adverbs that are not formed with -*ly* but are identical in form to corresponding adjectives (e.g. *runs faster, hits hardest, hold it tighter*).
- some independent adverbs (e.g. *often* and *soon*).

Adverbs ending in -*ly* formed from adjectives (e.g. *richly, softly, wisely*) generally do not have -er and -est forms but appear as *more softly, most wisely*, etc.

3. Sentences

A sentence is a group of words that makes complete sense, contains a main verb, and when written begins with a capital letter and ends with a full stop (or the equivalent such as a question mark or an exclamation mark). Some groups of words vary from these rules and are still normally regarded as sentences, for example answers to questions: 'Could you close the window?' 'Sure.'

There are three basic kinds of sentence:

- a simple sentence normally contains one statement:

    The train should be here soon.

- a compound sentence contains more than one statement, normally joined by a conjunction such as *and* or *but*:

    I have looked at the evidence and I have to say it is not sufficient.

    He was at the meeting but said very little.

- a complex sentence contains a main clause and one or more subordinate clauses, such as a conditional clause beginning with *if* or a relative clause introduced by *which* or *who*:

    The story would make headlines if it ever became public.

    This is a matter which the lawyers will have to resolve.

Getting words in the right order

The normal order of the key elements of an English sentence is subject – verb – object or complement (if any) – adverb or adverb phrase (if any):

    Kate had seen a large grey rat in the cellar.

The boys always went to the cinema on Tuesday.

However, the order is sometimes changed by a process called 'inversion':

    Here comes the train.

    'Hey,' shouted the woman.

Each of these elements can consist of a single word or a group of words. Because English has so few inflections (word endings that change a word's grammatical role), the order of words is an essential part of meaning; change the order and you often change the meaning.

There are more detailed rules of word order that we normally follow without thinking (for example, an adverb phrase referring to place normally comes before one referring to time, as with *to the cinema* and *on Tuesday* in the example above).

Normal sentence order is often reversed in questions, except when the question begins with an interrogative word such as *who* and *what*:

    Did Thomas remember to take his passport?

    Was your father there?

    Who said that?

Indirect questions should follow the word order of statements and should not be followed by a question mark. For example, it is non-standard to say:

- ✖ I asked them what did they want to do?
- ✖ Tell me how old are you?

The correct forms are:

- ☑ I asked them what they wanted to do
- ☑ Tell me how old you are.

Sometimes a word or phrase that normally occurs later in the sentence is brought to the beginning for emphasis:

    On Tuesday we went to London.

    Suddenly the door flew open.

    Great literature this is not.

Relative clauses: using words like *who* and *when*

A relative clause is one connected to a main clause by a relative pronoun or adjective such as *who* or *whom, which, whose*, or *that*, or by a relative adverb such as *when* and *where*. (These words, apart from *that*, are collectively called *wh-* words, and a *wh-*word means any of these.) Most problems with this kind of clause are to do with the choice between *that* and a *wh-* word, principally *which, who*, or *whom*. For much of the time *that* is interchangeable with any of these words, and it is the more usual choice, especially in relation to *which*, in everyday writing and conversation:

    She held out the hand that was hurt.

or She held out the hand which was hurt.

    The man who had spoken to us then walked in.

or The man that had spoken to us then walked in.

There are two types of relative clause, called 'restrictive' and 'non-restrictive'. A restrictive clause gives essential information about a noun or noun phrase that comes before. In the sentence above, 'the hand' is defined as 'the one that (or which) was hurt'. By contrast, in the sentence She held out her hand, which I clasped in both of mine, the information in the relative clause introduced by *which* is extra information that could be left out without affecting the structure or meaning of the sentence. This type is called a non-restrictive clause. A restrictive clause can be introduced by *that*, *which*, *who*, or *whose* and is not normally preceded by a comma, whereas a non-restrictive clause is normally introduced by *which*, *who*, or *whose* (and not usually *that*), and is preceded by a comma.

A non-restrictive clause introduced by a *wh-* word can apply to a whole clause and not just the preceding noun or noun phrase:

> The sun came out, which was nice.

Sometimes *that* is more idiomatic than *which*, for example when the construction is based on an impersonal *it* or an indefinite pronoun such as *anything*:

> There is something that I forgot to mention.
> Is there anything that you want?

That is also more usual when *which* already occurs earlier in the sentence in another role, for example as an interrogative word:

> Which is the one that you want?

(In all these types involving a preference for *that*, leaving out the relative word altogether is common: see **ELLIPSIS** below. But use of *which* in any of these sentences would be unnatural.)

Leaving words out: ellipsis

In some sentences, a verb and other words can be left out when they can be understood from what has gone before or comes later in the sentence. This process is called *ellipsis*:

> It had been a good party. An unforgettable party, actually. And still was.

Here, there is ellipsis of *it had been* in the second sentence and of *it* in the third. Ellipsis happens most often in conversation in expressions such as Told you so (= I told you so) and Sounds fine to me (= It or that sounds fine to me), and also occurs in all kinds of spoken and written English. This practice is standard in informal English.

Other common types of ellipsis are that of the subject of a verb (I just pick up wood in a leisurely way, stack it, and slowly rake the bark into heaps), and the verb itself after *to* (Knowledge didn't really advance, it only seemed to) or after an auxiliary verb (We must and will rectify the situation).

You can use ellipsis when the words left out can reasonably be supplied by the hearer or reader from the rest of the sentence without causing confusion. Ellipsis is less satisfactory, and in some cases not possible, when the omitted word does not have the same form and function as it does where it is present in the sentence:

> ☒ Our officials ought to manage things better than they have been.

(The word to be supplied is *managed*, not *manage*.)

> ☒ No state has or can adopt such measures.

(The word to be supplied is *adopted*, not *adopt*.)

> ☒ The budget must be equal or greater than the total cost of supplying the product.

(The word *equal* should be followed by *to* and not *than*.)

Cases where the number (singular or plural) changes should also be avoided:

> ☐ The ringleader was hanged and his followers imprisoned.

(The word needed before 'imprisoned' is *were*, not *was*.)

The relative pronoun *that* or *which* is routinely left out informally, especially when a final preposition refers back:

> It reminded him of the house he used to live in.

The verb *be* is often omitted, especially in informal English, in cases such as

> They are sorry for what they did and anxious to make amends.
> We're leaving now and catching the nine o'clock train.

But when *be* is used as an auxiliary verb and as a linking verb in the same sentence, it must be repeated because its role is different:

> The bill was overtaken by the election and its postponement was welcome.

Ambiguity

When words have more than one meaning it is not always clear which meaning is intended in a particular statement. For example, if someone says to you that you should 'check your speed', this could mean either 'reduce your speed' or 'look and see what your speed is', because the verb *check* has both these key meanings.

Some forms of sentence structure and word order can also lead to more than one meaning being possible. This situation, called ambiguity, is normally unintentional, although ambiguity is sometimes used deliberately, for example in advertising. In speech, ambiguity is often avoided by the rise and fall of the voice as you speak. In writing, the context will often make the right meaning clear, but not always.

Typical ambiguities in everyday language usually involve:

- the association of a word or phrase with the wrong part of the sentence in so-called 'misrelated constructions':

> ☐ The council plans to notify parents whose children are affected by post.

(where *by post* should be placed after *notify*)

> ☐ The claims were regarded as mere posturing by the management.

(where *by the management* should be placed after *regarded*)

- the unclear application of a negative, especially in statements of intention or reason:

> ☐ She did not go out to water the plants.

(which can mean either that she did not go out at all, or that she did go out but not to water the plants)

- lack of clarity about how far a modifying word applies:

[?] The boy was wearing old jeans and trainers.

(in which it is unclear whether the jeans and trainers were old or just the jeans)

- words or expressions that have more than one meaning or function:

    [?] Visiting friends can be tiresome

    [?] The Minister appealed to her supporters.

- a pronoun with wrong or unclear reference:

    [?] If the children don't like their toys, get rid of them.

The normal position of intensifying or emphasising adverbs, such as *even*, *usually*, and in particular *only*, is between the subject and its verb, or after an auxiliary verb such as *has* and *are*, although the words they refer to often occur later in the sentence:

☑ The company has even admitted that it was negligent.

☑ In those days, you only applied to one college.

In written English, these adverbs are sometimes placed close to the actual words they refer to, especially when another modifying word occurs in their normal position, and in contexts, such as legal language, in which precision is more important than a pleasing style:

☑ The public interest is properly served only where companies pursue the traditional goal of maximising profit.

Beginning sentences with *and* and *but*

It is not wrong to begin a sentence with a conjunction such as *and* or *but*. The practice is common in literature and can be effective:

ARTHUR: Must you with hot irons burn out both mine eyes?
HUBERT: Young boy, I must.
ARTHUR: And will you?
HUBERT: And I will.

(Shakespeare, *King John*)

It is also used for other rhetorical purposes, especially to denote surprise (And are you really going?) and sometimes just to introduce an improvised afterthought (I'm going to swim. And don't you dare watch).

Negatives and double negatives

A repeated negative of the type He never did no harm to no one is incorrect to the point of being regarded as illiterate in current English. However, it surprises many people, who regard double negatives as self-evidently wrong, that they were once regarded as reinforcing each other and were an integral feature of standard English, found in Chaucer, Shakespeare, and other writers up to the 17th century. For some reason the logic then changed, and a sequence of negatives came to be regarded as cancelling each other out.

By contrast, a double negative is acceptable when it is used with intentional cancelling effect as a figure of speech, as in It has not gone unnoticed (= It most certainly has been noticed).

Double negatives also occur, especially in speech, in uses of the type You can't not go (= you cannot consider not going, i.e. you have to go), in which *not go* is effectively a single idea expressed in a verb phrase.

Subjunctive

The subjunctive is a special form (or mood) of a verb expressing a wish or possibility instead of fact. It has a limited role in English:

It was suggested he wait till the next morning.
Fundamentalist Islam … decrees that men and women be strictly segregated.

In these sentences, the verbs *wait* (in the first) and *be* (in the second) are in the subjunctive; the ordinary forms (called the indicative) would be *waits* and *are*.

There are other typical uses of the subjunctive:

- after *if* (or *as if*, *as though*, *unless*) in hypothetical conditions:

    Each was required to undertake that if it were chosen it would place work here.

- *be* or *were* at the beginning of a clause with the subject following:

    Were I to get drunk, it would help me in the fight.
    All books, be they fiction or non-fiction, should provide entertainment in some form or other.

- in certain fixed expressions and phrases, e.g. *be that as it may*, *come what may*, *perish the thought*, *so be it*, and others.

In most cases, an alternative construction (e.g. with *should* or *might*) can also be used:

It was suggested that he should wait till the next morning.

In negative constructions, *not* (or *never* etc.) is normally placed before the subjunctive verb:

Again he insisted that you not be followed.

4. Agreement

When we use words together in sentences, we often have to change their form so that they produce the right grammar and meaning. In the sentence John wants me to give you these flowers, *wants* is the form of the verb *want* that agrees with its subject *John* and *give* is the form that goes with *to*. The word *these* is a plural form to agree with its noun *flowers*, and the pronoun *me* is in the first person because it refers to the speaker. This process of making words fit the context of sentences is called 'agreement'.

For most of the time we apply the rules of agreement instinctively, but problems can arise. Sometimes words have special meanings that do not seem to correspond to their grammatical form. When we mix words about with other words in sentences we can easily lose mental track and link the wrong words together, especially in conversation when we have less time to think.

In some sentences, especially longer ones, the subject can be singular but separated from its verb by other words that happen to be in the plural. This can lead you to put the verb in the plural as well, and this is incorrect:

- ☒ The consequence of long periods of inactivity or situations in which patients cannot look after themselves are often quite severe and long-lasting.

Here, the string of plural nouns coming before the main verb *are* has caused the writer to lose sight of the real subject of the sentence, which is *consequence*. To make this sentence correct, we have three choices: to change *consequence* to *consequences*, to change *are* to *is*, or to recast the sentence more simply, e.g.:

- ☑ Long periods of inactivity or situations in which patients cannot look after themselves can often have quite severe and long-lasting consequences.

Agreement within phrases

Awkward phrases

Some expressions can cause uncertainty because they are grammatically ambiguous or combine seemingly contradictory roles, for example phrases such as *more than one* and *either or both*:

> More than one dealer has shown an interest in the painting.

The meaning is clearly plural, but the grammar remains singular because *one* is closer to the verb as well as being the dominant word in its phrase (we could not say More than one dealer have shown an interest in the painting).

- ❓ The purchaser gets a licence to use either or both products.

Here there is a problem of agreement with the following noun, because *either* calls for the singular form *product* whereas *both* calls for the plural form *products*; *both* wins out because it is closer to the noun. Usually a better solution is to adjust or recast the sentence to avoid the problem altogether:

- ☑ The purchaser gets a licence to use either or both of the products.

We find a similar problem with *one or more*:

- ❓ To qualify you must be responsible for one or more children aged under 16.

Again a small adjustment gets round the difficulty:

- ☑ To qualify you must be responsible for at least one child under 16.

Compound subjects

Two nouns joined by *and* are normally treated as plural:

> Speed and accuracy are top of the list.

> His mum and dad are meeting him at the station.

But when the two nouns form a phrase that can be regarded as a single unit, they are sometimes (or, when the unity is very strong, always) treated as singular even when one of them is plural:

> Fish and chips is my favourite meal.

This Romeo and Juliet is the best I have seen.

This practice can extend to concepts that are distinct in themselves but are regarded as a single item in a particular sentence:

- ❓ The hurt and disbelief of parents' friends and families is already quite real.
- ❓ The extent and severity of drug use in the city has been a severe shock.

When a singular noun forming the subject of a sentence is followed by an additional element tagged on by means of a phrase such as *as well as*, *accompanied by*, or *together with*, the following verb should be singular and not plural, since the singular noun is by itself the true subject:

> The little girl, together with her friend Kerry, was busy filling her bucket with sand.

(but note The little girl and her friend Kerry were busy filling their buckets with sand.)

> Your booking form, accompanied by a cheque or card details, needs to reach us by the end of January.

Singular and plural

Another kind of problem is the mismatch between a word's form and its meaning. Here are some typical cases:

Singular nouns treated as plural

Some nouns are singular in form but are used with a verb that can be either singular or plural, or in some cases only plural. The commonest of these are the collective nouns which stand for a group or collection of people or things, such as *audience, committee, crew, family, generation, government, group, jury, team*, and many others.

The general rule with words like these is to treat them as singular when the emphasis is on the group as a whole and as plural when the emphasis is on the individuals that form the group. The choice affects the form of the following verb and any pronouns such as *he, she, they*, or *their* that are used to refer to the noun:

> (*singular*) Each succeeding generation of gallery visitors finds it easier to recognise Cubist subject-matter.

> A group of four young men in overalls was standing close to him.

> (*plural*) The jury retired at the end of the day to consider their verdict.

> A handful of bathers were bobbing about in the waves.

Collective nouns representing a large or indeterminate number of people, such as *government, mob*, and *staff*, are treated in British English as either singular or plural with little effective difference, but in American English the singular is always used:

> The government is / are under increasing pressure to deal with the backlog of asylum seekers.

When there is a choice, the important point is to avoid a mixture of singular and plural forms:

- ☒ The committee has decided to postpone their decision.

Here, *has decided* and *their* both refer to the same word *committee*, but one is singular and the other is plural.

Names of countries often behave like collective nouns, and can be followed by plural verbs, when they denote the people or representatives of the country:

> Germany continue to defend their policy on food imports.
> France play Brazil in the final on Saturday.

Some collective nouns are fully plural, taking plural verbs and being used with plural determiners such as *these* and *many*:

> Many people agree that some form of control is needed.
> By and large the police do a good job.

Plural nouns treated as singular

Other nouns are plural in form but are treated as singular, either always or in some meanings. Chief among these are the names of branches of knowledge or science, such as *acoustics* and *mathematics*, activities such as *billiards* and *gymnastics*, and diseases such as *measles*:

> Acoustics is taught as part of the extended course.

The plural noun *acoustics* is equivalent to the singular expression *the subject of acoustics*; but note the plural agreement in The cathedral's acoustics are spectacularly good for this kind of music, where *acoustics* has a different meaning that is physical rather than conceptual.

> The figures show that measles is on the increase.

Here, *measles* is equivalent to the notional subject *disease* or *illness*. In more casual conversation, this pattern extends to other plurals:

> If he bought a small chips, he'd have enough for some chocolate too.

(where a word such as *bag* or *portion* is the notional subject).

Other plural nouns, such as *data*, *media*, and *agenda*, are now commonly treated as singular. Depending on their meaning, they are either countable nouns, which can be used with *a* or *an* and have plural forms, e.g. *agendas*, or mass nouns, which do not have a plural form but are used in the singular with words such as *this* and *much*:

> The media has lost interest in the subject.
> This data is in a form that can be used by other institutions.
> The Prime Minister has set himself a formidable agenda.

Some plural words adopted unchanged from other languages, such as *spaghetti* and *graffiti*, develop singular meanings:

> The furniture had been damaged and graffiti was daubed on the walls.

There are also words, such as *means*, that are plural in form but can function as singular (even to the extent that you can say *a means*) or plural depending on the words used with them:

> (*singular*) Complaints are valuable as a means of identifying where improvements can be made.
> (*plural*) Various means are being sought to revive public interest in the scheme.

Subjects and objects

People often wonder what to do when the subject of the verb *be* is singular and the part that follows the verb (the complement) is plural. The answer is that the verb should generally agree with its subject, regardless of what comes after the verb:

> The only traffic is ox-carts and bicycles.

There is usually no problem when the reverse situation occurs, with the subject in the plural and the complement in the singular:

> These huge biographies are usually a mistake nowadays.

When the subject is a singular collective noun, the verb may be in the plural, following the usual pattern with such nouns:

> Its prey are other small animals.

When the subject is the relative pronoun *what*, the verb is singular:

> What I'm really interested in is the objects in this house.

Indefinite pronouns

Pronouns such as *each*, *either*, *neither*, and *none* are called indefinite pronouns. When used on their own like a noun, they can vary between singular and plural depending on whether the emphasis is on the individuals or on the collection or group as a whole:

> (*singular*) Either is preferable to muddling through with neither.
> Neither the chairman nor the chief executive is planning any dramatic gestures.
> None of them has had enough practical experience to run the company.
> (*plural*) They each carry several newspapers.
> Neither his mother nor his father earn much money now.
> None of the staff were aware of the ransom demand.

Like all pronouns these words (apart from *none*) can also come before nouns, as in *each person* and *neither house*. In this role they are classed, like *every*, as determiners, and they are then always singular:

> Each party has members in the Federal National Assembly.
> Neither suggestion is the right one.

Plural pronouns used in the singular

You may sometimes be unsure about what possessive word (*his*, *her*, etc.) to put in the place indicated by the question mark in the example that follows:

> Every student should hand in ? assignment by Tuesday.

Here, *every* can stand for a male or female person with correspondingly different forms of possessive word. The safest option is to put *his or her*:

> Every student should hand in his or her assignment by Tuesday.

But this can be awkward, especially when the sentence continues for some time with repeated references back to the original subject. In cases like this it is now acceptable to use a plural form of pronoun to refer back to an indefinite pronoun, so as to avoid having to specify gender at all when this is unknown or irrelevant:

> Every student should hand in their assignment by Tuesday.

This is a great deal neater, and is supported historically: the use of *they* and *their* in this way used to be common in English until people took against it in the 19th century, along with other grammatical superstitions that arose then. But there is an alternative that gets round the problem altogether, by putting the whole sentence in the plural:

> All students should hand in their assignments by Tuesday.

This option is worth remembering, but you have to keep the sentence in the singular when you use singular indefinite pronouns such as *anyone* or *somebody*:

> ☑ Does anyone want their tea now?

either ... or ... *and* neither ... nor ...

A problem arises when one of the alternatives in an *either ... or ... or neither ... nor ...* construction is singular and the other plural. Here, the normal choice is to make the verb agree with the one closer to it:

> ☑ Either the twins or their mother is responsible for this.

But often a better solution is to recast the sentence to avoid the problem:

> ☑ Either the twins are responsible for this or their mother is.

A mixture of persons normally has to be resolved by this kind of rephrasing:

> ? Neither you nor I am / are / is the right person.

is better as

> ☑ You are not the right person, and neither am I.

(or ... and nor am I.)

Personal pronouns

> It's a tiny bit boring, between you and me.

I, we, he, she, and *they* are subjective pronouns, which act as the subjects of verbs, while *me, us, him, her,* and *them* are objective, acting as the objects of verbs and prepositions. In the sentence above, therefore, *me* is correct, since the preposition *between* refers to both *you* and *me* and *I* has to be the subject of a sentence. The same applies to other prepositions used in this way (such as *for* and *with*):

> The boys are coming with Gavin and me.

After the verb *be* it is more natural and usual to use *me, us, him, her,* or *they* (the objective pronouns), although what follows *be* is not an object but a complement:

> I said it was only me.
>
> That's us sitting on the bench.
>
> Is it them you wanted to see?

The subjective forms (*I, we, he, she,* or *they*) are not wrong but often sound stilted, especially the first-person forms *I* and *we*:

> ? I said it was only I.
>
> ? That's we sitting on the bench.

It is however usual to use the subjective forms when a relative clause (introduced by *who* or *that*) follows:

> ☑ It was I who did it.

(It was me who did it, and especially ? It was me that did it, are much more informal in tone.)

5. Punctuation

The purpose of punctuation is to make writing clear. Bad punctuation is like a badly laid out timetable: the information may be correct but the way it is organised can clarify or obscure it. Like other aspects of language, punctuation has changed over the centuries; modern practice was influenced by the development of printing in the 15th and 16th centuries, which had the effect of standardising a practice that before then had been haphazard and unreliable.

There are several ways in which punctuation makes writing clearer:

- it can clarify the structure of continuous writing (full stop, comma, colon, semicolon, and brackets).
- it can indicate words that form something other than a statement (question mark, exclamation mark, quotation marks).
- it can show how words relate to each other (apostrophe, hyphen).
- it can indicate that a group of letters is an abbreviation (full stop) or that letters are missing (apostrophe).

Full stop

The principal use of the full stop (also called point, full point, and period) is to mark the end of a sentence that is a statement:

> Bernard went over to the bookcase and took down an atlas.

This applies to sentences when they are not complete statements or contain ellipsis, as in the opening of Dickens's *Bleak House*:

> London. Michaelmas term lately over, and the Lord Chancellor sitting in Lincoln's Hall. Implacable November weather.

If the sentence is a question or exclamation, the mark used is the question mark or exclamation mark, which include a full stop in their forms (see further on the **QUESTION MARK** and **EXCLAMATION MARK** below).

Comma

The role of the comma is to give detail to the structure of sentences and to make their meaning clear by marking off words that either do or do not belong together. It usually represents the natural breaks and pauses that you make in speech, and operates at phrase level and word level:

at phrase level You should use a comma to mark off parts of a sentence that are separated by conjunctions (*and, but, yet,* etc.). This is especially important when there is a change or repetition of the subject:

> Attempts to block him failed, and he went ahead on 23 June.
>
> Mokosh could foretell the future, and she could change herself into any form she pleased.

The use of a comma in these cases is especially important when the sentence is a long one:

> Readings are taken at points on a grid marked out on the ground, and the results are usually plotted in the form of computer-drawn diagrams.

(It may be preferable to use two sentences here.)

It is not normally correct to join the clauses of a compound sentence without a conjunction:

> ☒ His was the last house, the road ended with him.

(In this sentence, the comma should either be replaced by a semicolon, or retained and followed by *and*.)

It is also incorrect to separate a subject from its verb with a single comma:

> ☒ Those with the lowest incomes and no other means, should get the most support.

(Remove the comma.)

A comma also separates parts of a sentence that balance or complement each other, and can introduce direct speech, especially in continuation of dialogue:

> Parliament is not dissolved, only prorogued.
>
> He was getting better, but not as fast as his doctor wished.
>
> Then Laura said, 'Do you mean that?'

An important function of the comma is to prevent ambiguity or momentary misunderstanding:

> A hundred feet below, the woman in the red dress was gazing up at them.
>
> Mr Hogg said that he had shot, himself, as a small boy.

Commas are used in pairs to separate elements in a sentence that are asides or not part of the main statement:

> All history, of course, is the history of wars.
>
> By then, however, it was very close to being dark.

It is important to remember *both* the commas in cases like this. Using only one can be worse than none at all:

> ☒ By then, however it was very close to being dark.

Commas are also used to separate a relative clause (one beginning with *which*, *who*, *whom*, or *whose*) when this is adding extra information and could be removed from the sentence without changing the meaning or producing nonsense:

> The money, which totals more than half a million, comes from three anonymous donors.

(See the section on **SENTENCES**.)

But they are not used when the clause begins with *which* or *that* and is essential to the meaning by identifying a person or thing just mentioned:

> What have you done with the money that I gave you?

The difference between these two types of relative clause is explained in the section on sentences.

A single comma sometimes follows adverbs (such as *already*, *moreover*, and *yesterday*), phrases, and subordinate clauses that come at the beginning of a sentence:

> Moreover, they had lied about where they had been.

> Next morning, the air glittered and the palm tree stood upright in the sun.
>
> When the sun began to sink, she could take the riverside walk to the hotel and join her friends.

In all these cases and many others this comma is optional, but one or more is always needed with *however* when it means 'by contrast' or 'on the other hand':

> However, a good deal of discretion is left in the hands of area managers.

at word level A comma is used to separate adjectives having the same range of reference coming before a noun:

> a cold, damp, badly heated room
>
> a ruthless, manipulative person

The comma can be replaced by *and* between a pair of adjectives to make a stronger effect:

> a ruthless and manipulative person

The comma is omitted when the adjectives have a different range of reference (for example, size and colour) or when the last adjective has a closer relation to the noun:

> his baggy green jacket
>
> a distinguished foreign politician
>
> a dear little baby

Commas are used to separate items in a list or sequence:

> The visitors were given tea, scones, and cake.

The comma before *and* is regarded by many people as unnecessary and left out; this dictionary always includes one. There are cases where the final comma is essential for clarity (for example, where one of the items in the list is a pair joined by *and*), and sometimes not having one produces ambiguity:

> ☑ For breakfast they wanted tea, toast and marmalade, and eggs.
>
> ☒ I would like to thank my parents, Anne Smith and God.

Leave out the comma between nouns that occur together in the same grammatical role in a sentence (called apposition):

> My friend Judge Peters was not at home.
>
> Her daughter Mary became a nurse.

But use one when the noun is a piece of extra information that could be removed from the sentence without any noticeable effect on the meaning:

> His father, Humphrey V. Roe, was not so fortunate.

Semicolon

The semicolon is the punctuation mark that causes most trouble in ordinary writing, and it is the one least noticeable if you skim the pages of a modern novel. But if you use it carefully, it can be extremely helpful.

Its main role is to mark a grammatical separation that is stronger in effect than a comma but less strong than a full stop. Normally the two parts of a sentence divided by a semicolon balance each other, as distinct from leading from one to the other (in which case a colon is usually more suitable, as explained below):

> The sky grew bright with sunset; the earth glowed, and his face also with its own light.

Honey looked up and glared; the man scurried away.

You can also use it as a stronger division in a sentence that already contains commas:

> What has crippled me? Was it my grandmother, frowning on my childish affection and turning it to formality and cold courtesy; or my timid, fearful mother, in awe of everyone including, finally, me; or was it my wife's infidelities, or my own?

Colon

The colon tends to be used much more in formal print than in everyday writing. Whereas a semicolon links two balanced statements, a colon leads from the first statement to the second. Typically it links a general or introductory statement to an example, a cause to an effect, or a premise to a conclusion. (In many cases a conjunction such as 'so' or 'for example' could be introduced between the two halves.)

> He was being made to feel more part of the family: the children kissed him goodnight, like a third parent.
>
> I feel angry: do I look angry?

You also use a colon to introduce a list:

> The price includes the following: travel to London, flight to Venice, hotel accommodation, and excursions.

A colon can sometimes give more emphasis or drama to a statement in direct speech:

> Dobson told them: 'He has been arrested.'

In American English, a colon follows the initial greeting in a letter (Dear Ms Jones:), where in British English you would normally use a comma.

Brackets

The brackets you will use most often in writing are round brackets or parentheses ( ).

You use round brackets:

- to show explanations and additional comment:

> She let herself plan out what she would say, what her tone could be (easy but serious), how much need she could show (fatigue, strained loyalty).
>
> A verbal noun (also called a gerund) is a form of a verb ending in -ing.

- to show optional words, implying doubt or caution about them:

> There are many (apparent) difficulties.

- to give references and statistical information:

> a brass-rubbing of Sir Toby and Lady Falconer (c.1428)
>
> If music be the food of love (Shakespeare, *Twelfth Night*)

Square brackets [ ] are mostly used in formal printing. Their main use is to enclose extra information provided, often by someone other than the writer of the surrounding text, such as an editor, to clarify an obscure point or identity:

> When Charles had spoken to Henry, he [Henry] withdrew graciously.

Dash

In formal printing there are two types of dash: the en-rule (–) and the longer em-rule (—). Most word-processing programs are able to distinguish the two lengths of rule, but in ordinary writing no distinction is usually made. In printing, the en-rule has certain special uses (e.g. to mark a range of numbers, as in pages 34–6), whereas the em-rule is the one corresponding to the dash in general use.

The principal uses of the dash are:

- a single dash is used to introduce an explanation or expansion of what comes before it:

> It is a kind of irony of history that I should write about the French Revolution in the very country where it has had the least impact—I mean England, of course.

- a pair of dashes is used to indicate asides and parentheses, forming a more distinct break than commas would:

> Helen has only seen her father once in her adult life and—until her flight from Grassdale—her brother is a virtual stranger to her.

Question mark

The main use of the question mark (?) is to indicate a direct question:

> Are they leaving tomorrow?
>
> What time is it?

You can sometimes use it even when the question is put in the form of a statement:

> They told you that?
>
> Surely it's the same one?
>
> I wonder if you can help me?

You should not use a question mark in indirect questions in which the question is reported rather than expressed (He asked what time it was), but you should use it in tag questions of the kind She's much taller now, isn't she?.

A question mark is conventionally placed before a word about which there is some doubt, e.g. uncertain locations on maps and uncertain dates (Thomas Tallis, ?1505–85).

Exclamation mark

An exclamation mark (!) shows in writing what you would normally say loudly or strongly in speech, to attract attention or to tell someone what to do. You will most often use it:

- to mark a command or warning:

> Go to your room!
>
> Be careful!

- to indicate the expression of a strong feeling of absurdity, surprise, approval, dislike, regret, etc., especially after *how* or *what*:

> How awful!
>
> Aren't they odd!

Why, Archie, you're wet!

- to express a wish or a feeling of regret:

  I'd love to come!

  If only I had known!

- in speech, to indicate someone calling out or shouting:

  Outside Edith's house, someone knocked. 'Edith!'

  'You're only shielding her.' 'Shielding her!' His voice rose to a shriek.

The exclamation mark also occurs quite often in literature, especially in poetry, to express a strong feeling or idea:

  O, weep for Adonais! (Shelley)

  Ah! parted lips and little pearly teeth, Wide eyes, snub noses, shorts, divided skirts! (Betjeman)

In ordinary writing, you do not often need to use the exclamation mark in this way. Avoid using it just to add a false sense of drama or sensation to writing that is otherwise routine or unexciting.

Quotation marks

The main use of quotation marks (also called inverted commas) is to indicate direct speech and quotations. In writing it is common to use double quotation marks (" "), and in printing practice varies between the double and single style (' '). Single marks are more often used in Britain and double marks in America. The guidelines that follow reflect practice in British English, with indications of any variations in American English.

In direct speech and quotations, the closing quotation mark normally comes after a final full stop, and after any other punctuation that forms part of the quotation, such as an exclamation mark:

  Christie nodded her head as she said, 'A fine proposal this is, I must say.'

  Then they shouted, 'Watch out!'

When the quoted speech is followed or interrupted by a reporting verb such as *say*, *shout*, etc., the punctuation that divides the sentence is put inside the quotation marks:

  'No,' he said, slamming the suitcase shut.

  'You must have read my mind,' she said, 'a good strong cup of tea is just what I need.'

If a quoted word or phrase comes at the end of a sentence or coincides with a comma, the punctuation that belongs to the sentence as a whole is placed outside the quotation marks:

  What is a 'gigabyte'?

  No one should 'follow a multitude to do evil', as the Scripture says.

In American English, however, it is usual to place quotation marks outside the sentence punctuation (and note the more characteristic double quotation marks):

  No one should "follow a multitude to do evil," as the Scripture says.

When a quotation occurs within a quotation, the inner quotation is put in double quotation marks if the main quotation is in single marks (or vice versa, especially in American practice):

  'Have you any idea,' he asked, 'what a "gigabyte" is?' (British)

  "Have you any idea," he asked, "what a 'gigabyte' is?" (American)

Apostrophe

The principal role of the apostrophe is to indicate a possessive, as in **Tessa's house** and **the town's mayor**. For its conventional role to indicate omitted letters, see below.

Singular nouns form the possessive by adding *'s* (**the dog's barks** = one dog), and plural nouns ending in *s* add an apostrophe after the *s* (**the dogs' barks** = more than one dog).

When a plural noun ends in a letter other than *s*, the possessive is formed by adding *'s*: **the children's games**, **the oxen's hoofs**, etc.

Beware of the so-called 'grocers' apostrophe', an apostrophe wrongly applied to an ordinary plural, particularly in words ending in *-o* but also in quite harmless words such as *apples* and *pears* (e.g. ✖ **pear's 30p a pound**).

Beware also of confusing the possessive *whose* with *who's*, which is a contraction of *who is* (e.g. ✖ **Who's turn is it?**).

There is a problem with names ending in *-s*, because of the awkward sound that can result. Practice varies, but the best course is to add *'s* to names that end in *s* when you would pronounce the resulting form with an extra *s* in speech (e.g. *Charles's*, *Dickens's*, *Thomas's*, *The Times's*); and omit *'s* when the name is normally pronounced without the extra *s* (e.g. *Bridges'*, *Connors'*, *Mars'*, *Herodotus'*). With French names ending in (silent) *-s* or *-x*, add *'s* (e.g. *Dumas's*, *le Roux's*) and pronounce the modified word with a final *-z*.

An apostrophe should not be used in the pronouns *hers*, *its*, *ours*, *yours*, and *theirs*:

  ☑ **a friend of yours**

  ✖ **a friend of your's**

Be careful to distinguish *its* from *it's*. *Its* (no apostrophe) is a possessive meaning 'belonging to it', whereas *it's* (with an apostrophe) is a contraction meaning 'it is':

  ☑ **Give the cat its dinner.**

  ✖ **Give the cat it's dinner.**

  ☑ **It's hard to know where to start.**

  ☑ **It's been raining.**

An apostrophe is no longer normally used in the plural of abbreviated forms (e.g. **several MPs were standing around**), although it is used in the possessive (e.g. **the BBC's decision to go ahead with the broadcast**). It is used in plurals when clarity calls for it, e.g. **dot your i's and cross your t's**. The apostrophe is also rapidly disappearing in company names and other commercial uses, e.g. *Barclays Bank*, *Citizens Advice Bureau*.

Another important use of the apostrophe is to mark contractions such as *I'll*, *they've*, *couldn't*, and *she's*, and informally also in contractions involving nouns (e.g. **The joke's on them**).

The apostrophe is no longer needed in words that were originally shortened forms but are now treated as words in their own right, e.g. *cello*, *flu*, *phone*, and *plane*. Other words retain them in their spelling, usually in the middle of words rather than at the beginning, e.g. *fo'c'sle*, *ne'er-do-well*, *o'er*, *rock 'n' roll*.

Hyphen

In print, a hyphen is half the length of a dash, but in writing there is often little noticeable difference. While the dash has the purpose of separating words and groups of words, the hyphen is meant to link words and parts of words (apart from its use as a printing convention to split a word at the end of a line). Although the use of hyphens is very variable in English, the following guidelines reflect generally agreed principles.

As a so-called 'spelling hyphen', the hyphen is used to join two or more words so as to form a single word (often called a compound word), e.g. *free-for-all*, *multi-ethnic*, and *right-handed*, and words having a grammatical relationship which form a compound, e.g. *dive-bomb* (based on 'to bomb by making a dive'), *load-bearing* (based on 'bearing a load'), *punch-drunk* (based on 'drunk from a punch'). Straightforward noun compounds are now much more often spelt either as two words (*boiling point*, *credit card*, *focus group*, *garden party*) or as one, even when this involves a collision of consonants, which used to be a reason for putting in the hyphen (*database*, *earring*, *breaststroke*, *radioisotope*). However, there are two cases in which a compound spelt as two words is made into a hyphened form or a one-word form:

■ when a verb phrase such as *hold up* or *kick back* is made into a noun (*hold-up*, *kick-back*).

■ when a noun compound is made into a verb (e.g. *a date stamp* but *to date-stamp*).

A hyphen is often used:

■ to join a prefix ending in a vowel (such as *co-* and *neo-*) to another word (e.g. *co-opt*, *neo-Impressionism*), although one-word forms are becoming more usual (*cooperate*, *neoclassical*).

■ to avoid ambiguity by separating a prefix from the main word, e.g. to distinguish *re-cover* (= provide with a new cover) from *recover* and *re-sign* (= sign again) from *resign*.

■ to join a prefix to a name or designation, e.g. *anti-Christian*, *ex-husband*. There is no satisfactory way of dealing with the type *ex-Prime Minister*, in which the second element is itself a compound, except to rely on the tendency of readers to use their knowledge of the world to choose the natural meaning. A second hyphen, e.g. *ex-Prime-Minister*, is not standard.

■ to stand for a common second element in all but the last word of a list, e.g. **two-, three-, or fourfold**.

■ to clarify meanings in groups of words which might otherwise be unclear or ambiguous:

The library is reducing its purchase of hard-covered books.

Twenty-odd people came to the meeting.

There will be special classes for French-speaking children.

You should also use a hyphen to clarify the meaning of a compound that is normally spelled as separate words, when it is used before a noun: an **up-to-date record** but **the record is up to date**.

But there is no need to insert a hyphen between an adverb ending in *-ly* and an adjective qualified by it, even when they come before the noun: a **highly competitive market**, **recently published material**. When the adverb does not end in *-ly*, however, a hyphen is normally required to make the meaning clear: a **well-known woman**, an **ill-defined topic**.

Other uses of punctuation

Abbreviations (full stop)

Abbreviations are increasingly spelled without full stops when they are made up of all capital letters (*AGM*, *NNE*, *TUC*) or a mixture of capital and small letters (*BSc*, *Ms*). But full stops are more usual when the abbreviation is made up entirely of small letters, because in this form they are less immediately recognisable as abbreviations rather than words (*a.o.b.*, *p.m.*, *t.b.a.*). Shortenings, or abbreviations consisting of the first few letters of words, are usually spelled with a final full point (*co.*, *Oct.*, *cert.*), but those where the abbreviation ends with the last letter of the word tend not to be (*Dr*, *Dept*).

If an abbreviation with a full stop comes at the end of a sentence, another full stop is not added when the full stop of the abbreviation is the last character: **Bring your own pens, pencils, rulers, etc.** but **Bring your own things (pens, pencils, rulers, etc.).**

Number markers

Full stops are routinely used between units of money (£11.99, $27.50), before decimals (10.5%), and between hours and minutes (10.30 a.m.; American English uses a colon as in 10:30 a.m.).

Commas are used in numbers of four or more figures, to separate each group of three consecutive figures starting from the right (e.g. 14,236,681). Omit the comma when giving house numbers in addresses (**44 High Street**), and in dates (**27 July 2001**).

Internet and email addresses

A number of punctuation marks, including the full stop, are used as parts of Internet and email addresses. A typical Internet address, also known as a *URL* or 'uniform resource locator', takes the form of an expression like:

http://www.readersdigest.co.uk

All addresses on the World Wide Web begin with *http*, standing for 'hypertext transfer protocol', followed by *www* (separated by a colon and two forward slashes). The 'domain name' forming the rest of the address identifies a particular organisation (e.g. *readersdigest*). The extensions *co* and *uk* are letter codes indicating (in this case) a commercial organisation based in Great Britain.

An email address usually looks something like this:

gbeditorial@readersdigest.co.uk

The first part, e.g. *gbeditorial*, is the user's particular name. It is followed, after the 'at-sign' @, by the name of the system or server on which they are located.

As a full stop is a significant part of a domain name, you should be careful when punctuating a sentence which contains an Internet or email address. To avoid introducing a possible error, it is customary to omit the full stop at the end of a sentence ending with such an address.

6. Spelling

Changes in spelling

Before the invention of printing in the 15th century, English and other European languages had no regularity of spelling and usage was largely based on personal preference. At first the development of printed books added to the problem, with printers (many of them not English) using different spellings of the same word even in the same passage of text. For example, Caxton—the first English printer—spelled *book* as *booke* and *boke* within a few lines of each other. Even people's names were not spelled consistently (*Shakespeare*, for example, appeared as *Shakspere*, *Shakespear*, etc.). It was not until the 17th century, when the first dictionaries were written, that some order was brought to bear on this chaos.

Many words, therefore, have changed their spelling over centuries of use. Words derived from French that we spell with *-re* at the end (e.g. *theatre* and *lustre*) used to be spelled with the ending *-er*, and these forms (e.g. *theater* and *luster*) have survived in American English. There have been dozens of ways of spelling the word *through* (including *thourth*, *thurght*, and *thorght*), all now obsolete. If you look at letters written in the 18th century, you will find people writing *teaze* for *tease* and *happyness* for *happiness*, and signing themselves *your dutifull daughter*. *Duty* itself has had many forms, including *deuty*, *dewite*, and *dewtie*.

Even now, English is full of irregularities of spelling. The same sounds can be written in different ways (such as -oo- in *moon*, *threw*, *through*, and *lute*), and the same group of letters can stand for different sounds (such as -ough in *bough*, *though*, *through*, *enough*, and *cough*). Various proposals have been made over the years for reforms (some dating back to the 16th century) that would make spelling more straightforward for the benefit of native speakers and foreign learners alike. Among the most famous proposals were those of Isaac Pitman (the inventor of shorthand) and the playwright George Bernard Shaw, who left money in his will to finance the development of a new alphabet that could more consistently reflect the ways in which words are pronounced.

There are two serious problems with all these proposals for reforming the alphabet. First, there is the question of managing the change and getting people to use the new system. Second, English is pronounced in different accents, and so the question arises of which accent should provide the model on which the reformed alphabet is based. There are other difficulties: for example, which spelling to adopt when more than one is available for a particular sound (e.g. *ou* as in *count* or *ow* as in *cow*), and the objection that phonetic spelling would obscure word origins and connections, especially in groups of words in which the stress pattern changes, e.g. *adore*, *adoration* and *nation*, *national*. In any case, no machinery for reform exists, and it is unlikely that significant change can be achieved except by the weight of ordinary usage.

A major cause of confusion is the exceptional tolerance English has for different spellings of the same word. This works in unpredictable ways, so that *banister*, *bannister* and *judgement*, *judgment* are all permitted spellings whereas *accomodation* is not a permitted variant of *accommodation* nor *millenium* of *millennium*, even though these rejected forms are very common.

Difficult spellings

The tables following give examples of some of the most commonly misspelled and confused words. Systematic problems occur in words belonging to a certain type (e.g. the formation of nouns from verbs ending in *-edge*, such as *acknowledgement* and *judgement*) and in the inflection of words (e.g. the plural of nouns ending in *-o* such as *potato* and *solo*, and the *-ed* and *-ing* forms of verbs such as *benefit* and *unravel*). Some of these difficulties have been addressed in the section on **INFLECTION**.

The best-known spelling rule is 'i before e except after c'. This is generally valid when the combination is pronounced -ee-, as in *believe*, *brief*, *fiend*, *hygiene*, *niece*, *priest*, *siege*, and in *ceiling*, *deceive*, *conceit*, *receipt*, *receive*. There are exceptions: *caffeine*, *codeine*, *protein* (all formed from elements ending in *-e* followed by *-in* or *-ine*); *plebeian*, and *seize*.

The rule is not valid when the syllable is pronounced in other ways, as in *beige*, *freight*, *neighbour*, *sleigh*, *veil*, *vein*, and *weigh* (all pronounced as in *lake*), in *eiderdown*, *feisty*, *height*, *heist*, *kaleidoscope*, and *sleight* (all pronounced as in *like*), and in words in which the *i* and *e* are pronounced as separate vowels, e.g. *holier*, *occupier*.

Different spellings, related meaning, different parts of speech

word 1	part of speech	word 2	part of speech
annexe	noun	annex	verb
dependant	noun	dependent	verb
envelope	noun	envelop	verb
licence	noun	license	verb
practice	noun	practise	verb
thief	noun	thieve	verb
wreath	noun	wreathe	verb

Guide to good English

Frequently misspelled words

word	comment	word	comment	word	comment
accommodate, accommodation, etc.	two cs, two ms	embarrass, embarrassment, etc.	two rs, two s's	minuscule	not *miniscule*
acquaint, acquire, etc.	*acq-*	enthral	one *l*	mischievous	not *-ievious*
ageing	preferred to *aging*	fulfil	one final *l*; American also *fulfill*	misspell	two s's
aggressive, aggression, etc.	two gs, two s's	gauge	*-au-* not *-ua-*	necessary	one c, two s's
appal	two ps, one *l*; American also *appall*	guarantee	*-ua-* not *-au-*	niece	*i* before *e*
		guard, guardian, etc.	*-ua-* not *-au-*	occurrence	two cs, two rs
appalling	two ps, two *l*s	harass, harassment, etc.	one r, two s's	parliament	*-ia-* in second syllable
artefact	*arte-* preferred to *arti-*	hygienic	*i* before *e*	privilege	ends *-ilege*
attach	not *-atch*	independent	ends *-ent*, noun and adjective	questionnaire	two ns
besiege	*i* before *e*	install	two *l*s	receive	*e* before *i*
biased	preferred to *biassed*	instalment	one *l*; American *installment*	recommend	one c, two ms
commemorate	two ms followed by one m	itinerary	ends *-erary*	rhythm	begins *rh-*
committee	two ms, two ts	judgement	*-dge-* preferred form	seize	*e* before *i*
consensus	not *concensus*	manoeuvre	*-oeu-*; American *maneuver*	separate	*-par-* not *-per-*
desperate	*-per-* not *-par-*			siege	*i* before *e*
detach	not *-atch*	medieval	*-ev-* preferred to *-aev-*	sieve	*i* before *e*
disappear	one s, two p's	Mediterranean	one t, two rs	skilful	single *l*s; American also *skillful*
disappoint	one s, two p's	memento	*mem-* not *mom-*	supersede	not *-cede*
ecstasy	ends *-asy*	millennium	two *l*s, two ns	suppress	not *sur-*, two ps
eighth	two hs	millionaire	two *l*s, one n	surprise	begins *sur-*
		miniature	*-ia-* in second syllable	threshold	one h
				unwieldy	not *-wieldly*
				wilful	single *l*s
				withhold	two hs

Frequently confused words

Different spellings, same or close pronunciation, different meanings

word 1	meaning	word 2	meaning
aural	relating to the ear and hearing	oral	relating to the mouth and speaking
breach	a gap or break, to make a break	breech	part of a gun or cannon
canvas	material for tents and sails	canvass	to seek opinions or solicit votes
chord	a group of notes in music	cord	string or rope
complacent	smug and self-satisfied	complaisant	willing to please
complement	addition that completes, to add in a way that improves	compliment	expression of praise, to express praise for
council	advisory or administrative body	counsel	adviser, barrister in court, to give professional advice
desert	waterless area of sand (stress on first syllable), to abandon (stress on second syllable)	dessert	sweet course of meal (stress on second syllable)
discreet	circumspect	discrete	distinct
draft	preliminary sketch etc.	draught	air current, quantity of liquid
draw	to make a picture of, to pull, to have an equal score	drawer	a compartment in a desk or chest
ensure	to make sure	insure	to take out insurance on
faint	hard to see or hear	feint	a pretended blow, to make a pretended blow, denoting paper with faint lines
flair	a natural ability	flare	a burst of flame or light, to give a sudden light, to become angry
forbear (verb)	to desist from	forebear (noun)	ancestor
forego	to go before	forgo	to go without
forever	continually	for ever	eternally
grisly	causing revulsion	grizzly	as in *grizzly bear*
hoard	store of valuables	horde	large group of people (usually unwelcome)
its	possessive word, as in *the cat licked its paws*	it's	= it is or it has
loath	reluctant or unwilling	loathe	to dislike greatly
naught	chiefly in *come to naught* and *set at naught*	nought	the digit 0, nothing
naval	relating to a navy	navel	umbilicus
ordinance	an authoritative order	ordnance	mounted guns, military stores
palate	roof of the mouth, sense of taste	palette	artist's mixing board
principal	first or main, chief person	principle	basis of belief or action
shear	to cut wool off, to cut	sheer	to swerve or avoid, utter or complete (as in *sheer delight*)
stationary	not moving	stationery	writing materials
storey	part of a building on one level	story	account of imaginary events
straight	extending without a curve or bend	strait	narrow passage of water
who's	= who is	whose	possessive word, as in *whose house is this?*

7. Capital letters

Capital letters mark special uses of words. They emphasise a significant point in writing, especially the beginning of a sentence, and distinguish special kinds of words, for example proper names. They also occur in some abbreviations.

You should always use a capital letter:

- to begin a new sentence, or a quotation within a sentence.
- at the start of proper names and personal names (*New York, Alison, Churchill*).
- in certain special cases, e.g. the personal pronoun *I* and the exclamation *O*.

Beyond these elementary rules, practice and usage is not consistent. The following is based on a consensus of practice in British English. Capital letters are used for:

- prefixes and titles forming part of names referring to one person: *the Duke of Wellington, Sir Bob Geldof, Her Majesty the Queen, Queen Elizabeth the Queen Mother, His Excellency the American Ambassador.* When the reference is general, i.e. to many such people, a capital is not used: every king of England from William I to Richard II (where *king* is a common noun like *monarch* or *sovereign*).
- titles of office-holders when these refer to a particular holder: I have an appointment with the Mayor and He was appointed Bishop of Durham; but not when the reference is general or descriptive: He wanted to be a bishop and When I become mayor.
- recognised and official place-names: *Northern Ireland* (but *northern England*, which is simply descriptive), *Western Australia, South Africa, New England, the Straits of Gibraltar, Plymouth Sound, London Road* (when it is an address; but Take the London road, i.e. the road to London, when it is descriptive).
- compass directions when these are abbreviated (*N, NNE, SW*) or when denoting a recognised region (prosperity in the South).
- names of peoples and languages and derived words directly relating to them (*Irishman, German, Swahili*).
- names of months and days (*July, Tuesday, Christmas Day, the Annunciation*).
- names of events and periods of time: *the Bronze Age, the Middle Ages, the Renaissance, the First World War* (but *the 1914–18 war* is generally regarded as descriptive).
- names of institutions, when these are regarded as identifying rather than describing: *Christianity, Buddhism, Islam, Marxism, the (Roman) Catholic Church, the House of Lords.*
- names of ships and vehicles: *Cutty Sark, HMS Dreadnought, the US bomber Enola Gay:* see next section. Note also *a Boeing, a Renault,* which are trademarks.
- words referring to the deity of a religion (*God, Father, Allah, Almighty*), although the use of capitals in possessive words (as in in His name) is no longer common.
- proprietary names or trademarks: *Anadin, Cow & Gate,*

Kleenex, Persil. A capital initial should strictly also be used when the reference is generic (e.g. can you lend me a Biro?), but in practice this is more common in published print than in general writing. A verb formed from a proprietary name is spelled with a small initial, as in *to hoover* and *to xerox*.

Abbreviations and initialisms are usually spelled with capitals, whether they refer to institutions or are more generic (*BBC, MPs*); but acronyms, which are pronounced like words and tend to behave like words, often become wholly or partly lower-case (*Nato, radar, Aids*).

Words derived from proper names

You should use a capital letter when the word still has a direct reference to the original name: *Christian* (noun and adjective), *Machiavellian, Shakespearian.* But a small initial is used when the reference is remote or indirect: *arabic letters, french windows, mackintosh, wellington boot;* and when the sense is an attribute or quality suggested by the proper name: *chauvinistic, herculean, titanic.*

Verbs follow the same rule: *Americanise, Romanise,* but *bowdlerise, galvanise, pasteurise.* The guide in this area is the extent to which the name on which the word is based is present in the meaning used, as it clearly is with *Shakespearian* but not with *titanic* (which many people use without knowing about the mythological Titans from which the word is derived).

8. Italics

Italics are *a style of sloping type, like this,* and are used in printing for a number of special purposes (in ordinary writing you can underline words instead).

The principal uses of italics are:

- for titles of books, plays, longer poems, films, works of art, etc.: *Harry Potter and the Philosopher's Stone, A Midsummer Night's Dream, Paradise Lost, Four Weddings and a Funeral, The Laughing Cavalier.*
- for names of newspapers, magazines, and journals: *The Daily Express, Reader's Digest, Cosmopolitan.*
- for names of ships and vehicles: *Ark Royal, Concorde.*
- to denote foreign words and phrases that are not yet regarded as English: *echt, film noir, joie de vivre, magnum opus.* This practice is becoming less common, and many dictionaries (including this one) print them in ordinary roman type.
- to show emphasis: 'Oh, come on, it can't be *that* bad.'

9. Pronunciation

English, like all languages, is spoken in different accents depending on region and to a certain extent on social class. When English is taught in schools and to foreigners, there needs to be a standard for pronunciation, and this is usually based on the so-called 'Received Pronunciation', the accent used by educated people in south-east England. This is not to say that the speech of London is superior to the speech of Birmingham and Glasgow, just that it has become institutionalised as the practical basis for giving information about the language. The standard is not static, however, but subject to gradual change.

The way we pronounce English words today often differs considerably from the way they were pronounced in the past. Major changes have occurred to patterns of speech over the centuries. In the 15th century, between the times of Chaucer and Shakespeare, a process called the 'Great Vowel Shift' resulted in many vowels being pronounced differently. The word *life*, for example, had been pronounced as we now pronounce *leaf*, and words such as *fame* and *name* had been pronounced more like *farmer*. The number of long vowel sounds (such as the sound in *deed* as distinct from *dead*) was reduced from seven to the five which we use today (roughly the sounds as in *bean, barn, born, boon,* and *burn*). All this, and other changes in the language, explain why it is much more difficult to understand someone reading Chaucer than to hear a play by Shakespeare.

Other changes in the way we pronounce words have occurred much more recently. Within the last hundred years, the words listed below have all changed from the first pronunciation given to the second:

word	old pronunciation	current pronunciation	type of change
acoustic	əkowstik	əkoostik	change in second syllable
armada	aamaydə	aamaadə	change in second syllable
demonstrate	dəmonstrayt	demmənstrayt	change of stress
hygiene	hīji-een	hījeen	change from three syllables to two
protein	prōtee-in	prōteen	change from three syllables to two
syndrome	sindrəmi	sindrōm	change from three syllables to two
vagary	vəgairi	vaygəri	change of stress

Some older pronunciations that have been superseded in British English have survived in American English, for example *leisure* (British **lezh**ə, American **leezh**ə) and *laboratory* (which has second-syllable stress in British English and first-syllable stress in American English).

Much more recently, there has been a change of pronunciation in words ending in *-eity*, such as *deity* and *spontaneity*. These are tending to be pronounced as **-ay**-iti rather than the more traditional **-ee**-iti. You may find that some people dislike this change.

Stress patterns

Most of the problems of pronunciation in modern English are to do with stress, especially in longer words. In words of more than three syllables the stress is usually placed in the middle of the word, as in *archaeology*, *contemporary*, and *personality*. This is generally true of words that are extensions or derivatives of words with an earlier stress (compare **photograph** and **photography**, **explore** and *exploration*). Exceptions include **matrimony**, **consequently**, **presidency** (and other nouns ending in *-ency*), and **lamentable**, which are all stressed on the first syllable.

With a handful of words the position of the stress has become unstable. Traditionally they have been stressed on the first syllable, but you will hear them more and more with a stress on a later syllable, usually the second. In other cases the stress has moved from a second to a later syllable (e.g. *centrifugal*). These words are:

traditional	alternative	traditional	alternative
applicable	ap**plic**able	for**mid**able	formi**dab**le
cen**trif**ugal	centri**fug**al	**har**assment	ha**rass**ment
controversy	con**trov**ersy	**hos**pitable	hos**pit**able
despicable	des**pic**able	**kil**ometre	ki**lom**etre
exquisite	ex**quis**ite	mu**nic**ipal	mu**ni**cipal

To these we can add adverbs ending in *-arily*, in which the stress is moving to the end of the word under the influence of American practice:

traditional	alternative	traditional	alternative
primarily	prim**ar**ily	**temp**orarily	tempor**ar**ily
necessarily	necess**ar**ily	**vol**untarily	volunt**ar**ily

The stress is also moving to the end in some shorter words:

traditional	alternative	traditional	alternative
decade	dec**ade**	**har**ass	ha**rass**

Oddly enough there is another group of words in which the stress is tending to move in the other direction, i.e. towards the beginning of the word:

traditional	alternative	traditional	alternative
dis**pute**	**dis**pute	re**search**	**res**earch
con**tribute**	**con**tribute	ro**mance**	**rom**ance
dis**tribute**	**dis**tribute		

In some cases, notably *dispute* and *research*, this trend may be influenced by practice in other words that are used in the same form as both nouns and verbs (such as *record*, which is pronounced **rec**ord as a noun and re**cord** as a verb; also *conflict, insult, protest,* and others).

Controversial pronunciations

There are a number of words, not belonging to a particular type, with alternative pronunciations that are controversial:

word	traditional	alternative
dissect	di**sekt**	d**ī**sekt
finance	fi**nanss**	**fī**nans
forehead	**forr**id	**for**hed
privacy	**privv**əsi	**prī**vəsi
project	**proj**ekt	**prō**jekt
zoology	zō-**oll**əji	zōō-**oll**əji

And others that you should be careful not to mispronounce:

word	comment
asphalt	not ash-
deteriorate	pronounce all five syllables
government	pronounce the first n
mischievous	not -ievious
ophthalmic	of- not op-
prerogative	pronounce the first r
pronunciation	pronun- not pronoun-
secretary	pronounce the first r
twelfth	pronounce the f

Intrusive r

When a word ends in a silent (i.e. unpronounced) r and is followed by a vowel, the r is then pronounced, as in *hearing* and *far away*. But it is incorrect to make an r sound when there is no r at the end of the word, as in *draw-r-ing* for *drawing* and *law-r-and-order* for *law and order*. In the spoken sentence *Emma is near at hand*, an r sound is intrusive and wrong between *Emma* and *is* (where there is no r) but is justified between *near* and *at* (where there is an r).

Pronouncing middle t

The way the *t* sound is pronounced in words such as *butter* and *Saturday* is also changing, and this causes unease among those who prefer traditional pronunciations. The alternatives to a full sounding of the *t* are:

- a softening to a sound more like *d* (as in American English)
- a sounding at the back of the throat (a 'glottal stop', as in *buh-er* and *sa-er-day*, often associated with the East London accent)

Neither of these is fully accepted in Britain, and the second is especially controversial, because rightly or wrongly many people regard it as an uneducated form of speech.

10. Abbreviations

There are many kinds of abbreviations in English, and they all serve the same general purpose: to express a word or name in a shorter form, either for convenience or to give it a special meaning or status. The main types of abbreviation you will encounter and want to use are:

- initialisms (e.g. *BBC, MP, UN*)
- acronyms (e.g. *Aids, radar*)
- shortenings (e.g. *bike, pub, rhino,* and *Tues., Prof.*)
- contractions (e.g. *Dr, St*)

Initialisms

Initialisms (e.g. *a.m., BBC, MP, UN, VDU*) are abbreviations based on the initial letters (or sometimes other letters) of the words they stand for. They are usually pronounced as separate letters. Many are names of institutions and organisations, and are generally used in place of the full form of the name (e.g. *British Broadcasting Corporation, United Nations*). Abbreviations of compass points (e.g. *NNW* = north–north–west) are also initialisms. Others are names of everyday things whose full forms are too ungainly for general use (such as *VDU* = visual display unit) or technical terms for which the full forms are not normally used (such as *DNA* = deoxyribonucleic acid); initialisms of this kind are sometimes classified as nouns rather than as abbreviations.

The practice of marking this type of abbreviation with full stops (as in *B.B.C., M.P., N.N.W.*) has largely disappeared, although you will still find it in some older printing. The style recommended here is to omit full stops when all the initials are capitals and in other cases that are familiar or established, for example names of academic degrees (*DPhil, MSc*) and names of government departments (*DoE* = Department of the Environment).

When this type of abbreviation needs a plural form, you add an –s without an apostrophe (e.g. *MPs* rather than *MP's*). Possessives are formed in the usual way (e.g. *MP's* singular, *MPs'* plural):

> The MPs met in the conference room the same afternoon.
> Our MP's majority was cut by half. (one MP)
> This is the MPs' meeting room. (more than one MP)

Acronyms

Acronyms (e.g. *Aids, quango, radar, Unesco*) are initialisms that have gone one stage further and become words in their own right. They tend to be written with small letters, they can form plurals like ordinary words (when the meaning allows this), and they are pronounced as syllables rather than as the sequence of letters from which they are made. In many cases the full forms on which they are based are not used at all, except in technical explanations of the terms. For example, *laser* is based on the term *light amplification by stimulated emission of radiation*, which never occurs in its own right in ordinary language.

Some acronyms, especially the names of organisations, start off as ordinary abbreviations (often with full stops) and develop into acronyms. Others are deliberately contrived to become pronounceable words that relate to the activity of the institution (e.g. *ASH* = Action on Smoking and Health). Some have humorous connotations, for example *Nimby* (= not in my back yard, for a person who objects to the siting of a new development near where they live) and *WYSIWYG* (= what you see is what you get).

Some abbreviations are treated as both initialisms and acronyms (e.g. *VAT* = value added tax, which can be pronounced as its three letters or as a single word 'vat').

Shortenings

Shortenings are words that are cut off either at the end or at the beginning (or both). There are two kinds: those that form words in their own right (sometimes called 'clippings', such as *flu* and *vet*) and those that have the status of abbreviations (such as *Tues.* and *Prof.*).

Word shortenings

In the 18th century, major literary figures such as Joseph Addison and Alexander Pope regarded shortenings of words as bad style, but they are now a common feature of English and few people object to them. In some cases (e.g. *bus, cello, fridge, gym, vet,* and *zoo*) they have become the normal word to use, while the full forms on which they are based (*omnibus, violoncello, refrigerator, gymnasium, veterinary surgeon,* and *zoological gardens*) are generally reserved for formal contexts, such as names and titles.

Some shortenings have ousted the original words completely; we always refer now to a *cab* or a *taxi* and never to a *cabriolet* or *taximeter cab*. Other shortenings have special meanings or connotations not shared by the full form (e.g. *prep* refers to school work done at home, *quad* refers to a quadrangle in a college, and *spec* is used in the idiom *on spec*). On the other hand, some shortenings (such as *ad, info, ref,* and *telly*) still seem casual and should only be used in informal contexts.

The marking of shortened forms with apostrophes (as in *'cello* and *'flu*) has largely disappeared. It was never good practice, since *flu* results from removal of letters in two places and not one. But you will occasionally come across it in older printing. The nautical word *fo'c's'le* (= forecastle) is an exception, because it looks odd without apostrophes; but *bo'sun* (= boatswain) tends now to be written as *bosun*.

Abbreviation shortenings

The other kind of shortening consists of forms that serve as abbreviations rather than as words. Examples are days of the week (*Weds.* = Wednesday) and months of the year (*Sept.* = September), single-letter abbreviations such as *p.* (= page) and *l.* (= line) followed by a number reference, and technical abbreviations such as *lat.* (= latitude). These are normally spelled with a full stop. Some single-letter abbreviations double the letter to form a plural, e.g. *pp.* (= pages). Initials in names can be written with or without full stops (*M. Smith* or *M Smith*), but in handwriting a full stop is more usual as this is clearer.

Contractions

Contractions are a type of shortening in which letters from the middle of the word are omitted. This is common in some titles put before names (*Dr* = doctor, *Mr* = Mister, *St* = saint). The abbreviation *no.* (= number) is a contraction of the Latin word *numero* (a form of the word *numerus*). These contractions are simply conventions and do not imply any particular level of formality or informality. Where the last letter of the contraction is the same as that of the longer form, it is now usual not to mark the contraction with a full stop, except to avoid confusion with other words (as with *no.*).

Another kind of contraction is the type *don't* (= do not), *we've* (= we have), *shouldn't* (= should not), and so on, in which two words are merged together with an apostrophe marking the missing letters. This type of contraction reflects the practice of ordinary conversation and is normal in everyday writing, such as a note or a personal letter, or in recording conversation. In more formal writing, such as a business letter or a letter applying for a job, you should avoid these contractions as they tend to imply a familiarity with the person reading the letter that is not always suitable:

> ? I'll be available for an interview at any time if you're able to consider me.

> ☑ I shall be available for interview at any time if you are able to consider me.

Longer contractions, such as *could've* (= could have) and double contractions such as *mightn't've* (= might not have) occur from time to time in print but it is best to avoid them.

Units and symbols

Abbreviations for weights and measures, and abbreviations used in science, are usually written without full stops, e.g. *ft* (= foot or feet), *cm* (= centimetre or centimetres), *lb* (= pound or pounds weight), *kg* (= kilogram or kilograms), *MHz* (= megahertz), *mph* (= miles per hour). But some non-metric units are written with a full stop when leaving it out would be awkward or confusing, e.g. *in.* (= inch or inches), *mi.* (= mile or miles).

Plural forms are usually the same as the singular, e.g. *1 cm* and *50 cm*, but *yd* (= yard) tends to have a plural form *yds* (= yards).

Chemical symbols, such as *As* (= arsenic) and *Sn* (= tin) are always written without a full stop.

---

11. What words mean

Changes of meaning

New meanings

Words change their meanings even in relatively short periods of time. Some words change so drastically that they come to mean virtually the opposite of their original meaning, for example *nice*. You can still talk about a *nice distinction* (meaning 'a fine or subtle one') as well as a *nice day*, a *nice dinner*, a *nice rest*, and all sorts of things that are pleasant or enjoyable. And you may be surprised to know that the earliest meaning of *nice*, no longer used, was 'foolish' or 'stupid'.

Words develop whole new areas of meaning. For example, *check* has three core meanings: the meaning in chess, 'to threaten your opponent's king' (which is one of the earliest meanings of the word), the meaning 'to restrain' (**All these distractions did not check their progress too much**) and the meaning 'to verify' which is now the most common (**Her father went to check that the door was locked**). The verb *start* has two core meanings: 'to jump in surprise' (**The old woman started at the noise**) and 'to begin' (**We will start the work next week**).

Exchanges of meaning

Some words even change back to earlier meanings: a famous and troublesome example is provided by the pair *disinterested* and *uninterested*, which for several centuries have swapped two meanings based on different meanings of the word *interest*: 'not have any interest', i.e. 'not curious or wishing to know more', and 'not having an interest', i.e. 'not being involved' or 'impartial'.

In current usage *uninterested* has the first of these meanings:

> Paul showed her his work but she seemed uninterested.

and *disinterested* has the second meaning:

> A solicitor's ability to give disinterested advice is a fundamental element of his or her relationship with you, the client.

Most people now consider it wrong to use *disinterested* to mean 'not interested':

> ☒ He'd been so disinterested in her progress during six years of primary school that he'd only ever visited the school once.

Words earning their keep

When a word is no longer needed or useful it will either disappear or develop a new and more useful meaning. The verb *decimate* is a case in point: it is no longer needed in its original meaning 'to kill every tenth person' (usually as a military punishment) and has developed a new meaning, 'to kill in large numbers':

> ? Henry decided to lead what remained of his army, decimated by illness contracted at the siege, to Calais.

It has even produced a figurative meaning in which no physical killing or destruction takes place at all:

> ? Some matches were cancelled and attendances at those that went ahead were decimated.

Weakened meanings

There is a group of adjectives, such as *dreadful* and *terrific*, with basic meanings that are rooted in very strong feelings and emotions (in these cases, *dread* and *terror*). Some are used to describe something good or enjoyable and others to describe something bad or unpleasant:

- (bad) *awful, diabolical, dreadful, frightful, terrible*
- (good) *fabulous, fantastic, incredible, marvellous, terrific, tremendous*

Nowadays, a *fantastic film* is more likely to mean 'a very good or enjoyable film' than 'a film based on fantasy' (which is the original meaning of *fantastic*), and an *awful experience* is more likely to mean 'a very unpleasant experience' than 'an experience that gives you a feeling of awe or wonder' (which is the original meaning of *awful*). Words like these lose their power with use, and *awful* has gone a stage further in expressions such as *an awful lot* or *an awful shame*:

> ? The introduction of council tax is going to hurt an awful lot of people and there is no point in pretending otherwise.

The corresponding adverbs (such as *awfully*, *dreadfully*, and *incredibly*) have weakened in meaning to little more than 'extremely' or 'very':

> ? Once they were out of the building and had time to recover, they realised they had been incredibly lucky.

The result of this weakening of meaning is that such words no longer make much impact. They are all right in everyday conversation, and it would be difficult to avoid them. But if you want to sound convincing and make a real impression, you should use other words, such as *excellent, remarkable, spectacular, outstanding, exceptional, extraordinary, momentous*, or *phenomenal*.

If you need a strengthening adverb, you will often find that a simpler word such as *extremely, exceedingly, exceptionally*, or sometimes, as with feelings, *intensely* or *acutely*, will be more effective:

> ☑ Once they were out of the building and had time to recover, they realised they had been extremely lucky.

Another result of the meaning change is that words like *fabulous* and *fantastic* make no impact when you want to use them in their traditional meanings:

> ? She hung on his every word, looking terrified as Jack's fantastic story unfolded.

Here, the writer means the story sounded like fantasy, and was not just wonderful or exciting, which is what many readers will understand because of the way *fantastic* is so often used.

If there is any doubt about your real meaning being misunderstood, it is better to use other words that do not involve this kind of uncertainty, such as *bizarre, fanciful*, or *imaginative*; even a simpler word like *strange* can be much more effective:

> ☑ She hung on his every word, looking terrified as Jack's strange story unfolded.

Special meanings

Some words with special or semi-technical meanings, such as *dilemma* and *alibi*, tend to develop more general meanings that not everyone accepts or likes. Strictly speaking, a *dilemma* is a difficult choice or predicament involving two possibilities:

> ☑ The authority faces the familiar dilemma of cutting public services or increasing local taxes.

Avoid the word if you simply mean 'problem' or 'difficulty':

> ☒ The dilemma arose because the doctor coming from outside the area could not get there until 6.30, and the crematorium mortuary closed at 4.30.

An *alibi* is a legal term for evidence of where an accused person was at the time of a crime:

> ☑ Joseph had done nothing about contacting his old friend until he needed an alibi for the night of the murder.

Guide to good English

Again, avoid the word if you simply mean 'excuse' or 'pretext':

- ☒ Other politically imposed demands, such as the requirement to keep prices down, provide management with a plausible alibi for failing to meet their targets.

The table below shows some other words that have controversial meanings and need care in use.

word	main meaning	controversial meaning
aggravate	to make worse	to annoy
alibi	evidence that a person was elsewhere	an excuse or pretext
anticipate	to forestall or prevent	to expect
crescendo	an increasing noise or excitement	a climax
decimate	to kill one in ten of	to kill or destroy a large proportion of
dilemma	a difficult choice between two or more alternatives	a problem
feasible	able to be done	likely or probable
fulsome	excessive, cloying (praise)	extravagant (praise)
ironic	showing irony	strange, paradoxical
majority	the larger or largest number (the majority of people)	the largest part (the majority of the time)
obscene	indecent, tending to deprave	offensive or outrageous (obscene salary increases)
pristine	in its original condition	completely clean, spotless
transpire	to come to be known, to emerge	to happen

Confusable meanings

The table opposite shows many more words that are commonly confused, with a summary of their main meanings.

Pairs of words that are close in both form and meaning are the most likely to be confused. For example, *fortuitous* means 'happening by chance' and *fortunate* means 'happening by good chance'. *Regrettable* means 'to be regretted' and *regretful* means 'having regrets'; they are often confused especially in their adverb forms *regrettably* and *regretfully*. *Prevaricate* means 'to be evasive' and *procrastinate* means 'to put off action', and the two meanings overlap in a way that makes it possible to use either of them in many contexts although their precise meanings are different.

Tautology

Tautology is the repetition of the same idea or meaning in a phrase or sentence, as in *a free gift* (all gifts are free), *a new innovation*, and *to return again*. Some tautologies are contained within a small group of words such as a noun phrase (e.g. *future prospects*, *past history*, *no other alternative*, *the general consensus*). This kind of tautology is common, especially in the rapid flow of speech, and some have become idiomatic (such as *free gift* and *past history*).

Others occur in the way sentences are put together:

- ☒ The activities of the club are not limited only to golf.
- ☒ There is no need for undue haste.

The words *only* and *undue* can be dropped from their sentence

without any loss of sense because their meanings are contained in other words. This kind of tautology is not good style and you should avoid it in ordinary language, especially in writing.

Euphemism

A euphemism is a milder or vaguer word or phrase used in place of one that might seem too harsh or embarrassing in a particular context. The commonest subjects for euphemism are bodily functions (*to relieve yourself*), sexual activity (*to make love*), death (*to pass away*), economics (*downsizing*), and violence (*to do away with*).

We all need to resort to this kind of language in order to respect people's sensitivities, and our own. But there are two kinds of euphemisms that are questionable:

- euphemisms that blur the meaning or cause confusion (e.g. *cloakroom* for *lavatory*).
- euphemisms that attempt to show unpleasant activities in a more positive light (e.g. *ethnic cleansing* for the wholesale killing of peoples).

Some euphemisms have become official clichés, e.g. *helping the police with their inquiries* (= under interrogation and imminent arrest), or are only suitable as jokes, e.g. *tired and emotional* (= drunk).

Synonyms and antonyms

Synonyms are words that are identical or close in meaning, such as the pair *close* and *shut*, or the trio *begin*, *start*, and *commence*. English is rich in synonyms, often because words entered it from other languages (especially Old Norse during the Viking raids of the 9th and 10th centuries and French after the Norman Conquest in 1066), and failed to drive out those already in use. For example, *close* is a Middle English (13th-century) word derived from Old French, and joined the existing Old English word *shut*. Because French was the language of government in England after the Norman Conquest, some of the words taken from French are more formal than their Old English counterparts, for example, *commence* instead of *begin*, or *purchase* instead of *buy*.

Other pairs of words have their own special areas of use; for example, *kill* is a general word whereas *slay* is literary or rhetorical, and *little* implies an affection or intimacy not present in the more neutral word *small* (compare *a little child* and *a small child*). *Baby* is a general word for a newborn child, *infant* has a special meaning, and *neonate* is used chiefly in medical contexts.

Many words are loosely described as synonyms although their meanings are close rather than identical, and they are not always used in identical ways (e.g. *entreat* and *implore*, *leave* and *depart*). The words *danger* and *risk* have close meanings, and can be substituted for each other in some sentences:

- ☑ There was a danger of the roof collapsing.
- ☑ There was a risk of the roof collapsing.

word 1	meaning	word 2	meaning
adherence	(to belief etc.)	adhesion	sticking
admission	(general meanings)	admittance	right to be admitted
adverse	unfavourable	averse	opposed
affect	cause a change in	effect	bring about
alternate	one after another	alternative	available instead
ambiguous	(statements etc.)	ambivalent	(feelings etc.)
amend	change	emend	alter (a text etc.)
amoral	having no moral sense	immoral	not conforming to moral standards
appraise	assess the quality of	apprise	inform
avoid	keep away from	evade	avoid by guile
biannual	twice a year	biennial	every two years
censor	act as censor of	censure	criticise harshly
climactic	forming a climax	climatic	relating to climate
coherent	logical and clear	cohesive	sticking
complacent	self-satisfied	complaisant	too willing to please
compose	constitute	comprise	consist of
continual	happening constantly or repeatedly	continuous	going on without a break
credible	believable	credulous	too ready to believe
decided	unquestionable	decisive	conclusive
definite	clear and distinct	definitive	decisive, authoritative
defuse	remove the fuse from, reduce tension in	diffuse	spread out, not clear or concise
deprecate	disapprove of	depreciate	lower in value
discomfit	disconcert	discomfort	make uneasy
disinterested	impartial	uninterested	not interested
enormity	extreme seriousness, grave crime	enormousness	great size or scale
especially	in particular, above all	specially	for a special purpose
exceptionable	open to objection	exceptional	unusually good
flaunt	display ostentatiously	flout	disregard (rules etc.)
fortuitous	happening by chance	fortunate	happening by good chance, lucky
flounder	(of a person) struggle or be in confusion	founder	(of an undertaking) fail or come to nothing
gourmand	glutton	gourmet	food connoisseur
illegal	against the law	illicit	not allowed
imply	suggest strongly	infer	deduce or conclude
impracticable	not able to be done	impractical	not practical
incredible	not believable	incredulous	unwilling to believe
ingenious	well thought out	ingenuous	innocent, honest
intense	extreme in force or degree	intensive	thorough or concentrated
interment	burial	internment	being interned
loose	not fixed; unfasten or relax	lose	be deprived of or no longer have
luxuriant	lush	luxurious	comfortable and rich
masterful	powerful, domineering	masterly	highly skilful
militate	have force (against)	mitigate	make less severe
observance	keeping a law or custom etc.	observation	perception, remark
occupant	person in a vehicle etc.	occupier	person living in a property
official	having authorised status etc.	officious	aggressive in asserting authority
perquisite	special right or privilege	prerequisite	(something) needed in advance
perspicacious	having a ready understanding, perceptive	perspicuous	clearly expressed
pitiable	deserving pity	pitiful	causing pity, contemptible
practicable	able to be done	practical	effective or realistic, (of a person) skilled at manual tasks
precipitate	headlong	precipitous	abruptly steep
prescribe	recommend with authority, issue a prescription	proscribe	forbid or condemn
prevaricate	act evasively	procrastinate	defer action
purposely	intentionally	purposefully	resolutely
refute	prove to be false	repudiate	reject or disown
regrettable	causing regret, undesirable	regretful	feeling regret
sensual	gratifying the body sexually	sensuous	gratifying the senses as distinct from the intellect
sociable	friendly and willing to mix with people	social	relating to society
titillate	excite pleasantly	titivate	adorn or smarten
tortuous	twisting, devious	torturous	causing torture, tormenting
triumphal	done or made to celebrate a victory	triumphant	victorious, jubilant after a victory
turbid	(of a liquid) cloudy; confused	turgid	swollen or congested, tediously pompous
unsociable	not willing to mix with people	unsocial	socially inconvenient
venal	open to bribery, corrupt	venial	(of a sin) minor

But there are cases where you cannot use one for the other:

- ☑ Julia was no longer in danger and went back into the house.
- ☒ Julia was no longer in risk and went back into the house.
- ☐ Julia was no longer at risk and went back into the house.

- ☑ Your house is at risk if you do not keep up payments on your mortgage.
- ☒ Your house is at danger if you do not keep up payments on your mortgage.
- ☐ Your house is in danger if you do not keep up payments on your mortgage.

The question marks are there in the last of each set because *in danger* usually implies a physical threat and does not mean quite the same as *at risk*, which usually implies a non-physical threat such as legal action.

Other synonyms are more restricted in use than the words they might replace. For example, *enquire* and *request* are considered to be synonyms of *ask*, but their effect is more formal and they are not always interchangeable even for the same general meaning:

- ☑ Kate went to ask what happened next.
- ☑ Kate went to enquire what happened next.

- ☑ I'll go and ask them to stop.
- ☑ I'll go and request them to stop.

- ☑ The headteacher asked the mayor if he would give the prizes.
- ☒ The headteacher requested the mayor if he would give the prizes.
- ☐ The headteacher requested the mayor to give the prizes.

The second of the last three sentences is ungrammatical, and the third, with its grammar corrected, does not convey the meaning of the original wording. It is important to take note of any labels in the dictionary entries (such as *formal, informal,* and *archaic*) that tell you about the words and how suitable they are in a particular piece of speaking or writing.

Some words have synonyms that are really euphemisms, or ways of saying something unpleasant in a more pleasant way (see above), such as *pass away* or *perish* for *die*. You need to be careful when you use synonyms of this type as the effect can sometimes be artificial and coy.

Synonyms are most useful as more exact or descriptive alternatives for very generalised words. The following sentences all contain the adjective *nice*, which is one of the most overworked words in English:

> He wished her a nice time in Paris.
> We are hoping tomorrow will be a nice day.
> Frank always seems such a nice man.

In ordinary conversation *nice* will often be quite adequate in these sentences, but in more continuous speaking and writing it is useful to find alternatives to avoid repeating the same word too often. Anyone hearing or reading the word *nice* over and over again will become tired of it. Instead of *nice* in the three sentences you can say:

> He wished her an enjoyable (or agreeable or pleasant) time in Paris.
> We are hoping tomorrow will be a fine (or sunny or warm or pleasant) day.
> Frank always seems such a likeable (or kind or generous or pleasant) man.

Notice that *pleasant* is possible in all three sentences. It is often an improvement on *nice* but because it too is so versatile it is liable to be overused just as *nice* is.

There are some idiomatic uses in which nice cannot be replaced on a word-for-word basis:

> The house looked nice and tidy again.
> Go and have a nice little sleep.

Other synonyms are not really equivalents at all but are special kinds of a more general word. There is no synonym for the word *bed* (in its furniture meaning): words like *berth, bunk, divan,* and *futon* are not alternatives for the word *bed* but types of bed, and you can only use them when you mean that particular type (and even then you will be changing the emphasis). There is no synonym for *sing*: words like *chant, croon,* and *warble* mean particular kinds of singing but not singing in general.

Antonyms are words that are opposite in meaning, such as *allow* and *forbid, alive* and *dead*. Compared with synonyms, there are far fewer antonyms in language, because not all words allow opposite meaning (even *give* and *take* are only approximately opposite, and in some contexts are not opposite at all). Obviously concrete nouns such as *bed* and *floor* cannot have opposites, nor can classifying words such as *circular* and *German*.

12. Idioms

An idiom is a group of words with a meaning that cannot be worked out from the individual words, such as *in a nutshell* and *go to the dogs*. Some idioms (like the two just mentioned) are based on a distinct image, while others are made up of words that would normally make no sense together, such as *hard put to it, up to date,* and *go in for*. The last of these, consisting of a verb and an adverb or preposition or both, is known as a phrasal verb.

Questions arise about the use of idioms in two principal areas: when an idiom becomes a cliché, and how idiom affects grammar.

Idioms and clichés

Clichés are phrases that have become used so often that they convey no real conviction or in some cases no meaning at all, and they can usually be replaced by a simpler expression. Examples of clichés are *at the end of the day, leave no stone unturned,* and *not to put too fine a point on it*. The rapid growth of broadcasting, and of such exchanges as political interviews and panel discussions, has tended to highlight the use of clichés as a signal of evasion or insincerity, perceived or real. You should try to avoid them in ordinary English if only because of these associations.

Single words, such as *actually* and *definitely* used merely as fillers, are sometimes regarded as clichés, but they serve to show emphasis and maintain continuity in discourse:

> Actually, I think you are wrong.

Here, the opening adverb is a kind of call to attention, and serves a practical purpose even if it does not add anything to the literal meaning.

Idioms and grammar

Idioms do not always follow the normal rules of grammar. An expression can be idiomatic (that is, sound natural to a native speaker) or grammatical—or both or neither. It was not me, How's tricks?, and There is heaps of time are idiomatic but ungrammatical or apparently so. The answer was staring me in the eyes and The wind blew coldly are grammatical but unidiomatic. She was made leader and They all but died are both grammatical and idiomatic, and Don't you go without you tell me is neither.

Idioms form an important part of everyday language. They can appear to violate the strict rules of grammar, and this is a legitimate use of language; impeccably correct grammar does not by itself make good English.

13. Figures of speech

A figure of speech is a special way of using language to make it more interesting or colourful. Most figures of speech involve substituting one word or phrase for another, when the one you replace is not forceful enough or you need a stronger image than ordinary language can provide:

> We look across the room at James, screened from us by people, an ebb and flow of bodies through which we glimpse James, sitting with his book.

The writer could have said, more simply, that James was *partly hidden from us by people moving across the room*. But the language of water and the tides enriches the meaning and gives us a powerful image of movement from the real world that conveys the meaning much more vividly.

In fact we are doing this all the time in everyday language. When we talk about the *mouth* of a river, a *blanket* of fog, *music* to our ears, or plans bearing *fruit*, we are not referring to a mouth in its literal meaning, nor to an actual blanket, nor to real music or edible fruit. These so-called 'figurative' meanings are figures of speech as much as the *ebb and flow of bodies* in the literary example above. They allow the basic stock of words to take on new layers of meaning that effectively double their usefulness, as well as enriching the language by producing interesting or attractive mental images.

Idioms too are often miniature figures of speech of the type called metaphor, e.g. *get the green light, have one foot in the grave, be over the moon, take the rough with the smooth.*

Comparisons: similes and metaphors

The most common figures of speech in ordinary language are comparisons called similes and metaphors. A simile (pronounced **simm**ili, from the Latin word *similis* meaning 'like') is a comparison that is spoken or spelled out explicitly, usually with the words *as* or *like*. Here are some examples:

> Mother Francis had fought like a tiger for the small bundle she had rescued from the cottage.
> The local papers printed pictures of the pair grinning like village idiots.

Everyday English is full of idioms that are similes established by usage (although in some the association is not obvious): *as bold as brass, fit as a fiddle, sell like hot cakes.*

A metaphor (pronounced **mett**əfor, from the Greek word *metaphora* meaning 'transfer' or 'substitution') goes a stage further and says that the person or thing actually *is* what they are being compared to, so that we have:

> He was a giant among sportsmen.

Sometimes there is a thin line dividing simile and metaphor:

> (*simile*) She laughed and said he was behaving like a baby.
> (*metaphor*) She laughed and said what a baby he was.
> (*simile*) The music is like a vast cathedral of sound.
> (*metaphor*) The music is a vast cathedral of sound.

Many proverbs are types of extended metaphor: *a stitch in time saves nine, every cloud has a silver lining, look before you leap.*

Mixed metaphor

Because a metaphor is based on a very specific image, you need to be careful when you continue with what you are saying, to avoid introducing another metaphor that clashes with the first. The effect of this can often be ridiculous or funny. This is not ungrammatical but it can be distracting and is poor style:

> He has been made a sacrificial lamb for taking the lid off a can of worms.

It is also a good idea to avoid a mixture of metaphors and idioms that are incongruous or strange-sounding together:

> It will take a year to iron out all the bugs.
> The grass roots in the Party are pretty cheesed off.

It is easy to fall into this trap in ordinary conversation, but you should take care in writing, when there is more time to think about what you are saying.

Not saying what you mean: irony

Irony (pronounced **ī**rəni, from the Greek word *eironeia* meaning 'pretended ignorance') means several things. In everyday language it refers to the practice of saying something by using words that are the opposite of what you really mean. This creates a special effect and is often more striking than saying what you mean directly. When you look out of the window at the pouring rain and exclaim 'What a lovely day!', you are using a form of irony. To make sure you are not misunderstood, you would normally adopt a special tone of voice that differs from the one you would use in a literal meaning.

Understatement

Understatement is substituting a weak term or description for a stronger one. It is common in ordinary speech and writing:

> 'The head wound is just a scratch,' she said after a moment.

We often use understatement for social rather than stylistic reasons, for example to spare the hearer's feelings or because the plain truth might be unwelcome or alarming. Here, language comes to our aid, allowing us to say something other than what we really mean and still convey what is essentially valid.

There is a special form of understatement, called litotes (pronounced līᴛōᴇᴇz, from a Greek word *litos* meaning 'plain' or 'meagre'), in which a positive statement is replaced by a negative form of its opposite:

> I shan't be sorry to get home at last.

> It is not uncommon for patients to recover completely in a matter of days.

> Such high profits were no mean achievement in the present economic climate.

Exaggeration

Exaggeration is the opposite of understatement: substituting a strong term or description for a weaker one. As a figure of speech it is called hyperbole (pronounced hī**per**bəli, from a Greek word meaning 'throwing beyond'). This is an exaggerated statement that is not meant to be taken literally but creates an extreme effect:

> He had told her a thousand times and still she forgot it.

> Simon was tired and dispirited. He had been waiting for ages.

Some everyday idioms are based on exaggeration and are therefore a kind of ready-made hyperbole: *floods of tears, loads of money, having the time of your life, light years away*.

Contrasts

Oxymoron (pronounced oksi**mōr**on, derived from Greek words for 'sharp' and 'dull') is a figure of speech in which you use words of opposite meaning for special effect, e.g. *bitter-sweet, being cruel to be kind, a cheerful pessimist*. This type does not occur often and tends to be limited to a few phrases.

14. Varieties of English

Standard English

Standard English is the form of English most widely accepted and understood in an English-speaking country. It is usually based on the educated speech of a particular area (in England, the south-east), but it can be spoken in many accents. It is used in newspapers and broadcasting and is the form normally given in dictionaries and taught to learners of English.

Standard English does not just mean 'formal English'. There are levels of formality (called 'register') in Standard English as well as in other varieties. A word or use is 'non-standard' when it does not belong at any level to standard English, for example the word *ain't* and the gender-free pronoun *themself*.

Nor does Standard English mean 'British English'. Different varieties of English exist in North America, the Caribbean, Australia and New Zealand, the Indian subcontinent, south-east Asia, and southern Africa.

A variety is different from a dialect. A dialect is confined to a particular place or region, is often related to social class and ethnic origin, and varies from the standard language in having special items of vocabulary and rules of grammar.

American English

American English differs from British English in vocabulary, spelling and inflection, idiom, grammar, pronunciation, and even (in minor ways) punctuation. Some of the more significant differences are due to uses that disappeared in British English but survived in American English. Examples are the use of *gotten* as a past participle of *get*, and the use of *theater* and other spellings in *-er*, where British English has changed to spellings in *-re*. Other differences are due to developments in American English after it went its own way.

Vocabulary

There are well known differences in British and American vocabulary, such as American *shoestring*, British *shoelace* (but British English shares the idiom *on a shoestring*), and British *lorry*, American *truck*. American English is a major source of new vocabulary in British English, although some borrowings are disliked by some, such as the sentence adverb *hopefully*, and phrase-based words such as *ongoing*. Whole areas of vocabulary development, such as the political correctness movement, tend to be even more controversial. Relatively few terms have spread from British to American English, more notable examples being *central heating, miniskirt*, and *kiss of life*.

Spelling

Some spelling differences concern particular words and are not applied systematically (e.g. American English *aluminum, maneuver, pajamas*). The principal systematic differences in British English and American English spelling are:

■ use of the simple vowel *-e-* in place of *-ae-* and *-oe-*, as in ameba and estrogen. This practice has influenced British spellings in words such as encyclopedia and fetus, and is spreading further.

- use of -ense instead of -ence as a noun ending, as in defense, pretense, and license (noun).
- use of -er instead of -re as a noun ending in many words, as in center and theater (but not in acre, massacre, mediocre, and ogre).
- use of -or instead of -our as a noun ending, as in color and harbor.
- use of -l- instead of -ll- in verbal inflections, as in instal, rivaled, and traveler, and conversely use of -ll- instead of -l-, as in installment and skillful.
- reduction of final -ogue to -og, as in analog and catalog.
- preference for -ize instead of -ise in verbs that allow both, as in civilize and privatize.
- use of -z- occasionally instead of -s- in other words, such as analyze and cozy.

Grammar

There are significant differences of grammar, although these rarely affect understanding. American English favours more strongly than does British English the type Did you go? rather than Have you been?, I don't have rather than I haven't got, They just left rather than They've just left, I didn't use (or used) to rather than I used not to, and Let's not rather than Don't let's (as in Let's not stay here), although some of these American forms are becoming more common in British use.

There are differences in the way prepositions are used. For example, American English has out the window and off of the floor where standard British English has out of the window and off the floor.

Pronunciation

In pronunciation, as in spelling, there are particular differences and systematic differences. Examples of the first are schedule (sk- in American English, sh- in British English) and tomato (təmaytō in American English, təmaatō in British English). Systematic differences include the following:

- the letter r is pronounced or partly pronounced when it occurs in the middle of a word whether or not it is followed by a vowel, whereas typically it is not in British pronunciation, as in hard and rare.
- the vowel a is pronounced as in had, not as in hard in words such as after, can't, dance, and path.
- pronunciation of short o as in box is closer to ah as in barks.
- pronunciation of u as in tube is closer to oo as in boob.
- pronunciation of er in words such as clerk rhymes with murk, not with mark as in British English.
- pronunciation of the final syllables -ile (as in fertile and hostile) is -əl, not -īl as in British English.
- pronunciation of t following n and followed by an unstressed syllable (as in mental and twenty) is much less marked in American English than in British English.

15. Formal and informal language

Written and spoken English

The different contexts and levels of formality in which English is used are called registers. At a broad level English, like all languages, varies from the formal and technical to the informal and casual. Register also takes account of the various types of communication, such as conversation, informal writing, journalism and broadcasting, and formal writing including essays, speeches, and academic books. In conversation, for example, use of the personal pronouns I and you is relatively high, contractions such as I've, you're, and don't predominate over the fuller forms, and colloquial and slang words occur regularly. In more formal writing, colloquialisms are uncommon, the indefinite personal pronoun one is more likely to be used than the less formal you, upon is likely to be used as well as on, and more formal words such as ascertain and desirous are likely to occur.

Slang and informal language

The term slang is first recorded in the 1750s, shortly after the publication of Samuel Johnson's Dictionary of the English Language in 1755 (in which the disapproving term 'low word' is used instead). But the existence of words that are highly informal or are associated with a particular social group or occupation is much older, and this type of vocabulary has been commented on, usually unfavourably, for centuries.

Modern dictionaries tend to use the label 'informal' for vocabulary that would once have been termed 'slang', using 'slang' for the informal vocabulary of particular groups of people, for example military slang. In general, informal vocabulary typically includes extensions of meanings of established words and especially idioms and phrases (e.g. to do in = to kill), shortenings of words (e.g. fab from fabulous and cred from credibility), compound formations (e.g. airhead and couch potato), and blends (e.g. ginormous from gigantic and enormous), as well as special processes such as rhyming slang (e.g. butcher's = butcher's hook = look) and back slang, in which words are reversed (e.g. yob = boy).

Slang is at the extreme end of informality, has a strong element of metaphor or verbal imagery, and has the capacity to shock. In English, slang has strong group or class associations. Its origins often lie in the language of particular occupations or social groups, such as racing, the criminal world, the armed forces, and youth (e.g. ace, cool, and wicked). Informal and slang uses are especially prevalent in subjects in which direct language is regarded as improper or unsocial, such as death (to snuff it), sexual activity (to screw), and bodily functions (to pee).

Much informal vocabulary is short-lived, and relatively few words and uses pass into standard English. Exceptions include bogus, clever, flog, joke, prim, rogue, sheer (as in sheer joy), snob, and tip (meaning a gratuity), which were all classed by Samuel Johnson as 'low words'. Conversely some words that were once standard have passed into vulgar slang (e.g. *arse*, *shit*, and *tit*).

Choosing the right level of formality

Variation of formality in language is like different styles of dress. Each mode of writing and speaking calls for its own different kind of language. At one extreme there is the language of legal documents, business, and academic textbooks; at the other there is everyday conversation, with a broad range between. The language of broadcasting and journalism, in particular, has become much less formal in recent years, to such an extent as to annoy those who identify formality with high language standards.

Choice of vocabulary differs according to register. At the most formal end, a machine might be said to be *malfunctioning*; in a neutral or everyday register it will be described as *not working*, and at the informal extreme it will be said to be *bust* or *kaput*. Formal words are usual in instructions and notices: *alight* (from a bus or train), *conveyance* (for *vehicle*), *enquire* (rather than *ask*), *notify* (rather than *tell*), and *select* (rather than *choose*). In more general contexts, *purchase* is more formal than *buy*, *edifice* than *building*, *endeavour* than *try*, and *purloin* than *steal*. The language of technical writing has its own terminology; for example, *gravid*, meaning pregnant, occurs only in medicine and biology. Most of these formal words can be turned on their heads and made to look affected or silly in trivial or jocular use (Do you really live in this edifice?).

No one style of vocabulary and grammar is superior to another; it is their appropriateness to the occasion that matters.

Archaisms

Archaisms are words and phrases that no longer form a part of everyday language but are still used for special effect, normally in literature. Some are more usable in modern English than others; we can do without *peradventure* and *afore* but perhaps find a good use for *erstwhile*, *goodly*, *nay*, *perchance*, and *unbeknown*:

> In fact, unbeknown to them, Franco had played a crucial role in the failure.

The centuries-old prefix *a-* (as in *birds aflutter* and *out a-hunting*) is still used to good effect, especially to give an archaic flavour in contexts rooted in the past:

> Spectators would fall a-talking of the fashionableness of bicycling.

You are most likely to find archaisms in literature, e.g. If Mimi's cup runneth over, it runneth over with decency rather than with anything more vital (Anita Brookner, in an Old Testament allusion to Psalms 23:5), and The whole creation groaneth and travaileth in pain together (Iris Murdoch, in a New Testament allusion to Romans 8:22).

Archaic word forms also occur in titles, for example *The Compleat Girl* (by Mary McCarthy, 1963, in allusion to Isaak Walton's *The Compleat Angler*), and *Whitaker's Almanack* (which preserves an older spelling of *almanac*).

Jargon and gobbledegook

Every sphere of activity develops its own jargon to enable its participants to communicate effectively with one another; medicine, law, gastronomy, sociology, and computing are well known examples. Other domains, such as journalism, use special words and idioms that are not normally found in general use; these do not so much baffle as cause irritation to those who like their language to be straightforward: *probe* for *investigation* or *investigate*, *quiz* for *interrogate*, *package* for *deal*, and *swap* for *transplant* in the medical sense. But these too serve a purpose in allowing concise expression in a limited space, especially in headlines (Baby heart swap drama).

In some contexts, especially in law, the need for precision requires the use of special terminology because it has to stand up to constant scrutiny. Problems arise when members of these professions need to communicate with the public at large; then, jargon can easily become gobbledegook. Plain English, i.e. ordinary English that everyone can understand, requires clarity as well as accuracy and should avoid convoluted, obfuscating language typified by the use of such words as *aforementioned*, *in the event of*, *thereto*, *pursuant to*, and *incumbent on*. The following extract is from a letter addressed by a local authority to a tenant about house repairs:

> Find attached a draft programme for the anticipated commencement date on your property and we anticipate that the work will take three or four days to complete. Your next contact will be by the contractor … who will contact you individually about a week prior to the start at your house. If you anticipate any problems with access arrangements or require any further information, please do not hesitate to call.

A plainer version with the gobbledegook removed is as follows:

> I attach a programme which shows the likely starting date for work on your property. We expect the work will take three or four days to complete. You will hear next from the contractor … who will contact you about a week before work at your house begins. Please call … if you think the contractor will have any problems with access to your house, or if you need any more information.

(Examples are from M. Cutts, *The Plain English Guide*, 1995.)

---

16. Language sensitivities

Offensive language

Words and language have the power of upsetting and offending people. Sometimes this is deliberate, and the issue is then a social or political one rather than one of language. If you use any of the well-known 'four-letter' words in an abusive way, you are using the most offensive English words that have general reference. The type of words that get used in this way change from one age to another: in the past they have been words about death and money; in our own day they are words about sex and bodily functions.

There are other words that are offensive in themselves (usually informal words such as *git* and *nerd*). But there are words and uses that can cause offence unintentionally. You may either not realise that there is a danger of causing offence at all, or you may not realise how offensive a particular expression can be. Because you find a word in a dictionary does not mean it is safe to use it. Dictionaries exist to give information about all kinds of words and, like this one, they are careful to warn the reader in some way when a particular word is derogatory or offensive.

Stereotypes

Among the commonest types of offensiveness in language are stereotypes based on race, ethnic origin, religion, gender, and other characteristics. These stereotypes are very old in English (and occur in Shakespeare, for example). Usually they have more to do with popular prejudices and associations about people than with historical truth. Calling a woman a *bitch* or a *cow* is much more offensive than calling a man a *dog* or a *weasel* (uses that are now dated precisely because they have little effect). Calling a man an *old woman* is less obviously offensive but is more likely to upset people than it used to be.

Names for peoples

You should also be very careful in using slang or informal names for peoples. Some words can be fairly harmless or even affectionate (e.g. *Brit* = 'someone British', *Yank* = 'an American') and a lot depends on the tone of voice, the context in which you use the word, and how well you know the person or people who hear or read what you are saying. Others are much stronger in effect and will always cause offence (*dago* = 'a Spaniard', *Jap* = 'a Japanese', *Yid* = 'a Jew').

Nigger was always a highly offensive term for a black-skinned person, and was meant to be. Now *Negro* (and the feminine form *Negress*) are also regarded as offensive both in Britain and in America, and since the 1960s the term *black* (with a small initial letter) has replaced them. In Britain, the term *Paki* for a person from Pakistan or the Indian subcontinent generally is one of the most offensive ethnic terms in use.

Words based on disability

Another kind of use that causes great offence is that based on people's physical or mental disabilities. Calling someone *spastic* to mean 'stupid or incompetent', or using *cretin* to mean 'a stupid person', insults groups of people who suffer from the actual disabilities denoted by the first meanings of these words. So serious is the insult that the words cannot be used any more in their first meanings, because the offensive overtones have rubbed off on them. This means that we have to use alternative words, for example *person with cerebral palsy* instead of *spastic* and *person with Down's syndrome* instead of *mongol*.

Sexism and gender issues

Language is full of occasions in which gender can cause problems:

- when we need to refer to people of either sex (the 'he or she'

problem). Traditionally, masculine forms have been used, but this is no longer as acceptable as it was.

- when there is a feminine form of a word for a role or occupation, without any real need for it (mainly words ending in *-ess* and *-woman*).
- when pairs of words for men and women have different associations (for example, *bachelor* sounds romantic whereas *spinster* sounds dreary, *gentleman* is respectful whereas *lady* can sound condescending or affected, *master* always denotes authority whereas *mistress* has a meaning that implies submission).
- when neutral words that we need to apply generally are masculine in form (such as *mankind* and *man-made*).
- when we refer to men and women in different ways (for example, calling a male person a *man* and a female person a *girl*).

Some of the more specific words are falling out of use. We now talk about *cleaners* and not *charwomen*, and we would say that someone was *unmarried* rather than calling them a *bachelor* or *spinster*. Useful neutral occupational terms have come into use, including *firefighter*, *flight attendant*, and *police officer*. *Mankind* is steadily giving way to *humankind*.

There are other ways in which we can be careful about the way we use gender in language:

- we can avoid using he to mean 'he or she':
    - [?] Anyone who wants to take part should give his name to the secretary.
    - [✓] Anyone who wants to take part should give his or her name to the secretary.
    - [✓] Anyone who wants to take part should give their name to the secretary.
    - [✓] Those who want to take part should give their names to the secretary.

You will find more about this in the section on **AGREEMENT**.

- we can take care to match the tone and style of masculine and feminine references:
    - [?] 95 per cent of the audience were ladies, and 5 per cent were men.
    - [✓] 95 per cent of the audience were women, and 5 per cent were men.
- we can avoid words that are strongly masculine in form when they are meant to have a general reference:
    - [?] There's no man-made noise here, just the pounding of surf.
    - [✓] There's no human noise here, just the pounding of surf.

Occupational words

For many centuries in English terms for occupations have had masculine and feminine forms, such as *actor* and *actress*, *manager* and *manageress*, and *usher* and *usherette*. The way these words are formed, by adding a feminine suffix to a masculine word, suggests that the female forms are a kind of afterthought, and that the male form is the standard one. (This is less true of pairs such as *chairman* and *chairwoman*.) Today, people see less need to identify men and women in this way.

-ess *and* -ette

Words ending in *-ess* for feminine roles and occupations are very old in English, with early forms recorded from the 14th century or even earlier (e.g. *countess, duchess, mistress*). Those that are used as titles are not a problem in modern English, nor are *goddess, heiress, postmistress, waitress*, and some others. But you need to remember that some titles (e.g. *ambassadress* and *mayoress*) usually refer to the wife of the official rather than to a woman who holds the office herself, who would be called by the *-or* forms (*ambassador, mayor*). Others are considered acceptable in specific contexts (e.g. *manageress* when referring to a restaurant or hotel) though not generally.

The *-ess* words that now cause most offence are (on racial grounds) *Jewess* and *Negress*, and (on gender grounds) *air hostess, authoress, poetess, proprietress*, and *stewardess*. For most of these there are alternatives that you can use, either the traditional masculine forms (*author, manager, poet, proprietor*) or completely different terms (*flight attendant*). You will see many more neutral words used in job advertisements (e.g. *salesperson* and *spokesperson*), which need to avoid charges of sex discrimination for legal reasons.

Feminine words ending in *-ette* (e.g. *usherette*) and *-enne* (e.g. *comedienne*) are usually seen as the most patronising of all these forms and you should avoid them. Many of them are disappearing anyway.

It is also best to avoid expressions such as *woman* (or *lady*) *doctor*, which imply that a male is normal in this role, unless there are special reasons for specifying the gender. The same now goes, in reverse, for *male nurse*.

-man, -woman, *and* -person

You should use words ending in *-man*, such as *chairman* and *craftsman*, only when you are referring to a man. Some words in *-man* are still very common because the occupation they describe is still done mainly by men. For example, *postal worker* is the neutral term for people working in the post office but *postman* is still the usual term for the person who delivers post because that person is usually a man.

The use of *-person* as a gender-neutral suffix denoting occupations instead of *-man* began in the 1970s with *chairperson* and *spokesperson*. It has spread to other words (for example *barperson* and *salesperson*) only slowly, partly because these constructions can be awkward and cumbersome and partly because terms ending in *-woman* are often preferred (*spokeswoman*, for example).

Political correctness

All these sensitivities about language have been hugely increased by the movement called political correctness (or PC), which began in the 1980s in America. It goes a lot further than the type of uses we have been looking at so far by targeting language that causes offence in much less direct ways, in expressions such as *the black economy* and *being blind to something* (= 'unwilling to recognise it'), and to other words that might offend various groups more by the coincidence of words than a deliberate use of them.

Political correctness also tries to find alternative words that give a more positive aspect to negative or undesirable qualities, replacing *failure* with *achievement deficiency*, *disabled* with *differently abled*, and *unemployed* with *non-waged*. Disabilities and other human difficulties are expressed with the more positive-sounding word *challenged*: backward and educationally subnormal become *intellectually challenged*, short becomes *vertically challenged*, and disabled becomes *physically challenged*.

Words pick up their flavour from their meaning and use. In time all these words will go the way of the words they are replacing: *challenged* is already a common component of jokes and insults (*culinarily challenged, facially challenged*).

Without going to the extremes of PC, you should apply consideration and common sense in all uses of words, striking a balance between avoiding unnecessary offence and communicating effectively.

17. Split infinitives and other superstitions

In language, a superstition is a belief that is not based on reason or logic in grammar or usage. Many of the superstitions mentioned here date back to the 19th century, when self-appointed guardians of the language started to write new rules which were largely based on their knowledge of Latin grammar and had little to do with the ways of English. An example is the rule that you should not end a sentence with a preposition (e.g. **The chair is for sitting on**), which is true in Latin but often unrealistic in English.

Earlier generations had their own superstitions. In the 18th century, the lexicographer Samuel Johnson listed among his dislikes the 'low words' (as he called them) *bogus, coax, joke, flog, prim, rogue, snob,* and *spree*. All these are now part of general vocabulary. Henry Fowler, the famous lexicographer and the author of *A Dictionary of Modern English Usage*, published in 1926, had his list too, among them *cachet, caption, coastal,* and *malnutrition*. Again, all these are now familiar words. He also insisted that words formed on Latin plurals, such as *agenda* and *data*, should be used as plural nouns. Since then, *agenda* has developed a meaning that makes it a singular noun (e.g. **The agenda for the meeting is on the table**), and *data*, a word transformed by the computer age, is going the same way (e.g. **Our data is backed up every evening**): see the section on **AGREEMENT**.

Some other superstitions have already been mentioned:

- not beginning a sentence with *and* or *but*: see **SENTENCES**.
- not ending a sentence with a preposition: see **PARTS OF SPEECH**.
- *hopefully* and *thankfully* as sentence adverbs: see **PARTS OF SPEECH**.

Split infinitives

An infinitive is a form of the verb with *to* (such as *to love, to kill*), and a split infinitive occurs when a word or phrase comes between *to* and the verb (*to really love, to cruelly and brutally kill*). Examples of split infinitives can be found in Middle English (the form of English that arose in the 12th century after the Norman Conquest) but it went out of fashion from the 16th century to the end of the 18th. There are no split infinitives in Shakespeare. During the 19th century it came back into favour, and can be found in the work of well-known writers, for example Byron:

> To sit on rocks to muse o'er flood and fell, To slowly trace the forest's shady scene.

The idea that a split infinitive is wrong is fairly recent, and the term itself is not recorded until the end of the 19th century. Before that, no one cared much about it. There is no grammatical reason for always keeping the two parts of an infinitive together. The argument that *to* and the verb form a unit is not strong, being based on a spurious analogy with Latin, in which infinitives consist of only one word (e.g. *amare* 'to love'), and it does not agree with other verb patterns in English. For example, we regularly separate a verb from an auxiliary verb in uses such as I have never said so and We are constantly trying.

But just because we may split the infinitive does not mean that we always should. The normal position for an adverb is often before or after it, not within it:

☑ We talked about how everything was going to suddenly change.

The normal order is:

☑ We talked about how everything was suddenly going to change.

The adverb can also come after the infinitive:

☑ Your mother would like you to telephone her immediately.

However, there are cases where the adverb has to go immediately before the verb to make the meaning clear:

☑ Police are trying to strictly regulate the flow of traffic in the town centre.

Here, alternatives produce an awkward style and rhythm:

☑ Police are trying to regulate strictly the flow of traffic in the town centre.

Avoiding a split infinitive can lead to results that are just as unnatural, often stylistically poor, and in some cases ambiguous or misleading:

☑ He considers it unwise to attempt radically to alter taxes on large cars.

☑ She used secretly to admire him.

☑ It should be the Government's task quietly to advocate such a comprehensive strategy with our American allies.

In these examples the adverbs have a close association with their verbs, and separating them blurs the meaning as well as producing a poor rhythm.

In some cases, the adverb becomes attached to the wrong verb:

☒ It was in Paris that the wartime alliance began finally to break up.

☒ They are planning quietly to scrap the regulations.

In the first example, *finally* refers to the breaking up and not to the beginning. More seriously, in the second example, it is not clear whether the planning or the scrapping is being done quietly.

When an intensifying adverb such as *actually, even, ever, further, just*, or *quite* really belongs with a verb that happens to be an infinitive, it is usually better (and sometimes necessary) to place it between *to* and the verb:

☑ I want to really study, I want to be a scholar.

☑ She was wondering what it would have been like to really know him.

☑ In face of all this Patrick managed to quite like him.

☑ He'd never be able to fully comprehend what had happened.

In the first example, you could say *I really want to study*, but the meaning would be different. In the last example, some people might insist on saying ☑ He'd never be able fully to comprehend what had happened, but this is unnatural and unidiomatic. A more satisfactory alternative is:

☑ He'd never be able to comprehend fully what had happened.

There are two particular types of split infinitive that you should avoid:

- when the part that comes between is a phrase:

  ☒ You two shared a curious ability to without actually saying anything make me feel dirty.

  There is an exception to this, when words such as 'more than' come before the verb:

  ☑ Prices are likely to more than double.

  Here, the words *more than double* effectively form a single verb, and so in a sense this is not a split infinitive at all.

- when there is a negative word:

  ☒ I will try to never do it again.

  ☑ I will try never to do it again.

Different from *not* different to

The adjective *different* can be followed by three linking words: *from, to*, and *than*. Of these, the only one that everyone accepts is *from*:

> She was quite different from her brother.

> His political opinions were different from mine.

The argument runs that because we say that one thing *differs from* another, we should say that one thing is *different from* another. But English does not always work as logically as this. For example, we say *accord with* but *according to*. In actual use, as distinct from the theory, different is followed by *to* as often as it is by *from*:

> It was no different to any other day except that the shop was very busy.

It is less often followed by *than*, which is more common in American English:

> The court rules that electronic materials are very different than a copy printed in paper form.

It is tempting to use *than* when a clause follows, although it can often be rephrased:

☑ I am very different now than I was ten years ago.

☑ I am very different from what I was ten years ago.

There are occasions when *from* is inelegant and *to* or even *than* is more natural, especially when *different* is separated from the continuation it relates to:

☑ He looked no different at first to other boys Margaret had known.

☑ I found that a meadow seen against the light was an entirely different tone of green to the same meadow facing the light.

☑ A false sense of security which makes drivers behave quite differently on motorways than on ordinary roads.

None *takes a singular verb*

None is not a shortening of *no one* but a later form of an Old English pronoun. The rule, sometimes heard, that it should always be followed by a singular verb is another superstition.

In fact it may be followed by a singular or a plural verb, depending on the sense. When the main idea is of a single person or thing, a singular form is used. In other words, *none* is equivalent to *not one* (person or thing):

☑ A fear which we cannot know, which we cannot face, which none understands.

☑ She is rather difficult to describe physically, for none of her features is particularly striking.

You also use the singular form when *none* refers to something that cannot be plural:

☑ None of this was a matter of treachery.

When the main idea is of several people or things considered together, a plural form is used. Then *none* is equivalent to *not any* (people or things):

☑ None of our fundamental problems have been solved.

☑ Though she had many affairs, none were light-hearted romances.

It might help to think of *none* as behaving like *no*, which can be singular and plural (*no time, no car, no books, no friends*).

1: Countries & principal dependencies

Countries of the world

Country	Person (name in general use)	Related adjective (in general use)	Currency unit	Abbreviation (Olympics)
Afghanistan	Afghan	Afghan	afghani = 100 puls	AFG
Albania	Albanian	Albanian	lek = 100 qindarka	ALB
Algeria	Algerian	Algerian	dinar = 100 centimes	ALG
America (see United States of America)				
Andorra	Andorran	Andorran	French franc, Spanish peseta	AND
Angola	Angolan	Angolan	kwanza = 100 lwei	ANG
Antigua and Barbuda	Antiguan, Barbudan	Antiguan, Barbudan	dollar = 100 cents	ANT
Argentina	Argentinian	Argentine or Argentinian	peso = 10,000 australes	ARG
Armenia	Armenian	Armenian	dram = 100 luma	ARM
Australia	Australian	Australian	dollar = 100 cents	AUS
Austria	Austrian	Austrian	schilling = 100 groschen	AUT
Azerbaijan	Azerbaijani	Azerbaijani	manat = 100 gopik	AZE
Bahamas	Bahamian	Bahamian	dollar = 100 cents	BAH
Bahrain	Bahraini	Bahraini	dinar = 1,000 fils	BRN
Bangladesh	Bangladeshi	Bangladeshi	taka = 100 poisha	BAN
Barbados	Barbadian	Barbadian	dollar = 100 cents	BAR
Belarus	Belorussian or Byelorussian	Belorussian or Byelorussian	Belorussian rouble	BLR
Belgium	Belgian	Belgian	franc = 100 centimes	BEL
Belize	Belizian	Belizian	dollar = 100 cents	BIZ
Benin	Beninese	Beninese	African franc	BEN
Bhutan	Bhutanese	Bhutanese	ngultrum = 100 chetrum, Indian rupee	BHU
Bolivia	Bolivian	Bolivian	boliviano = 100 centavos	BOL
Bosnia-Herzegovina	Bosnian	Bosnian	dinar = 100 paras	BIH
Botswana	Tswana	Botswanan	pula = 100 thebe	BOT
Brazil	Brazilian	Brazilian	real = 100 centavos	BRA
Brunei	Bruneian	Bruneian	dollar = 100 sen	BRU
Bulgaria	Bulgarian	Bulgarian	lev = 100 stotinki	BUL
Burkina	Burkinese	Burkinese	African franc	BUR
Burma (officially called Myanmar)	Burmese	Burmese	kyat = 100 pyas	MYA
Burundi	Burundian	Burundian	franc = 100 centimes	BDI
Cambodia	Cambodian	Cambodian	riel = 100 sen	CAM
Cameroon	Cameroonian	Cameroonian	African franc	CMR
Canada	Canadian	Canadian	dollar = 100 cents	CAN
Cape Verde Islands	Cape Verdean	Cape Verdean	escudo = 100 centavos	CPV
Central African Republic			African franc	CAF
Chad	Chadian	Chadian	African franc	CHA
Chile	Chilean	Chilean	peso = 100 centavos	CHI
China	Chinese	Chinese	yuan = 10 jiao or 100 fen	CHN
Colombia	Colombian	Colombian	peso = 100 centavos	COL
Comoros	Comoran	Comoran	African franc	COM
Congo	Congolese	Congolese	African franc	CGO
Congo, Democratic Republic of (Zaire)	Congolese	Congolese	zaire = 100 makuta	ZAI
Costa Rica	Costa Rican	Costa Rican	colón = 100 centimos	CRC
Croatia	Croat or Croatian	Croat or Croatian	kuna = 100 lipa	CRO
Cuba	Cuban	Cuban	peso = 100 centavos	CUB
Cyprus	Cypriot	Cypriot	pound = 100 cents	CYP

Country	Person (name in general use)	Related adjective (in general use)	Currency unit	Abbreviation (Olympics)
Czech Republic	Czech	Czech	koruna = 100 haleru	CZE
Denmark	Dane	Danish	krone = 100 øre	DEN
Djibouti	Djiboutian	Djiboutian	franc = 100 centimes	DJI
Dominica	Dominican	Dominican	dollar = 100 cents	DMA
Dominican Republic	Dominican	Dominican	peso = 100 centavos	DOM
Ecuador	Ecuadorean	Ecuadorean	sucre = 100 centavos	ECU
Egypt	Egyptian	Egyptian	pound = 100 piastres or 1,000 milliemes	EGY
El Salvador	Salvadorean	Salvadorean	colón = 100 centavos	ESA
Equatorial Guinea	Equatorial Guinean	Equatorial Guinean	African franc	GEQ
Eritrea	Eritrean	Eritrean	Ethiopian birr	ERI
Estonia	Estonian	Estonian	kroon = 100 sents	EST
Ethiopia	Ethiopian	Ethiopian	birr = 100 cents	ETH
Fiji	Fijian	Fijian	dollar = 100 cents	FIJ
Finland	Finn	Finnish	markka = 100 penniä	FIN
France	Frenchman, Frenchwoman	French	franc = 100 centimes	FRA
Gabon	Gabonese	Gabonese	African franc	GAB
Gambia, the	Gambian	Gambian	dalasi = 100 butut	GAM
Georgia	Georgian	Georgian	lari = 100 tetri	GEO
Germany	German	German	Deutschmark = 100 pfennig	GER
Ghana	Ghanaian	Ghanaian	cedi = 100 pesewas	GHA
Greece	Greek	Greek	drachma = 100 leptae	GRE
Grenada	Grenadian	Grenadian	dollar = 100 cents	GRN
Guatemala	Guatemalan	Guatemalan	quetzal = 100 centavos	GUA
Guinea	Guinean	Guinean	franc = 100 centimes	GUI
Guinea-Bissau			peso = 100 centavos	GNB
Guyana	Guyanese	Guyanese	dollar = 100 cents	GUY
Haiti	Haitian	Haitian	gourde = 100 centimes	HAI
Holland (see Netherlands)				
Honduras	Honduran	Honduran	lempira = 100 centavos	HON
Hungary	Hungarian	Hungarian	forint = 100 filler	HUN
Iceland	Icelander	Icelandic	krona = 100 aurar	ISL
India	Indian	Indian	rupee = 100 paisa	IND
Indonesia	Indonesian	Indonesian	rupiah = 100 sen	INA
Iran	Iranian	Iranian	rial = 100 dinars	IRI
Iraq	Iraqi	Iraqi	dinar = 1,000 fils	IRQ
Ireland, Republic of	Irishman[1], Irishwoman[1]	Irish	pound (punt) = 100 pence	IRL
Israel	Israeli	Israeli	shekel = 100 agora	ISR
Italy	Italian	Italian	lira = 100 centesemi	ITA
Ivory Coast	Ivorian	Ivorian	African franc	CIV
Jamaica	Jamaican	Jamaican	dollar = 100 cents	JAM
Japan	Japanese	Japanese	yen = 100 sen	JPN
Jordan	Jordanian	Jordanian	dinar = 1,000 fils	JOR
Kazakhstan	Kazakh	Kazakh	tenge = 100 teins	KAZ
Kenya	Kenyan	Kenyan	shilling = 100 cents	KEN
Kiribati		Kiribati	dollar = 100 cents	
Kuwait	Kuwaiti	Kuwaiti	dinar = 1,000 fils	KUW
Kyrgyzstan	Kyrgyz	Kyrgyz	som = 100 tiyin	KGZ
Laos	Laotian	Laotian	kip = 100 ats	LAO
Latvia	Latvian	Latvian	lat = 100 santims	LAT
Lebanon	Lebanese	Lebanese	pound = 100 piastres	LIB
Lesotho	Mosotho, pl. Basotho	Lesothan	loti = 100 lisente	LES
Liberia	Liberian	Liberian	dollar = 100 cents	LBR

[1] May also denote a person from Northern Ireland.

Country	Person (name in general use)	Related adjective (in general use)	Currency unit	Abbreviation (Olympics)
Libya	Libyan	Libyan	dinar = 1,000 dirhams	LBA
Liechtenstein	Liechtensteiner		franc = 100 centimes	LIE
Lithuania	Lithuanian	Lithuanian	litas = 100 centas	LTU
Luxembourg	Luxembourger		franc = 100 centimes	LUX
Macedonia	Macedonian	Macedonian	denar	MKD
Madagascar	Malagasay or Madagascan	Malagasay or Madagascan	franc malgache = 100 centimes	MAD
Malawi	Malawian	Malawian	kwacha = 100 tambala	MAW
Malaysia	Malaysian	Malaysian	dollar (ringgit) = 100 sen	MAS
Maldives	Maldivian	Maldivian	rufiyaa = 100 laris	MDV
Mali	Malian	Malian	African franc	MLI
Malta	Maltese	Maltese	lira = 100 cents	MLT
Marshall Islands	Marshallese	Marshallese	US dollar	
Mauritania	Mauritanian	Mauritanian	ouguiya = 5 khoums	MTN
Mauritius	Mauritian	Mauritian	rupee = 100 cents	MRI
Mexico	Mexican	Mexican	peso = 100 centavos	MEX
Micronesia, Federated States of	Micronesian	Micronesian	US dollar	FSM
Moldova	Moldovan	Moldovan	leu = 100 bani	MDA
Monaco	Monégasque or Monacan	Monégasque or Monacan	franc = 100 centimes	MON
Mongolia	Mongolian	Mongolian	tugrik = 100 mongos	MGL
Montenegro (see Yugoslavia)				
Morocco	Moroccan	Moroccan	dirham = 100 centimes	MAR
Mozambique	Mozambican	Mozambican	metical = 100 centavos	MOZ
Myanmar (see Burma)				
Namibia	Namibian	Namibian	rand = 100 cents	NAM
Nauru	Nauruan	Nauruan	Australian dollar	NRU
Nepal	Nepalese	Nepalese	rupee = 100 paisa	NEP
Netherlands, the	Dutchman, Dutchwoman, or Netherlander	Dutch	guilder = 100 cents	NED
New Zealand	New Zealander		dollar = 100 cents	NZL
Nicaragua	Nicaraguan	Nicaraguan	cordoba = 100 centavos	NCA
Niger	Nigerien	Nigerien	African franc	NIG
Nigeria	Nigerian	Nigerian	naira = 100 kobo	NGR
North Korea	North Korean	North Korean	won = 100 jun	PRK
Norway	Norwegian	Norwegian	krone = 100 øre	NOR
Oman	Omani	Omani	rial = 1,000 baiza	OMA
Pakistan	Pakistani	Pakistani	rupee = 100 paisa	PAK
Panama	Panamanian	Panamanian	balboa = 100 centésimos	PAN
Papua New Guinea	Papua New Guinean or Guinean	Papua New Guinean or Guinean	kina = 100 toea	PNG
Paraguay	Paraguayan	Paraguayan	guarani = 100 centimos	PAR
Peru	Peruvian	Peruvian	nuevo sol = 100 cents	PER
Philippines	Filipino, Filipina	Filipino or Philippine	peso = 100 centavos	PHI
Poland	Pole	Polish	zloty = 100 groszy	POL
Portugal	Portuguese	Portuguese	escudo = 100 centavos	POR
Qatar	Qatari	Qatari	riyal = 100 dirhams	QAT
Romania	Romanian	Romanian	leu = 100 bani	ROM
Russia	Russian	Russian	rouble = 100 copecks	RUS
Rwanda	Rwandan	Rwandan	franc = 100 centimes	RWA
St Kitts and Nevis			dollar = 100 cents	SKN
St Lucia	St Lucian	St Lucian	dollar = 100 cents	LCA
St Vincent and the Grenadines	Vincentian, Grenadian	Vincentian, Grenadian	dollar = 100 cents	VIN
Samoa	Samoan	Samoan	tala = 100 sene	SAM
San Marino			Italian lira	SMR
São Tomé and Príncipe			dobra = 100 centavos	STP
Saudi Arabia	Saudi Arabian or Saudi	Saudi Arabian or Saudi	riyal = 20 qursh or 100 halalas	KSA

1: Countries & principal dependencies

Country	Person (name in general use)	Related adjective (in general use)	Currency unit	Abbreviation (Olympics)
Senegal	Senegalese	Senegalese	African franc	SEN
Serbia (see Yugoslavia)				
Seychelles, the	Seychellois	Seychellois	rupee = 100 cents	SEY
Sierra Leone	Sierra Leonian	Sierra Leonian	leone = 100 cents	SLE
Singapore	Singaporean	Singaporean	dollar = 100 cents	SIN
Slovakia	Slovak	Slovak	koruna = 100 haleru	SVK
Slovenia	Slovene *or* Slovenian	Slovene *or* Slovenian	tolar = 100 stotins	SLO
Solomon Islands	Solomon Islander		dollar = 100 cents	SOL
Somalia	Somali	Somali	shilling = 100 cents	SOM
South Africa	South African	South African	rand = 100 cents	RSA
South Korea	South Korean	South Korean	won = 100 jeon	KOR
Spain	Spaniard	Spanish	peseta = 100 centimos	ESP
Sri Lanka	Sri Lankan	Sri Lankan	rupee = 100 cents	SRI
Sudan	Sudanese	Sudanese	dinar = 10 pounds	SUD
Suriname	Surinamer *or* Surinamese	Surinamese	guilder = 100 cents	SUR
Swaziland	Swazi	Swazi	lilangeni = 100 cents	SWZ
Sweden	Swede	Swedish	krona = 100 öre	SWE
Switzerland	Swiss	Swiss	franc = 100 centimes	SUI
Syria	Syrian	Syrian	pound = 100 piastres	SYR
Taiwan	Taiwanese	Taiwanese	New Taiwan dollar = 100 cents	TPE
Tajikistan	Tajik *or* Tadjik	Tajik *or* Tadjik	Russian rouble	TJK
Tanzania	Tanzanian	Tanzanian	shilling = 100 cents	TAN
Thailand	Thai	Thai	baht = 100 satangs	THA
Togo	Togolese	Togolese	African franc	TOG
Tonga	Tongan	Tongan	pa'anga = 100 seniti	TGA
Trinidad and Tobago	Trinidadian, Tobagonian	Trinidadian, Tobagonian	dollar = 100 cents	TRI
Tunisia	Tunisian	Tunisian	dinar = 1,000 milliemes	TUN
Turkey	Turk	Turkish	lira = 100 kurus	TUR
Turkmenistan	Turkmen *or* Turkoman	Turkmen *or* Turkoman	manat = 100 tenge	TKM
Tuvalu	Tuvaluan	Tuvaluan	dollar = 100 cents	
Uganda	Ugandan	Ugandan	shilling = 100 cents	UGA
Ukraine	Ukrainian	Ukrainian	hryvna = 100 kopiykas	UKR
United Arab Emirates			dirham = 100 fils	UAE
United Kingdom	Briton	British	pound = 100 pence	GBR
United States of America	American	American	dollar = 100 cents	USA
Uruguay	Uruguayan	Uruguayan	peso = 100 centésimos	URU
Uzbekistan	Uzbek	Uzbek	som	UZB
Vanuatu	Vanuatuan	Vanuatuan	vatu = 100 centimes	VAN
Vatican City		Vatican	Italian lira	
Venezuela	Venezuelan	Venezuelan	bolivar = 100 centimos	VEN
Vietnam	Vietnamese	Vietnamese	dong = 10 hao or 100 xu	VIE
Yemen	Yemeni	Yemeni	riyal = 100 fils	YEM
Yugoslavia (Montenegro, Serbia)	Yugoslav	Yugoslav	dinar = 100 paras	YUG
Zaire (see Congo, Democratic Republic of)				
Zambia	Zambian	Zambian	kwacha = 100 ngwee	ZAM
Zimbabwe	Zimbabwean	Zimbabwean	dollar = 100 cents	ZIM

Principal dependencies

Country	Person (name in general use)	Related adjective (in general use)	Currency unit	Abbreviation (Olympics)
American Samoa (US)	American Samoan	American Samoan	US dollar	ASA
Anguilla (UK)	Anguillan	Anguillan	East Caribbean dollar	
Aruba (Netherlands)			florin	ARU
Bermuda (UK)	Bermudan or Bermudian	Bermudan or Bermudian	dollar	BER
Cayman Islands (UK)			dollar	CAY
Christmas Island (Australia)			Australian dollar	
Cocos Islands (Australia)			Australian dollar	
Cook Islands (NZ)			NZ dollar	COK
Faeroe Islands (Denmark)	Faeroese or Faroese	Faeroese or Faroese	Danish krone	
Falkland Islands (UK)	Falkland Islander		pound	
French Guiana (France)			French franc	
French Polynesia (France)			Pacific franc	
Gibraltar (UK)	Gibraltarian	Gibraltarian	pound	
Greenland (Denmark)	Greenlander		Danish krone	
Guadeloupe (France)	Guadeloupian	Guadeloupian	French franc	
Guam (US)	Guamanian	Guamanian	US dollar	GUM
Martinique (France)			French franc	
Mayotte (France)			French franc	
Montserrat (UK)			East Caribbean dollar	
Netherlands Antilles (Netherlands)			guilder	AHO
New Caledonia (France)	New Caledonian	New Caledonian	Pacific franc	
Niue (NZ)			NZ dollar	
Norfolk Island (Australia)			Australian dollar	
Northern Marianas (US)			US dollar	
Palau (US)			US dollar	PLW
Pitcairn Islands (UK)	Pitcairn Islander		NZ dollar	
Puerto Rico (US)	Puerto Rican	Puerto Rican	US dollar	PUR
Réunion (France)			French franc	
St Helena and dependencies (UK)			pound	
St Pierre and Miquelon (France)			French franc	
Svalbard (Norway)			Norwegian krone	
Turks and Caicos Islands (UK)			US dollar	
Virgin Islands (US)	Virgin Islander		US dollar	ISV
Virgin Islands, British (UK)	Virgin Islander		US dollar	IVB
Wallis and Futuna Islands (France)			French franc	
Western Sahara (Morocco)			Moroccan dirham	

The Commonwealth

The Commonwealth is a free association of the 54 sovereign independent states listed below, together with their associated states and dependencies.

Antigua and Barbuda	Cyprus	Kiribati	New Zealand	Seychelles, the	Tuvalu
Australia	Dominica	Lesotho	Nigeria	Sierra Leone	Uganda
Bahamas	Fiji	Malawi	Pakistan (suspended 1999)	Singapore	United Kingdom
Bangladesh	Gambia, the	Malaysia		Solomon Islands	Vanuatu
Barbados	Ghana	Maldives	Papua New Guinea	South Africa	Zambia
Belize	Grenada	Malta	St Kitts and Nevis	Sri Lanka	Zimbabwe
Botswana	Guyana	Mauritius	St Lucia	Swaziland	
Brunei	India	Mozambique	St Vincent and the Grenadines	Tanzania	
Cameroon	Jamaica	Namibia		Tonga	
Canada	Kenya	Nauru	Samoa	Trinidad and Tobago	

States and territories of Australia

State

New South Wales
Northern Territory
Queensland
South Australia
Tasmania
Victoria
Western Australia

Australian Capital Territory

Provinces and territories of Canada

(with postal abbreviations)

Province

Alberta (AB)
British Columbia (BC)
Manitoba (MB)
New Brunswick (NB)
Newfoundland and Labrador (NF)
Nova Scotia (NS)
Ontario (ON)
Prince Edward Island (PE)
Quebec (QC)
Saskatchewan (SK)

Northwest Territories (NT)
Nunavut (NT)
Yukon Territory (YT)

States of the United States of America

State	Related adjective/noun	Popular name	Postal abbreviation
Alabama	Alabaman	Yellowhammer State, Heart of Dixie, Cotton State	AL
Alaska	Alaskan	Great Land	AK
Arizona	Arizonan	Grand Canyon State	AZ
Arkansas	Arkansan	Land of Opportunity	AR
California	Californian	Golden State	CA
Colorado	Coloradan	Centennial State	CO
Connecticut	—	Constitution State, Nutmeg State	CT
Delaware	Delawarean	First State, Diamond State	DE
Florida	Floridian	Sunshine State	FL
Georgia	Georgian	Empire State of the South, Peach State	GA
Hawaii	Hawaiian	Aloha State	HI
Idaho	Idahoan	Gem State	ID
Illinois	Illinoisan	Prairie State	IL
Indiana	Indianan	Hoosier State	IN
Iowa	Iowan	Hawkeye State	IA
Kansas	Kansan	Sunflower State	KS
Kentucky	Kentuckian	Bluegrass State	KY
Louisiana	Louisianan or Louisianian	Pelican State	LA
Maine	Mainer (*noun*)	Pine Tree State	ME
Maryland	Marylander (*noun*)	Old Line State, Free State	MD
Massachusetts	—	Bay State, Old Colony	MA
Michigan	Michigander (*noun*)	Great Lake State, Wolverine State	MI
Minnesota	Minnesotan	North Star State, Gopher State	MN
Mississippi	Mississippian	Magnolia State	MS
Missouri	Missourian	Show Me State	MO
Montana	Montanan	Treasure State	MT
Nebraska	Nebraskan	Cornhusker State	NE
Nevada	Nevadan	Sagebrush State, Battleborn State, Silver State	NV
New Hampshire	New Hampshirite (*noun*)	Granite State	NH
New Jersey	New Jerseyan or New Jerseyite (*noun*)	Garden State	NJ
New Mexico	New Mexican	Land of Enchantment	NM
New York	New Yorker (*noun*)	Empire State	NY
North Carolina	North Carolinian	Tar Heel State, Old North State	NC
North Dakota	North Dakotan	Peace Garden State	ND
Ohio	Ohioan	Buckeye State	OH
Oklahoma	Oklahoman	Sooner State	OK
Oregon	Oregonian	Beaver State	OR
Pennsylvania	Pennsylvanian	Keystone State	PA
Rhode Island	Rhode Islander (*noun*)	Little Rhody, Ocean State	RI
South Carolina	South Carolinian	Palmetto State	SC
South Dakota	South Dakotan	Coyote State, Sunshine State	SD
Tennessee	Tennesseean	Volunteer State	TN
Texas	Texan	Lone Star State	TX
Utah	Utahan	Beehive State	UT
Vermont	Vermonter (*noun*)	Green Mountain State	VT
Virginia	Virginian	Old Dominion	VA
Washington	Washingtonian	Evergreen State	WA
West Virginia	West Virginian	Mountain State	WV
Wisconsin	Wisconsinite (*noun*)	Badger State	WI
Wyoming	Wyomingite (*noun*)	Equality	WY

Arabic, Hebrew, Greek, and Russian alphabets

Arabic

Alone	Final	Medial	Initial		
ا	ا			'alif	'
ب	ب	ب	ب	bā'	b
ت	ت	ت	ت	tā'	t
ث	ث	ث	ث	thā'	th
ج	ج	ج	ج	jīm	j
ح	ح	ح	ح	ḥā'	ḥ
خ	خ	خ	خ	khā'	kh
د	د			dāl	d
ذ	ذ			dhāl	dh
ر	ر			rā'	r
ز	ز			zāy	z
س	س	س	س	sīn	s
ش	ش	ش	ش	shīn	sh
ص	ص	ص	ص	ṣād	ṣ
ض	ض	ض	ض	ḍād	ḍ
ط	ط	ط	ط	ṭā'	ṭ
ظ	ظ	ظ	ظ	ẓā'	ẓ
ع	ع	ع	ع	'ayn	'
غ	غ	غ	غ	ghayn	gh
ف	ف	ف	ف	fā'	f
ق	ق	ق	ق	qāf	q
ك	ك	ك	ك	kāf	k
ل	ل	ل	ل	lām	l
م	م	م	م	mīm	m
ن	ن	ن	ن	nūn	n
ه	ه	ه	ه	hā'	h
و	و			wāw	w
ي	ي	ي	ي	yā'	y

Hebrew

א	'aleph	'
ב	beth	b, bh
ג	gimel	g, gh
ד	daleth	d, dh
ה	he	h
ו	waw	w
ז	zayin	z
ח	heth	ḥ
ט	teth	ṭ
י	yodh	y
כ ך	kaph	k, kh
ל	lamedh	l
מ ם	mem	m
נ ן	nun	n
ס	samekh	s
ע	'ayin	'
פ ף	pe	p, ph
צ ץ	sadhe	ṣ
ק	qoph	q
ר	resh	r
שׂ	śin	ś
שׁ	shin	sh
ת	taw	t, th

Greek

Α α	alpha	a
Β β	beta	b
Γ γ	gamma	g
Δ δ	delta	d
Ε ε	epsilon	e
Ζ ζ	zeta	z
Η η	eta	ē
Θ θ	theta	th
Ι ι	iota	i
Κ κ	kappa	k
Λ λ	lambda	l
Μ μ	mu	m
Ν ν	nu	n
Ξ ξ	xi	x
Ο ο	omicron	o
Π π	pi	p
Ρ ρ	rho	r, rh
Σ σ ς	sigma	s
Τ τ	tau	t
Υ υ	upsilon	u
Φ φ	phi	ph
Χ χ	chi	kh
Ψ ψ	psi	ps
Ω ω	omega	ō

Russian

А а	a
Б б	b
В в	v
Г г	g
Д д	d
Е е	e, ye
Ё ё	yo
Ж ж	zh
З з	z
И и	i
Й й	ĭ
К к	k
Л л	l
М м	m
Н н	n
О о	o
П п	p
Р р	r
С с	s
Т т	t
У у	u
Ф ф	f
Х х	kh
Ц ц	ts
Ч ч	ch
Ш ш	sh
Щ щ	shch
Ъ ъ	″ ('hard sign')
Ы ы	y
Ь ь	′ ('soft sign')
Э э	e
Ю ю	yu
Я я	ya

Punctuation marks

( )	brackets, parentheses
< >	angle brackets
[ ]	square brackets
{	brace
•	bullet
†	dagger, obelisk
‡	double dagger/diesis
★	asterisk/star
/	solidus/oblique/slash/virgule
§	section
~	swung dash
...	ellipsis/suspension points
¶	paragraph

Accents & diacritical marks

′	é	acute
°	å	bolle
˘	ŭ	breve
،	ç	cedilla
^	ê	circumflex
··	ö	umlaut/diaeresis
`	è	grave
ˇ	č	háček
‾	ō	macron
/	ø	streg
~	ñ	tilde

Phonetic alphabet

A	Alpha
B	Bravo
C	Charlie
D	Delta
E	Echo
F	Foxtrot
G	Golf
H	Hotel
I	India
J	Juliet
K	Kilo
L	Lima
M	Mike
N	November
O	Oscar
P	Papa
Q	Quebec
R	Romeo
S	Sierra
T	Tango
U	Uniform
V	Victor
W	Whisky
X	X-ray
Y	Yankee
Z	Zulu

Typefaces

	serif	sans serif	slab serif
roman	A	A	A
italic	A	A	A
bold face	A	A	A
light face	A	A	A

swash capitals	A B C D
upper case/ capital letters	A B C D
lower case/ small letters	a b c d e
ascenders	
x-height	**badge**
descender	

A selection of typefaces in 11pt size

American Typewriter
Bembo
Centaur
Gill Sans
Helvetica
Meta
Photina
Times
Walbaum

3: Weights and measures

British and American, with metric equivalents

Linear measure

1 inch	= 25.4 millimetres exactly
1 foot = 12 inches	= 0.3048 metre exactly
1 yard = 3 feet	= 0.9144 metre exactly
1 (statute) mile = 1,760 yards	= 1.609 kilometres
1 int. nautical mile = 1.150779 miles	= 1.852 kilometres exactly

Square measure

1 square inch	= 6.45 sq. centimetres
1 square foot = 144 sq. in.	= 9.29 sq. decimetres
1 square yard = 9 sq. ft	= 0.836 sq. metre
1 acre = 4,840 sq. yd	= 0.405 hectare
1 square mile = 640 acres	= 259 hectares

Cubic measure

1 cubic inch	= 16.4 cu. centimetres
1 cubic foot = 1,728 cu. in.	= 0.0283 cu. metre
1 cubic yard = 27 cu. ft	= 0.765 cu. metre

Capacity measure

British

1 fluid oz = 1.7339 cu. in.	= 0.0284 litre
1 gill = 5 fluid oz	= 0.1421 litre
1 pint = 20 fluid oz = 34.68 cu. in.	= 0.568 litre
1 quart = 2 pints	= 1.136 litres
1 gallon = 4 quarts	= 4.546 litres
1 peck = 2 gallons	= 9.092 litres
1 bushel = 4 pecks	= 36.4 litres

American dry

1 pint = 33.60 cu. in.	= 0.550 litre
1 quart = 2 pints	= 1.101 litres
1 peck = 8 quarts	= 8.81 litres
1 bushel = 4 pecks	= 35.3 litres

American liquid

1 pint = 16 fluid oz = 28.88 cu. in.	= 0.473 litre
1 quart = 2 pints	= 0.946 litre
1 gallon = 4 quarts	= 3.785 litres

Avoirdupois weight

1 grain	= 0.065 gram
1 dram	= 1.772 grams
1 ounce = 16 drams	= 28.35 grams
1 pound = 16 ounces = 7,000 grains	= 0.4536 kilogram (0.45359237 exactly)
1 stone = 14 pounds	= 6.35 kilograms
1 hundredweight = 112 pounds	= 50.80 kilograms
1 short ton = 2,000 pounds	= 0.907 tonne
1 (long) ton = 20 hundredweight	= 1.016 tonnes

Metric, with British equivalents

Linear measure

1 millimetre	= 0.039 inch
1 centimetre = 10 mm	= 0.394 inch
1 decimetre = 10 cm	= 3.94 inches
1 metre = 100 cm	= 1.094 yards
1 kilometre = 1,000 m	= 0.6214 mile

Square measure

1 square centimetre	= 0.155 sq. inch
1 square metre = 10,000 sq. cm	= 1.196 sq. yards
1 are = 100 square metres	= 119.6 sq. yards
1 hectare = 100 ares	= 2.471 acres
1 square kilometre = 100 hectares	= 0.386 sq. mile

Cubic measure

1 cubic centimetre	= 0.061 cu. inch
1 cubic metre = 1,000,000 cu. cm	= 1.308 cu. yards

Capacity measure

1 millilitre	= 0.002 pint (British)
1 centilitre = 10 ml	= 0.018 pint
1 decilitre = 10 cl	= 0.176 pint
1 litre = 1000 ml	= 1.76 pints
1 decalitre = 10 l	= 2.20 gallons
1 hectolitre = 100 l	= 2.75 bushels
1 kilolitre = 1,000 l	= 3.44 quarters

Weight

1 milligram	= 0.015 grain
1 centigram = 10 mg	= 0.154 grain
1 decigram = 100 mg	= 1.543 grains
1 gram = 1000 mg	= 15.43 grains
1 decagram = 10 g	= 5.64 drams
1 hectogram = 100 g	= 3.527 ounces
1 kilogram = 1,000 g	= 2.205 pounds
1 tonne (metric ton) = 1,000 kg	= 0.984 (long) ton

4: Symbols, shapes, and elements

Mathematical symbols

$+$	plus or positive
$-$	minus or negative
$\pm$	plus or minus, positive or negative
$\times$	multiplied by
$\div$	divided by
$=$	equal to
$\equiv$	identically equal to
$\neq$	not equal to
$\not\equiv$	not identically equal to
$\approx$	approximately equal to
$\sim$	of the order of or similar to
$>$	greater than
$<$	less than
$\not>$	not greater than
$\not<$	not less than
$\geq$	greater than or equal to
$\leq$	less than or equal to
$\gg$	much greater than
$\ll$	much less than
$\sqrt{}$	square root
∞	infinity
$\propto$	proportional to
$\sum$	sum of
$\prod$	product of
Δ	difference
$\therefore$	therefore
$\angle$	angle
$\parallel$	parallel to
$\perp$	perpendicular to
$:$	is to

Shapes and forms in mathematics

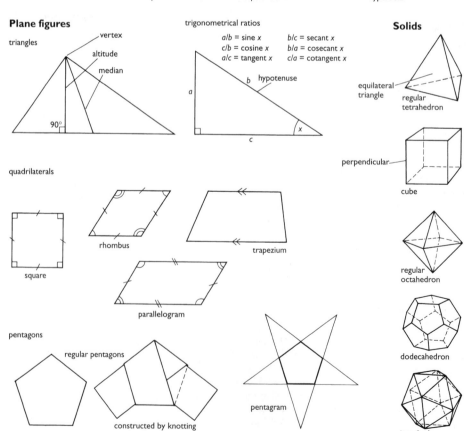

Circles and cones

circle
— radius, diameter, semicircle, circumference, centre, quadrant, chord, segment, sector, arc

evolute and involute
— 2 (involute of 1), 1 (evolute of 2), tangent to 1

conic sections
— circle, ellipse, parabola, hyperbola

Plane figures

triangles
— vertex, altitude, median, 90°

trigonometrical ratios

$a/b = \text{sine } x$ $b/c = \text{secant } x$
$c/b = \text{cosine } x$ $b/a = \text{cosecant } x$
$a/c = \text{tangent } x$ $c/a = \text{cotangent } x$

— hypotenuse, a, b, c, x

quadrilaterals
— square, rhombus, trapezium, parallelogram

pentagons
— regular pentagons, constructed by knotting a strip of paper, pentagram

Solids
— equilateral triangle, regular tetrahedron, perpendicular, cube, regular octahedron, dodecahedron, icosahedron

Chemical elements

Element	Symbol	Atomic number	Description
Actinium	Ac	89	metal, radioactive
Aluminium	Al	13	metal
Americium	Am	95	metal, radioactive
Antimony	Sb	51	metal
Argon	Ar	18	noble gas
Arsenic	As	33	metal
Astatine	At	85	halogen, non-metal, radioactive
Barium	Ba	56	metal
Berkelium	Bk	97	metal, radioactive
Beryllium	Be	4	metal
Bismuth	Bi	83	metal
Bohrium	Bh	107	very unstable, radioactive
Boron	B	5	non-metal
Bromine	Br	35	halogen, liquid
Cadmium	Cd	48	metal
Caesium	Cs	55	alkali metal
Calcium	Ca	20	metal
Californium	Cf	98	metal, radioactive
Carbon	C	6	non-metal
Cerium	Ce	58	metal
Chlorine	Cl	17	halogen, gas
Chromium	Cr	24	metal
Cobalt	Co	27	metal
Copper	Cu	29	metal
Curium	Cm	96	metal, radioactive
Dubnium	Db	105	very unstable, radioactive
Dysprosium	Dy	66	metal
Einsteinium	Es	99	very unstable, radioactive
Erbium	Er	68	metal
Europium	Eu	63	metal
Fermium	Fm	100	very unstable, radioactive
Fluorine	F	9	halogen, gas
Francium	Fr	87	alkali metal, radioactive
Gadolinium	Gd	64	metal
Gallium	Ga	31	metal
Germanium	Ge	32	semiconductor
Gold	Au	79	metal
Hafnium	Hf	72	metal
Hassium	Hs	108	very unstable, radioactive
Helium	He	2	noble gas
Holmium	Ho	67	metal
Hydrogen	H	1	gas
Indium	In	49	metal
Iodine	I	53	halogen, non-metal
Iridium	Ir	77	metal
Iron	Fe	26	metal
Krypton	Kr	36	noble gas
Lanthanum	La	57	metal
Lawrencium	Lr	103	very unstable, radioactive
Lead	Pb	82	metal
Lithium	Li	3	alkali metal
Lutetium	Lu	71	metal
Magnesium	Mg	12	metal
Manganese	Mn	25	metal
Meitnerium	Mt	109	very unstable, radioactive
Mendelevium	Md	101	very unstable, radioactive
Mercury	Hg	80	metal, liquid
Molybdenum	Mo	42	metal
Neodymium	Nd	60	metal
Neon	Ne	10	noble gas
Neptunium	Np	93	metal, radioactive
Nickel	Ni	28	metal
Niobium	Nb	41	metal
Nitrogen	N	7	gas
Nobelium	No	102	very unstable, radioactive
Osmium	Os	76	metal
Oxygen	O	8	gas
Palladium	Pd	46	metal
Phosphorus	P	15	non-metal
Platinum	Pt	78	metal
Plutonium	Pu	94	metal, radioactive
Polonium	Po	84	metal, radioactive
Potassium	K	19	alkali metal
Praseodymium	Pr	59	metal
Promethium	Pm	61	metal, radioactive
Protactinium	Pa	91	metal, radioactive
Radium	Ra	88	metal, radioactive
Radon	Rn	86	noble gas, radioactive
Rhenium	Re	75	metal
Rhodium	Rh	45	metal
Rubidium	Rb	37	alkali metal
Ruthenium	Ru	44	metal
Rutherfordium	Rf	104	very unstable, radioactive
Samarium	Sm	62	metal
Scandium	Sc	21	metal
Seaborgium	Sg	106	very unstable, radioactive
Selenium	Se	34	semiconductor
Silicon	Si	14	semiconductor
Silver	Ag	47	metal
Sodium	Na	11	alkali metal
Strontium	Sr	38	metal
Sulphur	S	16	non-metal
Tantalum	Ta	73	metal
Technetium	Tc	43	metal, radioactive
Tellurium	Te	52	semiconductor
Terbium	Tb	65	metal
Thallium	Tl	81	metal
Thorium	Th	90	metal, radioactive
Thulium	Tm	69	metal
Tin	Sn	50	metal
Titanium	Ti	22	metal
Tungsten	W	74	metal
Uranium	U	92	metal, radioactive
Vanadium	V	23	metal
Xenon	Xe	54	noble gas
Ytterbium	Yb	70	metal
Yttrium	Y	39	metal
Zinc	Zn	30	metal
Zirconium	Zr	40	metal

5: Planets, constellations, and star signs

Planets

Planet	Related adjective
Mercury	Mercurian
Venus	Venusian
Earth	terrestrial, earthly
Mars	Martian
Jupiter	Jovian
Saturn	Saturnian
Uranus	Uranian
Neptune	Neptunian
Pluto	Plutonian

Major non-Zodiac constellations

Astronomical name	Common name
Andromeda	—
Aquila	Eagle
Auriga	Charioteer
Boötes	Herdsman
Canis Major	Great Dog
Canis Minor	Little Dog
Carina	Keel
Cassiopeia	—
Centaurus	Centaur
Cepheus	—
Cetus	Whale
Crux (Australis)	Southern Cross
Cygnus	Swan
Draco	Dragon
Eridanus	River
Hercules	—
Hydra	Water Snake *or* Sea Monster
Lacerta	Lizard
Lyra	Lyre
Ophiuchus	Serpent Bearer
Orion	Hunter
Pegasus	—
Perseus	—
Puppis	Poop *or* Stern
Ursa Major	Great Bear
Ursa Minor	Little Bear
Vela	Sails

Signs of the Zodiac

Aries Ram
(March 21–April 20)

Taurus Bull
(April 21–May 20)

Gemini Twins
(May 21–June 20)

Cancer Crab
(June 21–July 21)

Leo Lion
(July 22–August 21)

Virgo Virgin
(August 22–September 21)

Libra Scales
(September 22–October 22)

Scorpio Scorpion
(October 23–November 21)

Sagittarius Archer
(November 22–December 20)

Capricorn Goat
(December 21–January 19)

Aquarius Water Bearer
(January 20– February 18)

Pisces Fish
(February 19–March 20)

Time periods

Name	Period
bicentennial	200 years
biennial	2 years
century	100 years
decade	10 years
centennial	every 100 years
decennial	every 10 years
leap year	366 days
millennium	1,000 years
month	28–31 days
Olympiad	every 4 years
quadrennial	every 4 years
quadricentennial	every 400 years
quincentennial	every 500 years
quinquennial	every 5 years
septennial	every 7 years
sesquicentennial	every 150 years
sexcentenary	600 years
sexennial	every 6 years
tercentenary	300 years
triennial	every 3 years
vicennial	every 20 years
week	7 days
year	365 days *or* 12 months *or* 52 weeks

Time intervals

annual	occurring every year
biannual	occurring twice a year
bimonthly	occurring every two months *or* twice a month
biweekly	every two weeks *or* twice a week
diurnal	daily, of each day
perennial	lasting through a year *or* several years
semi-annual	occurring twice a year
semi-diurnal	twice a day
semi-weekly	twice a week
trimonthly	every three months
triweekly	every three weeks *or* three times a week
thrice weekly	three times a week

Wedding anniversaries

Year	Traditional
1st	Paper
2nd	Cotton
3rd	Leather
4th	Linen (silk)
5th	Wood
6th	Iron
7th	Wool (copper)
8th	Bronze
9th	Pottery (china)
10th	Tin (aluminium)
11th	Steel
12th	Silk
13th	Lace
14th	Ivory
15th	Crystal
20th	China
25th	Silver
30th	Pearl
35th	Coral (jade)
40th	Ruby
45th	Sapphire
50th	Gold
55th	Emerald
60th	Diamond

Major divisions of geological time

Era	Period	Epoch	Duration
Cenozoic	Quaternary	Holocene	100,000 BP to present
		Pleistocene	2 mya–100,000 BP
	Tertiary	Pliocene	5–2 mya
		Miocene	24–5 mya
		Oligocene	38–24 mya
		Eocene	55–38 mya
		Palaeocene	65–55 mya
Mesozoic	Cretaceous		144–65 mya
	Jurassic		213–144 mya
	Triassic		248–213 mya
	Permian		286–248 mya
	Carboniferous		360–286 mya
Palaeozoic	Devonian		408–360 mya
	Silurian		438–408 mya
	Ordovician		505–438 mya
	Cambrian		590–505 mya
	Precambrian		4,600–590 mya

(BP = before present;
mya = millions of years ago)
All figures are approximate and based on currently available evidence.

7: Animals and collective nouns

Collective nouns

Many of these terms belong to 15th-century lists of 'proper terms', notably that in the *Book of St Albans* attributed to Dame Juliana Barnes (1486). Many of these are fanciful or humorous terms which probably never had any real currency, but have been taken up by antiquarian writers, notably Joseph Strutt in *Sports and Pastimes of England* (1801).

Animals

a shrewdness of apes
a chattering *or* clattering of choughs
a rag *or* rake of colts
a covert of coots
a cowardice of curs
a trip of dotterel
a flight *or* dole *or* piteousness of doves
a raft *or* bunch *or* paddling of ducks on water
a fling of dunlins
a gang of elk
a charm *or* chirm of finches
a pack *or* covey of grouse
a cast of hawks
a siege of herons
a desert of lapwing
an exaltation *or* a bevy of larks
a tiding of magpies
a sord *or* suit of mallard
a richesse of martens
a barren of mules
a watch of nightingales
a covey of partridges
a muster of peacocks
a head *or* nye of pheasants

a kit of pigeons flying together
a stand *or* wing *or* congregation of plovers
a rush *or* flight of pochards
a covey of ptarmigan
a bevy *or* drift of quail
a string of racehorses
an unkindness of ravens
a bevy of roe deer
a parliament *or* building of rooks
a hill of ruffs
a dopping of sheldrake
a wisp *or* walk of snipe
a host of sparrows
a murmuration of starlings
a flight of swallows
a game of swans; a wedge of swans in the air
a spring of teal
a bunch *or* knob *or* raft of waterfowl
a company *or* trip of wigeon
a destruction of wild cats
a bunch *or* trip *or* plump *or* knob (less than 30) of wildfowl
a drift of wild pigs
a fall of woodcock

People

a blush of boys
a drunkship of cobblers
a hastiness of cooks
a stalk of foresters
an observance of hermits
a bevy of ladies
a faith of merchants
a superfluity of nuns
a malapertness (= impertinence) of pedlars
a pity of prisoners
a glozing (= fawning) of taverners

Collective and other terms for animals

Animal	Group	Male	Female	Young	Related adjective	Home or menagerie
ass, donkey	herd, drove	jack, jackass, dicky	jenny	foal, colt (male), filly (female)	asinine	–
badger	cete*	boar	sow	cub	meline	sett (or set)
bee	swarm	–	–	–	apian	apiary, hive
bear	sloth*	–	–	cub	ursine	–
bird	flock	cock	hen	chick, fledgling	avian	nest, roost; aviary
cat	litter or kindle* (of kittens)	tom, gib-cat (usually castrated)	queen, tabby	kitten	feline	cattery; lair or den (wild cats)
cattle	herd, drove, drift; team or yoke (oxen)	bull, ox (castrated)	cow	calf, stirk, bullock (male), heifer (female), steer (castrated male)	bovine, taurine (bulls)	byre
chicken	brood, clutch	–	–	chick	–	–
deer	herd	buck, stag, hart	doe, hind	fawn, calf, kid; pricket or brocket (male)	cervine	–
dog	pack; kennel (of hounds); litter (of pups)	dog, hound	bitch	pup, puppy, whelp	canine	kennel
elephant	herd	bull	cow	calf	elephantine	–
ferret	business*	dog, buck, jack, hob	bitch, doe, jill	kit	musteline	–
fish	shoal	–	–	fry (pl.)	piscine	–
fox	skulk*	dog	vixen	cub	vulpine	earth, lair
frog	–	–	–	tadpole	ranine, batrachian, anuran, salientian	–
goat	flock, herd, tribe	billy, buck	nanny, doe	kid	caprine, hircine	–
goose	gaggle, skein	gander	–	gosling	anserine	–
hare	down*, husk*, trip*	buck, jack	doe, puss	leveret	leporine	form
horse	herd, stable, team, troop; rag* or rake* (of colts)	stallion, horse, sire, gelding (castrated)	mare, dam	foal, colt (male), filly (female)	equine	stable, paddock, stall, stud
kangaroo	troop, herd, mob	buck, boomer	doe, blue flier	joey	maropine	–
leopard	leap*	leopard	leopardess	cub	pardine	–
lion	pride	lion	lioness	cub	leonine	den
mole	labour*	–	–	–	talpine	burrow, fortress, tunnel
monkey	troop, tribe	–	–	–	simian	–
otter	–	dog	bitch	cub	lutrine	holt, lodge
pig, boar	herd, sounder (of wild pigs), farrow (of piglets)	boar, hog (castrated)	sow, gilt	piglet, pigling, squeaker, shoat (N. Amer.), gilt (female)	porcine, suilline	pen, sty
polecat	–	hob	jill	kit	musteline	–
rabbit	–	buck	doe	kitten	oryctolagine	warren, burrow, coneygarth (historical)
rat	–	buck	doe	nestling	murine	–
rhinoceros	crash*	bull	cow	calf	rhinocerotic	–
seal	herd	bull	cow	pup, cub	phocine	rookery
sheep	flock, drove, trip, herd	ram, tup, wether (castrated)	ewe	lamb, teg, hog	ovine	fold
snake	–	–	–	–	anguine, ophidian	den, nest
squirrel	–	–	–	nestling	sciurine	drey
tiger	–	tiger	tigress	cub	tigrine	lair
whale	pod, school, herd	bull	cow	calf	cetacean	–
wolf	pack, rout*	dog	bitch	cub, whelp	lupine	lair, den
zebra	herd	stallion	mare	foal, colt (male), filly (female)	zebrine	–

*Words marked * are obsolete or fanciful terms having little real currency, perhaps belonging more appropriately to the lists on p. 1190.*

8: Architecture

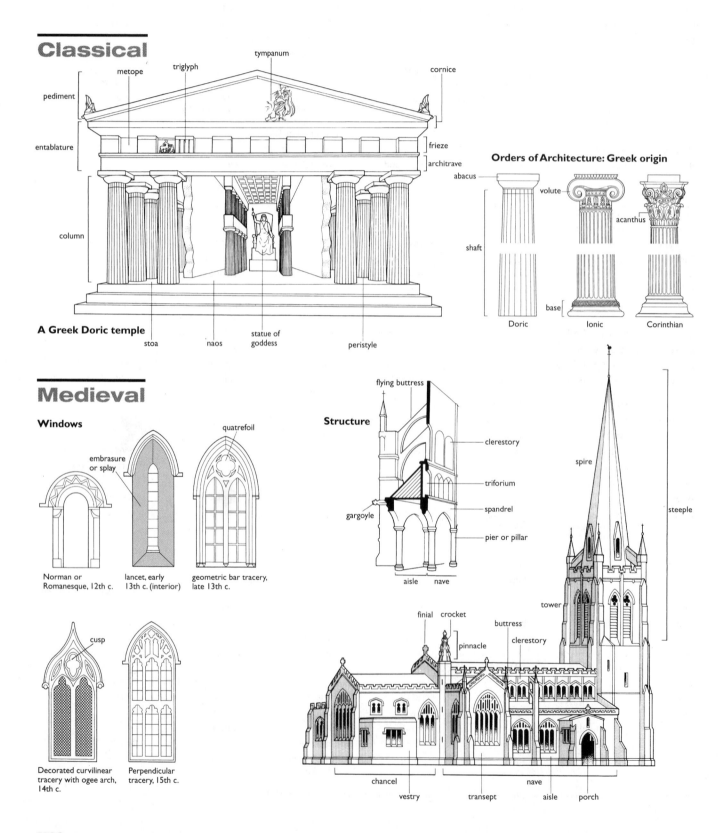

Classical

A Greek Doric temple

- pediment
- metope
- triglyph
- tympanum
- cornice
- entablature
- frieze
- architrave
- column
- stoa
- naos
- statue of goddess
- peristyle

Orders of Architecture: Greek origin

- abacus
- volute
- acanthus
- shaft
- base

Doric   Ionic   Corinthian

Medieval

Windows

- embrasure or splay
- quatrefoil

Norman or Romanesque, 12th c.

lancet, early 13th c. (interior)

geometric bar tracery, late 13th c.

- cusp

Decorated curvilinear tracery with ogee arch, 14th c.

Perpendicular tracery, 15th c.

Structure

- flying buttress
- clerestory
- triforium
- spandrel
- gargoyle
- pier or pillar
- aisle
- nave

- spire
- steeple
- tower
- finial
- crocket
- pinnacle
- buttress
- clerestory
- chancel
- vestry
- transept
- nave
- aisle
- porch